The Writer's Brief Handbook

THIRD EDITION

Alfred Rosa
UNIVERSITY OF VERMONT

Paul Eschholz
UNIVERSITY OF VERMONT

Allyn and Bacon

BOSTON   LONDON   TORONTO   SYDNEY   TOKYO   SINGAPORE

Vice President: Eben W. Ludlow
Developmental Editor: Harriett Prentiss
Series Editorial Assistant: Linda M. D'Angelo
Senior Marketing Manager: Lisa Kimball
Composition and Prepress Buyer: Linda Cox
Manufacturing Buyer: Suzanne Lareau
Cover Administrator: Linda Knowles
Cover Designer: Susan Paradise
Production Administrator: Susan Brown
Editorial-Production Service: Matrix Productions Inc.
Interior Design: Carol Somberg/Omegatype Typography, Inc.

Library of Congress Cataloging-in-Publication Data
Rosa, Alfred F.
    The writer's brief handbook / Alfred Rosa, Paul Eschholz.—3rd
ed.
        p.   cm.
    Includes bibliographical references and index.
    ISBN 0-205-28512-0
    1. English language—Rhetoric—Handbooks, manuals, etc.
    2. English language—Grammar—Handbooks, manuals, etc.
    I. Eschholz, Paul A.   II. Title.
PE1408.R675   1998
808'.042—dc21   97-48700
                                                                  CIP

Printed in the United States of America
10 9 8 7 6 5 4 3 2 1   01 00 99 98

Acknowledgments appear after the index, on a page that constitutes a continuation of the copyright page.

To the Student

You can find what you are looking for in *The Writer's Brief Handbook* in a number of ways. Suppose you have a question about whether to use a singular or plural verb in your sentence. First, locate the Editing for Grammar section in the Quick Reference Guide at the front of the book. Then flip to the EDIT tab, turn the divider page to the outline, and find Subject–verb agreement (EDIT 1). Look under this heading until you find Identifying subjects (EDIT 1a, page 119, reproduced below). Until you are familiar with the contents of the various chapters, you will also use the Detailed Contents beginning on page v or the Index at the end of the book to help you find the answer to a question.

Page tab indicates the chapter title (EDIT) and the number of the section (1a).

Running head and page number indicate the subject discussed on this page.

Section number and title.

EDIT 1

Boldface key terms are defined in text.

Subject–Verb Agreement

In grammar, **subject–verb agreement** refers to the correspondence in form between a verb and its subject. Every verb in a clause or sentence must agree in *number* and *person* with its subject. That is, make a verb singular if its subject is singular; make a verb plural if its subject is plural. Also, make a verb agree in person (that is, the doer of the action—first person, second person, third person) with its grammatical subject.

Examples illustrate the point of the section.

SINGULAR THIRD PERSON SUBJECT AND SINGULAR VERB
Overcrowding causes many of the discipline problems in our schools.

PLURAL THIRD PERSON SUBJECT AND PLURAL VERB
Hurricanes destroy millions of dollars worth of property each year.

Normally, we do not think twice about subject–verb agreement. A few constructions, however, can be troublesome. In most cases, the problem results from not having correctly identified the subject of the sentence.

Subsection headings indicate the main rules or conventions.

EDIT 1a To choose the correct verb form, identify the subject of the sentence.

Cross-references indicate where related information can be found.

Sometimes intervening word groups obscure the relationship between the subject (S) and the verb in a sentence. When the relationship is not clear, the culprit is usually an intervening prepositional phrase. Mentally block off all the prepositional phrases in a sentence, and see what is left. One of these leftover words must be the subject because a subject can never be in a prepositional phrase. (See GRAM 3a.)

Part of speech/sentence labels highlight featured words or word groups in sentences.

The first three weeks of basic training is the worst.
[The plural subject *weeks* takes a plural verb.]

Another word group that can cause confusion about subject–verb agreement is the subordinate clause. (See GRAM 4.) Neither the subject nor the verb of a sentence will ever be in a subordinate clause.

Handwritten corrections show revisions and corrections.

Taking mood-altering drugs, although they sometimes provide great medical benefits, are generally criticized by the public.
[The singular subject *taking* takes a singular verb.]

Bracketed explanations provide reasons for changes.

Detailed Contents

esl ESL Basics

sent Sentences

edit Editing for Grammar

word **Word Choice**

punct Punctuation

mech Mechanics

argue/lit Writing an Argumentative Essay/ Writing about Literature

lib The Library

other docu **Other Systems of Documentation**

🖥 Computer Tips

Preface

The Writer's Brief Handbook, Third Edition, is a compact, easy-to-use guide to writing. It offers clear definitions of important terms and concepts as well as helpful explanations of the rules and principles underlying effective written English. We believe *The Writer's Brief Handbook* is the best concise yet comprehensive reference available for today's college writers, and for good reason. Notice its important features:

- **User-Friendly, Multi-faceted Access System.** The more students consult *The Writer's Brief Handbook,* the more user-friendly they will find it. The Quick Reference Guide, which is keyed to the tabbed dividers with their complete chapter outlines, along with the Detailed Table of Contents and the Index make it as easy as possible to locate information.

- **Writing Process Orientation.** *The Writer's Brief Handbook* covers all stages of the writing process in depth: generating ideas, drafting, revising, editing, and proofreading. A sample student paper is presented with annotations and commentary.

- **Clearly Stated Learning Objectives.** Students can now find a list of what they are supposed to learn from each section of the *Handbook* on the tabbed divider page for that section.

- **Comprehensive Chapter on Effective Paragraphs.** Unique to brief handbooks, this chapter is illustrated with student and professional examples and helps students write better paragraphs.

- **More Student and Professional Writing Examples than Any Other Handbook.** Bountiful and carefully chosen examples establish realistic expectations for students' writing performance. Handwritten corrections of errors immediately convey where an error occurs in an example and how to correct it.

- **New Tabbed Section on Argumentation and Writing about Literature.** Two new annotated student papers illustrate the advice given for writing argumentative essays or papers that analyze a literary text.

- **Self-Contained ESL Section.** A comprehensive, easy-to-use chapter answers ESL questions without requiring students to search throughout the book. This chapter offers students for whom English is not their native language help with verb forms, nouns, adjectives and adverbs, prepositional phrases, parts of sentences, and word groups.

- **More Computer Tips.** Yet more Computer Tips, strategically positioned in shaded boxes throughout the text, remind students how to take full advantage of their personal computers while writing.

- **More Advice on Avoiding Bias in Writing.** An extensive section on avoiding bias and sexism offers students strategies for eliminating racial, ethnic, and gender bias in their writing.

- **Manuscript Format Chapter.** A tabbed section on manuscript formatting provides basic guidelines for academic manuscripts using either MLA or APA style as well as such essential business documents as letters, résumés, and memos. Helpful advice on page design, improving readability, and creating visuals is presented.

- **Enlarged Library Section on Using Electronic Resources.** *The Writer's Brief Handbook* is still the only brief handbook to offer a separate tabbed section on using the library. This section, which provides a sound introduction to the resources of the college library, has been expanded to include electronic research. Students are shown what is available to them on the World Wide Web, how to use search engines and subject directories to locate worthwhile websites, and how to download and print files.

- **Expanded Instruction for Using Online Sources for Writers of Research Papers.** Numerous examples and illustrations show how students can use online sources to complement print sources in their research. Students are shown how to locate and evaluate online sources, compile a preliminary bibliography of these sources, and take notes online. A sample student research paper in the MLA style, with annotations and commentary, accompanies this chapter.

- **Latest MLA, ACW, APA, and Chicago Documentation Guidelines.** Two separate documentation sections provide extensive models of correct citation format. Now included in the MLA DOCU section are references to Janice Walker's ACW web site for electronic citations. New to the OTHER DOCU section are the guidelines for using the *Chicago Manual of Style* citation system. Also included in OTHER DOCU is a sample student research paper in APA style. New in-text directories in both sections help students quickly locate the particular type of source they are trying to document.

- **More Help for Students.** A separate publication, *Exercise Book to Accompany The Writer's Brief Handbook,* is designed for those students who need extra practice with paragraphs, grammar, punctuation, mechanics, manuscript format, library resources, and research documentation styles. The exercises are keyed to the chapters of the *Handbook* so that students can consult the *Handbook* as they work. The exercises provide practice at both sentence and paragraph levels. An answer key to the *Exercise Book* is available to instructors.

Acknowledgments

During the writing and rewriting of the *Handbook*, we have benefited immensely from honest and wise advice from teachers of writing around the country. We are happy to acknowledge them here publicly:

Joseph A. Alvarez, Central Piedmont Community College; Kathleen Balutansky, Saint Michael's College; John Boly, Marquette University; Michal Brody, University of Texas at Austin; Virginia Chappell, Marquette University; Nancy C. DeJoy, Millikin University; Roberta Henson, Indiana Wesleyan University; Theresa M. Jackson, Western Iowa Tech Community College; Joan Karbach, Tri-State University; Mark Madigan, Nazareth College of Rochester; Kathleen Mahnke, Saint Michael's College; Anne Righton Malone, University of New Hampshire; Aisha F. Saidi, Boston College; Beckey Stamm, Columbus State Community College; Amy Ulmer, Pasadena City College; Karen Peterson Welch, University of Wisconsin–Eau Claire.

Closer to home, we would like to thank our colleagues at the University of Vermont for creating a responsive environment in which to work. We have especially benefited from discussions with colleagues who have used the text in their writing classes and have shared student responses with us: Joe Won, Alex Vardamis, Barry Snyder, Lynne Hefferon, Brian Kent, Frank Manchel, Michael Stanton, Nicole Aljoe, Jamie Ebersole, Cara Simone-Bader, and Dick Sweterlitsch. We appreciate all that we have learned over the years from our writing students, especially Pat LaRose, Andy Pellett, and Lauri Coulombe, whose essays appear in this text. Thanks should also go to Brooke Bailey of Florida State University, whose APA paper was written for a course taught by Sarah Eschholz. Special recognition goes to Michal Brody for help with ESL materials. Hope Greenberg and Martha Day helped with Web research; and Xia Li and Nancy Crane, our university reference librarians and authors of *Electronic Style: A Guide to Citing Electronic Information,* were very generous with their advice. Once again, Chris Bray, our former graduate student, genial friend, and author of the *Exercise Book* that accompanies this *Handbook,* has lent his considerable linguistic and computer expertise to the entire project.

It has been our pleasure to collaborate once again with Eben Ludlow, our friend and editor at Allyn & Bacon. His wisdom and years of experience as an editor continue to play a major role in making this *Handbook* the success it is. His editorial assistant, Linda D'Angelo, has always been friendly and professional in facilitating the writing and production of this revision. It is always a delight to work with a person who is simply the best at what she does, and nowhere is this more true than in the person of Harriett Prentiss, our development editor. We consider her both a friend and a colleague. At Allyn & Bacon, Sue Brown, our production editor, held together a tight schedule and complicated steps in the design and production processes with admirable skill and professionalism. We would also like to thank our other friends on the Allyn & Bacon team—Lisa Kimball, Sandi Kirshner, John Gilman, Doug Day, Sarita Uribe, Jennifer Quigley-Harris, and Bill Barke—for their enthusiastic support of our work on *The Writer's Brief Handbook.*

A.R.
P.E.

comp

Composing

Learning Objectives

After reading this section, you should:

- know how to plan a writing assignment, taking audience and purpose into account;
- understand the back-and-forth nature of the writing process;
- know the difference between revising, editing, and proofreading;
- be able to conduct a peer conference as part of revising your work.

Composing

A good prose composition, regardless of its length, is purposeful and well organized. In the following essay, H. Allen Smith humorously explains a life experience we've all had.

Claude Fetridge's Infuriating Law

Fetridge's Law, in simple language, states that important things that are supposed to happen do not happen, especially when people are looking; or, conversely, things that are supposed not to happen do happen, especially when people are looking. Thus a dog that will jump through a hoop a thousand times a day for his owner will not jump through a hoop when a neighbor is called to watch; and a baby that will say "Dada" in the presence of its proud parents will, when friends are summoned, either clam up or screech like a jaybird.

Fetridge's Law takes its name from a onetime radio engineer named Claude Fetridge. Back in 1936, Mr. Fetridge thought up the idea of broadcasting the flight of the famous swallows from San Juan de Capistrano mission in Southern California. As is well known, the swallows depart from the mission each year on St. John's Day, October 23, and return on March 19, St. Joseph's Day. Claude Fetridge conceived the idea of broadcasting the flutter of wings of the departing swallows on October 23. His company went to considerable expense to set up its equipment at the mission; then, with the whole nation waiting anxiously for the soul-stirring event, it was discovered that this year the swallows, out of sheer orneriness, had departed a day ahead of schedule. Thus did a flock of birds lend immortality to Claude Fetridge.

Television sets, of course, are often subject to the workings of Fetridge's Law. If a friend tells me he is going to appear on a television show and asks me to watch it, I groan inwardly, knowing this is going to cost me money. The moment his show comes on the air, my screen will snow up or acquire the look of an old-school-tie pattern. I turn it off and call the repairman. He travels three miles to my house and turns the set on. The picture emerges bright and clear, the contrast exactly right, a better picture than I've ever had before. It's that way always and forever, days without end.

An attractive woman neighbor of mine drives her husband to the railroad station every morning. On rare occasions she has been late getting her backfield in motion, and hasn't had time to get dressed. These times she has thrown a coat over her nightgown and, wearing bedroom slippers, headed for the depot. Fetridge's Law always seems to give her trouble. Once she clashed fenders with another car on the highway and had to go to the police station in her night shift. Twice she has had motor trouble in the depot plaza, requiring that she get out of her car in robe and slippers and pincurlers. The last I heard, she was considering sleeping in her street clothes.

Fetridge's Law operates fiercely in the realm of dentistry. In my own case, I have often noted that whenever I develop a raging toothache it is a Sunday and the dentists are all on the golf course. Not long ago, my toothache hung on through the weekend, and Monday morning it was still throbbing and pulsating like a diesel locomotive. I called my dentist, proclaiming an emergency, and drove to his office. As I was going up the stairway, the ache suddenly vanished. By the time I got into his chair, I was confused and embarrassed and unable to tell him with certainty which tooth it was that had been killing me. The X-ray showed no shady spots, though it would have several if he had pointed the thing at my brain. Claude Fetridge's law clearly has its good points; it can exasperate, but it can also cure toothaches.

From the title, in which the word *infuriating* arouses our interest to the amusing examples he uses, H. Allen Smith focuses every element of his essay on one purpose—to define Fetridge's Law and explain why it is so irrational and thus infuriating.

Writers like H. Allen Smith do not rely on luck or inspiration to produce an effective piece of writing. Good writers plan, write, revise, edit, and proofread. Keep in mind, however, that the writing process is rarely as simple and straightforward as this. Usually the process is recursive, moving back and forth among the four stages. Moreover, writing is very personal—no two people go about it exactly the same way. Still, it is possible to describe steps in the writing process and thereby have a reassuring and reliable method for undertaking a writing task and writing a good composition.

COMP 1

Writing with a Computer

Throughout *The Writer's Brief Handbook,* but most frequently in COMP, you will find suggestions to help you make the most of writing with a computer. You do not need a computer to write, of course, but many students prefer to work on one. The computer tips are labeled **C-Tip** and are found in the shaded boxes in the text. The tips are not meant to be exhaustive, nor are they a substitute for the directions and advice offered by your computer manual; rather, the tips serve as a bridge between the instruction in writing and the many ways a computer can facilitate the composing process. Here, to begin with, are some general computer tips.

C-Tip

Saving files

The best tip anyone can give you about using a computer is this: *always* save your work as you compose. Make it a habit to press the save key periodically. By doing so you will not lose your work because of a general power failure or because your computer crashes.

Backing up files

Almost as important as periodically saving your files is making a backup copy of your finished work. Preferably, do this on a diskette and not on your hard drive; if your hard drive fails, you can simply run the diskette on another computer.

Saving drafts

Rather than revising the same draft over and over again, keep each draft intact. Copy your file and designate it filename 1, filename 2, filename 3, and so on. The point is that if you want to return to an earlier draft at a later stage, you will have it. An earlier organizational pattern or a particular phrasing may have been the best after all.

Using school computers

If you plan to use your school's computer lab, check the hours it is open and keep in mind that other students will probably want computer time just when you do. Leave enough time in your schedule to be flexible.

Keeping supplies

Keep a supply of spare diskettes on hand in order to make backup copies. (It is also a good idea to have a spare ribbon or toner cartridge.)

COMP 2

Planning

The planning stage of the writing process encompasses everything you do before you actually begin to write. In planning, you:

a. analyze the writing task,
b. choose a subject,
c. focus on a topic,
d. generate ideas and collect information,
e. formulate a thesis statement,
f. determine your purpose,
g. analyze your audience, and
h. make an outline.

Each of these activities is discussed in detail in this section.

COMP 2a Analyze the writing task.

Much of your college writing will be in response to very specific assignments: your physical science professor may ask you to write a paper presenting pro and con evidence of the greenhouse effect. With such a narrowed topic, you can move ahead to collecting information and formulating a thesis, a one- or two-sentence statement of your main idea. At other times your instructor may assign only a general subject and ask you to choose a particular aspect of it to write on. For example, your American history teacher may assign a paper on World War II, giving you the opportunity to choose a specific topic (say, the internment of Japanese-Americans) and develop your own thesis (asserting this act was unjustified and the result of unfounded fears).

Sometimes your instructor will allow you to write on any subject that interests you. In such a case, you may already have an idea for a paper in mind (why you oppose any form of testing for substance abuse in the workplace, for instance). What happens, however, when you are free to choose your own subject and you cannot think of anything to write about? If you find yourself in this situation, follow the advice set forth in the rest of this section. We give many approaches to selecting a suitable subject and topic; one will work for you.

COMP 2b Choose a subject.

A **subject** is a general field of knowledge; farming, clothing, business, ecology, and transportation are all subjects. You may know a great deal about the subject of your essay, or you may simply be curious about an area and wish to expand your knowledge of it.

If you are free to choose your own subject, begin by asking yourself these questions: "What do I really care about?" "What am I interested in?" "What do I know something about?" "What do I want to learn about?" Your answers to these questions will provide you with potentially good subjects. Resist the temptation to seize the first subject that comes to mind. Take your time. Review the possibilities, and then pick the one subject that most appeals to you and best suits your audience. (See COMP 2g.)

COMP 2c   Focus on a topic.

A **topic** is the specific aspect of a subject on which the writer focuses. Subjects such as literature, television, and sports are too broad to be dealt with adequately in a short composition. Even books focus on only aspects of these and other subject areas. The writer's task is to select a manageable topic within the chosen or assigned subject area. Thus, if your subject is sports, you might choose as your topic rules violations in college sports recruiting, violence in ice hockey, types of fan behavior, the psychology of marathon runners, or the growth of sports medicine.

In moving from a subject to a particular topic, take into account any length or format constraints and the amount of time you have to write. These are practical considerations that affect the scope of your topic.

The following examples illustrate how to limit a topic:

farming → livestock → cows → dairy cow diseases → parasite control in dairy cows

music → classical → Haydn → symphonies → Haydn's Symphony 101

advertising → TV advertising → TV advertising of food → TV advertising of cereals → TV advertising of high-fiber cereals

Notice that each successive topic is more limited than the one before it. Moving from general to specific, the topics become appropriate for essay-length work.

COMP 2d   Generate ideas and collect information.

Ideas and information lie at the heart of good prose. Ideas grow from information; information (facts and details) supports ideas. To inform and intellectually stimulate your readers, gather as many ideas and as much specific information as you can about your topic. If you try to write before doing so, you run the risk of producing a shallow, boring draft. Good strategies for generating ideas and collecting information—and for beginning to make connections within the body of information you accumulate—include asking questions, brainstorming, clustering, keeping a journal, researching, rehearsing ideas, visualizing your topic, and stimulating your creativity.

Asking questions

Ask questions about your topic to discover areas for exploration and development. The newspaper reporter's 5Ws and an H—*Who?*, *What?*, *Where?*, *When?*, *Why?*, and *How?*—are excellent questions to start with. Also, questions usually give rise to yet more questions. Every set of questions will vary with the topic and with the person formulating them. Here is one sample set for echinacea, a popular medicinal herb:

1. *Who* discovered it?
2. *What* does it look like?
3. *Where* was it discovered?
4. *When* was it discovered?
5. *Why* did it take so long to be discovered?
6. *How* can I get some of it?
   a. How much does it cost?
   b. Are there limitations on how much I can buy?
   c. Who sells it?
   d. Where can I buy it?
   e. Can I resell it?

 C-Tip

Saving key questions

Develop a master file of key questions that you ask yourself at various stages of the writing process: questions about your subject, your topic, various drafts you write, and so forth. Leave several lines between the questions. This way you can copy (and rename) the file each time you begin an assignment, typing in answers and notes as you work and keeping the original for use again. Over time, you will find yourself revising your master file questions as you discover more about your personal writing style.

Brainstorming

If you already know something about your topic, you might begin collecting ideas by **brainstorming,** listing the things you know in no particular order. Freely associate one idea with another; let your mind take you in whatever direction it will. Try not to censor yourself or edit your brainstorming because you simply do not know what will emerge or how valuable it might be in the end. Write quickly. Do not worry about spelling or punctuation; abbreviate. Also, because all your ideas may not occur during one brainstorming session, keep your list over several days, adding new thoughts as they come to you. Here is a typical brainstorming list.

Animal Rights

animals are living beings, too

they have nervous systems so they feel pain

questionable experiments—proving the obvious, duplicative

some medical experiments nec., but only when no alternatives
    are available

computer models instead

also in vitro and membrane tests

Nat. Cancer Inst. reduced its use of animals 95% by using in
    vitro tests

cosmetic companies—Draize eye test

household product testing (lethal dose test for detergents,
    shampoo, etc.)

fur belongs on animals

steel jaw traps—animals chew off legs

dogs/cats caught, too

progress made—legislation against inhumane traps

some cosmetic companies quit using Draize; consumer
    protest

puppy mills

spay/neuter—the answer to pet overpopulation

When you complete your brainstorming list, number or color-code the entries that closely relate to one another. This is *sorting*, the first step in thinking about possible organizational patterns and outlining.

Brainstorming

Brainstorming on a computer stimulates your thinking because it allows you to keep up with your thoughts, especially if you are a fast typist. Moreover, because a computer is a new medium for capturing your thoughts, it may take you down more imaginative paths.

Try brainstorming with your screen switched off or turned down low. Because brainstorming relies on free-association (the presence of one idea suggesting another), some people find that looking at what they have written inhibits rather than stimulates their thinking. If you try this, every so often turn on the screen momentarily to make sure nothing has gone wrong technically and that you are actually capturing your thoughts. When you are done, turn on the screen to see what you have and print it out if you wish.

Clustering

Another strategy for generating ideas and gathering information is **clustering.** Put your topic, or a key word or phrase about your topic, in the center of a sheet of paper and draw a circle around it. (The example on page 9 shows the topic *gun control* in the center.) Draw four or five (or more) lines out from this circle, and jot down main ideas about your topic; draw circles around them. Repeat the process by drawing lines from the secondary circles and adding examples, details, and maybe questions you have. Or you may find yourself pursuing one line of thought through many add-on circles before beginning a new cluster. Do whatever works for you. As with brainstorming, keep writing—do not stop to think about being neat or capitalizing correctly.

Clustering allows you to generate material and sort it into meaningful groupings at the same time. Again, sorting is the first step to outlining.

Public safety

Political assassinations

Link to drugs

Why needed?

Home accidents

"Saturday Night Specials"

Second amendment issue

Argues for better law enforcement

Gun control

NRA Why anti?

Gun industry

Past attempts

Erosion of personal freedoms

Pending legislation

Legislation

Liberals vs. conservatives

1968 Gun Control Act

Brady Bill

Who is Brady?

Provisions of act

Why?

C-Tip

Clustering

If your computer has graphics capability, try clustering on screen. Use balloons, boxes, tree diagrams, and lines to diagram and group your ideas. This can be fun as well as productive.

Keeping a journal

Many people find their best ideas come when they are not actually working on a writing assignment, so they have learned to keep a **journal.** They carry a little notebook to record thoughts and observations, bits of overheard conversation, ironies, insights, and interesting facts and statistics from newspaper and magazine articles.

Freewriting

Journals are also useful for doing **freewriting.** Freewriting is simply writing for a brief uninterrupted period of time—say, five or ten minutes—on anything that comes into your mind. It is a way of getting your mind working and easing into the writing task. Start with a blank sheet of paper or computer screen and write as quickly as you can without stopping for any reason whatsoever. Don't worry about punctuation or spelling. Write as if you were talking to your best friend. If you run dry, don't stop; repeat the last few things you wrote or write, "I have nothing to write" over and over again, and you'll be surprised—writing with more content will begin to emerge. Once you have become comfortable with open-ended freewriting, you can move to more focused freewriting in which you write about a specific aspect of your topic. By freewriting regularly, you will come to feel more natural and comfortable about writing.

Researching

You may sometimes want to supplement what you know about your topic with **research.** This does not necessarily mean formal library work (see LIB). Firsthand observations and interviews with people knowledgeable about your topic are also forms of research and usually more up to date. Whatever your form of research, take careful notes (see RESCH 2c), so you can accurately paraphrase an author or quote interviewees.

Rehearsing ideas

Some writers find it helpful to **rehearse** what they are going to write before committing their thoughts to paper. Simply, rehearsal is running ideas or phrasings, even sentences, through your mind until they are fairly well crafted and then transferring them to paper. The image of the writer, pencil in hand, staring off into space, perhaps best captures the essence of this technique. Rehearsing may suit your personality and the way you think. Moreover, because it is a thoughtful practice, rehearsing may help you generate ideas. Sometimes rehearsing may even be oral. Try taking ten or fifteen minutes to talk your way through your paper with a roommate or friend.

Visualizing topics

Some experts believe that a large part of our thinking is **visual**—done through images. Tapping into those images can be a productive way of developing your ideas. For example, if you wish to describe an ancient pueblo, visualizing one you recently visited in New Mexico can make your task easier. Imagining that pueblo can also lead you to yet more images of what life must have been like there.

Thinking creatively

There are many definitions of **creativity,** but, in one way or another, creativity involves moving beyond what is generally regarded as normal or expected. To push an idea one step further, to make a connection not easily recognized by others, to step to one side of your topic and see it in a new light, to ask a question no one else would, to arrive at a fresh insight is to be creative. Creativity and inspired thinking are within the reach of most writers if they take the writing process seriously and work hard.

COMP 2e   Formulate a thesis statement.

Having generated ideas and information, you are ready to begin organizing your thoughts. At this stage you must commit to a controlling idea, a **thesis.** The thesis of a prose composition is its main idea, the point it is trying to make. The thesis is often expressed in one or two sentences called a **thesis statement:**

> The whole language approach to teaching reading best serves the needs of all children by equipping them with a well-rounded understanding of language and a variety of strategies for decoding it.
> —Michelle Whalen, student

The thesis statement should not be confused with a **purpose statement.** While a thesis statement makes an assertion about your topic, a purpose statement is about what you are trying to do in the paper:

> I plan to explain why the whole language approach to teaching children to read is better than the phonics approach.

A thesis statement should be:

    a. more general than the ideas and facts used to support it,
    b. focused enough to be covered in the space allotted, and
    c. the most important point you make about your topic.

A thesis statement should not be a question but an assertion (see ARGUE 1). If you find yourself writing a question for a thesis statement, answer the question first and then write your statement.

An effective strategy for developing a thesis statement is to begin by writing: *What I want to say is that....*

> *What I want to say is that* unless language barriers between patients and health care providers are bridged many patients' lives in our nation's most culturally diverse cities will be endangered.

Later, you can delete the formulaic opening and you will be left with a thesis statement.

> Unless language barriers between patients and health care providers are bridged many patients' lives in our nation's most culturally diverse cities will be endangered.

The thesis statement is usually set forth near the beginning of the composition, sometimes after a few sentences that establish a context. In the beginning of an essay on the harmful effects of disposable diapers, Lisa Denis builds a context for the last sentence in which she presents her thesis statement:

> Picture yourself having to change a child's diaper. I'll bet you don't see yourself using a cloth diaper and pins. The use of disposable diapers has become the norm in today's fast-paced society. But the fact is we have no idea of the damage they do. Disposable diapers are expensive, potentially harmful to babies, and environmentally unsound; the time has come to put an end to their use.
>
> —Lisa Denis, student

COMP 2f Determine your purpose for writing.

Implied in your thesis statement is your **purpose,** the answer you give the question, "What am I trying to accomplish in this composition?" Being clear about your purpose helps you choose the best supporting details and arrange them in the most effective order. (See PARA 3a.) For example, Lisa Denis ends her paragraph with the thesis statement that it is time to stop using disposable diapers because they are harmful, especially to the environment, a statement she will try to prove in order to persuade her readers. At the editing stage, keeping your purpose in mind helps you use language with an awareness of the effect you want it to have on your readers. (See COMP 4b and WORD 1.)

Generally, nonfiction writing has one of three purposes: (1) to express the writer's thoughts and feelings about a life experience, (2) to inform readers by explaining something about the world around them, or (3) to persuade readers to some belief or action.

Writing from experience

In writing from experience, or writing expressively, you put your thoughts and feelings before all other concerns. When you express yourself about what it felt like to turn eighteen, describe the relationship you have with your father, narrate a camping experience you had with a friend, or share an insight you had about the career you want to pursue, you are writing from experience. The first purpose of expressive writing is, therefore, to clarify life's experiences, and the second purpose is to communicate what you learn to someone else. That is not to say expressive writing is not immensely appealing to readers; the reflections of a thoughtful and sensitive writer illuminate the reader's experiences and clarify his or her own feelings and ideas. Here, for example, are the reflections of a writer on her ambitious nature:

> I've always liked ambitious people, and many of my closest friends have had grandiose dreams. I like such people, not because I am desperate to be buddies with a future secretary of state but because I find ambitious people entertaining, interesting to talk to, and fun to watch. And, of course, I like such people because I am ambitious myself, and I would rather not feel apologetic about it.   —Perri Klass, "Ambition"

Writing to inform

Informative writing focuses on the world outside the writer—the events, people, places, things, and ideas in the *objective* or *real world*. In informative writing you report, explain, analyze, define, classify, compare, describe a process, or get at causes and effects. (See PARA 2b.) Informative writing is the kind most often found in newspaper and magazine articles and nonfiction books. Informative writing encompasses everything from an article on better parenting, your chemistry textbook, and a news update on an approaching hurricane to a senate subcommittee report on housing, a travel guide, and a computer manual.

The following example of informative writing provides useful information about the South:

> To the visitor the South looks uniform and cohesive, but this is misleading. There are many Souths. The Englishness of colonial Virginia plantations is very different from the Spanish flavor of Florida's St. Augustine or the French bouquet of the bayou region of Louisiana.
> —Parke Rouse Jr. "The Old South Way of Life:
> America's Most Colorful Region"

Writing to persuade

In writing to persuade you attempt to influence your reader's thinking and attitudes toward a subject or issue and sometimes move him or her to a particular course of action. Persuasive writing uses logical reasoning and authoritative evidence and testimony, and sometimes emotionally charged language and examples. (See WORD 1b.)

> Physicians and nurses often assume that pain is not a problem unless the patient or family brings it up. If the patient is stoical and trying not to be a "bother," then the pain and unnecessary suffering continue.…
> Not wanting to "bug" the healthcare team is a natural reaction. However, the control of pain contributes to a person's physical and emotional wellbeing. And that is the goal toward which the healthcare team, the patient, and the family are all working.
> —Alexandra Beebe, "The Family:
> Important Participants in Cancer Pain Control"

Most of the writing that you do in college will be informative and some will be persuasive in character; occasionally you may be asked to write from experience. Often you will use some combination of these types of writing in a single composition. For example, as a political science student you may find yourself informing your readers about our foreign policy in Central America, expressing your own beliefs about its effects, telling of an experience you had in Central America, and attempting to persuade your readers that changes are needed.

COMP 2g Analyze your audience.

Having arrived at a thesis statement and decided on your purpose for writing, it is time to consider your **audience** or intended readership. Students often mistakenly assume their instructor is their only audience. Though it is true that your teacher will read your composition, do not forget the other students in your class. They, after all, make up the writing community to which you belong.

Use the following list of questions to identify your audience so that you can make appropriate decisions on content, sentence structure (see SENT 1–7), and word choice (see WORD 1 and 2).

AUDIENCE QUESTIONS

- Who are my readers?
- Is my audience specialized (my chemistry lab partners, other Macintosh computer users) or general (literate adults)?
- What do I know about my audience (age; sex; amount of education; religious, social, economic, and political attitudes)?
- What does my audience know about my subject? What is their knowledge level—expert or novice?
- What does my audience need to know that I can tell them?
- Will my audience have misconceptions that I can clarify?
- What is my relationship to my audience: Boss? Equal? Subordinate?
- How will my audience respond to what I have to say (interested, open-minded, resistant, hostile)?
- Is there any specialized language my audience needs or that I should avoid?
- What do I want my audience to do? How can I help them?
- How should I sound—formal or informal?

The best writers empathize with their readers. They try to see things as their readers might, recognize and understand their problems and address them, and appeal to their emotions, their rational faculties, and their humanity.

COMP 2h Make an outline.

Organize your material so as to present a logical sequence or flow of ideas and provide the strongest support for your thesis statement. Begin by making an informal outline. State your title, purpose, and thesis at the top. List the three parts of your essay—introduction, body, conclusion. Select those ideas from your brainstorming or clustering activities that are essential to your thesis; these will form the body of your essay.

INFORMAL OUTLINE

Title: Signs of the times: Bumper Stickers

Purpose: Informative: to explain the purpose of bumper stickers.

Thesis: Bumper stickers express people's beliefs, interests, and attitudes.

1. Introduction
2. Body--types of bumper stickers arranged in order of increasing social and cultural significance
   a. Advertising on bumper stickers--examples
   b. Humorous bumper stickers--examples
   c. Ethnic and religious statements on bumper stickers--examples
   d. Environmental, political, and social issues on bumper stickers-- examples
3. Conclusion

Following is the formal outline for the Annotated Student Essay in COMP 6. Andy Pellett, a student at the University of Vermont, prepared this outline to submit with his essay.

FORMAL OUTLINE

Title: The Perils of AstroTurf

Purpose: Persuasive: to argue against the use of artificial turf.

Thesis: Artificial turf affects the natural play of the game and causes injuries.

I. Arguments for artificial turf
   A. AstroTurf saves money.
      1. Counterargument: installation costs are high.
      2. Counterargument: artificial turf needs to be replaced more frequently, which further increases costs.
   B. AstroTurf increases traction, especially during inclement weather.
      1. Counterargument: Football and baseball are meant to be played in all kinds of weather.
      2. Counterargument: Fans' satisfaction is increased by seeing their teams playing in inclement weather.

II. Arguments against artificial turf

   A. Artificial turf causes the ball to hop unnaturally, affecting player statistics and game strategy.

   B. Artificial turf causes player injuries.

III. Conclusion: If we stick with real grass, we cannot go wrong.

In writing a formal outline, follow these rules:

1. Include the title, a statement of purpose, and the thesis statement.
2. Write in complete sentences unless your meaning is immediately clear from a phrase.
3. Divide each category into at least two subcategories. The reason for this is simple: you cannot logically divide something into fewer than two parts.
4. Observe the traditional formal outline pattern. Notice how each new level of specificity is given a new letter or number designation.

    I.
     A.
     B.
       1.
       2.
         a.
         b.
           (1)
           (2)
             (a)
             (b)
    II.

 C-Tip

Outlining

Develop a master outline file that can be copied for use with each writing project. Fill it in on the screen. Having a master file assures correct outline form (roman numerals, letters, and numerals), and using a word processor makes it easy to revise your outline during the writing process—adding, deleting, and rearranging ideas as you develop your composition, all without the chore of retyping each time.

COMP 3

Writing a Draft

Sometimes we are so eager to get on with the actual writing that we begin before we are ready, and the results are disappointing. Before beginning to write, therefore, ask yourself, "Am I ready to write? Is there a point to what I'm trying to say?" If you have done a thorough job of gathering ideas and information, if you feel you can accomplish the purpose of your paper, and if you are comfortable with your organizational plan, your answer will be "yes."

If, however, you feel uneasy, review the steps in the planning stage to get at the cause of your uneasiness. Do you need to gather more information? Sharpen your thesis? Rethink your purpose? Refine your organization? Now is the time to engage in critical thinking, to evaluate and clarify your writing plan. Time spent at this juncture is time well spent, and although it may not exactly feel as if you are making progress, you are making critical decisions that will affect the outcome of your composition.

COMP 3a   Choose a good title.

When you write your title is a matter of preference. Some people like to write it first, using it as a banner to guide the rest of the writing. Others prefer to write it last, after they have seen the final development of their ideas. Either way, when you decide to write your title, instead of trying to create *the* best one, brainstorm about a half dozen so you can choose among them.

A good title announces your subject and prepares your reader for the approach you take. For example, "Why We Crave Horror Movies" by Stephen King is an essay that delivers what its title promises: it explains what for many people is a difficult phenomenon to understand. A good title also hooks your reader. It sets up a question that makes your reader want to read on for an answer. Some titles, such as "Cholesterol" or "The Campus Bookstore" are merely labels. They are not bad, but they do not grab the reader's interest the way these titles do: "Never Get Sick in July" (why is July worse than other months?); "When Television Is a School for Criminals" (do criminals get ideas by watching television?).

C-Tip

Capturing titles

As you work on your composition, titles will occur to you. Do not lose your good ideas. Designate an area at the beginning or end of your file and label it "Title Ideas," so that when a good idea comes along, you can quickly move to that area of the file and type it in. Then, when it comes time to decide on a title, you will have some possibilities and will not have to start from scratch.

COMP 3b   Write the body of your composition.

In writing a draft, your main concern is to get your ideas down on paper. To a certain extent, let the topic take you where it will. Keep writing and do not be overly concerned about the exact wording or whether you punctuate correctly; concentrate on producing a lively flow of ideas and information. Be alert to new ideas about your topic, ideas that are fresh and potentially fruitful. You will revise and edit later.

Try writing the body of your paper in two stages. First, concentrate on the paragraphs and look at each individually. Do you provide enough details and examples? Second, look at the paragraphs as a group. Do the paragraphs work together as a unit? Do you need transitions to connect the individual parts logically and make them flow smoothly?

As you write the draft, be mindful of your outline but do not become a slave to it. You may find yourself departing from the outline

C-Tip

Triple-spacing for revision

If you triple-space between lines, you can easily make handwritten revisions on a printout (hard copy). Carry your hard copy with you to read at odd moments; sometimes when you are relaxed and not feeling pressed to produce, you will get new insights into your topic. Before printing out a final copy, type changes, reformat, and double-space your file.

because you discover something new about your subject through writing about it. Let this happen, but make an "X" or a note in the margin indicating that you may be deviating from your plan. These notes will remind you of what you were thinking as you wrote and allow you to reconsider those thoughts in revising.

COMP 3c Pay special attention to your beginning and ending.

No matter how you attract your reader's attention—with an anecdote, startling fact, pertinent question—your introduction should clearly relate to your thesis. For this reason, even though the temptation is to get it just right from the outset so you feel you are off to a good start, you may find it best to draft a workable beginning and then revise it after you have written and revised the body of your composition. When the body is in final form, you may have an even better idea how to introduce it to your readers.

A good conclusion does more than indicate the end of your composition. You may use it to inspire your reader to some action or new way of thinking, or you may want to drive home a point you made in your introduction by giving another particularly apt example or by repeating a key word or phrase to remind the reader of where you began your composition. You may also use your conclusion to summarize what you have written, but never in a mechanical way and not with such expressions as *In summary, In conclusion,* or *As you can see.*

See the essays on pages 1–2 and 28–31 of this section for examples of good beginnings and endings.

COMP 4

Revising

When you have finished writing your draft, give it an honest appraisal. Focus on the large issues of thesis, purpose, content, organization, and paragraph structure that affect your entire composition. It would be counterproductive to look at grammar and punctuation, for example, if the elements that make an essay "go" need work. Suppose you inherit an old car. Anyone can see that it badly needs a new paint job, but should you spend the money to have the work done if you do not know whether the car runs? What if you discover after you have invested in a paint job that the engine needs extensive repairs or, worse yet, is not worth fixing at all? So it is with writing. First you **revise**—work on the large issues that clarify your purpose and improve your organization—and then you **edit**—check for correctness and style.

No one—*no one*—produces perfect prose on the first draft. As economist John Kenneth Galbraith once wrote about his writing, "there are days when the result is so bad that no fewer than five revisions are required. In contrast, when I am greatly inspired, only four revisions are required."

COMP 4a Revise the largest elements of your composition first.

Revision is best done by asking yourself questions about what you have written. Otherwise, you can stare at a draft for a good long time, wondering what you should be looking for. Begin by reading, preferably aloud, what you have written. Reading aloud forces you to pay attention to every single word; you are more likely to catch lapses in the logical flow of thought. Then ask yourself the questions in the Checklist for Revising Large Elements, using the cross-referenced sections for help.

Checklist for Revising Large Elements

1. Is my topic well focused? (See COMP 2c.)
2. Does my thesis statement clearly identify my topic and make an assertion about it? (See COMP 2e.)
3. Is my organizational pattern the best one given my purpose? Have I tried alternative patterns of organization? (See COMP 2h.)
4. Are my paragraphs effective? Do my topic sentences relate to my thesis? Do they support my thesis? (See PARA 1 and 3.)
5. Do I have enough supporting details, and are my examples well chosen to support my thesis? (See PARA 2b.)
6. Do I accomplish my purpose? (See COMP 2f.)
7. How effective is my beginning? Ending? (See COMP 3c.)
8. Do I have a good title? (See COMP 3a.)

In answering these questions you may discover that parts of your paper bear little or no relationship to your thesis and purpose. You may need to rearrange your examples for greater impact. Or perhaps you need a transition between paragraphs. All this is good. Revision is a process, and effective writing is the result of thoughtful revision.

COMP 4b   Revise your sentences and diction.

Having revised the largest elements of your composition, turn next to the sentences themselves. Again, the best approach is to ask yourself specific questions. Use the Checklist for Revising Sentences.

Checklist for Revising Sentences

1. Do my sentences convey my thoughts clearly? (See SENT 2 and 4.)
2. Do I subordinate less important ideas to more important ones? (See SENT 5.)
3. Do my sentences emphasize the most important part of the thought? (See SENT 6.)
4. Are they varied? (See SENT 7.)
5. Are my sentences complete sentences? Have I unintentionally written any sentence fragments? (See EDIT 5.)
6. Are any of my sentences comma splices or run-ons? (See EDIT 6.)

You may find that some of your sentences are long and rambling and that others are short and choppy, giving the impression that your thoughts are disconnected. Perhaps you shifted focus within some sentences or used the same sentence pattern throughout most of your composition. Sentence problems like these may drive you to reconsider paragraphs you previously thought were effective. Again, all this is good. Writing is recursive, moving back and forth between larger and smaller elements and among the various stages.

C-Tip

Saving material

You never know when sections of text (more than a few phrases or sentences), references, or quotations you wish to delete from a draft may later prove useful, sometimes even after you have completed an assignment. Block off the material you want to delete, and move it to the end of your file in a section labeled "Supplementary Material." When you are finished writing, print only up to that point, saving the file with the supplementary material intact.

Now look at your **diction** or use of words. Do you use the word *tedious* when you mean *dull*? Do you use *man* when you mean *human*? Do you use three words when one would do? To revise for diction, ask yourself the questions in the Checklist for Revising Diction, using the cross-referenced sections for help.

Checklist for Revising Diction

1. Is my diction exact, with each word meaning precisely what I think it does? (See WORD 1, 5, and 6.)
2. Do I engage my reader with concrete nouns and strong action verbs? (See WORD 1c.)
3. Do I use appropriate language, avoiding slang, regional language, pompous language, and doublespeak? (See WORD 2.)
4. Is my language unbiased? (See WORD 3.)
5. Is my writing fresh and forceful or burdened by unnecessary words? (See WORD 4.)
6. Have I committed any usage errors? (See WORD 7)

Following is the next-to-final draft of Andy Pellett's opening paragraph of the Annotated Student Essay in COMP 6. It shows how he revised his sentences and diction.

> As a sports fan, ⟨*purist and a*⟩ ~~who thinks of himself as a sports purist,~~ I am ~~wary~~ ⟨*suspicious*⟩
> of changes ~~that occur~~ in ⟨*my favorite*⟩ pastimes ~~that I love~~, namely, baseball and
> football, ~~and~~ ⟨*I*⟩ in the past two decades, there have been many new
> developments—⟨*S*⟩ome ~~of these have been~~ good and some ~~not so good~~ ⟨*bad.*⟩
> ⟨*But t*⟩ ~~The~~ most disturbing change ~~I have seen, however, has been~~ ⟨*is*⟩ the ~~use~~ ⟨*introduction*⟩
> of artificial turf as a surface ⟨*playing*⟩ ~~on which to play~~ because it makes the
> games unnatural and causes injuries.

Some aspects of editing allow for personal choice. Another writer, for example, might have changed the opening of the first sentence to *As a sports fan who is also a purist*. Both revisions solve the problem of wordiness. Certain revision changes, however, are questions of correctness and thus are not open to choice. These are questions of grammar, punctuation, and mechanics (capitalization and spelling).

COMP 4c   Conduct peer conferences

An excellent way to improve your essay is to discuss it with a fellow student or friend in a conference. In turn, you can sharpen your critical skills by reading for a classmate.

Observe the following guidelines if you are critiquing someone's work:

- When the writer gives you a copy of the paper, set aside the time to read it. Make notes right on the paper to refer to during the conference.
- Be sure you understand the essay. Read it carefully. If you are confused, ask yourself if the problem is in the essay or whether you're missing something.
- At the beginning of the conference, ask the writer to briefly state the purpose of the essay and point out the thesis statement. If you and the writer disagree, discuss possible reasons.
- Rather than dictating changes, ask questions that lead the writer to reconsider parts of the draft.
- Ask the most important questions first so that if time is limited, you can be the most help in the shortest time. For example, tackle problems with purpose and thesis before discussing transitions or a particular word choice.
- Be supportive. The way you word your comments is as important as the comments themselves (not "This is a dumb example" but "This example is not as good as the others"). At the same time, you should be honest or you won't be much help.

As the writer of an essay that is being critiqued, follow these guidelines:

- Give a copy of your paper to your reviewer in advance of your meeting.
- As the conference proceeds, take brief notes on your own copy of your paper ("rephrase thesis statement," "clarify paragraph 3," "consider reworking title").
- Be attentive and listen carefully. Don't waste time arguing over issues. Take everything in and evaluate comments later.
- If your reader misunderstands something, ask why—don't just explain what you meant. Trying to understand your reader's point of view will help you rewrite more clearly.
- Consider all your reader's comments carefully, but make only the changes that you agree with. Retain ownership of your work.
- Show your appreciation for the time your reader took to help you improve your work. ("Thanks, I found this session worthwhile.")

COMP 5

Editing

Having revised your paper, you are now ready to edit it. In other words, having made it right, you now want to make it correct.

COMP 5a When you edit, check grammar, punctuation, and mechanics (capitalization and spelling).

Editing errors creep into your composition in two ways. First, there are the inadvertent errors. You know how to capitalize proper nouns, but rushing to get down your thoughts you write *spanish* instead of *Spanish.*

Second, there are genuine errors—mistakes you make because you don't know better. The best way to catch errors of this sort is to know yourself as a writer, and to take seriously the feedback you get from friends and teachers, and to use your *Handbook.* If you have trouble remembering which punctuation goes inside quotation marks and which does not, you are on your way to correcting the error. Simply check your *Handbook* during editing. For easy access to the information you need, use the tab indicators, the table of contents, or the index.

The more you know yourself as a writer, the more you will develop a sense of what does not seem to sound or look quite right. Which is correct, *none are* or *none is?* Is *receive* spelled *ei* or *ie?* Turn to the appropriate section of the *Handbook* for the answer.

COMP 5b Prepare the final copy.

Having revised and edited your work, you are ready to prepare the final copy of your composition. Consult FORMAT 1 and 2 for details. The sample essay in COMP 6 shows what your final draft should look like.

COMP 5c Proofread the final copy.

Always proofread thoroughly. You don't want to use *there* when you want *their.* Many such seemingly small matters add up. If you are aware that you frequently make particular kinds of errors (in comma usage or subject–verb agreement, for instance), read your manuscript once for each problem.

Use the Checklist for Proofreading to ask questions as you proof-read your composition.

Checklist for Proofreading

1. Did my manuscript print out as I expected it to? Is it properly line-spaced? Is all the text legible?
2. Have I left out words or unnecessarily repeated words or phrases? Have I overlooked any errors in grammar or punctuation?
3. Have I misspelled or mistyped any words? Has my spell-checker approved a properly spelled word but not the word I need? (See MECH 6, C-Tip: Spell-Checker, p. 235.)
4. Will I need to reprint my composition, or will my instructor allow me to handwrite minor corrections?

Check for spelling slips by reading lines of your manuscript backward. This allows you to read the words out of context and to view them separately, so your eye picks up errors you ordinarily pass over when reading for content.

Finally, it is a good idea to keep your notes and early drafts along with a copy of your submitted manuscript until your graded assignment is returned.

COMP 6

Annotated Student Essay

Student Andy Pellett was asked to write an argument on a topic of his own choosing. He knew from past experience that to write a good paper he should write about something he cares about. He also knew that he should allow himself a reasonable amount of time to find such a topic and gather his ideas. An avid sports fan, Andy decided to write about some aspect of sports. He considered and rejected several possibilities—including professional salaries, Olympic basketball teams, and sports heroes in advertising—before deciding that his topic would be artificial playing surfaces. From what he had read in the popular press and from his own observations, Andy disliked artificial playing surfaces, and he thought he could develop his essay on the thesis that such surfaces are bad for athletes and sports. His purpose would be to argue against their use.

Having focused on a topic, Andy began brainstorming on his computer for ideas, facts, examples, arguments, and counterarguments —anything that came to mind. When he felt he had amassed enough information, he began to sort it out. He saw that his material essentially broke down into two categories, pro and con. So, in making a rough outline of an organizational pattern, he decided to demonstrate first the weaknesses of the arguments put forth in favor of artificial turf and then present his own strong arguments against the use of artificial turf.

Andy was ready to write his first draft. He wrote quickly, keeping his organizational plan in mind but aiming primarily to get his thoughts down on paper. Now, with something drafted, he was in a position to assess how it could be improved. In reading his first draft, Andy realized he had failed to mention an important objection to artificial turf (the high cost of installation and replacement). He saw that his second and third paragraphs were really on the same topic, so he combined them. He also found places where phrases could be added to make his meaning clearer. Finally, he rearranged the sentences in his fifth paragraph and decided to wait until the very end to bring up his argument about injuries.

Next, Andy turned to his title. He wanted a title that would arouse curiosity, that would make people want to read what he had to say. He checked the list of titles he had begun building when he first started his paper and chose "The Perils of AstroTurf." He also put a lot of thought into the way his essay began and concluded. He was happy with his beginning but decided to lighten his ending by adding a comment made by Richie Allen.

When he was satisfied with his revisions, Andy began to edit. He referred to his *Handbook* to delete several vague words that had crept into his essay and to fix subject–verb agreement and comma-splice problems. Before printing a final copy, Andy proofread his paper and then used his spelling/typing checker (see MECH 6, C-Tip: Spell-Checker, p. 235).

The final draft of Andy's paper appears on the following pages. We have annotated it to highlight features that may be helpful to you as a writer. The paper may not be perfect, but Andy can be proud of learning how the steps in the composing process work. He now knows how to move systematically from large conceptual issues down to smaller technical matters, saving him time and frustration. No longer does he wonder where to start and what to do next. With more practice, Andy will make the process, if not always quicker and easier, at least more familiar and rewarding.

Pellett 1

Title: Indicates the main idea of the essay in a catchy way.

The Perils of AstroTurf

Andy Pellett

As a purist and a sports fan, I am suspicious of changes in my favorite pastimes, namely, baseball and football. In the past two decades, there have been many new developments--some good and some bad. But the

Thesis statement: Sets up a clear expectation ⟶ in the reader's mind.

most disturbing change is the introduction of artificial turf as a playing surface, because it makes the games unnatural and causes injuries.

Diction: Changing *artificial turf* to *fake grass* is calculated (no one likes "fake" things).

This fake grass first appeared on the sporting scene in 1966. The grass in the Houston Astrodome was dying, so in desperation owners replaced it with artificial turf. This new surface, manufactured by the Monsanto Company, was appropriately called AstroTurf. Since then, the living grass

Audience: Andy provides background information for his general audience.

in the stadiums and playing fields everywhere has been replaced with one form of artificial turf or another, usually made of green nylon fibers stitched over a cushioned polyester mat. AstroTurf is still the most common.

What's so great about artificial turf? If real grass was good enough for the sports heroes of yesteryear, why shouldn't it be good enough for those of today? The

Organization: ⟶ Andy announces two basic arguments.

proponents of artificial turf have at least two basic arguments.

The first argument uses a familiar line of reasoning: artificial turf saves money. The field needs less maintenance, and rain water drains easily through small holes in the mat. Also, the field can be used for more than one sport. A football game won't tear up the turf, making it possible to play a baseball game on the same field a day later.

This argument, however, overlooks several important problems. The cost of laying down a new synthetic field is very high--close to a million dollars. In addition, artificial turf deteriorates in appearance and condition. Tobacco juice spit onto the ground soaks in; on AstroTurf it makes an ugly stain that gives groundskeepers fits. In 1971, the artificial turf in Miami's Orange Bowl was decoratively painted for the Super Bowl. After the game, the paint couldn't be removed and remained on the field for months. For these and other reasons, older fake fields may have to be resurfaced. Such resurfacing increases, not decreases, the cost of field maintenance.

The second argument proponents of AstroTurf make is that traction is increased by artificial turf, thereby making it easier to play in inclement weather. But why should we make it easier to play in bad weather? A game like football is a tough sport, and playing in horrible conditions exemplifies that toughness. Most fans enjoy watching two football teams battle it out, with mud covering every part of their uniforms. Baseball, like football, was meant to be played outside on the grass, and, if we take the natural element out of the sport, we lose a sense of drama.

Transition: The use of *however* sets up Andy's refutation.

Paragraph development: Andy supports his argument with specific examples.

Pellett 3

Organization:
Transitional paragraph bridges the two halves of Andy's composition; it looks back, re-stating that the arguments for AstroTurf are weak, and ahead, promising two strong arguments against it.

It is evident that arguments in favor of artificial turf ignore some important facts. Furthermore, these arguments appear even weaker when compared to the arguments put forth by the detractors of AstroTurf. Opponents of artificial turf make essentially two arguments: artificial turf causes the ball to hop unnaturally, which affects team statistics and strategy, and artificial turf causes injuries to players.

Diction: Figurative language (a simile) creates a vivid image to drive home how artificial turf makes the whole game artificial.

In the major leagues the baseball diamond has been turned into a basketball court by the hard surface. The ball rockets off the turf as if being fired from a cannon. It rolls faster and farther than on natural grass, allowing for more extra-base hits.

Dialog: Speech makes the debate more realistic and captures the reader's attention with its unexpected use in a straight prose piece.

"Great," some fans will say. "We like to see more offense." But a baseball player's performance is measured by statistics. So it really isn't fair for a weak hitter to acquire more extra-base hits just because he plays on artificial turf. Strategy is also affected. An outfielder must play back to prevent the ball from caroming over his head. This allows cheap bloop singles that ordinarily would be caught. And what about when the batter grounds the ball into the turf in front of home plate? Normally this play should be an out; but by the time the ball comes down, the batter is standing on first with a "Monsanto single."

Organization:
Andy ends with player injuries because he feels it is his strongest argument.

The other problem with AstroTurf is injuries. Athletes have complained that artificial turf is responsible for everything from friction burns to broken bones. Because of

Pellett 4

the hard surface, athletes must make adaptations in their running style, which can often result in painful foot ailments. Also, the increased traction of AstroTurf means that when a player plants his foot, it won't slide at all. Therefore, if a player is in an awkward position with his feet planted and he gets hit, serious knee injuries can result. Billy Sims of the Detroit Lions blamed his season-ending knee injury on the artificial turf. Years ago, Gale Sayers blamed artificial turf for delaying his comeback from a knee injury.

Paragraph development: Andy has specific examples to support his point.

My fervent, yet probably unrealistic, hope is that artificial turf will be banned. There never was any controversy when real grass was the only surface on which outdoor games were played. If we stick with natural substances, we can't go wrong. Trying to improve on nature only causes trouble. Richie Allen, a former baseball player, probably said it best: "If my horse can't eat it, I don't want to play on it."

Conclusion: A natural outgrowth of the arguments against artificial turf.

para

Paragraphs

Learning Objectives

After reading this section, you should:

- understand what makes a paragraph unified;
- be able to use various strategies to develop your ideas;
- know different ways of achieving coherence within and between paragraphs.

Paragraphs

In many ways the paragraph is an essay in miniature. The paragraph has a topic sentence that states the main idea of the paragraph in the same way that the thesis statement presents the main point of the essay. Like the well-written essay, the well-written paragraph is *unified* —all sentences relate to the main idea (PARA 1); it is well *developed*— there is representative and sufficient supporting detail (PARA 2); and it is *coherent*—ideas and sentences flow logically and smoothly (PARA 3).

The following paragraph on the life cycle of neighborhoods by student Kevin Cunningham is an example of a well-written paragraph.

> Neighborhoods are often assigned human characteristics, one of which is a life cycle: they have a birth, a youth, a middle age, and an old age. A neighborhood is built and settled by young, vibrant people, proud of their sturdy new homes. Together, residents and houses mature as families grow larger and additions get built on. Eventually, though, the neighborhood begins to show its age. Buildings sag a little, houses aren't repaired as quickly, and maintenance slips. The neighborhood may grow poorer as the young and upwardly mobile find new jobs and move away, while the older and less successful inhabitants remain. —Kevin Cunningham, student

Cunningham provides a clear topic sentence that explains what he means by a life cycle. He then goes on to describe the stages of that cycle and the process by which one stage leads to the next. Cunningham maintains unity by excluding anything that does not directly relate to the concept of the life cycle. He achieves coherence by ordering his sentences to flow smoothly without breaks in rhythm or meaning and by using transitional words (*and, as, eventually, while*).

PARA 1

Unity

In a unified paragraph all sentences relate to the topic sentence by explaining it with supporting details. You should eliminate all sentences that stray from the point of the topic sentence.

PARA 1a Write a topic sentence.

The **topic sentence** presents the main idea of the paragraph. It is also called the *controlling idea* because it limits the subject of the paragraph and, like the thesis statement, suggests ways of developing the thought. The topic sentence of each paragraph should be an outgrowth of the essay's thesis statement. (See COMP 2e.)

TOPIC SENTENCE	IMPLIED STRATEGY OF DEVELOPMENT
There were three classes of people in medieval society.	You will *name* the three classes and *describe* each one.
What is a "best friend"?	You will *define* "best friend."
After the Civil War, America was not the same country it had been before.	You will *contrast* life in America before and after the Civil War.

Usually, the topic sentence appears at or near the beginning of the paragraph; this way, you let your reader know the direction of thought and function of the other sentences in the paragraph. The topic sentence may, however, come anywhere in the paragraph, particularly if you want to create a special effect.

In the following paragraph, the topic sentence (shown in italics) comes first, and the anecdote that follows illustrates how bees astonish us.

> *Bees are filled with astonishments, confounding anyone who studies them, producing volumes of anecdotes.* A lady of our acquaintance visited her sister, who raised honeybees in northern California. They left their car on a side road, suited up in protective gear, and walked across the fields to have a look at the hives. For reasons unknown, the bees were in a furious mood that afternoon, attacking in platoons, settling on them from all sides. Let us walk away slowly, advised the beekeeper sister, they'll give it up sooner or later. They walked until bee-free, then circled the fields and went back to the car, and found bees there, waiting for them.   —Lewis Thomas, "Clever Animals"

The topic sentence may be most effective at the end of the paragraph, when the writer wishes to create a sense of drama or suspense or when, as in the following paragraph, the main idea is introduced by a convincing example.

> Chicken soup or beef soup. Which is masculine and which is feminine? In English, neither chicken nor beef soup has formal gender. Yet most people find the question easy to answer: chicken soup is feminine and beef soup is masculine, and that unanimity demonstrates how vast

is the task of stamping out sexist words. *That effort, while constructive, remains superficial; deep within the language lurks the powerful force of Hidden Gender.*
—Jack Rosenthal, "Gender Benders"

Topic sentences are explicitly stated in most paragraphs, but on occasion, particularly in narrative or descriptive paragraphs, a writer may merely *imply* a controlling idea. In the following paragraph, the writer carefully chooses details that will lead the reader to arrive at the main idea without the writer's having to state it specifically. Leading the reader along until the point *dawns* on him or her can often have a much greater impact than a straightforward statement.

> You are standing on the threshold of time in as sacred a place as any in the world. It's where the life of the land and the life of the water converge in biological blur. These are the wetlands—the swamps and the mudflats that sometimes smell like rotten eggs. These are the marshes, clogged with weeds, swarming with bugs, teeming with beautiful life. This is where the moon moves the water in shallow ebbs and floods; where the sun pierces down to the ooze and the nutrients flow in a strange and marvelous way. Nowhere else except here in these sopping grounds is there so much life in so much concentration. But the life is dwindling. And as these lands start to go—you do, too.
> —Sierra Club, "Threshold of Time"

Through cumulative detail that strongly appeals to the senses, this writer conveys the controlling idea that marshes and wetlands are fascinating and ecologically important, and people ought to be concerned about them. The controlling idea is conveyed even though it is not explicitly stated.

C-Tip

Boldfacing topic sentences

To check for unity and coherence while drafting your paragraphs, boldface or underline the topic sentence in each of your paragraphs. By calling special attention to each topic sentence, you see how the other sentences in the paragraph relate to the topic sentence and to each other.

PARA 1b　Relate all sentences to the controlling idea.

A paragraph is unified when all its sentences develop, or expand on, the central idea in some way. No sentence is off the topic. In the following student paragraph by Nancy Shafran, the sentences that violate paragraph unity are italicized.

> NONUNIFIED
>
> When I was growing up, one of the places I enjoyed most was the cherry tree in the back yard. *Behind the yard was an alley and then more houses.* Every summer when the cherries began to ripen, I used to spend hours high in the tree, picking and eating the sweet, sun-warmed cherries. *My mother always worried about my falling out of the tree, but I never did.* But I had some competition for the cherries—flocks of birds that enjoyed them as much as I did and would perch all over the tree, devouring the fruit whenever I wasn't there. I used to wonder why the grown-ups never ate any of the cherries; but actually, when the birds and I had finished, there weren't many left.　　　　—Nancy Shafran, student

In contrast, every sentence in the following paragraph develops the topic sentence; it is a unified paragraph.

> UNIFIED
>
> My husband and I often joke that the reason we have stayed married for so long is that we continually mystify each other with responses and attitudes that are plainly due to our different backgrounds. For years I frustrated him with unpredictable silences and accusing looks. I felt a great reluctance to tell him what I wanted or what needed to be done in the home. I was inwardly furious that I was being put into the position of having to *tell* him what to do. I felt my femaleness, in the Japanese sense, was being degraded. I did not want to be the authority. That would be humiliating for him and for me. He, on the other hand, considering the home to be under my dominion, in the American sense, did not dare to impose on me what he wanted. He wanted me to tell him or make a list, like his parents did in his home.
> 　　　　—Jeanne Wakatsuki Houston, "Living in Two Cultures"

The plan of the paragraph is clear: Houston's first sentence states her belief that culture shapes our attitudes and our responses. Then she gives reasons:

1. She could not talk to her husband, so she remained silent and gave accusing looks.
2. She did not want the authority of having to tell him what to do.
3. Her femaleness, in the Japanese sense, was threatened by his attitude.

4. He considered, in the American sense, that the woman ran the house.
5. He did not want to impinge on her role.
6. He wanted to be told what to do or be given a list.

Testing for unity

If you think that there are sentences in any of your paragraphs that may be extraneous and might be eliminated, block them off, move them out of the paragraph, and read the new paragraph. If the paragraph is tight, with no gaps in logic, eliminate the sentences permanently.

PARA 2

Development

Whether it is first or last or someplace in the middle, whether it is explicitly stated or merely implied, the topic sentence is the point of departure for writing an effective paragraph. How you **develop**—clarify and support—your topic sentence depends on how you answer the question, "Why or how is this so?" Consider, for example, the following topic sentence:

Neat people are especially vicious with mail.

Applying the question, "Why or how is this so?" suggests a strategy for development: the writer needs to tell how "neat people are vicious with mail."

> *Neat people are especially vicious with mail.* They never go through their mail unless they are standing directly over a trash can. If the trash can is beside the mailbox, even better. All ads, catalogs, pleas for charitable contributions, church bulletins, and money-saving coupons go straight into the trash can without being opened. All letters from home, postcards from Europe, bills and paychecks are opened, immediately responded to, then dropped in the trash can. Neat people keep their receipts only for tax purposes. That's it. No sentimental salvaging of birthday cards or the last letter a dying relative ever wrote. Into the trash it goes. —Suzanne Britt, "Neat People vs. Sloppy People"

PARA 2a Develop paragraphs fully.

In expository prose (prose that explains), a paragraph is typically 100–150 words. Longer paragraphs appear in professional journals that discuss new or highly complex information requiring in-depth explanation and evidence. Paragraphs are shorter in newspapers and magazines where the print column is narrow and needs to be broken more often and where the subject matter is less demanding of the reader.

Occasionally a paragraph is too long and needs to be divided or restructured for clarity. The more common problem is the underdeveloped paragraph that leaves the reader wanting more information. To be sure you have provided enough information to enlighten and convince the reader—and thus communicate all you intend—ask a friend to read your composition and point out anything that is not explained clearly or fully enough.

A paragraph may be only a sentence or two long and still be well developed. Such paragraphs often function as transitions from one section of a composition to another. Sometimes, too, as in the following example, a very short paragraph is used to emphasize a point.

> Then Mr. Hoover, running for reelection with a weary momentum, came up with another beauty. He said grass would grow in the streets if Roosevelt were elected. He should have looked. Grass was already growing in the streets. Farmers dumped milk, burned crops to keep prices from collapsing. Armed neighbors guarded homes against mortgage-foreclosing sheriffs. Grass was growing not only in the streets but between the rusting tracks of factory railroad sidings.
>
> There wasn't much doubt of the election's outcome. In Dizzy Dean's immortal words, Franklin D. Roosevelt slud home.
>
> —John Steinbeck, *A Primer on the Thirties*

In his next paragraph, one of normal length, Steinbeck continues by discussing Roosevelt's presidency.

PARA 2b Use the strategy implied in your topic sentence to develop your paragraph.

Narration

To **narrate** is to tell what happened. Because narration is storytelling, it usually follows a chronological pattern, as in the following example. However, the sequence of events can be rearranged for special effect. (See PARA 3a.)

The angel of the candy counter had found me out at last, and was exacting excruciating penance for the stolen Milky Ways, Mounds, Mr. Goodbars and Hersheys with Almonds. I had two cavities that were rotten to the gums. The pain was beyond the bailiwick of crushed aspirins or oil of cloves. Only one thing could help me, so I prayed earnestly that I be allowed to sit under the house and have the building collapse on my left jaw. Since there was no Negro dentist in Stamps, nor doctor either, for that matter, Momma had dealt with previous toothaches by pulling them out (a string tied to the tooth with the other looped over her fist), pain killers and prayer. In this particular instance the medicine had proved ineffective; there wasn't enough enamel left to hook a string on, and the prayers were being ignored because the Balancing Angel was blocking their passage.

—Maya Angelou, "Momma, the Dentist, and Me"

Description

To **describe** is to create a verbal picture of a person, place, thing, or even a mood or idea. Description relies on specific and concrete details to create sensory impressions for the reader. (See WORD 1c and PARA 3a, Spatial Order.) In the following paragraph the author describes her father.

He was a tall, crooked-tooth, curly-haired man, who smelled of Lucky Strikes and St. Johns Bay Rum shaving lotion. He was the only father who wore penny loafers on business trips, a Mousketeer hat to pick up my brother on his first movie date, and had the delicious gall to invite the richest girl in my class (she had her own pool but an exclusive number of invitations) to come on over to the house ("When you're free, of course") and watch our lawn sprinklers.

—Phyllis Theroux, "My Father, the Prince"

Exemplification

One of the best ways to convince a reader of the validity of a generalization in the topic sentence is to provide **examples**—specific instances of what you are talking about. In the following paragraph, Teale enumerates eleven superstitions to support the generalization in his topic sentence—that country people have many superstitious ways of predicting what kind of winter it will be.

In the folklore of the country, numerous superstitions relate to winter weather. Back-country farmers examine their husks—the thicker the husk, the colder the winter. They watch the acorn crop—the more acorns, the more severe the season. They observe where white-faced hornets place their paper nests—the higher they are, the deeper will be the snow. They examine the size and shape and color of the spleens of butchered hogs for clues to the severity of the season. They keep track of the blooming of the dogwood in the spring—the more abundant the blooms, the more bitter the cold in January. When chipmunks carry their tails high and squirrels have heavier fur, the superstitious gird themselves for a long, hard winter. Without any scientific basis, a wider-than-usual black band on a woolly-bear caterpillar is accepted as a sign that winter will arrive early and stay late. Even the way a cat sits beside the stove carries its message to the credulous. According to a belief once widely held in the Ozarks, a cat sitting with its tail to the fire indicates very cold weather is on the way.   —Edwin Way Teale, "Wandering through Winter"

Sometimes a single, extended example is more effective.

I have always wondered why my best friends were so important to me; but it wasn't until recently that something happened to make me really understand my relationship with my best friends. My father died, and this was a crisis for me. Most of my friends gave me their condolences. But my best friends did more than that: they actually supported me. They called long distance to see how I was and what I needed, to try to help me work out my problems or simply to talk. Two of my best friends even took time from their spring break and, along with two other best friends, attended my father's memorial service; none of my other friends came. Since then, these are the only people who have continued to worry about me and talk about my father. I know that whenever I need someone, they will be there and willing to help me. I know also that whenever they need help, I will be ready to do the same for them.   —Howard Solomon Jr., student

Facts, statistics, reasons

A **fact** is a piece of information with objective reality. **Statistics** are numerical facts. A **reason** is a statement offered as a logical explanation or justification. Facts, statistics, and reasons can be used singly or in combination, as in the following example.

The whale is the most astonishing animal the earth has ever known. It does not merely inspire superlatives—it is a living superlative. Some whales are much larger than the gigantic dinosaurs of the Mesozoic. It would take 25 elephants, or 2,000 human beings, to equal the weight of a single blue whale; its tongue alone weighs as much as an elephant. The blue whale is as long as four buses placed end to end. The skeleton weighs 18 tons, its blubber 30, its meat 44. When it blows at the ocean's surface, the spout looks for all the world like a new cloud in the sky.
            —Jacques-Yves Cousteau and Yves Paccalet, *The Assault on Whales*

Definition

Depending on your audience, or sometimes your subject, you may need to **define** key words in your composition. Sometimes this can be done in a sentence or two, or even parenthetically. Occasionally you may want to provide an extended definition (as in the example that follows). To define a term, first place it in a class of similar items and then show how it is different from the others in that class. For example, a *wrist watch* is in the class of *devices for telling time* and is differentiated from other items in this class because it is relatively small and *worn on the wrist*.

Disorder, alas, is the natural order of things in the universe. There is even a precise measure of the amount of disorder, called entropy. Unlike almost every other physical property (motion, gravity, energy), entropy does not work both ways. It can only increase. Once it's created it can never be destroyed. The road to disorder is a one-way street.

—K.C. Cole, "Entropy"

Process analysis

There are two types of process analyses: *informational* and *instructional.* **Informational process analysis** explains how something works—how blood moves through the circulatory system or how tides occur. The following explanation of how champagne was first made and how it has been made ever since is informational.

The next time you find an excuse to break open a bottle of champagne—be it New Year's, a wedding, or a whim—you might raise your effervescent glass in solemn thanks to one blind Benedictine monk who made it all possible. Three centuries ago there lived in northern France a great blender of wines, Dom Perignon, who served as cellar-master at the Benedictine Abbey of Hautvillers for forty-seven years. For some reason that we may never know, this monk decided one day to seal his bottles with cork instead of the usual cloth soaked in oil. The carbon dioxide that is produced during fermentation could pass through the cloth, but was imprisoned by the new stopper. The result: a sparkling wine.   —Caroline Sutton, "How Did They Discover Champagne?"

Instructional process analysis gives directions on how to do something and usually follows a time pattern—first you do this and then you do this. (See PARA 3a, Chronological Order.) Gladstone's paragraph is instructional, telling step by step how to build a good fireplace fire.

Though "experts" differ as to the best technique to follow when building a fire, one generally accepted method consists of first laying a generous amount of crumpled newspaper on the hearth between the andirons. Kindling wood is then spread generously over this layer of newspaper and one of the thickest logs is placed across the back of the andirons. This should be as close to the back of the fireplace as possible, but not quite touching it. A second log is then placed an inch or so in front of this, and a few additional sticks of kindling are laid across these two. A third log is then placed on top to form a sort of pyramid with air spaces between all logs so that flames can lick freely up between them.   —Bernard Gladstone, "How to Build a Fire in a Fireplace"

Comparison and contrast

The purpose of any **comparison and contrast** is to make clear the similarities between dissimilar objects or the differences between similar ones. A comparison-contrast follows one of two basic patterns: AA/BB or AB/AB. In the first pattern, all the characteristics of A are presented, followed by all the characteristics of B. In the second pattern, one characteristic of A is compared or contrasted with its counterpart in B, the next characteristic of A with its counterpart in B, and so forth. Use the AA/BB pattern if you think the reader can remember all the points of A while reading about B; if not, the AB/AB pattern is probably a better choice.

In the following paragraph, Rodriguez uses the AA/BB pattern to compare how his mother and father publicly conversed in English with the way they spoke Spanish at home.

> In public, my father and mother spoke a hesitant, accented, not always grammatical English. And they would have to strain—their bodies tense—to catch the sense of what was rapidly said by *los gringos*. At home they spoke Spanish. The language of their Mexican past sounded in counterpoint to the English of public society. The words would come quickly, with ease. Conveyed through those sounds was the pleasing, soothing, consoling reminder of being at home.
> —Richard Rodriguez, "Private Language, Public Language"

In her essay on communicating with family and friends, Goodman uses the AB/AB alternating pattern of development.

> Sometimes I think the telephone call is as earthbound as daily dialogue, while a letter is an exchange of gifts. On the telephone you talk; in a letter you tell. There is a pace to letter writing and reading that doesn't come from the telephone company but from our own inner rhythm.
> —Ellen Goodman, "Life in a Bundle of Letters"

Analogy

An **analogy** is a special kind of comparison. It explains something unfamiliar by comparing it to something familiar, thereby enabling the reader to understand the difficult subject. In the following paragraph, some common causes of marital despair are explained using a weather analogy.

> Even though each broken marriage is unique, we can still find the common perils, the common causes for marital despair. Each marriage has crisis points and each marriage tests endurance, the capacity for both intimacy and change. Outside pressures such as job loss, illness, infertility, trouble with a child, care of aging parents, and all the other plagues of life hit marriage the way hurricanes blast our shores. Some marriages survive these storms and others don't. Marriages fail, however, not simply because of the outside weather but because the inner climate becomes too hot or too cold, too turbulent or too stupefying.
>
> —Anne Roiphe, "Why Marriages Fail"

Division and Classification

To **classify** is to categorize, to group people, ideas, facts—anything—on the basis of some system. The *basis of classification* is an integral part of the process. In the following paragraph, a student divides stereo buyers into four categories on the basis of why they buy. (In subsequent paragraphs he discusses each type in detail.)

> As stereo equipment gets better and prices go down, stereo systems are becoming household necessities rather than luxuries. People are buying stereos by the thousands. During my year as a stereo salesman, I witnessed this boom firsthand. I dealt with hundreds of customers, and it didn't take long for me to learn that people buy stereos for different reasons. Eventually, though, I was able to divide all the stereo buyers into four basic categories: the wattage buyer, the quality buyer, the price buyer, and the looks buyer.   —Gerald Cleary, student

Cause and effect

A **cause-and-effect** paragraph shows the relationship between events. The focus may be on cause by naming it in the topic sentence and following with its effects; or the focus may be the other way around, with an effect given in the topic sentence followed by its causes. The author begins the following paragraph on soap operas with an effect and follows with the reasons for it.

> It should not be surprising that all sorts of Americans—not only the bed- and house-ridden—find solace in the mythically stable communities of soap operas. Some soap communities, after all, have lasted over thirty years. All potential viewers are members of a society that has been in constant transformation through geographic mobility and the loss of extended families. Loneliness, we are repeatedly told, has become pandemic in America, and the longing for community is a palpable need. Whether through religion, clubs, associations, or support groups—or through daily immersion in a favorite soap—many Americans search for some kind of communal life to counter varying degrees of social isolation and alienation.
>
> —Ruth Rosen, "Search for Yesterday"

Mixed strategies

Often, logic dictates that you use a combination of strategies to develop your topic sentence. In the paragraph that follows, the writer uses cause and effect, informational process analysis, statistics, and a hypothetical case in point (a kind of example) to develop her topic sentence, *They [cockroaches] reproduce at a truly amazing rate.*

> Cockroaches give credence to the old adage that there is safety in numbers. They reproduce at a truly amazing rate. About two months after mating, a new generation of cockroaches is born. One cockroach can produce about two dozen offspring each time it mates. To get some idea of their reproductive power, imagine that you start with three pairs of cockroaches that mate. Approximately three weeks after mating the females lay their eggs, which hatch some forty-five days later. If we assume two dozen eggs from each female, the first generation would number seventy-two offspring. These roaches would continue to multiply geometrically so that by year's end the colony's population would total more than ten thousand cockroaches. Stopping the process is almost impossible because even if we annihilate the adult population, a new generation still in egg form would be in the making.
>
> —Courtney Smith, student

PARA 3

Coherence

When something *coheres*, it fits together and makes sense. **Coherence** in a paragraph is achieved when the sentences flow smoothly from one to another without awkward breaks in rhythm or meaning.

Coherence is achieved by arranging sentences in the most effective order, using transitional words and phrases, repeating key words and phrases, and using parallel structures. These techniques knit the sentences of a paragraph into a tight structure. Coherence is also a feature of the essay as a whole and is achieved by using transitions to link paragraphs. As originally written, the following paragraph lacked coherence; it seemed to jump from idea to idea. In the revision, coherence is achieved by (1) repositioning a sentence, (2) repeating a key phrase, and (3) adding a transition.

In comparison to other parts of the world—Mexico, India, and Africa, for example—America does not have widespread poverty. That we are the richest and most technologically advanced of all nations, however, makes the poverty we have seem all the more surprising and incongruous. We have poor people among the elderly, minorities, mentally ill, and children. As the great historian Arnold Toynbee so succinctly said: "The worst country to be poor in is America." Some of our poor people have clothing, appliances, radios, televisions, furniture, and housing that would make the ~~people~~ *poor* of other countries envious. *But w*~~We~~ also have *poor* people who are homeless (including runaway teenagers) and without adequate food.

PARA 3a Arrange sentences in the most effective order.

At the most basic level, coherence in a paragraph comes from organizing the ideas and facts in a sensible pattern. Sentences in a paragraph are usually arranged according to one of three patterns: (1) a *chronological (time) order*, (2) a *spatial order*, or (3) some *logical order*. The most suitable arrangement depends on purpose, subject, and audience. Whichever pattern you choose, follow it consistently and thoughtfully to knit the ideas and elements of your paragraph into a seamless whole that your reader can easily follow.

Chronological order

Chronological order, or *time order,* presents events as they occurred. A personal story, a report on an automobile accident or historical event, and the steps in a process, for example, would naturally be related in chronological order. In the following paragraph, the author uses chronological order to tell about a disturbing memory.

> I clearly remember my sixth birthday because Dad was in the hospital with pneumonia. He was working so hard he paid very little attention to his health. As a result, he spent almost the entire summer before I entered the first grade in the hospital. Mom visited him nightly. On my birthday I was allowed to see him. I have memories of sitting happily in the lobby of the hospital talking to the nurses, telling them with a big smile that I was going to see my dad because it was my birthday. I couldn't wait to see him because children under 12 were not allowed to visit patients, so I had not seen him in a long time. When I entered the hospital room, I saw tubes inserted into his nose and needles stuck in his arm. He was very, very thin. I was frightened and wanted to cry, but I was determined to have a good visit. So I stayed for a while, and he wished me a happy birthday. When it was time to go, I kissed him good-bye and waited until I left his room to cry.
> —Grace Ming-Yee Wai, "Chinese Puzzle"

Spatial order

Spatial order is used to describe a person, place, or thing. The writer begins at a particular point and moves methodically in one direction—say, from top to bottom, left to right, far to near, front to back, outside to inside, or, as in the following paragraph, the center of the room to the walls.

> The old store, lighted only by three fifty-watt bulbs, smelled of coal and baking bread. In the middle of the rectangular room, where the oak floor sagged a little, stood an iron stove. To the right was a wooden table with an unfinished game of checkers and a stool made from an apple-tree stump. On the shelves around the walls sat earthen jugs with corncob stoppers, a few canned goods, and some of the two thousand old clocks and clockworks Thurmond Watts owned. Only one was ticking; the others he just looked at. I asked how long he'd been in the store.   —William Least Heat-Moon, "Nameless, Tennessee"

Logical order

A **logical pattern** of organization can take many forms, depending on the subject matter and the writer's purpose. In organizing a paragraph, it may be most logical to move from the easiest to understand aspects of the subject to the most difficult, from the least important examples to the most important, from the specific to the general or from the general to the specific, or from the least controversial elements to the most controversial, to name just a few possible patterns.

The following paragraph begins with a strong but general topic sentence; each sentence thereafter narrows the subject until the last zeroes in on the writer's point.

> There is scarcely a corner of human affairs that Shakespeare doesn't touch upon, nor a topic for which he fails to supply a memorable quote. All of this has led, predictably, to every trade and profession claiming him for their own. There have been any number of attempts to prove that before he turned his hand to writing plays he was a lawyer, a soldier, a physician, an astronomer, a printer, a sportsman, a gardener, and heaven alone knows what else. And of all of these guesses as to what he did at Stratford before coming to his London career, one that seems nearest the mark is gardening. This does not mean, of course, that he would tramp off of a morning, spade and hoe slung over his shoulder like a pikeman's weapons, to delve in the soil of Lord So-and-so's gardens and orchards. What it does imply is that Shakespeare was a countryman long familiar with the growth of plants in woodlands, fields, and cottage and kitchen gardens. He may well have tended a garden of his own.
>
> —Frank J. Anderson, "Shakespeare in the Garden"

PARA 3b Use transitional words and phrases.

Transitional words and phrases connect units of thought—within a sentence, between sentences, and among paragraphs. In other words, **transitions** signal relationships and thus can be categorized by their functions. In revising your composition (see COMP 4), check that you use a transition everywhere one is needed to establish a logical connection between ideas, and that you use the correct transitional word. For example, do not use *also* (showing an addition) when you really want *similarly* (to compare two things), or *however* (showing contrast) when you really need *although* (to show concession).

The following list presents some of the more common transitional words and expressions categorized by meaning (some words are listed in more than one category because their meaning varies with context):

ADDITION   and, again, too, also, in addition, further, furthermore, moreover, besides

CAUSE AND EFFECT   therefore, consequently, thus, accordingly, as a result, hence, then, so

COMPARISON   similarly, likewise, by comparison

CONCESSION   although, to be sure, granted, of course, it is true, to tell the truth, certainly, with the exception of, although this may be true, even though, naturally

CONTRAST   but, however, at the same time, in contrast, on the contrary, on the other hand, yet, nevertheless, after all, in spite of, conversely, still

EXAMPLE   for example, for instance, one case of

TIME   afterward, later, earlier, subsequently, at the same time, immediately, this time, until now, shortly, currently, lately, in the meantime

PLACE   elsewhere, here, above, below, farther on, there, beyond, nearby, opposite to, around

CLARIFICATION   that is, in other words, in simpler terms, to put it differently, simply stated, partly, actually, in fact

SEQUENCE   first, second, third [NOT firstly, secondly, and so on], next, finally, following, then, in time

SUMMARY   in conclusion, to conclude, to summarize, in brief, in short

The transitional words and phrases in the following paragraph are italicized. To test how important they are in showing relationships among the ideas in the paragraph, try omitting them or substituting others.

> In America, *of course,* social distinctions have never been so sharp as they are in England. We find it somewhat easier to rise in the world, to move into social environments unknown to our parents. This is possible, *partly,* because speech differences are slighter; *conversely,* speech differences are slighter because this is possible. *But* speech differences do exist. If you've spent all your life driving a cab in Philly and, having inherited a fortune, move to San Francisco's Nob Hill, you will find that your language is different, perhaps embarrassingly so, from that of your new acquaintances.   —Paul Roberts, "Speech Communities"

PARA 3c   Repeat key words and phrases.

Repetition is another way of knitting together a paragraph. The strategic repeating of key words and phrases improves coherence by keeping the main point in front of the reader in the most obvious way. The repeated key word is italicized.

> Tears of hurt and frustration pricked at the corner of my eyes as the now-familiar pain seared my leg. I sat down and looked around the colorless room: *beige* walls, *beige* ceiling, *beige* floor tiles. In one

corner was a small cot with a *beige* bedspread, and in the opposite corner a sink, mirror, and *beige* waste basket. The shades were drawn and the lights were much dimmer than they had been in the hall. Gradually I relaxed and waited. —Laura LaPierre, student

PARA 3d   Use parallel structure.

Parallel structure is repetition of a certain kind; it is repetition in a series. Parallelism can occur on the word, phrase, clause, or whole-sentence level. (See SENT 1.) In the following paragraph, the writer uses parallelism to knit the sentences into a seamless whole; sentences 1 through 4 use one pattern of parallelism, and sentences 5 and 6 another. The parallel structures are italicized.

(1) *The herring gull is a creature of sufficient* ingenuity that if he picks up a mussel with a shell too hard for his beak to break, he will carry it to a height and drop it on a hard rock. (2) *He is a creature of sufficient* loyalty and perception to guarantee that he will never attack his own mate, and will recognize her among dozens flying into the colony at a distance to defy human binoculars. (3) *He is a creature of sufficient* social sophistication that, while many arrive in the spring already paired, definite areas in the colony which Tinbergen calls "clubs" will be set aside as meeting places for the unpaired. (4) *He is a creature* also, as we have seen, of such sensitive social adjustment that the arriving flock will make "decisions" of mood and readiness as if it were one being. (5) *So dependent is the herring gull* on the community of his citizenship that he would probably be unable to breed were he to return in the spring to the wrong gull town. (6) *So powerful and incomprehensible is his attachment* for home that, like the albatross, a pair may return year after year to nest in precisely the same spot, although the North Sea's winter storms will have effaced all landmarks to guide his eye.
—Robert Ardrey, "Herring Gull"

PARA 3e   Use transitions to link paragraphs.

Just as transitions are used to link sentences within a paragraph, so are they used to link paragraphs themselves. Because each new paragraph indicates a further progression of thought in the composition, transitions help the reader follow along. In the passage that follows, the writer uses transitions to link her first and second paragraphs and her second and third paragraphs; the transitions are italicized.

In high schools and colleges, women must develop support for female sports leadership in their communities. Toward that end, they should work with athletic directors, school administrations, and service and professional organizations to bring about needed changes.

Furthermore, women should not hesitate to cause a stir in athletic circles. They need to follow the example of the Black Coaches Association, a collegiate organization, and use a consolidated female network to help each other find jobs and serve as a pressure group for the recognition of women coaches.

In addition, they must be willing to use lawsuits, affirmative action, and boycotts to protest discrimination.

—Judith Jenkins George, "Women Coaches Are an Endangered Species"

 -Tip

Testing for transitional words

Test the coherence of your composition by putting the transitional words and phrases in boldface or underlining them. If you have surprisingly few, you may need to strengthen the connections between your thoughts by adding transitions, both within paragraphs and between them.

gram

Grammar Essentials

Learning Objectives

After reading this section, you should:

- be able to identify the parts of speech in a sentence;
- be able to identify the subject and predicate of a sentence;
- recognize different kinds of phrases and clauses;
- be able to classify sentences by structure or purpose.

Grammar Essentials

Studying grammar will help you write better in two ways. First, because there is never simply one way to write a sentence, but many ways to present the same thought, knowing the parts of speech and how they function in sentences gives you the power to write exactly what you mean. Second, if you understand how words function in sentences, you are better able to identify why a sentence is confused, awkward, or not as clear as you had hoped. Studying grammar, then, allows you to look at sentences in a new light, both when you compose and when you revise.

GRAM 1

Parts of Speech

Because English has more than 600,000 words, we group them in categories that share common characteristics in order to make it easier to talk about language. In grammar, these groupings are called *parts of speech*. English has eight parts of speech: *verbs* (V), *nouns* (N), *pronouns* (PRO), *adjectives* (ADJ), *adverbs* (ADV), *prepositions* (PREP), *conjunctions* (CONJ), and *interjections* (INTJ). A word may be a member of more than one category, however, depending on its use in a particular sentence.

ADJ
She had a *sound* plan.

N
They sailed across the *sound*.

V
The warrior will *sound* the horn.

GRAM 1a Verbs

A **verb** (V) expresses action (*run, think*) or a state of being (*is, become, seem*). A complete verb is composed of the **main verb** (MV) itself and any **helping verbs** (HV) that may be used with it. The most commonly used helping (auxiliary) verbs are the nine **modals:** *may, might, shall, will, would, must, should, can, could.* Modals express how the writer feels about an action. Modals express probability, necessity or obligation, or ability. (See ESL 1a.)

> HV   MV
> He *may wash* the dishes. [probability]
>
> HV   MV
> He *should wash* the dishes. [obligation]
>
> HV   MV
> He *can wash* the dishes. [ability]

Other helping verbs include the forms of *have, be, do, used to,* and *ought to.*

> HV   MV
> He *is washing* the dishes.
>
> HV   MV
> He *did wash* the dishes.
>
> HV   MV
> He *used to wash* the dishes.

Forms of verbs

All verbs have five forms, with the exception of *be,* which has eight forms. The first three of the five verb forms are called the *principal parts of a verb.*

1. **BASE FORM OR INFINITIVE**	*(to) talk/write*	*(to) be*
2. **PAST TENSE**	*I talked/wrote*	*was, were*
3. **PAST PARTICIPLE**	*I have talked/written*	*been*
4. **-s FORM OR PRESENT TENSE**	*He/she/it talks/writes*	*am, is, are*
5. **PRESENT PARTICIPLE**	*I am talking/writing*	*being*

The infinitive is made up of *to* and the base form (*to see, to believe*).

Most verbs in English are **regular** (*talk, talked, talked*), but a few are **irregular** (*write, wrote, written*). (See EDIT 2a and 2b.)

Intransitive, transitive, and linking verbs

A verb can be *intransitive, transitive,* or *linking,* depending on whether it takes an object or complement and, if so, what kind. (See GRAM 2c and 2d.)

An **intransitive verb** has a **subject** (S) but does not require an object or complement to complete its meaning.

> S   V
> Nobody *cares.*

A **transitive verb,** as its name indicates, transfers its action from the subject to the object of the sentence. Transitive verbs always take a **direct object** (DO) and sometimes an **indirect object** (IO) to complete their meaning.

> S   V   DO
> The waves *lashed* the shore.
> S   V   IO   DO
> Maria *gave* her mother flowers.

A **linking verb** (LV) connects the subject to a **predicate noun** (PN), which renames the subject, or a **predicate adjective** (PA), which describes the subject.

>   S   LV   PN
> Jamaica Kincaid *is* a writer.
> S   LV   PA
> The grapefruit *is* sour.

Verbals

Sometimes a verb does not function as a verb in a sentence. In this case, it is called a **verbal.** There are three types of verbals: *gerunds, participles* (both past and present), and *infinitives.* Verbals are usually used in phrases. (See GRAM 3b.)

GERUND

> N
> *Swimming* is my favorite sport.

PRESENT PARTICIPLE

> ADJ
> *Swimming* out to the raft, he got a cramp.

PAST PARTICIPLE

> ADJ
> His *cramped* leg still aches.

INFINITIVE

> N
> Bob is learning *to swim.*

GRAM 1b   Nouns

A **noun** (N) is the name of a person, place, thing, quality, action, or idea.

George, Brazil, chair, beauty, flight, mercy

Most nouns are made plural or possessive or both by *inflections*, or changes in form.

SINGULAR	PLURAL	SINGULAR POSSESSIVE	PLURAL POSSESSIVE
boy	boys	boy's	boys'
woman	women	woman's	women's
tennis	—	tennis's	—
society	societies	society's	societies'
New York	—	New York's	—

Nouns can be divided into the following subclasses:

Proper nouns name specific people, places, and things, and they are capitalized. (See MECH 1b.)

Katharine Hepburn, South Africa, Statue of Liberty

Common nouns name all items that are not proper nouns.

dog, paper, stoves

Abstract nouns name ideas, qualities, and other intangibles. (See WORD 1c.)

fear, freedom, neglect

Concrete nouns name tangible items. (See WORD 1c.) We experience concrete nouns through the five senses.

bottle, telephone, letters

Collective nouns name groups. If a collective noun refers to the group as a whole, it takes a singular verb. If it refers to the individual members of that group, it takes a plural verb. (See EDIT 1d.)

army, communities, herd

Count nouns name items that can be counted. Frequently count nouns are accompanied by an adjective indicating how many are referred to.

one dollar, twenty-four pills, a half-dozen sandwiches

Noncount nouns name items that come in quantities that are not capable of being counted. (See ESL 2a.) Most such nouns fall into certain categories.

> *Food:* butter, flour, milk, sugar
> *Nonfood bulk materials:* asphalt, gold, oxygen, snow
> *Abstractions:* anger, love, pity, stress

GRAM 1c Pronouns

A **pronoun** (PRO) is a word that takes the place of a noun in a sentence. While there are vast numbers of nouns in English, there are only about one hundred pronouns. The noun that a pronoun replaces is called its **antecedent.** (See EDIT 3a and 3b.) Pronouns are divided into the following groups:

Personal pronouns refer to specific persons, places, or things. The **case** of a personal pronoun refers to its function in a sentence. (See EDIT 3c.)

> *Singular:* I, me, you, he, she, him, her, it
> *Plural:* we, us, you, they, them

Possessive pronouns show ownership by persons, places, or things.

> *Singular:* my, mine, your, yours, his, her, hers, its
> *Plural:* our, ours, your, yours, their, theirs

Demonstrative pronouns point out the nouns that they replace.

> this, that, these, those

Indefinite pronouns refer to nonspecific persons or things. (See EDIT 1f.)

> all, any, anybody, anyone, anything, both, everybody, everyone, everything, few, many, no one, nothing, somebody, someone, something, several, some

Interrogative pronouns introduce questions.

> who(ever), whom(ever), whose, which(ever), what(ever)

Relative pronouns join a dependent clause to a noun.

> who(ever), whom(ever), whose, which, that

Intensive and **reflexive pronouns** consist of a personal pronoun plus *-self* or *-selves.* An intensive pronoun refers back to a noun or another pronoun for emphasis (I did it *myself*); a reflexive pronoun refers back to the subject for emphasis or to complete the meaning (I washed *myself*).

Singular: myself, yourself, himself, herself, itself
Plural: ourselves, yourselves, themselves

GRAM 1d   Adjectives

An **adjective** (ADJ) is a word that modifies or qualifies a noun or pronoun. An adjective tells what kind, how many, or which one.

N
brass trombones [what kind]
N
seventy-six trombones [how many]
PRO
the older one [which one]

Adjectives change form by adding *-er* or *-est* or are preceded by *more* or *most* to form the comparative and the superlative. (See EDIT 4e.)

POSITIVE	COMPARATIVE	SUPERLATIVE
silly	sillier	silliest
powerful	more powerful	most powerful

Articles are considered to be adjectives. There are two types of articles: **definite** (*the*) and **indefinite** (*a, an*).

GRAM 1e   Adverbs

An **adverb** (ADV) modifies a verb, an adjective, or another adverb. Adverbs tell where, when, how, why, under what circumstances, and to what extent.

He drove *nearby*. [where]

He drove *yesterday*. [when]

He drove *carefully*. [how]

He drove *because* he had to. [why]

He drove *while* tired. [under what circumstances]

He drove *quite* carefully. [to what extent]

Adverbs are frequently made from adjectives by adding *-ly* (*roughly, quickly*), but not all adverbs end in *-ly* (*first, not, very*). Like adjectives, adverbs can also signify degrees of comparison (*-er/-est*, *more/less*, and *most/least*). (See EDIT 4e.)

POSITIVE	COMPARATIVE	SUPERLATIVE
near	nearer	nearest
frequently	more frequently	most frequently

GRAM 1f Prepositions

A **preposition** (PREP) comes before a noun or pronoun to create a phrase that modifies another word in the sentence. The noun or the pronoun is called the **object of the preposition** (OP), and the phrase that is created is called a **prepositional phrase**. Prepositions show relationships between objects and ideas in a sentence. (See GRAM 3a.)

                        PREP OP
She spilled the soda *on him*. [*On him* is the prepositional phrase.]

Here is a list of the most common prepositions:

about	beside	near	than
above	between	next	through
across	but	of	till
after	by	off	to
along	concerning	on	toward
among	considering	opposite	under
around	despite	out	underneath
as	down	over	unlike
at	during	past	until
before	except	respecting	upon
behind	for	round	with
below	in	since	without

GRAM 1g Conjunctions

A **conjunction** (CONJ), like a preposition, shows the relationship between parts of a sentence. There are three kinds of conjunctions— *coordinating, subordinating,* and *correlative*—and conjunctive adverbs.

A **coordinating conjunction** connects words, phrases, and clauses of equal rank.

and   for   or   yet   but   nor   so

Leslie *and* Hal caught perch, *but* they didn't get any lake trout *or* pike.

A **subordinating conjunction** introduces a subordinate clause (SC) and connects it to a main clause (MC). (See GRAM 4.)

after	before	so	when
although	even if	than	where
as	if	that	whereas
as if	in order that	though	wherever
as though	rather than	unless	whether
because	since	until	while

    SC   MC   SC

Unless we hurry, we won't arrive *before* the concert starts.

Correlative conjunctions work in pairs to connect words, phrases, clauses, and whole sentences.

both/and	neither/nor	not only/but also
either/or	not/but	whether/or

We will be *neither* swayed *nor* delayed in our deliberations.

Conjunctive adverbs can function in two ways. First, they can serve as transitional expressions to connect units of thought. (See PARA 3b and PUNCT 1f.)

Meanwhile, Todd was home making Lisa's favorite dinner.

[*Meanwhile* connects Todd's actions to the previous statement.]

Second, conjunctive adverbs can link main clauses (MC). (See PUNCT 2b.)

                   MC

Lisa thought she'd surprise Todd by picking up a pizza for dinner; *meanwhile,*

     MC

Todd was home making her favorite—fried chicken.

Here is a list of common conjunctive adverbs:

accordingly	finally	likewise	specifically
also	furthermore	meanwhile	still
anyway	hence	moreover	then
besides	however	nevertheless	thereafter
certainly	incidentally	now	therefore
consequently	indeed	otherwise	thus
conversely	instead	similarly	undoubtedly

GRAM 1h Interjections

An **interjection** (INTJ) is a word or phrase used to express emotion or attract attention. Interjections are independent units not grammatically connected to a sentence, and they are always followed by an exclamation point (see PUNCT 6c) or a comma (see PUNCT 1i).

Hey! There's a parade coming.

Oh well, maybe we can do better next time.

GRAM 2

Parts of Sentences

A **sentence** is a word or group of words that contains a subject and predicate and expresses a complete thought. A sentence has two basic parts, a *subject* (S) and a *predicate* (P). The predicate includes the *verb* (V), *direct object* (DO), *indirect object* (IO), *predicate noun* (PN), *predicate adjective* (PA), and *object complement* (OC).

Most English sentences follow one of these six patterns:

$$\text{S} \overbrace{\boxed{\text{V}}}^{\text{P}}$$
Speed kills.

$$\text{S} \overbrace{\boxed{\text{V} \quad \text{DO}}}^{\text{P}}$$
Birds eat berries.

$$\text{S} \overbrace{\boxed{\text{V} \quad \text{IO} \quad \text{DO}}}^{\text{P}}$$
Dad wrote me a letter.

$$\text{S} \overbrace{\boxed{\text{V} \quad \text{PN}}}^{\text{P}}$$
She is a firefighter.

$$\text{S} \overbrace{\boxed{\text{V} \quad \text{PA}}}^{\text{P}}$$
The soldier is brave.

$$\text{S} \overbrace{\boxed{\text{V} \quad \text{DO} \quad \text{OC}}}^{\text{P}}$$
The movie made us sad.

GRAM 2a   Subjects

The **subject** (S) of a sentence is the person or thing the sentence is about.

Fear eroded our confidence.

The **simple subject** is the noun or pronoun alone.

A *Jeep* is my first choice.

The **complete subject** is the simple subject and all words associated with it.

A teal green Jeep with leather interior is my first choice.

A **compound subject** is made up of two or more simple subjects.

Sticks and stones broke his bones.

GRAM 2b   Predicates

The **simple predicate** of a sentence is made up of the verb and any helping verbs. (See GRAM 1a.)

The ship *was turning* in the harbor.

The **complete predicate** of a sentence is the simple predicate and its modifiers and complements.

The ship *was turning in the harbor.*

The **compound predicate** is made up of two or more predicates that have the same subject.

Tiger Woods *won the Master's and inspired young golfers.*

GRAM 2c   Objects

A **direct object** (DO) is the noun, pronoun, or verbal (see GRAM 1a) that receives the action of the verb.

He kissed *her.*

An **indirect object** (IO) is the noun, pronoun, or verbal that tells *to* whom or *for* whom something is done.

The coach gave *Melissa* another chance.

To test whether a word is a direct or indirect object, insert *to* or *for* into the sentence. If the sentence makes sense, the word is an indirect object.

The coach gave another chance *to Melissa.*

GRAM 2d   Complements

A **complement** is a word or word group that completes the sense of a verb and adds to the meaning of a subject. Linking verbs can take a complement that is either a predicate noun or a predicate adjective. (See GRAM 1a.) Transitive verbs that take a direct object can also take an object complement (OC), which refers to or modifies the direct object.

DO⎯⎯⎯OC

My brother painted his car bright green.

GRAM 3

Phrases

The phrase is the most common word group we use in writing. A **phrase,** unlike a clause, does not have a subject and a predicate. A phrase is used as a single part of speech—that is, as a noun, a verb, an adjective, or an adverb. There are four kinds of phrases: *prepositional, verbal* (including gerund, participle, and infinitive phrases), *appositive,* and *absolute.*

GRAM 3a   Prepositional phrases

A **prepositional phrase** consists of a preposition (a word such as *to, with, after,* or *between*) and its object, which is always a noun or pronoun. In sentences, prepositional phrases usually function as adjectives or adverbs, but in some instances they can function as nouns.

ADJ

The chapter *on photosynthesis* is fully illustrated.

ADV

Many Canadians go to Florida *in the winter.*

N

After two o'clock would be most convenient for me.

GRAM 3b Verbal phrases

When a verb does not function as a verb in a sentence, it is called a **verbal.** (See GRAM 1a.) Verbals are usually used in phrases. There are three kinds of verbal phrases: *gerund, participial,* and *infinitive.*

A **gerund phrase** consists of an *-ing* form of a verb (*brewing, flying, joking, studying*) with any modifier(s) and/or object(s). A gerund phrase always functions as a noun in a sentence. It can, therefore, serve as a subject, a predicate noun, a direct object, an indirect object, or an object of a preposition in a sentence.

S
All this fancy cooking takes time.

PN
Rick's main recreation is *lifting weights.*

OP
I believe in *telling the truth.*

A **participial phrase** consists of a present participle (*-ing* form of a verb) or past participle (*-ed* form of a verb) with its auxiliary, modifier(s), object(s), and complement(s). A participial phrase always functions as an adjective in a sentence.

ADJ
The girl *riding the mountain bike* is my cousin.

ADJ
Having finished his work for the day, the carpenter went home.

An **infinitive phrase** consists of the word *to* and the base form of the verb (*stop, attempt, march, liberate*) with its modifier(s) and object(s), if any. An infinitive phrase can function as an adjective, an adverb, or a noun in a sentence.

ADJ
These are the shoes *to wear* for hiking.

ADV
Sam couldn't wait *to eat his ice cream.*

N
Karen and Larry love *to golf.*

GRAM 3c Appositive phrases

An *appositive* is a noun or noun equivalent. An **appositive phrase** is a noun or noun equivalent, together with any modifier(s), that directly follows (or precedes) another noun or noun equivalent. Unlike an adjective, which modifies a noun or noun equivalent, an appositive phrase identifies or explains. Most appositive phrases contain nonessential or parenthetical information and are, therefore, set off by commas.

The Special Olympics, *games for disabled children,* celebrated its thirtieth anniversary in 1997.

A women's rights activist, Oprah Winfrey sets an excellent example.

GRAM 3d Absolute phrases

An **absolute phrase** is a noun or noun equivalent, followed in most cases by a participial phrase. An absolute phrase modifies a clause or sentence, not just a word as all other types of phrases do.

Joseph received six job offers, *his first concert having won rave reviews.*

Her truck packed with all her belongings, Phoebe set out for Oregon.

GRAM 4

Clauses

A **clause** is a group of words that contains a subject and a predicate. A **main clause,** or **independent clause,** can stand alone as a complete sentence.

Janie bought Ted's old Volkswagen.

It had a good engine but a rusted body.

A **subordinate clause,** or **dependent clause,** in contrast, cannot stand alone as a sentence because it is an incomplete thought.

When I cook, I use a lot of garlic.

If you don't like garlic, you can substitute onions.

GRAM 4a   Adjective clauses

An **adjective clause** (also called a **relative clause**) modifies a noun or pronoun. Usually it immediately follows the word or words modified and is introduced by a relative pronoun—*who, whom, whose, which, that, whoever, whomever,* or *whatever* (see GRAM 1c)—or by the subordinating conjunction *when* or *where* (see GRAM 1g).

Ted's old Volkswagen, *which had a badly rusted body,* still ran like a dream.

My grandmother remembers a time *when Volkswagens were not on the market.*

If the relative pronoun or subordinating conjunction (the subordinator) introducing an adjective clause does not function as the subject of the subordinate clause, you can omit it. In fact, omitting it picks up the pace of the sentence.

The Volkswagen ~~that~~ Janie saw at the car show was carefully restored.

If the subordinator is the subject of the adjective clause, you can usually rewrite the sentence to eliminate unneeded words.

marble
A statue of Pocahontas~~, which is made of marble,~~ is in the park.
∧

GRAM 4b   Adverb clauses

An **adverb clause** modifies a verb, an adjective, or an adverb. It is always introduced by a subordinating conjunction, such as *if, after, when, though, since, where,* or *while.* (See GRAM 1g.) An adverb clause answers the questions posed by the words *when, where, why,* or *how.*

The children looked for coins under the bleachers *after the game was over.*

GRAM 4c   Noun clauses

A **noun clause** can function any way that a noun does—as a subject, a predicate adjective, a predicate noun, a direct or an indirect object, an object complement, an object of a preposition, or an appositive (A). (See GRAM 1b.) A relative pronoun (*who, whom, whose, which, that, whoever, whomever,* or *whatever*) usually introduces a noun clause.

S
[Whoever said so] must be telling the truth.

DO
No one knows [what his name is.]

PN
One condition of Bill's employment was [that he shave off his beard.]

A
The news [that both sides called a ceasefire] took everyone by surprise.

GRAM 5

Types of Sentences

Sentences can be classified either in terms of the kinds of clauses they contain (grammatically) or in terms of their purpose (rhetorically). Becoming aware of types of sentences allows you to vary your writing style to suit your audience, content, and purpose. You will find, too, that sentence variety holds a reader's interest. How boring it is to read all simple sentences! In contrast, after many longer sentences, a punchy short sentence adds force to a key point. (See SENT 7.)

GRAM 5a Classification by structure

Simple sentences

A **simple sentence** consists of one main clause and no subordinate clauses.

Reading and writing are the primary goals of early education.

A simple sentence is not necessarily short, however, because the subject or the predicate—or both—may be compound or have many modifiers. The following example consists of one main clause; the subject is *Fort Benning* and the verb is *is*. The rest of the sentence is made up of descriptive details.

Fort Benning, Georgia, is a 285-square-mile ecological filigree of long-needle pine forests, ridges, swamps, clay banks, and foot-high anthills bordering lonesome pre–Civil War cemeteries, and networks of dirt trails and two-lane macadam highways named for long-forgotten heroes.   —Donald Smith

Compound sentences

A **compound sentence** consists of two or more main clauses and no subordinate clauses. The main clauses may be joined by a coordinating conjunction (*and, but, or, for, nor, so,* or *yet*) and a comma; by a semicolon; by a semicolon and a transitional word (*however, nevertheless, therefore*); or by a correlative conjunction such as *either/or, both/and.*

                        MC

A mall in Minnesota may resemble one in Florida or Arizona but shoppers

      MC

there look different.

Complex sentences

A **complex sentence** consists of one main clause and one or more subordinate clauses.

                    SC   MC

If we don't become stewards of our environment, our lives will change.

Compound-complex sentences

A **compound-complex sentence** consists of two or more main clauses and at least one subordinate clause.

                           SC

Even though many cities and towns along the Mississippi River were

                  MC   MC

prepared, the flood waters were devastating, and many lives were lost.

GRAM 5b   Classification by purpose

A **declarative sentence** makes a statement. In expository prose, most sentences are declarative. An **interrogative sentence** asks a question. It customarily ends with a question mark. An **imperative sentence** gives a command, makes a request, or offers advice. Usually *you* is the understood subject. An **exclamatory sentence** indicates intense emotion or excitement and ends with an exclamation point. Sometimes exclamations are not complete sentences.

DECLARATIVE	Betsy bought new running shoes.
INTERROGATIVE	Did Sarah get a job as a lifeguard?
IMPERATIVE	Please pass the salt and pepper.
EXCLAMATORY	What a movie!

esl

ESL Basics

Learning Objectives

After reading this section, you should:

- have greater mastery of auxiliary verbs;
- better understand the use of nouns, quantifiers, articles, adjectives, and adverbs;
- have greater mastery of prepositional phrases;
- be more proficient in using word groups and writing different kinds of sentences in English.

ESL Basics

Mastering a language, whether it is your own or a second language, is an ongoing process. This unit is designed to help students of English as a second language (ESL) with the most frequent problems in writing grammatically correct, idiomatic English.

ESL 1

Verbs

Verb constructions formed with helping verbs (auxiliaries) and modals can be troublesome for nonnative speakers. This section provides information about these constructions. (See GRAM 1a for more about verbs.)

ESL 1a Use modal auxiliaries correctly.

Modals (M) are verbs that are used with a main verb (MV) to suggest various judgments by the writer or speaker about the action of the main verb. (See GRAM 1a for more about modals.)

<pre>   M   MV</pre>
You *should* see a doctor.

[The modal *should* expresses the writer's feeling that the action is necessary or urgent.]

Modals express the following ideas about an action or event:

NECESSITY OR OBLIGATION must, should

ABILITY can, could

PROBABILITY OR LIKELIHOOD will, would, should, could, may, might,

[*Will* expresses the most certainty of a future event, *might* expresses the least]

Follow these six rules for writing verb phrases with modals.

1. **Use the base form of the main verb after modals that express ideas about the present or the future.**

   The modals *can, could, may, might, must, should,* and *will* can be used with the base form of the verb to write about the present or the future.

   <pre>   swim   compete</pre>
   Jeff can ~~swimming~~ very well. He should ~~competes~~.

2. **Do not omit *shall* or *will* to express the future, even in sentences with adverbs that indicate future time.**

> The coach ^will^ phone Bob soon. I am sure he ^will^ get to play first base this year.

You can also use *going to* or the present progressive to express the future. (See EDIT 2c.)

3. **Use only one modal with each main verb.**

The following sentence expresses two ideas that are normally suggested by modals. However, the expression *be able to* must substitute for the modal *can*.

> I might ^be able to^ ~~can~~ join the swimming team this year.

The following phrases can be used with modals. Their meanings are similar to modals.

have to	They may *have to* leave early.
be obliged to	He might *be obliged to* pay that bill.
be able to	I will *be able to* get to the theater by 8 p.m.

4. **Use *could, was able to, had to* and *was obliged to* plus the base form of the main verb to write about the past.**

> Two years ago he ^could not^ ~~cannot~~ read.

5. **Use *would* plus the base form of the main verb to write about a habitual action in the past.**

> When I was a child, I ^would^ ~~will~~ always try to go barefoot in summer.

See page 92 for how to use *would* and *might* in reported speech.

6. **When the modal is followed by a main verb in the perfect or progressive tense, use the base form of the auxiliaries *have* or *be*.**

> Ann should not ^have^ ~~had~~ quit school. She ^is^ looking for a job now.

ESL 1b Form the perfect tenses correctly.

The **perfect tenses** in English are useful for talking about two moments or periods of time in the same sentence. The perfect tenses are created by combining a form of *have* with the past participle of the main verb. (See EDIT 2c for more information about perfect tenses.)

PRESENT PERFECT Use present perfect to talk about an action that was begun in the past and continues into the present or to talk about an action that was completed in the past but still affects the present.

Luis and Lupe *have lived* here for ten years. (They still do.)

SIMPLE PAST

Luis and Lupe *lived* here for ten years. (They don't any more.)

PAST PERFECT Use past perfect to talk about one past action that occurred *before* another past action.

We already *had started* dinner when the Smiths arrived. (We started before they arrived.)

SIMPLE PAST

We *started* dinner when the Smiths arrived. (First they arrived, then we started.)

FUTURE PERFECT Use future perfect to talk about one future action that will occur before another future action.

All the snow *will have melted* by April. (The focus is on the process of the melting and the sentence encompasses all the time between now and April.)

SIMPLE FUTURE

All the snow *will melt* by April. (The focus is on the completion of the melting in the future.)

Sometimes, as in the present perfect example just given, the difference in meaning is clear. Often, however, there is no difference at all or the difference is very slight. When you're not sure which tense is correct, ask a native English speaker for an opinion.

ESL 1c Form and use the progressive tenses correctly.

The **progressive tenses** consist of a form of the auxiliary verb *be* (*am, is, are, was, were, being, be,* or *been*) plus the present participle of the main verb.

The progressive tenses usually refer to action that is in progress. The present progressive is also used for speaking about the future and referring to temporary conditions. The progressive tenses use a form of the auxiliary verb *be* (*am, is, are, was were, being, be,* or *been*) plus the present participle of the main verb. (See EDIT 2c for more information about progressive tenses.)

PRESENT PROGRESSIVE

Haroon is *building* a new house. [action in progress]

Arletha's parents *are moving* to California next year. [future action]

I *am taking* the bus this week while the mechanic fixes my car. [temporary condition]

PAST PROGRESSIVE

Sheila *was washing* her hair at midnight.

FUTURE PROGRESSIVE

We *will be traveling* to Montreal soon.

The following four points will help you form the progressive tenses correctly.

1. **Use a form of *be* with the progressive.**

   are
   Several of us working on the same project.

2. **Make sure the auxiliary verb *be* agrees with its subject.**

   is
   The number of work-study scholarships ~~are~~ increasing.

(Review subject–verb agreement in EDIT 1.)

3. **Use the auxiliary verb *have* in the present perfect progressive.**

   has
   Ari been cooking all day for the party.

   have
   Elliot and Craig been restoring an old Chevy on weekends.

4. Learn which verbs are usually not used in the progressive.

Certain verbs are *typically* not used in the progressive tenses (though there are exceptions). These verbs fall into the following categories:

LINKING VERBS AND VERBS THAT INDICATE QUALITIES OR STATES OF BEING appear, be, become, have, seem

Cheng ~~was seeming~~ sick all morning. *(seemed)*

VERBS THAT SHOW INTELLECTUAL STATES, EMOTIONS, OR ATTITUDES believe, disagree, dislike, hate, imagine, intend, know, like, pity, prefer, realize, suppose, think, understand, want, wish, wonder

I ~~am knowing~~ those formulas perfectly. *(know)*

VERBS THAT SHOW SENSE PERCEPTIONS feel, hear, see, smell, taste

The milk ~~is smelling~~ sour. *(smells)*

ESL 1d Form the passive voice correctly.

The **passive voice** of a verb (V) consists of a form of *be* (*am, is, are, was, were, being, be,* or *been*) plus the past participle of the main verb. In a sentence in the passive voice, the subject (S) *receives* the action; it does not *do* the action. (Read about the passive voice in SENT 6c, WORD 4e, EDIT 2f, and SENT 3d.)

Diamonds and gold *are mined* in South Africa.

Keep the following three points in mind to form the passive voice correctly.

1. Use the past participle, not the base form or past tense, to form the passive voice.

Pay particular attention to past participles of irregular verbs. (See EDIT 2a.)

Many electronic parts are ~~manufacture~~ in southeast Asia. *(manufactured)*

In my family, clothing was ~~wore~~ by all three children and then ~~gave~~ to the church. *(worn ... given)*

2. **Identify the subject and make sure the auxiliary verb** *be* **agrees with it.**

Coffee and dessert ~~was~~ *served* at the poetry reading.
(were written above was)

3. **Use only transitive verbs in the passive voice.**

A **transitive** verb, unlike an **intransitive** one, always takes a direct object (DO). (Review transitive and intransitive verbs in GRAM 1a.)

TRANSITIVE

      S   V   DO

Brett Favre *led* his team to victory.

[The direct object, *team,* receives the action of the verb *led.*]

In the passive voice, the object of the action becomes the grammatical subject of the sentence.

     S   V

The team *was led* to victory by Brett Favre.

INTRANSITIVE

     V

Sylvia *seems* forgetful lately.

[The verb *seems* has no direct object. *Forgetful* is a predicate adjective that describes the subject, *Sylvia.*]

Because intransitive verbs have no direct object, you cannot form the passive voice with them. If you are not sure whether a verb is transitive, check your dictionary.

ESL 1e   Use two-word verbs correctly.

Two-word verbs consist of a main verb plus a particle (a preposition or adverb). Note that the particle changes the meaning of a verb completely.

let down [disappoint]

let out [free]

These combinations of verb + particle are **idiomatic;** that is, the separate meanings of the verb and the particle do not predict their meaning when they are combined into a two-word verb.

Like other verbs, two-word verbs may be either transitive or intransitive.

TRANSITIVE   come across [find], let down [disappoint], tell off [rebuke]
INTRANSITIVE   catch on [understand], crop up [occur], give in [yield]

Transitive two-word verbs are either **inseparable** or **separable**. The verb and particle of inseparable two-word verbs are never separated by the direct object. However, the verb and particle of separable two-word verbs are sometimes separated by the direct object. There is no way of telling which two-word verbs are inseparable and which are separable except by noting how a writer handles the object of these verbs. You must, therefore, note this distinction when you learn each new two-word verb.

Follow these four rules in placing the direct object of transitive two-word verbs.

1. **Do not separate the verb and particle of inseparable two-word verbs. Place the noun or pronoun after the particle.**

   Olga does not *take after* her older sister.
   Olga does not *take after* her.

2. **When the object of a *separable* two-word verb is a noun, place it either between the main verb and the particle or after the particle.**

   We *turned* the offer *down*.
   We *turned down* the offer.

3. **When the object of a separable two-word verb is a pronoun, place the object only between the verb and the particle.**

   We *turned* it *down* because it came too late.

4. **Learn some common separable and inseparable transitive two-word verbs.**

   SEPARABLE

   fill out an application/*fill* it *out*   (to complete)
   give up smoking/*give* it *up*   (to quit)

look up some words/*look* them *up*	(to find, usually in a book)
put out a fire/*put* it *out*	(to extinguish)
tear down a house/*tear* one *down*	(to destroy or demolish)
throw away the paper/*throw* it *away*	(to put in the garbage)
try on some clothes/*try* some *on*	(to put on and examine)
turn down the TV/*turn* it *down*	(to reduce)
turn up the volume/*turn* it *up*	(to increase)

INSEPARABLE

call on a student/*call on* her	(to ask someone to speak)
come across an article/ *come across* it	(to encounter something by chance)
get over a cold/*get over* it	(to recover)
hear from an old friend/ *hear from* him	(to receive a communication)
look after his mother/ *look after* her	(to take care of)
look through an encyclopedia/ *look through* it	(to browse)
pick on someone smaller/ *pick on* someone	(to harass or bother)
run into a neighbor/ *run into* her	(to encounter somebody by chance)
take after a grandparent/ *take after* him	(to be, act, or look like)

ESL 1f   Learn which verbs are followed by an infinitive and which verbs are followed by a gerund.

Infinitives and **gerunds** are *verbals*, words formed from verbs. **Verbals** can function in a sentence as nouns, adjectives, or clauses. (See GRAM 1a.) Infinitives and gerunds can both be used as nouns and, therefore, can follow main verbs as direct objects. Some main verbs can be followed by either an infinitive or a gerund. However, some must be followed by an infinitive and others must be followed by a gerund.

The following six rules list common verbs and phrases associated with each of these verbals. They also give help in correctly using infinitives and gerunds as objects.

1. Use an infinitive with *to* after these common verbs:

agree	come	have	mean	refuse
arrange	decide	hope	offer	wait
beg	deserve	intend	plan	want
claim	expect	manage	promise	wish

to participate
Keith refused ~~participating~~ in the discussion.

2. Learn which verbs are followed by a noun or pronoun object and an infinitive with *to*.

Some verbs are followed by two objects—a noun or pronoun that receives the action of the verb and then the infinitive. The following verbs have a noun or pronoun object as well as an infinitive object:

advise	convince	invite	persuade	tell
allow	forbid	order	remind	urge
cause	instruct	permit	require	warn

our neighbors
We persuaded ˄ to come with us.
us
The Embassy invited ˄ to attend a reception in the Princess's honor.

The following verbs may either take a noun or pronoun object or be followed directly by an infinitive:

allow	cause	force	help	want
ask	expect	get	need	would like

I *would like* dessert.
I *would like* it.
I *would like* to go.

EXCEPTION: When *allow* does not have a noun or pronoun object, it is followed by a gerund.

Many companies no longer allow *smoking* on their premises.

3. Use *let, make,* and *have* correctly.

When *let* means "allow," *make* means "force," and *have* means "cause," they are followed by a noun or pronoun object (O) and the infinitive without *to.*

Customs officials *let* Martha *pass* through without inspecting her _O

luggage. They did not *make* her *show* them her briefcase, either.

Tom *had* the barber *cut* his hair much shorter this time.

4. Use a gerund after the following verbs:

admit	delay	imagine	postpone	resist
allow	deny	keep	practice	risk
appreciate	discuss	mind	prevent	stop
avoid	enjoy	miss	regret	suggest
consider	finish	permit	remember	tolerate

I enjoyed ~~to meet~~ your family. *(meeting)*

The government no longer allows ~~to smoke~~ in government offices. *(smoking)*

EXCEPTION: *Allow* is followed by an infinitive when it has a noun or pronoun object.

I don't allow anyone ~~smoking~~ in the house. *(to smoke)*

5. Use a gerund after certain verbs plus a preposition.

The following phrases are frequently followed by gerunds:

accuse someone of	be responsible for	feel like
apologize for	be tired of	insist on
approve of	be used to	look forward to
be afraid of	believe in	object to
be capable of	depend on	talk about
be interested in	dream of	think about

Sue *is responsible for* preparing the financial data.

(See EDIT 3c for gerunds modified by a possessive pronoun.)

6. **Use either an infinitive or a gerund after the following verbs:**

begin	hate	love	start
continue	like	prefer	

The store cannot *continue to raise* prices.

The store cannot *continue raising* prices.

EXCEPTIONS: When *begin* and *start* are used in the progressive tenses, they can only be followed by an infinitive.

Lani is beginning ~~enjoying~~ her dance class.
to enjoy

After some verbs, such as *remember, stop,* and *try,* the infinitive and the gerund have different meanings.

Sid remembers *going* to the bank on Friday.
[Sid remembers that he went to the bank last Friday.]

Sid remembers *to go* to the bank on Friday.
[Sid remembers that he must go to the bank every Friday.]

ESL 2

Nouns, Quantifiers, and Articles

Two important categories of nouns are *noncount nouns* and *count nouns*. **Noncount nouns** name things that cannot be counted separately, such as *air* and *water*. **Count nouns** name things that can be counted separately, such as *students* and *chairs*. (See GRAM 1b for more about noncount nouns and count nouns.) This section contains information about some features of noncount and count nouns. It also gives help in using quantifiers (such as *a little* and *a few*), the indefinite article *a/an*, and the definite article *the*.

ESL 2a Identify and use noncount nouns correctly.

Most noncount nouns fall into one of several categories. Learning these categories and some of the nouns associated with each one will help you recognize and use these nouns correctly.

1. **Learn to identify noncount nouns.**

   Many nouns in the following categories are noncount nouns:

   NAMES OF FOODS   beef, bread, cauliflower

   LIQUIDS, POWDERS, GRAINS   milk, dust, sand

   AREAS OF KNOWLEDGE   biology, economics, history

   IDEAS AND EMOTIONS   beauty, hatred, truth

   OTHER NONCOUNT NOUNS   (These are not obvious, so you must learn them.) clothes, furniture, information, machinery, money, news

2. **Do not make noncount nouns plural.**

   luggage
   I checked my ~~luggages~~ on the plane.

   A **partitive** is a phrase that indicates the units of something; for example, *a piece of* luggage, *a pound of* sugar, *a gallon of* gasoline. When a partitive is used with a noncount noun, the noun itself remains singular, even when the partitive is plural.

   I had two pieces of luggage~~s~~ with me.

3. **Do not use the indefinite article *a/an* with noncount nouns.**

   Use no article when the noun has a general meaning.

   Gasoline
   ~~A gasoline~~ becomes more expensive during holiday weekends.

   Use *some* or *the* when the noun has a specific identity that is known to your reader.

   some
   I bought ~~a~~ gasoline yesterday.

ESL 2b   Use the correct quantifiers for noncount nouns and count nouns.

A **quantifier** is a word or phrase that tells how much or how many of something. It can be used instead of an article.

1. **Use the appropriate quantifiers for noncount and count nouns.**

NONCOUNT NOUNS	COUNT NOUNS
a little salt	*a few* students
too much poverty	*too many* cars
a great deal of confidence	*three* instructors

2. **Learn which quantifiers can be used with both noncount and count nouns**

NONCOUNT NOUNS	COUNT NOUNS
enough money	*enough* quarters
some furniture	*some* chairs
a lot of bread	*a lot of* oranges

To ask questions regarding quantity, use "How much?" with non-count nouns and "How many?" with count nouns.

How much salad should I make?

How many foreign cars were sold in the United States last year?

ESL 2c Use the indefinite article *a* or *an* before a singular count noun when you do not specify which one.

It's hot in here. Please open *a* window. [any of several windows]

Use *a* before words beginning with a consonant sound and *an* before words beginning with a vowel sound.

a *user*	an *hour* from now
an *advertising* agency	a *happy* family

Notice that *an* is used before a silent *h* (*hour*) and *a* is used before an *h* with a consonant sound (*happy*).

ESL 2d Learn when to use the definite article *the*.

The following six rules explain when to use the **definite article** *the*.

1. **Use the definite article before nouns that refer to something the reader already knows about or that is obvious from the context.**

Please open ˄window. [The reader knows which window.]

the

2. **Use the definite article after the first time a noun is mentioned.**

   FIRST MENTION

   Fill a large pot with *water.*

   SUBSEQUENT MENTION

   Bring $\overset{the}{\wedge}$ water to a rolling boil.

3. **Use the definite article for items of unique reference.**

   California borders on $\overset{the}{\wedge}$ Pacific Ocean.

   $\overset{The}{\wedge}$ Women's Suffrage Movement achieved its goal in 1920.

4. **Use the definite article with the superlative form of adjectives.**

   $\overset{The\ best}{\wedge}$ ~~Best~~ way to paint a house is to hire a professional to do it.

5. **Use the definite article with nouns that are described by restrictive phrases or clauses.**

   Restrictive phrases and **restrictive clauses** answer the question "Which one?" or "Which ones?" about the noun they modify.

   $\overset{The\ woman}{\wedge}$ ~~A woman~~ *on the left* is the chairperson.

   $\overset{The\ person}{\wedge}$ ~~A person~~ *who began the consumer rights movement* was Ralph Nader.

6. **Do not use the definite article for the following:**

   PEOPLES' NAMES

   Please tell ~~the~~ Asif to come into my office.

   ABBREVIATIONS FOR UNIVERSITIES AND BUSINESSES

   Johnetta goes to ~~the~~ NYU.

   Zarenna works for ~~the~~ IBM.

GENERALIZATIONS

Vegetables
~~The vegetables~~ are good for you.

LANGUAGES OR SUBJECTS OF STUDY

Chitra is taking ~~the~~ history this semester.

SPORTS

Baseball
~~The baseball~~ is America's national sport.

HOLIDAYS OR RELIGIOUS OCCASIONS

~~The~~ Easter is in April this year.

PHRASES WITH *BED, CHURCH, CLASS, SCHOOL, TOWN, OR WORK*

Yael goes to ~~the~~ work in the afternoon.

CONTINENTS, COUNTRIES, STATES, CITIES, TOWNS, LAKES, STREETS

~~The~~ Australia is the smallest continent.

Many tourists visit ~~the~~ Washington, DC, each year.

EXCEPTIONS:　Countries whose name includes *of: the United States of America, the Commonwealth of Independent States, the People's Republic of China, the Republic of the Philippines.*

ESL 3

Adjectives and Adverbs

Adjectives and *adverbs* modify or describe other elements in a sentence. An **adjective** shows the quality or number of a noun. An **adverb** modifies a verb, an adjective, another adverb, or a clause. This section gives information about placing adjectives and adverbs in sentences. (See GRAM 1d and 1e for more about adjectives and adverbs.)

ESL 3a   Use correct word order when you modify a noun with more than one adjective.

a small oval   tall red brick
~~an oval small~~ gem   five ~~red brick tall~~ buildings

The following word order is typically used when more than one adjective precedes a noun:

1. Article, possessive adjective, or quantifier: *a/an, the, my, people's, five, some*
2. Number or comparative or superlative form of the adjective: *two, first, older, slowest*
3. Evaluative adjective that can be modified by *very: beautiful, committed, delicious*
4. Size: *big, small, long, short*
5. Shape: *round, square, triangular*
6. Age: *modern, nineteenth-century, ancient, new, old*
7. Color: *red, green, mauve*
8. Nationality: *German, Chinese, Mexican*
9. Religion: *Protestant, Jewish, Muslim, Buddhist*
10. Material: *wood, brick, gold*
11. Noun used as an adjective: *student* lounge, *music* program, *dining room* furniture

NOTE: Using more than two or three adjectives to modify a noun is usually awkward. Focus on the most important qualities and choose your descriptive words carefully.

ESL 3b   Learn the different meanings of present and past participles.

Present participles and past participles are verbals that are often used as adjectives. (See GRAM 1a for more about verbals.) Their meanings are quite different:

PRESENT PARTICIPLE

My friend Jake is *annoying*. [Jake causes annoyance.]

PAST PARTICIPLE

My friend Jake is *annoyed*.* [Jake experiences annoyances.]

*NOTE: This sentence is in the present tense. The past participle, which is an adjective in this sentence, does not indicate past tense.

When you use participles to describe moods or feelings such as the following, check a dictionary or ask a native speaker for help:

annoying/annoyed   exhausting/exhausted
boring/bored   interesting/interested
confusing/confused   frightening/frightened
depressing/depressed   refreshing/refreshed
discouraging/discouraged surprising/surprised
exciting/excited   tiring/tired

                              interesting
Our tour of the Roman ruins was ~~interested~~.

          interested
I am very ~~interesting~~ in learning to play the piano.

            exhausting   refreshed
Lisa's trip was ~~exhausted~~, but she returned ~~refreshing~~ by the experience.

ESL 3c Place adverbs correctly in sentences.

The position of an adverb in a sentence depends on what element of the sentence the adverb modifies. There are two basic types of adverbs: adverbs of frequency tell *how often* and adverbs of manner tell *how*. Remember these five rules regarding placement of adverbs in a sentence.

1. **Place adverbs of frequency, such as** *always, often, never,* **and** *usually,* **after the verb** *be.*

   Julio Iglesias's music is *usually* very romantic.

2. **Place adverbs of frequency before verbs other than** *be.*

   Unknown evils *always* lurk in the cemetery at midnight.

3. **Some adverbs modify adjectives (ADJ) or other adverbs (ADV). Place these adverbs of manner in front of the adjective or other adverb that they modify.**

                            ADJ
   Icy roads are *extremely* dangerous, day or night.

                            ADV
   We were going *too* fast for the road conditions.

EXCEPTION: The adverb *enough* follows the adjective or adverb that it modifies.

ADJ

We were not careful *enough* on such icy roads.

4. **Other adverbs may be placed before or after the verb or at the beginning or end of the sentence.**

Mina *tactfully* avoided the subject.

The Clean Air Act passed *easily*.

Slowly and *carefully*, he eased the car out of the parking space.

Check with a native speaker if you are not sure where to place the adverb in a sentence.

5. **Do not place an adverb between a verb and its direct object.**

gladly

We signed ~~gladly~~ his petition to get on the ballot.

ESL 4

Prepositions and Prepositional Phrases

A preposition (PREP) shows a relationship between objects or ideas in a sentence. The relationship can be in space (spatial), in time (temporal), or in manner.

Spatial: Ravi's room is *next to* the candy machine.
Temporal: Dr. Bey has her office hours *before* class.
Manner: They eat french fries *with* lots of ketchup.

A **prepositional phrase** contains a preposition followed by one of the items in the relationship, usually a noun or noun phrase. (See GRAM 1f and GRAM 3a for more about prepositions.)

ESL 4a   Learn the correct prepositions for the meanings you want to convey.

Not all languages have prepositions. Languages that do have them usually have fewer prepositions than English does, and the meanings of prepositions in other languages often do not correspond to the meanings of English prepositions. Moreover, most English prepositions have more than one meaning. (He left *at* 4:00. I live *at* 28 DeForest Heights.) For these reasons, English prepositions can be difficult to learn. When you are unsure of which preposition to use, consult your dictionary or ask a native speaker.

at/in
Yesterday I worked all day ~~to~~ the library.

[*To* is used to show direction with motion verbs, as in the sentence *I go to school every day. Work* does not show motion.]

in
Susan and Frank live ~~at~~ Chicago.

[*At* is used with exact addresses, as in the sentence *Susan and Frank live at 55 Summit Street. In* is used with the names of cities and states. Chicago is a city.]

ESL 4b   Do not omit necessary prepositions.

Prepositions are needed at the beginning of prepositional phrases. Without them, nouns that are not direct objects can be mistaken for direct objects. In addition, important information can be lost.

in
My father has been living ʌ this house for many years.

[A preposition is needed in front of *this house* to show that it is not the direct object of *has been living*. The preposition *in* helps explain where *my father* has been living.]

to
Yesterday we went ʌ the store.

[A preposition is needed in front of *the store* to show that it is not the direct object of *went*. The preposition *to* helps explain where we went.]

ESL 4c   Do not add extra words to prepositional phrases or create prepositional phrases when you do not need them.

A prepositional phrase is not always necessary to complete the meaning of a sentence. When one is necessary, it should contain only a preposition followed by its object. Subjects and verbs should not be included in prepositional phrases.

Peter is learning English by ~~he~~ listening to the radio.

[This prepositional phrase contains a preposition, a subject, and an object. Only a preposition and an object are necessary.]

ESL 4d Remember that infinitives cannot be used as the objects of prepositions.

The object in a prepositional phrase is always a pronoun or some form of noun, such as a noun phrase (*the dog*), noun clause (*what the dog wanted*), or gerund phrase (*barking*). Infinitives (*to bark*) cannot be used as objects of prepositions.

These heavy boots are especially designed for ~~to hike~~.

hiking

ESL 4e Learn some common compound prepositions.

Whereas some prepositions consist of one word, others are two or more words. Prepositions of two or more words are called **compound prepositions** (C PREP).

PREP
I like to walk *by* myself.
C PREP
I walk *next to* the sea.

COMMON COMPOUND PREPOSITIONS

according to	contrary to	next to
along with	due to	on behalf of
apart from	for the purpose of	on top of
as a result of	in addition to	out of
as far as	in back of	prior to
aside from	in contrast to/with	regardless of
as well as	in favor of	subsequent to
away from	in front of	together with
because of	in spite of	up to
by means of	instead of	with regard to

ESL 4f Learn some common adjective + preposition combinations.

Certain adjective + preposition combinations have special meanings and are very common.

Marta is *fond* ~~for~~ chocolate.
(of)

Adam is *interested* ~~about~~ Russian history.
(in)

COMMON ADJECTIVE + PREPOSITION COMBINATIONS

(un)accustomed to	conscious of	(dis)pleased with
associated with	dedicated to	proud of
aware of	different from	qualified for
based on	equal to	(dis)satisfied with
(in)capable of	fond of	surprised by, about
committed to	interested in	(un)worthy of
composed of	(un)known for	

ESL 5

Parts of Sentences

Every sentence has a subject and a predicate. (See GRAM 2a and 2b.)

ESL 5a Every sentence must have a verb, even when the meaning is understood.

English requires a main verb in each clause or sentence, even when the meaning is clear without it. Sentences need *be* to link a subject with a prepositional phrase or a predicate adjective.

The conference ∧ in New York this year. New Yorkers ∧ very friendly.
(is) *(are)*

ESL 5b Every sentence or independent clause has one, and only one, subject.

The weather, which started out cloudy, ~~it~~ improved later in the day.

[Even though the subject, *weather*, is separated from the verb *improved* by a descriptive clause, it should not be repeated.]

Miami has two soccer leagues. ∧ ~~Has~~ plans to add two more.
(It has)

ESL 5c   Use expletives correctly.

In most English sentences, the subject is first and the verb and other parts of the predicate follow it. (Review parts of sentences in GRAM 2.) However, a subject may be postponed until later in the sentence. In this case, an **expletive** (*there, here,* or *it*) at the beginning of the sentence substitutes for the postponed subject. (See EDIT 1g for more about expletives.)

Expletives are used in the following ways:

There is a common expletive used to indicate that a particular phenomenon exists.

> S
> *There* is a large Hmong community in Minneapolis.
>
> [The subject, *a large Hmong community,* is placed after the verb.]

The expletive *here* usually introduces information.

> S
> *Here* are a few ways to be an effective language learner.

The pronoun *it* often functions as an expletive when the deferred subject is a noun clause or phrase.

> S
> *It* is tragic to watch our tropical rain forests disappearing.
>
> [The subject is the entire noun phrase.]

> S
> *It* is not enough that we have good intentions.
>
> [The subject is the noun clause *that we have good intentions.*]

Follow these three guidelines for writing correct sentences with expletives:

1. **When you use *there* or *here* as an expletive, check that the verb agrees with the deferred subject.**

   Singular subjects require singular verbs; plural subjects require plural verbs.

   > SING.   PLURAL
   > Here is a turkey sandwich for your lunch, and here are some cookies.

2. **Use the expletive *it* when talking about a condition or when there is no other subject.**

It is
∧~~Is~~ wonderful to see you.

It is
∧~~Is~~ raining again.

3. **Remember to use a form of the verb *be* with expletives.**

are
There ~~have~~ many discount outlet stores in Kenosha.

ESL 6

Special Problems

This section gives information on word order and verb tenses in questions, reported speech, and conditional sentences. (See GRAM 4 for additional information on clauses.)

ESL 6a Use the correct word order for questions.

Word order in English questions is very important and follows pre-dictable patterns. Questions that take a "yes/no" answer begin with an auxiliary. When there is one verb in a basic tense, use a form of *do* (*do, does, did*), followed by the subject.

Does Simone play the piano?   Do her brothers also play?

"Yes/no" questions in progressive or perfect tenses, or ones that have modals, begin with the appropriate auxiliary or modal, followed by the subject.

Have you bought your books yet?   Can you swim?

When there is a question word (*who, what, where, when, why,* or *how*), it comes first, followed by the auxiliary. (See ESL 6b for *who* or *what* questions that do not require an auxiliary.)

Where does Professor Long's class meet?

This is the basic word order for English questions; the items in parentheses are optional:

(question word)	auxiliary	subject	(main verb)	(everything else)
	Are	they		hungry?
How long	has	Eun	worked	for IBM?
Who			teaches	calculus?
Who	is		teaching	calculus?

ESL 6b Use the correct word order and helping verbs for questions with *who, whom,* and *what.*

Who and *what* can be used in questions as either subjects or objects. However, notice the differences in the ways questions are formed when *who* and *what* are used as subjects and when they are used as objects.

1. **In questions with *who* or *what* as subject, use the word order of declarative sentences. Do not use a helping verb.**

QUESTION	DECLARATIVE SENTENCE
S	S
Who saw him?	*We* saw him clearly.
S	S
What causes lower back pain?	*Weak stomach muscles* cause it in most cases.

   NOTE: *Who* and *what* are always treated as singular and take singular verbs.

2. **In questions with *who(m)* or *what* as objects, use forms of *do* as helping verbs, and use an interrogative word order with the object at the beginning.**

   O   O
   Whom do they usually *hire?* They usually hire *students.*

   O   O
   What did they *decide?* They decided *to approve the project.*

ESL 6c Use correct word order in indirect questions.

Review declarative and interrogative sentences in GRAM 5b. When direct questions become part of another declarative sentence, they are called **indirect questions.**

DIRECT QUESTION	INDIRECT QUESTION
Does it rain a lot in Idaho?	I am not sure *whether it rains a lot in Idaho.*
Could Native Americans use tools at that time?	Archaeologists do not know *if Native Americans could use tools at that time.*
Where were the first Native Americans from?	This article discusses *where the first Native Americans were from.*
Where did they go?	The map shows *where they went.*

When you use indirect questions in your writing, watch for the following three differences between indirect questions and direct questions:

1. **For indirect questions, use the word order of declarative sentences, not the word order of direct questions.**

   The article discusses where ~~were they~~ they were from.

2. **Introduce indirect "yes/no" questions with *if* or *whether* and use the appropriate form of the main verb.**

   Do not use *do, does,* or *did* and the base form of the verb, as you would with a question.

   I don't know ~~did they explore~~ if they explored North America.

   Introduce indirect questions that have modal verbs with *if* or *whether.*

   The author is not sure ~~could Native Americans~~ whether Native Americans could navigate by the stars.

3. **Use the punctuation that is correct for the entire sentence.**

   No Native Americans remember why their tribes built the mounds?.

   [This is a declarative sentence, so punctuate it with a period.]

ESL 6d   Use the correct verb tense in reported speech.

Writers report someone else's words either by direct quotation or by reported speech. In **direct quotation,** the writer gives the speaker's exact words, enclosed in quotation marks. In **reported speech** (indirect quotation), the writer restates the speaker's words and embeds them in a clause. (Review tense in EDIT 2d and shifts between direct and indirect quotations in SENT 3e.) Changing a speaker's exact words into reported speech requires the following changes in the sentence:

1. **Change present tense in direct quotations to past tense in reported speech.**

   Change auxiliary verbs *do* and *does* to *did*.

DIRECT QUOTATION	REPORTED SPEECH
"I *assign* several short essays," Professor Lyons told us.	Professor Lyons told us that she *assigned* several short essays.
"I *do not require* a research paper," Professor Lyons assured us.	Professor Lyons assured us she *did not require* a research paper.*

   *NOTE: You may omit *that* at the beginning of the clause for reported speech.

2. **Change present perfect or past tense to past perfect.**

DIRECT QUOTATION	REPORTED SPEECH
Petra said, "I *have studied* acting for four years."	Petra said that she *had studied* acting for four years.
Ben said, "I *lost* my car keys."	Ben said he *had lost* his car keys.

3. **Change present progressive to past progressive.**

DIRECT QUOTATION	REPORTED SPEECH
"*I'm working* part time to earn money for tuition," I said.	I said I *was working* part time to earn money for tuition.

4. **Change *can* to *could*, *will* to *would*, and *may* to *might*. Do not change other modals.**

DIRECT QUOTATION	REPORTED SPEECH
The Mayor said, "We *can't* raise taxes."	The Mayor said that the town *couldn't* raise taxes.
"I *will* try to obtain federal funds," he told the audience.	He told the audience that he *would* try to obtain federal funds.
"However," he cautioned, "I *may* not be successful."	However, he cautioned that he *might* not be successful.

5. **Report "yes/no" questions with *if* or *whether*.**

DIRECT QUOTATION	REPORTED SPEECH
"Can we expect to know soon?" asked one reporter.	One reporter asked *if* we could expect to know soon.

6. **Report "or" questions with** *whether.*

DIRECT QUOTATION

He asked, "Are you going to meet here or in Washington?"

REPORTED SPEECH

He asked *whether* the Mayor was going to meet here or in Washington.

7. **Use the infinitive with** *to* **to report commands.**

DIRECT QUOTATION

The Mayor told the reporter, "*Wait* until next week for that announcement."

REPORTED SPEECH

The Mayor told the reporter *to wait* until next week for that announcement.

ESL 6e Use the correct verb tenses in conditional sentences.

In a **conditional sentence,** if a certain fact exists, then another related fact may also exist.

When population increases, the demand for health services also increases.

[An increase in population is one cause of an increase in the demand for health services.]

There are usually two clauses in a conditional sentence, a *main clause* (MC) and a *subordinate clause* (SC) that begins with *if, when, whenever,* or *unless.* The verb tenses in these clauses can be confusing because the normal meanings of the tenses do not always apply. In one type of conditional sentence, for example, the past tense is used to speculate about events in the future.

SC | MC
If you wear my size, you can borrow my jacket.

[The present tense is used to speak about the property]

SC | MC
If you wore my size, you could borrow my jacket.

[The past tense is used to speak about the future.]

Here are some rules to help you write correct conditional sentences.

1. **Determine what kind of condition you are writing about.**

First, determine the time frame—past, present, or future. Then determine whether the conditions you are describing are real or unreal. The most common types of conditional sentences are presented here.

In **present and past real conditions,** the conditions stated in both the subordinate and the main clause actually exist or existed.

SC   MC
When air warms, it rises.

SC   MC
Whenever the pollen count increased, my brother got hay fever.

Future real conditions predict situations that are likely to occur if a condition is met.

SC   MC
If you travel by freighter, expect an adventure.

Present and future unreal conditions speculate about untrue or unlikely situations in the present or future.

SC   MC
If I were* on vacation, we could spend more time together.

[I am not on vacation, so we can't spend more time together.]

NOTE: With the verb *be* use *were* for all subjects in the *if* clause.

Past unreal conditions speculate about situations in the past that did not occur.

SC   MC
If the plumber had fixed the leak, the cellar would not have flooded.

[The plumber did not fix the leak, and the cellar flooded.]

2. **For present and past real conditions, use the same tense in both clauses.**

SC   MC
If Tina *reads* for a long time, she *gets* a headache.

SC   MC
Whenever Kennedy *spoke,* the audience *was* spellbound.

3. **For future real conditions, use the following tenses:**

SUBORDINATE CLAUSE	MAIN CLAUSE
If or *unless* + present tense*	*can, may, might, should,* or *will* + base form

SC   MC

If you *leave* by eight o'clock, you *can* still catch your plane.

*NOTE: For future real conditions, use the present tense, not the future, in the subordinate clause, even though this clause expresses a future condition.

4. **For present and future unreal conditions, use the following verb tenses:**

SUBORDINATE CLAUSE   MAIN CLAUSE
If + past tense*   *could, might,* or *would* + base form

SC   MC

If I *had* my dictionary, I *could* check the spelling for you.

[Because I do not have my dictionary, I will not be able to check the spelling.]

SC   MC

If I *were*** in charge, things *might* be different.

[Because I'm not in charge, things will probably stay the same.]

MC   SC

Jorge *would* get up on time if he *set* his alarm clock at night.

[Because Jorge does not set his alarm, he will not get up on time.]

*NOTE: For present and future unreal conditions, past verb forms do not express action in the past. Instead, the past form is used to show that events are unlikely or imagined.

**NOTE: With the verb *be* remember to use *were* for all subjects in the *if* clause.

5. **For past unreal conditions, use the following verb tenses:**

SUBORDINATE CLAUSE   MAIN CLAUSE
If + past perfect*   *could have, might have,* or *would have* + past participle

SC   MC

If I *had done* my laundry, I *would have had* clean socks.

[I did not do my laundry, so I do not have clean socks.]

*NOTE: In past unreal conditions, the past perfect does not have its usual meaning of an event prior to another event in the past. Instead, it is used to speculate about something that did not occur or that was unreal in the past.

ESL 7

Confusing Words and Phrases

Some words and phrases in English are particularly confusing to ESL learners. Two of these are *do* and *make: Do* usually means "to complete" or "to perform." *Make* usually means "to create," 'to construct," or "to produce." Both are verbs.

The children *do* their homework before going outside.

[The children *complete* their homework first.]

Greg *makes* dinner almost every night.

[Greg *creates* or *puts together* the dinner.]

Two other particularly confusing words are *too* and *very. Too* implies a negative result. *Very* does not imply a negative result. Both are adverbs.

This book is *too* long to read in one day.

[It is *impossible* to read the book in one day.]

This book is *very* long, but I must read it all today.

[It is *possible* to read the book in one day.]

Certain words and phrases are also usage problems for native speakers. Some of the most common are presented in the Glossary of Usage in WORD 7.

sent

Sentences

Learning Objectives

After reading this section, you should:

- write more unified, logical, and varied sentences;
- be able to use parallelism, subordination, and coordination to express your ideas;
- be familiar with different ways of achieving emphasis in your writing;
- recognize problems with modifiers;
- recognize inappropriate shifts (for example, in verb tense).

Sentences

SENT 1

Parallelism

Improve the coherence and clarify the meaning of your sentences by using **parallelism;** that is, use parallel grammatical form to reinforce parallel ideas.

BALANCE A WORD WITH A WORD

I see one-third of the nation *ill-housed, ill-clad,* and *ill-nourished.*
—Franklin D. Roosevelt

BALANCE A PHRASE WITH A PHRASE

It's much easier to write *a solemn book* than *a funny book.*
—Fran Lebowitz

BALANCE A CLAUSE WITH A CLAUSE

I never write "metropolis" for seven cents because I can get the same price for "city"; I never write "policeman" because I can get the same money for "cop."
—Mark Twain

SENT 1a Use parallel constructions with coordinating conjunctions (*and, but, or, nor, for, yet, so*).

to appeal
The lawyer chose not to criticize the judge but ~~appealed~~ the decision.

provides companionship
A seeing eye dog announces danger, insures mobility, and ~~is a companion~~.

To emphasize parallel structures, repeat an article (*a, an, the*), a preposition, the sign of the infinitive (*to*), or the first word of a long phrase or clause.

a
Timothy wanted a promotion and salary increase.
^

to
Kim had real doubts—to go or stay.
^

97

SENT 1b Use parallel constructions with correlative conjunctions (*either/or, neither/nor, not only/but also, both/and, whether/or*).

He was neither a good host nor ~~someone who could tell a good story~~. _{a good storyteller.}

The couple behind us who kept whispering were both inattentive and ~~not showing good manners~~. _{rude.}

SENT 1c Use parallel constructions in comparisons that use *than* or *as*.

I would rather resign than ~~agreeing~~ to an unethical solution. _{agree}

Seeing is as good as ~~to believe~~. _{believing.}

SENT 2

Misplaced and Dangling Modifiers

The words, phrases, and clauses that function as modifiers in a sentence can usually be moved around, so place them carefully to avoid unintentionally confusing—or amusing—your reader. There are basically two types of problems that arise with modifiers: the **misplaced modifier** and the **dangling modifier**.

MISPLACED The waiter brought a steak to the young man *covered with mushrooms.*
[*Covered with mushrooms* is misplaced.]

REVISED The waiter brought a steak *covered with mushrooms* to the young man.
[The steak, not the man, was covered with mushrooms.]

DANGLING *Flying over the mountain tops,* several herds of deer could be seen.
[*Flying over the mountain tops* is dangling.]

REVISED *Flying over the mountain tops,* we could see several herds of deer.
[We, not the deer, were flying.]

Because most English sentences depend heavily on word order for meaning, modifiers should be placed as close as possible to the words they modify. We see this in the preceding sentences. Notice, in the following sentences, how the position of one word—*just*—can change the meaning.

Just he said that he dented the fender. [No one else said it.]

He *just* said that he dented the fender.
[He said it a short while ago, or he said no more.]

He said *just* that he dented the fender. [He said no more.]

He said that *just* he dented the fender. [No one else was involved.]

He said that he *just* dented the fender.
[He dented it a short while ago, or he did not do more damage.]

He said that he dented *just* the fender.
[He dented no more than the fender.]

SENT 2a   Place modifiers where they will be most effective.

1. **Place adverbs such as *just, only, even, hardly, nearly,* and *merely* directly before the words they modify.**

   nearly
   He missed his appointment. nearly.
   ^   ^

2. **Place prepositional phrases used as adjectives after the words they modify. (See GRAM 3a.)**

   with holes in it
   Dana wore an old shirt for painting. with holes in it.
                        ^   ^

3. **Place prepositional phrases used as adverbs near the words they modify. (See GRAM 3a.)**

   in a hurry
   Mary left for a vacation. in a hurry.
           ^   ^

4. **Place adjective clauses near the words they modify. (See GRAM 4a.)**

> *who was wearing a bathing suit*
> The actress was walking the poodle. ~~who was wearing a bathing suit.~~

5. **Be alert for squinting modifiers.**

A **squinting modifier** looks in two directions; that is, it appears to modify both the word it follows and the word it precedes.

> *badly*
> The passenger who was hurt ~~badly~~ needed help.

[Placed after *hurt, badly* modifies both *hurt* and *needed*. When *badly* is placed before *hurt,* the sentence says several passengers were hurt and one seriously.]

> *badly.*
> The passenger who was hurt ~~badly~~ needed help.

[Moving *badly* to modify *needed* communicates that only one passenger was hurt but seriously.]

6. **Keep the main verb and all auxiliaries and modals as close together as possible. (See GRAM 1a.)**

> *have*
> We ~~have~~ never before had such a tremendous interest in the right-to-
>
> die issue.

[The complete verb is *have had.*]

7. **Do not split infinitives. (See GRAM 1a.)**

> The president instructed his advisory board to ~~very carefully~~ analyze the
> *very carefully*
> new economic report.

SENT 2b Connect a dangling modifier to the main part of the sentence.

A **dangling modifier,** occurs when a participle, a gerund, an infinitive phrase (see GRAM 3b), or an **elliptical clause** (one with some words implied rather than stated) does not logically relate to the main part of the sentence. Dangling modifiers are usually at the beginning of a sentence; the doer of the action is unstated. To eliminate a dangling modifier, (1) state the subject immediately after the dangling phrase or (2) give the dangling phrase a subject.

was noticed by him.
Walking on the ceiling, ~~he noticed~~ a very large insect.

[The subject has been stated immediately after the dangling participial phrase. However, since the new sentence is in the passive voice and awkwardly phrased, it would be a good idea to revise further.]

He noticed a very large insect *walking on the ceiling.*

A   was walking on the ceiling, he noticed.
~~Walking on the ceiling, he noticed~~ A very large insect.

[The dangling participial phrase has been given a subject.]

the students began
After sitting down, the exam ~~began~~.

[The implied subject of the dangling gerund is explicitly stated.]

you need
To run well, good running shoes ~~are needed~~.

[The implied subject of the dangling infinitive phrase is explicitly stated.]

they are
Keep beating the eggs until fluffy.

[Here, *they are* substitutes for "the eggs are," which is implied but not stated in this elliptical clause.]

SENT 3

Shifts

Abrupt or inappropriate **shifts**—changes from first-person to third-person, from past to present tense, or from informal to formal diction, for example—weaken the logic of your writing or obscure your meaning. At the very least, such inconsistencies confuse and therefore slow down your reader. Inappropriate shifts most often occur within a sentence, but sometimes they happen between one sentence and the next.

SENT 3a Use pronouns that are consistent in person and number.

Shifts in **person** most commonly occur between first-person pronouns (*I, we, me, us, my, our*), second-person pronouns (*you, your, yours*), and second-person and third-person pronouns (*he, she, it, they, him, her, them, his, hers, its, their, theirs*).

First-person pronouns highlight the writer and are appropriate for writing based on personal experience. Second-person pronouns direct attention to the reader and are appropriate for directions and other how-to types of writing. Third-person pronouns highlight the subject and are used in most informative writing situations, which generally includes academic writing. (See COMP 2f.)

we
We were told ~~you~~ could take pack burros to the bottom of the canyon.

[Because the writer is not addressing the reader directly, the shift from first-person *we* to the second-person *you* is inappropriate.]

you
If you eat sensibly and watch your fat intake, ~~most people~~ should be

your
able to maintain ~~their~~ desired weight.

[The shift from second-person to third-person pronouns causes confusion. Because the writer is addressing the reader directly, *you* is appropriate throughout.]

Sometimes, in an effort to be formal or scholarly, writers use the indefinite pronoun *one,* as in "Nothing makes one realize the mystery of nature so much as viewing the northern lights." Because most people find such phrasings unnatural—even pretentious (see WORD 2c)—writers then find themselves shifting between *one* and first person or second person.

me
Viewing the northern lights makes ~~one~~ realize the mystery of nature, and knowing the scientific explanation makes me appreciate the spectacle all the more.

[It is much more natural to speak in the first-person throughout.]

Most shifts in **number**—the singular and plural forms of nouns and pronouns—occur when a plural pronoun is used to refer to a singular noun or vice versa. (See EDIT 1i.)

students take
When ~~a student takes~~ an exam, they should read all the questions carefully.

[By changing *student takes* to *students take,* the writer eliminates the unnecessary shift in number and avoids the *he/she* issue. See EDIT 3a.]

The Organization of American States has not achieved economic unity in

the western hemisphere; ~~they have~~ *it has* succeeded in other areas, however.

[Because *Organization of American States* is singular, the pronoun in the second main clause needs to be singular as well.]

SENT 3b Maintain the same verb tense.

The verb tense in a sentence indicates when the action is taking place. Shifting from one tense to another without a logical reason causes readers to wonder what you really mean. (See EDIT 2c and 2d.)

Margaret always stayed at the Algonquin Hotel; she ~~finds~~ *found* the rooms spacious and beautifully decorated.

[Putting both verbs in the past tense clarifies that Margaret no longer stays at the Algonquin.]

SENT 3c Maintain the same mood.

Verbs in English have three **moods:** the *indicative,* the *imperative,* and the *subjunctive.* (See EDIT 2e.) Problems with inconsistency usually occur with the imperative mood.

In learning to hit a golf ball, take a full back swing, and ~~it is also~~

~~important to~~ keep your eye on the ball.

[Eliminating *it is also important to* avoids the unnecessary shift from the imperative to the indicative mood.]

SENT 3d Keep subject and voice consistent.

Inconsistencies in the subject of a sentence (see GRAM 2a) and the voice (see EDIT 2f) often go hand in hand, resulting in awkwardness and confusion.

We could see the widespread effects of the drought as ~~the farm was~~ *we*

approached ~~,~~ *the farm.*

[Moving from the active voice in the main clause to the passive voice in the subordinate clause results in the confusing shift of subject from *we* to *farm.*]

Sometimes a shift in subject and voice creates a *dangling modifier*—a modifying phrase or clause that is not logically connected to any word in the sentence. (See SENT 2b.)

we could see
Exhausted, our final destination ~~could be seen~~ clearly in the distance.
                               ^

[*Exhausted* is a dangling modifier because it does not logically relate to the subject of the main clause (the destination is not exhausted); in the corrected main clause, the subject *we* tells who is exhausted.]

SENT 3e Avoid unnecessary shifts from direct to indirect quotation.

In **direct quotation** the writer gives a speaker's words verbatim—that is, word for word—in quotation marks. In **indirect quotation,** or **reported speech,** the writer paraphrases or summarizes what the speaker said.

DIRECT QUOTATION
The aerobics instructor said, "Let's really raise those knees!"

INDIRECT QUOTATION
The aerobics instructor said we should raise our knees higher.

A shift from direct to indirect quotation or vice versa can be confusing.

Our instructor said work stations had to be cleaned at the end of each
                                          had to be reported.
lab session and ~~report~~ all test-tube breakage.
                                                 ^

This example can also be revised to maintain consistent direct quotation.

Our instructor said, "Clean your work stations at the end of each lab session and report all test-tube breakage."

SENT 3f Keep tone and style consistent.

Unnecessary shifts in **tone**—the attitude or stance the writer takes toward the subject and audience—and in **style**—the writer's manner of expression—call attention to themselves and away from the intended meaning. For example, a reader would be surprised by an unexpected shift from a reverent to a sarcastic tone or from a flowery to a simple style. In most cases, such inconsistencies are matters of appropriate word choice. (See WORD 2.) Choose words carefully to achieve a consistent tone and style.

> The fact that some large industrial plants are not conforming to clean-air
> laws ~~ticks off~~ *angers* many people.

[*Ticks off* is a slang expression and contrasts sharply with the more formal and objective tone established at the beginning of the sentence. *Angers, worries,* or *alarms* is a better word choice.]

> John and Stefano climbed into the leaky old rowboat and rowed out to
> the middle of the lake to ~~reenact the ancient rivalry in which man and~~
>
> ~~fish do battle~~ *fish.*

[*To reenact the ancient rivalry in which man and fish do battle* is stylistically too poetic or elevated for the rest of this simple, straightforward sentence.]

SENT 3g   Maintain the same point of view.

An abrupt shift from one **point of view**—the angle from which events are viewed—to another perspective can be unsettling. An event can be viewed from any number of angles: from the inside or the outside, the front or the back, or above or below, for example. The key is to be consistent.

> The theater-goers applauded wildly at the end of *Cats,* ~~and~~ *while outside* the taxis
> lined up to take them away.

[The abrupt shift from inside to outside the theater is disconcerting; adding *while outside* prepares the reader for the change in point of view.]

SENT 4

Unified and Logical Sentences

In a **unified** sentence, all parts—words, phrases, and clauses—work together to achieve the effect you desire. A unified sentence is composed in such a manner that if its components were rearranged or changed, its purpose would not be achieved as effectively. Because we usually think faster than we write, however, we can easily neglect to include information that will make a sentence complete and clear. Or sometimes we do not put all the details we have in mind in the best order or fail to choose the best ones to make our point. Sometimes, too, we mentally make logical connections that we do not capture in writing, leaving our readers unable to follow our line of thought. For example, in the following sentence, notice how a cause-and-effect relationship is merely hinted at in the original version, whereas the revision clearly establishes the logical relationship for the reader.

The mail-order business is growing very fast in this country, ~~and~~ *because* many

people don't have time to shop.

In some sentences that lack unity, however, no logical relationship can be established between the ideas; in this case it is best to make two sentences.

DISJOINTED   The White House, set afire by the British in 1814, is located on Pennsylvania Avenue in Washington, DC.

REVISED   The White House is located on Pennsylvania Avenue in Washington, DC. The British set fire to the building in 1814.

SENT 4a   Use only relevant details.

Details make writing vivid and interesting, but details that have no connection to the central idea of a sentence only obscure that idea. Also, irrelevant details can bore and distract your reader.

The *Apollo 16* Space Mission left earth on April 16, 1972, ~~with its three-man crew~~ spent three days on the moon, and returned successfully on April 27, 1972.

SENT 4b   Avoid mixed or illogical constructions.

Sentences can be illogical for many reasons, but, as might be expected, certain kinds of constructions occur more frequently than others. Here are some guidelines for avoiding the most common problems.

1. Be sure the subject and predicate are related.

Faulty predication occurs when the subject and the predicate of a sentence are not sensibly related. (See GRAM 2a and 2b.)

done
The casting for the school play was ~~selected~~ by the director.

[*The casting was done* OR *the cast was selected,* but not both in the same sentence.]

2. Check your use of linking verbs.

A linking verb should not be used to equate elements that cannot be equated logically.

high.
The cost of a college education is ~~expensive~~.

[*The cost is high* OR *a college education is expensive,* but not both in the same sentence.]

A linking verb should not be used to introduce an adverbial clause. (See GRAM 4b.) This most often happens with *is when, is where,* and *the reason is because* constructions.

In a
A double-dip recession, ~~is where~~ the economy recovers for a short time, then dips once again.

[A *double-dip recession* is an event, not a place.]

~~The reason~~ I love math ~~is~~ because it's challenging.

[The linking verb *is* requires a subject complement, and here, what follows is an adverbial clause.]

An appositive, or noun substitute (see GRAM 3c), should be equal to the noun for which it stands.

vice presidency,
Ms. Martindale was given a promotion, a ~~vice president~~, for being so successful in sales.

[A *vice president* is a person; what is needed here is the name of the position.]

3. Keep figures of speech consistent.

We mix figures of speech (see WORD 1e) more often when we speak than when we write because we do not think out an entire sentence in advance. Still, the error also occurs in writing.

We were sailing along smoothly, until we ran into a roadblock. *rough seas.*

[A *roadblock* relates to land travel and is inconsistent with *sailing.*]

4. Make all parts of a sentence agree in number. (See SENT 3a.)

A police officer stopped our car, but they did not arrest us. *she*

[*A police officer* is singular; *they* is plural.]

5. Avoid double negatives.

It is a convention of standard English to use only one negative to negate. Avoid using a negative modifier (*no, not,* or *never*) with other negative words (such as *no one, nobody, nothing, none, neither,* and *nowhere*).

You can't say nothing that will change his mind. *anything*

[*Not* (in *can't*) and *nothing* are the two negatives.]

A double negative is acceptable, however, if the intent is to make a positive statement in a dramatic way.

Everyone agreed that she wasn't unaware of what she was doing.

SENT 5

Subordination and Coordination

As writers we impose emphasis on what we write to distinguish important ideas from lesser supporting details or to convey that ideas are equally important. We use **subordination** to make one idea less important than another. We use **coordination** to balance equal ideas and give equal emphasis.

Subordination emphasizes the important idea in a sentence by putting it in the main clause and the less important ideas in dependent phrases or clauses. (See GRAM 3 and 4.) In the following sentence, for example, because Jacoby wishes to emphasize that readers snicker at quotations attributed to cab drivers, she puts that idea in an independent clause and subordinates the rest of the thought under the subordinating conjunction *because.*

> Readers tend to snicker at newspaper stories with quotations attributed to taxi drivers, because the anonymous "cab driver quote" is a device much favored by reporters who are too lazy to ask any real people for their opinions. —Susan Jacoby

In the following example, the writer uses coordination to indicate that both ideas—what Lynn bought and how she paid for it—are equally important; thus, each is presented in a main clause.

Lynn bought a classic '57 Chevy/, ~~She~~ paid cash for it.
and she

SENT 5a Use subordination to group short, choppy sentences into larger units of thought.

Besides being stylistically monotonous, short, choppy sentences give equal importance to all your ideas, but only rarely are all your ideas equally important. You communicate more clearly if you show how your thoughts are related. Use one of the following four strategies for subordinating supporting details to the main idea (see also SENT 7a):

1. **Subordinate with an adjective or a phrase that functions as an adjective. (See GRAM 1d, 3a, and 3b.)**

   The football players, stood in the rain. ~~They were exhausted. They were covered with mud~~.
   exhausted and covered with mud,

   [The minor ideas, *exhausted* and *covered with mud,* are now subordinated.]

2. **Subordinate with an adverb or a phrase that functions as an adverb. (See GRAM 3a and 3b.)**

   ~~Remove~~ the spark plugs, ~~Clean~~ them with a wire brush/, ~~Reinstall~~ them.
   After removing   *and cleaning*   *carefully reinstall*

   ~~Be careful.~~

   [The minor idea *carefully* has been subordinated to the main point, the instructions.]

3. Subordinate with an adverb clause. (See GRAM 4b.)

When she   *she*
~~She~~ was thirty years old~~,~~ ~~She~~ made her first solo flight across the Atlantic.

[The less important thought, *thirty years old,* has been subordinated to the main point, what she achieved.]

4. Subordinate with an appositive or appositive phrase. (See GRAM 3c.)

The
~~There were two~~ winners~~,~~ ~~Their names were~~ Pamela and Jorge~~,~~ ~~They~~

couldn't attend the banquet.

[Because the main idea is that the winners couldn't attend, we're only incidentally interested in their names. Therefore, *Pamela and Jorge* has been subordinated.]

SENT 5b   Do not subordinate excessively.

In an effort to avoid short, choppy sentences, do not go overboard in the other direction and subordinate excessively. Your sentence will trail on and lose its effectiveness. Eliminate excessive subordination by using modifiers—phrases as well as words—or by breaking the sentence into two.

The ship~~, low in the water with cargo and silently creeping along,~~ en-

rising
tered the channel, which glittered from the light of the sun. ~~that was just~~

~~rising~~ Low in the water with cargo, it silently crept along.

[By breaking the sentence into two and changing the clause *that was just rising* to an adjective, the writing becomes more forceful.]

SENT 5c   Use coordination to put ideas of equal importance in grammatical structures of equal weight.

There are three ways to coordinate ideas in a sentence. Join the independent clauses by:

1. using a comma and a coordinating conjunction (*and, but, or, for, nor, so,* or *yet*—see GRAM 1g),

2. using a semicolon (see PUNCT 2a), or
3. using a set of correlative conjunctions, such as *either/or, neither/nor, not only/but also* (see GRAM 1g).

SENT 6

Emphasis

Inexperienced writers sometimes try to emphasize the most important ideas in a sentence by using italics, exclamation points, or intensifiers such as *truly* and *incredibly.* These are mechanical and unimaginative devices, however, and they actually have a numbing effect after a while. Instead, use subordination (see SENT 5) and a variety of other techniques presented in this section to sharpen the focus of your ideas and thereby heighten the interest of your readers.

SENT 6a   Achieve emphasis by placing the most important words and phrases at the beginning or end of a sentence.

The most emphatic part of a sentence is the end; the second most emphatic part is the beginning; the least emphatic part is the middle. Less important ideas and qualifying phrases such as *for the most part, as I see it,* and *in a sense* should be buried in the middle of the sentence, placed at the front, or—often best—eliminated.

When our two best players were injured, our hockey team was, de- *in a sense,*

feated, *in a sense.*

According to experts, children's
Children's carseats should be placed in the back seat, *according to experts.*

SENT 6b   Place ideas that occur in a series in a logical and climactic order.

lost control,
Wendell went off the road, *lost control,* and hit a tree.

[Losing control happened first and so should be stated first.]

SENT 6c   Use the active rather than the passive voice.

The **active voice** of a verb (see WORD 4e, EDIT 2f, and SENT 3d) is emphatic because it stresses the doer of an action; the **passive voice** of a verb, on the other hand, stresses the receiver of an action.

PASSIVE   Our sailboat was pushed by high winds onto the rocks, where it was torn to pieces by the waves.

ACTIVE   High winds pushed our sailboat onto the rocks, where the waves tore it to pieces.

Sometimes, however, the receiver of an action needs to be emphasized. In this case, of course, use the passive voice. Here, for example, how quickly the house sold is the point, not who sold it.

Our house was sold the day it went on the market.

SENT 6d   Repeat important words for emphasis.

Repeating a key word, phrase, or fact to keep an idea before the reader can be a very effective strategy. Repetition and parallelism (see SENT 1) are frequently found together in writing, though they are not necessary to one another.

Victory at all costs, *victory* in spite of all terror, *victory* however long and hard the road may be; for without *victory* there is no survival.
                                                                —Winston Churchill

SENT 6e   Occasionally use a short, dramatic sentence.

A short declarative sentence (see GRAM 5b), especially when it follows a longer, more involved sentence, can startle the reader and thus achieve emphasis.

The executive suite on the thirty-fifth floor of the Columbia Broadcasting System skyscraper in Manhattan is a tasteful blend of dark wood paneling, expensive abstract paintings, thick carpets, and pleasing colors. *It has the quiet look of power.*
                                                                —David Wise

SENT 6f Achieve emphasis by using periodic sentences.

In a **periodic sentence,** modifying phrases and clauses build to the main idea, which is placed at the end, closest to the period (hence its name). Periodic sentences are emphatic because they keep the reader in suspense until the main idea is reached, and because they do not appear frequently in modern prose.

Most sentences we write are *loose sentences;* that is, the main idea is expressed immediately, and subsequent phrases and clauses trail behind, providing details and qualifications.

LOOSE We put on our galoshes and walked up the sunny side of Fifth Avenue to Central Park on the afternoon of the first day of spring, when the gutters were still heaped high with Monday's snow but the sky itself had been swept clean.

PERIODIC On the afternoon of the first day of spring, when the gutters were still heaped with Monday's snow but the sky itself had been swept clean, we put on our galoshes and walked up the sunny side of Fifth Avenue to Central Park.

—John Updike

Both types of sentences are correct, but you gain emphasis by occasionally using a periodic sentence.

SENT 6g Achieve emphasis by using balanced constructions.

In most **balanced constructions,** similar ideas are presented in grammatically similar constructions. (See SENT 1.) Emphasis can be achieved, however, by doing the unexpected—placing contrasting ideas in grammatically similar constructions.

Hard practices are required for easy games.

[The expectation is that a similar idea will follow in a similar construction (*hard practices/difficult games*); instead, the unexpected contrasting idea (*easy games*) emphasizes the author's point.]

SENT 7

Sentence Variety

A series of sentences that are all the same length and that follow the same basic pattern is boring. **Sentence variety** adds interest to your writing. However, you should seek variety in sentence structure not as an end in itself but as a more accurate means of reflecting your thoughts. Just as you do not think in a mechanical and monotonous way, so too you should not write mechanical and monotonous sentences. (See GRAM 5.)

The techniques discussed in this section are all good options for adding variety to your writing. Use them to put your thoughts into sentences that suit your purpose (see COMP 2f) and your audience (see COMP 2g).

SENT 7a Avoid the overuse of short simple sentences.

The following passages both describe the city of Vancouver. Although their content is essentially the same, the first is monotonous because it is made up of a series of simple sentences of nearly the same length; the second is interesting because it is made up of sentences of varying structure and length.

CHOPPY AND MONOTONOUS

Water surrounds Vancouver on all sides. The snow-crowned Coast Mountains ring the city on the northeast. Vancouver has a floating quality of natural loveliness. There is a curved beach at English Bay. This beach is in the shape of a half-moon. Residential high rises stand behind the beach. They are pale tones of beige, blue, and ice-cream pink. Turn-of-the-century houses of painted wood frown upward at the glitter of the office towers. Any urban glare is softened by folds of green lawns, flowers, fountains, and trees. Such landscaping appears to be unplanned. It links Vancouver to its ultimate treasure of greenness. The treasure is thousand-acre Stanley Park.

INTERESTING

Surrounded by water on three sides and ringed to the northeast by the snow-covered Coast Mountains, Vancouver has a floating quality of natural loveliness. At English Bay, the half-moon curve of the beach is backed by high rises in pale tones of beige, blue, and ice-cream pink. Turn-of-the-century houses of painted wood frown upward at the glitter of office towers. Yet any urban glare is quickly softened by folds of green lawns, flowers, fountains, and trees that in a seemingly unplanned fashion link Vancouver to its ultimate treasure of greenness—thousand-acre Stanley Park.   —Veronica Thomas, "Vancouver"

If you tend to write short, simple sentences, study the following five ways of combining sentences to make your writing more interesting.

1. **Use subordinating and coordinating conjunctions to relate and connect ideas. (See GRAM 1g.)**

    After touring   *and seeing*   *Robert*
    ~~Robert went on a tour of~~ the hospital, ~~He saw~~ many sick people. ~~He~~ had
                                              and
    a greater appreciation for the work doctors do, ~~He had a greater appre-~~
                            which he
    ~~ciation~~ for his own good health, ~~He~~ had taken ~~his good health~~ for

    granted.

2. **Use modifiers effectively.**

    Instead of writing separate descriptive statements, combine modifiers to convey a more graphic picture in a single sentence. (See SENT 5a.)

                    old, dilapidated
    Martha bought the house. ~~It was old. It was dilapidated.~~

3. **Use a semicolon (see PUNCT 2a) or colon (see PUNCT 3a) to link closely related ideas.**

                                              i
    This novel is not one of her better works; It is ill-conceived and badly

    written.

    Four students won the essay contest: ~~The winners were~~ Mike, Susan,

    Alfie, and Cathy.

4. **Use parallel constructions. (See SENT 1.)**

> Georgene liked the dress. It was her favorite style. ~~The color was also~~
> *and*
> ~~her favorite.~~
> *color.*

5. **Use absolute constructions. (See GRAM 3d.)**

> ~~We were~~ stuck in traffic. ~~We~~ sat for forty minutes. ~~We~~ missed the opening
> *S* *w* *and*
> kick-off.

SENT 7b Vary your sentence openings.

More than half of all sentences in English begin with the subject. (See GRAM 2a.) However, if all, or nearly all, the sentences in a given passage begin this way, the effect is monotonous.

Consider the different ways in which the following sentence can be rewritten to vary its beginning and add interest:

> Passengers partied in the ballroom and did not know that the ship had hit an iceberg.

1. Begin with a participle, a gerund, or an infinitive. (See GRAM 3b.)

> *Partying* in the ballroom, the passengers did not know that the ship had hit an iceberg.

2. Begin with a prepositional phrase. (See GRAM 3a.)

> *In the ballroom,* the passengers partied, not knowing that the ship had hit an iceberg.

3. Begin with a subordinate clause. (See GRAM 4a and 4b.)

> *As they partied in the ballroom,* the passengers did not know that the ship had hit an iceberg.

4. Begin with a coordinating conjunction. (See GRAM 1g.)

> *And* the passengers, partying in the ballroom, did not know that the ship had hit an iceberg.

5. Begin with an expletive. (See EDIT 1g.)

> *There* were passengers partying in the ballroom who did not know the ship had hit an iceberg.

Another way of changing the usual subject–verb–object order of sentences is simply to **invert**—or reverse—the natural order. Do not, though, seek variety at the expense of proper emphasis.

USUAL ORDER	INVERTED ORDER
Subject–Predicate	Predicate–Subject
The water gushed out.	Out gushed the water.
Subject–Verb–Predicate	Object–Subject–Verb
I never promised that.	That I never promised.
Subject–Linking Verb–Complement	Complement–Subject–Linking Verb
They would never be happy.	Happy they would never be.

SENT 7c Do not overuse compound sentences.

A series of compound sentences (see GRAM 5a), especially with the main clauses connected by *and,* gives an impression of haste and thoughtlessness. Like a series of short, simple sentences (see SENT 7a), too many compound sentences bore the reader. When you revise, look for *ands* used as coordinating conjunctions. If you find that you overuse *and,* try the following four methods to bring important ideas into focus and make it easier for the reader to follow your thought.

1. **Change a compound sentence into a simple sentence with a modifier(s) or an appositive. (See GRAM 3c.)**

   SIMPLE SENTENCE WITH A MODIFIER

   The hiking trail, ~~was~~ nearly five miles long, and ~~it was~~ wonderfully scenic, ~~and it~~ was popular with young campers.

   SIMPLE SENTENCE WITH AN APPOSITIVE

   brilliant
   My brother, is a heart surgeon, ~~and he is brilliant, and he~~ is on the staff of Massachusetts General Hospital.

2. **Change a compound sentence into a simple sentence with a compound predicate. (See GRAM 2b.)**

   SIMPLE SENTENCE WITH A COMPOUND PREDICATE

   Tony grabbed his tennis racket, and ~~he~~ jumped in the car.

3. **Change a compound sentence into a simple sentence with a phrase or phrases. (See GRAM 5a.)**

   SIMPLE SENTENCE WITH A PHRASE

   Super Stores have a great variety of merchandise, ~~and the prices are~~ *with good prices.*

   ~~good.~~

4. **Change a compound sentence into a complex sentence. (See GRAM 5a.)**

   COMPLEX SENTENCE

   Because my
   ∧~~My~~ computer was broken, ~~and~~ I had to write my report in longhand.

edit

Editing for Grammar

Learning Objectives

After reading this section, you should:

- recognize subject–verb agreement errors;
- use verbs and pronouns correctly;
- use adjectives and adverbs correctly;
- recognize fragments, comma splices, and run-on sentences.

Editing for Grammar

EDIT 1

Subject–Verb Agreement

In grammar, **subject–verb agreement** refers to the correspondence in form between a verb and its subject. Every verb in a clause or sentence must agree in *number* and *person* with its subject. That is, make a verb singular if its subject is singular; make a verb plural if its subject is plural. Also, make a verb agree in person (that is, the doer of the action— first person, second person, third person) with its grammatical subject.

SINGULAR THIRD PERSON SUBJECT AND SINGULAR VERB

Overcrowding causes many of the discipline problems in our schools.

PLURAL THIRD PERSON SUBJECT AND PLURAL VERB

Hurricanes destroy millions of dollars worth of property each year.

Normally, we do not think twice about subject–verb agreement. A few constructions, however, can be troublesome. In most cases, the problem results from not having correctly identified the subject of the sentence.

EDIT 1a To choose the correct verb form, identify the subject of the sentence.

Sometimes intervening word groups obscure the relationship between the subject (S) and the verb in a sentence. When the relationship is not clear, the culprit is usually an intervening prepositional phrase. Mentally block off all the prepositional phrases in a sentence, and see what is left. One of these leftover words must be the subject because a subject can never be in a prepositional phrase. (See GRAM 3a.)

S   are
The first three weeks of basic training ~~is~~ the worst.

[The plural subject *weeks* takes a plural verb.]

Another word group that can cause confusion about subject–verb agreement is the subordinate clause. (See GRAM 4.) Neither the subject nor the verb of a sentence will ever be in a subordinate clause.

S
Taking mood-altering drugs, although they sometimes provide great

is
medical benefits, ~~are~~ generally criticized by the public.

[The singular subject *taking* takes a singular verb.]

A problem can also arise from the use of such expressions as *along with, as well as, in addition to, including,* and *together with.* Again, look elsewhere for the subject of the sentence.

> ~~s~~
> The cost of medication as well as doctors' fees ~~are~~ a problem for retired people.
> *is*
>
> [The singular subject *cost* takes a singular verb.]

Thus, if you mentally block off all the prepositional phrases, subordinate clauses, and miscellaneous expressions in a sentence, the subject and verb will pop out by process of elimination.

> Unless it rains, *I plan* on leaving as late as possible, along with all the other vacationers.

Finally, when you invert normal word order, be especially careful to identify the subject correctly. (See SENT 7b.)

> *have* s
> From his research ~~has~~ come three promising anti-cancer drugs.
>
> [The plural subject *drugs* takes a plural verb.]

EDIT 1b Use a plural verb with most compound subjects joined by *and.*

In most cases, compound subjects are clearly plural and clearly take a plural verb.

> s s *were*
> Their television and their camera ~~was~~ stolen.

However, when singular subjects joined by *and* are preceded by *each, every, no, nothing,* or *many a(n),* use a singular verb.

> *is*
> Every chair and every couch ~~are~~ on sale this week.
>
> [Every *single* chair and every *single* couch (each) is on sale.]

> *is*
> No bicycling and no hitchhiking ~~are~~ permitted on U.S. Highway 20.
>
> [Neither *one,* or nothing—*no thing* (singular)—is permitted.]

If the two parts of a compound subject, whether singular or plural, express a single idea or refer to a single person, use a singular verb.

is
Ham and eggs ~~are~~ my favorite breakfast.

[The subject *ham and eggs* is considered a single dish and takes a singular verb.]

knows
His son and partner ~~know~~ all the facts about the incident.

[His son is also his partner. If they were different people, *know* would be correct.]

EDIT 1c If subjects joined by *either/or* or *neither/nor* differ in number or person, make the verb agree with the subject that is closest to it.

are
Neither the instructor nor the students ~~is~~ satisfied with the classroom.

[One singular subject (*instructor*) and one plural subject (*students*) are joined by *nor*; make the verb agree with the closer subject (*students*), which is plural.]

have
Either Mary or I ~~has~~ to report the broken window.

[One third-person subject (*Mary*) and one first-person subject (*I*) are joined by *or*; make the verb agree with the closer subject (*I*, which is first person).]

EDIT 1d When a collective noun used as a subject regards a group as a unit, use a singular verb. When it refers to the individual members of a group, use a plural verb.

Collective nouns are singular in form but can have a plural meaning; for example, *band, jury, family, minority, majority*. (See GRAM 1b.) They may take either a singular or a plural verb, depending on whether you are considering the group as a unit or in terms of its individual members.

> The *committee gives* its report today.
>
> [*Committee* is considered a unit because all the members are acting as one in giving a single report; a singular verb is used.]
>
> The *committee give* their reports today.
>
> [The individual members of the committee will each give a report; *committee* has a plural meaning so the verb must be plural.]

To be consistent in sentences containing collective nouns, make pronoun references to the noun singular or plural as well.

> The *team plans* to fly to Indianapolis for *its* next game.
>
> [*Team* is considered a single entity (they are all on the same plane); use a singular verb and a singular pronoun.]
>
> The *team plan* to fly to Indianapolis for *their* next game.
>
> [The *team* is considered in terms of individuals traveling separately and arriving at different times; use a plural verb and a plural pronoun.]

EDIT 1e When a relative pronoun (*who, which, or that*) is the subject, make the verb agree with the pronoun's antecedent.

Usually, verb agreement is not a problem with relative pronouns. (See GRAM 1c.)

> A *politician who votes* pro-labor gets elected.
>
> [The singular noun *politician* is the antecedent of *who;* use a singular verb.]
>
> *Politicians who vote* pro-labor get elected.
>
> [The antecedent of *who* is *politicians,* which is plural; use a plural verb.]

However, when the phrase *one of the* or *the only one of the* is part of the sentence, identifying the antecedent takes extra care.

> She is one of the *senators who* always *vote* pro-labor.
>
> [The antecedent of *who* is *senators* because the sense is that more than one senator votes a particular way; the verb, therefore, is plural.]

She is the only *one* of the senators *who* always *votes* pro-labor.

[The antecedent of *who* is *one* because she is the only senator who votes a particular way; the verb, therefore, is singular.]

EDIT 1f When an indefinite pronoun is the subject, choose a singular or plural verb, depending on the number of the indefinite pronoun.

Indefinite pronouns are a problem area of subject–verb agreement in English. Their usage is changing in several respects, presenting writers with new choices.

1. **Use a singular verb with a singular indefinite pronoun (***another, anybody, anyone, anything, each, either, everybody, everyone, everything, neither, none, no one, nothing, one, somebody, someone, something***).**

   Somebody has to decide whether to paint the kitchen this year.

   [One person (*one body*) will make the decision.]

2. **Use a plural verb with a plural indefinite pronoun (***both, few, many, several***).**

   I spent the afternoon shopping for a camera, but *few were* reasonably priced.

   [Not many, but more than one, were available.]

3. **With indefinite pronouns that can be either singular or plural (***all, any, some***), use a singular or plural verb, depending on the word the indefinite pronoun refers to.**

   All of the *wheat* is harvested.

   All of the *fields are* plowed.

   [Because *wheat* is singular, *all* takes a singular verb. Because *fields* is plural, *all* takes a plural verb.]

EDIT 1g   When a sentence begins with the expletive *there* or *here*, make the verb agree in number with the subject.

Expletives are words that stand in for a subject that is deferred until later in the sentence. In addition to *there* and *here*, the pronoun *it* can also function as an expletive, but *it* always takes a singular verb.

> *are*
> There ~~is~~ stone, brick, and tile fireplaces in Blenheim Castle.

EDIT 1h   Make linking verbs agree in number with their subjects, not with their complements.

A **subject complement** (see GRAM 2d) renames or describes the subject and is, therefore, sometimes confused with it.

> s   *is*
> His main interest ~~are~~ stamps.

[The subject, *interest,* is singular, so the verb must be singular; *stamps* is the complement.]

EDIT 1i   When the subject noun is in the form of a plural but is singular in meaning, use a singular verb.

Nouns that are plural in form but singular in meaning take singular verbs. Examples of such nouns include *athletics, mathematics, measles, mumps, news, physics,* and *politics.*

> s   *was*
> Measles ~~were~~ a serious childhood disease until a vaccine was developed.

Some nouns, however, end in *s* and are singular in meaning but take plural verbs: *eyeglasses, pants, pliers, scissors, trousers, tweezers.*

> s   *are*
> The scissors ~~is~~ on the table.

If you are uncertain whether to use a singular or a plural verb with a particular noun, consult your desk dictionary.

EDIT 1j When the title of a poem, short story, play, or book is the subject of a sentence, use a singular verb, even if the title is plural in form.

> s   is
> *The Canterbury Tales* ~~are~~ by Chaucer.

EDIT 1k When a word used as a word is the subject, use a singular verb.

The number (singular or plural) of the word used as a word is unimportant; the sentence is about a single thing so use a singular verb.

> s   is
> *Octopi* ~~are~~ one of the plural forms of *octopus*.

EDIT 1l When the subject of a sentence is a noun clause, use a singular verb.

> s
> That he actually bought a new jeep *surprises* me.

[The verb is singular because the noun clause refers to a single thing: *it* (singular) surprises me.]

Noun clauses that begin with *what* are the exception. If the subject of the sentence is plural and the verb is a linking verb, use a plural verb with a *what* clause.

> are   s
> What worries him more than anything else ~~is~~ his low grades in his major.

EDIT 2

Verbs: Form, Tense, Mood, and Voice

EDIT 2a Use the principal parts of irregular verbs correctly.

English verbs are either *regular* or *irregular* in form. (See GRAM 1a.) Quite simply, a **regular verb** is one that forms both the past tense and the past participle by adding *-ed* to the base form (*walk, walked, walked*). Regular verbs rarely cause problems; it is **irregular verbs** that can be tricky because they have different forms for the past tense and past participle (*sing, sang, sung*).

> Americans usually *sing* the national anthem before sporting events.
>
> Mariah Carey *sang* the national anthem at the football game.
>
> Garth Brooks had *sung* the anthem the year before.

The most frequently used of the approximately two hundred irregular verbs in English are identified in the following list. For some, two acceptable forms are given; they usually represent regional variations. For example, *dove* is the accepted past-tense form of *dive* in much of the northern United States, but *dived* is the accepted form in much of the South.

COMMON IRREGULAR VERBS

INFINITIVE	PAST TENSE	PAST PARTICIPLE
awake	awoke	awakened
be	was	been
bear [to carry]	bore	borne
bear [to give birth]	bore	born
become	became	become
begin	began	begun
bend	bent	bent
bet	bet	bet
bite	bit	bitten, bit
blow	blew	blown
break	broke	broken
bring	brought	brought
build	built	built
burst	burst	burst
catch	caught	caught

INFINITIVE	PAST TENSE	PAST PARTICIPLE
choose	chose	chosen
come	came	come
cost	cost	cost
cut	cut	cut
deal	dealt	dealt
dig	dug	dug
dive	dived, dove	dived
do	did	done
drag	dragged	dragged
draw	drew	drawn
dream	dreamed, dreamt	dreamed, dreamt
drink	drank	drunk
drive	drove	driven
eat	ate	eaten
fall	fell	fallen
feel	felt	felt
find	found	found
fit	fit, fitted	fit, fitted
fly	flew	flown
forbid	forbade, forbad	forbidden
forget	forgot	forgotten, forgot
freeze	froze	frozen
get	got	got, gotten
give	gave	given
go	went	gone
grow	grew	grown
hang [to suspend]	hung	hung
hang [to execute]	hanged	hanged
hear	heard	heard
hit	hit	hit
hurt	hurt	hurt
know	knew	known
lay [to put]	laid	laid
lead	led	led
lend	lent	lent
let	let	let
lie [to recline]	lay	lain
light	lighted, lit	lighted, lit
lose	lost	lost
pay	paid	paid
put	put	put
ride	rode	ridden
ring	rang	rung
rise	rose	risen
run	ran	run

INFINITIVE	PAST TENSE	PAST PARTICIPLE
say	said	said
see	saw	seen
set [to place]	set	set
shake	shook	shaken
shine	shone, shined	shone, shined
shrink	shrank	shrunk
shut	shut	shut
sing	sang	sung
sink	sank	sunk
sit [to be seated]	sat	sat
slay	slew	slain
speak	spoke	spoken
split	split	split
spread	spread	spread
spring	sprang	sprung
steal	stole	stolen
strike	struck	struck, stricken
swear	swore	sworn
swim	swam	swum
take	took	taken
teach	taught	taught
tear	tore	torn
throw	threw	thrown
wake	woke, waked	waked, woken
wear	wore	worn
win	won	won
write	wrote	written

If you are not certain about the form of a particular verb, consult your desk dictionary. Most dictionaries list all three principal parts of irregular verbs and the infinitive form of regular verbs.

EDIT 2b Use *lay* and *lie* and *set* and *sit* correctly.

Writers often confuse the irregular verbs *lay* (to put down) and *lie* (to recline) and *set* (to put something somewhere) and *sit* (to take a seat).

INFINITIVE	PAST TENSE	PAST PARTICIPLE
lay	laid	laid
lie	lay	lain
set	set	set
sit	sat	sat

Lay and *set* are transitive verbs (see GRAM 1a) and require a direct object to complete their meaning. *Lie* and *sit* are intransitive verbs (see GRAM 1a), and therefore do not take a direct object (DO).

>   laid   DO
> I ~~lay~~ the package down on the table in the hall yesterday.

>   lie
> I'm going to ~~lay~~ down for an hour before dinner.

>   set   DO
> You can ~~sit~~ the groceries on the kitchen counter.

>   sit
> Ms. Lane asked the class to ~~set~~ quietly.

Another pair of irregular verbs that causes problems is *hang* (to execute a person) and *hang* (to suspend an object).

>   hanged
> The prisoner was ~~hung~~ at dawn yesterday.

>   hung   DO
> The curator ~~hanged~~ the African masks in the entrance.

EDIT 2c   Use the correct verb tense to convey your meaning.

The **tense** of a verb indicates when an action is taking place. In English there are three basic tenses—*present, past,* and *future.* Each tense also has a *perfect,* a *progressive,* and a *perfect progressive* form.

Present tense

Use the **present tense** to express an action occurring in the present, a habitual action, or a fact or general truth. Also use the present tense in describing or discussing an artistic work.

PRESENT TIME ACTION   Sarah Lynn *works* at Bell Labs.

HABITUAL ACTION   Tom *empties* the trash barrels every morning.

FACT   Water *boils* at 212°F.

GENERAL TRUTH   It *is* always better to be honest.

LITERARY WORK   Tragically, King Lear *trusts* Goneril and Regan.

The **literary** or **historical present tense** refers to the use of the present tense for events that have occurred in the past for the special purpose of making the events or fictional happenings come alive. Do not lapse into the past tense out of habit because you are writing about something that has already happened in your reading.

> *endures*
> Harriet Jacobs ~~endured~~ the degradation of slavery and eventually
> *gains*
> ~~gained~~ her freedom with the help of abolitionist-feminist friends.

The present tense can also be used to indicate actions that will take place at some future time.

> Susan *leaves* for Chapel Hill on Saturday.

Present perfect

Use the **present perfect tense** to describe (1) an action that occurred in the past but continues into or affects the present, or (2) an action that occurred at no specific time in the past. The present perfect is formed by combining a present form of *have* with the past participle.

> She *has taught* master classes in violin for over ten years.
>
> Some small recording studios *have produced* big hits.

Present progressive

To show an action that is ongoing at the time of speaking or writing, use the **present progressive**—the present participle of the verb with the present of the helping verb *to be*.

> Tom *is emptying* the trash barrels right now.

The present progressive can also be used to show actions that will take place at some future time.

> We *are going* to camp at both Yellowstone and Yosemite.

Present perfect progressive

To show the length of time an action is in progress, use the **present perfect progressive**—the present form of *have* together with *been* and the present participle of the verb.

> Ellen *has been working* at Babbage's for three years.

Past tense

Use the **past tense** to describe an action that occurred entirely in the past.

Sam *filed* his income tax forms early this year.

Past perfect

Use the **past perfect** to describe an action that preceded another action when both occurred in the past. The past perfect is formed by combining a past form of *have* with the past participle of the verb.

Everyone *had eaten* before I arrived.

Past progressive

To show continuing action in the past, use the **past progressive**—the present participle of the verb with the past of the helping verb *be*.

Matthew *was visiting* his grandparents in Nebraska.

Past perfect progressive

To show the length of time an action was in progress, use the **past perfect progressive**—the past form of *have* together with *been* and the present participle of the verb.

Cindy *had been playing* the piano before she took up the guitar.

Future tense

Use the **future tense** to describe an action that will take place in the future. The future tense is formed by combining *will* with the base form of the verb.

The Hillgroves *will take* their vacation in August this year.

English has additional ways of expressing future time; see the preceding discussions of present tense and present progressive.

Future perfect

Use the **future perfect tense** to describe an action that will be completed before another future event.

Ashley *will have accumulated* seventy credits in engineering by the end of the semester.

Future progressive

To show a continuing action in the future, use the **future progressive**—the present participle of the verb with the future of the helping verb *be*.

Astronomers *will be looking* for meteor showers over the southern horizon this spring.

Future perfect progressive

To show the length of time an action will be in progress, use the **future perfect progressive**—*will have been* with the present participle of the verb.

I *will have been collecting* teddy bears for ten years at my next birthday.

EDIT 2d   Use sequences of tense forms that are logically related.

How do you know which tense to use? You logically relate the time expressed by verbs in the main clauses with the time expressed by verbs in subordinate clauses, infinitives, or participles.

gave
The tiger jumped through the flaming hoop when the trainer ~~gives~~ the command.

Mixing tenses does not make a logical statement: you cannot have the tiger jumping in the past and the trainer giving the command in the present. Put both verbs in the past tense to show that both actions already happened, or put both verbs in the present tense to indicate it is a habitual action. (See SENT 3b.)

Subordinate clauses

You may use any verb tense in your subordinate clause (SC) that is compatible with the intended meaning of your sentence. (See GRAM 5a.)

MC	SC

The entrance march *will begin* after the wedding guests *have taken* their seats in the church.

[The future tense is used in the main clause (MC) to show an anticipated action; the present perfect tense is used in the subordinate clause to show that the seating of the guests will precede the march.]

MC SC

Some optimistic economists *believe* that the stock market soon *will top*

the 10,000 mark.

[The present tense is used in the main clause to show what economists currently believe; the future tense is used in the subordinate clause to show that the stock market's performance is anticipated at some future time.]

However, when the verb in the main clause is in the past or past perfect tense, you must also use the past or past perfect tense in the subordinate clause.

MC SC

The Celtics *had put* the game out of reach before the Rockets *changed*

their strategy.

[The past perfect is used in the main clause to show that the Celtics' action preceded the Rockets' action.]

When a general truth is presented in the subordinate clause, the present tense is used even though the verb in the main clause is in the past or past perfect.

SC

We *learned* in business ethics that power *corrupts.*

[The verb in the subordinate clause is in the present tense because *power corrupts* is a general truth.]

Infinitives

Use the **present infinitive** (*to praise, to drink*) to express action that occurs at the same time as or later than that of the main verb.

Marta tried *to improve* her tennis game.

[The present infinitive is used because Marta's improvement occurs at the same time as she tries.]

Mike wanted *to eat* the ice cream, but he was on a diet.

[The present infinitive is used because Mike's desire to eat the ice cream occurred after he'd begun his diet.]

Use the **present perfect infinitive** (*to have praised, to have drunk*) to express action that occurs prior to that of the main verb.

> I would like *to have attended* the Tori Amos concert last weekend.
>
> [The present perfect infinitive is used because attendance at the concert is in the past while the wishing or liking occurs in the present.]

Participles

Use the **present participle** (*praising, drinking*) to express action happening at the same time as that of the main verb.

> *Bicycling* across campus, Jan lost her bracelet.
>
> [The present participle is used because Jan lost her bracelet at the same time she was bicycling.]

Use the **present perfect participle** (*having praised, having drunk*) for action occurring prior to that of the main verb.

> *Having driven* two hundred miles nonstop, Rob stopped to stretch.
>
> [The present perfect participle is used because the driving occurs before the stopping.]

EDIT 2e Use verbs in the correct mood.

The three **moods** of a verb—*indicative, imperative,* and *subjunctive*—reveal the writer's intent; that is, how the writer views a thought or action. For example, it is a verb's mood that shows the writer is making a statement and not simply expressing a wish.

Use the **indicative mood** to make a statement or ask a question. Verb tense in the indicative mood depends on context. (See EDIT 2c.)

Use the **imperative mood** to give an order. Verbs in the imperative mood are always in the present tense except for *be*, which is used in the base form. Usually the subject *you* is understood.

> *Gargle* with salt water.
>
> *Be* at the airport by noon.

Use the **subjunctive mood** in *that* clauses expressing demands, resolutions, or requests and to express a condition contrary to fact or a wish. With *that* clauses, use the base form of the verb (*agree, be, farm, vote*) whether the subject is singular or plural.

The manager asked that he lists his qualifications for the job.

         be
The coach required that players ~~are~~ dressed one hour prior to the game.

Use *were* to express a wish and in contrary-to-fact clauses beginning with *if.*

         were
Coach Kray wished his new center ~~was~~ taller.

 were
If I ~~was~~ younger, I would go to law school.

EDIT 2f Use the active voice.

Voice indicates whether the subject of a sentence is the actor or the receiver of the action. (See SENT 6c.) In the **active voice,** the subject of the sentence does the acting; in the **passive voice,** the subject is acted upon.

ACTIVE VOICE

The National Rifle Association *opposes* gun-control legislation.

PASSIVE VOICE

Gun control legislation *is opposed* by the National Rifle Association.

Use the active voice in most of your writing; it is more concise, direct, and forceful than the passive voice. To change a sentence from passive to active voice, simply make the actor the subject of the sentence and eliminate unnecessary words.

The students selected
 ∧"Poverty and Homelessness" ~~was selected~~ as the theme for next year's

lecture series,~~by the students.~~
    ∧

When the action itself is what is important or you wish to minimize the importance of the actor, use the passive voice. The passive voice is often used in scientific and technical writing to emphasize processes and events rather than individuals.

Three drops of boric acid *were added* to the solution.

Investigative teams *were sent* by the Centers for Disease Control.

When you want to highlight the recipient of an action rather than the performer, use the passive voice.

Nolan Ryan, a sure-bet Hall of Famer, *was traded* by the New York Mets early in his career.

EDIT 3

Pronoun Problems

A **pronoun** takes the place of a noun in a sentence. (See GRAM 1c.) Pronoun problems fall into three general categories: problems with agreement (a pronoun must agree with the noun to which it refers), referent problems (a pronoun must clearly refer to another word), and case problems (a writer must know when to use *I* and when to use *me*, when to use *who* and when to use *whom*). The issues of agreement, reference, and case can produce sexist language, lack of clarity, or an impression of carelessness.

EDIT 3a A pronoun must agree with its antecedent in gender, number, and person.

A pronoun must agree with its **antecedent,** the noun to which it refers. (See GRAM 1c.) Personal pronouns must agree in gender, number, and person.

1. Be aware of sexist use of pronouns.

Traditionally, a masculine, singular pronoun has been used to agree with indefinite antecedents (such as *anyone, someone,* and *everyone*) and to refer to generic antecedents (such as *employee, student, patient, traveler,* or *applicant*). But *anyone* can be female or male, and women are employees (or students, patients, travelers, applicants), too. The use of masculine pronouns to refer to both females and males is unacceptable because it is **sexist;** that is, such usage leaves out women as a segment of society or diminishes their presence. (See WORD 3.) Instead, use *he or she, his or her*. Or, in an extended piece of writing, alternate in a balanced way the use of *he* and *she* throughout. Sometimes the best solution is to rewrite the sentence to put it in the plural or to avoid the problem altogether.

UNACCEPTABLE BECAUSE IT IS SEXIST

If *anyone* wants to buy a basketball season ticket, *he* will have to sign up before Friday.

UNACCEPTABLE BECAUSE IT IS GRAMMATICALLY INCORRECT

If *anyone* wants to buy a basketball season ticket, *they* will have to sign up before Friday.

REWRITTEN USING *HE OR SHE*

If *anyone* wants to buy a basketball season ticket, *he or she* will have to sign up before Friday.

REWRITTEN IN THE PLURAL

If any *students* want to buy basketball season *tickets, they* will have to sign up before Friday.

REWRITTEN TO AVOID THE PRONOUNS

All basketball season tickets must be reserved before Friday.

REWRITTEN IN THE SECOND PERSON

If *you* want to buy a basketball season ticket, *you* must sign up before Friday.

REWRITTEN WITH A RELATIVE PRONOUN

Anyone who wants to buy a basketball season ticket must sign up before Friday.

2. **Let the meaning of a collective noun (family, majority, choir, jury, faculty) determine whether pronouns that refer to it should be singular or plural.**

If a collective noun (see GRAM 1b) is understood as a unit, it takes a singular pronoun; if it is understood in terms of its individual members, it takes a plural pronoun.

The band started to play ~~their~~ its first number.

[The band as a unit is playing the same song; use a singular pronoun.]

The band agreed to pay for ~~its~~ their own uniforms.

[The individual members came to an agreement; use a plural pronoun.]

3. **Disregard gender and use a plural pronoun to refer to two or more singular antecedents that are connected by *and*.**

Antecedents joined by *and* form a compound subject and take a plural pronoun whether the antecedents are singular or plural. Gender is not an issue.

Dinah and Jack were exhausted after ~~her and his~~ chemistry final.
(their)

4. **When two or more antecedents are connected by *or, nor, either/or,* or *neither/nor,* and one is singular and the other is plural, use a pronoun that agrees with the closer antecedent.**

Neither the judge nor the lawyers were willing to discuss ~~his~~ reactions to the verdict.
(their)
[Use a plural pronoun because the nearest antecedent, *lawyers,* is plural.]

When a compound antecedent has both a male and a female component, make the pronouns consistent in both gender and the order presented.

Neither Dinah nor Jack was really confident about ~~their~~ grades.
(her or his)
[Use *her or his* in that order because *Dinah* is used first.]

5. **Use a singular pronoun to refer to such antecedents as *each, anyone, everybody, either, sort, kind,* or *someone*.**

In speech and informal writing, some people use plural pronouns with these antecedents, but formal English requires singular pronouns to be grammatically correct.

When someone doesn't understand, ~~they~~ should ask the instructor for help.
(he or she)

6. **Use *who* or *whom* to refer to persons; use *that* and *which* to refer to animals and things.**

The chef, ~~which~~ was trained in France, will make her famous Trout Amandine.
(who)

The bicyclist swerved to avoid the dog ~~who~~ had wandered into the street.
(that)

Who can be used with an animal that has a name, however.

> who
> Burt is a friendly dog ~~which~~ likes to bark.

EDIT 3b Be sure a pronoun's antecedent is clear.

To avoid repeating nouns in our speech and writing, we use pronouns as noun substitutes. (See GRAM 1c.) The noun for which a pronoun is substituted is called its **antecedent** or **referent**.

> she   her
> As Laurie opened the envelope, ~~Laurie~~ held ~~Laurie's~~ breath.

When the relationship between a pronoun and its antecedent is unclear, the message is inaccurate or ambiguous (has two or more meanings).

1. Place a pronoun as close to its antecedent as possible.

The more words that intervene between the antecedent and the pronoun, the more chance there is for confusion.

> who had never had much self-confidence,
> Cathy, was surprised she had been voted president by her classmates/.
>   ^   ^
> ~~who had never had much self-confidence~~\

2. Make every pronoun clearly refer to a specific antecedent.

If a pronoun can refer to either one of two antecedents, ambiguity exists. Either repeat the antecedent or rewrite the sentence.

> mother's
> Liz told her mother that her sweater had a hole in it.
>   ^
> Liz said to her mother, "Your sweater has a hole in it."

It is not acceptable to put the referent in parentheses following the pronoun.

3. When using *it* as a pronoun referent, check that the antecedent is unmistakable.

If there is more than one possible antecedent for the pronoun *it*, ambiguity results.

> the car.
> When Alex drove the car through the garage door, he badly damaged ~~it.~~
>   ^

4. Use *this, that, which,* and *such* judiciously to refer to a general idea in a preceding clause or sentence.

If an idea is relatively simple, no confusion results from such a construction. If the pronoun refers to a broader or more general idea, however, vagueness can result. To correct the problem either substitute a noun for the pronoun or provide an antecedent to which the pronoun can clearly refer.

One plumber supervised while the other one did the work,~~which~~ is normal.

a procedure that ∧

5. Make every pronoun refer to a stated, not an implied, antecedent.

Every time you use a pronoun in a sentence, you should be able to point to its noun equivalent. If you cannot, use a noun instead.

Because the hurricane was a potential danger to coastal communities, ~~they~~ were told to evacuate.

inhabitants

[*They* has no clearly stated antecedent; it does not refer to the hurricane or the communities.]

Sometimes a word or phrase, modifier, or possessive that implies a noun is mistaken for an antecedent.

In ~~Langston Hughes's~~ "Salvation," ~~he~~ tells how his family tried to save him from sin when he was a boy.

Langston Hughes

[*He* has no clearly stated antecedent; *he* could be an unnamed narrator or, as is the case, Hughes himself.]

6. The pronouns *it, they,* and *you* must have an antecedent.

In speech, we often get more involved in what we have to say than in how we say it. For example, we use *it, they,* and *you* loosely, without specific antecedents, and our listeners do not mind. But in written English, when these pronouns lack an antecedent, the writer gives an impression of vagueness and carelessness.

~~On the news, it~~ said the earthquake hit 6.5 on the Richter scale.

The newscaster

In the book, ~~they wrote that~~ Coach is a cocaine addict.

If ~~the driver is~~ ^{you are} not careful, you can easily miss the exit for San Jose.

EDIT 3c Use pronouns in the correct case.

In English the **case** or form of a personal pronoun is dictated by the grammatical function it serves in a sentence. In the **subjective case,** pronouns function as subjects or subject complements (see GRAM 1c); in the **objective case,** pronouns function as direct objects, indirect objects, or objects of prepositions; and in the **possessive case,** pronouns show ownership.

SUBJECTIVE	OBJECTIVE	POSSESSIVE
I	me	my, mine
you	you	your, yours
he	him	his, his
she	her	her, hers
it	it	its
we	us	our, ours
they	them	their, theirs
who	whom	whose

The pronouns *I, he, she, we, they,* and *who* have different forms in all three cases, whereas the pronouns *you* and *it* have a distinctive case form only for the possessive. Rule 3 below explains why there are two forms of the possessive case for most personal pronouns.

1. **Use the subjective case of pronouns (*I, you, he, she, it, we, they, who*) for subjects and subject complements.**

   Marge and ~~me~~ ^I shared expenses on the trip to Mexico.

   [*I* is part of the compound subject of the verb *shared.*]

   The guy Maria dated is ~~him~~ ^{he.}

   [*He* is the complement of the subject *guy.*]

Because we are lax about using the subjective case of pronouns for subject complements in speech, you may think being grammatically correct sounds unnatural. (See GRAM 2a and 2d.) If so, rewrite the sentence to put the pronoun in the subject position.

> He is the guy Maria dated.

2. **Use the objective case of pronouns (*me, you, him, her, it, us, them, whom, whomever*) for direct objects, indirect objects, and objects of prepositions.**

   her
   The dean invited ~~she~~ and Miguel to represent the student body in Washington.

   [*Her* is the direct object of the verb *invited*.]

   me
   Peter sent Alice, Diane, and ~~I~~ flowers.

   [*Me* is the indirect object of the verb *sent*.]

   me
   Between you and ~~I~~, Sharon's plan is best.

   [*Me* is the object of the preposition *between*.]

Also see GRAM 2c and 3a.

3. **Use one of the two forms of the possessive case of pronouns to show ownership.**

   When a pronoun precedes a noun, use the first form of the possessive case (*my, your, his, her, its, our, their, whose*) to show ownership.

   > *My* notebook has a red cover.

   Use the second form of the possessive case, if there is one (*mine, yours, his, hers, ours, theirs*), when the pronoun follows a verb and does not precede a noun.

   > The notebook with the red cover is *mine*.

4. **Use the possessive case of pronouns to modify gerunds.**

   Pronouns that modify a gerund take the first form of the possessive case (*my, your, his, her, its, our, their, whose*).

   His
   ~~Him~~ returning to college showed great maturity.

   our
   The car salesperson understood ~~us~~ wanting a good deal.

5. **Use the correct case for pronouns in compound constructions.**

To choose the correct pronoun in a compound construction, identify its function in the sentence: is it a subject or object? Test your choice by mentally blocking off the entire compound construction *except* the pronoun in question. Then read the remaining sentence aloud.

My three housemates and ~~me~~ ^I do the cooking.

[Read aloud: *Me do the cooking.* You can hear the error; revise to put the pronoun in the subjective case, *I.*]

Allison sent Max and ~~she~~ ^{her} an invitation to the open house.

[Read aloud: *Allison sent she the invitation.* You can hear the error; revise to use the objective case.]

The French Society appointed Karen and ~~I~~ ^{me} co-chairpersons for the coming term.

[Read aloud: *The society appointed I.* Again, you can hear the error; revise to use the objective case.]

Everyone had the surf-and-turf special except Danielle and ~~I~~ ^{me.}

[The preposition *except* requires the objective case.]

6. **Use the correct case for pronouns in appositives.**

An **appositive** is a noun or noun equivalent that directly follows, or sometimes precedes, another noun or noun equivalent and serves to amplify its meaning. (See SENT 5c.) Because an appositive has the same grammatical function as the noun or pronoun it explains, describes, or identifies, the appositive must be in the same case.

Two members of the debate team, Sara and ~~me~~ ^{I,} received certificates.

[*Sara and I* is in apposition to the subject *two members;* use the subjective case.]

Let's you and ~~I~~ ^{me} cut lab this afternoon and go surfing.

[*You and me* are in apposition to *us,* the object of the verb *let;* use the objective case.]

7. Use the correct case for pronouns in *as* and *than* comparisons.

When making comparisons using *as* or *than*, writers sometimes omit words because they trust their readers will readily understand what is being said.

William ate more hot dogs than I~~ate hot dogs~~.

Because the comparison being made is quite clear, the rest of the clause can be omitted.

However, the case of the pronoun depends on its function in the implied clause. One way to choose the right pronoun is to supply the implied sentence parts. If the pronoun in question is the subject of the implied or understood clause, use the subjective case.

Philip thinks about clothes more than ~~me~~ I.

[The complete understood clause is *than I think about clothes.*]

If the pronoun in question functions as an object in the implied clause, use the objective case.

My father gives my younger sister as big an allowance as ~~I~~ me.

[The complete understood clause is *as he gives me.*]

8. Use the objective case for pronouns (*me, you, him, her, it, us, them, whom*) that function as subjects or objects of infinitives.

Infinitives (*to* plus a verb) present an exception to the rule that the subjective case is used for subjects: subjects of infinitives are always in the objective case.

Mother asked Tim and ~~I~~ me to peel the potatoes.

[*Me* is the subject of the infinitive *to peel.*]

My sister named her new baby Leslie, so I expected ~~he~~ him to be a ~~she~~ her.

[*Him* is the subject of the infinitive *to be,* and *her* is its object; the objective case is used in each instance.]

9. Use *who* or *whom* according to how the word functions in its own clause.

Who and *whom* are interrogative pronouns (along with *whose*, which is rarely a problem for writers). *Who* is the subjective case and *whom* is the objective case.

As interrogative pronouns, *who* and *whom* commonly begin questions. But which one should you use? To determine the case of the interrogative pronoun, determine its function in the clause. Sometimes it helps to recast the question in your head or to answer the question.

> Who
>
> ~~Whom~~ among the generals led the Allied forces on D-Day?
>
> [Answer the question: he led the forces, not *him* led the forces, so use the subjective case *who*.]
>
> Whom
>
> ~~Who~~ is the detective speaking to now?
>
> [Answer the question: the detective is speaking to *him*, so use the objective case *whom*.]

As relative pronouns, *who, whoever, whom,* and *whomever* are also used to introduce subordinate clauses. (See GRAM 4.) The case of the pronoun depends on its function within the subordinate clause, regardless of the clause's function in the sentence as a whole. Use *who* and *whoever* for subjects; use *whom* or *whomever* for all objects. Use *whoever* or *whomever* when there is no specific noun or noun equivalent referent for the pronoun. To test your choice of pronoun, mentally block off the subordinate clause in question, and then read it aloud to determine whether the relative pronoun is functioning as subject or object in the subordinate clause.

> who
> He did not remember ~~whom~~ was president in 1976.
>
> whoever
> The Barnes Prize is awarded to ~~whomever~~ has the highest grade-point average in physics.
>
> [Remember that the case of the relative pronoun is determined by its function in the subordinate clause. Here, the relative pronoun is the subject of the verb *has,* so the subjective case is required—*whoever.* The entire subordinate clause is the object of the preposition *to.*]
>
> whomever
> Frank said he would select ~~whoever~~ he wanted.

Do not be confused by expressions such as *I believe, she thinks,* and *we know* that frequently follow *who* or *whom* in a subordinate clause. When you block off a subordinate clause containing one of these expressions, leave out the expression (*we know* in the example that follows) when reading aloud.

> who
> I plan to call only the people ~~whom~~ we know will want to come.

If *whom* sounds too formal or stiff for a particular writing situation, omit the pronoun if possible.

The female vocalist ~~whom~~ I like best is Whitney Houston.

EDIT 4

Adjectives and Adverbs

Adjectives and **adverbs** are modifiers—that is, they limit or qualify the meaning of other words. (See GRAM 1d and 1e.) There are, however, important differences between the two, and they cannot be used interchangeably.

If you have questions about the correct form of a modifier or whether a particular word is an adjective or an adverb, consult your desk dictionary.

EDIT 4a   Use adverbs, not adjectives, to modify verbs, adjectives, and other adverbs.

To avoid inadvertently using an adjective when an adverb is called for, pay attention to what is being modified. If it is a verb (V), an adjective (ADJ), or an adverb (ADV), use an adverb.

The gold dome *shone brightly* in the dazzling sunshine.

It is worth a special trip to see her *really unusual* collection of masks.

In informal spoken English, *real* is often used to mean "very": we had a *real* good time last night. In formal written English, however, this construction is not acceptable. (See WORD 2a.)

Gary runs *incredibly fast* for a big man.

EDIT 4b   Use an adjective, not an adverb, after a linking verb to modify the subject.

Because the subject of a sentence is always a noun (N) or noun substitute (PRON) and only adjectives—not adverbs—modify nouns, use an adjective after a linking verb to modify, or complement, a subject.

The *photography* in the new Audubon movie is *spectacular*.

Commonly used linking verbs include *be, become, appear, grow, seem, remain,* and *prove.*

PRON ⌒ ADJ
He seems *happy.*

N⌒ADJ
Sales remained *steady* from Thanksgiving through Christmas.

The verbs *feel, look, smell,* and *taste* can function as either linking verbs or action verbs. (See GRAM 1a.) If you are describing a state of being, the verb is functioning as a linking verb (LV) and you must use an adjective. If you are describing an action, use an adverb to modify the verb.

N⌒ LV ⌒ADJ
The *dentist* looked *curious.*

[In this sentence, the dentist appears inquisitive; *looked* is a linking verb and the adjective *curious* is used to describe his state of being.]

V⌒ADV
The dentist *looked* curiously at my chipped tooth.

[Here, the dentist is performing an action. He is looking at something in a curious way; *looked* is an action verb, and an adverb modifies it.]

EDIT 4c Use *bad/badly* and *good/well* correctly.

Two commonly misused adjective/adverb pairs are *bad/badly* and *good/well.* Errors usually occur when there is a linking verb in the sentence, but you should have no trouble if you remember that *bad* is always an adjective and *badly* is always an adverb. Also, *good* is always an adjective, but *well* can function as either an adjective or an adverb.

N⌒ LV *bad*
Anne felt ~~badly~~ about not inviting Peggy and Jeff.

[To describe Anne's state of being, use the adjective *bad;* to say she *felt badly* describes her sense of touch, which is not the issue here.]

N⌒ LV
good
Pork chops taste especially ~~well~~ with applesauce.

[Use the adjective *good* to modify the chops; *taste* is a linking verb.]

V⌒ *well*
Shake the juice ~~good~~ before drinking.

[Use the adverb *well* to modify the verb *shake.*]

As an adjective, *well* has several meanings.

All is *well* with my family. [satisfactory or pleasing]

Mark is not a *well* man. [sound in body and mind]

It is *well* that we did not go to the show. [proper or fitting]

EDIT 4d **Use the form of the demonstrative adjective that agrees with the noun it modifies.**

A singular demonstrative adjective (*this, that*) is used to modify a singular noun; a plural demonstrative adjective (*these, those*) is used to modify a plural noun. Demonstrative adjectives (see GRAM 1d) rarely cause problems for writers, with one exception: phrases such as *kind of, sort of,* and *type of*. In these constructions, the demonstrative adjective modifies the noun *kind, sort,* or *type,* and so must agree with it in number.

WITH SINGULAR NOUNS	WITH PLURAL NOUNS
this/that kind	these/those kinds
this/that sort	these/those sorts
this/that type	these/those types

kinds
We are looking for these ~~kind~~ of apples.

sorts
Those ~~sort~~ of questions come up during orientation every year.

EDIT 4e **Use the comparative and superlative forms of adjectives and adverbs correctly.**

Adjectives and adverbs have three forms: the **positive** (used to describe: *big, vigorously*), the **comparative** (used to compare two things: *bigger, more vigorously*), and the **superlative** (used to compare three or more things: *biggest, most vigorously*).

With few exceptions, one-syllable and many two-syllable adjectives form the comparative by adding *-er* and the superlative by adding *-est*. Adjectives with three or more syllables, as well as some two-syllable adjectives, use *more* and *most,* or *less* and *least,* to form the comparative and the superlative, respectively.

POSITIVE	COMPARATIVE	SUPERLATIVE
fast	faster	fastest
fancy	fancier OR more (less) fancy	fanciest OR most (least) fancy
beautiful	more beautiful	most beautiful

A few adjectives have irregular comparative and superlative forms.

good	better	best
bad	worse	worst

Several adjectives, because of their meaning, do not make sense as comparatives or superlatives. Among them are *perfect* and *unique;* that is, a thing either is or is not unique or perfect.

That's the most ~~unique~~ unusual ring I ever saw.

Her ring is ~~very~~ unique.

Most adverbs form the comparative and superlative by adding *more* and *most* (or *less* and *least*); a few short adverbs add *-er* and *-est.*

POSITIVE	COMPARATIVE	SUPERLATIVE
quick	quicker OR more (less) quickly	quickest OR most (least) quickly
safely	more (less) safely	most (least) safely

A few adverbs have irregular comparative and superlative forms.

well	better	best
badly	worse	worst

Use the comparative form to compare two things.

Which of the two candidates is ~~most~~ more qualified in your estimation?

Use the superlative to compare three or more things.

The javelin thrower's third attempt was her ~~less~~ least successful.

Be alert for double comparatives or double superlatives; that is, using *more* or *most* (or *less* or *least*) after already adding *-er* or *-est* to the adjective or adverb in question.

According to college polls, the ~~most~~ sexiest actor is Brad Pitt.

Tuesday was all the ~~more~~ gloomier because I failed a pop quiz.

EDIT 5

Fragments

A **sentence fragment** is a part of a sentence presented as if it were a complete sentence. That is, it begins with a capital letter and ends with a period, question mark, or exclamation point, but it does not include one of the two essential elements required of a grammatically complete sentence, a subject and a verb. A sentence fragment gives our readers a "fragment" of our thought, not our complete thought. Usually fragments occur unintentionally and are correctable; under certain circumstances, however, you may want to use a fragment intentionally.

The most common types of sentence fragments are (1) *phrases*, (2) *subordinate clauses*, (3) *appositives*, and (4) *parts of compound predicates* capitalized and punctuated as if they were complete sentences. (See GRAM 2, 3, and 4.)

You can eliminate sentence fragments in one of two ways: (1) join the fragment to a sentence nearby, or (2) develop the fragment itself into a complete sentence. In joining a fragment to a sentence, you may need a comma, a colon, a dash, or no punctuation at all. A dash and a colon indicate a more definite break in thought than a comma; a colon is expected before items in a series. (See PUNCT 3b.)

REVISING WITH A COMMA

He has many hobbies, including stamp collecting, bird watching, and vegetable gardening.

REVISING WITH A COLON

We had a traditional Thanksgiving dinner: turkey with stuffing, cranberry sauce, gravy, mashed potatoes, and pumpkin pie.

REVISING WITH A DASH

Dolores washes her hair twice a day—much too often.

REVISING WITHOUT PUNCTUATION

with
Tina would rather have tea/~~With~~ lemon.

EDIT 5a Join a phrase fragment to an existing sentence, or rewrite the fragment as a sentence.

A **phrase fragment** lacks either a subject or a complete verb or both.

We left Rome and traveled northward to the picturesque little hill towns
We also went
of Italy.~~Also~~ to Florence and Venice.

Often a verbal—an infinitive, gerund, or participle—is mistaken as the verb. (See GRAM 1a.)

Fourteen of us went on the desert survival trip,~~H~~hiking into Death Valley and traveling only after dark.

EDIT 5b Join a subordinate clause fragment to an existing sentence, or rewrite the fragment as a sentence.

A **subordinate clause** contains both a subject and a predicate, but it is introduced by a **subordinator,** either a subordinating conjunction (*after, because, rather than, as, if;* see GRAM 1g) or a relative pronoun (*that, which, who, whom, what;* see GRAM 1c), and therefore is not an independent sentence.

The president met with his staff every week,~~So~~ *so* that problems were rarely ignored.

Problems
The president met with his staff every week. ~~So that problems~~ were rarely ignored.

EDIT 5c Make an appositive fragment part of a sentence.

An **appositive phrase** is a noun or noun equivalent that identifies or explains another noun or noun equivalent. (See GRAM 3c.)

Marco read two good books during his vacation, Scott O'Dell's *Island of*
the *Blue Dolphins* and N. Scott Momaday's *House Made of Dawn*.

EDIT 5d Keep a compound predicate within a single sentence.

A **compound predicate** is made up of two or more predicates that have the same subject. (See GRAM 2b.)

but
I wanted to buy both Madonna albums, ~~But~~ had enough money to get

only one.
[The fragment has been made part of a compound predicate.]

but I
I wanted to buy both Madonna albums, ~~But~~ had enough money to buy

only one.
[The sentence has been rewritten as a compound sentence (see GRAM 5a) by converting the fragment into an independent clause with the addition of a subject, *I.*]

EDIT 5e Use sentence fragments intentionally to add emphasis and to write realistic dialog.

Sentence fragments are not always wrong. In fact, if not overused, a sentence fragment can add emphasis.

SENTENCE	DELIBERATE FRAGMENT
Would I change my major now? No, I wouldn't.	Change my major now? No!

Sentence fragments are most commonly used in conversation, in advertising, and in descriptive and fictional writing. To write realistic dialog, include some sentence fragments. An actual conversation, for example, might proceed this way:

"Go skiing yesterday?"
"Yes."
"Where?"
"Wing Hollow."
"Crowded?"
"About a fifteen-minute wait for the big chair."
"Icy?"
"Not really—just in spots."

In descriptive and fictional writing, fragments can be used to set mood or tone. In the following passage, O'Brien uses fragments to set a mood of anticipation for the coming of winter.

A narrow road and the first tentative fall of snow. A light fall that is merely preparatory and does not yet make life cumbersome for the people or the herds. Around each clapboard house a belt of trees, and around the younger trees wooden V's to protect the trunks from the heavier snow.   —Edna O'Brien, "Ways"

In the kind of written English that appears in quality newspapers and magazines and in textbooks, referred to as **edited standard English,** certain phrases can stand alone even though they are fragments: *And now, to summarize. So much for that argument. One final example.* Except for such occasional transitional expressions, however, readers expect the sentences of expository prose to follow the usual subject—verb–(object) pattern (see GRAM 2); deviations from this pattern, being unexpected, are very noticeable.

EDIT 6

Comma Splices and Fused Sentences

A **comma splice,** or *comma fault,* occurs when a writer uses only a comma or a comma and a conjunctive adverb to join two or more main clauses.

COMMA SPLICES

The legislators could not agree on the bill, they had to stay in session.

The legislators could not agree on the bill, therefore, they had to stay in session.

A **fused sentence,** or *run-on sentence,* occurs when no punctuation and no coordinating conjunction appear between two or more main clauses.

FUSED SENTENCE

The legislators could not agree on the bill they had to stay in session.

There are four main ways to correct comma splices and fused sentences:

1. Make the main clauses into separate sentences.
2. Use a semicolon.
3. Use a comma and a coordinating conjunction.
4. Subordinate one main clause to the others.

An example of each remedy follows:

1. The legislators could not agree on the bill. They had to stay in session.
2. The legislators could not agree on the bill; therefore, they had to stay in session.
3. The legislators could not agree on the bill, so they had to stay in session.
4. Because the legislators could not agree on the bill, they had to stay in session.

EDIT 6a   Separate comma splices and fused sentences with a period.

When the ideas expressed in the two main clauses are not closely related, make each clause a separate sentence.

CORRECTED COMMA SPLICE

I had to buy new sneakers, ~~my~~ My mother threw away my old pair.

CORRECTED RUN-ON SENTENCE

The sun finally rose ~~it~~ It was light enough to see where we were.

EDIT 6b   Connect sentences in comma splices and fused sentences with a semicolon.

When the ideas expressed in the two main clauses are close and the relationship between them is obvious without a coordinating conjunction, use a semicolon to join them.

CORRECTED COMMA SPLICE

The delegates to the convention were disorganized,̷;they needed some-

one to lead them.

CORRECTED RUN-ON SENTENCE

Our bike trip will be through sparsely settled country, I think I'll take a

bike repair course.

EDIT 6c   Connect comma splices and fused sentences with a comma and a coordinating conjunction (*and, but, or, nor, for, so, yet*).

If the two ideas are equally important and you want to avoid two short sentences, use this method of correction.

CORRECTED COMMA SPLICE

Many countries signed the treaty, but the United States did not.

CORRECTED RUN-ON SENTENCE

It was 95 degrees in the shade, but I'd promised to mow the lawn.

Using the right coordinating conjunction (see GRAM 1g) will also focus and clarify your meaning.

EDIT 6d   Make one of the sentences in a comma splice or fused sentence a subordinate clause.

This method of correction is often the best choice because it offers the greatest variety of possible revisions. You can choose the subordinating conjunction that conveys exactly what you mean and puts the emphasis where you want it in the sentence. (See GRAM 1g and SENT 5.)

CORRECTED COMMA SPLICE

Because the The fog came on suddenly, we couldn't find the dock.

[*Because* indicates a one-on-one cause-and-effect relationship.]

CORRECTED RUN-ON SENTENCE

When the
˄T͟h͟e fog came on suddenly, we couldn't find the dock.

[*When* also establishes cause, but more in a sense of bad timing.]

CORRECTED COMMA SPLICE

Even though the
˄T͟h͟e water was murky, we found the lost anchor.

[*Even though* indicates success despite the odds.]

CORRECTED RUN-ON SENTENCE

Though the
˄T͟h͟e water was murky, we found the lost anchor.

[*Though* also establishes a contrary situation, but not with the same intensity.]

Other methods of revision are also possible. Master the preceding four main methods of correcting comma splices and run-on sentences, but experiment, too. Here are some other ways the last example sentence could be rewritten.

OTHER POSSIBLE REVISIONS

Regardless of the murky water, we found the anchor.
[We paid no attention to the murky water.]

The murky water did not prevent us from finding the lost anchor.
[We overcame the obstacle of the murky water.]

We found the lost anchor even though the water was murky.
[Emphasis is on finding the anchor.]

word

Word Choice

Learning Objectives

After reading this section, you should:

- use words more exactly and appropriately;
- be able to identify bias in writing;
- recognize wordiness;
- use a dictionary and thesaurus to improve your writing;
- be aware of commonly confused words.

Word Choice

WORD 1

Exactness

Mark Twain wrote, "The difference between the almost right word and the right word is really a large matter—'tis the difference between the lightning-bug and the lightning." It is not enough merely to come close to saying what you want to say; imprecise **word choice,** or **diction,** not only fails to express your intended meaning but also runs the risk of confusing your reader. To use words precisely, you need not have a large vocabulary, but it is necessary that you know the correct meanings of the words you do use.

WORD 1a Choose words that accurately denote what you want to say.

The **denotation** of a word is its literal meaning or dictionary definition. Most of the time you will have no trouble with denotation, but problems can occur when words are close in meaning or sound a lot alike.

uninterested.
Bill could tell by the look on Judy's face that she was ~~disinterested.~~

[*Disinterested* means "unbiased by personal interest"; *uninterested* means "having no interest."]

anecdotes
Dave Barry's ~~antidotes~~ have made him an international celebrity.

[An *antidote* is "a medicine for countering the effects of poison"; an *anecdote* is "a short narrative concerning an interesting event."]

Consult your desk dictionary if you are not sure you are using the correct word. (See WORD 5.)

WORD 1b Choose words with connotations that suit your purpose.

Words have connotative as well as denotative meanings. **Connotations** are the associations or emotional overtones that words have acquired through the years. For example, the word *hostage* denotes a person who is given or held as security for the fulfillment of certain conditions or terms, but it connotes images of suffering, loneliness, torture, fear, deprivation, starvation, anxiety, and other private images based on our individual associations. Because many words in English have the same meanings—*strength, potency, force,* and *might* all denote "power"—your task as a writer in any given situation is to choose the word with connotations that best suit your purpose. (See COMP 2f.) Note how this writer uses connotations to suit her purpose.

Our mayor's ~~actions~~ *antics* make me think he's unfit for office.

[*Antics*, which means "ludicrous acts or actions," is a word more appropriate to the writer's purpose.]

WORD 1c Use specific and concrete words to engage your reader.

Words can be classified as relatively general or specific, abstract or concrete. **General words** name groups or classes of objects, qualities, or actions. **Specific words** name individual objects, qualities, or actions within a class or group. For example, *dessert* is a class of food, and *pie* is more specific than *dessert* but more general than *pecan pie*.

Abstract words refer to ideas, concepts, qualities, and conditions—*love, anger, beauty, youth, wisdom, honesty,* and *sincerity,* for example. **Concrete words** name things you can see, hear, taste, touch, or smell. *Pancake, rocking chair, sailboat, sulfur, sandpaper, smog, cow,* and *soda* are all concrete words.

General and abstract words fail to create in the reader's mind the kind of vivid response that concrete, specific words do. Always question the words you choose. If, for example, you are describing a party, is it enough to say the party was *wonderful?* How wonderful? Why was it wonderful? When was it wonderful? In what ways was it wonderful? Wonderful for whom? The following two paragraphs describe the same party. Based on the use of specific and concrete words, would you like to have attended this party?

> Some friends of ours told us they went to a party a few nights ago. They had fun seeing old friends and they danced a lot, especially a new dance that everybody is doing. There was quite a bit of food. They didn't get home until late.

Or would you prefer to have gone to this party?

> Debbie and Carl went to a great party last Friday. It was a birthday party for an old high school friend, Al Larson. They saw many old friends and met some of Al's friends they hadn't met before. They danced all night and even learned the Texas two-step. There was a huge

buffet, with platters of roast beef, turkey, and cheese, cold pasta, and all kinds of salads, topped off by a double-chocolate birthday cake for Al. Debbie and Carl had such a good time they didn't get home until nearly two in the morning.

WORD 1d Use idioms correctly.

An **idiom** is an expression whose meaning cannot be explained simply by the definitions of the individual words in it. For example, compare the meanings of the italicized words in the following sentences as individual words and as idiomatic expressions:

Julia was *beside herself* with envy.

[She wasn't having an out-of-body experience; she was extremely envious.]

Wear a hat or you'll *catch a cold.*

[You don't literally stop or restrain a cold; you become infected with cold germs.]

Idioms like these present no problems; they roll off the tongue practically as a single word (*roll off the tongue* is another idiom). Idiomatic expressions with prepositions, however, are less clear-cut. If you do not choose the correct preposition, your reader will probably still know what you mean, but your sentence will sound somehow strange. Consider these examples:

Gabe was rewarded ~~by~~ with an "A" for the hours he put into his lab report.

We're going ~~by~~ to Aunt Rose's for dinner tonight.

If you are unsure of which preposition to use in an idiom, consult your desk dictionary under the entry for the main word, not the preposition. Some idiomatic expressions using prepositions are identified in the following list:

agree *to* a plan
agree *on* a procedure
agree *in* principle
agree *with* someone
angry *with* someone [NOT angry *at*]
concern *about* something [IN THE SENSE OF *worried*]

concern *for* someone
concern *with* something [IN THE SENSE OF *be of interest*]
concur *in* a decision
concur *with* someone
different *from* theirs
different *than* they were
go *to* [NOT go *by*]
oblivious *of* her presence
oblivious *to* noise
off [NOT off *of*]
parallel *with* or *to* something
parallel *between* one thing and another
rewarded *by* someone
rewarded *for* something
rewarded *with* something
superior *to* [NOT superior *than*]
sure *to* [NOT sure *and*]
try *to* [NOT try *and*]
type *of* [NOT type of *a*]
vary *from* another
vary *in* detail
vary *with* something
wait *for* a person [NOT wait *on*]
wait *in* line [NOT wait *on*]

WORD 1e Use figurative language to make your writing fresh and strong.

In **figurative language** we speak imaginatively rather than in a literal (strict) sense. While we tend to associate figurative language with poetry, in fact we constantly use it in our daily speech.

The way Gretzky was firing the puck last night, *our net looked ten feet wide.*

You'd have to be a *Nobel laureate* to figure out these directions.

Figurative language not only brings freshness and color to writing but also helps clarify ideas. **Figures of speech** are particular kinds of figurative language. A **simile,** for example, is an explicit comparison between two essentially different ideas or objects using *like* or *as.*

Canada geese sweep across the hills and valleys like a formation of strategic bombers. —Benjamin B. Bachman

A **metaphor** also makes a comparison between dissimilar ideas or objects but without *like* or *as*.

> She was very old and small and she walked slowly in the dark pine shadows, moving a little from side to side in her steps, with the balanced heaviness and lightness of a pendulum in a grandfather clock.
>
> —Eudora Welty

An **extended metaphor** takes full advantage of the richness of a comparison by using several sentences or even a whole paragraph to develop a particular comparison.

> The point is that you have to strip down your writing before you can build it back up. You must know what the essential tools are and what job they were designed to do. If I may belabor the metaphor of carpentry, it is first necessary to be able to saw wood neatly and to drive nails. Later you can bevel the edges or add elegant finials, if that is your taste. But you can never forget that you are practicing a craft that is based on certain principles. If the nails are weak, your house will collapse. If your verbs are weak and your syntax is rickety, your sentences will fall apart. —William Zinsser, *On Writing Well*

In **personification** the writer attributes human qualities to animals or inanimate objects.

> Exclamation points are the most irritating of all. Look! they say, look at what I just said! How amazing is my thought!
>
> —Lewis Thomas, "Notes on Punctuation"

In each of the preceding examples, the writer more vividly communicates an idea or the essence of an object by comparing it to something concrete and familiar. In all cases, too, the figurative language grows out of the writer's thinking, reflecting the way he or she sees the material. Be similarly honest in your use of figurative language, or you risk sounding pompous or contrived. Check that your figurative language is not illogical or mixed. (See SENT 4b.)

WORD 1f Replace clichés with fresh language.

Imagine your roommate returns from an evening out, and you ask her, "How was the concert?" She replies, "The concert was okay, but they had us *packed* in there *like sardines*. How was your evening?" And you reply, "Well, I finished my term paper, but the noise *drove me crazy*. This dorm is a real *zoo*."

At one time the italicized expressions were vivid and colorful, but through constant use they have lost their life and energy. Expressions that are predictable and dull are termed **clichés** (trite expressions). If an expression comes too quickly to mind and sounds as if you've heard it before, the chances are you have. Replace clichés and over-worked expressions with fresh figurative language. (See WORD 1e.) How many of the following clichés have you heard lately?

arrived at the scene	in one fell swoop
at long last	it stands to reason
believe it or not	last but not least
better late than never	lodge a complaint
cool, calm, and collected	proves conclusively
crystal clear	rear its ugly head
few and far between	rude awakening
first and foremost	sadder but wiser
for all intents and purposes	sneaking suspicion
foreseeable future	step in the right direction
hit the spot	the bottom line
in no uncertain terms	the last straw

WORD 2

Appropriateness

In choosing how to say something, use words in keeping with your subject and be sensitive to the needs and feelings of your audience. In other words, strive for an **appropriate tone.** Ask yourself, "Does my choice of words support the seriousness of my subject?" "Do I make my subject sound more serious than it really is?" "Do I keep my audience at too great a distance from me, or do I make my readers uncomfortable because I try to get too close to them?"

Not only do you want to establish an appropriate tone, you also want to maintain that tone consistently throughout and not lapse into one that is more or less formal (see WORD 2a), for example, or perhaps pretentious (see WORD 2c) or voguish (see WORD 2e).

WORD 2a Choose a degree of formality appropriate to your subject and audience.

In **informal writing**—an e-mail message or short memo, for ex-ample—the tone may be informal and reflect the way that people who know each other talk to one another. Informal writing is characterized by simple sentences, contractions (*can't, doesn't*), and conversational words (*get around to it* rather than *do, show up* rather than *arrive*). Usually, the emphasis is more on the relationship between the writer and the audience than between the writer and the subject. Informal writing is used in the following note.

> Sorry I can't make tomorrow's meeting, Sally. I have to grab a plane this afternoon for Dallas and troubleshoot for those guys down there. I should be back Thursday night. Talk to you Friday.

In **formal writing**—a letter of application, a class assignment, or a research report—the tone you adopt and the words you choose to create that tone should be serious and not casual. In formal writing the relationship between the writer and the subject is paramount. Unlike informal writing, formal writing does not use contractions and often employs more complex sentences and a more sophisticated—but not stilted or old-fashioned—vocabulary.

Formal writing is used in the following paragraph from a *World Monitor* report.

> Western-style wedding ceremonies have become the fashion in South Korea—to such an extent that there are reportedly only five places in the capital of Seoul that perform conventional Korean weddings. Arguments arise over the materialism associated with the quasi-Western rituals. —*World Monitor*

WORD 2b Use standard English.

Standard English, both spoken and written, is the English used by educators, civic leaders, and professionals in all fields, and is the language of the media.

Nonstandard English differs from standard English in its use of fairly simple sentence structures, double negatives (*can't see no* for *can't see any*), unusual vocabulary (*spigot* for *faucet*), and unconventional spelling (*nite* for *night*), pronunciation (*yourn* for *yours*), and grammar (*I be going* for *I am going*). Nonstandard English is as acceptable and functional as standard English if it is used within the social and regional contexts that it is found. It is not acceptable where standard English is required.

Slang is the unconventional, informal language of particular subgroups—street gangs, soldiers, or college students, for example; it is not generally known to all members of society. Moreover, slang terms quickly come into and go out of existence, making communication among groups even more difficult. For example, the term *cat's pajamas*, meaning "something special," as in *He thought she was the cat's pajamas*, is no longer used and not readily understood. Slang, or code words, such as *diss, NIMBY,* and *dork,* are, therefore, unacceptable in most writing.

> upset
> Linda was ~~bummed~~ when she got her grades.

Regional expressions are common to a specific geographical area of the country. For example, in New England, the expression, *let's see how this sugars off,* means "let's see how this turns out." The expression derives from the process of boiling down maple sap to make maple syrup, a traditional activity in the Northeast. Like slang, however, regionalisms, while colorful, are not widely known and can leave your reader wondering about your exact meaning, especially when the sentence provides no context.

> miserly.
> He's real ~~chintzy~~

> NOTE: Nonstandard English, slang, and regionalisms may, of course, be used where specifically called for, especially in dialog, to delineate character and locate the action geographically.

WORD 2c Avoid pretentious language, euphemisms, and doublespeak.

To be direct and clear, avoid pretentious language, euphemisms, and doublespeak. **Pretentious language** is ornate, pompous, or falsely poetic and, therefore, inappropriate in most writing. It speaks louder than the message it is trying to convey.

> PRETENTIOUS Of all the wondrous natural metamorphoses with which May beguiles, perhaps none is so revered as the verdant canopy of new leaves spread by the trees.

> DIRECT Of all the changes that come in May, perhaps none is as wonderful as the new leaves budding on the trees.

Euphemism comes from the Greek word *euphemismos,* meaning "to speak with good words." A euphemism, then, is a mild or vague term substituted when the speaker or writer fears more direct wording might be offensive. For example, we say *portly* or *full-figured* instead of *fat, inexpensive* instead of *cheap.* And when employers reduce the number of people they employ, they call it *downsizing.* However it is put, though, these people no longer have jobs.

Sometimes evasive language goes beyond simply trying not to hurt people's feelings. Language purposely used to hide the truth is **doublespeak,** a term first used by George Orwell in his futuristic novel *1984.* For example, when our country's military officials referred to the bombing of villages during the Vietnam War as *limited duration protective reaction strikes,* the intent was to deceive. Similarly, when salespeople refer to a used car as *pre-owned* and advertisers offer a *free gift* with a purchase, they mean to obscure the truth rather than reveal it. Not only should we avoid using doublespeak, but we should also be wary when others use it.

WORD 2d Use technical language only where appropriate.

Every trade and profession has its own special vocabulary. For example, all printers know the meanings of the terms *flush left, run in,* and *extra leading,* which all refer to the position of type on a printed page. Technical terms allow professionals to communicate quickly and accurately among themselves. When technical language is used to communicate with a general audience, however, it is considered **jargon** and is inappropriate. It is far better for a doctor in communicating with a patient to use *swelling* instead of *edema, capable of preventing disease* instead of *prophylactic,* and *heart attack* instead of *myocardial infarction.*

Jargon also refers to abstract, unintelligible, self-important phrasing that conveys an attitude of wanting to set oneself apart with special knowledge of a field. It should also be avoided.

JARGON   Group modalities are effectively utilized in the educational setting during the formative years to restructure behavioral play relationships.

REVISED   Children are taught in school to get along with each other when they play in groups.

To test for jargon, ask yourself, "Have I used the simplest terms available without any loss in communication?"

WORD 2e Avoid vogue words.

Vogue words are words that suddenly and frequently appear in the language of newscasters, politicians, and other public figures until we soon find ourselves using them. One reason for their popularity is that once a vogue word enters the media it is picked up by yet other members of the media who give it even greater currency. Because vogue words are used so frequently within a short period of time, they lose their freshness and appeal quickly, disappearing as inexplicably as they became popular. Some current vogue terms are *soccer moms, venue, tweak, edgy, factoid,* and *virtual.* Until recently we might have included *sound bite, shock economics,* and *pushing the envelope.*

If Eric doesn't get a good grade on the final, he's ~~toast~~ could fail the course.

WORD 3

Bias in Writing

A **bias,** or slanted outlook, may be favorable or unfavorable and without good reason either way. Language carries certain biases within it because of the historical circumstances surrounding its development and the ways people have used it. Dominant groups within cultures have often used language to maintain their superior positions and to disempower others. For example, African-Americans have been referred to by such abusive terms as *boy* (adult male), *darky, nigger, spade,* and *blood.* Calling a woman *gal, little woman, the Mrs.,* or *honey* is patronizing, and in certain circumstances, abusive. Language that disempowers groups may be blatant or subtle, as the following examples show.

The ~~Yanks~~ Americans and ~~Japs~~ Japanese were on opposite sides in World War II.

Many ~~Indians~~ Native Americans are taking new pride in cultural traditions.

The immigrants came to America at the turn of the century seeking a

better way of life, ~~for themselves, their wives, and their children.~~
[Women and children were also immigrants, not lesser beings.]

Not only can language deny equality, it can deny individuality as well. Assuming that all nurses are women and all pilots are men or that the president of a company is a man and the secretary to the president is a woman may lead you astray. To assume that all young people are immature or unreasonable or reckless is no better than assuming that all middle-aged people are out of touch, or that all people in their later years are senile, infirm, and crotchety. Not all Latinos have dark complexions. Not all Italians have black hair. Not all Southerners are Protestants. Not all East Asians are good at math and science. To assume so is to fall prey to stereotypes, to take from people their individuality and uniqueness, to deny reality.

How can we avoid bias in language? The best way is to cultivate a sense of the equality of all people regardless of their age, gender, race, religion, country of origin, or sexual orientation.

Call the president's office and ask ~~his girl~~ the secretary to schedule an appointment.

Which player is Kate O'Flaherty? ~~The redhead?~~

~~For someone in his fifties,~~ He's remarkably fit.

We must also make an effort not to reinforce stereotypes, intentionally or subconsciously. Edit your writing to eliminate all inadvertent expressions and terms that promote inequality or stereotypes or that may offend your readers by making inappropriate assumptions. More specifically, we can learn how people want to be referred to and respect their wishes. Realize, though, that even the way people wish to be referred to may change and sometimes rather quickly.

Voter turnout among ~~blacks~~ African-Americans hit a record-high.

Josh, who's ~~handicapped~~ physically disabled, is a great basketball player.

Josh plays a great game of basketball from his wheelchair.

[The emphasis is on Josh's skill rather than his disability, which is, nevertheless, still recognized.]

Most often, however, there is no need to mention a particular characteristic of a group or an individual. Simply state the idea without interjecting irrelevant comments.

Josh, ~~who's physically handicapped,~~ is a great basketball player.

About seventy-five ~~homosexual~~ students attended the dance at the student center.

Trudy ~~is divorced and~~ lives in Chicago with her children.

The following list identifies some common sexist terms and alternative usages.

AVOIDING SEXIST TERMS

Instead of	Use
anchorman	anchor
bellboy	bellhop
chairman	chair, head, moderator, chairperson
clergyman	member of the clergy
congressman	congressional representative
fireman	fire fighter
forefather	ancestor, forebear
freshman	first-year student, student
landlord/landlady	proprietor, property owner, owner
mailman	letter carrier, postal worker
male nurse	nurse
man, mankind	humans, humankind, humanity, people
manpower	staff, human resources
middleman	go-between
newsman	reporter, journalist
policeman	police officer, officer
salesman	sales associate, sales representative, salesperson
stewardess	flight attendant, cabin attendant
waitress	waiter, server

For a discussion of how to avoid using sexist pronouns, see EDIT 3a.

WORD 4

Conciseness

Conciseness in writing is not necessarily a function of the length of your sentences. A long sentence can be concise and a short sentence wordy. Wordiness occurs when you have words that contribute little to the meaning of your sentence and at the same time overshadow those parts of the sentence that carry the meaning. Concise writing lets your meaning shine through regardless of the length of your sentences.

WORD 4a   Focus on subjects and verbs.

The essence of a sentence is its subject and its verb. The subject identifies who or what the sentence is about and the verb indicates the subject's action or state of being. Sentences often lose their conciseness because the actor that should be identified by the subject and the action that should be conveyed by the verb are lost in weak language or buried in other parts of the sentence.

> The *aim* of college athletics *is* the promotion of individual achievement, teamwork, and school spirit.

> College *athletics promotes* individual achievement, teamwork, and school spirit.

Once you become more conscious of your subjects and verbs you can use the following editing techniques to identify and eliminate the clutter in each of your sentences.

WORD 4b Eliminate redundancies.

Too often unnecessary repetition creeps into writing and distracts the reader. Have you ever written *purple in color, decided in my mind,* or *end result?* Redundancies enter writing in several guises; edit by deleting words or using synonyms.

Sometimes our intent is to add emphasis, but the net effect is extra words that contribute nothing to meaning.

> We reviewed the basic ~~and fundamental~~ principles of public speaking.

Sometimes we repeat an idea using different words, thinking we are being extra clear when really we are just saying the same thing twice, not better.

> The supermarket ~~where people buy their groceries~~ extended its hours.

Sometimes we repeat a noun when we could use a pronoun.

> Jordan passed the ball to Pippen, who tipped ~~the ball~~ *it* in the basket.

WORD 4c Delete empty words and phrases.

In strong writing, every word carries its own weight. Cut empty words or phrases that add little or nothing to your meaning.

> *Linguistics*
> ~~The area of linguistics~~ attracts researchers from many disciplines.

> *The*
> ~~In my opinion, the~~ orchestra performed ~~really~~ well.

> *outstanding.*
> John Lee Hooker's rendition of "Night Train" is ~~very good~~
> [Or use *excellent, exceptional, first rate,* and so on.]

Look for these other empty words and phrases as you edit:

apparently, seemingly [unless there is a discrepancy between what something is and how it appears]
basically
essentially
for all intents and purposes
generally
in some ways
I think, I feel, I believe
it seems to me
kind of, sort of [unless you are classifying]
tend to
various
virtually

WORD 4d Reduce inflated expressions to their core meanings.

Wanting to sound serious or knowledgeable, we sometimes use expressions that we think important or authoritative people use. We write *at this point in time* (instead of *now*) or *in the event that* (instead of *if*). Actually we sound pompous—as important and authoritative people do when they use inflated phrases. An expert *who is also a good writer* writes simply and directly. Reduce an inflated phrase to its core meaning. Often this will be a simple preposition or conjunction; at other times it may be a single, more precise word.

We were late ~~on account of the fact that~~ *because* the bus broke down.

He asked his cousin for a loan ~~in the neighborhood of~~ *of about* $75.

She ~~has the capability of performing~~ *performs* well under pressure.

Professor Trent ~~had an effect upon~~ *influenced* my decision to major in Anthropology.

We just hired two ~~people who have a complete knowledge of~~ personal computers/ *experts*.

Other inflated expressions that can be reduced to a word or two include the following:

WORDY	CONCISE
at this point in time	now
by means of	by
due to the fact that	because
for the purpose of	for
for the simple reason that	because
in order to	to
in spite of the fact that	even though, although
in the event that	if
in today's society	today, now
it is important that, it is necessary that	must
on the occasion of	when
prior to, in anticipation of	before
until such time as	until
with regard to	about

WORD 4e Reduce clutter by converting clauses to phrases.

You can often tighten your prose by converting clauses to phrases.

Orange juice ~~that is~~ made from concentrate is not as good as fresh squeezed.

[Subordinate clause converted to a verbal phrase.]

Spin doctors, ~~who are~~ people who manipulate the news media, appeared after the governor gave her speech.

[Subordinate clause converted to an appositive phrase.]

Sometimes a clause or phrase can be converted to a single word.

The ∧spectators, ~~who had become noisy~~∧ booed the referee's call.
noisy

[Subordinate clause converted to a single adjective.]

WORD 4f Use strong verbs and the active voice.

Strong verbs energize writing by vividly describing the action in each of your sentences.

The new study ~~deals with~~ the need for childcare in America.
evaluates

The lawyer ~~gave an explanation of~~ the jury selection process.
explained

When you encounter one of the following weak verbs, replace it with a strong descriptive verb.

is, are, was, were, will be	add
have, has, had	involve
deal with	concern
make	reflect
give	provide
do	become
use	go

The **active voice** emphasizes the actor in a sentence; the **passive voice** the receiver of the action.

tornado flattened the
The ^ grain elevators, ~~were flattened by the tornado~~

Avoid *there is* and *it is*. While necessary in references to time and weather, expletive constructions often add unnecessary words to your sentences.

Many　　　　　　　　　　　　　　　　　　　*followed*
~~There were many~~ peaceful demonstrations ~~following~~ the execution.

Note that when you eliminate an expletive you also give your sentence a specific subject and an action verb.

Combine sentences. Look for opportunities to combine the contents of two or more related sentences into one concise sentence.

WORDY Hector hopes to get many hours of overtime work. He assembles cars at the local General Motors plant. The General Motors plant has just been awarded two large government contracts.

CONCISE Hector hopes to get many hours of overtime work assembling cars at the local General Motors plant which has just been awarded two large government contracts.

WORD 5

The Dictionary

All good college desk dictionaries—including *The American Heritage Dictionary* (Second College Edition), *Random House Webster's College Dictionary*, *Webster's Tenth New Collegiate Dictionary*, and *Webster's New World Dictionary*—contain much useful information. It is worth spending some time learning just what your dictionary can do for you.

To use your dictionary efficiently—that is, to retrieve information quickly and accurately—become familiar with how the main entry for a word is organized. The sample entry for *regard* that appears opposite is

DICTIONARY ENTRY

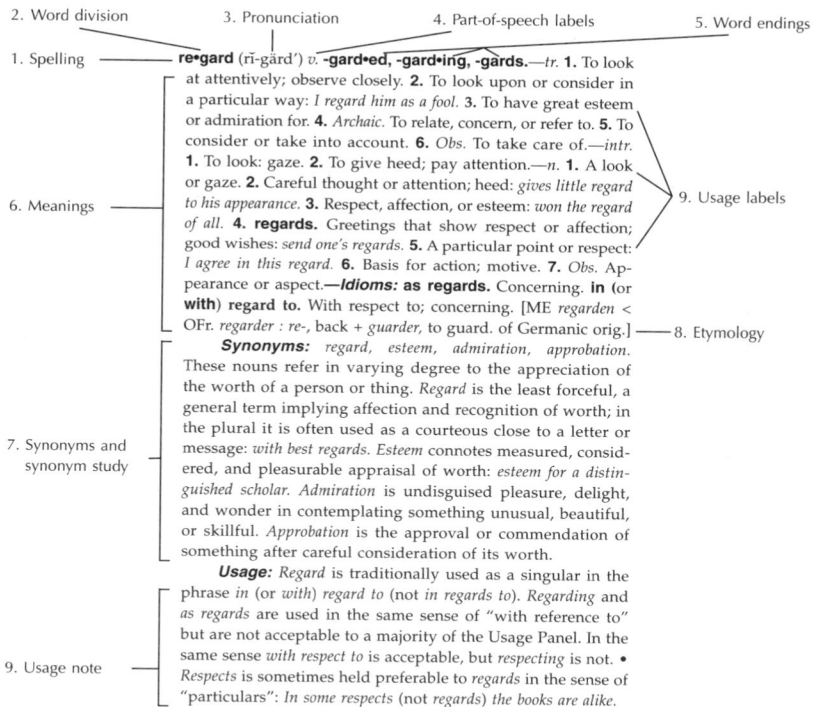

2. Word division   3. Pronunciation   4. Part-of-speech labels   5. Word endings

1. Spelling

re•gard (rĭ-gärd') *v.* **-gard•ed, -gard•ing, -gards.**—*tr.* **1.** To look at attentively; observe closely. **2.** To look upon or consider in a particular way: *I regard him as a fool.* **3.** To have great esteem or admiration for. **4.** *Archaic.* To relate, concern, or refer to. **5.** To consider or take into account. **6.** *Obs.* To take care of.—*intr.* **1.** To look: gaze. **2.** To give heed; pay attention.—*n.* **1.** A look or gaze. **2.** Careful thought or attention; heed: *gives little regard to his appearance.* **3.** Respect, affection, or esteem: *won the regard of all.* **4. regards.** Greetings that show respect or affection; good wishes: *send one's regards.* **5.** A particular point or respect: *I agree in this regard.* **6.** Basis for action; motive. **7.** *Obs.* Appearance or aspect.—***Idioms: as regards.*** Concerning. **in** (or **with**) **regard to.** With respect to; concerning. [ME *regarden* < OFr. *regarder* : *re*-, back + *guarder*, to guard. of Germanic orig.]

6. Meanings

9. Usage labels

8. Etymology

Synonyms: *regard, esteem, admiration, approbation.* These nouns refer in varying degree to the appreciation of the worth of a person or thing. *Regard* is the least forceful, a general term implying affection and recognition of worth; in the plural it is often used as a courteous close to a letter or message: *with best regards. Esteem* connotes measured, considered, and pleasurable appraisal of worth: *esteem for a distinguished scholar. Admiration* is undisguised pleasure, delight, and wonder in contemplating something unusual, beautiful, or skillful. *Approbation* is the approval or commendation of something after careful consideration of its worth.

7. Synonyms and synonym study

Usage: *Regard* is traditionally used as a singular in the phrase *in* (or *with*) *regard to* (not *in regards to*). *Regarding* and *as regards* are used in the same sense of "with reference to" but are not acceptable to a majority of the Usage Panel. In the same sense *with respect to* is acceptable, but *respecting* is not. • *Respects* is sometimes held preferable to *regards* in the sense of "particulars": *In some respects* (not *regards*) *the books are alike.*

9. Usage note

taken from *The American Heritage Dictionary* (Second College Edition). Note the kinds of information in an entry.

1. Spelling

The main entry word, in boldface type, gives the correct spelling. When two or more spellings are given, the first is preferred (*traveler,* also *traveller*). Foreign words and phrases that have not been Anglicized are italicized (*au courant*) to indicate that you should underline them in your writing. Also, words that are capitalized are capitalized in the entry (*Quaker,* but not *pasteurized*).

2. Word division

The main entry word is divided into syllables to show how to break it properly at the end of a line. Syllabication is indicated by centered periods as in *dic•tion•ar•y*. Compound words are indicated as two words, with a hyphen, or as a single word.

> free fall
> free-liv•ing
> free•load•er

3. Pronunciation

The pronunciation of a word is usually set off by parentheses or slashes. The pronunciation itself is written phonologically in sound symbols that are explained in the front matter as well as at the bottom of each two-page spread throughout the dictionary. An accent mark (´) indicates the most heavily stressed syllable: *character* (ka´r•ik•tar). Pay attention to pronunciation to avoid spelling errors from added letters (*athletics* not *atheletics*), omitted letters (*candidate* not *canidate*), incorrect vowels (*introduce* not *intraduce*), or transposed letters (*cavalry* not *calvary*).

4. Part-of-speech and other grammatical labels

Part-of-speech and grammatical labels are abbreviated.

adj.	adjective	*pl.*	plural
adv.	adverb	*prep.*	preposition
conj.	conjunction	*pron.*	pronoun
interj.	interjection	*sing.*	singular
intr.	intransitive verb	*tr.*	transitive verb
n.	noun	*v.*	verb

When a word functions as more than one part of speech, the entry separately lists each part of speech followed by its definition. The word *regard*, for example, can be used as a transitive and an intransitive verb as well as a noun.

5. Word endings

The principal parts are always given for both regular and irregular verbs (*regarded, regarding,* or *bring, brought, bringing*). Generally speaking, whenever there is an irregular form or inflection or a question of spelling, the dictionary provides the plurals of nouns (*hooves* for *hoof*) and the comparative and superlative forms for adjectives (*nice, nicer, nicest*) and adverbs (*badly, worse, worst*).

6. Meanings

Most dictionaries give definitions in the order of their frequency of use. If a definition is restricted in its use to a particular subject, such as *medicine, mining,* or *music,* the definition will be so labeled. Most dictionaries also provide an example sentence or quotation to illustrate how the word is used in context. This is particularly helpful to you as a writer in deciding on the appropriateness of a particular word.

7. Synonyms and antonyms

Synonyms, words with almost the same meaning, are frequently provided. *The American Heritage Dictionary* also provides synonym studies like the one for *regard* in our sample entry. Synonyms—and especially synonym studies—help a writer discriminate among words with very similar meanings, such as *regard, esteem, admiration,* and *approbation.* Occasionally **antonyms,** words with opposite meanings, are also given.

8. Etymology

Etymology refers to a word's origin and historical development. The etymology of a word usually appears in brackets immediately after the meanings; see the etymology for *regard* in the sample entry. The abbreviations used are defined in the dictionary's front-matter section.

9. Special usage labels and usage notes

There are three types of special labels:

TIME LABELS *Obs.* [obsolete] and *Archaic*

GEOGRAPHICAL LABELS *Regional, Chiefly Brit., So. Afr.,* *CanF* [Canadian French]

STYLE LABELS *Nonstandard, Informal, Slang, Obscene, Offensive*

In our sample entry, one meaning of *regard* is given as *Archaic* (belonging to another time), whereas two are given as *Obs.* (no longer in use).

Special usage notes are sometimes included; such notes are based on experts' analysis of usage in current printed materials. The usage notes for *regard* advise using it in the singular and avoiding confusion with the word *respect.*

WORD 6

The Thesaurus

If you are not sure you are using the best word to say just what you mean, check a thesaurus, or book of synonyms (words with similar meanings) and antonyms (words with opposite meanings). *Roget's International Thesaurus* is the classic reference work; it is available in inexpensive paperback editions as well as in software formats. Some users find the thesaurus as it has been traditionally organized a bit difficult to use, so the editors of *The American Heritage Dictionary* developed an easy-to-use version, *Roget's II: The New Thesaurus*. Here is a typical entry:

acknowledge *verb*

1. To recognize, often reluctantly, the reality or truth of: *He acknowledged his mistake.*

2. To express recognition of: *acknowledged his duty toward his family.*

1. **Syns:** admit, allow, avow, concede, confess, fess up (*Slang*), grant, own (up). **Near-ants:** disallow, disavow, disown, nix (*Slang*), reject; contradict, impugn, negate. **Ant:** deny.

2. **Syns:** admit, recognize.

As helpful as a thesaurus can be, you should use it with great care. You do not want to use a word with a denotation or connotation that does not suit your purpose. If you have doubts about the exact meaning of a word you wish to use, consult your desk dictionary. Also, do not use the thesaurus merely to dress up your prose. Use simple, correct words instead of inappropriate fancy words.

WORD 7

Glossary of Usage

The following glossary of usage is a handy reference guide to pairs of confusing words (*disinterested, uninterested*), frequently misspelled words (*their, there, they're*), words that cause agreement problems (*data, phenomena*), nonstandard words and phrases (*alright, is when*), and informal usages (*lots, real*).

Many of the usage problems discussed here are also treated in other parts of the text; use the index to locate them. If you have a usage problem not covered here, consult your desk dictionary.

a, an   Use *a* before words that begin with a consonant sound, even if the word begins with a vowel: *a book, a ladder, a unique choice.* Use *an* before a word that begins with a vowel sound, even if the word begins with a consonant: *an idea, an unlikely candidate, an hour.* With a word that begins with a hard *h*, use *a: a hotel, a hamster, a hotdog.* But with a word that begins with an unpronounced *h*, use *an: an hour, an honor, an honest mistake.*

accept, except   *Accept* is a verb that means "to receive." *Except* is usually a preposition that means "other than" or "with the exclusion of." *Carla will accept all the invitations except Jason's.*

adapt, adopt *Adapt* means "to adjust oneself to." *Adopt* means "to choose as one's own." *We will help our adopted child adapt to life in a new country.*

advice, advise *Advice* is a noun and means "opinion about a course of action." *Advise* is a verb and means "to offer advice." *She advised her roommate to seek advice.*

affect, effect *Affect* as a verb means "to influence." *Staring at a computer screen can affect your eyesight.* *Effect* as a noun means "result." *Painting the kitchen yellow brought about the effect she wanted.* *Effect* as a verb means "to bring about." *Negotiation was the only way to effect the release of the hostages.*

ain't *Ain't* is a nonstandard contraction for *am not, is not, has not,* and *have not* and is avoided by most writers. *I am not* [NOT *ain't*] *going tonight.*

all ready, already *All ready* means "prepared." *The swimmers were all ready to start.* *Already* means "previously or before." *We had already finished dessert when Raphael picked up his salad fork.*

all right, alright *All right* is always written as two words, just as *all wrong* is. *Alright* is nonstandard English. *It's all right* [NOT *alright*] *if we meet at the restaurant.*

allusion, illusion, delusion An *allusion* is "an implied or indirect reference." *The lawyer made an allusion to a mystery by Agatha Christie.* An *illusion* is "a false concept" or "deceptive impression." *The magician was a master of illusion.* A *delusion* is "a mistaken belief," usually as a result of psychological problems. *He suffered the delusion of thinking he was Napoleon.*

a lot, alot *A lot* is two words, not one. *I ate a lot* [NOT *alot*] *of cake.*

altogether, all together *Altogether* means "completely." *That's altogether wrong.* *All together* means "in a group." *All together now, "Row, row, row your boat."*

alumnus/alumni, alumna/alumnae Latin masculine and feminine (singular and plural) terms for the graduate(s) of an institution. Whereas most institutions use the singular forms to refer to a particular graduate, they refer to their graduates in the aggregate as *alumni,* leaving many women to wonder why the masculine term should prevail. Perhaps this is the reason *alum/alums* is gaining popularity. *They were both University of Denver alumni* [OR *alums*].

among, between Use *among* for three or more persons or things. *You can choose among several research topics.* Use *between* when there are only two persons or things. *The choice is between coffee and tea.*

amount, number *Amount* refers to things in bulk or mass. *A staggering amount of trash filled the basement.* *Number* refers to things that are countable. *A number of students were given parking tickets.*

and/or An awkward and sometimes imprecise example of legal or business usage that is best avoided in college writing. Although it appears that two choices are represented here, there are actually three: *Mr. Hayes told Marcia that she would receive a promotion and/or raise.* In nonbusiness language, write *Mr. Hayes told Marcia she would receive a promotion or a raise or both.*

anxious, eager *Anxious* is often used when *eager* is the appropriate choice. *Anxious* means "filled with worry and apprehension." *Eager* means "looking forward with pleasure." *I am eager* [NOT *anxious*] *to see the Hockney exhibit.*

anyone, any one *Anyone* means "any person at all." *Any one* refers to a particular person or thing in a group. *Anyone in the room can select any one of these gifts.* The distinction also applies to *everyone/every one* and *someone/some one.*

anyway, any way *Anyway* means "nevertheless." *Anyway, who cares? Any way* means "by whatever means." *He'll go any way he can.*

anyways, anywheres Nonstandard forms of *anyway* and *anywhere*. *Ted's going anyway* [NOT *anyways*].

as, like See **like, as, as if.**

awhile, a while Use the adverb, *awhile,* to modify a verb. *Rest awhile, if you like.* Use the article and noun, *a while,* as the object of a preposition. *We went to the park for a while.*

bad, badly *Bad* is an adjective and *badly* is an adverb. *I feel bad that Cathy didn't go.* (If you *felt badly* your sense of touch would be faulty.) *His car was badly damaged.* (See GRAM 1d, 1e, and EDIT 4c.)

being that, being as (how) Nonstandard expressions used in place of the subordinating conjunctions *because* or *since*. *Because* [NOT *being that*] *Patrick had to go to work early, he couldn't give her a ride.*

beside, besides *Beside* is a preposition meaning "next to" or "at the side of." *The first lady sat beside the president. Besides* is an adverb or a preposition meaning "in addition" or "moreover." *Besides free admission, you get a discount at the museum gift shop with membership.*

between, among See **among, between.**

between you and me, between you and I The preposition *between* always takes the objective case *me: The argument is between you and me* [NOT *you and I*].

bring, take Use *bring* when something is being moved toward the speaker. *Bring your calculator to class tomorrow.* Use *take* when something is being moved away from the speaker. *Would you please take these bottles to the recycling center?*

burst, bursted, bust, busted Use *burst. Bursted* is nonstandard and *bust* and *busted* are slang. *The stands burst into one big cheer when Casey came to bat.*

can, may *Can* means "having ability." *She can play chess.* *May* indicates "having permission." *The children may watch television.*

cannot, can not Always use *cannot.*

can't hardly A double negative, this usage should be avoided. Use *can hardly* instead. *I can hardly* [NOT *can't hardly*] *wait for graduation.*

climactic, climatic *Climactic* means "of or pertaining to climax." *Tiger Woods ended the tournament with a climactic hole-in-one. Climatic* means "of or pertaining to climate." *California enjoys climatic stability.*

compare to, compare with *Compare to* means "to represent as similar." *The human brain is often compared to a computer. Compare with* means "to examine the character or quality of two things to see how they are similar or different." *Muhammad Ali's boxing style has been compared with Joe Frazier's.*

complement, compliment *Complement* is a verb and means "to fill out or make whole." *Her lyrics complement his music. Compliment* means "to praise or congratulate." *She always compliments her students when they perform well.*

consensus of opinion *Consensus* means "general agreement," so the phrase is redundant. *Consensus* [NOT *of opinion*] *was reached before the deadline.*

contact When *contact* is used to mean "get in touch with," it is acceptable in speech and informal writing but not in formal writing. In formal writing, use the verbs *talk, write, call, telephone, e-mail. Call* [NOT *contact*] *your adviser.*

continual, continuous *Continual* means "recurring at intervals, intermittently." *Max continually tells the story of how we met. Continuous* means "occurring without interruption, incessantly." *She was plagued by a continuous ringing in her ears.*

could of Nonstandard for *could have. Craig could have* [NOT *could of*] *gone to summer school.*

criteria *Criteria* means "standards or tests on which judgments can be based" and is the plural of *criterion. There is only one criterion for admittance: age. Professor Kim explained the criteria for receiving an* A.

data *Data* means "pieces of information" and is the plural of *datum,* which is now rarely used, except in formal writing. Some writers treat *data* as both singular and plural; careful writers treat it as plural only. *The national census data were gathered last year.* For the singular of data, many writers prefer "a piece of data" to *datum.*

different from, different than Use *different from* in most instances. *This chili recipe is much different from mine.* Use *different than* if a clause follows. *The exam was different than what I expected.*

disinterested, uninterested *Disinterested* means "free of self-interest or bias." *She was a disinterested observer at the trial. Uninterested* means "without interest." *I'm uninterested in classical music but love opera.*

don't   *Don't* is an acceptable contraction for *do not* but not for *does not. You don't want to go, and she doesn't* [NOT *don't*] *want to stay.*

due to   *Due to* means "owing to" or "because of." It is acceptable as an adjective phrase following some form of the verb *to be: His death was due to natural causes. Due to* is not acceptable as a preposition meaning "because of." *Our flight was grounded because of* [NOT *due to*] *bad weather.*

eager, anxious   See **anxious, eager.**

effect, affect   See **affect, effect.**

e.g.   This is the Latin abbreviation for *exempli gratia,* meaning "for example." It is acceptable in parenthetical comments (*e.g.,* red, yellow, and blue), but outside parentheses, *for example* should be spelled out. *Our house, for example, needs a new roof.* (Both *e.g.* and *for example* are always followed by a comma.)

emigrate from, immigrate to   *Emigrate* means "to leave one country or area for another" and takes the preposition *from. All of my grandparents emigrated from Italy. Immigrate* means "to enter and settle permanently in another country" and takes the preposition *to. They immigrated to America in the 1890s.*

eminent, immanent, imminent   Close in pronunciation, these three words have very different meanings. *Eminent* means "outstanding, as in reputation." *Daniel Webster was an eminent lawyer.* "Immanent" means "existing within, inherent." *Transcendentalists believed that God was immanent in nature. Imminent* means "about to happen." *Volcanologists knew Mt. Kilauea's eruption was imminent.*

enthused, enthusiastic   *Enthused* is not widely accepted as an adjective meaning "showing enthusiasm." Use *enthusiastic* instead. *He gets enthusiastic* [NOT *enthused*] *about three things—breakfast, lunch, and dinner.*

etc.   *Etc.* (*et cetera*) is Latin for "and other things." Do not use *and etc.* because it is redundant. Also, do not use *etc.* to refer to people. Actually, it is stylistically preferable to use the expression *and so on* instead of *etc. Try varying your routine at the gym with the treadmill, stairs, rower, and so on.*

everyone, every one   See **anyone, any one.**

except, accept   See **accept, except.**

farther, further   Use *farther* when distance is involved. *The sailboat drifted farther away.* Use *further* to mean "more" or "to a greater extent." *The neurologist inquired further into Renee's medical history.*

fewer, less   *Fewer* means "amounting to a small number." *Less* is a comparative of "little." Use *fewer* with items that can be counted, and *less* with amounts. *With fewer* [NOT *less*] *tourists in town, there was less traffic congestion.*

further See **farther, further.**

goes (for **says** or **said**) *Goes* is nonstandard for "says" or "said." *She said* [NOT *goes*], *"I want you to help me."*

good, well *Good* as an adjective means "having positive or desirable qualities." *Well* as an adverb means "in a good manner, correctly." *The old Corvette not only looked good, but it ran well.* Use *well* in matters of health. *Do you feel well?* (See EDIT 4c.)

hanged, hung *Hanged* is the past tense and past participle of *hang*, meaning "to execute." *He was convicted and hanged. Hung* is the past tense and past participle of *hang*, meaning "to fasten, attach, or suspend." *Scarlet and gold banners hung from the pulpit.* (See EDIT 2a.)

he/she, his/her See EDIT 3a for a full discussion of these pronouns and sexist language. See WORD 3 for a discussion of bias in writing.

hisself, theirselves *Hisself* and *theirselves* are nonstandard for *himself* and *themselves. Doug can open up the cabin by himself* [NOT *hisself*].

hopefully *Hopefully* means "in a hopeful way." Do not use *hopefully* without indicating *who* is being hopeful. *The machinists look hopefully to the end of the strike.* Or, better because it is more direct, *The machinists hope the strike ends soon.* [NOT *Hopefully, the strike will be over soon.*]

hung See **hanged, hung.**

i.e. This Latin abbreviation for *id est* means "that is." It is used only within parentheses. *Arne Naess popularized "deep ecology"; that is,* [NOT *i.e.,*] *philosophic ecology.* (A comma is usually required after *i.e.* and after *that is.*)

illusion, allusion See **allusion, illusion, delusion.**

immanent See **eminent, immanent, imminent.**

imminent See **eminent, immanent, imminent.**

imply, infer *Imply* means "to hint" or "to express indirectly." *In her annual address the president implied she would retire soon. Infer* means "to conclude from evidence." *From what the financial officer said, students inferred it would be more difficult to get loans.*

incredible, incredulous *Incredible* means "unbelievable." *Incredulous* means "disbelieving." *The judge was incredulous that the defense attorney was so incredibly unprepared.*

individual, person *Individual* is a de-personalized term and should not be substituted for *person. A person* [NOT *individual*] *at high risk should get booster vaccinations.*

infer, imply See **imply, infer.**

ingenious, ingenuous *Ingenious* means "clever." *She offered an ingenious solution. Ingenuous* means "without sophistication." *His manner was ingenuous.*

in regards to A mixture of *in regard to* and *as regards*. Use one phrase or the other. Both, however, sound very formal, if not inflated; use *about* instead. *Talk to your commanding officer about* [NOT *in regards to*] *reenlisting.*

inside of, outside of Acceptable if the meaning intended is "beyond (or within) the boundaries of." *The tornado hit outside of town.* Do not use either term to mean "except" or "besides." *Except for* [NOT *outside of*] *Dr. Alvarez, the entire staff was present.*

irregardless Nonstandard for *regardless. Regardless* [NOT *irregardless*], *wear neon if you run at night.*

is when, is where Do not use *when* and *where* after *is* in definitions. *Scuttling a ship is a process by which* [NOT *is when*] *holes are cut in its bottom to sink it.*

its, it's *Its* is the possessive form of *it. It's* is the contraction of *it is*. Test whether you are using the correct spelling by inserting the words *it is. The Alaskan wolf is losing more of its* [NOT *it's*] *habitat every year.*

kind(s), sort(s), type(s) Use the singular forms in singular constructions. *This kind of paint gives the best results.* Use the plural with plural constructions. *These kinds of paints give the worst results.* Notice that all elements must be singular (*this, kind, paint*) or all must be plural (*these, kinds, paints*).

kind of, sort of, type of Used colloquially, these expressions mean "rather" or "somewhat." They are acceptable in speech but can add unnecessary words in writing. *I was somewhat* [NOT *kind of*] *disappointed by the low attendance.* Or, simply, *I was disappointed by the low attendance.* (See WORD 4b.) When you use these expressions to classify, which is acceptable in formal writing, do not use an *a. That kind of* [NOT *kind of a*] *potato is best for baking.*

lay, lie *Lay* means "to put" or "to place" and always takes an object (principal parts: *lay, laid*, and *laid*). *Lie* means "to recline" and is an intransitive verb, meaning it does not take an object (principal parts: *lie, lay*, and *lain*). Usage errors occur because the present tense of *lay* and the past tense of *lie* are both *lay. Lie* [NOT *lay*] *down immediately. The minute she lay* [NOT *laid*] *down, she fell asleep. Lay the carpet carefully.*

leave, let *Leave* means "to go away" or "to exit." Do not use *leave* to mean "permit." Use *let* instead. *Let* [NOT *leave*] *him do his homework.*

less, fewer See **fewer, less.**

liable, likely *Liable* means "legally obligated" or "responsible." *Hank was liable for his credit-card charges.* Do not use *liable* for *likely*, which means "having a high probability of occurring or being true." *The incumbent is likely* [NOT *liable*] *to win.*

like, as, as if   *Like* is a preposition expressing similarity. *She looks like Julia Roberts.* *As* and *as if* are subordinating conjunctions and are used to introduce dependent clauses. (See GRAM 4.) *As* [NOT *like*] *he said, he was out of town at the time.*

likely, liable   See **liable, likely.**

loose, lose   *Loose* is an adjective meaning "not tightly." *Lose* is a verb and means "to be unable to find" or "to be defeated in a game." Confusion between the two words comes about as much from misspelling as from misuse. *Did you lose the top button? It looked loose.*

lots, lots of   *Lots* and *lots of* are widely used informal substitutes for *a lot, much, a great deal,* and *many.* They should be avoided in formal writing. *Our family goes to many* [NOT *lots of*] *basketball games.* See also **a lot, alot.**

may, can   See **can, may.**

may of   Nonstandard for *may have. Mother may have* [NOT *may of*] *already paid that bill.*

media, medium   *Media* is the plural of *medium,* meaning "a publication or broadcast." *Television is the medium that most influences the American people.*

might of   Nonstandard for *might have. Betsy might have* [NOT *might of*] *sent the flowers.*

myself, himself/herself, yourself   These are reflexive pronouns (*I saw myself reflected in the store window.*) or intensive pronouns (*I myself would let bygones be bygones.*). Do not, however, use them as substitutes for *me, he/she,* or *you.* (See GRAM 1c.) *Packages arrived for Maria and me* [NOT *myself*].

none   *None* is singular (meaning "no one") and takes a singular verb: *None of us is* [NOT *are*] *packed yet.* (See EDIT 1f.)

nowheres   Nonstandard for *nowhere.* See **anywhere, anywheres.**

number, amount   See **amount, number.**

off of, off from   The *of* and *from* are redundant. *The cans fell off* [NOT *off of* OR *off from*] *the shelf.*

OK, O.K., okay   In formal speech and writing use a word such as *approval* or *agreement* instead. *Our zoning board approved* [NOT *okayed*] *the new subdivision.*

outside of, inside of   See **inside of, outside of.**

people, persons   Use *people* to refer to a group of individuals that are uncounted and anonymous. *The gates opened, and the people* [NOT *persons*] *rushed in.* When referring to a countable number, you may use *people* or *persons,* though *persons* is usually preceded by a specific number. *Only three persons* [OR *people*] *asked questions.* Sometimes *per-*

sons sounds inflated; the more commonly used word is *people*. *Not many people* [RATHER THAN *persons*] *asked questions afterwards.*

per   *Per* means "each." It is acceptable to use *per* in expressions such as "per person" and "per gallon" but not otherwise. Use "by," "a," or "in accordance with" instead. *In accordance with* [NOT *per*] *Murphy's Law, if something could go wrong, it did.*

percent, per cent, percentage   *Percent* (the preferred spelling) or *per cent* means "out of each hundred" and is usually preceded by a specific number. *Fifty-six percent of the voters rejected Amendment 12. Percentage* means "portion" or "part of." *A greater-than-expected percentage of Democrats turned out to vote.*

phenomena   *Phenomena* means "observable facts or events" and is the plural of *phenomenon*. There is no such word as *phenomenas*. *Edgar Allan Poe's short stories are filled with strange phenomena.*

plus   *Plus* means "added to": *The bill was $90 plus tax.* Do not use *plus* to link independent clauses. *Lethal injection is cruel and unusual punishment, and* [NOT *plus*] *it does not deter murderers.*

practical, practicable   *Practical* means "serving a purpose, useful." *Practicable* means "capable of being done, feasible." *Walking a tightrope between the skyscrapers is practicable but hardly practical.*

principal, principle   As an adjective *principal* means "first or foremost, chief." *Myron is the principal cellist.* As a noun *principal* means "leader" or "a sum of money as distinguished from interest or profit." *Mr. Marcotte is the new principal. The idea is to live off the interest and not the principal. Principle* is always a noun and means "a truth, or basic assumption." *She lives by the principle that less is more.*

quote, quotation   *Quote* is a verb, *quotation* a noun. In formal writing, do not use *quote* as a shortened form of *quotation*. *His term paper was a string of quotations* [NOT *quotes*].

real, really   In speech, *real* is used for "very" or "extremely." In formal writing, use *really*. *Jay Leno is really* [NOT *real*] *funny.* Avoid overusing the adverb. (See WORD 4b.)

reason is because, reason why   These expressions are awkward and redundant. Simply omit them. *I'm not going away for my vacation because I don't have the money.* [NOT *The reason why I'm not going away for my vacation is because I don't have the money.*] (See WORD 4a.)

sensual, sensuous   *Sensual* pertains to bodily or sexual pleasure. *Balanchine's choreography is so sensual. Sensuous* means "appealing to the senses." *The smell of bread baking is positively sensuous.*

set, sit   These two verbs are often confused. *Set* means "to put something down" and takes a direct object (principal parts: *set, set, set*);

sit means "to rest or be seated" (principal parts: *sit, sat, sat*). *Sit here, and set your popcorn on that little table.* (See EDIT 2b.)

shall, will *Shall* was once the preferred helping verb in the first-person singular and plural, but today *will* is generally acceptable. *I will* [NOT *shall*] *visit Aunt Kate when I'm in Atlanta. Shall* is still used with polite questions. *Shall* [NOT *will*] *we eat?*

should of Nonstandard for *should have. We should have* [NOT *should of*] *phoned first.*

sit, set See **set, sit.**

someone, some one See **anyone, any one.**

somewheres Nonstandard for *somewhere.* See **anywhere, anywheres.**

sort of, kind of See **kind of, sort of.**

stationary, stationery *Stationary* means "not moving, fixed." *Stationery* means "writing tools, such as paper and envelopes." Confusion about the two terms comes as much from misspelling as misuse. *Personalized stationery* [NOT *stationary*] *is less expensive than you'd think.*

such Overused as an intensifier. Avoid in formal writing situations. *It was* [NOT *such*] *a beautiful sunset.*

sure Used in speech as an adverb meaning "surely" or "certainly." In formal writing, use *surely* or *certainly. The arts in Eastern Europe will surely* [NOT *sure*] *flourish under democracy.*

sure and Nonstandard. Use *sure to* instead. *Be sure to* [NOT *sure and*] *proofread business letters carefully.*

than, then *Than* is a conjunction used in a clause of comparison or inequality. *I would rather have ice cream than* [not *then*] *cake. Then* is an adverb used to indicate past or future time. *We'll do our errands and then have lunch.*

that, which *That* is always used to introduce restrictive clauses. *The cowboy poetry that I heard last night was very funny. Which* is used to introduce nonrestrictive clauses. *His morals, which are questionable, should not influence our opinion of this novel.*

their, there, they're *Their* is a possessive pronoun. *Their sidewalk is always shoveled in winter. There* means "at or in that place." *We'll call when we get there. There* is also an expletive (*there is/are . . .*). *There is reason to believe Gwen is in Mexico. They're* is a contraction for "they are." *They're at their house now.*

theirself, theirselves See **hisself, theirselves.**

them, them there Nonstandard when used in place of *those. Those* [NOT *them*] *Appaloosas have beautiful markings.*

these/those kinds, sorts, types See **kind(s), sort(s), type(s).**

this here, that there, these here Nonstandard. Simply omit the *here* and *there* in these phrases. *This* [NOT *This here*] *German Shepherd is very good with children.*

to, too, two   Perhaps more of a spelling than a usage problem. *To* is a preposition, *too* is an adverb, and *two* a number. *Two tickets to a Metallica concert are two too many for my parents.*

toward, towards   Both versions are acceptable. *Toward* is preferred in the United States. *We rowed steadily toward shore.*

try and   Nonstandard. Use *try to* instead. *Try to* [NOT *Try and*] *be on time.*

uninterested, disinterested   See **disinterested, uninterested.**

unique   Like *perfect, straight, round,* and *complete, unique* is an absolute. There are no degrees of uniqueness; either something is one-of-a-kind or it isn't. *Very unique* is not only illogical but an overused intensifier. *Dilbert's cartoons are unique* [NOT *very unique*] *in their ridiculous humor.*

use, utilize   *Use* means "the act of employing something." *Utilize* means "to make use of." *Use* is simpler and more direct; *utilize* sounds inflated. *I used* [NOT *utilized*] *my credit card to buy the stereo.*

use to, suppose to   Nonstandard. Be sure to use a *d* with *use* and *suppose. Jessica used* [NOT *use*] *to date my brother.*

wait on   *Wait on* means "to serve" and should not be used when the desired meaning is "wait for." *We waited for* [NOT *on*] *Liz, but she never showed up.*

ways   Colloquial; use *way* when designating a distance. *You have a way* [NOT *ways*] *to go before you get to I-85.*

where   Colloquial for *that. I read that* [NOT *where*] *buying imported goods leads to unemployment.*

where . . . at   Redundant. Omit the *at. Where are they now?* [NOT *Where are they at now?*]

which, that   See **that, which.**

which, who, whose, that   Generally use *who* or *whose* to refer to people, except in an expression such as *That's an idea whose time has come.* Use *which* or *that* to refer to things. Do not use *which* to refer to people. *It was the tall man with red hair who* [NOT *which*] *witnessed the robbery.* [See EDIT 3a.]

while   *While* usually designates time and should not be used as a substitute for *and* or *but. He shopped for groceries while she waited in the car. Julia was convinced but* [NOT *while*] *Paul remained skeptical.*

who's, whose   *Who's* is a contraction of *who is. Whose* is a possessive pronoun. *Whose* [NOT *who's*] *volleyball is this?*

will, shall   See **shall, will.**

would of   Nonstandard for *would have. I would have* [NOT *would of*] *worn a tuxedo.*

your, you're   *Your* is a possessive pronoun. *You're* is a contraction of *you are. You're* [NOT *your*] *waitlisted for the 6:00 p.m. flight.*

Punctuation

Learning Objectives

After reading this section, you should:

- be able to use commas correctly;
- know when to use semicolons and colons;
- use apostrophes and quotation marks correctly;
- use end punctuation and other punctuation marks correctly.

Punctuation

PUNCT

PUNCT 1

The Comma

Commas help communicate meaning by eliminating possible misreadings. Consider this sentence:

> After telephoning Paul Lee James went to the library.

Depending upon where you put the comma, it could be James, Lee James, or Paul Lee James who goes to the library.

> After telephoning Paul Lee, James went to the library.
>   ^

> After telephoning Paul, Lee James went to the library.
>   ^

> After telephoning, Paul Lee James went to the library.
>   ^

Commas are used to mark the natural pauses of speech.

> Fish, rice, and mangoes are mainstays of the diet in Thailand.

In fact, reading a sentence aloud may sometimes help you place a comma correctly, but the only reliable route to correct comma use is knowledge of basic sentence structure. (See GRAM 2, 3, 4, and 5.)

Rules governing punctuation change over time to reflect changes in style and taste. Today writers use fewer commas than in the past without sacrificing clarity or meaning. The following comma rules sum up current practice while acknowledging variations and important exceptions.

As you study the rules, keep in mind that the comma, of all the marks of punctuation, has the greatest variety of uses, yet in every case, it functions in one of two basic ways—to *separate* or to *enclose* elements in a sentence.

PUNCT 1a Use a comma to separate independent clauses joined by a coordinating conjunction (*and, but, for, nor, or, so,* and *yet*).

Place a comma before a coordinating conjunction that joins two or more independent or main clauses. (See GRAM 4.)

> We stopped for lunch at McDonald's, and we both had salad.
>   ^

> We knew the Natalie Cole concert would be popular, so we bought our
> tickets early.   ^

EXCEPTION: It is acceptable to omit the comma, especially before *and* or *or*, when the main clauses in a compound sentence are short and there is no possibility of misreading.

Show me a hero and I will write you a tragedy.   —F. Scott Fitzgerald

When main clauses linked by a coordinating conjunction already contain commas or are especially long, use a semicolon instead.

Dr. Martin Luther King Jr., impressed people with his visionary ideas, courage in the face of death, and powerful presence/; and many who heard him speak in the 1960s still vividly remember him.

For a full discussion of the use of the semicolon, see PUNCT 2.

Be careful not to use a comma to separate compound elements that are not independent clauses. (See PUNCT 1m.)

Wanda washed the dishes/ and the pots in the sink.

PUNCT 1b Use a comma to set off an introductory group of words.

The most common introductory word groups are adverbial clauses, prepositional phrases, verbal phrases, and absolute phrases. The comma signals the end of the introductory group of words and the beginning of the sentence proper.

Adverbial clauses

Introductory clauses that function as adverbs tell when, where, why, how, or under what terms the central action of the sentence takes place. (See GRAM 4b.)

When electric power fails, hospitals rely on emergency generators.

EXCEPTION: If the introductory clause is short and there is no chance of misreading, the comma may be omitted.

After George moved we haven't seen him.

In the following sentence, which also begins with a short introductory clause, the comma is needed to make clear that Allison was not eating the birds.

> While Allison ate, the birds sang outside her window.

If commas are used consistently after introductory clauses, no sentence will be misread.

Prepositional phrases

Set off a lengthy introductory prepositional phrase (four words or more) or a series of prepositional phrases with a comma to signal that the main part of the sentence is about to begin. (See GRAM 3a.)

> After a delicious and perhaps too bountiful Thanksgiving dinner, Grandpa took a nap.

> In his book on Nepal, Trank tells how he came to live there.

As a general rule, a short introductory prepositional phrase is not followed by a comma.

> On weekends we like to sleep late.

Verbal phrases

Set off an introductory verbal phrase, whether short or long, with a comma. **Verbals**—gerunds, participles, and infinitives—are verbs that act as nouns, adjectives, or adverbs. (See GRAM 1a and 3b.)

> GERUND   By working out every day, Maria made the team.
>
> PARTICIPLE   Excited about her exam scores, Pam called her parents.
>
> INFINITIVE   To get elected to public office, a candidate must have a well-managed and well-funded campaign.

At times a single-word verbal may be used as an introductory comment. It, too, is always followed by a comma.

> Huffing, Carlos arrived to see the train pull away.

Absolute phrases

An **absolute phrase** modifies an entire statement. (See GRAM 3d.) Setting it off with commas helps the reader understand that it refers to all the rest of the sentence.

Everything considered, we chose a perfect day for the picnic.

The view of the mountains was superb, the sun shining brightly on the snow-covered peaks.

PUNCT 1c Use commas to set off nonrestrictive adjective phrases and clauses and appositives.

Adjective phrases and clauses and appositives are either restrictive or nonrestrictive. A **restrictive** phrase, clause, or appositive contains essential information that limits—or restricts—the meaning of the noun or pronoun it describes. Because a restrictive phrase or clause is essential to the meaning of the sentence, do not set it off with commas.

The woman, *wearing the green print dress,* is a shoplifter.

[The adjective phrase is essential (restrictive) and thus should not be set off with commas; without it, we have no way of identifying which woman is the shoplifter.]

Nonrestrictive adjective phrases and clauses

When an adjective phrase (see GRAM 3a) or clause (see GRAM 4) is not required to identify the noun or pronoun it modifies, it is **nonrestrictive;** this means you can omit the element without changing the meaning of the sentence. Therefore, you should set it off by commas whether it occurs at the beginning, the middle, or the end of a sentence.

NONRESTRICTIVE PHRASE

Awake since dawn, the nervous groom tossed and turned.

NONRESTRICTIVE CLAUSE

Utopian literature, which was popular during the last quarter of the nineteenth century, seems to emerge at times of social and political upheaval.

NONRESTRICTIVE CLAUSE

Kate hiked the Long Trail, which runs from Maine to Georgia.

To test whether or not a phrase or clause is essential, mentally block it off and read the sentence without it. If the sentence still makes sense, then the phrase or clause is nonrestrictive and should be set off by commas.

Sometimes a phrase or clause can be construed either way, restrictive or nonrestrictive, and it is the writer's use of commas—or not—that conveys the intended meaning.

NONRESTRICTIVE CLAUSE

My brother, who lives in Denver, is studying hotel management.

[As a nonrestrictive clause, *who lives in Denver* indicates the writer has only one brother.]

RESTRICTIVE CLAUSE

My brother who lives in Denver is studying hotel management.

[As a restrictive clause, *who lives in Denver* indicates the writer has more than one brother and wishes to identify the one under discussion by where he lives.]

Nonrestrictive appositives

An **appositive** renames or extends the meaning of a nearby noun or word group. (See GRAM 3c.) Most appositives are nonrestrictive and, therefore, are set off with commas.

Barry, the waiter at The Fishbowl, is a senior.

These trees, elms, have a fungus and must be cut down.

Nonrestrictive appositives that contain commas are set off with dashes rather than commas to prevent confusion. (See PUNCT 6d.) Restrictive appositives are never set off by commas.

Lise Mueller's collection/ *Alive Together*/ won the 1997 Pulitzer Prize for poetry.

As a test, restate the sentence without the appositive. If the sentence does not make sense, the appositive is restrictive and should not be set off with commas. Here *Alive Together* restricts the meaning of *collection*.

PUNCT 1d Use a comma to separate parallel words, phrases, and clauses in a series.

Rob bought his calculator, textbooks, and diskettes at the campus bookstore.

The horses trotted down the hill, across the meadow, and into the barn.

The manager told Liz she could have the job if she would work the evening shift, if she would work overtime on short notice, and if she would supply her own uniform.

Although it is not wrong to omit the comma before the final conjunction in a series, most writers prefer always to use the final comma to avoid any risk of confusion or misreading.

CLEAR   Willa Cather wrote poetry, fiction and nonfiction.

CONFUSING   The new tank tops were yellow, purple, red and white.
          [Are there red *and* white tank tops or tank tops that are both *red and white*?]

If the items in a series are joined by conjunctions—usually for emphasis—omit the commas completely.

I know someone who drinks Coke at breakfast and lunch and dinner.

PUNCT 1e Use a comma to separate coordinate adjectives. Do not use a comma with cumulative adjectives.

The mountain climber wore *hot, itchy* socks.

The *dark, muddy, smelly* swamp was infested with mosquitoes.

The adjectives in these examples are called **coordinate adjectives** because each one modifies a noun separately. Coordinate adjectives can be joined with *and* (hot *and* itchy; dark *and* muddy *and* smelly), and their order can be changed without altering the meaning of the sentence (*the muddy, dark, smelly swamp*). Coordinate adjectives are separated by commas.

Adjectives in a series that modify the adjectives that follow them as well as a noun or pronoun are called **cumulative adjectives.** Cumulative adjectives need no commas between them.

Angela sewed *two large denim* patches on the knees of her jeans.

[The adjectives are not separated by commas because *denim* modifies *patches, large* modifies *denim patches,* and *two* modifies *large denim patches.*]

You can test whether commas are needed with a series of adjectives by trying to join them with *and* or by changing their order. If you are testing cumulative adjectives, nonidiomatic sentences result.

NONIDIOMATIC

Angela sewed two and large and denim patches on the knees of her jeans.

Angela sewed denim large two patches on the knees of her jeans.

PUNCT 1f Use a comma to set off parenthetical, interrogative, and transitional expressions.

Parenthetical expressions are inserted in a sentence to qualify, explain, or give the writer's point of view.

In some kinds of writing, especially formal writing, contractions are frowned upon.

The lawyer's objection was overruled, unfortunately.

Interrogative expressions or tags are used at the end of sentences, almost as an afterthought.

The university has a policy about cars on campus, doesn't it?

Transitional expressions (see PARA 3b) such as *in other words, on the contrary, in summary,* and *for example* can occur at the beginning or end of a sentence or in the middle of an independent clause.

As a matter of fact, the expedition will be extremely dangerous.

A turkey sandwich, for example, is a healthy lunch.

When a conjunctive adverb functions as a transitional expression, it is set off with commas (see GRAM 1g).

You should, therefore, keep your credit cards in a safe place.

PUNCT 1g Use a comma to set off contrasted elements.

Expressions that indicate a contrast or contradiction usually begin with *not, nor, but,* or *unlike.*

Ulysses S. Grant was a successful general, not a successful president.

The steelworkers, unlike management, wanted a shorter workweek.

PUNCT 1h Use commas to set off speech tags such as *she said.*

Speech tags are words or expressions that attribute direct quotations to a speaker. (See PUNCT 5a.) Speech tags can introduce, interrupt, or follow a direct quotation.

The umpire yelled, "You're out!"

"Push the red button," she explained, "to record your message."

"I am staying with a family in Madrid," writes Sybil.

PUNCT 1i Use a comma to set off mild interjections, words of direct address, and the words *yes* and *no.*

Well, I think a compromise is in order.

Your sculpture of the wild horse is excellent, Susan.

Yes, we'll meet you at the gym tomorrow.

Sometimes interjections express strong emotion and require an exclamation point. (See PUNCT 6c.)

PUNCT 1j Use commas according to accepted practice with titles and degrees, names, dates, addresses, place names, measurements, numbers, and personal letters.

TITLES, DEGREES, AND EXTRA NAME ELEMENTS

Dr. Richard Steele, director of admissions at Bowdoin College, reports that applications are up.

Priscilla French, D.V.M., has a practice in Miami.

REVERSED NAMES

Lobo, Rebecca

Stowe, Harriet Beecher

DATES

On Friday, February 28, 1999, Sarah will be twenty-seven years old.

EXCEPTION: Omit the commas when the date is inverted (*28 February 1999*) or when only the month and year are given.

America entered World War II in December 1941.

ADDRESSES

Aneela's new address is 1166 Fifield Street, St. Paul, MN 55100.

For more information, write to Lee Dougherty at the Department of Natural Resources, Alabama State University, Montgomery, AL 36101.

PLACE NAMES

United's flight 404 leaves Boston, Massachusetts, on Sunday morning and arrives in Paris, France, that evening.

MEASUREMENTS AND NUMBERS

The Colemans' baby weighed seven pounds, three ounces at birth.

As an eighth grader Michael was already six feet, two inches tall.

CBS received over 12,500 letters after the Arafat interview.

SALUTATIONS AND COMPLIMENTARY CLOSINGS IN PERSONAL LETTERS

Dear Max,   Sincerely,

Dear Grandma and Grandpa,   Warm wishes,

PUNCT 1k Use commas to prevent confusion or misreading.

Occasionally you need to use a comma for no other reason but to make the meaning of a sentence clear.

To Marilyn, Franklin was the one responsible for the accident.
^

As soon as we got on, the train pulled out of the station.
^

After all, slavery was a major factor in the Civil War.
^

PUNCT 1l Use commas to indicate an omitted word or words.

To show the omission of an understood word or words, use a comma.

Joe enjoyed poker; Betty, bridge.
^

Jan is taking the 10:45 train; Atsuko, the 2:22; and Bob, the 5:03.
^   ^

PUNCT 1m Avoid unnecessary commas.

Overpunctuating by using commas where they are not needed can be as confusing to your reader as omitting necessary commas. Unnecessary commas break the flow of your prose by separating parts of your sentences that should not be separated. For example, if you separate a subject and its verb or an adjective and the word it modifies with commas, your reader must spend time figuring out which ideas go together instead of simply following your thought. In addition to observing the *do* rules of comma use, become familiar with the following seven situations in which you do not use a comma.

1. **Do not place a comma between a subject and its verb.**

   The candidates who fail to file timely financial reports/are subject to fines.

2. **Do not place a comma between a verb and its complement(s).**

   Calvin Coolidge announced/ that he would not seek reelection in 1928.

3. **Do not place a comma between an adjective and a noun or between an adverb and an adjective.**

Affirmative Action is a sensitive, difficult/ issue.

The Guthrie Theater attracts many extremely/ talented actors.

4. **Do not place a comma between compound elements that are not independent clauses. (See PUNCT 1a.)**

Martin picked up his suit at the cleaners/ and had a prescription filled.

To sell/ or not to sell is the question stock speculators face daily.

5. **Do not place a comma before the initial item or after the last item in a series or after the words** *such as* **or** *like.* **(See PUNCT 1d.)**

Technical innovations, strong characterizations, and intriguing plots/ make *Star Trek* a classic series.

She reads popular magazines such as/ *Time, Money,* and *People.*

6. **Do not use commas with cumulative adjectives. (See PUNCT 1e.)**

The taxi company ordered five/ new/ yellow sedans.

An exhibit of classic/ Chinese art is opening at the Hillyer this week.

7. **Do not use commas to set off restrictive modifiers. (See PUNCT 1c and 1f.)**

Perhaps/ the reporter can give us more information.

Blood enters pulmonary circulation/ from the right ventricle/ and travels through the pulmonary arteries to the lungs.

Great breakthroughs are made by scientists/ who are willing to take risks.

Find the history of the word/ *trick/* in the *Oxford English Dictionary.*

8. **Do not use a comma before** *than.*

Coming in third is definitely more satisfying for me/ than placing any farther back.

9. **Do not use a comma after a coordinating conjunction.**

The Yankees won the pennant last year but/ not this year.

10. **Do not use a comma before a parenthesis.**

Use the current name of the publisher/ (for example, Harcourt Brace), not the name at the time of publication.

11. **Do not use a comma with an indirect quotation.**

When I got through voice mail, the secretary said/ that she would take a message.

12. **Do not use a comma with a question mark or exclamation point.**

"I love you!/" she shouted across Grand Central Station.

PUNCT 2

The Semicolon

For a mark of punctuation with essentially only two uses, the **semicolon** may be the most misunderstood mark of all, often being confused with the colon and the period. The semicolon is used with major sentence elements of equal grammatical rank. A semicolon *joins* main clauses not joined by a coordinating conjunction, and it *separates* phrases and clauses containing other punctuation. Sometimes the semicolon is called a *weak period* because it marks a weaker separation or stop than the period. If two main clauses are particularly closely related, use a semicolon, especially if the two sentences are short. You are never wrong, however, to use a period.

Gazpacho is only the first course; The complete dinner is five courses.

PUNCT 2a Use a semicolon to join closely related main clauses when a coordinating conjunction (*and, but, for, nor, or, so, yet*) is not used.

A semicolon joining two main clauses indicates a strong connection between the content of the two clauses, a connection that would be lessened if a period were used instead.

Anatomy is not destiny; it is simply anatomy.
— Elizabeth Janeway

In fact, whenever independent clauses are connected without a coordinating conjunction, a semicolon *must* be used. A comma alone is not sufficient. Simply using a comma to join two independent clauses creates the error commonly known as the *comma splice.* (See EDIT 6b.)

The new cars are really disappointing/; they all look alike.

In general, when two independent clauses are joined by a coordinating conjunction, a comma—not a semicolon—is used to punctuate the resulting compound sentence. (See PUNCT 1a.) If, however, at least one of the independent clauses contains some form of internal punctuation, then you may elect to use a semicolon.

PUNCT 2b   **Use a semicolon to join main clauses when a transitional expression or conjunctive adverb introduces the second main clause.**

Cal-Edison recently instituted several new environmental policies; *for example*, it now offers customers a number of incentives to do home energy audits.

There are no telephones or radios at Rio Caliente; *however,* television is available by satellite hookup.

NOTE: Be careful not to mistake coordinating conjunctions (*and, but, for, nor, or, so,* and *yet*) for transitional expressions or conjunctive adverbs. A comma is used when a coordinating conjunction joins two main clauses. For a list of commonly used transitional expressions, see PARA 3b; for a list of commonly used conjunctive adverbs, see GRAM 1g.

PUNCT 2c   **Use semicolons to join items in a series containing other punctuation.**

In the following example, the semicolons help the reader distinguish major sentence elements and thus quickly and accurately understand the writer's intended meaning.

The works in the American novel course include Hawthorne's *The Scarlet Letter,* with the love triangle of Hester Prynne, Arthur Dimmesdale, and Roger Chillingworth; Melville's *Moby-Dick,* with the monomaniacal Captain Ahab; and Chopin's *The Awakening,* with the heroic struggle of Edna Pontellier.

PUNCT 2d Do not use the semicolon to join structures of unequal grammatical rank.

The sentence elements joined by a semicolon must always be of equal grammatical rank. Semicolons are most often incorrectly used between an independent clause and a phrase, between an independent clause and a subordinate clause, and between an independent clause and a list. (See GRAM 3 and 4.)

While vacationing in Arizona/, Bill saw friends in Yuma.

Polly took a short nap/, which she deserved after babysitting all day.

The grocery store carried difficult to find fruits and vegetables/: Asian

pears, star fruit, anise, and bok choy.

PUNCT 3

The Colon

Use the **colon** after an independent clause to direct your reader's attention forward to the word(s), phrase(s), or clause(s) that follows it.

PUNCT 3a Use a colon to link independent clauses when the second illustrates, interprets, or explains the first.

I am a man who at the precocious age of thirty-five experienced an astonishing revelation: it is better to be a success than a failure.
—Norman Podhoretz

[After reading the independent clause before the colon, the reader wants an explanation of the "astonishing revelation," which Podhoretz then provides.]

The writer has the option to capitalize the first word of the independent clause following a colon but should be consistent within a single composition. (See MECH 1f.)

PUNCT 3b Use a colon after an independent clause that introduces a series.

Camp Winnipesaukee offers several waterfront activities: swimming, canoeing, fishing, windsurfing, and water skiing.

When you use *the following* or *as follows* to introduce a series, use a colon.

The following constitutes a basic personal reference library: a college dictionary, an almanac, a thesaurus, an atlas, and an English handbook.

PUNCT 3c Use a colon after an independent clause to draw attention to an appositive.

In the Mideast, public attention focused on one thing: peace.

PUNCT 3d Use a colon after an independent clause to introduce a direct quotation.

A colon is always used to introduce a long quotation. If the quotation is longer than four typed lines, it is set off from the text. (See PUNCT 5a.) Although the colon is optional with shorter quotations, it is still a good idea to use one because the colon focuses the reader's attention on the quotation.

I'll always remember the Chinese proverb I learned in the ninth-grade: "I hear and I forget. I see and I remember. I do and I understand."

PUNCT 3e Use a colon to mark conventional separations between the following elements.

SALUTATION AND BODY OF A BUSINESS LETTER Dear Manager:

CHAPTER AND VERSE IN A BIBLICAL CITATION Ruth 2:3

TITLE AND SUBTITLE *The Army of the Potomac: A Stillness at Appomattox*

DATE AND PAGE IN BIBLIOGRAPHIC ENTRIES *Time* 27 October 1997: 62-72

PLACE AND PUBLISHER IN BIBLIOGRAPHIC ENTRIES Boston: Allyn and Bacon

For a complete discussion of business letters, see FORMAT 3a; for bibliographic entries, see MLA DOCU 2 and OTHER DOCU 2 and 4.

PUNCT 3f   Do not misuse colons.

If you remember that a complete independent clause must *always* precede a colon, you will avoid the most common misuses of the colon. Do not use a colon to separate a verb and its object, a verb and its complement, or a preposition and its object.

We need to buy/ lettuce, peppers, onions, cucumbers, and carrots.

The candidates for Student Association president are/ Steven Holden, Julie Dwire, and Amy Besette.

The vendors had an interesting selection of/ reed baskets, alpaca sweaters, silver jewelry, and terra-cotta pots.

PUNCT 4

The Apostrophe

Although we commonly say that an **apostrophe** (') is used to show possession, actual possession or ownership is only one kind of relationship indicated.

a dollar's worth = something worth a dollar

Oates's latest novel = the most recent novel written by Oates

a day's march = a march that takes a day

a two weeks' vacation = a vacation that lasts two weeks

my cousin's new boat = the new boat owned by my cousin

Apostrophes are also used to indicate omitted letters and numerals and to form the plurals of letters, numbers, abbreviations, and words used as words.

EXCEPTION: The apostrophe may be omitted in forming the plural of an abbreviation or number (ATMs, VCRs, 1990s, 80s).

PUNCT 4a Use an apostrophe to mark the possessive case of nouns and indefinite pronouns.

The following five rules for forming the possessive case of nouns and indefinite pronouns (see GRAM 1c) are based on the sound and/or letter with which a word ends.

1. **Add an 's to form the possessive of singular and plural nouns and indefinite pronouns that do not end in *s* or with an *s* or a *z* sound.**

   Joanne's house   that man's car
   anybody's guess   those men's cars

2. **Add 's to form the possessive of singular nouns ending in *s* or with an *s* or *z* sound.**

   Keats's poetry   Konrad Lorenz's research
   the boss's car   the prince's cloak

   Add only an apostrophe if an extra *s* would create awkward pronunciation.

   Moses' word   Euripides' plays

3. **Add only an apostrophe to form the possessive of plural nouns ending in *s* or with an *s* or a *z* sound.**

   the boys' coats   the Smiths' house
   the dogs' bones   the golfers' tour

4. **To form the possessive of compound nouns, add 's to only the last word.**

   my mother-in-law's clock   the runner-up's prize

5. **To show joint ownership, make only the last noun possessive.**

   Tom and Jennifer's house [Tom and Jennifer own the house together.]

   To show individual ownership, make both nouns possessive.

   Tom's and Jennifer's philosophies [Tom and Jennifer have different philosophies.]

PUNCT 4b Use an apostrophe to indicate omitted letters or numbers in contractions.

In the following examples the apostrophe replaces one or more omitted letters or numbers:

I'm [I am]   fish 'n' chips [fish and chips]
OK'd [okayed]   the earthquake of '94 [1994]

We use contractions in informal speech and writing all the time. In formal situations, however, most contemporary writers use contractions sparingly or not at all.

PUNCT 4c Use an apostrophe to form the plural of letters, numbers, abbreviations, and words cited as words.

Your *m*'s look like *w*'s.

Count to 999 by 3's. (also 3s or threes)

Most banks have ATM's today. (also ATMs)

I've heard enough of your *no*'s for a while.

Note that the letter, number, or word used as a word is italicized, but the *s* following the apostrophe is not. (See MECH 4c.)
The apostrophe is not used to form the plural of a decade.

The 1970s had much in common with the 1920s.

PUNCT 4d Do not misuse apostrophes.

1. **Do not use the apostrophe with the possessive pronouns *his, hers, its, ours, yours, theirs*.**

   The pizza with anchovies is all your̸s.

2. **Do not confuse possessive pronouns with contractions that look or sound similar.**

   its   it's (it is)
   whose   who's (who is)
   your   you're (you are)
   their   they're (they are)

3. **Follow the established usage for apostrophes in the names of organizations.**

Some organizations omit the apostrophe from their names.

Veterans Administration

United States Postal Service [OR U.S. Postal Service]

Women's Health Center

If you are uncertain about whether to use an apostrophe, check your dictionary or publications by the organization in question.

PUNCT 5

Quotation Marks

Quotation marks are used in pairs to signal the start and the end of a direct quotation, to enclose titles of short works, and to indicate words used as words.

PUNCT 5a Use double quotation marks (" ") to enclose direct quotations.

Direct quotations are written or spoken words repeated verbatim and need to be in quotation marks. Integrate quotations of four or fewer typed lines of prose or three or fewer lines of poetry into the text of your paper.

It was Kahlil Gibran who said, "Work is love made visible."

Walt Whitman boldly states, "I too am not a bit tamed, I too am untranslatable, / I sound my barbaric yawp over the roofs of the world."

[The slash (/) marks the end of a line of poetry; see PUNCT 6h.]

Block off prose quotations that are longer than four typed lines and poetry quotations that are more than three lines. (See RESCH 4c.) Do not use quotation marks with blocked-off quotations.

Indirect quotations, which report what someone has said instead of citing that person's exact words, are never placed within quotation marks.

DIRECT QUOTATION
Hector said, "I can't remember where I left my biology book."

INDIRECT QUOTATION
Hector told me he couldn't remember where he'd left his biology book.

Set off speech tags such as *she said* and *I replied* with commas. (See PUNCT 1h.) When you use quotation marks to indicate dialog, the directly quoted speech of two or more people, signal a change of speaker by beginning a new paragraph. The following dialog between a T-shirt shop owner and a young boy is taken from a student essay about a childhood experience when the writer discovered just how hot *hot* can be.

> "First I heat the iron up to 1,000 degrees. Then I . . . ."
>
> "One thousand degrees!" I thought to myself. "Could that burn off a finger? Or a whole hand? But what if it was so hot you wouldn't even feel it?" I had to find out.
>
> "Whoa, you don't want to get too close to that. It will give you a nasty burn," the shopkeeper said, catching me closing in on the iron.
>
> "Oh, sorry, I didn't know," I answered apologetically, hiding my true intention of sneaking just a touch.

PUNCT 5b   Use single quotation marks (' ') to enclose quotations within quotations.

Professor Cohen said, "I shall always remember Ellery Sedgwick's advice, 'Autobiographies ought to begin with the second chapter.' "

PUNCT 5c   Use quotation marks to indicate the titles of short written works, chapters of books, songs, and episodes of radio and television series.

ARTICLE Patricia thought "Closing the Recycling Loop" was especially helpful for her paper.

ESSAY We wrote a short paper on Emerson's "Self-Reliance."

SHORT STORY Stephen Crane captures the power of the ocean in "The Open Boat."

POEM In "Farm for Sale" Frances Frost depicts the despair of the Depression years in rural America.

CHAPTER I think "The Sermon" is the most memorable chapter from Melville's *Moby-Dick.*

SONG Elton John sings "Candle in the Wind."

EPISODE Viewers selected "The Trouble with Tribbles" as their favorite *Star Trek* show of all time.

Use italics or underlining for the names of longer works—including the names of newspapers and magazines and the titles of books, plays, films, and television or radio series. (See MECH 4a.)

PUNCT 5d Quotation marks may be used to indicate words used as words or words used in a special sense.

I finally understand the difference between "mean" and "median."

The mayor acknowledged that the "ghetto problem" was in fact his problem.

Although italics or underlining is still preferred to quotation marks for words used as words, quotation marks are also considered acceptable. (See MECH 4c.)

PUNCT 5e When using other marks of punctuation in combination with quotation marks, observe the following conventions.

1. **Commas and periods are *always* placed inside quotation marks.**

"Now," the conductor said, "let's add the violins."

2. **Colons and semicolons are *always* placed outside quotation marks.**

Mount Rushmore is a striking memorial to four Presidential "giants": George Washington, Thomas Jefferson, Abraham Lincoln, Theodore Roosevelt.

All domestic flights are now designated "no smoking"; the rule is clearly posted and strictly policed.

3. **Question marks and exclamation points are placed inside quotation marks when they apply to the quoted material; they are placed outside when they apply to the whole sentence.**

Harriet said, "Will you meet me at Bloomingdale's?"

Did Harriet say, "I'll meet you at Bloomingdale's"?

The defendant jumped to his feet shouting, "That's a lie!"

Stop whispering "The Star Spangled Banner"! Sing it out proudly!

PUNCT 5f Do not misuse quotation marks.

Because quotation marks direct attention to the words they enclose, use them judiciously to avoid diminishing the intended effect. Do not use quotation marks around nicknames, slang, technical terms, or after the word *so-called.*

The kids all called her "Bunny."

Lost World is a "cool" movie.

In weaving class we learned about the "warp" and the "weft."

Also, do not use quotation marks with indirect quotations. (See PUNCT 5a.)

Coach Barnett told his players "to be on time for practice."

Finally, do not use quotation marks around the titles of your papers. (See FORMAT 2.)

PUNCT 6

Other Punctuation Marks

PUNCT 6a The period

1. **Use a period to mark the end of all sentences except direct questions and exclamations.**

It is no secret that most sentences in English end with a **period,** but sometimes choosing between a period and a question mark or between a period and an exclamation point can be tricky. If your sentence tells of a question that was asked as opposed to asking the question directly, end that sentence with a period.

INDIRECT QUESTION

Mary asked when Annie Dillard had written *Pilgrim at Tinker Creek.*

Reserve the exclamation point for sentences that express strong emotion or deserve special emphasis. Otherwise, for a straightforward statement or command, use a period.

STATEMENT   Last month the Ford dealership sold forty-seven new cars.

COMMAND   Put your dishes in the sink when you finish eating.

On occasion you might put a polite or mild request in the form of a question, but if your intent is not to ask a question—that is, not to offer the reader the choice of saying "yes" or "no"—you can use a period. (See PUNCT 6b.)

2. Use a period after most abbreviations.

Use periods with standard abbreviations.

STANDARD ABBREVIATIONS		INITIALS	
Rev.	Reverend	B.A. (OR BA)	Bachelor of Arts
etc.	et cetera	A.D. (OR AD)	*Anno Domini*
Inc.	Incorporated	R.N. (OR RN)	Registered Nurse
St.	Street	a.m. (OR A.M.)	*ante meridiem*
Nov.	November	Ph.D. (OR PhD)	Doctor of
Dr.	Doctor		Philosophy
Capt.	Captain	C.P.A. (OR CPA)	Certified Public Accountant
		e.g.	*exempli gratia*

When an abbreviation falls at the end of a sentence, use only one period.

At graduation ceremonies in May, Andrea was awarded her Ph.D.

Acronyms are abbreviations that are usually pronounced as words (UNESCO) or sounded as letters (FBI) and written without periods.

ESP	extrasensory perception
TV	television
CARE	Cooperative for American Relief to Everywhere
TNT	trinitrotoluene
KO	knock out
MS	multiple sclerosis
NBA	National Basketball Association
IRS	Internal Revenue Service
USA (OR U.S.A.)	United States of America
NAFTA	North American Free Trade Agreement
JFK	John Fitzgerald Kennedy

Periods are not used with the U.S. Postal Service's abbreviations for states. (See FORMAT 3a.)

AR   CA   FL   MI   ND   TX   WA   WY

NOTE: Because usage varies regarding different kinds of abbreviations, it is always a good idea to consult your college dictionary or a style manual when you are uncertain about a particular one.

3. Use a period to mark divisions in citations to literary works.

When referring to works of literature by such divisions as act, scene, and line, use separating periods and no intervening spaces.

Macbeth III.ii.25–32 [act, scene, lines]

Paradise Lost XI.47–63 [book, lines]

John 10.3–10 [chapter, verses]

PUNCT 6b　The question mark

1. Use a question mark after all direct questions.

The **question mark** is the conventional form of punctuation to use with a direct question.

What's for dinner tonight?

When direct questions occur in a series, you may choose to use multiple question marks, indicating that a separate answer is expected for each question.

Did you call the meeting? Reserve a room? Order refreshments?

When a direct question occurs within a declarative sentence, use a question mark at the end of the question and a period at the end of the sentence.

"Where do you recommend we go to dinner tonight?" Gary inquired.

Use a question mark only if the question ends the sentence.

Maddy asked, "Where are the tennis balls?"

When written in the form of a question, polite requests may be followed by a question mark, though usage varies.

Will you please lock the door when you leave tonight?

Sometimes you will encounter a mixed sentence in which the first half seems declarative and the last half interrogative. If the gist is essentially interrogative—as in the following example—end the sentence with a question mark.

The grocery store is convenient, but is it always well-stocked?

In the following sentence, however, the gist is essentially declarative, so a period should be used.

We watched *The X-Files* last weekend, didn't we.

2. Use a question mark to indicate doubt or unverifiable information.

If you are uncertain about the accuracy or correctness of a word, number, or date, indicate your doubt by using a parenthetical question mark.

Ferdinand Magellan, born in 1480(?), commanded the Spanish expedition that was first to circumnavigate the world.

PUNCT 6c The exclamation point

Use an exclamation point after an interjection or at the end of a sentence that deserves special emphasis or expresses strong emotion. Use **exclamation points** sparingly to express strong feelings, surprise, or disbelief.

"Ouch!" he screamed.

The results of the survey are alarming!

If you think you need an exclamation point to add weight to a simple statement of fact, think instead about revising to get emphasis. (See SENT 6.) Like garlic or pepper, exclamation points lose their effect when overused. And the use of double or even triple exclamation points or an exclamation point in combination with other end punctuation adds nothing but clutter to a sentence.

PUNCT 6d The dash

Use **dashes** to emphasize part of a sentence or to set it off for clarity. They lose their intended effect, however, when used indiscriminately as substitutes for commas, semicolons, or periods.

On your computer or typewriter, use two unspaced hyphens (--) to form a dash (—); do not leave a space before the first hyphen or after the second hyphen.

CORRECT The shellfish--shrimp, lobster, clams, oysters, and mussels--at Bishop's is the freshest in town.

1. **Use dashes to highlight parenthetical material, informal explanations, and afterthoughts that warrant emphasis.**

Ads for bank credit cards and department stores refer to "convenient terms"--meaning 18 percent annual interest rates payable at the convenience of the creditor. —*Time* magazine

Our civilization is decadent, and our language--so the argument runs--must inevitably share in the general collapse. —George Orwell

2. **Use dashes to set off appositives that contain internal commas.**

Usually a nonrestrictive appositive is set off with commas (see PUNCT 1c), but if the appositive itself contains commas, use dashes to clarify how this one part of the sentence fits into the whole.

All our preparations for spring break--choosing the best vacation package, shopping for new clothes, getting to the tanning salon--made it hard to study for midterms.

3. **Use dashes to signal a dramatic reversal of thought or tone.**

He was a terrific father--when he was out of town.

PUNCT 6e Parentheses

Parentheses indicate helpful but not essential information. Avoid overusing parentheses or it will appear that your paper is cluttered with nonessential information. As you write and revise, check to see if you can elevate some parenthetical elements to part of the text by using commas (see PUNCT 1c and 1f) or to see if you can give stronger emphasis with dashes (see PUNCT 6d). Perhaps some details are so nonessential they can be dropped altogether.

Anita Jennings, (president of Harris Bank), thinks treasury notes are a good investment.
[Elevate the parenthetical material to an appositive.]

Each year 25,000—(some studies claim as many as 50,000)—Americans die in alcohol-related accidents.

[Elevate the parenthetical material to highlight the higher figure.]

Write your answers neatly ~~(and clearly)~~ in the left column.

[If your writing is neat, it will be clear; the nonessential *and clearly* can be omitted.]

1. Use parentheses to enclose supplementary or interpretive information, asides, and afterthoughts.

The average homemaker works just under one hundred hours a week at a variety of jobs (purchasing agent, cook, cleaner, economist, chauffeur, and so on) with no annual salary and little recognition.

For almost ten years (and that's ten years too long), American soldiers fought in Vietnam.

When a grammatically complete sentence is presented parenthetically, the end punctuation is placed within the closing parenthesis.

If you have kids, then you have all kinds of breakfast cereal in the house. When I was a kid, it was Rice Krispies, the breakfast cereal that went snap, crackle, and pop. (That's one hell of a claim for a product that is supposed to offer nutritional benefits.) Or Wheaties, the breakfast of champions, whatever that means. —Paul Stevens

2. Use parentheses to enclose numbers or letters used to mark a series in a sentence.

Bacteria are divided into three groups based on shape: (1) spheres, (2) rods, and (3) spirals.

PUNCT 6f   Brackets

1. Use brackets to add or substitute a clarifying comment in quoted material.

The environmentalist Rachel Carson believes that "problems [with controlling insects] arose with the intensification of agriculture—the devotion of immense acreages to a single crop."

[By using brackets to insert the kinds of problems Carson is referring to, the writer avoids having to quote an extended passage.]

One film critic believed that "after the first encounter with the Wizard, [the tin man] ~~he~~ was even more determined to get what he wanted."

[*The tin man* is substituted for *he* to identify which character the reviewer meant.]

2. **Use brackets to indicate that an error was made in the original material.**

The Latin word *sic*, meaning "thus," appears within brackets in a direct quotation to indicate that you recognize an error in the original and are letting it stand.

In one episode of "All in the Family" Archie Bunker was heard to say, "We got a regular Edna St. Louis [sic] Millay here."

[Here *sic* indicates that *St. Louis* actually appeared in the script and that it was the name-dropping Archie, and not the writer, who got the poet Edna St. Vincent Millay's name wrong.]

3. **Use brackets around parenthetical material already within a parenthesis.**

The literary Realists (led by William Dean Howells [1837–1920]) dominated American letters during the last half of the nineteenth century.

PUNCT 6g   The ellipsis mark

The **ellipsis mark** is three spaced periods (. . .) that indicates the writer has omitted words from quoted material.

The Secretary of Transportation said that "drivers . . . must learn to use seat belts, because seat belts save lives."

An ellipsis mark tells the reader that you have omitted the part of a quotation that is not pertinent to your point; at the same time, it shows that you are not misrepresenting the person being quoted.

When using an ellipsis, leave a space at the beginning of the omission, a space between each of the three periods, and a space before continuing with the quotation.

1. **Use an ellipsis mark to signal that you have omitted one word or whole sentences from a quoted passage.**

If omitted words within the original passage follow some form of internal or end punctuation, retain that punctuation, and then insert the ellipsis mark.

> Youth is impulsive. When our young men grow angry . . . and disfigure their faces with black paint, it denotes that their hearts are black, . . . and our old men and old women are unable to restrain them. . . . Thus it was when the white men first began to push our forefathers further westward. But let us hope that the hostilities between us may never return.
>
> —Chief Seattle, "My People"

Do not use an ellipsis mark at the beginning of a quotation or at the end unless you have deleted words from the end of the final sentence. In that case, retain the final punctuation, and then add the ellipsis.

> "At the beginning of the Olivier *Hamlet* film, we are told by Olivier's disembodied voice that this is the story of a man who could not make up his mind. Plays do not normally do this sort of self-foretelling. . . ."
> —Bert O. States, *Great Reckonings in Little Rooms*

2. **Indicate the omission of a full line or more of poetry or paragraphs of prose with a single typed line of spaced periods.**

> I shall be telling this with a sigh
> . . . .
> Two roads diverged in a wood, and I—
> I took the one less traveled by,
> And that has made all the difference.
> —Robert Frost, "The Road Not Taken"

3. **Use an ellipsis mark to indicate an incomplete statement or a deliberate pause when writing dialog.**

> I used the phrase "social responsibility," and they yelled: "What's that word you say, boy?"
> "Social responsibility," I said.
> "What?"
> "Social . . ."
> "Louder."
> ". . . responsibility." —Ralph Ellison, *The Invisible Man*

PUNCT 6h The slash

1. Use a slash to indicate options or alternative words.

> Marty took physics pass/fail.
>
> Every member of the band is responsible for his/her own uniform.

Do not leave a space either before or after the **slash** when separating options. Although spelling out *his or her* is preferable to using *his/her* to avoid the sexist pronoun *his*, both can become awkward and repetitious in an extended piece of writing. For alternative strategies, see EDIT 3a.

2. Use a slash to mark off two or three lines of poetry when you run them into your text.

> Emily Dickinson captures the paradox of success in the opening lines: "Success is counted sweetest / By those who ne'er succeed."

Leave one space both before and after the slash when quoting poetry. When quoting four or more lines of poetry, set them off from the text as a block. (See RESCH 4c.)

3. Use a slash to indicate a fraction that is not on your keyboard.

> 5 3/4   4 1/2   27/64

mech

Mechanics

Learning Objectives

After reading this section, you should:

- be able to use capitals and abbreviations correctly;
- understand the use of numbers, italics/underlining, and the hyphen in writing;
- be a better speller.

Mechanics

MECH 1

Capitals

In English, **proper nouns**—the names of specific people, places, and things—are capitalized, and **common nouns**—all other nouns—are not capitalized.

PROPER NOUNS	COMMON NOUNS
Atlanta	city
LeAnn Rimes	singer
Wall Street Journal	newspaper
Americorps	government program
History 271	course

Also, the first word of an English sentence is capitalized, as are important words in a title. The rules for capitalization are quite clear-cut; even the cases involving optional capitalization are clearly defined. If you have a question about a particular word, consult your college dictionary.

MECH 1a   Capitalize proper nouns.

NAMES AND NICKNAMES OF PEOPLE

Helen Keller	Franklin D. Roosevelt	Calamity Jane
Bill Cosby	Shoeless Joe Jackson	Princess Diana
Jackie Joyner-Kersee	William Least Heat-Moon	Malcolm X

GEOGRAPHIC PLACE NAMES

Rocky Mountains	Nile River	Isle of Man
Beijing	the Lone Star State	the Far East

Do not capitalize points of the compass unless they are used to refer to specific geographic places.

Jake went east for the holidays.

Jake drove to the Northeast to see the colorful leaves.

NAMES OF CELESTIAL BODIES

Venus   the North Star   Orion   Halley's Comet

RACES, NATIONALITIES, AND LANGUAGES

Native American	Caucasian	Japanese
Latino	Dane	African-American
Latin	Hebrew	Slavic

217

NAMES OF TRADEMARKS

Ping-Pong	Xerox	Levi's
Jello	HotBot	Coke
WordPerfect	Kleenex	Alka-Seltzer

Follow company or product style for innovative use of capitals in names. Do not capitalize products used with brand names.

Kleenex tissues   Scotch tape   Dodge truck

NAMES OF SPECIFIC SHIPS, PLANES, AND SPACECRAFT (See MECH 4b)

Titanic   Enola Gay   Enterprise

NAMES OF HISTORICAL EVENTS, PERIODS, DOCUMENTS, AND TREATIES

French Revolution	the Black Death	World War II
the Sixties	the Renaissance	the Depression
the U.S. Constitution	Treaty of Versailles	Magna Carta

Do not capitalize recently ascribed names of political, cultural, or scientific periods.

cold war   civil rights movement   space age

Do not capitalize centuries, as in *thirteenth century* or *twentieth century*.

NAMES OF ORGANIZATIONS, CORPORATIONS, INSTITUTIONS, AND GOVERNMENT AGENCIES AND COURTS

Salvation Army	Phi Beta Kappa	Planned Parenthood
Republican Party	Howard University	Ford Foundation
Kraft Foods	Citibank	Digital
Food and Drug Administration	U.S. Court of Claims	Mayo Clinic

When a common noun is part of a name, capitalize it.

Xerox Corporation   Ohio River   Canadian Pacific Railroad

With plurals, however, do not capitalize common nouns.

Shubert and Houseman theaters

Fox and Hudson rivers

United and American airlines

Do not capitalize words such as *a, an,* or *the* when used with proper nouns.

For the New York Yankees, the 1980s were one long slump.

NAMES OF THE DAYS OF THE WEEK, MONTHS OF THE YEAR, HOLIDAYS

Saturday   October   Labor Day

But do not capitalize the names of the seasons.

Saro has an internship in Washington this summer.

NAMES OF RELIGIONS, RELIGIOUS PRACTITIONERS, RELIGIOUS CEREMONIES, HOLY BOOKS, HOLY DAYS, AND WORDS USED TO REFER TO THE DEITY

Catholicism	Passover	Ramadan
Buddhist	Book of Mormon	God

PERSONIFICATION

Because I could not stop for Death—
He kindly stopped for me—

—Emily Dickinson, "Because I
could not stop for Death"

MECH 1b   Capitalize words derived from proper nouns.

Shakespearean	Victorian	Leninism
Christian	Arabian	Israeli

MECH 1c   Capitalize abbreviations of organizations, government agencies, call letters for radio and television stations, and acronyms (words formed from the initial letters of a name).

AFL-CIO	NCAA	IBM	BART	PC
KOST-FM	WCAX-TV	USMC	AIDS	CD-ROM

MECH 1d   Capitalize titles, words denoting family relationships when they precede the name of the person, and epithets (words or phrases used to describe a prominent characteristic).

Senator Jeffords	Great Grandmother Eliza
Reverend King	Honest Abe [epithet for Abraham Lincoln]
Dean Drake	Old Hickory [epithet for Andrew Jackson]

Do not capitalize a title that follows a proper noun.

Daniel Inouye, the senator from Hawaii, voted with the majority.

Madeline Sprague, director of personnel at General Electric, is responsible for all new hirings.

When you use titles of world figures alone, capitalization is optional.

The President [OR president] spoke to the reporters.

Capitalize a word indicating a family relationship when it is substituted for a proper noun.

Did Father call me?

If you are simply referring to a relative, no capitalization is required.

My mother collects stamps.

MECH 1e   Capitalize the first word of a sentence and the first word of a deliberate sentence fragment functioning as a sentence.

The ramshackle cabin was a welcome sight.

Superb acting.

MECH 1f   When an independent clause occurs after a colon, capitalizing the first word is optional.

The pennant race is too close to call: the [OR The] Red Sox and the Yankees will battle until the last day of the season.

Whether you choose to capitalize or not, however, be consistent within a composition.

MECH 1g   Capitalize the first word of a quoted sentence.

In an article on nuclear winter, Carl Sagan states, "Except for fools and madmen, everyone knows that nuclear war would be an unprecedented human catastrophe."

Do not capitalize the first word of a quoted sentence when it is blended into the main sentence.

Barbara Myerhoff has written that "our species can be characterized as *Homo narrans,* humankind as storyteller."

If you interrupt a quoted sentence with some words of explanation, do not capitalize the first word of the quotation after the break.

"Debunking but sympathetic," says *Publishers Weekly*, "this is an engrossing biography of Frank Lloyd Wright."

MECH 1h In quoting poetry, capitalize the first word of every line unless the poet does otherwise.

For the man who should loose me is dead,
Fighting with the Duke in Flanders,
In a pattern called a war.
Christ! What are patterns for?

— Amy Lowell, "Patterns"

what if a much of a which of a wind
gives the truth to summer's lie;

—e. e. cummings, "what if a much of a which of a wind"

MECH 1i Capitalize the first and last words and all other important words in the titles and subtitles of works such as books, magazine articles, films, and compact discs.

Unless they are the first or last word of a title or subtitle, do not capitalize articles (*a, an, the*), coordinating conjunctions (*and, but, or, for, nor, so, yet*), or prepositions (*in, at, of, near, from,* and so on).

BOOK
Bird by Bird

BOOK TITLE: SUBTITLE
A Passion for Excellence: The Leadership Difference

PLAY
The Adding Machine

SHORT STORY
"The Story of an Hour"

POEM
"The Love Song of J. Alfred Prufrock"

FILM
Amistad

PAINTING OR SCULPTURE
Homage to the Square

ARTICLE
"What's Wrong with Black English?"

COMIC STRIP
Hagar the Horrible

SONG
"On the Wings of Love"

COMPACT DISC OR RECORD ALBUM
The Rite of Spring

MECH 1j Capitalize the personal pronoun *I* and the interjection *O*.

The minute I got home, I collapsed on the couch.

"Hear, O Israel."

Do not capitalize the interjection *oh* unless it comes at the beginning of a sentence.

MECH 1k Do not capitalize words unnecessarily.

Only capitalize when it is conventional to do so. Here are rules for avoiding several of the most common errors with capitalization.

1. **Do not capitalize the names of academic subjects, except languages.**

Josie is taking chemistry, math, philosophy, German, and English.

The names of specific courses, however, are capitalized.

New students are required to take Race and Culture.

2. **Do not capitalize school terms or academic years.**

fall semester [NOT Fall Semester]
senior year [NOT Senior year]

3. **Capitalize only the first word in the complimentary close of a letter.**

Fondly,   Sincerely yours,   All best wishes,

4. **Do not capitalize common nouns to highlight them or give them special emphasis.**

We had fun at the company picnic. [NOT Company]

As a university student, I can use interlibrary loans. [NOT University]

5. **Do not capitalize computer terms.**

Many computer terms are English words with new meanings.

access	database [ALSO data base]	e-mail	mouse
debug	hard copy	laptop	online

Brand names of hardware (IBM, Apple, Dell) and software (WordPerfect, Lotus 1-2-3, Window98) are capitalized. Names of commercial online services (America Online, MS Network) and other resources (the Internet, the World Wide Web) should also be capitalized.

MECH 2

Abbreviations

Except for conventional usages, avoid **abbreviations** in formal writing, and that includes your college essays and exams. Spell out the names of holidays, names of days and months, addresses (street, state, country), names of academic subjects and subdivisions of books, units of measurement, names of academic departments, and parts of a business or institution's name (unless the abbreviation is part of the official name).

> _department_   _Christmas_   _December_
> The shipping ~~dept.~~ is having its ~~Xmas~~ party on ~~Dec.~~ 20.
>
> _sociology_   _Mount_   _Junior_
> Dana is a ~~soc.~~ major at ~~Mt.~~ Ida ~~Jr.~~ College.
>
> _Avenue_
> Park ~~Ave.~~ is a one-way street.
>
> _chapter_
> Read ~~ch.~~ 17 tonight.
>
> _dozen_
> Noah sent a ~~doz.~~ red roses.

If you have questions about how a word is abbreviated, consult your desk dictionary. Most dictionaries have a separate list of abbreviations.

MECH 2a Abbreviate academic, governmental, military, and religious titles when they are followed by a proper noun.

Rev. D. H. Shaw   Adm. Hyman Rickover
Dr. Virginia Wu   Hon. Langdon Crane
Assoc. Prof. Helen Murphy   St. Joan of Arc

Do not use title abbreviations without a person's complete name.

Sitting in the front row was Gen. ^Colin^ Powell. [OR General Powell]

Prof. ^Janet^ McGinness mused, "Will we ever know?"

[OR Professor McGinness]

When no proper noun is given, write the title.

The doctor took my grandmother's hand and smiled.

MECH 2b Abbreviate *Jr., Sr.,* and degrees such as *D.D., Ph.D., D.V.M., M.D.,* and *LL.D.* after proper names.

Gerald R. Brown Sr.   Elizabeth Luria, Ph.D.
Eleanor T. Bates, D.D.   Michael Kaplan, D.V.M.

It is also acceptable, according to MLA, to omit periods and spaces in some abbreviations, especially those made up of capital letters (MD, DVM, PhD, LLD).
Use a title either before or after a name, not twice.

INCORRECT Dr. Laura Keller, M.D.

CORRECT Dr. Laura Keller OR Laura Keller, M.D.

MECH 2c Use the conventional abbreviations *A.D., B.C., a.m., p.m., no.,* and *$* only with specific years, times, numbers, or amounts.

32 B.C. [OR B.C.E.*]   A.D. 1812 [OR C.E.*]   10,000 B.P.†
8 a.m. [OR A.M.]   6:30 p.m. [OR P.M.]
no. 33 [OR No.] $250

Driving straight through, Lee should be home by 7 a.m.

Always use B.C. after the date and A.D. before the date.

*Before Common Era and Common Era   †Before the Present

MECH 2d Use conventional abbreviations for organizations, corporations, government agencies, states, and countries.

By convention, certain names are abbreviated with capital letters and no periods. Here are some of the most common:

NAACP	NATO	FHA	CARE	NY
NCAA	IBM	IRS	USA [OR U.S.A.]	TN
YWCA	UPS	HUD	UK [OR U.K.]	ID

If your readers may be unfamiliar with an abbreviation you wish to use throughout an essay, write out the complete name the first time you use it with the abbreviation immediately following in parentheses: *United Press International (UPI)*. Then use the abbreviation in the rest of the essay. (See PUNCT 6a for using periods with abbreviations. See FORMAT 3, pages 259–260, for standard U.S. Postal abbreviations.)

MECH 2e Use scholarly Latin abbreviations such as *c., cf.,* and *et al.* in scholarly and technical writing and limit use of general Latin abbreviations in informal writing.

ABBREVIATION	LATIN	ENGLISH
c.	*circa*	about
cf.	*confer*	compare
e.g.	*exempli gratia*	for example
et al.	*et alia*	and others
etc.	*et cetera*	and so forth
i.e.	*id est*	that is
vs. [OR v.]	*versus*	versus
N.B.	*nota bene*	note well

Because not everyone is familiar with Latin abbreviations, keep them to a minimum and present them parenthetically. If you cannot present them parenthetically, write out the English equivalent.

Basic spices (e.g., basil, dill, oregano) come with the deluxe cabinet.

Janet calls herself a "Jeopard"; i.e., someone who never misses *Jeopardy*.

Do not use the ampersand (&) in formal or academic writing. (See WORD 7 for further information about *e.g.*, *etc.*, and *i.e.*)

MECH 3

Numbers

MECH 3a Spell out numbers of one or two words; use figures for all other numbers and amounts.

Judson found 35 old photographs at a garage sale.
thirty-five

Raspberries are on sale for two dollars and ninety nine cents.
$2.99.

However, when you give more than one number in a sentence or paragraph and at least one of those numbers is expressed by figures, then all numbers should be expressed by figures, regardless of other rules.

Of the 3,779 seniors, ninety-six were from New York, ninety-eight from Florida, and 428 from California.
96 ... *98*

In business and technical writing, numbers are sometimes preferred to words for brevity and clarity.

MECH 3b When two separate numbers appear together, spell out one and use figures for the other for clarity.

In our literature class we wrote six five-page papers.
6

MECH 3c Follow convention in using figures.

DATES
November 14, 1976   32 B.C. [OR 32 B.C.E.]   A.D. 60 [OR C.E. 60]
the nineteenth century [NOT the 19th century]
1970s [ALSO the seventies or '70s]

When the year is not given in a date, the forms *1st, 2nd, 3rd, 4th,* and so on can be used.

Our anniversary is April 20th.

TIME
5:30 a.m. [OR half-past five in the morning]
3 p.m. [OR three o'clock in the afternoon]

ADDRESSES
16 Third Avenue [NOT Sixteen Third Avenue]
328 West 128th Street

PAGE AND DIVISION NUMBERS IN BOOKS
page 67   chapter 2   volume 1

PLAYS
Act 4, scene 2 [OR Act IV, scene ii]

FRACTIONS, DECIMALS, AND PERCENTAGES
33 1/3   3.26 kilometers   75 percent [OR 75%]

However, fractions of less than one are normally written out: *one-third, three-eighths.*

NUMBERS IN SCORES AND STATISTICS
The score was Cleveland 8, Minnesota 3. [OR 8 to 3, OR 8–3]
Boulder Junction voted 173–125 against new taxes.
The survey shows that 7 players out of 10 prefer Nike.

EXACT MEASUREMENTS OR COUNTS
6.32 miles
1.87 pounds
32,753 people in attendance

EXACT AMOUNTS OF MONEY
$19.99
$20 [OR twenty dollars]
$56,007.68

LARGE ROUND NUMBERS
4.7 million
263 million
35 billion

IDENTIFICATION NUMBERS
Channel 3   Interstate 91   Room 27   #10772683

MECH 3d Spell out a number at the beginning of a sentence.

One hundred fifty-seven
~~157~~ passengers were stranded at the airport.

If you think the sentence is awkward, revise so that the number does not appear at the beginning.

The storm stranded 157 passengers at the airport.

MECH 4

Italics/Underlining

Italics is a typestyle in which the letters slant to the right and are more scriptlike than the letters of standard typestyles. Italics are used, by convention, for the titles of certain types of works and, because of their visual contrast, to give emphasis. In a handwritten or typed paper, <u>continuous underlining</u> indicates italics.

 C-Tip

Underlining/italic typeface

On your computer use the command for underlining to indicate italics. Or, if your word-processing program has a command for italic typeface and your printer is capable of producing it, you can simply italicize.

MECH 4a Underline (italicize) the titles of works issued separately; that is, those that are not a part of a larger work.

BOOK <u>Blue Highways</u>
PLAY <u>The Glass Menagerie</u>
FILM <u>Titanic</u>
RADIO OR TELEVISION SERIES <u>Home Improvement</u>

COMIC STRIP Doonesbury

MAGAZINE Portable Computing

JOURNAL American Scholar

NEWSPAPER Village Voice

LONG POEM Paradise Lost

LONG MUSICAL COMPOSITION Phantom of the Opera

PAINTING OR SCULPTURE Mona Lisa

COMPACT DISC OR RECORD ALBUM Abbey Road

Enclose the titles of shorter works such as poems, essays, and newspaper articles in quotation marks. (See PUNCT 5c.)

Do not underline (italicize) or put in quotation marks the Bible, books of the Bible, and titles of legal documents.

Bible [NOT Bible]

Ecclesiastes [NOT Ecclesiastes]

Bill of Rights [NOT Bill of Rights]

Do not underline (italicize) or put in quotation marks the titles of academic, business, or other types of papers and reports.

Personification in Emily Dickinson's Poetry

1999 Marketing Plan

MECH 4b Underline (italicize) the names of ships, planes, trains, and spacecraft.

Delta Queen   Spirit of St. Louis   Mir

Orient Express   Viking 7   Challenger

MECH 4c Underline (italicize) numbers, letters, and words referred to as such or used as illustrations.

A large gold 10 was painted on the door.

The letter e is the most frequently used letter in the English language.

Did you know the word piano is a shortened form of pianoforte?

Although underlining (italicizing) is preferred, quotation marks are sometimes used. (See PUNCT 5d.)

MECH 4d Underline (italicize) foreign words and phrases that have not been Anglicized.

Whether a foreign word should be underlined (italicized) depends on how widely it is used by speakers of English. Many foreign words have become part of the English language and are not, therefore, underlined. Consult your dictionary if you are unsure. *Webster's New Collegiate Dictionary*, for example, lists foreign words that should be italicized in a separate section entitled "Foreign Words and Phrases."

<u>pax vobiscum</u> [Latin: "peace be with you"]
<u>mano a mano</u> [Italian: "hand to hand"]
<u>chérie</u> [French: "dear one, darling"]
café au lait [NOT <u>café au lait</u>]
bon voyage [NOT <u>bon voyage</u>]
du jour [NOT <u>du jour</u>]

MECH 4e Underline (italicize) a word or words for emphasis, but do so sparingly.

For example, writers sometimes underline (italicize) the key word in their argument.

The time to face many of the problems of divorce is <u>before</u> marriage.
—Louise Montague

Underlining for emphasis can be effective but only when it is not overused. If too many words in a sentence or paragraph are underlined, none will stand out as more important. Every time you underline a word ask yourself if there is another way of achieving the emphasis you desire. Can you reorder the ideas in your sentence (see SENT 6a) or add telling details instead?

Louis Armstrong was a ^<u>brilliant</u>^ jazz musician.
technically *and stylistically innovative*

MECH 5

The Hyphen

The **hyphen** is a versatile mark. Use it to form compound words; to add certain prefixes, suffixes, and letters to words; and to divide words. Do not confuse the hyphen (-) with the dash (--). (See PUNCT 6d.)

And do not overuse the hyphen; learn the following rules for the hyphen so that you use it correctly.

MECH 5a Use a hyphen to form certain compound words.

A **compound word** is made up of two or more words that function as a single word or expression. Some compound words are two separate words (*half brother*); some are one word (*stepmother*); and some are two or more hyphenated words (*half-moon, father-in-law*). Sometimes the only way to be sure which form is correct is to consult your dictionary. If you cannot find an entry in your dictionary, treat the compound as two words.

> Police blamed the incident on two or three rabble ▪rousers.
>   ^

> Mr. Rodriguez is strictly interested in the bottom/line.

MECH 5b Use a hyphen to join two or more words serving as a single adjective before a noun.

When you put two or more words together to function as an adjective before a noun, hyphenate them; when you use these words after a noun, do not hyphenate them.

HYPHENATED FORM	NONHYPHENATED FORM
brand-new car	The car is brand new.
nineteenth-century literature	The literature of the nineteenth century
eighteen-year-old woman	The woman is eighteen years old.
all-but-indestructible toy	The toy is all but indestructible.

When a descriptive phrase functions as a noun, it is hyphenated.

> I drink instant coffee, but fresh-perked is better.

Do not hyphenate when the first word of a descriptive phrase is an adverb ending in -*ly*.

> frequently used dictionary   widely known fact

Use suspended hyphens with a series of single-hyphenated modifiers before a noun.

> At Disney World, visitors can buy one-, two-, or three-day passes.

MECH 5c Use a hyphen with compound numbers from twenty-one through ninety-nine and with written fractions.

twenty-five   three-fourths

MECH 5d Use a hyphen to avoid ambiguity and awkward combinations or repetitions of letters.

Hyphens prevent confusion between words otherwise spelled the same.

resign [to relinquish]
re-sign [to sign again]

recount [to narrate the facts]
re-count [to count again]

Hyphens prevent mispronunciation and difficulty in reading doubled or tripled letters.

co-worker [NOT coworker]
anti-inflammatory [NOT antiinflammatory]
de-emphasize [NOT deemphasize]
ball-like [NOT balllike]

MECH 5e Use a hyphen with the prefixes *all-*, *ex-*, *great-*, and *self-*, and with the suffix *-elect.*

all-city   ex-fighter   great-grandfather
self-appointed   governor-elect

Also use a hyphen between a prefix and a proper noun.

anti-Semitic   post-World War II   pro-Central America
un-American   pre-Columbian

And use a hyphen to join a single letter to a word.

T-square   L-shaped   U-turn

MECH 5f Use a hyphen to signal that a word is divided and continued on the next line.

Political candidates who want the respect of the elec-
torate should take firm positions on such important
and controversial issues as campaign financing, unemployment, and the national debt.

C-Tip

Hyphenating words at the end of lines

Most word-processing programs have the capacity to hyphenate words at the end of lines. Before you use this feature, check that the hyphenation pattern of your word-processing program hyphenates only between syllables; some programs break at the margin however the word falls. Also, watch for proper names (which should not be hyphenated) because a program cannot identify them as such and will therefore hyphenate them.

In general, avoid hyphenating at the end of a line, but when there is not enough space for the full word without violating the right-hand margin, refer to the following seven rules for correct hyphenation.

1. Divide words between syllables.

Mary Ellen could not remember whether her Sierra Club ~~memb-~~ mem-
~~bership~~ bership
~~ership~~ had expired.

If you are uncertain about the syllabification of a particular word, consult your desk dictionary.

2. Divide a word that is already a hyphenated compound at the point of hyphenation or carry it entirely to the next line.

With the slow economy more Americans are becoming ~~bud-~~ budget-
conscious.
~~get-conscious.~~

3. If a consonant has been doubled in adding *-ing* to a word, divide between the doubled consonant.

The state legislature approved a bill that would outlaw ~~bett-~~ betting
~~ing~~ on boxing matches.

But if the word already ends in a double consonant, divide at the suffix:

Cut the chilled pastry dough into small squares, put a little apricot ~~fil-~~ filling
~~ling~~ in the middle of each, and pinch the corners together.

4. Do not divide one-syllable words.

With 200 students in the band and over 300 in various choral ~~grou~~
groups
~~ps,~~ it isn't easy to schedule practice times.
⌄

5. Do not divide a word so that one letter is left at the end of a line or fewer than three letters at the beginning of a line; carry it entirely to the next line.

I'll have some turkey and mashed potatoes, but I don't want ~~a-~~
any
~~ny~~ dressing or gravy.
⌄

6. Do not divide any one word within a proper noun, and do not divide a first name from a middle initial.

Despite the bad weather, over 1,000 people turned out to hear Elie ~~Wie-~~
Wiesel
~~sel~~ lecture.
⌄

7. Do not separate a contraction.

shouldn't
After lengthy discussion, the university trustees decided they ~~should-~~
⌄
~~n't~~ invest in environmentally unfriendly companies.

MECH 6

Spelling

Americans have had a high regard for the ability to spell correctly since Noah Webster wrote *The American Spelling Book* in 1787. And while there is little correlation, if any, between spelling and intelligence, many people consider poor spelling symptomatic of some greater deficiency. At the least, poor spelling distracts the reader from the content of your writing and gives a general impression of carelessness. There is no reason, however, why someone has to remain a poor speller.

There are several things you can do to improve your spelling. First, keep your desk dictionary handy when writing, and check the spelling of any words about which you feel uncertain. Second, proof-read: you will be pleasantly surprised by the number of obvious, minor errors you catch. Finally, because spelling problems differ from one writer to the next, keep a list of the words you continually mis-spell at the front of your dictionary. By practicing correct spelling, your list will get shorter and shorter.

 C-Tip

Spell-Checker

Many word-processing programs have a Spell-Checker. This feature is useful, but it can give a false sense of security. While a Spell-Checker catches spelling errors, it often does not catch a lot of other problems: for example, homophones (words that sound alike but are not the same: *to, two, too*), omitted words, part of a word that you typed inad-vertently (*bout* for *about*), or a correctly spelled word but one that you did not intend (*worm* when *word* was intended).

MECH 6a   Distinguish between words that sound alike but have different meanings and spellings.

Words such as *cereal* and *serial* or *symbol* and *cymbal* that sound alike but have different spellings and meanings are called **homo-phones.** These and other frequently confused words are listed here:

accept	*v.,* to receive
except	*prep.,* to exclude
advice	*n.,* recommendation
advise	*v.,* to give information
affect	*v.,* to influence
effect	*n.,* the result
all ready	everyone is prepared
already	*adv.,* by this time
all together	as a group
altogether	*adv.,* entirely, completely

altar	*n.*, place of worship
alter	*v.*, to change
ascent	*n.*, movement up
assent	*n.*, agreement; *v.*, to agree
breath	*n.*, air drawn into lungs
breathe	*v.*, to take a breath
capital	*n.*, official seat of government; accumulated wealth; uppercase letter; crime
Capitol	the building in Washington, DC
choose	*v.*, to select
chose	past tense of *choose*
cite	*v.*, to quote or use as example
site	*n.*, location
sight	*n.*, vision; *v.*, to see
coarse	*adj.*, rough; crude
course	*n.*, a route; a program of instruction
complement	*n.*, that which completes
compliment	*n.*, praise
council	*n.*, an assembly
counsel	*n.*, a lawyer; *v.*, to advise
decent	*adj.*, respectable
descent	*n.*, the act of going down an incline
dissent	*n.*, disagreement
desert	*n.*, arid region; *v.*, abandon
dessert	*n.*, final course of meal
dual	*adj.*, twofold
duel	*n.*, a fight; *v.*, to fight
dying	*adj.*, ceasing to live
dyeing	*v.*, process of coloring fabrics
eminent	*adj.*, distinguished
immanent	*adj.*, remaining within
imminent	*adj.*, about to happen
foreword	*n.*, a preface
forward	*adv.*, ahead
formally	*adv.*, in a formal manner
formerly	*adv.*, in time past
forth	*adj.*, forward
fourth	*adj.*, referring to the number 4
implicit	*adj.*, implied
explicit	*adj.*, distinctly stated

incredible	*adj.,* unbelievable
incredulous	*adj.,* unwilling to believe
its	possessive form of *it*
it's	contraction of *it is*
lie	*v.,* to be at rest; *n.,* an untrue statement
lye	*n.,* a strong alkaline solution
loose	*adj.,* not fastened
lose	*v.,* to mislay; to fail to win
pair	*n.,* two of something that go together
pare	*v.,* to trim or shave off
pear	*n.,* fruit
past	*n.,* time gone by
passed	*v.,* past tense of *pass,* to go by
peace	*n.,* not war
piece	*n.,* a portion
personal	*adj.,* pertaining to a particular individual
personnel	*n.,* body of persons employed in the same place
principal	*n.,* a school official; in finance, a capital sum; *adj.,* most important
principle	*n.,* a basic law or rule of conduct
stationary	*adj.,* not movable
stationery	*n.,* writing paper
steal	*v.,* to take without permission
steel	*n., adj.,* referring to metal
than	*conj.,* used in comparisons
then	*adv.,* at that time
their	possessive form of *they*
they're	contraction of *they are*
there	*adv.,* at or in that place
to	*prep.,* toward
too	*adv.,* also, excessively
two	the number 2
vain	*adj.,* futile; excessively proud
vane	*n.,* object that indicates wind direction
vein	*n.,* blood vessel
whose	possessive form of *who*
who's	contraction of *who is*
your	possessive form of *you*
you're	contraction of *you are*

MECH 6b   Learn the basic spelling rules.

Learn the basic rules of spelling that apply to large groups of words. Investing a little time now will pay off many times over in your college career and later in life.

1. Use the traditional rhyme for *ie* and *ei* spellings.

Write *i* before *e*
Except after *c*
Or when sounded like *ay*
As in *neighbor* or *weigh*.

IE	EI AFTER C	EI PRONOUNCED AS AY
believe	ceiling	neighbor
chief	deceit	reign
grieve	perceive	veil
siege	receive	vein
yield		

Exceptions	Exception
either	financier
neither	
forfeit	
leisure	
seize	
sovereign	
weird	

2. Drop a final *e* before adding a suffix beginning with a vowel, but not before a suffix beginning with a consonant.

SUFFIX BEGINNING WITH A VOWEL	Exceptions
fame + ous = famous	dyeing
desire + able = desirable	gluey
hope + ing = hoping	hoeing

SUFFIX BEGINNING WITH A CONSONANT	Exceptions
achieve + ment = achievement	acknowledgment
hope + ful = hopeful	argument
love + ly = lovely	judgment
	awful
	duly
	ninth
	truly
	wholly

Retain the final *e* after a soft *c* or *g*.

> courage + ous = courageous
> exchange + able = exchangeable
> notice + able = noticeable

3. Double a final consonant before a suffix beginning with a vowel if the word is one syllable and ends in a consonant preceded by a single vowel.

> swim + ing = swimming
> fit + ed = fitted
> set + ing = setting

But:

> feed + ing = feeding

> [Here the word is one syllable and ends in a consonant, but there is a double vowel, *ee*.]

4. Double a final consonant before a suffix beginning with a vowel if the word ends in an accented syllable and a consonant preceded by a single vowel.

> commit + ing = committing
> occur + ed = occurred
> abhor + ent = abhorrent

But:

> benefit + ed = benefited

> [The word ends in a consonant that is preceded by a single vowel, but it does not end in an accented syllable.]

5. Change a final *y* preceded by a consonant to *i* before adding a suffix. Keep the final *y* when it is preceded by a vowel.

FINAL Y PRECEDED BY A CONSONANT	EXCEPTIONS
beauty + ful = beautiful	essay + ist = essayist
embody + ment = embodiment	study + ing = studying
modify + er = modifier	
lonely + ness = loneliness	

FINAL *Y* PRECEDED BY
A VOWEL

array + ed = arrayed
buy + er = buyer
obey + ing = obeying
sway + ed = swayed

EXCEPTIONS

day + ly = daily
gay + ety = gaiety
lay + ed = laid
pay + ed = paid
say + ed = said

6. **Most nouns form the plural by adding -*s* or -*es* to the singular.**

Add -*s* to most nouns.

stick + s = sticks
pattern + s = patterns
elephant + s = elephants

Add -*es* if the noun ends in -*s*, -*sh*, -*ch*, -*x*, or -*z*.

pass + es = passes   tax + es = taxes
brush + es = brushes   buzz + es = buzzes
peach + es = peaches

If the noun ends in *y* preceded by a consonant, change the *y* to *i* and add -*es*.

spy + es = spies
inventory + es = inventories
penny + es = pennies

7. **Follow convention in forming the plurals for nouns that do not follow the -*s* or -*es* pattern.**

For nouns ending in *o* preceded by a consonant, add -*es*.

tomato + es = tomatoes   embargo + es = embargoes
echo + es = echoes   buffalo + es = buffaloes

Some nouns ending in *f* or *fe* form the plural by adding -*s*, while others change the *f* to *v* and add -*es*.

-*S*	-*ES*
roof + s = roofs	wharf + es = wharves
safe + s = safes	wife + es = wives
chief + s = chiefs	hoof + es = hooves

Some nouns form their plurals by changing internal vowels.

SINGULAR	PLURAL
foot	feet
mouse	mice
woman	women

Plural forms of foreign borrowings usually retain the plural of the original language.

SINGULAR	PLURAL
datum	data
tableau	tableaux
appendix	appendices [OR appendixes]

Some foreign borrowings, however, have an Anglicized plural in addition to the plural of the original language; both forms are acceptable.

SINGULAR	PLURAL	
formula	formulae	formulas
index	indices	indexes
syllabus	syllabi	syllabuses

Some nouns make no changes to form the plural.

SINGULAR	PLURAL
deer	deer
fish	fish [OR fishes]
swine	swine

8. **Form the plurals of compound words by adding -s to the end of the word except when the first word is more important.**

SINGULAR	PLURAL
mastermind	masterminds
passer-by	passers-by
editor-in-chief	editors-in-chief

MECH 6c Watch for commonly misspelled words in your writing.

Following is a list of words that college students frequently use and commonly misspell.

COMMONLY MISSPELLED WORDS

abbreviate	accidental	acquire	a lot
absence	accommodate	acquittal	altogether
absorption	accompany	across	always
absurd	accomplishment	additionally	amateur
abundance	accumulation	address	among
academic	accustom	aggravate	analysis
accede	achievement	allotted	analyze
acceptable	acknowledge	all right	annual
accessible	acquaint	almost	answer

apartment
apologies
apparatus
apparently
appearance
appreciate
appropriate
argument
arising
arouse
arrange
article
ascend
associate
athletic
attendance
audience
authority
auxiliary
awkward

bachelor
balance
barbarous
bargain
basis
becoming
beginning
behavior
belief
beneficial
boundary
brilliance
bulletin
bureau
burial
business

cafeteria
calendar
candidate
capitalism
carburetor
career
category
certain
changeable

character
choose
chosen
commission
commit
committee
comparative
competitive
completely
compulsory
concede
conceivable
concentrate
conference
conqueror
conscience
conscientious
conscious
considerably
continuous
controversial
convenient
counsel
courteous
criticism
criticize
curiosity
curriculum
cylindrical

decision
definitely
dependent
describe
description
despair
desperate
diction
difference
dilemma
disagree
disappear
disappointment
disastrous
discipline
dissatisfied
dissipate

dominant
dormitory

efficient
eighth
eligible
elimination
embarrassment
eminent
enthusiastic
entrance
environment
equipped
equivalency
erroneous
escape
exaggerate
exceed
excellent
exceptionally
exercise
existence
experience
explanation
extraordinary
extremely

fallacy
familiar
fascinate
fictitious
foreign
frantically
friend
fundamental
further

generally
grammar
guarantee
guard
guidance

harass
height
heroine
hindrance

humorous
hungrily
hypocrisy

idea
illiterate
imaginary
imagination
imitation
immediately
impromptu
incident
incredible
indefinite
indispensable
inevitable
infinite
ingenious
initiation
intellectual
intelligence
interesting
interpretation
involve
irrelevant
irresistible

jealousy

knowledge

laboratory
legitimate
lightning
literature
liveliest
loneliness
luxury

magazine
maintenance
maneuver
marriage
mathematics
meant
medieval
miniature

mortgage
mysterious

necessary
nevertheless
ninety
noticeable

obligation
obstacle
occasion
occurrence
omission
operate
opinion
opportunity
optimistic
original
outrageous

pamphlets
parallel
paralyze
particular
peer

permanent
permissible
perseverance
physical
politics
practical
precedence
predominant
preference
prejudice
preparation
prevalent
privilege
probably
proceed
profession
prominent
pronunciation
propaganda
prove
psychology

quantity
quizzes

recede
recognize
recommend
reference
referred
regard
religious
repetition
representation
restaurant
rhythm
ridiculous

sacrifice
sandwich
schedule
secretary
separate
severely
similar
simultaneous
soliloquy
sophomore
special

species
strictly
succeed
superscede
surprise
syllable

temperament
tendency
thorough
tragedy
tries
Tuesday
typical
tyranny

unanimous
until

vengeance
villain

whether
written

format

Essentials of Formatting

Learning Objectives

After reading this section, you should:

- be able to format your papers on a computer and prepare visuals;
- be able to distinguish between MLA and APA styles of formatting;
- be able to format business letters, résumés, and memos.

Essentials of Formatting

The arrival of the information age has brought with it a flood of written material. It is not surprising, therefore, that people are paying more attention to the presentation of written materials. Formatting—improving readability through good page design—helps the reader understand your message by highlighting content and organization. Today's word-processing software makes it easy to format your written work. You can use different type sizes or styles for emphasis and even insert tables and graphs to help your reader visualize information. The same word-processing software also makes it easier to prepare the conventional formats required for academic manuscripts, business letters, résumés, and memos. *when in doubt*

"keep it simple"

FORMAT 1

Basic Computer Formatting Options

With all the formatting capabilities available on even the most basic computer software, how do you decide what to do? The answer lies in the piece of writing itself. What is the subject matter? A research paper in the humanities, for example, must follow MLA guidelines. (See FORMAT 2.) How long is the paper? Would headings make it more readable? What is your purpose, and who is your audience? Is your topic very complicated? Would a list instead of an extended narrative paragraph help your reader understand a particular point better? Aside from these questions, there are, of course, such fundamental matters as setting margins and choosing a text typeface.

FORMAT 1a Basic page design

Formatting of any kind of writing begins with four basic decisions: margins, line spacing, type style, and type size.

Margins and line spacing

Unless your instructor tells you otherwise, leave a one-inch margin at the top and bottom of the page and on the right and left sides. (Some instructors prefer a one and one-half inch margin on the left.) Leave a ragged (uneven) margin on the right, because a justified (even) margin causes odd spacing between words and too many hyphenated words at the ends of lines.

Most academic writing is double spaced. Long research papers or reports may be line-and-a-half spaced so that they are readable but not any longer than necessary. Memos are usually single spaced to be sure they fit on a single page, the preferred length in the business world.

 C-Tip

Using templates to work smart

Many word-processing programs provide templates—model formats—for letters, memos, and reports. You can customize a template by changing the margins, for example, or the type style. (Be careful not to destroy the original template by saving your template and giving it the exact same name.)

Using a template allows you to be consistent in formatting written work, and it saves you time.

Type styles and sizes

Use familiar styles (Courier, Times Roman, Helvetica, Geneva) in a standard 10- or 12-point size. Do not use a script typeface or all italics or capitals for your main text; they are too difficult to read. If you have headings and subheadings, use the same type style, though you may slightly increase the point size.

When you have made your basic page design choices, you may want to print out a sample page. Adequate margins and a type style and size that do not call attention to themselves will transmit your message most effectively.

FORMAT 1b Improving readability

Use the formatting capabilities of your computer to improve the readability of long and complex pieces of writing.

Headings and subheadings

There is no substitute for good organization in a piece of writing, but in the case of long or complex research papers and reports, the use of headings and sometimes even subheadings can enhance readability. Headings and subheadings break an extended piece of writing into visibly distinct sections, allowing the reader to enter and exit your train of thought, to stand back and see what has gone before and what is to come. Headings serve as a road map for reading.

Consistency is very important in using headings. First, you must be consistent in how you phrase headings. Most headings are a single word, usually a noun (for example, Gardens), or phrase (Types of Gardens). Often they are gerund phrases (Mulching the Garden). Headings may also be questions, which are then answered in that section (When should you prune roses?). Whichever type of heading you start with, however, you must continue using that type throughout your paper. If you are using both headings and subheadings, you can make all your headings one type (say, single word nouns) and all your subheadings another type (perhaps gerund phrases).

You must also be consistent in the type style and size of your headings. Suppose your text type is 10-point Helvetica. All your headings should also be Helvetica, but you might put your main headings in 14 point and your subheadings in 12 point. You have some options in how you present your headings: boldface (heavier type), underlining, italics or bold italics, all capitals, and capitals and lower case.

Types of Stress [bold]

<u>Types of Stress</u> [underline]

Types of Stress [italics]

Types of Stress [bold italics]

TYPES OF STRESS [all caps]

As with phrasing, you may choose one style for headings and another for subheadings. Again, though, you must be consistent in whichever you choose.

Finally, you must be consistent in the placement of headings. By convention, main headings are usually centered and subheadings are at the left margin.

Main Heading

Subheading

Headings can improve the readability of a long or complex piece of writing, but they must be used judiciously. Too many headings and levels of subheadings can be distracting or annoying. Every heading should introduce a major concept, not a minor point.

Lists

One way to make an extended piece of writing more manageable for your reader is to break it into sections with headings and subheadings. You can also help your reader by pulling material out of the text narrative and presenting it as a more visually accessible list. Some types of material lend themselves to listmaking more than others, of course. Steps in a process, categories, and how-to instructions naturally fit into a list.

Set off a list by indenting from the left margin. You can draw attention to the individual items in your list with graphic symbols, such as bullets (large, solid dots •), squares (▪), or dashes (—). Graphic symbols are a good idea if the items in your list run over one line; in this case, it is also a good idea to indent the second line. See how indentation and graphics work in this example:

Experts say there are four major ways to relieve stress:

- consider whether you are accurately appraising the situation,

- use your problem-solving skills to take action,

- seek the support of family and friends, and

- pay attention to your health by eating right, getting enough exercise, and going to bed at a regular time.

This example also shows that you should introduce a list with a colon (see PUNCT 3b), put a comma after each item, and end with a period. Note, too, that the phrasing should be parallel. (See SENT 1a.) In this list, every item begins with a verb: consider, use, seek, pay.

A final note: Do not overuse lists. As with heads, they are only effective if used purposefully.

FORMAT 1c   Using visuals

Visuals—charts and graphs, tables, and diagrams—can add a new dimension to your writing. They allow a reader to visualize as well as read the information you are presenting.

Types of visuals

Different types of visuals serve different purposes. **Charts** and **graphs** show relationships among numerical data. A **pie chart** is a circular graph; it shows a whole and the percentages that make up the whole. A **bar graph** uses bars, usually vertical, to indicate frequency or quantity; it is useful for showing large-scale size or mass comparisons. A **line graph** shows finely delineated data in a continuum, such as age, speed, or temperature. Overlaid lines in a line graph highlight points of intersection and deviation.

Following are examples of a pie chart, bar graph, and line graph. The same data—total units sold—are used in all three examples to show that the kind of information you want to present determines the type of visual you must use.

A **table** is useful for summarizing large amounts of information, either numerical data or text narrative. Because tables are columnar,

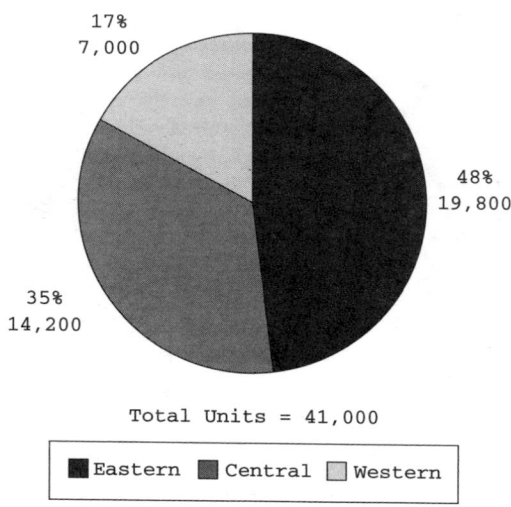

VeloPazzo Software:
Percent of Total Sales and
Number of Units by Region for 1999

17%
7,000

48%
19,800

35%
14,200

Total Units = 41,000

■ Eastern ■ Central □ Western

PIE CHART

VeloPazzo Software:
Regional Contributions to
Total Monthly Unit Sales for 1999

■ Eastern ▨ Central □ Western

BAR GRAPH

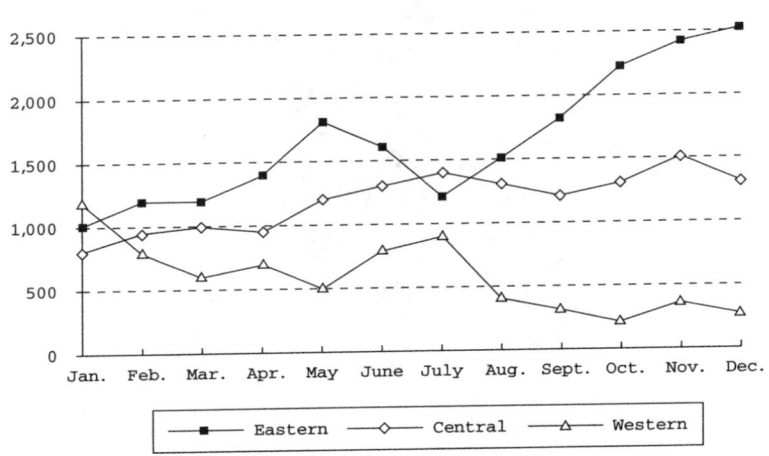

VeloPazzo Software:
Monthly Unit Sales by Region for 1999

■ Eastern ◇ Central △ Western

LINE GRAPH

they are also useful for making comparisons. See the tables on pages 54, 126, and 225.

A **diagram,** or drawing, is a concise visual representation of an object or idea that would take many words to convey. The diagram of clustering on page 9, for example, allows the reader to see quickly how ideas and information can be generated using this strategy.

Incorporating visuals

You can create your own visuals with computer graphic software, or you can use visuals you find in your research sources. If you use visuals someone else created, you must give proper credit. The acknowledgment should be placed directly beneath the visual and should include the name of the creator of the visual and the place and date of publication. The acknowledgment should also be included in your list of Works Cited.

Be sure that your visuals are properly sized (neither too large to fit within your margins nor too small to be legible), placed as close after (never before) the text to which they refer, and that the quality of your reproduction does not defeat the purpose of the visual aids. Better not to use a visual at all than to use one that confuses rather than enhances your message.

FORMAT 2

Formatting Academic Manuscripts Following MLA and APA Guidelines

The standard formatting guide for written work in English and the humanities is the Modern Language Association's *MLA Handbook for Writers of Research Papers,* 4th ed. (New York: MLA, 1995). For a model paper written according to MLA format, see RESCH 5. The standard guide for the social sciences is the *Publication Manual of the American Psychological Association,* 4th ed. (Washington, D.C.: APA, 1994). For a model paper written in the APA style, see OTHER DOCU 3.

The following guidelines are for formatting a manuscript according to MLA style. Wherever APA formatting style differs from MLA guidelines, information is provided.

General instructions

For academic purposes use 8½″ × 11″, 20-pound white paper. Leave a one-inch margin at the top and bottom of the page and on the right and left sides. Double-space the text of the paper including set-off quotations, information notes, and the entries on the Works Cited page. (See RESCH 5.) Do not justify (make even) the right-hand margin.

For your final copy, a letter-quality printer, such as a laser printer, gives the cleanest printout. If you use a dot-matrix printer, be sure to use its letter-quality setting and a fresh ribbon. If you use continuous-feed paper, remove the perforated strips from the sides of the paper, separate the pages, and use a paper clip (do not staple) to secure the pages. Finally, be sure you keep both a paper copy and an electronic copy of your paper.

Title and title page

Do not underline, put quotation marks around, or put a period at the end of the title of your paper. Capitalize the first letter of all words in the title except articles (*a, an*), coordinating conjunctions (*and, but, for, nor, or, so, yet*), and prepositions of four or fewer letters (*in, till, over*), unless your title begins with an article or preposition, in which case the word should be capitalized.

If your instructor does not require a separate title page, center your title on the first page of the paper. Double-space between your title and the first sentence. In addition, papers without a title page should display your name, course information, and the date in the upper-left corner of the first page, as shown in the sample page format on page 253.

If your instructor requires a title page, place the title fifteen lines from the top and center it. Approximately six lines below the title, center the word *by*, skip two more lines, and center your name. About twenty lines below your name, place the course title, professor's name, and date, all centered and double spaced. Do not number the title page. For a sample MLA title page, see page 323.

APA formatting requires a title page and that it be numbered. The page number should be placed one-half inch from the top of the page and one inch from the right edge of the page. Before the page number, and separated from it by five spaces, type a shortened title (usually the first three words of the title). Center the title on the page about 15 lines from the top. Double-space and type your name and the course information directly under the title. For a sample title page in APA format, see page 367.

SAMPLE PAGE FORMAT

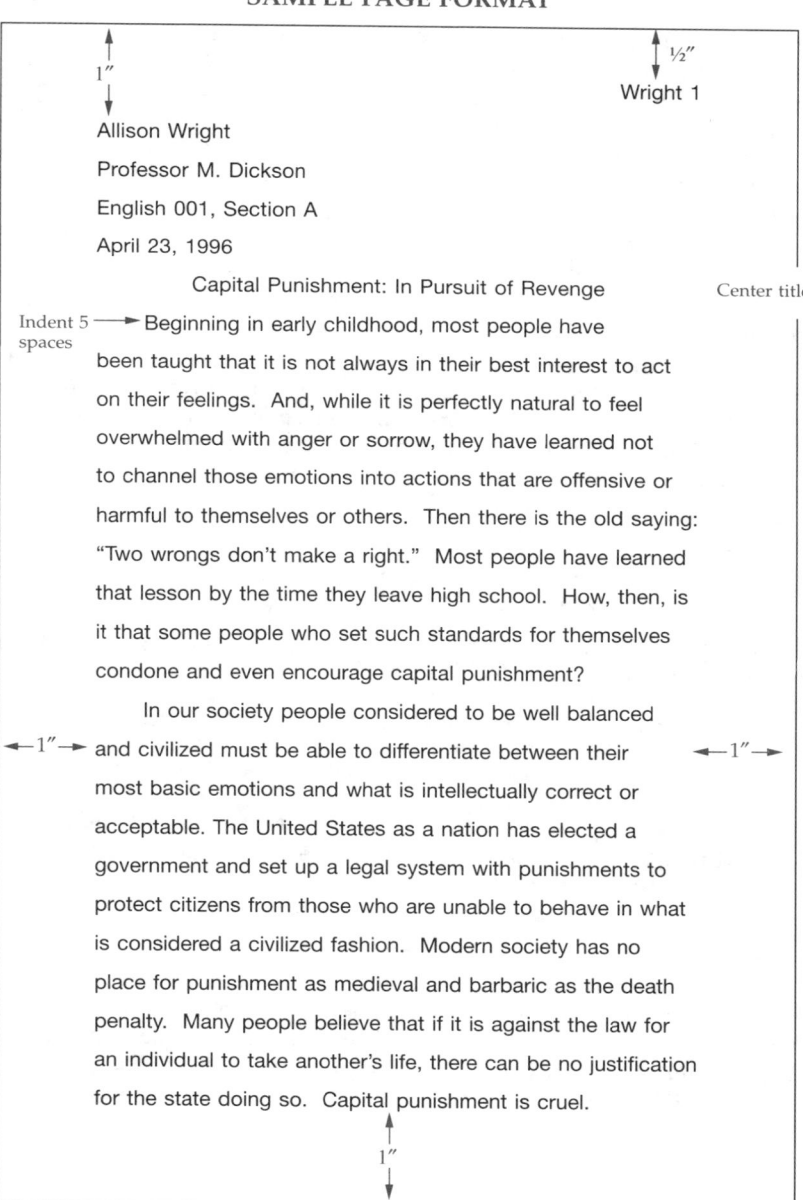

1″

½″

Wright 1

Allison Wright

Professor M. Dickson

English 001, Section A

April 23, 1996

Capital Punishment: In Pursuit of Revenge   Center title

Indent 5 → Beginning in early childhood, most people have
spaces

been taught that it is not always in their best interest to act

on their feelings. And, while it is perfectly natural to feel

overwhelmed with anger or sorrow, they have learned not

to channel those emotions into actions that are offensive or

harmful to themselves or others. Then there is the old saying:

"Two wrongs don't make a right." Most people have learned

that lesson by the time they leave high school. How, then, is

it that some people who set such standards for themselves

condone and even encourage capital punishment?

     In our society people considered to be well balanced

←1″→ and civilized must be able to differentiate between their   ←1″→

most basic emotions and what is intellectually correct or

acceptable. The United States as a nation has elected a

government and set up a legal system with punishments to

protect citizens from those who are unable to behave in what

is considered a civilized fashion. Modern society has no

place for punishment as medieval and barbaric as the death

penalty. Many people believe that if it is against the law for

an individual to take another's life, there can be no justification

for the state doing so. Capital punishment is cruel.

1″

Outline or abstract

An outline is not required by either MLA or APA formats. If your instructor requires an outline, see the MLA model in the student essay on page 324 for style suggestions. The outline should be presented after the title page.

Some instructors who follow APA formatting require an abstract, or brief summary (not exceeding 100 words) of your paper. Your abstract should state your thesis, the major points of your argument, and the conclusions you draw. The abstract should be placed after the title page and numbered as *page 2*.

Headings and subheadings

MLA format has no specific style requirements for heads. APA, however, has set forth requirements. The most important requirement is that heads are to be upper- and lowercase and centered. Subheadings are to be placed at the left-hand margin and underlined; they should also be upper- and lowercase. Do not number heads.

Indentation

Indent the first line of each paragraph five spaces. For prose or poetry set off from the text, follow these MLA guidelines:

1. If you quote more than four typed lines of prose, indent ten spaces from the left margin and double-space. (The right margin remains the same, one inch.) Do not use quotation marks. See page 330 for an example.
2. If you quote four or more lines of poetry, indent ten spaces from the left margin. (The right margin remains at one inch.) Do not double-space, and present poetry exactly as it is in the original. (See MECH 1h.)

APA style requires that quotations of more than forty words be indented five to seven spaces from the left margin and double spaced. Do not use quotation marks.

Page numbers

Use arabic numerals (1, 2, 3 . . .) for page numbers together with your last name. Place your last name and the page number in the upper right corner of each page, approximately one-half inch from the top and one inch from the right edge of the page (for example, Smith 1). Do not use the word *page* or its abbreviations *p., pp.,* or use a period or any other mark of punctuation. Number all pages of your paper, including the last.

APA style requires a header, or a shortened title (usually the first three words), on each manuscript page. The header and the page number should be separated by five spaces. The page number should be one inch from the right edge of the paper. (See OTHER DOCU 3.)

C-Tip

Using the header option

Use the header option on your word-processing program to create a heading of your last name and page number for MLA format or shortened title and page number for APA format that will automatically appear on each page of your essay. Remember to activate the consecutive numbering function if it is a separate option.

Spacing for punctuation

Observe the conventions for spacing after punctuation marks: two spaces after punctuation at the end of a sentence; one space after a comma, colon, and a semicolon and between the three periods in an ellipsis. Type dashes by using two hyphens with no space before or after.

APA style differs significantly here. It calls for one space after all marks of punctuation, including end punctuation.

FORMAT 3

Formatting Business Documents

FORMAT 3a Business letters

In the past, **business letters** were formal and stiff, with standardized phrasings and exaggerated courtesy. Today, courtesy is just as important in a business letter, but modern business practice allows for a relaxed tone. Clarity is imperative; there should be no confusion over the message you are sending, and your writing should be grammatically correct and free of clichés, jargon, and other inappropriate language. (See WORD 2 and 3.) Finally, business letters follow the conventional formats outlined here.

Format

Three patterns are used to format business letters today: **full block, modified block,** and **indented** (see page 257). Select the format appropriate for your purpose: full block is the most formal, whereas indented is the least formal. A job application letter, for example, is best presented in the full block pattern.

All business letters should be typed on unlined white paper and on one side of the page only. Use one-inch margins on the left and right sides. Single-space the letter except where indicated in the accompanying sample layouts of the three patterns. A sample letter of application in the full block pattern is shown on page 258.

Return address

Unless you are using letterhead stationery on which your name or your company's name and address are imprinted, include your return address and the date. Their placement depends on the format you have chosen (see the sample layouts).

Inside address

In all formats, type the name, title, and address of the person to whom you are writing at the left margin.

Salutation

The salutation is a word or phrase of greeting that conventionally comes before the body of a letter (such as *Dear Mr. Sampson*). If you do not know the name of the person you are addressing, use *Dear Sir or Madame*, the person's position (*Dear Manager* or *Dear Director of Personnel*), or the name of the company (*Dear Klein Refrigeration*). If you are addressing a woman and do not know her marital status or the way she prefers to be addressed, use *Ms.* If a title is necessary, put it after the person's name, separated by a comma (not on a separate line); capitalize the title. A colon follows the salutation.

Body

The body of a business letter begins at the left margin in the full block and modified block formats. If you are using the indented pattern, indent each paragraph five spaces.

Close

The first word (and *only* the first word) of the close begins with a capital letter. Customary closes include *Sincerely, Sincerely yours,* and

SAMPLE BUSINESS LETTER FORMATS

Full block

6–12 spaces

2–4 spaces

2–4 spaces
2–4 spaces

2 spaces

2–4 spaces

2–4 spaces

Indented

6–12 spaces

2–4 spaces

2–4 spaces
2–4 spaces

2 spaces

2–4 spaces

2–4 spaces

Modified block

6–12 spaces

2–4 spaces

2–4 spaces
2–4 spaces

2 spaces

2–4 spaces

2–4 spaces

SAMPLE LETTER OF APPLICATION: FULL BLOCK PATTERN

512 Living/Learning Center
University of Vermont   ⎤——— Return address
Burlington, VT 05401
November 1, 1998

Mr. Harold Sampson, Director
Management Training Program
Acme Insurance Group   ⎤——— Inside address
100 Asylum Street
Hartford, CT 06100

Dear Mr. Sampson: ◄——— Salutation

Through the Career Development Office of the University
of Vermont, I have learned that you have openings in your
Management Training Program. Your program interests me
very much, and I would like to apply for a position in it.

On May 12, 1999, I will graduate from the School of Business
Administration with a major in insurance. I believe that the
number and variety of courses I have taken in both insurance
and marketing qualify me to apply for your program.

In addition to my coursework, I have worked summers and part-
time during the school year as a clerk for Mr. Hugh Johnson of
your Burlington office. I have also accompanied Mr. Johnson at   Body
various times when he called upon clients. I feel, therefore, that I
have practical experience as well as theoretical experience on
which to base my choice of career in the insurance management
field.

My résumé is enclosed. I can also provide you with the names of
individuals who can give you assessments of my efficiency and
dependability as a worker.

I would be pleased to travel to Hartford to meet with you should
you feel it necessary. You may call me at (802) 555-1234 or write
me at the above address.

Sincerely yours, ◄——————— Close

James M. Morton ◄——— Signature

James M. Morton

Encl. Résumé
cc: Career Development Office   ⎤——— Notations

Yours truly. Put a comma after the close. The placement of the close depends on the format you have chosen (see the sample layouts).

Name and signature

Four spaces beneath the close, type your name (and your title, if you have one, on a separate line) and then place your signature above the typed name (see the sample letter of application).

Special notations

Other information may follow the signature, and should be abbreviated as follows:

NOTATION	MEANING
JMN: as JMN/as	The writer's initials are given in capital letters and the typist's in lowercase letters for reference.
CC Stephen Smith cc: Stephen Smith	A copy of the letter is being sent to Stephen Smith.
Enclosure Encl.	The recipient is alerted that something besides the letter is enclosed in the envelope.

Postal abbreviations

Use the standard postal abbreviations in your return address and the inside address.

Alabama	AL	Kentucky	KY
Alaska	AK	Louisiana	LA
Arizona	AZ	Maine	ME
Arkansas	AR	Maryland	MD
California	CA	Massachusetts	MA
Colorado	CO	Michigan	MI
Connecticut	CT	Minnesota	MN
Delaware	DE	Mississippi	MS
District of Columbia	DC	Missouri	MO
Florida	FL	Montana	MT
Georgia	GA	Nebraska	NB
Guam	GU	Nevada	NV
Hawaii	HI	New Hampshire	NH
Idaho	ID	New Jersey	NJ
Illinois	IL	New Mexico	NM
Indiana	IN	New York	NY
Iowa	IA	North Carolina	NC
Kansas	KS	North Dakota	ND

Ohio	OH	Texas	TX
Oklahoma	OK	Utah	UT
Oregon	OR	Vermont	VT
Pennsylvania	PA	Virgin Islands	VI
Puerto Rico	PR	Virginia	VA
Rhode Island	RI	Washington	WA
South Carolina	SC	West Virginia	WV
South Dakota	SD	Wisconsin	WI
Tennessee	TN	Wyoming	WY

FORMAT 3b   Résumés

A **résumé** tells a prospective employer of your qualifications for a particular position. Because your chances of getting a job interview—the first step in getting a job—rest, in large part, on how well your résumé communicates your training and experience, your skills and abilities, you will want to think carefully about what information to include and how to present it. Your résumé should reveal why you are the ideal candidate for the position.

In preparing your résumé and getting ready for a job search, you may find it helpful to read *What Color Is Your Parachute?* by Richard N. Bolles (Ten Speed Press, 1998), an excellent job-search guide. Also, consult with your college's placement office. A sample résumé is shown on page 261.

A résumé follows a conventional format and includes the following categories of information:

Name, address, phone number

Center your name at the top of the résumé. Give both your present address and permanent home address, with phone numbers for both, including area codes.

Job objective, position sought

As concisely as possible, describe the position you are seeking.

Education

Give the name of the institution you graduated from, the year you received your degree, the type of degree, your major and minor, and,

SAMPLE RÉSUMÉ

James Michael Morton

Present address:	Permanent address:
512 Living/Learning Center	1065 Peer Avenue
University of Vermont	Clifton, NJ 07013
Burlington, VT 05401	(201) 555-1212
(802) 555-1234	

Job Objective   Position in a management training program in the insurance industry with the goal of becoming an insurance executive.

Education

1995-99   B.S., May 1999, University of Vermont (expected)

Major: insurance

Minor: marketing

Grade average: 3.50

Awards, Honors   Dean's list for last four semesters.

Recipient of the Dean's Scholarship, School of Business Administration, senior year.

Employment

1998-1999   Part-time employment during the academic year: office worker and sales assistant for the Acme Insurance Group, Burlington, Vermont. Supervisor: Mr. Hugh Johnson.

1998   Summer: Office assistant for Acme Insurance Group, Burlington, Vermont. Supervisor: Mr. Hugh Johnson.

1995-97   Summer: Proofreader for the Burlington Free Press.

Activities   Sigma Phi Epsilon, Business Manager (1997), President (1998-99); intramural volleyball; peer tutor.

Skills   MS-DOS, WordPerfect, Microsoft Word, PageMaker, Lotus 1-2-3, Q&A.

References   Center for Career Development
University of Vermont
Burlington, VT 05405
(802) 555-3450

if you like, your grade-point average. Include other educational experiences if they are pertinent to the position you are seeking.

Awards and honors

Include awards and honors that show you are a superior student or have special talents or leadership abilities.

Employment

List the jobs you have held, starting with the most recent. If your responsibilities are not clear from your job titles, briefly outline what they were. Include the name of your supervisor.

Activities

List the campus organizations, volunteer groups, and collegiate sports in which you participated and name or describe the positions of responsibility you held.

Skills

List the computer operating systems and programs with which you are familiar. If you have desktop publishing experience or have worked with graphics or cameras, add that information. Other skills might include sales, telemarketing, academic research, laboratory research, political campaigning, data collection and entry, programming, and science or social science fieldwork.

References

You can either indicate where your references are on file (if your institution provides this service) or list the names, addresses, and phone numbers of your references.

FORMAT 3c   Memos

A memo is a brief, usually one-page, written communication between workers within the same office or company. Memos are used for a wide variety of communications: queries and answers, reminders, calls for meetings, and announcements affecting products, services, and personnel, for example. It is a good idea to cover only one topic in a memo so that your receiver can take action on it if necessary, and then file it in the proper file.

SAMPLE MEMO

MEMO

University of Vermont
Department of English

To: Members of the Department of English
From: Alan Broughton   *AB*
Date: April 27, 1998
Subject: Move to University Heights

Here is more information concerning our move.

Before the move, we will have at least one work-study student to help us. This student's primary duty will be to help pack the main office, but he/she will also be available to help with your needs.

Here is the moving schedule:
- week of May 4 = classroom furniture (so we will be ready for the opening of summer school on May 11),
- week of May 11 = main office,
- week of May 18 = faculty offices, on a floor-by-floor basis.

Computers will be moved by the Computer Technology office. This will require careful coordination with the moving company so that only one group is working in an office at a time.

Movers will transport furniture, files, and books. Plan to take personal or fragile objects home and move them into your new office yourself.

I'll keep you informed as I learn more. Meanwhile, thanks for your continued good humor during this hectic time.

Memos follow a conventional format. A company or organization may even supply special printed stationery for memos with the company logo at the top and the headings:

To:

From:

Date:

Subject:

You can add a CC: (copy) to send a copy to someone, and it can come after the To: or at the very end of the memo.

In writing a memo, use your own voice. Be natural but to the point. Courtesy is also important; use "please" and "thanks." Sign your name or initials next to your name or at the end of the memo.

argue/
lit

Writing an Argumentative Essay/ Writing about Literature

Learning Objectives

After reading this section, you should:

- understand how writing an argument is different from other writing;

- know some techniques for providing evidence, making appeals, and refuting the opposition;

- understand the importance of establishing credibility;

- know some basic questions to ask in analyzing a piece of literature;

- know the conventions for writing about literature;

- be able to write about literature using quotations from the text and secondary sources.

Writing an Argumentative Essay

argue / lit

Writing About Literature

Writing an Argumentative Essay

A written argument tries to convince a reader to agree with a particular point of view or take a particular course of action. The writer takes a stand on an issue; provides supporting evidence; appeals logically, emotionally, and ethically to the reader; and carefully uses language to move the reader to agree.

In many ways, writing an argument is like writing any other kind of composition. At the beginning, you need to choose a subject and generate ideas. You may sketch an outline to organize your ideas. After you write a draft, you need to revise and, finally, edit. (See COMP 2, 3, 4, and 5.) At the same time, an argument has a slightly different kind of thesis statement, provides some special kinds of evidence, answers the opposition's arguments, and pays special attention to establishing the writer's *credibility*, the belief that the writer is worth hearing.

ARGUE 1

Develop an Argumentative Thesis

The thesis statement of an argumentative essay is an **assertion**—a claim made about a debatable issue that can be supported with evidence. An assertion cannot be a statement of fact because a fact is provable or verifiable. A fact is either true or false.

Fact: Harry S. Truman was the thirty-third president. (You can check an encyclopedia to find out whether Truman was the thirty-third president or not.]

Assertion: Harry S. Truman was a great president. [This statement can never be proven true or false; it remains an opinion. If you provide enough good evidence, you can convince your reader that it is *valid*—that it logically follows from the evidence.]

The assertion in an argumentative essay is not just any opinion. It is an assertion on which there is a legitimate and recognized difference of opinion. For example, few people would dispute that falling in love is a rare and intense experience, that crime rates should be reduced, or that computers are changing our world. These assertions are not, therefore, generally arguable. But not everyone would agree that women experience love more intensely than men, that imprisonment deters crime, or that computers are changing the world for the better. There are differences of opinion on these assertions, and that makes them arguable. These last assertions would make good argumentative thesis statements. Each would, of course, have to be supported with ample and solid evidence.

ARGUE 2

Provide Sufficient and Appropriate Evidence

Evidence is information used to support an assertion. There are various kinds of evidence.

FORMS OF EVIDENCE

Facts: statements that can be verified (*Surinam is located on the northeast coast of South America.*)

Statistics: facts expressed in numerical form (*The violent crime rate has fallen 30 percent over the last five years.*)

Examples: specific cases in point (*Some students, Jaime and Kris for example, could not attend the meeting.*)

Expert testimony: the judgment of an authority (*The U.S. Surgeon General has declared that smoking causes cancer.*)

Research finding: result of a scientific study (*Child psychologist Karen Wynn has shown that five-month-old babies know simple arithmetic.*)

The amount and quality of the evidence you use to support your assertions will determine your success in convincing your readers. Your evidence should be:

- accurate (reliable, correctly interpreted and honestly communicated, current),
- complete (full and presented in the proper context),
- meaningful (specific and pertinent),
- representative (reflecting the larger body of information it is drawn from),
- appropriate (neither too sophisticated nor too simple for your subject and audience).

ARGUE 3

Make Appropriate Appeals

An effective argument can appeal to the reader in three basic ways—through logic, emotion, and ethics.

ARGUE 3a Use logical appeals.

Being reasonable is the most important requirement of argumentative writing. Perhaps nothing is more convincing to a reader than a good, clear, logical approach to an issue. Two basic ways we reason are **induction** and **deduction,** patterns of thinking we use so naturally that we are virtually unaware of them.

When you reason inductively, you generalize from specific pieces of information. Suppose you want to buy a camera but don't know which one is best for you. You would probably learn all you could about the different kinds of cameras on the market—their cost, features, available options. You would talk to friends who own cameras to find out which are easy to use and dependable. You might visit camera shops and read photography magazines. Finally, from all the specific evidence you gather, you would make a generalization—called an *inductive leap*—about which camera is right for you.

Deductive reasoning is more formal and complex than inductive reasoning. It moves in the opposite direction—from the general to the specific. Deductive logic follows the pattern of the **syllogism,** a simple three-part argument consisting of a major premise, a minor premise, and a conclusion. If the premises are true and the reasoning is valid, the syllogism is said to be *sound:*

    a. All humans are mortal. (*major premise*)
    b. Alessandro is a human. (*minor premise*)
    c. Therefore, Alessandro is mortal. (*conclusion*)

A syllogism will fail to work if either premise is untrue:

    a. All living creatures are mammals. (*major premise*)
    b. A lobster is a living creature. (*minor premise*)
    c. A lobster is a mammal. (*conclusion*)

The problem is immediately apparent. The major premise is false: many living creatures are not mammals, and a lobster happens to be one of them. Consequently, the conclusion is false and the syllogism is invalid.

BLEND Logic AND EMOTION
Artistic Judgement.

A syllogism can also fail to work even if both premises are true, but the reasoning is not valid:

   a. All college students read books. (*major premise*)
   b. Liz reads books. (*minor premise*)
   c. Liz is a college student. (*conclusion*)

Logical Fallacies

A logical fallacy is an error in reasoning that renders an argument invalid and untrue. Here are some of the more common fallacies:

OVERSIMPLIFICATION. Offering simple solutions to complex problems. "If mothers would stay home to raise their children, we would have fewer juvenile delinquents." There are many reasons for juvenile delinquency. What evidence is there that working mothers is one of the reasons?

NON SEQUITUR ("It does not follow"). A conclusion that does not follow from the premises. "If we can put a man on the moon, we ought to be able to find a cure for AIDS." Success in space does not guarantee success in medical science or any other field.

POST HOC, ERGO PROPTER HOC ("After this, therefore because of this"). Confusing coincidence with causation. Because one event comes after another, it does not mean the first event caused the second. "Every time I wear my orange sweater to one of our games, we win." One fan's clothing does not determine whether or not the team wins.

BEGGING THE QUESTION. Assuming what needs to be proven. "If you love your country, you will vote Republican." What is meant by "loving your country"? In fact, once that question is answered, it may be that loving your country means voting for the Democratic candidate.

FALSE ANALOGY. Making a connection between two logically unrelated ideas. "Eating crackers in bed is like driving with your foot on the clutch." Both may be bad habits, but are otherwise unconnected.

EITHER/OR THINKING. Seeing an issue as having only two sides. "If I cannot make the starting team, there is no use trying out at all." Not everyone can be a starter, and there is value in being on the team otherwise. Besides, practice and being a good team player might lead to a starting position.

Both premises in the syllogism are true, but the syllogism is invalid because it does not take into account that not all people who read books are in college. If the minor premise were "Liz is a college student," then the conclusion "Liz reads books" would logically follow and the syllogism would be sound, that is, both valid and true.

It is fairly easy to see the problems in a deductive argument when its premises and conclusion are presented in the simple form of a syllogism. It is more difficult to see errors in logic when the argument is presented in essay form. But if you can reduce an argument, whether made by you or an opponent, to its major and minor premises, and then test the truth of each premise as well as the validity of the form of the syllogism, you can determine the soundness of that argument.

ARGUE 3b   Use emotional appeals.

While some experts think there is no place in an argument for emotional appeals, others believe that as humans we are not merely logical machines, that our emotional responses to issues are important to us and sway our thinking on issues. When an editorial writer argues for stricter community leash laws by telling about a child bitten by a dog, she appeals to our fears for our own safety. Such fears can change minds. When a student writer argues for greater participation in campus volunteer activities by describing the satisfaction she gets from preparing meals for residents at the local Ronald McDonald House, she appeals to our sense of caring and, as a result, she may change our minds about volunteering. Emotional appeals are not a substitute for sound reasoning, but an effective addition.

ARGUE 3c   Use ethical appeals.

Ethical appeals are based on the credibility and, to some extent, the morals of the writer. This idea comes from Aristotle and Cicero, two classical theorists who believed that speakers must be credible and that they should argue only for worthwhile causes. To them, using argumentative skills in the service of a questionable cause was not acceptable.

But how do you establish credibility? There are three basic ways. First, be knowledgeable about your subject. Knowledge can either be first hand (you are capable of explaining how to change the oil in a car because you have been doing it yourself for years), or it can come from someone else who has first-hand knowledge. For example, if you want to argue that a good daycare center has a low ratio of children to caregivers, but you are not an expert in daycare, you can cite research studies and quote experts.

Secondly, establish credibility by taking the opposition into account. This does not mean you have to agree with the opposition. (See ARGUE 4.) Rather, by acknowledging that there are arguments on both sides, you establish yourself as a reasonable person.

Third, maintain a fair and even tone. Back up your assertions with solid evidence instead of spouting generalities. Use language sincerely and carefully: be aware of connotative meanings and avoid pretentious words and doublespeak. (See WORD 1b and WORD 2c.) At all times, show respect for the intelligence and interest of your reader.

ARGUE 4

Refute the Opposition's Arguments

You will not have much trouble convincing readers who already agree with your assertions. But what about those who are skeptical or think differently from you? You need to discover who they are and what they believe by talking to them and reading what they have written. Once you understand the other side's position, you can refute it. You can present evidence to counter the opposing argument, show why you think its evidence is incomplete or distorted, why its reasoning is faulty, or why the conclusions drawn do not fit the evidence. Again, do your research, be reasonable, and agree where you can but take issue where you must.

ARGUE 5

Consider Your Audience

When you consider the audience for your argument, first ask yourself the basic audience questions you ask for any kind of writing.

(See COMP 2g.) But then remind yourself that you are arguing a point and that not everyone will agree with you. In fact, your readers will likely range from extremely sympathetic and accepting to extremely hostile and resistant—with many possibilities in between. It is therefore important in writing an argument that you try to anticipate what your different readers' responses will be at every turn (especially your opponents' responses) and shape your argument accordingly. (See ARGUE 6.)

ARGUE 6

Organize the Elements of an Argumentative Essay

Here is a checklist of questions to ask yourself as you write, organize, and revise your argumentative essay:

- Have you properly introduced the issue that is the focus of your paper? Do you provide necessary background information for your readers and explain why your issue is important?
- What is your assertion and where in your paper have you placed it? Would it be more effective if placed elsewhere?
- Have you used enough evidence? Is the evidence accurate, reliable, and up to date? Does the evidence support your assertions?
- Have you made appropriate appeals to your readers? Have you established your credibility?
- Is your reasoning sound? Have you checked for logical fallacies?
- Are the points in your argument arranged in the most effective organizational pattern (simplest to most complex, least important to most important, most familiar to least familiar, and so on)?
- Have you taken into account the opposition's arguments? Do you do this at the best possible point in your paper? Are you thorough and fair in your refutation?
- Is your conclusion strong? Is it more than just a summary? Does it grow naturally out of your assertions, evidence, and your reasoning?

ARGUE 7

Annotated Student Argumentative Essay

Course information presented in upper left corner. (See FORMAT 2.)

Marcie Turple

English I

Mr. Rosa

October 20, 1998

Title centered.

Dying To Look Good

Introduction states problem.

Americans are obsessed with thinness--even at the risk of dying. In the 1930's, people took dinitrophenol, an industrial poison, to lose weight. It boosted metabolism but caused blindness and some deaths. Since then dieters have used thyroid hormone injections, amphetamines, and liquid protein diets--all of which were directly traced to some deaths

In-text citations to two works by the same author include abbreviated titles. (See MLA DOCU 1.)

(Kolata, "Fearful Price" 3). Most recently, dieters embraced fen-phen, a combination of fenfluramine or dextenfluramine and phentermine. In September, 1997, however, the makers took the two "fen" drugs off the market at the request of the Food and Drug Administration because fen-phen was linked to heart valve damage and death (Kolata, "Companies Recall" 1).

Transition to argumentative thesis.

Haven't we Americans learned our lesson about diets by now? Apparently not. When fen-phen was withdrawn, one woman said, " If the treatment killed me, at least I would fit in my coffin" (Cowley and Springen 46). But there is no magic way to lose weight--no pill, no crash diet plan.

Turple 2

The only way to permanent weight loss is through sensible eating and exercise.

Pills and crash diets don't work for several reasons. First, the body can't tell the difference between dieting and starving during a famine. So when the body doesn't get enough food, metabolism slows down to conserve energy. At the first increase in calories, weight gain is rapid because the body is still functioning at a lower metabolism.

Then there is the psychological effect of dieting. According to University of Toronto psychologist Janet Polivy, "If you're told you can't have something, then that's what you want. You want it so much, in fact, that you become preoccupied with food at the expense of emotional stability" (qtd. in Fraser 56).

Polivy and a colleague, Peter Herman, also did research which showed that people on diets binge-eat more often than people not on diets (Fraser 56). In one study, they gave dieters and non-dieters milk shakes and then offered them a snack. Dieters ate much more of the snack than non-dieters. Polivy and Herman noted that subjects were not eating according to whether they were full or not, but whether they were being "good" or "bad" on their diets. If they'd gone off their diets with a fattening milkshake, they seemed to reason, why not just keep eating?

The best way to lose weight is to eat sensibly and exercise. Choose a well-balanced, low fat-diet and watch

Thesis statement is an assertion on which opinion differs.

Writer provides expert testimony as one logical appeal.

Writer provides research findings as another logical appeal.

Writer uses a fair and even tone to establish credibility.

Turple 3

calories, but don't become obsessive. You should also
exercise regularly. Walking for 30 to 45 minutes three to five
times a week, for example, will raise your metabolism and
help you lose weight faster. If you want to exercise more
vigorously, it's a good idea to assess your fitness level to
be sure you don't do yourself more harm than good (Koop).

Writer states
the opposition's
argument and
refutes it with
an example.

Easy to say, but it takes so long to lose weight by
eating sensibly, and there are so many temptations to go
off a diet. Besides, it's hard to fit exercising into an already
busy schedule. Isn't it easier to just get a pill? Sure, if you
don't mind risking your life, and if you think you'll be the
one who really will keep off the weight. The fact is that
pills and crash diets simply do not work. The television talk
show host Oprah Winfrey is a perfect example. In 1988, she
lost 76 pounds on a liquid diet. Within two years, she was
back to 200. Over the last few years, though, Oprah has
stabilized her weight at 150--not ultra-thin--by eating
sensibly and exercising (Fraser 58).

Conclusion
grows naturally
out of assertion
and evidence.

The challenge with losing weight is that we may know
what's best for us, but we want instant results. With fen-
phen off the market, how many Americans will take a
sensible approach to losing weight? And how many will
just wait for the next diet pill? The FDA is, in fact, expected
to approve a new diet drug some time in 1998 (Cowley and
Springen 48), Unfortunately, there will probably be a lot of
people just dying to use it.

Turple 4

Works Cited

Cowley, Geoffrey, and Karen Springen. "After Fen-Phen." <u>Newsweek</u> 29 Sept. 1997: 46-48.

Fraser, Laura. "Say Good-Bye to Dieting." <u>Health</u> Apr. 1997: 56+.

Kolata, Gina. "Companies Recall 2 Top Diet Drugs at F.D.A.'s Urging." <u>New York Times</u> 16 Sept. 1997, natl. ed.: A1+.

Kolata, Gina. "The Fearful Price of Getting Thin." <u>New York Times</u> 13 July 1997, natl. ed.: E-3.

Koop, C. Everett. "Assess Your Fitness Level." <u>Healthy Weight for Life: Shape Up America</u>. 10 Oct. 1997 <http://www2.shapeup.org/sua/health-fitness/assess.htm>.

The heading *Works Cited* is centered at the top of the page.

Turple uses MLA style for her list of works cited. She begins the list on a new page.

The correct forms for various kinds of sources are given in MLA DOCU 2.

Writing about Literature

In some of your college courses, your instructor will ask you to read a piece of literature—a short story, poem, play, or novel—and respond to it in writing. Your first step in completing the assignment will be to read the work closely. As you interact with the text, you will begin to make connections, see patterns, and finally generate possible meanings. Ultimately, whatever interpretations you make will have to be supported by examples from the text.

On one level, writing about literature gives you the opportunity to demonstrate your understanding and appreciation of the work. On a deeper level, such an assignment allows you to learn something about art and human experience.

LIT 1

Carefully Read and Analyze the Literary Text

You are aiming to extract the full meaning of a piece of literature which is rarely yielded on a first reading. You should, therefore, allow yourself enough time to read the text *at least* twice. Sometimes, however, as in the case of a novel, this is not always possible. It is a good idea, if the book is your own, to annotate as you read. Jot down questions ("Why would she do that?"—about a character) or reactions ("Why does this author write such long sentences?") in the margin. Underline or highlight what seem to be important lines or passages.

Your goal in the first reading is to get an overall feel for the text. You want to find out what the text is about, where it is going, and how it gets there. Along the way, you'll form some first impressions of what it all means. Your second reading will be quite different. You are now ready to dig deeper—to analyze the various parts and relate the parts to the whole. You will want to carefully examine passages that were puzzling on your first reading. You will want to test your first impressions against the words on the page, developing and deepening your understanding of what the text means—or changing your mind about it.

As you analyze the text, you will want to examine its basic elements. The following list outlines basic literary elements and some questions to get you thinking logically and creatively about what you read and what it means:

Genre: the type of work—novel, novella, short story, play, poem, essay, or film.

- What kind of work is it—a science fiction novel, an autobiography, a sonnet, or a one-act play, for example? What expectations are created by your recognition of the genre?
- What conventions—established techniques, practices, or devices—characterize this type of work?

Plot: the pattern or sequence of events in a literary work.

- What happens in the story? Does the action occur in chronological order or are there flashbacks?
- What is the central conflict? What other conflicts occur?
- How are the events related to one another?
- Are there any subplots?

Character: the people the writer creates.

- Who are the central people in the story, play, or poem, and what seems to motivate them?
- How do the characters interact? How are their conflicts resolved?
- What do the characters reveal about themselves and others in what they do, say, and think?
- Do any of the characters change? What, if anything, have they learned about themselves from their experiences?

Setting: the time (historical period or season) and place (locale) against which the action takes place.

- What does the setting contribute to the writer's meaning?
- What is the social/cultural context for the work?
- What is the importance of scene changes when they occur?

Point of view: the perspective from which the story is told.

- Who is the narrator? Is the story being told by a character—in the first person (*I, we*), third person (*he, she, it, they*) or omniscient voice?
- Is the narrator reliable? How do you know? If the narrator is not reliable, how is your understanding of the story affected?
- What is the significance of the writer's choice of a narrator and point of view?
- In a poem, who is the speaker, and to whom is this person speaking?

Theme: the main idea or meaning of the work.

- What does the work tell you about the meaning of life, the way people think and behave?
- How do the other literary elements in this list work together to develop this meaning for you?

Tone: the feelings presented, the predominant mood as conveyed through the writer's choice of words.

- What attitude do you hear in the words of the story, play, or poem?
- Is the writer ironic?
- In what ways is the tone appropriate for the theme of the work? For the audience?

Imagery: descriptive details and figurative language appealing to the five senses.

- To which of your senses does the writer's imagery appeal?
- What patterns, if any, do you find in the imagery? Does recurring imagery seem symbolic to you?
- What metaphors, similes, and personifications does the writer use? How do these figures contribute to the meaning of the work?

LIT 2

Observe the Conventions for Writing about Literature

As you work on your essay, observe the **conventions**—or widely accepted practices—for writing about a literary text. Adhering to these conventions focuses your readers on the content of your paper and not on the details of your presentation.

- Avoid unnecessary and extended plot summaries. You can assume that your readers have read the piece of literature you are discussing. Your paper should therefore analyze and interpret the work and present any conclusions you wish to draw, not retell the story.
- Use literary terms accurately. Remember, for example, that an *essay* is not a *story*, the *speaker* or *narrator* is not necessarily the *author*, and that a group of lines in a poem is a *stanza* and not a *paragraph*. If you have questions about the use of a particular term, ask your instructor or consult one of the many dictionaries of literary terms available in your library.
- Use *suggests* or *implies* when you are attributing a particular meaning to a writer. Be careful not to claim absolute knowledge about a writer's intentions or meaning.
- Support your points with specific references to the text you are writing about—summarize an important scene, describe the atmosphere/setting, or paraphrase (or quote) what a character says. Be sparing, however, in your use of quotations. (See LIT 3. For specific advice about using quotations as well as paraphrase and summary, see RESCH 2c.)

- Give the page number parenthetically when you are citing a passage from a work of fiction or nonfiction; the line number(s) for a poem; the act, scene, and line numbers for a play; and book, chapter, and verse for the Bible. (See MLA DOCU 1, pp. 337–343.) In all cases, be sure to integrate evidence smoothly into your paper. (See LIT 3.)
- Use the present tense when discussing works of literature. (See EDIT 2c.)
- Use the past tense when you are talking about historical events, presenting biographical material about the writer, or referring to events that occur prior to the time of the story's central action.
- Use a writer's or critic's full name the first time you mention it. Thereafter, use only the last name.
- Underline or use italics for the titles of novels, novellas, plays, and films. (See MECH 4a.) Enclose the titles of short stories, poems, essays, and songs in quotation marks. (See PUNCT 5c.)
- If you use the work of others to support your analysis, you must acknowledge the source. Introduce each quotation, paraphrase, or summary by reference to the source in a signal phrase, and follow the borrowed material with parenthetical documentation. (See RESCH 4b.)
- Use the MLA documentation style, including in-text parenthetical citations (see MLA DOCU 1) and include a list of Works Cited (see MLA DOCU 2).

LIT 3

Use Quotations Purposefully and Effectively

Using quotations purposefully means using only those that truly support your interpretation. Using quotations effectively means reserving direct quotation for important ideas stated in vivid, imaginative, and memorable language or for revealing statements by characters themselves. When you are considering using a quotation, ask yourself these questions:

- How well does the quotation illustrate or support my analysis?
- Is this quotation the best evidence of the point I am making?
- Why am I quoting the text instead of saying this in my own words?

Resist the temptation to use quotations simply because they sound good or because you think you do not have "enough" of them in your paper. Finally, remember the good use of quotation gives your paper authority.

Whenever you quote, you need to tell how the quotation relates to your point. Do not leave it to your readers to guess your intent. Introduce each quotation and draw a conclusion from it. Integrate quotations into the flow of your paper so that they are not stylistically jarring. Consider the following uses of quotations in a student paper on the short stories of Edgar Allan Poe.

WEAK

Poe often uses specific details from the settings of his stories to suggest the psychological states of his characters. For example, in describing the "barely perceptible fissure" (237), he prefigures Roderick's mental disintegration.

EFFECTIVE

Poe often uses specific details from the settings of his stories to suggest the psychological states of his characters. In "The Fall of the House of Usher," for example, the narrator's description of the "barely perceptible fissure" (237) in the front wall of the Usher mansion prefigures Roderick's own mental disintegration.

Naming the short story and identifying the words as those of the narrator provide more of a context for the quotation. Stating that the fissure was in the front wall of the Usher mansion makes explicit the comparison between setting and psychological state. (For additional examples of integrating notations from literary texts, see RESCH 4c and MLA DOCU 1.)

Finally, use quotation marks around all passages borrowed word for word. (See PUNCT 5a.)

LIT 4

Annotated Student Literary Essay

Lauri D. Coulombe, a student, wrote a paper in response to novelist Julia Alvarez's short story "Snow." She supports her interpretation of the story by paraphrasing and quoting from Alvarez's text. She also draws on secondary sources to lend additional support to her ideas. Coulombe's essay follows the manuscript format guidelines of the MLA (see FORMAT 2) and illustrates correct MLA documentation style (see MLA DOCU). Her essay immediately follows the text of Alvarez's story.

Snow

Julia Alvarez

Our first year in New York we rented a small apartment with a Catholic school nearby, taught by the Sisters of Charity, hefty women in long black gowns and bonnets that made them look peculiar, like dolls in mourning. I liked them a lot, especially my grandmotherly fourth grade teacher, Sister Zoe. I had a lovely name, she said, and she had me teach the whole class how to pronounce it. *Yo-lan-da.* As the only immigrant in my class, I was put in a special seat in the first row by the window, apart from the other children so that Sister Zoe could tutor me without disturbing them. Slowly, she enunciated the new words I was to repeat: *laundromat, cornflakes, subway, snow.*

Soon I picked up enough English to understand holocaust was in the air. Sister Zoe explained to a wide-eyed classroom what was happening in Cuba. Russian missiles were being assembled, trained supposedly on New York City. President Kennedy, looking worried too, was on the television at home, explaining we might have to go to war against the Communists. At school, we had air-raid drills: an ominous bell would go off and we'd file into the hall, fall to the floor, cover our heads with our coats, and imagine our hair falling out, the bones in our arms going soft. At home, Mami and my sisters and I said a rosary for world peace. I heard new vocabulary: *nuclear bomb, radioactive fallout, bomb shelter.* Sister Zoe explained how it would happen. She drew a picture of a mushroom on the blackboard and dotted a flurry of chalkmarks for the dusty fallout that would kill us all.

The months grew cold, November, December. It was dark when I got up in the morning, frosty when I followed my breath to school. One morning as I sat at my desk daydreaming out the window, I saw dots in the air like the ones Sister Zoe had drawn—random at first, then lots and lots. I shrieked, "Bomb! Bomb!" Sister Zoe jerked around, her full black skirt ballooning as she hurried to my side. A few girls began to cry.

But then Sister Zoe's shocked look faded. "Why, Yolanda dear, that's snow!" She laughed. "Snow."

"Snow," I repeated. I looked out the window warily. All my life I had heard about white crystals that fell out of American skies in the winter. From my desk I watched the fine powder dust the sidewalk and parked cars below. Each flake was different, Sister Zoe said, like a person, irreplaceable and beautiful.

Coulombe 1

Lauri D. Coulombe

English 11

Ms. Prentiss

March 15, 1998

(Re)-producing Annihilation

When asked to comment on the purpose of "Snow,"
Julia Alvarez said, "I thought I might best 'prove' the
destructiveness of nuclear weapons if I showed how a
simple, poignant, and 'natural' moment becomes in this
nuclear age a moment of possible holocaust for a child"
(Gillespie, Singleton, and Becker 39). In "Snow," the child is
Yolanda, an immigrant who has moved to New York at the
height of the cold war, and the destructive "moment" is,
ironically, Yolanda's first experience with snow. This moment,
which should produce joy, produces hysteria because of the
fear of nuclear war that permeated America in the 1950s
and 60s. The fear that the Russians might drop an atomic
bomb at any time even penetrated the classroom where
Yolanda learns that "holocaust was in the air . . . an ominous
bell would go off and we'd file into the hall, fall to the floor,
cover our heads with our coats, and imagine our hair falling
out, the bones in our arms going soft" (Alvarez 87). Alvarez
not only conveys the fear of this period and accomplishes
her purpose--to prove the destructiveness of nuclear
weapons--but she goes a step further to show that it is
ultimately impossible to understand what nuclear war would

Course information presented in upper left corner. (See FORMAT 2.)

Title centered.

In-text citation with authors' names and page number in parentheses. (See MLA DOCU 1.)

Writer uses present tense to discuss story.

Writer quotes text to show children's fear but doesn't over quote.

Writer presents thesis.

Coulombe 2

mean without experiencing it. She develops her theme through the use of irony.

The most obvious irony lies in the difference between the length of the story and the subject of the story: Alvarez deals with mass destruction in one page. Nuclear holocaust is one of the most profound threats we can consider, yet Alvarez addresses it in minimal space.

Another important instance of irony is Alvarez's expression--in words--of the inability of words to produce understanding and reality. Knowing the words "snow" and "radioactive fallout" does not prepare Yolanda to understand either one. Similarly, we believe that because we have the words to name or describe something that we understand it. But Yolanda reminds us that words are merely labels, not reality: knowing the word "snow" does not produce an understanding of "snow." In the same way, knowing the words "nuclear holocaust" does not produce an understanding of "nuclear holocaust." We can no more grasp the meaning of "holocaust" through words than Yolanda can grasp the meaning of "snow" before she experiences it. Even being alive when the world was as political scientist Marcus Pohlmann observes, "closer to annihilation than at any time in its history" (337), does not convey the experience of annihilation. Herein lies the ultimate irony: we can never understand what nuclear holocaust would mean because experiencing it means dying from it.

Writer presents first example of irony.

Writer presents second example of irony.

Writer uses secondary source to comment on cold war era.

In-text citation with the author's full name given in a single phrase and the page number in parentheses.

Coulombe 3

<table>
<tr><td>

Writer quotes
description of
nuclear cloud to
show similarity
to snow.

</td><td>

A final irony stems from Sister Zoe's drawing of a
mushroom cloud. She "dotted a flurry of chalkmarks for
the dusty fallout that would kill us all (87)," on the board.
When Yolanda looks out the window and sees white "dots"
like those on the chalkboard falling from the sky, she cries,

</td></tr>
<tr><td>

Writer presents
third example
of irony.

</td><td>

"Bomb!" (87). It is ironic that Yolanda confuses snow with
the ashes from nuclear fallout because one is a blanket
of protection and life and the other of destruction and
death. And in a further twist Sister Zoe tells the children
that each snowflake is "like a person, irreplaceable and
beautiful" (87).

</td></tr>
<tr><td>

Conclusion pre-
sents the central
point the writer
wants to leave
with readers.

</td><td>

Through irony, Alvarez shows us that it is the
individuality of each one of us that will be annihilated if
we ever come to know nuclear holocaust in the same
way that Yolanda comes to know snow--through first-
hand experience. Though the fear that permeated the
50s and 60s is mostly forgotten, and though we can never
understand nuclear destruction through words alone, we
must keep trying. Otherwise, we may be destined to repeat
the history we long to forget.

</td></tr>
</table>

Coulombe 4

Works Cited

Alvarez, Julia. "Snow." <u>Flash Fiction: Very Short Stories</u>. Ed.
James Thomas, Denise Thomas, and Tom Hazuka.
New York: Norton, 1992. 86-87.

Gillespie, Sheena, Robert Singleton, and Robert Becker.
<u>The Writer's Craft</u>. Glenview, IL: Scott, Foresman,
1989.

Pohlmann, Marcus D. "Constraining Presidents at the Brink:
The Cuban Missile Crisis." <u>Presidential Studies
Quarterly</u> 19 (1989): 337-46.

The heading *Works Cited* is centered at the top of the page.

Coulombe uses MLA style for her list of works cited. The list begins on a new page.

The correct MLA forms for various kinds of publications are given in MLA DOCU 2.

lib

The Library

Learning Objectives

After reading this section, you should:

- be familiar with the kinds of reference books and periodical indexes available in your library;
- be able to use computerized periodical indexes;
- be able to use card and computer catalogs;
- know what is available for online research.

The Library

Your college library is a storehouse of information, and learning how to retrieve information from it is a basic part of your education. If your college library provides guided tours, avail yourself of the opportunity; if not, obtain a map showing the location of your library's various holdings. In either case, learn to ask for help. Reference librarians are trained specialists in information retrieval and will soon have you feeling at home in your college's library. If you learn early in your college career how to use the library efficiently, you will save yourself time and frustration and greatly enhance the quality of your education.

Generally, most libraries offer four types of resources: (1) reference books, (2) periodicals, (3) books in the general collection, and (4) computer databases and the Internet.

LIB 1

Reference Books

The **reference section** of a library houses encyclopedias, dictionaries, abstracts, atlases, yearbooks, handbooks, almanacs, catalogs, bibliographies, indexes, biographical guides, and other types of reference works. As you begin your research project, use one or more of these reference books to get an overview of your subject.

For a comprehensive descriptive guide to all reference books published in the world, see Eugene P. Sheehy's *Guide to Reference Books*. If you cannot locate a particular reference book or if you are simply looking for general assistance, do not hesitate to talk about your research project with your reference librarian. Finally, be aware that reference books are usually not allowed to circulate, so plan your library time accordingly.

LIB 2

Periodicals

The term **periodicals** refers to magazines, journals, and newspapers; that is, materials published on a regular basis (daily, weekly, monthly, yearly, or at some other time interval).

LIB 2a   Periodical indexes

To locate articles in periodicals, use a **periodical index,** which is usually found in the reference section of the library. Unless you are trying to locate a particular article by a particular author or know of an author who generally writes on a particular subject, start your search under subject headings.

The most widely used index to periodicals is the *Readers' Guide to Periodical Literature* (1900–present). The *Readers' Guide* annually indexes nearly two hundred periodicals of popular interest, such as *Newsweek, Harper's, Sports Illustrated,* and *Scientific American.* Monthly paperback supplements keep the *Readers' Guide* current throughout the year. *Readers' Guide* lists articles both by subject and by author in alphabetical order with cross-references to related subject headings.

The subject and author entries from the *Readers' Guide* for two articles that student Patricia LaRose consulted while writing her documented research paper (see pp. 323–335) follow. As you can see, all the information needed to locate an article is provided.

SUBJECT ENTRY FROM THE *READERS' GUIDE*

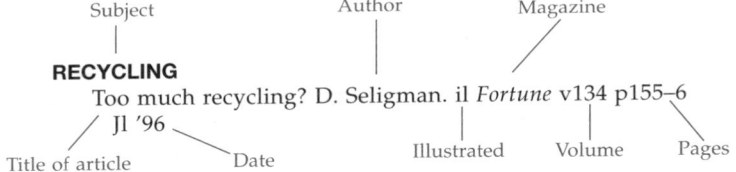

Subject   Author   Magazine

RECYCLING
   Too much recycling? D. Seligman. il *Fortune* v134 p155–6
   Jl '96

Title of article   Date   Illustrated   Volume   Pages

AUTHOR ENTRY FROM THE *READERS' GUIDE*

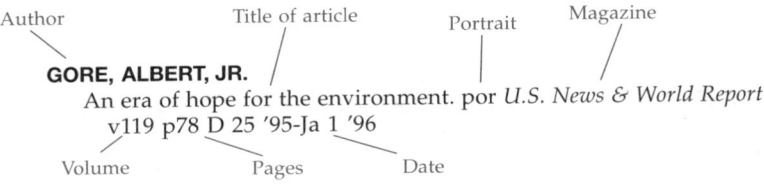

Author   Title of article   Portrait   Magazine

GORE, ALBERT, JR.
   An era of hope for the environment. por *U.S. News & World Report* v119 p78 D 25 '95-Ja 1 '96

Volume   Pages   Date

Articles from major newspapers can be located in any of the following representative newspaper indexes: [London] *Times Index, National Newspaper Index, NewsBank, New York Times Index, Wall Street Journal Index.*

Specialized periodical indexes list articles that have appeared in technical and scholarly journals or government publications. They are organized in much the same way as the *Readers' Guide*. Remember that your reference librarian is always available to help you locate specialized periodical indexes for your particular subject.

LIB 2b Computerized periodical indexes

Most libraries offer online and CD-ROM (**C**ompact **D**isc—**R**ead **O**nly **M**emory) computer database versions of periodical indexes. Computer searches can save you valuable time in locating articles—time that you can use in reading what you find.

To use a computerized periodical index, type in the access codes explained in the opening menu on the terminal screen. You can begin your search for articles by author, title, or subject keywords. At any time, if you have a problem, ask a reference librarian for help.

Bibliographic records of potentially useful articles will appear on the screen. In some cases you can access an abstract or even the full text of an article. He is a sample full-record display:

FULL RECORD DISPLAY SCREEN

Database identified

Subject being searched

Publication information for item #64

Summary of article

```
* * * * * * * * * * * * * * * * * Full Record Display * * * * * * * * * * * * * * * * *
    DATABASE: ReadGuideAbs          LIMITED TO:
    SEARCH: su:recycling

    Record 64 of 961___YOUR LIBRARY (VTU) MAY OWN THIS ITEM ___
  ( Page 1 of 3)

        AUTHOR: Grove, Noel.
         TITLE: Recycling.
        SOURCE: National Geographic v. 186 (July '94) p. 92–115 il.
   STANDARD NO: 0027–9358
          DATE: 1994
   RECORD TYPE: art
      CONTENTS: feature article
      ABSTRACT: Not since World War II have Americans been so fervent about
                recycling. The renewed interest in recycling stems from a num-
                ber of concerns, including loss of landfill space, contamination
                of groundwater by landfills, dwindling natural resources, and,
                possibly, a growing comprehension of America's unmatched
                waste production—200 million tons a year. The rapidly evolv-
                ing recycling industry nonetheless struggles with acceptance
                and financing. Economic arguments against it point to the ex-
                pense of implementing recycling programs and the difficulty of
                selling recycled materials, which often pile up unused. Sup-
                porters of recycling contend, however, that it just takes time for
                regional markets to evolve and close the loop from manufac-
                turer to consumer and back to manufacturer again. Various re-
                cycling programs around the country are discussed.
       SUBJECT: Recycling (Waste, etc.).
```

After reading the abstract, LaRose decided that this article looked helpful, and that she wanted to read it in its entirety. Therefore she printed the screen to preserve a complete bibliographic record for later reference.

LIB 3

Books

LIB 3a The card catalog

The **card catalog**—drawers of 3 × 5-inch cards—is an alphabetical index of a library's holdings. It lists all books, bound periodicals (issues for one year are bound in a single volume), pamphlets, and other printed documents housed in the library. Many libraries have a separate catalog for periodical holdings as well.

Every work in the library is classified three ways in the card catalog: by author, by title, and by subject. Here is a sample subject card:

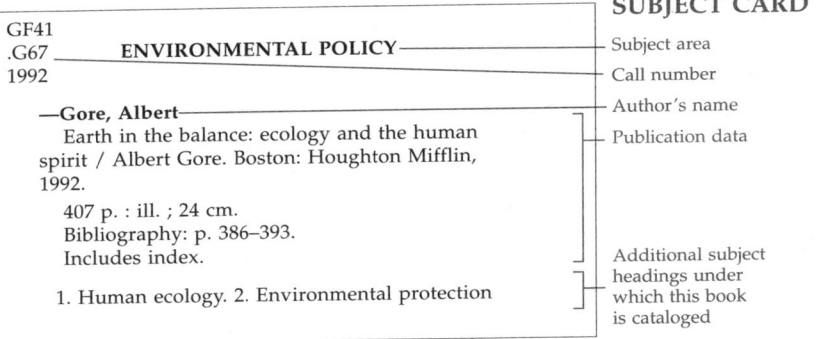

```
                                                            SUBJECT CARD
 GF41
 .G67 _____ ENVIRONMENTAL POLICY _____ Subject area
 1992                                                       Call number

   —Gore, Albert—_____ Author's name
     Earth in the balance: ecology and the human          Publication data
   spirit / Albert Gore. Boston: Houghton Mifflin,
   1992.
       407 p. : ill. ; 24 cm.
       Bibliography: p. 386–393.
       Includes index.                                     Additional subject
                                                           headings under
     1. Human ecology. 2. Environmental protection         which this book
                                                           is cataloged
```

Every library card provides the book's **call number,** which you need to locate the book in the library stacks. It also provides publication data and related card catalog subject headings you may wish to pursue. If you think you want to consult a particular book, write down the book's call number, author, title, and publication data on a 3 x 5-inch card. Note whether the book has a **bibliography** (a list of readings on the subject) or cross-reference subject headings; both provide additional source leads.

LIB 3b The computer catalog

If your college library has computerized its holdings, it no longer uses the traditional card catalog. The **computer catalog** gives the same immediate three-way access to the library's holdings—by subject, author, and title—and, in many cases, provides access by key words or combinations of key words.

The "keyword," option greatly increases the scope and possibilities of your search. LaRose started her search by entering the subject *garbage*. Within moments, her search had netted 12 entries.

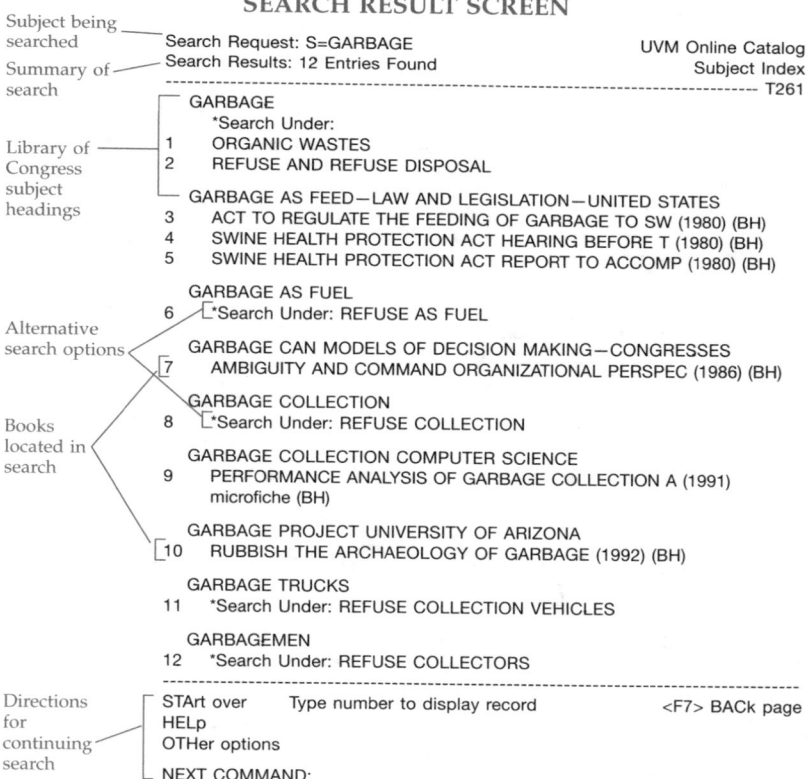

SEARCH RESULT SCREEN

Subject being searched

Summary of search

Library of Congress subject headings

Alternative search options

Books located in search

Directions for continuing search

Search Request: S=GARBAGE   UVM Online Catalog
Search Results: 12 Entries Found   Subject Index
--- T261

```
    GARBAGE
        *Search Under:
  1     ORGANIC WASTES
  2     REFUSE AND REFUSE DISPOSAL

    GARBAGE AS FEED—LAW AND LEGISLATION—UNITED STATES
  3     ACT TO REGULATE THE FEEDING OF GARBAGE TO SW (1980) (BH)
  4     SWINE HEALTH PROTECTION ACT HEARING BEFORE T (1980) (BH)
  5     SWINE HEALTH PROTECTION ACT REPORT TO ACCOMP (1980) (BH)

    GARBAGE AS FUEL
  6     *Search Under: REFUSE AS FUEL

    GARBAGE CAN MODELS OF DECISION MAKING—CONGRESSES
  7     AMBIGUITY AND COMMAND ORGANIZATIONAL PERSPEC (1986) (BH)

    GARBAGE COLLECTION
  8     *Search Under: REFUSE COLLECTION

    GARBAGE COLLECTION COMPUTER SCIENCE
  9     PERFORMANCE ANALYSIS OF GARBAGE COLLECTION A (1991)
        microfiche (BH)

    GARBAGE PROJECT UNIVERSITY OF ARIZONA
  10    RUBBISH THE ARCHAEOLOGY OF GARBAGE (1992) (BH)

    GARBAGE TRUCKS
  11    *Search Under: REFUSE COLLECTION VEHICLES

    GARBAGEMEN
  12    *Search Under: REFUSE COLLECTORS
--------------------------------------------------------------------------------
    STArt over        Type number to display record          <F7> BACk page
    HELp
    OTHer options
    NEXT COMMAND:
```

LaRose quickly reviewed these entries and noted that "Refuse and Refuse Disposal" and "Refuse Collection" were subject headings she should search later. She also wanted to take a closer look at item 10, so she typed in the number *10* and pressed *Enter*.

The information that appears on the terminal screen is almost exactly the same as on a 3×5-inch subject card in a card catalog. Most computer catalogs also tell you if a book is available or, if checked out, when it is due back. Some terminals have printers so you can get a printout of a title's complete bibliographic information. Below is the printout for item 10.

BOOK RECORD SCREEN

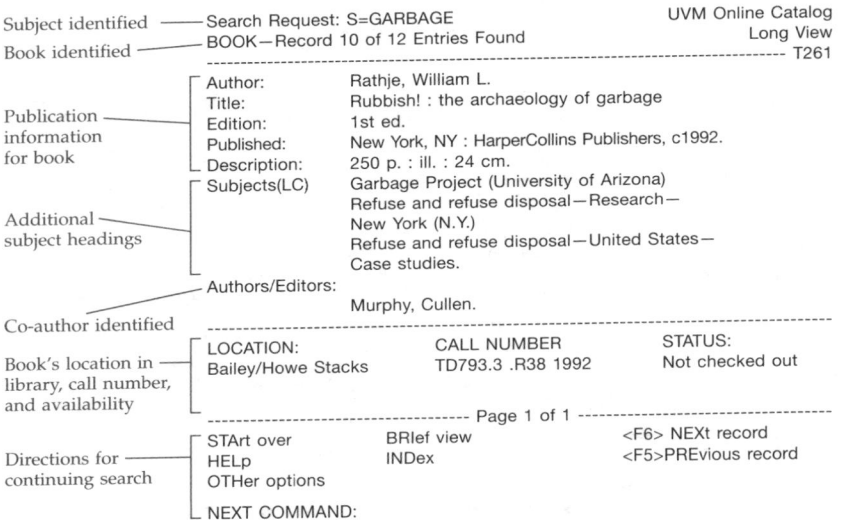

Subject identified ——— Search Request: S=GARBAGE   UVM Online Catalog
Book identified ——— BOOK—Record 10 of 12 Entries Found   Long View
--- T261

Author: Rathje, William L.
Title: Rubbish! : the archaeology of garbage
Publication ——— Edition: 1st ed.
information   Published: New York, NY : HarperCollins Publishers, c1992.
for book   Description: 250 p. : ill. : 24 cm.
Subjects(LC)   Garbage Project (University of Arizona)
                 Refuse and refuse disposal—Research—
Additional ——— New York (N.Y.)
subject headings Refuse and refuse disposal—United States—
                 Case studies.
Authors/Editors:
                 Murphy, Cullen.
Co-author identified —
Book's location in ——— LOCATION: CALL NUMBER   STATUS:
library, call number, Bailey/Howe Stacks TD793.3 .R38 1992   Not checked out
and availability
------------------------------------ Page 1 of 1 -----------------------------------
STArt over   BRIef view   <F6> NEXt record
Directions for ——— HELp   INDex   <F5>PREvious record
continuing search OTHer options
NEXT COMMAND:

LIB 3c The *Library of Congress Subject Headings (LCSH)*

Your library uses conventional headings to catalog its holdings, just as a telephone book lists *pharmacies* (not *drug stores*) and *service stations* (not *gas stations*). Sometimes these headings are not immediately obvious. For example, if you are looking for books about test-tube babies, you might not know that they are listed under *fertilization in vitro, human,* and not under *test-tube babies.*

If your subject headings are not yielding much information, try the **Library of Congress Subject Headings (LCSH)**, a four-volume reference work that lists the subject headings libraries use to catalog their holdings. Even if you are not having trouble finding what you are looking for, it is still a good idea to check the *LCSH*. The main entry there might help you limit or focus your subject or suggest a new and more interesting aspect of that subject.

If your research subject were *recovery of waste materials* or *waste reuse,* you would discover that there is nothing in the computer catalog under these headings. A check of the *LCSH* under these headings would cross-reference you to *recycling,* for which there is almost a half-column of related terms and subheadings. Abbreviations are explained at the beginning of each *LCSH* volume. Many computer catalogs have had the *Library of Congress Subject Headings* incorporated into the search systems for subject searches (see the "Search Result Screen" on p. 291).

LIB 4

Conducting Research on the Internet

Research today is both easier and more difficult than it was when print resources in the library were your only choices. Now, with the Internet, you can access resources anywhere in the world twenty-four hours a day, seven days a week. Finding the materials that you want, however, can be a challenge. Because there are no librarians in cyberspace, you need to know how the Internet works—where the information is stored and how to retrieve it. Most experts agree that the Internet should not supplant, but complement, traditional print sources. First, a great deal of scholarship is not available on the Web. And second, because anyone can publish on the Web, reliability and bias can be real problems. (See RESCH 2b for evaluating online sources.)

LIB 4a   Access the World Wide Web.

Netscape Navigator and other browsers make it possible to move around the Web easily with the aid of a mouse, to view color graphics, and to jump easily from one website or location to another by clicking on text and graphic links. Each website has a unique address known as a URL (Uniform Resource Locator), Here, for example, is the URL for the *Librarian's Index to the Internet:*

http://www.sunsite.berkeley.edu/InternetIndex/

NOTE: When entering or copying a URL be sure to reproduce accurately every symbol, punctuation mark, and letter (including case).

LIB 4b   Plan an Internet search strategy.

To do an Internet search, you must know about search engines and subject directories. A **search engine** is a program that enables you to locate information sources on the Internet, including websites. When you type in a keyword, the search engine goes looking for websites that match your term. The problem with keyword searches is that they can sometimes produce tens of thousands of matches, making it very difficult to find those of immediate value. An alternate, and sometimes more efficient, approach is to use the subject directory provided by most search engines. Once you choose a subject in the directory, you can click your mouse to narrow the subdirectories and eventually arrive at a list of sites closely related to your topic. At that point you can do a keyword search.

Suppose you are researching Jackie Robinson's move from the Negro Baseball League into the majors in the 1940s, and you are using the search engine called Yahoo! (http://www.yahoo.com/). This is the subject directory that would appear on your screen:

YAHOO!

New   Cool   Today's News   More Yahoos

Looking for a   Free Cruise to Monaco Grand Prix   Win Signed
Job? Home? Date?   autoweb.com   Seinfeld Script

[   ] Search options

Yahoo! Online - $14.95 a month Internet access - sign up today

Yellow Pages - **White Pages** / People Search - Maps - Classifieds - Personals - Chat - Email
Shopping - My Yahoo! - News - Sports - Weather - Stock Quotes - **more...**

- **Arts and Humanities**
  Architecture, Photography, Literature...

- **Business and Economy** [Xtra!]
  Companies, Finance, Employment...

- **Computers and Internet** [Xtra!]
  Internet, WWW, Software, Multimedia...

- **Education**
  Universities, K-12, College Entrance...

- **Entertainment** [Xtra!]
  Cool Links, Movies, Music, Humor...

- **Government**
  Military, Politics [Xtra!], Law, Taxes...

- **Health** [Xtra!]
  Medicine, Drugs, Diseases, Fitness...

- **News and Media** [Xtra!]
  Current Events, Magazines, TV, Newspapers...

- **Recreation and Sports** [Xtra!]
  Sports, Games, Travel, Autos, Outdoors...

- **Reference**
  Libraries, Dictionaries, Phone Numbers...

- **Regional**
  Countries, Regions, U.S. States...

- **Science**
  CS, Biology, Astronomy, Engineering...

- **Social Science**
  Anthropology, Sociology, Economics...

- **Society and Culture**
  People, Environment, Religion...

You would click on recreational activities. When that screen appears, you would click on Sports. This takes you to a screen that lists 120 individual sports. For baseball alone there are 3,266 websites.

When you click on Baseball, you see a listing of sites related to the national pastime.

Because you are interested in events that occurred some time ago, the "History" option is a natural. Clicking on History takes you to a screen where you find a link to a site entitled "Crossing the Color Barrier."

Top:Recreation:Sports:Baseball:History

[ ] Search | Options

(•) Search all of Yahoo ( ) Search only in **History**

- Canadian Baseball Hall of Fame and Museum - Official site includes inductee biographies, a quiz, selection criteria, merchandise and more.
- Conlon, Charles - from 1904 to 1942 this baseball photographer immortalized the sport's greatest players.
- Crossing The Color Barrier - information about Jackie Robinson, Larry Doby, Henry Thompson, Willard Brown and Dan Bankhead, the first five African Americans to play in the major leagues.
- Early Baseball Pictures on the World Wide Web
- History of Baseball
- Home Plate: Baseball in the 1930's - original research, writing, statistics, and book reviews about major league and minor league baseball during the 1930s.

Clicking on this site presents replicas of baseball cards of five famous African-American players. Here is Jackie Robinson's card.

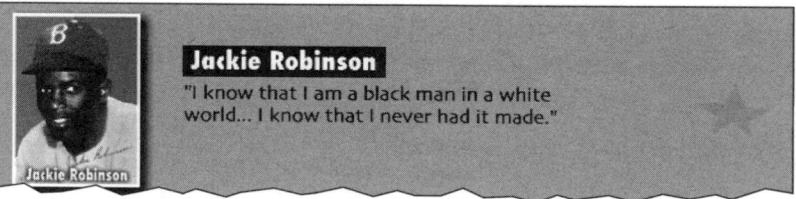

Jackie Robinson

"I know that I am a black man in a white world... I know that I never had it made."

Clicking on a card gives you a biography of that player. Finally, there is a link to "Links to other Jackie Robinson sites" as well as suggestions for further reading. Following are excerpts from two screens:

AFROameric@'s Online Black History Museum - A terrific online biography of Jackie Robinson

Negro Leagues Baseball Page - Learn about the leagues where African American ballplayers competed before tumbling the color barrier.

Total Baseball - The online home of the Official Encyclopedia of Major League Baseball. Good stats and information.

The Official Jackie Robinson Site - (CMG Worldwide) From the people who represent Jackie Robinson's name, with a welcome from Jackie's widow, Rachel Robinson.

The Jackie Robinson Society - A variety of interesting material from an official student group at the University of Texas.

The Baseball Hall of Fame - The Mecca of baseball information and history. Explore the Jackie Robinson resources page. An extensive bibliography of books and articles.

The National Archives Feature Document on Jackie Robinson - Fascinating information and lesson plans for teachers including correspondence between Jackie and Presidents Eisenhower, Kennedy and Johnson.

Sports Illustrated for Kids online feature on Jackie Robinson

The subject directories on the homepages of search engines also make it easy to browse various subjects and topics, a big help if you are undecided about a research topic or simply want to see if there is enough material to supplement your other library research.

LIB 4c   Use search engines to find Internet sources.

You should try more than one search engine in your research, because each one yields slightly different results. You can get to search engines easily by using the Net Search function at the bottom of your browser.

 C-Tip

Search engines

You will get the most out of your favorite search engines if you click on the *Help* button and spend a few minutes learning how they work. For example, what kind of search tips (logical connectors such as AND, OR, and NOT; quotation marks; and other specialized symbols) does the engine use? How does the engine search the Web, and in what order does it present the results? Knowing how to get the most out of your search engine makes you a more efficient and thorough researcher.

Following is a list of popular search engines:

All-in-one <http://www.albany.net/allinone/>
> This search engine searches all other search engines for websites. A fill-in search form is provided for your requests.

Altavista <http://www.altavista.digital.com>
> Fast and comprehensive, this search engine indexes millions of sites and is, therefore, useful for retrieving well-narrowed or hard-to-find topics.

InfoSeek <http://guide.infoseek.com>
> A reliable search engine using keyword, concept, and related terms. Recommended for Usenet Newsgroups searches.

Lycos <http://www.lycos.com>
> Indexing over 90 percent of websites, Lycos allows you to search FTP and Gopher sites but not Usenet Newsgroups.

WebCrawler <http://wc3.webcrawler.com>
> One of the fastest search engines because it is selective. Search results are ranked by frequency of occurrence of keyword.

Netscape's Net Search
> <http://home.netscape.com/home/internetsearch.html>
> Easily accessed on Netscape's taskbar, Net Search is a jump station to Web search engines and useful in beginning a search.

LIB 4d Use subject directories to focus your Internet search.

In addition to the subject directories provided on the homepages of most search engines, a number of websites contain more comprehensive and sophisticated subject directories. The following "stand-alone" directories can be helpful to your research. They can be reached at their Web addresses.

The Argus Clearinghouse <http://www.clearinghouse.net/>
A directory of detailed subject guides, each containing links compiled by experts in their fields. An excellent place to begin your research.

Galaxy <http://www.einet.net/>
An extensive database of subject-classified links with descriptive titles in lieu of annotations.

INFOMINE: Scholarly Internet Resource Collections <http://lib-www.ucr.edu/>
Nearly 10,000 subject-classified links to Internet sites, helpful to both students and scholars.

The Internet Public Library Reference Center <http://www.ipl.org/ref/>
Librarians have annotated this list of subject-classified links provided by the School of Information at the University of Michigan.

Liszt <http://www.liszt.com/>
A well-managed database of discussion lists that also provides useful information on how to select and subscribe. Searchable by category and topic.

Scholarly Journals Distributed by the World Wide Web, by Robert C. Spragg <http://info.lib.uh.edu/wj/webjour.html>
An alphabetical listing of links to scholarly journals on the Internet.

U.S. Federal Government Agencies: A List of Federal Agencies on the Internet <http://www.lib.lsu.edu/gov/fedgov.html>
A hierarchically arranged list of Internet links to government agencies and their subagencies.

The World Wide Web Virtual Library Subject Catalog <http://www.w3.org/pub/DataSources/bySubject/overview.html>
A large directory of guides to subject-classified links with limited annotations.

Yahoo! <http://www.yahoo.com/>
A huge, regularly updated database of subject-classified sites with informative annotations. Searchable by keywords in URLs, titles, or descriptions.

LIB 4e Use newsgroups, listservs, and synchronous sources.

A **newsgroup** is a group of people interested in a particular topic who read and post messages on an electronic bulletin board. The board is open to the general public.

A **listserv** is similar to a newsgroup but restricted to people who subscribe to it. Members of a listserv routinely receive all the postings of the list as e-mail messages. Members usually have more than passing interest in the topic and stand ready to answer research queries and discuss the finer points of the topic of the listserv.

A **synchronous** source is one in which information is being exchanged in "real time," or simultaneously. Two popular synchronous communications are IRCs (Internet Relay Chat groups) and MOOs (Multi-user domain, object-oriented groups). The Daedalus Group's Educational Information MOO Site is available at <http://www.daedalus.com/net/border.html>.

These forms of electronic communication allow you to pursue very specific questions about your topic when you are well into the research process. You also receive information rapidly or, in the case of synchronous communication, in real time, much as you would in a telephone conversation. To find out if there is a newsgroup or listserv in the area of your research, consult Tile.Net's website: <http://www.tile.net>.

resch

The Research Paper

Learning Objectives

After reading this section, you should:

- understand the research process well enough to set a realistic schedule for completing all the steps;
- be able to use your library's print and online resources for research;
- understand the importance of taking accurate notes and when to summarize, paraphrase, and quote directly;
- know how to integrate quotations into your paper;
- understand the importance of crediting others' ideas.

The Research Paper

$\mathbb{T}$ he **library research paper** is an essential part of a college education and for good reason: in writing a library paper you acquire a number of indispensable research skills that you can adapt to other assignments in college and to situations in life after graduation.

The real value of a library paper, however, goes beyond acquiring basic research skills; it is a unique hands-on learning experience. The purpose of a research paper is not to present a collection of quotations that show you can report what others have said about your topic. Rather, your goal is to analyze, evaluate, and synthesize the materials you research—to take ownership of your topic, and thereby learn how to do so with any topic. You learn how to view the results of research from your own perspective and arrive at an informed opinion of a topic. That, after all, is the mark of an educated person.

RESCH 1

Planning

In writing a library research paper, you draw heavily on what you learned about writing short essays. (See COMP.) You decide on a purpose, develop a thesis, consider your audience, marshal your evidence, write a first draft, revise and edit the paper, prepare the final copy, and proofread. The only new ingredient here is research. In addition to all the stages of writing a composition, a library research paper involves locating sources, evaluating those sources, reading to gather information, taking notes, and documenting your sources. A research project easily spans several weeks. So as not to lose track of time and find yourself facing an impossible deadline at the last moment, establish a realistic deadline for each key task, and stick to your schedule.

RESCH 1a Set a schedule and follow it.

A library research project can be broken down into eight key tasks or stages. By thinking of the research paper as a multi-staged process, you avoid becoming overwhelmed by the size of the undertaking. If your instructor has given you five weeks to complete your project, consider the following time allotments:

1. Choose a suitable research topic or question (2 days).
2. Prepare a working bibliography (4 days).
3. Develop a preliminary thesis and make a working outline (2 days).
4. Take complete and accurate notes (5–6 days).
5. Arrive at a final thesis and modify your outline (2 days).
6. Write a first draft, citing sources (8–9 days).

7. Revise your paper and proof citations, including the list of works cited (7 days).
8. Prepare your final copy and proofread (2 days).

Your schedule, like the preceding one, should allow at least a few days to accommodate unforeseen needs or delays.

The research process is by nature recursive, meaning that you may find yourself returning to one or more of the earlier steps no matter how carefully you plan and carry out each step. For example, while writing a first draft, you may discover that you need certain statistics to support a point you want to make. You return to the library. That means time spent locating the right source before you can finish drafting your paper.

RESCH 1b   Choose a suitable research topic or question.

The first step in the research process—**selecting a suitable topic**—may be the most important task in the entire research paper project. A clearly focused topic makes researching and writing the paper manageable and the likelihood of sound—even exciting—results possible.

Sometimes your instructor will assign a topic or give you a list of topics from which to choose. Be sure that you understand what your instructor is asking for and that the topic you select from the list really interests you. But what happens when you are allowed to choose your own topic and nothing comes to mind immediately? Relax. Spend a day or two brainstorming (see COMP 2d) and observing what interests you. Jot down interesting contemporary or historical persons, important social issues, intriguing political happenings, noteworthy medical and scientific discoveries, environmental crises, artistic movements and achievements, controversies in sports, economic issues in a global setting, puzzling moral and ethical issues—in short, anything that interests you or that you want to know more about.

In compiling your list of possible research subjects, you will find that one or two subjects interest you more than the others. These are worth pursuing further. However, avoid subjects for which there are not sufficient research materials in your college library. That is, avoid subjects so recent or so obscure that very little has been published about them anywhere (for example, Which partner gets frozen embryos in a divorce settlement?), subjects based almost exclusively on your own experiences (What are my personal religious beliefs, and why?), subjects that are highly speculative (What if money spent on Mars exploration had been spent on programs for social improvement?), and subjects that are too technical for your general audience (How is laser technology used in medicine?).

Having settled on a general subject (see COMP 2b), you now need to limit that subject to a manageable topic. It cannot be emphasized enough that your topic should feel right from the very start. Do not select a topic because you think it will be easy to write about—too often seemingly easy topics turn out to be the most difficult to write on. Also do not select a topic just because it is popular. Rather, choose a topic that genuinely interests you and that is manageable given your time and resources. Finally, if you have any doubts about your topic, consult with your instructor about its suitability for the assignment.

One effective way of focusing on a topic is to brainstorm by asking some specific questions about your subject (See COMP 2c and 2d.) At the start of her research project, Patricia LaRose, the student who wrote the sample research paper in RESCH 5, chose *recycling paper waste in the United States* as her subject and brainstormed the following list of possible **research questions** on her computer:

> How serious is our paper waste problem?
>
> How much of our paper waste is currently being recycled?
>
> Is recycling paper waste an economic or an environmental issue?
>
> Should Americans be required to recycle household paper waste?
>
> What are the problems of collecting waste paper?
>
> What is currently being done with old newspapers and telephone books?
>
> What is made from recycled paper?
>
> Do newspapers use recycled newsprint?
>
> If we don't recycle old newspapers, what will be the impact on
>
> > our environment?
>
> Should we concentrate on recycling non-biodegradable wastes first?

Each question narrows the general subject area, suggesting a more manageable research project. Also, simply phrasing your topic as a question gives you a starting point; that is, if you think in terms of a *research question*, your work has focus and direction from the outset. A one- or two-sentence answer to your research question often provides you with a preliminary thesis statement (see COMP 2e). Finally, when you are ready to begin planning your paper, you can approach the task in terms of exploring and answering your research question.

LaRose reviewed her list and found she kept returning to the question about what Americans do with their old newspapers and telephone books. At this point LaRose was ready to head to the library and start her research.

RESCH 2

Conducting Library Research

Your library research will involve working with both print sources and online sources. In both cases, though, the process is essentially the same: you are winnowing sources from many to the best few. (For a discussion of the resources available in most college libraries, see LIB.)

RESCH 2a Use the library's print sources.

Previewing print sources

Although you want to be thorough in your research, you will soon realize that you do not have the time to read every source. Rather, you must preview your sources to decide which you will read, which you will skim, and which you will simply eliminate.

GUIDELINES FOR PREVIEWING PRINT SOURCES

1. Although a book or article may be about your subject, eliminate it if it is not directly related to your research question.
2. Do not spend time with material that is obviously outdated (for example, a source on nuclear energy from the 1960s).
3. Check tables of contents and indexes in books to locate relevant material quickly.
4. Read the abstract or opening paragraph or two of an article to see if it is what you are looking for; if you are still unsure, quickly skim the piece.

One last piece of advice: at this early stage of research, it is better to err on the side of listing too many sources rather than later having to find the ones you discarded too hastily.

Developing a working bibliography

For each work that you think might be helpful, make a separate bibliography card, using a 3 × 5-inch index card. As your collection of bibliography cards grows, alphabetize the cards by the authors' last names. Using separate cards for each book or article allows you to edit your working bibliography continually, dropping sources that are not helpful for one reason or another and adding new ones.

Make sure you record *all* the necessary information about each source for which you make a bibliography card. You will use the cards to compile the **final bibliography,** or the **list of Works Cited,** for your paper. (See MLA DOCU 2 and OTHER DOCU 2 and 4.) For books, record the following information:

> All authors; any editors or translators
> Title and subtitle
> Edition (if not the first)
> Publication data: city, publishing company, and date
> Call number

For periodical articles, record the following information:

> All authors
> Title and subtitle
> Title of journal, magazine, or newspaper
> Volume and issue numbers
> Date and page numbers

Sample bibliography cards

BIBLIOGRAPHY CARD: ARTICLE

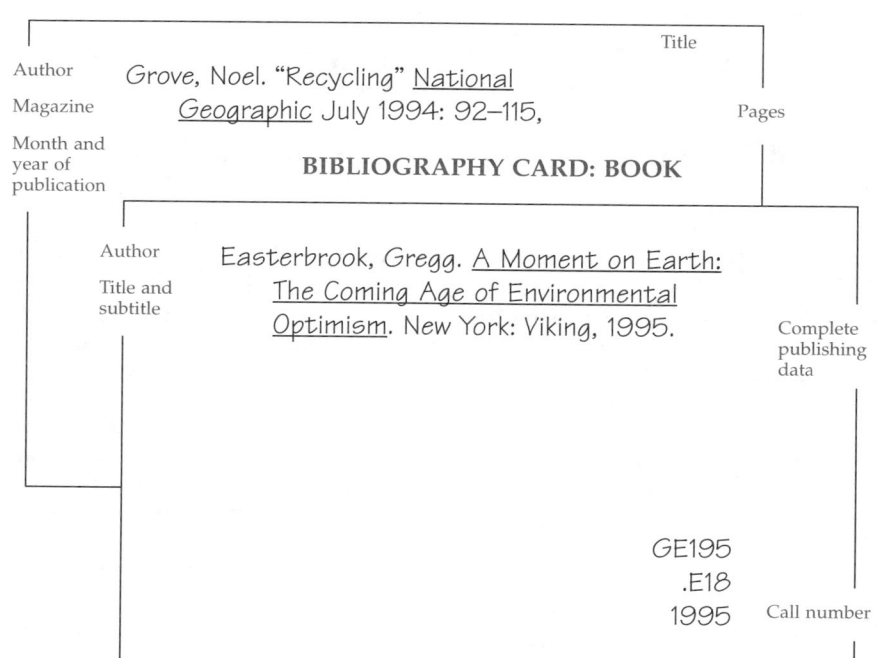

Title

Author   *Grove, Noel. "Recycling"* <u>National</u>
Magazine   <u>Geographic</u> July 1994: 92–115,   Pages
Month and
year of
publication   **BIBLIOGRAPHY CARD: BOOK**

Author   Easterbrook, Gregg. <u>A Moment on Earth</u>:
Title and   <u>The Coming Age of Environmental</u>
subtitle   <u>Optimism</u>. New York: Viking, 1995.   Complete
                                                                publishing
                                                                data

                                              GE195
                                               .E18
                                              1995   Call number

Using correct bibliographic form ensures that your entries are complete, reduces the chance of introducing careless errors, and saves time when you are ready to prepare your final bibliography. For specific directions on how to write bibliographic entries for various other types of sources, consult MLA DOCU 2 and OTHER DOCU 2 and 4.

Evaluating your print sources

Before beginning to take notes, evaluate your sources for their relevance and reliability in helping you answer your research question. Look for the writers' main ideas (do not lapse into reading material just because it seems interesting). Also look for information about the authors themselves, information that will indicate their authority and perspective on the issue.

QUESTIONS FOR EVALUATING PRINT SOURCES

1. Does your source clearly relate to your research question?
2. Is your source too abstract, too general, or too technical for your needs?
3. Does your source reflect current thinking and research in the field?
4. Does your source promote a particular view, or is it meant to inform?
5. What biases, if any, does your source exhibit?
6. Is the author of your source an authority on the issue? Do other writers mention the author of your source in their work?

RESCH 2b   Use the library's online sources.

Previewing websites

The abundance of print sources available in your library does not even approach the number of online sources available to you. Your library is local, but the Internet is a global network of computers and computer users. You can access information stored on computers anywhere in the world, and communicate with people worldwide who might have information on your research topic.

Given the abundance of Internet sources, the key to successful online research is identifying the websites and other online sources that will help you the most. (See LIB 4.) Use the following questions to weed out sources that hold no promise (we focus on websites here because you will find yourself using them most often).

QUESTIONS FOR PREVIEWING WEBSITES

1. Scan the homepage of the site. Do the contents and links appear to be related to your research topic?

2. Can you identify the author of the site? Are the author's credentials available?

3. Has the site been updated within the last six months? (This information is usually given at the bottom of the homepage.)

 C-Tip

Using bookmarks

Take a few minutes to learn how to use your Web browser's bookmarks or hotlist feature. This feature allows you to electronically capture website addresses of potentially useful sources. By merely clicking on an address in your bookmarks, you can revisit a site quickly and as often as you need. Later, as your research project develops and the number of sites you collect increases, you may want to categorize the bookmarks by subtopics of your research question.

Remember, too, that the copy and paste feature of your Web browser enables you to accurately capture website addresses in your working bibliography, thus eliminating the possibility of error.

Developing a working bibliography

Just as for print sources, you must maintain accurate records for the online sources you use. You can record each online source on a 3×5-inch card, or you can set up a separate file where you maintain an ongoing research log. Either way, this is the information you need for each source:

All authors or sponsoring agents

Title and subtitle of the document

Title of longer work to which the document belongs (if applicable)

Document date (or date last modified)

Date you accessed the site

Publishing data (place: publisher, date) for print version (if available)

Address of the site, URL or network path (see LIB 4)

Evaluating your online sources

The quality of sources on the Internet varies tremendously. You will, therefore, want to evaluate the sites in your working bibliography carefully.

Questions for Evaluating Websites

Identify the Type of Web Page

Who hosts the website? Often the top-level domain name indicates the source of information provided. These are the most common top-level domain names:

com	Business/commercial
edu	Educational institution
gov	Government
mil	Military
net	Various types of networks
org	Nonprofit organization

Authority/Author

Is it clear what individual or company is responsible for the site?

Can you verify if the site is sanctioned officially by an organization or company?

What are the author's or company's qualifications for writing on this subject?

Is there a way to verify the legitimacy of this individual or company (for example, are there links to a homepage or résumé)?

Purpose and Audience

What appears to be the author's or sponsor's purpose in publishing this website?

Who is the intended audience?

Objectivity

Are advertising, opinion, and factual information clearly distinguished?

What biases, if any, can you detect?

Accuracy

Is important information documented through links so that it can be verified in other sources?

Is the text well written and free of careless errors in spelling and grammar?

Coverage and Currency

Is there any indication that the site is still under construction?

For sources with print equivalents, is the Web version more or less extensive?

How detailed is the treatment of the topic?

Is there any indication of the currency of the information (date of last update or statement regarding frequency of updates)?

Are the graphics helpful, or are they simply window dressing?

Downloading Web files to disk

When you find a useful website for your paper, you may want to download the entire file to disk so that you can refer to it later offline. If you are working in the library, downloading cuts down your time on-line and allows other students to access online materials. Downloading is also insurance against a source being removed from the Internet.

 *C-Tip*

Downloading a website file

To download a website using Netscape, for example, go into the File menu and use the Save As option, and then save the file using its URL name or renaming it. If you save the file with an .htm or .html extension, you can re-open the file directly with Netscape.

If you are more comfortable working with hard copy, you can print documents directly from the online website or from your down-loaded file. Hard copy is easier to read than a computer screen, and it allows you to mark it up as you analyze it. If the printout does not include the title of the site, the URL, and the date you accessed it, make a handwritten notation of this information on the printout because you will need it later when you compile your list of Works Cited.

RESCH 2c Systematically take complete and accurate notes of your reading.

Having collected a number of print and online sources that look helpful in researching your topic, you are ready to begin taking notes. As you work through your sources, look for pertinent facts, opinions, statistics, and examples. But look especially for connections among ideas and recurring themes. Keep in mind that you are not merely collecting information but analyzing and synthesizing what you find.

Jot down the patterns you see—and the pieces that do not fit in. By looking at evidence on both sides, you will refine your topic and begin to see possible organizational plans. If you find yourself thinking in terms of the paper's main units or general movement and direction, make a rough outline. Having some sense of your paper's shape can, in turn, direct further research efforts. And remember, you are always free to modify your thinking as you conduct your research.

Now for some practical advice on **taking notes:** first and most important, be systematic. As a rule, write one note on a card, and use cards of uniform size (preferably 4 × 6-inch index cards because they are large enough to accommodate a long note on a single card and small enough to be easily handled and conveniently carried). More important, when you get to planning and writing your paper, you will be able to organize your notes according to your organizational plan. Furthermore, should you alter your outline, you can easily reorder your cards to reflect the changes.

The quality of your research paper will be determined by the quality—and not the quantity—of your notes. In fact, try not to take too many notes. Novice researchers often write down anything and everything that looks remotely usable only to discover later that most of their notes are irrelevant. Besides being a waste of valuable research time, too many note cards make it difficult to glean what is important from what is not. Before taking a note ask yourself, "How exactly does this material help prove or disprove my thesis?" You might even try envisioning where you could use the information in your paper.

A useful note card has three essential parts and one optional part.

Elements of a note card

1. **Topic heading** In the upper left corner of the note card, write a topic heading—a key word or phrase that describes the contents of the note—and underline it for easy identification. Thoughtful topic headings make it easy to organize your notes and then outline your paper.
2. **Note** Take the note as a summary, a paraphrase, or a direct quotation (explained on the following pages).
3. **Source** Record the author's last name and the page number on which you found the information; this is enough information because you have the full reference in your preliminary bibliography.
4. **Comment** (*optional*) Record any thoughts you have on the source or on how the material might be used. Do not trust ideas like these to your memory. Be sure to separate these comments or in some other way indicate that your commentary is not part of your actual note.

Whether to summarize, paraphrase, or quote directly largely depends upon the nature of the item and the way you envision using it in your paper.

Summary

When you **summarize** material from a source, you capture in your own words the essential idea of a passage or of an entire chapter or article in highly condensed form. Summaries are particularly useful when you are working with lengthy, detailed arguments or long passages of descriptive background information. You can distill a chapter or more into a paragraph or several paragraphs into a sentence or two.

Following are two paragraphs from a book source that LaRose used in researching her paper and the summary note she took.

> The *Titanic* sank twenty minutes after hitting an iceberg. The ship's reckless captain failed to appreciate that over 90 percent of an iceberg is hidden from view; even though the iceberg looked far away to the ship's stunned passengers, its submerged base had poked a fatal hole through the *Titanic*'s hull.
>
> Waste is like an iceberg. Ninety-five percent of it is hidden from view; the four pounds of discards we put in our trash cans each day represent only a fraction of our total waste. And, like icebergs, our wastepiles pose major obstacles to our path of resource conservation. They can sink us if we don't reduce their threat. We can't melt icebergs, but we can trim waste.
>
> —Arthur H. Purcell, *The Waste Watchers* (Garden City, NY: Anchor Books, 1980), 14–15

SUMMARY NOTE CARD

<u>Waste problem</u>

Purcell likens waste to an iceberg. Because we are not aware of the size/amount of our waste, the danger is greater than we think.

Purcell, pp. 14–15

Paraphrase

When you **paraphrase** a source, you restate the information in your own words instead of quoting the source directly. Unlike a summary, which is a short version of the essential information in the original, a paraphrase presents the information in the original in approximately the same number of words, but the wording is your own. That is, a paraphrase should closely parallel the presentation of ideas in the original but not use the same words or sentence structure as the original. To do so would be to plagiarize. (See RESCH 4d.)

Following are the original source and LaRose's paraphrase note card.

> Curbside recycling did not begin in earnest until the mid-1980s, when the national recycling rate was 3 percent. Today the rate hovers around 22 percent. Some 3,700 U.S. curbside collection programs existed in 1993 vs. 600 five years before. Some of these programs are expensive turkeys; most are affordable and successful. As a result, even with ever-increasing consumption in several major categories of consumer products, the amount of materials sent to municipal landfills peaked in the late 1980s and has been declining since. Already, several states and cities have recycling levels as high as those found in Japan. New Jersey has gone from a standing start to recycling 53 percent of municipal wastes, under a program whose target was 25 percent. Seattle recycles about 50 percent, the level achieved in Tokyo.
>
> —Gregg Easterbrook, "Good News from Planet Earth,"
> *USA Weekend* 14–16 Apr. 1995: 5.

PARAPHRASE NOTE CARD

> <u>Curbside recycling efforts</u>
>
> Curbside recycling programs have had a tremendous impact on the problems of waste disposal in this country. Since its inception in the mid-1980s, curbside recycling has risen from 3 percent to almost 22 percent today. And in the years 1988 through 1993 curbside collection programs increased more than sixfold. Not coincidentally, Americans have managed to keep landfill deposits down while their rate of consumption continues to rise. The state of New Jersey and the city of Seattle have model recycling programs, rivaling the results already achieved in Japan.
>
> Easterbrook, p. 5

In most cases it is better to summarize or paraphrase source materials—restating them in your own words—than it is to quote them verbatim (word for word). In the paraphrase note card, for example, LaRose says "in the years 1988 through 1993, curbside collection programs increased more than sixfold" so as to avoid Easterbrook's wording "Some 3,700 U.S. curbside collection programs existed in 1993 vs.

600 five years before." LaRose's reconceptualization of the figures shows that she has captured the idea in her own words. Paraphrasing requires that you think about an idea and understand it.

Direct quotation

When you **directly quote** your source, you copy the words of your source *exactly*, putting all quoted material in quotation marks. When you take a direct quotation note, carefully check for accuracy, including punctuation and capitalization. (See PUNCT 5.) Be selective about what you choose to quote. Reserve direct quotation for important ideas stated in memorable language, for especially clear explanations by authorities, and for proponents' arguments conveyed in their own words.

Following are a source LaRose quoted directly because of its startling specificity and the quotation note card she wrote.

> In those eight tons of garbage and dirt cover there were fewer than sixteen pounds of fast-food packaging; in other words, only about a tenth of one percent of the landfills' contents by weight consisted of fast-food packaging. Less than one percent of the contents by weight was disposable diapers. The entire category of things made from plastic accounted for less than 5 percent of the landfills' contents by weight, and only 12 percent by volume. The real culprit in every landfill is plain old paper—non-fast-food paper, and mostly paper that isn't for packaging. Paper accounts for 40 to 50 percent of everything we throw away, both by weight and by volume.
> —William L. Rathje, "Rubbish!" *The Atlantic Monthly* Dec. 1989: 102

QUOTATION NOTE CARD

<u>Paper waste</u>

"In those eight tons of garbage and dirt cover there were fewer than sixteen pounds of fast-food packaging; in other words, only about a tenth of one percent of the landfills' contents by weight consisted of fast-food packaging. Less than one percent of the contents by weight was disposable diapers. The entire category of things made from plastic accounted for less than 5 percent of the landfills' contents by weight, and only 12 percent by volume. The real culprit in every landfill is plain old paper—non-fast-food paper, and mostly paper that isn't for packaging. Paper accounts for 40 to 50 percent of everything we throw away, both by weight and by volume."

Rathje, p. 102

What if LaRose had chosen to use only part of the statement as a direct quotation? She could combine summary or paraphrase with quotation as in the following note card. Notice that LaRose is careful to put quotation marks around all words that are quoted directly.

QUOTATION AND SUMMARY NOTE CARD

<u>Paper waste</u>

A team of landfill archeologists made some surprising discoveries when they analyzed eight tons of garbage taken from several sites. Fast-food packaging, disposable diapers, and plastic items were not as plentiful as some environmentalists suspected. "The real culprit in every landfill is plain old paper— non-fast-food paper, and mostly paper that isn't for packaging. Paper accounts for 40 to 50 percent of everything we throw away, both by weight and by volume."

Rathje, p. 102

 C-Tip

Note Taking on the Internet

You can easily and accurately capture passages of text from the Internet by copying them into a separate computer file on your hard drive or diskette. In Netscape, for example, use your mouse to highlight the part of the text you want to save, and then use the copy and paste features to add it to your file of research notes. You can use the same commands to capture bibliographic information. (See RESCH 2b.)

In taking notes, it is extremely important that you be accurate. Check all direct quotations against the wording of the original source, and double-check your paraphrases to be sure you have not inadvertently used the writer's wording or sentence structure. If you are careful at the note-taking stage, you greatly reduce your chances of committing *plagiarism*—the unacknowledged use of someone else's ideas or wording. Plagiarism is discussed in depth in RESCH 4d, but it is important in note-taking because inadvertent plagiarism often begins at this stage. The writer is always held responsible for plagiarism, no matter how inadvertent.

RESCH 2d Use interviews, questionnaires, and other community sources to supplement your library research.

Some research topics lend themselves to another type of research—community-based research. Often we become so involved with our reading in the library that we forget about the rich research possibilities in our communities. As LaRose was learning more and more about recycling efforts at the national level, she wondered what was happening at the state and local levels. She identified several local authorities and interviewed them, gathering information she could use in her paper. (See RESCH 5.) Another student writing a research paper on the nature of friendship came up with the idea of finding out what other students thought. He constructed a brief six-item questionnaire and administered it to everyone in his dormitory. He was able to use the results of this questionnaire to support several key points in his research paper. Finally, a third student who was researching the Ronald McDonald House Foundation visited the local Ronald McDonald House. There she not only spoke with staff and families staying in the facility, she also received an assortment of publications about the foundation that gave her a great deal of up-to-date information. So, as you are working your way through your library resources, be thinking about research opportunities that await you in your community.

RESCH 3

Organizing the Research Paper

Having taken notes on the connections, patterns, and recurring or opposing ideas, opinions, and facts in your sources, you are now ready to develop an organizational plan for the position you want to take in your paper.

RESCH 3a Formulate a final thesis.

The first step in developing an overall plan for your paper is reevaluating your preliminary thesis. Do you want to commit to it? Or, in the course of doing research and note-taking, has your thesis evolved? This is what happened to LaRose. She found in the course of doing research that her preliminary thesis—*Americans are currently collecting more old newsprint than they can recycle*—had shifted focus. From wanting to find out what is being done with old newspapers and telephone books, LaRose found herself more specifically interested in the uses of old newsprint. This shift in focus was, of course, reflected in her note-taking: she had many notes under the topic headings *uses for recycled newsprint, the recycling process, the enormous amount of waste, collection efforts,* and *future uses.*

True to the recursive nature of research (see RESCH 1a), then, LaRose reformulated her thesis. She decided to take a much stronger, more argumentative position in her final thesis: *To stem the tide of the tremendous newspaper waste problem, Americans must find long-term uses for old newsprint that are environmentally and economically sustainable.*

At this time, too, LaRose thought about her purpose—whether her paper would be largely informative or persuasive. (See COMP 2f.) Initially, she intended to write an informative report on the status of newsprint recycling efforts. Now, though, based on her research, she decided to add a persuasive edge to her paper; she thought it important to urge her readers to make recycling part of their lifestyle.

RESCH 3b Develop a working outline.

With a final thesis in mind, you are ready to sort your note cards by topic headings and develop a **working outline.** You may want to take this working outline in steps, starting with a brief list of what you will cover and in what order. It is a quick way of concretizing your thinking. You can start with your scratch outline if you made one while taking notes. This is the list LaRose created:

1. Newsprint as a major problem--the enormous amount of waste
2. Efforts to collect and recycle old newsprint
3. The process of recycling old newsprint
4. Uses for recycled newsprint--what's currently being done
5. What needs to be done--future uses of recycled newsprint

From your list, move on to create an informal outline. (See COMP 2h.) Use the examples, quotations, figures and statistics, and other facts and ideas you collected in your research to flesh out your main ideas. This working outline will serve as your plan for writing the initial draft of your paper. As the name implies, the *working* outline can itself change as you write. The outline you submit with your paper is a final, cleaned-up version of your working outline—the one that reflects all the changes you made while drafting and revising. LaRose's final outline is included with her research paper in RESCH 5.

RESCH 4

Writing the Research Paper

Writing and revising a research paper is like writing and revising an essay or a composition (see COMP), with one difference—you are relying more heavily on information collected from various sources. You will want to learn, then, how to integrate your research findings into your paper without plagiarizing and how to document your sources correctly.

RESCH 4a Document your sources using the MLA style or APA style.

Whenever you use information from a note card, you must cite your source in the paper. Your citations must consistently follow an established system of documentation, such as that of the Modern Language Association (MLA style) or the American Psychological Association (APA style). Your instructor will tell you which to use.

But before we discuss the *do's* of correct documentation, keep one *don't* in mind: do not clutter your paper with citations for facts or common knowledge. For example, it is common knowledge that Sandra Day O'Connor is the first woman to serve on the Supreme Court and that the Soviet Union ceased to exist in 1992. Look for *repeated* facts. LaRose, for example, quickly discovered in her research that most of her sources pointed to the 1980s as the decade that conservationists first pushed for recycling newsprint. Because this was a fact that could be objectively verified, and because many sources mentioned the fact as baseline knowledge, LaRose decided it was common knowledge and thus did not document it in her paper.

There are two main elements of documentation in a research paper. The **in-text citation** is placed within the body of the paper. (See MLA DOCU 1 and OTHER DOCU 1.) The **list of works cited,** which provides complete publication data on your sources, is placed at the end of the paper. (See MLA DOCU 2 and OTHER DOCU 2.)

In-text citations usually consist of the author's last name and a page reference. Often the author's name is given in an introductory or signal phrase at the beginning of the borrowed material and only the page reference is given in parentheses at the end. If the author's name is not given at the beginning, put it in the parentheses together with the page number. The parenthetical reference signals the end of the borrowed material and directs readers to the list of works cited should they want to pursue a source.

IN-TEXT CITATION (MLA STYLE)

According to Leslie Pardue, Earth Care Paper Company sells a variety of recycled paper products, as well as educational materials on recycling for classroom use (56).

WORKS CITED ENTRY (MLA STYLE)

Pardue, Leslie. "What Goes Around Comes Around: A Look at Paper

Recycling." E Magazine Mar.-Apr. 1990: 54-56.

For a complete discussion of MLA-style in-text citations, see MLA DOCU 1. If your instructor asks you to use *Chicago Manual* documentation style, see OTHER DOCU 4; if your instructor prefers APA style, consult OTHER DOCU 1.

RESCH 4b   Integrate quotations smoothly.

When you refer to borrowed material in your research paper, whether by summary, paraphrase, or direct quotation, it is best to introduce the material with a **signal phrase,** which alerts the reader that the borrowed information is about to be stated. Signal phrases (such as, *according to Leslie Pardue*) help the reader follow your train of thought. They also tell the reader who is speaking and, in the case of summaries and paraphrases, signal phrases indicate exactly where your ideas end and someone else's begin. Without a signal phrase to integrate a quotation into the flow of your paper, the quotation seems to come from nowhere and jars the reader. Consider the following examples:

UNANNOUNCED QUOTATION

Most Americans think that we are producing more trash per person than ever, that plastic is a huge problem, and that paper biodegrades quickly in landfills. "The biggest challenge we will face is to recognize that the conventional wisdom about garbage is often wrong" (Rathje 99).

INTEGRATED QUOTATION

Most Americans think that we are producing more trash per person than ever, that plastic is a huge problem, and that paper biodegrades quickly in landfills. William L. Rathje, director of the Garbage Project at the University of Arizona, views the issue differently; he believes that "the biggest challenge we will face is to recognize that the conventional wisdom about garbage is often wrong" (99).

The quotation in the second example is integrated into the text not only by means of a signal phrase, but in two other ways as well. By mentioning the speaker's authority and that he "views the issue differently," LaRose provides even more of a context for the reader to understand how the quotation fits into the discussion.

How well you integrate a quotation, paraphrase, or summary into your paper also depends partly on your choice of signal phrase, in particular, the verb in the signal phrase. It is the verb that conveys the tone and intent of the writer being cited. If a source is arguing, use the verb *argue* (or *asserts, claims,* or *contends*); if a source contests a particular position or fact, use *disagrees* (or *denies, disputes, refutes,* or *rejects*); if a source agrees with a particular position or fact, use *concurs* (or *admits, concedes,* or *grants*). By using verbs that are specific to the situation in your paper, you help the reader process and organize the information you are presenting and thereby better understand your use of the quotation. Also, by choosing verbs carefully, you avoid the monotony of repeating the overworked *notes, says, states,* or *writes*. For advice on integrating quotations from literary texts, see LIT 3, RESCH 4c, and MLA DOCU 1.

RESCH 4c   Set off long quotations.

Set off or block prose quotations that are longer than four lines to help your reader more clearly see the quotation as a whole. Verse quotations are set off when longer than three lines. Set-off quotations are indented ten spaces from the left margin and double-spaced; no quotation marks are necessary because the format itself indicates the passage is a quotation. When you are quoting two or more paragraphs from the same source, indent the first line of each paragraph three additional spaces.

Patricia LaRose quotes a lengthy passage from Purcell in her research paper because his vivid description and concrete facts capture the drama and proportions of Garden State Paper's recycling efforts. (See RESCH 5, p. 330.) The impact on the reader is much greater than if LaRose had summarized or paraphrased instead.

The following example is taken from student Karen Bellitto's library research paper on John Updike's story "A Sense of Shelter."

> Fearing rejection from his fellow high school seniors, William chooses to sit with the more accepting juniors, who tend to look up to him as an older student. In addition, Updike sharply contrasts William's behavior with that of the character he loves, Mary, who is more adventurous. Critic A.S.G. Edwards explains this contrast:
>
>> On each of the three occasions she appears, Updike presents her <u>going away</u> from William's world, away from the classroom, out of the soda bar, and finally out of the school itself. This final encounter effectively dramatizes the nature of the contrasting characters: Mary's steady progression through and finally away from the school out into the cold world more appropriate to her greater experience and maturity is set against William's hurried retreat into the womb-like warmth of the school. (467)

The colon following Bellitto's sentence introducing the quotation indicates that the quotation is closely related to what precedes it. Note that, unlike an integrated quotation in which the parenthetical citation is inside the end punctuation, with a long quotation the parenthetical citation goes outside the final punctuation, according to MLA style.

On occasion, long quotations contain more information than you need to use. In such situations you can use an ellipsis mark (see PUNCT 6g) to show that you omitted material from the original text, in this way keeping the quotation to the point and as short as possible.

Another mark of punctuation that is useful when working with quotations is brackets. (See PUNCT 6f.) These squared parentheses allow you to insert your own words into a quotation to explain a pronoun reference, for example, or to change a verb tense to fit your text.

According to Rathje, "There are no ways of dealing with it [garbage] that haven't been known for many thousands of years" (100).

RESCH 4d Credit other people's ideas to avoid plagiarism.

The importance of honesty and accuracy in doing library research cannot be stressed enough. Any material borrowed word-for-word must be placed within quotation marks and properly cited; any idea, explanation, or argument you borrow in a summary or paraphrase must be documented, and it must be clear where the borrowed material begins and ends. In short, to use someone else's ideas in their original form or in an altered form without proper acknowledgment is **plagiarism.** And plagiarism is a serious offense regardless of whether it occurs intentionally or accidentally.

A little attention and effort at certain stages in the research process can go a long way in eliminating the possibility of inadvertent plagiarism. At the note-taking stage, check what you record on your note card against the original, paying particular attention to word choice and word order, especially if you are paraphrasing. It is not enough simply to use a synonym here or there and think it is a paraphrase; you must restate the idea in your own words, using your own style. At the drafting stage, check whenever you incorporate a source into your paper, be careful to put quotation marks around material taken verbatim, and double-check your text against your note card—or better yet, against the original source if you have it on hand.

The following example illustrates how plagiarism can occur when care is not taken in the wording or sentence structure of a paraphrase. Finally, an acceptable paraphrase of the original source is given.

ORIGINAL SOURCE

In theory, recycled paper should be cheaper, since it turns garbage that someone would otherwise have to pay to dispose of into a marketable commodity.   —Leslie Pardue, "What Goes Around Comes Around,"
E Magazine Mar.-Apr. 1990: 56

UNACCEPTABLY CLOSE WORDING

Turning someone's garbage into a marketable product while avoiding the costs of disposal would seem in theory to make recycled paper less expensive (Pardue 56).

UNACCEPTABLY CLOSE SENTENCE STRUCTURE

It seems only reasonable that recycled paper would be less expensive because it turns someone's waste that would have to be landfilled into a new product (Pardue 56).

ACCEPTABLE PARAPHRASE

By eliminating landfill costs, recycling, according to Pardue, should enable people to produce paper that is less expensive than paper made from virgin pulp (56).

If at any time while you are taking notes or writing your paper you have a question about plagiarism, it is your responsibility to consult your instructor for clarification and guidance before proceeding.

RESCH 5

Annotated Student Research Paper

Patricia LaRose, a student, wrote the research paper that appears on the following pages. Her paper is the product of a sustained research and writing effort that stretched over a period of five weeks. Beginning with her choice of a research question, LaRose stayed on task as she prepared a working bibliography, took notes, reformulated her thesis, made a working outline, and wrote an initial draft. She took her rough draft through several revisions before arriving at the final copy presented here.

LaRose used the MLA guidelines for manuscript preparation presented in FORMAT 2. She also used the MLA style of in-text citations (MLA DOCU 1), informational endnotes (MLA DOCU 3), and list of works cited (MLA DOCU 2) to document her research paper. LaRose was required to include a title page (FORMAT 2) and a final outline (COMP 2h) with her paper (some instructors—as well as the MLA guidelines—do not require these items).

Recycling Used Newsprint:

Coming to Terms with an Environmental Problem

Title is centered
and placed
about a third of
the way down
the page.

by

Patricia LaRose

Six lines below
the title, center *by*,
skip two lines,
and center your
name.

English 001, Section G

Professor P. Eschholz

April 1, 1999

Course information is centered
and double-spaced.

LaRose ii

Outline

Annotation: *Title piques readers' interest and announces the writer's topic (See COMP 3a.)*

Title: Recycling Used Newsprint: Coming to Terms with an Environmental Problem

Annotation: *Thesis answers the research question. (See RESCH 1b.)*

Thesis: To stem the tide of newspaper waste, Americans will have to find long-term uses for old newsprint that are environmentally and economically sustainable.

Annotation: *Purpose is to inform and urge reform. (See COMP 2f and RESCH 3a.)*

Purpose: To show there is a serious problem with newspaper waste in the United States and to explore some environmentally and economically sound solutions.

Annotation: *Introduction conveys the writer's strategy for developing the thesis.*

Introduction: Trash disposal, especially of old newsprint, is one of America's most pressing environmental problems. It is not enough simply to recognize the problem and start recycling programs; long-term uses for old newsprint must be identified and developed.

Annotation: *Topic outline; for an example of a sentence outline, see COMP 2h.*

I. Recycling old newspapers in the 1980s

   A. Success of early collection efforts

   B. Low demand for old newsprint

   C. Programs needed to meet projected supply

II. Current uses for old newsprint

   A. Egg cartons

   B. Paperboard

   C. Kitty litter

   D. Cellulose flowerpots

   E. Cereal boxes

   F. Corrugated cardboard boxes

   G. Books

LaRose iii

Writer's last name and the page number appear in the upper-right corner, one-half inch from the top of the page.

H. Home insulation

I. Wallboard

J. Animal bedding

III. Problems of recycling newsprint as newsprint

IV. Using recycled newsprint as newsprint

    A. Newspapers currently using recycled newsprint

    B. Prospects for the future

Conclusion: In a world of shrinking resources, we must increase pressure on the newspaper industry to recycle old newsprint for use as newsprint and to save our limited supply of virgin pulp for more critical uses.

Conclusion presents the central point the writer wants to leave with readers.

RESCH

5

LaRose 1

Recycling Used Newsprint: Coming to

Terms with an Environmental Problem

Title is centered.

Almost ten years ago, television viewers were shocked at

the pictures of a barge load of trash from Babylon, New York,

as it made its odyssey up and down the eastern seaboard.

At every port it was turned away with the cry that there was

"no room at the inn," while an entourage of seagulls nibbled

away at its decaying cargo. It may have been the first time

most Americans were forced to come face-to-face with the

unpleasant fact that trash is one of our most pressing

problems. The United States is a "throw-away society"

according to Jim Hightower, commissioner of agriculture in

Florida, that every year tosses out "41 million tons of food

and yard waste, 13 million tons of metals, 12 million tons of

glass, and 10 million tons of plastic" (xv-xvi).

Anecdotal
introductory
paragraph
grabs readers'
attention and
involves them
in the issue.

In-text citation
with the
author's name
given in a signal
phrase and the
page number
given in
parentheses.
LaRose uses
MLA-style
documentation.

For a long time Americans identified plastic and

styrofoam as the chief culprits, and perhaps justifiably

so because they are not biodegradable. But with all

the attention we have paid to them, we have ignored a

problem that is even worse. Noel Grove reports that paper

waste accounts for more than 70 million tons annually--

approximately 37 percent of our nation's waste--and that

50 million tons winds up in landfills (112). This is enough

paper waste to fill 2.5 million trailer trucks to the brim.

The problem is not expected to lessen. The Environmental

Protection Agency calculates that paper waste deposited

in landfills will reach 66 million tons by the year 2000

Paraphrase of a
source with the
author's name
in a signal
phrase and the
page number
in parentheses.
LaRose could
have presented
these landfill
statistics
graphically as
a pie chart. (see
FORMAT 1c.)

LaRose 2

(Carra 223). By most estimates Americans consume about 580 pounds of paper per person, more than any other nation in the world, and only about 25 percent of it is recycled.

As this paper blitz fills dumps, it is also emptying forests. Each Christmas Americans, according to one study, consume 11 million trees just for paper to wrap presents, and this gift-wrap in turn results in 62,500 tons of waste in dumps and landfills (Eller). William L. Rathje, director of the Garbage Project at the University of Arizona, reports that telephone books from the city of Phoenix alone accounted for 6,000 tons of waste in 1989 (102). The real culprit, however, is old newsprint (ONP). According to Rathje, newspapers account for the greatest amount of paper waste, using up 10-18 percent of the area of the typical landfill by volume (102). Every week in the United States an estimated half million trees are consumed to produce Sunday newspapers. To stem the tide of the tremendous newspaper waste problem, Americans must find long-term uses for old newsprint that are environmentally and economically sustainable.

In the early 1980s conservationists called for the recycling of newspaper along with other solid wastes. The results surpassed expectations. Elizabeth A. Brown reports that in 1988 almost one-third of the 13.6 million tons of newsprint used in the United States was collected after use from consumers (12). Collection efforts proved

Citation of a one-page article needs only the author's name in parentheses.

To establish Rathje's authority on the subject, LaRose gives his title in the signal phrase.

By establishing the immensity of the problem, LaRose has prepared readers for her thesis: long-term solutions are needed.

LaRose 3

so successful that by the early 1990s the supply of ONP exceeded the demand for it.

LaRose defines "recycling loop" for her general audience. (See COMP 2g.)

Instead of entering the recycling loop--the cycle that takes a product from the consumer to the recycling bin to a manufacturer and back again to the consumer for use[1]-- much of the ONP eventually ended up in our nation's landfills. Even today, only about 35 percent of it is truly recycled, that is, reused. The question is no longer, "How will we get people to recycle their used newspapers?" Instead we must ask, "What do we do with old newsprint now that we've collected it?"

Raised note number 1 indicates there is an informational note at the end of the paper.

There has always been a market for old newsprint for the manufacture of such recycled paper products as egg cartons and paperboard. But while people are looking for new ways to use the growing supply of old newsprint, Americans cannot let up on collection efforts. In fact, to make recycling easy for citizens, many towns have instituted curbside sorting. According to environmental reporter Gregg Easterbrook, "some 3,700 U.S. curbside collection programs existed in 1993" and the prospect is for more ("Good News" 5). Other cities and towns,

In citing one of two works by the same author, LaRose gives a shortened title in the parenthetical citation.

Louis Blumberg and Robert Gottlieb note, have already passed ordinances making it an offense punishable by fine to throw old newspapers out with the garbage (208). In most cases these strategies and regulations are only finger-in-the-dike solutions for keeping the mounting stacks of ONP out of our nation's landfills. Programs that will use

In citing a work by multiple authors, LaRose gives both names in the signal phrase.

LaRose 4

current as well as projected future supplies of ONP need to be developed and implemented.

In many places, such efforts are already under way or in the planning stage. In a personal interview, William McGrath of the Vermont Agency of Natural Resources mentioned several possible uses that are being actively explored. Manufacturers are experimenting with using old newspapers in the production of kitty litter. Another use is the manufacture of flowerpots from cellulose--a wood by-product--rather than plastic. The American Forest and Paper Association reports that recovered newsprint is now being used to make "cereal boxes, corrugated cardboard boxes, books, and insulating materials."[2] An upswing in the construction of new homes and commercial buildings would also increase the use of old newspapers for such needed products as wallboard (Lipschutzhe). In the agricultural sector, the Pennsylvania Department of Environmental Protection notes that farmers are finding shredded newspaper an ideal alternative to more expensive animal beddings. All of these potential uses, however, do not begin to exhaust the supply of ONP.

Most experts agree that for sheer volume and reliability of use--and to save our forests--newsprint is the best use of recycled newsprint (Lipschutzhe). And because newspaper publishers create the bulk of the problem, many environmentalists and economists believe that it makes sense that the newspapers themselves take

Using personal interviews to supplement print sources is good research.

No parenthetical page number is given because the online source is not paginated.

After cataloging the uses and potential uses of old newsprint, LaRose describes its best use in the most emphatic position, last. (See SENT 6a.)

LaRose 5

LaRose wisely uses several sources to justify what she claims is the best use of recycled newsprint. LaRose could have opted to present these statistics as a visual. (See FORMAT 1c.)

the lead in solving it. Leslie Pardue observes that "it has been estimated that if recycled paper were used instead of virgin pulp in the production of a single Sunday edition of the New York Times, some 75,000 trees would be saved" (54). Or, looked at from another perspective, "using one ton of 100 percent post-consumer recycled paper saves 17 trees, 3.3 cubic yards of landfill space, 4,100 kilowatt-hours of electricity, 7,000 gallons of water, and approximately 60 pounds of air-polluting effluents" (Shaw 6).

As obvious as this solution appears, it will not be easy to implement. Recycling newsprint for use as newsprint presents myriad problems: it is expensive; it pollutes; and markets for recycled newsprint are scarce. In spite of these problems, many newspapers have taken the lead in the use of ONP. For example, The Los Angeles Times, Arthur H. Purcell reports, receives much of its recycled newsprint from the Garden State Paper Company, a model plant and portent of things to come:

LaRose indents a long quotation ten spaces and double-spaces the text. She omits quotation marks. (See RESCH 4c.)

Ellipses indicate the writer has left out words from the original source. (See PUNCT 6g.)

You will see newly produced, high-quality newsprint spinning off in giant twenty-foot wide rolls at the rate of forty feet per second. Hundreds of yards past the steaming troughs of pulp you discover the source of the raw materials used to make the pulp that forms the newsprint. The source is 100 per cent discarded newspapers. . . . Nine times a day, a giant bucket drops over 35 tons of these papers into the pulping machinery.

LaRose 6

The result is over 300 tons of new, perfectly usable
newsprint every day. (85-86)

If this is a true indication of what can be done, the
outlook is good. Easterbrook shares this optimistic outlook,
citing a Tellus Institute study that showed "recycled-paper
manufacturing was five times more profitable than virgin-
paper production" (<u>Moment</u> 415). As the supply of recycled
newsprint becomes more reliable and the quality more
consistent, more newspapers are likely to increase the
recycled content of their papers.

Newspaper people themselves have seen that recycled
newsprint is the wave of the future. Lawmakers, as Grove
observes, have also lent a helping hand:

> Legislation is helping to force the change. Twelve
> states and the District of Columbia now require
> that newspapers be printed on paper that contains
> some recycled fiber. In 15 more states publishers
> have agreed to do this voluntarily. (113)

The American Forest and Paper Association reported in 1997
that "a little more than one-third of the ONP that is recovered
is recycled into newsprint."

There is no denying that the United States is a throw-
away society, but "a throw-away society is not a sustainable
society" (Hightower xv). Americans simply cannot afford
the dollars or the resources to become complacent in the
assumption that someone else is taking care of the problem.
Government and industry will have to work together to come

Citation in parentheses comes after the end punctuation in a long, set-off quotation.

LaRose signals her conclusion by returning to the idea of a "throw-away society" that was introduced in the opening paragraph.

In her conclusion, LaRose (1) answers her research question, (2) summarizes the body of her paper, (3) tells readers what they can do to help with the problem, and (4) provides closure. LaRose's conclusion shows she has assimilated her research and arrived at an informed opinion on a subject that concerns her.

up with better uses of our limited resources. One possibility that might balance the scales of opportunity would be cutting the subsidies to the timber industry or offering similar incentives to manufacturers of recycled newsprint. It might be wiser still to discontinue subsidies altogether. As Vice President Al Gore argues, we need to question federal policies and subsidies that "encourage further destruction of a critical natural resource" (194). In a world of shrinking resources, it makes sense to recycle old newsprint for use as newsprint and to save the limited supply of virgin pulp for other more critical uses.

In the future American consumers must remain steadfast in their good habits of recycling and of purchasing recycled products. They must continue to pressure the newspaper industry to use more recycled newsprint so that paper manufacturers will continue to invest in the technology and facilities needed to recycle old newsprint in an environmentally safe and economically sound way.

LaRose 8

Notes

[1] For a thorough explanation of the processes involved in recycling paper, see Hagerty, Pavoni, and Heer (58-62); Pardue (54-55); and Randolph. Kent Shaw provides a complete discussion of what is meant by "recycling loop" (1, 6).

[2] Besides providing a potentially huge market for ONP, cellulosic insulation has extremely high insulating properties. For a complete discussion of the advantages and disadvantages of cellulosic insulation, see Purcell (157-62).

Information notes provide additional material or sources of interest to readers.

The notes appear on a separate numbered page immediately after the text and before the list of works cited. (See MLA DOCU 4.)

LaRose double-spaces within and between note entries; she leaves a space but does not put a period after the superscript number.

LaRose 9

Works Cited

American Forest and Paper Association. "Old Newspapers."

    Recycling. 21 May 1997. 9 Sept. 1997 <http://www.

    afandpa.org/Recycling/Paper/index.html#OldNewspapers>.

Blumberg, Louis, and Robert Gottlieb. War on Waste: Can

    America Win Its Battle with Garbage? Washington:

    Island, 1989.

Brown, Elizabeth A. "Paper Recycling Catches on Slowly."

    Christian Science Monitor 14 Nov. 1989: 12-13.

Carra, Joseph S. "Municipal Solid Waste and Sanitary

    Landfilling in the United States of America." International

    Perspectives on Municipal Solid Wastes and Sanitary

    Landfilling. Ed. Joseph S. Carra and Raffaello Cossu.

    San Diego: Academic, 1990. 221-34.

Easterbrook, Gregg. "Good News from Planet Earth." USA

    Weekend 14-16 Apr. 1995: 4-6.

---. A Moment on the Earth: The Coming Age of

    Environmental Optimism. New York: Viking, 1995.

Eller, Daryn. "Spare the Wrappings: Give Trees a Chance."

    Longevity Dec. 1990: 96.

Gore, Al. Earth in the Balance: Ecology and the Human Spirit.

    New York: Plume, 1993.

Grove, Noel. "Recycling." National Geographic July 1994:

    92-115.

Hagerty, D. Joseph, Joseph L. Pavoni, and John E. Heer, Jr.

    Solid Waste Management. New York: Van Nostrand,

    1973.

The heading *Works Cited* is centered at the top of the page.

LaRose uses MLA style for her list of works cited. The list begins on a new page. The first line of each entry begins at the left margin; subsequent lines are indented five spaces. Double-space within entries as well as between entries.

The correct MLA forms for various other kinds of publications are given in MLA DOCU 2; APA forms are given in OTHER DOCU 2.

LaRose 10

Hightower, Jim. Foreword. <u>War on Waste: Can America Win</u>
　　<u>Its Battle with Garbage?</u> By Louis Blumberg and Robert
　　Gottlieb. Washington: Island, 1989. xv-xviii.

Lipschutzhe, Neal. "Recycling Efforts Outpace Capacity to Use
　　Old Papers." <u>Wall Street Journal</u> 1 Oct. 1990: B7.

McGrath, William. Personal interview. 11 Jan. 1993.

Pardue, Leslie. "What Goes Around Comes Around:
　　A Look at Paper Recycling." <u>E Magazine</u>
　　Mar.-Apr. 1990: 54-56.

Pennsylvania Department of Environmental Protection.
　　"Newsprint as Animal Bedding." <u>Pennsylvania</u>
　　<u>Homepage</u>. Aug. 1995. 4 Sept. 1997 <http://www.dep.
　　state.pa.us/dep/deputate/airwaste/wm/recycle/Facts/
　　ANMALB>.

Purcell, Arthur H. <u>The Waste Watchers: A Citizen's Handbook</u>
　　<u>for Conserving Energy and Resources</u>. Garden City:
　　Anchor, 1980.

Randolph, John. "Recycling of Materials." <u>The New Grolier</u>
　　<u>Multimedia Encyclopedia</u>. CD-ROM. Danbury: Grolier
　　Electronic, 1992.

Rathje, William L. "Rubbish!" <u>Atlantic Monthly</u> Dec. 1989:
　　99-106, 108-9.

Shaw, Kent. "Closing the Recycling Loop." <u>Burlington Free</u>
　　<u>Press</u> 26 Nov. 1990, Business Monday: 1+.

mla docu

MLA-Style Documentation

Learning Objectives

After reading this section, you should:

- know how to use MLA in-text citations in your research paper;

- understand how to assemble a list of Works Cited and use the correct formats for books, periodicals, CD-ROMs, and online sources;

- be familiar with the ACW style for citing Internet sources;

- be able to include information notes in your research paper

MLA-Style Documentation

In writing a research paper, you are using the information and ideas of others. Whenever you directly quote, summarize, or paraphrase another person's thoughts and ideas, or use facts and statistics that are not commonly known, you must properly acknowledge your source.

The documentation system recommended by the Modern Language Association (MLA) in the *MLA Handbook for Writers of Research Papers,* 4th edition (1995) is discussed and illustrated in this section. The MLA system is used primarily, although not exclusively, in English and the humanities. We also discuss the Alliance for Computers and Writing (ACW) guidelines for citing electronic sources. The system recommended by the American Psychological Association (APA) is used in the social sciences. We discuss that system in the following section, OTHER DOCU. Other disciplines have their own style manuals; see pages 381–382 for a listing.

MLA DOCU 1

MLA In-Text Citations

In 1984 the MLA adopted the in-text system for documentation. **In-text citations** are easy to use and informative because they immediately let readers know the source of a citation without breaking the flow of the paper. If readers want to consult the source themselves later, complete publication data are provided at the end of the paper in a **List of Works Cited.** (See MLA DOCU 2.) The student paper in RESCH 5 uses the MLA documentation system.

Most MLA-style in-text citations require only the author's last name and a page reference. The customary way to integrate this information into your text is to give an introductory signal phrase mentioning the author's name at the beginning of the sentence (see RESCH 4b) and then the page number parenthetically at the end of the borrowed material. If the author's name is not given in the signal phrase, it must appear parenthetically with the page number.

The following examples show correct MLA in-text citation form for different kinds of sources. Note that the end punctuation comes after the parenthetical citation; no *p.* for *page* is used; and there is no punctuation between author and page number.

1. AUTHOR MENTIONED IN A SIGNAL PHRASE

When the author's name is given in a signal phrase, give only the page reference in parentheses.

> Rich argues that the Napoleonic Wars were "world wars in the sense that they involved all the great powers of that era" (18).

2. AUTHOR NOT MENTIONED IN A SIGNAL PHRASE

If the author's name is not given in a signal phrase, it must appear with the page reference in parentheses.

> As one authority in diplomatic history argues, the Napoleonic Wars were "world wars in the sense that they involved all the great powers of that era" (Rich 18).

3. TWO OR MORE WORKS BY THE SAME AUTHOR

When you borrow material from two or more works by the same author, your citation must direct the reader to the correct publication. You can do this in one of three ways.

Give the title in the signal phrase.

> In "Politics and the English Language," Orwell claims that "political language is designed to make lies sound truthful and murder respectable" (508).

Give the title parenthetically at the end in an abbreviated form.

Orwell claims that "political language is designed to make lies sound truthful and murder respectable" ("Politics" 508).

In the absence of a signal phrase, put the author's name, the title, and the page reference in parentheses.

After killing the elephant, "I often wondered whether any of the others grasped that I had done it solely to avoid looking a fool" (Orwell, "Shooting" 46-47).

4. TWO OR THREE AUTHORS

As with single-author works, you have the option of including the last names of the authors in the signal phrase or in the parentheses.

Miller and Swift argue that "masculine and feminine are as sexist as any words can be because they invoke cultural stereotypes" (176).

Probability theory is a prerequisite for advanced work in the social sciences at colleges and universities today (Hoel, Port, and Stone 27-54).

5. MORE THAN THREE AUTHORS

For works with more than three authors, include only the last name of the first author followed by the Latin phrase *et al.* (meaning "and others").

"As a whole <u>Gulliver's Travels</u> has the multiple intentions of a masterpiece" (Baugh et al. 865).

6. AUTHORS WITH SAME LAST NAME

To avoid confusion when using two or more authors with the same last name, give each author's first name and last name in all references.

Donald H. Graves believes successful teachers of writing have firm control of the twin crafts, teaching and writing (5-6).

Other educators have developed ways in which teachers can transfer this control to their students (Richard L. Graves 239).

7. CORPORATE AUTHOR

A **corporate author** is an institution, company, agency, or organization that is credited with authorship of a work. Treat the name just as you would an individual, giving it in the signal phrase or in parentheses. The first time a corporate name is used, it must be spelled out (National Organization for Women). However, if it has a commonly used abbreviation (NOW), give the abbreviation in parentheses immediately after the first reference to the organization. Thereafter you can simply use the abbreviation in the text.

The National Rifle Association (NRA) opposes legislation--including the

recent Brady Bill--that seeks to restrict the sale of handguns (4-17).

8. UNKNOWN AUTHOR

When the author of a work is not given, use the complete title of the work in a signal phrase or a shortened version in the parenthetical reference.

According to the article "It's Raining Pennies--But Not from Heaven," the

penny, "is under attack as a public nuisance" (31).

The penny, "is under attack as a public nuisance" ("It's Raining Pennies" 31).

9. MULTIVOLUME WORK

If you use material from more than one volume of a multivolume work in your research paper, include the volume number followed by a colon and then the page number in your parenthetical citations.

Manchel has little doubt that "the basic metaphorical images of the American

Dream grew out of seventeenth-century European Utopian visions" (2: 1046).

10. AN ENTIRE WORK

To reference a whole book or article, give the author's name in the signal phrase or parenthetically; no page numbers are needed.

Peggy Noonan argues for the historical importance of political speeches.

Although political speeches are everyday fare in the United States, their

historical importance should not be overlooked (Noonan).

11. FICTION, POETRY, DRAMA, AND THE BIBLE

Because the Bible and literary works are often available in different editions, you need to include information that will help your readers locate the particular reference in the edition that they have access to.

FICTION

In citing a passage from a work of fictional prose, give the page number of the edition you are using and then give the part or chapter number.

> Edna Pontellier, the heroine of Chopin's The Awakening, stands alone in triumph at the novel's end. In the words of the narrator, "How strange and awful it seemed to stand naked under the sky!" (301; ch. 39).

POETRY

For poems, first give the part or division reference, if there is one, and then the line numbers. Use a period with no space between.

> In "Song of Myself" Whitman emerges larger than life itself:
>
> > Walt Whitman, a kosmos, of Manhattan the son,
> >
> > Turbulent, fleshy, sensual, eating, drinking, and breeding,
> >
> > No sentimentalist, no stander above men and women or
> >
> > > apart from them,
> >
> > No more modest than immodest. (24.1-4)

DRAMA

For plays, include the act, scene, and lines in your citation. Use periods without spaces to separate these three items and, unless your instructor directs otherwise, use arabic instead of roman numerals.

> Shakespeare's King Lear projects his own misery when he asks the Fool, "What, has his own daughters brought him to this pass? / Couldst thou save nothing? Didst thou give them all?" (3.4.61-62).

The slash (/) indicates the end of one line and the beginning of the next. (See PUNCT 6h.)

BIBLE

In citing the Bible, provide book, chapter, and verse. As with drama citations, use periods to separate these items. The books of the Bible may be abbreviated in the parenthetical citation but not when part of your text.

In the gospel according to St. Matthew, Christ begins his Sermon on the Mount by declaring who are the blessed (5.3-12).

Later in his sermon, Christ gives his listeners what we now know as the Lord's Prayer (Matt. 6.9-13).

12. WORK FROM AN ANTHOLOGY

In citing a work from an anthology, give the name of the writer of the piece you are using—not the editor of the anthology—in your signal phrase or parenthetical citation.

Ostriker argues that "women poets have been employing anatomical imagery both more frequently and more intimately than their male counterparts" (248).

13. A SOURCE QUOTED IN ANOTHER SOURCE

It is always better to take your material from original sources when they are available. Sometimes only indirect sources are available. If you need to cite someone quoted in a work written by another person, begin your parenthetical citation with *qtd. in* (for "quoted in").

To Boris Yeltsin, "Gorbachev was a communist, is a communist, and will always be a communist" (qtd. in Edwards 15).

14. TWO OR MORE SOURCES IN A SINGLE CITATION

When acknowledging more than one source in a single parenthetical citation, separate the citations with a semicolon.

Environmentalists contend that solid waste disposal will be America's--if not the world's--most pressing problem in the next decade (Blumberg and Gottlieb 117; Rathje 99).

15. INTERVIEW

To cite a personal interview, simply give the person's name in a signal phrase or parenthetically.

The folklorist Jan Brunvald discussed how difficult it is to trace the origins of these popular, widely circulated stories.

The origins of urban legends are extremely difficult to trace (Brunvald).

16. AN ELECTRONIC SOURCE

Some electronic sources use paragraph numbers instead of page numbers. For paragraph numbers, use the abbreviations "par." or "para."

Cloning promises medical breakthroughs (Meagher, par. 2)

If a source provides no page or paragraph number, give only the author's name.

MLA DOCU 2

MLA List of Works Cited

The MLA-style list of **works cited** is a listing of the sources you cite in your paper. It is not a list of all the sources you checked, just the ones you actually cite. The list of works cited is placed on a separate page at the end of your paper. To assemble a list of works cited for your paper, follow these three simple steps:

1. Sort through your working bibliography, pulling the cards for those sources you actually cited in your research paper (see RESCH 2a and 2b); file or discard the others.
2. Alphabetize the cited source cards by the authors' last names. If the author is unknown, alphabetize by the first word in the title, not counting *a, an,* or *the*.
3. You are now ready to prepare your list of works cited. Start the first line of each entry at the left margin and indent subsequent lines five spaces.This way authors' names stand out at the left margin, and your readers can readily spot the source they are seeking. Double-space both within and between entries.

See the sample research paper in RESCH 5 for an example of how the list of works cited should appear on the page.

Directory to MLA List of Works Cited

(continued)

BOOKS

1. BASIC FORMAT FOR A BOOK WITH ONE AUTHOR

Croft, Robert W. <u>Anne Tyler: A Bio-Bibliography</u>. Westport: Greenwood, 1995.

This illustrates the basic book format: a period followed by two spaces after both author and title, a colon between place (city) of publication and publisher, a comma between publisher and date of publication, and a period at the end. The underlining of the title is continuous (not broken). You may shorten the publisher's name (*Greenwood* for

Greenwood Press in the above example). Omit *Publisher, Co., Inc.,* and use *UP* for *University Press.* Give the most recent year of publication.

2. TWO OR THREE AUTHORS

Young Bear, Severt, and R. D. Theisz. <u>Standing in the Light: A Lakota Way</u>

    <u>of Seeing</u>. Lincoln: U Nebraska P, 1994.

The name of the first author is the only one reversed; separate the names with commas.

Brunas, Michael, John Brunas, and Tom Weaver. <u>Universal Horrors: The</u>

    <u>Studio's Classic Films, 1931-1946</u>. Jefferson: McFarland, 1990.

3. MORE THAN THREE AUTHORS

Bloom, Harold, et al. <u>Deconstruction & Criticism</u>. New York:

    Continuum, 1979.

Give the first author listed on the title page followed by the Latin phrase *et al.* (meaning "and others").

4. AUTHOR WITH AN EDITOR

Fisher, Dorothy Canfield. <u>The Bedquilt and Other Stories</u>. Ed. Mark J.

    Madigan. Columbia: U of Missouri P, 1996.

Use the capitalized abbreviation *Ed.* for "edited by."

5. EDITORS

Gwertzman, Bernard, and Michael T. Kaufman, eds. <u>The Collapse</u>

    <u>of Communism</u>. New York: Random, 1990.

If you are citing an entire edited collection and not just a work in it, use the lowercase abbreviation *ed.* for "editor" or *eds.* for "editors."

6. TRANSLATION

Kafka, Franz. <u>The Penal Colony: Stories and Short Pieces</u>. Trans.

    Willa Muir and Edwin Muir. New York: Schocken, 1984.

The translator of an authored text is cited after the title; use the abbreviation *Trans.* for "translated by."

7. CORPORATE AUTHOR

English Language Center, Brigham Young University. <u>Expeditions into</u>

<u>English: Grammar 1</u>. Englewood Cliffs: Prentice, 1991.

Treat a corporate author—an institution, company, agency, or organization that is credited with authorship—just as you would an individual.

8. UNKNOWN AUTHOR

<u>Children of the Dragon: The Story of Tiananmen Square</u>.

New York: Collier-Macmillan, 1990.

In the absence of a named author on the title page, start the entry with the title of the work. In the list of works cited, the entry is alphabetized by the first word of the title in the list of works cited (omitting *a, an,* or *the*).

9. TWO OR MORE WORKS BY THE SAME AUTHOR

Dillard, Annie. <u>An American Childhood</u>. New York: Harper, 1987.

---. "Death of a Moth." <u>Harper's</u> May 1976: 47-48.

---. <u>The Living: A Novel</u>. New York: HarperCollins, 1992.

When you cite more than one work by the same author in your paper, list the works alphabetically by title. Give the author's name in the first entry, but in subsequent entries use three unspaced hyphens followed by a period and two spaces for the name.

10. EDITION OTHER THAN FIRST

Aitchison, Jean. <u>Language Change: Process or Decay?</u> 2nd ed.

Cambridge: Cambridge UP, 1991.

Give the number of the edition (1st, 2nd, 3rd) followed by *ed.* immediately after the title.

11. REPUBLISHED BOOK

Wharton, Edith. <u>The House of Mirth</u>. 1905. Introd. Cynthia Griffin Wolff.

New York: Penguin, 1985.

Give the publication date for the original edition (you can find this information on the copyright page), but complete publication data only for the reprint, even if the publisher is different. If the republished book includes a new introduction or other interpretive material, add that information after the original publication date.

12. WORK IN MORE THAN ONE VOLUME

Manchel, Frank. Film Study: An Analytical Bibliography. 4 vols. Rutherford:

Fairleigh Dickinson UP, 1990-91.

Give the number of volumes after the title, using the abbreviation *vols.* This multivolume work was published over a two-year period. If you use only a particular volume, name it specifically before the city and publisher; although not required, the total number of volumes may be added at the end of the entry as follows:

Manchel, Frank. Film Study: An Analytical Bibliography. Vol. 2. Rutherford:

Fairleigh Dickinson UP. 1990-91. 4 vols.

13. WORK IN A SERIES

Magistrale, Tony. Stephen King: The Second Decade, Danse Macabre

to The Dark Half. Twayne's United States Authors Series 599.

New York: Maxwell Macmillan International, 1992.

After the title of the work, give the series' name and, if available, the work's number in the series.

14. WORK IN AN ANTHOLOGY

Dao, Bei. "13 Happiness Street." Contemporary Literature of Asia. Ed. Arthur

W. Biddle, Gloria Bien, and Vinay Dharwadker. Upper Saddle River, NJ:

Prentice, 1996. 281-92.

First give the title of the work, then the title and editor(s) of the anthology. Cite the pages on which the work appears after the publication data.

15. PREFACE, INTRODUCTION, FOREWORD, OR AFTERWORD

Douglas, Ann. Introduction. Uncle Tom's Cabin or, Life Among the Lowly.

By Harriet Beecher Stowe. New York: Penguin, 1981. 7-36.

When your reference is to the author of interpretive or critical material (such as a preface or an introduction) in a book by someone else, cite this author first and then the work and its author. Give the inclusive page numbers after the publication data.

16. ENCYCLOPEDIAS AND OTHER REFERENCE WORKS

Preuss, Harry G. "Nutrition." Encyclopedia Americana. 1994 ed.

Complete publication information is not needed for standard reference works, but you should include complete publication information for less well known works. If an article is unsigned, begin with the title. If a reference work is not arranged alphabetically, supply the page numbers.

PERIODICALS

17. ARTICLE IN A MONTHLY MAGAZINE

Norman, Geraldine. "Russia's Rocky Past." Arts & Antiques Oct. 1997:
94-99.

This example illustrates the basic MLA-style format for articles in periodicals: periods and two spaces follow the author and title; a colon appears after the date; and a period is placed at the end. With the exception of May, June, and July, abbreviate the month. If the article is numbered continuously, give the inclusive page numbers. If not, give the first page and a plus sign (+) to indicate that paging is discontinuous.

18. ARTICLE IN A WEEKLY MAGAZINE

McLeod, Scott. "The Nile's Other Kingdom." Time 15 Sept. 1997: 102-06.

Give the day, month, and year in that order without punctuation for weekly publications. If an article is unsigned, start your entry with the title.

19. ARTICLE IN A JOURNAL PAGINATED BY VOLUME

Flower, Dean. "Desegregating the Syllabus." Hudson Review
46 (1994): 683-93.

To locate an article in a journal that continues page numbers throughout a given year, the reader needs the volume number, the year, and the page numbers.

20. ARTICLE IN A JOURNAL PAGINATED BY ISSUE

Deegan, James G. "Gender and Pedagogy in Soviet Education: The

Inherited Context." International Education 22.2 (1993): 46-69.

Separate the volume number and the issue number with a period.

21. ARTICLE IN A DAILY NEWSPAPER

Broad, William J. "Another Possible Climate Culprit: The Sun." New York

Times 23 Sept. 1997, New England final ed.: C1+.

If there is a section letter, give it before the page number.

22. ARTICLE IN A WEEKLY NEWSPAPER

Lieb, Kristin. "Minority Students Get Help in Seeking Advanced

Degrees." Chronicle of Higher Education 5 Aug. 1992: A27-28.

23. EDITORIALS AND LETTERS TO THE EDITOR

Gough, Patricia B. "Moving Beyond the Myth." Editorial. Phi Delta Kappan

76 (1994): 99.

Begin an unsigned editorial with the title.

Although many newspapers and magazines give titles to letters to the editor, these titles are not part of the entry.

Diem, Bui. Letter. Washington Post 11 May 1995: A22.

24. BOOK REVIEW

Angell, Roger. "Designated Hero." Rev. of Jackie Robinson, by Arnold

Rampersad. New Yorker 15 Sept. 1997: 82-88.

If the review has no title, simply begin with *Rev.* after the author's name.

25. FILM REVIEW

Holden, Stephen. "A Love Affair Kept All in the Family." Rev. of The House

of Yes, dir. Mark Waters. New York Times 10 Oct. 1997: B10.

WORLD WIDE WEB SOURCES

The following guidelines for citing information retrieved from the World Wide Web are based on the very latest advice of the MLA as drawn from the *MLA Style Manual and Guide to Scholarly Publishing* (1998), as well as from the MLA's Web site <http://www.mla.org>. All of the following elements, if they are available and relevant, should be included in the reference. All items should be followed by a period with the exception of the date the site is accessed.

- *Name of the author,* editor, compiler, or translator of the source (if available and relevant), reversed for alphabetizing and followed by an abbreviation, such as *ed.,* if appropriate
- *Title of a poem,* short story, article, or similar short work within a scholarly project, database, or periodical (in quotation marks); or title of a posting to a discussion list or forum (taken from the subject line and put in quotation marks), followed by the description *Online posting*
- *Title of a book* (underlined)
- *Name of the editor,* compiler, or translator of the text (if relevant and if not cited earlier), preceded by the appropriate abbreviation, such as *Ed.*
- *Publication information* for any print version of the source
- *Title of the scholarly project,* database, periodical, or professional or personal site (underlined); or, for professional or personal site with no title, a description such as *Home page*
- *Name of the editor* of the scholarly project or database (if available)
- *Version number of the source* (if not part of the title) or, for a journal, the volume number, issue number, or other identifying number
- *Date of electronic publication,* or the latest update, or of posting
- *For a posting to a discussion list or forum, the name of the list or forum*
- *The number range or total number of pages,* paragraphs, or other sections, if they are numbered
- *Name of any institution or organization* sponsoring or associated with the Web site
- *Date when the researcher accessed the source*
- *Electronic address,* or URL, of the source (in angle brackets)

26. SCHOLARLY PROJECT

Electrifying the Renaissance: Hypertext, Literature, and the World Wide
Web. Mar. 1997. U. California, Santa Barbara. 4 Feb. 1998
<http://humanitas.ucsb.edu/depts/english/english/coursework/rar>.

27. PROFESSIONAL SITE

National Council of Teachers of English. Urbana, IL. 25 Mar. 1998 <http://www.ncte.org/about/>.

28. PERSONAL SITE

Cavrak, Steve. Home page. 15 Jan. 1998 <http://www.uvm.edu/~sjc/>.

29. BOOK

Butler, Josephine E. The Education and Employment of Women. Liverpool, 1868. Victorian Women Writers Project. Ed. Perry Willett. June, 1996. Indiana U. 4 Feb. 1998 <http://www.indiana.edu/~letrs/vwwwp/butler/educ.html>.

30. POETRY

Dunn, Stephen. "In the House." New and Selected Poems 1974-1994. New York, 1994. Poetry Daily, The Poetry Daily Association, Charlottesville, VA. 4 Feb. 1998 <http://www.cstone.net~poems/sele1dwn.htm>.

31. ARTICLE IN A REFERENCE DATABASE

"e. e. cummings." Encyclopedia.com. 1994. The Concise Columbia Electronic Encyclopedia, Third Edition. 9 Sept. 1997 <wysiwyg://Body.30/http://www.encyclopedia.com/articles/03328.htm>.

32. ARTICLE IN A JOURNAL

McKee, Patricia. "Spacing and Placing in Toni Morrison's Sula." Modern Fiction Studies 42.1 (1996): 30 pp. 5 Feb. 1998 <http://muse.jhu.edu/journals/modern_fiction_studies/V042/42.1mckee.html>.

33. ARTICLE IN A MAGAZINE

Holloway, Marguerite. "Pattie." Wired 5.12 Dec. 1997 <http://www.wired.com/wired/5.12/maes.html>.

34. POSTING TO A DISCUSSION LIST

Preston, Dennis R. "Re: basketball terms." Online posting. 8 Nov. 1997. American Dialect Society. 1 Mar. 1998 <http://www2.et.byu.edu/~lilliek/ads/index.htm>.

35. FILE TRANSFER PROTOCOL (FTP), TELNET, OR GOPHER SITE

Dartmouth College. "The Dante Project." Oct. 1988. 25 Sept. 1997

    <telnet://library.dartmouth.edu>.

ACW-STYLE CITATIONS FOR ELECTRONIC SOURCES

Your instructor may recommend that you follow guidelines developed by Janice R. Walker of the University of South Florida for documenting certain Internet sources. The following is Walker's basic citation model:

Author's Lastname, Author's Firstname. "Title of Document." Title of

    Complete Work (if applicable). Version or File Number (if applicable).

    Document date or date of last revision (if different from access date).

    Protocol and address, access path or directories (date of access).

The Alliance for Computers and Writing (ACW) has endorsed Walker's model. For current recommendations as well as new developments in ACW style, visit Walker's web site at <http://www.cas.usf.edu/english/walker/mla.html>.

OTHER SOURCES

36. CD-ROM UPDATED PERIODICALLY

Some CD-ROM databases are updated on a regular basis because they cover publications that are themselves published periodically. Your entry in the Works Cited list should include the publication information for the print source, followed by the title of the database (underlined), publication medium (CD-ROM), name of vendor, and the electronic publication date.

James, Caryn. "An Army Family as Strong as Its Weakest Link."

    New York Times 16 Sept. 1994, late ed.: C8. New York Times

    Ondisc. CD-ROM. UMI-Proquest. Oct. 1994.

37. CD-ROM RELEASED IN A SINGLE EDITION

Some CD-ROM databases are not routinely updated; in fact, they are issued much as books are. Cite these electronic sources as you would a book, being careful to add the publication medium.

"Proactive." The Oxford English Dictionary. 2nd ed. CD-ROM. Oxford:

    Oxford UP, 1992.

38. ONLINE MATERIAL FROM A COMPUTER SERVICE

When you access research materials through an online computer service such as BRS, DIALOG, America Online, or Nexis, you should include the following information in your works cited entry: author's name, title and publication data for print source, title of the database (underlined), publication medium (Online), name of the computer service, and date you accessed the file. If an access or order number is available, include it.

> Kappel-Smith, Diana. "Fickle Desert Blooms: Opulent One Year, No-Shows
>
> the Next." Smithsonian Magazine (Mar. 1995): 9 pp. Online. America
>
> Online. 18 Apr. 1998.

39. PAMPHLET

> NRA Institute for Legislative Action. The Myth of the "Saturday Night
>
> Special." Washington: NRA, 1989.

Treat a pamphlet like a book. Underline the title. When no author is given, start your entry with the title of the pamphlet.

> Education: How Can Schools and Communities Work Together to Meet the
>
> Challenge? Pomfret: Study Circles Resource Center, 1995.

40. GOVERNMENT PUBLICATION

> United States. Government Printing Office. Style Manual. Washington:
>
> GPO, 1984.

Give the government, the agency, and the title with a period and two spaces after each. The publisher is the Government Printing Office (GPO).

41. UNPUBLISHED DISSERTATION

> Taranto, Cheryl T. "Political Songsters for the Presidential Campaign of
>
> 1860." Diss. Louisiana State U, 1994.

Give the title of an unpublished dissertation in quotation marks followed by a period, two spaces, the abbreviation *Diss.*, the name of the degree-granting university, and the year. Treat a published dissertation as you would a book with the dissertation information after the title.

42. LECTURE OR PUBLIC PRESENTATION

> Bennett, Kristin. "Bottled Water: The Business of the 1990s." Business and
>
> Management Lecture Series. Merrimack College, North Andover, MA.
>
> 14 Feb. 1998.

Give the name of the sponsoring organization or series, the location, and the date.

43. LETTER

Proulx, E. Annie. Letter to the author. 22 Jan. 1995.

44. E-MAIL COMMUNICATION

Quigley-Harris, Jennifer. "Book Fair." E-mail to A. Rosa. 23 Sept. 1998.

45. LEGAL REFERENCE

R.A.V., Petitioner v. City of St. Paul, Minnesota. U.S. Law Week. 60 LW 4667.

    U.S. Supreme Ct. 1992.

Give the name of the case, the source of the opinion, the court in which the opinion was delivered, and the date.

46. INTERVIEW

Gore, Tipper. Personal interview. 23 July 1997.

47. FILM OR VIDEO

The Taming of the Shrew. Dir. Franco Zeffirelli. Perf. Richard Burton and

    Elizabeth Taylor. Columbia, 1966.

An Oral Historian's Work. With Edward D. Ives. Videocassette. Northeast

    Archives of Folklore and Oral History, 1987.

48. TELEVISION OR RADIO PROGRAM

"Shakespearean Putdowns." Narr. Robert Siegel and Linda Wertheimer. All

    Things Considered. Natl. Public Radio. WBUR, Boston.

    6 Apr. 1994.

49. STAGE PLAY, OPERA, OR CONCERT PERFORMANCE

Il Trovatore. By Giuseppe Verdi. Cond. Simone Young. Perf. June Anderson.

    Metropolitan Opera House, New York. 17 Feb. 1998.

50. WORK OF ART

Botticelli, Sandro. Birth of Venus. Uffizi Gallery, Florence.

51. RECORDING

Braxton, Toni. Secrets. LaFace, 1996.

52. CARTOON

Koren, Edward. Cartoon. New Yorker 3 Oct. 1994: 54.

53. MAP OR CHART

Philadelphia. Map. New York: H. M. Gousha, 1994.

54. ADVERTISEMENT

Bose. Advertisement. Atlantic Monthly Jan. 1995: 79.

MLA DOCU 3

MLA Information Notes

Information notes come in two forms: content notes and bibliographic notes. Content notes allow the researcher to give readers additional information without digressing from the point at hand, while bibliographic notes provide helpful sources for additional reading not cited in the paper itself. Information notes are optional in a research project. They may be presented at the foot of the page on which they appear or on a separate page at the end of the paper but before the list of works cited. Indicate an information note by placing a raised (superscript) arabic numeral at the end of the sentence or passage to which the note refers. Number notes consecutively throughout the paper.

TEXT

Instead of entering the recycling loop--the cycle that takes a product from the consumer to the recycling bin to a manufacturer and back again to the consumer for use[1]--most old newsprint (ONP) sits in storehouses and trailer trucks with no place to go.

INFORMATION NOTE

[1] For a thorough explanation of the processes involved in recycling paper, see Hagerty, Pavoni, and Heer (58-62); Pardue (54-55); and Randolph.

other
docu

Other Systems of Documentation

Learning Objectives

After reading this section, you should:

- know how to use APA in-text citations in a research paper;

- understand how to assemble a list of references and correctly cite books, periodicals, CD-ROMs, online sources, and other sources;

- be familiar with the *Chicago Manual* style of documentation;

- know what other style manuals are available for various academic disciplines.

Other Systems of Documentation

In writing a research paper you are using the information and ideas of others. Whenever you directly quote, summarize, or paraphrase another person's thoughts and ideas, or use facts and statistics that are not commonly known or believed, you must properly acknowledge your source.

OTHER DOCU 1

APA In-Text Citations

Like the Modern Language Association (MLA) style of documentation (see MLA DOCU), the American Psychological Association (APA) style uses brief in-text citations to refer the reader to full bibliographic information in a list of references at the end of the paper. However, there are several format differences between MLA and APA. The following recommendations are based on the *Publication Manual of the American Psychological Association,* 4th edition (1994).

An APA in-text citation gives the author's last name and the year of publication. In the case of a quotation, include the page number (a page number for a paraphrase or summary is optional). Use commas to separate items in the parentheses.

Directory to APA In-Text Citations

1. PARAPHRASE OR SUMMARY WITH AUTHOR'S NAME IN TEXT

Give the year of publication in parentheses immediately after the author's name.

Milstein (1990) believes that the grizzly bear, Dall sheep, and golden eagle are in danger if we do not curb poaching in our national parks.

2. PARAPHRASE OR SUMMARY WITHOUT AUTHOR'S NAME IN TEXT

Give the author and year of publication in parentheses at the end of the cited material.

The grizzly bear, Dall sheep, and golden eagle are in danger if we do not curb poaching in our national parks (Milstein, 1990).

3. QUOTATION WITH AUTHOR'S NAME IN TEXT

Give the year of publication in parentheses immediately after the author's name, and put the page number at the end of the quotation.

According to Milstein (1990), "as part of a recent Washington State wilderness bill, Congress upped the maximum fine for wildlife crimes at Olympic National Park from $500 to $25,000" (p. 125).

4. QUOTATION WITHOUT AUTHOR'S NAME IN TEXT

Give the author, year of publication, and page number in parentheses at the end of the citation.

During one federal sting operation in North Carolina, "agents bought about 1,200 bear claws, on their way to becoming jewelry; 102 feet, an exotic delicacy; 320 gallbladders, considered a panacea in the Orient; 18 heads; 18 hides; and one live bear cub" (Milstein, 1990, p. 122).

5. A WORK WITH TWO AUTHORS

List both authors' names in the text with the year of publication immediately following, or put both names in a parenthetical citation. In this case, note that the ampersand (&) is used instead of *and.*

The resurgence of recycling in the 1980s can be traced to the confrontations between incineration and landfill projects (Blumberg & Gottlieb, 1989).

6. A WORK WITH THREE TO FIVE AUTHORS

Give all authors' last names in the text or parentheses in your *first* citation only; use an ampersand (&) instead of *and* in the parenthetical citation.

> Liberation begins with an awareness that we all are to some degree prisoners of our own language (Clark, Eschholz, & Rosa, 1997).

In subsequent citations, use only the first author's name and *et al.* (Latin for "and others").

> Clark et al. (1997) maintain that language is one of humankind's greatest achievements and most important resources.

7. A WORK WITH SIX OR MORE AUTHORS

In all citations, use the first author's name followed by *et al.*

> Cognitive behavior therapy is now recognized as an effective intervention for disturbed body image in young women (Rosen et al., 1989).

8. AUTHOR UNKNOWN

When the author is unknown, use the title of the piece in the text, or give a shortened title in a parenthetical citation.

> In <u>Children of the Dragon: The Story of Tiananmen Square</u> (1990) the interconnections of the events leading up to the bloody massacre in June 1989 are presented in detail.

> The interconnections of the events leading up to the bloody massacre in China in June 1989 are presented in detail (<u>Children of the Dragon</u>, 1990).

9. CORPORATE AUTHOR

With corporate authorship, give the full name of the institution, agency, or organization in the text together with an abbreviation in brackets in the first citation.

> According to Internal Revenue Service (IRS) (1997) regulations, two new tax credits for education-related expenses exist.

> Under the new regulations, there are two tax credits for education-related expenses (Internal Revenue Service [IRS], 1997).

In subsequent citations the abbreviation is sufficient both in the text and parenthetically.

10. TWO OR MORE AUTHORS WITH THE SAME LAST NAME

When using references by two or more authors with the same last name, include initials with all references.

A survey completed by P. J. Babin (1998) showed that sales of cellular car phones tripled in the last five years.

11. MORE THAN ONE WORK IN A PARENTHETICAL CITATION

When acknowledging more than one source in a parenthetical citation, present the sources in the order in which they appear in your list of references (i.e., alphabetically); separate the citations with a semicolon.

Environmentalists contend that solid waste disposal will be America's--if not the world's--most pressing problem in the decade of the 1990s (Blumberg & Gottlieb, 1989; Rathje, 1989).

12. INTERVIEWS, LETTERS, MEMOS, E-MAIL, AND TELEPHONE CONVERSATIONS

Bennett and Ulrich (letter, June 29, 1998) are confident that their study on the effects of secondary smoke will be completed by the end of the year.

Do not include these items in your list of references.

OTHER DOCU 2

APA-Style References

In APA style, the alphabetical list of works cited that appears at the end of a research paper is called *References*. The following guidelines give the basic format for APA-style references:

1. Reverse *all* authors' names within each entry, and use initials, not first names.
2. Name all authors; do not use *et al.* Use an ampersand (&) instead of *and* in naming the second or last of several authors.
3. Give the date of publication in parentheses after the last author's name, followed by a period.
4. Underline the titles and subtitles of books and periodicals, but do not put quotation marks around titles of articles.
5. Capitalize only the first word of book and article titles and subtitles and any proper nouns. Capitalize the titles of periodicals according to standard rules (see MECH 1i).

6. When referring to a state in the place of publication, use postal service abbreviations (Springfield, IL:).
7. Use the abbreviations *p.* or *pp.* for page numbers of all publications except scholarly journals.
8. Entries can be presented one of two ways: with a paragraph indent or with a hanging indent. Ask your teacher which form to use. Either way, all the same information is included and you should double-space throughout. Here is the same entry shown both ways:

✓ **Paragraph indent:** indent only the first line 5 spaces:

5 spaces ⊢──▶ National Association for the Advancement of Colored

People. (1994). Beyond the Rodney King story: An

investigation of police conduct in minority communities.

Boston: Northeastern University Press.

Hanging indent: do not indent first line; indent all subsequent lines 5 spaces.

National Association for the Advancement of Colored

5 spaces ⊢──▶ People. (1994). Beyond the Rodney King story:

5 spaces ⊢──▶ An investigation of police conduct in minority com-

5 spaces ⊢──▶ munities. Boston: Northeastern University Press.

Following are sample APA-style references for the types of sources you are most likely to encounter.

Directory to APA List of References

Books

(continued)

BOOKS

1. BASIC FORMAT FOR A BOOK WITH ONE AUTHOR

Katznelson, I. (1992). Marxism and the city. New York: Oxford University Press.

2. TWO OR MORE AUTHORS

Davison, J., & Davison, L. (1994). To make a house a home: Four generations
    of American women and the houses they lived in. New York:
    Random House.

Debold, E., Wilson, M., & Malave, I. (1993). Mother daughter revolution: From
    good girls to great women. New York: Bantam Books.

3. CORPORATE AUTHOR

National Association for the Advancement of Colored People. (1994).
    Beyond the Rodney King story: An investigation of police conduct in
    minority communities. Boston: Northeastern University Press.

4. AUTHOR UNKNOWN

Children of the dragon: The story of Tiananmen Square. (1990). New York:
Collier.

5. EDITOR

Singer, R. N., Murphey, M., & Tennant, L. K. (Eds.). (1993). Handbook of
research on sport psychology. New York: Macmillan.

6. WORK IN AN ANTHOLOGY

Pinderhughes, E. (1995). Biracial identity--Asset or handicap? In
H. W. Harris, H. C. Blue, & E. E. H. Griffith (Eds.), Racial and
ethnic identity: Psychological development and creative expression
(pp. 163-179). New York: Routledge.

7. EDITION OTHER THAN FIRST

Polsby, N. W., & Wildavsky, A. (1991). Presidential elections: Contemporary
strategies of American electoral politics (2nd ed.). New York: Free Press.

8. TRANSLATION

Kafka, F. (1984). The penal colony: Stories and short pieces (W. E. Muir,
Trans.). New York: Schocken.

9. MULTIVOLUME WORK

Cassidy, F. G., & Hall, J. H. (Eds.). (1985). Dictionary of American regional
English (Vols. 1-3). Cambridge: Harvard University Press.

10. TWO OR MORE WORKS BY THE SAME AUTHOR

Sheehy, G. (1988). Character: America's search for leadership. New York:
William Morrow.

Sheehy, G. (1992). The silent passage: Menopause. New York: Random
House.

Sheehy, G. (1995). Passages 2000: The revolution of second adulthood. New
York: Random House.

When listing two or more works by the same author, arrange
them chronologically by year of publication, starting with the one

published earliest. Repeat the author's name including any initials for all entries. If two or more works by the same author were published in the same year, use lowercase letters to differentiate them: (1992a), (1992b), (1992c).

PERIODICALS

11. ARTICLE IN A JOURNAL PAGINATED BY VOLUME

Izraeli, D. N. (1993). They have eyes and see not: Gender politics in the Diaspora Museum. Psychology of Women Quarterly, 17, 515-523.

12. ARTICLE IN A JOURNAL PAGINATED BY ISSUE

Lachman, S. J. (1993). Psychology and riots. Psychology: A Journal of Human Behavior, 30(3/4), 16-23.

13. ARTICLE IN A MONTHLY MAGAZINE

Klingel, H. (1995, April). The South Bronx bounces back. Smithsonian, 26, pp. 100-111.

14. ARTICLE IN A WEEKLY MAGAZINE

Como, J. (1995, April 17). Hero storyteller. National Review, 47, pp. 53-56, 72.

15. ARTICLE IN A NEWSPAPER

Haveman, J. (1995, April 20). Indian tribes resist idea of state grants. The Washington Post, p. 19A.

16. EDITORIAL

Cole E., & Rothblum, E. D. (1991). [Editorial]. Women and Therapy: A Feminist Quarterly, 11(2), 1-2.

17. LETTER TO THE EDITOR

Seeley, D. S. (1991). "What's left?" is the wrong question [Letter to the editor]. Social Policy, 21(4), 60.

18. BOOK REVIEW

Retish, P. (1992). [Review of The troubled adolescent]. Journal of Pediatric Psychology, 17, 245-246.

ELECTRONIC SOURCES

Your goal with an electronic reference is to both credit the author and enable a reader to retrieve the source. APA recommends that you provide as much information as you can, including a specific retrieval path. For sources not covered in the following models, consult Li and Crane's (1996) *Electronic Style: A Guide to Citing Electronic Information* in the reference section of your library. Or consult Li and Crane's 1997 online version: *Electronic Sources: APA Style of Citation* (http://www.uvm.edu/~ncrane/estyles/apa.html).

19. CD-ROM, TAPE, OR DISKETTE

Randolph, J. (1992). Recycling of materials. In The New Grolier Multimedia

Encyclopedia. [CD-ROM] Available: Danbury, CT: Grolier Electronic

Waldron, A. (1989, March 14). Writers and alcohol Washington Post. [CD-ROM]

Available: 1994 SIRS/SIRS 1989 Alcohol - No. 4/48A.

20. ONLINE MATERIAL FROM A COMPUTER SERVICE

James, C. (1994, September 16). An army family as strong as its

weakest link. The New York Times [Online], p. C8.

Available: NEXIS/NEWS/NYT [1995, May 17]

21. INTERNET

Derian, J. D. (1994, September). Cyber-deterrence. Wired [Online] 2(9).

Available: http://www/wired.com/Etext/index.html File: Cyber-deterrence:

The US army fights tomorrow's war today [1997, October 15]

OTHER SOURCES

22. GOVERNMENT PUBLICATION

Internal Revenue Service. (1994). Your federal income tax (Publication 17).

Washington, DC: U.S. Government Printing Office.

23. DISSERTATION ABSTRACT

Erwin, L. K. (1990). The politics of anti-feminism: The pro-family movement

in Canada (Doctoral dissertation, York University, 1990). Dissertation

Abstracts International, 51, 3237-A.

24. COMPUTER SOFTWARE

Q-Corp. Q-Notes: Electronic note-taking [Computer Software]. (1997).

  Needham Heights, MA: Allyn & Bacon.

25. VIDEO

Schmiechen, B. (Producer), & Adelman, L. (Director). (1978). Controlling

  interest: The world of the multinational corporation [Videotape]. San

  Francisco, CA: California Newsreel.

OTHER DOCU 3

Annotated Student APA-Style Research Paper

Brooke Bailey, a student at Florida State University, wrote the research paper that appears on the following pages while enrolled in a criminal justice class. Early in the course, Bailey became interested in the relationship between public opinion and Supreme Court decisions. So for her first paper, she decided to research the studies that had been done on public opinion and the Supreme Court in the area of capital punishment.

Bailey used the APA guidelines for manuscript preparation presented in FORMAT 2. She also used the APA style of in-text citations (OTHER DOCU 1) and references (OTHER DOCU 2) to document her research paper. Bailey was required to include a title page (FORMAT 2) with her paper.

Public Opinion   1   Identification heading: short title and page.

Public Opinion and the Death Penalty

Brooke Bailey

Criminal Justice 4700: Introduction to Research Methods

Professor S. Eschholz

July 27, 1997

Full title of paper, writer's name, and course information are centered and double-spaced.

Short title and
page number.

Title is centered.

Authors' names
given in text
followed by date
in parentheses.

For a direct
quotation, the
writer gives the
page number
preceded by "p."

Questions
highlight main
issues the paper
will address.

When author's
name is not
given in the text,
it is given
parenthetically
with the date.

Public Opinion and the Death Penalty

Public opinion greatly influences decisions made by the
Supreme Court. In fact, public opinion even influences which
cases the Court will address. Is this good or bad? On the
one hand, "we the people" are the backbone of our court
system. Murphy and Tanehaus (1990) believe that "the
stability, even the continual existence, of a constitutional
democracy depends heavily on public opinion" (p. 991). On
the other hand, public opinion changes with the times--with
changes in social and economic conditions. The question,
then, is, to what extent should the Supreme Court be guided
by public opinion? And specifically, to what extent should
Supreme Court rulings on the death penalty--a very subjective
issue--be guided by public opinion?

Let's look first at the question of public opinion and
the death penalty. Gallup poll statistics from 1936 to 1994
show a stable and currently increasing level of support for
the death penalty. The only exception was a brief period
in the early 1960s, likely due to the new civil rights
movement (Erskine, 1970). In the 1960s, a proportionally
small but very vocal segment of the population had a lot
to say about civil rights issues. During this period, the
Supreme Court heard an abundance of civil rights cases,
which introduced the idea that a vocal minority can have
just as much influence when it comes to public opinion as
a surveyed majority.

Public Opinion   3

   The volatile 60s social climate brought the death
penalty case of <u>Furman v. Georgia</u> (1972) before a liberal
and very public-sensitive Supreme Court. In a landmark
decision, the Court declared that the way Georgia imposed
the death penalty was in violation of the 8th Amendment
against cruel and unusual punishment. The Court did not,
however, pronounce the death penalty itself unconstitutional,
and its decision applied only to Georgia, though other states
quickly scrambled to change their statutes to avoid being
in the same position as Georgia (Branham, 1994). In the
concurrence, Justice Marshall wrote that "the law should be
guided only by informed public opinion" (Vidmar & Ellsworth,
1974, pp. 1247-1248). Thus, the Court recognized the
importance of pubic opinion, even though it could not
determine to what extent public opinion determined
the constitutionality of the death penalty (Sarat & Vidmar,
1976).

   Two years later, in <u>Gregg v. Georgia</u> (1974), the Court
mandated that Georgia's new capital punishment law must
separate information given to a jury for determining guilt or
innocence from highly personal information needed in a
sentencing decision (Schmalleger, 1993). In other words,
it approved Georgia's new death penalty. Furthermore,
the majority opinion written for the case, according to
Schmalleger (1994), cited the "strong showing of public
support for the death penalty following <u>Furman</u> to mean

Writer presents
first court case.

Ampersand
joins the two
authors' names
in parentheses
followed by
date and page
numbers.

Writer presents
second court
case.

Paraphrase - in your own words

that death was still a socially and culturally acceptable penalty" (p. 369). For the first time, the Court recognized the significance of public opinion in deciding the legitimacy of the death penalty.

The Supreme Court--by virtue of being the highest court in the land--deals with the most important and controversial issues our society faces. The Court either upholds, overturns, modifies, or further interprets a disputed law or policy, even though the decisions rendered rarely apply to all jurisdictions. But the Court's feelings about a particular issue can be inferred from their rulings. "Thus, in Furman v. Georgia it was believed that the Court was against the death penalty for murder, while in Gregg v. Georgia it was believed to be for the death penalty for murder" (Marshall, 1987, p. 150).

Before and after these monumental cases, Gallup polls were conducted to gauge the nation's attitudes towards the death penalty. In a poll taken in March 1972--just before Furman--50% of those surveyed approved of the death penalty for murder, while 41% disapproved, and 9% had no opinion. In November 1972--after the Furman decision-- 57% approved, 32% disapproved, and 11% had no opinion. Approval of the death penalty increased even though the Supreme Court ruled that it had been unconstitutionally imposed. The most significant numbers, however, come from the poll taken in April 1976, just prior to the Gregg decision.

Writer presents clear statement of author's conclusions.

Writer introduces Gallup Poll study to highlight relationship between public opinion and court decision.

This survey indicated that 62% of the population approved of the death penalty, while only 27% disapproved and 11% had no opinion (Marshall, 1987). The notable increase of public support for capital punishment was followed soon after by the Supreme Court approval of the revised Georgia statutes on this issue.

But the influence of public opinion on the Court is not as linear as it may appear. In fact, the effect that these two entities have on each other may best be explained as circular: The public vindicates its support for capital punishment based upon the idea of justice as it is carried out by the courts, while the courts look to the people to justify their decisions. Thus, in the Gregg case, the Court could validate its support of the death penalty in the willingness of legislatures to authorize capital punishment, of juries to impose it, and of the general public to support it (Sarat, 1976). The public, in turn, could validate its support of the death penalty by citing the Court's decision (Casper, 1976),

Another important case that dealt with the death penalty specifically was McClesky v. Kemp (Marshall, 1987). This case, also in Georgia, brought the notion of racial disparity to the attention of the Court. Wrightsman, Neitzel, and Fortune (1994) believe that the issue was whether or not the death penalty discriminated against blacks or, more specifically, against persons who killed whites. Over a decade after the Furman case, the Supreme

Writer introduces third court case.

The word *and* is used between the authors' names in the text.

OTHER DOCU 3 *Annotated Student APA-Style Research Paper*

Court was still wading in muddy waters when it came to

The writer highlights a surprising conclusion.

public opinion on racial issues and the death penalty. In a surprising decision the Court held that "a simple showing of racial discrepancy in the application of the death penalty does not indicate a constitutional violation" (Schmalleger, 1993, p. 366).

Cases like <u>Furman v. Georgia</u> and <u>Gregg v. Georgia</u> stand as historical examples of how the opinions of a nation on subjective issues like the death penalty can affect which cases are brought before the Supreme Court and what decision is handed down. But is public opinion on the death penalty informed and educated, or is it guided by a desire for retribution and vengeance (Sarat & Vidmar, 1978)? Studies show that "the views of an informed public vary greatly from those of an uninformed public" (Branham, 1994, p. 104).

Writer is careful to put borrowed descriptor in quotes.

Further, support for the death penalty "diminishes substantially" when the public is fully aware of the penalty and its consequences (Branham, 1994, p. 109).

Writer concludes by highlighting the gap between the Court's ideal and the reality of the situation.

Despite the Court's ideal--that only informed public opinion should guide the law--the evidence seems to show that majority or vocal minority carry the most weight. In the future, perhaps the Court should look at the reasons behind people's feelings towards capital punishment and determine whether, as Sarat and Vidmar (1976) question, "public sentiment is an acceptable indicator of evolving standards of decency" (p. 171). As the Supreme Court itself recognized in <u>Weems v. United States</u>, another death penalty case, "time . . . brings into existence new conditions and purposes, and the interpretation of what constitutes cruel and unusual punishment may change as public opinion becomes enlightened by human justice" (Vidmar & Ellsworth, 1974, p. 1246). Perhaps the best way to enlighten the public is by not validating its majority or vocal minority opinions.

The heading
References is
centered at the
top of the page.

Writer follows
APA guidelines
for list of
references.

The list begins
on a new page,
and all entries
are given in
alphabetical
order by
authors' last
names.

The first line
of each entry
begins at the
left margin;
subsequent lines
are indented five
spaces.

Double space
within entries as
well as between
entries.

The correct
forms for
various other
kinds of
publications
are given in
OTHER DOCU 2.

References

Branham, L. S. (1994). Sentencing, corrections, and
    prisoners' rights. St. Paul, MN: West, pp. 104-109.

Casper, J. D. (1976). The supreme court and national policy
    making. American Political Science Review, 70(1),
    50-63.

Erskine, H. (1970). The polls: Capital punishment. Public
    Opinion Quarterly, 34, 290.

Marshall, T. (1987). The Supreme Court as an opinion leader:
    Court decisions and the mass public. American Politics
    Quarterly, 15, 147.

Murphy, W., & Tanehaus, J. (1990). Publicity, public opinion,
    and the Court. Northwestern University Law Review, 84,
    995-1020.

Sarat, A., & Vidmar, N. (1976). Public opinion, the death
    penalty, and the Eighth Amendment: Testing the
    Marshall hypothesis. Wisconsin Law Review, 171.

Schmalleger, F. (1993). Criminal justice today. Englewood
    Cliffs, NJ: Prentice-Hall, 1993.

Vidmar, N., & Ellsworth, P. (1974). Public opinion and the
    death penalty. Stanford Law Review, 26, 1245-1270.

Wrightsman, L. S., Nietzel, M., & Fortune, W. H. (1994).
    Psychology and the legal system. Pacific Grove, CA.:
    Brooks/Cole.

OTHER DOCU 4

Chicago Manual *Documentation Style*

The *Chicago Manual of Style* recommends the use of endnotes and accepts footnotes as an alternative. **Endnotes** are presented together at the "end" of the paper, whereas **footnotes** are found on the bottom or "foot" of the page on which the citations occur. A raised arabic numeral is placed immediately after the item being acknowledged. Number endnotes or footnotes consecutively throughout the paper.

The first time you cite a source, provide complete publication data including the page number for the material you are quoting, paraphrasing, or summarizing. For subsequent references, you can use a shortened version of the citation. (See OTHER DOCU 4b.) Provide complete publication data, including inclusive page numbers for articles in the bibliography entry. For endnotes, indent the first line 5 spaces and bring all subsequent lines flush left to the margin. Single-space within each endnote and double-space between notes. To compile your list of references, called the Bibliography, start each entry flush left and indent subsequent lines 5 spaces (see OTHER DOCU 4a). Single-space within each entry and double-space between entries.

TEXT CITATION FORMAT

And there are those environmentalists who believe that the real garbage crisis may be "the lack of reliable information and the persistence of misinformation."[1]

ENDNOTE OR FOOTNOTE FORMAT

1. William L. Rathje, "Rubbish!" The Atlantic Monthly, December 1989, 99.

BIBLIOGRAPHY FORMAT

Rathje, William L. "Rubbish!" The Atlantic Monthly, December 1989, 99-109.

OTHER DOCU 4a *Chicago Manual* endnotes (or footnotes) and bibliography entries

The following are model citations for the most commonly used research sources. The endnote and bibliography entry for each source appear together for easy access.

Directory to *Chicago Manual* Note and Bibliography Models

Books

Periodicals

Electronic Sources

Other Sources

BOOKS

1. ONE AUTHOR

　　1. Michael Ferber, The Poetry of Shelley (New York: Penguin Books, 1993), 173.

Ferber, Michael. The Poetry of Shelley. New York: Penguin Books, 1993.

2. TWO OR THREE AUTHORS

    2. Kate Fullbrook and Edward Fullbrook, <u>Simone de Beauvoir and Jean-Paul Sartre: The Remaking of a Twentieth Century Legend</u> (New York: Basic Books, 1994), 119.

Fullbrook, Kate, and Edward Fullbrook. <u>Simone de Beauvoir and Jean-Paul Sartre: The Remaking of a Twentieth Century Legend</u>. New York: Basic Books, 1994.

3. FOUR OR MORE AUTHORS

    3. Harold Bloom and others, <u>Deconstruction and Criticism</u> (New York: Seabury Press, 1979), 133.

Bloom, H., P. de Man, G. H. Hartman, and J. H. Miller. <u>Deconstruction and Criticism</u>. New York: Seabury Press, 1979.

4. AUTHOR WITH AN EDITOR

    4. William Shakespeare, <u>Antony and Cleopatra</u>, ed. Michael Neill (New York: Oxford University Press, 1994), 71.

Shakespeare, William. <u>Antony and Cleopatra</u>. Edited by Michael Neill. New York: Oxford University Press, 1994.

5. EDITOR

    5. A. Wayne Glowka and Donald M. Lance, eds., <u>Language Variation in North American English: Research and Teaching</u> (New York: Modern Language Association of America, 1993), 354.

Glowka, A. Wayne, and Donald M. Lance, eds., <u>Language Variation in North American English: Research and Teaching</u>. New York: Modern Language Association of America, 1993.

6. UNKNOWN AUTHOR

    6. <u>The Vermont Almanac</u> (Middlebury, Vt.: Regional Facts, 1993), 17-26.

<u>The Vermont Almanac</u>. Middlebury, Vt.: Regional Facts, 1993.

7. EDITION OTHER THAN FIRST

7. William Zinsser, On Writing Well, 5th ed. (New York: HarperPerennial, 1994), 70-72.

Zinsser, William. On Writing Well. 5th ed. New York: HarperPerennial, 1994.

8. WORK IN MORE THAN ONE VOLUME

8. J. B. Schneewind, Moral Philosophy from Montaigne to Kant: An Anthology (New York: Cambridge University Press, 1990), 1:630.

Schneewind, J. B. Moral Philosophy from Montaigne to Kant: An Anthology. Vol. 1. New York: Cambridge University Press, 1990.

9. WORK FROM AN ANTHOLOGY

9. Rita Dove, "Parsley," in New Worlds of Literature, eds. Jerome Beaty and J. Paul Hunter (New York: W. W. Norton, 1989), 502.

Dove, Rita. "Parsley." In New Worlds of Literature edited by Jerome Beaty and J. Paul Hunter, 502. New York: W. W. Norton, 1989.

PERIODICALS

10. ARTICLE IN A JOURNAL PAGINATED BY VOLUME

10. Harold Fromm, "My Science Wars," Hudson Review 49 (1997): 601.

Fromm, Harold. "My Science Wars." Hudson Review 49 (1997): 599-609.

11. ARTICLE IN A JOURNAL PAGINATED BY ISSUE

11. Michael Lobel, "Warhol's Closet," Art Journal 55, no. 4 (1996): 47.

Lobel, Michael. "Warhol's Closet." Art Journal 55, no. 4 (1996): 42-50.

12. ARTICLE IN A MAGAZINE

12. David Zane Mairowitz, "Fascism a la Mode," Harper's, October 1997, 61.

Mairowitz, David Zane. "Fascism a la Mode." Harper's, October 1997, 59-67.

13. UNSIGNED ARTICLE

13. "Pompeii: Will the City Go From Dust to Dust?" Newsweek, 1 September 1997, 8.

"Pompeii: Will the City Go From Dust to Dust?" Newsweek. 1 September 1997, 8.

14. ARTICLE IN A NEWSPAPER

14. William J. Broad, "Another Possible Climate Culprit: The Sun," New York Times, 23 September 1997, C1.

Broad, William J. "Another Possible Climate Culprit: The Sun." New York Times, 23 September 1997, C1.

ELECTRONIC SOURCES

15. SOURCE ON CD-ROM

15. Caryn James, "An Army Family as Strong as Its Weakest Link," in The New York Times, 16 September 1994, C8, New York Times Ondisc [CD-ROM], UMI-ProQuest, October 1997.

James, Caryn. "An Army Family as Strong as Its Weakest Link." New York Times, 16 September 1994, C8. New York Times Ondisc [CD-ROM], UMI-ProQuest, October 1997.

16. ONLINE SOURCE

16. Catherine Yoes, "The Science Fiction Web Project: Adventures in Teaching with Storyspace," in Computers, Writing, Rhetoric and Literature [electronic journal], accessed 1 October 1997; available from http://www.cwrl.utexas.edu/~cwrl/v2nl/yoes/yoes.html.

Yoes, Catherine. "The Science Fiction Web Project: Adventures in Teaching with Storyspace." Computers, Writing, Rhetoric and Literature [electronic journal]. Accessed 1 October 1997. Available from http://www.cwrl.utexas.edu/~cwrl/v2n1/yoes/yoes.html.

16. Mark Twain, The Adventures of Tom Sawyer [book online], (Hartford: American Publishing Company, 1876) Carnegie Mellon University, accessed, 16 May 1998; available from http://www.cs.cmu.edu/Web/People/rgs/sawyr-table.html

Twain, Mark. The Adventures of Tom Sawyer [book online], (Hartford: American Publishing Company, 1876). Carnegie Mellon University. Accessed 16 May 1998. Available from http://www.cs.cmu.edu/Web/People/rgs/sawyr-table.html

OTHER SOURCES

17. GOVERNMENT PUBLICATION

17. U.S. Bureau of the Census, Poverty in the United States, Current Population Reports, Ser. P-60, No. 163 (Washington, D.C.: GPO, 1989), 33.

U.S. Bureau of the Census. Poverty in the United States, Current Population Reports, Ser. P-60, No. 163. Washington, D.C.: GPO, 1989.

18. INTERVIEW, LETTER, OR E-MAIL

18. Carol Hosford, telephone interview by author, 7 April 1998.

Hosford, Carol. Telephone interview by author, 7 April 1998.

18. E. Annie Proulx, letter to author, 22 January 1998.

Proulx, E. Annie. Letter to author, 22 January 1998.

18. Harriett Prentiss, e-mail to E. Ludlow, 17 February 1998.

Prentiss, Harriett. E-mail to E. Ludlow, 17 February 1998.

19. FILM OR VIDEOTAPE

19. Forrest Gump, dir. Robert Zemeckis, with Tom Hanks and Sally Field, 2 hr. 15 min., Paramount, 1994, videocassette.

Forrest Gump. Directed by Robert Zemeckis, with Tom Hanks and Sally Field. 2 hr. 15 min. Paramount, 1994. Videocassette.

OTHER DOCU 4b   Subsequent references

After you cite a source for the first time in a paper and fully document it, all **subsequent references** to that source are shortened. For most notes give the author's last name followed by a comma, and the page number. If no author is given, use a shortened title.

> 20. Dove, 502.
>
> 21. Vermont Almanac, 225.

If you cite two or more works by the same author or works by authors with identical last names, include a shortened title.

> 22. Emerson, "Literature and Change," 10.
>
> 23. Emerson, Representative Men, 17.

The abbreviation "ibid." (Latin for *in the same place*) can be used to refer to the work cited in the previous note. When citing the same page you should use *Ibid.* alone. When citing a different page you must include the page number.

> 24. Ibid.
>
> 25. Ibid., 217.

OTHER DOCU 5

Other Documentation Styles

Many academic disciplines publish a style manual for their particular system of documentation. You will find these manuals in the reference section of the library.

American Chemical Society. *American Chemical Society Style Guide: A Manual for Authors and Editors.* 2nd ed. Washington: Amer. Chemical Soc., 1986.

American Institute of Physics. *Style Manual: Instructions to Authors and Volume Editors for the Preparation of AIP Book Manuscript.* 5th ed. New York: Amer. Instit. of Physics, 1995.

American Mathematical Society. *The AMS Author Handbook: General Instructions for Preparing Manuscripts.* Providence: Amer. Mathematical Soc., 1994.

American Political Science Association. *Style Manual for Political Science.* Rev. ed. Washington: Amer. Political Science Assn., 1993.

American Psychological Association. *Publication Manual of the American Psychological Association.* 4th ed. Washington: Amer. Psychological Assn., 1994.

Associated Press Staff. *Associated Press Stylebook and Libel Manual.* Reading, MA: Addison, 1994.

Bates, Robert L., Rex Buchanan, and Marla Adkins-Heljeson, eds. *Geowriting: A Guide to Writing, Editing, and Printing in Earth Science.* 5th ed. Alexandria, VA: American Geological Institute, 1992.

The Bluebook: A Uniform System of Citation. Comp. editors of Columbia Law Review et al. 16th ed. Cambridge, MA: Harvard Law Review Association, 1996.

Chicago Editorial Staff. *The Chicago Manual of Style.* 14th ed. Chicago: U of Chicago P, 1993.

Council of Biology Editors Style Manual Committee. *Scientific Style and Format: The CBE Manual for Authors, Editors, and Publishers.* 6th ed. New York: Cambridge U P, 1994.

Gibaldi, Joseph. *MLA Handbook for Writers of Research Papers.* 4th ed. New York: MLA, 1995.

Holoman, D. Kern, ed. *Writing About Music: A Style Sheet from the Editors of 19th-Century Music.* Berkeley: U of California P, 1988.

Linguistics Society of America. "LSA Style Sheet." Published yearly in the December issue of the *LSA Bulletin.*

Turabian, Kate L. *A Manual for Writers of Term Papers, Theses, and Dissertations.* 6th ed. Chicago: U of Chicago P, 1996.

Index

Acknowledgments

Pages 16–17, 23, 28–31: Andy Pellet, "The Perils of Astroturf."

Page 173: American Heritage Dictionary, entry for "regard." Copyright © 1997 Houghton Mifflin Company. Reproduced by permission from *The American Heritage Dictionary, Second College Edition.*

Page 176: Roget's II: The New Thesaurus, entry for "acknowledge." Copyright © 1988 by Houghton Mifflin Company. Reproduced by permission from *Roget's II: The New Thesaurus, Expanded Edition.*

Page 215: Robert Frost, "The Road Not Taken." From: *The Poetry of Robert Frost,* edited by Edward Connery Lathem, Copyright 1944 by Robert Frost, Copyright 1916, © 1969 by Henry Holt and Company, Inc. Reprinted by permission of Henry Holt and Company, Inc., and Jonathan Cape.

Pages 216, 219: Emily Dickinson, "Success is counted sweetest." Reprinted by permission of the publishers and the Trustees of Amherst College from *The Poems of Emily Dickinson,* Thomas H. Johnson, ed., Cambridge, Mass.: The Belknap Press of Harvard University Press, Copyright © 1951, 1955, 1979, 1983 by the President and Fellows of Harvard College.

Page 221: E. E. Cummings, "what if a much of a which of a wind." The lines from "what if a much of a which of a wind", copyright 1944, © 1972, 1991 by the Trustees for the E. E. Cummings Trust, from *Complete Poems: 1904–1962* by E. E. Cummings, Edited by George J. Firmage. Reprinted by permission of Liveright Publishing Corporation.

Page 281: Julia Alvarez, "Snow." From *How the Garcia Girls Lost Their Accents.* Copyright © 1991 by Julia Alvarez. Published by Plume, an imprint of Dutton Signet, a division of Penguin USA and originally in hardcover by Algonquin Books of Chapel Hill. Reprinted by permission of Susan Bergholz Literary Services, New York. All rights reserved.

Pages 282–285: Lauri Coulombe, "(Re)-producing Annihilation."

Page 288: Readers' Guide to Periodical Literature 1996, entries for "Recycling," "Too much recycling?," and "Gore, Albert, Jr." Reprinted by permission of H. W. Wilson.

Pages 289, 291, 292: ONLINE COMPUTER LIBRARY CENTER, INC., screens from FirstSearch database, copyrighted by Online Computer Library Center, Inc. FirstSearch is a registered trademark of OCLC Online Computer Library Center, Incorporated, reprinted by permission. Bibliographic records in OCLC format from Online Union Catalog, reprinted by permission.

Page 290: LIBRARY OF CONGRESS, subject catalog card for Albert Gore, *Earth in the Balance: Ecology and the Human Spirit.* Reprinted by permission.

Pages 294, 295, 296: Text and artwork copyright © 1998 by Yahoo! Inc. All rights reserved. Yahoo! and the Yahoo! logo are trademarks of Yahoo! Inc.

Pages 303, 311, 312, 313, 314, 316, 319, 323–335: Patricia LaRose, "Recycling Used Newsprint: Coming to Terms with an Environmental Problem."

Page 353: Walker, Janice R. "MLA-Style Citations of Electronic Sources." Version 1.2, revised Nov. 1997. http://www.cas.usf.edu/english/walker/mla/html (16 February 1998).

Pages 367–374: Brooke Bailey, "Public Opinion and the Death Penalty."

2021

ICD-10-CM
FOR PHYSICIANS

Jackie L. Koesterman, CPC
Coding and Reimbursement Specialist
JDK Medical Coding EDU, LLC
Grand Forks, North Dakota

BUCK'S

INCLUDES
NETTER'S
ANATOMY
ART

ELSEVIER

Elsevier
3251 Riverport Lane
St. Louis, Missouri 63043

BUCK'S 2021 ICD-10-CM FOR PHYSICIANS

ISBN: 978-0-323-76280-9

Previous editions copyrighted 2020, 2019, 2018, 2017, 2016, 2015, 2014, 2013, 2010.

International Standard Book Number: 978-0-323-76280-9

Senior Content Strategist: Brandi Graham
Senior Content Development Manager: Luke E. Held
Senior Content Development Specialist: Joshua S. Rapplean
Publishing Services Manager: Julie Eddy
Senior Project Manager: Tracey Schriefer
Senior Book Designer: Maggie Reid

Printed in Canada

Working together
to grow libraries in
developing countries

www.elsevier.com • www.bookaid.org

Last digit is the print number: 9 8 7 6 5 4 3 2 1

DEDICATION

To all the brave medical coders who transitioned the nation into a new coding system.
Decades of waiting finally concluded with the implementation of I-10,
and you have been the pioneers leading the way.

With greatest appreciations for your efforts!

Carol J. Buck, MS

CONTENTS

ICD-10-CM

GUIDE TO USING THE 2021 ICD-10-CM FOR PHYSICIANS

Medical coding has long been a part of the health care profession. Through the years medical coding systems have become more complex and extensive. Today, medical coding is an intricate and immense process that is present in every health care setting. The increased use of electronic submissions for health care services only increases the need for coders who understand the coding process.

2021 ICD-10-CM for Physicians, Professional Edition was developed to help meet the needs of coding professionals at all levels by offering a comprehensive coding text at a reasonable price.

All material strictly adheres to the latest government versions available at the time of printing. Updates from the *Definitions of Medicare Code Edits* (MCE) will be posted to the companion website (www. codingupdates.com) when available.

Illustrations and Items

The ICD-10-CM Tabular List contains illustrations, pictures, and items to assist you in understanding difficult terminology, diseases/conditions, or coding in a specific category. Items are always printed in ░░░░░░ ink so that the added material is not mistaken for official notations or instructions. ░░░░░░ ink is used for other annotations in the text. Your ideas on what other descriptions or illustrations should be in future editions of this text are always appreciated.

Instructional Notations

Includes Notes

Includes
The word "Includes" appears immediately under certain categories to further define, or give examples of, the content of the category.

Excludes Notes

The ICD-10-CM has two types of excludes notes. Each note has a different definition for use, but they are both similar in that they indicate that codes excluded from each other are independent of each other.

Excludes1
A type 1 Excludes note is a pure excludes. It means "NOT CODED HERE!" An Excludes1 note indicates that the code excluded should never be used at the same time as the code above the Excludes1 note. An Excludes1 is for use when two conditions cannot occur together, such as a congenital form versus an acquired form of the same condition.

Excludes2
A type 2 Excludes note represents "NOT INCLUDED HERE." An Excludes2 note indicates that the condition excluded is not part of the condition it is excluded from, but a patient may have both conditions at the same time. When an Excludes2 note appears under a code, it is acceptable to use both the code and the excluded code together.

Code First/Use Additional Code notes (etiology/manifestation paired codes)

Certain conditions have both an underlying etiology and multiple body system manifestations due to the underlying etiology. For such conditions the ICD-10-CM has a coding convention that requires the underlying condition be sequenced first, followed by the manifestation. Wherever such a combination exists, there is a "use additional code" note at the etiology code, and a "code first" note at the manifestation code. These instructional notes indicate the proper sequencing order of the codes, etiology followed by manifestation.

In most cases the manifestation codes will have in the code title, "in diseases classified elsewhere." Codes with this title are a component of the etiology/manifestation convention. The code title indicates that it is a manifestation code. "In diseases classified elsewhere" codes are never permitted to be used as first-listed or principal diagnosis codes. They must be used in conjunction with an underlying condition code, and they must be listed following the underlying condition.

Use additional
The words indicate an instructional note that another code may be needed.

Code first
The words indicate an instructional note that directs the coder to sequence the underlying condition before the manifestation.

Code also
A "code also" note instructs that two codes may be required to fully describe a condition, but the sequencing of the two codes is discretionary, depending on the severity of the conditions and the reason for the encounter.

7th characters and placeholder X

For codes less than 6 characters that require a 7th character, a placeholder X should be assigned for all characters less than 6. The 7th character must always be the 7th character of a code.

Annotated

Throughout the manual, revisions, additions, and deleted codes or words are indicated by the following symbols:

➡ **Revised:** Revisions within the line or code from the previous edition are indicated by the arrow.

▶ **New:** Additions to the previous edition are indicated by the triangle.

~~deleted~~ **Deleted:** Deletions from the previous edition are struck through.

ICD-10-CM Tabular List Symbols

● **Use Additional Character(s):** The red stop sign cautions that the code requires additional character(s) to ensure the greatest specificity.

X For codes less than 6 characters that require a 7th character, a placeholder X should be assigned for all characters less than 6. The 7th character must always be the 7th character of a code.

OGCR The *Official Guidelines for Coding and Reporting* symbol includes the placement of a portion of a guideline as that guideline pertains to the code by which it is located. The complete OGCR are located in Part I.

🅗 The **Hierarchical condition category (HCC)** was initiated in 2004 for the reimbursement for patients with Medicare Advantage plans (Medicare Part C). HCC is based on a list of chronic or severity of illness diagnosis codes that CMS uses to determine reimbursements to Medicare Advantage plans. The HCC risk adjustment factor data is calculated for an entire year for encounters of the patient's care.

▷ **Manifestation Code:** Describes the manifestation of an underlying disease, not the disease itself, and therefore should not be assigned as a principal diagnosis, according to the *Definitions of Medicare Code Edits* (MCE).

Age conflict: The *Definitions of Medicare Code Edits* (MCE) detects inconsistencies between a patient's age and diagnosis. For example, a 5-year-old patient with benign prostatic hypertrophy or a 78-year-old pregnant female.

The diagnosis is clinically and virtually impossible in a patient of the stated age. Therefore, either the diagnosis or the age is presumed to be incorrect. There are four age categories for diagnoses in the *Definitions of Medicare Code Edits* (MCE):

N • Newborn. Age of 0 years; a subset of diagnoses intended only for newborns and neonates (e.g., fetal distress, perinatal jaundice).

P • Pediatric. Age range is 0-17 years inclusive (e.g., Reye's syndrome, routine child health exam).

M • Maternity. Age range is 12-55 years inclusive (e.g., diabetes in pregnancy, antepartum pulmonary complication).

A • Adult. Age range is 15-124 years inclusive (e.g., senile delirium, mature cataract).

♀♂ **Sex conflict:** *Definitions of Medicare Code Edits* (MCE) detects inconsistencies between a patient's sex and any diagnosis or procedure on the patient's record. For example, a male patient with cervical cancer (diagnosis) or a female patient with a prostatectomy (procedure). In both instances, the indicated diagnosis or the procedure conflicts with the stated sex of the patient. Therefore, either the patient's diagnosis, procedure, or sex is presumed to be incorrect.

Key words

Highlight identifies key words within similar code descriptions in a particular category.

Coding Clinic Identifies the year, quarter, and page number that presents information about an ICD-10-CM code in the American Hospital Association's *Coding Clinic®* for ICD-10-CM.

Visit codingupdates.com for the full list of 2019 Present on Admission codes.

SYMBOLS AND CONVENTIONS

ICD-10-CM Tabular

Use Additional Character(s): The red stop sign cautions you that the code requires additional character(s) to ensure greatest specificity.

Volume 1, Tabular List

● **K22** **Other diseases of esophagus**

Excludes2 esophageal varices (I85.-)

X ● **V00.01** **Pedestrian on foot injured in collision with roller-skater**

A02.20 **Localized salmonella infection, unspecified**

Unacceptable Principal Diagnosis: These codes have a blue dot before them and are not permitted as a first-listed or principal diagnosis. They must be assigned in conjunction with an underlying condition code, and they must be listed following the underlying condition.

● **B95.0** **Streptococcus, group A, as the cause of diseases classified elsewhere**

A48.3 **Toxic shock syndrome**
Use additional code to identify the organism (B95, B96)

Placeholder X: The red X reminds you that for codes less than 6 characters that require a 7th character, a placeholder X should be assigned to all characters less than 6.

Unspecified: These codes are for use when the information in the medical record is insufficient to assign a more specific code. For those categories for which an unspecified code is not provided, the "other specified" code may represent both other and unspecified.

Use additional code: Located at the etiology code and directs you to assign a manifestation code.

Code first indicates the etiology code is to be first-listed before the manifestation code.

B39 **Histoplasmosis**
Code first associated AIDS (B20)

Notes define terms or give coding instructions.

E34.0 **Carcinoid syndrome**
Note: May be used as an additional code to identify functional activity associated with a carcinoid tumor.

Codes or index entries are for purposes of illustration only and may not be current.

OGCR Section I.C.6.B.5.

Neoplasm Related Pain Code G89.3 is assigned to pain documented as being related, associated or due to cancer, primary or secondary malignancy, or tumor. This code is assigned regardless of whether the pain is acute or chronic.

OGCR: The *Official Guidelines for Coding and Reporting* are placed near the codes to which they refer and are highlighted.

I70.2 **Atherosclerosis of native arteries of the extremities**
Mönckeberg's (medial) sclerosis

Use additional code, if applicable, to identify chronic total occlusion of artery of extremity (I70.92)

code, if applicable, directs the coder to other conditions that may be appropriate to report.

I74 **Arterial embolism and thrombosis**
Includes   embolic infarction
embolic occlusion
thrombotic infarction
thrombotic occlusion

The word "and" should be interpreted to mean either "and" or "or" when it appears in a statement.

Bold typeface is used on all codes and titles.

I83.001 **Varicose veins of unspecified lower extremity with ulcer of thigh**

"with" should be interpreted to mean "associated with" or "due to."

K73.2 **Chronic active hepatitis, not elsewhere classified**

"not elsewhere classified" or **NEC** identifies a code that is assigned only when the information at hand specifies a condition for which no more specific code is available.

"not otherwise specified" or **NOS** is equivalent to unspecified.

W13.9 **Fall from, out of or through building, not otherwise specified**

Codes or index entries are for purposes of illustration only and may not be current.

Excludes1 means "NOT CODED HERE!" An Excludes1 note indicates that the code excluded should never be assigned at the same time as the code above the Excludes1 note.

Includes: This note appears immediately under a three-character code title to further define, or give examples of, the content.

Codes titled "other" or "other specified" are for use when the information in the medical record provides detail for which a specific code does not exist.

Pediatric Age, Ø-17, according to the *Definitions of Medicare Code Edits* (MCE).

Females Only according to the *Definitions of Medicare Code Edits* (MCE).

M19 Other and unspecified osteoarthritis
  Excludes1   polyarthritis (M15.-)
  Excludes2   arthrosis of spine (M47.-)
         hallux rigidus (M20.2)
         osteoarthritis of spine (M47.-)

AØ6 Amebiasis
  Includes   infection due to Entamoeba histolytica

E26.Ø1 Conn's syndrome
         Code also adrenal adenoma (D35.Ø)

E25.8 Other adrenogenital disorders

OØØ.2 Ovarian pregnancy   M

PØ2.2Ø Newborn (suspected to be) affected by unspecified morphological and functional abnormalities of placenta   N

L21.Ø Seborrhea capitis
         Cradle cap   P

G3Ø.1 Alzheimer's disease with late onset   A

B37.3 Candidiasis of vulva and vagina ♀

C6Ø.1 Malignant neoplasm of glans penis ♂

Excludes2 represents "NOT INCLUDED HERE." An Excludes2 note indicates that the condition excluded is not part of the condition represented by the code, but a patient may have both conditions at the same time and it is acceptable to use both the code and the excluded code together, when appropriate.

Code also instructs that two codes may be required to fully describe a condition, but this note does not provide sequencing direction.

Maternity DX (Diagnosis) for ages 12-55 according to the *Definitions of Medicare Code Edits* (MCE).

Newborn, Age Ø, according to the *Definitions of Medicare Code Edits* (MCE).

Adult Age, 15-124, according to the *Definitions of Medicare Code Edits* (MCE).

Males Only according to the *Definitions of Medicare Code Edits* (MCE).

Codes or index entries are for purposes of illustration only and may not be current.

Manifestation according to the *Definitions of Medicare Code Edits* (MCE).

▶ *H22 Disorders of iris and ciliary body in diseases classified elsewhere*

Code first *underlying disease, such as:*
gout (M1A-, M10.-)

Key Term Highlight identifies key words within similar code descriptions in a particular category.

F10.21   Alcohol dependence, **in remission** ◄

Coding Clinic identifies the year, quarter, and page number that presents information about an ICD-10-PCS code in the American Hospital Association's *Coding Clinic®*.

B96.5   Pseudomonas (aeruginosa) (mallei) (pseudomallei) as the cause of diseases classified elsewhere
▶ Coding Clinic: 2015, Q1, P18

Codes or index entries are for purposes of illustration only and may not be current.

Alphabetic Index

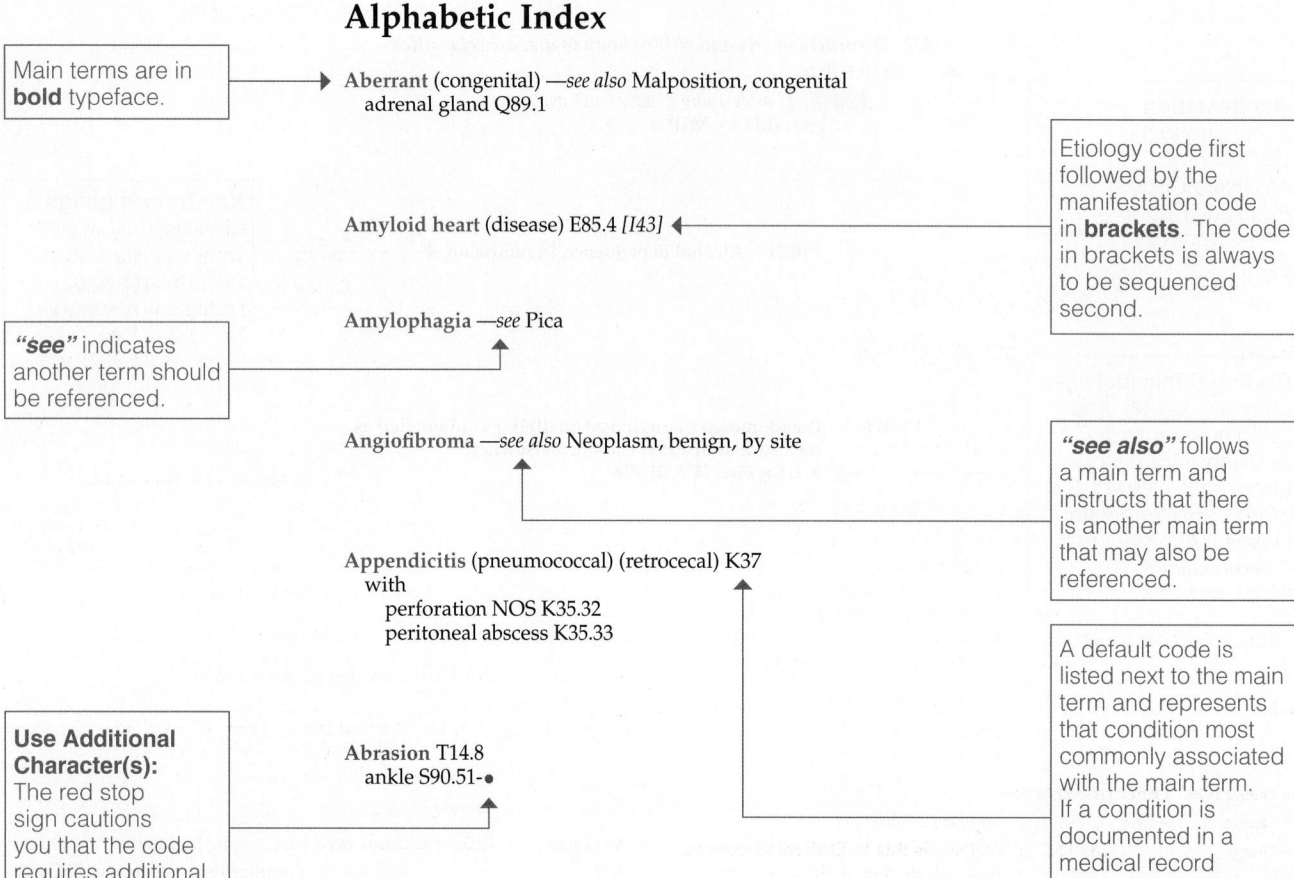

Main terms are in **bold** typeface.

Aberrant (congenital) —*see also* Malposition, congenital
   adrenal gland Q89.1

Etiology code first followed by the manifestation code in **brackets**. The code in brackets is always to be sequenced second.

Amyloid heart (disease) E85.4 *[I43]*

Amylophagia —*see* Pica

"see" indicates another term should be referenced.

Angiofibroma —*see also* Neoplasm, benign, by site

"see also" follows a main term and instructs that there is another main term that may also be referenced.

Appendicitis (pneumococcal) (retrocecal) K37
   with
      perforation NOS K35.32
      peritoneal abscess K35.33

A default code is listed next to the main term and represents that condition most commonly associated with the main term. If a condition is documented in a medical record without any additional information, such as acute or chronic, the default code should be assigned.

Use Additional Character(s):
The red stop sign cautions you that the code requires additional character(s) to ensure greatest specificity.

Abrasion T14.8
   ankle S90.51-•

Codes or index entries are for purposes of illustration only and may not be current.

No Change **CHAPTER 1**

No Change **CERTAIN INFECTIOUS AND PARASITIC DISEASES (A00-B99)**

No Change **RICKETTSIOSES (A75-A79)**

No Change **A75** Typhus fever

No Change **A75.3** Typhus fever due to Rickettsia tsutsugamushi

Add Typhus fever due to Orientia Tsutsugamushi (scrub typhus)

No Change **A77** Spotted fever [tick-borne rickettsioses]

No Change **A77.4** Ehrlichiosis

No Change **A77.49** Other ehrlichiosis

Add Ehrlichiosis due to E. ewingii

Add Ehrlichiosis due to E. muris euclairensis

No Change **A77.8** Other spotted fevers

Add Rickettsia 364D/R. philipii (Pacific Coast tick fever)

Add Spotted fever due to Rickettsia africae (African tick bite fever)

Add Spotted fever due to Rickettsia parkeri

No Change **A79** Other rickettsioses

No Change **A79.8** Other specified rickettsioses

No Change **A79.81** Rickettsiosis due to Ehrlichia sennetsu

Add Rickettsiosis due to Neorickettsia sennetsu

No Change **VIRAL AND PRION INFECTIONS OF THE CENTRAL NERVOUS SYSTEM (A80-A89)**

No Change **A84** Tick-borne viral encephalitis

No Change **A84.8** Other tick-borne viral encephalitis

Delete Louping ill

Delete Powassan virus disease

Add **A84.81** Powassan virus disease

Add **A84.89** Other tick-borne viral encephalitis

Add Louping ill

Add *Code first, if applicable, transfusion related infection (T80.22-)*

No Change **OTHER VIRAL DISEASES (B25-B34)**

No Change **B34** Viral infection of unspecified site

No Change **B34.2** Coronavirus infection, unspecified

Add **Excludes1** COVID-19 (U07.1)

No Change **MYCOSES (B35-B49)**

No Change **B48** Other mycoses, not elsewhere classified

No Change **B48.4** Penicillosis

Add Talaromycosis

No Change **PROTOZOAL DISEASES (B50-B64)**

No Change **B60** Other protozoal diseases, not elsewhere classified

No Change **B60.0** Babesiosis

Delete Piroplasmosis

Add **B60.00** Babesiosis, unspecified

Add Babesiosis due to unspecified Babesia species

Add Piroplasmosis, unspecified

Add **B60.01** Babesiosis due to Babesia microti

Add Infection due to B. microti

Add **B60.02** Babesiosis due to Babesia duncani

Add Infection due to B. duncani and B. duncani-type species

Add **B60.03** Babesiosis due to Babesia divergens

Add Babesiosis due to Babesia MO-1

Add Infection due to B. divergens and B. divergens-like strains

Add **B60.09** Other babesiosis

Add Babesiosis due to Babesia KO-1

Add Babesiosis due to Babesia venatorum

Add Infection due to other Babesia species

Add Infection due to other protozoa of the order Piroplasmida

Add Other piroplasmosis

No Change **CHAPTER 2**

No Change **NEOPLASMS (C00-D49)**

No Change **MALIGNANT NEOPLASMS OF LYMPHOID, HEMATOPOIETIC AND RELATED TISSUE (C81-C96)**

No Change **C93** Monocytic leukemia

No Change **C93.1** Chronic myelomonocytic leukemia

Add *Code also, if applicable, eosinophilia (D72.18)*

No Change **BENIGN NEOPLASMS, EXCEPT BENIGN NEUROENDOCRINE TUMORS (D10-D36)**

No Change **D21** Other benign neoplasms of connective and other soft tissue

No Change **D21.6** Benign neoplasm of connective and other soft tissue of trunk, unspecified

Revise from Benign neoplasm of connective and other soft tissue back NOS

Revise to Benign neoplasm of connective and other soft tissue of back NOS

No Change **NEOPLASMS OF UNCERTAIN BEHAVIOR, POLYCYTHEMIA VERA AND MYELODYSPLASTIC SYNDROMES (D37-D48)**

No Change **D47** Other neoplasms of uncertain behavior of lymphoid, hematopoietic and related tissue

No Change **D47.Z** Other specified neoplasms of uncertain behavior of lymphoid, hematopoietic and related tissue

No Change **D47.Z2** Castleman disease

No Change *Code also if applicable human herpesvirus 8 infection (B10.89)*

No Change **Excludes2**

Revise from Kaposi›s sarcoma (C46-)

Revise to Kaposi's sarcoma (C46.-)

No Change **CHAPTER 3**

No Change **DISEASES OF THE BLOOD AND BLOOD-FORMING ORGANS AND CERTAIN DISORDERS INVOLVING THE IMMUNE MECHANISM (D50-D89)**

No Change **HEMOLYTIC ANEMIAS (D55-D59)**

No Change	**D55**	**Anemia due to enzyme disorders**
No Change	**D55.2**	**Anemia due to disorders of glycolytic enzymes**
No Change		**Excludes1**
Revise from		disorders of glycolysis not associated with anemia (E74.8)
Revise to		disorders of glycolysis not associated with anemia (E74.81-)

No Change	**D57**	**Sickle-cell disorders**
No Change	**D57.0**	**Hb-SS disease with crisis**
Revise from		Sickle-cell disease NOS with crisis
Revise to		Sickle-cell disease with crisis
No Change		**D57.00 Hb-SS disease with crisis, unspecified**
Add		Hb-SS disease with (painful) crisis NOS
Add		Hb-SS disease with vasoocclusive pain NOS
Add		**D57.03 Hb-SS disease with cerebral vascular involvement**
Add		Code also, if applicable, cerebral infarction (I63.-)
Add		**D57.09 Hb-SS disease with crisis with other specified complication**
Add		Use additional code to identify complications, such as:
Add		cholelithiasis (K80.-)
Add		priapism (N48.32)
No Change	**D57.2**	**Sickle-cell/Hb-C disease**
No Change		**D57.21 Sickle-cell/Hb-C disease with crisis**
Add		**D57.213 Sickle-cell/Hb-C disease with cerebral vascular involvement**
Add		Code also, if applicable, cerebral infarction (I63.-)
Add		**D57.218 Sickle-cell/Hb-C disease with crisis with other specified complication**
Add		Use additional code to identify complications, such as:
Add		cholelithiasis (K80.-)
Add		priapism (N48.32)
No Change		**D57.219 Sickle-cell/Hb-C disease with crisis, unspecified**
Add		Sickle-cell/Hb-C disease with vasoocclusive pain NOS
No Change	**D57.4**	**Sickle-cell thalassemia**
Revise from		**D57.41 Sickle-cell thalassemia with crisis**
Revise to		**D57.41 Sickle-cell thalassemia, unspecified, with crisis**
Add		Sickle-cell thalassemia with (painful) crisis NOS
Revise from		Sickle-cell thalassemia with vasoocclusive pain
Revise to		Sickle-cell thalassemia with vasoocclusive pain NOS
Revise from		**D57.411 Sickle-cell thalassemia with acute chest syndrome**
Revise to		**D57.411 Sickle-cell thalassemia, unspecified, with acute chest syndrome**

Revise from		**D57.412 Sickle-cell thalassemia with splenic sequestration**
Revise to		**D57.412 Sickle-cell thalassemia with, unspecified, splenic sequestration**
Add		**D57.413 Sickle-cell thalassemia, unspecified, with cerebral vascular involvement**
Add		Code also, if applicable cerebral infarction (I63.-)
Add		**D57.418 Sickle-cell thalassemia, unspecified, with crisis with other specified complication**
Add		Use additional code to identify complications, such as:
Add		cholelithiasis (K80.-)
Add		priapism (N48.32)
Revise from		**D57.419 Sickle-cell thalassemia with crisis, unspecified**
Revise to		**D57.419 Sickle-cell thalassemia with, unspecified, crisis**
Revise from		Sickle-cell thalassemia with crisis NOS
Revise to		Sickle-cell thalassemia with (painful) crisis NOS
Add		Sickle-cell thalassemia with vasoocclusive pain
Add	**D57.42**	**Sickle-cell thalassemia beta zero without crisis**
Add		HbS-beta zero without crisis
Add		Sickle-cell beta zero without crisis
Add	**D57.43**	**Sickle-cell thalassemia beta zero with crisis**
Add		HbS-beta zero with crisis
Add		Sickle-cell beta zero with crisis
Add		**D57.431 Sickle-cell thalassemia beta zero with acute chest syndrome**
Add		HbS-beta zero with acute chest syndrome
Add		Sickle-cell beta zero with acute chest syndrome
Add		**D57.432 Sickle-cell thalassemia beta zero with splenic sequestration**
Add		HbS-beta zero with splenic sequestration
Add		Sickle-cell beta zero with splenic sequestration
Add		**D57.433 Sickle-cell thalassemia beta zero with cerebral vascular involvement**
Add		HbS-beta zero with cerebral vascular involvement
Add		Sickle-cell beta zero with cerebral vascular involvement
Add		Code also, if applicable cerebral infarction (I63.-)
Add		**D57.438 Sickle-cell thalassemia beta zero with crisis with other specified complication**
Add		HbS-beta zero with other specified complication
Add		Sickle-cell beta zero with other specified complication
Add		Use additional code to identify complications, such as:
Add		cholelithiasis (K80.-)
Add		priapism (N48.32)

Add	**D57.439**	**Sickle-cell thalassemia beta zero with crisis, unspecified**
Add		HbS-beta zero with other specified complication
Add		Sickle-cell beta zero with crisis unspecified
Add		Sickle-cell thalassemia beta zero with (painful) crisis NOS
Add		Sickle-cell thalassemia beta zero with vasoocclusive pain
Add	**D57.44**	**Sickle-cell thalassemia beta plus without crisis**
Add		HbS-beta plus without crisis
Add		Sickle-cell beta plus without crisis
Add	**D57.45**	**Sickle-cell thalassemia beta plus with crisis**
Add		HbS-beta plus with crisis
Add		Sickle-cell beta plus with crisis
Add	**D57.451**	**Sickle-cell thalassemia beta plus with acute chest syndrome**
Add		HbS-beta plus with acute chest syndrome
Add		Sickle-cell beta plus with acute chest syndrome
Add	**D57.452**	**Sickle-cell thalassemia beta plus with splenic sequestration**
Add		HbS-beta plus with splenic sequestration
Add		Sickle-cell beta plus with splenic sequestration
Add	**D57.453**	**Sickle-cell thalassemia beta plus with cerebral vascular involvement**
Add		HbS-beta plus with cerebral vascular involvement
Add		Sickle-cell beta plus with cerebral vascular involvement
Add		Code also, if applicable cerebral infarction (I63.-)
Add	**D57.458**	**Sickle-cell thalassemia beta plus with crisis with other specified complication**
Add		HbS-beta plus with crisis with other specified complication
Add		Sickle-cell beta plus with crisis with other specified complication
Add		Use additional code to identify complications, such as:
Add		cholelithiasis (K80.-)
Add		priapism (N48.32)
Add	**D57.459**	**Sickle-cell thalassemia beta plus with crisis, unspecified**
Add		HbS-beta plus with crisis with unspecified complication
Add		Sickle-cell beta plus with crisis with unspecified complication
Add		Sickle-cell thalassemia beta plus with (painful) crisis NOS
Add		Sickle-cell thalassemia beta plus with vasoocclusive pain

No Change	**D57.8**	**Other sickle-cell disorders**
No Change	**D57.81**	**Other sickle-cell disorders with crisis**
Add	**D57.813**	**Other sickle-cell disorders with cerebral vascular involvement**
Add		Code also, if applicable: cerebral infarction (I63.-)
Add	**D57.818**	**Other sickle-cell disorders with crisis with other specified complication**
Add		Use additional code to identify complications, such as:
Add		cholelithiasis (K80.-)
Add		priapism (N48.32)
No Change	**D57.819**	**Other sickle-cell disorders with crisis, unspecified**
Add		Other sickle-cell disorders with vasooclusive pain NOS
No Change **D59**		**Acquired hemolytic anemia**
No Change	**D59.1**	**Other autoimmune hemolytic anemias**
No Change		Autoimmune hemolytic disease (cold type) (warm type)
No Change		Chronic cold hemagglutinin disease
No Change		Cold agglutinin disease
No Change		Cold agglutinin hemoglobinuria
No Change		Cold type (secondary) (symptomatic) hemolytic anemia
Delete		Warm type (secondary) (symptomatic) hemolytic anemia
Delete	**Excludes1**	Evans syndrome (D69.41)
Delete		hemolytic disease of newborn (P55.-)
Delete		paroxysmal cold hemoglobinuria (D59.6)
Add	**Excludes2**	Evans syndrome (D69.41)
Add		hemolytic disease of newborn (P55.-)
Add		paroxysmal cold hemoglobinuria (D59.6)
Add	**D59.10**	**Autoimmune hemolytic anemia, unspecified**
Add	**D59.11**	**Warm autoimmune hemolytic anemia**
Add		Warm type (primary) (secondary) (symptomatic) autoimmune hemolytic anemia
Add		Warm type autoimmune hemolytic disease
Add	**D59.12**	**Cold autoimmune hemolytic anemia**
Add		Chronic cold hemagglutinin disease
Add		Cold agglutinin disease
Add		Cold agglutinin hemoglobinuria
Add		Cold type (primary) (secondary) (symptomatic) autoimmune hemolytic anemia
Add		Cold type autoimmune hemolytic disease
Add	**D59.13**	**Mixed type autoimmune hemolytic anemia**
Add		Mixed type autoimmune hemolytic disease
Add		Mixed type, cold and warm, (primary) (secondary) (symptomatic) autoimmune hemolyticanemia
Add	**D59.19**	**Other autoimmune hemolytic anemia**

No Change   **APLASTIC AND OTHER ANEMIAS AND OTHER BONE MARROW FAILURE SYNDROMES (D60-D64)**

No Change **D61**   Other aplastic anemias and other bone marrow failure syndromes
Delete   **Excludes1** neutropenia (D70.-)
Add   **Excludes2** neutropenia (D70.-)

No Change   **OTHER DISORDERS OF BLOOD AND BLOOD-FORMING ORGANS (D70-D77)**

No Change **D72**   Other disorders of white blood cells
No Change **D72.1**   Eosinophilia
Delete   Allergic eosinophilia
Delete   Hereditary eosinophilia
Delete   **Excludes1** Löffler's syndrome (J82)
No Change   pulmonary eosinophilia (J82)
Add   **Excludes2** Löffler's syndrome (J82)
Add   pulmonary eosinophilia (J82)
Add   **D72.10**   Eosinophilia, unspecified
Add   **D72.11**   Hypereosinophilic syndrome [HES]
Add   **D72.110** Idiopathic hypereosinophilic syndrome [IHES]
Add   **D72.111** Lymphocytic Variant Hypereosinophilic Syndrome [LHES]
No Change
Add   Lymphocyte variant hypereosinophilia
Add   Code also, if applicable, any associated lymphocytic neoplastic disorder
Add   **D72.118** Other hypereosinophilic syndrome
Add   Episodic angioedema with eosinophilia
Add   Gleich's syndrome
Add   **D72.119** Hypereosinophilic syndrome [HES], unspecified
Add   **D72.12**   Drug rash with eosinophilia and systemic symptoms syndrome
Add   DRESS syndrome
Add   Use additional code for adverse effect, if applicable, to identify drug (T36-T50 with fifth or sixth character 5)
Add   **D72.18**   Eosinophilia in diseases classified elsewhere
Add   *Code first* underlying disease, such as:
Add   chronic myelomonocytic leukemia (C93.1-)
Add   **D72.19**   Other eosinophilia
Add   Familial eosinophilia
Add   Hereditary eosinophilia

No Change   **CERTAIN DISORDERS INVOLVING THE IMMUNE MECHANISM (D80-D89)**

No Change **D84**   Other immunodeficiencies
No Change **D84.8**   Other specified immunodeficiencies
Add   **D84.81**   Immunodeficiency due to conditions classified elsewhere
Add   Code first underlying condition, such as:
Add   chromosomal abnormalities (Q90-Q99)
Add   diabetes mellitus (E08-E13)
Add   malignant neoplasms (C00-C96)
Add   **Excludes1** certain disorders involving the immune mechanism (D80-D83, D84.0, D84.1, D84.9)
Add   human immunodeficiency virus [HIV] disease (B20)

Add   **D84.82**   Immunodeficiency due to drugs and external causes
Add   **D84.821**   Immunodeficiency due to drugs
Add   Immunodeficiency due to (current or past) medication
Add   Use additional code for adverse effect if applicable, to identify adverse effect of drug (T36-T50 with fifth or six character 5)
Add   Use additional code, if applicable, for associated long term (current) drug therapy drug or medication such as:
Add   long term (current) drug therapy systemic steroids (Z79.52)
Add   other long term (current) drug therapy (Z79.899)
Add   **D84.822**   Immunodeficiency due to external causes
Add   Code also, if applicable, radiological procedure and radiotherapy (Y84.2)
Add   Use additional code for external cause such as:
Add   exposure to ionizing radiation (W88)
Add   **D84.89**   Other immunodeficiencies
No Change **D84.9**   Immunodeficiency, unspecified
Add   Immunocompromised NOS
Add   Immunodeficient NOS
Add   Immunosuppressed NOS]

No Change **D89**   Other disorders involving the immune mechanism, not elsewhere classified
No Change **D89.8**   Other specified disorders involving the immune mechanism, not elsewhere classified
Add   **D89.83**   Cytokine release syndrome
Add   *Code first* underlying cause, such as:
Add   complications following infusion, transfusion and therapeutic injection (T80.89-)
Add   complications of transplanted organs and tissue (T86.-)
Add   Use additional code to identify associated manifestations
Add   **D89.831**   Cytokine release syndrome, grade 1
Add   **D89.832**   Cytokine release syndrome, grade 2
Add   **D89.833**   Cytokine release syndrome, grade 3
Add   **D89.834**   Cytokine release syndrome, grade 4
Add   **D89.835**   Cytokine release syndrome, grade 5
Add   **D89.839**   Cytokine release syndrome, grade unspecified

No Change **CHAPTER 4**

No Change **ENDOCRINE, NUTRITIONAL AND METABOLIC DISEASES (E00-E89)**

No Change   **METABOLIC DISORDERS (E70-E88)**

No Change   **Excludes1**
Revise from   Ehlers-Danlos syndrome (Q79.6-)
Revise to   Ehlers-Danlos syndromes (Q79.6-)

No Change **E70**   Disorders of aromatic amino-acid metabolism

No Change   **E70.8**   Other disorders of aromatic amino-acid metabolism

Add   **E70.81**   **Aromatic L-amino acid decarboxylase deficiency**
Add   AADC deficiency

Add   **E70.89**   **Other disorders of aromatic amino-acid metabolism**

No Change **E74**   Other disorders of carbohydrate metabolism

No Change   **E74.8**   Other specified disorders of carbohydrate metabolism
Delete   Essential pentosuria
Delete   Renal glycosuria

Add   **E74.81**   **Disorders of glucose transport, not elsewhere classified**

Add   **E74.810**   **Glucose transporter protein type 1 deficiency**
Add   De Vivo syndrome
Add   Glucose transport defect, blood-brain barrier
Add   GLUT1 deficiency
Add   GLUT1 deficiency syndrome 1, infantile onset
Add   GLUT1 deficiency syndrome 2, childhood onset

Add   **E74.818**   **Other disorders of glucose transport**
Add   (Familial) renal glycosuria

Add   **E74.819**   **Disorders of glucose transport, unspecified**

Add   **E74.89**   **Other specified disorders of carbohydrate metabolism**
Add   Essential pentosuria

No Change **E86**   Volume depletion
Delete   **Excludes1**   hypovolemic shock NOS (R57.1)
Add   **Excludes2**   hypovolemic shock NOS (R57.1)

No Change **E88**   Other and unspecified metabolic disorders
No Change   **E88.0**   Disorders of plasma-protein metabolism, not elsewhere classified
Delete   **Excludes1**   disorder of lipoprotein metabolism (E78.-)
Add   **Excludes2**   disorder of lipoprotein metabolism (E78.-)

No Change **CHAPTER 5**

No Change **MENTAL, BEHAVIORAL AND NEURODEVELOPMENTAL DISORDERS (F01-F99)**

No Change   **MENTAL AND BEHAVIORAL DISORDERS DUE TO PSYCHOACTIVE SUBSTANCE USE (F10-F19)**

No Change **F10**   Alcohol related disorders
No Change   **F10.1**   Alcohol abuse
Add   **F10.13**   Alcohol abuse, with withdrawal
Add   **F10.130**   **Alcohol abuse with withdrawal, uncomplicated**
Add   **F10.131**   **Alcohol abuse with withdrawal delirium**

Add   **F10.132**   **Alcohol abuse with withdrawal with perceptual disturbance**
Add   **F10.139**   **Alcohol abuse with withdrawal, unspecified**

No Change   **F10.9**   Alcohol use, unspecified
Add   **F10.93**   **Alcohol use, unspecified with withdrawal**
Add   **F10.930**   **Alcohol use, unspecified with withdrawal, uncomplicated**
Add   **F10.931**   **Alcohol use, unspecified with withdrawal delirium**
Add   **F10.932**   **Alcohol use, unspecified with withdrawal with perceptual disturbance**
Add   **F10.939**   **Alcohol use, unspecified with withdrawal, unspecified**

No Change **F11**   Opioid related disorders
No Change   **F11.1**   Opioid abuse
Add   **F11.13**   Opioid abuse with withdrawal

No Change **F12**   Cannabis related disorders
No Change   **F12.1**   Cannabis abuse
Add   **F12.13**   Cannabis abuse with withdrawal

No Change **F13**   Sedative, hypnotic, or anxiolytic related disorders
No Change   **F13.1**   Sedative, hypnotic or anxiolytic-related abuse
Add   **F13.13**   Sedative, hypnotic or anxiolytic abuse with withdrawal
Add   **F13.130**   **Sedative, hypnotic or anxiolytic abuse with withdrawal, uncomplicated**
Add   **F13.131**   **Sedative, hypnotic or anxiolytic abuse with withdrawal delirium**
Add   **F13.132**   **Sedative, hypnotic or anxiolytic abuse with withdrawal with perceptual disturbance**
Add   **F13.139**   **Sedative, hypnotic or anxiolytic abuse with withdrawal, unspecified**

No Change **F14**   Cocaine related disorders
No Change   **F14.1**   Cocaine abuse
Add   **F14.13**   Cocaine abuse, unspecified with withdrawal
No Change   **F14.9**   Cocaine use, unspecified
Add   **F14.93**   Cocaine use, unspecified with withdrawal

No Change **F15**   Other stimulant related disorders
No Change   **F15.1**   Other stimulant abuse
Add   **F15.13**   Other stimulant abuse with withdrawal

No Change **F19**   Other psychoactive substance related disorders
No Change   **F19.1**   Other psychoactive substance abuse
Add   **F19.13**   Other psychoactive substance abuse with withdrawal
Add   **F19.130**   **Other psychoactive substance abuse with withdrawal, uncomplicated**
Add   **F19.131**   **Other psychoactive substance abuse with withdrawal delirium**
Add   **F19.132**   **Other psychoactive substance abuse with withdrawal with perceptual disturbance**
Add   **F19.139**   **Other psychoactive substance abuse with withdrawal, unspecified**

No Change	**DISORDERS OF ADULT PERSONALITY AND BEHAVIOR (F60-F69)**	

No Change **F60**   Specific personality disorders
No Change   **F60.5   Obsessive-compulsive personality disorder**
No Change   **Excludes2**
Revise from   obsessive-compulsive disorder (F42-)
Revise to   obsessive-compulsive disorder (F42.-)

No Change	**BEHAVIORAL AND EMOTIONAL DISORDERS WITH ONSET USUALLY OCCURRING IN CHILDHOOD AND ADOLESCENCE (F90-F98)**

No Change **F98**   Other behavioral and emotional disorders with onset usually occurring in childhood and adolescence
No Change   **Excludes2**
Revise from   obsessive-compulsive disorder (F42-)
Revise to   obsessive-compulsive disorder (F423-)
No Change   **F98.4   Stereotyped movement disorders**
No Change   **Excludes2**
Revise from   compulsions in obsessive-compulsive disorder (F42-)
Revise to   compulsions in obsessive-compulsive disorder (F42.-)

No Change **CHAPTER 6**

No Change **DISEASES OF THE NERVOUS SYSTEM (G00-G99)**

No Change	**SYSTEMIC ATROPHIES PRIMARILY AFFECTING THE CENTRAL NERVOUS SYSTEM (G10-G14)**

No Change **G11**   Hereditary ataxia
No Change   **G11.1   Early-onset cerebellar ataxia**
Delete   Early-onset cerebellar ataxia with essential tremor
Delete   Early-onset cerebellar ataxia with myoclonus [Hunt's ataxia]
Delete   Early-onset cerebellar ataxia with retained tendon reflexes
Delete   Friedreich's ataxia (autosomal recessive)
Delete   X-linked recessive spinocerebellar ataxia
Add   **G11.10 Early-onset cerebellar ataxia, unspecified**
Add   **G11.11 Friedreich ataxia**
Add   Autosomal recessive Friedreich ataxia
Add   Friedreich ataxia with retained reflexes
Add   **G11.19 Other early-onset cerebellar ataxia**
Add   Early-onset cerebellar ataxia with essential tremor
Add   Early-onset cerebellar ataxia with myoclonus [Hunt's ataxia]
Add   Early-onset cerebellar ataxia with retained tendon reflexes
Add   X-linked recessive spinocerebellar ataxia

No Change	**EXTRAPYRAMIDAL AND MOVEMENT DISORDERS (G20-G26)**

No Change **G20**   Parkinson's disease
Add   Use additional code to identify:
Add   dementia with behavioral disturbance (F02.81)
Add   dementia without behavioral disturbance (F02.80)

No Change	**EPISODIC AND PAROXYSMAL DISORDERS (G40-G47)**

No Change **G40**   Epilepsy and recurrent seizures
No Change   **G40.4   Other generalized epilepsy and epileptic syndromes**
Add   **G40.42   Cyclin-Dependent Kinase-Like 5 Deficiency Disorder**
No Change   CDKL5
Add   Use additional code, if known, to identify associated manifestations, such as:
Add   cortical blindness (H47.61-)
Add   global developmental delay (F88)
No Change   **G40.8   Other epilepsy and recurrent seizures**
Add   **G40.83   Dravet syndrome**
Add   Polymorphic epilepsy in infancy (PMEI)
Add   Severe myoclonic epilepsy in infancy (SMEI)
Add   **G40.833   Dravet syndrome, intractable, with status epilepticus**
Add   **G40.834   Dravet syndrome, intractable, without status epilepticus**
Add   Dravet syndrome NOS

No Change **G43**   Migraine
No Change   **Excludes1**
Revise from   headache NOS (R51)
Revise to   headache NOS (R51.9)

No Change **G44**   Other headache syndromes
No Change   **Excludes1**
Revise from   headache NOS (R51)
Revise to   headache NOS (R51.9)
No Change   **G44.8   Other specified headache syndromes**
Add   **Excludes2**   headache with orthostatic or positional component, not elsewhere classified (R51.0)

No Change	**DISEASES OF MYONEURAL JUNCTION AND MUSCLE (G70-G73)**

No Change **G71**   Primary disorders of muscles
No Change   **G71.2   Congenital myopathies**
Delete   Central core disease
Delete   Fiber-type disproportion
Delete   Minicore disease
Delete   Multicore disease
Delete   Myotubular (centronuclear) myopathy
Delete   Nemaline myopathy
Delete   **Excludes1**   arthrogryposis multiplex congenita (Q74.3)
Add   **Excludes2**   arthrogryposis multiplex congenita (Q74.3)
Add   **G71.20   Congenital myopathy, unspecifed**
Add   **G71.21   Nemaline myopathy**
Add   **G71.22   Centronuclear myopathy**
Add   **G71.220   X-linked myotubular myopathy**
Add   Myotubular (centronuclear) myopathy
Add   **G71.228   Other centronuclear myopathy**
Add   Autosomal centronuclear myopathy
Add   Autosomal dominant centronuclear myopathy
Add   Autosomal recessive centronuclear myopathy
Add   Centronuclear myopathy, NOS
Add   **G71.29   Other congenital myopathy**
Add   Central core disease
Add   Minicore disease
Add   Multicore disease
Add   Multiminicore disease

No Change		**OTHER DISORDERS OF THE NERVOUS SYSTEM (G89-G99)**
No Change	**G89**	**Pain, not elsewhere classified**
No Change		**Excludes2** localized pain, unspecified type - code to pain by site, such as:
Revise from		headache (R51)
Revise to		headache (R51.9)
No Change	**G92**	**Toxic encephalopathy**
Revise from		*Code first if applicable, drug induced (T36-T50)*
Revise to		*Code first if applicable, drug induced (T36-T50) or use (T51-T65) to identify toxic agent*
No Change	**G93**	**Other disorders of brain**
No Change		**G93.2 Benign intracranial hypertension**
Add		Pseudotumor
Add		**Excludes1** obstructive hydrocephalus (G91.1)
No Change		**G93.4 Other and unspecified encephalopathy**
Delete		**Excludes1** toxic (metabolic) encephalopathy (G92)
Add		**Excludes2** toxic (metabolic) encephalopathy (G92)
No Change	**G96**	**Other disorders of central nervous system**
No Change		**G96.0 Cerebrospinal fluid leak**
Add		Code also if applicable:
Add		intracranial hypotension (G96.81-)
Add		**G96.00 Cerebrospinal fluid leak, unspecified**
Add		Code also if applicable:
Add		head injury (S00.- to S09.-)
Add		**G96.01 Cranial cerebrospinal fluid leak, spontaneous**
Add		Otorrhea due to spontaneous cerebrospinal fluid CSF leak
Add		Rhinorrhea due to spontaneous cerebrospinal fluid CSF leak
Add		Spontaneous cerebrospinal fluid leak from skull base
Add		**G96.02 Spinal cerebrospinal fluid leak, spontaneous**
Add		Spontaneous cerebrospinal fluid leak from spine
Add		**G96.08 Other cranial cerebrospinal fluid leak**
Add		Postoperative cranial cerebrospinal fluid leak
Add		Traumatic cranial cerebrospinal fluid leak
Add		Code also if applicable:
Add		head injury (S00.- to S09.-)
Add		**G96.09 Other spinal cerebrospinal fluid leak**
Add		Other spinal CSF leak
Add		Postoperative spinal cerebrospinal fluid leak
Add		Traumatic spinal cerebrospinal fluid leak
Add		Code also if applicable:
Add		head injury (S00.- to S09.-)
No Change		**G96.1 Disorders of meninges, not elsewhere classified**
No Change		**G96.11 Dural tear**
Add		Code also intracranial hypotension, if applicable (G96.81-)
No Change		**G96.19 Other disorders of meninges, not elsewhere classified**
Add		**G96.191 Perineural cyst**
Add		Cervical nerve root cyst
Add		Lumbar nerve root cyst
Add		Sacral nerve root cyst
Add		Tarlov cyst
Add		Thoracic nerve root cyst
Add		**G96.198 Other disorders of meninges, not elsewhere classified**

No Change		**G96.8 Other specified disorders of central nervous system**
Add		**G96.81 Intracranial hypotension**
Add		Code also any associated diagnoses, such as:
Add		Brachial amyotrophy (G54.5)
Add		Cerebrospinal fluid leak from spine (G96.02)
Add		Cranial nerve disorders in diseases classified elsewhere (G53)
Add		Nerve root and compressions in diseases classified elsewhere (G55)
Add		Nonpyogenic thrombosis of intracranial venous system (I67.6)
Add		Nontraumatic intracerebral hemorrhage (I61.-)
Add		Nontraumatic subdural hemorrhage (I62.0-)
Add		Other and unspecified cord compression (G95.2-)
Add		Other secondary parkinsonism (G21.8)
Add		Reversible cerebrovascular vasoconstriction syndrome (I67.841)
Add		Spinal cord herniation (G95.89)
Add		Stroke (I63.-)
Add		Syringomyelia (G95.0)
Add		**G96.810 Intracranial hypotension, unspecified**
Add		**G96.811 Intracranial hypotension, spontaneous**
Add		**G96.819 Other intracranial hypotension**
Add		**G96.89 Other specified disorders of central nervous system**
No Change	**G97**	**Intraoperative and postprocedural complications and disorders of nervous system, not elsewhere classified**
No Change		**G97.0 Cerebrospinal fluid leak from spinal puncture**
Add		Code also any associated diagnoses or complications, such as:
Add		intracranial hypotension following a procedure (G97.83-G97.84)
No Change		**G97.1 Other reaction to spinal and lumbar puncture**
No Change		Headache due to lumbar puncture
Add		Other reaction to spinal dural puncture
Add		Code also, if applicable, any associated headache with orthostatic component (R51.0)
No Change		**G97.2 Intracranial hypotension following ventricular shunting**
Add		Code also any associated diagnoses or complications
No Change		**G97.4 Accidental puncture and laceration of a nervous system organ or structure during a procedure**
No Change		**G97.41 Accidental puncture or laceration of dura during a procedure**
Add		Code also any associated diagnoses or complications
No Change		**G97.8 Other intraoperative and postprocedural complications and disorders of nervous system**
Add		**G97.83 Intracranial hypotension following lumbar cerebrospinal fluid shunting**
Add		Code also any associated diagnoses or complications
Add		**G97.84 Intracranial hypotension following other procedure**
Add		Code also, if applicable:
Add		accidental puncture or laceration of dura during a procedure (G97.41)
Add		cerebrospinal fluid leak from spinal puncture (G97.0)

No Change **CHAPTER 7**

No Change **DISEASES OF THE EYE AND ADNEXA (H00-H59)**

No Change **DISORDERS OF SCLERA, CORNEA, IRIS AND CILIARY BODY (H15-H22)**

No Change H18   Other disorders of cornea
No Change   H18.5   Hereditary corneal dystrophies
No Change   H18.50   Unspecified hereditary corneal dystrophies
Add   H18.501   Unspecified hereditary corneal dystrophies, right eye
Add   H18.502   Unspecified hereditary corneal dystrophies, left eye
Add   H18.503   Unspecified hereditary corneal dystrophies, bilateral
Add   H18.509   Unspecified hereditary corneal dystrophies, unspecified eye
No Change   H18.51   Endothelial corneal dystrophy
No Change   Fuchs' dystrophy
Add   H18.511   Endothelial corneal dystrophy, right eye
Add   H18.512   Endothelial corneal dystrophy, left eye
Add   H18.513   Endothelial corneal dystrophy, bilateral
Add   H18.519   Endothelial corneal dystrophy, unspecified eye
No Change   H18.52   Epithelial (juvenile) corneal dystrophy
Add   H18.521   Epithelial (juvenile) corneal dystrophy, right eye
Add   H18.522   Epithelial (juvenile) corneal dystrophy, left eye
Add   H18.523   Epithelial (juvenile) corneal dystrophy, bilateral
Add   H18.529   Epithelial (juvenile) corneal dystrophy, unspecified eye
No Change   H18.53   Granular corneal dystrophy
Add   H18.531   Granular corneal dystrophy, right eye
Add   H18.532   Granular corneal dystrophy, left eye
Add   H18.533   Granular corneal dystrophy, bilateral
Add   H18.539   Granular corneal dystrophy, unspecified eye
No Change   H18.54   Lattice corneal dystrophy
Add   H18.541   Lattice corneal dystrophy, right eye
Add   H18.542   Lattice corneal dystrophy, left eye
Add   H18.543   Lattice corneal dystrophy, bilateral
Add   H18.549   Lattice corneal dystrophy, unspecified eye
No Change   H18.55   Macular corneal dystrophy
Add   H18.551   Macular corneal dystrophy, right eye
Add   H18.552   Macular corneal dystrophy, left eye
Add   H18.553   Macular corneal dystrophy, bilateral
Add   H18.559   Macular corneal dystrophy, unspecified eye
No Change   H18.59   Other hereditary corneal dystrophies
Add   H18.591   Other hereditary corneal dystrophies, right eye
Add   H18.592   Other hereditary corneal dystrophies, left eye
Add   H18.593   Other hereditary corneal dystrophies, bilateral
Add   H18.599   Other hereditary corneal dystrophies, unspecified eye

No Change **OTHER DISORDERS OF EYE AND ADNEXA (H55-H57)**

No Change H55   Nystagmus and other irregular eye movements
No Change   H55.8   Other irregular eye movements
Revise from   H55.81   Saccadic eye movements
Add   H55.81   Deficient saccadic eye movements
Add   H55.82   Deficient smooth pursuit eye movements

No Change **CHAPTER 9**

No Change **DISEASES OF THE CIRCULATORY SYSTEM (I00-I99)**

No Change **HYPERTENSIVE DISEASES (I10-I16)**

No Change I11   Hypertensive heart disease
Revise from   **Includes**   any condition in I50.-, I51.4-I51.9 due to hypertension
Revise to   **Includes**   any condition in I50.- or I51.4-I51.7, I51.89, I51.9 due to hypertension

No Change **PULMONARY HEART DISEASE AND DISEASES**
No Change **OF PULMONARY CIRCULATION (I26-I28)**

No Change I27   Other pulmonary heart diseases
No Change   I27.2   Other secondary pulmonary hypertension
No Change   I27.29   Other secondary pulmonary hypertension
No Change   Code also other associated disorders, if known, such as:
Revise from   chronic myeloid leukemia
No Change   (C92.10- C92.22)
Revise to   chronic myeloid leukemia (C92.10-C92.22)

No Change **OTHER FORMS OF HEART DISEASE (I30-I52)**

No Change I46   Cardiac arrest
Delete   **Excludes1**   cardiogenic shock (R57.0)
Add   **Excludes2**   cardiogenic shock (R57.0)

No Change **CEREBROVASCULAR DISEASES (I60-I69)**

No Change I63   Cerebral infarction
Add   **Excludes1**   neonatal cerebral infarction (P91.82-)

No Change **DISEASES OF ARTERIES, ARTERIOLES AND CAPILLARIES (I70-I79)**

No Change I70   Atherosclerosis
No Change   I70.2   Atherosclerosis of native arteries of the extremities
No Change   I70.22   Atherosclerosis of native arteries of extremities with rest pain
Add   **Includes**   chronic limb-threatening ischemia NOS of native arteries of extremities
Add   chronic limb-threatening ischemia of native arteries of extremities with rest pain
Add   critical limb ischemia NOS of native arteries of extremities
Add   critical limb ischemia of native arteries of extremities with rest pain

No Change	I70.23	**Atherosclerosis of native arteries of right leg with ulceration**
Add	**Includes**	chronic limb-threatening ischemia of native arteries of right leg with ulceration
Add		critical limb ischemia of native arteries of right leg with ulceration
No Change	I70.24	**Atherosclerosis of native arteries of left leg with ulceration**
Add	**Includes**	chronic limb-threatening ischemia of native arteries of left leg with ulceration
Add		critical limb ischemia of native arteries of left leg with ulceration
No Change	I70.26	**Atherosclerosis of native arteries of extremities with gangrene**
Add	**Includes**	chronic limb-threatening ischemia of native arteries of extremities with gangrene
Add		critical limb ischemia of native arteries of extremities with gangrene
No Change	I70.3	**Atherosclerosis of unspecified type of bypass graft(s) of the extremities**
No Change	I70.32	**Atherosclerosis of unspecified type of bypass graft(s) of the extremities with rest pain**
Add	**Includes**	chronic limb-threatening ischemia NOS of unspecified type of bypass graft(s) of the extremities
Add		chronic limb-threatening ischemia of unspecified type of bypass graft(s) of the extremities with rest pain, right leg
Add		critical limb ischemia NOS of unspecified type of bypass graft(s) of the extremities
Add		critical limb ischemia of unspecified type of bypass graft(s) of the extremities with rest pain
No Change	I70.33	**Atherosclerosis of unspecified type of bypass graft(s) of the right leg with ulceration**
Add	**Includes**	chronic limb-threatening ischemia of unspecified type of bypass graft(s) of the right leg with ulceration
Add		critical limb ischemia of unspecified type of bypass graft(s) of the right leg with ulceration

No Change	I70.34	**Atherosclerosis of unspecified type of bypass graft(s) of the left leg with ulceration**
Add	**Includes**	chronic limb-threatening ischemia of unspecified type of bypass graft(s) of the left leg with ulceration
Add		critical limb ischemia of unspecified type of bypass graft(s) of the left leg with ulceration
No Change	I70.36	**Atherosclerosis of unspecified type of bypass graft(s) of the extremities with gangrene**
Add	**Includes**	chronic limb-threatening ischemia of unspecified type of bypass graft(s) of the extremities with gangrene
Add		critical limb ischemia of unspecified type of bypass graft(s) of the extremities with gangrene
No Change	I70.4	**Atherosclerosis of autologous vein bypass graft(s) of the extremities**
No Change	I70.42	**Atherosclerosis of autologous vein bypass graft(s) of the extremities with rest pain**
Add	**Includes**	chronic limb-threatening ischemia NOS of autologous vein bypass graft(s) of the extremities
Add		chronic limb-threatening ischemia of autologous vein bypass graft(s) of the extremities with rest pain
Add		critical limb ischemia NOS of autologous vein bypass graft(s) of the extremities
Add		critical limb ischemia of autologous vein bypass graft(s) of the extremities with rest pain
No Change	I70.43	**Atherosclerosis of autologous vein bypass graft(s) of the right leg with ulceration**
Add	**Includes**	chronic limb-threatening ischemia of autologous vein bypass graft(s) of the right leg with ulceration
Add		critical limb ischemia of autologous vein bypass graft(s) of the right leg with ulceration

No Change	I70.44		Atherosclerosis of autologous vein bypass graft(s) of the left leg with ulceration
Add		**Includes**	chronic limb-threatening ischemia of autologous vein bypass graft(s) of the left leg with ulceration
Add			critical limb ischemia of autologous vein bypass graft(s) of the left leg with ulceration
No Change	I70.46		Atherosclerosis of autologous vein bypass graft(s) of the extremities with gangrene
Add		**Includes**	chronic limb-threatening ischemia of autologous vein bypass graft(s) of the extremities with gangrene
Add			critical limb ischemia of autologous vein bypass graft(s) of the extremities with gangrene
No Change	I70.5		Atherosclerosis of nonautologous biological bypass graft(s) of the extremities
No Change	I70.52		Atherosclerosis of nonautologous biological bypass graft(s) of the extremities with rest pain
Add		**Includes**	chronic limb-threatening ischemia NOS of nonautologous biological bypass graft(s) of the extremities
Add			chronic limb-threatening ischemia of nonautologous biological bypass graft(s) of the extremities with rest pain
Add			critical limb ischemia NOS of nonautologous biological bypass graft(s) of the extremities
Add			critical limb ischemia of nonautologous biological bypass graft(s) of the extremities with rest pain
No Change	I70.53		Atherosclerosis of nonautologous biological bypass graft(s) of the right leg with ulceration
Add		**Includes**	chronic limb-threatening ischemia of nonautologous biological bypass graft(s) of the right leg with ulceration
Add			critical limb ischemia of nonautologous biological bypass graft(s) of the right leg with ulceration

No Change	I70.54		Atherosclerosis of nonautologous biological bypass graft(s) of the left leg with ulceration
Add		**Includes**	chronic limb-threatening ischemia of nonautologous biological bypass graft(s) of the left leg with ulceration
Add			critical limb ischemia of nonautologous biological bypass graft(s) of the left leg with ulceration
No Change	I70.56		Atherosclerosis of nonautologous biological bypass graft(s) of the extremities with gangrene
Add		**Includes**	chronic limb-threatening ischemia of nonautologous biological bypass graft(s) of the extremities with gangrene
Add			critical limb ischemia of nonautologous biological bypass graft(s) of the extremities with gangrene
No Change	I70.6		Atherosclerosis of nonbiological bypass graft(s) of the extremities
No Change	I70.62		Atherosclerosis of nonbiological bypass graft(s) of the extremities with rest pain
Add		**Includes**	chronic limb-threatening ischemia NOS of nonbiological bypass graft(s) of the extremities
Add			chronic limb-threatening ischemia of nonbiological bypass graft(s) of the extremities with rest pain
Add			critical limb ischemia NOS of nonbiological bypass graft(s) of the extremities
Add			critical limb ischemia of nonbiological bypass graft(s) of the extremities with rest pain
No Change	I70.63		Atherosclerosis of nonbiological bypass graft(s) of the right leg with ulceration
Add		**Includes**	chronic limb-threatening ischemia of nonbiological bypass graft(s) of the right leg with ulceration
Add			critical limb ischemia of nonbiological bypass graft(s) of the right leg with ulceration
No Change	I70.64		Atherosclerosis of nonbiological bypass graft(s) of the left leg with ulceration
Add		**Includes**	chronic limb-threatening ischemia of nonbiological bypass graft(s) of the left leg with ulceration
Add			critical limb ischemia of nonbiological bypass graft(s) of the left leg with ulceration

No Change	I70.66		Atherosclerosis of nonbiological bypass graft(s) of the extremities with gangrene	
Add		Includes	chronic limb-threatening ischemia of nonbiological bypass graft(s) of the extremities with gangrene	
Add			critical limb ischemia of nonbiological bypass graft(s) of the extremities with gangrene	
No Change	I70.7		Atherosclerosis of other type of bypass graft(s) of the extremities	
No Change	I70.72		Atherosclerosis of other type of bypass graft(s) of the extremities with rest pain	
Add		Includes	chronic limb-threatening ischemia NOS of other type of bypass graft(s) of the extremities	
Add			chronic limb-threatening ischemia of other type of bypass graft(s) of the extremities with rest pain	
Add			critical limb ischemia NOS of other type of bypass graft(s) of the extremities	
Add			critical limb ischemia of other type of bypass graft(s) of the extremities with rest pain	
No Change	I70.73		Atherosclerosis of other type of bypass graft(s) of the right leg with ulceration	
Add		Includes	chronic limb-threatening ischemia of other type of bypass graft(s) of the right leg with ulceration	
Add			critical limb ischemia of other type of bypass graft(s) of the right leg with ulceration	
No Change	I70.74		Atherosclerosis of other type of bypass graft(s) of the left leg with ulceration	
Add		Includes	chronic limb-threatening ischemia of other type of bypass graft(s) of the left leg with ulceration	
Add			critical limb ischemia of other type of bypass graft(s) of the left leg with ulceration	
No Change	I70.76		Atherosclerosis of other type of bypass graft(s) of the extremities with gangrene	
Add		Includes	chronic limb-threatening ischemia of other type of bypass graft(s) of the extremities with gangrene	
Add			critical limb ischemia of other type of bypass graft(s) of the extremities with gangrene	

No Change **CHAPTER 10**

No Change

DISEASES OF THE RESPIRATORY SYSTEM (J00-J99)

No Change	**ACUTE UPPER RESPIRATORY INFECTIONS (J00-J06)**		
Delete	Excludes1	influenza virus with other respiratory manifestations (J09.X2, J10.1, J11.1)	
No Change J00	Acute nasopharyngitis [common cold]		
Add	Excludes1	influenza virus with other respiratory manifestations (J09.X2, J10.1, J11.1)	
No Change J02	Acute pharyngitis		
No Change	J02.9	Acute pharyngitis, unspecified	
Add		Excludes1	influenza virus with other respiratory manifestations (J09.X2, J10.1, J11.1)
No Change J03	Acute tonsillitis		
No Change	J03.9	Acute tonsillitis, unspecified	
Add		Excludes1	influenza virus with other respiratory manifestations (J09.X2, J10.1, J11.1)
No Change J04	Acute laryngitis and tracheitis		
Add	Code also influenza, if present, such as:		
Add	influenza due to identified novel influenza A virus with other respiratory manifestations (J09.X2)		
Add	influenza due to other identified influenza virus with other respiratory manifestations (J10.1)		
Add	influenza due to unidentified influenza virus with other respiratory manifestations (J11.1)		
No Change J05	Acute obstructive laryngitis [croup] and epiglottitis		
Add	Code also if present, such as:		
Add	influenza due to identified novel influenza A virus with other respiratory manifestations (J09.X2)		
Add	influenza due to other identified influenza virus with other respiratory manifestations (J10.1)		
Add	influenza due to unidentified influenza virus with other respiratory manifestations (J11.1)		
No Change J06	Acute upper respiratory infections of multiple and unspecified sites		
Add	Excludes1	influenza virus with other respiratory manifestations (J09.X2, J10.1, J11.1)	
No Change	**INFLUENZA AND PNEUMONIA (J09-J18)**		
No Change J10	Influenza due to other identified influenza virus		
Add	Includes	influenza A (non-novel)	
Add		influenza B	
Add		influenza C	
No Change J18	Pneumonia, unspecified organism		
No Change	Excludes1		
Revise from		usual interstitial pneumonia (J84.17)	
Revise to		usual interstitial pneumonia (J84.178)	
No Change	**CHRONIC LOWER RESPIRATORY DISEASES (J40-J47)**		
No Change J43	Emphysema		
Delete	Excludes1	traumatic subcutaneous emphysema (T79.7)	
Add	Excludes2	traumatic subcutaneous emphysema (T79.7)	
No Change J45	Asthma		
No Change	Use additional code to identify:		
Add	eosinophilic asthma (J82.83)		

No Change		**LUNG DISEASES DUE TO EXTERNAL AGENTS (J60-J70)**
No Change	J70	**Respiratory conditions due to other external agents**
No Change	J70.5	**Respiratory conditions due to smoke inhalation**
Delete		Smoke inhalation NOS
Delete		**Excludes1** smoke inhalation due to chemicals, gases, fumes and vapors (J68.9)
Add		*Code first smoke inhalation (T59.81-)*
Add		**Excludes2** smoke inhalation due to chemicals, gases, fumes and vapors (J68.9)

No Change		**OTHER RESPIRATORY DISEASES PRINCIPALLY AFFECTING**
No Change		**THE INTERSTITIUM (J80-J84)**
No Change	J82	**Pulmonary eosinophilia, not elsewhere classified**
Delete		Allergic pneumonia
Delete		Eosinophilic asthma
Delete		Eosinophilic pneumonia
Delete		Löffler's pneumonia
Delete		Tropical (pulmonary) eosinophilia NOS
Delete		**Excludes1** pulmonary eosinophilia due to aspergillosis (B44.-)
Delete		pulmonary eosinophilia due to drugs (J70.2-J70.4)
Delete		pulmonary eosinophilia due to specified parasitic infection (B50-B83)
Delete		pulmonary eosinophilia due to systemic connective tissue disorders (M30-M36)
Delete		pulmonary infiltrate NOS (R91.8)
Add		**Excludes2** pulmonary eosinophilia due to aspergillosis (B44.-)
Add		pulmonary eosinophilia due to drugs (J70.2-J70.4)
Add		pulmonary eosinophilia due to specified parasitic infection (B50-B83)
Add		pulmonary eosinophilia due to systemic connective tissue disorders (M30-M36)
Add		pulmonary infiltrate NOS (R91.8)
Add	J82.8	**Pulmonary eosinophilia, not elsewhere classified**
Add	J82.81	**Chronic eosinophilic pneumonia**
Add		Eosinophilic pneumonia, NOS
Add	J82.82	**Acute eosinophilic pneumonia**
Add	J82.83	**Eosinophilic asthma**
Add		*Code first asthma, by type, such as:*
Add		mild intermittent asthma (J45.2-)
Add		mild persistent asthma (J45.3-)
Add		moderate persistent asthma (J45.4-)
Add		severe persistent asthma (J45.5-)
Add	J82.89	**Other pulmonary eosinophilia, not elsewhere classified**
Add		Allergic pneumonia
Add		Löffler's pneumonia
Add		Tropical (pulmonary) eosinophilia NOS

No Change J84		Other interstitial pulmonary diseases
No Change	J84.1	Other interstitial pulmonary diseases with fibrosis
No Change	J84.17	Other interstitial pulmonary diseases with fibrosis in diseases classified elsewhere
Delete		Interstitial pneumonia (nonspecific) (usual) due to collagen vascular disease
Delete		Interstitial pneumonia (nonspecific) (usual) in diseases classified elsewhere
Delete		Organizing pneumonia due to collagen vascular disease
Delete		Organizing pneumonia in diseases classified elsewhere
Delete		*Code first underlying disease, such as:*
Delete		progressive systemic sclerosis (M34.0)
Delete		rheumatoid arthritis (M05.00-M06.9)
Delete		systemic lupus erythematosis (M32.0-M32.9)
Add	J84.170	**Interstitial lung disease with progressive fibrotic phenotype in diseases classified elsewhere**
Add		Progressive fibrotic interstitial lung disease
Add		*Code first underlying disease, such as:*
Add		lung diseases due to external agents (J60-J70)
Add		rheumatoid arthritis (M05.00-M06.9)
Add		sarcoidosis (D86)
Add		systemic connective tissue disorders (M30-M36)
Add	J84.178	**Other interstitial pulmonary diseases with fibrosis in diseases classified elsewhere**
Add		Interstitial pneumonia (nonspecific) (usual) due to collagen vascular disease
Add		Interstitial pneumonia (nonspecific) (usual) in diseases classified elsewhere
Add		Organizing pneumonia due to collagen vascular disease
Add		Organizing pneumonia in diseases classified elsewhere
Add		*Code first underlying disease, such as:*
Add		progressive systemic sclerosis (M34.0)
Add		rheumatoid arthritis (M05.00-M06.9)
Add		systemic lupus erythematosis (M32.0-M32.9)

No Change **CHAPTER 11**

No Change ## DISEASES OF THE DIGESTIVE SYSTEM (K00-K95)

No Change **DISEASES OF ESOPHAGUS, STOMACH AND DUODENUM (K20-K31)**

No Change **K20 Esophagitis**
No Change **Excludes1**
Revise from   esophagitis with gastro-esophageal reflux disease (K21.0)
Revise to   esophagitis with gastro-esophageal reflux disease (K21.0-)
Revise from   reflux esophagitis (K21.0)
Revise to   reflux esophagitis (K21.0-)
No Change   **K20.8 Other esophagitis**
Delete   Abscess of esophagus
Add   **K20.80 Other esophagitis without bleeding**
Add   Abscess of esophagus
Add   Other esophagitis NOS
Add   **K20.81 Other esophagitis with bleeding**
No Change   **K20.9 Esophagitis, unspecified**
Delete   Esophagitis NOS
Add   **K20.90 Esophagitis, unspecified without bleeding**
Add   Esophagitis NOS
Add   **K20.91 Esophagitis, unspecified with bleeding**

No Change **K21 Gastro-esophageal reflux disease**
No Change   **K21.0 Gastro-esophageal reflux disease with esophagitis**
Delete   Reflux esophagitis
Add   **K21.00 Gastro-esophageal reflux disease with esophagitis, without bleeding**
Add   Reflux esophagitis
Add   **K21.01 Gastro-esophageal reflux disease with esophagitis, with bleeding**

No Change **OTHER DISEASES OF INTESTINES (K55-K64)**

No Change **K56 Paralytic ileus and intestinal obstruction without hernia**
Delete   **Excludes1** stenosis of anus or rectum (K62.4)
Add   **Excludes2** stenosis of anus or rectum (K62.4)
No Change   **K56.6 Other and unspecified intestinal obstruction**
No Change   **K56.60 Unspecified intestinal obstruction**
Delete   **Excludes1** intestinal obstruction due to specified condition-code to condition

No Change **K57 Diverticular disease of intestine**
No Change   **K57.0 Diverticulitis of small intestine with perforation and abscess**
Delete   Diverticulitis of small intestine with peritonitis
No Change   **K57.2 Diverticulitis of large intestine with perforation and abscess**
Delete   Diverticulitis of colon with peritonitis
No Change   **K57.4 Diverticulitis of both small and large intestine with perforation and abscess**
Delete   Diverticulitis of both small and large intestine with peritonitis
No Change   **K57.8 Diverticulitis of intestine, part unspecified, with perforation and abscess**
Delete   Diverticulitis of intestine NOS with peritonitis

No Change   **K59.8 Other specified functional intestinal disorders**
Delete   Atony of colon
Delete   Pseudo-obstruction (acute) (chronic) of intestine
Add   **K59.81 Ogilvie syndrome**
Add   Acute colonic pseudo-obstruction (ACPO)
Add   **K59.89 Other specified functional intestinal disorders**
Add   Atony of colon
Add   Pseudo-obstruction (acute) (chronic) of intestine

No Change **K62 Other diseases of anus and rectum**
No Change   **K62.7 Radiation proctitis**
Revise from   Use additional code to identify the type of radiation (W90.-)
Revise to   Use additional code to identify the type of radiation (W88.-)
Add   or radiation therapy (Y84.2)

No Change **DISEASES OF LIVER (K70-K77)**

No Change **K74 Fibrosis and cirrhosis of liver**
No Change   **K74.0 Hepatic fibrosis**
Add   *Code first* underlying liver disease, such as:
Add   nonalcoholic steatohepatitis (NASH) (K75.81)
Add   **K74.00 Hepatic fibrosis, unspecified**
Add   **K74.01 Hepatic fibrosis, early fibrosis**
Add   Hepatic fibrosis, stage F1 or stage F2
Add   **K74.02 Hepatic fibrosis, advanced fibrosis**
Add   Hepatic fibrosis, stage F3
Add   **Excludes1** cirrhosis of liver (K74.6-)
Add   hepatic fibrosis, stage F4 (K74.6-)

No Change **K75 Other inflammatory liver diseases**
No Change   **K75.8 Other specified inflammatory liver diseases**
No Change   **K75.81 Nonalcoholic steatohepatitis (NASH)**
Add   Use additional code, if applicable, hepatic fibrosis (K74.0-)

No Change **DISORDERS OF GALLBLADDER, BILIARY TRACT AND PANCREAS (K80–K87)**

No Change **K80 Cholelithiasis**
No Change   **K80.4 Calculus of bile duct with cholecystitis**
Add   Code also fistula of bile duct (K83.3)

No Change **CHAPTER 12**

No Change ## DISEASES OF THE SKIN AND SUBCUTANEOUS TISSUE (L00-L99)

No Change **RADIATION-RELATED DISORDERS OF THE SKIN**
No Change **AND SUBCUTANEOUS TISSUE (L55-L59)**

No Change **L57 Skin changes due to chronic exposure to nonionizing radiation**
Revise from   Use additional code to identify the source of the ultraviolet radiation (W89)
Revise to   Use additional code to identify the source of the ultraviolet radiation (W89), or other nonionizing radiation (W90)

No Change	**INTRAOPERATIVE AND POSTPROCEDURAL COMPLICATIONS OF SKIN AND SUBCUTANEOUS TISSUE (L76)**

No Change **L98** Other disorders of skin and subcutaneous tissue, not elsewhere classified

No Change L98.4 **Non-pressure chronic ulcer of skin, not elsewhere classified**

Revise from **Excludes2** varicose ulcer (I83.0-I82.2)

Revise to **Excludes2** varicose ulcer (I83.0-I83.93)

No Change **CHAPTER 13**

No Change

DISEASES OF THE MUSCULOSKELETAL SYSTEM AND CONNECTIVE TISSUE (M00-M99)

No Change   **INFECTIOUS ARTHROPATHIES (M00-M02)**

No Change **M00** Pyogenic arthritis

Add **Excludes2** infection and inflammatory reaction due to internal joint prosthesis (T84.5-)

No Change **M00.0** **Staphylococcal arthritis and polyarthritis**

Delete **Excludes2** infection and inflammatory reaction due to internal joint prosthesis (T84.5-)

No Change   **INFLAMMATORY POLYARTHROPATHIES (M05-M14)**

No Change **M05** Rheumatoid arthritis with rheumatoid factor

No Change **M05.7** Rheumatoid arthritis with rheumatoid factor without organ or systems involvement

Add **M05.7A** Rheumatoid arthritis with rheumatoid factor of other specified site without organ orsystems involvement

No Change **M05.8** Other rheumatoid arthritis with rheumatoid factor

Add **M05.8A** Other rheumatoid arthritis with rheumatoid factor of other specified site

No Change **M06** Other rheumatoid arthritis

No Change **M06.0** Rheumatoid arthritis without rheumatoid factor

Add **M06.0A** Rheumatoid arthritis without rheumatoid factor, other specified site

No Change **M06.8** Other specified rheumatoid arthritis

Add **M06.8A** Other specified rheumatoid arthritis, other specified site

No Change **M08** Juvenile arthritis

No Change **M08.0** Unspecified juvenile rheumatoid arthritis

Add **M08.0A** Unspecified juvenile rheumatoid arthritis, other specified site

No Change **M08.2** Juvenile rheumatoid arthritis with systemic onset

Add **M08.2A** Juvenile rheumatoid arthritis with systemic onset, other specified site

No Change **M08.4** Pauciarticular juvenile rheumatoid arthritis

Add **M08.4A** Pauciarticular juvenile rheumatoid arthritis, other specified site

No Change **M08.9** Juvenile arthritis, unspecified

Add **M08.9A** Juvenile arthritis, unspecified, other specified site

No Change   **OSTEOARTHRITIS (M15-M19)**

No Change **M19** Other and unspecified osteoarthritis

No Change **M19.0** Primary osteoarthritis of other joints

Add **M19.09** Primary osteoarthritis, other specified site

No Change **M19.1** Post-traumatic osteoarthritis of other joints

Add **M19.19** Post-traumatic osteoarthritis, other specified site

No Change **M19.2** Secondary osteoarthritis of other joints

Add **M19.29** Secondary osteoarthritis, other specified site

---

No Change	**OTHER JOINT DISORDERS (M20-M25)**

No Change **M21** Other acquired deformities of limbs

No Change **M21.1** Varus deformity, not elsewhere classified

Revise from **Excludes1** tibia vara (M92.5)

Revise to **Excludes1** tibia vara (M92.51-) -)

No Change **M22** Disorder of patella

Delete **Excludes1** traumatic dislocation of patella (S83.0-)

Add **Excludes2** traumatic dislocation of patella (S83.0-)

No Change **M23** Internal derangement of knee

Delete **Excludes1** current injury - see injury of knee and lower leg (S80-S89)

Delete recurrent dislocation or subluxation of joints (M24.4)

Delete recurrent dislocation or subluxation of patella (M22.0-M22.1)

Add **Excludes2** current injury - see injury of knee and lower leg (S80-S89)

Add recurrent dislocation or subluxation of joints (M24.4)

Add recurrent dislocation or subluxation of patella (M22.0-M22.1)

No Change **M24** Other specific joint derangements

No Change **M24.1** Other articular cartilage disorders

Add **M24.19** Other articular cartilage disorders, other specified site

No Change **M24.2** Disorder of ligament

Add **M24.29** Disorder of ligament, other specified site

No Change **M24.3** Pathological dislocation of joint, not elsewhere classified

Add **M24.39** Pathological dislocation of other specified joint, not elsewhere classified

No Change **M24.4** Recurrent dislocation of joint

Add **M24.49** Recurrent dislocation, other specified joint

No Change **M24.5** Contracture of joint

Add **M24.59** Contracture, other specified joint

No Change **M24.6** Ankylosis of joint

Add **M24.69** Ankylosis, other specified joint

No Change **M24.8** Other specific joint derangements, not elsewhere classified

Add **M24.89** Other specific joint derangement of other specified joint, not elsewhere classified

No Change **M25** Other joint disorder, not elsewhere classified

No Change **M25** Other joint disorder, not elsewhere classified

Add **M25.39** Other instability of joint [new]

No Change **M25.5** Pain in joint

Add **M25.59** Pain in other specified joint

No Change **M25.6** Stiffness of joint, not elsewhere classified

Add **M25.69** Stiffness of other specified joint, not elsewhere classified

No Change	**DENTOFACIAL ANOMALIES [INCLUDING MALOCCLUSION] AND OTHER DISORDERS OF JAW (M26-M27)**

No Change **M26** Dentofacial anomalies [including malocclusion]

No Change **M26.6** Temporomandibular joint disorders

Add **M26.64** Arthritis of temporomandibular joint

Add **M26.641** Arthritis of right temporomandibular joint

Add **M26.642** Arthritis of left temporomandibular joint

Add **M26.643** Arthritis of bilateral temporomandibular joint

Add **M26.649** Arthritis of unspecified temporomandibular joint

Add	M26.65		Arthropathy of temporomandibular joint
Add		M26.651	Arthropathy of right temporomandibular joint
Add		M26.652	Arthropathy of left temporomandibular joint
Add		M26.653	Arthropathy of bilateral temporomandibular joint
Add		M26.659	Arthropathy of unspecified temporomandibular joint

SYSTEMIC CONNECTIVE TISSUE DISORDERS (M30-M36)
No Change

No Change **M30 Polyarteritis nodosa and related conditions**

No Change **M30.1 Polyarteritis with lung involvement [Churg-Strauss**

Add   Eosinophilic granulomatosis with polyangiitis [EGPA]

No Change **M31 Other necrotizing vasculopathies**

No Change **M31.3 Wegener's granulomatosis**

Add   Granulomatosis with polyangiitis

No Change **M35 Other systemic involvement of connective tissue**

No Change **M35.7 Hypermobility syndrome**

Revise from   **Excludes1** Ehlers-Danlos syndrome (Q79.6-)

Revise to   **Excludes1** Ehlers-Danlos syndromes (Q79.6-)

DISORDERS OF BONE DENSITY AND STRUCTURE (M80-M85)
No Change

No Change **M80 Osteoporosis with current pathological fracture**

No Change **M80.0 Age-related osteoporosis with current pathological fracture**

Add   M80.0A Age-related osteoporosis with current pathological fracture, other site

No Change **M80.8 Other osteoporosis with current pathological fracture**

Add   M80.8A Other osteoporosis with current pathological fracture, other site

CHONDROPATHIES (M91-M94)
No Change

No Change **M92 Other juvenile osteochondrosis**

No Change **M92.5 Juvenile osteochondrosis of tibia and fibula**

Delete   Osteochondrosis (juvenile) of proximal tibia [Blount]

Delete   Osteochondrosis (juvenile) of tibial tubercle [Osgood-Schlatter]

Delete   Tibia vara

Revise from M92.50 Juvenile osteochondrosis of tibia and fibula, unspecified leg

Revise to M92.50 Unspecified juvenile osteochondrosis of tibia and fibula

Add   M92.501 Unspecified juvenile osteochondrosis, right leg

Add   M92.502 Unspecified juvenile osteochondrosis, left leg

Add   M92.503 Unspecified juvenile osteochondrosis, bilateral leg

Add   M92.509 Unspecified juvenile osteochondrosis, unspecified leg

Revise from M92.51 Juvenile osteochondrosis of tibia and fibula, right leg

Revise to M92.51 Juvenile osteochondrosis of proximal tibia

Add   Blount disease

Add   Tibia vara

Add   M92.511 Juvenile osteochondrosis of proximal tibia, right leg

Add   M92.512 Juvenile osteochondrosis of proximal tibia, left leg

Add   M92.513 Juvenile osteochondrosis of proximal tibia, bilateral

Add   M92.519 Juvenile osteochondrosis of proximal tibia, unspecified leg

Revise from M92.52 Juvenile osteochondrosis of tibia and fibula, left leg

Revise to M92.52 Juvenile osteochondrosis of tibia tubercle

Add   Osgood-Schlatter disease

Add   M92.521 Juvenile osteochondrosis of tibia tubercle, right leg

Add   M92.522 Juvenile osteochondrosis of tibia tubercle, left leg

Add   M92.523 Juvenile osteochondrosis of tibia tubercle, bilateral

Add   M92.529 Juvenile osteochondrosis of tibia tubercle, unspecified leg

Add   M92.59 Other juvenile osteochondrosis of tibia and fibula

Add   M92.591 Other juvenile osteochondrosis of tibia and fibula, right leg

Add   M92.592 Other juvenile osteochondrosis of tibia and fibula, left leg

Add   M92.593 Other juvenile osteochondrosis of tibia and fibula, bilateral

Add   M92.599 Other juvenile osteochondrosis of tibia and fibula, unspecified leg

No Change **CHAPTER 14**

No Change **DISEASES OF THE GENITOURINARY SYSTEM (N00-N99)**

GLOMERULAR DISEASES (N00-N08)
No Change

No Change **N00 Acute nephritic syndrome**

No Change **N00.5 Acute nephritic syndrome with diffuse mesangiocapillary glomerulonephritis**

Add   **Excludes1** Acute nephritic syndrome with C3 glomerulonephritis (N00.A)

Add   Acute nephritic syndrome with C3 glomerulopathy (N00.A)

No Change **N00.6 Acute nephritic syndrome with dense deposit disease**

Add   Acute nephritic syndrome with C3 glomerulopathy with dense deposit disease

Add **N00.A Acute nephritic syndrome with C3 glomerulonephritis**

Add   Acute nephritic syndrome with C3 glomerulopathy, NOS

Add   **Excludes1** Acute nephritic syndrome (with C3 glomerulopathy) with dense deposit disease(N00.6)

No Change **N01 Rapidly progressive nephritic syndrome**

No Change **N01.5 Rapidly progressive nephritic syndrome with diffuse mesangiocapillary glomerulonephritis**

Add   **Excludes1** Rapidly progressive nephritic syndrome with C3 glomerulonephritis (N01.A)

Add   Rapidly progressive nephritic syndrome with C3 glomerulopathy (N01.A)

No Change **N01.6 Rapidly progressive nephritic syndrome with dense deposit disease**

Add   Rapidly progressive nephritic syndrome with C3 glomerulopathy with dense deposit disease

Add	**N01.A**	**Rapidly progressive nephritic syndrome with C3 glomerulonephritis**
Add		Rapidly progressive nephritic syndrome with C3 glomerulopathy, NOS
Add		**Excludes1** Rapidly progressive nephritic syndrome (with C3 glomerulopathy) with dense deposit disease (N01.6)

No Change	**N02**	**Recurrent and persistent hematuria**
No Change	**N02.5**	**Recurrent and persistent hematuria with diffuse mesangiocapillary glomerulonephritis**
Add		**Excludes1** Recurrent and persistent hematuria with C3 glomerulonephritis (N02.A)
Add		Recurrent and persistent hematuria with C3 glomerulopathy (N02.A)
No Change	**N02.6**	**Recurrent and persistent hematuria with dense deposit disease**
Add		Recurrent and persistent hematuria with C3 glomerulopathy with dense deposit disease
Add	**N02.A**	**Recurrent and persistent hematuria with C3 glomerulonephritis**
Add		Recurrent and persistent hematuria with C3 glomerulopathy
Add		**Excludes1** Recurrent and persistent hematuria (with C3 glomerulopathy) with dense deposit disease (N02.6)

No Change	**N03**	**Chronic nephritic syndrome**
No Change	**N03.5**	**Chronic nephritic syndrome with diffuse mesangiocapillary glomerulonephritis**
Add		**Excludes1** Chronic nephritic syndrome with C3 glomerulonephritis (N03.A)
Add		Chronic nephritic syndrome with C3 glomerulopathy (N03.A)
No Change	**N03.6**	**Chronic nephritic syndrome with dense deposit disease**
Add		Chronic nephritic syndrome with C3 glomerulopathy with dense deposit disease
Add	**N03.A**	**Chronic nephritic syndrome with C3 glomerulonephritis**
Add		Chronic nephritic syndrome with C3 glomerulopathy
Add		**Excludes1** Chronic nephritic syndrome (with C3 glomerulopathy) with dense deposit disease(N03.6)

No Change	**N04**	**Nephrotic syndrome**
No Change	**N04.5**	**Nephrotic syndrome with diffuse mesangiocapillary glomerulonephritis**
Add		**Excludes1** Nephrotic syndrome with C3 glomerulonephritis (N04.A)
Add		Nephrotic syndrome with C3 glomerulopathy (N04.A)
No Change	**N04.6**	**Nephrotic syndrome with dense deposit disease**
Add		Nephrotic syndrome with C3 glomerulopathy with dense deposit disease
Add	**N04.A**	**Nephrotic syndrome with C3 glomerulonephritis**
Add		Nephrotic syndrome with C3 glomerulopathy
Add		**Excludes1** Nephrotic syndrome (with C3 glomerulopathy) with dense deposit disease (N04.6)

No Change	**N05**	**Unspecified nephritic syndrome**
No Change	**N05.5**	**Unspecified nephritic syndrome with diffuse mesangiocapillary glomerulonephritis**
Add		**Excludes1** Unspecified nephritic syndrome with C3 glomerulonephritis (N05.A)
Add		Unspecified nephritic syndrome with C3 glomerulopathy (N05.A)

No Change	**N05.6**	**Unspecified nephritic syndrome with dense deposit disease**
Add		Unspecified nephritic syndrome with C3 glomerulopathy with dense deposit disease
Add	**N05.A**	**Unspecified nephritic syndrome with C3 glomerulonephritis**
Add		Unspecified nephritic syndrome with C3 glomerulopathy
Add		**Excludes1** Unspecified nephritic syndrome (with C3 glomerulopathy) with dense deposit disease(N05.6)

No Change	**N06**	**Isolated proteinuria with specified morphological lesion**
No Change	**N06.5**	**Isolated proteinuria with diffuse mesangiocapillary glomerulonephritis**
Add		**Excludes1** Isolated proteinuria with C3 glomerulonephritis (N06.A)
Add		Isolated proteinuria with C3 glomerulopathy (N06.A)
No Change	**N06.6**	**Isolated proteinuria with dense deposit disease**
Add		Isolated proteinuria with C3 glomerulopathy with dense deposit disease
Add	**N06.A**	**Isolated proteinuria with C3 glomerulonephritis**
Add		Isolated proteinuria with C3 glomerulopathy
Add		**Excludes1** Isolated proteinuria (with C3 glomerulopathy) with dense deposit disease (N06.6)
No Change		

No Change	**N07**	**Hereditary nephropathy, not elsewhere classified**
No Change	**N07.5**	**Hereditary nephropathy, not elsewhere classified with diffuse mesangiocapillary glomerulonephritis**
Add		**Excludes1** Hereditary nephropathy, not elsewhere classified with C3 glomerulonephritis (N07.A)
Add		Hereditary nephropathy, not elsewhere classified with C3 glomerulopathy (N07.A)
No Change	**N07.6**	**Hereditary nephropathy, not elsewhere classified with dense deposit disease**
Add		Hereditary nephropathy, not elsewhere classified with C3 glomerulopathy with dense deposit disease
Add	**N07.A**	**Hereditary nephropathy, not elsewhere classified with C3 glomerulonephritis**
Add		Hereditary nephropathy, not elsewhere classified with C3 glomerulopathy
Add		**Excludes1** Hereditary nephropathy, not elsewhere classified (with C3 glomerulopathy) with dense deposit disease (N07.6)

No Change		**ACUTE KIDNEY FAILURE AND CHRONIC KIDNEY DISEASE (N17-N19)**
No Change	**N18**	**Chronic kidney disease (CKD)**
No Change		**N18.3** **Chronic kidney disease, stage 3 (moderate)**
Add		**N18.30** **Chronic kidney disease, stage 3 unspecified**
Add		**N18.31** **Chronic kidney disease, stage 3a**
Add		**N18.32** **Chronic kidney disease, stage 3b**

No Change		**UROLITHIASIS (N20-N23)**
No Change	**N20**	**Calculus of kidney and ureter**
No Change		**N20.1** **Calculus of ureter**
Add		Calculus of the ureteropelvic junction

No Change		**DISORDERS OF BREAST (N60-N65)**
No Change N61	Inflammatory disorders of breast
Add	N61.2	Granulomatous mastitis
Add		N61.20	Granulomatous mastitis, unspecified breast
Add		N61.21	Granulomatous mastitis, right breast
Add		N61.22	Granulomatous mastitis, left breast
Add		N61.23	Granulomatous mastitis, bilateral breast

No Change CHAPTER 15

No Change   PREGNANCY, CHILDBIRTH, AND THE PUERPERIUM (O00-O9A)

No Change   MATERNAL CARE RELATED TO THE FETUS AND AMNIOTIC CAVITY AND POSSIBLE DELIVERY PROBLEMS (O30-O48)

No Change O34   Maternal care for abnormality of pelvic organs

No Change   O34.2   Maternal care due to uterine scar from previous surgery

No Change   O34.21   Maternal care for scar from previous cesarean delivery

Add   O34.218   Maternal care for other type scar from previous cesarean delivery

Add   Mid-transverse T incision

Add   O34.22   Maternal care for cesarean scar defect (isthmocele)

No Change   OTHER OBSTETRIC CONDITIONS, NOT ELSEWHERE CLASSIFIED (O94-O9A)

No Change O99   Other maternal diseases classifiable elsewhere but complicating pregnancy, childbirth and the puerperium

No Change   O99.2   Endocrine, nutritional and metabolic diseases complicating pregnancy, childbirth and the puerperium

Revise from   Conditions in E00-E88

Revise to   Conditions in E00-E89

No Change   O99.3   Mental disorders and diseases of the nervous system complicating pregnancy, childbirth and the puerperium

No Change   O99.34   Other mental disorders complicating pregnancy, childbirth, and the puerperium

Revise from   Conditions in F01-F09, F20-F99 and F54-F99

Revise to   Conditions in F01-F09, F20-F52 and F54-F99

No Change   O99.8   Other specified diseases and conditions complicating pregnancy, childbirth and the puerperium

No Change   O99.89   Other specified diseases and conditions complicating pregnancy, childbirth and the puerperium

Add   O99.891   Other specified diseases and conditions complicating pregnancy

Add   O99.892   Other specified diseases and conditions complicating childbirth

Add   O99.893   Other specified diseases and conditions complicating puerperium

No Change CHAPTER 16

No Change   CERTAIN CONDITIONS ORIGINATING IN THE PERINATAL PERIOD (P00-P96)

No Change   NEWBORN AFFECTED BY MATERNAL FACTORS AND BY COMPLICATIONS OF PREGNANCY, LABOR, AND DELIVERY (P00–P04)

No Change P00   Newborn affected by maternal conditions that may be unrelated to present pregnancy

No Change   P00.8   Newborn affected by other maternal conditions

No Change   P00.89   Newborn affected by other maternal conditions

Add   Use additional code to identify infectious agent, if known

No Change   OTHER DISORDERS ORIGINATING IN THE PERINATAL PERIOD (P90-P96)

No Change P91   Other disturbances of cerebral status of newborn

No Change   P91.0   Neonatal cerebral ischemia

Add   **Excludes1**   Neonatal cerebral infarction (P91.82-)

No Change   P91.8   Other specified disturbances of cerebral status of newborn

Add   P91.82   Neonatal cerebral infarction

Add   Neonatal stroke

Add   Perinatal arterial ischemic stroke

Add   Perinatal cerebral infarction

Add   **Excludes1**   cerebral infarction (I63.-)

Add   **Excludes2**   intracranial hemorrhage of newborn (P52.-)

Add   P91.821   Neonatal cerebral infarction, right side of brain

Add   P91.822   Neonatal cerebral infarction, left side of brain

Add   P91.823   Neonatal cerebral infarction, bilateral

Add   P91.829   Neonatal cerebral infarction, unspecified side

No Change CHAPTER 17

No Change   CONGENITAL MALFORMATIONS, DEFORMATIONS, AND CHROMOSOMAL ABNORMALITIES (Q00-Q99)

No Change   CLEFT LIP AND CLEFT PALATE (Q35-Q37)

Delete   **Excludes1**   Robin's syndrome (Q87.0)

Add   **Excludes2**   Robin's syndrome (Q87.0)

No Change   CONGENITAL MALFORMATIONS OF GENITAL ORGANS (Q50-Q56)

No Change Q51   Congenital malformations of uterus and cervix

No Change   Q51.2   Other doubling of uterus

Delete   Q51.20   Other doubling of uterus, unspecified

No Change   Septate uterus, unspecified

Revise from   Q51.21   Other complete doubling of uterus

Revise to   Q51.21   Complete doubling of uterus

Revise from   Q51.22   Other partial doubling of uterus

Revise to   Q51.22   Partial doubling of uterus

Revise from   Q51.28   Other doubling of uterus, other specified

Revise to   Q51.28   Other and unspecified doubling of uterus

Revise from   Septate uterus, other specified

Revise to   Septate uterus NOS

No Change		**OTHER CONGENITAL MALFORMATIONS (Q80–Q89)**	
No Change	Q82	Other congenital malformations of skin	
No Change		Q82.8	Other specified congenital malformations of skin
Revise from		**Excludes1**	Ehlers-Danlos syndrome (Q79.6-)
Revise to		**Excludes1**	Ehlers-Danlos syndromes (Q79.6-)

No Change **CHAPTER 18**

No Change
SYMPTOMS, SIGNS, AND ABNORMAL CLINICAL AND LABORATORY FINDINGS, NOT ELSEWHERE CLASSIFIED (R00–R99)

No Change		**SYMPTOMS AND SIGNS INVOLVING THE NERVOUS AND MUSCULOSKELETAL SYSTEMS (R25-R29)**	
No Change	R29	Other symptoms and signs involving the nervous and musculoskeletal systems	
No Change		R29.7	National Institutes of Health Stroke Scale (NIHSS) score
Revise from			*Code first the type of cerebral infarction (I63-*
Revise to			*Code first the type of cerebral infarction (I63.-)*
No Change		**SYMPTOMS AND SIGNS INVOLVING COGNITION, PERCEPTION, EMOTIONAL STATE AND BEHAVIOR (R40-R46)**	
No Change	R44	Other symptoms and signs involving general sensations and perceptions	
Revise from		**Excludes1**	alcoholic hallucinations (F1.5)
Revise to		**Excludes1**	alcoholic hallucinations (F10.151, F10.251, F10.951)
Revise from			hallucinations in drug psychosis (F11-F19 with .5)
Revise to			hallucinations in drug psychosis (F11-F19 with fifth to sixth characters 51)
No Change	R46	Symptoms and signs involving appearance and behavior	
No Change		R46.8	Other symptoms and signs involving appearance and behavior
No Change		R46.81	Obsessive-compulsive behavior
Revise from			**Excludes1** obsessive-compulsive disorder (F42-)
Revise to			**Excludes1** obsessive-compulsive disorder (F42.-)

No Change		**GENERAL SYMPTOMS AND SIGNS (R50-R69)**	
No Change	R51	Headache	
Delete			Facial pain NOS
Delete		**Excludes1**	atypical face pain (G50.1)
Delete			migraine and other headache syndromes (G43-G44)
Delete			trigeminal neuralgia (G50.0)
Add		**Excludes2**	atypical face pain (G50.1)
Add			migraine and other headache syndromes (G43-G44)
Add			trigeminal neuralgia (G50.0)
Add		R51.0	Headache with orthostatic component, not elsewhere classified
Add			Headache with positional component, not elsewhere classified
Add		R51.9	Headache, unspecified
Add			Facial pain NOS
No Change	R52	Pain, unspecified	
No Change		**Excludes1**	localized pain, unspecified type - code to pain by site, such as:
Revise from			headache (R51)
Revise to			headache (R51.9)

No Change	R53	Malaise and fatigue	
No Change		R53.1	Weakness
Revise from		**Excludes1**	muscle weakness (M62.8-)
Revise to		**Excludes1**	muscle weakness (generalized) (M62.81)
No Change		**ABNORMAL FINDINGS ON EXAMINATION OF BLOOD, WITHOUT DIAGNOSIS (R70-R79)**	
No Change	R74	Abnormal serum enzyme levels	
No Change		R74.0	Nonspecific elevation of levels of transaminase and lactic acid dehydrogenase [LDH]
Add			R74.01 Elevation of levels of liver transaminase levels
Add			Elevation of levels of alanine transaminase (ALT)
Add			Elevation of levels of aspartate transaminase (AST)
Add			R74.02 Elevation of levels of lactic acid dehydrogenase [LDH]
No Change		**ABNORMAL FINDINGS ON EXAMINATION OF URINE, WITHOUT DIAGNOSIS (R80-R82)**	
No Change	R81	Glycosuria	
Revise from		**Excludes1**	renal glycosuria (E74.8)
Revise to		**Excludes1**	renal glycosuria (E74.818)

No Change **CHAPTER 19**

No Change
INJURY, POISONING AND CERTAIN OTHER CONSEQUENCES OF EXTERNAL CAUSES (S00-T88)

No Change		**INJURIES TO THE HEAD (S00-S09)**	
No Change	S06	Intracranial injury	
No Change		S06.3	Focal traumatic brain injury
Delete			**Excludes1** focal cerebral edema (S06.1)
Add			**Excludes2** focal cerebral edema (S06.1)
No Change		**INJURIES TO THE THORAX (S20-S29)**	
No Change	S20	Superficial injury of thorax	
No Change		S20.2	Contusion of thorax
No Change			S20.21 Contusion of front wall of thorax
Add			S20.213 Contusion of bilateral front wall of thorax
Add			S20.214 Contusion of middle front wall of thorax
No Change			S20.22 Contusion of back wall of thorax
Add			S20.223 Contusion of bilateral back wall of thorax
Add			S20.224 Contusion of middle back wall of thorax
No Change		S20.3	Other and unspecified superficial injuries of front wall of thorax
No Change			S20.30 Unspecified superficial injuries of front wall of thorax
Add			S20.303 Unspecified superficial injuries of bilateral front wall of thorax
Add			S20.304 Unspecified superficial injuries of middle front wall of thorax
No Change			S20.31 Abrasion of front wall of thorax
Add			S20.313 Abrasion of bilateral front wall of thorax
Add			S20.314 Abrasion of middle front wall of thorax

No Change	S20.32	Blister (nonthermal) of front wall of thorax
Add	S20.323	Blister (nonthermal) of bilateral front wall of thorax
Add	S20.324	Blister (nonthermal) of middle front wall of thorax
No Change	S20.34	External constriction of front wall of thorax
Add	S20.343	External constriction of bilateral front wall of thorax
Add	S20.344	External constriction of middle front wall of thorax
No Change	S20.35	Superficial foreign body of front wall of thorax
Add	S20.353	Superficial foreign body of bilateral front wall of thorax
Add	S20.354	Superficial foreign body of middle front wall of thorax
No Change	S20.36	Insect bite (nonvenomous) of front wall of thorax
Add	S20.363	Insect bite (nonvenomous) of bilateral front wall of thorax
Add	S20.364	Insect bite (nonvenomous) of middle front wall of thorax
No Change	S20.37	Other superficial bite of front wall of thorax
Add	S20.373	Other superficial bite of bilateral front wall of thorax
Add	S20.374	Other superficial bite of middle front wall of thorax

INJURIES TO THE KNEE AND LOWER LEG (S80-S89)
No Change

No Change	S83		Dislocation and sprain of joints and ligaments of knee
Delete		**Excludes1**	derangement of patella (M22.0-M22.3)
Delete			injury of patellar ligament (tendon) (S76.1-)
Delete			internal derangement of knee (M23.-)
Delete			old dislocation of knee (M24.36)
Delete			pathological dislocation of knee (M24.36)
Delete			recurrent dislocation of knee (M22.0)
Add		**Excludes2**	derangement of patella (M22.0-M22.3)
Add			injury of patellar ligament (tendon) (S76.1-)
Add			internal derangement of knee (M23.-)
Add			old dislocation of knee (M24.36)
Add			pathological dislocation of knee (M24.36)
Add			recurrent dislocation of knee (M22.0)

POISONING BY, ADVERSE EFFECTS OF AND UNDERDOSING OF DRUGS MEDICAMENTS AND BIOLOGICAL SUBSTANCES (T36-T50)
No Change

Add		**Excludes2**	immunodeficiency due to drugs (D84.821)
No Change	T40		Poisoning by, adverse effect of and underdosing of narcotics and psychodysleptics [hallucinogens]
No Change		T40.4	Poisoning by, adverse effect of and underdosing of other synthetic narcotics
Delete		T40.4X	Poisoning by, adverse effect of and underdosing of other synthetic narcotics
Delete		T40.4X1	Poisoning by other synthetic narcotics, accidental (unintentional)
			Poisoning by other synthetic narcotics NOS
Delete		T40.4X2	Poisoning by other synthetic narcotics, intentional self-harm A, S

Delete		T40.4X3	Poisoning by other synthetic narcotics, assault
Delete		T40.4X4	Poisoning by other synthetic narcotics, undetermined
Delete		T40.4X5	Adverse effect of other synthetic narcotics
Delete		T40.4X6	Underdosing of other synthetic narcotics
Add	T40.41		Poisoning by, adverse effect of and underdosing of fentanyl or fentanyl analogs
Add		T40.411	Poisoning by fentanyl or fentanyl analogs, accidental (unintentional)
Add		T40.412	Poisoning by fentanyl or fentanyl analogs, intentional self-harm
Add		T40.413	Poisoning by fentanyl or fentanyl analogs, assault
Add		T40.414	Poisoning by fentanyl or fentanyl analogs, undetermined
Add		T40.415	Adverse effect of fentanyl or fentanyl analogs
Add		T40.416	Underdosing of fentanyl or fentanyl analogs
Add	T40.42		Poisoning by, adverse effect of and underdosing of tramadol
Add		T40.421	Poisoning by tramadol, accidental (unintentional)
Add		T40.422	Poisoning by tramadol, intentional self-harm
Add		T40.423	Poisoning by tramadol, assault
Add		T40.424	Poisoning by tramadol, undetermined
Add		T40.425	Adverse effect of tramadol
Add		T40.426	Underdosing of tramadol
Add	T40.49		Poisoning by, adverse effect of and underdosing of other synthetic narcotics
Add		T40.491	Poisoning by other synthetic narcotics, accidental (unintentional)
Add		T40.492	Poisoning by other synthetic narcotics, intentional self-harm
Add		T40.493	Poisoning by other synthetic narcotics, assault
Add		T40.494	Poisoning by other synthetic narcotics, undetermined
Add		T40.495	Adverse effect of other synthetic narcotics
Add		T40.496	Underdosing of other synthetic narcotics

CERTAIN EARLY COMPLICATIONS OF TRAUMA (T79)
No Change

No Change	T79		Certain early complications of trauma, not elsewhere classified
No Change		T79.7	Traumatic subcutaneous emphysema
Delete		**Excludes1**	emphysema NOS (J43)
Delete			emphysema (subcutaneous) resulting from a procedure (T81.82)
Add		**Excludes2**	emphysema NOS (J43)
Add			emphysema (subcutaneous) resulting from a procedure (T81.82)

No Change	**COMPLICATIONS OF SURGICAL AND MEDICAL CARE NOT ELSEWHERE CLASSIFIED (T80-T88)**	

No Change **T84** Complications of internal orthopedic prosthetic devices, implants and grafts

No Change   **T84.0** Mechanical complication of internal joint prosthesis

No Change   **T84.01** Broken internal joint prosthesis

Revise from   **Excludes1** periprosthetic joint implant fracture (M97-)

Revise to   **Excludes1** periprosthetic joint implant fracture (M97.-)

No Change **T86** Complications of transplanted organs and tissue

No Change   **T86.8** Complications of other transplanted organs and tissues

No Change   **T86.84** Complications of corneal transplant

No Change   **T86.840** Corneal transplant rejection

Add   **T86.8401** Corneal transplant rejection, right eye

Add   **T86.8402** Corneal transplant rejection, left eye

Add   **T86.8403** Corneal transplant rejection, bilateral

Add   **T86.8409** Corneal transplant rejection, unspecified eye

No Change   **T86.841** Corneal transplant failure

Add   **T86.8411** Corneal transplant failure, right eye

Add   **T86.8412** Corneal transplant failure, left eye

Add   **T86.8419** Corneal transplant failure, unspecified eye

No Change   **T86.842** Corneal transplant infection

Add   **T86.8421** Corneal transplant infection, right eye

Add   **T86.8422** Corneal transplant infection, left eye

Add   **T86.8423** Corneal transplant infection, bilateral

Add   **T86.8429** Corneal transplant infection, unspecified eye

No Change   **T86.848** Other complications of corneal transplant

Add   **T86.8481** Other complications of corneal transplant, right eye

Add   **T86.8482** Other complications of corneal transplant, left eye

Add   **T86.8483** Other complications of corneal transplant, bilateral

Add   **T86.8489** Other complications of corneal transplant, unspecified eye

No Change   **T86.849** Unspecified complication of corneal transplant

Add   **T86.8491** Unspecified complication of corneal transplant, right eye

Add   **T86.8492** Unspecified complication of corneal transplant, left eye

Add   **T86.8493** Unspecified complication of corneal transplant, bilateral

Add   **T86.8499** Unspecified complication of corneal transplant, unspecified eye

No Change # CHAPTER 20

No Change # EXTERNAL CAUSES OF MORBIDITY (V00-Y99)

No Change	**PEDESTRIAN INJURED IN TRANSPORT ACCIDENT (V00-V09)**	

No Change **V00** Pedestrian conveyance accident

No Change   **V00.0** Pedestrian on foot injured in collision with pedestrian conveyance

Add   **V00.03** Pedestrian on foot injured in collision with standing micro-mobility pedestrian conveyance

Add   **V00.031** Pedestrian on foot injured in collision with rider of standing electric scooter

Add   **V00.038** Pedestrian on foot injured in collision with rider of other standing micro-mobility pedestrian conveyance

Add   Pedestrian on foot injured in collision with rider of hoverboard

Add   Pedestrian on foot injured in collision with rider of segway

No Change   **V00.8** Accident on other pedestrian conveyance

Add   **V00.84** Accident with standing micro-mobility pedestrian conveyance

Add   **V00.841** Fall from standing electric scooter

Add   **V00.842** Pedestrian on standing electric scooter colliding with stationary object

Add   **V00.848** Other accident with standing micro-mobility pedestrian conveyance

Add   Accident with hoverboard

Add   Accident with segway

No Change **V01** Pedestrian injured in collision with pedal cycle

No Change   **V01.0** Pedestrian injured in collision with pedal cycle in nontraffic accident

Add   **V01.03** Pedestrian on standing micro-mobility pedestrian conveyance injured in collision with pedal cycle in nontraffic accident

Add   **V01.031** Pedestrian on standing electric scooter injured in collision with pedal cycle in nontraffic accident

Add   **V01.038** Pedestrian on other standing micro-mobility pedestrian conveyance injured in collision with pedal cycle in nontraffic accident

Add   Pedestrian on hoverboard injured in collision with pedal cycle in nontraffic accident

Add   Pedestrian on segway injured in collision with pedal cycle in nontraffic accident

No Change	V01.1	Pedestrian injured in collision with pedal cycle in traffic accident
Add	V01.13	Pedestrian on standing micro-mobility pedestrian conveyance injured in collision with pedal cycle in traffic accident
Add	V01.131	Pedestrian on standing electric scooter injured in collision with pedal cycle in traffic accident
Add	V01.138	Pedestrian on other standing micro-mobility pedestrian conveyance injured in collision with pedal cycle in traffic accident
Add		Pedestrian on hoverboard injured in collision with pedal cycle in traffic accident
Add		Pedestrian on segway injured in collision with pedal cycle in traffic accident
No Change	V01.9	Pedestrian injured in collision with pedal cycle, unspecified whether traffic or nontraffic accident
Add	V01.93	Pedestrian on standing micro-mobility pedestrian conveyance injured in collision with pedal cycle, unspecified whether traffic or nontraffic accident
Add	V01.931	Pedestrian on standing electric scooter injured in collision with pedal cycle, unspecified whether traffic or nontraffic accident
Add	V01.938	Pedestrian on other standing micro-mobility pedestrian conveyance injured in collision with pedal cycle, unspecified whether traffic or nontraffic accident
Add		Pedestrian on hoverboard injured in collision with pedal cycle, unspecified whether traffic or nontraffic accident
Add		Pedestrian on segway injured in collision with pedal cycle, unspecified whether traffic or nontraffic accident
No Change	V02	Pedestrian injured in collision with two- or three-wheeled motor vehicle
No Change	V02.0	Pedestrian injured in collision with two- or three-wheeled motor vehicle in nontraffic accident
Add	V02.03	Pedestrian on standing micro-mobility pedestrian conveyance injured in collision with two- or three-wheeled motor vehicle in nontraffic accident
Add	V02.031	Pedestrian on standing electric scooter injured in collision with two- or three-wheeled motor vehicle in nontraffic accident
Add	V02.038	Pedestrian on other standing micro-mobility pedestrian conveyance injured in collision with two- or three-wheeled motor vehicle in nontraffic accident
Add		Pedestrian on hoverboard injured in collision with two-or three wheeled motor vehicle in nontraffic accident
Add		Pedestrian on segway injured in collision with two- or three-wheeled motor vehicle in nontraffic accident

No Change	V02.1	Pedestrian injured in collision with two- or three-wheeled motor vehicle in traffic accident
Add	V02.13	Pedestrian on standing micro-mobility pedestrian conveyance injured in collision with two- or three-wheeled motor vehicle in traffic accident
Add	V02.131	Pedestrian on standing electric scooter injured in collision with two- or three-wheeled motor vehicle in traffic accident
Add	V02.138	Pedestrian on other standing micro-mobility pedestrian conveyance injured in collision with two- or three-wheeled motor vehicle in traffic accident
Add		Pedestrian on hoverboard injured in collision with two-or three wheeled motor vehicle in traffic accident
Add		Pedestrian on segway injured in collision with two- or three-wheeled motor vehicle in traffic accident
No Change	V02.9	Pedestrian injured in collision with two- or three-wheeled motor vehicle, unspecified whether traffic or nontraffic accident
Add	V02.93	Pedestrian on standing micro-mobility pedestrian conveyance injured in collision with two-or three-wheeled motor vehicle, unspecified whether traffic or nontraffic accident
Add	V02.931	Pedestrian on standing electric scooter injured in collision with two- or three wheeled motor vehicle, unspecified whether traffic or nontraffic accident
Add	V02.938	Pedestrian on other standing micro-mobility pedestrian conveyance injured in collision with two- or three wheeled motor vehicle, unspecified whether traffic or nontraffic accident
Add		Pedestrian on hoverboard injured in collision with two-three-wheeled motor vehicle, unspecified whether traffic or nontraffic accident
Add		Pedestrian on segway injured in collision with two- or three wheeled motor vehicle, unspecified whether traffic or nontraffic accident
No Change	V03	Pedestrian injured in collision with car, pick-up truck or van
No Change	V03.0	Pedestrian injured in collision with car, pick-up truck or van in nontraffic accident
Add	V03.03	Pedestrian on standing micro-mobility pedestrian conveyance injured in collision with car, pick-up or van in nontraffic accident
Add	V03.031	Pedestrian on standing electric scooter injured in collision with car, pick-up or van in nontraffic accident

Add		V03.038	Pedestrian on other standing micro-mobility pedestrian conveyance injured in collision with car, pick-up or van in nontraffic accident
Add			Pedestrian on hoverboard injured in collision with car, pick-up or van in nontraffic accident
Add			Pedestrian on segway injured in collision with car, pick-up or van in nontraffic accident
No Change	V03.1		Pedestrian injured in collision with car, pick-up truck or van in traffic accident
Add	V03.13		Pedestrian on standing micro-mobility pedestrian conveyance injured in collision with car, pick-up or van in traffic accident
Add		V03.131	Pedestrian on standing electric scooter injured in collision with car, pick-up or van in traffic accident
Add		V03.138	Pedestrian on other standing micro-mobility pedestrian conveyance injured in collision with car, pick-up or van in traffic accident
Add			Pedestrian on hoverboard injured in collision with car, pick-up or van in traffic accident
Add			Pedestrian on segway injured in collision with car, pick-up or van in traffic accident
No Change	V03.9		Pedestrian injured in collision with car, pick-up truck or van, unspecified whether traffic or nontraffic accident
Add	V03.93		Pedestrian on standing micro-mobility pedestrian conveyance injured in collision with car, pick-up or van, unspecified whether traffic or nontraffic accident
Add		V03.931	Pedestrian on standing electric scooter injured in collision with car, pick-up or van, unspecified whether traffic or nontraffic accident
Add		V03.938	Pedestrian on other standing micro-mobility pedestrian conveyance injured in collision with car, pick-up or van, unspecified whether traffic or nontraffic accident
Add			Pedestrian on hoverboard injured in collision with car, pick-up or van, unspecified whether traffic or nontraffic accident
Add			Pedestrian on segway injured in collision with car, pick-up or van, unspecified whether traffic or nontraffic accident

No Change	V04		Pedestrian injured in collision with heavy transport vehicle or bus
No Change	V04.0		Pedestrian injured in collision with heavy transport vehicle or bus in nontraffic accident
Add	V04.03		Pedestrian on standing micro-mobility pedestrian conveyance injured in collision with heavy transport vehicle or bus in nontraffic accident
Add		V04.031	Pedestrian on standing electric scooter injured in collision with heavy transport vehicle or bus in nontraffic accident
Add		V04.038	Pedestrian on other standing micro-mobility pedestrian conveyance injured in collision with heavy transport vehicle or bus in nontraffic accident
Add			Pedestrian on hoverboard injured in collision with heavy transport vehicle or bus in nontraffic accident
Add			Pedestrian on segway injured in collision with heavy transport vehicle or bus in nontraffic accident
No Change	V04.1		Pedestrian injured in collision with heavy transport vehicle or bus in traffic accident
Add	V04.13		Pedestrian on standing micro-mobility pedestrian conveyance injured in collision with heavy transport vehicle or bus in traffic accident
Add		V04.131	Pedestrian on standing electric scooter injured in collision with heavy transport vehicle or bus in traffic accident
Add		V04.138	Pedestrian on other standing micro-mobility pedestrian conveyance injured in collision with heavy transport vehicle or bus in traffic accident
Add			Pedestrian on hoverboard injured in collision with heavy transport vehicle or bus in traffic accident
Add			Pedestrian on segway injured in collision with heavy transport vehicle or bus in traffic accident
No Change	V04.9		Pedestrian injured in collision with heavy transport vehicle or bus, unspecified whether traffic or nontraffic accident
Add	V04.93		Pedestrian on standing micro-mobility pedestrian conveyance injured in collision with heavy transport vehicle or bus, unspecified whether traffic or nontraffic accident
Add		V04.931	Pedestrian on standing electric scooter injured in collision with heavy transport vehicle or bus, unspecified whether traffic or nontraffic accident

Add	V04.938	Pedestrian on other standing micro-mobility pedestrian conveyance injured in collision with heavy transport vehicle or bus, unspecified whether traffic or nontraffic accident
Add		Pedestrian on hoverboard injured in collision with heavy transport vehicle or bus, unspecified whether traffic or nontraffic accident
Add		Pedestrian on segway injured in collision with heavy transport vehicle or bus, unspecified whether traffic or nontraffic accident

No Change **V05** Pedestrian injured in collision with railway train or railway vehicle

No Change	V05.0	Pedestrian injured in collision with railway train or railway vehicle in nontraffic accident
Add	V05.03	Pedestrian on standing micro-mobility pedestrian conveyance injured in collision with railway train or railway vehicle in nontraffic accident
Add	V05.031	Pedestrian on standing electric scooter injured in collision with railway train or railway vehicle in nontraffic accident
Add	V05.038	Pedestrian on other standing micro-mobility pedestrian conveyance injured in collision with railway train or railway vehicle in nontraffic accident
Add		Pedestrian on hoverboard injured in collision with railway train or railway vehicle in nontraffic accident
Add		Pedestrian on segway injured in collision with railway train or railway vehicle in nontraffic accident
No Change	V05.1	Pedestrian injured in collision with railway train or railway vehicle in traffic accident
Add	V05.13	Pedestrian on standing micro-mobility pedestrian conveyance injured in collision with railway train or railway vehicle in traffic accident
Add	V05.131	Pedestrian on standing electric scooter injured in collision with railway train or railway vehicle in traffic accident
Add	V05.138	Pedestrian on other standing micro-mobility pedestrian conveyance injured in collision with railway train or railway vehicle in traffic accident
Add		Pedestrian on hoverboard injured in collision with railway train or railway vehicle in traffic accident
Add		Pedestrian on segway injured in collision with railway train or railway vehicle in traffic accident

No Change	V05.9	Pedestrian injured in collision with railway train or railway vehicle, unspecified whether traffic or nontraffic accident
Add	V05.93	Pedestrian on standing micro-mobility pedestrian conveyance injured in collision with railway train or railway vehicle, unspecified whether traffic or nontraffic accident
Add	V05.931	Pedestrian on standing electric scooter injured in collision with railway train or railway vehicle, unspecified whether traffic or nontraffic accident
Add	V05.938	Pedestrian on other standing micro-mobility pedestrian conveyance injured in collision with railway train or railway vehicle, unspecified whether traffic or nontraffic accident
Add		Pedestrian on hoverboard injured in collision with railway train or railway vehicle, unspecified whether traffic or nontraffic accident
Add		Pedestrian on segway injured in collision with railway train or railway vehicle, unspecified whether traffic or nontraffic accident

No Change **V06** Pedestrian injured in collision with other nonmotor vehicle

No Change	V06.0	Pedestrian injured in collision with other nonmotor vehicle in nontraffic accident
Add	V06.03	Pedestrian on standing micro-mobility pedestrian conveyance injured in collision with other nonmotor vehicle in nontraffic accident
Add	V06.031	Pedestrian on standing electric scooter injured in collision with other nonmotor vehicle in nontraffic accident
Add	V06.038	Pedestrian on other standing micro-mobility pedestrian conveyance injured in collision with other nonmotor vehicle in nontraffic accident
Add		Pedestrian on hoverboard injured in collision with other nonmotor vehicle in nontraffic accident
Add		Pedestrian on segway injured in collision with other nonmotor vehicle in nontraffic accident
No Change	V06.1	Pedestrian injured in collision with other nonmotor vehicle in traffic accident
Add	V06.13	Pedestrian on standing micro-mobility pedestrian conveyance injured in collision with other nonmotor vehicle in traffic accident
Add	V06.131	Pedestrian on standing electric scooter injured in collision with other nonmotor vehicle in traffic accident

Add   V06.138 Pedestrian on other standing micro-mobility pedestrian conveyance injured in collision with other nonmotor vehicle in traffic accident

Add   Pedestrian on hoverboard injured in collision with other nonmotor vehicle in traffic accident

Add   Pedestrian on segway injured in collision with other nonmotor vehicle in traffic accident

No Change   V06.9 Pedestrian injured in collision with other nonmotor vehicle, unspecified whether traffic or nontraffic accident

Add   V06.93 Pedestrian on standing micro-mobility pedestrian conveyance injured in collision with other nonmotor vehicle, unspecified whether traffic or nontraffic accident

Add   V06.931 Pedestrian on standing electric scooter injured in collision with other nonmotor vehicle, unspecified whether traffic or nontraffic accident

Add   V06.938 Pedestrian on other standing micro-mobility pedestrian conveyance injured in collision with other nonmotor vehicle, unspecified whether traffic or nontraffic accident

Add   Pedestrian on hoverboard injured in collision with other nonmotor, unspecified whether traffic or nontraffic accident

Add   Pedestrian on segway injured in collision with other nonmotor vehicle, unspecified whether traffic or nontraffic accident

No Change   **EXPOSURE TO ELECTRIC CURRENT, RADIATION AND EXTREME AMBIENT AIR TEMPERATURE AND PRESSURE (W85-W99)**

No Change W89 Exposure to man-made visible and ultraviolet light
Delete   Excludes1 exposure to sunlight (X32)
Add   Excludes2 exposure to sunlight (X32)

No Change W90 Exposure to other nonionizing radiation
Delete   Excludes1 exposure to sunlight (X32)
Add   Excludes2 exposure to sunlight (X32)

No Change   **MEDICAL DEVICES ASSOCIATED WITH ADVERSE INCIDENTS IN DIAGNOSTIC AND THERAPEUTIC USE (Y70-Y82)**

No Change Y77 Ophthalmic devices associated with adverse incidents
No Change   Y77.1 Therapeutic (nonsurgical) and rehabilitative ophthalmic devices associated with adverse incidents
Add   Y77.11 Contact lens associated with adverse incidents
Add   Rigid gas permeable contact lens associated with adverse incidents
Add   Soft (hydrophilic) contact lens associated with adverse incidents
Add   Y77.19 Other therapeutic (nonsurgical) and rehabilitative ophthalmic devices associated with adverse incidents

No Change   **SUPPLEMENTARY FACTORS RELATED TO CAUSES OF MORBIDITY CLASSIFIED ELSEWHERE (Y90-Y99)**

No Change Y92 Place of occurrence of the external cause
No Change   Y92.0 Non-institutional (private) residence as the place of occurrence of the external cause
No Change   Y92.00 Unspecified non-institutional (private) residence as the place of occurrence of the external cause
Add   Y92.002 Bathroom of unspecified non-institutional (private) residence single-family(private) house as the place of occurrence of the external cause
Add   Y92.002 Bathroom of unspecified non-institutional (private) residence as the place of occurrence of the external cause

No Change **CHAPTER 21**

No Change **FACTORS INFLUENCING HEALTH STATUS AND CONTACT WITH HEALTH SERVICES (Z00-Z99)**

No Change **PERSONS ENCOUNTERING HEALTH SERVICES FOR EXAMINATIONS (Z00-Z13)**

No Change Z03 Encounter for medical observation for suspected diseases and conditions ruled out
No Change   Z03.8 Encounter for observation for other suspected diseases and conditions ruled out
Add   Z03.82 Encounter for observation for suspected foreign body ruled out
Add   Excludes1 retained foreign body (Z18.-)
Add   retained foreign body in eyelid (H02.81)
Add   residual foreign body in soft tissue (M79.5)
Add   Excludes2 confirmed foreign body ingestion or aspiration including:
Add   foreign body in alimentary tract (T18)
Add   foreign body in ear (T16)
Add   foreign body on external eye (T15)
Add   foreign body in respiratory tract (T17)
Add   Z03.821 Encounter for observation for suspected ingested foreign body ruled out
Add   Z03.822 Encounter for observation for suspected aspirated (inhaled) foreign body ruled out
Add   Z03.823 Encounter for observation for suspected inserted (injected) foreign body ruled out
Add   Encounter for observation for suspected inserted (injected) foreign body in eye ruled out
Add   Encounter for observation for suspected inserted (injected) foreign body in orifice ruled out
Add   Encounter for observation for suspected inserted (injected) foreign body in skin ruled out

No Change	**PERSONS ENCOUNTERING HEALTH SERVICES IN CIRCUMSTANCES RELATED TO REPRODUCTION (Z30-Z39)**	
No Change	Z33	**Pregnant state**
No Change	Z33.1	**Pregnant state, incidental**
Add		Pregnancy NOS

No Change	**BODY MASS INDEX [BMI] (Z68)**	
No Change	Z68	**Body mass index [BMI]**
Revise from	Z68.1	**Body mass index (BMI) 19.9 or less, adult**
Revise to	Z68.1	**Body mass index [BMI] 19.9 or less, adult**
Revise from	Z68.2	**Body mass index (BMI) 20-29, adult**
Revise to	Z68.2	**Body mass index [BMI] 20-29, adult**
Revise from	Z68.20	**Body mass index (BMI) 20.0-20.9, adult**
Revise to	Z68.20	**Body mass index [BMI] 20.0-20.9, adult**
Revise from	Z68.21	**Body mass index (BMI) 21.0-21.9, adult**
Revise to	Z68.21	**Body mass index [BMI] 21.0-21.9, adult**
Revise from	Z68.22	**Body mass index (BMI) 22.0-22.9, adult**
Revise to	Z68.22	**Body mass index [BMI] 22.0-22.9, adult**
Revise from	Z68.23	**Body mass index (BMI) 23.0-23.9, adult**
Revise to	Z68.23	**Body mass index [BMI] 23.0-23.9, adult**
Revise from	Z68.24	**Body mass index (BMI) 24.0-24.9, adult**
Revise to	Z68.24	**Body mass index [BMI] 24.0-24.9, adult**
Revise from	Z68.25	**Body mass index (BMI) 25.0-25.9, adult**
Revise to	Z68.25	**Body mass index [BMI] 25.0-25.9, adult**
Revise from	Z68.26	**Body mass index (BMI) 26.0-26.9, adult**
Revise to	Z68.26	**Body mass index [BMI] 26.0-26.9, adult**
Revise from	Z68.27	**Body mass index (BMI) 27.0-27.9, adult**
Revise to	Z68.27	**Body mass index [BMI] 27.0-27.9, adult**
Revise from	Z68.28	**Body mass index (BMI) 28.0-28.9, adult**
Revise to	Z68.28	**Body mass index [BMI] 28.0-28.9, adult**
Revise from	Z68.29	**Body mass index (BMI) 29.0-29.9, adult**
Revise to	Z68.29	**Body mass index [BMI] 29.0-29.9, adult**
Revise from	Z68.3	**Body mass index (BMI) 30-39, adult**
Revise to	Z68.3	**Body mass index [BMI] 30-39, adult**
Revise from	Z68.30	**Body mass index (BMI) 30.0-30.9, adult**
Revise to	Z68.30	**Body mass index [BMI] 30.0-30.9, adult**
Revise from	Z68.31	**Body mass index (BMI) 31.0-31.9, adult**
Revise to	Z68.31	**Body mass index [BMI] 31.0-31.9, adult**
Revise from	Z68.32	**Body mass index (BMI) 32.0-32.9, adult**
Revise to	Z68.32	**Body mass index [BMI] 32.0-32.9, adult**
Revise from	Z68.33	**Body mass index (BMI) 33.0-33.9, adult**
Revise to	Z68.33	**Body mass index [BMI] 33.0-33.9, adult**
Revise from	Z68.34	**Body mass index (BMI) 34.0-34.9, adult**
Revise to	Z68.34	**Body mass index [BMI] 34.0-34.9, adult**
Revise from	Z68.35	**Body mass index (BMI) 35.0-35.9, adult**
Revise to	Z68.35	**Body mass index [BMI] 35.0-35.9, adult**
Revise from	Z68.36	**Body mass index (BMI) 36.0-36.9, adult**
Revise to	Z68.36	**Body mass index [BMI] 36.0-36.9, adult**
Revise from	Z68.37	**Body mass index (BMI) 37.0-37.9, adult**
Revise to	Z68.37	**Body mass index [BMI] 37.0-37.9, adult**
Revise from	Z68.38	**Body mass index (BMI) 38.0-38.9, adult**
Revise to	Z68.38	**Body mass index [BMI] 38.0-38.9, adult**
Revise from	Z68.39	**Body mass index (BMI) 39.0-39.9, adult**
Revise to	Z68.39	**Body mass index [BMI] 39.0-39.9, adult**
Revise from	Z68.4	**Body mass index (BMI) 40 or greater, adult**
Revise to	Z68.4	**Body mass index [BMI] 40 or greater, adult**
Revise from	Z68.41	**Body mass index (BMI) 40.0-44.9, adult**
Revise to	Z68.41	**Body mass index [BMI] 40.0-44.9, adult**
Revise from	Z68.42	**Body mass index (BMI) 45.0-49.9, adult**
Revise to	Z68.42	**Body mass index [BMI] 45.0-49.9, adult**

Revise from	Z68.43	**Body mass index (BMI) 50.0-59.9, adult**
Revise to	Z68.43	**Body mass index [BMI] 50.0-59.9, adult**
Revise from	Z68.44	**Body mass index (BMI) 60.0-69.9, adult**
Revise to	Z68.44	**Body mass index [BMI] 60.0-69.9, adult**
Revise from	Z68.45	**Body mass index (BMI) 70 or greater, adult**
Revise to	Z68.45	**Body mass index [BMI] 70 or greater, adult**
Revise from	Z68.5	**Body mass index (BMI) pediatric**
Revise to	Z68.5	**Body mass index [BMI] pediatric**
Revise from	Z68.51	**Body mass index (BMI) pediatric, less than 5th percentile for age**
Revise to	Z68.51	**Body mass index [BMI] pediatric, less than 5th percentile for age**
Revise from	Z68.52	**Body mass index (BMI) pediatric, 5th percentile to less than 85th percentile for age**
Revise to	Z68.52	**Body mass index [BMI] pediatric, 5th percentile to less than 85th percentile for age**
Revise from	Z68.53	**Body mass index (BMI) pediatric, 85th percentile to less than 95th percentile for age**
Revise to	Z68.53	**Body mass index [BMI] pediatric, 85th percentile to less than 95th percentile for age**
Revise from	Z68.54	**Body mass index (BMI) pediatric, greater than or equal to 95th percentile for age**
Revise to	Z68.54	**Body mass index [BMI] pediatric, greater than or equal to 95th percentile for age**

No Change	**PERSONS WITH POTENTIAL HEALTH HAZARDS RELATED TO FAMILY AND PERSONAL HISTORY AND CERTAIN CONDITIONS INFLUENCING HEALTH STATUS (Z77-Z99)**	
No Change	Z79	**Long term (current) drug therapy**
Delete	**Excludes2**	long term (current) use of oral antidiabetic drugs (Z79.84)
Delete		long term (current) use of oral hypoglycemic drugs (Z79.84)
No Change	Z79.4	**Long term (current) use of insulin**
Add	**Excludes1**	long term (current) use of oral antidiabetic drugs (Z79.84)
Add		long term (current) use of oral hypoglycemic drugs (Z79.84)
No Change	Z85	**Personal history of malignant neoplasm**
No Change	Z85.8	**Personal history of malignant neoplasms of other organs and systems**
No Change	Z85.81	**Personal history of malignant neoplasm of lip, oral cavity, and pharynx**
Add		Conditions classifiable to C00-C14
No Change	Z85.83	**Personal history of malignant neoplasm of bone and soft tissue**
Add		Conditions classifiable to C40-C41; C45-C49
No Change	Z85.84	**Personal history of malignant neoplasm of eye and nervous tissue**
Add		Conditions classifiable to C69-C72
No Change	Z85.85	**Personal history of malignant neoplasm of endocrine glands**
Add		Conditions classifiable to C73-C75
No Change	Z85.89	**Personal history of malignant neoplasm of other organs and systems**
Add		Conditions classifiable to C7A.098, C76, C77-C79

No Change	Z88	Allergy status to drugs, medicaments and biological substances
Revise from	Z88.1	Allergy status to other antibiotic agents status
Revise to	Z88.1	Allergy status to other antibiotic agents
Revise from	Z88.2	Allergy status to sulfonamides status
Revise to	Z88.2	Allergy status to sulfonamides
Revise from	Z88.3	Allergy status to other anti-infective agents status
Revise to	Z88.3	Allergy status to other anti-infective agents
Revise from	Z88.4	Allergy status to anesthetic agent status
Revise to	Z88.4	Allergy status to anesthetic agent
Revise from	Z88.5	Allergy status to narcotic agent status
Revise to	Z88.5	Allergy status to narcotic agent
Revise from	Z88.6	Allergy status to analgesic agent status
Revise to	Z88.6	Allergy status to analgesic agent
Revise from	Z88.7	Allergy status to serum and vaccine status
Revise to	Z88.7	Allergy status to serum and vaccine
Revise from	Z88.8	Allergy status to other drugs, medicaments and biological substances status
Revise to	Z88.8	Allergy status to other drugs, medicaments and biological substances
Revise from	Z88.9	Allergy status to unspecified drugs, medicaments and biological substances status
Revise to	Z88.9	Allergy status to unspecified drugs, medicaments and biological substances

No Change **CHAPTER 22**

No Change **CODES FOR SPECIAL PURPOSES (U00–U85)**

No Change   This chapter contains the following blocks:

Add

U00–U49	Provisional assignment of new diseases of uncertain etiology or emergency use

Add

PROVISIONAL ASSIGNMENT OF NEW DISEASES OF UNCERTAIN ETIOLOGY OR EMERGENCY USE (U00–U49)

Add	U07	Emergency use of U07
Add	U07.0	Vaping-related disorder
Add		Dabbing related lung damage
Add		Dabbing related lung injury
Add		E-cigarette, or vaping, product use associated lung injury [EVALI]
Add		Electronic cigarette related lung damage
Add		Electronic cigarette related lung injury
Add		Use additional code to identify manifestations, such as:
Add		abdominal pain (R10.84)
Add		acute respiratory distress syndrome (J80)
Add		diarrhea (R19.7)
Add		drug-induced interstitial lung disorder (J70.4)
Add		lipoid pneumonia (J69.1)
Add		weight loss (R63.4)
Add	U07.1	COVID-19
Add		Use additional code to identify pneumonia or other manifestations
Add		**Excludes1** coronavirus infection, unspecified (B34.2)
Add		coronavirus as the cause of diseases classified elsewhere (B97.2-)
Add		pneumonia due to SARS-associated coronavirus (J12.81)

PART I

Introduction

ICD-10-CM Official Guidelines for Coding and Reporting FY2021
(October 1, 2020 - September 30, 2021)

Narrative changes appear in **bold** text
Items <u>underlined</u> have been moved within the guidelines since the 2020 version
Italics are used to indicate revisions to heading changes

The Centers for Medicare and Medicaid Services (CMS) and the National Center for Health Statistics (NCHS), two departments within the U.S. Federal Government's Department of Health and Human Services (DHHS), provide the following guidelines for coding and reporting using the International Classification of Diseases, 10th Revision, Clinical Modification (ICD-10-CM). These guidelines should be used as a companion document to the official version of the ICD-10-CM as published on the NCHS website. The ICD-10-CM is a morbidity classification published by the United States for classifying diagnoses and reason for visits in all health care settings. The ICD-10-CM is based on the ICD-10, the statistical classification of disease published by the World Health Organization (WHO).

These guidelines have been approved by the four organizations that make up the Cooperating Parties for the ICD-10-CM: the American Hospital Association (AHA), the American Health Information Management Association (AHIMA), CMS, and NCHS.

These guidelines are a set of rules that have been developed to accompany and complement the official conventions and instructions provided within the ICD-10-CM itself. The instructions and conventions of the classification take precedence over guidelines. These guidelines are based on the coding and sequencing instructions in the Tabular List and Alphabetic Index of ICD-10-CM, but provide additional instruction. Adherence to these guidelines when assigning ICD-10-CM diagnosis codes is required under the Health Insurance Portability and Accountability Act (HIPAA). The diagnosis codes (Tabular List and Alphabetic Index)

have been adopted under HIPAA for all health care settings. A joint effort between the health care provider and the coder is essential to achieve complete and accurate documentation, code assignment, and reporting of diagnoses and procedures. These guidelines have been developed to assist both the health care provider and the coder in identifying those diagnoses that are to be reported. The importance of consistent, complete documentation in the medical record cannot be overemphasized. Without such documentation accurate coding cannot be achieved. The entire record should be reviewed to determine the specific reason for the encounter and the conditions treated.

The term "encounter" is used for all settings, including hospital admissions. In the context of these guidelines, the term "provider" is used throughout the guidelines to mean physician or any qualified health care practitioner who is legally accountable for establishing the patient's diagnosis. Only this set of guidelines, approved by the Cooperating Parties, is official.

The guidelines are organized into sections. Section I includes the structure and conventions of the classification and general guidelines that apply to the entire classification, and chapter-specific guidelines that correspond to the chapters as they are arranged in the classification. Section II includes guidelines for selection of principal diagnosis for non-outpatient settings. Section III includes guidelines for reporting additional diagnoses in non-outpatient settings. Section IV is for outpatient coding and reporting. It is necessary to review all sections of the guidelines to fully understand all of the rules and instructions needed to code properly.

ICD-10-CM Official Guidelines for Coding and Reporting

Section I. Conventions, General Coding Guidelines and Chapter Specific Guidelines

A. Conventions for the ICD-10-CM
1. The Alphabetic Index and Tabular List
2. Format and Structure:
3. Use of codes for reporting purposes
4. Placeholder character
5. 7th Characters
6. Abbreviations
   a. Alphabetic Index abbreviations
   b. Tabular List abbreviations
7. Punctuation
8. Use of "and"
9. Other and Unspecified codes
   a. "Other" codes
   b. "Unspecified" codes
10. Includes Notes
11. Inclusion terms
12. Excludes Notes
   a. Excludes1
   b. Excludes2
13. Etiology/manifestation convention ("code first", "use additional code" and "in diseases classified elsewhere" notes)
14. "And"
15. "With"
16. "See" and "See Also"
17. "Code also note"
18. Default codes
19. Code assignment and Clinical Criteria

B. General Coding Guidelines
1. Locating a code in the ICD-10-CM
2. Level of Detail in Coding
3. Code or codes from A00.0 through T88.9, Z00-Z99.8
4. Signs and symptoms
5. Conditions that are an integral part of a disease process
6. Conditions that are not an integral part of a disease process
7. Multiple coding for a single condition
8. Acute and Chronic Conditions
9. Combination Code
10. Sequela (Late Effects)
11. Impending or Threatened Condition
12. Reporting Same Diagnosis Code More than Once
13. Laterality
14. Documentation *by Clinicians Other than the Patient's Provider*
15. Syndromes
16. Documentation of Complications of Care
17. Borderline Diagnosis
18. Use of Sign/Symptom/Unspecified Codes
19. Coding for Healthcare Encounters in Hurricane Aftermath
   a. Use of External Cause of Morbidity Codes
   b. Sequencing of External Causes of Morbidity Codes
   c. Other External Causes of Morbidity Code Issues
   d. Use of Z codes

C. Chapter-Specific Coding Guidelines
1. Chapter 1: Certain Infectious and Parasitic Diseases (A00-B99, *U07.1*)
   a. Human Immunodeficiency Virus (HIV) Infections
   b. Infectious agents as the cause of diseases classified to other chapters
   c. Infections resistant to antibiotics
   d. Sepsis, Severe Sepsis, and Septic Shock
   e. Methicillin Resistant *Staphylococcus aureus* (MRSA) Conditions
   f. Zika virus infection
   g. Coronavirus infections
2. Chapter 2: Neoplasms (C00-D49)
   a. Treatment directed at the malignancy
   b. Treatment of secondary site
   c. Coding and sequencing of complications
   d. Primary malignancy previously excised
   e. Admissions/Encounters involving chemotherapy, immunotherapy and radiation therapy
   f. Admission/encounter to determine extent of malignancy
   g. Symptoms, signs, and abnormal findings listed in Chapter 18 associated with neoplasms
   h. Admission/encounter for pain control/management
   i. Malignancy in two or more noncontiguous sites
   j. Disseminated malignant neoplasm, unspecified
   k. Malignant neoplasm without specification of site
   l. Sequencing of neoplasm codes
   m. Current malignancy versus personal history of malignancy
   n. Leukemia, Multiple Myeloma, and Malignant Plasma Cell Neoplasms in remission versus personal history
   o. Aftercare following surgery for neoplasm
   p. Follow-up care for completed treatment of a malignancy
   q. Prophylactic organ removal for prevention of malignancy
   r. Malignant neoplasm associated with transplanted organ
3. Chapter 3: Disease of the Blood and Blood-Forming Organs and Certain Disorders Involving the Immune Mechanism (D50-D89)
4. Chapter 4: Endocrine, Nutritional, and Metabolic Diseases (E00-E89)
   a. Diabetes mellitus
5. Chapter 5: Mental, Behavioral, and Neurodevelopmental disorders (F01 – F99)
   a. Pain disorders related to psychological factors
   b. Mental and behavioral disorders due to psychoactive substance use
   c. Factitious Disorder
6. Chapter 6: Diseases of the Nervous System (G00-G99)
   a. Dominant/nondominant side
   b. Pain - Category G89
7. Chapter 7: Diseases of the Eye and Adnexa (H00-H59)
   a. Glaucoma
   b. Blindness
8. Chapter 8: Diseases of the Ear and Mastoid Process (H60-H95)

GUIDELINES (ICD-10-CM)

Section II. Selection of Principal Diagnosis

A. Codes for symptoms, signs, and ill-defined conditions
B. Two or more interrelated conditions, each potentially meeting the definition for principal diagnosis
C. Two or more diagnoses that equally meet the definition for principal diagnosis
D. Two or more comparative or contrasting conditions
E. A symptom(s) followed by contrasting/comparative diagnoses
F. Original treatment plan not carried out
G. Complications of surgery and other medical care
H. Uncertain Diagnosis
I. Admission from Observation Unit
   1. Admission Following Medical Observation
   2. Admission Following Post-Operative Observation
J. Admission from Outpatient Surgery
K. Admissions/Encounters for Rehabilitation

Section III. Reporting Additional Diagnoses

A. Previous conditions
B. Abnormal findings
C. Uncertain Diagnosis

Section IV. Diagnostic Coding and Reporting Guidelines for Outpatient Services

A. Selection of first-listed condition
   1. Outpatient Surgery
   2. Observation Stay
B. Codes from A00.0 through T88.9, Z00-Z99
C. Accurate reporting of ICD-10-CM diagnosis codes
D. Codes that describe symptoms and signs
E. Encounters for circumstances other than a disease or injury
F. Level of Detail in Coding
   1. ICD-10-CM codes with 3, 4, 5, 6, or 7 characters
   2. Use of full number of characters required for a code
G. ICD-10-CM code for the diagnosis, condition, problem, or other reason for encounter/visit
H. Uncertain diagnosis
I. Chronic diseases
J. Code all documented conditions that coexist
K. Patients receiving diagnostic services only
L. Patients receiving therapeutic services only
M. Patients receiving preoperative evaluations only
N. Ambulatory surgery
O. Routine outpatient prenatal visits
P. Encounters for general medical examinations with abnormal findings
Q. Encounters for routine health screenings

Appendix I: Present on Admission Reporting Guidelines

Section I. Conventions, General Coding Guidelines, and Chapter Specific Guidelines

The conventions, general guidelines, and chapter-specific guidelines are applicable to all health care settings unless otherwise indicated. The conventions and instructions of the classification take precedence over guidelines.

A. **Conventions for the ICD-10-CM**
   The conventions for the ICD-10-CM are the general rules for use of the classification independent of the guidelines. These conventions are incorporated within the Alphabetic Index and Tabular List of the ICD-10-CM as instructional notes.

   1. **The Alphabetic Index and Tabular List**
      The ICD-10-CM is divided into the Alphabetic Index, an alphabetical list of terms and their corresponding code, and the Tabular List, a structured list of codes divided into chapters based on body system or condition. The Alphabetic Index consists of the following parts: the Index of Diseases and Injury, the Index of External Causes of Injury, the Table of Neoplasms, and the Table of Drugs and Chemicals.
      See Section I.C2. General guidelines
      See Section I.C.19. Adverse effects, poisoning, underdosing and toxic effects

   2. **Format and Structure:**
      The ICD-10-CM Tabular List contains categories, subcategories and codes. Characters for categories, subcategories and codes may be either a letter or a number. All categories are 3 characters. A 3-character category that has no further subdivision is equivalent to a code. Subcategories are either 4 or 5 characters. Codes may be 3, 4, 5, 6 or 7 characters. That is, each level of subdivision after a category is a subcategory. The final level of subdivision is a code. Codes that have applicable 7th characters are still referred to as codes, not subcategories. A code that has an applicable 7th character is considered invalid without the 7th character.
      The ICD-10-CM uses an indented format for ease in reference

   3. **Use of codes for reporting purposes**
      For reporting purposes only codes are permissible, not categories or subcategories, and any applicable 7th character is required.

   4. **Placeholder character**
      The ICD-10-CM utilizes a placeholder character "X". The "X" is used as a placeholder at certain codes to allow for future expansion. An example of this is at the poisoning, adverse effect and underdosing codes, categories T36-T50. Where a placeholder exists, the X must be used in order for the code to be considered a valid code.

   5. **7th Characters**
      Certain ICD-10-CM categories have applicable 7th characters. The applicable 7th character is required for all codes within the category, or as the notes in the Tabular List instruct. The 7th character must always be the 7th character in the data field. If a code that requires a 7th character is not 6 characters, a placeholder X must be used to fill in the empty characters.

   6. **Abbreviations**
      a. **Alphabetic Index abbreviations**
         NEC "Not elsewhere classifiable"
         This abbreviation in the Alphabetic Index represents "other specified". When a

specific code is not available for a condition the Alphabetic Index directs the coder to the "other specified" code in the Tabular List.

NOS "Not otherwise specified"
This abbreviation is the equivalent of unspecified.

b. Tabular List abbreviations

NEC "Not elsewhere classifiable"
This abbreviation in the Tabular List represents "other specified". When a specific code is not available for a condition, the Tabular List includes an NEC entry under a code to identify the code as the "other specified" code.

NOS "Not otherwise specified"
This abbreviation is the equivalent of unspecified.

7. Punctuation

[ ] Brackets are used in the Tabular List to enclose synonyms, alternative wording or explanatory phrases. Brackets are used in the Alphabetic Index to identify manifestation codes.

( ) Parentheses are used in both the Alphabetic Index and Tabular List to enclose supplementary words that may be present or absent in the statement of a disease or procedure without affecting the code number to which it is assigned. The terms within the parentheses are referred to as nonessential modifiers. The nonessential modifiers in the Alphabetic Index to Diseases apply to subterms following a main term except when a nonessential modifier and a subentry are mutually exclusive, the subentry takes precedence. For example, in the ICD-10-CM Alphabetic Index under the main term Enteritis, "acute" is a nonessential modifier and "chronic" is a subentry. In this case, the nonessential modifier "acute" does not apply to the subentry "chronic".

: Colons are used in the Tabular List after an incomplete term which needs one or more of the modifiers following the colon to make it assignable to a given category.

8. Use of "and".

See Section I.A.14. Use of the term "And"

9. Other and Unspecified codes

a. "Other" codes

Codes titled "other" or "other specified" are for use when the information in the medical record provides detail for which a specific code does not exist. Alphabetic Index entries with NEC in the line designate "other" codes in the Tabular List. These Alphabetic Index entries represent specific disease entities for which no specific code exists so the term is included within an "other" code.

b. "Unspecified" codes

Codes titled "unspecified" are for use when the information in the medical record is insufficient to assign a more specific code. For those categories for which an unspecified code is not provided, the "other specified" code may represent both other and unspecified.

See Section I.B.18 Use of signs/symptoms/unspecified codes

10. Includes Notes

This note appears immediately under a 3-character code title to further define, or give examples of, the content of the category.

11. Inclusion terms

List of terms is included under some codes. These terms are the conditions for which that code is to be used. The terms may be synonyms of the code title, or, in the case of "other specified" codes, the terms are a list of the various conditions assigned to that code. The inclusion terms are not necessarily exhaustive. Additional terms found only in the Alphabetic Index may also be assigned to a code.

12. Excludes Notes

The ICD-10-CM has two types of excludes notes. Each type of note has a different definition for use but they are all similar in that they indicate that codes excluded from each other are independent of each other.

a. Excludes1

A type 1 Excludes note is a pure excludes note. It means "NOT CODED HERE!" An Excludes1 note indicates that the code excluded should never be used at the same time as the code above the Excludes1 note. An Excludes1 is used when two conditions cannot occur together, such as a congenital form versus an acquired form of the same condition.

An exception to the Excludes1 definition is the circumstance when the two conditions are unrelated to each other. If it is not clear whether the two conditions involving an Excludes1 note are related or not, query the provider. For example, code F45.8, Other somatoform disorders, has an Excludes1 note for "sleep related teeth grinding (G47.63)" because "teeth grinding" is an inclusion term under F45.8. Only one of these two codes should be assigned for teeth grinding. However, psychogenic dysmenorrhea is also an inclusion term under F45.8, and a patient could have both this condition and sleep-related teeth grinding. In this case, the two conditions are clearly unrelated to each other, and so it would be appropriate to report F45.8 and G47.63 together.

b. Excludes2

A Type 2 Excludes note represents "Not included here." An excludes2 note indicates that the condition excluded is not part of the condition represented by the code, but a patient may have both conditions at the same time. When an Excludes2 note appears under a code, it is acceptable to use both the code and the excluded code together, when appropriate.

GUIDELINES (ICD-10-CM)

13. **Etiology/manifestation convention ("code first", "use additional code" and "in diseases classified elsewhere" notes)**

Certain conditions have both an underlying etiology and multiple body system manifestations due to the underlying etiology. For such conditions, the ICD-10-CM has a coding convention that requires the underlying condition be sequenced first, if applicable, followed by the manifestation. Wherever such a combination exists, there is a "use additional code" note at the etiology code, and a "code first" note at the manifestation code. These instructional notes indicate the proper sequencing order of the codes, etiology followed by manifestation.

In most cases the manifestation codes will have in the code title, "in diseases classified elsewhere." Codes with this title are a component of the etiology/manifestation convention. The code title indicates that it is a manifestation code. "In diseases classified elsewhere" codes are never permitted to be used as first-listed or principal diagnosis codes. They must be used in conjunction with an underlying condition code and they must be listed following the underlying condition. See category F02, Dementia in other diseases classified elsewhere, for an example of this convention.

There are manifestation codes that do not have "in diseases classified elsewhere" in the title. For such codes, there is a "use additional code" note at the etiology code and a "code first" note at the manifestation code and the rules for sequencing apply.

In addition to the notes in the Tabular List, these conditions also have a specific Alphabetic Index entry structure. In the Alphabetic Index both conditions are listed together with the etiology code first followed by the manifestation codes in brackets. The code in brackets is always to be sequenced second.

An example of the etiology/manifestation convention is dementia in Parkinson's disease. In the Alphabetic Index, code G20 is listed first, followed by code F02.80 or F02.81 in brackets. Code G20 represents the underlying etiology, Parkinson's disease, and must be sequenced first, whereas code F02.80 and F02.81 represent the manifestation of dementia in diseases classified elsewhere, with or without behavioral disturbance.

"Code first" and "Use additional code" notes are also used as sequencing rules in the classification for certain codes that are not part of an etiology/manifestation combination.

See Section I.B.7. Multiple coding for a single condition.

14. **"And"**

The word "and" should be interpreted to mean either "and" or "or" when it appears in a title.

For example, cases of "tuberculosis of bones", "tuberculosis of joints" and "tuberculosis of bones and joints" are classified to subcategory A18.0, Tuberculosis of bones and joints.

15. **"With"**

The word "with" or "in" should be interpreted to mean "associated with" or "due to" when it appears in a code title, the Alphabetic Index, (either under a main term or subterm) or an instructional note in the Tabular List. The classification presumes a causal relationship between the two conditions linked by these terms in the Alphabetic Index or Tabular List. These conditions should be coded as related even in the absence of provider documentation explicitly linking them, unless the documentation clearly states the conditions are unrelated or when another guideline exists that specifically requires a documented linkage between two conditions (e.g., sepsis guideline for "acute organ dysfunction that is not clearly associated with the sepsis").

For conditions not specifically linked by these relational terms in the classification or when a guideline requires that a linkage between two conditions be explicitly documented provider documentation must link the conditions in order to code them as related.

The word "with" in the Alphabetic Index is sequenced immediately following the main term or subterm, not in alphabetical order.

16. **"See" and "See Also"**

The "see" instruction following a main term in the Alphabetic Index indicates that another term should be referenced. It is necessary to go to the main term referenced with the "see" note to locate the correct code.

A "see also" instruction following a main term in the Alphabetic Index instructs that there is another main term that may also be referenced that may provide additional Alphabetic Index entries that may be useful. It is not necessary to follow the "see also" note when the original main term provides the necessary code.

17. **"Code also" note**

A "code also" note instructs that two codes may be required to fully describe a condition, but this note does not provide sequencing direction. The sequencing depends on the circumstances of the encounter.

18. **Default codes**

A code listed next to a main term in the ICD-10-CM Alphabetic Index is referred to as a default code. The default code represents that condition that is most commonly associated with the main term, or is the unspecified code for the condition. If a condition is documented in a medical record (for example, appendicitis) without any additional information, such as acute or chronic, the default code should be assigned.

19. **Code assignment and Clinical Criteria**

The assignment of a diagnosis code is based on the provider's diagnostic statement that the condition exists. The provider's statement that the patient has a particular condition is sufficient. Code assignment is not based on clinical criteria used by the provider to establish the diagnosis.

B. General Coding Guidelines

1. Locating a code in the ICD-10-CM

To select a code in the classification that corresponds to a diagnosis or reason for visit documented in a medical record, first locate the term in the Alphabetic Index, and then verify the code in the Tabular List. Read and be guided by instructional notations that appear in both the Alphabetic Index and the Tabular List.

It is essential to use both the Alphabetic Index and Tabular List when locating and assigning a code. The Alphabetic Index does not always provide the full code. Selection of the full code, including laterality and any applicable 7th character can only be done in the Tabular List. A dash (-) at the end of an Alphabetic Index entry indicates that additional characters are required. Even if a dash is not included at the Alphabetic Index entry, it is necessary to refer to the Tabular List to verify that no 7th character is required.

2. Level of Detail in Coding

Diagnosis codes are to be used and reported at their highest number of characters available.

ICD-10-CM diagnosis codes are composed of codes with 3, 4, 5, 6, or 7 characters. Codes with three characters are included in ICD-10-CM as the heading of a category of codes that may be further subdivided by the use of 4th and/or 5th characters and/or 6th characters, which provide greater detail.

A 3-character code is to be used only if it is not further subdivided. A code is invalid if it has not been coded to the full number of characters required for that code, including the 7th character, if applicable.

3. Code or codes from A00.0 through T88.9, Z00-Z99.8

The appropriate code or codes from A00.0 through T88.9, Z00-Z99.8 must be used to identify diagnoses, symptoms, conditions, problems, complaints or other reason(s) for the encounter/visit.

4. Signs and symptoms

Codes that describe symptoms and signs, as opposed to diagnoses, are acceptable for reporting purposes when a related definitive diagnosis has not been established (confirmed) by the provider. Chapter 18 of ICD-10-CM, Symptoms, Signs, and Abnormal Clinical and Laboratory Findings, Not Elsewhere Classified (codes R00.0 - R99) contains many, but not all codes for symptoms.

See Section I.B.18 Use of signs/symptoms/ unspecified codes

5. Conditions that are an integral part of a disease process

Signs and symptoms that are associated routinely with a disease process should not be assigned as additional codes, unless otherwise instructed by the classification.

6. Conditions that are not an integral part of a disease process

Additional signs and symptoms that may not be associated routinely with a disease process should be coded when present.

7. Multiple coding for a single condition

In addition to the etiology/manifestation convention that requires two codes to fully describe a single condition that affects multiple body systems, there are other single conditions that also require more than one code. "Use additional code" notes are found in the Tabular List at codes that are not part of an etiology/manifestation pair where a secondary code is useful to fully describe a condition. The sequencing rule is the same as the etiology/manifestation pair, "use additional code" indicates that a secondary code should be added, if known.

For example, for bacterial infections that are not included in Chapter 1, a secondary code from category B95, Streptococcus, Staphylococcus, and Enterococcus, as the cause of diseases classified elsewhere, or B96, Other bacterial agents as the cause of diseases classified elsewhere, may be required to identify the bacterial organism causing the infection. A "use additional code" note will normally be found at the infectious disease code, indicating a need for the organism code to be added as a secondary code.

"Code first" notes are also under certain codes that are not specifically manifestation codes but may be due to an underlying cause. When there is a "code first" note and an underlying condition is present, the underlying condition should be sequenced first, if known.

"Code, if applicable, any causal condition first," notes indicate that this code may be assigned as a principal diagnosis when the causal condition is unknown or not applicable. If a causal condition is known, then the code for that condition should be sequenced as the principal or first-listed diagnosis.

Multiple codes may be needed for sequela, complication codes and obstetric codes to more fully describe a condition. See the specific guidelines for these conditions for further instruction.

8. Acute and Chronic Conditions

If the same condition is described as both acute (subacute) and chronic, and separate subentries exist in the Alphabetic Index at the same indentation level, code both and sequence the acute (subacute) code first.

9. Combination Code

A combination code is a single code used to classify:
Two diagnoses, or
A diagnosis with an associated secondary process (manifestation)
A diagnosis with an associated complication
Combination codes are identified by referring to subterm entries in the Alphabetic Index and by reading the inclusion and exclusion notes in the Tabular List.

Assign only the combination code when that code fully identifies the diagnostic conditions involved or when the Alphabetic Index so directs. Multiple coding should not be used when the classification provides a combination code that clearly identifies all of the elements documented in the diagnosis. When the combination code lacks necessary specificity in describing the manifestation or complication, an additional code should be used as a secondary code.

10. **Sequela (Late Effects)**
A sequela is the residual effect (condition produced) after the acute phase of an illness or injury has terminated. There is no time limit on when a sequela code can be used. The residual may be apparent early, such as in cerebral infarction, or it may occur months or years later, such as that due to a previous injury. Examples of sequela include: scar formation resulting from a burn, deviated septum due to a nasal fracture, and infertility due to tubal occlusion from old tuberculosis. Coding of sequela generally requires two codes sequenced in the following order: the condition or nature of the sequela is sequenced first. The sequela code is sequenced second.

An exception to the above guidelines are those instances where the code for the sequela is followed by a manifestation code identified in the Tabular List and title, or the sequela code has been expanded (at the 4th, 5th, or 6th character levels) to include the manifestation(s). The code for the acute phase of an illness or injury that led to the sequela is never used with a code for the late effect.

See Section I.C.9. Sequelae of cerebrovascular disease
See Section I.C.15. Sequelae of complication of pregnancy, childbirth and the puerperium
See Section I.C.19. Application of 7th characters for Chapter 19

11. **Impending or Threatened Condition**
Code any condition described at the time of discharge as "impending" or "threatened" as follows:

If it did occur, code as confirmed diagnosis.

If it did not occur, reference the Alphabetic Index to determine if the condition has a subentry term for "impending" or "threatened" and also reference main term entries for "Impending" and for "Threatened."

If the subterms are listed, assign the given code.

If the subterms are not listed, code the existing underlying condition(s) and not the condition described as impending or threatened.

12. **Reporting Same Diagnosis Code More Than Once**
Each unique ICD-10-CM diagnosis code may be reported only once for an encounter. This applies to bilateral conditions when there are no distinct codes identifying laterality or two different conditions classified to the same ICD-10-CM diagnosis code.

13. **Laterality**
Some ICD-10-CM codes indicate laterality, specifying whether the condition occurs on the left, right or is bilateral. If no bilateral code is provided and the condition is bilateral, assign separate codes for both the left and right side. If the side is not identified in the medical record, assign the code for the unspecified side.

When a patient has a bilateral condition and each side is treated during separate encounters, assign the "bilateral" code (as the condition still exists on both sides), including for the encounter to treat the first side. For the second encounter for treatment after one side has previously been treated and the condition no longer exists on that side, assign the appropriate unilateral code for the side where the condition still exists (e.g., cataract surgery performed on each eye in separate encounters). The bilateral code would not be assigned for the subsequent encounter, as the patient no longer has the condition in the previously-treated site. If the treatment on the first side did not completely resolve the condition, then the bilateral code would still be appropriate.

14. **Documentation by Clinicians Other than the Patient's Provider**
Code assignment is based on the documentation by patient's provider (i.e., physician or other qualified healthcare practitioner legally accountable for establishing the patient's diagnosis). There are a few exceptions, such as codes for the Body Mass Index (BMI), depth of non-pressure chronic ulcers, pressure ulcer stage, coma scale, and NIH stroke scale (NIHSS) codes, code assignment may be based on medical record documentation from clinicians who are not the patient's provider (i.e., physician or other qualified healthcare practitioner legally accountable for establishing the patient's diagnosis), since this information is typically documented by other clinicians involved in the care of the patient (e.g., a dietitian often documents the BMI, a nurse often documents the pressure ulcer stages, and an emergency medical technician often documents the coma scale). However, the associated diagnosis (such as overweight, obesity, acute stroke, or pressure ulcer) must be documented by the patient's provider. If there is conflicting medical record documentation, either from the same clinician or different clinicians, the patient's attending provider should be queried for clarification.

For social determinants of health, such as information found in categories Z55-Z65, Persons with potential health hazards related to socioeconomic and psychosocial circumstances, code assignment may be based on medical record documentation from clinicians involved in the care of the patient who are not the patient's provider since this information represents social information, rather than medical diagnoses.

Patient self-reported documentation may also be used to assign codes for social determinants of health, as long as the patient self-reported information is signed-off by and incorporated into the health record by either a clinician or provider.

The BMI, coma scale, and NIHSS codes and categories Z55-Z65 should only be reported as secondary diagnoses.

15. Syndromes

Follow the Alphabetic Index guidance when coding syndromes. In the absence of Alphabetic Index guidance, assign codes for the documented manifestations of the syndrome. Additional codes for manifestations that are not an integral part of the disease process may also be assigned when the condition does not have a unique code.

16. Documentation of Complications of Care

Code assignment is based on the provider's documentation of the relationship between the condition and the care or procedure, unless otherwise instructed by the classification. The guideline extends to any complications of care, regardless of the chapter the code is located in. It is important to note that not all conditions that occur during or following medical care or surgery are classified as complications. There must be a cause-and-effect relationship between the care provided and the condition, and an indication in the documentation that it is a complication. Query the provider for clarification, if the complication is not clearly documented.

17. Borderline Diagnosis

If the provider documents a "borderline" diagnosis at the time of discharge, the diagnosis is coded as confirmed, unless the classification provides a specific entry (e.g., borderline diabetes). If a borderline condition has a specific index entry in ICD-10-CM, it should be coded as such. Since borderline conditions are not uncertain diagnoses, no distinction is made between the care setting (inpatient versus outpatient). Whenever the documentation is unclear regarding a borderline condition, coders are encouraged to query for clarification.

18. Use of Sign/Symptom/Unspecified Codes

Sign/symptom and "unspecified" codes have acceptable, even necessary, uses. While specific diagnosis codes should be reported when they are supported by the available medical record documentation and clinical knowledge of the patient's health condition, there are instances when signs/symptoms or unspecified codes are the best choices for accurately reflecting the healthcare encounter. Each healthcare encounter should be coded to the level of certainty known for that encounter.

If a definitive diagnosis has not been established by the end of the encounter, it is appropriate to report codes for sign(s) and/or symptom(s) in lieu of a definitive diagnosis. When sufficient clinical information isn't known or available about a particular health condition to assign a more specific code, it is acceptable to report the appropriate "unspecified" code (e.g., a diagnosis of pneumonia has been determined, but not the specific type). Unspecified codes should be reported when they are the codes that most accurately reflect what is known about the patient's condition at the time of that particular encounter. It would be inappropriate to select a specific code that is not supported by the medical record documentation or conduct medically unnecessary diagnostic testing in order to determine a more specific code.

19. Coding for Healthcare Encounters in Hurricane Aftermath

a. Use of External Cause of Morbidity Codes

An external cause of morbidity code should be assigned to identify the cause of the injury(ies) incurred as a result of the hurricane. The use of external cause of morbidity codes is supplemental to the application of ICD-10-CM codes. External cause of morbidity codes are never to be recorded as a principal diagnosis (first-listed in non-inpatient settings). The appropriate injury code should be sequenced before any external cause codes. The external cause of morbidity codes capture how the injury or health condition happened (cause), the intent (unintentional or accidental; or intentional, such as suicide or assault), the place where the event occurred, the activity of the patient at the time of the event, and the person's status (e.g., civilian, military). They should not be assigned for encounters to treat hurricane victims' medical conditions when no injury, adverse effect or poisoning is involved. External cause of morbidity codes should be assigned for each encounter for care and treatment of the injury. External cause of morbidity codes may be assigned in all health care settings. For the purpose of capturing complete and accurate ICD-10-CM data in the aftermath of the hurricane, a healthcare setting should be considered as any location where medical care is provided by licensed healthcare professionals.

b. Sequencing of External Causes of Morbidity Codes

Codes for cataclysmic events, such as a hurricane, take priority over all other external cause codes except child and adult abuse and terrorism and should be sequenced before other external cause of injury codes. Assign as many external cause of morbidity codes as necessary to fully explain each cause. For example, if an injury occurs as a result of a building collapse during the hurricane, external cause codes for both the hurricane and the building collapse should be assigned, with the external causes code for hurricane being sequenced as the first external cause code. For injuries incurred as a direct result of the hurricane, assign the appropriate code(s) for the injuries, followed by the code X37.0-, Hurricane (with the appropriate 7th character), and any other applicable external cause of injury codes. Code X37.0- also should be assigned when an injury is incurred as a result of flooding caused by a levee breaking related to the hurricane. Code X38.-, Flood (with the appropriate 7th character), should be assigned when an injury is from flooding resulting directly from the storm. Code X36.Ø.-, Collapse of dam or man-made structure, should not be assigned when the cause of the collapse is due to the hurricane. Use of code X36.Ø- is limited to collapses of man-made structures due to earth surface movements, not due to storm surges directly from a hurricane.

c. Other External Causes of Morbidity Code Issues

For injuries that are not a direct result of the hurricane, such as an evacuee that has incurred an injury as a result of a motor vehicle accident, assign the appropriate external cause of morbidity code(s) to describe the cause of the injury, but do not assign code X37.Ø-, Hurricane. If it is not clear whether the injury was a direct result of the hurricane, assume the injury is due to the hurricane and assign code X37.Ø-, Hurricane, as well as any other applicable external cause of morbidity codes. In addition to code X37.Ø-, Hurricane, other possible applicable external cause of morbidity codes include:

W54.Ø- Bitten by dog
X3Ø- Exposure to excessive natural heat
X31- Exposure to excessive natural cold
X38- Flood

d. Use of Z codes

Z codes (other reasons for healthcare encounters) may be assigned as appropriate to further explain the reasons for presenting for healthcare services, including transfers between healthcare facilities. The ICD-10-CM Official Guidelines for Coding and Reporting identify which codes maybe assigned as principal or first-listed diagnosis only, secondary diagnosis only, or principal/first-listed or secondary (depending on the circumstances). Possible applicable Z codes include:

Z59.Ø Homelessness
Z59.1 Inadequate housing
Z59.5 Extreme poverty
Z75.1 Person awaiting admission to adequate facility elsewhere
Z75.3 Unavailability and inaccessibility of health-care facilities
Z75.4 Unavailability and inaccessibility of other helping agencies
Z76.2 Encounter for health supervision and care of other healthy infant and child
Z99.12 Encounter for respirator [ventilator] dependence during power failure

The external cause of morbidity codes and the Z codes listed above are not an all-inclusive list. Other codes may be applicable to the encounter based upon the documentation. Assign as many codes as necessary to fully explain each healthcare encounter. Since patient history information may be very limited, use any available documentation to assign the appropriate external cause of morbidity and Z codes.

C. Chapter-Specific Coding Guidelines

In addition to general coding guidelines, there are guidelines for specific diagnoses and/or conditions in the classification. Unless otherwise indicated, these guidelines apply to all health care settings. Please refer to Section II for guidelines on the selection of principal diagnosis.

1. Chapter 1: Certain Infectious and Parasitic Diseases (AØØ-B99, *U07.1*)

a. Human Immunodeficiency Virus (HIV) Infections

1) Code only confirmed cases

Code only confirmed cases of HIV infection/illness. This is an exception to the hospital inpatient guideline Section II, H.

In this context, "confirmation" does not require documentation of positive serology or culture for HIV; the provider's diagnostic statement that the patient is HIV positive, or has an HIV-related illness is sufficient.

2) Selection and sequencing of HIV codes

(a) Patient admitted for HIV-related condition

If a patient is admitted for an HIV-related condition, the principal diagnosis should be B2Ø, Human immunodeficiency virus [HIV] disease followed by additional diagnosis codes for all reported HIV-related conditions.

(b) Patient with HIV disease admitted for unrelated condition

If a patient with HIV disease is admitted for an unrelated condition (such as a traumatic injury), the code for the unrelated condition (e.g., the nature of injury code) should be the principal diagnosis. Other diagnoses would be B2Ø followed by additional diagnosis codes for all reported HIV-related conditions.

(c) Whether the patient is newly diagnosed

Whether the patient is newly diagnosed or has had previous admissions/encounters for HIV conditions is irrelevant to the sequencing decision.

(d) Asymptomatic human immunodeficiency virus

Z21, Asymptomatic human immunodeficiency virus [HIV] infection status, is to be applied when the patient without any documentation of symptoms is listed as being "HIV positive," "known HIV," "HIV test positive," or similar terminology. Do not use this code if the term "AIDS" is used or if the patient is treated for any HIV-related illness or is described as having any condition(s) resulting from his/her HIV positive status; use B2Ø in these cases.

(e) Patients with inconclusive HIV serology

Patients with inconclusive HIV serology, but no definitive diagnosis or manifestations of the illness, may be assigned code R75, Inconclusive laboratory evidence of human immunodeficiency virus [HIV].

(f) Previously diagnosed HIV-related illness

Patients with any known prior diagnosis of an HIV-related illness should be coded to B20. Once a patient has developed an HIV-related illness, the patient should always be assigned code B20 on every subsequent admission/encounter. Patients previously diagnosed with any HIV illness (B20) should never be assigned to R75 or Z21, Asymptomatic human immunodeficiency virus [HIV] infection status.

(g) HIV Infection in Pregnancy, Childbirth and the Puerperium

During pregnancy, childbirth or the puerperium, a patient admitted (or presenting for a health care encounter) because of an HIV-related illness should receive a principal diagnosis code of O98.7-, Human immunodeficiency [HIV] disease complicating pregnancy, childbirth and the puerperium, followed by B20 and the code(s) for the HIV-related illness(es). Codes from Chapter 15 always take sequencing priority.

Patients with asymptomatic HIV infection status admitted (or presenting for a health care encounter) during pregnancy, childbirth, or the puerperium should receive codes of O98.7- and Z21.

(h) Encounters for testing for HIV

If a patient is being seen to determine his/her HIV status, use code Z11.4, Encounter for screening for human immunodeficiency virus [HIV]. Use additional codes for any associated high-risk behavior.

If a patient with signs or symptoms is being seen for HIV testing, code the signs and symptoms. An additional counseling code Z71.7, Human immunodeficiency virus [HIV] counseling, may be used if counseling is provided during the encounter for the test.

When a patient returns to be informed of his/her HIV test results and the test result is negative, use code Z71.7, Human immunodeficiency virus [HIV] counseling.

If the results are positive, see previous guidelines and assign codes as appropriate.

b. Infectious agents as the cause of diseases classified to other chapters

Certain infections are classified in chapters other than Chapter 1 and no organism is identified as part of the infection code. In these instances, it is necessary to use an additional code from Chapter 1 to identify the organism. A code from category B95, Streptococcus, Staphylococcus, and Enterococcus as the cause of diseases classified to other chapters, B96, Other bacterial agents as the cause of diseases classified to other chapters, or B97, Viral agents as the cause of diseases classified to other chapters, is to be used as an additional code to identify the organism. An instructional note will be found at the infection code advising that an additional organism code is required.

c. Infections resistant to antibiotics

Many bacterial infections are resistant to current antibiotics. It is necessary to identify all infections documented as antibiotic resistant. Assign a code from category Z16, Resistance to antimicrobial drugs, following the infection code only if the infection code does not identify drug resistance.

d. Sepsis, Severe Sepsis, and Septic Shock

1) Coding of Sepsis and Severe Sepsis

(a) Sepsis

For a diagnosis of sepsis, assign the appropriate code for the underlying systemic infection. If the type of infection or causal organism is not further specified, assign code A41.9, Sepsis, unspecified organism.

A code from subcategory R65.2, Severe sepsis, should not be assigned unless severe sepsis or an associated acute organ dysfunction is documented.

(i) Negative or inconclusive blood cultures and sepsis
Negative or inconclusive blood cultures do not preclude a diagnosis of sepsis in patients with clinical evidence of the condition, however, the provider should be queried.

(ii) Urosepsis
The term urosepsis is a nonspecific term. It is not to be considered synonymous with sepsis. It has no default code in the Alphabetic Index. Should a provider use this term, he/she must be queried for clarification.

(iii) Sepsis with organ dysfunction
If a patient has sepsis and associated acute organ dysfunction or multiple organ dysfunction (MOD), follow the instructions for coding severe sepsis.

(iv) Acute organ dysfunction that is not clearly associated with the sepsis
If a patient has sepsis and an acute organ dysfunction, but the medical record documentation indicates that the acute organ dysfunction is related to a medical condition other than the sepsis, do not assign a code from subcategory R65.2, Severe sepsis. An acute organ dysfunction must be associated with the sepsis in order to assign the severe sepsis code. If the documentation is not clear as to whether an acute organ dysfunction is related to the sepsis or another medical condition, query the provider.

(b) Severe sepsis

The coding of severe sepsis requires a minimum of 2 codes: first a code for the underlying systemic infection, followed by a code from subcategory

R65.2, Severe sepsis. If the causal organism is not documented, assign code A41.9, Sepsis, unspecified organism, for the infection. Additional code(s) for the associated acute organ dysfunction are also required.

Due to the complex nature of severe sepsis, some cases may require querying the provider prior to assignment of the codes.

2) Septic shock

(a) Septic shock generally refers to circulatory failure associated with severe sepsis, and therefore, it represents a type of acute organ dysfunction.

For all cases of septic shock, the code for the systemic infection should be sequenced first, followed by code R65.21, Severe sepsis with septic shock or code T81.12, Postprocedural septic shock. Any additional codes for the other acute organ dysfunctions should also be assigned. As noted in the sequencing instructions in the Tabular List, the code for septic shock cannot be assigned as a principal diagnosis.

3) Sequencing of severe sepsis

If severe sepsis is present on admission, and meets the definition of principal diagnosis, the underlying systemic infection should be assigned as principal diagnosis followed by the appropriate code from subcategory R65.2 as required by the sequencing rules in the Tabular List. A code from subcategory R65.2 can never be assigned as a principal diagnosis.

When severe sepsis develops during an encounter (it was not present on admission) the underlying systemic infection and the appropriate code from subcategory R65.2 should be assigned as secondary diagnoses.

Severe sepsis may be present on admission but the diagnosis may not be confirmed until sometime after admission. If the documentation is not clear whether severe sepsis was present on admission, the provider should be queried.

4) Sepsis or severe sepsis with a localized infection

If the reason for admission is sepsis or severe sepsis and a localized infection, such as pneumonia or cellulitis, a code(s) for the underlying systemic infection should be assigned first and the code for the localized infection should be assigned as a secondary diagnosis. If the patient has severe sepsis, a code from subcategory R65.2 should also be assigned as a secondary diagnosis. If the patient is admitted with a localized infection, such as pneumonia, and sepsis/severe sepsis doesn't develop until after admission, the localized infection should be assigned first, followed by the appropriate sepsis/severe sepsis codes.

5) Sepsis due to a postprocedural infection

(a) Documentation of causal relationship

As with all postprocedural complications, code assignment is based on the provider's documentation of the relationship between the infection and the procedure.

(b) Sepsis due to a postprocedural infection

For infections following a procedure, a code from T81.40, to T81.43. Infection following a procedure, or a code from O86.00 to O86.03, Infection of obstetric surgical wound, that identifies the site of the infection should be coded first, if known. Assign an additional code for sepsis following a procedure (T81.44) or sepsis following an obstetrical procedure (O86.04). Use an additional code to identify the infectious agent. If the patient has severe sepsis the appropriate code from subcategory R65.2 should also be assigned with the additional code(s) for any acute organ dysfunction.

For infections following infusion, transfusion, therapeutic injection, or immunization, a code from subcategory T80.2, Infections following infusion, transfusion, and therapeutic injection, or code T88.0-, Infection following immunization, should be coded first, followed by the code for the specific infection. If the patient has severe sepsis, the appropriate code from subcategory R65.2 should also be assigned, with the additional codes(s) for any acute organ dysfunction.

(c) Postprocedural infection and postprocedural septic shock

If a postprocedural infection has resulted in postprocedural septic shock, assign the codes indicated above for sepsis due to a postprocedural infection, followed by code T81.12-, Postprocedural septic shock. Do not assign code R65.21, Severe sepsis with septic shock. Additional code(s) should be assigned for any acute organ dysfunction.

6) Sepsis and severe sepsis associated with a noninfectious process (condition)

In some cases a noninfectious process (condition), such as trauma, may lead to an infection which can result in sepsis or severe sepsis. If sepsis or severe sepsis is documented as associated with a noninfectious condition, such as a burn or serious injury, and this condition meets the definition for principal diagnosis, the code for the noninfectious condition should be sequenced first, followed by the code for the resulting infection. If severe sepsis is present, a code from subcategory R65.2 should also be assigned with any associated organ dysfunction(s) codes. It is not necessary to assign a code from subcategory R65.1, Systemic inflammatory response syndrome (SIRS) of non-infectious origin, for these cases.

If the infection meets the definition of principal diagnosis it should be sequenced before the non-infectious condition. When both the associated non-infectious condition and the infection meet the definition of principal diagnosis either may be assigned as principal diagnosis.

Only one code from category R65, Symptoms and signs specifically associated with systemic inflammation and infection, should be assigned. Therefore, when a non-infectious condition leads to an infection resulting in severe sepsis, assign the appropriate code from subcategory R65.2, Severe sepsis. Do not additionally assign a code from subcategory R65.1, Systemic inflammatory response syndrome (SIRS) of non-infectious origin.

See Section I.C.18. SIRS due to non-infectious process

7) Sepsis and septic shock complicating abortion, pregnancy, childbirth, and the puerperium

See Section I.C.15. Sepsis and septic shock complicating abortion, pregnancy, childbirth and the puerperium

8) Newborn sepsis
See Section I.C.16. f. Bacterial sepsis of Newborn

e. Methicillin Resistant Staphylococcus aureus (MRSA) Conditions

1) Selection and sequencing of MRSA codes

(a) Combination codes for MRSA infection
When a patient is diagnosed with an infection that is due to methicillin resistant *Staphylococcus aureus* (MRSA), and that infection has a combination code that includes the causal organism (e.g., sepsis, pneumonia) assign the appropriate combination code for the condition (e.g., code A41.02, Sepsis due to Methicillin resistant Staphylococcus aureus or code J15.212, Pneumonia due to Methicillin resistant Staphylococcus aureus). Do not assign code B95.62, Methicillin resistant Staphylococcus aureus infection as the cause of diseases classified elsewhere, as an additional code because the combination code includes the type of infection and the MRSA organism. Do not assign a code from subcategory Z16.11, Resistance to penicillins, as an additional diagnosis.

See Section C.1. for instructions on coding and sequencing of sepsis and severe sepsis.

(b) Other codes for MRSA infection
When there is documentation of a current infection (e.g., wound infection, stitch abscess, urinary tract infection) due to MRSA, and that infection does not have a combination code that includes the causal organism, assign the appropriate code to identify the condition along with code B95.62, Methicillin resistant Staphylococcus aureus infection as the cause of diseases classified elsewhere for the MRSA infection. Do not assign a code from subcategory Z16.11, Resistance to penicillins.

(c) Methicillin susceptible Staphylococcus aureus (MSSA) and MRSA colonization
The condition or state of being colonized or carrying MSSA or MRSA is called colonization or carriage, while an individual person is described as being colonized or being a carrier. Colonization means that MSSA or MSRA is present on or in the body without necessarily causing illness. A positive MRSA colonization test might be documented by the provider as "MRSA screen positive" or "MRSA nasal swab positive".

Assign code Z22.322, Carrier or suspected carrier of Methicillin resistant Staphylococcus

aureus, for patients documented as having MRSA colonization. Assign code Z22.321, Carrier or suspected carrier of Methicillin susceptible Staphylococcus aureus, for patients documented as having MSSA colonization. Colonization is not necessarily indicative of a disease process or as the cause of a specific condition the patient may have unless documented as such by the provider.

(d) MRSA colonization and infection
If a patient is documented as having both MRSA colonization and infection during a hospital admission, code Z22.322, Carrier or suspected carrier of Methicillin resistant Staphylococcus aureus, and a code for the MRSA infection may both be assigned.

f. Zika virus infections

1) Code only confirmed cases
Code only a confirmed diagnosis of Zika virus (A92.5, Zika virus disease) as documented by the provider. This is an exception to the hospital inpatient guideline Section II, H.

In this context, "confirmation" does not require documentation of the type of test performed; the provider's diagnostic statement that the condition is confirmed is sufficient. This code should be assigned regardless of the stated mode of transmission.

If the provider documents "suspected", "possible" or "probable" Zika, do not assign code A92.5. Assign a code(s) explaining the reason for encounter (such as fever, rash, or joint pain) or Z20.821, Contact with and (suspected) exposure to Zika virus.

g. Coronavirus infections

1) COVID-19 infection (infection due to SARS-CoV-2)

(a) Code only confirmed cases
Code only a confirmed diagnosis of the 2019 novel coronavirus disease (COVID-19) as documented by the provider or documentation of a positive COVID19 test result. For a confirmed diagnosis, assign code U07.1, COVID-19. This is an exception to the hospital inpatient guideline Section II, H. In this context, "confirmation" does not require documentation of a positive test result for COVID-19; the provider's documentation that the individual has COVID-19 is sufficient.

If the provider documents "suspected," "possible," "probable," or "inconclusive" COVID-19, do not assign code U07.1. Instead, code the signs and symptoms reported. See guideline I.C.1.g.1.g.

(b) Sequencing of codes
When COVID-19 meets the definition of principal diagnosis, code U07.1, COVID-19, should be sequenced first, followed by the appropriate codes for associated manifestations, except when another guideline requires that certain codes be sequenced first, such as obstetrics, sepsis, or transplant complications.

For a COVID-19 infection that progresses to sepsis, see Section I.C.1.d. Sepsis, Severe Sepsis, and Septic Shock

See Section I.C.15.s. for COVID-19 infection in pregnancy, childbirth, and the puerperium

See Section I.C.16.h. for COVID-19 infection in newborn

For a COVID-19 infection in a lung transplant patient, see Section I.C.19.g.3.a. Transplant complications other than kidney.

(c) Acute respiratory manifestations of COVID-19

When the reason for the encounter/admission is a respiratory manifestation of COVID-19, assign code U07.1, COVID-19, as the principal/first-listed diagnosis and assign code(s) for the respiratory manifestation(s) as additional diagnoses.

The following conditions are examples of common respiratory manifestations of COVID-19.

(i) Pneumonia
For a patient with pneumonia confirmed as due to COVID-19, assign codes U07.1, COVID-19, and J12.89, Other viral pneumonia.

(ii) Acute bronchitis
For a patient with acute bronchitis confirmed as due to COVID-19, assign codes U07.1, and J20.8, Acute bronchitis due to other specified organisms.

Bronchitis not otherwise specified (NOS) due to COVID-19 should be coded using code U07.1 and J40, Bronchitis, not specified as acute or chronic.

(iii) Lower respiratory infection
If the COVID-19 is documented as being associated with a lower respiratory infection, not otherwise specified (NOS), or an acute respiratory infection, NOS, codes U07.1 and J22, Unspecified acute lower respiratory infection, should be assigned.

If the COVID-19 is documented as being associated with a respiratory infection, NOS, codes U07.1 and J98.8, Other specified respiratory disorders, should be assigned.

(iv) Acute respiratory distress syndrome
For acute respiratory distress syndrome (ARDS) due to COVID-19, assign codes U07.1, and J80, Acute respiratory distress syndrome.

(v) Acute respiratory failure
For acute respiratory failure due to COVID-19, assign code U07.1, and code J96.0-, Acute respiratory failure.

(d) Non-respiratory manifestations of COVID-19

When the reason for the encounter/admission is a non-respiratory manifestation (e.g., viral enteritis) of COVID-19, assign code U07.1, COVID-19, as the principal/first-listed diagnosis and assign code(s) for the manifestation(s) as additional diagnoses.

(e) Exposure to COVID-19

For asymptomatic individuals with actual or suspected exposure to COVID-19, assign code Z20.828, Contact with and (suspected) exposure to other viral communicable diseases.

For symptomatic individuals with actual or suspected exposure to COVID-19 and the infection has been ruled out, or test results are inconclusive or unknown, assign code Z20.828, Contact with and (suspected) exposure to other viral communicable diseases. See guideline I.C.21.c.1, Contact/Exposure, for additional guidance regarding the use of category Z20 codes.

If COVID-19 is confirmed, see guideline I.C.1.g.1.a.

(f) Screening for COVID-19

During the COVID-19 pandemic, a screening code is generally not appropriate. For encounters for COVID-19 testing, including preoperative testing, code as exposure to COVID-19 (guideline I.C.1.g.1.e).

Coding guidance will be updated as new information concerning any changes in the pandemic status becomes available.

(g) Signs and symptoms without definitive diagnosis of COVID-19

For patients presenting with any signs/symptoms associated with COVID-19 (such as fever, etc.) but a definitive diagnosis has not been established, assign the appropriate code(s) for each of the presenting signs and symptoms such as:

- R05 Cough
- R06.02 Shortness of breath
- R50.9 Fever, unspecified

If a patient with signs/symptoms associated with COVID-19 also has an actual or suspected contact with or exposure to COVID-19, assign Z20.828, Contact with and (suspected) exposure to other viral communicable diseases, as an additional code.

(h) Asymptomatic individuals who test positive for COVID-19

For asymptomatic individuals who test positive for COVID-19, see guideline I.C.1.g.1.a. Although the individual is asymptomatic, the individual has tested positive and is considered to have the COVID-19 infection.

(i) Personal history of COVID-19

For patients with a history of COVID-19, assign code Z86.19, Personal history of other infectious and parasitic diseases.

(j) Follow-up visits after COVID-19 infection has resolved

For individuals who previously had COVID-19 and are being seen for follow-up evaluation, and COVID-19 test results are negative, assign codes Z09, Encounter for follow-up examination after completed treatment for conditions other than malignant neoplasm, and Z86.19, Personal history of other infectious and parasitic diseases.

(k) Encounter for antibody testing

For an encounter for antibody testing that is not being performed to confirm a current COVID-19 infection, nor is a follow-up test after resolution of COVID-19, assign Z01.84, Encounter for antibody response examination.

Follow the applicable guidelines above if the individual is being tested to confirm a current COVID-19 infection.

For follow-up testing after a COVID-19 infection, see guideline I.C.1.g.1.j.

2. **Chapter 2: Neoplasms (C00-D49)**
General guidelines

Chapter 2 of the ICD-10-CM contains the codes for most benign and all malignant neoplasms. Certain benign neoplasms, such as prostatic adenomas, may be found in the specific body system chapters. To properly code a neoplasm it is necessary to determine from the record if the neoplasm is benign, in-situ, malignant, or of uncertain histologic behavior. If malignant, any secondary (metastatic) sites should also be determined.

Primary malignant neoplasms overlapping site boundaries

A primary malignant neoplasm that overlaps two or more contiguous (next to each other) sites should be classified to the subcategory/code .8 ("overlapping lesion"), unless the combination is specifically indexed elsewhere. For multiple neoplasms of the same site that are not contiguous such as tumors in different quadrants of the same breast, codes for each site should be assigned.

Malignant neoplasm of ectopic tissue

Malignant neoplasms of ectopic tissue are to be coded to the site of origin mentioned (e.g., ectopic pancreatic malignant neoplasms involving the stomach are coded to malignant neoplasm of pancreas, unspecified) (C25.9).

The neoplasm table in the Alphabetic Index should be referenced first. However, if the histological term is documented, that term should be referenced first, rather than going immediately to the Neoplasm Table, in order to determine which column in the Neoplasm Table is appropriate. For example, if the documentation indicates "adenoma," refer to the term in the Alphabetic Index to review the entries under this term and the instructional note to "see also neoplasm, by site, benign." The table provides the proper code based on the type of neoplasm and the site. It is important to select the proper column in the table

that corresponds to the type of neoplasm. The Tabular List should then be referenced to verify that the correct code has been selected from the table and that a more specific site code does not exist.

See Section I.C.21. Factors influencing health status and contact with health services, Status, for information regarding Z15.0, codes for genetic susceptibility to cancer.

a. Treatment directed at the malignancy

If the treatment is directed at the malignancy, designate the malignancy as the principal diagnosis.

The only exception to this guideline is if a patient admission/encounter is solely for the administration of chemotherapy, immunotherapy or external beam radiation therapy, assign the appropriate Z51.— code as the first-listed or principal diagnosis, and the diagnosis or problem for which the service is being performed as a secondary diagnosis.

b. Treatment of secondary site

When a patient is admitted because of a primary neoplasm with metastasis and treatment is directed toward the secondary site only, the secondary neoplasm is designated as the principal diagnosis even though the primary malignancy is still present.

c. Coding and sequencing of complications

Coding and sequencing of complications associated with the malignancies or with the therapy thereof are subject to the following guidelines:

1) Anemia associated with malignancy

When admission/encounter is for management of an anemia associated with the malignancy, and the treatment is only for anemia, the appropriate code for the malignancy is sequenced as the principal or first-listed diagnosis followed by the appropriate code for the anemia (such as code D63.0, Anemia in neoplastic disease).

2) Anemia associated with chemotherapy, immunotherapy and radiation therapy

When the admission/encounter is for management of an anemia associated with an adverse effect of the administration of chemotherapy or immunotherapy and the only treatment is for the anemia, the anemia code is sequenced first followed by the appropriate codes for the neoplasm and the adverse effect (T45.1X5, Adverse effect of antineoplastic and immunosuppressive drugs).

When the admission/encounter is for management of an anemia associated with an adverse effect of radiotherapy, the anemia code should be sequenced first, followed by the appropriate neoplasm code and code Y84.2, Radiological procedure and radiotherapy as the cause of abnormal reaction of the patient, or of later complication, without mention of misadventure at the time of the procedure.

3) Management of dehydration due to the malignancy

When the admission/encounter is for management of dehydration due to the malignancy and only the dehydration is being treated (intravenous rehydration), the dehydration is sequenced first, followed by the code(s) for the malignancy.

4) Treatment of a complication resulting from a surgical procedure

When the admission/encounter is for treatment of a complication resulting from a surgical procedure, designate the complication as the principal or first-listed diagnosis if treatment is directed at resolving the complication.

d. Primary malignancy previously excised

When a primary malignancy has been previously excised or eradicated from its site and there is no further treatment directed to that site and there is no evidence of any existing primary malignancy, at that site a code from category Z85, Personal history of malignant neoplasm, should be used to indicate the former site of the malignancy. Any mention of extension, invasion, or metastasis to another site is coded as a secondary malignant neoplasm to that site. The secondary site may be the principal or first-listed diagnosis with the Z85 code used as a secondary code.

e. Admissions/Encounters involving chemotherapy, immunotherapy and radiation therapy

1) Episode of care involves surgical removal of neoplasm

When an episode of care involves the surgical removal of a neoplasm, primary or secondary site, followed by adjunct chemotherapy or radiation treatment during the same episode of care, the code for the neoplasm should be assigned as principal or first-listed diagnosis.

2) Patient admission/encounter solely for administration of chemotherapy, immunotherapy and radiation therapy

If a patient admission/encounter is solely for the administration of chemotherapy, immunotherapy or external beam radiation therapy assign code Z51.0, Encounter for antineoplastic radiation therapy, or Z51.11, Encounter for antineoplastic chemotherapy, or Z51.12, Encounter for antineoplastic immunotherapy as the first-listed or principal diagnosis. If a patient receives more than one of these therapies during the same admission more than one of these codes may be assigned, in any sequence.

The malignancy for which the therapy is being administered should be assigned as a secondary diagnosis.

If a patient admission/encounter is for the insertion or implantation of radioactive elements (e.g., brachytherapy) the appropriate code for the malignancy is sequenced as the principal or first-listed diagnosis. Code Z51.0 should not be assigned.

3) Patient admitted for radiation therapy, chemotherapy or immunotherapy and develops complications

When a patient is admitted for the purpose of external beam radiotherapy, immunotherapy or chemotherapy and develops complications such as uncontrolled nausea and vomiting or dehydration, the principal or first-listed diagnosis is Z51.0, Encounter for antineoplastic radiation therapy, or Z51.11, Encounter for antineoplastic chemotherapy, or Z51.12, Encounter for antineoplastic immunotherapy followed by any codes for the complications.

When a patient is admitted for the purpose of insertion or implantation of radioactive elements (e.g., brachytherapy) and develops complications such as uncontrolled nausea and vomiting or dehydration, the principal or first-listed diagnosis is the appropriate code for the malignancy followed by any codes for the complications.

f. Admission/encounter to determine extent of malignancy

When the reason for admission/encounter is to determine the extent of the malignancy, or for a procedure such as paracentesis or thoracentesis, the primary malignancy or appropriate metastatic site is designated as the principal or first-listed diagnosis, even though chemotherapy or radiotherapy is administered.

g. Symptoms, signs, and abnormal findings listed in Chapter 18 associated with neoplasms

Symptoms, signs, and ill-defined conditions listed in Chapter 18 characteristic of, or associated with, an existing primary or secondary site malignancy cannot be used to replace the malignancy as principal or first-listed diagnosis, regardless of the number of admissions or encounters for treatment and care of the neoplasm.

See Section I.C.21. Factors influencing health status and contact with health services, Encounter for prophylactic organ removal.

h. Admission/encounter for pain control/ management

See Section I.C.6. for information on coding admission/ encounter for pain control/management.

i. Malignancy in two or more noncontiguous sites

A patient may have more than one malignant tumor in the same organ. These tumors may represent different primaries or metastatic disease, depending on the site. Should the documentation be unclear, the provider should be queried as to the status of each tumor so that the correct codes can be assigned.

j. Disseminated malignant neoplasm, unspecified

Code C80.0, Disseminated malignant neoplasm, unspecified, is for use only in those cases where the patient has advanced metastatic disease and no known primary or secondary sites are specified. It should not be used in place of assigning codes for the primary site and all known secondary sites.

k. Malignant neoplasm without specification of site

Code C80.1, Malignant (primary) neoplasm, unspecified, equates to Cancer, unspecified. This code should only be used when no determination can be made as to the primary site of a malignancy. This code should rarely be used in the inpatient setting.

l. Sequencing of neoplasm codes

1) Encounter for treatment of primary malignancy

If the reason for the encounter is for treatment of a primary malignancy, assign the malignancy as the principal/first-listed diagnosis. The primary site is to be sequenced first, followed by any metastatic sites.

2) Encounter for treatment of secondary malignancy

When an encounter is for a primary malignancy with metastasis and treatment is directed toward the metastatic (secondary) site(s) only, the metastatic site(s) is designated as the principal/first-listed diagnosis. The primary malignancy is coded as an additional code.

3) Malignant neoplasm in a pregnant patient

When a pregnant woman has a malignant neoplasm, a code from subcategory O9A.1-, Malignant neoplasm complicating pregnancy, childbirth, and the puerperium, should be sequenced first, followed by the appropriate code from Chapter 2 to indicate the type of neoplasm.

4) Encounter for complication associated with a neoplasm

When an encounter is for management of a complication associated with a neoplasm, such as dehydration, and the treatment is only for the complication, the complication is coded first, followed by the appropriate code(s) for the neoplasm.

The exception to this guideline is anemia. When the admission/encounter is for management of an anemia associated with the malignancy, and the treatment is only for anemia, the appropriate code for the malignancy is sequenced as the principal or first-listed diagnosis followed by code D63.0, Anemia in neoplastic disease.

5) Complication from surgical procedure for treatment of a neoplasm

When an encounter is for treatment of a complication resulting from a surgical procedure performed for the treatment of the neoplasm, designate the complication as the principal/first-listed diagnosis. See the guideline regarding the coding of a current malignancy versus personal history to determine if the code for the neoplasm should also be assigned.

6) Pathologic fracture due to a neoplasm

When an encounter is for a pathological fracture due to a neoplasm, and the focus of treatment is the fracture, a code from subcategory M84.5, Pathological fracture in neoplastic disease, should be sequenced first, followed by the code for the neoplasm.

If the focus of treatment is the neoplasm with an associated pathological fracture, the neoplasm code should be sequenced first, followed by a code from M84.5 for the pathological fracture.

m. Current malignancy versus personal history of malignancy

When a primary malignancy has been excised but further treatment, such as an additional surgery for the malignancy, radiation therapy or chemotherapy is directed to that site, the primary malignancy code should be used until treatment is completed.

When a primary malignancy has been previously excised or eradicated from its site, there is no further treatment (of the malignancy) directed to that site, and there is no evidence of any existing primary malignancy at that site, a code from category Z85, Personal history of malignant neoplasm, should be used to indicate the former site of the malignancy.

Codes from subcategories Z85.0 – Z85.85 should only be assigned for the former site of a primary malignancy, not the site of a secondary malignancy. Code Z85.89, may be assigned for the former site(s) of either a primary or secondary malignancy.

See Section I.C.21. Factors influencing health status and contact with health services, History (of)

n. Leukemia, Multiple Myeloma, and Malignant Plasma Cell Neoplasms in remission versus personal history

The categories for leukemia, and category C90, Multiple myeloma and malignant plasma cell neoplasms, have codes indicating whether or not the leukemia has achieved remission. There are also codes Z85.6, Personal history of leukemia, and Z85.79, Personal history of other malignant neoplasms of lymphoid, hematopoietic and related tissues. If the documentation is unclear, as to whether the leukemia has achieved remission, the provider should be queried.

See Section I.C.21. Factors influencing health status and contact with health services, History (of)

o. Aftercare following surgery for neoplasm

See Section I.C.21. Factors influencing health status and contact with health services, Aftercare

p. Follow-up care for completed treatment of a malignancy

See Section I.C.21. Factors influencing health status and contact with health services, Follow-up

q. Prophylactic organ removal for prevention of malignancy

See Section I.C. 21, Factors influencing health status and contact with health services, Prophylactic organ removal

r. Malignant neoplasm associated with transplanted organ

A malignant neoplasm of a transplanted organ should be coded as a transplant complication. Assign first the appropriate code from category T86.-, Complications of transplanted organs and tissue, followed by code C80.2, Malignant neoplasm associated with transplanted organ. Use an additional code for the specific malignancy.

3. **Chapter 3: Disease of the blood and blood-forming organs and certain disorders involving the immune mechanism (D50-D89)**
Reserved for future guideline expansion

4. **Chapter 4: Endocrine, Nutritional, and Metabolic Diseases (E00-E89)**

   a. **Diabetes mellitus**
   The diabetes mellitus codes are combination codes that include the type of diabetes mellitus, the body system affected, and the complications affecting that body system. As many codes within a particular category as are necessary to describe all of the complications of the disease may be used. They should be sequenced based on the reason for a particular encounter. Assign as many codes from categories E08 – E13 as needed to identify all of the associated conditions that the patient has.

   1) **Type of diabetes**
   The age of a patient is not the sole determining factor, though most type 1 diabetics develop the condition before reaching puberty. For this reason type 1 diabetes mellitus is also referred to as juvenile diabetes.

   2) **Type of diabetes mellitus not documented**
   If the type of diabetes mellitus is not documented in the medical record the default is E11.-, Type 2 diabetes mellitus.

   3) **Diabetes mellitus and the use of insulin, oral hypoglycemics,** *and injectable non-insulin drugs*
   If the documentation in a medical record does not indicate the type of diabetes but does indicate that the patient uses insulin, code E11, Type 2 diabetes mellitus, should be assigned. An additional code should be assigned from category Z79 to identify the long-term (current) use of insulin or oral hypoglycemic drugs. If the patient is treated with both oral medications and insulin, only the code for long-term (current) use of insulin should be assigned. **If the patient is treated with both insulin and an injectable non-insulin antidiabetic drug, assign codes Z79.4, Long-term (current) use of insulin, and Z79.899, Other long term (current) drug therapy. If the patient is treated with both oral hypoglycemic drugs and an injectable non-insulin antidiabetic drug, assign codes Z79.84, Long-term (current) use of oral hypoglycemic drugs, and Z79.899, Other long-term (current) drug therapy.** Code Z79.4 should not be assigned if insulin is given temporarily to bring a type 2 patient's blood sugar under control during an encounter.

   4) **Diabetes mellitus in pregnancy and gestational diabetes**
   See Section I.C.15. Diabetes mellitus in pregnancy.
   See Section I.C.15. Gestational (pregnancy induced) diabetes

   5) **Complications due to insulin pump malfunction**

      (a) **Underdose of insulin due to insulin pump failure**
      An underdose of insulin due to an insulin pump failure should be assigned to a code from subcategory T85.6, Mechanical complication of other specified internal and external prosthetic devices, implants and grafts, that specifies the type of pump malfunction, as the principal or first-listed code, followed by code T38.3X6-, Underdosing of insulin and oral hypoglycemic [antidiabetic] drugs. Additional codes for the type of diabetes mellitus and any associated complications due to the underdosing should also be assigned.

      (b) **Overdose of insulin due to insulin pump failure**
      The principal or first-listed code for an encounter due to an insulin pump malfunction resulting in an overdose of insulin, should also be T85.6-, Mechanical complication of other specified internal and external prosthetic devices, implants and grafts, followed by code T38.3X1-, Poisoning by insulin and oral hypoglycemic [antidiabetic] drugs, accidental (unintentional).

   6) **Secondary diabetes mellitus**
   Codes under categories E08, Diabetes mellitus due to underlying condition, E09, Drug or chemical induced diabetes mellitus and E13, Other specified diabetes mellitus, identify complications/ manifestations associated with secondary diabetes mellitus. Secondary diabetes is always caused by another condition or event (e.g., cystic fibrosis, malignant neoplasm of pancreas, pancreatectomy, adverse effect of drug, or poisoning).

      (a) **Secondary diabetes mellitus and the use of insulin or hypoglycemic drugs**
      For patients with secondary diabetes mellitus who routinely use insulin or oral hypoglycemic drugs, an additional code from category Z79 should be assigned to identify the long-term (current) use of insulin or oral hypoglycemic drugs. If the patient is treated with both oral medications and insulin, only the code for long-term (current) use of insulin should be assigned. Code Z79.4 should not be assigned if insulin is given temporarily to bring a type 2 patient's blood sugar under control during an encounter.

      (b) **Assigning and sequencing secondary diabetes codes and its causes**
      The sequencing of the secondary diabetes codes in relationship to codes for the cause of the diabetes is based on the Tabular List instructions for categories E08, E09 and E13.

         (i) **Secondary diabetes mellitus due to pancreatectomy** For postpancreatectomy diabetes mellitus (lack of insulin due to the surgical removal of all or part of the pancreas), assign code E89.1, Postprocedural hypoinsulinemia. Assign a code from category E13 and a code from subcategory Z90.41-, Acquired absence of pancreas, as additional codes.

         (ii) **Secondary diabetes due to drugs** Secondary diabetes may be caused by an adverse effect of correctly

GUIDELINES (ICD-10-CM)

administered medications,
poisoning or sequela of poisoning.
See Section I.C.19.e for coding of adverse effects and poisoning, and Section I.C.20 for external cause code reporting.

5. Chapter 5: Mental, Behavioral and Neurodevelopmental disorders (F01 – F99)

a. Pain disorders related to psychological factors

Assign code F45.41, for pain that is exclusively related to psychological disorders. As indicated by the Excludes1 note under category G89, a code from category G89 should not be assigned with code F45.41

Code F45.42, Pain disorders with related psychological factors, should be used with a code from category G89, Pain, not elsewhere classified, if there is documentation of a psychological component for a patient with acute or chronic pain.
See Section I.C.6. Pain

b. Mental and behavioral disorders due to psychoactive substance use

1) In Remission

Selection of codes for "in remission" for categories F10-F19, Mental and behavioral disorders due to psychoactive substance use (categories F10-F19 with -11, -.21) requires the provider's clinical judgment. The appropriate codes for "in remission" are assigned only on the basis of provider documentation (as defined in the Official Guidelines for Coding and Reporting), unless otherwise instructed by the classification.

Mild substance use disorders in early or sustained remission are classified to the appropriate codes for substance abuse in remission, and moderate or severe substance use disorders in early or sustained remission are classified to the appropriate codes for substance dependence in remission.

2) Psychoactive Substance Use, Abuse and Dependence

When the provider documentation refers to use, abuse and dependence of the same substance (e.g., alcohol, opioid, cannabis, etc.), only one code should be assigned to identify the pattern of use based on the following hierarchy:
- If both use and abuse are documented, assign only the code for abuse
- If both abuse and dependence are documented, assign only the code for dependence
- If use, abuse and dependence are all documented, assign only the code for dependence
- If both use and dependence are documented, assign only the code for dependence.

3) Psychoactive Substance Use, Unspecified

As with all other unspecified diagnoses, the codes for unspecified psychoactive substance use disorders (F10.9-, F11.9-, F12.9-, F13.9-, F14.9-, F15.9-, F16.9-, F18.9-, F19.9-) should only be assigned based on provider documentation and when they meet the definition of a reportable diagnosis (see Section III, Reporting Additional Diagnoses). These codes are to be used only when the psychoactive substance use is associated with a physical **disorder included in chapter 5 (such as sexual dysfunction and sleep disorder), or a** mental or behavioral disorder, and such a relationship is documented by the provider.

c. Factitious Disorder

Factitious disorder imposed on self or Munchausen's syndrome is a disorder in which a person falsely reports or causes his or her own physical or psychological signs or symptoms. For patients with documented factitious disorder on self or Munchausen's syndrome, assign the appropriate code from subcategory F68.1-, Factitious disorder imposed on self.

Munchausen's syndrome by proxy (MSBP) is a disorder in which a caregiver (perpetrator) falsely reports or causes an illness or injury in another person (victim) under his or her care, such as a child, an elderly adult, or a person who has a disability. The condition is also referred to as "factitious disorder imposed on another" or "factitious disorder by proxy." The perpetrator, not the victim, receives this diagnosis. Assign code F68.A, Factitious disorder imposed on another, to the perpetrator's record. For the victim of a patient suffering from MSBP, assign the appropriate code from categories T74, Adult and child abuse, neglect and other maltreatment, confirmed, or T76, Adult and child abuse, neglect and other maltreatment, suspected.
See Section I.C.19.f. Adult and child abuse, neglect and other maltreatment

6. Chapter 6: Diseases of the Nervous System (G00-G99)

a. Dominant/nondominant side

Codes from category G81, Hemiplegia and hemiparesis, and subcategories, G83.1, Monoplegia of lower limb, G83.2, Monoplegia of upper limb, and G83.3, Monoplegia, unspecified, identify whether the dominant or nondominant side is affected. Should the affected side be documented, but not specified as dominant or nondominant, and the classification system does not indicate a default, code selection is as follows:
- For ambidextrous patients, the default should be dominant.
- If the left side is affected, the default is non-dominant.
- If the right side is affected, the default is dominant.

b. Pain - Category G89

1) General coding information

Codes in category G89, Pain, not elsewhere classified, may be used in conjunction with codes from other categories and chapters to provide more detail about acute or chronic pain and neoplasm-related pain, unless otherwise indicated below.

If the pain is not specified as acute or chronic, post-thoracotomy, postprocedural, or neoplasm-related, do not assign codes from category G89.

A code from category G89 should not be assigned if the underlying (definitive) diagnosis is known, unless the reason for the encounter is pain control/management and not management of the underlying condition.

When an admission or encounter is for a procedure aimed at treating the underlying condition (e.g., spinal fusion, kyphoplasty), a code for the underlying condition (e.g., vertebral fracture, spinal stenosis) should be assigned as the principal diagnosis. No code from category G89 should be assigned.

(a) Category G89 Codes as Principal or First-Listed Diagnosis

Category G89 codes are acceptable as principal diagnosis or the first-listed code:

- When pain control or pain management is the reason for the admission/encounter (e.g., a patient with displaced intervertebral disc, nerve impingement and severe back pain presents for injection of steroid into the spinal canal). The underlying cause of the pain should be reported as an additional diagnosis, if known.
- When a patient is admitted for the insertion of a neurostimulator for pain control, assign the appropriate pain code as the principal or first-listed diagnosis. When an admission or encounter is for a procedure aimed at treating the underlying condition and a neurostimulator is inserted for pain control during the same admission/encounter, a code for the underlying condition should be assigned as the principal diagnosis and the appropriate pain code should be assigned as a secondary diagnosis.

(b) Use of Category G89 Codes in Conjunction with Site-Specific Pain Codes

(i) Assigning Category G89 and Site-Specific Pain Codes

Codes from category G89 may be used in conjunction with codes that identify the site of pain (including codes from Chapter 18) if the category G89 code provides additional information. For example, if the code describes the site of the pain, but does not fully describe whether the pain is acute or chronic, then both codes should be assigned.

(ii) Sequencing of Category G89 Codes with Site-Specific Pain Codes

The sequencing of category G89 codes with site-specific pain codes (including Chapter 18 codes), is dependent on the circumstances of the encounter/admission as follows:

- If the encounter is for pain control or pain management, assign the code from category G89 followed by the code identifying the specific site of pain (e.g., encounter for pain management for acute neck pain from trauma is assigned code G89.11, Acute pain due to

trauma, followed by code M54.2, Cervicalgia, to identify the site of pain).
- If the encounter is for any other reason except pain control or pain management, and a related definitive diagnosis has not been established (confirmed) by the provider, assign the code for the specific site of pain first, followed by the appropriate code from category G89.

2) Pain due to devices, implants and grafts
See Section I.C.19. Pain due to medical devices

3) Postoperative Pain

The provider's documentation should be used to guide the coding of postoperative pain, as well as *Section III. Reporting Additional Diagnoses* and *Section IV. Diagnostic Coding and Reporting in the Outpatient Setting.*

The default for post-thoracotomy and other postoperative pain not specified as acute or chronic is the code for the acute form.

Routine or expected postoperative pain immediately after surgery should not be coded.

(a) Postoperative pain not associated with specific postoperative complication

Postoperative pain not associated with a specific postoperative complication is assigned to the appropriate postoperative pain code in category G89.

(b) Postoperative pain associated with specific postoperative complication

Postoperative pain associated with a specific postoperative complication (such as painful wire sutures) is assigned to the appropriate code(s) found in Chapter 19, Injury, poisoning, and certain other consequences of external causes. If appropriate, use additional code(s) from category G89 to identify acute or chronic pain (G89.18 or G89.28).

4) Chronic pain

Chronic pain is classified to subcategory G89.2. There is no time frame defining when pain becomes chronic pain. The provider's documentation should be used to guide use of these codes.

5) Neoplasm Related Pain

Code G89.3 is assigned to pain documented as being related, associated or due to cancer, primary or secondary malignancy, or tumor. This code is assigned regardless of whether the pain is acute or chronic.

This code may be assigned as the principal or first-listed code when the stated reason for the admission/encounter is documented as pain control/pain management. The underlying neoplasm should be reported as an additional diagnosis.

When the reason for the admission/encounter is management of the neoplasm and the pain associated with the neoplasm is also documented, code G89.3 may be assigned as an additional diagnosis. It is not necessary to assign an additional code for the site of the pain.

See Section I.C.2 for instructions on the sequencing of neoplasms for all other stated reasons for the admission/ encounter (except for pain control/pain management).

6) Chronic pain syndrome

Central pain syndrome (G89.0) and chronic pain syndrome (G89.4) are different than the term "chronic pain," and therefore codes should only be used when the provider has specifically documented this condition.

See Section I.C.5. Pain disorders related to psychological factors

7. Chapter 7: Diseases of the Eye and Adnexa (H00-H59)

a. Glaucoma

1) Assigning Glaucoma Codes

Assign as many codes from category H40, Glaucoma, as needed to identify the type of glaucoma, the affected eye, and the glaucoma stage.

2) Bilateral glaucoma with same type and stage

When a patient has bilateral glaucoma and both eyes are documented as being the same type and stage, and there is a code for bilateral glaucoma, report only the code for the type of glaucoma, bilateral, with the seventh character for the stage.

When a patient has bilateral glaucoma and both eyes are documented as being the same type and stage, and the classification does not provide a code for bilateral glaucoma (i.e., subcategories H40.10, H40.11 and H40.20) report only one code for the type of glaucoma with the appropriate seventh character for the stage.

3) Bilateral glaucoma stage with different types or stages

When a patient has bilateral glaucoma and each eye is documented as having a different type or stage, and the classification distinguishes laterality, assign the appropriate code for each eye rather than the code for bilateral glaucoma.

When a patient has bilateral glaucoma and each eye is documented as having a different type, and the classification does not distinguish laterality (i.e., subcategories H40.10, H40.11 and H40.20), assign one code for each type of glaucoma with the appropriate 7th character for the stage.

When a patient has bilateral glaucoma and each eye is documented as having the same type, but different stage, and the classification does not distinguish laterality (i.e., subcategories H40.10, H40.11 and H40.20), assign a code for the type of glaucoma for each eye with the 7th character for the specific glaucoma stage documented for each eye.

4) Patient admitted with glaucoma and stage evolves during the admission

If a patient is admitted with glaucoma and the stage progresses during the admission, assign the code for highest stage documented.

5) Indeterminate stage glaucoma

Assignment of the 7th character "4" for "indeterminate stage" should be based on the clinical documentation. The 7th character "4" is used for glaucomas whose stage cannot be clinically determined. This 7th character should not be confused with the 7th character "0", unspecified, which should be assigned when there is no documentation regarding the stage of the glaucoma.

b. Blindness

If "blindness" or "low vision" of both eyes is documented but the visual impairment category is not documented, assign code H54.3, Unqualified visual loss, both eyes. If "blindness" or "low vision" in one eye is documented but the visual impairment category is not documented, assign a code from H54.6-, Unqualified visual loss, one eye. If "blindness" or "visual loss" is documented without any information about whether one or both eyes are affected, assign code H54.7, Unspecified visual loss.

8. Chapter 8: Diseases of the Ear and Mastoid Process (H60-H95)

Reserved for future guideline expansion

9. Chapter 9: Diseases of the Circulatory System (I00-I99)

a. Hypertension

The classification presumes a causal relationship between hypertension and heart involvement and between hypertension and kidney involvement, as the two conditions are linked by the term "with" in the Alphabetic Index. These conditions should be coded as related even in the absence of provider documentation explicitly linking them, unless the documentation clearly states the conditions are unrelated.

For hypertension and conditions not specifically linked by relational terms such as "with," "associated with" or "due to" in the classification, provider documentation must link the conditions in order to code them as related.

1) Hypertension with Heart Disease

Hypertension with heart conditions classified to I50.- or I51.4-I51.7, I51.89, I51.9, are assigned to, a code from category I11, Hypertensive heart disease. Use additional code(s) from category I50, Heart failure, to identify the type(s) of heart failure in those patients with heart failure.

The same heart conditions (I50.-, I51.4-I51.7, I51.89, I51.9) with hypertension are coded separately if the provider has documented they are unrelated to the hypertension. Sequence according to the circumstances of the admission/encounter.

2) Hypertensive Chronic Kidney Disease

Assign codes from category I12, Hypertensive chronic kidney disease, when both hypertension and a condition classifiable to category N18, Chronic kidney disease (CKD), are present. CKD should not be coded as hypertensive if the provider indicates the CKD is not related to the hypertension.

The appropriate code from category N18 should be used as a secondary code with a code from category I12 to identify the stage of chronic kidney disease.

See Section I.C.14. Chronic kidney disease.

If a patient has hypertensive chronic kidney disease and acute renal failure, the acute renal failure **should also be coded. Sequence according to the circumstances of the admission/encounter.**

3) Hypertensive Heart and Chronic Kidney Disease

Assign codes from combination category I13, Hypertensive heart and chronic kidney disease, when there is hypertension with both heart and kidney involvement. If heart failure is present, assign an additional code from category I50 to identify the type of heart failure.

The appropriate code from category N18, Chronic kidney disease, should be used as a secondary code with a code from category I13 to identify the stage of chronic kidney disease.

See Section I.C.14. Chronic kidney disease.

The codes in category I13, Hypertensive heart and chronic kidney disease, are combination codes that include hypertension, heart disease and chronic kidney disease. The Includes note at I13 specifies that the conditions included at I11 and I12 are included together in I13. If a patient has hypertension, heart disease and chronic kidney disease then a code from I13 should be used, not individual codes for hypertension, heart disease and chronic kidney disease, or codes from I11 or I12.

For patients with both acute renal failure and chronic kidney disease **the** acute renal failure **should also be coded. Sequence according to the circumstances of the admission/encounter.**

4) Hypertensive Cerebrovascular Disease

For hypertensive cerebrovascular disease, first assign the appropriate code from categories I60-I69, followed by the appropriate hypertension code.

5) Hypertensive Retinopathy

Subcategory H35.0, Background retinopathy and retinal vascular changes, should be used with a code from category I10 – I15, Hypertensive disease to include the systemic hypertension. The sequencing is based on the reason for the encounter.

6) Hypertension, Secondary

Secondary hypertension is due to an underlying condition. Two codes are required: one to identify the underlying etiology and one from category I15 to identify the hypertension. Sequencing of codes is determined by the reason for admission/ encounter.

7) Hypertension, Transient

Assign code R03.0, Elevated blood pressure reading without diagnosis of hypertension, unless patient has an established diagnosis of hypertension. Assign code O13.-, Gestational [pregnancy-induced] hypertension without significant proteinuria, or O14.-, Pre-eclampsia, for transient hypertension of pregnancy.

8) Hypertension, Controlled

This diagnostic statement usually refers to an existing state of hypertension under control

by therapy. Assign the appropriate code from categories I10-I15, Hypertensive diseases.

9) Hypertension, Uncontrolled

Uncontrolled hypertension may refer to untreated hypertension or hypertension not responding to current therapeutic regimen. In either case, assign the appropriate code from categories I10-I15, Hypertensive diseases.

10) Hypertensive Crisis

Assign a code from category I16, Hypertensive crisis, for documented hypertensive urgency, hypertensive emergency or unspecified hypertensive crisis. Code also any identified hypertensive disease (I10-I15). The sequencing is based on the reason for the encounter.

11) Pulmonary Hypertension

Pulmonary hypertension is classified to category I27, Other pulmonary heart diseases. For secondary pulmonary hypertension (I27.1, I27.2-), code also any associated conditions or adverse effects of drugs or toxins. The sequencing is based on the reason for the encounter, except for adverse effects of drugs.

See Section I.C.19.e

b. Atherosclerotic Coronary Artery Disease and Angina

ICD-10-CM has combination codes for atherosclerotic heart disease with angina pectoris. The subcategories for these codes are I25.11, Atherosclerotic heart disease of native coronary artery with angina pectoris and I25.7, Atherosclerosis of coronary artery bypass graft(s) and coronary artery of transplanted heart with angina pectoris.

When using one of these combination codes it is not necessary to use an additional code for angina pectoris. A causal relationship can be assumed in a patient with both atherosclerosis and angina pectoris, unless the documentation indicates the angina is due to something other than the atherosclerosis.

If a patient with coronary artery disease is admitted due to an acute myocardial infarction (AMI), the AMI should be sequenced before the coronary artery disease.

See Section I.C.9. Acute myocardial infarction (AMI)

c. Intraoperative and Postprocedural Cerebrovascular Accident

Medical record documentation should clearly specify the cause-and-effect relationship between the medical intervention and the cerebrovascular accident in order to assign a code for intraoperative or postprocedural cerebrovascular accident.

Proper code assignment depends on whether it was an infarction or hemorrhage and whether it occurred intraoperatively or postoperatively. If it was a cerebral hemorrhage, code assignment depends on the type of procedure performed.

d. Sequelae of Cerebrovascular Disease

1) Category I69, Sequelae of Cerebrovascular disease

Category I69 is used to indicate conditions classifiable to categories I60-I67 as the causes of sequela (neurologic deficits), themselves classified elsewhere. These "late effects" include neurologic deficits that persist after initial onset of conditions classifiable to categories I60-I67. The neurologic deficits caused by cerebrovascular disease may be present from the onset or may arise at any time after the onset of the condition classifiable to categories I60-I67.

Codes from category I69, Sequelae of cerebrovascular disease, that specify hemiplegia, hemiparesis and monoplegia identify whether the dominant or nondominant side is affected. Should the affected side be documented, but not specified as dominant or nondominant, and the classification system does not indicate a default, code selection is as follows:

- For ambidextrous patients, the default should be dominant.
- If the left side is affected, the default is non-dominant.
- If the right side is affected, the default is dominant.

2) Codes from category I69 with codes from I60-I67

Codes from category I69 may be assigned on a health care record with codes from I60-I67, if the patient has a current cerebrovascular disease and deficits from an old cerebrovascular disease.

3) Codes from category I69 and Personal history of transient ischemic attack (TIA) and cerebral infarction (Z86.73)

Codes from category I69 should not be assigned if the patient does not have neurologic deficits.

See Section I.C.21. 4. History (of) for use of personal history codes

e. Acute myocardial infarction (AMI)

1) Type 1 ST elevation myocardial infarction (STEMI) and non ST elevation myocardial infarction (NSTEMI)

The ICD-10-CM codes for type 1 acute myocardial infarction (AMI) identify the site, such as anterolateral wall or true posterior wall. Subcategories I21.0-I21.2 and code I21.3 are used for type 1 ST elevation myocardial infarction (STEMI). Code I21.4, Non-ST elevation (NSTEMI) myocardial infarction, is used for type 1 non ST elevation myocardial infarction (NSTEMI) and nontransmural MIs.

If a type 1 NSTEMI evolves to STEMI, assign the STEMI code. If a type 1 STEMI converts to NSTEMI due to thrombolytic therapy, it is still coded as STEMI.

For encounters occurring while the myocardial infarction is equal to, or less than, 4 weeks old, including transfers to another acute setting or a postacute setting, and the myocardial infarction meets the definition for "other diagnoses" (see Section III, Reporting Additional Diagnoses), codes from category I21 may continue to be reported. For encounters after the 4 week time frame and the patient is still receiving care related to the myocardial infarction, the appropriate aftercare code should be assigned, rather than a code from category I21. For old or healed myocardial infarctions not requiring further care, code I25.2, Old myocardial infarction, may be assigned.

2) Acute myocardial infarction, unspecified

Code I21.9, Acute myocardial infarction, unspecified, is the default for unspecified acute myocardial infarction or unspecified type. If only type 1 STEMI or transmural MI without the site is documented, assign code I21.3, ST elevation (STEMI) myocardial infarction of unspecified site.

3) AMI documented as nontransmural or subendocardial but site provided

If an AMI is documented as nontransmural or subendocardial, but the site is provided, it is still coded as a subendocardial AMI.

See Section I.C.21.3 for information on coding status post administration of tPA in a different facility within the last 24 hours.

4) Subsequent acute myocardial infarction

A code from category I22, Subsequent ST elevation (STEMI) and non ST elevation (NSTEMI) myocardial infarction, is to be used when a patient who has suffered a type 1 or unspecified AMI has a new AMI within the 4 week time frame of the initial AMI. A code from category I22 must be used in conjunction with a code from category I21. The sequencing of the I22 and I21 codes depends on the circumstances of the encounter.

Do not assign code I22 for subsequent myocardial infarctions other than type 1 or unspecified. For subsequent type 2 AMI assign only code I21.A1. For subsequent type 4 or type 5 AMI, assign only code I21.A9.

If a subsequent myocardial infarction of one type occurs within 4 weeks of a myocardial infarction of a different type, assign the appropriate codes from category I21 to identify each type. Do not assign a code from I22. Codes from category I22 should only be assigned if both the initial and subsequent myocardial infarctions are type 1 or unspecified.

5) Other Types of Myocardial Infarction

The ICD-10-CM provides codes for different types of myocardial infarction. Type 1 myocardial infarctions are assigned to codes I21.0-I21.4.

Type 2 myocardial infarction (myocardial infarction due to demand ischemia or secondary to ischemic imbalance) is assigned to code I21.A1, Myocardial infarction type 2 with the underlying cause coded first. Do not assign code I24.8, Other forms of acute ischemic heart disease, for the demand ischemia. If a type 2 AMI is described as NSTEMI or STEMI, only assign code I21.A1. Codes I21.01-I21.4 should only be assigned for type 1 AMIs.

Acute myocardial infarctions type 3, 4a, 4b, 4c, and 5 are assigned to code I21.A9, Other myocardial infarction type.

The "Code also" and "Code first" notes should be followed related to complications, and for coding of postprocedural myocardial infarctions during or following cardiac surgery.

10. **Chapter 10: Diseases of the Respiratory System (J00–J99, *U07.1*)**

a. **Chronic Obstructive Pulmonary Disease [COPD] and Asthma**

1) **Acute exacerbation of chronic obstructive bronchitis and asthma**

The codes in categories J44 and J45 distinguish between uncomplicated cases and those in acute exacerbation. An acute exacerbation is a worsening or a decompensation of a chronic condition. An acute exacerbation is not equivalent to an infection superimposed on a chronic condition, though an exacerbation may be triggered by an infection.

b. **Acute Respiratory Failure**

1) **Acute respiratory failure as principal diagnosis**

A code from subcategory J96.0, Acute respiratory failure, or subcategory J96.2, Acute and chronic respiratory failure, may be assigned as a principal diagnosis when it is the condition established after study to be chiefly responsible for occasioning the admission to the hospital, and the selection is supported by the Alphabetic Index and Tabular List. However, chapter-specific coding guidelines (such as obstetrics, poisoning, HIV, newborn) that provide sequencing direction take precedence.

2) **Acute respiratory failure as secondary diagnosis**

Respiratory failure may be listed as a secondary diagnosis if it occurs after admission, or if it is present on admission, but does not meet the definition of principal diagnosis.

3) **Sequencing of acute respiratory failure and another acute condition**

When a patient is admitted with respiratory failure and another acute condition (e.g., myocardial infarction, cerebrovascular accident, aspiration pneumonia), the principal diagnosis will not be the same in every situation. This applies whether the other acute condition is a respiratory or nonrespiratory condition. Selection of the principal diagnosis will be dependent on the circumstances of admission. If both the respiratory failure and the other acute condition are equally responsible for occasioning the admission to the hospital, and there are no chapter-specific sequencing rules, the guideline regarding two or more diagnoses that equally meet the definition for principal diagnosis *(Section II, C.)* may be applied in these situations.

If the documentation is not clear as to whether acute respiratory failure and another condition are equally responsible for occasioning the admission, query the provider for clarification.

c. **Influenza due to certain identified influenza viruses**

Code only confirmed cases of influenza due to certain identified influenza viruses (category J09), and due to other identified influenza virus (category J10). This is an exception to the hospital inpatient guideline Section II, H. (Uncertain Diagnosis).

In this context, "confirmation" does not require documentation of positive laboratory testing specific for avian or other novel influenza A or other identified influenza virus. However, coding should be based on the provider's diagnostic statement that the patient has avian influenza, or other novel influenza A, for category J09, or has another particular identified strain of influenza, such as H1N1 or H3N2, but not identified as novel or variant, for category J10.

If the provider records "suspected" or "possible" or "probable" avian influenza, or novel influenza, or other identified influenza, then the appropriate influenza code from category J11, Influenza due to unidentified influenza virus, should be assigned. A code from category J09, Influenza due to certain identified influenza viruses, should not be assigned nor should a code from category J10, Influenza due to other identified influenza virus.

d. **Ventilator associated Pneumonia**

1) **Documentation of Ventilator associated Pneumonia**

As with all procedural or postprocedural complications, code assignment is based on the provider's documentation of the relationship between the condition and the procedure.

Code J95.851, Ventilator associated pneumonia, should be assigned only when the provider has documented ventilator associated pneumonia (VAP). An additional code to identify the organism (e.g., Pseudomonas aeruginosa, code B96.5) should also be assigned. Do not assign an additional code from categories J12-J18 to identify the type of pneumonia.

Code J95.851 should not be assigned for cases where the patient has pneumonia and is on a mechanical ventilator and the provider has not specifically stated that the pneumonia is ventilator-associated pneumonia. If the documentation is unclear as to whether the patient has a pneumonia that is a complication attributable to the mechanical ventilator, query the provider.

2) **Ventilator associated Pneumonia Develops after Admission**

A patient may be admitted with one type of pneumonia (e.g., code J13, Pneumonia due to Streptococcus pneumonia) and subsequently develop VAP. In this instance, the principal diagnosis would be the appropriate code from categories J12-J18 for the pneumonia diagnosed at the time of admission. Code J95.851, Ventilator associated pneumonia, would be assigned as an additional diagnosis when the provider has also documented the presence of ventilator associated pneumonia.

e. **Vaping-related disorders**

For patients presenting with condition(s) related to vaping, assign code U07.0, Vaping-related disorder, as the principal diagnosis. For lung injury due to vaping, assign only code U07.0. Assign additional codes for other manifestations,

such as acute respiratory failure (subcategory J96.0-) or pneumonitis (code J68.0).

Associated respiratory signs and symptoms due to vaping, such as cough, shortness of breath, etc., are not coded separately, when a definitive diagnosis has been established. However, it would be appropriate to code separately any gastrointestinal symptoms, such as diarrhea and abdominal pain.

11. **Chapter 11: Diseases of the Digestive System (K00-K95)**
   Reserved for future guideline expansion

12. **Chapter 12: Diseases of the Skin and Subcutaneous Tissue (L00-L99)**
   a. **Pressure ulcer stage codes**
      1) **Pressure ulcer stages**
      Codes in category L89, Pressure ulcer, identify the site and stage of the pressure ulcer.

      The ICD-10-CM classifies pressure ulcer stages based on severity, which is designated by stages 1-4, deep tissue pressure injury, unspecified stage, and unstageable.

      Assign as many codes from category L89 as needed to identify all the pressure ulcers the patient has, if applicable.
      See Section I.B.14 for pressure ulcer stage documentation by clinicians other than patient's provider

      2) **Unstageable pressure ulcers**
      Assignment of the code for unstageable pressure ulcer (L89.--0) should be based on the clinical documentation. These codes are used for pressure ulcers whose stage cannot be clinically determined (e.g., the ulcer is covered by eschar or has been treated with a skin or muscle graft). This code should not be confused with the codes for unspecified stage (L89.--9). When there is no documentation regarding the stage of the pressure ulcer, assign the appropriate code for unspecified stage (L89.9).

      3) **Documented pressure ulcer stage**
      Assignment of the pressure ulcer stage code should be guided by clinical documentation of the stage or documentation of the terms found in the Alphabetic Index. For clinical terms describing the stage that are not found in the Alphabetic Index, and there is no documentation of the stage, the provider should be queried.

      4) **Patients admitted with pressure ulcers documented as healed**
      No code is assigned if the documentation states that the pressure ulcer is completely healed at the time of admission.

      5) **Pressure ulcers documented as healing**
      Pressure ulcers described as healing should be assigned the appropriate pressure ulcer stage code based on the documentation in the medical record. If the documentation does not provide information about the stage of the healing pressure ulcer, assign the appropriate code for unspecified stage.

      If the documentation is unclear as to whether the patient has a current (new) pressure ulcer or if

the patient is being treated for a healing pressure ulcer, query the provider.

      For ulcers that were present on admission but healed at the time of discharge, assign the code for the site and stage of the pressure ulcer at the time of admission.

      6) **Patient admitted with pressure ulcer evolving into another stage during the admission**
      If a patient is admitted to an inpatient hospital with a pressure ulcer at one stage and it progresses to a higher stage, two separate codes should be assigned: one code for the site and stage of the ulcer on admission and a second code for the same ulcer site and the highest stage reported during the stay.

      7) **Pressure-induced deep tissue damage**
      For pressure-induced deep tissue damage or deep tissue pressure injury, assign only the appropriate code for pressure-induced deep tissue damage (L89.--6).

   b. **Non-Pressure Chronic Ulcers**
      1) **Patients admitted with non-pressure ulcers documented as healed**
      No code is assigned if the documentation states that the non-pressure ulcer is completely healed at the time of admission.

      2) **Non-pressure ulcers documented as healing**
      Non-pressure ulcers described as healing should be assigned the appropriate non-pressure ulcer code based on the documentation in the medical record. If the documentation does not provide information about the severity of the healing non-pressure ulcer, assign the appropriate code for unspecified severity.

      If the documentation is unclear as to whether the patient has a current (new) non-pressure ulcer or if the patient is being treated for a healing non-pressure ulcer, query the provider.

      For ulcers that were present on admission but healed at the time of discharge, assign the code for the site and severity of the non-pressure ulcer at the time of admission.

      3) **Patient admitted with non-pressure ulcer that progresses to another severity level during the admission**
      If a patient is admitted to an inpatient hospital with a non-pressure ulcer at one severity level and it progresses to a higher severity level, two separate codes should be assigned: one code for the site and severity level of the ulcer on admission and a second code for the same ulcer site and the highest severity level reported during the stay.
      See Section I.B.14 for pressure ulcer stage documentation by clinicians other than patient's provider

13. **Chapter 13: Diseases of the Musculoskeletal System and Connective Tissue (M00-M99)**
   a. **Site and laterality**
   Most of the codes within Chapter 13 have site and laterality designations. The site represents

the bone, joint or the muscle involved. For some conditions where more than one bone, joint or muscle is usually involved, such as osteoarthritis, there is a "multiple sites" code available. For categories where no multiple site code is provided and more than one bone, joint or muscle is involved, multiple codes should be used to indicate the different sites involved.

1) Bone versus joint

For certain conditions, the bone may be affected at the upper or lower end (e.g., avascular necrosis of bone, M87, Osteoporosis, M80, M81). Though the portion of the bone affected may be at the joint, the site designation will be the bone, not the joint.

b. Acute traumatic versus chronic or recurrent musculoskeletal conditions

Many musculoskeletal conditions are a result of previous injury or trauma to a site, or are recurrent conditions. Bone, joint or muscle conditions that are the result of a healed injury are usually found in Chapter 13. Recurrent bone, joint or muscle conditions are also usually found in Chapter 13. Any current, acute injury should be coded to the appropriate injury code from Chapter 19. Chronic or recurrent conditions should generally be coded with a code from Chapter 13. If it is difficult to determine from the documentation in the record which code is best to describe a condition, query the provider.

c. Coding of Pathologic Fractures

Seventh character A is for use as long as the patient is receiving active treatment for the fracture. While the patient may be seen by a new or different provider over the course of treatment for a pathological fracture, assignment of the 7th character is based on whether the patient is undergoing active treatment and not whether the provider is seeing the patient for the first time.

Seventh character, D is to be used for encounters after the patient has completed active treatment for the fracture and is receiving routine care for the fracture during the healing or recovery phase. The other 7th characters, listed under each subcategory in the Tabular List, are to be used for subsequent encounters for treatment of problems associated with the healing, such as malunions, nonunions, and sequelae.

Care for complications of surgical treatment for fracture repairs during the healing or recovery phase should be coded with the appropriate complication codes.

See Section I.C.19. Coding of traumatic fractures

d. Osteoporosis

Osteoporosis is a systemic condition, meaning that all bones of the musculoskeletal system are affected. Therefore, site is not a component of the codes under category M81, Osteoporosis without current pathological fracture. The site codes under category M80, Osteoporosis with current pathological fracture, identify the site of the fracture, not the osteoporosis.

1) Osteoporosis without pathological fracture

Category M81, Osteoporosis without current pathological fracture, is for use for patients with osteoporosis who do not currently have a pathologic fracture due to the osteoporosis, even if they have had a fracture in the past. For patients with a history of osteoporosis fractures, status code Z87.310, Personal history of (healed) osteoporosis fracture, should follow the code from M81.

2) Osteoporosis with current pathological fracture

Category M80, Osteoporosis with current pathological fracture, is for patients who have a current pathologic fracture at the time of an encounter. The codes under M80 identify the site of the fracture. A code from category M80, not a traumatic fracture code, should be used for any patient with known osteoporosis who suffers a fracture, even if the patient had a minor fall or trauma, if that fall or trauma would not usually break a normal, healthy bone.

14. Chapter 14: Diseases of Genitourinary System (N00-N99)

a. Chronic kidney disease

1) Stages of chronic kidney disease (CKD)

The ICD-10-CM classifies CKD based on severity. The severity of CKD is designated by stages 1-5. Stage 2, code N18.2, equates to mild CKD; stage 3, **codes N18.30-N18.32, equate** to moderate CKD; and stage 4, code N18.4, equates to severe CKD. Code N18.6, End stage renal disease (ESRD), is assigned when the provider has documented end-stage-renal disease (ESRD).

If both a stage of CKD and ESRD are documented, assign code N18.6 only.

2) Chronic kidney disease and kidney transplant status

Patients who have undergone kidney transplant may still have some form of chronic kidney disease (CKD) because the kidney transplant may not fully restore kidney function. Therefore, the presence of CKD alone does not constitute a transplant complication. Assign the appropriate N18 code for the patient's stage of CKD and code Z94.0, Kidney transplant status. If a transplant complication such as failure or rejection or other transplant complication is documented, see Section I.C.19.g for information on coding complications of a kidney transplant. If the documentation is unclear as to whether the patient has a complication of the transplant, query the provider.

3) Chronic kidney disease with other conditions

Patients with CKD may also suffer from other serious conditions, most commonly diabetes mellitus and hypertension. The sequencing of the CKD code in relationship to codes for other contributing conditions is based on the conventions in the Tabular List.

See I.C.9. Hypertensive chronic kidney disease.
See I.C.19. Chronic kidney disease and kidney transplant complications.

15. **Chapter 15: Pregnancy, Childbirth, and the Puerperium (O00-O9A)**

   a. **General Rules for Obstetric Cases**

   1) **Codes from Chapter 15 and sequencing priority**

   Obstetric cases require codes from Chapter 15, codes in the range O00-O9A, Pregnancy, Childbirth, and the Puerperium. Chapter 15 codes have sequencing priority over codes from other chapters. Additional codes from other chapters may be used in conjunction with Chapter 15 codes to further specify conditions. Should the provider document that the pregnancy is incidental to the encounter, then code Z33.1, Pregnant state, incidental, should be used in place of any Chapter 15 codes. It is the provider's responsibility to state that the condition being treated is not affecting the pregnancy.

   2) **Chapter 15 codes used only on the maternal record**

   Chapter 15 codes are to be used only on the maternal record, never on the record of the newborn.

   3) **Final character for trimester**

   The majority of codes in Chapter 15 have a final character indicating the trimester of pregnancy. The time frames for the trimesters are indicated at the beginning of the chapter. If trimester is not a component of a code it is because the condition always occurs in a specific trimester, or the concept of trimester of pregnancy is not applicable. Certain codes have characters for only certain trimesters because the condition does not occur in all trimesters, but it may occur in more than just one.

   Assignment of the final character for trimester should be based on the provider's documentation of the trimester (or number of weeks) for the current admission/encounter. This applies to the assignment of trimester for pre-existing conditions as well as those that develop during or are due to the pregnancy. The provider's documentation of the number of weeks may be used to assign the appropriate code identifying the trimester.

   Whenever delivery occurs during the current admission, and there is an "in childbirth" option for the obstetric complication being coded, the "in childbirth" code should be assigned.

   4) **Selection of trimester for inpatient admissions that encompass more than one trimester**

   In instances when a patient is admitted to a hospital for complications of pregnancy during one trimester and remains in the hospital into a subsequent trimester, the trimester character for the antepartum complication code should be assigned on the basis of the trimester when the complication developed, not the trimester of the discharge. If the condition developed prior to the current admission/encounter or represents a pre-existing condition, the trimester character for the trimester at the time of the admission/encounter should be assigned.

   5) **Unspecified trimester**

   Each category that includes codes for trimester has a code for "unspecified trimester." The "unspecified trimester" code should rarely be used, such as when the documentation in the record is insufficient to determine the trimester and it is not possible to obtain clarification.

   6) **7th character for Fetus Identification**

   Where applicable, a 7th character is to be assigned for certain categories (O31, O32, O33.3 - O33.6, O35, O36, O40, O41, O60.1, O60.2, O64, and O69) to identify the fetus for which the complication code applies.

   Assign 7th character "0":
   • For single gestations
   • When the documentation in the record is insufficient to determine the fetus affected and it is not possible to obtain clarification.
   • When it is not possible to clinically determine which fetus is affected.

   b. **Selection of OB Principal or First-listed Diagnosis**

   1) **Routine outpatient prenatal visits**

   For routine outpatient prenatal visits when no complications are present, a code from category Z34, Encounter for supervision of normal pregnancy, should be used as the first-listed diagnosis. These codes should not be used in conjunction with Chapter 15 codes.

   2) **Supervision of High-Risk Pregnancy**

   Codes from category O09, Supervision of high-risk pregnancy, are intended for use only during the prenatal period. For complications during the labor or delivery episode as a result of a high-risk pregnancy, assign the applicable complication codes from Chapter 15. If there are no complications during the labor or delivery episode, assign code O80, Encounter for full-term uncomplicated delivery.

   For routine prenatal outpatient visits for patients with high-risk pregnancies, a code from category O09, Supervision of high-risk pregnancy, should be used as the first-listed diagnosis. Secondary Chapter 15 codes may be used in conjunction with these codes if appropriate.

   3) **Episodes when no delivery occurs**

   In episodes when no delivery occurs, the principal diagnosis should correspond to the principal complication of the pregnancy which necessitated the encounter. Should more than one complication exist, all of which are treated or monitored, any of the complication codes may be sequenced first.

   4) **When a delivery occurs**

   When an obstetric patient is admitted and delivers during that admission, the condition that prompted the admission should be sequenced as the principal diagnosis. If multiple conditions prompted the admission, sequence the one most related to the delivery as the principal diagnosis. A code for any complication of the delivery should be assigned as an additional diagnosis. In cases

GUIDELINES (ICD-10-CM)

of cesarean delivery, if the patient was admitted with a condition that resulted in the performance of a cesarean procedure, that condition should be selected as the principal diagnosis. If the reason for the admission was unrelated to the condition resulting in the cesarean delivery, the condition related to the reason for the admission should be selected as the principal diagnosis.

5) Outcome of delivery

A code from category Z37, Outcome of delivery, should be included on every maternal record when a delivery has occurred. These codes are not to be used on subsequent records or on the newborn record.

c. Pre-existing conditions versus conditions due to the pregnancy

Certain categories in Chapter 15 distinguish between conditions of the mother that existed prior to pregnancy (pre-existing) and those that are a direct result of pregnancy. When assigning codes from Chapter 15, it is important to assess if a condition was pre-existing prior to pregnancy or developed during or due to the pregnancy in order to assign the correct code.

Categories that do not distinguish between pre-existing and pregnancy-related conditions may be used for either. It is acceptable to use codes specifically for the puerperium with codes complicating pregnancy and childbirth if a condition arises postpartum during the delivery encounter.

d. Pre-existing hypertension in pregnancy

Category O10, Pre-existing hypertension complicating pregnancy, childbirth and the puerperium, includes codes for hypertensive heart and hypertensive chronic kidney disease. When assigning one of the O10 codes that includes hypertensive heart disease or hypertensive chronic kidney disease, it is necessary to add a secondary code from the appropriate hypertension category to specify the type of heart failure or chronic kidney disease.

See Section I.C.9. Hypertension.

e. Fetal Conditions Affecting the Management of the Mother

1) Codes from categories O35 and O36

Codes from categories O35, Maternal care for known or suspected fetal abnormality and damage, and O36, Maternal care for other fetal problems, are assigned only when the fetal condition is actually responsible for modifying the management of the mother, i.e., by requiring diagnostic studies, additional observation, special care, or termination of pregnancy. The fact that the fetal condition exists does not justify assigning a code from this series to the mother's record.

2) In utero surgery

In cases when surgery is performed on the fetus, a diagnosis code from category O35, Maternal care for known or suspected fetal abnormality and damage, should be assigned identifying the fetal condition. Assign the appropriate procedure code for the procedure performed.

No code from Chapter 16, the perinatal codes, should be used on the mother's record to identify fetal conditions. Surgery performed in utero on a fetus is still to be coded as an obstetric encounter.

f. HIV Infection in Pregnancy, Childbirth and the Puerperium

During pregnancy, childbirth or the puerperium, a patient admitted because of an HIV-related illness should receive a principal diagnosis from subcategory O98.7-, Human immunodeficiency [HIV] disease complicating pregnancy, childbirth and the puerperium, followed by the code(s) for the HIV-related illness(es).

Patients with asymptomatic HIV infection status admitted during pregnancy, childbirth, or the puerperium should receive codes of O98.7- and Z21, Asymptomatic human immunodeficiency virus [HIV] infection status.

g. Diabetes mellitus in pregnancy

Diabetes mellitus is a significant complicating factor in pregnancy. Pregnant women who are diabetic should be assigned a code from category O24, Diabetes mellitus in pregnancy, childbirth, and the puerperium, first, followed by the appropriate diabetes code(s) (E08-E13) from Chapter 4.

h. Long-term use of insulin and oral hypoglycemics

See Section I.C.4.a.3 for information on the long term use of insulin and oral hypoglycemics.

i. Gestational (pregnancy induced) diabetes

Gestational (pregnancy induced) diabetes can occur during the second and third trimester of pregnancy in women who were not diabetic prior to pregnancy. Gestational diabetes can cause complications in the pregnancy similar to those of pre-existing diabetes mellitus. It also puts the woman at greater risk of developing diabetes after the pregnancy. Codes for gestational diabetes are in subcategory O24.4, Gestational diabetes mellitus. No other code from category O24, Diabetes mellitus in pregnancy, childbirth, and the puerperium, should be used with a code from O24.4.

The codes under subcategory O24.4 include diet controlled, insulin controlled, and controlled by oral hypoglycemic drugs. If a patient with gestational diabetes is treated with both diet and insulin, only the code for insulin-controlled is required. If a patient with gestational diabetes is treated with both diet and oral hypoglycemic medications, only the code for "controlled by oral hypoglycemic drugs" is required. Code Z79.4, Long-term (current) use of insulin or code Z79.84, Long-term (current) use of oral hypoglycemic drugs, should not be assigned with codes from subcategory O24.4.

An abnormal glucose tolerance in pregnancy is assigned a code from subcategory O99.81, Abnormal glucose complicating pregnancy, childbirth, and the puerperium.

j. Sepsis and septic shock complicating abortion, pregnancy, childbirth and the puerperium

When assigning a Chapter 15 code for sepsis complicating abortion, pregnancy, childbirth, and the puerperium, a code for the specific type of infection should be assigned as an additional diagnosis. If severe sepsis is present, a code from subcategory R65.2, Severe sepsis, and code(s) for associated organ dysfunction(s) should also be assigned as additional diagnoses.

k. Puerperal sepsis

Code O85, Puerperal sepsis, should be assigned with a secondary code to identify the causal organism (e.g., for a bacterial infection, assign a code from category B95-B96, Bacterial infections in conditions classified elsewhere). A code from category A40, Streptococcal sepsis, or A41, Other sepsis, should not be used for puerperal sepsis. If applicable, use additional codes to identify severe sepsis (R65.2-) and any associated acute organ dysfunction.

Code O85 should not be assigned for sepsis following an obstetrical procedure (See Section I.C.1.d.5.b., Sepsis due to a postprocedural infection).

l. Alcohol, tobacco and drug use during pregnancy, childbirth and the puerperium

1) Alcohol use during pregnancy, childbirth and the puerperium

Codes under subcategory O99.31, Alcohol use complicating pregnancy, childbirth, and the puerperium, should be assigned for any pregnancy case when a mother uses alcohol during the pregnancy or postpartum. A secondary code from category F10, Alcohol related disorders, should also be assigned to identify manifestations of the alcohol use.

2) Tobacco use during pregnancy, childbirth and the puerperium

Codes under subcategory O99.33, Smoking (tobacco) complicating pregnancy, childbirth, and the puerperium, should be assigned for any pregnancy case when a mother uses any type of tobacco product during the pregnancy or postpartum. A secondary code from category F17, Nicotine dependence, should also be assigned to identify the type of nicotine dependence.

3) Drug use during pregnancy, childbirth and the puerperium

Codes under subcategory O99.32, Drug use complicating pregnancy, childbirth, and the puerperium, should be assigned for any pregnancy case when a mother uses drugs during the pregnancy or postpartum. This can involve illegal drugs, or inappropriate use or abuse of prescription drugs. Secondary code(s) from categories F11-F16 and F18-F19 should also be assigned to identify manifestations of the drug use.

m. Poisoning, toxic effects, adverse effects and underdosing in a pregnant patient

A code from subcategory O9A.2, Injury, poisoning and certain other consequences of external causes complicating pregnancy, childbirth, and the puerperium, should be sequenced first, followed by the appropriate injury, poisoning, toxic effect, adverse effect or underdosing code, and then the additional code(s) that specifies the condition caused by the poisoning, toxic effect, adverse effect or underdosing.

See Section I.C.19. Adverse effects, poisoning, underdosing and toxic effects.

n. Normal Delivery, Code O80

1) Encounter for full term uncomplicated delivery

Code O80 should be assigned when a woman is admitted for a full-term normal delivery and delivers a single, healthy infant without any complications antepartum, during the delivery, or postpartum during the delivery episode. Code O80 is always a principal diagnosis. It is not to be used if any other code from Chapter 15 is needed to describe a current complication of the antenatal, delivery, or postnatal period. Additional codes from other chapters may be used with code O80 if they are not related to or are in any way complicating the pregnancy.

2) Uncomplicated delivery with resolved antepartum complication

Code O80 may be used if the patient had a complication at some point during the pregnancy, but the complication is not present at the time of the admission for delivery.

3) Outcome of delivery for O80

Z37.0, Single live birth, is the only outcome of delivery code appropriate for use with O80.

o. The Peripartum and Postpartum Periods

1) Peripartum and Postpartum periods

The postpartum period begins immediately after delivery and continues for 6 weeks following delivery. The peripartum period is defined as the last month of pregnancy to 5 months postpartum.

2) Peripartum and postpartum complication

A postpartum complication is any complication occurring within the 6-week period.

3) Pregnancy-related complications after 6-week period

Chapter 15 codes may also be used to describe pregnancy-related complications after the peripartum or postpartum period if the provider documents that a condition is pregnancy related.

4) Admission for routine postpartum care following delivery outside hospital

When the mother delivers outside the hospital prior to admission and is admitted for routine postpartum care and no complications are noted, code Z39.0, Encounter for care and examination of mother immediately after delivery, should be assigned as the principal diagnosis.

5) Pregnancy associated cardiomyopathy

Pregnancy associated cardiomyopathy, code O90.3, is unique in that it may be diagnosed in the third trimester of pregnancy but may continue to progress months after delivery. For this reason, it is referred to as peripartum cardiomyopathy. Code O90.3 is only for use when the cardiomyopathy develops as a result of pregnancy in a woman who did not have pre-existing heart disease.

p. Code O94, Sequelae of complication of pregnancy, childbirth, and the puerperium

1) Code O94

Code O94, Sequelae of complication of pregnancy, childbirth, and the puerperium, is for use in those cases when an initial complication of a pregnancy develops a sequelae requiring care or treatment at a future date.

2) After the initial postpartum period

This code may be used at any time after the initial postpartum period.

3) Sequencing of Code O94

This code, like all sequela codes, is to be sequenced following the code describing the sequelae of the complication.

q. Termination of Pregnancy and Spontaneous abortions

1) Abortion with Liveborn Fetus

When an attempted termination of pregnancy results in a liveborn fetus assign code Z33.2, Encounter for elective termination of pregnancy and a code from category Z37, Outcome of Delivery.

2) Retained Products of Conception following an abortion

Subsequent encounters for retained products of conception following a spontaneous abortion or elective termination of pregnancy, without complications are assigned O03.4, Incomplete spontaneous, abortion without complication or codes O07.4, Failed attempted termination of pregnancy without complication. This advice is appropriate even when the patient was discharged previously with a discharge diagnosis of complete abortion. If the patient has a specific complication associated with the spontaneous abortion or elective termination of pregnancy in addition to retained products of conception, assign the appropriate complication code (e.g., O03.-, O04.-, O07.-) instead of code O03.4 or O07.4

3) Complications leading to abortion

Codes from Chapter 15 may be used as additional codes to identify any documented complications of the pregnancy in conjunction with codes in categories in O04, O07 and O08.

r. Abuse in a pregnant patient

For suspected or confirmed cases of abuse of a pregnant patient, a code(s) from subcategories O9A.3, Physical abuse complicating pregnancy, childbirth, and the puerperium, O9A.4, Sexual abuse complicating pregnancy, childbirth, and the puerperium, and O9A.5, Psychological abuse complicating pregnancy, childbirth, and the puerperium, should be sequenced first, followed by the appropriate codes (if applicable) to identify any associated current injury due to physical abuse, sexual abuse, and the perpetrator of abuse.

See Section I.C.19. Adult and child abuse, neglect and other maltreatment.

s. *COVID-19 infection in pregnancy, childbirth, and the puerperium*

During pregnancy, childbirth or the puerperium, when COVID-19 is the reason for admission/ encounter, code O98.5-, Other viral diseases complicating pregnancy, childbirth and the puerperium, should be sequenced as the principal/first-listed diagnosis, and code U07.1, COVID-19, and the appropriate codes for associated manifestation(s) should be assigned as additional diagnoses. Codes from Chapter 15 always take sequencing priority.

If the reason for admission/encounter is unrelated to COVID-19 but the patient tests positive for COVID-19 during the admission/ encounter, the appropriate code for the reason for admission/encounter should be sequenced as the principal/first-listed diagnosis, and codes O98.5- and U07.1, as well as the appropriate codes for associated COVID-19 manifestations, should be assigned as additional diagnoses.

16. Chapter 16: Certain Conditions Originating in the Perinatal Period (P00-P96)

For coding and reporting purposes the perinatal period is defined as before birth through the 28th day following birth. The following guidelines are provided for reporting purposes

a. General Perinatal Rules

1) Use of Chapter 16 Codes

Codes in this chapter are for use on the maternal record. Codes from Chapter 15, the obstetric chapter, are never permitted on the newborn record. Chapter 16 codes may be used throughout the life of the patient if the condition is still present.

2) Principal Diagnosis for Birth Record

When coding the birth episode in a newborn record, assign a code from category Z38, Liveborn infants according to place of birth and type of delivery, as the principal diagnosis. A code from category Z38 is assigned only once, to a newborn at the time of birth. If a newborn is transferred to another institution, a code from category Z38 should not be used at the receiving hospital.

A code from category Z38 is used only on the newborn record, not on the mother's record.

3) Use of Codes from other Chapters with Codes from Chapter 16

Codes from other chapters may be used with codes from Chapter 16 if the codes from the other chapters provide more specific detail. Codes for signs and symptoms may be assigned when a definitive diagnosis has not been established. If the reason for the encounter is a perinatal condition, the code from Chapter 16 should be sequenced first.

4) Use of Chapter 16 Codes after the Perinatal Period

Should a condition originate in the perinatal period, and continue throughout the life of the patient, the perinatal code should continue to be used regardless of the patient's age.

5) Birth process or community acquired conditions

If a newborn has a condition that may be either due to the birth process or community acquired and the documentation does not indicate which it is, the default is due to the birth process and the code from Chapter 16 should be used. If the condition is community-acquired, a code from Chapter 16 should not be assigned.

For COVID-19 infection in a newborn, see guideline I.C.16.h.

6) Code all clinically significant conditions

All clinically significant conditions noted on routine newborn examination should be coded. A condition is clinically significant if it requires:

- clinical evaluation; or
- therapeutic treatment; or
- diagnostic procedures; or
- extended length of hospital stay; or
- increased nursing care and/or monitoring; or
- has implications for future health care needs

Note: The perinatal guidelines listed above are the same as the general coding guidelines for "additional diagnoses", except for the final point regarding implications for future health care needs. Codes should be assigned for conditions that have been specified by the provider as having implications for future health care needs.

b. Observation and Evaluation of Newborns for Suspected Conditions not Found

1) Use of Z05 codes

Assign a code from category Z05, Observation and evaluation of newborns and infants for suspected conditions ruled out, to identify those instances when a healthy newborn is evaluated for a suspected condition that is determined after study not to be present. Do not use a code from category Z05 when the patient has identified signs or symptoms of a suspected problem; in such cases code the sign or symptom.

2) Z05 on other than the birth record

A code from category Z05 may also be assigned as a principal or first-listed code for readmissions or encounters when the code from category Z38 code no longer applies. Codes from category Z05 are for use only for healthy newborns and infants for which no condition after study is found to be present.

3) Z05 on a birth record

A code from category Z05 is to be used as a secondary code after the code from category Z38,

Liveborn infants according to place of birth and type of delivery.

c. Coding Additional Perinatal Diagnoses

1) Assigning codes for conditions that require treatment

Assign codes for conditions that require treatment or further investigation, prolong the length of stay, or require resource utilization.

2) Codes for conditions specified as having implications for future health care needs

Assign codes for conditions that have been specified by the provider as having implications for future health care needs.

Note: This guideline should not be used for adult patients.

d. Prematurity and Fetal Growth Retardation

Providers utilize different criteria in determining prematurity. A code for prematurity should not be assigned unless it is documented. Assignment of codes in categories P05, Disorders of newborn related to slow fetal growth and fetal malnutrition, and P07, Disorders of newborn related to short gestation and low birth weight, not elsewhere classified, should be based on the recorded birth weight and estimated gestational age.

When both birth weight and gestational age are available, two codes from category P07 should be assigned, with the code for birth weight sequenced before the code for gestational age.

e. Low birth weight and immaturity status

Codes from category P07, Disorders of newborn related to short gestation and low birth weight, not elsewhere classified, are for use for a child or adult who was premature or had a low birth weight as a newborn and this is affecting the patient's current health status.

See Section I.C.21. Factors influencing health status and contact with health services, Status.

f. Bacterial Sepsis of Newborn

Category P36, Bacterial sepsis of newborn, includes congenital sepsis. If a perinate is documented as having sepsis without documentation of congenital or community acquired, the default is congenital and a code from category P36 should be assigned. If the P36 code includes the causal organism, an additional code from category B95, Streptococcus, Staphylococcus, and Enterococcus as the cause of diseases classified elsewhere, or B96, Other bacterial agents as the cause of diseases classified elsewhere, should not be assigned. If the P36 code does not include the causal organism, assign an additional code from category B96. If applicable, use additional codes to identify severe sepsis (R65.2-) and any associated acute organ dysfunction.

g. Stillbirth

Code P95, Stillbirth, is only for use in institutions that maintain separate records for stillbirths. No other code should be used with P95. Code P95 should not be used on the mother's record.

h. **COVID-19 Infection in Newborn**
For a newborn that tests positive for COVID-19, assign code U07.1, COVID-19, and the appropriate codes for associated manifestation(s) in neonates/newborns in the absence of documentation indicating a specific type of transmission. For a newborn that tests positive for COVID-19 and the provider documents the condition was contracted in utero or during the birth process, assign codes P35.8, Other congenital viral diseases, and U07.1, COVID-19. When coding the birth episode in a newborn record, the appropriate code from category Z38, Liveborn infants according to place of birth and type of delivery, should be assigned as the principal diagnosis.

17. **Chapter 17: Congenital Malformations, Deformations, and Chromosomal Abnormalities (Q00-Q99)**
Assign an appropriate code(s) from categories Q00-Q99, Congenital malformations, deformations, and chromosomal abnormalities when a malformation/deformation or chromosomal abnormality is documented. A malformation/deformation/or chromosomal abnormality may be the principal/first-listed diagnosis on a record or a secondary diagnosis.

When a malformation/deformation/or chromosomal abnormality does not have a unique code assignment, assign additional code(s) for any manifestations that may be present.

When the code assignment specifically identifies the malformation/deformation/or chromosomal abnormality, manifestations that are an inherent component of the anomaly should not be coded separately. Additional codes should be assigned for manifestations that are not an inherent component.

Codes from Chapter 17 may be used throughout the life of the patient. If a congenital malformation or deformity has been corrected, a personal history code should be used to identify the history of the malformation or deformity. Although present at birth, a malformation/deformation/or chromosomal abnormality may not be identified until later in life. Whenever the condition is diagnosed by the provider, it is appropriate to assign a code from codes Q00-Q99.

For the birth admission, the appropriate code from category Z38, Liveborn infants, according to place of birth and type of delivery, should be sequenced as the principal diagnosis, followed by any congenital anomaly codes, Q00-Q99.

18. **Chapter 18: Symptoms, Signs, and Abnormal Clinical and Laboratory Findings, Not Elsewhere Classified (R00-R99)**
Chapter 18 includes symptoms, signs, abnormal results of clinical or other investigative procedures, and ill-defined conditions regarding which no diagnosis classifiable elsewhere is recorded. Signs and symptoms that point to a specific diagnosis have been assigned to a category in other chapters of the classification.

a. **Use of symptom codes**
Codes that describe symptoms and signs are acceptable for reporting purposes when a related definitive diagnosis has not been established (confirmed) by the provider.

b. **Use of a symptom code with a definitive diagnosis code**
Codes for signs and symptoms may be reported in addition to a related definitive diagnosis when the sign or symptom is not routinely associated with that diagnosis, such as the various signs and symptoms associated with complex syndromes. The definitive diagnosis code should be sequenced before the symptom code.

Signs or symptoms that are associated routinely with a disease process should not be assigned as additional codes, unless otherwise instructed by the classification.

c. **Combination codes that include symptoms**
ICD-10-CM contains a number of combination codes that identify both the definitive diagnosis and common symptoms of that diagnosis. When using one of these combination codes, an additional code should not be assigned for the symptom.

d. **Repeated falls**
Code R29.6, Repeated falls, is for use for encounters when a patient has recently fallen and the reason for the fall is being investigated.

Code Z91.81, History of falling, is for use when a patient has fallen in the past and is at risk for future falls. When appropriate, both codes R29.6 and Z91.81 may be assigned together.

e. **Coma scale**
The coma scale codes (R40.2-) can be used in conjunction with traumatic brain injury codes. These codes are primarily for use by trauma registries, but they may be used in any setting where this information is collected. The coma scale codes should be sequenced after the diagnosis code(s).

These codes, one from each subcategory, are needed to complete the scale. The 7th character indicates when the scale was recorded. The 7th character should match for all three codes.

At a minimum, report the initial score documented on presentation at your facility. This may be a score from the emergency medicine technician (EMT) or in the emergency department. If desired, a facility may choose to capture multiple coma scale scores.

Assign code R40.24, Glasgow coma scale, total score, when only the total score is documented in the medical record and not the individual score(s).

Do not report codes for individual or total Glasgow coma scale scores for a patient with a medically induced coma or a sedated patient.

See Section I.B.14 for coma scale documentation by clinicians other than patient's provider

f. **Functional quadriplegia**
GUIDELINE HAS BEEN DELETED EFFECTIVE OCTOBER 1, 2017

g. SIRS due to Non-Infectious Process

The systemic inflammatory response syndrome (SIRS) can develop as a result of certain non-infectious disease processes, such as trauma, malignant neoplasm, or pancreatitis. When SIRS is documented with a noninfectious condition, and no subsequent infection is documented, the code for the underlying condition, such as an injury, should be assigned, followed by code R65.10, Systemic inflammatory response syndrome (SIRS) of non-infectious origin without acute organ dysfunction, or code R65.11, Systemic inflammatory response syndrome (SIRS) of non-infectious origin with acute organ dysfunction. If an associated acute organ dysfunction is documented, the appropriate code(s) for the specific type of organ dysfunction(s) should be assigned in addition to code R65.11. If acute organ dysfunction is documented, but it cannot be determined if the acute organ dysfunction is associated with SIRS or due to another condition (e.g., directly due to the trauma), the provider should be queried.

h. Death NOS

Code R99, Ill-defined and unknown cause of mortality, is only for use in the very limited circumstance when a patient who has already died is brought into an emergency department or other healthcare facility and is pronounced dead upon arrival. It does not represent the discharge disposition of death.

i. NIHSS Stroke Scale

The NIH stroke scale (NIHSS) codes (R29.7- -) can be used in conjunction with acute stroke codes (I63) to identify the patient's neurological status and the severity of the stroke. The stroke scale codes should be sequenced after the acute stroke diagnosis code(s).

At a minimum, report the initial score documented. If desired, a facility may choose to capture multiple stroke scale scores.

See Section I.B.14 for NIHSS stroke scale documentation by clinicians other than patient's provider

19. Chapter 19: Injury, Poisoning, and Certain Other Consequences of External Causes (S00-T88)

a. Application of 7th Characters in Chapter 19

Most categories in Chapter 19 have a 7th character requirement for each applicable code. Most categories in this chapter have three 7th character values (with the exception of fractures): A, initial encounter, D, subsequent encounter and S, sequela. Categories for traumatic fractures have additional 7th character values. While the patient may be seen by a new or different provider over the course of treatment for an injury, assignment of the 7th character is based on whether the patient is undergoing active treatment and not whether the provider is seeing the patient for the first time.

For complication codes, active treatment refers to treatment for the condition described by the code, even though it may be related to an earlier precipitating problem. For example, code T84.50XA, Infection and inflammatory reaction due to unspecified internal joint prosthesis, initial encounter, is used when active treatment is provided for the infection, even though the condition relates to the prosthetic device, implant or graft that was placed at a previous encounter.

7th character "A", initial encounter is used for each encounter where the patient is receiving active treatment for the condition.

7th character "D" subsequent encounter is used for encounters after the patient has completed active treatment of the condition and is receiving routine care for the condition during the healing or recovery phase.

The aftercare Z codes should not be used for aftercare for conditions such as injuries or poisonings, where 7th characters are provided to identify subsequent care. For example, for aftercare of an injury, assign the acute injury code with the 7th character "D" (subsequent encounter).

7th character "S", sequela, is for use for complications or conditions that arise as a direct result of a condition, such as scar formation after a burn. The scars are sequelae of the burn. When using 7th character "S", it is necessary to use both the injury code that precipitated the sequela and the code for the sequela itself. The "S" is added only to the injury code, not the sequela code. The 7th character "S" identifies the injury responsible for the sequela. The specific type of sequela (e.g., scar) is sequenced first, followed by the injury code.

See Section I.B.10. Sequelae, (Late Effects)

b. Coding of Injuries

When coding injuries, assign separate codes for each injury unless a combination code is provided, in which case the combination code is assigned. Codes from category T07, Unspecified multiple injuries should not be assigned in the inpatient setting unless information for a more specific code is not available. Traumatic injury codes (S00-T14.9) are not to be used for normal, healing surgical wounds or to identify complications of surgical wounds.

The code for the most serious injury, as determined by the provider and the focus of treatment, is sequenced first.

1) Superficial injuries

Superficial injuries such as abrasions or contusions are not coded when associated with more severe injuries of the same site.

2) Primary injury with damage to nerves/ blood vessels

When a primary injury results in minor damage to peripheral nerves or blood vessels, the primary injury is sequenced first with additional code(s) for injuries to nerves and spinal cord (such as category S04), and/or injury to blood vessels (such as category S15). When the primary injury is to the blood vessels or nerves, that injury should be sequenced first.

3) Iatrogenic injuries

Injury codes from Chapter 19 should not be assigned for injuries that occur during, or as a result of, a medical intervention. Assign the appropriate complication code(s).

c. Coding of Traumatic Fractures

The principles of multiple coding of injuries should be followed in coding fractures. Fractures of specified sites are coded individually by site in accordance with both the provisions within categories S02, S12, S22, S32, S42, S49, S52, S59, S62, S72, S79, S82, S89, S92 and the level of detail furnished by medical record content.

A fracture not indicated as open or closed should be coded to closed. A fracture not indicated whether displaced or not displaced should be coded to displaced.

More specific guidelines are as follows:

1) Initial vs. subsequent encounter for fractures

Traumatic fractures are coded using the appropriate 7th character for initial encounter (A, B, C) for each encounter where the patient is receiving active treatment for the fracture. The appropriate 7th character for initial encounter should also be assigned for a patient who delayed seeking treatment for the fracture or nonunion.

Fractures are coded using the appropriate 7th character for subsequent care for encounters after the patient has completed active treatment of the fracture and is receiving routine care for the fracture during the healing or recovery phase.

Care for complications of surgical treatment for fracture repairs during the healing or recovery phase should be coded with the appropriate complication codes.

Care of complications of fractures, such as malunion and nonunion, should be reported with the appropriate 7th character for subsequent care with nonunion (K, M, N,) or subsequent care with malunion (P, Q, R).

Malunion/nonunion: The appropriate 7th character for initial encounter should also be assigned for a patient who delayed seeking treatment for the fracture or nonunion.

The open fracture designations in the assignment of the 7th character for fractures of the forearm, femur and lower leg, including ankle are based on the Gustilo open fracture classification. When the Gustilo classification type is not specified for an open fracture, the 7th character for open fracture type I or II should be assigned (B, E, H, M, Q).

A code from category M80, not a traumatic fracture code, should be used for any patient with known osteoporosis who suffers a fracture, even if the patient had a minor fall or trauma, if that fall or trauma would not usually break a normal, healthy bone.

See Section I.C.13. Osteoporosis.

The aftercare Z codes should not be used for aftercare for traumatic fractures. For aftercare of a traumatic fracture, assign the acute fracture code with the appropriate 7th character.

2) Multiple fractures sequencing

Multiple fractures are sequenced in accordance with the severity of the fracture.

3) Physeal fractures

For physeal fractures, assign only the code identifying the type of physeal fracture. Do not assign a separate code to identify the specific bone that is fractured.

d. Coding of Burns and Corrosions

The ICD-10-CM makes a distinction between burns and corrosions. The burn codes are for thermal burns, except sunburns, that come from a heat source, such as a fire or hot appliance. The burn codes are also for burns resulting from electricity and radiation. Corrosions are burns due to chemicals. The guidelines are the same for burns and corrosions.

Current burns (T20-T25) are classified by depth, extent and by agent (X code). Burns are classified by depth as first degree (erythema), second degree (blistering), and third degree (full-thickness involvement). Burns of the eye and internal organs (T26-T28) are classified by site, but not by degree.

1) Sequencing of burn and related condition codes

Sequence first the code that reflects the highest degree of burn when more than one burn is present.

   a. When the reason for the admission or encounter is for treatment of external multiple burns, sequence first the code that reflects the burn of the highest degree.

   b. When a patient has both internal and external burns, the circumstances of admission govern the selection of the principal diagnosis or first-listed diagnosis.

   c. When a patient is admitted for burn injuries and other related conditions such as smoke inhalation and/or respiratory failure, the circumstances of admission govern the selection of the principal or first-listed diagnosis.

2) Burns of the same anatomic site

Classify burns of the same anatomic site and on the same side but of different degrees to the subcategory identifying the highest degree recorded in the diagnosis (e.g., for second and third degree burns of right thigh, assign only code T24.311-).

3) Non-healing burns

Non-healing burns are coded as acute burns.

Necrosis of burned skin should be coded as a non-healed burn.

4) Infected burn

For any documented infected burn site, use an additional code for the infection.

5) Assign separate codes for each burn site

When coding burns, assign separate codes for each burn site. Category T30, Burn and corrosion, body region unspecified is extremely vague and should rarely be used.

Codes for burns of "multiple sites" should only be assigned when the medical record documentation does not specify the individual sites.

6) Burns and corrosions classified according to extent of body surface involved

Assign codes from category T31, Burns classified according to extent of body surface involved, or T32, Corrosions classified according to extent of body surface involved, when the site of the burn is not specified or when there is a need for additional data. It is advisable to use category T31 as additional coding when needed to provide data for evaluating burn mortality, such as that needed by burn units. It is also advisable to use category T31 as an additional code for reporting purposes when there is mention of a third-degree burn involving 2Ø percent or more of the body surface.

Categories T31 and T32 are based on the classic "rule of nines" in estimating body surface involved: head and neck are assigned nine percent, each arm nine percent, each leg 18 percent, the anterior trunk 18 percent, posterior trunk 18 percent, and genitalia 1 percent. Providers may change these percentage assignments where necessary to accommodate infants and children who have proportionately larger heads than adults, and patients who have large buttocks, thighs, or abdomen that involve burns.

7) Encounters for treatment of sequela of burns

Encounters for the treatment of the late effects of burns or corrosions (i.e., scars or joint contractures) should be coded with a burn or corrosion code with the 7th character "S" for sequela.

8) Sequelae with a late effect code and current burn

When appropriate, both a code for a current burn or corrosion with 7th character "A" or "D" and a burn or corrosion code with 7th character "S" may be assigned on the same record (when both a current burn and sequelae of an old burn exist). Burns and corrosions do not heal at the same rate and a current healing wound may still exist with sequela of a healed burn or corrosion.

See Section I.B.1Ø. Sequela, (Late Effects)

9) Use of an external cause code with burns and corrosions

An external cause code should be used with burns and corrosions to identify the source and intent of the burn, as well as the place where it occurred.

e. Adverse Effects, Poisoning, Underdosing and Toxic Effects

Codes in categories T36-T65 are combination codes that include the substance that was taken as well as the intent. No additional external cause code is required for poisonings, toxic effects, adverse effects and underdosing codes.

1) Do not code directly from the Table of Drugs

Do not code directly from the Table of Drugs and Chemicals. Always refer back to the Tabular List.

2) Use as many codes as necessary to describe

Use as many codes as necessary to describe completely all drugs, medicinal or biological substances.

3) If the same code would describe the causative agent

If the same code would describe the causative agent for more than one adverse reaction, poisoning, toxic effect or underdosing, assign the code only once.

4) If two or more drugs, medicinal or biological substances

If two or more drugs, medicinal or biological substances are taken, code each individually unless a combination code is listed in the Table of Drugs and Chemicals.

If multiple unspecified drugs, medicinal or biological substances were taken, assign the appropriate code from subcategory T5Ø.91, Poisoning by, adverse effect of and underdosing of multiple unspecified drugs, medicaments and biological substances.

5) The occurrence of drug toxicity is classified in ICD-1Ø-CM as follows:

(a) Adverse Effect

When coding an adverse effect of a drug that has been correctly prescribed and properly administered, assign the appropriate code for the nature of the adverse effect followed by the appropriate code for the adverse effect of the drug (T36-T5Ø). The code for the drug should have a 5th or 6th character "5" (for example T36.ØX5-) Examples of the nature of an adverse effect are tachycardia, delirium, gastrointestinal hemorrhaging, vomiting, hypokalemia, hepatitis, renal failure, or respiratory failure.

(b) Poisoning

When coding a poisoning or reaction to the improper use of a medication (e.g., overdose, wrong substance given or taken in error, wrong route of administration), first assign the appropriate code from categories T36-T5Ø. The poisoning codes have an associated intent as their 5th or 6th character (accidental, intentional self-harm, assault and undetermined). If the intent of the poisoning is unknown or unspecified, code the intent as accidental intent. The undetermined intent is only for use if the documentation in the record specifies that the intent cannot be determined. Use additional code(s) for all manifestations of poisonings.

If there is also a diagnosis of abuse or dependence of the substance, the abuse or dependence is assigned as an additional code.

Examples of poisoning include:

(i) Error was made in drug prescription Errors made in drug prescription or in the administration of the drug by provider, nurse, patient, or other person.

(ii) Overdose of a drug intentionally taken If an overdose of a drug was intentionally taken or administered and resulted in drug toxicity, it would be coded as a poisoning.

(iii) Nonprescribed drug taken with correctly prescribed and properly administered drug.

If a nonprescribed drug or medicinal agent was taken in combination with a correctly prescribed and properly administered drug, any drug toxicity or other reaction resulting from the interaction of the two drugs would be classified as a poisoning.

(iv) Interaction of drug(s) and alcohol. When a reaction results from the interaction of a drug(s) and alcohol, this would be classified as poisoning.

See Section I.C.4. if poisoning is the result of insulin pump malfunctions.

(c) Underdosing

Underdosing refers to taking less of a medication than is prescribed by a provider or a manufacturer's instruction. Discontinuing the use of a prescribed medication on the patient's own initiative (not directed by the patient's provider) is also classified as an underdosing. For underdosing, assign the code from categories T36-T50 (5th or 6th character "6").

Codes for underdosing should never be assigned as principal or first-listed codes. If a patient has a relapse or exacerbation of the medical condition for which the drug is prescribed because of the reduction in dose, then the medical condition itself should be coded.

Noncompliance (Z91.12-, Z91.13- and Z91.14-) or complication of care (Y63.6-Y63.9) codes are to be used with an underdosing code to indicate intent, if known.

(d) Toxic Effects

When a harmful substance is ingested or comes in contact with a person, this is classified as a toxic effect. The toxic effect codes are in categories T51-T65.

Toxic effect codes have an associated intent: accidental, intentional self-harm, assault and undetermined.

f. Adult and child abuse, neglect and other maltreatment

Sequence first the appropriate code from categories T74 (Adult and child abuse, neglect and other maltreatment, confirmed) or T76 (Adult and child abuse, neglect and other maltreatment, suspected) for abuse, neglect and other maltreatment, followed by any accompanying mental health or injury code(s).

If the documentation in the medical record states abuse or neglect it is coded as confirmed (T74.-). It is coded as suspected if it is documented as suspected (T76.-).

For cases of confirmed abuse or neglect an external cause code from the assault section (X92-Y09) should be added to identify the cause of any physical injuries. A perpetrator code (Y07)

should be added when the perpetrator of the abuse is known. For suspected cases of abuse or neglect, do not report external cause or perpetrator code.

If a suspected case of abuse, neglect or mistreatment is ruled out during an encounter code Z04.71, Encounter for examination and observation following alleged physical adult abuse, ruled out, or code Z04.72, Encounter for examination and observation following alleged child physical abuse, ruled out, should be used, not a code from T76.

If a suspected case of alleged rape or sexual abuse is ruled out during an encounter code Z04.41, Encounter for examination and observation following alleged adult rape or code Z04.42, Encounter for examination and observation following alleged child rape, should be used, not a code from T76.

If a suspected case of forced sexual exploitation or forced labor exploitation is ruled out during an encounter, code Z04.81, Encounter for examination and observation of victim following forced sexual exploitation, or code Z04.82, Encounter for examination and observation of victim following forced labor exploitation, should be used, not a code from T76.

See Section I.C.15. Abuse in a pregnant patient.

g. Complications of care

1) General guidelines for complications of care

(a) Documentation of complications of care

See Section I.B.16. for information on documentation of complications of care.

2) Pain due to medical devices

Pain associated with devices, implants or grafts left in a surgical site (for example painful hip prosthesis) is assigned to the appropriate code(s) found in Chapter 19, Injury, poisoning, and certain other consequences of external causes. Specific codes for pain due to medical devices are found in the T code section of the ICD-10-CM. Use additional code(s) from category G89 to identify acute or chronic pain due to presence of the device, implant or graft (G89.18 or G89.28).

3) Transplant complications

(a) Transplant complications other than kidney

Codes under category T86, Complications of transplanted organs and tissues, are for use for both complications and rejection of transplanted organs. A transplant complication code is only assigned if the complication affects the function of the transplanted organ. Two codes are required to fully describe a transplant complication: the appropriate code from category T86 and a secondary code that identifies the complication.

Pre-existing conditions or conditions that develop after the transplant are not coded as complications unless they affect the function of the transplanted organs.

See Section I.C.21. for transplant organ removal status
See Section I.C.2. for malignant neoplasm associated with transplanted organ.

(b) Kidney transplant complications

Patients who have undergone kidney transplant may still have some form of chronic kidney disease (CKD) because the kidney transplant may not fully restore kidney function. Code T86.1- should be assigned for documented complications of a kidney transplant, such as transplant failure or rejection or other transplant complication. Code T86.1- should not be assigned for post kidney transplant patients who have chronic kidney (CKD) unless a transplant complication such as transplant failure or rejection is documented. If the documentation is unclear as to whether the patient has a complication of the transplant, query the provider.

Conditions that affect the function of the transplanted kidney, other than CKD, should be assigned a code from subcategory T86.1, Complications of transplanted organ, Kidney, and a secondary code that identifies the complication.

For patients with CKD following a kidney transplant, but who do not have a complication such as failure or rejection, *see Section I.C.14. Chronic kidney disease and kidney transplant status.*

4) Complication codes that include the external cause

As with certain other T codes, some of the complications of care codes have the external cause included in the code. The code includes the nature of the complication as well as the type of procedure that caused the complication. No external cause code indicating the type of procedure is necessary for these codes.

5) Complications of care codes within the body system chapters

Intraoperative and postprocedural complication codes are found within the body system chapters with codes specific to the organs and structures of that body system. These codes should be sequenced first, followed by a code(s) for the specific complication, if applicable.

Complication codes from the body system chapters should be assigned for intraoperative and postprocedural complications (e.g., the appropriate complication code from Chapter 9 would be assigned for a vascular intraoperative or postprocedural complication) unless the complication is specifically indexed to a T code in Chapter 19.

20. Chapter 20: External Causes of Morbidity (V00-Y99)

The external causes of morbidity codes should never be sequenced as the first-listed or principal diagnosis.

External cause codes are intended to provide data for injury research and evaluation of injury prevention strategies. These codes capture how the injury or health condition happened (cause), the intent (unintentional or accidental; or intentional, such as suicide or assault), the place where the event occurred the activity of the patient at the time of the event, and the person's status (e.g., civilian, military).

There is no national requirement for mandatory ICD-10-CM external cause code reporting. Unless a provider is subject to a state-based external cause code reporting mandate or these codes are required by a particular payer, reporting of ICD-10-CM codes in Chapter 20, External Causes of Morbidity, is not required. In the absence of a mandatory reporting requirement, providers are encouraged to voluntarily report external cause codes, as they provide valuable data for injury research and evaluation of injury prevention strategies.

a. General External Cause Coding Guidelines

1) Used with any code in the range of A00.0-T88.9, Z00-Z99

An external cause code may be used with any code in the range of A00.0-T88.9, Z00-Z99, classification that represents a health condition due to an external cause. Though they are most applicable to injuries, they are also valid for use with such things as infections or diseases due to an external source, and other health conditions, such as a heart attack that occurs during strenuous physical activity.

2) External cause code used for length of treatment

Assign the external cause code, with the appropriate 7th character (initial encounter, subsequent encounter or sequela) for each encounter for which the injury or condition is being treated.

Most categories in Chapter 20 have a 7th character requirement for each applicable code. Most categories in this chapter have three 7th character values: A, initial encounter, D, subsequent encounter and S, sequela. While the patient may be seen by a new or different provider over the course of treatment for an injury or condition, assignment of the 7th character for external cause should match the 7th character of the code assigned for the associated injury or condition for the encounter.

3) Use the full range of external cause codes

Use the full range of external cause codes to completely describe the cause, the intent, the place of occurrence and if applicable, the activity of the patient at the time of the event, and the patient's status, for all injuries, and other health conditions due to an external cause.

4) Assign as many external cause codes as necessary

Assign as many external cause codes as necessary to fully explain each cause. If only one external code can be recorded, assign the code most related to the principal diagnosis.

5) The selection of the appropriate external cause code

The selection of the appropriate external cause code is guided by the Alphabetic Index of External Causes and by Inclusion and Exclusion notes in the Tabular List.

6) External cause code can never be a principal diagnosis

An external cause code can never be a principal (first-listed) diagnosis.

7) Combination external cause codes

Certain of the external cause codes are combination codes that identify sequential events that result in an injury, such as a fall which results in striking against an object. The injury may be due to either event or both. The combination external cause code used should correspond to the sequence of events regardless of which caused the most serious injury.

8) No external cause code needed in certain circumstances

No external cause code from Chapter 2Ø is needed if the external cause and intent are included in a code from another chapter (e.g., T36.ØX1- Poisoning by penicillins, accidental (unintentional)).

b. Place of Occurrence Guideline

Codes from category Y92, Place of occurrence of the external cause, are secondary codes for use after other external cause codes to identify the location of the patient at the time of injury or other condition.

Generally, a place of occurrence code is assigned only once, at the initial encounter for treatment. However, in the rare instance that a new injury occurs during hospitalization, an additional place of occurrence code may be assigned. No 7th characters are used for Y92. Only one code from Y92 should be recorded on a medical record.

Do not use place of occurrence code Y92.9 if the place is not stated or is not applicable.

c. Activity Code

Assign a code from category Y93, Activity code, to describe the activity of the patient at the time the injury or other health condition occurred.

An activity code is used only once, at the initial encounter for treatment. Only one code from Y93 should be recorded on a medical record.

The activity codes are not applicable to poisonings, adverse effects, misadventures or sequela.

Do not assign Y93.9, Unspecified activity, if the activity is not stated.

A code from category Y93 is appropriate for use with external cause and intent codes if identifying the activity provides additional information about the event.

d. Place of Occurrence, Activity, and Status Codes Used with other External Cause Code

When applicable, place of occurrence, activity, and external cause status codes are sequenced after the main external cause code(s). Regardless of the number of external cause codes assigned, there should be only one place of occurrence code, one activity code, and one external cause status code assigned to an encounter.

e. If the Reporting Format Limits the Number of External Cause Codes

If the reporting format limits the number of external cause codes that can be used in reporting clinical data, report the code for the cause/intent most related to the principal diagnosis. If the format permits capture of additional external cause codes, the cause/intent, including medical misadventures,

of the additional events should be reported rather than the codes for place, activity, or external status.

f. Multiple External Cause Coding Guidelines

More than one external cause code is required to fully describe the external cause of an illness or injury. The assignment of external cause codes should be sequenced in the following priority:

If two or more events cause separate injuries, an external cause code should be assigned for each cause. The first-listed external cause code will be selected in the following order:

External codes for child and adult abuse take priority over all other external cause codes.
See Section I.C.19., Child and Adult abuse guidelines.

External codes for terrorism events take priority over all other external cause codes except child and adult abuse.

External cause codes for cataclysmic events take priority over all other external cause codes except child and adult abuse and terrorism.

External cause codes for transport accidents take priority over all other external cause codes except cataclysmic events, child and adult abuse and terrorism.

Activity and external cause status codes are assigned following all causal (intent) external cause codes.

The first-listed external cause code should correspond to the cause of the most serious diagnosis due to an assault, accident, or self-harm, following the order of hierarchy listed above.

g. Child and Adult Abuse Guideline

Adult and child abuse, neglect and maltreatment are classified as assault. Any of the assault codes may be used to indicate the external cause of any injury resulting from the confirmed abuse.

For confirmed cases of abuse, neglect and maltreatment, when the perpetrator is known, a code from YØ7, Perpetrator of maltreatment and neglect, should accompany any other assault codes.
See Section I.C.19. Adult and child abuse, neglect and other maltreatment

h. Unknown or Undetermined Intent Guideline

If the intent (accident, self-harm, assault) of the cause of an injury or other condition is unknown or unspecified, code the intent as accidental intent. All transport accident categories assume accidental intent.

1) Use of undetermined intent

External cause codes for events of undetermined intent are only for use if the documentation in the record specifies that the intent cannot be determined.

i. Sequelae (Late Effects) of External Cause Guidelines

1) Sequelae external cause codes

Sequela are reported using the external cause code with the 7th character "S" for sequela. These codes should be used with any report of a late effect or sequela resulting from a previous injury.
See Section I.B.1Ø. Sequela (Late Effects)

2) Sequela external cause code with a related current injury

A sequela external cause code should never be used with a related current nature of injury code.

3) Use of sequela external cause codes for subsequent visits

Use a late effect external cause code for subsequent visits when a late effect of the initial injury is being treated. Do not use a late effect external cause code for subsequent visits for follow-up care (e.g., to assess healing, to receive rehabilitative therapy) of the injury when no late effect of the injury has been documented.

j. Terrorism Guidelines

1) Cause of injury identified by the Federal Government (FBI) as terrorism

When the cause of an injury is identified by the Federal Government (FBI) as terrorism, the first-listed external cause code should be a code from category Y38, Terrorism. The definition of terrorism employed by the FBI is found at the inclusion note at the beginning of category Y38. Use additional code for place of occurrence (Y92.-). More than one Y38 code may be assigned if the injury is the result of more than one mechanism of terrorism.

2) Cause of an injury is suspected to be the result of terrorism

When the cause of an injury is suspected to be the result of terrorism a code from category Y38 should not be assigned. Suspected cases should be classified as assault.

3) Code Y38.9, Terrorism, secondary effects

Assign code Y38.9, Terrorism, secondary effects, for conditions occurring subsequent to the terrorist event. This code should not be assigned for conditions that are due to the initial terrorist act.

It is acceptable to assign code Y38.9 with another code from Y38 if there is an injury due to the initial terrorist event and an injury that is a subsequent result of the terrorist event.

k. External Cause Status

A code from category Y99, External cause status, should be assigned whenever any other external cause code is assigned for an encounter, including an Activity code, except for the events noted below. Assign a code from category Y99, External cause status, to indicate the work status of the person at the time the event occurred. The status code indicates whether the event occurred during military activity, whether a non-military person was at work, whether an individual including a student or volunteer was involved in a non-work activity at the time of the causal event.

A code from Y99, External cause status, should be assigned, when applicable, with other external cause codes, such as transport accidents and falls. The external cause status codes are not applicable to poisonings, adverse effects, misadventures or late effects.

Do not assign a code from category Y99 if no other external cause codes (cause, activity) are applicable for the encounter.

An external cause status code is used only once, at the initial encounter for treatment. Only one code from Y99 should be recorded on a medical record.

Do not assign code Y99.9, Unspecified external cause status, if the status is not stated.

21. Chapter 21: Factors Influencing Health Status and Contact with Health Services (Z00-Z99)

Note: The chapter-specific guidelines provide additional information about the use of Z codes for specified encounters.

a. Use of Z Codes in Any Healthcare Setting

Z codes are for use in any healthcare setting. Z codes may be used as either a first-listed (principal diagnosis code in the inpatient setting) or secondary code, depending on the circumstances of the encounter. Certain Z codes may only be used as first-listed or principal diagnosis.

b. Z Codes Indicate a Reason for an Encounter

Z codes are not procedure codes. A corresponding procedure code must accompany a Z code to describe any procedure performed.

c. Categories of Z Codes

1) Contact/Exposure

Category Z20 indicates contact with, and suspected exposure to, communicable diseases. These codes are for patients who are suspected to have been exposed to a disease by close personal contact with an infected individual or are in an area where a disease is epidemic.

Category Z77, Other contact with and (suspected) exposures hazardous to health, indicates contact with and suspected exposures hazardous to health.

Contact/exposure codes may be used as a first-listed code to explain an encounter for testing, or, more commonly, as a secondary code to identify a potential risk.

2) Inoculations and vaccinations

Code Z23 is for encounters for inoculations and vaccinations. It indicates that a patient is being seen to receive a prophylactic inoculation against a disease. Procedure codes are required to identify the actual administration of the injection and the type(s) of immunizations given. Code Z23 may be used as a secondary code if the inoculation is given as a routine part of preventive health care, such as a well-baby visit.

3) Status

Status codes indicate that a patient is either a carrier of a disease or has the sequelae or residual of a past disease or condition. This includes such things as the presence of prosthetic or mechanical devices resulting from past treatment. A status code is informative, because the status may affect the course of treatment and its outcome. A status code is distinct from a history code. The history code indicates that the patient no longer has the condition.

A status code should not be used with a diagnosis code from one of the body system chapters, if the diagnosis code includes the information provided by the status code. For example, code Z94.1, Heart transplant status, should not be used with a code from subcategory T86.2, Complications of heart transplant. The status code does not provide additional information. The complication code indicates that the patient is a heart transplant patient.

For encounters for weaning from a mechanical ventilator, assign a code from subcategory J96.1, Chronic respiratory failure, followed by code Z99.11, Dependence on respirator [ventilator] status.

The status Z codes/categories are:

Z14   Genetic carrier
Genetic carrier status indicates that a person carries a gene, associated with a particular disease, which may be passed to offspring who may develop that disease. The person does not have the disease and is not at risk of developing the disease.

Z15   Genetic susceptibility to disease Genetic susceptibility indicates that a person has a gene that increases the risk of that person developing the disease.

Codes from category Z15 should not be used as principal or first-listed codes. If the patient has the condition to which he/she is susceptible, and that condition is the reason for the encounter, the code for the current condition should be sequenced first. If the patient is being seen for follow-up after completed treatment for this condition, and the condition no longer exists, a follow-up code should be sequenced first, followed by the appropriate personal history and genetic susceptibility codes. If the purpose of the encounter is genetic counseling associated with procreative management, code Z31.5, Encounter for genetic counseling, should be assigned as the first-listed code, followed by a code from category Z15. Additional codes should be assigned for any applicable family or personal history.

Z16   Resistance to antimicrobial drugs
This code indicates that a patient has a condition that is resistant to antimicrobial drug treatment. Sequence the infection code first.

Z17   Estrogen receptor status
Z18   Retained foreign body fragments
Z19   Hormone sensitivity malignancy status
Z21   Asymptomatic HIV infection status This code indicates that a patient has tested positive for HIV but has manifested no signs or symptoms of the disease.

Z22   Carrier of infectious disease Carrier status indicates that a person harbors the specific organisms of a disease without manifest symptoms and is capable of transmitting the infection.

Z28.3   Underimmunization status
Z33.1   Pregnant state, incidental This code is a secondary code only for use when the pregnancy is in no way complicating the reason for visit. Otherwise, a code from the obstetric chapter is required.

Z66   Do not resuscitate
This code may be used when it is documented by the provider that a patient is on do not resuscitate status at any time during the stay.

Z67   Blood type
Z68   Body mass index (BMI)
BMI codes should only be assigned when there is an associated reportable diagnosis (such as obesity). Do not assign BMI codes during pregnancy.

See Section I.B.14 for BMI documentation by clinicians other than the patient's provider.

Z74.01   Bed confinement status
Z76.82   Awaiting organ transplant status
Z78   Other specified health status
Code Z78.1, Physical restraint status, may be used when it is documented by the provider that a patient has been put in restraints during the current encounter. Please note that this code should not be reported when it is documented by the provider that a patient is temporarily restrained during a procedure.

Z79   Long-term (current) drug therapy
Codes from this category indicate a patient's continuous use of a prescribed drug (including such things as aspirin therapy) for the long-term treatment of a condition or for prophylactic use. It is not for use for patients who have addictions to drugs. This subcategory is not for use of medications for detoxification or maintenance programs to prevent withdrawal symptoms (e.g., methadone maintenance for opiate dependence). Assign the appropriate code for the drug **use, abuse, or** dependence instead.

Assign a code from Z79 if the patient is receiving a medication for an extended period as a prophylactic measure (such as for the prevention of deep vein thrombosis) or as treatment of a chronic condition (such as arthritis) or a disease requiring a lengthy course of treatment (such as cancer). Do not assign a code from category Z79 for medication being administered for a brief period of time to treat an acute illness or injury (such as a course of antibiotics to treat acute bronchitis).

Z88   Allergy status to drugs, medicaments and biological substances Except: Z88.9, Allergy status to unspecified drugs, medicaments and biological substances status

Z89   Acquired absence of limb
Z90   Acquired absence of organs, not
        elsewhere classified
Z91.0- Allergy status, other than to drugs and
        biological substances
Z92.82 Status post administration of tPA (rtPA)
        in a different facility within the last 24
        hours prior to admission to a current
        facility Assign code Z92.82, Status post
        administration of tPA (rtPA) in a
        different facility within the last 24 hours
        prior to admission to current facility, as a
        secondary diagnosis when a patient is
        received by transfer into a facility and
        documentation indicates they were
        administered tissue plasminogen
        activator (tPA) within the last 24 hours
        prior to admission to the current facility.
        This guideline applies even if the patient
        is still receiving the tPA at the time they
        are received into the current facility. The
        appropriate code for the condition for
        which the tPA was administered (such
        as cerebrovascular disease or myocardial
        infarction) should be assigned first.
        Code Z92.82 is only applicable to the
        receiving facility record and not to the
        transferring facility record.
Z93   Artificial opening status
Z94   Transplanted organ and tissue status
Z95   Presence of cardiac and vascular
        implants and grafts
Z96   Presence of other functional implants
Z97   Presence of other devices
Z98   Other postprocedural states

Assign code Z98.85, Transplanted organ removal status, to indicate that a transplanted organ has been previously removed. This code should not be assigned for the encounter in which the transplanted organ is removed. The complication necessitating removal of the transplant organ should be assigned for that encounter.

See Section I.C.19. for information on the coding of organ transplant complications.

Z99   Dependence on enabling machines and
        devices, not elsewhere classified

Note: Categories Z89-Z90 and Z93-Z99 are for use only if there are no complications or malfunctions of the organ or tissue replaced, the amputation site or the equipment on which the patient is dependent.

4) History (of)

There are two types of history Z codes, personal and family. Personal history codes explain a patient's past medical condition that no longer exists and is not receiving any treatment, but that has the potential for recurrence, and therefore may require continued monitoring.

Family history codes are for use when a patient has a family member(s) who has had a particular disease that causes the patient to be at higher risk of also contracting the disease.

Personal history codes may be used in conjunction with follow-up codes and family history codes may be used in conjunction with screening codes to explain the need for a test or procedure. History codes are also acceptable on any medical record regardless of the reason for visit. A history of an illness, even if no longer present, is important information that may alter the type of treatment ordered.

The history Z code categories are:

Z80   Family history of primary malignant
        neoplasm
Z81   Family history of mental and behavioral
        disorders
Z82   Family history of certain disabilities and
        chronic diseases (leading to
        disablement)
Z83   Family history of other specific
        disorders
Z84   Family history of other conditions
Z85   Personal history of malignant neoplasm
Z86   Personal history of certain other
        diseases
Z87   Personal history of other diseases and
        conditions
Z91.4- Personal history of psychological
        trauma, not elsewhere classified
Z91.5   Personal history of self-harm
Z91.81 History of falling
Z91.82 Personal history of military
        deployment
Z92   Personal history of medical treatment
        Except: Z92.0, Personal history of
        contraception Except: Z92.82, Status
        post administration of tPA (rtPA) in a
        different facility within the last 24 hours
        prior to admission to a current facility

5) Screening

Screening is the testing for disease or disease precursors in seemingly well individuals so that early detection and treatment can be provided for those who test positive for the disease (e.g., screening mammogram).

The testing of a person to rule out or confirm a suspected diagnosis because the patient has some sign or symptom is a diagnostic examination, not a screening. In these cases, the sign or symptom is used to explain the reason for the test.

A screening code may be a first-listed code if the reason for the visit is specifically the screening exam. It may also be used as an additional code if the screening is done during an office visit for other health problems. A screening code is not necessary if the screening is inherent to a routine examination, such as a pap smear done during a routine pelvic examination.

Should a condition be discovered during the screening then the code for the condition may be assigned as an additional diagnosis.

The Z code indicates that a screening exam is planned. A procedure code is required to confirm that the screening was performed.

GUIDELINES (ICD-10-CM)

The screening Z codes/categories:

Z11   Encounter for screening for infectious and parasitic diseases

Z12   Encounter for screening for malignant neoplasms

Z13   Encounter for screening for other diseases and disorders Except: Z13.9, Encounter for screening, unspecified

Z36   Encounter for antenatal screening for mother

6) Observation

There are three observation Z code categories. They are for use in very limited circumstances when a person is being observed for a suspected condition that is ruled out. The observation codes are not for use if an injury or illness or any signs or symptoms related to the suspected condition are present. In such cases the diagnosis/symptom code is used with the corresponding external cause code.

The observation codes are **primarily** to be used as **a** principal/**first-listed** diagnosis. **An observation code may be assigned as a secondary diagnosis code when the patient is being observed for a condition that is ruled out and is unrelated** to the principal/first-listed diagnosis (e.g., patient presents for treatment following injuries sustained in a motor vehicle accident and is also observed for suspected COVID-19 infection that is subsequently ruled out). Also, when the principal diagnosis is required to be a code from category Z38, Liveborn infants according to place of birth and type of delivery, **then** a code from category Z05, Encounter for observation and evaluation of newborn for suspected diseases and conditions ruled out, is sequenced after the Z38 code. Additional codes may be used in addition to the observation code, but only if they are unrelated to the suspected condition being observed.

Codes from subcategory Z03.7 Encounter for suspected maternal and fetal conditions ruled out, may either be used as a first-listed or as an additional code assignment depending on the case. They are for use in very limited circumstances on a maternal record when an encounter is for a suspected maternal or fetal condition that is ruled out during that encounter (for example, a maternal or fetal condition may be suspected due to an abnormal test result). These codes should not be used when the condition is confirmed. In those cases, the confirmed condition should be coded. In addition, these codes are not for use if an illness or any signs or symptoms related to the suspected condition or problem are present. In such cases the diagnosis/symptom code is used.

Additional codes may be used in addition to the code from subcategory Z03.7, but only if they are unrelated to the suspected condition being evaluated.

Codes from subcategory Z03.7 may not be used for encounters for antenatal screening of mother. *See Section I.C.21. Screening.*

For encounters for suspected fetal condition that are inconclusive following testing and evaluation, assign the appropriate code from category O35, O36, O40 or O41.

The observation Z code categories:

Z03   Encounter for medical observation for suspected diseases and conditions ruled out

Z04   Encounter for examination and observation for other reasons Except: Z04.9, Encounter for examination and observation for unspecified reason

Z05   Encounter for observation and evaluation of newborn for suspected diseases and conditions ruled out

7) Aftercare

Aftercare visit codes cover situations when the initial treatment of a disease has been performed and the patient requires continued care during the healing or recovery phase, or for the long-term consequences of the disease. The aftercare Z code should not be used if treatment is directed at a current, acute disease. The diagnosis code is to be used in these cases.

Exceptions to this rule are codes Z51.0, Encounter for antineoplastic radiation therapy, and codes from subcategory Z51.1, Encounter for antineoplastic chemotherapy and immunotherapy. These codes are to be first-listed, followed by the diagnosis code when a patient's encounter is solely to receive radiation therapy, chemotherapy, or immunotherapy for the treatment of a neoplasm. If the reason for the encounter is more than one type of antineoplastic therapy, code Z51.0 and a code from subcategory Z51.1 may be assigned together, in which case one of these codes would be reported as a secondary diagnosis.

The aftercare Z codes should also not be used for aftercare for injuries. For aftercare of an injury, assign the acute injury code with the appropriate 7th character (for subsequent encounter).

The aftercare codes are generally first-listed to explain the specific reason for the encounter. An aftercare code may be used as an additional code when some type of aftercare is provided in addition to the reason for admission and no diagnosis code is applicable. An example of this would be the closure of a colostomy during an encounter for treatment of another condition.

Aftercare codes should be used in conjunction with other aftercare codes or diagnosis codes to provide better detail on the specifics of an aftercare encounter visit, unless otherwise directed by the classification. The sequencing of multiple aftercare codes depends on the circumstances of the encounter.

Certain aftercare Z code categories need a secondary diagnosis code to describe the resolving condition or sequelae. For others, the condition is included in the code title.

Additional Z code aftercare category terms include fitting and adjustment, and attention to artificial openings.

Status Z codes may be used with aftercare Z codes to indicate the nature of the aftercare. For example code Z95.1, Presence of aortocoronary bypass graft, may be used with code Z48.812, Encounter for surgical aftercare following surgery on the circulatory system, to indicate the surgery for which the aftercare is being performed. A status code should not be used when the aftercare code indicates the type of status, such as using Z43.0, Encounter for attention to tracheostomy, with Z93.0, Tracheostomy status.

The aftercare Z category/codes:

Z42 Encounter for plastic and reconstructive surgery following medical procedure or healed injury

Z43 Encounter for attention to artificial openings

Z44 Encounter for fitting and adjustment of external prosthetic device

Z45 Encounter for adjustment and management of implanted device

Z46 Encounter for fitting and adjustment of other devices

Z47 Orthopedic aftercare

Z48 Encounter for other postprocedural aftercare

Z49 Encounter for care involving renal dialysis

Z51 Encounter for other aftercare and medical care

8) Follow-up

The follow-up codes are used to explain continuing surveillance following completed treatment of a disease, condition, or injury. They imply that the condition has been fully treated and no longer exists. They should not be confused with aftercare codes, or injury codes with a 7th character for subsequent encounter, that explain ongoing care of a healing condition or its sequelae. Follow-up codes may be used in conjunction with history codes to provide the full picture of the healed condition and its treatment. The follow-up code is sequenced first, followed by the history code.

A follow-up code may be used to explain multiple visits. Should a condition be found to have recurred on the follow-up visit, then the diagnosis code for the condition should be assigned in place of the follow-up code.

The follow-up Z code categories:

Z08 Encounter for follow-up examination after completed treatment for malignant neoplasm

Z09 Encounter for follow-up examination after completed treatment for conditions other than malignant neoplasm

Z39 Encounter for maternal postpartum care and examination

9) Donor

Codes in category Z52, Donors of organs and tissues, are used for living individuals who are donating blood or other body tissue. These codes are only for individuals donating for others, not for self-donations. They are not used to identify cadaveric donations.

10) Counseling

Counseling Z codes are used when a patient or family member receives assistance in the aftermath of an illness or injury, or when support is required in coping with family or social problems.

The counseling Z codes/categories:

Z30.0- Encounter for general counseling and advice on contraception

Z31.5 Encounter for procreative genetic counseling

Z31.6- Encounter for general counseling and advice on procreation

Z32.2 Encounter for childbirth instruction

Z32.3 Encounter for childcare instruction

Z69 Encounter for mental health services for victim and perpetrator of abuse

Z70 Counseling related to sexual attitude, behavior and orientation

Z71 Persons encountering health services for other counseling and medical advice, not elsewhere classified
Note: Code Z71.84, Encounter for health counseling related to travel, is to be used for health risk and safety counseling for future travel purposes.

Z76.81 Expectant mother prebirth pediatrician visit

11) Encounters for Obstetrical and Reproductive Services

See Section I.C.15. Pregnancy, childbirth, and the puerperium, for further instruction on the use of these codes.

Z codes for pregnancy are for use in those circumstances when none of the problems or complications included in the codes from the Obstetrics chapter exist (a routine prenatal visit or postpartum care). Codes in category Z34, Encounter for supervision of normal pregnancy, are always first listed and are not to be used with any other code from the OB chapter.

Codes in category Z3A, Weeks of gestation, may be assigned to provide additional information about the pregnancy. Category Z3A codes should not be assigned for pregnancies with abortive outcomes (categories O00-O08), elective termination of pregnancy (code Z33.2), nor for postpartum conditions, as category Z3A is not applicable to these conditions. The date of the admission should be used to determine weeks of gestation for inpatient admissions that encompass more than one gestational week.

The outcome of delivery, category Z37, should be included on all maternal delivery records. It is always a secondary code. Codes in category Z37 should not be used on the newborn record.

GUIDELINES (ICD-10-CM)

Z codes for family planning (contraceptive) or procreative management and counseling should be included on an obstetric record either during the pregnancy or the postpartum stage, if applicable.

Z codes/categories for obstetrical and reproductive services:

Z30	Encounter for contraceptive management
Z31	Encounter for procreative management
Z32.2	Encounter for childbirth instruction
Z32.3	Encounter for childcare instruction
Z33	Pregnant state
Z34	Encounter for supervision of normal pregnancy
Z36	Encounter for antenatal screening of mother
Z3A	Weeks of gestation
Z37	Outcome of delivery
Z39	Encounter for maternal postpartum care and examination
Z76.81	Expectant mother prebirth pediatrician visit

12) Newborns and Infants

See Section I.C.16. Newborn (Perinatal) guidelines, for further instruction on the use of these codes.

Newborn Z codes/categories:

Z76.1	Encounter for health supervision and care of foundling
Z00.1-	Encounter for routine child health examination
Z38	Liveborn infants according to place of birth and type of delivery

13) Routine and Administrative Examinations

The Z codes allow for the description of encounters for routine examinations, such as, a general check-up, or, examinations for administrative purposes, such as, a pre-employment physical. The codes are not to be used if the examination is for diagnosis of a suspected condition or for treatment purposes. In such cases the diagnosis code is used. During a routine exam, should a diagnosis or condition be discovered, it should be coded as an additional code. Pre-existing and chronic conditions and history codes may also be included as additional codes as long as the examination is for administrative purposes and not focused on any particular condition.

Some of the codes for routine health examinations distinguish between "with" and "without" abnormal findings. Code assignment depends on the information that is known at the time the encounter is being coded. For example, if no abnormal findings were found during the examination, but the encounter is being coded before test results are back, it is acceptable to assign the code for "without abnormal findings." When assigning a code for "with abnormal findings," additional code(s) should be assigned to identify the specific abnormal finding(s).

Pre-operative examination and pre-procedural laboratory examination Z codes are for use only in those situations when a patient is being cleared for a procedure or surgery and no treatment is given.

The Z codes/categories for routine and administrative examinations:

Z00	Encounter for general examination without complaint, suspected or reported diagnosis
Z01	Encounter for other special examination without complaint, suspected or reported diagnosis
Z02	Encounter for administrative examination Except: Z02.9, Encounter for administrative examinations, unspecified
Z32.0-	Encounter for pregnancy test

14) Miscellaneous Z Codes

The miscellaneous Z codes capture a number of other health care encounters that do not fall into one of the other categories. Certain of these codes identify the reason for the encounter; others are for use as additional codes that provide useful information on circumstances that may affect a patient's care and treatment.

Prophylactic Organ Removal

For encounters specifically for prophylactic removal of an organ (such as prophylactic removal of breasts due to a genetic susceptibility to cancer or a family history of cancer), the principal or first-listed code should be a code from category Z40, Encounter for prophylactic surgery, followed by the appropriate codes to identify the associated risk factor (such as genetic susceptibility or family history).

If the patient has a malignancy of one site and is having prophylactic removal at another site to prevent either a new primary malignancy or metastatic disease, a code for the malignancy should also be assigned in addition to a code from subcategory Z40.0, Encounter for prophylactic surgery for risk factors related to malignant neoplasms. A Z40.0 code should not be assigned if the patient is having organ removal for treatment of a malignancy, such as the removal of the testes for the treatment of prostate cancer.

Miscellaneous Z codes/categories:

Z28	Immunization not carried out Except: Z28.3, Underimmunization status
Z29	Encounter for other prophylactic measures
Z40	Encounter for prophylactic surgery
Z41	Encounter for procedures for purposes other than remedying health state Except: Z41.9, Encounter for procedure for purposes other than remedying health state, unspecified
Z53	Persons encountering health services for specific procedures and treatment, not carried out
Z55	Problems related to education and literacy
Z56	Problems related to employment and unemployment
Z57	Occupational exposure to risk factors

Z58	Problems related to physical environment
Z59	Problems related to housing and economic circumstances
Z60	Problems related to social environment
Z62	Problems related to upbringing
Z63	Other problems related to primary support group, including family circumstances
Z64	Problems related to certain psychosocial circumstances
Z65	Problems related to other psychosocial circumstances
Z72	Problems related to lifestyle Note: These codes should be assigned only when the documentation specifies that the patient has an associated problem
Z73	Problems related to life management difficulty
Z74	Problems related to care provider dependency Except: Z74.01, Bed confinement status
Z75	Problems related to medical facilities and other health care
Z76.0	Encounter for issue of repeat prescription
Z76.3	Healthy person accompanying sick person
Z76.4	Other boarder to healthcare facility
Z76.5	Malingerer [conscious simulation]
Z91.1-	Patient's noncompliance with medical treatment and regimen
Z91.83	Wandering in diseases classified elsewhere
Z91.84-	Oral health risk factors
Z91.89	Other specified personal risk factors, not elsewhere classified

See Section I.B.14 for Z55-Z65 Persons with potential health hazards related to socioeconomic and psychosocial circumstances, documentation by clinicians other than the patient's provider

15) Nonspecific Z Codes

Certain Z codes are so non-specific, or potentially redundant with other codes in the classification, that there can be little justification for their use in the inpatient setting. Their use in the outpatient setting should be limited to those instances when there is no further documentation to permit more precise coding. Otherwise, any sign or symptom or any other reason for visit that is captured in another code should be used.

Nonspecific Z codes/categories:

Z02.9	Encounter for administrative examinations, unspecified
Z04.9	Encounter for examination and observation for unspecified reason
Z13.9	Encounter for screening, unspecified
Z41.9	Encounter for procedure for purposes other than remedying health state, unspecified
Z52.9	Donor of unspecified organ or tissue

Z86.59	Personal history of other mental and behavioral disorders
Z88.9	Allergy status to unspecified drugs, medicaments and biological substances status
Z92.0	Personal history of contraception

16) Z Codes That May Only be Principal/First-Listed Diagnosis

The following Z codes/categories may only be reported as the principal/first-listed diagnosis, except when there are multiple encounters on the same day and the medical records for the encounters are combined:

Z00	Encounter for general examination without complaint, suspected or reported diagnosis Except: Z00.6
Z01	Encounter for other special examination without complaint, suspected or reported diagnosis
Z02	Encounter for administrative examination
Z04	Encounter for examination and observation for other reasons
Z33.2	Encounter for elective termination of pregnancy
Z31.81	Encounter for male factor infertility in female patient
Z31.83	Encounter for assisted reproductive fertility procedure cycle
Z31.84	Encounter for fertility preservation procedure
Z34	Encounter for supervision of normal pregnancy
Z39	Encounter for maternal postpartum care and examination
Z38	Liveborn infants according to place of birth and type of delivery
Z40	Encounter for prophylactic surgery
Z42	Encounter for plastic and reconstructive surgery following medical procedure or healed injury
Z51.0	Encounter for antineoplastic radiation therapy
Z51.1-	Encounter for antineoplastic chemotherapy and immunotherapy
Z52	Donors of organs and tissues Except: Z52.9, Donor of unspecified organ or tissue
Z76.1	Encounter for health supervision and care of foundling
Z76.2	Encounter for health supervision and care of other healthy infant and child
Z99.12	Encounter for respirator [ventilator] dependence during power failure

22. *Chapter 22: Codes for Special Purposes (U00-U85)*

U07.0	**Vaping-related disorder (see Section I.C.10.e., Vaping-related disorders)**
U07.1	**COVID-19 (see Section I.C.1.g.1., COVID-19 infection)**

Section II. Selection of Principal Diagnosis

The circumstances of inpatient admission always govern the selection of principal diagnosis. The principal diagnosis is defined in the Uniform Hospital Discharge Data Set (UHDDS) as "that condition established after study to be chiefly responsible for occasioning the admission of the patient to the hospital for care."

The UHDDS definitions are used by hospitals to report inpatient data elements in a standardized manner. These data elements and their definitions can be found in the July 31, 1985, Federal Register (Vol. 50, No, 147), pp. 31038-40.

Since that time, the application of the UHDDS definitions has been expanded to include all nonoutpatient settings (acute care, short term, long-term care and psychiatric hospitals; home health agencies; rehab facilities; nursing homes, etc. . .). The UHDDS definitions also apply to hospice services (all levels of care).

In determining principal diagnosis, coding conventions in the ICD-10-CM, the Tabular List and Alphabetic Index take precedence over these official coding guidelines.

(See Section I.A., Conventions for the ICD-10-CM)

The importance of consistent, complete documentation in the medical record cannot be overemphasized. Without such documentation the application of all coding guidelines is a difficult, if not impossible, task.

A. Codes for symptoms, signs, and ill-defined conditions

Codes for symptoms, signs, and ill-defined conditions from Chapter 18 are not to be used as principal diagnosis when a related definitive diagnosis has been established.

B. Two or more interrelated conditions, each potentially meeting the definition for principal diagnosis.

When there are two or more interrelated conditions (such as diseases in the same ICD-10-CM chapter or manifestations characteristically associated with a certain disease) potentially meeting the definition of principal diagnosis, either condition may be sequenced first, unless the circumstances of the admission, the therapy provided, the Tabular List, or the Alphabetic Index indicate otherwise.

C. Two or more diagnoses that equally meet the definition for principal diagnosis

In the unusual instance when two or more diagnoses equally meet the criteria for principal diagnosis as determined by the circumstances of admission, diagnostic workup and/or therapy provided, and the Alphabetic Index, Tabular List, or another coding guidelines does not provide sequencing direction, any one of the diagnoses may be sequenced first.

D. Two or more comparative or contrasting conditions.

In those rare instances when two or more contrasting or comparative diagnoses are documented as "either/or" (or similar terminology), they are coded as if the diagnoses were confirmed and the diagnoses are sequenced according to the circumstances of the admission. If no further determination can be made as to which diagnosis should be principal, either diagnosis may be sequenced first.

E. A symptom(s) followed by contrasting/comparative diagnoses

GUIDELINE HAS BEEN DELETED EFFECTIVE OCTOBER 1, 2014

F. Original treatment plan not carried out

Sequence as the principal diagnosis the condition, which after study occasioned the admission to the hospital, even though treatment may not have been carried out due to unforeseen circumstances.

G. Complications of surgery and other medical care

When the admission is for treatment of a complication resulting from surgery or other medical care, the complication code is sequenced as the principal diagnosis. If the complication is classified to the T80-T88 series and the code lacks the necessary specificity in describing the complication, an additional code for the specific complication should be assigned.

H. Uncertain Diagnosis

If the diagnosis documented at the time of discharge is qualified as "probable," "suspected," "likely," "questionable," "possible," or "still to be ruled out," "compatible with," "consistent with," or other similar terms indicating uncertainty, code the condition as if it existed or was established. The bases for these guidelines are the diagnostic workup, arrangements for further workup or observation, and initial therapeutic approach that correspond most closely with the established diagnosis.

Note: This guideline is applicable only to inpatient admissions to short-term, acute, long-term care and psychiatric hospitals.

I. Admission from Observation Unit

1. Admission Following Medical Observation

When a patient is admitted to an observation unit for a medical condition, which either worsens or does not improve, and is subsequently admitted as an inpatient of the same hospital for this same medical condition, the principal diagnosis would be the medical condition which led to the hospital admission.

2. Admission Following Post-Operative Observation

When a patient is admitted to an observation unit to monitor a condition (or complication) that develops following outpatient surgery, and then is subsequently admitted as an inpatient of the same hospital, hospitals should apply the Uniform Hospital Discharge Data Set (UHDDS) definition of principal diagnosis as "that condition established after study to be chiefly responsible for occasioning the admission of the patient to the hospital for care."

J. Admission from Outpatient Surgery

When a patient receives surgery in the hospital's outpatient surgery department and is subsequently admitted for continuing inpatient care at the same hospital, the following guidelines should be followed in selecting the principal diagnosis for the inpatient admission:

- If the reason for the inpatient admission is a complication, assign the complication as the principal diagnosis.
- If no complication, or other condition, is documented as the reason for the inpatient admission, assign the reason for the outpatient surgery as the principal diagnosis.
- If the reason for the inpatient admission is another condition unrelated to the surgery, assign the unrelated condition as the principal diagnosis.

K. Admissions/Encounters for Rehabilitation

When the purpose for the admission/encounter is rehabilitation, sequence first the code for the condition for which the service is being performed. For example, for an admission/encounter for rehabilitation for right-sided dominant hemiplegia following a cerebrovascular infarction, report code I69.351, Hemiplegia and hemiparesis following cerebral infarction affecting right dominant side, as the first-listed or principal diagnosis.

If the condition for which the rehabilitation service is no longer present, report the appropriate aftercare code as the first-listed or principal diagnosis, unless the rehabilitation service is being provided following an injury. For rehabilitation services following active treatment of an injury, assign the injury code with the appropriate seventh character for subsequent encounter as the first-listed or principal diagnosis. For example, if a patient with severe degenerative osteoarthritis of the hip, underwent hip replacement and the current encounter/admission is for rehabilitation, report code Z47.1, Aftercare following joint replacement surgery, as the first-listed or principal diagnosis. If the patient requires rehabilitation post hip replacement for right intertrochanteric femur fracture, report code S72.141D, Displaced intertrochanteric fracture of right femur, subsequent encounter for closed fracture with routine healing, as the first-listed or principal diagnosis.

See Section I.C.21.c.7, Factors influencing health states and contact with health services, Aftercare.

See Section I.C.19.a, for additional information about the use of 7th characters for injury codes.

Section III. Reporting Additional Diagnoses

GENERAL RULES FOR OTHER (ADDITIONAL) DIAGNOSES

For reporting purposes the definition for "other diagnoses" is interpreted as additional conditions that affect patient care in terms of requiring:

clinical evaluation; or

therapeutic treatment; or

diagnostic procedures; or

extended length of hospital stay; or

increased nursing care and/or monitoring.

The UHDDS item #11-b defines Other Diagnoses as "all conditions that coexist at the time of admission, that

develop subsequently, or that affect the treatment received and/or the length of stay. Diagnoses that relate to an earlier episode which have no bearing on the current hospital stay are to be excluded." UHDDS definitions apply to inpatients in acute care, short-term, long term care and psychiatric hospital setting. The UHDDS definitions are used by acute care short-term hospitals to report inpatient data elements in a standardized manner. These data elements and their definitions can be found in the July 31, 1985, Federal Register (Vol. 50, No, 147), pp. 31038-40.

Since that time, the application of the UHDDS definitions has been expanded to include all nonoutpatient settings (acute care, short term, long term care and psychiatric hospitals; home health agencies; rehab facilities; nursing homes, etc. . .). The UHDDS definitions also apply to hospice services (all levels of care).

The following guidelines are to be applied in designating "other diagnoses" when neither the Alphabetic Index nor the Tabular List in ICD-10-CM provide direction. The listing of the diagnoses in the patient record is the responsibility of the attending provider.

A. Previous conditions

If the provider has included a diagnosis in the final diagnostic statement, such as the discharge summary or the face sheet, it should ordinarily be coded. Some providers include in the diagnostic statement resolved conditions or diagnoses and status-post procedures from previous admissions that have no bearing on the current stay. Such conditions are not to be reported and are coded only if required by hospital policy.

However, history codes (categories Z80-Z87) may be used as secondary codes if the historical condition or family history has an impact on current care or influences treatment.

B. Abnormal findings

Abnormal findings (laboratory, x-ray, pathologic, and other diagnostic results) are not coded and reported unless the provider indicates their clinical significance. If the findings are outside the normal range and the attending provider has ordered other tests to evaluate the condition or prescribed treatment, it is appropriate to ask the provider whether the abnormal finding should be added.

Please note: This differs from the coding practices in the outpatient setting for coding encounters for diagnostic tests that have been interpreted by a provider.

C. Uncertain Diagnosis

If the diagnosis documented at the time of discharge is qualified as "probable," "suspected," "likely," "questionable," "possible," or "still to be ruled out," "compatible with," "consistent with," or other similar terms indicating uncertainty, code the condition as if it existed or was established. The bases for these guidelines are the diagnostic workup, arrangements for further workup or observation, and initial therapeutic approach that correspond most closely with the established diagnosis.

Note: This guideline is applicable only to inpatient admissions to short-term, acute, long-term care and psychiatric hospitals.

Section IV. Diagnostic Coding and Reporting Guidelines for Outpatient Services

These coding guidelines for outpatient diagnoses have been approved for use by hospitals/ providers in coding and reporting hospital-based outpatient services and provider-based office visits. Guidelines in Section I, Conventions, general coding guidelines and chapter-specific guidelines, should also be applied for outpatient services and office visits.

Information about the use of certain abbreviations, punctuation, symbols, and other conventions used in the ICD-10-CM Tabular List (code numbers and titles), can be found in Section IA of these guidelines, under "Conventions Used in the Tabular List." Section I.B. contains general guidelines that apply to the entire classification. Section I.C. contains chapter-specific guidelines that correspond to the chapters as they are arranged in the classification. Information about the correct sequence to use in finding a code is also described in Section I.

The terms encounter and visit are often used interchangeably in describing outpatient service contacts and, therefore, appear together in these guidelines without distinguishing one from the other.

Though the conventions and general guidelines apply to all settings, coding guidelines for outpatient and provider reporting of diagnoses will vary in a number of instances from those for inpatient diagnoses, recognizing that:

The Uniform Hospital Discharge Data Set (UHDDS) definition of principal diagnosis does not apply to hospital-based outpatient services and provider-based office visits.

Coding guidelines for inconclusive diagnoses (probable, suspected, rule out, etc.) were developed for inpatient reporting and do not apply to outpatients.

A. Selection of first-listed condition

In the outpatient setting, the term first-listed diagnosis is used in lieu of principal diagnosis.

In determining the first-listed diagnosis the coding conventions of ICD-10-CM, as well as the general and disease specific guidelines take precedence over the outpatient guidelines.

Diagnoses often are not established at the time of the initial encounter/visit. It may take two or more visits before the diagnosis is confirmed.

The most critical rule involves beginning the search for the correct code assignment through the Alphabetic Index. Never begin searching initially in the Tabular List as this will lead to coding errors.

1. Outpatient Surgery

When a patient presents for outpatient surgery (same day surgery), code the reason for the surgery as the first-listed diagnosis (reason for the encounter), even if the surgery is not performed due to a contraindication.

2. Observation Stay

When a patient is admitted for observation for a medical condition, assign a code for the medical condition as the first-listed diagnosis.

When a patient presents for outpatient surgery and develops complications requiring admission to observation, code the reason for the surgery as the first reported diagnosis (reason for the encounter), followed by codes for the complications as secondary diagnoses.

B. Codes from A00.0 through T88.9, Z00-Z99

The appropriate code(s) from A00.0 through T88.9, Z00-Z99 must be used to identify diagnoses, symptoms, conditions, problems, complaints, or other reason(s) for the encounter/visit.

C. Accurate reporting of ICD-10-CM diagnosis codes

For accurate reporting of ICD-10-CM diagnosis codes, the documentation should describe the patient's condition, using terminology which includes specific diagnoses as well as symptoms, problems, or reasons for the encounter. There are ICD-10-CM codes to describe all of these.

D. Codes that describe symptoms and signs

Codes that describe symptoms and signs, as opposed to diagnoses, are acceptable for reporting purposes when a diagnosis has not been established (confirmed) by the provider. Chapter 18 of ICD-10-CM, Symptoms, Signs, and Abnormal Clinical and Laboratory Findings Not Elsewhere Classified (codes R00-R99) contains many, but not all codes for symptoms.

E. Encounters for circumstances other than a disease or injury

ICD-10-CM provides codes to deal with encounters for circumstances other than a disease or injury. The Factors Influencing Health Status and Contact with Health Services codes (Z00-Z99) are provided to deal with occasions when circumstances other than a disease or injury are recorded as diagnosis or problems.

See Section I.C.21., Factors influencing health status and contact with health services.

F. Level of Detail in Coding

1. ICD-10-CM codes with 3, 4, 5, 6 or 7 characters

ICD-10-CM is composed of codes with 3, 4, 5, 6 or 7 characters. Codes with three characters are included in ICD-10-CM as the heading of a category of codes that may be further subdivided by the use of 4th, 5th, 6th or 7th characters to provide greater specificity.

2. Use of full number of characters required for a code

A 3-character code is to be used only if it is not further subdivided. A code is invalid if it has not been coded to the full number of characters required for that code, including the 7th character, if applicable.

G. ICD-10-CM code for the diagnosis, condition, problem, or other reason for encounter/visit

List first the ICD-10-CM code for the diagnosis, condition, problem, or other reason for encounter/visit shown in the medical record to be chiefly responsible for the services provided. List additional codes that describe any coexisting conditions. In some cases the first-listed diagnosis may be a symptom when a diagnosis has not been established (confirmed) by the provider.

H. Uncertain diagnosis

Do not code diagnoses documented as "probable," "suspected," "questionable," "ruled out," "compatible with," "consistent with," or "working diagnosis" or other similar terms indicating uncertainty. Rather, code the condition(s) to the highest degree of certainty for that encounter/visit, such as symptoms, signs, abnormal test results, or other reason for the visit.

   Please note: This differs from the coding practices used by short-term, acute care, long-term care and psychiatric hospitals.

I. Chronic diseases

Chronic diseases treated on an ongoing basis may be coded and reported as many times as the patient receives treatment and care for the condition(s)

J. Code all documented conditions that coexist

Code all documented conditions that coexist at the time of the encounter/visit, and require or affect patient care treatment or management. Do not code conditions that were previously treated and no longer exist. However, history codes (categories Z80-Z87) may be used as secondary codes if the historical condition or family history has an impact on current care or influences treatment.

K. Patients receiving diagnostic services only

For patients receiving diagnostic services only during an encounter/visit, sequence first the diagnosis, condition, problem, or other reason for encounter/visit shown in the medical record to be chiefly responsible for the outpatient services provided during the encounter/visit. Codes for other diagnoses (e.g., chronic conditions) may be sequenced as additional diagnoses.

   For encounters for routine laboratory/radiology testing in the absence of any signs, symptoms, or associated diagnosis, assign Z01.89, Encounter for other specified special examinations. If routine testing is performed during the same encounter as a test to evaluate a sign, symptom, or diagnosis, it is appropriate to assign both the Z code and the code describing the reason for the non-routine test.

   For outpatient encounters for diagnostic tests that have been interpreted by a physician, and the final report is available at the time of coding, code any confirmed or definitive diagnosis(es) documented in the interpretation. Do not code related signs and symptoms as additional diagnoses.

   Please note: This differs from the coding practice in the hospital inpatient setting regarding abnormal findings on test results.

L. Patients receiving therapeutic services only

For patients receiving therapeutic services only during an encounter/visit, sequence first the diagnosis, condition, problem, or other reason for encounter/visit shown in the medical record to be chiefly responsible for the outpatient services provided during the encounter/visit. Codes for other diagnoses (e.g., chronic conditions) may be sequenced as additional diagnoses.

   The only exception to this rule is that when the primary reason for the admission/encounter is chemotherapy or radiation therapy, the appropriate Z code for the service is listed first, and the diagnosis or problem for which the service is being performed listed second.

M. Patients receiving preoperative evaluations only

For patients receiving preoperative evaluations only, sequence first a code from subcategory Z01.81, Encounter for pre-procedural examinations, to describe the pre-op consultations. Assign a code for the condition to describe the reason for the surgery as an additional diagnosis. Code also any findings related to the pre-op evaluation.

N. Ambulatory surgery

For ambulatory surgery, code the diagnosis for which the surgery was performed. If the postoperative diagnosis is known to be different from the preoperative diagnosis at the time the diagnosis is confirmed, select the postoperative diagnosis for coding, since it is the most definitive.

O. Routine outpatient prenatal visits

See Section I.C.15., Routine outpatient prenatal visits.

P. Encounters for general medical examinations with abnormal findings

The subcategories for encounters for general medical examinations, Z00.0- and encounter for routine child health examination, Z00.12-, provide codes for with and without abnormal findings. Should a general medical examination result in an abnormal finding, the code for general medical examination with abnormal finding should be assigned as the first-listed diagnosis. An examination with abnormal findings refers to a condition/diagnosis that is newly identified or a change in severity of a chronic condition (such as uncontrolled hypertension, or an acute exacerbation of chronic obstructive pulmonary disease) during a routine physical examination. A secondary code for the abnormal finding should also be coded.

Q. Encounters for routine health screenings

See Section I.C.21., Factors influencing health status and contact with health services, Screening

GUIDELINES (ICD-10-CM)

Appendix I
Present on Admission Reporting Guidelines

Introduction

These guidelines are to be used as a supplement to the *ICD-10-CM Official Guidelines for Coding and Reporting* to facilitate the assignment of the Present on Admission (POA) indicator for each diagnosis and external cause of injury code reported on claim forms (UB-04 and 837 Institutional).

These guidelines are not intended to replace any guidelines in the main body of the *ICD-10-CM Official Guidelines for Coding and Reporting*. The POA guidelines are not intended to provide guidance on when a condition should be coded, but rather, how to apply the POA indicator to the final set of diagnosis codes that have been assigned in accordance with Sections I, II, and III of the official coding guidelines. Subsequent to the assignment of the ICD-10-CM codes, the POA indicator should then be assigned to those conditions that have been coded.

As stated in the Introduction to the ICD-10-CM Official Guidelines for Coding and Reporting, a joint effort between the healthcare provider and the coder is essential to achieve complete and accurate documentation, code assignment, and reporting of diagnoses and procedures. The importance of consistent, complete documentation in the medical record cannot be overemphasized. Medical record documentation from any provider involved in the care and treatment of the patient may be used to support the determination of whether a condition was present on admission or not. In the context of the official coding guidelines, the term "provider" means a physician or any qualified healthcare practitioner who is legally accountable for establishing the patient's diagnosis.

These guidelines are not a substitute for the provider's clinical judgment as to the determination of whether a condition was/was not present on admission. The provider should be queried regarding issues related to the linking of signs/symptoms, timing of test results, and the timing of findings.

Please see the CDC website for the detailed list of ICD-10-CM codes that do not require the use of a POA indicator (https://www.cdc.gov/nchs/icd/icd10cm.htm) (https://www.cms.gov/Medicare/Coding/ICD10/2018-ICD-10-CM-and-GEMs.html). The codes and categories on this exempt list are for circumstances regarding the healthcare encounter or factors influencing health status that do not represent a current disease or injury or that describe conditions that are always present on admission.

General Reporting Requirements

All claims involving inpatient admissions to general acute care hospitals or other facilities that are subject to a law or regulation mandating collection of present on admission information.

Present on admission is defined as present at the time the order for inpatient admission occurs—conditions that develop during an outpatient encounter, including emergency department, observation, or outpatient surgery, are considered as present on admission.

POA indicator is assigned to principal and secondary diagnoses (as defined in Section II of the Official Guidelines for Coding and Reporting) and the external cause of injury codes.

Issues related to inconsistent, missing, conflicting or unclear documentation must still be resolved by the provider.

If a condition would not be coded and reported based on UHDDS definitions and current official coding guidelines, then the POA indicator would not be reported.

Reporting Options

Y - Yes

N - No

U - Unknown

W - Clinically undetermined

Unreported/Not used - (Exempt from POA reporting)

Reporting Definitions

Y = present at the time of inpatient admission

N = not present at the time of inpatient admission

U = documentation is insufficient to determine if conditus is present on admission

W = provider is unable to clinically determine whether condition was present on admission or not

Timeframe for POA Identification and Documentation

There is no required timeframe as to when a provider (per the definition of "provider" used in these guidelines) must identify or document a condition to be present on admission. In some clinical situations, it may not be possible for a provider to make a definitive diagnosis (or a condition may not be recognized or reported by the patient) for a period of time after admission. In some cases it may be several days before the provider arrives at a definitive diagnosis. This does not mean that the condition was not present on admission. Determination of whether the condition was present on admission or not will be based on the applicable POA guideline as identified in this document, or on the provider's best clinical judgment.

If at the time of code assignment the documentation is unclear as to whether a condition was present on admission or not, it is appropriate to query the provider for clarification.

Assigning the POA Indicator

Condition is on the "Exempt from Reporting" list

Leave the "present on admission" field blank if the condition is on the list of ICD-10-CM codes for which this field is not applicable. This is the only circumstance in which the field may be left blank.

POA Explicitly Documented

Assign "Y" for any condition the provider explicitly documents as being present on admission.

Assign "N" for any condition the provider explicitly documents as not present at the time of admission.

Conditions diagnosed prior to inpatient admission

Assign "Y" for conditions that were diagnosed prior to admission (example: hypertension, diabetes mellitus, asthma)

Conditions diagnosed during the admission but clearly present before admission

Assign "Y" for conditions diagnosed during the admission that were clearly present but not diagnosed until after admission occurred.

Diagnoses subsequently confirmed after admission are considered present on admission if at the time of admission they are documented as suspected, possible, rule out, differential diagnosis, or constitute an underlying cause of a symptom that is present at the time of admission.

Condition develops during outpatient encounter prior to inpatient admission

Assign "Y" for any condition that develops during an outpatient encounter prior to a written order for inpatient admission.

Documentation does not indicate whether condition was present on admission

Assign "U" when the medical record documentation is unclear as to whether the condition was present on admission. "U" should not be routinely assigned and used only in very limited circumstances. Coders are encouraged to query the providers when the documentation is unclear.

Documentation states that it cannot be determined whether the condition was or was not present on admission

Assign "W" when the medical record documentation indicates that it cannot be clinically determined whether or not the condition was present on admission.

Chronic condition with acute exacerbation during the admission

If a single code identifies both the chronic condition and the acute exacerbation, see POA guidelines pertaining to codes that contain multiple clinical concepts.

If a single code only identifies the chronic condition and not the acute exacerbation (e.g., acute exacerbation of chronic leukemia), assign "Y."

Conditions documented as possible, probable, suspected, or rule out at the time of discharge

If the final diagnosis contains a possible, probable, suspected, or rule out diagnosis, and this diagnosis was based on signs, symptoms or clinical findings suspected at the time of inpatient admission, assign "Y."

If the final diagnosis contains a possible, probable, suspected, or rule out diagnosis, and this diagnosis was based on signs, symptoms or clinical findings that were not present on admission, assign "N".

Conditions documented as impending or threatened at the time of discharge

If the final diagnosis contains an impending or threatened diagnosis, and this diagnosis is based on symptoms or clinical findings that were present on admission, assign "Y".

If the final diagnosis contains an impending or threatened diagnosis, and this diagnosis is based on symptoms or clinical findings that were not present on admission, assign "N".

Acute and Chronic Conditions

Assign "Y" for acute conditions that are present at time of admission and "N" for acute conditions that are not present at time of admission.

Assign "Y" for chronic conditions, even though the condition may not be diagnosed until after admission.

If a single code identifies both an acute and chronic condition, see the POA guidelines for codes that contain multiple clinical concepts.

Codes That Contain Multiple Clinical Concepts

Assign "N" if at least one of the clinical concepts included in the code was not present on admission (e.g., COPD with acute exacerbation and the exacerbation was not present on admission; gastric ulcer that does not start bleeding until after admission; asthma patient develops status asthmaticus after admission).

Assign "Y" if all of the clinical concepts included in the code were present on admission (e.g., duodenal ulcer that perforates prior to admission).

For infection codes that include the causal organism, assign "Y" if the infection (or signs of the infection) were present on admission, even though the culture results may not be known until after admission (e.g., patient is admitted with pneumonia and the provider documents Pseudomonas as the causal organism a few days later).

Same Diagnosis Code for Two or More Conditions

When the same ICD-10-CM diagnosis code applies to two or more conditions during the same encounter (e.g., two separate conditions classified to the same ICD-10-CM diagnosis code):

Assign "Y" if all conditions represented by the single ICD-10-CM code were present on admission (e.g., bilateral unspecified age-related cataracts).

Assign "N" if any of the conditions represented by the single ICD-10-CM code was not present on admission (e.g., traumatic secondary and recurrent hemorrhage and seroma is assigned to a single code T79.2, but only one of the conditions was present on admission).

Obstetrical conditions

Whether or not the patient delivers during the current hospitalization does not affect assignment of the POA indicator. The determining factor for POA assignment is whether the pregnancy complication or obstetrical condition described by the code was present at the time of admission or not.

If the pregnancy complication or obstetrical condition was present on admission (e.g., patient admitted in preterm labor), assign "Y".

If the pregnancy complication or obstetrical condition was not present on admission (e.g., 2nd degree laceration during delivery, postpartum hemorrhage that occurred during current hospitalization, fetal distress develops after admission), assign "N".

If the obstetrical code includes more than one diagnosis and any of the diagnoses identified by the code were not present on admission assign "N".

GUIDELINES (ICD-10-CM)

(e.g., Category O11, Pre-existing hypertension with pre-eclampsia)

Perinatal conditions

Newborns are not considered to be admitted until after birth. Therefore, any condition present at birth or that developed in utero is considered present at admission and should be assigned "Y". This includes conditions that occur during delivery (e.g., injury during delivery, meconium aspiration, exposure to streptococcus B in the vaginal canal).

Congenital conditions and anomalies

Assign "Y" for congenital conditions and anomalies except for categories Q00-Q99, Congenital anomalies, which are on the exempt list. Congenital conditions are always considered present on admission.

External cause of injury codes

Assign "Y" for any external cause code representing an external cause of morbidity that occurred prior to inpatient admission (e.g., patient fell out of bed at home, patient fell out of bed in emergency room prior to admission).

Assign "N" for any external cause code representing an external cause of morbidity that occurred during inpatient hospitalization (e.g., patient fell out of hospital bed during hospital stay, patient experienced an adverse reaction to a medication administered after inpatient admission).

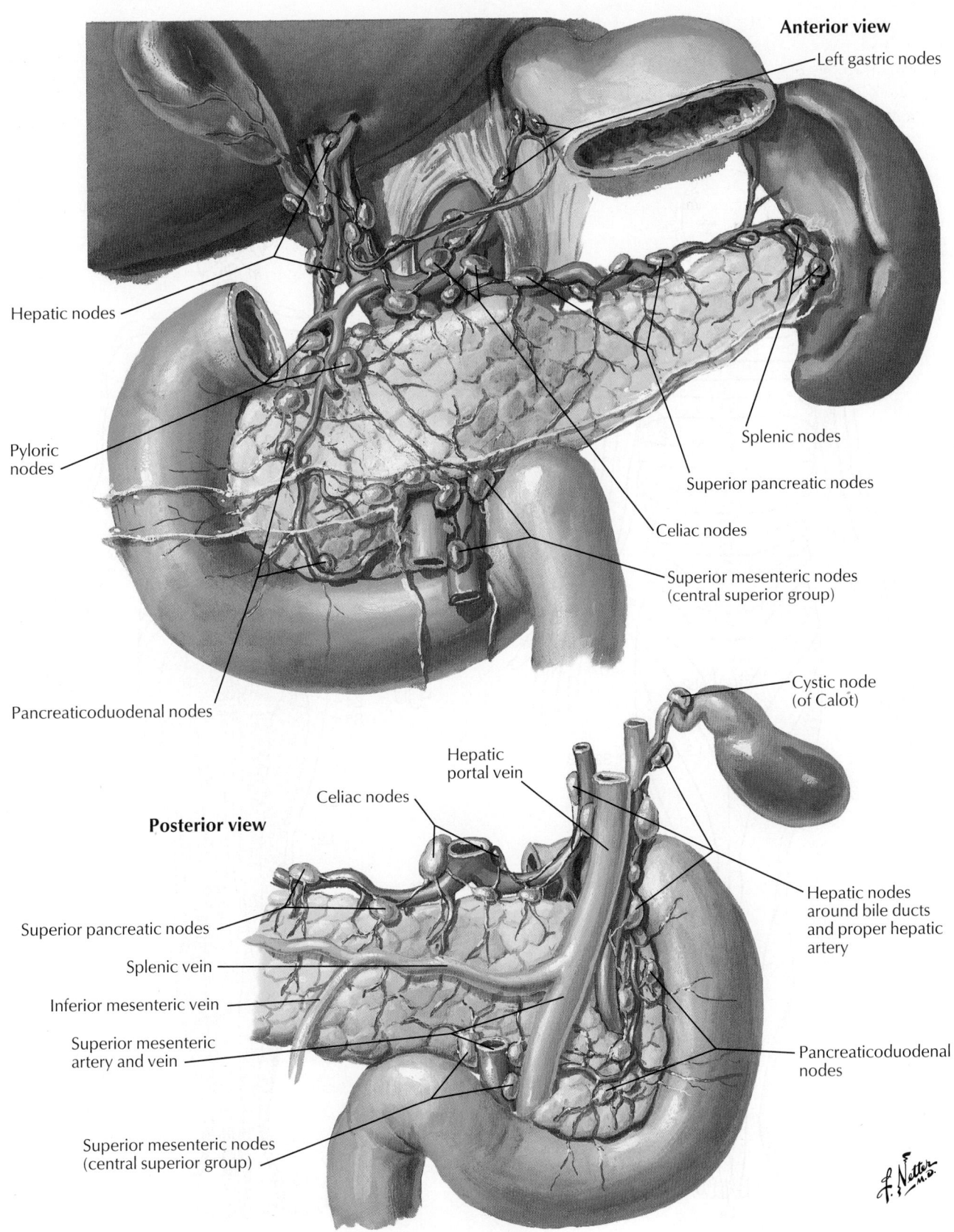

Anterior view

Left gastric nodes

Hepatic nodes

Pyloric nodes

Splenic nodes

Superior pancreatic nodes

Celiac nodes

Superior mesenteric nodes (central superior group)

Pancreaticoduodenal nodes

Cystic node (of Calot)

Hepatic portal vein

Celiac nodes

Posterior view

Hepatic nodes around bile ducts and proper hepatic artery

Superior pancreatic nodes

Splenic vein

Inferior mesenteric vein

Superior mesenteric artery and vein

Pancreaticoduodenal nodes

Superior mesenteric nodes (central superior group)

Plate 1 Lymph Vessels and Nodes of Pancreas. (Netter: Atlas of Human Anatomy, 4 ed, 2006, Saunders. Plate 315)

Levels of principal dermatomes

C5	Clavicles
C5, 6, 7	Lateral parts of upper limbs
C8, T1	Medial sides of upper limbs
C6	Thumb
C6, 7, 8	Hand
C8	Ring and little fingers
T4	Level of nipples
T10	Level of umbilicus
L1	Inguinal or groin regions
L1, 2, 3, 4	Anterior and inner surfaces of lower limbs
L4, 5, S1	Foot
L4	Medial side of great toe
S1, 2, L5	Posterior and other surfaces of lower limbs
S1	Lateral margin of foot and little toe
S2, 3, 4	Perineum

Plate 2 Schematic demarcation of Dermatomes. (Miller MD, Hart JA, MacKnight JM: Essential Orthopaedics, ed 2, Philadelphia, 2020, Elsevier.)

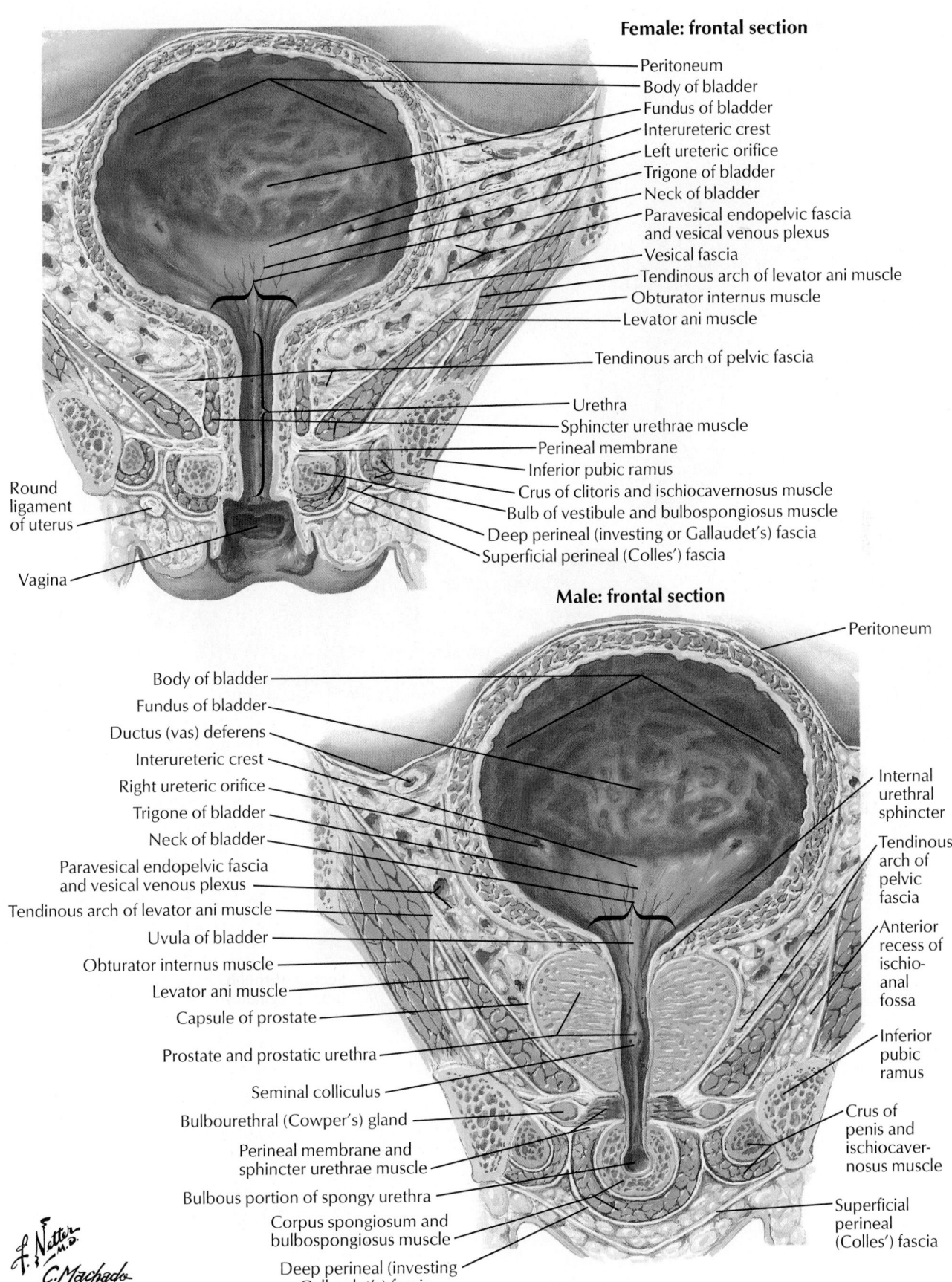

Female: frontal section

- Peritoneum
- Body of bladder
- Fundus of bladder
- Interureteric crest
- Left ureteric orifice
- Trigone of bladder
- Neck of bladder
- Paravesical endopelvic fascia and vesical venous plexus
- Vesical fascia
- Tendinous arch of levator ani muscle
- Obturator internus muscle
- Levator ani muscle
- Tendinous arch of pelvic fascia
- Urethra
- Sphincter urethrae muscle
- Perineal membrane
- Inferior pubic ramus
- Crus of clitoris and ischiocavernosus muscle
- Bulb of vestibule and bulbospongiosus muscle
- Deep perineal (investing or Gallaudet's) fascia
- Superficial perineal (Colles') fascia

- Round ligament of uterus
- Vagina

Male: frontal section

- Body of bladder
- Fundus of bladder
- Ductus (vas) deferens
- Interureteric crest
- Right ureteric orifice
- Trigone of bladder
- Neck of bladder
- Paravesical endopelvic fascia and vesical venous plexus
- Tendinous arch of levator ani muscle
- Uvula of bladder
- Obturator internus muscle
- Levator ani muscle
- Capsule of prostate
- Prostate and prostatic urethra
- Seminal colliculus
- Bulbourethral (Cowper's) gland
- Perineal membrane and sphincter urethrae muscle
- Bulbous portion of spongy urethra
- Corpus spongiosum and bulbospongiosus muscle
- Deep perineal (investing or Gallaudet's) fascia

- Peritoneum
- Internal urethral sphincter
- Tendinous arch of pelvic fascia
- Anterior recess of ischio-anal fossa
- Inferior pubic ramus
- Crus of penis and ischiocavernosus muscle
- Superficial perineal (Colles') fascia

Plate 3 Urinary Bladder: Female and Male. (Netter: Atlas of Human Anatomy, 4 ed, 2006, Saunders. Plate 366.)

ANATOMY ILLUSTRATIONS

Sites of ectopic implantation

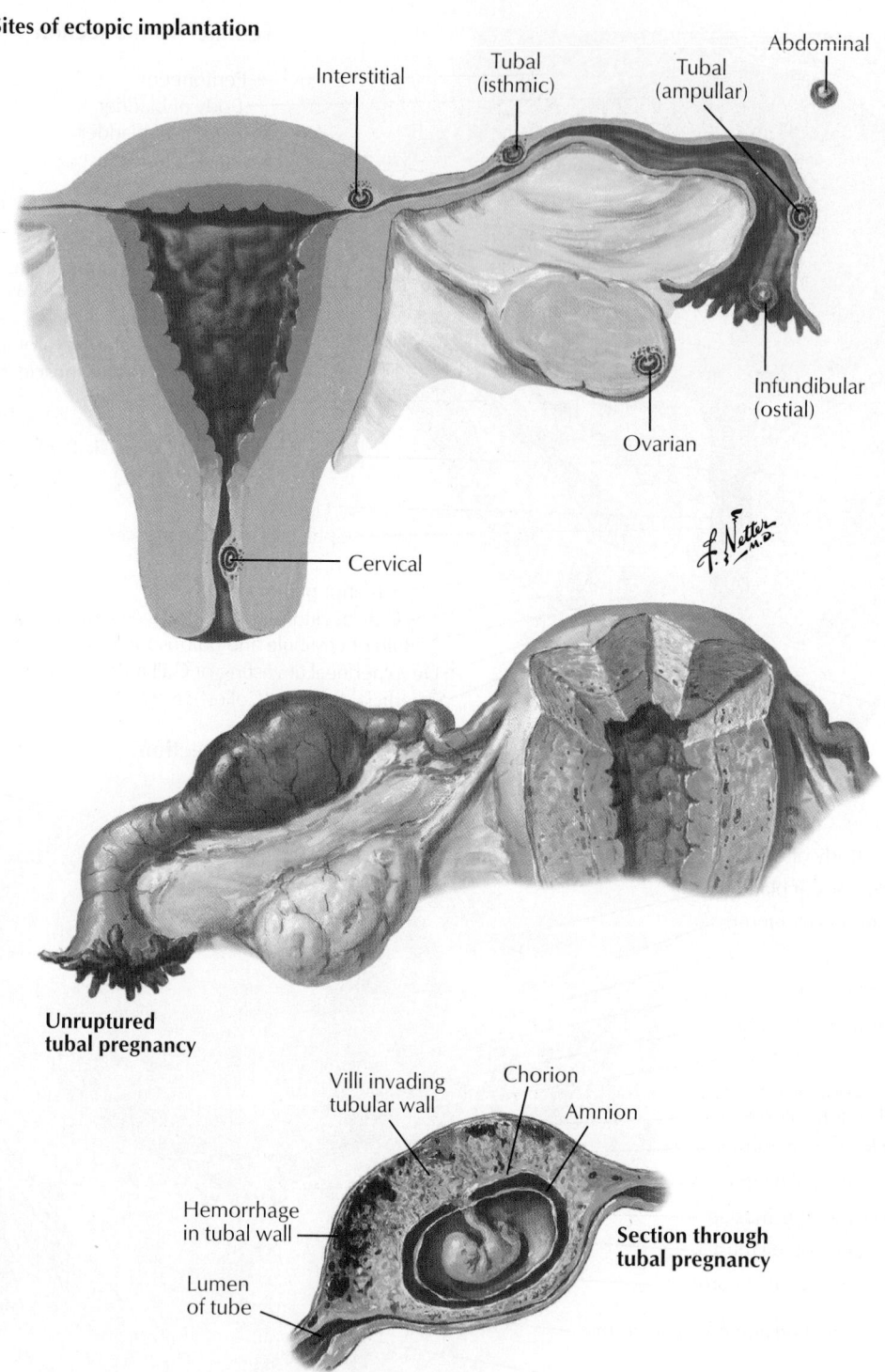

Interstitial

Tubal (isthmic)

Tubal (ampullar)

Abdominal

Infundibular (ostial)

Ovarian

Cervical

Unruptured tubal pregnancy

Villi invading tubular wall

Chorion

Amnion

Hemorrhage in tubal wall

Lumen of tube

Section through tubal pregnancy

Plate 4 Ectopic Pregnancy. (Netter: Atlas of Human Anatomy, 4 ed, 2006, Saunders. Plate 375)

Superficial
inguinal ring

External
spermatic fascia

Cremaster muscle
and fascia

Septum of scrotum
(formed by
dartos fascia)

Superficial
(dartos) fascia
of scrotum

Skin of scrotum

Skin of penis

Superficial fascia
of penis (Colles' fascia)

Deep (Buck's)
fascia of penis

Testicular artery

Ductus deferens

Artery to ductus deferens

Genital branch of
genitofemoral nerve

Pampiniform (venous) plexus

Epididymis

Appendix of epididymis

Appendix of testis

Testis (covered by visceral
layer of tunica vaginalis)

Parietal layer of tunica vaginalis

Superficial (dartos) fascia of scrotum

External spermatic fascia

Cremaster muscle and fascia

Internal spermatic fascia

Parietal layer of tunica vaginalis

Epididymis

Testis (covered by visceral layer of tunica vaginalis)

Skin of scrotum

Plate 5   Scrotum and Contents. (Netter: Atlas of Human Anatomy, 4 ed, 2006, Saunders. Plate 387)

I Olfactory

III Oculomotor

II Optic

IV Trochlear
VI Abducens

V Trigeminal

VII Facial

VIII Vestibulocochlear

X Vagus

XII Hypoglossal

IX
Glossopharyngeal

XI Accessory

Plate 6 Cranial Nerves (12 pairs) are known by their numbers (Roman numerals) and names. (Herlihy BL: The Human Body in Health and Illness, ed 6, St. Louis, 2018, Elsevier.)

Superior view

- Supratrochlear nerve
- Medial rectus muscle
- Superior oblique muscle
- Infratrochlear nerve
- Nasociliary nerve
- Trochlear nerve (IV)
- Common tendinous ring
- Ophthalmic nerve (V₁)
- Optic nerve (II)
- Internal carotid artery and nerve plexus
- Oculomotor nerve (III)
- Trochlear nerve (IV)
- Abducent nerve (VI)
- Tentorium cerebelli

- Medial branch } Supraorbital nerve
- Lateral branch
- Levator palpebrae superioris muscle
- Superior rectus muscle
- Lacrimal gland
- Lacrimal nerve
- Lateral rectus muscle
- Frontal nerve
- Maxillary nerve (V₂)
- Meningeal branch of maxillary nerve
- Mandibular nerve (V₃)
- Lesser petrosal nerve
- Meningeal branch of mandibular nerve
- Greater petrosal nerve
- Trigeminal (semilunar) ganglion
- Tentorial (meningeal) branch of ophthalmic nerve

Superior view:
levator palpebrae superioris, superior rectus, and superior oblique muscles partially cut away

- Supratrochlear nerve *(cut)*
- Supraorbital nerve branches *(cut)*
- Infratrochlear nerve
- Anterior ethmoidal nerve
- Optic nerve (II)
- Posterior ethmoidal nerve
- Superior branch of oculomotor nerve (III) *(cut)*
- Nasociliary nerve
- Internal carotid plexus
- Trochlear nerve (IV) *(cut)*
- Oculomotor nerve (III)
- Abducent nerve (VI)

- Long ciliary nerves
- Short ciliary nerves
- Lacrimal nerve
- Ciliary ganglion
- Parasympathetic root of ciliary ganglion (from inferior branch of oculomotor nerve)
- Sympathetic root of ciliary ganglion (from internal carotid plexus)
- Sensory root of ciliary ganglion (from nasociliary nerve)
- Branches to inferior and medial rectus muscles
- Abducent nerve (VI)
- Inferior branch of oculomotor nerve (III)
- Lacrimal nerve
- Frontal nerve *(cut)*
- Ophthalmic nerve (V₁)

Plate 7 Nerves of Orbit. (Netter: Atlas of Human Anatomy, 4 ed, 2006, Saunders. Plate 86)

Medial two lumbricals innervated by ulnar nerve

Proper palmar digital nerves (median nerve)

Cutaneous innervation of the median nerve in the hand

Cutaneous innervation of the palmar branch of the median nerve

Palmar view

Cutaneous innervation of the dorsal branch of the ulnar nerve

Dorsal view

Lateral two lumbricals innervated by median nerve

Proper palmar digital nerve (ulnar nerve)

Intrinsic muscles innervated by ulnar nerve except the thenar muscles and the two lateral lumbricals

Common palmar digital nerve

Hypothenar muscles innervated by ulnar nerve

Palmaris brevis

Deep branch of the ulnar nerve

Superficial branch of the ulnar nerve

Palmar branch of the ulnar nerve

Ulnar nerve

Ulna

Common palmar digital nerves (median nerve)

Thenar muscles innervated by median nerve

Recurrent branch of median nerve

Palmar branch of the median nerve

Median nerve

Radius

Cutaneous innervation of the superficial branch of the ulnar nerve in the hand

Cutaneous innervation of the palmar branch of the ulnar nerve

Palmar view

Cutaneous innervation of the median nerve in the hand

Dorsal view

Innervation of the hand, median and ulnar nerves (palmar view)

Plate 8 Innervation of the Hand: Median and Ulnar Nerves (From Drake RL, Vogl AW, Mitchell AWM, Tibbitts RM, Richardson PE: Gray's Atlas of Anatomy, ed 2, Philadelphia, 2015, Churchill Livingstone.)

Arteries and nerves of forearm (anterior view)

Biceps brachii

Posterior cutaneous nerve of forearm (cut) (from radial nerve)

Ulnar nerve

Medial cutaneous nerve of forearm (from medial cord of brachial plexus)

Median nerve

Brachial artery

Medial epicondyle

Lateral cutaneous nerve of forearm (cut) (from musculocutaneous nerve)

Bicipital aponeurosis

Biceps brachii tendon

Radial artery

Brachioradialis

Radial artery

Palmaris longus tendon

Median nerve

Thenar muscles

Palmar branch of median nerve

Palmar aponeurosis

Ulnar artery

Ulnar nerve

Brachioradialis tendon (cut)

Palmar branch of ulnar nerve

Hypothenar muscles

Superior ulnar collateral artery

Inferior ulnar collateral artery

Radial collateral artery

Brachial artery

Radial recurrent artery

Median nerve

Recurrent interosseous artery

Ulnar nerve

Humeral head of pronator teres (cut)

Posterior interosseous artery

Anterior ulnar recurrent artery

Humeral head of flexor carpi ulnaris

Posterior ulnar recurrent artery

Ulnar head of pronator teres

Ulnar artery

Anterior interosseous nerve

Anterior interosseous artery

Radial artery

Interosseous membrane

Flexor digitorum superficialis (cut)

Radial nerve

Brachial artery

Lateral epicondyle

Radial recurrent artery

Deep branch radial nerve

Radial artery

Supinator

Superficial branch radial nerve

Common interosseous artery

Posterior interosseous artery

Interosseous membrane

Pronator teres (cut)

Perforating branches of anterior interosseous artery

Flexor digitorum profundus

Median nerve

Flexor carpi radialis tendon (cut)

Flexor retinaculum

Superficial palmar branch of radial artery

Palmar branch of median nerve

Flexor carpi ulnaris tendon (cut)

Ulnar nerve

Palmar branch of ulnar nerve

Deep palmar branch of ulnar artery

Deep palmar arch

Superficial palmar arch

Anterior ulnar recurrent artery

Posterior ulnar recurrent artery

Common interosseous artery

Anterior interosseous artery

Ulnar artery

Radius

Ulna

Superficial palmar branch of radial artery

Pisiform

Superficial palmar arch

Deep palmar arch

Arteries and nerves of forearm (anterior view)

Plate 9 Arteries and Nerves of the Forearm (Anterior View) (From Drake RL, Vogl AW, Mitchell AWM, Tibbitts RM, Richardson PE: Gray's Atlas of Anatomy, ed 2, Philadelphia, 2015, Churchill Livingstone.)

ANATOMY ILLUSTRATIONS

Lateral cutaneous branch of subcostal nerve

Inguinal ligament (Poupart's)

Superficial circumflex iliac vein

Femoral branches of genitofemoral nerve

Lateral femoral cutaneous nerve

Saphenous opening (fossa ovalis)

Fascia lata

Anterior cutaneous branches of femoral nerve

Patellar nerve plexus

Branches of lateral sural cutaneous nerve (from common fibular [peroneal] nerve)

Deep fascia of leg (crural fascia)

Superficial fibular (peroneal) nerve
Medial dorsal cutaneous branch

Intermediate dorsal cutaneous branch

Small saphenous vein and lateral dorsal cutaneous nerve (from sural nerve)

Lateral dorsal digital nerve and vein of 5th toe

Dorsal metatarsal veins

Dorsal digital nerves and veins

Superficial epigastric vein

Ilioinguinal nerve (scrotal branch) (usually passes through superficial inguinal ring)

Genital branch of genitofemoral nerve

Femoral vein

Superficial external pudendal vein

Accessory saphenous vein

Great saphenous vein

Cutaneous branches of obturator nerve

Infrapatellar branch of saphenous nerve

Saphenous nerve (terminal branch of femoral nerve)

Great saphenous vein

Dorsal digital nerves

Dorsal venous arch

Dorsal digital nerve and vein of medial side of great toe

Dorsal digital branch of deep fibular (peroneal) nerve

ANATOMY ILLUSTRATIONS

Plate 10 Superficial Nerves and Veins of Lower Limb: Anterior View. (Netter: Atlas of Human Anatomy, 4 ed, 2006, Saunders. Plate 544)

Lateral cutaneous branch of iliohypogastric nerve

Iliac crest

Medial cluneal nerves (from dorsal rami of S1, 2, 3)

Superior cluneal nerves (from dorsal rami of L1, 2, 3)

Inferior cluneal nerves (from posterior femoral cutaneous nerve)

Perforating cutaneous nerve (from dorsal rami of S1, 2, 3)

Branches of posterior femoral cutaneous nerve

Branches of lateral femoral cutaneous nerve

Accessory saphenous vein

Branch of femoral cutaneous nerve

Branch of cutaneous branch of femoral nerve

Terminal branches of posterior femoral cutaneous nerve

Great saphenous vein

Lateral sural cutaneous nerve (from common fibular [peroneal] nerve)

Small saphenous vein

Sural communicating nerve

Branches of saphenous nerve

Medial sural cutaneous nerve (from tibial nerve)

Sural nerve

Lateral calcaneal branches of sural nerve

Lateral dorsal cutaneous nerve (continuation of sural nerve)

Medial calcaneal branches of tibial nerve

Plantar cutaneous branches of medial plantar nerve

Plantar cutaneous branches of lateral plantar nerve

ANATOMY ILLUSTRATIONS

Plate 11 Superficial Nerves and Veins of Lower Limb: Posterior View. (Netter: Atlas of Human Anatomy, 4 ed, 2006, Saunders. Plate 545)

Superficial dissections

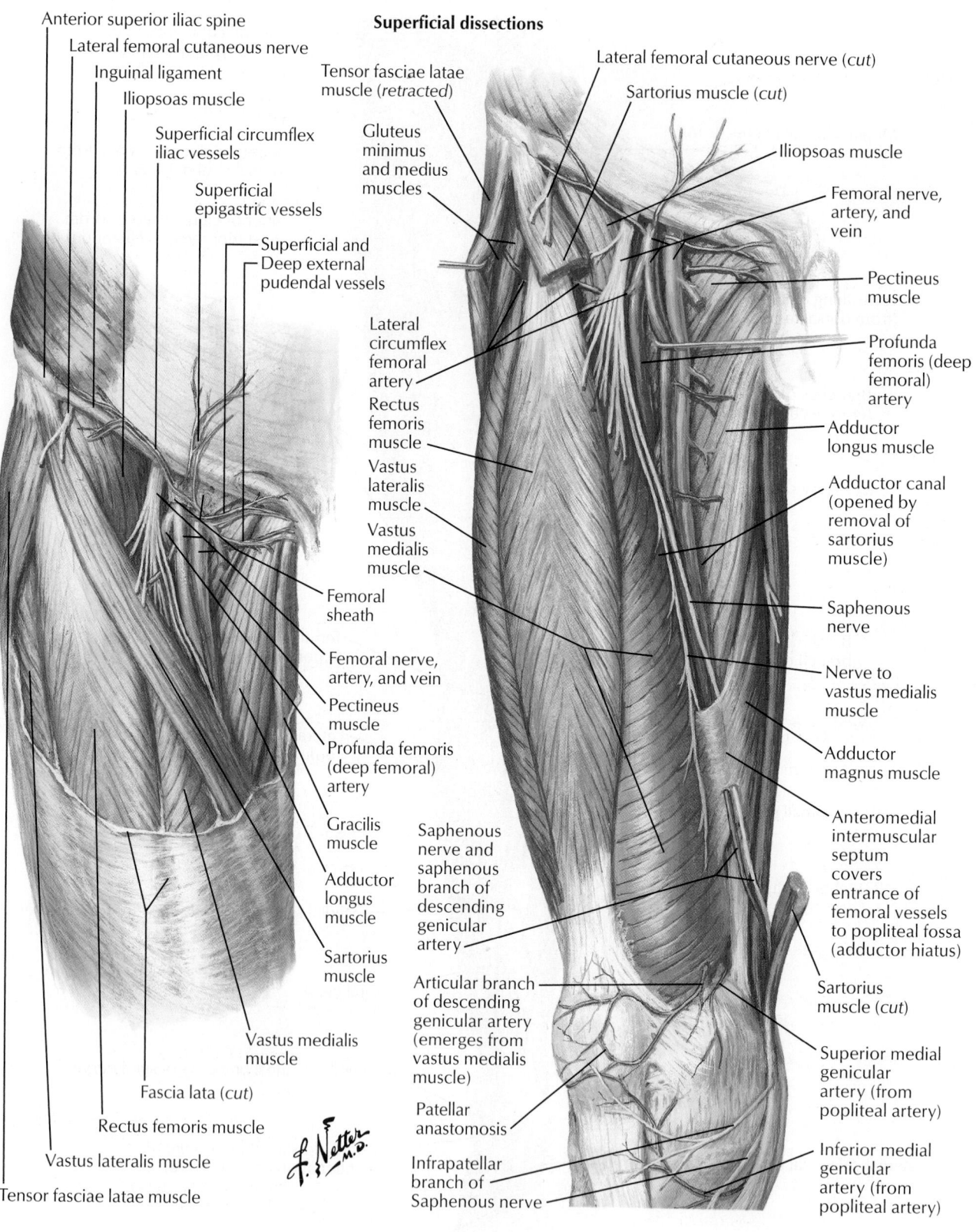

Anterior superior iliac spine

Lateral femoral cutaneous nerve

Inguinal ligament

Iliopsoas muscle

Superficial circumflex iliac vessels

Superficial epigastric vessels

Superficial and Deep external pudendal vessels

Tensor fasciae latae muscle (*retracted*)

Gluteus minimus and medius muscles

Lateral circumflex femoral artery

Rectus femoris muscle

Vastus lateralis muscle

Vastus medialis muscle

Femoral sheath

Femoral nerve, artery, and vein

Pectineus muscle

Profunda femoris (deep femoral) artery

Gracilis muscle

Adductor longus muscle

Sartorius muscle

Saphenous nerve and saphenous branch of descending genicular artery

Articular branch of descending genicular artery (emerges from vastus medialis muscle)

Patellar anastomosis

Infrapatellar branch of Saphenous nerve

Vastus medialis muscle

Fascia lata (*cut*)

Rectus femoris muscle

Vastus lateralis muscle

Tensor fasciae latae muscle

Lateral femoral cutaneous nerve (*cut*)

Sartorius muscle (*cut*)

Iliopsoas muscle

Femoral nerve, artery, and vein

Pectineus muscle

Profunda femoris (deep femoral) artery

Adductor longus muscle

Adductor canal (opened by removal of sartorius muscle)

Saphenous nerve

Nerve to vastus medialis muscle

Adductor magnus muscle

Anteromedial intermuscular septum covers entrance of femoral vessels to popliteal fossa (adductor hiatus)

Sartorius muscle (*cut*)

Superior medial genicular artery (from popliteal artery)

Inferior medial genicular artery (from popliteal artery)

F. Netter M.D.

Plate 12 Arteries and Nerves of Thigh: Anterior Views. (Netter: Atlas of Human Anatomy, 4 ed, 2006, Saunders. Plate 500)

Deep dissection

Deep circumflex iliac artery

Lateral femoral cutaneous nerve

Sartorius muscle (*cut*)

Iliopsoas muscle

Tensor fasciae latae muscle (*retracted*)

Gluteus medius and minimus muscles

Femoral nerve

Rectus femoris muscle (*cut*)

Ascending, transverse and descending branches of Lateral circumflex femoral artery

Medial circumflex femoral artery

Pectineus muscle (*cut*)

Profunda femoris (deep femoral) artery

Perforating branches

Adductor longus muscle (*cut*)

Vastus lateralis muscle

Vastus intermedius muscle

Rectus femoris muscle (*cut*)

Saphenous nerve

Anteromedial intermuscular septum (*opened*)

Vastus medialis muscle

Quadriceps femoris tendon

Patella and patellar anastomosis

Medial patellar retinaculum

Patellar ligament

External iliac artery and vein

Inguinal ligament (Poupart's)

Femoral artery and vein (*cut*)

Pectineus muscle (*cut*)

Obturator canal

Obturator externus muscle

Adductor longus muscle (*cut*)

Anterior branch and Posterior branch of obturator nerve

Quadratus femoris muscle

Adductor brevis muscle

Branches of posterior branch of obturator nerve

Adductor magnus muscle

Gracilis muscle

Cutaneous branch of obturator nerve

Femoral artery and vein (*cut*)

Descending genicular artery
Articular branch
Saphenous branch

Adductor hiatus

Sartorius muscle (*cut*)

Adductor magnus tendon

Adductor tubercle on medial epicondyle of femur

Superior medial genicular artery (from popliteal artery)

Infrapatellar branch of Saphenous nerve

Inferior medial genicular artery (from popliteal artery)

Plate 13 Arteries and Nerves of Thigh: Posterior View. (Netter: Atlas of Human Anatomy, 4 ed, 2006, Saunders. Plate 501)

65

ANATOMY ILLUSTRATIONS

Deep dissection

Superior cluneal nerves

Gluteus maximus muscle (*cut*)

Medial cluneal nerves

Inferior gluteal artery and nerve

Pudendal nerve

Nerve to obturator internus (and superior gemellus)

Posterior femoral cutaneous nerve

Sacrotuberous ligament

Ischial tuberosity

Inferior cluneal nerves (*cut*)

Adductor magnus muscle

Gracilis muscle

Sciatic nerve

Muscular branches of sciatic nerve

Semitendinosus muscle (*retracted*)

Semimembranosus muscle

Sciatic nerve

Articular branch

Adductor hiatus

Popliteal vein and artery

Superior medial genicular artery

Medial epicondyle of femur

Tibial nerve

Gastrocnemius muscle (medial head)

Medial sural cutaneous nerve

Small saphenous vein

Iliac crest

Gluteal aponeurosis and gluteus medius muscle (*cut*)

Superior gluteal artery and nerve

Gluteus minimus muscle

Tensor fasciae latae muscle

Piriformis muscle

Gluteus medius muscle (*cut*)

Superior gemellus muscle

Greater trochanter of femur

Obturator internus muscle

Inferior gemellus muscle

Gluteus maximus muscle (*cut*)

Quadratus femoris muscle

Medial circumflex femoral artery

Vastus lateralis muscle and iliotibial tract

Adductor minimus part of adductor magnus muscle

1st perforating artery (from profunda femoris artery)

Adductor magnus muscle

2nd and 3rd perforating arteries (from profunda femoris artery)

4th perforating artery (from profunda femoris artery)

Long head (*retracted*)
Short head } Biceps femoris muscle

Superior lateral genicular artery

Common fibular (peroneal) nerve

Plantaris muscle

Gastrocnemius muscle (lateral head)

Lateral sural cutaneous nerve

Plate 14 Arteries and Nerves of Thigh: Posterior View. (Netter: Atlas of Human Anatomy, 4 ed, 2006, Saunders. Plate 502)

ANATOMY ILLUSTRATIONS

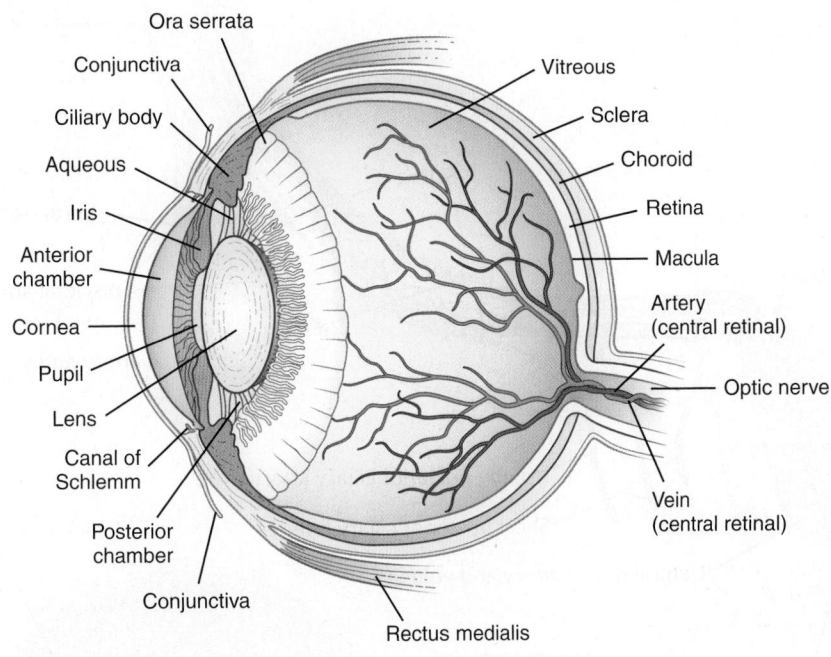

Ora serrata

Conjunctiva

Ciliary body

Aqueous

Iris

Anterior chamber

Cornea

Pupil

Lens

Canal of Schlemm

Posterior chamber

Conjunctiva

Rectus medialis

Vitreous

Sclera

Choroid

Retina

Macula

Artery (central retinal)

Optic nerve

Vein (central retinal)

Plate 15 Anatomy of the eye. (Dehn RW, Asprey DP: Essential Clinical Procedures, ed 3, Philadelphia, 2013, Saunders.)

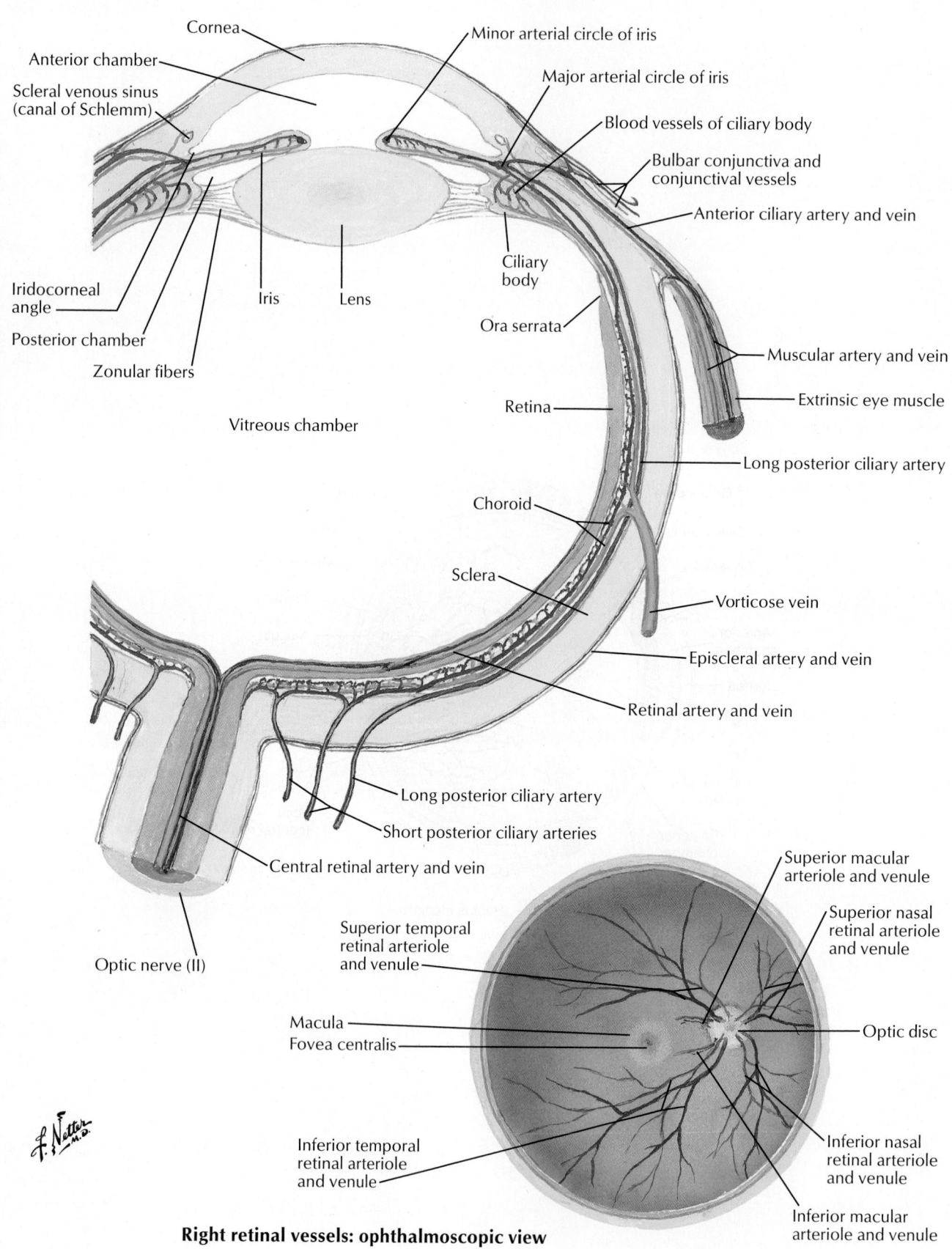

Cornea

Anterior chamber

Scleral venous sinus
(canal of Schlemm)

Minor arterial circle of iris

Major arterial circle of iris

Blood vessels of ciliary body

Bulbar conjunctiva and
conjunctival vessels

Anterior ciliary artery and vein

Iridocorneal
angle

Posterior chamber

Zonular fibers

Iris

Lens

Ciliary
body

Ora serrata

Muscular artery and vein

Extrinsic eye muscle

Long posterior ciliary artery

Vitreous chamber

Retina

Choroid

Sclera

Vorticose vein

Episcleral artery and vein

Retinal artery and vein

Long posterior ciliary artery

Short posterior ciliary arteries

Central retinal artery and vein

Optic nerve (II)

Superior temporal
retinal arteriole
and venule

Macula

Fovea centralis

Inferior temporal
retinal arteriole
and venule

Superior macular
arteriole and venule

Superior nasal
retinal arteriole
and venule

Optic disc

Inferior nasal
retinal arteriole
and venule

Inferior macular
arteriole and venule

Right retinal vessels: ophthalmoscopic view

Plate 16 Intrinsic Arteries and Veins of Eye. (Netter: Atlas of Human Anatomy, 4 ed, 2006, Saunders. Plate 90)

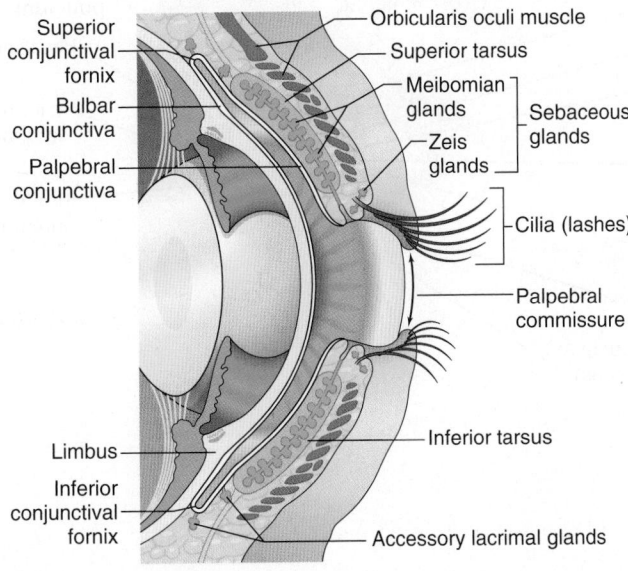

Plate 17 Anatomy of the conjunctiva and eyelids. (Kumar V, Abbas AK, Aster JC: Robbins and Cotran Pathologic Basis of Disease, ed 9, Philadelphia, 2015, Saunders.)

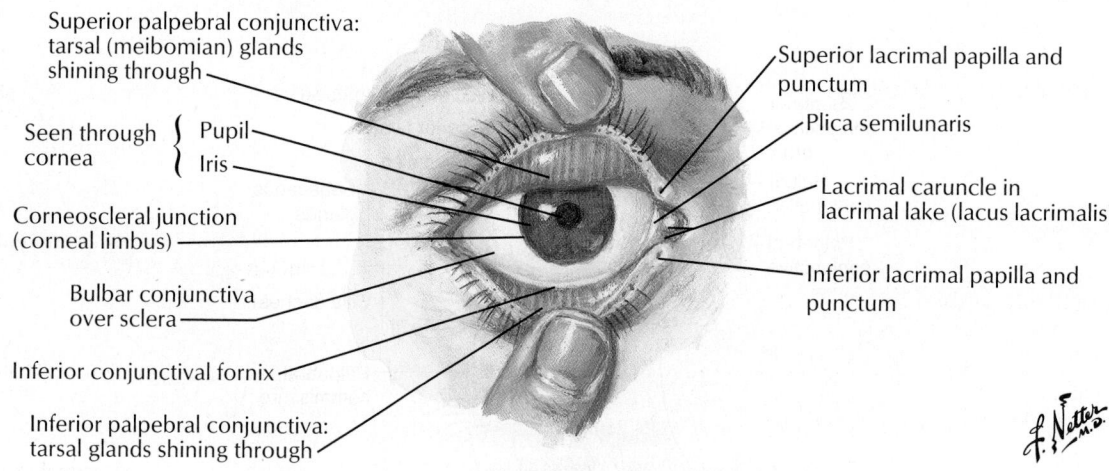

Superior palpebral conjunctiva: tarsal (meibomian) glands shining through

Seen through cornea { Pupil / Iris

Corneoscleral junction (corneal limbus)

Bulbar conjunctiva over sclera

Inferior conjunctival fornix

Inferior palpebral conjunctiva: tarsal glands shining through

Superior lacrimal papilla and punctum

Plica semilunaris

Lacrimal caruncle in lacrimal lake (lacus lacrimalis)

Inferior lacrimal papilla and punctum

Plate 18   Eyelid. (Netter: Atlas of Human Anatomy, 4 ed, 2006, Saunders. Plate 81, Upper)

Orbital part of lacrimal gland

Palpebral part of lacrimal gland

Excretory ducts of lacrimal gland

Plica semilunaris

Lacrimal caruncle

Inferior lacrimal papilla and punctum

Superior lacrimal papilla and punctum

Lacrimal canaliculi

Lacrimal sac

Nasolacrimal duct

Opening of nasolacrimal duct

Frontal bone (cut away)

Orbital part of lacrimal gland

Palpebral part of lacrimal gland

Excretory ducts of lacrimal gland

Plica semilunaris and lacrimal lake

Lacrimal caruncle

Inferior lacrimal papilla and punctum

Opening of nasolacrimal duct

Superior lacrimal papilla and punctum

Lacrimal canaliculi

Lacrimal sac

Nasolacrimal duct

Middle nasal concha

Nasal cavity

Inferior nasal concha (cut)

Inferior nasal meatus

Plate 19   Lacrimal Apparatus. (Netter: Atlas of Human Anatomy, 4 ed, 2006, Saunders. Plate 82)

Outer ear
- Pinna
- External auditory canal

Middle ear
- Tympanic membrane
- Ossicles: Malleus, incus, stapes
- Oval window

Inner ear
- Cochlea
- Auditory nerve

Brain
- Cerebrum

Plate 20 Pathway of Sound. (LaFleur Brooks D, LaFleur Brooks M: Basic Medical Language, ed 4, St. Louis, 2013, Mosby.)

Middle ear

Auditory ossicles

Stapes Malleus

Incus

Tympanic membrane (eardrum)

Eustachian tube

©Elsevier Collection

Plate 21 Middle ear structures. (©Elsevier Collection.)

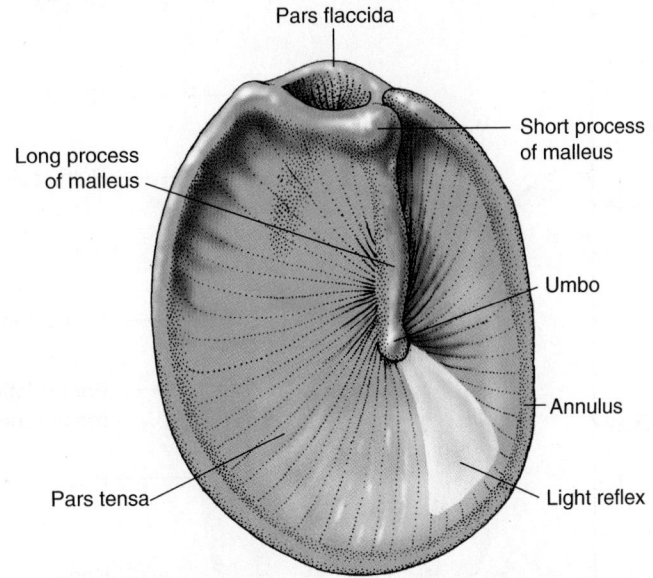

Pars flaccida

Short process
of malleus

Long process
of malleus

Umbo

Annulus

Pars tensa

Light reflex

Plate 22 Structural landmarks of tympanic membrane. (Ignatavicius DD, Workman ML: Medical-Surgical Nursing: Patient-Centered Collaborative Care, ed 7, St. Louis, 2013, Saunders.)

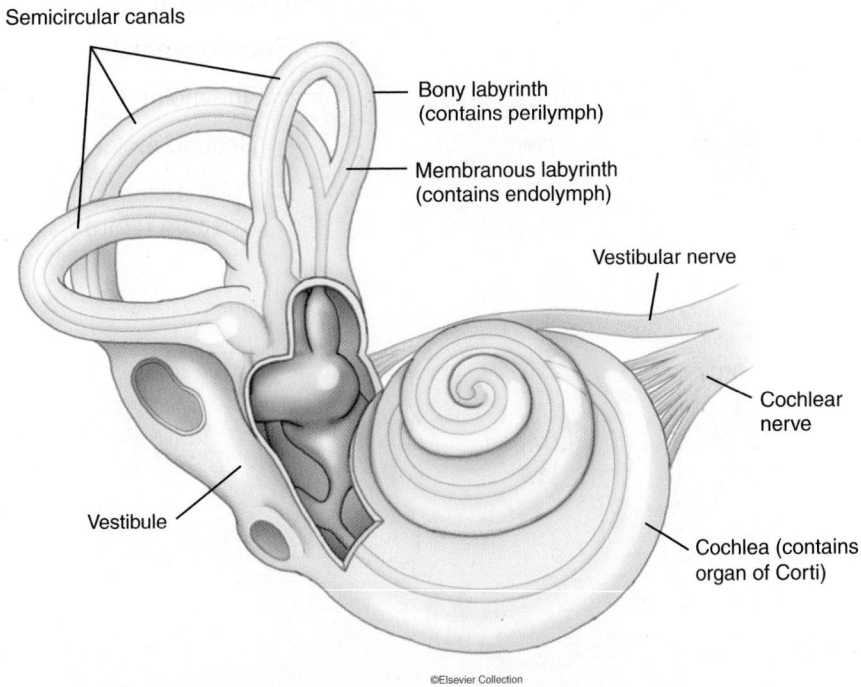

Semicircular canals

Bony labyrinth
(contains perilymph)

Membranous labyrinth
(contains endolymph)

Vestibular nerve

Cochlear
nerve

Vestibule

Cochlea (contains
organ of Corti)

©Elsevier Collection

Plate 23 Inner ear structures. (©Elsevier Collection.)

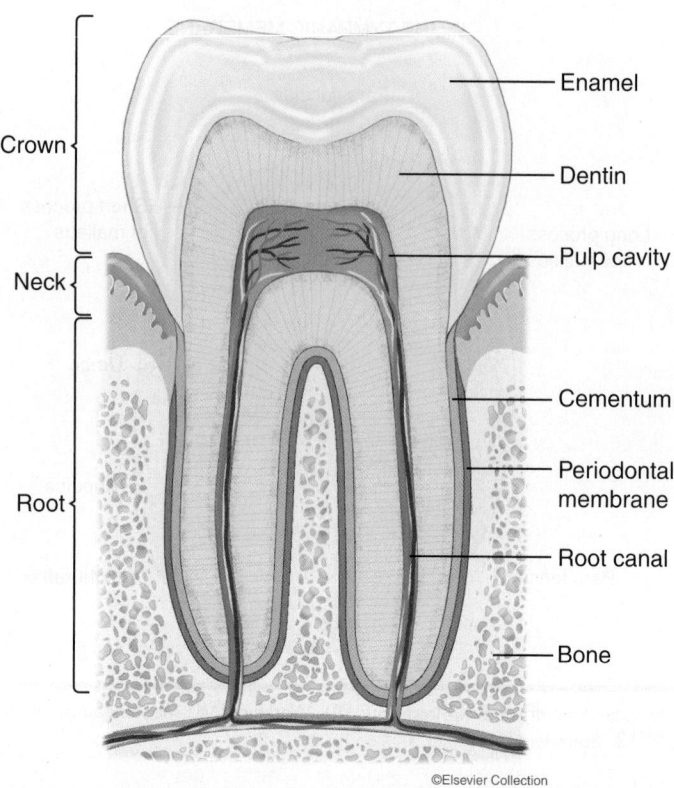

Crown

Neck

Root

Enamel

Dentin

Pulp cavity

Cementum

Periodontal membrane

Root canal

Bone

©Elsevier Collection

Plate 24　The Tooth. (©Elsevier Collection).

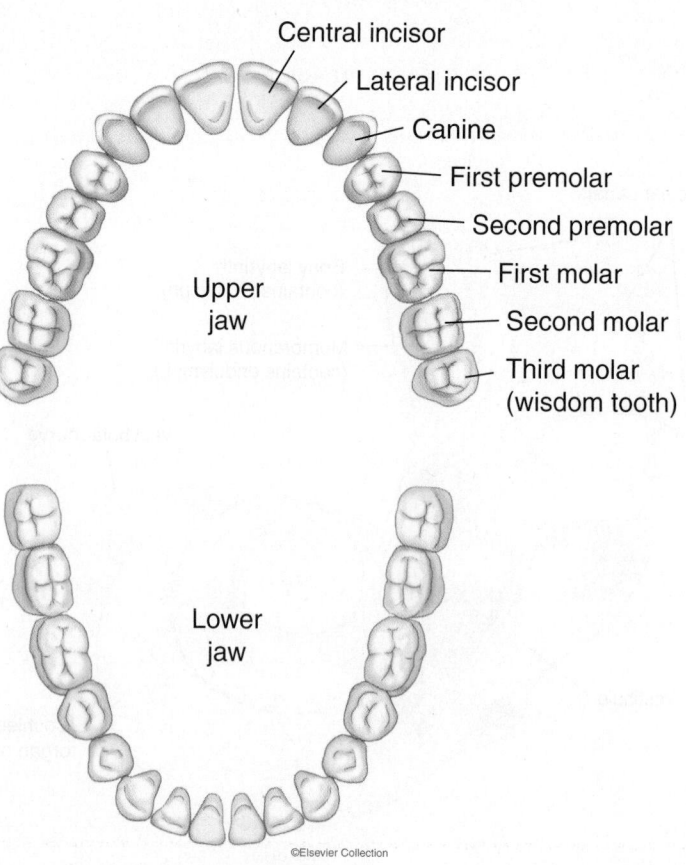

Central incisor

Lateral incisor

Canine

First premolar

Second premolar

First molar

Second molar

Third molar (wisdom tooth)

Upper jaw

Lower jaw

©Elsevier Collection

Plate 25　Adult Teeth. (©Elsevier Collection).

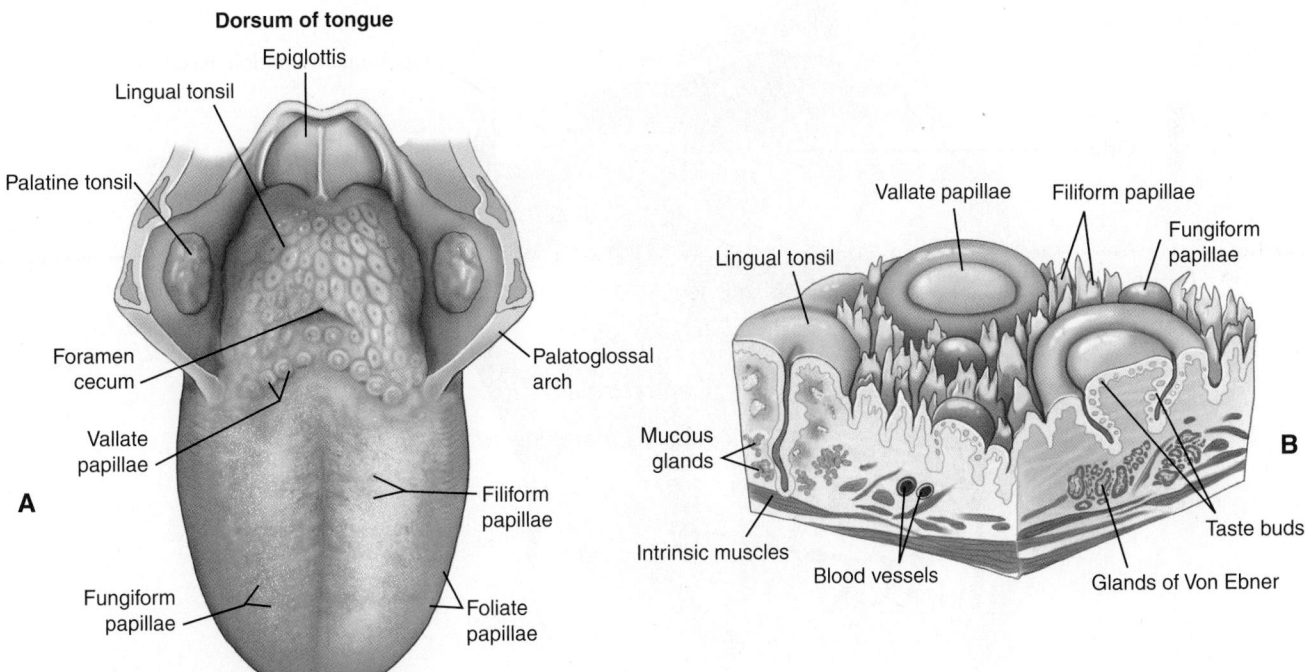

Dorsum of tongue

Epiglottis

Lingual tonsil

Palatine tonsil

Foramen cecum

Vallate papillae

A

Fungiform papillae

Filiform papillae

Foliate papillae

Palatoglossal arch

Vallate papillae

Filiform papillae

Fungiform papillae

Lingual tonsil

Mucous glands

Intrinsic muscles

Blood vessels

Taste buds

Glands of Von Ebner

B

© Elsevier Collection

Plate 26   A, Dorsal view of tongue showing the roughened large lingual tonsils on the posterior of the tongue and the foliate papillae on the side. B, Section of dorsal of the tongue showing a cutaway through lingual papillae and showing von Ebner's glands at the base of the vallate papilla. (Brand RW, Isselhard DE: Anatomy of Orofacial Structures: A Comprehensive Approach, ed 8, St. Louis, 2019, Elsevier.)

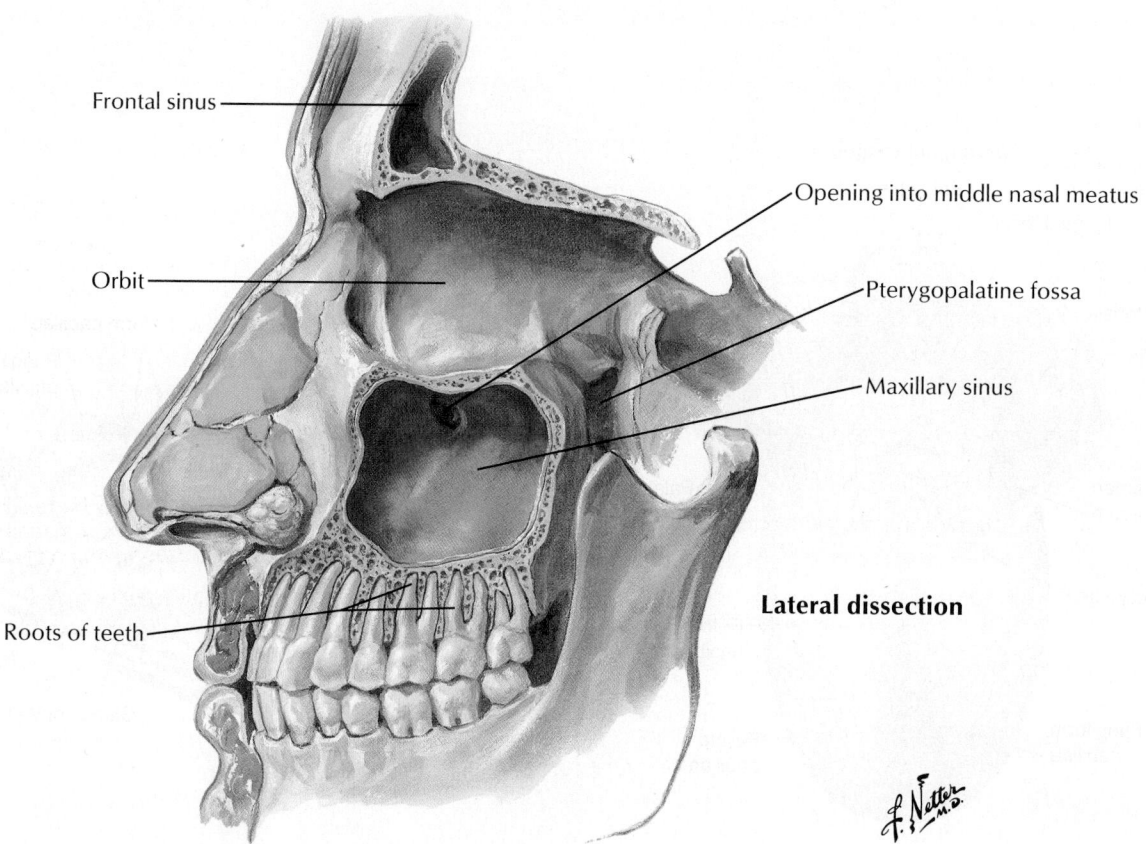

Frontal sinus

Orbit

Opening into middle nasal meatus

Pterygopalatine fossa

Maxillary sinus

Lateral dissection

Roots of teeth

Plate 27 Paranasal Sinuses. (Netter: Atlas of Human Anatomy, 4 ed, 2006, Saunders. Plate 49)

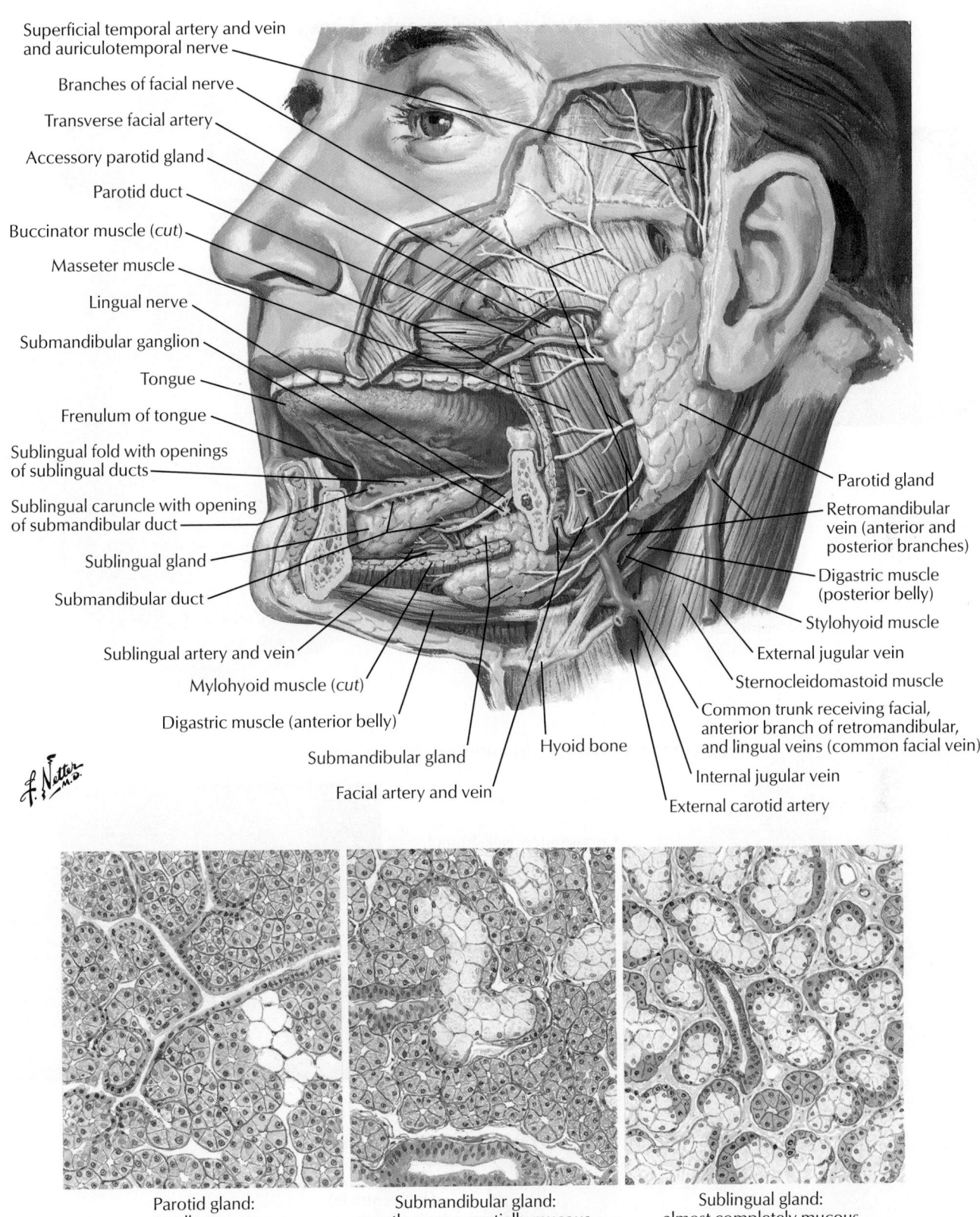

Superficial temporal artery and vein and auriculotemporal nerve

Branches of facial nerve

Transverse facial artery

Accessory parotid gland

Parotid duct

Buccinator muscle (*cut*)

Masseter muscle

Lingual nerve

Submandibular ganglion

Tongue

Frenulum of tongue

Sublingual fold with openings of sublingual ducts

Sublingual caruncle with opening of submandibular duct

Sublingual gland

Submandibular duct

Sublingual artery and vein

Mylohyoid muscle (*cut*)

Digastric muscle (anterior belly)

Submandibular gland

Facial artery and vein

Hyoid bone

Parotid gland

Retromandibular vein (anterior and posterior branches)

Digastric muscle (posterior belly)

Stylohyoid muscle

External jugular vein

Sternocleidomastoid muscle

Common trunk receiving facial, anterior branch of retromandibular, and lingual veins (common facial vein)

Internal jugular vein

External carotid artery

Parotid gland: totally serous

Submandibular gland: mostly serous, partially mucous

Sublingual gland: almost completely mucous

Plate 28 Salivary Glands. (Netter: Atlas of Human Anatomy, 4 ed, 2006, Saunders. Plate 61)

Coronary Arteries: Arteriographic Views

Right coronary artery: left anterior oblique view

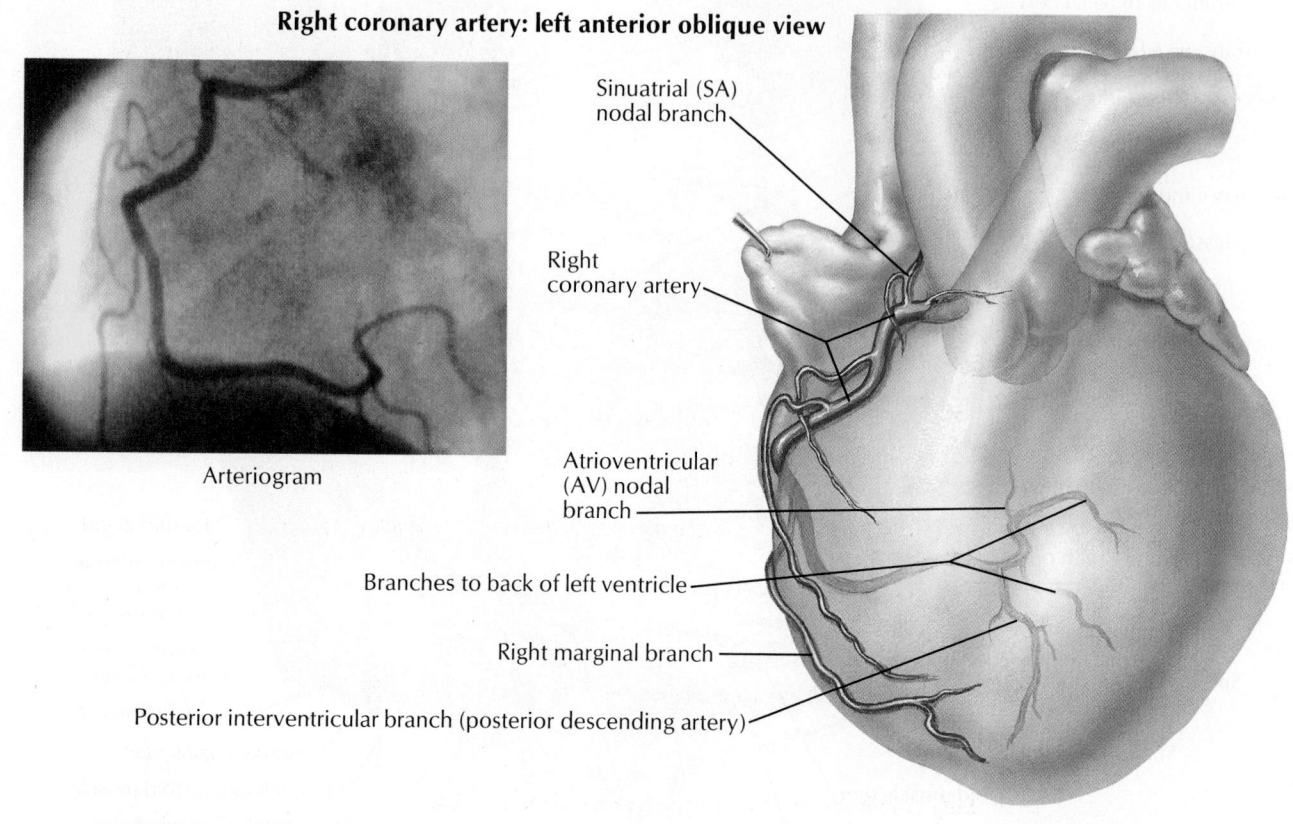

Arteriogram

Sinuatrial (SA) nodal branch

Right coronary artery

Atrioventricular (AV) nodal branch

Branches to back of left ventricle

Right marginal branch

Posterior interventricular branch (posterior descending artery)

Right coronary artery: right anterior oblique view

Sinuatrial (SA) nodal branch

Conus (arteriosus) branch

Right coronary artery

Right marginal branch

Arteriogram

Atrioventricular (AV) nodal branch

Right posterolateral branches (to back of left ventricle)

Posterior interventricular branch (posterior descending artery)

Plate 29 Coronary Arteries: Arteriographic Views. (Netter: Atlas of Human Anatomy, 4 ed, 2006, Saunders. Plate 218)

78

ANATOMY ILLUSTRATIONS

Left coronary artery: left anterior oblique view

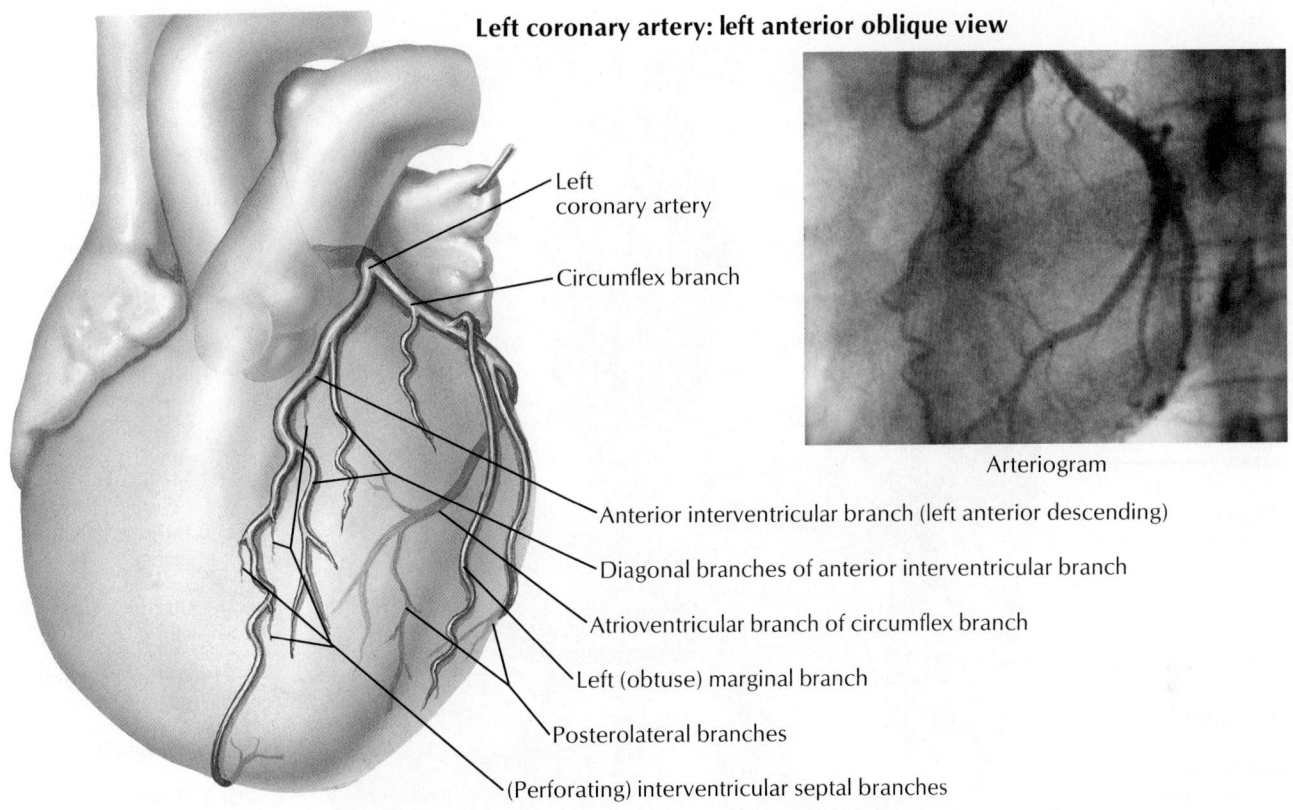

Left coronary artery

Circumflex branch

Arteriogram

Anterior interventricular branch (left anterior descending)

Diagonal branches of anterior interventricular branch

Atrioventricular branch of circumflex branch

Left (obtuse) marginal branch

Posterolateral branches

(Perforating) interventricular septal branches

Left coronary artery: right anterior oblique view

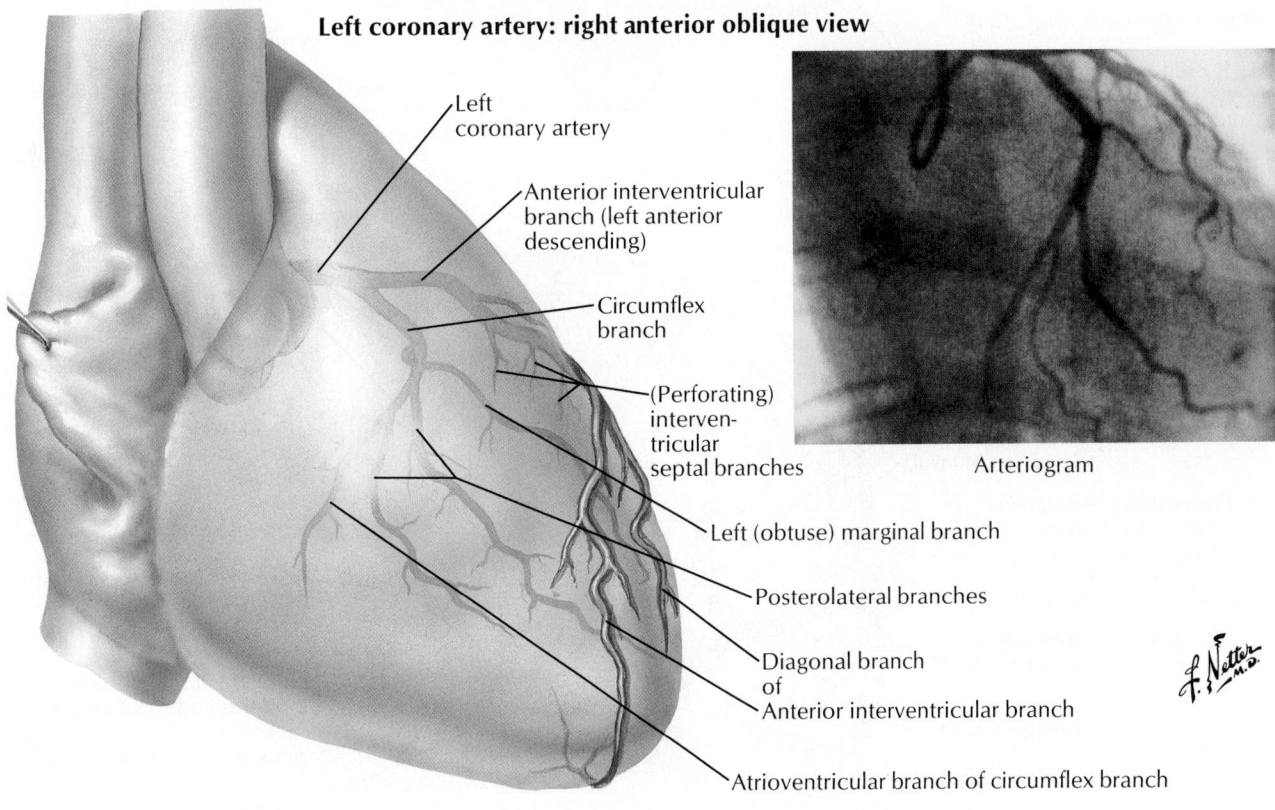

Left coronary artery

Anterior interventricular branch (left anterior descending)

Circumflex branch

(Perforating) interventricular septal branches

Arteriogram

Left (obtuse) marginal branch

Posterolateral branches

Diagonal branch of Anterior interventricular branch

Atrioventricular branch of circumflex branch

Plate 30 Coronary Arteries: Arteriographic Views. (Netter: Atlas of Human Anatomy, 4 ed, 2006, Saunders. Plate 219)

79

ANATOMY ILLUSTRATIONS

Corpus callosum

Anterolateral central (lenticulostriate) arteries

Lateral frontobasal (orbitofrontal) artery

Prefrontal artery

Precentral (pre-Rolandic) and central (Rolandic) sulcal arteries

Anterior parietal (postcentral sulcal) artery

Posterior parietal artery

Branch to angular gyrus

Temporal branches (anterior, middle, and posterior)

Middle cerebral artery and branches (deep in lateral cerebral [Sylvian] sulcus)

Anterior communicating artery

Posterior communicating artery

Anterior inferior cerebellar artery (AICA)

Posterior spinal artery

Paracentral artery

Medial frontal branches

Pericallosal artery

Callosomarginal artery

Polar frontal artery

Anterior cerebral arteries

Medial frontobasal (orbitofrontal) artery

Distal medial striate artery (recurrent artery of Heubner)

Internal carotid artery

Anterior choroidal artery

Posterior cerebral artery

Superior cerebellar artery

Basilar and pontine arteries

Labyrinthine (internal acoustic) artery

Vertebral artery

Posterior inferior cerebellar artery (PICA)

Anterior spinal artery

Corpus striatum (caudate and lentiform nuclei)

Anterolateral central (lenticulostriate) arteries

Insula (island of Reil)

Limen of insula

Precentral (pre-Rolandic), central (Rolandic) sulcal, and parietal arteries

Lateral cerebral (Sylvian) sulcus

Temporal branches of middle cerebral artery

Temporal lobe

Middle cerebral artery

Internal carotid artery

Falx cerebri

Callosomarginal arteries and Pericallosal arteries (branches of anterior cerebral arteries)

Trunk of corpus callosum

Internal capsule

Septum pellucidum

Rostrum of corpus callosum

Anterior cerebral arteries

Distal medial striate artery (recurrent artery of Heubner)

Anterior communicating artery

Optic chiasm

Plate 31   Arteries of Brain: Frontal View and Section. (Netter: Atlas of Human Anatomy, 4 ed, 2006, Saunders. Plate 141)

ANATOMY ILLUSTRATIONS

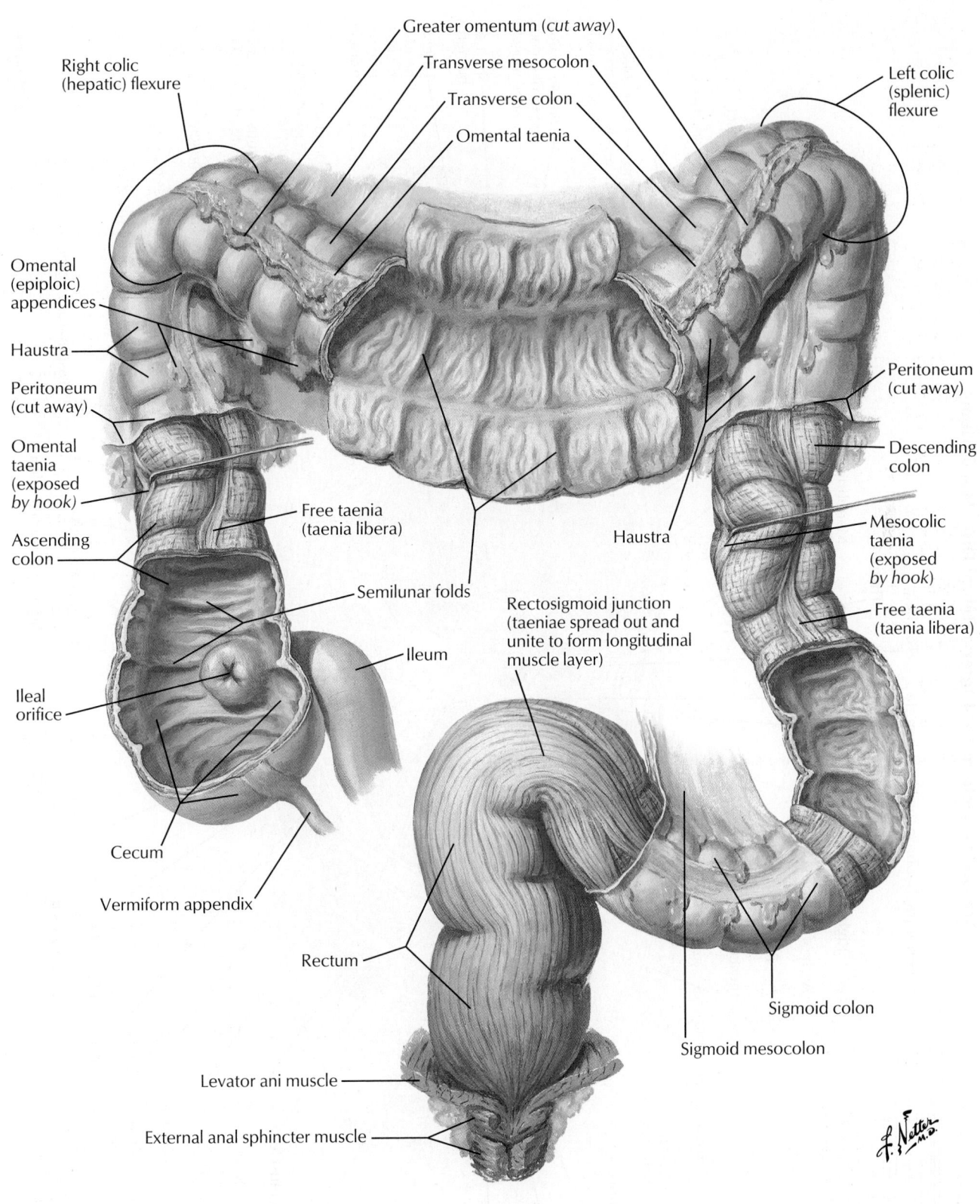

Right colic (hepatic) flexure

Omental (epiploic) appendices

Haustra

Peritoneum (cut away)

Omental taenia (exposed by hook)

Ascending colon

Ileal orifice

Cecum

Vermiform appendix

Rectum

Levator ani muscle

External anal sphincter muscle

Greater omentum (cut away)

Transverse mesocolon

Transverse colon

Omental taenia

Left colic (splenic) flexure

Free taenia (taenia libera)

Semilunar folds

Ileum

Rectosigmoid junction (taeniae spread out and unite to form longitudinal muscle layer)

Haustra

Peritoneum (cut away)

Descending colon

Mesocolic taenia (exposed by hook)

Free taenia (taenia libera)

Sigmoid colon

Sigmoid mesocolon

Plate 32 Mucosa and Musculature of Large Intestine. (Netter: Atlas of Human Anatomy, 4 ed, 2006, Saunders. Plate 284)

Transverse Section: T3-4 Intervertebral Disc, Manubrium

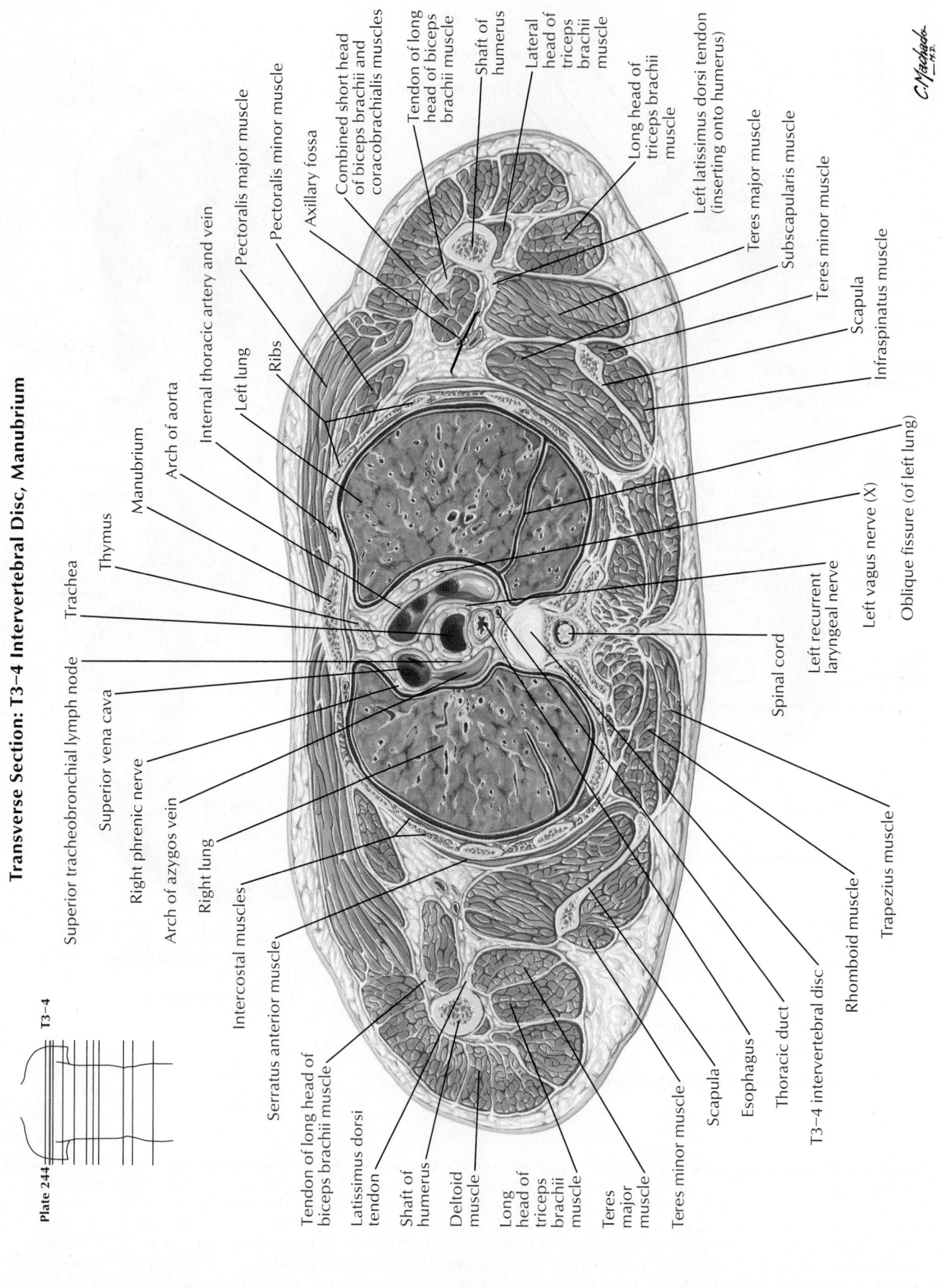

Plate 244

T3-4

Plate 33 Cross Section of Thorax at T3-4 Disc Level. (Netter: Atlas of Human Anatomy, 4 ed, 2006, Saunders. Plate 244)

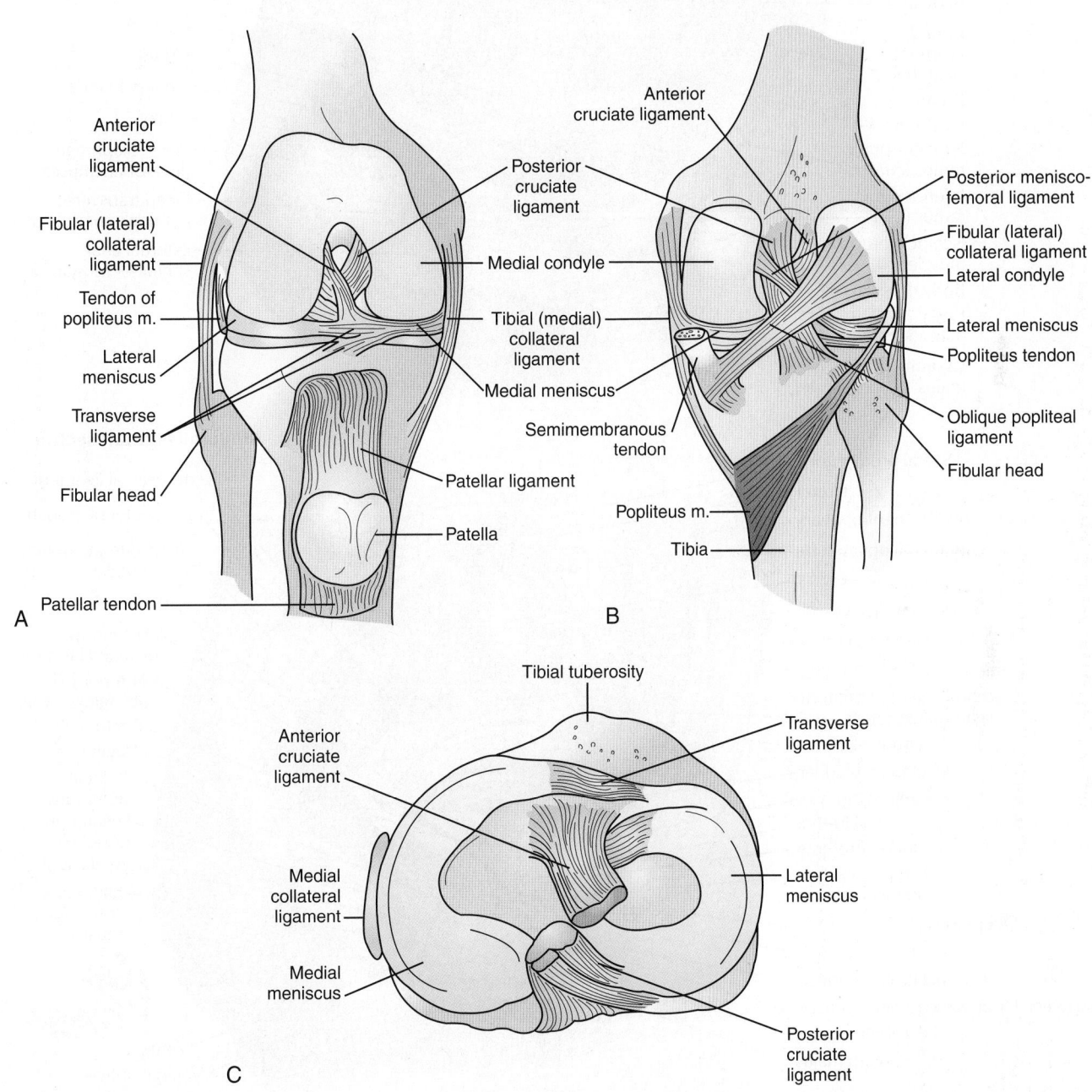

Plate 34 Knee joint opened; anterior, posterior, and proximal views. A, Anterior view of the knee joint, opened by folding the patella and patellar ligament inferiorly. On the lateral side is the fibular collateral ligament, separated by the popliteal tendon from the lateral meniscus. On the medial side, the tibial collateral ligament is attached to the medial meniscus. The anterior and posterior cruciate ligaments are seen between the femoral condyles. B, Posterior view of the opened knee joint with a more complete view of the posterior cruciate ligament. C, The femur is removed, showing the proximal (articular) end of the right tibia. On the medial side is the gently curved medial meniscus; on the lateral side is the more tightly curved lateral meniscus. The anterior end of the medial meniscus is anchored to the surface of the tibia by the transverse ligament. The cut ends of the anterior and posterior cruciate ligaments are shown, as well as the meniscofemoral ligament. (Fritz S: Mosby's Essential Sciences for Therapeutic Massage: Anatomy, Physiology, Biomechanics, and Pathology, ed 5, St. Louis, 2017, Elsevier.)

Paramedian (sagittal) dissection

Ureter
Uterine (fallopian) tube
Ovary
Ligament of ovary
Round ligament of uterus
Broad ligament (*cut*)
Superior pubic ramus (*cut*)
Inferior pubic ramus (*cut*)
Ischiocavernosus muscle
Body of clitoris
Labia minora
Labium majus

Rectouterine pouch (of Douglas)
Peritoneum (*cut edge*)
Vesicouterine pouch
Rectum
Ureter
Urinary bladder
Vagina
Pelvic diaphragm (levator ani muscle)
Deep transverse perineal muscle (*cut*)
External anal sphincter muscle

Median (sagittal) section

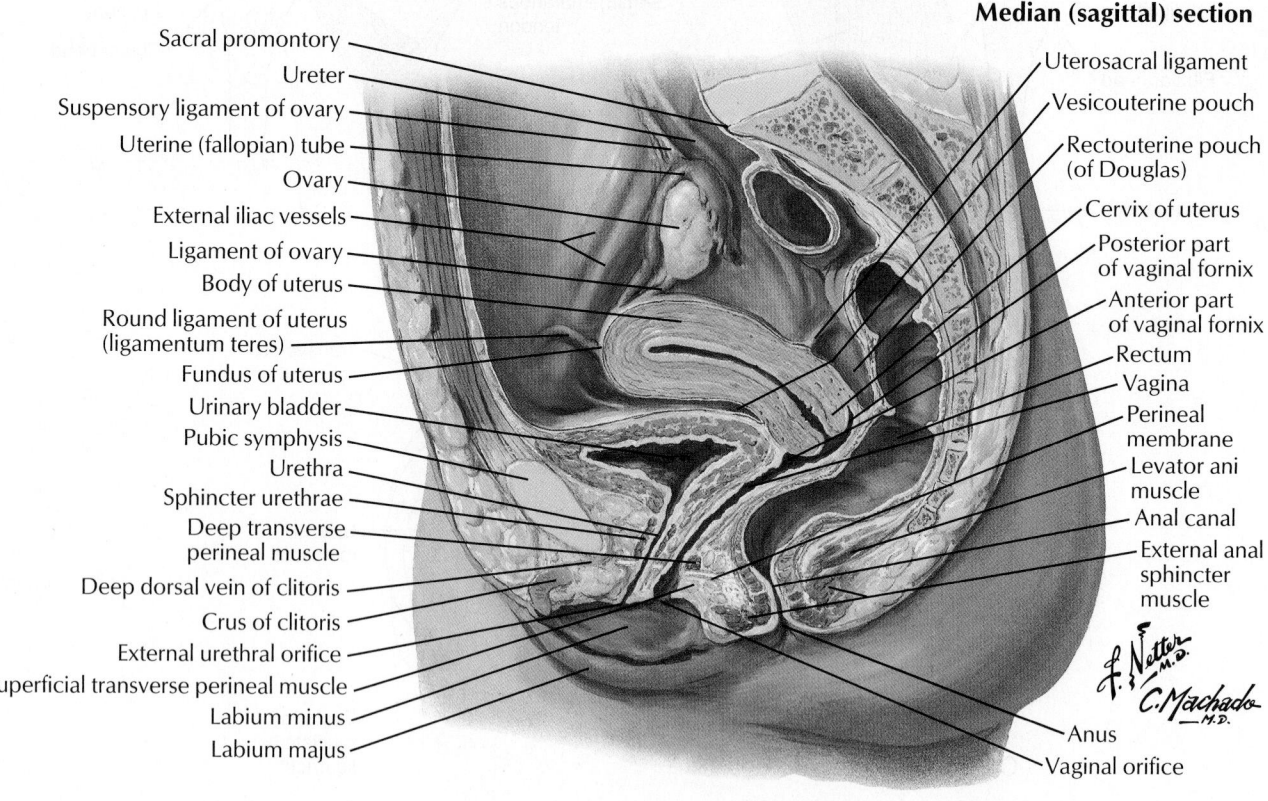

Sacral promontory
Ureter
Suspensory ligament of ovary
Uterine (fallopian) tube
Ovary
External iliac vessels
Ligament of ovary
Body of uterus
Round ligament of uterus (ligamentum teres)
Fundus of uterus
Urinary bladder
Pubic symphysis
Urethra
Sphincter urethrae
Deep transverse perineal muscle
Deep dorsal vein of clitoris
Crus of clitoris
External urethral orifice
Superficial transverse perineal muscle
Labium minus
Labium majus

Uterosacral ligament
Vesicouterine pouch
Rectouterine pouch (of Douglas)
Cervix of uterus
Posterior part of vaginal fornix
Anterior part of vaginal fornix
Rectum
Vagina
Perineal membrane
Levator ani muscle
Anal canal
External anal sphincter muscle
Anus
Vaginal orifice

Plate 35 Pelvic Viscera and Perineum: Female. (Netter: Atlas of Human Anatomy, 4 ed, 2006, Saunders. Plate 360)

PART II

Alphabetic Index

A

Aarskog's syndrome Q87.19
Abandonment —see Maltreatment
Abasia (-astasia) (hysterical) F44.4
Abderhalden-Kaufmann-Lignac syndrome
    (cystinosis) E72.04
Abdomen, abdominal —see also condition
    acute R10.0
    angina K55.1
    muscle deficiency syndrome Q79.4
Abdominalgia —see Pain, abdominal
Abduction contracture, hip or other joint —see
    Contraction, joint
Aberrant (congenital) —see also Malposition,
    congenital
    adrenal gland Q89.1
    artery (peripheral) Q27.8
        basilar NEC Q28.1
        cerebral Q28.3
        coronary Q24.5
        digestive system Q27.8
        eye Q15.8
        lower limb Q27.8
        precerebral Q28.1
        pulmonary Q25.79
        renal Q27.2
        retina Q14.1
        specified site NEC Q27.8
        subclavian Q27.8
        upper limb Q27.8
        vertebral Q28.1
    breast Q83.8
    endocrine gland NEC Q89.2
    hepatic duct Q44.5
    pancreas Q45.3
    parathyroid gland Q89.2
    pituitary gland Q89.2
    sebaceous glands, mucous membrane,
        mouth, congenital Q38.6
    spleen Q89.09
    subclavian artery Q27.8
    thymus (gland) Q89.2
    thyroid gland Q89.2
    vein (peripheral) NEC Q27.8
        cerebral Q28.3
        digestive system Q27.8
        lower limb Q27.8
        precerebral Q28.1
        specified site NEC Q27.8
        upper limb Q27.8
Aberration
    distantial —see Disturbance, visual
    mental F99
Abetalipoproteinemia E78.6
Abiotrophy R68.89
Ablatio, ablation
    retinae —see Detachment, retina
Ablepharia, ablepharon Q10.3
Abnormal, abnormality, abnormalities —see
        also Anomaly
    acid-base balance (mixed) E87.4
    albumin R77.0
    alphafetoprotein R77.2
    alveolar ridge K08.9
    anatomical relationship Q89.9
    apertures, congenital, diaphragm
        Q79.1
    auditory perception H93.29-●
        diplacusis —see Diplacusis
        hyperacusis —see Hyperacusis
        recruitment —see Recruitment, auditory
        threshold shift —see Shift, auditory
            threshold
    autosomes Q99.9
        fragile site Q95.5
    basal metabolic rate R94.8
    biosynthesis, testicular androgen
        E29.1
    bleeding time R79.1

Abnormal, abnormality, abnormalities —
    (Continued)
    blood level (of)
        cobalt R79.0
        copper R79.0
        iron R79.0
        lithium R78.89
        magnesium R79.0
        mineral NEC R79.0
        zinc R79.0
    blood pressure
        elevated R03.0
        low reading (nonspecific) R03.1
    blood sugar R73.09
    blood-gas level R79.81
    bowel sounds R19.15
        absent R19.11
        hyperactive R19.12
    brain scan R94.02
    breathing R06.9
    caloric test R94.138
    cerebrospinal fluid R83.9
        cytology R83.6
        drug level R83.2
        enzyme level R83.0
        hormones R83.1
        immunology R83.4
        microbiology R83.5
        nonmedicinal level R83.3
        specified type NEC R83.8
    chemistry, blood R79.9
        C-reactive protein R79.82
        drugs —see Findings, abnormal, in blood
        gas level R79.81
        minerals R79.0
        pancytopenia D61.818
        PTT R79.1
        specified NEC R79.89
        toxins —see Findings, abnormal, in
            blood
    chest sounds (friction) (rales) R09.89
    chromosome, chromosomal Q99.9
        with more than three X chromosomes,
            female Q97.1
        analysis result R89.8
            bronchial washings R84.8
            cerebrospinal fluid R83.8
            cervix uteri NEC R87.89
            nasal secretions R84.8
            nipple discharge R89.8
            peritoneal fluid R85.89
            pleural fluid R84.8
            prostatic secretions R86.8
            saliva R85.89
            seminal fluid R86.8
            sputum R84.8
            synovial fluid R89.8
            throat scrapings R84.8
            vagina R87.89
            vulva R87.89
            wound secretions R89.8
        dicentric replacement Q93.2
        ring replacement Q93.2
        sex Q99.8
            female phenotype Q97.9
                specified NEC Q97.8
            male phenotype Q98.9
                specified NEC Q98.8
            structural male Q98.6
        specified NEC Q99.8
    clinical findings NEC R68.89
    coagulation D68.9
        newborn, transient P61.6
        profile R79.1
        time R79.1
    communication —see Fistula
    conjunctiva, vascular H11.41-●
    coronary artery Q24.5
    cortisol-binding globulin E27.8
    course, eustachian tube Q17.8

Abnormal, abnormality, abnormalities —
    (Continued)
    creatinine clearance R94.4
    cytology
        anus R85.619
            atypical squamous cells cannot
                exclude high grade squamous
                intraepithelial lesion (ASC-H)
                R85.611
            atypical squamous cells of undetermined
                significance (ASC-US) R85.610
            cytologic evidence of malignancy
                R85.614
            high grade squamous intraepithelial
                lesion (HGSIL) R85.613
            human papillomavirus (HPV) DNA test
                high risk positive R85.81
                low risk postive R85.82
            inadequate smear R85.615
            low grade squamous intraepithelial
                lesion (LGSIL) R85.612
            satisfactory anal smear but lacking
                transformation zone R85.616
            specified NEC R85.618
            unsatisfactory smear R85.615
        female genital organs —see Abnormal,
            Papanicolaou (smear)
    dark adaptation curve H53.61
    dentofacial NEC —see Anomaly, dentofacial
    development, developmental Q89.9
        central nervous system Q07.9
    diagnostic imaging
        abdomen, abdominal region NEC R93.5
        biliary tract R93.2
        bladder R93.41
        breast R92.8
        central nervous system NEC R90.89
        cerebrovascular NEC R90.89
        coronary circulation R93.1
        digestive tract NEC R93.3
        gastrointestinal (tract) R93.3
        genitourinary organs R93.89
        head R93.0
        heart R93.1
        intrathoracic organ NEC R93.89
        kidney R93.42-●
        limbs R93.6
        liver R93.2
        lung (field) R91.8
        musculoskeletal system NEC R93.7
        renal pelvis R93.41
        retroperitoneum R93.5
        site specified NEC R93.89
        skin and subcutaneous tissue R93.89
    ➡skull R93.0
        testis R93.81-●
        urinary organs specified NEC R93.49
        ureter R93.41
    direction, teeth, fully erupted M26.30
    ear ossicles, acquired NEC H74.39-●
        ankylosis —see Ankylosis, ear ossicles
        discontinuity —see Discontinuity, ossicles,
            ear
        partial loss —see Loss, ossicles, ear (partial)
    Ebstein Q22.5
    echocardiogram R93.1
    echoencephalogram R90.81
    echogram —see Abnormal, diagnostic
        imaging
    electrocardiogram [ECG] [EKG] R94.31
    electroencephalogram [EEG] R94.01
    electrolyte —see Imbalance, electrolyte
    electromyogram [EMG] R94.131
    electro-oculogram [EOG] R94.110
    electrophysiological intracardiac studies
        R94.39
    electroretinogram [ERG] R94.111
    erythrocytes
        congenital, with perinatal jaundice D58.9
    feces (color) (contents) (mucus) R19.5

Abnormal, abnormality, abnormalities —
(Continued)
finding —see Findings, abnormal, without
diagnosis
fluid
amniotic —see Abnormal, specimen,
specified
cerebrospinal —see Abnormal,
cerebrospinal fluid
peritoneal —see Abnormal, specimen,
digestive organs
pleural —see Abnormal, specimen,
respiratory organs
synovial —see Abnormal, specimen,
specified
thorax (bronchial washings) (pleural
fluid) —see Abnormal, specimen,
respiratory organs
vaginal —see Abnormal, specimen, female
genital organs
form
teeth K00.2
uterus —see Anomaly, uterus
function studies
auditory R94.120
bladder R94.8
brain R94.09
cardiovascular R94.30
ear R94.128
endocrine NEC R94.7
eye NEC R94.118
kidney R94.4
liver R94.5
nervous system
central NEC R94.09
peripheral NEC R94.138
pancreas R94.8
placenta R94.8
pulmonary R94.2
special senses NEC R94.128
spleen R94.8
thyroid R94.6
vestibular R94.121
gait —see Gait
hysterical F44.4
gastrin secretion E16.4
globulin R77.1
cortisol-binding E27.8
thyroid-binding E07.89
glomerular, minor —see also N00-N07 with
fourth character .0 N05.0
glucagon secretion E16.3
glucose tolerance (test) (non-fasting)
R73.09
gravitational (G) forces or states (effect of)
T75.81
hair (color) (shaft) L67.9
specified NEC L67.8
hard tissue formation in pulp (dental)
K04.3
head movement R25.0
heart
rate R00.9
specified NEC R00.8
shadow R93.1
sounds NEC R01.2
hemoglobin (disease) —see also Disease,
hemoglobin D58.2
trait —see Trait, hemoglobin, abnormal
histology NEC R89.7
immunological findings R89.4
in serum R76.9
specified NEC R76.8
increase in appetite R63.2
involuntary movement —see Abnormal,
movement, involuntary
jaw closure M26.51
karyotype R89.8
kidney function test R94.4
knee jerk R29.2
leukocyte (cell) (differential) NEC D72.9

Abnormal, abnormality, abnormalities —
(Continued)
liver function test R94.5
loss of
height R29.890
weight R63.4
mammogram NEC R92.8
calcification (calculus) R92.1
microcalcification R92.0
Mantoux test R76.11
movement (disorder) —see also Disorder,
movement
head R25.0
involuntary R25.9
fasciculation R25.3
of head R25.0
spasm R25.2
specified type NEC R25.8
tremor R25.1
myoglobin (Aberdeen) (Annapolis) R89.7
neonatal screening P09
oculomotor study R94.113
palmar creases Q82.8
Papanicolaou (smear)
anus R85.619
atypical squamous cells cannot
exclude high grade squamous
intraepithelial lesion (ASC-H)
R85.611
atypical squamous cells of undetermined
significance (ASC-US) R85.610
cytologic evidence of malignancy
R85.614
high grade squamous intraepithelial
lesion (HGSIL) R85.613
human papillomavirus (HPV)
DNA test
high risk positive R85.81
low risk postive R85.82
inadequate smear R85.615
low grade squamous intraepithelial
lesion (LGSIL) R85.612
satisfactory anal smear but lacking
transformation zone R85.616
specified NEC R85.618
unsatisfactory smear R85.615
bronchial washings R84.6
cerebrospinal fluid R83.6
cervix R87.619
atypical squamous cells cannot
exclude high grade squamous
intraepithelial lesion (ASC-H)
R87.611
atypical squamous cells of undetermined
significance (ASC-US) R87.610
cytologic evidence of malignancy
R87.614
high grade squamous intraepithelial
lesion (HGSIL) R87.613
inadequate smear R87.615
low grade squamous intraepithelial
lesion (LGSIL) R87.612
non-atypical endometrial cells
R87.618
satisfactory cervical smear but
lacking transformation zone
R87.616
specified NEC R87.618
thin preparaton R87.619
unsatisfactory smear R87.615
nasal secretions R84.6
nipple discharge R89.6
peritoneal fluid R85.69
pleural fluid R84.6
prostatic secretions R86.6
saliva R85.69
seminal fluid R86.6
sites NEC R89.6
sputum R84.6
synovial fluid R89.6
throat scrapings R84.6

Abnormal, abnormality, abnormalities —
(Continued)
Papanicolaou (smear) (Continued)
vagina R87.629
atypical squamous cells cannot
exclude high grade squamous
intraepithelial lesion (ASC-H)
R87.621
atypical squamous cells of
undetermined significance
(ASC-US) R87.620
cytologic evidence of malignancy
R87.624
high grade squamous intraepithelial
lesion (HGSIL) R87.623
inadequate smear R87.625
low grade squamous intraepithelial
lesion (LGSIL) R87.622
specified NEC R87.628
thin preparation R87.629
unsatisfactory smear R87.625
vulva R87.69
wound secretions R89.6
partial thromboplastin time (PTT) R79.1
pelvis (bony) —see Deformity, pelvis
percussion, chest (tympany) R09.89
periods (grossly) —see Menstruation
phonocardiogram R94.39
plantar reflex R29.2
plasma
protein R77.9
specified NEC R77.8
viscosity R70.1
pleural (folds) Q34.0
posture R29.3
product of conception O02.9
specified type NEC O02.89
prothrombin time (PT) R79.1
pulmonary
artery, congenital Q25.79
function, newborn P28.89
test results R94.2
pulsations in neck R00.2
pupillary H21.56-•
function (reaction) (reflex) —see Anomaly,
pupil, function
radiological examination —see Abnormal,
diagnostic imaging
red blood cell(s) (morphology) (volume)
R71.8
reflex —see Reflex
renal function test R94.4
response to nerve stimulation R94.130
retinal correspondence H53.31
retinal function study R94.111
rhythm, heart —see also Arrhythmia
saliva —see Abnormal, specimen, digestive
organs
scan
kidney R94.4
liver R93.2
thyroid R94.6
secretion
gastrin E16.4
glucagon E16.3
semen, seminal fluid —see Abnormal,
specimen, male genital organs
serum level (of)
acid phosphatase R74.8
alkaline phosphatase R74.8
amylase R74.8
enzymes R74.9
specified NEC R74.8
lipase R74.8
triacylglycerol lipase R74.8
shape
gravid uterus —see Anomaly, uterus
sinus venosus Q21.1
size, tooth, teeth K00.2
spacing, tooth, teeth, fully erupted
M26.30

Abnormal, abnormality, abnormalities —
(Continued)
specimen
digestive organs (peritoneal fluid) (saliva)
R85.9
cytology R85.69
drug level R85.2
enzyme level R85.0
histology R85.7
hormones R85.1
immunology R85.4
microbiology R85.5
nonmedicinal level R85.3
specified type NEC R85.89
female genital organs (secretions) (smears)
R87.9
cytology R87.69
cervix R87.619
human papillomavirus (HPV) DNA
test
high risk positive R87.810
low risk positive R87.820
inadequate (unsatisfactory) smear
R87.615
non-atypical endometrial cells
R87.618
specified NEC R87.618
vagina R87.629
human papillomavirus (HPV) DNA
test
high risk positive R87.811
low risk positive R87.821
inadequate (unsatisfactory) smear
R87.625
vulva R87.69
drug level R87.2
enzyme level R87.0
histological R87.7
hormones R87.1
immunology R87.4
microbiology R87.5
nonmedicinal level R87.3
specified type NEC R87.89
male genital organs (prostatic secretions)
(semen) R86.9
cytology R86.6
drug level R86.2
enzyme level R86.0
histological R86.7
hormones R86.1
immunology R86.4
microbiology R86.5
nonmedicinal level R86.3
specified type NEC R86.8
nipple discharge —see Abnormal,
specimen, specified
respiratory organs (bronchial washings)
(nasal secretions) (pleural fluid)
(sputum) R84.9
cytology R84.6
drug level R84.2
enzyme level R84.0
histology R84.7
hormones R84.1
immunology R84.4
microbiology R84.5
nonmedicinal level R84.3
specified type NEC R84.8
specified organ, system and tissue NOS
R89.9
cytology R89.6
drug level R89.2
enzyme level R89.0
histology R89.7
hormones R89.1
immunology R89.4
microbiology R89.5
nonmedicinal level R89.3
specified type NEC R89.8
synovial fluid —see Abnormal, specimen,
specified

Abnormal, abnormality, abnormalities —
(Continued)
specimen (Continued)
thorax (bronchial washings) (pleural
fluids) —see Abnormal, specimen,
respiratory organs
vagina (secretion) (smear) R87.629
vulva (secretion) (smear) R87.69
wound secretion —see Abnormal,
specimen, specified
spermatozoa —see Abnormal, specimen, male
genital organs
sputum (amount) (color) (odor) R09.3
stool (color) (contents) (mucus) R19.5
bloody K92.1
guaiac positive R19.5
synchondrosis Q78.8
thermography —see also Abnormal,
diagnostic imaging R93.89
thyroid-binding globulin E07.89
tooth, teeth (form) (size) K00.2
toxicology (findings) R78.9
transport protein E88.09
tumor marker NEC R97.8
ultrasound results —see Abnormal, diagnostic
imaging
umbilical cord complicating delivery O69.9
urination NEC R39.198
urine (constituents) R82.90
bile R82.2
cytological examination R82.89
drugs R82.5
fat R82.0
glucose R81
heavy metals R82.6
hemoglobin R82.3
histological examination R82.89
ketones R82.4
microbiological examination (culture)
R82.79
myoglobin R82.1
positive culture R82.79
protein —see Proteinuria
specified substance NEC R82.998
chromoabnormality NEC R82.91
substances nonmedical R82.6
uterine hemorrhage —see Hemorrhage,
uterus
vectorcardiogram R94.39
visually evoked potential (VEP) R94.112
white blood cells D72.9
specified NEC D72.89
X-ray examination —see Abnormal,
diagnostic imaging
Abnormity (any organ or part) —see Anomaly
Abocclusion M26.29
hemolytic disease (newborn) P55.1
incompatibility reaction ABO —see
Complication(s), transfusion,
incompatibility reaction, ABO
Abolition, language R48.8
Aborter, habitual or recurrent —see Loss (of),
pregnancy, recurrent
Abortion (complete) (spontaneous) O03.9
with
retained products of conception —see
Abortion, incomplete
attempted (elective) (failed) O07.4
complicated by O07.30
afibrinogenemia O07.1
cardiac arrest O07.36
chemical damage of pelvic organ(s)
O07.34
circulatory collapse O07.31
cystitis O07.38
defibrination syndrome O07.1
electrolyte imbalance O07.33
embolism (air) (amniotic fluid) (blood
clot) (fat) (pulmonary) (septic)
(soap) O07.2
endometritis O07.0

Abortion (Continued)
attempted (Continued)
complicated by (Continued)
genital tract and pelvic infection O07.0
hemolysis O07.1
hemorrhage (delayed) (excessive) O07.1
infection
genital tract or pelvic O07.0
urinary tract tract O07.38
intravascular coagulation O07.1
laceration of pelvic organ(s) O07.34
metabolic disorder O07.33
oliguria O07.32
oophoritis O07.0
parametritis O07.0
pelvic peritonitis O07.0
perforation of pelvic organ(s) O07.34
renal failure or shutdown O07.32
salpingitis or salpingo-oophoritis O07.0
sepsis O07.37
shock O07.31
specified condition NEC O07.39
tubular necrosis (renal) O07.32
uremia O07.32
urinary tract infection O07.38
venous complication NEC O07.35
embolism (air) (amniotic fluid) (blood
clot) (fat) (pulmonary) (septic)
(soap) O07.2
complicated (by) (following) O03.80
afibrinogenemia O03.6
cardiac arrest O03.86
chemical damage of pelvic organ(s) O03.84
circulatory collapse O03.81
cystitis O03.88
defibrination syndrome O03.6
electrolyte imbalance O03.83
embolism (air) (amniotic fluid) (blood clot)
(fat) (pulmonary) (septic) (soap) O03.7
endometritis O03.5
genital tract and pelvic infection O03.5
hemolysis O03.6
hemorrhage (delayed) (excessive) O03.6
infection
genital tract or pelvic O03.5
urinary tract O03.88
intravascular coagulation O03.6
laceration of pelvic organ(s) O03.84
metabolic disorder O03.83
oliguria O03.82
oophoritis O03.5
parametritis O03.5
pelvic peritonitis O03.5
perforation of pelvic organ(s) O03.84
renal failure or shutdown O03.82
salpingitis or salpingo-oophoritis
O03.5
sepsis O03.87
shock O03.81
specified condition NEC O03.89
tubular necrosis (renal) O03.82
uremia O03.82
urinary tract infection O03.88
venous complication NEC O03.85
embolism (air) (amniotic fluid) (blood
clot) (fat) (pulmonary) (septic)
(soap) O03.7
failed —see Abortion, attempted
habitual or recurrent N96
with current abortion —see categories
O03-O04
without current pregnancy N96
care in current pregnancy O26.2-•
incomplete (spontaneous) O03.4
complicated (by) (following) O03.30
afibrinogenemia O03.1
cardiac arrest O03.36
chemical damage of pelvic organ(s)
O03.34
circulatory collapse O03.31
cystitis O03.38

Abortion *(Continued)*
  incomplete *(Continued)*
    complicated *(Continued)*
      defibrination syndrome O03.1
      electrolyte imbalance O03.33
      embolism (air) (amniotic fluid) (blood
        clot) (fat) (pulmonary) (septic)
        (soap) O03.2
      endometritis O03.0
      genital tract and pelvic infection O03.0
      hemolysis O03.1
      hemorrhage (delayed) (excessive) O03.1
      infection
        genital tract or pelvic O03.0
        urinary tract O03.38
      intravascular coagulation O03.1
      laceration of pelvic organ(s) O03.34
      metabolic disorder O03.33
      oliguria O03.32
      oophoritis O03.0
      parametritis O03.0
      pelvic peritonitis O03.0
      perforation of pelvic organ(s) O03.34
      renal failure or shutdown O03.32
      salpingitis or salpingo-oophoritis O03.0
      sepsis O03.37
      shock O03.31
      specified condition NEC O03.39
      tubular necrosis (renal) O03.32
      uremia O03.32
      urinary infection O03.38
      venous complication NEC O03.35
        embolism (air) (amniotic fluid) (blood
          clot) (fat) (pulmonary) (septic)
          (soap) O03.2
  induced (encounter for) Z33.2
    complicated by O04.80
      afibrinogenemia O04.6
      cardiac arrest O04.86
      chemical damage of pelvic organ(s)
        O04.84
      circulatory collapse O04.81
      cystitis O04.88
      defibrination syndrome O04.6
      electrolyte imbalance O04.83
      embolism (air) (amniotic fluid) (blood
        clot) (fat) (pulmonary) (septic)
        (soap) O04.7
      endometritis O04.5
      genital tract and pelvic infection O04.5
      hemolysis O04.6
      hemorrhage (delayed) (excessive) O04.6
      infection
        genital tract or pelvic O04.5
        urinary tract O04.88
      intravascular coagulation O04.6
      laceration of pelvic organ(s) O04.84
      metabolic disorder O04.83
      oliguria O04.82
      oophoritis O04.5
      parametritis O04.5
      pelvic peritonitis O04.5
      perforation of pelvic organ(s) O04.84
      renal failure or shutdown O04.82
      salpingitis or salpingo-oophoritis O04.5
      sepsis O04.87
      shock O04.81
      specified condition NEC O04.89
      tubular necrosis (renal) O04.82
      uremia O04.82
      urinary tract infection O04.88
      venous complication NEC O04.85
        embolism (air) (amniotic fluid) (blood
          clot) (fat) (pulmonary) (septic)
          (soap) O04.7
  ▶inevitable O03.4
  missed O02.1
  spontaneous —*see* Abortion (complete)
    (spontaneous)
    threatened O20.0
  threatened (spontaneous) O20.0

Abortion *(Continued)*
  tubal O00.10-●
    with intrauterine pregnancy O00.11-
Abortus fever A23.1
Aboulomania F60.7
Abrami's disease D59.8
Abramov-Fiedler myocarditis (acute isolated
  myocarditis) I40.1
Abrasion T14.8
  abdomen, abdominal (wall) S30.811
  alveolar process S00.512
  ankle S90.51-●
  antecubital space —*see* Abrasion, elbow
  anus S30.817
  arm (upper) S40.81-●
  auditory canal —*see* Abrasion, ear
  auricle —*see* Abrasion, ear
  axilla —*see* Abrasion, arm
  back, lower S30.810
  breast S20.11-●
  brow S00.81
  buttock S30.810
  calf —*see* Abrasion, leg
  canthus —*see* Abrasion, eyelid
  cheek S00.81
    internal S00.512
  chest wall —*see* Abrasion, thorax
  chin S00.81
  clitoris S30.814
  cornea S05.0-●
  costal region —*see* Abrasion, thorax
  dental K03.1
  digit(s)
    foot —*see* Abrasion, toe
    hand —*see* Abrasion, finger
  ear S00.41-●
  elbow S50.31-●
  epididymis S30.813
  epigastric region S30.811
  epiglottis S10.11
  esophagus (thoracic) S27.818
    cervical S10.11
  eyebrow —*see* Abrasion, eyelid
  eyelid S00.21-●
  face S00.81
  finger(s) S60.41-●
    index S60.41-●
    little S60.41-●
    middle S60.41-●
    ring S60.41-●
  flank S30.811
  foot (except toe(s) alone) S90.81-●
    toe —*see* Abrasion, toe
  forearm S50.81-●
    elbow only —*see* Abrasion, elbow
  forehead S00.81
  genital organs, external
    female S30.816
    male S30.815
  groin S30.811
  gum S00.512
  hand S60.51-●
  head S00.91
    ear —*see* Abrasion, ear
    eyelid —*see* Abrasion, eyelid
    lip S00.511
    nose S00.31
    oral cavity S00.512
    scalp S00.01
    specified site NEC S00.81
  heel —*see* Abrasion, foot
  hip S70.21-●
  inguinal region S30.811
  interscapular region S20.419
  jaw S00.81
  knee S80.21-●
  labium (majus) (minus) S30.814
  larynx S10.11
  leg (lower) S80.81-●
    knee —*see* Abrasion, knee
    upper —*see* Abrasion, thigh

Abrasion *(Continued)*
  lip S00.511
  lower back S30.810
  lumbar region S30.810
  malar region S00.81
  mammary —*see* Abrasion, breast
  mastoid region S00.81
  mouth S00.512
  nail
    finger —*see* Abrasion, finger
    toe —*see* Abrasion, toe
  nape S10.81
  nasal S00.31
  neck S10.91
    specified site NEC S10.81
    throat S10.11
  nose S00.31
  occipital region S00.01
  oral cavity S00.512
  orbital region —*see* Abrasion, eyelid
  palate S00.512
  palm —*see* Abrasion, hand
  parietal region S00.01
  pelvis S30.810
  penis S30.812
  perineum
    female S30.814
    male S30.810
  periocular area —*see* Abrasion, eyelid
  phalanges
    finger —*see* Abrasion, finger
    toe —*see* Abrasion, toe
  pharynx S10.11
  pinna —*see* Abrasion, ear
  popliteal space —*see* Abrasion, knee
  prepuce S30.812
  pubic region S30.810
  pudendum
    female S30.816
    male S30.815
  sacral region S30.810
  scalp S00.01
  scapular region —*see* Abrasion, shoulder
  scrotum S30.813
  shin —*see* Abrasion, leg
  shoulder S40.21-●
  skin NEC T14.8
  sternal region S20.319
  submaxillary region S00.81
  submental region S00.81
  subungual
    finger(s) —*see* Abrasion, finger
    toe(s) —*see* Abrasion, toe
  supraclavicular fossa S10.81
  supraorbital S00.81
  temple S00.81
  temporal region S00.81
  testis S30.813
  thigh S70.31-●
  thorax, thoracic (wall) S20.91
    back S20.41-●
    front S20.31-●
  throat S10.11
  thumb S60.31-●
  toe(s) (lesser) S90.416
    great S90.41-●
  tongue S00.512
  tooth, teeth (dentifrice) (habitual) (hard
    tissues) (occupational) (ritual)
    (traditional) K03.1
  trachea S10.11
  tunica vaginalis S30.813
  tympanum, tympanic membrane —*see*
    Abrasion, ear
  uvula S00.512
  vagina S30.814
  vocal cords S10.11
  vulva S30.814
  wrist S60.81-●
Abrism —*see* Poisoning, food, noxious,
  plant

Abruptio placentae O45.9-●
  with
    afibrinogenemia O45.01-●
    coagulation defect O45.00-●
      specified NEC O45.09-●
    disseminated intravascular coagulation
      O45.02-●
    hypofibrinogenemia O45.01-●
  specified NEC O45.8-●
Abruption, placenta —*see* Abruptio placentae
Abscess (connective tissue) (embolic) (fistulous)
    (infective) (metastatic) (multiple)
    (pernicious) (pyogenic) (septic) L02.91
  with
    diverticular disease (intestine) K57.80
      with bleeding K57.81
      large intestine K57.20
        with
          bleeding K57.21
          small intestine K57.40
            with bleeding K57.41
      small intestine K57.00
        with
          bleeding K57.01
          large intestine K57.40
            with bleeding K57.41
    lymphangitis - code by site under
      Abscess
  abdomen, abdominal
    cavity K65.1
    wall L02.211
  abdominopelvic K65.1
  accessory sinus —*see* Sinusitis
  adrenal (capsule) (gland) E27.8
  alveolar K04.7
    with sinus K04.6
  amebic A06.4
    brain (and liver or lung abscess) A06.6
    genitourinary tract A06.82
    liver (without mention of brain or lung
      abscess) A06.4
    lung (and liver) (without mention of brain
      abscess) A06.5
    specified site NEC A06.89
    spleen A06.89
  anerobic A48.0
  ankle —*see* Abscess, lower limb
  anorectal K61.2
  antecubital space —*see* Abscess, upper limb
  antrum (chronic) (Highmore) —*see* Sinusitis,
    maxillary
  anus K61.0
  apical (tooth) K04.7
    with sinus (alveolar) K04.6
  appendix K35.33
  areola (acute) (chronic) (nonpuerperal)
    N61.1
    puerperal, postpartum or gestational —*see*
      Infection, nipple
  arm (any part) —*see* Abscess, upper limb
  artery (wall) I77.89
  atheromatous I77.2
  auricle, ear —*see* Abscess, ear, external
  axilla (region) L02.41-●
    lymph gland or node L04.2
  back (any part, except buttock) L02.212
  Bartholin's gland N75.1
    with
      abortion —*see* Abortion, by type
        complicated by, sepsis
      ectopic or molar pregnancy O08.0
    following ectopic or molar pregnancy O08.0
  Bezold's —*see* Mastoiditis, acute
  bilharziasis B65.1
  bladder (wall) —*see* Cystitis, specified type
    NEC
  bone (subperiosteal) —*see also* Osteomyelitis,
    specified type NEC
    accessory sinus (chronic) —*see* Sinusitis
    chronic or old —*see* Osteomyelitis, chronic
    jaw (lower) (upper) M27.2

Abscess (*Continued*)
  bone (*Continued*)
    mastoid —*see* Mastoiditis, acute,
      subperiosteal
    petrous —*see* Petrositis
    spinal (tuberculous) A18.01
      nontuberculous —*see* Osteomyelitis,
        vertebra
  bowel K63.0
  brain (any part) (cystic) (otogenic) G06.0
    amebic (with abscess of any other site) A06.6
    gonococcal A54.82
    pheomycotic (chromomycotic) B43.1
    tuberculous A17.81
  breast (acute) (chronic) (nonpuerperal)
    N61.1
    newborn P39.0
    puerperal, postpartum, gestational —*see*
      Mastitis, obstetric, purulent
  broad ligament N73.2
    acute N73.0
    chronic N73.1
  Brodie's (localized) (chronic) M86.8X-●
  bronchi J98.09
  buccal cavity K12.2
  bulbourethral gland N34.0
  bursa M71.00
    ankle M71.07-●
    elbow M71.02-●
    foot M71.07-●
    hand M71.04-●
    hip M71.05-●
    knee M71.06-●
    multiple sites M71.09
    pharyngeal J39.1
    shoulder M71.01-●
    specified site NEC M71.08
    wrist M71.03-●
  buttock L02.31
  canthus —*see* Blepharoconjunctivitis
  cartilage —*see* Disorder, cartilage, specified
    type NEC
  cecum K35.33
  cerebellum, cerebellar G06.0
    sequelae G09
  cerebral (embolic) G06.0
    sequelae G09
  cervical (meaning neck) L02.11
    lymph gland or node L04.0
  cervix (stump) (uteri) —*see* Cervicitis
  cheek (external) L02.01
    inner K12.2
  chest J86.9
    with fistula J86.0
    wall L02.213
  chin L02.01
  choroid —*see* Inflammation, chorioretinal
  circumtonsillar J36
  cold (lung) (tuberculous) —*see also*
    Tuberculosis, abscess, lung
    articular —*see* Tuberculosis, joint
  colon (wall) K63.0
  colostomy K94.02
  conjunctiva —*see* Conjunctivitis, acute
  cornea H16.31-●
  corpus
    cavernosum N48.21
    luteum —*see* Oophoritis
  Cowper's gland N34.0
  cranium G06.0
  cul-de-sac (Douglas') (posterior) —*see*
    Peritonitis, pelvic, female
  cutaneous —*see* Abscess, by site
  dental K04.7
    with sinus (alveolar) K04.6
  dentoalveolar K04.7
    with sinus K04.6
  diaphragm, diaphragmatic K65.1
  Douglas' cul-de-sac or pouch —*see*
    Peritonitis, pelvic, female
  Dubois A50.59

Abscess (*Continued*)
  ear (middle) —*see also* Otitis, media,
    suppurative
    acute —*see* Otitis, media, suppurative, acute
    external H60.0-●
  entamebic —*see* Abscess, amebic
  enterostomy K94.12
  epididymis N45.4
  epidural G06.2
    brain G06.0
    spinal cord G06.1
  epiglottis J38.7
  epiploon, epiploic K65.1
  erysipelatous —*see* Erysipelas
  ➡ esophagus K20.80
  ethmoid (bone) (chronic) (sinus) J32.2
  external auditory canal —*see* Abscess, ear,
    external
  extradural G06.2
    brain G06.0
      sequelae G09
    spinal cord G06.1
  extraperitoneal K68.19
  eye —*see* Endophthalmitis, purulent
  eyelid H00.03-●
  face (any part, except ear, eye and nose) L02.01
  fallopian tube —*see* Salpingitis
  fascia M72.8
  fauces J39.1
  fecal K63.0
  femoral (region) —*see* Abscess, lower limb
  filaria, filarial —*see* Infestation, filarial
  finger (any) —*see also* Abscess, hand
    nail —*see* Cellulitis, finger
  foot L02.61-●
  forehead L02.01
  frontal sinus (chronic) J32.1
  gallbladder K81.0
  genital organ or tract
    female (external) N76.4
    male N49.9
      multiple sites N49.8
      specified NEC N49.8
  gestational mammary O91.11-●
  gestational subareolar O91.11-●
  gingival —*see* Periodontitis, localized
  gland, glandular (lymph) (acute) —*see*
    Lymphadenitis, acute
  gluteal (region) L02.31
  gonorrheal —*see* Gonococcus
  groin L02.214
  gum —*see* Periodontitis, localized
  hand L02.51-●
  head NEC L02.811
    face (any part, except ear, eye and nose)
      L02.01
  heart —*see* Carditis
  heel —*see* Abscess, foot
  helminthic —*see* Infestation, helminth
  hepatic (cholangitic) (hematogenic)
    (lymphogenic) (pylephlebitic) K75.0
    amebic A06.4
  hip (region) —*see* Abscess, lower limb
  horseshoe K61.31
  ileocecal K35.33
  ileostomy (bud) K94.12
  iliac (region) L02.214
    fossa K35.33
  infraclavicular (fossa) —*see* Abscess, upper
    limb
  inguinal (region) L02.214
    lymph gland or node L04.1
  intersphincteric K61.4
  intestine, intestinal NEC K63.0
    rectal K61.1
  intra-abdominal —*see also* Abscess,
    peritoneum K65.1
    following procedure T81.43
      obstetrical O86.03
  ➡ postprocedural T81.43
    retroperitoneal K68.11

▶ New   ➡ Revised   ~~deleted~~ Deleted   ● Use Additional Character(s)

Abscess *(Continued)*
  intracranial G06.0
  intramammary —*see* Abscess, breast
  intramuscular, following procedure T81.44
    obstetrical O86.02
  intraorbital —*see* Abscess, orbit
  intraperitoneal K65.1
  intrasphincteric (anus) K61.4
  intraspinal G06.1
  intratonsillar J36
  ischiorectal (fossa) (specified NEC) K61.39
  jaw (bone) (lower) (upper) M27.2
  joint —*see* Arthritis, pyogenic or pyemic
    spine (tuberculous) A18.01
      nontuberculous —*see* Spondylopathy, infective
  kidney N15.1
    with calculus N20.0
      with hydronephrosis N13.6
    puerperal (postpartum) O86.21
  knee —*see also* Abscess, lower limb
    joint M00.9
  labium (majus) (minus) N76.4
  lacrimal
    caruncle —*see* Inflammation, lacrimal, passages, acute
    gland —*see* Dacryoadenitis
    passages (duct) (sac) —*see* Inflammation, lacrimal, passages, acute
  lacunar N34.0
  larynx J38.7
  lateral (alveolar) K04.7
    with sinus K04.6
  leg (any part) —*see* Abscess, lower limb
  lens H27.8
  lingual K14.0
    tonsil J36
  lip K13.0
  Littre's gland N34.0
  liver (cholangitic) (hematogenic) (lymphogenic) (pylephlebitic) (pyogenic) K75.0
    amebic (due to Entamoeba histolytica) (dysenteric) (tropical) A06.4
      with
        brain abscess (and liver or lung abscess) A06.6
        lung abscess A06.5
  loin (region) L02.211
  lower limb L02.41-●
  lumbar (tuberculous) A18.01
    nontuberculous L02.212
  lung (miliary) (putrid) J85.2
    with pneumonia J85.1
      due to specified organism (*see* Pneumonia, in (due to))
    amebic (with liver abscess) A06.5
      with
        brain abscess A06.6
        pneumonia A06.5
  lymph, lymphatic, gland or node (acute) —*see also* Lymphadenitis, acute
    mesentery I88.0
  malar M27.2
  mammary gland —*see* Abscess, breast
  marginal, anus K61.0
  mastoid —*see* Mastoiditis, acute
  maxilla, maxillary M27.2
    molar (tooth) K04.7
      with sinus K04.6
    premolar K04.7
    sinus (chronic) J32.0
  mediastinum J85.3
  meibomian gland —*see* Hordeolum
  meninges G06.2
  mesentery, mesenteric K65.1
  mesosalpinx —*see* Salpingitis
  mons pubis L02.215
  mouth (floor) K12.2
  muscle —*see* Myositis, infective
  myocardium I40.0
  nabothian (follicle) —*see* Cervicitis
  nasal J32.9
  nasopharyngeal J39.1

Abscess *(Continued)*
  navel L02.216
    newborn P38.9
      with mild hemorrhage P38.1
      without hemorrhage P38.9
  neck (region) L02.11
    lymph gland or node L04.0
  nephritic —*see* Abscess, kidney
  nipple N61.1
    associated with
      lactation —*see* Pregnancy, complicated by
      pregnancy —*see* Pregnancy, complicated by
  nose (external) (fossa) (septum) J34.0
    sinus (chronic) —*see* Sinusitis
  omentum K65.1
  operative wound T81.49
  orbit, orbital —*see* Cellulitis, orbit
  otogenic G06.0
  ovary, ovarian (corpus luteum) —*see* Oophoritis
  oviduct —*see* Oophoritis
  palate (soft) K12.2
    hard M27.2
  palmar (space) —*see* Abscess, hand
  pancreas (duct) —*see* Pancreatitis, acute
  parafrenal N48.21
  parametric, parametrium N73.2
    acute N73.0
    chronic N73.1
  paranephric N15.1
  parapancreatic —*see* Pancreatitis, acute
  parapharyngeal J39.0
  pararectal K61.1
  parasinus —*see* Sinusitis
  parauterine (*see also* Disease, pelvis, inflammatory) N73.2
  paravaginal —*see* Vaginitis
  parietal region (scalp) L02.811
  parodontal —*see* Periodontitis, aggressive, localized
  parotid (duct) (gland) K11.3
    region K12.2
  pectoral (region) L02.213
  pelvis, pelvic
    female —*see* Disease, pelvis, inflammatory
    male, peritoneal K65.1
  penis N48.21
    gonococcal (accessory gland) (periurethral) A54.1
  perianal K61.0
  periapical K04.7
    with sinus (alveolar) K04.6
  periappendicular K35.33
  pericardial I30.1
  pericecal K35.33
  pericemental —*see* Periodontitis, aggressive, localized
  pericholecystic —*see* Cholecystitis, acute
  pericoronal —*see* Periodontitis, aggressive, localized
  peridental —*see* Periodontitis, aggressive, localized
  perimetric —*see also* Disease, pelvis, inflammatory N73.2
  perinephric, perinephritic —*see* Abscess, kidney
  perineum, perineal (superficial) L02.215
    urethra N34.0
  periodontal (parietal) —*see* Periodontitis, aggressive, localized
    apical K04.7
  periosteum, periosteal —*see also* Osteomyelitis, specified type NEC
    with osteomyelitis —*see also* Osteomyelitis, specified type NEC
    acute —*see* Osteomyelitis, acute
    chronic —*see* Osteomyelitis, chronic
  peripharyngeal J39.0
  peripleuritic J86.9
    with fistula J86.0
  periprostatic N41.2

Abscess *(Continued)*
  perirectal K61.1
  perirenal (tissue) —*see* Abscess, kidney
  perisinuous (nose) —*see* Sinusitis
  peritoneum, peritoneal (perforated) (ruptured) K65.1
    with appendicitis (*see also* Appendicitis) K35.33
    pelvic
      female —*see* Peritonitis, pelvic, female
      male K65.1
    postoperative T81.49
    puerperal, postpartum, childbirth O85
    tuberculous A18.31
  peritonsillar J36
  perityphlic K35.33
  periureteral N28.89
  periurethral N34.0
    gonococcal (accessory gland) (periurethral) A54.1
  periuterine —*see also* Disease, pelvis, inflammatory N73.2
  perivesical —*see* Cystitis, specified type NEC
  petrous bone —*see* Petrositis
  phagedenic NOS L02.91
    chancroid A57
  pharynx, pharyngeal (lateral) J39.1
  pilonidal L05.01
  pituitary (gland) E23.6
  pleura J86.9
    with fistula J86.0
  popliteal —*see* Abscess, lower limb
  postcecal K35.33
  postlaryngeal J38.7
  postnasal J34.0
  postoperative (any site) (*see also* Infection, postoperative wound) T81.49
    retroperitoneal K68.11
  postpharyngeal J39.0
  posttonsillar J36
  post-typhoid A01.09
  pouch of Douglas —*see* Peritonitis, pelvic, female
  premammary —*see* Abscess, breast
  prepatellar —*see* Abscess, lower limb
  prostate N41.2
    gonococcal (acute) (chronic) A54.22
  psoas muscle K68.12
  puerperal - code by site under Puerperal, abscess
  pulmonary —*see* Abscess, lung
  pulp, pulpal (dental) K04.01
    irreversible K04.02
    reversible K04.01
  rectovaginal septum K63.0
  rectovesical —*see* Cystitis, specified type NEC
  rectum K61.1
  renal —*see* Abscess, kidney
  retina —*see* Inflammation, chorioretinal
  retrobulbar —*see* Abscess, orbit
  retrocecal K65.1
  retrolaryngeal J38.7
  retromammary —*see* Abscess, breast
  retroperitoneal NEC K68.19
    postprocedural K68.11
  retropharyngeal J39.0
  retrouterine —*see* Peritonitis, pelvic, female
  retrovesical —*see* Cystitis, specified type NEC
  root, tooth K04.7
    with sinus (alveolar) K04.6
  round ligament —*see also* Disease, pelvis, inflammatory N73.2
  rupture (spontaneous) NOS L02.91
  sacrum (tuberculous) A18.01
    nontuberculous M46.28
  salivary (duct) (gland) K11.3
  scalp (any part) L02.811
  scapular —*see* Osteomyelitis, specified type NEC
  sclera —*see* Scleritis
  scrofulous (tuberculous) A18.2
  scrotum N49.2

Abscess *(Continued)*
  seminal vesicle N49.0
  septal, dental K04.7
    with sinus (alveolar) K04.6
  serous —*see* Periostitis
  shoulder (region) —*see* Abscess, upper limb
  sigmoid K63.0
  sinus (accessory) (chronic) (nasal) —*see also*
    Sinusitis
    intracranial venous (any) G06.0
  Skene's duct or gland N34.0
  skin —*see* Abscess, by site
  specified site NEC L02.818
  spermatic cord N49.1
  sphenoidal (sinus) (chronic) J32.3
  spinal cord (any part) (staphylococcal) G06.1
    tuberculous A17.81
  spine (column) (tuberculous) A18.01
    epidural G06.1
    nontuberculous —*see* Osteomyelitis,
      vertebra
  spleen D73.3
    amebic A06.89
  stitch T81.41
    following an obstetrical procedure O86.01
  subarachnoid G06.2
    brain G06.0
    spinal cord G06.1
  subareolar —*see* Abscess, breast
  subcecal K35.33
  subcutaneous —*see also* Abscess, by site
    following procedure T81.41
      obstetrical O86.01
    pheomycotic (chromomycotic) B43.2
  subdiaphragmatic K65.1
  subdural G06.2
    brain G06.0
      sequelae G09
    spinal cord G06.1
  sub-fascial, following an obstetrical
    procedure O86.02
  subgaleal L02.811
  subhepatic K65.1
  sublingual K12.2
    gland K11.3
  submammary —*see* Abscess, breast
  submandibular (region) (space) (triangle) K12.2
    gland K11.3
  submaxillary (region) L02.01
    gland K11.3
  submental L02.01
    gland K11.3
  subperiosteal —*see* Osteomyelitis, specified
    type NEC
  subphrenic K65.1
    following an obstetrical procedure O86.03
    postoperative T81.43
  suburethral N34.0
  sudoriparous L75.8
  supraclavicular (fossa) —*see* Abscess, upper
    limb
  supralevator K61.5
  suprapelvic, acute N73.0
  suprarenal (capsule) (gland) E27.8
  sweat gland L74.8
  tear duct —*see* Inflammation, lacrimal,
    passages, acute
  temple L02.01
  temporal region L02.01
  temporosphenoidal G06.0
  tendon (sheath) M65.00
    ankle M65.07-●
    foot M65.07-●
    forearm M65.03-●
    hand M65.04-●
    lower leg M65.06-●
    pelvic region M65.05-●
    shoulder region M65.01-●
    specified site NEC M65.08
    thigh M65.05-●
    upper arm M65.02-●
  testis N45.4
  thigh —*see* Abscess, lower limb

Abscess *(Continued)*
  thorax J86.9
    with fistula J86.0
  throat J39.1
  thumb —*see also* Abscess, hand
    nail —*see* Cellulitis, finger
  thymus (gland) E32.1
  thyroid (gland) E06.0
  toe (any) —*see also* Abscess, foot
    nail —*see* Cellulitis, toe
  tongue (staphylococcal) K14.0
  tonsil(s) (lingual) J36
  tonsillopharyngeal J36
  tooth, teeth (root) K04.7
    with sinus (alveolar) K04.6
    supporting structures NEC —*see*
      Periodontitis, aggressive, localized
  trachea J39.8
  trunk L02.219
    abdominal wall L02.211
    back L02.212
    chest wall L02.213
    groin L02.214
    perineum L02.215
    umbilicus L02.216
  tubal —*see* Salpingitis
  tuberculous —*see* Tuberculosis, abscess
  tubo-ovarian —*see* Salpingo-oophoritis
  tunica vaginalis N49.1
  umbilicus L02.216
  upper
    limb L02.41-●
    respiratory J39.8
  urethral (gland) N34.0
  urinary N34.0
  uterus, uterine (wall) —*see also* Endometritis
    ligament —*see also* Disease, pelvis,
      inflammatory N73.2
    neck —*see* Cervicitis
  uvula K12.2
  vagina (wall) —*see* Vaginitis
  vaginorectal —*see* Vaginitis
  vas deferens N49.1
  vermiform appendix K35.33
  vertebra (column) (tuberculous) A18.01
    nontuberculous —*see* Osteomyelitis, vertebra
  vesical —*see* Cystitis, specified type NEC
  vesico-uterine pouch —*see* Peritonitis, pelvic,
    female
  vitreous (humor) —*see* Endophthalmitis,
    purulent
  vocal cord J38.3
  von Bezold's —*see* Mastoiditis, acute
  vulva N76.4
  vulvovaginal gland N75.1
  web space —*see* Abscess, hand
  wound T81.49
  wrist —*see* Abscess, upper limb
Absence (of) (organ or part) (complete or partial)
  adrenal (gland) (congenital) Q89.1
    acquired E89.6
  albumin in blood E88.09
  alimentary tract (congenital) Q45.8
    upper Q40.8
  alveolar process (acquired) —*see* Anomaly,
    alveolar
  ankle (acquired) Z89.44-●
  anus (congenital) Q42.3
    with fistula Q42.2
  aorta (congenital) Q25.41
  appendix, congenital Q42.8
  arm (acquired) Z89.20-●
    above elbow Z89.22-●
      congenital (with hand present) —*see*
        Agenesis, arm, with hand present
      and hand —*see* Agenesis, forearm,
        and hand
    below elbow Z89.21-●
      congenital (with hand present) —*see*
        Agenesis, arm, with hand present
      and hand —*see* Agenesis, forearm,
        and hand

Absence *(Continued)*
  arm *(Continued)*
    congenital —*see* Defect, reduction, upper
      limb
    shoulder (following explantation of
      shoulder joint prosthesis) (joint) (with
      or without presence of antibiotic-
      impregnated cement spacer) Z89.23-●
    congenital (with hand present) —*see*
      Agenesis, arm, with hand present
  artery (congenital) (peripheral) Q27.8
    brain Q28.3
    coronary Q24.5
    pulmonary Q25.79
    specified NEC Q27.8
    umbilical Q27.0
  atrial septum (congenital) Q21.1
  auditory canal (congenital) (external) Q16.1
  auricle (ear), congenital Q16.0
  bile, biliary duct, congenital Q44.5
  bladder (acquired) Z90.6
    congenital Q64.5
  bowel sounds R19.11
  brain Q00.0
    part of Q04.3
  breast(s) (and nipple(s)) (acquired) Z90.1-●
    congenital Q83.8
  broad ligament Q50.6
  bronchus (congenital) Q32.4
  canaliculus lacrimalis, congenital Q10.4
  cerebellum (vermis) Q04.3
  cervix (acquired) (with uterus) Z90.710
    with remaining uterus Z90.712
    congenital Q51.5
  chin, congenital Q18.8
  cilia (congenital) Q10.3
    acquired —*see* Madarosis
  clitoris (congenital) Q52.6
  coccyx, congenital Q76.49
  cold sense R20.8
  congenital
    lumen —*see* Atresia
    organ or site NEC —*see* Agenesis
    septum —*see* Imperfect, closure
  corpus callosum Q04.0
  cricoid cartilage, congenital Q31.8
  diaphragm (with hernia), congenital Q79.1
  digestive organ(s) or tract, congenital Q45.8
    acquired NEC Z90.49
    upper Q40.8
  ductus arteriosus Q28.8
  duodenum (acquired) Z90.49
    congenital Q41.0
  ear, congenital Q16.9
    acquired H93.8-●
    auricle Q16.0
    external Q16.0
    inner Q16.5
    lobe, lobule Q17.8
    middle, except ossicles Q16.4
      ossicles Q16.3
    ossicles Q16.3
  ejaculatory duct (congenital) Q55.4
  endocrine gland (congenital) NEC Q89.2
    acquired E89.89
  epididymis (congenital) Q55.4
    acquired Z90.79
  epiglottis, congenital Q31.8
  esophagus (congenital) Q39.8
    acquired (partial) Z90.49
  eustachian tube (congenital) Q16.2
  extremity (acquired) Z89.9
    congenital Q73.0
    knee (following explantation of knee joint
      prosthesis) (joint) (with or without
      presence of antibiotic-impregnated
      cement spacer) Z89.52-●
    lower (above knee) Z89.619
      below knee Z89.51-●
    upper —*see* Absence, arm
  eye (acquired) Z90.01
    congenital Q11.1
    muscle (congenital) Q10.3

▶ New   ⇒ Revised   ~~deleted~~ Deleted   ● Use Additional Character(s)

Absence *(Continued)*
eyeball (acquired) Z90.01
eyelid (fold) (congenital) Q10.3
  acquired Z90.01
face, specified part NEC Q18.8
fallopian tube(s) (acquired) Z90.79
  congenital Q50.6
family member (causing problem in home)
  NEC —*see also* Disruption, family Z63.32
femur, congenital —*see* Defect, reduction,
  lower limb, longitudinal, femur
fibrinogen (congenital) D68.2
  acquired D65
finger(s) (acquired) Z89.02-●
  congenital —*see* Agenesis, hand
foot (acquired) Z89.43-●
  congenital —*see* Agenesis, foot
forearm (acquired) —*see* Absence, arm, below
  elbow
gallbladder (acquired) Z90.49
  congenital Q44.0
gamma globulin in blood D80.1
  hereditary D80.0
genital organs
  acquired (female) (male) Z90.79
  female, congenital Q52.8
   external Q52.71
   internal NEC Q52.8
  male, congenital Q55.8
genitourinary organs, congenital NEC
  female Q52.8
  male Q55.8
globe (acquired) Z90.01
  congenital Q11.1
glottis, congenital Q31.8
hand and wrist (acquired) Z89.11-●
  congenital —*see* Agenesis, hand
head, part (acquired) NEC Z90.09
heat sense R20.8
hip (following explantation of hip joint
  prosthesis) (joint) (with or without
  presence of antibiotic-impregnated
  cement spacer) Z89.62-●
hymen (congenital) Q52.4
ileum (acquired) Z90.49
  congenital Q41.2
immunoglobulin, isolated NEC D80.3
  IgA D80.2
  IgG D80.3
  IgM D80.4
incus (acquired) —*see* Loss, ossicles, ear
  congenital Q16.3
inner ear, congenital Q16.5
intestine (acquired) (small) Z90.49
  congenital Q41.9
   specified NEC Q41.8
  large Z90.49
   congenital Q42.9
    specified NEC Q42.8
iris, congenital Q13.1
jejunum (acquired) Z90.49
  congenital Q41.1
joint
  acquired
   hip (following explantation of hip joint
    prosthesis) (with or without
    presence of antibiotic-impregnated
    cement spacer) Z89.62-●
   knee (following explantation of knee
    joint prosthesis) (with or without
    presence of antibiotic-impregnated
    cement spacer) Z89.52-●
   shoulder (following explantation of
    shoulder joint prosthesis) (with or
    without presence of antibiotic-
    impregnated cement spacer)
    Z89.23-●
  congenital NEC Q74.8
kidney(s) (acquired) Z90.5
  congenital Q60.2
   bilateral Q60.1
   unilateral Q60.0

Absence *(Continued)*
knee (following explantation of knee joint
  prosthesis) (joint) (with or without
  presence of antibiotic-impregnated
  cement spacer) Z89.52-●
labyrinth, membranous Q16.5
larynx (congenital) Q31.8
  acquired Z90.02
leg (acquired) (above knee) Z89.61-●
  below knee (acquired) Z89.51-●
  congenital —*see* Defect, reduction, lower
   limb
lens (acquired) —*see also* Aphakia
  congenital Q12.3
  post cataract extraction Z98.4-●
limb (acquired) —*see* Absence, extremity
lip Q38.6
liver (congenital) Q44.7
lung (fissure) (lobe) (bilateral) (unilateral)
  (congenital) Q33.3
  acquired (any part) Z90.2
menstruation —*see* Amenorrhea
muscle (congenital) (pectoral) Q79.8
  ocular Q10.3
neck, part Q18.8
neutrophil —*see* Agranulocytosis
nipple(s) (with breast(s)) (acquired) Z90.1-●
  congenital Q83.2
nose (congenital) Q30.1
  acquired Z90.09
organ
  of Corti, congenital Q16.5
  or site, congenital NEC Q89.8
   acquired NEC Z90.89
osseous meatus (ear) Q16.4
ovary (acquired)
  bilateral Z90.722
  congenital
   bilateral Q50.02
   unilateral Q50.01
  unilateral Z90.721
oviduct (acquired)
  bilateral Z90.722
  congenital Q50.6
  unilateral Z90.721
pancreas (congenital) Q45.0
  acquired Z90.410
   complete Z90.410
   partial Z90.411
   total Z90.410
parathyroid gland (acquired) E89.2
  congenital Q89.2
patella, congenital Q74.1
penis (congenital) Q55.5
  acquired Z90.79
pericardium (congenital) Q24.8
pituitary gland (congenital) Q89.2
  acquired E89.3
prostate (acquired) Z90.79
  congenital Q55.4
pulmonary valve Q22.0
punctum lacrimale (congenital) Q10.4
radius, congenital —*see* Defect, reduction,
  upper limb, longitudinal, radius
rectum (congenital) Q42.1
  with fistula Q42.0
  acquired Z90.49
respiratory organ NOS Q34.9
rib (acquired) Z90.89
  congenital Q76.6
sacrum, congenital Q76.49
salivary gland(s), congenital Q38.4
scrotum, congenital Q55.29
seminal vesicles (congenital) Q55.4
  acquired Z90.79
septum
  atrial (congenital) Q21.1
  between aorta and pulmonary artery Q21.4
  ventricular (congenital) Q20.4
sex chromosome
  female phenotype Q97.8
  male phenotype Q98.8

Absence *(Continued)*
skull bone (congenital) Q75.8
  with
   anencephaly Q00.0
   encephalocele —*see* Encephalocele
   hydrocephalus Q03.9
    with spina bifida —*see* Spina bifida, by
     site, with hydrocephalus
   microcephaly Q02
spermatic cord, congenital Q55.4
spine, congenital Q76.49
spleen (congenital) Q89.01
  acquired Z90.81
sternum, congenital Q76.7
stomach (acquired) (partial) Z90.3
  congenital Q40.2
superior vena cava, congenital Q26.8
teeth, tooth (congenital) K00.0
  acquired (complete) K08.109
   class I K08.101
   class II K08.102
   class III K08.103
   class IV K08.104
   due to
    caries K08.139
     class I K08.131
     class II K08.132
     class III K08.133
     class IV K08.134
    periodontal disease K08.129
     class I K08.121
     class II K08.122
     class III K08.123
     class IV K08.124
    specified NEC K08.199
     class I K08.191
     class II K08.192
     class III K08.193
     class IV K08.194
    trauma K08.119
     class I K08.111
     class II K08.112
     class III K08.113
     class IV K08.114
   partial K08.409
    class I K08.401
    class II K08.402
    class III K08.403
    class IV K08.404
    due to
     caries K08.439
      class I K08.431
      class II K08.432
      class III K08.433
      class IV K08.434
     periodontal disease K08.429
      class I K08.421
      class II K08.422
      class III K08.423
      class IV K08.424
     specified NEC K08.499
      class I K08.491
      class II K08.492
      class III K08.493
      class IV K08.494
     trauma K08.419
      class I K08.411
      class II K08.412
      class III K08.413
      class IV K08.414
tendon (congenital) Q79.8
testis (congenital) Q55.0
  acquired Z90.79
thumb (acquired) Z89.01-●
  congenital —*see* Agenesis, hand
thymus gland Q89.2
thyroid (gland) (acquired) E89.0
  cartilage, congenital Q31.8
  congenital E03.1
toe(s) (acquired) Z89.42-●
  with foot —*see* Absence, foot and ankle
  congenital —*see* Agenesis, foot
  great Z89.41-●

Absence *(Continued)*
  tongue, congenital Q38.3
  trachea (cartilage), congenital Q32.1
  transverse aortic arch, congenital Q25.49
  tricuspid valve Q22.4
  umbilical artery, congenital Q27.0
  upper arm and forearm with hand present,
    congenital —*see* Agenesis, arm, with
    hand present
  ureter (congenital) Q62.4
    acquired Z90.6
  urethra, congenital Q64.5
  uterus (acquired) Z90.710
    with cervix Z90.710
    with remaining cervical stump Z90.711
    congenital Q51.0
  uvula, congenital Q38.5
  vagina, congenital Q52.0
  vas deferens (congenital) Q55.4
    acquired Z90.79
  vein (peripheral) congenital NEC Q27.8
    cerebral Q28.3
    digestive system Q27.8
    great Q26.8
    lower limb Q27.8
    portal Q26.5
    precerebral Q28.1
    specified site NEC Q27.8
    upper limb Q27.8
  vena cava (inferior) (superior), congenital
    Q26.8
  ventricular septum Q20.4
  vertebra, congenital Q76.49
  vulva, congenital Q52.71
  wrist (acquired) Z89.12-●
Absorbent system disease I87.8
Absorption
  carbohydrate, disturbance K90.49
  chemical —*see* Table of Drugs and Chemicals
    through placenta (newborn) P04.9
      environmental substance P04.6
      nutritional substance P04.5
      obstetric anesthetic or analgesic drug P04.0
  drug NEC —*see* Table of Drugs and Chemicals
    addictive
      through placenta (newborn) (*see also*
        Newborn, affected by, maternal,
        use of) P04.40
        cocaine P04.41
        hallucinogens P04.42
        specified drug NEC P04.49
    medicinal
      through placenta (newborn) P04.19
    through placenta (newborn) P04.19
      obstetric anesthetic or analgesic drug P04.0
  fat, disturbance K90.49
  pancreatic K90.3
  noxious substance —*see* Table of Drugs and
    Chemicals
  protein, disturbance K90.49
  starch, disturbance K90.49
  toxic substance —*see* Table of Drugs and
    Chemicals
  uremic —*see* Uremia
Abstinence symptoms, syndrome
  alcohol F10.239
    with delirium F10.231
  cocaine F14.23
  neonatal P96.1
  nicotine —*see* Dependence, drug, nicotine,
    with, withdrawal
  opioid F11.93
    with dependence F11.23
  psychoactive NEC F19.939
    with
      delirium F19.931
      dependence F19.239
        with
          delirium F19.231
          perceptual disturbance F19.232
        uncomplicated F19.230
      perceptual disturbance F19.932
    uncomplicated F19.930

Abstinence symptoms, syndrome *(Continued)*
  sedative F13.939
    with
      delirium F13.931
      dependence F13.239
        with
          delirium F13.231
          perceptual disturbance F13.232
        uncomplicated F13.230
      perceptual disturbance F13.932
    uncomplicated F13.930
  stimulant NEC F15.93
    with dependence F15.23
Abulia R68.89
Abulomania F60.7
Abuse
  adult —*see* Maltreatment, adult
    as reason for
      couple seeking advice (including
        offender) Z63.0
  alcohol (non-dependent) F10.10
    with
      anxiety disorder F10.180
      intoxication F10.129
        with delirium F10.121
        uncomplicated F10.120
      mood disorder F10.14
      other specified disorder F10.188
      psychosis F10.159
        delusions F10.150
        hallucinations F10.151
      sexual dysfunction F10.181
      sleep disorder F10.182
      unspecified disorder F10.19
      ▸withdrawal F10.139
        ▸with
          ▸perceptual disturbance F10.132
        ▸delirium F10.131
        ▸uncomplicated F10.130
    counseling and surveillance Z71.41
    in remission (early) (sustained) F10.11
  amphetamine (or related substance) —*see also*
    Abuse, drug, stimulant NEC
    stimulant NEC F15.10
      with
        anxiety disorder F15.180
        intoxication F15.129
          with
            delirium F15.121
            perceptual disturbance F15.122
      ▸withdrawal F15.13
  analgesics (non-prescribed) (over the counter)
    F55.8
  antacids F55.0
  antidepressants —*see* Abuse, drug,
    psychoactive NEC
  anxiolytic —*see* Abuse, drug, sedative
  barbiturates —*see* Abuse, drug, sedative
  caffeine —*see* Abuse, drug, stimulant NEC
  cannabis, cannabinoids —*see* Abuse, drug,
    cannabis
  child —*see* Maltreatment, child
  cocaine —*see* Abuse, drug, cocaine
  drug NEC (non-dependent) F19.10
    with sleep disorder F19.182
    amphetamine type —*see* Abuse, drug,
      stimulant NEC
    analgesics (non-prescribed) (over the
      counter) F55.8
    antacids F55.0
    antidepressants —*see* Abuse, drug,
      psychoactive NEC
    anxiolytics —*see* Abuse, drug, sedative
    barbiturates —*see* Abuse, drug, sedative
    caffeine —*see* Abuse, drug, stimulant NEC
    cannabis F12.10
      with
        anxiety disorder F12.180
        intoxication F12.129
          with
            delirium F12.121
            perceptual disturbance F12.122
          uncomplicated F12.120

Abuse *(Continued)*
  drug NEC *(Continued)*
    cannabis *(Continued)*
      with *(Continued)*
        other specified disorder F12.188
        psychosis F12.159
          delusions F12.150
          hallucinations F12.151
        unspecified disorder F12.19
        ▸withdrawal F12.13
      in remission (early) (sustained) F12.11
    cocaine F14.10
      with
        anxiety disorder F14.180
        intoxication F14.129
          with
            delirium F14.121
            perceptual disturbance F14.122
          uncomplicated F14.120
        mood disorder F14.14
        other specified disorder F14.188
        psychosis F14.159
          delusions F14.150
          hallucinations F14.151
        sexual dysfunction F14.181
        sleep disorder F14.182
        unspecified disorder F14.19
        ▸withdrawal F14.13
      in remission (early) (sustained)
        F14.11
    counseling and surveillance Z71.51
    hallucinogen F16.10
      with
        anxiety disorder F16.180
        flashbacks F16.183
        intoxication F16.129
          with
            delirium F16.121
            perceptual disturbance F16.122
          uncomplicated F16.120
        mood disorder F16.14
        other specified disorder F16.188
        perception disorder, persisting F16.183
        psychosis F16.159
          delusions F16.150
          hallucinations F16.151
        unspecified disorder F16.19
      in remission (early) (sustained) F16.11
    hashish —*see* Abuse, drug, cannabis
    herbal or folk remedies F55.1
    hormones F55.3
    hypnotics —*see* Abuse, drug, sedative
    inhalant F18.10
      with
        anxiety disorder F18.180
        dementia, persisting F18.17
        intoxication F18.129
          with delirium F18.121
          uncomplicated F18.120
        mood disorder F18.14
        other specified disorder F18.188
        psychosis F18.159
          delusions F18.150
          hallucinations F18.151
        unspecified disorder F18.19
      in remission (early) (sustained) F18.11
    in remission (early) (sustained) F19.11
    laxatives F55.2
    LSD —*see* Abuse, drug, hallucinogen
    marihuana —*see* Abuse, drug, cannabis
    morphine type (opioids) —*see* Abuse, drug,
      opioid
    opioid F11.10
      with
        intoxication F11.129
          with
            delirium F11.121
            perceptual disturbance F11.122
          uncomplicated F11.120
        mood disorder F11.14
        other specified disorder F11.188

▶ New   ⇒ Revised   ~~deleted~~ Deleted   ● Use Additional Character(s)

Abuse *(Continued)*
 drug NEC *(Continued)*
  opioid *(Continued)*
   with *(Continued)*
    psychosis F11.159
     delusions F11.150
     hallucinations F11.151
    sexual dysfunction F11.181
    sleep disorder F11.182
    unspecified disorder F11.19
   ▶withdrawal F11.13
   in remission (early) (sustained) F11.11
  PCP (phencyclidine) (or related substance) —
   see Abuse, drug, hallucinogen
  psychoactive NEC F19.10
   with
    amnestic disorder F19.16
    anxiety disorder F19.180
    dementia F19.17
    intoxication F19.129
     with
      delirium F19.121
      perceptual disturbance F19.122
     uncomplicated F19.120
    mood disorder F19.14
    other specified disorder F19.188
    psychosis F19.159
     delusions F19.150
     hallucinations F19.151
    sexual dysfunction F19.181
    sleep disorder F19.182
    unspecified disorder F19.19
   ▶withdrawal F19.139
    ▶with
     ▶perceptual disturbance F19.132
    ▶delirium F19.131
    ▶uncomplicated F19.130
  sedative, hypnotic or anxiolytic F13.10
   with
    anxiety disorder F13.180
    intoxication F13.129
     with delirium F13.121
     uncomplicated F13.120
    mood disorder F13.14
    other specified disorder F13.188
    psychosis F13.159
     delusions F13.150
     hallucinations F13.151
    sexual dysfunction F13.181
    sleep disorder F13.182
    unspecified disorder F13.19
   ▶withdrawal F13.139
    ▶with
     ▶perceptual disturbance F13.132
    ▶delirium F13.131
    ▶uncomplicated F13.130
   in remission (early) (sustained) F13.11
  solvent —*see* Abuse, drug, inhalant
  steroids F55.3
  stimulant NEC F15.10
   with
    anxiety disorder F15.180
    intoxication F15.129
     with
      delirium F15.121
      perceptual disturbance F15.122
     uncomplicated F15.120
    mood disorder F15.14
    other specified disorder F15.188
    psychosis F15.159
     delusions F15.150
     hallucinations F15.151
    sexual dysfunction F15.181
    sleep disorder F15.182
    unspecified disorder F15.19
   ▶withdrawal F15.13
   in remission (early) (sustained) F15.11
  tranquilizers —*see* Abuse, drug, sedative
  vitamins F55.4
 hallucinogens —*see* Abuse, drug, hallucinogen
 hashish —*see* Abuse, drug, cannabis

Abuse *(Continued)*
 herbal or folk remedies F55.1
 hormones F55.3
 hypnotic —*see* Abuse, drug, sedative
 inhalant —*see* Abuse, drug, inhalant
 laxatives F55.2
 LSD —*see* Abuse, drug, hallucinogen
 marihuana —*see* Abuse, drug, cannabis
 morphine type (opioids) —*see* Abuse, drug,
  opioid
 non-psychoactive substance NEC F55.8
  antacids F55.0
  folk remedies F55.1
  herbal remedies F55.1
  hormones F55.3
  laxatives F55.2
  steroids F55.3
  vitamins F55.4
 opioids —*see* Abuse, drug, opioid
 PCP (phencyclidine) (or related substance) —
  see Abuse, drug, hallucinogen
 physical (adult) (child) —*see* Maltreatment
 psychoactive substance —*see* Abuse, drug,
  psychoactive NEC
 psychological (adult) (child) —*see* Maltreatment
 sedative —*see* Abuse, drug, sedative
 sexual —*see* Maltreatment
 solvent —*see* Abuse, drug, inhalant
 steroids F55.3
 vitamins F55.4
Acalculia R48.8
 developmental F81.2
Acanthamebiasis (with) B60.10
 conjunctiva B60.12
 keratoconjunctivitis B60.13
 meningoencephalitis B60.11
 other specified B60.19
Acanthocephaliasis B83.8
Acanthocheilonemiasis B74.4
Acanthocytosis E78.6
Acantholysis L11.9
Acanthosis (acquired) (nigricans) L83
 benign Q82.8
 congenital Q82.8
 seborrheic L82.1
  inflamed L82.0
 tongue K14.3
Acapnia E87.3
Acarbia E87.2
Acardia, acardius Q89.8
Acardiacus amorphus Q89.8
Acardiotrophia I51.4
Acariasis B88.0
 scabies B86
Acarodermatitis (urticarioides) B88.0
Acarophobia F40.218
Acatalasemia, acatalasia E80.3
Acathisia (drug induced) G25.71
Accelerated atrioventricular conduction I45.6
Accentuation of personality traits (type A) Z73.1
Accessory (congenital)
 adrenal gland Q89.1
 anus Q43.4
 appendix Q43.4
 atrioventricular conduction I45.6
 auditory ossicles Q16.3
 auricle (ear) Q17.0
 biliary duct or passage Q44.5
 bladder Q64.79
 blood vessels NEC Q27.9
  coronary Q24.5
 bone NEC Q79.8
 breast tissue, axilla Q83.1
 carpal bones Q74.0
 cecum Q43.4
 chromosome(s) NEC (nonsex) Q92.9
  with complex rearrangements NEC Q92.5
   seen only at prometaphase Q92.8
  13 —*see* Trisomy, 13
  18 —*see* Trisomy, 18
  21 —*see* Trisomy, 21

Accessory *(Continued)*
 chromosome(s) NEC (nonsex) *(Continued)*
  partial Q92.9
  sex
   female phenotype Q97.8
 coronary artery Q24.5
 cusp(s), heart valve NEC Q24.8
  pulmonary Q22.3
 cystic duct Q44.5
 digit(s) Q69.9
 ear (auricle) (lobe) Q17.0
 endocrine gland NEC Q89.2
 eye muscle Q10.3
 eyelid Q10.3
 face bone(s) Q75.8
 fallopian tube (fimbria) (ostium) Q50.6
 finger(s) Q69.0
 foreskin N47.8
 frontonasal process Q75.8
 gallbladder Q44.1
 genital organ(s)
  female Q52.8
   external Q52.79
   internal NEC Q52.8
  male Q55.8
 genitourinary organs NEC Q89.8
  female Q52.8
  male Q55.8
 hallux Q69.2
 heart Q24.8
  valve NEC Q24.8
   pulmonary Q22.3
 hepatic ducts Q44.5
 hymen Q52.4
 intestine (large) (small) Q43.4
 kidney Q63.0
 lacrimal canal Q10.6
 leaflet, heart valve NEC Q24.8
 ligament, broad Q50.6
 liver Q44.7
  duct Q44.5
 lobule (ear) Q17.0
 lung (lobe) Q33.1
 muscle Q79.8
 navicular of carpus Q74.0
 nervous system, part NEC Q07.8
 nipple Q83.3
 nose Q30.8
 organ or site not listed —*see* Anomaly, by site
 ovary Q50.31
 oviduct Q50.6
 pancreas Q45.3
 parathyroid gland Q89.2
 parotid gland (and duct) Q38.4
 pituitary gland Q89.2
 preauricular appendage Q17.0
 prepuce N47.8
 renal arteries (multiple) Q27.2
 rib Q76.6
  cervical Q76.5
 roots (teeth) K00.2
 salivary gland Q38.4
 sesamoid bones Q74.8
  foot Q74.2
  hand Q74.0
 skin tags Q82.8
 spleen Q89.09
 sternum Q76.7
 submaxillary gland Q38.4
 tarsal bones Q74.2
 teeth, tooth K00.1
 tendon Q79.8
 thumb Q69.1
 thymus gland Q89.2
 thyroid gland Q89.2
 toes Q69.2
 tongue Q38.3
 tooth, teeth K00.1
 tragus Q17.0
 ureter Q62.5
 urethra Q64.79

A

▶ New   ⇒ Revised   ~~deleted~~ Deleted   ● Use Additional Character(s)

Accessory (Continued)
   urinary organ or tract NEC Q64.8
   uterus Q51.28
   vagina Q52.10
   valve, heart NEC Q24.8
      pulmonary Q22.3
   vertebra Q76.49
   vocal cords Q31.8
   vulva Q52.79
Accident
   birth —see Birth, injury
   cardiac —see Infarct, myocardium
   cerebral I63.9
   cerebrovascular (embolic) (ischemic)
      (thrombotic) I63.9
      aborted I63.9
      hemorrhagic —see Hemorrhage,
         intracranial, intracerebral
      old (without sequelae) Z86.73
         with sequelae (of) —see Sequelae,
            infarction, cerebral
   coronary —see Infarct, myocardium
   craniovascular I63.9
   vascular, brain I63.9
Accidental —see condition
Accommodation (disorder) —see also condition
   hysterical paralysis of F44.89
   insufficiency of H52.4
   paresis —see Paresis, of accommodation
   spasm —see Spasm, of accommodation
Accouchement —see Delivery
Accreta placenta O43.21-●
Accretio cordis (nonrheumatic) I31.0
Accretions, tooth, teeth K03.6
Acculturation difficulty Z60.3
Accumulation secretion, prostate N42.89
Acephalia, acephalism, acephalus, acephaly
   Q00.0
Acephalobrachia monster Q89.8
Acephalochirus monster Q89.8
Acephalogaster Q89.8
Acephalostomus monster Q89.8
Acephalothorax Q89.8
Acerophobia F40.298
Acetonemia R79.89
   in Type 1 diabetes E10.10
      with coma E10.11
Acetonuria R82.4
Achalasia (cardia) (esophagus) K22.0
   congenital Q39.5
   pylorus Q40.0
   sphincteral NEC K59.89
Ache(s) —see Pain
Acheilia Q38.6
Achillobursitis —see Tendinitis, Achilles
Achillodynia —see Tendinitis, Achilles
Achlorhydria, achlorhydric (neurogenic) K31.83
   anemia D50.8
   diarrhea K31.83
   psychogenic F45.8
   secondary to vagotomy K91.1
Achluophobia F40.228
Acholia K82.8
Acholuric jaundice (familial)
   (splenomegalic) —see also Spherocytosis
   acquired D59.8
Achondrogenesis Q77.0
Achondroplasia (osteosclerosis congenita) Q77.4
Achroma, cutis L80
Achromat (ism), achromatopsia (acquired)
   (congenital) H53.51
Achromia, congenital —see Albinism
Achromia parasitica B36.0
Achylia gastrica K31.89
   psychogenic F45.8
Acid
   burn —see Corrosion
   deficiency
      amide nicotinic E52
      ascorbic E54
      folic E53.8

Acid (Continued)
   deficiency (Continued)
      nicotinic E52
      pantothenic E53.8
   intoxication E87.2
   peptic disease K30
   phosphatase deficiency E83.39
   stomach K30
      psychogenic F45.8
Acidemia E87.2
   argininosuccinic E72.22
   isovaleric E71.110
   metabolic (newborn) P19.9
      first noted before onset of labor P19.0
      first noted during labor P19.1
      noted at birth P19.2
   methylmalonic E71.120
   pipecolic E72.3
   propionic E71.121
Acidity, gastric (high) K30
   psychogenic F45.8
Acidocytopenia —see Agranulocytosis
Acidocytosis D72.10
Acidopenia —see Agranulocytosis
Acidosis (lactic) (respiratory) E87.2
   in Type 1 diabetes E10.10
      with coma E10.11
   kidney, tubular N25.89
   lactic E87.2
   metabolic NEC E87.2
      hyperchloremic, of newborn P74.421
      with respiratory acidosis E87.4
      late, of newborn P74.0
   mixed metabolic and respiratory, newborn P84
   newborn P84
   renal (hyperchloremic) (tubular) N25.89
   respiratory E87.2
      complicated by
         metabolic
            acidosis E87.4
            alkalosis E87.4
Aciduria
   4-hydroxybutyric E72.81
   argininosuccinic E72.22
   gamma-hydroxybutyric E72.81
   glutaric (type I) E72.3
      type II E71.313
      type III E71.5-●
   orotic (congenital) (hereditary) (pyrimidine
      deficiency) E79.8
      anemia D53.0
Acladiosis (skin) B36.0
Aclasis, diaphyseal Q78.6
Acleistocardia Q21.1
Aclusion —see Anomaly, dentofacial,
   malocclusion
Acne L70.9
   artificialis L70.8
   atrophica L70.2
   cachecticorum (Hebra) L70.8
   conglobata L70.1
   cystic L70.0
   decalvans L66.2
   excoriée (des jeunes filles) L70.5
   frontalis L70.2
   indurata L70.0
   infantile L70.4
   keloid L73.0
   lupoid L70.2
   necrotic, necrotica (miliaris) L70.2
   neonatal L70.4
   nodular L70.0
   occupational L70.8
   picker's L70.5
   pustular L70.0
   rodens L70.2
   rosacea L71.9
   specified NEC L70.8
   tropica L70.3
   varioliformis L70.2
   vulgaris L70.0

Acnitis (primary) A18.4
Acosta's disease T70.29
Acoustic —see condition
Acousticophobia F40.298
ACPO (acute colonic pseudo-obstruction)
   K59.81
Acquired —see also condition
   immunodeficiency syndrome (AIDS) B20
Acrania Q00.0
Acroangiodermatitis I78.9
Acroasphyxia, chronic I73.89
Acrobystitis N47.7
Acrocephalopolysyndactyly Q87.0
Acrocephalosyndactyly Q87.0
Acrocephaly Q75.0
Acrochondrohyperplasia —see Syndrome,
   Marfan's
Acrocyanosis I73.89
   newborn P28.2
      meaning transient blue hands and feet -
         omit code
Acrodermatitis L30.8
   atrophicans (chronica) L90.4
   continua (Hallopeau) L40.2
   enteropathica (hereditary) E83.2
   Hallopeau's L40.2
   infantile papular L44.4
   perstans L40.2
   pustulosa continua L40.2
   recalcitrant pustular L40.2
Acrodynia —see Poisoning, mercury
Acromegaly, acromegalia E22.0
Acromelalgia I73.81
Acromicria, acromikria Q79.8
Acronyx L60.0
Acropachy, thyroid —see Thyrotoxicosis
Acroparesthesia (simple) (vasomotor) I73.89
Acropathy, thyroid —see Thyrotoxicosis
Acrophobia F40.241
Acroposthitis N47.7
Acroscleriasis, acroscleroderma,
   acrosclerosis —see Sclerosis, systemic
Acrosphacelus I96
Acrospiroma, eccrine —see Neoplasm, skin,
   benign
Acrostealgia —see Osteochondropathy
Acrotrophodynia —see Immersion
ACTH ectopic syndrome E24.3
Actinic —see condition
Actinobacillosis, actinobacillus A28.8
   mallei A24.0
   muris A25.1
Actinomyces israelii (infection) —see
   Actinomycosis
Actinomycetoma (foot) B47.1
Actinomycosis, actinomycotic A42.9
   with pneumonia A42.0
   abdominal A42.1
   cervicofacial A42.2
   cutaneous A42.89
   gastrointestinal A42.1
   pulmonary A42.0
   sepsis A42.7
   specified site NEC A42.89
Actinoneuritis G62.82
Action, heart
   disorder I49.9
   irregular I49.9
      psychogenic F45.8
Activated protein C resistance D68.51
Activation
   mast cell (disorder) (syndrome) D89.40
      idiopathic D89.42
      monoclonal D89.41
      secondary D89.43
      specified type NEC D89.49
Active —see condition
Acute —see also condition
   abdomen R10.0
   gallbladder —see Cholecystitis, acute
Acyanotic heart disease (congenital) Q24.9

Acystia Q64.5

Adair-Dighton syndrome (brittle bones and blue sclera, deafness) Q78.0

Adamantinoblastoma —see Ameloblastoma

Adamantinoma —see also Cyst, calcifying odontogenic
- long bones C40.90
  - lower limb C40.2-●
  - upper limb C40.0-●
- malignant C41.1
  - jaw (bone) (lower) C41.1
    - upper C41.0
- tibial C40.2-●

Adamantoblastoma —see Ameloblastoma

Adams-Stokes (-Morgagni) disease or syndrome I45.9

Adaption reaction —see Disorder, adjustment

Addiction —see also Dependence F19.20
- alcohol, alcoholic (ethyl) (methyl) (wood) (without remission) F10.20
  - with remission F10.21
- drug —see Dependence, drug
- ethyl alcohol (without remission) F10.20
  - with remission F10.21
- heroin —see Dependence, drug, opioid
- methyl alcohol (without remission) F10.20
  - with remission F10.21
- methylated spirit (without remission) F10.20
  - with remission F10.21
- morphine(-like substances) —see Dependence, drug, opioid
- nicotine —see Dependence, drug, nicotine
- opium and opioids —see Dependence, drug, opioid
- tobacco —see Dependence, drug, nicotine

Addisonian crisis E27.2

Addison's
- anemia (pernicious) D51.0
- disease (bronze) or syndrome E27.1
  - tuberculous A18.7
- keloid L94.0

Addison-Biermer anemia (pernicious) D51.0

Addison-Schilder complex E71.528

Additional —see also Accessory
- chromosome(s) Q99.8
  - 21 —see Trisomy, 21
  - sex —see Abnormal, chromosome, sex

Adduction contracture, hip or other joint —see Contraction, joint

Adenitis —see also Lymphadenitis
- acute, unspecified site L04.9
- axillary I88.9
  - acute L04.2
  - chronic or subacute I88.1
- Bartholin's gland N75.8
- bulbourethral gland —see Urethritis
- cervical I88.9
  - acute L04.0
  - chronic or subacute I88.1
- chancroid (Hemophilus ducreyi) A57
- chronic, unspecified site I88.1
- Cowper's gland —see Urethritis
- due to Pasteurella multocida (P. septica) A28.0
- epidemic, acute B27.09
- gangrenous L04.9
- gonorrheal NEC A54.89
- groin I88.9
  - acute L04.1
  - chronic or subacute I88.1
- infectious (acute) (epidemic) B27.09
- inguinal I88.9
  - acute L04.1
  - chronic or subacute I88.1
- lymph gland or node, except mesenteric I88.9
  - acute —see Lymphadenitis, acute
  - chronic or subacute I88.1
- mesenteric (acute) (chronic) (nonspecific) (subacute) I88.0

Adenitis (Continued)
- parotid gland (suppurative) —see Sialoadenitis
- salivary gland (any) (suppurative) —see Sialoadenitis
- scrofulous (tuberculous) A18.2
- Skene's duct or gland —see Urethritis
- strumous, tuberculous A18.2
- subacute, unspecified site I88.1
- sublingual gland (suppurative) —see Sialoadenitis
- submandibular gland (suppurative) —see Sialoadenitis
- submaxillary gland (suppurative) —see Sialoadenitis
- tuberculous —see Tuberculosis, lymph gland
- urethral gland —see Urethritis
- Wharton's duct (suppurative) —see Sialoadenitis

Adenoacanthoma —see Neoplasm, malignant, by site

Adenoameloblastoma —see Cyst, calcifying odontogenic

Adenocarcinoma —see also Neoplasm, malignant, by site
- acidophil
  - specified site —see Neoplasm, malignant, by site
  - unspecified site C75.1
- adrenal cortical C74.0-●
- alveolar —see Neoplasm, lung, malignant
- apocrine
  - breast —see Neoplasm, breast, malignant
  - in situ
    - breast D05.8-●
    - specified site NEC —see Neoplasm, skin, in situ
    - unspecified site D04.9
  - specified site NEC —see Neoplasm, skin, malignant
  - unspecified site C44.99
- basal cell
  - specified site —see Neoplasm, skin, malignant
  - unspecified site C08.9
- basophil
  - specified site —see Neoplasm, malignant, by site
  - unspecified site C75.1
- bile duct type C22.1
  - liver C22.1
  - specified site NEC —see Neoplasm, malignant, by site
  - unspecified site C22.1
- bronchiolar —see Neoplasm, lung, malignant
- bronchioloalveolar —see Neoplasm, lung, malignant
- ceruminous C44.29-●
- cervix, in situ (see also Carcinoma, cervix uteri, in situ) D06.9
- chromophobe
  - specified site —see Neoplasm, malignant, by site
  - unspecified site C75.1
- diffuse type
  - specified site —see Neoplasm, malignant, by site
  - unspecified site C16.9
- duct
  - infiltrating
    - with Paget's disease —see Neoplasm, breast, malignant
    - specified site —see Neoplasm, malignant, by site
    - unspecified site (female) C50.91-●
      - male C50.92-●
  - specified site —see Neoplasm, malignant, by site

Adenocarcinoma (Continued)
- duct (Continued)
  - unspecified site
    - female C56.9
    - male C61
- eosinophil
  - specified site —see Neoplasm, malignant, by site
  - unspecified site C75.1
- follicular
  - with papillary C73
  - moderately differentiated C73
  - specified site —see Neoplasm, malignant, by site
  - trabecular C73
  - unspecified site C73
  - well differentiated C73
- Hurthle cell C73
- in
  - adenomatous
    - polyposis coli C18.9
- infiltrating duct
  - with Paget's disease —see Neoplasm, breast, malignant
  - specified site —see Neoplasm, malignant, by site
  - unspecified site (female) C50.91-●
    - male C50.92-●
- inflammatory
  - specified site —see Neoplasm, malignant, by site
  - unspecified site (female) C50.91-●
    - male C50.92-●
- intestinal type
  - specified site —see Neoplasm, malignant, by site
  - unspecified site C16.9
- intracystic papillary
- intraductal
  - breast D05.1-●
  - noninfiltrating
    - breast D05.1-●
    - papillary
      - with invasion
        - specified site —see Neoplasm, malignant, by site
        - unspecified site (female) C50.91-●
          - male C50.92-●
      - breast D05.1-●
      - specified site NEC —see Neoplasm, in situ, by site
      - unspecified site D05.1-●
    - specified site NEC —see Neoplasm, in situ, by site
    - unspecified site D05.1-●
  - papillary
    - with invasion
      - specified site —see Neoplasm, malignant, by site
      - unspecified site (female) C50.91-●
        - male C50.92-●
    - breast D05.1-●
    - specified site —see Neoplasm, in situ, by site
    - unspecified site D05.1-●
  - specified site NEC —see Neoplasm, in situ, by site
  - unspecified site D05.1-●
- islet cell
  - with exocrine, mixed
    - specified site —see Neoplasm, malignant, by site
    - unspecified site C25.9
  - pancreas C25.4
  - specified site NEC —see Neoplasm, malignant, by site
  - unspecified site C25.4

Adenocarcinoma (Continued)
lobular
in situ
breast D05.0-●
specified site NEC —see Neoplasm, in
situ, by site
unspecified site D05.0-●
specified site —see Neoplasm, malignant,
by site
unspecified site (female) C50.91-●
male C50.92-●
mucoid —see also Neoplasm, malignant,
by site
cell
specified site —see Neoplasm,
malignant, by site
unspecified site C75.1
nonencapsulated sclerosing C73
papillary
with follicular C73
follicular variant C73
intraductal (noninfiltrating)
with invasion
specified site —see Neoplasm,
malignant, by site
unspecified site (female) C50.91-●
male C50.92-●
breast D05.1-●
specified site NEC —see Neoplasm, in
situ, by site
unspecified site D05.1-●
serous
specified site —see Neoplasm,
malignant, by site
unspecified site C56.9
papillocystic
specified site —see Neoplasm, malignant,
by site
unspecified site C56.9
pseudomucinous
specified site —see Neoplasm, malignant,
by site
unspecified site C56.9
renal cell C64-●
sebaceous —see Neoplasm, skin, malignant,
by site
serous —see also Neoplasm, malignant, by site
papillary
specified site —see Neoplasm,
malignant, by site
unspecified site C56.9
sweat gland —see Neoplasm, skin, malignant
water-clear cell C75.0
Adenocarcinoma-in-situ —see also Neoplasm,
in situ, by site
breast D05.9-●
Adenofibroma
clear cell —see Neoplasm, benign, by site
endometrioid D27.9
borderline malignancy D39.10
malignant C56-●
mucinous
specified site —see Neoplasm, benign, by
site
unspecified site D27.9
papillary
specified site —see Neoplasm, benign, by
site
unspecified site D27.9
prostate —see Enlargement, enlarged,
prostate
serous
specified site —see Neoplasm, benign, by
site
unspecified site D27.9
specified site —see Neoplasm, benign,
by site
unspecified site D27.9
Adenofibrosis
breast —see Fibroadenosis, breast
endometrioid N80.0

Adenoiditis (chronic) J35.02
with tonsillitis J35.03
acute J03.90
recurrent J03.91
specified organism NEC J03.80
recurrent J03.81
staphylococcal J03.80
recurrent J03.81
streptococcal J03.00
recurrent J03.01
Adenoids —see condition
Adenolipoma —see Neoplasm, benign,
by site
Adenolipomatosis, Launois-Bensaude E88.89
Adenolymphoma
specified site —see Neoplasm, benign, by site
unspecified site D11.9
Adenoma —see also Neoplasm, benign, by site
acidophil
specified site —see Neoplasm, benign, by
site
unspecified site D35.2
acidophil-basophil, mixed
specified site —see Neoplasm, benign, by
site
unspecified site D35.2
adrenal (cortical) D35.00
clear cell D35.00
compact cell D35.00
glomerulosa cell D35.00
heavily pigmented variant D35.00
mixed cell D35.00
alpha-cell
pancreas D13.7
specified site NEC —see Neoplasm, benign,
by site
unspecified site D13.7
alveolar D14.30
apocrine
breast D24-●
specified site NEC —see Neoplasm, skin,
benign, by site
unspecified site D23.9
basal cell D11.9
basophil
specified site —see Neoplasm, benign,
by site
unspecified site D35.2
basophil-acidophil, mixed
specified site —see Neoplasm, benign, by
site
unspecified site D35.2
beta-cell
pancreas D13.7
specified site NEC —see Neoplasm, benign,
by site
unspecified site D13.7
bile duct D13.4
common D13.5
extrahepatic D13.5
intrahepatic D13.4
specified site NEC —see Neoplasm, benign,
by site
unspecified site D13.4
black D35.00
bronchial D38.1
cylindroid type —see Neoplasm, lung,
malignant
ceruminous D23.2-●
chief cell D35.1
chromophobe
specified site —see Neoplasm, benign, by
site
unspecified site D35.2
colloid
specified site —see Neoplasm, benign, by
site
unspecified site D34
duct
eccrine, papillary —see Neoplasm, skin,
benign

Adenoma (Continued)
endocrine, multiple
single specified site —see Neoplasm,
uncertain behavior, by site
two or more specified sites D44-●
unspecified site D44.9
endometrioid —see also Neoplasm, benign
borderline malignancy —see Neoplasm,
uncertain behavior, by site
eosinophil
specified site —see Neoplasm, benign,
by site
unspecified site D35.2
fetal
specified site —see Neoplasm, benign, by
site
unspecified site D34
follicular
specified site —see Neoplasm, benign, by
site
unspecified site D34
hepatocellular D13.4
Hurthle cell D34
islet cell
pancreas D13.7
specified site NEC —see Neoplasm, benign,
by site
unspecified site D13.7
liver cell D13.4
macrofollicular
specified site —see Neoplasm, benign, by site
unspecified site D34
malignant, malignum —see Neoplasm,
malignant, by site
microcystic
pancreas D13.6
specified site NEC —see Neoplasm, benign,
by site
unspecified site D13.6
microfollicular
specified site —see Neoplasm, benign, by
site
unspecified site D34
mucoid cell
specified site —see Neoplasm, benign, by
site
unspecified site D35.2
multiple endocrine
single specified site —see Neoplasm,
uncertain behavior, by site
two or more specified sites D44-●
unspecified site D44.9
nipple D24-●
papillary —see also Neoplasm, benign, by site
eccrine —see Neoplasm, skin, benign, by
site
Pick's tubular
specified site —see Neoplasm, benign, by
site
unspecified site
female D27.9
male D29.20
pleomorphic
carcinoma in —see Neoplasm, salivary
gland, malignant
specified site —see Neoplasm,
malignant, by site
unspecified site C08.9
polypoid —see also Neoplasm, benign
adenocarcinoma in —see Neoplasm,
malignant, by site
adenocarcinoma in situ —see Neoplasm, in
situ, by site
prostate —see Neoplasm, benign, prostate
rete cell D29.20
sebaceous —see Neoplasm, skin, benign
Sertoli cell
specified site —see Neoplasm, benign, by site
unspecified site
female D27.9
male D29.20

▶ New   ⇒ Revised   ~~deleted~~ Deleted   ● Use Additional Character(s)

Adenoma *(Continued)*
  skin appendage —*see* Neoplasm, skin, benign
  sudoriferous gland —*see* Neoplasm, skin, benign
  sweat gland —*see* Neoplasm, skin, benign
  testicular
    specified site —*see* Neoplasm, benign, by site
    unspecified site
      female D27.9
      male D29.20
  tubular —*see also* Neoplasm, benign, by site
    adenocarcinoma in —*see* Neoplasm, malignant, by site
    adenocarcinoma in situ —*see* Neoplasm, in situ, by site
    Pick's
      specified site —*see* Neoplasm, benign
      unspecified site
        female D27.9
        male D29.20
  tubulovillous —*see also* Neoplasm, benign, by site
    adenocarcinoma in —*see* Neoplasm, malignant, by site
    adenocarcinoma in situ —*see* Neoplasm, in situ, by site
  villous —*see* Neoplasm, uncertain behavior, by site
    adenocarcinoma in —*see* Neoplasm, malignant, by site
    adenocarcinoma in situ —*see* Neoplasm, in situ, by site
  water-clear cell D35.1
Adenomatosis
  endocrine (multiple) E31.20
    single specified site —*see* Neoplasm, uncertain behavior, by site
  erosive of nipple D24-●
  pluriendocrine —*see* Adenomatosis, endocrine
  pulmonary D38.1
    malignant —*see* Neoplasm, lung, malignant
  specified site —*see* Neoplasm, benign, by site
  unspecified site D12.6
Adenomatous
  goiter (nontoxic) E04.9
    with hyperthyroidism —*see* Hyperthyroidism, with, goiter, nodular
    toxic —*see* Hyperthyroidism, with, goiter, nodular
Adenomyoma —*see also* Neoplasm, benign, by site
  prostate —*see* Enlarged, prostate
Adenomyometritis N80.0
Adenomyosis N80.0
Adenopathy (lymph gland) R59.9
  generalized R59.1
  inguinal R59.0
  localized R59.0
  mediastinal R59.0
  mesentery R59.0
  syphilitic (secondary) A51.49
  tracheobronchial R59.0
    tuberculous A15.4
      primary (progressive) A15.7
  tuberculous —*see also* Tuberculosis, lymph gland
    tracheobronchial A15.4
      primary (progressive) A15.7
Adenosalpingitis —*see* Salpingitis
Adenosarcoma —*see* Neoplasm, malignant, by site
Adenosclerosis I88.8
Adenosis (sclerosing) breast —*see* Fibroadenosis, breast
Adenovirus, as cause of disease classified elsewhere B97.0
Adentia (complete) (partial) —*see* Absence, teeth

Adherent —*see also* Adhesions
  labia (minora) N90.89
  pericardium (nonrheumatic) I31.0
    rheumatic I09.2
  placenta (with hemorrhage) O72.0
    without hemorrhage O73.0
  prepuce, newborn N47.0
  scar (skin) L90.5
  tendon in scar L90.5
Adhesions, adhesive (postinfective) K66.0
  with intestinal obstruction K56.50
    complete K56.52
    incomplete K56.51
    partial K56.51
  abdominal (wall) —*see* Adhesions, peritoneum
  appendix K38.8
  bile duct (common) (hepatic) K83.8
  bladder (sphincter) N32.89
  bowel —*see* Adhesions, peritoneum
  cardiac I31.0
    rheumatic I09.2
  cecum —*see* Adhesions, peritoneum
  cervicovaginal N88.1
    congenital Q52.8
    postpartal O90.89
      old N88.1
  cervix N88.1
  ciliary body NEC —*see* Adhesions, iris
  clitoris N90.89
  colon —*see* Adhesions, peritoneum
  common duct K83.8
  congenital —*see also* Anomaly, by site
    fingers —*see* Syndactylism, complex, fingers
    omental, anomalous Q43.3
    peritoneal Q43.3
    tongue (to gum or roof of mouth) Q38.3
  conjunctiva (acquired) H11.21-●
    congenital Q15.8
  cystic duct K82.8
  diaphragm —*see* Adhesions, peritoneum
  due to foreign body —*see* Foreign body
  duodenum —*see* Adhesions, peritoneum
  ear
    middle H74.1-●
  epididymis N50.89
  epidural —*see* Adhesions, meninges
  epiglottis J38.7
  eyelid H02.59
  female pelvis N73.6
  gallbladder K82.8
  globe H44.89
  heart I31.0
    rheumatic I09.2
  ileocecal (coil) —*see* Adhesions, peritoneum
  ileum —*see* Adhesions, peritoneum
  intestine —*see also* Adhesions, peritoneum
    with obstruction K56.50
      complete K56.52
      incomplete K56.51
      partial K56.51
  intra-abdominal —*see* Adhesions, peritoneum
  iris H21.50-●
    anterior H21.51-●
    goniosynechiae H21.52-●
    posterior H21.54-●
    to corneal graft T85.898
  joint —*see* Ankylosis
    knee M23.8X
    temporomandibular M26.61-●
  labium (majus) (minus), congenital Q52.5
  liver —*see* Adhesions, peritoneum
  lung J98.4
  mediastinum J98.59
  meninges (cerebral) (spinal) G96.12
    congenital Q07.8
    tuberculous (cerebral) (spinal) A17.0
  mesenteric —*see* Adhesions, peritoneum
  nasal (septum) (to turbinates) J34.89
  ocular muscle —*see* Strabismus, mechanical
  omentum —*see* Adhesions, peritoneum

Adhesions, adhesive *(Continued)*
  ovary N73.6
    congenital (to cecum, kidney or omentum) Q50.39
  paraovarian N73.6
  pelvic (peritoneal)
    female N73.6
      postprocedural N99.4
    male —*see* Adhesions, peritoneum
    postpartal (old) N73.6
    tuberculous A18.17
  penis to scrotum (congenital) Q55.8
  periappendiceal —*see also* Adhesions, peritoneum
  pericardium (nonrheumatic) I31.0
    focal I31.0
    rheumatic I09.2
    tuberculous A18.84
  pericholecystic K82.8
  perigastric —*see* Adhesions, peritoneum
  periovarian N73.6
  periprostatic N42.89
  perirectal —*see* Adhesions, peritoneum
  perirenal N28.89
  peritoneum, peritoneal (postinfective) K66.0
    with obstruction (intestinal) K56.50
      complete K56.52
      incomplete K56.51
      partial K56.51
    congenital Q43.3
    pelvic, female N73.6
      postprocedural N99.4
    postpartal, pelvic N73.6
    postprocedural K66.0
    to uterus N73.6
  peritubal N73.6
  periureteral N28.89
  periuterine N73.6
  perivesical N32.89
  perivesicular (seminal vesicle) N50.89
  pleura, pleuritic J94.8
    tuberculous NEC A15.6
  pleuropericardial J94.8
  postoperative (gastrointestinal tract) K66.0
    with obstruction —*see also* Obstruction, intestine, postoperative K91.30
    due to foreign body accidentally left in wound —*see* Foreign body, accidentally left during a procedure
    pelvic peritoneal N99.4
    urethra —*see* Stricture, urethra, postprocedural
    vagina N99.2
  postpartal, old (vulva or perineum) N90.89
  preputial, prepuce N47.5
  pulmonary J98.4
  pylorus —*see* Adhesions, peritoneum
  sciatic nerve —*see* Lesion, nerve, sciatic
  seminal vesicle N50.89
  shoulder (joint) —*see* Capsulitis, adhesive
  sigmoid flexure —*see* Adhesions, peritoneum
  spermatic cord (acquired) N50.89
    congenital Q55.4
  spinal canal G96.12
  stomach —*see* Adhesions, peritoneum
  subscapular —*see* Capsulitis, adhesive
  temporomandibular M26.61-●
  tendinitis —*see also* Tenosynovitis, specified type NEC
    shoulder —*see* Capsulitis, adhesive
  testis N44.8
  tongue, congenital (to gum or roof of mouth) Q38.3
    acquired K14.8
  trachea J39.8
  tubo-ovarian N73.6
  tunica vaginalis N44.8
  uterus N73.6
    internal N85.6
    to abdominal wall N73.6

Adhesions, adhesive *(Continued)*
  vagina (chronic) N89.5
    postoperative N99.2
  vitreomacular H43.82-●
  vitreous H43.89
  vulva N90.89
Adiaspiromycosis B48.8
Adie (-Holmes) pupil or syndrome —*see*
    Anomaly, pupil, function, tonic pupil
Adiponecrosis neonatorum P83.88
Adiposis —*see also* Obesity
  cerebralis E23.6
  dolorosa E88.2
Adiposity —*see also* Obesity
  heart —*see* Degeneration, myocardial
  localized E65
Adiposogenital dystrophy E23.6
Adjustment
  disorder —*see* Disorder, adjustment
  implanted device —*see* Encounter (for),
    adjustment (of)
  prosthesis, external —*see* Fitting
  reaction —*see* Disorder, adjustment
Administration of tPA (rtPA) in a different
    facility within the last 24 hours prior to
    admission to current facility Z92.82
Admission (for) —*see also* Encounter (for)
  adjustment (of)
    artificial
      arm Z44.00-●
        complete Z44.01-●
        partial Z44.02-●
      eye Z44.2
      leg Z44.10-●
        complete Z44.11-●
        partial Z44.12-●
    brain neuropacemaker Z46.2
      implanted Z45.42
    breast
      implant Z45.81
      prosthesis (external) Z44.3
    colostomy belt Z46.89
    contact lenses Z46.0
    cystostomy device Z46.6
    dental prosthesis Z46.3
    device NEC
      abdominal Z46.89
      implanted Z45.89
        cardiac Z45.09
          defibrillator (with synchronous
            cardiac pacemaker) Z45.02
          pacemaker (cardiac
            resynchronization therapy
            (CRT-P)) Z45.018
            pulse generator Z45.010
          resynchronization therapy
            defibrillator (CRT-D) Z45.02
        hearing device Z45.328
          bone conduction Z45.320
          cochlear Z45.321
        infusion pump Z45.1
        nervous system Z45.49
          CSF drainage Z45.41
          hearing device —*see* Admission,
            adjustment, device, implanted,
            hearing device
          neuropacemaker Z45.42
          visual substitution Z45.31
        specified NEC Z45.89
        vascular access Z45.2
        visual substitution Z45.31
      nervous system Z46.2
        implanted —*see* Admission,
          adjustment, device, implanted,
          nervous system
      orthodontic Z46.4
      prosthetic Z44.9
        arm —*see* Admission, adjustment,
          artificial, arm
        breast Z44.3
        dental Z46.3

Admission *(Continued)*
  adjustment *(Continued)*
    device NEC *(Continued)*
      prosthetic *(Continued)*
        eye Z44.2
        leg —*see* Admission, adjustment,
          artificial, leg
        specified type NEC Z44.8
      substitution
        auditory Z46.2
          implanted —*see* Admission,
            adjustment, device, implanted,
            hearing device
        nervous system Z46.2
          implanted —*see* Admission,
            adjustment, device, implanted,
            nervous system
        visual Z46.2
          implanted Z45.31
    urinary Z46.6
    hearing aid Z46.1
      implanted —*see* Admission, adjustment,
        device, implanted, hearing device
    ileostomy device Z46.89
    intestinal appliance or device NEC Z46.89
    neuropacemaker (brain) (peripheral nerve)
      (spinal cord) Z46.2
      implanted Z45.42
    orthodontic device Z46.4
    orthopedic (brace) (cast) (device) (shoes)
      Z46.89
    pacemaker (cardiac resynchronization
      therapy (CRT-P))
      cardiac Z45.018
        pulse generator Z45.010
      nervous system Z46.2
        implanted Z45.42
    portacath (port-a-cath) Z45.2
    prosthesis Z44.9
      arm —*see* Admission, adjustment,
        artificial, arm
      breast Z44.3
      dental Z46.3
      eye Z44.2
      leg —*see* Admission, adjustment,
        artificial, leg
      specified NEC Z44.8
    spectacles Z46.0
  aftercare (*see also* Aftercare) Z51.89
    postpartum
      immediately after delivery Z39.0
      routine follow-up Z39.2
    radiation therapy (antineoplastic) Z51.0
  attention to artificial opening (of) Z43.9
    artificial vagina Z43.7
    colostomy Z43.3
    cystostomy Z43.5
    enterostomy Z43.4
    gastrostomy Z43.1
    ileostomy Z43.2
    jejunostomy Z43.4
    nephrostomy Z43.6
    specified site NEC Z43.8
      intestinal tract Z43.4
      urinary tract Z43.6
    tracheostomy Z43.0
    ureterostomy Z43.6
    urethrostomy Z43.6
  breast augmentation or reduction Z41.1
  breast reconstruction following mastectomy
    Z42.1
  change of
    dressing (nonsurgical) Z48.00
    neuropacemaker device (brain) (peripheral
      nerve) (spinal cord) Z46.2
      implanted Z45.42
    surgical dressing Z48.01
  circumcision, ritual or routine (in absence of
    diagnosis) Z41.2
  clinical research investigation (control)
    (normal comparison) (participant) Z00.6

Admission *(Continued)*
  contraceptive management Z30.9
  cosmetic surgery NEC Z41.1
  counseling (*see also* Counseling)
    dietary Z71.3
    gestational carrier Z31.7
    HIV Z71.7
    human immunodeficiency virus Z71.7
    nonattending third party Z71.0
    procreative management NEC Z31.69
  delivery, full-term, uncomplicated O80
    cesarean, without indication O82
  desensitization to allergens Z51.6
  dietary surveillance and counseling Z71.3
  ear piercing Z41.3
  examination at health care facility (adult) —
      see also Examination Z00.00
    with abnormal findings Z00.01
    clinical research investigation (control)
      (normal comparison) (participant)
      Z00.6
    dental Z01.20
      with abnormal findings Z01.21
    donor (potential) Z00.5
    ear Z01.10
      with abnormal findings NEC Z01.118
      following failed vision screening
        Z01.020
        with abnormal findings Z01.021
    eye Z01.00
      with abnormal findings Z01.01
    general, specified reason NEC Z00.8
    hearing Z01.10
      with abnormal findings NEC Z01.118
      infant or child (over 28 days old) Z00.129
        with abnormal findings Z00.121
    postpartum checkup Z39.2
    psychiatric (general) Z00.8
      requested by authority Z04.6
    vision Z01.00
      with abnormal findings Z01.01
        following failed vision screening
          Z01.020
          with abnormal findings Z01.021
      infant or child (over 28 days old) Z00.129
        with abnormal findings Z00.121
  fitting (of)
    artificial
      arm —*see* Admission, adjustment,
        artificial, arm
      eye Z44.2
      leg —*see* Admission, adjustment,
        artificial, leg
    brain neuropacemaker Z46.2
      implanted Z45.42
    breast prosthesis (external) Z44.3
    colostomy belt Z46.89
    contact lenses Z46.0
    cystostomy device Z46.6
    dental prosthesis Z46.3
    dentures Z46.3
    device NEC
      abdominal Z46.89
      nervous system Z46.2
        implanted —*see* Admission,
          adjustment, device, implanted,
          nervous system
      orthodontic Z46.4
      prosthetic Z44.9
        breast Z44.3
        dental Z46.3
        eye Z44.2
      substitution
        auditory Z46.2
          implanted —*see* Admission,
            adjustment, device, implanted,
            hearing device
        nervous system Z46.2
          implanted —*see* Admission,
            adjustment, device, implanted,
            nervous system

▶ New   ⇒ Revised   ~~deleted~~ Deleted   ● Use Additional Character(s)

Admission *(Continued)*
  fitting (of) *(Continued)*
    device NEC *(Continued)*
      substitution *(Continued)*
        visual Z46.2
          implanted Z45.31
    hearing aid Z46.1
    ileostomy device Z46.89
    intestinal appliance or device NEC Z46.89
    neuropacemaker (brain) (peripheral nerve) (spinal cord) Z46.2
      implanted Z45.42
    orthodontic device Z46.4
    orthopedic device (brace) (cast) (shoes) Z46.89
    prosthesis Z44.9
      arm —*see* Admission, adjustment, artificial, arm
      breast Z44.3
      dental Z46.3
      eye Z44.2
      leg —*see* Admission, adjustment, artificial, leg
      specified type NEC Z44.8
    spectacles Z46.0
  follow-up examination Z09
  intrauterine device management Z30.431
    initial prescription Z30.014
  mental health evaluation Z00.8
    requested by authority Z04.6
  observation —*see* Observation
  Papanicolaou smear, cervix Z12.4
    for suspected malignant neoplasm Z12.4
  plastic and reconstructive surgery following medical procedure or healed injury NEC Z42.8
  plastic surgery, cosmetic NEC Z41.1
  postpartum observation
    immediately after delivery Z39.0
    routine follow-up Z39.2
  poststerilization (for restoration) Z31.0
    aftercare Z31.42
  procreative management Z31.9
  prophylactic (measure) —*see also* Encounter, prophylactic measures
    organ removal Z40.00
      breast Z40.01
      fallopian tube(s) Z40.03
        with ovary(s) Z40.02
      ovary(s) Z40.02
      specified organ NEC Z40.09
      testes Z40.09
    vaccination Z23
  psychiatric examination (general) Z00.8
    requested by authority Z04.6
  radiation therapy (antineoplastic) Z51.0
  reconstructive surgery following medical procedure or healed injury NEC Z42.8
  removal of
    cystostomy catheter Z43.5
    drains Z48.03
    dressing (nonsurgical) Z48.00
    implantable subdermal contraceptive Z30.46
    intrauterine contraceptive device Z30.432
    neuropacemaker (brain) (peripheral nerve) (spinal cord) Z46.2
      implanted Z45.42
    staples Z48.02
    surgical dressing Z48.01
    sutures Z48.02
    ureteral stent Z46.6
  respirator [ventilator] use during power failure Z99.12
  restoration of organ continuity (poststerilization) Z31.0
    aftercare Z31.42
  sensitivity test —*see also* Test, skin
    allergy NEC Z01.82
    Mantoux Z11.1

Admission *(Continued)*
  tuboplasty following previous sterilization Z31.0
    aftercare Z31.42
  vasoplasty following previous sterilization Z31.0
    aftercare Z31.42
  vision examination Z01.00
    with abnormal findings Z01.01
      following failed vision screening Z01.020
        with abnormal findings Z01.021
    infant or child (over 28 days old) Z00.129
      with abnormal findings Z00.121
  waiting period for admission to other facility Z75.1
Adnexitis (suppurative) —*see* Salpingo-oophoritis
Adolescent X-linked adrenoleukodystrophy E71.521
Adrenal (gland) —*see* condition
Adrenalism, tuberculous A18.7
Adrenalitis, adrenitis E27.8
  autoimmune E27.1
  meningococcal, hemorrhagic A39.1
Adrenarche, premature E27.0
Adrenocortical syndrome —*see* Cushing's, syndrome
Adrenogenital syndrome E25.9
  acquired E25.8
  congenital E25.0
  salt loss E25.0
Adrenogenitalism, congenital E25.0
Adrenoleukodystrophy E71.529
  neonatal E71.511
  X-linked E71.529
    Addison only phenotype E71.528
    Addison-Schilder E71.528
    adolescent E71.521
    adrenomyeloneuropathy E71.522
    childhood cerebral E71.520
    other specified E71.528
Adrenomyeloneuropathy E71.522
Adventitious bursa —*see* Bursopathy, specified type NEC
Adverse effect —*see* Table of Drugs and Chemicals, categories T36-T50, with 6th character 5
Advice —*see* Counseling
Adynamia (episodica) (hereditary) (periodic) G72.3
Aeration lung imperfect, newborn —*see* Atelectasis
Aerobullosis T70.3
Aerocele —*see* Embolism, air
Aerodermectasia
  subcutaneous (traumatic) T79.7
Aerodontalgia T70.29
Aeroembolism T70.3
Aerogenes capsulatus infection A48.0
Aero-otitis media T70.0
Aerophagy, aerophagia (psychogenic) F45.8
Aerophobia F40.228
Aerosinusitis T70.1
Aerotitis T70.0
Affection —*see* Disease
Afibrinogenemia —*see also* Defect, coagulation D68.8
  acquired D65
  congenital D68.2
  following ectopic or molar pregnancy O08.1
  in abortion —*see* Abortion, by type, complicated by, afibrinogenemia
  puerperal O72.3
African
  sleeping sickness B56.9
  tick fever A68.1
  trypanosomiasis B56.9
    gambian B56.0
    rhodesian B56.1

Aftercare —*see also* Care Z51.89
  following surgery (for) (on)
    amputation Z47.81
    attention to
      drains Z48.03
      dressings (nonsurgical) Z48.00
        surgical Z48.01
      sutures Z48.02
    circulatory system Z48.812
    delayed (planned) wound closure Z48.1
    digestive system Z48.815
    explantation of joint prosthesis (staged procedure)
      hip Z47.32
      knee Z47.33
      shoulder Z47.31
    genitourinary system Z48.816
    joint replacement Z47.1
    neoplasm Z48.3
    nervous system Z48.811
    oral cavity Z48.814
    organ transplant
      bone marrow Z48.290
      heart Z48.21
      heart-lung Z48.280
      kidney Z48.22
      liver Z48.23
      lung Z48.24
      multiple organs NEC Z48.288
      specified NEC Z48.298
    orthopedic NEC Z47.89
    planned wound closure Z48.1
    removal of internal fixation device Z47.2
    respiratory system Z48.813
    scoliosis Z47.82
    sense organs Z48.810
    skin and subcutaneous tissue Z48.817
    specified body system
      circulatory Z48.812
      digestive Z48.815
      genitourinary Z48.816
      nervous Z48.811
      oral cavity Z48.814
      respiratory Z48.813
      sense organs Z48.810
      skin and subcutaneous tissue Z48.817
      teeth Z48.814
    specified NEC Z48.89
    spinal Z47.89
    teeth Z48.814
  fracture — code to fracture with seventh character D
  involving
    removal of
      drains Z48.03
      dressings (nonsurgical) Z48.00
      staples Z48.02
      surgical dressings Z48.01
      sutures Z48.02
  neuropacemaker (brain) (peripheral nerve) (spinal cord) Z46.2
    implanted Z45.42
  orthopedic NEC Z47.89
  postprocedural —*see* Aftercare, following surgery
After-cataract —*see* Cataract, secondary
Agalactia (primary) O92.3
  elective, secondary or therapeutic O92.5
Agammaglobulinemia (acquired (secondary)) (nonfamilial) D80.1
  with
    immunoglobulin-bearing B-lymphocytes D80.1
    lymphocytes D81.9
  autosomal recessive (Swiss type) D80.0
  Bruton's X-linked D80.0
  common variable (CVAgamma) D80.1
  congenital sex-linked D80.0
  hereditary D80.0
  lymphopenic D81.9
  Swiss type (autosomal recessive) D80.0

Agammaglobulinemia *(Continued)*
X-linked (with growth hormone deficiency) (Bruton) D80.0
Aganglionosis (bowel) (colon) Q43.1
Age (old) —*see* Senility
Agenesis
adrenal (gland) Q89.1
alimentary tract (complete) (partial) NEC Q45.8
upper Q40.8
anus, anal (canal) Q42.3
with fistula Q42.2
aorta Q25.41
appendix Q42.8
arm (complete) Q71.0-●
with hand present Q71.1-●
artery (peripheral) Q27.9
brain Q28.3
coronary Q24.5
pulmonary Q25.79
specified NEC Q27.8
umbilical Q27.0
auditory (canal) (external) Q16.1
auricle (ear) Q16.0
bile duct or passage Q44.5
bladder Q64.5
bone Q79.9
brain Q00.0
part of Q04.3
breast (with nipple present) Q83.8
with absent nipple Q83.0
bronchus Q32.4
canaliculus lacrimalis Q10.4
carpus —*see* Agenesis, hand
cartilage Q79.9
cecum Q42.8
cerebellum Q04.3
cervix Q51.5
chin Q18.8
cilia Q10.3
circulatory system, part NOS Q28.9
clavicle Q74.0
clitoris Q52.6
coccyx Q76.49
colon Q42.9
specified NEC Q42.8
corpus callosum Q04.0
cricoid cartilage Q31.8
diaphragm (with hernia) Q79.1
digestive organ(s) or tract (complete) (partial) NEC Q45.8
upper Q40.8
ductus arteriosus Q28.8
duodenum Q41.0
ear Q16.9
auricle Q16.0
lobe Q17.8
ejaculatory duct Q55.4
endocrine (gland) NEC Q89.2
epiglottis Q31.8
esophagus Q39.8
eustachian tube Q16.2
eye Q11.1
adnexa Q15.8
eyelid (fold) Q10.3
face
bones NEC Q75.8
specified part NEC Q18.8
fallopian tube Q50.6
femur —*see* Defect, reduction, lower limb, longitudinal, femur
fibula —*see* Defect, reduction, lower limb, longitudinal, fibula
finger (complete) (partial) —*see* Agenesis, hand
foot (and toes) (complete) (partial) Q72.3-●
forearm (with hand present) —*see* Agenesis, arm, with hand present
and hand Q71.2-●
gallbladder Q44.0
gastric Q40.2

Agenesis *(Continued)*
genitalia, genital (organ(s))
female Q52.8
external Q52.71
internal NEC Q52.8
male Q55.8
glottis Q31.8
hair Q84.0
hand (and fingers) (complete) (partial) Q71.3-●
heart Q24.8
valve NEC Q24.8
pulmonary Q22.0
hepatic Q44.7
humerus —*see* Defect, reduction, upper limb
hymen Q52.4
ileum Q41.2
incus Q16.3
intestine (small) Q41.9
large Q42.9
specified NEC Q42.8
iris (dilator fibers) Q13.1
jaw M26.09
jejunum Q41.1
kidney(s) (partial) Q60.2
bilateral Q60.1
unilateral Q60.0
labium (majus) (minus) Q52.71
labyrinth, membranous Q16.5
lacrimal apparatus Q10.4
larynx Q31.8
leg (complete) Q72.0-●
with foot present Q72.1-●
lower leg (with foot present) —*see* Agenesis, leg, with foot present
and foot Q72.2-●
lens Q12.3
limb (complete) Q73.0
lower —*see* Agenesis, leg
upper —*see* Agenesis, arm
lip Q38.0
liver Q44.7
lung (fissure) (lobe) (bilateral) (unilateral) Q33.3
mandible, maxilla M26.09
metacarpus —*see* Agenesis, hand
metatarsus —*see* Agenesis, foot
muscle Q79.8
eyelid Q10.3
ocular Q15.8
musculoskeletal system NEC Q79.8
nail(s) Q84.3
neck, part Q18.8
nerve Q07.8
nervous system, part NEC Q07.8
nipple Q83.2
nose Q30.1
nuclear Q07.8
organ
of Corti Q16.5
or site not listed —*see* Anomaly, by site
osseous meatus (ear) Q16.1
ovary
bilateral Q50.02
unilateral Q50.01
oviduct Q50.6
pancreas Q45.0
parathyroid (gland) Q89.2
parotid gland(s) Q38.4
patella Q74.1
pelvic girdle (complete) (partial) Q74.2
penis Q55.5
pericardium Q24.8
pituitary (gland) Q89.2
prostate Q55.4
punctum lacrimale Q10.4
radioulnar —*see* Defect, reduction, upper limb
radius —*see* Defect, reduction, upper limb, longitudinal, radius
rectum Q42.1
with fistula Q42.0

Agenesis *(Continued)*
renal Q60.2
bilateral Q60.1
unilateral Q60.0
respiratory organ NEC Q34.8
rib Q76.6
roof of orbit Q75.8
round ligament Q52.8
sacrum Q76.49
salivary gland Q38.4
scapula Q74.0
scrotum Q55.29
seminal vesicles Q55.4
septum
atrial Q21.1
between aorta and pulmonary artery Q21.4
ventricular Q20.4
shoulder girdle (complete) (partial) Q74.0
skull (bone) Q75.8
with
anencephaly Q00.0
encephalocele —*see* Encephalocele
hydrocephalus Q03.9
with spina bifida —*see* Spina bifida, by site, with hydrocephalus
microcephaly Q02
spermatic cord Q55.4
spinal cord Q06.0
spine Q76.49
spleen Q89.01
sternum Q76.7
stomach Q40.2
submaxillary gland(s) (congenital) Q38.4
tarsus —*see* Agenesis, foot
tendon Q79.8
testicle Q55.0
thymus (gland) Q89.2
thyroid (gland) E03.1
cartilage Q31.8
tibia —*see* Defect, reduction, lower limb, longitudinal, tibia
tibiofibular —*see* Defect, reduction, lower limb, specified type NEC
toe (and foot) (complete) (partial) —*see* Agenesis, foot
tongue Q38.3
trachea (cartilage) Q32.1
ulna —*see* Defect, reduction, upper limb, longitudinal, ulna
upper limb —*see* Agenesis, arm
ureter Q62.4
urethra Q64.5
urinary tract NEC Q64.8
uterus Q51.0
uvula Q38.5
vagina Q52.0
vas deferens Q55.4
vein(s) (peripheral) Q27.9
brain Q28.3
great NEC Q26.8
portal Q26.5
vena cava (inferior) (superior) Q26.8
vermis of cerebellum Q04.3
vertebra Q76.49
vulva Q52.71
Ageusia R43.2
Agitated —*see* condition
Agitation R45.1
Aglossia (congenital) Q38.3
Aglossia-adactylia syndrome Q87.0
Aglycogenosis E74.00
Agnosia (body image) (other senses) (tactile) R48.1
developmental F88
verbal R48.1
auditory R48.1
developmental F80.2
developmental F80.2
visual (object) R48.3

▶ New ⟱ Revised ~~deleted~~ Deleted ● Use Additional Character(s)

Agoraphobia F40.00
  with panic disorder F40.01
  without panic disorder F40.02
Agrammatism R48.8
Agranulocytopenia —see Agranulocytosis
Agranulocytosis (chronic) (cyclical) (genetic)
    (infantile) (periodic) (pernicious) (see also
    Neutropenia) D70.9
  congenital D70.0
  cytoreductive cancer chemotherapy sequela
    D70.1
  drug-induced D70.2
    due to cytoreductive cancer chemotherapy
      D70.1
  due to infection D70.3
  secondary D70.4
    drug-induced D70.2
      due to cytoreductive cancer
        chemotherapy D70.1
Agraphia (absolute) R48.8
  with alexia R48.0
  developmental F81.81
Ague (dumb) —see Malaria
Agyria Q04.3
Ahumada-del Castillo syndrome E23.0
Aichomophobia F40.298
AIDS (related complex) B20
Ailment heart —see Disease, heart
Ailurophobia F40.218
Ainhum (disease) L94.6
AIN —see Neoplasia, intraepithelial, anal
AIPHI (acute idiopathic pulmonary hemorrhage
    in infants (over 28 days old)) R04.81
Air
  anterior mediastinum J98.2
  compressed, disease T70.3
  conditioner lung or pneumonitis J67.7
  embolism (artery) (cerebral) (any site)
    T79.0
    with ectopic or molar pregnancy O08.2
    due to implanted device NEC —see
      Complications, by site and type,
      specified NEC
    following
      abortion —see Abortion by type,
        complicated by, embolism
      ectopic or molar pregnancy O08.2
    infusion, therapeutic injection or
      transfusion T80.0
    in pregnancy, childbirth or puerperium —
      see Embolism, obstetric
    traumatic T79.0
  hunger, psychogenic F45.8
  rarefied, effects of —see Effect, adverse, high
    altitude
  sickness T75.3
Airplane sickness T75.3
Akathisia (drug-induced) (treatment- induced)
    G25.71
  neuroleptic induced (acute) G25.71
  tardive G25.71
Akinesia R29.898
Akinetic mutism R41.89
Akureyri's disease G93.3
Alactasia, congenital E73.0
Alagille's syndrome Q44.7
Alastrim B03
Albers-Schönberg syndrome Q78.2
Albert's syndrome —see Tendinitis,
    Achilles
Albinism, albino E70.30
  with hematologic abnormality E70.339
    Chédiak-Higashi syndrome E70.330
    Hermansky-Pudlak syndrome E70.331
    other specified E70.338
  I E70.320
  II E70.321
  ocular E70.319
    autosomal recessive E70.311
    other specified E70.318
    X-linked E70.310

Albinism, albino (Continued)
  oculocutaneous E70.329
    other specified E70.328
    tyrosinase (ty) negative E70.320
    tyrosinase (ty) positive E70.321
  other specified E70.39
Albinismus E70.30
Albright (-McCune)(-Sternberg) syndrome
    Q78.1
Albuminous —see condition
Albuminuria, albuminuric (acute) (chronic)
    (subacute) —see also Proteinuria R80.9
  complicating pregnancy —see Proteinuria,
    gestational
  with
      gestational hypertension —see
        Pre-eclampsia
      pre-existing hypertension —see
        Hypertension, complicating
        pregnancy, pre-existing, with,
        pre-eclampsia
  gestational —see Proteinuria, gestational
    with
      gestational hypertension —see
        Pre-eclampsia
      pre-existing hypertension —see
        Hypertension, complicating
        pregnancy, pre-existing, with,
        pre-eclampsia
  orthostatic R80.2
  postural R80.2
  pre-eclamptic —see Pre-eclampsia
  scarlatinal A38.8
Albuminurophobia F40.298
Alcaptonuria E70.29
Alcohol, alcoholic, alcohol-induced
  addiction (without remission) F10.20
    with remission F10.21
  amnestic disorder, persisting F10.96
    with dependence F10.26
  anxiety disorder F10.980
  bipolar and related disorder F10.94
  brain syndrome, chronic F10.97
    with dependence F10.27
  cardiopathy I42.6
  counseling and surveillance
    Z71.41
    family member Z71.42
  delirium (acute) (tremens) (withdrawal)
    F10.231
    with intoxication F10.921
    in
        abuse F10.121
        dependence F10.221
  dementia F10.97
    with dependence F10.27
  depressive disorder F10.94
  deterioration F10.97
    with dependence F10.27
  hallucinosis (acute) F10.951
    in
        abuse F10.151
        dependence F10.251
  insanity F10.959
  intoxication (acute) (without dependence)
    F10.129
    with
        delirium F10.121
        dependence F10.229
          with delirium F10.221
          uncomplicated F10.220
        uncomplicated F10.120
  jealousy F10.988
  Korsakoff's, Korsakov's, Korsakow's F10.26
  liver K70.9
    acute —see Disease, liver, alcoholic,
      hepatitis
  major neurocognitive disorder, amnestic-
    confabulatory type F10.96
  major neurocognitive disorder, nonamnestic-
    confabulatory type F10.97

Alcohol, alcoholic, alcohol-induced (Continued)
  mania (acute) (chronic) F10.959
  mild neurocognitive disorder F10.988
  paranoia, paranoid (type) psychosis F10.950
  pellagra E52
  poisoning, accidental (acute) NEC —see
    Table of Drugs and Chemicals, alcohol,
    poisoning
  psychosis —see Psychosis, alcoholic
  psychotic disorder F10.959
  sexual dysfunction F10.981
  sleep disorder F10.982
  withdrawal (without convulsions) F10.239
    with delirium F10.231
Alcoholism (chronic) (without remission) F10.20
  with
      psychosis —see Psychosis, alcoholic
      remission F10.21
  Korsakov's F10.96
    with dependence F10.26
Alder (-Reilly) anomaly or syndrome
    (leukocyte granulation) D72.0
Aldosteronism E26.9
  familial (type I) E26.02
    glucocorticoid-remediable E26.02
  primary (due to (bilateral) adrenal
    hyperplasia) E26.09
  primary NEC E26.09
  secondary E26.1
  specified NEC E26.89
Aldosteronoma D44.10
Aldrich(-Wiskott) syndrome (eczema-
    thrombocytopenia) D82.0
Alektorophobia F40.218
Aleppo boil B55.1
Aleukemic —see condition Aleukia
  congenital D70.0
  hemorrhagica D61.9
    congenital D61.09
  splenica D73.1
Alexia R48.0
  developmental F81.0
  secondary to organic lesion R48.0
Algoneurodystrophy M89.00
  ankle M89.07-●
  foot M89.07-●
  forearm M89.03-●
  hand M89.04-●
  lower leg M89.06-●
  multiple sites M89.0-●
  shoulder M89.01-●
  specified site NEC M89.08
  thigh M89.05-●
  upper arm M89.02-●
Algophobia F40.298
Alienation, mental —see Psychosis
Alkalemia E87.3
Alkalosis E87.3
  metabolic E87.3
    with respiratory acidosis E87.4
  of newborn P74.41
  respiratory E87.3
Alkaptonuria E70.29
Allen-Masters syndrome N83.8
Allergy, allergic (reaction) (to) T78.40
  air-borne substance NEC (rhinitis) J30.89
  alveolitis (extrinsic) J67.9
    due to
        Aspergillus clavatus J67.4
        Cryptostroma corticale J67.6
        organisms (fungal, thermophilic
          actinomycete) growing in
          ventilation (air conditioning)
          systems J67.7
      specified type NEC J67.8
  anaphylactic reaction or shock T78.2
  angioneurotic edema T78.3
  animal (dander) (epidermal) (hair) (rhinitis)
    J30.81
  bee sting (anaphylactic shock) —see Toxicity,
    venom, arthropod, bee

Allergy, allergic *(Continued)*
 biological —*see* Allergy, drug
 colitis —*see also* Colitis, allergic K52.29
 dander (animal) (rhinitis) J30.81
 dandruff (rhinitis) J30.81
 dental restorative material (existing) K08.55
 dermatitis —*see* Dermatitis, contact, allergic
 diathesis —*see* History, allergy
 drug, medicament & biological (any)
   (external) (internal) T78.40
   correct substance properly administered —
     see Table of Drugs and Chemicals, by
     drug, adverse effect
   wrong substance given or taken NEC (by
     accident) —*see* Table of Drugs and
     Chemicals, by drug, poisoning
  due to pollen J30.1
 dust (house) (stock) (rhinitis) J30.89
   with asthma —*see* Asthma, allergic extrinsic
 eczema —*see* Dermatitis, contact, allergic
 epidermal (animal) (rhinitis) J30.81
 feathers (rhinitis) J30.89
 food (any) (ingested) NEC T78.1
   anaphylactic shock —*see* Shock,
     anaphylactic, due to food
   dermatitis —*see* Dermatitis, due to, food
   dietary counseling and surveillance Z71.3
   in contact with skin L23.6
   rhinitis J30.5
   status (without reaction) Z91.018
     eggs Z91.012
     milk products Z91.011
     peanuts Z91.010
     seafood Z91.013
     specified NEC Z91.018
 gastrointestinal —*see also* specific type of
   allergic reaction
   meaning colitis —*see also* Colitis, allergic)
     K52.29
   meaning gastroenteritis —*see also*
     Gastroenteritis, allergic) K52.29
   meaning other adverse food reaction not
     elsewhere classified T78.1
 grain J30.1
 grass (hay fever) (pollen) J30.1
   asthma —*see* Asthma, allergic extrinsic
 hair (animal) (rhinitis) J30.81
 history (of) —*see* History, allergy
 horse serum —*see* Allergy, serum
 inhalant (rhinitis) J30.89
   pollen J30.1
 kapok (rhinitis) J30.89
 medicine —*see* Allergy, drug
 milk protein —*see also* Allergy, food
     Z91.011
   anaphylactic reaction T78.07
   dermatitis L27.2
   enterocolitis syndrome K52.21
   enteropathy K52.22
   gastroenteritis K52.29
   gastroesophageal reflux —*see also* Reaction,
     adverse, food) K21.9
     ➡with esophagitis without bleeding
       K21.00
     ▶with bleeding K21.01
   proctocolitis K52.82
 nasal, seasonal due to pollen J30.1
 ➡pneumonia J82.89
 pollen (any) (hay fever) J30.1
   asthma —*see* Asthma, allergic extrinsic
 primrose J30.1
 primula J30.1
 proctocolitis K52.82
 purpura D69.0
 ragweed (hay fever) (pollen) J30.1
   asthma —*see* Asthma, allergic extrinsic
 rose (pollen) J30.1
 seasonal NEC J30.2
 Senecio jacobae (pollen) J30.1
 serum —*see also* Reaction, serum T80.69
   anaphylactic shock T80.59

Allergy, allergic *(Continued)*
 shock (anaphylactic) T78.2
   due to
     administration of blood and blood
       products T80.51
     adverse effect of correct medicinal
       substance properly administered
       T88.6
     immunization T80.52
     serum NEC T80.59
     vaccination T80.52
   specific NEC T78.49
 tree (any) (hay fever) (pollen) J30.1
   asthma —*see* Asthma, allergic extrinsic
 upper respiratory J30.9
 urticaria L50.0
 vaccine —*see* Allergy, serum
 wheat —*see* Allergy, food
Allescheriasis B48.2
Alligator skin disease Q80.9
Allocheiria, allochiria R20.8
Almeida's disease —*see*
   Paracoccidioidomycosis
Alopecia (hereditaria) (seborrheica) L65.9
 androgenic L64.9
   drug-induced L64.0
   specified NEC L64.8
 areata L63.9
   ophiasis L63.2
   specified NEC L63.8
   totalis L63.0
   universalis L63.1
 cicatricial L66.9
   specified NEC L66.8
 circumscripta L63.9
 congenital, congenitalis Q84.0
 due to cytotoxic drugs NEC L65.8
 mucinosa L65.2
 postinfective NEC L65.8
 postpartum L65.0
 premature L64.8
 specific (syphilitic) A51.32
 specified NEC L65.8
 syphilitic (secondary) A51.32
 totalis (capitis) L63.0
 universalis (entire body) L63.1
 X-ray L58.1
Alpers' disease G31.81
Alpine sickness T70.29
Alport syndrome Q87.81
ALTE (apparent life threatening event) in
   newborn and infant R68.13
Alteration (of), **Altered**
 awareness
   transient R40.4
   unintended under general anesthesia,
     during procedure T88.53
 mental status R41.82
 pattern of family relationships affecting child
     Z62.898
 sensation
   following
     cerebrovascular disease I69.998
       cerebral infarction I69.398
       intracerebral hemorrhage I69.198
       nontraumatic intracranial hemorrhage
         NEC I69.298
       specified disease NEC I69.898
       subarachnoid hemorrhage I69.098
Alternating —*see* condition
Altitude, high (effects) —*see* Effect, adverse,
   high altitude
Aluminosis (of lung) J63.0
Alveolitis
 allergic (extrinsic) —*see* Pneumonitis,
   hypersensitivity
 due to
   Aspergillus clavatus J67.4
   Cryptostroma corticale J67.6
 fibrosing (cryptogenic) (idiopathic)
     J84.112

Alveolitis *(Continued)*
 jaw M27.3
 sicca dolorosa M27.3
Alveolus, alveolar —*see* condition
Alymphocytosis D72.810
 thymic (with immunodeficiency) D82.1
Alymphoplasia, thymic D82.1
Alzheimer's disease or sclerosis —*see* Disease,
   Alzheimer's
Amastia (with nipple present) Q83.8
 with absent nipple Q83.0
Amathophobia F40.228
Amaurosis (acquired) (congenital) —*see also*
   Blindness
 fugax G45.3
 hysterical F44.6
 Leber's congenital H35.50
 uremic —*see* Uremia
Amaurotic idiocy (infantile) (juvenile) (late)
   E75.4
Amaxophobia F40.248
Ambiguous genitalia Q56.4
Amblyopia (congenital) (ex anopsia) (partial)
   (suppression) H53.00-●
 anisometropic —*see* Amblyopia, refractive
 deprivation H53.01-●
 hysterical F44.6
 nocturnal —*see also* Blindness, night
   vitamin A deficiency E50.5
 refractive H53.02-●
 strabismic H53.03-●
 suspect H53.04-●
 tobacco H53.8
 toxic NEC H53.8
 uremic —*see* Uremia
Ameba, amebic (histolytica) —*see also*
   Amebiasis
 abscess (liver) A06.4
Amebiasis A06.9
 with abscess —*see* Abscess, amebic
 acute A06.0
 chronic (intestine) A06.1
   with abscess —*see* Abscess, amebic
 cutaneous A06.7
 cutis A06.7
 cystitis A06.81
 genitourinary tract NEC A06.82
 hepatic —*see* Abscess, liver, amebic
 intestine A06.0
 nondysenteric colitis A06.2
 skin A06.7
 specified site NEC A06.89
Ameboma (of intestine) A06.3
Amelia Q73.0
 lower limb —*see* Agenesis, leg
 upper limb —*see* Agenesis, arm
Ameloblastoma —*see also* Cyst, calcifying
   odontogenic
 long bones C40.9-●
   lower limb C40.2-●
   upper limb C40.0-●
 malignant C41.1
   jaw (bone) (lower) C41.1
     upper C41.0
 tibial C40.2-●
Amelogenesis imperfecta K00.5
 nonhereditaria (segmentalis) K00.4
Amenorrhea N91.2
 hyperhormonal E28.8
 primary N91.0
 secondary N91.1
Amentia —*see* Disability, intellectual
 Meynert's (nonalcoholic) F04
American
 leishmaniasis B55.2
 mountain tick fever A93.2
Ametropia —*see* Disorder, refraction
AMH (asymptomatic microscopic hematuria)
   R31.21
Amianthosis J61
Amimia R48.8

Amino-acid disorder E72.9
  anemia D53.0
Aminoacidopathy E72.9
Aminoaciduria E72.9
Amnes (t)ic syndrome (post-traumatic) F04
  induced by
    alcohol F10.96
      with dependence F10.26
    psychoactive NEC F19.96
      with
        abuse F19.16
        dependence F19.26
    sedative F13.96
      with dependence F13.26
Amnesia R41.3
  anterograde R41.1
  auditory R48.8
  dissociative F44.0
    with dissociative fugue F44.1
  hysterical F44.0
  postictal in epilepsy —see Epilepsy
  psychogenic F44.0
  retrograde R41.2
  transient global G45.4
Amnion, amniotic —see condition
Amnionitis —see Pregnancy, complicated by
Amok F68.8
Amoral traits F60.89
Amphetamine (or other stimulant) —
    induced
  anxiety disorder F15.980
  bipolar and related disorder F15.94
  delirium F15.921
  depressive disorder F15.94
  obsessive-compulsive and related disorder
    F15.988
  psychotic disorder F15.959
  sexual dysfunction F15.981
  sleep disorder F15.982
  stimulant withdrawal F15.23
Ampulla
  lower esophagus K22.8
  phrenic K22.8
Amputation —see also Absence, by site,
    acquired
  neuroma (postoperative) (traumatic) —see
    Complications, amputation stump,
    neuroma
  stump (surgical)
    abnormal, painful, or with complication
      (late) —see Complications, amputation
      stump
    healed or old NOS Z89.9
  traumatic (complete) (partial)
    arm (upper) (complete) S48.91-•
      at
        elbow S58.01-•
          partial S58.02-•
        shoulder joint (complete) S48.01-•
          partial S48.02-•
      between
        elbow and wrist (complete) S58.11-•
          partial S58.12-•
        shoulder and elbow (complete)
          S48.11-•
          partial S48.12-•
      partial S48.92-•
    breast (complete) S28.21-•
      partial S28.22-•
    clitoris (complete) S38.211
      partial S38.212
    ear (complete) S08.11-•
      partial S08.12-•
    finger (complete) (metacarpophalangeal)
      S68.11-•
      index S68.11-•
      little S68.11-•
      middle S68.11-•
      partial S68.12-•
        index S68.12-•
        little S68.12-•

Amputation (Continued)
  traumatic (Continued)
    finger (Continued)
      partial (Continued)
        middle S68.12-•
        ring S68.12-•
      ring S68.11-•
      thumb —see Amputation, traumatic,
        thumb
      transphalangeal (complete) S68.61-•
        index S68.61-•
        little S68.61-•
        middle S68.61-•
        partial S68.62-•
          index S68.62-•
          little S68.62-•
          middle S68.62-•
          ring S68.62-•
        ring S68.61-•
    foot (complete) S98.91-•
      at ankle level S98.01-•
        partial S98.02-•
      midfoot S98.31-•
        partial S98.32-•
      partial S98.92-•
    forearm (complete) S58.91-•
      at elbow level (complete) S58.01-•
        partial S58.02-•
      between elbow and wrist (complete)
        S58.11-•
        partial S58.12-•
      partial S58.92-•
    genital organ(s) (external)
      female (complete) S38.211
        partial S38.212
      male
        penis (complete) S38.221
          partial S38.222
        scrotum (complete) S38.231
          partial S38.232
        testes (complete) S38.231
          partial S38.232
    hand (complete) (wrist level) S68.41-•
      finger(s) alone —see Amputation,
        traumatic, finger
      partial S68.42-•
      thumb alone —see Amputation,
        traumatic, thumb
      transmetacarpal (complete) S68.71-•
        partial S68.72-•
    head
      ear —see Amputation, traumatic, ear
      nose (partial) S08.812
        complete S08.811
      part S08.89
      scalp S08.0
    hip (and thigh) (complete) S78.91-•
      at hip joint (complete) S78.01-•
        partial S78.02-•
      between hip and knee (complete)
        S78.11-•
        partial S78.12-•
      partial S78.92-•
    labium (majus) (minus) (complete)
      S38.21-•
      partial S38.21-•
    leg (lower) S88.91-•
      at knee level S88.01-•
        partial S88.02-•
      between knee and ankle S88.11-•
        partial S88.12-•
      partial S88.92-•
    nose (partial) S08.812
      complete S08.811
    penis (complete) S38.221
      partial S38.222
    scrotum (complete) S38.231
      partial S38.232
    shoulder —see Amputation, traumatic, arm
      at shoulder joint —see Amputation,
        traumatic, arm, at shoulder joint

Amputation (Continued)
  traumatic (Continued)
    testes (complete) S38.231
      partial S38.232
    thigh —see Amputation, traumatic, hip
    thorax, part of S28.1
      breast —see Amputation, traumatic,
        breast
    thumb (complete) (metacarpophalangeal)
      S68.01-•
      partial S68.02-•
      transphalangeal (complete) S68.51-•
        partial S68.52-•
    toe (lesser) S98.13-•
      great S98.11-•
        partial S98.12-•
      more than one S98.21-•
        partial S98.22-•
      partial S98.14-•
    vulva (complete) S38.211
      partial S38.212
Amputee (bilateral) (old) Z89.9
Amsterdam dwarfism Q87.19
Amusia R48.8
  developmental F80.89
Amyelencephalus, amyelencephaly Q00.0
Amyelia Q06.0
Amygdalitis —see Tonsillitis
Amygdalolith J35.8
Amyloid heart (disease) E85.4 [I43]
Amyloidosis (generalized) (primary) E85.9
  with lung involvement E85.4 [J99]
  familial E85.2
  genetic E85.2
  heart E85.4 [I43]
  hemodialysis-associated E85.3
  light chain (AL) E85.81
  liver E85.4 [K77]
  localized E85.4
  neuropathic heredofamilial E85.1
  non-neuropathic heredofamilial E85.0
  organ limited E85.4
  Portuguese E85.1
  pulmonary E85.4 [J99]
  secondary systemic E85.3
  senile systemic (SSA) E85.82
  skin (lichen) (macular) E85.4 [L99]
  specified NEC E85.89
  subglottic E85.4 [J99]
  wild-type transthyretin-related (ATTR)
    E85.82
Amylopectinosis (brancher enzyme deficiency)
    E74.03
Amylophagia —see Pica
Amyoplasia congenita Q79.8
Amyotonia M62.89
  congenita G70.2
Amyotrophia, amyotrophy, amyotrophic G71.8
  congenita Q79.8
  diabetic —see Diabetes, amyotrophy
  lateral sclerosis G12.21
  neuralgic G54.5
  spinal progressive G12.25
Anacidity, gastric K31.83
  psychogenic F45.8
Anaerosis of newborn P28.89
Analbuminemia E88.09
Analgesia —see Anesthesia
Analphalipoproteinemia E78.6
Anaphylactic
  purpura D69.0
  shock or reaction —see Shock, anaphylactic
Anaphylactoid shock or reaction —see Shock,
  anaphylactic
Anaphylactoid syndrome of pregnancy
  O88.01-•
Anaphylaxis —see Shock, anaphylactic
Anaplasia cervix —see also Dysplasia, cervix
  N87.9
Anaplasmosis, human A77.49
Anarthria R47.1

Anasarca R60.1
  cardiac —see Failure, heart, congestive
  lung J18.2
  newborn P83.2
  nutritional E43
  pulmonary J18.2
  renal N04.9
Anastomosis
  aneurysmal —see Aneurysm
  arteriovenous ruptured brain I60.8
  intestinal K63.89
    complicated NEC K91.89
      involving urinary tract N99.89
  intracerebral I61.8
  intraparenchymal I61.8
  intraventricular I61.5
  retinal and choroidal vessels (congenital) Q14.8
  subarachnoid I60.8
Anatomical narrow angle H40.03-•
Ancylostoma, ancylostomiasis (braziliense)
    (caninum) (ceylanicum) (duodenale) B76.0
  Necator americanus B76.1
Andersen's disease (glycogen storage) E74.09
Anderson-Fabry disease E75.21
Andes disease T70.29
Andrews' disease (bacterid) L08.89
Androblastoma
  benign
    specified site —see Neoplasm, benign, by
        site
    unspecified site
      female D27.9
      male D29.20
  malignant
    specified site —see Neoplasm, malignant,
        by site
    unspecified site
      female C56.9
      male C62.90
  specified site —see Neoplasm, uncertain
      behavior, by site
  tubular
    with lipid storage
      specified site —see Neoplasm, benign,
          by site
      unspecified site
        female D27.9
        male D29.20
    specified site —see Neoplasm, benign,
        by site
    unspecified site
      female D27.9
      male D29.20
  unspecified site
    female D39.10
    male D40.10
Androgen insensitivity syndrome —see also
    Syndrome, androgen insensitivity E34.50
Androgen resistance syndrome —see also
    Syndrome, androgen insensitivity E34.50
Android pelvis Q74.2
  with disproportion (fetopelvic) O33.3
    causing obstructed labor O65.3
Androphobia F40.290
Anectasis, pulmonary (newborn) —see Atelectasis
Anemia (essential) (general) (hemoglobin
    deficiency) (infantile) (primary) (profound)
    D64.9
  with (due to) (in)
    disorder of
      anaerobic glycolysis D55.2
      pentose phosphate pathway D55.1
    koilonychia D50.9
  achlorhydric D50.8
  achrestic D53.1
  Addison (-Biermer) (pernicious) D51.0
  agranulocytic —see Agranulocytosis
  amino-acid-deficiency D53.0
  aplastic D61.9
    congenital D61.09
    drug-induced D61.1

Anemia (Continued)
  aplastic (Continued)
    due to
      drugs D61.1
      external agents NEC D61.2
      infection D61.2
      radiation D61.2
    idiopathic D61.3
    red cell (pure) D60.9
      chronic D60.0
      congenital D61.01
      specified type NEC D60.8
      transient D60.1
    specified type NEC D61.89
    toxic D61.2
  aregenerative
    congenital D61.09
  asiderotic D50.9
  atypical (primary) D64.9
  Baghdad spring D55.0
  Balantidium coli A07.0
  Biermer's (pernicious) D51.0
  blood loss (chronic) D50.0
    acute D62
  bothriocephalus B70.0 [D63.8]
  brickmaker's B76.9 [D63.8]
  cerebral I67.89
  childhood D58.9
  chlorotic D50.8
  chronic
    blood loss D50.0
    hemolytic D58.9
      idiopathic D59.9
    simple D53.9
  chronica congenita aregenerativa D61.09
  combined system disease NEC D51.0 [G32.0]
    due to dietary vitamin B12 deficiency
        D51.3 [G32.0]
  complicating pregnancy, childbirth
      or puerperium —see Pregnancy,
      complicated by (management affected
      by), anemia
  congenital P61.4
    aplastic D61.09
    due to isoimmunization NOS P55.9
    dyserythropoietic, dyshematopoietic D64.4
    following fetal blood loss P61.3
    Heinz body D58.2
    hereditary hemolytic NOS D58.9
    pernicious D51.0
    spherocytic D58.0
  Cooley's (erythroblastic) D56.1
  cytogenic D51.0
  deficiency D53.9
    2, 3 diphosphoglycurate mutase D55.2
    2, 3 PG D55.2
    6 phosphogluconate dehydrogenase D55.1
    6-PGD D55.1
    amino-acid D53.0
    combined B12 and folate D53.1
    enzyme D55.9
      drug-induced (hemolytic) D59.2
      glucose-6-phosphate dehydrogenase
          (G6PD) D55.0
      glycolytic D55.2
      nucleotide metabolism D55.3
      related to hexose monophosphate
          (HMP) shunt pathway NEC D55.1
      specified type NEC D55.8
    erythrocytic glutathione D55.1
    folate D52.9
      dietary D52.0
      drug-induced D52.1
    folic acid D52.9
      dietary D52.0
      drug-induced D52.1
    G SH D55.1
    G6PD D55.0
    GGS-R D55.1
    glucose-6-phosphate dehydrogenase D55.0
    glutathione reductase D55.1

Anemia (Continued)
  deficiency (Continued)
    glyceraldehyde phosphate dehydrogenase
        D55.2
    hexokinase D55.2
    iron D50.9
      secondary to blood loss (chronic) D50.0
    nutritional D53.9
      with
        poor iron absorption D50.8
        specified deficiency NEC D53.8
    phosphofructo-aldolase D55.2
    phosphoglycerate kinase D55.2
    PK D55.2
    protein D53.0
    pyruvate kinase D55.2
    transcobalamin II D51.2
    triose-phosphate isomerase D55.2
    vitamin B12 NOS D51.9
      dietary D51.3
      due to
        intrinsic factor deficiency D51.0
        selective vitamin B12 malabsorption
            with proteinuria D51.1
      pernicious D51.0
      specified type NEC D51.8
  Diamond-Blackfan (congenital hypoplastic)
      D61.01
  dibothriocephalus B70.0 [D63.8]
  dimorphic D53.1
  diphasic D53.1
  Diphyllobothrium (Dibothriocephalus) B70.0
      [D63.8]
  due to (in) (with)
    antineoplastic chemotherapy D64.81
    blood loss (chronic) D50.0
      acute D62
    chemotherapy, antineoplastic D64.81
    chronic disease classified elsewhere NEC
        D63.8
    chronic kidney disease D63.1
    deficiency
      amino-acid D53.0
      copper D53.8
      folate (folic acid) D52.9
        dietary D52.0
        drug-induced D52.1
      molybdenum D53.8
      protein D53.0
      zinc D53.8
    dietary vitamin B12 deficiency D51.3
    disorder of
      glutathione metabolism D55.1
      nucleotide metabolism D55.3
    drug —see Anemia, by type —see also Table
        of Drugs and Chemicals
    end stage renal disease D63.1
    enzyme disorder D55.9
    fetal blood loss P61.3
    fish tapeworm (D latum) infestation B70.0
        [D63.8]
    hemorrhage (chronic) D50.0
      acute D62
    impaired absorption D50.9
    loss of blood (chronic) D50.0
      acute D62
    myxedema E03.9 [D63.8]
    Necator americanus B76.1 [D63.8]
    prematurity P61.2
    selective vitamin B12 malabsorption with
        proteinuria D51.1
    transcobalamin II deficiency D51.2
  Dyke-Young type (secondary) (symptomatic)
      D59.19
  dyserythropoietic (congenital) D64.4
  dyshematopoietic (congenital) D64.4
  Egyptian B76.9 [D63.8]
  elliptocytosis —see Elliptocytosis
  enzyme-deficiency, drug-induced D59.2
  epidemic —see also Ancylostomiasis B76.9
      [D63.8]

▶ New   ⇒ Revised   ~~deleted~~ Deleted   • Use Additional Character(s)

Anemia *(Continued)*
  erythroblastic
    familial D56.1
    newborn —*see also* Disease, hemolytic
      P55.9
    of childhood D56.1
  erythrocytic glutathione deficiency D55.1
  erythropoietin-resistant anemia (EPO
    resistant anemia) D63.1
  Faber's (achlorhydric anemia) D50.9
  factitious (self-induced blood letting) D50.0
  familial erythroblastic D56.1
  Fanconi's (congenital pancytopenia) D61.09
  favism D55.0
  fish tapeworm (D. latum) infestation B70.0
    [D63.8]
  folate (folic acid) deficiency D52.9
  glucose-6-phosphate dehydrogenase (G6PD)
    deficiency D55.0
  glutathione-reductase deficiency D55.1
  goat's milk D52.0
  granulocytic —*see* Agranulocytosis
  Heinz body, congenital D58.2
  hemolytic D58.9
    acquired D59.9
      with hemoglobinuria NEC D59.6
      ⇒autoimmune NEC D59.19
      infectious D59.4
      specified type NEC D59.8
      toxic D59.4
    acute D59.9
      due to enzyme deficiency specified type
        NEC D55.8
    ⇒Lederer's D59.19
    ⇒autoimmune D59.10
      ▶cold D59.12
      drug-induced D59.0
      ▶mixed D59.13
      ▶warm D59.11
    chronic D58.9
      idiopathic D59.9
    ⇒cold type (secondary) (symptomatic)
      D59.12
    congenital (spherocytic) —*see*
      Spherocytosis
    due to
      cardiac conditions D59.4
      drugs (nonautoimmune) D59.2
        autoimmune D59.0
      enzyme disorder D55.9
        drug-induced D59.2
      presence of shunt or other internal
        prosthetic device D59.4
    familial D58.9
    hereditary D58.9
      due to enzyme disorder D55.9
        specified type NEC D55.8
      specified type NEC D58.8
    idiopathic (chronic) D59.9
    mechanical D59.4
    microangiopathic D59.4
    ▶mixed type (primary) (secondary)
      (symptomatic) D59.13
    nonautoimmune D59.4
      drug-induced D59.2
    nonspherocytic
      congenital or hereditary NEC D55.8
        glucose-6-phosphate dehydrogenase
          deficiency D55.0
        pyruvate kinase deficiency D55.2
        type
          I D55.1
          II D55.2
      type
        I D55.1
        II D55.2
    ▶primary
      ▶autoimmune
        ▶cold type D59.12
        ▶mixed type D59.13
        ▶warm type D59.11

Anemia *(Continued)*
  hemolytic *(Continued)*
    secondary D59.4
      ⇒autoimmune
        ▶cold type D59.12
        ▶mixed type D59.13
        ▶warm type D59.11
    specified (hereditary) type NEC D58.8
    Stransky-Regala type —*see also*
      Hemoglobinopathy D58.8
    symptomatic D59.4
      ⇒autoimmune
        ▶cold type D59.12
        ▶mixed type D59.13
        ▶warm type D59.11
    toxic D59.4
    ⇒warm type (primary) (secondary)
      (symptomatic) D59.11
  hemorrhagic (chronic) D50.0
    acute D62
  Herrick's D57.1
  hexokinase deficiency D55.2
  hookworm B76.9 [D63.8]
  hypochromic (idiopathic) (microcytic)
    (normoblastic) D50.9
    due to blood loss (chronic) D50.0
      acute D62
    familial sex-linked D64.0
    pyridoxine-responsive D64.3
    sideroblastic, sex-linked D64.0
  hypoplasia, red blood cells D61.9
    congenital or familial D61.01
  hypoplastic (idiopathic) D61.9
    congenital or familial (of childhood)
      D61.01
  hypoproliferative (refractive) D61.9
  idiopathic D64.9
    aplastic D61.3
    hemolytic, chronic D59.9
  in (due to) (with)
    chronic kidney disease D63.1
    end stage renal disease D63.1
    failure, kidney (renal) D63.1
    neoplastic disease —*see also* Neoplasm
      D63.0
  intertropical —*see also* Ancylostomiasis
    D63.8
  iron deficiency D50.9
    secondary to blood loss (chronic) D50.0
      acute D62
    specified type NEC D50.8
  Joseph-Diamond-Blackfan (congenital
    hypoplastic) D61.01
  ⇒Lederer's (hemolytic) D59.19
  leukoerythroblastic D61.82
  macrocytic D53.9
    nutritional D52.0
    tropical D52.8
  malarial (*see also* Malaria) B54 [D63.8]
  malignant (progressive) D51.0
  malnutrition D53.9
  marsh (*see also* Malaria) B54 [D63.8]
  Mediterranean (with other
    hemoglobinopathy) D56.9
  megaloblastic D53.1
    combined B12 and folate deficiency
      D53.1
    hereditary D51.1
    nutritional D52.0
    orotic aciduria D53.0
    refractory D53.1
    specified type NEC D53.1
  megalocytic D53.1
  microcytic (hypochromic) D50.9
    due to blood loss (chronic) D50.0
      acute D62
    familial D56.8
  microdrepanocytosis D57.40
  microelliptopoikilocytic (Rietti-Greppi-
    Micheli) D56.9
  miner's B76.9 [D63.8]

Anemia *(Continued)*
  myelodysplastic D46.9
  myelofibrosis D75.81
  myelogenous D64.89
  myelopathic D64.89
  myelophthisic D61.82
  myeloproliferative D47.Z9
  newborn P61.4
    due to
      ABO (antibodies, isoimmunization,
        maternal/fetal incompatibility)
        P55.1
      Rh (antibodies, isoimmunization,
        maternal/fetal incompatibility)
        P55.0
    following fetal blood loss P61.3
    posthemorrhagic (fetal) P61.3
  nonspherocytic hemolytic —*see* Anemia,
    hemolytic, nonspherocytic
  normocytic (infectional) D64.9
    due to blood loss (chronic) D50.0
      acute D62
    myelophthisic D61.82
  nutritional (deficiency) D53.9
    with
      poor iron absorption D50.8
      specified deficiency NEC D53.8
    megaloblastic D52.0
  of prematurity P61.2
  orotaciduric (congenital) (hereditary)
    D53.0
  osteosclerotic D64.89
  ovalocytosis (hereditary) —*see* Elliptocytosis
  paludal —*see also* Malaria B54 [D63.8]
  pernicious (congenital) (malignant)
    (progressive) D51.0
  pleochromic D64.89
    of sprue D52.8
  posthemorrhagic (chronic) D50.0
    acute D62
    newborn P61.3
  postoperative (postprocedural)
    due to (acute) blood loss D62
      chronic blood loss D50.0
    specified NEC D64.9
  postpartum O90.81
  pressure D64.89
  progressive D64.9
    malignant D51.0
    pernicious D51.0
  protein-deficiency D53.0
  pseudoleukemica infantum D64.89
  pure red cell D60.9
    congenital D61.01
  pyridoxine-responsive D64.3
  pyruvate kinase deficiency D55.2
  refractory D46.4
    with
      excess of blasts D46.20
        1 (RAEB 1) D46.21
        2 (RAEB 2) D46.22
        in transformation (RAEB T) —*see*
          Leukemia, acute myeloblastic
      hemochromatosis D46.1
      sideroblasts (ring) (RARS) D46.1
    without ring sideroblasts, so stated
      D46.0
    without sideroblasts without excess of
      blasts D46.0
    megaloblastic D53.1
    sideroblastic D46.1
    sideropenic D50.9
  Rietti-Greppi-Micheli D56.9
  scorbutic D53.2
  secondary to
    blood loss (chronic) D50.0
      acute D62
    hemorrhage (chronic) D50.0
      acute D62
  semiplastic D61.89
  sickle-cell —*see* Disease, sickle-cell

Anemia (Continued)
  sideroblastic D64.3
    hereditary D64.0
    hypochromic, sex-linked D64.0
    pyridoxine-responsive NEC D64.3
    refractory D46.1
    secondary (due to)
      disease D64.1
      drugs and toxins D64.2
    specified type NEC D64.3
  sideropenic (refractory) D50.9
    due to blood loss (chronic) D50.0
      acute D62
  simple chronic D53.9
  specified type NEC D64.89
  spherocytic (hereditary) —see Spherocytosis
  splenic D64.89
  splenomegalic D64.89
  stomatocytosis D58.8
  syphilitic (acquired) (late) A52.79 [D63.8]
  target cell D64.89
  thalassemia D56.9
  thrombocytopenic —see Thrombocytopenia
  toxic D61.2
  tropical B76.9 [D63.8]
    macrocytic D52.8
  tuberculous A18.89 [D63.8]
  vegan D51.3
  vitamin
    B6-responsive D64.3
    B12 deficiency (dietary) pernicious
      D51.0
  von Jaksch's D64.89
  Witts' (achlorhydric anemia) D50.8
Anemophobia F40.228
Anencephalus, anencephaly Q00.0
Anergasia —see Psychosis, organic
Anesthesia, anesthetic R20.0
  complication or reaction NEC —see also
    Complications, anesthesia T88.59
  due to
    correct substance properly
      administered —see Table of Drugs
      and Chemicals, by drug, adverse
      effect
    overdose or wrong substance given —see
      Table of Drugs and Chemicals, by
      drug, poisoning
    unintended awareness under general
      anesthesia during procedure
      T88.53
      personal history of Z92.84
  cornea H18.81-●
  dissociative F44.6
  functional (hysterical) F44.6
  hyperesthetic, thalamic G89.0
  hysterical F44.6
  local skin lesion R20.0
  sexual (psychogenic) F52.1
  shock (due to) T88.2
  skin R20.0
  testicular N50.9
Anetoderma (maculosum) (of) L90.8
  Jadassohn-Pellizzari L90.2
  Schweniger-Buzzi L90.1
Aneurin deficiency E51.9
Aneurysm (anastomotic) (artery) (cirsoid)
  (diffuse) (false) (fusiform) (multiple)
  (saccular) I72.9
  abdominal (aorta) I71.4
    ruptured I71.3
    syphilitic A52.01
  aorta, aortic (nonsyphilitic) I71.9
    abdominal I71.4
      ruptured I71.3
    arch I71.2
      ruptured I71.1
    arteriosclerotic I71.9
      ruptured I71.8
    ascending I71.2
      ruptured I71.1

Aneurysm (Continued)
  aorta, aortic (nonsyphilitic) (Continued)
    congenital Q25.43
    descending I71.9
      abdominal I71.4
        ruptured I71.3
      ruptured I71.8
      thoracic I71.2
        ruptured I71.1
    root Q25.43
    ruptured I71.8
    sinus, congenital Q25.43
    syphilitic A52.01
    thoracic I71.2
      ruptured I71.1
    thoracoabdominal I71.6
      ruptured I71.5
    thorax, thoracic (arch) I71.2
      ruptured I71.1
    transverse I71.2
      ruptured I71.1
    valve (heart) —see also Endocarditis, aortic
      I35.8
  arteriosclerotic I72.9
    cerebral I67.1
      ruptured —see Hemorrhage, intracranial,
        subarachnoid
  arteriovenous (congenital) —see also
    Malformation, arteriovenous
    acquired I77.0
      brain I67.1
        ruptured —see Aneurysm,
          arteriorvenous, brain, ruptured
      coronary I25.41
      pulmonary I28.0
    brain Q28.2
      ruptured I60.8
        intracerebral I61.8
        intraparenchymal I61.8
        intraventricular I61.5
        subarachnoid I60.8
    peripheral —see Malformation,
      arteriovenous, peripheral
    precerebral vessels Q28.0
    specified site NEC —see also Malformation,
      arteriovenous
    acquired I77.0
  basal —see Aneurysm, brain
  basilar (trunk) I72.5
  berry (congenital) (nonruptured) I67.1
    ruptured I60.7
  brain I67.1
    arteriosclerotic I67.1
      ruptured —see Hemorrhage, intracranial,
        subarachnoid
    arteriovenous (congenital) (nonruptured)
      Q28.2
      acquired I67.1
▶   ruptured —see Aneurysm,
        arteriorvenous, brain, ruptured
        I60.8-
▶   ruptured —see Aneurysm,
        arteriorvenous, brain, ruptured
        I60.8-
    berry (congenital) (nonruptured) I67.1
      ruptured —see also Hemorrhage,
        intracranial, subarachnoid I60.7
    congenital Q28.3
      aorta (root) (sinus) Q25.43
      ruptured I60.7
    meninges I67.1
      ruptured I60.8
    miliary (congenital) (nonruptured) I67.1
      ruptured —see also Hemorrhage,
        intracranial, subarachnoid I60.7
    mycotic I33.0
      ruptured —see Hemorrhage, intracranial,
        subarachnoid
    syphilitic (hemorrhage) A52.05
  cardiac (false) —see also Aneurysm, heart
    I25.3

Aneurysm (Continued)
  carotid artery (common) (external) I72.0
    internal (intracranial) I67.1
      extracranial portion I72.0
    ruptured into brain I60.0-●
    syphilitic A52.09
      intracranial A52.05
  cavernous sinus I67.1
    arteriovenous (congenital) (nonruptured)
      Q28.3
      ruptured I60.8
  celiac I72.8
  central nervous system, syphilitic A52.05
  cerebral —see Aneurysm, brain
  chest —see Aneurysm, thorax
  circle of Willis I67.1
    congenital Q28.3
      ruptured I60.6
    ruptured I60.6
  common iliac artery I72.3
  congenital (peripheral) Q27.8
    aorta (root) (sinus) Q25.43
    brain Q28.3
      ruptured I60.7
    coronary Q24.5
    digestive system Q27.8
    lower limb Q27.8
    pulmonary Q25.79
    retina Q14.1
    specified site NEC Q27.8
    upper limb Q27.8
  conjunctiva —see Abnormality, conjunctiva,
    vascular
  conus arteriosus —see Aneurysm, heart
  coronary (arteriosclerotic) (artery) I25.41
    arteriovenous, congenital Q24.5
    congenital Q24.5
    ruptured —see Infarct, myocardium
    syphilitic A52.06
    vein I25.89
  cylindroid (aorta) I71.9
    ruptured I71.8
    syphilitic A52.01
  ductus arteriosus Q25.0
  endocardial, infective (any valve) I33.0
  femoral (artery) (ruptured) I72.4
  gastroduodenal I72.8
  gastroepiploic I72.8
  heart (wall) (chronic or with a stated duration
    of over 4 weeks) I25.3
    valve —see Endocarditis
  hepatic I72.8
  iliac (common) (artery) (ruptured) I72.3
  infective I72.9
    endocardial (any valve) I33.0
  innominate (nonsyphilitic) I72.8
    syphilitic A52.09
  interauricular septum —see Aneurysm,
    heart
  interventricular septum —see Aneurysm,
    heart
  intrathoracic (nonsyphilitic) I71.2
    ruptured I71.1
    syphilitic A52.01
  lower limb I72.4
  lung (pulmonary artery) I28.1
  mediastinal (nonsyphilitic) I72.8
    syphilitic A52.09
  miliary (congenital) I67.1
    ruptured —see Hemorrhage, intracerebral,
      subarachnoid, intracranial
  mitral (heart) (valve) I34.8
  mural —see Aneurysm, heart
  mycotic I72.9
    endocardial (any valve) I33.0
    ruptured, brain —see Hemorrhage,
      intracerebral, subarachnoid
  myocardium —see Aneurysm, heart
  neck I72.0
  pancreaticoduodenal I72.8
  patent ductus arteriosus Q25.0

Aneurysm *(Continued)*
  peripheral NEC I72.8
    congenital Q27.8
      digestive system Q27.8
      lower limb Q27.8
      specified site NEC Q27.8
      upper limb Q27.8
  popliteal (artery) (ruptured) I72.4
  precerebral
    congenital (nonruptured) Q28.1
    specified site, NEC I72.5
  pulmonary I28.1
    arteriovenous Q25.72
      acquired I28.0
    syphilitic A52.09
    valve (heart) —*see* Endocarditis, pulmonary
  racemose (peripheral) I72.9
    congenital —*see* Aneurysm, congenital
  radial I72.1
  Rasmussen NEC A15.0
  renal (artery) I72.2
  retina —*see also* Disorder, retina,
      microaneurysms
    congenital Q14.1
    diabetic —*see* E08-E13 with .3-●
  sinus of Valsalva Q25.49
  specified NEC I72.8
  spinal (cord) I72.8
    syphilitic (hemorrhage) A52.09
  splenic I72.8
  subclavian (artery) (ruptured) I72.8
    syphilitic A52.09
  superior mesenteric I72.8
  syphilitic (aorta) A52.01
    central nervous system A52.05
    congenital (late) A50.54 *[I79.0]*
    spine, spinal A52.09
  thoracoabdominal (aorta) I71.6
    ruptured I71.5
    syphilitic A52.01
  thorax, thoracic (aorta) (arch) (nonsyphilitic)
      I71.2
    ruptured I71.1
    syphilitic A52.01
  traumatic (complication) (early), specified
      site —*see* Injury, blood vessel
  tricuspid (heart) (valve) I07.8
  ulnar I72.1
  upper limb (ruptured) I72.1
  valve, valvular —*see* Endocarditis
  visceral NEC I72.8
  venous —*see also* Varix I86.8
    congenital Q27.8
      digestive system Q27.8
      lower limb Q27.8
      specified site NEC Q27.8
      upper limb Q27.8
  ventricle —*see* Aneurysm, heart
  vertebral artery I72.6
  visceral NEC I72.8
Angelman syndrome Q93.51
Anger R45.4
Angiectasis, angiectopia I99.8
Angiitis I77.6
  allergic granulomatous M30.1
  hypersensitivity M31.0
  necrotizing M31.9
    specified NEC M31.8
  nervous system, granulomatous I67.7
Angina (attack) (cardiac) (chest) (heart)
    (pectoris) (syndrome) (vasomotor) I20.9
  with
    atherosclerotic heart disease —*see*
        Arteriosclerosis, coronary (artery)
    documented spasm I20.1
  abdominal K55.1
  accelerated —*see* Angina, unstable
  agranulocytic —*see* Agranulocytosis
  angiospastic —*see* Angina, with documented
      spasm
  aphthous B08.5

Angina *(Continued)*
  crescendo —*see* Angina, unstable
  croupous J05.0
  cruris I73.9
  de novo effort —*see* Angina, unstable
  diphtheritic, membranous A36.0
  equivalent I20.8
  exudative, chronic J37.0
  following acute myocardial infarction I23.7
  gangrenous diphtheritic A36.0
  intestinal K55.1
  Ludovici K12.2
  Ludwig's K12.2
  malignant diphtheritic A36.0
  membranous J05.0
    diphtheritic A36.0
    Vincent's A69.1
  mesenteric K55.1
  monocytic —*see* Mononucleosis, infectious
  of effort —*see* Angina, specified NEC
  phlegmonous J36
    diphtheritic A36.0
  post-infarctional I23.7
  pre-infarctional —*see* Angina, unstable
  Prinzmetal —*see* Angina, with documented
      spasm
  progressive —*see* Angina, unstable
  pseudomembranous A69.1
  pultaceous, diphtheritic A36.0
  spasm-induced —*see* Angina, with
      documented spasm
  specified NEC I20.8
  stable I20.8
  stenocardia —*see* Angina, specified NEC
  stridulous, diphtheritic A36.2
  tonsil J36
  trachealis J05.0
  unstable I20.0
  variant —*see* Angina, with documented spasm
  Vincent's A69.1
  worsening effort —*see* Angina, unstable
Angioblastoma —*see* Neoplasm, connective
    tissue, uncertain behavior
Angiocholecystitis —*see* Cholecystitis, acute
Angiocholitis —*see also* Cholecystitis, acute
    K83.09
Angiodysgenesis spinalis G95.19
Angiodysplasia (cecum) (colon) K55.20
  with bleeding K55.21
  duodenum (and stomach) K31.819
    with bleeding K31.811
  stomach (and duodenum) K31.819
    with bleeding K31.811
Angioedema (allergic) (any site) (with urticaria)
    T78.3
▶ episodic, with eosinophilia D72.118
  hereditary D84.1
Angioendothelioma —*see* Neoplasm, uncertain
    behavior, by site
  benign D18.00
    intra-abdominal D18.03
    intracranial D18.02
    skin D18.01
    specified site NEC D18.09
  bone —*see* Neoplasm, bone, malignant
  Ewing's —*see* Neoplasm, bone, malignant
Angioendotheliomatosis C85.8-●
Angiofibroma —*see also* Neoplasm, benign, by
    site
  juvenile
    specified site —*see* Neoplasm, benign, by
        site
    unspecified site D10.6
Angiohemophilia (A) (B) D68.0
Angioid streaks (choroid) (macula) (retina)
    H35.33
Angiokeratoma —*see* Neoplasm, skin, benign
  corporis diffusum E75.21
Angioleiomyoma —*see* Neoplasm, connective
    tissue, benign
Angiolipoma —*see also* Lipoma
  infiltrating —*see* Lipoma

Angioma —*see also* Hemangioma, by site
  capillary I78.1
  hemorrhagicum hereditaria I78.0
  intra-abdominal D18.03
  intracranial D18.02
  malignant —*see* Neoplasm, connective tissue,
      malignant
  plexiform D18.00
    intra-abdominal D18.03
    intracranial D18.02
    skin D18.01
    specified site NEC D18.09
  senile I78.1
  serpiginosum L81.7
  skin D18.01
  specified site NEC D18.09
  spider I78.1
  stellate I78.1
  venous Q28.3
Angiomatosis Q82.8
  bacillary A79.89
  encephalotrigeminal Q85.8
  hemorrhagic familial I78.0
  hereditary familial I78.0
  liver K76.4
Angiomyolipoma —*see* Lipoma
Angiomyoliposarcoma —*see* Neoplasm,
    connective tissue, malignant
Angiomyoma —*see* Neoplasm, connective
    tissue, benign
Angiomyosarcoma —*see* Neoplasm, connective
    tissue, malignant
Angiomyxoma —*see* Neoplasm, connective
    tissue, uncertain behavior
Angioneurosis F45.8
Angioneurotic edema (allergic) (any site) (with
    urticaria) T78.3
  hereditary D84.1
Angiopathia, angiopathy I99.9
  cerebral I67.9
    amyloid E85.4 *[I68.0]*
  diabetic (peripheral) —*see* Diabetes,
      angiopathy
  peripheral I73.9
    diabetic —*see* Diabetes, angiopathy
    specified type NEC I73.89
  retinae syphilitica A52.05
  retinae (juvenilis)
    diabetic —*see* Diabetes, retinopathy
    proliferative —*see* Retinopathy, proliferative
Angiosarcoma —*see also* Neoplasm, connective
    tissue, malignant
  liver C22.3
Angiosclerosis —*see* Arteriosclerosis
Angiospasm (peripheral) (traumatic) (vessel)
    I73.9
  brachial plexus G54.0
  cerebral G45.9
  cervical plexus G54.2
  nerve
    arm —*see* Mononeuropathy, upper limb
      axillary G54.0
      median —*see* Lesion, nerve, median
      ulnar —*see* Lesion, nerve, ulnar
    axillary G54.0
    leg —*see* Mononeuropathy, lower limb
    median —*see* Lesion, nerve, median
    plantar —*see* Lesion, nerve, plantar
    ulnar —*see* Lesion, nerve, ulnar
Angiospastic disease or edema I73.9
Angiostrongyliasis
  due to
    Parastrongylus
      cantonensis B83.2
      costaricensis B81.3
  intestinal B81.3
Anguillulosis —*see* Strongyloidiasis
Angulation
  cecum —*see* Obstruction, intestine
  coccyx (acquired) —*see also* subcategory M43.8
    congenital NEC Q76.49

A

Angulation *(Continued)*
  femur (acquired) —*see also* Deformity, limb,
      specified type NEC, thigh
    congenital Q74.2
  intestine (large) (small) —*see* Obstruction,
      intestine
  sacrum (acquired) —*see also* subcategory M43.8
    congenital NEC Q76.49
  sigmoid (flexure) —*see* Obstruction, intestine
  spine —*see* Dorsopathy, deforming,
      specified NEC
  tibia (acquired) —*see also* Deformity, limb,
      specified type NEC, lower leg
    congenital Q74.2
  ureter N13.5
    with infection N13.6
  wrist (acquired) —*see also* Deformity,
      limb, specified type NEC, forearm
    congenital Q74.0
Angulus infectiosus (lips) K13.0
Anhedonia R45.84
  sexual F52.0
Anhidrosis L74.4
Anhydration E86.0
Anhydremia E86.0
Anidrosis L74.4
Aniridia (congenital) Q13.1
Anisakiasis (infection) (infestation) B81.0
Anisakis larvae infestation B81.0
Aniseikonia H52.32
Anisocoria (pupil) H57.02
  congenital Q13.2
Anisocytosis R71.8
Anisometropia (congenital) H52.31
Ankle —*see* condition
Ankyloblepharon (eyelid) (acquired) —*see also*
    Blepharophimosis
  filiforme (adnatum) (congenital) Q10.3
  total Q10.3
Ankyloglossia Q38.1
Ankylosis (fibrous) (osseous) (joint) M24.60
  ankle M24.67-●
  arthrodesis status Z98.1
  cricoarytenoid (cartilage) (joint) (larynx) J38.7
  dental K03.5
  ear ossicles H74.31-●
  elbow M24.62-●
  foot M24.67-●
  hand M24.64-●
  hip M24.65-●
  incostapedial joint (infectional) —*see*
      Ankylosis, ear ossicles
  jaw (temporomandibular) M26.61-●
  knee M24.66-●
  lumbosacral (joint) M43.27
  postoperative (status) Z98.1
  produced by surgical fusion, status Z98.1
  sacro-iliac (joint) M43.28
  shoulder M24.61-●
▶ specified site NEC M24.69
  spine (joint) —*see also* Fusion, spine
    spondylitic —*see* Spondylitis, ankylosing
  surgical Z98.1
  temporomandibular M26.61-●
  tooth, teeth (hard tissues) K03.5
  wrist M24.63-●
Ankylostoma —*see* Ancylostoma
Ankylostomiasis —*see* Ancylostomiasis
Ankylurethria —*see* Stricture, urethra
Annular —*see also* condition
  detachment, cervix N88.8
  organ or site, congenital NEC —*see* Distortion
  pancreas (congenital) Q45.1
Anodontia (complete) (partial) (vera) K00.0
  acquired K08.10
Anomaly, anomalous (congenital) (unspecified
    type) Q89.9
  abdominal wall NEC Q79.59
  acoustic nerve Q07.8
  adrenal (gland) Q89.1
  Alder (-Reilly) (leukocyte granulation) D72.0

Anomaly, anomalous *(Continued)*
  alimentary tract Q45.9
    upper Q40.9
  alveolar M26.70
    hyperplasia M26.79
      mandibular M26.72
      maxillary M26.71
    hypoplasia M26.79
      mandibular M26.74
      maxillary M26.73
    ridge (process) M26.79
    specified NEC M26.79
  ankle (joint) Q74.2
  anus Q43.9
  aorta (arch) NEC Q25.40
    coarctation (preductal) (postductal) Q25.1
  aortic cusp or valve Q23.9
  appendix Q43.8
  apple peel syndrome Q41.1
  aqueduct of Sylvius Q03.0
    with spina bifida —*see* Spina bifida, with
        hydrocephalus
  arm Q74.0
  arteriovenous NEC
    coronary Q24.5
    gastrointestinal Q27.33
      acquired —*see* Angiodysplasia
  artery (peripheral) Q27.9
    basilar NEC Q28.1
    cerebral Q28.3
    coronary Q24.5
    digestive system Q27.8
    eye Q15.8
    great Q25.9
      specified NEC Q25.8
    lower limb Q27.8
    peripheral Q27.9
      specified NEC Q27.8
    pulmonary NEC Q25.79
    renal Q27.2
    retina Q14.1
    specified site NEC Q27.8
    subclavian Q27.8
      origin Q25.48
    umbilical Q27.0
    upper limb Q27.8
    vertebral NEC Q28.1
  aryteno-epiglottic folds Q31.8
  atrial
    bands or folds Q20.8
    septa Q21.1
  atrioventricular
    excitation I45.6
    septum Q21.0
  auditory canal Q17.8
  auricle
    ear Q17.8
      causing impairment of hearing Q16.9
    heart Q20.8
  Axenfeld's Q15.0
  back Q89.9
  band
    atrial Q20.8
    heart Q24.8
    ventricular Q24.8
  Bartholin's duct Q38.4
  biliary duct or passage Q44.5
  bladder Q64.70
    absence Q64.5
    diverticulum Q64.6
    exstrophy Q64.10
      cloacal Q64.12
      extroversion Q64.19
      specified type NEC Q64.19
      supravesical fissure Q64.11
    neck obstruction Q64.31
    specified type NEC Q64.79
  bone Q79.9
    arm Q74.0
    face Q75.9
    leg Q74.2

Anomaly, anomalous *(Continued)*
  bone *(Continued)*
    pelvic girdle Q74.2
    shoulder girdle Q74.0
    skull Q75.9
      with
        anencephaly Q00.0
        encephalocele —*see* Encephalocele
        hydrocephalus Q03.9
          with spina bifida —*see* Spina bifida,
              by site, with hydrocephalus
        microcephaly Q02
  brain (multiple) Q04.9
    vessel Q28.3
  breast Q83.9
  broad ligament Q50.6
  bronchus Q32.4
  bulbus cordis Q21.9
  bursa Q79.9
  canal of Nuck Q52.4
  canthus Q10.3
  capillary Q27.9
  cardiac Q24.9
    chambers Q20.9
      specified NEC Q20.8
    septal closure Q21.9
      specified NEC Q21.8
    valve NEC Q24.8
      pulmonary Q22.3
  cardiovascular system Q28.8
  carpus Q74.0
  caruncle, lacrimal Q10.6
  cascade stomach Q40.2
  cauda equina Q06.3
  cecum Q43.9
  cerebral Q04.9
    vessels Q28.3
  cervix Q51.9
  Chédiak-Higashi(-Steinbrinck) (congenital
      gigantism of peroxidase granules)
      E70.330
  cheek Q18.9
  chest wall Q67.8
    bones Q76.9
  chin Q18.9
  chordae tendineae Q24.8
  choroid Q14.3
    plexus Q07.8
  chromosomes, chromosomal Q99.9
    D (1) —*see* condition, chromosome 13
    E (3) —*see* condition, chromosome 18
    G —*see* condition, chromosome 21
    sex
      female phenotype Q97.8
      gonadal dysgenesis (pure) Q99.1
      Klinefelter's Q98.4
      male phenotype Q98.9
      Turner's Q96.9
    specified NEC Q99.8
  cilia Q10.3
  circulatory system Q28.9
  clavicle Q74.0
  clitoris Q52.6
  coccyx Q76.49
  colon Q43.9
  common duct Q44.5
  communication
    coronary artery Q24.5
    left ventricle with right atrium Q21.0
  concha (ear) Q17.3
  connection
    portal vein Q26.5
    pulmonary venous Q26.4
      partial Q26.3
      total Q26.2
    renal artery with kidney Q27.2
  cornea (shape) Q13.4
  coronary artery or vein Q24.5
  cranium —*see* Anomaly, skull
  cricoid cartilage Q31.8
  cystic duct Q44.5

▶ New ⇛ Revised ~~deleted~~ Deleted ● Use Additional Character(s)

Anomaly, anomalous (Continued)
  dental
    alveolar —see Anomaly, alveolar
    arch relationship M26.20
      specified NEC M26.29
  dentofacial M26.9
    alveolar —see Anomaly, alveolar
    dental arch relationship M26.20
      specified NEC M26.29
    functional M26.50
      specified NEC M26.59
    jaw-cranial base relationship M26.10
      asymmetry M26.12
        maxillary M26.11
      specified type NEC M26.19
    jaw size M26.00
      macrogenia M26.05
      mandibular
        hyperplasia M26.03
        hypoplasia M26.04
      maxillary
        hyperplasia M26.01
        hypoplasia M26.02
      microgenia M26.06
      specified type NEC M26.09
    malocclusion M26.4
      dental arch relationship NEC M26.29
      jaw-cranial base relationship —see
          Anomaly, dentofacial, jaw-cranial
          base relationship
      jaw size —see Anomaly, dentofacial, jaw
          size
      specified type NEC M26.89
    temporomandibular joint M26.60-●
      adhesions M26.61-●
      ankylosis M26.61-●
      arthralgia M26.62-●
      articular disc M26.63-●
      specified type NEC M26.69
    tooth position, fully erupted M26.30
      specified NEC M26.39
  dermatoglyphic Q82.8
  diaphragm (apertures) NEC Q79.1
  digestive organ(s) or tract Q45.9
    lower Q43.9
    upper Q40.9
  distance, interarch (excessive) (inadequate)
      M26.25
  distribution, coronary artery Q24.5
  ductus
    arteriosus Q25.0
    botalli Q25.0
  duodenum Q43.9
  dura (brain) Q04.9
    spinal cord Q06.9
  ear (external) Q17.9
    causing impairment of hearing Q16.9
    inner Q16.5
    middle (causing impairment of hearing)
        Q16.4
    ossicles Q16.3
  Ebstein's (heart) (tricuspid valve) Q22.5
  ectodermal Q82.9
  Eisenmenger's (ventricular septal defect)
      Q21.8
  ejaculatory duct Q55.4
  elbow Q74.0
  endocrine gland NEC Q89.2
  epididymis Q55.4
  epiglottis Q31.8
  esophagus Q39.9
  eustachian tube Q17.8
  eye Q15.9
    anterior segment Q13.9
      specified NEC Q13.89
    posterior segment Q14.9
      specified NEC Q14.8
    ptosis (eyelid) Q10.0
    specified NEC Q15.8
  eyebrow Q18.8
  eyelid Q10.3
    ptosis Q10.0

Anomaly, anomalous (Continued)
  face Q18.9
    bone(s) Q75.9
  fallopian tube Q50.6
  fascia Q79.9
  femur NEC Q74.2
  fibula NEC Q74.2
  finger Q74.0
  fixation, intestine Q43.3
  flexion (joint) NOS Q74.9
    hip or thigh Q65.89
  foot NEC Q74.2
    varus (congenital) Q66.3-●
  foramen
    Botalli Q21.1
    ovale Q21.1
  forearm Q74.0
  forehead Q75.8
  form, teeth K00.2
  fovea centralis Q14.1
  frontal bone —see Anomaly, skull
  gallbladder (position) (shape) (size)
      Q44.1
  Gartner's duct Q52.4
  gastrointestinal tract Q45.9
  genitalia, genital organ(s) or system
    female Q52.9
      external Q52.70
      internal NOS Q52.9
    male Q55.9
      hydrocele P83.5
      specified NEC Q55.8
  genitourinary NEC
    female Q52.9
    male Q55.9
  Gerbode Q21.0
  glottis Q31.8
  granulation or granulocyte, genetic
      (constitutional) (leukocyte) D72.0
  gum Q38.6
  gyri Q07.9
  hair Q84.2
  hand Q74.0
  hard tissue formation in pulp K04.3
  head —see Anomaly, skull
  heart Q24.9
    auricle Q20.8
    bands or folds Q24.8
    fibroelastosis cordis I42.4
    obstructive NEC Q22.6
    patent ductus arteriosus (Botalli) Q25.0
    septum Q21.9
      auricular Q21.1
      interatrial Q21.1
      interventricular Q21.0
        with pulmonary stenosis or atresia,
            dextraposition of aorta and
            hypertrophy of right ventricle
            Q21.3
      specified NEC Q21.8
      ventricular Q21.0
        with pulmonary stenosis or atresia,
            dextraposition of aorta and
            hypertrophy of right ventricle
            Q21.3
    tetralogy of Fallot Q21.3
    valve NEC Q24.8
      aortic
        bicuspid valve Q23.1
        insufficiency Q23.1
        stenosis Q23.0
          subaortic Q24.4
      mitral
        insufficiency Q23.3
        stenosis Q23.2
      pulmonary Q22.3
        atresia Q22.0
        insufficiency Q22.2
        stenosis Q22.1
          infundibular Q24.3
          subvalvular Q24.3

Anomaly, anomalous (Continued)
  heart (Continued)
    valve NEC (Continued)
      tricuspid
        atresia Q22.4
        stenosis Q22.4
      ventricle Q20.8
  heel NEC Q74.2
  Hegglin's D72.0
  hemianencephaly Q00.0
  hemicephaly Q00.0
  hemicrania Q00.0
  hepatic duct Q44.5
  hip NEC Q74.2
  hourglass stomach Q40.2
  humerus Q74.0
  hydatid of Morgagni
    female Q50.5
    male (epididymal) Q55.4
    testicular Q55.29
  hymen Q52.4
  hypersegmentation of neutrophils, hereditary
      D72.0
  hypophyseal Q89.2
  ileocecal (coil) (valve) Q43.9
  ileum Q43.9
  ilium NEC Q74.2
  integument Q84.9
    specified NEC Q84.8
  interarch distance (excessive) (inadequate)
      M26.25
  intervertebral cartilage or disc Q76.49
  intestine (large) (small) Q43.9
    with anomalous adhesions, fixation or
        malrotation Q43.3
  iris Q13.2
  ischium NEC Q74.2
  jaw —see Anomaly, dentofacial
    alveolar —see Anomaly, alveolar
    jaw-cranial base relationship —see Anomaly,
        dentofacial, jaw-cranial base relationship
  jejunum Q43.8
  joint Q74.9
    specified NEC Q74.8
  Jordan's D72.0
  kidney(s) (calyx) (pelvis) Q63.9
    artery Q27.2
    specified NEC Q63.8
  Klippel-Feil (brevicollis) Q76.1
  knee Q74.1
  labium (majus) (minus) Q52.70
  labyrinth, membranous Q16.5
  lacrimal apparatus or duct Q10.6
  larynx, laryngeal (muscle) Q31.9
    web (bed) Q31.0
  lens Q12.9
  leukocytes, genetic D72.0
    granulation (constitutional) D72.0
  lid (fold) Q10.3
  ligament Q79.9
    broad Q50.6
    round Q52.8
  limb Q74.9
    lower NEC Q74.2
      reduction deformity —see Defect,
          reduction, lower limb
    upper Q74.0
  lip Q38.0
  liver Q44.7
    duct Q44.5
  lower limb NEC Q74.2
  lumbosacral (joint) (region) Q76.49
    kyphosis —see Kyphosis, congenital
    lordosis —see Lordosis, congenital
  lung (fissure) (lobe) Q33.9
  mandible —see Anomaly, dentofacial
  maxilla —see Anomaly, dentofacial
  May (-Hegglin) D72.0
  meatus urinarius NEC Q64.79
  meningeal bands or folds Q07.9
    constriction of Q07.8
    spinal Q06.9

Anomaly, anomalous (Continued)
  meninges Q07.9
    cerebral Q04.8
    spinal Q06.9
  meningocele Q05.9
  mesentery Q45.9
  metacarpus Q74.0
  metatarsus NEC Q74.2
  middle ear Q16.4
    ossicles Q16.3
  mitral (leaflets) (valve) Q23.9
    insufficiency Q23.3
    specified NEC Q23.8
    stenosis Q23.2
  mouth Q38.6
  Müllerian —see also Anomaly, by site
    uterus NEC Q51.818
  multiple NEC Q89.7
  muscle Q79.9
    eyelid Q10.3
  musculoskeletal system, except limbs Q79.9
  myocardium Q24.8
  nail Q84.6
  narrowness, eyelid Q10.3
  nasal sinus (wall) Q30.8
  neck (any part) Q18.9
  nerve Q07.9
    acoustic Q07.8
    optic Q07.8
  nervous system (central) Q07.9
  nipple Q83.9
  nose, nasal (bones) (cartilage) (septum)
    (sinus) Q30.9
    specified NEC Q30.8
  ocular muscle Q15.8
  omphalomesenteric duct Q43.0
  opening, pulmonary veins Q26.4
  optic
    disc Q14.2
    nerve Q07.8
  opticociliary vessels Q13.2
  orbit (eye) Q10.7
  organ Q89.9
    of Corti Q16.5
  origin
    artery
      innominate Q25.8
      pulmonary Q25.79
      renal Q27.2
      subclavian Q25.48
  osseous meatus (ear) Q16.1
  ovary Q50.39
  oviduct Q50.6
  palate (hard) (soft) NEC Q38.5
  pancreas or pancreatic duct Q45.3
  papillary muscles Q24.8
  parathyroid gland Q89.2
  paraurethral ducts Q64.79
  parotid (gland) Q38.4
  patella Q74.1
  Pelger-Huët (hereditary hyposegmentation)
    D72.0
  pelvic girdle NEC Q74.2
  pelvis (bony) NEC Q74.2
    rachitic E64.3
  penis (glans) Q55.69
  pericardium Q24.8
  peripheral vascular system Q27.9
  Peter's Q13.4
  pharynx Q38.8
  pigmentation L81.9
    congenital Q82.8
  pituitary (gland) Q89.2
  pleural (folds) Q34.0
  portal vein Q26.5
    connection Q26.5
  position, tooth, teeth, fully erupted M26.30
    specified NEC M26.39
  precerebral vessel Q28.1
  prepuce Q55.69
  prostate Q55.4

Anomaly, anomalous (Continued)
  pulmonary Q33.9
    artery NEC Q25.79
    valve Q22.3
      atresia Q22.0
      insufficiency Q22.2
      specified type NEC Q22.3
      stenosis Q22.1
        infundibular Q24.3
        subvalvular Q24.3
    venous connection Q26.4
      partial Q26.3
      total Q26.2
  pupil Q13.2
    function H57.00
      anisocoria H57.02
      Argyll Robertson pupil H57.01
      miosis H57.03
      mydriasis H57.04
      specified type NEC H57.09
      tonic pupil H57.05-●
  pylorus Q40.3
  radius Q74.0
  rectum Q43.9
  reduction (extremity) (limb)
    femur (longitudinal) —see Defect,
      reduction, lower limb, longitudinal,
      femur
    fibula (longitudinal) —see Defect,
      reduction, lower limb, longitudinal,
      fibula
    lower limb —see Defect, reduction, lower
      limb
    radius (longitudinal) —see Defect,
      reduction, upper limb, longitudinal,
      radius
    tibia (longitudinal) —see Defect, reduction,
      lower limb, longitudinal, tibia
    ulna (longitudinal) —see Defect, reduction,
      upper limb, longitudinal, ulna
    upper limb —see Defect, reduction, upper
      limb
  refraction —see Disorder, refraction
  renal Q63.9
    artery Q27.2
    pelvis Q63.9
      specified NEC Q63.8
  respiratory system Q34.9
    specified NEC Q34.8
  retina Q14.1
  rib Q76.6
    cervical Q76.5
  Rieger's Q13.81
  rotation —see Malrotation
    hip or thigh Q65.89
  round ligament Q52.8
  sacroiliac (joint) NEC Q74.2
  sacrum NEC Q76.49
    kyphosis —see Kyphosis, congenital
    lordosis —see Lordosis, congenital
  saddle nose, syphilitic A50.57
  salivary duct or gland Q38.4
  scapula Q74.0
  scrotum —see Malformation, testis and
    scrotum
  sebaceous gland Q82.9
  seminal vesicles Q55.4
  sense organs NEC Q07.8
  sex chromosomes NEC —see also Anomaly,
    chromosomes
    female phenotype Q97.8
    male phenotype Q98.9
  shoulder (girdle) (joint) Q74.0
  sigmoid (flexure) Q43.9
  simian crease Q82.8
  sinus of Valsalva Q25.49
  skeleton generalized Q78.9
  skin (appendage) Q82.9
  skull Q75.9
    with
      anencephaly Q00.0
      encephalocele —see Encephalocele

Anomaly, anomalous (Continued)
  skull (Continued)
    with (Continued)
      hydrocephalus Q03.9
        with spina bifida —see Spina bifida, by
        site, with hydrocephalus
      microcephaly Q02
  specified organ or site NEC Q89.8
  spermatic cord Q55.4
  spine, spinal NEC Q76.49
    column NEC Q76.49
      kyphosis —see Kyphosis, congenital
      lordosis —see Lordosis, congenital
    cord Q06.9
    nerve root Q07.8
  spleen Q89.09
    agenesis Q89.01
  stenonian duct Q38.4
  sternum NEC Q76.7
  stomach Q40.3
  submaxillary gland Q38.4
  tarsus NEC Q74.2
  tendon Q79.9
  testis —see Malformation, testis and scrotum
  thigh NEC Q74.2
  thorax (wall) Q67.8
    bony Q76.9
  throat Q38.8
  thumb Q74.0
  thymus gland Q89.2
  thyroid (gland) Q89.2
    cartilage Q31.8
  tibia NEC Q74.2
    saber A50.56
  toe Q74.2
  tongue Q38.3
  tooth, teeth K00.9
    eruption K00.6
    position, fully erupted M26.30
    spacing, fully erupted M26.30
  trachea (cartilage) Q32.1
  tragus Q17.9
  tricuspid (leaflet) (valve) Q22.9
    atresia or stenosis Q22.4
    Ebstein's Q22.5
  Uhl's (hypoplasia of myocardium, right
    ventricle) Q24.8
  ulna Q74.0
  umbilical artery Q27.0
  union
    cricoid cartilage and thyroid cartilage
      Q31.8
    thyroid cartilage and hyoid bone Q31.8
    trachea with larynx Q31.8
  upper limb Q74.0
  urachus Q64.4
  ureter Q62.8
    obstructive NEC Q62.39
      cecoureterocele Q62.32
      orthotopic ureterocele Q62.31
  urethra Q64.70
    absence Q64.5
    double Q64.74
    fistula to rectum Q64.73
    obstructive Q64.39
      stricture Q64.32
    prolapse Q64.71
    specified type NEC Q64.79
  urinary tract Q64.9
  uterus Q51.9
    with only one functioning horn Q51.4
  uvula Q38.5
  vagina Q52.4
  valleculae Q31.8
  valve (heart) NEC Q24.8
    coronary sinus Q24.5
    inferior vena cava Q24.8
    pulmonary Q22.3
    sinus coronario Q24.5
    venae cavae inferioris Q24.8
  vas deferens Q55.4

▶ New   ⇒ Revised   ~~deleted~~ Deleted   ● Use Additional Character(s)

Anomaly, anomalous *(Continued)*
  vascular Q27.9
    brain Q28.3
    ring Q25.45
  vein(s) (peripheral) Q27.9
    brain Q28.3
    cerebral Q28.3
    coronary Q24.5
    developmental Q28.3
    great Q26.9
      specified NEC Q26.8
  vena cava (inferior) (superior) Q26.9
  venous —*see* Anomaly, vein(s)
  venous return Q26.8
  ventricular
    bands or folds Q24.8
    septa Q21.0
  vertebra Q76.49
    kyphosis —*see* Kyphosis, congenital
    lordosis —*see* Lordosis, congenital
  vesicourethral orifice Q64.79
  vessel(s) Q27.9
    optic papilla Q14.2
    precerebral Q28.1
  vitelline duct Q43.0
  vitreous body or humor Q14.0
  vulva Q52.70
  wrist (joint) Q74.0
Anomia R48.8
Anonychia (congenital) Q84.3
  acquired L60.8
Anophthalmos, anophthalmus (congenital)
    (globe) Q11.1
  acquired Z90.01
Anopia, anopsia H53.46-●
  quadrant H53.46-●
Anorchia, anorchism, anorchidism Q55.0
Anorexia R63.0
  hysterical F44.89
  nervosa F50.00
    atypical F50.9
    binge-eating type F50.2
      with purging F50.02
    restricting type F50.01
Anorgasmy, psychogenic (female)
    F52.31
  male F52.32
Anosmia R43.0
  hysterical F44.6
  postinfectional J39.8
Anosognosia R41.89
Anosteoplasia Q78.9
Anovulatory cycle N97.0
Anoxemia R09.02
  newborn P84
Anoxia (pathological) R09.02
  altitude T70.29
  cerebral G93.1
    complicating
      anesthesia (general) (local) or other
        sedation T88.59
      in labor and delivery O74.3
      in pregnancy O29.21-●
      postpartum, puerperal O89.2
    delivery (cesarean) (instrumental)
      O75.4
    during a procedure G97.81
    newborn P84
    resulting from a procedure G97.82
  due to
    drowning T75.1
    high altitude T70.29
  heart —*see* Insufficiency, coronary
  intrauterine P84
  myocardial —*see* Insufficiency, coronary
  newborn P84
  spinal cord G95.11
  systemic (by suffocation) (low content in
    atmosphere) —*see* Asphyxia,
    traumatic
Anteflexion —*see* Anteversion

Antenatal
  care (normal pregnancy) Z34.90
  screening (encounter for) of mother —*see also*
    Encounter, antenatal screening Z36.9
Antepartum —*see* condition
Anterior —*see* condition
Antero-occlusion M26.220
Anteversion
  cervix —*see* Anteversion, uterus
  femur (neck), congenital Q65.89
  uterus, uterine (cervix) (postinfectional)
    (postpartal, old) N85.4
    congenital Q51.818
    in pregnancy or childbirth —*see* Pregnancy,
      complicated by
Anthophobia F40.228
Anthracosilicosis J60
Anthracosis (lung) (occupational) J60
  lingua K14.3
Anthrax A22.9
  with pneumonia A22.1
  cerebral A22.8
  colitis A22.2
  cutaneous A22.0
  gastrointestinal A22.2
  inhalation A22.1
  intestinal A22.2
  meningitis A22.8
  pulmonary A22.1
  respiratory A22.1
  sepsis A22.7
  specified manifestation NEC A22.8
Anthropoid pelvis Q74.2
  with disproportion (fetopelvic) O33.0
Anthropophobia F40.10
  generalized F40.11
Antibodies, maternal (blood group) —*see*
    Isoimmunization, affecting management of
    pregnancy
  anti-D —*see* Isoimmunization, affecting
    management of pregnancy, Rh
  newborn P55.0
Antibody
  anticardiolipin R76.0
    with
      hemorrhagic disorder D68.312
      hypercoagulable state D68.61
  antiphosphatidylglycerol R76.0
    with
      hemorrhagic disorder D68.312
      hypercoagulable state D68.61
  antiphosphatidylinositol R76.0
    with
      hemorrhagic disorder D68.312
      hypercoagulable state D68.61
  antiphosphatidylserine R76.0
    with
      hemorrhagic disorder D68.312
      hypercoagulable state D68.61
  antiphospholipid R76.0
    with
      hemorrhagic disorder D68.312
      hypercoagulable state D68.61
Anticardiolipin syndrome D68.61
Anticoagulant, circulating (intrinsic) —*see also* -
    Disorder, hemorrhagic D68.318
  drug-induced (extrinsic) —*see also* - Disorder,
    hemorrhagic D68.32
  iatrogenic D68.32
Antidiuretic hormone syndrome E22.2
Antimonial cholera —*see* Poisoning,
    antimony
Antiphospholipid
  antibody
    with hemorrhagic disorder D68.312
    syndrome D68.61
Antisocial personality F60.2
Antithrombinemia —*see* Circulating
    anticoagulants
Antithromboplastinemia D68.318
Antithromboplastinogenemia D68.318

Antitoxin complication or reaction —*see*
    Complications, vaccination
Antlophobia F40.228
Antritis J32.0
  maxilla J32.0
    acute J01.00
      recurrent J01.01
  stomach K29.60
    with bleeding K29.61
Antrum, antral —*see* condition
Anuria R34
  calculous (impacted) (recurrent) —*see also*
    Calculus, urinary N20.9
  following
    abortion —*see* Abortion by type
      complicated by, renal failure
    ectopic or molar pregnancy O08.4
  newborn P96.0
  postprocedural N99.0
  postrenal N13.8
  traumatic (following crushing) T79.5
Anus, anal —*see* condition
Anusitis K62.89
Anxiety F41.9
  depression F41.8
  episodic paroxysmal F41.0
  generalized F41.1
  hysteria F41.8
  neurosis F41.1
  panic type F41.0
  reaction F41.1
  separation, abnormal (of childhood) F93.0
  specified NEC F41.8
  state F41.1
Aorta, aortic —*see* condition
Aortectasia —*see* Ectasia, aorta
  with aneurysm —*see* Aneurysm, aorta
Aortitis (nonsyphilitic) (calcific) I77.6
  arteriosclerotic I70.0
  Doehle-Heller A52.02
  luetic A52.02
  rheumatic —*see* Endocarditis, acute,
    rheumatic
  specific (syphilitic) A52.02
  syphilitic A52.02
    congenital A50.54 *[I79.1]*
Apathetic thyroid storm —*see* Thyrotoxicosis
Apathy R45.3
Apeirophobia F40.228
Apepsia K30
  psychogenic F45.8
Aperistalsis, esophagus K22.0
Apertognathia M26.29
Apert's syndrome Q87.0
Aphagia R13.0
  psychogenic F50.9
Aphakia (acquired) (postoperative) H27.0-●
  congenital Q12.3
Aphasia (amnestic) (global) (nominal)
    (semantic) (syntactic) R47.01
  acquired, with epilepsy (Landau-Kleffner
    syndrome) —*see* Epilepsy, specified
    NEC
  auditory (developmental) F80.2
  developmental (receptive type) F80.2
    expressive type F80.1
    Wernicke's F80.2
  following
    cerebrovascular disease I69.920
      cerebral infarction I69.320
      intracerebral hemorrhage I69.120
      nontraumatic intracranial hemorrhage
        NEC I69.220
      specified disease NEC I69.820
      subarachnoid hemorrhage I69.020
  primary progressive G31.01 *[F02.80]*
    with behavioral disturbance G31.01
      [F02.81]
  progressive isolated G31.01 *[F02.80]*
    with behavioral disturbance G31.01
      [F02.81]

Aphasia (Continued)
  sensory F80.2
  syphilis, tertiary A52.19
  Wernicke's (developmental) F80.2
Aphonia (organic) R49.1
  hysterical F44.4
  psychogenic F44.4
Aphthae, aphthous —see also condition
  Bednar's K12.0
  cachectic K14.0
  epizootic B08.8
  fever B08.8
  oral (recurrent) K12.0
  stomatitis (major) (minor) K12.0
  thrush B37.0
  ulcer (oral) (recurrent) K12.0
    genital organ(s) NEC
      female N76.6
      male N50.89
    larynx J38.7
Apical —see condition
Apiphobia F40.218
Aplasia —see also Agenesis
  abdominal muscle syndrome Q79.4
  alveolar process (acquired) —see Anomaly,
      alveolar
    congenital Q38.6
  aorta (congenital) Q25.41
  axialis extracticalis (congenita) E75.29
  bone marrow (myeloid) D61.9
    congenital D61.01
  brain Q00.0
    part of Q04.3
  bronchus Q32.4
  cementum K00.4
  cerebellum Q04.3
  cervix (congenital) Q51.5
  congenital pure red cell D61.01
  corpus callosum Q04.0
  cutis congenita Q84.8
  erythrocyte congenital D61.01
  extracortical axial E75.29
  eye Q11.1
  fovea centralis (congenital) Q14.1
  gallbladder, congenital Q44.0
  iris Q13.1
  labyrinth, membranous Q16.5
  limb (congenital) Q73.8
    lower —see Defect, reduction, lower limb
    upper —see Agenesis, arm
  lung, congenital (bilateral) (unilateral)
      Q33.3
  pancreas Q45.0
  parathyroid-thymic D82.1
  Pelizaeus-Merzbacher E75.29
  penis Q55.5
  prostate Q55.4
  red cell (with thymoma) D60.9
    acquired D60.9
      due to drugs D60.9
    adult D60.9
    chronic D60.0
    congenital D61.01
    constitutional D61.01
    due to drugs D60.9
    hereditary D61.01
    of infants D61.01
    primary D61.01
    pure D61.01
      due to drugs D60.9
    specified type NEC D60.8
    transient D60.1
  round ligament Q52.8
  skin Q84.8
  spermatic cord Q55.4
  spleen Q89.01
  testicle Q55.0
  thymic, with immunodeficiency D82.1
  thyroid (congenital) (with myxedema) E03.1
  uterus Q51.0
  ventral horn cell Q06.1

Apnea, apneic (of) (spells) R06.81
  newborn NEC P28.4
    obstructive P28.4
    sleep (central) (obstructive) (primary) P28.3
  prematurity P28.4
  sleep G47.30
    central (primary) G47.31
      idiopathic G47.31
      in conditions classified elsewhere G47.37
    obstructive (adult) (pediatric) G47.33
      hypopnea G47.33
    primary central G47.31
    specified NEC G47.39
Apneumatosis, newborn P28.0
Apocrine metaplasia (breast) —see Dysplasia,
    mammary, specified type NEC
Apophysitis (bone) —see also
    Osteochondropathy
  calcaneus M92.8
  juvenile M92.9
Apoplectiform convulsions (cerebral ischemia)
    I67.82
Apoplexia, apoplexy, apoplectic
  adrenal A39.1
  heart (auricle) (ventricle) —see Infarct,
      myocardium
  heat T67.01
  hemorrhagic (stroke) —see Hemorrhage,
      intracranial
  meninges, hemorrhagic —see Hemorrhage,
      intracranial, subarachnoid
  uremic N18.9 [I68.8]
Appearance
  bizarre R46.1
  specified NEC R46.89
  very low level of personal hygiene R46.0
Appendage
  epididymal (organ of Morgagni) Q55.4
  intestine (epiploic) Q43.8
  preauricular Q17.0
  testicular (organ of Morgagni) Q55.29
Appendicitis (pneumococcal) (retrocecal) K37
  with
    gangrene K35.891
    perforation NOS K35.32
    peritoneal abscess K35.33
    peritonitis NEC K35.33
      generalized (with perforation or
          rupture) K35.20
        with abscess K35.21
      localized K35.30
        with
          gangrene K35.32
          perforation K35.32
            and abscess K35.33
      ruptured NOS (with localized
          peritonitis) K35.32
  acute (catarrhal) (fulminating) (gangrenous)
      (obstructive) (retrocecal) (suppurative)
      K35.80
    with
      gangrene K35.891
      peritoneal abscess K35.33
      peritonitis NEC K35.33
        generalized (with perforation or
            rupture) K35.20
          with abscess K35.21
        localized K35.30
          with
            gangrene K35.32
            perforation K35.32
              and abscess K35.33
    specified NEC K35.890
      with gangrene K35.891
  amebic A06.89
  chronic (recurrent) K36
  exacerbation —see Appendicitis, acute
  gangrenous —see Appendicitis, acute
  healed (obliterative) K36
  interval K36
  neurogenic K36

Appendicitis (Continued)
  obstructive K36
  recurrent K36
  relapsing K36
    ruptured NOS (with localized peritonitis)
        K35.32
  subacute (adhesive) K36
  subsiding K36
  suppurative —see Appendicitis, acute
  tuberculous A18.32
Appendicopathia oxyurica B80
Appendix, appendicular —see also condition
  epididymis Q55.4
  Morgagni
    female Q50.5
    male (epididymal) Q55.4
      testicular Q55.29
  testis Q55.29
Appetite
  depraved —see Pica
  excessive R63.2
  lack or loss —see also Anorexia R63.0
    nonorganic origin F50.89
    psychogenic F50.89
  perverted (hysterical) —see Pica
Apple peel syndrome Q41.1
Apprehension state F41.1
Apprehensiveness, abnormal F41.9
Approximal wear K03.0
Apraxia (classic) (ideational) (ideokinetic)
    (ideomotor) (motor) (verbal) R48.2
  following
    cerebrovascular disease I69.990
      cerebral infarction I69.390
      intracerebral hemorrhage I69.190
      nontraumatic intracranial hemorrhage
          NEC I69.290
      specified disease NEC I69.890
      subarachnoid hemorrhage I69.090
  oculomotor, congenital H51.8
Aptyalism K11.7
Apudoma —see Neoplasm, uncertain behavior,
    by site
Aqueous misdirection H40.83-●
Arabicum elephantiasis —see Infestation, filarial
Arachnitis —see Meningitis
Arachnodactyly —see Syndrome, Marfan's
Arachnoiditis (acute) (adhesive) (basal) (brain)
    (cerebrospinal) —see Meningitis
Arachnophobia F40.210
Arboencephalitis, Australian A83.4
Arborization block (heart) I45.5
ARC (AIDS-related complex) B20
Arch
  aortic Q25.49
  bovine Q25.49
Arches —see condition
Arcuate uterus Q51.810
Arcuatus uterus Q51.810
Arcus (cornea) senilis —see Degeneration,
    cornea, senile
Arc-welder's lung J63.4
Areflexia R29.2
Areola —see condition
Argentaffinoma —see also Neoplasm, uncertain
    behavior, by site
  malignant —see Neoplasm, malignant, by site
  syndrome E34.0
Argininemia E72.21
Arginosuccinic aciduria E72.22
Argyll Robertson phenomenon, pupil or
    syndrome (syphilitic) A52.19
  atypical H57.09
  nonsyphilitic H57.09
Argyria, argyriasis
  conjunctival H11.13-●
  from drug or medicament —see Table of
      Drugs and Chemicals, by substance
Argyrosis, conjunctival H11.13-●
Arhinencephaly Q04.1
Ariboflavinosis E53.0

▶ New   ⇒ Revised   ~~deleted~~ Deleted   ● Use Additional Character(s)

Arm —*see* condition
Arnold-Chiari disease, obstruction or syndrome (type II) Q07.00
  with
    hydrocephalus Q07.02
      with spina bifida Q07.03
    spina bifida Q07.01
      with hydrocephalus Q07.03
  type III —*see* Encephalocele
  type IV Q04.8
Aromatic amino-acid metabolism disorder E70.9
  specified NEC E70.89
Arousals, confusional G47.51
Arrest, arrested
  cardiac I46.9
    complicating
      abortion —*see* Abortion, by type, complicated by, cardiac arrest
      anesthesia (general) (local) or other sedation —*see* Table of Drugs and Chemicals, by drug
        in labor and delivery O74.2
        in pregnancy O29.11-●
        postpartum, puerperal O89.1
      delivery (cesarean) (instrumental) O75.4
    due to
      cardiac condition I46.2
      specified condition NEC I46.8
    intraoperative I97.71-●
    newborn P29.81
    personal history, successfully resuscitated Z86.74
    postprocedural I97.12-●
      obstetric procedure O75.4
  cardiorespiratory —*see* Arrest, cardiac
  circulatory —*see* Arrest, cardiac
  deep transverse O64.0
  development or growth
    bone —*see* Disorder, bone, development or growth
    child R62.50
    tracheal rings Q32.1
  epiphyseal
    complete
      femur M89.15-●
      humerus M89.12-●
      tibia M89.16-●
      ulna M89.13-●
      forearm M89.13-●
        specified NEC M89.13-●
        ulna —*see* Arrest, epiphyseal, by type, ulna
      lower leg M89.16-●
        specified NEC M89.168
        tibia —*see* Arrest, epiphyseal, by type, tibia
    partial
      femur M89.15-●
      humerus M89.12-●
      tibia M89.16-●
      ulna M89.13-●
    specified NEC M89.18
  granulopoiesis —*see* Agranulocytosis
  growth plate —*see* Arrest, epiphyseal
  heart —*see* Arrest, cardiac
  legal, anxiety concerning Z65.3
  physeal —*see* Arrest, epiphyseal
  respiratory R09.2
    newborn P28.81
  sinus I45.5
  spermatogenesis (complete) —*see* Azoospermia
    incomplete —*see* Oligospermia
  transverse (deep) O64.0
Arrhenoblastoma
  benign
    specified site —*see* Neoplasm, benign, by site
    unspecified site
      female D27.9
      male D29.20

Arrhenoblastoma (*Continued*)
  malignant
    specified site —*see* Neoplasm, malignant, by site
    unspecified site
      female C56.9
      male C62.90
  specified site —*see* Neoplasm, uncertain behavior, by site
  unspecified site
    female D39.10
    male D40.10
Arrhythmia (auricle)(cardiac) (juvenile)(nodal) (reflex)(supraventricular)(transitory) (ventricle) I49.9
  block I45.9
  extrasystolic I49.49
  newborn
    bradycardia P29.12
    occurring before birth P03.819
      before onset of labor P03.810
      during labor P03.811
    tachycardia P29.11
  psychogenic F45.8
  sinus I49.8
  specified NEC I49.8
  vagal R55
  ventricular re-entry I47.0
Arrillaga-Ayerza syndrome (pulmonary sclerosis with pulmonary hypertension) I27.0
Arsenical pigmentation L81.8
  from drug or medicament —*see* Table of Drugs and Chemicals
Arsenism —*see* Poisoning, arsenic
Arterial —*see* condition
Arteriofibrosis —*see* Arteriosclerosis
Arteriolar sclerosis —*see* Arteriosclerosis
Arteriolith —*see* Arteriosclerosis
Arteriolitis I77.6
  necrotizing, kidney I77.5
  renal —*see* Hypertension, kidney
Arteriolosclerosis —*see* Arteriosclerosis
Arterionephrosclerosis —*see* Hypertension, kidney
Arteriopathy I77.9
  cerebral autosomal dominant, with subcortical infarcts and leukoencephalopathy (CADASIL) I67.850
Arteriosclerosis, arteriosclerotic (diffuse) (obliterans) (of) (senile) (with calcification) I70.90
  with
    chronic limb-threatening ischemia —*see* Arteriosclerosis, with critical limb ischemia
    critical limb ischemia
      bypass graft I70.329
        autologous vein graft I70.429
          leg I70.429
            with
              gangrene (and intermittent claudication, rest pain, and ulcer) I70.469
              rest pain (and intermittent claudication) I70.429
            bilateral I70.423
              with
                gangrene (and intermittent claudication, rest pain, and ulcer) I70.463
                rest pain (and intermittent claudication) I70.423
            left I70.422
              with
                gangrene (and intermittent claudication, rest pain, and ulcer) I70.462
                rest pain (and intermittent claudication) I70.422

Arteriosclerosis, arteriosclerotic (*Continued*)
  chronic limb-threatening ischemia (*Continued*)
    critical limb ischemia (*Continued*)
      bypass graft (*Continued*)
        autologous vein graft (*Continued*)
          leg (*Continued*)
            left (*Continued*)
              with (*Continued*)
                ulceration (and intermittent claudication and rest pain) I70.449
                  ankle I70.443
                  calf I70.442
                  foot site NEC I70.445
                  heel I70.444
                  lower leg NEC I70.448
                  mid foot I70.444
                  thigh I70.441
            right I70.421
              with
                gangrene (and intermittent claudication, rest pain, and ulcer) I70.461
                rest pain (and intermittent claudication) I70.421
                ulceration (and intermittent claudication and rest pain) I70.439
                  ankle I70.433
                  calf I70.432
                  foot site NEC I70.435
                  heel I70.434
                  lower leg NEC I70.438
                  midfoot I70.434
                  thigh I70.431
        leg I70.329
          with
            gangrene (and intermittent claudication, rest pain, and ulcer) I70.369
            rest pain (and intermittent claudication) I70.329
          bilateral I70.323
            with
              gangrene (and intermittent claudication, rest pain, and ulcer) I70.363
              rest pain (and intermittent claudication) I70.323
          left I70.322
            with
              rest pain (and intermittent claudication) I70.322
              ulceration (and intermittent claudication and rest pain) I70.349
                ankle I70.343
                calf I70.342
                foot site NEC I70.345
                heel I70.344
                lower leg NEC I70.348
                midfoot I70.344
                thigh I70.341
          right I70.321
            with
              gangrene (and intermittent claudication, rest pain, and ulcer) I70.361
              rest pain (and intermittent claudication) I70.321
              ulceration (and intermittent claudication and rest pain) I70.339
                ankle I70.333
                calf I70.332
                foot site NEC I70.335
                heel I70.334
                lower leg NEC I70.338
                midfoot I70.334
                thigh I70.331

▶ New   ⮕ Revised   ~~deleted~~ Deleted   ● Use Additional Character(s)

Arteriosclerosis, arteriosclerotic (Continued)
  chronic limb-threatening ischemia (Continued)
    critical limb ischemia (Continued)
      bypass graft (Continued)
       ▶nonautologous biological graft I70.529
        ▶leg I70.529
         ▶with
          ▶gangrene (and intermittent claudication, rest pain, and ulcer) I70.569
          ▶rest pain (and intermittent claudication) I70.529
        ▶bilateral I70.523
         ▶with
          ▶gangrene (and intermittent claudication, rest pain, and ulcer) I70.563
          ▶rest pain (and intermittent claudication) I70.523
        ▶left I70.522
         ▶with
          ▶gangrene (and intermittent claudication, rest pain, and ulcer) I70.562
          ▶rest pain (and intermittent claudication) I70.522
          ▶ulceration (and intermittent claudication and rest pain) I70.549
           ▶ankle I70.543
           ▶calf I70.542
           ▶foot site NEC I70.545
           ▶heel I70.544
           ▶lower leg NEC I70.548
           ▶midfoot I70.544
           ▶thigh I70.541
        ▶right I70.521
         ▶with
          ▶gangrene (and intermittent claudication, rest pain, and ulcer) I70.561
          ▶rest pain (and intermittent claudication) I70.521
          ▶ulceration (and intermittent claudication and rest pain) I70.539
           ▶ankle I70.533
           ▶calf I70.532
           ▶foot site NEC I70.535
           ▶heel I70.534
           ▶lower leg NEC I70.538
           ▶midfoot I70.534
           ▶thigh I70.531
      ▶nonbiological graft I70.629
       ▶leg I70.629
        ▶with
         ▶gangrene (and intermittent claudication, rest pain, and ulcer) I70.669
         ▶rest pain (and intermittent claudication) I70.629
        ▶bilateral I70.623
         ▶with
          ▶gangrene (and intermittent claudication, rest pain, and ulcer) I70.663
          ▶rest pain (and intermittent claudication) I70.623
        ▶left I70.622
         ▶with
          ▶gangrene (and intermittent claudication, rest pain, and ulcer) I70.662
          ▶rest pain (and intermittent claudication) I70.622
          ▶ulceration (and intermittent claudication and rest pain) I70.649
           ▶ankle I70.643
           ▶calf I70.642

Arteriosclerosis, arteriosclerotic (Continued)
  chronic limb-threatening ischemia (Continued)
    critical limb ischemia (Continued)
      bypass graft (Continued)
       nonbiological graft (Continued)
        leg (Continued)
         left (Continued)
          with (Continued)
           ulceration (Continued)
            ▶foot site NEC I70.645
            ▶heel I70.644
            ▶lower leg NEC I70.648
            ▶midfoot I70.644
            ▶thigh I70.641
        ▶right I70.621
         ▶with
          ▶gangrene (and intermittent claudication, rest pain, and ulcer) I70.661
          ▶rest pain (and intermittent claudication) I70.621
          ▶ulceration (and intermittent claudication and rest pain) I70.639
           ▶ankle I70.633
           ▶calf I70.632
           ▶foot site NEC I70.635
           ▶heel I70.634
           ▶lower leg NEC I70.638
           ▶midfoot I70.634
           ▶thigh I70.631
      ▶specified graft NEC I70.729
       ▶leg I70.729
        ▶with
         ▶gangrene (and intermittent claudication, rest pain, and ulcer) I70.769
         ▶rest pain (and intermittent claudication) I70.729
        ▶bilateral I70.723
         ▶with
          ▶gangrene (and intermittent claudication, rest pain, and ulcer) I70.763
          ▶rest pain (and intermittent claudication) I70.723
        ▶left I70.722
         ▶with
          ▶gangrene (and intermittent claudication, rest pain, and ulcer) I70.762
          ▶rest pain (and intermittent claudication) I70.722
          ▶ulceration (and intermittent claudication and rest pain) I70.749
           ▶ankle I70.743
           ▶calf I70.742
           ▶foot site NEC I70.745
           ▶heel I70.744
           ▶lower leg NEC I70.748
           ▶midfoot I70.744
           ▶thigh I70.741
        ▶right I70.721
         ▶with
          ▶gangrene (and intermittent claudication, rest pain, and ulcer) I70.761
          ▶rest pain (and intermittent claudication) I70.721
          ▶ulceration (and intermittent claudication and rest pain) I70.739
           ▶ankle I70.733
           ▶calf I70.732
           ▶foot site NEC I70.735
           ▶heel I70.734
           ▶lower leg NEC I70.738
           ▶midfoot I70.734
           ▶thigh I70.731

Arteriosclerosis, arteriosclerotic (Continued)
  chronic limb-threatening ischemia (Continued)
    critical limb ischemia (Continued)
      ▶leg I70.229
       ▶with
        ▶gangrene (and intermittent claudication, rest pain, and ulcer) I70.269
        ▶rest pain (and intermittent claudication) I70.229
      ▶bilateral I70.223
       ▶with
        ▶gangrene (and intermittent claudication, rest pain, and ulcer) I70.263
        ▶rest pain (and intermittent claudication) I70.223
      ▶left I70.222
       ▶with
        ▶gangrene (and intermittent claudication, rest pain, and ulcer) I70.262
        ▶rest pain (and intermittent claudication) I70.222
        ▶ulceration (and intermittent claudication and rest pain) I70.249
         ▶ankle I70.243
         ▶calf I70.242
         ▶foot site NEC I70.245
         ▶heel I70.244
         ▶lower leg NEC I70.248
         ▶midfoot I70.244
         ▶thigh I70.241
      ▶right I70.221
       ▶with
        ▶gangrene (and intermittent claudication, rest pain, and ulcer) I70.261
        ▶rest pain (and intermittent claudication) I70.221
        ▶ulceration (and intermittent claudication and rest pain) I70.239
         ▶ankle I70.233
         ▶calf I70.232
         ▶foot site NEC I70.235
         ▶heel I70.234
         ▶lower leg NEC I70.238
         ▶midfoot I70.234
         ▶thigh I70.231
  aorta I70.0
  arteries of extremities —see Arteriosclerosis, extremities
  ▶with
    ▶chronic limb-threatening ischemia —see Arteriosclerosis, with critical limb ischemia
    ▶critical limb ischemia —see Arteriosclerosis, with critical limb ischemia
  brain I67.2
  bypass graft
  ▶with
    ▶chronic limb-threatening ischemia —see Arteriosclerosis, with critical limb ischemia
    ▶critical limb ischemia —see Arteriosclerosis, with critical limb ischemia
    coronary —see Arteriosclerosis, coronary, bypass graft
    extremities —see Arteriosclerosis, extremities, bypass graft
  cardiac —see Disease, heart, ischemic, atherosclerotic
  cardiopathy —see Disease, heart, ischemic, atherosclerotic
  cardiorenal —see Hypertension, cardiorenal

▶ New   ⇒ Revised   ~~deleted~~ Deleted   ● Use Additional Character(s)

Arteriosclerosis, arteriosclerotic *(Continued)*
  cardiovascular —*see* Disease, heart, ischemic, atherosclerotic
  carotid —*see also* Occlusion, artery, carotid I65.2-●
  central nervous system I67.2
  cerebral I67.2
  cerebrovascular I67.2
  coronary (artery) I25.10
    bypass graft I25.810
      with
        angina pectoris I25.709
          with documented spasm I25.701
          specified type NEC I25.708
          unstable I25.700
        ischemic chest pain I25.709
    autologous artery I25.810
      with
        angina pectoris I25.729
          with documented spasm I25.721
          specified type I25.728
          unstable I25.720
        ischemic chest pain I25.729
    autologous vein I25.810
      with
        angina pectoris I25.719
          with documented spasm I25.711
          specified type I25.718
          unstable I25.710
        ischemic chest pain I25.719
    nonautologous biological I25.810
      with
        angina pectoris I25.739
          with documented spasm I25.731
          specified type I25.738
          unstable I25.730
        ischemic chest pain I25.739
    specified type NEC I25.810
      with
        angina pectoris I25.799
          with documented spasm I25.791
          specified type I25.798
          unstable I25.790
        ischemic chest pain I25.799
    due to
      calcified coronary lesion (severely) I25.84
      lipid rich plaque I25.83
    native vessel
      with
        angina pectoris I25.119
          with documented spasm I25.111
          specified type NEC I25.118
          unstable I25.110
        ischemic chest pain I25.119
    transplanted heart I25.811
      bypass graft I25.812
        with
          angina pectoris I25.769
            with documented spasm I25.761
            specified type I25.768
            unstable I25.760
          ischemic chest pain I25.769
      native coronary artery I25.811
        with
          angina pectoris I25.759
            with documented spasm I25.751
            specified type I25.758
            unstable I25.750
          ischemic chest pain I25.759
  extremities (native arteries) I70.209
    ▶with
      ▶chronic limb-threatening ischemia —*see*
        Arteriosclerosis, with critical limb ischemia
      ▶critical limb ischemia —*see*
        Arteriosclerosis, with critical limb ischemia

Arteriosclerosis, arteriosclerotic *(Continued)*
  extremities *(Continued)*
    bypass graft I70.309
    ▶with
      ▶chronic limb-threatening ischemia —*see* Arteriosclerosis, with critical limb ischemia
      ▶critical limb ischemia —*see* Arteriosclerosis, with critical limb ischemia
    autologous vein graft I70.409
      leg I70.409
        with
          gangrene (and intermittent claudication, rest pain and ulcer) I70.469
          intermittent claudication I70.419
          rest pain (and intermittent claudication) I70.429
        bilateral I70.403
          with
            gangrene (and intermittent claudication, rest pain and ulcer) I70.463
            intermittent claudication I70.413
            rest pain (and intermittent claudication) I70.423
          specified type NEC I70.493
        left I70.402
          with
            gangrene (and intermittent claudication, rest pain and ulcer) I70.462
            intermittent claudication I70.412
            rest pain (and intermittent claudication) I70.422
            ulceration (and intermittent claudication and rest pain) I70.449
              ankle I70.443
              calf I70.442
              foot site NEC I70.445
              heel I70.444
              lower leg NEC I70.448
              midfoot I70.444
              thigh I70.441
          specified type NEC I70.492
        right I70.401
          with
            gangrene (and intermittent claudication, rest pain and ulcer) I70.461
            intermittent claudication I70.411
            rest pain (and intermittent claudication) I70.421
            ulceration (and intermittent claudication and rest pain) I70.439
              ankle I70.433
              calf I70.432
              foot site NEC I70.435
              heel I70.434
              lower leg NEC I70.438
              midfoot I70.434
              thigh I70.431
          specified type NEC I70.491
      specified type NEC I70.499
    specified NEC I70.408
      with
        gangrene (and intermittent claudication, rest pain and ulcer) I70.468
        intermittent claudication I70.418
        rest pain (and intermittent claudication) I70.428
        ulceration (and intermittent claudication and rest pain) I70.45
      specified type NEC I70.498

Arteriosclerosis, arteriosclerotic *(Continued)*
  extremities *(Continued)*
    bypass graft *(Continued)*
      leg I70.309
        with
          gangrene (and intermittent claudication, rest pain and ulcer) I70.369
          intermittent claudication I70.319
          rest pain (and intermittent claudication) I70.329
        bilateral I70.303
          with
            gangrene (and intermittent claudication, rest pain and ulcer) I70.363
            intermittent claudication I70.313
            rest pain (and intermittent claudication) I70.323
          specified type NEC I70.393
        left I70.302
          with
            gangrene (and intermittent claudication, rest pain and ulcer) I70.362
            intermittent claudication I70.312
            rest pain (and intermittent claudication) I70.322
            ulceration (and intermittent claudication and rest pain) I70.349
              ankle I70.343
              calf I70.342
              foot site NEC I70.345
              heel I70.344
              lower leg NEC I70.348
              midfoot I70.344
              thigh I70.341
          specified type NEC I70.392
        right I70.301
          with
            gangrene (and intermittent claudication, rest pain and ulcer) I70.361
            intermittent claudication I70.311
            rest pain (and intermittent claudication) I70.321
            ulceration (and intermittent claudication and rest pain) I70.339
              ankle I70.333
              calf I70.332
              foot site NEC I70.335
              heel I70.334
              lower leg NEC I70.338
              midfoot I70.334
              thigh I70.331
          specified type NEC I70.391
      specified type NEC I70.399
    nonautologous biological graft I70.509
      leg I70.509
        with
          gangrene (and intermittent claudication, rest pain and ulcer) I70.569
          intermittent claudication I70.519
          rest pain (and intermittent claudication) I70.529
        bilateral I70.503
          with
            gangrene (and intermittent claudication, rest pain and ulcer) I70.563
            intermittent claudication I70.513
            rest pain (and intermittent claudication) I70.523
          specified type NEC I70.593

Arteriosclerosis, arteriosclerotic (Continued)
  extremities (Continued)
    bypass graft (Continued)
      nonautologous biological graft
          (Continued)
        leg (Continued)
          left I70.502
            with
              gangrene (and intermittent
                  claudication, rest pain and
                  ulcer) I70.562
              intermittent claudication
                  I70.512
              rest pain (and intermittent
                  claudication) I70.522
              ulceration (and intermittent
                  claudication and rest
                  pain) I70.549
                ankle I70.543
                calf I70.542
                foot site NEC I70.545
                heel I70.544
                lower leg NEC I70.548
                midfoot I70.544
                thigh I70.541
              specified type NEC
                  I70.592
          right I70.501
            with
              gangrene (and intermittent
                  claudication, rest pain and
                  ulcer) I70.561
              intermittent claudication
                  I70.511
              rest pain (and intermittent
                  claudication) I70.521
              ulceration (and intermittent
                  claudication and rest
                  pain) I70.539
                ankle I70.533
                calf I70.532
                foot site NEC I70.535
                heel I70.534
                lower leg NEC I70.538
                midfoot I70.534
                thigh I70.531
              specified type NEC I70.591
          specified type NEC I70.599
        specified NEC I70.508
          with
            gangrene (and intermittent
                claudication, rest pain and
                ulcer) I70.568
            intermittent claudication
                I70.518
            rest pain (and intermittent
                claudication) I70.528
            ulceration (and intermittent
                claudication and rest pain)
                I70.55
          specified type NEC I70.598
      nonbiological graft I70.609
        leg I70.609
          with
            gangrene (and intermittent
                claudication, rest pain and
                ulcer) I70.669
            intermittent claudication
                I70.619
            rest pain (and intermittent
                claudication) I70.629
          bilateral I70.603
            with
              gangrene (and intermittent
                  claudication, rest pain and
                  ulcer) I70.663
              intermittent claudication
                  I70.613
              rest pain (and intermittent
                  claudication) I70.623
            specified type NEC I70.693

Arteriosclerosis, arteriosclerotic (Continued)
  extremities (Continued)
    bypass graft (Continued)
      nonbiological graft (Continued)
        leg (Continued)
          left I70.602
            with
              gangrene (and intermittent
                  claudication, rest pain and
                  ulcer) I70.662
              intermittent claudication
                  I70.612
              rest pain (and intermittent
                  claudication) I70.622
              ulceration (and intermittent
                  claudication and rest
                  pain) I70.649
                ankle I70.643
                calf I70.642
                foot site NEC I70.645
                heel I70.644
                lower leg NEC I70.648
                midfoot I70.644
                thigh I70.641
              specified type NEC I70.692
          right I70.601
            with
              gangrene (and intermittent
                  claudication, rest pain and
                  ulcer) I70.661
              intermittent claudication
                  I70.611
              rest pain (and intermittent
                  claudication) I70.621
              ulceration (and intermittent
                  claudication and rest
                  pain) I70.639
                ankle I70.633
                calf I70.632
                foot site NEC I70.635
                heel I70.634
                lower leg NEC I70.638
                midfoot I70.634
                thigh I70.631
              specified type NEC I70.691
          specified type NEC I70.699
        specified NEC I70.608
          with
            gangrene (and intermittent
                claudication, rest pain and
                ulcer) I70.668
            intermittent claudication I70.618
            rest pain (and intermittent
                claudication) I70.628
            ulceration (and intermittent
                claudication and rest pain)
                I70.65
          specified type NEC I70.698
      specified graft NEC I70.709
        leg I70.709
          with
            gangrene (and intermittent
                claudication, rest pain and
                ulcer) I70.769
            intermittent claudication I70.719
            rest pain (and intermittent
                claudication) I70.729
          bilateral I70.703
            with
              gangrene (and intermittent
                  claudication, rest pain and
                  ulcer) I70.763
              intermittent claudication I70.713
              rest pain (and intermittent
                  claudication) I70.723
            specified type NEC I70.793
          left I70.702
            with
              gangrene (and intermittent
                  claudication, rest pain and
                  ulcer) I70.762

Arteriosclerosis, arteriosclerotic (Continued)
  extremities (Continued)
    bypass graft (Continued)
      specified graft NEC (Continued)
        leg (Continued)
          left (Continued)
            with (Continued)
              intermittent claudication I70.712
              rest pain (and intermittent
                  claudication) I70.722
              ulceration (and intermittent
                  claudication and rest
                  pain) I70.749
                ankle I70.743
                calf I70.742
                foot site NEC I70.745
                heel I70.744
                lower leg NEC I70.748
                midfoot I70.744
                thigh I70.741
              specified type NEC I70.792
          right I70.701
            with
              gangrene (and intermittent
                  claudication, rest pain and
                  ulcer) I70.761
              intermittent claudication I70.711
              rest pain (and intermittent
                  claudication) I70.721
              ulceration (and intermittent
                  claudication and rest
                  pain) I70.739
                ankle I70.733
                calf I70.732
                foot site NEC I70.735
                heel I70.734
                lower leg NEC I70.738
                midfoot I70.734
                thigh I70.731
              specified type NEC I70.791
          specified type NEC I70.799
        specified NEC I70.708
          with
            gangrene (and intermittent
                claudication, rest pain and
                ulcer) I70.768
            intermittent claudication I70.718
            rest pain (and intermittent
                claudication) I70.728
            ulceration (and intermittent
                claudication and rest pain)
                I70.75
          specified type NEC I70.798
      specified NEC I70.308
        with
          gangrene (and intermittent
              claudication, rest pain and
              ulcer) I70.368
          intermittent claudication I70.318
          rest pain (and intermittent
              claudication) I70.328
          ulceration (and intermittent
              claudication and rest pain)
              I70.35
        specified type NEC I70.398
    leg I70.209
      with
        gangrene (and intermittent
            claudication, rest pain and ulcer)
            I70.269
        intermittent claudication I70.219
        rest pain (and intermittent
            claudication) I70.229
      bilateral I70.203
        with
          gangrene (and intermittent
              claudication, rest pain and
              ulcer) I70.263
          intermittent claudication I70.213
          rest pain (and intermittent
              claudication) I70.223
        specified type NEC I70.293

▶ New   ⮕ Revised   ~~deleted~~ Deleted   ● Use Additional Character(s)

Arteriosclerosis, arteriosclerotic (Continued)
  extremities (Continued)
    leg (Continued)
      left I70.202
        with
          gangrene (and intermittent
            claudication, rest pain and
            ulcer) I70.262
          intermittent claudication I70.212
          rest pain (and intermittent
            claudication) I70.222
          ulceration (and intermittent
            claudication and rest pain)
            I70.249
            ankle I70.243
            calf I70.242
            foot site NEC I70.245
            heel I70.244
            lower leg NEC I70.248
            midfoot I70.244
            thigh I70.241
        specified type NEC I70.292
      right I70.201
        with
          gangrene (and intermittent
            claudication, rest pain and
            ulcer) I70.261
          intermittent claudication I70.211
          rest pain (and intermittent
            claudication) I70.221
          ulceration (and intermittent
            claudication and rest pain)
            I70.239
            ankle I70.233
            calf I70.232
            foot site NEC I70.235
            heel I70.234
            lower leg NEC I70.238
            midfoot I70.234
            thigh I70.231
        specified type NEC I70.291
      specified type NEC I70.299
    specified site NEC I70.208
      with
        gangrene (and intermittent claudication,
          rest pain and ulcer) I70.268
        intermittent claudication I70.218
        rest pain (and intermittent
          claudication) I70.228
        ulceration (and intermittent
          claudication and rest pain) I70.25
      specified type NEC I70.298
  generalized I70.91
  heart (disease) —see Arteriosclerosis,
    coronary (artery)
  kidney —see Hypertension, kidney
  medial —see Arteriosclerosis, extremities
  mesenteric (artery) K55.1
  Mönckeberg's —see Arteriosclerosis,
    extremities
  myocarditis I51.4
  peripheral (of extremities) —see
    Arteriosclerosis, extremities
  pulmonary (idiopathic) I27.0
  renal (arterioles) —see also Hypertension,
    kidney
    artery I70.1
  retina (vascular) I70.8 [H35.0-●]
  specified artery NEC I70.8
  spinal (cord) G95.19
  vertebral (artery) I67.2
Arteriospasm I73.9
Arteriovenous —see condition
Arteritis I77.6
  allergic M31.0
  aorta (nonsyphilitic) I77.6
    syphilitic A52.02
  aortic arch M31.4
  brachiocephalic M31.4
  brain I67.7
    syphilitic A52.04

Arteritis (Continued)
  cerebral I67.7
  in
      diseases classified elsewhere I68.2
      systemic lupus erythematosus M32.19
    listerial A32.89
    syphilitic A52.04
    tuberculous A18.89
  coronary (artery) I25.89
    rheumatic I01.8
      chronic I09.89
    syphilitic A52.06
  cranial (left) (right), giant cell M31.6
  deformans —see Arteriosclerosis
  giant cell NEC M31.6
    with polymyalgia rheumatica M31.5
  necrosing or necrotizing M31.9
    specified NEC M31.8
  nodosa M30.0
  obliterans —see Arteriosclerosis
  pulmonary I28.8
  rheumatic —see Fever, rheumatic
  senile —see Arteriosclerosis
  suppurative I77.2
  syphilitic (general) A52.09
    brain A52.04
    coronary A52.06
    spinal A52.09
  temporal, giant cell M31.6
  young female aortic arch syndrome M31.4
Artery, arterial —see also condition
  abscess I77.89
  single umbilical Q27.0
Arthralgia (allergic) —see also Pain, joint
  in caisson disease T70.3
  temporomandibular M26.62
Arthritis, arthritic (acute) (chronic)
    (nonpyogenic) (subacute) M19.90
  allergic —see Arthritis, specified form NEC
  ankylosing (crippling) (spine) —see also
      Spondylitis, ankylosing
    sites other than spine —see Arthritis,
        specified form NEC
  atrophic —see Osteoarthritis
    spine —see Spondylitis, ankylosing
  back —see Spondylopathy, inflammatory
  blennorrhagic (gonococcal) A54.42
  Charcot's —see Arthropathy, neuropathic
    diabetic —see Diabetes, arthropathy,
        neuropathic
    syringomyelic G95.0
  chylous (filarial) —see also category M01 B74.9
  climacteric (any site) NEC —see Arthritis,
      specified form NEC
  crystal (-induced) —see Arthritis, in, crystals
  deformans —see Osteoarthritis
  degenerative —see Osteoarthritis
  due to or associated with
    acromegaly E22.0
    brucellosis —see Brucellosis
    caisson disease T70.3
    diabetes —see Diabetes, arthropathy
    dracontiasis —see also category M01 B72
    enteritis NEC
      regional —see Enteritis, regional
      erysipelas —see also category M01 A46
    erythema
      epidemic A25.1
      nodosum L52
    filariasis NOS B74.9
    glanders A24.0
    helminthiasis —see also category M01 B83.9
    hemophilia D66 [M36.2]
    Henoch-(Schönlein) purpura D69.0 [M36.4]
    human parvovirus —see also category M01
      B97.6
    infectious disease NEC —see category M01
    leprosy (see also category M01) —see also
        Leprosy A30.9
    Lyme disease A69.23
    mycobacteria —see also category M01 A31.8

Arthritis, arthritic (Continued)
  due to or associated with (Continued)
    parasitic disease NEC —see also category
        M01 B89
    paratyphoid fever (see also category M01)
        —see also Fever, paratyphoid A01.4
    rat bite fever —see also category M01 A25.1
    regional enteritis —see Enteritis, regional
    respiratory disorder NOS J98.9
    serum sickness —see also Reaction, serum
        T80.69
    syringomyelia G95.0
    typhoid fever A01.04
  epidemic erythema A25.1
  febrile —see Fever, rheumatic
  gonococcal A54.42
  gouty (acute) —see Gout
  in (due to)
    acromegaly —see also subcategory
        M14.8-● E22.0
    amyloidosis —see also subcategory
        M14.8-● E85.4
    bacterial disease —see also subcategory
        M01 A49.9
    Behçet's syndrome M35.2
    caisson disease —see also subcategory
        M14.8-● T70.3
    coliform bacilli (Escherichia coli) —see
        Arthritis, in, pyogenic organism NEC
    crystals M11.9
      dicalcium phosphate —see Arthritis, in,
          crystals, specified type NEC
      hydroxyapatite M11.0-●
      pyrophosphate —see Arthritis, in,
          crystals, specified type NEC
      specified type NEC M11.80
        ankle M11.87-●
        elbow M11.82-●
        foot joint M11.87-●
        hand joint M11.84-●
        hip M11.85-●
        knee M11.86-●
        multiple sites M11.8-●
        shoulder M11.81-●
        vertebrae M11.88
        wrist M11.83-●
    dermatoarthritis, lipoid E78.81
    dracontiasis (dracunculiasis) —see also
        category M01 B72
    endocrine disorder NEC —see also
        subcategory M14.8-● E34.9
    enteritis, infectious NEC —see also category
        M01 A09
      specified organism NEC —see also
          category M01 A08.8
    erythema
      multiforme —see also subcategory
          M14.8-● L51.9
      nodosum —see also subcategory M14.8-●
          L52
    gout —see Gout
    helminthiasis NEC —see also category M01
        B83.9
    hemochromatosis —see also subcategory
        M14.8-● E83.118
    hemoglobinopathy NEC D58.2 [M36.3]
    hemophilia NEC D66 [M36.2]
    Hemophilus influenzae M00.8-● [B96.3]
    Henoch(-Schönlein) purpura D69.0 [M36.4]
    hyperparathyroidism NEC —see also
        subcategory M14.8-● E21.3
    hypersensitivity reaction NEC T78.49
        [M36.4]
    hypogammaglobulinemia —see also
        subcategory M14.8-● D80.1
    hypothyroidism NEC —see also
        subcategory M14.8-● E03.9
    infection —see Arthritis, pyogenic or
        pyemic
      spine —see Spondylopathy, infective
    infectious disease NEC —see category M01

Arthritis, arthritic *(Continued)*
  in *(Continued)*
    leprosy —*see also* category M01 A30.9
    leukemia NEC C95.9-• *[M36.1]*
    lipoid dermatoarthritis E78.81
    Lyme disease A69.23
    Mediterranean fever, familial —*see also* subcategory M14.8-• M04.1
    Meningococcus A39.83
    metabolic disorder NEC —*see also* subcategory M14.8-• E88.9
    multiple myelomatosis C90.0-• *[M36.1]*
    mumps B26.85
    mycosis NEC —*see also* category M01 B49
    myelomatosis (multiple) C90.0-• *[M36.1]*
    neurological disorder NEC G98.0
    ochronosis —*see also* subcategory M14.8-• E70.29
    O'nyong-nyong —*see also* category M01 A92.1
    parasitic disease NEC —*see also* category M01 B89
    paratyphoid fever —*see also* category M01 A01.4
    Pseudomonas —*see* Arthritis, pyogenic, bacterial NEC
    psoriasis L40.50
    pyogenic organism NEC —*see* Arthritis, pyogenic, bacterial NEC
    Reiter's disease —*see* Reiter's disease
    respiratory disorder NEC —*see also* subcategory M14.8-• J98.9
    reticulosis, malignant —*see also* subcategory M14.8-• C86.0
    rubella B06.82
    Salmonella (arizonae) (cholerae-suis) (enteritidis) (typhimurium) A02.23
    sarcoidosis D86.86
    specified bacteria NEC —*see* Arthritis, pyogenic, bacterial NEC
    sporotrichosis B42.82
    syringomyelia G95.0
    thalassemia NEC D56.9 *[M36.3]*
    tuberculosis —*see* Tuberculosis, arthritis
    typhoid fever A01.04
    urethritis, Reiter's —*see* Reiter's disease
    viral disease NEC —*see also* category M01 B34.9
  infectious or infective —*see also* Arthritis, pyogenic or pyemic
    spine —*see* Spondylopathy, infective
  juvenile M08.90
    with systemic onset —*see* Still's disease
    ankle M08.97-•
    elbow M08.92-•
    foot joint M08.97-•
    hand joint M08.94-•
    hip M08.95-•
    knee M08.96-•
    multiple site M08.99
    pauciarticular M08.40
      ankle M08.47-•
      elbow M08.42-•
      foot joint M08.47-•
      hand joint M08.44-•
      hip M08.45-•
      knee M08.46-•
      shoulder M08.41-•
    ▶ specified site NEC M08.4A
      vertebrae M08.48
      wrist M08.43-•
    psoriatic L40.54
    rheumatoid —*see* Arthritis, rheumatoid, juvenile
    shoulder M08.91-•
   ▶ specified site NEC M08.9A
    specified type NEC M08.80
      ankle M08.87-•
      elbow M08.82-•
      foot joint M08.87-•

Arthritis, arthritic *(Continued)*
  juvenile *(Continued)*
    specified type NEC *(Continued)*
      hand joint M08.84-•
      hip M08.85-•
      knee M08.86-•
      multiple site M08.89
      shoulder M08.81-•
      specified joint NEC M08.88
      vertebrae M08.88
      wrist M08.83-•
    vertebra M08.98
    wrist M08.93-•
  meaning osteoarthritis —*see* Osteoarthritis
  meningococcal A39.83
  menopausal (any site) NEC —*see* Arthritis, specified form NEC
  mutilans (psoriatic) L40.52
  mycotic NEC —*see also* category M01 B49
  neuropathic (Charcot) —*see* Arthropathy, neuropathic
    diabetic —*see* Diabetes, arthropathy, neuropathic
    nonsyphilitic NEC G98.0
    syringomyelic G95.0
  ochronotic —*see also* subcategory M14.8-• E70.29
  palindromic (any site) —*see* Rheumatism, palindromic
  pneumococcal M00.10
    ankle M00.17-•
    elbow M00.12-•
    foot joint —*see* Arthritis, pneumococcal, ankle
    hand joint M00.14-•
    hip M00.15-•
    knee M00.16-•
    multiple site M00.19
    shoulder M00.11-•
    vertebra M00.18
    wrist M00.13-•
  postdysenteric —*see* Arthropathy, postdysenteric
  postmeningococcal A39.84
  postrheumatic, chronic —*see* Arthropathy, postrheumatic, chronic
  primary progressive —*see also* Arthritis, specified form NEC
    spine —*see* Spondylitis, ankylosing
  psoriatic L40.50
  purulent (any site except spine) —*see* Arthritis, pyogenic or pyemic
    spine —*see* Spondylopathy, infective
  pyogenic or pyemic (any site except spine) M00.9
    bacterial NEC M00.80
      ankle M00.87-•
      elbow M00.82-•
      foot joint —*see* Arthritis, pyogenic, bacterial NEC, ankle
      hand joint M00.84-•
      hip M00.85-•
      knee M00.86-•
      multiple site M00.89
      shoulder M00.81-•
      vertebra M00.88
      wrist M00.83-•
    pneumococcal —*see* Arthritis, pneumococcal
    spine —*see* Spondylopathy, infective
    staphylococcal —*see* Arthritis, staphylococcal
    streptococcal —*see* Arthritis, streptococcal NEC
    pneumococcal —*see* Arthritis, pneumococcal
  reactive —*see* Reiter's disease
  rheumatic —*see also* Arthritis, rheumatoid
    acute or subacute —*see* Fever, rheumatic

Arthritis, arthritic *(Continued)*
  rheumatoid M06.9
    with
      carditis —*see* Rheumatoid, carditis
      endocarditis —*see* Rheumatoid, carditis
      heart involvement NEC —*see* Rheumatoid, carditis
      lung involvement —*see* Rheumatoid, lung
      myocarditis —*see* Rheumatoid, carditis
      myopathy —*see* Rheumatoid, myopathy
      pericarditis —*see* Rheumatoid, carditis
      polyneuropathy —*see* Rheumatoid, polyneuropathy
      rheumatoid factor —*see* Arthritis, rheumatoid, seropositive
      splenoadenomegaly and leukopenia — *see* Felty's syndrome
      vasculitis —*see* Rheumatoid, vasculitis
      visceral involvement NEC —*see* Rheumatoid, arthritis, with involvement of organs NEC
    juvenile (with or without rheumatoid factor) M08.00
   ▶ with systemic onset —*see* Still's disease
    ankle M08.07-•
    elbow M08.02-•
    foot joint M08.07-•
    hand joint M08.04-•
    hip M08.05-•
    knee M08.06-•
    multiple site M08.09
    shoulder M08.01-•
   ▶ specified site NEC M08.0A
    vertebra M08.08
    wrist M08.03-•
    seronegative M06.00
      ankle M06.07-•
      elbow M06.02-•
      foot joint M06.07-•
      hand joint M06.04-•
      hip M06.05-•
      knee M06.06-•
      multiple sites M06.09
      shoulder M06.01-•
   ▶ specified site NEC M06.0A
      vertebra M06.08
      wrist M06.03-•
    seropositive M05.9
      without organ involvement M05.70
        ankle M05.77-•
        elbow M05.72-•
        foot joint M05.77-•
        hand joint M05.74-•
        hip M05.75-•
        knee M05.76-•
        multiple sites M05.79
        shoulder M05.71-•
     ▶ specified site NEC M05.7A
        vertebra —*see* Spondylitis, ankylosing
        wrist M05.73-•
    specified NEC M05.80
      ankle M05.87-•
      elbow M05.82-•
      foot joint M05.87-•
      hand joint M05.84-•
      hip M05.85-•
      knee M05.86-•
      multiple sites M05.89
   ▶ specified site NEC M05.8A
      shoulder M05.81-•
      vertebra —*see* Spondylitis, ankylosing
      wrist M05.83-•
    specified type NEC M06.80
      ankle M06.87-•
      elbow M06.82-•
      foot joint M06.87-•
      hand joint M06.84-•
      hip M06.85-•
      knee M06.86-•
      multiple site M06.89
      shoulder M06.81-•

▶ New   ⇒ Revised   ~~deleted~~ Deleted   • Use Additional Character(s)

Arthritis, arthritic *(Continued)*
rheumatoid *(Continued)*
specified type NEC *(Continued)*
▶specified site NEC M06.8A
vertebra M06.88
wrist M06.83-●
spine —*see* Spondylitis, ankylosing
rubella B06.82
scorbutic —*see also* subcategory M14.8-● E54
senile or senescent —*see* Osteoarthritis
septic (any site except spine) —*see* Arthritis,
pyogenic or pyemic
spine —*see* Spondylopathy, infective
serum (nontherapeutic) (therapeutic) —*see*
Arthropathy, postimmunization
specified form NEC M13.80
ankle M13.87-●
elbow M13.82-●
foot joint M13.87-●
hand joint M13.84-●
hip M13.85-●
knee M13.86-●
multiple site M13.89
shoulder M13.81-●
specified joint NEC M13.88
wrist M13.83-●
�B spine —*see also* Spondylosis
infectious or infective NEC —*see*
Spondylopathy, infective
Marie-Strümpell —*see* Spondylitis,
ankylosing
pyogenic —*see* Spondylopathy, infective
rheumatoid —*see* Spondylitis, ankylosing
traumatic (old) —*see* Spondylopathy,
traumatic
tuberculous A18.01
staphylococcal M00.00
ankle M00.07-●
elbow M00.02-●
foot joint —*see* Arthritis, staphylococcal,
ankle
hand joint M00.04-●
hip M00.05-●
knee M00.06-●
multiple site M00.09
shoulder M00.01-●
vertebra M00.08
wrist M00.03-●
streptococcal NEC M00.20
ankle M00.27-●
elbow M00.22-●
foot joint —*see* Arthritis, streptococcal, ankle
hand joint M00.24-●
hip M00.25-●
knee M00.26-●
multiple site M00.29
shoulder M00.21-●
vertebra M00.28
wrist M00.23-●
suppurative —*see* Arthritis, pyogenic or
pyemic
syphilitic (late) A52.16
congenital A50.55 *[M12.80]*
syphilitica deformans (Charcot) A52.16
▶temporomandibular joint M26.65-●
toxic of menopause (any site) —*see* Arthritis,
specified form NEC
transient —*see* Arthropathy, specified form
NEC
traumatic (chronic) —*see* Arthropathy,
traumatic
tuberculous A18.02
spine A18.01
uratic —*see* Gout
urethritica (Reiter's) —*see* Reiter's disease
vertebral —*see* Spondylopathy, inflammatory
villous (any site) —*see* Arthropathy, specified
form NEC
Arthrocele —*see* Effusion, joint
Arthrodesis status Z98.1
Arthrodynia —*see also* Pain, joint

Arthrodysplasia Q74.9
Arthrofibrosis, joint —*see* Ankylosis
Arthrogryposis (congenital) Q68.8
multiplex congenita Q74.3
Arthrokatadysis M24.7
Arthropathy *(see also* Arthritis) M12.9
Charcot's —*see* Arthropathy, neuropathic
diabetic —*see* Diabetes, arthropathy,
neuropathic
syringomyelic G95.0
cricoarytenoid J38.7
crystal(-induced) —*see* Arthritis, in, crystals
diabetic NEC —*see* Diabetes, arthropathy
distal interphalangeal, psoriatic L40.51
enteropathic M07.60
ankle M07.67-●
elbow M07.62-●
foot joint M07.67-●
hand joint M07.64-●
hip M07.65-●
knee M07.66-●
multiple site M07.69
shoulder M07.61-●
vertebra M07.68
wrist M07.63-●
following intestinal bypass M02.00
ankle M02.07-●
elbow M02.02-●
foot joint M02.07-●
hand joint M02.04-●
hip M02.05-●
knee M02.06-●
multiple site M02.09
shoulder M02.01-●
vertebra M02.08
wrist M02.03-●
gouty —*see also* Gout
in (due to)
Lesch-Nyhan syndrome E79.1
[M14.8-●]
sickle-cell disorders D57-● *[M14.8-●]*
hemophilic NEC D66 *[M36.2]*
in (due to)
hyperparathyroidism NEC E21.3
[M14.8-●]
metabolic disease NOS E88.9 *[M14.8-●]*
in (due to)
acromegaly E22.0 *[M14.8-●]*
amyloidosis E85.4 *[M14.8-●]*
blood disorder NOS D75.9 *[M36.3]*
diabetes —*see* Diabetes, arthropathy
endocrine disease NOS E34.9 *[M14.8-●]*
erythema
multiforme L51.9 *[M14.8-●]*
nodosum L52 *[M14.8-●]*
hemochromatosis E83.118 *[M14.8-●]*
hemoglobinopathy NEC D58.2 *[M36.3]*
hemophilia NEC D66 *[M36.2]*
Henoch-Schönlein purpura D69.0 *[M36.4]*
hyperthyroidism E05.90 *[M14.8-●]*
hypothyroidism E03.9 *[M14.8-●]*
infective endocarditis I33.0 *[M12.80]*
leukemia NEC C95.9-● *[M36.1]*
malignant histiocytosis C96.A *[M36.1]*
metabolic disease NOS E88.9 *[M14.8-●]*
multiple myeloma C90.0-● *[M36.1]*
neoplastic disease NOS *(see also* Neoplasm)
D49.9 *[M36.1]*
nutritional deficiency —*see also*
subcategory M14.8-● E63.9
psoriasis NOS L40.50
sarcoidosis D86.86
syphilis (late) A52.77
congenital A50.55 *[M12.80]*
thyrotoxicosis —*see also* subcategory
M14.8-● E05.90
ulcerative colitis K51.90 *[M07.60]*
viral hepatitis (postinfectious) NEC B19.9
[M12.80]
Whipple's disease —*see also* subcategory
M14.8-● K90.81

Arthropathy *(Continued)*
Jaccoud —*see* Arthropathy, postrheumatic,
chronic
juvenile —*see* Arthritis, juvenile
psoriatic L40.54
mutilans (psoriatic) L40.52
neuropathic (Charcot) M14.60
ankle M14.67-●
diabetic —*see* Diabetes, arthropathy,
neuropathic
elbow M14.62-●
foot joint M14.67-●
hand joint M14.64-●
hip M14.65-●
knee M14.66-●
multiple site M14.69
nonsyphilitic NEC G98.0
shoulder M14.61-●
syringomyelic G95.0
vertebra M14.68
wrist M14.63-●
osteopulmonary —*see* Osteoarthropathy,
hypertrophic, specified NEC
postdysenteric M02.10
ankle M02.17-●
elbow M02.12-●
foot joint M02.17-●
hand joint M02.14-●
hip M02.15-●
knee M02.16-●
multiple site M02.19
shoulder M02.11-●
vertebra M02.18
wrist M02.13-●
postimmunization M02.20
ankle M02.27-●
elbow M02.22-●
foot joint M02.27-●
hand joint M02.24-●
hip M02.25-●
knee M02.26-●
multiple site M02.29
shoulder M02.21-●
vertebra M02.28
wrist M02.23-●
postinfectious NEC B99 *[M12.80]*
in (due to)
enteritis due to Yersinia enterocolitica
A04.6 *[M12.80]*
syphilis A52.77
viral hepatitis NEC B19.9 *[M12.80]*
postrheumatic, chronic (Jaccoud)
M12.00
ankle M12.07-●
elbow M12.02-●
foot joint M12.07-●
hand joint M12.04-●
hip M12.05-●
knee M12.06-●
multiple site M12.09
shoulder M12.01-●
specified joint NEC M12.08
vertebrae M12.08
wrist M12.03-●
psoriatic NEC L40.59
interphalangeal, distal L40.51
reactive M02.9
in (due to)
infective endocarditis I33.0
[M02.9]
specified type NEC M02.80
ankle M02.87-●
elbow M02.82-●
foot joint M02.87-●
hand joint M02.84-●
hip M02.85-●
knee M02.86-●
multiple site M02.89
shoulder M02.81-●
vertebra M02.88
wrist M02.83-●

Arthropathy *(Continued)*
  specified form NEC M12.80
    ankle M12.87-●
    elbow M12.82-●
    foot joint M12.87-●
    hand joint M12.84-●
    hip M12.85-●
    knee M12.86-●
    multiple site M12.89
    shoulder M12.81-●
    specified joint NEC M12.88
    vertebrae M12.88
    wrist M12.83-●
  syringomyelic G95.0
  tabes dorsalis A52.16
  tabetic A52.16
▶ temporomandibular joint M26.65-●
  transient —*see* Arthropathy, specified form
      NEC
  traumatic M12.50
    ankle M12.57-●
    elbow M12.52-●
    foot joint M12.57-●
    hand joint M12.54-●
    hip M12.55-●
    knee M12.56-●
    multiple site M12.59
    shoulder M12.51-●
    specified joint NEC M12.58
    vertebrae M12.58
    wrist M12.53-●
Arthropyosis —*see* Arthritis, pyogenic or
    pyemic
Arthrosis (deformans) (degenerative)
    (localized) —*see also* Osteoarthritis
    M19.90
  spine —*see* Spondylosis
Arthus' phenomenon or reaction T78.41
  due to
    drug —*see* Table of Drugs and Chemicals,
      by drug
Articular —*see* condition
Articulation, reverse (teeth) M26.24
Artificial
  insemination complication —*see*
      Complications, artificial, fertilization
  opening status (functioning) (without
      complication) Z93.9
    anus (colostomy) Z93.3
    colostomy Z93.3
    cystostomy Z93.50
      appendico-vesicostomy Z93.52
      cutaneous Z93.51
      specified NEC Z93.59
    enterostomy Z93.4
    gastrostomy Z93.1
    ileostomy Z93.2
    intestinal tract NEC Z93.4
    jejunostomy Z93.4
    nephrostomy Z93.6
    specified site NEC Z93.8
    tracheostomy Z93.0
    ureterostomy Z93.6
    urethrostomy Z93.6
    urinary tract NEC Z93.6
    vagina Z93.8
  vagina status Z93.8
Arytenoid —*see* condition
Asbestosis (occupational) J61
ASC-H (atypical squamous cells cannot exclude
    high grade squamous intraepithelial lesion
    on cytologic smear)
  anus R85.611
  cervix R87.611
  vagina R87.621
ASC-US (atypical squamous cells of
    undetermined significance on cytologic
    smear)
  anus R85.610
  cervix R87.610
  vagina R87.620

Ascariasis B77.9
  with
    complications NEC B77.89
    intestinal complications B77.0
    pneumonia, pneumonitis B77.81
Ascaridosis, ascaridiasis —*see* Ascariasis
Ascaris (infection) (infestation)
    (lumbricoides) —*see* Ascariasis
Ascending —*see* condition
Aschoff's bodies —*see* Myocarditis, rheumatic
Ascites (abdominal) R18.8
  cardiac —*see also* Failure, heart, right I50.810
  chylous (nonfilarial) I89.8
    filarial —*see* Infestation, filarial
  due to
    cirrhosis, alcoholic K70.31
    hepatitis
      alcoholic K70.11
      chronic active K71.51
    S. japonicum B65.2
  heart —*see also* Failure, heart, right I50.810
  malignant R18.0
  pseudochylous R18.8
  syphilitic A52.74
  tuberculous A18.31
Aseptic —*see* condition
Asherman's syndrome N85.6
Asialia K11.7
Asiatic cholera —*see* Cholera
Asimultagnosia (simultanagnosia) R48.3
Askin's tumor —*see* Neoplasm, connective
    tissue, malignant
Asocial personality F60.2
Asomatognosia R41.4
Aspartylglucosaminuria E77.1
Asperger's disease or syndrome F84.5
Aspergilloma —*see* Aspergillosis
Aspergillosis (with pneumonia) B44.9
  bronchopulmonary, allergic B44.81
  disseminated B44.7
  generalized B44.7
  pulmonary NEC B44.1
    allergic B44.81
    invasive B44.0
  specified NEC B44.89
  tonsillar B44.2
Aspergillus (flavus) (fumigatus) (infection)
    (terreus) —*see* Aspergillosis
Aspermatogenesis —*see* Azoospermia
Aspermia (testis) —*see* Azoospermia
Asphyxia, asphyxiation (by) R09.01
  antenatal P84
  birth P84
  bunny bag —*see* Asphyxia, due to,
      mechanical threat to breathing, trapped
      in bed clothes
  crushing S28.0
  drowning T75.1
  gas, fumes, or vapor —*see* Table of Drugs and
      Chemicals
  inhalation —*see* Inhalation
  intrauterine P84
  local I73.00
    with gangrene I73.01
  mucus —*see also* Foreign body, respiratory
      tract, causing asphyxia
  newborn P84
  pathological R09.01
  postnatal P84
    mechanical —*see* Asphyxia, due to,
        mechanical threat to breathing
  prenatal P84
  reticularis R23.1
  strangulation —*see* Asphyxia, due to,
      mechanical threat to breathing
  submersion T75.1
  traumatic T71.9
    due to
      crushed chest S28.0
      foreign body (in) —*see* Foreign body,
          respiratory tract, causing asphyxia

Asphyxia, asphyxiation *(Continued)*
  traumatic *(Continued)*
    due to *(Continued)*
      low oxygen content of ambient air
          T71.20
        due to
          being trapped in
            low oxygen environment
                T71.29
            in car trunk T71.221
              circumstances undetermined
                  T71.224
              done with intent to harm by
                  another person T71.223
                  self T71.222
            in refrigerator T71.231
              circumstances undetermined
                  T71.234
              done with intent to
                  harm by
                  another person T71.233
                  self T71.232
      cave-in T71.21
    mechanical threat to breathing
        (accidental) T71.191
      circumstances undetermined T71.194
      done with intent to harm by
          another person T71.193
          self T71.192
      hanging T71.161
        circumstances undetermined
            T71.164
        done with intent to harm by
            another person T71.163
            self T71.162
      plastic bag T71.121
        circumstances undetermined T71.124
        done with intent to harm by
            another person T71.123
            self T71.122
      smothering
        in furniture T71.151
          circumstances undetermined
              T71.154
          done with intent to harm by
              another person T71.153
              self T71.152
        under
          another person's body T71.141
            circumstances undetermined
                T71.144
            done with intent to harm
                T71.143
          pillow T71.111
            circumstances undetermined
                T71.114
            done with intent to harm by
                another person T71.113
                self T71.112
        trapped in bed clothes T71.131
          circumstances undetermined
              T71.134
          done with intent to harm by
              another person T71.133
              self T71.132
  vomiting, vomitus —*see* Foreign body,
      respiratory tract, causing asphyxia
Aspiration
  amniotic (clear) fluid (newborn) P24.10
    with
      pneumonia (pneumonitis) P24.11
      respiratory symptoms P24.11
  blood
    newborn (without respiratory symptoms)
        P24.20
      with
        pneumonia (pneumonitis) P24.21
        respiratory symptoms P24.21
    specified age NEC —*see* Foreign body,
        respiratory tract
  bronchitis J69.0

▶ New　⇛ Revised　~~deleted~~ Deleted　● Use Additional Character(s)

Aspiration *(Continued)*
  food or foreign body (with asphyxiation) —
      see Asphyxia, food
  liquor (amnii) (newborn) P24.10
    with
      pneumonia (pneumonitis) P24.11
      respiratory symptoms P24.11
  meconium (newborn) (without respiratory
      symptoms) P24.00
    with
      pneumonitis (pneumonitis) P24.01
      respiratory symptoms P24.01
  milk (newborn) (without respiratory
      symptoms) P24.30
    with
      pneumonia (pneumonitis) P24.31
      respiratory symptoms P24.31
    specified age NEC —*see* Foreign body,
        respiratory tract
  mucus —*see also* Foreign body, by site,
      causing asphyxia
    newborn P24.10
      with
        pneumonia (pneumonitis) P24.11
        respiratory symptoms P24.11
  neonatal P24.9
    specific NEC (without respiratory
        symptoms) P24.80
      with
        pneumonia (pneumonitis) P24.81
        respiratory symptoms P24.81
  newborn P24.9
    specific NEC (without respiratory
        symptoms) P24.80
      with
        pneumonia (pneumonitis) P24.81
        respiratory symptoms P24.81
  pneumonia J69.0
  pneumonitis J69.0
  syndrome of newborn —*see* Aspiration, by
      substance, with pneumonia
  vernix caseosa (newborn) P24.80
    with
      pneumonia (pneumonitis) P24.81
      respiratory symptoms P24.81
  vomitus —*see also* Foreign body, respiratory
      tract
    newborn (without respiratory symptoms)
        P24.30
      with
        pneumonia (pneumonitis) P24.31
        respiratory symptoms P24.31
Asplenia (congenital) Q89.01
  postsurgical Z90.81
Assam fever B55.0
Assault, sexual —*see* Maltreatment
Assmann's focus NEC A15.0
Astasia (-abasia) (hysterical) F44.4
Asteatosis cutis L85.3
Astereognosia, astereognosis R48.1
Asterixis R27.8
  in liver disease K71.3
Asteroid hyalitis —*see* Deposit, crystalline
Asthenia, asthenic R53.1
  cardiac —*see also* Failure, heart I50.9
    psychogenic F45.8
  cardiovascular —*see also* Failure, heart I50.9
    psychogenic F45.8
  heart —*see also* Failure, heart I50.9
    psychogenic F45.8
  hysterical F44.4
  myocardial —*see also* Failure, heart I50.9
    psychogenic F45.8
  nervous F48.8
  neurocirculatory F45.8
  neurotic F48.8
  psychogenic F48.8
  psychoneurotic F48.8
  psychophysiologic F48.8
  reaction (psychophysiologic) F48.8
  senile R54

Asthenopia —*see also* Discomfort, visual
  hysterical F44.6
  psychogenic F44.6
Asthenospermia —*see* Abnormal, specimen,
    male genital organs
Asthma, asthmatic (bronchial) (catarrh)
    (spasmodic) J45.909
  with
    chronic obstructive bronchitis J44.9
      with
        acute lower respiratory infection
            J44.0
        exacerbation (acute) J44.1
    chronic obstructive pulmonary disease
        J44.9
      with
        acute lower respiratory infection
            J44.0
        exacerbation (acute) J44.1
    exacerbation (acute) J45.901
    hay fever —*see* Asthma, allergic extrinsic
    rhinitis, allergic —*see* Asthma, allergic
        extrinsic
    status asthmaticus J45.902
  allergic extrinsic J45.909
    with
      exacerbation (acute) J45.901
      status asthmaticus J45.902
  atopic —*see* Asthma, allergic extrinsic
  cardiac —*see* Failure, ventricular, left
  cardiobronchial I50.1
  childhood J45.909
    with
      exacerbation (acute) J45.901
      status asthmaticus J45.902
  chronic obstructive J44.9
    with
      acute lower respiratory infection J44.0
      exacerbation (acute) J44.1
  collier's J60
  cough variant J45.991
  detergent J69.8
  due to
    detergent J69.8
    inhalation of fumes J68.3
➡ eosinophilic J82.83
  extrinsic, allergic —*see* Asthma, allergic
      extrinsic
  grinder's J62.8
  hay —*see* Asthma, allergic extrinsic
  heart I50.1
  idiosyncratic —*see* Asthma, nonallergic
  intermittent (mild) J45.20
    with
      exacerbation (acute) J45.21
      status asthmaticus J45.22
  intrinsic, nonallergic —*see* Asthma,
      nonallergic
  Kopp's E32.8
  late-onset J45.909
    with
      exacerbation (acute) J45.901
      status asthmaticus J45.902
  mild intermittent J45.20
    with
      exacerbation (acute) J45.21
      status asthmaticus J45.22
  mild persistent J45.30
    with
      exacerbation (acute) J45.31
      status asthmaticus J45.32
  Millar's (laryngismus stridulus) J38.5
  miner's J60
  mixed J45.909
    with
      exacerbation (acute) J45.901
      status asthmaticus J45.902
  moderate persistent J45.40
    with
      exacerbation (acute) J45.41
      status asthmaticus J45.42

Asthma, asthmatic *(Continued)*
  nervous —*see* Asthma, nonallergic
  nonallergic (intrinsic) J45.909
    with
      exacerbation (acute) J45.901
      status asthmaticus J45.902
  persistent
    mild J45.30
      with
        exacerbation (acute) J45.31
        status asthmaticus J45.32
    moderate J45.40
      with
        exacerbation (acute) J45.41
        status asthmaticus J45.42
    severe J45.50
      with
        exacerbation (acute) J45.51
        status asthmaticus J45.52
  platinum J45.998
  pneumoconiotic NEC J64
  potter's J62.8
  predominantly allergic J45.909
  psychogenic F54
➡ pulmonary eosinophilic J82.83
  red cedar J67.8
  Rostan's I50.1
  sandblaster's J62.8
  sequoiosis J67.8
  severe persistent J45.50
    with
      exacerbation (acute) J45.51
      status asthmaticus J45.52
  specified NEC J45.998
  stonemason's J62.8
  thymic E32.8
  tuberculous —*see* Tuberculosis, pulmonary
  Wichmann's (laryngismus stridulus) J38.5
  wood J67.8
Astigmatism (compound) (congenital)
    H52.20-●
  irregular H52.21-●
  regular H52.22-●
Astraphobia F40.220
Astroblastoma
  specified site —*see* Neoplasm, malignant, by
      site
  unspecified site C71.9
Astrocytoma (cystic)
  anaplastic
    specified site —*see* Neoplasm, malignant,
        by site
    unspecified site C71.9
  fibrillary
    specified site —*see* Neoplasm, malignant,
        by site
    unspecified site C71.9
  fibrous
    specified site —*see* Neoplasm, malignant,
        by site
    unspecified site C71.9
  gemistocytic
    specified site —*see* Neoplasm, malignant,
        by site
    unspecified site C71.9
  juvenile
    specified site —*see* Neoplasm, malignant,
        by site
    unspecified site C71.9
  pilocytic
    specified site —*see* Neoplasm, malignant,
        by site
    unspecified site C71.9
  piloid
    specified site —*see* Neoplasm, malignant,
        by site
    unspecified site C71.9
  protoplasmic
    specified site —*see* Neoplasm, malignant,
        by site
    unspecified site C71.9

Astrocytoma *(Continued)*
  specified site NEC —*see* Neoplasm,
    malignant, by site
  subependymal D43.2
    giant cell
      specified site —*see* Neoplasm, uncertain
        behavior, by site
      unspecified site D43.2
    specified site —*see* Neoplasm, uncertain
      behavior, by site
    unspecified site D43.2
  unspecified site C71.9
Astroglioma
  specified site —*see* Neoplasm, malignant, by
    site
  unspecified site C71.9
Asymbolia R48.8
Asymmetry —*see also* Distortion
  between native and reconstructed breast N65.1
  face Q67.0
  jaw (lower) —*see* Anomaly, dentofacial, jaw-
    cranial base relationship, asymmetry
Asynergia, asynergy R27.8
  ventricular I51.89
Asystole (heart) —*see* Arrest, cardiac
At risk
  for
    dental caries Z91.849
      high Z91.843
      low Z91.841
      moderate Z91.842
    falling Z91.81
Ataxia, ataxy, ataxic R27.0
  acute R27.8
▶ autosomal recessive Friedreich G11.11
  brain (hereditary) G11.9
  cerebellar (hereditary) G11.9
    with defective DNA repair G11.3
    alcoholic G31.2
  ➡ early-onset G11.10
    ▶ with
      ▶ essential tremor G11.19
      ▶ myoclonus [Hunt's ataxia] G11.19
      ▶ retained tendon reflexes G11.19
    in
      alcoholism G31.2
      myxedema E03.9 *[G13.2]*
      neoplastic disease —*see also* Neoplasm
        D49.9 *[G32.81]*
      specified disease NEC G32.81
    late-onset (Marie's) G11.2
  cerebral (hereditary) G11.9
  congenital nonprogressive G11.0
  family, familial —*see* Ataxia, hereditary
  following
    cerebrovascular disease I69.993
      cerebral infarction I69.393
      intracerebral hemorrhage I69.193
      nontraumatic intracranial hemorrhage
        NEC I69.293
      specified disease NEC I69.893
      subarachnoid hemorrhage I69.093
  ➡ Friedreich's (heredofamilial) (cerebellar)
    (spinal) G11.11
  gait R26.0
    hysterical F44.4
  general R27.8
  gluten M35.9 *[G32.81]*
    with celiac disease K90.0 *[G32.81]*
  hereditary G11.9
    with neuropathy G60.2
    cerebellar —*see* Ataxia, cerebellar
    spastic G11.4
    specified NEC G11.8
  ➡ spinal (Friedreich's) G11.11
  heredofamilial —*see* Ataxia, hereditary
  ➡ Hunt's G11.19
  hysterical F44.4
  locomotor (progressive) (syphilitic) (partial)
    (spastic) A52.11
    diabetic —*see* Diabetes, ataxia

Ataxia, ataxy, ataxic *(Continued)*
  Marie's (cerebellar) (heredofamilial)
    (late- onset) G11.2
  nonorganic origin F44.4
  nonprogressive, congenital G11.0
  psychogenic F44.4
  Roussy-Lévy G60.0
  Sanger-Brown's (hereditary) G11.2
  spastic hereditary G11.4
  spinal
    ➡ hereditary (Friedreich's) G11.11
      progressive (syphilitic) A52.11
  ➡ spinocerebellar, X-linked recessive
    G11.19
  telangiectasia (Louis-Bar) G11.3
Ataxia-telangiectasia (Louis-Bar) G11.3
Atelectasis (massive) (partial) (pressure)
    (pulmonary) J98.11
  newborn P28.10
    due to resorption P28.11
    partial P28.19
    primary P28.0
    secondary P28.19
  primary (newborn) P28.0
  tuberculous —*see* Tuberculosis, pulmonary
Atelocardia Q24.9
Atelomyelia Q06.1
Atheroembolism
  of
    extremities
      lower I75.02-●
      upper I75.01-●
    kidney I75.81
    specified NEC I75.89
Atheroma, atheromatous —*see also*
    Arteriosclerosis I70.90
  aorta, aortic I70.0
    valve —*see also* Endocarditis,
      aortic I35.8
  aorto-iliac I70.0
  artery —*see* Arteriosclerosis
  basilar (artery) I67.2
  carotid (artery) (common) (internal)
    I67.2
  cerebral (arteries) I67.2
  coronary (artery) I25.10
    with angina pectoris —*see* Arteriosclerosis,
      coronary (artery)
  degeneration —*see* Arteriosclerosis
  heart, cardiac —*see* Disease, heart, ischemic,
    atherosclerotic
  mitral (valve) I34.8
  myocardium, myocardial —*see* Disease, heart,
    ischemic, atherosclerotic
  pulmonary valve (heart) —*see also*
    Endocarditis, pulmonary I37.8
  tricuspid (heart) (valve) I36.8
  valve, valvular —*see* Endocarditis
  vertebral (artery) I67.2
Atheromatosis —*see* Arteriosclerosis
Atherosclerosis —*see also* Arteriosclerosis
  coronary
    artery I25.10
      with angina pectoris —*see*
        Arteriosclerosis, coronary (artery),
      due to
        calcified coronary lesion (severely)
          I25.84
        lipid rich plaque I25.83
  transplanted heart I25.811
    bypass graft I25.812
      with angina pectoris —*see*
        Arteriosclerosis, coronary (artery)
    native coronary artery I25.811
      with angina pectoris —*see*
        Arteriosclerosis, coronary (artery)
Athetosis (acquired) R25.8
  bilateral (congenital) G80.3
  congenital (bilateral) (double) G80.3
  double (congenital) G80.3
  unilateral R25.8

Athlete's
  foot B35.3
  heart I51.7
Athrepsia E41
Athyrea (acquired) —*see also* Hypothyroidism
  congenital E03.1
Atonia, atony, atonic
  bladder (sphincter) (neurogenic) N31.2
  capillary I78.8
  ➡ cecum K59.89
    psychogenic F45.8
  colon —*see* Atony, intestine
  congenital P94.2
  esophagus K22.8
  ➡ intestine K59.89
    psychogenic F45.8
  stomach K31.89
    neurotic or psychogenic F45.8
  uterus (during labor) O62.2
    with hemorrhage (postpartum) O72.1
    postpartum (with hemorrhage) O72.1
      without hemorrhage O75.89
Atopy —*see* History, allergy
Atransferrinemia, congenital E88.09
Atresia, atretic
  alimentary organ or tract NEC Q45.8
    upper Q40.8
  ani, anus, anal (canal) Q42.3
    with fistula Q42.2
  aorta (ring) Q25.29
  aortic (orifice) (valve) Q23.0
    arch Q25.21
    congenital with hypoplasia of ascending
      aorta and defective development of
      left ventricle (with mitral stenosis)
      Q23.4
    in hypoplastic left heart syndrome Q23.4
  aqueduct of Sylvius Q03.0
    with spina bifida —*see* Spina bifida, with
      hydrocephalus
  artery NEC Q27.8
    cerebral Q28.3
    coronary Q24.5
    digestive system Q27.8
    eye Q15.8
    lower limb Q27.8
    pulmonary Q25.5
    specified site NEC Q27.8
    umbilical Q27.0
    upper limb Q27.8
  auditory canal (external) Q16.1
  bile duct (common) (congenital) (hepatic)
    Q44.2
    acquired —*see* Obstruction, bile duct
  bladder (neck) Q64.39
    obstruction Q64.31
  bronchus Q32.4
  cecum Q42.8
  cervix (acquired) N88.2
    congenital Q51.828
    in pregnancy or childbirth —*see* Anomaly,
      cervix, in pregnancy or childbirth
      causing obstructed labor O65.5
  choana Q30.0
  colon Q42.9
    specified NEC Q42.8
  common duct Q44.2
  cricoid cartilage Q31.8
  cystic duct Q44.2
    acquired K82.8
      with obstruction K82.0
  digestive organs NEC Q45.8
  duodenum Q41.0
  ear canal Q16.1
  ejaculatory duct Q55.4
  epiglottis Q31.8
  esophagus Q39.0
    with tracheoesophageal fistula Q39.1
  eustachian tube Q17.8
  fallopian tube (congenital) Q50.6
    acquired N97.1

▶ New   ➡ Revised   ~~deleted~~ Deleted   ● Use Additional Character(s)

Atresia, atretic (*Continued*)
  follicular cyst N83.0-●
  foramen of
    Luschka Q03.1
      with spina bifida —*see* Spina bifida, with
        hydrocephalus
    Magendie Q03.1
      with spina bifida —*see* Spina bifida, with
        hydrocephalus
  gallbladder Q44.1
  genital organ
    external
      female Q52.79
      male Q55.8
    internal
      female Q52.8
      male Q55.8
  glottis Q31.8
  gullet Q39.0
    with tracheoesophageal fistula Q39.1
  heart valve NEC Q24.8
    pulmonary Q22.0
    tricuspid Q22.4
  hymen Q52.3
    acquired (postinfective) N89.6
  ileum Q41.2
  intestine (small) Q41.9
    large Q42.9
      specified NEC Q42.8
  iris, filtration angle Q15.0
  jejunum Q41.1
  lacrimal apparatus Q10.4
  larynx Q31.8
  meatus urinarius Q64.33
  mitral valve Q23.2
    in hypoplastic left heart syndrome Q23.4
  nares (anterior) (posterior) Q30.0
  nasopharynx Q34.8
  nose, nostril Q30.0
    acquired J34.89
  organ or site NEC Q89.8
  osseous meatus (ear) Q16.1
  oviduct (congenital) Q50.6
    acquired N97.1
  parotid duct Q38.4
    acquired K11.8
  pulmonary (artery) Q25.5
    valve Q22.0
  pulmonic Q22.0
  pupil Q13.2
  rectum Q42.1
    with fistula Q42.0
  salivary duct Q38.4
    acquired K11.8
  sublingual duct Q38.4
    acquired K11.8
  submandibular duct Q38.4
    acquired K11.8
  submaxillary duct Q38.4
    acquired K11.8
  thyroid cartilage Q31.8
  trachea Q32.1
  tricuspid valve Q22.4
  ureter Q62.10
    pelvic junction Q62.11
    vesical orifice Q62.12
  ureteropelvic junction Q62.11
  ureterovesical orifice Q62.12
  urethra (valvular) Q64.39
    stricture Q64.32
  urinary tract NEC Q64.8
  uterus Q51.818
    acquired N85.8
  vagina (congenital) Q52.4
    acquired (postinfectional) (senile) N89.5
  vas deferens Q55.3
  vascular NEC Q27.8
    cerebral Q28.3
    digestive system Q27.8
    lower limb Q27.8
    specified site NEC Q27.8
    upper limb Q27.8

Atresia, atretic (*Continued*)
  vein NEC Q27.8
    digestive system Q27.8
    great Q26.8
    lower limb Q27.8
    portal Q26.5
    pulmonary Q26.4
      partial Q26.3
      total Q26.2
    specified site NEC Q27.8
    upper limb Q27.8
  vena cava (inferior) (superior) Q26.8
  vesicourethral orifice Q64.31
  vulva Q52.79
    acquired N90.5
Atrichia, atrichosis —*see* Alopecia
Atrophia —*see also* Atrophy
  cutis senilis L90.8
    due to radiation L57.8
  gyrata of choroid and retina H31.23
  senilis R54
    dermatological L90.8
      due to radiation (nonionizing) (solar)
        L57.8
  unguium L60.3
    congenita Q84.6
Atrophie blanche (en plaque) (de Milian) L95.0
Atrophoderma, atrophodermia (of) L90.9
  diffusum (idiopathic) L90.4
  maculatum L90.8
    et striatum L90.8
      due to syphilis A52.79
    syphilitic A51.39
  neuriticum L90.8
  Pasini and Pierini L90.3
  pigmentosum Q82.1
  reticulatum symmetricum faciei L66.4
  senile L90.8
    due to radiation (nonionizing) (solar) L57.8
  vermiculata (cheeks) L66.4
Atrophy, atrophic (of)
  adrenal (capsule) (gland) E27.49
    primary (autoimmune) E27.1
  alveolar process or ridge (edentulous) K08.20
  anal sphincter (disuse) N81.84
  appendix K38.8
  arteriosclerotic —*see* Arteriosclerosis
  bile duct (common) (hepatic) K83.8
  bladder N32.89
    neurogenic N31.8
  blanche (en plaque) (of Milian) L95.0
  bone (senile) NEC —*see also* Disorder, bone,
    specified type NEC
    due to
      tabes dorsalis (neurogenic) A52.11
  brain (cortex) (progressive) G31.9
    frontotemporal circumscribed G31.01
      [F02.80]
      with behavioral disturbance G31.01
        [F02.81]
    senile NEC G31.1
  breast N64.2
    obstetric —*see* Disorder, breast, specified
      type NEC
  buccal cavity K13.79
  cardiac —*see* Degeneration, myocardial
  cartilage (infectional) (joint) —*see* Disorder,
    cartilage, specified NEC
  cerebellar —*see* Atrophy, brain
  cerebral —*see* Atrophy, brain
  cervix (mucosa) (senile) (uteri) N88.8
    menopausal N95.8
  Charcot-Marie-Tooth G60.0
  choroid (central) (macular) (myopic) (retina)
    H31.10-●
    diffuse secondary H31.12-●
    gyrate H31.23
    senile H31.11-●
  ciliary body —*see* Atrophy, iris
  conjunctiva (senile) H11.89
  corpus cavernosum N48.89

Atrophy, atrophic (*Continued*)
  cortical —*see* Atrophy, brain
  cystic duct K82.8
  Déjérine-Thomas G23.8
  disuse NEC —*see* Atrophy, muscle
  Duchenne-Aran G12.21
  ear H93.8-●
  edentulous alveolar ridge K08.20
  endometrium (senile) N85.8
    cervix N88.8
  enteric K63.89
  epididymis N50.89
  eyeball —*see* Disorder, globe, degenerated
    condition, atrophy
  eyelid (senile) —*see* Disorder, eyelid,
    degenerative
  facial (skin) L90.9
  fallopian tube (senile) N83.32-●
    with ovary N83.33-●
  fascioscapulohumeral (Landouzy-Déjérine)
    G71.02
  fatty, thymus (gland) E32.8
  gallbladder K82.8
  gastric K29.40
    with bleeding K29.41
  gastrointestinal K63.89
  glandular I89.8
  globe H44.52-●
  gum —*see* Recession, gingival
  hair L67.8
  heart (brown) —*see* Degeneration, myocardial
  hemifacial Q67.4
    Romberg G51.8
  infantile E41
    paralysis, acute —*see* Poliomyelitis,
      paralytic
  intestine K63.89
  iris (essential) (progressive) H21.26-●
    specified NEC H21.29
  kidney (senile) (terminal) —*see also* Sclerosis,
    renal N26.1
    congenital or infantile Q60.5
      bilateral Q60.4
      unilateral Q60.3
    hydronephrotic —*see* Hydronephrosis
  lacrimal gland (primary) H04.14-●
    secondary H04.15-●
  Landouzy-Déjérine G71.02
  laryngitis, infective J37.0
  larynx J38.7
  Leber's optic (hereditary) H47.22
  lip K13.0
  liver (yellow) K72.90
    with coma K72.91
    acute, subacute K72.00
      with coma K72.01
    chronic K72.10
      with coma K72.11
  lung (senile) J98.4
  macular (dermatological) L90.8
    syphilitic, skin A51.39
      striated A52.79
  mandible (edentulous) K08.20
    minimal K08.21
    moderate K08.22
    severe K08.23
  maxilla K08.20
    minimal K08.24
    moderate K08.25
    severe K08.26
  muscle, muscular (diffuse) (general)
    (idiopathic) (primary) M62.50
    ankle M62.57-●
    Duchenne-Aran G12.21
    foot M62.57-●
    forearm M62.53-●
    hand M62.54-●
    infantile spinal G12.0
    lower leg M62.56-●
    multiple sites M62.59
    myelopathic —*see* Atrophy, muscle, spinal

Atrophy, atrophic *(Continued)*
  muscle, muscular *(Continued)*
    myotonic G71.11
    neuritic G58.9
    neuropathic (peroneal) (progressive)
        G60.0
    pelvic (disuse) N81.84
    peroneal G60.0
    progressive (bulbar) G12.21
        adult G12.1
        infantile (spinal) G12.0
        spinal G12.25
            adult G12.1
            infantile G12.0
    pseudohypertrophic G71.02
    shoulder region M62.51-•
    specified site NEC M62.58
    spinal G12.9
        adult form G12.1
        Aran-Duchenne G12.21
        childhood form, type II G12.1
        distal G12.1
        hereditary NEC G12.1
        infantile, type I (Werdnig-Hoffmann)
            G12.0
        juvenile form, type III (Kugelberg-
            Welander) G12.1
        progressive G12.25
        scapuloperoneal form G12.1
        specified NEC G12.8
    syphilitic A52.78
    thigh M62.55-•
    upper arm M62.52-•
  myocardium —*see* Degeneration, myocardial
  myometrium (senile) N85.8
    cervix N88.8
  myopathic NEC —*see* Atrophy, muscle
  myotonia G71.11
  nail L60.3
  nasopharynx J31.1
  nerve —*see also* Disorder, nerve
    abducens —*see* Strabismus, paralytic, sixth
        nerve
    accessory G52.8
    acoustic or auditory —*see* subcategory
        H93.3
    cranial G52.9
        eighth (auditory) —*see* subcategory
            H93.3
        eleventh (accessory) G52.8
        fifth (trigeminal) G50.8
        first (olfactory) G52.0
        fourth (trochlear) —*see* Strabismus,
            paralytic, fourth nerve
        second (optic) H47.20
        sixth (abducens) —*see* Strabismus,
            paralytic, sixth nerve
        tenth (pneumogastric) (vagus) G52.2
        third (oculomotor) —*see* Strabismus,
            paralytic, third nerve
        twelfth (hypoglossal) G52.3
    hypoglossal G52.3
    oculomotor —*see* Strabismus, paralytic,
        third nerve
    olfactory G52.0
    optic (papillomacular bundle)
        syphilitic (late) A52.15
            congenital A50.44
    pneumogastric G52.2
    trigeminal G50.8
    trochlear —*see* Strabismus, paralytic,
        fourth nerve
    vagus (pneumogastric) G52.2
  neurogenic, bone, tabetic A52.11
  nutritional E41
  old age R54
  olivopontocerebellar G23.8
  optic (nerve) H47.20
    glaucomatous H47.23-•
    hereditary H47.22
    primary H47.21-•

Atrophy, atrophic *(Continued)*
  optic *(Continued)*
    specified type NEC H47.29-•
    syphilitic (late) A52.15
        congenital A50.44
  orbit H05.31-•
  ovary (senile) N83.31-•
    with fallopian tube N83.33-•
  oviduct (senile) —*see* Atrophy, fallopian tube
  palsy, diffuse (progressive) G12.22
  pancreas (duct) (senile) K86.89
  parotid gland K11.0
  pelvic muscle N81.84
  penis N48.89
  pharynx J39.2
  pluriglandular E31.8
    autoimmune E31.0
  polyarthritis M15.9
  prostate N42.89
  pseudohypertrophic (muscle) G71.02
  renal —*see also* Sclerosis, renal N26.1
  retina, retinal (postinfectional) H35.89
  rhinitis J31.0
  salivary gland K11.0
  scar L90.5
  sclerosis, lobar (of brain) G31.09 *[F02.80]*
    with behavioral disturbance G31.09 *[F02.81]*
  scrotum N50.89
  seminal vesicle N50.89
  senile R54
    due to radiation (nonionizing) (solar) L57.8
  skin (patches) (spots) L90.9
    degenerative (senile) L90.8
    due to radiation (nonionizing) (solar) L57.8
    senile L90.8
  spermatic cord N50.89
  spinal (acute) (cord) G95.89
    muscular —*see* Atrophy, muscle, spinal
    paralysis G12.20
        acute —*see* Poliomyelitis, paralytic
        meaning progressive muscular atrophy
            G12.25
  spine (column) —*see* Spondylopathy,
      specified NEC
  spleen (senile) D73.0
  stomach K29.40
    with bleeding K29.41
  striate (skin) L90.6
    syphilitic A52.79
  subcutaneous L90.9
  sublingual gland K11.0
  submandibular gland K11.0
  submaxillary gland K11.0
  Sudeck's —*see* Algoneurodystrophy
  suprarenal (capsule) (gland) E27.49
    primary E27.1
  systemic affecting central nervous system
      in
        myxedema E03.9 *[G13.2]*
        neoplastic disease —*see also* Neoplasm
            D49.9 *[G13.1]*
        specified disease NEC G13.8
  tarso-orbital fascia, congenital Q10.3
  testis N50.89
  thenar, partial —*see* Syndrome, carpal tunnel
  thymus (fatty) E32.8
  thyroid (gland) (acquired) E03.4
    with cretinism E03.1
    congenital (with myxedema) E03.1
  tongue (senile) K14.8
    papillae K14.4
  trachea J39.8
  tunica vaginalis N50.89
  turbinate J34.89
  tympanic membrane (nonflaccid) H73.82-•
    flaccid H73.81-•
  upper respiratory tract J39.8
  uterus, uterine (senile) N85.8
    cervix N88.8
    due to radiation (intended effect) N85.8
        adverse effect or misadventure N99.89

Atrophy, atrophic *(Continued)*
  vagina (senile) N95.2
  vas deferens N50.89
  vascular I99.8
  vertebra (senile) —*see* Spondylopathy,
      specified NEC
  vulva (senile) N90.5
  Werdnig-Hoffmann G12.0
  yellow —*see* Failure, hepatic
Attack, attacks
  with alteration of consciousness (with
      automatisms) —*see* Epilepsy,
      localization-related, symptomatic, with
      complex partial seizures
  without alteration of consciousness —
      see Epilepsy, localization-related,
      symptomatic, with simple partial
      seizures
  Adams-Stokes I45.9
  akinetic —*see* Epilepsy, generalized, specified
      NEC
  angina —*see* Angina
  atonic —*see* Epilepsy, generalized, specified
      NEC
  benign shuddering G25.83
  cataleptic —*see* Catalepsy
  coronary —*see* Infarct, myocardium
  cyanotic, newborn P28.2
  drop NEC R55
  epileptic —*see* Epilepsy
  heart —*see* infarct, myocardium
  hysterical F44.9
  jacksonian —*see* Epilepsy, localization-
      related, symptomatic, with simple
      partial seizures
  myocardium, myocardial —*see* Infarct,
      myocardium
  myoclonic —*see* Epilepsy, generalized,
      specified NEC
  panic F41.0
  psychomotor —*see* Epilepsy, localization-
      related, symptomatic, with complex
      partial seizures
  salaam —*see* Epilepsy, spasms
  schizophreniform, brief F23
  shuddering, benign G25.83
  Stokes-Adams I45.9
  syncope R55
  transient ischemic (TIA) G45.9
    specified NEC G45.8
  unconsciousness R55
    hysterical F44.89
  vasomotor R55
  vasovagal (paroxysmal) (idiopathic) R55
Attention (to)
  artificial
    opening (of) Z43.9
        digestive tract NEC Z43.4
            colon Z43.3
            ilium Z43.2
            stomach Z43.1
        specified NEC Z43.8
        trachea Z43.0
        urinary tract NEC Z43.6
            cystostomy Z43.5
            nephrostomy Z43.6
            ureterostomy Z43.6
            urethrostomy Z43.6
        vagina Z43.7
  colostomy Z43.3
  cystostomy Z43.5
  deficit disorder or syndrome F98.8
    with hyperactivity —*see* Disorder,
        attention-deficit hyperactivity
  gastrostomy Z43.1
  ileostomy Z43.2
  jejunostomy Z43.4
  nephrostomy Z43.6
  surgical dressings Z48.01
  sutures Z48.02
  tracheostomy Z43.0

▶ New   ⟹ Revised   ~~deleted~~ Deleted   • Use Additional Character(s)

Attention *(Continued)*
 ureterostomy Z43.6
 urethrostomy Z43.6
Attrition
 gum —*see* Recession, gingival
 tooth, teeth (excessive) (hard tissues) K03.0
Atypical, atypism —*see also* condition
 cells (on cytolgocial smear) (endocervical)
  (endometrial) (glandular)
  cervix R87.619
  vagina R87.629
 cervical N87.9
 endometrium N85.9
  hyperplasia N85.00
 parenting situation Z62.9
Auditory —*see* condition
Aujeszky's disease B33.8
Aurantiasis, cutis E67.1
Auricle, auricular —*see also* condition
 cervical Q18.2
Auriculotemporal syndrome G50.8
Austin Flint murmur (aortic insufficiency)
 I35.1
Australian
 Q fever A78
 X disease A83.4
Autism, autistic (childhood) (infantile) F84.0
 atypical F84.9
 spectrum disorder F84.0
Autodigestion R68.89
Autoerythrocyte sensitization (syndrome)
 D69.2
Autographism L50.3
Autoimmune
 disease (systemic) M35.9
 inhibitors to clotting factors D68.311
 lymphoproliferative syndrome [ALPS]
  D89.82
 thyroiditis E06.3
Autointoxication R68.89
Automatism G93.89
 with temporal sclerosis G93.81
 epileptic —*see* Epilepsy, localization- related,
  symptomatic, with complex partial
  seizures
 paroxysmal, idiopathic —*see* Epilepsy,
  localization-related, symptomatic, with
  complex partial seizures

Autonomic, autonomous
 bladder (neurogenic) N31.2
 hysteria seizure F44.5
Autosensitivity, erythrocyte D69.2
Autosensitization, cutaneous L30.2
Autosome —*see* condition by chromosome
 involved
Autotopagnosia R48.1
Autotoxemia R68.89
Autumn —*see* condition
Avellis' syndrome G46.8
Aversion
 oral R63.3
  newborn P92.-●
  nonorganic origin F98.2
 sexual F52.1
Aviator's
 disease or sickness —*see* Effect, adverse, high
  altitude
 ear T70.0
Avitaminosis (multiple) —*see also* Deficiency,
 vitamin E56.9
 B E53.9
  with
   beriberi E51.11
   pellagra E52
 B2 E53.0
 B6 E53.1
 B12 E53.8
 D E55.9
  with rickets E55.0
 G E53.0
 K E56.1
 nicotinic acid E52
AVNRT (atrioventricular nodal re-entrant
 tachycardia) I47.1
AVRT (atrioventricular nodal re-entrant
 tachycardia) I47.1
Avulsion (traumatic)
 blood vessel —*see* Injury, blood vessel
 bone —*see* Fracture, by site
 cartilage —*see also* Dislocation, by site
  symphyseal (inner), complicating delivery
   O71.6
 external site other than limb —*see* Wound,
  open, by site
 eye S05.7-●

Avulsion *(Continued)*
 head (intracranial)
  external site NEC S08.89
  scalp S08.0
 internal organ or site —*see* Injury, by site
 joint —*see also* Dislocation, by site
  capsule —*see* Sprain, by site
 kidney S37.06-●
 ligament —*see* Sprain, by site
 limb —*see also* Amputation, traumatic,
  by site
  skin and subcutaneous tissue —*see* Wound,
   open, by site
 muscle —*see* Injury, muscle
 nerve (root) —*see* Injury, nerve
 scalp S08.0
 skin and subcutaneous tissue —*see* Wound,
  open, by site
 spleen S36.032
 symphyseal cartilage (inner), complicating
  delivery O71.6
 tendon —*see* Injury, muscle
 tooth S03.2
Awareness of heart beat R00.2
Axenfeld's
 anomaly or syndrome Q15.0
 degeneration (calcareous) Q13.4
Axilla, axillary —*see also* condition
 breast Q83.1
Axonotmesis —*see* Injury, nerve
Ayerza's disease or syndrome (pulmonary
  artery sclerosis with pulmonary
  hypertension) I27.0
Azoospermia (organic) N46.01
 due to
  drug therapy N46.021
  efferent duct obstruction N46.023
  infection N46.022
  radiation N46.024
  specified cause NEC N46.029
  systemic disease N46.025
Azotemia R79.89
 meaning uremia N19
Aztec ear Q17.3
Azygos
 continuation inferior vena cava Q26.8
 lobe (lung) Q33.1

B

Baastrup's disease —see Kissing spine
▶ Babesiosis B60.00
  due to
    ▶ Babesia
      ▶ divergens B60.03
      ▶ duncani B60.02
      ▶ KO-1 B60.09
      ▶ microti B60.01
      ▶ MO-1 B60.03
      ▶ species
        ▶ unspecified B60.00
      ▶ venatorum B60.09
    ▶ specified NEC B60.09
Babington's disease (familial hemorrhagic
  telangiectasia) I78.0
Babinski's syndrome A52.79
Baby
  crying constantly R68.11
  floppy (syndrome) P94.2
Bacillary —see condition
Bacilluria R82.71
Bacillus —see also Infection, bacillus
  abortus infection A23.1
  anthracis infection A22.9
  coli infection —see also Escherichia coli B96.20
  Flexner's A03.1
  mallei infection A24.0
  Shiga's A03.0
  suipestifer infection —see Infection, salmonella
Back —see condition
Backache (postural) M54.9
  sacroiliac M53.3
  specified NEC M54.89
Backflow —see Reflux
Backward reading (dyslexia) F81.0
Bacteremia R78.81
  with sepsis —see Sepsis
Bactericholia —see Cholecystitis, acute
Bacterid, bacteride (pustular) L40.3
Bacterium, bacteria, bacterial
  agent NEC, as cause of disease classified
    elsewhere B96.89
  in blood —see Bacteremia
  in urine —see Bacteriuria
Bacteriuria, bacteruria R82.71
  asymptomatic R82.71
Bacteroides
  fragilis, as cause of disease classified
    elsewhere B96.6
Bad
  heart —see Disease, heart
  trip
    due to drug abuse —see Abuse, drug,
      hallucinogen
    due to drug dependence —see Dependence,
      drug, hallucinogen
Baelz's disease (cheilitis glandularis
  apostematosa) K13.0
Baerensprung's disease (eczema marginatum)
  B35.6
Bagasse disease or pneumonitis J67.1
Bagassosis J67.1
Baker's cyst —see Cyst, Baker's
Bakwin-Krida syndrome (metaphyseal
  dysplasia) Q78.5
Balancing side interference M26.56
Balanitis (circinata) (erosiva) (gangrenosa)
  (phagedenic) (vulgaris) N48.1
  amebic A06.82
  candidal B37.42
  due to Haemophilus ducreyi A57
  gonococcal (acute) (chronic) A54.23
  xerotica obliterans N48.0
Balanoposthitis N47.6
  gonococcal (acute) (chronic) A54.23
  ulcerative (specific) A63.8
Balanorrhagia —see Balanitis
Balantidiasis, balantidiosis A07.0
Bald tongue K14.4

Baldness —see also Alopecia
  male-pattern —see Alopecia, androgenic
Balkan grippe A78
Balloon disease —see Effect, adverse, high
  altitude
Balo's disease (concentric sclerosis) G37.5
Bamberger-Marie disease —see Osteoarthropathy,
  hypertrophic, specified type NEC
Bancroft's filariasis B74.0
Band(s)
  adhesive —see Adhesions, peritoneum
  anomalous or congenital —see also Anomaly,
    by site
    heart (atrial) (ventricular) Q24.8
    intestine Q43.3
    omentum Q43.3
  cervix N88.1
  constricting, congenital Q79.8
  gallbladder (congenital) Q44.1
  intestinal (adhesive) —see Adhesions,
    peritoneum
  obstructive
    intestine K56.50
      complete K56.52
      incomplete K56.51
      partial K56.51
    peritoneum K56.50
      complete K56.52
      incomplete K56.51
      partial K56.51
  periappendiceal, congenital Q43.3
  peritoneal (adhesive) —see Adhesions,
    peritoneum
  uterus N73.6
    internal N85.6
  vagina N89.5
Bandemia D72.825
Bandl's ring (contraction), complicating
  delivery O62.4
Bangkok hemorrhagic fever A91
Bang's disease (brucella abortus) A23.1
Bankruptcy, anxiety concerning Z59.8
Bannister's disease T78.3
  hereditary D84.1
Banti's disease or syndrome (with cirrhosis)
  (with portal hypertension) K76.6
Bar, median, prostate —see Enlargement,
  enlarged, prostate
Barcoo disease or rot —see Ulcer, skin
Barlow's disease E54
Barodontalgia T70.29
Baron Münchausen syndrome —see Disorder,
  factitious
Barosinusitis T70.1
Barotitis T70.0
Barotrauma T70.29
  odontalgia T70.29
  otitic T70.0
  sinus T70.1
Barraquer (-Simons) disease or syndrome
  (progressive lipodystrophy) E88.1
Barré-Guillain disease or syndrome G61.0
Barré-Liéou syndrome (posterior cervical
  sympathetic) M53.0
Barrel chest M95.4
Barrett's
  disease —see Barrett's, esophagus
  esophagus K22.70
    with dysplasia K22.719
      high grade K22.711
      low grade K22.710
    without dysplasia K22.70
  syndrome —see Barrett's, esophagus
  ulcer K22.10
    with bleeding K22.11
    without bleeding K22.10
Barth syndrome E78.71
Bársony (-Polgár) (-Teschendorf) syndrome
  (corkscrew esophagus) K22.4
Bartholinitis (suppurating) N75.8
  gonococcal (acute) (chronic) (with abscess)
    A54.1

Bartonellosis A44.9
  cutaneous A44.1
  mucocutaneous A44.1
  specified NEC A44.8
  systemic A44.0
Barton's fracture S52.56-●
Bartter's syndrome E26.81
Basal —see condition
Basan's (hidrotic) ectodermal dysplasia Q82.4
Baseball finger —see Dislocation, finger
Basedow's disease (exophthalmic goiter) —see
  Hyperthyroidism, with, goiter
Basic —see condition
Basilar —see condition
Bason's (hidrotic) ectodermal dysplasia Q82.4
Basopenia —see Agranulocytosis
Basophilia D72.824
Basophilism (cortico-adrenal) (Cushing's)
  (pituitary) E24.0
Bassen-Kornzweig disease or syndrome E78.6
Bat ear Q17.5
Bateman's
  disease B08.1
  purpura (senile) D69.2
Bathing cramp T75.1
Bathophobia F40.248
Batten (-Mayou) disease E75.4
  retina E75.4 [H36]
Batten-Steiner syndrome G71.11
Battered —see Maltreatment
Battey Mycobacterium infection A31.0
Battle exhaustion F43.0
Battledore placenta O43.19-●
Baumgarten-Cruveilhier cirrhosis, disease or
  syndrome K74.69
Bauxite fibrosis (of lung) J63.1
Bayle's disease (general paresis) A52.17
Bazin's disease (primary) (tuberculous) A18.4
Beach ear —see Swimmer's, ear
Beaded hair (congenital) Q84.1
Béal conjunctivitis or syndrome B30.2
Beard's disease (neurasthenia) F48.8
Beat(s)
  atrial, premature I49.1
  ectopic I49.49
  elbow —see Bursitis, elbow
  escaped, heart I49.49
  hand —see Bursitis, hand
  knee —see Bursitis, knee
  premature I49.40
    atrial I49.1
    auricular I49.1
    supraventricular I49.1
Beau's
  disease or syndrome —see Degeneration,
    myocardial
  lines (transverse furrows on fingernails) L60.4
Bechterev's syndrome —see Spondylitis,
  ankylosing
Beck's syndrome (anterior spinal artery
  occlusion) I65.8
Becker's
  cardiomyopathy I42.8
  disease
    idiopathic mural endomyocardial disease
      I42.3
    myotonia congenita, recessive form G71.12
  dystrophy G71.01
  pigmented hairy nevus D22.5
Beckwith-Wiedemann syndrome Q87.3
Bed confinement status Z74.01
Bed sore —see Ulcer, pressure, by site
Bedbug bite(s) —see Bite(s), by site, superficial,
  insect
Bedclothes, asphyxiation or suffocation
  by —see Asphyxia, traumatic, due to,
    mechanical, trapped
Bednar's
  aphthae K12.0
  tumor —see Neoplasm, malignant, by site
Bedridden Z74.01

▶ New   ⇒ Revised   ~~deleted~~ Deleted   ● Use Additional Character(s)

Bedsore —*see* Ulcer, pressure, by site
Bedwetting —*see* Enuresis
Bee sting (with allergic or anaphylactic shock) —
    see Toxicity, venom, arthropod, bee
Beer drinker's heart (disease) I42.6
Begbie's disease (exophthalmic goiter) —*see*
    Hyperthyroidism, with, goiter
Behavior
    antisocial
        adult Z72.811
        child or adolescent Z72.810
    disorder, disturbance —*see* Disorder, conduct
    disruptive —*see* Disorder, conduct
    drug seeking Z76.5
    inexplicable R46.2
    marked evasiveness R46.5
    obsessive-compulsive R46.81
    overactivity R46.3
    poor responsiveness R46.4
    self-damaging (life-style) Z72.89
    sleep-incompatible Z72.821
    slowness R46.4
    specified NEC R46.89
    strange (and inexplicable) R46.2
    suspiciousness R46.5
    type A pattern Z73.1
    undue concern or preoccupation with
        stressful events R46.6
    verbosity and circumstantial detail obscuring
        reason for contact R46.7
Behcet's disease or syndrome M35.2
Behr's disease —*see* Degeneration, macula
Beigel's disease or morbus (white piedra)
    B36.2
Bejel A65
Bekhterev's syndrome —*see* Spondylitis,
    ankylosing
Belching —*see* Eructation
Bell's
    mania F30.8
    palsy, paralysis G51.0
        infant or newborn P11.3
    spasm G51.3-•
Bence Jones albuminuria or proteinuria NEC
    R80.3
Bends T70.3
Benedikt's paralysis or syndrome G46.3
Benign (*see also* condition)
    prostatic hyperplasia —*see* Hyperplasia,
        prostate
Bennett's fracture (displaced) S62.21-•
Benson's disease —*see* Deposit, crystalline
Bent
    back (hysterical) F44.4
    nose M95.0
        congenital Q67.4
Bereavement (uncomplicated) Z63.4
Bergeron's disease (hysterical chorea) F44.4
Berger's disease —*see* Nephropathy, IgA
Beriberi (dry) E51.11
    heart (disease) E51.12
    polyneuropathy E51.11
    wet E51.12
        involving circulatory system E51.11
Berlin's disease or edema (traumatic) S05.8X-•
Berlock (berloque) dermatitis L56.2
Bernard-Horner syndrome G90.2
Bernard-Soulier disease or thrombopathia D69.1
Bernhardt (-Roth) disease —*see*
    Mononeuropathy, lower limb, meralgia
    paresthetica
Bernheim's syndrome —*see* Failure, heart,
    right
Bertielliasis B71.8
Berylliosis (lung) J63.2
Besnier-Boeck (-Schaumann) disease —*see*
    Sarcoidosis
Besnier's
    lupus pernio D86.3
    prurigo L20.0
Bestiality F65.89
Best's disease H35.50

Beta-mercaptolactate-cysteine disulfiduria
    E72.09
Betalipoproteinemia, broad or floating E78.2
Betting and gambling Z72.6
    pathological (compulsive) F63.0
Bezoar T18.9
    intestine T18.3
    stomach T18.2
Bezold's abscess —*see* Mastoiditis, acute
Bianchi's syndrome R48.8
Bicornate or bicornis uterus Q51.3
    in pregnancy or childbirth O34.00
        causing obstructed labor O65.5
Bicuspid aortic valve Q23.1
Biedl-Bardet syndrome Q87.89
Bielschowsky (-Jansky) disease E75.4
Biermer's (pernicious) anemia or disease D51.0
Biett's disease L93.0
Bifid (congenital)
    apex, heart Q24.8
    clitoris Q52.6
    kidney Q63.8
    nose Q30.2
    patella Q74.1
    scrotum Q55.29
    toe NEC Q74.2
    tongue Q38.3
    ureter Q62.8
    uterus Q51.3
    uvula Q35.7
Biforis uterus (suprasimplex) Q51.3
Bifurcation (congenital)
    gallbladder Q44.1
    kidney pelvis Q63.8
    renal pelvis Q63.8
    rib Q76.6
    tongue, congenital Q38.3
    trachea Q32.1
    ureter Q62.8
    urethra Q64.74
    vertebra Q76.49
Big spleen syndrome D73.1
Bigeminal pulse R00.8
Bilateral —*see* condition
Bile
    duct —*see* condition
    pigments in urine R82.2
Bilharziasis —*see also* Schistosomiasis
    chyluria B65.0
    cutaneous B65.3
    galacturia B65.0
    hematochyluria B65.0
    intestinal B65.1
    lipemia B65.9
    lipuria B65.0
    oriental B65.2
    piarhemia B65.9
    pulmonary NOS B65.9 [J99]
        pneumonia B65.9 [J17]
    tropical hematuria B65.0
    vesical B65.0
Biliary —*see* condition
Bilirubin metabolism disorder E80.7
    specified NEC E80.6
Bilirubinemia, familial nonhemolytic E80.4
Bilirubinuria R82.2
Biliuria R82.2
Bilocular stomach K31.2
Binswanger's disease I67.3
Biparta, bipartite
    carpal scaphoid Q74.0
    patella Q74.1
    vagina Q52.10
Bird
    face Q75.8
    fancier's disease or lung J67.2
Birt-Hogg-Dube syndrome Q87.89
Birth
    complications in mother —*see* Delivery,
        complicated
    compression during NOS P15.9

Birth (*Continued*)
    defect —*see* Anomaly
    immature (less than 37 completed weeks) —
        see Preterm, newborn
        extremely (less than 28 completed
            weeks) —*see* Immaturity, extreme
    inattention, at or after —*see* Maltreatment,
        child, neglect
    injury NOS P15.9
        basal ganglia P11.1
        brachial plexus NEC P14.3
        brain (compression) (pressure) P11.2
        central nervous system NOS P11.9
        cerebellum P11.1
        cerebral hemorrhage P10.1
        external genitalia P15.5
        eye P15.3
        face P15.4
        fracture
            bone P13.9
                specified NEC P13.8
            clavicle P13.4
            femur P13.2
            humerus P13.3
            long bone, except femur P13.3
            radius and ulna P13.3
            skull P13.0
            spine P11.5
            tibia and fibula P13.3
        intracranial P11.2
            laceration or hemorrhage P10.9
                specified NEC P10.8
        intraventricular hemorrhage P10.2
        laceration
            brain P10.1
            by scalpel P15.8
            peripheral nerve P14.9
        liver P15.0
        meninges
            brain P11.1
            spinal cord P11.5
        nerve
            brachial plexus P14.3
            cranial NEC (except facial) P11.4
            facial P11.3
            peripheral P14.9
            phrenic (paralysis) P14.2
        paralysis
            facial nerve P11.3
            spinal P11.5
        penis P15.5
        rupture
            spinal cord P11.5
        scalp P12.9
        scalpel wound P15.8
        scrotum P15.5
        skull NEC P13.1
            fracture P13.0
        specified type NEC P15.8
        spinal cord P11.5
        spine P11.5
        spleen P15.1
        sternomastoid (hematoma) P15.2
        subarachnoid hemorrhage P10.3
        subcutaneous fat necrosis P15.6
        subdural hemorrhage P10.0
        tentorial tear P10.4
        testes P15.5
        vulva P15.5
    lack of care, at or after —*see* Maltreatment,
        child, neglect
    neglect, at or after —*see* Maltreatment, child,
        neglect
    palsy or paralysis, newborn, NOS (birth
        injury) P14.9
    premature (infant) —*see* Preterm, newborn
    shock, newborn P96.89
    trauma —*see* Birth, injury
    weight
        4000 grams to 4499 grams P08.1
        4500 grams or more P08.0

Birth *(Continued)*
  weight *(Continued)*
    low (2499 grams or less) —*see* Low,
      birthweight
        extremely (999 grams or less) —*see* Low,
          birthweight, extreme
Birthmark Q82.5
Bisalbuminemia E88.09
Biskra's button B55.1
Bite(s) (animal) (human)
  abdomen, abdominal
    wall S31.159
      with penetration into peritoneal cavity
        S31.659
      epigastric region S31.152
        with penetration into peritoneal cavity
          S31.652
      left
        lower quadrant S31.154
          with penetration into peritoneal
            cavity S31.654
        upper quadrant S31.151
          with penetration into peritoneal
            cavity S31.651
      periumbilic region S31.155
        with penetration into peritoneal cavity
          S31.655
      right
        lower quadrant S31.153
          with penetration into peritoneal
            cavity S31.653
        upper quadrant S31.150
          with penetration into peritoneal
            cavity S31.650
      superficial NEC S30.871
        insect S30.861
    alveolar (process) —*see* Bite, oral cavity
    amphibian (venomous) —*see* Venom, bite,
      amphibian
    animal —*see also* Bite, by site
      venomous —*see* Venom
    ankle S91.05-●
      superficial NEC S90.57-●
        insect S90.56-●
    antecubital space —*see* Bite, elbow
    anus S31.835
      superficial NEC S30.877
        insect S30.867
    arm (upper) S41.15-●
      lower —*see* Bite, forearm
      superficial NEC S40.87-●
        insect S40.86-●
    arthropod NEC —*see* Venom, bite, arthropod
    auditory canal (external) (meatus) —
      see Bite, ear
    auricle, ear —*see* Bite, ear
    axilla —*see* Bite, arm
    back —*see also* Bite, thorax, back
      lower S31.050
        with penetration into retroperitoneal
          space S31.051
        superficial NEC S30.870
          insect S30.860
    bedbug —*see* Bite(s), by site, superficial,
      insect
    breast S21.05-●
      superficial NEC S20.17-●
        insect S20.16-●
    brow —*see* Bite, head, specified site NEC
    buttock S31.805
      left S31.825
      right S31.815
      superficial NEC S30.870
        insect S30.860
    calf —*see* Bite, leg
    canaliculus lacrimalis —*see* Bite, eyelid
    canthus, eye —*see* Bite, eyelid
    centipede —*see* Toxicity, venom, arthropod,
      centipede
    cheek (external) S01.45-●
      internal —*see* Bite, oral cavity
      superficial NEC S00.87
        insect S00.86

Bite *(Continued)*
  chest wall —*see* Bite, thorax
  chigger B88.0
  chin —*see* Bite, head, specified site NEC
  clitoris —*see* Bite, vulva
  costal region —*see* Bite, thorax
  digit(s)
    hand —*see* Bite, finger
    toe —*see* Bite, toe
  ear (canal) (external) S01.35-●
    superficial NEC S00.47-●
      insect S00.46-●
  elbow S51.05-●
    superficial NEC S50.37-●
      insect S50.36-●
  epididymis —*see* Bite, testis
  epigastric region —*see* Bite, abdomen
  epiglottis —*see* Bite, neck, specified site NEC
  esophagus, cervical S11.25
    superficial NEC S10.17
      insect S10.16
  eyebrow —*see* Bite, eyelid
  eyelid S01.15-●
    superficial NEC S00.27-●
      insect S00.26-●
  face NEC —*see* Bite, head, specified site NEC
  finger(s) S61.259
    with
      damage to nail S61.359
    index S61.258
      with
        damage to nail S61.358
      left S61.251
        with
          damage to nail S61.351
      right S61.250
        with
          damage to nail S61.350
      superficial NEC S60.478
        insect S60.46-●
    little S61.25-●
      with
        damage to nail S61.35-●
      superficial NEC S60.47-●
        insect S60.46-●
    middle S61.25-●
      with
        damage to nail S61.35-●
      superficial NEC S60.47-●
        insect S60.46-●
    ring S61.25-●
      with
        damage to nail S61.35-●
      superficial NEC S60.47-●
        insect S60.46-●
    superficial NEC S60.479
      insect S60.469
    thumb —*see* Bite, thumb
  flank —*see* Bite, abdomen, wall
  flea —*see* Bite, by site, superficial,
    insect
  foot (except toe(s) alone) S91.35-●
    superficial NEC S90.87-●
      insect S90.86-●
    toe —*see* Bite, toe
  forearm S51.85-●
    elbow only —*see* Bite, elbow
    superficial NEC S50.87-●
      insect S50.86-●
  forehead —*see* Bite, head, specified site
    NEC
  genital organs, external
    female S31.552
      superficial NEC S30.876
        insect S30.866
      vagina and vulva —*see* Bite, vulva
    male S31.551
      penis —*see* Bite, penis
      scrotum —*see* Bite, scrotum
      superficial NEC S30.875
        insect S30.865
      testes —*see* Bite, testis
  groin —*see* Bite, abdomen, wall

Bite *(Continued)*
  gum —*see* Bite, oral cavity
  hand S61.45-●
    finger —*see* Bite, finger
    superficial NEC S60.57-●
      insect S60.56-●
    thumb —*see* Bite, thumb
  head S01.95
    cheek —*see* Bite, cheek
    ear —*see* Bite, ear
    eyelid —*see* Bite, eyelid
    lip —*see* Bite, lip
    nose —*see* Bite, nose
    oral cavity —*see* Bite, oral cavity
    scalp —*see* Bite, scalp
    specified site NEC S01.85
      superficial NEC S00.87
        insect S00.86
    superficial NEC S00.97
      insect S00.96
    temporomandibular area —*see* Bite, cheek
  heel —*see* Bite, foot
  hip S71.05-●
    superficial NEC S70.27-●
      insect S70.26-●
  hymen S31.45
  hypochondrium —*see* Bite, abdomen, wall
  hypogastric region —*see* Bite, abdomen, wall
  inguinal region —*see* Bite, abdomen, wall
  insect —*see* Bite, by site, superficial, insect
  instep —*see* Bite, foot
  interscapular region —*see* Bite, thorax, back
  jaw —*see* Bite, head, specified site NEC
  knee S81.05-●
    superficial NEC S80.27-●
      insect S80.26-●
  labium (majus) (minus) —*see* Bite, vulva
  lacrimal duct —*see* Bite, eyelid
  larynx S11.015
    superficial NEC S10.17
      insect S10.16
  leg (lower) S81.85-●
    ankle —*see* Bite, ankle
    foot —*see* Bite, foot
    knee —*see* Bite, knee
    superficial NEC S80.87-●
      insect S80.86-●
    toe —*see* Bite, toe
    upper —*see* Bite, thigh
  lip S01.551
    superficial NEC S00.571
      insect S00.561
  lizard (venomous) —*see* Venom, bite, reptile
  loin —*see* Bite, abdomen, wall
  lower back —*see* Bite, back, lower
  lumbar region —*see* Bite, back, lower
  malar region —*see* Bite, head, specified site
    NEC
  mammary —*see* Bite, breast
  marine animals (venomous) —*see* Toxicity,
    venom, marine animal
  mastoid region —*see* Bite, head, specified site
    NEC
  mouth —*see* Bite, oral cavity
  nail
    finger —*see* Bite, finger
    toe —*see* Bite, toe
  nape —*see* Bite, neck, specified site NEC
  nasal (septum) (sinus) —*see* Bite, nose
  nasopharynx —*see* Bite, head, specified site
    NEC
  neck S11.95
    involving
      cervical esophagus —*see* Bite,
        esophagus, cervical
      larynx —*see* Bite, larynx
      pharynx —*see* Bite, pharynx
      thyroid gland S11.15
      trachea —*see* Bite, trachea
    specified site NEC S11.85
      superficial NEC S10.87
        insect S10.86

▶ New   ⇒ Revised   ~~deleted~~ Deleted   ● Use Additional Character(s)

Bite *(Continued)*
  neck *(Continued)*
    superficial NEC S10.97
      insect S10.96
    throat S11.85
      superficial NEC S10.17
        insect S10.16
  nose (septum) (sinus) S01.25
    superficial NEC S00.37
      insect S00.36
  occipital region —*see* Bite, scalp
  oral cavity S01.552
    superficial NEC S00.572
      insect S00.562
  orbital region —*see* Bite, eyelid
  palate —*see* Bite, oral cavity
  palm —*see* Bite, hand
  parietal region —*see* Bite, scalp
  pelvis S31.050
    with penetration into retroperitoneal space S31.051
    superficial NEC S30.870
      insect S30.860
  penis S31.25
    superficial NEC S30.872
      insect S30.862
  perineum
    female —*see* Bite, vulva
    male —*see* Bite, pelvis
  periocular area (with or without lacrimal passages) —*see* Bite, eyelid
  phalanges
    finger —*see* Bite, finger
    toe —*see* Bite, toe
  pharynx S11.25
    superficial NEC S10.17
      insect S10.16
  pinna —*see* Bite, ear
  poisonous —*see* Venom
  popliteal space —*see* Bite, knee
  prepuce —*see* Bite, penis
  pubic region —*see* Bite, abdomen, wall
  rectovaginal septum —*see* Bite, vulva
  red bug B88.0
  reptile NEC —*see also* Venom, bite, reptile
    nonvenomous —*see* Bite, by site
    snake —*see* Venom, bite, snake
  sacral region —*see* Bite, back, lower
  sacroiliac region —*see* Bite, back, lower
  salivary gland —*see* Bite, oral cavity
  scalp S01.05
    superficial NEC S00.07
      insect S00.06
  scapular region —*see* Bite, shoulder
  scrotum S31.35
    superficial NEC S30.873
      insect S30.863
  sea-snake (venomous) —*see* Toxicity, venom, snake, sea snake
  shin —*see* Bite, leg
  shoulder S41.05-●
    superficial NEC S40.27-●
      insect S40.26-●
  snake —*see also* Venom, bite, snake
    nonvenomous —*see* Bite, by site
  spermatic cord —*see* Bite, testis
  spider (venomous) —*see* Toxicity, venom, spider
    nonvenomous —*see* Bite, by site, superficial, insect
  sternal region —*see* Bite, thorax, front
  submaxillary region —*see* Bite, head, specified site NEC
  submental region —*see* Bite, head, specified site NEC
  subungual
    finger(s) —*see* Bite, finger
    toe —*see* Bite, toe
  superficial —*see* Bite, by site, superficial
  supraclavicular fossa S11.85

Bite *(Continued)*
  supraorbital —*see* Bite, head, specified site NEC
  temple, temporal region —*see* Bite, head, specified site NEC
  temporomandibular area —*see* Bite, cheek
  testis S31.35
    superficial NEC S30.873
      insect S30.863
  thigh S71.15-●
    superficial NEC S70.37-●
      insect S70.36-●
  thorax, thoracic (wall) S21.95
    back S21.25-●
      with penetration into thoracic cavity S21.45-●
    breast —*see* Bite, breast
    front S21.15-●
      with penetration into thoracic cavity S21.35-●
    superficial NEC S20.97
      back S20.47-●
      front S20.37-●
      insect S20.96
        back S20.46-●
        front S20.36-●
  throat —*see* Bite, neck, throat
  thumb S61.05-●
    with
      damage to nail S61.15-●
    superficial NEC S60.37-●
      insect S60.36-●
  thyroid S11.15
    superficial NEC S10.87
      insect S10.86
  toe(s) S91.15-●
    with
      damage to nail S91.25-●
    great S91.15-●
      with
        damage to nail S91.25-●
    lesser S91.15-●
      with
        damage to nail S91.25-●
    superficial NEC S90.47-●
      great S90.47-●
      insect S90.46-●
        great S90.46-●
  tongue S01.552
  trachea S11.025
    superficial NEC S10.17
      insect S10.16
  tunica vaginalis —*see* Bite, testis
  tympanum, tympanic membrane —*see* Bite, ear
  umbilical region S31.155
  uvula —*see* Bite, oral cavity
  vagina —*see* Bite, vulva
  venomous —*see* Venom
  vocal cords S11.035
    superficial NEC S10.17
      insect S10.16
  vulva S31.45
    superficial NEC S30.874
      insect S30.864
  wrist S61.55-●
    superficial NEC S60.87-●
      insect S60.86-●
Biting, cheek or lip K13.1
Biventricular failure (heart) I50.82
Björck (-Thorson) syndrome (malignant carcinoid) E34.0
Black
  death A20.9
  eye S00.1-●
  hairy tongue K14.3
  heel (foot) S90.3-●
  lung (disease) J60
  palm (hand) S60.22-●
Blackfan-Diamond anemia or syndrome (congenital hypoplastic anemia) D61.01

Blackhead L70.0
Blackout R55
Bladder —*see* condition
Blast (air) (hydraulic) (immersion) (underwater)
  blindness S05.8X-●
  injury
    abdomen or thorax —*see* Injury, by site
    ear (acoustic nerve trauma) —*see* Injury, nerve, acoustic, specified type NEC
    syndrome NEC T70.8
Blastoma —*see* Neoplasm, malignant, by site
  pulmonary —*see* Neoplasm, lung, malignant
Blastomycosis, blastomycotic B40.9
  Brazilian —*see* Paracoccidioidomycosis
  cutaneous B40.3
  disseminated B40.7
  European —*see* Cryptococcosis
  generalized B40.7
  keloidal B48.0
  North American B40.9
  primary pulmonary B40.0
  pulmonary B40.2
    acute B40.0
    chronic B40.1
  skin B40.3
  South American —*see* Paracoccidioidomycosis
  specified NEC B40.89
Bleb(s) R23.8
  emphysematous (lung) (solitary) J43.9
  endophthalmitis H59.43
  filtering (vitreous), after glaucoma surgery Z98.83
  inflamed (infected), postprocedural H59.40
    stage 1 H59.41
    stage 2 H59.42
    stage 3 H59.43
  lung (ruptured) J43.9
    congenital —*see* Atelectasis
    newborn P25.8
  subpleural (emphysematous) J43.9
Blebitis, postprocedural H59.40
  stage 1 H59.41
  stage 2 H59.42
  stage 3 H59.43
Bleeder (familial) (hereditary) —*see* Hemophilia
Bleeding —*see also* Hemorrhage
  anal K62.5
  anovulatory N97.0
  atonic, following delivery O72.1
  capillary I78.8
    puerperal O72.2
  contact (postcoital) N93.0
  due to uterine subinvolution N85.3
  ear —*see* Otorrhagia
  excessive, associated with menopausal onset N92.4
  familial —*see* Defect, coagulation
  following intercourse N93.0
  gastrointestinal K92.2
  hemorrhoids —*see* Hemorrhoids
  intermenstrual (regular) N92.3
    irregular N92.1
  intraoperative —*see* Complication, intraoperative, hemorrhage
  irregular N92.6
  menopausal N92.4
  newborn, intraventricular —*see* Newborn, affected by, hemorrhage, intraventricular
  nipple N64.59
  nose R04.0
  ovulation N92.3
  perimenopausal N92.4
  postclimacteric N95.0
  postcoital N93.0
  postmenopausal N95.0
  postoperative —*see* Complication, postprocedural, hemorrhage
  preclimacteric N92.4
  pre-pubertal vaginal N93.1
  puberty (excessive, with onset of menstrual periods) N92.2

Bleeding *(Continued)*
  rectum, rectal K62.5
    newborn P54.2
  tendencies —*see* Defect, coagulation
  throat R04.1
  tooth socket (post-extraction) K91.840
  umbilical stump P51.9
  uterus, uterine NEC N93.9
    climacteric N92.4
    dysfunctional or functional N93.8
    menopausal N92.4
    preclimacteric or premenopausal N92.4
    unrelated to menstrual cycle N93.9
  vagina, vaginal (abnormal) N93.9
    dysfunctional or functional N93.8
    newborn P54.6
    pre-pubertal N93.1
  vicarious N94.89
Blennorrhagia, blennorrhagic —*see* Gonorrhea
Blennorrhea (acute) (chronic) —*see also*
      Gonorrhea
  inclusion (neonatal) (newborn) P39.1
  lower genitourinary tract (gonococcal) A54.00
  neonatorum (gonococcal ophthalmia) A54.31
Blepharelosis —*see* Entropion
Blepharitis (angularis) (ciliaris) (eyelid)
      (marginal) (nonulcerative) H01.009
  herpes zoster B02.39
  left H01.006
    lower H01.005
    upper H01.004
    upper and lower H01.00B
  right H01.003
    lower H01.002
    upper H01.001
    upper and lower H01.00A
  squamous H01.029
    left H01.026
      lower H01.025
      upper H01.024
      upper and lower H01.02B
    right H01.023
      lower H01.022
      upper H01.021
      upper and lower H01.02A
  ulcerative H01.019
    left H01.016
      lower H01.015
      upper H01.014
      upper and lower H01.01B
    right H01.013
      lower H01.012
      upper H01.011
      upper and lower H01.01B
Blepharochalasis H02.30
  congenital Q10.0
  left H02.36
    lower H02.35
    upper H02.34
  right H02.33
    lower H02.32
    upper H02.31
Blepharoclonus H02.59
Blepharoconjunctivitis H10.50-●
  angular H10.52-●
  contact H10.53-●
  ligneous H10.51-●
Blepharophimosis (eyelid) H02.529
  congenital Q10.3
  left H02.526
    lower H02.525
    upper H02.524
  right H02.523
    lower H02.522
    upper H02.521
Blepharoptosis H02.40-●
  congenital Q10.0
  mechanical H02.41-●
  myogenic H02.42-●
  neurogenic H02.43-●
  paralytic H02.43-●
Blepharopyorrhea, gonococcal A54.39

Blepharospasm G24.5
  drug induced G24.01
Blighted ovum O02.0
Blind —*see also* Blindness
  bronchus (congenital) Q32.4
  loop syndrome K90.2
    congenital Q43.8
  sac, fallopian tube (congenital) Q50.6
  spot, enlarged —*see* Defect, visual field,
      localized, scotoma, blind spot area
  tract or tube, congenital NEC —*see* Atresia,
      by site
Blindness (acquired) (congenital) (both eyes)
      H54.0X-●
  blast S05.8X-●
  color —*see* Deficiency, color vision
  concussion S05.8X-●
  cortical H47.619
    left brain H47.612
    right brain H47.611
  day H53.11
  due to injury (current episode) S05.9-●
    sequelae — code to injury with seventh
        character S
  eclipse (total) —*see* Retinopathy, solar
  emotional (hysterical) F44.6
  face H53.16
  hysterical F44.6
  legal (both eyes) (USA definition) H54.8
  mind R48.8
  night H53.60
    abnormal dark adaptation curve H53.61
    acquired H53.62
    congenital H53.63
    specified type NEC H53.69
    vitamin A deficiency E50.5
  one eye (other eye normal) H54.40
    left (normal vision on right) H54.42-●
      low vision on right H54.12-●
    low vision, other eye H54.10
    right (normal vision on left) H54.41-●
      low vision on left H54.11-●
  psychic R48.8
  river B73.01
  snow —*see* Photokeratitis
  sun, solar —*see* Retinopathy, solar
  transient —*see* Disturbance, vision, subjective,
      loss, transient
  traumatic (current episode) S05.9-●
  word (developmental) F81.0
    acquired R48.0
    secondary to organic lesion R48.0
Blister (nonthermal)
  abdominal wall S30.821
  alveolar process S00.522
  ankle S90.52-●
  antecubital space —*see* Blister, elbow
  anus S30.827
  arm (upper) S40.82-●
  auditory canal —*see* Blister, ear
  auricle —*see* Blister, ear
  axilla —*see* Blister, arm
  back, lower S30.820
  beetle dermatitis L24.89
  breast S20.12-●
  brow S00.82
  calf —*see* Blister, leg
  canthus —*see* Blister, eyelid
  cheek S00.82
    internal S00.522
  chest wall —*see* Blister, thorax
  chin S00.82
  costal region —*see* Blister, thorax
  digit(s)
    foot —*see* Blister, toe
    hand —*see* Blister, finger
  due to burn —*see* Burn, by site, second degree
  ear S00.42-●
  elbow S50.32-●
  epiglottis S10.12
  esophagus, cervical S10.12
  eyebrow —*see* Blister, eyelid

Blister *(Continued)*
  eyelid S00.22-●
  face S00.82
  fever B00.1
  finger(s) S60.429
    index S60.42-●
    little S60.42-●
    middle S60.42-●
    ring S60.42-●
  foot (except toe(s) alone) S90.82-●
    toe —*see* Blister, toe
  forearm S50.82-●
    elbow only —*see* Blister, elbow
  forehead S00.82
  fracture - omit code
  genital organ
    female S30.826
    male S30.825
  gum S00.522
  hand S60.52-●
  head S00.92
    ear —*see* Blister, ear
    eyelid —*see* Blister, eyelid
    lip S00.521
    nose S00.32
    oral cavity S00.522
    scalp S00.02
    specified site NEC S00.82
  heel —*see* Blister, foot
  hip S70.22-●
  interscapular region S20.429
  jaw S00.82
  knee S80.22-●
  larynx S10.12
  leg (lower) S80.82-●
    knee —*see* Blister, knee
    upper —*see* Blister, thigh
  lip S00.521
  malar region S00.82
  mammary —*see* Blister, breast
  mastoid region S00.82
  mouth S00.522
  multiple, skin, nontraumatic R23.8
  nail
    finger —*see* Blister, finger
    toe —*see* Blister, toe
  nasal S00.32
  neck S10.92
    specified site NEC S10.82
    throat S10.12
  nose S00.32
  occipital region S00.02
  oral cavity S00.522
  orbital region —*see* Blister, eyelid
  palate S00.522
  palm —*see* Blister, hand
  parietal region S00.02
  pelvis S30.820
  penis S30.822
  periocular area —*see* Blister, eyelid
  phalanges
    finger —*see* Blister, finger
    toe —*see* Blister, toe
  pharynx S10.12
  pinna —*see* Blister, ear
  popliteal space —*see* Blister, knee
  scalp S00.02
  scapular region —*see* Blister, shoulder
  scrotum S30.823
  shin —*see* Blister, leg
  shoulder S40.22-●
  sternal region S20.329
  submaxillary region S00.82
  submental region S00.82
  subungual
    finger(s) —*see* Blister, finger
    toe(s) —*see* Blister, toe
  supraclavicular fossa S10.82
  supraorbital S00.82
  temple S00.82
  temporal region S00.82
  testis S30.823

▶ New   ➡ Revised   ~~deleted~~ Deleted   ● Use Additional Character(s)

Blister (Continued)
  thermal —see Burn, second degree, by site
  thigh S70.32-●
  thorax, thoracic (wall) S20.92
    back S20.42-●
    front S20.32-●
  throat S10.12
  thumb S60.32-●
  toe(s) S90.42-●
    great S90.42-●
  tongue S00.522
  trachea S10.12
  tympanum, tympanic membrane —see Blister,
    ear
  upper arm —see Blister, arm (upper)
  uvula S00.522
  vagina S30.824
  vocal cords S10.12
  vulva S30.824
  wrist S60.82-●
Bloating R14.0
Bloch-Sulzberger disease or syndrome Q82.3
Block, blocked
  alveolocapillary J84.10
  arborization (heart) I45.5
  arrhythmic I45.9
  atrioventricular (incomplete) (partial) I44.30
    with atrioventricular dissociation I44.2
    complete I44.2
      congenital Q24.6
    congenital Q24.6
    first degree I44.0
    second degree (types I and II) I44.1
    specified NEC I44.39
    third degree I44.2
    types I and II I44.1
  auriculoventricular —see Block,
    atrioventricular
  bifascicular (cardiac) I45.2
  bundle-branch (complete) (false) (incomplete)
    I45.4
    bilateral I45.2
    left I44.7
      with right bundle branch block I45.2
      hemiblock I44.60
        anterior I44.4
        posterior I44.5
      incomplete I44.7
        with right bundle branch block I45.2
    right I45.10
      with
        left bundle branch block I45.2
        left fascicular block I45.2
      specified NEC I45.19
    Wilson's type I45.19
  cardiac I45.9
  conduction I45.9
    complete I44.2
  fascicular (left) I44.60
    anterior I44.4
    posterior I44.5
    right I45.0
    specified NEC I44.69
  foramen Magendie (acquired) G91.1
    congenital Q03.1
      with spina bifida —see Spina bifida, by
        site, with hydrocephalus
  heart I45.9
    bundle branch I45.4
      bilateral I45.2
    complete (atrioventricular) I44.2
    congenital Q24.6
    first degree (atrioventricular) I44.0
    second degree (atrioventricular) I44.1
    specified type NEC I45.5
    third degree (atrioventricular) I44.2
  hepatic vein I82.0
  intraventricular (nonspecific) I45.4
    bundle branch
      bilateral I45.2
  kidney N28.9
    postcystoscopic or postprocedural N99.0

Block, blocked (Continued)
  Mobitz (types I and II) I44.1
  myocardial —see Block, heart
  nodal I45.5
  organ or site, congenital NEC —see Atresia,
    by site
  portal (vein) I81
  second degree (types I and II) I44.1
  sinoatrial I45.5
  sinoauricular I45.5
  third degree I44.2
  trifascicular I45.3
  tubal N97.1
  vein NOS I82.90
  Wenckebach (types I and II) I44.1
Blockage —see Obstruction
Blocq's disease F44.4
Blood
  constituents, abnormal R78.9
  disease D75.9
  donor —see Donor, blood
  dyscrasia D75.9
    with
      abortion —see Abortion, by type,
        complicated by, hemorrhage
      ectopic pregnancy O08.1
      molar pregnancy O08.1
      following ectopic or molar pregnancy
        O08.1
      newborn P61.9
      puerperal, postpartum O72.3
  flukes NEC —see Schistosomiasis
  in
    feces K92.1
      occult R19.5
    urine —see Hematuria
  mole O02.0
  occult in feces R19.5
  pressure
    decreased, due to shock following injury
      T79.4
    examination only Z01.30
    fluctuating I99.8
    high —see Hypertension
      borderline R03.0
      incidental reading, without diagnosis of
        hypertension R03.0
    low —see also Hypotension
      incidental reading, without diagnosis of
        hypotension R03.1
  spitting —see Hemoptysis
  staining cornea —see Pigmentation, cornea,
    stromal
  transfusion
    reaction or complication —see
        Complications, transfusion
  type
    A (Rh positive) Z67.10
      Rh negative Z67.11
    AB (Rh positive) Z67.30
      Rh negative Z67.31
    B (Rh positive) Z67.20
      Rh negative Z67.21
    O (Rh positive) Z67.40
      Rh negative Z67.41
    Rh (positive) Z67.90
      negative Z67.91
  vessel rupture —see Hemorrhage
  vomiting —see Hematemesis
Blood-forming organs, disease D75.9
Bloodgood's disease —see Mastopathy,
  cystic
Bloom (-Machacek)(-Torre) syndrome Q82.8
⇒ **Blount disease or osteochondrosis**
  M92.51-●
Blue
  baby Q24.9
  diaper syndrome E72.09
  dome cyst (breast) —see Cyst, breast
  dot cataract Q12.0
  nevus D22.9

Blue (Continued)
  sclera Q13.5
    with fragility of bone and deafness Q78.0
  toe syndrome I75.02-●
Blueness —see Cyanosis
Blues, postpartal O90.6
  baby O90.6
Blurring, visual H53.8
Blushing (abnormal) (excessive) R23.2
BMI —see Body, mass index
Boarder, hospital NEC Z76.4
  accompanying sick person Z76.3
  healthy infant or child Z76.2
    foundling Z76.1
Bockhart's impetigo L01.02
Bodechtel-Guttman disease (subacute
  sclerosing panencephalitis) A81.1
Boder-Sedgwick syndrome (ataxia-
  telangiectasia) G11.3
Body, bodies
  Aschoff's —see Myocarditis, rheumatic
  asteroid, vitreous —see Deposit, crystalline
  cytoid (retina) —see Occlusion, artery, retina
  drusen (degenerative) (macula) (retinal) —see
    also Degeneration, macula, drusen
    optic disc —see Drusen, optic disc
  foreign —see Foreign body
  loose
    joint, except knee —see Loose, body, joint
      knee M23.4-●
    sheath, tendon —see Disorder, tendon,
      specified type NEC
  mass index (BMI)
    adult
      19.9 or less Z68.1
      20.0-20.9 Z68.20
      21.0-21.9 Z68.21
      22.0-22.9 Z68.22
      23.0-23.9 Z68.23
      24.0-24.9 Z68.24
      25.0-25.9 Z68.25
      26.0-26.9 Z68.26
      27.0-27.9 Z68.27
      28.0-28.9 Z68.28
      29.0-29.9 Z68.29
      30.0-30.9 Z68.30
      31.0-31.9 Z68.31
      32.0-32.9 Z68.32
      33.0-33.9 Z68.33
      34.0-34.9 Z68.34
      35.0-35.9 Z68.35
      36.0-36.9 Z68.36
      37.0-37.9 Z68.37
      38.0-38.9 Z68.38
      39.0-39.9 Z68.39
      40.0-44.9 Z68.41
      45.0-49.9 Z68.42
      50.0-59.9 Z68.43
      60.0-69.9 Z68.44
      70 and over Z68.45
    pediatric
      5th percentile to less than 85th percentile
        for age Z68.52
      85th percentile to less than 95th
        percentile for age Z68.53
      greater than or equal to ninety-fifth
        percentile for age Z68.54
      less than fifth percentile for age
        Z68.51
  Mooser's A75.2
  rice —see also Loose, body, joint
    knee M23.4-●
  rocking F98.4
Boeck's
  disease or sarcoid —see Sarcoidosis
  lupoid (miliary) D86.3
Boerhaave's syndrome (spontaneous
  esophageal rupture) K22.3
Boggy
  cervix N88.8
  uterus N85.8

Boil —*see also* Furuncle, by site
   Aleppo B55.1
   Baghdad B55.1
   Delhi B55.1
   lacrimal
      gland —*see* Dacryoadenitis
      passages (duct) (sac) —*see* Inflammation,
         lacrimal, passages, acute
   Natal B55.1
   orbit, orbital —*see* Abscess, orbit
   tropical B55.1
Bold hives —*see* Urticaria
Bombé, iris —*see* Membrane, pupillary
Bone —*see* condition
Bonnevie-Ullrich syndrome —*see also* Turner's
   syndrome Q87.19
Bonnier's syndrome —*see* subcategory H81.8
Bonvale dam fever T73.3
Bony block of joint —*see* Ankylosis
BOOP (bronchiolitis obliterans organized
   pneumonia) J84.89
Borderline
   diabetes mellitus R73.03
   hypertension R03.0
   osteopenia M85.8-●
   pelvis, with obstruction during labor O65.1
   personality F60.3
Borna disease A83.9
Bornholm disease B33.0
Boston exanthem A88.0
Botalli, ductus (patent) (persistent) Q25.0
Bothriocephalus latus infestation B70.0
Botulism (foodborne intoxication) A05.1
   infant A48.51
   non-foodborne A48.52
   wound A48.52
Bouba —*see* Yaws
Bouchard's nodes (with arthropathy) M15.2
Bouffée délirante F23
Bouillaud's disease or syndrome (rheumatic
   heart disease) I01.9
Bourneville's disease Q85.1
Boutonniere deformity (finger) —*see*
   Deformity, finger, boutonniere
Bouveret (-Hoffmann) syndrome (paroxysmal
   tachycardia) I47.9
Bovine heart —*see* Hypertrophy, cardiac
Bowel —*see* condition
Bowen's
   dermatosis (precancerous) —*see* Neoplasm,
     skin, in situ
   disease —*see* Neoplasm, skin, in situ
   epithelioma —*see* Neoplasm, skin, in situ
   type
     epidermoid carcinoma-in-situ —*see*
       Neoplasm, skin, in situ
     intraepidermal squamous cell carcinoma —
       see Neoplasm, skin, in situ
Bowing
   femur —*see also* Deformity, limb, specified
     type NEC, thigh
     congenital Q68.3
   fibula —*see also* Deformity, limb, specified
     type NEC, lower leg
     congenital Q68.4
   forearm —*see* Deformity, limb, specified type
     NEC, forearm
   leg(s), long bones, congenital Q68.5
   radius —*see* Deformity, limb, specified type
     NEC, forearm
   tibia —*see also* Deformity, limb, specified type
     NEC, lower leg
     congenital Q68.4
Bowleg(s) (acquired) M21.16-●
   congenital Q68.5
   rachitic E64.3
Boyd's dysentery A03.2
Brachial —*see* condition
Brachycardia R00.1
Brachycephaly Q75.0
Bradley's disease A08.19

Bradyarrhythmia, cardiac I49.8
Bradycardia (sinoatrial) (sinus) (vagal) R00.1
   neonatal P29.12
   reflex G90.09
   tachycardia syndrome I49.5
Bradykinesia R25.8
Bradypnea R06.89
Bradytachycardia I49.5
Brailsford's disease or osteochondrosis —*see*
   Osteochondrosis, juvenile, radius
Brain —*see also* condition
   death G93.82
   syndrome —*see* Syndrome, brain
Branched-chain amino-acid disorder E71.2
Branchial —*see* condition
   cartilage, congenital Q18.2
Branchiogenic remnant (in neck) Q18.0
Brandt's syndrome (acrodermatitis
   enteropathica) E83.2
Brash (water) R12
Bravais-Jacksonian epilepsy —*see* Epilepsy,
   localization-related, symptomatic, with
   simple partial seizures
Braxton Hicks contractions —*see* False, labor
Brazilian leishmaniasis B55.2
BRBPR K62.5
Break, retina (without detachment) H33.30-●
   with retinal detachment —*see* Detachment,
     retina
   horseshoe tear H33.31-●
   multiple H33.33-●
   round hole H33.32-●
Breakdown
   device, graft or implant —*see also*
     Complications, by site and type,
     mechanical T85.618
     arterial graft NEC —*see* Complication,
       cardiovascular device, mechanical,
       vascular
     breast (implant) T85.41
     catheter NEC T85.618
       cystostomy T83.010
       dialysis (renal) T82.41
         intraperitoneal T85.611
       Hopkins T83.018
       ileostomy T83.018
       infusion NEC T82.514
         cranial T85.610
         epidural T85.610
         intrathecal T85.610
         spinal T85.610
         subarachnoid T85.610
         subdural T85.610
       nephrostomy T83.012
       urethral indwelling T83.011
       urinary NEC T83.018
       urostomy T83.018
     electronic (electrode) (pulse generator)
       (stimulator)
       bone T84.310
       cardiac T82.119
         electrode T82.110
         pulse generator T82.111
         specified type NEC T82.118
       nervous system —*see* Complication,
         prosthetic device, mechanical,
         electronic nervous system stimulator
       urinary —*see* Complication,
         genitourinary, device, urinary,
         mechanical
     fixation, internal (orthopedic) NEC —
       see Complication, fixation device,
       mechanical
     gastrointestinal —*see* Complications,
       prosthetic device, mechanical,
       gastrointestinal device
     genital NEC T83.418
       intrauterine contraceptive device T83.31
       penile prosthesis (cylinder) (implanted)
        (pump) (resevoir) T83.410
       testicular prosthesis T83.411

Breakdown (*Continued*)
   device, graft or implant (*Continued*)
     heart NEC —*see* Complication,
       cardiovascular device, mechanical
     intrathecal infusion pump T85.615
     joint prosthesis —*see* Complications…, joint
       prosthesis, internal, mechanical, by site
     nervous system, specified device NEC
       T85.615
     ocular NEC —*see* Complications, prosthetic
       device, mechanical, ocular device
     orthopedic NEC —*see* Complication,
       orthopedic, device, mechanical
     specified NEC T85.618
     subcutaneous device pocket
       nervous system prosthetic device,
         implant, or graft T85.890
       other internal prosthetic device, implant,
         or graft T85.898
     sutures, permanent T85.612
       used in bone repair —*see* Complications,
         fixation device, internal
         (orthopedic), mechanical
     urinary NEC T83.118
       graft T83.21
       sphincter, implanted T83.111
       stent (ileal conduit) (nephroureteral)
        T83.113
       ureteral indwelling T83.112
     vascular NEC —*see* Complication,
       cardiovascular device, mechanical
     ventricular intracranial shunt T85.01
   nervous F48.8
   perineum O90.1
   respirator J95.850
     specified NEC J95.859
   ventilator J95.850
     specified NEC J95.859
Breast —*see also* condition
   buds E30.1
     in newborn P96.89
   dense R92.2
   nodule —*see also* Lump, breast N63.0
Breath
   foul R19.6
   holder, child R06.89
   holding spell R06.89
   shortness R06.02
Breathing
   labored —*see* Hyperventilation
   mouth R06.5
     causing malocclusion M26.5
   periodic R06.3
     high altitude G47.32
Breathlessness R06.81
Breda's disease —*see* Yaws
Breech presentation (mother) O32.1
   causing obstructed labor O64.1
   footling O32.8
     causing obstructed labor O64.8
   incomplete O32.8
     causing obstructed labor O64.8
Breisky's disease N90.4
Brennemann's syndrome I88.0
Brenner
   tumor (benign) D27.9
     borderline malignancy D39.1-●
     malignant C56
     proliferating D39.1
Bretonneau's disease or angina A36.0
Breus' mole O02.0
Brevicollis Q76.49
Brickmakers' anemia B76.9 *[D63.8]*
Bridge, myocardial Q24.5
Bright red blood per rectum (BRBPR)
   K62.5
Bright's disease —*see also* Nephritis
   arteriosclerotic —*see* Hypertension, kidney
Brill (-Zinsser) disease (recrudescent typhus)
   A75.1
Brill-Symmers' disease C82.90

Brion-Kayser disease —*see* Fever, parathyroid
Briquet's disorder or syndrome F45.0
Brissaud's
  infantilism or dwarfism E23.0
  motor-verbal tic F95.2
Brittle
  bones disease Q78.0
  nails L60.3
    congenital Q84.6
Broad —*see also* condition
  beta disease E78.2
  ligament laceration syndrome N83.8
Broad- or floating-betalipoproteinemia E78.2
Brock's syndrome (atelectasis due to enlarged
    lymph nodes) J98.19
Brocq-Duhring disease (dermatitis
    herpetiformis) L13.0
Brodie's abscess or disease M86.8X-●
Broken
  arches —*see also* Deformity, limb, flat foot
  arm (meaning upper limb) —*see* Fracture, arm
  back —*see* Fracture, vertebra
  bone —*see* Fracture
  implant or internal device —*see*
      Complications, by site and type,
      mechanical
  leg (meaning lower limb) —*see* Fracture, leg
  nose S02.2
  tooth, teeth —*see* Fracture, tooth
Bromhidrosis, bromidrosis L75.0
Bromidism, bromism G92
  chronic (dependence) F13.20
  due to
    correct substance properly administered —
        see Table of Drugs and Chemicals, by
        drug, adverse effect
    overdose or wrong substance given
        or taken —*see* Table of Drugs and
        Chemicals, by drug, poisoning
Bromidrosiphobia F40.298
Bronchi, bronchial —*see* condition
Bronchiectasis (cylindrical) (diffuse) (fusiform)
    (localized) (saccular) J47.9
  with
    acute
      bronchitis J47.0
      lower respiratory infection J47.0
    exacerbation (acute) J47.1
  congenital Q33.4
  tuberculous NEC —*see* Tuberculosis,
      pulmonary
Bronchiolectasis —*see* Bronchiectasis
Bronchiolitis (acute) (infective) (subacute) J21.9
  with
    bronchospasm or obstruction J21.9
    influenza, flu or grippe —*see* Influenza,
        with, respiratory manifestations NEC
  chemical (chronic) J68.4
    acute J68.0
  chronic (fibrosing) (obliterative) J44.9
  due to
    external agent —*see* Bronchitis, acute,
        due to
    human metapneumovirus J21.1
    respiratory syncytial virus (RSV) J21.0
    specified organism NEC J21.8
  fibrosa obliterans J44.9
  influenzal —*see* Influenza, with, respiratory
      manifestations NEC
  obliterans J42
    with organizing pneumonia (BOOP) J84.89
  obliterative (chronic) (subacute) J44.9
    due to chemicals, gases, fumes or vapors
        (inhalation) J68.4
    due to fumes or vapors J68.4
  respiratory, interstitial lung disease J84.115
Bronchitis (diffuse) (fibrinous) (hypostatic)
    (infective) (membranous) J40
  with
    influenza, flu or grippe —*see* Influenza,
        with, respiratory manifestations NEC

Bronchitis (*Continued*)
  with (*Continued*)
    obstruction (airway) (lung) J44.9
    tracheitis (15 years of age and above) J40
      acute or subacute J20.9
      chronic J42
      under 15 years of age J20.9
  acute or subacute (with bronchospasm or
      obstruction) J20.9
    with
      bronchiectasis J47.0
      chronic obstructive pulmonary disease
          J44.0
    chemical (due to gases, fumes or vapors)
        J68.0
    due to
      fumes or vapors J68.0
      Haemophilus influenzae J20.1
      Mycoplasma pneumoniae J20.0
      radiation J70.0
      specified organism NEC J20.8
      Streptococcus J20.2
      virus
        coxsackie J20.3
        echovirus J20.7
        parainfluenzae J20.4
        respiratory syncytial (RSV) J20.5
        rhinovirus J20.6
    viral NEC J20.8
  allergic (acute) J45.909
    with
      exacerbation (acute) J45.901
      status asthmaticus J45.902
  arachidic T17.528
  ⟫aspiration (due to food and vomit) J69.0
  asthmatic J45.9
    chronic J44.9
      with
        acute lower respiratory infection J44.0
        exacerbation (acute) J44.1
  capillary —*see* Pneumonia, broncho
  caseous (tuberculous) A15.5
  Castellani's A69.8
  catarrhal (15 years of age and above) J40
    acute —*see* Bronchitis, acute
    chronic J41.0
    under 15 years of age J20.9
  chemical (acute) (subacute) J68.0
    chronic J68.4
    due to fumes or vapors J68.0
      chronic J68.4
  chronic J42
    with
      airways obstruction J44.9
      tracheitis (chronic) J42
    asthmatic (obstructive) J44.9
    catarrhal J41.0
    chemical (due to fumes or vapors) J68.4
    due to
      chemicals, gases, fumes or vapors
          (inhalation) J68.4
      radiation J70.1
      tobacco smoking J41.0
    emphysematous J44.9
    mucopurulent J41.1
    non-obstructive J41.0
    obliterans J44.9
    obstructive J44.9
    purulent J41.1
    simple J41.0
  croupous —*see* Bronchitis, acute
  due to gases, fumes or vapors (chemical)
      J68.0
  emphysematous (obstructive) J44.9
  exudative —*see* Bronchitis, acute
  fetid J41.1
  grippal —*see* Influenza, with, respiratory
      manifestations NEC
  in those under 15 years age —*see* Bronchitis,
      acute
    chronic —*see* Bronchitis, chronic

Bronchitis (*Continued*)
  influenzal —*see* Influenza, with, respiratory
      manifestations NEC
  mixed simple and mucopurulent J41.8
  moulder's J62.8
  mucopurulent (chronic) (recurrent) J41.1
    acute or subacute J20.9
    simple (mixed) J41.8
  obliterans (chronic) J44.9
  obstructive (chronic) (diffuse) J44.9
  pituitous J41.1
  pneumococcal, acute or subacute J20.2
  pseudomembranous, acute or subacute —*see*
      Bronchitis, acute
  purulent (chronic) (recurrent) J41.1
    acute or subacute —*see* Bronchitis, acute
  putrid J41.1
  senile (chronic) J42
  simple and mucopurulent (mixed) J41.8
  smokers' J41.0
  spirochetal NEC A69.8
  subacute —*see* Bronchitis, acute
  suppurative (chronic) J41.1
    acute or subacute —*see* Bronchitis, acute
  tuberculous A15.5
  under 15 years of age —*see* Bronchitis, acute
    chronic —*see* Bronchitis, chronic
  viral NEC, acute or subacute —*see also*
      Bronchitis, acute J20.8
Bronchoalveolitis J18.0
Bronchoaspergillosis B44.1
Bronchocele meaning goiter E04.0
Broncholithiasis J98.09
  tuberculous NEC A15.5
Bronchomalacia J98.09
  congenital Q32.2
Bronchomycosis NOS B49 [*J99*]
  candidal B37.1
Bronchopleuropneumonia —*see* Pneumonia,
    broncho
Bronchopneumonia —*see* Pneumonia, broncho
Bronchopneumonitis —*see* Pneumonia,
    broncho
Bronchopulmonary —*see* condition
Bronchopulmonitis —*see* Pneumonia, broncho
Bronchorrhagia (*see* Hemoptysis)
Bronchorrhea J98.09
  acute J20.9
  chronic (infective) (purulent) J42
Bronchospasm (acute) J98.01
  with
    bronchiolitis, acute J21.9
    bronchitis, acute (conditions in J20) —*see*
        Bronchitis, acute
  due to external agent —*see* condition,
      respiratory, acute, due to
  exercise induced J45.990
Bronchospirochetosis A69.8
  Castellani A69.8
Bronchostenosis J98.09
Bronchus —*see* condition
Brontophobia F40.220
Bronze baby syndrome P83.88
Brooke's tumor —*see* Neoplasm, skin, benign
Brown enamel of teeth (hereditary) K00.5
Brown's sheath syndrome H50.61-●
Brown-Séquard disease, paralysis or
    syndrome G83.81
Bruce sepsis A23.9
Brucellosis (infection) A23.9
  abortus A23.1
  canis A23.3
  dermatitis A23.9
  melitensis A23.0
  mixed A23.8
  sepsis A23.9
    melitensis A23.0
    specified NEC A23.8
  suis A23.2
Bruck-de Lange disease Q87.19
Bruck's disease —*see* Deformity, limb

▶ New   ⇒ Revised   ~~deleted~~ Deleted   ● Use Additional Character(s)

Burn *(Continued)*
  extent *(Continued)*
    20-29 percent T31.20
      with 0-9 percent third degree burns T31.20
      with 10-19 percent third degree burns T31.21
      with 20-29 percent third degree burns T31.22
    30-39 percent T31.30
      with 0-9 percent third degree burns T31.30
      with 10-19 percent third degree burns T31.31
      with 20-29 percent third degree burns T31.32
      with 30-39 percent third degree burns T31.33
    40-49 percent T31.40
      with 0-9 percent third degree burns T31.40
      with 10-19 percent third degree burns T31.41
      with 20-29 percent third degree burns T31.42
      with 30-39 percent third degree burns T31.43
      with 40-49 percent third degree burns T31.44
    50-59 percent T31.50
      with 0-9 percent third degree burns T31.50
      with 10-19 percent third degree burns T31.51
      with 20-29 percent third degree burns T31.52
      with 30-39 percent third degree burns T31.53
      with 40-49 percent third degree burns T31.54
      with 50-59 percent third degree burns T31.55
    60-69 percent T31.60
      with 0-9 percent third degree burns T31.60
      with 10-19 percent third degree burns T31.61
      with 20-29 percent third degree burns T31.62
      with 30-39 percent third degree burns T31.63
      with 40-49 percent third degree burns T31.64
      with 50-59 percent third degree burns T31.65
      with 60-69 percent third degree burns T31.66
    70-79 percent T31.70
      with 0-9 percent third degree burns T31.70
      with 10-19 percent third degree burns T31.71
      with 20-29 percent third degree burns T31.72
      with 30-39 percent third degree burns T31.73
      with 40-49 percent third degree burns T31.74
      with 50-59 percent third degree burns T31.75
      with 60-69 percent third degree burns T31.76
      with 70-79 percent third degree burns T31.77
    80-89 percent T31.80
      with 0-9 percent third degree burns T31.80
      with 10-19 percent third degree burns T31.81
      with 20-29 percent third degree burns T31.82
      with 30-39 percent third degree burns T31.83
      with 40-49 percent third degree burns T31.84

Burn *(Continued)*
  extent *(Continued)*
    80-89 percent T31.80 *(Continued)*
      with 50-59 percent third degree burns T31.85
      with 60-69 percent third degree burns T31.86
      with 70-79 percent third degree burns T31.87
      with 80-89 percent third degree burns T31.88
    90 percent or more T31.90
      with 0-9 percent third degree burns T31.90
      with 10-19 percent third degree burns T31.91
      with 20-29 percent third degree burns T31.92
      with 30-39 percent third degree burns T31.93
      with 40-49 percent third degree burns T31.94
      with 50-59 percent third degree burns T31.95
      with 60-69 percent third degree burns T31.96
      with 70-79 percent third degree burns T31.97
      with 80-89 percent third degree burns T31.98
      with 90 percent or more third degree burns T31.99
  extremity —*see* Burn, limb
  eye(s) and adnexa T26.4-●
    with resulting rupture and destruction of eyeball T26.2-●
    conjunctival sac —*see* Burn, cornea
    cornea —*see* Burn, cornea
    lid —*see* Burn, eyelid
    periocular area —*see* Burn, eyelid
    specified site NEC T26.3-●
  eyeball —*see* Burn, eye
  eyelid(s) T26.0-●
    chemical —*see* Corrosion, eyelid
  face —*see* Burn, head
  finger T23.029
    first degree T23.129
    left T23.022
      first degree T23.122
      second degree T23.222
      third degree T23.322
    multiple sites (without thumb) T23.039
      with thumb T23.049
        first degree T23.149
        left T23.042
          first degree T23.142
          second degree T23.242
          third degree T23.342
        right T23.041
          first degree T23.141
          second degree T23.241
          third degree T23.341
        second degree T23.249
        third degree T23.349
      first degree T23.139
      left T23.032
        first degree T23.132
        second degree T23.232
        third degree T23.332
      right T23.031
        first degree T23.131
        second degree T23.231
        third degree T23.331
      second degree T23.239
      third degree T23.339
    right T23.021
      first degree T23.121
      second degree T23.221
      third degree T23.321
    second degree T23.229
    third degree T23.329
  flank —*see* Burn, abdominal wall

Burn *(Continued)*
  foot T25.029
    first degree T25.129
    left T25.022
      first degree T25.122
      second degree T25.222
      third degree T25.322
    multiple with ankle —*see* Burn, lower, limb, multiple, ankle and foot
    right T25.021
      first degree T25.121
      second degree T25.221
      third degree T25.321
    second degree T25.229
    third degree T25.329
  forearm T22.019
    first degree T22.119
    left T22.012
      first degree T22.112
      second degree T22.212
      third degree T22.312
    right T22.011
      first degree T22.111
      second degree T22.211
      third degree T22.311
    second degree T22.219
    third degree T22.319
  forehead T20.06
    first degree T20.16
    second degree T20.26
    third degree T20.36
  fourth degree - code as Burn, third degree, by site
  friction —*see* Burn, by site
  from swallowing caustic or corrosive substance NEC —*see* Corrosion, by site
  full thickness skin loss - code as Burn, third degree, by site
  gastrointestinal tract NEC T28.2
    from swallowing caustic or corrosive substance T28.7
  genital organs
    external
      female T21.07
        first degree T21.17
        second degree T21.27
        third degree T21.37
      male T21.06
        first degree T21.16
        second degree T21.26
        third degree T21.36
    internal T28.3
      from caustic or corrosive substance T28.8
  groin —*see* Burn, abdominal wall
  hand(s) T23.009
    back —*see* Burn, dorsum of hand
    finger —*see* Burn, finger
    first degree T23.109
    left T23.002
      first degree T23.102
      second degree T23.202
      third degree T23.302
    multiple sites with wrist T23.099
      first degree T23.199
      left T23.092
        first degree T23.192
        second degree T23.292
        third degree T23.392
      right T23.091
        first degree T23.191
        second degree T23.291
        third degree T23.391
      second degree T23.299
      third degree T23.399
    palm —*see* Burn, palm
    right T23.001
      first degree T23.101
      second degree T23.201
      third degree T23.301

Burn *(Continued)*
  hand *(Continued)*
    second degree T23.209
    third degree T23.309
    thumb —*see* Burn, thumb
  head (and face) (and neck) T20.00
    cheek —*see* Burn, cheek
    chin —*see* Burn, chin
    ear —*see* Burn, ear
    eye(s) only —*see* Burn, eye
    first degree T20.10
    forehead —*see* Burn, forehead
    lip —*see* Burn, lip
    multiple sites T20.09
      first degree T20.19
      second degree T20.29
      third degree T20.39
    neck —*see* Burn, neck
    nose —*see* Burn, nose
    scalp —*see* Burn, scalp
    second degree T20.20
    third degree T20.30
  hip(s) —*see* Burn, thigh
  inhalation —*see* Burn, respiratory tract
    caustic or corrosive substance (fumes) —*see*
      Corrosion, respiratory tract
  internal organ(s) T28.40
    alimentary tract T28.2
      esophagus T28.1
    eardrum T28.41
    esophagus T28.1
    from caustic or corrosive substance
      (swallowing) NEC —*see* Corrosion,
      by site
    genitourinary T28.3
    mouth T28.0
    pharynx T28.0
    respiratory tract —*see* Burn, respiratory
      tract
    specified organ NEC T28.49
  interscapular region —*see* Burn, back,
    upper
  intestine (large) (small) T28.2
  knee T24.029
    first degree T24.129
    left T24.022
      first degree T24.122
      second degree T24.222
      third degree T24.322
    right T24.021
      first degree T24.121
      second degree T24.221
      third degree T24.321
    second degree T24.229
    third degree T24.329
  labium (majus) (minus) —*see* Burn, genital
    organs, external, female
  lacrimal apparatus, duct, gland or sac —*see*
    Burn, eye, specified site NEC
  larynx T27.0
    with lung T27.1
  leg(s) (lower) (upper) —*see* Burn, lower,
    limb
  lightning —*see* Burn, by site
  limb(s)
    lower (except ankle or foot alone) —*see*
      Burn, lower, limb
    upper —*see* Burn, upper limb
  lip(s) T20.02
    first degree T20.12
    second degree T20.22
    third degree T20.32
  lower
    back —*see* Burn, back
    limb T24.009
      ankle —*see* Burn, ankle
      calf —*see* Burn, calf
      first degree T24.109
      foot —*see* Burn, foot
      hip —*see* Burn, thigh
      knee —*see* Burn, knee

Burn *(Continued)*
  lower *(Continued)*
    limb *(Continued)*
      left T24.002
        first degree T24.102
        second degree T24.202
        third degree T24.302
      multiple sites, except ankle and foot
        T24.099
        ankle and foot T25.099
          first degree T25.199
          left T25.092
            first degree T25.192
            second degree T25.292
            third degree T25.392
          right T25.091
            first degree T25.191
            second degree T25.291
            third degree T25.391
          second degree T25.299
          third degree T25.399
        first degree T24.199
        left T24.092
          first degree T24.192
          second degree T24.292
          third degree T24.392
        right T24.091
          first degree T24.191
          second degree T24.291
          third degree T24.391
        second degree T24.299
        third degree T24.399
      right T24.001
        first degree T24.101
        second degree T24.201
        third degree T24.301
      second degree T24.209
      thigh —*see* Burn, thigh
      third degree T24.309
      toe —*see* Burn, toe
  lung (with larynx and trachea) T27.1
  mouth T28.0
  neck T20.07
    first degree T20.17
    second degree T20.27
    third degree T20.37
  nose (septum) T20.04
    first degree T20.14
    second degree T20.24
    third degree T20.34
  ocular adnexa —*see* Burn, eye
  orbit region —*see* Burn, eyelid
  palm T23.059
    first degree T23.159
    left T23.052
      first degree T23.152
      second degree T23.252
      third degree T23.352
    right T23.051
      first degree T23.151
      second degree T23.251
      third degree T23.351
    second degree T23.259
    third degree T23.359
  partial thickness - code as Burn, degree,
    by site
  pelvis —*see* Burn, trunk
  penis —*see* Burn, genital organs, external,
    male
  perineum
    female —*see* Burn, genital organs, external,
      female
    male —*see* Burn, genital organs, external,
      male
  periocular area —*see* Burn, eyelid
  pharynx T28.0
  rectum T28.2
  respiratory tract T27.3
    larynx —*see* Burn, larynx
    specified part NEC T27.2
    trachea —*see* Burn, trachea

Burn *(Continued)*
  sac, lacrimal —*see* Burn, eye, specified site
    NEC
  scalp T20.05
    first degree T20.15
    second degree T20.25
    third degree T20.35
  scapular region T22.069
    first degree T22.169
    left T22.062
      first degree T22.162
      second degree T22.262
      third degree T22.362
    right T22.061
      first degree T22.161
      second degree T22.261
      third degree T22.361
    second degree T22.269
    third degree T22.369
  sclera —*see* Burn, eye, specified site NEC
  scrotum —*see* Burn, genital organs, external,
    male
  shoulder T22.059
    first degree T22.159
    left T22.052
      first degree T22.152
      second degree T22.252
      third degree T22.352
    right T22.051
      first degree T22.151
      second degree T22.251
      third degree T22.351
    second degree T22.259
    third degree T22.359
  stomach T28.2
  temple —*see* Burn, head
  testis —*see* Burn, genital organs, external, male
  thigh T24.019
    first degree T24.119
    left T24.012
      first degree T24.112
      second degree T24.212
      third degree T24.312
    right T24.011
      first degree T24.111
      second degree T24.211
      third degree T24.311
    second degree T24.219
    third degree T24.319
  thorax (external) —*see* Burn, trunk
  throat (meaning pharynx) T28.0
  thumb(s) T23.019
    first degree T23.119
    left T23.012
      first degree T23.112
      second degree T23.212
      third degree T23.312
    multiple sites with fingers T23.049
      first degree T23.149
      left T23.042
        first degree T23.142
        second degree T23.242
        third degree T23.342
      right T23.041
        first degree T23.141
        second degree T23.241
        third degree T23.341
      second degree T23.249
      third degree T23.349
    right T23.011
      first degree T23.111
      second degree T23.211
      third degree T23.311
    second degree T23.219
    third degree T23.319
  toe T25.039
    first degree T25.139
    left T25.032
      first degree T25.132
      second degree T25.232
      third degree T25.332

▶ New   ⇨ Revised   ~~deleted~~ Deleted   ● Use Additional Character(s)

Burn *(Continued)*
  toe *(Continued)*
    right T25.031
      first degree T25.131
      second degree T25.231
      third degree T25.331
    second degree T25.239
    third degree T25.339
  tongue T28.0
  tonsil(s) T28.0
  trachea T27.0
    with lung T27.1
  trunk T21.00
    abdominal wall —*see* Burn, abdominal wall
    anus —*see* Burn, buttock
    axilla —*see* Burn, upper limb
    back —*see* Burn, back
    breast —*see* Burn, chest wall
    buttock —*see* Burn, buttock
    chest wall —*see* Burn, chest wall
    first degree T21.10
    flank —*see* Burn, abdominal wall
    genital
      female —*see* Burn, genital organs, external, female
      male —*see* Burn, genital organs, external, male
    groin —*see* Burn, abdominal wall
    interscapular region —*see* Burn, back, upper
    labia —*see* Burn, genital organs, external, female
    lower back —*see* Burn, back
    penis —*see* Burn, genital organs, external, male
    perineum
      female —*see* Burn, genital organs, external, female
      male —*see* Burn, genital organs, external, male
    scapula region —*see* Burn, scapular region
    scrotum —*see* Burn, genital organs, external, male
    second degree T21.20
    specified site NEC T21.09
      first degree T21.19
      second degree T21.29
      third degree T21.39
    testes —*see* Burn, genital organs, external, male
    third degree T21.30
    upper back —*see* Burn, back, upper
    vulva —*see* Burn, genital organs, external, female
  unspecified site with extent of body surface involved specified
    less than 10 percent T31.0
    10-19 percent (0-9 percent third degree) T31.10
      with 10-19 percent third degree T31.11
    20-29 percent (0-9 percent third degree) T31.20
      with
        10-19 percent third degree T31.21
        20-29 percent third degree T31.22
    30-39 percent (0-9 percent third degree) T31.30
      with
        10-19 percent third degree T31.31
        20-29 percent third degree T31.32
        30-39 percent third degree T31.33
    40-49 percent (0-9 percent third degree) T31.40
      with
        10-19 percent third degree T31.41
        20-29 percent third degree T31.42
        30-39 percent third degree T31.43
        40-49 percent third degree T31.44

Burn *(Continued)*
  unspecified site with extent of body surface involved specified *(Continued)*
    50-59 percent (0-9 percent third degree) T31.50
      with
        10-19 percent third degree T31.51
        20-29 percent third degree T31.52
        30-39 percent third degree T31.53
        40-49 percent third degree T31.54
        50-59 percent third degree T31.55
    60-69 percent (0-9 percent third degree) T31.60
      with
        10-19 percent third degree T31.61
        20-29 percent third degree T31.62
        30-39 percent third degree T31.63
        40-49 percent third degree T31.64
        50-59 percent third degree T31.65
        60-69 percent third degree T31.66
    70-79 percent (0-9 percent third degree) T31.70
      with
        10-19 percent third degree T31.71
        20-29 percent third degree T31.72
        30-39 percent third degree T31.73
        40-49 percent third degree T31.74
        50-59 percent third degree T31.75
        60-69 percent third degree T31.76
        70-79 percent third degree T31.77
    80-89 percent (0-9 percent third degree) T31.80
      with
        10-19 percent third degree T31.81
        20-29 percent third degree T31.82
        30-39 percent third degree T31.83
        40-49 percent third degree T31.84
        50-59 percent third degree T31.85
        60-69 percent third degree T31.86
        70-79 percent third degree T31.87
        80-89 percent third degree T31.88
    90 percent or more (0-9 percent third degree) T31.90
      with
        10-19 percent third degree T31.91
        20-29 percent third degree T31.92
        30-39 percent third degree T31.93
        40-49 percent third degree T31.94
        50-59 percent third degree T31.95
        60-69 percent third degree T31.96
        70-79 percent third degree T31.97
        80-89 percent third degree T31.98
        90-99 percent third degree T31.99
  upper limb T22.00
    above elbow —*see* Burn, above elbow
    axilla —*see* Burn, axilla
    elbow —*see* Burn, elbow
    first degree T22.10
    forearm —*see* Burn, forearm
    hand —*see* Burn, hand
    interscapular region —*see* Burn, back, upper
    multiple sites T22.099
      first degree T22.199
      left T22.092
        first degree T22.192
        second degree T22.292
        third degree T22.392
      right T22.091
        first degree T22.191
        second degree T22.291
        third degree T22.391
      second degree T22.299
      third degree T22.399
    scapular region —*see* Burn, scapular region
    second degree T22.20
    shoulder —*see* Burn, shoulder
    third degree T22.30
    wrist —*see* Burn, wrist
  uterus T28.3
  vagina T28.3

Burn *(Continued)*
  vulva —*see* Burn, genital organs, external, female
  wrist T23.079
    first degree T23.179
    left T23.072
      first degree T23.172
      second degree T23.272
      third degree T23.372
    multiple sites with hand T23.099
      first degree T23.199
      left T23.092
        first degree T23.192
        second degree T23.292
        third degree T23.392
      right T23.091
        first degree T23.191
        second degree T23.291
        third degree T23.391
      second degree T23.299
      third degree T23.399
    right T23.071
      first degree T23.171
      second degree T23.271
      third degree T23.371
    second degree T23.279
    third degree T23.379
Burnett's syndrome E83.52
Burning
  feet syndrome E53.9
  sensation R20.8
  tongue K14.6
Burn-out (state) Z73.0
Burns' disease or osteochondrosis —*see* Osteochondrosis, juvenile, ulna
Bursa —*see* condition
Bursitis M71.9
  Achilles —*see* Tendinitis, Achilles
  adhesive —*see* Bursitis, specified NEC
  ankle —*see* Enthesopathy, lower limb, ankle, specified type NEC
  calcaneal —*see* Enthesopathy, foot, specified type NEC
  collateral ligament, tibial —*see* Bursitis, tibial collateral
  due to use, overuse, pressure —*see also* Disorder, soft tissue, due to use, specified type NEC
    specified NEC —*see* Disorder, soft tissue, due to use, specified NEC
  Duplay's M75.0
  elbow NEC M70.3-●
    olecranon M70.2-●
  finger —*see* Disorder, soft tissue, due to use, specified type NEC, hand
  foot —*see* Enthesopathy, foot, specified type NEC
  gonococcal A54.49
  gouty —*see* Gout
  hand M70.1-●
  hip NEC M70.7-●
    trochanteric M70.6-●
  infective NEC M71.10
    abscess —*see* Abscess, bursa
    ankle M71.17-●
    elbow M71.12-●
    foot M71.17-●
    hand M71.14-●
    hip M71.15-●
    knee M71.16-●
    multiple sites M71.19
    shoulder M71.11-●
    specified site NEC M71.18
    wrist M71.13-●
  ischial —*see* Bursitis, hip
  knee NEC M70.5-●
    prepatellar M70.4-●
  occupational NEC —*see also* Disorder, soft tissue, due to, use
  olecranon —*see* Bursitis, elbow, olecranon
  pharyngeal J39.1

Bursitis *(Continued)*
  popliteal —*see* Bursitis, knee
  prepatellar M70.4-●
  radiohumeral M77.8
  rheumatoid M06.20
    ankle M06.27-●
    elbow M06.22-●
    foot joint M06.27-●
    hand joint M06.24-●
    hip M06.25-●
    knee M06.26-●
    multiple site M06.29
    shoulder M06.21-●
    vertebra M06.28
    wrist M06.23-●
  scapulohumeral —*see* Bursitis, shoulder
  semimembranous muscle (knee) —*see*
      Bursitis, knee
  shoulder M75.5-●
    adhesive —*see* Capsulitis, adhesive
  specified NEC M71.50
    ankle M71.57-●
    due to use, overuse or pressure —*see*
        Disorder, soft tissue, due to, use
    elbow M71.52-●
    foot M71.57-●
    hand M71.54-●

Bursitis *(Continued)*
  specified NEC *(Continued)*
    hip M71.55-●
    knee M71.56-●
    shoulder —*see* Bursitis, shoulder
    specified site NEC M71.58
    tibial collateral M76.4-●
    wrist M71.53-●
  subacromial —*see* Bursitis, shoulder
  subcoracoid —*see* Bursitis, shoulder
  subdeltoid —*see* Bursitis, shoulder
  syphilitic A52.78
  Thornwaldt, Tornwaldt J39.2
  tibial collateral M76.4-●
  toe —*see* Enthesopathy, foot, specified type
      NEC
  trochanteric (area) —*see* Bursitis, hip,
      trochanteric
  wrist —*see* Bursitis, hand
Bursopathy M71.9
  specified type NEC M71.80
    ankle M71.87-●
    elbow M71.82-●
    foot M71.87-●
    hand M71.84-●
    hip M71.85-●
    knee M71.86-●

Bursopathy *(Continued)*
  specified type NEC *(Continued)*
    multiple sites M71.89
    shoulder M71.81-●
    specified site NEC M71.88
    wrist M71.83-●
Burst stitches or sutures (complication of
    surgery) T81.31
  external operation wound T81.31
  internal operation wound T81.32
Buruli ulcer A31.1
Bury's disease L95.1
Buschke's
  ➡disease —*see* Cryptococcosis by site
  scleredema —*see* Sclerosis, systemic
➡Busse-Buschke disease —*see* Cryptococcosis by
    site
Buttock —*see* condition
Button
  Biskra B55.1
  Delhi B55.1
  oriental B55.1
Buttonhole deformity (finger) —*see* Deformity,
    finger, boutonniere
Bwamba fever A92.8
Byssinosis J66.0
Bywaters' syndrome T79.5

▶ New   ➡ Revised   ~~deleted~~ Deleted   ● Use Additional Character(s)

C

Cachexia R64
  cancerous R64
  cardiac —see Disease, heart
  dehydration E86.0
  due to malnutrition R64
  exophthalmic —see Hyperthyroidism
  heart —see Disease, heart
  hypophyseal E23.0
  hypopituitary E23.0
  lead —see Poisoning, lead
  malignant R64
  marsh —see Malaria
  nervous F48.8
  old age R54
  paludal —see Malaria
  pituitary E23.0
  renal N28.9
  saturnine —see Poisoning, lead
  senile R54
  Simmonds' E23.0
  splenica D73.0
  strumipriva E03.4
  tuberculous NEC —see Tuberculosis
CADASIL (cerebral autosomal dominant arteriopathy with subcortical infarcts and leukoencephalopathy) I67.850
Café au lait spots L81.3
Caffeine-induced
  anxiety disorder F15.980
  sleep disorder F15.982
Caffey's syndrome Q78.8
Caisson disease T70.3
Cake kidney Q63.1
Caked breast (puerperal, postpartum) O92.79
Calabar swelling B74.3
Calcaneal spur —see Spur, bone, calcaneal
Calcaneo-apophysitis M92.8
Calcareous —see condition
Calcicosis J62.8
Calciferol (vitamin D) deficiency E55.9
  with rickets E55.0
Calcification
  adrenal (capsule) (gland) E27.49
    tuberculous E35 [B90.8]
  aorta I70.0
  artery (annular) —see Arteriosclerosis
  auricle (ear) —see Disorder, pinna, specified type NEC
  basal ganglia G23.8
  bladder N32.89
    due to Schistosoma hematobium B65.0
  brain (cortex) —see Calcification, cerebral
  bronchus J98.09
  bursa M71.40
    ankle M71.47-●
    elbow M71.42-●
    foot M71.47-●
    hand M71.44-●
    hip M71.45-●
    knee M71.46-●
    multiple sites M71.49
    shoulder M75.3-●
    specified site NEC M71.48
    wrist M71.43-●
  cardiac —see Degeneration, myocardial
  cerebral (cortex) G93.89
    artery I67.2
  cervix (uteri) N88.8
  choroid plexus G93.89
  conjunctiva —see Concretion, conjunctiva
  corpora cavernosa (penis) N48.89
  cortex (brain) —see Calcification, cerebral
  dental pulp (nodular) K04.2
  dentinal papilla K00.4
  fallopian tube N83.8
  falx cerebri G96.198
  gallbladder K82.8
  general E83.59
  heart —see also Degeneration, myocardial
    valve —see Endocarditis

Calcification (Continued)
  idiopathic infantile arterial (IIAC) Q28.8
  intervertebral cartilage or disc (postinfective) —see Disorder, disc, specified NEC
  intracranial —see Calcification, cerebral
  joint —see Disorder, joint, specified type NEC
  kidney N28.89
    tuberculous N29 [B90.1]
  larynx (senile) J38.7
  lens —see Cataract, specified NEC
  lung (active) (postinfectional) J98.4
    tuberculous B90.9
  lymph gland or node (postinfectional) I89.8
    tuberculous —see also Tuberculosis, lymph gland B90.8
  mammographic R92.1
  massive (paraplegic) —see Myositis, ossificans, in, quadriplegia
  medial —see Arteriosclerosis, extremities
  meninges (cerebral) (spinal) G96.198
  metastatic E83.59
  Mönckeberg's —see Arteriosclerosis, extremities
  muscle M61.9
    due to burns —see Myositis, ossificans, in, burns
    paralytic —see Myositis, ossificans, in, quadriplegia
    specified type NEC M61.40
      ankle M61.47-●
      foot M61.47-●
      forearm M61.43-●
      hand M61.44-●
      lower leg M61.46-●
      multiple sites M61.49
      pelvic region M61.45-●
      shoulder region M61.41-●
      specified site NEC M61.48
      thigh M61.45-●
      upper arm M61.42-●
  myocardium, myocardial —see Degeneration, myocardial
  ovary N83.8
  pancreas K86.89
  penis N48.89
  periarticular —see Disorder, joint, specified type NEC
  pericardium —see also Pericarditis I31.1
  pineal gland E34.8
  pleura J94.8
    postinfectional J94.8
    tuberculous NEC B90.9
  pulpal (dental) (nodular) K04.2
  sclera H15.89
  spleen D73.89
  subcutaneous L94.2
  suprarenal (capsule) (gland) E27.49
  tendon (sheath) —see also Tenosynovitis, specified type NEC
    with bursitis, synovitis or tenosynovitis —see Tendinitis, calcific
  trachea J39.8
  ureter N28.89
  vitreous —see Deposit, crystalline
Calcified —see Calcification
Calcinosis (interstitial) (tumoral) (universalis) E83.59
  with Raynaud's phenomenon, esophageal dysfunction, sclerodactyly, telangiectasia (CREST syndrome) M34.1
  circumscripta (skin) L94.2
  cutis L94.2
Calciphylaxis —see also Calcification, by site E83.59
Calcium
  deposits —see Calcification, by site
  metabolism disorder E83.50
  salts or soaps in vitreous —see Deposit, crystalline

Calciuria R82.994
Calculi —see Calculus
Calculosis, intrahepatic —see Calculus, bile duct
Calculus, calculi, calculous
  ampulla of Vater —see Calculus, bile duct
  anuria (impacted) (recurrent) —see also Calculus, urinary N20.9
  appendix K38.1
  bile duct (common) (hepatic) K80.50
    with
      calculus of gallbladder —see Calculus, gallbladder and bile duct
      cholangitis K80.30
        with
          cholecystitis —see Calculus, bile duct, with cholecystitis
          obstruction K80.31
        acute K80.32
          with
            chronic cholangitis K80.36
              with obstruction K80.37
            obstruction K80.33
        chronic K80.34
          with
            acute cholangitis K80.36
              with obstruction K80.37
            obstruction K80.35
      cholecystitis (with cholangitis) K80.40
        with obstruction K80.41
        acute K80.42
          with
            chronic cholecystitis K80.46
              with obstruction K80.47
            obstruction K80.43
        chronic K80.44
          with
            acute cholecystitis K80.46
              with obstruction K80.47
            obstruction K80.45
      obstruction K80.51
  biliary —see also Calculus, gallbladder
    specified NEC K80.80
      with obstruction K80.81
  bilirubin, multiple —see Calculus, gallbladder
  bladder (encysted) (impacted) (urinary) (diverticulum) N21.0
  bronchus J98.09
  calyx (kidney) (renal) —see Calculus, kidney
  cholesterol (pure) (solitary) —see Calculus, gallbladder
  common duct (bile) —see Calculus, bile duct
  conjunctiva —see Concretion, conjunctiva
  cystic N21.0
    duct —see Calculus, gallbladder
  dental (subgingival) (supragingival) K03.6
  diverticulum
    bladder N21.0
    kidney N20.0
  epididymis N50.89
  gallbladder K80.20
    with
      bile duct calculus —see Calculus, gallbladder and bile duct
      cholecystitis K80.10
        with obstruction K80.11
        acute K80.00
          with
            chronic cholecystitis K80.12
              with obstruction K80.13
            obstruction K80.01
        chronic K80.10
          with
            acute cholecystitis K80.12
              with obstruction K80.13
            obstruction K80.11
        specified NEC K80.18
          with obstruction K80.19
      obstruction K80.21

Calculus, calculi, calculous *(Continued)*
  gallbladder and bile duct K80.70
    with
      cholecystitis K80.60
        with obstruction K80.61
        acute K80.62
          with
            chronic cholecystitis K80.66
              with obstruction K80.67
            obstruction K80.63
          chronic K80.64
            with
              acute cholecystitis K80.66
                with obstruction K80.67
              obstruction K80.65
        obstruction K80.71
  hepatic (duct) —*see* Calculus, bile duct
  hepatobiliary K80.80
    with obstruction K80.81
  ileal conduit N21.8
  intestinal (impaction) (obstruction) K56.49
  kidney (impacted) (multiple) (pelvis)
      (recurrent) (staghorn) N20.0
    with calculus, ureter N20.2
    congenital Q63.8
  lacrimal passages —*see* Dacryolith
  liver (impacted) —*see* Calculus, bile duct
  lung J98.4
  mammographic R92.1
  nephritic (impacted) (recurrent) —*see*
      Calculus, kidney
  nose J34.89
  pancreas (duct) K86.89
  parotid duct or gland K11.5
  pelvis, encysted —*see* Calculus, kidney
  prostate N42.0
  pulmonary J98.4
  pyelitis (impacted) (recurrent) N20.0
    with hydronephrosis N13.6
  pyelonephritis (impacted) (recurrent) —*see*
      category N20
    with hydronephrosis N13.6
  renal (impacted) (recurrent) —*see* Calculus,
      kidney
  salivary (duct) (gland) K11.5
  seminal vesicle N50.89
  staghorn —*see* Calculus, kidney
  Stensen's duct K11.5
  stomach K31.89
  sublingual duct or gland K11.5
    congenital Q38.4
  submandibular duct, gland or region K11.5
  submaxillary duct, gland or region K11.5
  suburethral N21.8
  tonsil J35.8
  tooth, teeth (subgingival) (supragingival) K03.6
  tunica vaginalis N50.89
  ureter (impacted) (recurrent) N20.1
    with calculus, kidney N20.2
      with hydronephrosis N13.2
        with infection N13.6
  ▶ureteropelvic junction N20.1
  urethra (impacted) N21.1
  urinary (duct) (impacted) (passage) (tract)
      N20.9
    with hydronephrosis N13.2
      with infection N13.6
    in (due to)
    lower N21.9
      specified NEC N21.8
  vagina N89.8
  vesical (impacted) N21.0
  Wharton's duct K11.5
  xanthine E79.8 [N22]
Calicectasis N28.89
Caliectasis N28.89
California
  disease B38.9
  encephalitis A83.5
Caligo cornea —*see* Opacity, cornea, central
Callositas, callosity (infected) L84

Callus (infected) L84
  bone —*see* Osteophyte
    excessive, following fracture - code as
        Sequelae of fracture
CALME (childhood asymmetric labium majus
    enlargement) N90.61
Calorie deficiency or malnutrition —*see also*
    Malnutrition E46
Calvé-Perthes disease —*see* Legg-Calve-Perthes
    disease
Calvé's disease —*see* Osteochondrosis, juvenile,
    spine
Calvities —*see* Alopecia, androgenic
Cameroon fever —*see* Malaria
Camptocormia (hysterical) F44.4
Camurati-Engelmann syndrome Q78.3
Canal —*see also* condition
  atrioventricular common Q21.2
Canaliculitis (lacrimal) (acute) (subacute)
    H04.33-●
  Actinomyces A42.89
  chronic H04.42-●
Canavan's disease E75.29
Canceled procedure (surgical) Z53.9
  because of
    contraindication Z53.09
      smoking Z53.01
    left against medical advice (AMA) Z53.29
    patient's decision Z53.20
      for reasons of belief or group pressure
          Z53.1
      specified reason NEC Z53.29
    specified reason NEC Z53.8
Cancer —*see also* Neoplasm, by site, malignant
  bile duct type, liver C22.1
  blood —*see* Leukemia
  breast —*see also* Neoplasm, breast, malignant
      C50.91-●
  hepatocellular C22.0
  lung —*see also* Neoplasm, lung, malignant
      C34.90-●
  ovarian —*see also* Neoplasm, ovary,
      malignant C56.9-●
  unspecified site (primary) C80.1
Cancer (o)phobia F45.29
Cancerous —*see* Neoplasm, malignant, by site
Cancrum oris A69.0
Candidiasis, candidal B37.9
  balanitis B37.42
  bronchitis B37.1
  cheilitis B37.83
  congenital P37.5
  cystitis B37.41
  disseminated B37.7
  endocarditis B37.6
  enteritis B37.82
  esophagitis B37.81
  intertrigo B37.2
  lung B37.1
  meningitis B37.5
  mouth B37.0
  nails B37.2
  neonatal P37.5
  onychia B37.2
  oral B37.0
  osteomyelitis B37.89
  otitis externa B37.84
  paronychia B37.2
  perionyxis B37.2
  pneumonia B37.1
  proctitis B37.82
  pulmonary B37.1
  pyelonephritis B37.49
  sepsis B37.7
  skin B37.2
  specified site NEC B37.89
  stomatitis B37.0
  systemic B37.7
  urethritis B37.41
  urogenital site NEC B37.49
  vagina B37.3
  vulva B37.3
  vulvovaginitis B37.3

Candidid L30.2
Candidosis —*see* Candidiasis
Candiru infection or infestation B88.8
Canities (premature) L67.1
  congenital Q84.2
Canker (mouth) (sore) K12.0
  rash A38.9
Cannabinosis J66.2
Cannabis induced
  anxiety disorder F12.980
  psychotic disorder F12.959
  sleep disorder F12.988
Canton fever A75.9
Cantrell's syndrome Q87.89
Capillariasis (intestinal) B81.1
  hepatic B83.8
Capillary —*see* condition
Caplan's syndrome —*see* Rheumatoid, lung
Capsule —*see* condition
Capsulitis (joint) —*see also* Enthesopathy
  adhesive (shoulder) M75.0-●
  hepatic K65.8
  labyrinthine —*see* Otosclerosis, specified NEC
  thyroid E06.9
Caput
  crepitus Q75.8
  medusae I86.8
  succedaneum P12.81
Car sickness T75.3
Carapata (disease) A68.0
Carate —*see* Pinta
Carbon lung J60
Carbuncle L02.93
  abdominal wall L02.231
  anus K61.0
  auditory canal, external —*see* Abscess, ear,
      external
  auricle ear —*see* Abscess, ear, external
  axilla L02.43-●
  back (any part) L02.232
  breast N61.1
  buttock L02.33
  cheek (external) L02.03
  chest wall L02.233
  chin L02.03
  corpus cavernosum N48.21
  ear (any part) (external) (middle) —*see*
      Abscess, ear, external
  external auditory canal —*see* Abscess, ear,
      external
  eyelid —*see* Abscess, eyelid
  face NEC L02.03
  femoral (region) —*see* Carbuncle, lower limb
  finger —*see* Carbuncle, hand
  flank L02.231
  foot L02.63-●
  forehead L02.03
  genital —*see* Abscess, genital
  gluteal (region) L02.33
  groin L02.234
  hand L02.53-●
  head NEC L02.831
  heel —*see* Carbuncle, foot
  hip —*see* Carbuncle, lower limb
  kidney —*see* Abscess, kidney
  knee —*see* Carbuncle, lower limb
  labium (majus) (minus) N76.4
  lacrimal
    gland —*see* Dacryoadenitis
    passages (duct) (sac) —*see* Inflammation,
        lacrimal, passages, acute
  leg —*see* Carbuncle, lower limb
  lower limb L02.43-●
  malignant A22.0
  navel L02.236
  neck L02.13
  nose (external) (septum) J34.0
  orbit, orbital —*see* Abscess, orbit
  palmar (space) —*see* Carbuncle, hand
  partes posteriores L02.33
  pectoral region L02.233
  penis N48.21

▶ New   ⇒ Revised   ~~deleted~~ Deleted   ● Use Additional Character(s)

Carbuncle (Continued)
    perineum L02.235
    pinna —see Abscess, ear, external
    popliteal —see Carbuncle, lower limb
    scalp L02.831
    seminal vesicle N49.0
    shoulder —see Carbuncle, upper limb
    specified site NEC L02.838
    temple (region) L02.03
    thumb —see Carbuncle, hand
    toe —see Carbuncle, foot
    trunk L02.239
      abdominal wall L02.231
      back L02.232
      chest wall L02.233
      groin L02.234
      perineum L02.235
      umbilicus L02.236
    umbilicus L02.236
    upper limb L02.43-•
    urethra N34.0
    vulva N76.4
Carbunculus —see Carbuncle
Carcinoid (tumor) —see Tumor, carcinoid
Carcinoidosis E34.0
Carcinoma (malignant) —see also Neoplasm,
    by site, malignant
    acidophil
      specified site —see Neoplasm, malignant,
        by site
      unspecified site C75.1
    acidophil-basophil, mixed
      specified site —see Neoplasm, malignant,
        by site
      unspecified site C75.1
    adnexal (skin) —see Neoplasm, skin, malignant
    adrenal cortical C74.0-•
    alveolar —see Neoplasm, lung, malignant
      cell —see Neoplasm, lung, malignant
    ameloblastic C41.1
      upper jaw (bone) C41.0
    apocrine
      breast —see Neoplasm, breast, malignant
      specified site NEC —see Neoplasm, skin,
        malignant
      unspecified site C44.99
    basal cell (pigmented) (see also Neoplasm,
      skin, malignant) C44.91
      fibro-epithelial —see Neoplasm, skin,
        malignant
      morphea —see Neoplasm, skin, malignant
      multicentric —see Neoplasm, skin,
        malignant
    basaloid
    basal-squamous cell, mixed —see Neoplasm,
      skin, malignant
    basophil
      specified site —see Neoplasm, malignant,
        by site
      unspecified site C75.1
    basophil-acidophil, mixed
      specified site —see Neoplasm, malignant,
        by site
      unspecified site C75.1
    basosquamous —see Neoplasm, skin, malignant
    bile duct
      with hepatocellular, mixed C22.0
      liver C22.1
      specified site NEC —see Neoplasm,
        malignant, by site
      unspecified site C22.1
    branchial or branchiogenic C10.4
    bronchial or bronchogenic —see Neoplasm,
      lung, malignant
    bronchiolar —see Neoplasm, lung, malignant
    bronchioloalveolar —see Neoplasm, lung,
      malignant
    C cell
      specified site —see Neoplasm, malignant,
        by site
      unspecified site C73
    ceruminous C44.29-•

Carcinoma (Continued)
    cervix uteri
      in situ D06.9
        endocervix D06.0
        exocervix D06.1
        specified site NEC D06.7
    chorionic
      specified site —see Neoplasm, malignant,
        by site
      unspecified site
        female C58
        male C62.90
    chromophobe
      specified site —see Neoplasm, malignant,
        by site
      unspecified site C75.1
    cloacogenic
      specified site —see Neoplasm, malignant,
        by site
      unspecified site C21.2
    diffuse type
      specified site —see Neoplasm, malignant,
        by site
      unspecified site C16.9
    duct (cell)
      with Paget's disease —see Neoplasm,
        breast, malignant
      infiltrating
        with lobular carcinoma (in situ)
          specified site —see Neoplasm,
            malignant, by site
          unspecified site (female) C50.91-•
            male C50.92-•
        specified site —see Neoplasm,
          malignant, by site
        unspecified site (female) C50.91-•
          male C50.92-•
    ductal
      with lobular
        specified site —see Neoplasm,
          malignant, by site
        unspecified site (female) C50.91-•
          male C50.92-•
    ductular, infiltrating
      specified site —see Neoplasm, malignant,
        by site
      unspecified site (female) C50.91-•
        male C50.92-•
    embryonal
      liver C22.7
    endometrioid
      specified site —see Neoplasm, malignant,
        by site
      unspecified site
        female C56.9
        male C61
    eosinophil
      specified site —see Neoplasm, malignant,
        by site
      unspecified site C75.1
    epidermoid —see also Neoplasm, skin
      malignant
      in situ, Bowen's type —see Neoplasm, skin,
        in situ
    fibroepithelial, basal cell —see Neoplasm,
      skin, malignant
    follicular
      with papillary (mixed) C73
      moderately differentiated C73
      pure follicle C73
      specified site —see Neoplasm, malignant,
        by site
      trabecular C73
      unspecified site C73
      well differentiated C73
    generalized, with unspecified primary site
      C80.0
    glycogen-rich —see Neoplasm, breast,
      malignant
    granulosa cell C56-•
    hepatic cell C22.0

Carcinoma (Continued)
    hepatocellular C22.0
      with bile duct, mixed C22.0
      fibrolamellar C22.0
    hepatocholangiolitic C22.0
    Hurthle cell C73
    in
      adenomatous
        polyposis coli C18.9
      pleomorphic adenoma —see Neoplasm,
        salivary glands, malignant
      situ —see Carcinoma-in-situ
    infiltrating
      duct
        with lobular
          specified site —see Neoplasm,
            malignant, by site
          unspecified site (female) C50.91-•
            male C50.92-•
        with Paget's disease —see Neoplasm,
          breast, malignant
        specified site —see Neoplasm,
          malignant
        unspecified site (female) C50.91-•
          male C50.92-•
      ductular
        specified site —see Neoplasm,
          malignant
        unspecified site (female) C50.91-•
          male C50.92-•
      lobular
        specified site —see Neoplasm,
          malignant
        unspecified site (female) C50.91-•
          male C50.92-•
    inflammatory
      specified site —see Neoplasm, malignant
      unspecified site (female) C50.91-•
        male C50.92-•
    intestinal type
      specified site —see Neoplasm, malignant,
        by site
      unspecified site C16.9
    intracystic
      noninfiltrating —see Neoplasm, in situ,
        by site
    intraductal (noninfiltrating)
      with Paget's disease —see Neoplasm,
        breast, malignant
      breast D05.1-•
      papillary
        with invasion
          specified site —see Neoplasm,
            malignant, by site
          unspecified site (female) C50.91-•
            male C50.92-•
        breast D05.1-•
        specified site NEC —see Neoplasm,
          in situ, by site
        unspecified site (female) D05.1-•
      specified site NEC —see Neoplasm,
        in situ, by site
      unspecified site (female) D05.1-•
    intraepidermal —see Neoplasm, in situ
      squamous cell, Bowen's type —see
        Neoplasm, skin, in situ
    intraepithelial —see Neoplasm, in situ,
      by site
      squamous cell —see Neoplasm, in situ,
        by site
    intraosseous C41.1
      upper jaw (bone) C41.0
    islet cell
      with exocrine, mixed
        specified site —see Neoplasm,
          malignant, by site
        unspecified site C25.9
      pancreas C25.4
      specified site NEC —see Neoplasm,
        malignant, by site
      unspecified site C25.4

Carcinoma *(Continued)*
  juvenile, breast —*see* Neoplasm, breast, malignant
  large cell
    small cell
      specified site —*see* Neoplasm, malignant, by site
      unspecified site C34.90
  Leydig cell (testis)
    specified site —*see* Neoplasm, malignant, by site
    unspecified site
      female C56.9
      male C62.90
  lipid-rich (female) C50.91-•
    male C50.92-•
  liver cell C22.0
  liver NEC C22.7
  lobular (infiltrating)
    with intraductal
      specified site —*see* Neoplasm, malignant, by site
      unspecified site (female) C50.91-•
        male C50.92-•
    noninfiltrating
      breast D05.0-•
      specified site NEC —*see* Neoplasm, in situ, by site
      unspecified site D05.0-•
    specified site —*see* Neoplasm, malignant, by site
    unspecified site (female) C50.91-•
      male C50.92-•
  medullary
    with
      amyloid stroma
        specified site —*see* Neoplasm, malignant, by site
        unspecified site C73
      lymphoid stroma
        specified site —*see* Neoplasm, malignant, by site
        unspecified site (female) C50.91-•
          male C50.92-•
  Merkel cell C4A.9
    anal margin C4A.51
    anal skin C4A.51
    canthus C4A.1-•
    ear and external auricular canal C4A.2-•
    external auricular canal C4A.2-•
    eyelid, including canthus C4A.1-•
    face C4A.30
      specified NEC C4A.39
    hip C4A.7-•
    lip C4A.0
    lower limb, including hip C4A.7-•
    neck C4A.4
    nodal presentation C7B.1
    nose C4A.31
    overlapping sites C4A.8
    perianal skin C4A.51
    scalp C4A.4
    secondary C7B.1
    shoulder C4A.6-•
    skin of breast C4A.52
    trunk NEC C4A.59
    upper limb, including shoulder C4A.6-•
    visceral metastatic C7B.1
  metastatic —*see* Neoplasm, secondary
  metatypical —*see* Neoplasm, skin, malignant
  morphea, basal cell —*see* Neoplasm, skin, malignant
  mucoid
    cell
      specified site —*see* Neoplasm, malignant, by site
      unspecified site C75.1
  neuroendocrine —*see also* Tumor, neuroendocrine
    high grade, any site C7A.1
    poorly differentiated, any site C7A.1

Carcinoma *(Continued)*
  nonencapsulated sclerosing C73
  noninfiltrating
    intracystic —*see* Neoplasm, in situ, by site
    intraductal
      breast D05.1-•
      papillary
        breast D05.1-•
        specified site NEC —*see* Neoplasm, in situ, by site
        unspecified site D05.1-•
      specified site —*see* Neoplasm, in situ, by site
      unspecified site D05.1-•
    lobular
      breast D05.0-•
      specified site NEC —*see* Neoplasm, in situ, by site
      unspecified site (female) D05.0-•
  oat cell
    specified site —*see* Neoplasm, malignant, by site
    unspecified site C34.90
  odontogenic C41.1
    upper jaw (bone) C41.0
  papillary
    with follicular (mixed) C73
    follicular variant C73
    intraductal (noninfiltrating)
      with invasion
        specified site —*see* Neoplasm, malignant, by site
        unspecified site (female) C50.91-•
          male C50.92-•
      breast D05.1-•
      specified site NEC —*see* Neoplasm, in situ, by site
      unspecified site D05.1-•
    serous
      specified site —*see* Neoplasm, malignant, by site
      surface
        specified site —*see* Neoplasm, malignant, by site
        unspecified site C56.9
      unspecified site C56.9
  papillocystic
    specified site —*see* Neoplasm, malignant, by site
    unspecified site C56.9
  parafollicular cell
    specified site —*see* Neoplasm, malignant, by site
    unspecified site C73
  pilomatrix —*see* Neoplasm, skin, malignant
  pseudomucinous
    specified site —*see* Neoplasm, malignant, by site
    unspecified site C56.9
  renal cell C64-•
  Schmincke —*see* Neoplasm, nasopharynx, malignant
  Schneiderian
    specified site —*see* Neoplasm, malignant, by site
    unspecified site C30.0
  sebaceous —*see* Neoplasm, skin, malignant
  secondary —*see also* Neoplasm, secondary, by site
    Merkel cell C7B.1
  secretory, breast —*see* Neoplasm, breast, malignant
  serous
    papillary
      specified site —*see* Neoplasm, malignant, by site
      unspecified site C56.9
    surface, papillary
      specified site —*see* Neoplasm, malignant, by site
      unspecified site C56.9

Carcinoma *(Continued)*
  Sertoli cell
    specified site —*see* Neoplasm, malignant, by site
    unspecified site C62.90
      female C56.9
      male C62.90
  skin appendage —*see* Neoplasm, skin, malignant
  small cell
    fusiform cell
      specified site —*see* Neoplasm, malignant, by site
      unspecified site C34.90
    intermediate cell
      specified site —*see* Neoplasm, malignant, by site
      unspecified site C34.90
    large cell
      specified site —*see* Neoplasm, malignant, by site
      unspecified site C34.90
  solid
    with amyloid stroma
      specified site —*see* Neoplasm, malignant, by site
      unspecified site C73
    microinvasive
      specified site —*see* Neoplasm, malignant, by site
      unspecified site C53.9
  sweat gland —*see* Neoplasm, skin, malignant
  theca cell C56.-•
  thymic C37
  unspecified site (primary) C80.1
  water-clear cell C75.0
Carcinoma-in-situ —*see also* Neoplasm, in situ, by site
  breast NOS D05.9-•
    specified type NEC D05.8-•
  epidermoid —*see also* Neoplasm, in situ, by site
    with questionable stromal invasion
      cervix D06.9
      specified site NEC —*see* Neoplasm, in situ, by site
      unspecified site D06.9
    Bowen's type —*see* Neoplasm, skin, in situ
  intraductal
    breast D05.1-•
    specified site NEC —*see* Neoplasm, in situ, by site
    unspecified site D05.1-•
  lobular
    with
      infiltrating duct
        breast (female) C50.91-•
          male C50.92-•
        specified site NEC —*see* Neoplasm, malignant
        unspecified site (female) C50.91-•
          male C50.92-•
      intraductal
        breast D05.8-•
        specified site NEC —*see* Neoplasm, in situ, by site
        unspecified site (female) D05.8-•
    breast D05.0-•
    specified site NEC —*see* Neoplasm, in situ, by site
    unspecified site D05.0-•
  squamous cell —*see also* Neoplasm, in situ, by site
    with questionable stromal invasion
      cervix D06.9
      specified site NEC —*see* Neoplasm, in situ, by site
      unspecified site D06.9
Carcinomaphobia F45.29

Carcinomatosis C80.0
  peritonei C78.6
  unspecified site (primary) (secondary) C80.0
Carcinosarcoma —see Neoplasm, malignant,
    by site
  embryonal —see Neoplasm, malignant, by site
Cardia, cardial —see condition
Cardiac —see also condition
  death, sudden —see Arrest, cardiac
  pacemaker
    in situ Z95.0
      management or adjustment Z45.018
  tamponade I31.4
Cardialgia —see Pain, precordial
Cardiectasis —see Hypertrophy, cardiac
Cardiochalasia K21.9
Cardiomalacia I51.5
Cardiomegalia glycogenica diffusa E74.02 [I43]
Cardiomegaly —see also Hypertrophy, cardiac
  congenital Q24.8
  glycogen E74.02 [I43]
  idiopathic I51.7
Cardiomyoliposis I51.5
Cardiomyopathy (familial) (idiopathic) I42.9
  alcoholic I42.6
  amyloid E85.4 [I43]
    transthyretin-related (ATTR) familial E85.4
        [I43]
  arteriosclerotic —see Disease, heart, ischemic,
      atherosclerotic
  beriberi E51.12
  cobalt-beer I42.6
  congenital I42.4
  congestive I42.0
  constrictive NOS I42.5
  dilated I42.0
  due to
    alcohol I42.6
    beriberi E51.12
    cardiac glycogenosis E74.02 [I43]
    drugs I42.7
    external agents NEC I42.7
➡ Friedreich's ataxia G11.11
    myotonia atrophica G71.11 [I43]
    progressive muscular dystrophy G71.09
        [I43]
  glycogen storage E74.02 [I43]
  hypertensive —see Hypertension, heart
  hypertrophic (nonobstructive) I42.2
    obstructive I42.1
      congenital Q24.8
  in
    Chagas' disease (chronic) B57.2
      acute B57.0
    sarcoidosis D86.85
  ischemic I25.5
  metabolic E88.9 [I43]
    thyrotoxic E05.90 [I43]
      with thyroid storm E05.91 [I43]
  newborn I42.8
    congenital I42.4
  non-ischemic (see also by cause) I42.8
  nutritional E63.9 [I43]
    beriberi E51.12
  obscure of Africa I42.8
  peripartum O90.3
  postpartum O90.3
  restrictive NEC I42.5
  rheumatic I09.0
  secondary I42.9
  specified NEC I42.8
  stress induced I51.81
  takotsubo I51.81
  thyrotoxic E05.90 [I43]
    with thyroid storm E05.91 [I43]
  toxic NEC I42.7
  transthyretin-related (ATTR) familial amyloid
      E85.4
  tuberculous A18.84
  viral B33.24
Cardionephritis —see Hypertension,
    cardiorenal

Cardionephropathy —see Hypertension,
    cardiorenal
Cardionephrosis —see Hypertension, cardiorenal
Cardiopathia nigra I27.0
Cardiopathy —see also Disease, heart I51.9
  idiopathic I42.9
  mucopolysaccharidosis E76.3 [I52]
Cardiopericarditis —see Pericarditis
Cardiophobia F45.29
Cardiorenal —see condition
Cardiorrhexis —see Infarct, myocardium
Cardiosclerosis —see Disease, heart, ischemic,
    atherosclerotic
Cardiosis —see Disease, heart
Cardiospasm (esophagus) (reflex) (stomach)
    K22.0
  congenital Q39.5
    with megaesophagus Q39.5
Cardiostenosis —see Disease, heart
Cardiosymphysis I31.0
Cardiovascular —see condition
Carditis (acute) (bacterial) (chronic) (subacute)
    I51.89
  meningococcal A39.50
  rheumatic —see Disease, heart, rheumatic
  rheumatoid —see Rheumatoid, carditis
  viral B33.20
Care (of) (for) (following)
  child (routine) Z76.2
  family member (handicapped) (sick)
    creating problem for family Z63.6
    provided away from home for holiday
        relief Z75.5
    unavailable, due to
      absence (person rendering care)
          (sufferer) Z74.2
      inability (any reason) of person
          rendering care Z74.2
  foundling Z76.1
  holiday relief Z75.5
  improper —see Maltreatment
  lack of (at or after birth) (infant) —see
      Maltreatment, child, neglect
  lactating mother Z39.1
  palliative Z51.5
  postpartum
    immediately after delivery Z39.0
    routine follow-up Z39.2
  respite Z75.5
  unavailable, due to
    absence of person rendering care Z74.2
    inability (any reason) of person rendering
        care Z74.2
  well-baby Z76.2
Caries
  bone NEC A18.03
  dental (dentino enamel junction) (early
      childhood) (of dentine) (pre-eruptive)
      (recurrent) (to the pulp) K02.9
    arrested (coronal) (root) K02.3
    chewing surface
      limited to enamel K02.51
      penetrating into dentin K02.52
      penetrating into pulp K02.53
    coronal surface
      chewing surface
        limited to enamel K02.51
        penetrating into dentin K02.52
        penetrating into pulp K02.53
      pit and fissure surface
        limited to enamel K02.51
        penetrating into dentin K02.52
        penetrating into pulp K02.53
      smooth surface
        limited to enamel K02.61
        penetrating into dentin K02.62
        penetrating into pulp K02.63
    pit and fissure surface
      limited to enamel K02.51
      penetrating into dentin K02.52
      penetrating into pulp K02.53

Caries (Continued)
  dental (Continued)
    primary, cervical origin K02.52
    root K02.7
    smooth surface
      limited to enamel K02.61
      penetrating into dentin K02.62
      penetrating into pulp K02.63
  external meatus —see Disorder, ear, external,
      specified type NEC
  hip (tuberculous) A18.02
  initial (tooth)
    chewing surface K02.51
    pit and fissure surface K02.51
    smooth surface K02.61
  knee (tuberculous) A18.02
  labyrinth —see subcategory H83.8
  limb NEC (tuberculous) A18.03
  mastoid process (chronic) —see Mastoiditis,
      chronic
    tuberculous A18.03
  middle ear —see subcategory H74.8
  nose (tuberculous) A18.03
  orbit (tuberculous) A18.03
  ossicles, ear —see Abnormal, ear ossicles
  petrous bone —see Petrositis
  root (dental) (tooth) K02.7
  sacrum (tuberculous) A18.01
  spine, spinal (column) (tuberculous) A18.01
  syphilitic A52.77
    congenital (early) A50.02 [M90.80]
  tooth, teeth —see Caries, dental
  tuberculous A18.03
  vertebra (column) (tuberculous) A18.01
Carious teeth —see Caries, dental
Carneous mole O02.0
Carnitine insufficiency E71.40
Carotenemia (dietary) E67.1
Carotenosis (cutis) (skin) E67.1
Carotid body or sinus syndrome G90.01
Carotidynia G90.01
Carpal tunnel syndrome —see Syndrome,
    carpal tunnel
Carpenter's syndrome Q87.0
Carpopedal spasm —see Tetany
Carr-Barr-Plunkett syndrome Q97.1
Carrier (suspected) of
  amebiasis Z22.1
  bacterial disease NEC Z22.39
    diphtheria Z22.2
    intestinal infectious NEC Z22.1
      typhoid Z22.0
    meningococcal Z22.31
    sexually transmitted Z22.4
    specified NEC Z22.39
    staphylococcal (Methicillin susceptible)
        Z22.321
      Methicillin resistant Z22.322
    streptococcal Z22.338
      group B Z22.330
        complicating pregnancy or delivery
            O99.82-●
    typhoid Z22.0
  cholera Z22.1
  diphtheria Z22.2
  gastrointestinal pathogens NEC Z22.1
  genetic Z14.8
    cystic fibrosis Z14.1
    hemophilia A (asymptomatic) Z14.01
      symptomatic Z14.02
  gestational, pregnant Z33.1
  gonorrhea Z22.4
  HAA (hepatitis Australian-antigen) B18.8
  HB (c)(s)-AG B18.1
  hepatitis (viral) B18.9
    Australia-antigen (HAA) B18.8
    B surface antigen (HBsAg) B18.1
      with acute delta- (super)infection B17.0
    C B18.2
    specified NEC B18.8
  human T-cell lymphotropic virus type-1
      (HTLV-1) infection Z22.6

Carrier of *(Continued)*
  infectious organism Z22.9
    specified NEC Z22.8
  meningococci Z22.31
  Salmonella typhosa Z22.0
  serum hepatitis —*see* Carrier, hepatitis
  staphylococci (Methicillin susceptible) Z22.321
    Methicillin resistant Z22.322
  streptococci Z22.338
    group B Z22.330
      complicating pregnancy or delivery O99.82-●
  syphilis Z22.4
  typhoid Z22.0
  venereal disease NEC Z22.4
Carrion's disease A44.0
Carter's relapsing fever (Asiatic) A68.1
Cartilage —*see* condition
Caruncle (inflamed)
  conjunctiva (acute) —*see* Conjunctivitis, acute
  labium (majus) (minus) N90.89
  lacrimal —*see* Inflammation, lacrimal, passages
  myrtiform N89.8
  urethral (benign) N36.2
Cascade stomach K31.2
Caseation lymphatic gland (tuberculous) A18.2
Cassidy (-Scholte) syndrome (malignant carcinoid) E34.0
Castellani's disease A69.8
Castration, traumatic, male S38.231
Casts in urine R82.998
Cat
  cry syndrome Q93.4
  ear Q17.3
  eye syndrome Q92.8
Catabolism, senile R54
Catalepsy (hysterical) F44.2
  schizophrenic F20.2
Cataplexy (idiopathic) —*see* Narcolepsy
Cataract (cortical) (immature) (incipient) H26.9
  with
    neovascularization —*see* Cataract, complicated
  age-related —*see* Cataract, senile
  anterior
    and posterior axial embryonal Q12.0
    pyramidal Q12.0
  associated with
    galactosemia E74.21 *[H28]*
    myotonic disorders G71.19 *[H28]*
  blue Q12.0
  central Q12.0
  cerulean Q12.0
  complicated H26.20
    with
      neovascularization H26.21-●
      ocular disorder H26.22-●
      glaucomatous flecks H26.23-●
  congenital Q12.0
  coraliform Q12.0
  coronary Q12.0
  crystalline Q12.0
  diabetic —*see* Diabetes, cataract
  drug-induced H26.3-●
  due to
    ocular disorder —*see* Cataract, complicated
    radiation H26.8
  electric H26.8
  extraction status Z98.4-●
  glass-blower's H26.8
  heat ray H26.8
  heterochromic —*see* Cataract, complicated
  hypermature —*see* Cataract, senile, morgagnian type
  in (due to)
    chronic iridocyclitis —*see* Cataract, complicated
    diabetes —*see* Diabetes, cataract
    endocrine disease E34.9 *[H28]*
    eye disease —*see* Cataract, complicated

Cataract *(Continued)*
  in (due to) *(Continued)*
    hypoparathyroidism E20.9 *[H28]*
    malnutrition-dehydration E46 *[H28]*
    metabolic disease E88.9 *[H28]*
    myotonic disorders G71.19 *[H28]*
    nutritional disease E63.9 *[H28]*
  infantile —*see* Cataract, presenile
  irradiational —*see* Cataract, specified NEC
  juvenile —*see* Cataract, presenile
  malnutrition-dehydration E46 *[H28]*
  morgagnian —*see* Cataract, senile, morgagnian type
  myotonic G71.19 *[H28]*
  myxedema E03.9 *[H28]*
  nuclear
    embryonal Q12.0
    sclerosis —*see* Cataract, senile, nuclear
  presenile H26.00-●
    combined forms H26.06-●
    cortical H26.01-●
    lamellar —*see* Cataract, presenile, cortical
    nuclear H26.03-●
    specified NEC H26.09
    subcapsular polar (anterior) H26.04-●
      posterior H26.05-●
    zonular —*see* Cataract, presenile, cortical
  secondary H26.40
    Soemmering's ring H26.41-●
    specified NEC H26.49-●
    to eye disease —*see* Cataract, complicated
  senile H25.9
    brunescens —*see* Cataract, senile, nuclear
    combined forms H25.81-●
    coronary —*see* Cataract, senile, incipient
    cortical H25.01-●
    hypermature —*see* Cataract, senile, morgagnian type
    incipient (mature) (total) H25.09-●
      cortical —*see* Cataract, senile, cortical
      subcapsular —*see* Cataract, senile, subcapsular
    morgagnian type (hypermature) H25.2-●
    nuclear (sclerosis) H25.1-●
    polar subcapsular (anterior) (posterior) — *see* Cataract, senile, incipient
    punctate —*see* Cataract, senile, incipient
    specified NEC H25.89
    subcapsular polar (anterior) H25.03-●
      posterior H25.04-●
  snowflake —*see* Diabetes, cataract
  specified NEC H26.8
  toxic —*see* Cataract, drug-induced
  traumatic H26.10-●
    localized H26.11-●
    partially resolved H26.12-●
    total H26.13-●
  zonular (perinuclear) Q12.0
Cataracta —*see also* Cataract
  brunescens —*see* Cataract, senile, nuclear
  centralis pulverulenta Q12.0
  cerulea Q12.0
  complicata —*see* Cataract, complicated
  congenita Q12.0
  coralliformis Q12.0
  coronaria Q12.0
  diabetic —*see* Diabetes, cataract
  membranacea
    accreta —*see* Cataract, secondary
    congenita Q12.0
  nigra —*see* Cataract, senile, nuclear
  sunflower —*see* Cataract, complicated
Catarrh, catarrhal (acute) (febrile) (infectious) (inflammation) *(see also* condition) J00
  bronchial —*see* Bronchitis
  chest —*see* Bronchitis
  chronic J31.0
  due to congenital syphilis A50.03
  enteric —*see* Enteritis
  eustachian H68.009
  fauces —*see* Pharyngitis

Catarrh, catarrhal *(Continued)*
  gastrointestinal —*see* Enteritis
  gingivitis K05.00
    nonplaque induced K05.01
    plaque induced K05.00
  hay —*see* Fever, hay
  intestinal —*see* Enteritis
  larynx, chronic J37.0
  liver B15.9
    with hepatic coma B15.0
  lung —*see* Bronchitis
  middle ear, chronic —*see* Otitis, media, nonsuppurative, chronic, serous
  mouth K12.1
  nasal (chronic) —*see* Rhinitis
  nasobronchial J31.1
  nasopharyngeal (chronic) J31.1
    acute J00
  pulmonary —*see* Bronchitis
  spring (eye) (vernal) —*see* Conjunctivitis, acute, atopic
  summer (hay) —*see* Fever, hay
  throat J31.2
  tubotympanal —*see also* Otitis, media, nonsuppurative
    chronic —*see* Otitis, media, nonsuppurative, chronic, serous
Catatonia (schizophrenic) F20.2
Catatonic
  disorder due to known physiologic condition F06.1
  schizophrenia F20.2
  stupor R40.1
Cat-scratch —*see also* Abrasion
  disease or fever A28.1
Cauda equina —*see* condition
Cauliflower ear M95.1-●
Causalgia (upper limb) G56.4-●
  lower limb G57.7-●
Cause
  external, general effects T75.89
Caustic burn —*see* Corrosion, by site
Cavare's disease (familial periodic paralysis) G72.3
Cave-in, injury
  crushing (severe) —*see* Crush
  suffocation —*see* Asphyxia, traumatic, due to low oxygen, due to cave-in
Cavernitis (penis) N48.29
Cavernositis N48.29
Cavernous —*see* condition
Cavitation of lung —*see also* Tuberculosis, pulmonary
  nontuberculous J98.4
Cavities, dental —*see* Caries, dental
Cavity
  lung —*see* Cavitation of lung
  optic papilla Q14.2
  pulmonary —*see* Cavitation of lung
Cavovarus foot, congenital Q66.1-●
Cavus foot (congenital) Q66.7-●
  acquired —*see* Deformity, limb, foot, specified NEC
Cazenave's disease L10.2
▶**CDKL5 (Cyclin-Dependent Kinase-Like 5 Deficiency Disorder)** G40.42
Cecitis K52.9
  with perforation, peritonitis, or rupture K65.8
Cecoureterocele Q62.32
Cecum —*see* condition
Celiac
  artery compression syndrome I77.4
  disease (with steatorrhea) K90.0
  infantilism K90.0
Cell(s), cellular —*see also* condition
  in urine R82.998
Cellulitis (diffuse) (phlegmonous) (septic) (suppurative) L03.90
  abdominal wall L03.311
  anaerobic A48.0
  ankle —*see* Cellulitis, lower limb
  anus K61.0

▶ New   ⇒ Revised   ~~deleted~~ Deleted   ● Use Additional Character(s)

Cellulitis *(Continued)*
arm —*see* Cellulitis, upper limb
auricle (ear) —*see* Cellulitis, ear
axilla L03.11-●
back (any part) L03.312
breast (acute) (nonpuerperal) (subacute)
    N61.0
    nipple N61.0
broad ligament
    acute N73.0
buttock L03.317
cervical (meaning neck) L03.221
cervix (uteri) —*see* Cervicitis
cheek (external) L03.211
    internal K12.2
chest wall L03.313
chronic L03.90
clostridial A48.0
corpus cavernosum N48.22
digit
    finger —*see* Cellulitis, finger
    toe —*see* Cellulitis, toe
Douglas' cul-de-sac or pouch
    acute N73.0
drainage site (following operation) T81.49
ear (external) H60.1-●
eosinophilic (granulomatous) L98.3
erysipelatous —*see* Erysipelas
external auditory canal —*see* Cellulitis, ear
eyelid —*see* Abscess, eyelid
face NEC L03.211
finger (intrathecal) (periosteal)
    (subcutaneous) (subcuticular) L03.01-●
foot —*see* Cellulitis, lower limb
gangrenous —*see* Gangrene
genital organ NEC
    female (external) N76.4
    male N49.9
        multiple sites N49.8
        specified NEC N49.8
gluteal (region) L03.317
gonococcal A54.89
groin L03.314
hand —*see* Cellulitis, upper limb
head NEC L03.811
    face (any part, except ear, eye and nose)
        L03.211
heel —*see* Cellulitis, lower limb
hip —*see* Cellulitis, lower limb
jaw (region) L03.211
knee —*see* Cellulitis, lower limb
labium (majus) (minus) —*see* Vulvitis
lacrimal passages —*see* Inflammation,
    lacrimal, passages
larynx J38.7
leg —*see* Cellulitis, lower limb
lip K13.0
lower limb L03.11-●
    toe —*see* Cellulitis, toe
mouth (floor) K12.2
multiple sites, so stated L03.90
nasopharynx J39.1
navel L03.316
    newborn P38.9
        with mild hemorrhage P38.1
        without hemorrhage P38.9
neck (region) L03.221
nipple (acute) (nonpuerperal) (subacute) N61.0
nose (septum) (external) J34.0
orbit, orbital H05.01-●
palate (soft) K12.2
pectoral (region) L03.313
pelvis, pelvic (chronic)
    female —*see also* Disease, pelvis,
        inflammatory N73.2
        acute N73.0
    following ectopic or molar pregnancy O08.0
    male K65.0
penis N48.22
perineal, perineum L03.315
periorbital L03.213

Cellulitis *(Continued)*
perirectal K61.1
peritonsillar J36
periurethral N34.0
periuterine —*see also* Disease, pelvis,
    inflammatory N73.2
    acute N73.0
pharynx J39.1
preseptal L03.213
rectum K61.1
retroperitoneal K68.9
round ligament
    acute N73.0
scalp (any part) L03.811
scrotum N49.2
seminal vesicle N49.0
shoulder —*see* Cellulitis, upper limb
specified site NEC L03.818
submandibular (region) (space) (triangle)
    K12.2
    gland K11.3
submaxillary (region) K12.2
    gland K11.3
thigh —*see* Cellulitis, lower limb
thumb (intrathecal) (periosteal)
    (subcutaneous) (subcuticular) —*see*
    Cellulitis, finger
toe (intrathecal) (periosteal) (subcutaneous)
    (subcuticular) L03.03-●
tonsil J36
trunk L03.319
    abdominal wall L03.311
    back (any part) L03.312
    buttock L03.317
    chest wall L03.313
    groin L03.314
    perineal, perineum L03.315
    umbilicus L03.316
tuberculous (primary) A18.4
umbilicus L03.316
upper limb L03.11-●
    axilla —*see* Cellulitis, axilla
    finger —*see* Cellulitis, finger
    thumb —*see* Cellulitis, finger
vaccinal T88.0
vocal cord J38.3
vulva —*see* Vulvitis
wrist —*see* Cellulitis, upper limb
Cementoblastoma, benign —*see* Cyst,
    calcifying odontogenic
Cementoma —*see* Cyst, calcifying odontogenic
Cementoperiostitis —*see* Periodontitis
Cementosis K03.4
Central auditory processing disorder H93.25
Central pain syndrome G89.0
Cephalematocele, cephal (o)hematocele
    newborn P52.8
        birth injury P10.8
        traumatic —*see* Hematoma, brain
Cephalematoma, cephalhematoma (calcified)
    newborn (birth injury) P12.0
    traumatic —*see* Hematoma, brain
Cephalgia, cephalalgia —*see also* Headache
    histamine G44.009
        intractable G44.001
        not intractable G44.009
    trigeminal autonomic (TAC) NEC G44.099
        intractable G44.091
        not intractable G44.099
Cephalic —*see* condition
Cephalitis —*see* Encephalitis
Cephalocele —*see* Encephalocele
Cephalomenia N94.89
Cephalopelvic —*see* condition
Cerclage (with cervical incompetence) in
    pregnancy —*see* Incompetence, cervix, in
    pregnancy
Cerebellitis —*see* Encephalitis
Cerebellum, cerebellar —*see* condition
Cerebral —*see* condition
Cerebritis —*see* Encephalitis

Cerebro-hepato-renal syndrome Q87.89
Cerebromalacia —*see* Softening, brain
    sequelae of cerebrovascular disease I69.398
Cerebroside lipidosis E75.22
Cerebrospasticity (congenital) G80.1
Cerebrospinal —*see* condition
Cerebrum —*see* condition
Ceroid-lipofuscinosis, neuronal E75.4
Cerumen (accumulation) (impacted) H61.2-●
Cervical —*see also* condition
    auricle Q18.2
    dysplasia in pregnancy —*see* Abnormal,
        cervix, in pregnancy or childbirth
    erosion in pregnancy —*see* Abnormal, cervix,
        in pregnancy or childbirth
    fibrosis in pregnancy —*see* Abnormal, cervix,
        in pregnancy or childbirth
    fusion syndrome Q76.1
    rib Q76.5
    shortening (complicating pregnancy) O26.87-●
Cervicalgia M54.2
Cervicitis (acute) (chronic) (nonvenereal)
    (senile (atrophic)) (subacute) (with
    ulceration) N72
    with
        abortion —*see* Abortion, by type complicated
            by genital tract and pelvic infection
        ectopic pregnancy O08.0
        molar pregnancy O08.0
    chlamydial A56.09
    gonococcal A54.03
    herpesviral A60.03
    puerperal (postpartum) O86.11
    syphilitic A52.76
    trichomonal A59.09
    tuberculous A18.16
Cervicocolpitis (emphysematosa) (*see also*
    Cervicitis) N72
Cervix —*see* condition
Cesarean delivery, previous, affecting
    management of pregnancy O34.219
    classical (vertical) scar O34.212
    ▶isthmocele O34.22
    low transverse scar O34.211
    ▶mid-transverse T incision O34.218
    ▶scar
        ▶defect (isthmocele) O34.22
        ▶specified type NEC O34.218
Céstan (-Chenais) **paralysis or syndrome** G46.3
Céstan-Raymond syndrome I65.8
Cestode infestation B71.9
    specified type NEC B71.8
Cestodiasis B71.9
Chabert's disease A22.9
Chacaleh E53.8
Chafing L30.4
Chagas' (-Mazza) **disease** (chronic) B57.2
    with
        cardiovascular involvement NEC B57.2
        digestive system involvement B57.30
            megacolon B57.32
            megaesophagus B57.31
            other specified B57.39
        megacolon B57.32
        megaesophagus B57.31
        myocarditis B57.2
        nervous system involvement B57.40
            meningitis B57.41
            meningoencephalitis B57.42
            other specified B57.49
        specified organ involvement NEC B57.5
    acute (with) B57.1
        cardiovascular NEC B57.0
        myocarditis B57.0
Chagres fever B50.9
Chairridden Z74.09
Chalasia (cardiac sphincter) K21.9
Chalazion H00.19
    left H00.16
        lower H00.15
        upper H00.14

Chalazion *(Continued)*
- right H00.13
  - lower H00.12
  - upper H00.11
Chalcosis —*see also* Disorder, globe, degenerative, chalcosis
- cornea —*see* Deposit, cornea
- crystalline lens —*see* Cataract, complicated
- retina H35.89
Chalicosis (pulmonum) J62.8
Chancre (any genital site) (hard) (hunterian) (mixed) (primary) (seronegative) (seropositive) (syphilitic) A51.0
- congenital A50.07
- conjunctiva NEC A51.2
- Ducrey's A57
- extragenital A51.2
- eyelid A51.2
- lip A51.2
- nipple A51.2
- Nisbet's A57
- of
  - carate A67.0
  - pinta A67.0
  - yaws A66.0
- palate, soft A51.2
- phagedenic A57
- simple A57
- soft A57
  - bubo A57
  - palate A51.2
- urethra A51.0
- yaws A66.0
Chancroid (anus) (genital) (penis) (perineum) (rectum) (urethra) (vulva) A57
Chandler's disease (osteochondritis dissecans, hip) —*see* Osteochondritis, dissecans, hip
Change(s) (in) (of) —*see also* Removal
- arteriosclerotic —*see* Arteriosclerosis
- bone —*see also* Disorder, bone
  - diabetic —*see* Diabetes, bone change
- bowel habit R19.4
- cardiorenal (vascular) —*see* Hypertension, cardiorenal
- cardiovascular —*see* Disease, cardiovascular
- circulatory I99.9
- cognitive (mild) (organic) R41.89
- color, tooth, teeth
  - during formation K00.8
  - posteruptive K03.7
- contraceptive device Z30.433
- corneal membrane H18.30
  - Bowman's membrane fold or rupture H18.31-●
  - Descemet's membrane
    - fold H18.32-●
    - rupture H18.33-●
- coronary —*see* Disease, heart, ischemic
- degenerative, spine or vertebra —*see* Spondylosis
- dental pulp, regressive K04.2
- dressing (nonsurgical) Z48.00
  - surgical Z48.01
- heart —*see* Disease, heart
- hip joint —*see* Derangement, joint, hip
- hyperplastic larynx J38.7
- hypertrophic
  - nasal sinus J34.89
  - turbinate, nasal J34.3
  - upper respiratory tract J39.8
- indwelling catheter Z46.6
- inflammatory —*see also* Inflammation
  - sacroiliac M46.1
- job, anxiety concerning Z56.1
- joint —*see* Derangement, joint
- life —*see* Menopause
- mental status R41.82
- minimal (glomerular) —*see also* N00-N07
  - with fourth character .0 N05.0
- myocardium, myocardial —*see* Degeneration, myocardial - of life —*see* Menopause
- pacemaker Z45.018
  - pulse generator Z45.010

Change *(Continued)*
- personality (enduring) F68.8
  - due to (secondary to)
    - general medical condition F07.0
    - secondary (nonspecific) F60.89
- regressive, dental pulp K04.2
- renal —*see* Disease, renal
- retina H35.9
  - myopic —*see also* Myopia, degenerative H44.2-●
- sacroiliac joint M53.3
- senile —*see also* condition R54
- sensory R20.8
- skin R23.9
  - acute, due to ultraviolet radiation L56.9
    - specified NEC L56.8
  - chronic, due to nonionizing radiation L57.9
    - specified NEC L57.8
  - cyanosis R23.0
  - flushing R23.2
  - pallor R23.1
  - petechiae R23.3
  - specified change NEC R23.8
  - swelling —*see* Mass, localized
  - texture R23.4
- trophic
  - arm —*see* Mononeuropathy, upper limb
  - leg —*see* Mononeuropathy, lower limb
- vascular I99.9
- vasomotor I73.9
- voice R49.9
  - psychogenic F44.4
  - specified NEC R49.8
Changing sleep-work schedule, affecting sleep G47.26
Changuinola fever A93.1
Chapping skin T69.8
Charcot-Marie-Tooth disease, paralysis or syndrome G60.0
Charcot's
- arthropathy —*see* Arthropathy, neuropathic
- cirrhosis K74.3
- disease (tabetic arthropathy) A52.16
- joint (disease) (tabetic) A52.16
  - diabetic —*see* Diabetes, with, arthropathy
  - syringomyelic G95.0
- syndrome (intermittent claudication) I73.9
CHARGE association Q89.8
Charley-horse (quadriceps) M62.831
- traumatic (quadriceps) S76.11-●
Charlouis' disease —*see* Yaws
Cheadle's disease E54
Checking (of)
- cardiac pacemaker (battery) (electrode(s)) Z45.018
  - pulse generator Z45.010
- implantable subdermal contraceptive Z30.46
- intrauterine contraceptive device Z30.431
- wound Z48.0-●
  - due to injury - code to Injury, by site, using appropriate seventh character for subsequent encounter
Check-up —*see* Examination
Chédiak-Higashi (-Steinbrinck) **syndrome** (congenital gigantism of peroxidase granules) E70.330
Cheek —*see* condition
Cheese itch B88.0
Cheese-washer's lung J67.8
Cheese-worker's lung J67.8
Cheilitis (acute) (angular) (catarrhal) (chronic) (exfoliative) (gangrenous) (glandular) (infectional) (suppurative) (ulcerative) (vesicular) K13.0
- actinic (due to sun) L56.8
  - other than from sun L59.8
- candidal B37.83
Cheilodynia K13.0
Cheiloschisis —*see* Cleft, lip
Cheilosis (angular) K13.0
- with pellagra E52
- due to
  - vitamin B2 (riboflavin) deficiency E53.0

Cheiromegaly M79.89
Cheiropompholyx L30.1
Cheloid —*see* Keloid
Chemical burn —*see* Corrosion, by site
Chemodectoma —*see* Paraganglioma, nonchromaffin
Chemosis, conjunctiva —*see* Edema, conjunctiva
Chemotherapy (session) (for)
- cancer Z51.11
- neoplasm Z51.11
Cherubism M27.8
Chest —*see* condition
Cheyne-Stokes breathing (respiration) R06.3
Chiari's
- disease or syndrome (hepatic vein thrombosis) I82.0
- malformation
  - type I G93.5
  - type II —*see* Spina bifida
- net Q24.8
Chicago disease B40.9
Chickenpox —*see* Varicella
Chiclero ulcer or sore B55.1
Chigger (infestation) B88.0
Chignon (disease) B36.8
- newborn (from vacuum extraction) (birth injury) P12.1
Chilaiditi's syndrome (subphrenic displacement, colon) Q43.3
Chilblain(s) (lupus) T69.1
Child
- custody dispute Z65.3
Childbirth —*see* Delivery
Childhood
- cerebral X-linked adrenoleukodystrophy E71.520
- period of rapid growth Z00.2
Chill(s) R68.83
- with fever R50.9
- without fever R68.83
- congestive in malarial regions B54
Chilomastigiasis A07.8
Chimera 46,XX/46,XY Q99.0
Chin —*see* condition
Chinese dysentery A03.9
Chionophobia F40.228
Chitral fever A93.1
Chlamydia, chlamydial A74.9
- cervicitis A56.09
- conjunctivitis A74.0
- cystitis A56.01
- endometritis A56.11
- epididymitis A56.19
- female
  - pelvic inflammatory disease A56.11
  - pelviperitonitis A56.11
- orchitis A56.19
- peritonitis A74.81
- pharyngitis A56.4
- proctitis A56.3
- psittaci (infection) A70
- salpingitis A56.11
- sexually-transmitted infection NEC A56.8
- specified NEC A74.89
- urethritis A56.01
- vulvovaginitis A56.02
Chlamydiosis —*see* Chlamydia
Chloasma (skin) (idiopathic) (symptomatic) L81.1
- eyelid H02.719
  - hyperthyroid E05.90 *[H02.719]*
    - with thyroid storm E05.91 *[H02.719]*
  - left H02.716
    - lower H02.715
    - upper H02.714
  - right H02.713
    - lower H02.712
    - upper H02.711
Chloroma C92.3-●
Chlorosis D50.9
- Egyptian B76.9 *[D63.8]*
- miner's B76.9 *[D63.8]*

▶ New ⟹ Revised ~~deleted~~ Deleted ● Use Additional Character(s)

Chlorotic anemia D50.8
Chocolate cyst (ovary) N80.1
Choked
  disc or disk —see Papilledema
  on food, phlegm, or vomitus NOS —see
    Foreign body, by site
  while vomiting NOS —see Foreign body, by
    site
Chokes (resulting from bends) T70.3
Choking sensation R09.89
Cholangiectasis K83.8
Cholangiocarcinoma
  with hepatocellular carcinoma, combined
    C22.0
  liver C22.1
  specified site NEC —see Neoplasm,
    malignant, by site
  unspecified site C22.1
Cholangiohepatitis K83.8
  due to fluke infestation B66.1
Cholangiohepatoma C22.0
Cholangiolitis (acute) (chronic) (extrahepatic)
    (gangrenous) (intrahepatic) K83.09
  paratyphoidal —see Fever, paratyphoid
  typhoidal A01.09
Cholangioma D13.4
  malignant —see Cholangiocarcinoma
Cholangitis (ascending) (primary) (recurrent)
    (sclerosing) (secondary) (stenosing)
    (suppurative) K83.09
  with calculus, bile duct —see Calculus, bile
    duct, with cholangitis
  chronic nonsuppurative destructive K74.3
  primary K83.09
    sclerosing K83.01
  sclerosing K83.09
Cholecystectasia K82.8
Cholecystitis K81.9
  with
    calculus, stones in
      bile duct (common) (hepatic) —
        see Calculus, bile duct, with
        cholecystitis
      cystic duct —see Calculus, gallbladder,
        with cholecystitis
      gallbladder —see Calculus, gallbladder,
        with cholecystitis
    choledocholithiasis —see Calculus, bile
      duct, with cholecystitis
    cholelithiasis —see Calculus, gallbladder,
      with cholecystitis
    gangrene of gallbladder K82.A1
    perforation of gallbladder K82.A2
  acute (emphysematous) (gangrenous)
    (suppurative) K81.0
    with
      calculus, stones in
        cystic duct —see Calculus, gallbladder,
          with cholecystitis, acute
        gallbladder —see Calculus, gallbladder,
          with cholecystitis, acute
      choledocholithiasis —see Calculus, bile
        duct, with cholecystitis, acute
      cholelithiasis —see Calculus, gallbladder,
        with cholecystitis, acute
      chronic cholecystitis K81.2
        with gallbladder calculus K80.12
          with obstruction K80.13
  chronic K81.1
    with acute cholecystitis K81.2
      with gallbladder calculus K80.12
        with obstruction K80.13
    emphysematous (acute) —see Cholecystitis,
      acute
    gangrenous —see Cholecystitis, acute
    paratyphoidal, current A01.4
    suppurative —see Cholecystitis, acute
    typhoidal A01.09
Cholecystolithiasis —see Calculus, gallbladder
Choledochitis (suppurative) K83.09
Choledocholith —see Calculus, bile duct

Choledocholithiasis (common duct) (hepatic
    duct) —see Calculus, bile duct
  cystic —see Calculus, gallbladder
  typhoidal A01.09
Cholelithiasis (cystic duct) (gallbladder)
    (impacted) (multiple) —see Calculus,
    gallbladder
  bile duct (common) (hepatic) —see Calculus,
    bile duct
  hepatic duct —see Calculus, bile duct
  specified NEC K80.80
    with obstruction K80.81
Cholemia —see also Jaundice
  familial (simple) (congenital) E80.4
  Gilbert's E80.4
Choleperitoneum, choleperitonitis K65.3
Cholera (Asiatic) (epidemic) (malignant) A00.9
  antimonial —see Poisoning, antimony
  classical A00.0
  due to Vibrio cholerae 01 A00.9
    biovar cholerae A00.0
    biovar eltor A00.1
    el tor A00.1
  el tor A00.1
Cholerine —see Cholera
Cholestasis NEC K83.1
  with hepatocyte injury K71.0
  due to total parenteral nutrition (TPN) K76.89
  pure K71.0
Cholesteatoma (ear) (middle) (with reaction)
    H71.9-●
  attic H71.0-●
  external ear (canal) H60.4-●
  mastoid H71.2-●
  postmastoidectomy cavity (recurrent) —see
    Complications, postmastoidectomy,
    recurrent cholesteatoma
  recurrent (postmastoidectomy) —see
    Complications, postmastoidectomy,
    recurrent cholesteatoma
  tympanum H71.1-●
Cholesteatosis, diffuse H71.3-●
Cholesteremia E78.00
Cholesterin in vitreous —see Deposit, crystalline
Cholesterol
  deposit
    retina H35.89
    vitreous —see Deposit, crystalline
  elevated (high) E78.00
    with elevated (high) triglycerides E78.2
    screening for Z13.220
  imbibition of gallbladder K82.4
Cholesterolemia (essential) (pure) E78.00
  familial E78.01
  hereditary E78.01
Cholesterolosis, cholesterosis (gallbladder)
    K82.4
  cerebrotendinous E75.5
Cholocolic fistula K82.3
Choluria R82.2
Chondritis M94.8X9
  aurical H61.03-●
  costal (Tietze's) M94.0
  external ear H61.03-●
  patella, posttraumatic —see Chondromalacia,
    patella
  pinna H61.03-●
  purulent M94.8X-●
  tuberculous NEC A18.02
    intervertebral A18.01
Chondroblastoma —see also Neoplasm, bone,
    benign
  malignant —see Neoplasm, bone, malignant
Chondrocalcinosis M11.20
  ankle M11.27-●
  elbow M11.22-●
  familial M11.10
    ankle M11.17-●
    elbow M11.12-●
    foot joint M11.17-●
    hand joint M11.14-●

Chondrocalcinosis (Continued)
  familial (Continued)
    hip M11.15-●
    knee M11.16-●
    multiple site M11.19
    shoulder M11.11-●
    vertebrae M11.18
    wrist M11.13-●
  foot joint M11.27-●
  hand joint M11.24-●
  hip M11.25-●
  knee M11.26-●
  multiple site M11.29
  shoulder M11.21-●
  specified type NEC M11.20
    ankle M11.27-●
    elbow M11.22-●
    foot joint M11.27-●
    hand joint M11.24-●
    hip M11.25-●
    knee M11.26-●
    multiple site M11.29
    shoulder M11.21-●
    vertebrae M11.28
    wrist M11.23-●
  vertebrae M11.28
  wrist M11.23-●
Chondrodermatitis nodularis helicis or
    anthelicis —see Perichondritis, ear
Chondrodysplasia Q78.9
  with hemangioma Q78.4
  calcificans congenita Q77.3
  fetalis Q77.4
  metaphyseal (Jansen's) (McKusick's)
    (Schmid's) Q78.8
  punctata Q77.3
Chondrodystrophy, chondrodystrophia
    (familial) (fetalis) (hypoplastic) Q78.9
  calcificans congenita Q77.3
  myotonic (congenital) G71.13
  punctata Q77.3
Chondroectodermal dysplasia Q77.6
Chondrogenesis imperfecta Q77.4
Chondrolysis M94.35-●
Chondroma —see also Neoplasm, cartilage,
    benign
  juxtacortical —see Neoplasm, bone, benign
  periosteal —see Neoplasm, bone, benign
Chondromalacia (systemic) M94.20
  acromioclavicular joint M94.21-●
  ankle M94.27-●
  elbow M94.22-●
  foot joint M94.27-●
  glenohumeral joint M94.21-●
  hand joint M94.24-●
  hip M94.25-●
  knee M94.26-●
    patella M22.4-●
  multiple sites M94.29
  patella M22.4-●
  rib M94.28
  sacroiliac joint M94.259
  shoulder M94.21-●
  sternoclavicular joint M94.21-●
  vertebral joint M94.28
  wrist M94.23-●
Chondromatosis —see also Neoplasm, cartilage,
    uncertain behavior
  internal Q78.4
Chondromyxosarcoma —see Neoplasm,
    cartilage, malignant
Chondro-osteodysplasia (Morquio-Brailsford
    type) E76.219
Chondro-osteodystrophy E76.29
Chondro-osteoma —see Neoplasm, bone, benign
Chondropathia tuberosa M94.0
Chondrosarcoma —see Neoplasm, cartilage,
    malignant
  juxtacortical —see Neoplasm, bone, malignant
  mesenchymal —see Neoplasm, connective
    tissue, malignant
  myxoid —see Neoplasm, cartilage, malignant

Chordee (nonvenereal) N48.89
  congenital Q54.4
  gonococcal A54.09
Chorditis (fibrinous) (nodosa) (tuberosa) J38.2
Chordoma —see Neoplasm, vertebral (column),
    malignant
Chorea (chronic) (gravis) (posthemiplegic)
    (senile) (spasmodic) G25.5
  with
    heart involvement I02.0
      active or acute (conditions in I01-•) I02.0
        rheumatic I02.9
          with valvular disorder I02.0
      rheumatic heart disease (chronic) (inactive)
          (quiescent) — code to rheumatic heart
          condition involved
  drug-induced G25.4
  habit F95.8
  hereditary G10
  Huntington's G10
  hysterical F44.4
  minor I02.9
    with heart involvement I02.0
  progressive G25.5
    hereditary G10
  rheumatic (chronic) I02.9
    with heart involvement I02.0
  Sydenham's I02.9
    with heart involvement —see Chorea, with
        rheumatic heart disease
  nonrheumatic G25.5
Choreoathetosis (paroxysmal) G25.5
Chorioadenoma (destruens) D39.2
Chorioamnionitis O41.12-•
Chorioangioma D26.7
Choriocarcinoma —see Neoplasm, malignant,
    by site
  combined with
    embryonal carcinoma —see Neoplasm,
        malignant, by site
    other germ cell elements —see Neoplasm,
        malignant, by site
    teratoma —see Neoplasm, malignant, by site
  specified site —see Neoplasm, malignant, by
      site
  unspecified site
    female C58
    male C62.90
Chorioencephalitis (acute) (lymphocytic)
    (serous) A87.2
Chorioepithelioma —see Choriocarcinoma
Choriomeningitis (acute) (lymphocytic)
    (serous) A87.2
Chorionepithelioma —see Choriocarcinoma
Chorioretinitis —see also Inflammation,
    chorioretinal
  disseminated —see also Inflammation,
      chorioretinal, disseminated
    in neurosyphilis A52.19
  Egyptian B76.9 [D63.8]
  focal —see also Inflammation, chorioretinal,
      focal
  histoplasmic B39.9 [H32]
  in (due to)
    histoplasmosis B39.9 [H32]
    syphilis (secondary) A51.43
      late A52.71
    toxoplasmosis (acquired) B58.01
      congenital (active) P37.1 [H32]
    tuberculosis A18.53
  juxtapapillary, juxtapapillaris —see
      Inflammation, chorioretinal, focal,
      juxtapapillary
  leprous A30.9 [H32]
  miner's B76.9 [D63.8]
  progressive myopia (degeneration) —see also
      Myopia, degenerative H44.2-•
  syphilitic (secondary) A51.43
    congenital (early) A50.01 [H32]
      late A50.32
    late A52.71
  tuberculous A18.53

Chorioretinopathy, central serous H35.71-•
Choroid —see condition
Choroideremia H31.21
Choroiditis —see Chorioretinitis
Choroidopathy —see Disorder, choroid
Choroidoretinitis —see Chorioretinitis
Choroidoretinopathy, central serous —see
    Chorioretinopathy, central serous
Christian-Weber disease M35.6
Christmas disease D67
Chromaffinoma —see also Neoplasm, benign,
    by site
  malignant —see Neoplasm, malignant, by site
Chromatopsia —see Deficiency, color vision
Chromhidrosis, chromidrosis L75.1
Chromoblastomycosis —see Chromomycosis
Chromoconversion R82.91
Chromomycosis B43.9
  brain abscess B43.1
  cerebral B43.1
  cutaneous B43.0
  skin B43.0
  specified NEC B43.8
  subcutaneous abscess or cyst B43.2
Chromophytosis B36.0
Chromosome —see condition by chromosome
    involved
  D (1) —see condition, chromosome 13
  E (3) —see condition, chromosome 18
  G —see condition, chromosome 21
Chromotrichomycosis B36.8
Chronic —see condition
  fracture —see Fracture, pathological
Churg-Strauss syndrome M30.1
Chyle cyst, mesentery I89.8
Chylocele (nonfilarial) I89.8
  filarial —see also Infestation, filarial B74.9
      [N51]
  tunica vaginalis N50.89
    filarial —see also Infestation, filarial B74.9
        [N51]
Chylomicronemia (fasting) (with
    hyperprebetalipoproteinemia) E78.3
Chylopericardium I31.3
  acute I30.9
Chylothorax (nonfilarial) I89.8
  filarial —see also Infestation, filarial B74.9 [J91.8]
Chylous —see condition
Chyluria (nonfilarial) R82.0
  due to
    bilharziasis B65.0
    Brugia (malayi) B74.1
      timori B74.2
    schistosomiasis (bilharziasis) B65.0
    Wuchereria (bancrofti) B74.0
  filarial —see Infestation, filarial
Cicatricial (deformity) —see Cicatrix
Cicatrix (adherent) (contracted) (painful)
    (vicious) —see also Scar L90.5
  adenoid (and tonsil) J35.8
  alveolar process M26.79
  anus K62.89
  auricle —see Disorder, pinna, specified type
      NEC
  bile duct (common) (hepatic) K83.8
  bladder N32.89
  bone —see Disorder, bone, specified type NEC
  brain G93.89
  cervix (postoperative) (postpartal) N88.1
  common duct K83.8
  cornea H17.9
    tuberculous A18.59
  duodenum (bulb), obstructive K31.5
  esophagus K22.2
  eyelid —see Disorder, eyelid function
  hypopharynx J39.2
  lacrimal passages —see Obstruction, lacrimal
  larynx J38.7
  lung J98.4
  middle ear —see subcategory H74.8
  mouth K13.79

Cicatrix (Continued)
  muscle M62.89
    with contracture —see Contraction, muscle
        NEC
  nasopharynx J39.2
  palate (soft) K13.79
  penis N48.89
  pharynx J39.2
  prostate N42.89
  rectum K62.89
  retina —see Scar, chorioretinal
  semilunar cartilage —see Derangement,
      meniscus
  seminal vesicle N50.89
  skin L90.5
    infected L08.89
    postinfective L90.5
    tuberculous B90.8
  specified site NEC L90.5
  throat J39.2
  tongue K14.8
  tonsil (and adenoid) J35.8
  trachea J39.8
  tuberculous NEC B90.9
  urethra N36.8
  uterus N85.8
  vagina N89.8
    postoperative N99.2
  vocal cord J38.3
  wrist, constricting (annular) L90.5
CIDP (chronic inflammatory demyelinating
    polyneuropathy) G61.81
CIN —see Neoplasia, intraepithelial, cervix
CINCA (chronic infantile neurological,
    cutaneous and articular syndrome)
    M04.2
Cinchonism —see Deafness, ototoxic
  correct substance properly administered —see
      Table of Drugs and Chemicals, by drug,
      adverse effect
  overdose or wrong substance given
      or taken —see Table of Drugs and
      Chemicals, by drug, poisoning
Circle of Willis —see condition
Circular —see condition
Circulating anticoagulants —see also - Disorder,
    hemorrhagic D68.318
  due to drugs —see also - Disorder,
      hemorrhagic D68.32
  following childbirth O72.3
Circulation
  collateral, any site I99.8
  defective (lower extremity) I99.9
    congenital Q28.9
  embryonic Q28.9
  failure (peripheral) R57.9
    newborn P29.89
  fetal, persistent P29.38
  heart, incomplete Q28.9
Circulatory system —see condition
Circulus senilis (cornea) —see Degeneration,
    cornea, senile
Circumcision (in absence of medical indication)
    (ritual) (routine) Z41.2
Circumscribed —see condition
Circumvallate placenta O43.11-•
Cirrhosis, cirrhotic (hepatic) (liver) K74.60
  alcoholic K70.30
    with ascites K70.31
  atrophic —see Cirrhosis, liver
  Baumgarten-Cruveilhier K74.69
  biliary (cholangiolitic) (cholangitic)
      (hypertrophic) (obstructive)
      (pericholangiolitic) K74.5
    due to
      Clonorchiasis B66.1
      flukes B66.3
    primary K74.3
    secondary K74.4
  cardiac (of liver) K76.1
  Charcot's K74.3

▶ New   ⇒ Revised   ~~deleted~~ Deleted   • Use Additional Character(s)

Cirrhosis, cirrhotic *(Continued)*
  cholangiolitic, cholangitic, cholostatic
      (primary) K74.3
  congestive K76.1
  Cruveilhier-Baumgarten K74.69
  cryptogenic (liver) K74.69
  due to
      hepatolenticular degeneration E83.01
      Wilson's disease E83.01
      xanthomatosis E78.2
  fatty K76.0
      alcoholic K70.0
  Hanot's (hypertrophic) K74.3
  hepatic —*see* Cirrhosis, liver
  hypertrophic K74.3
  Indian childhood K74.69
  kidney —*see* Sclerosis, renal
  Laennec's K70.30
      with ascites K70.31
      alcoholic K70.30
          with ascites K70.31
      nonalcoholic K74.69
  liver K74.60
      alcoholic K70.30
          with ascites K70.31
      fatty K70.0
      congenital P78.81
      syphilitic A52.74
  lung (chronic) J84.10
  macronodular K74.69
      alcoholic K70.30
          with ascites K70.31
  micronodular K74.69
      alcoholic K70.30
          with ascites K70.31
  mixed type K74.69
  monolobular K74.3
  nephritis —*see* Sclerosis, renal
  nutritional K74.69
      alcoholic K70.30
          with ascites K70.31
  obstructive —*see* Cirrhosis, biliary
  ovarian N83.8
  pancreas (duct) K86.89
  pigmentary E83.110
  portal K74.69
      alcoholic K70.30
          with ascites K70.31
  postnecrotic K74.69
      alcoholic K70.30
          with ascites K70.31
  pulmonary J84.10
  renal —*see* Sclerosis, renal
  spleen D73.2
  stasis K76.1
  Todd's K74.3
  unilobar K74.3
  xanthomatous (biliary) K74.5
      due to xanthomatosis (familial) (metabolic)
          (primary) E78.2
Cistern, subarachnoid R93.0
Citrullinemia E72.23
Citrullinuria E72.23
Civatte's disease or poikiloderma L57.3
Clam digger's itch B65.3
Clammy skin R23.1
Clap —*see* Gonorrhea
Clarke-Hadfield syndrome (pancreatic
      infantilism) K86.89
Clark's paralysis G80.9
Clastothrix L67.8
Claude Bernard-Horner syndrome G90.2
      traumatic —*see* Injury, nerve, cervical
          sympathetic
Claude's disease or syndrome G46.3
Claudicatio venosa intermittens I87.8
Claudication (intermittent) I73.9
  cerebral (artery) G45.9
  spinal cord (arteriosclerotic) G95.19
      syphilitic A52.09
  venous (axillary) I87.8

Claustrophobia F40.240
Clavus (infected) L84
Clawfoot (congenital) Q66.89
  acquired —*see* Deformity, limb, clawfoot
Clawhand (acquired) —*see also* Deformity, limb,
      clawhand
  congenital Q68.1
Clawtoe (congenital) Q66.89
  acquired —*see* Deformity, toe, specified NEC
Clay eating —*see* Pica
Cleansing of artificial opening —*see* Attention
      to, artificial, opening
Cleft (congenital) —*see also* Imperfect, closure
  alveolar process M26.79
  branchial (persistent) Q18.2
  cyst Q18.0
      fistula Q18.0
      sinus Q18.0
  cricoid cartilage, posterior Q31.8
  foot Q72.7
  hand Q71.6
  lip (unilateral) Q36.9
      with cleft palate Q37.9
          hard Q37.1
              with soft Q37.5
          soft Q37.3
              with hard Q37.5
      bilateral Q36.0
          with cleft palate Q37.8
              hard Q37.0
                  with soft Q37.4
              soft Q37.2
                  with hard Q37.4
      median Q36.1
  nose Q30.2
  palate Q35.9
      with cleft lip (unilateral) Q37.9
          bilateral Q37.8
      hard Q35.1
          with
              cleft lip (unilateral) Q37.1
                  bilateral Q37.0
              soft Q35.5
                  with cleft lip (unilateral) Q37.5
                      bilateral Q37.4
      medial Q35.5
      soft Q35.3
          with
              cleft lip (unilateral) Q37.3
                  bilateral Q37.2
              hard Q35.5
                  with cleft lip (unilateral) Q37.5
                      bilateral Q37.4
  penis Q55.69
  scrotum Q55.29
  thyroid cartilage Q31.8
  uvula Q35.7
Cleidocranial dysostosis Q74.0
Cleptomania F63.2
Clicking hip (newborn) R29.4
Climacteric (female) —*see also* Menopause
  arthritis (any site) NEC —*see* Arthritis,
      specified form NEC
  depression (single episode) F32.89
      recurrent episode F33.8
  male (symptoms) (syndrome) NEC N50.89
  melancholia (single episode) F32.89
      recurrent episode F33.8
  paranoid state F22
  polyarthritis NEC —*see* Arthritis, specified
      form NEC
  symptoms (female) N95.1
Clinical research investigation (clinical trial)
      (control subject) (normal comparison)
      (participant) Z00.6
Clitoris —*see* condition Cloaca (persistent)
      Q43.7
Clonorchiasis, clonorchis infection (liver)
      B66.1
Clonus R25.8
Closed bite M26.29

Clostridium (C.) perfringens, as cause of
      disease classified elsewhere B96.7
Closure
  congenital, nose Q30.0
  cranial sutures, premature Q75.0
  defective or imperfect NEC —*see* Imperfect,
      closure
  fistula, delayed —*see* Fistula
  foramen ovale, imperfect Q21.1
  hymen N89.6
  interauricular septum, defective Q21.1
  interventricular septum, defective Q21.0
  lacrimal duct —*see also* Stenosis, lacrimal,
      duct
      congenital Q10.5
  nose (congenital) Q30.0
      acquired M95.0
  of artificial opening —*see* Attention to,
      artificial, opening
  primary angle, without glaucoma damage
      H40.06-●
  vagina N89.5
  valve —*see* Endocarditis
  vulva N90.5
Clot (blood) —*see also* Embolism
  artery (obstruction) (occlusion) —*see*
      Embolism
  bladder N32.89
  brain (intradural or extradural) —*see*
      Occlusion, artery, cerebral
  circulation I74.9
  heart —*see also* Infarct, myocardium
      not resulting in infarction I51.3
  vein —*see* Thrombosis
Clouded state R40.1
  epileptic —*see* Epilepsy, specified NEC
  paroxysmal —*see* Epilepsy, specified NEC
Cloudy antrum, antra J32.0
Clouston's (hidrotic) ectodermal dysplasia
      Q82.4
Clubbed nail pachydermoperiostosis M89.40
      [L62]
Clubbing of finger(s) (nails) R68.3
Clubfinger R68.3
  congenital Q68.1
Clubfoot (congenital) Q66.89
  acquired —*see* Deformity, limb, clubfoot
  equinovarus Q66.0-●
  paralytic —*see* Deformity, limb, clubfoot
Clubhand (congenital) (radial) Q71.4-●
  acquired —*see* Deformity, limb, clubhand
Clubnail R68.3
  congenital Q84.6
Clump, kidney Q63.1
Clumsiness, clumsy child syndrome F82
Cluttering F98.81
Clutton's joints A50.51 [M12.80]
Coagulation, intravascular (diffuse)
      (disseminated) —*see also* Defibrination
      syndrome
  complicating abortion —*see* Abortion, by
      type, complicated by, intravascular
      coagulation
  following ectopic or molar pregnancy
      O08.1
Coagulopathy —*see also* Defect, coagulation
  consumption D65
  intravascular D65
      newborn P60
Coalition
  calcaneo-scaphoid Q66.89
  tarsal Q66.89
Coalminer's
  elbow —*see* Bursitis, elbow, olecranon
  lung or pneumoconiosis J60
Coalworker's lung or pneumoconiosis
      J60
Coarctation
  aorta (preductal) (postductal) Q25.1
  pulmonary artery Q25.71
Coated tongue K14.3

Coats' disease (exudative retinopathy) —*see*
    Retinopathy, exudative
Cocaine-induced
    anxiety disorder F14.980
    bipolar and related disorder F14.94
    depressive disorder F14.94
    obsessive-compulsive and related disorder
        F14.988
    psychotic disorder F14.959
    sleep disorder F14.982
    sexual dysfunction F14.981
Cocainism —*see* Disorder, cocaine use
Coccidioidomycosis B38.9
    cutaneous B38.3
    disseminated B38.7
    generalized B38.7
    meninges B38.4
    prostate B38.81
    pulmonary B38.2
        acute B38.0
        chronic B38.1
    skin B38.3
    specified NEC B38.89
Coccidioidosis —*see* Coccidioidomycosis
Coccidiosis (intestinal) A07.3
Coccydynia, coccygodynia M53.3
Coccyx —*see* condition
Cochin-China diarrhea K90.1
Cockayne's syndrome Q87.19
Cocked up toe —*see* Deformity, toe, specified
    NEC
Cock's peculiar tumor L72.3
Codman's tumor —*see* Neoplasm, bone, benign
Coenurosis B71.8
Coffee-worker's lung J67.8
Cogan's syndrome H16.32-•
    oculomotor apraxia H51.8
Coitus, painful (female) N94.10
    male N53.12
    psychogenic F52.6
Cold J00
    with influenza, flu, or grippe —*see* Influenza,
        with, respiratory manifestations NEC
➠agglutinin disease or hemoglobinuria
        (chronic) D59.12
    bronchial —*see* Bronchitis
    chest —*see* Bronchitis
    common (head) J00
    effects of T69.9
        specified effect NEC T69.8
    excessive, effects of T69.9
        specified effect NEC T69.8
    exhaustion from T69.8
    exposure to T69.9
        specified effect NEC T69.8
    head J00
    injury syndrome (newborn) P80.0
    on lung —*see* Bronchitis
    rose J30.1
➠sensitivity, auto-immune D59.12
    symptoms J00
    virus J00
Coldsore B00.1
Colibacillosis A49.8
    as the cause of other disease (*see also*
        Escherichia coli) B96.20
    generalized A41.50
Colic (bilious) (infantile) (intestinal) (recurrent)
    (spasmodic) R10.83
    abdomen R10.83
        psychogenic F45.8
    appendix, appendicular K38.8
    bile duct —*see* Calculus, bile duct
    biliary —*see* Calculus, bile duct
    common duct —*see* Calculus, bile duct
    cystic duct —*see* Calculus, gallbladder
    Devonshire NEC —*see* Poisoning, lead
    gallbladder —*see* Calculus, gallbladder
    gallstone —*see* Calculus, gallbladder
        gallbladder or cystic duct —*see* Calculus,
            gallbladder

Colic (*Continued*)
    hepatic (duct) —*see* Calculus, bile duct
    hysterical F45.8
    kidney N23
    lead NEC —*see* Poisoning, lead
    mucous K58.9
        with diarrhea K58.0
        psychogenic F54
    nephritic N23
    painter's NEC —*see* Poisoning, lead
    pancreas K86.89
    psychogenic F45.8
    renal N23
    saturnine NEC —*see* Poisoning, lead
    ureter N23
    urethral N36.8
        due to calculus N21.1
    uterus NEC N94.89
        menstrual —*see* Dysmenorrhea
    worm NOS B83.9
Colicystitis —*see* Cystitis
Colitis (acute) (catarrhal) (chronic)
    (noninfective) (hemorrhagic) (*see also*
        Enteritis) K52.9
    allergic K52.29
        with
            food protein-induced enterocolitis
                syndrome K52.21
            proctocolitis K52.82
    amebic (acute) —*see also* Amebiasis A06.0
        nondysenteric A06.2
    anthrax A22.2
    bacillary —*see* Infection, Shigella
    balantidial A07.0
    Clostridium difficile
        not specified as recurrent A04.72
        recurrent A04.71
    coccidial A07.3
    collagenous K52.831
    cystica superficialis K52.89
    dietary counseling and surveillance (for) Z71.3
    dietetic —*see also* Colitis, allergic K52.29
    drug-induced K52.1
    due to radiation K52.0
    eosinophilic K52.82
    food hypersensitivity —*see also* Colitis,
        allergic K52.29
    giardial A07.1
    granulomatous —*see* Enteritis, regional, large
        intestine
    infectious —*see* Enteritis, infectious
    indeterminate, so stated K52.3
    ischemic K55.9
        acute (subacute) —*see also* Ischemia,
            intestine, acute K55.039
        chronic K55.1
        due to mesenteric artery insufficiency K55.1
        fulminant (acute) —*see also* Ischemia,
            intestine, acute K55.039
    left sided K51.50
        with
            abscess K51.514
            complication K51.519
                specified NEC K51.518
            fistula K51.513
            obstruction K51.512
            rectal bleeding K51.511
    lymphocytic K52.832
    membranous
        psychogenic F54
    microscopic K52.839
        specified NEC K52.838
    mucous —*see* Syndrome, irritable, bowel
        psychogenic F54
    noninfective K52.9
        specified NEC K52.89
    polyposa —*see* Polyp, colon, inflammatory
    protozoal A07.9
    pseudomembranous
        not specified as recurrent A04.72
        recurrent A04.71

Colitis (*Continued*)
    pseudomucinous —*see* Syndrome, irritable,
        bowel
    regional —*see* Enteritis, regional, large intestine
        infectious A09
    segmental —*see* Enteritis, regional, large
        intestine
    septic —*see* Enteritis, infectious
    spastic K58.9
        with diarrhea K58.0
        psychogenic F54
    staphylococcal A04.8
        foodborne A05.0
    subacute ischemic —*see also* Ischemia,
        intestine, acute K55.039
    thromboulcerative —*see also* Ischemia,
        intestine, acute K55.039
    toxic NEC K52.1
        due to Clostridium difficile
            not specified as recurrent A04.72
            recurrent A04.71
    transmural —*see* Enteritis, regional, large
        intestine
    trichomonal A07.8
    tuberculous (ulcerative) A18.32
    ulcerative (chronic) K51.90
        with
            complication K51.919
                abscess K51.914
                fistula K51.913
                obstruction K51.912
                rectal bleeding K51.911
                specified complication NEC K51.918
        enterocolitis —*see* Enterocolitis, ulcerative
        ileocolitis —*see* Ileocolitis, ulcerative
        mucosal proctocolitis —*see* Proctocolitis,
            mucosal
        proctitis —*see* Proctitis, ulcerative
        pseudopolyposis —*see* Polyp, colon,
            inflammatory
        psychogenic F54
        rectosigmoiditis —*see* Rectosigmoiditis,
            ulcerative
        specified type NEC K51.80
            with
                complication K51.819
                    abscess K51.814
                    fistula K51.813
                    obstruction K51.812
                    rectal bleeding K51.811
                    specified complication NEC K51.818
Collagenosis, collagen disease (nonvascular)
    (vascular) M35.9
    cardiovascular I42.8
    reactive perforating L87.1
    specified NEC M35.8
Collapse R55
    adrenal E27.2
    cardiorespiratory R57.0
    cardiovascular R57.0
        newborn P29.89
    circulatory (peripheral) R57.9
        during or after labor and delivery O75.1
        following ectopic or molar pregnancy O08.3
        newborn P29.89
    during or
        after labor and delivery O75.1
        resulting from a procedure, not elsewhere
            classified T81.10
    external ear canal —*see* Stenosis, external ear
        canal
    general R55
    heart —*see* Disease, heart
    heat T67.1
    hysterical F44.89
    labyrinth, membranous (congenital) Q16.5
    lung (massive) —*see also* Atelectasis J98.19
        pressure due to anesthesia (general) (local)
            or other sedation T88.2
            during labor and delivery O74.1
            in pregnancy O29.02-•
            postpartum, puerperal O89.09

Collapse *(Continued)*
  myocardial —*see* Disease, heart
  nervous F48.8
  neurocirculatory F45.8
  nose M95.0
  postoperative T81.10
  pulmonary —*see also* Atelectasis J98.19
    newborn —*see* Atelectasis
  trachea J39.8
  tracheobronchial J98.09
  valvular —*see* Endocarditis
  vascular (peripheral) R57.9
    during or after labor and delivery O75.1
    following ectopic or molar pregnancy O08.3
    newborn P29.89
  vertebra M48.50-•
    cervical region M48.52-•
    cervicothoracic region M48.53-•
    in (due to)
      metastasis —*see* Collapse, vertebra, in,
        specified disease NEC
      osteoporosis —*see also* Osteoporosis
        M80.88
        cervical region M80.88
        cervicothoracic region M80.88
        lumbar region M80.88
        lumbosacral region M80.88
        multiple sites M80.88
        occipito-atlanto-axial region M80.88
        sacrococcygeal region M80.88
        thoracic region M80.88
        thoracolumbar region M80.88
      specified disease NEC M48.50-•
        cervical region M48.52-•
        cervicothoracic region M48.53-•
        lumbar region M48.56-•
        lumbosacral region M48.57-•
        occipito-atlanto-axial region M48.51-•
        sacrococcygeal region M48.58-•
        thoracic region M48.54-•
        thoracolumbar region M48.55-•
    lumbar region M48.56-•
    lumbosacral region M48.57-•
    occipito-atlanto-axial region M48.51-•
    sacrococcygeal region M48.58-•
    thoracic region M48.54-•
    thoracolumbar region M48.55-•
Collateral —*see also* condition
  circulation (venous) I87.8
  dilation, veins I87.8
Colles' fracture S52.53-•
Collet (-Sicard) syndrome G52.7
Collier's asthma or lung J60
Collodion baby Q80.2
Colloid nodule (of thyroid) (cystic) E04.1
Coloboma (iris) Q13.0
  eyelid Q10.3
  fundus Q14.8
  lens Q12.2
  optic disc (congenital) Q14.2
    acquired H47.31-•
Coloenteritis —*see* Enteritis
Colon —*see* condition
Colonization
  MRSA (Methicillin resistant Staphylococcus
    aureus) Z22.322
  MSSA (Methicillin susceptible
    Staphylococcus aureus) Z22.321
  status —*see* Carrier (suspected) of
Coloptosis K63.4
Color blindness —*see* Deficiency, color vision
Colostomy
  attention to Z43.3
  fitting or adjustment Z46.89
  malfunctioning K94.03
  status Z93.3
Colpitis (acute) —*see* Vaginitis
Colpocele N81.5
Colpocystitis —*see* Vaginitis
Colpospasm N94.2
Column, spinal, vertebral —*see* condition

Coma R40.20
  with
    motor response (none) R40.231
      abnormal R40.233
      abnormal extensor posturing to pain or
        noxious stimuli (<2 years of age)
        R40.232
      abnormal flexure posturing to pain or
        noxious stimuli (0-5 years of age)
        R40.233
      extension R40.232
      extensor posturing to pain or noxious
        stimuli (2-5 years of age) R40.232
      flexion/decorticate posturing
        (<2 years of age) R40.233
      flexion withdrawal R40.234
      localizes pain (2-5 years of age) R40.235
      normal or spontaneous movement
        (<2 years of age) R40.236
      obeys commands (2-5 years of age)
        R40.236
      score of
        1 R40.231
        2 R40.232
        3 R40.233
        4 R40.234
        5 R40.235
        6 R40.236
      withdraws from pain or noxious stimuli
        (0-5 years of age) R40.234
      withdraws to touch (<2 years of age)
        R40.235
    opening of eyes (never) R40.211
      in response to
        pain R40.212
        sound R40.213
      score of
        1 R40.211
        2 R40.212
        3 R40.213
        4 R40.214
      spontaneous R40.214
    verbal response (none) R40.221
      confused conversation R40.224
      cooing or babbling or crying
        appropriately (<2 years of age)
        R40.225
      inappropriate crying or screaming
        (<2 years of age) R40.223
      inappropriate words R40.223
      inappropriate words (2-5 years of age)
        R40.224
      incomprehensible sounds (2-5 years of
        age) R40.222
      incomprehensible words R40.222
      irritable cries (<2 years of age) R40.224
      moans/grunts to pain; restless
        (<2 years old) R40.222
      oriented R40.225
      score of
        1 R40.221
        2 R40.222
        3 R40.223
        4 R40.224
        5 R40.225
      screaming (2-5 years of age) R40.223
      uses appropriate words (2-5 years of
        age) R40.225
  eclamptic —*see* Eclampsia
  epileptic —*see* Epilepsy
  Glasgow, scale score —*see* Glasgow coma
    scale
  hepatic —*see* Failure, hepatic, by type, with
    coma
  hyperglycemic (diabetic) —*see* Diabetes, by
    type, with hyperosmolarity, with coma
  hyperosmolar (diabetic) —*see* Diabetes, by
    type, with hyperosmolarity, with coma
  hypoglycemic (diabetic) —*see* Diabetes, by
    type, with hypoglycemia, with coma
  nondiabetic E15

Coma *(Continued)*
  in diabetes —*see* Diabetes, coma
  insulin-induced —*see* Coma, hypoglycemic
  ketoacidotic (diabetic) —*see* Diabetes, by
    type, with ketoacidosis, with coma
  myxedematous E03.5
  newborn P91.5
  persistent vegetative state R40.3
  specified NEC, without documented
    Glasgow coma scale score, or with
    partial Glasgow coma scale score
    reported R40.244
Comatose —*see* Coma
Combat fatigue F43.0
Combined —*see* condition
Comedo, comedones (giant) L70.0
Comedocarcinoma —*see also* Neoplasm, breast,
  malignant
  noninfiltrating
    breast D05.8-•
    specified site —*see* Neoplasm, in situ, by site
    unspecified site D05.8-•
Comedomastitis —*see* Ectasia, mammary duct
Comminuted fracture - code as Fracture, closed
Common
  arterial trunk Q20.0
  atrioventricular canal Q21.2
  atrium Q21.1
  cold (head) J00
  truncus (arteriosus) Q20.0
  variable immunodeficiency —*see*
    Immunodeficiency, common variable
  ventricle Q20.4
Commotio, commotion (current)
  brain —*see* Injury, intracranial, concussion
  cerebri —*see* Injury, intracranial, concussion
  retinae S05.8X-•
  spinal cord —*see* Injury, spinal cord, by region
  spinalis —*see* Injury, spinal cord, by region
Communication
  between
    base of aorta and pulmonary artery Q21.4
    left ventricle and right atrium Q20.5
    pericardial sac and pleural sac Q34.8
    pulmonary artery and pulmonary vein,
      congenital Q25.72
  congenital between uterus and digestive or
    urinary tract Q51.7
Compartment syndrome (deep) (posterior)
  (traumatic) T79.A0
  abdomen T79.A3
  lower extremity (hip, buttock, thigh, leg, foot,
    toes) T79.A2
  nontraumatic
    abdomen M79.A3
    lower extremity (hip, buttock, thigh, leg,
      foot, toes) M79.A2-•
    specified site NEC M79.A9
    upper extremity (shoulder, arm, forearm,
      wrist, hand, fingers) M79.A1-•
  specified site NEC T79.A9
  upper extremity (shoulder, arm, forearm,
    wrist, hand, fingers) T79.A1
Compensation
  failure —*see* Disease, heart
  neurosis, psychoneurosis —*see* Disorder,
    factitious
Complaint —*see also* Disease
  bowel, functional K59.9
    psychogenic F45.8
  intestine, functional K59.9
    psychogenic F45.8
  kidney —*see* Disease, renal
  miners' J60
Complete —*see* condition
Complex
  Addison-Schilder E71.528
  cardiorenal —*see* Hypertension, cardiorenal
  Costen's M26.69
  disseminated mycobacterium avium-
    intracellulare (DMAC) A31.2

Complex *(Continued)*
    Eisenmenger's (ventricular septal defect) I27.83
    hypersexual F52.8
    jumped process, spine —*see* Dislocation, vertebra
    primary, tuberculous A15.7
    Schilder-Addison E71.528
    subluxation (vertebral) M99.19
        abdomen M99.19
        acromioclavicular M99.17
        cervical region M99.11
        cervicothoracic M99.11
        costochondral M99.18
        costovertebral M99.18
        head region M99.10
        hip M99.15
        lower extremity M99.16
        lumbar region M99.13
        lumbosacral M99.13
        occipitocervical M99.10
        pelvic region M99.15
        pubic M99.15
        rib cage M99.18
        sacral region M99.14
        sacrococcygeal M99.14
        sacroiliac M99.14
        specified NEC M99.19
        sternochondral M99.18
        sternoclavicular M99.17
        thoracic region M99.12
        thoracolumbar M99.12
        upper extremity M99.17
    Taussig-Bing (transposition, aorta and overriding pulmonary artery) Q20.1
Complication(s) (from) (of)
    accidental puncture or laceration during a procedure (of) —*see* Complications, intraoperative (intraprocedural), puncture or laceration
    amputation stump (surgical) (late) NEC T87.9
        dehiscence T87.81
        infection or inflammation T87.40
            lower limb T87.4-●
            upper limb T87.4-●
        necrosis T87.50
            lower limb T87.5-●
            upper limb T87.5-●
        neuroma T87.30
            lower limb T87.3-●
            upper limb T87.3-●
        specified type NEC T87.89
    anastomosis (and bypass) —*see also* Complications, prosthetic device or implant
        intestinal (internal) NEC K91.89
            involving urinary tract N99.89
        urinary tract (involving intestinal tract) N99.89
        vascular —*see* Complications, cardiovascular device or implant
    anesthesia, anesthetic —*see also* Anesthesia, complication T88.59
        brain, postpartum, puerperal O89.2
        cardiac
            in
                labor and delivery O74.2
                pregnancy O29.19-●
            postpartum, puerperal O89.1
        central nervous system
            in
                labor and delivery O74.3
                pregnancy O29.29-●
            postpartum, puerperal O89.2
        difficult or failed intubation T88.4
            in pregnancy O29.6-●
        failed sedation (conscious) (moderate) during procedure T88.52
        general, unintended awareness during procedure T88.53
        hyperthermia, malignant T88.3
        hypothermia T88.51
        intubation failure T88.4

Complication *(Continued)*
    anesthesia, anesthetic *(Continued)*
        malignant hyperthermia T88.3
        pulmonary
            in
                labor and delivery O74.1
                pregnancy NEC O29.09-●
            postpartum, puerperal O89.09
        shock T88.2
        spinal and epidural
            in
                labor and delivery NEC O74.6
                  headache O74.5
                pregnancy NEC O29.5X-●
            postpartum, puerperal NEC O89.5
                headache O89.4
        unintended awareness under general anesthesia during procedure T88.53
    anti-reflux device —*see* Complications, esophageal anti-reflux device
    aortic (bifurcation) graft —*see* Complications, graft, vascular
    aortocoronary (bypass) graft —*see* Complications, coronary artery (bypass) graft
    aortofemoral (bypass) graft —*see* Complications, extremity artery (bypass) graft
    arteriovenous
        fistula, surgically created T82.9
            embolism T82.818
            fibrosis T82.828
            hemorrhage T82.838
            infection or inflammation T82.7
            mechanical
                breakdown T82.510
                displacement T82.520
                leakage T82.530
                malposition T82.520
                obstruction T82.590
                perforation T82.590
                protrusion T82.590
            pain T82.848
            specified type NEC T82.898
            stenosis T82.858
            thrombosis T82.868
        shunt, surgically created T82.9
            embolism T82.818
            fibrosis T82.828
            hemorrhage T82.838
            infection or inflammation T82.7
            mechanical
                breakdown T82.511
                displacement T82.521
                leakage T82.531
                malposition T82.521
                obstruction T82.591
                perforation T82.591
                protrusion T82.591
            pain T82.848
            specified type NEC T82.898
            stenosis T82.858
            thrombosis T82.868
    arthroplasty —*see* Complications, joint prosthesis
    artificial
        fertilization or insemination N98.9
            attempted introduction (of)
                embryo in embryo transfer N98.3
                ovum following in vitro fertilization N98.2
            hyperstimulation of ovaries N98.1
            infection N98.0
            specified NEC N98.8
        heart T82.9
            embolism T82.817
            fibrosis T82.827
            hemorrhage T82.837
            infection or inflammation T82.7
            mechanical
                breakdown T82.512
                displacement T82.522
                leakage T82.532

Complication *(Continued)*
    artificial *(Continued)*
        heart *(Continued)*
            mechanical *(Continued)*
                malposition T82.522
                obstruction T82.592
                perforation T82.592
                protrusion T82.592
            pain T82.847
            specified type NEC T82.897
            stenosis T82.857
            thrombosis T82.867
         opening
            cecostomy —*see* Complications, colostomy
            colostomy —*see* Complications, colostomy
            cystostomy —*see* Complications, cystostomy
            enterostomy —*see* Complications, enterostomy
            gastrostomy —*see* Complications, gastrostomy
            ileostomy —*see* Complications, enterostomy
            jejunostomy —*see* Complications, enterostomy
            nephrostomy —*see* Complications, stoma, urinary tract
            tracheostomy —*see* Complications, tracheostomy
            ureterostomy —*see* Complications, stoma, urinary tract
            urethrostomy —*see* Complications, stoma, urinary tract
    balloon implant or device
        gastrointestinal T85.9
            embolism T85.818
            fibrosis T85.828
            hemorrhage T85.838
            infection and inflammation T85.79
            pain T85.848
            specified type NEC T85.898
            stenosis T85.858
            thrombosis T85.868
        vascular (counterpulsation) T82.9
            embolism T82.818
            fibrosis T82.828
            hemorrhage T82.838
            infection or inflammation T82.7
            mechanical
                breakdown T82.513
                displacement T82.523
                leakage T82.533
                malposition T82.523
                obstruction T82.593
                perforation T82.593
                protrusion T82.593
            pain T82.848
            specified type NEC T82.898
            stenosis T82.858
            thrombosis T82.868
    bariatric procedure
        gastric band procedure K95.09
            infection K95.01
        specified procedure NEC K95.89
            infection K95.81
    bile duct implant (prosthetic) T85.9
        embolism T85.818
        fibrosis T85.828
        hemorrhage T85.838
        infection and inflammation T85.79
        mechanical
            breakdown T85.510
            displacement T85.520
            malfunction T85.510
            malposition T85.520
            obstruction T85.590
            perforation T85.590
            protrusion T85.590
            specified NEC T85.590
        pain T85.848
        specified type NEC T85.898

▶ New   ➡ Revised   ~~deleted~~ Deleted   ● Use Additional Character(s)

Complication *(Continued)*
  bile duct implant *(Continued)*
    stenosis T85.858
    thrombosis T85.868
  bladder device (auxiliary) —*see*
      Complications, genitourinary, device or
      implant, urinary system
  bleeding (postoperative) —*see* Complication,
      postoperative, hemorrhage
    intraoperative —*see* Complication,
      intraoperative, hemorrhage
  blood vessel graft —*see* Complications, graft,
      vascular
  bone
    device NEC T84.9
      embolism T84.81
      fibrosis T84.82
      hemorrhage T84.83
      infection or inflammation T84.7
      mechanical
        breakdown T84.318
        displacement T84.328
        malposition T84.328
        obstruction T84.398
        perforation T84.398
        protrusion T84.398
      pain T84.84
      specified type NEC T84.89
      stenosis T84.85
      thrombosis T84.86
    graft —*see* Complications, graft, bone
    growth stimulator (electrode) —*see*
        Complications, electronic stimulator
        device, bone
    marrow transplant —*see* Complications,
        transplant, bone, marrow
  brain neurostimulator (electrode) —*see*
      Complications, electronic stimulator
      device, brain
  breast implant (prosthetic) T85.9
    capsular contracture T85.44
    embolism T85.818
    fibrosis T85.828
    hemorrhage T85.838
    infection and inflammation T85.79
    mechanical
      breakdown T85.41
      displacement T85.42
      leakage T85.43
      malposition T85.42
      obstruction T85.49
      perforation T85.49
      protrusion T85.49
      specified NEC T85.49
    pain T85.848
    specified type NEC T85.898
    stenosis T85.858
    thrombosis T85.868
  bypass —*see also* Complications, prosthetic
      device or implant
    aortocoronary —*see* Complications,
        coronary artery (bypass) graft
    arterial —*see also* Complications, graft,
        vascular
      extremity —*see* Complications, extremity
          artery (bypass) graft
  cardiac —*see also* Disease, heart
    device, implant or graft T82.9
      embolism T82.817
      fibrosis T82.827
      hemorrhage T82.837
      infection or inflammation T82.7
        valve prosthesis T82.6
      mechanical
        breakdown T82.519
          specified device NEC T82.518
        displacement T82.529
          specified device NEC T82.528
        leakage T82.539
          specified device NEC T82.538
        malposition T82.529
          specified device NEC T82.528

Complication *(Continued)*
  cardiac *(Continued)*
    device, implant or graft *(Continued)*
      mechanical *(Continued)*
        obstruction T82.599
          specified device NEC T82.598
        perforation T82.599
          specified device NEC T82.598
        protrusion T82.599
          specified device NEC T82.598
      pain T82.847
      specified type NEC T82.897
      stenosis T82.857
      thrombosis T82.867
  cardiovascular device, graft or implant T82.9
    aortic graft —*see* Complications, graft,
        vascular
    arteriovenous
      fistula, artificial —*see* Complication,
          arteriovenous, fistula, surgically
          created
      shunt —*see* Complication, arteriovenous,
          shunt, surgically created
    artificial heart —*see* Complication,
        artificial, heart
    balloon (counterpulsation) device —*see*
        Complication, balloon implant,
        vascular
    carotid artery graft —*see* Complications,
        graft, vascular
    coronary bypass graft —*see* Complication,
        coronary artery (bypass) graft
    dialysis catheter (vascular) —*see*
        Complication, catheter, dialysis
    electronic T82.9
      electrode T82.9
        embolism T82.817
        fibrosis T82.827
        hemorrhage T82.837
        infection T82.7
        mechanical
          breakdown T82.110
          displacement T82.120
          leakage T82.190
          obstruction T82.190
          perforation T82.190
          protrusion T82.190
          specified type NEC T82.190
        pain T82.847
        specified NEC T82.897
        stenosis T82.857
        thrombosis T82.867
      embolism T82.817
      fibrosis T82.827
      hemorrhage T82.837
      infection T82.7
      mechanical
        breakdown T82.119
        displacement T82.129
        leakage T82.199
        obstruction T82.199
        perforation T82.199
        protrusion T82.199
        specified type NEC T82.199
      pain T82.847
      pulse generator T82.9
        embolism T82.817
        fibrosis T82.827
        hemorrhage T82.837
        infection T82.7
        mechanical
          breakdown T82.111
          displacement T82.121
          leakage T82.191
          obstruction T82.191
          perforation T82.191
          protrusion T82.191
          specified type NEC T82.191
        pain T82.847
        specified NEC T82.897
        stenosis T82.857
        thrombosis T82.867

Complication *(Continued)*
  cardiovascular device, graft or implant
      (Continued)
    electronic *(Continued)*
      specified condition NEC T82.897
      specified device NEC T82.9
        embolism T82.817
        fibrosis T82.827
        hemorrhage T82.837
        infection T82.7
        mechanical
          breakdown T82.118
          displacement T82.128
          leakage T82.198
          obstruction T82.198
          perforation T82.198
          protrusion T82.198
          specified type NEC T82.198
        pain T82.847
        specified NEC T82.897
        stenosis T82.857
        thrombosis T82.867
      stenosis T82.857
      thrombosis T82.867
    extremity artery graft —*see* Complication,
        extremity artery (bypass) graft
    femoral artery graft —*see* Complication,
        extremity artery (bypass) graft
    heart
      transplant —*see* Complication,
          transplant, heart
      valve —*see* Complication, prosthetic
          device, heart valve
        graft —*see* Complication, heart, valve,
            graft
    heart-lung transplant —*see* Complication,
        transplant, heart, with lung
    infection or inflammation T82.7
    umbrella device —*see* Complication,
        umbrella device, vascular
    vascular graft (or anastomosis) —*see*
        Complication, graft, vascular
  carotid artery (bypass) graft —*see*
      Complications, graft, vascular
  catheter (device) NEC —*see also*
      Complications, prosthetic device or
      implant
    cranial infusion
      infection and inflammation T85.735
      mechanical
        breakdown T85.610
        displacement T85.620
        leakage T85.630
        malfunction T85.690
        malposition T85.620
        obstruction T85.690
        perforation T85.690
        protrusion T85.690
        specified NEC T85.690
    cystostomy T83.9
      embolism T83.81
      fibrosis T83.82
      hemorrhage T83.83
      infection and inflammation T83.510
      mechanical
        breakdown T83.010
        displacement T83.020
        leakage T83.030
        malposition T83.020
        obstruction T83.090
        perforation T83.090
        protrusion T83.090
        specified NEC T83.090
      pain T83.84
      specified type NEC T83.89
      stenosis T83.85
      thrombosis T83.86
    dialysis (vascular) T82.9
      embolism T82.818
      fibrosis T82.828
      hemorrhage T82.838

Complication (Continued)
  catheter NEC (Continued)
    dialysis (Continued)
      infection and inflammation T82.7
      intraperitoneal —see Complications,
        catheter, intraperitoneal
      mechanical
        breakdown T82.41
        displacement T82.42
        leakage T82.43
        malposition T82.42
        obstruction T82.49
        perforation T82.49
        protrusion T82.49
      pain T82.848
      specified type NEC T82.898
      stenosis T82.858
      thrombosis T82.868
    epidural infusion T85.9
      embolism T85.810
      fibrosis T85.820
      hemorrhage T85.830
      infection and inflammation T85.735
      mechanical
        breakdown T85.610
        displacement T85.620
        leakage T85.630
        malfunction T85.610
        malposition T85.620
        obstruction T85.690
        perforation T85.690
        protrusion T85.690
        specified NEC T85.690
      pain T85.840
      specified type NEC T85.890
      stenosis T85.850
      thrombosis T85.860
    intraperitoneal dialysis T85.9
      embolism T85.818
      fibrosis T85.828
      hemorrhage T85.838
      infection and inflammation T85.71
      mechanical
        breakdown T85.611
        displacement T85.621
        leakage T85.631
        malfunction T85.611
        malposition T85.621
        obstruction T85.691
        perforation T85.691
        protrusion T85.691
        specified NEC T85.691
      pain T85.848
      specified type NEC T85.898
      stenosis T85.858
      thrombosis T85.868
    intrathecal infusion
      infection and inflammation T85.735
      mechanical
        breakdown T85.610
        displacement T85.620
        leakage T85.630
        malfunction T85.690
        malposition T85.620
        obstruction T85.690
        perforation T85.690
        protrusion T85.690
        specified NEC T85.690
    intravenous infusion T82.9
      embolism T82.818
      fibrosis T82.828
      hemorrhage T82.838
      infection or inflammation T82.7
      mechanical
        breakdown T82.514
        displacement T82.524
        leakage T82.534
        malposition T82.524
        obstruction T82.594
        perforation T82.594
        protrusion T82.594
      pain T82.848

Complication (Continued)
  catheter NEC (Continued)
    intravenous infusion (Continued)
      specified type NEC T82.898
      stenosis T82.858
      thrombosis T82.868
    spinal infusion
      infection and inflammation T85.735
      mechanical
        breakdown T85.610
        displacement T85.620
        leakage T85.630
        malfunction T85.690
        malposition T85.620
        obstruction T85.690
        perforation T85.690
        protrusion T85.690
        specified NEC T85.690
    subarachnoid infusion
      infection and inflammation
        T85.735
      mechanical
        breakdown T85.610
        displacement T85.620
        leakage T85.630
        malfunction T85.690
        malposition T85.620
        obstruction T85.690
        perforation T85.690
        protrusion T85.690
        specified NEC T85.690
    subdural infusion T85.9
      embolism T85.810
      fibrosis T85.820
      hemorrhage T85.830
      infection and inflammation T85.735
      mechanical
        breakdown T85.610
        displacement T85.620
        leakage T85.630
        malfunction T85.610
        malposition T85.620
        obstruction T85.690
        perforation T85.690
        protrusion T85.690
        specified NEC T85.690
      pain T85.840
      specified type NEC T85.890
      stenosis T85.850
      thrombosis T85.860
    urethral T83.9
      displacement T83.028
      embolism T83.81
      fibrosis T83.82
      hemorrhage T83.83
      indwelling
        breakdown T83.011
        displacement T83.021
        infection and inflammation T83.511
        leakage T83.031
        specified complication NEC T83.091
      infection and inflammation T83.511
      leakage T83.038
      malposition T83.028
      mechanical
        breakdown T83.011
      obstruction (mechanical) T83.091
      pain T83.84
      perforation T83.091
      protrusion T83.091
      specified type NEC T83.091
      stenosis T83.85
      thrombosis T83.86
    urinary NEC
      breakdown T83.018
      displacement T83.028
      infection and inflammation T83.518
      leakage T83.038
      specified complication NEC T83.098
  cecostomy (stoma) —see Complications,
    colostomy

Complication (Continued)
  cesarean delivery wound NEC O90.89
    disruption O90.0
    hematoma O90.2
    infection (following delivery) O86.00
  chemotherapy (antineoplastic) NEC T88.7
  chin implant (prosthetic) —see Complication,
    prosthetic device or implant, specified
    NEC
  circulatory system I99.8
    intraoperative I97.88
    postprocedural I97.89
      following cardiac surgery —see also
        Infarct, myocardium, associated with
        revascularization procedure I97.19-•
        postcardiotomy syndrome I97.0
      hypertension I97.3
      lymphedema after mastectomy I97.2
      postcardiotomy syndrome I97.0
      specified NEC I97.89
  colostomy (stoma) K94.00
    hemorrhage K94.01
    infection K94.02
    malfunction K94.03
    mechanical K94.03
    specified complication NEC K94.09
  contraceptive device, intrauterine —
    see Complications, intrauterine,
    contraceptive device
  cord (umbilical) —see Complications,
    umbilical cord
  corneal graft —see Complications, graft, cornea
  coronary artery (bypass) graft T82.9
    atherosclerosis —see Arteriosclerosis,
      coronary (artery)
    embolism T82.818
    fibrosis T82.828
    hemorrhage T82.838
    infection and inflammation T82.7
    mechanical
      breakdown T82.211
      displacement T82.212
      leakage T82.213
      malposition T82.212
      obstruction T82.218
      perforation T82.218
      protrusion T82.218
      specified NEC T82.218
    pain T82.848
    specified type NEC T82.898
    stenosis T82.858
    thrombosis T82.868
  counterpulsation device (balloon), intra-
    aortic —see Complications, balloon
    implant, vascular
  cystostomy (stoma) N99.518
    catheter —see Complications, catheter,
      cystostomy
    hemorrhage N99.510
    infection N99.511
    malfunction N99.512
    specified type NEC N99.518
  delivery —see also Complications, obstetric
    O75.9
    procedure (instrumental) (manual)
      (surgical) O75.4
    specified NEC O75.89
  dialysis (peritoneal) (renal) —see also
    Complications, infusion
    catheter (vascular) —see Complication,
      catheter, dialysis
      peritoneal, intraperitoneal —see
        Complications, catheter,
        intraperitoneal
  dorsal column (spinal) neurostimulator —see
    Complications, electronic stimulator
    device, spinal cord
  drug NEC T88.7
  ear procedure —see also Disorder, ear
    intraoperative H95.88-•
      hematoma —see Complications,
        intraoperative, hematoma (of), ear

▶ New   ⇒ Revised   ~~deleted~~ Deleted   • Use Additional Character(s)

Complication *(Continued)*
  ear procedure *(Continued)*
    intraoperative *(Continued)*
      hemorrhage —*see* Complications,
        intraoperative, hemorrhage (of), ear
      laceration —*see* Complications,
        intraoperative, puncture or
        laceration..., ear
      seroma —*see* Complications,
        postprocedural, seroma (of),
        mastoid process
      specified NEC H95.88-●
    postoperative H95.89-●
      external ear canal stenosis H95.81-●
      hematoma —*see* Complications,
        postprocedural, hemorrhage
        (hematoma) (of), ear
      hemorrhage —*see* Complications,
        postprocedural, hemorrhage
        (hematoma) (of), ear
      postmastoidectomy —*see* Complications,
        postmastoidectomy
      specified NEC H95.89-●
  ectopic pregnancy O08.9
    damage to pelvic organs O08.6
    embolism O08.2
    genital infection O08.0
    hemorrhage (delayed) (excessive) O08.1
    metabolic disorder O08.5
    renal failure O08.4
    shock O08.3
    specified type NEC O08.0
    venous complication NEC O08.7
  electronic stimulator device
    bladder (urinary) —*see* Complications,
      electronic stimulator device, urinary
    bone T84.9
      breakdown T84.310
      displacement T84.320
      embolism T84.81
      fibrosis T84.82
      hemorrhage T84.83
      infection or inflammation T84.7
      malfunction T84.310
      malposition T84.320
      mechanical NEC T84.390
      obstruction T84.390
      pain T84.84
      perforation T84.390
      protrusion T84.390
      specified type NEC T84.89
      stenosis T84.85
      thrombosis T84.86
    brain T85.9
      embolism T85.810
      fibrosis T85.820
      hemorrhage T85.830
      infection and inflammation T85.731
      mechanical
        breakdown T85.110
        displacement T85.120
        leakage T85.190
        malposition T85.120
        obstruction T85.190
        perforation T85.190
        protrusion T85.190
        specified NEC T85.190
      pain T85.840
      specified type NEC T85.890
      stenosis T85.850
      thrombosis T85.860
    cardiac (defibrillator) (pacemaker) —*see*
      Complications, cardiovascular device
      or implant, electronic
    generator (brain) (gastric) (peripheral)
      (sacral) (spinal)
      breakdown T85.113
      displacement T85.123
      leakage T85.193
      malposition T85.123
      obstruction T85.193

Complication *(Continued)*
  electronic stimulator device *(Continued)*
    generator *(Continued)*
      perforation T85.193
      protrusion T85.193
      specified type NEC T85.193
    muscle T84.9
      breakdown T84.418
      displacement T84.428
      embolism T84.81
      fibrosis T84.82
      hemorrhage T84.83
      infection or inflammation T84.7
      mechanical NEC T84.498
      pain T84.84
      specified type NEC T84.89
      stenosis T84.85
      thrombosis T84.86
    nervous system T85.9
      brain —*see* Complications, electronic
        stimulator device, brain
      cranial nerve —*see* Complications,
        electronic stimulator device,
        peripheral nerve
      embolism T85.810
      fibrosis T85.820
      gastric nerve —*see* Complications,
        electronic stimulator device,
        peripheral nerve
      hemorrhage T85.830
      infection and inflammation T85.738
      mechanical
        breakdown T85.118
        displacement T85.128
        leakage T85.199
        malposition T85.128
        obstruction T85.199
        perforation T85.199
        protrusion T85.199
        specified NEC T85.199
      pain T85.840
      peripheral nerve —*see* Complications,
        electronic stimulator device,
        peripheral nerve
      sacral nerve —*see* Complications,
        electronic stimulator device,
        peripheral nerve
      specified type NEC T85.890
      spinal cord —*see* Complications, electronic
        stimulator device, spinal cord
      stenosis T85.850
      thrombosis T85.860
      vagal nerve —*see* Complications,
        electronic stimulator device,
        peripheral nerve
    peripheral nerve T85.9
      embolism T85.810
      fibrosis T85.820
      hemorrhage T85.830
      infection and inflammation T85.732
      mechanical
        breakdown T85.111
        displacement T85.121
        leakage T85.191
        malposition T85.121
        obstruction T85.191
        perforation T85.191
        protrusion T85.191
        specified NEC T85.191
      pain T85.840
      specified type NEC T85.890
      stenosis T85.850
      thrombosis T85.860
    spinal cord T85.9
      embolism T85.810
      fibrosis T85.820
      hemorrhage T85.830
      infection and inflammation T85.733
      mechanical
        breakdown T85.112
        displacement T85.122

Complication *(Continued)*
  electronic stimulator device *(Continued)*
    spinal cord *(Continued)*
      mechanical *(Continued)*
        leakage T85.192
        malposition T85.122
        obstruction T85.192
        perforation T85.192
        protrusion T85.192
        specified NEC T85.192
      pain T85.840
      specified type NEC T85.890
      stenosis T85.850
      thrombosis T85.860
    urinary T83.9
      embolism T83.81
      fibrosis T83.82
      hemorrhage T83.83
      infection and inflammation T83.598
      mechanical
        breakdown T83.110
        displacement T83.120
        malposition T83.120
        perforation T83.190
        protrusion T83.190
        specified NEC T83.190
      pain T83.84
      specified type NEC T83.89
      stenosis T83.85
      thrombosis T83.86
  electroshock therapy T88.9
    specified NEC T88.8
  endocrine E34.9
    postprocedural
      adrenal hypofunction E89.6
      hypoinsulinemia E89.1
      hypoparathyroidism E89.2
      hypopituitarism E89.3
      hypothyroidism E89.0
      ovarian failure E89.40
        asymptomatic E89.40
        symptomatic E89.41
      specified NEC E89.89
      testicular hypofunction E89.5
  endodontic treatment NEC M27.59
  enterostomy (stoma) K94.10
    hemorrhage K94.11
    infection K94.12
    malfunction K94.13
    mechanical K94.13
    specified complication NEC K94.19
  episiotomy, disruption O90.1
  esophageal anti-reflux device T85.9
    embolism T85.818
    fibrosis T85.828
    hemorrhage T85.838
    infection and inflammation T85.79
    mechanical
      breakdown T85.511
      displacement T85.521
      malfunction T85.511
      malposition T85.521
      obstruction T85.591
      perforation T85.591
      protrusion T85.591
      specified NEC T85.591
    pain T85.848
    specified type NEC T85.898
    stenosis T85.858
    thrombosis T85.868
  esophagostomy K94.30
    hemorrhage K94.31
    infection K94.32
    malfunction K94.33
    mechanical K94.33
    specified complication NEC K94.39
  extracorporeal circulation T80.90
  extremity artery (bypass) graft T82.9
    arteriosclerosis —*see* Arteriosclerosis,
      extremities, bypass graft
    embolism T82.818
    fibrosis T82.828

Complication (Continued)
 extremity artery (bypass) graft (Continued)
  hemorrhage T82.838
  infection and inflammation T82.7
  mechanical
   breakdown T82.318
    femoral artery T82.312
   displacement T82.328
    femoral artery T82.322
   leakage T82.338
    femoral artery T82.332
   malposition T82.328
    femoral artery T82.322
   obstruction T82.398
    femoral artery T82.392
   perforation T82.398
    femoral artery T82.392
   protrusion T82.398
    femoral artery T82.392
  pain T82.848
  specified type NEC T82.898
  stenosis T82.858
  thrombosis T82.868
 eye H57.9
  corneal graft —see Complications, graft,
   cornea
  implant (prosthetic) T85.9
   embolism T85.818
   fibrosis T85.828
   hemorrhage T85.838
   infection and inflammation T85.79
   mechanical
    breakdown T85.318
    displacement T85.328
    leakage T85.398
    malposition T85.328
    obstruction T85.398
    perforation T85.398
    protrusion T85.398
    specified NEC T85.398
   pain T85.848
   specified type NEC T85.898
   stenosis T85.858
   thrombosis T85.868
  intraocular lens —see Complications,
   intraocular lens
  orbital prosthesis —see Complications,
   orbital prosthesis
 female genital N94.9
  device, implant or graft NEC —see
   Complications, genitourinary, device
   or implant, genital tract
 femoral artery (bypass) graft —see
   Complication, extremity artery (bypass)
   graft
 fixation device, internal (orthopedic) T84.9
  infection and inflammation T84.60
   arm T84.61-●
    humerus T84.61-●
    radius T84.61-●
    ulna T84.61-●
   leg T84.629
    femur T84.62-●
    fibula T84.62-●
    tibia T84.62-●
   specified site NEC T84.69
   spine T84.63
  mechanical
   breakdown
    limb T84.119
     carpal T84.210
     femur T84.11-●
     fibula T84.11-●
     humerus T84.11-●
     metacarpal T84.210
     metatarsal T84.213
     phalanx
      foot T84.213
      hand T84.210
     radius T84.11-●
     tarsal T84.213

Complication (Continued)
 fixation device, internal (Continued)
  mechanical (Continued)
   breakdown (Continued)
    limb (Continued)
     tibia T84.11-●
     ulna T84.11-●
    specified bone NEC T84.218
    spine T84.216
   displacement
    limb T84.129
     carpal T84.220
     femur T84.12-●
     fibula T84.12-●
     humerus T84.12-●
     metacarpal T84.220
     metatarsal T84.223
     phalanx
      foot T84.223
      hand T84.220
     radius T84.12-●
     tarsal T84.223
     tibia T84.12-●
     ulna T84.12-●
    specified bone NEC T84.228
    spine T84.226
   malposition —see Complications,
    fixation device, internal,
    mechanical, displacement
   obstruction —see Complications, fixation
    device, internal, mechanical,
    specified type NEC
   perforation —see Complications, fixation
    device, internal, mechanical,
    specified type NEC
   protrusion —see Complications, fixation
    device, internal, mechanical,
    specified type NEC
   specified type NEC
    limb T84.199
     carpal T84.290
     femur T84.19-●
     fibula T84.19-●
     humerus T84.19-●
     metacarpal T84.290
     metatarsal T84.293
     phalanx
      foot T84.293
      hand T84.290
     radius T84.19-●
     tarsal T84.293
     tibia T84.19-●
     ulna T84.19-●
    specified bone NEC T84.298
    vertebra T84.296
  specified type NEC T84.89
   embolism T84.81
   fibrosis T84.82
   hemorrhage T84.83
   pain T84.84
   specified complication NEC T84.89
   stenosis T84.85
   thrombosis T84.86
 following
  acute myocardial infarction NEC I23.8
   aneurysm (false) (of cardiac wall)
    (of heart wall) (ruptured) I23.3
   angina I23.7
   atrial
    septal defect I23.1
    thrombosis I23.6
   cardiac wall rupture I23.3
   chordae tendinae rupture I23.4
   defect
    septal
     atrial (heart) I23.1
     ventricular (heart) I23.2
   hemopericardium I23.0
   papillary muscle rupture I23.5
   rupture
    cardiac wall I23.3
     with hemopericardium I23.0

Complication (Continued)
 following (Continued)
  acute myocardial infarction NEC
   (Continued)
    rupture (Continued)
     chordae tendineae I23.4
     papillary muscle I23.5
    specified NEC I23.8
    thrombosis
     atrium I23.6
     auricular appendage I23.6
     ventricle (heart) I23.6
    ventricular
     septal defect I23.2
     thrombosis I23.6
  ectopic or molar pregnancy O08.9
   cardiac arrest O08.81
   sepsis O08.82
   specified type NEC O08.89
   urinary tract infection O08.83
  termination of pregnancy —see Abortion
 gastrointestinal K92.9
  bile duct prosthesis —see Complications,
   bile duct implant
  esophageal anti-reflux device —see
   Complications, esophageal
   anti-reflux device
  postoperative
   colostomy —see Complications, colostomy
   dumping syndrome K91.1
   enterostomy —see Complications,
    enterostomy
   gastrostomy —see Complications,
    gastrostomy
   malabsorption NEC K91.2
   obstruction —see also Obstruction,
    intestine, postoperative K91.30
   postcholecystectomy syndrome K91.5
   specified NEC K91.89
   vomiting after GI surgery K91.0
  prosthetic device or implant
   bile duct prosthesis —see Complications,
    bile duct implant
   esophageal anti-reflux device —see
    Complications, esophageal
    anti-reflux device
   specified type NEC
    embolism T85.818
    fibrosis T85.828
    hemorrhage T85.838
    mechanical
     breakdown T85.518
     displacement T85.528
     malfunction T85.518
     malposition T85.528
     obstruction T85.598
     perforation T85.598
     protrusion T85.598
     specified NEC T85.598
    pain T85.848
    specified complication NEC T85.898
    stenosis T85.858
    thrombosis T85.868
 gastrostomy (stoma) K94.20
  hemorrhage K94.21
  infection K94.22
  malfunction K94.23
  mechanical K94.23
  specified complication NEC K94.29
 genitourinary
  device or implant T83.9
   genital tract T83.9
    infection or inflammation T83.69
    intrauterine contraceptive device —see
     Complications, intrauterine,
     contraceptive device
    mechanical —see Complications, by
     device, mechanical
    mesh —see Complications, prosthetic
     device or implant, mesh
    penile prosthesis —see Complications,
     prosthetic device, penile

▶ New   ⇒ Revised   ~~deleted~~ Deleted   ● Use Additional Character(s)

Complication *(Continued)*
  genitourinary *(Continued)*
    device or implant *(Continued)*
      genital tract *(Continued)*
        specified type NEC T83.89
          embolism T83.81
          fibrosis T83.82
          hemorrhage T83.83
          pain T83.84
          specified complication NEC T83.89
          stenosis T83.85
          thrombosis T83.86
        vaginal mesh —*see* Complications,
          prosthetic device or implant, mesh
      urinary system T83.9
        cystostomy catheter —*see*
          Complication, catheter,
          cystostomy
        electronic stimulator —*see*
          Complications, electronic
          stimulator device, urinary
        indwelling urethral catheter —*see*
          Complications, catheter, urethral,
          indwelling
        infection or inflammation T83.598
          indwelling urethral catheter T83.511
        kidney transplant —*see* Complication,
          transplant, kidney
        organ graft —*see* Complication, graft,
          urinary organ
        specified type NEC T83.89
          embolism T83.81
          fibrosis T83.82
          hemorrhage T83.83
          mechanical T83.198
            breakdown T83.118
            displacement T83.128
            malfunction T83.118
            malposition T83.128
            obstruction T83.198
            perforation T83.198
            protrusion T83.198
            specified NEC T83.198
        sphincter, implanted T83.191
        stent (ileal conduit) (nephroureteral)
          T83.193
        ureteral indwelling T83.192
        pain T83.84
        specified complication NEC T83.89
        stenosis T83.85
        thrombosis T83.86
        sphincter implant —*see* Complications,
          implant, urinary sphincter
  postprocedural
    pelvic peritoneal adhesions N99.4
    renal failure N99.0
    specified NEC N99.89
    stoma —*see* Complications, stoma,
      urinary tract
    urethral stricture —*see* Stricture, urethra,
      postprocedural
    vaginal
      adhesions N99.2
      vault prolapse N99.3
  graft (bypass) (patch) —*see also*
    Complications, prosthetic device or
    implant
    aorta —*see* Complications, graft, vascular
    arterial —*see* Complication, graft, vascular
    bone T86.839
      failure T86.831
      infection T86.832
      mechanical T84.318
        breakdown T84.318
        displacement T84.328
        protrusion T84.398
        specified type NEC T84.398
      rejection T86.830
      specified type NEC T86.838
    carotid artery —*see* Complications, graft,
      vascular

Complication *(Continued)*
  graft *(Continued)*
    ➠cornea T86.849-
      ➠failure T86.841-
      ➠infection T86.842-
      mechanical T85.398
        breakdown T85.318
        displacement T85.328
        protrusion T85.398
        specified type NEC T85.398
      ➠rejection T86.840-
      retroprosthetic membrane T85.398
      ➠specified type NEC T86.848-
    femoral artery (bypass) —*see* Complication,
      extremity artery (bypass) graft
    genital organ or tract —*see* Complications,
      genitourinary, device or implant,
      genital tract
    muscle T84.9
      breakdown T84.410
      displacement T84.420
      embolism T84.81
      fibrosis T84.82
      hemorrhage T84.83
      infection and inflammation T84.7
      mechanical NEC T84.490
      pain T84.84
      specified type NEC T84.89
      stenosis T84.85
      thrombosis T84.86
    nerve —*see* Complication, prosthetic device
      or implant, specified NEC
    skin —*see* Complications, prosthetic device
      or implant, skin graft
    tendon T84.9
      breakdown T84.410
      displacement T84.420
      embolism T84.81
      fibrosis T84.82
      hemorrhage T84.83
      infection and inflammation T84.7
      mechanical NEC T84.490
      pain T84.84
      specified type NEC T84.89
      stenosis T84.85
      thrombosis T84.86
    urinary organ T83.9
      embolism T83.81
      fibrosis T83.82
      hemorrhage T83.83
      infection and inflammation T83.598
        indwelling urethral catheter T83.511
      mechanical
        breakdown T83.21
        displacement T83.22
        erosion T83.24
        exposure T83.25
        leakage T83.23
        malposition T83.22
        obstruction T83.29
        perforation T83.29
        protrusion T83.29
        specified NEC T83.29
      pain T83.84
      specified type NEC T83.89
      stenosis T83.85
      thrombosis T83.86
    vascular T82.9
      embolism T82.818
      femoral artery —*see* Complication,
        extremity artery (bypass) graft
      fibrosis T82.828
      hemorrhage T82.838
      mechanical
        breakdown T82.319
          aorta (bifurcation) T82.310
          carotid artery T82.311
          specified vessel NEC T82.318
        displacement T82.329
          aorta (bifurcation) T82.320
          carotid artery T82.321
          specified vessel NEC T82.328

Complication *(Continued)*
  graft *(Continued)*
    vascular *(Continued)*
      mechanical *(Continued)*
        leakage T82.339
          aorta (bifurcation) T82.330
          carotid artery T82.331
          specified vessel NEC T82.338
        malposition T82.329
          aorta (bifurcation) T82.320
          carotid artery T82.321
          specified vessel NEC T82.328
        obstruction T82.399
          aorta (bifurcation) T82.390
          carotid artery T82.391
          specified vessel NEC T82.398
        perforation T82.399
          aorta (bifurcation) T82.390
          carotid artery T82.391
          specified vessel NEC T82.398
        protrusion T82.399
          aorta (bifurcation) T82.390
          carotid artery T82.391
          specified vessel NEC T82.398
      pain T82.848
      specified complication NEC T82.898
      stenosis T82.858
      thrombosis T82.868
  heart I51.9
    assist device
      infection and inflammation T82.7
    following acute myocardial infarction —
      see Complications, following, acute
      myocardial infarction
    postoperative —*see* Complications,
      circulatory system
    transplant —*see* Complication, transplant,
      heart
      and lung(s) —*see* Complications,
        transplant, heart, with lung
    valve
      graft (biological) T82.9
        embolism T82.817
        fibrosis T82.827
        hemorrhage T82.837
        infection and inflammation T82.7
        mechanical T82.228
          breakdown T82.221
          displacement T82.222
          leakage T82.223
          malposition T82.222
          obstruction T82.228
          perforation T82.228
          protrusion T82.228
        pain T82.847
        specified type NEC T82.897
        stenosis T82.857
        thrombosis T82.867
      prosthesis T82.9
        embolism T82.817
        fibrosis T82.827
        hemorrhage T82.837
        infection or inflammation T82.6
        mechanical T82.09
          breakdown T82.01
          displacement T82.02
          leakage T82.03
          malposition T82.02
          obstruction T82.09
          perforation T82.09
          protrusion T82.09
        pain T82.847
        specified type NEC T82.897
          mechanical T82.09
        stenosis T82.857
        thrombosis T82.867
  hematoma
    intraoperative —*see* Complication,
      intraoperative, hemorrhage
    postprocedural —*see* Complication,
      postprocedural, hematoma
  hemodialysis —*see* Complications, dialysis

Complication *(Continued)*
  hemorrhage
    intraoperative —*see* Complication,
      intraoperative, hemorrhage
    postprocedural —*see* Complication,
      postprocedural, hemorrhage
  ileostomy (stoma) —*see* Complications,
    enterostomy
  immunization (procedure) —*see*
    Complications, vaccination
  implant —*see also* Complications, by site and
    type
    urinary sphincter T83.9
      embolism T83.81
      fibrosis T83.82
      hemorrhage T83.83
      infection and inflammation T83.591
      mechanical
        breakdown T83.111
        displacement T83.121
        leakage T83.191
        malposition T83.121
        obstruction T83.191
        perforation T83.191
        protrusion T83.191
        specified NEC T83.191
      pain T83.84
      specified type NEC T83.89
      stenosis T83.85
      thrombosis T83.86
  infusion (procedure) T80.90
    air embolism T80.0
    blood —*see* Complications, transfusion
    catheter —*see* Complications, catheter
    infection T80.29
    pump —*see* Complications, cardiovascular,
      device or implant
    sepsis T80.29
    serum reaction —*see also* Reaction, serum
      T80.69
      anaphylactic shock —*see also* Shock,
        anaphylactic T80.59
    specified type NEC T80.89
  inhalation therapy NEC T81.81
  injection (procedure) T80.90
    drug reaction —*see* Reaction, drug
    infection T80.29
    sepsis T80.29
    serum (prophylactic) (therapeutic) —*see*
      Complications, vaccination
    specified type NEC T80.89
    vaccine (any) —*see* Complications,
      vaccination
  inoculation (any) —*see* Complications,
    vaccination
  insulin pump
    infection and inflammation T85.72
    mechanical
      breakdown T85.614
      displacement T85.624
      leakage T85.633
      malposition T85.624
      obstruction T85.694
      perforation T85.694
      protrusion T85.694
      specified NEC T85.694
  intestinal pouch NEC K91.858
  intraocular lens (prosthetic) T85.9
    embolism T85.818
    fibrosis T85.828
    hemorrhage T85.838
    infection and inflammation T85.79
    mechanical
      breakdown T85.21
      displacement T85.22
      malposition T85.22
      obstruction T85.29
      perforation T85.29
      protrusion T85.29
      specified NEC T85.29
    pain T85.848
    specified type NEC T85.898

Complication *(Continued)*
  intraocular lens *(Continued)*
    stenosis T85.858
    thrombosis T85.868
  intraoperative (intraprocedural)
    cardiac arrest —*see also* Infarct,
      myocardium, associated with
      revascularization procedure
      during cardiac surgery I97.710
      during other surgery I97.711
    cardiac functional disturbance NEC —*see*
      also Infarct, myocardium, associated
      with revascularization procedure
      during cardiac surgery I97.790
      during other surgery I97.791
    hemorrhage (hematoma) (of)
      circulatory system organ or structure
        during cardiac bypass I97.411
        during cardiac catheterization I97.410
        during other circulatory system
          procedure I97.418
        during other procedure I97.42
      digestive system organ
        during procedure on digestive system
          K91.61
        during procedure on other organ
          K91.62
      ear
        during procedure on ear and mastoid
          process H95.21
        during procedure on other organ
          H95.22
      endocrine system organ or structure
        during procedure on endocrine
          system organ or structure E36.01
        during procedure on other organ
          E36.02
      eye and adnexa
        during ophthalmic procedure H59.11-●
        during other procedure H59.12-●
      genitourinary organ or structure
        during procedure on genitourinary
          organ or structure N99.61
        during procedure on other organ
          N99.62
      mastoid process
        during procedure on ear and mastoid
          process H95.21
        during procedure on other organ
          H95.22
      musculoskeletal structure
        during musculoskeletal surgery
          M96.810
        during non-orthopedic surgery
          M96.811
        during orthopedic surgery M96.810
      nervous system
        during a nervous system procedure
          G97.31
        during other procedure G97.32
      respiratory system
        during other procedure J95.62
        during procedure on respiratory
          system organ or structure
          J95.61
      skin and subcutaneous tissue
        during a dermatologic procedure
          L76.01
        during a procedure on other organ
          L76.02
      spleen
        during a procedure on other organ
          D78.02
        during a procedure on the spleen
          D78.01
    puncture or laceration (accidental)
      (unintentional) (of)
      brain
        during a nervous system procedure
          G97.48
        during other procedure G97.49

Complication *(Continued)*
  intraoperative *(Continued)*
    puncture or laceration *(Continued)*
      circulatory system organ or structure
        during circulatory system procedure
          I97.51
        during other procedure I97.52
      digestive system
        during procedure on digestive system
          K91.71
        during procedure on other organ K91.72
      ear
        during procedure on ear and mastoid
          process H95.31
        during procedure on other organ
          H95.32
      endocrine system organ or structure
        during procedure on endocrine
          system organ or structure E36.11
        during procedure on other organ E36.12
      eye and adnexa
        during ophthalmic procedure H59.21-●
        during other procedure H59.22-●
      genitourinary organ or structure
        during procedure on genitourinary
          organ or structure N99.71
        during procedure on other organ
          N99.72
      mastoid process
        during procedure on ear and mastoid
          process H95.31
        during procedure on other organ
          H95.32
      musculoskeletal structure
        during musculoskeletal surgery
          M96.820
        during non-orthopedic surgery
          M96.821
        during orthopedic surgery M96.820
      nervous system
        during a nervous system procedure
          G97.48
        during other procedure G97.49
      respiratory system
        during other procedure J95.72
        during procedure on respiratory
          system organ or structure J95.71
      skin and subcutaneous tissue
        during a dermatologic procedure
          L76.11
        during a procedure on other organ
          L76.12
      spleen
        during a procedure on other organ
          D78.12
        during a procedure on the spleen
          D78.11
    specified NEC
      circulatory system I97.88
      digestive system K91.81
      ear H95.88
      endocrine system E36.8
      eye and adnexa H59.88
      genitourinary system N99.81
      mastoid process H95.88
      musculoskeletal structure M96.89
      nervous system G97.81
      respiratory system J95.88
      skin and subcutaneous tissue L76.81
      spleen D78.81
  intraperitoneal catheter (dialysis)
    (infusion) —*see* Complications, catheter,
    intraperitoneal
  intrathecal infusion pump
    infection and inflammation T85.738
    mechanical
      breakdown T85.615
      displacement T85.625
      leakage T85.635
      malfunction T85.695
      malposition T85.625
      obstruction T85.695

▶ New   ⇒ Revised   ~~deleted~~ Deleted   ● Use Additional Character(s)

Complication *(Continued)*
  intrathecal infusion pump *(Continued)*
    mechanical *(Continued)*
      perforation T85.695
      protrusion T85.695
      specified NEC T85.695
  intrauterine
    contraceptive device
      embolism T83.81
      fibrosis T83.82
      hemorrhage T83.83
      infection and inflammation T83.69
      mechanical
        breakdown T83.31
        displacement T83.32
        malposition T83.32
        obstruction T83.39
        perforation T83.39
        protrusion T83.39
        specified NEC T83.39
      pain T83.84
      specified type NEC T83.89
      stenosis T83.85
      thrombosis T83.86
    procedure (fetal), to newborn P96.5
  jejunostomy (stoma) —*see* Complications,
    enterostomy
  joint prosthesis, internal T84.9
    breakage (fracture) T84.01-●
    dislocation T84.02-●
    fracture T84.01-●
    infection or inflammation T84.50
      hip T84.5-●
      knee T84.5-●
      specified joint NEC T84.59
    instability T84.02-●
    malposition —*see* Complications, joint
      prosthesis, mechanical, displacement
    mechanical
      breakage, broken T84.01-●
      dislocation T84.02-●
      fracture T84.01-●
      instability T84.02-●
      leakage —*see* Complications, joint
        prosthesis, mechanical, specified
        NEC
      loosening T84.039
        hip T84.03-●
        knee T84.03-●
        specified joint NEC T84.038
      obstruction —*see* Complications, joint
        prosthesis, mechanical, specified
        NEC
      perforation —*see* Complications, joint
        prosthesis, mechanical, specified
        NEC
        osteolysis T84.059
          hip T84.05-●
          knee T84.05-●
          other specified joint T84.058
        periprosthetic T84.059
      protrusion —*see* Complications, joint
        prosthesis, mechanical, specified
        NEC
      specified complication NEC T84.099
        hip T84.09-●
        knee T84.09-●
        other specified joint T84.098
      subluxation T84.02-●
      wear of articular bearing surface T84.069
        hip T84.06-●
        knee T84.06-●
        other specified joint T84.068
    specified joint NEC T84.89
      embolism T84.81
      fibrosis T84.82
      hemorrhage T84.83
      pain T84.84
      specified complication NEC T84.89
      stenosis T84.85
      thrombosis T84.86
    subluxation T84.02-●

Complication *(Continued)*
  kidney transplant —*see* Complications,
    transplant, kidney
  labor O75.9
    specified NEC O75.89
  liver transplant (immune or nonimmune) —
    see Complications, transplant,
    liver
  lumbar puncture G97.1
    cerebrospinal fluid leak G97.0
    headache or reaction G97.1
  lung transplant —*see* Complications,
    transplant, lung
    and heart —*see* Complications, transplant,
      lung, with heart
  male genital N50.9
    device, implant or graft —*see*
      Complications, genitourinary,
      device or implant, genital tract
    postprocedural or postoperative —*see*
      Complications, genitourinary,
      postprocedural
    specified NEC N99.89
  mastoid (process) procedure
    intraoperative H95.88-●
      hematoma —*see* Complications,
        intraoperative, hemorrhage
        (hematoma) (of), mastoid process
      hemorrhage —*see* Complications,
        intraoperative, hemorrhage
        (hematoma) (of), mastoid process
      laceration —*see* Complications,
        intraoperative, puncture or
        laceration..., mastoid process
      specified NEC H95.88-●
    postmastoidectomy —*see* Complications,
      postmastoidectomy
    postoperative H95.89-●
      external ear canal stenosis H95.81-●
      hematoma —*see* Complications...,
        postprocedural, hematoma (of),
        mastoid process
      hemorrhage —*see* Complications...,
        postprocedural, hemorrhage (of),
        mastoid process
      postmastoidectomy —*see* Complications,
        postmastoidectomy
      seroma —*see* Complications,
        postprocedural, seroma (of),
        mastoid process
      specified NEC H95.89-●
  mastoidectomy cavity —*see* Complications,
    postmastoidectomy
  mechanical —*see* Complications, by site and
    type, mechanical
  medical procedures (*see also* Complication(s),
    intraoperative) T88.9
  metabolic E88.9
    postoperative E89.89
      specified NEC E89.89
  molar pregnancy NOS O08.9
    damage to pelvic organs O08.6
    embolism O08.2
    genital infection O08.0
    hemorrhage (delayed) (excessive) O08.1
    metabolic disorder O08.5
    renal failure O08.4
    shock O08.3
    specified type NEC O08.0
    venous complication NEC O08.7
  musculoskeletal system —*see also*
    Complication, intraoperative
    (intraprocedural), by site
    device, implant or graft NEC —*see*
      Complications, orthopedic, device or
      implant
    internal fixation (nail) (plate) (rod) —*see*
      Complications, fixation device,
      internal
    joint prosthesis —*see* Complications, joint
      prosthesis

Complication *(Continued)*
  musculoskeletal system *(Continued)*
    postoperative (postprocedural) M96.89
      with osteoporosis —*see* Osteoporosis
      fracture following insertion of device —
        see Fracture, following insertion of
        orthopedic implant, joint prosthesis
        or bone plate
      joint instability after prosthesis removal
        M96.89
      lordosis M96.4
      postlaminectomy syndrome NEC M96.1
        kyphosis M96.2
      pseudarthrosis M96.0
      specified complication NEC M96.89
    post radiation M96.89
      kyphosis M96.3
      scoliosis M96.5
      specified complication NEC M96.89
  nephrostomy (stoma) —*see* Complications,
    stoma, urinary tract, external NEC
  nervous system G98.8
    central G96.9
    device, implant or graft —*see also*
      Complication, prosthetic device or
      implant, specified NEC
      electronic stimulator (electrode(s)) —*see*
        Complications, electronic stimulator
        device
      specified NEC
        infection and inflammation T85.738
        mechanical T85.695
          breakdown T85.615
          displacement T85.625
          leakage T85.635
          malfunction T85.695
          malposition T85.625
          obstruction T85.695
          perforation T85.695
          protrusion T85.695
          specified NEC T85.695
      ventricular shunt —*see* Complications,
        ventricular shunt
    electronic stimulator (electrode(s)) —*see*
      Complications, electronic stimulator
      device
    postprocedural G97.82
      intracranial hypotension G97.2
      specified NEC G97.82
      spinal fluid leak G97.0
  newborn, due to intrauterine (fetal)
    procedure P96.5
  nonabsorbable (permanent) sutures —*see*
    Complication, sutures, permanent
  obstetric O75.9
    procedure (instrumental) (manual)
      (surgical) specified NEC O75.4
    specified NEC O75.89
    surgical wound NEC O90.89
      hematoma O90.2
      infection O86.00
  ocular lens implant —*see* Complications,
    intraocular lens
  ophthalmologic
    postprocedural bleb —*see* Blebitis
  orbital prosthesis T85.9
    embolism T85.818
    fibrosis T85.828
    hemorrhage T85.838
    infection and inflammation T85.79
    mechanical
      breakdown T85.31-●
      displacement T85.32-●
      malposition T85.32-●
      obstruction T85.39-●
      perforation T85.39-●
      protrusion T85.39-●
      specified NEC T85.39-●
    pain T85.848
    specified type NEC T85.898
    stenosis T85.858
    thrombosis T85.868

Complication *(Continued)*
  organ or tissue transplant (partial) (total) —
      see Complications, transplant
  orthopedic —*see also* Disorder, soft tissue
    device or implant T84.9
      bone
          device or implant —*see* Complication,
              bone, device NEC
          graft —*see* Complication, graft, bone
      breakdown T84.418
      displacement T84.428
      electronic bone stimulator —*see*
          Complications, electronic stimulator
          device, bone
      embolism T84.81
      fibrosis T84.82
      fixation device —*see* Complication,
          fixation device, internal
      hemorrhage T84.83
      infection or inflammation T84.7
      joint prosthesis —*see* Complication, joint
          prosthesis, internal
      malfunction T84.418
      malposition T84.428
      mechanical NEC T84.498
      muscle graft —*see* Complications, graft,
          muscle
      obstruction T84.498
      pain T84.84
      perforation T84.498
      protrusion T84.498
      specified complication NEC T84.89
      stenosis T84.85
      tendon graft —*see* Complications, graft,
          tendon
      thrombosis T84.86
    fracture (following insertion of device) —
        see Fracture, following insertion of
        orthopedic implant, joint prosthesis or
        bone plate
    postprocedural M96.89
      fracture —*see* Fracture, following
          insertion of orthopedic implant,
          joint prosthesis or bone plate
      postlaminectomy syndrome NEC M96.1
        kyphosis M96.3
        lordosis M96.4
      postradiation
        kyphosis M96.2
        scoliosis M96.5
      pseudarthrosis post-fusion M96.0
      specified type NEC M96.89
  pacemaker (cardiac) —*see* Complications,
      cardiovascular device or implant,
      electronic
  pancreas transplant —*see* Complications,
      transplant, pancreas
  penile prosthesis (implant) —*see*
      Complications, prosthetic device, penile
  perfusion NEC T80.90
  perineal repair (obstetrical) NEC O90.89
    disruption O90.1
    hematoma O90.2
    infection (following delivery) O86.09
  phototherapy T88.9
    specified NEC T88.8
  postmastoidectomy NEC H95.19-●
    cyst, mucosal H95.13-●
    granulation H95.12-●
    inflammation, chronic H95.11-●
    recurrent cholesteatoma H95.0-●
  postoperative —*see* Complications,
      postprocedural
    circulatory —*see* Complications, circulatory
        system
    ear —*see* Complications, ear
    endocrine —*see* Complications,
        endocrine
    eye —*see* Complications, eye
    lumbar puncture G97.1
      cerebrospinal fluid leak G97.0

Complication *(Continued)*
  postoperative *(Continued)*
    nervous system (central) (peripheral) —*see*
        Complications, nervous system
    respiratory system —*see* Complications,
        respiratory system
  postprocedural —*see also* Complications,
      surgical procedure
    cardiac arrest —*see also* Infarct,
        myocardium, associated with
        revascularization procedure
      following cardiac surgery I97.120
      following other surgery I97.121
    cardiac functional disturbance NEC —*see
        also* Infarct, myocardium, associated
        with revascularization procedure
      following cardiac surgery I97.190
      following other surgery I97.191
    cardiac insufficiency
      following cardiac surgery I97.110
      following other surgery I97.111
    chorioretinal scars following retinal
        surgery H59.81-●
    following cataract surgery
      cataract (lens) fragments H59.02-●
      cystoid macular edema H59.03-●
      specified NEC H59.09-●
      vitreous (touch) syndrome H59.01-●
    heart failure
      following cardiac surgery I97.130
      following other surgery I97.131
    hematoma (of)
      circulatory system organ or structure
        following cardiac bypass I97.631
        following cardiac catheterization
            I97.630
        following other circulatory system
            procedure I97.638
        following other procedure I97.621
      digestive system
        following procedure on digestive
            system K91.870
        following procedure on other organ
            K91.871
      ear
        following other procedure H95.52
        following procedure on ear and
            mastoid process H95.51
      endocrine system
        following endocrine system procedure
            E89.820
        following other procedure E89.821
      eye and adnexa
        following ophthalmic procedure
            H59.33-●
        following other procedure H59.34-●
      genitourinary organ or structure
        following procedure on genitourinary
            organ or structure N99.840
        following procedure on other organ
            N99.841
      mastoid process
        following other procedure H95.52
        following procedure on ear and
            mastoid process H95.51
      musculoskeletal structure
        following musculoskeletal surgery
            M96.840
        following non-orthopedic surgery
            M96.841
        following orthopedic surgery M96.840
      nervous system
        following nervous system procedure
            G97.61
        following other procedure G97.62
      respiratory system
        following other procedure J95.861
        following procedure on respiratory
            system organ or structure J95.860
      skin and subcutaneous tissue
        following dermatologic procedure
            L76.31

Complication *(Continued)*
  postprocedural *(Continued)*
    hematoma *(Continued)*
      skin and subcutaneous tissue *(Continued)*
        following procedure on other organ
            L76.32
      spleen
        following procedure on other organ
            D78.32
        following procedure on the spleen
            D78.31
    hemorrhage (of)
      circulatory system organ or structure
        following cardiac bypass I97.611
        following cardiac catheterization
            I97.610
        following other circulatory system
            procedure I97.618
        following other procedure I97.620
      digestive system
        following procedure on digestive
            system K91.840
        following procedure on other organ
            K91.841
      ear
        following other procedure H95.42
        following procedure on ear and
            mastoid process H95.41
      endocrine system
        following endocrine system procedure
            E89.810
        following other procedure E89.811
      eye and adnexa
        following ophthalmic procedure
            H59.31-●
        following other procedure H59.32-●
      genitourinary organ or structure
        following procedure on genitourinary
            organ or structure N99.820
        following procedure on other organ
            N99.821
      mastoid process
        following other procedure H95.42
        following procedure on ear and
            mastoid process H95.41
      musculoskeletal structure
        following musculoskeletal surgery
            M96.830
        following non-orthopedic surgery
            M96.831
        following orthopedic surgery M96.830
      nervous system
        following nervous system procedure
            G97.51
        following other procedure G97.52
      respiratory system
        following other procedure J95.831
        following procedure on respiratory
            system organ or structure J95.830
      skin and subcutaneous tissue
        following dermatologic procedure
            L76.21
        following a procedure on other organ
            L76.22
      spleen
        following procedure on other organ
            D78.22
        following procedure on the spleen
            D78.21
    seroma (of)
      circulatory system organ or structure
        following cardiac bypass I97.641
        following cardiac catheterization
            I97.640
        following other circulatory system
            procedure I97.648
        following other procedure I97.622
      digestive system
        following procedure on digestive
            system K91.872
        following procedure on other organ
            K91.873

▶ New   ⇒ Revised   ~~deleted~~ Deleted   ● Use Additional Character(s)

Complication *(Continued)*
  postprocedural *(Continued)*
    seroma *(Continued)*
      ear
        following other procedure H95.54
        following procedure on ear and
          mastoid process H95.53
      endocrine system
        following endocrine system procedure
          E89.822
        following other procedure E89.823
      eye and adnexa
        following ophthalmic procedure
          H59.35-●
        following other procedure H59.36-●
      genitourinary organ or structure
        following procedure on genitourinary
          organ or structure N99.842
        following procedure on other organ
          N99.843
      mastoid process
        following other procedure H95.54
        following procedure on ear and
          mastoid process H95.53
      musculoskeletal structure
        following musculoskeletal surgery
          M96.842
        following non-orthopedic surgery
          M96.843
        following orthopedic surgery M96.842
      nervous system
        following nervous system procedure
          G97.63
        following other procedure G97.64
      respiratory system
        following other procedure J95.863
        following procedure on respiratory
          system organ or structure J95.862
      skin and subcutaneous tissue
        following dermatologic procedure
          L76.33
        following procedure on other organ
          L76.34
      spleen
        following procedure on other organ
          D78.34
        following procedure on the spleen
          D78.33
    specified NEC
      circulatory system I97.89
      digestive K91.89
      ear H95.89
      endocrine E89.89
      eye and adnexa H59.89
      genitourinary N99.89
      mastoid process H95.89
      metabolic E89.89
      musculoskeletal structure M96.89
      nervous system G97.82
      respiratory system J95.89
      skin and subcutaneous tissue L76.82
      spleen D78.89
  pregnancy NEC —*see* Pregnancy,
    complicated by
  prosthetic device or implant T85.9
    bile duct —*see* Complications, bile duct
      implant
    breast —*see* Complications, breast
      implant
    bulking agent
      ureteral
        erosion T83.714
        exposure T83.724
      urethral
        erosion T83.713
        exposure T83.723
    cardiac and vascular NEC —*see*
      Complications, cardiovascular device
      or implant
    corneal transplant —*see* Complications,
      graft, cornea

Complication *(Continued)*
  prosthetic device or implant *(Continued)*
    electronic nervous system stimulator —*see*
      Complications, electronic stimulator
      device
    epidural infusion catheter —*see*
      Complications, catheter, epidural
    esophageal anti-reflux device —*see*
      Complications, esophageal anti-reflux
      device
    genital organ or tract —*see* Complications,
      genitourinary, device or implant,
      genital tract
      specified NEC T83.79
    heart valve —*see* Complications, heart,
      valve, prosthesis
    infection or inflammation T85.79
      intestine transplant T86.892
      liver transplant T86.43
      lung transplant T86.812
      pancreas transplant T86.892
      skin graft T86.822
    intraocular lens —*see* Complications,
      intraocular lens
    intraperitoneal (dialysis) catheter —
      see Complications, catheter,
      intraperitoneal
    joint —*see* Complications, joint prosthesis,
      internal
    mechanical NEC T85.698
      dialysis catheter (vascular) —*see also*
        Complication, catheter, dialysis,
        mechanical
        peritoneal —*see* Complication, catheter,
          intraperitoneal, mechanical
      gastrointestinal device T85.598
      ocular device T85.398
      subdural (infusion) catheter T85.690
      suture, permanent T85.692
        that for bone repair —*see*
          Complications, fixation device,
          internal (orthopedic), mechanical
      ventricular shunt
        breakdown T85.01
        displacement T85.02
        leakage T85.03
        malposition T85.02
        obstruction T85.09
        perforation T85.09
        protrusion T85.09
        specified NEC T85.09
    mesh
      erosion (to surrounding organ or tissue)
        T83.718
        urethral (into pelvic floor muscles)
          T83.712
        vaginal (into pelvic floor muscles)
          T83.711
      exposure (into surrounding organ or
        tissue) T83.728
        urethral (through urethral wall)
          T83.722
        vaginal (into vagina) (through vaginal
          wall) T83.721
    orbital —*see* Complications, orbital
      prosthesis
    penile T83.9
      embolism T83.81
      fibrosis T83.82
      hemorrhage T83.83
      infection and inflammation T83.61
      mechanical
        breakdown T83.410
        displacement T83.420
        leakage T83.490
        malposition T83.420
        obstruction T83.490
        perforation T83.490
        protrusion T83.490
        specified NEC T83.490
      pain T83.84

Complication *(Continued)*
  prosthetic device or implant *(Continued)*
    penile *(Continued)*
      specified type NEC T83.89
      stenosis T83.85
      thrombosis T83.86
    prosthetic materials NEC
      erosion (to surrounding organ or tissue)
        T83.718
      exposure (into surrounding organ or
        tissue) T83.728
    skin graft T86.829
      artificial skin or decellularized
        allodermis
        embolism T85.818
        fibrosis T85.828
        hemorrhage T85.838
        infection and inflammation T85.79
        mechanical
          breakdown T85.613
          displacement T85.623
          malfunction T85.613
          malposition T85.623
          obstruction T85.693
          perforation T85.693
          protrusion T85.693
          specified NEC T85.693
        pain T85.848
        specified type NEC T85.898
        stenosis T85.858
        thrombosis T85.868
      failure T86.821
      infection T86.822
      rejection T86.820
      specified NEC T86.828
    sling
      urethral (female) (male)
        erosion T83.712
        exposure T83.722
    specified NEC T85.9
      embolism T85.818
      fibrosis T85.828
      hemorrhage T85.838
      infection and inflammation T85.79
      mechanical
        breakdown T85.618
        displacement T85.628
        leakage T85.638
        malfunction T85.618
        malposition T85.628
        obstruction T85.698
        perforation T85.698
        protrusion T85.698
        specified NEC T85.698
      pain T85.848
      specified type NEC T85.898
      stenosis T85.858
      thrombosis T85.868
    subdural infusion catheter —*see*
      Complications, catheter, subdural
    sutures —*see* Complications, sutures
    urinary organ or tract NEC —*see*
      Complications, genitourinary, device
      or implant, urinary system
    vascular —*see* Complications,
      cardiovascular device or implant
    ventricular shunt —*see* Complications,
      ventricular shunt (device)
  puerperium —*see* Puerperal
  puncture, spinal G97.1
    cerebrospinal fluid leak G97.0
    headache or reaction G97.1
  pyelogram N99.89
  radiation
    kyphosis M96.2
    scoliosis M96.5
  reattached
    extremity (infection) (rejection)
      lower T87.1X-●
      upper T87.0X-●
    specified body part NEC T87.2

Complication *(Continued)*
  reconstructed breast
    asymmetry between native and
        reconstructed breast N65.1
    deformity N65.0
    disproportion between native and
        reconstructed breast N65.1
    excess tissue N65.0
    misshappen N65.0
  reimplant NEC —*see also* Complications,
        prosthetic device or implant
    limb (infection) (rejection) —*see*
        Complications, reattached,
        extremity
    organ (partial) (total) —*see* Complications,
        transplant
    prosthetic device NEC —*see* Complications,
        prosthetic device
  renal N28.9
    allograft —*see* Complications, transplant,
        kidney
    dialysis —*see* Complications, dialysis
  respirator
    mechancial J95.850
      specified NEC J95.859
  respiratory system J98.9
    device, implant or graft —*see*
        Complication, prosthetic device or
        implant, specified NEC
    lung transplant —*see* Complications,
        prosthetic device or implant, lung
        transplant
    postoperative J95.89
      air leak J95.812
      Mendelson's syndrome (chemical
          pneumonitis) J95.4
      pneumothorax J95.811
      pulmonary insufficiency (acute) (after
          nonthoracic surgery) J95.2
        chronic J95.3
        following thoracic surgery J95.1
      respiratory failure (acute) J95.821
        acute and chronic J95.822
      specified NEC J95.89
      subglottic stenosis J95.5
      tracheostomy complication —*see*
          Complications, tracheostomy
    therapy T81.89
  sedation during labor and delivery O74.9
    cardiac O74.2
    central nervous system O74.3
    pulmonary NEC O74.1
  shunt —*see also* Complications, prosthetic
        device or implant
    arteriovenous —*see* Complications,
        arteriovenous, shunt
    ventricular (communicating) —*see*
        Complications, ventricular shunt
  skin
    graft T86.829
      failure T86.821
      infection T86.822
      rejection T86.820
      specified type NEC T86.828
  spinal
    anesthesia —*see* Complications, anesthesia,
        spinal
    catheter (epidural) (subdural) —*see*
        Complications, catheter
    puncture or tap G97.1
      cerebrospinal fluid leak G97.0
      headache or reaction G97.1
  stent
    bile duct —*see* Complications, bile duct
        prosthesis
    ureteral indwelling
      breakdown T83.112
      displacement T83.122
      leakage T83.192
      malposition T83.122

Complication *(Continued)*
  stent *(Continued)*
    ureteral indwelling *(Continued)*
      obstruction T83.192
      perforation T83.192
      protrusion T83.192
      specified NEC T83.192
    urinary (ileal conduit) (nephroureteral)
        T83.193
      embolism T83.81
      fibrosis T83.82
      hemorrhage T83.83
      infection and inflammation T83.593
      mechanical
        breakdown T83.113
        displacement T83.123
        leakage T83.193
        malposition T83.123
        obstruction T83.193
        perforation T83.193
        protrusion T83.193
        specified NEC T83.193
      pain T83.84
      specified type NEC T83.89
      stenosis T83.85
      thrombosis T83.86
    vascular
      end stent stenosis —*see* Restenosis,
          stent
      in stent stenosis —*see* Restenosis, stent
  stoma
    digestive tract
      colostomy —*see* Complications,
          colostomy
      enterostomy —*see* Complications,
          enterostomy
      esophagostomy —*see* Complications,
          esophagostomy
      gastrostomy —*see* Complications,
          gastrostomy
    urinary tract N99.528
      continent N99.538
        hemorrhage N99.530
        herniation N99.533
        infection N99.531
        malfunction N99.532
        specified type NEC N99.538
        stenosis N99.534
      cystostomy —*see* Complications,
          cystostomy
      external NOS N99.528
      hemorrhage N99.520
      herniation N99.523
      incontinent N99.528
        hemorrhage N99.520
        herniation N99.523
        infection N99.521
        malfunction N99.522
        specified type NEC N99.528
        stenosis N99.524
      infection N99.521
      malfunction N99.522
      specified type NEC N99.528
      stenosis N99.524
  stomach banding —*see* Complication(s),
        bariatric procedure
  stomach stapling —*see* Complication(s),
        bariatric procedure
  surgical material, nonabsorbable —*see*
        Complication, suture, permanent
  surgical procedure (on) T81.9
    amputation stump (late) —*see*
        Complications, amputation stump
    cardiac —*see* Complications, circulatory
        system
    cholesteatoma, recurrent —*see*
        Complications, postmastoidectomy,
        recurrent cholesteatoma
    circulatory (early) —*see* Complications,
        circulatory system

Complication *(Continued)*
  surgical procedure *(Continued)*
    digestive system —*see* Complications,
        gastrointestinal
    dumping syndrome (postgastrectomy)
        K91.1
    ear —*see* Complications, ear
    elephantiasis or lymphedema I97.89
        postmastectomy I97.2
    emphysema (surgical) T81.82
    endocrine —*see* Complications, endocrine
    eye —*see* Complications, eye
    fistula (persistent postoperative) T81.83
    foreign body inadvertently left in wound
        (sponge) (suture) (swab) —*see* Foreign
        body, accidentally left during a
        procedure
    gastrointestinal —*see* Complications,
        gastrointestinal
    genitourinary NEC N99.89
    hematoma
      intraoperative —*see* Complication,
          intraoperative, hemorrhage
      postprocedural —*see* Complication,
          postprocedural, hematoma
    hemorrhage
      intraoperative —*see* Complication,
          intraoperative, hemorrhage
      postprocedural —*see* Complication,
          postprocedural, hemorrhage
    hepatic failure K91.82
    hyperglycemia (postpancreatectomy) E89.1
    hypoinsulinemia (postpancreatectomy)
        E89.1
    hypoparathyroidism
        (postparathyroidectomy) E89.2
    hypopituitarism (posthypophysectomy)
        E89.3
    hypothyroidism (post-thyroidectomy)
        E89.0
    intestinal obstruction —*see also*
        Obstruction, intestine, postoperative
        K91.30
    intracranial hypotension following
        ventricular shunting
        (ventriculostomy) G97.2
    lymphedema I97.89
        postmastectomy I97.2
    malabsorption (postsurgical) NEC K91.2
      osteoporosis —*see* Osteoporosis,
          postsurgical malabsorption
    mastoidectomy cavity NEC —*see*
        Complications, postmastoidectomy
    metabolic E89.89
      specified NEC E89.89
    musculoskeletal —*see* Complications,
        musculoskeletal system
    nervous system (central) (peripheral) —*see*
        Complications, nervous system
    ovarian failure E89.40
      asymptomatic E89.40
      symptomatic E89.41
    peripheral vascular —*see* Complications,
        surgical procedure, vascular
    postcardiotomy syndrome I97.0
    postcholecystectomy syndrome K91.5
    postcommissurotomy syndrome I97.0
    postgastrectomy dumping syndrome K91.1
    postlaminectomy syndrome NEC M96.1
        kyphosis M96.3
    postmastectomy lymphedema syndrome
        I97.2
    postmastoidectomy cholesteatoma —*see*
        Complications, postmastoidectomy,
        recurrent cholesteatoma
    postvagotomy syndrome K91.1
    postvalvulotomy syndrome I97.0
    pulmonary insufficiency (acute) J95.2
      chronic J95.3
      following thoracic surgery J95.1

▶ New   ⇒ Revised   ~~deleted~~ Deleted   ● Use Additional Character(s)

Complication *(Continued)*
  surgical procedure *(Continued)*
    reattached body part —*see* Complications, reattached
    respiratory —*see* Complications, respiratory system
    shock (hypovolemic) T81.19
    spleen (postoperative) D78.89
      intraoperative D78.81
    stitch abscess T81.41
    subglottic stenosis (postsurgical) J95.5
    testicular hypofunction E89.5
    transplant —*see* Complications, organ or tissue transplant
    urinary NEC N99.89
    vaginal vault prolapse (posthysterectomy) N99.3
    vascular (peripheral)
      artery T81.719
        mesenteric T81.710
        renal T81.711
        specified NEC T81.718
      vein T81.72
    wound infection T81.49
  suture, permanent (wire) NEC T85.9
    with repair of bone —*see* Complications, fixation device, internal
    embolism T85.818
    fibrosis T85.828
    hemorrhage T85.838
    infection and inflammation T85.79
    mechanical
      breakdown T85.612
      displacement T85.622
      malfunction T85.612
      malposition T85.622
      obstruction T85.692
      perforation T85.692
      protrusion T85.692
      specified NEC T85.692
    pain T85.848
    specified type NEC T85.898
    stenosis T85.858
    thrombosis T85.868
  tracheostomy J95.00
    granuloma J95.09
    hemorrhage J95.01
    infection J95.02
    malfunction J95.03
    mechanical J95.03
    obstruction J95.03
    specified type NEC J95.09
    tracheo-esophageal fistula J95.04
  transfusion (blood) (lymphocytes) (plasma) T80.92
    air embolism T80.0
    circulatory overload E87.71
    febrile nonhemolytic transfusion reaction R50.84
    hemochromatosis E83.111
    hemolysis T80.89
    hemolytic reaction (antigen unspecified) T80.919
    incompatibility reaction (antigen unspecified) T80.919
      ABO T80.30
        delayed serologic (DSTR) T80.39
        hemolytic transfusion reaction (HTR) (unspecified time after transfusion) T80.319
        acute (AHTR) (less than 24 hours after transfusion) T80.310
        delayed (DHTR) (24 hours or more after transfusion) T80.311
        specified NEC T80.39
      acute (antigen unspecified) T80.910
      delayed (antigen unspecified) T80.911
      delayed serologic (DSTR) T80.89

Complication *(Continued)*
  transfusion *(Continued)*
    incompatibility reaction *(Continued)*
      Non-ABO (minor antigens (Duffy) (K) (Kell) (Kidd) (Lewis) (M) (N) (P) (S)) T80.A0
        delayed serologic (DSTR) T80.A9
        hemolytic transfusion reaction (HTR) (unspecified time after transfusion) T80.A19
        acute (AHTR) (less than 24 hours after transfusion) T80.A10
        delayed (DHTR) (24 hours or more after transfusion) T80.A11
        specified NEC T80.A9
      Rh (antigens (C) (c) (D) (E) (e)) (factor) T80.40
        delayed serologic (DSTR) T80.49
        hemolytic transfusion reaction (HTR) (unspecified time after transfusion) T80.419
        acute (AHTR) (less than 24 hours after transfusion) T80.410
        delayed (DHTR) (24 hours or more after transfusion) T80.411
        specified NEC T80.49
    infection T80.29
      acute T80.22
    reaction NEC T80.89
    sepsis T80.29
    shock T80.89
  transplant T86.90
    bone T86.839
      failure T86.831
      infection T86.832
      rejection T86.830
      specified type NEC T86.838
    bone marrow T86.00
      failure T86.02
      infection T86.03
      rejection T86.01
      specified type NEC T86.09
    ➠cornea T86.849-
      ➠failure T86.841-
      ➠infection T86.842-
      ➠rejection T86.840-
      ➠specified type NEC T86.848-
    failure T86.92
    heart T86.20
      with lung T86.30
      cardiac allograft vasculopathy T86.290
        failure T86.32
        infection T86.33
        rejection T86.31
        specified type NEC T86.39
      failure T86.22
      infection T86.23
      rejection T86.21
      specified type NEC T86.298
    infection T86.93
    intestine T86.859
      failure T86.851
      infection T86.852
      rejection T86.850
      specified type NEC T86.858
    kidney T86.10
      failure T86.12
      infection T86.13
      rejection T86.11
      specified type NEC T86.19
    liver T86.40
      failure T86.42
      infection T86.43
      rejection T86.41
      specified type NEC T86.49
    lung T86.819
      with heart T86.30
        failure T86.32
        infection T86.33
        rejection T86.31
        specified type NEC T86.39

Complication *(Continued)*
  transplant *(Continued)*
    lung *(Continued)*
      failure T86.811
      infection T86.812
      rejection T86.810
      specified type NEC T86.818
    malignant neoplasm C80.2
    pancreas T86.899
      failure T86.891
      infection T86.892
      rejection T86.890
      specified type NEC T86.898
    peripheral blood stem cells T86.5
    post-transplant lymphoproliferative disorder (PTLD) D47.Z1
    rejection T86.91
    skin T86.829
      failure T86.821
      infection T86.822
      rejection T86.820
      specified type NEC T86.828
    specified
      tissue T86.899
        failure T86.891
        infection T86.892
        rejection T86.890
        specified type NEC T86.898
      type NEC T86.99
    stem cell (from peripheral blood) (from umbilical cord) T86.5
    umbilical cord stem cells T86.5
  trauma (early) T79.9
    specified NEC T79.8
  ultrasound therapy NEC T88.9
  umbilical cord NEC
    complicating delivery O69.9
      specified NEC O69.89
  umbrella device, vascular T82.9
    embolism T82.818
    fibrosis T82.828
    hemorrhage T82.838
    infection or inflammation T82.7
    mechanical
      breakdown T82.515
      displacement T82.525
      leakage T82.535
      malposition T82.525
      obstruction T82.595
      perforation T82.595
      protrusion T82.595
    pain T82.848
    specified type NEC T82.898
    stenosis T82.858
    thrombosis T82.868
  urethral catheter —*see* Complications, catheter, urethral, indwelling
  vaccination T88.1
    anaphylaxis NEC T80.52
    arthropathy —*see* Arthropathy, postimmunization
    cellulitis T88.0
    encephalitis or encephalomyelitis G04.02
    infection (general) (local) NEC T88.0
    meningitis G03.8
    myelitis G04.02
    protein sickness T80.62
    rash T88.1
    reaction (allergic) T88.1
      serum T80.62
    sepsis T88.0
    serum intoxication, sickness, rash, or other serum reaction NEC T80.62
      anaphylactic shock T80.52
    shock (allergic) (anaphylactic) T80.52
    vaccinia (generalized) (localized) T88.1
  vas deferens device or implant —*see* Complications, genitourinary, device or implant, genital tract

Complication (Continued)
- vascular I99.9
  - device or implant T82.9
    - embolism T82.818
    - fibrosis T82.828
    - hemorrhage T82.838
    - infection or inflammation T82.7
    - mechanical
      - breakdown T82.519
        - specified device NEC T82.518
      - displacement T82.529
        - specified device NEC T82.528
      - leakage T82.539
        - specified device NEC T82.538
      - malposition T82.529
        - specified device NEC T82.528
      - obstruction T82.599
        - specified device NEC T82.598
      - perforation T82.599
        - specified device NEC T82.598
      - protrusion T82.599
        - specified device NEC T82.598
    - pain T82.848
    - specified type NEC T82.898
    - stenosis T82.858
    - thrombosis T82.868
  - dialysis catheter —see Complication, catheter, dialysis
  - following infusion, therapeutic injection or transfusion T80.1
  - graft T82.9
    - embolism T82.818
    - fibrosis T82.828
    - hemorrhage T82.838
    - mechanical
      - breakdown T82.319
        - aorta (bifurcation) T82.310
        - carotid artery T82.311
        - specified vessel NEC T82.318
      - displacement T82.329
        - aorta (bifurcation) T82.320
        - carotid artery T82.321
        - specified vessel NEC T82.328
      - leakage T82.339
        - aorta (bifurcation) T82.330
        - carotid artery T82.331
        - specified vessel NEC T82.338
      - malposition T82.329
        - aorta (bifurcation) T82.320
        - carotid artery T82.321
        - specified vessel NEC T82.328
      - obstruction T82.399
        - aorta (bifurcation) T82.390
        - carotid artery T82.391
        - specified vessel NEC T82.398
      - perforation T82.399
        - aorta (bifurcation) T82.390
        - carotid artery T82.391
        - specified vessel NEC T82.398
      - protrusion T82.399
        - aorta (bifurcation) T82.390
        - carotid artery T82.391
        - specified vessel NEC T82.398
    - pain T82.848
    - specified complication NEC T82.898
    - stenosis T82.858
    - thrombosis T82.868
  - postoperative —see Complications, postoperative, circulatory
  - vena cava device (filter) (sieve) (umbrella) — see Complications, umbrella device, vascular
- ventilation therapy NEC T81.81
- ventilator
  - mechanical J95.850
    - specified NEC J95.859
- ventricular (communicating) shunt (device) T85.9
  - embolism T85.810
  - fibrosis T85.820
  - hemorrhage T85.830

Complication (Continued)
- ventricular shunt (Continued)
  - infection and inflammation T85.730
  - mechanical
    - breakdown T85.01
    - displacement T85.02
    - leakage T85.03
    - malposition T85.02
    - obstruction T85.09
    - perforation T85.09
    - protrusion T85.09
    - specified NEC T85.09
  - pain T85.840
  - specified type NEC T85.890
  - stenosis T85.850
  - thrombosis T85.860
- wire suture, permanent (implanted) —see Complications, suture, permanent

Compressed air disease T70.3

Compression
- with injury - code by Nature of injury
- artery I77.1
  - celiac, syndrome I77.4
- brachial plexus G54.0
- brain (stem) G93.5
  - due to
    - contusion (diffuse) —see Injury, intracranial, diffuse
    - focal —see Injury, intracranial, focal
    - injury NEC —see Injury, intracranial, diffuse
    - traumatic —see Injury, intracranial, diffuse
- bronchus J98.09
- cauda equina G83.4
- celiac (artery) (axis) I77.4
- cerebral —see Compression, brain
- cervical plexus G54.2
- cord
  - spinal —see Compression, spinal
  - umbilical —see Compression, umbilical cord
- cranial nerve G52.9
  - eighth —see subcategory H93.3
  - eleventh G52.8
  - fifth G50.8
  - first G52.0
  - fourth —see Strabismus, paralytic, fourth nerve
  - ninth G52.1
  - second —see Disorder, nerve, optic
  - seventh G51.8
  - sixth —see Strabismus, paralytic, sixth nerve
  - tenth G52.2
  - third —see Strabismus, paralytic, third nerve
  - twelfth G52.3
- diver's squeeze T70.3
- during birth (newborn) P15.9
- esophagus K22.2
- eustachian tube —see Obstruction, eustachian tube, cartilaginous
- facies Q67.1
- fracture
  - nontraumatic NOS —see Collapse, vertebra
  - pathological —see Fracture, pathological
  - traumatic —see Fracture, traumatic
- heart —see Disease, heart
- intestine —see Obstruction, intestine
- laryngeal nerve, recurrent G52.2
  - with paralysis of vocal cords and larynx J38.00
    - bilateral J38.02
    - unilateral J38.01
- lumbosacral plexus G54.1
- lung J98.4
- lymphatic vessel I89.0
- medulla —see Compression, brain
- nerve —see also Disorder, nerve G58.9
  - arm NEC —see Mononeuropathy, upper limb

Compression (Continued)
- nerve (Continued)
  - axillary G54.0
  - cranial —see Compression, cranial nerve
  - leg NEC —see Mononeuropathy, lower limb
  - median (in carpal tunnel) —see Syndrome, carpal tunnel
  - optic —see Disorder, nerve, optic
  - plantar —see Lesion, nerve, plantar
  - posterior tibial (in tarsal tunnel) —see Syndrome, tarsal tunnel
  - root or plexus NOS (in) G54.9
    - intervertebral disc disorder NEC — see Disorder, disc, with, radiculopathy
    - with myelopathy —see Disorder, disc, with, myelopathy
    - neoplastic disease —see also Neoplasm D49.9 [G55]
    - spondylosis —see Spondylosis, with radiculopathy
  - sciatic (acute) —see Lesion, nerve, sciatic
  - sympathetic G90.8
  - traumatic —see Injury, nerve
  - ulnar —see Lesion, nerve, ulnar
  - upper extremity NEC —see Mononeuropathy, upper limb
- spinal (cord) G95.20
  - by displacement of intervertebral disc NEC —see also Disorder, disc, with, myelopathy
  - nerve root NOS G54.9
    - due to displacement of intervertebral disc NEC —see Disorder, disc, with, radiculopathy
    - with myelopathy —see Disorder, disc, with, myelopathy
  - specified NEC G95.29
  - spondylogenic (cervical) (lumbar, lumbosacral) (thoracic) —see Spondylosis, with myelopathy NEC
  - anterior —see Syndrome, anterior, spinal artery, compression
  - traumatic —see Injury, spinal cord, by region
- subcostal nerve (syndrome) —see Mononeuropathy, upper limb, specified NEC
- sympathetic nerve NEC G90.8
- syndrome T79.5
- trachea J39.8
- ulnar nerve (by scar tissue) —see Lesion, nerve, ulnar
- umbilical cord
  - complicating delivery O69.2
    - cord around neck O69.1
    - prolapse O69.0
    - specified NEC O69.2
- ureter N13.5
- vein I87.1
- vena cava (inferior) (superior) I87.1

Compulsion, compulsive
- gambling F63.0
- neurosis F42.8
- personality F60.5
- states F42.8
- swearing F42.8
  - in Gilles de la Tourette's syndrome F95.2
- tics and spasms F95.9

Concato's disease (pericardial polyserositis) A19.9
- nontubercular I31.1
- pleural —see Pleurisy, with effusion

Concavity chest wall M95.4

Concealed penis Q55.64

Concern (normal) about sick person in family Z63.6

Concrescence (teeth) K00.2

Concretio cordis I31.1
- rheumatic I09.2

▶ New   ⇒ Revised   ~~deleted~~ Deleted   ● Use Additional Character(s)

Concretion —see also Calculus
  appendicular K38.1
  canaliculus —see Dacryolith
  clitoris N90.89
  conjunctiva H11.12-●
  eyelid —see Disorder, eyelid, specified type
      NEC
  lacrimal passages —see Dacryolith
  prepuce (male) N47.8
  salivary gland (any) K11.5
  seminal vesicle N50.89
  tonsil J35.8
Concussion (brain) (cerebral) (current)
      S06.0X9
  with
    loss of consciousness of 30 minutes or less
        S06.0X1
    loss of consciousness of unspecified
        duration S06.0X9
  blast (air) (hydraulic) (immersion)
      (underwater)
    abdomen or thorax —see Injury, blast, by
        site
    ear with acoustic nerve injury —see Injury,
        nerve, acoustic, specified type NEC
  cauda equina S34.3
  conus medullaris S34.02
  ocular S05.8X-●
  spinal (cord)
    cervical S14.0
    lumbar S34.01
    sacral S34.02
    thoracic S24.0
  syndrome F07.81
  without loss of consciousness S06.0X0
Condition —see Disease
Conditions arising in the perinatal period —
    see Newborn, affected by
Conduct disorder —see Disorder, conduct
Condyloma A63.0
  acuminatum A63.0
  gonorrheal A54.09
  latum A51.31
  syphilitic A51.31
    congenital A50.07
  venereal, syphilitic A51.31
Conflagration —see also Burn
  asphyxia (by inhalation of gases, fumes or
      vapors) —see also Table of Drugs and
      Chemicals T59.9-●
Conflict (with) —see also Discord
  family Z73.9
  marital Z63.0
    involving divorce or estrangement Z63.5
  parent-child Z62.820
    parent-adopted child Z62.821
    parent-biological child Z62.820
    parent-foster child Z62.822
  social role NEC Z73.5
Confluent —see condition
Confusion, confused R41.0
  epileptic F05
  mental state (psychogenic) F44.89
  psychogenic F44.89
  reactive (from emotional stress, psychological
      trauma) F44.89
Confusional arousals G47.51
Congelation T69.9
Congenital —see also condition
  aortic septum Q25.49
  intrinsic factor deficiency D51.0
  malformation —see Anomaly
Congestion, congestive
  bladder N32.89
  bowel K63.89
  brain G93.89
  breast N64.59
  bronchial J98.09
  catarrhal J31.0
  chest R09.89
  chill, malarial —see Malaria

Congestion, congestive (Continued)
  circulatory NEC I99.8
  duodenum K31.89
  eye —see Hyperemia, conjunctiva
  facial, due to birth injury P15.4
  general R68.89
  glottis J37.0
  heart —see Failure, heart, congestive
  hepatic K76.1
  hypostatic (lung) —see Edema, lung
  intestine K63.89
  kidney N28.89
  labyrinth —see subcategory H83.8
  larynx J37.0
  liver K76.1
  lung R09.89
    active or acute —see Pneumonia
  malaria, malarial —see Malaria
  nasal R09.81
  nose R09.81
  orbit, orbital —see also Exophthalmos
    inflammatory (chronic) —see Inflammation,
        orbit
  ovary N83.8
  pancreas K86.89
  pelvic, female N94.89
  pleural J94.8
  prostate (active) N42.1
  pulmonary —see Congestion, lung
  renal N28.89
  retina H35.81
  seminal vesicle N50.1
  spinal cord G95.19
  spleen (chronic) D73.2
  stomach K31.89
  trachea —see Tracheitis
  urethra N36.8
  uterus N85.8
    with subinvolution N85.3
  venous (passive) I87.8
  viscera R68.89
Congestive —see Congestion
Conical
  cervix (hypertrophic elongation) N88.4
  cornea —see Keratoconus
  teeth K00.2
Conjoined twins Q89.4
Conjugal maladjustment Z63.0
  involving divorce or estrangement Z63.5
Conjunctiva —see condition
Conjunctivitis (staphylococcal) (streptococcal)
      NOS H10.9
  Acanthamoeba B60.12
  acute H10.3-●
    atopic H10.1-●
    chemical —see also Corrosion, cornea
        H10.21-●
    mucopurulent H10.02-●
      follicular H10.01-●
    pseudomembranous H10.22-●
    serous except viral H10.23-●
      viral —see Conjunctivitis, viral
    toxic H10.21-●
  adenoviral (acute) (follicular) B30.1
  allergic (acute) —see Conjunctivitis, acute,
      atopic
    chronic H10.45
      vernal H10.44
  anaphylactic —see Conjunctivitis, acute,
      atopic
  Apollo B30.3
  atopic (acute) —see Conjunctivitis, acute,
      atopic
  Béal's B30.2
  blennorrhagic (gonococcal) (neonatorum)
      A54.31
  chemical (acute) —see also Corrosion, cornea
      H10.21-●
  chlamydial A74.0
    due to trachoma A71.1
    neonatal P39.1

Conjunctivitis (Continued)
  chronic (nodosa) (petrificans) (phlyctenular)
      H10.40-●
    allergic H10.45
      vernal H10.44
    follicular H10.43-●
    giant papillary H10.41-●
    simple H10.42-●
    vernal H10.44
  coxsackievirus 24 B30.3
  diphtheritic A36.86
  due to
    dust —see Conjunctivitis, acute, atopic
    filariasis B74.9
    mucocutaneous leishmaniasis B55.2
  enterovirus type 70 (hemorrhagic) B30.3
  epidemic (viral) B30.9
    hemorrhagic B30.3
  gonococcal (neonatorum) A54.31
  granular (trachomatous) A71.1
    sequelae (late effect) B94.0
  hemorrhagic (acute) (epidemic) B30.3
  herpes zoster B02.31
  in (due to)
    Acanthamoeba B60.12
    adenovirus (acute) (follicular) B30.1
    Chlamydia A74.0
    coxsackievirus 24 B30.3
    diphtheria A36.86
    enterovirus type 70 (hemorrhagic) B30.3
    filariasis B74.9
    gonococci A54.31
    herpes (simplex) virus B00.53
      zoster B02.31
    infectious disease NEC B99
    meningococci A39.89
    mucocutaneous leishmaniasis B55.2
    rosacea H10.82-●
    syphilis (late) A52.71
    zoster B02.31
  inclusion A74.0
  infantile P39.1
    gonococcal A54.31
  Koch-Weeks' —see Conjunctivitis, acute,
      mucopurulent
  light —see Conjunctivitis, acute, atopic
  ligneous —see Blepharoconjunctivitis,
      ligneous
  meningococcal A39.89
  mucopurulent —see Conjunctivitis, acute,
      mucopurulent
  neonatal P39.1
    gonococcal A54.31
  Newcastle B30.8
  of Béal B30.2
  parasitic
    filariasis B74.9
    mucocutaneous leishmaniasis B55.2
  Parinaud's H10.89
  petrificans H10.89
  rosacea H10.82-●
  specified NEC H10.89
  swimming-pool B30.1
  trachomatous A71.1
    acute A71.0
    sequelae (late effect) B94.0
  traumatic NEC H10.89
  tuberculous A18.59
  tularemic A21.1
  tularensis A21.1
  viral B30.9
    due to
      adenovirus B30.1
      enterovirus B30.3
    specified NEC B30.8
Conjunctivochalasis H11.82-●
Connective tissue —see condition
Conn's syndrome E26.01
Conradi (-Hunermann) disease Q77.3
Consanguinity Z84.3
  counseling Z71.89

Conscious simulation (of illness) Z76.5
Consecutive —see condition
Consolidation lung (base) —see Pneumonia,
lobar
Constipation (atonic) (neurogenic) (simple)
(spastic) K59.00
chronic K59.09
idiopathic K59.04
drug-induced K59.03
functional K59.04
outlet dysfunction K59.02
psychogenic F45.8
slow transit K59.01
specified NEC K59.09
Constitutional —see also condition
substandard F60.7
Constitutionally substandard F60.7
Constriction —see also Stricture
auditory canal —see Stenosis, external ear
canal
bronchial J98.09
duodenum K31.5
esophagus K22.2
external
abdomen, abdominal (wall) S30.841
alveolar process S00.542
ankle S90.54-●
antecubital space —see Constriction,
external, forearm
arm (upper) S40.84-●
auricle —see Constriction, external, ear
axilla —see Constriction, external, arm
back, lower S30.840
breast S20.14-●
brow S00.84
buttock S30.840
calf —see Constriction, external, leg
canthus —see Constriction, external, eyelid
cheek S00.84
internal S00.542
chest wall —see Constriction, external,
thorax
chin S00.84
clitoris S30.844
costal region —see Constriction, external,
thorax
digit(s)
foot —see Constriction, external, toe
hand —see Constriction, external, finger
ear S00.44-●
elbow S50.34-●
epididymis S30.843
epigastric region S30.841
esophagus, cervical S10.14
eyebrow —see Constriction, external, eyelid
eyelid S00.24-●
face S00.84
finger(s) S60.44-●
index S60.44-●
little S60.44-●
middle S60.44-●
ring S60.44-●
flank S30.841
foot (except toe(s) alone) S90.84-●
toe —see Constriction, external, toe
forearm S50.84-●
elbow only —see Constriction, external,
elbow
forehead S00.84
genital organs, external
female S30.846
male S30.845
groin S30.841
gum S00.542
hand S60.54-●
head S00.94
ear —see Constriction, external, ear
eyelid —see Constriction, external, eyelid
lip S00.541
nose S00.34
oral cavity S00.542

Constriction (Continued)
external (Continued)
head (Continued)
scalp S00.04
specified site NEC S00.84
heel —see Constriction, external, foot
hip S70.24-●
inguinal region S30.841
interscapular region S20.449
jaw S00.84
knee S80.24-●
labium (majus) (minus) S30.844
larynx S10.14
leg (lower) S80.84-●
knee —see Constriction, external, knee
upper —see Constriction, external, thigh
lip S00.541
lower back S30.840
lumbar region S30.840
malar region S00.84
mammary —see Constriction, external,
breast
mastoid region S00.84
mouth S00.542
nail
finger —see Constriction, external, finger
toe —see Constriction, external, toe
nasal S00.34
neck S10.94
specified site NEC S10.84
throat S10.14
nose S00.34
occipital region S00.04
oral cavity S00.542
orbital region —see Constriction, external,
eyelid
palate S00.542
palm —see Constriction, external, hand
parietal region S00.04
pelvis S30.840
penis S30.842
perineum
female S30.844
male S30.840
periocular area —see Constriction, external,
eyelid
phalanges
finger —see Constriction, external, finger
toe —see Constriction, external, toe
pharynx S10.14
pinna —see Constriction, external, ear
popliteal space —see Constriction, external,
knee
prepuce S30.842
pubic region S30.840
pudendum
female S30.846
male S30.845
sacral region S30.840
scalp S00.04
scapular region —see Constriction,
external, shoulder
scrotum S30.843
shin —see Constriction, external, leg
shoulder S40.24-●
sternal region S20.349
submaxillary region S00.84
submental region S00.84
subungual
finger(s) —see Constriction, external,
finger
toe(s) —see Constriction, external, toe
supraclavicular fossa S10.84
supraorbital S00.84
temple S00.84
temporal region S00.84
testis S30.843
thigh S70.34-●
thorax, thoracic (wall) S20.94
back S20.44-●
front S20.34-●

Constriction (Continued)
external (Continued)
throat S10.14
thumb S60.34-●
toe(s) (lesser) S90.44-●
great S90.44-●
tongue S00.542
trachea S10.14
tunica vaginalis S30.843
uvula S00.542
vagina S30.844
vulva S30.844
wrist S60.84-●
gallbladder —see Obstruction, gallbladder
intestine —see Obstruction, intestine
larynx J38.6
congenital Q31.8
specified NEC Q31.8
subglottic Q31.1
organ or site, congenital NEC —see Atresia,
by site
prepuce (acquired) (congenital) N47.1
pylorus (adult hypertrophic) K31.1
congenital or infantile Q40.0
newborn Q40.0
ring dystocia (uterus) O62.4
spastic —see also Spasm
ureter N13.5
ureter N13.5
with infection N13.6
urethra —see Stricture, urethra
visual field (peripheral) (functional) —see
Defect, visual field
Constrictive —see condition
Consultation
without complaint or sickness Z71.9
feared complaint unfounded Z71.1
specified reason NEC Z71.89
medical —see Counseling, medical
religious Z71.81
specified reason NEC Z71.89
spiritual Z71.81
Consumption —see Tuberculosis
Contact (with) —see also Exposure (to)
acariasis Z20.7
AIDS virus Z20.6
air pollution Z77.110
algae and algae toxins Z77.121
algae bloom Z77.121
anthrax Z20.810
aromatic (hazardous) compounds NEC
Z77.028
aromatic amines Z77.020
aromatic dyes NOS Z77.028
arsenic Z77.010
asbestos Z77.090
bacterial disease NEC Z20.818
benzene Z77.021
blue-green algae bloom Z77.121
body fluids (potentially hazardous) Z77.21
brown tide Z77.121
chemicals (chiefly nonmedicinal) (hazardous)
NEC Z77.098
cholera Z20.09
chromium compounds Z77.018
communicable disease Z20.9
bacterial NEC Z20.818
specified NEC Z20.89
viral NEC Z20.828
Zika virus Z20.821
cyanobacteria bloom Z77.121
dyes Z77.098
Escherichia coli (E. coli) Z20.01
fiberglass —see Table of Drugs and
Chemicals, fiberglass
German measles Z20.4
gonorrhea Z20.2
hazardous metals NEC Z77.018
hazardous substances NEC Z77.29
hazards in the physical environment NEC
Z77.128
hazards to health NEC Z77.9

▶ New   ⇒ Revised   ~~deleted~~ Deleted   ● Use Additional Character(s)

Contact *(Continued)*
　HIV Z20.6
　HTLV-III/LAV Z20.6
　human immunodeficiency virus (HIV) Z20.6
　infection Z20.9
　　specified NEC Z20.89
　infestation (parasitic) NEC Z20.7
　intestinal infectious disease NEC Z20.09
　　Escherichia coli (E. coli) Z20.01
　lead Z77.011
　meningococcus Z20.811
　mold (toxic) Z77.120
　nickel dust Z77.018
　noise Z77.122
　parasitic disease Z20.7
　pediculosis Z20.7
　pfiesteria piscicida Z77.121
　poliomyelitis Z20.89
　pollution
　　air Z77.110
　　environmental NEC Z77.118
　　soil Z77.112
　　water Z77.111
　polycyclic aromatic hydrocarbons Z77.028
　rabies Z20.3
　radiation, naturally occurring NEC Z77.123
　radon Z77.123
　red tide (Florida) Z77.121
　rubella Z20.4
　sexually-transmitted disease Z20.2
　smallpox (laboratory) Z20.89
　syphilis Z20.2
　tuberculosis Z20.1
　uranium Z77.012
　varicella Z20.820
　venereal disease Z20.2
　viral disease NEC Z20.828
　viral hepatitis Z20.5
　water pollution Z77.111
　Zika virus Z20.821
Contamination, food —*see* Intoxication,
　foodborne
Contraception, contraceptive
　advice Z30.09
　counseling Z30.09
　device (intrauterine) (in situ) Z97.5
　　causing menorrhagia T83.83
　　checking Z30.431
　　complications —*see* Complications,
　　　intrauterine, contraceptive device
　　in place Z97.5
　　initial prescription Z30.014
　　reinsertion Z30.433
　　removal Z30.432
　　replacement Z30.433
　emergency (postcoital) Z30.012
　initial prescription Z30.019
　　barrier Z30.018
　　diaphragm Z30.018
　　injectable Z30.013
　　intrauterine device Z30.014
　　pills Z30.011
　　postcoital (emergency) Z30.012
　　specified type NEC Z30.018
　　subdermal implantable Z30.017
　　transdermal patch hormonal Z30.016
　　vaginal ring hormonal Z30.015
　maintenance Z30.40
　　barrier Z30.49
　　diaphragm Z30.49
　　examination Z30.8
　　injectable Z30.42
　　intrauterine device Z30.431
　　pills Z30.41
　　specified type NEC Z30.49
　　subdermal implantable Z30.46
　　transdermal patch hormonal Z30.45
　　vaginal ring hormonal Z30.44
　management Z30.9
　　specified NEC Z30.8
　postcoital (emergency) Z30.012
　prescription Z30.019
　　repeat Z30.40

Contraception, contraceptive *(Continued)*
　sterilization Z30.2
　surveillance (drug) —*see* Contraception,
　　maintenance
Contraction(s), contracture, contracted
　Achilles tendon —*see also* Short, tendon,
　　Achilles
　　congenital Q66.89
　amputation stump (surgical) (flexion) (late)
　　next proximal joint T87.89
➡ anus K59.89
　bile duct (common) (hepatic) K83.8
　bladder N32.89
　　neck or sphincter N32.0
　bowel, cecum, colon or intestine, any part —
　　see Obstruction, intestine
　Braxton Hicks —*see* False, labor
　breast implant, capsular T85.44
　bronchial J98.09
　burn (old) —*see* Cicatrix
　cervix —*see* Stricture, cervix
　cicatricial —*see* Cicatrix
　conjunctiva, trachomatous, active A71.1
　　sequelae (late effect) B94.0
　Dupuytren's M72.0
　eyelid —*see* Disorder, eyelid function
　fascia (lata) (postural) M72.8
　　Dupuytren's M72.0
　　palmar M72.0
　　plantar M72.2
　finger NEC —*see also* Deformity, finger
　　congenital Q68.1
　　joint —*see* Contraction, joint, hand
　flaccid —*see* Contraction, paralytic
　gallbladder K82.0
　heart valve —*see* Endocarditis
　hip —*see* Contraction, joint, hip
　hourglass
　　bladder N32.89
　　　congenital Q64.79
　　gallbladder K82.0
　　　congenital Q44.1
　　stomach K31.89
　　　congenital Q40.2
　　　psychogenic F45.8
　　uterus (complicating delivery) O62.4
　hysterical F44.4
　internal os —*see* Stricture, cervix
　joint (abduction) (acquired) (adduction)
　　(flexion) (rotation) M24.50
　　ankle M24.57-●
　　congenital NEC Q68.8
　　　hip Q65.89
　　elbow M24.52-●
　　foot joint M24.57-●
　　hand joint M24.54-●
　　hip M24.55-●
　　　congenital Q65.89
　　hysterical F44.4
　　knee M24.56-●
　　shoulder M24.51-●
➤　specified site NEC M24.59
　　wrist M24.53-●
　kidney (granular) (secondary) N26.9
　　congenital Q63.8
　　hydronephritic —*see* Hydronephrosis
　　　Page N26.2
　　pyelonephritic —*see* Pyelitis, chronic
　　tuberculous A18.11
　ligament —*see also* Disorder, ligament
　　congenital Q79.8
　muscle (postinfective) (postural) NEC M62.40
　　with contracture of joint —*see* Contraction,
　　　joint
　　ankle M62.47-●
　　congenital Q79.8
　　　sternocleidomastoid Q68.0
　　extraocular —*see* Strabismus
　　eye (extrinsic) —*see* Strabismus
　　foot M62.47-●
　　forearm M62.43-●
　　hand M62.44-●

Contraction, contracture, contracted
　(Continued)
　muscle *(Continued)*
　　hysterical F44.4
　　ischemic (Volkmann's) T79.6
　　lower leg M62.46-●
　　multiple sites M62.49
　　pelvic region M62.45-●
　　posttraumatic —*see* Strabismus, paralytic
　　psychogenic F45.8
　　　conversion reaction F44.4
　　shoulder region M62.41-●
　　specified site NEC M62.48
　　thigh M62.45-●
　　upper arm M62.42-●
　neck —*see* Torticollis
　ocular muscle —*see* Strabismus
　organ or site, congenital NEC —*see* Atresia,
　　by site
　outlet (pelvis) —*see* Contraction, pelvis
　palmar fascia M72.0
　paralytic
　　joint —*see* Contraction, joint
　　muscle —*see also* Contraction, muscle NEC
　　　ocular —*see* Strabismus, paralytic
　pelvis (acquired) (general) M95.5
　　with disproportion (fetopelvic) O33.1
　　　causing obstructed labor O65.1
　　　inlet O33.2
　　　mid-cavity O33.3
　　　outlet O33.3
　plantar fascia M72.2
　premature
　　atrium I49.1
　　auriculoventricular I49.49
　　heart I49.49
　　junctional I49.2
　　supraventricular I49.1
　　ventricular I49.3
　prostate N42.89
　pylorus NEC —*see also* Pylorospasm
　　psychogenic F45.8
➡ rectum, rectal (sphincter) K59.89
　ring (Bandl's) (complicating delivery) O62.4
　scar —*see* Cicatrix
　spine —*see* Dorsopathy, deforming
　sternocleidomastoid (muscle), congenital
　　Q68.0
　stomach K31.89
　　hourglass K31.89
　　　congenital Q40.2
　　　psychogenic F45.8
　　psychogenic F45.8
　tendon (sheath) M62.40
　　with contracture of joint —*see* Contraction,
　　　joint
　　Achilles —*see* Short, tendon, Achilles
　　ankle M62.47-●
　　　Achilles —*see* Short, tendon, Achilles
　　foot M62.47-●
　　forearm M62.43-●
　　hand M62.44-●
　　lower leg M62.46-●
　　multiple sites M62.49
　　neck M62.48
　　pelvic region M62.45-●
　　shoulder region M62.41-●
　　specified site NEC M62.48
　　thigh M62.45-●
　　thorax M62.48
　　trunk M62.48
　　upper arm M62.42-●
　toe —*see* Deformity, toe, specified NEC
　ureterovesical orifice (postinfectional) N13.5
　　with infection N13.6
　urethra —*see also* Stricture, urethra
　　orifice N32.0
　uterus N85.8
　　abnormal NEC O62.9
　　clonic (complicating delivery) O62.4
　　dyscoordinate (complicating delivery) O62.4

Contraction, contracture, contracted
(Continued)
  uterus *(Continued)*
    hourglass (complicating delivery) O62.4
    hypertonic O62.4
    hypotonic NEC O62.2
    inadequate
      primary O62.0
      secondary O62.1
    incoordinate (complicating delivery) O62.4
    poor O62.2
    tetanic (complicating delivery) O62.4
  vagina (outlet) N89.5
  vesical N32.89
    neck or urethral orifice N32.0
  visual field —*see* Defect, visual field,
    generalized
  Volkmann's (ischemic) T79.6
Contusion (skin surface intact) T14.8
  abdomen, abdominal (muscle) (wall) S30.1
  adnexa, eye NEC S05.8X-●
  adrenal gland S37.812
  alveolar process S00.532
  ankle S90.0-●
  antecubital space —*see* Contusion, forearm
  anus S30.3
  arm (upper) S40.02-●
    lower (with elbow) —*see* Contusion,
      forearm
  auditory canal —*see* Contusion, ear
  auricle —*see* Contusion, ear
  axilla —*see* Contusion, arm, upper
  back —*see also* Contusion, thorax, back
    lower S30.0
  bile duct S36.13
  bladder S37.22
  bone NEC T14.8
  brain (diffuse) —*see* Injury, intracranial, diffuse
    focal —*see* Injury, intracranial, focal
  brainstem S06.38-●
  breast S20.0-●
  broad ligament S37.892
  brow S00.83
  buttock S30.0
  canthus, eye S00.1-●
  cauda equina S34.3
  cerebellar, traumatic S06.37-●
  cerebral S06.33-●
    left side S06.32-●
    right side S06.31-●
  cheek S00.83
    internal S00.532
  chest (wall) —*see* Contusion, thorax
  chin S00.83
  clitoris S30.23
  colon —*see* Injury, intestine, large, contusion
  common bile duct S36.13
  conjunctiva S05.1-●
    with foreign body (in conjunctival sac) —
      see Foreign body, conjunctival sac
  conus medullaris (spine) S34.139
  cornea —*see* Contusion, eyeball
    with foreign body —*see* Foreign body,
      cornea
  corpus cavernosum S30.21
  cortex (brain) (cerebral) —*see* Injury,
    intracranial, diffuse
    focal —*see* Injury, intracranial, focal
  costal region —*see* Contusion, thorax
  cystic duct S36.13
  diaphragm S27.802
  duodenum S36.420
  ear S00.43-●
  elbow S50.0-●
    with forearm —*see* Contusion, forearm
  epididymis S30.22
  epigastric region S30.1
  epiglottis S10.0
  esophagus (thoracic) S27.812
    cervical S10.0
  eyeball S05.1-●

Contusion *(Continued)*
  eyebrow S00.1-●
  eyelid (and periocular area) S00.1-●
  face NEC S00.83
  fallopian tube S37.529
    bilateral S37.522
    unilateral S37.521
  femoral triangle S30.1
  finger(s) S60.00
    with damage to nail (matrix) S60.10
    index S60.02-●
      with damage to nail S60.12-●
    little S60.05-●
      with damage to nail S60.15-●
    middle S60.03-●
      with damage to nail S60.13-●
    ring S60.04-●
      with damage to nail S60.14-●
    thumb —*see* Contusion, thumb
  flank S30.1
  foot (except toe(s) alone) S90.3-●
    toe —*see* Contusion, toe
  forearm S50.1-●
    elbow only —*see* Contusion, elbow
  forehead S00.83
  gallbladder S36.122
  genital organs, external
    female S30.202
    male S30.201
  globe (eye) —*see* Contusion, eyeball
  groin S30.1
  gum S00.532
  hand S60.22-●
    finger(s) —*see* Contusion, finger
    wrist —*see* Contusion, wrist
  head S00.93
    ear —*see* Contusion, ear
    eyelid —*see* Contusion, eyelid
    lip S00.531
    nose S00.33
    oral cavity S00.532
    scalp S00.03
    specified part NEC S00.83
  heart —*see also* Injury, heart S26.91
  heel —*see* Contusion, foot
  hepatic duct S36.13
  hip S70.0-●
  ileum S36.428
  iliac region S30.1
  inguinal region S30.1
  interscapular region S20.229
  intra-abdominal organ S36.92
    colon —*see* Injury, intestine, large, contusion
    liver S36.112
    pancreas —*see* Contusion, pancreas
    rectum S36.62
    small intestine —*see* Injury, intestine, small,
      contusion
    specified organ NEC S36.892
    spleen —*see* Contusion, spleen
    stomach S36.32
  iris (eye) —*see* Contusion, eyeball
  jaw S00.83
  jejunum S36.428
  kidney S37.01-●
    major (greater than 2 cm) S37.02-●
    minor (less than 2 cm) S37.01-●
  knee S80.0-●
  labium (majus) (minus) S30.23
  lacrimal apparatus, gland or sac S05.8X-●
  larynx S10.0
  leg (lower) S80.1-●
    knee —*see* Contusion, knee
  lens —*see* Contusion, eyeball
  lip S00.531
  liver S36.112
  lower back S30.0
  lumbar region S30.0
  lung S27.329
    bilateral S27.322
    unilateral S27.321

Contusion *(Continued)*
  malar region S00.83
  mastoid region S00.83
  membrane, brain —*see* Injury, intracranial,
    diffuse
    focal —*see* Injury, intracranial, focal
  mesentery S36.892
  mesosalpinx S37.892
  mouth S00.532
  muscle —*see* Contusion, by site
  nail
    finger —*see* Contusion, finger, with
      damage to nail
    toe —*see* Contusion, toe, with damage to
      nail
  nasal S00.33
  neck S10.93
    specified site NEC S10.83
    throat S10.0
  nerve —*see* Injury, nerve
  newborn P54.5
  nose S00.33
  occipital
    lobe (brain) —*see* Injury, intracranial,
      diffuse
      focal —*see* Injury, intracranial,
        focal
    region (scalp) S00.03
  orbit (region) (tissues) S05.1-●
  ovary S37.429
    bilateral S37.422
    unilateral S37.421
  palate S00.532
  pancreas S36.229
    body S36.221
    head S36.220
    tail S36.222
  parietal
    lobe (brain) —*see* Injury, intracranial,
      diffuse
      focal —*see* Injury, intracranial, focal
    region (scalp) S00.03
  pelvic organ S37.92
    adrenal gland S37.812
    bladder S37.22
    fallopian tube —*see* Contusion, fallopian
      tube
    kidney —*see* Contusion, kidney
    ovary —*see* Contusion, ovary
    prostate S37.822
    specified organ NEC S37.892
    ureter S37.12
    urethra S37.32
    uterus S37.62
  pelvis S30.0
  penis S30.21
  perineum
    female S30.23
    male S30.0
  periocular area S00.1-●
  peritoneum S36.81
  periurethral tissue —*see* Contusion,
    urethra
  pharynx S10.0
  pinna —*see* Contusion, ear
  popliteal space —*see* Contusion, knee
  prepuce S30.21
  prostate S37.822
  pubic region S30.1
  pudendum
    female S30.202
    male S30.201
  quadriceps femoris —*see* Contusion, thigh
  rectum S36.62
  retroperitoneum S36.892
  round ligament S37.892
  sacral region S30.0
  scalp S00.03
    due to birth injury P12.3
  scapular region —*see* Contusion, shoulder
  sclera —*see* Contusion, eyeball

► New   ⇒ Revised   ~~deleted~~ Deleted   ● Use Additional Character(s)

Contusion (*Continued*)
scrotum S30.22
seminal vesicle S37.892
shoulder S40.01-•
skin NEC T14.8
small intestine —*see* Injury, intestine, small, contusion
spermatic cord S30.22
spinal cord —*see* Injury, spinal cord, by region
cauda equina S34.3
conus medullaris S34.139
spleen S36.029
major S36.021
minor S36.020
sternal region S20.219
stomach S36.32
subconjunctival S05.1-•
subcutaneous NEC T14.8
submaxillary region S00.83
submental region S00.83
subperiosteal NEC T14.8
subungual
finger —*see* Contusion, finger, with damage to nail
toe —*see* Contusion, toe, with damage to nail
supraclavicular fossa S10.83
supraorbital S00.83
suprarenal gland S37.812
temple (region) S00.83
temporal
lobe (brain) —*see* Injury, intracranial, diffuse
focal —*see* Injury, intracranial, focal
region S00.83
testis S30.22
thigh S70.1-•
thorax (wall) S20.20
back S20.22-•
front S20.21-•
throat S10.0
thumb S60.01-•
with damage to nail S60.11-•
toe(s) (lesser) S90.12-•
with damage to nail S90.22-•
great S90.11-•
with damage to nail S90.21-•
tongue S00.532
trachea (cervical) S10.0
thoracic S27.52
tunica vaginalis S30.22
tympanum, tympanic membrane —*see* Contusion, ear
ureter S37.12
urethra S37.32
urinary organ NEC S37.892
uterus S37.62
uvula S00.532
vagina S30.23
vas deferens S37.892
vesical S37.22
vocal cord(s) S10.0
vulva S30.23
wrist S60.21-•
Conus (congenital) (any type) Q14.8
cornea —*see* Keratoconus
medullaris syndrome G95.81
Conversion hysteria, neurosis or reaction F44.9
Converter, tuberculosis (test reaction) R76.11
Conviction (legal), anxiety concerning Z65.0
with imprisonment Z65.1
Convulsions (idiopathic) —*see also* Seizure(s) R56.9
apoplectiform (cerebral ischemia) I67.82
dissociative F44.5
epileptic —*see* Epilepsy
epileptiform, epileptoid —*see* Seizure, epileptiform

Convulsions (*Continued*)
ether (anesthetic) —*see* Table of Drugs and Chemicals, by drug
febrile R56.00
with status epilepticus G40.901
complex R56.01
with status epilepticus G40.901
simple R56.00
hysterical F44.5
infantile P90
epilepsy —*see* Epilepsy
jacksonian —*see* Epilepsy, localization-related, symptomatic, with simple partial seizures
myoclonic G25.3
newborn P90
obstetrical (nephritic) (uremic) —*see* Eclampsia
paretic A52.17
post traumatic R56.1
psychomotor —*see* Epilepsy, localization-related, symptomatic, with complex partial seizures
recurrent R56.9
reflex R25.8
scarlatinal A38.8
tetanus, tetanic —*see* Tetanus
thymic E32.8
Convulsive —*see also* Convulsions
Cooley's anemia D56.1
Coolie itch B76.9
Cooper's
disease —*see* Mastopathy, cystic
hernia —*see* Hernia, abdomen, specified site NEC
Copra itch B88.0
Coprophagy F50.89
Coprophobia F40.298
Coproporphyria, hereditary E80.29
Cor
biloculare Q20.8
bovis, bovinum —*see* Hypertrophy, cardiac
pulmonale (chronic) I27.81
acute I26.09
triatriatum, triatrium Q24.2
triloculare Q20.8
biatrium Q20.4
biventriculare Q21.1
Corbus' disease (gangrenous balanitis) N48.1
Cord —*see also* condition
around neck
complicating delivery O69.81
with compression O69.1
bladder G95.89
tabetic A52.19
Cordis ectopia Q24.8
Corditis (spermatic) N49.1
Corectopia Q13.2
Cori's disease (glycogen storage) E74.03
Corkhandler's disease or lung J67.3
Corkscrew esophagus K22.4
Corkworker's disease or lung J67.3
Corn (infected) L84
Cornea —*see also* condition
donor Z52.5
plana Q13.4
Cornelia de Lange syndrome Q87.19
Cornu cutaneum L85.8
Cornual gestation or pregnancy O00.80
with intrauterine pregnancy O00.81
Coronary (artery) —*see* condition
~~Coronavirus, as cause of disease classified elsewhere B97.29~~
~~SARS-associated B97.21~~
▶**Coronavirus** (infection)
▶as cause of disease classified elsewhere B97.29
▶coronavirus-19 U07.1
▶COVID-19 U07.1
▶SARS-associated B97.21
Corpora —*see also* condition
amylacea, prostate N42.89
cavernosa —*see* condition

Corpulence —*see* Obesity
Corpus —*see* condition
Corrected transposition Q20.5
Corrosion (injury) (acid) (caustic) (chemical) (lime) (external) (internal) T30.4
abdomen, abdominal (muscle) (wall) T21.42
first degree T21.52
second degree T21.62
third degree T21.72
above elbow T22.439
first degree T22.539
left T22.432
first degree T22.532
second degree T22.632
third degree T22.732
right T22.431
first degree T22.531
second degree T22.631
third degree T22.731
second degree T22.639
third degree T22.739
alimentary tract NEC T28.7
ankle T25.419
first degree T25.519
left T25.412
first degree T25.512
second degree T25.612
third degree T25.712
multiple with foot —*see* Corrosion, lower, limb, multiple, ankle and foot
right T25.411
first degree T25.511
second degree T25.611
third degree T25.711
second degree T25.619
third degree T25.719
anus —*see* Corrosion, buttock
arm(s) (meaning upper limb(s)) —*see* Corrosion, upper limb
axilla T22.449
first degree T22.549
left T22.442
first degree T22.542
second degree T22.642
third degree T22.742
right T22.441
first degree T22.541
second degree T22.641
third degree T22.741
second degree T22.649
third degree T22.749
back (lower) T21.44
first degree T21.54
second degree T21.64
third degree T21.74
upper T21.43
first degree T21.53
second degree T21.63
third degree T21.73
blisters - code as Corrosion, second degree, by site
breast(s) —*see* Corrosion, chest wall
buttock(s) T21.45
first degree T21.55
second degree T21.65
third degree T21.75
calf T24.439
first degree T24.539
left T24.432
first degree T24.532
second degree T24.632
third degree T24.732
right T24.431
first degree T24.531
second degree T24.631
third degree T24.731
second degree T24.639
third degree T24.739
canthus (eye) —*see* Corrosion, eyelid
cervix T28.8

Corrosion (Continued)
  cheek T20.46
    first degree T20.56
    second degree T20.66
    third degree T20.76
  chest wall T21.41
    first degree T21.51
    second degree T21.61
    third degree T21.71
  chin T20.43
    first degree T20.53
    second degree T20.63
    third degree T20.73
  colon T28.7
  conjunctiva (and cornea) —see Corrosion, cornea
  cornea (and conjunctiva) T26.6-●
  deep necrosis of underlying tissue - code as Corrosion, third degree, by site
  dorsum of hand T23.469
    first degree T23.569
    left T23.462
      first degree T23.562
      second degree T23.662
      third degree T23.762
    right T23.461
      first degree T23.561
      second degree T23.661
      third degree T23.761
    second degree T23.669
    third degree T23.769
  ear (auricle) (external) (canal) T20.41
    drum T28.91
    first degree T20.51
    second degree T20.61
    third degree T20.71
  elbow T22.429
    first degree T22.529
    left T22.422
      first degree T22.522
      second degree T22.622
      third degree T22.722
    right T22.421
      first degree T22.521
      second degree T22.621
      third degree T22.721
    second degree T22.629
    third degree T22.729
  entire body —see Corrosion, multiple body regions
  epidermal loss - code as Corrosion, second degree, by site
  epiglottis T27.4
  erythema, erythematous - code as Corrosion, first degree, by site
  esophagus T28.6
  extent (percentage of body surface)
    less than 10 percent T32.0
    10-19 percent (0-9 percent third degree) T32.10
      with 10-19 percent third degree T32.11
    20-29 percent (0-9 percent third degree) T32.20
      with
        10-19 percent third degree T32.21
        20-29 percent third degree T32.22
    30-39 percent (0-9 percent third degree) T32.30
      with
        10-19 percent third degree T32.31
        20-29 percent third degree T32.32
        30-39 percent third degree T32.33
    40-49 percent (0-9 percent third degree) T32.40
      with
        10-19 percent third degree T32.41
        20-29 diercent third degree T32.42
        30-39 percent third degree T32.43
        40-49 percent third degree T32.44

Corrosion (Continued)
  extent (Continued)
    50-59 percent (0-9 percent third degree) T32.50
      with
        10-19 percent third degree T32.51
        20-29 percent third degree T32.52
    50-59 percent (Continued)
      with (Continued)
        30-39 percent third degree T32.53
        40-49 percent third degree T32.54
        50-59 percent third degree T32.55
    60-69 percent (0-9 percent third degree) T32.60
      with
        10-19 percent third degree T32.61
        20-29 percent third degree T32.62
        30-39 percent third degree T32.63
        40-49 percent third degree T32.64
        50-59 percent third degree T32.65
        60-69 percent third degree T32.66
    70-79 percent (0-9 percent third degree) T32.70
      with
        10-19 percent third degree T32.71
        20-29 percent third degree T32.72
        30-39 percent third degree T32.73
        40-49 percent third degree T32.74
        50-59 percent third degree T32.75
        60-69 percent third degree T32.76
        70-79 percent third degree T32.77
    80-89 percent (0-9 percent third degree) T32.80
      with
        10-19 percent third degree T32.81
        20-29 percent third degree T32.82
        30-39 percent third degree T32.83
        40-49 percent third degree T32.84
        50-59 percent third degree T32.85
        60-69 percent third degree T32.86
        70-79 percent third degree T32.87
        80-89 percent third degree T32.88
    90 percent or more (0-9 percent third degree) T32.90
      with
        10-19 percent third degree T32.91
        20-29 percent third degree T32.92
        30-39 percent third degree T32.93
        40-49 percent third degree T32.94
        50-59 percent third degree T32.95
        60-69 percent third degree T32.96
        70-79 percent third degree T32.97
        80-89 percent third degree T32.98
        90-99 percent third degree T32.99
  extremity —see Corrosion, limb
  eye(s) and adnexa T26.9-●
    with resulting rupture and destruction of eyeball T26.7-●
    conjunctival sac —see Corrosion, cornea
    cornea —see Corrosion, cornea
    lid —see Corrosion, eyelid
    periocular area —see Corrosion eyelid
    specified site NEC T26.8-●
  eyeball —see Corrosion, eye
  eyelid(s) T26.5-●
  face —see Corrosion, head
  finger T23.429
    first degree T23.529
    left T23.422
      first degree T23.522
      second degree T23.622
      third degree T23.722
    multiple sites (without thumb) T23.439
      with thumb T23.449
        first degree T23.549
        left T23.442
          first degree T23.542
          second degree T23.642
          third degree T23.742

Corrosion (Continued)
  finger (Continued)
    multiple sites (Continued)
      with thumb (Continued)
        right T23.441
          first degree T23.541
          second degree T23.641
          third degree T23.741
        second degree T23.649
        third degree T23.749
      first degree T23.539
      left T23.432
        first degree T23.532
        second degree T23.632
        third degree T23.732
      right T23.431
        first degree T23.531
        second degree T23.631
        third degree T23.731
      second degree T23.639
      third degree T23.739
    right T23.421
      first degree T23.521
      second degree T23.621
      third degree T23.721
    second degree T23.629
    third degree T23.729
  flank —see Corrosion, abdomen
  foot T25.429
    first degree T25.529
    left T25.422
      first degree T25.522
      second degree T25.622
      third degree T25.722
    multiple with ankle —see Corrosion, lower, limb, multiple, ankle and foot
    right T25.421
      first degree T25.521
      second degree T25.621
      third degree T25.721
    second degree T25.629
    third degree T25.729
  forearm T22.419
    first degree T22.519
    left T22.412
      first degree T22.512
      second degree T22.612
      third degree T22.712
    right T22.411
      first degree T22.511
      second degree T22.611
      third degree T22.711
    second degree T22.619
    third degree T22.719
  forehead T20.46
    first degree T20.56
    second degree T20.66
    third degree T20.76
  fourth degree - code as Corrosion, third degree, by site
  full thickness skin loss - code as Corrosion, third degree, by site
  gastrointestinal tract NEC T28.7
  genital organs
    external
      female T21.47
        first degree T21.57
        second degree T21.67
        third degree T21.77
      male T21.46
        first degree T21.56
        second degree T21.66
        third degree T21.76
    internal T28.8
  groin —see Corrosion, abdominal wall
  hand(s) T23.409
    back —see Corrosion, dorsum of hand
    finger —see Corrosion, finger
    first degree T23.509
    left T23.402
      first degree T23.502
      second degree T23.602
      third degree T23.702

▶ New   ⇒ Revised   ~~deleted~~ Deleted   ● Use Additional Character(s)

Corrosion *(Continued)*
  hand(s) *(Continued)*
    multiple sites with wrist T23.499
      first degree T23.599
      left T23.492
        first degree T23.592
        second degree T23.692
        third degree T23.792
      right T23.491
        first degree T23.591
        second degree T23.691
        third degree T23.791
      second degree T23.699
      third degree T23.799
    palm —*see* Corrosion, palm
    right T23.401
      first degree T23.501
      second degree T23.601
      third degree T23.701
    second degree T23.609
    third degree T23.709
    thumb —*see* Corrosion, thumb
  head (and face) (and neck) T20.40
    cheek —*see* Corrosion, cheek
    chin —*see* Corrosion, chin
    ear —*see* Corrosion, ear
    eye(s) only —*see* Corrosion, eye
    first degree T20.50
    forehead —*see* Corrosion, forehead
    lip —*see* Corrosion, lip
    multiple sites T20.49
      first degree T20.59
      second degree T20.69
      third degree T20.79
    neck —*see* Corrosion, neck
    nose —*see* Corrosion, nose
    scalp —*see* Corrosion, scalp
    second degree T20.60
    third degree T20.70
  hip(s) —*see* Corrosion, lower, limb
  inhalation —*see* Corrosion, respiratory
    tract
  internal organ(s) *(see also* Corrosion, by site)
    T28.90
    alimentary tract T28.7
      esophagus T28.6
    esophagus T28.6
    genitourinary T28.8
    mouth T28.5
    pharynx T28.5
    specified organ NEC T28.99
  interscapular region —*see* Corrosion, back,
    upper
  intestine (large) (small) T28.7
  knee T24.429
    first degree T24.529
    left T24.422
      first degree T24.522
      second degree T24.622
      third degree T24.722
    right T24.421
      first degree T24.521
      second degree T24.621
      third degree T24.721
    second degree T24.629
    third degree T24.729
  labium (majus) (minus) —*see* Corrosion,
    genital organs, external, female
  lacrimal apparatus, duct, gland or sac —*see*
    Corrosion, eye, specified site NEC
  larynx T27.4
    with lung T27.5
  leg(s) (meaning lower limb(s)) —*see*
    Corrosion, lower limb
  limb(s)
    lower —*see* Corrosion, lower, limb
    upper —*see* Corrosion, upper limb
  lip(s) T20.42
    first degree T20.52
    second degree T20.62
    third degree T20.72

Corrosion *(Continued)*
  lower
    back —*see* Corrosion, back
    limb T24.409
      ankle —*see* Corrosion, ankle
      calf —*see* Corrosion, calf
      first degree T24.509
      foot —*see* Corrosion, foot
      hip —*see* Corrosion, thigh
      knee —*see* Corrosion, knee
      left T24.402
        first degree T24.502
        second degree T24.602
        third degree T24.702
      multiple sites, except ankle and foot
        T24.499
        ankle and foot T25.499
          first degree T25.599
          left T25.492
            first degree T25.592
            second degree T25.692
            third degree T25.792
          right T25.491
            first degree T25.591
            second degree T25.691
            third degree T25.791
          second degree T25.699
          third degree T25.799
        first degree T24.599
        left T24.492
          first degree T24.592
          second degree T24.692
          third degree T24.792
        right T24.491
          first degree T24.591
          second degree T24.691
          third degree T24.791
        second degree T24.699
        third degree T24.799
      right T24.401
        first degree T24.501
        second degree T24.601
        third degree T24.701
      second degree T24.609
      thigh —*see* Corrosion, thigh
      third degree T24.709
  lung (with larynx and trachea) T27.5
  mouth T28.5
  neck T20.47
    first degree T20.57
    second degree T20.67
    third degree T20.77
  nose (septum) T20.44
    first degree T20.54
    second degree T20.64
    third degree T20.74
  ocular adnexa —*see* Corrosion, eye
  orbit region —*see* Corrosion, eyelid
  palm T23.459
    first degree T23.559
    left T23.452
      first degree T23.552
      second degree T23.652
      third degree T23.752
    right T23.451
      first degree T23.551
      second degree T23.651
      third degree T23.751
    second degree T23.659
    third degree T23.759
  partial thickness - code as Corrosion,
    unspecified degree, by site
  pelvis —*see* Corrosion, trunk
  penis —*see* Corrosion, genital organs,
    external, male
  perineum
    female —*see* Corrosion, genital organs,
      external, female
    male —*see* Corrosion, genital organs,
      external, male
  periocular area —*see* Corrosion, eyelid

Corrosion *(Continued)*
  pharynx T28.5
  rectum T28.7
  respiratory tract T27.7
    larynx —*see* Corrosion, larynx
    specified part NEC T27.6
    trachea —*see* Corrosion, larynx
  sac, lacrimal —*see* Corrosion, eye,
    specified site NEC
  scalp T20.45
    first degree T20.55
    second degree T20.65
    third degree T20.75
  scapular region T22.469
    first degree T22.569
    left T22.462
      first degree T22.562
      second degree T22.662
      third degree T22.762
    right T22.461
      first degree T22.561
      second degree T22.661
      third degree T22.761
    second degree T22.669
    third degree T22.769
  sclera —*see* Corrosion, eye, specified site NEC
  scrotum —*see* Corrosion, genital organs,
    external, male
  shoulder T22.459
    first degree T22.559
    left T22.452
      first degree T22.552
      second degree T22.652
      third degree T22.752
    right T22.451
      first degree T22.551
      second degree T22.651
      third degree T22.751
    second degree T22.659
    third degree T22.759
  stomach T28.7
  temple —*see* Corrosion, head
  testis —*see* Corrosion, genital organs,
    external, male
  thigh T24.419
    first degree T24.519
    left T24.412
      first degree T24.512
      second degree T24.612
      third degree T24.712
    right T24.411
      first degree T24.511
      second degree T24.611
      third degree T24.711
    second degree T24.619
    third degree T24.719
  thorax (external) —*see* Corrosion, trunk
  throat (meaning pharynx) T28.5
  thumb(s) T23.419
    first degree T23.519
    left T23.412
      first degree T23.512
      second degree T23.612
      third degree T23.712
    multiple sites with fingers T23.449
      first degree T23.549
      left T23.442
        first degree T23.542
        second degree T23.642
        third degree T23.742
      right T23.441
        first degree T23.541
        second degree T23.641
        third degree T23.741
      second degree T23.649
      third degree T23.749
    right T23.411
      first degree T23.511
      second degree T23.611
      third degree T23.711
    second degree T23.619
    third degree T23.719

Corrosion (Continued)
toe T25.439
  first degree T25.539
  left T25.432
    first degree T25.532
    second degree T25.632
    third degree T25.732
  right T25.431
    first degree T25.531
    second degree T25.631
    third degree T25.731
  second degree T25.639
  third degree T25.739
tongue T28.5
tonsil(s) T28.5
total body —see Corrosion, multiple body
  regions
trachea T27.4
  with lung T27.5
trunk T21.40
  abdominal wall —see Corrosion,
    abdominal wall
  anus —see Corrosion, buttock
  axilla —see Corrosion, upper limb
  back —see Corrosion, back
  breast —see Corrosion, chest wall
  buttock —see Corrosion, buttock
  chest wall —see Corrosion, chest wall
  first degree T21.50
  flank —see Corrosion, abdominal wall
  genital
    female —see Corrosion, genital organs,
      external, female
    male —see Corrosion, genital organs,
      external, male
  groin —see Corrosion, abdominal wall
  interscapular region —see Corrosion, back,
    upper
  labia —see Corrosion, genital organs,
    external, female
  lower back —see Corrosion, back
  penis —see Corrosion, genital organs,
    external, male
  perineum
    female —see Corrosion, genital organs,
      external, female
    male —see Corrosion, genital organs,
      external, male
  scapular region —see Corrosion, upper
    limb
  scrotum —see Corrosion, genital organs,
    external, male
  second degree T21.60
  shoulder —see Corrosion, upper limb
  specified site NEC T21.49
    first degree T21.59
    second degree T21.69
    third degree T21.79
  testes —see Corrosion, genital organs,
    external, male
  third degree T21.70
  upper back —see Corrosion, back, upper
  vagina T28.8
  vulva —see Corrosion, genital organs,
    external, female
unspecified site with extent of body surface
  involved specified
  less than 10 percent T32.0
  10-19 percent (0-9 percent third degree)
    T32.10
    with 10-19 percent third degree T32.11
  20-29 percent (0-9 percent third degree)
    T32.20
    with
      10-19 percent third degree T32.21
      20-29 percent third degree T32.22
  30-39 percent (0-9 percent third degree)
    T32.30
    with
      10-19 percent third degree T32.31
      20-29 percent third degree T32.32
      30-39 percent third degree T32.33

Corrosion (Continued)
unspecified site with extent of body surface
  involved specified (Continued)
  40-49 percent (0-9 percent third degree)
    T32.40
    with
      10-19 percent third degree T32.41
      20-29 percent third degree T32.42
      30-39 percent third degree T32.43
      40-49 percent third degree T32.44
  50-59 percent (0-9 percent third degree)
    T32.50
    with
      10-19 percent third degree T32.51
      20-29 percent third degree T32.52
      30-39 percent third degree T32.53
      40-49 percent third degree T32.54
      50-59 percent third degree T32.55
  60-69 percent (0-9 percent third degree)
    T32.60
    with
      10-19 percent third degree T32.61
      20-29 percent third degree T32.62
      30-39 percent third degree T32.63
      40-49 percent third degree T32.64
      50-59 percent third degree T32.65
      60-69 percent third degree T32.66
  70-79 percent (0-9 percent third degree)
    T32.70
    with
      10-19 percent third degree T32.71
      20-29 percent third degree T32.72
      30-39 percent third degree T32.73
      40-49 percent third degree T32.74
      50-59 percent third degree T32.75
      60-69 percent third degree T32.76
      70-79 percent third degree T32.77
  80-89 percent (0-9 percent third degree)
    T32.80
    with
      10-19 percent third degree T32.81
      20-29 percent third degree T32.82
      30-39 percent third degree T32.83
      40-49 percent third degree T32.84
      50-59 percent third degree T32.85
      60-69 percent third degree T32.86
      70-79 percent third degree T32.87
      80-89 percent third degree T32.88
  90 percent or more (0-9 percent third
    degree) T32.90
    with
      10-19 percent third degree T32.91
      20-29 percent third degree T32.92
      30-39 percent third degree T32.93
      40-49 percent third degree T32.94
      50-59 percent third degree T32.95
      60-69 percent third degree T32.96
      70-79 percent third degree T32.97
      80-89 percent third degree T32.98
      90-99 percent third degree T32.99
upper limb (axilla) (scapular region) T22.40
  above elbow —see Corrosion, above elbow
  axilla —see Corrosion, axilla
  elbow —see Corrosion, elbow
  first degree T22.50
  forearm —see Corrosion, forearm
  hand —see Corrosion, hand
  interscapular region —see Corrosion, back,
    upper
  multiple sites T22.499
    first degree T22.599
    left T22.492
      first degree T22.592
      second degree T22.692
      third degree T22.792
    right T22.491
      first degree T22.591
      second degree T22.691
      third degree T22.791
    second degree T22.699
    third degree T22.799

Corrosion (Continued)
upper limb (axilla) (scapular region)
  (Continued)
  scapular region —see Corrosion, scapular
    region
  second degree T22.60
  shoulder —see Corrosion, shoulder
  third degree T22.70
  wrist —see Corrosion, hand
uterus T28.8
vagina T28.8
vulva —see Corrosion, genital organs,
  external, female
wrist T23.479
  first degree T23.579
  left T23.472
    first degree T23.572
    second degree T23.672
    third degree T23.772
  multiple sites with hand T23.499
    first degree T23.599
    left T23.492
      first degree T23.592
      second degree T23.692
      third degree T23.792
    right T23.491
      first degree T23.591
      second degree T23.691
      third degree T23.791
    second degree T23.699
    third degree T23.799
  right T23.471
    first degree T23.571
    second degree T23.671
    third degree T23.771
  second degree T23.679
  third degree T23.779
Corrosive burn —see Corrosion
Corsican fever —see Malaria
Cortical —see condition
Cortico-adrenal —see condition
Coryza (acute) J00
  with grippe or influenza —see Influenza,
    with, respiratory manifestations
    NEC
  syphilitic
    congenital (chronic) A50.05
Costen's syndrome or complex M26.69
Costiveness —see Constipation
Costochondritis M94.0
Cot death R99
Cotard's syndrome F22
Cotia virus B08.8
Cotton wool spots (retinal) H35.81
Cotungo's disease —see Sciatica
Cough (affected) (chronic) (epidemic) (nervous)
  R05
  with hemorrhage —see Hemoptysis
  bronchial R05
    with grippe or influenza —see Influenza,
      with, respiratory manifestations
      NEC
  functional F45.8
  hysterical F45.8
  laryngeal, spasmodic R05
  psychogenic F45.8
  smokers' J41.0
  tea taster's B49
Counseling (for) Z71.9
  abuse NEC
    perpetrator Z69.82
    victim Z69.81
  alcohol abuser Z71.41
    family Z71.42
  child abuse
    nonparental
      perpetrator Z69.021
      victim Z69.020
    parental
      perpetrator Z69.011
      victim Z69.010

▶ New   ⇨ Revised   deleted Deleted   ● Use Additional Character(s)

Counseling *(Continued)*
  consanguinity Z71.89
  contraceptive Z30.09
  dietary Z71.3
  drug abuser Z71.51
    family member Z71.52
  exercise Z71.82
  family Z71.89
  fertility preservation (prior to cancer therapy)
      (prior to removal of gonads) Z31.62
  for non-attending third party Z71.0
    related to sexual behavior or orientation
        Z70.2
  genetic
    nonprocreative Z71.83
    procreative NEC Z31.5
  gestational carrier Z31.7
  health (advice) (education) (instruction) —*see*
      Counseling, medical
    risk for travel (international) Z71.84
  human immunodeficiency virus (HIV) Z71.7
  impotence Z70.1
  insulin pump use Z46.81
  medical (for) Z71.9
    boarding school resident Z59.3
    consanguinity Z71.89
    feared complaint and no disease found Z71.1
    human immunodeficiency virus (HIV) Z71.7
    institutional resident Z59.3
    on behalf of another Z71.0
      related to sexual behavior or orientation
          Z70.2
    person living alone Z60.2
    specified reason NEC Z71.89
  natural family planning
    procreative Z31.61
    to avoid pregnancy Z30.02
  perpetrator (of)
    abuse NEC Z69.82
    child abuse
      non-parental Z69.021
      parental Z69.011
    rape NEC Z69.82
    spousal abuse Z69.12
  procreative NEC Z31.69
    fertility preservation (prior to cancer
        therapy) (prior to removal of
        gonads) Z31.62
    using natural family planning Z31.61
  promiscuity Z70.1
  rape victim Z69.81
  religious Z71.81
  safety for travel (international) Z71.84
  sex, sexual (related to) Z70.9
    attitude(s) Z70.0
    behavior or orientation Z70.1
    combined concerns Z70.3
    non-responsiveness Z70.1
    on behalf of third party Z70.2
    specified reason NEC Z70.8
  specified reason NEC Z71.89
  spiritual Z71.81
  spousal abuse (perpetrator) Z69.12
    victim Z69.11
  substance abuse Z71.89
    alcohol Z71.41
    drug Z71.51
    tobacco Z71.6
  travel (international) Z71.84
  tobacco use Z71.6
  use (of)
    insulin pump Z46.81
  victim (of)
    abuse Z69.81
    child abuse
      by parent Z69.010
      non-parental Z69.020
    rape NEC Z69.81
Coupled rhythm R00.8
Couvelaire syndrome or uterus (complicating
    delivery) O45.8X-●
Cowperitis —*see* Urethritis

Cowper's gland —*see* condition
Cowpox B08.010
  due to vaccination T88.1
Coxa
  magna M91.4-●
  plana M91.2-●
  valga (acquired) —*see also* Deformity, limb,
      specified type NEC, thigh
    congenital Q65.81
    sequelae (late effect) of rickets E64.3
  vara (acquired) —*see also* Deformity, limb,
      specified type NEC, thigh
    congenital Q65.82
    sequelae (late effect) of rickets E64.3
Coxalgia, coxalgic (nontuberculous) —*see also*
    Pain, joint, hip
  tuberculous A18.02
Coxitis —*see* Monoarthritis, hip
Coxsackie (virus) (infection) B34.1
  as cause of disease classified elsewhere B97.11
  carditis B33.20
  central nervous system NEC A88.8
  endocarditis B33.21
  enteritis A08.39
  meningitis (aseptic) A87.0
  myocarditis B33.22
  pericarditis B33.23
  pharyngitis B08.5
  pleurodynia B33.0
  specific disease NEC B33.8
Crabs, meaning pubic lice B85.3
Crack baby P04.41
Cracked nipple N64.0
  associated with
    lactation O92.13
    pregnancy O92.11-●
    puerperium O92.12
Cracked tooth K03.81
Cradle cap L21.0
Craft neurosis F48.8
Cramp(s) R25.2
  abdominal —*see* Pain, abdominal
  bathing T75.1
  colic R10.83
    psychogenic F45.8
  due to immersion T75.1
  fireman T67.2
  heat T67.2
  immersion T75.1
  intestinal —*see* Pain, abdominal
    psychogenic F45.8
  leg, sleep related G47.62
  limb (lower) (upper) NEC R25.2
    sleep related G47.62
  linotypist's F48.8
    organic G25.89
  muscle (limb) (general) R25.2
    due to immersion T75.1
    psychogenic F45.8
  occupational (hand) F48.8
    organic G25.89
  salt-depletion E87.1
  sleep related, leg G47.62
  stoker's T67.2
  swimmer's T75.1
  telegrapher's F48.8
    organic G25.89
  typist's F48.8
    organic G25.89
  uterus N94.89
    menstrual —*see* Dysmenorrhea
  writer's F48.8
    organic G25.89
Cranial —*see* condition
Craniocleidodysostosis Q74.0
Craniofenestria (skull) Q75.8
Craniolacunia (skull) Q75.8
Craniopagus Q89.4
Craniopathy, metabolic M85.2
Craniopharyngeal —*see* condition
Craniopharyngioma D44.4
Craniorachischisis (totalis) Q00.1

Cranioschisis Q75.8
Craniostenosis Q75.0
Craniosynostosis Q75.0
Craniotabes (cause unknown) M83.8
  neonatal P96.3
  rachitic E64.3
  syphilitic A50.56
Cranium —*see* condition
Craw-craw —*see* Onchocerciasis
Creaking joint —*see* Derangement, joint,
    specified type NEC
Creeping
  eruption B76.9
  palsy or paralysis G12.22
Crenated tongue K14.8
Creotoxism A05.9
Crepitus
  caput Q75.8
  joint —*see* Derangement, joint, specified type
      NEC
Crescent or conus choroid, congenital Q14.3
CREST syndrome M34.1
Cretin, cretinism (congenital) (endemic)
    (nongoitrous) (sporadic) E00.9
  pelvis
    with disproportion (fetopelvic) O33.0
      causing obstructed labor O65.0
  type
    hypothyroid E00.1
    mixed E00.2
    myxedematous E00.1
    neurological E00.0
Creutzfeldt-Jakob disease or syndrome (with
    dementia) A81.00
  familial A81.09
  iatrogenic A81.09
  specified NEC A81.09
  sporadic A81.09
  variant (vCJD) A81.01
Crib death R99
Cribriform hymen Q52.3
Cri-du-chat syndrome Q93.4
Crigler-Najjar disease or syndrome E80.5
Crime, victim of Z65.4
Crimean hemorrhagic fever A98.0
Criminalism F60.2
Crisis
  abdomen R10.0
  acute reaction F43.0
  addisonian E27.2
  adrenal (cortical) E27.2
  celiac K90.0
  Dietl's N13.8
  emotional —*see also* Disorder, adjustment
    acute reaction to stress F43.0
    specific to childhood and adolescence F93.8
  glaucomatocyclitic —*see* Glaucoma,
      secondary, inflammation
  heart —*see* Failure, heart
  nitritoid I95.2
    correct substance properly administered —
        see Table of Drugs and Chemicals, by
        drug, adverse effect
    overdose or wrong substance given
        or taken —*see* Table of Drugs and
        Chemicals, by drug, poisoning
  oculogyric H51.8
    psychogenic F45.8
  Pel's (tabetic) A52.11
  psychosexual identity F64.2
  renal N28.0
  sickle-cell D57.00
    with
      acute chest syndrome D57.01
    ▶cerebral vascular involvement D57.03
    ▶crisis (painful) D57.00
      ▶with complication specified NEC
          D57.09
      splenic sequestration D57.02
    ▶vasoocclusive pain D57.00
  state (acute reaction) F43.0

Crisis *(Continued)*
  tabetic A52.11
  thyroid —*see* Thyrotoxicosis with thyroid
        storm
  thyrotoxic —*see* Thyrotoxicosis with thyroid
        storm
Crocq's disease (acrocyanosis) I73.89
Crohn's disease —*see* Enteritis, regional
Crooked septum, nasal J34.2
Cross syndrome E70.328
Crossbite (anterior) (posterior) M26.24
Cross-eye —*see* Strabismus, convergent
        concomitant
Croup, croupous (catarrhal) (infectious)
        (inflammatory) (nondiphtheritic) J05.0
  bronchial J20.9
  diphtheritic A36.2
  false J38.5
  spasmodic J38.5
      diphtheritic A36.2
  stridulous J38.5
      diphtheritic A36.2
Crouzon's disease Q75.1
Crowding, tooth, teeth, fully erupted M26.31
CRST syndrome M34.1
Cruchet's disease A85.8
Cruelty in children —*see also* Disorder, conduct
Crural ulcer —*see* Ulcer, lower limb
Crush, crushed, crushing T14.8
  abdomen S38.1
  ankle S97.0-●
  arm (upper) (and shoulder) S47.-●
  axilla —*see* Crush, arm
  back, lower S38.1
  buttock S38.1
  cheek S07.0
  chest S28.0
  cranium S07.1
  ear S07.0
  elbow S57.0-●
  extremity
    lower
      ankle —*see* Crush, ankle
      below knee —*see* Crush, leg
      foot —*see* Crush, foot
      hip —*see* Crush, hip
      knee —*see* Crush, knee
      thigh —*see* Crush, thigh
      toe —*see* Crush, toe
    upper
      below elbow S67.9-●
      elbow —*see* Crush, elbow
      finger —*see* Crush, finger
      forearm —*see* Crush, forearm
      hand —*see* Crush, hand
      thumb —*see* Crush, thumb
      upper arm —*see* Crush, arm
      wrist —*see* Crush, wrist
  face S07.0
  finger(s) S67.1-●
    with hand (and wrist) —*see* Crush, hand,
        specified site NEC
    index S67.19-●
    little S67.19-●
    middle S67.19-●
    ring S67.19-●
    thumb —*see* Crush, thumb
  foot S97.8-●
    toe —*see* Crush, toe
  forearm S57.8-●
  genitalia, external
    female S38.002
      vagina S38.03
      vulva S38.03
    male S38.001
      penis S38.01
      scrotum S38.02
      testis S38.02
  hand (except fingers alone) S67.2-●
    with wrist S67.4-●
  head S07.9
    specified NEC S07.8

Crush, crushed, crushing *(Continued)*
  heel —*see* Crush, foot
  hip S77.0-●
    with thigh S77.2-●
  internal organ (abdomen, chest, or pelvis)
        NEC T14.8
  knee S87.0-●
  labium (majus) (minus) S38.03
  larynx S17.0
  leg (lower) S87.8-●
    knee —*see* Crush, knee
  lip S07.0
  lower
    back S38.1
    leg —*see* Crush, leg
  neck S17.9
  nerve —*see* Injury, nerve
  nose S07.0
  pelvis S38.1
  penis S38.01
  scalp S07.8
  scapular region —*see* Crush, arm
  scrotum S38.02
  severe, unspecified site T14.8
  shoulder (and upper arm) —*see* Crush, arm
  skull S07.1
  syndrome (complication of trauma) T79.5
  testis S38.02
  thigh S77.1-●
    with hip S77.2-●
  throat S17.8
  thumb S67.0-●
    with hand (and wrist) —*see* Crush, hand,
        specified site NEC
  toe(s) S97.10-●
    great S97.11-●
    lesser S97.12-●
  trachea S17.0
  vagina S38.03
  vulva S38.03
  wrist S67.3-●
    with hand S67.4-●
Crusta lactea L21.0
Crusts R23.4
Crutch paralysis —*see* Injury, brachial plexus
Cruveilhier-Baumgarten cirrhosis, disease or
        syndrome K74.69
Cruveilhier's atrophy or disease G12.8
Crying (constant) (continuous) (excessive)
  child, adolescent, or adult R45.83
  infant (baby) (newborn) R68.11
Cryofibrinogenemia D89.2
Cryoglobulinemia (essential) (idiopathic)
        (mixed) (primary) (purpura) (secondary)
        (vasculitis) D89.1
  with lung involvement D89.1 *[J99]*
Cryptitis (anal) (rectal) K62.89
Cryptococcosis, cryptococcus (infection)
        (neoformans) B45.9
  bone B45.3
  cerebral B45.1
  cutaneous B45.2
  disseminated B45.7
  generalized B45.7
  meningitis B45.1
  meningocerebralis B45.1
  osseous B45.3
  pulmonary B45.0
  skin B45.2
  specified NEC B45.8
Cryptopapillitis (anus) K62.89
Cryptophthalmos Q11.2
  syndrome Q87.0
Cryptorchid, cryptorchism, cryptorchidism
        Q53.9
  bilateral Q53.20
    abdominal Q53.211
    perineal Q53.22
  unilateral Q53.10
    abdominal Q53.111
    perineal Q53.12

Cryptosporidiosis A07.2
  hepatobiliary B88.8
  respiratory B88.8
Cryptostromosis J67.6
Crystalluria R82.998
Cubitus
  congenital Q68.8
  valgus (acquired) M21.0-●
    congenital Q68.8
    sequelae (late effect) of rickets E64.3
  varus (acquired) M21.1-●
    congenital Q68.8
    sequelae (late effect) of rickets E64.3
Cultural deprivation or shock Z60.3
Curling esophagus K22.4
Curling's ulcer —*see* Ulcer, peptic, acute
Curschmann (-Batten) (-Steinert) disease or
        syndrome G71.11
Curse, Ondine's —*see* Apnea, sleep
Curvature
  organ or site, congenital NEC —*see* Distortion
  penis (lateral) Q55.61
  Pott's (spinal) A18.01
  radius, idiopathic, progressive (congenital)
        Q74.0
  spine (acquired) (angular) (idiopathic)
        (incorrect) (postural) —*see* Dorsopathy,
        deforming
    congenital Q67.5
    due to or associated with
      Charcot-Marie-Tooth disease —*see also*
        subcategory M49.8 G60.0
      osteitis
        deformans M88.88
        fibrosa cystica —*see also* subcategory
            M49.8 E21.0
      tuberculosis (Pott's curvature) A18.01
  sequelae (late effect) of rickets E64.3
  tuberculous A18.01
Cushingoid due to steroid therapy E24.2
  correct substance properly administered —*see*
        Table of Drugs and Chemicals, by drug,
        adverse effect
  overdose or wrong substance given
        or taken —*see* Table of Drugs and
        Chemicals, by drug, poisoning
Cushing's
  syndrome or disease E24.9
    drug-induced E24.2
    iatrogenic E24.2
    pituitary-dependent E24.0
    specified NEC E24.8
  ulcer —*see* Ulcer, peptic, acute
Cusp, Carabelli - omit code
Cut (external) —*see also* Laceration
  muscle —*see* Injury, muscle
Cutaneous —*see also* condition
  hemorrhage R23.3
  larva migrans B76.9
Cutis —*see also* condition
  hyperelastica Q82.8
    acquired L57.4
  laxa (hyperelastica) —*see* Dermatolysis
  marmorata R23.8
  osteosis L94.2
  pendula —*see* Dermatolysis
  rhomboidalis nuchae L57.2
  verticis gyrata Q82.8
    acquired L91.8
Cyanosis R23.0
  due to
    patent foramen botalli Q21.1
    persistent foramen ovale Q21.1
  enterogenous D74.8
  paroxysmal digital —*see* Raynaud's disease
    with gangrene I73.01
  retina, retinal H35.89
Cyanotic heart disease I24.9
  congenital Q24.9
Cycle
  anovulatory N97.0
  menstrual, irregular N92.6

▶ New   ⇒ Revised   ~~deleted~~ Deleted   ● Use Additional Character(s)

Cyclencephaly Q04.9
Cyclical vomiting, in migraine (see also
    Vomiting, cyclical) G43.A0
  psychogenic F50.89
Cyclitis —see also Iridocyclitis H20.9
  chronic —see Iridocyclitis, chronic
  Fuchs' heterochromic H20.81-●
  granulomatous —see Iridocyclitis, chronic
  lens-induced —see Iridocyclitis,
    lens-induced
  posterior H30.2-●
Cycloid personality F34.0
Cyclophoria H50.54
Cyclopia, cyclops Q87.0
Cyclopism Q87.0
Cyclosporiasis A07.4
Cyclothymia F34.0
Cyclothymic personality F34.0
Cyclotropia H50.41-●
Cylindroma —see also Neoplasm, malignant,
  by site
  eccrine dermal —see Neoplasm, skin, benign
  skin —see Neoplasm, skin, benign
Cylindruria R82.998
Cynanche
  diphtheritic A36.2
  tonsillaris J36
Cynophobia F40.218
Cynorexia R63.2
Cyphosis —see Kyphosis
Cyprus fever —see Brucellosis
Cyst (colloid) (mucous) (simple) (retention)
  adenoid (infected) J35.8
  adrenal gland E27.8
    congenital Q89.1
  air, lung J98.4
  allantoic Q64.4
  alveolar process (jaw bone) M27.40
  amnion, amniotic O41.8X-●
  aneurysmal M27.49
  anterior
    chamber (eye) —see Cyst, iris
    nasopalatine K09.1
  antrum J34.1
  anus K62.89
  apical (tooth) (periodontal) K04.8
  appendix K38.8
  arachnoid, brain (acquired) G93.0
    congenital Q04.6
  arytenoid J38.7
  Baker's M71.2-●
    ruptured M66.0
    tuberculous A18.02
  Bartholin's gland N75.0
  bile duct (common) (hepatic) K83.5
  bladder (multiple) (trigone) N32.89
  blue dome (breast) —see Cyst, breast
  bone (local) NEC M85.60
    aneurysmal M85.50
      ankle M85.57-●
      foot M85.57-●
      forearm M85.53-●
      hand M85.54-●
      jaw M27.49
      lower leg M85.56-●
      multiple site M85.59
      neck M85.58
      rib M85.58
      shoulder M85.51-●
      skull M85.58
      specified site NEC M85.58
      thigh M85.55-●
      toe M85.57-●
      upper arm M85.52-●
      vertebra M85.58
    solitary M85.40
      ankle M85.47-●
      fibula M85.46-●
      foot M85.47-●
      hand M85.44-●
      humerus M85.42-●

Cyst (Continued)
  bone NEC (Continued)
    solitary (Continued)
      jaw M27.49
      neck M85.48
      pelvis M85.45-●
      radius M85.43-●
      rib M85.48
      shoulder M85.41-●
      skull M85.48
      specified site NEC M85.48
      tibia M85.46-●
      toe M85.47-●
      ulna M85.43-●
      vertebra M85.48
    specified type NEC M85.60
      ankle M85.67-●
      foot M85.67-●
      forearm M85.63-●
      hand M85.64-●
      jaw M27.40
        developmental (nonodontogenic) K09.1
          odontogenic K09.0
        latent M27.0
      lower leg M85.66-●
      multiple site M85.69
      neck M85.68
      rib M85.68
      shoulder M85.61-●
      skull M85.68
      specified site NEC M85.68
      thigh M85.65-●
      toe M85.67-●
      upper arm M85.62-●
      vertebra M85.68
  brain (acquired) G93.0
    congenital Q04.6
    hydatid B67.99 [G94]
    third ventricle (colloid), congenital
      Q04.6
  branchial (cleft) Q18.0
  branchiogenic Q18.0
  breast (benign) (blue dome) (pedunculated)
    (solitary) N60.0-●
    involution —see Dysplasia, mammary,
      specified type NEC
    sebaceous —see Dysplasia, mammary,
      specified type NEC
  broad ligament (benign) N83.8
  bronchogenic (mediastinal) (sequestration)
    J98.4
    congenital Q33.0
  buccal K09.8
  bulbourethral gland N36.8
  bursa, bursal NEC M71.30
    with rupture —see Rupture, synovium
    ankle M71.37-●
    elbow M71.32-●
    foot M71.37-●
    hand M71.34-●
    hip M71.35-●
    multiple sites M71.39
    pharyngeal J39.2
    popliteal space —see Cyst, Baker's
    shoulder M71.31-●
    specified site NEC M71.38
    wrist M71.33-●
  calcifying odontogenic D16.5
    upper jaw (bone) (maxilla) D16.4
  canal of Nuck (female) N94.89
    congenital Q52.4
  canthus —see Cyst, conjunctiva
  carcinomatous —see Neoplasm, malignant,
    by site
  cauda equina G95.89
  cavum septi pellucidi —see Cyst, brain
  celomic (pericardium) Q24.8
  cerebellopontine (angle) —see Cyst, brain
  cerebellum —see Cyst, brain
  cerebral —see Cyst, brain
  cervical lateral Q18.0

Cyst (Continued)
  cervix NEC N88.8
    embryonic Q51.6
    nabothian N88.8
  chiasmal optic NEC —see Disorder, optic,
    chiasm
  chocolate (ovary) N80.1
  choledochus, congenital Q44.4
  chorion O41.8X-●
  choroid plexus G93.0
    congenital Q04.6
  ciliary body —see Cyst, iris
  clitoris N90.7
  colon K63.89
  common (bile) duct K83.5
  congenital NEC Q89.8
    adrenal gland Q89.1
    epiglottis Q31.8
    esophagus Q39.8
    fallopian tube Q50.4
    kidney Q61.00
      more than one (multiple) Q61.02
        specified as polycystic Q61.3
          adult type Q61.2
          infantile type NEC Q61.19
            collecting duct dilation Q61.11
      solitary Q61.01
    larynx Q31.8
    liver Q44.6
    lung Q33.0
    mediastinum Q34.1
    ovary Q50.1
    oviduct Q50.4
    periurethral (tissue) Q64.79
    prepuce Q55.69
    salivary gland (any) Q38.4
    sublingual Q38.6
    submaxillary gland Q38.6
    thymus (gland) Q89.2
    tongue Q38.3
    ureterovesical orifice Q62.8
    vulva Q52.79
  conjunctiva H11.44-●
  cornea H18.89-●
  corpora quadrigemina G93.0
  corpus
    albicans N83.29-●
    luteum (hemorrhagic) (ruptured) N83.1-●
  Cowper's gland (benign) (infected) N36.8
  cranial meninges G93.0
  craniobuccal pouch E23.6
  craniopharyngeal pouch E23.6
  cystic duct K82.8
  Cysticercus —see Cysticercosis
  Dandy-Walker Q03.1
    with spina bifida —see Spina bifida
  dental (root) K04.8
    developmental K09.0
    eruption K09.0
    primordial K09.0
  dentigerous (mandible) (maxilla) K09.0
  dermoid —see Neoplasm, benign, by site
    with malignant transformation C56.-●
    implantation
      external area or site (skin) NEC L72.0
      iris —see Cyst, iris, implantation
      vagina N89.8
      vulva N90.7
    mouth K09.8
    oral soft tissue K09.8
    sacrococcygeal —see Cyst, pilonidal
  developmental K09.1
    odontogenic K09.0
    oral region (nonodontogenic) K09.1
    ovary, ovarian Q50.1
  dura (cerebral) G93.0
    spinal G96.198
  ear (external) Q18.1
  echinococcal —see Echinococcus
  embryonic
    cervix uteri Q51.6
    fallopian tube Q50.4
    vagina Q52.4

Cyst (Continued)
   endometrium, endometrial (uterus) N85.8
     ectopic —see Endometriosis
   enterogenous Q43.8
   epidermal, epidermoid (inclusion) (see also
     Cyst, skin) L72.0
     mouth K09.8
     oral soft tissue K09.8
   epididymis N50.3
   epiglottis J38.7
   epiphysis cerebri E34.8
   epithelial (inclusion) L72.0
   epoophoron Q50.5
   eruption K09.0
   esophagus K22.8
   ethmoid sinus J34.1
   external female genital organs NEC N90.7
   eye NEC H57.89
     congenital Q15.8
   eyelid (sebaceous) H02.829
     infected —see Hordeolum
     left H02.826
       lower H02.825
       upper H02.824
     right H02.823
       lower H02.822
       upper H02.821
   fallopian tube N83.8
     congenital Q50.4
   fimbrial (twisted) Q50.4
   fissural (oral region) K09.1
   follicle (graafian) (hemorrhagic) N83.0-●
     nabothian N88.8
   follicular (atretic) (hemorrhagic) (ovarian)
     N83.0-●
     dentigerous K09.0
     odontogenic K09.0
     skin L72.9
     specified NEC L72.8
   frontal sinus J34.1
   gallbladder K82.8
   ganglion —see Ganglion
   Gartner's duct Q52.4
   gingiva K09.0
   gland of Moll —see Cyst, eyelid
   globulomaxillary K09.1
   graafian follicle (hemorrhagic) N83.0-●
   granulosal lutein (hemorrhagic) N83.1-●
   hemangiomatous D18.00
     intra-abdominal D18.03
     intracranial D18.02
     skin D18.01
     specified site NEC D18.09
   hemorrhagic M27.49
   hydatid —see also Echinococcus B67.90
     brain B67.99 [G94]
     liver —see also Cyst, liver, hydatid B67.8
     lung NEC B67.99 [J99]
     Morgagni
       female Q50.5
       male (epididymal) Q55.4
         testicular Q55.29
     specified site NEC B67.99
   hymen N89.8
     embryonic Q52.4
   hypopharynx J39.2
   hypophysis, hypophyseal (duct) (recurrent)
     E23.6
     cerebri E23.6
   implantation (dermoid)
     external area or site (skin) NEC L72.0
     iris —see Cyst, iris, implantation
     vagina N89.8
     vulva N90.7
   incisive canal K09.1
   inclusion (epidermal) (epithelial)
     (epidermoid) (squamous) L72.0
     not of skin - code under Cyst, by site
   intestine (large) (small) K63.89
   intracranial —see Cyst, brain
   intraligamentous —see also Disorder, ligament
     knee —see Derangement, knee

Cyst (Continued)
   intrasellar E23.6
   iris H21.309
     exudative H21.31-●
     idiopathic H21.30-●
     implantation H21.32-●
     parasitic H21.33-●
     pars plana (primary) H21.34-●
       exudative H21.35-●
   jaw (bone) M27.40
     aneurysmal M27.49
     developmental (odontogenic) K09.0
     fissural K09.1
     hemorrhagic M27.49
     traumatic M27.49
   joint NEC —see Disorder, joint, specified type
     NEC
   kidney (acquired) N28.1
     calyceal —see Hydronephrosis
     congenital Q61.00
     more than one (multiple) Q61.02
       specified as polycystic Q61.3
         adult type (autosomal dominant)
           Q61.2
         infantile type (autosomal recessive)
           NEC Q61.19
             collecting duct dilation Q61.11
     pyelogenic —see Hydronephrosis
     simple N28.1
     solitary (single) Q61.01
       acquired N28.1
   labium (majus) (minus) N90.7
     sebaceous N90.7
   lacrimal —see also Disorder, lacrimal system,
     specified NEC
     gland H04.13-●
     passages or sac —see Disorder, lacrimal
       system, specified NEC
   larynx J38.7
   lateral periodontal K09.0
   lens H27.8
     congenital Q12.8
   lip (gland) K13.0
   liver (idiopathic) (simple) K76.89
     congenital Q44.6
     hydatid B67.8
       granulosus B67.0
       multilocularis B67.5
   lung J98.4
     congenital Q33.0
     giant bullous J43.9
   lutein N83.1-●
   lymphangiomatous D18.1
   lymphoepithelial, oral soft tissue K09.8
   macula —see Degeneration, macula, hole
   malignant —see Neoplasm, malignant, by site
   mammary gland —see Cyst, breast
   mandible M27.40
     dentigerous K09.0
     radicular K04.8
   maxilla M27.40
     dentigerous K09.0
     radicular K04.8
   medial, face and neck Q18.8
   median
     anterior maxillary K09.1
     palatal K09.1
   mediastinum, congenital Q34.1
   meibomian (gland) —see Chalazion
     infected —see Hordeolum
   membrane, brain G93.0
   meninges (cerebral) G93.0
     spinal G96.198
   meniscus, knee —see Derangement, knee,
     meniscus, cystic
   mesentery, mesenteric K66.8
     chyle I89.8
   mesonephric duct
     female Q50.5
     male Q55.4
   milk N64.89

Cyst (Continued)
   Morgagni (hydatid)
     female Q50.5
     male (epididymal) Q55.4
       testicular Q55.29
   mouth K09.8
   Müllerian duct Q50.4
     appendix testis Q55.29
     cervix Q51.6
     fallopian tube Q50.4
     female Q50.4
     male Q55.29
     prostatic utricle Q55.4
     vagina (embryonal) Q52.4
   multilocular (ovary) D39.10
     benign —see Neoplasm, benign, by site
   myometrium N85.8
   nabothian (follicle) (ruptured) N88.8
   nasoalveolar K09.1
   nasolabial K09.1
   nasopalatine (anterior) (duct) K09.1
   nasopharynx J39.2
   neoplastic —see Neoplasm, uncertain
     behavior, by site
     benign —see Neoplasm, benign, by site
   ▶nerve root
     ▶cervical G96.191
     ▶lumbar G96.191
     ▶sacral G96.191
     ▶thoracic G96.191
   ⇒nervous system NEC G96.89
   neuroenteric (congenital) Q06.8
   nipple —see Cyst, breast
   nose (turbinates) J34.1
     sinus J34.1
   odontogenic, developmental K09.0
   omentum (lesser) K66.8
     congenital Q45.8
   ora serrata —see Cyst, retina, ora serrata
   oral
     region K09.9
       developmental (nonodontogenic) K09.1
       specified NEC K09.8
     soft tissue K09.9
       specified NEC K09.8
   orbit H05.81-●
   ovary, ovarian (twisted) N83.20-●
     adherent N83.20-●
     chocolate N80.1
     corpus
       albicans N83.29-●
       luteum (hemorrhagic) N83.1-●
     dermoid D27.9
     developmental Q50.1
     due to failure of involution NEC N83.20-●
     endometrial N80.1
     follicular (graafian) (hemorrhagic) N83.0-●
     hemorrhagic N83.20-●
     in pregnancy or childbirth O34.8-●
       with obstructed labor O65.5
     multilocular D39.10
     pseudomucinous D27.9
     retention N83.29-●
     serous N83.20-●
     specified NEC N83.29-●
     theca lutein (hemorrhagic) N83.1-●
     tuberculous A18.18
   oviduct N83.8
   palate (median) (fissural) K09.1
   palatine papilla (jaw) K09.1
   pancreas, pancreatic (hemorrhagic) (true) K86.2
     congenital Q45.2
     false K86.3
   paralabral
     hip M24.85-●
     shoulder S43.43-●
   paramesonephric duct Q50.4
     female Q50.4
     male Q55.29
   paranephric N28.1
   paraphysis, cerebri, congenital Q04.6
   parasitic B89
   parathyroid (gland) E21.4

▶ New   ⇒ Revised   deleted Deleted   ● Use Additional Character(s)

Cyst *(Continued)*
  paratubal N83.8
  paraurethral duct N36.8
  paroophoron Q50.5
  parotid gland K11.6
  parovarian Q50.5
  pelvis, female N94.89
    in pregnancy or childbirth O34.8-●
      causing obstructed labor O65.5
  penis (sebaceous) N48.89
  periapical K04.8
  pericardial (congenital) Q24.8
    acquired (secondary) I31.8
  pericoronal K09.0
▶ perineural G96.191
  periodontal K04.8
    lateral K09.0
  peripelvic (lymphatic) N28.1
  peritoneum K66.8
    chylous I89.8
  periventricular, acquired, newborn P91.1
  pharynx (wall) J39.2
  pilar L72.11
  pilonidal (infected) (rectum) L05.91
    with abscess L05.01
    malignant C44.59-●
  pituitary (duct) (gland) E23.6
  placenta O43.19-●
  pleura J94.8
  popliteal —*see* Cyst, Baker's
  porencephalic Q04.6
    acquired G93.0
  postanal (infected) —*see* Cyst, pilonidal
  postmastoidectomy cavity (mucosal) —*see*
      Complications, postmastoidectomy, cyst
  preauricular Q18.1
  prepuce N47.4
    congenital Q55.69
  primordial (jaw) K09.0
  prostate N42.83
  pseudomucinous (ovary) D27.9
  pupillary, miotic H21.27-●
  radicular (residual) K04.8
  radiculodental K04.8
  ranular K11.8
  Rathke's pouch E23.6
  rectum (epithelium) (mucous) K62.89
  renal —*see* Cyst, kidney
  residual (radicular) K04.8
  retention (ovary) N83.29-●
    salivary gland K11.6
  retina H33.19-●
    ora serrata H33.11-●
    parasitic H33.12-●
  retroperitoneal K68.9
  sacrococcygeal (dermoid) —*see* Cyst,
      pilonidal
  salivary gland or duct (mucous extravasation
      or retention) K11.6
  Sampson's N80.1
  sclera H15.89
  scrotum L72.9
    sebaceous L72.3
  sebaceous (duct) (gland) L72.3
    breast —*see* Dysplasia, mammary, specified
        type NEC
    eyelid —*see* Cyst, eyelid
    genital organ NEC
      female N94.89
      male N50.89
    scrotum L72.3
  semilunar cartilage (knee) (multiple) —*see*
      Derangement, knee, meniscus, cystic
  seminal vesicle N50.89
  serous (ovary) N83.20-●
  sinus (accessory) (nasal) J34.1
  Skene's gland N36.8
  skin L72.9
    breast —*see* Dysplasia, mammary, specified
        type NEC
    epidermal, epidermoid L72.0
    epithelial L72.0
    eyelid —*see* Cyst, eyelid

Cyst *(Continued)*
  skin *(Continued)*
    genital organ NEC
      female N90.7
      male N50.89
    inclusion L72.0
    scrotum L72.9
    sebaceous L72.3
    sweat gland or duct L74.8
  solitary
    bone —*see* Cyst, bone, solitary
    jaw M27.40
    kidney N28.1
  spermatic cord N50.89
  sphenoid sinus J34.1
➡ spinal meninges G96.198
  spleen NEC D73.4
    congenital Q89.09
    hydatid —*see also* Echinococcus B67.99 *[D77]*
  Stafne's M27.0
  subarachnoid intrasellar R93.0
  subcutaneous, pheomycotic (chromomycotic)
      B43.2
  subdural (cerebral) G93.0
➡ spinal cord G96.198
  sublingual gland K11.6
  submandibular gland K11.6
  submaxillary gland K11.6
  suburethral N36.8
  suprarenal gland E27.8
  suprasellar —*see* Cyst, brain
  sweat gland or duct L74.8
  synovial —*see also* Cyst, bursa
    ruptured —*see* Rupture, synovium
▶ Tarlov G96.191
  tarsal —*see* Chalazion
  tendon (sheath) —*see* Disorder, tendon,
      specified type NEC
  testis N44.2
    tunica albuginea N44.1
  theca lutein (ovary) N83.1-●
  Thornwaldt's J39.2
  thymus (gland) E32.8
  thyroglossal duct (infected) (persistent) Q89.2
  thyroid (gland) E04.1
  thyrolingual duct (infected) (persistent) Q89.2
  tongue K14.8
  tonsil J35.8
  tooth —*see* Cyst, dental
  Tornwaldt's J39.2
  trichilemmal (proliferating) L72.12
  trichodermal L72.12
  tubal (fallopian) N83.8
    inflammatory —*see* Salpingitis, chronic
  tubo-ovarian N83.8
    inflammatory N70.13
  tunica
    albuginea testis N44.1
    vaginalis N50.89
  turbinate (nose) J34.1
  Tyson's gland N48.89
  urachus, congenital Q64.4
  ureter N28.89
  ureterovesical orifice N28.89
  urethra, urethral (gland) N36.8
  uterine ligament N83.8
  uterus (body) (corpus) (recurrent)
      N85.8
    embryonic Q51.818
      cervix Q51.6
  vagina, vaginal (implantation) (inclusion)
      (squamous cell) (wall) N89.8
    embryonic Q52.4
  vallecula, vallecular (epiglottis) J38.7
  vesical (orifice) N32.89
  vitreous body H43.89
  vulva (implantation) (inclusion) N90.7
    congenital Q52.79
    sebaceous gland N90.7
  vulvovaginal gland N90.7
  wolffian
    female Q50.5
    male Q55.4

Cystadenocarcinoma —*see* Neoplasm,
    malignant, by site
  bile duct C22.1
  endometrioid —*see* Neoplasm, malignant,
      by site
    specified site —*see* Neoplasm, malignant,
        by site
    unspecified site
      female C56.9
      male C61
  mucinous
    papillary
      specified site —*see* Neoplasm,
          malignant, by site
      unspecified site C56.9
    specified site —*see* Neoplasm, malignant,
        by site
    unspecified site C56.9
  papillary
    mucinous
      specified site —*see* Neoplasm,
          malignant, by site
      unspecified site C56.9
    pseudomucinous
      specified site —*see* Neoplasm,
          malignant, by site
      unspecified site C56.9
    serous
      specified site —*see* Neoplasm,
          malignant, by site
      unspecified site C56.9
    specified site —*see* Neoplasm, malignant,
        by site
    unspecified site C56.9
  pseudomucinous
    papillary
      specified site —*see* Neoplasm,
          malignant, by site
      unspecified site C56.9
    specified site —*see* Neoplasm, malignant,
        by site
    unspecified site C56.9
  serous
    papillary
      specified site —*see* Neoplasm,
          malignant, by site
      unspecified site C56.9
    specified site —*see* Neoplasm, malignant,
        by site
    unspecified site C56.9
Cystadenofibroma
  clear cell —*see* Neoplasm, benign, by site
  endometrioid D27.9
    borderline malignancy D39.1-●
    malignant C56.-●
  mucinous
    specified site —*see* Neoplasm, benign, by site
    unspecified site D27.9
  serous
    specified site —*see* Neoplasm, benign, by site
    unspecified site D27.9
  specified site —*see* Neoplasm, benign, by site
  unspecified site D27.9
Cystadenoma —*see also* Neoplasm, benign, by
    site
  bile duct D13.4
  endometrioid —*see* Neoplasm, benign, by site
    borderline malignancy —*see* Neoplasm,
        uncertain behavior, by site
  malignant —*see* Neoplasm, malignant, by site
  mucinous
    borderline malignancy
      ovary C56.-●
      specified site NEC —*see* Neoplasm,
          uncertain behavior, by site
      unspecified site C56.9
    papillary
      borderline malignancy
        ovary C56.-●
        specified site NEC —*see* Neoplasm,
            uncertain behavior, by site
      unspecified site C56.9

Cystadenoma (Continued)
  mucinous (Continued)
    papillary (Continued)
      specified site —see Neoplasm, benign,
        by site
      unspecified site D27.9
    specified site —see Neoplasm, benign, by site
    unspecified site D27.9
  papillary
    borderline malignancy
      ovary C56-●
      specified site NEC —see Neoplasm,
        uncertain behavior, by site
      unspecified site C56.9
    lymphomatosum
      specified site —see Neoplasm, benign,
        by site
      unspecified site D11.9
    mucinous
      borderline malignancy
        ovary C56.-●
        specified site NEC —see Neoplasm,
          uncertain behavior, by site
        unspecified site C56.9
      specified site —see Neoplasm, benign,
        by site
      unspecified site D27.9
    pseudomucinous
      borderline malignancy
        ovary C56.-●
        specified site NEC —see Neoplasm,
          uncertain behavior, by site
        unspecified site C56.9
      specified site —see Neoplasm, benign,
        by site
      unspecified site D27.9
    serous
      borderline malignancy
        ovary C56.-●
        specified site NEC —see Neoplasm,
          uncertain behavior, by site
        unspecified site C56.9
      specified site —see Neoplasm, benign,
        by site
      unspecified site D27.9
    specified site —see Neoplasm, benign, by site
    unspecified site D27.9
  pseudomucinous
    borderline malignancy
      ovary C56.-●
      specified site NEC —see Neoplasm,
        uncertain behavior, by site
      unspecified site C56.9
    papillary
      borderline malignancy
        ovary C56.-●
        specified site NEC —see Neoplasm,
          uncertain behavior, by site
        unspecified site C56.9
      specified site —see Neoplasm, benign,
        by site
      unspecified site D27.9
    specified site —see Neoplasm, benign, by site
    unspecified site D27.9
  serous
    borderline malignancy
      ovary C56.-●
      specified site NEC —see Neoplasm,
        uncertain behavior, by site
      unspecified site C56.9
    papillary
      borderline malignancy
        ovary C56.-●
        specified site NEC —see Neoplasm,
          uncertain behavior, by site
        unspecified site C56.9
      specified site —see Neoplasm, benign,
        by site
      unspecified site D27.9
    specified site —see Neoplasm, benign, by site
    unspecified site D27.9

Cystathionine synthase deficiency E72.11
Cystathioninemia E72.19
Cystathioninuria E72.19
Cystic —see also condition
  breast (chronic) —see Mastopathy, cystic
  corpora lutea (hemorrhagic) N83.1-●
  duct —see condition
  eyeball (congenital) Q11.0
  fibrosis —see Fibrosis, cystic
  kidney (congenital) Q61.9
    adult type Q61.2
    infantile type NEC Q61.19
      collecting duct dilatation Q61.11
    medullary Q61.5
  liver, congenital Q44.6
  lung disease J98.4
    congenital Q33.0
  mastitis, chronic —see Mastopathy, cystic
  medullary, kidney Q61.5
  meniscus —see Derangement, knee,
    meniscus, cystic
  ovary N83.20-●
Cysticercosis, cysticerciasis B69.9
  with
    epileptiform fits B69.0
    myositis B69.81
  brain B69.0
  central nervous system B69.0
  cerebral B69.0
  ocular B69.1
  specified NEC B69.89
Cysticercus cellulose infestation —see
  Cysticercosis
Cystinosis (malignant) E72.04
Cystinuria E72.01
Cystitis (exudative) (hemorrhagic) (septic)
    (suppurative) N30.90
  with
    fibrosis —see Cystitis, chronic, interstitial
    hematuria N30.91
    leukoplakia —see Cystitis, chronic,
      interstitial
    malakoplakia —see Cystitis, chronic,
      interstitial
    metaplasia —see Cystitis, chronic, interstitial
    prostatitis N41.3
  acute N30.00
    with hematuria N30.01
    of trigone N30.30
      with hematuria N30.31
  allergic —see Cystitis, specified type NEC
  amebic A06.81
  bilharzial B65.9 [N33]
  blennorrhagic (gonococcal) A54.01
  bullous —see Cystitis, specified type NEC
  calculous N21.0
  chlamydial A56.01
  chronic N30.20
    with hematuria N30.21
    interstitial N30.10
      with hematuria N30.11
    of trigone N30.30
      with hematuria N30.31
    specified NEC N30.20
      with hematuria N30.21
  cystic (a) —see Cystitis, specified type NEC
  diphtheritic A36.85
  echinococcal
    granulosus B67.39
    multilocularis B67.69
  emphysematous —see Cystitis, specified type
    NEC
  encysted —see Cystitis, specified type NEC
  eosinophilic —see Cystitis, specified type
    NEC
  follicular —see Cystitis, of trigone
  gangrenous —see Cystitis, specified type
    NEC
  glandularis —see Cystitis, specified type
    NEC

Cystitis (Continued)
  gonococcal A54.01
  incrusted —see Cystitis, specified type
    NEC
  interstitial (chronic) —see Cystitis, chronic,
    interstitial
  irradiation N30.40
    with hematuria N30.41
  irritation —see Cystitis, specified type
    NEC
  malignant —see Cystitis, specified type
    NEC
  of trigone N30.30
    with hematuria N30.31
  panmural —see Cystitis, chronic, interstitial
  polyposa —see Cystitis, specified type NEC
  prostatic N41.3
  puerperal (postpartum) O86.22
  radiation —see Cystitis, irradiation
  specified type NEC N30.80
    with hematuria N30.81
  subacute —see Cystitis, chronic
  submucous —see Cystitis, chronic, interstitial
  syphilitic (late) A52.76
  trichomonal A59.03
  tuberculous A18.12
  ulcerative —see Cystitis, chronic, interstitial
Cystocele (-urethrocele)
  female N81.10
    with prolapse of uterus —see Prolapse,
      uterus
    lateral N81.12
    midline N81.11
    paravaginal N81.12
  in pregnancy or childbirth O34.8-●
    causing obstructed labor O65.5
  male N32.89
Cystolithiasis N21.0
Cystoma —see also Neoplasm, benign, by site
  endometrial, ovary N80.1
  mucinous
    specified site —see Neoplasm, benign, by site
    unspecified site D27.9
  serous
    specified site —see Neoplasm, benign, by site
    unspecified site D27.9
  simple (ovary) N83.29-●
Cystoplegia N31.2
Cystoptosis N32.89
Cystopyelitis —see Pyelonephritis
Cystorrhagia N32.89
Cystosarcoma phyllodes D48.6-●
  benign D24-●
  malignant —see Neoplasm, breast, malignant
Cystostomy
  attention to Z43.5
  complication —see Complications, cystostomy
  status Z93.50
    appendico-vesicostomy Z93.52
    cutaneous Z93.51
    specified NEC Z93.59
Cystourethritis —see Urethritis
Cystourethrocele —see also Cystocele
  female N81.10
    with uterine prolapse —see Prolapse,
      uterus
    lateral N81.12
    midline N81.11
    paravaginal N81.12
  male N32.89
Cytomegalic inclusion disease
  congenital P35.1
Cytomegalovirus infection B25.9
Cytomycosis (reticuloendothelial) B39.4
Cytopenia D75.9
  refractory
    with multilineage dysplasia D46.A
      and ring sideroblasts (RCMD RS) D46.B
Czerny's disease (periodic hydrarthrosis of the
  knee) —see Effusion, joint, knee

▶ New   ⇨ Revised   ~~deleted~~ Deleted   ● Use Additional Character(s)

D

Daae (-Finsen) disease (epidemic pleurodynia) B33.0
Dabney's grip B33.0
Da Costa's syndrome F45.8
Dacryoadenitis, dacryadenitis H04.00-●
 acute H04.01-●
 chronic H04.02-●
Dacryocystitis H04.30-●
 acute H04.32-●
 chronic H04.41-●
 neonatal P39.1
 phlegmonous H04.31-●
 syphilitic A52.71
  congenital (early) A50.01
 trachomatous, active A71.1
  sequelae (late effect) B94.0
Dacryocystoblenorrhea —see Inflammation, lacrimal, passages, chronic
Dacryocystocele —see Disorder, lacrimal system, changes
Dacryolith, dacryolithiasis H04.51-●
Dacryoma —see Disorder, lacrimal system, changes
Dacryopericystitis —see Dacryocystitis
Dacryops H04.11-●
Dacryostenosis —see also Stenosis, lacrimal
 congenital Q10.5
Dactylitis
 bone —see Osteomyelitis
 sickle-cell D57.00
  Hb C D57.219
  Hb SS D57.00
  specified NEC D57.819
 skin L08.9
 syphilitic A52.77
 tuberculous A18.03
Dactylolysis spontanea (ainhum) L94.6
Dactylosymphysis Q70.9
 fingers —see Syndactylism, complex, fingers
 toes —see Syndactylism, complex, toes
Damage
 arteriosclerotic —see Arteriosclerosis
 brain (nontraumatic) G93.9
  anoxic, hypoxic G93.1
   resulting from a procedure G97.82
  child NEC G80.9
  due to birth injury P11.2
 cardiorenal (vascular) —see Hypertension, cardiorenal
 cerebral NEC —see Damage, brain
 coccyx, complicating delivery O71.6
 coronary —see Disease, heart, ischemic
 deep tissue, pressure-induced —see also L89
  with final character .6
 eye, birth injury P15.3
 liver (nontraumatic) K76.9
  alcoholic K70.9
  due to drugs —see Disease, liver, toxic
  toxic —see Disease, liver, toxic
▶lung
 ▶dabbing (related) U07.0
 ▶electronic cigarette (related) U07.0
 ▶vaping (associated) (device) (product) (use) U07.0
 medication T88.7
▶organ
 ▶dabbing (related) U07.0
 ▶electronic cigarette (related) U07.0
 ▶vaping (associated) (device) (product) (use) U07.0
 pelvic
  joint or ligament, during delivery O71.6
  organ NEC
   during delivery O71.5
   following ectopic or molar pregnancy O08.6
 renal —see Disease, renal
 subendocardium, subendocardial —see Degeneration, myocardial
 vascular I99.9

Dana-Putnam syndrome (subacute combined sclerosis with pernicious anemia) —see Degeneration, combined
Danbolt (-Cross) syndrome (acrodermatitis enteropathica) E83.2
Dandruff L21.0
Dandy-Walker syndrome Q03.1
 with spina bifida —see Spina bifida
Danlos' syndrome (see also Syndrome, Ehler-Danlos) Q79.60
Darier (-White) disease (congenital) Q82.8
 meaning erythema annulare centrifugum L53.1
Darier-Roussy sarcoid D86.3
Darling's disease or histoplasmosis B39.4
Darwin's tubercle Q17.8
Dawson's (inclusion body) encephalitis A81.1
De Beurmann (-Gougerot) disease B42.1
De la Tourette's syndrome F95.2
De Lange's syndrome Q87.19
De Morgan's spots (senile angiomas) I78.1
De Quervain's
 disease (tendon sheath) M65.4
 syndrome E34.51
 thyroiditis (subacute granulomatous thyroiditis) E06.1
De Toni-Fanconi (-Debré) syndrome E72.09
 with cystinosis E72.04
Dead
 fetus, retained (mother) O36.4
  early pregnancy O02.1
 labyrinth —see subcategory H83.2
 ovum, retained O02.0
Deaf nonspeaking NEC H91.3
Deafmutism (acquired) (congenital) NEC H91.3
 hysterical F44.6
 syphilitic, congenital —see also subcategory H94.8 A50.09
Deafness (acquired) (complete) (hereditary) (partial) H91.9-●
 with blue sclera and fragility of bone Q78.0
 auditory fatigue —see Deafness, specified type NEC
 aviation T70.0
  nerve injury —see Injury, nerve, acoustic, specified type NEC
 boilermaker's —see subcategory H83.3
 central —see Deafness, sensorineural
 conductive H90.2
  and sensorineural
   mixed H90.8
    bilateral H90.6
  bilateral H90.0
  unilateral H90.1-●
   with restricted hearing on the contralateral side H90.A-●
 congenital H90.5
  with blue sclera and fragility of bone Q78.0
 due to toxic agents —see Deafness, ototoxic
 emotional (hysterical) F44.6
 functional (hysterical) F44.6
 high frequency H91.9-●
 hysterical F44.6
 low frequency H91.9-●
 mental R48.8
 mixed conductive and sensorineural H90.8
  bilateral H90.6
  unilateral H90.7-●
 nerve —see Deafness, sensorineural
 neural —see Deafness, sensorineural
 noise-induced —see also subcategory H83.3
  nerve injury —see Injury, nerve, acoustic, specified type NEC
 nonspeaking H91.3
 ototoxic —see subcategory H91.0
 perceptive —see Deafness, sensorineural
 psychogenic (hysterical) F44.6
 sensorineural H90.5
  and conductive
   mixed H90.8
    bilateral H90.6
  bilateral H90.3

Deafness (Continued)
 sensorineural (Continued)
  unilateral H90.4-●
   with restricted hearing on the contralateral side H90.A-●
  sensory —see Deafness, sensorineural
  specified type NEC —see subcategory H91.8
  sudden (idiopathic) H91.2-●
  syphilitic A52.15
  transient ischemic H93.01-●
  traumatic —see Injury, nerve, acoustic, specified type NEC
  word (developmental) H93.25
Death (cause unknown) (of) (unexplained) (unspecified cause) R99
 brain G93.82
 cardiac (sudden) (with successful resuscitation) — code to underlying disease
  family history of Z82.41
  personal history of Z86.74
 family member (assumed) Z63.4
Debility (chronic) (general) (nervous) R53.81
 congenital or neonatal NOS P96.9
 nervous R53.81
 old age R54
 senile R54
Débove's disease (splenomegaly) R16.1
Decalcification
 bone —see Osteoporosis
 teeth K03.89
Decapsulation, kidney N28.89
Decay
 dental —see Caries, dental
 senile R54
 tooth, teeth —see Caries, dental
Deciduitis (acute)
 following ectopic or molar pregnancy O08.0
Decline (general) —see Debility
 cognitive, age-associated R41.81
Decompensation
 cardiac (acute) (chronic) —see Disease, heart
 cardiovascular —see Disease, cardiovascular
 heart —see Disease, heart
 hepatic —see Failure, hepatic
 myocardial (acute) (chronic) —see Disease, heart
 respiratory J98.8
Decompression sickness T70.3
Decrease (d)
 absolute neutrophile count —see Neutropenia
 blood
  platelets —see Thrombocytopenia
  pressure R03.1
   due to shock following
    injury T79.4
    operation T81.19
 estrogen E28.39
  postablative E89.40
   asymptomatic E89.40
   symptomatic E89.41
 fragility of erythrocytes D58.8
 function
  lipase (pancreatic) K90.3
  ovary in hypopituitarism E23.0
  parenchyma of pancreas K86.89
  pituitary (gland) (anterior) (lobe) E23.0
   posterior (lobe) E23.0
 functional activity R68.89
 glucose R73.09
 hematocrit R71.0
 hemoglobin R71.0
 leukocytes D72.819
  specified NEC D72.818
 libido R68.82
 lymphocytes D72.810
 platelets D69.6
 respiration, due to shock following injury T79.4
 sexual desire R68.82
 tear secretion NEC —see Syndrome, dry eye

Decrease *(Continued)*
  tolerance
    fat K90.49
    glucose R73.09
    pancreatic K90.3
    salt and water E87.8
  vision NEC H54.7
  white blood cell count D72.819
    specified NEC D72.818
Decubitus (ulcer) —*see* Ulcer, pressure, by site
  cervix N86
Deepening acetabulum —*see* Derangement,
    joint, specified type NEC, hip
Defect, defective Q89.9
  3-beta-hydroxysteroid dehydrogenase E25.0
  11-hydroxylase E25.0
  21-hydroxylase E25.0
  abdominal wall, congenital Q79.59
  antibody immunodeficiency D80.9
  aorticopulmonary septum Q21.4
  atrial septal (ostium secundum type) Q21.1
    following acute myocardial infarction
        (current complication) I23.1
    ostium primum type Q21.2
  atrioventricular
    canal Q21.2
    septum Q21.2
  auricular septal Q21.1
  bilirubin excretion NEC E80.6
  biosynthesis, androgen (testicular) E29.1
  bulbar septum Q21.0
  catalase E80.3
  cell membrane receptor complex (CR3) D71
  circulation I99.9
    congenital Q28.9
    newborn Q28.9
  coagulation (factor) —*see also* Deficiency,
      factor D68.9
    with
      ectopic pregnancy O08.1
      molar pregnancy O08.1
    acquired D68.4
    antepartum with hemorrhage —*see*
        Hemorrhage, antepartum, with
        coagulation defect
    due to
      liver disease D68.4
      vitamin K deficiency D68.4
    hereditary NEC D68.2
    intrapartum O67.0
    newborn, transient P61.6
    postpartum O99.13
      with hemorrhage O72.3
    specified type NEC D68.8
  complement system D84.1
  conduction (heart) I45.9
    bone —*see* Deafness, conductive
  congenital, organ or site not listed —*see*
      Anomaly, by site
  coronary sinus Q21.1
  cushion, endocardial Q21.2
  degradation, glycoprotein E77.1
  dental bridge, crown, fillings —*see* Defect,
      dental restoration
  dental restoration K08.50
    specified NEC K08.59
  dentin (hereditary) K00.5
  Descemet's membrane, congenital Q13.89
  developmental —*see also* Anomaly
    cauda equina Q06.3
  diaphragm
    with elevation, eventration or hernia —*see*
        Hernia, diaphragm
    congenital Q79.1
      with hernia Q79.0
      gross (with hernia) Q79.0
  ectodermal, congenital Q82.9
  Eisenmenger's Q21.8
  enzyme
    catalase E80.3
    peroxidase E80.3

Defect, defective *(Continued)*
  esophagus, congenital Q39.9
  extensor retinaculum M62.89
  fibrin polymerization D68.2
  filling
    bladder R93.41
    kidney R93.42-●
    renal pelvis R93.41
    stomach R93.3
    ureter R93.41
    urinary organs, specified NEC R93.49
  GABA (gamma aminobutyric acid) metabolic
      E72.81
  Gerbode Q21.0
▶glucose transport, blood-brain barrier E74.810
  glycoprotein degradation E77.1
  Hageman (factor) D68.2
  hearing —*see* Deafness
  high grade F70
  interatrial septal Q21.1
  interauricular septal Q21.1
  interventricular septal Q21.0
    with dextroposition of aorta, pulmonary
        stenosis and hypertrophy of right
        ventricle Q21.3
    in tetralogy of Fallot Q21.3
  learning (specific) —*see* Disorder, learning
  lymphocyte function antigen-1 (LFA-1) D84.0
  lysosomal enzyme, post-translational
      modification E77.0
  major osseous M89.70
    ankle M89.77-●
    carpus M89.74-●
    clavicle M89.71-●
    femur M89.75-●
    fibula M89.76-●
    fingers M89.74-●
    foot M89.77-●
    forearm M89.73-●
    hand M89.74-●
    humerus M89.72-●
    lower leg M89.76-●
    metacarpus M89.74-●
    metatarsus M89.77-●
    multiple sites M89.79
    pelvic region M89.75-●
    pelvis M89.75-●
    radius M89.73-●
    scapula M89.71-●
    shoulder region M89.71-●
    specified NEC M89.78
    tarsus M89.77-●
    thigh M89.75-●
    tibia M89.76-●
    toes M89.77-●
    ulna M89.73-●
  mental —*see* Disability, intellectual
  modification, lysosomal enzymes, post-
      translational E77.0
  obstructive, congenital
    renal pelvis Q62.39
    ureter Q62.39
      atresia —*see* Atresia, ureter
      cecoureterocele Q62.32
      megaureter Q62.2
      orthotopic ureterocele Q62.31
  osseous, major M89.70
    ankle M89.77-●
    carpus M89.74-●
    clavicle M89.71-●
    femur M89.75-●
    fibula M89.76-●
    fingers M89.74-●
    foot M89.77-●
    forearm M89.73-●
    hand M89.74-●
    humerus M89.72-●
    lower leg M89.76-●
    metacarpus M89.74-●
    metatarsus M89.77-●
    multiple sites M89.9

Defect, defective *(Continued)*
  osseous, major *(Continued)*
    pelvic region M89.75-●
    pelvis M89.75-●
    radius M89.73-●
    scapula M89.71-●
    shoulder region M89.71-●
    specified NEC M89.78
    tarsus M89.77-●
    thigh M89.75-●
    tibia M89.76-●
    toes M89.77-●
    ulna M89.73-●
  osteochondral NEC —*see also* Deformity
      M95.8-●
  ostium
    primum Q21.2
    secundum Q21.1
  peroxidase E80.3
  placental blood supply —*see* Insufficiency,
      placental
  platelets, qualitative D69.1
    constitutional D68.0
  postural NEC, spine —*see* Dorsopathy,
      deforming
  reduction
    limb Q73.8
      lower Q72.9-●
        absence —*see* Agenesis, leg
          foot —*see* Agenesis, foot
        longitudinal
          femur Q72.4-●
          fibula Q72.6-●
          tibia Q72.5-●
        specified type NEC Q72.89-●
        split foot Q72.7-●
      specified type NEC Q73.8
      upper Q71.9-●
        absence —*see* Agenesis, arm
          forearm —*see* Agenesis, forearm
          hand —*see* Agenesis, hand
        lobster-claw hand Q71.6-●
        longitudinal
          radius Q71.4-●
          ulna Q71.5-●
        specified type NEC Q71.89-●
  renal pelvis Q63.8
    obstructive Q62.39
  respiratory system, congenital Q34.9
  restoration, dental K08.50
    specified NEC K08.59
  retinal nerve bundle fibers H35.89
  septal (heart) NOS Q21.9
    acquired (atrial) (auricular) (ventricular)
        (old) I51.0
    atrial Q21.1
      concurrent with acute myocardial
          infarction —*see* Infarct,
          myocardium
      following acute myocardial infarction
          (current complication) I23.1
    ventricular —*see also* Defect, ventricular
        septal Q21.0
  sinus venosus Q21.1
➡speech —*see* Disorder, speech
    developmental F80.9
    specified NEC R47.89
  Taussig-Bing (aortic transposition and
      overriding pulmonary artery)
      Q20.1
  teeth, wedge K03.1
  vascular (local) I99.9
    congenital Q27.9
  ventricular septal Q21.0
    concurrent with acute myocardial
        infarction —*see* Infarct,
        myocardium
    following acute myocardial infarction
        (current complication) I23.2
    in tetralogy of Fallot Q21.3
  vision NEC H54.7

▶ New   ⇒ Revised   ~~deleted~~ Deleted   ● Use Additional Character(s)

Defect, defective (Continued)
  visual field H53.40
    bilateral
      heteronymous H53.47
      homonymous H53.46-●
    generalized contraction H53.48-●
    localized
      arcuate H53.43-●
      scotoma (central area) H53.41-●
        blind spot area H53.42-●
      sector H53.43-●
      specified type NEC H53.45-●
  voice R49.9
    specified NEC R49.8
  wedge, tooth, teeth (abrasion) K03.1
Deferentitis N49.1
  gonorrheal (acute) (chronic) A54.23
Defibrination (syndrome) D65
  antepartum —see Hemorrhage, antepartum,
    with coagulation defect, disseminated
    intravascular coagulation
  following ectopic or molar pregnancy O08.1
  intrapartum O67.0
  newborn P60
  postpartum O72.3
Deficiency, deficient
  3-beta hydroxysteroid dehydrogenase E25.0
  11-hydroxylase E25.0
  21-hydroxylase E25.0
  5-alpha reductase (with male
    pseudohermaphroditism) E29.1
▶AADC (aromatic L-amino acid
    decarboxylase) E70.81
  abdominal muscle syndrome Q79.4
  AC globulin (congenital) (hereditary) D68.2
    acquired D68.4
  accelerator globulin (Ac G) (blood) D68.2
  acid phosphatase E83.39
  activating factor (blood) D68.2
  ADA2 (adenosine deaminase 2) D81.32
  adenosine deaminase (ADA) D81.30
    with severe combined immunodeficiency
      (SCID) D81.31
    partial (type 1) D81.39
    specified NEC D81.39
    type 1 (without SCID) (without severe
      combined immunodeficiency) D81.39
    type 2 D81.32
  aldolase (hereditary) E74.19
  alpha-1-antitrypsin E88.01
  amino-acids E72.9
  anemia —see Anemia
  aneurin E51.9
  antibody with
    hyperimmunoglobulinemia D80.6
    near-normal immunoglobins D80.6
  antidiuretic hormone E23.2
  anti-hemophilic
    factor (A) D66
      B D67
      C D68.1
    globulin (AHG) NEC D66
  antithrombin (antithrombin III) D68.59
▶aromatic L-amino acid decarboxylase
    (AADC) E70.81
  ascorbic acid E54
  attention (disorder) (syndrome) F98.8
    with hyperactivity —see Disorder,
      attention-deficit hyperactivity
  autoprothrombin
    I D68.2
    II D67
    C D68.2
  beta-glucuronidase E76.29
  biotin E53.8
  biotin-dependent carboxylase D81.819
  biotinidase D81.810
  brancher enzyme (amylopectinosis) E74.03
  C1 esterase inhibitor (C1-INH) D84.1
  calciferol E55.9
    with
      adult osteomalacia M83.8
      rickets —see Rickets

Deficiency, deficient (Continued)
  calcium (dietary) E58
  calorie, severe E43
    with marasmus E41
      and kwashiorkor E42
  cardiac —see Insufficiency, myocardial
  carnitine E71.40
    due to
      hemodialysis E71.43
      inborn errors of metabolism E71.42
      Valproic acid therapy E71.43
    iatrogenic E71.43
    muscle palmityltransferase E71.314
    primary E71.41
    secondary E71.448
  carotene E50.9
▶central nervous system G96.89
  ceruloplasmin (Wilson) E83.01
  choline E53.8
  Christmas factor D67
  chromium E61.4
  clotting (blood) —see also Deficiency,
    coagulation factor D68.9
  clotting factor NEC (hereditary) —see also
    Deficiency, factor D68.2
  coagulation NOS D68.9
    with
      ectopic pregnancy O08.1
      molar pregnancy O08.1
    acquired (any) D68.4
    antepartum hemorrhage —see Hemorrhage,
      antepartum, with coagulation defect
    clotting factor NEC —see also Deficiency,
      factor D68.2
    due to
      hyperprothrombinemia D68.4
      liver disease D68.4
      vitamin K deficiency D68.4
    newborn, transient P61.6
    postpartum O72.3
    specified NEC D68.8
  cognitive F09
  color vision H53.50
    achromatopsia H53.51
    acquired H53.52
    deuteranomaly H53.53
    protanomaly H53.54
    specified type NEC H53.59
    tritanomaly H53.55
  combined glucocorticoid and
    mineralocorticoid E27.49
  contact factor D68.2
  copper (nutritional) E61.0
  corticoadrenal E27.40
    primary E27.1
  craniofacial axis Q75.0
  cyanocobalamin E53.8
  debrancher enzyme (limit dextrinosis) E74.03
  dehydrogenase
    long chain/very long chain acyl CoA E71.310
    medium chain acyl CoA E71.311
    short chain acyl CoA E71.312
  diet E63.9
  dihydropyrimidine dehydrogenase (DPD)
    E88.89
  disaccharidase E73.9
  edema —see Malnutrition, severe
  endocrine E34.9
  energy-supply —see Malnutrition
  enzymes, circulating NEC E88.09
  ergosterol E55.9
    with
      adult osteomalacia M83.8
      rickets —see Rickets
  essential fatty acid (EFA) E63.0
▶eye movements
  ▶saccadic H55.81
  ▶smooth pursuit H55.82
  factor —see also Deficiency, coagulation
    Hageman D68.2
    I (congenital) (hereditary) D68.2

Deficiency, deficient (Continued)
  factor (Continued)
    II (congenital) (hereditary) D68.2
    IX (congenital) (functional) (hereditary)
      (with functional defect) D67
    multiple (congenital) D68.8
      acquired D68.4
    V (congenital) (hereditary) D68.2
    VII (congenital) (hereditary) D68.2
    VIII (congenital) (functional) (hereditary)
      (with functional defect) D66
      with vascular defect D68.0
    X (congenital) (hereditary) D68.2
    XI (congenital) (hereditary) D68.1
    XII (congenital) (hereditary) D68.2
    XIII (congenital) (hereditary) D68.2
    femoral, proximal focal (congenital) —
      see Defect, reduction, lower limb,
      longitudinal, femur
    fibrin-stabilizing factor (congenital)
      (hereditary) D68.2
      acquired D68.4
    fibrinase D68.2
    fibrinogen (congenital) (hereditary) D68.2
      acquired D65
    folate E53.8
    folic acid E53.8
    foreskin N47.3
    fructokinase E74.11
    fructose 1,6-diphosphatase E74.19
    fructose-1-phosphate aldolase E74.19
    GABA (gamma aminobutyric acid)
      transaminase E72.81
    GABA-T (gamma aminobutyric acid
      transaminase) E72.81
    galactokinase E74.29
    galactose-1-phosphate uridyl transferase
      E74.29
    gammaglobulin in blood D80.1
      hereditary D80.0
    glass factor D68.2
    glucocorticoid E27.49
      mineralocorticoid E27.49
    glucose-6-phosphatase E74.01
    glucose-6-phosphate dehydrogenase anemia
      anemia D55.0
      without anemia D75.A
  ▶glucose transporter protein type 1 E74.810
    glucuronyl transferase E80.5
  ▶Glut1 E74.810
    glycogen synthetase E74.09
    gonadotropin (isolated) E23.0
    growth hormone (idiopathic) (isolated) E23.0
    Hageman factor D68.2
    hemoglobin D64.9
    hepatophosphorylase E74.09
    homogentisate 1,2-dioxygenase E70.29
    hormone
      anterior pituitary (partial) NEC E23.0
        growth E23.0
      growth (isolated) E23.0
      pituitary E23.0
      testicular E29.1
    hypoxanthine-(guanine)-
      phosphoribosyltransferase (HG-PRT)
      (total HG-PRT) E79.1
    immunity D84.9
  ▶cell-mediated D84.89
      with thrombocytopenia and eczema
        D82.0
      combined D81.9
      humoral D80.9
      IgA (secretory) D80.2
      IgG D80.3
      IgM D80.4
    immuno —see Immunodeficiency
    immunoglobulin, selective
      A (IgA) D80.2
      G (IgG) (subclasses) D80.3
      M (IgM) D80.4
    inositol (B complex) E53.8

Deficiency, deficient *(Continued)*
  intrinsic
    factor (congenital) D51.0
    sphincter N36.42
      with urethral hypermobility N36.43
  iodine E61.8
    congenital syndrome —*see* Syndrome,
      iodine-deficiency, congenital
  iron E61.1
    anemia D50.9
  kalium E87.6
  kappa-light chain D80.8
  labile factor (congenital) (hereditary) D68.2
    acquired D68.4
  lacrimal fluid (acquired) —*see also* Syndrome,
      dry eye
    congenital Q10.6
  lactase
    congenital E73.0
    secondary E73.1
  Laki-Lorand factor D68.2
  lecithin cholesterol acyltransferase E78.6
  lipocaic K86.89
  lipoprotein (familial) (high density) E78.6
  liver phosphorylase E74.09
  lysosomal alpha-1, 4 glucosidase E74.02
  magnesium E61.2
  major histocompatibility complex
    class I D81.6
    class II D81.7
  manganese E61.3
  menadione (vitamin K) E56.1
    newborn P53
  mental (familial) (hereditary) —*see* Disability,
      intellectual
  methylenetetrahydrofolate reductase
      (MTHFR) E72.12
  mevalonate kinase M04.1
  mineral NEC E61.8
  mineralocorticoid E27.49
    with glucocorticoid E27.49
  molybdenum (nutritional) E61.5
  moral F60.2
  multiple nutrient elements E61.7
  multiple sulfatase (MSD) E75.26
  muscle
    carnitine (palmityltransferase) E71.314
    phosphofructokinase E74.09
  myoadenylate deaminase E79.2
  myocardial —*see* Insufficiency, myocardial
  myophosphorylase E74.04
  NADH diaphorase or reductase (congenital)
      D74.0
  NADH-methemoglobin reductase
      (congenital) D74.0
  natrium E87.1
  niacin (amide) (-tryptophan) E52
  nicotinamide E52
  nicotinic acid E52
  number of teeth —*see* Anodontia
  nutrient element E61.9
    multiple E61.7
    specified NEC E61.8
  nutrition, nutritional E63.9
    sequelae —*see* Sequelae, nutritional
      deficiency
    specified NEC E63.8
  of interleukin 1 receptor antagonist [DIRA]
      M04.8
  ornithine transcarbamylase E72.4
  ovarian E28.39
  oxygen —*see* Anoxia
  pantothenic acid E53.8
  parathyroid (gland) E20.9
  perineum (female) N81.89
  phenylalanine hydroxylase E70.1
  phosphoenolpyruvate carboxykinase E74.4
  phosphofructokinase E74.19
▶ phosphomannomutase E74.818
▶ phosphomannose isomerase E74.818
▶ phosphomannosyl mutase E74.818

Deficiency, deficient *(Continued)*
  phosphorylase kinase, liver E74.09
  pituitary hormone (isolated) E23.0
  plasma thromboplastin
    antecedent (PTA) D68.1
    component (PTC) D67
  plasminogen (type 1) (type 2) E88.02
  platelet NEC D69.1
    constitutional D68.0
  polyglandular E31.8
    autoimmune E31.0
  potassium (K) E87.6
  prepuce N47.3
  proaccelerin (congenital) (hereditary)
      D68.2
    acquired D68.4
  proconvertin factor (congenital) (hereditary)
      D68.2
    acquired D68.4
  protein —*see also* Malnutrition E46
    anemia D53.0
    C D68.59
    S D68.59
  prothrombin (congenital) (heredItary)
      D68.2
    acquired D68.4
  Prower factor D68.2
  pseudocholinesterase E88.09
  PTA (plasma thromboplastin antecedent)
      D68.1
  PTC (plasma thromboplastin component)
      D67
  purine nucleoside phosphorylase (PNP)
      D81.5
  pyracin (alpha) (beta) E53.1
  pyridoxal E53.1
  pyridoxamine E53.1
  pyridoxine (derivatives) E53.1
  pyruvate
    carboxylase E74.4
    dehydrogenase E74.4
  riboflavin (vitamin B2) E53.0
  salt E87.1
  secretion
    ovary E28.39
    salivary gland (any) K11.7
    urine R34
  selenium (dietary) E59
  serum antitrypsin, familial E88.01
  short stature homeobox gene (SHOX)
    with
      dyschondrosteosis Q78.8
      short stature (idiopathic) E34.3
      Turner's syndrome Q96.9
  sodium (Na) E87.1
  SPCA (factor VII) D68.2
  sphincter, intrinsic N36.42
    with urethral hypermobility N36.43
  stable factor (congenital) (hereditary)
      D68.2
    acquired D68.4
  Stuart-Prower (factor X) D68.2
  succinic semialdehyde dehydrogenase
      E72.81
  sucrase E74.39
  sulfatase E75.26
  sulfite oxidase E72.19
  thiamin, thiaminic (chloride) E51.9
    beriberi (dry) E51.11
      wet E51.12
  thrombokinase D68.2
    newborn P53
  thyroid (gland) —*see* Hypothyroidism
  tocopherol E56.0
  tooth bud K00.0
  transcobalamine II (anemia) D51.2
  vanadium E61.6
  vascular I99.9
  vasopressin E23.2
  vertical ridge K06.8
  viosterol —*see* Deficiency, calciferol

Deficiency, deficient *(Continued)*
  vitamin (multiple) NOS E56.9
    A E50.9
      with
        Bitot's spot (corneal) E50.1
        follicular keratosis E50.8
        keratomalacia E50.4
        manifestations NEC E50.8
        night blindness E50.5
        scar of cornea, xerophthalmic E50.6
        xeroderma E50.8
        xerophthalmia E50.7
        xerosis
          conjunctival E50.0
            and Bitot's spot E50.1
          cornea E50.2
            and ulceration E50.3
      sequelae E64.1
    B (complex) NOS E53.9
      with
        beriberi (dry) E51.11
          wet E51.12
        pellagra E52
    B1 NOS E51.9
      beriberi (dry) E51.11
        with circulatory system
          manifestations E51.11
        wet E51.12
    B12 E53.8
    B2 (riboflavin) E53.0
    B6 E53.1
    C E54
      sequelae E64.2
    D E55.9
      with
        adult osteomalacia M83.8
        rickets —*see* Rickets
      25-hydroxylase E83.32
    E E56.0
    folic acid E53.8
    G E53.0
    group B E53.9
      specified NEC E53.8
    H (biotin) E53.8
    K E56.1
      of newborn P53
    nicotinic E52
    P E56.8
    PP (pellagra-preventing) E52
    specified NEC E56.8
    thiamin E51.9
      beriberi —*see* Beriberi
  zinc, dietary E60
Deficit —*see also* Deficiency
  attention and concentration R41.840
    following
      cerebral infarction I69.310
      cerebrovascular disease I69.910
        specified disease NEC I69.810
      nontraumatic
        intracerebral hemorrhage I69.110
        specified intracranial hemorrhage
          NEC I69.210
        subarachnoid hemorrhage I69.010
    disorder —*see* Attention, deficit
  cognitive
    communication R41.841
    emotional
      following
        cerebral infarction I69.315
        cerebrovascular disease I69.915
          specified disease NEC I69.815
        nontraumatic
          intracerebral hemorrhage I69.115
          specified intracranial hemorrhage
            NEC I69.215
          subarachnoid hemorrhage I69.015
      following
        cerebral infarction I69.319
        cerebrovascular disease I69.919
          specified disease NEC I69.819

▶ New   ⟱ Revised   ~~deleted~~ Deleted   ● Use Additional Character(s)

Deficit *(Continued)*
  cognitive *(Continued)*
    following *(Continued)*
      nontraumatic
        intracerebral hemorrhage I69.119
        specified intracranial hemorrhage
          NEC I69.219
        subarachnoid hemorrhage I69.019
    social
      following
        cerebral infarction I69.315
        cerebrovascular disease I69.915
          specified disease NEC I69.815
        nontraumatic
          intracerebral hemorrhage I69.115
          specified intracranial hemorrhage
            NEC I69.215
          subarachnoid hemorrhage
            I69.015
  cognitive NEC R41.89
    following
      cerebral infarction I69.318
      cerebrovascular disease I69.918
        specified disease NEC I69.818
      nontraumatic
        intracerebral hemorrhage I69.118
        specified intracranial hemorrhage
          NEC I69.218
        subarachnoid hemorrhage I69.018
  concentration R41.840
  executive function R41.844
    following
      cerebral infarction I69.314
      cerebrovascular disease I69.914
        specified disease NEC I69.814
      nontraumatic
        intracerebral hemorrhage I69.114
        specified intracranial hemorrhage
          NEC I69.214
        subarachnoid hemorrhage
          I69.014
  frontal lobe R41.844
    following
      cerebral infarction I69.314
      cerebrovascular disease I69.914
        specified disease NEC I69.814
      nontraumatic
        intracerebral hemorrhage I69.114
        specified intracranial hemorrhage
          NEC I69.214
        subarachnoid hemorrhage
          I69.014
  memory
    following
      cerebral infarction I69.311
      cerebrovascular disease I69.911
        specified disease NEC I69.811
      nontraumatic
        intracerebral hemorrhage
          I69.111
        specified intracranial hemorrhage
          NEC I69.211
        subarachnoid hemorrhage I69.011
  neurologic NEC R29.818
    ischemic
      reversible (RIND) I63.9
        prolonged (PRIND) I63.9
  oxygen R09.02
  prolonged reversible ischemic neurologic
    (PRIND) I63.9
  psychomotor R41.843
    following
      cerebral infarction I69.313
      cerebrovascular disease I69.913
        specified disease NEC I69.813
      nontraumatic
        intracerebral hemorrhage I69.113
        specified intracranial hemorrhage
          NEC I69.213
        subarachnoid hemorrhage
          I69.013

Deficit *(Continued)*
  visuospatial R41.842
    following
      cerebral infarction I69.312
      cerebrovascular disease I69.912
        specified disease NEC I69.812
      nontraumatic
        intracerebral hemorrhage I69.112
        specified intracranial hemorrhage
          NEC I69.212
        subarachnoid hemorrhage
          I69.012
Deflection
  radius —*see* Deformity, limb, specified type
    NEC, forearm
  septum (acquired) (nasal) (nose) J34.2
  spine —*see* Curvature, spine
  turbinate (nose) J34.2
Defluvium
  capillorum —*see* Alopecia
  ciliorum —*see* Madarosis
  unguium L60.8
Deformity Q89.9
  abdomen, congenital Q89.9
  abdominal wall
    acquired M95.8
    congenital Q79.59
  acquired (unspecified site) M95.9
  adrenal gland Q89.1
  alimentary tract, congenital Q45.9
    upper Q40.9
  ankle (joint) (acquired) —*see also* Deformity,
    limb, lower leg
    abduction —*see* Contraction, joint, ankle
    congenital Q68.8
    contraction —*see* Contraction, joint, ankle
    specified type NEC —*see* Deformity, limb,
      foot, specified NEC
  anus (acquired) K62.89
    congenital Q43.9
  aorta (arch) (congenital) Q25.40
    acquired I77.89
  aortic
    arch, acquired I77.89
    cusp or valve (congenital) Q23.8
      acquired —*see also* Endocarditis, aortic
        I35.8
  arm (acquired) (upper) —*see also* Deformity,
    limb, upper arm
    congenital Q68.8
    forearm —*see* Deformity, limb, forearm
  artery (congenital) (peripheral) NOS Q27.9
    acquired I77.89
    coronary (acquired) I25.9
      congenital Q24.5
    umbilical Q27.0
  atrial septal Q21.1
  auditory canal (external) (congenital) —*see*
    also Malformation, ear, external
    acquired —*see* Disorder, ear, external,
      specified type NEC
  auricle
    ear (congenital) —*see also* Malformation,
      ear, external
      acquired —*see* Disorder, pinna,
        deformity
  back —*see* Dorsopathy, deforming
  bile duct (common) (congenital) (hepatic)
    Q44.5
    acquired K83.8
  biliary duct or passage (congenital) Q44.5
    acquired K83.8
  bladder (neck) (trigone) (sphincter)
    (acquired) N32.89
    congenital Q64.79
  bone (acquired) NOS M95.9
    congenital Q79.9
    turbinate M95.0
  brain (congenital) Q04.9
    acquired G93.89
    reduction Q04.3

Deformity *(Continued)*
  breast (acquired) N64.89
    congenital Q83.9
    reconstructed N65.0
  bronchus (congenital) Q32.4
    acquired NEC J98.09
  bursa, congenital Q79.9
  canaliculi (lacrimalis) (acquired) —*see also*
    Disorder, lacrimal system, changes
    congenital Q10.6
  canthus, acquired —*see* Disorder, eyelid,
    specified type NEC
  capillary (acquired) I78.8
  cardiovascular system, congenital Q28.9
  caruncle, lacrimal (acquired) —*see also*
    Disorder, lacrimal system, changes
    congenital Q10.6
  cascade, stomach K31.2
  cecum (congenital) Q43.9
    acquired K63.89
  cerebral, acquired G93.89
    congenital Q04.9
  cervix (uterus) (acquired) NEC N88.8
    congenital Q51.9
  cheek (acquired) M95.2
    congenital Q18.9
  chest (acquired) (wall) M95.4
    congenital Q67.8
    sequelae (late effect) of rickets E64.3
  chin (acquired) M95.2
    congenital Q18.9
  choroid (congenital) Q14.3
    acquired H31.8
    plexus Q07.8
    ⇒acquired G96.198
  cicatricial —*see* Cicatrix
  cilia, acquired —*see* Disorder, eyelid,
    specified type NEC
  clavicle (acquired) M95.8
    congenital Q68.8
  clitoris (congenital) Q52.6
    acquired N90.89
  clubfoot —*see* Clubfoot
  coccyx (acquired) —*see* subcategory
    M43.8
  colon (congenital) Q43.9
    acquired K63.89
  concha (ear), congenital —*see also*
    Malformation, ear, external
    acquired —*see* Disorder, pinna, deformity
  cornea (acquired) H18.70
    congenital Q13.4
    descemetocele —*see* Descemetocele
    ectasia —*see* Ectasia, cornea
    specified NEC H18.79-●
    staphyloma —*see* Staphyloma, cornea
  coronary artery (acquired) I25.9
    congenital Q24.5
  cranium (acquired) —*see* Deformity, skull
  cricoid cartilage (congenital) Q31.8
    acquired J38.7
  cystic duct (congenital) Q44.5
    acquired K82.8
  Dandy-Walker Q03.1
    with spina bifida —*see* Spina bifida
  diaphragm (congenital) Q79.1
    acquired J98.6
  digestive organ NOS Q45.9
  ductus arteriosus Q25.0
  duodenal bulb K31.89
  duodenum (congenital) Q43.9
    acquired K31.89
  dura —*see* Deformity, meninges
  ear (acquired) —*see also* Disorder, pinna,
    deformity
    congenital (external) Q17.9
      internal Q16.5
      middle Q16.4
        ossicles Q16.3
      ossicles Q16.3
  ectodermal (congenital) NEC Q84.9

Deformity (Continued)

ejaculatory duct (congenital) Q55.4
  acquired N50.89
elbow (joint) (acquired) —see also Deformity, limb, upper arm
  congenital Q68.8
  contraction —see Contraction, joint, elbow
endocrine gland NEC Q89.2
epididymis (congenital) Q55.4
  acquired N50.89
epiglottis (congenital) Q31.8
  acquired J38.7
esophagus (congenital) Q39.9
  acquired K22.8
eustachian tube (congenital) NEC Q17.8
eye, congenital Q15.9
eyebrow (congenital) Q18.8
eyelid (acquired) —see also Disorder, eyelid, specified type NEC
  congenital Q10.3
face (acquired) M95.2
  congenital Q18.9
fallopian tube, acquired N83.8
femur (acquired) —see Deformity, limb, specified type NEC, thigh
fetal
  with fetopelvic disproportion O33.7
    causing obstructed labor O66.3
finger (acquired) M20.00-●
  boutonniere M20.02-●
  congenital Q68.1
  flexion contracture —see Contraction, joint, hand
  mallet finger M20.01-●
  specified NEC M20.09-●
  swan-neck M20.03-●
flexion (joint) (acquired) —see also Deformity, limb, flexion M21.20
  congenital NOS Q74.9
  hip Q65.89
foot (acquired) —see also Deformity, limb, lower leg
  cavovarus (congenital) Q66.1-●
  congenital NOS Q66.9-●
    specified type NEC Q66.89
  specified type NEC —see Deformity, limb, foot, specified NEC
  valgus (congenital) Q66.6
    acquired —see Deformity, valgus, ankle
  varus (congenital) NEC Q66.3-●
    acquired —see Deformity, varus, ankle
forearm (acquired) —see also Deformity, limb, forearm
  congenital Q68.8
forehead (acquired) M95.2
  congenital Q75.8
frontal bone (acquired) M95.2
  congenital Q75.8
gallbladder (congenital) Q44.1
  acquired K82.8
gastrointestinal tract (congenital) NOS Q45.9
  acquired K63.89
genitalia, genital organ(s) or system NEC
  female (congenital) Q52.9
    acquired N94.89
    external Q52.70
  male (congenital) Q55.9
    acquired N50.89
globe (eye) (congenital) Q15.8
  acquired H44.89
gum, acquired NEC K06.8
hand (acquired) —see Deformity, limb, hand
  congenital Q68.1
head (acquired) M95.2
  congenital Q75.8
heart (congenital) Q24.9
  septum Q21.9
    auricular Q21.1
    ventricular Q21.0
  valve (congenital) NEC Q24.8
    acquired —see Endocarditis

Deformity (Continued)

heel (acquired) —see Deformity, foot
hepatic duct (congenital) Q44.5
  acquired K83.8
hip (joint) (acquired) —see also Deformity, limb, thigh
  congenital Q65.9
  due to (previous) juvenile osteochondrosis —see Coxa, plana
  flexion —see Contraction, joint, hip
hourglass —see Contraction, hourglass
humerus (acquired) M21.82-●
  congenital Q74.0
hypophyseal (congenital) Q89.2
ileocecal (coil) (valve) (acquired) K63.89
  congenital Q43.9
ileum (congenital) Q43.9
  acquired K63.89
ilium (acquired) M95.5
  congenital Q74.2
integument (congenital) Q84.9
intervertebral cartilage or disc (acquired) — see Disorder, disc, specified NEC
intestine (large) (small) (congenital) NOS Q43.9
  acquired K63.89
intrinsic minus or plus (hand) —see Deformity, limb, specified type NEC, forearm
iris (acquired) H21.89
  congenital Q13.2
ischium (acquired) M95.5
  congenital Q74.2
jaw (acquired) (congenital) M26.9
joint (acquired) NEC M21.90
  congenital Q68.8
  elbow M21.92-●
  hand M21.94-●
  hip M21.95-●
  knee M21.96-●
  shoulder M21.92-●
  wrist M21.93-●
kidney(s) (calyx) (pelvis) (congenital) Q63.9
  acquired N28.89
  artery (congenital) Q27.2
    acquired I77.89
Klippel-Feil (brevicollis) Q76.1
knee (acquired) NEC —see also Deformity, limb, lower leg
  congenital Q68.2
labium (majus) (minus) (congenital) Q52.79
  acquired N90.89
lacrimal passages or duct (congenital) NEC Q10.6
  acquired —see Disorder, lacrimal system, changes
larynx (muscle) (congenital) Q31.8
  acquired J38.7
  web (glottic) Q31.0
leg (upper) (acquired) NEC —see also Deformity, limb, thigh
  congenital Q68.8
  lower leg —see Deformity, limb, lower leg
lens (acquired) H27.8
  congenital Q12.9
lid (fold) (acquired) —see also Disorder, eyelid, specified type NEC
  congenital Q10.3
ligament (acquired) —see Disorder, ligament
  congenital Q79.9
limb (acquired) M21.90
  clawfoot M21.53-●
  clawhand M21.51-●
  clubfoot M21.54-●
  clubhand M21.52-●
  congenital, except reduction deformity Q74.9
  flat foot M21.4-●
  flexion M21.20
    ankle M21.27-●
    elbow M21.22-●

Deformity (Continued)

limb (Continued)
  flexion (Continued)
    finger M21.24-●
    hip M21.25-●
    knee M21.26-●
    shoulder M21.21-●
    toe M21.27-●
    wrist M21.23-●
  foot
    claw —see Deformity, limb, clawfoot
    club —see Deformity, limb, clubfoot
    drop M21.37-●
    flat —see Deformity, limb, flat foot
    specified NEC M21.6X-●
  forearm M21.93-●
  hand M21.94-●
  lower leg M21.96-●
  specified type NEC M21.80
    forearm M21.83-●
    lower leg M21.86-●
    thigh M21.85-●
    upper arm M21.82-●
  thigh M21.95-●
  unequal length M21.70
    short site is
      femur M21.75-●
      fibula M21.76-●
      humerus M21.72-●
      radius M21.73-●
      tibia M21.76-●
      ulna M21.73-●
  upper arm M21.92-●
  valgus —see Deformity, valgus
  varus —see Deformity, varus
  wrist drop M21.33-●
lip (acquired) NEC K13.0
  congenital Q38.0
liver (congenital) Q44.7
  acquired K76.89
lumbosacral (congenital) (joint) (region) Q76.49
  acquired —see subcategory M43.8
  kyphosis —see Kyphosis, congenital
  lordosis —see Lordosis, congenital
lung (congenital) Q33.9
  acquired J98.4
lymphatic system, congenital Q89.9
Madelung's (radius) Q74.0
mandible (acquired) (congenital) M26.9
maxilla (acquired) (congenital) M26.9
meninges or membrane (congenital) Q07.9
  cerebral Q04.8
    ➡acquired G96.198
  ➡spinal cord (congenital) G96.198
    ➡acquired G96.198
metacarpus (acquired) —see Deformity, limb, forearm
  congenital Q74.0
metatarsus (acquired) —see Deformity, foot
  congenital Q66.9-●
middle ear (congenital) Q16.4
  ossicles Q16.3
mitral (leaflets) (valve) I05.8
  parachute Q23.2
  stenosis, congenital Q23.2
mouth (acquired) K13.79
  congenital Q38.6
multiple, congenital NEC Q89.7
muscle (acquired) M62.89
  congenital Q79.9
    sternocleidomastoid Q68.0
musculoskeletal system (acquired) M95.9
  congenital Q79.9
  specified NEC M95.8
nail (acquired) L60.8
  congenital Q84.6
nasal —see Deformity, nose
neck (acquired) M95.3
  congenital Q18.9
    sternocleidomastoid Q68.0

▶ New   ➡ Revised   ~~deleted~~ Deleted   ● Use Additional Character(s)

Deformity *(Continued)*
  nervous system (congenital) Q07.9
  nipple (congenital) Q83.9
    acquired N64.89
  nose (acquired) (cartilage) M95.0
    bone (turbinate) M95.0
    congenital Q30.9
      bent or squashed Q67.4
    saddle M95.0
      syphilitic A50.57
    septum (acquired) J34.2
      congenital Q30.8
    sinus (wall) (congenital) Q30.8
      acquired M95.0
    syphilitic (congenital) A50.57
      late A52.73
  ocular muscle (congenital) Q10.3
    acquired —*see* Strabismus, mechanical
  opticociliary vessels (congenital) Q13.2
  orbit (eye) (acquired) H05.30
    atrophy —*see* Atrophy, orbit
    congenital Q10.7
    due to
      bone disease NEC H05.32-●
      trauma or surgery H05.33-●
    enlargement —*see* Enlargement, orbit
    exostosis —*see* Exostosis, orbit
  organ of Corti (congenital) Q16.5
  ovary (congenital) Q50.39
    acquired N83.8
  oviduct, acquired N83.8
  palate (congenital) Q38.5
    acquired M27.8
    cleft (congenital) —*see* Cleft, palate
  pancreas (congenital) Q45.3
    acquired K86.89
  parathyroid (gland) Q89.2
  parotid (gland) (congenital) Q38.4
    acquired K11.8
  patella (acquired) —*see* Disorder, patella,
      specified NEC
  pelvis, pelvic (acquired) (bony) M95.5
    with disproportion (fetopelvic) O33.0
      causing obstructed labor O65.0
    congenital Q74.2
    rachitic sequelae (late effect) E64.3
  penis (glans) (congenital) Q55.69
    acquired N48.89
  pericardium (congenital) Q24.8
    acquired —*see* Pericarditis
  pharynx (congenital) Q38.8
    acquired J39.2
  pinna, acquired —*see also* Disorder, pinna,
      deformity
    congenital Q17.9
  pituitary (congenital) Q89.2
  posture —*see* Dorsopathy, deforming
  prepuce (congenital) Q55.69
    acquired N47.8
  prostate (congenital) Q55.4
    acquired N42.89
  pupil (congenital) Q13.2
    acquired —*see* Abnormality, pupillary
  pylorus (congenital) Q40.3
    acquired K31.89
  rachitic (acquired), old or healed E64.3
  radius (acquired) —*see also* Deformity, limb,
      forearm
    congenital Q68.8
  rectum (congenital) Q43.9
    acquired K62.89
  reduction (extremity) (limb), congenital (*see
      also* condition and site) Q73.8
    brain Q04.3
    lower —*see* Defect, reduction, lower limb
    upper —*see* Defect, reduction, upper limb
  renal —*see* Deformity, kidney
  respiratory system (congenital) Q34.9
  rib (acquired) M95.4
    congenital Q76.6
      cervical Q76.5

Deformity *(Continued)*
  rotation (joint) (acquired) —*see* Deformity,
      limb, specified site NEC
    congenital Q74.9
    hip —*see* Deformity, limb, specified type
        NEC, thigh
      congenital Q65.89
  sacroiliac joint (congenital) Q74.2
    acquired —*see* subcategory M43.8
  sacrum (acquired) —*see* subcategory M43.8
  saddle
    back —*see* Lordosis
    nose M95.0
      syphilitic A50.57
  salivary gland or duct (congenital) Q38.4
    acquired K11.8
  scapula (acquired) M95.8
    congenital Q68.8
  scrotum (congenital) —*see also* Malformation,
      testis and scrotum
    acquired N50.89
  seminal vesicles (congenital) Q55.4
    acquired N50.89
  septum, nasal (acquired) J34.2
  shoulder (joint) (acquired) —*see* Deformity,
      limb, upper arm
    congenital Q74.0
    contraction —*see* Contraction, joint,
        shoulder
  sigmoid (flexure) (congenital) Q43.9
    acquired K63.89
  skin (congenital) Q82.9
  skull (acquired) M95.2
    congenital Q75.8
      with
        anencephaly Q00.0
        encephalocele —*see* Encephalocele
        hydrocephalus Q03.9
          with spina bifida —*see* Spina bifida,
              by site, with hydrocephalus
        microcephaly Q02
  soft parts, organs or tissues (of pelvis)
    in pregnancy or childbirth NEC O34.8-●
      causing obstructed labor O65.5
  spermatic cord (congenital) Q55.4
    acquired N50.89
    torsion —*see* Torsion, spermatic cord
  spinal —*see* Dorsopathy, deforming
    column (acquired) —*see* Dorsopathy,
        deforming
    congenital Q67.5
    cord (congenital) Q06.9
      acquired G95.89
    nerve root (congenital) Q07.9
  spine (acquired) —*see also* Dorsopathy,
      deforming
    congenital Q67.5
    rachitic E64.3
    specified NEC —*see* Dorsopathy,
        deforming, specified NEC
  spleen
    acquired D73.89
    congenital Q89.09
  Sprengel's (congenital) Q74.0
  sternocleidomastoid (muscle), congenital
      Q68.0
  sternum (acquired) M95.4
    congenital NEC Q76.7
  stomach (congenital) Q40.3
    acquired K31.89
  submandibular gland (congenital) Q38.4
  submaxillary gland (congenital) Q38.4
    acquired K11.8
  talipes —*see* Talipes
  testis (congenital) —*see also* Malformation,
      testis and scrotum
    acquired N44.8
    torsion —*see* Torsion, testis
  thigh (acquired) —*see also* Deformity, limb,
      thigh
    congenital NEC Q68.8

Deformity *(Continued)*
  thorax (acquired) (wall) M95.4
    congenital Q67.8
    sequelae of rickets E64.3
  thumb (acquired) —*see also* Deformity, finger
    congenital NEC Q68.1
  thymus (tissue) (congenital) Q89.2
  thyroid (gland) (congenital) Q89.2
    cartilage Q31.8
    acquired J38.7
  tibia (acquired) —*see also* Deformity, limb,
      specified type NEC, lower leg
    congenital NEC Q68.8
    saber (syphilitic) A50.56
  toe (acquired) M20.6-●
    congenital Q66.9-●
    hallux rigidus M20.2-●
    hallux valgus M20.1-●
    hallux varus M20.3-●
    hammer toe M20.4-●
    specified NEC M20.5X-●
  tongue (congenital) Q38.3
    acquired K14.8
  tooth, teeth K00.2
  trachea (rings) (congenital) Q32.1
    acquired J39.8
  transverse aortic arch (congenital)
      Q25.49
  tricuspid (leaflets) (valve) I07.8
    atresia or stenosis Q22.4
    Ebstein's Q22.5
  trunk (acquired) M95.8
    congenital Q89.9
  ulna (acquired) —*see also* Deformity, limb,
      forearm
    congenital NEC Q68.8
  urachus, congenital Q64.4
  ureter (opening) (congenital) Q62.8
    acquired N28.89
  urethra (congenital) Q64.79
    acquired N36.8
  urinary tract (congenital) Q64.9
    urachus Q64.4
  uterus (congenital) Q51.9
    acquired N85.8
  uvula (congenital) Q38.5
  vagina (acquired) N89.8
    congenital Q52.4
  valgus NEC M21.00
    ankle M21.07-●
    elbow M21.02-●
    hip M21.05-●
    knee M21.06-●
  valve, valvular (congenital) (heart) Q24.8
    acquired —*see* Endocarditis
  varus NEC M21.10
    ankle M21.17-●
    elbow M21.12-●
    hip M21.15
    knee M21.16-●
    tibia —*see* Osteochondrosis, juvenile, tibia
  vas deferens (congenital) Q55.4
    acquired N50.89
  vein (congenital) Q27.9
    great Q26.9
  vertebra —*see* Dorsopathy, deforming
  vertical talus (congenital) Q66.80
    left foot Q66.82
    right foot Q66.81
  vesicourethral orifice (acquired) N32.89
    congenital NEC Q64.79
  vessels of optic papilla (congenital) Q14.2
  visual field (contraction) —*see* Defect, visual
      field
  vitreous body, acquired H43.89
  vulva (congenital) Q52.79
    acquired N90.89
  wrist (joint) (acquired) —*see also* Deformity,
      limb, forearm
    congenital Q68.8
    contraction —*see* Contraction, joint, wrist

Degeneration, degenerative
adrenal (capsule) (fatty) (gland) (hyaline)
  (infectional) E27.8
amyloid —see also Amyloidosis E85.9
anterior cornua, spinal cord G12.29
anterior labral S43.49-●
aorta, aortic I70.0
  fatty I77.89
aortic valve (heart) —see Endocarditis,
  aortic
arteriovascular —see Arteriosclerosis
artery, arterial (atheromatous) (calcareous) —
  see also Arteriosclerosis
  cerebral, amyloid E85.4 [I68.0]
  medial —see Arteriosclerosis, extremities
articular cartilage NEC —see Derangement,
  joint, articular cartilage, by site
atheromatous —see Arteriosclerosis
basal nuclei or ganglia G23.9
  specified NEC G23.8
bone NEC —see Disorder, bone, specified
  type NEC
brachial plexus G54.0
brain (cortical) (progressive) G31.9
  alcoholic G31.2
  arteriosclerotic I67.2
  childhood G31.9
    specified NEC G31.89
  cystic G31.89
    congenital Q04.6
  in
    alcoholism G31.2
    beriberi E51.2
    cerebrovascular disease I67.9
    congenital hydrocephalus Q03.9
      with spina bifida —see also Spina
        bifida
    Fabry-Anderson disease E75.21
    Gaucher's disease E75.22
    Hunter's syndrome E76.1
    lipidosis
      cerebral E75.4
      generalized E75.6
    mucopolysaccharidosis —see
      Mucopolysaccharidosis
    myxedema E03.9 [G32.89]
    neoplastic disease —see also Neoplasm
      D49.6 [G32.89]
    Niemann-Pick disease E75.249 [G32.89]
    sphingolipidosis E75.3 [G32.89]
    vitamin B12 deficiency E53.8 [G32.89]
  senile NEC G31.1
breast N64.89
Bruch's membrane —see Degeneration,
  choroid
capillaries (fatty) I78.8
  amyloid E85.89 [I79.8]
cardiac —see also Degeneration, myocardial
  valve, valvular —see Endocarditis
cardiorenal —see Hypertension, cardiorenal
cardiovascular —see also Disease,
  cardiovascular
  renal —see Hypertension, cardiorenal
cerebellar NOS G31.9
  alcoholic G31.2
  primary (hereditary) (sporadic) G11.9
cerebral —see Degeneration, brain
cerebrovascular I67.9
  due to hypertension I67.4
cervical plexus G54.2
cervix N88.8
  due to radiation (intended effect) N88.8
    adverse effect or misadventure N99.89
chamber angle H21.21-●
changes, spine or vertebra —see Spondylosis
chorioretinal —see also Degeneration, choroid
  hereditary H31.20
choroid (colloid) (drusen) H31.10-●
  atrophy —see Atrophy, choroidal
  hereditary —see Dystrophy, choroidal,
    hereditary

Degeneration, degenerative *(Continued)*
ciliary body H21.22-●
cochlear —see subcategory H83.8
combined (spinal cord) (subacute) E53.8
  [G32.0]
  with anemia (pernicious) D51.0 [G32.0]
    due to dietary vitamin B12 deficiency
      D51.3 [G32.0]
  in (due to)
    vitamin B12 deficiency E53.8 [G32.0]
    anemia D51.9 [G32.0]
conjunctiva H11.10
  concretions —see Concretion, conjunctiva
  deposits —see Deposit, conjunctiva
  pigmentations —see Pigmentation,
    conjunctiva
  pinguecula —see Pinguecula
  xerosis —see Xerosis, conjunctiva
cornea H18.40
  calcerous H18.43
    band keratopathy H18.42-●
  familial, hereditary —see Dystrophy, cornea
  hyaline (of old scars) H18.49
  keratomalacia —see Keratomalacia
  nodular H18.45-●
  peripheral H18.46-●
  senile H18.41-●
  specified type NEC H18.49
cortical (cerebellar) (parenchymatous) G31.89
  alcoholic G31.2
  diffuse, due to arteriopathy I67.2
corticobasal G31.85
cutis L98.8
  amyloid E85.4 [L99]
dental pulp K04.2
disc disease —see Degeneration,
  intervertebral disc NEC
dorsolateral (spinal cord) —see Degeneration,
  combined
extrapyramidal G25.9
eye, macular —see also Degeneration, macula
  congenital or hereditary —see Dystrophy,
    retina
facet joints —see Spondylosis
fatty
  liver NEC K76.0
    alcoholic K70.0
grey matter (brain) (Alpers') G31.81
heart —see also Degeneration, myocardial
  amyloid E85.4 [I43]
  atheromatous —see Disease, heart,
    ischemic, atherosclerotic
  ischemic —see Disease, heart, ischemic
hepatolenticular (Wilson's) E83.01
hepatorenal K76.7
hyaline (diffuse) (generalized)
  localized —see Degeneration, by site
infrapatellar fat pad M79.4
intervertebral disc NOS
  with
    myelopathy —see Disorder, disc, with,
      myelopathy
    radiculitis or radiculopathy —see
      Disorder, disc, with, radiculopathy
  cervical, cervicothoracic —see Disorder,
    disc, cervical, degeneration
    with
      myelopathy —see Disorder, disc,
        cervical, with myelopathy
      neuritis, radiculitis or
        radiculopathy —see Disorder,
        disc, cervical, with neuritis
  lumbar region M51.36
    with
      myelopathy M51.06
      neuritis, radiculitis, radiculopathy or
        sciatica M51.16
  lumbosacral region M51.37
    with
      neuritis, radiculitis, radiculopathy or
        sciatica M51.17

Degeneration, degenerative *(Continued)*
intervertebral disc *(Continued)*
  sacrococcygeal region M53.3
  thoracic region M51.34
    with
      myelopathy M51.04
      neuritis, radiculitis, radiculopathy
        M51.14
  thoracolumbar region M51.35
    with
      myelopathy M51.05
      neuritis, radiculitis, radiculopathy
        M51.15
intestine, amyloid E85.4
iris (pigmentary) H21.23-●
ischemic —see Ischemia
joint disease —see Osteoarthritis
kidney N28.89
  amyloid E85.4 [N29]
  cystic, congenital Q61.9
  fatty N28.89
  polycystic Q61.3
    adult type (autosomal dominant)
      Q61.2
    infantile type (autosomal recessive) NEC
      Q61.19
      collecting duct dilatation Q61.11
Kuhnt-Junius —see also Degeneration, macula
  H35.32-●
lens —see Cataract
lenticular (familial) (progressive) (Wilson's)
  (with cirrhosis of liver) E83.01
liver (diffuse) NEC K76.89
  amyloid E85.4 [K77]
  cystic K76.89
    congenital Q44.6
  fatty NEC K76.0
    alcoholic K70.0
  hypertrophic K76.89
  parenchymatous, acute or subacute K72.00
    with coma K72.01
  pigmentary K76.89
  toxic (acute) K71.9
lung J98.4
lymph gland I89.8
  hyaline I89.8
macula, macular (acquired) (age-related)
  (senile) H35.30
  angioid streaks H35.33
  atrophic age-related H35.31-●
  congenital or hereditary —see Dystrophy,
    retina
  cystoid H35.35-●
  drusen H35.36-●
  dry age-related H35.31-●
  exudative H35.32-●
  hole H35.34-●
  nonexudative H35.31-●
  puckering H35.37-●
  toxic H35.38-●
  wet age-related H35.32-●
membranous labyrinth, congenital (causing
  impairment of hearing) Q16.5
meniscus —see Derangement, meniscus
mitral —see Insufficiency, mitral
Mönckeberg's —see Arteriosclerosis,
  extremities
motor centers, senile G31.1
multi-system G90.3
mural —see Degeneration, myocardial
muscle (fatty) (fibrous) (hyaline)
  (progressive) M62.89
  heart —see Degeneration, myocardial
myelin, central nervous system G37.9
myocardial, myocardium (fatty) (hyaline)
  (senile) I51.5
  with rheumatic fever (conditions in I00)
    I09.0
    active, acute or subacute I01.2
      with chorea I02.0
    inactive or quiescent (with chorea) I09.0

▶ New   ⟹ Revised   ~~deleted~~ Deleted   ● Use Additional Character(s)

Degeneration, degenerative *(Continued)*
  myocardial, myocardium *(Continued)*
    hypertensive —*see* Hypertension, heart
    rheumatic —*see* Degeneration, myocardial,
        with rheumatic fever
    syphilitic A52.06
  nasal sinus (mucosa) J32.9
    frontal J32.1
    maxillary J32.0
  nerve —*see* Disorder, nerve
  nervous system G31.9
    alcoholic G31.2
    amyloid E85.4 *[G99.8]*
    autonomic G90.9
    fatty G31.89
    specified NEC G31.89
  nipple N64.89
  olivopontocerebellar (hereditary) (familial)
      G23.8
  osseous labyrinth —*see* subcategory H83.8
  ovary N83.8
    cystic N83.20-●
    microcystic N83.20-●
  pallidal pigmentary (progressive) G23.0
  pancreas K86.89
    tuberculous A18.83
  penis N48.89
  pigmentary (diffuse) (general)
    localized —*see* Degeneration, by site
    pallidal (progressive) G23.0
  pineal gland E34.8
  pituitary (gland) E23.6
  popliteal fat pad M79.4
  posterolateral (spinal cord) —*see*
      Degeneration, combined
  pulmonary valve (heart) I37.8
  pulp (tooth) K04.2
  pupillary margin H21.24-●
  renal —*see* Degeneration, kidney
  retina H35.9
    hereditary (cerebroretinal) (congenital)
        (juvenile) (macula) (peripheral)
        (pigmentary) —*see* Dystrophy, retina
    Kuhnt-Junius —*see also* Degeneration,
        macula H35.32-●
    macula (cystic) (exudative) (hole)
        (nonexudative) (pseudohole) (senile)
        (toxic) —*see* Degeneration, macula
    peripheral H35.40
      lattice H35.41-●
      microcystoid H35.42-●
      paving stone H35.43-●
      secondary
        pigmentary H35.45-●
        vitreoretinal H35.46-●
      senile reticular H35.44-●
    pigmentary (primary) —*see also* Dystrophy,
        retina
      secondary —*see* Degeneration, retina,
          peripheral, secondary
    posterior pole —*see* Degeneration, macula
  saccule, congenital (causing impairment of
      hearing) Q16.5
  senile R54
    brain G31.1
    cardiac, heart or myocardium —*see*
        Degeneration, myocardial
    motor centers G31.1
    vascular —*see* Arteriosclerosis
  sinus (cystic) —*see also* Sinusitis
    polypoid J33.1
  skin L98.8
    amyloid E85.4 *[L99]*
    colloid L98.8
  spinal (cord) G31.89
    amyloid E85.4 *[G32.89]*
    combined (subacute) —*see* Degeneration,
        combined
    dorsolateral —*see* Degeneration, combined
    familial NEC G31.89
    fatty G31.89

Degeneration, degenerative *(Continued)*
  spinal *(Continued)*
    funicular —*see* Degeneration, combined
    posterolateral —*see* Degeneration,
        combined
    subacute combined —*see* Degeneration,
        combined
    tuberculous A17.81
  spleen D73.0
    amyloid E85.4 *[D77]*
  stomach K31.89
  striatonigral G23.2
  suprarenal (capsule) (gland) E27.8
  synovial membrane (pulpy) —*see* Disorder,
      synovium, specified type NEC
  tapetoretinal —*see* Dystrophy, retina
  thymus (gland) E32.8
    fatty E32.8
  thyroid (gland) E07.89
  tricuspid (heart) (valve) I07.9
  tuberculous NEC —*see* Tuberculosis
  turbinate J34.89
  uterus (cystic) N85.8
  vascular (senile) —*see* Arteriosclerosis
    hypertensive —*see* Hypertension
  vitreoretinal, secondary —*see* Degeneration,
      retina, peripheral, secondary, vitreoretinal
  vitreous (body) H43.81-●
  Wallerian —*see* Disorder, nerve
  Wilson's hepatolenticular E83.01
Deglutition
  paralysis R13.0
    hysterical F44.4
  pneumonia J69.0
Degos' disease I77.89
Dehiscence (of)
  amputation stump T87.81
  cesarean wound O90.0
  closure of
    cornea T81.31
    craniotomy T81.32
    fascia (muscular) (superficial) T81.32
    internal organ or tissue T81.32
    laceration (external) (internal) T81.33
    ligament T81.32
    mucosa T81.31
    muscle or muscle flap T81.32
    ribs or rib cage T81.32
    skin and subcutaneous tissue (full-
        thickness) (superficial) T81.31
    skull T81.32
    sternum (sternotomy) T81.32
    tendon T81.32
    traumatic laceration (external) (internal)
        T81.33
  episiotomy O90.1
  operation wound NEC T81.31
    external operation wound (superficial)
        T81.31
    internal operation wound (deep)
        T81.32
  perineal wound (postpartum) O90.1
  traumatic injury wound repair T81.33
  wound T81.30
    traumatic repair T81.33
Dehydration E86.0
  newborn P74.1
Déjérine-Roussy syndrome G93.89
Déjérine-Sottas disease or neuropathy
    (hypertrophic) G60.0
Déjérine-Thomas atrophy G23.8
Delay, delayed
  any plane in pelvis
    complicating delivery O66.9
  birth or delivery NOS O63.9
  closure, ductus arteriosus (Botalli) P29.38
  coagulation —*see* Defect, coagulation
  conduction (cardiac) (ventricular)
      I45.9
  delivery, second twin, triplet, etc
      O63.2

Delay, delayed *(Continued)*
  development R62.50
    global F88
    intellectual (specific) F81.9
    language F80.9
      due to hearing loss F80.4
    learning F81.9
    pervasive F84.9
    physiological R62.50
      specified stage NEC R62.0
    reading F81.0
    sexual E30.0
    speech F80.9
      due to hearing loss F80.4
    spelling F81.81
  ejaculation F52.32
  gastric emptying K30
  menarche E30.0
  menstruation (cause unknown) N91.0
  milestone R62.0
  passage of meconium (newborn)
      P76.0
  primary respiration P28.9
  puberty (constitutional) E30.0
  separation of umbilical cord P96.82
  sexual maturation, female E30.0
  sleep phase syndrome G47.21
  union, fracture —*see* Fracture, by site
  vaccination Z28.9
Deletion(s)
  autosome Q93.9
    identified by fluorescence in situ
        hybridization (FISH) Q93.89
    identified by in situ hybridization (ISH)
        Q93.89
  chromosome
    with complex rearrangements NEC
        Q93.7
    part of NEC Q93.59
    seen only at prometaphase Q93.89
    short arm
      4 Q93.3
      5p Q93.4
      22q11.2 Q93.81
    specified NEC Q93.89
  long arm chromosome 18 or 21 Q93.89
    with complex rearrangements NEC Q93.7
  microdeletions NEC Q93.88
Delhi boil or button B55.1
Delinquency (juvenile) (neurotic) F91.8
  group Z72.810
Delinquent immunization status Z28.3
Delirious (acute or subacute) (not alcohol or
    drug-induced) (with dementia) R41.0
  alcoholic (acute) (tremens) (withdrawal)
      F10.921
    with intoxication F10.921
      in
        abuse F10.121
        dependence F10.221
  due to (secondary to)
    alcohol
      intoxication F10.921
        in
          abuse F10.121
          dependence F10.221
      withdrawal F10.231
    amphetamine intoxication F15.921
      in
        abuse F15.121
        dependence F15.221
    anxiolytic
      intoxication F13.921
        in
          abuse F13.121
          dependence F13.221
      withdrawal F13.231
    cannabis intoxication (acute) F12.921
      in
        abuse F12.121
        dependence F12.221

Delirious *(Continued)*
 due to *(Continued)*
  cocaine intoxication (acute) F14.921
   in
    abuse F14.121
    dependence F14.221
  general medical condition F05
  hallucinogen intoxication F16.921
   in
    abuse F16.121
    dependence F16.221
  hypnotic
   intoxication F13.921
    in
     abuse F13.121
     dependence F13.221
   withdrawal F13.231
  inhalant intoxication (acute) F18.921
   in
    abuse F18.121
    dependence F18.221
  multiple etiologies F05
  opioid intoxication (acute) F11.921
   in
    abuse F11.121
    dependence F11.221
  other (or unknown) substance
    F19.921
  phencyclidine intoxication (acute)
    F16.921
   in
    abuse F16.121
    dependence F16.221
  psychoactive substance NEC intoxication
    (acute) F19.921
   in
    abuse F19.121
    dependence F19.221
  sedative
   intoxication F13.921
    in
     abuse F13.121
     dependence F13.221
   withdrawal F13.231
  unknown etiology R41.0
 exhaustion F43.0
 hysterical F44.89
 postprocedural (postoperative) F05
 puerperal F05
 thyroid —*see* Thyrotoxicosis with thyroid
   storm
 traumatic —*see* Injury, intracranial
 tremens (alcohol-induced) F10.231
  sedative-induced F13.231
Delivery (childbirth) (labor)
 arrested active phase O62.1
 cesarean (for)
  without indication O82
  abnormal
   pelvis (bony) (deformity) (major) NEC
     with disproportion (fetopelvic)
      O33.0
     with obstructed labor O65.0
    presentation or position O32.9
  abruptio placentae —*see also* Abruptio
    placentae Ø45.9-●
  acromion presentation O32.2
  atony, uterus O62.2
  breech presentation O32.1
   incomplete O32.8
  brow presentation O32.3
  cephalopelvic disproportion O33.9
  cerclage O34.3-●
  chin presentation O32.3
  cicatrix of cervix O34.4-●
  contracted pelvis (general)
   inlet O33.2
   outlet O33.3
  cord presentation or prolapse
    O69.0
  cystocele O34.8-●

Delivery *(Continued)*
 cesarean *(Continued)*
  deformity (acquired) (congenital)
   pelvic organs or tissues NEC O34.8-●
   pelvis (bony) NEC O33.0
  disproportion NOS O33.9
  eclampsia —*see* Eclampsia
  face presentation O32.3
  failed
   forceps O66.5
   induction of labor O61.9
    instrumental O61.1
    mechanical O61.1
    medical O61.0
    specified NEC O61.8
    surgical O61.1
   trial of labor NOS O66.40
    following previous cesarean delivery
      O66.41
   vacuum extraction O66.5
   ventouse O66.5
  fetal-maternal hemorrhage O43.01-●
  hemorrhage (intrapartum) O67.9
   with coagulation defect O67.0
   specified cause NEC O67.8
  high head at term O32.4
  hydrocephalic fetus O33.6
  incarceration of uterus O34.51-●
  incoordinate uterine action O62.4
  increased size, fetus O33.5
  inertia, uterus O62.2
   primary O62.0
   secondary O62.1
  ►isthmocele O34.22
  lateroversion, uterus O34.59-●
  mal lie O32.9
  malposition
   fetus O32.9
   pelvic organs or tissues NEC O34.8-●
   uterus NEC O34.59-●
  malpresentation NOS O32.9
  oblique presentation O32.2
  occurring after 37 completed weeks of
    gestation but before 39 completed
    weeks gestation due to (spontaneous)
    onset of labor O75.82
  oversize fetus O33.5
  pelvic tumor NEC O34.8-●
  placenta previa O44.0-●
   complete O44.0-●
    with hemorrhage O44.1-●
  placental insufficiency O36.51-●
  planned, occurring after 37 completed
    weeks of gestation but before 39
    completed weeks gestation due to
    (spontaneous) onset of labor O75.82
  polyp, cervix O34.4-●
   causing obstructed labor O65.5
  poor dilatation, cervix O62.0
  pre-eclampsia O14.94
   mild O14.04
   moderate O14.04
   severe O14.14
    with hemolysis, elevated liver
      enzymes and low platelet count
      (HELLP) O14.24
  previous
   cesarean delivery O34.219
    classical (vertical) scar O34.212
    ►isthmocele O34.22
    low transverse scar O34.211
   ►mid-transverse T incision O34.218
   ►scar
    ►defect (isthmocele) O34.22
    ►specified type NEC O34.218
   surgery (to)
    cervix O34.4-●
    gynecological NEC O34.8-●
    rectum O34.7-●
    uterus O34.29
    vagina O34.6-●

Delivery *(Continued)*
 cesarean *(Continued)*
  prolapse
   arm or hand O32.2
   uterus O34.52-●
  prolonged labor NOS O63.9
  rectocele O34.8-●
  retroversion
   uterus O34.53-●
  rigid
   cervix O34.4-●
   pelvic floor O34.8-●
   perineum O34.7-●
   vagina O34.6-●
   vulva O34.7-●
  sacculation, pregnant uterus O34.59-●
  scar(s)
   cervix O34.4-●
   cesarean delivery O34.219
    classical (vertical) O34.212
    ►isthmocele O34.22
    low transverse O34.211
   ►mid-transverse T incision O34.218
   ►scar
    ►defect (isthmocele) O34.22
    ►specified type NEC O34.218
  ►defect (isthmocele) O34.22
  transmural uterine O34.29
  uterus O34.29
  Shirodkar suture in situ O34.3-●
  shoulder presentation O32.2
  stenosis or stricture, cervix O34.4-●
  streptococcus group B (GBS) carrier state
    O99.824
  transmural uterine scar O34.29
  transverse presentation or lie O32.2
  tumor, pelvic organs or tissues NEC O34.8-●
   cervix O34.4-●
  umbilical cord presentation or prolapse
    O69.0
 completely normal case O80
 complicated O75.9
  by
   abnormal, abnormality (of)
    forces of labor O62.9
     specified type NEC O62.8
    glucose O99.814
    uterine contractions NOS O62.9
   abruptio placentae —*see also* Abruptio
     placentae O45.9-●
   abuse
    physical O9A.32
    psychological O9A.52
    sexual O9A.42
   adherent placenta O72.0
    without hemorrhage O73.0
   alcohol use O99.314
   anemia (pre-existing) O99.02
   anesthetic death O74.8
   annular detachment of cervix O71.3
   atony, uterus O62.2
   attempted vacuum extraction and
     forceps O66.5
   Bandl's ring O62.4
   bariatric surgery status O99.844
   biliary tract disorder O26.62
   bleeding —*see* Delivery, complicated by,
     hemorrhage
   blood disorder NEC O99.12
   cervical dystocia (hypotonic) O62.2
    primary O62.0
    secondary O62.1
   circulatory system disorder O99.42
   compression of cord (umbilical) NEC
     O69.2
  ⇒condition NEC O99.892
   contraction, contracted ring O62.4
   cord (umbilical)
    around neck
     with compression O69.1
     without compression O69.81

Delivery *(Continued)*
  complicated *(Continued)*
    by *(Continued)*
      cord *(Continued)*
        bruising O69.5
        complication O69.9
          specified NEC O69.89
        compression NEC O69.2
        entanglement O69.2
          without compression O69.82
        hematoma O69.5
        presentation O69.0
        prolapse O69.0
        short O69.3
        thrombosis (vessels) O69.5
        vascular lesion O69.5
      Couvelaire uterus O45.8X-●
      damage to (injury to) NEC
        perineum O71.82
        periurethral tissue O71.82
        vulva O71.82
      delay following rupture of membranes
          (spontaneous) —*see* Pregnancy,
          complicated by, premature rupture
          of membranes
      depressed fetal heart tones O76
      diabetes O24.92
        gestational O24.429
          diet controlled O24.420
          insulin controlled O24.424
          oral drug controlled (antidiabetic)
              (hypoglycemic) O24.425
        pre-existing O24.32
          specified NEC O24.82
          type 1 O24.02
          type 2 O24.12
      diastasis recti (abdominis) O71.89
      dilatation
        bladder O66.8
        cervix incomplete, poor or slow O62.0
      ➠disease NEC O99.892
      disruptio uteri —*see* Delivery,
          complicated by, rupture, uterus
      drug use O99.324
      dysfunction, uterus NOS O62.9
        hypertonic O62.4
        hypotonic O62.2
          primary O62.0
          secondary O62.1
        incoordinate O62.4
      eclampsia O15.1
      embolism (pulmonary) —*see* Embolism,
          obstetric
      endocrine, nutritional or metabolic
          disease NEC O99.284
      failed
        attempted vaginal birth after previous
            cesarean delivery O66.41
        induction of labor O61.9
          instrumental O61.1
          mechanical O61.1
          medical O61.0
          specified NEC O61.8
          surgical O61.1
        trial of labor O66.40
      female genital mutilation O65.5
      fetal
        abnormal acid-base balance O68
        acidemia O68
        acidosis O68
        alkalosis O68
        death, early O02.1
        deformity O66.3
        heart rate or rhythm (abnormal) (non-
            reassuring) O76
        hypoxia O77.8
        stress O77.9
          due to drug administration O77.1
          electrocardiographic evidence of
              O77.8
          specified NEC O77.8
          ultrasound evidence of O77.8

Delivery *(Continued)*
  complicated *(Continued)*
    by *(Continued)*
      fever during labor O75.2
      gastric banding status O99.844
      gastric bypass status O99.844
      gastrointestinal disease NEC O99.62
      gestational
        diabetes O24.429
          diet controlled O24.420
          insulin (and diet) controlled
              O24.424
          oral drug controlled (antidiabetic)
              (hypoglycemic) O24.425
        edema O12.04
          with proteinuria O12.24
        proteinuria O12.14
      gonorrhea O98.22
      hematoma O71.7
        ischial spine O71.7
        pelvic O71.7
        vagina O71.7
        vulva or perineum O71.7
      hemorrhage (uterine) O67.9
        associated with
          afibrinogenemia O67.0
          coagulation defect O67.0
          hyperfibrinolysis O67.0
          hypofibrinogenemia O67.0
        due to
          low implantation of placenta
              O44.5-●
          low-lying placenta O44.5-●
          placenta previa O44.1-●
            marginal O44.3-●
            partial O44.3-●
          premature separation of placenta
              (normally implanted) (*see also*
              Abruptio placentae) O45.9-●
          retained placenta O72.0
          uterine leiomyoma O67.8
        placenta NEC O67.8
        postpartum NEC (atonic) (immediate)
            O72.1
          with retained or trapped placenta
              O72.0
          delayed O72.2
          secondary O72.2
          third stage O72.0
      hourglass contraction, uterus O62.4
      hypertension, hypertensive (pre-
          existing) —*see* Hypertension,
          complicated by, childbirth (labor)
      hypotension O26.5-●
      incomplete dilatation (cervix)
          O62.0
      incoordinate uterus contractions
          O62.4
      inertia, uterus O62.2
        during latent phase of labor O62.0
        primary O62.0
        secondary O62.1
      infection (maternal) O98.92
        carrier state NEC O99.834
        gonorrhea O98.22
        human immunodeficiency virus (HIV)
            O98.72
        sexually transmitted NEC O98.32
        specified NEC O98.82
        syphilis O98.12
        tuberculosis O98.02
        viral hepatitis O98.42
        viral NEC O98.52
      injury (to mother) (*see also* Delivery,
          complicated, by, damage to)
          O71.9
        nonobstetric O9A.22
          caused by abuse —*see* Delivery,
              complicated by, abuse
      intrauterine fetal death, early O02.1
      inversion, uterus O71.2

Delivery *(Continued)*
  complicated *(Continued)*
    by *(Continued)*
      laceration (perineal) O70.9
        anus (sphincter) O70.4
          with third degree laceration —*see
              also* Delivery, complicated, by,
              laceration, perineum, third
              degree O70.20
            with mucosa O70.3
          without third degree laceration
              O70.4
        bladder (urinary) O71.5
        bowel O71.5
        cervix (uteri) O71.3
        fourchette O70.0
        hymen O70.0
        labia O70.0
        pelvic
          floor O70.1
          organ NEC O71.5
        perineum, perineal O70.9
          first degree O70.0
          fourth degree O70.3
          muscles O70.1
          second degree O70.1
          skin O70.0
          slight O70.0
          third degree O70.20
            with
              both external anal sphincter
                  (EAS) and internal anal
                  sphincter (IAS) torn (IIIc)
                  O70.23
              less than 50% of external anal
                  sphincter (EAS) thickness
                  torn (IIIa) O70.21
              more than 50% external anal
                  sphincter (EAS) thickness
                  torn (IIIb) O70.22
            IIIa O70.21
            IIIb O70.22
            IIIc O70.23
        peritoneum (pelvic) O71.5
        rectovaginal (septum) (without
            perineal laceration) O71.4
          with perineum —*see also* Delivery,
              complicated, by, laceration,
              perineum, third degree
              O70.20
            with anal or rectal mucosa
                O70.3
        specified NEC O71.89
        sphincter ani —*see* Delivery,
            complicated, by, laceration, anus
            (sphincter)
        urethra O71.5
        uterus O71.81
          before labor O71.81
        vagina, vaginal (deep) (high)
            (without perineal laceration)
            O71.4
          with perineum O70.0
            muscles, with perineum O70.1
        vulva O70.0
      liver disorder O26.62
      malignancy O9A.12
      malnutrition O25.2
      malposition, malpresentation
        without obstruction O32.9 —*see
            also* Delivery, complicated by,
            obstruction
        breech O32.1
        compound O32.6
        face (brow) (chin) O32.3
        footling O38.8
        high head O32.4
        oblique O32.2
        specified NEC O32.8
        transverse O32.2
        unstable lie O32.0

▶ New   ⇒ Revised   ~~deleted~~ Deleted   ● Use Additional Character(s)

Dementia *(Continued)*
  in *(Continued)*
    Alzheimer's disease —*see* Disease, Alzheimer's
    arteriosclerotic brain disease —*see* Dementia, vascular
    cerebral lipidoses E75.-● *[F02.80]*
      with behavioral disturbance E75.-● *[F02.81]*
    Creutzfeldt-Jakob disease —*see also* Creutzfeldt-Jakob disease or syndrome (with dementia) A81.00
    epilepsy G40.-● *[F02.80]*
      with behavioral disturbance G40.-● *[F02.81]*
    hepatolenticular degeneration E83.01 *[F02.80]*
      with behavioral disturbance E83.01 *[F02.81]*
    human immunodeficiency virus (HIV) disease B20 *[F02.80]*
      with behavioral disturbance B20 *[F02.81]*
    Huntington's disease or chorea G10 *[F02.80]*
      with behavioral disturbance G10 *[F02.81]*
    hypercalcemia E83.52 *[F02.80]*
      with behavioral disturbance E83.52 *[F02.81]*
    hypothyroidism, acquired E03.9 *[F02.80]*
      with behavioral disturbance E03.9 *[F02.81]*
      due to iodine deficiency E01.8 *[F02.80]*
        with behavioral disturbance E01.8 *[F02.81]*
    inhalants F18.97
      with dependence F18.27
    multiple
      etiologies F03
      sclerosis G35 *[F02.80]*
        with behavioral disturbance G35 *[F02.81]*
    neurosyphilis A52.17 *[F02.80]*
      with behavioral disturbance A52.17 *[F02.81]*
      juvenile A50.49 *[F02.80]*
        with behavioral disturbance A50.49 *[F02.81]*
    niacin deficiency E52 *[F02.80]*
      with behavioral disturbance E52 *[F02.81]*
    paralysis agitans G20 *[F02.80]*
      with behavioral disturbance G20 *[F02.81]*
    Parkinson's disease G20 *[F02.80]*
    pellagra E52 *[F02.80]*
      with behavioral disturbance E52 *[F02.81]*
    Pick's G31.01 *[F02.80]*
      with behavioral disturbance G31.01 *[F02.81]*
    polyarteritis nodosa M30.0 *[F02.80]*
      with behavioral disturbance M30.0 *[F02.81]*
    psychoactive drug F19.97
      with dependence F19.27
      inhalants F18.97
        with dependence F18.27
      sedatives, hypnotics or anxiolytics F13.97
        with dependence F13.27
    sedatives, hypnotics or anxiolytics F13.97
      with dependence F13.27
    systemic lupus erythematosus M32.-● *[F02.80]*
      with behavioral disturbance M32.-● *[F02.81]*
    trypanosomiasis
      African B56.9 *[F02.80]*
        with behavioral disturbance B56.9 *[F02.81]*
    unknown etiology F03
    vitamin B12 deficiency E53.8 *[F02.80]*
      with behavioral disturbance E53.8 *[F02.81]*

Dementia *(Continued)*
  vitamin B12 deficiency *(Continued)*
    volatile solvents F18.97
      with dependence F18.27
  infantile, infantilis F84.3
  Lewy body G31.83 *[F02.80]*
    with behavioral disturbance G31.83 *[F02.81]*
  multi-infarct —*see* Dementia, vascular
  paralytica, paralytic (syphilitic) A52.17 *[F02.80]*
    with behavioral disturbance A52.17 *[F02.81]*
    juvenilis A50.45
  paretic A52.17
  praecox —*see* Schizophrenia
  presenile F03
    Alzheimer's type —*see* Disease, Alzheimer's, early onset
  primary degenerative F03
  progressive, syphilitic A52.17
  senile F03
    with acute confusional state F05
    Alzheimer's type —*see* Disease, Alzheimer's, late onset
    depressed or paranoid type F03
  vascular (acute onset) (mixed) (multi-infarct) (subcortical) F01.50
    with behavioral disturbance F01.51
Demineralization, bone —*see* Osteoporosis
Demodex folliculorum (infestation) B88.0
Demophobia F40.248
Demoralization R45.3
Demyelination, demyelinization
  central nervous system G37.9
    specified NEC G37.8
  corpus callosum (central) G37.1
  disseminated, acute G36.9
    specified NEC G36.8
  global G35
  in optic neuritis G36.0
Dengue (classical) (fever) A90
  hemorrhagic A91
  sandfly A93.1
Dennie-Marfan syphilitic syndrome A50.45
Dens evaginatus, in dente or invaginatus K00.2
Dense breasts R92.2
Density
  increased, bone (disseminated) (generalized) (spotted) —*see* Disorder, bone, density and structure, specified type NEC
  lung (nodular) J98.4
Dental —*see also* condition
  examination Z01.20
    with abnormal findings Z01.21
  restoration
    aesthetically inadequate or displeasing K08.56
    defective K08.50
      specified NEC K08.59
    failure of marginal integrity K08.51
    failure of periodontal anatomical integrity K08.54
Dentia praecox K00.6
Denticles (pulp) K04.2
Dentigerous cyst K09.0
Dentin
  irregular (in pulp) K04.3
  opalescent K00.5
  secondary (in pulp) K04.3
  sensitive K03.89
Dentinogenesis imperfecta K00.5
Dentinoma —*see* Cyst, calcifying odontogenic
Dentition (syndrome) K00.7
  delayed K00.6
  difficult K00.7
  precocious K00.6
  premature K00.6
  retarded K00.6

Dependence (on) (syndrome) F19.20
  with remission F19.21
  alcohol (ethyl) (methyl) (without remission) F10.20
    with
      amnestic disorder, persisting F10.26
      anxiety disorder F10.280
      dementia, persisting F10.27
      intoxication F10.229
        with delirium F10.221
        uncomplicated F10.220
      mood disorder F10.24
      psychotic disorder F10.259
        with
          delusions F10.250
          hallucinations F10.251
      remission F10.21
      sexual dysfunction F10.281
      sleep disorder F10.282
      specified disorder NEC F10.288
      withdrawal F10.239
        with
          delirium F10.231
          perceptual disturbance F10.232
        uncomplicated F10.230
    counseling and surveillance Z71.41
  amobarbital —*see* Dependence, drug, sedative
  amphetamine(s) (type) —*see* Dependence, drug, stimulant NEC
  amytal (sodium) —*see* Dependence, drug, sedative
  analgesic NEC F55.8
  anesthetic (agent) (gas) (general) (local) NEC —*see* Dependence, drug, psychoactive NEC
  anxiolytic NEC —*see* Dependence, drug, sedative
  barbital(s) —*see* Dependence, drug, sedative
  barbiturate(s) (compounds) (drugs classifiable to T42) —*see* Dependence, drug, sedative
  benzedrine —*see* Dependence, drug, stimulant NEC
  bhang —*see* Dependence, drug, cannabis
  bromide(s) NEC —*see* Dependence, drug, sedative
  caffeine —*see* Dependence, drug, stimulant NEC
  cannabis (sativa) (indica) (resin) (derivatives) (type) —*see* Dependence, drug, cannabis
  chloral (betaine) (hydrate) —*see* Dependence, drug, sedative
  chlordiazepoxide —*see* Dependence, drug, sedative
  coca (leaf) (derivatives) —*see* Dependence, drug, cocaine
  cocaine —*see* Dependence, drug, cocaine
  codeine —*see* Dependence, drug, opioid
  combinations of drugs F19.20
  dagga —*see* Dependence, drug, cannabis
  demerol —*see* Dependence, drug, opioid
  dexamphetamine —*see* Dependence, drug, stimulant NEC
  dexedrine —*see* Dependence, drug, stimulant NEC
  dextromethorphan —*see* Dependence, drug, opioid
  dextromoramide —*see* Dependence, drug, opioid
  dextro-nor-pseudo-ephedrine —*see* Dependence, drug, stimulant NEC
  dextrorphan —*see* Dependence, drug, opioid
  diazepam —*see* Dependence, drug, sedative
  dilaudid —*see* Dependence, drug, opioid
  D-lysergic acid diethylamide —*see* Dependence, drug, hallucinogen

Dependence *(Continued)*
 drug NEC F19.20
  with sleep disorder F19.282
  cannabis F12.20
   with
    anxiety disorder F12.280
    intoxication F12.229
     with
      delirium F12.221
       perceptual disturbance F12.222
     uncomplicated F12.220
    other specified disorder F12.288
    psychosis F12.259
     delusions F12.250
     hallucinations F12.251
    unspecified disorder F12.29
    withdrawal F12.23
   in remission F12.21
  cocaine F14.20
   with
    anxiety disorder F14.280
    intoxication F14.229
     with
      delirium F14.221
       perceptual disturbance F14.222
     uncomplicated F14.220
    mood disorder F14.24
    other specified disorder F14.288
    psychosis F14.259
     delusions F14.250
     hallucinations F14.251
    sexual dysfunction F14.281
    sleep disorder F14.282
    unspecified disorder F14.29
    withdrawal F14.23
   in remission F14.21
   withdrawal symptoms in newborn P96.1
  counseling and surveillance Z71.51
  hallucinogen F16.20
   with
    anxiety disorder F16.280
    flashbacks F16.283
    intoxication F16.229
     with delirium F16.221
     uncomplicated F16.220
    mood disorder F16.24
    other specified disorder F16.288
    perception disorder, persisting F16.283
    psychosis F16.259
     delusions F16.250
     hallucinations F16.251
    unspecified disorder F16.29
   in remission F16.21
  in remission F19.21
  inhalant F18.20
   with
    anxiety disorder F18.280
    dementia, persisting F18.27
    intoxication F18.229
     with delirium F18.221
     uncomplicated F18.220
    mood disorder F18.24
    other specified disorder
     F18.288
    psychosis F18.259
     delusions F18.250
     hallucinations F18.251
    unspecified disorder F18.29
   in remission F18.21
  nicotine F17.200
   with disorder F17.209
    in remission F17.201
    specified disorder NEC
     F17.208
    withdrawal F17.203
   chewing tobacco F17.220
    with disorder F17.229
     in remission F17.221
     specified disorder NEC
      F17.228
     withdrawal F17.223

Dependence *(Continued)*
 drug NEC *(Continued)*
  nicotine *(Continued)*
   cigarettes F17.210
    with disorder F17.219
     in remission F17.211
     specified disorder NEC F17.218
     withdrawal F17.213
   specified product NEC F17.290
    with disorder F17.299
     remission F17.291
     specified disorder NEC F17.298
     withdrawal F17.293
  opioid F11.20
   with
    intoxication F11.229
     with
      delirium F11.221
       perceptual disturbance F11.222
     uncomplicated F11.220
    mood disorder F11.24
    other specified disorder F11.288
    psychosis F11.259
     delusions F11.250
     hallucinations F11.251
    sexual dysfunction F11.281
    sleep disorder F11.282
    unspecified disorder F11.29
    withdrawal F11.23
   in remission F11.21
  psychoactive NEC F19.20
   with
    amnestic disorder F19.26
    anxiety disorder F19.280
    dementia F19.27
    intoxication F19.229
     with
      delirium F19.221
       perceptual disturbance F19.222
     uncomplicated F19.220
    mood disorder F19.24
    other specified disorder F19.288
    psychosis F19.259
     delusions F19.250
     hallucinations F19.251
    sexual dysfunction F19.281
    sleep disorder F19.282
    unspecified disorder F19.29
    withdrawal F19.239
     with
      delirium F19.231
       perceptual disturbance F19.232
     uncomplicated F19.230
  sedative, hypnotic or anxiolytic F13.20
   with
    amnestic disorder F13.26
    anxiety disorder F13.280
    dementia, persisting F13.27
    intoxication F13.229
     with delirium F13.221
     uncomplicated F13.220
    mood disorder F13.24
    other specified disorder F13.288
    psychosis F13.259
     delusions F13.250
     hallucinations F13.251
    sexual dysfunction F13.281
    sleep disorder F13.282
    unspecified disorder F13.29
    withdrawal F13.239
     with
      delirium F13.231
       perceptual disturbance F13.232
     uncomplicated F13.230
   in remission F13.21
  stimulant NEC F15.20
   with
    anxiety disorder F15.280
    intoxication F15.229
     with
      delirium F15.221
       perceptual disturbance F15.222
     uncomplicated F15.220

Dependence *(Continued)*
 methyl *(Continued)*
  stimulant NEC *(Continued)*
   with *(Continued)*
     mood disorder F15.24
     other specified disorder F15.288
     psychosis F15.259
      delusions F15.250
      hallucinations F15.251
     sexual dysfunction F15.281
     sleep disorder F15.282
     unspecified disorder F15.29
     withdrawal F15.23
    in remission F15.21
  ethyl
   alcohol (without remission) F10.20
    with remission F10.21
   bromide —*see* Dependence, drug,
    sedative
   carbamate F19.20
   chloride F19.20
   morphine —*see* Dependence, drug, opioid
  ganja —*see* Dependence, drug, cannabis
  glue (airplane) (sniffing) —*see* Dependence,
    drug, inhalant
  glutethimide —*see* Dependence, drug,
    sedative
  hallucinogenics —*see* Dependence, drug,
    hallucinogen
  hashish —*see* Dependence, drug, cannabis
  hemp —*see* Dependence, drug, cannabis
  heroin (salt) (any) —*see* Dependence, drug,
    opioid
  hypnotic NEC —*see* Dependence, drug,
    sedative
  Indian hemp —*see* Dependence, drug,
    cannabis
  inhalants —*see* Dependence, drug, inhalant
  khat —*see* Dependence, drug, stimulant NEC
  laudanum —*see* Dependence, drug, opioid
  LSD (-25) (derivatives) —*see* Dependence,
    drug, hallucinogen
  luminal —*see* Dependence, drug, sedative
  lysergic acid —*see* Dependence, drug,
    hallucinogen
  maconha —*see* Dependence, drug, cannabis
  marihuana —*see* Dependence, drug, cannabis
  meprobamate —*see* Dependence, drug,
    sedative
  mescaline —*see* Dependence, drug,
    hallucinogen
  methadone —*see* Dependence, drug, opioid
  methamphetamine(s) —*see* Dependence,
    drug, stimulant NEC
  methaqualone —*see* Dependence, drug,
    sedative
  methyl
   alcohol (without remission) F10.20
    with remission F10.21
   bromide —*see* Dependence, drug, sedative
   morphine —*see* Dependence, drug, opioid
   phenidate —*see* Dependence, drug,
    stimulant NEC
   sulfonal —*see* Dependence, drug, sedative
  morphine (sulfate) (sulfite) (type) —*see*
    Dependence, drug, opioid
  narcotic (drug) NEC —*see* Dependence, drug,
    opioid
  nembutal —*see* Dependence, drug, sedative
  neraval —*see* Dependence, drug, sedative
  neravan —*see* Dependence, drug, sedative
  neurobarb —*see* Dependence, drug, sedative
  nicotine —*see* Dependence, drug, nicotine
  nitrous oxide F19.20
  nonbarbiturate sedatives and tranquilizers
    with similar effect —*see* Dependence,
    drug, sedative
 on
  artificial heart (fully implantable)
    (mechanical) Z95.812
  aspirator Z99.0

▶ New   ⇨ Revised   ~~deleted~~ Deleted   ● Use Additional Character(s)

Dependence *(Continued)*
  on *(Continued)*
    care provider (because of) Z74.9
      impaired mobility Z74.09
      need for
        assistance with personal care Z74.1
        continuous supervision Z74.3
      no other household member able to
        render care Z74.2
      specified reason NEC Z74.8
    machine Z99.89
      enabling NEC Z99.89
      specified type NEC Z99.89
    renal dialysis (hemodialysis) (peritoneal)
      Z99.2
    respirator Z99.11
    ventilator Z99.11
    wheelchair Z99.3
  opiate —*see* Dependence, drug, opioid
  opioids —*see* Dependence, drug, opioid
  opium (alkaloids) (derivatives) (tincture) —
    see Dependence, drug, opioid
  oxygen (long-term) (supplemental) Z99.81
  paraldehyde —*see* Dependence, drug,
    sedative
  paregoric —*see* Dependence, drug, opioid
  PCP (phencyclidine) (or related substance) —
    see Dependence, drug, hallucinogen
  pentobarbital —*see* Dependence, drug,
    sedative
  pentobarbitone (sodium) —*see* Dependence,
    drug, sedative
  pentothal —*see* Dependence, drug, sedative
  peyote —*see* Dependence, drug, hallucinogen
  phencyclidine (PCP) (or related substance) —
    see Dependence, drug, hallucinogen
  phenmetrazine —*see* Dependence, drug,
    stimulant NEC
  phenobarbital —*see* Dependence, drug,
    sedative
  polysubstance F19.20
  psilocibin, psilocin, psilocyn, psilocyline —*see*
    Dependence, drug, hallucinogen
  psychostimulant NEC —*see* Dependence,
    drug, stimulant NEC
  secobarbital —*see* Dependence, drug, sedative
  seconal —*see* Dependence, drug, sedative
  sedative NEC —*see* Dependence, drug,
    sedative
  specified drug NEC —*see* Dependence, drug
  stimulant NEC —*see* Dependence, drug,
    stimulant NEC
  substance NEC —*see* Dependence, drug
  supplemental oxygen Z99.81
  tobacco —*see* Dependence, drug, nicotine
    counseling and surveillance Z71.6
  tranquilizer NEC —*see* Dependence, drug,
    sedative
  vitamin B6 E53.1
  volatile solvents —*see* Dependence, drug,
    inhalant
Dependency
  care-provider Z74.9
  passive F60.7
  reactions (persistent) F60.7
Depersonalization (in neurotic state) (neurotic)
  (syndrome) F48.1
Depletion
  extracellular fluid E86.9
  plasma E86.1
  potassium E87.6
    nephropathy N25.89
  salt or sodium E87.1
    causing heat exhaustion or prostration
      T67.4
    nephropathy N28.9
  volume NOS E86.9
Deployment (current) (military) status Z56.82
  in theater or in support of military war,
    peacekeeping and humanitarian
    operations Z56.82

Deployment *(Continued)*
  personal history of Z91.82
    military war, peacekeeping and
      humanitarian deployment (current or
      past conflict) Z91.82
  returned from Z91.82
Depolarization, premature I49.40
  atrial I49.1
  junctional I49.2
  specified NEC I49.49
  ventricular I49.3
Deposit
  bone in Boeck's sarcoid D86.89
  calcareous, calcium —*see* Calcification
  cholesterol
    retina H35.89
    vitreous (body) (humor) —*see* Deposit,
      crystalline
  conjunctiva H11.11-●
  cornea H18.00-●
    argentous H18.02-●
    due to metabolic disorder H18.03-●
    Kayser-Fleischer ring H18.04-●
    pigmentation —*see* Pigmentation, cornea
  crystalline, vitreous (body) (humor) H43.2-●
  hemosiderin in old scars of cornea —*see*
    Pigmentation, cornea, stromal
  metallic in lens —*see* Cataract, specified NEC
  skin R23.8
  tooth, teeth (betel) (black) (green) (materia
    alba) (orange) (tobacco) K03.6
  urate, kidney —*see* Calculus, kidney
Depraved appetite —*see* Pica
Depressed
  HDL cholesterol E78.6
Depression (acute) (mental) F32.9
  agitated (single episode) F32.2
  anaclitic —*see* Disorder, adjustment
  anxiety F41.8
    persistent F34.1
  arches —*see also* Deformity, limb, flat foot
  atypical (single episode) F32.89
    recurrent episode F33.8
  basal metabolic rate R94.8
  bone marrow D75.89
  central nervous system R09.2
  cerebral R29.818
    newborn P91.4
  cerebrovascular I67.9
  chest wall M95.4
  climacteric (single episode) F32.89
    recurrent episode F33.8
  endogenous (without psychotic symptoms)
    F33.2
    with psychotic symptoms F33.3
  functional activity R68.89
  hysterical F44.89
  involutional (single episode) F32.89
    recurrent episode F33.8
  major F32.9
    with psychotic symptoms F32.3
    recurrent —*see* Disorder, depressive,
      recurrent
  manic-depressive —*see* Disorder, depressive,
    recurrent
  masked (single episode) F32.89
  medullary G93.89
  menopausal (single episode) F32.89
    recurrent episode F33.8
  metatarsus —*see* Depression, arches
  monopolar F33.9
  nervous F34.1
  neurotic F34.1
  nose M95.0
  postnatal (NOS) F53.0
  postpartum (NOS) F53.0
  post-psychotic of schizophrenia F32.89
  post-schizophrenic F32.89
  psychogenic (reactive) (single episode)
    F32.9
  psychoneurotic F34.1

Depression *(Continued)*
  psychotic (single episode) F32.3
    recurrent F33.3
  reactive (psychogenic) (single episode) F32.9
    psychotic (single episode) F32.3
  recurrent —*see* Disorder, depressive, recurrent
  respiratory center G93.89
  seasonal —*see* Disorder, depressive, recurrent
  senile F03
  severe, single episode F32.2
  situational F43.21
  skull Q67.4
  specified NEC (single episode) F32.89
  sternum M95.4
  visual field —*see* Defect, visual field
  vital (recurrent) (without psychotic
    symptoms) F33.2
    with psychotic symptoms F33.3
    single episode F32.2
Deprivation
  cultural Z60.3
  effects NOS T73.9
    specified NEC T73.8
  emotional NEC Z65.8
    affecting infant or child —*see*
      Maltreatment, child, psychological
  food T73.0
  protein —*see* Malnutrition
  sleep Z72.820
  social Z60.4
    affecting infant or child —*see*
      Maltreatment, child, psychological
  specified NEC T73.8
  vitamins —*see* Deficiency, vitamin
  water T73.1
Derangement
  ankle (internal) —*see* Derangement, joint,
    ankle
  cartilage (articular) NEC —*see* Derangement,
    joint, articular cartilage, by site
    recurrent —*see* Dislocation, recurrent
  cruciate ligament, anterior, current injury —
    see Sprain, knee, cruciate, anterior
  elbow (internal) —*see* Derangement, joint,
    elbow
  hip (joint) (internal) (old) —*see* Derangement,
    joint, hip
  joint (internal) M24.9
    ankylosis —*see* Ankylosis
    articular cartilage M24.10
      ankle M24.17-●
      elbow M24.12-●
      foot M24.17-●
      hand M24.14-●
      hip M24.15-●
      knee NEC M23.9-●
      loose body —*see* Loose, body
      shoulder M24.11-●
      ▶specified site NEC M24.19
      wrist M24.13-●
    contracture —*see* Contraction, joint
    current injury —*see also* Dislocation
      knee, meniscus or cartilage —*see* Tear,
      meniscus
    dislocation
      pathological —*see* Dislocation,
        pathological
      recurrent —*see* Dislocation, recurrent
    knee —*see* Derangement, knee
    ligament —*see* Disorder, ligament
    loose body —*see* Loose, body
    recurrent —*see* Dislocation, recurrent
    specified type NEC M24.80
      ankle M24.87-●
      elbow M24.82-●
      foot joint M24.87-●
      hand joint M24.84-●
      hip M24.85-●
      shoulder M24.81-●
      ▶specified site NEC M24.89
      wrist M24.83-●
    temporomandibular M26.69

Derangement (Continued)

- knee (recurrent) M23.9-●
  - ligament disruption, spontaneous M23.60-●
    - anterior cruciate M23.61-●
    - capsular M23.67-●
    - instability, chronic M23.5-●
    - lateral collateral M23.64-●
    - medial collateral M23.63-●
    - posterior cruciate M23.62-●
  - loose body M23.4-●
  - meniscus M23.30-●
    - cystic M23.00-●
      - lateral M23.002
        - anterior horn M23.04-●
        - posterior horn M23.05-●
        - specified NEC M23.06-●
      - medial M23.005
        - anterior horn M23.01-●
        - posterior horn M23.02-●
        - specified NEC M23.03-●
    - degenerate —see Derangement, knee, meniscus, specified NEC
    - detached —see Derangement, knee, meniscus, specified NEC
    - due to old tear or injury M23.20-●
      - lateral M23.20-●
        - anterior horn M23.24-●
        - posterior horn M23.25-●
        - specified NEC M23.26-●
      - medial M23.20-●
        - anterior horn M23.21-●
        - posterior horn M23.22-●
        - specified NEC M23.23-●
    - retained —see Derangement, knee, meniscus, specified NEC
    - specified NEC M23.30-●
      - lateral M23.30-●
        - anterior horn M23.34-●
        - posterior horn M23.35-●
        - specified NEC M23.36-●
      - medial M23.30-●
        - anterior horn M23.31-●
        - posterior horn M23.32-●
        - specified NEC M23.33-●
    - old M23.8X-●
    - specified NEC —see subcategory M23.8
  - low back NEC —see Dorsopathy, specified NEC
  - meniscus —see Derangement, knee, meniscus
  - mental —see Psychosis
  - patella, specified NEC —see Disorder, patella, derangement NEC
  - semilunar cartilage (knee) —see Derangement, knee, meniscus, specified NEC
  - shoulder (internal) —see Derangement, joint, shoulder

Dercum's disease E88.2

Derealization (neurotic) F48.1

Dermal —see condition

Dermaphytid —see Dermatophytosis

Dermatitis (eczematous) L30.9

- ab igne L59.0
- acarine B88.0
- actinic (due to sun) L57.8
  - other than from sun L59.8
- allergic —see Dermatitis, contact, allergic
- ambustionis, due to burn or scald —see Burn
- amebic A06.7
- ammonia L22
- arsenical (ingested) L27.8
- artefacta L98.1
  - psychogenic F54
- atopic L20.9
  - psychogenic F54
  - specified NEC L20.89
- autoimmune progesterone L30.8
- berlock, berloque L56.2
- blastomycotic B40.3

Dermatitis (Continued)

- blister beetle L24.89
- bullous, bullosa L13.9
  - mucosynechial, atrophic L12.1
  - seasonal L30.8
  - specified NEC L13.8
- calorica L59.0
  - due to burn or scald —see Burn
- caterpillar L24.89
- cercarial B65.3
- combustionis L59.0
  - due to burn or scald —see Burn
- congelationis T69.1
- contact (occupational) L25.9
  - allergic L23.9
    - due to
      - adhesives L23.1
      - cement L23.5
      - chemical products NEC L23.5
      - chromium L23.0
      - cosmetics L23.2
      - dander (cat) (dog) L23.81
      - drugs in contact with skin L23.3
      - dyes L23.4
      - food in contact with skin L23.6
      - hair (cat) (dog) L23.81
      - insecticide L23.5
      - metals L23.0
      - nickel L23.0
      - plants, non-food L23.7
      - plastic L23.5
      - rubber L23.5
      - specified agent NEC L23.89
  - due to
    - cement L25.3
    - chemical products NEC L25.3
    - cosmetics L25.0
    - dander (cat) (dog) L23.81
    - drugs in contact with skin L25.1
    - dyes L25.2
    - food in contact with skin L25.4
    - hair (cat) (dog) L23.81
    - plants, non-food L25.5
    - specified agent NEC L25.8
  - irritant L24.9
    - due to
      - cement L24.5
      - chemical products NEC L24.5
      - cosmetics L24.3
      - detergents L24.0
      - drugs in contact with skin L24.4
      - food in contact with skin L24.6
      - oils and greases L24.1
      - plants, non-food L24.7
      - solvents L24.2
      - specified agent NEC L24.89
- contusiformis L52
- ▶desquamative L30.8
- diabetic —see E08-E13 with .620
- diaper L22
- diphtheritica A36.3
- dry skin L85.3
- due to
  - acetone (contact) (irritant) L24.2
  - acids (contact) (irritant) L24.5
  - adhesive(s) (allergic) (contact) (plaster) L23.1
    - irritant L24.5
  - alcohol (irritant) (skin contact) (substances in category T51) L24.2
    - taken internally L27.8
  - alkalis (contact) (irritant) L24.5
  - arsenic (ingested) L27.8
  - carbon disulfide (contact) (irritant) L24.2
  - caustics (contact) (irritant) L24.5
  - cement (contact) L25.3
  - cereal (ingested) L27.2
  - chemical(s) NEC L25.3
    - taken internally L27.8
  - chlorocompounds L24.2
  - chromium (contact) (irritant) L24.81

Dermatitis (Continued)

- due to (Continued)
  - coffee (ingested) L27.2
  - cold weather L30.8
  - cosmetics (contact) L25.0
    - allergic L23.2
    - irritant L24.3
  - cyclohexanes L24.2
  - dander (cat) (dog) L23.81
  - Demodex species B88.0
  - Dermanyssus gallinae B88.0
  - detergents (contact) (irritant) L24.0
  - dichromate L24.81
  - drugs and medicaments (generalized) (internal use) L27.0
    - external —see Dermatitis, due to, drugs, in contact with skin
    - in contact with skin L25.1
      - allergic L23.3
      - irritant L24.4
    - localized skin eruption L27.1
    - specified substance —see Table of Drugs and Chemicals
  - dyes (contact) L25.2
    - allergic L23.4
    - irritant L24.89
  - epidermophytosis —see Dermatophytosis
  - esters L24.2
  - external irritant NEC L24.9
  - fish (ingested) L27.2
  - flour (ingested) L27.2
  - food (ingested) L27.2
    - in contact with skin L25.4
  - fruit (ingested) L27.2
  - furs (allergic) (contact) L23.81
  - glues —see Dermatitis, due to, adhesives
  - glycols L24.2
  - greases NEC (contact) (irritant) L24.1
  - hair (cat) (dog) L23.81
  - hot
    - objects and materials —see Burn
    - weather or places L59.0
  - hydrocarbons L24.2
  - infrared rays L59.8
  - ingestion, ingested substance L27.9
    - chemical NEC L27.8
    - drugs and medicaments —see Dermatitis, due to, drugs
    - food L27.2
    - specified NEC L27.8
  - insecticide in contact with skin L24.5
  - internal agent L27.9
    - drugs and medicaments (generalized) —see Dermatitis, due to, drugs
    - food L27.2
  - irradiation —see Dermatitis, due to, radioactive substance
  - ketones L24.2
  - lacquer tree (allergic) (contact) L23.7
  - light (sun) NEC L57.8
    - acute L56.8
    - other L59.8
  - Liponyssoides sanguineus B88.0
  - low temperature L30.8
  - meat (ingested) L27.2
  - metals, metal salts (contact) (irritant) L24.81
  - milk (ingested) L27.2
  - nickel (contact) (irritant) L24.81
  - nylon (contact) (irritant) L24.5
  - oils NEC (contact) (irritant) L24.1
  - paint solvent (contact) (irritant) L24.2
  - petroleum products (contact) (irritant) (substances in T52) L24.2
  - plants NEC (contact) L25.5
    - allergic L23.7
    - irritant L24.7
  - plasters (adhesive) (any) (allergic) (contact) L23.1
    - irritant L24.5
  - plastic (contact) L25.3

▶ New   ⇒ Revised   ~~deleted~~ Deleted   ● Use Additional Character(s)

Dermatitis *(Continued)*
  due to *(Continued)*
    preservatives (contact) —*see* Dermatitis, due to, chemical, in contact with skin
    primrose (allergic) (contact) L23.7
    primula (allergic) (contact) L23.7
    radiation L59.8
      nonionizing (chronic exposure) L57.8
        sun NEC L57.8
          acute L56.8
      radioactive substance L58.9
        acute L58.0
        chronic L58.1
      radium L58.9
        acute L58.0
        chronic L58.1
    ragweed (allergic) (contact) L23.7
    Rhus (allergic) (contact) (diversiloba) (radicans) (toxicodendron) (venenata) (verniciflua) L23.7
    rubber (contact) L24.5
    Senecio jacobaea (allergic) (contact) L23.7
    solvents (contact) (irritant) (substances in categories T52) L24.2
    specified agent NEC (contact) L25.8
      allergic L23.89
      irritant L24.89
    sunshine NEC L57.8
      acute L56.8
    tetrachlorethylene (contact) (irritant) L24.2
    toluene (contact) (irritant) L24.2
    turpentine (contact) L24.2
    ultraviolet rays (sun NEC) (chronic exposure) L57.8
      acute L56.8
    vaccine or vaccination L27.0
      specified substance —*see* Table of Drugs and Chemicals
    varicose veins —*see* Varix, leg, with, inflammation
    X-rays L58.9
      acute L58.0
      chronic L58.1
  dyshydrotic L30.1
  dysmenorrheica N94.6
  escharotica —*see* Burn
  exfoliative, exfoliativa (generalized) L26
    neonatorum L00
  eyelid —*see also* Dermatosis, eyelid
    allergic H01.119
      left H01.116
        lower H01.115
        upper H01.114
      right H01.113
        lower H01.112
        upper H01.111
    contact —*see* Dermatitis, eyelid, allergic
    due to
      Demodex species B88.0
      herpes (zoster) B02.39
        simplex B00.59
    eczematous H01.139
      left H01.136
        lower H01.135
        upper H01.134
      right H01.133
        lower H01.132
        upper H01.131
  facta, factitia, factitial L98.1
    psychogenic F54
  flexural NEC L20.82
  friction L30.4
  fungus B36.9
    specified type NEC B36.8
  gangrenosa, gangrenous infantum L08.0
  harvest mite B88.0
  heat L59.0

Dermatitis *(Continued)*
  herpesviral, vesicular (ear) (lip) B00.1
  herpetiformis (bullous) (erythematous) (pustular) (vesicular) L13.0
    juvenile L12.2
    senile L12.0
  hiemalis L30.8
  hypostatic, hypostatica —*see* Varix, leg, with, inflammation
  infectious eczematoid L30.3
  infective L30.3
  irritant —*see* Dermatitis, contact, irritant
  Jacquet's (diaper dermatitis) L22
  Leptus B88.0
  lichenified NEC L28.0
  medicamentosa (generalized) (internal use) —*see* Dermatitis, due to drugs
  mite B88.0
  multiformis L13.0
    juvenile L12.2
  napkin L22
  neurotica L13.0
  nummular L30.0
  papillaris capillitii L73.0
  pellagrous E52
  perioral L71.0
  photocontact L56.2
  polymorpha dolorosa L13.0
  pruriginosa L13.0
  pruritic NEC L30.8
  psychogenic F54
  purulent L08.0
  pustular
    contagious B08.02
    subcorneal L13.1
  pyococcal L08.0
  pyogenica L08.0
  repens L40.2
  Ritter's (exfoliativa) L00
  Schamberg's L81.7
  schistosome B65.3
  seasonal bullous L30.8
  seborrheic L21.9
    infantile L21.1
    specified NEC L21.8
  sensitization NOS L23.9
  septic L08.0
  solare L57.8
  specified NEC L30.8
  stasis I87.2
    with
      varicose ulcer —*see* Varix, leg, with ulcer, with inflammation
      varicose veins —*see* Varix, leg, with, inflammation
    due to postthrombotic syndrome —*see* Syndrome, postthrombotic
  suppurative L08.0
  traumatic NEC L30.4
  trophoneurotica L13.0
  ultraviolet (sun) (chronic exposure) L57.8
    acute L56.8
  varicose —*see* Varix, leg, with, inflammation
  vegetans L10.1
  verrucosa B43.0
  vesicular, herpesviral B00.1
Dermatoarthritis, lipoid E78.81
Dermatochalasis, eyelid H02.839
  left H02.836
    lower H02.835
    upper H02.834
  right H02.833
    lower H02.832
    upper H02.831
Dermatofibroma (lenticulare) —*see* Neoplasm, skin, benign
  protuberans —*see* Neoplasm, skin, uncertain behavior
Dermatofibrosarcoma (pigmented) (protuberans) —*see* Neoplasm, skin, malignant

Dermatographia L50.3
Dermatolysis (exfoliativa) (congenital) Q82.8
  acquired L57.4
  eyelids —*see* Blepharochalasis
  palpebrarum —*see* Blepharochalasis
  senile L57.4
Dermatomegaly NEC Q82.8
Dermatomucosomyositis M33.10
  with
    myopathy M33.12
    respiratory involvement M33.11
    specified organ involvement NEC M33.19
Dermatomycosis B36.9
  furfuracea B36.0
  specified type NEC B36.8
Dermatomyositis (acute) (chronic) —*see also* Dermatopolymyositis
  adult —*see also* Dermatomyositis, specified NEC M33.10
  in (due to) neoplastic disease —*see also* Neoplasm D49.9 *[M36.0]*
  juvenile M33.00
    with
      myopathy M33.02
      respiratory involvement M33.01
      specified organ involvement NEC M33.09
    without myopathy M33.03
  specified NEC M33.10
    with
      myopathy M33.12
      respiratory involvement M33.11
      specified organ involvement NEC M33.19
    without myopathy M33.13
Dermatoneuritis of children —*see* Poisoning, mercury
Dermatophilosis A48.8
Dermatophytid L30.2
Dermatophytide —*see* Dermatophytosis
Dermatophytosis (epidermophyton) (infection) (Microsporum) (tinea) (Trichophyton) B35.9
  beard B35.0
  body B35.4
  capitis B35.0
  corporis B35.4
  deep-seated B35.8
  disseminated B35.8
  foot B35.3
  granulomatous B35.8
  groin B35.6
  hand B35.2
  nail B35.1
  perianal (area) B35.6
  scalp B35.0
  specified NEC B35.8
Dermatopolymyositis M33.90
  with
    myopathy M33.92
    respiratory involvement M33.91
    specified organ involvement NEC M33.99
  in neoplastic disease —*see also* Neoplasm D49.9 *[M36.0]*
  juvenile M33.00
    with
      myopathy M33.02
      respiratory involvement M33.01
      specified organ involvement NEC M33.09
    specified NEC M33.10
      myopathy M33.12
      respiratory involvement M33.11
      specified organ involvement NEC M33.19
    without myopathy M33.93
Dermatopolyneuritis —*see* Poisoning, mercury
Dermatorrhexis (*see also* Syndrome, Ehlers-Danlos) Q79.60
  acquired L57.4
Dermatosclerosis —*see also* Scleroderma
  localized L94.0

Dermatosis L98.9
  Andrews' L08.89
  Bowen's —*see* Neoplasm, skin, in situ
  bullous L13.9
    specified NEC L13.8
  exfoliativa L26
  eyelid (noninfectious)
    dermatitis —*see* Dermatitis, eyelid
    discoid lupus erythematosus —*see* Lupus,
      erythematosus, eyelid
    xeroderma —*see* Xeroderma, acquired,
      eyelid
  factitial L98.1
  febrile neutrophilic L98.2
  gonococcal A54.89
  herpetiformis L13.0
    juvenile L12.2
  linear IgA L13.8
  menstrual NEC L98.8
  neutrophilic, febrile L98.2
  occupational —*see* Dermatitis, contact
  papulosa nigra L82.1
  pigmentary L81.9
    progressive L81.7
    Schamberg's L81.7
  psychogenic F54
  purpuric, pigmented L81.7
  pustular, subcorneal L13.1
  transient acantholytic L11.1
Dermographia, dermographism L50.3
Dermoid (cyst) —*see also* Neoplasm, benign,
    by site
  with malignant transformation C56-•
  due to radiation (nonionizing) L57.8
Dermopathy
  infiltrative with thyrotoxicosis —*see*
    Thyrotoxicosis
  nephrogenic fibrosing L90.8
Dermophytosis —*see* Dermatophytosis
Descemetocele H18.73-•
Descemet's membrane —*see* condition
Descending —*see* condition
Descensus uteri —*see* Prolapse, uterus
Desert
  rheumatism B38.0
  sore —*see* Ulcer, skin
Desertion (newborn) —*see* Maltreatment
Desmoid (extra-abdominal) (tumor) —*see*
    Neoplasm, connective tissue, uncertain
    behavior
  abdominal D48.1
Despondency F32.9
Desquamation, skin R23.4
Destruction, destructive —*see also* Damage
  articular facet —*see also* Derangement, joint,
      specified type NEC
    knee M23.8X-•
    vertebra —*see* Spondylosis
  bone —*see also* Disorder, bone, specified type
      NEC
    syphilitic A52.77
  joint —*see also* Derangement, joint, specified
      type NEC
    sacroiliac M53.3
  rectal sphincter K62.89
  septum (nasal) J34.89
  tuberculous NEC —*see* Tuberculosis
  tympanum, tympanic membrane
      (nontraumatic) —*see* Disorder, tympanic
      membrane, specified NEC
  vertebral disc —*see* Degeneration,
      intervertebral disc
Destructiveness —*see also* Disorder,
    conduct
  adjustment reaction —*see* Disorder,
    adjustment
Desultory labor O62.2
Detachment
  cartilage —*see* Sprain
  cervix, annular N88.8
    complicating delivery O71.3

Detachment *(Continued)*
  choroid (old) (postinfectional) (simple)
      (spontaneous) H31.40-•
    hemorrhagic H31.41-•
    serous H31.42-•
  ligament —*see* Sprain
  meniscus (knee) —*see also* Derangement,
      knee, meniscus, specified NEC
    current injury —*see* Tear, meniscus
    due to old tear or injury —*see*
      Derangement, knee, meniscus, due to
      old tear
  retina (without retinal break) (serous)
      H33.2-•
    with retinal:
      break H33.00-•
        giant H33.03-•
        multiple H33.02-•
        single H33.01-•
      dialysis H33.04-•
    pigment epithelium —*see* Degeneration,
      retina, separation of layers, pigment
      epithelium detachment
    rhegmatogenous —*see* Detachment, retina,
      with retinal, break
    specified NEC H33.8
    total H33.05-•
    traction H33.4-•
  vitreous (body) H43.81
Detergent asthma J69.8
Deterioration
  epileptic F06.8
  general physical R53.81
  heart, cardiac —*see* Degeneration,
    myocardial
  mental —*see* Psychosis
  myocardial, myocardium —*see* Degeneration,
    myocardial
  senile (simple) R54
Deuteranomaly (anomalous trichromat) H53.53
Deuteranopia (complete) (incomplete) H53.53
Development
  abnormal, bone Q79.9
  arrested R62.50
    bone —*see* Arrest, development or growth,
      bone
    child R62.50
    due to malnutrition E45
  defective, congenital —*see also* Anomaly, by
      site
    cauda equina Q06.3
    left ventricle Q24.8
      in hypoplastic left heart syndrome Q23.4
    valve Q24.8
      pulmonary Q22.3
  delayed (*see also* Delay, development) R62.50
    arithmetical skills F81.2
    language (skills) (expressive) F80.1
    learning skill F81.9
    mixed skills F88
    motor coordination F82
    reading F81.0
    specified learning skill NEC F81.89
    speech F80.9
    spelling F81.81
    written expression F81.81
  imperfect, congenital —*see also* Anomaly, by
      site
    heart Q24.9
    lungs Q33.6
  incomplete
    bronchial tree Q32.4
    organ or site not listed —*see* Hypoplasia,
      by site
    respiratory system Q34.9
  sexual, precocious NEC E30.1
  tardy, mental (*see also* Disability, intellectual)
      F79
Developmental —*see* condition
  testing, infant or child —*see* Examination,
      child

Devergie's disease (pityriasis rubra pilaris)
    L44.0
Deviation (in)
  conjugate palsy (eye) (spastic) H51.0
  esophagus (acquired) K22.8
  eye, skew H51.8
  midline (jaw) (teeth) (dental arch) M26.29
    specified site NEC —*see* Malposition
  nasal septum J34.2
    congenital Q67.4
  opening and closing of the mandible M26.53
  organ or site, congenital NEC —*see*
    Malposition, congenital
  septum (nasal) (acquired) J34.2
    congenital Q67.4
  sexual F65.9
    bestiality F65.89
    erotomania F52.8
    exhibitionism F65.2
    fetishism, fetishistic F65.0
      transvestism F65.1
    frotteurism F65.81
    masochism F65.51
    multiple F65.89
    necrophilia F65.89
    nymphomania F52.8
    pederosis F65.4
    pedophilia F65.4
    sadism, sadomasochism F65.52
    satyriasis F52.8
    specified type NEC F65.89
    transvestism F64.1
    voyeurism F65.3
  teeth, midline M26.29
  trachea J39.8
  ureter, congenital Q62.61
Device
  cerebral ventricle (communicating) in situ
    Z98.2
  contraceptive —*see* Contraceptive, device
  drainage, cerebrospinal fluid, in situ Z98.2
Devic's disease G36.0
Devil's
  grip B33.0
  pinches (purpura simplex) D69.2
Devitalized tooth K04.99
Devonshire colic —*see* Poisoning, lead
Dextraposition, aorta Q20.3
  in tetralogy of Fallot Q21.3
Dextrinosis, limit (debrancher enzyme
    deficiency) E74.03
Dextrocardia (true) Q24.0
  with
    complete transposition of viscera
      Q89.3
    situs inversus Q89.3
Dextrotransposition, aorta Q20.3
d-glycericacidemia E72.59
Dhat syndrome F48.8
Dhobi itch B35.6
Di George's syndrome D82.1
Di Guglielmo's disease C94.0-•
Diabetes, diabetic (mellitus) (sugar) E11.9
  with
    amyotrophy E11.44
    arthropathy NEC E11.618
    autonomic (poly)neuropathy E11.43
    cataract E11.36
    Charcot's joints E11.610
    chronic kidney disease E11.22
    circulatory complication NEC E11.59
    complication E11.8
      specified NEC E11.69
    dermatitis E11.620
    foot ulcer E11.621
    gangrene E11.52
    gastroparalysis E11.43
    gastroparesis E11.43
    glomerulonephrosis, intracapillary E11.21
    glomerulosclerosis, intercapillary E11.21
    hyperglycemia E11.65

▶ New   ⇒ Revised   ~~deleted~~ Deleted   • Use Additional Character(s)

Diabetes, diabetic *(Continued)*
  with *(Continued)*
    hyperosmolarity E11.00
      with coma E11.01
    hypoglycemia E11.649
      with coma E11.641
    ketoacidosis E11.10
      with coma E11.11
    kidney complications NEC E11.29
    Kimmelstiel-Wilson disease E11.21
    loss of protective sensation (LOPS) —*see*
      Diabetes, by type, with neuropathy
    mononeuropathy E11.41
    myasthenia E11.44
    necrobiosis lipoidica E11.620
    nephropathy E11.21
    neuralgia E11.42
    neurologic complication NEC E11.49
    neuropathic arthropathy E11.610
    neuropathy E11.40
    ophthalmic complication NEC E11.39
    oral complication NEC E11.638
    osteomyelitis E11.69
    periodontal disease E11.630
    peripheral angiopathy E11.51
      with gangrene E11.52
    polyneuropathy E11.42
    renal complication NEC E11.29
    renal tubular degeneration E11.29
    retinopathy E11.319
      with macular edema E11.311
        resolved following treatment
        E11.37
      nonproliferative E11.329
        with macular edema E11.321
        mild E11.329
          with macular edema E11.321
        moderate E11.339
          with macular edema E11.331
        severe E11.349
          with macular edema E11.341
      proliferative E11.359
        with
          combined traction retinal
            detachment and
            rhegmatogenous retinal
            detachment E11.354
          macular edema E11.351
          stable proliferative diabetic
            retinopathy E11.355
          traction retinal detachment
            involving the macula E11.352
          traction retinal detachment not
            involving the macula E11.353
    skin complication NEC E11.628
    skin ulcer NEC E11.622
  brittle —*see* Diabetes, type 1
  bronzed E83.110
  complicating pregnancy —*see* Pregnancy,
    complicated by, diabetes
  dietary counseling and surveillance Z71.3
  due to
    autoimmune process —*see* Diabetes, type 1
    immune mediated pancreatic islet
      beta-cell destruction —*see* Diabetes,
      type 1
  due to drug or chemical E09.9
    with
      amyotrophy E09.44
      arthropathy NEC E09.618
      autonomic (poly)neuropathy E09.43
      cataract E09.36
      Charcot's joints E09.610
      chronic kidney disease E09.22
      circulatory complication NEC E09.59
      complication E09.8
        specified NEC E09.69
      dermatitis E09.620
      foot ulcer E09.621
      gangrene E09.52
      gastroparalysis E09.43

Diabetes, diabetic *(Continued)*
  due to drug or chemical *(Continued)*
    with *(Continued)*
      gastroparesis E09.43
      glomerulonephrosis, intracapillary
        E09.21
      glomerulosclerosis, intercapillary E09.21
      hyperglycemia E09.65
      hyperosmolarity E09.00
        with coma E09.01
      hypoglycemia E09.649
        with coma E09.641
      ketoacidosis E09.10
        with coma E09.11
      kidney complications NEC E09.29
      Kimmelstiel-Wilson disease E09.21
      mononeuropathy E09.41
      myasthenia E09.44
      necrobiosis lipoidica E09.620
      nephropathy E09.21
      neuralgia E09.42
      neurologic complication NEC E09.49
      neuropathic arthropathy E09.610
      neuropathy E09.40
      ophthalmic complication NEC E09.39
      oral complication NEC E09.638
      periodontal disease E09.630
      peripheral angiopathy E09.51
        with gangrene E09.52
      polyneuropathy E09.42
      renal complication NEC E09.29
      renal tubular degeneration E09.29
      retinopathy E09.319
        with macular edema E09.311
          resolved following treatment
          E09.37
        nonproliferative E09.329
          with macular edema E09.321
          mild E09.329
            with macular edema E09.321
          moderate E09.339
            with macular edema E09.331
          severe E09.349
            with macular edema E09.341
        proliferative E09.359
          with
            combined traction retinal
              detachment and
              rhegmatogenous retinal
              detachment E09.354
            macular edema E09.351
            stable proliferative diabetic
              retinopathy E09.355
            traction retinal detachment
              involving the macula
              E09.352
            traction retinal detachment not
              involving the macula
              E09.353
    skin complication NEC E09.628
    skin ulcer NEC E09.622
  due to underlying condition E08.9
    with
      amyotrophy E08.44
      arthropathy NEC E08.618
      autonomic (poly)neuropathy E08.43
      cataract E08.36
      Charcot's joints E08.610
      chronic kidney disease E08.22
      circulatory complication NEC E08.59
      complication E08.8
        specified NEC E08.69
      dermatitis E08.620
      foot ulcer E08.621
      gangrene E08.52
      gastroparalysis E08.43
      gastroparesis E08.43
      glomerulonephrosis, intracapillary
        E08.21
      glomerulosclerosis, intercapillary E08.21
      hyperglycemia E08.69

Diabetes, diabetic *(Continued)*
  due to underlying condition *(Continued)*
    with *(Continued)*
      hyperosmolarity E08.00
        with coma E08.01
      hypoglycemia E08.649
        with coma E08.641
      ketoacidosis E08.10
        with coma E08.11
      kidney complications NEC E08.29
      Kimmelstiel-WIlson disease E08.21
      mononeuropathy E08.41
      myasthenia E08.44
      necrobiosis lipoidica E08.620
      nephropathy E08.21
      neuralgia E08.42
      neurologic complication NEC E08.49
      neuropathic arthropathy E08.610
      neuropathy E08.40
      ophthalmic complication NEC
        E08.39
      oral complication NEC E08.638
      periodontal disease E08.630
      peripheral angiopathy E08.51
        with gangrene E08.52
      polyneuropathy E08.42
      renal complication NEC E08.29
      renal tubular degeneration E08.29
      retinopathy E08.319
        with macular edema E08.311
          resolved following treatment
          E08.37
        nonproliferative E08.329
          with macular edema E08.321
          mild E08.329
            with macular edema E08.321
          moderate E08.339
            with macular edema E08.331
          severe E08.349
            with macular edema E08.341
        proliferative E08.359
          with
            combined traction retinal
              detachment and
              rhegmatogenous retinal
              detachment E08.354
            macular edema E08.351
            stable proliferative diabetic
              retinopathy E08.355
            traction retinal detachment
              involving the macula
              E08.352
            traction retinal detachment not
              involving the macula
              E08.353
    skin complication NEC E08.628
    skin ulcer NEC E08.622
  gestational (in pregnancy) O24.419
    affecting newborn P70.0
    diet-controlled O24.410
    in childbirth O24.429
      diet-controlled O24.420
      insulin (and diet) controlled O24.424
      oral drug controlled (antidiabetic)
        (hypoglycemic) O24.425
    insulin (and diet) controlled O24.414
    oral drug controlled (antidiabetic)
      (hypoglycemic) O24.415
    puerperal O24.439
      diet-controlled O24.430
      insulin (and diet) controlled O24.434
      oral drug controlled (antidiabetic)
        (hypoglycemic) O24.435
  hepatogenous E13.9
  idiopathic —*see* Diabetes, type 1
  inadequately controlled — code to Diabetes,
    by type, with hyperglycemia
  insipidus E23.2
    nephrogenic N25.1
    pituitary E23.2
    vasopressin resistant N25.1

► New   ➛ Revised   ~~deleted~~ Deleted   ● Use Additional Character(s)

Diabetes, diabetic (Continued)
  type 2 (Continued)
    with (Continued)
      skin complication NEC E11.628
      skin ulcer NEC E11.622
    uncontrolled
      meaning
        hyperglycemia —see Diabetes, by type,
          with, hyperglycemia
        hypoglycemia —see Diabetes, by type,
          with, hypoglycemia
Diacyclothrombopathia D69.1
Diagnosis deferred R69
Dialysis (intermittent) (treatment)
  noncompliance (with) Z91.15
  renal (hemodialysis) (peritoneal), status Z99.2
  retina, retinal —see Detachment, retina, with
    retinal, dialysis
Diamond-Blackfan anemia (congenital
  hypoplastic) D61.01
Diamond-Gardener syndrome
  (autoerythrocyte sensitization) D69.2
Diaper rash L22
Diaphoresis (excessive) R61
Diaphragm —see condition
Diaphragmalgia R07.1
Diaphragmatitis, diaphragmitis J98.6
Diaphysial aclasis Q78.6
Diaphysitis —see Osteomyelitis, specified type
  NEC
Diarrhea, diarrheal (disease) (infantile)
  (inflammatory) R19.7
  achlorhydric K31.83
  allergic K52.29
    due to
      colitis —see Colitis, allergic
      enteritis —see Enteritis, allergic
  amebic —see also Amebiasis A06.0
    with abscess —see Abscess, amebic
    acute A06.0
    chronic A06.1
    nondysenteric A06.2
  bacillary —see Dysentery, bacillary
  balantidial A07.0
  cachectic NEC K52.89
  Chilomastix A07.8
  choleriformis A00.1
  chronic (noninfectious) K52.9
  coccidial A07.3
  Cochin-China K90.1
    strongyloidiasis B78.0
  Dientamoeba A07.8
  dietetic —see also Diarrhea, allergic K52.29
  drug-induced K52.1
  due to
    bacteria A04.9
      specified NEC A04.8
    Campylobacter A04.5
    Capillaria philippinensis B81.1
    Clostridium difficile
      not specified as recurrent A04.72
      recurrent A04.71
    Clostridium perfringens (C) (F) A04.8
    Cryptosporidium A07.2
    drugs K52.1
    Escherichia coli A04.4
      enteroaggregative A04.4
      enterohemorrhagic A04.3
      enteroinvasive A04.2
      enteropathogenic A04.0
      enterotoxigenic A04.1
      specified NEC A04.4
    food hypersensitivity —see also Diarrhea,
      allergic K52.29
    Necator americanus B76.1
    S. japonicum B65.2
    specified organism NEC A08.8
      bacterial A04.8
      viral A08.39
    Staphylococcus A04.8
    Trichuris trichiuria B79

Diarrhea, diarrheal (Continued)
  due to (Continued)
    virus —see Enteritis, viral
    Yersinia enterocolitica A04.6
  dysenteric A09
  endemic A09
  epidemic A09
  flagellate A07.9
  Flexner's (ulcerative) A03.1
  functional K59.1
    following gastrointestinal surgery
      K91.89
    psychogenic F45.8
  Giardia lamblia A07.1
  giardial A07.1
  hill K90.1
  infectious A09
  malarial —see Malaria
  mite B88.0
  mycotic NEC B49
  neonatal (noninfectious) P78.3
  nervous F45.8
  neurogenic K59.1
  noninfectious K52.9
  postgastrectomy K91.1
  postvagotomy K91.1
  protozoal A07.9
    specified NEC A07.8
  psychogenic F45.8
  specified
    bacterium NEC A04.8
    virus NEC A08.39
  strongyloidiasis B78.0
  toxic K52.1
  trichomonal A07.8
  tropical K90.1
  tuberculous A18.32
  viral —see Enteritis, viral
Diastasis
  cranial bones M84.88
    congenital NEC Q75.8
  joint (traumatic) —see Dislocation
  muscle M62.00
    ankle M62.07-●
    congenital Q79.8
    foot M62.07-●
    forearm M62.03-●
    hand M62.04-●
    lower leg M62.06-●
    pelvic region M62.05-●
    shoulder region M62.01-●
    specified site NEC M62.08
    thigh M62.05-●
    upper arm M62.02-●
  recti (abdomen)
    complicating delivery O71.89
    congenital Q79.59
Diastema, tooth, teeth, fully erupted
  M26.32
Diastematomyelia Q06.2
Diataxia, cerebral G80.4
Diathesis
  allergic —see History, allergy
  bleeding (familial) D69.9
  cystine (familial) E72.00
  gouty —see Gout
  hemorrhagic (familial) D69.9
    newborn NEC P53
  spasmophilic R29.0
Diaz's disease or osteochondrosis (juvenile)
  (talus) —see Osteochondrosis, juvenile,
  tarsus
Dibothriocephalus, dibothriocephaliasis
  (latus) (infection) (infestation) B70.0
  larval B70.1
Dicephalus, dicephaly Q89.4
Dichotomy, teeth K00.2
Dichromat, dichromatopsia (congenital) —see
  Deficiency, color vision
Dichuchwa A65
Dicroceliasis B66.2

Didelphia, didelphys —see Double uterus
Didymytis N45.1
  with orchitis N45.3
Dietary
  inadequacy or deficiency E63.9
  surveillance and counseling Z71.3
Dietl's crisis N13.8
Dieulafoy lesion (hemorrhagic)
  duodenum K31.82
  esophagus K22.8
  intestine (colon) K63.81
  stomach K31.82
Difficult, difficulty (in)
  acculturation Z60.3
  feeding R63.3
    newborn P92.9
      breast P92.5
      specified NEC P92.8
    nonorganic (infant or child) F98.29
  intubation, in anesthesia T88.4
  mechanical, gastroduodenal stoma K91.89
    causing obstruction —see also Obstruction,
      intestine, postoperative K91.30
  micturition
    need to immediately re-void R39.191
    position dependent R39.192
    specified NEC R39.198
  reading (developmental) F81.0
    secondary to emotional disorders F93.9
  spelling (specific) F81.81
    with reading disorder F81.89
    due to inadequate teaching Z55.8
  swallowing —see Dysphagia
  walking R26.2
  work
    conditions NEC Z56.5
    schedule Z56.3
Diffuse —see condition
DiGeorge's syndrome (thymic hypoplasia)
  D82.1
Digestive —see condition
Dihydropyrimidine dehydrogenase disease
  (DPD) E88.89
Diktyoma —see Neoplasm, malignant, by site
Dilaceration, tooth K00.4
Dilatation
▶anus K59.89
    venule —see Hemorrhoids
  aorta (focal) (general) —see Ectasia, aorta
    with aneurysm —see Aneurysm, aorta
    congenital Q25.44
  artery —see Aneurysm
  bladder (sphincter) N32.89
    congenital Q64.79
  blood vessel I99.8
  bronchial J47.9
    with
      exacerbation (acute) J47.1
      lower respiratory infection J47.0
  calyx (due to obstruction) —see
    Hydronephrosis
  capillaries I78.8
  cardiac (acute) (chronic) —see also
    Hypertrophy, cardiac
    congenital Q24.8
      valve NEC Q24.8
        pulmonary Q22.3
    valve —see Endocarditis
  cavum septi pellucidi Q06.8
  cervix (uteri) —see also Incompetency, cervix
    incomplete, poor, slow complicating
      delivery O62.0
  colon K59.39
    congenital Q43.1
    psychogenic F45.8
    toxic K59.31
  common duct (acquired) K83.8
    congenital Q44.5
  cystic duct (acquired) K82.8
    congenital Q44.5
  duct, mammary —see Ectasia, mammary duct

Dilatation *(Continued)*
⟱duodenum K59.89
esophagus K22.8
  congenital Q39.5
  due to achalasia K22.0
eustachian tube, congenital Q17.8
gallbladder K82.8
gastric —*see* Dilatation, stomach
heart (acute) (chronic) —*see also* Hypertrophy,
    cardiac
  congenital Q24.8
  valve —*see* Endocarditis
⟱ileum K59.89
  psychogenic F45.8
⟱jejunum K59.89
  psychogenic F45.8
kidney (calyx) (collecting structures) (cystic)
    (parenchyma) (pelvis) (idiopathic)
    N28.89
lacrimal passages or duct —*see* Disorder,
    lacrimal system, changes
lymphatic vessel I89.0
mammary duct —*see* Ectasia, mammary
    duct
Meckel's diverticulum (congenital) Q43.0
  malignant —*see* Table of Neoplasms, small
    intestine, malignant
myocardium (acute) (chronic) —*see*
    Hypertrophy, cardiac organ or site,
    congenital NEC —*see* Distortion
pancreatic duct K86.89
pericardium —*see* Pericarditis
pharynx J39.2
prostate N42.89
pulmonary
  artery (idiopathic) I28.8
  valve, congenital Q22.3
pupil H57.04
rectum K59.39
saccule, congenital Q16.5
salivary gland (duct) K11.8
sphincter ani K62.89
stomach K31.89
  acute K31.0
  psychogenic F45.8
submaxillary duct K11.8
trachea, congenital Q32.1
ureter (idiopathic) N28.82
  congenital Q62.2
  due to obstruction N13.4
urethra (acquired) N36.8
vasomotor I73.9
vein I86.8
ventricular, ventricle (acute) (chronic) —*see
    also* Hypertrophy, cardiac
  cerebral, congenital Q04.8
venule NEC I86.8
vesical orifice N32.89
Dilated, dilation —*see* Dilatation
Diminished, diminution
hearing (acuity) —*see* Deafness
sense or sensation (cold) (heat) (tactile)
    (vibratory) R20.8
vision NEC H54.7
vital capacity R94.2
Diminuta taenia B71.0
Dimitri-Sturge-Weber disease Q85.8
Dimple
congenital sacral Q82.6
parasacral Q82.6
pilonidal or postanal —*see* Cyst, pilonidal
Dioctophyme renalis (infection) (infestation)
  B83.8
Dipetalonemiasis B74.4
Diphallus Q55.69
Diphtheria, diphtheritic (gangrenous)
  (hemorrhagic) A36.9
carrier (suspected) Z22.2
cutaneous A36.3
faucial A36.0
infection of wound A36.3

Diphtheria, diphtheritic *(Continued)*
laryngeal A36.2
myocarditis A36.81
nasal, anterior A36.89
nasopharyngeal A36.1
neurological complication A36.89
pharyngeal A36.0
specified site NEC A36.89
tonsillar A36.0
Diphyllobothriasis (intestine) B70.0
larval B70.1
Diplacusis H93.22-●
Diplegia (upper limbs) G83.0
congenital (cerebral) G80.8
facial G51.0
lower limbs G82.20
spastic G80.1
Diplococcus, diplococcal —*see* condition
Diplopia H53.2
Dipsomania F10.20
with
    psychosis —*see* Psychosis, alcoholic
  remission F10.21
Dipylidiasis B71.1
DIRA (deficiency of interleukin 1 receptor
  antagonist) M04.8
Direction, teeth, abnormal, fully erupted
  M26.30
Dirofilariasis B74.8
Dirt-eating child F98.3
Disability, disabilities
heart —*see* Disease, heart
intellectual F79
  with
    autistic features F84.9
  mild (I.Q. 50-69) F70
  moderate (I.Q. 35-49) F71
  profound (I.Q. under 20) F73
  severe (I.Q. 20-34) F72
  specified level NEC F78
knowledge acquisition F81.9
learning F81.9
limiting activities Z73.6
spelling, specific F81.81
Disappearance of family member Z63.4
Disarticulation —*see* Amputation
meaning traumatic amputation —*see*
    Amputation, traumatic
Discharge (from)
abnormal finding in —*see* Abnormal, specimen
breast (female) (male) N64.52
diencephalic autonomic idiopathic —*see*
    Epilepsy, specified NEC
ear —*see also* Otorrhea
  blood —*see* Otorrhagia
excessive urine R35.8
nipple N64.52
penile R36.9
postnasal R09.82
prison, anxiety concerning Z65.2
urethral R36.9
  without blood R36.0
  hematospermia R36.1
vaginal N89.8
Discitis, diskitis M46.40
cervical region M46.42
cervicothoracic region M46.43
lumbar region M46.46
lumbosacral region M46.47
multiple sites M46.49
occipito-atlanto-axial region M46.41
pyogenic —*see* Infection, intervertebral
    disc, pyogenic
sacrococcygeal region M46.48
thoracic region M46.44
thoracolumbar region M46.45
Discoid
meniscus (congenital) Q68.6
semilunar cartilage (congenital) —*see*
    Derangement, knee, meniscus,
    specified NEC

Discoloration
nails L60.8
teeth (posteruptive) K03.7
  during formation K00.8
Discomfort
chest R07.89
visual H53.14-●
Discontinuity, ossicles, ear H74.2-●
Discord (with)
boss Z56.4
classmates Z55.4
counselor Z64.4
employer Z56.4
family Z63.8
fellow employees Z56.4
in-laws Z63.1
landlord Z59.2
lodgers Z59.2
neighbors Z59.2
probation officer Z64.4
social worker Z64.4
teachers Z55.4
workmates Z56.4
Discordant connection
atrioventricular (congenital) Q20.5
ventriculoarterial Q20.3
Discrepancy
centric occlusion maximum intercuspation
  M26.55
leg length (acquired) —*see* Deformity, limb,
    unequal length
  congenital —*see* Defect, reduction, lower
    limb
uterine size date O26.84-●
Discrimination
ethnic Z60.5
political Z60.5
racial Z60.5
religious Z60.5
sex Z60.5
Disease, diseased —*see also* Syndrome
absorbent system I87.8
acid-peptic K30
Acosta's T70.29
Adams-Stokes (-Morgagni) (syncope with
    heart block) I45.9
Addison's anemia (pernicious) D51.0
adenoids (and tonsils) J35.9
adrenal (capsule) (cortex) (gland) (medullary)
  E27.9
  hyperfunction E27.0
  specified NEC E27.8
ainhum L94.6
airway
  obstructive, chronic J44.9
    due to
      cotton dust J66.0
      specific organic dusts NEC J66.8
  reactive —*see* Asthma
akamushi (scrub typhus) A75.3
Albers-Schönberg (marble bones) Q78.2
Albert's —*see* Tendinitis, Achilles
alimentary canal K63.9
alligator-skin Q80.9
  acquired L85.0
alpha heavy chain C88.3
alpine T70.29
altitude T70.20
alveolar ridge
  edentulous K06.9
    specified NEC K06.8
alveoli, teeth K08.9
Alzheimer's G30.9 [F02.80]
  with behavioral disturbance G30.9 [F02.81]
  early onset G30.0 [F02.80]
    with behavioral disturbance G30.0 [F02.81]
  late onset G30.1 [F02.80]
    with behavioral disturbance G30.1 [F02.81]
  specified NEC G30.8 [F02.80]
    with behavioral disturbance G30.8
      [F02.81]

▶ New   ⟱ Revised   ~~deleted~~ Deleted   ● Use Additional Character(s)

Disease, diseased *(Continued)*
  amyloid —*see* Amyloidosis
  Andersen's (glycogenosis IV) E74.09
  Andes T70.29
  Andrews' (bacterid) L08.89
  angiospastic I73.9
    cerebral G45.9
    vein I87.8
  anterior
    chamber H21.9
    horn cell G12.29
  antiglomerular basement membrane
      (anti-GBM) antibody M31.0
    tubulo-interstitial nephritis N12
  antral —*see* Sinusitis, maxillary
  anus K62.9
    specified NEC K62.89
  aorta (nonsyphilitic) I77.9
    syphilitic NEC A52.02
  aortic (heart) (valve) I35.9
    rheumatic I06.9
  Apollo B30.3
  aponeuroses —*see* Enthesopathy
  appendix K38.9
    specified NEC K38.8
  aqueous (chamber) H21.9
  Arnold-Chiari —*see* Arnold-Chiari disease
  arterial I77.9
    occlusive —*see* Occlusion, by site
      due to stricture or stenosis I77.1
    peripheral I73.9
  arteriocardiorenal —*see* Hypertension,
      cardiorenal
  arteriolar (generalized) (obliterative) I77.9
  arteriorenal —*see* Hypertension, kidney
  arteriosclerotic —*see also* Arteriosclerosis
    cardiovascular —*see* Disease, heart,
      ischemic, atherosclerotic
    coronary (artery) —*see* Disease, heart,
      ischemic, atherosclerotic
    heart —*see* Disease, heart, ischemic,
      atherosclerotic
  artery I77.9
    cerebral I67.9
    coronary I25.10
      with angina pectoris —*see*
        Arteriosclerosis, coronary
        (artery)
    peripheral I73.9
  arthropod-borne NOS (viral) A94
    specified type NEC A93.8
  atticoantral, chronic H66.20
    left H66.22
      with right H66.23
    right H66.21
      with left H66.23
  auditory canal —*see* Disorder, ear, external
  auricle, ear NEC —*see* Disorder, pinna
  Australian X A83.4
  autoimmune (systemic) NOS M35.9
  ⮞hemolytic D59.10
    ▶cold type (primary) (secondary)
        (symptomatic) D59.12
      drug-induced D59.0
    ▶mixed type (primary) (secondary)
        (symptomatic) D59.13
    ▶warm type (primary) (secondary)
        (symptomatic) D59.11
    thyroid E06.3
  autoinflammatory M04.9
    NOD2-associated M04.8
    specified type NEC M04.8
  aviator's —*see* Effect, adverse, high altitude
  Ayerza's (pulmonary artery sclerosis with
      pulmonary hypertension) I27.0
  Babington's (familial hemorrhagic
      telangiectasia) I78.0
  bacterial A49.9
    specified NEC A48.8
    zoonotic A28.9
      specified type NEC A28.8

Disease, diseased *(Continued)*
  Baelz's (cheilitis glandularis apostematosa)
      K13.0
  bagasse J67.1
  balloon —*see* Effect, adverse, high altitude
  Bang's (brucella abortus) A23.1
  Bannister's T78.3
  barometer makers' —*see* Poisoning, mercury
  Barraquer (-Simons') (progressive
      lipodystrophy) E88.1
  Barrett's —*see* Barrett's, esophagus
  Bartholin's gland N75.9
  basal ganglia G25.9
    degenerative G23.9
      specified NEC G23.8
    specified NEC G25.89
  Basedow's (exophthalmic goiter) —*see*
      Hyperthyroidism, with, goiter (diffuse)
  Bateman's B08.1
  Batten-Steinert G71.11
  Battey A31.0
  Beard's (neurasthenia) F48.8
  Becker
    idiopathic mural endomyocardial I42.3
    myotonia congenita G71.12
  Begbie's (exophthalmic goiter) —*see*
      Hyperthyroidism, with, goiter (diffuse)
  behavioral, organic F07.9
  Beigel's (white piedra) B36.2
  Benson's —*see* Deposit, crystalline
  Bernard-Soulier (thrombopathy) D69.1
  Bernhardt (-Roth) —*see* Mononeuropathy,
      lower limb, meralgia paresthetica
  Biermer's (pernicious anemia) D51.0
  bile duct (common) (hepatic) K83.9
    with calculus, stones —*see* Calculus, bile
        duct
    specified NEC K83.8
  biliary (tract) K83.9
    specified NEC K83.8
  Billroth's —*see* Spina bifida
  bird fancier's J67.2
  black lung J60
  bladder N32.9
    in (due to)
      schistosomiasis (bilharziasis) B65.0 *[N33]*
    specified NEC N32.89
  bleeder's D66
  blood D75.9
    forming organs D75.9
    vessel I99.9
  Bloodgood's —*see* Mastopathy, cystic
▶ Blount M92.51-●
  Bodechtel-Guttmann (subacute sclerosing
      panencephalitis) A81.1
  bone —*see also* Disorder, bone
    aluminum M83.4
    fibrocystic NEC
      jaw M27.49
  bone-marrow D75.9
  Borna A83.9
  Bornholm (epidemic pleurodynia) B33.0
  Bouchard's (myopathic dilatation of the
      stomach) K31.0
  Bouillaud's (rheumatic heart disease) I01.9
  Bouveret (-Hoffmann) (paroxysmal
      tachycardia) I47.9
  bowel K63.9
    functional K59.9
      psychogenic F45.8
  brain G93.9
    arterial, artery I67.9
    arteriosclerotic I67.2
    congenital Q04.9
    degenerative —*see* Degeneration, brain
    inflammatory —*see* Encephalitis
    organic G93.9
      arteriosclerotic I67.2
    parasitic NEC B71.9 *[G94]*

Disease, diseased *(Continued)*
  brain *(Continued)*
    senile NEC G31.1
    specified NEC G93.89
  breast *(see also* Disorder, breast) N64.9
    cystic (chronic) —*see* Mastopathy, cystic
    fibrocystic —*see* Mastopathy, cystic
    Paget's
      female, unspecified side C50.91-●
      male, unspecified side C50.92-●
    specified NEC N64.89
  Breda's —*see* Yaws
  Bretonneau's (diphtheritic malignant angina)
      A36.0
  Bright's —*see* Nephritis
    arteriosclerotic —*see* Hypertension, kidney
  Brill's (recrudescent typhus) A75.1
  Brill-Zinsser (recrudescent typhus) A75.1
  Brion-Kayser —*see* Fever, paratyphoid
  broad
    beta E78.2
    ligament (noninflammatory) N83.9
      inflammatory —*see* Disease, pelvis,
          inflammatory
      specified NEC N83.8
  Brocq-Duhring (dermatitis herpetiformis)
      L13.0
  Brocq's
    meaning
      dermatitis herpetiformis L13.0
      prurigo L28.2
  bronchopulmonary J98.4
  bronchus NEC J98.09
  bronze Addison's E27.1
    tuberculous A18.7
  budgerigar fancier's J67.2
  Buerger's (thromboangiitis obliterans)
      I73.1
  bullous L13.9
    chronic of childhood L12.2
    specified NEC L13.8
  Bürger-Grütz (essential familial
      hyperlipemia) E78.3
  bursa —*see* Bursopathy
  caisson T70.3
  California —*see* Coccidioidomycosis
  capillaries I78.9
    specified NEC I78.8
  Carapata A68.0
  cardiac —*see* Disease, heart
  cardiopulmonary, chronic I27.9
  cardiorenal (hepatic) (hypertensive)
      (vascular) —*see* Hypertension,
      cardiorenal
  cardiovascular (atherosclerotic) I25.10
    with angina pectoris —*see* Arteriosclerosis,
        coronary (artery),
    congenital Q28.9
    hypertensive —*see* Hypertension, heart
    newborn P29.9
      specified NEC P29.89
    renal (hypertensive) —*see* Hypertension,
        cardiorenal
    syphilitic (asymptomatic) A52.00
  cartilage —*see* Disorder, cartilage
  Castellani's A69.8
  Castleman (unicentric) (multicentric)
      D47.Z2
    HHV-8-associated —*see also* Herpesvirus,
        human, 8 D47.Z2
  cat-scratch A28.1
  Cavare's (familial periodic paralysis) G72.3
  cecum K63.9
  celiac (adult) (infantile) (with steatorrhea)
      K90.0
  cellular tissue L98.9
  ⮞central core G71.29
  cerebellar, cerebellum —*see* Disease, brain
  cerebral —*see also* Disease, brain
    degenerative —*see* Degeneration, brain
  cerebrospinal G96.9

Disease, diseased (Continued)
cerebrovascular I67.9
  acute I67.89
    embolic I63.4-●
    thrombotic I63.3-●
  arteriosclerotic I67.2
  hereditary NEC I67.858
  specified NEC I67.89
cervix (uteri) (noninflammatory) N88.9
  inflammatory —see Cervicitis
  specified NEC N88.8
Chabert's A22.9
Chandler's (osteochondritis dissecans, hip) —
  see Osteochondritis, dissecans, hip
Charlouis —see Yaws
Chédiak-Steinbrinck (-Higashi) (congenital
  gigantism of peroxidase granules) E70.330
chest J98.9
Chiari's (hepatic vein thrombosis) I82.0
Chicago B40.9
Chignon B36.8
chigo, chigoe B88.1
childhood granulomatous D71
Chinese liver fluke B66.1
chlamydial A74.9
  specified NEC A74.89
cholecystic K82.9
choroid H31.9
  specified NEC H31.8
Christmas D67
chronic bullous of childhood L12.2
chylomicron retention E78.3
ciliary body H21.9
  specified NEC H21.89
circulatory (system) NEC I99.8
  newborn P29.9
  syphilitic A52.00
    congenital A50.54
coagulation factor deficiency (congenital) —
  see Defect, coagulation
coccidioidal —see Coccidioidomycosis
cold
  ▸agglutinin or hemoglobinuria D59.12
    paroxysmal D59.6
  ▸hemagglutinin (chronic) D59.12
collagen NOS (nonvascular) (vascular) M35.9
  specified NEC M35.8
colon K63.9
  functional K59.9
    congenital Q43.2
  ischemic —see also Ischemia, intestine,
    acute K55.039
colonic inflammatory bowel, unclassified
  (IBDU) K52.3
combined system —see Degeneration,
  combined
compressed air T70.3
Concato's (pericardial polyserositis) A19.9
  nontubercular I31.1
  pleural —see Pleurisy, with effusion
conjunctiva H11.9
  chlamydial A74.0
  specified NEC H11.89
  viral B30.9
    specified NEC B30.8
connective tissue, systemic (diffuse) M35.9
  in (due to)
    hypogammaglobulinemia D80.1 [M36.8]
    ochronosis E70.29 [M36.8]
  specified NEC M35.8
Conor and Bruch's (boutonneuse fever) A77.1
Cooper's —see Mastopathy, cystic
Cori's (glycogenosis III) E74.03
corkhandler's or corkworker's J67.3
cornea H18.9
  specified NEC H18.89-●
coronary (artery) —see Disease, heart,
  ischemic, atherosclerotic
  congenital Q24.5
  ostial, syphilitic (aortic) (mitral)
    (pulmonary) A52.03

Disease, diseased (Continued)
corpus cavernosum N48.9
  specified NEC N48.89
Cotugno's —see Sciatica
▸COVID-19 U07.1
coxsackie (virus) NEC B34.1
cranial nerve NOS G52.9
Creutzfeldt-Jakob —see Creutzfeldt-Jakob
  disease or syndrome
Crocq's (acrocyanosis) I73.89
Crohn's —see Enteritis, regional
Curschmann G71.11
cystic
  breast (chronic) —see Mastopathy, cystic
  kidney, congenital Q61.9
  liver, congenital Q44.6
  lung J98.4
    congenital Q33.0
cytomegalic inclusion (generalized) B25.9
  with pneumonia B25.0
  congenital P35.1
cytomegaloviral B25.9
  specified NEC B25.8
Czerny's (periodic hydrarthrosis of the
  knee) —see Effusion, joint, knee
Daae (-Finsen) (epidemic pleurodynia) B33.0
Darling's —see Histoplasmosis capsulati
Débove's (splenomegaly) R16.1
deer fly —see Tularemia
Degos' I77.8
demyelinating, demyelinizating (nervous
  system) G37.9
  multiple sclerosis G35
  specified NEC G37.8
dense deposit —see also N00-N07 with fourth
  character .6 N05.6
deposition, hydroxyapatite —see Disease,
  hydroxyapatite deposition
de Quervain's (tendon sheath) M65.4
  thyroid (subacute granulomatous
    thyroiditis) E06.1
Devergie's (pityriasis rubra pilaris) L44.0
Devic's G36.0
diaphorase deficiency D74.0
diaphragm J98.6
diarrheal, infectious NEC A09
digestive system K92.9
  specified NEC K92.89
disc, degenerative —see Degeneration,
  intervertebral disc
discogenic —see also Displacement,
  intervertebral disc NEC
  with myelopathy —see Disorder, disc, with,
    myelopathy
diverticular —see Diverticula
Dubois (thymus) A50.59 [E35]
Duchenne-Griesinger G71.01
Duchenne's
  muscular dystrophy G71.01
  pseudohypertrophy, muscles G71.01
ductless glands E34.9
Duhring's (dermatitis herpetiformis) L13.0
duodenum K31.9
  specified NEC K31.89
Dupré's (meningism) R29.1
Dupuytren's (muscle contracture) M72.0
Durand-Nicholas-Favre (climatic bubo) A55
Duroziez's (congenital mitral stenosis) Q23.2
ear —see Disorder, ear
Eberth's —see Fever, typhoid
Ebola (virus) A98.4
Ebstein's heart Q22.5
Echinococcus —see Echinococcus
echovirus NEC B34.1
Eddowes' (brittle bones and blue sclera)
  Q78.0
edentulous (alveolar) ridge K06.9
  specified NEC K06.8
Edsall's T67.2
Eichstedt's (pityriasis versicolor) B36.0
Eisenmenger's (irreversible) I27.83

Disease, diseased (Continued)
Ellis-van Creveld (chondroectodermal
  dysplasia) Q77.6
end stage renal (ESRD) N18.6
  due to hypertension I12.0
endocrine glands or system NEC E34.9
endomyocardial (eosinophilic) I42.3
English (rickets) E55.0
enteroviral, enterovirus NEC B34.1
  central nervous system NEC A88.8
epidemic B99.9
  specified NEC B99.8
epididymis N50.9
Erb (-Landouzy) G71.02
Erdheim-Chester (ECD) E88.89
esophagus K22.9
  functional K22.4
  psychogenic F45.8
  specified NEC K22.8
Eulenburg's (congenital paramyotonia)
  G71.19
eustachian tube —see Disorder, eustachian
  tube
external
  auditory canal —see Disorder, ear,
    external
  ear —see Disorder, ear, external
extrapyramidal G25.9
  specified NEC G25.89
eye H57.9
  anterior chamber H21.9
  inflammatory NEC H57.89
  muscle (external) —see Strabismus
  specified NEC H57.89
  syphilitic —see Oculopathy, syphilitic
eyeball H44.9
  specified NEC H44.89
eyelid —see Disorder, eyelid
  specified NEC —see Disorder, eyelid,
    specified type NEC
eyeworm of Africa B74.3
facial nerve (seventh) G51.9
  newborn (birth injury) P11.3
Fahr (of brain) G23.8
Fahr Volhard (of kidney) I12.-●
fallopian tube (noninflammatory) N83.9
  inflammatory —see Salpingo-oophoritis
  specified NEC N83.8
familial periodic paralysis G72.3
Fanconi's (congenital pancytopenia) D61.09
fascia NEC —see also Disorder, muscle
  inflammatory —see Myositis
  specified NEC M62.89
Fauchard's (periodontitis) —see Periodontitis
Favre-Durand-Nicolas (climatic bubo) A55
Fede's K14.0
Feer's —see Poisoning, mercury
female pelvic inflammatory —see also Disease,
  pelvis, inflammatory N73.9
  syphilitic (secondary) A51.42
  tuberculous A18.17
Fernels' (aortic aneurysm) I71.9
fibrocaseous of lung —see Tuberculosis,
  pulmonary
fibrocystic —see Fibrocystic disease
Fiedler's (leptospiral jaundice) A27.0
fifth B08.3
file-cutter's —see Poisoning, lead
fish-skin Q80.9
  acquired L85.0
Flajani (-Basedow) (exophthalmic goiter) —
  see Hyperthyroidism, with, goiter
  (diffuse)
flax-dresser's J66.1
fluke —see Infestation, fluke
foot and mouth B08.8
foot process N04.9
Forbes' (glycogenosis III) E74.03
Fordyce-Fox (apocrine miliaria) L75.2
Fordyce's (ectopic sebaceous glands) (mouth)
  Q38.6

Disease, diseased *(Continued)*
  Forestier's (rhizomelic pseudopolyarthritis)
      M35.3
    meaning ankylosing hyperostosis —*see*
        Hyperostosis, ankylosing
  Fothergill's
    neuralgia —*see* Neuralgia, trigeminal
    scarlatina anginosa A38.9
  Fournier (gangrene) N49.3
    female N76.89
  fourth B08.8
  Fox (-Fordyce) (apocrine miliaria) L75.2
  Francis' —*see* Tularemia
  Franklin C88.2
  Frei's (climatic bubo) A55
  Friedreich's
    ⟿combined systemic or ataxia G11.11
    myoclonia G25.3
  frontal sinus —*see* Sinusitis, frontal
  fungus NEC B49
  Gaisböck's (polycythemia hypertonica) D75.1
  gallbladder K82.9
    calculus —*see* Calculus, gallbladder
    cholecystitis —*see* Cholecystitis
    cholesterolosis K82.4
    fistula —*see* Fistula, gallbladder
    hydrops K82.1
    obstruction —*see* Obstruction, gallbladder
    perforation K82.2
    specified NEC K82.8
  gamma heavy chain C88.2
  Gamna's (siderotic splenomegaly) D73.2
  Gamstorp's (adynamia episodica hereditaria)
      G72.3
  Gandy-Nanta (siderotic splenomegaly) D73.2
  ganister J62.8
  gastric —*see* Disease, stomach
  gastroesophageal reflux (GERD) K21.9
    ⟿with esophagitis (without bleeding) K21.00
    ▶with bleeding K21.01
  gastrointestinal (tract) K92.9
    amyloid E85.4
    functional K59.9
      psychogenic F45.8
    specified NEC K92.89
  Gee (-Herter) (-Heubner) (-Thaysen)
      (nontropical sprue) K90.0
  genital organs
    female N94.9
    male N50.9
  Gerhardt's (erythromelalgia) I73.81
  Gibert's (pityriasis rosea) L42
  Gierke's (glycogenosis I) E74.01
  Gilles de la Tourette's (motor-verbal tic) F95.2
  gingiva K06.9
    plaque induced K05.00
    specified NEC K06.8
  gland (lymph) I89.9
  Glanzmann's (hereditary hemorrhagic
      thrombasthenia) D69.1
  glass-blower's (cataract) —*see* Cataract,
      specified NEC
    salivary gland hypertrophy K11.1
  Glisson's —*see* Rickets
  globe H44.9
    specified NEC H44.89
  glomerular —*see also* Glomerulonephritis
    with edema —*see* Nephrosis
    acute —*see* Nephritis, acute
    chronic —*see* Nephritis, chronic
    minimal change N05.0
    rapidly progressive N01.9
  glycogen storage E74.00
    Andersen's E74.09
    Cori's E74.03
    Forbes' E74.03
    generalized E74.00
    glucose-6-phosphatase deficiency E74.01
    heart E74.02 *[I43]*
    hepatorenal E74.09
    Hers' E74.09

Disease, diseased *(Continued)*
  glycogen storage *(Continued)*
    liver and kidney E74.09
    McArdle's E74.04
    muscle phosphofructokinase E74.09
    myocardium E74.02 *[I43]*
    Pompe's E74.02
    Tauri's E74.09
    type 0 E74.09
    type I E74.01
    type II E74.02
    type III E74.03
    type IV E74.09
    type V E74.04
    type VI-XI E74.09
    Von Gierke's E74.01
  Goldstein's (familial hemorrhagic
      telangiectasia) I78.0
  gonococcal NOS A54.9
  graft-versus-host (GVH) D89.813
    acute D89.810
    acute on chronic D89.812
    chronic D89.811
  grainhandler's J67.8
  granulomatous (childhood) (chronic) D71
  Graves' (exophthalmic goiter) —*see*
      Hyperthyroidism, with, goiter (diffuse)
  Griesinger's —*see* Ancylostomiasis
  Grisel's M43.6
  Gruby's (tinea tonsurans) B35.0
  Guillain-Barré G61.0
  Guinon's (motor-verbal tic) F95.2
  gum K06.9
  gynecological N94.9
  H (Hartnup's) E72.02
  Haff —*see* Poisoning, mercury
  Hageman (congenital factor XII deficiency)
      D68.2
  hair (color) (shaft) L67.9
    follicles L73.9
      specified NEC L73.8
  Hamman's (spontaneous mediastinal
      emphysema) J98.2
  hand, foot and mouth B08.4
  Hansen's —*see* Leprosy
  Hantavirus, with pulmonary manifestations
      B33.4
    with renal manifestations A98.5
  Harada's H30.81-●
  Hartnup (pellagra-cerebellar ataxia-renal
      aminoaciduria) E72.02
  Hart's (pellagra-cerebellar ataxia-renal
      aminoaciduria) E72.02
  Hashimoto's (struma lymphomatosa) E06.3
  Hb —*see* Disease, hemoglobin
  heart (organic) I51.9
    with
      pulmonary edema (acute) —*see also*
          Failure, ventricular, left I50.1
      rheumatic fever (conditions in I00)
        active I01.9
          with chorea I02.0
          specified NEC I01.8
        inactive or quiescent (with chorea)
            I09.9
          specified NEC I09.89
    amyloid E85.4 *[I43]*
    aortic (valve) I35.9
    arteriosclerotic or sclerotic (senile) —
        see Disease, heart, ischemic,
        atherosclerotic
    artery, arterial —*see* Disease, heart,
        ischemic, atherosclerotic
    beer drinkers' I42.6
    beriberi (wet) E51.12
    black I27.0
    congenital Q24.9
      cyanotic Q24.9
      specified NEC Q24.8
    coronary —*see* Disease, heart, ischemic
    cryptogenic I51.9

Disease, diseased *(Continued)*
  heart *(Continued)*
    fibroid —*see* Myocarditis
    functional I51.89
      psychogenic F45.8
    glycogen storage E74.02 *[I43]*
    gonococcal A54.83
    hypertensive —*see* Hypertension, heart
    hyperthyroid —*see also* Hyperthyroidism
        E05.90 *[I43]*
      with thyroid storm E05.91 *[I43]*
    ischemic (chronic or with a stated duration
        of over 4 weeks) I25.9
      atherosclerotic (of) I25.10
        with angina pectoris —*see*
            Arteriosclerosis, coronary (artery)
        coronary artery bypass graft —*see*
            Arteriosclerosis, coronary
            (artery),
        cardiomyopathy I25.5
        diagnosed on ECG or other special
            investigation, but currently
            presenting no symptoms I25.6
        silent I25.6
        specified form NEC I25.89
    kyphoscoliotic I27.1
    meningococcal A39.50
      endocarditis A39.51
      myocarditis A39.52
      pericarditis A39.53
    mitral I05.9
      specified NEC I05.8
    muscular —*see* Degeneration, myocardial
    psychogenic (functional) F45.8
    pulmonary (chronic) I27.9
      in schistosomiasis B65.9 *[I52]*
      specified NEC I27.89
    rheumatic (chronic) (inactive) (old)
        (quiescent) (with chorea) I09.9
      active or acute I01.9
        with chorea (acute) (rheumatic)
            (Sydenham's) I02.0
      specified NEC I09.89
    senile —*see* Myocarditis
    syphilitic A52.06
      aortic A52.03
        aneurysm A52.01
      congenital A50.54 *[I52]*
    thyrotoxic —*see also* Thyrotoxicosis E05.90
        [I43]
      with thyroid storm E05.91 *[I43]*
    valve, valvular (obstructive)
        (regurgitant) —*see also* Endocarditis
      congenital NEC Q24.8
        pulmonary Q22.3
    vascular —*see* Disease, cardiovascular
  heavy chain NEC C88.2
    alpha C88.3
    gamma C88.2
    mu C88.2
  Hebra's
    pityriasis
      maculata et circinata L42
      rubra pilaris L44.0
    prurigo L28.2
  hematopoietic organs D75.9
  hemoglobin or Hb
    abnormal (mixed) NEC D58.2
      with thalassemia D56.9
    AS genotype D57.3
    Bart's D56.0
    C (Hb-C) D58.2
      with other abnormal hemoglobin NEC
          D58.2
      elliptocytosis D58.1
      Hb-S D57.2-●
      sickle-cell D57.2-●
      thalassemia D56.8
    Constant Spring D58.2
    D (Hb-D) D58.2
    E (Hb-E) D58.2

Disease, diseased *(Continued)*
  hemoglobin or Hb *(Continued)*
    E-beta thalassemia D56.5
    elliptocytosis D58.1
    H (Hb-H) (thalassemia) D56.0
      with other abnormal hemoglobin NEC
        D56.9
      Constant Spring D56.0
    I thalassemia D56.9
    M D74.0
    S or SS D57.1
    ▶with
      ▶acute chest syndrome D57.01
      ▶cerebral vascular involvement D57.03
      ▶crisis (painful) D57.00
        ▶with complication specified NEC
          D57.09
      ▶splenic sequestration D57.02
      ▶vasoocclusive pain D57.00
    ▶beta plus D57.44
      ▶with
        ▶acute chest syndrome D57.451
        ▶cerebral vascular involvement
          D57.453
        ▶crisis D57.459
        ▶with specified complication NEC
          D57.458
        ▶splenic sequestration D57.452
        ▶vasoocclusive pain D57.459
      ▶without crisis D57.44
    ▶beta zero D57.42
      ▶with
        ▶acute chest syndrome D57.431
        ▶cerebral vascular involvement
          D57.433
        ▶crisis D57.439
        ▶with specified complication NEC
          D57.438
        ▶splenic sequestration D57.432
        ▶vasoocclusive pain D57.439
      ▶without crisis D57.42
    SC D57.2-●
    SD D57.8-●
    SE D57.8-●
    spherocytosis D58.0
    unstable, hemolytic D58.2
  hemolytic (newborn) P55.9
   ⇒autoimmune D59.10
    ▶cold type (primary) (secondary)
      (symptomatic) D59.12
    ▶mixed type (primary) (secondary)
      (symptomatic) D59.13
    ▶warm type (primary) (secondary)
      (symptomatic) D59.11
    drug-induced D59.0
    due to or with
      incompatibility
        ABO (blood group) P55.1
        blood (group) (Duffy) (K) (Kell)
          (Kidd) (Lewis) (M) (S) NEC P55.8
        Rh (blood group) (factor) P55.0
        Rh negative mother P55.0
    specified type NEC P55.8
    unstable hemoglobin D58.2
  hemorrhagic D69.9
    newborn P53
  Henoch (-Schönlein) (purpura nervosa) D69.0
  hepatic —*see* Disease, liver
  hepatobiliary K83.9
    toxic K71.9
  hepatolenticular E83.01
  heredodegenerative NEC
    spinal cord G95.89
  herpesviral, disseminated B00.7
  Hers' (glycogenosis VI) E74.09
  Herter (-Gee) (-Heubner) (nontropical sprue)
    K90.0
  Heubner-Herter (nontropical sprue) K90.0
  high fetal gene or hemoglobin thalassemia
    D56.9
  Hildenbrand's —*see* Typhus

Disease, diseased *(Continued)*
  hip (joint) M25.9
    congenital Q65.89
    suppurative M00.9
    tuberculous A18.02
  His (-Werner) (trench fever) A79.0
  Hodgson's I71.2
    ruptured I71.1
  Holla —*see* Spherocytosis
  hookworm B76.9
    specified NEC B76.8
  host-versus-graft D89.813
    acute D89.810
    acute on chronic D89.812
    chronic D89.811
  human immunodeficiency virus (HIV) B20
  Huntington's G10
    with dementia G10 *[F02.80]*
  Hutchinson's (cheiropompholyx) —*see*
    Hutchinson's disease
  hyaline (diffuse) (generalized)
    membrane (lung) (newborn) P22.0
      adult J80
  hydatid —*see* Echinococcus
  hydroxyapatite deposition M11.00
    ankle M11.07-●
    elbow M11.02-●
    foot joint M11.07-●
    hand joint M11.04-●
    hip M11.05-●
    knee M11.06-●
    multiple site M11.09
    shoulder M11.01-●
    vertebra M11.08
    wrist M11.03-●
  hyperkinetic —*see* Hyperkinesia
  hypertensive —*see* Hypertension
  hypophysis E23.7
  Iceland G93.3
  I-cell E77.0
  immune D89.9
  immunoproliferative (malignant) C88.9
    small intestinal C88.3
    specified NEC C88.8
  inclusion B25.9
    salivary gland B25.9
  infectious, infective B99.9
    congenital P37.9
      specified NEC P37.8
      viral P35.9
        specified type NEC P35.8
    specified NEC B99.8
  inflammatory
    penis N48.29
      abscess N48.21
      cellulitis N48.22
    prepuce N47.7
      balanoposthitis N47.6
    tubo-ovarian —*see* Salpingo-oophoritis
  intervertebral disc —*see also* Disorder, disc
    with myelopathy —*see* Disorder, disc, with,
      myelopathy
    cervical, cervicothoracic —*see* Disorder,
      disc, cervical
      with
        myelopathy —*see* Disorder, disc,
          cervical, with myelopathy
        neuritis, radiculitis or
          radiculopathy —*see* Disorder,
          disc, cervical, with neuritis
        specified NEC —*see* Disorder, disc,
          cervical, specified type NEC
    lumbar (with)
      myelopathy M51.06
      neuritis, radiculitis, radiculopathy or
        sciatica M51.16
      specified NEC M51.86
    lumbosacral (with)
      neuritis, radiculitis, radiculopathy or
        sciatica M51.17
      specified NEC M51.87

Disease, diseased *(Continued)*
  intervertebral disc *(Continued)*
    specified NEC —*see* Disorder, disc,
      specified NEC
    thoracic (with)
      myelopathy M51.04
      neuritis, radiculitis or radiculopathy
        M51.14
      specified NEC M51.84
    thoracolumbar (with)
      myelopathy M51.05
      neuritis, radiculitis or radiculopathy
        M51.15
      specified NEC M51.85
  intestine K63.9
    functional K59.9
      psychogenic F45.8
    ⇒specified NEC K59.89
    organic K63.9
    protozoal A07.9
    specified NEC K63.89
  iris H21.9
    specified NEC H21.89
  iron metabolism or storage E83.10
  island (scrub typhus) A75.3
  itai-itai —*see* Poisoning, cadmium
  Jakob-Creutzfeldt —*see* Creutzfeldt-Jakob
    disease or syndrome
  jaw M27.9
    fibrocystic M27.49
    specified NEC M27.8
  jigger B88.1
  joint —*see also* Disorder, joint
    Charcot's —*see* Arthropathy, neuropathic
      (Charcot)
    degenerative —*see* Osteoarthritis
      multiple M15.9
      spine —*see* Spondylosis
    hypertrophic —*see* Osteoarthritis
    sacroiliac M53.3
    specified NEC —*see* Disorder, joint,
      specified type NEC
    spine NEC —*see* Dorsopathy
    suppurative —*see* Arthritis, pyogenic or
      pyemic
  Jourdain's (acute gingivitis) K05.00
    nonplaque induced K05.01
    plaque induced K05.00
  Kaschin-Beck (endemic polyarthritis)
    M12.10
    ankle M12.17-●
    elbow M12.12-●
    foot joint M12.17-●
    hand joint M12.14-●
    hip M12.15-●
    knee M12.16-●
    multiple site M12.19
    shoulder M12.11-●
    vertebra M12.18
    wrist M12.13-●
  Katayama B65.2
  Kedani (scrub typhus) A75.3
  Keshan E59
  kidney (functional) (pelvis) N28.9
    chronic N18.9
      hypertensive —*see* Hypertension, kidney
      stage 1 N18.1
      stage 2 (mild) N18.2
     ⇒stage 3 (moderate) N18.30
        ▶stage 3a N18.31
        ▶stage 3b N18.32
      stage 4 (severe) N18.4
      stage 5 N18.5
    complicating pregnancy —*see* Pregnancy,
      complicated by, renal disease
    cystic (congenital) Q61.9
    diabetic —*see* E08-E13 with .22
    fibrocystic (congenital) Q61.8
    hypertensive —*see* Hypertension, kidney
    in (due to)
      schistosomiasis (bilharziasis) B65.9 *[N29]*

    ▶ New   ⇒ Revised   ~~deleted~~ Deleted   ● Use Additional Character(s)

Disease, diseased *(Continued)*
  kidney *(Continued)*
    multicystic Q61.4
    polycystic Q61.3
      adult type Q61.2
      childhood type NEC Q61.19
        collecting duct dilatation Q61.11
    Kimmelstiel (-Wilson) (intercapillary polycystic (congenital) glomerulosclerosis) —*see* E08-E13 with .21
    Kimura D21.9
      specified site (see Neoplasm, connective tissue benign)
    Kinnier Wilson's (hepatolenticular degeneration) E83.01
    kissing —*see* Mononucleosis, infectious
    Klebs' —*see also* Glomerulonephritis N05.- •
    Klippel-Feil (brevicollis) Q76.1
    Köhler-Pellegrini-Stieda (calcification, knee joint) —*see* Bursitis, tibial collateral
    Kok Q89.8
    König's (osteochondritis dissecans) —*see* Osteochondritis, dissecans
    Korsakoff's (nonalcoholic) F04
      alcoholic F10.96
        with dependence F10.26
    Kostmann's (infantile genetic agranulocytosis) D70.0
    kuru A81.81
    Kyasanur Forest A98.2
    labyrinth, ear —*see* Disorder, ear, inner
    lacrimal system —*see* Disorder, lacrimal system
    Lafora's —*see* Epilepsy, generalized, idiopathic
    Lancereaux-Mathieu (leptospiral jaundice) A27.0
    Landry's G61.0
    Larrey-Weil (leptospiral jaundice) A27.0
    larynx J38.7
    legionnaires' A48.1
      nonpneumonic A48.2
    Lenegre's I44.2
    lens H27.9
      specified NEC H27.8
    Lev's (acquired complete heart block) I44.2
    Lewy body (dementia) G31.83 *[F02.80]*
      with behavioral disturbance G31.83 *[F02.81]*
    Lichtheim's (subacute combined sclerosis with pernicious anemia) D51.0
    Lightwood's (renal tubular acidosis) N25.89
    Lignac's (cystinosis) E72.04
    lip K13.0
    lipid-storage E75.6
      specified NEC E75.5
    Lipschütz's N76.6
    liver (chronic) (organic) K76.9
      alcoholic (chronic) K70.9
        acute —*see* Disease, liver, alcoholic, hepatitis
        cirrhosis K70.30
          with ascites K70.31
        failure K70.40
          with coma K70.41
        fatty liver K70.0
        fibrosis K70.2
        hepatitis K70.10
          with ascites K70.11
        sclerosis K70.2
      cystic, congenital Q44.6
      drug-induced (idiosyncratic) (toxic) (predictable) (unpredictable) —*see* Disease, liver, toxic
      end stage K72.90
        due to hepatitis —*see* Hepatitis
      fatty, nonalcoholic (NAFLD) K76.0
        alcoholic K70.0
      fibrocystic (congenital) Q44.6
      fluke
        Chinese B66.1
        oriental B66.1
        sheep B66.3

Disease, diseased *(Continued)*
  liver *(Continued)*
    gestational alloimmune (GALD) P78.84
    glycogen storage E74.09 *[K77]*
    in (due to)
      schistosomiasis (bilharziasis) B65.9 *[K77]*
    inflammatory K75.9
      alcoholic K70.1
      specified NEC K75.89
    polycystic (congenital) Q44.6
    toxic K71.9
      with
        cholestasis K71.0
        cirrhosis (liver) K71.7
        fibrosis (liver) K71.7
        focal nodular hyperplasia K71.8
        hepatic granuloma K71.8
        hepatic necrosis K71.10
          with coma K71.11
        hepatitis NEC K71.6
          acute K71.2
          chronic
            active K71.50
              with ascites K71.51
            lobular K71.4
            persistent K71.3
        lupoid K71.50
          with ascites K71.51
        peliosis hepatis K71.8
        veno-occlusive disease (VOD) of liver K71.8
    veno-occlusive K76.5
  Lobo's (keloid blastomycosis) B48.0
  Lobstein's (brittle bones and blue sclera) Q78.0
  Ludwig's (submaxillary cellulitis) K12.2
  lumbosacral region M53.87
  lung J98.4
    black J60
    congenital Q33.9
    cystic J98.4
      congenital Q33.0
  ▶ dabbing (related) U07.0
  ▶ electronic cigarette (related) U07.0
    fibroid (chronic) —*see* Fibrosis, lung
    fluke B66.4
      oriental B66.4
    in
      amyloidosis E85.4 *[J99]*
      sarcoidosis D86.0
      Sjögren's syndrome M35.02
      systemic
        lupus erythematosus M32.13
        sclerosis M34.81
    interstitial J84.9
    of childhood, specified NEC J84.848
    respiratory bronchiolitis J84.115
    specified NEC J84.89
  ▶ with progressive fibrotic phenotype, in diseases classified elsewhere J84.170
  ⇨ obstructive (chronic) J44.9
    with
      acute
        bronchitis J44.0
        exacerbation NEC J44.1
        lower respiratory infection J44.0
      alveolitis, allergic J67.9
      asthma J44.9
      bronchiectasis J47.9
        with
          exacerbation (acute) J47.1
          lower respiratory infection J47.0
      bronchitis J44.9
        with
          exacerbation (acute) J44.1
          lower respiratory infection J44.0
      emphysema J43.9
      hypersensitivity pneumonitis J67.9
    decompensated J44.1
      with
        exacerbation (acute) J44.1

Disease, diseased *(Continued)*
  lung *(Continued)*
    polycystic J98.4
      congenital Q33.0
    rheumatoid (diffuse) (interstitial) —*see* Rheumatoid, lung
  ▶ vaping (associated) (device) (product) (use) U07.0
  Lutembacher's (atrial septal defect with mitral stenosis) Q21.1
  Lyme A69.20
  lymphatic (gland) (system) (channel) (vessel) I89.9
  lymphoproliferative D47.9
    specified NEC D47.Z9
    T-gamma D47.Z9
    X-linked D82.3
  Magitot's M27.2
  malarial —*see* Malaria
  malignant —*see also* Neoplasm, malignant, by site
  Manson's B65.1
  maple bark J67.6
  maple-syrup-urine E71.0
  Marburg (virus) A98.3
  Marion's (bladder neck obstruction) N32.0
  Marsh's (exophthalmic goiter) —*see* Hyperthyroidism, with, goiter (diffuse)
  mastoid (process) —*see* Disorder, ear, middle
  Mathieu's (leptospiral jaundice) A27.0
  Maxcy's A75.2
  McArdle (-Schmid-Pearson) (glycogenosis V) E74.04
  mediastinum J98.59
  medullary center (idiopathic) (respiratory) G93.89
  Meige's (chronic hereditary edema) Q82.0
  meningococcal —*see* Infection, meningococcal
  mental F99
    organic F09
  mesenchymal M35.9
  mesenteric embolic —*see also* Ischemia, intestine, acute K55.039
  metabolic, metabolism E88.9
    bilirubin E80.7
  metal-polisher's J62.8
  metastatic —*see also* Neoplasm, secondary, by site C79.9
  microvascular — code to condition
  microvillus
    atrophy Q43.8
    inclusion (MVD) Q43.8
  middle ear —*see* Disorder, ear, middle
  Mikulicz' (dryness of mouth, absent or decreased lacrimation) K11.8
  Milroy's (chronic hereditary edema) Q82.0
  Minamata —*see* Poisoning, mercury
  ⇨ minicore G71.29
  Minor's G95.19
  Minot's (hemorrhagic disease, newborn) P53
  Minot-von Willebrand-Jürgens (angiohemophilia) D68.0
  Mitchell's (erythromelalgia) I73.81
  mitral (valve) I05.9
    nonrheumatic I34.9
  mixed connective tissue M35.1
  moldy hay J67.0
  Monge's T70.29
  Morgagni-Adams-Stokes (syncope with heart block) I45.9
  Morgagni's (syndrome) (hyperostosis frontalis interna) M85.2
  Morton's (with metatarsalgia) —*see* Lesion, nerve, plantar
  Morvan's G60.8
  motor neuron (bulbar) (mixed type) (spinal) G12.20
    amyotrophic lateral sclerosis G12.21
    familial G12.24
    progressive bulbar palsy G12.22
    specified NEC G12.29

Disease, diseased (Continued)
- moyamoya I67.5
- mu heavy chain disease C88.2
- multicore G71.29
- multiminicore G71.29
- muscle —see also Disorder, muscle
  - inflammatory —see Myositis
  - ocular (external) —see Strabismus
- musculoskeletal system, soft tissue —see also Disorder, soft tissue
  - specified NEC —see Disorder, soft tissue, specified type NEC
- mushroom workers' J67.5
- mycotic B49
- myelodysplastic, not classified C94.6
- myeloproliferative, not classified C94.6
  - chronic D47.1
- myocardium, myocardial —see also Degeneration, myocardial I51.5
  - primary (idiopathic) I42.9
- myoneural G70.9
- Naegeli's D69.1
- nails L60.9
  - specified NEC L60.8
- Nairobi (sheep virus) A93.8
- nasal J34.9
- nemaline body G71.21
- nerve —see Disorder, nerve
- nervous system G98.8
  - autonomic G90.9
  - central G96.9
    - specified NEC G96.89
  - congenital Q07.9
  - parasympathetic G90.9
  - specified NEC G98.8
  - sympathetic G90.9
  - vegetative G90.9
- neuromuscular system G70.9
- Newcastle B30.8
- Nicolas (-Durand)-Favre (climatic bubo) A55
- nipple N64.9
  - Paget's C50.01-●
    - female C50.01-●
    - male C50.02-●
- Nishimoto (-Takeuchi) I67.5
- nonarthropod-borne NOS (viral) B34.9
  - enterovirus NEC B34.1
- nonautoimmune hemolytic D59.4
  - drug-induced D59.2
- Nonne-Milroy-Meige (chronic hereditary edema) Q82.0
- nose J34.9
- nucleus pulposus —see Disorder, disc
- nutritional E63.9
- oast-house-urine E72.19
  - ocular
    - herpesviral B00.50
    - zoster B02.30
- obliterative vascular I77.1
- Ohara's —see Tularemia
- Opitz's (congestive splenomegaly) D73.2
- Oppenheim-Urbach (necrobiosis lipoidica diabeticorum) —see E08-E13 with .620
- optic nerve NEC —see Disorder, nerve, optic
  - orbit —see Disorder, orbit
- organ
  - dabbing (related) U07.0
  - electronic cigarette (related) U07.0
  - vaping (associated) (device) (product) (use) U07.0
- Oriental liver fluke B66.1
- Oriental lung fluke B66.4
- Ormond's N13.5
- Oropouche virus A93.0
- Osler-Rendu (familial hemorrhagic telangiectasia) I78.0
- osteofibrocystic E21.0
- Otto's M24.7
- outer ear —see Disorder, ear, external

Disease, diseased (Continued)
- ovary (noninflammatory) N83.9
  - cystic N83.20-●
  - inflammatory —see Salpingo-oophoritis
  - polycystic E28.2
  - specified NEC N83.8
- Owren's (congenital) —see Defect, coagulation
- pancreas K86.9
  - cystic K86.2
  - fibrocystic E84.9
  - specified NEC K86.89
- panvalvular I08.9
  - specified NEC I08.8
- parametrium (noninflammatory) N83.9
- parasitic B89
  - cerebral NEC B71.9 [G94]
  - intestinal NOS B82.9
  - mouth B37.0
  - skin NOS B88.9
  - specified type —see Infestation
  - tongue B37.0
- parathyroid (gland) E21.5
  - specified NEC E21.4
- Parkinson's G20
- parodontal K05.6
- Parrot's (syphilitic osteochondritis) A50.02
- Parry's (exophthalmic goiter) —see Hyperthyroidism, with, goiter (diffuse)
- Parson's (exophthalmic goiter) —see Hyperthyroidism, with, goiter (diffuse)
- Paxton's (white piedra) B36.2
- pearl-worker's —see Osteomyelitis, specified type NEC
- Pellegrini-Stieda (calcification, knee joint) — see Bursitis, tibial collateral
- pelvis, pelvic
  - female NOS N94.9
    - specified NEC N94.89
  - gonococcal (acute) (chronic) A54.24
  - inflammatory (female) N73.9
    - acute N73.0
    - chlamydial A56.11
    - chronic N73.1
    - specified NEC N73.8
    - syphilitic (secondary) A51.42
      - late A52.76
    - tuberculous A18.17
  - organ, female N94.9
  - peritoneum, female NEC N94.89
- penis N48.9
  - inflammatory N48.29
    - abscess N48.21
    - cellulitis N48.22
  - specified NEC N48.89
- periapical tissues NOS K04.90
- periodontal K05.6
  - specified NEC K05.5
- periosteum —see Disorder, bone, specified type NEC
- peripheral
  - arterial I73.9
  - autonomic nervous system G90.9
  - nerves —see Polyneuropathy
  - vascular NOS I73.9
- peritoneum K66.9
  - pelvic, female NEC N94.89
  - specified NEC K66.8
- persistent mucosal (middle ear) H66.20
  - left H66.22
    - with right H66.23
  - right H66.21
    - with left H66.23
- Petit's —see Hernia, abdomen, specified site NEC
- pharynx J39.2
  - specified NEC J39.2
- Phocas' —see Mastopathy, cystic
- photochromogenic (acid-fast bacilli) (pulmonary) A31.0
  - nonpulmonary A31.9

Disease, diseased (Continued)
- Pick's G31.01 [F02.80]
  - with behavioral disturbance G31.01 [F02.81]
    - brain G31.01 [F02.80]
      - with behavioral disturbance G31.01 [F02.81]
  - of pericardium (pericardial pseudocirrhosis of liver) I31.1
- pigeon fancier's J67.2
- pineal gland E34.8
- pink —see Poisoning, mercury
- Pinkus' (lichen nitidus) L44.1
- pinworm B80
- Piry virus A93.8
- pituitary (gland) E23.7
- pituitary-snuff-taker's J67.8
- pleura (cavity) J94.9
  - specified NEC J94.8
- pneumatic drill (hammer) T75.21
- Pollitzer's (hidradenitis suppurativa) L73.2
- polycystic
  - kidney or renal Q61.3
    - adult type Q61.2
    - childhood type NEC Q61.19
      - collecting duct dilatation Q61.11
  - liver or hepatic Q44.6
  - lung or pulmonary J98.4
    - congenital Q33.0
  - ovary, ovaries E28.2
  - spleen Q89.09
- polyethylene T84.05-●
- Pompe's (glycogenosis II) E74.02
- Posadas-Wernicke B38.9
- Potain's (pulmonary edema) —see Edema, lung
- prepuce N47.8
  - inflammatory N47.7
    - balanoposthitis N47.6
- Pringle's (tuberous sclerosis) Q85.1
- prion, central nervous system A81.9
  - specified NEC A81.89
- prostate N42.9
  - specified NEC N42.89
- protozoal B64
  - acanthamebiasis —see Acanthamebiasis
  - African trypanosomiasis —see African trypanosomiasis
  - babesiosis —(see also Babesiosis) B60.00
  - Chagas disease —see Chagas disease
  - intestine, intestinal A07.9
  - leishmaniasis —see Leishmaniasis
  - malaria —see Malaria
  - naegleriasis B60.2
  - pneumocystosis B59
  - specified organism NEC B60.8
  - toxoplasmosis —see Toxoplasmosis
- pseudo-Hurler's E77.0
- psychiatric F99
- psychotic —see Psychosis
- Puente's (simple glandular cheilitis) K13.0
- puerperal —see also Puerperal O90.89
- pulmonary —see also Disease, lung
  - artery I28.9
  - chronic obstructive J44.9
    - with
      - acute bronchitis J44.0
      - exacerbation (acute) J44.1
      - lower respiratory infection (acute) J44.0
    - decompensated J44.1
      - with
        - exacerbation (acute) J44.1
  - heart I27.9
    - specified NEC I27.89
  - hypertensive (vascular) —see also Hypertension, pulmonary I27.20
    - primary (idiopathic) I27.0
  - valve I37.9
    - rheumatic I09.89
- pulp (dental) NOS K04.90

▶ New ⇒ Revised ~~deleted~~ Deleted ● Use Additional Character(s)

Disease, diseased *(Continued)*
  pulseless M31.4
  Putnam's (subacute combined sclerosis with pernicious anemia) D51.0
  Pyle (-Cohn) (metaphyseal dysplasia) Q78.5
  ragpicker's or ragsorter's A22.1
  Raynaud's —*see* Raynaud's disease
  reactive airway —*see* Asthma
  Reclus' (cystic) —*see* Mastopathy, cystic
  rectum K62.9
    specified NEC K62.89
  Refsum's (heredopathia atactica polyneuritiformis) G60.1
  renal (functional) (pelvis) —*see also* Disease, kidney N28.9
    with
      edema —*see* Nephrosis
      glomerular lesion —*see* Glomerulonephritis
        with edema —*see* Nephrosis
      interstitial nephritis N12
    acute N28.9
    chronic —*see also* Disease, kidney, chronic N18.9
    cystic, congenital Q61.9
    diabetic —*see* E08-E13 with .22
    end-stage (failure) N18.6
      due to hypertension I12.0
    fibrocystic (congenital) Q61.8
    hypertensive —*see* Hypertension, kidney
    lupus M32.14
    phosphate-losing (tubular) N25.0
    polycystic (congenital) Q61.3
      adult type Q61.2
      childhood type NEC Q61.19
        collecting duct dilatation Q61.11
    rapidly progressive N01.9
    subacute N01.9
  Rendu-Osler-Weber (familial hemorrhagic telangiectasia) I78.0
  renovascular (arteriosclerotic) —*see* Hypertension, kidney
  respiratory (tract) J98.9
    acute or subacute NOS J06.9
      due to
        chemicals, gases, fumes or vapors (inhalation) J68.3
        external agent J70.9
          specified NEC J70.8
        radiation J70.0
        smoke inhalation J70.5
      noninfectious J39.8
    chronic NOS J98.9
      due to
        chemicals, gases, fumes or vapors J68.4
        external agent J70.9
          specified NEC J70.8
        radiation J70.1
      newborn P27.9
        specified NEC P27.8
    due to
      chemicals, gases, fumes or vapors J68.9
        acute or subacute NEC J68.3
        chronic J68.4
      external agent J70.9
        specified NEC J70.8
      newborn P28.9
        specified type NEC P28.89
    upper J39.9
      acute or subacute J06.9
      noninfectious NEC J39.8
      specified NEC J39.8
      streptococcal J06.9
  retina, retinal H35.9
    Batten's or Batten-Mayou E75.4 [H36]
    specified NEC H35.89
  rheumatoid —*see* Arthritis, rheumatoid
  rickettsial NOS A79.9
    specified type NEC A79.89
  Riga (-Fede) (cachectic aphthae) K14.0
  Riggs' (compound periodontitis) —*see* Periodontitis
  Ritter's L00

Disease, diseased *(Continued)*
  Rivalta's (cervicofacial actinomycosis) A42.2
  ▶ rod body G71.21
  Robles' (onchocerciasis) B73.01
  Roger's (congenital interventricular septal defect) Q21.0
  Rosenthal's (factor XI deficiency) D68.1
  Ross River B33.1
  Rossbach's (hyperchlorhydria) K31.89
    psychogenic F45.8
  Rotes Quérol —*see* Hyperostosis, ankylosing
  Roth (-Bernhardt) —*see* Mononeuropathy, lower limb, meralgia paresthetica
  Runeberg's (progressive pernicious anemia) D51.0
  sacroiliac NEC M53.3
  salivary gland or duct K11.9
    inclusion B25.9
    specified NEC K11.8
    virus B25.9
  sandworm B76.9
  Schimmelbusch's —*see* Mastopathy, cystic
  Schmorl's —*see* Schmorl's disease or nodes
  Schönlein (-Henoch) (purpura rheumatica) D69.0
  Schottmüller's —*see* Fever, paratyphoid
  Schultz's (agranulocytosis) —*see* Agranulocytosis
  Schwalbe-Ziehen-Oppenheim G24.1
  Schwartz-Jampel G71.13
  sclera H15.9
    specified NEC H15.89
  scrofulous (tuberculous) A18.2
  scrotum N50.9
  sebaceous glands L73.9
  semilunar cartilage, cystic —*see also* Derangement, knee, meniscus, cystic
  seminal vesicle N50.9
  serum NEC —*see also* Reaction, serum T80.69
  sexually transmitted A64
    anogenital
      herpesviral infection —*see* Herpes, anogenital
      warts A63.0
    chancroid A57
    chlamydial infection —*see* Chlamydia
    gonorrhea —*see* Gonorrhea
    granuloma inguinale A58
    specified organism NEC A63.8
    syphilis —*see* Syphilis
    trichomoniasis —*see* Trichomoniasis
  Sézary C84.1- •
  shimamushi (scrub typhus) A75.3
  shipyard B30.0
  sickle-cell D57.1
  ▶ with
    ▶ acute chest syndrome D57.01
    ▶ cerebral vascular involvement D57.03
    ▶ crisis (painful) D57.00
      ▶ with complication specified NEC D57.09
    ▶ splenic sequestration D57.02
    ▶ vasoocclusive pain D57.00
    ~~with crisis (vasoocclusive pain) D57.00~~
    ~~with~~
      ~~acute chest syndrome D57.01~~
      ~~splenic sequestration D57.02~~
  elliptocytosis D57.8- •
  Hb-C D57.20
  ▶ with
    ▶ acute chest syndrome D57.211
    ▶ cerebral vascular involvement D57.213
    ▶ crisis (painful) D57.219
      ▶ with specified complication NEC D57.218
    ▶ splenic sequestration D57.212
    ▶ vasoocclusive pain D57.219
    ~~with crisis (vasoocclusive pain) D57.219~~
    ~~with~~
      ~~acute chest syndrome D57.211~~
      ~~splenic sequestration D57.212~~
    without crisis D57.20

Disease, diseased *(Continued)*
  sickle-cell *(Continued)*
    Hb-SD D57.80
    ▶ with
      ▶ acute chest syndrome D57.811
      ▶ cerebral vascular involvement D57.813
      ▶ crisis (painful) D57.819
        ▶ with complication specified NEC D57.818
      ▶ splenic sequestration D57.812
      ▶ vasoocclusive pain D57.819
    ▶ without crisis D57.80
    ~~with crisis D57.819~~
      ~~with~~
        ~~acute chest syndrome D57.811~~
        ~~splenic sequestration D57.812~~
    Hb-SE D57.80
    ▶ with
      ▶ acute chest syndrome D57.811
      ▶ cerebral vascular involvement D57.813
      ▶ crisis (painful) D57.819
        ▶ with complication specified NEC D57.818
      ▶ splenic sequestration D57.812
      ▶ vasoocclusive pain D57.819
    ▶ without crisis D57.80
    ~~with crisis D57.819~~
      ~~with~~
        ~~acute chest syndrome D57.811~~
        ~~splenic sequestration D57.812~~
    specified NEC D57.80
    ▶ with
      ▶ acute chest syndrome D57.811
      ▶ cerebral vascular involvement D57.813
      ▶ crisis (painful) D57.819
        ▶ with complication specified NEC D57.818
      ▶ splenic sequestration D57.812
      ▶ vasoocclusive pain D57.819
    ▶ without crisis D57.80
    ~~with crisis D57.819~~
      ~~with~~
        ~~acute chest syndrome D57.811~~
        ~~splenic sequestration D57.812~~
    spherocytosis D57.80
    ▶ with
      ▶ acute chest syndrome D57.811
      ▶ cerebral vascular involvement D57.813
      ▶ crisis (painful) D57.819
        ▶ with complication specified NEC D57.818
      ▶ splenic sequestration D57.812
      ▶ vasoocclusive pain D57.819
    ▶ without crisis D57.80
    ~~with crisis D57.819~~
      ~~with~~
        ~~acute chest syndrome D57.811~~
        ~~splenic sequestration D57.812~~
    thalassemia D57.40
    ▶ with
      ▶ acute chest syndrome D57.411
      ▶ cerebral vascular involvement D57.413
      ▶ crisis (painful) D57.419
        ▶ with specified complication NEC D57.418
      ▶ splenic sequestration D57.412
      ▶ vasoocclusive pain D57.419
    ▶ beta plus D57.44
    ▶ with
      ▶ acute chest syndrome D57.451
      ▶ cerebral vascular involvement D57.453
      ▶ crisis D57.459
        ▶ with specified complication NEC D57.458
      ▶ splenic sequestration D57.452
      ▶ vasoocclusive pain D57.459
    ▶ without crisis D57.44

Disease, diseased (Continued)
sickle-cell (Continued)
  thalassemia (Continued)
    ▶ beta zero D57.42
      ▶ with
        ▶ acute chest syndrome D57.431
        ▶ cerebral vascular involvement
          D57.433
        ▶ crisis D57.439
          ▶ with specified complication NEC
            D57.438
        ▶ splenic sequestration D57.432
        ▶ vasoocclusive pain D57.439
      ▶ without crisis D57.42
    with crisis (vasoocclusive pain) D57.419
      with
        acute chest syndrome D57.411
        splenic sequestration D57.412
    without crisis D57.40
silo-filler's J68.8
  bronchitis J68.0
  pneumonitis J68.0
  pulmonary edema J68.1
simian B B00.4
Simons' (progressive lipodystrophy) E88.1
sin nombre virus B33.4
sinus —see Sinusitis
Sirkari's B55.0
sixth B08.20
  due to human herpesvirus 6 B08.21
  due to human herpesvirus 7 B08.22
skin L98.9
  due to metabolic disorder NEC E88.9 [L99]
  specified NEC L98.8
slim (HIV) B20
small vessel I73.9
Sneddon-Wilkinson (subcorneal pustular
  dermatosis) L13.1
South African creeping B88.0
spinal (cord) G95.9
  congenital Q06.9
  specified NEC G95.89
spine —see also Spondylopathy
  joint —see Dorsopathy
  tuberculous A18.01
spinocerebellar (hereditary) G11.9
  specified NEC G11.8
spleen D73.9
  amyloid E85.4 [D77]
  organic D73.9
  polycystic Q89.09
  postinfectional D73.89
sponge-diver's —see Toxicity, venom, marine
  animal, sea anemone
Startle Q89.8
Steinert's G71.11
Sticker's (erythema infectiosum) B08.3
Stieda's (calcification, knee joint) —see
  Bursitis, tibial collateral
Stokes' (exophthalmic goiter) —see
  Hyperthyroidism, with, goiter (diffuse)
Stokes-Adams (syncope with heart block)
  I45.9
stomach K31.9
  functional, psychogenic F45.8
  specified NEC K31.89
stonemason's J62.8
storage
  glycogen —see Disease, glycogen storage
  mucopolysaccharide —see
    Mucopolysaccharidosis
striatopallidal system NEC G25.89
Stuart-Prower (congenital factor X deficiency)
  D68.2
Stuart's (congenital factor X deficiency) D68.2
subcutaneous tissue —see Disease, skin
supporting structures of teeth K08.9
  specified NEC K08.89
suprarenal (capsule) (gland) E27.9
  hyperfunction E27.0
  specified NEC E27.8

Disease, diseased (Continued)
sweat glands L74.9
  specified NEC L74.8
Sweeley-Klionsky E75.21
Swift (-Feer) —see Poisoning, mercury
swimming-pool granuloma A31.1
Sylvest's (epidemic pleurodynia) B33.0
sympathetic nervous system G90.9
synovium —see Disorder, synovium
syphilitic —see Syphilis
systemic tissue mast cell D47.02
tanapox (virus) B08.71
Tangier E78.6
Tarral-Besnier (pityriasis rubra pilaris) L44.0
Tauri's E74.09
tear duct —see Disorder, lacrimal system
tendon, tendinous —see also Disorder, tendon
  nodular —see Trigger finger
terminal vessel I73.9
testis N50.9
thalassemia Hb-S —see Disease, sickle-cell,
  thalassemia
Thaysen-Gee (nontropical sprue) K90.0
Thomsen G71.12
throat J39.2
  septic J02.0
thromboembolic —see Embolism
thymus (gland) E32.9
  specified NEC E32.8
thyroid (gland) E07.9
  heart —see also Hyperthyroidism E05.90 [I43]
    with thyroid storm E05.91 [I43]
  specified NEC E07.8
Tietze's M94.0
tongue K14.9
  specified NEC K14.89
tonsils, tonsillar (and adenoids) J35.9
tooth, teeth K08.9
  hard tissues K03.9
    specified NEC K03.89
  pulp NEC K04.99
  specified NEC K08.89
Tourette's F95.2
trachea NEC J39.8
tricuspid I07.9
  nonrheumatic I36.9
triglyceride-storage E75.5
trophoblastic —see Mole, hydatidiform
tsutsugamushi A75.3
tube (fallopian) (noninflammatory) N83.9
  inflammatory —see Salpingitis
  specified NEC N83.8
tuberculous NEC —see Tuberculosis
tubo-ovarian (noninflammatory) N83.9
  inflammatory —see Salpingo-oophoritis
  specified NEC N83.8
tubotympanic, chronic —see Otitis, media,
  suppurative, chronic, tubotympanic
tubulo-interstitial N15.9
  specified NEC N15.8
tympanum —see Disorder, tympanic
  membrane
Uhl's Q24.8
Underwood's (sclerema neonatorum) P83.0
Unverricht (-Lundborg) —see Epilepsy,
  generalized, idiopathic
Urbach-Oppenheim (necrobiosis lipoidica
  diabeticorum) —see E08-E13 with .620
ureter N28.9
  in (due to)
    schistosomiasis (bilharziasis) B65.0 [N29]
urethra N36.9
  specified NEC N36.8
urinary (tract) N39.9
  bladder N32.9
    specified NEC N32.89
  specified NEC N39.8
uterus (noninflammatory) N85.9
  infective —see Endometritis
  inflammatory —see Endometritis
  specified NEC N85.8

Disease, diseased (Continued)
uveal tract (anterior) H21.9
  posterior H31.9
vagabond's B85.1
vagina, vaginal (noninflammatory) N89.9
  inflammatory NEC N76.89
  specified NEC N89.8
valve, valvular I38
  multiple I08.9
    specified NEC I08.8
van Creveld-von Gierke (glycogenosis I)
  E74.01
vas deferens N50.9
vascular I99.9
  arteriosclerotic —see Arteriosclerosis
  ciliary body NEC —see Disorder, iris,
    vascular
  hypertensive —see Hypertension
  iris NEC —see Disorder, iris, vascular
  obliterative I77.1
    peripheral I73.9
  occlusive I99.8
  peripheral (occlusive) I73.9
    in diabetes mellitus —see E08-E13 with .51
vasomotor I73.9
vasospastic I73.9
vein I87.9
venereal —see also Disease, sexually
  transmitted A64
  chlamydial NEC A56.8
    anus A56.3
    genitourinary NOS A56.2
    pharynx A56.4
    rectum A56.3
  fifth A55
  sixth A55
  specified nature or type NEC A63.8
vertebra, vertebral —see also Spondylopathy
  disc —see Disorder, disc
vibration —see Vibration, adverse effects
viral, virus —see also Disease, by type of virus
  B34.9
  arbovirus NOS A94
  arthropod-borne NOS A94
  congenital P35.9
    specified NEC P35.8
  Hanta (with renal manifestations)
    (Dobrava) (Puumala) (Seoul) A98.5
    with pulmonary manifestations (Andes)
      (Bayou) (Bermejo) (Black Creek
      Canal) (Choclo) (Juquitiba) (Laguna
      negra) (Lechiguanas) (New York)
      (Oran) (Sin nombre) B33.4
  Hantaan (Korean hemorrhagic fever) A98.5
  human immunodeficiency (HIV) B20
  Kunjin A83.4
  nonarthropod-borne NOS B34.9
  ⇒ Powassan A84.81
  Rocio (encephalitis) A83.6
  Sin nombre (Hantavirus) (cardio)-
    pulmonary syndrome B33.4
  Tahyna B33.8
  vesicular stomatitis A93.8
vitreous H43.9
  specified NEC H43.89
vocal cord J38.3
Volkmann's, acquired T79.6
von Eulenburg's (congenital paramyotonia)
  G71.19
von Gierke's (glycogenosis I) E74.01
von Graefe's —see Strabismus, paralytic,
  ophthalmoplegia, progressive
von Willebrand (-Jürgens) (angiohemophilia)
  D68.0
Vrolik's (osteogenesis imperfecta) Q78.0
vulva (noninflammatory) N90.9
  inflammatory NEC N76.89
  specified NEC N90.89
Wallgren's (obstruction of splenic vein with
  collateral circulation) I87.8
Wassilieff's (leptospiral jaundice) A27.0

▶ New   ⇒ Revised   ~~deleted~~ Deleted   ● Use Additional Character(s)

Disease, diseased (Continued)
  wasting NEC R64
    due to malnutrition E41
  Waterhouse-Friderichsen A39.1
  Wegner's (syphilitic osteochondritis) A50.02
  Weil's (leptospiral jaundice of lung) A27.0
  Weir Mitchell's (erythromelalgia) I73.81
  Werdnig-Hoffmann G12.0
  Wermer's E31.21
  Werner-His (trench fever) A79.0
  Werner-Schultz (neutropenic splenomegaly)
    D73.81
  Wernicke-Posadas B38.9
  whipworm B79
  white blood cells D72.9
    specified NEC D72.89
  white matter R90.82
  white-spot, meaning lichen sclerosus et
    atrophicus L90.0
    penis N48.0
    vulva N90.4
  Wilkie's K55.1
  Wilkinson-Sneddon (subcorneal pustular
    dermatosis) L13.1
  Willis' —see Diabetes
  Wilson's (hepatolenticular degeneration) E83.01
  woolsorter's A22.1
  yaba monkey tumor B08.72
  yaba pox (virus) B08.72
  Zika virus A92.5
  zoonotic, bacterial A28.9
    congenital P35.4
    specified type NEC A28.8
Disfigurement (due to scar) L90.5
Disgerminoma —see Dysgerminoma
DISH (diffuse idiopathic skeletal
  hyperostosis) —see Hyperostosis,
  ankylosing
Disinsertion, retina —see Detachment, retina
Dislocatable hip, congenital Q65.6
Dislocation (articular)
  with fracture —see Fracture
  acromioclavicular (joint) S43.10-●
    with displacement
      100%-200% S43.12-●
      more than 200% S43.13-●
    inferior S43.14-●
    posterior S43.15-●
  ankle S93.0-●
  astragalus —see Dislocation, ankle
  atlantoaxial S13.121
  atlantooccipital S13.111
  atloidooccipital S13.111
  breast bone S23.29
  capsule, joint code by site under Dislocation
  carpal (bone) —see Dislocation, wrist
  carpometacarpal (joint) NEC S63.05-●
    thumb S63.04-●
  cartilage (joint) - code by site under
    Dislocation
  cervical spine (vertebra) —see Dislocation,
    vertebra, cervical
  chronic —see Dislocation, recurrent
  clavicle —see Dislocation, acromioclavicular
    joint
  coccyx S33.2
  congenital NEC Q68.8
  coracoid —see Dislocation, shoulder
  costal cartilage S23.29
  costochondral S23.29
  cricoarytenoid articulation S13.29
  cricothyroid articulation S13.29
  dorsal vertebra —see Dislocation, vertebra,
    thoracic
  ear ossicle —see Discontinuity, ossicles, ear
  elbow S53.10-●
    congenital Q68.8
    pathological —see Dislocation, pathological
      NEC, elbow
    radial head alone —see Dislocation, radial
      head

Dislocation (Continued)
  elbow (Continued)
    recurrent —see Dislocation, recurrent,
      elbow
    traumatic S53.10-●
      anterior S53.11-●
      lateral S53.14-●
      medial S53.13-●
      posterior S53.12-●
      specified type NEC S53.19-●
  eye, nontraumatic —see Luxation, globe
  eyeball, nontraumatic —see Luxation, globe
  femur
    distal end —see Dislocation, knee
    proximal end —see Dislocation, hip
  fibula
    distal end —see Dislocation, ankle
    proximal end —see Dislocation, knee
  finger S63.25-●
    index S63.25-●
    interphalangeal S63.27-●
      distal S63.29-●
        index S63.29-●
        little S63.29-●
        middle S63.29-●
        ring S63.29-●
      index S63.27-●
      little S63.27-●
      middle S63.27-●
      proximal S63.28-●
        index S63.28-●
        little S63.28-●
        middle S63.28-●
        ring S63.28-●
      ring S63.27-●
    little S63.25-●
    metacarpophalangeal S63.26-●
      index S63.26-●
      little S63.26-●
      middle S63.26-●
      ring S63.26-●
    middle S63.25-●
    recurrent —see Dislocation, recurrent,
      finger
    ring S63.25-●
    thumb —see Dislocation, thumb
  foot S93.30-●
    recurrent —see Dislocation, recurrent,
      foot
    specified site NEC S93.33-●
    tarsal joint S93.31-●
    tarsometatarsal joint S93.32-●
    toe —see Dislocation, toe
  fracture —see Fracture
  glenohumeral (joint) —see Dislocation,
    shoulder
  glenoid —see Dislocation, shoulder
  habitual —see Dislocation, recurrent
  hip S73.00-●
    anterior S73.03-●
      obturator S73.02-●
    central S73.04-●
    congenital (total) Q65.2
      bilateral Q65.1
      partial Q65.5
        bilateral Q65.4
        unilateral Q65.3-●
      unilateral Q65.0-●
    developmental M24.85-●
    pathological —see Dislocation, pathological
      NEC, hip
    posterior S73.01-●
    recurrent —see Dislocation, recurrent,
      hip
  humerus, proximal end —see Dislocation,
    shoulder
  incomplete —see Subluxation, by site
  incus —see Discontinuity, ossicles,
    ear
  infracoracoid —see Dislocation,
    shoulder

Dislocation (Continued)
  innominate (pubic junction) (sacral
    junction) S33.39
    acetabulum —see Dislocation, hip
  interphalangeal (joint(s))
    finger S63.279
      distal S63.29-●
        index S63.29-●
        little S63.29-●
        middle S63.29-●
        ring S63.29-●
      index S63.27-●
      little S63.27-●
      middle S63.27-●
      proximal S63.28-●
        index S63.28-●
        little S63.28-●
        middle S63.28-●
        ring S63.28-●
      ring S63.27-●
    foot or toe —see Dislocation, toe
    thumb S63.12-●
  jaw (cartilage) (meniscus) S03.0-●
  joint prosthesis —see Complications, joint
    prosthesis, mechanical, displacement,
    by site
  knee S83.106
    cap —see Dislocation, patella
    congenital Q68.2
    old M23.8X-●
    patella —see Dislocation, patella
    pathological —see Dislocation, pathological
      NEC, knee
    proximal tibia
      anteriorly S83.11-●
      laterally S83.14-●
      medially S83.13-●
      posteriorly S83.12-●
    recurrent —see also Derangement, knee,
      specified NEC
    specified type NEC S83.19-●
  lacrimal gland H04.16-●
  lens (complete) H27.10-●
    anterior H27.12-●
    congenital Q12.1
    ocular implant —see Complications,
      intraocular lens
    partial H27.11-●
    posterior H27.13-●
    traumatic S05.8X-●
  ligament code by site under Dislocation
  lumbar (vertebra) —see Dislocation, vertebra,
    lumbar
  lumbosacral (vertebra) —see also Dislocation,
    vertebra, lumbar
    congenital Q76.49
  mandible S03.0-●
  meniscus (knee) —see Tear, meniscus
    other sites code by site under
      Dislocation
  metacarpal (bone)
    distal end —see Dislocation, finger
    proximal end S63.06-●
  metacarpophalangeal (joint)
    finger S63.26-●
      index S63.26-●
      little S63.26-●
      middle S63.26-●
      ring S63.26-●
    thumb S63.11-●
  metatarsal (bone) —see Dislocation, foot
  metatarsophalangeal (joint(s)) —see
    Dislocation, toe
  midcarpal (joint) S63.03-●
  midtarsal (joint) —see Dislocation, foot
  neck S13.20
    specified site NEC S13.29
    vertebra —see Dislocation, vertebra,
      cervical
  nose (septal cartilage) S03.1
  occipitoatloid S13.111

Dislocation (*Continued*)

old —*see* Derangement, joint, specified type NEC
ossicles, ear —*see* Discontinuity, ossicles, ear
partial —*see* Subluxation, by site
patella S83.006
  congenital Q74.1
  lateral S83.01-•
  recurrent (nontraumatic) M22.0-•
    incomplete M22.1-•
  specified type NEC S83.09-•
pathological NEC M24.30
  ankle M24.37-•
  elbow M24.32-•
  foot joint M24.37-•
  hand joint M24.34-•
  hip M24.35-•
  knee M24.36-•
  lumbosacral joint —*see* subcategory M53.2
  pelvic region —*see* Dislocation, pathological, hip
  sacroiliac —*see* subcategory M53.2
  shoulder M24.31-•
▶ specified site NEC M24.39
  wrist M24.33-•
pelvis NEC S33.30
  specified NEC S33.39
phalanx
  finger or hand —*see* Dislocation, finger
  foot or toe —*see* Dislocation, toe
prosthesis, internal —*see* Complications, prosthetic device, by site, mechanical
radial head S53.006
  anterior S53.01-•
  posterior S53.02-•
  specified type NEC S53.09-•
radiocarpal (joint) S63.02-•
radiohumeral (joint) —*see* Dislocation, radial head
radioulnar (joint)
  distal S63.01-•
  proximal —*see* Dislocation, elbow
radius
  distal end —*see* Dislocation, wrist
  proximal end —*see* Dislocation, radial head
recurrent M24.40
  ankle M24.47-•
  elbow M24.42-•
  finger M24.44-•
  foot joint M24.47-•
  hand joint M24.44-•
  hip M24.45-•
  knee M24.46-•
    patella —*see* Dislocation, patella, recurrent
  patella —*see* Dislocation, patella, recurrent
  sacroiliac —*see* subcategory M53.2
  shoulder M24.41-•
▶ specified site NEC M24.49
  toe M24.47-•
  vertebra —*see also* subcategory M43.5
    atlantoaxial M43.4
      with myelopathy M43.3
  wrist M24.43-•
rib (cartilage) S23.29
sacrococcygeal S33.2
sacroiliac (joint) (ligament) S33.2
  congenital Q74.2
  recurrent —*see* subcategory M53.2
sacrum S33.2
scaphoid (bone) (hand) (wrist) —*see* Dislocation, wrist
  foot —*see* Dislocation, foot
scapula —*see* Dislocation, shoulder, girdle, scapula
semilunar cartilage, knee —*see* Tear, meniscus
septal cartilage (nose) S03.1
septum (nasal) (old) J34.2
sesamoid bone code by site under Dislocation

Dislocation (*Continued*)

shoulder (blade) (ligament) (joint) (traumatic) S43.006
  acromioclavicular —*see* Dislocation, acromioclavicular
  chronic —*see* Dislocation, recurrent, shoulder
  congenital Q68.8
  girdle S43.30-•
    scapula S43.31-•
    specified site NEC S43.39-•
  humerus S43.00-•
    anterior S43.01-•
    inferior S43.03-•
    posterior S43.02-•
  pathological —*see* Dislocation, pathological NEC, shoulder
  recurrent —*see* Dislocation, recurrent, shoulder
  specified type NEC S43.08-•
spine
  cervical —*see* Dislocation, vertebra, cervical
  congenital Q76.49
  due to birth trauma P11.5
  lumbar —*see* Dislocation, vertebra, lumbar
  thoracic —*see* Dislocation, vertebra, thoracic
spontaneous —*see* Dislocation, pathological
sternoclavicular (joint) S43.206
  anterior S43.21-•
  posterior S43.22-•
sternum S23.29
subglenoid —*see* Dislocation, shoulder
symphysis pubis S33.4
talus —*see* Dislocation, ankle
tarsal (bone(s)) (joint(s)) —*see* Dislocation, foot
tarsometatarsal (joint(s)) —*see* Dislocation, foot
temporomandibular (joint) S03.0-•
thigh, proximal end —*see* Dislocation, hip
thorax S23.20
  specified site NEC S23.29
  vertebra —*see* Dislocation, vertebra
thumb S63.10-•
  interphalangeal joint —*see* Dislocation, interphalangeal (joint), thumb
  metacarpophalangeal joint —*see* Dislocation, metacarpophalangeal (joint), thumb
thyroid cartilage S13.29
tibia
  distal end —*see* Dislocation, ankle
  proximal end —*see* Dislocation, knee
tibiofibular (joint)
  distal —*see* Dislocation, ankle
  superior —*see* Dislocation, knee
toe(s) S93.106
  great S93.10-•
    interphalangeal joint S93.11-•
    metatarsophalangeal joint S93.12-•
  interphalangeal joint S93.119
  lesser S93.106
    interphalangeal joint S93.11-•
    metatarsophalangeal joint S93.12-•
  metatarsophalangeal joint S93.12-•
tooth S03.2
trachea S23.29
ulna
  distal end S63.07-•
  proximal end —*see* Dislocation, elbow
ulnohumeral (joint) —*see* Dislocation, elbow
vertebra (articular process) (body) (traumatic)
  cervical S13.101
    atlantoaxial joint S13.121
    atlantooccipital joint S13.111
    atloidooccipital joint S13.111
    joint between
      C0 and C1 S13.111
      C1 and C2 S13.121

Dislocation (*Continued*)

vertebra (*Continued*)
  cervical (*Continued*)
    joint between (*Continued*)
      C2 and C3 S13.131
      C3 and C4 S13.141
      C4 and C5 S13.151
      C5 and C6 S13.161
      C6 and C7 S13.171
      C7 and T1 S13.181
    occipitoatloid joint S13.111
    congenital Q76.49
  lumbar S33.101
    joint between
      L1 and L2 S33.111
      L2 and L3 S33.121
      L3 and L4 S33.131
      L4 and L5 S33.141
  nontraumatic —*see* Displacement, intervertebral disc
  partial —*see* Subluxation, by site
  recurrent NEC —*see* subcategory M43.5
  thoracic S23.101
    joint between
      T1 and T2 S23.111
      T2 and T3 S23.121
      T3 and T4 S23.123
      T4 and T5 S23.131
      T5 and T6 S23.133
      T6 and T7 S23.141
      T7 and T8 S23.143
      T8 and T9 S23.151
      T9 and T10 S23.153
      T10 and T11 S23.161
      T11 and T12 S23.163
      T12 and L1 S23.171
wrist (carpal bone) S63.006
  carpometacarpal joint —*see* Dislocation, carpometacarpal (joint)
  distal radioulnar joint —*see* Dislocation, radioulnar (joint), distal
  metacarpal bone, proximal —*see* Dislocation, metacarpal (bone), proximal end
  midcarpal —*see* Dislocation, midcarpal (joint)
  radiocarpal joint —*see* Dislocation, radiocarpal (joint)
  recurrent —*see* Dislocation, recurrent, wrist
  specified site NEC S63.09-•
  ulna —*see* Dislocation, ulna, distal end
xiphoid cartilage S23.29
Disorder (of) —*see also* Disease
acantholytic L11.9
  specified NEC L11.8
acute
  psychotic —*see* Psychosis, acute
  stress F43.0
adjustment (grief) F43.20
  with
    anxiety F43.22
      with depressed mood F43.23
    conduct disturbance F43.24
      with emotional disturbance F43.25
    depressed mood F43.21
      with anxiety F43.23
    other specified symptom F43.29
adrenal (capsule) (gland) (medullary) E27.9
  specified NEC E27.8
adrenogenital E25.9
  drug-induced E25.8
  iatrogenic E25.8
  idiopathic E25.8
adult personality (and behavior) F69
  specified NEC F68.8
affective (mood) —*see* Disorder, mood
aggressive, unsocialized F91.1

▶ New   ➡ Revised   ~~deleted~~ Deleted   • Use Additional Character(s)

Disorder *(Continued)*
  alcohol-related F10.99
    with
      amnestic disorder, persisting
        F10.96
      anxiety disorder F10.980
      dementia, persisting F10.97
      intoxication F10.929
        with delirium F10.921
        uncomplicated F10.920
      mood disorder F10.94
      other specified F10.988
      psychotic disorder F10.959
        with
          delusions F10.950
          hallucinations F10.951
      sexual dysfunction F10.981
      sleep disorder F10.982
  alcohol use
    mild F10.10
      with
        alcohol-induced
          anxiety disorder F10.180
          bipolar and related disorder
            F10.14
          depressive disorder F10.14
          psychotic disorder F10.159
          sexual dysfunction F10.181
          sleep disorder F10.182
        alcohol intoxication F10.129
          delirium F10.121
      in remission (early) (sustained)
        F10.11
    moderate or severe F10.20
      with
        alcohol-induced
          anxiety disorder F10.280
          bipolar and related disorder
            F10.24
          depressive disorder F10.24
          major neurocognitive disorder,
            amnestic-confabulatory type
            F10.26
          major neurocognitive disorder,
            nonamnestic-confabulatory
            type F10.27
          mild neurocognitive disorder
            F10.288
          psychotic disorder F10.259
          sexual dysfunction F10.281
          sleep disorder F10.282
         alcohol intoxication F10.229
          delirium F10.221
      in remission (early) (sustained)
        F10.21
  allergic —*see* Allergy
  alveolar NEC J84.09
  amino-acid
    cystathioninuria E72.19
    cystinosis E72.04
    cystinuria E72.01
    glycinuria E72.09
    homocystinuria E72.11
    metabolism —*see* Disturbance,
      metabolism, amino-acid
    specified NEC E72.89
    neonatal, transitory P74.8
    renal transport NEC E72.09
    transport NEC E72.09
  amnesic, amnestic
    alcohol-induced F10.96
      with dependence F10.26
    due to (secondary to) general medical
      condition F04
    psychoactive NEC-induced F19.96
      with
        abuse F19.16
        dependence F19.26
    sedative, hypnotic or anxiolytic-•
      induced F13.96
      with dependence F13.26

Disorder *(Continued)*
  amphetamine-type substance use
    mild F15.10
      in remission (early) (sustained) F15.11
    moderate F15.20
      in remission (early) (sustained) F15.21
    severe F15.20
      in remission (early) (sustained) F15.21
  amphetamine (or other stimulant) use
    mild
      with
        amphetamine (or other stimulant)
          -induced
          anxiety disorder F15.180
          bipolar and related disorder F15.14
          depressive disorder F15.14
          obsessive-compulsive and related
            disorder F15.188
          psychotic disorder F15.159
          sexual dysfunction F15.181
        amphetamine, cocaine, or other
          stimulant intoxication
          with perceptual disturbances
            F15.122
          without perceptual disturbances
            F15.129
        intoxication delirium F15.121
    moderate or severe
      with
        amphetamine (or other stimulant)
          -induced
          anxiety disorder F15.280
          obsessive-compulsive and related
            disorder F15.288
          sexual dysfunction F15.281
          bipolar and related disorder F15.24
          depressive disorder F15.24
          psychotic disorder F15.259
        amphetamine, cocaine, or other
          stimulant intoxication
          with perceptual disturbances
            F15.222
          without perceptual disturbances
            F15.229
        intoxication delirium F15.221
  anaerobic glycolysis with anemia D55.2
  anxiety F41.9
    due to (secondary to)
      alcohol F10.980
        in
          abuse F10.180
          dependence F10.280
      amphetamine F15.980
        in
          abuse F15.180
          dependence F15.280
      anxiolytic F13.980
        in
          abuse F13.180
          dependence F13.280
      caffeine F15.980
        in
          abuse F15.180
          dependence F15.280
      cannabis F12.980
        in
          abuse F12.180
          dependence F12.280
      cocaine F14.980
        in
          abuse F14.180
          dependence F14.180
      general medical condition F06.4
      hallucinogen F16.980
        in
          abuse F16.180
          dependence F16.280
      hypnotic F13.980
        in
          abuse F13.180
          dependence F13.280

Disorder *(Continued)*
  anxiety *(Continued)*
    due to *(Continued)*
      inhalant F18.980
        in
          abuse F18.180
          dependence F18.280
      phencyclidine F16.980
        in
          abuse F16.180
          dependence F16.280
      psychoactive substance NEC
        F19.980
        in
          abuse F19.180
          dependence F19.280
      sedative F13.980
        in
          abuse F13.180
          dependence F13.280
      volatile solvents F18.980
        in
          abuse F18.180
          dependence F18.280
    generalized F41.1
    illness F45.21
    mixed
      with depression (mild) F41.8
      specified NEC F41.3
    organic F06.4
    phobic F40.9
      of childhood F40.8
    specified NEC F41.8
  aortic valve —*see* Endocarditis, aortic
  aromatic amino-acid metabolism E70.9
  ➡specified NEC E70.89
  arteriole NEC I77.89
  artery NEC I77.89
  articulation —*see* Disorder, joint
  attachment (childhood)
    disinhibited F94.2
    reactive F94.1
  attention-deficit hyperactivity (adolescent)
    (adult) (child) F98.8
    combined
      presentation F90.2
      type F90.2
    hyperactive
      impulsive presentation F90.1
      type F90.1
    inattentive
      presentation F90.0
      type F90.0
    specified type NEC F90.8
  attention-deficit without hyperactivity
    (adolescent) (adult) (child) F90.0
  auditory processing (central) H93.25
  autism spectrum F84.0
  autistic F84.0
  autoimmune D89.89
  autonomic nervous system G90.9
    specified NEC G90.8
  avoidant
    child or adolescent F40.10
    restrictive food intake F50.82
  balance
    acid-base E87.8
      mixed E87.4
    electrolyte E87.8
    fluid NEC E87.8
  behavioral (disruptive) —*see* Disorder,
    conduct
  beta-amino-acid metabolism E72.89
  bile acid and cholesterol metabolism
    E78.70
    Barth syndrome E78.71
    other specified E78.79
    Smith-Lemli-Opitz syndrome
      E78.72
  bilirubin excretion E80.6
  binge eating F50.81

Disorder *(Continued)*
  binocular
    movement H51.9
      convergence
        excess H51.12
        insufficiency H51.11
      internuclear ophthalmoplegia —*see*
        Ophthalmoplegia, internuclear
      palsy of conjugate gaze H51.Ø
      specified type NEC H51.8
    vision NEC —*see* Disorder, vision, binocular
  bipolar (I) (type 1) F31.9
    and related due to a known physiological
      condition
      with
        manic features FØ6.33
        manic- or hypomanic-like episodes
          FØ6.33
        mixed features FØ6.34
    current (or most recent) episode
      depressed F31.9
        with psychotic features F31.5
        without psychotic features
          F31.3Ø
          mild F31.31
          moderate F31.32
          severe (without psychotic features)
            F31.4
            with psychotic features
              F31.5
      hypomanic F31.Ø
      manic F31.9
        with psychotic features F31.2
        without psychotic features
          F31.1Ø
          mild F31.11
          moderate F31.12
          severe (without psychotic features)
            F31.13
            with psychotic features
              F31.2
      mixed F31.6Ø
        mild F31.61
        moderate F31.62
        severe (without psychotic features)
          F31.63
        with psychotic features F31.64
        severe depression (without psychotic
          features) F31.4
        with psychotic features F31.5
    II (type 2) F31.81
    in remission (currently) F31.7Ø
      in full remission
        most recent episode
          depressed F31.76
          hypomanic F31.72
          manic F31.74
          mixed F31.78
      in partial remission
        most recent episode
          depressed F31.75
          hypomanic F31.71
          manic F31.73
          mixed F31.77
    organic FØ6.3Ø
    single manic episode F3Ø.9
      mild F3Ø.11
      moderate F3Ø.12
      hhsevere (without psychotic symptoms)
        F3Ø.13
      with psychotic symptoms F3Ø.2
    specified NEC F31.89
  bladder N32.9
    functional NEC N31.9
    in schistosomiasis B65.Ø [N33]
    specified NEC N32.89
  bleeding D68.9
  blood D75.9
    in congenital early syphilis A5Ø.Ø9
      [D77]
  body dysmorphic F45.22

Disorder *(Continued)*
  bone M89.9
    continuity M84.9
      specified type NEC M84.8Ø
        ankle M84.87-•
        fibula M84.86-•
        foot M84.87-•
        hand M84.84-•
        humerus M84.82-•
        neck M84.88
        pelvis M84.859
        radius M84.83-•
        rib M84.88
        shoulder M84.81-•
        skull M84.88
        thigh M84.85-•
        tibia M84.86-•
        ulna M84.83-•
        vertebra M84.88
    density and structure M85.9
      cyst —*see also* Cyst, bone, specified type
        NEC
        aneurysmal —*see* Cyst, bone,
          aneurysmal
        solitary —*see* Cyst, bone, solitary
      diffuse idiopathic skeletal
        hyperostosis —*see* Hyperostosis,
          ankylosing
      fibrous dysplasia (monostotic) —*see*
        Dysplasia, fibrous, bone
      fluorosis —*see* Fluorosis, skeletal
      hyperostosis of skull M85.2
      osteitis condensans —*see* Osteitis,
        condensans
      specified type NEC M85.8-•
        ankle M85.87-•
        foot M85.87-•
        forearm M85.83-•
        hand M85.84-•
        lower leg M85.86-•
        multiple sites M85.89
        neck M85.88
        rib M85.88
        shoulder M85.81-•
        skull M85.88
        thigh M85.85-•
        upper arm M85.82-•
        vertebra M85.88
    development and growth NEC M89.2Ø
      carpus M89.24-•
      clavicle M89.21-•
      femur M89.25-•
      fibula M89.26-•
      finger M89.24-•
      humerus M89.22-•
      ilium M89.259
      ischium M89.259
      metacarpus M89.24-•
      metatarsus M89.27-•
      multiple sites M89.29
      neck M89.28
      radius M89.23-•
      rib M89.28
      scapula M89.21-•
      skull M89.28
      tarsus M89.27-•
      tibia M89.26-•
      toe M89.27-•
      ulna M89.23-•
      vertebra M89.28
    specified type NEC M89.8X-•
  brachial plexus G54.Ø
  branched-chain amino-acid metabolism E71.2
    specified NEC E71.19
  breast N64.9
    agalactia —*see* Agalactia
    associated with
      lactation O92.7Ø
        specified NEC O92.79
      pregnancy O92.2Ø
        specified NEC O92.29

Disorder *(Continued)*
  breast *(Continued)*
    associated with *(Continued)*
      puerperium O92.2Ø
        specified NEC O92.29
    cracked nipple —*see* Cracked nipple
    galactorrhea —*see* Galactorrhea
    hypogalactia O92.4
    lactation disorder NEC O92.79
    mastitis —*see* Mastitis
    nipple infection —*see* Infection, nipple
    retracted nipple —*see* Retraction, nipple
    specified type NEC N64.89
  Briquet's F45.Ø
  bullous, in diseases classified elsewhere L14
  caffeine use
    mild
      with
        caffeine-induced
          anxiety disorder F15.18Ø
          sleep disorder F15.182
    moderate or severe
      with
        caffeine-induced
          anxiety disorder F15.28Ø
          sleep disorder F15.282
  cannabis use
    mild F12.1Ø
      with
        cannabis-induced
          anxiety disorder F12.18Ø
          psychotic disorder F12.159
          sleep disorder F12.188
        cannabis intoxication delirium
          F12.121
          with perceptual disturbances
            F12.122
          without perceptual disturbances
            F12.129
      in remission (early) (sustained) F12.11
    moderate or severe F12.2Ø
      with
        cannabis-induced
          anxiety disorder F12.28Ø
          psychotic disorder F12.259
          sleep disorder F12.288
        cannabis intoxication
          with perceptual disturbances
            F12.222
          without perceptual disturbances
            F12.229
        delirium F12.221
      in remission (early) (sustained) F12.21
  carbohydrate
    absorption, intestinal NEC E74.39
    metabolism (congenital) E74.9
  ➡specified NEC E74.89
  cardiac, functional I51.89
  carnitine metabolism E71.4Ø
  cartilage M94.9
    articular NEC —*see* Derangement, joint,
      articular cartilage
    chondrocalcinosis —*see*
      Chondrocalcinosis
    specified type NEC M94.8X-•
      articular —*see* Derangement, joint,
        articular cartilage
      multiple sites M94.8XØ
  catatonia (due to known physiological
    condition) (with another mental
    disorder) FØ6.1
  catatonic
    due to (secondary to) known physiological
      condition FØ6.1
    organic FØ6.1
  central auditory processing H93.25
  cervical
    region NEC M53.82
    root (nerve) NEC G54.2
  character NOS F6Ø.9
  childhood disintegrative NEC F84.3

▶ New   ⟹ Revised   ~~deleted~~ Deleted   • Use Additional Character(s)

Disorder *(Continued)*
  cholesterol and bile acid metabolism E78.70
    Barth syndrome E78.71
    other specified E78.79
    Smith-Lemli-Opitz syndrome E78.72
  choroid H31.9
    atrophy —*see* Atrophy, choroid
    degeneration —*see* Degeneration, choroid
    detachment —*see* Detachment, choroid
    dystrophy —*see* Dystrophy, choroid
    hemorrhage —*see* Hemorrhage, choroid
    rupture —*see* Rupture, choroid
    scar —*see* Scar, chorioretinal
    solar retinopathy —*see* Retinopathy, solar
    specified type NEC H31.8
  ciliary body —*see* Disorder, iris
    degeneration —*see* Degeneration, ciliary
      body
  coagulation (factor) *(see also* Defect,
    coagulation) D68.9
    newborn, transient P61.6
  cocaine use
    mild F14.10
      with
        amphetamine, cocaine, or other
          stimulant intoxication
          with perceptual disturbances
            F14.122
          without perceptual disturbances
            F14.129
        cocaine-induced
          anxiety disorder F14.180
          bipolar and related disorder
            F14.14
          depressive disorder F14.14
          obsessive-compulsive and related
            disorder F14.188
          psychotic disorder F14.159
          sexual dysfunction F14.181
          sleep disorder F14.182
        cocaine intoxication delirium F14.121
      in remission (early) (sustained) F14.11
    moderate or severe F14.20
      with
        amphetamine, cocaine, or other
          stimulant intoxication
          with perceptual disturbances
            F14.222
          without perceptual disturbances
            F14.229
        cocaine-induced
          anxiety disorder F14.280
          bipolar and related disorder
            F14.24
          depressive disorder F14.24
          obsessive-compulsive and related
            disorder F14.288
          psychotic disorder F14.259
          sexual dysfunction F14.281
          sleep disorder F14.282
        cocaine intoxication delirium F14.221
      in remission (early) (sustained) F14.21
  coccyx NEC M53.3
  cognitive F09
    due to (secondary to) general medical
      condition F09
    persisting R41.89
      due to
        alcohol F10.97
          with dependence F10.27
        anxiolytics F13.97
          with dependence F13.27
        hypnotics F13.97
          with dependence F13.27
        sedatives F13.97
          with dependence F13.27
        specified substance NEC
          F19.97
          with
            abuse F19.17
            dependence F19.27

Disorder *(Continued)*
  communication F80.9
    social pragmatic F80.82
  conduct (childhood) F91.9
    adjustment reaction —*see* Disorder,
      adjustment
    adolescent onset type F91.2
    childhood onset type F91.1
    compulsive F63.9
    confined to family context F91.0
    depressive F91.8
    group type F91.2
    hyperkinetic —*see* Disorder, attention-
      deficit hyperactivity
    oppositional defiance F91.3
    socialized F91.2
    solitary aggressive type F91.1
    specified NEC F91.8
    unsocialized (aggressive) F91.1
  conduction, heart I45.9
  ➡ congenital glycosylation (CDG) E74.89
  conjunctiva H11.9
    infection —*see* Conjunctivitis
  connective tissue, localized L94.9
    specified NEC L94.8
  conversion (functional neurological symptom
    disorder)
    with
      abnormal movement F44.4
      anesthesia or sensory loss F44.6
      attacks or seizures F44.5
      mixed symptoms F44.7
      special sensory symptoms F44.6
      speech symptoms F44.4
      swallowing symptoms F44.4
      weakness or paralysis F44.4
  convulsive (secondary) —*see* Convulsions
  cornea H18.9
    deformity —*see* Deformity, cornea
    degeneration —*see* Degeneration, cornea
    deposits —*see* Deposit, cornea
    due to contact lens H18.82-•
      specified as edema —*see* Edema, cornea
    edema —*see* Edema, cornea
    keratitis —*see* Keratitis
    keratoconjunctivitis —*see*
      Keratoconjunctivitis
    membrane change —*see* Change, corneal
      membrane
    neovascularization —*see*
      Neovascularization, cornea
    scar —*see* Opacity, cornea
    specified type NEC H18.89-•
    ulcer —*see* Ulcer, cornea
  corpus cavernosum N48.9
  cranial nerve —*see* Disorder, nerve, cranial
  ▶ Cyclin-Dependent Kinase-Like 5 Deficiency
    (CDKL5) G40.42
  cyclothymic F34.0
  defiant oppositional F91.3
  delusional (persistent) (systematized) F22
    induced F24
  depersonalization F48.1
  depressive F32.9
    due to known physiological condition
      with
        depressive features F06.31
        major depressive-like episode F06.32
        mixed features F06.34
    major F32.9
      with psychotic symptoms F32.3
      in remission (full) F32.5
        partial F32.4
      recurrent F33.9
        with psychotic features F33.3
      single episode F32.9
        mild F32.0
        moderate F32.1
        severe (without psychotic symptoms)
          F32.2
          with psychotic symptoms F32.3

Disorder *(Continued)*
  depressive *(Continued)*
    organic F06.31
    persistent F34.1
    recurrent F33.9
      current episode
        mild F33.0
        moderate F33.1
        severe (without psychotic symptoms)
          F33.2
          with psychotic symptoms F33.3
      in remission F33.40
        full F33.42
        partial F33.41
      specified NEC F33.8
      single episode —*see* Episode, depressive
    specified NEC F32.89
  developmental F89
    arithmetical skills F81.2
    coordination (motor) F82
    expressive writing F81.81
    language F80.9
      expressive F80.1
      mixed receptive and expressive
        F80.2
      receptive type F80.2
      specified NEC F80.89
    learning F81.9
      arithmetical F81.2
      reading F81.0
    mixed F88
    motor coordination or function F82
    pervasive F84.9
      specified NEC F84.8
    phonological F80.0
    reading F81.0
    scholastic skills —*see also* Disorder,
      learning
      mixed F81.89
    specified NEC F88
    speech F80.9
      articulation F80.0
      specified NEC F80.89
    written expression F81.81
  diaphragm J98.6
  digestive (system) K92.9
    newborn P78.9
      specified NEC P78.89
    postprocedural —*see* Complication,
      gastrointestinal
    psychogenic F45.8
  disc (intervertebral) M51.9
    with
      myelopathy
        cervical region M50.00
        cervicothoracic region M50.03
        high cervical region M50.01
        lumbar region M51.06
        mid-cervical region M50.020
        sacrococcygeal region M53.3
        thoracic region M51.04
        thoracolumbar region M51.05
      radiculopathy
        cervical region M50.10
        cervicothoracic region M50.13
        high cervical region M50.11
        lumbar region M51.16
        lumbosacral region M51.17
        mid-cervical region M50.120
        sacrococcygeal region M53.3
        thoracic region M51.14
        thoracolumbar region M51.15
    cervical M50.90
      with
        myelopathy M50.00
          C2-C3 M50.01
          C3-C4 M50.01
          C4-C5 M50.021
          C5-C6 M50.022
          C6-C7 M50.023
          C7-T1 M50.03

Disorder *(Continued)*
  disc *(Continued)*
    cervical *(Continued)*
      with *(Continued)*
        myelopathy *(Continued)*
          cervicothoracic region M50.03
          high cervical region M50.01
          mid-cervical region M50.020
        neuritis, radiculitis or radiculopathy
          M50.10
          C2-C3 M50.11
          C3-C4 M50.11
          C4-C5 M50.121
          C5-C6 M50.122
          C6-C7 M50.123
          C7-T1 M50.13
          cervicothoracic region M50.13
          high cervical region M50.11
          mid-cervical region M50.120
      C2-C3 M50.91
      C3-C4 M50.91
      C4-C5 M50.921
      C5-C6 M50.922
      C6-C7 M50.923
      C7-T1 M50.93
      cervicothoracic region M50.93
      degeneration M50.30
        C2-C3 M50.31
        C3-C4 M50.31
        C4-C5 M50.321
        C5-C6 M50.322
        C6-C7 M50.323
        C7-T1 M50.33
        cervicothoracic region M50.33
        high cervical region M50.31
        mid-cervical region M50.320
      displacement M50.20
        C2-C3 M50.21
        C3-C4 M50.21
        C4-C5 M50.221
        C5-C6 M50.222
        C6-C7 M50.223
        C7-T1 M50.23
        cervicothoracic region M50.23
        high cervical region M50.21
        mid-cervical region M50.220
      high cervical region M50.91
      mid-cervical region M50.920
      specified type NEC M50.80
        C2-C3 M50.81
        C3-C4 M50.81
        C4-C5 M50.821
        C5-C6 M50.822
        C6-C7 M50.823
        C7-T1 M50.83
        cervicothoracic region M50.83
        high cervical region M50.81
        mid-cervical region M50.820
    specified NEC
      lumbar region M51.86
      lumbosacral region M51.87
      sacrococcygeal region M53.3
      thoracic region M51.84
      thoracolumbar region M51.85
  disinhibited attachment (childhood) F94.2
  disintegrative, childhood NEC F84.3
  disruptive F91.9
    mood dysregulation F34.81
    specified NEC F91.8
  disruptive behavior —*see* Disorder, conduct
  dissocial personality F60.2
  dissociative F44.9
    affecting
      motor function F44.4
        and sensation F44.7
      sensation F44.6
        and motor function F44.7
    brief reactive F43.0
    due to (secondary to) general medical
      condition F06.8
    mixed F44.7

Disorder *(Continued)*
  dissociative *(Continued)*
    organic F06.8
    other specified NEC F44.89
  double heterozygous sickling —*see* Disease,
    sickle-cell
  dream anxiety F51.5
  drug induced hemorrhagic D68.32
  drug related F19.99
    abuse —*see* Abuse, drug
    dependence —*see* Dependence, drug
  dysmorphic body F45.22
  dysthymic F34.1
  ear H93.9-●
    bleeding —*see* Otorrhagia
    deafness —*see* Deafness
    degenerative H93.09-●
    discharge —*see* Otorrhea
    external H61.9-●
      auditory canal stenosis —*see* Stenosis,
        external ear canal
      exostosis —*see* Exostosis, external ear
        canal
      impacted cerumen —*see* Impaction,
        cerumen
      otitis —*see* Otitis, externa
      perichondritis —*see* Perichondritis, ear
      pinna —*see* Disorder, pinna
      specified type NEC H61.89-●
        in diseases classified elsewhere
          H62.8X-●
    inner H83.9-●
      vestibular dysfunction —*see* Disorder,
        vestibular function
    middle H74.9-●
      adhesive H74.1-●
      ossicle —*see* Abnormal, ear ossicles
      polyp —*see* Polyp, ear (middle)
      specified NEC, in diseases classified
        elsewhere H75.8-●
    postprocedural —*see* Complications, ear,
      procedure
    specified NEC, in diseases classified
      elsewhere H94.8-●
  eating (adult) (psychogenic) F50.9
    anorexia —*see* Anorexia
    binge F50.81
    bulimia F50.2
    child F98.29
      pica F98.3
      rumination disorder F98.21
    pica F50.89
      childhood F98.3
  electrolyte (balance) NEC E87.8
    with
      abortion —*see* Abortion by type
        complicated by specified condition
          NEC
      ectopic pregnancy O08.5
      molar pregnancy O08.5
    acidosis (metabolic) (respiratory) E87.2
    alkalosis (metabolic) (respiratory) E87.3
  elimination, transepidermal L87.9
    specified NEC L87.8
  emotional (persistent) F34.9
    of childhood F93.9
      specified NEC F93.8
  endocrine E34.9
    postprocedural E89.89
    specified NEC E89.89
  erectile (male) (organic) —*see also*
    Dysfunction, sexual, male, erectile N52.9
    nonorganic F52.21
  erythematous —*see* Erythema
  esophagus K22.9
    functional K22.4
    psychogenic F45.8
  eustachian tube H69.9-●
    infection —*see* Salpingitis, eustachian
    obstruction —*see* Obstruction, eustachian
      tube

Disorder *(Continued)*
  eustachian tube *(Continued)*
    patulous —*see* Patulous, eustachian tube
    specified NEC H69.8-●
  exhibitionistic F65.2
  extrapyramidal G25.9
    in diseases classified elsewhere —*see*
      category G26
    specified type NEC G25.89
  eye H57.9
    postprocedural —*see* Complication,
      postprocedural, eye
  eyelid H02.9
    cyst —*see* Cyst, eyelid
    degenerative H02.70
      chloasma —*see* Chloasma, eyelid
      madarosis —*see* Madarosis
      specified type NEC H02.79
      vitiligo —*see* Vitiligo, eyelid
      xanthelasma —*see* Xanthelasma
    dermatochalasis —*see* Dermato-chalasis
    edema —*see* Edema, eyelid
    elephantiasis —*see* Elephantiasis, eyelid
    foreign body, retained —*see* Foreign body,
      retained, eyelid
    function H02.59
      abnormal innervation syndrome —
        see Syndrome, abnormal
        innervation
      blepharochalasis —*see* Blepharochalasis
      blepharoclonus —*see* Blepharoclonus
      blepharophimosis —*see*
        Blepharophimosis
      blepharoptosis —*see* Blepharoptosis
      lagophthalmos —*see* Lagophthalmos
      lid retraction —*see* Retraction, lid
    hypertrichosis —*see* Hypertrichosis,
      eyelid
    specified type NEC H02.89
    vascular H02.879
      left H02.876
        lower H02.875
        upper H02.874
      right H02.873
        lower H02.872
        upper H02.871
  factitious
    by proxy F68.A
    imposed on another F68.A
    imposed on self F68.10
      with predominantly
        psychological symptoms F68.11
          with physical symptoms F68.13
        physical symptoms F68.12
          with psychological symptoms
            F68.13
  factor, coagulation —*see* Defect,
    coagulation
  fatty acid
    metabolism E71.30
      specified NEC E71.39
    oxidation
      LCAD E71.310
      MCAD E71.311
      SCAD E71.312
      specified deficiency NEC E71.318
  feeding (infant or child) —*see also* Disorder,
    eating R63.3-●
    or eating disorder F50.9
    specified NEC F50.9
  feigned (with obvious motivation)
    Z76.5
    without obvious motivation —
      see Disorder, factitious
  female
    hypoactive sexual desire F52.0
    orgasmic F52.31
    sexual interest/arousal F52.22
  fetishistic F65.0
  fibroblastic M72.9
    specified NEC M72.8

▶ New   ⇒ Revised   ~~deleted~~ Deleted   ● Use Additional Character(s)

Disorder *(Continued)*
fluency
adult onset F98.5
childhood onset F80.81
following
cerebral infarction I69.323
cerebrovascular disease I69.923
specified disease NEC I69.823
intracerebral hemorrhage I69.123
nontraumatic intracranial hemorrhage
NEC I69.223
subarachnoid hemorrhage I69.023
in conditions classified elsewhere
R47.82
fluid balance E87.8
follicular (skin) L73.9
specified NEC L73.8
frotteuristic F65.81
fructose metabolism E74.10
essential fructosuria E74.11
fructokinase deficiency E74.11
fructose-1, 6-diphosphatase deficiency
E74.19
hereditary fructose intolerance E74.12
other specified E74.19
functional polymorphonuclear neutrophils
D71
gallbladder, biliary tract and pancreas in
diseases classified elsewhere K87
gambling F63.0
gamma aminobutyric acid (GABA)
metabolism E72.81
gamma-glutamyl cycle E72.89
gastric (functional) K31.9
motility K30
psychogenic F45.8
secretion K30
gastrointestinal (functional) NOS K92.9
newborn P78.9
psychogenic F45.8
gender-identity or -role F64.9
childhood F64.2
effect on relationship F66
of adolescence or adulthood F64.0
nontranssexual F64.8
specified NEC F64.8
uncertainty F66
genito-pelvic pain penetration F52.6
genitourinary system
female N94.9
male N50.9
psychogenic F45.8
globe H44.9
degenerated condition H44.50
absolute glaucoma H44.51-●
atrophy H44.52-●
leucocoria H44.53-●
degenerative H44.30
chalcosis H44.31-●
myopia —*see also* Myopia, degenerative
H44.2-●
siderosis H44.32-●
specified type NEC H44.39-●
endophthalmitis —*see* Endophthalmitis
foreign body, retained —*see* Foreign body,
intraocular, old, retained
hemophthalmos —*see* Hemophthalmos
hypotony H44.40
due to
ocular fistula H44.42-●
specified disorder NEC H44.43-●
flat anterior chamber H44.41-●
primary H44.44-●
luxation —*see* Luxation, globe
specified type NEC H44.89
glomerular (in) N05.9
amyloidosis E85.4 *[N08]*
cryoglobulinemia D89.1 *[N08]*
disseminated intravascular coagulation
D65 *[N08]*
Fabry's disease E75.21 *[N08]*

Disorder *(Continued)*
glomerular *(Continued)*
familial lecithin cholesterol acyltransferase
deficiency E78.6 *[N08]*
Goodpasture's syndrome M31.0
hemolytic-uremic syndrome D59.3
Henoch (-Schönlein) purpura D69.0
[N08]
malariae malaria B52.0
microscopic polyangiitis M31.7 *[N08]*
multiple myeloma C90.0-● *[N08]*
mumps B26.83
schistosomiasis B65.9 *[N08]*
sepsis NEC A41.-● *[N08]*
streptococcal A40.-● *[N08]*
sickle-cell disorders D57.-● *[N08]*
strongyloidiasis B78.9 *[N08]*
subacute bacterial endocarditis I33.0
[N08]
syphilis A52.75
systemic lupus erythematosus M32.14
thrombotic thrombocytopenic purpura
M31.1 *[N08]*
Waldenström macroglobulinemia C88.0
[N08]
Wegener's granulomatosis M31.31
gluconeogenesis E74.4
glucosaminoglycan metabolism —
see Disorder, metabolism,
glucosaminoglycan
▶glucose transport E74.819
▶specified NEC E74.818
glycine metabolism E72.50
d-glycericacidemia E72.59
hyperhydroxyprolinemia E72.59
hyperoxaluria R82.992
primary E72.53
hyperprolinemia E72.59
non-ketotic hyperglycinemia E72.51
oxalosis E72.53
oxaluria E72.53
sarcosinemia E72.59
trimethylaminuria E72.52
glycoprotein metabolism E77.9
specified NEC E77.8
habit (and impulse) F63.9
involving sexual behavior NEC F65.9
specified NEC F63.89
hallucinogen use
mild F16.10
with
hallucinogen-induced
anxiety disorder F16.180
bipolar and related disorder
F16.14
depressive disorder F16.14
psychotic disorder F16.159
hallucinogen intoxication delirium
F16.121
other hallucinogen intoxication
F16.129
in remission (early) (sustained) F16.11
moderate or severe F16.20
with
hallucinogen-induced
anxiety disorder F16.280
bipolar and related disorder
F16.24
depressive disorder F16.24
psychotic disorder F16.259
hallucinogen intoxication delirium
F16.221
other hallucinogen intoxication
F16.229
in remission (early) (sustained)
F16.21
heart action I49.9
hematological D75.9
newborn (transient) P61.9
specified NEC P61.8
hematopoietic organs D75.9

Disorder *(Continued)*
hemorrhagic NEC D69.9
drug-induced D68.32
due to
extrinsic circulating anticoagulants
D68.32
increase in
anti-IIa D68.32
anti-Xa D68.32
intrinsic
circulating anticoagulants D68.318
increase in
antithrombin D68.318
anti-VIIIa D68.318
anti-IXa D68.318
anti-XIa D68.318
following childbirth O72.3
hemostasis —*see* Defect, coagulation
histidine metabolism E70.40
histidinemia E70.41
other specified E70.49
hoarding F42.3
hyperkinetic —*see* Disorder, attention-deficit
hyperactivity
hyperleucine-isoleucinemia E71.19
hypervalinemia E71.19
hypoactive sexual desire F52.0
hypochondriacal F45.20
body dysmorphic F45.22
neurosis F45.21
other specified F45.29
identity
dissociative F44.81
illness anxiety F45.21
of childhood F93.8
immune mechanism (immunity) D89.9
specified type NEC D89.89
impaired renal tubular function N25.9
specified NEC N25.89
impulse (control) F63.9
inflammatory
pelvic, in diseases classified elsewhere —
see category N74
penis N48.29
abscess N48.21
cellulitis N48.22
inhalant use
mild F18.10
with
inhalant-induced
anxiety disorder F18.180
depressive disorder F18.14
major neurocognitive disorder
F18.17
mild neurocognitive disorder
F18.188
psychotic disorder F18.159
inhalant intoxication F18.129
inhalant intoxication delirium F18.121
in remission (early) (sustained) F18.11
moderate or severe F18.20
with
inhalant-induced
anxiety disorder F18.280
depressive disorder F18.24
major neurocognitive disorder
F18.27
mild neurocognitive disorder
F18.288
psychotic disorder F18.259
inhalant intoxication F18.229
inhalant intoxication delirium F18.221
in remission (early) (sustained) F18.21
integument, newborn P83.9
specified NEC P83.88
intermittent explosive F63.81
internal secretion pancreas —*see* Increased,
secretion, pancreas, endocrine
intestine, intestinal
carbohydrate absorption NEC E74.39
postoperative K91.2

Disorder *(Continued)*
  intestine, intestinal *(Continued)*
    functional NEC K59.9
      postoperative K91.89
    psychogenic F45.8
    vascular K55.9
      chronic K55.1
      specified NEC K55.8
  intraoperative (intraprocedural) —*see*
    Complications, intraoperative
  involuntary emotional expression (IEED) F48.2
  iris H21.9
    adhesions —*see* Adhesions, iris
    atrophy —*see* Atrophy, iris
    chamber angle recession —*see* Recession,
      chamber angle
    cyst —*see* Cyst, iris
    degeneration —*see* Degeneration, iris
    in diseases classified elsewhere H22
    iridodialysis —*see* Iridodialysis
    iridoschisis —*see* Iridoschisis
    miotic pupillary cyst —*see* Cyst, pupillary
    pupillary
      abnormality —*see* Abnormality, pupillary
      membrane —*see* Membrane, pupillary
    specified type NEC H21.89
    vascular NEC H21.1X-●
  iron metabolism E83.10
    specified NEC E83.19
  isovaleric acidemia E71.110
  jaw, developmental M27.0
    temporomandibular —*see also* Anomaly,
      dentofacial, temporomandibular joint
      M26.60-●
  joint M25.9
    derangement —*see* Derangement, joint
    effusion —*see* Effusion, joint
    fistula —*see* Fistula, joint
    hemarthrosis —*see* Hemarthrosis
    instability —*see* Instability, joint
    osteophyte —*see* Osteophyte
    pain —*see* Pain, joint
    psychogenic F45.8
    specified type NEC M25.80
      ankle M25.87-●
      elbow M25.82-●
      foot joint M25.87-●
      hand joint M25.84-●
      hip M25.85-●
      knee M25.86-●
      shoulder M25.81-●
      wrist M25.83-●
    stiffness —*see* Stiffness, joint
  ketone metabolism E71.32
  kidney N28.9
    functional (tubular) N25.9
    in
      schistosomiasis B65.9 *[N29]*
    tubular function N25.9
    specified NEC N25.89
  lacrimal system H04.9
    changes H04.69
      fistula —*see* Fistula, lacrimal
    gland H04.19
      atrophy —*see* Atrophy, lacrimal gland
      cyst —*see* Cyst, lacrimal, gland
      dacryops —*see* Dacryops
      dislocation —*see* Dislocation, lacrimal
        gland
      dry eye syndrome —*see* Syndrome, dry
        eye
      infection —*see* Dacryoadenitis
      granuloma —*see* Granuloma, lacrimal
      inflammation —*see* Inflammation, lacrimal
      obstruction —*see* Obstruction, lacrimal
      specified NEC H04.89
  lactation NEC O92.79
  language (developmental) F80.9
    expressive F80.1
    mixed receptive and expressive F80.2
    receptive F80.2

Disorder *(Continued)*
  late luteal phase dysphoric N94.89
  learning (specific) F81.9
    acalculia R48.8
    alexia R48.0
    mathematics F81.2
    reading F81.0
    specified
      with impairment in
        mathematics F81.2
        reading F81.0
        written expression F81.81
    specified NEC F81.89
    spelling F81.81
    written expression F81.81
  lens H27.9
    aphakia —*see* Aphakia
    cataract —*see* Cataract
    dislocation —*see* Dislocation, lens
    specified type NEC H27.8
  ligament M24.20
    ankle M24.27-●
    attachment, spine —*see* Enthesopathy,
      spinal
    elbow M24.22-●
    foot joint M24.27-●
    hand joint M24.24-●
    hip M24.25-●
    knee —*see* Derangement, knee, specified
      NEC
    shoulder M24.21-●
 ▶ specified site NEC M24.29
    vertebra M24.28
    wrist M24.23-●
  ligamentous attachments —*see also*
    Enthesopathy
    spine —*see* Enthesopathy, spinal
  lipid
    metabolism, congenital E78.9
    storage E75.6
      specified NEC E75.5
  lipoprotein
    deficiency (familial) E78.6
    metabolism E78.9
      specified NEC E78.89
  liver K76.9
    malarial B54 *[K77]*
  low back —*see also* Dorsopathy, specified NEC
  lumbosacral
    plexus G54.1
    root (nerve) NEC G54.4
  lung, interstitial, drug-induced J70.4
    acute J70.2
    chronic J70.3
 ▶ dabbing (related) U07.0
 ▶ e-cigarette (related) U07.0
 ▶ electronic cigarette (related) U07.0
 ▶ vaping (associated) (device) (product)
    (related) (use) U07.0
  lymphoproliferative, post-transplant (PTLD)
    D47.Z1
  lysine and hydroxylysine metabolism E72.3
  major neurocognitive —*see* Dementia, in
    (due to)
  male
    erectile (organic) —*see also* Dysfunction,
      sexual, male, erectile N52.9
      nonorganic F52.21
    hypoactive sexual desire F52.0
    orgasmic F52.32
  manic F30.9
    organic F06.33
  mast cell activation —*see* Activation, mast cell
  mastoid —*see also* Disorder, ear, middle
    postprocedural —*see* Complications, ear,
      procedure
 ▶ meninges, specified type NEC G96.198
  meniscus —*see* Derangement, knee,
    meniscus
  menopausal N95.9
    specified NEC N95.8

Disorder *(Continued)*
  menstrual N92.6
    psychogenic F45.8
    specified NEC N92.5
  mental (or behavioral) (nonpsychotic) F99
    due to (secondary to)
      amphetamine
        due to drug abuse —*see* Abuse, drug,
          stimulant
        due to drug dependence —*see*
          Dependence, drug, stimulant
      brain disease, damage and dysfunction
        F09
      caffeine use
        due to drug abuse —*see* Abuse, drug,
          stimulant
        due to drug dependence —*see*
          Dependence, drug, stimulant
      cannabis use
        due to drug abuse —*see* Abuse, drug,
          cannabis
        due to drug dependence —*see*
          Dependence, drug, cannabis
      general medical condition F09
      sedative or hypnotic use
        due to drug abuse —*see* Abuse, drug,
          sedative
        due to drug dependence —*see*
          Dependence, drug, sedative
      tobacco (nicotine) use —*see* Dependence,
        drug, nicotine
    following organic brain damage F07.9
      frontal lobe syndrome F07.0
      personality change F07.0
      postconcussional syndrome F07.81
      specified NEC F07.89
    infancy, childhood or adolescence F98.9
    neurotic —*see* Neurosis
    organic or symptomatic F09
    presenile, psychotic F03
    problem NEC
    psychoneurotic —*see* Neurosis
    psychotic —*see* Psychosis
    puerperal F53.0
    senile, psychotic NEC F03
  metabolic, amino acid, transitory, newborn
    P74.8
  metabolism NOS E88.9
    amino-acid E72.9
      aromatic E70.9
        albinism —*see* Albinism
        histidine E70.40
          histidinemia E70.41
          other specified E70.49
        hyperphenylalaninemia E70.1
          classical phenylketonuria E70.0
 ➡   other specified E70.89
        tryptophan E70.5
        tyrosine E70.20
          hypertyrosinemia E70.21
          other specified E70.29
      branched chain E71.2
        3-methylglutaconic aciduria E71.111
        hyperleucine-isoleucinemia E71.19
        hypervalinemia E71.19
        isovaleric acidemia E71.110
        maple syrup urine disease E71.0
        methylmalonic acidemia E71.120
        organic aciduria NEC E71.118
        other specified E71.19
        proprionate NEC E71.128
        proprionic acidemia E71.121
      glycine E72.50
        d-glycericacidemia E72.59
        hyperhydroxyprolinemia E72.59
        hyperoxaluria R82.992
          primary E72.53
        hyperprolinemia E72.59
        non-ketotic hyperglycinemia
          E72.51
        other specified E72.59

Disorder *(Continued)*
  metabolism *(Continued)*
    amino-acid *(Continued)*
      glycine *(Continued)*
        sarcosinemia E72.59
        trimethylaminuria E72.52
      hydroxylysine E72.3
      lysine E72.3
      ornithine E72.4
      other specified E72.89
        beta-amino acid E72.89
        gamma-glutamyl cycle E72.89
      straight-chain E72.89
      sulfur-bearing E72.10
        homocystinuria E72.11
        methylenetetrahydrofolate reductase deficiency E72.12
      other specified E72.19
    bile acid and cholesterol metabolism E78.70
    bilirubin E80.7
      specified NEC E80.6
    calcium E83.50
      hypercalcemia E83.52
      hypocalcemia E83.51
      other specified E83.59
    carbohydrate E74.9
    ⟹specified NEC E74.89
    cholesterol and bile acid metabolism E78.70
    congenital E88.9
    copper E83.00
      specified type NEC E83.09
      Wilson's disease E83.01
    cystinuria E72.01
    fructose E74.10
    galactose E74.20
    glucosaminoglycan E76.9
      mucopolysaccharidosis —*see* Mucopolysaccharidosis
      specified NEC E76.8
    glutamine E72.89
    glycine E72.50
    glycogen storage (hepatorenal) E74.09
    glycoprotein E77.9
      specified NEC E77.8
    glycosaminoglycan E76.9
      specified NEC E76.8
    in labor and delivery O75.89
    iron E83.10
    isoleucine E71.19
    leucine E71.19
    lipoid E78.9
    lipoprotein E78.9
      specified NEC E78.89
    magnesium E83.40
      hypermagnesemia E83.41
      hypomagnesemia E83.42
      other specified E83.49
    mineral E83.9
      specified NEC E83.89
    mitochondrial E88.40
      MELAS syndrome E88.41
      MERRF syndrome (myoclonic epilepsy associated with ragged-red fibers) E88.42
      other specified E88.49
    ornithine E72.4
    phosphatases E83.30
    phosphorus E83.30
      acid phosphatase deficiency E83.39
      hypophosphatasia E83.39
      hypophosphatemia E83.39
        familial E83.31
      other specified E83.39
      pseudovitamin D deficiency E83.32
    plasma protein NEC E88.09
    porphyrin —*see* Porphyria
    postprocedural E89.89
      specified NEC E89.89
    purine E79.9
      specified NEC E79.8

Disorder *(Continued)*
  metabolism *(Continued)*
    pyrimidine E79.9
      specified NEC E79.8
    pyruvate E74.4
    serine E72.89
    sodium E87.8
    specified NEC E88.89
    threonine E72.89
    valine E71.19
    zinc E83.2
  methylmalonic acidemia E71.120
  micturition NEC —*see also* Difficulty, micturition R39.198
    feeling of incomplete emptying R39.14
    hesitancy R39.11
    poor stream R39.12
    psychogenic F45.8
    split stream R39.13
    straining R39.16
    urgency R39.15
  mild neurocognitive G31.84
  mitochondrial metabolism E88.40
  mitral (valve) —*see* Endocarditis, mitral
  mixed
    anxiety and depressive F41.8
    of scholastic skills (developmental) F81.89
    receptive expressive language F80.2
  mood F39
    bipolar —*see* Disorder, bipolar
    depressive —*see* Disorder, depressive
    due to (secondary to)
      alcohol F10.94
      amphetamine F15.94
        in
          abuse F15.14
          dependence F15.24
      anxiolytic F13.94
        in
          abuse F13.14
          dependence F13.24
      cocaine F14.94
        in
          abuse F14.14
          dependence F14.24
      general medical condition F06.30
      hallucinogen F16.94
        in
          abuse F16.14
          dependence F16.24
      hypnotic F13.94
        in
          abuse F13.14
          dependence F13.24
      inhalant F18.94
        in
          abuse F18.14
          dependence F18.24
      opioid F11.94
        in
          abuse F11.14
          dependence F11.24
      phencyclidine (PCP) F16.94
        in
          abuse F16.14
          dependence F16.24
      physiological condition F06.30
        with
          depressive features F06.31
          major depressive-like episode F06.32
          manic features F06.33
          mixed features F06.34
      psychoactive substance NEC F19.94
        in
          abuse F19.14
          dependence F19.24
      sedative F13.94
        in
          abuse F13.14
          dependence F13.24

Disorder *(Continued)*
  mood *(Continued)*
    due to *(Continued)*
      volatile solvents F18.94
        in
          abuse F18.14
          dependence F18.24
    manic episode F30.9
      with psychotic symptoms F30.2
      without psychotic symptoms F30.10
        mild F30.11
        moderate F30.12
        severe F30.13
      in remission (full) F30.4
        partial F30.3
      specified type NEC F30.8
    organic F06.30
      right hemisphere F07.89
    persistent F34.9
      cyclothymia F34.0
      dysthymia F34.1
      specified type NEC F34.89
    recurrent F39
    right hemisphere organic F07.89
  movement G25.9
    drug-induced G25.70
      akathisia G25.71
      specified NEC G25.79
    hysterical F44.4
    in diseases classified elsewhere —*see* category G26
    periodic limb G47.61
      sleep related G47.61
    sleep related NEC G47.69
    specified NEC G25.89
    stereotyped F98.4
    treatment-induced G25.9
  multiple personality F44.81
  muscle M62.9
    attachment, spine —*see* Enthesopathy, spinal
    in trichinellosis —*see* Trichinellosis, with muscle disorder
    psychogenic F45.8
    specified type NEC M62.89
    tone, newborn P94.9
      specified NEC P94.8
  muscular
    attachments —*see also* Enthesopathy
      spine —*see* Enthesopathy, spinal
    urethra N36.44
  musculoskeletal system, soft tissue —*see* Disorder, soft tissue
    postprocedural M96.89
    psychogenic F45.8
  myoneural G70.9
    due to lead G70.1
    specified NEC G70.89
    toxic G70.1
  myotonic NEC G71.19
  nail, in diseases classified elsewhere L62
  neck region NEC —*see* Dorsopathy, specified NEC
  neonatal onset multisystemic inflammatory (NOMID) M04.2
  nerve G58.9
    abducent NEC —*see* Strabismus, paralytic, sixth nerve
    accessory G52.8
    acoustic —*see* subcategory H93.3
    auditory —*see* subcategory H93.3
    auriculotemporal G50.8
    axillary G54.0
    cerebral —*see* Disorder, nerve, cranial
    cranial G52.9
      eighth —*see* subcategory H93.3
      eleventh G52.8
      fifth G50.9
      first G52.0
      fourth NEC —*see* Strabismus, paralytic, fourth nerve

Disorder *(Continued)*
  nerve *(Continued)*
    cranial *(Continued)*
      multiple G52.7
      ninth G52.1
      second NEC —*see* Disorder, nerve, optic
      seventh NEC G51.8
      sixth NEC —*see* Strabismus, paralytic, sixth nerve
      specified NEC G52.8
      tenth G52.2
      third NEC —*see* Strabismus, paralytic, third nerve
      twelfth G52.3
    entrapment —*see* Neuropathy, entrapment
    facial G51.9
      specified NEC G51.8
    femoral —*see* Lesion, nerve, femoral
    glossopharyngeal NEC G52.1
    hypoglossal G52.3
    intercostal G58.0
    lateral
      cutaneous of thigh —*see* Mononeuropathy, lower limb, meralgia paresthetica
      popliteal —*see* Lesion, nerve, popliteal
    lower limb —*see* Mononeuropathy, lower limb
    medial popliteal —*see* Lesion, nerve, popliteal, medial
    median NEC —*see* Lesion, nerve, median
    multiple G58.7
    oculomotor NEC —*see* Strabismus, paralytic, third nerve
    olfactory G52.0
    optic NEC H47.09-●
      hemorrhage into sheath —*see* Hemorrhage, optic nerve
      ischemic H47.01-●
    peroneal —*see* Lesion, nerve, popliteal
    phrenic G58.8
    plantar —*see* Lesion, nerve, plantar
    pneumogastric G52.2
    posterior tibial —*see* Syndrome, tarsal tunnel
    radial —*see* Lesion, nerve, radial
    recurrent laryngeal G52.2
    root G54.9
      cervical G54.2
      lumbosacral G54.1
      specified NEC G54.8
      thoracic G54.3
    sciatic NEC —*see* Lesion, nerve, sciatic
    specified NEC G58.8
      lower limb —*see* Mononeuropathy, lower limb, specified NEC
      upper limb —*see* Mononeuropathy, upper limb, specified NEC
    sympathetic G90.9
    tibial —*see* Lesion, nerve, popliteal, medial
    trigeminal G50.9
      specified NEC G50.8
    trochlear NEC —*see* Strabismus, paralytic, fourth nerve
    ulnar —*see* Lesion, nerve, ulnar
    upper limb —*see* Mononeuropathy, upper limb
    vagus G52.2
  nervous system G98.8
    autonomic (peripheral) G90.9
      specified NEC G90.8
    central G96.9
    ➡ specified NEC G96.89
    parasympathetic G90.9
    specified NEC G98.8
    sympathetic G90.9
    vegetative G90.9

Disorder *(Continued)*
  neurocognitive R41.9
    major
      with
        aggressive behavior F01.51
        combative behavior F01.51
        violent behavior F01.51
      due to vascular disease, with behavioral disturbance F01.51
      in (due to) (other diseases classified elsewhere) —*see also* Dementia, in (due to) F02.80
        with
          aggressive behavior F02.81
          combative behavior F02.81
          violent behavior F02.81
        without behavioral disturbance F01.50
    mild G31.84
  neurodevelopmental F89
    specified NEC F88
  neurohypophysis NEC E23.3
  neurological NEC R29.818
  neuromuscular G70.9
    hereditary NEC G71.9
    specified NEC G70.89
    toxic G70.1
  neurotic F48.9
    specified NEC F48.8
  neutrophil, polymorphonuclear D71
  nightmare F51.5
  non-rapid eye movement sleep arousal
    sleep terror type F51.4
    sleepwalking type F51.3
  nose J34.9
    specified NEC J34.89
  obsessive-compulsive F42.9
    and related disorder due to a known physiological condition F06.8
  odontogenesis NOS K00.9
  opioid use
    with
      opioid-induced psychotic disorder F11.959
        with
          delusions F11.950
          hallucinations F11.951
    due to drug abuse —*see* Abuse, drug, opioid
    due to drug dependence —*see* Dependence, drug, opioid
    mild F11.10
      with
        opioid-induced
          anxiety disorder F11.188
          depressive disorder F11.14
          sexual dysfunction F11.181
        opioid intoxication
          with perceptual disturbances F11.122
          delirium F11.121
          without perceptual disturbances F11.129
      in remission (early) (sustained) F11.11
    moderate or severe F11.20
      with
        opioid-induced
          anxiety disorder F11.288
          anxiety disorder F11.988
          depressive disorder F11.24
          depressive disorder F11.94
          sexual dysfunction F11.281
          sexual dysfunction F11.981
        opioid intoxication
          with perceptual disturbances F11.222
          delirium F11.221
          without perceptual disturbances F11.229
      in remission (early) (sustained) F11.21
  oppositional defiant F91.3

Disorder *(Continued)*
  optic
    chiasm H47.49
      due to
        inflammatory disorder H47.41
        neoplasm H47.42
        vascular disorder H47.43
    disc H47.39-●
      coloboma —*see* Coloboma, optic disc
      drusen —*see* Drusen, optic disc
      pseudopapilledema —*see* Pseudopapilledema
    radiations —*see* Disorder, visual, pathway
    tracts —*see* Disorder, visual, pathway
  orbit H05.9
    cyst —*see* Cyst, orbit
    deformity —*see* Deformity, orbit
    edema —*see* Edema, orbit
    enophthalmos —*see* Enophthalmos
    exophthalmos —*see* Exophthalmos
    hemorrhage —*see* Hemorrhage, orbit
    inflammation —*see* Inflammation, orbit
    myopathy —*see* Myopathy, extraocular muscles
    retained foreign body —*see* Foreign body, orbit, old
    specified type NEC H05.89
  organic
    anxiety F06.4
    catatonic F06.1
    delusional F06.2
    dissociative F06.8
    emotionally labile (asthenic) F06.8
    mood (affective) F06.30
    schizophrenia-like F06.2
  orgasmic (female) F52.31
    male F52.32
  ornithine metabolism E72.4
  overanxious F41.1
    of childhood F93.8
  pain
    with related psychological factors F45.42
    exclusively related to psychological factors F45.41
    genito-pelvic penetration disorder F52.6
  pancreatic internal secretion E16.9
    specified NEC E16.8
  panic F41.0
    with agoraphobia F40.01
  papulosquamous L44.9
    in diseases classified elsewhere L45
    specified NEC L44.8
  paranoid F22
    induced F24
    shared F24
  paraphilic F65.9
    specified NEC F65.89
  parathyroid (gland) E21.5
    specified NEC E21.4
  parietoalveolar NEC J84.09
  paroxysmal, mixed R56.9
  patella M22.9-●
    chondromalacia —*see* Chondromalacia, patella
    derangement NEC M22.3X-●
    recurrent
      dislocation —*see* Dislocation, patella, recurrent
      subluxation —*see* Dislocation, patella, recurrent, incomplete
    specified NEC M22.8X-●
  patellofemoral M22.2X-●
  pedophilic F65.4
  pentose phosphate pathway with anemia D55.1
  perception, due to hallucinogens F16.983
    in
      abuse F16.183
      dependence F16.283
  peripheral nervous system NEC G64

▶ New   ⇨ Revised   ~~deleted~~ Deleted   ● Use Additional Character(s)

Disorder *(Continued)*
  peroxisomal E71.50
    biogenesis
      neonatal adrenoleukodystrophy
        E71.511
      specified disorder NEC E71.518
      Zellweger syndrome E71.510
    rhizomelic chondrodysplasia punctata
      E71.540
    specified form NEC E71.548
      group 1 E71.518
      group 2 E71.53
      group 3 E71.542
    X-linked adrenoleukodystrophy E71.529
      adolescent E71.521
      adrenomyeloneuropathy E71.522
      childhood E71.520
      specified form NEC E71.528
    Zellweger-like syndrome E71.541
  persistent
    (somatoform) pain F45.41
    affective (mood) F34.9
  personality —*see also* Personality F60.9
    affective F34.0
    aggressive F60.3
    amoral F60.2
    anankastic F60.5
    antisocial F60.2
    anxious F60.6
    asocial F60.2
    asthenic F60.7
    avoidant F60.6
    borderline F60.3
    change (secondary) due to general medical
      condition F07.0
    compulsive F60.5
    cyclothymic F34.0
    dependent (passive) F60.7
    depressive F34.1
    dissocial F60.2
    emotional instability F60.3
    expansive paranoid F60.0
    explosive F60.3
    following organic brain damage F07.9
    histrionic F60.4
    hyperthymic F34.0
    hypothymic F34.1
    hysterical F60.4
    immature F60.89
    inadequate F60.7
    labile F60.3
    mixed (nonspecific) F60.89
    moral deficiency F60.2
    narcissistic F60.81
    negativistic F60.89
    obsessional F60.5
    obsessive (-compulsive) F60.5
    organic F07.9
    overconscientious F60.5
    paranoid F60.0
    passive (-dependent) F60.7
    passive-aggressive F60.89
    pathological NEC F60.9
    pseudosocial F60.2
    psychopathic F60.2
    schizoid F60.1
    schizotypal F21
    self-defeating F60.7
    specified NEC F60.89
    type A F60.5
    unstable (emotional) F60.3
  pervasive, developmental F84.9
  phencyclidine use
    mild F16.10
      with
        phencyclidine-induced
          anxiety disorder F16.180
          bipolar and related disorder
            F16.14
          depressive disorder F16.14
          psychotic disorder F16.159

Disorder *(Continued)*
  phencyclidine use *(Continued)*
    mild *(Continued)*
      with *(Continued)*
        phencyclidine intoxication F16.129
        phencyclidine intoxication delirium
          F16.121
      in remission (early) (sustained) F16.11
    moderate or severe F16.20
      with
        phencyclidine-induced
          anxiety disorder F16.280
          bipolar and related disorder F16.24
          depressive disorder F16.24
          psychotic disorder F16.259
        phencyclidine intoxication F16.229
        phencyclidine intoxication delirium
          F16.221
      in remission (early) (sustained) F16.21
  phobic anxiety, childhood F40.8
  phosphate-losing tubular N25.0
  pigmentation L81.9
    choroid, congenital Q14.3
    diminished melanin formation L81.6
    iron L81.8
    specified NEC L81.8
  pinna (noninfective) H61.10-●
    deformity, acquired H61.11-●
    hematoma H61.12-●
    perichondritis —*see* Perichondritis, ear
    specified type NEC H61.19-●
  pituitary gland E23.7
    iatrogenic (postprocedural) E89.3
    specified NEC E23.6
  platelets D69.1
  plexus G54.9
    specified NEC G54.8
  polymorphonuclear neutrophils D71
  porphyrin metabolism —*see* Porphyria
  postconcussional F07.81
  posthallucinogen perception F16.983
    in
      abuse F16.183
      dependence F16.283
  postmenopausal N95.9
    specified NEC N95.8
  postprocedural (postoperative) —*see*
    Complications, postprocedural
  post-transplant lymphoproliferative D47.z1
  post-traumatic stress (PTSD) F43.10
    acute F43.11
    chronic F43.12
  premenstrual dysphoric (PMDD) F32.81
  prepuce N47.8
  propionic acidemia E71.121
  prostate N42.9
    specified NEC N42.89
  psychogenic NOS —*see also* condition F45.9
    anxiety F41.8
    appetite F50.9
    asthenic F48.8
    cardiovascular (system) F45.8
    compulsive F42.8
    cutaneous F54
    depressive F32.9
    digestive (system) F45.8
    dysmenorrheic F45.8
    dyspneic F45.8
    endocrine (system) F54
    eye NEC F45.8
    feeding —*see* Disorder, eating
    functional NEC F45.8
    gastric F45.8
    gastrointestinal (system) F45.8
    genitourinary (system) F45.8
    heart (function) (rhythm) F45.8
    hyperventilatory F45.8
    hypochondriacal —*see* Disorder,
      hypochondriacal
    intestinal F45.8
    joint F45.8

Disorder *(Continued)*
  psychogenic NOS *(Continued)*
    learning F81.9
    limb F45.8
    lymphatic (system) F45.8
    menstrual F45.8
    micturition F45.8
    monoplegic NEC F44.4
    motor F44.4
    muscle F45.8
    musculoskeletal F45.8
    neurocirculatory F45.8
    obsessive F42.8
    occupational F48.8
    organ or part of body NEC F45.8
    paralytic NEC F44.4
    phobic F40.9
    physical NEC F45.8
    rectal F45.8
    respiratory (system) F45.8
    rheumatic F45.8
    sexual (function) F52.9
    skin (allergic) (eczematous) F54
    sleep F51.9
    specified part of body NEC F45.8
    stomach F45.8
  psychological F99
    associated with
      disease classified elsewhere F54
      sexual
        development F66
        relationship F66
        uncertainty about gender identity F64.9
  psychomotor NEC F44.4
    hysterical F44.4
  psychoneurotic —*see also* Neurosis
    mixed NEC F48.8
  psychophysiologic —*see* Disorder,
    somatoform
  psychosexual F65.9
    development F66
    identity of childhood F64.2
  psychosomatic NOS —*see* Disorder,
    somatoform
    multiple F45.0
    undifferentiated F45.1
  psychotic —*see* Psychosis
    transient (acute) F23
  puberty E30.9
    specified NEC E30.8
  pulmonary (valve) —*see* Endocarditis,
    pulmonary
  purine metabolism E79.9
  pyrimidine metabolism E79.9
  pyruvate metabolism E74.4
  reactive attachment (childhood) F94.1
  reading R48.0
    developmental (specific) F81.0
  receptive language F80.2
  receptor, hormonal, peripheral —*see also*
    Syndrome, androgen insensitivity E34.50
  recurrent brief depressive F33.8
  reflex R29.2
  refraction H52.7
    aniseikonia H52.32
    anisometropia H52.31
    astigmatism —*see* Astigmatism
    hypermetropia —*see* Hypermetropia
    myopia —*see* Myopia
    presbyopia H52.4
    specified NEC H52.6
  relationship F68.8
    due to sexual orientation F66
  REM sleep behavior G47.52
  renal function, impaired (tubular) N25.9
  resonance R49.9
    specified NEC R49.8
  respiratory function, impaired —*see also*
    Failure, respiration
    postprocedural —*see* Complication,
      postoperative, respiratory system
    psychogenic F45.8

Disorder *(Continued)*
  retina H35.9
    angioid streaks H35.33
    changes in vascular appearance H35.01-•
    degeneration —*see* Degeneration, retina
    dystrophy (hereditary) —*see* Dystrophy, retina
    edema H35.81
    hemorrhage —*see* Hemorrhage, retina
    ischemia H35.82
    macular degeneration —*see* Degeneration, macula
    microaneurysms H35.04-•
    microvascular abnormality NEC H35.09
    neovascularization —*see* Neovascularization, retina
    retinopathy —*see* Retinopathy
    separation of layers H35.70
      central serous chorioretinopathy H35.71-•
      pigment epithelium detachment (serous) H35.72-•
        hemorrhagic H35.73-•
    specified type NEC H35.89
    telangiectasis —*see* Telangiectasis, retina
    vasculitis —*see* Vasculitis, retina
  retroperitoneal K68.9
  right hemisphere organic affective F07.89
  rumination (infant or child) F98.21
  sacrum, sacrococcygeal NEC M53.3
  schizoaffective F25.9
    bipolar type F25.0
    depressive type F25.1
    manic type F25.0
    mixed type F25.0
    specified NEC F25.8
  schizoid of childhood F84.5
  schizophrenia spectrum and other psychotic disorder F29
    specified NEC F28
  schizophreniform F20.81
    brief F23
  schizotypal (personality) F21
  secretion, thyrocalcitonin E07.0
  sedative, hypnotic, or anxiolytic use
    mild F13.10
      with
        sedative, hypnotic, or anxiolytic-induced
          anxiety disorder F13.180
          bipolar and related disorder F13.14
          depressive disorder F13.14
          psychotic disorder F13.159
          sexual dysfunction F13.181
        sedative, hypnotic, or anxiolytic intoxication F13.129
        sedative, hypnotic, or anxiolytic intoxication delirium F13.121
      in remission (early) (sustained) F13.11
    moderate or severe F13.20
      with
        sedative, hypnotic, or anxiolytic-induced
          anxiety disorder F13.280
          bipolar and related disorder F13.24
          depressive disorder F13.24
          major neurocognitive disorder F13.27
          mild neurocognitive disorder F13.288
          psychotic disorder F13.259
          sexual dysfunction F13.281
        sedative, hypnotic, or anxiolytic intoxication F13.229
        sedative, hypnotic, or anxiolytic intoxication delirium F13.221
      in remission (early) (sustained) F13.21
  seizure —*see also* Epilepsy G40.909
    intractable G40.919
      with status epilepticus G40.911
  semantic pragmatic F80.89
    with autism F84.0

Disorder *(Continued)*
  sense of smell R43.1
    psychogenic F45.8
  separation anxiety, of childhood F93.0
  sexual
    arousal, female F52.22
    aversion F52.1
    function, psychogenic F52.9
    interest/arousal, female F52.22
    masochism F65.51
    maturation F66
    nonorganic F52.9
    preference —*see also* Deviation, sexual F65.9
      fetishistic transvestism F65.1
    relationship F66
    sadism F65.52
  shyness, of childhood and adolescence F40.10
  sibling rivalry F93.8
  sickle-cell (sickling) (homozygous) —*see* Disease, sickle-cell
    heterozygous D57.3
    specified type NEC D57.8-•
    trait D57.3
  sinus (nasal) J34.9
    specified NEC J34.89
  skin L98.9
    atrophic L90.9
      specified NEC L90.8
    granulomatous L92.9
      specified NEC L92.8
    hypertrophic L91.9
      specified NEC L91.8
    infiltrative NEC L98.6
    newborn P83.9
      specified NEC P83.88
    picking F42.4
    psychogenic (allergic) (eczematous) F54
  sleep G47.9
    breathing-related —*see* Apnea, sleep
    circadian rhythm G47.20
      advance sleep phase type G47.22
      delayed sleep phase type G47.21
      due to
        alcohol
          abuse F10.182
          dependence F10.282
          use F10.982
        amphetamines
          abuse F15.182
          dependence F15.282
          use F15.982
        caffeine
          abuse F15.182
          dependence F15.282
          use F15.982
        cocaine
          abuse F14.182
          dependence F14.282
          use F14.982
        drug NEC
          abuse F19.182
          dependence F19.282
          use F19.982
        opioid
          abuse F11.182
          dependence F11.282
          use F11.982
        psychoactive substance NEC
          abuse F19.182
          dependence F19.282
          use F19.982
        sedative, hypnotic, or anxiolytic
          abuse F13.182
          dependence F13.282
          use F13.982
        stimulant NEC
          abuse F15.182
          dependence F15.282
          use F15.982
      free running type G47.24

Disorder *(Continued)*
  sleep *(Continued)*
    circadian rhythm *(Continued)*
      in conditions classified elsewhere G47.27
      irregular sleep wake type G47.23
      jet lag type G47.25
      non-24-hour sleep-wake type G47.24
      shift work type G47.26
      specified NEC G47.29
      due to
        alcohol
          abuse F10.182
          dependence F10.282
          use F10.982
        amphetamine
          abuse F15.182
          dependence F15.282
          use F15.982
        anxiolytic
          abuse F13.182
          dependence F13.282
          use F13.982
        caffeine
          abuse F15.182
          dependence F15.282
          use F15.982
        cocaine
          abuse F14.182
          dependence F14.282
          use F14.982
        drug NEC
          abuse F19.182
          dependence F19.282
          use F19.982
        hypnotic
          abuse F13.182
          dependence F13.282
          use F13.982
        opioid
          abuse F11.182
          dependence F11.282
          use F11.982
        psychoactive substance NEC
          abuse F19.182
          dependence F19.282
          use F19.982
        sedative
          abuse F13.182
          dependence F13.282
          use F13.982
        stimulant NEC
          abuse F15.182
          dependence F15.282
          use F15.982
    emotional F51.9
    excessive somnolence —*see* Hypersomnia
    hypersomnia type —*see* Hypersomnia
    initiating or maintaining —*see* Insomnia
    nightmares F51.5
    nonorganic F51.9
      specified NEC F51.8
    parasomnia type G47.50
    specified NEC G47.8
    terrors F51.4
    walking F51.3
  sleep-wake pattern or schedule —*see also* Disorder, sleep, circadian rhythm G47.9
    specified NEC G47.8
  social
    anxiety (of childhood) F40.10
      generalized F40.11
    functioning in childhood F94.9
      specified NEC F94.8
    pragmatic F80.82
  soft tissue M79.9
    ankle M79.9
    due to use, overuse and pressure M70.90
      ankle M70.97-•
      bursitis —*see* Bursitis
      foot M70.97-•

▶ New   ⟹ Revised   ~~deleted~~ Deleted   • Use Additional Character(s)

Disorder *(Continued)*
  soft tissue *(Continued)*
    due to use, overuse and pressure
      (Continued)
      forearm M70.93-●
      hand M70.94-●
      lower leg M70.96-●
      multiple sites M70.99
      pelvic region M70.95-●
      shoulder region M70.91-●
      specified site NEC M70.98
      specified type NEC M70.80
        ankle M70.87-●
        foot M70.87-●
        forearm M70.83-●
        hand M70.84-●
        lower leg M70.86-●
        multiple sites M70.89
        pelvic region M70.85-●
        shoulder region M70.81-●
        specified site NEC M70.88
        thigh M70.85-●
        upper arm M70.82-●
      thigh M70.95-●
      upper arm M70.92-●
    foot M79.9
    forearm M79.9
    hand M79.9
    lower leg M79.9
    multiple sites M79.9
    occupational —*see* Disorder, soft tissue,
      due to use, overuse and pressure
    pelvic region M79.9
    shoulder region M79.9
    specified type NEC M79.89
    thigh M79.9
    upper arm M79.9
  somatic symptom F45.1
  somatization F45.0
  somatoform F45.9
    pain (persistent) F45.41
    somatization (multiple) (long-lasting)
      F45.0
    specified NEC F45.8
    undifferentiated F45.1
  somnolence, excessive —*see* Hypersomnia
  specific
    arithmetical F81.2
    developmental, of motor F82
    reading F81.0
    speech and language F80.9
    spelling F81.81
    written expression F81.81
  speech R47.9
    articulation (functional) (specific) F80.0
    developmental F80.9
    specified NEC R47.89
  speech-sound F80.0
  spelling (specific) F81.81
  spine —*see also* Dorsopathy
    ligamentous or muscular attachments,
      peripheral —*see* Enthesopathy, spinal
    specified NEC —*see* Dorsopathy, specified
      NEC
  stereotyped, habit or movement F98.4
  stimulant use (other) (unspecified)
    mild F15.10
      in remission (early) (sustained) F15.11
    moderate or severe F15.20
      in remission (early) (sustained) F15.21
  stomach (functional) —*see* Disorder, gastric
  stress F43.9
    acute F43.0
    post-traumatic F43.10
      acute F43.11
      chronic F43.12
  substance use (other) (unknown)
    mild F19.10
      with substance-induced
        anxiety disorder F19.180
        bipolar and related disorder F19.14

Disorder *(Continued)*
  substance use (other) (unknown) *(Continued)*
    mild *(Continued)*
      with substance-induced*(Continued)*
        depressive disorder F19.14
        major neurocognitive disorder F19.17
        mild neurocognitive disorder F19.188
        obsessive-compulsive and related
          disorder F19.188
        sexual dysfunction F19.181
      substance intoxication F19.129
      substance intoxication delirium F19.121
    moderate or severe F19.20
      with substance-induced
        anxiety disorder F19.280
        bipolar and related disorder F19.24
        depressive disorder F19.24
        major neurocognitive disorder F19.27
        mild neurocognitive disorder F19.288
        obsessive-compulsive and related
          disorder F19.288
        sexual dysfunction F19.281
      in remission (early) (sustained) F19.21
      substance intoxication F19.229
      substance intoxication delirium F19.221
  sulfur-bearing amino-acid metabolism
    E72.10
  sweat gland (eccrine) L74.9
    apocrine L75.9
      specified NEC L75.8
    specified NEC L74.8
  synovium M67.90
    acromioclavicular M67.91-●
    ankle M67.97-●
    elbow M67.92-●
    foot M67.97-●
    forearm M67.93-●
    hand M67.94-●
    hip M67.95-●
    knee M67.96-●
    multiple sites M67.99
    rupture —*see* Rupture, synovium
    shoulder M67.91-●
    specified type NEC M67.80
      acromioclavicular M67.81-●
      ankle M67.87-●
      elbow M67.82-●
      foot M67.87-●
      hand M67.84-●
      hip M67.85-●
      knee M67.86-●
      multiple sites M67.89
      wrist M67.83-●
    synovitis —*see* Synovitis
    upper arm M67.92-●
    wrist M67.93-●
  temperature regulation, newborn P81.9
    specified NEC P81.8
  temporomandibular joint M26.60-●
  tendon M67.90
    acromioclavicular M67.91-●
    ankle M67.97-●
    contracture —*see* Contracture, tendon
    elbow M67.92-●
    foot M67.97-●
    forearm M67.93-●
    hand M67.94-●
    hip M67.95-●
    knee M67.96-●
    multiple sites M67.99
    rupture —*see* Rupture, tendon
    shoulder M67.91-●
    specified type NEC M67.80
      acromioclavicular M67.81-●
      ankle M67.87-●
      elbow M67.82-●
      foot M67.87-●
      hand M67.84-●
      hip M67.85-●
      knee M67.86-●
      multiple sites M67.89

Disorder *(Continued)*
  tendon *(Continued)*
    specified type NEC *(Continued)*
      trunk M67.88
      wrist M67.83-●
    synovitis —*see* Synovitis
    tendinitis —*see* Tendinitis
    tenosynovitis —*see* Tenosynovitis
    trunk M67.98
    upper arm M67.92-●
    wrist M67.93-●
  thoracic root (nerve) NEC G54.3
  thyrocalcitonin hypersecretion E07.0
  thyroid (gland) E07.9
    function NEC, neonatal, transitory P72.2
    iodine-deficiency related E01.8
    specified NEC E07.89
  tic —*see* Tic
  tobacco use
    chewing tobacco (mild) (moderate) (severe)
      in remission (early) (sustained) F17.221
    cigarettes (mild) (moderate) (severe)
      in remission (early) (sustained) F17.211
    mild F17.200
      in remission (early) (sustained) F17.201
    moderate F17.200
      in remission (early) (sustained) F17.201
    severe F17.200
      in remission (early) (sustained) F17.201
    specified product NEC (mild) (moderate)
      (severe)
      in remission (early) (sustained) F17.291
  tooth K08.9
    development K00.9
      specified NEC K00.8
    eruption K00.6
  Tourette's F95.2
  trance and possession F44.89
  transvestic F65.1
  trauma and stressor-related F43.9
    other specified F43.8
  tricuspid (valve) —*see* Endocarditis, tricuspid
  tryptophan metabolism E70.5
  tubular, phosphate-losing N25.0
  tubulo-interstitial (in)
    brucellosis A23.9 *[N16]*
    cystinosis E72.04
    diphtheria A36.84
    glycogen storage disease E74.00 *[N16]*
    leukemia NEC C95.9-● *[N16]*
    lymphoma NEC C85.9-● *[N16]*
    mixed cryoglobulinemia D89.1 *[N16]*
    multiple myeloma C90.0-● *[N16]*
    Salmonella infection A02.25
    sarcoidosis D86.84
    sepsis A41.9 *[N16]*
      streptococcal A40.9 *[N16]*
    systemic lupus erythematosus M32.15
    toxoplasmosis B58.83
    transplant rejection T86.91 *[N16]*
    Wilson's disease E83.01 *[N16]*
  tubulo-renal function, impaired N25.9
    specified NEC N25.89
  tympanic membrane H73.9-●
    atrophy —*see* Atrophy, tympanic membrane
    infection —*see* Myringitis
    perforation —*see* Perforation, tympanum
    specified NEC H73.89-●
  unsocialized aggressive F91.1
  urea cycle metabolism E72.20
    argininemia E72.21
    arginosuccinic aciduria E72.22
    citrullinemia E72.23
    ornithine transcarbamylase deficiency
      E72.4
    other specified E72.29
  ureter (in) N28.9
    schistosomiasis B65.0 *[N29]*
    tuberculosis A18.11
  urethra N36.9
    specified NEC N36.8

Disorder *(Continued)*

urinary system N39.9
  specified NEC N39.8
valve, heart
  aortic —*see* Endocarditis, aortic
  mitral —*see* Endocarditis, mitral
  pulmonary —*see* Endocarditis, pulmonary
  rheumatic
    aortic —*see* Endocarditis, aortic,
      rheumatic
    mitral —*see* Endocarditis, mitral
    pulmonary —*see* Endocarditis,
      pulmonary, rheumatic
    tricuspid —*see* Endocarditis, tricuspid
  tricuspid —*see* Endocarditis, tricuspid
vestibular function H81.9-●
  specified NEC —*see* subcategory H81.8
    in diseases classified elsewhere H82.-●
  vertigo —*see* Vertigo
vision, binocular H53.30
  abnormal retinal correspondence H53.31
  diplopia H53.2
  fusion with defective stereopsis H53.32
  simultaneous perception H53.33
  suppression H53.34
visual
  cortex
    blindness H47.619
      left brain H47.612
      right brain H47.611
      due to
        inflammatory disorder H47.629
          left brain H47.622
          right brain H47.621
        neoplasm H47.639
          left brain H47.632
          right brain H47.631
        vascular disorder H47.649
          left brain H47.642
          right brain H47.641
  pathway H47.9
    due to
      inflammatory disorder H47.51-●
      neoplasm H47.52-●
      vascular disorder H47.53-●
    optic chiasm —*see* Disorder, optic,
      chiasm
vitreous body H43.9
  crystalline deposits —*see* Deposit,
    crystalline
  degeneration —*see* Degeneration, vitreous
  hemorrhage —*see* Hemorrhage, vitreous
  opacities —*see* Opacity, vitreous
  prolapse —*see* Prolapse, vitreous
  specified type NEC H43.89
voice R49.9
  specified type NEC R49.8
volatile solvent use
  due to drug abuse —*see* Abuse, drug,
    inhalant
  due to drug dependence —*see* Dependence,
    drug, inhalant
voyeuristic F65.3
white blood cells D72.9
  specified NEC D72.89
withdrawing, child or adolescent
  F40.10
Disorientation R41.0
Displacement, displaced
acquired traumatic of bone, cartilage, joint,
  tendon NEC —*see* Dislocation
adrenal gland (congenital) Q89.1
appendix, retrocecal (congenital) Q43.8
auricle (congenital) Q17.4
bladder (acquired) N32.89
  congenital Q64.19
brachial plexus (congenital) Q07.8
brain stem, caudal (congenital) Q04.8
canaliculus (lacrimalis), congenital Q10.6
cardia through esophageal hiatus (congenital)
  Q40.1

Displacement, displaced *(Continued)*

cerebellum, caudal (congenital) Q04.8
cervix —*see* Malposition, uterus
colon (congenital) Q43.3
device, implant or graft —*see also*
  Complications, by site and type,
  mechanical T85.628
  arterial graft NEC —*see* Complication,
    cardiovascular device, mechanical,
    vascular
  breast (implant) T85.42
  catheter NEC T85.628
    dialysis (renal) T82.42
      intraperitoneal T85.621
    infusion NEC T82.524
      spinal (epidural) (subdural) T85.620
    urinary
      cystostomy T83.020
      Hopkins T83.028
      ileostomy T83.028
      indwelling T83.021
      nephrostomy T83.022
      specified NEC T83.028
      urostomy T83.028
  electronic (electrode) (pulse generator)
    (stimulator) —*see* Complication,
    electronic stimulator
  fixation, internal (orthopedic) NEC —
    see Complication, fixation device,
    mechanical
  gastrointestinal —*see* Complications,
    prosthetic device, mechanical,
    gastrointestinal device
  genital NEC T83.428
    intrauterine contraceptive device (string)
      T83.32
    penile prosthesis (cylinder) (implanted)
      (pump) (resevoir) T83.420
    testicular prosthesis T83.421
  heart NEC —*see* Complication,
    cardiovascular device, mechanical
  joint prosthesis —*see* Complications, joint
    prosthesis, mechanical
  ocular —*see* Complications, prosthetic
    device, mechanical, ocular device
  orthopedic NEC —*see* Complication,
    orthopedic, device or graft,
    mechanical
  specified NEC T85.628
  urinary NEC T83.128
    graft T83.22
    sphincter, implanted T83.121
    stent (ileal conduit) (nephroureteral)
      T83.123
    ureteral indwelling T83.122
  vascular NEC —*see* Complication,
    cardiovascular device, mechanical
  ventricular intracranial shunt T85.02
electronic stimulator
  bone T84.320
  cardiac —*see* Complications, cardiac
    device, electronic
  nervous system —*see* Complication,
    prosthetic device, mechanical,
    electronic nervous system
    stimulator
  urinary —*see* Complications, electronic
    stimulator, urinary
esophageal mucosa into cardia of stomach,
  congenital Q39.8
esophagus (acquired) K22.8
  congenital Q39.8
eyeball (acquired) (lateral) (old) —*see*
  Displacement, globe
  congenital Q15.8
  current —*see* Avulsion, eye
fallopian tube (acquired) N83.4-●
  congenital Q50.6
  opening (congenital) Q50.6
gallbladder (congenital) Q44.1
gastric mucosa (congenital) Q40.2

Displacement, displaced *(Continued)*

globe (acquired) (old) (lateral) H05.21-●
  current —*see* Avulsion, eye
heart (congenital) Q24.8
  acquired I51.89
hymen (upward) (congenital) Q52.4
intervertebral disc NEC
  with myelopathy —*see* Disorder, disc, with,
    myelopathy
  cervical, cervicothoracic (with)
    M50.20
    myelopathy —*see* Disorder, disc,
      cervical, with myelopathy
    neuritis, radiculitis or radiculopathy —
      see Disorder, disc, cervical, with
      neuritis
  due to trauma —*see* Dislocation, vertebra
  lumbar region M51.26
    with
      neuritis, radiculitis, radiculopathy or
        sciatica M51.16
  lumbosacral region M51.27
    with
      myelopathy M51.07
      neuritis, radiculitis, radiculopathy or
        sciatica M51.17
  sacrococcygeal region M53.3
  thoracic region M51.24
    with
      myelopathy M51.04
      neuritis, radiculitis, radiculopathy
        M51.14
  thoracolumbar region M51.25
    with
      myelopathy M51.05
      neuritis, radiculitis, radiculopathy
        M51.15
intrauterine device (string) T83.32
kidney (acquired) N28.83
  congenital Q63.2
lachrymal, lacrimal apparatus or duct
  (congenital) Q10.6
lens, congenital Q12.1
macula (congenital) Q14.1
Meckel's diverticulum Q43.0
  malignant —*see* Table of Neoplasms, small
    intestine, malignant
nail (congenital) Q84.6
  acquired L60.8
opening of Wharton's duct in mouth Q38.4
organ or site, congenital NEC —*see*
  Malposition, congenital
ovary (acquired) N83.4-●
  congenital Q50.39
  free in peritoneal cavity (congenital)
    Q50.39
  into hernial sac N83.4-●
oviduct (acquired) N83.4-●
  congenital Q50.6
parathyroid (gland) E21.4
parotid gland (congenital) Q38.4
punctum lacrimale (congenital) Q10.6
sacro-iliac (joint) (congenital) Q74.2
  current injury S33.2
  old —*see* subcategory M53.2
salivary gland (any) (congenital) Q38.4
spleen (congenital) Q89.09
stomach, congenital Q40.2
sublingual duct Q38.4
tongue (downward) (congenital) Q38.3
tooth, teeth, fully erupted M26.30
  horizontal M26.33
  vertical M26.34
trachea (congenital) Q32.1
ureter or ureteric opening or orifice
  (congenital) Q62.62
uterine opening of oviducts or fallopian tubes
  Q50.6
uterus, uterine —*see* Malposition, uterus
ventricular septum Q21.0
  with rudimentary ventricle Q20.4

Disproportion
  between native and reconstructed breast
      N65.1
  fiber-type G71.20
    congenital G71.29
Disruptio uteri —*see* Rupture, uterus
Disruption (of)
  ciliary body NEC H21.89
  closure of
    cornea T81.31
    craniotomy T81.32
    fascia (muscular) (superficial) T81.32
    internal organ or tissue T81.32
    laceration (external) (internal) T81.33
    ligament T81.32
    mucosa T81.31
    muscle or muscle flap T81.32
    ribs or rib cage T81.32
    skin and subcutaneous tissue (full-
        thickness) (superficial) T81.31
    skull T81.32
    sternum (sternotomy) T81.32
    tendon T81.32
    traumatic laceration (external) (internal)
        T81.33
  family Z63.8
    due to
      absence of family member due to
          military deployment Z63.31
      absence of family member NEC
          Z63.32
      alcoholism and drug addiction in
          family Z63.72
      bereavement Z63.4
      death (assumed) or disappearance of
          family member Z63.4
      divorce or separation Z63.5
      drug addiction in family Z63.72
      return of family member from military
          deployment (current or past
          conflict) Z63.71
      stressful life events NEC Z63.79
  iris NEC H21.89
  ligament(s) —*see also* Sprain
    knee
      current injury —*see* Dislocation, knee
      old (chronic) —*see* Derangement, knee,
          ligament, instability, chronic
      spontaneous NEC —*see* Derangement,
          knee, disruption ligament
  ossicular chain —*see* Discontinuity, ossicles,
      ear
  pelvic ring (stable) S32.810
    unstable S32.811
  traumatic injury wound repair T81.33
  wound T81.30
    episiotomy O90.1
    operation T81.31
      cesarean O90.0
      external operation wound (superficial)
          T81.31
      internal operation wound (deep)
          T81.32
    perineal (obstetric) O90.1
  traumatic injury repair T81.33
Dissatisfaction with
  employment Z56.9
  school environment Z55.4
Dissecting —*see* condition
Dissection
  aorta I71.00
    abdominal I71.02
    thoracic I71.01
    thoracoabdominal I71.03
  artery I77.70
    basilar (trunk) I77.75
    carotid I77.71
    cerebral (nonruptured) I67.0
      ruptured —*see* Hemorrhage, intracranial,
          subarachnoid
    coronary I25.42

Dissection *(Continued)*
  artery *(Continued)*
    extremity
      lower I77.77
      upper I77.76
    iliac I77.72
    precerebral
      congenital (nonruptured) Q28.1
      specified site NEC I77.75
    renal I77.73
    specified NEC I77.79
    vertebral I77.74
  precerebral artery, congenital (nonruptured)
      Q28.1
    Heartland A93.8
  traumatic —*see* Wound, open, by site
  vascular I99.8
  wound —*see* Wound, open
Disseminated —*see* condition
Dissociation
  auriculoventricular or atrioventricular (AV)
      (any degree) (isorhythmic) I45.89
    with heart block I44.2
  interference I45.89
Dissociative reaction, state F44.9
Dissolution, vertebra —*see* Osteoporosis
Distension, distention
  abdomen R14.0
  bladder N32.89
  cecum K63.89
  colon K63.89
  gallbladder K82.8
  intestine K63.89
  kidney N28.89
  liver K76.89
  seminal vesicle N50.89
  stomach K31.89
    acute K31.0
    psychogenic F45.8
  ureter —*see* Dilatation, ureter
  uterus N85.8
Distoma hepaticum infestation B66.3
Distomiasis B66.9
  bile passages B66.3
  hemic B65.9
  hepatic B66.3
    due to Clonorchis sinensis B66.1
  intestinal B66.5
  liver B66.3
    due to Clonorchis sinensis B66.1
  lung B66.4
  pulmonary B66.4
Distomolar (fourth molar) K00.1
Disto-occlusion (Division I) (Division II)
    M26.212
Distortion(s) (congenital)
  adrenal (gland) Q89.1
  arm NEC Q68.8
  bile duct or passage Q44.5
  bladder Q64.79
  brain Q04.9
  cervix (uteri) Q51.9
  chest (wall) Q67.8
    bones Q76.8
  clavicle Q74.0
  clitoris Q52.6
  coccyx Q76.49
  common duct Q44.5
  coronary Q24.5
  cystic duct Q44.5
  ear (auricle) (external) Q17.3
    inner Q16.5
    middle Q16.4
      ossicles Q16.3
  endocrine NEC Q89.2
  eustachian tube Q17.8
  eye (adnexa) Q15.8
  face bone(s) NEC Q75.8
  fallopian tube Q50.6
  femur NEC Q68.8
  fibula NEC Q68.8

Distortion *(Continued)*
  finger(s) Q68.1
  foot Q66.9-●
  genitalia, genital organ(s)
    female Q52.8
      external Q52.79
      internal NEC Q52.8
  gyri Q04.8
  hand bone(s) Q68.1
  heart (auricle) (ventricle) Q24.8
    valve (cusp) Q24.8
  hepatic duct Q44.5
  humerus NEC Q68.8
  hymen Q52.4
  intrafamilial communications Z63.8
  jaw NEC M26.89
  labium (majus) (minus) Q52.79
  leg NEC Q68.8
  lens Q12.8
  liver Q44.7
  lumbar spine Q76.49
    with disproportion O33.8
      causing obstructed labor O65.0
  lumbosacral (joint) (region) Q76.49
    kyphosis —*see* Kyphosis, congenital
    lordosis —*see* Lordosis, congenital
  nerve Q07.8
  nose Q30.8
  organ
    of Corti Q16.5
    or site not listed —*see* Anomaly, by site
      ossicles, ear Q16.3
  oviduct Q50.6
  pancreas Q45.3
  parathyroid (gland) Q89.2
  pituitary (gland) Q89.2
  radius NEC Q68.8
  sacroiliac joint Q74.2
  sacrum Q76.49
  scapula Q74.0
  shoulder girdle Q74.0
  skull bone(s) NEC Q75.8
    with
      anencephalus Q00.0
      encephalocele —*see* Encephalocele
      hydrocephalus Q03.9
        with spina bifida —*see* Spina bifida,
            with hydrocephalus
      microcephaly Q02
  spinal cord Q06.8
  spine Q76.49
    kyphosis —*see* Kyphosis, congenital
    lordosis —*see* Lordosis, congenital
  spleen Q89.09
  sternum NEC Q76.7
  thorax (wall) Q67.8
    bony Q76.8
  thymus (gland) Q89.2
  thyroid (gland) Q89.2
  tibia NEC Q68.8
  toe(s) Q66.9-●
  tongue Q38.3
  trachea (cartilage) Q32.1
  ulna NEC Q68.8
  ureter Q62.8
  urethra Q64.79
    causing obstruction Q64.39
  uterus Q51.9
  vagina Q52.4
  vertebra Q76.49
    kyphosis —*see* Kyphosis, congenital
    lordosis —*see* Lordosis, congenital
  visual —*see also* Disturbance, vision
    shape and size H53.15
  vulva Q52.79
  wrist (bones) (joint) Q68.8
Distress
  abdomen —*see* Pain, abdominal
  acute respiratory R06.03
    syndrome (adult) (child) J80
  epigastric R10.13

Distress *(Continued)*
  fetal P84
    complicating pregnancy —*see* Stress, fetal
  gastrointestinal (functional) K30
    psychogenic F45.8
  intestinal (functional) NOS K59.9
    psychogenic F45.8
  maternal, during labor and delivery O75.0
  relationship, with spouse or intimate partner
    Z63.0
  respiratory (adult) (child) R06.03
    newborn P22.9
      specified NEC P22.8
    orthopnea R06.01
    psychogenic F45.8
    shortness of breath R06.02
    specified type NEC R06.09
Distribution vessel, atypical Q27.9
  coronary artery Q24.5
  precerebral Q28.1
Districhiasis L68.8
Disturbance(s) —*see also* Disease
  absorption K90.9
    calcium E58
    carbohydrate K90.49
    fat K90.49
      pancreatic K90.3
    protein K90.49
    starch K90.49
    vitamin —*see* Deficiency, vitamin
  acid-base equilibrium E87.8
    mixed E87.4
  activity and attention (with hyperkinesis) —
    see Disorder, attention-deficit
    hyperactivity
  amino acid transport E72.00
  assimilation, food K90.9
  auditory nerve, except deafness —*see*
    subcategory H93.3
  behavior —*see* Disorder, conduct
  blood clotting (mechanism) —*see also* Defect,
    coagulation D68.9
  cerebral
    nerve —*see* Disorder, nerve, cranial
    status, newborn P91.9
      specified NEC P91.88
  circulatory I99.9
  conduct —*see also* Disorder, conduct F91.9
    adjustment reaction —*see* Disorder,
      adjustment
    compulsive F63.9
    disruptive F91.9
    hyperkinetic —*see* Disorder, attention-
      deficit hyperactivity
    socialized F91.2
    specified NEC F91.8
    unsocialized F91.1
  coordination R27.8
  cranial nerve —*see* Disorder, nerve, cranial
  deep sensibility —*see* Disturbance, sensation
  digestive K30
    psychogenic F45.8
  electrolyte —*see also* Imbalance, electrolyte
    newborn, transitory P74.49
      hyperammonemia P74.6
      hyperchloremia P74.421
      hyperchloremic metabolic acidosis
        P74.421
      hypochloremia P74.422
      potassium balance
        hyperkalemia P74.31
        hypokalemia P74.32
      sodium balance
        hypernatremia P74.21
        hyponatremia P74.22
      specified type NEC P74.49
  emotions specific to childhood and
    adolescence F93.9
    with
      anxiety and fearfulness NEC F93.8
      elective mutism F94.0

Disturbance *(Continued)*
  emotions specific to childhood and
    adolescence *(Continued)*
    with *(Continued)*
      oppositional disorder F91.3
      sensitivity (withdrawal) F40.10
      shyness F40.10
      social withdrawal F40.10
    involving relationship problems F93.8
    mixed F93.8
    specified NEC F93.8
  endocrine (gland) E34.9
    neonatal, transitory P72.9
      specified NEC P72.8
  equilibrium R42
  fructose metabolism E74.10
  gait —*see* Gait
    hysterical F44.4
    psychogenic F44.4
  gastrointestinal (functional) K30
    psychogenic F45.8
  habit, child F98.9
  hearing, except deafness and tinnitus —*see*
    Abnormal, auditory perception
  heart, functional (conditions in I44-I50)
    due to presence of (cardiac) prosthesis
      I97.19-●
    postoperative I97.89
      cardiac surgery —*see also* Infarct,
        myocardium, associated with
        revascularization procedure I97.19-●
  hormones E34.9
  innervation uterus (parasympathetic)
    (sympathetic) N85.8
  keratinization NEC
    gingiva K05.10
      nonplaque induced K05.11
      plaque induced K05.10
    lip K13.0
    oral (mucosa) (soft tissue) K13.29
    tongue K13.29
  learning (specific) —*see* Disorder, learning
  memory —*see* Amnesia
    mild, following organic brain damage F06.8
  mental F99
    associated with diseases classified
      elsewhere F54
  metabolism E88.9
    with
      abortion —*see* Abortion, by type with
        other specified complication
      ectopic pregnancy O08.5
      molar pregnancy O08.5
    amino-acid E72.9
      aromatic E70.9
      branched-chain E71.2
      straight-chain E72.89
      sulfur-bearing E72.10
    ammonia E72.20
    arginine E72.21
    arginosuccinic acid E72.22
    carbohydrate E74.9
    cholesterol E78.9
    citrulline E72.23
    cystathionine E72.19
    general E88.9
    glutamine E72.89
    histidine E70.40
    homocystine E72.19
    hydroxylysine E72.3
    in labor or delivery O75.89
    iron E83.10
    lipoid E78.9
    lysine E72.3
    methionine E72.19
    neonatal, transitory P74.9
      calcium and magnesium P71.9
        specified type NEC P71.8
      carbohydrate metabolism P70.9
        specified type NEC P70.8
      specified NEC P74.8

Disturbance *(Continued)*
  metabolism *(Continued)*
    ornithine E72.4
    phosphate E83.39
    sodium NEC E87.8
    threonine E72.89
    tryptophan E70.5
    tyrosine E70.20
    urea cycle E72.20
  motor R29.2
  nervous, functional R45.0
  neuromuscular mechanism (eye), due to
    syphilis A52.15
  nutritional E63.9
    nail L60.3
  ocular motion H51.9
    psychogenic F45.8
  oculogyric H51.8
    psychogenic F45.8
  oculomotor H51.9
    psychogenic F45.8
  olfactory nerve R43.1
  optic nerve NEC —*see* Disorder, nerve, optic
  oral epithelium, including tongue NEC
    K13.29
  perceptual due to
    alcohol withdrawal F10.232
    amphetamine intoxication F15.922
      in
        abuse F15.122
        dependence F15.222
    anxiolytic withdrawal F13.232
    cannabis intoxication (acute) F12.922
      in
        abuse F12.122
        dependence F12.222
    cocaine intoxication (acute) F14.922
      in
        abuse F14.122
        dependence F14.222
    hypnotic withdrawal F13.232
    opioid intoxication (acute) F11.922
      in
        abuse F11.122
        dependence F11.222
    phencyclidine intoxication (acute) F16.122
    sedative withdrawal F13.232
  personality (pattern) (trait) —*see also*
    Disorder, personality F60.9
    following organic brain damage F07.9
  polyglandular E31.9
    specified NEC E31.8
  potassium balance, newborn
    hyperkalemia P74.31
    hypokalemia P74.32
  psychogenic F45.9
  psychomotor F44.4
  psychophysical visual H53.16
  pupillary —*see* Anomaly, pupil, function
  reflex R29.2
  rhythm, heart I49.9
  salivary secretion K11.7
  sensation (cold) (heat) (localization) (tactile
    discrimination) (texture) (vibratory)
    NEC R20.9
    hysterical F44.6
    skin R20.9
      anesthesia R20.0
      hyperesthesia R20.3
      hypoesthesia R20.1
      paresthesia R20.2
      specified type NEC R20.8
    smell R43.9
      and taste (mixed) R43.8
      anosmia R43.0
      parosmia R43.1
      specified NEC R43.8
    taste R43.9
      and smell (mixed) R43.8
      parageusia R43.2
      specified NEC R43.8

▶ New   ⇨ Revised   ~~deleted~~ Deleted   ● Use Additional Character(s)

Dorsopathy *(Continued)*
  specified NEC *(Continued)*
    occipito-atlanto-axial region M53.81
    sacrococcygeal region M53.88
    thoracic region M53.84
    thoracolumbar region M53.85
Double
  albumin E88.09
  aortic arch Q25.45
  auditory canal Q17.8
  auricle (heart) Q20.8
  bladder Q64.79
  cervix Q51.820
    with doubling of uterus (and vagina)
      Q51.10
      with obstruction Q51.11
  inlet ventricle Q20.4
  kidney with double pelvis (renal) Q63.0
  meatus urinarius Q64.75
  monster Q89.4
  outlet
    left ventricle Q20.2
    right ventricle Q20.1
  pelvis (renal) with double ureter Q62.5
  tongue Q38.3
  ureter (one or both sides) Q62.5
    with double pelvis (renal) Q62.5
  urethra Q64.74
  urinary meatus Q64.75
➡ uterus Q51.28
    with
      doubling of cervix (and vagina)
        Q51.10
        with obstruction Q51.11
    complete Q51.21
    in pregnancy or childbirth O34.0-•
      causing obstructed labor O65.5
    partial Q51.22
    specified NEC Q51.28
  vagina Q52.10
    with doubling of uterus (and cervix)
      Q51.10
      with obstruction Q51.11
  vision H53.2
  vulva Q52.79
Douglas' pouch, cul-de-sac —*see* condition
Down syndrome Q90.9
  meiotic nondisjunction Q90.0
  mitotic nondisjunction Q90.1
  mosaicism Q90.1
  translocation Q90.2
DPD (dihydropyrimidine dehydrogenase
  deficiency) E88.89
Dracontiasis B72
Dracunculiasis, dracunculosis B72
Dream state, hysterical F44.89
Drepanocytic anemia —*see* Disease,
  sickle-cell
Dresbach's syndrome (elliptocytosis)
  D58.1
Dreschlera (hawaiiensis) (infection)
  B43.8
Dressler's syndrome I24.1
Drift, ulnar —*see* Deformity, limb, specified
  type NEC, forearm
Drinking (alcohol)
  excessive, to excess NEC (without
    dependence) F10.10
    habitual (continual) (without remission)
      F10.20
      with remission F10.21
Drip, postnasal (chronic) R09.82
  due to
    allergic rhinitis —*see* Rhinitis, allergic
    common cold J00
    gastroesophageal reflux —*see* Reflux,
      gastroesophageal
    nasopharyngitis —*see* Nasopharyngitis
    other known condition — code to
      condition
    sinusitis —*see* Sinusitis

Droop
  facial R29.810
    cerebrovascular disease I69.992
      cerebral infarction I69.392
      intracerebral hemorrhage I69.192
      nontraumatic intracranial hemorrhage
        NEC I69.292
      specified disease NEC I69.892
      subarachnoid hemorrhage I69.092
Drop (in)
  attack NEC R55
  finger —*see* Deformity, finger
  foot —*see* Deformity, limb, foot, drop
  hematocrit (precipitous) R71.0
  hemoglobin R71.0
  toe —*see* Deformity, toe, specified NEC
  wrist —*see* Deformity, limb, wrist drop
Dropped heart beats I45.9
Dropsy, dropsical —*see also* Hydrops
  abdomen R18.8
  brain —*see* Hydrocephalus
  cardiac, heart —*see* Failure, heart, congestive
  gangrenous —*see* Gangrene
  heart —*see* Failure, heart, congestive
  kidney —*see* Nephrosis
  lung —*see* Edema, lung
  newborn due to isoimmunization P56.0
  pericardium —*see* Pericarditis
Drowned, drowning (near) T75.1
Drowsiness R40.0
Drug
  abuse counseling and surveillance Z71.51
  addiction —*see* Dependence
  dependence —*see* Dependence
  habit —*see* Dependence
  harmful use —*see* Abuse, drug
  induced fever R50.2
  overdose —*see* Table of Drugs and Chemicals,
    by drug, poisoning
  poisoning —*see* Table of Drugs and
    Chemicals, by drug, poisoning
  resistant organism infection —*see also*
    Resistant, organism, to, drug Z16.30
  therapy
    long term (current) (prophylactic) —*see*
      Therapy, drug long-term (current)
      (prophylactic)
    short term - omit code
  wrong substance given or taken in error —*see*
    Table of Drugs and Chemicals, by drug,
    poisoning
Drunkenness (without dependence) F10.129
  acute in alcoholism F10.229
  chronic (without remission) F10.20
    with remission F10.21
  pathological (without dependence) F10.129
    with dependence F10.229
  sleep F51.9
Drusen
  macula (degenerative) (retina) —*see*
    Degeneration, macula, drusen
  optic disc H47.32-•
Dry, dryness —*see also* condition
  larynx J38.7
  mouth R68.2
    due to dehydration E86.0
  nose J34.89
  socket (teeth) M27.3
  throat J39.2
DSAP L56.5
Duane's syndrome H50.81-•
Dubin-Johnson disease or syndrome E80.6
Dubois' disease (thymus gland) A50.59 *[E35]*
Dubowitz' syndrome Q87.19
Duchenne-Aran muscular atrophy G12.21
Duchenne-Griesinger disease G71.01
Duchenne's
  disease or syndrome
    motor neuron disease G12.22
    muscular dystrophy G71.01
  locomotor ataxia (syphilitic) A52.11

Duchenne's *(Continued)*
  paralysis
    birth injury P14.0
    due to or associated with
      motor neuron disease G12.22
      muscular dystrophy G71.01
Ducrey's chancre A57
Duct, ductus —*see* condition
Duhring's disease (dermatitis herpetiformis)
  L13.0
Dullness, cardiac (decreased) (increased) R01.2
Dumb ague —*see* Malaria
Dumbness —*see* Aphasia
Dumdum fever B55.0
Dumping syndrome (postgastrectomy) K91.1
Duodenitis (nonspecific) (peptic) K29.80
  with bleeding K29.81
Duodenocholangitis —*see* Cholangitis
Duodenum, duodenal —*see* condition
Duplay's bursitis or periarthritis —*see*
  Tendinitis, calcific, shoulder
Duplication, duplex —*see also* Accessory
  alimentary tract Q45.8
  anus Q43.4
  appendix (and cecum) Q43.4
  biliary duct (any) Q44.5
  bladder Q64.79
  cecum (and appendix) Q43.4
  cervix Q51.820
  chromosome NEC
    with complex rearrangements NEC Q92.5
    seen only at prometaphase Q92.8
  cystic duct Q44.5
  digestive organs Q45.8
  esophagus Q39.8
  frontonasal process Q75.8
  intestine (large) (small) Q43.4
  kidney Q63.0
  liver Q44.7
  pancreas Q45.3
  penis Q55.69
  respiratory organs NEC Q34.8
  salivary duct Q38.4
  spinal cord (incomplete) Q06.2
  stomach Q40.2
Dupré's disease (meningism) R29.1
Dupuytren's contraction or disease M72.0
Durand-Nicolas-Favre disease A55
Durotomy (inadvertent) (incidental) G97.41
Duroziez's disease (congenital mitral stenosis)
  Q23.2
Dutton's relapsing fever (West African) A68.1
Dwarfism E34.3
  achondroplastic Q77.4
  congenital E34.3
  constitutional E34.3
  hypochondroplastic Q77.4
  hypophyseal E23.0
  infantile E34.3
  Laron-type E34.3
  Lorain (-Levi) type E23.0
  metatropic Q77.8
  nephrotic-glycosuric (with
    hypophosphatemic rickets) E72.09
  nutritional E45
  pancreatic K86.89
  pituitary E23.0
  renal N25.0
  thanatophoric Q77.1
➡ Dyke-Young anemia (secondary)
  (symptomatic) D59.19
Dysacusis —*see* Abnormal, auditory
  perception
Dysadrenocortism E27.9
  hyperfunction E27.0
Dysarthria R47.1
  following
    cerebral infarction I69.322
    cerebrovascular disease I69.922
      specified disease NEC I69.822
    intracerebral hemorrhage I69.122

Dysarthria *(Continued)*
  following *(Continued)*
    nontraumatic intracranial hemorrhage
        NEC I69.222
    subarachnoid hemorrhage I69.022
Dysautonomia (familial) G90.1
Dysbarism T70.3
Dysbasia R26.2
  angiosclerotica intermittens I73.9
  hysterical F44.4
  lordotica (progressiva) G24.1
  nonorganic origin F44.4
  psychogenic F44.4
Dysbetalipoproteinemia (familial) E78.2
Dyscalculia R48.8
  developmental F81.2
Dyschezia K59.00
Dyschondroplasia (with hemangiomata) Q78.4
Dyschromia (skin) L81.9
Dyscollagenosis M35.9
Dyscranio-pygo-phalangy Q87.0
Dyscrasia
  blood (with) D75.9
    antepartum hemorrhage —*see* Hemorrhage,
        antepartum, with coagulation defect
    intrapartum hemorrhage O67.0
    newborn P61.9
      specified type NEC P61.8
    puerperal, postpartum O72.3
  polyglandular, pluriglandular E31.9
Dysendocrinism E34.9
Dysentery, dysenteric (catarrhal) (diarrhea)
    (epidemic) (hemorrhagic) (infectious)
    (sporadic) (tropical) A09
  abscess, liver A06.4
  amebic —*see also* Amebiasis A06.0
    with abscess —*see* Abscess, amebic
    acute A06.0
    chronic A06.1
  arthritis —*see also* category M01 A09
    bacillary —*see also* category M01 A03.9
  bacillary A03.9
    arthritis —*see also* category M01 A03.9
    Boyd A03.2
    Flexner A03.1
    Schmitz (-Stutzer) A03.0
    Shiga (-Kruse) A03.0
    Shigella A03.9
      boydii A03.2
      dysenteriae A03.0
      flexneri A03.1
      group A A03.0
      group B A03.1
      group C A03.2
      group D A03.3
      sonnei A03.3
      specified type NEC A03.8
    Sonne A03.3
    specified type NEC A03.8
  balantidial A07.0
  Balantidium coli A07.0
  Boyd's A03.2
  candidal B37.82
  Chilomastix A07.8
  Chinese A03.9
  coccidial A07.3
  Dientamoeba (fragilis) A07.8
  Embadomonas A07.8
  Entamoeba, entamebic —*see* Dysentery,
      amebic
  Flexner-Boyd A03.2
  Flexner's A03.1
  Giardia lamblia A07.1
  Hiss-Russell A03.1
  Lamblia A07.1
  leishmanial B55.0
  malarial —*see* Malaria
  metazoal B82.0
  monilial B37.82
  protozoal A07.9
  Salmonella A02.0

Dysentery, dysenteric *(Continued)*
  schistosomal B65.1
  Schmitz (-Stutzer) A03.0
  Shiga (-Kruse) A03.0
  Shigella NOS —*see* Dysentery, bacillary
  Sonne A03.3
  strongyloidiasis B78.0
  trichomonal A07.8
  viral —*see also* Enteritis, viral A08.4
Dysequilibrium R42
Dysesthesia R20.8
  hysterical F44.6
Dysfibrinogenemia (congenital) D68.2
Dysfunction
  adrenal E27.9
    hyperfunction E27.0
  autonomic
    due to alcohol G31.2
    somatoform F45.8
  bladder N31.9
    neurogenic NOS —*see* Dysfunction,
        bladder, neuromuscular
    neuromuscular NOS N31.9
      atonic (motor) (sensory) N31.2
      autonomous N31.2
      flaccid N31.2
      nonreflex N31.2
      reflex N31.1
      specified NEC N31.8
      uninhibited N31.0
  bleeding, uterus N93.8
  cerebral G93.89
  colon K59.9
    psychogenic F45.8
  colostomy K94.03
  cystic duct K82.8
  cystostomy (stoma) —*see* Complications,
      cystostomy
  ejaculatory N53.19
    anejaculatory orgasm N53.13
    painful N53.12
    premature F52.4
    retarded N53.11
  endocrine NOS E34.9
  endometrium N85.8
  enterostomy K94.13
  erectile —*see* Dysfunction, sexual, male,
      erectile
  gallbladder K82.8
  gastrostomy (stoma) K94.23
  gland, glandular NOS E34.9
    meibomian, of eyelid -*see* Dysfunction,
        meibomian gland
  heart I51.89
  hemoglobin D75.89
  hepatic K76.89
  hypophysis E23.7
  hypothalamic NEC E23.3
  ileostomy (stoma) K94.13
  jejunostomy (stoma) K94.13
  kidney —*see* Disease, renal
  labyrinthine —*see* subcategory H83.2
  left ventricular, following sudden emotional
      stress I51.81
  liver K76.89
  male —*see* Dysfunction, sexual, male
  meibomian gland, of eyelid H02.889
    left H02.886
      lower H02.885
      upper H02.884
      upper and lower eyelids H02.88B
    right H02.883
      lower H02.882
      upper H02.881
      upper and lower eyelids H02.88A
  orgasmic (female) F52.31
    male F52.32
  ovary E28.9
    specified NEC E28.8
  papillary muscle I51.89
  parathyroid E21.4

Dysfunction *(Continued)*
  physiological NEC R68.89
    psychogenic F59
  pineal gland E34.8
  pituitary (gland) E23.3
  platelets D69.1
  polyglandular E31.9
    specified NEC E31.8
  psychophysiologic F59
  psychosexual F52.9
    with
      dyspareunia F52.6
      premature ejaculation F52.4
      vaginismus F52.5
  pylorus K31.9
  rectum K59.9
    psychogenic F45.8
  reflex (sympathetic) —*see* Syndrome, pain,
      complex regional I
  segmental —*see* Dysfunction, somatic
  senile R54
  sexual (due to) R37
    alcohol F10.981
    amphetamine F15.981
      in
        abuse F15.181
        dependence F15.281
    anxiolytic F13.981
      in
        abuse F13.181
        dependence F13.281
    cocaine F14.981
      in
        abuse F14.181
        dependence F14.281
    excessive sexual drive F52.8
    failure of genital response (male) F52.21
      female F52.22
    female N94.9
      aversion F52.1
      dyspareunia N94.10
        psychogenic F52.6
      frigidity F52.22
      nymphomania F52.8
      orgasmic F52.31
      psychogenic F52.9
        aversion F52.1
        dyspareunia F52.6
        frigidity F52.22
        nymphomania F52.8
        orgasmic F52.31
        vaginismus F52.5
      vaginismus N94.2
        psychogenic F52.5
    hypnotic F13.981
      in
        abuse F13.181
        dependence F13.281
    inhibited orgasm (female) F52.31
      male F52.32
    lack
      of sexual enjoyment F52.1
      or loss of sexual desire F52.0
    male N53.9
      anejaculatory orgasm N53.13
      ejaculatory N53.19
        painful N53.12
        premature F52.4
        retarded N53.11
      erectile N52.9
        drug induced N52.2
        due to
          disease classified elsewhere N52.1
          drug N52.2
        postoperative (postprocedural) N52.39
          following
            cryotherapy N52.37
            interstitial seed therapy N52.36
            prostate ablative therapy N52.37
            prostatectomy N52.34
              radical N52.31

Dysfunction *(Continued)*
  sexual *(Continued)*
    male *(Continued)*
      erectile *(Continued)*
        postoperative *(Continued)*
          following *(Continued)*
            radiation therapy N52.35
            radical cystectomy N52.32
            ultrasound ablative therapy N52.37
            urethral surgery N52.33
        psychogenic F52.21
        specified cause NEC N52.8
        vasculogenic
          arterial insufficiency N52.01
            with corporo-venous occlusive N52.03
          corporo-venous occlusive N52.02
            with arterial insufficiency N52.03
      impotence —*see* Dysfunction, sexual, male, erectile
      psychogenic F52.9
        aversion F52.1
        erectile F52.21
        orgasmic F52.32
        premature ejaculation F52.4
        satyriasis F52.8
        specified type NEC F52.8
      specified type NEC N53.8
    nonorganic F52.9
      specified NEC F52.8
    opioid F11.981
      in
        abuse F11.181
        dependence F11.281
    orgasmic dysfunction (female) F52.31
      male F52.32
    premature ejaculation F52.4
    psychoactive substances NEC F19.981
      in
        abuse F19.181
        dependence F19.281
    psychogenic F52.9
    sedative F13.981
      in
        abuse F13.181
        dependence F13.281
    sexual aversion F52.1
    vaginismus (nonorganic) (psychogenic) F52.5
  sinoatrial node I49.5
  somatic M99.09
    abdomen M99.09
    acromioclavicular M99.07
    cervical region M99.01
    cervicothoracic M99.01
    costochondral M99.08
    costovertebral M99.08
    head region M99.00
    hip M99.05
    lower extremity M99.06
    lumbar region M99.03
    lumbosacral M99.03
    occipitocervical M99.00
    pelvic region M99.05
    pubic M99.05
    rib cage M99.08
    sacral region M99.04
    sacrococcygeal M99.04
    sacroiliac M99.04
    specified NEC M99.09
    sternochondral M99.08
    sternoclavicular M99.07
    thoracic region M99.02
    thoracolumbar M99.02
    upper extremity M99.07
  somatoform autonomic F45.8
  stomach K31.89
    psychogenic F45.8
  suprarenal E27.9
    hyperfunction E27.0

Dysfunction *(Continued)*
  symbolic R48.9
    specified type NEC R48.8
  temporomandibular (joint) M26.69
    joint-pain syndrome M26.62-●
  testicular (endocrine) E29.9
    specified NEC E29.8
  thymus E32.9
  thyroid E07.9
  ureterostomy (stoma) —*see* Complications, stoma, urinary tract
  urethrostomy (stoma) —*see* Complications, stoma, urinary tract
  uterus, complicating delivery O62.9
    hypertonic O62.4
    hypotonic O62.2
      primary O62.0
      secondary O62.1
  ventricular I51.9
    with congestive heart failure —*see also* Failure, heart I50.9
    left, reversible, following sudden emotional stress I51.81
Dysgenesis
  gonadal (due to chromosomal anomaly) Q96.9
    pure Q99.1
  renal Q60.5
    bilateral Q60.4
    unilateral Q60.3
  reticular D72.0
  tidal platelet D69.3
Dysgerminoma
  specified site —*see* Neoplasm, malignant, by site
  unspecified site
    female C56.9
    male C62.90
Dysgeusia R43.2
Dysgraphia R27.8
Dyshidrosis, dysidrosis L30.1
Dyskaryotic cervical smear R87.619
Dyskeratosis L85.8
  cervix —*see* Dysplasia, cervix
  congenital Q82.8
  uterus NEC N85.8
Dyskinesia G24.9
  biliary (cystic duct or gallbladder) K82.8
  drug induced
    orofacial G24.01
  esophagus K22.4
  hysterical F44.4
➡ intestinal K59.89
  nonorganic origin F44.4
  orofacial (idiopathic) G24.4
    drug induced G24.01
  psychogenic F44.4
  subacute, drug induced G24.01
  tardive G24.01
    neuroleptic induced G24.01
  trachea J39.8
  tracheobronchial J98.09
Dyslalia (developmental) F80.0
Dyslexia R48.0
  developmental F81.0
Dyslipidemia E78.5
  depressed HDL cholesterol E78.6
  elevated fasting triglycerides E78.1
Dysmaturity —*see also* Light for dates
  pulmonary (newborn) (Wilson-Mikity) P27.0
Dysmenorrhea (essential) (exfoliative) N94.6
  congestive (syndrome) N94.6
  primary N94.4
  psychogenic F45.8
  secondary N94.5
Dysmetabolic syndrome X E88.81
Dysmetria R27.8
Dysmorphism (due to)
  alcohol Q86.0
  exogenous cause NEC Q86.8
  hydantoin Q86.1
  warfarin Q86.2

Dysmorphophobia (nondelusional) F45.22
  delusional F22
Dysnomia R47.01
Dysorexia R63.0
  psychogenic F50.89
Dysostosis
  cleidocranial, cleidocranialis Q74.0
  craniofacial Q75.1
  Fairbank's (idiopathic familial generalized osteophytosis) Q78.9
  mandibulofacial (incomplete) Q75.4
  multiplex E76.01
  oculomandibular Q75.5
Dyspareunia (female) N94.10
  deep N94.12
  male N53.12
  nonorganic F52.6
  psychogenic F52.6
  secondary N94.19
  specified NEC N94.19
  superficial (introital) N94.11
Dyspepsia R10.13
  atonic K30
  functional (allergic) (congenital) (gastrointestinal) (occupational) (reflex) K30
➡ intestinal K59.89
  nervous F45.8
  neurotic F45.8
  psychogenic F45.8
Dysphagia R13.10
  cervical R13.19
  following
    cerebral infarction I69.391
    cerebrovascular disease I69.991
      specified NEC I69.891
    intracerebral hemorrhage I69.191
    nontraumatic intracranial hemorrhage NEC I69.291
    specified disease NEC I69.891
    subarachnoid hemorrhage I69.091
  functional (hysterical) F45.8
  hysterical F45.8
  nervous (hysterical) F45.8
  neurogenic R13.19
  oral phase R13.11
  oropharyngeal phase R13.12
  pharyngeal phase R13.13
  pharyngoesophageal phase R13.14
  psychogenic F45.8
  sideropenic D50.1
  spastica K22.4
  specified NEC R13.19
Dysphagocytosis, congenital D71
Dysphasia R47.02
  developmental
    expressive type F80.1
    receptive type F80.2
  following
    cerebrovascular disease I69.921
      cerebral infarction I69.321
      intracerebral hemorrhage I69.121
    nontraumatic intracranial hemorrhage NEC I69.221
      specified disease NEC I69.821
      subarachnoid hemorrhage I69.021
Dysphonia R49.0
  functional F44.4
  hysterical F44.4
  psychogenic F44.4
  spastica J38.3
Dysphoria
  gender F64.9
    in
      adolescence and adulthood F64.0
      children F64.2
    specified NEC F64.8
    postpartal O90.6
Dyspituitarism E23.3

▶ New   ➡ Revised   ~~deleted~~ Deleted   ● Use Additional Character(s)

Dysplasia —*see also* Anomaly
  acetabular, congenital Q65.89
  alveolar capillary, with vein misalignment
    J84.843
  anus (histologically confirmed) (mild)
    (moderate) K62.82
    severe D01.3
  arrhythmogenic right ventricular I42.8
  arterial, fibromuscular I77.3
  asphyxiating thoracic (congenital) Q77.2
  brain Q07.9
  bronchopulmonary, perinatal P27.1
  cervix (uteri) N87.9
    mild N87.0
    moderate N87.1
    severe D06.9
  chondroectodermal Q77.6
  colon D12.6
  craniometaphyseal Q78.58
  dentinal K00.5
  diaphyseal, progressive Q78.3
  dystrophic Q77.5
  ectodermal (anhidrotic) (congenital)
    (hereditary) Q82.4
    hydrotic Q82.8
  epithelial, uterine cervix —*see* Dysplasia,
    cervix
  eye (congenital) Q11.2
  fibrous
    bone NEC (monostotic) M85.00
      ankle M85.07-●
      foot M85.07-●
      forearm M85.03-●
      hand M85.04-●
      lower leg M85.06-●
      multiple site M85.09
      neck M85.08
      rib M85.08
      shoulder M85.01-●
      skull M85.08
      specified site NEC M85.08
      thigh M85.05-●
      toe M85.07-●
      upper arm M85.02-●
      vertebra M85.08
    diaphyseal, progressive Q78.3
    jaw M27.8
    polyostotic Q78.1
  florid osseous —*see also* Cyst, calcifying
    odontogenic
  high grade, focal D12.6
  hip, congenital Q65.89
  joint, congenital Q74.8
  kidney Q61.4
    multicystic Q61.4
  leg Q74.2
  lung, congenital (not associated with short
    gestation) Q33.6
  mammary (gland) (benign) N60.9-●
    cyst (solitary) —*see* Cyst, breast
    cystic —*see* Mastopathy, cystic
    duct ectasia —*see* Ectasia, mammary duct
    fibroadenosis —*see* Fibroadenosis, breast
    fibrosclerosis —*see* Fibrosclerosis, breast
    specified type NEC N60.8-●
  metaphyseal Q78.5
  muscle Q79.8
  oculodentodigital Q87.0
  periapical (cemental) (cemento-osseous) —*see*
    Cyst, calcifying odontogenic
  periosteum —*see* Disorder, bone, specified
    type NEC
  polyostotic fibrous Q78.1
  prostate —*see also* Neoplasia, intraepithelial,
    prostate N42.30
    severe D07.5
    specified NEC N42.39
  renal Q61.4
    multicystic Q61.4
  retinal, congenital Q14.1
  right ventricular, arrhythmogenic I42.8

Dysplasia (*Continued*)
  septo-optic Q04.4
  skin L98.8
  spinal cord Q06.1
  spondyloepiphyseal Q77.7
  thymic, with immunodeficiency D82.1
  vagina N89.3
    mild N89.0
    moderate N89.1
    severe NEC D07.2
  vulva N90.3
    mild N90.0
    moderate N90.1
    severe NEC D07.1
Dysplasminogenemia E88.02
Dyspnea (nocturnal) (paroxysmal) R06.00
  asthmatic (bronchial) J45.909
    with
      bronchitis J45.909
        with
          exacerbation (acute) J45.901
          status asthmaticus J45.902
        chronic J44.9
      exacerbation (acute) J45.901
      status asthmaticus J45.902
    cardiac —*see* Failure, ventricular, left
  cardiac —*see* Failure, ventricular, left
  functional F45.8
  hyperventilation R06.4
  hysterical F45.8
  newborn P28.89
  psychogenic F45.8
  shortness of breath R06.02
  specified type NEC R06.09
Dyspraxia R27.8
  developmental (syndrome) F82
Dysproteinemia E88.09
Dysreflexia, autonomic G90.4
Dysrhythmia
  cardiac I49.9
    newborn
      bradycardia P29.12
      occurring before birth P03.819
        before onset of labor P03.810
        during labor P03.811
      tachycardia P29.11
    postoperative I97.89
  cerebral or cortical —*see* Epilepsy
Dyssomnia —*see* Disorder, sleep
Dyssynergia
  biliary K83.8
  bladder sphincter N36.44
  cerebellaris myoclonica (Hunt's ataxia) G11.19
Dysthymia F34.1
Dysthyroidism E07.9
Dystocia O66.9
  affecting newborn P03.1
  cervical (hypotonic) O62.2
    affecting newborn P03.6
    primary O62.0
    secondary O62.1
  contraction ring O62.4
  fetal O66.9
    abnormality NEC O66.3
    conjoined twins O66.3
    oversize O66.2
  maternal O66.9
  positional O64.9
  shoulder (girdle) O66.0
    causing obstructed labor O66.0
  uterine NEC O62.4
Dystonia G24.9
  cervical G24.3
  deformans progressiva G24.1
  drug induced NEC G24.09
    acute G24.02
    specified NEC G24.09
  familial G24.1
  idiopathic G24.1
    familial G24.1
    nonfamilial G24.2
    orofacial G24.4

Dystonia (*Continued*)
  lenticularis G24.8
  musculorum deformans G24.1
  neuroleptic induced (acute) G24.02
  orofacial (idiopathic) G24.4
  oromandibular G24.4
    due to drug G24.01
  specified NEC G24.8
  torsion (familial) (idiopathic) G24.1
    acquired G24.8
    genetic G24.1
    symptomatic (nonfamilial) G24.2
Dystonic movements R25.8
Dystrophy, dystrophia
  adiposogenital E23.6
  autosomal recessive, childhood type,
    muscular dystrophy resembling
    Duchenne or Becker G71.01
  Becker's type G71.01
  cervical sympathetic G90.2
  choroid (hereditary) H31.20
    central areolar H31.22
    choroideremia H31.21
    gyrate atrophy H31.23
    specified type NEC H31.29
  cornea (hereditary) H18.50-●
    endothelial H18.51-●
    epithelial H18.52-●
    granular H18.53-●
    lattice H18.54-●
    macular H18.55-●
    specified type NEC H18.59-●
  Duchenne's type G71.01
  due to malnutrition E45
  Erb's G71.02
  Fuchs' H18.51-●
  Gower's muscular G71.01
  hair L67.8
  infantile neuraxonal G31.89
  Landouzy-Déjérine G71.02
  Leyden-Möbius G71.09
  muscular G71.00
    autosomal recessive, childhood type,
      muscular dystrophy resembling
      Duchenne or Becker G71.01
    benign (Becker type) G71.01
      scapuloperoneal with early contractures
        [Emery-Dreifuss] G71.09
    congenital (hereditary) (progressive) (with
      specific morphological abnormalities
      of the muscle fiber) G71.09
      myotonic G71.11
    distal G71.09
    Duchenne type G71.01
    Emery-Dreifuss G71.09
    Erb type G71.02
    facioscapulohumeral G71.02
    Gower's G71.01
    hereditary (progressive) G71.09
    Landouzy-Déjérine type G71.02
    limb-girdle G71.09
    myotonic G71.11
    progressive (hereditary) G71.09
      Charcot-Marie (-Tooth) type G60.0
    pseudohypertrophic (infantile) G71.01
    scapulohumeral G71.02
    scapuloperoneal G71.09
    severe (Duchenne type) G71.01
    specified type NEC G71.09
  myocardium, myocardial —*see*
    Degeneration, myocardial
  nail L60.3
    congenital Q84.6
  nutritional E45
  ocular G71.09
  oculocerebrorenal E72.03
  oculopharyngeal G71.09
  ovarian N83.8
  polyglandular E31.8
  reflex (neuromuscular) (sympathetic) —
    see Syndrome, pain, complex regional I

Dystrophy, dystrophia *(Continued)*
   retinal (hereditary) H35.50
     in
       lipid storage disorders E75.6 *[H36]*
       systemic lipidoses E75.6 *[H36]*
     involving
       pigment epithelium H35.54
       sensory area H35.53
     pigmentary H35.52
     vitreoretinal H35.51

Dystrophy, dystrophia *(Continued)*
   Salzmann's nodular —*see* Degeneration,
     cornea, nodular
   scapuloperoneal G71.09
   skin NEC L98.8
   sympathetic (reflex) —*see* Syndrome, pain,
     complex regional I
     cervical G90.2
   tapetoretinal H35.54

Dystrophy, dystrophia *(Continued)*
   thoracic, asphyxiating Q77.2
   unguium L60.3
     congenital Q84.6
   vitreoretinal H35.51
   vulva N90.4
   yellow (liver) —*see* Failure, hepatic
Dysuria R30.0
   psychogenic F45.8

▶ New   ⇒ Revised   ~~deleted~~ Deleted   ● Use Additional Character(s)

E

Eales' disease H35.06-●
Ear —*see also* condition
　piercing Z41.3
　tropical NEC B36.9 *[H62.40]*
　　in
　　　aspergillosis B44.89
　　　candidiasis B37.84
　　　moniliasis B37.84
　　wax (impacted) H61.20
　　　left H61.22
　　　　with right H61.23
　　　right H61.21
　　　　with left H61.23
Earache —*see* subcategory H92.0
Early satiety R68.81
Eaton-Lambert syndrome—*see* Syndrome, Lambert-Eaton
Eberth's disease (typhoid fever) A01.00
Ebola virus disease A98.4
Ebstein's anomaly or syndrome (heart) Q22.5
Eccentro-osteochondrodysplasia E76.29
Ecchondroma —*see* Neoplasm, bone, benign
Ecchondrosis D48.0
Ecchymosis R58
　conjunctiva —*see* Hemorrhage, conjunctiva
　eye (traumatic) —*see* Contusion, eyeball
　eyelid (traumatic) —*see* Contusion, eyelid
　newborn P54.5
　spontaneous R23.3
　traumatic —*see* Contusion
Echinococciasis —*see* Echinococcus
Echinococcosis —*see* Echinococcus
Echinococcus (infection) B67.90
　granulosus B67.4
　　bone B67.2
　　liver B67.0
　　lung B67.1
　　multiple sites B67.32
　　specified site NEC B67.39
　　thyroid B67.31
　liver NOS B67.8
　　granulosus B67.0
　　multilocularis B67.5
　lung NEC B67.99
　　granulosus B67.1
　　multilocularis B67.69
　multilocularis B67.7
　　liver B67.5
　　multiple sites B67.61
　　specified site NEC B67.69
　specified site NEC B67.99
　　granulosus B67.39
　　multilocularis B67.69
　thyroid NEC B67.99
　　granulosus B67.31
　　multilocularis B67.69 *[E35]*
Echinorhynchiasis B83.8
Echinostomiasis B66.8
Echolalia R48.8
Echovirus, as cause of disease classified elsewhere B97.12
Eclampsia, eclamptic (coma) (convulsions) (delirium) (with hypertension) NEC O15.9
　complicating
　　labor and delivery O15.1
　　postpartum O15.2
　　pregnancy O15.0-●
　　puerperium O15.2
Economic circumstances affecting care Z59.9
Economo's disease A85.8
Ectasia, ectasis
　annuloaortic I35.8
　aorta I77.819
　　with aneurysm —*see* Aneurysm, aorta
　　abdominal I77.811
　　thoracic I77.810
　　thoracoabdominal I77.812
　breast —*see* Ectasia, mammary duct
　capillary I78.8
　cornea H18.71-●

Ectasia, ectasis *(Continued)*
　gastric antral vascular (GAVE) K31.819
　　with hemorrhage K31.811
　　without hemorrhage K31.819
　mammary duct N60.4-●
　salivary gland (duct) K11.8
　sclera —*see* Sclerectasia
Ecthyma L08.0
　contagiosum B08.02
　gangrenosum L08.0
　infectiosum B08.02
Ectocardia Q24.8
Ectodermal dysplasia (anhidrotic) Q82.4
Ectodermosis erosiva pluriorificialis L51.1
Ectopic, ectopia (congenital)
　abdominal viscera Q45.8
　　due to defect in anterior abdominal wall Q79.59
　ACTH syndrome E24.3
　adrenal gland Q89.1
　anus Q43.5
　atrial beats I49.1
　beats I49.49
　　atrial I49.1
　　ventricular I49.3
　bladder Q64.10
　bone and cartilage in lung Q33.5
　brain Q04.8
　breast tissue Q83.8
　cardiac Q24.8
　cerebral Q04.8
　cordis Q24.8
　endometrium —*see* Endometriosis
　gastric mucosa Q40.2
　gestation —*see* Pregnancy, by site
　heart Q24.8
　hormone secretion NEC E34.2
　kidney (crossed) (pelvis) Q63.2
　lens, lentis Q12.1
　mole —*see* Pregnancy, by site
　organ or site NEC —*see* Malposition, congenital
　pancreas Q45.3
　pregnancy —*see* Pregnancy, ectopic
　pupil —*see* Abnormality, pupillary
　renal Q63.2
　sebaceous glands of mouth Q38.6
　spleen Q89.09
　testis Q53.00
　　bilateral Q53.02
　　unilateral Q53.01
　thyroid Q89.2
　tissue in lung Q33.5
　ureter Q62.63
　ventricular beats I49.3
　vesicae Q64.10
Ectromelia Q73.8
　lower limb —*see* Defect, reduction, limb, lower, specified type NEC
　upper limb —*see* Defect, reduction, limb, upper, specified type NEC
Ectropion H02.109
　cervix N86
　　with cervicitis N72
　congenital Q10.1
　eyelid H02.109
　　cicatricial H02.119
　　　left H02.116
　　　　lower H02.115
　　　　upper H02.114
　　　right H02.113
　　　　lower H02.112
　　　　upper H02.111
　　congenital Q10.1
　　left H02.106
　　　lower H02.105
　　　upper H02.104
　　mechanical H02.129
　　　left H02.126
　　　　lower H02.125
　　　　upper H02.124

Ectropion *(Continued)*
　eyelid *(Continued)*
　　mechanical *(Continued)*
　　　right H02.123
　　　　lower H02.122
　　　　upper H02.121
　　paralytic H02.159
　　　left H02.156
　　　　lower H02.155
　　　　upper H02.154
　　　right H02.153
　　　　lower H02.152
　　　　upper H02.151
　　right H02.103
　　　lower H02.102
　　　upper H02.101
　　senile H02.139
　　　left H02.136
　　　　lower H02.135
　　　　upper H02.134
　　　right H02.133
　　　　lower H02.132
　　　　upper H02.131
　　spastic H02.149
　　　left H02.146
　　　　lower H02.145
　　　　upper H02.144
　　　right H02.143
　　　　lower H02.142
　　　　upper H02.141
　iris H21.89
　lip (acquired) K13.0
　　congenital Q38.0
　urethra N36.8
　uvea H21.89
Eczema (acute) (chronic) (erythematous) (fissum) (rubrum) (squamous) *(see also* Dermatitis) L30.9
　contact —*see* Dermatitis, contact
　dyshydrotic L30.1
　external ear —*see* Otitis, externa, acute, eczematoid
　flexural L20.82
　herpeticum B00.0
　hypertrophicum L28.0
　hypostatic —*see* Varix, leg, with, inflammation
　impetiginous L01.1
　infantile (due to any substance) L20.83
　　intertriginous L21.1
　　seborrheic L21.1
　intertriginous NEC L30.4
　　infantile L21.1
　intrinsic (allergic) L20.84
　lichenified NEC L28.0
　marginatum (hebrae) B35.6
　pustular L30.3
　stasis I87.2
　　with varicose veins —*see* Varix, leg, with, inflammation
　vaccination, vaccinatum T88.1
　varicose —*see* Varix, leg, with, inflammation
Eczematid L30.2
Eddowes (-Spurway) syndrome Q78.0
Edema, edematous (infectious) (pitting) (toxic) R60.9
　with nephritis —*see* Nephrosis
　allergic T78.3
　amputation stump (surgical) (sequelae (late effect)) T87.89
　angioneurotic (allergic) (any site) (with urticaria) T78.3
　　hereditary D84.1
　angiospastic I73.9
　Berlin's (traumatic) S05.8X-●
　brain (cytotoxic) (vasogenic) G93.6
　　due to birth injury P11.0
　　newborn (anoxia or hypoxia) P52.4
　　　birth injury P11.0
　　traumatic —*see* Injury, intracranial, cerebral edema
　cardiac —*see* Failure, heart, congestive

Edema, edematous (Continued)
cardiovascular —see Failure, heart, congestive
cerebral —see Edema, brain
cerebrospinal —see Edema, brain
cervix (uteri) (acute) N88.8
   puerperal, postpartum O90.89
chronic hereditary Q82.0
circumscribed, acute T78.3
   hereditary D84.1
conjunctiva H11.42-●
cornea H18.2-●
   idiopathic H18.22-●
   secondary H18.23-●
     due to contact lens H18.21-●
due to
   lymphatic obstruction I89.0
   salt retention E87.0
epiglottis —see Edema, glottis
essential, acute T78.3
   hereditary D84.1
extremities, lower —see Edema, legs
eyelid NEC H02.849
   left H02.846
     lower H02.845
     upper H02.844
   right H02.843
     lower H02.842
     upper H02.841
familial, hereditary Q82.0
famine —see Malnutrition, severe
generalized R60.9
glottis, glottic, glottidis (obstructive) (passive)
   J38.4
   allergic T78.3
     hereditary D84.1
heart —see Failure, heart, congestive
heat T67.7
hereditary Q82.0
inanition —see Malnutrition, severe
intracranial G93.6
iris H21.89
joint —see Effusion, joint
larynx —see Edema, glottis
legs R60.0
   due to venous obstruction I87.1
   hereditary Q82.0
localized R60.0
   due to venous obstruction I87.1
lower limbs —see Edema, legs
lung J81.1
   with heart condition or failure —see
     Failure, ventricular, left
   acute J81.0
   chemical (acute) J68.1
     chronic J68.1
   chronic J81.1
     due to
       chemicals, gases, fumes or vapors
         (inhalation) J68.1
       external agent J70.9
         specified NEC J70.8
       radiation J70.1
   due to
     chemicals, fumes or vapors (inhalation)
       J68.1
     external agent J70.9
       specified NEC J70.8
     high altitude T70.29
     near drowning T75.1
     radiation J70.0
   meaning failure, left ventricle I50.1
lymphatic I89.0
   due to mastectomy I97.2
macula H35.81
   cystoid, following cataract surgery —see
     Complications, postprocedural,
     following cataract surgery
   diabetic —see Diabetes, by type, with,
     retinopathy, with macular edema
malignant —see Gangrene, gas
Milroy's Q82.0

Edema, edematous (Continued)
nasopharynx J39.2
newborn P83.30
   hydrops fetalis —see Hydrops, fetalis
   specified NEC P83.39
nutritional —see also Malnutrition, severe
   with dyspigmentation, skin and hair E40
optic disc or nerve —see Papilledema
orbit H05.22-●
pancreas K86.89
papilla, optic —see Papilledema
penis N48.89
periodic T78.3
   hereditary D84.1
pharynx J39.2
pulmonary —see Edema, lung
Quincke's T78.3
   hereditary D84.1
renal —see Nephrosis
retina H35.81
   diabetic —see Diabetes, by type, with,
     retinopathy, with macular edema
salt E87.0
scrotum N50.89
seminal vesicle N50.89
spermatic cord N50.89
spinal (cord) (vascular) (nontraumatic) G95.19
starvation —see Malnutrition, severe
stasis —see Hypertension, venous, (chronic)
subglottic —see Edema, glottis
supraglottic —see Edema, glottis
testis N44.8
tunica vaginalis N50.89
vas deferens N50.89
vulva (acute) N90.89
Edentulism —see Absence, teeth, acquired
Edsall's disease T67.2
Educational handicap Z55.9
   specified NEC Z55.8
Edward's syndrome —see Trisomy, 18
Effect, adverse
   abnormal gravitational (G) forces or states
     T75.81
   abuse —see Maltreatment
   air pressure T70.9
     specified NEC T70.8
   altitude (high) —see Effect, adverse, high
     altitude
   anesthesia —see also Anesthesia T88.59
     in labor and delivery O74.9
     local, toxic
       in labor and delivery O74.4-●
       in pregnancy NEC O29.3-●
       postpartum, puerperal O89.3
     postpartum, puerperal O89.9
     specified NEC T88.59
       in labor and delivery O74.8
       postpartum, puerperal O89.8
     spinal and epidural T88.59
       headache T88.59
         in labor and delivery O74.5
         postpartum, puerperal O89.4
       specified NEC
         in labor and delivery O74.6
         postpartum, puerperal O89.5
   antitoxin —see Complications, vaccination
   atmospheric pressure T70.9
     due to explosion T70.8
     high T70.3
     low —see Effect, adverse, high altitude
     specified effect NEC T70.8
   biological, correct substance properly
     administered —see Effect, adverse, drug
   blood (derivatives) (serum) (transfusion) —
     see Complications, transfusion
   chemical substance —see Table of Drugs and
     Chemicals
   cold (temperature) (weather) T69.9
     chilblains T69.1
     frostbite —see Frostbite
     specified effect NEC T69.8

Effect, adverse (Continued)
   drugs and medicaments T88.7
     specified drug —see Table of Drugs and
       Chemicals, by drug, adverse effect
     specified effect — code to condition
   electric current, electricity (shock) T75.4
     burn —see Burn
   exertion (excessive) T73.3
   exposure —see Exposure
   external cause NEC T75.89
   foodstuffs T78.1
     allergic reaction —see Allergy, food
       causing anaphylaxis —see Shock,
         anaphylactic, due to food
     noxious —see Poisoning, food, noxious
   gases, fumes, or vapors T59.9-●
     specified agent —see Table of Drugs and
       Chemicals
   glue (airplane) sniffing
     due to drug abuse —see Abuse, drug,
       inhalant
     due to drug dependence —see Dependence,
       drug, inhalant
   heat —see Heat
   high altitude NEC T70.29
     anoxia T70.29
     on
       ears T70.0
       sinuses T70.1
     polycythemia D75.1
   high pressure fluids T70.4
   hot weather —see Heat
   hunger T73.0
   immersion, foot —see Immersion
   immunization —see Complications,
     vaccination
   immunological agents —see Complications,
     vaccination
   infrared (radiation) (rays) NOS T66
     dermatitis or eczema L59.8
   infusion —see Complications, infusion
   lack of care of infants —see Maltreatment,
     child
   lightning —see Lightning
   medical care T88.9
     specified NEC T88.8
   medicinal substance, correct, properly
     administered —see Effect, adverse, drug
   motion T75.3
   noise, on inner ear —see subcategory H83.3
   overheated places —see Heat
   psychosocial, of work environment Z56.5
   radiation (diagnostic) (infrared) (natural
     source) (therapeutic) (ultraviolet) (X-ray)
     NOS T66
     dermatitis or eczema —see Dermatitis, due
       to, radiation
     fibrosis of lung J70.1
     pneumonitis J70.0
     pulmonary manifestations
       acute J70.0
       chronic J70.1
     skin L59.9
   radioactive substance NOS
     dermatitis or eczema —see Radiodermatitis
   reduced temperature T69.9
     immersion foot or hand —see Immersion
     specified effect NEC T69.8
   serum NEC (see also Reaction, serum) T80.69
   specified NEC T78.8
     external cause NEC T75.89
   strangulation —see Asphyxia, traumatic
   submersion T75.1
   thirst T73.1
   toxic —see Toxicity
   transfusion —see Complications, transfusion
   ultraviolet (radiation) (rays) NOS T66
     burn —see Burn
     dermatitis or eczema —see Dermatitis, due
       to, ultraviolet rays
       acute L56.8

▶ New ⇒ Revised ~~deleted~~ Deleted ● Use Additional Character(s)

Effect, adverse *(Continued)*
  vaccine (any) —*see* Complications, vaccination
  vibration —*see* Vibration, adverse effects
  water pressure NEC T70.9
    specified NEC T70.8
  weightlessness T75.82
  whole blood —*see* Complications, transfusion
  work environment Z56.5
Effect(s) (of) (from) —*see* Effect, adverse NEC
Effects, late —*see* Sequelae
Effluvium
  anagen L65.1
  telogen L65.0
Effort syndrome (psychogenic) F45.8
Effusion
  amniotic fluid —*see* Pregnancy, complicated
      by, prematue rupture of membranes
  brain (serous) G93.6
  bronchial —*see* Bronchitis
  cerebral G93.6
  cerebrospinal —*see also* Meningitis
    vessel G93.6
  chest —*see* Effusion, pleura
  chylous, chyliform (pleura) J94.0
  intracranial G93.6
  joint M25.40
    ankle M25.47-●
    elbow M25.42-●
    foot joint M25.47-●
    hand joint M25.44-●
    hip M25.45-●
    knee M25.46-●
    shoulder M25.41-●
    specified joint NEC M25.48
    wrist M25.43-●
  malignant pleural J91.0
  meninges —*see* Meningitis
  pericardium, pericardial (noninflammatory)
      I31.3
    acute —*see* Pericarditis, acute
  peritoneal (chronic) R18.8
  pleura, pleurisy, pleuritic, pleuropericardial
      J90
    chylous, chyliform J94.0
    due to systemic lupus erythematosis
        M32.13
    in conditions classified elsewhere J91.8
    influenzal —*see* Influenza, with, respiratory
        manifestations NEC
    malignant J91.0
    newborn P28.89
    tuberculous NEC A15.6
      primary (progressive) A15.7
  spinal —*see* Meningitis
  thorax, thoracic —*see* Effusion, pleura
Egg shell nails L60.3
  congenital Q84.6
EGPA (eosinophilic granulomatosis with
    polyangiitis) M30.1
Egyptian splenomegaly B65.1
Ehlers-Danlos syndrome *(see also* Syndrome,
    Ehlers-Danlos) Q79.60
Ehrlichiosis A77.40
  due to
    E. chafeensis A77.41
    E. ewingii A77.49
    E. muris euclairensis A77.49
    E. sennetsu A79.81
    specified organism NEC A77.49
Eichstedt's disease B36.0
Eisenmenger's
  complex or syndrome I27.83
  defect Q21.8
Ejaculation
  delayed F52.32
  painful N53.12
  premature F52.4
  retarded N53.11
  retrograde N53.14
  semen, painful N53.12
    psychogenic F52.6

Ekbom's syndrome (restless legs) G25.81
Ekman's syndrome (brittle bones and blue
    sclera) Q78.0
Elastic skin Q82.8
  acquired L57.4
Elastofibroma —*see* Neoplasm, connective
    tissue, benign
Elastoma (juvenile) Q82.8
  Miescher's L87.2
Elastomyofibrosis I42.4
Elastosis
  actinic, solar L57.8
  atrophicans (senile) L57.4
  perforans serpiginosa L87.2
  senilis L57.4
Elbow —*see* condition
Electric current, electricity, effects (concussion)
    (fatal) (nonfatal) (shock) T75.4
  burn —*see* Burn
Electric feet syndrome E53.8
Electrocution T75.4
  from electroshock gun (taser) T75.4
Electrolyte imbalance E87.8
  with
    abortion —*see* Abortion by type,
        complicated by, electrolyte imbalance
    ectopic pregnancy O08.5
    molar pregnancy O08.5
Elephantiasis (nonfilarial) I89.0
  arabicum —*see* Infestation, filarial
  bancroftian B74.0
  congenital (any site) (hereditary) Q82.0
  due to
    Brugia (malayi) B74.1
      timori B74.2
    mastectomy I97.2
    Wuchereria (bancrofti) B74.0
  eyelid H02.859
    left H02.856
      lower H02.855
      upper H02.854
    right H02.853
      lower H02.852
      upper H02.851
  filarial, filariensis —*see* Infestation, filarial
  glandular I89.0
  graecorum A30.9
  lymphangiectatic I89.0
  lymphatic vessel I89.0
    due to mastectomy I97.2
  scrotum (nonfilarial) I89.0
  streptococcal I89.0
  surgical I97.89
    postmastectomy I97.2
  telangiectodes I89.0
  vulva (nonfilarial) N90.89
Elevated, elevation
  alanine transaminase (ALT) R74.01
  ALT (alanine transaminase) R74.01
  antibody titer R76.0
  aspartate transaminase (AST) R74.01
  AST (aspartate transaminase) R74.01
  basal metabolic rate R94.8
  blood pressure —*see also* Hypertension
    reading (incidental) (isolated) (nonspecific),
        no diagnosis of hypertension R03.0
  blood sugar R73.9
  body temperature (of unknown origin) R50.9
  C-reactive protein (CRP) R79.82
  cancer antigen 125 [CA 125] R97.1
  carcinoembryonic antigen [CEA] R97.0
  cholesterol E78.00
    with high triglycerides E78.2
  conjugate, eye H51.0
  diaphragm, congenital Q79.1
  erythrocyte sedimentation rate R70.0
  fasting glucose R73.01
  fasting triglycerides E78.1
  finding on laboratory examination —*see*
      Findings, abnormal, inconclusive,
      without diagnosis, by type of exam

Elevated, elevation *(Continued)*
  GFR (glomerular filtration rate) —*see*
      Findings, abnormal, inconclusive,
      without diagnosis, by type of exam
  glucose tolerance (oral) R73.02
  immunoglobulin level R76.8
  indoleacetic acid R82.5
  lactic acid dehydrogenase (LDH) level
      R74.02
  leukocytes D72.829
  lipoprotein a (Lp(a)) level E78.41
  liver function
    study R94.5
    test R79.89
      alkaline phosphatase R74.8
      aminotransferase R74.01
      bilirubin R17
      hepatic enzyme R74.8
      lactate dehydrogenase R74.02
  (Lp(a)) (lipoprotein(a)) E78.41
  lymphocytes D72.820
  prostate specific antigen [PSA] R97.20
  Rh titer —*see* Complication(s), transfusion,
      incompatibility reaction, Rh (factor)
  scapula, congenital Q74.0
  sedimentation rate R70.0
  SGOT R74.01
  SGPT R74.01
  transaminase level R74.01
  triglycerides E78.1
    with high cholesterol E78.2
  troponin R77.8
  tumor associated antigens [TAA] NEC R97.8
  tumor specific antigens [TSA] NEC R97.8
  urine level of
    17-ketosteroids R82.5
    catecholamine R82.5
    indoleacetic acid R82.5
    steroids R82.5
    vanillylmandelic acid (VMA) R82.5
  venous pressure I87.8
  white blood cell count D72.829
    specified NEC D72.828
Elliptocytosis (congenital) (hereditary) D58.1
  Hb C (disease) D58.1
  hemoglobin disease D58.1
  sickle-cell (disease) D57.8-●
    trait D57.3
Ellison-Zollinger syndrome E16.4
Ellis-van Creveld syndrome
    (chondroectodermal dysplasia) Q77.6
Elongated, elongation (congenital) —*see also*
    Distortion
  bone Q79.9
  cervix (uteri) Q51.828
    acquired N88.4
    hypertrophic N88.4
  colon Q43.8
  common bile duct Q44.5
  cystic duct Q44.5
  frenulum, penis Q55.69
  labia minora (acquired) N90.69
  ligamentum patellae Q74.1
  petiolus (epiglottidis) Q31.8
  tooth, teeth K00.2
  uvula Q38.6
Eltor cholera A00.1
Emaciation (due to malnutrition) E43
Embadomoniasis A07.8
Embedded tooth, teeth K01.0
  root only K08.3
Embolic —*see* condition
Embolism (multiple) (paradoxical) I74.9
  air (any site) (traumatic) T79.0
    following
      abortion —*see* Abortion by type
          complicated by embolism
      ectopic pregnancy O08.2
      infusion, therapeutic injection or
          transfusion T80.0
      molar pregnancy O08.2

Embolism *(Continued)*
　air *(Continued)*
　　following *(Continued)*
　　　procedure NEC
　　　　artery T81.719
　　　　　mesenteric T81.710
　　　　　renal T81.711
　　　　　specified NEC T81.718
　　　　vein T81.72
　　　in pregnancy, childbirth or puerperium —
　　　　see Embolism, obstetric
　amniotic fluid (pulmonary) —*see also*
　　Embolism, obstetric
　　following
　　　abortion —*see* Abortion by type
　　　　complicated by embolism
　　　ectopic pregnancy O08.2
　　　molar pregnancy O08.2
　aorta, aortic I74.10
　　abdominal I74.09
　　　saddle I74.01
　　bifurcation I74.09
　　saddle I74.01
　　thoracic I74.11
　artery I74.9
　　auditory, internal I65.8
　　basilar —*see* Occlusion, artery, basilar
　　carotid (common) (internal) —*see*
　　　Occlusion, artery, carotid
　　cerebellar (anterior inferior) (posterior
　　　inferior) (superior) I66.3
　　cerebral —*see* Occlusion, artery, cerebral
　　choroidal (anterior) I65.8
　　communicating posterior I65.8
　　coronary —*see also* Infarct, myocardium
　　　not resulting in infarction I24.0
　　extremity I74.4
　　　lower I74.3
　　　upper I74.2
　　hypophyseal I65.8
　　iliac I74.5
　　limb I74.4
　　　lower I74.3
　　　upper I74.2
　　mesenteric (with gangrene) —*see also*
　　　Ischemia, intestine, acute K55.09
　　ophthalmic —*see* Occlusion, artery, retina
　　peripheral I74.4
　　pontine I65.8
　　precerebral —*see* Occlusion, artery,
　　　precerebral
　　pulmonary —*see* Embolism, pulmonary
　　renal N28.0
　　retinal —*see* Occlusion, artery, retina
　　septic I76
　　specified NEC I74.8
　　vertebral —*see* Occlusion, artery, vertebral
　basilar (artery) I65.1
　blood clot
　　following
　　　abortion —*see* Abortion by type
　　　　complicated by embolism
　　　ectopic or molar pregnancy O08.2
　　in pregnancy, childbirth or puerperium —
　　　see Embolism, obstetric
　brain —*see also* Occlusion, artery, cerebral
　　following
　　　abortion —*see* Abortion by type
　　　　complicated by embolism
　　　ectopic or molar pregnancy O08.2
　　puerperal, postpartum, childbirth —*see*
　　　Embolism, obstetric
　capillary I78.8
　cardiac —*see also* Infarct, myocardium
　　not resulting in infarction I51.3
　carotid (artery) (common) (internal) —*see*
　　Occlusion, artery, carotid
　cavernous sinus (venous) —*see* Embolism,
　　intracranial venous sinus
　cerebral —*see* Occlusion, artery, cerebral
　cholesterol —*see* Atheroembolism

Embolism *(Continued)*
　coronary (artery or vein) (systemic) —*see*
　　Occlusion, coronary
　due to device, implant or graft —*see also*
　　Complications, by site and type,
　　specified NEC
　　arterial graft NEC T82.818
　　breast (implant) T85.818
　　catheter NEC T85.818
　　　dialysis (renal) T82.818
　　　　intraperitoneal T85.818
　　　infusion NEC T82.818
　　　　spinal (epidural) (subdural) T85.810
　　　urinary (indwelling) T83.81
　　electronic (electrode) (pulse generator)
　　　(stimulator)
　　　bone T84.81
　　　cardiac T82.817
　　　nervous system (brain) (peripheral
　　　　nerve) (spinal) T85.810
　　　urinary T83.81
　　fixation, internal (orthopedic) NEC T84.81
　　gastrointestinal (bile duct) (esophagus)
　　　T85.818
　　genital NEC T83.81
　　heart (graft) (valve) T82.817
　　joint prosthesis T84.81
　　ocular (corneal graft) (orbital implant)
　　　T85.818
　　orthopedic (bone graft) NEC T86.838
　　specified NEC T85.818
　　urinary (graft) NEC T83.81
　　vascular NEC T82.818
　　ventricular intracranial shunt T85.810
　extremities
　　lower —*see* Embolism, vein, lower
　　　extremity
　　　arterial I74.3
　　upper I74.2
　eye H34.9
　fat (cerebral) (pulmonary) (systemic) T79.1
　　complicating delivery —*see* Embolism,
　　　obstetric
　　following
　　　abortion —*see* Abortion by type
　　　　complicated by embolism
　　　ectopic or molar pregnancy O08.2
　following
　　abortion —*see* Abortion by type
　　　complicated by embolism
　　ectopic or molar pregnancy O08.2
　　infusion, therapeutic injection or transfusion
　　　air T80.0
　heart (fatty) —*see also* Infarct, myocardium
　　not resulting in infarction I51.3
　hepatic (vein) I82.0
　in pregnancy, childbirth or puerperium —*see*
　　Embolism, obstetric
　intestine (artery) (vein) (with gangrene) —*see*
　　also Ischemia, intestine, acute K55.039
　intracranial —*see also* Occlusion, artery,
　　cerebral
　　venous sinus (any) G08
　　　nonpyogenic I67.6
　intraspinal venous sinuses or veins G08
　　nonpyogenic G95.19
　kidney (artery) N28.0
　lateral sinus (venous) —*see* Embolism,
　　intracranial, venous sinus
　leg —*see* Embolism, vein, lower extremity
　　arterial I74.3
　longitudinal sinus (venous) —*see* Embolism,
　　intracranial, venous sinus
　lung (massive) —*see* Embolism, pulmonary
　meninges I66.8
　mesenteric (artery) (vein) (with gangrene) —
　　see also Ischemia, intestine, acute K55.059
　obstetric (in) (pulmonary)
　　childbirth O88.22
　　　air O88.02
　　　amniotic fluid O88.12

Embolism *(Continued)*
　obstetric *(Continued)*
　　childbirth *(Continued)*
　　　blood clot O88.22
　　　fat O88.82
　　　pyemic O88.32
　　　septic O88.32
　　　specified type NEC O88.82
　　pregnancy O88.21-●
　　　air O88.01-●
　　　amniotic fluid O88.11-●
　　　blood clot O88.21-●
　　　fat O88.81-●
　　　pyemic O88.31-●
　　　septic O88.31-●
　　　specified type NEC O88.81-●
　　puerperal O88.23
　　　air O88.03
　　　amniotic fluid O88.13
　　　blood clot O88.23
　　　fat O88.83
　　　pyemic O88.33
　　　septic O88.33
　　　specified type NEC O88.83
　ophthalmic —*see* Occlusion, artery, retina
　penis N48.81
　peripheral artery NOS I74.4
　pituitary E23.6
　popliteal (artery) I74.3
　portal (vein) I81
　postoperative, postprocedural
　　artery T81.719
　　　mesenteric T81.710
　　　renal T81.711
　　　specified NEC T81.718
　　vein T81.72
　precerebral artery —*see* Occlusion, artery,
　　precerebral
　puerperal —*see* Embolism, obstetric
　pulmonary (acute) (artery) (vein) I26.99
　　with acute cor pulmonale I26.09
　　chronic I27.82
　　following
　　　abortion —*see* Abortion by type
　　　　complicated by embolism
　　　ectopic or molar pregnancy O08.2
　　healed or old Z86.711
　　in pregnancy, childbirth or puerperium —
　　　see Embolism, obstetric
　　multiple subsegmental without acute cor
　　　pulmonale I26.94
　　personal history of Z86.711
　　saddle I26.92
　　　with acute cor pulmonale I26.02
　　septic I26.90
　　　with acute cor pulmonale I26.01
　　single subsegmental without acute cor
　　　pulmonale I26.93
　　subsegmental NOS I26.93
　pyemic (multiple) I76
　　following
　　　abortion —*see* Abortion by type
　　　　complicated by embolism
　　　ectopic or molar pregnancy O08.2
　　Hemophilus influenzae A41.3
　　pneumococcal A40.3
　　　with pneumonia J13
　　puerperal, postpartum, childbirth
　　　(any organism) —*see* Embolism,
　　　obstetric
　　specified organism NEC A41.89
　　staphylococcal A41.2
　　streptococcal A40.9
　renal (artery) N28.0
　　vein I82.3
　retina, retinal —*see* Occlusion, artery,
　　retina
　saddle
　　abdominal aorta I74.01
　　pulmonary artery I26.92
　　　with acute cor pulmonale I26.02

Embolism *(Continued)*
  septic (arterial) I76
    complicating abortion —*see* Abortion, by
      type, complicated by, embolism
    sinus —*see* Embolism, intracranial, venous
      sinus
    soap complicating abortion —*see* Abortion,
      by type, complicated by, embolism
  spinal cord G95.19
    pyogenic origin G06.1
  spleen, splenic (artery) I74.8
  upper extremity I74.2
  vein (acute) I82.90
    antecubital I82.61-●
      chronic I82.71-●
    axillary I82.A1-●
      chronic I82.A2-●
    basilic I82.61-●
      chronic I82.71-●
    brachial I82.62-●
      chronic I82.72-●
    brachiocephalic (innominate) I82.290
      chronic I82.291
    cephalic I82.61-●
      chronic I82.71-●
    chronic I82.91
    deep (DVT) I82.40-●
      calf I82.4Z-●
        chronic I82.5Z-●
      lower leg I82.4Z-●
        chronic I82.5Z-●
      thigh I82.4Y-●
        chronic I82.5Y-●
      upper leg I82.4Y
        chronic I82.5y--●
    femoral I82.41-●
      chronic I82.51-●
    iliac (iliofemoral) I82.42-●
      chronic I82.52-●
    innominate I82.290
      chronic I82.291
    internal jugular I82.C1-●
      chronic I82.C2-●
    lower extremity
      deep I82.40-●
        chronic I82.50-●
          specified NEC I82.49-●
            chronic NEC I82.59-●
      distal
        deep I82.4Z-●
      proximal
        deep I82.4Y-●
          chronic I82.5Y-●
      superficial I82.81-●
    popliteal I82.43-●
      chronic I82.53-●
    radial I82.62-●
      chronic I82.72-●
    renal I82.3
    saphenous (greater) (lesser) I82.81-●
    specified NEC I82.890
      chronic NEC I82.891
    subclavian I82.B1-●
      chronic I82.B2-●
    thoracic NEC I82.290
      chronic I82.291
    tibial I82.44-●
      chronic I82.54-●
    ulnar I82.62-●
      chronic I82.72-●
    upper extremity I82.60-●
      chronic I82.70-●
      deep I82.62-●
        chronic I82.72-●
      superficial I82.61-●
        chronic I82.71-●
  vena cava
    inferior (acute) I82.220
      chronic I82.221
    superior (acute) I82.210
      chronic I82.211

Embolism *(Continued)*
  venous sinus G08
  vessels of brain —*see* Occlusion, artery,
    cerebral
Embolus —*see* Embolism
Embryoma —*see also* Neoplasm, uncertain
  behavior, by site
  benign —*see* Neoplasm, benign, by site
  kidney C64.-●
  liver C22.0
  malignant —*see also* Neoplasm, malignant,
    by site
    kidney C64.-●
    liver C22.0
    testis C62.9-●
      descended (scrotal) C62.1-●
      undescended C62.0-●
  testis C62.9-●
    descended (scrotal) C62.1-●
    undescended C62.0-●
Embryonic
  circulation Q28.9
  heart Q28.9
  vas deferens Q55.4
Embryopathia NOS Q89.9
Embryotoxon Q13.4
Emesis —*see* Vomiting
Emotional lability R45.86
Emotionality, pathological F60.3
Emotogenic disease —*see* Disorder,
  psychogenic
Emphysema (atrophic) (bullous) (chronic)
  (interlobular) (lung) (obstructive)
  (pulmonary) (senile) (vesicular) J43.9
  cellular tissue (traumatic) T79.7
    surgical T81.82
  centrilobular J43.2
  compensatory J98.3
  congenital (interstitial) P25.0
  conjunctiva H11.89
  connective tissue (traumatic) T79.7
    surgical T81.82
  due to chemicals, gases, fumes or vapors J68.4
  eyelid(s) —*see* Disorder, eyelid, specified type
    NEC
    surgical T81.82
    traumatic T79.7
  interstitial J98.2
    congenital P25.0
    perinatal period P25.0
  laminated tissue T79.7
    surgical T81.82
  mediastinal J98.2
    newborn P25.2
  orbit, orbital —*see* Disorder, orbit, specified
    type NEC
  panacinar J43.1
  panlobular J43.1
  specified NEC J43.8
  subcutaneous (traumatic) T79.7
    nontraumatic J98.2
    postprocedural T81.82
    surgical T81.82
  surgical T81.82
  thymus (gland) (congenital) E32.8
  traumatic (subcutaneous) T79.7
  unilateral J43.0
Empty nest syndrome Z60.0
Empyema (acute) (chest) (double) (pleura)
  (supradiaphragmatic) (thorax) J86.9
  with fistula J86.0
  accessory sinus (chronic) —*see* Sinusitis
  antrum (chronic) —*see* Sinusitis, maxillary
  brain (any part) —*see* Abscess, brain
  ethmoidal (chronic) (sinus) —*see* Sinusitis,
    ethmoidal
  extradural —*see* Abscess, extradural
  frontal (chronic) (sinus) —*see* Sinusitis, frontal
  gallbladder K81.0
  mastoid (process) (acute) —*see* Mastoiditis,
    acute
  maxilla, maxillary M27.2

Empyema *(Continued)*
  sinus (chronic) —*see* Sinusitis, maxillary
  nasal sinus (chronic) —*see* Sinusitis
  sinus (accessory) (chronic) (nasal) —*see*
    Sinusitis
  sphenoidal (sinus) (chronic) —*see* Sinusitis,
    sphenoidal
  subarachnoid —*see* Abscess, extradural
  subdural —*see* Abscess, subdural
  tuberculous A15.6
  ureter —*see* Ureteritis
  ventricular —*see* Abscess, brain
En coup de sabre lesion L94.1
Enamel pearls K00.2
Enameloma K00.2
Enanthema, viral B09
Encephalitis (chronic) (hemorrhagic)
  (idiopathic) (nonepidemic) (spurious)
  (subacute) G04.90
  acute —*see also* Encephalitis, viral A86
    disseminated G04.00
      infectious G04.01
      noninfectious G04.81
      postimmunization (postvaccination)
        G04.02
      postinfectious G04.01
    inclusion body A85.8
    necrotizing hemorrhagic G04.30
      postimmunization G04.32
      postinfectious G04.31
      specified NEC G04.39
  arboviral, arbovirus NEC A85.2
  arthropod-borne NEC (viral) A85.2
  Australian A83.4
  California (virus) A83.5
  Central European (tick-borne) A84.1
  Czechoslovakian A84.1
  Dawson's (inclusion body) A81.1
  diffuse sclerosing A81.1
  disseminated, acute G04.00
  due to
    cat scratch disease A28.1
    human immunodeficiency virus (HIV)
      disease B20 *[G05.3]*
    malaria —*see* Malaria
    rickettsiosis —*see* Rickettsiosis
    smallpox inoculation G04.02
    typhus —*see* Typhus
  Eastern equine A83.2
  endemic (viral) A86
  epidemic NEC (viral) A86
  equine (acute) (infectious) (viral) A83.9
    Eastern A83.2
    Venezuelan A92.2
    Western A83.1
  Far Eastern (tick-borne) A84.0
  following vaccination or other immunization
    procedure G04.02
  herpes zoster B02.0
  herpesviral B00.4
    due to herpesvirus 6 B10.01
    due to herpesvirus 7 B10.09
    specified NEC B10.09
  Ilheus (virus) A83.8
  in (due to)
    actinomycosis A42.82
    adenovirus A85.1
    African trypanosomiasis B56.9 *[G05.3]*
    Chagas' disease (chronic) B57.42
    cytomegalovirus B25.8
    enterovirus A85.0
    herpes (simplex) virus B00.4
      due to herpesvirus 6 B10.01
      due to herpesvirus 7 B10.09
      specified NEC B10.09
    infectious disease NEC B99 *[G05.3]*
    influenza —*see* Influenza, with,
      encephalopathy
    listeriosis A32.12
    measles B05.0
    mumps B26.2
    naegleriasis B60.2

Encounter *(Continued)*
  antenatal screening *(Continued)*
    fetal growth retardation Z36.4
    fetal lung maturity Z36.84
    fetal macrosomia Z36.88
    hydrops fetalis Z36.81
    intrauterine growth restriction (IUGR)/
      small-for-dates Z36.4
    isoimmunization Z36.5
    large-for-dates Z36.88
    malformations Z36.3
    non-visualized anatomy on a previous scan
      Z36.2
    nuchal translucency Z36.82
    raised alphafetoprotein level Z36.1
    risk of pre-term labor Z36.86
    specified type NEC Z36.89
    specified follow-up NEC Z36.2
    specified genetic defects NEC Z36.8A
    Streptococcus B Z36.85
    suspected anomaly Z36.3
    uncertain dates Z36.87
  assisted reproductive fertility procedure cycle
    Z31.83
  blood typing Z01.83
    Rh typing Z01.83
  breast augmentation or reduction Z41.1
  breast implant exchange (different material)
    (different size) Z45.81
  breast reconstruction following mastectomy
    Z42.1
  check-up —*see* Examination
  chemotherapy for neoplasm Z51.11
  colonoscopy, screening Z12.11
  counseling —*see* Counseling
  delivery, full-term, uncomplicated O80
    cesarean, without indication O82
  desensitization to allergens Z51.6
  ear piercing Z41.3
  examination —*see* Examination
  expectant parent(s) (adoptive) pre-birth
    pediatrician visit Z76.81
  fertility preservation procedure (prior to
    cancer therapy) (prior to removal of
    gonads) Z31.84
  fitting (of) —*see* Fitting (and adjustment) (of)
  genetic
    counseling
      nonprocreative Z71.83
      procreative Z31.5
    testing —*see* Test, genetic
  hearing conservation and treatment Z01.12
  immunotherapy for neoplasm Z51.12
  in vitro fertilization cycle Z31.83
  instruction (in)
    child care (postpartal) (prenatal) Z32.3
    childbirth Z32.2
    natural family planning
      procreative Z31.61
      to avoid pregnancy Z30.02
  insulin pump titration Z46.81
  joint prosthesis insertion following prior
    explantation of joint prosthesis (staged
    procedure)
    hip Z47.32
    knee Z47.33
    shoulder Z47.31
  laboratory (as part of a general medical
    examination) Z00.00
    with abnormal findings Z00.01
  mental health services (for)
    abuse NEC
      perpetrator Z69.82
      victim Z69.81
    child abuse
      nonparental
        perpetrator Z69.021
        victim Z69.020
      parental
        perpetrator Z69.011
        victim Z69.010

Encounter *(Continued)*
  mental health services *(Continued)*
    child neglect
      nonparental
        perpetrator Z69.021
        victim Z69.020
      parental
        perpetrator Z69.011
        victim Z69.010
    child psychological abuse
      nonparental
        perpetrator Z69.021
        victim Z69.020
      parental
        perpetrator Z69.011
        victim Z69.010
    child sexual abuse
      nonparental
        perpetrator Z69.021
        victim Z69.020
      parental
        perpetrator Z69.011
        victim Z69.010
    non-spousal adult abuse
      perpetrator Z69.82
      victim Z69.81
    spousal or partner
      abuse
        perpetrator Z69.12
        victim Z69.11
      neglect
        perpetrator Z69.12
        victim Z69.11
      psychological abuse
        perpetrator Z69.12
        victim Z69.11
      violence
        perpetrator (physical) (sexual)
          Z69.12
        victim (physical) Z69.11
          sexual Z69.81
  observation (for) (ruled out)
    exposure to (suspected)
      anthrax Z03.810
      biological agent NEC Z03.818
  pediatrician visit, by expectant parent(s)
    (adoptive) Z76.81
  placental sample (taken vaginally) —*see also*
    Encounter, antenatal screening Z36.9
  plastic and reconstructive surgery following
    medical procedure or healed injury NEC
    Z42.8
  pregnancy
    supervision of —*see* Pregnancy,
      supervision of
    test Z32.00
      result negative Z32.02
      result positive Z32.01
  procreative management and counseling for
    gestational carrier Z31.7
  prophylactic measures Z29.9
    antivenin Z29.12
    fluoride administration Z29.3
    immunotherapy for respiratory syncytial
      virus (RSV) Z29.11
    rabies immune globin Z29.14
    Rho (D) immune globulin Z29.13
    specified NEC Z29.8
  radiation therapy (antineoplastic) Z51.0
  radiological (as part of a general medical
    examination) Z00.00
    with abnormal findings Z00.01
  reconstructive surgery following medical
    procedure or healed injury NEC
    Z42.8
  removal (of) —*see also* Removal
    artificial
      arm Z44.00-•
        complete Z44.01-•
        partial Z44.02-•
      eye Z44.2-•

Encounter *(Continued)*
  removal *(Continued)*
    artificial *(Continued)*
      leg Z44.10-•
        complete Z44.11-•
        partial Z44.12-•
    breast implant Z45.81
      tissue expander (with or without
        synchronous insertion of permanent
        implant) Z45.81
    device Z46.9
      specified NEC Z46.89
    external
      fixation device — code to fracture with
        seventh character D
      prosthesis, prosthetic device Z44.9
        breast Z44.3-•
        specified NEC Z44.8
    implanted device NEC Z45.89
    insulin pump Z46.81
    internal fixation device Z47.2
    myringotomy device (stent) (tube) Z45.82
    nervous system device NEC Z46.2
      brain neuropacemaker Z46.2
      visual substitution device Z46.2
        implanted Z45.31
    non-vascular catheter Z46.82
    orthodontic device Z46.4
    stent
      ureteral Z46.6
    urinary device Z46.6
  repeat cervical smear to confirm findings of
    recent normal smear following initial
    abnormal smear Z01.42
  respirator [ventilator] use during power
    failure (Z99.12)
  Rh typing Z01.83
  screening —*see* Screening
  specified NEC Z76.89
  sterilization Z30.2
  suspected condition, ruled out
    amniotic cavity and membrane Z03.71
    cervical shortening Z03.75
    fetal anomaly Z03.73
    fetal growth Z03.74
    maternal and fetal conditions NEC
      Z03.79
    oligohydramnios Z03.71
    placental problem Z03.72
    polyhydramnios Z03.71
  suspected exposure (to), ruled out
    anthrax Z03.810
    biological agents NEC Z03.818
  termination of pregnancy, elective Z33.2
  testing —*see* Test
  therapeutic drug level monitoring Z51.81
  titration, insulin pump Z46.81
  to determine fetal viability of pregnancy
    O36.80
  training
    insulin pump Z46.81
  X-ray of chest (as part of a general medical
    examination Z00.00)
    with abnormal findings Z00.01
Encystment —*see* Cyst
Endarteritis (bacterial, subacute) (infective)
  I77.6
  brain I67.7
  cerebral or cerebrospinal I67.7
  deformans —*see* Arteriosclerosis
  embolic —*see* Embolism
  obliterans —*see also* Arteriosclerosis
    pulmonary I28.8
  pulmonary I28.8
  retina —*see* Vasculitis, retina
  senile —*see* Arteriosclerosis
  syphilitic A52.09
    brain or cerebral A52.04
    congenital A50.54 *[I79.8]*
  tuberculous A18.89
Endemic —*see* condition

Endocarditis (chronic) (marantic) (nonbacterial) (thrombotic) (valvular) I38
  with rheumatic fever (conditions in I00)
    active —see Endocarditis, acute, rheumatic
    inactive or quiescent (with chorea) I09.1
  acute or subacute I33.9
    infective I33.0
    rheumatic (aortic) (mitral) (pulmonary) (tricuspid) I01.1
      with chorea (acute) (rheumatic) (Sydenham's) I02.0
  aortic (heart) (nonrheumatic) (valve) I35.8
    with
      mitral disease I08.0
        with tricuspid (valve) disease I08.3
          active or acute I01.1
            with chorea (acute) (rheumatic) (Sydenham's) I02.0
        rheumatic fever (conditions in I00)
          active —see Endocarditis, acute, rheumatic
          inactive or quiescent (with chorea) I06.9
      tricuspid (valve) disease I08.2
        with mitral (valve) disease I08.3
    acute or subacute I33.9
    arteriosclerotic I35.8
    rheumatic I06.9
      with mitral disease I08.0
        with tricuspid (valve) disease I08.3
          active or acute I01.1
            with chorea (acute) (rheumatic) (Sydenham's) I02.0
      active or acute I01.1
        with chorea (acute) (rheumatic) (Sydenham's) I02.0
    specified NEC I06.8
    specified cause NEC I35.8
    syphilitic A52.03
  arteriosclerotic I38
  atypical verrucous (Libman-Sacks) M32.11
  bacterial (acute) (any valve) (subacute) I33.0
  candidal B37.6
  congenital Q24.8
  constrictive I33.0
  Coxiella burnetii A78 [I39]
  Coxsackie B33.21
  due to
    prosthetic cardiac valve T82.6
    Q fever A78 [I39]
    Serratia marcescens I33.0
    typhoid (fever) A01.02
  gonococcal A54.83
  infectious or infective (acute) (any valve) (subacute) I33.0
  lenta (acute) (any valve) (subacute) I33.0
  Libman-Sacks M32.11
  listerial A32.82
  Löffler's I42.3
  malignant (acute) (any valve) (subacute) I33.0
  meningococcal A39.51
  mitral (chronic) (double) (fibroid) (heart) (inactive) (valve) (with chorea) I05.9
    with
      aortic (valve) disease I08.0
        with tricuspid (valve) disease I08.3
          active or acute I01.1
            with chorea (acute) (rheumatic) (Sydenham's) I02.0
        rheumatic fever (conditions in I00)
          active —see Endocarditis, acute, rheumatic
          inactive or quiescent (with chorea) I05.9
      tricuspid (valve) disease I08.1
        with aortic (valve) disease I08.3
    active or acute I01.1
      with chorea (acute) (rheumatic) (Sydenham's) I02.0
    bacterial I33.0

Endocarditis (Continued)
  mitral (Continued)
    arteriosclerotic I34.8
    nonrheumatic I34.8
      acute or subacute I33.9
    specified NEC I05.8
  monilial B37.6
  multiple valves I08.9
    specified disorders I08.8
  mycotic (acute) (any valve) (subacute) I33.0
  pneumococcal (acute) (any valve) (subacute) I33.0
  pulmonary (chronic) (heart) (valve) I37.8
    with rheumatic fever (conditions in I00)
      active —see Endocarditis, acute, rheumatic
      inactive or quiescent (with chorea) I09.89
        with aortic, mitral or tricuspid disease I08.8
    acute or subacute I33.9
      rheumatic I01.1
        with chorea (acute) (rheumatic) (Sydenham's) I02.0
    arteriosclerotic I37.8
    congenital Q22.2
    rheumatic (chronic) (inactive) (with chorea) I09.89
      active or acute I01.1
        with chorea (acute) (rheumatic) (Sydenham's) I02.0
    syphilitic A52.03
  purulent (acute) (any valve) (subacute) I33.0
  Q fever A78 [I39]
  rheumatic (chronic) (inactive) (with chorea) I09.1
    active or acute (aortic) (mitral) (pulmonary) (tricuspid) I01.1
      with chorea (acute) (rheumatic) (Sydenham's) I02.0
  rheumatoid —see Rheumatoid, carditis
  septic (acute) (any valve) (subacute) I33.0
  streptococcal (acute) (any valve) (subacute) I33.0
  subacute —see Endocarditis, acute
  suppurative (acute) (any valve) (subacute) I33.0
  syphilitic A52.03
  toxic I33.9
  tricuspid (chronic) (heart) (inactive) (rheumatic) (valve) (with chorea) I07.9
    with
      aortic (valve) disease I08.2
        mitral (valve) disease I08.3
      mitral (valve) disease I08.1
        aortic (valve) disease I08.3
      rheumatic fever (conditions in I00)
        active —see Endocarditis, acute, rheumatic
        inactive or quiescent (with chorea) I07.8
    active or acute I01.1
      with chorea (acute) (rheumatic) (Sydenham's) I02.0
    arteriosclerotic I36.8
    nonrheumatic I36.8
      acute or subacute I33.9
    specified cause, except rheumatic I36.8
  tuberculous —see Tuberculosis, endocarditis
  typhoid A01.02
  ulcerative (acute) (any valve) (subacute) I33.0
  vegetative (acute) (any valve) (subacute) I33.0
  verrucous (atypical) (nonbacterial) (nonrheumatic) M32.11
Endocardium, endocardial —see also condition
  cushion defect Q21.2
Endocervicitis —see also Cervicitis
  due to intrauterine (contraceptive) device T83.69
  hyperplastic N72
Endocrine —see condition
Endocrinopathy, pluriglandular E31.9

Endodontic
  overfill M27.52
  underfill M27.53
Endodontitis K04.01
  irreversible K04.02
  reversible K04.01
Endomastoiditis —see Mastoiditis
Endometrioma N80.9
Endometriosis N80.9
  appendix N80.5
  bladder N80.8
  bowel N80.5
  broad ligament N80.3
  cervix N80.0
  colon N80.5
  cul-de-sac (Douglas') N80.3
  exocervix N80.0
  fallopian tube N80.2
  female genital organ NEC N80.8
  gallbladder N80.8
  in scar of skin N80.6
  internal N80.0
  intestine N80.5
  lung N80.8
  myometrium N80.0
  ovary N80.1
  parametrium N80.3
  pelvic peritoneum N80.3
  peritoneal (pelvic) N80.3
  rectovaginal septum N80.4
  rectum N80.5
  round ligament N80.3
  skin (scar) N80.6
  specified site NEC N80.8
  stromal D39.0
  thorax N80.8
  umbilicus N80.8
  uterus (internal) N80.0
  vagina N80.4
  vulva N80.8
Endometritis (decidual) (nonspecific) (purulent) (senile (atrophic) (suppurative) N71.9
  with ectopic pregnancy O08.0
  acute N71.0
  blenorrhagic (gonococcal) (acute) (chronic) A54.24
  cervix, cervical (with erosion or ectropion) — see also Cervicitis
    hyperplastic N72
  chlamydial A56.11
  chronic N71.1
  following
    abortion —see Abortion by type complicated by genital infection
    ectopic or molar pregnancy O08.0
  gonococcal, gonorrheal (acute) (chronic) A54.24
  hyperplastic —see also Hyperplasia, endometrial N85.00-●
    cervix N72
  puerperal, postpartum, childbirth O86.12
  subacute N71.0
  tuberculous A18.17
Endometrium —see condition
Endomyocardiopathy, South African I42.3
Endomyocarditis —see Endocarditis
Endomyofibrosis I42.3
Endomyometritis —see Endometritis
Endopericarditis —see Endocarditis
Endoperineuritis —see Disorder, nerve
Endophlebitis —see Phlebitis
Endophthalmia —see Endophthalmitis, purulent
Endophthalmitis (acute) (infective) (metastatic) (subacute) H44.009
  bleb associated H59.4 —see also Bleb, inflamed (infected), postprocedural
  gonorrheal A54.39
  in (due to)
    cysticercosis B69.1
    onchocerciasis B73.01
    toxocariasis B83.0

▶ New   ⇒ Revised   ~~deleted~~ Deleted   ● Use Additional Character(s)

Endophthalmitis *(Continued)*
  panuveitis —*see* Panuveitis
  parasitic H44.12-•
  purulent H44.00-•
    panophthalmitis —*see* Panophthalmitis
    vitreous abscess H44.02-•
  specified NEC H44.19
  sympathetic —*see* Uveitis, sympathetic
Endosalpingioma D28.2
Endosalpingiosis N94.89
Endosteitis —*see* Osteomyelitis
Endothelioma, bone —*see* Neoplasm, bone, malignant
Endotheliosis (hemorrhagic infectional) D69.8
Endotoxemia — code to condition
Endotrachelitis —*see* Cervicitis
Engelmann (-Camurati) syndrome Q78.3
English disease —*see* Rickets
Engman's disease L30.3
Engorgement
  breast N64.59
    newborn P83.4
    puerperal, postpartum O92.79
  lung (passive) —*see* Edema, lung
  pulmonary (passive) —*see* Edema, lung
  stomach K31.89
  venous, retina —*see* Occlusion, retina, vein, engorgement
Enlargement, enlarged —*see also* Hypertrophy
  adenoids J35.2
    with tonsils J35.3
  alveolar ridge K08.89
    congenital —*see* Anomaly, alveolar
  apertures of diaphragm (congenital) Q79.1
  gingival K06.1
  heart, cardiac —*see* Hypertrophy, cardiac
  labium majus, childhood asymmetric (CALME) N90.61
  lacrimal gland, chronic H04.03-•
  liver —*see* Hypertrophy, liver
  lymph gland or node R59.9
    generalized R59.1
    localized R59.0
  orbit H05.34-•
  organ or site, congenital NEC —*see* Anomaly, by site
  parathyroid (gland) E21.0
  pituitary fossa R93.0
  prostate N40.0
    with lower urinary tract symptoms (LUTS) N40.1
    without lower urinary tract symptoms (LUTS) N40.0
  sella turcica R93.0
  spleen —*see* Splenomegaly
  thymus (gland) (congenital) E32.0
  thyroid (gland) —*see* Goiter
  tongue K14.8
  tonsils J35.1
    with adenoids J35.3
  uterus N85.2
  vestibular aqueduct Q16.5
Enophthalmos H05.40-•
  due to
    orbital tissue atrophy H05.41-•
    trauma or surgery H05.42-•
Enostosis M27.8
Entamebic, entamebiasis —*see* Amebiasis
Entanglement
  umbilical cord(s) O69.82
    with compression O69.2
    around neck (with compression) O69.81
      with compression O69.1
      without compression O69.81
    of twins in monoamniotic sac O69.2
    without compression O69.82
Enteralgia —*see* Pain, abdominal
Enteric —*see* condition

Enteritis (acute) (diarrheal) (hemorrhagic) (noninfective) K52.9
  adenovirus A08.2
  aertrycke infection A02.0
  allergic K52.29
    with
      eosinophilic gastritis or gastroenteritis K52.81
      food protein-induced enterocolitis syndrome K52.21
      food protein-induced enteropathy K52.22
      FPIES K52.21
  amebic (acute) A06.0
    with abscess —*see* Abscess, amebic
    chronic A06.1
      with abscess —*see* Abscess, amebic
      nondysenteric A06.2
    nondysenteric A06.2
  astrovirus A08.32
  bacillary NOS A03.9
  bacterial A04.9
    specified NEC A04.8
  calicivirus A08.31
  candidal B37.82
  Chilomastix A07.8
  choleriformis A00.1
  chronic (noninfectious) K52.9
    ulcerative —*see* Colitis, ulcerative
  cicatrizing (chronic) —*see* Enteritis, regional, small intestine
  Clostridium
    botulinum (food poisoning) A05.1
    difficile
      not specified as recurrent A04.72
      recurrent A04.71
  coccidial A07.3
  coxsackie virus A08.39
  dietetic —*see also* Enteritis, allergic K52.29
  drug-induced K52.1
  due to
    astrovirus A08.32
    calicivirus A08.31
    coxsackie virus A08.39
    drugs K52.1
    echovirus A08.39
    enterovirus NEC A08.39
    food hypersensitivity —*see also* Enteritis, allergic K52.29
    infectious organism (bacterial) (viral) —*see* Enteritis, infectious
    torovirus A08.39
    Yersinia enterocolitica A04.6
  echovirus A08.39
  eltor A00.1
  enterovirus NEC A08.39
  eosinophilic K52.81
  epidemic (infectious) A09
  fulminant —*see also* Ischemia, intestine, acute K55.019
  gangrenous —*see* Enteritis, infectious
  giardial A07.1
  infectious NOS A09
    due to
      adenovirus A08.2
      Aerobacter aerogenes A04.8
      Arizona (bacillus) A02.0
      bacteria NOS A04.9
        specified NEC A04.8
      Campylobacter A04.5
      Clostridium difficile
        not specified as recurrent A04.72
        recurrent A04.71
      Clostridium perfringens A04.8
      Enterobacter aerogenes A04.8
      enterovirus A08.39
      Escherichia coli A04.4
        enteroaggregative A04.4
        enterohemorrhagic A04.3
        enteroinvasive A04.2
        enteropathogenic A04.0
        enterotoxigenic A04.1
        specified NEC A04.4

Enteritis *(Continued)*
  infectious NOS *(Continued)*
    due to *(Continued)*
      specified
        bacteria NEC A04.8
        virus NEC A08.39
      Staphylococcus A04.8
      virus NEC A08.4
        specified type NEC A08.39
      Yersinia enterocolitica A04.6
    specified organism NEC A08.8
  influenzal —*see* Influenza, with, digestive manifestations
  ischemic K55.9
    acute —*see also* Ischemia, intestine, acute K55.019
    chronic K55.1
  microsporidial A07.8
  mucomembranous, myxomembranous —*see* Syndrome, irritable bowel
  mucous —*see* Syndrome, irritable bowel
  necroticans A05.2
  necrotizing of newborn —*see* Enterocolitis, necrotizing, in newborn
  neurogenic —*see* Syndrome, irritable bowel
  newborn necrotizing —*see* Enterocolitis, necrotizing, in newborn
  noninfectious K52.9
  norovirus A08.11
  parasitic NEC B82.9
  paratyphoid (fever) —*see* Fever, paratyphoid
  protozoal A07.9
    specified NEC A07.8
  radiation K52.0
  regional (of) K50.90
    with
      complication K50.919
        abscess K50.914
        fistula K50.913
        intestinal obstruction K50.912
        rectal bleeding K50.911
        specified complication NEC K50.918
    colon —*see* Enteritis, regional, large intestine
    duodenum —*see* Enteritis, regional, small intestine
    ileum —*see* Enteritis, regional, small intestine
    jejunum —*see* Enteritis, regional, small intestine
    large bowel —*see* Enteritis, regional, large intestine
    large intestine (colon) (rectum) K50.10
      with
        complication K50.119
          abscess K50.114
          fistula K50.113
          intestinal obstruction K50.112
          rectal bleeding K50.111
          small intestine (duodenum) (ileum) (jejunum) involvement K50.80
            with
              complication K50.819
                abscess K50.814
                fistula K50.813
                intestinal obstruction K50.812
                rectal bleeding K50.811
                specified complication NEC K50.818
          specified complication NEC K50.118
    rectum —*see* Enteritis, regional, large intestine
    small intestine (duodenum) (ileum) (jejunum) K50.00
      with
        complication K50.019
          abscess K50.014
          fistula K50.013
          intestinal obstruction K50.012

Enteritis (Continued)
  regional (Continued)
    small intestine (Continued)
      with (Continued)
        complication (Continued)
          large intestine (colon) (rectum)
            involvement K50.80
            with
              complication K50.819
                abscess K50.814
                fistula K50.813
                intestinal obstruction
                  K50.812
                rectal bleeding K50.811
                specified complication NEC
                  K50.818
          rectal bleeding K50.011
          specified complication NEC
            K50.018
  rotaviral A08.0
  Salmonella, salmonellosis (arizonae)
    (cholerae-suis) (enteritidis)
    (typhimurium) A02.0
  segmental —see Enteritis, regional
  septic A09
  Shigella —see Infection, Shigella
  small round structured NEC A08.19
  spasmodic, spastic —see Syndrome, irritable
    bowel
  staphylococcal A04.8
    due to food A05.0
  torovirus A08.39
  toxic NEC K52.1
    due to Clostridium difficile
      not specified as recurrent A04.72
      recurrent A04.71
  trichomonal A07.8
  tuberculous A18.32
  typhosa A01.00
  ulcerative (chronic) —see Colitis, ulcerative
  viral A08.4
    adenovirus A08.2
    enterovirus A08.39
    Rotavirus A08.0
    small round structured NEC A08.19
    specified NEC A08.39
    virus specified NEC A08.39
Enterobiasis B80
Enterobius vermicularis (infection) (infestation)
  B80
Enterocele —see also Hernia, abdomen
  pelvic, pelvis (acquired) (congenital) N81.5
  vagina, vaginal (acquired) (congenital)
    NEC N81.5
Enterocolitis —see also Enteritis K52.9
  due to Clostridium difficile
    not specified as recurrent A04.72
    recurrent A04.71
  fulminant ischemic —see also Ischemia,
    intestine, acute K55.059
  granulomatous —see Enteritis, regional
  hemorrhagic (acute) —see also Ischemia,
    intestine, acute K55.059
    chronic K55.1
  infectious NEC A09
  ischemic K55.9
  necrotizing K55.30
    with
      perforation K55.33
      pneumatosis K55.32
      and perforation K55.33
    due to Clostridium difficile
      not specified as recurrent A04.72
      recurrent A04.71
    in non-newborn K55.30
      stage 1 (without pneumatosis, without
        perforation) K55.31
      stage 2 (with pneumatosis, without
        perforation) K55.32
      stage 3 (with pneumatosis, with
        perforation) K55.33

Enterocolitis (Continued)
  necrotizing (Continued)
    in newborn P77.9
      stage 1 (without pneumatosis, without
        perforation) P77.1
      stage 2 (with pneumatosis, without
        perforation) P77.2
      stage 3 (with pneumatosis, with
        perforation) P77.3
    without pneumatosis or perforation K55.31
  noninfectious K52.9
    newborn —see Enterocolitis, necrotizing, in
      newborn
  pseudomembranous (newborn)
    not specified as recurrent A04.72
    recurrent A04.71
  radiation K52.0
    newborn —see Enterocolitis, necrotizing, in
      newborn
  ulcerative (chronic) —see Pancolitis,
    ulcerative (chronic)
Enterogastritis —see Enteritis
Enteropathy K63.9
  celiac-gluten-sensitive K90.0
    non-celiac K90.41
  food protein-induced K52.22
  hemorrhagic, terminal —see also Ischemia,
    intestine, acute K55.059
  protein-losing K90.49
Enteroperitonitis —see Peritonitis
Enteroptosis K63.4
Enterorrhagia K92.2
Enterospasm —see also Syndrome, irritable,
  bowel
  psychogenic F45.8
Enterostenosis —see also Obstruction, intestine,
  specified NEC K56.699
Enterostomy
  complication —see Complication,
    enterostomy
  status Z93.4
Enterovirus, as cause of disease classified
  elsewhere B97.10
  coxsackievirus B97.11
  echovirus B97.12
  other specified B97.19
Enthesopathy (peripheral) M77.5-•
  Achilles tendinitis —see Tendinitis, Achilles
  ankle and tarsus M77.9
    specified type NEC —see Enthesopathy,
      foot, specified type NEC
  anterior tibial syndrome M76.81-•
  calcaneal spur —see Spur, bone, calcaneal
  elbow region M77.8
    lateral epicondylitis —see Epicondylitis,
      lateral
    medial epicondylitis —see Epicondylitis,
      medial
  foot NEC M77.8
    metatarsalgia —see Metatarsalgia
    specified type NEC M77.5-•
  forearm M77.8
  gluteal tendinitis —see Tendinitis, gluteal
  hand M77.8
  hip —see Enthesopathy, lower limb, specified
    type NEC
  iliac crest spur —see Spur, bone, iliac crest
  iliotibial band syndrome —see Syndrome,
    iliotibial band
  knee —see Enthesopathy, lower limb, lower
    leg, specified type NEC
  lateral epicondylitis —see Epicondylitis,
    lateral
  lower limb (excluding foot) M76.9
    Achilles tendinitis —see Tendinitis, Achilles
    ankle and tarsus M77.5-
      specified type NEC - see Enthesopathy,
        foot, specified type NEC
    anterior tibial syndrome M76.81-•
    gluteal tendinitis —see Tendinitis, gluteal
    iliac crest spur —see Spur, bone, iliac crest

Enthesopathy (Continued)
  lower limb (Continued)
    iliotibial band syndrome —see Syndrome,
      iliotibial band
    patellar tendinitis —see Tendinitis, patellar
    pelvic region —see Enthesopathy, lower
      limb, specified type NEC
    peroneal tendinitis —see Tendinitis,
      peroneal
    posterior tibial syndrome M76.82-•
    psoas tendinitis —see Tendinitis, psoas
    specified type NEC M76.89-•
    tibial collateral bursitis —see Bursitis, tibial
      collateral
  medial epicondylitis —see Epicondylitis,
    medial
  multiple sites M77.8
  patellar tendinitis —see Tendinitis, patellar
  pelvis M77.8
  periarthritis of wrist —see Periarthritis, wrist
  peroneal tendinitis —see Tendinitis, peroneal
  posterior tibial syndrome M76.82-•
  psoas tendinitis —see Tendinitis, psoas
  shoulder M77.8
  shoulder region —see Lesion, shoulder
  specified site NEC M77.9
  specified type NEC M77.8
  spinal M46.00
    cervical region M46.02
    cervicothoracic region M46.03
    lumbar region M46.06
    lumbosacral region M46.07
    multiple sites M46.09
    occipito-atlanto-axial region M46.01
    sacrococcygeal region M46.08
    thoracic region M46.04
    thoracolumbar region M46.05
  tibial collateral bursitis —see Bursitis, tibial
    collateral
  upper arm M77.8
  wrist and carpus NEC M77.8
    calcaneal spur —see Spur, bone, calcaneal
    periarthritis of wrist —see Periarthritis,
      wrist
Entomophobia F40.218
Entomophthoromycosis B46.8
Entrance, air into vein —see Embolism, air
Entrapment, nerve —see Neuropathy, entrapment
Entropion (eyelid) (paralytic) H02.009
  cicatricial H02.019
    left H02.016
      lower H02.015
      upper H02.014
    right H02.013
      lower H02.012
      upper H02.011
  congenital Q10.2
  left H02.006
    lower H02.005
    upper H02.004
  mechanical H02.029
    left H02.026
      lower H02.025
      upper H02.024
    right H02.023
      lower H02.022
      upper H02.021
  right H02.003
    lower H02.002
    upper H02.001
  senile H02.039
    left H02.036
      lower H02.035
      upper H02.034
    right H02.033
      lower H02.032
      upper H02.031
  spastic H02.049
    left H02.046
      lower H02.045
      upper H02.044

▶ New   ⇨ Revised   deleted Deleted   • Use Additional Character(s)

Entropion (Continued)
  spastic (Continued)
    right H02.043
      lower H02.042
      upper H02.041
Enucleated eye (traumatic, current) S05.7-●
Enuresis R32
  functional F98.0
  habit disturbance F98.0
  nocturnal N39.44
    psychogenic F98.0
  nonorganic origin F98.0
  psychogenic F98.0
Eosinopenia —see Agranulocytosis
Eosinophilia (allergic) (idiopathic) (secondary) D72.10
  with
    angiolymphoid hyperplasia (ALHE) D18.01
  familial D72.19
  hereditary D72.19
  in disease classified elsewhere D72.18
  infiltrative —see Eosinophilia, pulmonary
  Löffler's J82.89
  peritoneal —see Peritonitis, eosinophilic
  pulmonary NEC J82.89
    acute J82.82
    asthmatic J82.83
    chronic J82.81
  specified NEC D72.19
  tropical (pulmonary) J82.89
Eosinophilia-myalgia syndrome M35.8
Ependymitis (acute) (cerebral) (chronic) (granular) —see Encephalomyelitis
Ependymoblastoma
  specified site —see Neoplasm, malignant, by site
  unspecified site C71.9
Ependymoma (epithelial) (malignant)
  anaplastic
    specified site —see Neoplasm, malignant, by site
    unspecified site C71.9
  benign
    specified site —see Neoplasm, benign, by site
    unspecified site D33.2
  myxopapillary D43.2
    specified site —see Neoplasm, uncertain behavior, by site
    unspecified site D43.2
  papillary D43.2
    specified site —see Neoplasm, uncertain behavior, by site
    unspecified site D43.2
  specified site —see Neoplasm, malignant, by site
  unspecified site C71.9
Ependymopathy G93.89
Ephelis, ephelides L81.2
Epiblepharon (congenital) Q10.3
Epicanthus, epicanthic fold (eyelid) (congenital) Q10.3
Epicondylitis (elbow)
  lateral M77.1-●
  medial M77.0-●
Epicystitis —see Cystitis
Epidemic —see condition
Epidermidalization, cervix —see Dysplasia, cervix
Epidermis, epidermal —see condition
Epidermodysplasia verruciformis B07.8
Epidermolysis
  bullosa (congenital) Q81.9
    acquired L12.30
      drug-induced L12.31
      specified cause NEC L12.35
    dystrophica Q81.2
    letalis Q81.1
    simplex Q81.0
    specified NEC Q81.8

Epidermolysis (Continued)
  necroticans combustiformis L51.2
    due to drug —see Table of Drugs and Chemicals, by drug
Epidermophytid —see Dermatophytosis
Epidermophytosis (infected) —see Dermatophytosis
Epididymis —see condition
Epididymitis (acute) (nonvenereal) (recurrent) (residual) N45.1
  with orchitis N45.3
  blennorrhagic (gonococcal) A54.23
  caseous (tuberculous) A18.15
  chlamydial A56.19
  filarial —see also Infestation, filarial B74.9 [N51]
  gonococcal A54.23
  syphilitic A52.76
  tuberculous A18.15
Epididymo-orchitis —see also Epididymitis N45.3
Epidural —see condition
Epigastrium, epigastric —see condition
Epigastrocele —see Hernia, ventral
Epiglottis —see condition
Epiglottitis, epiglottiditis (acute) J05.10
  with obstruction J05.11
  chronic J37.0
Epignathus Q89.4
Epilepsia partialis continua —see also Kozhevnikof's epilepsy G40.1-●
Epilepsy, epileptic, epilepsia (attack) (cerebral) (convulsion) (fit) (seizure) G40.909

> Note: the following terms are to be considered equivalent to intractable: pharmacoresistant (pharmacologically resistant), treatment resistant, refractory (medically) and poorly controlled

  with
    complex partial seizures —see Epilepsy, localization-related, symptomatic, with complex partial seizures
    grand mal seizures on awakening — see Epilepsy, generalized, specified NEC
    myoclonic absences —see Epilepsy, generalized, specified NEC
    myoclonic-astatic seizures —see Epilepsy, generalized, specified NEC
    simple partial seizures —see Epilepsy, localization-related, symptomatic, with simple partial seizures
  akinetic —see Epilepsy, generalized, specified NEC
  benign childhood with centrotemporal EEG spikes —see Epilepsy, localization-related, idiopathic
  benign myoclonic in infancy G40.80-●
  Bravais-jacksonian —see Epilepsy, localization-related, symptomatic, with simple partial seizures
  childhood
    with occipital EEG paroxysms —see Epilepsy, localization-related, idiopathic
    absence G40.A09
      intractable G40.A19
        with status epilepticus G40.A11
        without status epilepticus G40.A19
      not intractable G40.A09
        with status epilepticus G40.A01
        without status epilepticus G40.A09
  climacteric —see Epilepsy, specified NEC
  cysticercosis B69.0
  deterioration (mental) F06.8
  due to syphilis A52.19
  focal —see Epilepsy, localization-related, symptomatic, with simple partial seizures

Epilepsy, epileptic, epilepsia (Continued)
  generalized
    idiopathic G40.309
      intractable G40.319
        with status epilepticus G40.311
        without status epilepticus G40.319
      not intractable G40.309
        with status epilepticus G40.301
        without status epilepticus G40.309
    specified NEC G40.409
      intractable G40.419
        with status epilepticus G40.411
        without status epilepticus G40.419
      not intractable G40.409
        with status epilepticus G40.401
        without status epilepticus G40.409
  impulsive petit mal —see Epilepsy, juvenile myoclonic
  intractable G40.919
    with status epilepticus G40.911
    without status epilepticus G40.919
  juvenile absence G40.A09
    intractable G40.A19
      with status epilepticus G40.A11
      without status epilepticus G40.A19
    not intractable G40.A09
      with status epilepticus G40.A01
      without status epilepticus G40.A09
  juvenile myoclonic G40.B11
    intractable G40.B19
      with status epilepticus G40.B11
      without status epilepticus G40.B19
    not intractable G40.B09
      with status epilepticus G40.B01
      without status epilepticus G40.B09
  localization-related (focal) (partial)
    idiopathic G40.009
      with seizures of localized onset G40.009
        intractable G40.019
          with status epilepticus G40.011
          without status epilepticus G40.019
        not intractable G40.009
          with status epilepticus G40.001
          without status epilepticus G40.009
    symptomatic
      with complex partial seizures G40.209
        intractable G40.219
          with status epilepticus G40.211
          without status epilepticus G40.219
        not intractable G40.209
          with status epilepticus G40.201
          without status epilepticus G40.209
      with simple partial seizures G40.109
        intractable G40.119
          with status epilepticus G40.111
          without status epilepticus G40.119
        not intractable G40.109
          with status epilepticus G40.101
          without status epilepticus G40.109
  myoclonus, myoclonic —see also Epilepsy, generalized, specified NEC
  progressive —see Epilepsy, generalized, idiopathic
  severe, in infancy (SMEI) G40.83-●
  not intractable G40.909
    with status epilepticus G40.901
    without status epilepticus G40.909
  on awakening —see Epilepsy, generalized, specified NEC
  parasitic NOS B71.9 [G94]
  partialis continua —see also Kozhevnikof's epilepsy G40.1-●
  peripheral —see Epilepsy, specified NEC
  polymorphic, in infancy (PMEI) G40.83-●
  procursiva —see Epilepsy, localization-related, symptomatic, with simple partial seizures
  progressive (familial) myoclonic —see Epilepsy, generalized, idiopathic

Epilepsy, epileptic, epilepsia (Continued)
reflex —see Epilepsy, specified NEC
related to
alcohol G40.509
not intractable G40.509
with status epilepticus G40.501
without status epliepticus G40.509
drugs G40.509
not intractable G40.509
with status epilepticus G40.501
without status epliepticus G40.509
external causes G40.509
not intractable G40.509
with status epilepticus G40.501
without status epliepticus G40.509
hormonal changes G40.509
not intractable G40.509
with status epilepticus G40.501
without status epliepticus G40.509
sleep deprivation G40.509
not intractable G40.509
with status epilepticus G40.501
without status epliepticus G40.509
stress G40.509
not intractable G40.509
with status epilepticus G40.501
without status epliepticus G40.509
somatomotor —see Epilepsy, localization-
related, symptomatic, with simple
partial seizures
somatosensory —see Epilepsy, localization-
related, symptomatic, with simple
partial seizures
spasms G40.822
intractable G40.824
with status epilepticus G40.823
without status epilepticus G40.824
not intractable G40.822
with status epilepticus G40.821
without status epilepticus G40.822
specified NEC G40.802
intractable G40.804
with status epilepticus G40.803
without status epilepticus G40.804
not intractable G40.802
with status epilepticus G40.801
without status epilepticus G40.802
syndromes
generalized
idiopathic G40.309
intractable G40.319
with status epilepticus G40.311
without status epilepticus G40.319
not intractable G40.309
with status epilepticus G40.301
without status epilepticus G40.309
specified NEC G40.409
intractable G40.419
with status epilepticus G40.411
without status epilepticus G40.419
not intractable G40.409
with status epilepticus G40.401
without status epilepticus G40.409
localization-related (focal) (partial)
idiopathic G40.009
with seizures of localized onset
G40.009
intractable G40.019
with status epilepticus G40.011
without status epilepticus
G40.019
not intractable G40.009
with status epilepticus G40.001
without status epilepticus
G40.009
symptomatic
with complex partial seizures
G40.209
intractable G40.219
with status epilepticus G40.211
without status epilepticus G40.219

Epilepsy, epileptic, epilepsia (Continued)
syndromes (Continued)
localization-related (Continued)
symptomatic (Continued)
with complex partial seizures
(Continued)
not intractable G40.209
with status epilepticus G40.201
without status epilepticus
G40.209
with simple partial seizures G40.109
intractable G40.119
with status epilepticus G40.111
without status epilepticus
G40.119
not intractable G40.109
with status epilepticus G40.101
without status epilepticus
G40.109
specified NEC G40.802
intractable G40.804
with status epilepticus G40.803
without status epilepticus G40.804
not intractable G40.802
with status epilepticus G40.801
without status epilepticus G40.802
tonic (-clonic) —see Epilepsy, generalized,
specified NEC
twilight F05
uncinate (gyrus) —see Epilepsy, localization-
related, symptomatic, with complex
partial seizures
Unverricht (-Lundborg) (familial myoclonic) —
see Epilepsy, generalized, idiopathic
visceral —see Epilepsy, specified NEC
visual —see Epilepsy, specified NEC
Epiloia Q85.1
Epimenorrhea N92.0
Epipharyngitis —see Nasopharyngitis
Epiphora H04.20-●
due to
excess lacrimation H04.21-●
insufficient drainage H04.22-●
Epiphyseal arrest —see Arrest, epiphyseal
Epiphyseolysis, epiphysiolysis —see
Osteochondropathy
Epiphysitis —see also Osteochondropathy
juvenile M92.9
syphilitic (congenital) A50.02
Epiplocele —see Hernia, abdomen
Epiploitis —see Peritonitis
Epiplosarcomphalocele —see Hernia,
umbilicus
Episcleritis (suppurative) H15.10-●
in (due to)
syphilis A52.71
tuberculosis A18.51
nodular H15.12-●
periodica fugax H15.11-●
angioneurotic —see Edema, angioneurotic
syphilitic (late) A52.71
tuberculous A18.51
Episode
affective, mixed F39
depersonalization (in neurotic state) F48.1
depressive F32.9
major F32.9
mild F32.0
moderate F32.1
severe (without psychotic symptoms)
F32.2
with psychotic symptoms F32.3
recurrent F33.9
brief F33.8
specified NEC F32.89
hypomanic F30.8
manic F30.9
with
psychotic symptoms F30.2
remission (full) F30.4
partial F30.3

Episode (Continued)
manic (Continued)
without psychotic symptoms F30.10
mild F30.11
moderate F30.12
severe (without psychotic symptoms)
F30.13
with psychotic symptoms F30.2
other specified F30.8
recurrent F31.89
psychotic F23
organic F06.8
schizophrenic (acute) NEC, brief F23
Epispadias (female) (male) Q64.0
Episplenitis D73.89
Epistaxis (multiple) R04.0
hereditary I78.0
vicarious menstruation N94.89
Epithelioma (malignant) —see also Neoplasm,
malignant, by site
adenoides cysticum —see Neoplasm, skin,
benign
basal cell —see Neoplasm, skin, malignant
benign —see Neoplasm, benign, by site
Bowen's —see Neoplasm, skin, in situ
calcifying, of Malherbe —see Neoplasm, skin,
benign
external site —see Neoplasm, skin, malignant
intraepidermal, Jadassohn —see Neoplasm,
skin, benign
squamous cell —see Neoplasm, malignant,
by site
Epitheliomatosis pigmented Q82.1
Epitheliopathy, multifocal placoid pigment
H30.14-●
Epithelium, epithelial —see condition
Epituberculosis (with atelectasis) (allergic)
A15.7
Eponychia Q84.6
Epstein's
nephrosis or syndrome —see Nephrosis
pearl K09.8
Epulis (gingiva) (fibrous) (giant cell) K06.8
Equinia A24.0
Equinovarus (congenital) (talipes) Q66.0-●
acquired —see Deformity, limb, clubfoot
Equivalent
convulsive (abdominal) —see Epilepsy,
specified NEC
epileptic (psychic) —see Epilepsy,
localization-related, symptomatic, with
complex partial seizures
Erb (-Duchenne) paralysis (birth injury)
(newborn) P14.0
Erb's
disease G71.02
palsy, paralysis (brachial) (birth) (newborn)
P14.0
spinal (spastic) syphilitic A52.17
pseudohypertrophic muscular dystrophy
G71.02
Erb-Goldflam disease or syndrome G70.00
with exacerbation (acute) G70.01
in crisis G70.01
Erdheim's syndrome (acromegalic
macrospondylitis) E22.0
Erection, painful (persistent) —see Priapism
Ergosterol deficiency (vitamin D) E55.9
with
adult osteomalacia M83.8
rickets —see Rickets
Ergotism —see also Poisoning, food, noxious,
plant
from ergot used as drug (migraine therapy) —
see Table of Drugs and Chemicals
Erosio interdigitalis blastomycetica B37.2
Erosion
artery I77.2
without rupture I77.89
bone —see Disorder, bone, density and
structure, specified NEC

▶ New   ⇒ Revised   ~~deleted~~ Deleted   ● Use Additional Character(s)

Erosion (Continued)
bronchus J98.09
cartilage (joint) —see Disorder, cartilage, specified type NEC
cervix (uteri) (acquired) (chronic) (congenital) N86
  with cervicitis N72
cornea (nontraumatic) —see Ulcer, cornea
  recurrent H18.83-●
  traumatic —see Abrasion, cornea
dental (idiopathic) (occupational) (due to diet, drugs or vomiting) K03.2
duodenum, postpyloric —see Ulcer, duodenum
esophagus K22.10
  with bleeding K22.11
gastric —see Ulcer, stomach
gastrojejunal —see Ulcer, gastrojejunal
implanted mesh —see Complications, prosthetic devise or implant, mesh
intestine K63.3
lymphatic vessel I89.8
pylorus, pyloric (ulcer) —see Ulcer, stomach
spine, aneurysmal A52.09
stomach —see Ulcer, stomach
subcutaneous device pocket
  nervous system prosthetic device, implant, or graft T85.890
  other internal prosthetic device, implant, or graft T85.898
teeth (idiopathic) (occupational) (due to diet, drugs or vomiting) K03.2
urethra N36.8
uterus N85.8
Erotomania F52.8
Error
metabolism, inborn —see Disorder, metabolism
refractive —see Disorder, refraction
Eructation R14.2
nervous or psychogenic F45.8
Eruption
creeping B76.9
drug (generalized) (taken internally) L27.0
  fixed L27.1
  in contact with skin —see Dermatitis, due to drugs
  localized L27.1
Hutchinson, summer L56.4
Kaposi's varicelliform B00.0
napkin L22
polymorphous light (sun) L56.4
recalcitrant pustular L13.8
ringed R23.8
skin (nonspecific) R21
  creeping (meaning hookworm) B76.9
  due to inoculation/vaccination (generalized) —see also Dermatitis, due to, vaccine L27.0
    localized L27.1
  erysipeloid A26.0
  feigned L98.1
  Kaposi's varicelliform B00.0
  lichenoid L28.0
  meaning dermatitis —see Dermatitis
  toxic NEC L53.0
tooth, teeth, abnormal (incomplete) (late) (premature) (sequence) K00.6
vesicular R23.8
Erysipelas (gangrenous) (infantile) (newborn) (phlegmonous) (suppurative) A46
external ear A46 [H62.40]
puerperal, postpartum O86.89
Erysipeloid A26.9
cutaneous (Rosenbach's) A26.0
disseminated A26.8
sepsis A26.7
specified NEC A26.8
Erythema, erythematous (infectional) (inflammation) L53.9
ab igne L59.0
annulare (centrifugum) (rheumaticum) L53.1

Erythema, erythematous (Continued)
arthriticum epidemicum A25.1
brucellum —see Brucellosis
chronic figurate NEC L53.3
chronicum migrans (Borrelia burgdorferi) A69.20
diaper L22
due to
  chemical NEC L53.0
    in contact with skin L24.5
  drug (internal use) —see Dermatitis, due to, drugs
elevatum diutinum L95.1
endemic E52
epidemic, arthritic A25.1
figuratum perstans L53.3
gluteal L22
heat - code by site under Burn, first degree
ichthyosiforme congenitum bullous Q80.3
in diseases classified elsewhere L54
induratum (nontuberculous) L52
  tuberculous A18.4
infectiosum B08.3
intertrigo L30.4
iris L51.9
marginatum L53.2
  in (due to) acute rheumatic fever I00
medicamentosum —see Dermatitis, due to, drugs
migrans A26.0
  chronicum A69.20
  tongue K14.1
multiforme (major) (minor) L51.9
  bullous, bullosum L51.1
  conjunctiva L51.1
  nonbullous L51.0
  pemphigoides L12.0
  specified NEC L51.8
napkin L22
neonatorum P83.88
  toxic P83.1
nodosum L52
  tuberculous A18.4
palmar L53.8
pernio T69.1
rash, newborn P83.88
scarlatiniform (recurrent) (exfoliative) L53.8
solare L55.0
specified NEC L53.8
toxic, toxicum NEC L53.0
  newborn P83.1
tuberculous (primary) A18.4
Erythematous, erythematosus —see condition
Erythermalgia (primary) I73.81
Erythralgia I73.81
Erythrasma L08.1
Erythredema (polyneuropathy) —see Poisoning, mercury
Erythremia (acute) C94.0-●
chronic D45
secondary D75.1
Erythroblastopenia —see also Aplasia, red cell D60.9
congenital D61.01
Erythroblastophthisis D61.09
Erythroblastosis (fetalis) (newborn) P55.9
due to
  ABO (antibodies) (incompatibility) (isoimmunization) P55.1
  Rh (antibodies) (incompatibility) (isoimmunization) P55.0
Erythrocyanosis (crurum) I73.89
Erythrocythemia —see Erythremia
Erythrocytosis (megalosplenic) (secondary) D75.1
familial D75.0
oval, hereditary —see Elliptocytosis
secondary D75.1
stress D75.1

Erythroderma (secondary) —see also Erythema L53.9
bullous ichthyosiform, congenital Q80.3
desquamativum L21.1
ichthyosiform, congenital (bullous) Q80.3
neonatorum P83.88
psoriaticum L40.8
Erythrodysesthesia, palmar plantar (PPE) L27.1
Erythrogenesis imperfecta D61.09
Erythroleukemia C94.0-●
Erythromelalgia I73.81
Erythrophagocytosis D75.89
Erythrophobia F40.298
Erythroplakia, oral epithelium, and tongue K13.29
Erythroplasia (Queyrat) D07.4
specified site —see Neoplasm, skin, in situ
unspecified site D07.4
Escherichia coli (E. coli), as cause of disease classified elsewhere B96.20
non-O157 Shiga toxin-producing (with known O group) B96.22
non-Shiga toxin-producing B96.29
O157 with confirmation of Shiga toxin when H antigen is unknown, or is not H7 B96.21
O157:H- (nonmotile) with confirmation of Shiga toxin B96.21
~~O157:H7 with or without confirmation of Shiga toxin-production B96.21~~
Shiga toxin-producing (with unspecified O group) (STEC) B96.23
O157 B96.21
O157:H7 with or without confirmation of Shiga toxin-production B96.21
~~specified NEC B96.22~~
specified NEC B96.29
Esophagismus K22.4
⇒ **Esophagitis** (acute) (alkaline) (chemical) (chronic) (infectional) (necrotic) (peptic) (postoperative) (without bleeding) K20.90
▶ with bleeding K20.91
candidal B37.81
⇒ due to gastrointestinal reflux disease (without bleeding) K21.00
  ▶ with bleeding K21.01
eosinophilic K20.0
⇒ reflux K21.00
⇒ specified NEC (without bleeding) K20.80
  ▶ with bleeding K21.81
tuberculous A18.83
ulcerative K22.10
  with bleeding K22.11
Esophagocele K22.5
Esophagomalacia K22.8
Esophagospasm K22.4
Esophagostenosis K22.2
Esophagostomiasis B81.8
Esophagotracheal —see condition
Esophagus —see condition
Esophoria H50.51
convergence, excess H51.12
divergence, insufficiency H51.8
Esotropia —see Strabismus, convergent concomitant
Espundia B55.2
Essential —see condition
Esthesioneuroblastoma C30.0
Esthesioneurocytoma C30.0
Esthesioneuroepithelioma C30.0
Esthiomene A55
Estivo-autumnal malaria (fever) B50.9
Estrangement (marital) Z63.5
parent-child NEC Z62.890
Estriasis —see Myiasis
Ethanolism —see Alcoholism
Etherism —see Dependence, drug, inhalant
Ethmoid, ethmoidal —see condition

Ethmoiditis (chronic) (nonpurulent)
    (purulent) —*see also* Sinusitis, ethmoidal
influenzal —*see* Influenza, with, respiratory
    manifestations NEC
    Woakes' J33.1
Ethylism —*see* Alcoholism
Eulenburg's disease (congenital paramyotonia)
    G71.19
Eumycetoma B47.0
Eunuchoidism E29.1
    hypogonadotropic E23.0
European blastomycosis —*see* Cryptococcosis
Eustachian —*see* condition
Evaluation (for) (of)
    development state
        adolescent Z00.3
        period of
            delayed growth in childhood Z00.70
                with abnormal findings Z00.71
            rapid growth in childhood Z00.2
        puberty Z00.3
    growth and developmental state (period of
        rapid growth) Z00.2
        delayed growth Z00.70
            with abnormal findings Z00.71
    mental health (status) Z00.8
        requested by authority Z04.6
    period of
        delayed growth in childhood Z00.70
            with abnormal findings Z00.71
        rapid growth in childhood Z00.2
    suspected condition —*see* Observation
Evans syndrome D69.41
Event
    apparent life threatening in newborn and
        infant (ALTE) R68.13
    brief resolved unexplained event (BRUE)
        R68.13
Eventration —*see also* Hernia, ventral
    colon into chest —*see* Hernia, diaphragm
    diaphragm (congenital) Q79.1
Eversion
    bladder N32.89
    cervix (uteri) N86
        with cervicitis N72
    foot NEC —*see also* Deformity, valgus, ankle
        congenital Q66.6
    punctum lacrimale (postinfectional) (senile)
        H04.52-•
    ureter (meatus) N28.89
    urethra (meatus) N36.8
    uterus N81.4
Evidence
    cytologic
        of malignancy on anal smear R85.614
        of malignancy on cervical smear R87.614
        of malignancy on vaginal smear R87.624
Evisceration
    birth injury P15.8
    traumatic NEC
        eye —*see* Enucleated eye
Evulsion —*see* Avulsion
Ewing's sarcoma or tumor —*see* Neoplasm,
    bone, malignant
Examination (for) (following) (general) (of)
    (routine) Z00.00
    with abnormal findings Z00.01
    abuse, physical (alleged), ruled out
        adult Z04.71
        child Z04.72
    adolescent (development state) Z00.3
    alleged rape or sexual assault (victim), ruled
        out
        adult Z04.41
        child Z04.42
    allergy Z01.82
    annual (adult) (periodic) (physical) Z00.00
        with abnormal findings Z00.01
        gynecological Z01.419
            with abnormal findings Z01.411
    antibody response Z01.84

Examination (*Continued*)
    blood —*see* Examination, laboratory
    blood pressure Z01.30
        with abnormal findings Z01.31
    cancer staging —*see* Neoplasm, malignant,
        by site
    cervical Papanicolaou smear Z12.4
        as part of routine gynecological
            examination Z01.419
            with abnormal findings Z01.411
    child (over 28 days old) Z00.129
        with abnormal findings Z00.121
        under 28 days old —*see* Newborn,
            examination
    clinical research control or normal
        comparison (control) (participant)
        Z00.6
    contraceptive (drug) maintenance (routine)
        Z30.8
        device (intrauterine) Z30.431
    dental Z01.20
        with abnormal findings Z01.21
    developmental —*see* Examination, child
    donor (potential) Z00.5
    ear Z01.10
        with abnormal findings NEC Z01.118
    eye Z01.00
        with abnormal findings Z01.01
        following failed vision screening Z01.020
            with abnormal findings Z01.021
    following
        accident NEC Z04.3
            transport Z04.1
            work Z04.2
        assault, alleged, ruled out
            adult Z04.71
            child Z04.72
        motor vehicle accident Z04.1
        treatment (for) Z09
            combined NEC Z09
                fracture Z09
                    malignant neoplasm Z08
                malignant neoplasm Z08
                mental disorder Z09
            specified condition NEC Z09
    follow-up (routine) (following) Z09
        chemotherapy NEC Z09
            malignant neoplasm Z08
        fracture Z09
        malignant neoplasm Z08
        postpartum Z39.2
        psychotherapy Z09
        radiotherapy NEC Z09
            malignant neoplasm Z08
        surgery NEC Z09
            malignant neoplasm Z08
    forced sexual exploitation Z04.81
    forced labor exploitation Z04.82
    gynecological Z01.419
        with abnormal findings Z01.411
        for contraceptive maintenance Z30.8
    health —*see* Examination, medical
    hearing Z01.10
        with abnormal findings NEC Z01.118
        infant or child (over 28 days old) Z00.129
            with abnormal findings Z00.121
        following failed hearing screening
            Z01.110
    immunity status testing Z01.84
    laboratory (as part of a general medical
        examination) Z00.00
        with abnormal findings Z00.01
        preprocedural Z01.812
    lactating mother Z39.1
    medical (adult) (for) (of) Z00.00
        with abnormal findings Z00.01
        administrative purpose only Z02.9
            specified NEC Z02.89
        admission to
            armed forces Z02.3
            old age home Z02.2

Examination (*Continued*)
    medical (*Continued*)
        admission to (*Continued*)
            prison Z02.89
            residential institution Z02.2
            school Z02.0
                following illness or medical treatment
                    Z02.0
            summer camp Z02.89
        adoption Z02.82
        blood alcohol or drug level Z02.83
        camp (summer) Z02.89
        clinical research, normal subject (control)
            (participant) Z00.6
        control subject in clinical research (normal
            comparison) (participant) Z00.6
        donor (potential) Z00.5
        driving license Z02.4
        general (adult) Z00.00
            with abnormal findings Z00.01
        immigration Z02.89
        insurance purposes Z02.6
        marriage Z02.89
        medicolegal reasons NEC Z04.89
        naturalization Z02.89
        participation in sport Z02.5
        paternity testing Z02.81
        population survey Z00.8
        pre-employment Z02.1
        pre-operative —*see* Examination,
            pre-procedural
        pre-procedural
            cardiovascular Z01.810
            respiratory Z01.811
            specified NEC Z01.818
        preschool children
            for admission to school Z02.0
        prisoners
            for entrance into prison Z02.89
        recruitment for armed forces Z02.3
        specified NEC Z00.8
        sport competition Z02.5
    medicolegal reason NEC Z04.89
        forced sexual exploitation Z04.81
        forced labor exploitation Z04.82
    newborn —*see* Newborn, examination
    pelvic (annual) (periodic) Z01.419
        with abnormal findings Z01.411
    period of rapid growth in childhood Z00.2
    periodic (adult) (annual) (routine) Z00.00
        with abnormal findings Z00.01
    physical (adult) —*see also* Examination,
        medical Z00.00
        sports Z02.5
    postpartum
        immediately after delivery Z39.0
        routine follow-up Z39.2
    pre-chemotherapy (antineoplastic) Z01.818
    prenatal (normal pregnancy) —*see also*
        Pregnancy, normal Z34.9-•
    pre-procedural (pre-operative)
        cardiovascular Z01.810
        laboratory Z01.812
        respiratory Z01.811
        specified NEC Z01.818
    prior to chemotherapy (antineoplastic) Z01.818
    psychiatric NEC Z00.8
        follow-up not needing further care Z09
        requested by authority Z04.6
    radiological (as part of a general medical
        examination) Z00.00
        with abnormal findings Z00.01
    repeat cervical smear to confirm findings of
        recent normal smear following initial
        abnormal smear Z01.42
    skin (hypersensitivity) Z01.82
    special —*see also* Examination, by type Z01.89
        specified type NEC Z01.89
    specified type or reason NEC Z04.89
    teeth Z01.20
        with abnormal findings Z01.21

▶ New   ⟾ Revised   ~~deleted~~ Deleted   • Use Additional Character(s)

Examination *(Continued)*
  urine —*see* Examination, laboratory
  vision Z01.00
    with abnormal findings Z01.01
    following failed vision screening Z01.020
      with abnormal findings Z01.021
    infant or child (over 28 days old) Z00.129
      with abnormal findings Z00.121
Exanthem, exanthema —*see also* Rash
  with enteroviral vesicular stomatitis B08.4
  Boston A88.0
  epidemic with meningitis A88.0 *[G02]*
  subitum B08.20
    due to human herpesvirus 6 B08.21
    due to human herpesvirus 7 B08.22
  viral, virus B09
    specified type NEC B08.8
Excess, excessive, excessively
  alcohol level in blood R78.0
  androgen (ovarian) E28.1
  attrition, tooth, teeth K03.0
  carotene, carotin (dietary) E67.1
  cold, effects of T69.9
    specified effect NEC T69.8
  convergence H51.12
  crying
    in child, adolescent, or adult R45.83
    in infant R68.11
  development, breast N62
  divergence H51.8
  drinking (alcohol) NEC (without
      dependence) F10.10
    habitual (continual) (without remission)
      F10.20
  eating R63.2
  estrogen E28.0
  fat —*see also* Obesity
    in heart —*see* Degeneration, myocardial
    localized E65
  foreskin N47.8
  gas R14.0
  glucagon E16.3
  heat —*see* Heat
  intermaxillary vertical dimension of fully
      erupted teeth M26.37
  interocclusal distance of fully erupted teeth
      M26.37
  kalium E87.5
  large
    colon K59.39
      congenital Q43.8
    infant P08.0
    organ or site, congenital NEC —*see*
        Anomaly, by site
  long
    organ or site, congenital NEC —*see*
        Anomaly, by site
  menstruation (with regular cycle) N92.0
    with irregular cycle N92.1
  napping Z72.821
  natrium E87.0
  number of teeth K00.1
  nutrient (dietary) NEC R63.2
  potassium (K) E87.5
  salivation K11.7
  secretion —*see also* Hypersecretion
    milk O92.6
    sputum R09.3
    sweat R61
  sexual drive F52.8
  short
    organ or site, congenital NEC —*see*
        Anomaly, by site
    umbilical cord in labor or delivery O69.3
  skin L98.7
    and subcutaneous tissue L98.7
    eyelid (acquired) —*see* Blepharochalasis
      congenital Q10.3
  sodium (Na) E87.0
  spacing of fully erupted teeth M26.32
  sputum R09.3

Excess, excessive, excessively *(Continued)*
  sweating R61
  thirst R63.1
    due to deprivation of water T73.1
  tuberosity of jaw M26.07
  vitamin
    A (dietary) E67.0
      administered as drug (prolonged
          intake) —*see* Table of Drugs and
          Chemicals, vitamins, adverse
          effect
      overdose or wrong substance given
          or taken —*see* Table of Drugs and
          Chemicals, vitamins, poisoning
    D (dietary) E67.3
      administered as drug (prolonged
          intake) —*see* Table of Drugs and
          Chemicals, vitamins, adverse
          effect
      overdose or wrong substance given
          or taken —*see* Table of Drugs and
          Chemicals, vitamins, poisoning
  weight
    gain R63.5
    loss R63.4
Excitability, abnormal, under minor stress
    (personality disorder) F60.3
Excitation
  anomalous atrioventricular I45.6
  psychogenic F30.8
  reactive (from emotional stress, psychological
      trauma) F30.8
Excitement
  hypomanic F30.8
  manic F30.9
  mental, reactive (from emotional stress,
      psychological trauma) F30.8
  state, reactive (from emotional stress,
      psychological trauma) F30.8
Excoriation (traumatic) —*see also* Abrasion
  neurotic L98.1
  skin picking disorder F42.4
Exfoliation
  due to erythematous conditions according to
      extent of body surface involved L49.0
    10-19 percent of body surface L49.1
    20-29 percent of body surface L49.2
    30-39 percent of body surface L49.3
    40-49 percent of body surface L49.4
    50-59 percent of body surface L49.5
    60-69 percent of body surface L49.6
    70-79 percent of body surface L49.7
    80-89 percent of body surface L49.8
    90-99 percent of body surface L49.9
    less than 10 percent of body surface L49.0
  teeth, due to systemic causes K08.0
Exfoliative —*see* condition
Exhaustion, exhaustive (physical NEC) R53.83
  battle F43.0
  cardiac —*see* Failure, heart
  delirium F43.0
  due to
    cold T69.8
    excessive exertion T73.3
    exposure T73.2
    neurasthenia F48.8
  heart —*see* Failure, heart
  heat —*see also* Heat, exhaustion T67.5
    due to
      salt depletion T67.4
      water depletion T67.3
  maternal, complicating delivery O75.81
  mental F48.8
  myocardium, myocardial —*see* Failure, heart
  nervous F48.8
  old age R54
  psychogenic F48.8
  psychosis F43.0
  senile R54
  vital NEC Z73.0
Exhibitionism F65.2

Exocervicitis —*see* Cervicitis
Exomphalos Q79.2
  meaning hernia —*see* Hernia, umbilicus
Exophoria H50.52
  convergence, insufficiency H51.11
  divergence, excess H51.8
Exophthalmos H05.2-●
  congenital Q15.8
  constant NEC H05.24-●
  displacement, globe —*see* Displacement,
      globe
  due to thyrotoxicosis (hyperthyroidism) —*see*
      Hyperthyroidism, with, goiter (diffuse)
  dysthyroid —*see* Hyperthyroidism, with,
      goiter (diffuse)
  goiter —*see* Hyperthyroidism, with, goiter
      (diffuse)
  intermittent NEC H05.25-●
  malignant —*see* Hyperthyroidism, with,
      goiter (diffuse)
  orbital
    edema —*see* Edema, orbit
    hemorrhage —*see* Hemorrhage, orbit
  pulsating NEC H05.26-●
  thyrotoxic, thyrotropic —*see*
      Hyperthyroidism, with, goiter (diffuse)
Exostosis —*see also* Disorder, bone
  cartilaginous —*see* Neoplasm, bone, benign
  congenital (multiple) Q78.6
  external ear canal H61.81-●
  gonococcal A54.49
  jaw (bone) M27.8
  multiple, congenital Q78.6
  orbit H05.35-●
  osteocartilaginous —*see* Neoplasm, bone,
      benign
  syphilitic A52.77
Exotropia —*see* Strabismus, divergent
    concomitant
Explanation of
  investigation finding Z71.2
  medication Z71.89
Exposure (to) —*see also* Contact, with
    T75.89
  acariasis Z20.7
  AIDS virus Z20.6
  air pollution Z77.110
  algae and algae toxins Z77.121
  algae bloom Z77.121
  anthrax Z20.810
  aromatic amines Z77.020
  aromatic (hazardous) compounds NEC
      Z77.028
  aromatic dyes NOS Z77.028
  arsenic Z77.010
  asbestos Z77.090
  bacterial disease NEC Z20.818
  benzene Z77.021
  blue-green algae bloom Z77.121
  body fluids (potentially hazardous)
      Z77.21
  brown tide Z77.121
  chemicals (chiefly nonmedicinal) (hazardous)
      NEC Z77.098
  cholera Z20.09
  chromium compounds Z77.018
  cold, effects of T69.9
    specified effect NEC T69.8
  communicable disease Z20.9
    bacterial NEC Z20.818
    specified NEC Z20.89
    viral NEC Z20.828
    Zika virus Z20.821
  cyanobacteria bloom Z77.121
  disaster Z65.5
  discrimination Z60.5
  dyes Z77.098
  effects of T73.9
  environmental tobacco smoke (acute)
      (chronic) Z77.22
  Escherichia coli (E. coli) Z20.01

Exposure *(Continued)*
  exhaustion due to T73.2
  fiberglass —*see* Table of Drugs and
    Chemicals, fiberglass
  German measles Z20.4
  gonorrhea Z20.2
  hazardous metals NEC Z77.018
  hazardous substances NEC Z77.29
  hazards in the physical environment NEC
    Z77.128
  hazards to health NEC Z77.9
  human immunodeficiency virus (HIV)
    Z20.6
  human T-lymphotropic virus type-1 (HTLV-1)
    Z20.89
  implanted
    mesh —*see* Complications, prosthetic
      device or implant, mesh
    prosthetic materials NEC —*see*
      Complications, prosthetic materials
      NEC
  infestation (parasitic) NEC Z20.7
  intestinal infectious disease NEC Z20.09
    Escherichia coli (E. coli) Z20.01
  lead Z77.011
  meningococcus Z20.811
  mold (toxic) Z77.120
  nickel dust Z77.018
  noise Z77.122
  occupational
    air contaminants NEC Z57.39
    dust Z57.2
    environmental tobacco smoke Z57.31
    extreme temperature Z57.6
    noise Z57.0
    radiation Z57.1
    risk factors Z57.9
      specified NEC Z57.8
    toxic agents (gases) (liquids) (solids)
      (vapors) in agriculture Z57.4
    toxic agents (gases) (liquids) (solids)
      (vapors) in industry NEC Z57.5
    vibration Z57.7
  parasitic disease NEC Z20.7
  pediculosis Z20.7

Exposure *(Continued)*
  persecution Z60.5
  pfiesteria piscicida Z77.121
  poliomyelitis Z20.89
  pollution
    air Z77.110
    environmental NEC Z77.118
    soil Z77.112
    water Z77.111
  polycyclic aromatic hydrocarbons
    Z77.028
  prenatal (drugs) (toxic chemicals) —*see*
    Newborn, affected by, noxious
    substances transmitted via placenta or
    breast milk
  rabies Z20.3
  radiation, naturally occurring NEC
    Z77.123
  radon Z77.123
  red tide (Florida) Z77.121
  rubella Z20.4
  second hand tobacco smoke (acute) (chronic)
    Z77.22
    in the perinatal period P96.81
  sexually-transmitted disease Z20.2
  smallpox (laboratory) Z20.89
  syphilis Z20.2
  terrorism Z65.4
  torture Z65.4
  tuberculosis Z20.1
  uranium Z77.012
  varicella Z20.820
  venereal disease Z20.2
  viral disease NEC Z20.828
  war Z65.5
  water pollution Z77.111
  Zika virus Z20.821
Exsanguination —*see* Hemorrhage
Exstrophy
  abdominal contents Q45.8
  bladder Q64.10
    cloacal Q64.12
    specified type NEC Q64.19
    supravesical fissure Q64.11
Extensive —*see* condition

Extra —*see also* Accessory
  marker chromosomes (normal individual)
    Q92.61
    in abnormal individual Q92.62
  rib Q76.6
    cervical Q76.5
Extrasystoles (supraventricular) I49.49
  atrial I49.1
  auricular I49.1
  junctional I49.2
  ventricular I49.3
Extrauterine gestation or pregnancy —*see*
  Pregnancy, by site
Extravasation
  blood R58
  chyle into mesentery I89.8
  pelvicalyceal N13.8
  pyelosinus N13.8
  urine (from ureter) R39.0
  vesicant agent
    antineoplastic chemotherapy T80.810
    other agent NEC T80.818
Extremity —*see* condition, limb
Extrophy —*see* Exstrophy
Extroversion
  bladder Q64.19
  uterus N81.4
    complicating delivery O71.2
    postpartal (old) N81.4
Extruded tooth (teeth) M26.34
Extrusion
  breast implant (prosthetic) T85.42
  eye implant (globe) (ball) T85.328
  intervertebral disc —*see* Displacement,
    intervertebral disc
  ocular lens implant (prosthetic) —*see*
    Complications, intraocular lens
  vitreous —*see* Prolapse, vitreous
Exudate
  pleural —*see* Effusion, pleura
  retina H35.89
Exudative —*see* condition
Eye, eyeball, eyelid —*see* condition
Eyestrain —*see* Disturbance, vision, subjective
Eyeworm disease of Africa B74.3

▶ New   ⇒ Revised   ~~deleted~~ Deleted   ● Use Additional Character(s)

F

Faber's syndrome (achlorhydric anemia) D50.9
Fabry (-Anderson) disease E75.21
▶Facet syndrome M47.89-●
Faciocephalalgia, autonomic —see also
    Neuropathy, peripheral, autonomic G90.09
Factor(s)
  psychic, associated with diseases classified
      elsewhere F54
  psychological
    affecting physical conditions F54
    or behavioral
      affecting general medical condition F54
      associated with disorders or diseases
        classified elsewhere F54
Fahr disease (of brain) G23.8
Fahr Volhard disease (of kidney) I12.-●
Failure, failed
  abortion —see Abortion, attempted
  aortic (valve) I35.8
    rheumatic I06.8
  attempted abortion —see Abortion, attempted
  biventricular I50.82
    due to left heart failure I50.814
  bone marrow —see Anemia, aplastic
  cardiac —see Failure, heart
  cardiorenal (chronic) —see also Failure, renal,
    and Failure, heart I50.9
    hypertensive I13.2
  cardiorespiratory (see also Failure, heart)
    R09.2
  cardiovascular (chronic) —see Failure, heart
  cerebrovascular I67.9
  cervical dilatation in labor O62.0
  circulation, circulatory (peripheral) R57.9
    newborn P29.89
  compensation —see Disease, heart
  compliance with medical treatment or
    regimen —see Noncompliance
  congestive —see Failure, heart, congestive
  dental implant (endosseous) M27.69
    due to
      failure of dental prosthesis M27.63
      lack of attached gingiva M27.62
      occlusal trauma (poor prosthetic design)
        M27.62
      parafunctional habits M27.62
      periodontal infection (peri-implantitis)
        M27.62
      poor oral hygiene M27.62
    osseointegration M27.61
      due to
        complications of systemic disease
          M27.61
        poor bone quality M27.61
      iatrogenic M27.61
    post-osseointegration
      biological M27.62
      due to complications of systemic disease
        M27.62
      iatrogenic M27.62
      mechanical M27.63
    pre-integration M27.61
    pre-osseointegration M27.61
    specified NEC M27.69
  descent of head (at term) of pregnancy
    (mother) O32.4
  endosseous dental implant —see Failure,
    dental implant
  engagement of head (term of pregnancy)
    (mother) O32.4
  erection (penile) —see also Dysfunction,
    sexual, male, erectile N52.9
    nonorganic F52.21
  examination(s), anxiety concerning Z55.2
  expansion terminal respiratory units
    (newborn) (primary) P28.0
  forceps NOS (with subsequent cesarean
    delivery) O66.5

Failure, failed (Continued)
  gain weight (child over 28 days old) R62.51
    adult R62.7
    newborn P92.6
  genital response (male) F52.21
    female F52.22
  heart (acute) (senile) (sudden) I50.9
    with
      acute pulmonary edema —see Failure,
        ventricular, left
      decompensation —see also Failure, heart,
        by type as diastolic or systolic,
        acute and chronic I50.9
      dilatation —see Disease, heart
      hypertension —see Hypertension, heart
      normal ejection fraction —see Failure,
        heart, diastolic
      preserved ejection fraction —see Failure,
        heart, diastolic
      reduced ejection fraction —see Failure,
        heart, systolic
    arteriosclerotic I70.90
    biventricular I50.82
      due to left heart failure I50.814
    combined left-right sided I50.82
      due to left heart failure I50.814
    compensated —see also Failure, heart, by
      type as diastolic or systolic, chronic
      I50.9
    complicating
      anesthesia (general) (local) or other
        sedation
        in labor and delivery O74.2
        in pregnancy O29.12-●
        postpartum, puerperal O89.1
      delivery (cesarean) (instrumental) O75.4
    congestive I50.9
      with rheumatic fever (conditions in I00)
        active I01.8
        inactive or quiescent (with chorea)
          I09.81
      newborn P29.0
      rheumatic (chronic) (inactive) (with
        chorea) I09.81
        active or acute I01.8
          with chorea I02.0
    decompensated —see also Failure, heart, by
      type as diastolic or systolic, acute and
      chronic I50.9
    degenerative —see Degeneration,
      myocardial
    diastolic (congestive) (left ventricular)
      I50.30
      acute (congestive) I50.31
        and (on) chronic (congestive) I50.33
      chronic (congestive) I50.32
        and (on) acute (congestive) I50.33
      combined with systolic (congestive)
        I50.40
        acute (congestive) I50.41
          and (on) chronic (congestive) I50.43
        chronic (congestive) I50.42
          and (on) acute (congestive) I50.43
    due to presence of cardiac prosthesis I97.13-●
    end stage —see also Failure, heart, by type
      as diastolic or systolic, chronic I50.84
    following cardiac surgery I97.13-●
    high output NOS I50.83
    hypertensive —see Hypertension, heart
    left (ventricular) —see also Failure,
      ventricular, left
      combined diastolic and systolic —see
        Failure, heart, diastolic, combined
        with systolic
      diastolic —see Failure, heart, diastolic
      systolic —see Failure, heart, systolic
    low output (syndrome) NOS I50.9
    newborn P29.0
    organic —see Disease, heart
    peripartum O90.3

Failure, failed (Continued)
  heart (Continued)
    postprocedural I97.13-●
    rheumatic (chronic) (inactive) I09.9
    right (isolated) (ventricular) I50.810
      acute I50.811
        and (on) chronic I50.813
      chronic I50.812
        and acute I50.813
      secondary to left heart failure I50.814
    specified NEC I50.89

> Note: heart failure stages A, B, C, and
> D are based on the American College of
> Cardiology and American Heart Association
> stages of heart failure, which complement
> and should not be confused with the New
> York Heart Association Classification of
> Heart Failure, into Class I, Class II, Class III,
> and Class IV

    stage A Z91.89
    stage B (see also Failure, heart, by type as
      diastolic or systolic) I50.9
    stage C (see also Failure, heart, by type as
      diastolic or systolic) I50.9
    stage D (see also Failure, heart, by type as
      diastolic or systolic, chronic) I50.84
    systolic (congestive) (left ventricular)
      I50.20
      acute (congestive) I50.21
        and (on) chronic (congestive) I50.23
      chronic (congestive) I50.22
        and (on) acute (congestive) I50.23
      combined with diastolic (congestive)
        I50.40
        acute (congestive) I50.41
          and (on) chronic (congestive)
            I50.43
        chronic (congestive) I50.42
          and (on) acute (congestive) I50.43
    thyrotoxic (see also Thyrotoxicosis) E05.90
      [I43]
      with
        high output (see also Thyrotoxicosis)
          I50.83
        thyroid storm E05.91 [I43]
          high output (see also
            Thyrotoxicosis) I50.83
    valvular —see Endocarditis
  hepatic K72.90
    with coma K72.91
    acute or subacute K72.00
      with coma K72.01
      due to drugs K71.10
        with coma K71.11
    alcoholic (acute) (chronic) (subacute)
      K70.40
      with coma K70.41
    chronic K72.10
      with coma K72.11
      due to drugs (acute) (subacute) (chronic)
        K71.11
        with coma K71.11
    due to drugs (acute) (subacute) (chronic)
      K71.10
      with coma K71.11
    postprocedural K91.82
  hepatorenal K76.7
  induction (of labor) O61.9
    abortion —see Abortion, attempted
    by
      oxytocic drugs O61.0
      prostaglandins O61.0
    instrumental O61.1
    mechanical O61.1
    medical O61.0
    specified NEC O61.8
    surgical O61.1

Failure, failed *(Continued)*
 intubation during anesthesia T88.4
  in pregnancy O29.6-●
  labor and delivery O74.7
  postpartum, puerperal O89.6
 involution, thymus (gland) E32.0
 kidney —*see also* Disease, kidney, chronic N19
  acute —*see also* Failure, renal, acute
   N17.9-●
  diabetic —*see* E08-E13 with .22
 lactation (complete) O92.3
  partial O92.4
 Leydig's cell, adult E29.1
 liver —*see* Failure, hepatic
 menstruation at puberty N91.0
 mitral I05.8
 myocardial, myocardium —*see also* Failure,
   heart I50.9
  chronic —*see also* Failure, heart, congestive
   I50.9
  congestive —*see also* Failure, heart,
   congestive I50.9
 orgasm (female) (psychogenic) F52.31
  male F52.32
 ovarian (primary) E28.39
  iatrogenic E89.40
   asymptomatic E89.40
   symptomatic E89.41
  postprocedural (postablative)
    (postirradiation) (postsurgical) E89.40
   asymptomatic E89.40
   symptomatic E89.41
 ovulation causing infertility N97.0
 polyglandular, autoimmune E31.0
 prosthetic joint implant —*see* Complications,
   joint prosthesis, mechanical, breakdown,
   by site
 renal N19
  with
   tubular necrosis (acute) N17.0
  acute N17.9
   with
    cortical necrosis N17.1
    medullary necrosis N17.2
    tubular necrosis N17.0
   specified NEC N17.8
  chronic N18.9
   hypertensive —*see* Hypertension, kidney
  congenital P96.0
  end stage (chronic) N18.6
   due to hypertension I12.0
  following
   abortion —*see* Abortion by type
     complicated by specified
     condition NEC
   crushing T79.5
   ectopic or molar pregnancy O08.4
   labor and delivery (acute) O90.4
  hypertensive —*see* Hypertension, kidney
  postprocedural N99.0
 respiration, respiratory J96.9
  with
   hypercapnia J96.92
   hypercarbia J96.02
   hypoxia J96.91
  acute J96.00
   with
    hypercapnia J96.02
    hypercarbia J96.92
    hypoxia J96.01
  acute and (on) chronic J96.20
   with
    hypercapnia J96.22
    hypercarbia J96.22
    hypoxia J96.21
  center G93.89
  chronic J96.10
   with
    hypercapnia J96.12
    hypercarbia J96.12
    hypoxia J96.11

Failure, failed *(Continued)*
 respiration, respiratory *(Continued)*
  newborn P28.5
  postprocedural (acute) J95.821
   acute and chronic J95.822
 rotation
  cecum Q43.3
  colon Q43.3
  intestine Q43.3
  kidney Q63.2
 sedation (conscious) (moderate) during
   procedure T88.52
  history of Z92.83
 segmentation —*see also* Fusion
  fingers —*see* Syndactylism, complex,
   fingers
  vertebra Q76.49
   with scoliosis Q76.3
 seminiferous tubule, adult E29.1
 senile (general) R54
 sexual arousal (male) F52.21
  female F52.22
 testicular endocrine function E29.1
 to thrive (child over 28 days old) R62.51
  adult R62.7
  newborn P92.6
 transplant T86.92
  bone T86.831
   marrow T86.02
  ➡ cornea T86.841-●
  heart T86.22
   with lung(s) T86.32
  intestine T86.851
  kidney T86.12
  liver T86.42
  lung(s) T86.811
   with heart T86.32
  pancreas T86.891
  skin (allograft) (autograft) T86.821
  specified organ or tissue NEC T86.891
  stem cell (peripheral blood) (umbilical
   cord) T86.5
 trial of labor (with subsequent cesarean
   delivery) O66.40
  following previous cesarean delivery
   O66.41
 tubal ligation N99.89
 urinary —*see* Disease, kidney, chronic
 vacuum extraction NOS (with subsequent
   cesarean delivery) O66.5
 vasectomy N99.89
 ventouse NOS (with subsequent cesarean
   delivery) O66.5
 ventricular —*see also* Failure, heart I50.9
  left —*see also* Failure, heart, left I50.1
   with rheumatic fever (conditions
    in I00)
    active I01.8
     with chorea I02.0
    inactive or quiescent (with chorea)
     I09.81
   rheumatic (chronic) (inactive) (with
    chorea) I09.81
    active or acute I01.8
     with chorea I02.0
  right —*see* Failure, heart, right
 vital centers, newborn P91.88
Fainting (fit) R55
Fallen arches —*see* Deformity, limb, flat foot
Falling, falls (repeated) R29.6
 any organ or part —*see* Prolapse
Fallopian
 insufflation Z31.41
 tube —*see* condition
Fallot's
 pentalogy Q21.8
 tetrad or tetralogy Q21.3
 triad or trilogy Q22.3
False —*see also* condition
 croup J38.5
 joint —*see* Nonunion, fracture

False *(Continued)*
 labor (pains) O47.9
  at or after 37 completed weeks of gestation
   O47.1
  before 37 completed weeks of gestation
   O47.0-●
 passage, urethra (prostatic) N36.5
 pregnancy F45.8
Family, familial —*see also* condition
 disruption Z63.8
  involving divorce or separation
   Z63.5
 Li-Fraumeni (syndrome) Z15.01
 planning advice Z30.09
 problem Z63.9
  specified NEC Z63.8
 retinoblastoma C69.2-●
Famine (effects of) T73.0
 edema —*see* Malnutrition, severe
Fanconi (-de Toni)(-Debré) syndrome
  E72.09
 with cystinosis E72.04
Fanconi's anemia (congenital pancytopenia)
  D61.09
Farber's disease or syndrome E75.29
Farcy A24.0
Farmer's
 lung J67.0
 skin L57.8
Farsightedness —*see* Hypermetropia
Fascia —*see* condition
Fasciculation R25.3
Fasciitis M72.9
 diffuse (eosinophilic) M35.4
 infective M72.8
  necrotizing M72.6
 necrotizing M72.6
 nodular M72.4
 perirenal (with ureteral obstruction)
   N13.5
  with infection N13.6
 plantar M72.2
 specified NEC M72.8
 traumatic (old) M72.8
  current - code by site under Sprain
Fascioliasis B66.3
Fasciolopsis, fasciolopsiasis (intestinal)
  B66.5
Fascioscapulohumeral myopathy G71.02
Fast pulse R00.0
Fat
 embolism —*see* Embolism, fat
 excessive —*see also* Obesity
  in heart —*see* Degeneration, myocardial
 in stool R19.5
 localized (pad) E65
  heart —*see* Degeneration, myocardial
  knee M79.4
  retropatellar M79.4
 necrosis
  breast N64.1
  mesentery K65.4
  omentum K65.4
 pad E65
  knee M79.4
Fatigue R53.83
 auditory deafness —*see* Deafness
 chronic R53.82
 combat F43.0
 general R53.83
  psychogenic F48.8
 heat (transient) T67.6
 muscle M62.89
 myocardium —*see* Failure, heart
 neoplasm-related R53.0
 nervous, neurosis F48.8
 operational F48.8
 psychogenic (general) F48.8
 senile R54
 voice R49.8
Fatness —*see* Obesity

▶ New   ⇨ Revised   ~~deleted~~ Deleted   ● Use Additional Character(s)

Fatty —*see also* condition
  apron E65
  degeneration —*see* Degeneration, fatty
  heart (enlarged) —*see* Degeneration,
    myocardial
  liver NEC K76.0
    alcoholic K70.0
    nonalcoholic K76.0
  necrosis —*see* Degeneration, fatty
Fauces —*see* condition
Fauchard's disease (periodontitis) —*see*
    Periodontitis
Faucitis J02.9
Favism (anemia) D55.0
Favus —*see* Dermatophytosis
Fazio-Londe disease or syndrome
    G12.1
Fear complex or reaction F40.9
Fear of —*see* Phobia
Feared complaint unfounded Z71.1
Febris, febrile —*see also* Fever
  flava —*see also* Fever, yellow A95.9
  melitensis A23.0
  pestis —*see* Plague
  recurrens —*see* Fever, relapsing
  rubra A38.9
Fecal
  incontinence R15.9
  smearing R15.1
  soiling R15.1
  urgency R15.2
Fecalith (impaction) K56.41
  appendix K38.1
  congenital P76.8
Fede's disease K14.0
Feeble rapid pulse due to shock following
    injury T79.4
Feeble-minded F70
Feeding
  difficulties R63.3
  problem R63.3
    newborn P92.9
      specified NEC P92.8
    nonorganic (adult) —*see* Disorder,
      eating
Feeling (of)
  foreign body in throat R09.89
Feer's disease —*see* Poisoning, mercury
Feet —*see* condition
Feigned illness Z76.5
Feil-Klippel syndrome (brevicollis) Q76.1
Feinmesser's (hidrotic) ectodermal dysplasia
    Q82.4
Felinophobia F40.218
Felon —*see also* Cellulitis, digit
  with lymphangitis —*see* Lymphangitis,
    acute, digit
Felty's syndrome M05.00
  ankle M05.07-●
  elbow M05.02-●
  foot joint M05.07-●
  hand joint M05.04-●
  hip M05.05-●
  knee M05.06-●
  multiple site M05.09
  shoulder M05.01-●
  vertebra —*see* Spondylitis, ankylosing
  wrist M05.03-●
Female genital cutting status —*see* Female
    genital mutilation status (FGM)
Female genital mutilation status (FGM)
    N90.810
  specified NEC N90.818
  type I (clitorectomy status) N90.811
  type II (clitorectomy with excision
    of labia minora status)
    N90.812
  type III (infibulation status)
    N90.813
  type IV N90.818
Femur, femoral —*see* condition

Fenestration, fenestrated —*see also* Imperfect,
    closure
  aortico-pulmonary Q21.4
  cusps, heart valve NEC Q24.8
    pulmonary Q22.3
  pulmonic cusps Q22.3
Fernell's disease (aortic aneurysm) I71.9
Fertile eunuch syndrome E23.0
Fetid
  breath R19.6
  sweat L75.0
Fetishism F65.0
  transvestic F65.1
Fetus, fetal —*see also* condition
  alcohol syndrome (dysmorphic) Q86.0
  compressus O31.0-●
  hydantoin syndrome Q86.1
  lung tissue P28.0
  papyraceous O31.0-●
Fever (inanition) (of unknown origin)
    (persistent) (with chills) (with rigor) R50.9
  abortus A23.1
  Aden (dengue) A90
  ▶African tick bite A77.8
  African tick-borne A68.1
  American
    mountain (tick) A93.2
    spotted A77.0
  aphthous B08.8
  arbovirus, arboviral A94
    hemorrhagic A94
    specified NEC A93.8
  Argentinian hemorrhagic A96.0
  Assam B55.0
  Australian Q A78
  Bangkok hemorrhagic A91
  Barmah forest A92.8
  Bartonella A44.0
  bilious, hemoglobinuric B50.8
  blackwater B50.8
  blister B00.1
  Bolivian hemorrhagic A96.1
  Bonvale dam T73.3
  boutonneuse A77.1
  brain —*see* Encephalitis
  Brazilian purpuric A48.4
  breakbone A90
  Bullis A77.0
  Bunyamwera A92.8
  Burdwan B55.0
  Bwamba A92.8
  Cameroon —*see* Malaria
  Canton A75.9
  catarrhal (acute) J00
    chronic J31.0
  cat-scratch A28.1
  Central Asian hemorrhagic A98.0
  cerebral —*see* Encephalitis
  cerebrospinal meningococcal A39.0
  Chagres B50.9
  Chandipura A92.8
  Changuinola A93.1
  Charcot's (biliary) (hepatic) (intermittent) —
    see Calculus, bile duct
  Chikungunya (viral) (hemorrhagic) A92.0
  Chitral A93.1
  Colombo —*see* Fever, paratyphoid
  Colorado tick (virus) A93.2
  congestive (remittent) —*see* Malaria
  Congo virus A98.0
  continued malarial B50.9
  Corsican —*see* Malaria
  Crimean-Congo hemorrhagic A98.0
  Cyprus —*see* Brucellosis
  dandy A90
  deer fly —*see* Tularemia
  dengue (virus) A90
    hemorrhagic A91
    sandfly A93.1
  desert B38.0
  drug induced R50.2

Fever *(Continued)*
  due to
    conditions classified elsewhere R50.81
    heat T67.01
  enteric A01.00
  enteroviral exanthematous (Boston
    exanthem) A88.0
  ephemeral (of unknown origin) R50.9
  epidemic hemorrhagic A98.5
  erysipelatous —*see* Erysipelas
  estivo-autumnal (malarial) B50.9
  famine A75.0
  five day A79.0
  following delivery O86.4
  Fort Bragg A27.89
  gastroenteric A01.00
  gastromalarial —*see* Malaria
  Gibraltar —*see* Brucellosis
  glandular —*see* Mononucleosis, infectious
  Guama (viral) A92.8
  Haverhill A25.1
  hay (allergic) J30.1
    with asthma (bronchial) J45.909
      with
        exacerbation (acute) J45.901
        status asthmaticus J45.902
      due to
        allergen other than pollen J30.89
        pollen, any plant or tree J30.1
  heat (effects) T67.01
  hematuric, bilious B50.8
  hemoglobinuric (malarial) (bilious) B50.8
  hemorrhagic (arthropod-borne) NOS A94
    with renal syndrome A98.5
    arenaviral A96.9
      specified NEC A96.8
    Argentinian A96.0
    Bangkok A91
    Bolivian A96.1
    Central Asian A98.0
    Chikungunya A92.0
    Crimean-Congo A98.0
    dengue (virus) A91
    epidemic A98.5
    Junin (virus) A96.0
    Korean A98.5
    Kyasanur forest A98.2
    Machupo (virus) A96.1
    mite-borne A93.8
    mosquito-borne A92.8
    Omsk A98.1
    Philippine A91
    Russian A98.5
    Singapore A91
    Southeast Asia A91
    Thailand A91
    tick-borne NEC A93.8
    viral A99
      specified NEC A98.8
  hepatic —*see* Cholecystitis
  herpetic —*see* Herpes
  icterohemorrhagic A27.0
  Indiana A93.8
  infective B99.9
    specified NEC B99.8
  intermittent (bilious) —*see also* Malaria
    of unknown origin R50.9
    pernicious B50.9
  iodide R50.2
  Japanese river A75.3
  jungle —*see also* Malaria
    yellow A95.0
  Junin (virus) hemorrhagic A96.0
  Katayama B65.2
  kedani A75.3
  Kenya (tick) A77.1
  Kew Garden A79.1
  Korean hemorrhagic A98.5
  Lassa A96.2
  Lone Star A77.0
  Machupo (virus) hemorrhagic A96.1

Fever (Continued)
  malaria, malarial —see Malaria
  Malta A23.9
  Marseilles A77.1
  marsh —see Malaria
  Mayaro (viral) A92.8
  Mediterranean —see also Brucellosis A23.9
    familial M04.1
    tick A77.1
  meningeal —see Meningitis
  Meuse A79.0
  Mexican A75.2
  mianeh A68.1
  miasmatic —see Malaria
  mosquito-borne (viral) A92.9
    hemorrhagic A92.8
  mountain —see also Brucellosis
    meaning Rocky Mountain spotted fever
      A77.0
    tick (American) (Colorado) (viral) A93.2
  Mucambo (viral) A92.8
  mud A27.9
  Neapolitan —see Brucellosis
  neutropenic D70.9
  newborn P81.9
    environmental P81.0
  Nine-Mile A78
  non-exanthematous tick A93.2
  North Asian tick-borne A77.2
  Omsk hemorrhagic A98.1
  O'nyong-nyong (viral) A92.1
  Oropouche (viral) A93.0
  Oroya A44.0
▶ pacific coast tick A77.8
  paludal —see Malaria
  Panama (malarial) B50.9
  Pappataci A93.1
  paratyphoid A01.4
    A A01.1
    B A01.2
    C A01.3
  parrot A70
  periodic (Mediterranean) M04.1
  persistent (of unknown origin) R50.9
  petechial A39.0
  pharyngoconjunctival B30.2
  Philippine hemorrhagic A91
  phlebotomus A93.1
  Piry (virus) A93.8
  Pixuna (viral) A92.8
  Plasmodium ovale B53.0
  polioviral (nonparalytic) A80.4
  Pontiac A48.2
  postimmunization R50.83
  postoperative R50.82
    due to infection T81.40
  posttransfusion R50.84
  postvaccination R50.83
  presenting with conditions classified
      elsewhere R50.81
  pretibial A27.89
  puerperal O86.4
  Q A78
  quadrilateral A78
  quartan (malaria) B52.9
  Queensland (coastal) (tick) A77.3
  quintan A79.0
  rabbit —see Tularemia
  rat-bite A25.9
    due to
      Spirillum A25.0
      Streptobacillus moniliformis A25.1
  recurrent —see Fever, relapsing
  relapsing (Borrelia) A68.9
    Carter's (Asiatic) A68.1
    Dutton's (West African) A68.1
    Koch's A68.9
    louse-borne A68.0
    Novy's
      louse-borne A68.0
      tick-borne A68.1

Fever (Continued)
  relapsing (Borrelia) (Continued)
    Obermeyer's (European) A68.0
    tick-borne A68.1
  remittent (bilious) (congestive) (gastric) —see
      Malaria
  rheumatic (active) (acute) (chronic) (subacute)
      I00
    with central nervous system involvement
      I02.9
    active with heart involvement —see
      category I01
    inactive or quiescent with
      cardiac hypertrophy I09.89
      carditis I09.9
      endocarditis I09.1
        aortic (valve) I06.9
          with mitral (valve) disease I08.0
        mitral (valve) I05.9
          with aortic (valve) disease I08.0
        pulmonary (valve) I09.89
        tricuspid (valve) I07.8
      heart disease NEC I09.89
      heart failure (congestive) (conditions in
        category I50.) I09.81
    ⟹left ventricular failure (conditions in
        I50.1-I50.4-) I09.81
      myocarditis, myocardial degeneration
        (conditions in I51.4) I09.0
      pancarditis I09.9
      pericarditis I09.2
  Rift Valley (viral) A92.4
  Rocky Mountain spotted A77.0
  rose J30.1
  Ross River B33.1
  Russian hemorrhagic A98.5
  San Joaquin (Valley) B38.0
  sandfly A93.1
  Sao Paulo A77.0
  scarlet A38.9
  seven day (leptospirosis) (autumnal)
      (Japanese) A27.89
    dengue A90
  shin-bone A79.0
  Singapore hemorrhagic A91
  solar A90
  Songo A98.5
  sore B00.1
  South African tick-bite A68.1
  Southeast Asia hemorrhagic A91
  spinal —see Meningitis
  spirillary A25.0
  splenic —see Anthrax
  spotted A77.9
    American A77.0
    Brazilian A77.0
    cerebrospinal meningitis A39.0
    Colombian A77.0
    due to Rickettsia
    ▶africae (African tick bite fever) A77.8
      australis A77.3
      conorii A77.1
    ▶parkeri A77.8
      rickettsii A77.0
      sibirica A77.2
      specified type NEC A77.8
    Ehrlichiosis A77.40
      due to
        E. chafeensis A77.41
        specified organism NEC A77.49
    Rocky Mountain A77.0
  steroid R50.2
  streptobacillary A25.1
  subtertian B50.9
  Sumatran mite A75.3
  sun A90
  swamp A27.9
  swine A02.8
  sylvatic, yellow A95.0
  Tahyna B33.8
  tertian —see Malaria, tertian

Fever (Continued)
  Thailand hemorrhagic A91
  thermic T67.01
  three-day A93.1
  tick
    American mountain A93.2
    Colorado A93.2
    Kemerovo A93.8
    Mediterranean A77.1
    mountain A93.2
    nonexanthematous A93.2
    Quaranfil A93.8
  tick-bite NEC A93.8
  tick-borne (hemorrhagic) NEC A93.8
  trench A79.0
  tsutsugamushi A75.3
  typhogastric A01.00
  typhoid (abortive) (hemorrhagic)
      (intermittent) (malignant) A01.00
    complicated by
      arthritis A01.04
      heart involvement A01.02
      meningitis A01.01
      osteomyelitis A01.05
      pneumonia A01.03
      specified NEC A01.09
  typhomalarial —see Malaria
  typhus —see Typhus (fever)
  undulant —see Brucellosis
  unknown origin R50.9
  uveoparotid D86.89
  valley B38.0
  Venezuelan equine A92.2
  vesicular stomatitis A93.8
  viral hemorrhagic —see Fever, hemorrhagic,
      by type of virus
  Volhynian A79.0
  Wesselsbron (viral) A92.8
  West
    African B50.8
    Nile (viral) A92.30
      with
        complications NEC A92.39
        cranial nerve disorders A92.32
        encephalitis A92.31
        encephalomyelitis A92.31
        neurologic manifestation NEC
          A92.32
        optic neuritis A92.32
        polyradiculitis A92.32
  Whitmore's —see Melioidosis
  Wolhynian A79.0
  worm B83.9
  yellow A95.9
    jungle A95.0
    sylvatic A95.0
    urban A95.1
  Zika virus A92.5
Fibrillation
  atrial or auricular (established) I48.91
    chronic I48.20
      persistent I48.19
    paroxysmal I48.0
    permanent I48.21
    persistent (chronic) (NOS) (other) I48.19
      longstanding I48.11
  cardiac I49.8
  heart I49.8
  muscular M62.89
  ventricular I49.01
Fibrin
  ball or bodies, pleural (sac) J94.1
  chamber, anterior (eye) (gelatinous
      exudate) —see Iridocyclitis, acute
Fibrinogenolysis —see Fibrinolysis
Fibrinogenopenia D68.8
  acquired D65
  congenital D68.2
Fibrinolysis (hemorrhagic) (acquired) D65
  antepartum hemorrhage —see Hemorrhage,
      antepartum, with coagulation defect

Fibrinolysis *(Continued)*
  following
    abortion —*see* Abortion by type
      complicated by hemorrhage
    ectopic or molar pregnancy O08.1
  intrapartum O67.0
  newborn, transient P60
  postpartum O72.3
Fibrinopenia (hereditary) D68.2
  acquired D68.4
Fibrinopurulent —*see* condition
Fibrinous —*see* condition
Fibroadenoma
  cellular intracanalicular D24-●
  giant D24-●
  intracanalicular
    cellular D24-●
    giant D24-●
    specified site —*see* Neoplasm, benign, by
      site
    unspecified site D24-●
  juvenile D24-●
  pericanalicular
    specified site —*see* Neoplasm, benign, by
      site
    unspecified site D24-●
  phyllodes D24-●
  prostate D29.1
  specified site NEC —*see* Neoplasm, benign,
    by site
  unspecified site D24-●
Fibroadenosis, breast (chronic) (cystic) (diffuse)
  (periodic) (segmental) N60.2-●
Fibroangioma —*see also* Neoplasm, benign, by
  site
  juvenile
    specified site —*see* Neoplasm, benign, by
      site
    unspecified site D10.6
Fibrochondrosarcoma —*see* Neoplasm,
  cartilage, malignant
Fibrocystic
  disease —*see also* Fibrosis, cystic
    breast —*see* Mastopathy, cystic
    jaw M27.49
    kidney (congenital) Q61.8
    liver Q44.6
    pancreas E84.9
  kidney (congenital) Q61.8
Fibrodysplasia ossificans progressiva —*see*
  Myositis, ossificans, progressiva
Fibroelastosis (cordis) (endocardial)
  (endomyocardial) I42.4
Fibroid (tumor) —*see also* Neoplasm, connective
  tissue, benign
  disease, lung (chronic) —*see* Fibrosis, lung
  heart (disease) —*see* Myocarditis
  in pregnancy or childbirth O34.1-●
    causing obstructed labor O65.5
  induration, lung (chronic) —*see* Fibrosis, lung
  lung —*see* Fibrosis, lung
  pneumonia (chronic) —*see* Fibrosis, lung
  uterus —*see also* Leiomyoma, uterus D25.9
Fibrolipoma —*see* Lipoma
Fibroliposarcoma —*see* Neoplasm, connective
  tissue, malignant
Fibroma —*see also* Neoplasm, connective tissue,
  benign
  ameloblastic —*see* Cyst, calcifying odontogenic
  bone (nonossifying) —*see* Disorder, bone,
    specified type NEC
    ossifying —*see* Neoplasm, bone, benign
  cementifying —*see* Neoplasm, bone, benign
  chondromyxoid —*see* Neoplasm, bone,
    benign
  desmoplastic —*see* Neoplasm, connective
    tissue, uncertain behavior
  durum —*see* Neoplasm, connective tissue,
    benign
  fascial —*see* Neoplasm, connective tissue,
    benign

Fibroma *(Continued)*
  invasive —*see* Neoplasm, connective tissue,
    uncertain behavior
  molle —*see* Lipoma
  myxoid —*see* Neoplasm, connective tissue,
    benign
  nasopharynx, nasopharyngeal (juvenile)
    D10.6
  nonosteogenic (nonossifying) —*see* Dysplasia,
    fibrous
  odontogenic (central) —*see* Cyst, calcifying
    odontogenic
  ossifying —*see* Neoplasm, bone, benign
  periosteal —*see* Neoplasm, bone, benign
  soft —*see* Lipoma
Fibromatosis M72.9
  abdominal —*see* Neoplasm, connective tissue,
    uncertain behavior
  aggressive —*see* Neoplasm, connective tissue,
    uncertain behavior
  congenital generalized —*see* Neoplasm,
    connective tissue, juvenile, uncertain behavior
  Dupuytren's M72.0
  gingival K06.1
  palmar (fascial) M72.0
  plantar (fascial) M72.2
  pseudosarcomatous (proliferative)
    (subcutaneous) M72.4
  retroperitoneal D48.3
  specified NEC M72.8
Fibromyalgia M79.7
Fibromyoma —*see also* Neoplasm, connective
  tissue, benign
  uterus (corpus) —*see also* Leiomyoma, uterus
    in pregnancy or childbirth —*see* Fibroid, in
      pregnancy or childbirth
    causing obstructed labor O65.5
Fibromyositis M79.7
Fibromyxolipoma D17.9
Fibromyxoma —*see* Neoplasm, connective
  tissue, benign
Fibromyxosarcoma —*see* Neoplasm, connective
  tissue, malignant
Fibro-odontoma, ameloblastic —*see* Cyst,
  calcifying odontogenic
Fibro-osteoma —*see* Neoplasm, bone, benign
Fibroplasia, retrolental H35.17
Fibropurulent —*see* condition
Fibrosarcoma —*see also* Neoplasm, connective
  tissue, malignant
  ameloblastic C41.1
    upper jaw (bone) C41.0
  congenital —*see* Neoplasm, connective tissue,
    malignant
  fascial —*see* Neoplasm, connective tissue,
    malignant
  infantile —*see* Neoplasm, connective tissue,
    malignant
  odontogenic C41.1
    upper jaw (bone) C41.0
  periosteal —*see* Neoplasm, bone, malignant
Fibrosclerosis
  breast N60.3-●
  multifocal M35.5
  penis (corpora cavernosa) N48.6
Fibrosis, fibrotic
  adrenal (gland) E27.8
  amnion O41.8X-●
  anal papillae K62.89
  arteriocapillary —*see* Arteriosclerosis
  bladder N32.89
    interstitial —*see* Cystitis, chronic,
      interstitial
    localized submucosal —*see* Cystitis,
      chronic, interstitial
    panmural —*see* Cystitis, chronic, interstitial
  breast —*see* Fibrosclerosis, breast
  capillary —*see also* Arteriosclerosis I70.90
    lung (chronic) —*see* Fibrosis, lung
  cardiac —*see* Myocarditis
  cervix N88.8

Fibrosis, fibrotic *(Continued)*
  chorion O41.8X-●
  corpus cavernosum (sclerosing) N48.6
  cystic (of pancreas) E84.9
    with
      distal intestinal obstruction syndrome
        E84.19
      fecal impaction E84.19
      intestinal manifestations NEC E84.19
      pulmonary manifestations E84.0
      specified manifestations NEC E84.8
  due to device, implant or graft —*see also*
    Complications, by site and type,
    specified NEC T85.828
    arterial graft NEC T82.828
    breast (implant) T85.828
    catheter NEC T85.828
      dialysis (renal) T82.828
        intraperitoneal T85.828
      infusion NEC T82.828
        spinal (epidural) (subdural)
          T85.820
      urinary (indwelling) T83.82
    electronic (electrode) (pulse generator)
      (stimulator)
      bone T84.82
      cardiac T82.827
      nervous system (brain) (peripheral
        nerve) (spinal) T85.820
      urinary T83.82
    fixation, internal (orthopedic) NEC T84.82
    gastrointestinal (bile duct) (esophagus)
      T85.828
    genital NEC T83.82
    heart NEC T82.827
    joint prosthesis T84.82
    ocular (corneal graft) (orbital implant)
      NEC T85.828
    orthopedic NEC T84.82
    specified NEC T85.828
    urinary NEC T83.82
    vascular NEC T82.828
    ventricular intracranial shunt T85.820
  ejaculatory duct N50.89
  endocardium —*see* Endocarditis
  endomyocardial (tropical) I42.3
  epididymis N50.89
  eye muscle —*see* Strabismus, mechanical
  heart —*see* Myocarditis
  hepatic —*see* Fibrosis, liver
  hepatolienal (portal hypertension) K76.6
  hepatosplenic (portal hypertension) K76.6
  infrapatellar fat pad M79.4
  intrascrotal N50.89
  kidney N26.9
  ➡ liver K74.00
    with sclerosis K74.2
    ▶ advanced K74.02
    alcoholic K70.2
    ▶ early K74.01
    ▶ stage
      ▶ F1 or F2 K74.01
      ▶ F3 K74.02
  lung (atrophic) (chronic) (confluent)
    (massive) (perialveolar) (peribronchial)
    J84.10
    with
      anthracosilicosis J60
      anthracosis J60
      asbestosis J61
      bagassosis J67.1
      bauxite J63.1
      berylliosis J63.2
      byssinosis J66.0
      calcicosis J62.8
      chalicosis J62.8
      dust reticulation J64
      farmer's lung J67.0
      ganister disease J62.8
      graphite J63.3
      pneumoconiosis NOS J64

Fibrosis, fibrotic *(Continued)*
  lung *(Continued)*
    with *(Continued)*
      siderosis J63.4
      silicosis J62.8
    capillary J84.10
    congenital P27.8
    diffuse (idiopathic) J84.10
      chemicals, gases, fumes or vapors
          (inhalation) J68.4
      interstitial J84.10
        acute J84.114
      talc J62.0
    following radiation J70.1
    idiopathic J84.112
    postinflammatory J84.10
    silicotic J62.8
    tuberculous —*see* Tuberculosis, pulmonary
  lymphatic gland I89.8
  median bar —*see* Hyperplasia, prostate
  mediastinum (idiopathic) J98.59
  meninges G96.198
  myocardium, myocardial —*see* Myocarditis
  ovary N83.8
  oviduct N83.8
  pancreas K86.89
  penis NEC N48.6
  pericardium I31.0
  perineum, in pregnancy or childbirth O34.7-•
    causing obstructed labor O65.5
  pleura J94.1
  popliteal fat pad M79.4
  prostate (chronic) —*see* Hyperplasia, prostate
  pulmonary —*see also* Fibrosis, lung J84.10
    congenital P27.8
    idiopathic J84.112
  rectal sphincter K62.89
  retroperitoneal, idiopathic (with ureteral
      obstruction) N13.5
    with infection N13.6
  sclerosing mesenteric (idiopathic) K65.4
  scrotum N50.89
  seminal vesicle N50.89
  senile R54
  skin L90.5
  spermatic cord N50.89
  spleen D73.89
    in schistosomiasis (bilharziasis) B65.9 [D77]
  subepidermal nodular —*see* Neoplasm, skin,
      benign
  submucous (oral) (tongue) K13.5
  testis N44.8
    chronic, due to syphilis A52.76
  thymus (gland) E32.8
  tongue, submucous K13.5
  tunica vaginalis N50.89
  uterus (non-neoplastic) N85.8
  vagina N89.8
  valve, heart —*see* Endocarditis
  vas deferens N50.89
  vein I87.8
Fibrositis (periarticular) M79.7
  nodular, chronic (Jaccoud's) (rheumatoid) —
      see Arthropathy, postrheumatic, chronic
Fibrothorax J94.1
Fibrotic —*see* Fibrosis
Fibrous —*see* condition
Fibroxanthoma —*see also* Neoplasm, connective
    tissue, benign
  atypical —*see* Neoplasm, connective tissue,
      uncertain behavior
  malignant —*see* Neoplasm, connective tissue,
      malignant
Fibroxanthosarcoma —*see* Neoplasm,
    connective tissue, malignant
Fiedler's
  disease (icterohemorrhagic leptospirosis) A27.0
  myocarditis (acute) I40.1
Fifth disease B08.3
  venereal A55
Filaria, filarial, filariasis —*see* Infestation, filarial

Filatov's disease —*see* Mononucleosis,
    infectious
File-cutter's disease —*see* Poisoning, lead
Filling defect
  biliary tract R93.2
  bladder R93.41
  duodenum R93.3
  gallbladder R93.2
  gastrointestinal tract R93.3
  intestine R93.3
  kidney R93.42-•
  stomach R93.3
  ureter R93.41
  urinary organs, specified NEC R93.49
Fimbrial cyst Q50.4
Financial problem affecting care NOS Z59.9
  bankruptcy Z59.8
  foreclosure on loan Z59.8
**Findings, abnormal, inconclusive, without
    diagnosis** —*see also* Abnormal
  17-ketosteroids, elevated R82.5
  acetonuria R82.4
  alcohol in blood R78.0
  anisocytosis R71.8
  antenatal screening of mother O28.9
    biochemical O28.1
    chromosomal O28.5
    cytological O28.2
    genetic O28.5
    hematological O28.0
    radiological O28.4
    specified NEC O28.8
    ultrasonic O28.3
  antibody titer, elevated R76.0
  anticardiolipin antibody R76.0
  antiphosphatidylglycerol antibody R76.0
  antiphosphatidylinositol antibody R76.0
  antiphosphatidylserine antibody R76.0
  antiphospholipid antibody R76.0
  bacteriuria R82.71
  bicarbonate E87.8
  bile in urine R82.2
  blood sugar R73.09
    high R73.9
    low (transient) E16.2
  body fluid or substance, specified NEC R88.8
  casts, urine R82.998
  catecholamines R82.5
  cells, urine R82.998
  chloride E87.8
  cholesterol E78.9
    high E78.00
      with high triglycerides E78.2
  chyluria R82.0
  cloudy
    dialysis effluent R88.0
    urine R82.90
  creatinine clearance R94.4
  crystals, urine R82.998
  culture
    blood R78.81
    positive —*see* Positive, culture
  echocardiogram R93.1
  electrolyte level, urinary R82.998
  function study NEC R94.8
    bladder R94.8
    endocrine NEC R94.7
      thyroid R94.6
    kidney R94.4
    liver R94.5
    pancreas R94.8
    placenta R94.8
    pulmonary R94.2
    spleen R94.8
  gallbladder, nonvisualization R93.2
  glucose (tolerance test) (non-fasting) R73.09
  glycosuria R81
  heart
    shadow R93.1
    sounds R01.2
  hematinuria R82.3

**Findings, abnormal, inconclusive, without
    diagnosis** *(Continued)*
  hematocrit drop (precipitous) R71.0
  hemoglobinuria R82.3
  human papillomavirus (HPV) DNA test
      positive
    cervix
      high risk R87.810
      low risk R87.820
    vagina
      high risk R87.811
      low risk R87.821
  in blood (of substance not normally found in
      blood) R78.9
    addictive drug NEC R78.4
    alcohol (excessive level) R78.0
    cocaine R78.2
    hallucinogen R78.3
    heavy metals (abnormal level) R78.79
    lead R78.71
    lithium (abnormal level) R78.89
    opiate drug R78.1
    psychotropic drug R78.5
    specified substance NEC R78.89
    steroid agent R78.6
  indoleacetic acid, elevated R82.5
  ketonuria R82.4
  lactic acid dehydrogenase (LDH) R74.02
  liver function test R79.89
  mammogram NEC R92.8
    calcification (calculus) R92.1
    inconclusive result (due to dense breasts)
        R92.2
    microcalcification R92.0
  mediastinal shift R93.89
  melanin, urine R82.998
  myoglobinuria R82.1
  neonatal screening P09
  nonvisualization of gallbladder R93.2
  odor of urine NOS R82.90
  Papanicolaou cervix R87.619
    non-atypical endometrial cells R87.618
  pneumoencephalogram R93.0
  poikilocytosis R71.8
  potassium (deficiency) E87.6
    excess E87.5
  PPD R76.11
  radiologic (X-ray) R93.89
    abdomen R93.5
    biliary tract R93.2
    breast R92.8
    gastrointestinal tract R93.3
    genitourinary organs R93.89
    head R93.0
    inconclusive due to excess body fat of
        patient R93.9
    intrathoracic organs NEC R93.1
    musculoskeletal
      limbs R93.6
      other than limb R93.7
    placenta R93.89
    retroperitoneum R93.5
    skin R93.89
    skull R93.0
    subcutaneous tissue R93.89
    testis R93.81-•
  red blood cell (count) (morphology) (sickling)
      (volume) R71.8
  scan NEC R94.8
    bladder R94.8
    bone R94.8
    kidney R94.4
    liver R93.2
    lung R94.2
    pancreas R94.8
    placental R94.8
    spleen R94.8
    thyroid R94.6
  sedimentation rate, elevated R70.0
  SGOT R74.01
  SGPT R74.01

▶ New   ⇒ Revised   ~~deleted~~ Deleted   • Use Additional Character(s)

Findings, abnormal, inconclusive, without
  diagnosis (Continued)
  sodium (deficiency) E87.1
    excess E87.0
  specified body fluid NEC R88.8
  stress test R94.39
  thyroid (function) (metabolic rate) (scan)
    (uptake) R94.6
  ➡transaminase (level) R74.01
  triglycerides E78.9
    high E78.1
      with high cholesterol E78.2
  tuberculin skin test (without active
    tuberculosis) R76.11
  urine R82.90
    acetone R82.4
    bacteria R82.71
    bile R82.2
    casts or cells R82.998
    chyle R82.0
    culture positive R82.79
    glucose R81
    hemoglobin R82.3
    ketone R82.4
    sugar R81
  vanillylmandelic acid (VMA), elevated
    R82.5
  vectorcardiogram (VCG) R94.39
  ventriculogram R93.0
  white blood cell (count) (differential)
    (morphology) D72.9
  xerography R92.8
Finger —see condition
Fire, Saint Anthony's —see Erysipelas
Fire-setting
  pathological (compulsive) F63.1
Fish hook stomach K31.89
Fishmeal-worker's lung J67.8
Fissure, fissured
  anus, anal K60.2
    acute K60.0
    chronic K60.1
    congenital Q43.8
  ear, lobule, congenital Q17.8
  epiglottis (congenital) Q31.8
  larynx J38.7
    congenital Q31.8
  lip K13.0
    congenital —see Cleft, lip
  nipple N64.0
    associated with
      lactation O92.13
      pregnancy O92.11-●
      puerperium O92.12
  nose Q30.2
  palate (congenital) —see Cleft, palate
  skin R23.4
  spine (congenital) —see also Spina bifida
    with hydrocephalus —see Spina bifida, by
      site, with hydrocephalus
  tongue (acquired) K14.5
    congenital Q38.3
Fistula (cutaneous) L98.8
  abdomen (wall) K63.2
    bladder N32.2
    intestine NEC K63.2
    ureter N28.89
    uterus N82.5
  abdominorectal K63.2
  abdominosigmoidal K63.2
  abdominothoracic J86.0
  abdominouterine N82.5
    congenital Q51.7
  abdominovesical N32.2
  accessory sinuses —see Sinusitis
  actinomycotic —see Actinomycosis
  alveolar antrum —see Sinusitis, maxillary
  alveolar process K04.6
  anorectal K60.5
  antrobuccal —see Sinusitis, maxillary
  antrum —see Sinusitis, maxillary

Fistula (Continued)
  anus, anal (recurrent) (infectional) K60.3
    congenital Q43.6
      with absence, atresia and stenosis Q42.2
    tuberculous A18.32
  aorta-duodenal I77.2
  appendix, appendicular K38.3
  arteriovenous (acquired) (nonruptured) I77.0
    brain I67.1
      congenital Q28.2
        ruptured —see Fistula, arteriovenous,
          brain, ruptured
      ruptured I60.8
        intracerebral I61.8
        intraparenchymal I61.8
        intraventricular I61.5
        subarachnoid I60.8
    cerebral —see Fistula, arteriovenous, brain
    congenital (peripheral) —see also
      Malformation, arteriovenous
      brain Q28.2
        ruptured —see Fistula, arteriovenous,
          brain, ruptured
      coronary Q24.5
      pulmonary Q25.72
    coronary I25.41
      congenital Q24.5
    pulmonary I28.0
      congenital Q25.72
    surgically created (for dialysis) Z99.2
      complication —see Complication,
        arteriovenous, fistula, surgically
        created
    traumatic —see Injury, blood vessel
  artery I77.2
  aural (mastoid) —see Mastoiditis, chronic
  auricle —see also Disorder, pinna, specified
    type NEC
    congenital Q18.1
  Bartholin's gland N82.8
  bile duct (common) (hepatic) K83.3
  ➡with calculus, stones —see also Calculus,
      bile duct K83.3
  biliary (tract) —see Fistula, bile duct
  bladder (sphincter) NEC —see also Fistula,
    vesico- N32.2
    into seminal vesicle N32.2
  bone —see also Disorder, bone, specified type
    NEC
    with osteomyelitis, chronic —see
      Osteomyelitis, chronic, with draining
      sinus
  brain G93.89
    arteriovenous (acquired) (see Fistula,
      arteriovenous, brain) I67.1
    congenital Q28.2
  branchial (cleft) Q18.0
  branchiogenous Q18.0
  breast N61.0
    puerperal, postpartum or gestational, due
      to mastitis (purulent) —see Mastitis,
      obstetric, purulent
  bronchial J86.0
  bronchocutaneous, bronchomediastinal,
    bronchopleural, bronchopleuromediastinal
    (infective) J86.0
    tuberculous NEC A15.5
  bronchoesophageal J86.0
    congenital Q39.2
      with atresia of esophagus Q39.1
  bronchovisceral J86.0
  buccal cavity (infective) K12.2
  cecosigmoidal K63.2
  cecum K63.2
  ➡cerebrospinal (fluid) G96.08
  cervical, lateral Q18.1
  cervicoaural Q18.1
  cervicosigmoidal N82.4
  cervicovesical N82.1
  cervix N82.8
  chest (wall) J86.0

Fistula (Continued)
  cholecystenteric —see Fistula, gallbladder
  cholecystocolic —see Fistula, gallbladder
  cholecystocolonic —see Fistula, gallbladder
  cholecystoduodenal —see Fistula, gallbladder
  cholecystogastric —see Fistula, gallbladder
  cholecystointestinal —see Fistula, gallbladder
  choledochoduodenal —see Fistula, bile duct
  cholocolic K82.3
  coccyx —see Sinus, pilonidal
  colon K63.2
  colostomy K94.09
  colovesical N32.1
  common duct —see Fistula, bile duct
  congenital, site not listed —see Anomaly, by
    site
  coronary, arteriovenous I25.41
    congenital Q24.5
  costal region J86.0
  cul-de-sac, Douglas' N82.8
  cystic duct —see also Fistula, gallbladder
    congenital Q44.5
  dental K04.6
  diaphragm J86.0
  duodenum K31.6
  ear (external) (canal) —see Disorder, ear,
    external, specified type NEC
  enterocolic K63.2
  enterocutaneous K63.2
  enterouterine N82.4
    congenital Q51.7
  enterovaginal N82.4
    congenital Q52.2
    large intestine N82.3
    small intestine N82.2
  enterovesical N32.1
  epididymis N50.89
    tuberculous A18.15
  esophagobronchial J86.0
    congenital Q39.2
      with atresia of esophagus Q39.1
  esophagocutaneous K22.8
  esophagopleural-cutaneous J86.0
  esophagotracheal J86.0
    congenital Q39.2
      with atresia of esophagus Q39.1
  esophagus K22.8
    congenital Q39.2
      with atresia of esophagus Q39.1
  ethmoid —see Sinusitis, ethmoidal
  eyeball (cornea) (sclera) —see Disorder, globe,
    hypotony
  eyelid H01.8
  fallopian tube, external N82.5
  fecal K63.2
    congenital Q43.6
  from periapical abscess K04.6
  frontal sinus —see Sinusitis, frontal
  gallbladder K82.3
    with calculus, cholelithiasis, stones —see
      Calculus, gallbladder
  gastric K31.6
  gastrocolic K31.6
    congenital Q40.2
    tuberculous A18.32
  gastroenterocolic K31.6
  gastroesophageal K31.6
  gastrojejunal K31.6
  gastrojejunocolic K31.6
  genital tract (female) N82.9
    specified NEC N82.8
    to intestine NEC N82.4
    to skin N82.5
  hepatic artery-portal vein, congenital Q26.6
  hepatopleural J86.0
  hepatopulmonary J86.0
  ileorectal or ileosigmoidal K63.2
  ileovaginal N82.2
  ileovesical N32.1
  ileum K63.2
  in ano K60.3
    tuberculous A18.32

Fistula *(Continued)*
    inner ear (labyrinth) —*see* subcategory H83.1
    intestine NEC K63.2
    intestinocolonic (abdominal) K63.2
    intestinoureteral N28.89
    intestinouterine N82.4
    intestinovaginal N82.4
      large intestine N82.3
      small intestine N82.2
    intestinovesical N32.1
    ischiorectal (fossa) K61.39
    jejunum K63.2
    joint M25.10
      ankle M25.17-●
      elbow M25.12-●
      foot joint M25.17-●
      hand joint M25.14-●
      hip M25.15-●
      knee M25.16-●
      shoulder M25.11-●
      specified joint NEC M25.18
      tuberculous —*see* Tuberculosis, joint
      vertebrae M25.18
      wrist M25.13-●
    kidney N28.89
    labium (majus) (minus) N82.8
    labyrinth —*see* subcategory H83.1
    lacrimal (gland) (sac) H04.61-●
    lacrimonasal duct —*see* Fistula, lacrimal
    laryngotracheal, congenital Q34.8
    larynx J38.7
    lip K13.0
      congenital Q38.0
    lumbar, tuberculous A18.01
    lung J86.0
    lymphatic I89.8
    mammary (gland) N61.0
    mastoid (process) (region) —*see* Mastoiditis,
      chronic
    maxillary J32.0
    medial, face and neck Q18.8
    mediastinal J86.0
    mediastinobronchial J86.0
    mediastinocutaneous J86.0
    middle ear —*see* subcategory H74.8
    mouth K12.2
    nasal J34.89
      sinus —*see* Sinusitis
    nasopharynx J39.2
    nipple N64.0
    nose J34.89
    oral (cutaneous) K12.2
      maxillary J32.0
      nasal (with cleft palate) —*see* Cleft, palate
    orbit, orbital —*see* Disorder, orbit, specified
      type NEC
    oroantral J32.0
    oviduct, external N82.5
    palate (hard) M27.8
    pancreatic K86.89
    pancreaticoduodenal K86.89
    parotid (gland) K11.4
      region K12.2
    penis N48.89
    perianal K60.3
    pericardium (pleura) (sac) —*see* Pericarditis
    pericecal K63.2
    perineorectal K60.4 perineosigmoidal K63.2
    perineosigmoidal K63.2
    perineum, perineal (with urethral
      involvement) NEC N36.0
      tuberculous A18.13
      ureter N28.89
    perirectal K60.4
      tuberculous A18.32
    peritoneum K65.9
    pharyngoesophageal J39.2
    pharynx J39.2
      branchial cleft (congenital) Q18.0
    pilonidal (infected) (rectum) —*see* Sinus,
      pilonidal

Fistula *(Continued)*
    pleura, pleural, pleurocutaneous,
      pleuroperitoneal J86.0
      tuberculous NEC A15.6
    pleuropericardial I31.8
    portal vein-hepatic artery, congenital Q26.6
    postauricular H70.81-●
    postoperative, persistent T81.83
      specified site —*see* Fistula, by site
    preauricular (congenital) Q18.1
    prostate N42.89
    pulmonary J86.0
      arteriovenous I28.0
        congenital Q25.72
      tuberculous —*see* Tuberculosis, pulmonary
    pulmonoperitoneal J86.0
    rectolabial N82.4
    rectosigmoid (intercommunicating) K63.2
    rectoureteral N28.89
    rectourethral N36.0
      congenital Q64.73
    rectouterine N82.4
      congenital Q51.7
    rectovaginal N82.3
      congenital Q52.2
      tuberculous A18.18
    rectovesical N32.1
      congenital Q64.79
    rectovesicovaginal N82.3
    rectovulval N82.4
      congenital Q52.79
    rectum (to skin) K60.4
      congenital Q43.6
        with absence, atresia and stenosis Q42.0
      tuberculous A18.32
    renal N28.89
    retroauricular —*see* Fistula, postauricular
    salivary duct or gland (any) K11.4
      congenital Q38.4
    scrotum (urinary) N50.89
      tuberculous A18.15
    semicircular canals —*see* subcategory H83.1
    sigmoid K63.2
      to bladder N32.1
    sinus —*see* Sinusitis
    skin L98.8
      to genital tract (female) N82.5
    splenocolic D73.89
    stercoral K63.2
    stomach K31.6
    sublingual gland K11.4
    submandibular gland K11.4
    submaxillary (gland) K11.4
      region K12.2
    thoracic J86.0
      duct I89.8
    thoracoabdominal J86.0
    thoracogastric J86.0
    thoracointestinal J86.0
    thorax J86.0
    thyroglossal duct Q89.2
    thyroid E07.89
    trachea, congenital (external) (internal) Q32.1
    tracheoesophageal J86.0
      congenital Q39.2
        with atresia of esophagus Q39.1
      following tracheostomy J95.04
    traumatic arteriovenous —*see* Injury, blood
      vessel, by site
    tuberculous - code by site under Tuberculosis
    typhoid A01.09
    umbilicourinary Q64.8
    urachus, congenital Q64.4
    ureter (persistent) N28.89
    ureteroabdominal N28.89
    ureterorectal N28.89
    ureterosigmoido-abdominal N28.89
    ureterovaginal N82.1
    ureterovesical N32.2
    urethra N36.0
      congenital Q64.79
      tuberculous A18.13

Fistula *(Continued)*
    urethroperineal N36.0
    urethroperineovesical N32.2
    urethrorectal N36.0
      congenital Q64.73
    urethroscrotal N50.89
    urethrovaginal N82.1
    urethrovesical N32.2
    urinary (tract) (persistent) (recurrent)
      N36.0
    uteroabdominal N82.5
      congenital Q51.7
    uteroenteric, uterointestinal N82.4
      congenital Q51.7
    uterorectal N82.4
      congenital Q51.7
    uteroureteric N82.1
    uterourethral Q51.7
    uterovaginal N82.8
    uterovesical N82.1
      congenital Q51.7
    uterus N82.8
    vagina (postpartal) (wall) N82.8
    vaginocutaneous (postpartal) N82.5
    vaginointestinal NEC N82.4
      large intestine N82.3
      small intestine N82.2
    vaginoperineal N82.5
    vasocutaneous, congenital Q55.7
    vesical NEC N32.2
    vesicoabdominal N32.2
    vesicocervicovaginal N82.1
    vesicocolic N32.1
    vesicocutaneous N32.2
    vesicoenteric N32.1
    vesicointestinal N32.1
    vesicometrorectal N82.4
    vesicoperineal N32.2
    vesicorectal N32.1
      congenital Q64.79
    vesicosigmoidal N32.1
    vesicosigmoidovaginal N82.3
    vesicoureteral N32.2
    vesicoureterovaginal N82.1
    vesicourethral N32.2
    vesicourethrorectal N32.1
    vesicouterine N82.1
      congenital Q51.7
    vesicovaginal N82.0
    vulvorectal N82.4
      congenital Q52.79
Fit R56.9
    epileptic —*see* Epilepsy
    fainting R55
    hysterical F44.5
    newborn P90
Fitting (and adjustment) (of)
    artificial
      arm —*see* Admission, adjustment, artificial,
        arm
        breast Z44.3
        eye Z44.2
        leg —*see* Admission, adjustment, artificial,
        leg
    automatic implantable cardiac defibrillator
      (with synchronous cardiac pacemaker)
      Z45.02
    brain neuropacemaker Z46.2
      implanted Z45.42
    cardiac defibrillator —*see* Fitting (and
      adjustment) (of), automatic implantable
      cardiac defibrillator
    catheter, non-vascular Z46.82
    colostomy belt Z46.89
    contact lenses Z46.0
    CRT-D (resynchronization therapy
      defibrillator) Z45.02
    CRT-P (cardiac resynchronization therapy
      pacemaker) Z45.018
      pulse generator Z45.010
    cystostomy device Z46.6

▶ New   ⇒ Revised   ~~deleted~~ Deleted   ● Use Additional Character(s)

Fitting (Continued)
  defibrillator, cardiac —see Fitting (and
      adjustment) (of), automatic implantable
      cardiac defibrillator
  dentures Z46.3
  device NOS Z46.9
    abdominal Z46.89
    gastrointestinal NEC Z46.59
    implanted NEC Z45.89
    nervous system Z46.2
      implanted —see Admission, adjustment,
          device, implanted, nervous system
    orthodontic Z46.4
    orthoptic Z46.0
    orthotic Z46.89
    prosthetic (external) Z44.9
      breast Z44.3
      dental Z46.3
      eye Z44.2
      specified NEC Z44.8
    specified NEC Z46.89
    substitution
      auditory Z46.2
        implanted —see Admission,
            adjustment, device, implanted,
            hearing device
      nervous system Z46.2
        implanted —see Admission,
            adjustment, device, implanted,
            nervous system
      visual Z46.2
        implanted Z45.31
    urinary Z46.6
  gastric lap band Z46.51
  gastrointestinal appliance NEC Z46.59
  glasses (reading) Z46.0
  hearing aid Z46.1
  ileostomy device Z46.89
  insulin pump Z46.81
  intestinal appliance NEC Z46.89
  myringotomy device (stent) (tube) Z45.82
  neuropacemaker Z46.2
    implanted Z45.42
  non-vascular catheter Z46.82
  orthodontic device Z46.4
  orthopedic device (brace) (cast) (corset)
      (shoes) Z46.89
  pacemaker (cardiac) (cardiac
      resynchronization therapy (CRT-P))
      Z45.018
    nervous system (brain) (peripheral nerve)
        (spinal cord) Z46.2
      implanted Z45.42
    pulse generator Z45.010
  portacath (port-a-cath) Z45.2
  prosthesis (external) Z44.9
    arm —see Admission, adjustment, artificial,
        arm
    breast Z44.3
    dental Z46.3
    eye Z44.2
    leg —see Admission, adjustment, artificial,
        leg
    specified NEC Z44.8
  spectacles Z46.0
  wheelchair Z46.89
Fitzhugh-Curtis syndrome
  due to
    Chlamydia trachomatis A74.81
    Neisseria gonorrhorea (gonococcal
        peritonitis) A54.85
Fitz's syndrome (acute hemorrhagic
    pancreatitis) —see also Pancreatitis,
    acute K85.80
Fixation
  joint —see Ankylosis
  larynx J38.7
  stapes —see Ankylosis, ear ossicles
    deafness —see Deafness, conductive
  uterus (acquired) —see Malposition, uterus
  vocal cord J38.3

Flabby ridge K06.8
Flaccid —see also condition
  palate, congenital Q38.5
Flail
  chest S22.5-●
    newborn (birth injury) P13.8
  joint (paralytic) M25.20
    ankle M25.27-●
    elbow M25.22-●
    foot joint M25.27-●
    hand joint M25.24-●
    hip M25.25-●
    knee M25.26-●
    shoulder M25.21-●
    specified joint NEC M25.28
    wrist M25.23-●
Flajani's disease —see Hyperthyroidism, with,
    goiter (diffuse)
Flap, liver K71.3
Flashbacks (residual to hallucinogen use)
    F16.283
Flat
  chamber (eye) —see Disorder, globe,
      hypotony, flat anterior chamber
  chest, congenital Q67.8
  foot (acquired) (fixed type) (painful)
      (postural) —see also Deformity, limb,
      flat foot
    congenital (rigid) (spastic (everted))
        Q66.5-●
    rachitic sequelae (late effect) E64.3
  organ or site, congenital NEC —see Anomaly,
      by site
  pelvis M95.5
    with disproportion (fetopelvic) O33.0
      causing obstructed labor O65.0
    congenital Q74.2
Flatau-Schilder disease G37.0
Flatback syndrome M40.30
  lumbar region M40.36
  lumbosacral region M40.37
  thoracolumbar region M40.35
Flattening
  head, femur M89.8X5
  hip —see Coxa, plana
  lip (congenital) Q18.8
  nose (congenital) Q67.4
    acquired M95.0
Flatulence R14.3
  psychogenic F45.8
Flatus R14.3
  vaginalis N89.8
Flax-dresser's disease J66.1
Flea bite —see Injury, bite, by site, superficial,
    insect
Flecks, glaucomatous (subcapsular) —see
    Cataract, complicated
Fleischer (-Kayser) ring (cornea) H18.04-●
Fleshy mole O02.0
Flexibilitas cerea —see Catalepsy
Flexion
  amputation stump (surgical) T87.89
  cervix —see Malposition, uterus
  contracture, joint —see Contraction, joint
  deformity, joint —see also Deformity, limb,
      flexion M21.20
    hip, congenital Q65.89
  uterus —see also Malposition, uterus
    lateral —see Lateroversion, uterus
Flexner-Boyd dysentery A03.2
Flexner's dysentery A03.1
Flexure —see Flexion
Flint murmur (aortic insufficiency) I35.1
Floater, vitreous —see Opacity, vitreous
Floating
  cartilage (joint) —see also Loose, body, joint
    knee —see Derangement, knee, loose body
  gallbladder, congenital Q44.1
  kidney N28.89
    congenital Q63.8
  spleen D73.89

Flooding N92.0
Floor —see condition
Floppy
  baby syndrome (nonspecific) P94.2
  iris syndrome (intraoperative) (IFIS) H21.81
  nonrheumatic mitral valve syndrome I34.1
Flu —see also Influenza
  avian —see also Influenza, due to, identified
      novel influenza A virus J09.X2
  bird —see also Influenza, due to, identified
      novel influenza A virus J09.X2
  intestinal NEC A08.4
  swine (viruses that normally cause infections
      in pigs) —see also Influenza, due to,
      identified novel influenza A virus J09.X2
Fluctuating blood pressure I99.8
Fluid
  abdomen R18.8
  chest J94.8
  heart —see Failure, heart, congestive
  joint —see Effusion, joint
  loss (acute) E86.9
  lung —see Edema, lung
  overload E87.70
    specified NEC E87.79
  peritoneal cavity R18.8
  pleural cavity J94.8
  retention R60.9
Flukes NEC —see also Infestation, fluke
  blood NEC —see Schistosomiasis
  liver B66.3
Fluor (vaginalis) N89.8
  trichomonal or due to Trichomonas
      (vaginalis) A59.00
Fluorosis
  dental K00.3
  skeletal M85.10
    ankle M85.17-●
    foot M85.17-●
    forearm M85.13-●
    hand M85.14-●
    lower leg M85.16-●
    multiple site M85.19
    neck M85.18
    rib M85.18
    shoulder M85.11-●
    skull M85.18
    specified site NEC M85.18
    thigh M85.15-●
    toe M85.17-●
    upper arm M85.12-●
    vertebra M85.18
Flush syndrome E34.0
Flushing R23.2
  menopausal N95.1
Flutter
  atrial or auricular I48.92
    atypical I48.4
      type I I48.3
      type II I48.4
    typical I48.3
  heart I49.8
    atrial or auricular I48.92
      atypical I48.4
        type I I48.3
        type II I48.4
      typical I48.3
    ventricular I49.02
  ventricular I49.02
FNHTR (febrile nonhemolytic transfusion
    reaction) R50.84
Fochier's abscess - code by site under Abscess
Focus, Assmann's —see Tuberculosis,
    pulmonary
Fogo selvagem L10.3
Foix-Alajouanine syndrome G95.19
Fold, folds (anomalous) —see also Anomaly,
    by site
  Descemet's membrane —see Change, corneal
      membrane, Descemet's, fold
  epicanthic Q10.3
  heart Q24.8

▶ New   ⇒ Revised   ~~deleted~~ Deleted   ● Use Additional Character(s)

▶ New   ⇒ Revised   deleted Deleted   ● Use Additional Character(s)

Foreign body *(Continued)*
entering through orifice *(Continued)*
gum T18.0
Highmore's antrum T17.0
hypopharynx —*see* Foreign body, pharynx
ileum T18.3
intestine (small) T18.3
large T18.4
lacrimal apparatus (punctum) —*see*
Foreign body, entering through orifice,
eye, specified part NEC
large intestine T18.4
larynx —*see* Foreign body, larynx
lung —*see* Foreign body, respiratory tract,
specified site NEC
maxillary sinus T17.0
mouth T18.0
nasal sinus T17.0
nasopharynx —*see* Foreign body, pharynx
nose (passage) T17.1
nostril T17.1
oral cavity T18.0
palate T18.0
penis T19.4
pharynx —*see* Foreign body, pharynx
piriform sinus —*see* Foreign body, pharynx
rectosigmoid (junction) T18.5
rectum T18.5
respiratory tract —*see* Foreign body,
respiratory tract
sinus (accessory) (frontal) (maxillary)
(nasal) T17.0
piriform —*see* Foreign body, pharynx
small intestine T18.3
stomach T18.2
suffocation by —*see* Foreign body, by site
tear ducts or glands —*see* Foreign body,
entering through orifice, eye, specified
part NEC
throat —*see* Foreign body, pharynx
tongue T18.0
tonsil, tonsillar (fossa) —*see* Foreign body,
pharynx
trachea —*see* Foreign body, trachea
ureter T19.8
urethra T19.0
uterus (any part) T19.3
vagina T19.2
vulva T19.2
esophagus T18.108
causing
injury NEC T18.108
food (bone) (seed) T18.128
gastric contents (vomitus) T18.118
specified type NEC T18.198
tracheal compression T18.100
food (bone) (seed) T18.120
gastric contents (vomitus) T18.110
specified type NEC T18.190
feeling of, in throat R09.89
fragment —*see* Retained, foreign body
fragments (type of)
genitourinary tract T19.9
bladder T19.1
multiple parts T19.8
penis T19.4
specified site NEC T19.8
urethra T19.0
uterus T19.3
IUD Z97.5
vagina T19.2
contraceptive device Z97.5
vulva T19.2
granuloma (old) (soft tissue) —*see also*
Granuloma, foreign body
skin L92.3
in
laceration —*see* Laceration, by site, with
foreign body
puncture wound —*see* Puncture, by site,
with foreign body
soft tissue (residual) M79.5

Foreign body *(Continued)*
inadvertently left in operation wound —*see*
Foreign body, accidentally left during a
procedure
ingestion, ingested NOS T18.9
inhalation or inspiration —*see* Foreign body,
by site
internal organ, not entering through a natural
orifice - code as specific injury with
foreign body
intraocular S05.5-●
old, retained (nonmagnetic) H44.70-●
anterior chamber H44.71-●
ciliary body H44.72-●
iris H44.72-●
lens H44.73-●
magnetic H44.60-●
anterior chamber H44.61-●
ciliary body H44.62-●
iris H44.62-●
lens H44.63-●
posterior wall H44.64-●
specified site NEC H44.69-●
vitreous body H44.65-●
posterior wall H44.74-●
specified site NEC H44.79-●
vitreous body H44.75-●
iris —*see* Foreign body, intraocular
lacrimal punctum —*see* Foreign body,
entering through orifice, eye, specified
part NEC
larynx T17.308
causing
asphyxiation T17.300
food (bone) (seed) T17.320
gastric contents (vomitus) T17.310
specified type NEC T17.390
injury NEC T17.308
food (bone) (seed) T17.328
gastric contents (vomitus) T17.318
specified type NEC T17.398
lens —*see* Foreign body, intraocular
ocular muscle S05.4-●
old, retained —*see* Foreign body, orbit, old
old or residual
soft tissue (residual) M79.5
operation wound, left accidentally —*see*
Foreign body, accidentally left during a
procedure
orbit S05.4-●
old, retained H05.5-●
pharynx T17.208
causing
asphyxiation T17.200
food (bone) (seed) T17.220
gastric contents (vomitus)
T17.210
specified type NEC T17.290
injury NEC T17.208
food (bone) (seed) T17.228
gastric contents (vomitus)
T17.218
specified type NEC T17.298
respiratory tract T17.908
bronchioles —*see* Foreign body, respiratory
tract, specified site NEC
bronchus —*see* Foreign body, bronchus
causing
asphyxiation T17.900
food (bone) (seed) T17.920
gastric contents (vomitus) T17.910
specified type NEC T17.990
injury NEC T17.908
food (bone) (seed) T17.928
gastric contents (vomitus) T17.918
specified type NEC T17.998
larynx —*see* Foreign body, larynx
lung —*see* Foreign body, respiratory tract,
specified site NEC
multiple parts —*see* Foreign body,
respiratory tract, specified site NEC

Foreign body *(Continued)*
respiratory tract *(Continued)*
nasal sinus T17.0
nasopharynx —*see* Foreign body,
pharynx
nose T17.1
nostril T17.1
pharynx —*see* Foreign body, pharynx
specified site NEC T17.808
causing
asphyxiation T17.800
food (bone) (seed) T17.820
gastric contents (vomitus) T17.810
specified type NEC T17.890
injury NEC T17.808
food (bone) (seed) T17.828
gastric contents (vomitus) T17.818
specified type NEC T17.898
throat —*see* Foreign body, pharynx
trachea —*see* Foreign body, trachea
retained (old) (nonmagnetic) (in)
anterior chamber (eye) —*see* Foreign body,
intraocular, old, retained, anterior
chamber
magnetic —*see* Foreign body, intraocular,
old, retained, magnetic, anterior
chamber
ciliary body —*see* Foreign body,
intraocular, old, retained, ciliary body
magnetic —*see* Foreign body, intraocular,
old, retained, magnetic, ciliary body
eyelid H02.819
left H02.816
lower H02.815
upper H02.814
right H02.813
lower H02.812
upper H02.811
fragments —*see* Retained, foreign body
fragments (type of)
globe —*see* Foreign body, intraocular, old,
retained
magnetic —*see* Foreign body, intraocular,
old, retained, magnetic
intraocular —*see* Foreign body, intraocular,
old, retained
magnetic —*see* Foreign body, intraocular,
old, retained, magnetic
iris —*see* Foreign body, intraocular, old,
retained, iris
magnetic —*see* Foreign body, intraocular,
old, retained, magnetic, iris
lens —*see* Foreign body, intraocular, old,
retained, lens
magnetic —*see* Foreign body, intraocular,
old, retained, magnetic, lens
muscle —*see* Foreign body, retained, soft
tissue
orbit —*see* Foreign body, orbit, old
posterior wall of globe —*see* Foreign body,
intraocular, old, retained, posterior
wall
magnetic —*see* Foreign body, intraocular,
old, retained, magnetic, posterior
wall
retrobulbar —*see* Foreign body, orbit, old,
retrobulbar
soft tissue M79.5
vitreous —*see* Foreign body, intraocular,
old, retained, vitreous body
magnetic —*see* Foreign body, intraocular,
old, retained, magnetic, vitreous
body
retina S05.5-●
superficial, without open wound
abdomen, abdominal (wall) S30.851
alveolar process S00.552
ankle S90.55-●
antecubital space —*see* Foreign body,
superficial, forearm
anus S30.857

Foreign body (Continued)
   superficial, without open wound (Continued)
     arm (upper) S40.85-•
     auditory canal —see Foreign body,
      superficial, ear
     auricle —see Foreign body, superficial, ear
     axilla —see Foreign body, superficial, arm
     back, lower S30.850
     breast S20.15-•
     brow S00.85
     buttock S30.850
     calf —see Foreign body, superficial, leg
     canthus —see Foreign body, superficial,
      eyelid
     cheek S00.85
      internal S00.552
     chest wall —see Foreign body, superficial,
      thorax
     chin S00.85
     clitoris S30.854
     costal region —see Foreign body,
      superficial, thorax
     digit(s)
      foot —see Foreign body, superficial, toe
      hand —see Foreign body, superficial,
       finger
     ear S00.45-•
     elbow S50.35-•
     epididymis S30.853
     epigastric region S30.851
     epiglottis S10.15
     esophagus, cervical S10.15
     eyebrow —see Foreign body, superficial,
      eyelid
     eyelid S00.25-•
     face S00.85
     finger(s) S60.459
      index S60.45-•
      little S60.45-•
      middle S60.45-•
      ring S60.45-•
     flank S30.851
     foot (except toe(s) alone) S90.85-•
      toe —see Foreign body, superficial, toe
     forearm S50.85-•
      elbow only —see Foreign body,
       superficial, elbow
     forehead S00.85
     genital organs, external
      female S30.856
      male S30.855
     groin S30.851
     gum S00.552
     hand S60.55-•
     head S00.95
      ear —see Foreign body, superficial, ear
      eyelid —see Foreign body, superficial,
       eyelid
      lip S00.551
      nose S00.35
      oral cavity S00.552
      scalp S00.05
      specified site NEC S00.85
     heel —see Foreign body, superficial, foot
     hip S70.25-•
     inguinal region S30.851
     interscapular region S20.459
     jaw S00.85
     knee S80.25-•
     labium (majus) (minus) S30.854
     larynx S10.15
     leg (lower) S80.85-•
      knee —see Foreign body, superficial, knee
      upper —see Foreign body, superficial,
       thigh
     lip S00.551
     lower back S30.850
     lumbar region S30.850
     malar region S00.85
     mammary —see Foreign body, superficial,
      breast

Foreign body (Continued)
   superficial, without open wound (Continued)
     mastoid region S00.85
     mouth S00.552
     nail
      finger —see Foreign body, superficial,
       finger
      toe —see Foreign body, superficial, toe
     nape S10.85
     nasal S00.35
     neck S10.95
      specified site NEC S10.85
      throat S10.15
     nose S00.35
     occipital region S00.05
     oral cavity S00.552
     orbital region —see Foreign body,
      superficial, eyelid
     palate S00.552
     palm —see Foreign body, superficial,
      hand
     parietal region S00.05
     pelvis S30.850
     penis S30.852
     perineum
      female S30.854
      male S30.850
     periocular area —see Foreign body,
      superficial, eyelid
     phalanges
      finger —see Foreign body, superficial,
       finger
      toe —see Foreign body, superficial, toe
     pharynx S10.15
     pinna —see Foreign body, superficial, ear
     popliteal space —see Foreign body,
      superficial, knee
     prepuce S30.852
     pubic region S30.850
     pudendum
      female S30.856
      male S30.855
     sacral region S30.850
     scalp S00.05
     scapular region —see Foreign body,
      superficial, shoulder
     scrotum S30.853
     shin —see Foreign body, superficial, leg
     shoulder S40.25-•
     sternal region S20.359
     submaxillary region S00.85
     submental region S00.85
     subungual
      finger(s) —see Foreign body, superficial,
       finger
      toe(s) —see Foreign body, superficial,
       toe
     supraclavicular fossa S10.85
     supraorbital S00.85
     temple S00.85
     temporal region S00.85
     testis S30.853
     thigh S70.35-•
     thorax, thoracic (wall) S20.95
      back S20.45-•
      front S20.35-•
     throat S10.15
     thumb S60.35-•
     toe(s) (lesser) S90.456
      great S90.45-•
     tongue S00.552
     trachea S10.15
     tunica vaginalis S30.853
     tympanum, tympanic membrane —see
      Foreign body, superficial, ear
     uvula S00.552
     vagina S30.854
     vocal cords S10.15
     vulva S30.854
     wrist S60.85-•
   swallowed T18.9

Foreign body (Continued)
   trachea T17.408
     causing
      asphyxiation T17.400
       food (bone) (seed) T17.420
       gastric contents (vomitus) T17.410
       specified type NEC T17.490
      injury NEC T17.408
       food (bone) (seed) T17.428
       gastric contents (vomitus) T17.418
       specified type NEC T17.498
   type of fragment —see Retained, foreign body
     fragments (type of)
   vitreous (humor) S05.5-•
Forestier's disease (rhizomelic
   pseudopolyarthritis) M35.3-•
   meaning ankylosing hyperostosis —see
     Hyperostosis, ankylosing
Formation
   hyalin in cornea —see Degeneration, cornea
   sequestrum in bone (due to infection) —see
     Osteomyelitis, chronic
   valve
     colon, congenital Q43.8
     ureter (congenital) Q62.39
Formication R20.2
Fort Bragg fever A27.89
Fossa —see also condition
   pyriform —see condition
Foster-Kennedy syndrome H47.14-•
Fothergill's
   disease (trigeminal neuralgia) —see also
     Neuralgia, trigeminal
   scarlatina anginosa A38.9
Foul breath R19.6
Foundling Z76.1
Fournier disease or gangrene N49.3
   female N76.89
Fourth
   cranial nerve —see condition
   molar K00.1
Foville's (peduncular) disease or syndrome G46.3
Fox (-Fordyce) disease (apocrine miliaria) L75.2
FPIES (food protein-induced enterocolitis
   syndrome) K52.21
Fracture, burst —see Fracture, traumatic, by site
Fracture, chronic —see Fracture, pathological,
   by site
Fracture, insufficiency —see Fracture,
   pathological, by site
Fracture, nontraumatic, NEC
   atypical
     femur M84.750-•
      complete
       oblique M84.759
        left side M84.758
        right side M84.757
       transverse M84.756
        left side M84.755
        right side M84.754
      incomplete M84.753
       left side M84.752
       right side M84.751
Fracture, pathological (pathologic) —see also
   Fracture, traumatic M84.40
   ankle M84.47-•
   carpus M84.44-•
   clavicle M84.41-•
   compression (not due to trauma) —see also
     Collapse, vertebra M48.50-•
   dental implant M27.63
   dental restorative material K08.539
     with loss of material K08.531
     without loss of material K08.530
   due to
     neoplastic disease NEC —see also
      Neoplasm M84.50
      ankle M84.57-•
      carpus M84.54-•
      clavicle M84.51-•
      femur M84.55-•

▶ New   ⇛ Revised   ~~deleted~~ Deleted   • Use Additional Character(s)

Fracture, pathological (Continued)
  due to (Continued)
    neoplastic disease NEC (Continued)
      fibula M84.56-●
      finger M84.54-●
      hip M84.559
      humerus M84.52-●
      ilium M84.550
      ischium M84.550
      metacarpus M84.54-●
      metatarsus M84.57-●
      neck M84.58
      pelvis M84.550
      radius M84.53-●
      rib M84.58
      scapula M84.51-●
      skull M84.58
      specified site NEC M84.58
      tarsus M84.57-●
      tibia M84.56-●
      toe M84.57-●
      ulna M84.53-●
      vertebra M84.58
    osteoporosis M80.00
      disuse —see Osteoporosis, specified type
        NEC, with pathological fracture
      drug-induced —see Osteoporosis, drug
        induced, with pathological fracture
      idiopathic —see Osteoporosis, specified
        type NEC, with pathological
        fracture
      postmenopausal —see Osteoporosis,
        postmenopausal, with pathological
        fracture
      postoophorectomy —see Osteo-
        porosis, postoophorectomy, with
        pathological fracture
      postsurgical malabsorption —see
        Osteoporosis, specified type NEC,
        with pathological fracture
      specified cause NEC —see Osteoporosis,
        specified type NEC, with
        pathological fracture
    specified disease NEC M84.60
      ankle M84.67-●
      carpus M84.64-●
      clavicle M84.61-●
      femur M84.65-●
      fibula M84.66-●
      finger M84.64-●
      hip M84.65-●
      humerus M84.62-●
      ilium M84.650
      ischium M84.650
      metacarpus M84.64-●
      metatarsus M84.67-●
      neck M84.68
      radius M84.63-●
      rib M84.68
      scapula M84.61-●
      skull M84.68
      tarsus M84.67-●
      tibia M84.66-●
      toe M84.67-●
      ulna M84.63-●
      vertebra M84.68
  femur M84.45-●
  fibula M84.46-●
  finger M84.44-●
  hip M84.459
  humerus M84.42-●
  ilium M84.454
  ischium M84.454
  joint prosthesis —see Complications, joint
    prosthesis, mechanical, breakdown, by
    site
  periprosthetic —see Fracture, pathological,
    periprosthetic
  metacarpus M84.44-●
  metatarsus M84.47-●
  neck M84.48

Fracture, pathological (Continued)
  pelvis M84.454
  periprosthetic M97.9
    ankle M97.2-●
    elbow M97.4-●
    finger M97.8
    hip M97.0-●
    knee M97.1-●
    other specified joint M97.8
    shoulder M97.3-●
    spinal joint M97.8
    toe joint M97.8
    wrist joint M97.8
  radius M84.43-●
  restorative material (dental) K08.539
    with loss of material K08.531
    without loss of material K08.530
  rib M84.48
  scapula M84.41-●
  skull M84.48
  tarsus M84.47-●
  tibia M84.46-●
  toe M84.47-●
  ulna M84.43-●
  vertebra M84.48
Fracture, traumatic (abduction) (adduction)
  (separation) —see also Fracture,
    pathological T14.8
  acetabulum S32.40-●
    column
      anterior (displaced) (iliopubic) S32.43-●
        nondisplaced S32.436
      posterior (displaced) (ilioischial)
        S32.443
        nondisplaced S32.44-●
    dome (displaced) S32.48-●
      nondisplaced S32.48
    specified NEC S32.49-●
    transverse (displaced) S32.45-●
      with associated posterior wall fracture
        (displaced) S32.46-●
        nondisplaced S32.46-●
      nondisplaced S32.45-●
    wall
      anterior (displaced) S32.41-●
        nondisplaced S32.41-●
      medial (displaced) S32.47-●
        nondisplaced S32.47-●
      posterior (displaced) S32.42-●
        with associated transverse fracture
          (displaced) S32.46-●
          nondisplaced S32.46-●
        nondisplaced S32.42-●
  acromion —see Fracture, scapula, acromial
    process
  ankle S82.899
    bimalleolar (displaced) S82.84-●
      nondisplaced S82.84-●
    lateral malleolus only (displaced) S82.6-●
      nondisplaced S82.6-●
    medial malleolus (displaced) S82.5-●
      associated with Maisonneuve's
        fracture —see Fracture,
        Maisonneuve's
      nondisplaced S82.5-●
    talus —see Fracture, tarsal, talus
    trimalleolar (displaced) S82.85-●
      nondisplaced S82.85-●
  arm (upper) —see also Fracture, humerus,
    shaft
    humerus —see Fracture, humerus
    radius —see Fracture, radius
    ulna —see Fracture, ulna
  astragalus —see Fracture, tarsal, talus
  atlas —see Fracture, neck, cervical vertebra,
    first
  axis —see Fracture, neck, cervical vertebra,
    second
  back —see Fracture, vertebra
  Barton's —see Barton's fracture
  base of skull —see Fracture, skull, base

Fracture, traumatic (Continued)
  basicervical (basal) (femoral) S72.0
  Bennett's —see Bennett's fracture
  bimalleolar —see Fracture, ankle,
    bimalleolar
  blow-out S02.3-●
  bone NEC T14.8
    birth injury P13.9
    following insertion of orthopedic implant,
      joint prosthesis or bone plate —see
      Fracture, following insertion of
      orthopedic implant, joint prosthesis or
      bone plate
    in (due to) neoplastic disease NEC —
      see Fracture, pathological, due to,
      neoplastic disease
    pathological (cause unknown) —see
      Fracture, pathological
  breast bone —see Fracture, sternum
  ▶ buckle —see Fracture, by site, torus
  bucket handle (semilunar cartilage) —see
    Tear, meniscus
  burst —see Fracture, traumatic, by site
  calcaneus —see Fracture, tarsal, calcaneus
  carpal bone(s) S62.10-●
    capitate (displaced) S62.13-●
      nondisplaced S62.13-●
    cuneiform —see Fracture, carpal bone,
      triquetrum
    hamate (body) (displaced) S62.143
      hook process (displaced) S62.15-●
        nondisplaced S62.15-●
      nondisplaced S62.14-●
    larger multangular —see Fracture, carpal
      bones, trapezium
    lunate (displaced) S62.12-●
      nondisplaced S62.12-●
    navicular S62.00-●
      distal pole (displaced) S62.01-●
        nondisplaced S62.01-●
      middle third (displaced) S62.02-●
        nondisplaced S62.02-●
      proximal third (displaced) S62.03-●
        nondisplaced S62.03-●
      volar tuberosity —see Fracture, carpal
        bones, navicular, distal pole
    os magnum —see Fracture, carpal bones,
      capitate
    pisiform (displaced) S62.16-●
      nondisplaced S62.16-●
    semilunar —see Fracture, carpal bones,
      lunate
    smaller multangular —see Fracture, carpal
      bones, trapezoid
    trapezium (displaced) S62.17-●
      nondisplaced S62.17-●
    trapezoid (displaced) S62.18-●
      nondisplaced S62.18-●
    triquetrum (displaced) S62.11-●
      nondisplaced S62.11-●
    unciform —see Fracture, carpal bones,
      hamate
  cervical —see Fracture, vertebra, cervical
  clavicle S42.00-●
    acromial end (displaced) S42.03-●
      nondisplaced S42.03-●
    birth injury P13.4
    lateral end —see Fracture, clavicle, acromial
      end
    shaft (displaced) S42.02-●
      nondisplaced S42.02-●
    sternal end (anterior) (displaced) S42.01-●
      nondisplaced S42.01-●
      posterior S42.01-●
  coccyx S32.2
  collapsed —see Collapse, vertebra
  collar bone —see Fracture, clavicle
  Colles' —see Colles' fracture
  coronoid process —see Fracture, ulna, upper
    end, coronoid process
  corpus cavernosum penis S39.840

Fracture, traumatic *(Continued)*
  costochondral cartilage S23.41
  costochondral, costosternal junction —*see*
    Fracture, rib
  cranium —*see* Fracture, skull
  cricoid cartilage S12.8
  cuboid (ankle) —*see* Fracture, tarsal, cuboid
  cuneiform
    foot —*see* Fracture, tarsal, cuneiform
    wrist —*see* Fracture, carpal, triquetrum
  delayed union —*see* Delay, union, fracture
  dental restorative material K08.539
    with loss of material K08.531
    without loss of material K08.530
  due to
    birth injury —*see* Birth, injury, fracture
    osteoporosis —*see* Osteoporosis, with
      fracture
  Dupuytren's —*see* Fracture, ankle, lateral
    malleolus
  elbow S42.40-●
  ethmoid (bone) (sinus) —*see* Fracture, skull,
    base
  face bone S02.92
  fatigue —*see also* Fracture, stress
    vertebra M48.40
      cervical region M48.42
      cervicothoracic region M48.43
      lumbar region M48.46
      lumbosacral region M48.47
      occipito-atlanto-axial region M48.41
      sacrococcygeal region M48.48
      thoracic region M48.44
      thoracolumbar region M48.45
  femur, femoral S72.9-●
    basicervical (basal) S72.0
    birth injury P13.2
    capital epiphyseal S79.01-●
    condyles, epicondyles —*see* Fracture,
      femur, lower end
    distal end —*see* Fracture, femur, lower end
    epiphysis
      head —*see* Fracture, femur, upper end,
        epiphysis
      lower —*see* Fracture, femur, lower end,
        epiphysis
      upper —*see* Fracture, femur, upper end,
        epiphysis
    following insertion of implant, prosthesis
      or plate M96.66-●
    head —*see* Fracture, femur, upper end,
      head
    intertrochanteric —*see* Fracture, femur,
      trochanteric
    intratrochanteric —*see* Fracture, femur,
      trochanteric
    lower end S72.40-●
      condyle (displaced) S72.41-●
        lateral (displaced) S72.42-●
          nondisplaced S72.42-●
        medial (displaced) S72.43-●
          nondisplaced S72.43-●
        nondisplaced S72.41-●
      epiphysis (displaced) S72.44-●
        nondisplaced S72.44-●
      physeal S79.10-●
        Salter-Harris
          Type I S79.11-●
          Type II S79.12-●
          Type III S79.13-●
          Type IV S79.14-●
        specified NEC S79.19-●
      specified NEC S72.49-●
      supracondylar (displaced) S72.45-●
        with intracondylar extension
          (displaced) S72.46-●
          nondisplaced S72.46-●
        nondisplaced S72.45-●
      torus S72.47-●
    neck —*see* Fracture, femur, upper end,
      neck

Fracture, traumatic *(Continued)*
  femur, femoral *(Continued)*
    pertrochanteric —*see* Fracture, femur,
      trochanteric
    shaft (lower third) (middle third) (upper
      third) S72.30-●
      comminuted (displaced) S72.35-●
        nondisplaced S72.35-●
      oblique (displaced) S72.33-●
        nondisplaced S72.33-●
      segmental (displaced) S72.36-●
        nondisplaced S72.36-●
      specified NEC S72.39-●
      spiral (displaced) S72.34-●
        nondisplaced S72.34-●
      transverse (displaced) S72.32-●
        nondisplaced S72.32-●
    specified site NEC —*see* subcategory
      S72.8
    subcapital (displaced) S72.01-●
    subtrochanteric (region) (section)
      (displaced) S72.2-●
      nondisplaced S72.2-●
    transcervical —*see* Fracture, femur,
      midcervical
    transtrochanteric —*see* Fracture, femur,
      trochanteric
    trochanteric S72.10-●
      apophyseal (displaced) S72.13-●
        nondisplaced S72.13-●
      greater trochanter (displaced) S72.11-●
        nondisplaced S72.11-●
      intertrochanteric (displaced) S72.14-●
        nondisplaced S72.14-●
      lesser trochanter (displaced) S72.12-●
        nondisplaced S72.12-●
    upper end S72.00-●
      apophyseal (displaced) S72.13-●
        nondisplaced S72.13-●
      cervicotrochanteric —*see* Fracture,
        femur, upper end, neck, base
      epiphysis (displaced) S72.02-●
        nondisplaced S72.02-●
      head S72.05-●
        articular (displaced) S72.06-●
          nondisplaced S72.06-●
        specified NEC S72.09-●
      intertrochanteric (displaced)
        S72.14-●
        nondisplaced S72.14-●
      intracapsular S72.01-●
      midcervical (displaced) S72.03-●
        nondisplaced S72.03-●
      neck S72.00-●
        base (displaced) S72.04-●
          nondisplaced S72.04-●
        specified NEC S72.09-●
      pertrochanteric —*see* Fracture, femur,
        upper end, trochanteric
      physeal S79.00-●
        Salter-Harris type I S79.01-●
        specified NEC S79.09-●
      subcapital (displaced) S72.01-●
      subtrochanteric (displaced) S72.2-●
        nondisplaced S72.2-●
      transcervical —*see* Fracture, femur,
        upper end, midcervical
      trochanteric S72.10-●
        greater (displaced) S72.11-●
          nondisplaced S72.11-●
        lesser (displaced) S72.12-●
          nondisplaced S72.12-●
  fibula (shaft) (styloid) S82.40-●
    comminuted (displaced) S82.45-●
      nondisplaced S82.45-●
    following insertion of implant, prosthesis
      or plate M96.67-●
    involving ankle or malleolus —*see*
      Fracture, fibula, lateral malleolus
    lateral malleolus (displaced) S82.6-●
      nondisplaced S82.6-●

Fracture, traumatic *(Continued)*
  fibula (shaft) (styloid) *(Continued)*
    lower end
      physeal S89.30-●
        Salter-Harris
          Type I S89.31-●
          Type II S89.32-●
        specified NEC S89.39-●
      specified NEC S82.83-●
      torus S82.82-●
    oblique (displaced) S82.43-●
      nondisplaced S82.43-●
    segmental (displaced) S82.46-●
      nondisplaced S82.46-●
    specified NEC S82.49-●
    spiral (displaced) S82.44-●
      nondisplaced S82.44-●
    transverse (displaced) S82.42-●
      nondisplaced S82.42-●
    upper end
      physeal S89.20-●
        Salter-Harris
          Type I S89.21-●
          Type II S89.22-●
        specified NEC S89.29-●
      specified NEC S82.83-●
      torus S82.81-●
  finger (except thumb) S62.60-●
    distal phalanx (displaced) S62.63-●
      nondisplaced S62.66-●
    index S62.60-●
      distal phalanx (displaced) S62.63-●
        nondisplaced S62.66-●
      middle phalanx (displaced) S62.62-●
        nondisplaced S62.65-●
      proximal phalanx (displaced) S62.61-●
        nondisplaced S62.64-●
    little S62.60-●
      distal phalanx (displaced) S62.63-●
        nondisplaced S62.66-●
      middle phalanx (displaced) S62.62-●
        nondisplaced S62.65-●
      proximal phalanx (displaced) S62.61-●
        nondisplaced S62.64-●
    middle phalanx (displaced) S62.62-●
      nondisplaced S62.65-●
    middle S62.60-●
      distal phalanx (displaced) S62.63-●
        nondisplaced S62.66-●
      middle phalanx (displaced) S62.62-●
        nondisplaced S62.65-●
      proximal phalanx (displaced) S62.61-●
        nondisplaced S62.64-●
    proximal phalanx (displaced) S62.61-●
      nondisplaced S62.64-●
    ring S62.60-●
      distal phalanx (displaced) S62.63-●
        nondisplaced S62.66-●
      middle phalanx (displaced) S62.62-●
        nondisplaced S62.65-●
      proximal phalanx (displaced) S62.61-●
        nondisplaced S62.64-●
    thumb —*see* Fracture, thumb
  following insertion (intraoperative)
    (postoperative) of orthopedic implant,
    joint prosthesis or bone plate M96.69
    femur M96.66-●
    fibula M96.67-●
    humerus M96.62-●
    pelvis M96.65
    radius M96.63-●
    specified bone NEC M96.69
    tibia M96.67-●
    ulna M96.63-●
  foot S92.90-●
    astragalus —*see* Fracture, tarsal, talus
    calcaneus —*see* Fracture, tarsal, calcaneus
    cuboid —*see* Fracture, tarsal, cuboid
    cuneiform —*see* Fracture, tarsal, cuneiform
    metatarsal —*see* Fracture, metatarsal
    navicular —*see* Fracture, tarsal, navicular

▶ New ⇒ Revised ~~deleted~~ Deleted ● Use Additional Character(s)

Fracture, traumatic *(Continued)*
foot *(Continued)*
sesamoid S92.81-•
specified NEC S92.81-•
talus —*see* Fracture, tarsal, talus
tarsal —*see* Fracture, tarsal
toe —*see* Fracture, toe
forearm S52.9-•
radius —*see* Fracture, radius
ulna —*see* Fracture, ulna
fossa (anterior) (middle) (posterior) S02.19
fragility —*see* Fracture, pathological, due to
osteoporosis
frontal (bone) (skull) S02.0
sinus S02.19
glenoid (cavity) (scapula) —*see* Fracture,
scapula, glenoid cavity
greenstick —*see* Fracture, by site
hallux —*see* Fracture, toe, great
hand S62.9-•
carpal —*see* Fracture, carpal bone
finger (except thumb) —*see* Fracture,
finger
metacarpal —*see* Fracture, metacarpal
navicular (scaphoid) (hand) —*see* Fracture,
carpal bone, navicular
thumb —*see* Fracture, thumb
healed or old
with complications - code by Nature of the
complication
heel bone —*see* Fracture, tarsal, calcaneus
Hill-Sachs S42.29-•
hip —*see* Fracture, femur, neck
humerus S42.30-•
anatomical neck —*see* Fracture, humerus,
upper end
articular process —*see* Fracture, humerus,
lower end
capitellum —*see* Fracture, humerus, lower
end, condyle, lateral
distal end —*see* Fracture, humerus, lower
end
epiphysis
lower —*see* Fracture, humerus, lower
end, physeal
upper —*see* Fracture, humerus, upper
end, physeal
external condyle —*see* Fracture, humerus,
lower end, condyle, lateral
following insertion of implant, prosthesis
or plate M96.62-•
great tuberosity —*see* Fracture, humerus,
upper end, greater tuberosity
intercondylar —*see* Fracture, humerus,
lower end
internal epicondyle —*see* Fracture, humerus,
lower end, epicondyle, medial
lesser tuberosity —*see* Fracture, humerus,
upper end, lesser tuberosity
lower end S42.40-•
condyle
lateral (displaced) S42.45-•
nondisplaced S42.45-•
medial (displaced) S42.46-•
nondisplaced S42.46-•
epicondyle
lateral (displaced) S42.43-•
nondisplaced S42.43-•
medial (displaced) S42.44-•
incarcerated S42.44-•
nondisplaced S42.44-•
physeal S49.10-•
Salter-Harris
Type I S49.11-•
Type II S49.12-•
Type III S49.13-•
Type IV S49.14-•
specified NEC S49.19-•
specified NEC (displaced)
S42.49-•
nondisplaced S42.49-•

Fracture, traumatic *(Continued)*
humerus *(Continued)*
lower end *(Continued)*
supracondylar (simple) (displaced)
S42.41-•
with intercondylar fracture —*see*
Fracture, humerus, lower end
comminuted (displaced) S42.42-•
nondisplaced S42.42-•
nondisplaced S42.41-•
torus S42.48-•
transcondylar (displaced) S42.47-•
nondisplaced S42.47-•
proximal end —*see* Fracture, humerus,
upper end
shaft S42.30-•
comminuted (displaced) S42.35-•
nondisplaced S42.35-•
greenstick S42.31-•
oblique (displaced) S42.33-•
nondisplaced S42.33-•
segmental (displaced) S42.36-•
nondisplaced S42.36-•
specified NEC S42.39-•
spiral (displaced) S42.34-•
nondisplaced S42.34-•
transverse (displaced) S42.32-•
nondisplaced S42.32-•
supracondylar —*see* Fracture, humerus,
lower end
surgical neck —*see* Fracture, humerus,
upper end, surgical neck
trochlea —*see* Fracture, humerus, lower
end, condyle, medial
tuberosity —*see* Fracture, humerus, upper
end
upper end S42.20-•
anatomical neck —*see* Fracture,
humerus, upper end, specified NEC
articular head —*see* Fracture, humerus,
upper end, specified NEC
epiphysis —*see* Fracture, humerus,
upper end, physeal
greater tuberosity (displaced) S42.25-•
nondisplaced S42.25-•
lesser tuberosity (displaced) S42.26-•
nondisplaced S42.26-•
physeal S49.00-•
Salter-Harris
Type I S49.01-•
Type II S49.02-•
Type III S49.03-•
Type IV S49.04-•
specified NEC S49.09-•
specified NEC (displaced) S42.29-•
nondisplaced S42.29-•
surgical neck (displaced) S42.21-•
four-part S42.24-•
nondisplaced S42.21-•
three-part S42.23-•
two-part (displaced) S42.22-•
nondisplaced S42.22-•
torus S42.27-•
transepiphyseal —*see* Fracture, humerus,
upper end, physeal
hyoid bone S12.8
ilium S32.30-•
with disruption of pelvic ring —*see*
Disruption, pelvic ring
avulsion (displaced) S32.31-•
nondisplaced S32.31-•
specified NEC S32.39-•
impaction, impacted - code as Fracture, by
site
innominate bone —*see* Fracture, ilium
instep —*see* Fracture, foot
ischium S32.60-•
with disruption of pelvic ring —*see*
Disruption, pelvic ring
avulsion (displaced) S32.61-•
nondisplaced S32.61-•
specified NEC S32.69-•

Fracture, traumatic *(Continued)*
jaw (bone) (lower) —*see* Fracture, mandible
upper —*see* Fracture, maxilla
joint prosthesis —*see* Complications, joint
prosthesis, mechanical, breakdown,
by site
periprosthetic —*see* Fracture, traumatic,
periprosthetic
knee cap —*see* Fracture, patella
larynx S12.8
late effects —*see* Sequelae, fracture
leg (lower) S82.9-•
ankle —*see* Fracture, ankle
femur —*see* Fracture, femur
fibula —*see* Fracture, fibula
malleolus —*see* Fracture, ankle
patella —*see* Fracture, patella
specified site NEC S82.89-•
tibia —*see* Fracture, tibia
lumbar spine —*see* Fracture, vertebra, lumbar
lumbosacral spine S32.9
Maisonneuve's (displaced) S82.86-•
nondisplaced S82.86-•
malar bone —*see also* Fracture, maxilla
S02.400
left side S02.40B
right side S02.40A
malleolus —*see* Fracture, ankle
malunion —*see* Fracture, by site
mandible (lower jawbone) S02.609
alveolus S02.67-•
angle (of jaw) S02.65-•
body, unspecified S02.600-•
left side S02.602
right side S02.601
condylar process S02.61-•
coronoid process S02.63-•
ramus, unspecified S02.64-•
specified site NEC S02.69
subcondylar process S02.62-•
symphysis S02.66
manubrium (sterni) S22.21
dissociation from sternum S22.23
march —*see* Fracture, traumatic, stress, by site
maxilla, maxillary (bone) (sinus) (superior)
(upper jaw) S02.401
alveolus S02.42
inferior —*see* Fracture, mandible
LeFort I S02.411
LeFort II S02.412
LeFort III S02.413
left side S02.40D
right side S02.40C
metacarpal S62.309
base (displaced) S62.319
nondisplaced S62.349
fifth S62.30-•
base (displaced) S62.31-•
nondisplaced S62.34-•
neck (displaced) S62.33-•
nondisplaced S62.36-•
shaft (displaced) S62.32-•
nondisplaced S62.35-•
specified NEC S62.398
first S62.20-•
base NEC (displaced) S62.23-•
nondisplaced S62.23-•
Bennett's —*see* Bennett's fracture
neck (displaced) S62.25-•
nondisplaced S62.25-•
shaft (displaced) S62.24-•
nondisplaced S62.24-•
specified NEC S62.29-•
fourth S62.30-•
base (displaced) S62.31-•
nondisplaced S62.34-•
neck (displaced) S62.33-•
nondisplaced S62.36-•
shaft (displaced) S62.32-•
nondisplaced S62.35-•
specified NEC S62.39-•

Fracture, traumatic *(Continued)*
  metacarpal *(Continued)*
    neck (displaced) S62.33-●
      nondisplaced S62.36-●
    Rolando's —*see* Rolando's fracture
    second S62.30-●
      base (displaced) S62.31-●
        nondisplaced S62.34-●
      neck (displaced) S62.33-●
        nondisplaced S62.36-●
      shaft (displaced) S62.32-●
        nondisplaced S62.35-●
      specified NEC S62.39-●
    shaft (displaced) S62.32-●
      nondisplaced S62.35-●
    specified NEC S62.399
    third S62.30-●
      base (displaced) S62.31-●
        nondisplaced S62.34-●
      neck (displaced) S62.33-●
        nondisplaced S62.36-●
      shaft (displaced) S62.32-●
        nondisplaced S62.35-●
      specified NEC S62.39-●
▶ metaphyseal —*see* Fracture, traumatic, by
    site, shaft
  metastatic —*see* Fracture, pathological,
    due to, neoplastic disease —*see also*
    Neoplasm
  metatarsal bone S92.30-●
    fifth (displaced) S92.35-●
      nondisplaced S92.35-●
    first (displaced) S92.31-●
      nondisplaced S92.31-●
    fourth (displaced) S92.34-●
      nondisplaced S92.34-●
    physeal S99.10-●
      Salter-Harris
        Type I S99.11-●
        Type II S99.12-●
        Type III S99.13-●
        Type IV S99.14-●
      specified NEC S99.19-●
    second (displaced) S92.32-●
      nondisplaced S92.32-●
    third (displaced) S92.33-●
      nondisplaced S92.33-●
  Monteggia's —*see* Monteggia's fracture
  multiple
    hand (and wrist) NEC —*see* Fracture,
      by site
    ribs —*see* Fracture, rib, multiple
  nasal (bone(s)) S02.2
  navicular (scaphoid) (foot) —*see also* Fracture,
    tarsal, navicular
    hand —*see* Fracture, carpal, navicular
  neck S12.9
    cervical vertebra S12.9
      fifth (displaced) S12.400
        nondisplaced S12.401
        specified type NEC (displaced)
          S12.490
          nondisplaced S12.491
      first (displaced) S12.000
        burst (stable) S12.01
          unstable S12.02
        lateral mass (displaced)
          S12.040
          nondisplaced S12.041
        nondisplaced S12.001
        posterior arch (displaced)
          S12.030
          nondisplaced S12.031
        specified type NEC (displaced)
          S12.090
          nondisplaced S12.091
      fourth (displaced) S12.300
        nondisplaced S12.301
        specified type NEC (displaced)
          S12.390
          nondisplaced S12.391

Fracture, traumatic *(Continued)*
  neck *(Continued)*
    cervical vertebra *(Continued)*
      second (displaced) S12.100
        dens (anterior) (displaced) (type II)
          S12.110
          nondisplaced S12.112
          posterior S12.111
          specified type NEC (displaced)
            S12.120
            nondisplaced S12.121
        nondisplaced S12.101
        specified type NEC (displaced)
          S12.190
          nondisplaced S12.191
      seventh (displaced) S12.600
        nondisplaced S12.601
        specified type NEC (displaced)
          S12.690
          nondisplaced S12.691
      sixth (displaced) S12.500
        nondisplaced S12.501
        specified type NEC (displaced)
          S12.590
          nondisplaced S12.591
      third (displaced) S12.200
        nondisplaced S12.201
        specified type NEC (displaced)
          S12.290
          nondisplaced S12.291
    hyoid bone S12.8
    larynx S12.8
    specified site NEC S12.8
    thyroid cartilage S12.8
    trachea S12.8
  neoplastic NEC —*see* Fracture, pathological,
    due to, neoplastic disease
  neural arch —*see* Fracture, vertebra
  newborn —*see* Birth, injury, fracture
  nontraumatic —*see* Fracture, pathological
  nonunion —*see* Nonunion, fracture
  nose, nasal (bone) (septum) S02.2
  occiput —*see* Fracture, skull, base,
    occiput
  odontoid process —*see* Fracture, neck,
    cervical vertebra, second
  olecranon (process) (ulna) —*see* Fracture,
    ulna, upper end, olecranon process
  orbit, orbital (bone) (region) S02.85
    floor (blow-out) S02.3-●
    roof S02.12-●
    wall S02.85
      lateral S02.84-●
      medial S02.83-●
  os
    calcis —*see* Fracture, tarsal,
      calcaneus
    magnum —*see* Fracture, carpal,
      capitate
    pubis —*see* Fracture, pubis
  palate S02.8-●
  parietal bone (skull) S02.0
  patella S82.00-●
    comminuted (displaced) S82.04-●
      nondisplaced S82.04-●
    longitudinal (displaced) S82.02-●
      nondisplaced S82.02-●
    osteochondral (displaced) S82.01-●
      nondisplaced S82.01-●
    specified NEC S82.09-●
    transverse (displaced) S82.03-●
      nondisplaced S82.03-●
  pedicle (of vertebral arch) —*see* Fracture,
    vertebra
  pelvis, pelvic (bone) S32.9
    acetabulum —*see* Fracture, acetabulum
    circle —*see* Disruption, pelvic ring
    following insertion of implant, prosthesis
      or plate M96.65
    ilium —*see* Fracture, ilium
    ischium —*see* Fracture, ischium

Fracture, traumatic *(Continued)*
  pelvis, pelvic *(Continued)*
    multiple
      with disruption of pelvic ring (circle) —
        see Disruption, pelvic ring
      without disruption of pelvic ring (circle)
        S32.82
    pubis —*see* Fracture, pubis
    sacrum —*see* Fracture, sacrum
    specified site NEC S32.89
  periprosthetic, around internal prosthetic
    joint M97.9
    ankle M97.2-●
    elbow M97.4-●
    finger M97.8
    hip M97.0-●
    knee M97.1-●
    shoulder M97.3-●
    specified joint NEC M97.8
    spine M97.8
    toe M97.8
    wrist M97.8
  phalanx
    foot —*see* Fracture, toe
    hand —*see* Fracture, finger
  pisiform —*see* Fracture, carpal, pisiform
  pond —*see* Fracture, skull
  prosthetic device, internal —*see*
    Complications, prosthetic device, by site,
    mechanical
  pubis S32.50-●
    with disruption of pelvic ring —*see*
      Disruption, pelvic ring
    specified site NEC S32.59-●
    superior rim S32.59-●
  radius S52.9-●
    distal end —*see* Fracture, radius, lower end
    following insertion of implant, prosthesis
      or plate M96.63-●
    head —*see* Fracture, radius, upper end,
      head
    lower end S52.50-●
      Barton's —*see* Barton's fracture
      Colles' —*see* Colles' fracture
      extraarticular NEC S52.55-●
      intraarticular NEC S52.57-●
      physeal S59.20-●
        Salter-Harris
          Type I S59.21-●
          Type II S59.22-●
          Type III S59.23-●
          Type IV S59.24-●
        specified NEC S59.29-●
      Smith's —*see* Smith's fracture
      specified NEC S52.59-●
      styloid process (displaced) S52.51-●
        nondisplaced S52.51-●
      torus S52.52-●
    neck —*see* Fracture, radius, upper end
    proximal end —*see* Fracture, radius, upper
      end
    shaft S52.30-●
      bent bone S52.38-●
      comminuted (displaced) S52.35-●
        nondisplaced S52.35-●
      Galeazzi's —*see* Galeazzi's fracture
      greenstick S52.31-●
      oblique (displaced) S52.33-●
        nondisplaced S52.33-●
      segmental (displaced) S52.36-●
        nondisplaced S52.36-●
      specified NEC S52.39-●
      spiral (displaced) S52.34-●
        nondisplaced S52.34-●
      transverse (displaced) S52.32-●
        nondisplaced S52.32-●
    upper end S52.10-●
      head (displaced) S52.12-●
        nondisplaced S52.12-●
      neck (displaced) S52.13-●
        nondisplaced S52.13-●

▶ New   ➡ Revised   ~~deleted~~ Deleted   ● Use Additional Character(s)

Fracture, traumatic *(Continued)*
  radius *(Continued)*
    upper end *(Continued)*
      physeal S59.10-●
        Salter-Harris
          Type I S59.11-●
          Type II S59.12-●
          Type III S59.13-●
          Type IV S59.14-●
        specified NEC S59.19-●
      specified NEC S52.18-●
      torus S52.11-●
  ramus
    inferior or superior, pubis —*see* Fracture,
      pubis
    mandible —*see* Fracture, mandible
  restorative material (dental)
    K08.539
    with loss of material K08.531
    without loss of material K08.530
  rib S22.3-●
    with flail chest —*see* Flail, chest
    multiple S22.4-●
      with flail chest —*see* Flail, chest
  root, tooth —*see* Fracture, tooth
  sacrum S32.10
    specified NEC S32.19
    Type
      1 S32.14
      2 S32.15
      3 S32.16
      4 S32.17
    Zone
      I S32.119
        displaced (minimally) S32.111
          severely S32.112
        nondisplaced S32.110
      II S32.129
        displaced (minimally) S32.121
          severely S32.122
        nondisplaced S32.120
      III S32.139
        displaced (minimally) S32.131
          severely S32.132
        nondisplaced S32.130
  scaphoid (hand) —*see also* Fracture, carpal,
    navicular
    foot —*see* Fracture, tarsal, navicular
  scapula S42.10-●
    acromial process (displaced) S42.12-●
      nondisplaced S42.12-●
    body (displaced) S42.11-●
      nondisplaced S42.11-●
    coracoid process (displaced) S42.13-●
      nondisplaced S42.13-●
    glenoid cavity (displaced) S42.14-●
      nondisplaced S42.14-●
    neck (displaced) S42.15-●
      nondisplaced S42.15-●
    specified NEC S42.19-●
  semilunar bone, wrist —*see* Fracture, carpal,
    lunate
  sequelae —*see* Sequelae, fracture
  sesamoid bone
    foot S92.81-●
    hand —*see* Fracture, carpal
    other —*see* Fracture, traumatic, by site
  shepherd's —*see* Fracture, tarsal, talus
  shoulder (girdle) S42.9-●
    blade —*see* Fracture, scapula
  sinus (ethmoid) (frontal) S02.19
  skull S02.91
    base S02.10-●
      occiput S02.119
        condyle S02.113
          type I S02.110
            left side S02.11B
            right side S02.11A
          type II S02.111
            left side S02.11D
            right side S02.11C

Fracture, traumatic *(Continued)*
  skull *(Continued)*
    base *(Continued)*
      occiput *(Continued)*
        condyle *(Continued)*
          type III S02.112
            left side S02.11F
            right side S02.11E
          specified NEC S02.118
            left side S02.11H
            right side S02.11G
      specified NEC S02.19-●
    birth injury P13.0
    frontal bone S02.0
    parietal bone S02.0
    specified site NEC S02.8
    temporal bone S02.19
    vault S02.0
  Smith's —*see* Smith's fracture
  sphenoid (bone) (sinus) S02.19
  spine —*see* Fracture, vertebra
  spinous process —*see* Fracture, vertebra
  spontaneous (cause unknown) —*see* Fracture,
    pathological
  stave (of thumb) —*see* Fracture, metacarpal,
    first
  sternum S22.20
    with flail chest —*see* Flail, chest
    body S22.22
    manubrium S22.21
    xiphoid (process) S22.24
  stress M84.30
    ankle M84.37-●
    carpus M84.34-●
    clavicle M84.31-●
    femoral neck M84.359
    femur M84.35-●
    fibula M84.36-●
    finger M84.34-●
    hip M84.359
    humerus M84.32-●
    ilium M84.350
    ischium M84.350
    metacarpus M84.34-●
    metatarsus M84.37-●
    neck —*see* Fracture, fatigue, vertebra
    pelvis M84.350
    radius M84.33-●
    rib M84.38
    scapula M84.31-●
    skull M84.38
    tarsus M84.37-●
    tibia M84.36-●
    toe M84.37-●
    ulna M84.33-●
    vertebra —*see* Fracture, fatigue, vertebra
  supracondylar, elbow —*see* Fracture,
    humerus, lower end, supracondylar
  symphysis pubis —*see* Fracture, pubis
  talus (ankle bone) —*see* Fracture, tarsal,
    talus
  tarsal bone(s) S92.20-●
    astragalus —*see* Fracture, tarsal, talus
    calcaneus S92.00-●
      anterior process (displaced)
        S92.02-●
        nondisplaced S92.02-●
      body (displaced) S92.01-●
        nondisplaced S92.01-●
      extraarticular NEC (displaced)
        S92.05-●
        nondisplaced S92.05-●
      intraarticular (displaced) S92.06-●
        nondisplaced S92.06-●
      physeal S99.00-●
        Salter-Harris
          Type I S99.01-●
          Type II S99.02-●
          Type III S99.03-●
          Type IV S99.04-●
        specified NEC S99.09-●

Fracture, traumatic *(Continued)*
  tarsal bone(s) *(Continued)*
    calcaneus *(Continued)*
      tuberosity (displaced) S92.04-●
        avulsion (displaced) S92.03-●
          nondisplaced S92.03-●
        nondisplaced S92.04-●
    cuboid (displaced) S92.21-●
      nondisplaced S92.21-●
    cuneiform
      intermediate (displaced) S92.23-●
        nondisplaced S92.23-●
      lateral (displaced) S92.22-●
        nondisplaced S92.22-●
      medial (displaced) S92.24-●
        nondisplaced S92.24-●
    navicular (displaced) S92.25-●
      nondisplaced S92.25-●
    scaphoid —*see* Fracture, tarsal, navicular
    talus S92.10-●
      avulsion (displaced) S92.15-●
        nondisplaced S92.15-●
      body (displaced) S92.12-●
        nondisplaced S92.12-●
      dome (displaced) S92.14-●
        nondisplaced S92.14-●
      head (displaced) S92.12-●
        nondisplaced S92.12-●
      lateral process (displaced)
        S92.14-●
        nondisplaced S92.14-●
      neck (displaced) S92.11-●
        nondisplaced S92.11-●
      posterior process (displaced)
        S92.13-●
        nondisplaced S92.13-●
      specified NEC S92.19-●
  temporal bone (styloid) S02.19
  thorax (bony) S22.9
    with flail chest —*see* Flail, chest
    rib S22.3-●
      multiple S22.4-●
        with flail chest —*see* Flail, chest
    sternum S22.20
      body S22.22
      manubrium S22.21
      xiphoid process S22.24
    vertebra (displaced) S22.009
      burst (stable) S22.001
        unstable S22.002
      eighth S22.069
        burst (stable) S22.061
          unstable S22.062
        specified type NEC S22.068
        wedge compression S22.060
      eleventh S22.089
        burst (stable) S22.081
          unstable S22.082
        specified type NEC S22.088
        wedge compression S22.080
      fifth S22.059
        burst (stable) S22.051
          unstable S22.052
        specified type NEC S22.058
        wedge compression S22.050
      first S22.019
        burst (stable) S22.011
          unstable S22.012
        specified type NEC S22.018
        wedge compression S22.010
      fourth S22.049
        burst (stable) S22.041
          unstable S22.042
        specified type NEC S22.048
        wedge compression S22.040
      ninth S22.079
        burst (stable) S22.071
          unstable S22.072
        specified type NEC S22.078
        wedge compression S22.070
      nondisplaced S22.001

▶ New   ⇒ Revised   ~~deleted~~ Deleted   ● Use Additional Character(s)

Fracture, traumatic *(Continued)*
  vertebra, vertebral *(Continued)*
    metastatic —*see* Collapse, vertebra, in,
      specified disease NEC —*see also*
      Neoplasm
    newborn (birth injury) P11.5
    sacrum S32.10
      specified NEC S32.19
      Type
        1 S32.14
        2 S32.15
        3 S32.16
        4 S32.17
      Zone
        I S32.119
          displaced (minimally) S32.111
            severely S32.112
          nondisplaced S32.110
        II S32.129
          displaced (minimally) S32.121
            severely S32.122
          nondisplaced S32.120
        III S32.139
          displaced (minimally) S32.131
            severely S32.132
          nondisplaced S32.130
    thoracic —*see* Fracture, thorax, vertebra
  vertex S02.0
  vomer (bone) S02.2
  wrist S62.10-●
    carpal —*see* Fracture, carpal bone
    navicular (scaphoid) (hand) —*see* Fracture,
      carpal, navicular
  xiphisternum, xiphoid (process) S22.24
  zygoma S02.442
    left side S02.40F
    right side S02.40E
Fragile, fragility
  autosomal site Q95.5
  bone, congenital (with blue sclera) Q78.0
  capillary (hereditary) D69.8
  hair L67.8
  nails L60.3
  non-sex chromosome site Q95.5
  X chromosome Q99.2
Fragilitas
  crinium L67.8
  ossium (with blue sclerae) (hereditary) Q78.0
  unguium L60.3
    congenital Q84.6
Fragments, cataract (lens), following cataract
  surgery H59.02-●
  retained foreign body —*see* Retained, foreign
    body fragments (type of)
Frailty (frail) R54
  mental R41.81
Frambesia, frambesial (tropica) —*see also* Yaws
  initial lesion or ulcer A66.0
  primary A66.0
Frambeside
  gummatous A66.4
  of early yaws A66.2
Frambesioma A66.1
Franceschetti-Klein (-Wildervanck) disease or
  syndrome Q75.4
Francis' disease —*see* Tularemia
Franklin disease C88.2
Frank's essential thrombocytopenia D69.3
Fraser's syndrome Q87.0
Freckle(s) L81.2
  malignant melanoma in —*see* Melanoma
  melanotic (Hutchinson's) —*see* Melanoma,
    in situ
  retinal D49.81
Frederickson's hyperlipoproteinemia, type
  I and V E78.3
  IIA E78.00
  IIB and III E78.2
  IV E78.1
Freeman Sheldon syndrome Q87.0
Freezing —*see also* Effect, adverse, cold T69.9

Freiberg's disease (infraction of metatarsal head
  or osteochondrosis) —*see* Osteochondrosis,
  juvenile, metatarsus
Frei's disease A55
Fremitus, friction, cardiac R01.2
Frenum, frenulum
  external os Q51.828
  tongue (shortening) (congenital) Q38.1
Frequency micturition (nocturnal) R35.0
  psychogenic F45.8
Frey's syndrome
  auriculotemporal G50.8
  hyperhidrosis L74.52
Friction
  burn —*see* Burn, by site
  fremitus, cardiac R01.2
  precordial R01.2
  sounds, chest R09.89
Friderichsen-Waterhouse syndrome or disease
  A39.1
Friedländer's B (bacillus) NEC —*see also*
  condition A49.8
Friedreich's
  ⇛ataxia G11.11
  ⇛combined systemic disease G11.11
  facial hemihypertrophy Q67.4
  ⇛sclerosis (cerebellum) (spinal cord)
    G11.11
Frigidity F52.22
Fröhlich's syndrome E23.6
Frontal —*see also* condition
  lobe syndrome F07.0
Frostbite (superficial) T33.90
  with
    partial thickness skin loss —*see* Frostbite
      (superficial), by site
    tissue necrosis T34.90
  abdominal wall T33.3
    with tissue necrosis T34.3
  ankle T33.81-●
    with tissue necrosis T34.81-●
  arm T33.4-●
  with tissue necrosis T34.4-●
    finger(s) —*see* Frostbite, finger
    hand —*see* Frostbite, hand
    wrist —*see* Frostbite, wrist
  ear T33.01-●
    with tissue necrosis T34.01-●
  face T33.09
    with tissue necrosis T34.09
  finger T33.53-●
    with tissue necrosis T34.53-●
  foot T33.82-●
    with tissue necrosis T34.82-●
  hand T33.52-●
    with tissue necrosis T34.52-●
  head T33.09
    with tissue necrosis T34.09
    ear —*see* Frostbite, ear
    nose —*see* Frostbite, nose
  hip (and thigh) T33.6-●
    with tissue necrosis T34.6-●
  knee T33.7-●
    with tissue necrosis T34.7-●
  leg T33.9-●
    with tissue necrosis T34.9-●
    ankle —*see* Frostbite, ankle
    foot —*see* Frostbite, foot
    knee —*see* Frostbite, knee
    lower T33.7-●
      with tissue necrosis T34.7-●
    thigh —*see* Frostbite, hip
    toe —*see* Frostbite, toe
  limb
    lower T33.99
      with tissue necrosis T34.99
    upper —*see* Frostbite, arm
  neck T33.1
    with tissue necrosis T34.1
  nose T33.02
    with tissue necrosis T34.02

Frostbite *(Continued)*
  pelvis T33.3
    with tissue necrosis T34.3
  specified site NEC T33.99
    with tissue necrosis T34.99
  thigh —*see* Frostbite, hip
  thorax T33.2
    with tissue necrosis T34.2
  toes T33.83-●
    with tissue necrosis T34.83-●
  trunk T33.99
    with tissue necrosis T34.99
  wrist T33.51-●
    with tissue necrosis T34.51-●
Frotteurism F65.81
Frozen —*see also* Effect, adverse, cold T69.9
  pelvis (female) N94.89
    male K66.8
  shoulder —*see* Capsulitis, adhesive
Fructokinase deficiency E74.11
Fructose 1,6 diphosphatase deficiency E74.19
Fructosemia (benign) (essential) E74.12
Fructosuria (benign) (essential) E74.11
Fuchs'
  black spot (myopic) —*see also* Myopia,
    degenerative H44.2-●
  ⇛dystrophy (corneal endothelium) H18.51-●
  heterochromic cyclitis —*see* Cyclitis, Fuchs'
    heterochromic
Fucosidosis E77.1
Fugue R68.89
  dissociative F44.1
  hysterical (dissociative) F44.1
  postictal in epilepsy —*see* Epilepsy
  reaction to exceptional stress (transient)
    F43.0
Fulminant, fulminating —*see* condition
Functional —*see also* condition
  bleeding (uterus) N93.8
Functioning, intellectual, borderline R41.83
Fundus —*see* condition
Fungemia NOS B49
Fungus, fungous
  cerebral G93.89
  disease NOS B49
  infection —*see* Infection, fungus
Funiculitis (acute) (chronic) (endemic)
  N49.1
  gonococcal (acute) (chronic) A54.23
  tuberculous A18.15
Funnel
  breast (acquired) M95.4
    congenital Q67.6
    sequelae (late effect) of rickets E64.3
  chest (acquired) M95.4
    congenital Q67.6
    sequelae (late effect) of rickets E64.3
  pelvis (acquired) M95.5
    with disproportion (fetopelvic) O33.3
      causing obstructed labor O65.3
    congenital Q74.2
FUO (fever of unknown origin) R50.9
Furfur L21.0
  microsporon B36.0
Furrier's lung J67.8
Furrowed K14.5
  nail(s) (transverse) L60.4
    congenital Q84.6
  tongue K14.5
    congenital Q38.3
Furuncle L02.92
  abdominal wall L02.221
  ankle —*see* Furuncle, lower limb
  antecubital space —*see* Furuncle, upper
    limb
  anus K61.0
  arm —*see* Furuncle, upper limb
  auditory canal, external —*see* Abscess, ear,
    external
  auricle (ear) —*see* Abscess, ear, external
  axilla (region) L02.42-●

Furuncle *(Continued)*
  back (any part) L02.222
  breast N61.1
  buttock L02.32
  cheek (external) L02.02
  chest wall L02.223
  chin L02.02
  corpus cavernosum N48.21
  ear, external —*see* Abscess, ear, external
  external auditory canal —*see* Abscess, ear, external
  eyelid —*see* Abscess, eyelid
  face L02.02
  femoral (region) —*see* Furuncle, lower limb
  finger —*see* Furuncle, hand
  flank L02.221
  foot L02.62-•
  forehead L02.02
  gluteal (region) L02.32
  groin L02.224
  hand L02.52-•
  head L02.821
    face L02.02
  hip —*see* Furuncle, lower limb
  kidney —*see* Abscess, kidney
  knee —*see* Furuncle, lower limb
  labium (majus) (minus) N76.4
  lacrimal
    gland —*see* Dacryoadenitis
    passages (duct) (sac) —*see* Inflammation, lacrimal, passages, acute
  leg (any part) —*see* Furuncle, lower limb
  lower limb L02.42-•
  malignant A22.0
  mouth K12.2
  navel L02.226
  neck L02.12
  nose J34.0
  orbit, orbital —*see* Abscess, orbit
  palmar (space) —*see* Furuncle, hand
  partes posteriores L02.32
  pectoral region L02.223
  penis N48.21
  perineum L02.225

Furuncle *(Continued)*
  pinna —*see* Abscess, ear, external
  popliteal —*see* Furuncle, lower limb
  prepatellar —*see* Furuncle, lower limb
  scalp L02.821
  seminal vesicle N49.0
  shoulder —*see* Furuncle, upper limb
  specified site NEC L02.828
  submandibular K12.2
  temple (region) L02.02
  thumb —*see* Furuncle, hand
  toe —*see* Furuncle, foot
  trunk L02.229
    abdominal wall L02.221
    back L02.222
    chest wall L02.223
    groin L02.224
    perineum L02.225
    umbilicus L02.226
  umbilicus L02.226
  upper limb L02.42-•
  vulva N76.4
Furunculosis —*see* Furuncle
Fused —*see* Fusion, fused
Fusion, fused (congenital)
  astragaloscaphoid Q74.2
  atria Q21.1
  auditory canal Q16.1
  auricles, heart Q21.1
  binocular with defective stereopsis H53.32
  bone Q79.8
  cervical spine M43.22
  choanal Q30.0
  commissure, mitral valve Q23.2
  cusps, heart valve NEC Q24.8
    mitral Q23.2
    pulmonary Q22.1
    tricuspid Q22.4
  ear ossicles Q16.3
  fingers Q70.0-•
  hymen Q52.3
  joint (acquired) —*see also* Ankylosis
    congenital Q74.8
  kidneys (incomplete) Q63.1
  labium (majus) (minus) Q52.5

Fusion, fused *(Continued)*
  larynx and trachea Q34.8
  limb, congenital Q74.8
    lower Q74.2
    upper Q74.0
  lobes, lung Q33.8
  lumbosacral (acquired) M43.27
    arthrodesis status Z98.1
    congenital Q76.49
    postprocedural status Z98.1
  nares, nose, nasal, nostril(s) Q30.0
  organ or site not listed —*see* Anomaly, by site
  ossicles Q79.9
    auditory Q16.3
  pulmonic cusps Q22.1
  ribs Q76.6
  sacroiliac (joint) (acquired) M43.28
    arthrodesis status Z98.1
    congenital Q74.2
    postprocedural status Z98.1
  spine (acquired) NEC M43.20
    arthrodesis status Z98.1
    cervical region M43.22
    cervicothoracic region M43.23
    congenital Q76.49
    lumbar M43.26
    lumbosacral region M43.27
    occipito-atlanto-axial region M43.21
    postoperative status Z98.1
    sacrococcygeal region M43.28
    thoracic region M43.24
    thoracolumbar region M43.25
  sublingual duct with submaxillary duct at opening in mouth Q38.4
  testes Q55.1
  toes Q70.2
  tooth, teeth K00.2
  trachea and esophagus Q39.8
  twins Q89.4
  vagina Q52.4
  ventricles, heart Q21.0
  vertebra (arch) —*see* Fusion, spine
  vulva Q52.5
Fusospirillosis (mouth) (tongue) (tonsil) A69.1
Fussy baby R68.12

▶ New   ⇒ Revised   ~~deleted~~ Deleted   • Use Additional Character(s)

G

Gain in weight (abnormal) (excessive) —see also
　　Weight, gain
Gaisböck's disease (polycythemia hypertonica)
　　D75.1
Gait abnormality R26.9
　　ataxic R26.0
　　falling R29.6
　　hysterical (ataxic) (staggering) F44.4
　　paralytic R26.1
　　spastic R26.1
　　specified type NEC R26.89
　　staggering R26.0
　　unsteadiness R26.81
　　walking difficulty NEC R26.2
Galactocele (breast) N64.89
　　puerperal, postpartum O92.79
Galactokinase deficiency E74.29
Galactophoritis N61.0
　　gestational, puerperal, postpartum O91.2-●
Galactorrhea O92.6
　　not associated with childbirth N64.3
Galactosemia (classic) (congenital) E74.21
Galactosuria E74.29
Galacturia R82.0
　　schistosomiasis (bilharziasis) B65.0
GALD (gestational alloimmune liver disease)
　　P78.84
Galeazzi's fracture S52.37-●
Galen's vein —see condition
Galeophobia F40.218
Gall duct —see condition
Gallbladder —see also condition
　　acute K81.0
Gallop rhythm R00.8
Gallstone (colic) (cystic duct) (gallbladder)
　　(impacted) (multiple) —see also Calculus,
　　gallbladder
　　with
　　　cholecystitis —see Calculus, gallbladder,
　　　　with cholecystitis
　　bile duct (common) (hepatic) —see Calculus,
　　　bile duct
　　causing intestinal obstruction K56.3
　　specified NEC K80.80
　　　with obstruction K80.81
Gambling Z72.6
　　pathological (compulsive) F63.0
Gammopathy (of undetermined significance
　　[MGUS]) D47.2
　　associated with lymphoplasmacytic dyscrasia
　　　D47.2
　　monoclonal D47.2
　　polyclonal D89.0
Gamna's disease (siderotic splenomegaly)
　　D73.1
Gamophobia F40.298
Gampsodactylia (congenital) Q66.7-●
Gamstorp's disease (adynamia episodica
　　hereditaria) G72.3
Gandy-Nanta disease (siderotic splenomegaly)
　　D73.1
Gang
　　membership offenses Z72.810
Gangliocytoma D36.10
Ganglioglioma —see Neoplasm, uncertain
　　behavior, by site
Ganglion (compound) (diffuse) (joint) (tendon
　　(sheath)) M67.40
　　ankle M67.47-●
　　foot M67.47-●
　　forearm M67.43-●
　　hand M67.44-●
　　lower leg M67.46-●
　　multiple sites M67.49
　　of yaws (early) (late) A66.6
　　pelvic region M67.45-●
　　periosteal —see Periostitis
　　shoulder region M67.41-●
　　specified site NEC M67.48

Ganglion (Continued)
　　thigh region M67.45-●
　　tuberculous A18.09
　　upper arm M67.42-●
　　wrist M67.43-●
Ganglioneuroblastoma —see Neoplasm, nerve,
　　malignant
Ganglioneuroma D36.10
　　malignant —see Neoplasm, nerve, malignant
Ganglioneuromatosis D36.10
Ganglionitis
　　fifth nerve —see Neuralgia, trigeminal
　　gasserian (postherpetic) (postzoster)
　　　B02.21
　　geniculate G51.1
　　　newborn (birth injury) P11.3
　　　postherpetic, postzoster B02.21
　　herpes zoster B02.21
　　postherpetic geniculate B02.21
Gangliosidosis E75.10
　　GM1 E75.19
　　GM2 E75.00
　　　other specified E75.09
　　　Sandhoff disease E75.01
　　　Tay-Sachs disease E75.02
　　GM3 E75.19
　　mucolipidosis IV E75.11
Gangosa A66.5
Gangrene, gangrenous (connective tissue)
　　(dropsical) (dry) (moist) (skin) (ulcer) —see
　　also Necrosis I96
　　with diabetes (mellitus) —see Diabetes,
　　　gangrene
　　abdomen (wall) I96
　　alveolar M27.3
　　appendix K35.80
　　　with
　　　　peritonitis, localized (see also
　　　　　Appendicitis) K35.31
　　arteriosclerotic (general) (senile) —see
　　　Arteriosclerosis, extremities, with,
　　　gangrene
　　auricle I96
　　Bacillus welchii A48.0
　　bladder (infectious) —see Cystitis, specified
　　　type NEC
　　bowel, cecum, or colon —see Gangrene,
　　　intestine
　　Clostridium perfringens or welchii A48.0
　　cornea H18.89-●
　　corpora cavernosa N48.29
　　　noninfective N48.89
　　cutaneous, spreading I96
　　decubital —see Ulcer, pressure, by site
　　diabetic (any site) —see Diabetes, gangrene
　　emphysematous —see Gangrene, gas
　　epidemic —see Poisoning, food, noxious,
　　　plant
　　epididymis (infectional) N45.1
　　erysipelas —see Erysipelas
　　extremity (lower) (upper) I96
　　Fournier N49.3
　　　female N76.89
　　fusospirochetal A69.0
　　gallbladder —see Cholecystitis, acute
　　gas (bacillus) A48.0
　　　following
　　　　abortion —see Abortion by type
　　　　　complicated by infection
　　　　ectopic or molar pregnancy O08.0
　　glossitis K14.0
　　hernia —see Hernia, by site, with gangrene
　　intestine, intestinal (hemorrhagic)
　　　(massive) —see also Infarct, intestine
　　　K55.069
　　　with
　　　　mesenteric embolism —see also Infarct,
　　　　　intestine K55.069
　　　　obstruction —see Obstruction, intestine
　　laryngitis J04.0
　　limb (lower) (upper) I96

Gangrene, gangrenous (Continued)
　　lung J85.0
　　　spirochetal A69.8
　　lymphangitis I89.1
　　Meleney's (synergistic) —see Ulcer, skin
　　mesentery —see also Infarct, intestine
　　　K55.069
　　　with
　　　　embolism —see also Infarct, intestine
　　　　　K55.069
　　　　intestinal obstruction —see Obstruction,
　　　　　intestine
　　mouth A69.0
　　ovary —see Oophoritis
　　pancreas —see Pancreatitis, acute
　　penis N48.29
　　　noninfective N48.89
　　perineum I96
　　pharynx —see also Pharyngitis
　　　Vincent's A69.1
　　presenile I73.1
　　progressive synergistic —see Ulcer, skin
　　pulmonary J85.0
　　pulpal (dental) K04.1
　　quinsy J36
　　Raynaud's (symmetric gangrene) I73.01
　　retropharyngeal J39.2
　　scrotum N49.3
　　　noninfective N50.89
　　senile (atherosclerotic) —see Arteriosclerosis,
　　　extremities, with, gangrene
　　spermatic cord N49.1
　　　noninfective N50.89
　　spine I96
　　spirochetal NEC A69.8
　　spreading cutaneous I96
　　stomatitis A69.0
　　symmetrical I73.01
　　testis (infectional) N45.2
　　　noninfective N44.8
　　throat —see also Pharyngitis
　　　diphtheritic A36.0
　　　Vincent's A69.1
　　thyroid (gland) E07.89
　　tooth (pulp) K04.1
　　tuberculous NEC —see Tuberculosis
　　tunica vaginalis N49.1
　　　noninfective N50.89
　　umbilicus I96
　　uterus —see Endometritis
　　uvulitis K12.2
　　vas deferens N49.1
　　　noninfective N50.89
　　vulva N76.89
Ganister disease J62.8
Ganser's syndrome (hysterical) F44.89
Gardner-Diamond syndrome (autoerythrocyte
　　sensitization) D69.2
Gargoylism E76.01
Garré's disease, osteitis (sclerosing),
　　osteomyelitis —see Osteomyelitis,
　　specified type NEC
Garrod's pad, knuckle M72.1
Gartner's duct
　　cyst Q52.4
　　persistent Q50.6
Gas R14.3
　　asphyxiation, inhalation, poisoning,
　　　suffocation NEC —see Table of Drugs
　　　and Chemicals
　　excessive R14.0
　　gangrene A48.0
　　　following
　　　　abortion —see Abortion by type
　　　　　complicated by infection
　　　　ectopic or molar pregnancy O08.0
　　on stomach R14.0
　　pains R14.1
Gastralgia —see also Pain, abdominal
Gastrectasis K31.0
　　psychogenic F45.8

Gastric —*see* condition
Gastrinoma
  malignant
    pancreas C25.4
    specified site NEC —*see* Neoplasm,
      malignant, by site
    unspecified site C25.4
  specified site —*see* Neoplasm, uncertain
    behavior
  unspecified site D37.9
Gastritis (simple) K29.70
  with bleeding K29.71
  acute (erosive) K29.00
    with bleeding K29.01
  alcoholic K29.20
    with bleeding K29.21
  allergic K29.60
    with bleeding K29.61
  atrophic (chronic) K29.40
    with bleeding K29.41
  chronic (antral) (fundal) K29.50
    with bleeding K29.51
    atrophic K29.40
      with bleeding K29.41
    superficial K29.30
      with bleeding K29.31
  dietary counseling and surveillance Z71.3
  due to diet deficiency E63.9
  eosinophilic K52.81
  giant hypertrophic K29.60
    with bleeding K29.61
  granulomatous K29.60
    with bleeding K29.61
  hypertrophic (mucosa) K29.60
    with bleeding K29.61
  nervous F54
  spastic K29.60
    with bleeding K29.61
  specified NEC K29.60
    with bleeding K29.61
  superficial chronic K29.30
    with bleeding K29.31
  tuberculous A18.83
  viral NEC A08.4
Gastrocarcinoma —*see* Neoplasm, malignant,
  stomach
Gastrocolic —*see* condition
Gastrodisciasis, gastrodiscoidiasis B66.8
Gastroduodenitis K29.90
  with bleeding K29.91
  virus, viral A08.4
    specified type NEC A08.39
Gastrodynia —*see* Pain, abdominal
Gastroenteritis (acute) (chronic) (noninfectious)
  (*see also* Enteritis) K52.9
  allergic K52.29
  with
    eosinophilic gastritis or gastroenteritis
      K52.81
    food protein-induced enterocolitis
      syndrome K52.21
    food protein-induced enteropathy K52.22
  dietetic —*see also* Gastroenteritis, allergic
    K52.29
  drug-induced K52.1
  due to
    Cryptosporidium A07.2
    drugs K52.1
    food poisoning —*see* Intoxication,
      foodborne
    radiation K52.0
  eosinophilic K52.81
  epidemic (infectious) A09
  food hypersensitivity —*see also*
    Gastroenteritis, allergic K52.29
  infectious —*see* Enteritis, infectious
  influenzal —*see* Influenza, with
    gastroenteritis
  noninfectious K52.9
    specified NEC K52.89
  rotaviral A08.0

Gastroenteritis (Continued)
  Salmonella A02.0
  toxic K52.1
  viral NEC A08.4
    acute infectious A08.39
      type Norwalk A08.11
    infantile (acute) A08.39
    Norwalk agent A08.11
    rotaviral A08.0
    severe of infants A08.39
    specified type NEC A08.39
Gastroenteropathy —*see also* Gastroenteritis
  K52.9
  acute, due to Norovirus A08.11
  acute, due to Norwalk agent A08.11
  infectious A09
Gastroenteroptosis K63.4
Gastroesophageal laceration-hemorrhage
  syndrome K22.6
Gastrointestinal —*see* condition
Gastrojejunal —*see* condition
Gastrojejunitis —*see also* Enteritis K52.9
Gastrojejunocolic —*see* condition
Gastroliths K31.89
Gastromalacia K31.89
Gastroparalysis K31.84
  diabetic —*see* Diabetes, gastroparalysis
Gastroparesis K31.84
  diabetic —*see* Diabetes, by type, with
    gastroparesis
Gastropathy K31.9
  congestive portal K31.89
  erythematous K29.70
  exudative K90.89
  portal hypertensive K31.89
Gastroptosis K31.89
Gastrorrhagia K92.2
  psychogenic F45.8
Gastroschisis (congenital) Q79.3
Gastrospasm (neurogenic) (reflex) K31.89
  neurotic F45.8
  psychogenic F45.8
Gastrostaxis —*see* Gastritis, with bleeding
Gastrostenosis K31.89
Gastrostomy
  attention to Z43.1
  status Z93.1
Gastrosuccorrhea (continuous) (intermittent)
  K31.89
  neurotic F45.8
  psychogenic F45.8
Gatophobia F40.218
Gaucher's disease or splenomegaly (adult)
  (infantile) E75.22
Gee (-Herter)(-Thaysen) disease (nontropical
  sprue) K90.0
Gélineau's syndrome G47.419
  with cataplexy G47.411
Gemination, tooth, teeth K00.2
Gemistocytoma
  specified site —*see* Neoplasm, malignant, by
    site
  unspecified site C71.9
General, generalized —*see* condition
Genetic
  carrier (status)
    cystic fibrosis Z14.1
    hemophilia A (asymptomatic) Z14.01
      symptomatic Z14.02
    specified NEC Z14.8
  susceptibility to disease NEC Z15.89
    malignant neoplasm Z15.09
      breast Z15.01
      endometrium Z15.04
      ovary Z15.02
      prostate Z15.03
      specified NEC Z15.09
    multiple endocrine neoplasia Z15.81
Genital —*see* condition
Genito-anorectal syndrome A55
Genitourinary system —*see* condition

Genu
  congenital Q74.1
  extrorsum (acquired) —*see also* Deformity,
    varus, knee
    congenital Q74.1
    sequelae (late effect) of rickets E64.3
  introrsum (acquired) —*see also* Deformity,
    valgus, knee
    congenital Q74.1
    sequelae (late effect) of rickets E64.3
  rachitic (old) E64.3
  recurvatum (acquired) —*see also* Deformity,
    limb, specified type NEC, lower leg
    congenital Q68.2
    sequelae (late effect) of rickets E64.3
  valgum (acquired) (knock-knee) M21.06-●
    congenital Q74.1
    sequelae (late effect) of rickets E64.3
  varum (acquired) (bowleg) M21.16-●
    congenital Q74.1
    sequelae (late effect) of rickets E64.3
Geographic tongue K14.1
Geophagia —*see* Pica
Geotrichosis B48.3
  stomatitis B48.3
Gephyrophobia F40.242
Gerbode defect Q21.0
GERD (gastroesophageal reflux disease) K21.9
Gerhardt's
  disease (erythromelalgia) I73.81
  syndrome (vocal cord paralysis)
    J38.00
    bilateral J38.02
    unilateral J38.01
German measles —*see also* Rubella
  exposure to Z20.4
Germinoblastoma (diffuse) C85.9-●
  follicular C82.9-●
Germinoma —*see* Neoplasm, malignant, by site
Gerontoxon —*see* Degeneration, cornea, senile
Gerstmann-Sträussler-Scheinker syndrome
  (GSS) A81.82
Gerstmann's syndrome R48.8
  developmental F81.2
Gestation (period) —*see also* Pregnancy
  ectopic —*see* Pregnancy, by site
  multiple O30.9-●
    greater than quadruplets —*see* Pregnancy,
      multiple (gestation), specified NEC
    specified NEC —*see* Pregnancy, multiple
      (gestation), specified NEC
Gestational
  mammary abscess O91.11-●
  purulent mastitis O91.11-●
  subareolar abscess O91.11-●
Ghon tubercle, primary infection A15.7
Ghost
  teeth K00.4
  vessels (cornea) H16.41-●
Ghoul hand A66.3
Gianotti-Crosti disease L44.4
Giant
  cell
    epulis K06.8
    peripheral granuloma K06.8
  esophagus, congenital Q39.5
  kidney, congenital Q63.3
  urticaria T78.3
    hereditary D84.1
Giardiasis A07.1
Gibert's disease or pityriasis L42
Giddiness R42
  hysterical F44.89
  psychogenic F45.8
Gierke's disease (glycogenosis I) E74.01
Gigantism (cerebral) (hypophyseal) (pituitary)
  E22.0
  constitutional E34.4
Gilbert's disease or syndrome E80.4
Gilchrist's disease B40.9
Gilford-Hutchinson disease E34.8

▶ New ⇒ Revised ~~deleted~~ Deleted ● Use Additional Character(s)

Gilles de la Tourette's disease or syndrome
(motor-verbal tic) F95.2
Gingivitis K05.10
acute (catarrhal) K05.00
necrotizing A69.1
nonplaque induced K05.01
plaque induced K05.00
chronic (desquamative) (hyperplastic)
(simple marginal) (pregnancy
associated) (ulcerative) K05.10
nonplaque induced K05.11
plaque induced K05.10
expulsiva —see Periodontitis
necrotizing ulcerative (acute) A69.1
pellagrous E52
acute necrotizing A69.1
Vincent's A69.1
Gingivoglossitis K14.0
Gingivopericementitis —see Periodontitis
Gingivosis —see Gingivitis, chronic
Gingivostomatitis K05.10
herpesviral B00.2
necrotizing ulcerative (acute) A69.1
Gland, glandular —see condition
Glanders A24.0
Glanzmann (-Naegeli) disease or
thrombasthenia D69.1
Glasgow coma scale
total score
3-8 R40.243
9-12 R40.242
13-15 R40.241
Glass-blower's disease (cataract) —see
Cataract, specified NEC
Glaucoma H40.9
with
increased episcleral venous pressure
H40.81-●
pseudoexfoliation of lens —see Glaucoma,
open angle, primary, capsular
absolute H44.51-●
angle-closure (primary) H40.20-●
acute (attack) (crisis) H40.21-●
chronic H40.22-●
intermittent H40.23-●
residual stage H40.24-●
borderline H40.00-●
capsular (with pseudoexfoliation of lens) —
see Glaucoma, open angle, primary,
capsular
childhood Q15.0
closed angle —see Glaucoma, angle-closure
congenital Q15.0
corticosteroid-induced —see Glaucoma,
secondary, drugs
hypersecretion H40.82-●
in (due to)
amyloidosis E85.4 [H42]
aniridia Q13.1 [H42]
concussion of globe —see Glaucoma,
secondary, trauma
dislocation of lens —see Glaucoma,
secondary
disorder of lens NEC —see Glaucoma,
secondary
drugs —see Glaucoma, secondary, drugs
endocrine disease NOS E34.9 [H42]
eye
inflammation —see Glaucoma,
secondary, inflammation
trauma —see Glaucoma, secondary,
trauma
hypermature cataract —see Glaucoma,
secondary
iridocyclitis —see Glaucoma, secondary,
inflammation
lens disorder —see Glaucoma, secondary,
Lowe's syndrome E72.03 [H42]
metabolic disease NOS E88.9 [H42]
ocular disorders NEC —see Glaucoma,
secondary

Glaucoma (Continued)
in (due to) (Continued)
onchocerciasis B73.02
pupillary block —see Glaucoma, secondary
retinal vein occlusion —see Glaucoma,
secondary
Rieger's anomaly Q13.81 [H42]
rubeosis of iris —see Glaucoma, secondary
tumor of globe —see Glaucoma, secondary
infantile Q15.0
low tension —see Glaucoma, open angle,
primary, low-tension
malignant H40.83-●
narrow angle —see Glaucoma, angle-closure
newborn Q15.0
noncongestive (chronic) —see Glaucoma,
open angle
nonobstructive —see Glaucoma, open angle
obstructive —see also Glaucoma,
angle-closure
due to lens changes —see Glaucoma,
secondary
open angle H40.10-●
primary H40.11-●
capsular (with pseudoexfoliation of lens)
H40.14-●
low-tension H40.12-●
pigmentary H40.13-●
residual stage H40.15-●
phacolytic —see Glaucoma, secondary
pigmentary —see Glaucoma, open angle,
primary, pigmentary
postinfectious —see Glaucoma, secondary,
inflammation
secondary (to) H40.5-●
drugs H40.6-●
inflammation H40.4-●
trauma H40.3-●
simple (chronic) H40.11-●
simplex H40.11-●
specified type NEC H40.89
suspect H40.00-●
syphilitic A52.71
traumatic —see also Glaucoma, secondary,
trauma
newborn (birth injury) P15.3
tuberculous A18.59
Glaucomatous flecks (subcapsular) —see
Cataract, complicated
Glazed tongue K14.4
Gleet (gonococcal) A54.01
Glénard's disease K63.4
Glioblastoma (multiforme)
with sarcomatous component
specified site —see Neoplasm, malignant,
by site
unspecified site C71.9
giant cell
specified site —see Neoplasm, malignant,
by site
unspecified site C71.9
specified site —see Neoplasm, malignant, by
site
unspecified site C71.9
Glioma (malignant)
astrocytic
specified site —see Neoplasm, malignant,
by site
unspecified site C71.9
mixed
specified site —see Neoplasm, malignant,
by site
unspecified site C71.9
nose Q30.8
specified site NEC —see Neoplasm,
malignant, by site
subependymal D43.2
specified site —see Neoplasm, uncertain
behavior, by site
unspecified site D43.2
unspecified site C71.9
Gliomatosis cerebri C71.0

Glioneuroma —see Neoplasm, uncertain
behavior, by site
Gliosarcoma
specified site —see Neoplasm, malignant, by
site
unspecified site C71.9
Gliosis (cerebral) G93.89
spinal G95.89
Glisson's disease —see Rickets
Globinuria R82.3
Globus (hystericus) F45.8
Glomangioma D18.00
intra-abdominal D18.03
intracranial D18.02
skin D18.01
specified site NEC D18.09
Glomangiomyoma D18.00
intra-abdominal D18.03
intracranial D18.02
skin D18.01
specified site NEC D18.09
Glomangiosarcoma —see Neoplasm, connective
tissue, malignant
Glomerular
disease in syphilis A52.75
nephritis —see Glomerulonephritis
Glomerulitis —see Glomerulonephritis
Glomerulonephritis —see also Nephritis N05.9
with
▶C3
▶glomerulonephritis N05.A
▶glomerulopathy N05.A
▶with dense deposit disease N05.6
edema —see Nephrosis
minimal change N05.0
minor glomerular abnormality N05.0
acute N00.9
chronic N03.9
crescentic (diffuse) NEC —see also N00-N07
with fourth character .7 N05.7
dense deposit —see also N00-N07 with fourth
character .6 N05.6
diffuse
crescentic —see also N00-N07 with fourth
character .7 N05.7
endocapillary proliferative —see also
N00N07 with fourth character .4 N05.4
membranous —see also N00-N07 with
fourth character .2 N05.2
mesangial proliferative —see also N00-N07
with fourth character .3 N05.3
mesangiocapillary —see also N00-N07 with
fourth character .5 N05.5
sclerosing N18.9
endocapillary proliferative (diffuse) NEC —
see also N00-N07 with fourth character
.4 N05.4
extracapillary NEC —see also N00-N07 with
fourth character .7 N05.7
focal (and segmental) —see also N00-N07 with
fourth character .1 N05.1
hypocomplementemic —
see Glomerulonephritis,
membranoproliferative
IgA —see Nephropathy, IgA
immune complex (circulating) NEC N05.8
in (due to)
amyloidosis E85.4 [N08]
bilharziasis B65.9 [N08]
cryoglobulinemia D89.1 [N08]
defibrination syndrome D65 [N08]
diabetes mellitus —see Diabetes,
glomerulosclerosis
disseminated intravascular coagulation
D65 [N08]
Fabry (-Anderson) disease E75.21 [N08]
Goodpasture's syndrome M31.0
hemolytic-uremic syndrome D59.3
Henoch (-Schönlein) purpura D69.0 [N08]
lecithin cholesterol acyltransferase
deficiency E78.6 [N08]

G

Glomerulonephritis *(Continued)*
  in *(Continued)*
    microscopic polyangiitis M31.7 *[N08]*
    multiple myeloma C90.0-• *[N08]*
    Plasmodium malariae B52.0
    schistosomiasis B65.9 *[N08]*
    sepsis A41.9-• *[N08]*
      streptococcal A40-• *[N08]*
    sickle-cell disorders D57.-• *[N08]*
    strongyloidiasis B78.9 *[N08]*
    subacute bacterial endocarditis I33.0
      [N08]
    syphilis (late) congenital A50.59 *[N08]*
    systemic lupus erythematosus M32.14
    thrombotic thrombocytopenic purpura
      M31.1 *[N08]*
    typhoid fever A01.09
    Waldenström macroglobulinemia C88.0
      [N08]
    Wegener's granulomatosis M31.31
  latent or quiescent N03.9
  lobular, lobulonodular —
    see Glomerulonephritis,
    membranoproliferative
  membranoproliferative (diffuse) (type 1
    or 3) —*see also* N00-N07 with fourth
    character .5 N05.5
    dense deposit (type 2) NEC —*see also*
      N00-N07 with fourth character .6
      N05.6
  membranous (diffuse) NEC —*see also*
    N00-N07 with fourth character .2 N05.2
  mesangial
    IgA/IgG —*see* Nephropathy, IgA
    proliferative (diffuse) NEC —*see also*
      N00-N07 with fourth character .3
      N05.3
  mesangiocapillary (diffuse) NEC —*see also*
    N00-N07 with fourth character .5 N05.5
  necrotic, necrotizing NEC —*see also* N00-N07
    with fourth character .8 N05.8
  nodular —*see* Glomerulonephritis,
    membranoproliferative
  poststreptococcal NEC N05.9
    acute N00.9
    chronic N03.9
    rapidly progressive N01.9
  proliferative NEC —*see also* N00-N07 with
    fourth character .8 N05.8
    diffuse (lupus) M32.14
  rapidly progressive N01.9
  sclerosing, diffuse N18.9
  specified pathology NEC —*see also* N00-N07
    with fourth character .8 N05.8
  subacute N01.9
Glomerulopathy —*see* Glomerulonephritis
Glomerulosclerosis —*see also* Sclerosis, renal
  intercapillary (nodular) (with diabetes) —*see*
    Diabetes, glomerulosclerosis
  intracapillary —*see* Diabetes, glomerulosclerosis
Glossagra K14.6
Glossalgia K14.6
Glossitis (chronic superficial) (gangrenous)
  (Moeller's) K14.0
  areata exfoliativa K14.1
  atrophic K14.4
  benign migratory K14.1
  cortical superficial, sclerotic K14.0
  Hunter's D51.0
  interstitial, sclerous K14.0
  median rhomboid K14.2
  pellagrous E52
  superficial, chronic K14.0
Glossocele K14.8
Glossodynia K14.6
  exfoliativa K14.4
Glossoncus K14.8
Glossopathy K14.9
Glossophytia K14.3
Glossoplegia K14.8
Glossoptosis K14.8

Glossopyrosis K14.6
Glossotrichia K14.3
Glossy skin L90.8
Glottis —*see* condition
Glottitis —*see also* Laryngitis J04.0
Glucagonoma
  pancreas
    benign D13.7
    malignant C25.4
    uncertain behavior D37.8
  specified site NEC
    benign —*see* Neoplasm, benign, by site
    malignant —*see* Neoplasm, malignant, by
      site
    uncertain behavior —*see* Neoplasm,
      uncertain behavior, by site
  unspecified site
    benign D13.7
    malignant C25.4
    uncertain behavior D37.8
Glucoglycinuria E72.51
Glucose-galactose malabsorption E74.39
Glue
  ear —*see* Otitis, media, nonsuppurative,
    chronic, mucoid
  sniffing (airplane) —*see* Abuse, drug, inhalant
    dependence —*see* Dependence, drug,
      inhalant
▶GLUT1 deficiency syndrome 1, infantile onset
  E74.810
▶GLUT1 deficiency syndrome 2, childhood
  onset E74.810
Glutaric aciduria E72.3
Glycinemia E72.51
Glycinuria (renal) (with ketosis) E72.09
Glycogen
  infiltration —*see* Disease, glycogen storage
  storage disease —*see* Disease, glycogen storage
Glycogenosis (diffuse) (generalized) —*see also*
  Disease, glycogen storage
  cardiac E74.02 *[I43]*
  diabetic, secondary —*see* Diabetes,
    glycogenosis, secondary
  pulmonary interstitial J84.842
Glycopenia E16.2
Glycosuria R81
▥renal (familial) E74.818
Gnathostoma spinigerum (infection)
  (infestation), gnathostomiasis (wandering
  swelling) B83.1
Goiter (plunging) (substernal) E04.9
  with
    hyperthyroidism (recurrent) —*see*
      Hyperthyroidism, with, goiter
    thyrotoxicosis —*see* Hyperthyroidism,
      with, goiter
  adenomatous —*see* Goiter, nodular
  cancerous C73
  congenital (nontoxic) E03.0
    diffuse E03.0
    parenchymatous E03.0
    transitory, with normal functioning P72.0
  cystic E04.2
    due to iodine-deficiency E01.1
  due to
    enzyme defect in synthesis of thyroid
      hormone E07.1
    iodine-deficiency (endemic) E01.2
  dyshormonogenetic (familial) E07.1
  endemic (iodine-deficiency) E01.2
    diffuse E01.0
    multinodular E01.1
  exophthalmic —*see* Hyperthyroidism, with,
    goiter
  iodine-deficiency (endemic) E01.2
    diffuse E01.0
    multinodular E01.1
    nodular E01.1
  lingual Q89.2
  lymphadenoid E06.3
  malignant C73

Goiter *(Continued)*
  multinodular (cystic) (nontoxic) E04.2
    toxic or with hyperthyroidism E05.20
      with thyroid storm E05.21
  neonatal NEC P72.0
  nodular (nontoxic) (due to) E04.9
    with
      hyperthyroidism E05.20
        with thyroid storm E05.21
      thyrotoxicosis E05.20
        with thyroid storm E05.21
    endemic E01.1
    iodine-deficiency E01.1
    sporadic E04.9
    toxic E05.20
      with thyroid storm E05.21
  nontoxic E04.9
    diffuse (colloid) E04.0
    multinodular E04.2
    simple E04.0
    specified NEC E04.8
    uninodular E04.1
  simple E04.0
  toxic —*see* Hyperthyroidism, with, goiter
  uninodular (nontoxic) E04.1
    toxic or with hyperthyroidism E05.10
      with thyroid storm E05.11
Goiter-deafness syndrome E07.1
Goldberg syndrome Q89.8
Goldberg-Maxwell syndrome E34.51
Goldblatt's hypertension or kidney I70.1
Goldenhar (-Gorlin) syndrome Q87.0
Goldflam-Erb disease or syndrome G70.00
  with exacerbation (acute) G70.01
  in crisis G70.01
Goldscheider's disease Q81.8
Goldstein's disease (familial hemorrhagic
  telangiectasia) I78.0
Golfer's elbow —*see* Epicondylitis, medial
Gonadoblastoma
  specified site —*see* Neoplasm, uncertain
    behavior, by site
  unspecified site
    female D39.10
    male D40.10
Gonecystitis —*see* Vesiculitis
Gongylonemiasis B83.8
Goniosynechiae —*see* Adhesions, iris,
  goniosynechiae
Gonococcemia A54.86
Gonococcus, gonococcal (disease) (infection)
  —*see also* condition A54.9
  anus A54.6
  bursa, bursitis A54.49
  conjunctiva, conjunctivitis (neonatorum)
    A54.31
  endocardium A54.83
  eye A54.30
    conjunctivitis A54.31
    iridocyclitis A54.32
    keratitis A54.33
    newborn A54.31
    other specified A54.39
  fallopian tubes (acute) (chronic) A54.24
  genitourinary (organ) (system) (tract) (acute)
    lower A54.00
      with abscess (accessory gland)
        (periurethral) A54.1
    upper —*see also* condition A54.29
  heart A54.83
  iridocyclitis A54.32
  joint A54.42
  lymphatic (gland) (node) A54.89
  meninges, meningitis A54.81
  musculoskeletal A54.40
    arthritis A54.42
    osteomyelitis A54.43
    other specified A54.49
    spondylopathy A54.41
  pelviperitonitis A54.24
  pelvis (acute) (chronic) A54.24

▶ New   ⇒ Revised   ~~deleted~~ Deleted   • Use Additional Character(s)

Gonococcus, gonococcal *(Continued)*
  pharynx A54.5
  proctitis A54.6
  pyosalpinx (acute) (chronic) A54.24
  rectum A54.6
  skin A54.89
  specified site NEC A54.89
  tendon sheath A54.49
  throat A54.5
  urethra (acute) (chronic) A54.01
    with abscess (accessory gland)
      (periurethral) A54.1
  vulva (acute) (chronic) A54.02
Gonocytoma
  specified site —*see* Neoplasm, uncertain
    behavior, by site
  unspecified site
    female D39.10
    male D40.10
Gonorrhea (acute) (chronic) A54.9
  Bartholin's gland (acute) (chronic) (purulent)
    A54.02
    with abscess (accessory gland)
      (periurethral) A54.1
  bladder A54.01
  cervix A54.03
  conjunctiva, conjunctivitis (neonatorum)
    A54.31
  contact Z20.2
  Cowper's gland (with abscess) A54.1
  exposure to Z20.2
  fallopian tube (acute) (chronic) A54.24
  kidney (acute) (chronic) A54.21
  lower genitourinary tract A54.00
    with abscess (accessory gland)
      (periurethral) A54.1
  ovary (acute) (chronic) A54.24
  pelvis (acute) (chronic) A54.24
    female pelvic inflammatory disease A54.24
  penis A54.09
  prostate (acute) (chronic) A54.22
  seminal vesicle (acute) (chronic) A54.23
  specified site not listed —*see also* Gonococcus
    A54.89
  spermatic cord (acute) (chronic) A54.23
  urethra A54.01
    with abscess (accessory gland)
      (periurethral) A54.1
  vagina A54.02
  vas deferens (acute) (chronic) A54.23
  vulva A54.02
Goodall's disease A08.19
Goodpasture's syndrome M31.0
Gopalan's syndrome (burning feet) E53.0
Gorlin-Chaudry-Moss syndrome Q87.0
Gottron's papules L94.4
Gougerot's syndrome (trisymptomatic) L81.7
Gougerot-Blum syndrome (pigmented
  purpuric lichenoid dermatitis) L81.7
Gougerot-Carteaud disease or syndrome
  (confluent reticulate papillomatosis) L83
Gouley's syndrome (constrictive pericarditis)
  I31.1
Goundou A66.6
Gout, chronic *(see also* Gout, gouty) M1A.9-●
  drug-induced M1A.20
    ankle M1A.27-●
    elbow M1A.22-●
    foot joint M1A.27-●
    hand joint M1A.24-●
    hip M1A.25-●
    knee M1A.26-●
    multiple site M1A.29-●
    shoulder M1A.21-●
    vertebrae M1A.28
    wrist M1A.23-●
  idiopathic M1A.00
    ankle M1A.07-●
    elbow M1A.02-●
    foot joint M1A.07-●
    hand joint M1A.04-●

Gout, chronic *(Continued)*
  idiopathic *(Continued)*
    hip M1A.05-●
    knee M1A.06-●
    multiple site M1A.09
    shoulder M1A.01-●
    vertebrae M1A.08
    wrist M1A.03-●
  in (due to) renal impairment M1A.30
    ankle M1A.37-●
    elbow M1A.32-●
    foot joint M1A.37-●
    hand joint M1A.34-●
    hip M1A.35-●
    knee M1A.36-●
    multiple site M1A.39
    shoulder M1A.31-●
    vertebrae M1A.38
    wrist M1A.33-●
  lead-induced M1A.10
    ankle M1A.17-●
    elbow M1A.12-●
    foot joint M1A.17-●
    hand joint M1A.14-●
    hip M1A.15-●
    knee M1A.16-●
    multiple site M1A.19
    shoulder M1A.11-●
    vertebrae M1A.18
    wrist M1A.13-●
  primary —*see* Gout, chronic, idiopathic
  saturnine —*see* Gout, chronic, lead-induced
  secondary NEC M1A.40
    ankle M1A.47-●
    elbow M1A.42-●
    foot joint M1A.47-●
    hand joint M1A.44-●
    hip M1A.45-●
    knee M1A.46-●
    multiple site M1A.49
    shoulder M1A.41-●
    vertebrae M1A.48
    wrist M1A.43-●
  syphilitic —*see also* subcategory M14.8-●
    A52.77
  tophi M1A.9
Gout, gouty (acute) (attack) (flare) —*see also*
  Gout, chronic M10.9-●
  drug-induced M10.20
    ankle M10.27-●
    elbow M10.22-●
    foot joint M10.27-●
    hand joint M10.24-●
    hip M10.25-●
    knee M10.26-●
    multiple site M10.29
    shoulder M10.21-●
    vertebrae M10.28
    wrist M10.23-●
  idiopathic M10.00
    ankle M10.07-●
    elbow M10.02-●
    foot joint M10.07-●
    hand joint M10.04-●
    hip M10.05-●
    knee M10.06-●
    multiple site M10.09
    shoulder M10.01-●
    vertebrae M10.08
    wrist M10.03-●
  in (due to) renal impairment M10.30
    ankle M10.37-●
    elbow M10.32-●
    foot joint M10.37-●
    hand joint M10.34-●
    hip M10.35-●
    knee M10.36-●
    multiple site M10.39
    shoulder M10.31-●
    vertebrae M10.38
    wrist M10.33-●

Gout, gouty *(Continued)*
  lead-induced M10.10
    ankle M10.17-●
    elbow M10.12-●
    foot joint M10.17-●
    hand joint M10.14-●
    hip M10.15-●
    knee M10.16-●
    multiple site M10.19
    shoulder M10.11-●
    vertebrae M10.18
    wrist M10.13-●
  primary —*see* Gout, idiopathic
  saturnine —*see* Gout, lead-induced
  secondary NEC M10.40
    ankle M10.47-●
    elbow M10.42-●
    foot joint M10.47-●
    hand joint M10.44-●
    hip M10.45-●
    knee M10.46-●
    multiple site M10.49
    shoulder M10.41-●
    vertebrae M10.48
    wrist M10.43-●
  syphilitic —*see also* subcategory M14.8-●
    A52.77
  tophi NEC —*see* Gout, chronic
Gower's
  muscular dystrophy G71.01
  syndrome (vasovagal attack) R55
Gradenigo's syndrome —*see* Otitis, media,
  suppurative, acute
Graefe's disease —*see* Strabismus, paralytic,
  ophthalmoplegia, progressive
Graft-versus-host disease D89.813
  acute D89.810
  acute on chronic D89.812
  chronic D89.811
Grain mite (itch) B88.0
Grainhandler's disease or lung J67.8
Grand mal —*see* Epilepsy, generalized,
  specified NEC
Grand multipara status only (not pregnant)
  Z64.1
  pregnant —*see* Pregnancy, complicated by,
    grand multiparity
Granite worker's lung J62.8
Granular —*see also* condition
  inflammation, pharynx J31.2
  kidney (contracting) —*see* Sclerosis, renal
  liver K74.69
Granulation tissue (abnormal) (excessive) L92.9
  postmastoidectomy cavity —*see*
    Complications, postmastoidectomy,
    granulation
Granulocytopenia (primary) (malignant) —*see*
  Agranulocytosis
Granuloma L92.9
  abdomen K66.8
    from residual foreign body L92.3
    pyogenicum L98.0
  actinic L57.5
  annulare (perforating) L92.0
  apical K04.5
  aural —*see* Otitis, externa, specified NEC
  beryllium (skin) L92.3
  bone
    eosinophilic C96.6
    from residual foreign body —*see*
      Osteomyelitis, specified type NEC
    lung C96.6
  brain (any site) G06.0
    schistosomiasis B65.9 *[G07]*
  canaliculus lacrimalis —*see* Granuloma,
    lacrimal
  candidal (cutaneous) B37.2
  cerebral (any site) G06.0
  coccidioidal (primary) (progressive) B38.7
    lung B38.1
    meninges B38.4

Granuloma (Continued)
colon K63.89
conjunctiva H11.22-●
dental K04.5
ear, middle —see Cholesteatoma
eosinophilic C96.6
bone C96.6
lung C96.6
oral mucosa K13.4
skin L92.2
eyelid H01.8
facial (e) L92.2
foreign body (in soft tissue) NEC M60.20
ankle M60.27-●
foot M60.27-●
forearm M60.23-●
hand M60.24-●
in operation wound —see Foreign body,
accidentally left during a procedure
lower leg M60.26-●
pelvic region M60.25-●
shoulder region M60.21-●
skin L92.3
specified site NEC M60.28
subcutaneous tissue L92.3
thigh M60.25-●
upper arm M60.22-●
gangraenescens M31.2
genito-inguinale A58
giant cell (central) (reparative) (jaw) M27.1
gingiva (peripheral) K06.8
gland (lymph) I88.8
hepatic NEC K75.3
in (due to)
berylliosis J63.2 [K77]
sarcoidosis D86.89
Hodgkin C81.9
ileum K63.89
infectious B99.9
specified NEC B99.8
inguinale (Donovan) (venereal) A58
intestine NEC K63.89
intracranial (any site) G06.0
intraspinal (any part) G06.1
iridocyclitis —see Iridocyclitis, chronic
jaw (bone) (central) M27.1
reparative giant cell M27.1
kidney —see also Infection, kidney N15.8
lacrimal H04.81-●
larynx J38.7
lethal midline (faciale (e)) M31.2
liver NEC —see Granuloma, hepatic
lung (infectious) —see also Fibrosis, lung
coccidioidal B38.1
eosinophilic C96.6
Majocchi's B35.8
malignant (facial (e)) M31.2
mandible (central) M27.1
midline (lethal) M31.2
monilial (cutaneous) B37.2
nasal sinus —see Sinusitis
operation wound T81.89
foreign body —see Foreign body,
accidentally left during a procedure
stitch T81.89
talc —see Foreign body, accidentally left
during a procedure
oral mucosa K13.4
orbit, orbital H05.11-●
paracoccidioidal B41.8
penis, venereal A58
periapical K04.5
peritoneum K66.8
due to ova of helminths NOS —see also
Helminthiasis B83.9 [K67]
postmastoidectomy cavity —see
Complications, postmastoidectomy,
recurrent cholesteatoma
prostate N42.89
pudendi (ulcerating) A58
pulp, internal (tooth) K03.3

Granuloma (Continued)
pyogenic, pyogenicum (of) (skin) L98.0
gingiva K06.8
maxillary alveolar ridge K04.5
oral mucosa K13.4
rectum K62.89
reticulohistiocytic D76.3
rubrum nasi L74.8
Schistosoma —see Schistosomiasis
septic (skin) L98.0
silica (skin) L92.3
sinus (accessory) (infective) (nasal) —see
Sinusitis
skin L92.9
from residual foreign body L92.3
pyogenicum L98.0
spine
syphilitic (epidural) A52.19
tuberculous A18.01
stitch (postoperative) T81.89
suppurative (skin) L98.0
swimming pool A31.1
talc —see also Granuloma, foreign body
in operation wound —see Foreign body,
accidentally left during a procedure
telangiectaticum (skin) L98.0
tracheostomy J95.09
trichophyticum B35.8
tropicum A66.4
umbilical P83.81
umbilicus P83.81
urethra N36.8
uveitis —see Iridocyclitis, chronic
vagina A58
venereum A58
vocal cord J38.3
Granulomatosis L92.9
▶with polyangiitis M31.3
▶eosinophilic, with polyangiitis [EGPA] M30.1
lymphoid C83.8-●
miliary (listerial) A32.89
necrotizing, respiratory M31.30
progressive septic D71
specified NEC L92.8
Wegener's M31.30
with renal involvement M31.31
Granulomatous tissue (abnormal) (excessive)
L92.9
Granulosis rubra nasi L74.8
Graphite fibrosis (of lung) J63.3
Graphospasm F48.8
organic G25.89
Grating scapula M89.8X1
Gravel (urinary) —see Calculus, urinary
Graves' disease —see Hyperthyroidism, with,
goiter
Gravis —see condition
Grawitz tumor C64.-●
Gray syndrome (newborn) P93.0
Grayness, hair (premature) L67.1
congenital Q84.2
Green sickness D50.8
Greenfield's disease
meaning
concentric sclerosis (encephalitis periaxialis
concentrica) G37.5
metachromatic leukodystrophy E75.25
Greenstick fracture - code as Fracture, by site
Grey syndrome (newborn) P93.0
Grief F43.21
prolonged F43.29
reaction —see also Disorder, adjustment F43.20
Griesinger's disease B76.0
Grinder's lung or pneumoconiosis J62.8
Grinding, teeth
psychogenic F45.8
sleep related G47.63
Grip
Dabney's B33.0
devil's B33.0
Grippe, grippal —see also Influenza
Balkan A78
summer, of Italy A93.1

Grisel's disease M43.6
Groin —see condition
Grooved tongue K14.5
Ground itch B76.9
Grover's disease or syndrome L11.1
Growing pains, children R29.898
Growth (fungoid) (neoplastic) (new) —see also
Neoplasm
adenoid (vegetative) J35.8
benign —see Neoplasm, benign, by site
malignant —see Neoplasm, malignant, by site
rapid, childhood Z00.2
secondary —see Neoplasm, secondary, by site
Gruby's disease B35.0
Gubler-Millard paralysis or syndrome G46.3
Guerin-Stern syndrome Q74.3
Guidance, insufficient anterior (occlusal) M26.54
Guillain-Barré disease or syndrome G61.0
sequelae G65.0
Guinea worms (infection) (infestation) B72
Guinon's disease (motor-verbal tic) F95.2
Gull's disease E03.4
Gum —see condition
Gumboil K04.7
with sinus K04.6
Gumma (syphilitic) A52.79
artery A52.09
cerebral A52.04
bone A52.77
of yaws (late) A66.6
brain A52.19
cauda equina A52.19
central nervous system A52.3
ciliary body A52.71
congenital A50.59
eyelid A52.71
heart A52.06
intracranial A52.19
iris A52.71
kidney A52.75
larynx A52.73
leptomeninges A52.19
liver A52.74
meninges A52.19
myocardium A52.06
nasopharynx A52.73
neurosyphilitic A52.3
nose A52.73
orbit A52.71
palate (soft) A52.79
penis A52.76
pericardium A52.06
pharynx A52.73
pituitary A52.79
scrofulous (tuberculous) A18.4
skin A52.79
specified site NEC A52.79
spinal cord A52.19
tongue A52.79
tonsil A52.73
trachea A52.73
tuberculous A18.4
ulcerative due to yaws A66.4
ureter A52.75
yaws A66.4
bone A66.6
Gunn's syndrome Q07.8
⇒**Gunshot wound** —see also Puncture, open
fracture - code as Fracture, by site
internal organs —see Injury, by site
Gynandrism Q56.0
Gynandroblastoma
specified site —see Neoplasm, uncertain
behavior, by site
unspecified site
female D39.10
male D40.10
Gynecological examination (periodic) (routine)
Z01.419
with abnormal findings Z01.411
Gynecomastia N62
Gynephobia F40.291
Gyrate scalp Q82.8

▶ New   ⇒ Revised   ~~deleted~~ Deleted   ● Use Additional Character(s)

H

H (Hartnup's) disease E72.02
Haas' disease or osteochondrosis (juvenile) (head of humerus) —see Osteochondrosis, juvenile, humerus
Habit, habituation
  bad sleep Z72.821
  chorea F95.8
  disturbance, child F98.9
  drug —see Dependence, drug
  irregular sleep Z72.821
  laxative F55.2
  spasm —see Tic
  tic —see Tic
Haemophilus (H.) influenzae, as cause of disease classified elsewhere B96.3
Haff disease —see Poisoning, mercury
Hageman's factor defect, deficiency or disease D68.2
Haglund's disease or osteochondrosis (juvenile) (os tibiale externum) —see Osteochondrosis, juvenile, tarsus
Hailey-Hailey disease Q82.8
Hair —see also condition
  plucking F63.3
    in stereotyped movement disorder F98.4
  tourniquet syndrome —see also Constriction, external, by site
    finger S60.44-●
    penis S30.842
    thumb S60.34-●
    toe S90.44-●
Hairball in stomach T18.2
Hair-pulling, pathological (compulsive) F63.3
Hairy black tongue K14.3
Half vertebra Q76.49
Halitosis R19.6
Hallerman-Streiff syndrome Q87.0
Hallervorden-Spatz disease G23.0
Hallopeau's acrodermatitis or disease L40.2
Hallucination R44.3
  auditory R44.0
  gustatory R44.2
  olfactory R44.2
  specified NEC R44.2
  tactile R44.2
  visual R44.1
Hallucinosis (chronic) F28
  alcoholic (acute) F10.951
    in
      abuse F10.151
      dependence F10.251
  drug-induced F19.951
    cannabis F12.951
    cocaine F14.951
    hallucinogen F16.151
    in
      abuse F19.151
        cannabis F12.151
        cocaine F14.151
        hallucinogen F16.151
        inhalant F18.151
        opioid F11.151
        sedative, anxiolytic or hypnotic F13.151
        stimulant NEC F15.151
      dependence F19.251
        cannabis F12.251
        cocaine F14.251
        hallucinogen F16.251
        inhalant F18.251
        opioid F11.251
        sedative, anxiolytic or hypnotic F13.251
        stimulant NEC F15.251
    inhalant F18.951
    opioid F11.951
    sedative, anxiolytic or hypnotic F13.951
    stimulant NEC F15.951
  organic F06.0

Hallux
  deformity (acquired) NEC M20.5X-●
  limitus M20.5X-●
  malleus (acquired) NEC M20.3-●
  rigidus (acquired) M20.2-●
    congenital Q74.2
    sequelae (late effect) of rickets E64.3
  valgus (acquired) M20.1-●
    congenital Q66.6
  varus (acquired) M20.3-●
    congenital Q66.3-●
Halo, visual H53.19
Hamartoma, hamartoblastoma Q85.9
  epithelial (gingival), odontogenic, central or peripheral —see Cyst, calcifying odontogenic
Hamartosis Q85.9
Hamman-Rich syndrome J84.114
Hammer toe (acquired) NEC —see also Deformity, toe, hammer toe
  congenital Q66.89
  sequelae (late effect) of rickets E64.3
Hand —see condition
Hand-foot syndrome L27.1
Handicap, handicapped
  educational Z55.9
    specified NEC Z55.8
Hand-Schüller-Christian disease or syndrome C96.5
Hanging (asphyxia) (strangulation) (suffocation) —see Asphyxia, traumatic, due to mechanical threat
Hangnail —see also Cellulitis, digit
  with lymphangitis —see Lymphangitis, acute, digit
Hangover (alcohol) F10.129
Hanhart's syndrome Q87.0
Hanot-Chauffard (-Troisier) syndrome E83.19
Hanot's cirrhosis or disease K74.3
Hansen's disease —see Leprosy
Hantaan virus disease (Korean hemorrhagic fever) A98.5
Hantavirus disease (with renal manifestations) (Dobrava) (Puumala) (Seoul) A98.5
  with pulmonary manifestations (Andes) (Bayou) (Bermejo) (Black Creek Canal) (Choclo) (Juquitiba) (Laguna negra) (Lechiguanas) (New York) (Oran) (Sin nombre) B33.4
Happy puppet syndrome Q93.59
Harada's disease or syndrome H30.81-●
Hardening
  artery —see Arteriosclerosis
  brain G93.89
Harelip (complete) (incomplete) —see Cleft, lip
Harlequin (newborn) Q80.4
Harley's disease D59.6
Harmful use (of)
  alcohol F10.10
  anxiolytics —see Abuse, drug, sedative
  cannabinoids —see Abuse, drug, cannabis
  cocaine —see Abuse, drug, cocaine
  drug —see Abuse, drug
  hallucinogens —see Abuse, drug, hallucinogen
  hypnotics —see Abuse, drug, sedative -
  opioids —see Abuse, drug, opioid
  PCP (phencyclidine) —see Abuse, drug, hallucinogen
  sedatives —see Abuse, drug, sedative
  stimulants NEC —see Abuse, drug, stimulant
Harris' lines —see Arrest, epiphyseal
Hartnup's disease E72.02
Harvester's lung J67.0
Harvesting ovum for in vitro fertilization Z31.83
Hashimoto's disease or thyroiditis E06.3
Hashitoxicosis (transient) E06.3
Hassal-Henle bodies or warts (cornea) H18.49
Haut mal —see Epilepsy, generalized, specified NEC

Haverhill fever A25.1
Hay fever —see also Fever, hay J30.1
Hayem-Widal syndrome D59.8
Haygarth's nodes M15.8
Haymaker's lung J67.0
Hb (abnormal)
  Bart's disease D56.0
  disease —see Disease, hemoglobin
  trait —see Trait
Head —see condition
⇒Headache R51.9
  ▶with
    ▶orthostatic component NEC R51.0
    ▶positional component NEC R51.0
  allergic NEC G44.89
  associated with sexual activity G44.82
⇒chronic daily R51.9
  cluster G44.009
    chronic G44.029
      intractable G44.021
      not intractable G44.029
    episodic G44.019
      intractable G44.011
      not intractable G44.019
    intractable G44.001
    not intractable G44.009
  cough (primary) G44.83
⇒daily chronic R51.9
  drug-induced NEC G44.40
    intractable G44.41
    not intractable G44.40
  exertional (primary) G44.84
  histamine G44.009
    intractable G44.001
    not intractable G44.009
  hypnic G44.81
  lumbar puncture G97.1
  medication overuse G44.40
    intractable G44.41
    not intractable G44.40
  menstrual —see Migraine, menstrual
  migraine (type) —see also Migraine G43.909
⇒nasal septum R51.9
  neuralgiform, short lasting unilateral, with conjunctival injection and tearing (SUNCT) G44.059
    intractable G44.051
    not intractable G44.059
  new daily persistent (NDPH) G44.52
  orgasmic G44.82
  periodic syndromes in adults and children G43.C0
    with refractory migraine G43.C1
      intractable G43.C1
      not intractable G43.C0
    without refractory migraine G43.C0
  postspinal puncture G97.1
  post-traumatic G44.309
    acute G44.319
      intractable G44.311
      not intractable G44.319
    chronic G44.329
      intractable G44.321
      not intractable G44.329
    intractable G44.301
    not intractable G44.309
  pre-menstrual —see Migraine, menstrual
  preorgasmic G44.82
  primary
    cough G44.83
    exertional G44.84
    stabbing G44.85
    thunderclap G44.53
  rebound G44.40
    intractable G44.41
    not intractable G44.40
  short lasting unilateral neuralgiform, with conjunctival injection and tearing (SUNCT) G44.059
    intractable G44.051
    not intractable G44.059
  specified syndrome NEC G44.89

Headache *(Continued)*
  spinal and epidural anesthesia - induced T88.59
    in labor and delivery O74.5
      in pregnancy O29.4-●
      postpartum, puerperal O89.4
  spinal fluid loss (from puncture) G97.1
  stabbing (primary) G44.85
  tension (-type) G44.209
    chronic G44.229
      intractable G44.221
      not intractable G44.229
    episodic G44.219
      intractable G44.211
      not intractable G44.219
    intractable G44.201
    not intractable G44.209
  thunderclap (primary) G44.53
  vascular NEC G44.1
Healthy
  infant
    accompanying sick mother Z76.3
    receiving care Z76.2
  person accompanying sick person Z76.3
Hearing examination Z01.10
  with abnormal findings NEC Z01.118
  infant or child (over 28 days old) Z00.129
    with abnormal findings Z00.121
  following failed hearing screening Z01.110
  for hearing conservation and treatment Z01.12
Heart —*see* condition
Heart beat
  abnormality R00.9
    specified NEC R00.8
  awareness R00.2
  rapid R00.0
  slow R00.1
Heartburn R12
  psychogenic F45.8
Heartland virus disease A93.8
Heat (effects) T67.9
  apoplexy T67.01
  burn —*see also* Burn L55.9
  collapse T67.1
  cramps T67.2
  dermatitis or eczema L59.0
  edema T67.7
  erythema - code by site under Burn, first degree
  excessive T67.9
    specified effect NEC T67.8
  exhaustion T67.5
    anhydrotic T67.3
    due to
      salt (and water) depletion T67.4
      water depletion T67.3
        with salt depletion T67.4
  fatigue (transient) T67.6
  fever T67.01
  hyperpyrexia T67.01
  prickly L74.0
  prostration —*see* Heat, exhaustion
  pyrexia T67.01
  rash L74.0
  specified effect NEC T67.8
  stroke T67.01
    exertional T67.02
    specified NEC T67.09
  sunburn —*see* Sunburn
  syncope T67.1
Heavy-for-dates NEC (infant) (4000g to 4499g) P08.1
  exceptionally (4500g or more) P08.0
Hebephrenia, hebephrenic (schizophrenia) F20.1
Heberden's disease or nodes (with arthropathy) M15.1
Hebra's
  pityriasis L26
  prurigo L28.2
Heel —*see* condition
Heerfordt's disease D86.89
Hegglin's anomaly or syndrome D72.0
Heilmeyer-Schoner disease D45

Heine-Medin disease A80.9
Heinz body anemia, congenital D58.2
Heliophobia F40.228
Heller's disease or syndrome F84.3
HELLP syndrome (hemolysis, elevated liver enzymes and low platelet count) O14.2-●
  complicating
    childbirth O14.24
    puerperium O14.25
Helminthiasis —*see also* Infestation, helminth
  Ancylostoma B76.0
  intestinal B82.0
    mixed types (types classifiable to more than one of the titles B65.0-B81.3 and B81.8) B81.4
    specified type NEC B81.8
  mixed types (intestinal) (types classifiable to more than one of the titles B65.0-B81.3 and B81.8) B81.4
  Necator (americanus) B76.1
  specified type NEC B83.8
Heloma L84
Hemangioblastoma —*see* Neoplasm, connective tissue, uncertain behavior
  malignant —*see* Neoplasm, connective tissue, malignant
Hemangioendothelioma —*see also* Neoplasm, uncertain behavior, by site
  benign D18.00
    intra-abdominal D18.03
    intracranial D18.02
    skin D18.01
    specified site NEC D18.09
  bone (diffuse) —*see* Neoplasm, bone, malignant
  epithelioid —*see also* Neoplasm, uncertain behavior, by site
    malignant —*see* Neoplasm, malignant, by site
  malignant —*see* Neoplasm, connective tissue, malignant
Hemangiofibroma —*see* Neoplasm, benign, by site
Hemangiolipoma —*see* Lipoma
Hemangioma D18.00
  arteriovenous D18.00
    intra-abdominal D18.03
    intracranial D18.02
    skin D18.01
    specified site NEC D18.09
  capillary I78.1
    intra-abdominal D18.03
    intracranial D18.02
    skin D18.01
    specified site NEC D18.09
  cavernous D18.00
    intra-abdominal D18.03
    intracranial D18.02
    skin D18.01
    specified site NEC D18.09
  epithelioid D18.00
    intra-abdominal D18.03
    intracranial D18.02
    skin D18.01
    specified site NEC D18.09
  histiocytoid D18.00
    intra-abdominal D18.03
    intracranial D18.02
    skin D18.01
    specified site NEC D18.09
  infantile D18.00
    intra-abdominal D18.03
    intracranial D18.02
    skin D18.01
    specified site NEC D18.09
  intra-abdominal D18.03
  intracranial D18.02
  intramuscular D18.00
    intra-abdominal D18.03
    intracranial D18.02
    skin D18.01
    specified site NEC D18.09

Hemangioma *(Continued)*
  intrathoracic structures D18.09
  juvenile D18.00
  malignant —*see* Neoplasm, connective tissue, malignant
  plexiform D18.00
    intra-abdominal D18.03
    intracranial D18.02
    skin D18.01
    specified site NEC D18.09
  racemose D18.00
    intra-abdominal D18.03
    intracranial D18.02
    skin D18.01
    specified site NEC D18.09
  sclerosing —*see* Neoplasm, skin, benign
  simplex D18.00
    intra-abdominal D18.03
    intracranial D18.02
    skin D18.01
    specified site NEC D18.09
  skin D18.01
  specified site NEC D18.09
  venous D18.00
    intra-abdominal D18.03
    intracranial D18.02
    skin D18.01
    specified site NEC D18.09
  verrucous keratotic D18.00
    intra-abdominal D18.03
    intracranial D18.02
    skin D18.01
    specified site NEC D18.09
Hemangiomatosis (systemic) I78.8
  involving single site —*see* Hemangioma
Hemangiopericytoma —*see also* Neoplasm, connective tissue, uncertain behavior
  benign —*see* Neoplasm, connective tissue, benign
  malignant —*see* Neoplasm, connective tissue, malignant
Hemangiosarcoma —*see* Neoplasm, connective tissue, malignant
Hemarthrosis (nontraumatic) M25.00
  ankle M25.07-●
  elbow M25.02-●
  foot joint M25.07-●
  hand joint M25.04-●
  hip M25.05-●
  in hemophilic arthropathy —*see* Arthropathy, hemophilic
  knee M25.06-●
  shoulder M25.01-●
  specified joint NEC M25.08
  traumatic —*see* Sprain, by site
  vertebrae M25.08
  wrist M25.03-●
Hematemesis K92.0
  with ulcer - code by site under Ulcer, with hemorrhage K27.4
  newborn, neonatal P54.0
    due to swallowed maternal blood P78.2
Hematidrosis L74.8
Hematinuria —*see also* Hemoglobinuria
  malarial B50.8
Hematobilia K83.8
Hematocele
  female NEC N94.89
    with ectopic pregnancy O00.90
      with intrauterine pregnancy O00.91
    ovary N83.8
  male N50.1
Hematochezia —*see also* Melena K92.1
Hematochyluria —*see also* Infestation, filarial
  schistosomiasis (bilharziasis) B65.0
Hematocolpos (with hematometra or hematosalpinx) N89.7
Hematocornea —*see* Pigmentation, cornea, stromal
Hematogenous —*see* condition

Hematoma (traumatic) (skin surface intact) —
    see also Contusion
  with
    injury of internal organs —*see* Injury, by site
    open wound —*see* Wound, open
  amputation stump (surgical) (late) T87.89
  aorta, dissecting I71.00
    abdominal I71.02
    thoracic I71.01
    thoracoabdominal I71.03
  aortic intramural —*see* Dissection, aorta
  arterial (complicating trauma) —*see* Injury,
    blood vessel, by site
  auricle —*see* Contusion, ear
    nontraumatic —*see* Disorder, pinna,
      hematoma
  birth injury NEC P15.8
  brain (traumatic)
    with
      cerebral laceration or contusion
        (diffuse) —*see* Injury, intracranial,
        diffuse
      focal —*see* Injury, intracranial, focal
    cerebellar, traumatic S06.37-●
    intracerebral, traumatic —*see* Injury,
      intracranial, intracerebral hemorrhage
    newborn NEC P52.4
      birth injury P10.1
    nontraumatic —*see* Hemorrhage,
      intracranial
    subarachnoid, arachnoid, traumatic —*see*
      Injury, intracranial, subarachnoid
      hemorrhage
    subdural, traumatic —*see* Injury,
      intracranial, subdural hemorrhage
  breast (nontraumatic) N64.89
  broad ligament (nontraumatic) N83.7
    traumatic S37.892
  cerebellar, traumatic S06.37-●
  cerebral —*see* Hematoma, brain
  cerebrum S06.36-●
    left S06.35-●
    right S06.34-●
  cesarean delivery wound O90.2
  complicating delivery (perineal) (pelvic)
    (vagina) (vulva) O71.7
  corpus cavernosum (nontraumatic) N48.89
  epididymis (nontraumatic) N50.1
  epidural (traumatic) —*see* Injury, intracranial,
    epidural hemorrhage
    spinal —*see* Injury, spinal cord, by region
  episiotomy O90.2
  face, birth injury P15.4
  genital organ NEC (nontraumatic)
    female (nonobstetric) N94.89
      traumatic S30.202
    male N50.1
      traumatic S30.201
  internal organs —*see* Injury, by site
  intracerebral, traumatic —*see* Injury,
    intracranial, intracerebral hemorrhage
  intraoperative —*see* Complications,
    intraoperative, hemorrhage
  labia (nontraumatic) (nonobstetric) N90.8
  liver (subcapsular) (nontraumatic) K76.89
    birth injury P15.0
  mediastinum —*see* Injury, intrathoracic
  mesosalpinx (nontraumatic) N83.7
    traumatic S37.898
  muscle - code by site under Contusion
  nontraumatic
    muscle M79.81
    soft tissue M79.81
  obstetrical surgical wound O90.2
  orbit, orbital (nontraumatic) —*see also*
    Hemorrhage, orbit
    traumatic —*see* Contusion, orbit
  pelvis (female) (nontraumatic) (nonobstetric)
    N94.89
    obstetric O71.7
    traumatic —*see* Injury, by site

Hematoma *(Continued)*
  penis (nontraumatic) N48.89
    birth injury P15.5
  perianal (nontraumatic) K64.5
  perineal S30.23
    complicating delivery O71.7
  perirenal —*see* Injury, kidney
  pinna —*see* Contusion, ear
    nontraumatic —*see* Disorder, pinna,
      hematoma
  placenta O43.89-●
  postoperative (postprocedural) —*see*
    Complication, postprocedural,
    hematoma
  retroperitoneal (nontraumatic) K66.1
    traumatic S36.892
  scrotum, superficial S30.22
    birth injury P15.5
  seminal vesicle (nontraumatic) N50.1
    traumatic S37.892
  spermatic cord (traumatic) S37.892
    nontraumatic N50.1
  spinal (cord) (meninges) —*see also* Injury,
    spinal cord, by region
    newborn (birth injury) P11.5
  spleen D73.5
    intraoperative —*see* Complications,
      intraoperative, hemorrhage, spleen
    postprocedural (postoperative) —*see*
      Complications, postprocedural,
      hemorrhage, spleen
  sternocleidomastoid, birth injury P15.2
  sternomastoid, birth injury P15.2
  subarachnoid (traumatic) —*see* Injury,
    intracranial, subarachnoid hemorrhage
    newborn (nontraumatic) P52.5
      due to birth injury P10.3
    nontraumatic —*see* Hemorrhage,
      intracranial, subarachnoid
  subdural (traumatic) —*see* Injury, intracranial,
    subdural hemorrhage
    newborn (localized) P52.8
      birth injury P10.0
    nontraumatic —*see* Hemorrhage,
      intracranial, subdural
  superficial, newborn P54.5
  testis (nontraumatic) N50.1
    birth injury P15.5
  tunica vaginalis (nontraumatic) N50.1
  umbilical cord, complicating delivery O69.5
  uterine ligament (broad) (nontraumatic) N83.7
    traumatic S37.892
  vagina (ruptured) (nontraumatic) N89.8
    complicating delivery O71.7
  vas deferens (nontraumatic) N50.1
    traumatic S37.892
  vitreous —*see* Hemorrhage, vitreous
  vulva (nontraumatic) (nonobstetric) N90.89
    complicating delivery O71.7
    newborn (birth injury) P15.5
Hematometra N85.7
  with hematocolpos N89.7
Hematomyelia (central) G95.19
  newborn (birth injury) P11.5
  traumatic T14.8
Hematomyelitis G04.90
Hematoperitoneum —*see* Hemoperitoneum
Hematophobia F40.230
Hematopneumothorax *(see* Hemothorax)
Hematopoiesis, cyclic D70.4
Hematoporphyria —*see* Porphyria
Hematorachis, hematorrhachis G95.19
  newborn (birth injury) P11.5
Hematosalpinx N83.6
  with
    hematocolpos N89.7
    hematometra N85.7
      with hematocolpos N89.7
  infectional —*see* Salpingitis
Hematospermia R36.1
Hematothorax *(see* Hemothorax)

Hematuria R31.9
  benign (familial) (of childhood) —*see also*
    Hematuria, idiopathic
    essential microscopic R31.1
  due to sulphonamide, sulfonamide —*see* Table
    of Drugs and Chemicals, by drug
  endemic —*see also* Schistosomiasis B65.0
  gross R31.0
  idiopathic N02.9
    with glomerular lesion
    ▶C3
      ▶glomerulonephritis N02.A
      ▶glomerulopathy N02.A
      ▶with dense deposit disease N02.6
      crescentic (diffuse) glomerulonephritis
        N02.7
      dense deposit disease N02.6
      endocapillary proliferative
        glomerulonephritis N02.4
      focal and segmental hyalinosis or
        sclerosis N02.1
      membranoproliferative (diffuse) N02.5
      membranous (diffuse) N02.2
      mesangial proliferative (diffuse) N02.3
      mesangiocapillary (diffuse) N02.5
      minor abnormality N02.0
      proliferative NEC N02.8
      specified pathology NEC N02.8
  intermittent —*see* Hematuria, idiopathic
  malarial B50.8
  microscopic NEC (with symptoms) R31.29
    asymptomatic R31.21
    benign essential R31.1
  paroxysmal —*see also* Hematuria, idiopathic
    nocturnal D59.5
  persistent —*see* Hematuria, idiopathic
  recurrent —*see* Hematuria, idiopathic
  tropical —*see also* Schistosomiasis B65.0
  tuberculous A18.13
Hemeralopia (day blindness) H53.11
  vitamin A deficiency E50.5
Hemi-akinesia R41.4
Hemianalgesia R20.0
Hemianencephaly Q00.0
Hemianesthesia R20.0
Hemianopia, hemianopsia (heteronymous)
  H53.47
  homonymous H53.46-●
  syphilitic A52.71
Hemiathetosis R25.8
Hemiatrophy R68.89
  cerebellar G31.9
  face, facial, progressive (Romberg) G51.8
  tongue K14.8
Hemiballism (us) G25.5
Hemicardia Q24.8
Hemicephalus, hemicephaly Q00.0
Hemichorea G25.5
Hemicolitis, left —*see* Colitis, left sided
Hemicrania
  congenital malformation Q00.0
  continua G44.51
  meaning migraine —*see also* Migraine G43.909
  paroxysmal G44.039
    chronic G44.049
      intractable G44.041
      not intractable G44.049
    episodic G44.039
      intractable G44.031
      not intractable G44.039
    intractable G44.031
    not intractable G44.039
Hemidystrophy —*see* Hemiatrophy
Hemiectromelia Q73.8
Hemihypalgesia R20.8
Hemihypesthesia R20.1
Hemi-inattention R41.4
Hemimelia Q73.8
  lower limb —*see* Defect, reduction, lower
    limb, specified type NEC
  upper limb —*see* Defect, reduction, upper
    limb, specified type NEC

Hemiparalysis —*see* Hemiplegia
Hemiparesis —*see* Hemiplegia
Hemiparesthesia R20.2
Hemiparkinsonism G20
Hemiplegia G81.9-•
  alternans facialis G83.89
  ascending NEC G81.90
    spinal G95.89
  congenital (cerebral) G80.8
    spastic G80.2
  embolic (current episode) I63.4-•
  flaccid G81.0-•
  following
    cerebrovascular disease I69.959
      cerebral infarction I69.35-•
      intracerebral hemorrhage I69.15-•
      nontraumatic intracranial hemorrhage
          NEC I69.25-•
      specified disease NEC I69.85-•
      stroke NOS I69.35-•
      subarachnoid hemorrhage I69.05-•
  hysterical F44.4
  newborn NEC P91.88
    birth injury P11.9
  spastic G81.1-•
    congenital G80.2
  thrombotic (current episode) I63.3-•
Hemisection, spinal cord —*see* Injury, spinal
    cord, by region
Hemispasm (facial) R25.2
Hemisporosis B48.8
Hemitremor R25.1
Hemivertebra Q76.49
  failure of segmentation with scoliosis Q76.3
  fusion with scoliosis Q76.3
Hemochromatosis E83.119
  with refractory anemia D46.1
  due to repeated red blood cell transfusion
      E83.111
  hereditary (primary) E83.110
  neonatal P78.84
  primary E83.110
  specified NEC E83.118
Hemoglobin —*see also* condition
  abnormal (disease) —*see* Disease, hemoglobin
  AS genotype D57.3
  Constant Spring D58.2
  E-beta thalassemia D56.5
  fetal, hereditary persistence (HPFH) D56.4
  H Constant Spring D56.0
  low NOS D64.9
  S (Hb S), heterozygous D57.3
Hemoglobinemia D59.9
  due to blood transfusion T80.89
  paroxysmal D59.6
    nocturnal D59.5
Hemoglobinopathy (mixed) D58.2
  with thalassemia D56.8
  sickle-cell D57.1
    with thalassemia D57.40
    ▶with
      ▶acute chest syndrome D57.411
      ▶cerebral vascular involvement D57.413
      ▶crisis (painful) D57.419
        ▶with specified complication NEC
            D57.418
      ▶splenic sequestration D57.412
      ▶vasoocclusive pain D57.419
    with crisis (vasoocclusive pain) D57.419
      with
        acute chest syndrome D57.411
        splenic sequestration D57.412
    without crisis D57.40
Hemoglobinuria R82.3
  with anemia, hemolytic, acquired (chronic)
      NEC D59.6
  ⇒cold (paroxysmal) (with Raynaud's
      syndrome) D59.6
    ▶agglutinin D59.12
  due to exertion or hemolysis NEC D59.6
  intermittent D59.6

Hemoglobinuria (*Continued*)
  malarial B50.8
  march D59.6
  nocturnal (paroxysmal) D59.5
  paroxysmal (cold) D59.6
    nocturnal D59.5
Hemolymphangioma D18.1
Hemolysis
  intravascular
    with
      abortion —*see* Abortion, by type,
          complicated by, hemorrhage
      ectopic or molar pregnancy O08.1
      hemorrhage
        antepartum —*see* Hemorrhage,
            antepartum, with coagulation
            defect
        intrapartum —*see also* Hemorrhage,
            complicating, delivery O67.0
    postpartum O72.3
  neonatal (excessive) P58.9
    specified NEC P58.8
Hemolytic —*see* condition
Hemopericardium I31.2
  following acute myocardial infarction
      (current complication) I23.0
  newborn P54.8
  traumatic —*see* Injury, heart, with
      hemopericardium
Hemoperitoneum K66.1
  infectional K65.9
  traumatic S36.899
    with open wound —*see* Wound, open, with
        penetration into peritoneal cavity
Hemophilia (classical) (familial) (hereditary)
    D66
  A D66
  B D67
  C D68.1
  acquired D68.311
  autoimmune D68.311
  calcipriva —*see also* Defect, coagulation
      D68.4
  nonfamilial —*see also* Defect, coagulation
      D68.4
  secondary D68.311
  vascular D68.0
Hemophthalmos H44.81-•
Hemopneumothorax —*see also* Hemothorax
  traumatic S27.2
Hemoptysis R04.2
  newborn P26.9
  tuberculous —*see* Tuberculosis, pulmonary
Hemorrhage, hemorrhagic (concealed) R58
  abdomen R58
  accidental antepartum —*see* Hemorrhage,
      antepartum
  acute idiopathic pulmonary, in infants
      R04.81
  adenoid J35.8
  adrenal (capsule) (gland) E27.49
    medulla E27.8
    newborn P54.4
  after delivery —*see* Hemorrhage, postpartum
  alveolar
    lung, newborn P26.8
    process K08.89
  alveolus K08.89
  amputation stump (surgical) T87.89
  anemia (chronic) D50.0
    acute D62
  antepartum (with) O46.90
    with coagulation defect O46.00-•
      afibrinogenemia O46.01-•
      disseminated intravascular coagulation
          O46.02-•
      hypofibrinogenemia O46.01-•
      specified defect NEC O46.09-•
    before 20 weeks gestation O20.9
      specified type NEC O20.8
      threatened abortion O20.0

Hemorrhage, hemorrhagic (*Continued*)
  antepartum (*Continued*)
    due to
      abruptio placenta —*see also* Abruptio
          placentae O45.9-•
      leiomyoma, uterus —*see* Hemorrhage,
          antepartum, specified cause NEC
      placenta previa O44.1-•
    specified cause NEC —*see* subcategory
        O46.8X-•
  anus (sphincter) K62.5
  apoplexy (stroke) —*see* Hemorrhage,
      intracranial, intracerebral
  arachnoid —*see* Hemorrhage, intracranial,
      subarachnoid
  artery R58
    brain —*see* Hemorrhage, intracranial,
        intracerebral
  basilar (ganglion) I61.0
  bladder N32.89
  bowel K92.2
    newborn P54.3
  brain (miliary) (nontraumatic) —*see*
      Hemorrhage, intracranial, intracerebral
    due to
      birth injury P10.1
      syphilis A52.05
    epidural or extradural (traumatic) —
        see Injury, intracranial, epidural
        hemorrhage
    newborn P52.4
      birth injury P10.1
    subarachnoid —*see* Hemorrhage,
        intracranial, subarachnoid
    subdural —*see* Hemorrhage, intracranial,
        subdural
  brainstem (nontraumatic) I61.3
    traumatic S06.38-•
  breast N64.59
  bronchial tube —*see* Hemorrhage, lung
  bronchopulmonary —*see* Hemorrhage, lung
  bronchus —*see* Hemorrhage, lung
  bulbar I61.5
  capillary I78.8
    primary D69.8
  cecum K92.2
  cerebellar, cerebellum (nontraumatic) I61.4
    newborn P52.6
    traumatic S06.37-•
  cerebral, cerebrum —*see also* Hemorrhage,
      intracranial, intracerebral
    lobe I61.1
    newborn (anoxic) P52.4
      birth injury P10.1
  cerebromeningeal I61.8
  cerebrospinal —*see* Hemorrhage, intracranial,
      intracerebral
  cervix (uteri) (stump) NEC N88.8
  chamber, anterior (eye) —*see* Hyphema
  childbirth —*see* Hemorrhage, complicating,
      delivery
  choroid H31.30-•
    expulsive H31.31-•
  ciliary body —*see* Hyphema
  cochlea —*see* subcategory H83.8
  colon K92.2
  complicating
    abortion —*see* Abortion, by type,
        complicated by, hemorrhage
    delivery O67.9
      associated with coagulation defect
          (afibrinogenemia) (DIC)
          (hyperfibrinolysis) O67.0
      specified cause NEC O67.8
    surgical procedure —*see* Hemorrhage,
        intraoperative
  conjunctiva H11.3-•
    newborn P54.8
  cord, newborn (stump) P51.9
  corpus luteum (ruptured) cyst N83.1-•
  cortical (brain) I61.1

▶ New   ⇒ Revised   ~~deleted~~ Deleted   • Use Additional Character(s)

Hemorrhage, hemorrhagic *(Continued)*
cranial —*see* Hemorrhage, intracranial
cutaneous R23.3
  due to autosensitivity, erythrocyte D69.2
  newborn P54.5
delayed
  following ectopic or molar pregnancy
    O08.1
  postpartum O72.2
diathesis (familial) D69.9
disease D69.9
  newborn P53
  specified type NEC D69.8
due to or associated with
  afibrinogenemia or other coagulation defect
    (conditions in categories D65-D69)
    antepartum —*see* Hemorrhage,
      antepartum, with coagulation
      defect
    intrapartum O67.0
dental implant M27.61
device, implant or graft —*see also*
    Complications, by site and type,
    specified NEC T85.838
  arterial graft NEC T82.838
  breast T85.838
  catheter NEC T85.838
    dialysis (renal) T82.838
      intraperitoneal T85.838
    infusion NEC T82.838
      spinal (epidural) (subdural)
        T85.830
    urinary (indwelling) T83.83
  electronic (electrode) (pulse generator)
    (stimulator)
    bone T84.83
    cardiac T82.837
    nervous system (brain) (peripheral
      nerve) (spinal) T85.830
    urinary T83.83
  fixation, internal (orthopedic) NEC
    T84.83
  gastrointestinal (bile duct) (esophagus)
    T85.838
  genital NEC T83.83
  heart NEC T82.837
  joint prosthesis T84.83
  ocular (corneal graft) (orbital implant)
    NEC T85.838
  orthopedic NEC T84.83
    bone graft T86.838
  specified NEC T85.838
  urinary NEC T83.83
  vascular NEC T82.838
  ventricular intracranial shunt T85.838
duodenum, duodenal K92.2
  ulcer —*see* Ulcer, duodenum, with
    hemorrhage
dura mater —*see* Hemorrhage, intracranial,
    subdural
endotracheal —*see* Hemorrhage, lung
epicranial subaponeurotic (massive), birth
    injury P12.2
epidural (traumatic) —*see also* Injury,
    intracranial, epidural hemorrhage
  nontraumatic I62.1
esophagus K22.8
  varix I85.01
    secondary I85.11
excessive, following ectopic gestation
    (subsequent episode) O08.1
extradural (traumatic) —*see* Injury,
    intracranial, epidural hemorrhage
  birth injury P10.8
  newborn (anoxic) (nontraumatic) P52.8
  nontraumatic I62.1
eye NEC H57.89
  fundus —*see* Hemorrhage, retina
  lid —*see* Disorder, eyelid, specified type
    NEC
fallopian tube N83.6

Hemorrhage, hemorrhagic *(Continued)*
fibrinogenolysis —*see* Fibrinolysis
fibrinolytic (acquired) —*see* Fibrinolysis
from
  ear (nontraumatic) —*see* Otorrhagia
  tracheostomy stoma J95.01
fundus, eye —*see* Hemorrhage, retina
funis —*see* Hemorrhage, umbilicus, cord
gastric —*see* Hemorrhage, stomach
gastroenteric K92.2
  newborn P54.3
gastrointestinal (tract) K92.2
  newborn P54.3
genital organ, male N50.1
genitourinary (tract) NOS R31.9
gingiva K06.8
globe (eye) —*see* Hemophthalmos
graafian follicle cyst (ruptured) N83.0-●
gum K06.8
heart I51.89
hypopharyngeal (throat) R04.1
intermenstrual (regular) N92.3
  irregular N92.1
internal (organs) NEC R58
  capsule I61.0
  ear —*see* subcategory H83.8
  newborn P54.8
intestine K92.2
  newborn P54.3
intra-abdominal R58
intra-alveolar (lung), newborn P26.8
intracerebral (nontraumatic) —*see*
    Hemorrhage, intracranial,
    intracerebral
intracranial (nontraumatic) I62.9
  birth injury P10.9
  epidural, nontraumatic I62.1
  extradural, nontraumatic I62.1
  intracerebral (nontraumatic) (in) I61.9
    brain stem I61.3
    cerebellum I61.4
    hemisphere I61.2
      cortical (superficial) I61.1
      subcortical (deep) I61.0
    intraoperative
      during a nervous system procedure
        G97.31
      during other procedure G97.32
    intraventricular I61.5
    multiple localized I61.6
    newborn P52.4
      birth injury P10.1
    postprocedural
      following a nervous system procedure
        G97.51
      following other procedure
        G97.52
    specified NEC I61.8
    superficial I61.1
    traumatic (diffuse) —*see* Injury,
      intracranial, diffuse
    focal —*see* Injury, intracranial, focal
  newborn P52.9
    specified NEC P52.8
  subarachnoid (nontraumatic) (from) I60.9
    intracranial (cerebral) artery I60.7
      anterior communicating I60.2
      basilar I60.4
      carotid siphon and bifurcation
        I60.0-●
      communicating I60.7
        anterior I60.2
        posterior I60.3-●
      middle cerebral I60.1-●
      posterior communicating I60.3-●
      specified artery NEC I60.6
      vertebral I60.5-●
    newborn P52.5
      birth injury P10.3
    specified NEC I60.8
    traumatic S06.6X-●

Hemorrhage, hemorrhagic *(Continued)*
intracranial *(Continued)*
  subdural (nontraumatic) I62.00
    acute I62.01
    birth injury P10.0
    chronic I62.03
    newborn (anoxic) (hypoxic) P52.8
      birth injury P10.0
    spinal G95.19
    subacute I62.02
    traumatic —*see* Injury, intracranial,
      subdural hemorrhage
  traumatic —*see* Injury, intracranial, focal
    brain injury
intramedullary NEC G95.19
intraocular —*see* Hemophthalmos
intraoperative, intraprocedural —*see*
    Complication, hemorrhage (hematoma),
    intraoperative (intraprocedural), by site
intrapartum —*see* Hemorrhage, complicating,
    delivery
intrapelvic
  female N94.89
  male K66.1
intraperitoneal K66.1
intrapontine I61.3
intraprocedural —*see* Complication,
    hemorrhage (hematoma), intraoperative
    (intraprocedural), by site
intrauterine N85.7
  complicating delivery —*see also* Hemorrhage,
    complicating, delivery O67.9
  postpartum —*see* Hemorrhage, postpartum
intraventricular I61.5
  newborn (nontraumatic) —*see also* Newborn,
    affected by, hemorrhage P52.3
    due to birth injury P10.2
    grade
      1 P52.0
      2 P52.1
      3 P52.21
      4 P52.22
intravesical N32.89
iris (postinfectional) (postinflammatory)
    (toxic) —*see* Hyphema
joint (nontraumatic) —*see* Hemarthrosis
kidney N28.89
knee (joint) (nontraumatic) —*see*
    Hemarthrosis, knee
labyrinth —*see* subcategory H83.8
lenticular striate artery I61.0
ligature, vessel —*see* Hemorrhage,
    postoperative
liver K76.89
lung R04.89
  newborn P26.9
    massive P26.1
    specified NEC P26.8
  tuberculous —*see* Tuberculosis, pulmonary
massive umbilical, newborn P51.0
mediastinum —*see* Hemorrhage, lung
medulla I61.3
membrane (brain) I60.8
  spinal cord —*see* Hemorrhage, spinal cord
meninges, meningeal (brain) (middle) I60.8
  spinal cord —*see* Hemorrhage, spinal cord
mesentery K66.1
metritis —*see* Endometritis
mouth K13.79
mucous membrane NEC R58
  newborn P54.8
muscle M62.89
nail (subungual) L60.8
nasal turbinate R04.0
  newborn P54.8
navel, newborn P51.9
newborn P54.9
  specified NEC P54.8
nipple N64.59
nose R04.0
  newborn P54.8

Hemorrhage, hemorrhagic *(Continued)*
- omentum K66.1
- optic nerve (sheath) H47.02-●
- orbit, orbital H05.23-●
- ovary NEC N83.8
- oviduct N83.6
- pancreas K86.89
- parathyroid (gland) (spontaneous) E21.4
- parturition —*see* Hemorrhage, complicating, delivery
- penis N48.89
- pericardium, pericarditis I31.2
- peritoneum, peritoneal K66.1
- peritonsillar tissue J35.8
  - due to infection J36
- petechial R23.3
  - due to autosensitivity, erythrocyte D69.2
- pituitary (gland) E23.6
- pleura —*see* Hemorrhage, lung
- polioencephalitis, superior E51.2
- polymyositis —*see* Polymyositis
- pons, pontine I61.3
- posterior fossa (nontraumatic) I61.8
  - newborn P52.6
- postmenopausal N95.0
- postnasal R04.0
- postoperative —*see* Complications, postprocedural, hemorrhage, by site
- postpartum NEC (following delivery of placenta) O72.1
  - delayed or secondary O72.2
  - retained placenta O72.0
  - third stage O72.0
- pregnancy —*see* Hemorrhage, antepartum
- preretinal —*see* Hemorrhage, retina
- prostate N42.1
- puerperal —*see* Hemorrhage, postpartum
  - delayed or secondary O72.2
- pulmonary R04.89
  - newborn P26.9
    - massive P26.1
    - specified NEC P26.8
  - tuberculous —*see* Tuberculosis, pulmonary
- purpura (primary) D69.3
- rectum (sphincter) K62.5
  - newborn P54.2
- recurring, following initial hemorrhage at time of injury T79.2
- renal N28.89
- respiratory passage or tract R04.9
  - specified NEC R04.89
- retina, retinal (vessels) H35.6-●
  - diabetic —*see* Diabetes, retinal, hemorrhage
- retroperitoneal R58
- scalp R58
- scrotum N50.1
- secondary (nontraumatic) R58
  - following initial hemorrhage at time of injury T79.2
- seminal vesicle N50.1
- skin R23.3
  - newborn P54.5
- slipped umbilical ligature P51.8
- spermatic cord N50.1
- spinal (cord) G95.19
  - newborn (birth injury) P11.5
- spleen D73.5
  - intraoperative —*see* Complications, intraoperative, hemorrhage, spleen
  - postprocedural —*see* Complications, postprocedural, hemorrhage, spleen
- stomach K92.2
  - newborn P54.3
  - ulcer —*see* Ulcer, stomach, with hemorrhage
- subarachnoid (nontraumatic) —*see* Hemorrhage, intracranial, subarachnoid
- subconjunctival —*see also* Hemorrhage, conjunctiva
  - birth injury P15.3
- subcortical (brain) I61.0

Hemorrhage, hemorrhagic *(Continued)*
- subcutaneous R23.3
- subdiaphragmatic R58
- subdural (acute) (nontraumatic) —*see* Hemorrhage, intracranial, subdural
- subependymal
  - newborn P52.0
    - with intraventricular extension P52.1
      - and intracerebral extension P52.22
- subgaleal P12.2
- subhyaloid —*see* Hemorrhage, retina
- subperiosteal —*see* Disorder, bone, specified type NEC
- subretinal —*see* Hemorrhage, retina
- subtentorial —*see* Hemorrhage, intracranial, subdural
- subungual L60.8
- suprarenal (capsule) (gland) E27.49
  - newborn P54.4
- tentorium (traumatic) NEC —*see* Hemorrhage, brain
  - newborn (birth injury) P10.4
- testis N50.1
- third stage (postpartum) O72.0
- thorax —*see* Hemorrhage, lung
- throat R04.1
- thymus (gland) E32.8
- thyroid (cyst) (gland) E07.89
- tongue K14.8
- tonsil J35.8
- trachea —*see* Hemorrhage, lung
- tracheobronchial R04.89
  - newborn P26.0
- traumatic — code to specific injury
  - cerebellar —*see* Hemorrhage, brain
  - intracranial —*see* Hemorrhage, brain
  - recurring or secondary (following initial hemorrhage at time of injury) T79.2
- tuberculous NEC —*see also* Tuberculosis, pulmonary A15.0
- tunica vaginalis N50.1
- ulcer - code by site under Ulcer, with hemorrhage K27.4
- umbilicus, umbilical
  - cord
    - after birth, newborn P51.9
    - complicating delivery O69.5
  - newborn P51.9
    - massive P51.0
    - slipped ligature P51.8
  - stump P51.9
- urethra (idiopathic) N36.8
- uterus, uterine (abnormal) N93.9
  - climacteric N92.4
  - complicating delivery —*see* Hemorrhage, complicating, delivery
  - dysfunctional or functional N93.8
  - intermenstrual (regular) N92.3
    - irregular N92.1
  - postmenopausal N95.0
  - postpartum —*see* Hemorrhage, postpartum
  - preclimacteric or premenopausal N92.4
  - prepubertal N93.8
  - pubertal N92.2
- vagina (abnormal) N93.9
  - newborn P54.6
- vas deferens N50.1
- vasa previa O69.4
- ventricular I61.5
- vesical N32.89
- viscera NEC R58
  - newborn P54.8
- vitreous (humor) (intraocular) H43.1-●
- vulva N90.89

Hemorrhoids (bleeding) (without mention of degree) K64.9
- 1st degree (grade/stage I) (without prolapse outside of anal canal) K64.0
- 2nd degree (grade/stage II) (that prolapse with straining but retract spontaneously) K64.1

Hemorrhoids *(Continued)*
- 3rd degree (grade/stage III) (that prolapse with straining and require manual replacement back inside anal canal) K64.2
- 4th degree (grade/stage IV) (with prolapsed tissue that cannot be manually replaced) K64.3
- complicating
  - pregnancy O22.4
  - puerperium O87.2
- external K64.4
  - with
    - thrombosis K64.5
- internal (without mention of degree) K64.8
- prolapsed K64.8
- skin tags
  - anus K64.4
  - residual K64.4
- specified NEC K64.8
- strangulated —*see also* Hemorrhoids, by degree K64.8
- thrombosed —*see also* Hemorrhoids, by degree K64.5
- ulcerated —*see also* Hemorrhoids, by degree K64.8
Hemosalpinx N83.6
- with
  - hematocolpos N89.7
  - hematometra N85.7
    - with hematocolpos N89.7
Hemosiderosis (dietary) E83.19
- pulmonary, idiopathic E83.1 *[J84.03]*
- transfusion T80.89
Hemothorax (bacterial) (nontuberculous) J94.2
- newborn P54.8
- traumatic S27.1
  - with pneumothorax S27.2
- tuberculous NEC A15.6
Henoch (-Schönlein) disease or syndrome (purpura) D69.0
Henpue, henpuye A66.6
Hepar lobatum (syphilitic) A52.74
Hepatalgia K76.89
Hepatitis K75.9
- acute B17.9
  - with coma K72.01
  - with hepatic failure —*see* Failure, hepatic
  - alcoholic —*see* Hepatitis, alcoholic
  - infectious B15.9
  - non-viral K72.0
  - viral B17.9
- alcoholic (acute) (chronic) K70.10
  - with ascites K70.11
- amebic —*see* Abscess, liver, amebic
- anicteric (viral) —*see* Hepatitis, viral
- antigen-associated (HAA) —*see* Hepatitis, B
- Australia-antigen (positive) —*see* Hepatitis, B
- autoimmune K75.4
- B B19.10
  - with hepatic coma B19.11
  - acute B16.9
    - with
      - delta-agent (coinfection) (without hepatic coma) B16.1
        - with hepatic coma B16.0
      - hepatic coma (without delta-agent coinfection) B16.2
  - chronic B18.1
    - with delta-agent B18.0
- bacterial NEC K75.89
- C (viral) B19.20
  - with hepatic coma B19.21
  - acute B17.10
    - with hepatic coma B17.11
  - chronic B18.2
- catarrhal (acute) B15.9
  - with hepatic coma B15.0
- cholangiolitic K75.89
- cholestatic K75.89

▶ New   ⇒ Revised   ~~deleted~~ Deleted   ● Use Additional Character(s)

Hepatitis *(Continued)*
  chronic K73.9
    active NEC K73.2
    lobular NEC K73.1
    persistent NEC K73.0
    specified NEC K73.8
  cytomegaloviral B25.1
  due to ethanol (acute) (chronic) —*see*
    Hepatitis, alcoholic
  epidemic B15.9
    with hepatic coma B15.0
  fulminant NEC (viral) —*see* Hepatitis,
    viral
  granulomatous NEC K75.3
  herpesviral B00.81
  history of
    B Z86.19
    C Z86.19
  homologous serum —*see* Hepatitis, viral,
    type B
  in (due to)
    mumps B26.81
    toxoplasmosis (acquired) B58.1
      congenital (active) P37.1 *[K77]*
  infectious, infective B15.9
    acute (subacute) B17.9
    chronic B18.9
  inoculation —*see* Hepatitis, viral, type B
  interstitial (chronic) K74.69
  lupoid NEC K75.2
  malignant NEC (with hepatic failure)
    K72.90
    with coma K72.91
  neonatal giant cell P59.29
  neonatal (idiopathic) (toxic) P59.29
  newborn P59.29
  postimmunization —*see* Hepatitis, viral,
    type B
  post-transfusion —*see* Hepatitis, viral,
    type B
  reactive, nonspecific K75.2
  serum —*see* Hepatitis, viral, type B
  specified type NEC
    with hepatic failure —*see* Failure, hepatic
  syphilitic (late) A52.74
    congenital (early) A50.08 *[K77]*
      late A50.59 *[K77]*
    secondary A51.45
  toxic —*see also* Disease, liver, toxic K71.6
  tuberculous A18.83
  viral, virus B19.9
    with hepatic coma B19.0
    acute B17.9
    chronic B18.9
      specified NEC B18.8
      type
        B B18.1
          with delta-agent B18.0
        C B18.2
    congenital P35.3
    coxsackie B33.8 *[K77]*
    cytomegalic inclusion B25.1
    in remission, any type — code to Hepatitis,
      chronic, by type
    non-A, non-B B17.8
    specified type NEC (with or without coma)
      B17.8
    type
      A B15.9
        with hepatic coma B15.0
      B B19.10
        with hepatic coma B19.11
        acute B16.9
          with
            delta-agent (coinfection) (without
              hepatic coma) B16.1
              with hepatic coma B16.0
            hepatic coma (without delta-
              agent coinfection) B16.2
        chronic B18.1
          with delta-agent B18.0

Hepatitis *(Continued)*
  viral, virus *(Continued)*
    type *(Continued)*
      C B19.20
        with hepatic coma B19.21
        acute B17.10
          with hepatic coma B17.11
        chronic B18.2
      E B17.2
      non-A, non-B B17.8
Hepatization lung (acute) —*see* Pneumonia,
  lobar
Hepatoblastoma C22.2
Hepatocarcinoma C22.0
Hepatocholangiocarcinoma C22.0
Hepatocholangioma, benign D13.4
Hepatocholangitis K75.89
Hepatolenticular degeneration E83.01
Hepatoma (malignant) C22.0
  benign D13.4
  embryonal C22.0
Hepatomegaly —*see also* Hypertrophy, liver
  with splenomegaly R16.2
  congenital Q44.7
  in mononucleosis
    gammaherpesviral B27.09
    infectious specified NEC B27.89
Hepatoptosis K76.89
Hepatorenal syndrome following labor and
  delivery O90.4
Hepatosis K76.89
Hepatosplenomegaly R16.2
  hyperlipemic (Bürger-Grütz type) E78.3 *[K77]*
Hereditary —*see* condition
Heredodegeneration, macular —*see* Dystrophy,
  retina
Heredopathia atactica polyneuritiformis G60.1
Heredosyphilis —*see* Syphilis, congenital
Herlitz' syndrome Q81.1
Hermansky-Pudlak syndrome E70.331
Hermaphrodite, hermaphroditism (true) Q56.0
  46,XX with streak gonads Q99.1
  46,XX/46,XY Q99.0
  46,XY with streak gonads Q99.1
  chimera 46,XX/46,XY Q99.0
Hernia, hernial (acquired) (recurrent) K46.9
  with
    gangrene —*see* Hernia, by site, with,
      gangrene
    incarceration —*see* Hernia, by site, with,
      obstruction
    irreducible —*see* Hernia, by site, with,
      obstruction
    obstruction —*see* Hernia, by site, with,
      obstruction
    strangulation —*see* Hernia, by site, with,
      obstruction
  abdomen, abdominal K46.9
    with
      gangrene (and obstruction) K46.1
      obstruction K46.0
    femoral —*see* Hernia, femoral
    incisional —*see* Hernia, incisional
    inguinal —*see* Hernia, inguinal
    specified site NEC K45.8
      with
        gangrene (and obstruction) K45.1
        obstruction K45.0
    umbilical —*see* Hernia, umbilical
    wall —*see* Hernia, ventral
  appendix —*see* Hernia, abdomen
  bladder (mucosa) (sphincter)
    congenital (female) (male) Q79.51
    female —*see* Cystocele
    male N32.89
  brain, congenital —*see* Encephalocele
  cartilage, vertebra —*see* Displacement,
    intervertebral disc
  cerebral, congenital —*see also* Encephalocele
    endaural Q01.8
  ciliary body (traumatic) S05.2-●

Hernia, hernial *(Continued)*
  colon —*see* Hernia, abdomen
  Cooper's —*see* Hernia, abdomen, specified
    site NEC
  crural —*see* Hernia, femoral
  diaphragm, diaphragmatic K44.9
    with
      gangrene (and obstruction) K44.1
      obstruction K44.0
    congenital Q79.0
  direct (inguinal) —*see* Hernia, inguinal
  diverticulum, intestine —*see* Hernia,
    abdomen
  double (inguinal) —*see* Hernia, inguinal,
    bilateral
  due to adhesions (with obstruction) K56.50
  epigastric —*see also* Hernia, ventral K43.9
  esophageal hiatus —*see* Hernia, hiatal
  external (inguinal) —*see* Hernia, inguinal
  fallopian tube N83.4-●
  fascia M62.89
  femoral K41.90
    with
      gangrene (and obstruction) K41.40
        not specified as recurrent K41.40
        recurrent K41.41
      obstruction K41.30
        not specified as recurrent K41.30
        recurrent K41.31
    bilateral K41.20
      with
        gangrene (and obstruction) K41.10
          not specified as recurrent K41.10
          recurrent K41.11
        obstruction K41.00
          not specified as recurrent K41.00
          recurrent K41.01
      not specified as recurrent K41.20
      recurrent K41.21
    not specified as recurrent K41.90
    recurrent K41.91
    unilateral K41.90
      with
        gangrene (and obstruction) K41.40
          not specified as recurrent K41.40
          recurrent K41.41
        obstruction K41.30
          not specified as recurrent K41.30
          recurrent K41.31
      not specified as recurrent K41.90
      recurrent K41.91
  foramen magnum G93.5
    congenital Q01.8
  funicular (umbilical) —*see also* Hernia,
    umbilicus
    spermatic (cord) —*see* Hernia, inguinal
  gastrointestinal tract —*see* Hernia, abdomen
  Hesselbach's —*see* Hernia, femoral, specified
    site NEC
  hiatal (esophageal) (sliding) K44.9
    with
      gangrene (and obstruction) K44.1
      obstruction K44.0
    congenital Q40.1
  hypogastric —*see* Hernia, ventral
  incarcerated —*see also* Hernia, by site, with
    obstruction
    with gangrene —*see* Hernia, by site, with
      gangrene
  incisional K43.92
    with
      gangrene (and obstruction) K43.1
      obstruction K43.0
  indirect (inguinal) —*see* Hernia, inguinal
  inguinal (direct) (external) (funicular)
    (indirect) (internal) (oblique) (scrotal)
    (sliding) K40.90
    with
      gangrene (and obstruction) K40.40
        not specified as recurrent K40.40
        recurrent K40.41

Hernia, hernial *(Continued)*
  inguinal *(Continued)*
    with *(Continued)*
      obstruction K40.30
        not specified as recurrent K40.30
        recurrent K40.31
    bilateral K40.20
      with
        gangrene (and obstruction)
          K40.10
          not specified as recurrent
            K40.10
          recurrent K40.11
        obstruction K40.00
          not specified as recurrent K40.00
          recurrent K40.01
      not specified as recurrent K40.20
      recurrent K40.21
    not specified as recurrent K40.90
    recurrent K40.91
    unilateral K40.90
      with
        gangrene (and obstruction) K40.40
          not specified as recurrent K40.40
          recurrent K40.41
        obstruction K40.30
          not specified as recurrent K40.30
          recurrent K40.31
      not specified as recurrent K40.90
      recurrent K40.91
  internal —*see also* Hernia, abdomen
    inguinal —*see* Hernia, inguinal
  interstitial —*see* Hernia, abdomen
  intervertebral cartilage or disc —*see*
    Displacement, intervertebral disc
  intestine, intestinal —*see* Hernia, by site
  intra-abdominal —*see* Hernia, abdomen
  iris (traumatic) S05.2-•
  irreducible —*see also* Hernia, by site, with
    obstruction
    with gangrene —*see* Hernia, by site, with
      gangrene
  ischiatic —*see* Hernia, abdomen, specified
    site NEC
  ischiorectal —*see* Hernia, abdomen, specified
    site NEC
  lens (traumatic) S05.2-•
  linea (alba) (semilunaris) —*see* Hernia,
    ventral
  Littre's —*see* Hernia, abdomen
  lumbar —*see* Hernia, abdomen, specified site
    NEC
  lung (subcutaneous) J98.4
  mediastinum J98.59
  mesenteric (internal) —*see* Hernia, abdomen
  midline —*see* Hernia, ventral
  muscle (sheath) M62.89
  nucleus pulposus —*see* Displacement,
    intervertebral disc
  oblique (inguinal) —*see* Hernia, inguinal
  obstructive —*see also* Hernia, by site, with
    obstruction
    with gangrene —*see* Hernia, by site, with
      gangrene
  obturator —*see* Hernia, abdomen, specified
    site NEC
  omental —*see* Hernia, abdomen
  ovary N83.4-•
  oviduct N83.4-•
  paraesophageal —*see also* Hernia, diaphragm
    congenital Q40.1
  parastomal K43.5
    with
      gangrene (and obstruction) K43.4
      obstruction K43.3
  paraumbilical —*see* Hernia, umbilicus
  perineal —*see* Hernia, abdomen, specified
    site NEC
  Petit's —*see* Hernia, abdomen, specified site
    NEC
  postoperative —*see* Hernia, incisional

Hernia, hernial *(Continued)*
  pregnant uterus —*see* Abnormal, uterus in
    pregnancy or childbirth
  prevesical N32.89
  properitoneal —*see* Hernia, abdomen,
    specified site NEC
  pudendal —*see* Hernia, abdomen, specified
    site NEC
  rectovaginal N81.6
  retroperitoneal —*see* Hernia, abdomen,
    specified site NEC
  Richter's —*see* Hernia, abdomen, with
    obstruction
  Rieux's, Riex's —*see* Hernia, abdomen,
    specified site NEC
  sac condition (adhesion) (dropsy)
    (inflammation) (laceration)
    (suppuration) - code by site under
    Hernia
  sciatic —*see* Hernia, abdomen, specified site
    NEC
  scrotum, scrotal —*see* Hernia, inguinal
  sliding (inguinal) —*see also* Hernia,
    inguinal
    hiatus —*see* Hernia, hiatal
  spigelian —*see* Hernia, ventral
  spinal —*see* Spina bifida
  strangulated —*see also* Hernia, by site, with
    obstruction
    with gangrene —*see* Hernia, by site, with
      gangrene
  subxiphoid —*see* Hernia, ventral
  supra-umbilicus —*see* Hernia, ventral
  tendon —*see* Disorder, tendon, specified type
    NEC
  Treitz's (fossa) —*see* Hernia, abdomen,
    specified site NEC
  tunica vaginalis Q55.29
  umbilicus, umbilical K42.9
    with
      gangrene (and obstruction) K42.1
      obstruction K42.0
  ureter N28.89
  urethra, congenital Q64.79
  urinary meatus, congenital Q64.79
  uterus N81.4
    pregnant —*see* Abnormal, uterus in
      pregnancy or childbirth
  vaginal (anterior) (wall) —*see* Cystocele
  Velpeau's —*see* Hernia, femoral
  ventral K43.9
    with
      gangrene (and obstruction) K43.7
      obstruction K43.6
    incisional K43.2
      with
        gangrene (and obstruction) K43.1
        obstruction K43.0
      recurrent —*see* Hernia, incisional
    specified NEC K43.9
      with
        gangrene (and obstruction) K43.7
        obstruction K43.6
  vesical
    congenital (female) (male) Q79.51
    female —*see* Cystocele
    male N32.89
  vitreous (into wound) S05.2-•
    into anterior chamber —*see* Prolapse,
      vitreous
Herniation —*see also* Hernia
  brain (stem) G93.5
  cerebral G93.5
  mediastinum J98.59
  nucleus pulposus —*see* Displacement,
    intervertebral disc
Herpangina B08.5
Herpes, herpesvirus, herpetic B00.9
  anogenital A60.9
    perianal skin A60.1
    rectum A60.1

Herpes, herpesvirus, herpetic *(Continued)*
  anogenital *(Continued)*
    urogenital tract A60.00
      cervix A60.03
      male genital organ NEC A60.02
      penis A60.01
      specified site NEC A60.09
      vagina A60.04
      vulva A60.04
  blepharitis (zoster) B02.39
    simplex B00.59
  circinatus B35.4
    bullosus L12.0
  conjunctivitis (simplex) B00.53
    zoster B02.31
  cornea B02.33
  encephalitis B00.4
    due to herpesvirus 6 B10.01
    due to herpesvirus 7 B10.09
    specified NEC B10.09
  eye (zoster) B02.30
    simplex B00.50
  eyelid (zoster) B02.39
    simplex B00.59
  facialis B00.1
  febrilis B00.1
  geniculate ganglionitis B02.21
  genital, genitalis A60.00
    female A60.09
    male A60.02
  gestational, gestationis O26.4-•
  gingivostomatitis B00.2
  human B00.9
    1 —*see* Herpes, simplex
    2 —*see* Herpes, simplex
    3 —*see* Varicella
    4 —*see* Mononucleosis, Epstein-Barr (virus)
    5 —*see* Disease, cytomegalic inclusion
      (generalized)
    6
      encephalitis B10.01
      specified NEC B10.81
    7
      encephalitis B10.09
      specified NEC B10.82
    8 B10.89
  infection NEC B10.89
    Kaposi's sarcoma associated B10.89
  iridocyclitis (simplex) B00.51
    zoster B02.32
  iris (vesicular erythema multiforme) L51.9
  iritis (simplex) B00.51
  Kaposi's sarcoma associated B10.89
  keratitis (simplex) (dendritic) (disciform)
    (interstitial) B00.52
    zoster (interstitial) B02.33
  keratoconjunctivitis (simplex) B00.52
    zoster B02.33
  labialis B00.1
  lip B00.1
  meningitis (simplex) B00.3
    zoster B02.1
  ophthalmicus (zoster) NEC B02.30
    simplex B00.50
  penis A60.01
  perianal skin A60.1
  pharyngitis, pharyngotonsillitis B00.2
  rectum A60.1
  scrotum A60.02
  sepsis B00.7
  simplex B00.9
    complicated NEC B00.89
    congenital P35.2
    conjunctivitis B00.53
    external ear B00.1
    eyelid B00.59
    hepatitis B00.81
    keratitis (interstitial) B00.52
    myleitis B00.82
    specified complication NEC B00.89
    visceral B00.89

▶ New   ⇒ Revised   ~~deleted~~ Deleted   • Use Additional Character(s)

Herpes, herpesvirus, herpetic *(Continued)*
 stomatitis B00.2
 tonsurans B35.0
 visceral B00.89
 vulva A60.04
 whitlow B00.89
 zoster —*see also* condition B02.9
  auricularis B02.21
  complicated NEC B02.8
  conjunctivitis B02.31
  disseminated B02.7
  encephalitis B02.0
  eye(lid) B02.39
  geniculate ganglionitis B02.21
  keratitis (interstitial) B02.33
  meningitis B02.1
  myelitis B02.24
  neuritis, neuralgia B02.29
  ophthalmicus NEC B02.30
  oticus B02.21
  polyneuropathy B02.23
  specified complication NEC B02.8
  trigeminal neuralgia B02.22
Herpesvirus (human) —*see* Herpes
Herpetophobia F40.218
Herrick's anemia —*see* Disease, sickle-cell
Hers' disease E74.09
Herter-Gee syndrome K90.0
Herxheimer's reaction R68.89
Hesitancy
 of micturition R39.11
 urinary R39.11
Hesselbach's hernia —*see* Hernia, femoral,
  specified site NEC
Heterochromia (congenital) Q13.2
 cataract —*see* Cataract, complicated
 cyclitis (Fuchs) —*see* Cyclitis, Fuchs'
  heterochromic
 hair L67.1
 iritis —*see* Cyclitis, Fuchs' heterochromic
 retained metallic foreign body
   (nonmagnetic) —*see* Foreign body,
   intraocular, old, retained
  magnetic —*see* Foreign body, intraocular,
   old, retained, magnetic
 uveitis —*see* Cyclitis, Fuchs' heterochromic
Heterophoria —*see* Strabismus, heterophoria
Heterophyes, heterophyiasis (small intestine)
  B66.8
Heterotopia, heterotopic —*see also* Malposition,
  congenital
 cerebralis Q04.8
Heterotropia —*see* Strabismus
Heubner-Herter disease K90.0
Hexadactylism Q69.9
HGSIL (cytology finding) (high grade
  squamous intraepithelial lesion on
  cytologic smear) (Pap smear finding)
 anus R85.613
 cervix R87.613
  biopsy (histology) finding — *see* Neoplasia,
   intraepithelial, cervix, grade II or
   grade III
 vagina R87.623
  biopsy (histology) finding — *see* Neoplasia,
   intraepithelial, vagina, grade II or
   grade III
Hibernoma —*see* Lipoma
Hiccup, hiccough R06.6
 epidemic B33.0
 psychogenic F45.8
Hidden penis (congenital) Q55.64
 acquired N48.83
Hidradenitis (axillaris) (suppurative)
  L73.2
Hidradenoma (nodular) —*see also* Neoplasm,
  skin, benign
 clear cell —*see* Neoplasm, skin, benign
 papillary —*see* Neoplasm, skin, benign
Hidrocystoma —*see* Neoplasm, skin,
  benign

High
 altitude effects T70.20
  anoxia T70.29
  on
    ears T70.0
    sinuses T70.1
  polycythemia D75.1
 arch
  foot Q66.7-●
  palate, congenital Q38.5
 arterial tension —*see* Hypertension
 basal metabolic rate R94.8
 blood pressure —*see also* Hypertension
  borderline R03.0
  reading (incidental) (isolated)
    (nonspecific), without diagnosis of
    hypertension R03.0
 cholesterol E78.00
  with high triglycerides E78.2
 diaphragm (congenital) Q79.1
 expressed emotional level within family Z63.8
 head at term O32.4
 palate, congenital Q38.5
 risk
  infant NEC Z76.2
  sexual behavior (heterosexual) Z72.51
   bisexual Z72.53
   homosexual Z72.52
 scrotal testis, testes
  bilateral Q53.23
  unilateral Q53.13
 temperature (of unknown origin) R50.9
 thoracic rib Q76.6
 triglycerides E78.1
  with high cholesterol E78.2
Hildenbrand's disease A75.0
Hilum —*see* condition
Hip —*see* condition
Hippel's disease Q85.8
Hippophobia F40.218
Hippus H57.09
Hirschsprung's disease or megacolon Q43.1
Hirsutism, hirsuties L68.0
Hirudiniasis
 external B88.3
 internal B83.4
Hiss-Russell dysentery A03.1
Histidinemia, histidinuria E70.41
Histiocytoma —*see also* Neoplasm, skin, benign
 fibrous —*see also* Neoplasm, skin, benign
   atypical —*see* Neoplasm, connective tissue,
    uncertain behavior
   malignant —*see* Neoplasm, connective
    tissue, malignant
Histiocytosis D76.3
 acute differentiated progressive C96.0
 Langerhans' cell NEC C96.6
  multifocal X
   multisystemic (disseminated) C96.0
   unisystemic C96.5
  pulmonary, adult (adult PLCH) J84.82
  unifocal (X) C96.6
 lipid, lipoid D76.3
  essential E75.29
 malignant C96.A
 mononuclear phagocytes NEC D76.1
  Langerhans' cells C96.6
 non-Langerhans cell D76.3
 polyostotic sclerosing D76.3
 sinus, with massive lymphadenopathy D76.3
 syndrome NEC D76.3
 X NEC C96.6
  acute (progressive) C96.0
  chronic C96.6
  multifocal C96.5
  multisystemic C96.0
  unifocal C96.6
Histoplasmosis B39.9
 with pneumonia NEC B39.2
 African B39.5
 American —*see* Histoplasmosis, capsulati

Histoplasmosis *(Continued)*
 capsulati B39.4
  disseminated B39.3
  generalized B39.3
  pulmonary B39.2
   acute B39.0
   chronic B39.1
 Darling's B39.4
 duboisii B39.5
 lung NEC B39.2
History
 family (of) —*see also* History, personal (of)
  alcohol abuse Z81.1
  allergy NEC Z84.89
  anemia Z83.2
  arthritis Z82.61
  asthma Z82.5
  blindness Z82.1
  cardiac death (sudden) Z82.41
  carrier of genetic disease Z84.81
  chromosomal anomaly Z82.79
  chronic
   disabling disease NEC Z82.8
   lower respiratory disease Z82.5
  colonic polyps Z83.71
  congenital malformations and
    deformations Z82.79
   polycystic kidney Z82.71
  consanguinity Z84.3
  deafness Z82.2
  diabetes mellitus Z83.3
  disability NEC Z82.8
  disease or disorder (of)
   allergic NEC Z84.89
   behavioral NEC Z81.8
   blood and blood-forming organs Z83.2
   cardiovascular NEC Z82.49
   chronic disabling NEC Z82.8
   digestive Z83.79
   ear NEC Z83.52
   elevated lipoprotein (a) (Lp(a)) Z83.430
   endocrine NEC Z83.49
   eye NEC Z83.518
    glaucoma Z83.511
   familial hypercholesterolemia Z83.42
   genitourinary NEC Z84.2
   glaucoma Z83.511
   hematological Z83.2
   immune mechanism Z83.2
   infectious NEC Z83.1
   ischemic heart Z82.49
   kidney Z84.1
   lipoprotein metabolism Z83.438
   mental NEC Z81.8
   metabolic Z83.49
   musculoskeletal NEC Z82.69
   neurological NEC Z82.0
   nutritional Z83.49
   parasitic NEC Z83.1
   psychiatric NEC Z81.8
   respiratory NEC Z83.6
   skin and subcutaneous tissue NEC Z84.0
   specified NEC Z84.89
  drug abuse NEC Z81.3
  elevated lipoprotein(a) (Lp (a)) Z83.430
  epilepsy Z82.0
  familial hypercholesterolemia Z83.42
  genetic disease carrier Z84.81
  glaucoma Z83.511
  hearing loss Z82.2
  human immunodeficiency virus (HIV)
    infection Z83.0
  Huntington's chorea Z82.0
  hyperlipidemia, familial combined Z83.438
  intellectual disability Z81.0
  leukemia Z80.6
  lipidemia NEC Z83.438
  malignant neoplasm (of) NOS Z80.9
   bladder Z80.52
   breast Z80.3
   bronchus Z80.1

▶ New   ⇒ Revised   ~~deleted~~ Deleted   ● Use Additional Character(s)

History *(Continued)*
  personal *(Continued)*
    in situ neoplasm
      breast Z86.000
      cervix uteri Z86.001
      digestive organs, specified NEC Z86.004
      esophagus Z86.003
      genital organs, specified NEC Z86.002
      melanoma Z86.006
      middle ear Z86.005
      oral cavity Z86.003
      respiratory system Z86.005
      skin Z86.007
      specified NEC Z86.008
      stomach Z86.003
    infection NEC Z86.19
      central nervous system Z86.61
      latent tuberculosis Z86.15
      Methicillin resistant Staphylococcus aureus (MRSA) Z86.14
      urinary (tract) Z87.41
    injury NEC Z87.828
    in utero procedure during pregnancy Z98.870
    in utero procedure while a fetus Z98.871
    irradiation Z92.3
    kidney stones Z87.442
    latent tuberculosis Z86.15
    leukemia Z85.6
    lymphoma (non-Hodgkin) Z85.72
    malignant melanoma (skin) Z85.820
    malignant neoplasm (of) Z85.9
      accessory sinuses Z85.22
      anus NEC Z85.048
        carcinoid Z85.040
      bladder Z85.51
      bone Z85.830
      brain Z85.841
      breast Z85.3
      bronchus NEC Z85.118
        carcinoid Z85.110
      carcinoid —*see* History, personal (of), malignant neoplasm, by site, carcinioid
      cervix Z85.41
      colon NEC Z85.038
        carcinoid Z85.030
      digestive organ Z85.00
        specified NEC Z85.09
      endocrine gland NEC Z85.858
      epididymis Z85.48
      esophagus Z85.01
      eye Z85.840
      gastrointestinal tract —*see* History, malignant neoplasm, digestive organ
      genital organ
        female Z85.40
          specified NEC Z85.44
        male Z85.45
          specified NEC Z85.49
      hematopoietic NEC Z85.79
      intrathoracic organ Z85.20-•
      kidney NEC Z85.528
        carcinoid Z85.520
      large intestine NEC Z85.038
        carcinoid Z85.030
      larynx Z85.21
      liver Z85.05
      lung NEC Z85.118
        carcinoid Z85.110
      mediastinum Z85.29
      Merkel cell Z85.821
      middle ear Z85.22
      nasal cavities Z85.22
      nervous system NEC Z85.848
      oral cavity Z85.819
        specified site NEC Z85.818
      ovary Z85.43
      pancreas Z85.07
      pelvis Z85.53

History *(Continued)*
  personal *(Continued)*
    malignant neoplasm (of) *(Continued)*
      pharynx Z85.819
        specified site NEC Z85.818
      pleura Z85.29
      prostate Z85.46
      rectosigmoid junction NEC Z85.048
        carcinoid Z85.040
      rectum NEC Z85.048
        carcinoid Z85.040
      respiratory organ Z85.20
      sinuses, accessory Z85.22
      skin NEC Z85.828
        melanoma Z85.820
        Merkel cell Z85.821
      small intestine NEC Z85.068
        carcinoid Z85.060
      soft tissue Z85.831
      specified site NEC Z85.89
      stomach NEC Z85.028
        carcinoid Z85.020
      testis Z85.47
      thymus NEC Z85.238
        carcinoid Z85.230
      thyroid Z85.850
      tongue Z85.810
      trachea Z85.12
      ureter Z85.54
      urinary organ or tract Z85.50
        specified NEC Z85.59
      uterus Z85.42
    maltreatment Z91.89
    medical treatment NEC Z92.89
    melanoma Z85.820
      in situ Z86.06
      malignant (skin) Z85.820
    meningitis Z86.61
    mental disorder Z86.59
    Merkel cell carcinoma (skin) Z85.821
    Methicillin resistant Staphylococcus aureus (MRSA) Z86.14
    military deployment Z91.82
    military war, peacekeeping and humanitarian deployment (current or past conflict) Z91.82
    myocardial infarction (old) I25.2
    neglect (in)
      adult Z91.412
      childhood Z62.812
    neoplasia
      anal intraepithelial, III [AIN III] Z86.004
      high-grade prostatic intraepithelial, III [HGPIN III] Z86.002
      vaginal intraepithelial, III [VAIN III] Z86.002
      vulvar intraepithelial, III [VIN III] Z86.002
    neoplasm
      benign Z86.018
        brain Z86.011
        colon polyp Z86.010
      in situ
        breast Z86.000
        cervix uteri Z86.001
        digestive organs, specified NEC Z86.004
        esophagus Z86.003
        genital organs, specified NEC Z86.002
        melanoma Z86.006
        middle ear Z86.005
        oral cavity Z86.003
        respiratory system Z86.005
        skin Z86.007
        specified NEC Z86.008
        stomach Z86.003
      malignant —*see* History of, malignant neoplasm
      uncertain behavior Z86.03
    nephrotic syndrome Z87.441
    nicotine dependence Z87.891
    noncompliance with medical treatment or regimen —*see* Noncompliance

History *(Continued)*
  personal *(Continued)*
    nutritional deficiency Z86.39
    obstetric complications Z87.59
      childbirth Z87.59
      pregnancy Z87.59
      pre-term labor Z87.51
      puerperium Z87.59
    osteoporosis fractures Z87.31
    parasuicide (attempt) Z91.5
    physical trauma NEC Z87.828
      self-harm or suicide attempt Z91.5
    pneumonia (recurrent) Z87.01
    poisoning NEC Z91.89
      self-harm or suicide attempt Z91.5
    poor personal hygiene Z91.89
    preterm labor Z87.51
    procedure during pregnancy Z98.870
    procedure while a fetus Z98.871
    prolonged reversible ischemic neurologic deficit (PRINO) Z86.73
    prostatic dysplasia Z87.430
    psychiatric disorder NEC Z87.89
    psychological
      abuse
        adult Z91.411
        child Z62.811
      trauma, specified NEC Z91.49
    radiation therapy Z92.3
    removal
      implant
        breast Z98.86
    renal calculi Z87.442
    respiratory condition NEC Z87.09
    retained foreign body fully removed Z87.821
    risk factors NEC Z91.89
    self-harm Z91.5
    self-poisoning attempt Z91.5
    sex reassignment Z87.890
    sleep-wake cycle problem Z72.821
    specified NEC Z87.898
    steroid therapy (systemic) Z92.241
      inhaled Z92.240
    stroke without residual deficits Z86.73
    substance abuse NEC F10-F19
    sudden cardiac arrest Z86.74
    sudden cardiac death successfully resuscitated Z86.74
    suicide attempt Z91.5
    surgery NEC Z98.890
      with uterine scar Z98.891
      sex reassignment Z87.890
      transplant —*see* Transplant
    thrombophlebitis Z86.72
    thrombosis (venous) Z86.718
      pulmonary Z86.711
    tobacco dependence Z87.891
    transient ischemic attack (TIA) without residual deficits Z86.73
    trauma (physical) NEC Z87.828
      psychological NEC Z91.49
      self-harm Z91.5
    traumatic brain injury Z87.820
    tuberculosis, latent infection Z86.15
    unhealthy sleep-wake cycle Z72.821
    unintended awareness under general anesthesia Z92.84
    urinary (recurrent) (tract) infection(s) Z87.440
    urinary calculi Z87.42
    uterine scar from previous surgery Z98.891
    vaginal dysplasia Z87.411
    venous thrombosis or embolism Z86.718
      pulmonary Z86.711
    vulvar dysplasia Z87.412
His-Werner disease A79.0
HIV —*see also* Human, immunodeficiency virus B20
  laboratory evidence (nonconclusive) R75
  nonconclusive test (in infants) R75
  positive, seropositive Z21
Hives (bold) —*see* Urticaria

Hoarseness R49.0
Hobo Z59.0
Hodgkin disease —*see* Lymphoma, Hodgkin
Hodgson's disease I71.2
  ruptured I71.1
Hoffa-Kastert disease E88.89
Hoffa's disease E88.89
Hoffmann-Bouveret syndrome I47.9
Hoffmann's syndrome E03.9 [*G73.7*]
Hole (round)
  macula H35.34-●
  retina (without detachment) —*see* Break,
    retina, round hole
    with detachment —*see* Detachment, retina,
      with retinal, break
Holiday relief care Z75.5
Hollenhorst's plaque —*see* Occlusion, artery,
  retina
Hollow foot (congenital) Q66.7-●
  acquired —*see* Deformity, limb, foot, specified
    NEC
Holoprosencephaly Q04.2
Holt-Oram syndrome Q87.2
Homelessness Z59.0
Homesickness —*see* Disorder, adjustment
Homocystinemia, homocystinuria E72.11
Homogentisate 1,2-dioxygenase deficiency
  E70.29
Homologous serum hepatitis (prophylactic)
  (therapeutic) —*see* Hepatitis, viral, type B
Honeycomb lung J98.4
  congenital Q33.0
Hooded
  clitoris Q52.6
  penis Q55.69
Hookworm (disease) (infection) (infestation)
  B76.9
  with anemia B76.9 [*D63.8*]
  specified NEC B76.8
Hordeolum (eyelid) (externum) (recurrent)
  H00.019
  internum H00.029
    left H00.026
      lower H00.025
      upper H00.024
    right H00.023
      lower H00.022
      upper H00.021
  left H00.016
    lower H00.015
    upper H00.014
  right H00.013
    lower H00.012
    upper H00.011
Horn
  cutaneous L85.8
  nail L60.2
    congenital Q84.6
Horner (-Claude Bernard) syndrome G90.2
  traumatic —*see* Injury, nerve, cervical
    sympathetic
Horseshoe kidney (congenital) Q63.1
Horton's headache or neuralgia G44.099
  intractable G44.091
  not intractable G44.099
Hospital hopper syndrome —*see* Disorder,
  factitious
Hospitalism in children —*see* Disorder,
  adjustment
Hostility R45.5
  towards child Z62.3
Hot flashes
  menopausal N95.1
Hourglass (contracture) —*see also* Contraction,
  hourglass
  stomach K31.89
    congenital Q40.2
    stricture K31.2
Household, housing circumstance affecting
  care Z59.9
  specified NEC Z59.8

Housemaid's knee —*see* Bursitis, prepatellar
Hudson (-Stähli) line (cornea) —*see*
  Pigmentation, cornea, anterior
Human
  bite (open wound) —*see also* Bite
    intact skin surface —*see* Bite, superficial
  herpesvirus —*see* Herpes
  immunodeficiency virus (HIV) disease
    (infection) B20
    asymptomatic status Z21
    contact Z20.6
    counseling Z71.7
    dementia B20 [*F02.80*]
      with behavioral disturbance B20
        [*F02.81*]
    exposure to Z20.6
    laboratory evidence R75
    type-2 (HIV 2) as cause of disease classified
      elsewhere B97.35
  papillomavirus (HPV)
    DNA test positive
      high risk
        cervix R87.810
        vagina R87.811
      low risk
        cervix R87.820
        vagina R87.821
    screening for Z11.51
  T-cell lymphotropic virus
    type-1 (HTLV-I) infection B33.3
      as cause of disease classified elsewhere
        B97.33
      carrier Z22.6
    type-2 (HTLV-II) as cause of disease
      classified elsewhere B97.34
Humidifier lung or pneumonitis J67.7
Humiliation (experience) in childhood Z62.898
Humpback (acquired) —*see* Kyphosis
Hunchback (acquired) —*see* Kyphosis
Hunger T73.0
  air, psychogenic F45.8
Hungry bone syndrome E83.81
Hunner's ulcer —*see* Cystitis, chronic, interstitial
Hunter's
  glossitis D51.0
  syndrome E76.1
Huntington's disease or chorea G10
  with dementia G10 [*F02.80*]
    with behavioral disturbance G10 [*F02.81*]
Hunt's
  disease or syndrome (herpetic geniculate
    ganglionitis) B02.21
  ➠dyssynergia cerebellaris myoclonica G11.19
  neuralgia B02.21
Hurler (-Scheie) disease or syndrome E76.02
Hurst's disease G36.1
Hurthle cell
  adenocarcinoma C73
  adenoma D34
  carcinoma C73
  tumor D34
Hutchinson-Boeck disease or syndrome —*see*
  Sarcoidosis
Hutchinson-Gilford disease or syndrome E34.8
Hutchinson's
  disease, meaning
    angioma serpiginosum L81.7
    pompholyx (cheiropompholyx) L30.1
    prurigo estivalis L56.4
    summer eruption or summer prurigo L56.4
    melanotic freckle —*see* Melanoma, in situ
      malignant melanoma in —*see* Melanoma
  teeth or incisors (congenital syphilis) A50.52
  triad (congenital syphilis) A50.53
Hyalin plaque, sclera, senile H15.89
Hyaline membrane (disease) (lung)
  (pulmonary) (newborn) P22.0
Hyalinosis
  cutis (et mucosae) E78.89
  focal and segmental (glomerular) —*see also*
    N00-N07 with fourth character .1 N05.1

Hyalitis, hyalosis, asteroid —*see also* Deposit,
  crystalline
  syphilitic (late) A52.71
Hydatid
  cyst or tumor —*see* Echinococcus
  mole —*see* Hydatidiform mole
  Morgagni
    female Q50.5
    male (epididymal) Q55.4
      testicular Q55.29
Hydatidiform mole (benign) (complicating
  pregnancy) (delivered) (undelivered) O01.9
  classical O01.0
  complete O01.0
  incomplete O01.1
  invasive D39.2
  malignant D39.2
  partial O01.1
Hydatidosis —*see* Echinococcus
Hydradenitis (axillaris) (suppurative) L73.2
Hydradenoma —*see* Hidradenoma
Hydramnios O40.-●
Hydrancephaly, hydranencephaly Q04.3
  with spina bifida —*see* Spina bifida, with
    hydrocephalus
Hydrargyrism NEC —*see* Poisoning, mercury
Hydrarthrosis —*see also* Effusion, joint
  gonococcal A54.42
  intermittent M12.40
    ankle M12.47-●
    elbow M12.42-●
    foot joint M12.47-●
    hand joint M12.44-●
    hip M12.45-●
    knee M12.46-●
    multiple site M12.49
    shoulder M12.41-●
    specified joint NEC M12.48
    wrist M12.43-●
  of yaws (early) (late) —*see also* subcategory
    M14.8-● A66.6
  syphilitic (late) A52.77
    congenital A50.55 [*M12.80*]
Hydremia D64.89
Hydrencephalocele (congenital) —*see*
  Encephalocele
Hydrencephalomeningocele (congenital) —*see*
  Encephalocele
Hydroa R23.8
  aestivale L56.4
  vacciniforme L56.4
Hydroadenitis (axillaris) (suppurative) L73.2
Hydrocalycosis —*see* Hydronephrosis
Hydrocele (spermatic cord) (testis) (tunica
  vaginalis) N43.3
  canal of Nuck N94.89
  communicating N43.2
    congenital P83.5
  congenital P83.5
  encysted N43.0
  female NEC N94.89
  infected N43.1
  newborn P83.5
  round ligament N94.89
  specified NEC N43.2
  spinalis —*see* Spina bifida
  vulva N90.89
Hydrocephalus (acquired) (external) (internal)
  (malignant) (recurrent) G91.9
  aqueduct Sylvius stricture Q03.0
  causing disproportion O33.6
    with obstructed labor O66.3
  communicating G91.0
  congenital (external) (internal) Q03.9
    with spina bifida Q05.4
      cervical Q05.0
      dorsal Q05.1
      lumbar Q05.2
      lumbosacral Q05.2
      sacral Q05.3
      thoracic Q05.1
      thoracolumbar Q05.1
    specified NEC Q03.8

▶ New   ⇨ Revised   ~~deleted~~ Deleted   ● Use Additional Character(s)

Hydrocephalus *(Continued)*
  due to toxoplasmosis (congenital) P37.1
  foramen Magendie block (acquired) G91.1
    congenital —*see also* Hydrocephalus,
      congenital Q03.1
  in (due to)
    infectious disease NEC B89 *[G91.4]*
    neoplastic disease NEC *(see also* Neoplasm)
      G91.4
    parasitic disease B89 *[G91.4]*
  newborn Q03.9
    with spina bifida —*see* Spina bifida, with
      hydrocephalus
  noncommunicating G91.1
  normal pressure G91.2
    secondary G91.0
  obstructive G91.1
  otitic G93.2
  post-traumatic NEC G91.3
  secondary G91.4
    post-traumatic G91.3
  specified NEC G91.8
  syphilitic, congenital A50.49
Hydrocolpos (congenital) N89.8
Hydrocystoma —*see* Neoplasm, skin, benign
Hydroencephalocele (congenital) —*see*
  Encephalocele
Hydroencephalomeningocele (congenital) —
  see Encephalocele
Hydrohematopneumothorax —*see* Hemothorax
Hydromeningitis —*see* Meningitis
Hydromeningocele (spinal) —*see also* Spina bifida
  cranial —*see* Encephalocele
Hydrometra N85.8
Hydrometrocolpos N89.8
Hydromicrocephaly Q02
Hydromphalos (since birth) Q45.8
Hydromyelia Q06.4
Hydromyelocele —*see* Spina bifida
Hydronephrosis (atrophic) (early)
    (functionless) (intermittent) (primary)
    (secondary) NEC N13.30
  with
    infection N13.6
    obstruction (by) (of)
      renal calculus N13.2
        with infection N13.6
      ureteral NEC N13.1
        with infection N13.6
        calculus N13.2
          with infection N13.6
      ureteropelvic junction (congenital) Q62.11
        acquired N13.0
          with infection N13.6
      ureteral stricture NEC N13.1
        with infection N13.6
  congenital Q62.0
  due to acquired occlusion of ureteropelvic
    junction N13.0
  specified type NEC N13.39
  tuberculous A18.11
Hydropericarditis —*see* Pericarditis
Hydropericardium —*see* Pericarditis
Hydroperitoneum R18.8
Hydrophobia —*see* Rabies
Hydrophthalmos Q15.0
Hydropneumohemothorax —*see* Hemothorax
Hydropneumopericarditis —*see* Pericarditis
Hydropneumopericardium —*see* Pericarditis
Hydropneumothorax J94.8
  traumatic —*see* Injury, intrathoracic, lung
  tuberculous NEC A15.6
Hydrops R60.9
  abdominis R18.8
  articulorum intermittens —*see* Hydrarthrosis,
    intermittent
  cardiac —*see* Failure, heart, congestive
  causing obstructed labor (mother) O66.3
  endolymphatic H81.0-•
  fetal —*see* Pregnancy, complicated by,
    hydrops, fetalis

Hydrops *(Continued)*
  fetalis P83.2
    due to
      ABO isoimmunization P56.0
      alpha thalassemia D56.0
      hemolytic disease P56.90
        specified NEC P56.99
      isoimmunization (ABO) (Rh) P56.0
      other specified nonhemolytic disease
        NEC P83.2
      Rh incompatibility P56.0
    during pregnancy —*see* Pregnancy,
      complicated by, hydrops, fetalis
  gallbladder K82.1
  joint —*see* Effusion, joint
  labyrinth H81.0
  newborn (idiopathic) P83.2
    due to
      ABO isoimmunization P56.0
      alpha thalassemia D56.0
      hemolytic disease P56.90
        specified NEC P56.99
      isoimmunization (ABO) (Rh) P56.0
      Rh incompatibility P56.0
  nutritional —*see* Malnutrition, severe
  pericardium —*see* Pericarditis
  pleura —*see* Hydrothorax
  spermatic cord —*see* Hydrocele
Hydropyonephrosis N13.6
Hydrorachis Q06.4
Hydrorrhea (nasal) J34.89
  pregnancy —*see* Rupture, membranes,
    premature
Hydrosadenitis (axillaris) (suppurative) L73.2
Hydrosalpinx (fallopian tube) (follicularis)
  N70.11
Hydrothorax (double) (pleura) J94.8
  chylous (nonfilarial) I89.8
    filarial —*see also* Infestation, filarial B74.9
      [J91.8]
  traumatic —*see* Injury, intrathoracic
  tuberculous NEC (non primary) A15.6
Hydroureter —*see also* Hydronephrosis
  N13.4
  with infection N13.6
  congenital Q62.39
Hydroureteronephrosis —*see* Hydronephrosis
Hydrourethra N36.8
Hydroxykynureninuria E70.89
Hydroxylysinemia E72.3
Hydroxyprolinemia E72.59
Hygiene, sleep
  abuse Z72.821
  inadequate Z72.821
  poor Z72.821
Hygroma (congenital) (cystic) D18.1
  praepatellare, prepatellar —*see* Bursitis,
    prepatellar
Hymen —*see* condition
Hymenolepis, hymenolepiasis (diminuta)
  (infection) (infestation) (nana) B71.0
Hypalgesia R20.8
Hyperacidity (gastric) K31.89
  psychogenic F45.8
Hyperactive, hyperactivity F90.9
  basal cell, uterine cervix —*see* Dysplasia,
    cervix
  bowel sounds R19.12
  cervix epithelial (basal) —*see* Dysplasia,
    cervix
  child F90.9
    attention deficit —*see* Disorder, attention-
      deficit hyperactivity
  detrusor muscle N32.81
  gastrointestinal K31.89
    psychogenic F45.8
  nasal mucous membrane J34.3
  stomach K31.89
  thyroid (gland) —*see* Hyperthyroidism
Hyperacusis H93.23-•
Hyperadrenalism E27.5

Hyperadrenocorticism E24.9
  congenital E25.0
  iatrogenic E24.2
    correct substance properly administered —
      see Table of Drugs and Chemicals, by
      drug, adverse effect
    overdose or wrong substance given
      or taken —*see* Table of Drugs and
      Chemicals, by drug, poisoning
  not associated with Cushing's syndrome E27.0
  pituitary-dependent E24.0
Hyperaldosteronism E26.9
  familial (type I) E26.02
  glucocorticoid-remediable E26.02
  primary (due to (bilateral) adrenal
    hyperplasia) E26.09
  primary NEC E26.09
  secondary E26.1
  specified NEC E26.89
Hyperalgesia R20.8
Hyperalimentation R63.2
  carotene, carotin E67.1
  specified NEC E67.8
  vitamin
    A E67.0
    D E67.3
Hyperaminoaciduria
  arginine E72.21
  cystine E72.01
  lysine E72.3
  ornithine E72.4
Hyperammonemia (congenital) E72.20
Hyperazotemia —*see* Uremia
Hyperbetalipoproteinemia (familial) E78.00
  with prebetalipoproteinemia E78.2
Hyperbilirubinemia
  constitutional E80.6
  familial conjugated E80.6
  neonatal (transient) —*see* Jaundice, newborn
Hypercalcemia, hypocalciuric, familial E83.52
Hypercalciuria, idiopathic R82.994
Hypercapnia R06.89
  newborn P84
Hypercarotenemia (dietary) E67.1
Hypercementosis K03.4
Hyperchloremia E87.8
Hyperchlorhydria K31.89
  neurotic F45.8
  psychogenic F45.8
Hypercholesterinemia —*see*
  Hypercholesterolemia
Hypercholesterolemia (essential) (primary)
  (pure) E78.00
  with hyperglyceridemia, endogenous E78.2
  dietary counseling and surveillance Z71.3
  familial E78.01
  hereditary E78.01
Hyperchylia gastrica, psychogenic F45.8
Hyperchylomicronemia (familial) (primary)
  E78.3
  with hyperbetalipoproteinemia E78.3
Hypercoagulable (state) D68.59
  activated protein C resistance D68.51
  antithrombin (III) deficiency D68.59
  factor V Leiden mutation D68.51
  primary NEC D68.59
  protein C deficiency D68.59
  protein S deficiency D68.59
  prothrombin gene mutation D68.52
  secondary D68.69
  specified NEC D68.69
Hypercoagulation (state) D68.59
Hypercorticalism, pituitary-dependent E24.0
Hypercorticosolism —*see* Cushing's, syndrome
Hypercorticosteronism E24.2
  correct substance properly administered —*see*
    Table of Drugs and Chemicals, by drug,
    adverse effect
  overdose or wrong substance given
    or taken —*see* Table of Drugs and
    Chemicals, by drug, poisoning

Hypercortisonism E24.2
  correct substance properly administered —see
    Table of Drugs and Chemicals, by drug,
    adverse effect
  overdose or wrong substance given
    or taken —see Table of Drugs and
    Chemicals, by drug, poisoning
Hyperekplexia Q89.8
Hyperelectrolytemia E87.8
Hyperemesis R11.10
  with nausea R11.2
  gravidarum (mild) O21.0
    with
      carbohydrate depletion O21.1
      dehydration O21.1
      electrolyte imbalance O21.1
      metabolic disturbance O21.1
      severe (with metabolic disturbance)
        O21.1
  projectile R11.12
  psychogenic F45.8
Hyperemia (acute) (passive) R68.89
  anal mucosa K62.89
  bladder N32.89
  cerebral I67.89
  conjunctiva H11.43-●
  ear internal, acute —see subcategory H83.0
  enteric K59.89
  eye —see Hyperemia, conjunctiva
  eyelid (active) (passive) —see Disorder,
    eyelid, specified type NEC
  intestine K59.89
  iris —see Disorder, iris, vascular
  kidney N28.89
  labyrinth —see subcategory H83.0
  liver (active) K76.89
  lung (passive) —see Edema, lung
  pulmonary (passive) —see Edema, lung
  renal N28.89
  retina H35.89
  stomach K31.89
Hyperesthesia (body surface) R20.3
  larynx (reflex) J38.7
    hysterical F44.89
  pharynx (reflex) J39.2
    hysterical F44.89
Hyperestrogenism (drug-induced) (iatrogenic)
  E28.0
Hyperexplexia Q89.8
Hyperfibrinolysis —see Fibrinolysis
Hyperfructosemia E74.19
Hyperfunction
  adrenal cortex, not associated with Cushing's
    syndrome E27.0
    medulla E27.5
      adrenomedullary E27.5
    virilism E25.9
      congenital E25.0
  ovarian E28.8
  pancreas K86.89
  parathyroid (gland) E21.3
  pituitary (gland) (anterior) E22.9
    specified NEC E22.8
  polyglandular E31.1
  testicular E29.0
Hypergammaglobulinemia D89.2
  polyclonal D89.0
  Waldenström D89.0
Hypergastrinemia E16.4
Hyperglobulinemia R77.1
Hyperglycemia, hyperglycemic (transient)
  R73.9
  coma —see Diabetes, by type, with coma
  postpancreatectomy E89.1
Hyperglyceridemia (endogenous) (essential)
  (familial) (hereditary) (pure) E78.1
  mixed E78.3
Hyperglycinemia (non-ketotic) E72.51
Hypergonadism
  ovarian E28.8
  testicular (primary) (infantile) E29.0

Hyperheparinemia D68.32
Hyperhidrosis, hyperidrosis R61
  focal
    primary L74.519
      axilla L74.510
      face L74.511
      palms L74.512
      soles L74.513
    secondary L74.52
  generalized R61
  localized
    primary L74.519
      axilla L74.510
      face L74.511
      palms L74.512
      soles L74.513
    secondary L74.52
  psychogenic F45.8
  secondary R61
    focal L74.52
Hyperhistidinemia E70.41
Hyperhomocysteinemia E72.11
Hyperhydroxyprolinemia E72.59
Hyperinsulinism (functional) E16.1
  with
    coma (hypoglycemic) E15
    encephalopathy E16.1 [G94]
  ectopic E16.1
  therapeutic misadventure (from
    administration of insulin) —see
    subcategory T38.3
Hyperkalemia E87.5
Hyperkeratosis —see also Keratosis L85.9
  cervix N88.0
  due to yaws (early) (late) (palmar or plantar)
    A66.3
  follicularis Q82.8
    penetrans (in cutem) L87.0
  palmoplantaris climacterica L85.1
  pinta A67.1
  senile (with pruritus) L57.0
  universalis congenita Q80.8
  vocal cord J38.3
  vulva N90.4
Hyperkinesia, hyperkinetic (disease) (reaction)
  (syndrome) (childhood) (adolescence) —
    see also Disorder, attention-deficit
    hyperactivity
  heart I51.89
Hyperleucine-isoleucinemia E71.19
Hyperlipemia, hyperlipidemia E78.5
  combined E78.2
    familial E78.49
  group
    A E78.00
    B E78.1
    C E78.2
    D E78.3
  mixed E78.2
  specified NEC E78.49
Hyperlipidosis E75.6
  hereditary NEC E75.5
Hyperlipoproteinemia E78.5
  Fredrickson's type
    I E78.3
    IIa E78.00
    IIb E78.2
    III E78.2
    IV E78.1
    V E78.3
  low-density-lipoprotein-type (LDL)
    E78.00
  very-low-density-lipoprotein-type (VLDL)
    E78.1
Hyperlucent lung, unilateral J43.0
Hyperlysinemia E72.3
Hypermagnesemia E83.41
  neonatal P71.8
Hypermenorrhea N92.0
Hypermethioninemia E72.19
Hypermetropia (congenital) H52.0-●

Hypermobility, hypermotility
  cecum —see Syndrome, irritable bowel
  coccyx —see subcategory M53.2
  colon —see Syndrome, irritable bowel
    psychogenic F45.8
  ileum K58.9
  intestine —see also Syndrome, irritable bowel
    K58.9
    psychogenic F45.8
  meniscus (knee) —see Derangement, knee,
    meniscus
  scapula —see Instability, joint, shoulder
  stomach K31.89
    psychogenic F45.8
  syndrome M35.7
  urethra N36.41
    with intrinsic sphincter deficiency N36.43
Hypernasality R49.21
Hypernatremia E87.0
Hypernephroma C64.-●
Hyperopia —see Hypermetropia
Hyperorexia nervosa F50.2
Hyperornithinemia E72.4
Hyperosmia R43.1
Hyperosmolality E87.0
Hyperostosis (monomelic) —see also Disorder,
  bone, density and structure, specified NEC
  ankylosing (spine) M48.10
    cervical region M48.12
    cervicothoracic region M48.13
    lumbar region M48.16
    lumbosacral region M48.17
    multiple sites M48.19
    occipito-atlanto-axial region M48.11
    sacrococcygeal region M48.18
    thoracic region M48.14
    thoracolumbar region M48.15
  cortical (skull) M85.2
    infantile M89.8X-●
  frontal, internal of skull M85.2
  interna frontalis M85.2
  skeletal, diffuse idiopathic —see
    Hyperostosis, ankylosing
  skull M85.2
    congenital Q75.8
  vertebral, ankylosing —see Hyperostosis,
    ankylosing
Hyperovarism E28.8
Hyperoxaluria (primary) R82.992
Hyperparathyroidism E21.3
  primary E21.0
  secondary (renal) N25.81
    non-renal E21.1
  specified NEC E21.2
  tertiary E21.2
Hyperpathia R20.8
Hyperperistalsis R19.2
  psychogenic F45.8
Hyperpermeability, capillary I78.8
Hyperphagia R63.2
Hyperphenylalaninemia NEC E70.1
Hyperphoria (alternating) H50.53
Hyperphosphatemia E83.39
Hyperpiesis, hyperpiesia —see Hypertension
Hyperpigmentation —see also Pigmentation
  melanin NEC L81.4
  postinflammatory L81.0
Hyperpinealism E34.8
Hyperpituitarism E22.9
Hyperplasia, hyperplastic
  adenoids J35.2
  adrenal (capsule) (cortex) (gland) E27.8
    with
      sexual precocity (male) E25.9
        congenital E25.0
      virilism, adrenal E25.9
        congenital E25.0
      virilization (female) E25.9
        congenital E25.0
    congenital E25.0
    salt-losing E25.0

▶ New   ⇒ Revised   ~~deleted~~ Deleted   ● Use Additional Character(s)

Hyperplasia, hyperplastic *(Continued)*
  adrenomedullary E27.5
  angiolymphoid, eosinophilia (ALHE)
    D18.01
  appendix (lymphoid) K38.0
  artery, fibromuscular I77.3
  bone —*see also* Hypertrophy, bone
    marrow D75.89
  breast —*see also* Hypertrophy, breast
    atypical, atypia N60.9-●
      ductal N60.9-●
      lobular N60.9-●
  C-cell, thyroid E07.0
  cementation (tooth) (teeth) K03.4
  cervical gland R59.0
  cervix (uteri) (basal cell) (endometrium)
    (polypoid) —*see also* Dysplasia, cervix
    congenital Q51.828
  clitoris, congenital Q52.6
  denture K06.2
  endocervicitis N72
  endometrium, endometrial (adenomatous)
    (cystic) (glandular) (glandular-cystic)
    (polypoid) N85.00
    with atypia N85.02
    benign N85.01
    cervix —*see* Dysplasia, cervix
    complex (without atypia) N85.01
    simple (without atypia) N85.01
  epithelial L85.9
    focal, oral, including tongue K13.29
    nipple N62
    skin L85.9
    tongue K13.29
    vaginal wall N89.3
  erythroid D75.89
  fibromuscular of artery (carotid)
    (renal) I77.3
  genital
    female NEC N94.89
    male N50.89
  gingiva K06.1
  glandularis cystica uteri (interstitialis) —*see*
    also Hyperplasia, endometrial N85.00-●
  gum K06.1
  hymen, congenital Q52.4
  irritative, edentulous (alveolar) K06.2
  jaw M26.09
    alveolar M26.79
    lower M26.03
      alveolar M26.72
    upper M26.01
      alveolar M26.71
  kidney (congenital) Q63.3
  labia N90.69
    epithelial N90.3
  liver (congenital) Q44.7
    nodular, focal K76.89
  lymph gland or node R59.9
  mandible, mandibular M26.03
    alveolar M26.72
    unilateral condylar M27.8
  maxilla, maxillary M26.01
    alveolar M26.71
  myometrium, myometrial N85.2
  neuroendocrine cell, of infancy J84.841
  nose
    lymphoid J34.89
    polypoid J33.9
  oral mucosa (irritative) K13.6
  organ or site, congenital NEC —*see* Anomaly,
    by site
  ovary N83.8
  palate, papillary (irritative) K13.6
  pancreatic islet cells E16.9
    alpha E16.8
      with excess
        gastrin E16.4
        glucagon E16.3
    beta E16.1
  parathyroid (gland) E21.0

Hyperplasia, hyperplastic *(Continued)*
  pharynx (lymphoid) J39.2
  prostate (adenofibromatous) (nodular)
    N40.0
    with lower urinary tract symptoms (LUTS)
      N40.1
    without lower urinary tract symptoms
      (LUTS) N40.0
  renal artery I77.89
  reticulo-endothelial (cell) D75.89
  salivary gland (any) K11.1
  Schimmelbusch's —*see* Mastopathy, cystic
  suprarenal capsule (gland) E27.8
  thymus (gland) (persistent) E32.0
  thyroid (gland) —*see* Goiter
  tonsils (faucial) (infective) (lingual)
    (lymphoid) J35.1
    with adenoids J35.3
  unilateral condylar M27.8
  uterus, uterine N85.2
    endometrium (glandular) —*see also*
      Hyperplasia, endometrial
      N85.00-●
  vulva N90.69
    epithelial N90.3
Hyperpnea —*see* Hyperventilation
Hyperpotassemia E87.5
Hyperprebetalipoproteinemia (familial)
  E78.1
Hyperprolactinemia E22.1
Hyperprolinemia (type I) (type II) E72.59
Hyperproteinemia E88.09
Hyperprothrombinemia, causing coagulation
  factor deficiency D68.4
Hyperpyrexia R50.9
  heat (effects) T67.01
  malignant, due to anesthetic T88.3
  rheumatic —*see* Fever, rheumatic
  unknown origin R50.9
Hyper-reflexia R29.2
Hypersalivation K11.7
Hypersecretion
  ACTH (not associated with Cushing's
    syndrome) E27.0
    pituitary E24.0
  adrenaline E27.5
  adrenomedullary E27.5
  androgen (testicular) E29.0
    ovarian (drug-induced) (iatrogenic) E28.1
  calcitonin E07.0
  catecholamine E27.5
  corticoadrenal E24.9
  cortisol E24.9
  epinephrine E27.5
  estrogen E28.0
  gastric K31.89
    psychogenic F45.8
  gastrin E16.4
  glucagon E16.3
  hormone(s)
    ACTH (not associated with Cushing's
      syndrome) E27.0
      pituitary E24.0
    antidiuretic E22.2
    growth E22.0
    intestinal NEC E34.1
    ovarian androgen E28.1
    pituitary E22.9
    testicular E29.0
    thyroid stimulating E05.80
      with thyroid storm E05.81
  insulin —*see* Hyperinsulinism
  lacrimal glands —*see* Epiphora
  medulloadrenal E27.5
  milk O92.6
  ovarian androgens E28.1
  salivary gland (any) K11.7
  thyrocalcitonin E07.0
  upper respiratory J39.8
Hypersegmentation, leukocytic, hereditary
  D72.0

Hypersensitive, hypersensitiveness,
  hypersensitivity —*see also* Allergy
  carotid sinus G90.01
  colon —*see* Irritable, colon
  drug T88.7
  gastrointestinal K52.29
    immediate K52.29
    psychogenic F45.8
  labyrinth —*see* subcategory H83.2
  pain R20.8
  pneumonitis —*see* Pneumonitis, allergic
  reaction T78.40
    upper respiratory tract NEC J39.3
Hypersomnia (organic) G47.10
  due to
    alcohol
      abuse F10.182
      dependence F10.282
      use F10.982
    amphetamines
      abuse F15.182
      dependence F15.282
      use F15.982
    caffeine
      abuse F15.182
      dependence F15.282
      use F15.982
    cocaine
      abuse F14.182
      dependence F14.282
      use F14.982
    drug NEC
      abuse F19.182
      dependence F19.282
      use F19.982
    medical condition G47.14
    mental disorder F51.13
    opioid
      abuse F11.182
      dependence F11.282
      use F11.982
    psychoactive substance NEC
      abuse F19.182
      dependence F19.282
      use F19.982
    sedative, hypnotic, or anxiolytic
      abuse F13.182
      dependence F13.282
      use F13.982
    stimulant NEC
      abuse F15.182
      dependence F15.282
      use F15.982
  idiopathic G47.11
    with long sleep time G47.11
    without long sleep time G47.12
  menstrual related G47.13
  nonorganic origin F51.11
    specified NEC F51.19
  not due to a substance or known
    physiological condition F51.11
    specified NEC F51.19
  primary F51.11
  recurrent G47.13
  specified NEC G47.19
Hypersplenia, hypersplenism D73.1
Hyperstimulation, ovaries (associated with
  induced ovulation) N98.1
Hypersusceptibility —*see* Allergy
Hypertelorism (ocular) (orbital) Q75.2
Hypertension, hypertensive (accelerated)
  (benign) (essential) (idiopathic)
  (malignant) (systemic) I10
  with
    heart failure (congestive) I11.0
    ➡ heart involvement (conditions in I50.- or
      I51.4-I51.7, I51.89, I51.9, due to
      hypertension) —*see* Hypertension,
      heart
    kidney involvement —*see* Hypertension,
      kidney

Hypertension, hypertensive (*Continued*)
  benign, intracranial G93.2
  borderline R03.0
  cardiorenal (disease) I13.10
    with heart failure I13.0
      with stage 1 through stage 4 chronic
        kidney disease I13.0
      with stage 5 or end stage renal disease
        I13.2
    without heart failure I13.10
      with stage 1 through stage 4 chronic
        kidney disease I13.10
      with stage 5 or end stage renal disease
        I13.11
  cardiovascular
    disease (arteriosclerotic) (sclerotic) —*see*
      Hypertension, heart
    renal (disease) —*see* Hypertension,
      cardiorenal
  chronic venous —*see* Hypertension, venous
    (chronic)
  complicating
    childbirth (labor) O16.4
      pre-existing O10.92
        with
          heart disease O10.12
            with renal disease O10.32
          pre-eclampsia O11.4
          renal disease O10.22
            with heart disease O10.32
          essential O10.02
      secondary O10.42
    pregnancy O16.-●
      with edema —*see also* Pre-eclampsia
        O14.9-●
      gestational (pregnancy induced)
        (without proteinuria) O13.-●
        with proteinuria O14.9-●
          mild pre-eclampsia O14.0-●
          moderate pre-eclampsia O14.0-●
          severe pre-eclampsia O14.1-●
            with hemolysis, elevated liver
              enzymes and low platelet
              count (HELLP) O14.2-●
      pre-existing O10.91-●
        with
          heart disease O10.11-●
            with renal disease O10.31-●
            pre-eclampsia —*see* category O11
          renal disease O10.21-●
            with heart disease O10.31-●
          essential O10.01-●
        secondary O10.41-●
      transient O13.-●
    puerperium pre-existing O16.5
      pre-existing
        with
          heart disease O10.13
            with renal disease O10.33
          pre-eclampsia O11.5
          renal disease O10.23
            with heart disease O10.33
          essential O10.03
      pregnancy-induced O13.9
      secondary O10.43
  crisis I16.9
  due to
    endocrine disorders I15.2
    pheochromocytoma I15.2
    renal disorders NEC I15.1
      arterial I15.0
    renovascular disorders I15.0
    specified disease NEC I15.8
  emergency I16.1
  encephalopathy I67.4
  gestational (without significant proteinuria)
    (pregnancy-induced) (transient) O13.-●
    with significant proteinuria —*see*
      Pre-eclampsia
    complicating
      delivery O13.4
      puerperium O13.5

Hypertension, hypertensive (*Continued*)
  Goldblatt's I70.1
  heart (disease) (conditions in I51.4-I51.9 due
    to hypertension) I11.9
    with
      heart failure (congestive) I11.0
      kidney disease (chronic) —*see*
        Hypertension, cardiorenal
  intracranial, benign G93.2
  kidney I12.9
    with
      heart disease —*see* Hypertension,
        cardiorenal
      stage 1 through stage 4 chronic kidney
        disease I12.9
      stage 5 chronic kidney disease (CKD) or
        end stage renal disease (ESRD)
        I12.0
  lesser circulation I27.0
  maternal O16.-●
  newborn P29.2
    pulmonary (persistent) P29.30
  ocular H40.05-●
  pancreatic duct — code to underlying
    condition
    with chronic pancreatitis K86.1
  portal (due to chronic liver disease)
    (idiopathic) K76.6
    gastropathy K31.89
    in (due to) schistosomiasis (bilharziasis)
      B65.9 [*K77*]
  postoperative I97.3
  psychogenic F45.8
  pulmonary NEC I27.20
    with
      cor pulmonale (chronic) I27.29
        acute I26.09
      right heart ventricular strain/failure
        I27.29
        acute I26.09
      right to left shunt related to congenital
        heart disease I27.83
      unclear multifactorial mechanisms
        I27.29
    arterial (associated) (drug-induced) (toxin-
      induced) I27.21
    chronic thromboembolic I27.24
    due to
      hematologic disorders I27.29
      left heart disease I27.22
      lung diseases and hypoxia I27.23
      metabolic disorders I27.29
      specified systemic disorders NEC I27.29
    group 1 (associated) (drug-induced) (toxin-
      induced) I27.21
    group 2 I27.22
    group 3 I27.23
    group 4 I27.24
    group 5 I27.29
    of newborn (persistent) P29.30
    secondary
      arterial I27.21
      specified NEC I27.29
    primary (idiopathic) I27.0
  renal —*see* Hypertension, kidney
  renovascular I15.0
  secondary NEC I15.9
    due to
      endocrine disorders I15.2
      pheochromocytoma I15.2
      renal disorders NEC I15.1
        arterial I15.0
      renovascular disorders I15.0
    specified NEC I15.8
  transient R03.0
    of pregnancy O13.●
  urgency I16.0
  venous (chronic)
    due to
      deep vein thrombosis —*see* Syndrome,
        postthrombotic

Hypertension, hypertensive (*Continued*)
  venous (*Continued*)
    idiopathic I87.309
      with
        inflammation I87.32-●
          with ulcer I87.33-●
        specified complication NEC I87.39-●
        ulcer I87.31-●
          with inflammation I87.33-●
      asymptomatic I87.30-●
Hypertensive urgency —*see* Hypertension
Hyperthecosis ovary E28.8
Hyperthermia (of unknown origin) —*see also*
  Hyperpyrexia
  malignant, due to anesthesia T88.3
  newborn P81.9
    environmental P81.0
Hyperthyroid (recurrent) —*see* Hyperthyroidism
Hyperthyroidism (latent) (pre-adult) (recurrent)
  E05.90
  with
    goiter (diffuse) E05.00
      with thyroid storm E05.01
      nodular (multinodular) E05.20
        with thyroid storm E05.21
        uninodular E05.10
          with thyroid storm E05.11
    storm E05.91
  due to ectopic thyroid tissue E05.30
    with thyroid storm E05.31
  neonatal, transitory P72.1
  specified NEC E05.80
    with thyroid storm E05.81
Hypertony, hypertonia, hypertonicity
  bladder N31.8
  congenital P94.1
  stomach K31.89
    psychogenic F45.8
  uterus, uterine (contractions) (complicating
    delivery) O62.4
Hypertrichosis L68.9
  congenital Q84.2
  eyelid H02.869
    left H02.866
      lower H02.865
      upper H02.864
    right H02.863
      lower H02.862
      upper H02.861
  lanuginosa Q84.2
    acquired L68.1
  localized L68.2
  specified NEC L68.8
Hypertriglyceridemia, essential E78.1
Hypertrophy, hypertrophic
  adenofibromatous, prostate —*see*
    Enlargement, enlarged, prostate
  adenoids (infective) J35.2
    with tonsils J35.3
  adrenal cortex E27.8
  alveolar process or ridge —*see* Anomaly,
    alveolar
  anal papillae K62.89
  artery I77.89
    congenital NEC Q27.8
      digestive system Q27.8
      lower limb Q27.8
      specified site NEC Q27.8
      upper limb Q27.8
  auricular —*see* Hypertrophy, cardiac
  Bartholin's gland N75.8
  bile duct (common) (hepatic) K83.8
  bladder (sphincter) (trigone) N32.89
  bone M89.30
    carpus M89.34-●
    clavicle M89.31-●
    femur M89.35-●
    fibula M89.36-●
    finger M89.34-●
    humerus M89.32-●
    ilium M89.359

▶ New   ⇒ Revised   ~~deleted~~ Deleted   ● Use Additional Character(s)

Hypertrophy, hypertrophic *(Continued)*
  bone *(Continued)*
    ischium M89.359
    metacarpus M89.34-•
    metatarsus M89.37-•
    multiple sites M89.39
    neck M89.38
    radius M89.33-•
    rib M89.38
    scapula M89.31-•
    skull M89.38
    tarsus M89.37-•
    tibia M89.36-•
    toe M89.37-•
    ulna M89.33-•
    vertebra M89.38
  brain G93.89
  breast N62
    cystic —*see* Mastopathy, cystic
    newborn P83.4
    pubertal, massive N62
    puerperal, postpartum —*see* Disorder,
        breast, specified type NEC
    senile (parenchymatous) N62
  cardiac (chronic) (idiopathic) I51.7
    with rheumatic fever (conditions in I00)
        active I01.8
        inactive or quiescent (with chorea) I09.89
    congenital NEC Q24.8
    fatty —*see* Degeneration, myocardial
    hypertensive —*see* Hypertension, heart
    rheumatic (with chorea) I09.89
        active or acute I01.8
            with chorea I02.0
    valve —*see* Endocarditis
  cartilage —*see* Disorder, cartilage, specified
      type NEC
  cecum —*see* Megacolon
  cervix (uteri) N88.8
    congenital Q51.828
    elongation N88.4
  clitoris (cirrhotic) N90.89
    congenital Q52.6
  colon —*see also* Megacolon
    congenital Q43.2
  conjunctiva, lymphoid H11.89
  corpora cavernosa N48.89
  cystic duct K82.8
  duodenum K31.89
  endometrium (glandular) —*see also*
      Hyperplasia, endometrial N85.00-•
    cervix N88.8
  epididymis N50.89
  esophageal hiatus (congenital) Q79.1
    with hernia —*see* Hernia, hiatal
  eyelid —*see* Disorder, eyelid, specified type
      NEC
  fat pad E65
    knee (infrapatellar) (popliteal) (prepatellar)
        (retropatellar) M79.4
  foot (congenital) Q74.2
  frenulum, frenum (tongue) K14.8
    lip K13.0
  gallbladder K82.8
  gastric mucosa K29.60
    with bleeding K29.61
  gland, glandular R59.9
    generalized R59.1
    localized R59.0
  gum (mucous membrane) K06.1
  heart (idiopathic) —*see also* Hypertrophy,
      cardiac
    valve —*see also* Endocarditis I38
  hemifacial Q67.4
  hepatic —*see* Hypertrophy, liver
  hiatus (esophageal) Q79.1
  hilus gland R59.0
  hymen, congenital Q52.4
  ileum K63.89
  intestine NEC K63.89
  jejunum K63.89

Hypertrophy, hypertrophic *(Continued)*
  kidney (compensatory) N28.81
    congenital Q63.3
  labium (majus) (minus) N90.60
  ligament —*see* Disorder, ligament
  lingual tonsil (infective) J35.1
    with adenoids J35.3
  lip K13.0
    congenital Q18.6
  liver R16.0
    acute K76.89
    cirrhotic —*see* Cirrhosis, liver
    congenital Q44.7
    fatty —*see* Fatty, liver
  lymph, lymphatic gland R59.9
    generalized R59.1
    localized R59.0
    tuberculous —*see* Tuberculosis, lymph
        gland
  mammary gland —*see* Hypertrophy, breast
  Meckel's diverticulum (congenital) Q43.0
    malignant —*see* Table of Neoplasms, small
        intestine, malignant
  median bar —*see* Hyperplasia, prostate
  meibomian gland —*see* Chalazion
  meniscus, knee, congenital Q74.1
  metatarsal head —*see* Hypertrophy, bone,
      metatarsus
  metatarsus —*see* Hypertrophy, bone,
      metatarsus
  mucous membrane
    alveolar ridge K06.2
    gum K06.1
    nose (turbinate) J34.3
  muscle M62.89
  muscular coat, artery I77.89
  myocardium —*see also* Hypertrophy, cardiac
    idiopathic I42.2
  myometrium N85.2
  nail L60.2
    congenital Q84.5
  nasal J34.89
    alae J34.89
    bone J34.89
    cartilage J34.89
    mucous membrane (septum) J34.3
    sinus J34.89
    turbinate J34.3
  nasopharynx, lymphoid (infectional) (tissue)
      (wall) J35.2
  nipple N62
  organ or site, congenital NEC —*see* Anomaly,
      by site - ovary N83.8
  palate (hard) M27.8
    soft K13.79
  pancreas, congenital Q45.3
  parathyroid (gland) E21.0
  parotid gland K11.1
  penis N48.89
  pharyngeal tonsil J35.2
  pharynx J39.2
    lymphoid (infectional) (tissue) (wall)
        J35.2
  pituitary (anterior) (fossa) (gland) E23.6
  prepuce (congenital) N47.8
    female N90.89
  prostate —*see* Enlargement, enlarged,
      prostate
    congenital Q55.4
  pseudomuscular G71.09
  pylorus (adult) (muscle) (sphincter) K31.1
    congenital or infantile Q40.0
  rectal, rectum (sphincter) K62.89
  rhinitis (turbinate) J31.0
  salivary gland (any) K11.1
    congenital Q38.4
  scaphoid (tarsal) —*see* Hypertrophy, bone,
      tarsus
  scar L91.0
  scrotum N50.89
  seminal vesicle N50.89

Hypertrophy, hypertrophic *(Continued)*
  sigmoid —*see* Megacolon
  skin L91.9
    specified NEC L91.8
  spermatic cord N50.89
  spleen —*see* Splenomegaly
  spondylitis —*see* Spondylosis
  stomach K31.89
  sublingual gland K11.1
  submandibular gland K11.1
  suprarenal cortex (gland) E27.8
  synovial NEC M67.20
    acromioclavicular M67.21-•
    ankle M67.27-•
    elbow M67.22-•
    foot M67.27-•
    hand M67.24-•
    hip M67.25-•
    knee M67.26-•
    multiple sites M67.29
    specified site NEC M67.28
    wrist M67.23-•
  tendon —*see* Disorder, tendon, specified type
      NEC
  testis N44.8
    congenital Q55.29
  thymic, thymus (gland) (congenital)
      E32.0
  thyroid (gland) —*see* Goiter
  toe (congenital) Q74.2
    acquired —*see also* Deformity, toe, specified
        NEC
  tongue K14.8
    congenital Q38.2
    papillae (foliate) K14.3
  tonsils (faucial) (infective) (lingual)
      (lymphoid) J35.1
    with adenoids J35.3
  tunica vaginalis N50.89
  ureter N28.89
  urethra N36.8
  uterus N85.2
    neck (with elongation) N88.4
    puerperal O90.89
  uvula K13.79
  vagina N89.8
  vas deferens N50.89
  vein I87.8
  ventricle, ventricular (heart) —*see also*
      Hypertrophy, cardiac
    congenital Q24.8
    in tetralogy of Fallot Q21.3
  verumontanum N36.8
  vocal cord J38.3
  vulva N90.60
    stasis (nonfilarial) N90.69
Hypertropia H50.2-•
Hypertyrosinemia E70.21
Hyperuricemia (asymptomatic) E79.0
Hyperuricosuria R82.993
Hypervalinemia E71.19
Hyperventilation (tetany) R06.4
  hysterical F45.8
  psychogenic F45.8
  syndrome F45.8
Hypervitaminosis (dietary) NEC E67.8
  A E67.0
    administered as drug (prolonged intake) —
        see Table of Drugs and Chemicals,
        vitamins, adverse effect
    overdose or wrong substance given
        or taken —*see* Table of Drugs and
        Chemicals, vitamins, poisoning
  B6 E67.2
  D E67.3
    administered as drug (prolonged intake) —
        see Table of Drugs and Chemicals,
        vitamins, adverse effect
    overdose or wrong substance given
        or taken —*see* Table of Drugs and
        Chemicals, vitamins, poisoning

Hypervitaminosis NEC (Continued)
  K E67.8
    administered as drug (prolonged intake) —
      see Table of Drugs and Chemicals,
      vitamins, adverse effect
    overdose or wrong substance given
      or taken —see Table of Drugs and
      Chemicals, vitamins, poisoning
Hypervolemia E87.70
  specified NEC E87.79
Hypesthesia R20.1
  cornea —see Anesthesia, cornea
Hyphema H21.0-●
  traumatic S05.1-●
Hypoacidity, gastric K31.89
  psychogenic F45.8
Hypoadrenalism, hypoadrenia E27.40
  primary E27.1
  tuberculous A18.7
Hypoadrenocorticism E27.40
  pituitary E23.0
  primary E27.1
Hypoalbuminemia E88.09
Hypoaldosteronism E27.40
Hypoalphalipoproteinemia E78.6
Hypobarism T70.29
Hypobaropathy T70.29
Hypobetalipoproteinemia (familial) E78.6
Hypocalcemia E83.51
  dietary E58
  neonatal P71.1
    due to cow's milk P71.0
    phosphate-loading (newborn) P71.1
Hypochloremia E87.8
Hypochlorhydria K31.89
  neurotic F45.8
  psychogenic F45.8
Hypochondria, hypochondriac,
  hypochondriasis (reaction) F45.21
  sleep F51.03
Hypochondrogenesis Q77.0
Hypochondroplasia Q77.4
Hypochromasia, blood cells D50.8
Hypodontia —see Anodontia
Hypocitraturia R82.991
Hypoeosinophilia D72.89
Hypoesthesia R20.1
Hypofibrinogenemia D68.8
  acquired D65
  congenital (hereditary) D68.2
Hypofunction
  adrenocortical E27.40
    drug-induced E27.3
    postprocedural E89.6
    primary E27.1
  adrenomedullary, postprocedural E89.6
  cerebral R29.818
  corticoadrenal NEC E27.40
  ⮕intestinal K59.89
  labyrinth —see subcategory H83.2
  ovary E28.39
  pituitary (gland) (anterior) E23.0
  testicular E29.1
    postprocedural (postsurgical)
      (postirradiation) (iatrogenic) E89.5
Hypogalactia O92.4
Hypogammaglobulinemia —see also
  Agammaglobulinemia D80.1
  hereditary D80.0
  nonfamilial D80.1
  transient, of infancy D80.7
Hypogenitalism (congenital) —see
  Hypogonadism
Hypoglossia Q38.3
Hypoglycemia (spontaneous) E16.2
  coma E15
    diabetic —see Diabetes, by type, with
      hypoglycemia, with coma
  diabetic —see Diabetes, hypoglycemia
  dietary counseling and surveillance
    Z71.3

Hypoglycemia (Continued)
  drug-induced E16.0
    with coma (nondiabetic) E15
  due to insulin E16.0
    with coma (nondiabetic) E15
      therapeutic misadventure —see
        subcategory T38.3
  functional, nonhyperinsulinemic E16.1
  iatrogenic E16.0
    with coma (nondiabetic) E15
  in infant of diabetic mother P70.1
    gestational diabetes P70.0
  infantile E16.1
  leucine-induced E71.19
  neonatal (transitory) P70.4
    iatrogenic P70.3
  reactive (not drug-induced) E16.1
  transitory neonatal P70.4
Hypogonadism
  female E28.39
  hypogonadotropic E23.0
  male E29.1
  ovarian (primary) E28.39
  pituitary E23.0
  testicular (primary) E29.1
Hypohidrosis, hypoidrosis L74.4
Hypoinsulinemia, postprocedural E89.1
Hypokalemia E87.6
Hypoleukocytosis —see Agranulocytosis
Hypolipoproteinemia (alpha) (beta) E78.6
Hypomagnesemia E83.42
  neonatal P71.2
Hypomania, hypomanic reaction F30.8
Hypomenorrhea —see Oligomenorrhea
Hypometabolism R63.8
Hypomotility
  gastrointestinal (tract) K31.89
    psychogenic F45.8
  ⮕intestine K59.89
    psychogenic F45.8
  stomach K31.89
    psychogenic F45.8
Hyponasality R49.22
Hyponatremia E87.1
Hypo-osmolality E87.1
Hypo-ovarianism, hypo-ovarism
  E28.39
Hypoparathyroidism E20.9
  familial E20.8
  idiopathic E20.0
  neonatal, transitory P71.4
  postprocedural E89.2
  specified NEC E20.8
Hypoperfusion (in)
  newborn P96.89
Hypopharyngitis —see Laryngopharyngitis
Hypophoria H50.53
Hypophosphatemia, hypophosphatasia
  (acquired) (congenital) (renal) E83.39
  familial E83.31
Hypophyseal, hypophysis —see also
  condition
  dwarfism E23.0
  gigantism E22.0
Hypopiesis —see Hypotension
Hypopinealism E34.8
Hypopituitarism (juvenile) E23.0
  drug-induced E23.1
  due to
    hypophysectomy E89.3
    radiotherapy E89.3
  iatrogenic NEC E23.1
  postirradiation E89.3
  postpartum O99.285
  postprocedural E89.3
Hypoplasia, hypoplastic
  adrenal (gland), congenital Q89.1
  alimentary tract, congenital Q45.8
    upper Q40.8
  anus, anal (canal) Q42.3
    with fistula Q42.2

Hypoplasia, hypoplastic (Continued)
  aorta, aortic Q25.42
    ascending, in hypoplastic left heart
      syndrome Q23.4
    valve Q23.1
      in hypoplastic left heart syndrome Q23.4
  areola, congenital Q83.8
  arm (congenital) —see Defect, reduction,
    upper limb
  artery (peripheral) Q27.8
    brain (congenital) Q28.3
    coronary Q24.5
    digestive system Q27.8
    lower limb Q27.8
    pulmonary Q25.79
      functional, unilateral J43.0
    retinal (congenital) Q14.1
    specified site NEC Q27.8
    umbilical Q27.0
    upper limb Q27.8
  auditory canal Q17.8
    causing impairment of hearing Q16.9
  biliary duct or passage Q44.5
  bone NOS Q79.9
    face Q75.8
    marrow D61.9
      megakaryocytic D69.49
    skull —see Hypoplasia, skull
  brain Q02
    gyri Q04.3
    part of Q04.3
  breast (areola) N64.82
  bronchus Q32.4
  cardiac Q24.8
  carpus —see Defect, reduction, upper limb,
    specified type NEC
  cartilage hair Q78.8
  cecum Q42.8
  cementum K00.4
  cephalic Q02
  cerebellum Q04.3
  cervix (uteri), congenital Q51.821
  clavicle (congenital) Q74.0
  coccyx Q76.49
  colon Q42.9
    specified NEC Q42.8
  corpus callosum Q04.0
  cricoid cartilage Q31.2
  digestive organ(s) or tract NEC Q45.8
    upper (congenital) Q40.8
  ear (auricle) (lobe) Q17.2
    middle Q16.4
  enamel of teeth (neonatal) (postnatal)
    (prenatal) K00.4
  endocrine (gland) NEC Q89.2
  endometrium N85.8
  epididymis (congenital) Q55.4
  epiglottis Q31.2
  erythroid, congenital D61.01
  esophagus (congenital) Q39.8
  eustachian tube Q17.8
  eye Q11.2
  eyelid (congenital) Q10.3
  face Q18.8
    bone(s) Q75.8
  femur (congenital) —see Defect, reduction,
    lower limb, specified type NEC
  fibula (congenital) —see Defect, reduction,
    lower limb, specified type NEC
  finger (congenital) —see Defect, reduction,
    upper limb, specified type NEC
  focal dermal Q82.8
  foot —see Defect, reduction, lower limb,
    specified type NEC
  gallbladder Q44.0
  genitalia, genital organ(s)
    female, congenital Q52.8
      external Q52.79
      internal NEC Q52.8
    in adiposogenital dystrophy E23.6
  glottis Q31.2

Hypoplasia, hypoplastic *(Continued)*
  hair Q84.2
  hand (congenital) —*see* Defect, reduction,
      upper limb, specified type NEC
  heart Q24.8
  humerus (congenital) —*see* Defect, reduction,
      upper limb, specified type NEC
  intestine (small) Q41.9
    large Q42.9
      specified NEC Q42.8
  jaw M26.09
    alveolar M26.79
    lower M26.04
      alveolar M26.74
    upper M26.02
      alveolar M26.73
  kidney(s) Q60.5
    bilateral Q60.4
    unilateral Q60.3
  labium (majus) (minus), congenital Q52.79
  larynx Q31.2
  left heart syndrome Q23.4
  leg (congenital) —*see* Defect, reduction, lower
      limb
  limb Q73.8
    lower (congenital) —*see* Defect, reduction,
        lower limb
    upper (congenital) —*see* Defect, reduction,
        upper limb
  liver Q44.7
  lung (lobe) (not associated with short
      gestation) Q33.6
    associated with immaturity, low birth
        weight, prematurity, or short gestation
        P28.0
  mammary (areola), congenital Q83.8
  mandible, mandibular M26.04
    alveolar M26.74
    unilateral condylar M27.8
  maxillary M26.02
    alveolar M26.73
  medullary D61.9
  megakaryocytic D69.49
  metacarpus —*see* Defect, reduction, upper
      limb, specified type NEC
  metatarsus —*see* Defect, reduction, lower
      limb, specified type NEC
  muscle Q79.8
  nail(s) Q84.6
  nose, nasal Q30.1
  optic nerve H47.03-●
  osseous meatus (ear) Q17.8
  ovary, congenital Q50.39
  pancreas Q45.0
  parathyroid (gland) Q89.2
  parotid gland Q38.4
  patella Q74.1
  pelvis, pelvic girdle Q74.2
  penis (congenital) Q55.62
  peripheral vascular system Q27.8
    digestive system Q27.8
    lower limb Q27.8
    specified site NEC Q27.8
    upper limb Q27.8
  pituitary (gland) (congenital) Q89.2
  pulmonary (not associated with short
      gestation) Q33.6
    artery, functional J43.0
    associated with short gestation P28.0
  radioulnar —*see* Defect, reduction, upper
      limb, specified type NEC
  radius —*see* Defect, reduction, upper limb
  rectum Q42.1
    with fistula Q42.0
  respiratory system NEC Q34.8
  rib Q76.6
  right heart syndrome Q22.6
  sacrum Q76.49
  scapula Q74.0
  scrotum Q55.1
  shoulder girdle Q74.0

Hypoplasia, hypoplastic *(Continued)*
  skin Q82.8
  skull (bone) Q75.8
    with
      anencephaly Q00.0
      encephalocele —*see* Encephalocele
      hydrocephalus Q03.9
        with spina bifida —*see* Spina bifida, by
            site, with hydrocephalus
      microcephaly Q02
  spinal (cord) (ventral horn cell) Q06.1
  spine Q76.49
  sternum Q76.7
  tarsus —*see* Defect, reduction, lower limb,
      specified type NEC
  testis Q55.1
  thymic, with immunodeficiency D82.1
  thymus (gland) Q89.2
    with immunodeficiency D82.1
  thyroid (gland) E03.1
    cartilage Q31.2
  tibiofibular (congenital) —*see* Defect,
      reduction, lower limb, specified type
      NEC
  toe —*see* Defect, reduction, lower limb,
      specified type NEC
  tongue Q38.3
  Turner's K00.4
  ulna (congenital) —*see* Defect, reduction,
      upper limb
  umbilical artery Q27.0
  unilateral condylar M27.8
  ureter Q62.8
  uterus, congenital Q51.811
  vagina Q52.4
  vascular NEC peripheral Q27.8
    brain Q28.3
    digestive system Q27.8
    lower limb Q27.8
    specified site NEC Q27.8
    upper limb Q27.8
  vein(s) (peripheral) Q27.8
    brain Q28.3
    digestive system Q27.8
    great Q26.8
    lower limb Q27.8
    specified site NEC Q27.8
    upper limb Q27.8
  vena cava (inferior) (superior) Q26.8
  vertebra Q76.49
  vulva, congenital Q52.79
  zonule (ciliary) Q12.8
Hypoplasminogenemia E88.02
Hypopnea, obstructive sleep apnea
    G47.33
Hypopotassemia E87.6
Hypoproconvertinemia, congenital
    (hereditary) D68.2
Hypoproteinemia E77.8
Hypoprothrombinemia (congenital)
    (hereditary) (idiopathic) D68.2
  acquired D68.4
  newborn, transient P61.6
Hypoptyalism K11.7
Hypopyon (eye) (anterior chamber) —*see*
    Iridocyclitis, acute, hypopyon
Hypopyrexia R68.0
Hyporeflexia R29.2
Hyposecretion
  ACTH E23.0
  antidiuretic hormone E23.2
  ovary E28.39
  salivary gland (any) K11.7
  vasopressin E23.2
Hyposegmentation, leukocytic, hereditary D72.0
Hyposiderinemia D50.9
Hypospadias Q54.9
  balanic Q54.0
  coronal Q54.0
  glandular Q54.0
  penile Q54.1

Hypospadias *(Continued)*
  penoscrotal Q54.2
  perineal Q54.3
  specified NEC Q54.8
Hypospermatogenesis —*see* Oligospermia
Hyposplenism D73.0
Hypostasis pulmonary, passive —*see* Edema,
    lung
Hypostatic —*see* condition
Hyposthenuria N28.89
Hypotension (arterial) (constitutional) I95.9
  chronic I95.89
  drug-induced I95.2
  due to (of) hemodialysis I95.3
  iatrogenic I95.89
  idiopathic (permanent) I95.0
  ▶intracranial G96.810
    ▶following
      ▶lumbar cerebrospinal fluid shunting
          G97.83
      ▶specified procedure NEC G97.84
      ▶ventricular shunting (ventriculostomy)
          G97.2
    ▶specified NEC G96.819
    ▶spontaneous G96.811
  ~~intracranial, following ventricular shunting~~
      ~~(ventriculostomy) G97.2~~
  intra-dialytic I95.3
  maternal, syndrome (following labor and
      delivery) O26.5-●
  neurogenic, orthostatic G90.3
  orthostatic (chronic) I95.1
    due to drugs I95.2
    neurogenic G90.3
  postoperative I95.81
  postural I95.1
  specified NEC I95.89
Hypothermia (accidental) T68
  due to anesthesia, anesthetic T88.51
  low environmental temperature T68
  neonatal P80.9
    environmental (mild) NEC P80.8
    mild P80.8
    severe (chronic) (cold injury syndrome)
        P80.0
    specified NEC P80.8
  not associated with low environmental
      temperature R68.0
Hypothyroidism (acquired) E03.9
  autoimmune —*see* Thyroiditis, autoimmune
  congenital (without goiter) E03.1
    with goiter (diffuse) E03.0
  due to
    exogenous substance NEC E03.2
    iodine-deficiency, acquired E01.8
      subclinical E02
    irradiation therapy E89.0
    medicament NEC E03.2
    P-aminosalicylic acid (PAS) E03.2
    phenylbutazone E03.2
    resorcinol E03.2
    sulfonamide E03.2
    surgery E89.0
    thiourea group drugs E03.2
  iatrogenic NEC E03.2
  iodine-deficiency (acquired) E01.8
    congenital —*see* Syndrome, iodine-
        deficiency, congenital
    subclinical E02
  neonatal, transitory P72.2
  postinfectious E03.3
  postirradiation E89.0
  postprocedural E89.0
  postsurgical E89.0
  specified NEC E03.8
  subclinical, iodine-deficiency related E02
Hypotonia, hypotonicity, hypotony
  bladder N31.2
  congenital (benign) P94.2
  eye —*see* Disorder, globe, hypotony
Hypotrichosis —*see* Alopecia

Hypotropia H50.2-●
Hypoventilation R06.89
  congenital central alveolar G47.35
  sleep related
    idiopathic nonobstructive alveolar
      G47.34
    in conditions classified elsewhere G47.36
Hypovitaminosis —*see* Deficiency, vitamin
Hypovolemia E86.1
  surgical shock T81.19
  traumatic (shock) T79.4

Hypoxemia R09.02
  newborn P84
  sleep related, in conditions classified
    elsewhere G47.36
Hypoxia —*see also* Anoxia R09.02
  cerebral, during a procedure NEC G97.81
    postprocedural NEC G97.82
  intrauterine P84
  myocardial —*see* Insufficiency, coronary
  newborn P84
  sleep-related G47.34

Hypsarhythmia —*see* Epilepsy, generalized,
  specified NEC
Hysteralgia, pregnant uterus O26.89-●
Hysteria, hysterical (conversion) (dissociative
  state) F44.9
  anxiety F41.8
  convulsions F44.5
  psychosis, acute F44.9
Hysteroepilepsy F44.5

I

IBDU (colonic inflammatory bowel dissease unclassified) K52.3
Ichthyoparasitism due to Vandellia cirrhosa B88.8
Ichthyosis (congenital) Q80.9
  acquired L85.0
  fetalis Q80.4
  hystrix Q80.8
  lamellar Q80.2
  lingual K13.29
  palmaris and plantaris Q82.8
  simplex Q80.0
  vera Q80.8
  vulgaris Q80.0
  X-linked Q80.1
Ichthyotoxism —*see* Poisoning, fish
  bacterial —*see* Intoxication, foodborne
Icteroanemia, hemolytic (acquired) D59.9
  congenital —*see* Spherocytosis
Icterus —*see also* Jaundice
  conjunctiva R17
  gravis, newborn P55.0
  hematogenous (acquired) D59.9
  hemolytic (acquired) D59.9
    congenital —*see* Spherocytosis
  hemorrhagic (acute) (leptospiral) (spirochetal) A27.0
    newborn P53
  infectious B15.9
    with hepatic coma B15.0
    leptospiral A27.0
    spirochetal A27.0
  neonatorum —*see* Jaundice, newborn
  newborn P59.9
  spirochetal A27.0
Ictus solaris, solis T67.01
Ideation
  homicidal R45.850
  suicidal R45.851
Identity disorder (child) F64.9
  gender role F64.2
  psychosexual F64.2
Idioglossia F80.0
Idiopathic —*see* condition
Idiot, idiocy (congenital) F73
  amaurotic (Bielschowsky(-Jansky)) (family) (infantile (late)) (juvenile (late)) (Vogt-Spielmeyer) E75.4
  microcephalic Q02
Id reaction (due to bacteria) L30.2
IgE asthma J45.909
IIAC (idiopathic infantile arterial calcification) Q28.8
Ileitis (chronic) (noninfectious) —*see also* Enteritis K52.9
  backwash —*see* Pancolitis, ulcerative (chronic)
  infectious A09
  regional (ulcerative) —*see* Enteritis, regional, small intestine
  segmental —*see* Enteritis, regional
  terminal (ulcerative) —*see* Enteritis, regional, small intestine
Ileocolitis —*see also* Enteritis K52.9
  infectious A09
  regional —*see* Enteritis, regional
  ulcerative K51.0-•
Ileostomy
  attention to Z43.2
  malfunctioning K94.13
  status Z93.2
    with complication —*see* Complications, enterostomy
Ileotyphus —*see* Typhoid
Ileum —*see* condition
Ileus (bowel) (colon) (inhibitory) (intestine) K56.7
  adynamic K56.0
  due to gallstone (in intestine) K56.3
  duodenal (chronic) K31.5

Ileus (*Continued*)
  gallstone K56.3
  mechanical NEC —*see also* Obstruction, intestine, specified K56.699
  meconium P76.0
    in cystic fibrosis E84.11
    meaning meconium plug (without cystic fibrosis) P76.0
  ➮myxedema K59.89
  neurogenic K56.0
    Hirschsprung's disease or megacolon Q43.1
  newborn
    due to meconium P76.0
      in cystic fibrosis E84.11
      meaning meconium plug (without cystic fibrosis) P76.0
    transitory P76.1
  obstructive —*see also* Obstruction, intestine, specified K56.699
  paralytic K56.0
  postoperative K91.89
Iliac —*see* condition
Iliotibial band syndrome M76.3-•
Illiteracy Z55.0
Illness—*see also* Disease R69
  manic-depressive —*see* Disorder, bipolar
Imbalance R26.89
  autonomic G90.8
  constituents of food intake E63.1
  electrolyte E87.8
    with
      abortion —*see* Abortion by type, complicated by, electrolyte imbalance
      molar pregnancy O08.5
    due to hyperemesis gravidarum O21.1
    following ectopic or molar pregnancy O08.5
    neonatal, transitory NEC P74.49
      potassium
        hyperkalemia P74.31
        hypokalemia P74.32
      sodium
        hypernatremia P74.21
        hyponatremia P74.22
  endocrine E34.9
  eye muscle NOS H50.9
  hormone E34.9
  hysterical F44.4
  labyrinth —*see* subcategory H83.2
  posture R29.3
  protein-energy —*see* Malnutrition
  sympathetic G90.8
Imbecile, imbecility (I.Q. 35-49) F71
Imbedding, intrauterine device T83.39
Imbibition, cholesterol (gallbladder) K82.4
Imbrication, teeth, fully erupted M26.30
Imerslund (-Gräsbeck) syndrome D51.1
Immature —*see also* Immaturity
  birth (less than 37 completed weeks) —*see* Preterm, newborn
  extremely (less than 28 completed weeks) —*see* Immaturity, extreme
  personality F60.89
Immaturity (less than 37 completed weeks) — *see also* Preterm, newborn
  extreme of newborn (less than 28 completed weeks of gestation) (less than 196 completed days of gestation) (unspecified weeks of gestation) P07.20
    gestational age
      23 completed weeks (23 weeks, 0 days through 23 weeks, 6 days) P07.22
      24 completed weeks (24 weeks, 0 days through 24 weeks, 6 days) P07.23
      25 completed weeks (25 weeks, 0 days through 25 weeks, 6 days) P07.24
      26 completed weeks (26 weeks, 0 days through 26 weeks, 6 days) P07.25
      27 completed weeks (27 weeks, 0 days through 27 weeks, 6 days) P07.26
      less than 23 completed weeks P07.21

Immaturity (*Continued*)
  fetus or infant light-for-dates —*see* Light-for-dates
  lung, newborn P28.0
  organ or site NEC —*see* Hypoplasia
  pulmonary, newborn P28.0
  reaction F60.89
  sexual (female) (male), after puberty E30.0
Immersion T75.1
  foot T69.02-•
  hand T69.01-•
Immobile, immobility
  complete, due to severe physical disability or frailty R53.2
  ➮intestine K59.89
  syndrome (paraplegic) M62.3
Immune reconstitution (inflammatory) syndrome [IRIS] D89.3
Immunization —*see also* Vaccination
  ABO —*see* Incompatibility, ABO
    in newborn P55.1
  appropriate for age
    child (over 28 days old) Z00.129
      with abnormal findings Z00.121
  complication —*see* Complications, vaccination
  encounter for Z23
  not done (not carried out) Z28.9
    because (of)
      acute illness of patient Z28.01
      allergy to vaccine (or component) Z28.04
      caregiver refusal Z28.82
      chronic illness of patient Z28.02
      contraindication NEC Z28.09
      delay in delivery of vaccine Z28.83
      group pressure Z28.1
      guardian refusal Z28.82
      immune compromised state of patient Z28.03
      lack of availability of vaccine Z28.83
      manufacturer delay of vaccine Z28.83
      parent refusal Z28.82
      patient's belief Z28.1
      patient had disease being vaccinated against Z28.81
      patient refusal Z28.21
      religious beliefs of patient Z28.1
      specified reason NEC Z28.89
        of patient Z28.29
      unavailability of vaccine Z28.83
      unspecified patient reason Z28.20
  Rh factor
    affecting management of pregnancy NEC O36.09-•
    anti-D antibody O36.01-•
    from transfusion —*see* Complication(s), transfusion, incompatibility reaction, Rh (factor)
▶**Immunocompromised NOS** D84.9
Immunocytoma C83.0-•
Immunodeficiency D84.9
  with
    adenosine-deaminase deficiency (*see also* Deficiency, adenosine deaminase) D81.30
    antibody defects D80.9
      specified type NEC D80.8
    hyperimmunoglobulinemia D80.6
    increased immunoglobulin M (IgM) D80.5
    major defect D82.9
      specified type NEC D82.8
    partial albinism D82.8
    short-limbed stature D82.2
    thrombocytopenia and eczema D82.0
  antibody with
    hyperimmunoglobulinemia D80.6
    near-normal immunoglobulins D80.6
  autosomal recessive, Swiss type D80.0

Immunodeficiency (Continued)
  combined D81.9
    biotin-dependent carboxylase D81.819
      biotinidase D81.810
      holocarboxylase synthetase D81.818
      specified type NEC D81.818
    severe (SCID) D81.9
      with
        low or normal B-cell numbers D81.2
        low T- and B-cell numbers D81.1
        reticular dysgenesis D81.0
      specified type NEC D81.89
  common variable D83.9
    with
      abnormalities of B-cell numbers and
        function D83.0
      autoantibodies to B- or T-cells D83.2
      immunoregulatory T-cell disorders
        D83.1
    specified type NEC D83.8
  due to
    conditions classified elsewhere D84.81
    drugs D84.821
    external causes D84.822
    medication (current or past) D84.821
  following hereditary defective response to
    Epstein-Barr virus (EBV) D82.3
  selective, immunoglobulin
    A (IgA) D80.2
    G (IgG) (subclasses) D80.3
    M (IgM) D80.4
  severe combined (SCID) D81.9
    due to adenosine deaminase deficiency
      D81.31
  specified type NEC D84.89
  X-linked, with increased IgM D80.5
Immunodeficient NOS D84.9
Immunosuppressed NOS D84.9
Immunotherapy (encounter for)
  antineoplastic Z51.12
Impaction, impacted
  bowel, colon, rectum —see also Impaction,
    fecal K56.49
    by gallstone K56.3
  calculus —see Calculus
  cerumen (ear) (external) H61.2-●
  cuspid —see Impaction, tooth
  dental (same or adjacent tooth) K01.1
  fecal, feces K56.41
  fracture —see Fracture, by site
  gallbladder —see Calculus, gallbladder
  gallstone(s) —see Calculus, gallbladder
    bile duct (common) (hepatic) —see
      Calculus, bile duct
    cystic duct —see Calculus, gallbladder
    in intestine, with obstruction (any part)
      K56.3
  intestine (calculous) NEC —see also
    Impaction, fecal K56.49
    gallstone, with ileus K56.3
  intrauterine device (IUD) T83.39
  molar —see Impaction, tooth
  shoulder, causing obstructed labor O66.0
  tooth, teeth K01.1
  turbinate J34.89
Impaired, impairment (function)
  auditory discrimination —see Abnormal,
    auditory perception
  cognitive, mild, so stated G31.84
  dual sensory Z73.82
  fasting glucose R73.01
  glucose tolerance (oral) R73.02
  hearing —see Deafness
  heart —see Disease, heart
  kidney N28.9
    disorder resulting from N25.9
      specified NEC N25.89
  liver K72.90
    with coma K72.91
  mastication K08.89
  mild cognitive, so stated G31.84

Impaired, impairment (Continued)
  mobility
    ear ossicles —see Ankylosis, ear ossicles
    requiring care provider Z74.09
  myocardium, myocardial —see Insufficiency,
    myocardial
  rectal sphincter R19.8
  renal (acute) (chronic) N28.9
    disorder resulting from N25.9
      specified NEC N25.89
  vision NEC H54.7
    both eyes H54.3
Impediment, speech (see also Disorder, speech)
    R47.9
  psychogenic (childhood) F98.8
  slurring R47.81
  specified NEC R47.89
Impending
  coronary syndrome I20.0
  delirium tremens F10.239
  myocardial infarction I20.0
Imperception auditory (acquired) —see also
    Deafness
  congenital H93.25
Imperfect
  aeration, lung (newborn) NEC —see
    Atelectasis
  closure (congenital)
    alimentary tract NEC Q45.8
      lower Q43.8
      upper Q40.8
    atrioventricular ostium Q21.2
    atrium (secundum) Q21.1
    branchial cleft NOS Q18.2
      cyst Q18.0
      fistula Q18.0
      sinus Q18.0
    choroid Q14.3
    cricoid cartilage Q31.8
    cusps, heart valve NEC Q24.8
      pulmonary Q22.3
    ductus
      arteriosus Q25.0
      Botalli Q25.0
    ear drum (causing impairment of hearing)
      Q16.4
    esophagus with communication to
      bronchus or trachea Q39.1
    eyelid Q10.3
    foramen
      botalli Q21.1
      ovale Q21.1
    genitalia, genital organ(s) or system
      female Q52.8
        external Q52.79
        internal NEC Q52.8
      male Q55.8
    glottis Q31.8
    interatrial ostium or septum Q21.1
    interauricular ostium or septum Q21.1
    interventricular ostium or septum Q21.0
    larynx Q31.8
    lip —see Cleft, lip
    nasal septum Q30.3
    nose Q30.2
    omphalomesenteric duct Q43.0
    optic nerve entry Q14.2
    organ or site not listed —see Anomaly,
      by site
    ostium
      interatrial Q21.1
      interauricular Q21.1
      interventricular Q21.0
    palate —see Cleft, palate
    preauricular sinus Q18.1
    retina Q14.1
    roof of orbit Q75.8
    sclera Q13.5
    septum
      aorticopulmonary Q21.4
      atrial (secundum) Q21.1

Imperfect (Continued)
  closure (Continued)
    septum (Continued)
      between aorta and pulmonary artery
        Q21.4
      heart Q21.9
      interatrial (secundum) Q21.1
      interauricular (secundum) Q21.1
      interventricular Q21.0
        in tetralogy of Fallot Q21.3
      nasal Q30.3
      ventricular Q21.0
        with pulmonary stenosis or atresia,
          dextraposition of aorta, and
          hypertrophy of right ventricle
          Q21.3
        in tetralogy of Fallot Q21.3
    skull Q75.0
      with
        anencephaly Q00.0
        encephalocele —see Encephalocele
        hydrocephalus Q03.9
          with spina bifida —see Spina bifida,
            by site, with hydrocephalus
        microcephaly Q02
    spine (with meningocele) —see Spina
      bifida
    trachea Q32.1
    tympanic membrane (causing impairment
      of hearing) Q16.4
    uterus Q51.818
    vitelline duct Q43.0
  erection —see Dysfunction, sexual, male,
    erectile
  fusion —see Imperfect, closure
  inflation, lung (newborn) —see Atelectasis
  posture R29.3
  rotation, intestine Q43.3
  septum, ventricular Q21.0
Imperfectly descended testis —see
    Cryptorchid
Imperforate (congenital) —see also Atresia
  anus Q42.3
    with fistula Q42.2
  cervix (uteri) Q51.828
  esophagus Q39.0
    with tracheoesophageal fistula Q39.1
  hymen Q52.3
  jejunum Q41.1
  pharynx Q38.8
  rectum Q42.1
    with fistula Q42.0
  urethra Q64.39
  vagina Q52.4
Impervious (congenital) —see also Atresia
  anus Q42.3
    with fistula Q42.2
  bile duct Q44.2
  esophagus Q39.0
    with tracheoesophageal fistula Q39.1
  intestine (small) Q41.9
    large Q42.9
      specified NEC Q42.8
  rectum Q42.1
    with fistula Q42.0
  ureter —see Atresia, ureter
  urethra Q64.39
Impetiginization of dermatoses L01.1
Impetigo (any organism) (any site) (circinate)
    (contagiosa) (simplex) (vulgaris) L01.00
  Bockhart's L01.02
  bullous, bullosa L01.03
  external ear L01.00 [H62.40]
  follicularis L01.02
  furfuracea L30.5
  herpetiformis L40.1
    nonobstetrical L40.1
  neonatorum L01.03
  nonbullous L01.01
  specified type NEC L01.09
  ulcerative L01.09

Impingement (on teeth)
   joint —*see* Disorder, joint, specified type NEC
   soft tissue
      anterior M26.81
      posterior M26.82
Implant, endometrial N80.9
Implantation
   anomalous —*see* Anomaly, by site
      ureter Q62.63
   cyst
      external area or site (skin) NEC L72.0
      iris —*see* Cyst, iris, implantation
      vagina N89.8
      vulva N90.7
   dermoid (cyst) —*see* Implantation, cyst
Impotence (sexual) N52.9
   counseling Z70.1
   organic origin —*see also* Dysfunction, sexual,
      male, erectile N52.9
   psychogenic F52.21
Impression, basilar Q75.8
Imprisonment, anxiety concerning Z65.1
Improper care (child) (newborn) —*see*
   Maltreatment
Improperly tied umbilical cord (causing
   hemorrhage) P51.8
Impulsiveness (impulsive) R45.87
Inability to swallow —*see* Aphagia
Inaccessible, inaccessibility
   health care NEC Z75.3
      due to
         waiting period Z75.2
            for admission to facility elsewhere
               Z75.1
      other helping agencies Z75.4
Inactive —*see* condition
Inadequate, inadequacy
   aesthetics of dental restoration K08.56
   biologic, constitutional, functional, or social
      F60.7
   development
      child R62.50
      genitalia
         after puberty NEC E30.0
         congenital
            female Q52.8
               external Q52.79
               internal Q52.8
            male Q55.8
      lungs Q33.6
         associated with short gestation P28.0
      organ or site not listed —*see* Anomaly, by
         site
   diet (causing nutritional deficiency)
      E63.9
   eating habits Z72.4
   environment, household Z59.1
   family support Z63.8
   food (supply) NEC Z59.4
      hunger effects T73.0
   functional F60.7
   household care, due to
      family member
         handicapped or ill Z74.2
         on vacation Z75.5
         temporarily away from home Z74.2
      technical defects in home Z59.1
      temporary absence from home of person
         rendering care Z74.2
   housing (heating) (space) Z59.1
   income (financial) Z59.6
   intrafamilial communication Z63.8
   material resources Z59.9
   mental —*see* Disability, intellectual
   parental supervision or control of child
      Z62.0
   personality F60.7
   pulmonary
      function R06.89
         newborn P28.5
      ventilation, newborn P28.5

Inadequate, inadequacy *(Continued)*
   sample of cytologic smear
      anus R85.615
      cervix R87.615
      vagina R87.625
   social F60.7
      insurance Z59.7
      skills NEC Z73.4
   supervision of child by parent Z62.0
   teaching affecting education Z55.8
   welfare support Z59.7
Inanition R64
   with edema —*see* Malnutrition, severe
   due to
      deprivation of food T73.0
      malnutrition —*see* Malnutrition
   fever R50.9
Inappropriate
   change in quantitative human chorionic
      gonadotropin (hCG) in early pregnancy
      O02.81
   diet or eating habits Z72.4
   level of quantitative human chorionic
      gonadotropin (hCG) for gestational age
      in early pregnancy O02.81
   secretion
      antidiuretic hormone (ADH) (excessive)
         E22.2
      deficiency E23.2
      pituitary (posterior) E22.2
Inattention at or after birth —*see* Neglect
Incarceration, incarcerated
   enterocele K46.0
      gangrenous K46.1
   epiplocele K46.0
      gangrenous K46.1
   exomphalos K42.0
      gangrenous K42.1
   hernia —*see also* Hernia, by site, with
      obstruction
      with gangrene —*see* Hernia, by site, with
         gangrene
   iris, in wound —*see* Injury, eye, laceration,
      with prolapse
   lens, in wound —*see* Injury, eye, laceration,
      with prolapse
   omphalocele K42.0
   prison, anxiety concerning Z65.1
   rupture —*see* Hernia, by site
   sarcoepiplocele K46.0
      gangrenous K46.1
   sarcoepiplomphalocele K42.0
      with gangrene K42.1
   uterus N85.8
      gravid O34.51-●
         causing obstructed labor O65.5
Incised wound
   external —*see* Laceration
   internal organs —*see* Injury, by site
Incision, incisional
   hernia K43.2
      with
         gangrene (and obstruction) K43.1
         obstruction K43.0
   surgical, complication —*see* Complications,
      surgical procedure
   traumatic
      external —*see* Laceration
      internal organs —*see* Injury, by site
Inclusion
   azurophilic leukocytic D72.0
   blennorrhea (neonatal) (newborn)
      P39.1
   gallbladder in liver (congenital) Q44.1
Incompatibility
   ABO
      affecting management of pregnancy
         O36.11-●
         anti-A sensitization O36.11-●
         anti-B sensitization O36.19-●
         specified NEC O36.19-●

Incompatibility *(Continued)*
   ABO *(Continued)*
      infusion or transfusion reaction —*see*
         Complication(s), transfusion,
         incompatibility reaction, ABO
      newborn P55.1
   blood (group) (Duffy) (K) (Kell) (Kidd)
      (Lewis) (M) (S) NEC
      affecting management of pregnancy
         O36.11-●
         anti-A sensitization O36.11-●
         anti-B sensitization O36.19-●
      infusion or transfusion reaction
         T80.89
      newborn P55.8
   divorce or estrangement Z63.5
   Rh (blood group) (factor) Z31.82
      affecting management of pregnancy NEC
         O36.09-●
         anti-D antibody O36.01-●
      infusion or transfusion reaction —*see*
         Complication(s), transfusion,
         incompatibility reaction, Rh (factor)
      newborn P55.0
   rhesus —*see* Incompatibility, Rh
Incompetency, incompetent, incompetence
   annular
      aortic (valve) —*see* Insufficiency, aortic
      mitral (valve) I34.0
      pulmonary valve (heart) I37.1
   aortic (valve) —*see* Insufficiency, aortic
   cardiac valve —*see* Endocarditis
   cervix, cervical (os) N88.3
      in pregnancy O34.3-●
   chronotropic I45.89
      with
         autonomic dysfunction G90.8
         ischemic heart disease I25.89
         left ventricular dysfunction I51.89
         sinus node dysfunction I49.8
   esophagogastric (junction) (sphincter) K22.0
   mitral (valve) —*see* Insufficiency, mitral
   pelvic fundus N81.89
   pubocervical tissue N81.82
   pulmonary valve (heart) I37.1
      congenital Q22.3
   rectovaginal tissue N81.83
   tricuspid (annular) (valve) —*see* Insufficiency,
      tricuspid
   valvular —*see* Endocarditis
      congenital Q24.8
   vein, venous (saphenous) (varicose) —*see*
      Varix, leg
Incomplete —*see also* condition
   bladder, emptying R33.9
   defecation R15.0
   expansion lungs (newborn) NEC —*see*
      Atelectasis
   rotation, intestine Q43.3
Inconclusive
   diagnostic imaging due to excess body fat of
      patient R93.9
   findings on diagnostic imaging of breast NEC
      R92.8
   mammogram (due to dense breasts) R92.2
Incontinence R32
   anal sphincter R15.9
   coital N39.491
   feces R15.9
      nonorganic origin F98.1
   insensible (urinary) N39.42
   overflow N39.490
   postural (urinary) N39.492
   psychogenic F45.8
   rectal R15.9
   reflex N39.498
   stress (female) (male) N39.3
      and urge N39.46
   urethral sphincter R32
   urge N39.41
      and stress (female) (male) N39.46

Incontinence (Continued)
  urine (urinary) R32
    continuous N39.45
    due to cognitive impairment, or severe
      physical disability or immobility
      R39.81
    functional R39.81
    insensible N39.42
    mixed (stress and urge) N39.46
    nocturnal N39.44
    nonorganic origin F98.0
    overflow N39.490
    post dribbling N39.43
    postural N39.492
    reflex N39.498
    specified NEC N39.498
    stress (female) (male) N39.3
      and urge N39.46
    total N39.498
    unaware N39.42
    urge N39.41
      and stress (female) (male) N39.46
Incontinentia pigmenti Q82.3
Incoordinate, incoordination
  esophageal-pharyngeal (newborn) —see
    Dysphagia
  muscular R27.8
  uterus (action) (contractions) (complicating
    delivery) O62.4
Increase, increased
  abnormal, in development R63.8
  androgens (ovarian) E28.1
  anticoagulants (antithrombin) (anti-VIIIa)
    (anti-IXa) (anti-Xa) (anti-XIa) —see
    Circulating anticoagulants
  cold sense R20.8
  estrogen E28.0
  function
    adrenal
      cortex —see Cushing's, syndrome
      medulla E27.5
    pituitary (gland) (anterior) (lobe) E22.9
      posterior E22.2
  heat sense R20.8
  intracranial pressure (benign) G93.2
  permeability, capillaries I78.8
  pressure, intracranial G93.2
  secretion
    gastrin E16.4
    glucagon E16.3
    pancreas, endocrine E16.9
      growth hormone-releasing hormone
        E16.8
      pancreatic polypeptide E16.8
      somatostatin E16.8
      vasoactive-intestinal polypeptide
        E16.8
  sphericity, lens Q12.4
  splenic activity D73.1
  venous pressure I87.8
    portal K76.6
Increta placenta O43.22-●
Incrustation, cornea, foreign body (lead)
  (zinc) —see Foreign body, cornea
Incyclophoria H50.54
Incyclotropia —see Cyclotropia
Indeterminate sex Q56.4
India rubber skin Q82.8
Indigestion (acid) (bilious) (functional)
  K30
  catarrhal K31.89
  due to decomposed food NOS A05.9
  nervous F45.8
  psychogenic F45.8
Indirect —see condition
Induratio penis plastica N48.6
Induration, indurated
  brain G93.89
  breast (fibrous) N64.51
    puerperal, postpartum O92.29
  broad ligament N83.8

Induration, indurated (Continued)
  chancre
    anus A51.1
    congenital A50.07
    extragenital NEC A51.2
  corpora cavernosa (penis) (plastic) N48.6
  liver (chronic) K76.89
  lung (black) (chronic) (fibroid) —see also
    Fibrosis, lung J84.10
    essential brown J84.03
  penile (plastic) N48.6
  phlebitic —see Phlebitis
  skin R23.4
Inebriety (without dependence) —see Alcohol,
  intoxication
Inefficiency, kidney N28.9
Inelasticity, skin R23.4
Inequality, leg (length) (acquired) —see also
  Deformity, limb, unequal length
  congenital —see Defect, reduction, lower limb
  lower leg —see Deformity, limb, unequal
    length
Inertia
  bladder (neurogenic) N31.2
  stomach K31.89
    psychogenic F45.8
  uterus, uterine during labor O62.2
    during latent phase of labor O62.0
    primary O62.0
    secondary O62.1
  vesical (neurogenic) N31.2
Infancy, infantile, infantilism —see also
  condition
  celiac K90.0
  genitalia, genitals (after puberty) E30.0
  Herter's (nontropical sprue) K90.0
  intestinal K90.0
  Lorain E23.0
  pancreatic K86.89
  pelvis M95.5
    with disproportion (fetopelvic) O33.1
      causing obstructed labor O65.1
  pituitary E23.0
  renal N25.0
  uterus —see Infantile, genitalia
Infant(s) —see also Infancy
  excessive crying R68.11
  irritable child R68.12
  lack of care —see Neglect
  liveborn (singleton) Z38.2
    born in hospital Z38.00
      by cesarean Z38.01
    born outside hospital Z38.1
    multiple NEC Z38.8
      born in hospital Z38.68
        by cesarean Z38.69
      born outside hospital Z38.7
    quadruplet Z38.8
      born in hospital Z38.63
        by cesarean Z38.64
      born outside hospital Z38.7
    quintuplet Z38.8
      born in hospital Z38.65
        by cesarean Z38.66
      born outside hospital Z38.7
    triplet Z38.8
      born in hospital Z38.61
        by cesarean Z38.62
      born outside hospital Z38.7
    twin Z38.5
      born in hospital Z38.30
        by cesarean Z38.31
      born outside hospital Z38.4
  of diabetic mother (syndrome of) P70.1
    gestational diabetes P70.0
Infantile —see also condition
  genitalia, genitals E30.0
  os, uterine E30.0
  penis E30.0
  testis E29.1
  uterus E30.0

Infantilism —see Infancy
Infarct, infarction
  adrenal (capsule) (gland) E27.49
  appendices epiploicae —see also Infarct,
    intestine K55.069
  bowel —see also Infarct, intestine K55.069
  brain (stem) —see Infarct, cerebral
  breast N64.89
  brewer's (kidney) N28.0
  cardiac —see Infarct, myocardium
  cerebellar —see Infarct, cerebral
  cerebral (acute) (chronic) (see also Occlusion,
    artery cerebral or precerebral, with
    infarction) I63.9-●
    aborted I63.9
    cortical I63.9
    due to
      cerebral venous thrombosis,
        nonpyogenic I63.6
      embolism
        cerebral arteries I63.4-●
        precerebral arteries I63.1-●
      occlusion NEC
        cerebral arteries I63.5-●
        precerebral arteries I63.2-●
        small artery I63.81
      stenosis NEC
        cerebral arteries I63.5-●
        precerebral arteries I63.2-●
        small artery I63.81
      thrombosis
        cerebral artery I63.3-●
        precerebral artery I63.0-●
    intraoperative
      during cardiac surgery I97.810
      during other surgery I97.811
    ▶neonatal P91.82-●
    ▶perinatal (arterial ischemic) P91.82-●
    postprocedural
      following cardiac surgery I97.820
      following other surgery I97.821
    specified NEC I63.89
  colon (acute) (agnogenic) (embolic)
    (hemorrhagic) (nonocclusive)
    (nonthrombotic) (occlusive) (segmental)
    (thrombotic) (with gangrene) —see also
    Infarct, intestine K55.049
  coronary artery —see Infarct, myocardium
  embolic —see Embolism
  fallopian tube N83.8
  gallbladder K82.8
  heart —see Infarct, myocardium
  hepatic K76.3
  hypophysis (anterior lobe) E23.6
  impending (myocardium) I20.0
  intestine (acute) (agnogenic) (embolic)
    (hemorrhagic) (nonocclusive)
    (nonthrombotic) (occlusive) (thrombotic)
    (with gangrene) K55.069
    diffuse K55.062
    focal K55.061
    large K55.049
      diffuse K55.042
      focal K55.041
    small K55.029
      diffuse K55.022
      focal K55.021
  kidney N28.0
  lacunar I63.81
  liver K76.3
  lung (embolic) (thrombotic) —see Embolism,
    pulmonary
  lymph node I89.8
  mesentery, mesenteric (embolic) (thrombotic)
    (with gangrene) —see also Infarct,
    intestine K55.069
  muscle (ischemic) M62.20
    ankle M62.27-●
    foot M62.27-●
    forearm M62.23-●
    hand M62.24-●

▶ New   ⇒ Revised   ~~deleted~~ Deleted   ● Use Additional Character(s)

Infarct, infarction *(Continued)*
  muscle *(Continued)*
    lower leg M62.26-●
    pelvic region M62.25-●
    shoulder region M62.21-●
    specified site NEC M62.28
    thigh M62.25-●
    upper arm M62.22-●
  myocardium, myocardial (acute) (with stated
      duration of 4 weeks or less) I21.9
    associated with revascularization
        procedure I21.A9
    diagnosed on ECG, but presenting no
        symptoms I25.2
    due to
      demand ischemia I21.A1
      ischemic imbalance I21.A1
    healed or old I25.2
    intraoperative —*see also* Infarct,
        myocardium, associated with
        revascularization procedure
      during cardiac surgery I97.790
      during other surgery I97.791
    non-Q wave I21.4
    non-ST elevation (NSTEMI) I21.4
      subsequent I22.2
    nontransmural I21.4
    past (diagnosed on ECG or other
        investigation, but currently presenting
        no symptoms) I25.2
    postprocedural —*see also* Infarct,
        myocardium, associated with
        revascularization procedure
      following cardiac surgery —*see also* Infarct,
          myocardium, type 4 or type 5 I97.190
      following other surgery I97.191
    Q wave —*see also* Infarct, myocardium, by
        site I21.3
    secondary to
      demand ischemia I21.A1
      ischemic imbalance I21.A1
    ST elevation (STEMI) I21.3
      anterior (anteroapical) (anterolateral)
          (anteroseptal) (Q wave) (wall) I21.09
        subsequent I22.0
      inferior (diaphragmatic) (inferolateral)
          (inferoposterior) (wall) NEC I21.19
        subsequent I22.1
      inferoposterior transmural (Q wave) I21.11
      involving
        coronary artery of anterior wall NEC
            I21.09
        coronary artery of inferior wall NEC
            I21.19
        diagonal coronary artery I21.02
        left anterior descending coronary
            artery I21.02
        left circumflex coronary artery I21.21
        left main coronary artery I21.01
        oblique marginal coronary artery I21.21
        right coronary artery I21.11
      lateral (apical-lateral) (basal-lateral)
          (high) I21.29
        subsequent I22.8
      posterior (posterobasal) (posterolateral)
          (posteroseptal) (true) I21.29
        subsequent I22.8
      septal I21.29
        subsequent I22.8
      specified NEC I21.29
        subsequent I22.8
      subsequent I22.9
    subsequent (recurrent) (reinfarction) I22.9
      anterior (anteroapical) (anterolateral)
          (anteroseptal) (wall) I22.0
      diaphragmatic (wall) I22.1
      inferior (diaphragmatic) (inferolateral)
          (inferoposterior) (wall) I22.1
      lateral (apical-lateral) (basal-lateral)
          (high) I22.8
      non-ST elevation (NSTEMI) I22.2

Infarct, infarction *(Continued)*
  myocardium, myocardial *(Continued)*
    subsequent *(Continued)*
      posterior (posterobasal) (posterolateral)
          (posteroseptal) (true) I22.8
      septal I22.8
      specified NEC I22.8
      ST elevation I22.9
        anterior (anteroapical) (anterolateral)
            (anteroseptal) (wall) I22.0
        inferior (diaphragmatic) (inferolateral)
            (inferoposterior) (wall) I22.1
        specified NEC I22.8
      subendocardial I22.2
      transmural I21.3
        anterior (anteroapical) (anterolateral)
            (anteroseptal) (wall) I22.0
        diaphragmatic (wall) I22.1
        inferior (diaphragmatic) (inferolateral)
            (inferoposterior) (wall) I22.1
        lateral (apical-lateral) (basal-lateral)
            (high) I22.8
        posterior (posterobasal) (posterolateral)
            (posteroseptal) (true) I22.8
        specified NEC I22.8
      type 1 —*see also* Infarction, myocardial,
          subsequent, by site, or by ST
          elevation or non-ST elevation I22.9
      type 2 I21.A1
      type 3 I21.A9
      type 4 I21.A9
      type 5 I21.A9
    syphilitic A52.06
    transmural I21.9
      anterior (anteroapical) (anterolateral)
          (anteroseptal) (Q wave) (wall) NEC
          I21.09
      inferior (diaphragmatic) (inferolateral)
          (inferoposterior) (Q wave) (wall)
          NEC I21.19
      inferoposterior (Q wave) I21.11
      lateral (apical-lateral) (basal-lateral)
          (high) NEC I21.29
      posterior (posterobasal) (posterolateral)
          (posteroseptal) (true) NEC I21.29
      septal NEC I21.29
      specified NEC I21.29
    type 1 —*see also* Infarction, myocardial,
        by site, or by ST elevation or non-ST
        elevation I21.9
    type 2 I21.A1
    type 3 I21.A9
    type 4 (a) (b) (c) I21.A9
    type 5 I21.A9
  nontransmural I21.4
  omentum —*see also* Infarct, intestine
      K55.069
  ovary N83.8
  pancreas K86.89
  papillary muscle —*see* Infarct, myocardium
  parathyroid gland E21.4
  pituitary (gland) E23.6
  placenta O43.81-●
  prostate N42.89
  pulmonary (artery) (vein) (hemorrhagic) —
      see Embolism, pulmonary
  renal (embolic) (thrombotic) N28.0
  retina, retinal (artery) —*see* Occlusion, artery,
      retina
  spinal (cord) (acute) (embolic) (nonembolic)
      G95.11
  spleen D73.5
    embolic or thrombotic I74.8
  subendocardial (acute) (nontransmural) I21.4
  suprarenal (capsule) (gland) E27.49
  testis N50.1
  thrombotic —*see also* Thrombosis
    artery, arterial —*see* Embolism
  thyroid (gland) E07.89
  ventricle (heart) —*see* Infarct, myocardium
Infecting —*see* condition

Infection, infected, infective (opportunistic)
    B99.9
  with
    drug resistant organism —*see* Resistance
        (to), drug —*see also* specific organism
    lymphangitis —*see* Lymphangitis
    organ dysfunction (acute) R65.20
      with septic shock R65.21
  abscess (skin) - code by site under Abscess
  Absidia —*see* Mucormycosis
  Acanthamoeba —*see* Acanthamebiasis
  Acanthocheilonema (perstans) (streptocerca)
      B74.4
  accessory sinus (chronic) —*see* Sinusitis
  achorion —*see* Dermatophytosis
  Acremonium falciforme B47.0
  acromioclavicular M00.9
  Actinobacillus (actinomycetem-comitans)
      A28.8
    mallei A24.0
    muris A25.1
  Actinomadura B47.1
  Actinomyces (israelii) —*see also*
      Actinomycosis A42.9
  Actinomycetales —*see* Actinomycosis
  actinomycotic NOS —*see* Actinomycosis
  adenoid (and tonsil) J03.90
    chronic J35.02
  adenovirus NEC
    as cause of disease classified elsewhere
        B97.0
    unspecified nature or site B34.0
  aerogenes capsulatus A48.0
  aertrycke —*see* Infection, salmonella
  alimentary canal NOS —*see* Enteritis,
      infectious
  Allescheria boydii B48.2
  Alternaria B48.8
  alveolus, alveolar (process) K04.7
  Ameba, amebic (histolytica) —*see* Amebiasis
  amniotic fluid, sac or cavity O41.10-●
    chorioamnionitis O41.12-●
    placentitis O41.14-●
  amputation stump (surgical) —*see*
      Complication, amputation stump,
      infection
  Ancylostoma (duodenalis) B76.0
  Anisakiasis, Anisakis larvae B81.0
  anthrax —*see* Anthrax
  antrum (chronic) —*see* Sinusitis, maxillary
  anus, anal (papillae) (sphincter) K62.89
  arbovirus (arbor virus) A94
    specified type NEC A93.8
  artificial insemination N98.0
  Ascaris lumbricoides —*see* Ascariasis
  Ascomycetes B47.0
  Aspergillus (flavus) (fumigatus) (terreus) —
      see Aspergillosis
  atypical
    acid-fast (bacilli) —*see* Mycobacterium,
        atypical
    mycobacteria —*see* Mycobacterium, atypical
    virus A81.9
      specified type NEC A81.89
  auditory meatus (external) —*see* Otitis,
      externa, infective
  auricle (ear) —*see* Otitis, externa, infective
  axillary gland (lymph) L04.2
  Bacillus A49.9
    abortus A23.1
    anthracis —*see* Anthrax
    Ducrey's (any location) A57
    Flexner's A03.1
    Friedländer's NEC A49.8
    gas (gangrene) A48.0
    mallei A24.0
    melitensis A23.0
    paratyphoid, paratyphosus A01.4
      A A01.1
      B A01.2
      C A01.3

Infection, infected, infective (Continued)
   Bacillus (Continued)
     Shiga (-Kruse) A03.0
     suipestifer —see Infection, salmonella
     swimming pool A31.1
     typhosa A01.00
     welchii —see Gangrene, gas
   bacterial NOS A49.9
     as cause of disease classified elsewhere
       B96.89
       Bacteroides fragilis [B. fragilis] B96.6
       Clostridium perfringens [C. perfringens]
         B96.7
       Enterobacter sakazakii B96.89
       Enterococcus B95.2
       Escherichia coli [E. coli] (see also
         Escherichia coli) B96.20
       Helicobacter pylori [H.pylori] B96.81
       Hemophilus influenzae [H. influenzae]
         B96.3
       Klebsiella pneumoniae [K. pneumoniae]
         B96.1
       Mycoplasma pneumoniae [M.
         pneumoniae] B96.0
       Proteus (mirabilis) (morganii) B96.4
       Pseudomonas (aeruginosa) (mallei)
         (pseudomallei) B96.5
       Staphylococcus B95.8
        aureus (methicillin susceptible)
         (MSSA) B95.61
         methicillin resistant (MRSA) B95.62
        specified NEC B95.7
       Streptococcus B95.5
        group A B95.0
        group B B95.1
        pneumoniae B95.3
        specified NEC B95.4
        Vibrio vulnificus B96.82
     specified NEC A48.8
   Bacterium
     paratyphosum A01.4
       A A01.1
       B A01.2
       C A01.3
     typhosum A01.00
   Bacteroides NEC A49.8
     fragilis, as cause of disease classified
       elsewhere B96.6
   Balantidium coli A07.0
   Bartholin's gland N75.8
   Basidiobolus B46.8
   bile duct (common) (hepatic) —see
     Cholangitis
   bladder —see Cystitis
   Blastomyces, blastomycotic —see also
     Blastomycosis
     brasiliensis —see Paracoccidioidomycosis
     dermatitidis —see Blastomycosis
     European —see Cryptococcosis
     Loboi B48.0
     North American B40.9
     South American —see
       Paracoccidioidomycosis
   bleb, postprocedure —see Blebitis
   bone —see Osteomyelitis
   Bordetella —see Whooping cough
   Borrelia bergdorfi A69.20
   brain —see also Encephalitis G04.90
     membranes —see Meningitis
     septic G06.0
     meninges —see Meningitis, bacterial
   branchial cyst Q18.0
   breast —see Mastitis
   bronchus —see Bronchitis
   Brucella A23.9
     abortus A23.1
     canis A23.3
     melitensis A23.0
     mixed A23.8
     specified NEC A23.8
     suis A23.2

Infection, infected, infective (Continued)
   Brugia (malayi) B74.1
     timori B74.2
   bursa —see Bursitis, infective
   buttocks (skin) L08.9
   Campylobacter, intestinal A04.5
     as cause of disease classified elsewhere
       B96.81
   Candida (albicans) (tropicalis) —see
     Candidiasis
   candiru B88.8
   Capillaria (intestinal) B81.1
     hepatica B83.8
     philippinensis B81.1
   cartilage —see Disorder, cartilage, specified
     type NEC
   catheter-related bloodstream (CRBSI)
     T80.211
   cat liver fluke B66.0
   cellulitis - code by site under Cellulitis
   central line-associated T80.219
     bloodstream (CLABSI) T80.211
     specified NEC T80.218
   Cephalosporium falciforme B47.0
   cerebrospinal —see Meningitis
   cervical gland (lymph) L04.0
   cervix —see Cervicitis
   cesarean delivery wound (puerperal)
     O86.00
   cestodes —see Infestation, cestodes
   chest J22
   Chilomastix (intestinal) A07.8
   Chlamydia, chlamydial A74.9
     anus A56.3
     genitourinary tract A56.2
       lower A56.00
       specified NEC A56.19
     lymphogranuloma A55
     pharynx A56.4
     psittaci A70
     rectum A56.3
     sexually transmitted NEC A56.8
   cholera —see Cholera
   Cladosporium
     bantianum (brain abscess) B43.1
     carrionii B43.0
     castellanii B36.1
     trichoides (brain abscess) B43.1
     werneckii B36.1
   Clonorchis (sinensis) (liver) B66.1
   Clostridium NEC
     bifermentans A48.0
     botulinum (food poisoning) A05.1
       infant A48.51
       wound A48.52
     difficile
       as cause of disease classified elsewhere
         B96.89
       foodborne (disease)
        not specified as recurrent A04.72
        recurrent A04.71
       gas gangrene A48.0
       necrotizing enterocolitis
        not specified as recurrent A04.72
        recurrent A04.71
       sepsis A41.4
     gas-forming NEC A48.0
     histolyticum A48.0
     novyi, causing gas gangrene A48.0
     oedematiens A48.0
     perfringens
       as cause of disease classified elsewhere
         B96.7
       due to food A05.2
       foodborne (disease) A05.2
       gas gangrene A48.0
       sepsis A41.4
     septicum, causing gas gangrene
       A48.0
     sordellii, causing gas gangrene
       A48.0

Infection, infected, infective (Continued)
   Clostridium NEC (Continued)
     welchii
       as cause of disease classified elsewhere
         B96.7
       foodborne (disease) A05.2
       gas gangrene A48.0
       necrotizing enteritis A05.2
       sepsis A41.4
   Coccidioides (immitis) —see
     Coccidioidomycosis
   colon —see Enteritis, infectious
   colostomy K94.02
   common duct —see Cholangitis
   congenital P39.9
     Candida (albicans) P37.5
     cytomegalovirus P35.1
     hepatitis, viral P35.3
     herpes simplex P35.2
     infectious or parasitic disease P37.9
       specified NEC P37.8
     listeriosis (disseminated) P37.2
     malaria NEC P37.4
       falciparum P37.3
     Plasmodium falciparum P37.3
     poliomyelitis P35.8
     rubella P35.0
     skin P39.4
     toxoplasmosis (acute) (subacute) (chronic)
       P37.1
     tuberculosis P37.0
     urinary (tract) P39.3
     vaccinia P35.8
     virus P35.9
       specified type NEC P35.8
   Conidiobolus B46.8
  ▶coronavirus-2019 U07.1
   coronavirus NEC B34.2
     as cause of disease classified elsewhere
       B97.29
     severe acute respiratory syndrome (SARS
       associated) B97.21
   corpus luteum —see Salpingo-oophoritis
   Corynebacterium diphtheriae —see
     Diphtheria
   cotia virus B08.8
  ▶COVID-19 U07.1
   Coxiella burnetii A78
   coxsackie —see Coxsackie
   Cryptococcus neoformans —see
     Cryptococcosis
   Cryptosporidium A07.2
   Cunninghamella —see Mucormycosis
   cyst —see Cyst
   cystic duct —see also Cholecystitis K81.9
   Cysticercus cellulosae —see Cysticercosis
   cytomegalovirus, cytomegaloviral B25.9
     congenital P35.1
     maternal, maternal care for (suspected)
       damage to fetus O35.3
     mononucleosis B27.10
       with
        complication NEC B27.19
        meningitis B27.12
        polyneuropathy B27.11
   delta-agent (acute), in hepatitis B carrier
     B17.0
   dental (pulpal origin) K04.7
   Deuteromycetes B47.0
   Dicrocoelium dendriticum B66.2
   Dipetalonema (perstans) (streptocerca) B74.4
   diphtherial —see Diphtheria
   Diphyllobothrium (adult) (latum) (pacificum)
     B70.0
     larval B70.1
   Diplogonoporus (grandis) B71.8
   Dipylidium caninum B67.4
   Dirofilaria B74.8
   Dracunculus medinensis B72
   Drechslera (hawaiiensis) B43.8
   Ducrey Haemophilus (any location) A57

▶ New   ⇒ Revised   deleted Deleted   ● Use Additional Character(s)

Infection, infected, infective *(Continued)*
  due to or resulting from
    artificial insemination N98.0
    ▶Babesia
      ▶divergens (-like) strain B60.03
      ▶duncani (-type) species B60.02
      ▶microti B60.01
      ▶species
        ▶specified NEC B60.09
    central venous catheter T80.219
      bloodstream T80.211
      exit or insertion site T80.212
      localized T80.212
      port or reservoir T80.212
      specified NEC T80.218
      tunnel T80.212
    device, implant or graft —*see also*
      Complications, by site and type,
      infection or inflammation T85.79
      arterial graft NEC T82.7
      breast (implant) T85.79
      catheter NEC T85.79
        dialysis (renal) T82.7
        ▶central line T80.211
          intraperitoneal T85.71
        infusion NEC T82.7
          cranial T85.735
          intrathecal T85.735
          spinal (epidural) (subdural) T85.735
          subarachnoid T85.735
        urinary T83.518
          cystostomy T83.510
          Hopkins T83.518
          ileostomy T83.518
          nephrostomy T83.512
          specified NEC T83.518
          urethral indwelling T83.511
          urostomy T83.518
      electronic (electrode) (pulse generator)
        (stimulator)
        bone T84.7
        cardiac T82.7
        nervous system T85.738
          brain T85.731
          cranial nerve T85.732
          gastric nerve T85.732
          generator pocket T85.734
          neurostimulator generator
            T85.734
          peripheral nerve T85.732
          sacral nerve T85.732
          spinal cord T85.733
          vagal nerve T85.732
        urinary T83.590
      fixation, internal (orthopedic) NEC —
        see Complication, fixation device,
        infection
      gastrointestinal (bile duct) (esophagus)
        T85.79
        neurostimulator electrode (lead)
          T85.732
      genital NEC T83.69
      heart NEC T82.7
        valve (prosthesis) T82.6
          graft T82.7
      joint prosthesis —*see* Complication, joint
        prosthesis, infection
      ocular (corneal graft) (orbital implant)
        NEC T85.79
      orthopedic NEC T84.7
      penile (cylinder) (pump) (resevoir)
        T83.61
      specified NEC T85.79
      testicular T83.62
      urinary NEC T83.598
        ileal conduit stent T83.593
        implanted neurostimulation T83.590
        implanted sphincter T83.591
        indwelling ureteral stent T83.592
        nephroureteral stent T83.593
        specified stent NEC T83.593

Infection, infected, infective *(Continued)*
  due to or resulting from *(Continued)*
    device, implant or graft *(Continued)*
      vascular NEC T82.7
      ventricular intracranial (communicating)
        shunt T85.730
    Hickman catheter T80.219
      bloodstream T80.211
      localized T80.212
      specified NEC T80.218
    immunization or vaccination
      T88.0
    infusion, injection or transfusion
      NEC T80.29
      acute T80.22
    injury NEC - code by site under Wound,
      open
    peripherally inserted central catheter
      (PICC) T80.219
      bloodstream T80.211
      localized T80.212
      specified NEC T80.218
    portacath (port-a-cath) T80.219
      bloodstream T80.211
      localized T80.212
      specified NEC T80.218
    ▶protozoa of the order Piroplasmida NEC
      B60.09
    pulmonary artery catheter —*see* Infection,
      due to or resulting from, central
      venous catheter
    surgery T81.40
    Swan Ganz catheter —*see* Infection, due
      to or resulting from, central venous
      catheter
    triple lumen catheter T80.219
      bloodstream T80.211
      localized T80.212
      specified NEC T80.218
    umbilical venous catheter T80.219
      bloodstream T80.211
      localized T80.212
      specified NEC T80.218
  during labor NEC O75.3
  ear (middle) —*see also* Otitis media
    external —*see* Otitis, externa, infective
    inner —*see* subcategory H83.0
  Eberthella typhosa A01.00
  Echinococcus —*see* Echinococcus
  echovirus
    as cause of disease classified elsewhere
      B97.12
    unspecified nature or site B34.1
  endocardium I33.0
  endocervix —*see* Cervicitis
  Entamoeba —*see* Amebiasis
  enteric —*see* Enteritis, infectious
  Enterobacter sakazakii B96.89
  Enterobius vermicularis B80
  enterostomy K94.12
  enterovirus B34.1
    as cause of disease classified elsewhere
      B97.10
      coxsackievirus B97.11
      echovirus B97.12
      specified NEC B97.19
  Entomophthora B46.8
  Epidermophyton —*see* Dermatophytosis
  epididymis —*see* Epididymitis
  episiotomy (puerperal) O86.09
  Erysipelothrix (insidiosa) (rhusiopathiae) —
    see Erysipeloid
  erythema infectiosum B08.3
  Escherichia (E.) coli NEC A49.8
    as cause of disease classified elsewhere —
      see also Escherichia coli B96.20
    congenital P39.8
      sepsis P36.4
    generalized A41.51
    intestinal —*see* Enteritis, infectious, due to,
      Escherichia coli

Infection, infected, infective *(Continued)*
  ethmoidal (chronic) (sinus) —*see* Sinusitis,
    ethmoidal
  eustachian tube (ear) —*see* Salpingitis,
    eustachian
  external auditory canal (meatus) NEC —*see*
    Otitis, externa, infective
  eye (purulent) —*see* Endophthalmitis, purulent
  eyelid —*see* Inflammation, eyelid
  fallopian tube —*see* Salpingo-oophoritis
  Fasciola (gigantica) (hepatica) (indica) B66.3
  Fasciolopsis (buski) B66.5
  filarial —*see* Infestation, filarial
  finger (skin) L08.9
    nail L03.01-●
      fungus B35.1
  fish tapeworm B70.0
    larval B70.1
  flagellate, intestinal A07.9
  fluke —*see* Infestation, fluke
  focal
    teeth (pulpal origin) K04.7
    tonsils J35.01
  Fonsecaea (compactum) (pedrosoi) B43.0
  food —*see* Intoxication, foodborne
  foot (skin) L08.9
    dermatophytic fungus B35.3
  Francisella tularensis —*see* Tularemia
  frontal (sinus) (chronic) —*see* Sinusitis, frontal
  fungus NOS B49
    beard B35.0
    dermatophytic —*see* Dermatophytosis
    foot B35.3
    groin B35.6
    hand B35.2
    nail B35.1
    pathogenic to compromised host only B48.8
    perianal (area) B35.6
    scalp B35.0
    skin B36.9
      foot B35.3
      hand B35.2
      toenails B35.1
  Fusarium B48.8
  gallbladder —*see* Cholecystitis
  gas bacillus —*see* Gangrene, gas
  gastrointestinal —*see* Enteritis, infectious
  generalized NEC —*see* Sepsis
  generator pocket, implanted electronic
    neurostimulator T85.734
  genital organ or tract
    female —*see* Disease, pelvis, inflammatory
    male N49.9
      multiple sites N49.8
      specified NEC N49.8
  Ghon tubercle, primary A15.7
  Giardia lamblia A07.1
  gingiva (chronic) K05.10
    acute K05.00
      nonplaque induced K05.01
      plaque induced K05.00
    nonplaque induced K05.11
    plaque induced K05.10
  glanders A24.0
  glenosporopsis B48.0
  Gnathostoma (spinigerum) B83.1
  Gongylonema B83.8
  gonococcal —*see* Gonococcus
  gram-negative bacilli NOS A49.9
  guinea worm B72
  gum (chronic) K05.10
    acute K05.00
      nonplaque induced K05.01
      plaque induced K05.00
    nonplaque induced K05.11
    plaque induced K05.10
  Haemophilus —*see* Infection, Hemophilus
  heart —*see* Carditis
  Helicobacter pylori A04.8
    as cause of disease classified elsewhere
      B96.81

Infection, infected, infective *(Continued)*
  helminths B83.9
    intestinal B82.0
      mixed (types classifiable to more than
        one of the titles B65.0-B81.3 and
        B81.8) B81.4
      specified type NEC B81.8
    specified type NEC B83.8
  Hemophilus
    aegyptius, systemic A48.4
    ducrey (any location) A57
    generalized A41.3
    influenzae NEC A49.2
      as cause of disease classified elsewhere
        B96.3
  herpes (simplex) —*see also* Herpes
    congenital P35.2
    disseminated B00.7
    zoster B02.9
  herpesvirus, herpesviral —*see* Herpes
  Heterophyes (heterophyes) B66.8
  hip (joint) NEC M00.9
    due to internal joint prosthesis
      left T84.52
      right T84.51
    skin NEC L08.9
  Histoplasma —*see* Histoplasmosis
    American B39.4
    capsulatum B39.4
  hookworm B76.9
  human
    papilloma virus A63.0
    T-cell lymphotropic virus type-1 (HTLV-1)
      B33.3
  hydrocele N43.0
  Hymenolepis B71.0
  hypopharynx —*see* Pharyngitis
  inguinal (lymph) glands L04.1
    due to soft chancre A57
  intervertebral disc, pyogenic M46.30
    cervical region M46.32
    cervicothoracic region M46.33
    lumbar region M46.36
    lumbosacral region M46.37
    multiple sites M46.39
    occipito-atlanto-axial region M46.31
    sacrococcygeal region M46.38
    thoracic region M46.34
    thoracolumbar region M46.35
  intestine, intestinal —*see* Enteritis, infectious
    specified NEC A08.8
  intra-amniotic affecting newborn NEC P39.2
▶ intrauterine inflammation O41.12-●
  Isospora belli or hominis A07.3
  Japanese B encephalitis A83.0
  jaw (bone) (lower) (upper) M27.2
  joint NEC M00.9
    due to internal joint prosthesis T84.50
  kidney (cortex) (hematogenous) N15.9
    with calculus N20.0
      with hydronephrosis N13.6
    following ectopic gestation O08.83
    pelvis and ureter (cystic) N28.85
    puerperal (postpartum) O86.21
    specified NEC N15.8
  Klebsiella (K.) pneumoniae NEC A49.8
    as cause of disease classified elsewhere
      B96.1
  knee (joint) NEC M00.9
    due to internal joint prosthesis
      left T84.54
      right T84.53
    joint M00.9
    skin L08.9
  Koch's —*see* Tuberculosis
  labia (majora) (minora) (acute) —*see* Vulvitis
  lacrimal
    gland —*see* Dacryoadenitis
    passages (duct) (sac) —*see* Inflammation,
      lacrimal, passages
  lancet fluke B66.2

Infection, infected, infective *(Continued)*
  larynx NEC J38.7
  leg (skin) NOS L08.9
  Legionella pneumophila A48.1
    nonpneumonic A48.2
  Leishmania —*see also* Leishmaniasis
    aethiopica B55.1
    braziliensis B55.2
    chagasi B55.0
    donovani B55.0
    infantum B55.0
    major B55.1
    mexicana B55.1
    tropica B55.1
  lentivirus, as cause of disease classified
    elsewhere B97.31
  Leptosphaeria senegalensis B47.0
  Leptospira interrogans A27.9
    autumnalis A27.89
    canicola A27.89
    hebdomadis A27.89
    icterohaemorrhagiae A27.0
    pomona A27.89
    specified type NEC A27.89
  leptospirochetal NEC —*see* Leptospirosis
  Listeria monocytogenes —*see also* Listeriosis
    congenital P37.2
  Loa loa B74.3
    with conjunctival infestation B74.3
    eyelid B74.3
  Loboa loboi B48.0
  local, skin (staphylococcal) (streptococcal)
    L08.9
    abscess - code by site under Abscess
    cellulitis - code by site under Cellulitis
    specified NEC L08.89
    ulcer —*see* Ulcer, skin
  Loefflerella mallei A24.0
  lung —*see also* Pneumonia J18.9
    atypical Mycobacterium A31.0
    spirochetal A69.8
    tuberculous —*see* Tuberculosis, pulmonary
    virus —*see* Pneumonia, viral
  lymph gland —*see also* Lymphadenitis, acute
    mesenteric I88.0
  lymphoid tissue, base of tongue or posterior
    pharynx, NEC (chronic) J35.03
  Madurella (grisea) (mycetomii) B47.0
  major
    following ectopic or molar pregnancy
      O08.0
    puerperal, postpartum, childbirth O85
  Malassezia furfur B36.0
  Malleomyces
    mallei A24.0
    pseudomallei (whitmori) —*see* Melioidosis
  mammary gland N61.0
  Mansonella (ozzardi) (perstans) (streptocerca)
    B74.4
  mastoid —*see* Mastoiditis
  maxilla, maxillary M27.2
    sinus (chronic) —*see* Sinusitis, maxillary
  mediastinum J98.51
  Medina (worm) B72
  meibomian cyst or gland —*see* Hordeolum
  meninges —*see* Meningitis, bacterial
  meningococcal —*see also* condition A39.9
    adrenals A39.1
    brain A39.81
    cerebrospinal A39.0
    conjunctiva A39.89
    endocardium A39.51
    heart A39.50
      endocardium A39.51
      myocardium A39.52
      pericardium A39.53
    joint A39.83
    meninges A39.0
    meningococcemia A39.4
      acute A39.2
      chronic A39.3

Infection, infected, infective *(Continued)*
  meningococcal *(Continued)*
    myocardium A39.52
    pericardium A39.53
    retrobulbar neuritis A39.82
    specified site NEC A39.89
  mesenteric lymph nodes or glands NEC
    I88.0
  Metagonimus B66.8
  metatarsophalangeal M00.9
  methicillin
    resistant Staphylococcus aureus (MRSA)
      A49.02
    susceptible Staphylococcus aureus (MSSA)
      A49.01
  Microsporum, microsporic —*see*
    Dermatophytosis
  mixed flora (bacterial) NEC A49.8
  Monilia —*see* Candidiasis
  Monosporium apiospermum B48.2
  mouth, parasitic B37.0
  Mucor —*see* Mucormycosis
  muscle NEC —*see* Myositis, infective
  mycelium NOS B49
  mycetoma B47.9
    actinomycotic NEC B47.1
    mycotic NEC B47.0
  Mycobacterium, mycobacterial —*see*
    Mycobacterium
  Mycoplasma NEC A49.3
    pneumoniae, as cause of disease classified
      elsewhere B96.0
  mycotic NOS B49
    pathogenic to compromised host only
      B48.8
    skin NOS B36.9
  myocardium NEC I40.0
  nail (chronic)
    with lymphangitis —*see* Lymphangitis,
      acute, digit
    finger L03.01-●
      fungus B35.1
    ingrowing L60.0
    toe L03.03-●
      fungus B35.1
  nasal sinus (chronic) —*see* Sinusitis
  nasopharynx —*see* Nasopharyngitis
  navel L08.82
  Necator americanus B76.1
  Neisseria —*see* Gonococcus
  Neotestudina rosatii B47.0
  newborn P39.9
    intra-amniotic NEC P39.2
    skin P39.4
    specified type NEC P39.8
  nipple N61.0
    associated with
      lactation O91.03
      pregnancy O91.01-●
      puerperium O91.02
  Nocardia —*see* Nocardiosis
  obstetrical surgical wound (puerperal)
    O86.00
    incisional site
      deep O86.02
      superficial O86.01
    organ and space site O86.03
    surgical site specified NEC O86.09
  Oesophagostomum (apiostomum)
    B81.8
  Oestrus ovis —*see* Myiasis
  Oidium albicans B37.9
  Onchocerca (volvulus) —*see* Onchocerciasis -
    oncovirus, as cause of disease classified
      elsewhere B97.32
  operation wound T81.49
  Opisthorchis (felineus) (viverrini) B66.0
  orbit, orbital —*see* Inflammation, orbit
  orthopoxvirus NEC B08.09
  ovary —*see* Salpingo-oophoritis
  Oxyuris vermicularis B80

▶ New   ⇒ Revised   ~~deleted~~ Deleted   ● Use Additional Character(s)

Infection, infected, infective *(Continued)*
  pancreas (acute) —*see* Pancreatitis, acute
    abscess —*see* Pancreatitis, acute
    specified NEC —*see also* Pancreatitis, acute
      K85.80
  papillomavirus, as cause of disease classified
    elsewhere B97.7
  papovavirus NEC B34.4
  Paracoccidioides brasiliensis —*see*
    Paracoccidioidomycosis
  Paragonimus (westermani) B66.4
  parainfluenza virus B34.8
  parameningococcus NOS A39.9
  parapoxvirus B08.60
    specified NEC B08.69
  parasitic B89
  Parastrongylus
    cantonensis B83.2
    costaricensis B81.3
    paratyphoid A01.4
      Type A A01.1
      Type B A01.2
      Type C A01.3
  paraurethral ducts N34.2
  parotid gland —*see* Sialoadenitis
  parvovirus NEC B34.3
    as cause of disease classified elsewhere
      B97.6
  Pasteurella NEC A28.0
    multocida A28.0
    pestis —*see* Plague
    pseudotuberculosis A28.0
    septica (cat bite) (dog bite) A28.0
    tularensis —*see* Tularemia
  pelvic, female —*see* Disease, pelvis,
    inflammatory
  Penicillium (marneffei) B48.4
  penis (glans) (retention) NEC N48.29
  periapical K04.5
  peridental, periodontal K05.20
    generalized —*see* Periodontitis, aggressive,
      generalized
    localized —*see* Periodontitis, aggressive,
      localized
  perinatal period P39.9
    specified type NEC P39.8
  perineal repair (puerperal) O86.09
  periorbital —*see* Inflammation, orbit
  perirectal K62.89
  perirenal —*see* Infection, kidney
  peritoneal —*see* Peritonitis
  periureteral N28.89
  Petriellidium boydii B48.2
  pharynx —*see also* Pharyngitis
    coxsackievirus B08.5
    posterior, lymphoid (chronic) J35.03
  Phialophora
    gougerotii (subcutaneous abscess or cyst)
      B43.2
    jeanselmei (subcutaneous abscess or cyst)
      B43.2
    verrucosa (skin) B43.0
  Piedraia hortae B36.3
  pinta A67.9
    intermediate A67.1
    late A67.2
    mixed A67.3
    primary A67.0
  pinworm B80
  pityrosporum furfur B36.0
  pleuro-pneumonia-like organism (PPLO)
    NEC A49.3
    as cause of disease classified elsewhere
      B96.0
  pneumococcus, pneumococcal NEC A49.1
    as cause of disease classified elsewhere
      B95.3
    generalized (purulent) A40.3
      with pneumonia J13
  Pneumocystis carinii (pneumonia) B59
  Pneumocystis jiroveci (pneumonia) B59

Infection, infected, infective *(Continued)*
  port or reservoir T80.212
  postoperative T81.40
  postoperative wound T81.49
  postprocedural T81.40
    surgical site
      deep incisional T81.42
      organ and space T81.43
      specified NEC T81.49
      superficial incisional T81.41
  postvaccinal T88.0
  prepuce NEC N47.7
    with penile inflammation N47.6
  prion —*see* Disease, prion, central nervous
    system
  prostate (capsule) —*see* Prostatitis
  Proteus (mirabilis) (morganii) (vulgaris) NEC
    A49.8
    as cause of disease classified elsewhere
      B96.4
  protozoal NEC B64
    intestinal A07.9
      specified NEC A07.8
    specified NEC B60.8
  Pseudoallescheria boydii B48.2
  Pseudomonas NEC A49.8
    as cause of disease classified elsewhere
      B96.5
    mallei A24.0
    pneumonia J15.1
    pseudomallei —*see* Melioidosis
  puerperal O86.4
    genitourinary tract NEC O86.89
    major or generalized O85
    minor O86.4
    specified NEC O86.89
  pulmonary —*see* Infection, lung
  purulent —*see* Abscess
  Pyrenochaeta romeroi B47.0
  Q fever A78
  rectum (sphincter) K62.89
  renal —*see also* Infection, kidney
    pelvis and ureter (cystic) N28.85
  reovirus, as cause of disease classified
    elsewhere B97.5
  respiratory (tract) NEC J98.8
    acute J22
    chronic J98.8
    influenzal (upper) (acute) —*see* Influenza,
      with, respiratory manifestations
      NEC
    lower (acute) J22
      chronic —*see* Bronchitis, chronic
    rhinovirus J00
    syncytial virus (RSV) —*see* Infection, virus,
      respiratory syncytial (RSV)
    upper (acute) NOS J06.9
      chronic J39.8
      streptococcal J06.9
      viral NOS J06.9
        due to respiratory syncytial virus
          (RSV) J06.9 *[B97.1]*
  resulting from
    presence of internal prosthesis, implant,
      graft —*see* Complications, by site and
      type, infection
  retortamoniasis A07.8
  retroperitoneal NEC K68.9
  retrovirus B33.3
    as cause of disease classified elsewhere
      B97.30
    human
      immunodeficiency, type 2 (HIV 2)
        B97.35
      T-cell lymphotropic
        type I (HTLV-I) B97.33
        type II (HTLV-II) B97.34
    lentivirus B97.31
    oncovirus B97.32
    specified NEC B97.39
  Rhinosporidium (seeberi) B48.1

Infection, infected, infective *(Continued)*
  rhinovirus
    as cause of disease classified elsewhere
      B97.89
    unspecified nature or site B34.8
  Rhizopus —*see* Mucormycosis
  rickettsial NOS A79.9
  roundworm (large) NEC B82.0
    Ascariasis —*see also* Ascariasis B77.9
  rubella —*see* Rubella
  Saccharomyces —*see* Candidiasis
  salivary duct or gland (any) —*see*
    Sialoadenitis
  Salmonella (aertrycke) (arizonae)
    (callinarum) (cholerae-suis) (enteritidis)
    (suipestifer) (typhimurium) A02.9
    with
      (gastro) enteritis A02.0
      sepsis A02.1
      specified manifestation NEC
        A02.8
    due to food (poisoning) A02.9
    hirschfeldii A01.3
    localized A02.20
      arthritis A02.23
      meningitis A02.21
      osteomyelitis A02.24
      pneumonia A02.22
      pyelonephritis A02.25
      specified NEC A02.29
    paratyphi A01.4
      A A01.1
      B A01.2
      C A01.3
    schottmuelleri A01.2
    typhi, typhosa —*see* Typhoid
  Sarcocystis A07.8
  scabies B86
  Schistosoma —*see* Infestation, Schistosoma
  scrotum (acute) NEC N49.2
  seminal vesicle —*see* Vesiculitis
  septic
    localized, skin —*see* Abscess
  sheep liver fluke B66.3
  Shigella A03.9
    boydii A03.2
    dysenteriae A03.0
    flexneri A03.1
    group
      A A03.0
      B A03.1
      C A03.2
      D A03.3
    Schmitz (-Stutzer) A03.0
    schmitzii A03.0
    shigae A03.0
    sonnei A03.3
    specified NEC A03.8
  shoulder (joint) NEC M00.9
    due to internal joint prosthesis
      T84.59
    skin NEC L08.9
  sinus (accessory) (chronic) (nasal) —*see also*
    Sinusitis
    pilonidal —*see* Sinus, pilonidal
    skin NEC L08.89
  Skene's duct or gland —*see* Urethritis
  skin (local) (staphylococcal) (streptococcal)
    L08.9
    abscess - code by site under Abscess
    cellulitis - code by site under Cellulitis
    due to fungus B36.9
      specified type NEC B36.8
    mycotic B36.9
      specified type NEC B36.8
    newborn P39.4
    ulcer —*see* Ulcer, skin
  slow virus A81.9
    specified NEC A81.89
  Sparganum (mansoni) (proliferum) (baxteri)
    B70.1

Infection, infected, infective (Continued)
  specific —*see also* Syphilis
    to perinatal period —*see* Infection,
      congenital
  specified NEC B99.8
  spermatic cord NEC N49.1
  sphenoidal (sinus) —*see* Sinusitis,
    sphenoidal
  spinal cord NOS —*see also* Myelitis G04.91
    abscess G06.1
    meninges —*see* Meningitis
    streptococcal G04.89
  Spirillum A25.0
  spirochetal NOS A69.9
    lung A69.8
    specified NEC A69.8
  Spirometra larvae B70.1
  spleen D73.89
  Sporotrichum, Sporothrix (schenckii) —*see*
    Sporotrichosis
  staphylococcal, unspecified site
    aureus (methicillin susceptible) (MSSA)
      A49.01
      methicillin resistant (MRSA) A49.02
    as cause of disease classified elsewhere
      B95.8
      aureus (methicillin susceptible) (MSSA)
        B95.61
        methicillin resistant (MRSA)
          B95.62
      specified NEC B95.7
    food poisoning A05.0
    generalized (purulent) A41.2
    pneumonia —*see* Pneumonia,
      staphylococcal
  Stellantchasmus falcatus B66.8
  streptobacillus moniliformis A25.1
  streptococcal NEC A49.1
    as cause of disease classified elsewhere
      B95.5
    B genitourinary complicating
      childbirth O98.82
      pregnancy O98.81-●
      puerperium O98.83
    congenital
      sepsis P36.10
        group B P36.0
        specified NEC P36.19
    generalized (purulent) A40.9
  Streptomyces B47.1
  Strongyloides (stercoralis) —*see*
    Strongyloidiasis
  stump (amputation) (surgical) —*see*
    Complication, amputation stump,
    infection
  subcutaneous tissue, local L08.9
  suipestifer —*see* Infection, salmonella
  swimming pool bacillus A31.1
  Taenia —*see* Infestation, Taenia
  Taeniarhynchus saginatus B68.1
  tapeworm —*see* Infestation,
    tapeworm
  tendon (sheath) —*see* Tenosynovitis, infective
    NEC
  Ternidens diminutus B81.8
  testis —*see* Orchitis
  threadworm B80
  throat —*see* Pharyngitis
  thyroglossal duct K14.8
  toe (skin) L08.9
    cellulitis L03.03-●
      fungus B35.1
    nail L03.03-●
      fungus B35.1
  tongue NEC K14.0
    parasitic B37.0
  tonsil (and adenoid) (faucial) (lingual)
    (pharyngeal) —*see* Tonsillitis
  tooth, teeth K04.7
    irreversible K04.02
    periapical K04.7

Infection, infected, infective (Continued)
  tooth, teeth (Continued)
    peridental, periodontal K05.20
      generalized —*see* Periodontitis,
        aggressive, generalized
      localized —*see* Periodontitis, aggressive,
        localized
    pulp K04.01
      irreversible K04.02
      reversible K04.01
  TORCH —*see* Infection, congenital
    without active infection P00.2
  Torula histolytica —*see* Cryptococcosis
  Toxocara (canis) (cati) (felis) B83.0
  Toxoplasma gondii —*see* Toxoplasma
  trachea, chronic J42
  trematode NEC —*see* Infestation, fluke
  trench fever A79.0
  Treponema pallidum —*see* Syphilis
  Trichinella (spiralis) B75
  Trichomonas A59.9
    cervix A59.09
    intestine A07.8
    prostate A59.02
    specified site NEC A59.8
    urethra A59.03
    urogenitalis A59.00
    vagina A59.01
    vulva A59.01
  Trichophyton, trichophytic —*see*
    Dermatophytosis
  Trichosporon (beigelii) cutaneum B36.2
  Trichostrongylus B81.2
  Trichuris (trichiura) B79
  Trombicula (irritans) B88.0
  Trypanosoma
    brucei
      gambiense B56.0
      rhodesiense B56.1
    cruzi —*see* Chagas' disease
  tubal —*see* Salpingo-oophoritis
  tuberculous
    latent (LTBI) Z22.7
    NEC —*see* Tuberculosis
  tubo-ovarian —*see* Salpingo-oophoritis
  tunica vaginalis N49.1
  tunnel T80.212
  tympanic membrane NEC —*see* Myringitis
  typhoid (abortive) (ambulant) (bacillus) —*see*
    Typhoid
  typhus A75.9
    flea-borne A75.2
    mite-borne A75.3
    recrudescent A75.1
    tick-borne A77.9
      African A77.1
      North Asian A77.2
  umbilicus L08.82
  ureter —*see* Ureteritis
  urethra —*see* Urethritis
  urinary (tract) N39.0
    bladder —*see* Cystitis
    complicating
      pregnancy O23.4-●
        specified type NEC O23.3-●
    kidney —*see* Infection, kidney
    newborn P39.3
    puerperal (postpartum) O86.20
    tuberculous A18.13
    urethra —*see* Urethritis
  uterus, uterine —*see* Endometritis
  vaccination T88.0
  vaccinia not from vaccination B08.011
  vagina (acute) —*see* Vaginitis
  varicella B01.9
  varicose veins —*see* Varix
  vas deferens NEC N49.1
  vesical —*see* Cystitis
  Vibrio
    cholerae A00.0
      El Tor A00.1

Infection, infected, infective (Continued)
  Vibrio (Continued)
    parahaemolyticus (food poisoning)
      A05.3
    vulnificus
      as cause of disease classified elsewhere
        B96.82
      foodborne intoxication A05.5
  Vincent's (gum) (mouth) (tonsil) A69.1
  virus, viral NOS B34.9
    adenovirus
      as cause of disease classified elsewhere
        B97.0
      unspecified nature or site B34.0
    arborvirus, arbovirus arthropod-borne
      A94
    as cause of disease classified elsewhere
      B97.89
      adenovirus B97.0
      coronavirus B97.29
        SARS-associated B97.21
      coxsackievirus B97.11
      echovirus B97.12
      enterovirus B97.10
        coxsackievirus B97.11
        echovirus B97.12
        specified NEC B97.19
      human
        immunodeficiency, type 2 (HIV 2)
          B97.35
        metapneumovirus B97.81
        T-cell lymphotropic,
          type I (HTLV-I) B97.33
          type II (HTLV-II) B97.34
      papillomavirus B97.7
      parvovirus B97.6
      reovirus B97.5
      respiratory syncytial (RSV) —*see*
        Infection virus, respiratory
        syncytial (RSV)
      retrovirus B97.30
        human
          immunodeficiency, type 2 (HIV 2)
            B97.35
          T-cell lymphotropic,
            type I (HTLV-I) B97.33
            type II (HTLV-II) B97.34
        lentivirus B97.31
        oncovirus B97.32
        specified NEC B97.39
      specified NEC B97.89
    central nervous system A89
      atypical A81.9
        specified NEC A81.89
      enterovirus NEC A88.8
        meningitis A87.0
      slow virus A81.9
        specified NEC A81.89
      specified NEC A88.8
    chest J98.8
    cotia B08.8
  ▶COVID-19 U07.1
    coxsackie —*see also* Infection, coxsackie
      B34.1
    as cause of disease classified elsewhere
      B97.11
    ECHO
      as cause of disease classified elsewhere
        B97.12
      unspecified nature or site B34.1
    encephalitis, tick-borne A84.9
    enterovirus, as cause of disease classified
      elsewhere B97.10
      coxsackievirus B97.11
      echovirus B97.12
      specified NEC B97.19
    exanthem NOS B09
    human metapneumovirus as cause of
      disease classified elsewhere B97.81
    human papilloma as cause of disease
      classified elsewhere B97.7

▶ New   ➡ Revised   ~~deleted~~ Deleted   ● Use Additional Character(s)

Infection, infected, infective (Continued)
  virus, viral NOS (Continued)
    intestine —see Enteritis, viral
    respiratory syncytial (RSV) —see Infection,
      virus, respiratory syncytial (RSV)
      bronchiolitis J21.0
      bronchitis J20.5
      bronchopneumonia J12.1
      otitis media H65.-● [B97.4]
      pneumonia J12.1
      upper respiratory infection J06.9
        [B97.4]
    rhinovirus
      as cause of disease classified elsewhere
        B97.89
      unspecified nature or site B34.8
    slow A81.9
      specified NEC A81.89
    specified type NEC B33.8
      as cause of disease classified elsewhere
        B97.89
      unspecified nature or site B34.8
    unspecified nature or site B34.9
    West Nile —see Virus, West Nile
  vulva (acute) —see Vulvitis
  West Nile —see Virus, West Nile
  whipworm B79
  worms B83.9
    specified type NEC B83.8
  Wuchereria (bancrofti) B74.0
    malayi B74.1
  yatapoxvirus B08.70
    specified NEC B08.79
  yeast (see also Candidiasis) B37.9
  yellow fever —see Fever, yellow
  Yersinia
    enterocolitica (intestinal) A04.6
    pestis —see Plague
    pseudotuberculosis A28.2
  Zeis' gland —see Hordeolum
  Zika virus A92.5
    congenital P35.4
  zoonotic bacterial NOS A28.9
  Zopfia senegalensis B47.0
Infective, infectious —see condition
Infertility
  female N97.9
    age-related N97.8
    associated with
      anovulation N97.0
      cervical (mucus) disease or anomaly
        N88.3
      congenital anomaly
        cervix N88.3
        fallopian tube N97.1
        uterus N97.2
        vagina N97.8
      dysmucorrhea N88.3
      fallopian tube disease or anomaly
        N97.1
      pituitary-hypothalamic origin
        E23.0
      specified origin NEC N97.8
      Stein-Leventhal syndrome E28.2
      uterine disease or anomaly N97.2
      vaginal disease or anomaly N97.8
    due to
      cervical anomaly N88.3
      fallopian tube anomaly N97.1
      ovarian failure E28.39
      Stein-Leventhal syndrome
        E28.2
      uterine anomaly N97.2
      vaginal anomaly N97.8
    nonimplantation N97.2
    origin
      cervical N88.3
      tubal (block) (occlusion) (stenosis)
        N97.1
      uterine N97.2
      vaginal N97.8

Infertility (Continued)
  male N46.9
    azoospermia N46.01
      extratesticular cause N46.029
        drug therapy N46.021
        efferent duct obstruction N46.023
        infection N46.022
        radiation N46.024
        specified cause NEC N46.029
        systemic disease N46.025
    oligospermia N46.11
      extratesticular cause N46.129
        drug therapy N46.121
        efferent duct obstruction N46.123
        infection N46.122
        radiation N46.124
        specified cause NEC N46.129
        systemic disease N46.125
    specified type NEC N46.8
Infestation B88.9
  Acanthocheilonema (perstans) (streptocerca)
    B74.4
  Acariasis B88.0
    demodex folliculorum B88.0
    sarcoptes scabiei B86
    trombiculae B88.0
  Agamofilaria streptocerca B74.4
  Ancylostoma, ankylostoma (braziliense)
    (caninum) (ceylanicum) (duodenale)
    B76.0
    americanum B76.1
    new world B76.1
  Anisakis larvae, anisakiasis B81.0
  arthropod NEC B88.2
  Ascaris lumbricoides —see Ascariasis
  Balantidium coli A07.0
  beef tapeworm B68.1
  Bothriocephalus (latus) B70.0
    larval B70.1
  broad tapeworm B70.0
    larval B70.1
  Brugia (malayi) B74.1
    timori B74.2
  candiru B88.8
  Capillaria
    hepatica B83.8
    philippinensis B81.1
  cat liver fluke B66.0
  cestodes B71.9
    diphyllobothrium —see Infestation,
      diphyllobothrium
    dipylidiasis B71.1
    hymenolepiasis B71.0
    specified type NEC B71.8
  chigger B88.0
  chigo, chigoe B88.1
  Clonorchis (sinensis) (liver) B66.1
  coccidial A07.3
  crab-lice B85.3
  Cysticercus cellulosae —see Cysticercosis
  Demodex (folliculorum) B88.0
  Dermanyssus gallinae B88.0
  Dermatobia (hominis) —see Myiasis
  Dibothriocephalus (latus) B70.0
    larval B70.1
  Dicrocoelium dendriticum B66.2
  Diphyllobothrium (adult) (latum) (intestinal)
    (pacificum) B70.0
    larval B70.1
  Diplogonoporus (grandis) B71.8
  Dipylidium caninum B67.4
  Distoma hepaticum B66.3
  dog tapeworm B67.4
  Dracunculus medinensis B72
  dragon worm B72
  dwarf tapeworm B71.0
  Echinococcus —see Echinococcus
  Echinostomum ilocanum B66.8
  Entamoeba (histolytica) —see Infection,
    Ameba
  Enterobius vermicularis B80

Infestation (Continued)
  eyelid
    in (due to)
      leishmaniasis B55.1
      loiasis B74.3
      onchocerciasis B73.09
      phthiriasis B85.3
    parasitic NOS B89
  eyeworm B74.3
  Fasciola (gigantica) (hepatica) (indica) B66.3
  Fasciolopsis (buski) (intestine) B66.5
  filarial B74.9
    bancroftian B74.0
    conjunctiva B74.9
    due to
      Acanthocheilonema (perstans)
        (streptocerca) B74.4
      Brugia (malayi) B74.1
        timori B74.2
      Dracunculus medinensis B72
      guinea worm B72
      loa loa B74.3
      Mansonella (ozzardi) (perstans)
        (streptocerca) B74.4
      Onchocerca volvulus B73.00
        eye B73.00
        eyelid B73.09
      Wuchereria (bancrofti) B74.0
    Malayan B74.1
    ozzardi B74.4
    specified type NEC B74.8
  fish tapeworm B70.0
    larval B70.1
  fluke B66.9
    blood NOS —see Schistosomiasis
    cat liver B66.0
    intestinal B66.5
    lancet B66.2
    liver (sheep) B66.3
      cat B66.0
      Chinese B66.1
      due to clonorchiasis B66.1
      oriental B66.1
    lung (oriental) B66.4
    sheep liver B66.3
    specified type NEC B66.8
  fly larvae —see Myiasis
  Gasterophilus (intestinalis) —see Myiasis
  Gastrodiscoides hominis B66.8
  Giardia lamblia A07.1
  Gnathostoma (spinigerum) B83.1
  Gongylonema B83.8
  guinea worm B72
  helminth B83.9
    angiostrongyliasis B83.2
      intestinal B81.3
    gnathostomiasis B83.1
    hirudiniasis, internal B83.4
    intestinal B82.0
      angiostrongyliasis B81.3
      anisakiasis B81.0
      ascariasis —see Ascariasis
      capillariasis B81.1
      cysticercosis —see Cysticercosis
      diphyllobothriasis —see Infestation,
        diphyllobothriasis
      dracunculiasis B72
      echinococcus —see Echinococcosis
      enterobiasis B80
      filariasis —see Infestation, filarial
      fluke —see Infestation, fluke
      hookworm —see Infestation, hookworm
      mixed (types classifiable to more than
        one of the titles B65.0-B81.3 and
        B81.8) B81.4
      onchocerciasis —see Onchocerciasis
      schistosomiasis —see Infestation,
        schistosoma
      specified
        cestode NEC —see Infestation, cestode
        type NEC B81.8

Infestation (Continued)

helminth (Continued)

intestinal (Continued)

strongyloidiasis —see Strongyloidiasis

taenia —see Infestation, taenia

trichinellosis B75

trichostrongyliasis B81.2

trichuriasis B79

specified type NEC B83.8

syngamiasis B83.3

visceral larva migrans B83.0

Heterophyes (heterophyes) B66.8

hookworm B76.9

ancylostomiasis B76.0

necatoriasis B76.1

specified type NEC B76.8

Hymenolepis (diminuta) (nana) B71.0

intestinal NEC B82.9

leeches (aquatic) (land) —see Hirudiniasis

Leishmania —see Leishmaniasis

lice, louse —see Infestation, Pediculus

Linguatula B88.8

Liponyssoides sanguineus B88.0

Loa loa B74.3

conjunctival B74.3

eyelid B74.3

louse —see Infestation, Pediculus

maggots —see Myiasis

Mansonella (ozzardi) (perstans) (streptocerca) B74.4

Medina (worm) B72

Metagonimus (yokogawai) B66.8

microfilaria streptocerca —see Onchocerciasis

eye B73.00

eyelid B73.09

mites B88.9

scabic B86

Monilia (albicans) —see Candidiasis

mouth B37.0

Necator americanus B76.1

nematode NEC (intestinal) B82.0

Ancylostoma B76.0

conjunctiva NEC B83.9

Enterobius vermicularis B80

Gnathostoma spinigerum B83.1

physaloptera B80

specified NEC B81.8

trichostrongylus B81.2

trichuris (trichuria) B79

Oesophagostomum (apiostomum) B81.8

Oestrus ovis —see also Myiasis B87.9

Onchocerca (volvulus) —see Onchocerciasis

Opisthorchis (felineus) (viverrini) B66.0

orbit, parasitic NOS B89

Oxyuris vermicularis B80

Paragonimus (westermani) B66.4

parasite, parasitic B89

eyelid B89

intestinal NOS B82.9

mouth B37.0

skin B88.9

tongue B37.0

Parastrongylus

cantonensis B83.2

costaricensis B81.3

Pediculus B85.2

body B85.1

capitis (humanus) (any site) B85.0

corporis (humanus) (any site) B85.1

head B85.0

mixed (classifiable to more than one of the titles B85.0-B85.3) B85.4

pubis (any site) B85.3

Pentastoma B88.8

Phthirus (pubis) (any site) B85.3

with any infestation classifiable to B85.0-B85.2 B85.4

pinworm B80

pork tapeworm (adult) B68.0

Infestation (Continued)

protozoal NEC B64

intestinal A07.9

specified NEC A07.8

specified NEC B60.8

pubic, louse B85.3

rat tapeworm B71.0

red bug B88.0

roundworm (large) NEC B82.0

Ascariasis —see also Ascariasis B77.9

sandflea B88.1

Sarcoptes scabiei B86

scabies B86

Schistosoma B65.9

bovis B65.8

cercariae B65.3

haematobium B65.0

intercalatum B65.8

japonicum B65.2

mansoni B65.1

mattheei B65.8

mekongi B65.8

specified type NEC B65.8

spindale B65.8

screw worms —see Myiasis

skin NOS B88.9

Sparganum (mansoni) (proliferum) (baxteri) B70.1

larval B70.1

specified type NEC B88.8

Spirometra larvae B70.1

Stellantchasmus falcatus B66.8

Strongyloides stercoralis —see Strongyloidiasis

Taenia B68.9

diminuta B71.0

echinococcus —see Echinococcus

mediocanellata B68.1

nana B71.0

saginata B68.1

solium (intestinal form) B68.0

larval form —see Cysticercosis

Taeniarhynchus saginatus B68.1

tapeworm B71.9

beef B68.1

broad B70.0

larval B70.1

dog B67.4

dwarf B71.0

fish B70.0

larval B70.1

pork B68.0

rat B71.0

Ternidens diminutus B81.8

Tetranychus molestissimus B88.0

threadworm B80

tongue B37.0

Toxocara (canis) (cati) (felis) B83.0

trematode(s) NEC —see Infestation, fluke

Trichinella (spiralis) B75

Trichocephalus B79

Trichomonas —see Trichomoniasis

Trichostrongylus B81.2

Trichuris (trichiura) B79

Trombicula (irritans) B88.0

Tunga penetrans B88.1

Uncinaria americana B76.1

Vandellia cirrhosa B88.8

whipworm B79

worms B83.9

intestinal B82.0

Wuchereria (bancrofti) B74.0

Infiltrate, infiltration

amyloid (generalized) (localized) —see Amyloidosis

calcareous NEC R89.7

localized —see Degeneration, by site

calcium salt R89.7

cardiac

fatty —see Degeneration, myocardial

glycogenic E74.02 [I43]

Infiltrate, infiltration (Continued)

corneal —see Edema, cornea

eyelid —see Inflammation, eyelid

glycogen, glycogenic —see Disease, glycogen storage

heart, cardiac

fatty —see Degeneration, myocardial

glycogenic E74.02 [I43]

inflammatory in vitreous H43.89

kidney N28.89

leukemic —see Leukemia

liver K76.89

fatty —see Fatty, liver NEC

glycogen —see also Disease, glycogen storage E74.03 [K77]

lung R91.8

▸eosinophilic —see Eosinophilia, pulmonary

lymphatic —see also Leukemia, lymphatic C91.9-●

gland I88.9

muscle, fatty M62.89

myocardium, myocardial

fatty —see Degeneration, myocardial

glycogenic E74.02 [I43]

on chest x-ray R91.8

pulmonary R91.8

▸with eosinophilia —see Eosinophilia, pulmonary

skin (lymphocytic) L98.6

thymus (gland) (fatty) E32.8

urine R39.0

vesicant agent

antineoplastic chemotherapy T80.810

other agent NEC T80.818

vitreous body H43.89

Infirmity R68.89

senile R54

Inflammation, inflamed, inflammatory (with exudation)

abducent (nerve) —see Strabismus, paralytic, sixth nerve

accessory sinus (chronic) —see Sinusitis

adrenal (gland) E27.8

alveoli, teeth M27.3

scorbutic E54

anal canal, anus K62.89

antrum (chronic) —see Sinusitis, maxillary

appendix —see Appendicitis

arachnoid —see Meningitis

areola N61.0

puerperal, postpartum or gestational —see Infection, nipple

areolar tissue NOS L08.9

artery —see Arteritis

auditory meatus (external) —see Otitis, externa

Bartholin's gland N75.8

bile duct (common) (hepatic) or passage —see Cholangitis

bladder —see Cystitis

bone —see Osteomyelitis

brain —see also Encephalitis

membrane —see Meningitis

breast N61.0

puerperal, postpartum, gestational —see Mastitis, obstetric

broad ligament —see Disease, pelvis, inflammatory

bronchi —see Bronchitis

catarrhal J00

cecum —see Appendicitis

cerebral —see also Encephalitis

membrane —see Meningitis

cerebrospinal

meningococcal A39.0

cervix (uteri) —see Cervicitis

chest J98.8

chorioretinal H30.9-●

cyclitis —see Cyclitis

disseminated H30.10-●

generalized H30.13-●

peripheral H30.12-●

posterior pole H30.11-●

▶ New ▸ Revised ~~deleted~~ Deleted ● Use Additional Character(s)

Inflammation, inflamed, inflammatory
(Continued)
 chorioretinal *(Continued)*
  epitheliopathy —*see* Epitheliopathy
  focal H30.00-●
   juxtapapillary H30.01-●
   macular H30.04-●
   paramacular —*see* Inflammation,
    chorioretinal, focal, macular
   peripheral H30.03-●
   posterior pole H30.02-●
   specified type NEC H30.89-●
 choroid —*see* Inflammation, chorioretinal
 chronic, postmastoidectomy cavity —*see*
  Complications, postmastoidectomy,
  inflammation
 colon —*see* Enteritis
 connective tissue (diffuse) NEC —*see*
  Disorder, soft tissue, specified type NEC
 cornea —*see* Keratitis
 corpora cavernosa N48.29
 cranial nerve —*see* Disorder, nerve, cranial
 Douglas' cul-de-sac or pouch (chronic) N73.0
 due to device, implant or graft —*see also*
  Complications, by site and type,
  infection or inflammation
  arterial graft T82.7
  breast (implant) T85.79
  catheter T85.79
   dialysis (renal) T82.7
    intraperitoneal T85.71
   infusion T82.7
    cranial T85.735
    intrathecal T85.735
    spinal (epidural) (subdural) T85.735
    subarachnoid T85.735
   urinary T83.518
    cystostomy T83.510
    Hopkins T83.518
    ileostomy T83.518
    nephrostomy T83.512
    specified NEC T83.518
    urethral indwelling T83.511
    urostomy T83.518
  electronic (electrode) (pulse generator)
   (stimulator)
   bone T84.7
   cardiac T82.7
   nervous system T85.738
    brain T85.731
    cranial nerve T85.732
    gastric nerve T85.732
    neurostimulator generator T85.734
    peripheral nerve T85.732
    sacral nerve T85.732
    spinal cord T85.733
    vagal nerve T85.732
   urinary T83.590
  fixation, internal (orthopedic) NEC —
   see Complication, fixation device,
   infection
  gastrointestinal (bile duct) (esophagus)
   T85.79
  neurostimulator electrode (lead) T85.732
  genital NEC T83.69
  heart NEC T82.7
   valve (prosthesis) T82.6
    graft T82.7
  joint prosthesis —*see* Complication, joint
   prosthesis, infection
  ocular (corneal graft) (orbital implant)
   NEC T85.79
  orthopedic NEC T84.7
  penile (cylinder) (pump) (resevoir) T83.61
   specified NEC T85.79
   testicular T83.62
  urinary NEC T83.598
   ileal conduit stent T83.593
   implanted neurostimulation T83.590
   implanted sphincter T83.591
   indwelling ureteral stent T83.592

Inflammation, inflamed, inflammatory
(Continued)
 due to device, implant or graft *(Continued)*
 (Continued)
  urinary NEC *(Continued)*
   nephroureteral stent T83.593
   specified stent NEC T83.593
  vascular NEC T82.7
  ventricular intracranial (communicating)
   shunt T85.730
 duodenum K29.80
  with bleeding K29.81
 dura mater —*see* Meningitis
 ear (middle) —*see also* Otitis, media
  external —*see* Otitis, externa
  inner —*see* subcategory H83.0
 epididymis —*see* Epididymitis
➡ esophagus —*see* Esophagitis
 ethmoidal (sinus) (chronic) —*see* Sinusitis,
  ethmoidal
 eustachian tube (catarrhal) —*see* Salpingitis,
  eustachian
 eyelid H01.9
  abscess —*see* Abscess, eyelid
  blepharitis —*see* Blepharitis
  chalazion —*see* Chalazion
  dermatosis (noninfectious) —*see*
   Dermatosis, eyelid
  hordeolum —*see* Hordeolum
  specified NEC H01.8
 fallopian tube —*see* Salpingo-oophoritis
 fascia —*see* Myositis
 follicular, pharynx J31.2
 frontal (sinus) (chronic) —*see* Sinusitis, frontal
 gallbladder —*see* Cholecystitis
 gastric —*see* Gastritis
 gastrointestinal —*see* Enteritis
 genital organ (internal) (diffuse)
  female —*see* Disease, pelvis, inflammatory
  male N49.9
   multiple sites N49.8
   specified NEC N49.8
 gland (lymph) —*see* Lymphadenitis
 glottis —*see* Laryngitis
 granular, pharynx J31.2
 gum K05.10
  nonplaque induced K05.11
  plaque induced K05.10
 heart —*see* Carditis
 hepatic duct —*see* Cholangitis
 ileoanal (internal) pouch K91.850
 ileum —*see also* Enteritis
  regional or terminal —*see* Enteritis, regional
 intestinal pouch K91.850
 intestine (any part) —*see* Enteritis
 jaw (acute) (bone) (chronic) (lower)
  (suppurative) (upper) M27.2
 joint NEC —*see* Arthritis
  sacroiliac M46.1
 kidney —*see* Nephritis
 knee (joint) M13.169
  tuberculous A18.02
 labium (majus) (minus) —*see* Vulvitis
 lacrimal
  gland —*see* Dacryoadenitis
  passages (duct) (sac) —*see also* Dacryocystitis
   canaliculitis —*see* Canaliculitis, lacrimal
 larynx —*see* Laryngitis
 leg NOS L08.9
 lip K13.0
 liver (capsule) —*see also* Hepatitis
  chronic K73.9
  suppurative K75.0
 lung (acute) —*see also* Pneumonia
  chronic J98.4
 lymphatic vessel —*see* Lymphangitis
 lymph gland or node —*see* Lymphadenitis
 maxilla, maxillary M27.2
  sinus (chronic) —*see* Sinusitis, maxillary
 membranes of brain or spinal cord —*see*
  Meningitis

Inflammation, inflamed, inflammatory
(Continued)
 meninges —*see* Meningitis
 mouth K12.1
 muscle —*see* Myositis
 myocardium —*see* Myocarditis
 nasal sinus (chronic) —*see* Sinusitis
 nasopharynx —*see* Nasopharyngitis
 navel L08.82
 nerve NEC —*see* Neuralgia
 nipple N61.0
  puerperal, postpartum or gestational —*see*
   Infection, nipple
 nose —*see* Rhinitis
 oculomotor (nerve) —*see* Strabismus,
  paralytic, third nerve
 optic nerve —*see* Neuritis, optic
 orbit (chronic) H05.10
  acute H05.00
   abscess —*see* Abscess, orbit
   cellulitis —*see* Cellulitis, orbit
   osteomyelitis —*see* Osteomyelitis, orbit
   periostitis —*see* Periostitis, orbital
   tenonitis —*see* Tenonitis, eye
  granuloma —*see* Granuloma, orbit
  myositis —*see* Myositis, orbital
 ovary —*see* Salpingo-oophoritis
 oviduct —*see* Salpingo-oophoritis
 pancreas (acute) —*see* Pancreatitis
 parametrium N73.0
 parotid region L08.9
 pelvis, female —*see* Disease, pelvis,
  inflammatory
 penis (corpora cavernosa) N48.29
 perianal K62.89
 pericardium —*see* Pericarditis
 perineum (female) (male) L08.9
 perirectal K62.89
 peritoneum —*see* Peritonitis
 periuterine —*see* Disease, pelvis, inflammatory
 perivesical —*see* Cystitis
 petrous bone (acute) (chronic) —*see* Petrositis
 pharynx (acute) —*see* Pharyngitis
 pia mater —*see* Meningitis
 pleura —*see* Pleurisy
 polyp, colon —*see also* Polyp, colon,
  inflammatory K51.40
 prostate —*see also* Prostatitis
  specified type NEC N41.8
 rectosigmoid —*see* Rectosigmoiditis
 rectum —*see also* Proctitis K62.89
 respiratory, upper —*see also* Infection,
  respiratory, upper J06.9
  acute, due to radiation J70.0
  chronic, due to external agent —*see*
   condition, respiratory, chronic, due to
  due to
   chemicals, gases, fumes or vapors
    (inhalation) J68.2
   radiation J70.1
 retina —*see* Chorioretinitis
 retrocecal —*see* Appendicitis
 retroperitoneal —*see* Peritonitis
 salivary duct or gland (any) (suppurative) —
  see Sialoadenitis
 scorbutic, alveoli, teeth E54
 scrotum N49.2
 seminal vesicle —*see* Vesiculitis
 sigmoid —*see* Enteritis
 sinus —*see* Sinusitis
 Skene's duct or gland —*see* Urethritis
 skin L08.9
 spermatic cord N49.1
 sphenoidal (sinus) —*see* Sinusitis, sphenoidal
 spinal
  cord —*see* Encephalitis
  membrane —*see* Meningitis
  nerve —*see* Disorder, nerve
 spine —*see* Spondylopathy, inflammatory
 spleen (capsule) D73.89
 stomach —*see* Gastritis

Inflammation, inflamed, inflammatory
(Continued)
subcutaneous tissue L08.9
suprarenal (gland) E27.8
synovial —*see* Tenosynovitis
tendon (sheath) NEC —*see* Tenosynovitis
testis —*see* Orchitis
throat (acute) —*see* Pharyngitis
thymus (gland) E32.8
thyroid (gland) —*see* Thyroiditis
tongue K14.0
tonsil —*see* Tonsillitis
trachea —*see* Tracheitis
trochlear (nerve) —*see* Strabismus, paralytic,
fourth nerve
tubal —*see* Salpingo-oophoritis
tuberculous NEC —*see* Tuberculosis
tubo-ovarian —*see* Salpingo-oophoritis
tunica vaginalis N49.1
tympanic membrane —*see* Tympanitis
umbilicus, umbilical L08.82
uterine ligament —*see* Disease, pelvis,
inflammatory
uterus (catarrhal) —*see* Endometritis
uveal tract (anterior) NOS —*see also*
Iridocyclitis
posterior —*see* Chorioretinitis
vagina —*see* Vaginitis
vas deferens N49.1
vein —*see also* Phlebitis
intracranial or intraspinal (septic) G08
thrombotic I80.9
leg —*see* Phlebitis, leg
lower extremity —*see* Phlebitis, leg
vocal cord J38.3
vulva —*see* Vulvitis
Wharton's duct (suppurative) —*see*
Sialoadenitis
Inflation, lung, imperfect (newborn) —*see*
Atelectasis
**Influenza (bronchial) (epidemic) (respiratory
(upper)) (unidentified influenza virus) J11.1**
with
digestive manifestations J11.2
encephalopathy J11.81
enteritis J11.2
gastroenteritis J11.2
gastrointestinal manifestations J11.2
laryngitis J11.1
myocarditis J11.82
otitis media J11.83
pharyngitis J11.1
pneumonia J11.00
specified type J11.08
respiratory manifestations NEC J11.1
specified manifestation NEC J11.89
▶A (non-novel) J10-●
A/H5N1 —*see also* Influenza, due to,
identified novel influenza A virus J09.X2
avian —*see also* Influenza, due to, identified
novel influenza A virus J09.X2
▶B J10-●
bird —*see also* Influenza, due to, identified
novel influenza A virus J09.X2
▶C J10-●
novel (2009) H1N1 influenza —*see also*
Influenza, due to, identified influenza
virus NEC J10.1
novel influenza A/H1N1 —*see also* Influenza,
due to, identified influenza virus NEC
J10.1
due to
avian (*see also* Influenza, due to, identified
novel influenza A virus) J09.X2
identified influenza virus NEC J10.1
with
digestive manifestations J10.2
encephalopathy J10.81
enteritis J10.2
gastroenteritis J10.2
gastrointestinal manifestations J10.2

Influenza *(Continued)*
due to *(Continued)*
identified influenza virus NEC *(Continued)*
with *(Continued)*
laryngitis J10.1
myocarditis J10.82
otitis media J10.83
pharyngitis J10.1
pneumonia (unspecified type) J10.00
with same identified influenza virus
J10.01
specified type NEC J10.08
respiratory manifestations NEC J10.1
specified manifestation NEC J10.89
identified novel influenza A virus J09.X2
with
digestive manifestations J09.X3
encephalopathy J09.X9
enteritis J09.X3
gastroenteritis J09.X3
gastrointestinal manifestations J09.X3
laryngitis J09.X2
myocarditis J09.X9
otitis media J09.X9
pharyngitis J09.X2
pneumonia J09.X1
respiratory manifestations NEC
J09.X2
specified manifestation NEC J09.X9
upper respiratory symptoms J09.X2
of other animal origin, not bird or swine (*see
also* Influenza, due to, identified novel
influenza A virus) J09.X2
swine (viruses that normally cause infections
in pigs) —*see also* Influenza, due to,
identified novel influenza A virus J09.X2
Influenza-like disease —*see* Influenza
Influenzal —*see* Influenza
Infraction, Freiberg's (metatarsal head) —*see*
Osteochondrosis, juvenile, metatarsus
Infraeruption of tooth (teeth) M26.34
**Infusion complication, misadventure, or
reaction** —*see* Complications, infusion
Ingestion
chemical —*see* Table of Drugs and Chemicals,
by substance, poisoning
drug or medicament
correct substance properly administered —
see Table of Drugs and Chemicals, by
drug, adverse effect
overdose or wrong substance given
or taken —*see* Table of Drugs and
Chemicals, by drug, poisoning
foreign body —*see* Foreign body, alimentary
tract
multiple drug —*see* Table of Drugs and
Chemicals, multiple
tularemia A21.3
Ingrowing
hair (beard) L73.1
nail (finger) (toe) L60.0
Inguinal —*see also* condition
testicle Q53.9
bilateral Q53.212
unilateral Q53.112
Inhalant-induced
anxiety disorder F18.980
depressive disorder F18.94
major neurocognitive disorder F18.97
mild neurocognitive disorder F18.988
psychotic disorder F18.959
Inhalation
anthrax A22.1
flame T27.3
food or foreign body —*see* Foreign body, by
site
⇒gases, fumes, or vapors T59.9-●
⇒specified agent NEC —*see* Table of Drugs
and Chemicals, by substance
T59.89-●
liquid or vomitus —*see* Asphyxia

Inhalation *(Continued)*
meconium (newborn) P24.00
with
with respiratory symptoms P24.01
pneumonia (pneumonitis) P24.01
mucus —*see* Asphyxia, mucus
oil or gasoline (causing suffocation) —*see*
Foreign body, by site
⇒smoke T59.81-●
▶with respiratory conditions J70.5
▶due to chemicals, gases, fumes and
vapors J68.9
~~due to chemicals, gases, fumes and vapors
J68.9~~
⇒steam T59.9-●
stomach contents or secretions —*see* Foreign
body, by site
due to anesthesia (general) (local) or other
sedation T88.59
in labor and delivery O74.0
in pregnancy O29.01-●
postpartum, puerperal O89.01
Inhibition, orgasm
female F52.31
male F52.32
Inhibitor, systemic lupus erythematosus
(presence of) D68.62
Iniencephalus, iniencephaly Q00.2
Injection, traumatic jet (air) (industrial) (water)
(paint or dye) T70.4
Injury —*see also* specified injury type T14.90
abdomen, abdominal S39.91
blood vessel —*see* Injury, blood vessel,
abdomen
cavity —*see* Injury, intra-abdominal
contusion S30.1
internal —*see* Injury, intra-abdominal
intra-abdominal organ —*see* Injury,
intra-abdominal
nerve —*see* Injury, nerve, abdomen
open —*see* Wound, open, abdomen
specified NEC S39.81
superficial —*see* Injury, superficial,
abdomen
Achilles tendon S86.00-●
laceration S86.02-●
specified type NEC S86.09-●
strain S86.01-●
acoustic, resulting in deafness —*see* Injury,
nerve, acoustic
adrenal (gland) S37.819
contusion S37.812
laceration S37.813
specified type NEC S37.818
alveolar (process) S09.93
ankle S99.91-●
contusion —*see* Contusion, ankle
dislocation —*see* Dislocation, ankle
fracture —*see* Fracture, ankle
nerve —*see* Injury, nerve, ankle
open —*see* Wound, open, ankle
specified type NEC S99.81-●
sprain —*see* Sprain, ankle
superficial —*see* Injury, superficial, ankle
anterior chamber, eye —*see* Injury, eye,
specified site NEC
anus —*see* Injury, abdomen
aorta (thoracic) S25.00
abdominal S35.00
laceration (minor) (superficial) S35.01
major S35.02
specified type NEC S35.09
laceration (minor) (superficial) S25.01
major S25.02
specified type NEC S25.09
arm (upper) S49.9-●
blood vessel —*see* Injury, blood vessel, arm
contusion —*see* Contusion, arm, upper
fracture —*see* Fracture, humerus
lower —*see* Injury, forearm
muscle —*see* Injury, muscle, shoulder

▶ New   ⇒ Revised   ~~deleted~~ Deleted   ● Use Additional Character(s)

Injury *(Continued)*
  arm *(Continued)*
    nerve —*see* Injury, nerve, arm
    open —*see* Wound, open, arm
    specified type NEC S49.8-●
    superficial —*see* Injury, superficial, arm
  artery (complicating trauma) —*see also* Injury,
    blood vessel, by site
    cerebral or meningeal —*see* Injury,
      intracranial
  auditory canal (external) (meatus) S09.91
  auricle, auris, ear S09.91
  axilla —*see* Injury, shoulder
  back —*see* Injury, back, lower
  bile duct S36.13
  birth —*see also* Birth, injury P15.9
  bladder (sphincter) S37.20
    at delivery O71.5
    contusion S37.22
    laceration S37.23
    obstetrical trauma O71.5
    specified type NEC S37.29
  blast (air) (hydraulic) (immersion)
    (underwater) NEC T14.8
    acoustic nerve trauma —*see* Injury, nerve,
      acoustic
    bladder —*see* Injury, bladder
    brain —*see* Concussion
    colon —*see* Injury, intestine, large, blast
      injury
    ear (primary) S09.31-●
      secondary S09.39-●
    generalized T70.8
    lung —*see* Injury, intrathoracic, lung, blast
      injury
    multiple body organs T70.8
    peritoneum S36.81
    rectum S36.61
    retroperitoneum S36.898
    small intestine S36.419
      duodenum S36.410
      specified site NEC S36.418
    specified
      intra-abdominal organ NEC S36.898
      pelvic organ NEC S37.899
  blood vessel NEC T14.8
    abdomen S35.9-●
      aorta —*see* Injury, aorta, abdominal
      celiac artery —*see* Injury, blood vessel,
        celiac artery
      iliac vessel —*see* Injury, blood vessel, iliac
      laceration S35.91
      mesenteric vessel —*see* Injury, mesenteric
      portal vein —*see* Injury, blood vessel,
        portal vein
      renal vessel —*see* Injury, blood vessel,
        renal
      specified vessel NEC S35.8X-●
      splenic vessel —*see* Injury, blood vessel,
        splenic
      vena cava —*see* Injury, vena cava,
        inferior
    ankle —*see* Injury, blood vessel, foot
    aorta (abdominal) (thoracic) —*see* Injury,
      aorta
    arm (upper) NEC S45.90-●
      forearm —*see* Injury, blood vessel,
        forearm
      laceration S45.91-●
      specified
        site NEC S45.80-●
          laceration S45.81-●
          specified type NEC S45.89-●
        type NEC S45.99-●
      superficial vein S45.30-●
        laceration S45.31-●
        specified type NEC S45.39-●
    axillary
      artery S45.00-●
        laceration S45.01-●
        specified type NEC S45.09-●

Injury *(Continued)*
  blood vessel NEC *(Continued)*
    axillary *(Continued)*
      vein S45.20-●
        laceration S45.21-●
        specified type NEC S45.29-●
    azygos vein —*see* Injury, blood vessel,
      thoracic, specified site NEC
    brachial
      artery S45.10-●
        laceration S45.11-●
        specified type NEC S45.19-●
      vein S45.20-●
        laceration S45.219
        specified type NEC S45.29-●
    carotid artery (common) (external)
      (internal, extracranial) S15.00-●
      internal, intracranial S06.8-●
      laceration (minor) (superficial) S15.01-●
        major S15.02-●
      specified type NEC S15.09-●
    celiac artery S35.219
      branch S35.299
        laceration (minor) (superficial) S35.291
          major S35.292
        specified NEC S35.298
      laceration (minor) (superficial) S35.211
        major S35.212
      specified type NEC S35.218
    cerebral —*see* Injury, intracranial
    deep plantar —*see* Injury, blood vessel,
      plantar artery
    digital (hand) —*see* Injury, blood vessel,
      finger
    dorsal
      artery (foot) S95.00-●
        laceration S95.01-●
        specified type NEC S95.09-●
      vein (foot) S95.20-●
        laceration S95.21-●
        specified type NEC S95.29-●
    due to accidental laceration during
      procedure —*see* Laceration, accidental
      complicating surgery
    extremity —*see* Injury, blood vessel, limb
    femoral
      artery (common) (superficial) S75.00-●
        laceration (minor) (superficial) S75.01-●
          major S75.02-●
        specified type NEC S75.09-●
      vein (hip level) (thigh level) S75.10-●
        laceration (minor) (superficial) S75.11-●
          major S75.12-●
        specified type NEC S75.19-●
    finger S65.50-●
      index S65.50-●
        laceration S65.51-●
        specified type NEC S65.59-●
      laceration S65.51-●
      little S65.50-●
        laceration S65.51-●
        specified type NEC S65.59-●
      middle S65.50-●
        laceration S65.51-●
        specified type NEC S65.59-●
      specified type NEC S65.59-●
      thumb —*see* Injury, blood vessel, thumb
    foot S95.90-●
      dorsal
        artery —*see* Injury, blood vessel,
          dorsal, artery
        vein —*see* Injury, blood vessel, dorsal,
          vein
      laceration S95.91-●
      plantar artery —*see* Injury, blood vessel,
        plantar artery
      specified
        site NEC S95.80-●
          laceration S95.81-●
          specified type NEC S95.89-●
        specified type NEC S95.99-●

Injury *(Continued)*
  blood vessel NEC *(Continued)*
    forearm S55.90-●
      laceration S55.91-●
      radial artery —*see* Injury, blood vessel,
        radial artery
      specified
        site NEC S55.80-●
          laceration S55.81-●
          specified type NEC S55.89-●
        type NEC S55.99-●
      ulnar artery —*see* Injury, blood vessel,
        ulnar artery
      vein S55.20-●
        laceration S55.21-●
        specified type NEC S55.29-●
    gastric
      artery —*see* Injury, mesenteric, artery,
        branch
      vein —*see* Injury, blood vessel, abdomen
    gastroduodenal artery —*see* Injury,
      mesenteric, artery, branch
    greater saphenous vein (lower leg level)
      S85.30-●
      hip (and thigh) level S75.20-●
        laceration (minor) (superficial) S75.21-●
          major S75.22-●
        specified type NEC S75.29-●
      laceration S85.31-●
      specified type NEC S85.39-●
    hand (level) S65.90-●
      finger —*see* Injury, blood vessel, finger
      laceration S65.91-●
      palmar arch —*see* Injury, blood vessel,
        palmar arch
      radial artery —*see* Injury, blood vessel,
        radial artery, hand
      specified
        site NEC S65.80-●
          laceration S65.81-●
          specified type NEC S65.89-●
        type NEC S65.99-●
      thumb —*see* Injury, blood vessel, thumb
      ulnar artery —*see* Injury, blood vessel,
        ulnar artery, hand
    head S09.0
      intracranial —*see* Injury, intracranial
      multiple S09.0
    hepatic
      artery —*see* Injury, mesenteric, artery
      vein —*see* Injury, vena cava, inferior
    hip S75.90-●
      femoral artery —*see* Injury, blood vessel,
        femoral, artery
      femoral vein —*see* Injury, blood vessel,
        femoral, vein
      greater saphenous vein —*see* Injury, blood
        vessel, greater saphenous, hip level
      laceration S75.91-●
      specified
        site NEC S75.80-●
          laceration S75.81-●
          specified type NEC S75.89-●
        type NEC S75.99-●
    hypogastric (artery) (vein) —*see* Injury,
      blood vessel, iliac
    iliac S35.5-●
      artery S35.51-●
      specified vessel NEC S35.5-●
      uterine vessel —*see* Injury, blood vessel,
        uterine
      vein S35.51-●
    innominate —*see* Injury, blood vessel,
      thoracic, innominate
    intercostal (artery) (vein) —*see* Injury,
      blood vessel, thoracic, intercostal
    jugular vein (external) S15.20-●
      internal S15.30-●
        laceration (minor) (superficial) S15.31-●
          major S15.32-●
        specified type NEC S15.39-●

Injury (Continued)
  blood vessel NEC (Continued)
    jugular vein (Continued)
      laceration (minor) (superficial) S15.21-●
        major S15.22-●
      specified type NEC S15.29-●
    leg (level) (lower) S85.90-●
      greater saphenous —see Injury, blood
        vessel, greater saphenous
      laceration S85.91-●
      lesser saphenous —see Injury, blood
        vessel, lesser saphenous
      peroneal artery —see Injury, blood
        vessel, peroneal artery
      popliteal
        artery —see Injury, blood vessel,
          popliteal, artery
        vein —see Injury, blood vessel,
          popliteal, vein
      specified
        site NEC S85.80-●
          laceration S85.81-●
          specified type NEC S85.89-●
        type NEC S85.99-●
      thigh —see Injury, blood vessel, hip
      tibial artery —see Injury, blood vessel,
        tibial artery
    lesser saphenous vein (lower leg level)
      S85.40-●
      laceration S85.41-●
      specified type NEC S85.49-●
    limb
      lower —see Injury, blood vessel, leg
      upper —see Injury, blood vessel, arm
    lower back —see Injury, blood vessel,
      abdomen
      specified NEC —see Injury, blood vessel,
        abdomen, specified, site NEC
    mammary (artery) (vein) —see Injury, blood
      vessel, thoracic, specified site NEC
    mesenteric (inferior) (superior)
      artery —see Injury, mesenteric, artery
      vein —see Injury, mesenteric, vein
    neck S15.9
      specified site NEC S15.8
    ovarian (artery) (vein) —see subcategory
      S35.8
    palmar arch (superficial) S65.20-●
      deep S65.30-●
        laceration S65.31-●
        specified type NEC S65.39-●
      laceration S65.21-●
      specified type NEC S65.29-●
    pelvis —see Injury, blood vessel, abdomen
      specified NEC —see Injury, blood vessel,
        abdomen, specified, site NEC
    peroneal artery S85.20-●
      laceration S85.21-●
      specified type NEC S85.29-●
    plantar artery (deep) (foot) S95.10-●
      laceration S95.11-●
      specified type NEC S95.19-●
    popliteal
      artery S85.00-●
        laceration S85.01-●
        specified type NEC S85.09-●
      vein S85.50-●
        laceration S85.51-●
        specified type NEC S85.59-●
    portal vein S35.319
      laceration S35.311
      specified type NEC S35.318
    precerebral —see Injury, blood vessel, neck
    pulmonary (artery) (vein) —see Injury,
      blood vessel, thoracic, pulmonary
    radial artery (forearm level) S55.10-●
      hand and wrist (level) S65.10-●
        laceration S65.11-●
        specified type NEC S65.19-●
      laceration S55.11-●
      specified type NEC S55.19-●

Injury (Continued)
  blood vessel NEC (Continued)
    renal
      artery S35.40-●
        laceration S35.41-●
        specified NEC S35.49-●
      vein S35.40-●
        laceration S35.41-●
        specified NEC S35.49-●
    saphenous vein (greater) (lower leg
      level) —see Injury, blood vessel,
      greater saphenous
    hip and thigh level —see Injury, blood
      vessel, greater saphenous, hip level
    lesser —see Injury, blood vessel, lesser
      saphenous
    shoulder
      specified NEC —see Injury, blood vessel,
        arm, specified site NEC
      superficial vein —see Injury, blood
        vessel, arm, superficial vein
    specified NEC T14.8
    splenic
      artery —see Injury, blood vessel, celiac
        artery, branch
      vein S35.329
        laceration S35.321
        specified NEC S35.328
    subclavian —see Injury, blood vessel,
      thoracic, innominate
    thigh —see Injury, blood vessel, hip
    thoracic S25.90
      aorta S25.00
        laceration (minor) (superficial)
          S25.01
          major S25.02
        specified type NEC S25.09
      azygos vein —see Injury, blood vessel,
        thoracic, specified, site NEC
      innominate
        artery S25.10-●
          laceration (minor) (superficial)
            S25.11-●
            major S25.12-●
          specified type NEC S25.19-●
        vein S25.30-●
          laceration (minor) (superficial)
            S25.31-●
            major S25.32-●
          specified type NEC S25.39-●
      intercostal S25.50-●
        laceration S25.51-●
        specified type NEC S25.59-●
      laceration S25.91
      mammary vessel —see Injury, blood
        vessel, thoracic, specified, site NEC
      pulmonary S25.40-●
        laceration (minor) (superficial)
          S25.41-●
          major S25.42-●
        specified type NEC S25.49-●
      specified
        site NEC S25.80-●
          laceration S25.81-●
          specified type NEC S25.89-●
        type NEC S25.99
      subclavian —see Injury, blood vessel,
        thoracic, innominate
      vena cava (superior) S25.20
        laceration (minor) (superficial)
          S25.21
          major S25.22
        specified type NEC S25.29
    thumb S65.40-●
      laceration S65.41-●
      specified type NEC S65.49-●
    tibial artery S85.10-●
      anterior S85.13-●
        laceration S85.14-●
        specified injury NEC S85.15-●
      laceration S85.11-●

Injury (Continued)
  blood vessel NEC (Continued)
    tibial artery (Continued)
      posterior S85.16-●
        laceration S85.17-●
        specified injury NEC S85.18-●
      specified injury NEC S85.12-●
    ulnar artery (forearm level) S55.00-●
      hand and wrist (level) S65.00-●
        laceration S65.01-●
        specified type NEC S65.09-●
      laceration S55.01-●
      specified type NEC S55.09-●
    upper arm (level) —see Injury, blood vessel,
      arm
      superficial vein —see Injury, blood
        vessel, arm, superficial vein
    uterine S35.5-●
      artery S35.53-●
      vein S35.53-●
    vena cava —see Injury, vena cava
    vertebral artery S15.10-●
      laceration (minor) (superficial)
        S15.11-●
        major S15.12-●
      specified type NEC S15.19-●
    wrist (level) —see Injury, blood vessel,
      hand
  brachial plexus S14.3
    newborn P14.3
  brain (traumatic) S06.9-●
    diffuse (axonal) S06.2X-●
    focal S06.30-●
  brainstem S06.38-●
  breast NOS S29.9
  broad ligament —see Injury, pelvic organ,
    specified site NEC
  bronchus, bronchi —see Injury, intrathoracic,
    bronchus
  brow S09.90
  buttock S39.92
  canthus, eye S05.90
  cardiac plexus —see Injury, nerve, thorax,
    sympathetic
  cauda equina S34.3
  cavernous sinus —see Injury, intracranial
  cecum —see Injury, colon
  celiac ganglion or plexus —see Injury, nerve,
    lumbosacral, sympathetic
  cerebellum —see Injury, intracranial
  cerebral —see Injury, intracranial
  cervix (uteri) —see Injury, uterus
  cheek (wall) S09.93
  chest —see Injury, thorax
  childbirth (newborn) —see also Birth, injury
    maternal NEC O71.9
  chin S09.93
  choroid (eye) —see Injury, eye, specified site
    NEC
  clitoris S39.94
  coccyx —see also Injury, back, lower
    complicating delivery O71.6
  colon —see Injury, intestine, large
  common bile duct —see Injury, liver
  conjunctiva (superficial) —see Injury, eye,
    conjunctiva
  conus medullaris —see Injury, spinal, sacral
  cord
    spermatic (pelvic region) S37.898
      scrotal region S39.848
    spinal —see Injury, spinal cord, by region
  cornea —see Injury, eye, specified site NEC
    abrasion —see Injury, eye, cornea,
      abrasion
  cortex (cerebral) —see also Injury, intracranial
    visual —see Injury, nerve, optic
  costal region NEC S29.9
  costochondral NEC S29.9
  cranial
    cavity —see Injury, intracranial
    nerve —see Injury, nerve, cranial

▶ New   ⇒ Revised   ~~deleted~~ Deleted   ● Use Additional Character(s)

Injury *(Continued)*
crushing —*see* Crush
cutaneous sensory nerve
cystic duct —*see* Injury, liver
deep tissue —*see* Contusion, by site
➡ meaning pressure ulcer —*see* Ulcer,
pressure L89 with final character .6
delivery (newborn) P15.9
maternal NEC O71.9
Descemet's membrane —*see* Injury, eyeball,
penetrating
diaphragm —*see* Injury, intrathoracic,
diaphragm
duodenum —*see* Injury, intestine, small,
duodenum
ear (auricle) (external) (canal) S09.91
abrasion —*see* Abrasion, ear
bite —*see* Bite, ear
blister —*see* Blister, ear
bruise —*see* Contusion, ear
contusion —*see* Contusion, ear
external constriction —*see* Constriction,
external, ear
hematoma —*see* Hematoma, ear
inner —*see* Injury, ear, middle
laceration —*see* Laceration, ear
middle S09.30-●
blast —*see* Injury, blast, ear
specified NEC S09.39-●
puncture —*see* Puncture, ear
superficial —*see* Injury, superficial, ear
eighth cranial nerve (acoustic or auditory) —
see Injury, nerve, acoustic
elbow S59.90-●
contusion —*see* Contusion, elbow
dislocation —*see* Dislocation, elbow
fracture —*see* Fracture, ulna, upper
end
open —*see* Wound, open, elbow
specified NEC S59.80-●
sprain —*see* Sprain, elbow
superficial —*see* Injury, superficial,
elbow
eleventh cranial nerve (accessory) —*see*
Injury, nerve, accessory
epididymis S39.94
epigastric region S39.91
epiglottis NEC S19.89
esophageal plexus —*see* Injury, nerve, thorax,
sympathetic
esophagus (thoracic part) —*see also* Injury,
intrathoracic, esophagus
cervical NEC S19.85
eustachian tube S09.30-●
eye S05.9-●
avulsion S05.7-●
ball —*see* Injury, eyeball
conjunctiva S05.0-●
cornea
abrasion S05.0-●
laceration S05.3-●
with prolapse S05.2-●
lacrimal apparatus S05.8X-●
orbit penetration S05.4-●
specified site NEC S05.8X-●
eyeball S05.8X-●
contusion S05.1-●
penetrating S05.6-●
with
foreign body S05.5-●
prolapse or loss of intraocular tissue
S05.2-●
without prolapse or loss of intraocular
tissue S05.3-●
specified type NEC S05.8-●
eyebrow S09.93
eyelid S09.93
abrasion —*see* Abrasion, eyelid
contusion —*see* Contusion, eyelid
open —*see* Wound, open, eyelid
face S09.93

Injury *(Continued)*
fallopian tube S37.509
bilateral S37.502
blast injury S37.512
contusion S37.522
laceration S37.532
specified type NEC S37.592
blast injury (primary) S37.519
bilateral S37.512
secondary —*see* Injury, fallopian tube,
specified type NEC
unilateral S37.511
contusion S37.529
bilateral S37.522
unilateral S37.521
laceration S37.539
bilateral S37.532
unilateral S37.531
specified type NEC S37.599
bilateral S37.592
unilateral S37.591
unilateral S37.501
blast injury S37.511
contusion S37.521
laceration S37.531
specified type NEC S37.591
fascia —*see* Injury, muscle
fifth cranial nerve (trigeminal) —*see* Injury,
nerve, trigeminal
finger (nail) S69.9-●
blood vessel —*see* Injury, blood vessel,
finger
contusion —*see* Contusion, finger
dislocation —*see* Dislocation, finger
fracture —*see* Fracture, finger
muscle —*see* Injury, muscle, finger
nerve —*see* Injury, nerve, digital, finger
open —*see* Wound, open, finger
specified NEC S69.8-●
sprain —*see* Sprain, finger
superficial —*see* Injury, superficial, finger
first cranial nerve (olfactory) —*see* Injury,
nerve, olfactory
flank —*see* Injury, abdomen
foot S99.92-●
blood vessel —*see* Injury, blood vessel,
foot
contusion —*see* Contusion, foot
dislocation —*see* Dislocation, foot
fracture —*see* Fracture, foot
muscle —*see* Injury, muscle, foot
open —*see* Wound, open, foot
specified type NEC S99.82-●
sprain —*see* Sprain, foot
superficial —*see* Injury, superficial, foot
forceps NOS P15.9
forearm S59.91-●
blood vessel —*see* Injury, blood vessel,
forearm
contusion —*see* Contusion, forearm
fracture —*see* Fracture, forearm
muscle —*see* Injury, muscle, forearm
nerve —*see* Injury, nerve, forearm
open —*see* Wound, open, forearm
specified NEC S59.81-●
superficial —*see* Injury, superficial, forearm
forehead S09.90
fourth cranial nerve (trochlear) —*see* Injury,
nerve, trochlear
gallbladder S36.129
contusion S36.122
laceration S36.123
specified NEC S36.128
ganglion
celiac, coeliac —*see* Injury, nerve,
lumbosacral, sympathetic
gasserian —*see* Injury, nerve, trigeminal
stellate —*see* Injury, nerve, thorax,
sympathetic
thoracic sympathetic —*see* Injury, nerve,
thorax, sympathetic

Injury *(Continued)*
gasserian ganglion —*see* Injury, nerve,
trigeminal
gastric artery —*see* Injury, blood vessel, celiac
artery, branch
gastroduodenal artery —*see* Injury, blood
vessel, celiac artery, branch
gastrointestinal tract —*see* Injury,
intra-abdominal
with open wound into abdominal cavity —
see Wound, open, with penetration
into peritoneal cavity
colon —*see* Injury, intestine, large
rectum —*see* Injury, intestine, large, rectum
with open wound into abdominal cavity
S36.61
small intestine —*see* Injury, intestine, small
specified site NEC —*see* Injury, intra-
abdominal, specified, site NEC
stomach —*see* Injury, stomach
genital organ(s)
external S39.94
specified NEC S39.848
internal S37.90
fallopian tube —*see* Injury, fallopian tube
ovary —*see* Injury, ovary
prostate —*see* Injury, prostate
seminal vesicle —*see* Injury, pelvis,
organ, specified site NEC
uterus —*see* Injury, uterus
vas deferens —*see* Injury, pelvis, organ,
specified site NEC
obstetrical trauma O71.9
gland
lacrimal laceration —*see* Injury, eye,
specified site NEC
salivary S09.93
thyroid NEC S19.84
globe (eye) S05.90
specified NEC S05.8X-●
groin —*see* Injury, abdomen
gum S09.90
hand S69.9-●
blood vessel —*see* Injury, blood vessel,
hand
contusion —*see* Contusion, hand
fracture —*see* Fracture, hand
muscle —*see* Injury, muscle, hand
nerve —*see* Injury, nerve, hand
open —*see* Wound, open, hand
specified NEC S69.8-●
sprain —*see* Sprain, hand
superficial —*see* Injury, superficial, hand
head S09.90
with loss of consciousness S06.9-●
specified NEC S09.8-●
heart S26.90
with hemopericardium S26.00
contusion S26.01
laceration (mild) S26.020
major S26.022
moderate S26.021
specified type NEC S26.09
without hemopericardium S26.10
contusion S26.11
laceration S26.12
specified type NEC S26.19
contusion S26.91
laceration S26.92
specified type NEC S26.99
heel —*see* Injury, foot
hepatic
artery —*see* Injury, blood vessel, celiac
artery, branch
duct —*see* Injury, liver
vein —*see* Injury, vena cava, inferior
hip S79.91-●
blood vessel —*see* Injury, blood vessel,
hip
contusion —*see* Contusion, hip
dislocation —*see* Dislocation, hip

Injury *(Continued)*
  hip *(Continued)*
    fracture —*see* Fracture, femur, neck
    muscle —*see* Injury, muscle, hip
    nerve —*see* Injury, nerve, hip
    open —*see* Wound, open, hip
    specified NEC S79.81-●
    sprain —*see* Sprain, hip
    superficial —*see* Injury, superficial, hip
  hymen S39.94
  hypogastric
    blood vessel —*see* Injury, blood vessel, iliac
    plexus —*see* Injury, nerve, lumbosacral,
        sympathetic
  ileum —*see* Injury, intestine, small
  iliac region S39.91
  instrumental (during surgery) —*see*
      Laceration, accidental complicating
      surgery
    birth injury —*see* Birth, injury
    nonsurgical —*see* Injury, by site
    obstetrical O71.9
      bladder O71.5
      cervix O71.3
      high vaginal O71.4
      perineal NOS O70.9
      urethra O71.5
      uterus O71.5
        with rupture or perforation O71.1
  internal T14.8
    aorta —*see* Injury, aorta
    bladder (sphincter) —*see* Injury, bladder
      with
        ectopic or molar pregnancy O08.6
        following ectopic or molar pregnancy
            O08.6
        obstetrical trauma O71.5
    bronchus, bronchi —*see* Injury,
        intrathoracic, bronchus
    cecum —*see* Injury, intestine, large
    cervix (uteri) —*see also* Injury, uterus
      with ectopic or molar pregnancy O08.6
      following ectopic or molar pregnancy
          O08.6
      obstetrical trauma O71.3
    chest —*see* Injury, intrathoracic
    gastrointestinal tract —*see* Injury,
        intra-abdominal
    heart —*see* Injury, heart
    intestine NEC —*see* Injury, intestine
    intrauterine —*see* Injury, uterus
    mesentery —*see* Injury, intra-abdominal,
        specified, site NEC
    pelvis, pelvic (organ) S37.90
      following ectopic or molar pregnancy
          (subsequent episode) O08.6
      obstetrical trauma NEC O71.5
        rupture or perforation O71.1
      specified NEC S39.83
    rectum —*see* Injury, intestine, large, rectum
    stomach —*see* Injury, stomach
    ureter —*see* Injury, ureter
    urethra (sphincter) following ectopic or
        molar pregnancy O08.6
    uterus —*see* Injury, uterus
  interscapular area —*see* Injury, thorax
  intestine
    large S36.509
      ascending (right) S36.500
        blast injury (primary) S36.510
          secondary S36.590
        contusion S36.520
        laceration S36.530
        specified type NEC S36.590
      blast injury (primary) S36.519
        ascending (right) S36.510
        descending (left) S36.512
        rectum S36.61
        sigmoid S36.513
        specified site NEC S36.518
        transverse S36.511

Injury *(Continued)*
  intestine *(Continued)*
    large *(Continued)*
      contusion S36.529
        ascending (right) S36.520
        descending (left) S36.522
        rectum S36.62
        sigmoid S36.523
        specified site NEC S36.528
        transverse S36.521
      descending (left) S36.502
        blast injury (primary) S36.512
          secondary S36.592
        contusion S36.522
        laceration S36.532
        specified type NEC S36.592
      laceration S36.539
        ascending (right) S36.530
        descending (left) S36.532
        rectum S36.63
        sigmoid S36.533
        specified site NEC S36.538
        transverse S36.531
      rectum S36.60
        blast injury (primary) S36.61
          secondary S36.69
        contusion S36.62
        laceration S36.63
        specified type NEC S36.69
      sigmoid S36.503
        blast injury (primary) S36.513
          secondary S36.593
        contusion S36.523
        laceration S36.533
        specified type NEC S36.593
      specified
        site NEC S36.508
          blast injury (primary)
              S36.518
            secondary S36.598
          contusion S36.528
          laceration S36.538
          specified type NEC S36.598
        type NEC S36.599
          ascending (right) S36.590
          descending (left) S36.592
          rectum S36.69
          sigmoid S36.593
          specified site NEC S36.598
          transverse S36.591
      transverse S36.501
        blast injury (primary) S36.511
          secondary S36.591
        contusion S36.521
        laceration S36.531
        specified type NEC S36.591
    small S36.409
      blast injury (primary) S36.419
        duodenum S36.410
        secondary S36.499
          duodenum S36.490
          specified site NEC S36.498
        specified site NEC S36.418
      contusion S36.429
        duodenum S36.420
        specified site NEC S36.428
      duodenum S36.400
        blast injury (primary) S36.410
          secondary S36.490
        contusion S36.420
        laceration S36.430
        specified NEC S36.490
      laceration S36.439
        duodenum S36.430
        specified site NEC S36.438
      specified
        site NEC S36.408
        type NEC S36.499
          duodenum S36.490
          specified site NEC
              S36.498

Injury *(Continued)*
  intra-abdominal S36.90
    adrenal gland —*see* Injury, adrenal gland
    bladder —*see* Injury, bladder
    colon —*see* Injury, intestine, large
    contusion S36.92
    fallopian tube —*see* Injury, fallopian tube
    gallbladder —*see* Injury, gallbladder
    intestine —*see* Injury, intestine
    kidney —*see* Injury, kidney
    laceration S36.93
    liver —*see* Injury, liver
    ovary —*see* Injury, ovary
    pancreas —*see* Injury, pancreas
    pelvic NOS S37.90
    peritoneum —*see* Injury, intra-abdominal,
        specified, site NEC
    prostate —*see* Injury, prostate
    rectum —*see* Injury, intestine, large, rectum
    retroperitoneum —*see* Injury, intra-
        abdominal, specified, site NEC
    seminal vesicle —*see* Injury, pelvis, organ,
        specified site NEC
    small intestine —*see* Injury, intestine, small
    specified
      pelvic S37.90
        specified
          site NEC S37.899
            specified type NEC S37.898
          type NEC S37.99
      site NEC S36.899
        contusion S36.892
        laceration S36.893
        specified type NEC S36.898
      type NEC S36.99
    spleen —*see* Injury, spleen
    stomach —*see* Injury, stomach
    ureter —*see* Injury, ureter
    urethra —*see* Injury, urethra
    uterus —*see* Injury, uterus
    vas deferens —*see* Injury, pelvis, organ,
        specified site NEC
  intracranial (traumatic) S06.9-●
    cerebellar hemorrhage, traumatic —*see*
        Injury, intracranial, focal
    cerebral edema, traumatic S06.1X-●
      diffuse S06.1X-●
      focal S06.1X-●
    diffuse (axonal) S06.2X-●
    epidural hemorrhage (traumatic)
        S06.4X-●
    focal brain injury S06.30-●
      contusion —*see* Contusion, cerebral
      laceration —*see* Laceration, cerebral
    intracerebral hemorrhage, traumatic
        S06.36-●
      left side S06.35-●
      right side S06.34-●
    subarachnoid hemorrhage, traumatic
        S06.6X-●
    subdural hemorrhage, traumatic
        S06.5X-●
  intraocular —*see* Injury, eyeball, penetrating
  intrathoracic S27.9
    bronchus S27.409
      bilateral S27.402
      blast injury (primary) S27.419
        bilateral S27.412
        secondary —*see* Injury, intrathoracic,
            bronchus, specified type NEC
        unilateral S27.411
      contusion S27.429
        bilateral S27.422
        unilateral S27.421
      laceration S27.439
        bilateral S27.432
        unilateral S27.431
      specified type NEC S27.499
        bilateral S27.492
        unilateral S27.491
      unilateral S27.401

▶ New   ⇨ Revised   ~~deleted~~ Deleted   ● Use Additional Character(s)

Injury (Continued)
   intrathoracic (Continued)
      diaphragm S27.809
         contusion S27.802
         laceration S27.803
         specified type NEC S27.808
      esophagus (thoracic) S27.819
         contusion S27.812
         laceration S27.813
         specified type NEC S27.818
      heart —see Injury, heart
      hemopneumothorax S27.2
      hemothorax S27.1
      lung S27.309
         aspiration J69.0
         bilateral S27.302
         blast injury (primary) S27.319
            bilateral S27.312
            secondary —see Injury, intrathoracic,
               lung, specified type NEC
            unilateral S27.311
         contusion S27.329
            bilateral S27.322
            unilateral S27.321
         laceration S27.339
            bilateral S27.332
            unilateral S27.331
         specified type NEC S27.399
            bilateral S27.392
            unilateral S27.391
         unilateral S27.301
      pleura S27.60
         laceration S27.63
         specified type NEC S27.69
      pneumothorax S27.0
      specified organ NEC S27.899
         contusion S27.892
         laceration S27.893
         specified type NEC S27.898
      thoracic duct —see Injury, intrathoracic,
         specified organ NEC
      thymus gland —see Injury, intrathoracic,
         specified organ NEC
      trachea, thoracic S27.50
         blast (primary) S27.51
         contusion S27.52
         laceration S27.53
         specified type NEC S27.59
   iris —see Injury, eye, specified site NEC
      penetrating —see Injury, eyeball,
         penetrating
   jaw S09.93
   jejunum —see Injury, intestine, small
   joint NOS T14.8
      old or residual —see Disorder, joint,
         specified type NEC
   kidney S37.00-●
      acute (nontraumatic) N17.9
      contusion —see Contusion, kidney
      laceration —see Laceration, kidney
      specified NEC S37.09-●
   knee S89.9-●
      contusion —see Contusion, knee
      dislocation —see Dislocation, knee
      meniscus (lateral) (medial) —see Sprain,
         knee, specified site NEC
         old injury or tear —see Derangement,
            knee, meniscus, due to old injury
      open —see Wound, open, knee
      specified NEC S89.8-●
      sprain —see Sprain, knee
      superficial —see Injury, superficial, knee
   labium (majus) (minus) S39.94
   labyrinth, ear S09.30-●
   lacrimal apparatus, duct, gland, or sac —see
      Injury, eye, specified site NEC
   larynx NEC S19.81
   leg (lower) S89.9-●
      blood vessel —see Injury, blood vessel, leg
      contusion —see Contusion, leg
      fracture —see Fracture, leg

Injury (Continued)
   leg (Continued)
      muscle —see Injury, muscle, leg
      nerve —see Injury, nerve, leg
      open —see Wound, open, leg
      specified NEC S89.8-●
      superficial —see Injury, superficial, leg
   lens, eye —see Injury, eye, specified site
      NEC
      penetrating —see Injury, eyeball,
         penetrating
   limb NEC T14.8
   lip S09.93
   liver S36.119
      contusion S36.112
      laceration S36.113
         major (stellate) S36.116
         minor S36.114
         moderate S36.115
      specified NEC S36.118
   lower back S39.92
      specified NEC S39.82
   lumbar, lumbosacral (region) S39.92
      plexus —see Injury, lumbosacral plexus
   lumbosacral plexus S34.4
   lung —see also Injury, intrathoracic, lung
      aspiration J69.0
   ▶ dabbing (related) U07.0
   ▶ electronic cigarette (related) U07.0
   ▶ EVALI - [e-cigarette, or vaping, product
      use associated] U07.0
      transfusion-related (TRALI) J95.84
   ▶ vaping (associated) (device) (product) (use)
      U07.0
   lymphatic thoracic duct —see Injury,
      intrathoracic, specified organ NEC
   malar region S09.93
   mastoid region S09.90
   maxilla S09.93
   mediastinum —see Injury, intrathoracic,
      specified organ NEC
   membrane, brain —see Injury, intracranial
   meningeal artery —see Injury, intracranial,
      subdural hemorrhage
   meninges (cerebral) —see Injury, intracranial
   mesenteric
      artery
         branch S35.299
            laceration (minor) (superficial) S35.291
               major S35.292
            specified NEC S35.298
         inferior S35.239
            laceration (minor) (superficial) S35.231
               major S35.232
            specified NEC S35.238
         superior S35.229
            laceration (minor) (superficial) S35.221
               major S35.222
            specified NEC S35.228
      plexus (inferior) (superior) —see Injury,
         nerve, lumbosacral, sympathetic
      vein
         inferior S35.349
            laceration S35.341
            specified NEC S35.348
         superior S35.339
            laceration S35.331
            specified NEC S35.338
   mesentery —see Injury, intra-abdominal,
      specified site NEC
   mesosalpinx —see Injury, pelvic organ,
      specified site NEC
   middle ear S09.30-●
   midthoracic region NOS S29.9
   mouth S09.93
   multiple NOS T07
   muscle (and fascia) (and tendon)
      abdomen S39.001
         laceration S39.021
         specified type NEC S39.091
         strain S39.011

Injury (Continued)
   muscle (Continued)
      abductor
         thumb, forearm level —see Injury,
            muscle, thumb, abductor
      adductor
         thigh S76.20-●
            laceration S76.22-●
            specified type NEC S76.29-●
            strain S76.21-●
      ankle —see Injury, muscle, foot
      anterior muscle group, at leg level (lower)
         S86.20-●
         laceration S86.22-●
         specified type NEC S86.29-●
         strain S86.21-●
      arm (upper) —see Injury, muscle,
         shoulder
      biceps (parts NEC) S46.20-●
         laceration S46.22-●
         long head S46.10-●
            laceration S46.12-●
            specified type NEC S46.19-●
            strain S46.11-●
         specified type NEC S46.29-●
         strain S46.21-●
      extensor
         finger(s) (other than thumb) —see Injury,
            muscle, finger by site, extensor
         forearm level, specified NEC —see
            Injury, muscle, forearm, extensor
         thumb —see Injury, muscle, thumb,
            extensor
         toe (large) (ankle level) (foot level) —see
            Injury, muscle, toe, extensor
      finger
         extensor (forearm level) S56.40-●
            hand level S66.309
               laceration S66.329
               specified type NEC S66.399
               strain S66.319
            laceration S56.429
            specified type NEC S56.499
            strain S56.419
         flexor (forearm level) S56.10-●
            hand level S66.109
               laceration S66.129
               specified type NEC S66.199
               strain S66.119
            laceration S56.129
            specified type NEC S56.199
            strain S56.119
         index
            extensor (forearm level)
               hand level S66.308
                  laceration S66.32-●
                  specified type NEC S66.39-●
                  strain S66.31-●
             specified type NEC S56.492-●
            flexor (forearm level)
               hand level S66.108
                  laceration S66.12-●
                  specified type NEC
                    S66.19-●
                  strain S66.11-●
             specified type NEC S56.19-●
             strain S56.11-●
            intrinsic S66.50-●
              laceration S66.52-●
              specified type NEC S66.59-●
              strain S66.51-●
         intrinsic S66.509
            laceration S66.529
            specified type NEC S66.599
            strain S66.519
         little
            extensor (forearm level)
               hand level S66.30-●
                  laceration S66.32-●
                  specified type NEC S66.39-●
                  strain S66.31-●

Injury (Continued)
  muscle (Continued)
    finger (Continued)
      little (Continued)
        extensor (Continued)
          laceration S56.42-●
          specified type NEC S56.49-●
          strain S56.41-●
        flexor (forearm level)
          hand level S66.10-●
            laceration S66.12-●
            specified type NEC S66.19-●
            strain S66.11-●
          laceration S56.12-●
          specified type NEC S56.19-●
          strain S56.11-●
        intrinsic S66.50-●
          laceration S66.52-●
          specified type NEC S66.59-●
          strain S66.51-●
      middle
        extensor (forearm level)
          hand level S66.30-●
            laceration S66.32-●
            specified type NEC S66.39-●
            strain S66.31-●
          laceration S56.42-●
          specified type NEC S56.49-●
          strain S56.41-●
        flexor (forearm level)
          hand level S66.10-●
            laceration S66.12-●
            specified type NEC S66.19-●
            strain S66.11-●
          laceration S56.12-●
          specified type NEC S56.19-●
          strain S56.11-●
        intrinsic S66.50-●
          laceration S66.52-●
          specified type NEC S66.59-●
          strain S66.51-●
      ring
        extensor (forearm level)
          hand level S66.30-●
            laceration S66.32-●
            specified type NEC S66.39-●
            strain S66.31-●
          laceration S56.42-●
          specified type NEC S56.49-●
          strain S56.41-●
        flexor (forearm level)
          hand level S66.10-●
            laceration S66.12-●
            specified type NEC S66.19-●
            strain S66.11-●
          laceration S56.12-●
          specified type NEC S56.19-●
          strain S56.11-●
        intrinsic S66.50-●
          laceration S66.52-●
          specified type NEC S66.59-●
          strain S66.51-●
    flexor
      finger(s) (other than thumb) — see Injury,
        muscle, finger
      forearm level, specified NEC —
        see Injury, muscle, forearm,
        flexor
      thumb —see Injury, muscle, thumb,
        flexor
      toe (long) (ankle level) (foot level) —see
        Injury, muscle, toe, flexor
    foot S96.90-●
      intrinsic S96.20-●
        laceration S96.22-●
        specified type NEC S96.29-●
        strain S96.21-●
      laceration S96.92-●

Injury (Continued)
  muscle (Continued)
    foot (Continued)
      long extensor, toe —see Injury, muscle,
        toe, extensor
      long flexor, toe —see Injury, muscle, toe,
        flexor
      specified
        site NEC S96.80-●
          laceration S96.82-●
          specified type NEC S96.89-●
          strain S96.81-●
        type NEC S96.99-●
      strain S96.91-●
    forearm (level) S56.90-●
      extensor S56.50-●
        laceration S56.52-●
        specified type NEC S56.59-●
        strain S56.51-●
      flexor S56.20-●
        laceration S56.22-●
        specified type NEC S56.29-●
        strain S56.21-●
      laceration S56.92-●
      specified S56.99-●
        site NEC S56.80-●
          laceration S56.82-●
          strain S56.81-●
        type NEC S56.89-●
      strain S56.91-●
    hand (level) S66.90-●
      laceration S66.92-●
      specified
        site NEC S66.80-●
          laceration S66.82-●
          specified type NEC S66.89-●
          strain S66.81-●
        type NEC S66.99-●
      strain S66.91-●
    head S09.10
      laceration S09.12
      specified type NEC S09.19
      strain S09.11
    hip NEC S76.00-●
      laceration S76.02-●
      specified type NEC S76.09-●
      strain S76.01-●
    intrinsic
      ankle and foot level —see Injury, muscle,
        foot, intrinsic
      finger (other than thumb) —see Injury,
        muscle, finger by site, intrinsic
      foot (level) —see Injury, muscle, foot,
        intrinsic
      thumb —see Injury, muscle, thumb,
        intrinsic
    leg (level) (lower) S86.90-●
      Achilles tendon —see Injury, Achilles
        tendon
      anterior muscle group —see Injury,
        muscle, anterior muscle group
      laceration S86.92-●
      peroneal muscle group —see Injury,
        muscle, peroneal muscle group
      posterior muscle group —see Injury,
        muscle, posterior muscle group,
        leg level
      specified
        site NEC S86.80-●
          laceration S86.82-●
          specified type NEC S86.89-●
          strain S86.81-●
        type NEC S86.99-●
      strain S86.91-●
    long
      extensor toe, at ankle and foot level —see
        Injury, muscle, toe, extensor
      flexor, toe, at ankle and foot level —see
        Injury, muscle, toe, flexor
      head, biceps —see Injury, muscle, biceps,
        long head

Injury (Continued)
  muscle (Continued)
    lower back S39.002
      laceration S39.022
      specified type NEC S39.092
      strain S39.012
    neck (level) S16.9
      laceration S16.2
      specified type NEC S16.8
      strain S16.1
    pelvis S39.003
      laceration S39.023
      specified type NEC S39.093
      strain S39.013
    peroneal muscle group, at leg level (lower)
      S86.30-●
      laceration S86.32-●
      specified type NEC S86.39-●
      strain S86.31-●
    posterior muscle (group)
      leg level (lower) S86.10-●
        laceration S86.12-●
        specified type NEC S86.19-●
        strain S86.11-●
      thigh level S76.30-●
        laceration S76.32-●
        specified type NEC S76.39-●
        strain S76.31-●
    quadriceps (thigh) S76.10-●
      laceration S76.12-●
      specified type NEC S76.19-●
      strain S76.11-●
    shoulder S46.90-●
      laceration S46.92-●
      rotator cuff —see Injury, rotator cuff
      specified site NEC S46.80-●
        laceration S46.82-●
        specified type NEC S46.89-●
        strain S46.81-●
      specified type NEC S46.99-●
      strain S46.91-●
    thigh NEC (level) S76.90-●
      adductor —see Injury, muscle, adductor,
        thigh
      laceration S76.92-●
      posterior muscle (group) —see Injury,
        muscle, posterior muscle, thigh level
      quadriceps —see Injury, muscle,
        quadriceps
      specified
        site NEC S76.80-●
          laceration S76.82-●
          specified type NEC S76.89-●
          strain S76.81-●
        type NEC S76.99-●
      strain S76.91-●
    thorax (level) S29.009
      back wall S29.002
      front wall S29.001
      laceration S29.029
        back wall S29.022
        front wall S29.021
      specified type NEC S29.099
        back wall S29.092
        front wall S29.091
      strain S29.019
        back wall S29.012
        front wall S29.011
    thumb
      abductor (forearm level) S56.30-●
        laceration S56.32-●
        specified type NEC S56.39-●
        strain S56.31-●
      extensor (forearm level) S56.30-●
        hand level S66.20-●
          laceration S66.22-●
          specified type NEC S66.29-●
          strain S66.21-●
        laceration S56.32-●
        specified type NEC S56.39-●
        strain S56.31-●

▶ New   ⇒ Revised   ~~deleted~~ Deleted   ● Use Additional Character(s)

Injury *(Continued)*
  muscle *(Continued)*
    thumb *(Continued)*
      flexor (forearm level) S56.00-●
        hand level S66.00-●
          laceration S66.02-●
          specified type NEC S66.09-●
          strain S66.01-●
        laceration S56.02-●
        specified type NEC S56.09-●
        strain S56.01-●
        wrist level —*see* Injury, muscle, thumb, flexor, hand level
      intrinsic S66.40-●
        laceration S66.42-●
        specified type NEC S66.49-●
        strain S66.41-●
    toe —*see also* Injury, muscle, foot
      extensor, long S96.10-●
        laceration S96.12-●
        specified type NEC S96.19-●
        strain S96.11-●
      flexor, long S96.00-●
        laceration S96.02-●
        specified type NEC S96.09-●
        strain S96.01-●
    triceps S46.30-●
      laceration S46.32-●
      specified type NEC S46.39-●
      strain S46.31-●
    wrist (and hand) level —*see* Injury, muscle, hand
  musculocutaneous nerve —*see* Injury, nerve, musculocutaneous
  myocardium —*see* Injury, heart
  nape —*see* Injury, neck
  nasal (septum) (sinus) S09.92
  nasopharynx S09.92
  neck S19.9
    specified NEC S19.80
      specified site NEC S19.89
  nerve NEC T14.8
    abdomen S34.9
      peripheral S34.6
      specified site NEC S34.8
    abducens S04.4-●
      contusion S04.4-●
      laceration S04.4-●
      specified type NEC S04.4-●
    abducent —*see* Injury, nerve, abducens
    accessory S04.7-●
      contusion S04.7-●
      laceration S04.7-●
      specified type NEC S04.7-●
    acoustic S04.6-●
      contusion S04.6-●
      laceration S04.6-●
      specified type NEC S04.6-●
    ankle S94.9-●
      cutaneous sensory S94.3-●
      specified site NEC —*see* subcategory S94.8
    anterior crural, femoral —*see* Injury, nerve, femoral
    arm (upper) S44.9-●
      axillary —*see* Injury, nerve, axillary
      cutaneous —*see* Injury, nerve, cutaneous, arm
      median —*see* Injury, nerve, median, upper arm
      musculocutaneous —*see* Injury, nerve, musculocutaneous
      radial —*see* Injury, nerve, radial, upper arm
      specified site NEC —*see* subcategory S44.8
      ulnar —*see* Injury, nerve, ulnar, arm
    auditory —*see* Injury, nerve, acoustic

Injury *(Continued)*
  nerve NEC *(Continued)*
    axillary S44.3-●
    brachial plexus —*see* Injury, brachial plexus
    cervical sympathetic S14.5
    cranial S04.9
      contusion S04.9
      eighth (acoustic or auditory) —*see* Injury, nerve, acoustic
      eleventh (accessory) —*see* Injury, nerve, accessory
      fifth (trigeminal) —*see* Injury, nerve, trigeminal
      first (olfactory) —*see* Injury, nerve, olfactory
      fourth (trochlear) —*see* Injury, nerve, trochlear
      laceration S04.9
      ninth (glossopharyngeal) —*see* Injury, nerve, glossopharyngeal
      second (optic) —*see* Injury, nerve, optic
      seventh (facial) —*see* Injury, nerve, facial
      sixth (abducent) —*see* Injury, nerve, abducens
      specified
        nerve NEC S04.89-●
          contusion S04.89-●
          laceration S04.89-●
          specified type NEC S04.89-●
        type NEC S04.9
      tenth (pneumogastric or vagus) —*see* Injury, nerve, vagus
      third (oculomotor) —*see* Injury, nerve, oculomotor
      twelfth (hypoglossal) —*see* Injury, nerve, hypoglossal
    cutaneous sensory
      ankle (level) S94.3-●
      arm (upper) (level) S44.5-●
      foot (level) —*see* Injury, nerve, cutaneous sensory, ankle
      forearm (level) S54.3-●
      hip (level) S74.2-●
      leg (lower level) S84.2-●
      shoulder (level) —*see* Injury, nerve, cutaneous sensory, arm
      thigh (level) —*see* Injury, nerve, cutaneous sensory, hip
    deep peroneal —*see* Injury, nerve, peroneal, foot
    digital
      finger S64.4-●
        index S64.49-●
        little S64.49-●
        middle S64.49-●
        ring S64.49-●
        thumb S64.3-●
      toe —*see* Injury, nerve, ankle, specified site NEC
    eighth cranial (acoustic or auditory) —*see* Injury, nerve, acoustic
    eleventh cranial (accessory) —*see* Injury, nerve, accessory
    facial S04.5-●
      contusion S04.5-●
      laceration S04.5-●
      newborn P11.3
      specified type NEC S04.5-●
    femoral (hip level) (thigh level) S74.1-●
    fifth cranial (trigeminal) —*see* Injury, nerve, trigeminal
    finger (digital) —*see* Injury, nerve, digital, finger
    first cranial (olfactory) —*see* Injury, nerve, olfactory
    foot S94.9-●
      cutaneous sensory S94.3-●
      deep peroneal S94.2-●
      lateral plantar S94.0-●

Injury *(Continued)*
  nerve NEC *(Continued)*
    foot *(Continued)*
      medial plantar S94.1-●
      specified site NEC —*see* subcategory S94.8
    forearm (level) S54.9-●
      cutaneous sensory —*see* Injury, nerve, cutaneous sensory, forearm
      median —*see* Injury, nerve, median
      radial —*see* Injury, nerve, radial
      specified site NEC —*see* subcategory S54.8
      ulnar —*see* Injury, nerve, ulnar
    fourth cranial (trochlear) —*see* Injury, nerve, trochlear
    glossopharyngeal S04.89-●
      specified type NEC S04.89-●
    hand S64.9-●
      median —*see* Injury, nerve, median, hand
      radial —*see* Injury, nerve, radial, hand
      specified NEC —*see* subcategory S64.8
      ulnar —*see* Injury, nerve, ulnar, hand
    hip (level) S74.9-●
      cutaneous sensory —*see* Injury, nerve, cutaneous sensory, hip
      femoral —*see* Injury, nerve, femoral
      sciatic —*see* Injury, nerve, sciatic
      specified site NEC —*see* subcategory S74.8
    hypoglossal S04.89-●
      specified type NEC S04.89-●
    lateral plantar S94.0-●
    leg (lower) S84.9-●
      cutaneous sensory —*see* Injury, nerve, cutaneous sensory, leg
      peroneal —*see* Injury, nerve, peroneal
      specified site NEC —*see* subcategory S84.8
      tibial —*see* Injury, nerve, tibial
      upper —*see* Injury, nerve, thigh
    lower
      back —*see* Injury, nerve, abdomen, specified site NEC
        peripheral —*see* Injury, nerve, abdomen, peripheral
      limb —*see* Injury, nerve, leg
    lumbar plexus —*see* Injury, nerve, lumbosacral, sympathetic
    lumbar spinal —*see* Injury, nerve, spinal, lumbar
    lumbosacral
      plexus —*see* Injury, nerve, lumbosacral, sympathetic
      sympathetic S34.5
    medial plantar S94.1-●
    median (forearm level) S54.1-●
      hand (level) S64.1-●
      upper arm (level) S44.1-●
      wrist (level) —*see* Injury, nerve, median, hand
    musculocutaneous S44.4-●
    musculospiral (upper arm level) —*see* Injury, nerve, radial, upper arm
    neck S14.9
      peripheral S14.4
      specified site NEC S14.8
      sympathetic S14.5
    ninth cranial (glossopharyngeal) —*see* Injury, nerve, glossopharyngeal
    oculomotor S04.1-●
      contusion S04.1-●
      laceration S04.1-●
      specified type NEC S04.1-●
    olfactory S04.81-●
      specified type NEC S04.81-●
    optic S04.01-●
      contusion S04.01-●
      laceration S04.01-●
      specified type NEC S04.01-●

Injury (Continued)

nerve NEC (Continued)

pelvic girdle —see Injury, nerve, hip

pelvis —see Injury, nerve, abdomen, specified site NEC

peripheral —see Injury, nerve, abdomen, peripheral

peripheral NEC T14.8

abdomen —see Injury, nerve, abdomen, peripheral

lower back —see Injury, nerve, abdomen, peripheral

neck —see Injury, nerve, neck, peripheral

pelvis —see Injury, nerve, abdomen, peripheral

specified NEC T14.8

peroneal (lower leg level) S84.1-●

foot S94.2-●

plexus

brachial —see Injury, brachial plexus

celiac, coeliac —see Injury, nerve, lumbosacral, sympathetic

mesenteric, inferior —see Injury, nerve, lumbosacral, sympathetic

sacral —see Injury, lumbosacral plexus

spinal

brachial —see Injury, brachial plexus

lumbosacral —see Injury, lumbosacral plexus

pneumogastric —see Injury, nerve, vagus

radial (forearm level) S54.2-●

hand (level) S64.2-●

upper arm (level) S44.2-●

wrist (level) —see Injury, nerve, radial, hand

root —see Injury, nerve, spinal, root

sacral plexus —see Injury, lumbosacral plexus

sacral spinal —see Injury, nerve, spinal, sacral

sciatic (hip level) (thigh level) S74.0-●

second cranial (optic) —see Injury, nerve, optic

seventh cranial (facial) —see Injury, nerve, facial

shoulder —see Injury, nerve, arm

sixth cranial (abducent) —see Injury, nerve, abducens

spinal

plexus —see Injury, nerve, plexus, spinal

root

cervical S14.2

dorsal S24.2

lumbar S34.21

sacral S34.22

thoracic —see Injury, nerve, spinal, root, dorsal

splanchnic —see Injury, nerve, lumbosacral, sympathetic

sympathetic NEC —see Injury, nerve, lumbosacral, sympathetic

cervical —see Injury, nerve, cervical sympathetic

tenth cranial (pneumogastric or vagus) — see Injury, nerve, vagus

thigh (level) —see Injury, nerve, hip

cutaneous sensory —see Injury, nerve, cutaneous sensory, hip

femoral —see Injury, nerve, femoral

sciatic —see Injury, nerve, sciatic

specified NEC —see Injury, nerve, hip

third cranial (oculomotor) —see Injury, nerve, oculomotor

thorax S24.9

peripheral S24.3

specified site NEC S24.8

sympathetic S24.4

thumb, digital —see Injury, nerve, digital, thumb

tibial (lower leg level) (posterior) S84.0-●

Injury (Continued)

nerve NEC (Continued)

toe —see Injury, nerve, ankle

trigeminal S04.3-●

contusion S04.3-●

laceration S04.3-●

specified type NEC S04.3-●

trochlear S04.2-●

contusion S04.2-●

laceration S04.2-●

specified type NEC S04.2-●

twelfth cranial (hypoglossal) —see Injury, nerve, hypoglossal

ulnar (forearm level) S54.0-●

arm (upper) (level) S44.0-●

hand (level) S64.0-●

wrist (level) —see Injury, nerve, ulnar, hand

vagus S04.89-●

specified type NEC S04.89-●

wrist (level) —see Injury, nerve, hand

ninth cranial nerve (glossopharyngeal) —see Injury, nerve, glossopharyngeal

nose (septum) S09.92

obstetrical O71.9

specified NEC O71.89

occipital (region) (scalp) S09.90

lobe —see Injury, intracranial

optic chiasm S04.02

optic radiation S04.03-●

optic tract and pathways S04.03-●

orbit, orbital (region) —see Injury, eye

penetrating (with foreign body) —see Injury, eye, orbit, penetrating

specified NEC —see Injury, eye, specified site NEC

ovary, ovarian S37.409

bilateral S37.402

contusion S37.422

laceration S37.432

specified type NEC S37.492

blood vessel —see Injury, blood vessel, ovarian

contusion S37.429

bilateral S37.422

unilateral S37.421

laceration S37.439

bilateral S37.432

unilateral S37.431

specified type NEC S37.499

bilateral S37.492

unilateral S37.491

unilateral S37.401

contusion S37.421

laceration S37.431

specified type NEC S37.491

palate (hard) (soft) S09.93

pancreas S36.209

body S36.201

contusion S36.221

laceration S36.231

major S36.261

minor S36.241

moderate S36.251

specified type NEC S36.291

contusion S36.229

head S36.200

contusion S36.220

laceration S36.230

major S36.260

minor S36.240

moderate S36.250

specified type NEC S36.290

laceration S36.239

major S36.269

minor S36.249

moderate S36.259

specified type NEC S36.299

tail S36.202

contusion S36.222

Injury (Continued)

pancreas (Continued)

tail (Continued)

laceration S36.232

major S36.262

minor S36.242

moderate S36.252

specified type NEC S36.292

parietal (region) (scalp) S09.90

lobe —see Injury, intracranial

patellar ligament (tendon) S76.10-●

laceration S76.12-●

specified NEC S76.19-●

strain S76.11-●

pelvis, pelvic (floor) S39.93

complicating delivery O70.1

joint or ligament, complicating delivery O71.6

organ S37.90

with ectopic or molar pregnancy O08.6

complication of abortion —see Abortion

contusion S37.92

following ectopic or molar pregnancy O08.6

laceration S37.93

obstetrical trauma NEC O71.5

specified

site NEC S37.899

contusion S37.892

laceration S37.893

specified type NEC S37.898

type NEC S37.99

specified NEC S39.83

penis S39.94

perineum S39.94

peritoneum S36.81

laceration S36.893

periurethral tissue —see Injury, urethra

complicating delivery O71.82

phalanges

foot —see Injury, foot

hand —see Injury, hand

pharynx NEC S19.85

pleura —see Injury, intrathoracic, pleura

plexus

brachial —see Injury, brachial plexus

cardiac —see Injury, nerve, thorax, sympathetic

celiac, coeliac —see Injury, nerve, lumbosacral, sympathetic

esophageal —see Injury, nerve, thorax, sympathetic

hypogastric —see Injury, nerve, lumbosacral, sympathetic

lumbar, lumbosacral —see Injury, lumbosacral plexus

mesenteric —see Injury, nerve, lumbosacral, sympathetic

pulmonary —see Injury, nerve, thorax, sympathetic

postcardiac surgery (syndrome) I97.0

prepuce S39.94

pressure

injury —see Ulcer, pressure, by site

prostate S37.829

contusion S37.822

laceration S37.823

specified type NEC S37.828

pubic region S39.94

pudendum S39.94

pulmonary plexus —see Injury, nerve, thorax, sympathetic

rectovaginal septum NEC S39.83

rectum —see Injury, intestine, large, rectum

retina —see Injury, eye, specified site NEC

penetrating —see Injury, eyeball, penetrating

retroperitoneal —see Injury, intra-abdominal, specified site NEC

Injury *(Continued)*
    rotator cuff (muscle(s)) (tendon(s)) S46.00-●
        laceration S46.02-●
        specified type NEC S46.09-●
        strain S46.01-●
    round ligament —*see* Injury, pelvic organ,
        specified site NEC
    sacral plexus —*see* Injury, lumbosacral
        plexus
    salivary duct or gland S09.93
    scalp S09.90
        newborn (birth injury) P12.9
            due to monitoring (electrode) (sampling
                incision) P12.4
            specified NEC P12.89
                caput succedaneum P12.81
    scapular region —*see* Injury, shoulder
    sclera —*see* Injury, eye, specified site NEC
        penetrating —*see* Injury, eyeball,
            penetrating
    scrotum S39.94
    second cranial nerve (optic) —*see* Injury,
        nerve, optic
    seminal vesicle —*see* Injury, pelvic organ,
        specified site NEC
    seventh cranial nerve (facial) —*see* Injury,
        nerve, facial
    shoulder S49.9-●
        blood vessel —*see* Injury, blood vessel,
            arm
        contusion —*see* Contusion, shoulder
        dislocation —*see* Dislocation, shoulder
        fracture —*see* Fracture, shoulder
        muscle —*see* Injury, muscle, shoulder
        nerve —*see* Injury, nerve, shoulder
        open —*see* Wound, open, shoulder
        specified type NEC S49.8-●
        sprain —*see* Sprain, shoulder girdle
        superficial —*see* Injury, superficial,
            shoulder
    sinus
        cavernous —*see* Injury, intracranial
        nasal S09.92
    sixth cranial nerve (abducent) —*see* Injury,
        nerve, abducens
    skeleton, birth injury P13.9
        specified part NEC P13.8
    skin NEC T14.8
        surface intact —*see* Injury, superficial
    skull NEC S09.90
    specified NEC T14.8
    spermatic cord (pelvic region) S37.898
        scrotal region S39.848
    spinal (cord)
        cervical (neck) S14.109
            anterior cord syndrome S14.139
                C1 level S14.131
                C2 level S14.132
                C3 level S14.133
                C4 level S14.134
                C5 level S14.135
                C6 level S14.136
                C7 level S14.137
                C8 level S14.138
            Brown-Séquard syndrome S14.149
                C1 level S14.141
                C2 level S14.142
                C3 level S14.143
                C4 level S14.144
                C5 level S14.145
                C6 level S14.146
                C7 level S14.147
                C8 level S14.148
            C1 level S14.101
            C2 level S14.102
            C3 level S14.103
            C4 level S14.104
            C5 level S14.105
            C6 level S14.106
            C7 level S14.107
            C8 level S14.108

Injury *(Continued)*
    spinal *(Continued)*
        cervical *(Continued)*
            central cord syndrome
                S14.129
                C1 level S14.121
                C2 level S14.122
                C3 level S14.123
                C4 level S14.124
                C5 level S14.125
                C6 level S14.126
                C7 level S14.127
                C8 level S14.128
            complete lesion S14.119
                C1 level S14.111
                C2 level S14.112
                C3 level S14.113
                C4 level S14.114
                C5 level S14.115
                C6 level S14.116
                C7 level S14.117
                C8 level S14.118
            concussion S14.0
            edema S14.0
            incomplete lesion specified NEC
                S14.159
                C1 level S14.151
                C2 level S14.152
                C3 level S14.153
                C4 level S14.154
                C5 level S14.155
                C6 level S14.156
                C7 level S14.157
                C8 level S14.158
            posterior cord syndrome S14.159
                C1 level S14.151
                C2 level S14.152
                C3 level S14.153
                C4 level S14.154
                C5 level S14.155
                C6 level S14.156
                C7 level S14.157
                C8 level S14.158
        dorsal —*see* Injury, spinal, thoracic
        lumbar S34.109
            complete lesion S34.119
                L1 level S34.111
                L2 level S34.112
                L3 level S34.113
                L4 level S34.114
                L5 level S34.115
            concussion S34.01
            edema S34.01
            incomplete lesion S34.129
                L1 level S34.121
                L2 level S34.122
                L3 level S34.123
                L4 level S34.124
                L5 level S34.125
            L1 level S34.101
            L2 level S34.102
            L3 level S34.103
            L4 level S34.104
            L5 level S34.105
         nerve root NEC
            cervical —*see* Injury, nerve, spinal, root,
                cervical
            dorsal —*see* Injury, nerve, spinal, root,
                dorsal
            lumbar S34.21
            sacral S34.22
            thoracic —*see* Injury, nerve, spinal, root,
                dorsal
        plexus
            brachial —*see* Injury, brachial
                plexus
            lumbosacral —*see* Injury, lumbosacral
                plexus
        sacral S34.139
            complete lesion S34.131
            incomplete lesion S34.132

Injury *(Continued)*
    spinal *(Continued)*
        thoracic S24.109
            anterior cord syndrome S24.139
                T1 level S24.131
                T2-T6 level S24.132
                T7-T10 level S24.133
                T11-T12 level S24.134
            Brown-Séquard syndrome
                S24.149
                T1 level S24.141
                T2-T6 level S24.142
                T7-T10 level S24.143
                T11-T12 level S24.144
            complete lesion S24.119
                T1 level S24.111
                T2-T6 level S24.112
                T7-T10 level S24.113
                T11-T12 level S24.114
            concussion S24.0
            edema S24.0
            incomplete lesion specified NEC
                S24.159
                T1 level S24.151
                T2-T6 level S24.152
                T7-T10 level S24.153
                T11-T12 level S24.154
            posterior cord syndrome S24.159
                T1 level S24.151
                T2-T6 level S24.152
                T7-T10 level S24.153
                T11-T12 level S24.154
            T1 level S24.101
            T2-T6 level S24.102
            T7-T10 level S24.103
            T11-T12 level S24.104
    splanchnic nerve —*see* Injury, nerve,
        lumbosacral, sympathetic
    spleen S36.00
        contusion S36.029
            major S36.021
            minor S36.020
        laceration S36.039
            major (massive) (stellate) S36.032
            moderate S36.031
            superficial (capsular) (minor) S36.030
        specified type NEC S36.09
    splenic artery —*see* Injury, blood vessel, celiac
        artery, branch
    stellate ganglion —*see* Injury, nerve, thorax,
        sympathetic
    sternal region S29.9
    stomach S36.30
        contusion S36.32
        laceration S36.33
        specified type NEC S36.39
    subconjunctival —*see* Injury, eye, conjunctiva
    subcutaneous NEC T14.8
    submaxillary region S09.93
    submental region S09.93
    subungual
        fingers —*see* Injury, hand
        toes —*see* Injury, foot
    superficial NEC T14.8
        abdomen, abdominal (wall) S30.92
            abrasion S30.811
            bite S30.871
                insect S30.861
            contusion S30.1
            external constriction S30.841
            foreign body S30.851
        abrasion —*see* Abrasion, by site
        adnexa, eye NEC —*see* Injury, eye,
            specified site NEC
        alveolar process —*see* Injury, superficial,
            oral cavity
        ankle S90.91-●
            abrasion —*see* Abrasion, ankle
            bite —*see* Bite, ankle
            blister —*see* Blister, ankle
            contusion —*see* Contusion, ankle

Injury (Continued)
  superficial NEC (Continued)
    ankle (Continued)
      external constriction —see Constriction,
        external, ankle
      foreign body —see Foreign body,
        superficial, ankle
    anus S30.98
    arm (upper) S40.92-●
      abrasion —see Abrasion, arm
      bite —see Bite, superficial, arm
      blister —see Blister, arm (upper)
      contusion —see Contusion, arm
      external constriction —see Constriction,
        external, arm
      foreign body —see Foreign body,
        superficial, arm
    auditory canal (external) (meatus) —see
      Injury, superficial, ear
    auricle —see Injury, superficial, ear
    axilla —see Injury, superficial, arm
    back —see also Injury, superficial, thorax,
      back
      lower S30.91
        abrasion S30.810
        contusion S30.0
        external constriction S30.840
        superficial
          bite NEC S30.870
            insect S30.860
          foreign body S30.850
    bite NEC —see Bite, superficial NEC, by
      site
    blister —see Blister, by site
    breast S20.10-●
      abrasion —see Abrasion, breast
      bite —see Bite, superficial, breast
      contusion —see Contusion, breast
      external constriction —see Constriction,
        external, breast
      foreign body —see Foreign body,
        superficial, breast
    brow —see Injury, superficial, head,
      specified NEC
    buttock S30.91
    calf —see Injury, superficial, leg
    canthus, eye —see Injury, superficial,
      periocular area
    cheek (external) —see Injury, superficial,
      head, specified NEC
      internal —see Injury, superficial, oral
        cavity
    chest wall —see Injury, superficial, thorax
    chin —see Injury, superficial, head NEC
    clitoris S30.95
    conjunctiva —see Injury, eye, conjunctiva
      with foreign body (in conjunctival
        sac) —see Foreign body,
        conjunctival sac
    contusion —see Contusion, by site
    costal region —see Injury, superficial,
      thorax
    digit(s)
      hand —see Injury, superficial, finger
    ear (auricle) (canal) (external) S00.40-●
      abrasion —see Abrasion, ear
      bite —see Bite, superficial, ear
      contusion —see Contusion, ear
      external constriction —see Constriction,
        external, ear
      foreign body —see Foreign body,
        superficial, ear
    elbow S50.90-●
      abrasion —see Abrasion, elbow
      bite —see Bite, superficial, elbow
      blister —see Blister, elbow
      contusion —see Contusion, elbow
      external constriction —see Constriction,
        external, elbow
      foreign body —see Foreign body,
        superficial, elbow

Injury (Continued)
  superficial NEC (Continued)
    epididymis S30.94
    epigastric region S30.92
    epiglottis —see Injury, superficial, throat
    esophagus
      cervical —see Injury, superficial,
        throat
      external constriction —see Constriction,
        external, by site
    extremity NEC T14.8
    eyeball NEC —see Injury, eye, specified
      site NEC
    eyebrow —see Injury, superficial,
      periocular area
    eyelid S00.20-●
      abrasion —see Abrasion, eyelid
      bite —see Bite, superficial, eyelid
      contusion —see Contusion, eyelid
      external constriction —see Constriction,
        external, eyelid
      foreign body —see Foreign body,
        superficial, eyelid
    face NEC —see Injury, superficial, head,
      specified NEC
    finger(s) S60.949
      abrasion —see Abrasion, finger
      bite —see Bite, superficial, finger
      blister —see Blister, finger
      contusion —see Contusion, finger
      external constriction —see Constriction,
        external, finger
      foreign body —see Foreign body,
        superficial, finger
      index S60.94-●
      insect bite —see Bite, by site, superficial,
        insect
      little S60.94-●
      middle S60.94-●
      ring S60.94-●
    flank S30.92
    foot S90.92-●
      abrasion —see Abrasion, foot
      bite —see Bite, foot
      blister —see Blister, foot
      contusion —see Contusion, foot
      external constriction —see Constriction,
        external, foot
      foreign body —see Foreign body,
        superficial, foot
    forearm S50.91-●
      abrasion —see Abrasion, forearm
      bite —see Bite, forearm, superficial
      blister —see Blister, forearm
      contusion —see Contusion, forearm
      elbow only —see Injury, superficial,
        elbow
      external constriction —see Constriction,
        external, forearm
      foreign body —see Foreign body,
        superficial, forearm
    forehead —see Injury, superficial, head
      NEC
    foreign body —see Foreign body,
      superficial
    genital organs, external
      female S30.97
      male S30.96
    globe (eye) —see Injury, eye, specified site
      NEC
    groin S30.92
    gum —see Injury, superficial, oral
      cavity
    hand S60.92-●
      abrasion —see Abrasion, hand
      bite —see Bite, superficial, hand
      contusion —see Contusion, hand
      external constriction —see Constriction,
        external, hand
      foreign body —see Foreign body,
        superficial, hand

Injury (Continued)
  superficial NEC (Continued)
    head S00.90
      ear —see Injury, superficial, ear
      eyelid —see Injury, superficial, eyelid
      nose S00.30
      oral cavity S00.502
      scalp S00.00
      specified site NEC S00.80
    heel —see Injury, superficial, foot
    hip S70.91-●
      abrasion —see Abrasion, hip
      bite —see Bite, superficial, hip
      blister —see Blister, hip
      contusion —see Contusion, hip
      external constriction —see Constriction,
        external, hip
      foreign body —see Foreign body,
        superficial, hip
    iliac region —see Injury, superficial,
      abdomen
    inguinal region —see Injury, superficial,
      abdomen
    insect bite —see Bite, by site, superficial,
      insect
    interscapular region —see Injury,
      superficial, thorax, back
    jaw —see Injury, superficial, head, specified
      NEC
    knee S80.91-●
      abrasion —see Abrasion, knee
      bite —see Bite, superficial, knee
      blister —see Blister, knee
      contusion —see Contusion, knee
      external constriction —see Constriction,
        external, knee
      foreign body —see Foreign body,
        superficial, knee
    labium (majus) (minus) S30.95
    lacrimal (apparatus) (gland) (sac) —see
      Injury, eye, specified site NEC
    larynx —see Injury, superficial, throat
    leg (lower) S80.92-●
      abrasion —see Abrasion, leg
      bite —see Bite, superficial, leg
      contusion —see Contusion, leg
      external constriction —see Constriction,
        external, leg
      foreign body —see Foreign body,
        superficial, leg
      knee —see Injury, superficial, knee
    limb NEC T14.8
    lip S00.501
    lower back S30.91
    lumbar region S30.91
    malar region —see Injury, superficial, head,
      specified NEC
    mammary —see Injury, superficial, breast
    mastoid region —see Injury, superficial,
      head, specified NEC
    mouth —see Injury, superficial, oral cavity
    muscle NEC T14.8
    nail NEC T14.8
      finger —see Injury, superficial, finger
      toe —see Injury, superficial, toe
    nasal (septum) —see Injury, superficial, nose
    neck S10.90
      specified site NEC S10.80
    nose (septum) S00.30
    occipital region —see Injury, superficial,
      scalp
    oral cavity S00.502
    orbital region —see Injury, superficial,
      periocular area
    palate —see Injury, superficial, oral
      cavity
    palm —see Injury, superficial, hand
    parietal region —see Injury, superficial,
      scalp
    pelvis S30.91
      girdle —see Injury, superficial, hip

▶ New   ⇒ Revised   ~~deleted~~ Deleted   ● Use Additional Character(s)

Injury (Continued)
  superficial NEC (Continued)
    penis S30.93
    perineum
      female S30.95
      male S30.91
    periocular area S00.20-●
      abrasion —see Abrasion, eyelid
      bite —see Bite, superficial, eyelid
      contusion —see Contusion, eyelid
      external constriction —see Constriction, external, eyelid
      foreign body —see Foreign body, superficial, eyelid
    phalanges
      finger —see Injury, superficial, finger
      toe —see Injury, superficial, toe
    pharynx —see Injury, superficial, throat
    pinna —see Injury, superficial, ear
    popliteal space —see Injury, superficial, knee
    prepuce S30.93
    pubic region S30.91
    pudendum
      female S30.97
      male S30.96
    sacral region S30.91
    scalp S00.00
    scapular region —see Injury, superficial, shoulder
    sclera —see Injury, eye, specified site NEC
    scrotum S30.94
    shin —see Injury, superficial, leg
    shoulder S40.91-●
      abrasion —see Abrasion, shoulder
      bite —see Bite, superficial, shoulder
      blister —see Blister, shoulder
      contusion —see Contusion, shoulder
      external constriction —see Constriction, external, shoulder
      foreign body —see Foreign body, superficial, shoulder
    skin NEC T14.8
    sternal region —see Injury, superficial, thorax, front
    subconjunctival —see Injury, eye, specified site NEC
    subcutaneous NEC T14.8
    submaxillary region —see Injury, superficial, head, specified NEC
    submental region —see Injury, superficial, head, specified NEC
    subungual
      finger(s) —see Injury, superficial, finger
      toe(s) —see Injury, superficial, toe
    supraclavicular fossa —see Injury, superficial, neck
    supraorbital —see Injury, superficial, head, specified NEC
    temple —see Injury, superficial, head, specified NEC
    temporal region —see Injury, superficial, head, specified NEC
    testis S30.94
    thigh S70.92-●
      abrasion —see Abrasion, thigh
      bite —see Bite, superficial, thigh
      blister —see Blister, thigh
      contusion —see Contusion, thigh
      external constriction —see Constriction, external, thigh
      foreign body —see Foreign body, superficial, thigh
    thorax, thoracic (wall) S20.90
      abrasion —see Abrasion, thorax
      back S20.40-●
      bite —see Bite, thorax, superficial
      blister —see Blister, thorax
      contusion —see Contusion, thorax
      external constriction —see Constriction, external, thorax

Injury (Continued)
  superficial NEC (Continued)
    thorax, thoracic (Continued)
      foreign body —see Foreign body, superficial, thorax
      front S20.30-●
      throat S10.10
        abrasion S10.11
        bite S10.17
          insect S10.16
        blister S10.12
        contusion S10.0
        external constriction S10.14
        foreign body S10.15
      thumb S60.93-●
        abrasion —see Abrasion, thumb
        bite —see Bite, superficial, thumb
        blister —see Blister, thumb
        contusion —see Contusion, thumb
        external constriction —see Constriction, external, thumb
        foreign body —see Foreign body, superficial, thumb
        insect bite —see Bite, by site, superficial, insect
        specified type NEC S60.39-●
      toe(s) S90.93-●
        abrasion —see Abrasion, toe
        bite —see Bite, toe
        blister —see Blister, toe
        contusion —see Contusion, toe
        external constriction —see Constriction, external, toe
        foreign body —see Foreign body, superficial, toe
        great S90.93-●
      tongue —see Injury, superficial, oral cavity
      tooth, teeth —see Injury, superficial, oral cavity
      trachea S10.10
      tunica vaginalis S30.94
      tympanum, tympanic membrane —see Injury, superficial, ear
      uvula —see Injury, superficial, oral cavity
      vagina S30.95
      vocal cords —see Injury, superficial, throat
      vulva S30.95
      wrist S60.91-●
    supraclavicular region —see Injury, neck
    supraorbital S09.93
    suprarenal gland (multiple) —see Injury, adrenal
    surgical complication (external or internal site) —see Laceration, accidental complicating surgery
    temple S09.90
    temporal region S09.90
    tendon —see also Injury, muscle, by site
      abdomen —see Injury, muscle, abdomen
      Achilles —see Injury, Achilles tendon
      lower back —see Injury, muscle, lower back
      pelvic organs —see Injury, muscle, pelvis
    tenth cranial nerve (pneumogastric or vagus) —see Injury, nerve, vagus
    testis S39.94
    thigh S79.92-●
      blood vessel —see Injury, blood vessel, hip
      contusion —see Contusion, thigh
      fracture —see Fracture, femur
      muscle —see Injury, muscle, thigh
      nerve —see Injury, nerve, thigh
      open —see Wound, open, thigh
      specified NEC S79.82-●
      superficial —see Injury, superficial, thigh
    third cranial nerve (oculomotor) —see Injury, nerve, oculomotor
    thorax, thoracic S29.9
      blood vessel —see Injury, blood vessel, thorax
      cavity —see Injury, intrathoracic

Injury (Continued)
  thorax, thoracic (Continued)
    dislocation —see Dislocation, thorax
    external (wall) S29.9
      contusion —see Contusion, thorax
      nerve —see Injury, nerve, thorax
      open —see Wound, open, thorax
      specified NEC S29.8
      sprain —see Sprain, thorax
      superficial —see Injury, superficial, thorax
    fracture —see Fracture, thorax
    internal —see Injury, intrathoracic
    intrathoracic organ —see Injury, intrathoracic
    sympathetic ganglion —see Injury, nerve, thorax, sympathetic
  throat —see also Injury, neck S19.9
  thumb S69.9-●
    blood vessel —see Injury, blood vessel, thumb
    contusion —see Contusion, thumb
    dislocation —see Dislocation, thumb
    fracture —see Fracture, thumb
    muscle —see Injury, muscle, thumb
    nerve —see Injury, nerve, digital, thumb
    open —see Wound, open, thumb
    specified NEC S69.8-●
    sprain —see Sprain, thumb
    superficial —see Injury, superficial, thumb
  thymus (gland) —see Injury, intrathoracic, specified organ NEC
  thyroid (gland) NEC S19.84
  toe S99.92-●
    contusion —see Contusion, toe
    dislocation —see Dislocation, toe
    fracture —see Fracture, toe
    muscle —see Injury, muscle, toe
    open —see Wound, open, toe
    specified type NEC S99.82-●
    sprain —see Sprain, toe
    superficial —see Injury, superficial, toe
  tongue S09.93
  tonsil S09.93
  tooth S09.93
  trachea (cervical) NEC S19.82
    thoracic —see Injury, intrathoracic, trachea, thoracic
  transfusion-related acute lung (TRALI) J95.84
  tunica vaginalis S39.94
  twelfth cranial nerve (hypoglossal) —see Injury, nerve, hypoglossal
  ureter S37.10
    contusion S37.12
    laceration S37.13
    specified type NEC S37.19
  urethra (sphincter) S37.30
    at delivery O71.5
    contusion S37.32
    laceration S37.33
    specified type NEC S37.38
  urinary organ S37.899
    contusion S37.92
    laceration S37.93
    specified
      site NEC S37.899
        contusion S37.892
        laceration S37.893
        specified type NEC S37.898
      type NEC S37.99
  uterus, uterine S37.60
    with ectopic or molar pregnancy O08.6
    blood vessel —see Injury, blood vessel, iliac
    contusion S37.62
    laceration S37.63
      cervix at delivery O71.3
    rupture associated with obstetrics —see Rupture, uterus
    specified type NEC S37.69
  uvula S09.93

▶ New   ⇒ Revised   ~~deleted~~ Deleted   ● Use Additional Character(s)

Injury *(Continued)*
  vagina S39.93
    abrasion S30.814
    bite S31.45
      insect S30.864
      superficial NEC S30.874
    contusion S30.23
    crush S38.03
    during delivery —*see* Laceration, vagina,
        during delivery
    external constriction S30.844
    insect bite S30.864
    laceration S31.41
      with foreign body S31.42
    open wound S31.40
    puncture S31.43
      with foreign body S31.44
    superficial S30.95
      foreign body S30.854
  vas deferens —*see* Injury, pelvic organ,
      specified site NEC
  vascular NEC T14.8
  vein —*see* Injury, blood vessel
  vena cava (superior) S25.20
    inferior S35.10
      laceration (minor) (superficial)
          S35.11
        major S35.12
      specified type NEC S35.19
    laceration (minor) (superficial) S25.21
      major S25.22
    specified type NEC S25.29
  vesical (sphincter) —*see* Injury, bladder
  visual cortex S04.04-●
  vitreous (humor) S05.90
    specified NEC S05.8X-●
  vocal cord NEC S19.83
  vulva S39.94
    abrasion S30.814
    bite S31.45
      insect S30.864
      superficial NEC S30.874
    contusion S30.23
    crush S38.03
    during delivery —*see* Laceration,
        perineum, female, during delivery
    external constriction S30.844
    insect bite S30.864
    laceration S31.41
      with foreign body S31.42
    open wound S31.40
    puncture S31.43
      with foreign body S31.44
    superficial S30.95
      foreign body S30.854
  whiplash (cervical spine) S13.4
  wrist S69.9-●
    blood vessel —*see* Injury, blood vessel,
        hand
    contusion —*see* Contusion, wrist
    dislocation —*see* Dislocation, wrist
    fracture —*see* Fracture, wrist
    muscle —*see* Injury, muscle, hand
    nerve —*see* Injury, nerve, hand
    open —*see* Wound, open, wrist
    specified NEC S69.8-●
    sprain —*see* Sprain, wrist
    superficial —*see* Injury, superficial, wrist
Inoculation —*see also* Vaccination
  complication or reaction —*see* Complications,
      vaccination
Insanity, insane —*see also* Psychosis
  adolescent —*see* Schizophrenia
  confusional F28
    acute or subacute F05
  delusional F22
  senile F03
Insect
  bite —*see* Bite, by site, superficial, insect
  venomous, poisoning NEC (by) —*see* Venom,
      arthropod

Insensitivity
  adrenocorticotropin hormone (ACTH)
      E27.49
  androgen E34.50
    complete E34.51
    partial E34.52
Insertion
  cord (umbilical) lateral or velamentous
      O43.12-●
  intrauterine contraceptive device (encounter
      for) —*see* Intrauterine contraceptive
      device
Insolation (sunstroke) T67.01
Insomnia (organic) G47.00
  without objective findings F51.02
  adjustment F51.02
  adjustment disorder F51.02
  behavioral, of childhood Z73.819
    combined type Z73.812
    limit setting type Z73.811
    sleep-onset association type Z73.810
  childhood Z73.819
  chronic F51.04
    somatized tension F51.04
  conditioned F51.04
  due to
    alcohol
      abuse F10.182
      dependence F10.282
      use F10.982
    amphetamines
      abuse F15.182
      dependence F15.282
      use F15.982
    anxiety disorder F51.05
    caffeine
      abuse F15.182
      dependence F15.282
      use F15.982
    cocaine
      abuse F14.182
      dependence F14.282
      use F14.982
    depression F51.05
    drug NEC
      abuse F19.182
      dependence F19.282
      use F19.982
    medical condition G47.01
    mental disorder NEC F51.05
    opioid
      abuse F11.182
      dependence F11.282
      use F11.982
    psychoactive substance NEC
      abuse F19.182
      dependence F19.282
      use F19.982
    sedative, hypnotic, or anxiolytic
      abuse F13.182
      dependence F13.282
      use F13.982
    stimulant NEC
      abuse F15.182
      dependence F15.282
      use F15.982
  fatal familial (FFI) A81.83
  idiopathic F51.01
  learned F51.3
  nonorganic origin F51.01
  not due to a substance or known
      physiological condition F51.01
    specified NEC F51.09
  paradoxical F51.03
  primary F51.01
  psychiatric F51.05
  psychophysiologic F51.04
  related to psychopathology F51.05
  short-term F51.02
  specified NEC G47.09
  stress-related F51.02
  transient F51.02

Inspiration
  food or foreign body —*see* Foreign body, by
      site
  mucus —*see* Asphyxia, mucus
Inspissated bile syndrome (newborn) P59.1
Instability
  emotional (excessive) F60.3
  joint (post-traumatic) M25.30
    ankle M25.37-●
    due to old ligament injury —*see* Disorder,
        ligament
    elbow M25.32-●
    flail —*see* Flail, joint
    foot M25.37-●
    hand M25.34-●
    hip M25.35-●
    knee M25.36-●
    lumbosacral —*see* subcategory M53.2
    prosthesis —*see* Complications, joint
        prosthesis, mechanical, displacement,
        by site
    sacroiliac —*see* subcategory M53.2
    secondary to
      old ligament injury —*see* Disorder,
          ligament
      removal of joint prosthesis M96.89
    shoulder (region) M25.31-●
  ▶specified site NEC M25.39
    spine —*see* subcategory M53.2
    wrist M25.33-●
  knee (chronic) M23.5-●
  lumbosacral —*see* subcategory M53.2
  nervous F48.8
  personality (emotional) F60.3
  spine —*see* Instability, joint, spine
  vasomotor R55
Institutional syndrome (childhood)
    F94.2
Institutionalization, affecting child
    Z62.22
  disinhibited attachment F94.2
Insufficiency, insufficient
  accommodation, old age H52.4
  adrenal (gland) E27.40
    primary E27.1
  adrenocortical E27.40
    drug-induced E27.3
    iatrogenic E27.3
    primary E27.1
  anatomic crown height K08.89
  anterior (occlusal) guidance M26.54
  anus K62.89
  aortic (valve) I35.1
    with
      mitral (valve) disease I08.0
        with tricuspid (valve) disease I08.3
      stenosis I35.2
      tricuspid (valve) disease I08.2
        with mitral (valve) disease I08.3
    congenital Q23.1
    rheumatic I06.1
      with
        mitral (valve) disease I08.0
          with tricuspid (valve) disease I08.3
        stenosis I06.2
          with mitral (valve) disease I08.0
            with tricuspid (valve) disease
                I08.3
          tricuspid (valve) disease I08.2
            with mitral (valve) disease I08.3
    specified cause NEC I35.1
    syphilitic A52.03
  arterial I77.1
    basilar G45.0
    carotid (hemispheric) G45.1
    cerebral I67.81
    coronary (acute or subacute) I24.8
    mesenteric K55.1
    peripheral I73.9
    precerebral (multiple) (bilateral) G45.2
    vertebral G45.0

▶ New   ⇒ Revised   ~~deleted~~ Deleted   ● Use Additional Character(s)

Insufficiency, insufficient *(Continued)*
  arteriovenous I99.8
  biliary K83.8
  cardiac —*see also* Insufficiency, myocardial
    due to presence of (cardiac) prosthesis
      I97.11-●
    postprocedural I97.11-●
  cardiorenal, hypertensive I13.2
  cardiovascular —*see* Disease, cardiovascular
  cerebrovascular (acute) I67.81
    with transient focal neurological signs and
      symptoms G45.8
  circulatory NEC I99.8
    newborn P29.89
  clinical crown length K08.89
  convergence H51.11
  coronary (acute or subacute) I24.8
    chronic or with a stated duration of over 4
      weeks I25.89
  corticoadrenal E27.40
    primary E27.1
  dietary E63.9
  divergence H51.8
  food T73.0
  gastroesophageal K22.8
  gonadal
    ovary E28.39
    testis E29.1
  heart —*see also* Insufficiency, myocardial
    newborn P29.0
    valve —*see* Endocarditis
  hepatic —*see* Failure, hepatic
  idiopathic autonomic G90.09
  interocclusal distance of fully erupted teeth
    (ridge) M26.36
  kidney N28.9
    acute N28.9
    chronic N18.9
  lacrimal (secretion) H04.12-●
    passages —*see* Stenosis, lacrimal
  liver —*see* Failure, hepatic
  lung —*see* Insufficiency, pulmonary
  mental (congenital) —*see* Disability,
    intellectual
  mesenteric K55.1
  mitral (valve) I34.0
    with
      aortic valve disease I08.0
        with tricuspid (valve) disease I08.3
      obstruction or stenosis I05.2
        with aortic valve disease I08.0
      tricuspid (valve) disease I08.1
        with aortic (valve) disease I08.3
    congenital Q23.3
    rheumatic I05.1
      with
        aortic valve disease I08.0
          with tricuspid (valve) disease I08.3
        obstruction or stenosis I05.2
          with aortic valve disease I08.0
            with tricuspid (valve) disease
              I08.3
        tricuspid (valve) disease I08.1
          with aortic (valve) disease I08.3
      active or acute I01.1
        with chorea, rheumatic (Sydenham's)
          I02.0
    specified cause, except rheumatic I34.0
  muscle —*see also* Disease, muscle
    heart —*see* Insufficiency, myocardial
  ocular NEC H50.9
  myocardial, myocardium (with
      arteriosclerosis) —*see also* Failure,
      heart I50.9
    with
      rheumatic fever (conditions in I00) I09.0
        active, acute or subacute I01.2
          with chorea I02.0
        inactive or quiescent (with chorea)
          I09.0
      congenital Q24.8

Insufficiency, insufficient *(Continued)*
  myocardial, myocardium *(Continued)*
    hypertensive —*see* Hypertension, heart
    newborn P29.0
    rheumatic I09.0
      active, acute, or subacute I01.2
    syphilitic A52.06
  nourishment T73.0
  pancreatic K86.89
    exocrine K86.81
  parathyroid (gland) E20.9
  peripheral vascular (arterial) I73.9
  pituitary E23.0
  placental (mother) O36.51-●
  platelets D69.6
  prenatal care affecting management of
    pregnancy O09.3-●
  progressive pluriglandular E31.0
  pulmonary J98.4
    acute, following surgery (nonthoracic)
      J95.2
      thoracic J95.1
    chronic, following surgery J95.3
    following
      shock J98.4
      trauma J98.4
    newborn P28.89
    valve I37.1
      with stenosis I37.2
      congenital Q22.2
      rheumatic I09.89
        with aortic, mitral or tricuspid (valve)
          disease I08.8
  pyloric K31.89
  renal (acute) N28.9
    chronic N18.9
  respiratory R06.89
    newborn P28.5
  rotation —*see* Malrotation
  sleep syndrome F51.12
  social insurance Z59.7
  suprarenal E27.40
    primary E27.1
  tarso-orbital fascia, congenital Q10.3
  testis E29.1
  thyroid (gland) (acquired) E03.9
    congenital E03.1
  tricuspid (valve) (rheumatic) I07.1
    with
      aortic (valve) disease I08.2
        with mitral (valve) disease I08.3
      mitral (valve) disease I08.1
        with aortic (valve) disease I08.3
      obstruction or stenosis I07.2
        with aortic (valve) disease I08.2
          with mitral (valve) disease I08.3
    congenital Q22.8
    nonrheumatic I36.1
      with stenosis I36.2
  urethral sphincter R32
  valve, valvular (heart) I38
    aortic —*see* Insufficiency, aortic (valve)
    mitral —*see* Insufficiency, mitral (valve)
    pulmonary —*see* Insufficiency, pulmonary,
      valve
    tricuspid —*see* Insufficiency, tricuspid
      (valve)
    congenital Q24.8
  vascular I99.8
    intestine K55.9
      acute —*see also* Ischemia, intestine, acute
        K55.059
    mesenteric K55.1
    peripheral I73.9
    renal —*see* Hypertension, kidney
  velopharyngeal
    acquired K13.79
    congenital Q38.8
  venous (chronic) (peripheral) I87.2
  ventricular —*see* Insufficiency, myocardial
  welfare support Z59.7

Insufflation, fallopian Z31.41
Insular —*see* condition
Insulinoma
  pancreas
    benign D13.7
    malignant C25.4
    uncertain behavior D37.8
  specified site
    benign —*see* Neoplasm, by site, benign
    malignant —*see* Neoplasm, by site,
      malignant
    uncertain behavior —*see* Neoplasm, by site,
      uncertain behavior
  unspecified site
    benign D13.7
    malignant C25.4
    uncertain behavior D37.8
Insuloma —*see* Insulinoma
Interference
  balancing side M26.56
  non-working side M26.56
Intermenstrual —*see* condition
Intermittent —*see* condition
Internal —*see* condition
Interrogation
  cardiac defibrillator (automatic) (implantable)
    Z45.02
  cardiac pacemaker Z45.018
  cardiac (event) (loop) recorder Z45.09
  infusion pump (implanted) (intrathecal) Z45.1
  neurostimulator Z46.2
Interruption
  aortic arch Q25.21
  phase-shift, sleep cycle —*see* Disorder, sleep,
    circadian rhythm
  sleep phase-shift, or 24 hour sleep-wake
    cycle —*see* Disorder, sleep, circadian
    rhythm
Interstitial —*see* condition
Intertrigo L30.4
  labialis K13.0
Intervertebral disc —*see* condition
Intestine, intestinal —*see* condition
Intolerance
  carbohydrate K90.49
  disaccharide, hereditary E73.0
  fat NEC K90.49
    pancreatic K90.3
  food K90.49
    dietary counseling and surveillance Z71.3
  fructose E74.10
    hereditary E74.12
  glucose(-galactose) E74.39
  gluten K90.01
  lactose E73.9
    specified NEC E73.8
  lysine E72.3
  milk NEC K90.49
    lactose E73.9
  protein K90.49
  starch NEC K90.49
  sucrose (-isomaltose) E74.31
Intoxicated NEC (without dependence) —*see*
  Alcohol, intoxication
Intoxication
  acid E87.2
  alcoholic (acute) (without dependence) —*see*
    Alcohol, intoxication
  alimentary canal K52.1
  amphetamine (without dependence) —*see*
    also Abuse, drug, stimulant, with
    intoxication
    stimulant NEC F15.10
      with
        anxiety disorder F15.180
        intoxication F15.129
          with
            delirium F15.121
            perceptual disturbance F15.122
      with dependence —*see* Dependence, drug,
        stimulant, with intoxication

Intoxication (*Continued*)
anxiolytic (acute) (without dependence) —*see* Abuse, drug, sedative, with intoxication
with dependence —*see* Dependence, drug, sedative, with intoxication
caffeine F15.929
with dependence —*see* Dependence, drug, stimulant, with intoxication
cannabinoids (acute) (without dependence) —*see* Use, cannabis, with intoxication
with
abuse —*see* Abuse, drug, cannabis, with intoxication
dependence —*see* Dependence, drug, cannabis, with intoxication
chemical —*see* Table of Drugs and Chemicals
via placenta or breast milk —*see* Absorption, chemical, through placenta
cocaine (acute) (without dependence) —*see* Abuse, drug, cocaine, with intoxication
with dependence —*see* Dependence, drug, cocaine, with intoxication
drug
acute (without dependence) —*see* Abuse, drug, by type with intoxication
with dependence —*see* Dependence, drug, by type with intoxication
addictive
via placenta or breast milk —*see* Absorption, drug, addictive, through placenta
newborn P93.8
gray baby syndrome P93.0
overdose or wrong substance given or taken —*see* Table of Drugs and Chemicals, by drug, poisoning
enteric K52.1
foodborne A05.9
bacterial A05.9
classical (Clostridium botulinum) A05.1
due to
Bacillus cereus A05.4
bacterium A05.9
specified NEC A05.8
Clostridium
botulinum A05.1
perfringens A05.2
welchii A05.2
Salmonella A02.9
with
(gastro) enteritis A02.0
localized infection(s) A02.20
arthritis A02.23
meningitis A02.21
osteomyelitis A02.24
pneumonia A02.22
pyelonephritis A02.25
specified NEC A02.29
sepsis A02.1
specified manifestation NEC A02.8
Staphylococcus A05.0
Vibrio
parahaemolyticus A05.3
vulnificus A05.5
enterotoxin, staphylococcal A05.0
noxious —*see* Poisoning, food, noxious
gastrointestinal K52.1
hallucinogenic (without dependence) — *see* Abuse, drug, hallucinogen, with intoxication
with dependence —*see* Dependence, drug, hallucinogen, with intoxication
hypnotic (acute) (without dependence) —*see* Abuse, drug, sedative, with intoxication
with dependence —*see* Dependence, drug, sedative, with intoxication

Intoxication (*Continued*)
inhalant (acute) (without dependence) —*see* Abuse, drug, inhalant, with intoxication
with dependence —*see* Dependence, drug, inhalant, with intoxication
meaning
inebriation —*see* category F10
poisoning —*see* Table of Drugs and Chemicals
methyl alcohol (acute) (without dependence) —*see* Alcohol, intoxication
opioid (acute) (without dependence) —*see* Abuse, drug, opioid, with intoxication
with dependence —*see* Dependence, drug, opioid, with intoxication
pathologic NEC (without dependence) —*see* Alcohol, intoxication
phencyclidine (without dependence) —*see* Abuse, drug, hallucinogen, with intoxication
with dependence —*see* Dependence, drug, hallucinogen, with intoxication
potassium (K) E87.5
psychoactive substance NEC (without dependence) —*see* Abuse, drug, psychoactive NEC, with intoxication
with dependence —*see* Dependence, drug, psychoactive NEC, with intoxication
sedative (acute) (without dependence) —*see* Abuse, drug, sedative, with intoxication
with dependence —*see* Dependence, drug, sedative, with intoxication
serum —*see also* Reaction, serum T80.69
uremic —*see* Uremia
volatile solvents (acute) (without dependence) —*see* Abuse, drug, inhalant, with intoxication
with dependence —*see* Dependence, drug, inhalant, with intoxication
water E87.79
Intraabdominal testis, testes
bilateral Q53.211
unilateral Q53.111
Intracranial —*see* condition
Intrahepatic gallbladder Q44.1
Intraligamentous —*see* condition
Intrathoracic —*see also* condition
kidney Q63.2
Intrauterine contraceptive device
checking Z30.431
in situ Z97.5
insertion Z30.430
immediately following removal Z30.433
management Z30.431
reinsertion Z30.433
removal Z30.432
replacement Z30.433
retention in pregnancy O26.3-●
Intraventricular —*see* condition
Intrinsic deformity —*see* Deformity
Intubation, difficult or failed T88.4
Intumescence, lens (eye) (cataract) —*see* Cataract
Intussusception (bowel) (colon) (enteric) (ileocecal) (ileocolic) (intestine) (rectum) K56.1
appendix K38.8
congenital Q43.8
ureter (with obstruction) N13.5
Invagination (bowel, colon, intestine or rectum) K56.1
Inversion
albumin-globulin (A-G) ratio E88.09
bladder N32.89
cecum —*see* Intussusception
cervix N88.8
chromosome in normal individual Q95.1
circadian rhythm —*see* Disorder, sleep, circadian rhythm

Inversion (*Continued*)
nipple N64.59
congenital Q83.8
gestational —*see* Retraction, nipple
puerperal, postpartum —*see* Retraction, nipple
nyctohemeral rhythm —*see* Disorder, sleep, circadian rhythm
optic papilla Q14.2
organ or site, congenital NEC —*see* Anomaly, by site
sleep rhythm —*see* Disorder, sleep, circadian rhythm
testis (congenital) Q55.29
uterus (chronic) (postinfectional) (postpartal, old) N85.5
postpartum O71.2
vagina (posthysterectomy) N99.3
ventricular Q20.5
Investigation —*see also* Examination Z04.9
clinical research subject (control) (normal comparison) (participant) Z00.6
Involuntary movement, abnormal R25.9
Involution, involutional —*see also* condition
breast, cystic —*see* Dysplasia, mammary, specified type NEC
depression (single episode) F32.89
recurrent episode F33.9
melancholia (single episode) F32.89
recurrent episode F33.8
ovary, senile —*see* Atrophy, ovary
thymus failure E32.8
I.Q.
under 20 F73
20-34 F72
35-49 F71
50-69 F70
IRDS (type I) P22.0
type II P22.1
Irideremia Q13.1
Iridis rubeosis —*see* Disorder, iris, vascular
Iridochoroiditis (panuveitis) —*see* Panuveitis
Iridocyclitis H20.9-●
acute H20.0-●
hypopyon H20.05-●
primary H20.01-●
recurrent H20.02-●
secondary (noninfectious) H20.04-●
infectious H20.03-●
chronic H20.1-●
due to allergy —*see* Iridocyclitis, acute, secondary
endogenous —*see* Iridocyclitis, acute, primary
Fuchs' —*see* Cyclitis, Fuchs' heterochromic
gonococcal A54.32
granulomatous —*see* Iridocyclitis, chronic
herpes, herpetic (simplex) B00.51
zoster B02.32
hypopyon —*see* Iridocyclitis, acute, hypopyon
in (due to)
ankylosing spondylitis M45.9
gonococcal infection A54.32
herpes (simplex) virus B00.51
zoster B02.32
infectious disease NOS B99
parasitic disease NOS B89 [*H22*]
sarcoidosis D86.83
syphilis A51.43
tuberculosis A18.54
zoster B02.32
lens-induced H20.2-●
nongranulomatous —*see* Iridocyclitis, acute
recurrent —*see* Iridocyclitis, acute, recurrent
rheumatic —*see* Iridocyclitis, chronic
subacute —*see* Iridocyclitis, acute
sympathetic —*see* Uveitis, sympathetic
syphilitic (secondary) A51.43
tuberculous (chronic) A18.54
Vogt-Koyanagi H20.82-●

▶ New　⇥ Revised　~~deleted~~ Deleted　● Use Additional Character(s)

Iridocyclochoroiditis (panuveitis) —*see* Panuveitis
Iridodialysis H21.53- •
Iridodonesis H21.89
Iridoplegia (complete) (partial) (reflex) H57.09
Iridoschisis H21.25- •
Iris —*see also* condition
  bombé —*see* Membrane, pupillary
Iritis —*see also* Iridocyclitis
  chronic —*see* Iridocyclitis, chronic
  diabetic —*see* E08-E13 with .39
  due to
    herpes simplex B00.51
    leprosy A30.9 [H22]
  gonococcal A54.32
  gouty —*see also* Gout, by type M10.9 [H22]
  granulomatous —*see* Iridocyclitis, chronic
  lens induced —*see* Iridocyclitis, lens-induced
  papulosa (syphilitic) A52.71
  rheumatic —*see* Iridocyclitis, chronic
  syphilitic (secondary) A51.43
    congenital (early) A50.01
    late A52.71
  tuberculous A18.54
Iron —*see* condition
Iron-miner's lung J63.4
Irradiated enamel (tooth, teeth) K03.89
Irradiation effects, adverse T66
Irreducible, irreducibility —*see* condition
Irregular, irregularity
  action, heart I49.9
  alveolar process K08.89
  bleeding N92.6
  breathing R06.89
  contour of cornea (acquired) —*see* Deformity, cornea
    congenital Q13.4
  contour, reconstructed breast N65.0
  dentin (in pulp) K04.3
  eye movements H55.89
    ▶deficient
      ▶saccadic H55.81
      ▶smooth H55.82
    nystagmus —*see* Nystagmus
    saccadic H55.81
  labor O62.2
  menstruation (cause unknown) N92.6
  periods N92.6
  prostate N42.9
  pupil —*see* Abnormality, pupillary
  reconstructed breast N65.0
  respiratory R06.89
  septum (nasal) J34.2
  shape, organ or site, congenital NEC —*see* Distortion
  sleep-wake pattern (rhythm) G47.23
Irritable, irritability R45.4
  bladder N32.89
  bowel (syndrome) K58.9
    with
      constipation K58.1
      diarrhea K58.0
    mixed K58.2
    psychogenic F45.8
    specified NEC K58.8
  bronchial —*see* Bronchitis
  cerebral, in newborn P91.3
  colon —*see also* Irritable, bowel K58.9
    with diarrhea K58.0
    psychogenic F45.8
  ⇒duodenum K59.89
  heart (psychogenic) F45.8
  hip —*see* Derangement, joint, specified type NEC, hip
  ⇒ileum K59.89
  infant R68.12
  ⇒jejunum K59.89
  ⇒rectum K59.89
  stomach K31.89
    psychogenic F45.8
  sympathetic G90.8
  urethra N36.8

Irritation
  anus K62.89
  axillary nerve G54.0
  bladder N32.89
  brachial plexus G54.0
  bronchial —*see* Bronchitis
  cervical plexus G54.2
  cervix —*see* Cervicitis
  choroid, sympathetic —*see* Endophthalmitis
  cranial nerve —*see* Disorder, nerve, cranial
  gastric K31.89
    psychogenic F45.8
  globe, sympathetic —*see* Uveitis, sympathetic
  labyrinth —*see* subcategory H83.2
  lumbosacral plexus G54.1
  meninges (traumatic) —*see* Injury, intracranial
    nontraumatic —*see* Meningismus
  nerve —*see* Disorder, nerve
  nervous R45.0
  penis N48.89
  perineum NEC L29.3
  peripheral autonomic nervous system G90.8
  peritoneum —*see* Peritonitis
  pharynx J39.2
  plantar nerve —*see* Lesion, nerve, plantar
  spinal (cord) (traumatic) —*see also* Injury, spinal cord, by region
    nerve G58.9
      root NEC —*see* Radiculopathy
    nontraumatic —*see* Myelopathy
  stomach K31.89
    psychogenic F45.8
  sympathetic nerve NEC G90.8
  ulnar nerve —*see* Lesion, nerve, ulnar
  vagina N89.8
Ischemia, ischemic I99.8
  bowel (transient)
    acute —*see also* Ischemia, intestine, acute K55.059
    chronic K55.1
    due to mesenteric artery insufficiency K55.1
  brain —*see* Ischemia, cerebral
  cardiac (*see* Disease, heart, ischemic)
  cardiomyopathy I25.5
  cerebral (chronic) (generalized) I67.82
    arteriosclerotic I67.2
    intermittent G45.9
    newborn P91.0
    recurrent focal G45.8
    transient G45.9
  colon chronic (due to mesenteric artery insufficiency) K55.1
  coronary —*see* Disease, heart, ischemic
  demand (coronary) —*see also* Angina I24.8
    with myocardial infarction I21.A1
    resulting in myocardial infarction I21.A1
  heart (chronic or with a stated duration of over 4 weeks) I25.9
    acute or with a stated duration of 4 weeks or less I24.9
    subacute I24.9
  infarction, muscle —*see* Infarct, muscle
  intestine (large) (small) (transient) K55.9
    acute K55.059
      diffuse K55.052
      focal K55.051
      large K55.039
        diffuse K55.032
        focal K55.031
      small K55.019
        diffuse K55.012
        focal K55.011
    chronic K55.1
    due to mesenteric artery insufficiency K55.1
  kidney N28.0
  ▶limb, critical —*see* Arteriosclerosis, with critical limb ischemia

Ischemia, ischemic (*Continued*)
  ▶limb-threatening, chronic —*see* Arteriosclerosis, with critical limb ischemia
  mesenteric, acute —*see also* Ischemia, intestine, acute K55.059
  muscle, traumatic T79.6
  myocardium, myocardial (chronic or with a stated duration of over 4 weeks) I25.9
    acute, without myocardial infarction I51.3
    silent (asymptomatic) I25.6
    transient of newborn P29.4
  renal N28.0
  retina, retinal —*see* Occlusion, artery, retina
  small bowel
    acute K55.019
      diffuse K55.012
      focal K55.011
    chronic K55.1
    due to mesenteric artery insufficiency K55.1
  spinal cord G95.11
  subendocardial —*see* Insufficiency, coronary
  supply (coronary) —*see also* Angina I25.9
    due to vasospasm I20.1
Ischial spine —*see* condition
Ischialgia —*see* Sciatica
Ischiopagus Q89.4
Ischium, ischial —*see* condition
Ischuria R34
Iselin's disease or osteochondrosis —*see* Osteochondrosis, juvenile, metatarsus
Islands of
  parotid tissue in
    lymph nodes Q38.6
    neck structures Q38.6
  submaxillary glands in
    fascia Q38.6
    lymph nodes Q38.6
    neck muscles Q38.6
Islet cell tumor, pancreas D13.7
Isoimmunization NEC —*see also* Incompatibility
  affecting management of pregnancy (ABO) (with hydrops fetalis) O36.11- •
    anti-A sensitization O36.11- •
    anti-B sensitization O36.19- •
    anti-c sensitization O36.09- •
    anti-C sensitization O36.09- •
    anti-e sensitization O36.09- •
    anti-E sensitization O36.09- •
    Rh NEC O36.09- •
      anti-D antibody O36.01- •
    specified NEC O36.19- •
  newborn P55.9
    with
      hydrops fetalis P56.0
      kernicterus P57.0
    ABO (blood groups) P55.1
    Rhesus (Rh) factor P55.0
    specified type NEC P55.8
Isolation, isolated
  dwelling Z59.8
  family Z63.79
  social Z60.4
Isoleucinosis E71.19
Isomerism atrial appendages (with asplenia or polysplenia) Q20.6
Isosporiasis, isosporosis A07.3
Isovaleric acidemia E71.110
Issue of
  medical certificate Z02.79
    for disability determination Z02.71
  repeat prescription (appliance) (glasses) (medicinal substance, medicament, medicine) Z76.0
    contraception —*see* Contraception

Itch, itching —*see also* Pruritus
   baker's L23.6
   barber's B35.0
   bricklayer's L24.5
   cheese B88.0
   clam digger's B65.3
   coolie B76.9
   copra B88.0
   dew B76.9
   dhobi B35.6
   filarial —*see* Infestation, filarial
   grain B88.0
   grocer's B88.0

Itch, itching (*Continued*)
   ground B76.9
   harvest B88.0
   jock B35.6
   Malabar B35.5
     beard B35.0
     foot B35.3
     scalp B35.0
   meaning scabies B86
   Norwegian B86
   perianal L29.0
   poultrymen's B88.0

Itch, itching (*Continued*)
   sarcoptic B86
   scabies B86
   scrub B88.0
   straw B88.0
   swimmer's B65.3
   water B76.9
   winter L29.8
Ivemark's syndrome (asplenia with congenital
   heart disease) Q89.01
Ivory bones Q78.2
Ixodiasis NEC B88.8

▶ New   ⇒ Revised   ~~deleted~~ Deleted   ● Use Additional Character(s)

J

Jaccoud's syndrome —*see* Arthropathy, postrheumatic, chronic
Jackson's
    membrane Q43.3
    paralysis or syndrome G83.89
    veil Q43.3
Jacquet's dermatitis (diaper dermatitis) L22
Jadassohn-Pellizari's disease or anetoderma L90.2
Jadassohn's
    blue nevus —*see* Nevus
    intraepidermal epithelioma —*see* Neoplasm, skin, benign
Jaffe-Lichtenstein (-Uehlinger) syndrome —*see* Dysplasia, fibrous, bone NEC
Jakob-Creutzfeldt disease or syndrome —*see* Creutzfeldt-Jakob disease or syndrome
Jaksch-Luzet disease D64.89
Jamaican
    neuropathy G92
    paraplegic tropical ataxic-spastic syndrome G92
Janet's disease F48.8
Janiceps Q89.4
Jansky-Bielschowsky amaurotic idiocy E75.4
Japanese
    B-type encephalitis A83.0
    river fever A75.3
Jaundice (yellow) R17
    acholuric (familial) (splenomegalic) —*see also* Spherocytosis
        acquired D59.8
    breast-milk (inhibitor) P59.3
    catarrhal (acute) B15.9
        with hepatic coma B15.0
    cholestatic (benign) R17
    due to or associated with
        delayed conjugation P59.8
            associated with (due to) preterm delivery P59.0
        preterm delivery P59.0
    epidemic (catarrhal) B15.9
        with hepatic coma B15.0
        leptospiral A27.0
        spirochetal A27.0
    familial nonhemolytic (congenital) (Gilbert) E80.4
        Crigler-Najjar E80.5
    febrile (acute) B15.9
        with hepatic coma B15.0
        leptospiral A27.0
        spirochetal A27.0
    hematogenous D59.9
    hemolytic (acquired) D59.9
        congenital —*see* Spherocytosis

Jaundice *(Continued)*
    hemorrhagic (acute) (leptospiral) (spirochetal) A27.0
    infectious (acute) (subacute) B15.9
        with hepatic coma B15.0
        leptospiral A27.0
        spirochetal A27.0
    leptospiral (hemorrhagic) A27.0
    malignant (without coma) K72.90
        with coma K72.91
    neonatal —*see* Jaundice, newborn
    newborn P59.9
        due to or associated with
            ABO
                antibodies P55.1
                incompatibility, maternal/fetal P55.1
                isoimmunization P55.1
            absence or deficiency of enzyme system for bilirubin conjugation (congenital) P59.8
            bleeding P58.1
            breast milk inhibitors to conjugation P59.3
                associated with preterm delivery P59.0
            bruising P58.0
            Crigler-Najjar syndrome E80.5
            delayed conjugation P59.8
                associated with preterm delivery P59.0
            drugs or toxins
                given to newborn P58.42
                transmitted from mother P58.41
            excessive hemolysis P58.9
                due to
                    bleeding P58.1
                    bruising P58.0
                    drugs or toxins
                        given to newborn P58.42
                        transmitted from mother P58.41
                    infection P58.2
                    polycythemia P58.3
                    swallowed maternal blood P58.5
                specified type NEC P58.8
            galactosemia E74.21
            Gilbert syndrome E80.4
            hemolytic disease P55.9
                ABO isoimmunization P55.1
                Rh isoimmunization P55.0
                specified NEC P55.8
            hepatocellular damage P59.20
                specified NEC P59.29
            hereditary hemolytic anemia P58.8
            hypothyroidism, congenital E03.1
            incompatibility, maternal/fetal NOS P55.9
            infection P58.2

Jaundice *(Continued)*
    newborn *(Continued)*
        due to or associated with *(Continued)*
            inspissated bile syndrome P59.1
            isoimmunization NOS P55.9
            mucoviscidosis E84.9
            polycythemia P58.3
            preterm delivery P59.0
            Rh
                antibodies P55.0
                incompatibility, maternal/fetal P55.0
                isoimmunization P55.0
            specified cause NEC P59.8
            swallowed maternal blood P58.5
        spherocytosis (congenital) D58.0
        nonhemolytic congenital familial (Gilbert) E80.4
        nuclear, newborn —*see also* Kernicterus of newborn P57.9
        obstructive —*see also* Obstruction, bile duct K83.1
        post-immunization —*see* Hepatitis, viral, type, B
        post-transfusion —*see* Hepatitis, viral, type, B
        regurgitation —*see also* Obstruction, bile duct K83.1
        serum (homologous) (prophylactic) (therapeutic) —*see* Hepatitis, viral, type, B
        spirochetal (hemorrhagic) A27.0
        symptomatic R17
            newborn P59.9
Jaw —*see* condition
Jaw-winking phenomenon or syndrome Q07.8
Jealousy
    alcoholic F10.988
    childhood F93.8
    sibling F93.8
Jejunitis —*see* Enteritis
Jejunostomy status Z93.4
Jejunum, jejunal —*see* condition
Jensen's disease —*see* Inflammation, chorioretinal, focal, juxtapapillary
Jerks, myoclonic G25.3
Jervell-Lange-Nielsen syndrome I45.81
Jeune's disease Q77.2
Jigger disease B88.1
Job's syndrome (chronic granulomatous disease) D71
Joint —*see also* condition
    mice —*see* Loose, body, joint
        knee M23.4-●
Jordan's anomaly or syndrome D72.0
Joseph-Diamond-Blackfan anemia (congenital hypoplastic) D61.01
Jungle yellow fever A95.0
Jüngling's disease —*see* Sarcoidosis
Juvenile —*see* condition

K

Kahler's disease C90.0-●
Kakke E51.11
Kala-azar B55.0
Kallmann's syndrome E23.0
Kanner's syndrome (autism) —see Psychosis, childhood
Kaposi's
  dermatosis (xeroderma pigmentosum) Q82.1
  lichen ruber L44.0
    acuminatus L44.0
  sarcoma
    colon C46.4
    connective tissue C46.1
    gastrointestinal organ C46.4
    lung C46.5-●
    lymph node (multiple) C46.3
    palate (hard) (soft) C46.2
    rectum C46.4
    skin (multiple sites) C46.0
    specified site NEC C46.7
    stomach C46.4
    unspecified site C46.9
  varicelliform eruption B00.0
    vaccinia T88.1
Kartagener's syndrome or triad (sinusitis, bronchiectasis, situs inversus) Q89.3
Karyotype
  with abnormality except iso (Xq) Q96.2
  45,X Q96.0
  46,X
    iso (Xq) Q96.1
  46,XX Q98.3
    with streak gonads Q50.32
    hermaphrodite (true) Q99.1
    male Q98.3
  46,XY
    with streak gonads Q56.1
    female Q97.3
    hermaphrodite (true) Q99.1
  47,XXX Q97.0
  47,XXY Q98.0
  47,XYY Q98.5
Kaschin-Beck disease —see Disease, Kaschin-Beck
Katayama's disease or fever B65.2
Kawasaki's syndrome M30.3
Kayser-Fleischer ring (cornea) (pseudosclerosis) H18.04-●
Kaznelson's syndrome (congenital hypoplastic anemia) D61.01
Kearns-Sayre syndrome H49.81-●
Kedani fever A75.3
Kelis L91.0
Kelly (-Patterson) syndrome (sideropenic dysphagia) D50.1
Keloid, cheloid L91.0
  acne L73.0
  Addison's L94.0
  cornea —see Opacity, cornea
  Hawkin's L91.0
  scar L91.0
Keloma L91.0
Kenya fever A77.1
Keratectasia —see also Ectasia, cornea
  congenital Q13.4
Keratinization of alveolar ridge mucosa
  excessive K13.23
  minimal K13.22
Keratinized residual ridge mucosa
  excessive K13.23
  minimal K13.22
Keratitis (nodular) (nonulcerative) (simple) (zonular) H16.9
  with ulceration (central) (marginal) (perforated) (ring) —see Ulcer, cornea
  actinic —see Photokeratitis
  arborescens (herpes simplex) B00.52
  areolar H16.11-●
  bullosa H16.8

Keratitis (Continued)
  deep H16.309
    specified type NEC H16.399
  dendritic (a) (herpes simplex) B00.52
  disciform (is) (herpes simplex) B00.52
    varicella B01.81
  filamentary H16.12-●
  gonococcal (congenital or prenatal) A54.33
  herpes, herpetic (simplex) B00.52
    zoster B02.33
  in (due to)
    acanthamebiasis B60.13
    adenovirus B30.0
    exanthema —see also Exanthem B09
    herpes (simplex) virus B00.52
    measles B05.81
    syphilis A50.31
    tuberculosis A18.52
    zoster B02.33
  interstitial (nonsyphilitic) H16.30-●
    diffuse H16.32-●
    herpes, herpetic (simplex) B00.52
      zoster B02.33
    sclerosing H16.33-●
    specified type NEC H16.39-●
    syphilitic (congenital) (late) A50.31
    tuberculous A18.52
  macular H16.11-●
  nummular H16.11-●
  oyster shuckers' H16.8
  parenchymatous —see Keratitis, interstitial
  petrificans H16.8
  postmeasles B05.81
  punctata
    leprosa A30.9 [H16.14-●]
    syphilitic (profunda) A50.31
  punctate H16.14-●
  purulent H16.8
  rosacea L71.8
  sclerosing H16.33-●
  specified type NEC H16.8
  stellate H16.11-●
  striate H16.11-●
  superficial H16.10-●
    with conjunctivitis —see Keratoconjunctivitis
    due to light —see Photokeratitis
  suppurative H16.8
  syphilitic (congenital) (prenatal) A50.31
  trachomatous A71.1
    sequelae B94.0
  tuberculous A18.52
  vesicular H16.8
  xerotic —see also Keratomalacia H16.8
    vitamin A deficiency E50.4
Keratoacanthoma L85.8
Keratocele —see Descemetocele
Keratoconjunctivitis H16.20-●
  Acanthamoeba B60.13
  adenoviral B30.0
  epidemic B30.0
  exposure H16.21-●
  herpes, herpetic (simplex) B00.52
    zoster B02.33
  in exanthema —see also Exanthem B09
  infectious B30.0
  lagophthalmic —see Keratoconjunctivitis, specified type NEC
  neurotrophic H16.23-●
  phlyctenular H16.25-●
  postmeasles B05.81
  shipyard B30.0
  sicca (Sjogren's) M35.0-●
    not Sjogren's H16.22-●
  specified type NEC H16.29-●
  tuberculous (phlyctenular) A18.52
  vernal H16.26-●
Keratoconus H18.60-●
  congenital Q13.4
  stable H18.61-●
  unstable H18.62-●

Keratocyst (dental) (odontogenic) —see Cyst, calcifying odontogenic
Keratoderma, keratodermia (congenital) (palmaris et plantaris) (symmetrical) Q82.8
  acquired L85.1
    in diseases classified elsewhere L86
  climactericum L85.1
  gonococcal A54.89
  gonorrheal A54.89
  punctata L85.2
  Reiter's —see Reiter's disease
Keratodermatocele —see Descemetocele
Keratoglobus H18.79
  congenital Q15.8
    with glaucoma Q15.0
Keratohemia —see Pigmentation, cornea, stromal
Keratoiritis —see also Iridocyclitis
  syphilitic A50.39
  tuberculous A18.54
Keratoma L57.0
  palmaris and plantaris hereditarium Q82.8
  senile L57.0
Keratomalacia H18.44-●
  vitamin A deficiency E50.4
Keratomegaly Q13.4
Keratomycosis B49
  nigrans, nigricans (palmaris) B36.1
Keratopathy H18.9
  band H18.42-●
  bullous H18.1-●
  bullous (aphakic), following cataract surgery H59.01-●
Keratoscleritis, tuberculous A18.52
Keratosis L57.0
  actinic L57.0
  arsenical L85.8
  congenital, specified NEC Q80.8
  female genital NEC N94.89
  follicularis Q82.8
    acquired L11.0
    congenita Q82.8
    et parafollicularis in cutem penetrans L87.0
    spinulosa (decalvans) Q82.8
    vitamin A deficiency E50.8
  gonococcal A54.89
  male genital (external) N50.89
  nigricans L83
  obturans, external ear (canal) —see Cholesteatoma, external ear
  palmaris et plantaris (inherited) (symmetrical) Q82.8
    acquired L85.1
  penile N48.89
  pharynx J39.2
  pilaris, acquired L85.8
  punctata (palmaris et plantaris) L85.2
  scrotal N50.89
  seborrheic L82.1
    inflamed L82.0
  senile L57.0
  solar L57.0
  tonsillaris J35.8
  vagina N89.4
  vegetans Q82.8
  vitamin A deficiency E50.8
  vocal cord J38.3
Kerato-uveitis —see Iridocyclitis
Kerion (celsi) B35.0
Kernicterus of newborn (not due to isoimmunization) P57.9
  due to isoimmunization (conditions in P55.0-P55.9) P57.0
  specified type NEC P57.8
Kerunoparalysis T75.09
Keshan disease E59
Ketoacidosis E87.2
  diabetic —see Diabetes, by type, with ketoacidosis
Ketonuria R82.4

▶ New   ⇒ Revised   ~~deleted~~ Deleted   ● Use Additional Character(s)

Ketosis NEC E88.89
  diabetic —see Diabetes, by type, with
    ketoacidosis
Kew Garden fever A79.1
Kidney —see condition
Kienböck's disease —see also Osteochondrosis,
    juvenile, hand, carpal lunate
  adult M93.1
Kimmelstiel (-Wilson) disease —see Diabetes,
    Kimmelstiel (-Wilson) disease
Kimura disease D21.9
  specified site (see Neoplasm, connective
    tissue benign)
Kink, kinking
  artery I77.1
  hair (acquired) L67.8
  ileum or intestine —see Obstruction,
    intestine
  Lane's —see Obstruction, intestine
  organ or site, congenital NEC —see Anomaly,
    by site
  ureter (pelvic junction) N13.5
    with
      hydronephrosis N13.1
        with infection N13.6
      pyelonephritis (chronic) N11.1
    congenital Q62.39
  vein(s) I87.8
    caval I87.1
    peripheral I87.1
Kinnier Wilson's disease (hepatolenticular
    degeneration) E83.01
Kissing spine M48.20
  cervical region M48.22
  cervicothoracic region M48.23
  lumbar region M48.26
  lumbosacral region M48.27
  occipito-atlanto-axial region M48.21
  thoracic region M48.24
  thoracolumbar region M48.25
Klatskin's tumor C24.0
Klauder's disease A26.8
Klebs' disease —see also Glomerulonephritis
    N05.-•
Klebsiella (K.) pneumoniae, as cause of
    disease classified elsewhere B96.1
Klein (e)-Levin syndrome G47.13
Kleptomania F63.2
Klinefelter's syndrome Q98.4
  karyotype 47,XXY Q98.0
  male with more than two X chromosomes
    Q98.1
Klippel-Feil deficiency, disease, or syndrome
    (brevicollis) Q76.1
Klippel's disease I67.2
Klippel-Trenaunay (-Weber) syndrome
    Q87.2
Klumpke (-Déjerine) palsy, paralysis (birth)
    (newborn) P14.1
Knee —see condition
Knock knee (acquired) M21.06-•
  congenital Q74.1

Knot(s)
  intestinal, syndrome (volvulus) K56.2
  surfer S89.8-•
  umbilical cord (true) O69.2
Knotting (of)
  hair L67.8
  intestine K56.2
Knuckle pad (Garrod's) M72.1
Koch's
  infection —see Tuberculosis
  relapsing fever A68.9
Koch-Weeks' conjunctivitis —see
    Conjunctivitis, acute, mucopurulent
Köebner's syndrome Q81.8
Köenig's disease (osteochondritis dissecans) —
    see Osteochondritis, dissecans
Köhler-Pellegrini-Steida disease or syndrome
    (calcification, knee joint) —see Bursitis,
    tibial collateral
Köhler's disease
  patellar —see Osteochondrosis, juvenile,
    patella
  tarsal navicular —see Osteochondrosis,
    juvenile, tarsus
Koilonychia L60.3
  congenital Q84.6
Kojevnikov's, epilepsy —see Kozhevnikof's
    epilepsy
Koplik's spots B05.9
Kopp's asthma E32.8
Korsakoff's (Wernicke) disease, psychosis or
    syndrome (alcoholic) F10.96
  with dependence F10.26
  drug-induced
    due to drug abuse —see Abuse, drug, by
      type, with amnestic disorder
    due to drug dependence —see Dependence,
      drug, by type, with amnestic disorder
  nonalcoholic F04
Korsakov's disease, psychosis or syndrome —
    see Korsakoff's disease
Korsakow's disease, psychosis or syndrome —
    see Korsakoff's disease
Kostmann's disease or syndrome (infantile
    genetic agranulocytosis) —see
    Agranulocytosis
Kozhevnikof's epilepsy G40.109
  intractable G40.119
    with status epilepticus G40.111
    without status epilepticus G40.119
  not intractable G40.109
    with status epilepticus G40.101
    without status epilepticus G40.109
Krabbe's
  disease E75.23
  syndrome, congenital muscle hypoplasia
    Q79.8
Kraepelin-Morel disease —see Schizophrenia
Kraft-Weber-Dimitri disease Q85.8
Kraurosis
  ani K62.89
  penis N48.0

Kraurosis (Continued)
  vagina N89.8
  vulva N90.4
Kreotoxism A05.9
Krukenberg's
  spindle —see Pigmentation, cornea, posterior
  tumor C79.6-•
Kufs' disease E75.4
Kugelberg-Welander disease G12.1
Kuhnt-Junius degeneration —see also
    Degeneration, macula H35.32-•
Kümmell's disease or spondylitis —see
    Spondylopathy, traumatic
Kupffer cell sarcoma C22.3
Kuru A81.81
Kussmaul's
  disease M30.0
  respiration E87.2
    in diabetic acidosis —see Diabetes, by type,
      with ketoacidosis
Kwashiorkor E40
  marasmic, marasmus type E42
Kyasanur Forest disease A98.2
Kyphoscoliosis, kyphoscoliotic (acquired) —
    see also Scoliosis M41.9
  congenital Q67.5
  heart (disease) I27.1
  sequelae of rickets E64.3
  tuberculous A18.01
Kyphosis, kyphotic (acquired) M40.209
  cervical region M40.202
  cervicothoracic region M40.203
  congenital Q76.419
    cervical region Q76.412
    cervicothoracic region Q76.413
    occipito-atlanto-axial region Q76.411
    thoracic region Q76.414
    thoracolumbar region Q76.415
  Morquio-Brailsford type (spinal) —see also
    subcategory M49.8 E76.219
  postlaminectomy M96.3
  postradiation therapy M96.2
  postural (adolescent) M40.00
    cervicothoracic region M40.03
    thoracic region M40.04
    thoracolumbar region M40.05
  secondary NEC M40.10
    cervical region M40.12
    cervicothoracic region M40.13
    thoracic region M40.14
    thoracolumbar region M40.15
  sequelae of rickets E64.3
  specified type NEC M40.299
    cervical region M40.292
    cervicothoracic region M40.293
    thoracic region M40.294
    thoracolumbar region M40.295
  syphilitic, congenital A50.56
  thoracic region M40.204
  thoracolumbar region M40.205
  tuberculous A18.01
Kyrle disease L87.0

L

Labia, labium —*see* condition
Labile
  blood pressure R09.89
  vasomotor system I73.9
Labioglossal paralysis G12.29
Labium leporinum —*see* Cleft, lip
Labor —*see* Delivery
Labored breathing —*see* Hyperventilation
Labyrinthitis (circumscribed) (destructive)
    (diffuse) (inner ear) (latent) (purulent)
    (suppurative) (*see also* subcategory)
    H83.0
  syphilitic A52.79
Laceration
  with abortion —*see* Abortion, by type,
      complicated by laceration of pelvic
      organs
  abdomen, abdominal
    wall S31.119
      with
        foreign body S31.129
        penetration into peritoneal cavity
          S31.619
          with foreign body S31.629
      epigastric region S31.112
        with
          foreign body S31.122
          penetration into peritoneal cavity
            S31.612
            with foreign body S31.622
      left
        lower quadrant S31.114
          with
            foreign body S31.124
            penetration into peritoneal cavity
              S31.614
              with foreign body S31.624
        upper quadrant S31.111
          with
            foreign body S31.121
            penetration into peritoneal cavity
              S31.611
              with foreign body S31.621
      periumbilic region S31.115
        with
          foreign body S31.125
          penetration into peritoneal cavity
            S31.615
            with foreign body S31.625
      right
        lower quadrant S31.113
          with
            foreign body S31.123
            penetration into peritoneal cavity
              S31.613
              with foreign body S31.623
        upper quadrant S31.110
          with
            foreign body S31.120
            penetration into peritoneal cavity
              S31.610
              with foreign body S31.620
  accidental, complicating surgery —*see*
      Complications, surgical, accidental
      puncture or laceration
  Achilles tendon S86.02-●
  adrenal gland S37.813
  alveolar (process) —*see* Laceration, oral cavity
  ankle S91.01-●
    with
      foreign body S91.02-●
  antecubital space —*see* Laceration, elbow
  anus (sphincter) S31.831
    with
      ectopic or molar pregnancy O08.6
      foreign body S31.832
    complicating delivery —*see* Delivery,
      complicated, by, laceration, anus
      (sphincter)

Laceration (*Continued*)
  anus (*Continued*)
    following ectopic or molar pregnancy
      O08.6
    nontraumatic, nonpuerperal —*see* Fissure,
      anus
  arm (upper) S41.11-●
    with foreign body S41.12-●
    lower —*see* Laceration, forearm
  auditory canal (external) (meatus) —*see*
    Laceration, ear
  auricle, ear —*see* Laceration, ear
  axilla —*see* Laceration, arm
  back —*see also* Laceration, thorax, back
    lower S31.010
      with
        foreign body S31.020
          with penetration into
            retroperitoneal space S31.021
        penetration into retroperitoneal space
          S31.011
  bile duct S36.13
  bladder S37.23
    with ectopic or molar pregnancy O08.6
    following ectopic or molar pregnancy
      O08.6
    obstetrical trauma O71.5
  blood vessel —*see* Injury, blood vessel
  bowel —*see also* Laceration, intestine
    with ectopic or molar pregnancy O08.6
    complicating abortion —*see* Abortion,
      by type, complicated by, specified
      condition NEC
    following ectopic or molar pregnancy
      O08.6
    obstetrical trauma O71.5
  brain (any part) (cortex) (diffuse)
    (membrane) —*see also* Injury,
    intracranial, diffuse
    during birth P10.8
      with hemorrhage P10.1
    focal —*see* Injury, intracranial, focal brain
      injury
  brainstem S06.38-●
  breast S21.01-●
    with foreign body S21.02-●
  broad ligament S37.893
    with ectopic or molar pregnancy O08.6
    following ectopic or molar pregnancy
      O08.6
    laceration syndrome N83.8
    obstetrical trauma O71.6
    syndrome (laceration) N83.8
  buttock S31.801
    with foreign body S31.802
    left S31.821
      with foreign body S31.822
    right S31.811
      with foreign body S31.812
  calf —*see* Laceration, leg
  canaliculus lacrimalis —*see* Laceration,
    eyelid
  canthus, eye —*see* Laceration, eyelid
  capsule, joint —*see* Sprain
  causing eversion of cervix uteri (old) N86
  central (perineal), complicating delivery
    O70.9
  cerebellum, traumatic S06.37-●
  cerebral S06.33-●
    during birth P10.8
      with hemorrhage P10.1
    left side S06.32-●
    right side S06.31-●
  cervix (uteri)
    with ectopic or molar pregnancy O08.6
    following ectopic or molar pregnancy
      O08.6
    nonpuerperal, nontraumatic N88.1
    obstetrical trauma (current) O71.3
    old (postpartal) N88.1
    traumatic S37.63

Laceration (*Continued*)
  cheek (external) S01.41-●
    with foreign body S01.42-●
    internal —*see* Laceration, oral cavity
  chest wall —*see* Laceration, thorax
  chin —*see* Laceration, head, specified site
    NEC
  chordae tendinae NEC I51.1
    concurrent with acute myocardial
      infarction —*see* Infarct, myocardium
    following acute myocardial infarction
      (current complication) I23.4
  clitoris —*see* Laceration, vulva
  colon —*see* Laceration, intestine, large,
    colon
  common bile duct S36.13
  cortex (cerebral) —*see* Injury, intracranial,
    diffuse
  costal region —*see* Laceration, thorax
  cystic duct S36.13
  diaphragm S27.803
  digit(s)
    foot —*see* Laceration, toe
    hand —*see* Laceration, finger
  duodenum S36.430
  ear (canal) (external) S01.31-●
    with foreign body S01.32-●
    drum S09.2-●
  elbow S51.01-●
    with
      foreign body S51.02-●
  epididymis —*see* Laceration, testis
  epigastric region —*see* Laceration, abdomen,
    wall, epigastric region
  esophagus K22.8
    traumatic
      cervical S11.21
        with foreign body S11.22
      thoracic S27.813
  eye (ball) S05.3-●
    with prolapse or loss of intraocular tissue
      S05.2-●
    penetrating S05.6-●
  eyebrow —*see* Laceration, eyelid
  eyelid S01.11-●
    with foreign body S01.12-●
  face NEC —*see* Laceration, head, specified
    site NEC
  fallopian tube S37.539
    bilateral S37.532
    unilateral S37.531
  finger(s) S61.219
    with
      damage to nail S61.319
        with
          foreign body S61.329
      foreign body S61.229
    index S61.218
      with
        damage to nail S61.318
          with
            foreign body S61.328
        foreign body S61.228
    left S61.211
      with
        damage to nail S61.311
          with
            foreign body S61.321
        foreign body S61.221
    right S61.210
      with
        damage to nail S61.310
          with
            foreign body S61.320
        foreign body S61.220
    little S61.218
      with
        damage to nail S61.318
          with
            foreign body S61.328
        foreign body S61.228

▶ New   ⟹ Revised   ~~deleted~~ Deleted   ● Use Additional Character(s)

Laceration *(Continued)*
 finger *(Continued)*
  little *(Continued)*
   left S61.217
    with
     damage to nail S61.317
      with
       foreign body S61.327
     foreign body S61.227
   right S61.216
    with
     damage to nail S61.316
      with
       foreign body S61.326
     foreign body S61.226
  middle S61.218
   with
    damage to nail S61.318
     with
      foreign body S61.328
    foreign body S61.228
   left S61.213
    with
     damage to nail S61.313
      with
       foreign body S61.323
     foreign body S61.223
   right S61.212
    with
     damage to nail S61.312
      with
       foreign body S61.322
     foreign body S61.222
  ring S61.218
   with
    damage to nail S61.318
     with
      foreign body S61.328
    foreign body S61.228
   left S61.215
    with
     damage to nail S61.315
      with
       foreign body S61.325
     foreign body S61.225
   right S61.214
    with
     damage to nail S61.314
      with
       foreign body S61.324
     foreign body S61.224
 flank S31.119
  with foreign body S31.129
 foot (except toe(s) alone) S91.319
  with foreign body S91.329
  left S91.312
   with foreign body S91.322
  right S91.311
   with foreign body S91.321
  toe —*see* Laceration, toe
 forearm S51.819
  with
   foreign body S51.829
  elbow only —*see* Laceration,
   elbow
  left S51.812
   with
    foreign body S51.822
  right S51.811
   with
    foreign body S51.821
 forehead S01.81
  with foreign body S01.82
 fourchette O70.0
  with ectopic or molar pregnancy
   O08.6
  complicating delivery O70.0
  following ectopic or molar pregnancy
   O08.6
 gallbladder S36.123

Laceration *(Continued)*
 genital organs, external
  female S31.512
   with foreign body S31.522
   vagina —*see* Laceration, vagina
   vulva —*see* Laceration, vulva
  male S31.511
   with foreign body S31.521
   penis —*see* Laceration, penis
   scrotum —*see* Laceration, scrotum
   testis —*see* Laceration, testis
 groin —*see* Laceration, abdomen, wall
 gum —*see* Laceration, oral cavity
 hand S61.419
  with
   foreign body S61.429
  finger —*see* Laceration, finger
  left S61.412
   with
    foreign body S61.422
  right S61.411
   with
    foreign body S61.421
  thumb —*see* Laceration, thumb
 head S01.91
  with foreign body S01.92
  cheek —*see* Laceration, cheek
  ear —*see* Laceration, ear
  eyelid —*see* Laceration, eyelid
  lip —*see* Laceration, lip
  nose —*see* Laceration, nose
  oral cavity —*see* Laceration, oral
   cavity
  scalp S01.01
   with foreign body S01.02
  specified site NEC S01.81
   with foreign body S01.82
  temporomandibular area —*see* Laceration,
   cheek
 heart —*see* Injury, heart, laceration
 heel —*see* Laceration, foot
 hepatic duct S36.13
 hip S71.019
  with foreign body S71.029
  left S71.012
   with foreign body S71.022
  right S71.011
   with foreign body S71.021
 hymen —*see* Laceration, vagina
 hypochondrium —*see* Laceration, abdomen,
  wall
 hypogastric region —*see* Laceration,
  abdomen, wall
 ileum S36.438
 inguinal region —*see* Laceration, abdomen,
  wall
 instep —*see* Laceration, foot
 internal organ —*see* Injury, by site
 interscapular region —*see* Laceration, thorax,
  back
 intestine
  large
   colon S36.539
    ascending S36.530
    descending S36.532
    sigmoid S36.533
    specified site NEC S36.538
   rectum S36.63
    transverse S36.531
  small S36.439
   duodenum S36.430
   specified site NEC S36.438
 intra-abdominal organ S36.93
  intestine —*see* Laceration, intestine
  liver —*see* Laceration, liver
  pancreas —*see* Laceration, pancreas
  peritoneum S36.81
  specified site NEC S36.893
  spleen —*see* Laceration, spleen
  stomach —*see* Laceration, stomach

Laceration *(Continued)*
 intracranial NEC —*see also* Injury,
  intracranial, diffuse
  birth injury P10.9
 jaw —*see* Laceration, head, specified site NEC
 jejunum S36.438
 joint capsule —*see* Sprain, by site
 kidney S37.03-●
  major (greater than 3 cm) (massive)
   (stellate) S37.06-●
  minor (less than 1 cm) S37.04-●
  moderate (1 to 3 cm) S37.05-●
  multiple S37.06-●
 knee S81.01-●
  with foreign body S81.02-●
 labium (majus) (minus) —*see* Laceration,
  vulva
 lacrimal duct —*see* Laceration, eyelid
 large intestine —*see* Laceration, intestine,
  large
 larynx S11.011
  with foreign body S11.012
 leg (lower) S81.819
  with foreign body S81.829
  foot —*see* Laceration, foot
  knee —*see* Laceration, knee
  left S81.812
   with foreign body S81.822
  right S81.811
   with foreign body S81.821
  upper —*see* Laceration, thigh
 ligament —*see* Sprain
 lip S01.511
  with foreign body S01.521
 liver S36.113
  major (stellate) S36.116
  minor S36.114
  moderate S36.115
 loin —*see* Laceration, abdomen, wall
 lower back —*see* Laceration, back, lower
 lumbar region —*see* Laceration, back, lower
 lung S27.339
  bilateral S27.332
  unilateral S27.331
 malar region —*see* Laceration, head, specified
  site NEC
 mammary —*see* Laceration, breast
 mastoid region —*see* Laceration, head,
  specified site NEC
 meninges —*see* Injury, intracranial, diffuse
 meniscus —*see* Tear, meniscus
 mesentery S36.893
 mesosalpinx S37.893
 mouth —*see* Laceration, oral cavity
 muscle —*see* Injury, muscle, by site,
  laceration
 nail
  finger —*see* Laceration, finger, with
   damage to nail
  toe —*see* Laceration, toe, with damage to nail
 nasal (septum) (sinus) —*see* Laceration, nose
 nasopharynx —*see* Laceration, head, specified
  site NEC
 neck S11.91
  with foreign body S11.92
  involving
   cervical esophagus S11.21
    with foreign body S11.22
   larynx —*see* Laceration, larynx
   pharynx —*see* Laceration, pharynx
   thyroid gland —*see* Laceration, thyroid
    gland
   trachea —*see* Laceration, trachea
  specified site NEC S11.81
   with foreign body S11.82
 nerve —*see* Injury, nerve
 nose (septum) (sinus) S01.21
  with foreign body S01.22
 ocular NOS S05.3-●
  adnexa NOS S01.11-●

Laceration (Continued)

oral cavity S01.512
  with foreign body S01.522
orbit (eye) —see Wound, open, ocular, orbit
ovary S37.439
  bilateral S37.432
  unilateral S37.431
palate —see Laceration, oral cavity
palm —see Laceration, hand
pancreas S36.239
  body S36.231
    major S36.261
    minor S36.241
    moderate S36.251
  head S36.230
    major S36.260
    minor S36.240
    moderate S36.250
  major S36.269
  minor S36.249
  moderate S36.259
  tail S36.232
    major S36.262
    minor S36.242
    moderate S36.252
pelvic S31.010
  with
    foreign body S31.020
      penetration into retroperitoneal cavity S31.021
    penetration into retroperitoneal cavity S31.011
  floor —see also Laceration, back, lower
    with ectopic or molar pregnancy O08.6
    complicating delivery O70.1
    following ectopic or molar pregnancy O08.6
    old (postpartal) N81.89
  organ S37.93
    with ectopic or molar pregnancy O08.6
    adrenal gland S37.813
    bladder S37.23
    fallopian tube —see Laceration, fallopian tube
    following ectopic or molar pregnancy O08.6
    kidney —see Laceration, kidney
    obstetrical trauma O71.5
    ovary —see Laceration, ovary
    prostate S37.823
    specified site NEC S37.893
    ureter S37.13
    urethra S37.33
    uterus S37.63
penis S31.21
  with foreign body S31.22
perineum
  female S31.41
    with
      ectopic or molar pregnancy O08.6
      foreign body S31.42
    during delivery O70.9
      first degree O70.0
      fourth degree O70.3
      second degree O70.1
      third degree —see also Delivery, complicated, by, laceration, perineum, third degree O70.20
    old (postpartal) N81.89
    postpartal N81.89
    secondary (postpartal) O90.1
  male S31.119
    with foreign body S31.129
periocular area (with or without lacrimal passages) —see Laceration, eyelid
peritoneum S36.893
periumbilic region —see Laceration, abdomen, wall, periumbilic

Laceration (Continued)

periurethral tissue —see Laceration, urethra
phalanges
  finger —see Laceration, finger
  toe —see Laceration, toe
pharynx S11.21
  with foreign body S11.22
pinna —see Laceration, ear
popliteal space —see Laceration, knee
prepuce —see Laceration, penis
prostate S37.823
pubic region S31.119
  with foreign body S31.129
pudendum —see Laceration, genital organs, external
rectovaginal septum —see Laceration, vagina
rectum S36.63
retroperitoneum S36.893
round ligament S37.893
sacral region —see Laceration, back, lower
sacroiliac region —see Laceration, back, lower
salivary gland —see Laceration, oral cavity
scalp S01.01
  with foreign body S01.02
scapular region —see Laceration, shoulder
scrotum S31.31
  with foreign body S31.32
seminal vesicle S37.893
shin —see Laceration, leg
shoulder S41.019
  with foreign body S41.029
  left S41.012
    with foreign body S41.022
  right S41.011
    with foreign body S41.021
small intestine —see Laceration, intestine, small
spermatic cord —see Laceration, testis
spinal cord (meninges) —see also Injury, spinal cord, by region
  due to injury at birth P11.5
  newborn (birth injury) P11.5
spleen S36.039
  major (massive) (stellate) S36.032
  moderate S36.031
  superficial (minor) S36.030
sternal region —see Laceration, thorax, front
stomach S36.33
submaxillary region —see Laceration, head, specified site NEC
submental region —see Laceration, head, specified site NEC
subungual
  finger(s) —see Laceration, finger, with damage to nail
  toe(s) —see Laceration, toe, with damage to nail
suprarenal gland —see Laceration, adrenal gland
temple, temporal region —see Laceration, head, specified site NEC
temporomandibular area —see Laceration, cheek
tendon —see Injury, muscle, by site, laceration
  Achilles S86.02-●
tentorium cerebelli —see Injury, intracranial, diffuse
testis S31.31
  with foreign body S31.32
thigh S71.11-●
  with foreign body S71.12-●
thorax, thoracic (wall) S21.91
  with foreign body S21.92
  back S21.22-●
    with penetration into thoracic cavity S21.42-●
  front S21.12-●
    with penetration into thoracic cavity S21.32-●

Laceration (Continued)

thorax, thoracic (Continued)
  back S21.21-●
    with
      foreign body S21.22-●
        with penetration into thoracic cavity S21.42-●
      penetration into thoracic cavity S21.41-●
  breast —see Laceration, breast
  front S21.11-●
    with
      foreign body S21.12-●
        with penetration into thoracic cavity S21.32-●
      penetration into thoracic cavity S21.31-●
thumb S61.019
  with
    damage to nail S61.119
      with
        foreign body S61.129
    foreign body S61.029
  left S61.012
    with
      damage to nail S61.112
        with
          foreign body S61.122
      foreign body S61.022
  right S61.011
    with
      damage to nail S61.111
        with
          foreign body S61.121
      foreign body S61.021
thyroid gland S11.11
  with foreign body S11.12
toe(s) S91.119
  with
    damage to nail S91.219
      with
        foreign body S91.229
    foreign body S91.129
  great S91.113
    with
      damage to nail S91.213
        with
          foreign body S91.223
      foreign body S91.123
    left S91.112
      with
        damage to nail S91.212
          with
            foreign body S91.222
        foreign body S91.122
    right S91.111
      with
        damage to nail S91.211
          with
            foreign body S91.221
        foreign body S91.121
  lesser S91.116
    with
      damage to nail S91.216
        with
          foreign body S91.226
      foreign body S91.126
    left S91.115
      with
        damage to nail S91.215
          with
            foreign body S91.225
        foreign body S91.125
    right S91.114
      with
        damage to nail S91.214
          with
            foreign body S91.224
        foreign body S91.124
tongue —see Laceration, oral cavity

▶ New   ⇒ Revised   ~~deleted~~ Deleted   ● Use Additional Character(s)

Laceration (Continued)
trachea S11.021
  with foreign body S11.022
tunica vaginalis —see Laceration, testis
tympanum, tympanic membrane —see
    Laceration, ear, drum
umbilical region S31.115
  with foreign body S31.125
ureter S37.13
urethra S37.33
  with or following ectopic or molar
    pregnancy O08.6
  obstetrical trauma O71.5
urinary organ NEC S37.893
uterus S37.63
  with ectopic or molar pregnancy O08.6
  following ectopic or molar pregnancy O08.6
  nonpuerperal, nontraumatic N85.8
  obstetrical trauma NEC O71.81
  old (postpartal) N85.8
uvula —see Laceration, oral cavity
vagina S31.41
  with
    ectopic or molar pregnancy O08.6
    foreign body S31.42
  during delivery O71.4
    with perineal laceration —see Laceration,
      perineum, female, during delivery
  following ectopic or molar pregnancy
    O08.6
  nonpuerperal, nontraumatic N89.8
  old (postpartal) N89.8
vas deferens S37.893
vesical —see Laceration, bladder
vocal cords S11.031
  with foreign body S11.032
vulva S31.41
  with
    ectopic or molar pregnancy O08.6
    foreign body S31.42
  complicating delivery O70.0
  following ectopic or molar pregnancy
    O08.6
  nonpuerperal, nontraumatic N90.89
  old (postpartal) N90.89
wrist S61.519
  with
    foreign body S61.529
  left S61.512
    with
      foreign body S61.522
  right S61.511
    with
      foreign body S61.521
Lack of
achievement in school Z55.3
adequate
  food Z59.4
  intermaxillary vertical dimension of fully
    erupted teeth M26.36
  sleep Z72.820
appetite (see Anorexia) R63.0
awareness R41.9
care
  in home Z74.2
  of infant (at or after birth) T76.02
    confirmed T74.02
cognitive functions R41.9
coordination R27.9
  ataxia R27.0
  specified type NEC R27.8
development (physiological) R62.50
  failure to thrive (child over 28 days old)
    R62.51
    adult R62.7
    newborn P92.6
  short stature R62.52
  specified type NEC R62.59
energy R53.83
financial resources Z59.6

Lack of (Continued)
food T73.0
growth R62.52
heating Z59.1
housing (permanent) (temporary) Z59.0
  adequate Z59.1
learning experiences in childhood Z62.898
leisure time (affecting life-style) Z73.2
material resources Z59.9
memory —see also Amnesia
  mild, following organic brain damage
    F06.8
ovulation N97.0
parental supervision or control of child
  Z62.0
person able to render necessary care
  Z74.2
physical exercise Z72.3
play experience in childhood Z62.898
posterior occlusal support M26.57
relaxation (affecting life-style) Z73.2
sexual
  desire F52.0
  enjoyment F52.1
shelter Z59.0
sleep (adequate) Z72.820
supervision of child by parent Z62.0
support, posterior occlusal M26.57
water T73.1
Lacrimal —see condition
Lacrimation, abnormal —see Epiphora
Lacrimonasal duct —see condition
Lactation, lactating (breast) (puerperal,
  postpartum)
associated
  cracked nipple O92.13
  retracted nipple O92.03
defective O92.4
disorder NEC O92.79
excessive O92.6
failed (complete) O92.3
  partial O92.4
mastitis NEC —see Mastitis, obstetric
mother (care and/or examination) Z39.1
nonpuerperal N64.3
Lacticemia, excessive E87.2
Lacunar skull Q75.8
Laennec's cirrhosis K70.30
  with ascites K70.31
  nonalcoholic K74.69
Lafora's disease —see Epilepsy, generalized,
  idiopathic
Lag, lid (nervous) —see Retraction, lid
Lagophthalmos (eyelid) (nervous) H02.209
bilateral, upper and lower eyelids H02.20C
cicatricial H02.219
  bilateral, upper and lower eyelids H02.21C
  left H02.216
    lower H02.215
    upper H02.214
    upper and lower eyelids H02.21B
  right H02.213
    lower H02.212
    upper H02.211
    upper and lower eyelids H02.21A
keratoconjunctivitis —see Keratoconjunctivitis
left H02.206
  lower H02.205
  upper H02.204
  upper and lower eyelids H02.20B
mechanical H02.229
  bilateral, upper and lower eyelids H02.22C
  left H02.226
    lower H02.225
    upper H02.224
    upper and lower eyelids H02.22B
  right H02.223
    lower H02.222
    upper H02.221
    upper and lower eyelids H02.22A

Lagophthalmos (Continued)
paralytic H02.239
  bilateral, upper and lower eyelids H02.23C
  left H02.236
    lower H02.235
    upper H02.234
    upper and lower eyelids H02.23B
  right H02.233
    lower H02.232
    upper H02.231
    upper and lower eyelids H02.23A
right H02.203
  lower H02.202
  upper H02.201
  upper and lower eyelids H02.20A
Laki-Lorand factor deficiency —see Defect,
  coagulation, specified type NEC
Lalling F80.0
Lambert-Eaton syndrome —see Syndrome,
  Lambert-Eaton
Lambliasis, lambliosis A07.1
Landau-Kleffner syndrome —see Epilepsy,
  specified NEC
Landouzy-Déjérine dystrophy or
  facioscapulohumeral atrophy G71.02
Landouzy's disease (icterohemorrhagic
  leptospirosis) A27.0
Landry-Guillain-Barré, syndrome or paralysis
  G61.0
Landry's disease or paralysis G61.0
Lane's
band Q43.3
kink —see Obstruction, intestine
syndrome K90.2
Langdon Down's syndrome —see Trisomy, 21
Lapsed immunization schedule status Z28.3
Large
baby (regardless of gestational age) (4000g to
  4499g) P08.1
ear, congenital Q17.1
physiological cup Q14.2
stature R68.89
Large-for-dates NEC (infant) (4000g to 4499g)
  P08.1
  affecting management of pregnancy O36.6-●
  exceptionally (4500g or more) P08.0
Larsen-Johansson disease
  orosteochondrosis —see Osteochondrosis,
    juvenile, patella
Larsen's syndrome (flattened facies and
  multiple congenital dislocations) Q74.8
Larva migrans
cutaneous B76.9
  Ancylostoma B76.0
visceral B83.0
Laryngeal —see condition
Laryngismus (stridulus) J38.5
congenital P28.89
diphtheritic A36.2
Laryngitis (acute) (edematous) (fibrinous)
  (infective) (infiltrative) (malignant)
  (membranous) (phlegmonous)
  (pneumococcal) (pseudomembranous)
  (septic) (subglottic) (suppurative)
  (ulcerative) J04.0
with
  influenza, flu, or grippe —see Influenza,
    with, laryngitis
  tracheitis (acute) —see Laryngotracheitis
atrophic J37.0
catarrhal J37.0
chronic J37.0
  with tracheitis (chronic) J37.1
diphtheritic A36.2
due to external agent —see Inflammation,
  respiratory, upper, due to
Hemophilus influenzae J04.0
H. influenzae J04.0
hypertrophic J37.0
influenzal —see Influenza, with, respiratory
  manifestations NEC

Laryngitis *(Continued)*
  obstructive J05.0
  sicca J37.0
  spasmodic J05.0
    acute J04.0
  streptococcal J04.0
  stridulous J05.0
  syphilitic (late) A52.73
    congenital A50.59 *[J99]*
      early A50.03 *[J99]*
  tuberculous A15.5
  Vincent's A69.1
Laryngocele (congenital) (ventricular) Q31.3
Laryngofissure J38.7
  congenital Q31.8
Laryngomalacia (congenital) Q31.5
Laryngopharyngitis (acute) J06.0
  chronic J37.0
  due to external agent —*see* Inflammation,
    respiratory, upper, due to
Laryngoplegia J38.00
  bilateral J38.02
  unilateral J38.01
Laryngoptosis J38.7
Laryngospasm J38.5
Laryngostenosis J38.6
Laryngotracheitis (acute) (Infectional)
  (infective) (viral) J04.2
  atrophic J37.1
  catarrhal J37.1
  chronic J37.1
  diphtheritic A36.2
  due to external agent —*see* Inflammation,
    respiratory, upper, due to
  Hemophilus influenzae J04.2
  hypertrophic J37.1
  influenzal —*see* Influenza, with, respiratory
    manifestations NEC
  pachydermic J38.7
  sicca J37.1
  spasmodic J38.5
    acute J05.0
  streptococcal J04.2
  stridulous J38.5
  syphilitic (late) A52.73
    congenital A50.59 *[J99]*
      early A50.03 *[J99]*
  tuberculous A15.5
  Vincent's A69.1
Laryngotracheobronchitis —*see* Bronchitis
Larynx, laryngeal —*see* condition
Lassa fever A96.2
Lassitude —*see* Weakness
Late
  talker R62.0
  walker R62.0
Late effect(s) —*see* Sequelae
Latent —*see* condition
Laterocession —*see* Lateroversion
Lateroflexion —*see* Lateroversion
Lateroversion
  cervix —*see* Lateroversion, uterus
  uterus, uterine (cervix) (postinfectional)
    (postpartal, old) N85.4
    congenital Q51.818
    in pregnancy or childbirth O34.59-•
Lathyrism —*see* Poisoning, food, noxious,
  plant
Launois' syndrome (pituitary gigantism) E22.0
Launois-Bensaude adenolipomatosis E88.89
Laurence-Moon (-Bardet)-Biedl syndrome
  Q87.89
Lax, laxity —*see also* Relaxation
  ligament (ous) —*see also* Disorder, ligament
    familial M35.7
    knee —*see* Derangement, knee
  skin (acquired) L57.4
    congenital Q82.8
Laxative habit F55.2
Lazy leukocyte syndrome D70.8
Lead miner's lung J63.6

Leak, leakage
  air NEC J93.82
    postprocedural J95.812
  amniotic fluid —*see* Rupture, membranes,
    premature
  blood (microscopic), fetal, into maternal
    circulation affecting management
    of pregnancy —*see* Pregnancy,
    complicated by
  cerebrospinal fluid G96.00
    cranial
      postoperative G96.08
      specified NEC G96.08
      spontaneous G96.01
      traumatic G96.08
    from spinal (lumbar) puncture G97.0
    spinal
      postoperative G96.09
      post-traumatic G96.09
      specified NEC G96.09
      spontaneous G96.02
    spontaneous
      from
      skull base G96.01
    spine G96.02
  CSF —*see* Leak, cerebrospinal fluid
  device, implant or graft —*see also*
    Complications, by site and type,
    mechanical
    arterial graft NEC —*see* Complication,
      cardiovascular device, mechanical,
      vascular
    breast (implant) T85.43
    catheter NEC T85.638
      dialysis (renal) T82.43
        intraperitoneal T85.631
      infusion NEC T82.534
        spinal (epidural) (subdural)
          T85.630
      urinary T83.038
        cystostomy T83.030
        Hopkins T83.038
        ileostomy T83.038
        indwelling T83.031
        nephrostomy T83.032
        specified NEC T83.038
        urostomy T83.038
    gastrointestinal —*see* Complications,
      prosthetic device, mechanical,
      gastrointestinal device
    genital NEC T83.498
      penile prosthesis (cylinder) (implanted)
        (pump) (resevoir) T83.490
      testicular prosthesis T83.491
    heart NEC —*see* Complication,
      cardiovascular device, mechanical
    joint prosthesis —*see* Complications, joint
      prosthesis, mechanical, specified NEC,
      by site
    ocular NEC —*see* Complications, prosthetic
      device, mechanical, ocular device
    orthopedic NEC —*see* Complication,
      orthopedic, device, mechanical
    persistent air J93.82
    specified NEC T85.638
    urinary NEC —*see also* Complication,
      genitourinary, device, urinary,
      mechanical
      graft T83.23
    vascular NEC —*see* Complication,
      cardiovascular device, mechanical
    ventricular intracranial shunt T85.03
  urine —*see* Incontinence
Leaky heart —*see* Endocarditis
Learning defect (specific) F81.9
Leather bottle stomach C16.9
Leber's
  congenital amaurosis H35.50
  optic atrophy (hereditary) H47.22
Lederer's anemia D59.19
Leeches (external) —*see* Hirudiniasis

Leg —*see* condition
Legg (-Calvé)-Perthes disease, syndrome or
  osteochondrosis M91.1-•
Legionellosis A48.1
  nonpneumonic A48.2
Legionnaires'
  disease A48.1
    nonpneumonic A48.2
    pneumonia A48.1
Leigh's disease G31.82
Leiner's disease L21.1
Leiofibromyoma —*see* Leiomyoma
Leiomyoblastoma —*see* Neoplasm, connective
  tissue, benign
Leiomyofibroma —*see also* Neoplasm,
  connective tissue, benign
  uterus (cervix) (corpus) D25.9
Leiomyoma —*see also* Neoplasm, connective
  tissue, benign
  bizarre —*see* Neoplasm, connective tissue,
    benign
  cellular —*see* Neoplasm, connective tissue,
    benign
  epithelioid —*see* Neoplasm, connective
    tissue, benign
  uterus (cervix) (corpus) D25.9
    intramural D25.1
    submucous D25.0
    subserosal D25.2
  vascular —*see* Neoplasm, connective tissue,
    benign
Leiomyoma, leiomyomatosis (intravascular) —
  see Neoplasm, connective tissue, uncertain
  behavior
Leiomyosarcoma —*see also* Neoplasm,
  connective tissue, malignant
  epithelioid —*see* Neoplasm, connective
    tissue, malignant
  myxoid —*see* Neoplasm, connective tissue,
    malignant
Leishmaniasis B55.9
  American (mucocutaneous) B55.2
    cutaneous B55.1
  Asian Desert B55.1
  Brazilian B55.2
  cutaneous (any type) B55.1
  dermal —*see also* Leishmaniasis, cutaneous
    post-kala-azar B55.0
  eyelid B55.1
  infantile B55.0
  Mediterranean B55.0
  mucocutaneous (American) (New World)
    B55.2
  naso-oral B55.2
  nasopharyngeal B55.2
  old world B55.1
  tegumentaria diffusa B55.1
  visceral B55.0
Leishmanoid, dermal —*see also* Leishmaniasis,
  cutaneous
  post-kala-azar B55.0
Lenegre's disease I44.2
Lengthening, leg —*see* Deformity, limb,
  unequal length
Lennert's lymphoma —*see* Lymphoma,
  Lennert's
Lennox-Gastaut syndrome G40.812
  intractable G40.814
    with status epilepticus G40.813
    without status epilepticus G40.814
  not intractable G40.812
    with status epilepticus G40.811
    without status epilepticus G40.812
Lens —*see* condition
Lenticonus (anterior) (posterior) (congenital)
  Q12.8
Lenticular degeneration, progressive E83.01
Lentiglobus (posterior) (congenital) Q12.8
Lentigo (congenital) L81.4
  maligna —*see also* Melanoma, in situ
    melanoma —*see* Melanoma

▶ New   ⇒ Revised   ~~deleted~~ Deleted   • Use Additional Character(s)

Lentivirus, as cause of disease classified
    elsewhere B97.31
Leontiasis
  ossium M85.2
  syphilitic (late) A52.78
    congenital A50.59
Lepothrix A48.8
Lepra —see Leprosy
Leprechaunism E34.8
Leprosy A30.-●
  with muscle disorder A30.9 [M63.80]
    ankle A30.9 [M63.87-●]
    foot A30.9 [M63.87-●]
    forearm A30.9 [M63.83-●]
    hand A30.9 [M63.84-●]
    lower leg A30.9 [M63.86-●]
    multiple sites A30.9 [M63.89]
    pelvic region A30.9 [M63.85-●]
    shoulder region A30.9 [M63.81-●]
    specified site NEC A30.9 [M63.88]
    thigh A30.9 [M63.85-●]
    upper arm A30.9 [M63.82-●]
  anesthetic A30.9
  BB A30.3
  BL A30.4
  borderline (infiltrated) (neuritic) A30.3
    lepromatous A30.4
    tuberculoid A30.2
  BT A30.2
  dimorphous (infiltrated) (neuritic) A30.3
  I A30.0
  indeterminate (macular) (neuritic) A30.0
  lepromatous (diffuse) (infiltrated) (macular)
    (neuritic) (nodular) A30.5
  LL A30.5
  macular (early) (neuritic) (simple) A30.9
  maculoanesthetic A30.9
  mixed A30.3
  neural A30.9
  nodular A30.5
  primary neuritic A30.3
  specified type NEC A30.8
  TT A30.1
  tuberculoid (major) (minor) A30.1
Leptocytosis, hereditary D56.9
Leptomeningitis (chronic) (circumscribed)
    (hemorrhagic) (nonsuppurative) —see
    Meningitis
➡ Leptomeningopathy G96.198
Leptospiral —see condition
Leptospirochetal —see condition
Leptospirosis A27.9
  canicola A27.89
  due to Leptospira interrogans serovar
    icterohaemorrhagiae A27.0
  icterohemorrhagica A27.0
  pomona A27.89
  Weil's disease A27.0
Leptus dermatitis B88.0
Leriche's syndrome (aortic bifurcation
    occlusion) I74.09
Leri's pleonosteosis Q78.8
Leri-Weill syndrome Q77.8
Lermoyez' syndrome —see Vertigo, peripheral
    NEC
Lesch-Nyhan syndrome E79.1
Leser-Trélat disease L82.1
  inflamed L82.0
Lesion(s) (nontraumatic)
  abducens nerve —see Strabismus, paralytic,
    sixth nerve
  alveolar process K08.9
  angiocentric immunoproliferative
    D47.Z9
  anorectal K62.9
  aortic (valve) I35.9
  auditory nerve —see subcategory
    H93.3
  basal ganglion G25.9
  bile duct —see Disease, bile duct
  biomechanical M99.9

Lesion (Continued)
  biomechanical (Continued)
    specified type NEC M99.89
      abdomen M99.89
      acromioclavicular M99.87
      cervical region M99.81
      cervicothoracic M99.81
      costochondral M99.88
      costovertebral M99.88
      head region M99.80
      hip M99.85
      lower extremity M99.86
      lumbar region M99.83
      lumbosacral M99.83
      occipitocervical M99.80
      pelvic region M99.85
      pubic M99.85
      rib cage M99.88
      sacral region M99.84
      sacrococcygeal M99.84
      sacroiliac M99.84
      specified NEC M99.89
      sternochondral M99.88
      sternoclavicular M99.87
      thoracic region M99.82
      thoracolumbar M99.82
      upper extremity M99.87
  bladder N32.9
  bone —see Disorder, bone
  brachial plexus G54.0
  brain G93.9
    congenital Q04.9
    vascular I67.9
      degenerative I67.9
      hypertensive I67.4
  buccal cavity K13.79
  calcified —see Calcification
  canthus —see Disorder, eyelid
  carate —see Pinta, lesions
  cardia K31.9
  cardiac —see also Disease, heart I51.9
    congenital Q24.9
    valvular —see Endocarditis
  cauda equina G83.4
  cecum K63.9
  cerebral —see Lesion, brain
  cerebrovascular I67.9
    degenerative I67.9
    hypertensive I67.4
  cervical (nerve) root NEC G54.2
  chiasmal —see Disorder, optic, chiasm
  chorda tympani G51.8
  coin, lung R91.1
  colon K63.9
  combined periodontic - endodontic K05.5
  congenital —see Anomaly, by site
  conjunctiva H11.9
  conus medullaris —see Injury, conus
    medullaris
  coronary artery —see Ischemia, heart
  cranial nerve G52.9
    eighth —see Disorder, ear
    eleventh G52.9
    fifth G50.9
    first G52.0
    fourth —see Strabismus, paralytic, fourth
      nerve
    seventh G51.9
    sixth —see Strabismus, paralytic, sixth nerve
    tenth G52.2
    twelfth G52.3
  cystic —see Cyst
  degenerative —see Degeneration
  duodenum K31.9
  edentulous (alveolar) ridge, associated with
    trauma, due to traumatic occlusion K06.2
  en coup de sabre L94.1
  eyelid —see Disorder, eyelid
  gasserian ganglion G50.8
  gastric K31.9
  gastroduodenal K31.9

Lesion (Continued)
  gastrointestinal K63.9
  gingiva, associated with trauma K06.2
  glomerular
    focal and segmental —see also N00-N07
      with fourth character .1 N05.1
    minimal change —see also N00-N07 with
      fourth character .0 N05.0
  heart (organic) —see Disease, heart
  hyperchromic, due to pinta (carate) A67.1
  hyperkeratotic —see Hyperkeratosis
  hypothalamic E23.7
  ileocecal K63.9
  ileum K63.9
  iliohypogastric nerve G57.8-●
  inflammatory —see Inflammation
  intestine K63.9
  intracerebral —see Lesion, brain
  intrachiasmal (optic) —see Disorder, optic,
    chiasm
  intracranial, space-occupying R90.0
  joint —see Disorder, joint
    sacroiliac (old) M53.3
  keratotic —see Keratosis
  kidney —see Disease, renal
  laryngeal nerve (recurrent) G52.2
  lip K13.0
  liver K76.9
  lumbosacral
    plexus G54.1
    root (nerve) NEC G54.4
  lung (coin) R91.1
  maxillary sinus J32.0
  mitral I05.9
  Morel-Lavallée —see Hematoma,
    by site
  motor cortex NEC G93.89
  mouth K13.79
  nerve G58.9
    femoral G57.2-●
    median G56.1-●
      carpal tunnel syndrome —see Syndrome,
        carpal tunnel
    plantar G57.6-●
    popliteal (lateral) G57.3-●
      medial G57.4-●
    radial G56.3-●
    sciatic G57.0-●
    spinal —see Injury, nerve, spinal
    ulnar G56.2-●
  nervous system, congenital Q07.9
  nonallopathic —see Lesion, biomechanical
  nose (internal) J34.89
  obstructive —see Obstruction
  obturator nerve G57.8-●
  oral mucosa K13.70
  organ or site NEC —see Disease, by site
  osteolytic —see Osteolysis
  peptic K27.9
  periodontal, due to traumatic occlusion K05.5
  pharynx J39.2
  pigment, pigmented (skin) L81.9
  pinta —see Pinta, lesions
  polypoid —see Polyp
  prechiasmal (optic) —see Disorder, optic,
    chiasm
  primary —see also Syphilis, primary A51.0
    carate A67.0
    pinta A67.0
    yaws A66.0
  pulmonary J98.4
    valve I37.9
  pylorus K31.9
  rectosigmoid K63.9
  retina, retinal H35.9
  sacroiliac (joint) (old) M53.3
  salivary gland K11.9
    benign lymphoepithelial K11.8
  saphenous nerve G57.8-●
  sciatic nerve G57.0-●
  secondary —see Syphilis, secondary

Lesion *(Continued)*
  shoulder (region) M75.9-●
    specified NEC M75.8-●
  sigmoid K63.9
  sinus (accessory) (nasal) J34.89
  skin L98.9
    suppurative L08.0
  SLAP S43.43-●
  spinal cord G95.9
    congenital Q06.9
  spleen D73.89
  stomach K31.9
  superior glenoid labrum S43.43-●
  syphilitic —*see* Syphilis
  tertiary —*see* Syphilis, tertiary
  thoracic root (nerve) NEC G54.3
  tonsillar fossa J35.9
  tooth, teeth K08.9
    white spot
      chewing surface K02.51
      pit and fissure surface K02.51
      smooth surface K02.61
  traumatic —*see* specific type of injury by site
  tricuspid (valve) I07.9
    nonrheumatic I36.9
  trigeminal nerve G50.9
  ulcerated or ulcerative —*see* Ulcer, skin
  uterus N85.9
  vagina N89.8
  vulva N90.89
  vagus nerve G52.2
  valvular —*see* Endocarditis
  vascular I99.9
    affecting central nervous system I67.9
    following trauma NEC T14.8
    umbilical cord, complicating delivery
      O69.5
  warty —*see* Verruca
  white spot (tooth)
    chewing surface K02.51
    pit and fissure surface K02.51
    smooth surface K02.61
Lethargic —*see* condition
Lethargy R53.83
Letterer-Siwe's disease C96.0
Leukemia, leukemic C95.9-●
  acute basophilic C94.8-●
  acute bilineal C95.0-●
  acute erythroid C94.0-●
  acute lymphoblastic C91.0-●
  acute megakaryoblastic C94.2-●
  acute megakaryocytic C94.2-●
  acute mixed lineage C95.0-●
  acute monoblastic (monoblastic/monocytic)
    C93.0-●
  acute monocytic (monoblastic/monocytic)
    C93.0-●
  acute myeloblastic (minimal differentiation)
    (with maturation) C92.0-●
  acute myeloid, NOS C92.0-●
    with
      11q23-abnormality C92.6-●
      dysplasia of remaining hematopoesis
        and/or myelodysplastic disease in
        its history C92.A-●
      multilineage dysplasia C92.A-●
      variation of MLL-gene C92.6-●
    M6 (a)(b) C94.0-●
    M7 C94.2-●
  acute myelomonocytic C92.5-●
  acute promyelocytic C92.4-●
  adult T-cell (HTLV-1-associated) (acute
    variant) (chronic variant)
    (lymphomatoid variant) (smouldering
    variant) C91.5-●
  aggressive NK-cell C94.8-●
  AML (1/ETO) (M0) (M1) (M2) (without a
    FAB classification) C92.0-●
  AML M3 C92.4-●
  AML M4 (Eo with inv(16) or t(16;16)) C92.5-●
  AML M5 C93.0-●

Leukemia, leukemic *(Continued)*
  AML M5a C93.0-●
  AML M5b C93.0-●
  AML Me with t (15;17) and variants C92.4-●
  atypical chronic myeloid, BCR/ABL-negative
    C92.2-●
  biphenotypic acute C95.0-●
  blast cell C95.0-●
  Burkitt-type, mature B-cell C91.A-●
▶ chronic eosinophilic (*see also* Syndrome,
    hypereosinophilic, myeloid) C94.8-●
  chronic lymphocytic, of B-cell type C91.1-●
  chronic monocytic C93.1-●
  chronic myelogenous (Philadelphia
    chromosome (Ph1) positive) (t(9;22))
    (q34;q11) (with crisis of blast cells)
    C92.1-●
  chronic myeloid, BCR/ABL-positive C92.1-●
    atypical, BCR/ABL-negative C92.2-●
  chronic myelomonocytic C93.1-●
  chronic neutrophilic D47.1
  CMML (-1) (-2) (with eosinophilia) C93.1-●
  granulocytic —*see also* Category C92 C92.9-●
  hairy-cell C91.4-●
  juvenile myelomonocytic C93.3-●
  lymphoid C91.9-●
    specified NEC C91.Z-●
  mast cell C94.3-●
  mature B-cell, Burkitt-type C91.A-●
  monocytic (subacute) C93.9-●
    specified NEC C93.Z-●
  myelogenous —*see also* Category
    C92 C92.9-●
  myeloid C92.9-●
    specified NEC C92.Z-●
  plasma cell C90.1-●
  plasmacytic C90.1-●
  prolymphocytic
    of B-cell type C91.3-●
    of T-cell type C91.6-●
  specified NEC C94.8-●
  stem cell, of unclear lineage C95.0-●
  subacute lymphocytic C91.9-●
  T-cell large granular lymphocytic C91.Z-●
  unspecified cell type C95.9-●
    acute C95.0-●
    chronic C95.1-●
Leukemoid reaction —*see also* Reaction,
    leukemoid D72.823-●
Leukoaraiosis (hypertensive) I67.81
Leukoariosis —*see* Leukoaraiosis
Leukocoria —*see* Disorder, globe, degenerated
    condition, leucocoria
Leukocytopenia D72.819
Leukocytosis D72.829
⇒ eosinophilic D72.19
Leukoderma, leukodermia NEC L81.5
  syphilitic A51.39
    late A52.79
Leukodystrophy E75.29
Leukoedema, oral epithelium K13.29
Leukoencephalitis G04.81
  acute (subacute) hemorrhagic G36.1
    postimmunization or postvaccinal
      G04.02
  postinfectious G04.01
  subacute sclerosing A81.1
  van Bogaert's (sclerosing) A81.1
Leukoencephalopathy —*see also*
    Encephalopathy G93.49
  Binswanger's I67.3
  heroin vapor G92
  metachromatic E75.25
  multifocal (progressive) A81.2
  postimmunization and postvaccinal
    G04.02
  progressive multifocal A81.2
  reversible, posterior G93.6
  van Bogaert's (sclerosing) A81.1
  vascular, progressive I67.3
Leukoerythroblastosis D75.9

Leukokeratosis —*see also* Leukoplakia
  mouth K13.21
  nicotina palati K13.24
  oral mucosa K13.21
  tongue K13.21
  vocal cord J38.3
Leukokraurosis vulva (e) N90.4
Leukoma (cornea) —*see also* Opacity, cornea
  adherent H17.0-●
  interfering with central vision —*see* Opacity,
    cornea, central
Leukomalacia, cerebral, newborn P91.2
  periventricular P91.2
Leukomelanopathy, hereditary D72.0
Leukonychia (punctata) (striata) L60.8
  congenital Q84.4
Leukopathia unguium L60.8
  congenital Q84.4
Leukopenia D72.819
  basophilic D72.818
  chemotherapy (cancer) induced D70.1
  congenital D70.0
  cyclic D70.0
  drug induced NEC D70.2
    due to cytoreductive cancer chemotherapy
      D70.1
  eosinophilic D72.818
  familial D70.0
  infantile genetic D70.0
  malignant D70.9
  periodic D70.0
  transitory neonatal P61.5
Leukopenic —*see* condition
Leukoplakia
  anus K62.89
  bladder (postinfectional) N32.89
  buccal K13.21
  cervix (uteri) N88.0
  esophagus K22.8
  gingiva K13.21
  hairy (oral mucosa) (tongue) K13.3
  kidney (pelvis) N28.89
  larynx J38.7
  lip K13.21
  mouth K13.21
  oral epithelium, including tongue (mucosa)
    K13.21
  palate K13.21
  pelvis (kidney) N28.89
  penis (infectional) N48.0
  rectum K62.89
  syphilitic (late) A52.79
  tongue K13.21
  ureter (postinfectional) N28.89
  urethra (postinfectional) N36.8
  uterus N85.8
  vagina N89.4
  vocal cord J38.3
  vulva N90.4
Leukorrhea N89.8
  due to Trichomonas (vaginalis)
    A59.00
  trichomonal A59.00
Leukosarcoma C85.9
Levocardia (isolated) Q24.1
  with situs inversus Q89.3
Levotransposition Q20.5
Lev's disease or syndrome (acquired complete
    heart block) I44.2
Levulosuria —*see* Fructosuria
Levurid L30.2
Lewy body (ies) (dementia) (disease)
    G31.83
Leyden-Moebius dystrophy G71.09
Leydig cell
  carcinoma
    specified site —*see* Neoplasm, malignant,
      by site
    unspecified site
      female C56.9-●
      male C62.9-●

▶ New　⇒ Revised　~~deleted~~ Deleted　● Use Additional Character(s)

Leydig cell (Continued)
  tumor
    benign
      specified site —see Neoplasm, benign,
        by site
      unspecified site
        female D27.-●
        male D29.2-●
    malignant
      specified site —see Neoplasm,
        malignant, by site
      unspecified site
        female C56.-●
        male C62.9-●
    specified site —see Neoplasm, uncertain
      behavior, by site
    unspecified site
      female D39.1-●
      male D40.1-●
Leydig-Sertoli cell tumor
  specified site —see Neoplasm, benign,
    by site
  unspecified site
    female D27.-●
    male D29.2-●
LGSIL (Low grade squamous intraepithelial
  lesion on cytologic smear of)
  anus R85.612
  cervix R87.612
  vagina R87.622
Liar, pathologic F60.2
Libido
  decreased R68.82
Libman-Sacks disease M32.11
Lice (infestation) B85.2
  body (Pediculus corporis) B85.1
  crab B85.3
  head (Pediculus capitis) B85.0
  mixed (classifiable to more than one of the
    titles B85.0-B85.3) B85.4
  pubic (Phthirus pubis) B85.3
Lichen L28.0
  albus L90.0
    penis N48.0
    vulva N90.4
  amyloidosis E85.4 [L99]
  atrophicus L90.0
    penis N48.0
    vulva N90.4
  congenital Q82.8
  myxedematosus L98.5
  nitidus L44.1
  pilaris Q82.8
    acquired L85.8
  planopilaris L66.1
  planus (chronicus) L43.9
    annularis L43.8
    bullous L43.1
    follicular L66.1
    hypertrophic L43.0
    moniliformis L44.3
    of Wilson L43.9
    specified NEC L43.8
    subacute (active) L43.3
    tropicus L43.3
  ruber
    acuminatus L44.0
    moniliformis L44.3
    planus L43.9
  sclerosus (et atrophicus) L90.0
    penis N48.0
    vulva N90.4
  scrofulosus (primary) (tuberculous) A18.4
  simplex (chronicus) (circumscriptus)
    L28.0
  striatus L44.2
  urticatus L28.2
Lichenification L28.0
Lichenoides tuberculosis (primary) A18.4
Lichtheim's disease or syndrome D51.0
Lien migrans D73.89

Ligament —see condition
Light
  for gestational age —see Light for dates
  headedness R42
Light-for-dates (infant) P05.00
  with weight of
    499 grams or less P05.01
    500-749 grams P05.02
    750-999 grams P05.03
    1000-1249 grams P05.04
    1250-1499 grams P05.05
    1500-1749 grams P05.06
    1750-1999 grams P05.07
    2000-2499 grams P05.08
    2500 grams and over P05.09
  affecting management of pregnancy O36.59-●
  and small-for-dates —see Small for dates
  specified NEC P05.09
Lightning (effects) (stroke) (struck by) T75.00
  burn —see Burn
  foot E53.8
  shock T75.01
  specified effect NEC T75.09
Lightwood-Albright syndrome N25.89
Lightwood's disease or syndrome (renal
  tubular acidosis) N25.89
Lignac (-de Toni) (-Fanconi) (-Debré) disease or
  syndrome E72.09
  with cystinosis E72.04
Ligneous thyroiditis E06.5
Likoff's syndrome I20.8
Limb —see condition
Limbic epilepsy personality syndrome F07.0
Limitation, limited
  activities due to disability Z73.6
  cardiac reserve —see Disease, heart
  eye muscle duction, traumatic —see
    Strabismus, mechanical
  mandibular range of motion M26.52
Lindau (-von Hippel) disease Q85.8
Line(s)
  Beau's L60.4
  Harris' —see Arrest, epiphyseal
  Hudson's (cornea) —see Pigmentation,
    cornea, anterior
  Stähli's (cornea) —see Pigmentation, cornea,
    anterior
Linea corneae senilis —see Change, cornea,
  senile
Lingua
  geographica K14.1
  nigra (villosa) K14.3
  plicata K14.5
  tylosis K13.29
Lingual —see condition
Linguatulosis B88.8
Linitis (gastric) plastica C16.9
Lip —see condition
Lipedema —see Edema
Lipemia —see also Hyperlipidemia
  retina, retinalis E78.3
Lipidosis E75.6
  cerebral (infantile) (juvenile) (late) E75.4
  cerebroretinal E75.4
  cerebroside E75.22
  cholesterol (cerebral) E75.5
  glycolipid E75.21
  hepatosplenomegalic E78.3
  sphingomyelin —see Niemann-Pick disease
    or syndrome
  sulfatide E75.29
Lipoadenoma —see Neoplasm, benign, by site
Lipoblastoma —see Lipoma
Lipoblastomatosis —see Lipoma
Lipochondrodystrophy E76.01
Lipochrome histiocytosis (familial) D71
Lipodermatosclerosis —see Varix, leg, with,
  inflammation
  ulcerated —see Varix, leg, with, ulcer, with
    inflammation by site
Lipodystrophia progressiva E88.1

Lipodystrophy (progressive) E88.1
  insulin E88.1
  intestinal K90.81
  mesenteric K65.4
Lipofibroma —see Lipoma
Lipofuscinosis, neuronal (with ceroidosis)
  E75.4
Lipogranuloma, sclerosing L92.8
Lipogranulomatosis E78.89
Lipoid —see also condition
  histiocytosis D76.3
    essential E75.29
  nephrosis N04.9
  proteinosis of Urbach E78.89
Lipoidemia —see Hyperlipidemia
Lipoidosis —see Lipidosis
Lipoma D17.9
  fetal D17.9
    fat cell D17.9
  infiltrating D17.9
  intramuscular D17.9
  pleomorphic D17.9
  site classification
    arms (skin) (subcutaneous) D17.2-●
    connective tissue D17.30
      intra-abdominal D17.5
      intrathoracic D17.4
      peritoneum D17.79
      retroperitoneum D17.79
      specified site NEC D17.39
      spermatic cord D17.6
    face (skin) (subcutaneous) D17.0
    genitourinary organ NEC D17.72
    head (skin) (subcutaneous) D17.0
    intra-abdominal D17.5
    intrathoracic D17.4
    kidney D17.71
    legs (skin) (subcutaneous) D17.2-●
    neck (skin) (subcutaneous) D17.0
    peritoneum D17.79
    retroperitoneum D17.79
    skin D17.30
      specified site NEC D17.39
    specified site NEC D17.79
    spermatic cord D17.6
    subcutaneous D17.30
      specified site NEC D17.39
    trunk (skin) (subcutaneous) D17.1
    unspecified D17.9
  spindle cell D17.9
Lipomatosis E88.2
  dolorosa (Dercum) E88.2
  fetal —see Lipoma
  Launois-Bensaude E88.89
Lipomyoma —see Lipoma
Lipomyxoma —see Lipoma
Lipomyxosarcoma —see Neoplasm, connective
  tissue, malignant
Lipoprotein metabolism disorder E78.9
Lipoproteinemia E78.5
  broad-beta E78.2
  floating-beta E78.2
  hyper-pre-beta E78.1
Liposarcoma —see also Neoplasm, connective
  tissue, malignant
  dedifferentiated —see Neoplasm, connective
    tissue, malignant
  differentiated type —see Neoplasm,
    connective tissue, malignant
  embryonal —see Neoplasm, connective tissue,
    malignant
  mixed type —see Neoplasm, connective
    tissue, malignant
  myxoid —see Neoplasm, connective tissue,
    malignant
  pleomorphic —see Neoplasm, connective
    tissue, malignant
  round cell —see Neoplasm, connective tissue,
    malignant
  well differentiated type —see Neoplasm,
    connective tissue, malignant

Liposynovitis prepatellaris E88.89
Lipping, cervix N86
Lipschütz disease or ulcer N76.6
Lipuria R82.0
  schistosomiasis (bilharziasis) B65.0
Lisping F80.0
Lissauer's paralysis A52.17
Lissencephalia, lissencephaly Q04.3
Listeriosis, listerellosis A32.9
  congenital (disseminated) P37.2
  cutaneous A32.0
  neonatal, newborn (disseminated) P37.2
  oculoglandular A32.81
  specified NEC A32.89
Lithemia E79.0
Lithiasis —see Calculus
Lithosis J62.8
Lithuria R82.998
Litigation, anxiety concerning Z65.3
Little leaguer's elbow —see Epicondylitis, medial
Little's disease G80.9
Littre's
  gland —see condition
  hernia —see Hernia, abdomen
Littritis —see Urethritis
Livedo (annularis) (racemosa) (reticularis) R23.1
Liver —see condition
Living alone (problems with) Z60.2
  with handicapped person Z74.2
Lloyd's syndrome —see Adenomatosis,
    endocrine
Loa loa, loaiasis, loasis B74.3
Lobar —see condition
Lobomycosis B48.0
Lobo's disease B48.0
Lobotomy syndrome F07.0
Lobstein (-Ekman) disease or syndrome Q78.0
Lobster-claw hand Q71.6-●
Lobulation (congenital) —see also Anomaly,
    by site
  kidney, Q63.1
  liver, abnormal Q44.7
  spleen Q89.09
Lobule, lobular —see condition
Local, localized —see condition
Locked twins causing obstructed labor O66.1
Locked-in state G83.5
Locking
  joint —see Derangement, joint, specified type
    NEC
    knee —see Derangement, knee
Lockjaw —see Tetanus
Löffler's
  endocarditis I42.3
⇒ eosinophilia J82.89
⇒ pneumonia J82.89
⇒ syndrome (eosinophilic pneumonitis) J82.89
Loiasis (with conjunctival infestation) (eyelid)
    B74.3
Lone Star fever A77.0
Long
  labor O63.9
    first stage O63.0
    second stage O63.1
  QT syndrome I45.81
Long-term (current) (prophylactic) drug
    therapy (use of)
  agents affecting estrogen receptors and
    estrogen levels NEC Z79.818
  anastrozole (Arimidex) Z79.811
  antibiotics Z79.2
    short-term use - omit code
  anticoagulants Z79.01
  anti-inflammatory, non-steroidal (NSAID)
    Z79.1
  antiplatelet Z79.02
  antithrombotics Z79.02
  aromatase inhibitors Z79.811
  aspirin Z79.82
  birth control pill or patch Z79.3
  bisphosphonates Z79.83

Long-term (Continued)
  contraceptive, oral Z79.3
  drug, specified NEC Z79.899
  estrogen receptor downregulators Z79.818
  Evista Z79.810
  exemestane (Aromasin) Z79.811
  Fareston Z79.810
  fulvestrant (Faslodex) Z79.818
  gonadotropin-releasing hormone (GnRH)
    agonist Z79.818
  goserelin acetate (Zoladex) Z79.818
  hormone replacement Z79.890
  insulin Z79.4
  letrozole (Femara) Z79.811
  leuprolide acetate (leuprorelin) (Lupron)
    Z79.818
  megestrol acetate (Megace) Z79.818
  methadone for pain management Z79.891
  Nolvadex Z79.810
  non-steroidal anti-inflammatories (NSAID)
    Z79.1
  opiate analgesic Z79.891
  oral
    antidiabetic Z79.84
    contraceptive Z79.3
    hypoglycemic Z79.84
  raloxifene (Evista) Z79.810
  selective estrogen receptor modulators
    (SERMs) Z79.810
  steroids
    inhaled Z79.51
    systemic Z79.52
  tamoxifen (Nolvadex) Z79.810
  toremifene (Fareston) Z79.810
Longitudinal stripes or grooves, nails L60.8
  congenital Q84.6
Loop
  intestine —see Volvulus
  vascular on papilla (optic) Q14.2
Loose —see also condition
  body
    joint M24.00
      ankle M24.07-●
      elbow M24.02-●
      hand M24.04-●
      hip M24.05-●
      knee M23.4-●
      shoulder (region) M24.01-●
      specified site NEC M24.08
      toe M24.07-●
      vertebra M24.08
      wrist M24.03-●
    knee M23.4-●
    sheath, tendon —see Disorder, tendon,
      specified type NEC
  cartilage —see Loose, body, joint
  skin and subcutaneous tissue (following
    bariatric surgery weight loss) (following
    dietary weight loss) L98.7
  tooth, teeth K08.89
Loosening
  aseptic
    joint prosthesis —see Complications, joint
      prosthesis, mechanical, loosening,
      by site
    epiphysis —see Osteochondropathy
  mechanical
    joint prosthesis —see Complications, joint
      prosthesis, mechanical, loosening,
      by site
Looser-Milkman (-Debray) syndrome M83.8
Lop ear (deformity) Q17.3
Lorain (-Levi) short stature syndrome E23.0
Lordosis M40.50
  acquired —see Lordosis, specified type NEC
  congenital Q76.429
    lumbar region Q76.426
    lumbosacral region Q76.427
    sacral region Q76.428
    sacrococcygeal region Q76.428
    thoracolumbar region Q76.425

Lordosis (Continued)
  lumbar region M40.56
  lumbosacral region M40.57
  postsurgical M96.4
  postural —see Lordosis, specified type NEC
  rachitic (late effect) (sequelae) E64.3
  sequelae of rickets E64.3
  specified type NEC M40.40
    lumbar region M40.46
    lumbosacral region M40.47
    thoracolumbar region M40.45
  thoracolumbar region M40.55
  tuberculous A18.01
Loss (of)
  appetite (see Anorexia) R63.0
    hysterical F50.89
    nonorganic origin F50.89
    psychogenic F50.89
  blood —see Hemorrhage
  bone —see Loss, substance of, bone
  consciousness, transient R55
    traumatic —see Injury, intracranial
  control, sphincter, rectum R15.9
    nonorganic origin F98.1
  elasticity, skin R23.4
  family (member) in childhood Z62.898
  fluid (acute) E86.9
  function of labyrinth —see subcategory H83.2
  hair, nonscarring —see Alopecia
  hearing —see also Deafness
    central NOS H90.5
    conductive H90.2
      bilateral H90.0
      unilateral
        with
          restricted hearing on the
            contralateral side H90.A1-●
          unrestricted hearing on the
            contralateral side H90.1-●
    mixed conductive and sensorineural
      hearing loss H90.8
      bilateral H90.6
      unilateral
        with
          restricted hearing on the
            contralateral side H90.A3-●
          unrestricted hearing on the
            contralateral side H90.7-●
    neural NOS H90.5
    perceptive NOS H90.5
    sensorineural NOS H90.5
      bilateral H90.3
      unilateral
        with
          restricted hearing on the
            contralateral side H90.A2-●
          unrestricted hearing on the
            contralateral side H90.4-●
    sensory NOS H90.5
  height R29.890
  limb or member, traumatic, current —see
    Amputation, traumatic
  love relationship in childhood Z62.898
  memory —see also Amnesia
    mild, following organic brain damage F06.8
  mind —see Psychosis
  occlusal vertical dimension of fully erupted
    teeth M26.37
  organ or part —see Absence, by site, acquired
  ossicles, ear (partial) H74.32-●
  parent in childhood Z63.4
  pregnancy, recurrent N96
    without current pregnancy N96
    care in current pregnancy O26.2-●
  recurrent pregnancy —see Loss, pregnancy,
    recurrent
  self-esteem, in childhood Z62.898
  sense of
    smell —see Disturbance, sensation, smell
    taste —see Disturbance, sensation, taste
    touch R20.8

▶ New   ⇒ Revised   ~~deleted~~ Deleted   ● Use Additional Character(s)

Loss *(Continued)*
  sensory R44.9
    dissociative F44.6
  sexual desire F52.0
  sight (acquired) (complete) (congenital) —*see* Blindness
  substance of
    bone —*see* Disorder, bone, density and structure, specified NEC
      horizontal alveolar K06.3
    cartilage —*see* Disorder, cartilage, specified type NEC
      auricle (ear) —*see* Disorder, pinna, specified type NEC
    vitreous (humor) H15.89
  tooth, teeth —*see* Absence, teeth, acquired
  vision, visual H54.7
    both eyes H54.3
    one eye H54.60
      left (normal vision on right) H54.62
      right (normal vision on left) H54.61
      specified as blindness —*see* Blindness
    subjective
      sudden H53.13-●
      transient H53.12-●
  vitreous —*see* Prolapse, vitreous
  voice —*see* Aphonia
  weight (abnormal) (cause unknown) R63.4
Louis-Bar syndrome (ataxia-telangiectasia) G11.3
▶Louping ill (encephalitis) A84.89
Louse, lousiness —*see* Lice
Low
  achiever, school Z55.3
  back syndrome M54.5
  basal metabolic rate R94.8
  birthweight (2499 grams or less) P07.10
    with weight of
      1000-1249 grams P07.14
      1250-1499 grams P07.15
      1500-1749 grams P07.16
      1750-1999 grams P07.17
      2000-2499 grams P07.18
    extreme (999 grams or less) P07.00
      with weight of
        499 grams or less P07.01
        500-749 grams P07.02
        750-999 grams P07.03
    for gestational age —*see* Light for dates
  blood pressure —*see also* Hypotension
    reading (incidental) (isolated) (nonspecific) R03.1
  cardiac reserve —*see* Disease, heart
  function —*see also* Hypofunction
    kidney N28.9
  hematocrit D64.9
  hemoglobin D64.9
  income Z59.6
  level of literacy Z55.0
  lying
    kidney N28.89
    organ or site, congenital —*see* Malposition, congenital
  output syndrome (cardiac) —*see* Failure, heart
  platelets (blood) —*see* Thrombocytopenia
  reserve, kidney N28.89
  salt syndrome E87.1
  self esteem R45.81
  set ears Q17.4
  vision H54.2X-
    one eye (other eye normal) H54.50
      left (normal vision on right) H54.52A-
      other eye blind —*see* Blindness
      right (normal vision on left) H54.511-
Low-density-lipoprotein-type (LDL) hyperlipoproteinemia E78.00
Lowe's syndrome E72.03
Lown-Ganong-Levine syndrome I45.6

LSD reaction (acute) (without dependence) F16.90
  with dependence F16.20
L-shaped kidney Q63.8
LTBI (lantent tuberculosis infection) Z22.7
Ludwig's angina or disease K12.2
Lues (venerea), luetic —*see* Syphilis
Luetscher's syndrome (dehydration) E86.0
Lumbago, lumbalgia M54.5
  with sciatica M54.4-●
  due to intervertebral disc disorder M51.17
  due to displacement, intervertebral disc M51.27
    with sciatica M51.17
Lumbar —*see* condition
Lumbarization, vertebra, congenital Q76.49
Lumbermen's itch B88.0
Lump —*see also* Mass
  breast N63.0
    axillary tail
      left N63.32
      right N63.31
    left
      lower inner quadrant N63.24
      lower outer quadrant N63.23
      overlapping quadrants N63.25
      unspecified quadrant N63.20
      upper inner quadrant N63.22
      upper outer quadrant N63.21
    right
      lower inner quadrant N63.14
      lower outer quadrant N63.13
      overlapping quadrants N63.15
      unspecified quadrant N63.10
      upper inner quadrant N63.12
      upper outer quadrant N63.11
    subareolar
      left N63.42
      right N63.41
Lunacy —*see* Psychosis
Lung —*see* condition
Lupoid (miliary) of Boeck D86.3
Lupus
  anticoagulant D68.62
    with
      hemorrhagic disorder D68.312
      hypercoagulable state D68.62
    finding without diagnosis R76.0
  discoid (local) L93.0
  erythematosus (discoid) (local) L93.0
    disseminated —*see* Lupus, erythematosus, systemic
    eyelid H01.129
      left H01.126
        lower H01.125
        upper H01.124
      right H01.123
        lower H01.122
        upper H01.121
    profundus L93.2
    specified NEC L93.2
    subacute cutaneous L93.1
    systemic M32.9
      with organ or system involvement M32.10
        endocarditis M32.11
        lung M32.13
        pericarditis M32.12
        renal (glomerular) M32.14
          tubulo-interstitial M32.15
        specified organ or system NEC M32.19
      drug-induced M32.0
      inhibitor (presence of) D68.62
        with
          hemorrhagic disorder D68.312
          hypercoagulable state D68.62
        finding without diagnosis R76.0
      specified NEC M32.8
  exedens A18.4

Lupus *(Continued)*
  hydralazine M32.0
    correct substance properly administered — *see* Table of Drugs and Chemicals, by drug, adverse effect
    overdose or wrong substance given or taken —*see* Table of Drugs and Chemicals, by drug, poisoning
  nephritis (chronic) M32.14
  nontuberculous, not disseminated L93.0
  panniculitis L93.2
  pernio (Besnier) D86.3
  systemic —*see* Lupus, erythematosus, systemic
  tuberculous A18.4
    eyelid A18.4
  vulgaris A18.4
    eyelid A18.4
Luteinoma D27.-●
Lutembacher's disease or syndrome (atrial septal defect with mitral stenosis) Q21.1
Luteoma D27.-●
Lutz (-Splendore-de Almeida) disease —*see* Paracoccidioidomycosis
Luxation —*see also* Dislocation
  eyeball (nontraumatic) —*see* Luxation, globe
    birth injury P15.3
  globe, nontraumatic H44.82-●
  lacrimal gland —*see* Dislocation, lacrimal gland
  lens (old) (partial) (spontaneous)
    congenital Q12.1
    syphilitic A50.39
Lycanthropy F22
Lyell's syndrome L51.2
  due to drug L51.2
    correct substance properly administered — *see* Table of Drugs and Chemicals, by drug, adverse effect
    overdose or wrong substance given or taken —*see* Table of Drugs and Chemicals, by drug, poisoning
Lyme disease A69.20
Lymph
  gland or node —*see* condition
  scrotum —*see* Infestation, filarial
Lymphadenitis I88.9
  with ectopic or molar pregnancy O08.0
  acute L04.9
    axilla L04.2
    face L04.0
    head L04.0
    hip L04.3
    limb
      lower L04.3
      upper L04.2
    neck L04.0
    shoulder L04.2
    specified site NEC L04.8
    trunk L04.1
  anthracosis (occupational) J60
  any site, except mesenteric I88.9
    chronic I88.1
    subacute I88.1
  breast
    gestational —*see* Mastitis, obstetric
    puerperal, postpartum (nonpurulent) O91.22
  chancroidal (congenital) A57
  chronic I88.1
    mesenteric I88.0
  due to
    Brugia (malayi) B74.1
      timori B74.2
    chlamydial lymphogranuloma A55
    diphtheria (toxin) A36.89
    lymphogranuloma venereum A55
    Wuchereria bancrofti B74.0
  following ectopic or molar pregnancy O08.0
  gonorrheal A54.89
  infective —*see* Lymphadenitis, acute

▶ New   ⇒ Revised   ~~deleted~~ Deleted   ● Use Additional Character(s)

Lymphoma *(Continued)*
   Hodgkin *(Continued)*
      nodular
         lymphocyte predominant C81.0-●
            sclerosis (classical) C81.1-●
   intravascular large B-cell C83.8-●
   Lennert's C84.4-●
   lymphoblastic (diffuse) C83.5-●
   lymphoblastic B-cell C83.5-●
   lymphoblastic T-cell C83.5-●
   lymphoepithelioid C84.4-●
   lymphoplasmacytic C83.0-●
      with IgM-production C88.0
   MALT C88.4
   mantle cell C83.1-●
   mature T-cell NEC C84.4-●
   mature T/NK-cell C84.9-●
      specified NEC C84.Z-●
   mediastinal (thymic) large B-cell
      C85.2-●
   Mediterranean C88.3

Lymphoma *(Continued)*
   mucosa-associated lymphoid tissue
      [MALT-lymphoma] C88.4
   NK/T cell C84.9-●
   nodal marginal zone C83.0-●
   non-follicular (diffuse) C83.9-●
      specified NEC C83.8-●
   non-Hodgkin —*see also* Lymphoma, by type
      C85.9-●
      specified NEC C85.8-●
   non-leukemic variant of B-CLL C83.0-●
   peripheral T-cell, not classified C84.4-●
   primary cutaneous
      anaplastic large cell C86.6
      CD30-positive large T-cell C86.6
   primary effusion B-cell C83.8-●
   SALT C88.4
   skin-associated lymphoid tissue
      [SALT-lymphoma] C88.4
   small cell B-cell C83.0-●
   splenic marginal zone C83.0-●

Lymphoma *(Continued)*
   subcutaneous panniculitis-like T-cell
      C86.3
   T-precursor C83.5-●
   true histiocytic C96.A
Lymphomatosis —*see* Lymphoma
Lymphopathia venereum, veneris A55
Lymphopenia D72.810
Lymphoplasmacytic leukemia —*see* Leukemia,
   chronic lymphocytic, B-cell type
Lymphoproliferation, X-linked disease D82.3
Lymphoreticulosis, benign (of inoculation)
   A28.1
Lymphorrhea I89.8
Lymphosarcoma (diffuse) —*see also* Lymphoma
   C85.9-●
Lymphostasis I89.8
Lypemania —*see* Melancholia
Lysine and hydroxylysine metabolism
   disorder E72.3
Lyssa —*see* Rabies

M

Macacus ear Q17.3
Maceration, wet feet, tropical (syndrome) T69.02-●
MacLeod's syndrome J43.0
Macrocephalia, macrocephaly Q75.3
Macrocheilia, macrochilia (congenital)Q18.6
Macrocolon —see also Megacolon Q43.1
Macrocornea Q15.8
  with glaucoma Q15.0
Macrocytic —see condition
Macrocytosis D75.89
Macrodactylia, macrodactylism (fingers) (thumbs) Q74.0
  toes Q74.2
Macrodontia K00.2
Macrogenia M26.05
Macrogenitosomia (adrenal) (male) (praecox) E25.9
  congenital E25.0
Macroglobulinemia (idiopathic) (primary) C88.0
  monoclonal (essential) D47.2
  Waldenström C88.0
Macroglossia (congenital) Q38.2
  acquired K14.8
Macrognathia, macrognathism (congenital) (mandibular) (maxillary) M26.09
Macrogyria (congenital) Q04.8
Macrohydrocephalus —see Hydrocephalus
Macromastia —see Hypertrophy, breast
Macrophthalmos Q11.3
  in congenital glaucoma Q15.0
Macropsia H53.15
Macrosigmoid K59.39
  congenital Q43.2
Macrospondylitis, acromegalic E22.0
Macrostomia (congenital) Q18.4
Macrotia (external ear) (congenital) Q17.1
Macula
  cornea, corneal —see Opacity, cornea
  degeneration (atrophic) (exudative) (senile) —see also Degeneration, macula
    hereditary —see Dystrophy, retina
Maculae ceruleae — B85.1
Maculopathy, toxic —see Degeneration, macula, toxic
Madarosis (eyelid) H02.729
  left H02.726
    lower H02.725
    upper H02.724
  right H02.723
    lower H02.722
    upper H02.721
Madelung's
  deformity (radius) Q74.0
  disease
    radial deformity Q74.0
    symmetrical lipomas, neck E88.89
Madness —see Psychosis
Madura
  foot B47.9
    actinomycotic B47.1
    mycotic B47.0
Maduromycosis B47.0
Maffucci's syndrome Q78.4
Magnesium metabolism disorder —see Disorder, metabolism, magnesium
Main en griffe (acquired) —see also Deformity, limb, clawhand
  congenital Q74.0
Maintenance (encounter for)
  antineoplastic chemotherapy Z51.11
  antineoplastic radiation therapy Z51.0
  methadone F11.20
Majocchi's
  disease L81.7
  granuloma B35.8
Major —see condition
Malabar itch (any site) B35.5

Malabsorption K90.9
  calcium K90.89
  carbohydrate K90.49
  disaccharide E73.9
  fat K90.49
  galactose E74.20
  glucose(-galactose) E74.39
  intestinal K90.9
    specified NEC K90.89
  isomaltose E74.31
  lactose E73.9
  methionine E72.19
  monosaccharide E74.39
  postgastrectomy K91.2
  postsurgical K91.2
  protein K90.49
  starch K90.49
  sucrose E74.39
  syndrome K90.9
    postsurgical K91.2
Malacia, bone (adult) M83.9
  juvenile —see Rickets
Malacoplakia
  bladder N32.89
  pelvis (kidney) N28.89
  ureter N28.89
  urethra N36.8
Malacosteon, juvenile —see Rickets
Maladaptation —see Maladjustment
Maladie de Roger Q21.0
Maladjustment
  conjugal Z63.0
    involving divorce or estrangement Z63.5
  educational Z55.4
  family Z63.9
  marital Z63.0
    involving divorce or estrangement Z63.5
  occupational NEC Z56.89
  simple, adult —see Disorder, adjustment
  situational —see Disorder, adjustment
  social Z60.9
    due to
      acculturation difficulty Z60.3
      discrimination and persecution (perceived) Z60.5
      exclusion and isolation Z60.4
      life-cycle (phase of life) transition Z60.0
      rejection Z60.4
      specified reason NEC Z60.8
Malaise R53.81
Malakoplakia —see Malacoplakia
Malaria, malarial (fever) B54
  with
    blackwater fever B50.8
      hemoglobinuric (bilious) B50.8
    hemoglobinuria B50.8
  accidentally induced (therapeutically) - code by type under Malaria
  algid B50.9
  cerebral B50.0 [G94]
  clinically diagnosed (without parasitological confirmation) B54
  congenital NEC P37.4
    falciparum P37.3
  congestion, congestive B54
  continued (fever) B50.9
  estivo-autumnal B50.9
  falciparum B50.9
    with complications NEC B50.8
      cerebral B50.0 [G94]
    severe B50.8
  hemorrhagic B54
  malariae B52.9
    with
      complications NEC B52.8
      glomerular disorder B52.0
  malignant (tertian) —see Malaria, falciparum
  mixed infections — code to first listed type in B50-B53
  ovale B53.0
  parasitologically confirmed NEC B53.8

Malaria, malarial (Continued)
  pernicious, acute —see Malaria, falciparum
  Plasmodium (P.)
    falciparum NEC —see Malaria, falciparum
    malariae NEC B52.9
      with Plasmodium
        falciparum (and or vivax) —see Malaria, falciparum
        vivax —see also Malaria, vivax and falciparum —see Malaria, falciparum
    ovale B53.0
      with Plasmodium malariae —see also Malaria, malariae
        and vivax —see also Malaria, vivax and falciparum —see Malaria, falciparum
    simian B53.1
      with Plasmodium malariae —see also Malaria, malariae
        and vivax —see also Malaria, vivax and falciparum —see Malaria, falciparum
    vivax NEC B51.9
      with Plasmodium falciparum —see Malaria, falciparum
  quartan —see Malaria, malariae
  quotidian —see Malaria, falciparum
  recurrent B54
  remittent B54
  specified type NEC (parasitologically confirmed) B53.8
  spleen B54
  subtertian (fever) —see Malaria, falciparum
  tertian (benign) —see also Malaria, vivax
    malignant B50.9
  tropical B50.9
  typhoid B54
  vivax B51.9
    with
      complications NEC B51.8
      ruptured spleen B51.0
Malassez's disease (cystic) N50.89
Malassimilation K90.9
Mal de los pintos —see Pinta
Mal de mer T75.3
Maldescent, testis Q53.9
  bilateral Q53.20
    abdominal Q53.211
    perineal Q53.22
  unilateral Q53.10
    abdominal Q53.111
    perineal Q53.12
Maldevelopment —see also Anomaly
  brain Q07.9
  colon Q43.9
  hip Q74.2
    congenital dislocation Q65.2
      bilateral Q65.1
      unilateral Q65.0-●
  mastoid process Q75.8
  middle ear Q16.4
    except ossicles Q16.4
    ossicles Q16.3
  ossicles Q16.3
  spine Q76.49
  toe Q74.2
Male type pelvis Q74.2
  with disproportion (fetopelvic) O33.3
    causing obstructed labor O65.3
Malformation (congenital) —see also Anomaly
  adrenal gland Q89.1
  affecting multiple systems with skeletal changes NEC Q87.5
  alimentary tract Q45.9
    specified type NEC Q45.8
    upper Q40.9
      specified type NEC Q40.8
  aorta Q25.40
    absence Q25.41
    aneurysm, congenital Q25.43

Malformation (Continued)

aorta (Continued)
aplasia Q25.41
atresia Q25.29
aortic arch Q25.21
coarctation (preductal) (postductal) Q25.1
dilatation, congenital Q25.44
hypoplasia Q25.42
patent ductus arteriosus Q25.0
specified type NEC Q25.49
stenosis Q25.1
supravalvular Q25.3
aortic valve Q23.9
specified NEC Q23.8
arteriovenous, aneurysmatic (congenital) Q27.30
brain Q28.2
ruptured I60.8
intracerebral I61.8
intraparenchymal I61.8
intraventricular I61.5
subarachnoid I60.8
cerebral (see Malformation, arteriovenous, brain) Q28.2
peripheral Q27.30
congenital Q27.33
digestive system —see Angiodysplasia
lower limb Q27.32
other specified site Q27.39
renal vessel Q27.34
upper limb Q27.31
precerebral vessels (nonruptured) Q28.0
auricle
ear (congenital) Q17.3
acquired H61.119
left H61.112
with right H61.113
right H61.111
with left H61.113
bile duct Q44.5
bladder Q64.79
aplasia Q64.5
diverticulum Q64.6
exstrophy —see Exstrophy, bladder
neck obstruction Q64.31
bone Q79.9
face Q75.9
specified type NEC Q75.8
skull Q75.9
specified type NEC Q75.8
brain (multiple) Q04.9
arteriovenous Q28.2
specified type NEC Q04.8
branchial cleft Q18.2
breast Q83.9
specified type NEC Q83.8
broad ligament Q50.6
bronchus Q32.4
bursa Q79.9
cardiac
chambers Q20.9
specified type NEC Q20.8
septum Q21.9
specified type NEC Q21.8
cerebral Q04.9
vessels Q28.3
cervix uteri Q51.9
specified type NEC Q51.828
Chiari
Type I G93.5
Type II Q07.01
choroid (congenital) Q14.3
plexus Q07.8
circulatory system Q28.9
cochlea Q16.5
cornea Q13.4
coronary vessels Q24.5
corpus callosum (congenital) Q04.0
diaphragm Q79.1
digestive system NEC, specified type NEC Q45.8

Malformation (Continued)

dura Q07.9
brain Q04.9
spinal Q06.9
ear Q17.9
causing impairment of hearing Q16.9
external Q17.9
accessory auricle Q17.0
causing impairment of hearing Q16.9
absence of
auditory canal Q16.1
auricle Q16.0
macrotia Q17.1
microtia Q17.2
misplacement Q17.4
misshapen NEC Q17.3
prominence Q17.5
specified type NEC Q17.8
inner Q16.5
middle Q16.4
absence of eustachian tube Q16.2
ossicles (fusion) Q16.3
ossicles Q16.3
specified type NEC Q17.8
epididymis Q55.4
esophagus Q39.9
specified type NEC Q39.8
eye Q15.9
lid Q10.3
specified NEC Q15.8
fallopian tube Q50.6
genital organ —see Anomaly, genitalia
great
artery Q25.9
aorta —see Malformation, aorta
pulmonary artery —see Malformation, pulmonary, artery
specified type NEC Q25.8
vein Q26.9
anomalous
portal venous connection Q26.5
pulmonary venous connection Q26.4
partial Q26.3
total Q26.2
persistent left superior vena cava Q26.1
portal vein-hepatic artery fistula Q26.6
specified type NEC Q26.8
vena cava stenosis, congenital Q26.0
gum Q38.6
hair Q84.2
heart Q24.9
specified type NEC Q24.8
integument Q84.9
specified type NEC Q84.8
internal ear Q16.5
intestine Q43.9
specified type NEC Q43.8
iris Q13.2
joint Q74.9
ankle Q74.2
lumbosacral Q76.49
sacroiliac Q74.2
specified type NEC Q74.8
kidney Q63.9
accessory Q63.0
giant Q63.3
horseshoe Q63.1
hydronephrosis Q62.0
malposition Q63.2
specified type NEC Q63.8
lacrimal apparatus Q10.6
lingual Q38.3
lip Q38.0
liver Q44.7
lung Q33.9
meninges or membrane (congenital) Q07.9
cerebral Q04.8
spinal (cord) Q06.9
middle ear Q16.4
ossicles Q16.3
mitral valve Q23.9
specified NEC Q23.8

Malformation (Continued)

Mondini's (congenital) (malformation, cochlea) Q16.5
mouth (congenital) Q38.6
multiple types NEC Q89.7
musculoskeletal system Q79.9
myocardium Q24.8
nail Q84.6
nervous system (central) Q07.9
nose Q30.9
specified type NEC Q30.8
optic disc Q14.2
orbit Q10.7
ovary Q50.39
palate Q38.5
parathyroid gland Q89.2
pelvic organs or tissues NEC
in pregnancy or childbirth O34.8-•
causing obstructed labor O65.5
penis Q55.69
aplasia Q55.5
curvature (lateral) Q55.61
hypoplasia Q55.62
pericardium Q24.8
peripheral vascular system Q27.9
specified type NEC Q27.8
pharynx Q38.8
precerebral vessels Q28.1
prostate Q55.4
pulmonary
arteriovenous Q25.72
artery Q25.9
atresia Q25.5
specified type NEC Q25.79
stenosis Q25.6
valve Q22.3
renal artery Q27.2
respiratory system Q34.9
retina Q14.1
scrotum —see Malformation, testis and scrotum
seminal vesicles Q55.4
sense organs NEC Q07.9
skin Q82.9
specified NEC Q89.8
spinal
cord Q06.9
nerve root Q07.8
spine Q76.49
kyphosis —see Kyphosis, congenital
lordosis —see Lordosis, congenital
spleen Q89.09
stomach Q40.3
specified type NEC Q40.2
teeth, tooth K00.9
tendon Q79.9
testis and scrotum Q55.20
aplasia Q55.0
hypoplasia Q55.1
polyorchism Q55.21
retractile testis Q55.22
scrotal transposition Q55.23
specified NEC Q55.29
thorax, bony Q76.9
throat Q38.8
thyroid gland Q89.2
tongue (congenital) Q38.3
hypertrophy Q38.2
tie Q38.1
trachea Q32.1
tricuspid valve Q22.9
specified type NEC Q22.8
umbilical cord NEC (complicating delivery) O69.89
umbilicus Q89.9
ureter Q62.8
agenesis Q62.4
duplication Q62.5
malposition —see Malposition, congenital, ureter
obstructive defect —see Defect, obstructive, ureter
vesico-uretero-renal reflux Q62.7

Malformation (*Continued*)
  urethra Q64.79
    aplasia Q64.5
    duplication Q64.74
    posterior valves Q64.2
    prolapse Q64.71
    stricture Q64.32
  urinary system Q64.9
  uterus Q51.9
    specified type NEC Q51.818
  vagina Q52.4
  vascular system, peripheral Q27.9
  vas deferens Q55.4
    atresia Q55.3
  venous —*see* Anomaly, vein(s)
  vulva Q52.70
Malfunction —*see also* Dysfunction
  cardiac electronic device T82.119
    electrode T82.110
    pulse generator T82.111
    specified type NEC T82.118
  catheter device NEC T85.618
    cystostomy T83.010
    dialysis (renal) (vascular) T82.41
      intraperitoneal T85.611
    infusion NEC T82.514
      cranial T85.610
      epidural T85.610
      intrathecal T85.610
      spinal T85.610
      subarachnoid T85.610
      subdural T85.610
    urinary —*see also* Breakdown, device,
      catheter T83.018
  colostomy K94.03
    valve K94.03
  cystostomy (stoma) N99.512
    catheter T83.010
  enteric stoma K94.13
  enterostomy K94.13
  esophagostomy K94.33
  gastroenteric K31.89
  gastrostomy K94.23
  ileostomy K94.13
    valve K94.13
  intrathecal infusion pump T85.615
  jejunostomy K94.13
  nervous system device, implant or graft,
    specified NEC T85.615
  pacemaker —*see* Malfunction, cardiac
    electronic device
  prosthetic device, internal —*see*
    Complications, prosthetic device, by site,
    mechanical
  tracheostomy J95.03
  urinary device NEC —*see* Complication,
    genitourinary, device, urinary,
    mechanical
  valve
    colostomy K94.03
    heart T82.09
    ileostomy K94.13
  vascular graft or shunt NEC —*see*
    Complication, cardiovascular device,
    mechanical, vascular
  ventricular (communicating shunt) T85.01
Malherbe's tumor —*see* Neoplasm, skin,
  benign
Malibu disease L98.8-●
Malignancy —*see also* Neoplasm, malignant,
  by site
  unspecified site (primary) C80.1
Malignant —*see* condition
Malingerer, malingering Z76.5
Mallet finger (acquired) —*see* Deformity, finger,
  mallet finger
  congenital Q74.0
  sequelae of rickets E64.3
Malleus A24.0
Mallory's bodies R89.7
Mallory-Weiss syndrome K22.6

Malnutrition E46
  degree
    first E44.1
    mild (protein) E44.1
    moderate (protein) E44.0
    second E44.0
    severe (protein-energy) E43
      intermediate form E42
        with
          kwashiorkor (and marasmus) E42
          marasmus E41
    third E43
  following gastrointestinal surgery K91.2
  intrauterine
    light-for-dates —*see* Light for dates
    small-for-dates —*see* Small for dates
  lack of care, or neglect (child) (infant) T76.02
    confirmed T74.02
  malignant E40
  protein E46
    calorie E46
      mild E44.1
      moderate E44.0
      severe E43
        intermediate form E42
          with
            kwashiorkor (and marasmus)
              E42
            marasmus E41
    energy E46
      mild E44.1
      moderate E44.0
      severe E43
        intermediate form E42
          with
            kwashiorkor (and marasmus)
              E42
            marasmus E41
  severe (protein-energy) E43
    with
      kwashiorkor (and marasmus) E42
      marasmus E41
Malocclusion (teeth) M26.4
  Angle's M26.219
    class I M26.211
    class II M26.212
    class III M26.213
  due to
    abnormal swallowing M26.59
    mouth breathing M26.59
    tongue, lip or finger habits M26.59
  temporomandibular (joint) M26.69
Malposition
  cervix —*see* Malposition, uterus
  congenital
    adrenal (gland) Q89.1
    alimentary tract Q45.8
      lower Q43.8
      upper Q40.8
    aorta Q25.49
    appendix Q43.8
    arterial trunk Q20.0
    artery (peripheral) Q27.8
      coronary Q24.5
      digestive system Q27.8
      lower limb Q27.8
      pulmonary Q25.79
      specified site NEC Q27.8
      upper limb Q27.8
    auditory canal Q17.8
      causing impairment of hearing Q16.9
    auricle (ear) Q17.4
      causing impairment of hearing Q16.9
    cervical Q18.2
    biliary duct or passage Q44.5
    bladder (mucosa) —*see* Exstrophy,
      bladder
    brachial plexus Q07.8
    brain tissue Q04.8
    breast Q83.8
    bronchus Q32.4

Malposition (*Continued*)
  congenital (*Continued*)
    cecum Q43.8
    clavicle Q74.0
    colon Q43.8
    digestive organ or tract NEC Q45.8
      lower Q43.8
      upper Q40.8
    ear (auricle) (external) Q17.4
      ossicles Q16.3
    endocrine (gland) NEC Q89.2
    epiglottis Q31.8
    eustachian tube Q17.8
    eye Q15.8
    facial features Q18.8
    fallopian tube Q50.6
    finger(s) Q68.1
      supernumerary Q69.0
    foot Q66.9-●
    gallbladder Q44.1
    gastrointestinal tract Q45.8
    genitalia, genital organ(s) or tract
      female Q52.8
        external Q52.79
        internal NEC Q52.8
      male Q55.8
    glottis Q31.8
    hand Q68.1
    heart Q24.8
      dextrocardia Q24.0
        with complete transposition of viscera
          Q89.3
    hepatic duct Q44.5
    hip (joint) Q65.89
    intestine (large) (small) Q43.8
      with anomalous adhesions, fixation or
        malrotation Q43.3
    joint NEC Q68.8
    kidney Q63.2
    larynx Q31.8
    limb Q68.8
      lower Q68.8
      upper Q68.8
    liver Q44.7
    lung (lobe) Q33.8
    nail(s) Q84.6
    nerve Q07.8
    nervous system NEC Q07.8
    nose, nasal (septum) Q30.8
    organ or site not listed —*see* Anomaly,
      by site
    ovary Q50.39
    pancreas Q45.3
    parathyroid (gland) Q89.2
    patella Q74.1
    peripheral vascular system Q27.8
    pituitary (gland) Q89.2
    respiratory organ or system NEC
      Q34.8
    rib (cage) Q76.6
      supernumerary in cervical region
        Q76.5
    scapula Q74.0
    shoulder Q74.0
    spinal cord Q06.8
    spleen Q89.09
    sternum NEC Q76.7
    stomach Q40.2
    symphysis pubis Q74.2
    thymus (gland) Q89.2
    thyroid (gland) (tissue) Q89.2
      cartilage Q31.8
    toe(s) Q66.9-●
      supernumerary Q69.2
    tongue Q38.3
    trachea Q32.1
    ureter Q62.60
      deviation Q62.61
      displacement Q62.62
      ectopia Q62.63
      specified type NEC Q62.69

▶ New   ⟹ Revised   ~~deleted~~ Deleted   ● Use Additional Character(s)

Malposition *(Continued)*
  congenital *(Continued)*
    uterus Q51.818
    vein(s) (peripheral) Q27.8
      great Q26.8
    vena cava (inferior) (superior) Q26.8
  device, implant or graft —*see also*
      Complications, by site and type,
      mechanical T85.628
    arterial graft NEC —*see* Complication,
      cardiovascular device, mechanical,
      vascular
    breast (implant) T85.42
    catheter NEC T85.628
      cystostomy T83.020
      dialysis (renal) T82.42
        intraperitoneal T85.621
      infusion NEC T82.524
        spinal (epidural) (subdural) T85.620
      urinary —*see also* Displacement, device,
        catheter, urinary T83.028
    electronic (electrode) (pulse generator)
        (stimulator)
      bone T84.320
      cardiac T82.129
        electrode T82.120
        pulse generator T82.121
        specified type NEC T82.128
      nervous system —*see* Complication,
        prosthetic device, mechanical,
        electronic nervous system
        stimulator
      urinary —*see* Complication,
        genitourinary, device, urinary,
        mechanical
    fixation, internal (orthopedic) NEC —
        see Complication, fixation device,
        mechanical
    gastrointestinal —*see* Complications,
        prosthetic device, mechanical,
        gastrointestinal device
    genital NEC T83.428
      intrauterine contraceptive device (string)
        T83.32
      penile prosthesis (cylinder) (implanted)
        (pump) (reservoir) T83.420
      testicular prosthesis T83.421
    heart NEC —*see* Complication,
        cardiovascular device, mechanical
    joint prosthesis —*see* Complication, joint
        prosthesis, mechanical
    ocular NEC —*see* Complications,
        prosthetic device, mechanical,
        ocular device
    orthopedic NEC —*see* Complication,
        orthopedic, device, mechanical
    specified NEC T85.628
    urinary NEC —*see also* Complication,
        genitourinary, device, urinary,
        mechanical
      graft T83.22
    vascular NEC —*see* Complication,
        cardiovascular device, mechanical
    ventricular intracranial shunt T85.02
  fetus —*see* Pregnancy, complicated by
      (management affected by), presentation,
      fetal
  gallbladder K82.8
  gastrointestinal tract, congenital Q45.8
  heart, congenital NEC Q24.8
  joint prosthesis —*see* Complications, joint
      prosthesis, mechanical, displacement,
      by site
  stomach K31.89
    congenital Q40.2
  tooth, teeth, fully erupted M26.30
  uterus (acute) (acquired) (adherent)
      (asymptomatic) (postinfectional)
      (postpartal, old) N85.4
    anteflexion or anteversion N85.4
      congenital Q51.818

Malposition *(Continued)*
  uterus *(Continued)*
    flexion N85.4
      lateral —*see* Lateroversion, uterus
    inversion N85.5
    lateral (flexion) (version) —*see*
        Lateroversion, uterus
    in pregnancy or childbirth —*see*
        subcategory O34.5
    retroflexion or retroversion —*see*
        Retroversion, uterus
Malposture R29.3
Malrotation
  cecum Q43.3
  colon Q43.3
  intestine Q43.3
  kidney Q63.2
Malta fever —*see* Brucellosis
Maltreatment
  adult
    abandonment
      confirmed T74.01
      suspected T76.01
    bullying
      confirmed T74.31
      suspected T76.31
    confirmed T74.91
    history of Z91.419
    intimidation (through social media)
      confirmed T74.31
      suspected T76.31
    neglect
      confirmed T74.01
      suspected T76.01
    physical abuse
      confirmed T74.11
      suspected T76.11
    psychological abuse
      confirmed T74.31
      history of Z91.411
      suspected T76.31
    sexual abuse
      confirmed T74.21
      suspected T76.21
    suspected T76.91
  child
    abandonment
      confirmed T74.02
      suspected T76.02
    bullying
      confirmed T74.32
      suspected T76.32
    confirmed T74.92
    history of —*see* History, personal (of),
        abuse
    intimidation (through social media)
      confirmed T74.32
      suspected T76.32
    neglect
      confirmed T74.02
      history of —*see* History, personal (of),
          abuse
      suspected T76.02
    physical abuse
      confirmed T74.12
      history of —*see* History, personal (of),
          abuse
      suspected T76.12
    psychological abuse
      confirmed T74.32
      history of —*see* History, personal (of),
          abuse
      suspected T76.32
    sexual abuse
      confirmed T74.22
      history of —*see* History, personal (of),
          abuse
      suspected T76.22
    suspected T76.92
  personal history of Z91.89
Maltworker's lung J67.4

Malunion, fracture —*see* Fracture, by site
Mammillitis N61.0
  puerperal, postpartum O91.02
Mammitis —*see* Mastitis
Mammogram (examination) Z12.39
  routine Z12.31
Mammoplasia N62
Management (of)
  bone conduction hearing device (implanted)
      Z45.320
  cardiac pacemaker NEC Z45.018
  cerebrospinal fluid drainage device Z45.41
  cochlear device (implanted) Z45.321
  contraceptive Z30.9
    specified NEC Z30.8
  implanted device Z45.9
    specified NEC Z45.89
  infusion pump Z45.1
  procreative Z31.9
    male factor infertility in female Z31.81
    specified NEC Z31.89
  prosthesis (external) —*see also* Fitting
      Z44.9
    implanted Z45.9
      specified NEC Z45.89
  renal dialysis catheter Z49.01
  vascular access device Z45.2
Mangled —*see* specified injury by site
Mania (monopolar) —*see also* Disorder, mood,
    manic episode
  with psychotic symptoms F30.2
  without psychotic symptoms F30.10
    mild F30.11
    moderate F30.12
    severe F30.13
  Bell's F30.8
  chronic (recurrent) F31.89
  hysterical F44.89
  puerperal F30.8
  recurrent F31.89
Manic depression F31.9
Manic-depressive insanity, psychosis, or
    syndrome —*see* Disorder, bipolar
Mannosidosis E77.1
Mansonelliasis, mansonellosis B74.4
Manson's
  disease B65.1
  schistosomiasis B65.1
Manual —*see* condition
Maple-bark-stripper's lung (disease) J67.6
Maple-syrup-urine disease E71.0
Marable's syndrome (celiac artery
    compression) I77.4
Marasmus E41
  due to malnutrition E41
  intestinal E41
  nutritional E41
  senile R54
  tuberculous NEC —*see* Tuberculosis
Marble
  bones Q78.2
  skin R23.8
Marburg virus disease A98.3
March
  fracture —*see* Fracture, traumatic, stress, by
      site
  hemoglobinuria D59.6
Marchesani (-Weill) syndrome Q87.0
Marchiafava (-Bignami) syndrome or disease
    G37.1
Marchiafava-Micheli syndrome D59.5
Marcus Gunn's syndrome Q07.8
Marfan's syndrome —*see* Syndrome, Marfan's
Marie-Bamberger disease —*see*
    Osteoarthropathy, hypertrophic, specified
    NEC
Marie-Charcot-Tooth neuropathic muscular
    atrophy G60.0
Marie's
  cerebellar ataxia (late-onset) G11.2
  disease or syndrome (acromegaly) E22.0

Marie-Strümpell arthritis, disease or
    spondylitis —see Spondylitis, ankylosing
Marion's disease (bladder neck obstruction)
    N32.0
Marital conflict Z63.0
Mark
    port wine Q82.5
    raspberry Q82.5
    strawberry Q82.5
    stretch L90.6
    tattoo L81.8
Marker heterochromatin —see Extra, marker
    chromosomes
Maroteaux-Lamy syndrome (mild) (severe)
    E76.29
Marrow (bone)
    arrest D61.9
    poor function D75.89
Marseilles fever A77.1
Marsh fever —see Malaria
Marshall's (hidrotic) ectodermal dysplasia
    Q82.4
Marsh's disease (exophthalmic goiter)
    E05.00
    with storm E05.01
Masculinization (female) with adrenal
    hyperplasia E25.9
    congenital E25.0
Masculinovoblastoma D27.-●
Masochism (sexual) F65.51
Mason's lung J62.8
Mass
    abdominal R19.00
        epigastric R19.06
        generalized R19.07
        left lower quadrant R19.04
        left upper quadrant R19.02
        periumbilic R19.05
        right lower quadrant R19.03
        right upper quadrant R19.01
        specified site NEC R19.09
    breast —see also Lump, breast N63.0
    chest R22.2
    cystic —see Cyst
    ear H93.8-●
    head R22.0
    intra-abdominal (diffuse) (generalized) —see
        Mass, abdominal
    kidney N28.89
    liver R16.0
    localized (skin) R22.9
        chest R22.2
        head R22.0
        limb
            lower R22.4-●
            upper R22.3-●
        neck R22.1
        trunk R22.2
    lung R91.8
    malignant —see Neoplasm, malignant,
        by site
    neck R22.1
    pelvic (diffuse) (generalized) —see Mass,
        abdominal
    specified organ NEC —see Disease, by site
    splenic R16.1
    substernal thyroid —see Goiter
    superficial (localized) R22.9
    umbilical (diffuse) (generalized) R19.09
Massive —see condition
Mast cell
    disease, systemic tissue D47.02
    leukemia C94.3-●
    neoplasm
        malignant C96.20
            specified type NEC C96.29
        of uncertain behavior NEC D47.09
    sarcoma C96.22
    tumor D47.09
Mastalgia N64.4
Masters-Allen syndrome N83.8

Mastitis (acute) (diffuse) (nonpuerperal)
    (subacute) N61.0
    with abscess N61.1
    chronic (cystic) —see Mastopathy, cystic
    cystic (Schimmelbusch's type) —see
        Mastopathy, cystic
    fibrocystic —see Mastopathy, cystic
    ▶ granulomatous N61.2-●
    infective N61.0
        newborn P39.0
    interstitial, gestational or puerperal —see
        Mastitis, obstetric
    neonatal (noninfective) P83.4
        infective P39.0
    obstetric (interstitial) (nonpurulent)
        associated with
            lactation O91.23
            pregnancy O91.21-●
            puerperium O91.22
        purulent
            associated with
                lactation O91.13
                pregnancy O91.11-●
                puerperium O91.12
    periductal —see Ectasia, mammary duct
    phlegmonous —see Mastopathy, cystic
    plasma cell —see Ectasia, mammary duct
    without abscess N61.0
Mastocytoma (extracutaneous) D47.09
    malignant C96.29
    solitary D47.01
Mastocytosis D47.09
    aggressive systemic C96.21
    cutaneous (diffuse) (maculopapular) D47.01
        congenital Q82.2
        of neonatal onset Q82.2
        of newborn onset Q82.2
    indolent systemic D47.02
    isolated bone marrow D47.02
    malignant C96.29
    systemic (indolent) (smoldering)
        with an associated hematological
            non-mast cell lineage disease (SM-
            AHNMD) D47.02
Mastodynia N64.4
Mastoid —see condition
Mastoidalgia —see subcategory H92.0
Mastoiditis (coalescent) (hemorrhagic)
    (suppurative) H70.9-●
    acute, subacute H70.00-●
        complicated NEC H70.09-●
        subperiosteal H70.01-●
    chronic (necrotic) (recurrent) H70.1-●
    in (due to)
        infectious disease NEC B99 [H75.0-●]
        parasitic disease NEC B89 [H75.0-●]
        tuberculosis A18.03
    petrositis —see Petrositis
    postauricular fistula —see Fistula,
        postauricular
    specified NEC H70.89-●
    tuberculous A18.03
Mastopathy, mastopathia N64.9
    chronica cystica —see Mastopathy, cystic
    cystic (chronic) (diffuse) N60.1
        with epithelial proliferation N60.3-●
    diffuse cystic —see Mastopathy, cystic
    estrogenic, oestrogenica N64.89
    ovarian origin N64.89
Mastoplasia, mastoplastia N62
Masturbation (excessive) F98.8
Maternal care (for) —see Pregnancy
    (complicated by) (management affected by)
Matheiu's disease (leptospiral jaundice) A27.0
Mauclaire's disease or osteochondrosis —see
    Osteochondrosis, juvenile, hand, metacarpal
Maxcy's disease A75.2
Maxilla, maxillary —see condition
May (-Hegglin) anomaly or syndrome D72.0
McArdle (-Schmid)(-Pearson) disease
    (glycogen storage) E74.04

McCune-Albright syndrome Q78.1
McQuarrie's syndrome (idiopathic familial
    hypoglycemia) E16.2
Meadow's syndrome Q86.1
Measles (black) (hemorrhagic) (suppressed)
    B05.9
    with
        complications NEC B05.89
        encephalitis B05.0
        intestinal complications B05.4
        keratitis (keratoconjunctivitis) B05.81
        meningitis B05.1
        otitis media B05.3
        pneumonia B05.2
    French —see Rubella
    German —see Rubella
    Liberty —see Rubella
Meatitis, urethral —see Urethritis
Meatus, meatal —see condition
Meat-wrappers' asthma J68.9
Meckel-Gruber syndrome Q61.9
Meckel's diverticulitis, diverticulum
    (displaced) (hypertrophic) Q43.0
Meconium
    ileus, newborn P76.0
        in cystic fibrosis E84.11
        meaning meconium plug (without cystic
            fibrosis) P76.0
    obstruction, newborn P76.0
        due to fecaliths P76.0
        in mucoviscidosis E84.11
    peritonitis P78.0
    plug syndrome (newborn) NEC P76.0
Median —see also condition
    arcuate ligament syndrome I77.4
    bar (prostate) (vesical orifice) —see
        Hyperplasia, prostate
    rhomboid glossitis K14.2
Mediastinal shift R93.89
Mediastinitis (acute) (chronic) J98.51
    syphilitic A52.73
    tuberculous A15.8
Mediastinopericarditis —see also Pericarditis
    acute I30.9
    adhesive I31.0
    chronic I31.8
    rheumatic I09.2
Mediastinum, mediastinal —see condition
Medicine poisoning —see Table of Drugs and
    Chemicals, by drug, poisoning
Mediterranean
    fever —see Brucellosis
        familial M04.1
        tick A77.1
    kala-azar B55.0
    leishmaniasis B55.0
    tick fever A77.1
Medulla —see condition
Medullary cystic kidney Q61.5
Medullated fibers
    optic (nerve) Q14.8
    retina Q14.1
Medulloblastoma
    desmoplastic C71.6
    specified site —see Neoplasm, malignant, by
        site
    unspecified site C71.6
Medulloepithelioma —see also Neoplasm,
    malignant, by site
    teratoid —see Neoplasm, malignant, by site
Medullomyoblastoma
    specified site —see Neoplasm, malignant, by
        site
    unspecified site C71.6
Meekeren-Ehlers-Danlos syndrome —see also
    Syndrome, Ehlers-Danlos Q79.6
Megacolon (acquired) (functional) (not
    Hirschsprung's disease) (in) K59.39
    Chagas' disease B57.32
    congenital, congenitum (aganglionic) Q43.1
    Hirschsprung's (disease) Q43.1

▶ New   ⇒ Revised   ~~deleted~~ Deleted   ● Use Additional Character(s)

Megacolon *(Continued)*
 toxic NEC K59.31
  due to Clostridium difficile
   not specified as recurrent A04.72
   recurrent A04.71
Megaesophagus (functional) K22.0
 congenital Q39.5
 in (due to) Chagas' disease B57.31
Megalencephaly Q04.5
Megalerythema (epidemic) B08.3
Megaloappendix Q43.8
Megalocephalus, megalocephaly NEC Q75.3
Megalocornea Q15.8
 with glaucoma Q15.0
Megalocytic anemia D53.1
Megalodactylia (fingers) (thumbs) (congenital)
 Q74.0
 toes Q74.2
Megaloduodenum Q43.8
Megaloesophagus (functional) K22.0
 congenital Q39.5
Megalogastria (acquired) K31.89
 congenital Q40.2
Megalophthalmos Q11.3
Megalopsia H53.15
Megalosplenia —*see* Splenomegaly
Megaloureter N28.82
 congenital Q62.2
Megarectum K62.89
Megasigmoid K59.39
 congenital Q43.2
Megaureter N28.82
 congenital Q62.2
Megavitamin-B6 syndrome E67.2
Megrim —*see* Migraine
Meibomian
 cyst, infected —*see* Hordeolum
 gland —*see* condition
 sty, stye —*see* Hordeolum
Meibomitis —*see* Hordeolum
Meige-Milroy disease (chronic hereditary
 edema) Q82.0
Meige's syndrome Q82.0
Melalgia, nutritional E53.8
Melancholia F32.9
 climacteric (single episode) F32.89
  recurrent episode F33.8
 hypochondriac F45.29
 intermittent (single episode) F32.89
  recurrent episode F33.8
 involutional (single episode) F32.89
  recurrent episode F33.8
 menopausal (single episode) F32.89
  recurrent episode F33.8
 puerperal F32.89
 reactive (emotional stress or trauma) F32.3
 recurrent F33.9
 senile F03
 stuporous (single episode) F32.89
  recurrent episode F33.8
Melanemia R79.89
Melanoameloblastoma —*see* Neoplasm, bone,
 benign
Melanoblastoma —*see* Melanoma
Melanocarcinoma —*see* Melanoma
Melanocytoma, eyeball D31.9-●
Melanocytosis, neurocutaneous Q82.8
Melanoderma, melanodermia L81.4
Melanodontia, infantile K03.89
Melanodontoclasia K03.89
Melanoepithelioma —*see* Melanoma
Melanoma (malignant) C43.9
 acral lentiginous, malignant —*see* Melanoma,
  skin, by site
 amelanotic —*see* Melanoma, skin, by site
 balloon cell —*see* Melanoma, skin, by site
 benign —*see* Nevus
 desmoplastic, malignant —*see* Melanoma,
  skin, by site
 epithelioid cell —*see* Melanoma, skin, by site
  with spindle cell, mixed —*see* Melanoma,
   skin, by site

Melanoma *(Continued)*
 in
  giant pigmented nevus —*see* Melanoma,
   skin, by site
  Hutchinson's melanotic freckle —*see*
   Melanoma, skin, by site
  junctional nevus —*see* Melanoma, skin,
   by site
  precancerous melanosis —*see* Melanoma,
   skin, by site
 in situ D03.9
  abdominal wall D03.59
  ala nasi D03.39
  ankle D03.7-●
  anus, anal (margin) (skin) D03.51
  arm D03.6-●
  auditory canal D03.2-●
  auricle (ear) D03.2-●
  auricular canal (external) D03.2-●
  axilla, axillary fold D03.59
  back D03.59
  breast D03.52
  brow D03.39
  buttock D03.59
  canthus (eye) D03.1-●
  cheek (external) D03.39
  chest wall D03.59
  chin D03.39
  choroid D03.8
  conjunctiva D03.8
  ear (external) D03.2-●
  external meatus (ear) D03.2-●
  eye D03.8
  eyebrow D03.39
  eyelid (lower) (upper) D03.1-●
  face D03.30
   specified NEC D03.39
  female genital organ (external) NEC D03.8
  finger D03.6-●
  flank D03.59
  foot D03.7-●
  forearm D03.6-●
  forehead D03.39
  foreskin D03.8
  gluteal region D03.59
  groin D03.59
  hand D03.6-●
  heel D03.7-●
  helix D03.2-●
  hip D03.7-●
  interscapular region D03.59
  iris D03.8
  jaw D03.39
  knee D03.7-●
  labium (majus) (minus) D03.8
  lacrimal gland D03.8
  leg D03.7-●
  lip (lower) (upper) D03.0
  lower limb NEC D03.7-●
  male genital organ (external) NEC D03.8
  nail D03.9
   finger D03.6-●
   toe D03.7-●
  neck D03.4
  nose (external) D03.39
  orbit D03.8
  penis D03.8
  perianal skin D03.51
  perineum D03.51
  pinna D03.2-●
  popliteal fossa or space D03.7-●
  prepuce D03.8
  pudendum D03.8
  retina D03.8
  retrobulbar D03.8
  scalp D03.4
  scrotum D03.8
  shoulder D03.6-●
  specified site NEC D03.8
  submammary fold D03.52
  temple D03.39

Melanoma *(Continued)*
 in situ *(Continued)*
  thigh D03.7-●
  toe D03.7-●
  trunk NEC D03.59
  umbilicus D03.59
  upper limb NEC D03.6-●
  vulva D03.8
 juvenile —*see* Nevus
 malignant, of soft parts except skin —*see*
  Neoplasm, connective tissue, malignant
 metastatic
  breast C79.81
  genital organ C79.82
  specified site NEC C79.89
 neurotropic, malignant —*see* Melanoma, skin,
  by site
 nodular —*see* Melanoma, skin, by site
 regressing, malignant —*see* Melanoma, skin,
  by site
 skin C43.9
  abdominal wall C43.59
  ala nasi C43.31
  ankle C43.7-●
  anus, anal (skin) C43.51
  arm C43.6-●
  auditory canal (external) C43.2-●
  auricle (ear) C43.2-●
  auricular canal (external) C43.2-●
  axilla, axillary fold C43.59
  back C43.59
  breast (female) (male) C43.52
  brow C43.39
  buttock C43.59
  canthus (eye) C43.1-●
  cheek (external) C43.39
  chest wall C43.59
  chin C43.39
  ear (external) C43.2-●
  elbow C43.6-●
  external meatus (ear) C43.2-●
  eyebrow C43.39
  eyelid (lower) (upper) C43.1-●
  face C43.30
   specified NEC C43.39
  female genital organ (external) NEC C51.9
  finger C43.6-●
  flank C43.59
  foot C43.7-●
  forearm C43.6-●
  forehead C43.39
  foreskin C60.0
  glabella C43.39
  gluteal region C43.59
  groin C43.59
  hand C43.6-●
  heel C43.7-●
  helix C43.2-●
  hip C43.7-●
  interscapular region C43.59
  jaw (external) C43.39
  knee C43.7-●
  labium C51.9
   majus C51.0
   minus C51.1
  leg C43.7-●
  lip (lower) (upper) C43.0
  lower limb NEC C43.7-●
  male genital organ (external) NEC C63.9
  nail
   finger C43.6-●
   toe C43.7-●
  nasolabial groove C43.39
  nates C43.59
  neck C43.4
  nose (external) C43.31
  overlapping site C43.8
  palpebra C43.1-●
  penis C60.9
  perianal skin C43.51
  perineum C43.51

M

Melanoma *(Continued)*
  skin *(Continued)*
    pinna C43.2-●
    popliteal fossa or space C43.7-●
    prepuce C60.0
    pudendum C51.9
    scalp C43.4
    scrotum C63.2
    shoulder C43.6-●
    skin NEC C43.9
    submammary fold C43.52
    temple C43.39
    thigh C43.7-●
    toe C43.7-●
    trunk NEC C43.59
    umbilicus C43.59
    upper limb NEC C43.6-●
    vulva C51.9
      overlapping sites C51.8
  spindle cell
    with epithelioid, mixed —*see* Melanoma,
      skin, by site
    type A C69.4-●
    type B C69.4-●
  superficial spreading —*see* Melanoma, skin,
    by site
Melanosarcoma —*see also* Melanoma
  epithelioid cell —*see* Melanoma
Melanosis L81.4
  addisonian E27.1
    tuberculous A18.7
  adrenal E27.1
  colon K63.89
  conjunctiva —*see* Pigmentation, conjunctiva
    congenital Q13.89
  cornea (presenile) (senile) —*see also*
    Pigmentation, cornea
    congenital Q13.4
  eye NEC H57.89
    congenital Q15.8
  lenticularis progressiva Q82.1
  liver K76.89
  precancerous —*see also* Melanoma, in situ
    malignant melanoma in —*see* Melanoma
  Riehl's L81.4
  sclera H15.89
    congenital Q13.89
  suprarenal E27.1
  tar L81.4
  toxic L81.4
Melanuria R82.998
MELAS syndrome E88.41
Melasma L81.1
  adrenal (gland) E27.1
  suprarenal (gland) E27.1
Melena K92.1
  with ulcer - code by site under Ulcer, with
    hemorrhage K27.4
  due to swallowed maternal blood P78.2
  newborn, neonatal P54.1
    due to swallowed maternal blood P78.2
Meleney's
  gangrene (cutaneous) —*see* Ulcer, skin
  ulcer (chronic undermining) —*see* Ulcer, skin
Melioidosis A24.9
  acute A24.1
  chronic A24.2
  fulminating A24.1
  pneumonia A24.1
  pulmonary (chronic) A24.2
    acute A24.1
    subacute A24.2
  sepsis A24.1
  specified NEC A24.3
  subacute A24.2
Melitensis, febris A23.0
Melkersson (-Rosenthal) syndrome G51.2
Mellitus, diabetes —*see* Diabetes
Melorheostosis (bone) —*see* Disorder, bone,
  density and structure, specified NEC
Meloschisis Q18.4

Melotia Q17.4
Membrana
  capsularis lentis posterior Q13.89
  epipapillaris Q14.2
Membranacea placenta O43.19-●
Membranaceous uterus N85.8
Membrane(s), membranous —*see also* condition
  cyclitic —*see* Membrane, pupillary
  folds, congenital —*see* Web
  Jackson's Q43.3
  over face of newborn P28.9
  premature rupture —*see* Rupture,
    membranes, premature
  pupillary H21.4-●
    persistent Q13.89
  retained (with hemorrhage) (complicating
    delivery) O72.2
    without hemorrhage O73.1
  secondary cataract —*see* Cataract, secondary
  unruptured (causing asphyxia) —*see*
    Asphyxia, newborn
  vitreous —*see* Opacity, vitreous, membranes
    and strands
Membranitis —*see* Chorioamnionitis
Memory disturbance, lack or loss —*see also*
    Amnesia
  mild, following organic brain damage F06.8
Menadione deficiency E56.1
Menarche
  delayed E30.0
  precocious E30.1
Mendacity, pathologic F60.2
Mendelson's syndrome (due to anesthesia) J95.4
  in labor and delivery O74.0
  in pregnancy O29.01-●
  obstetric O74.0
  postpartum, puerperal O89.01
Ménétrier's disease or syndrome K29.60
  with bleeding K29.61
Ménière's disease, syndrome or vertigo H81.0-●
Meninges, meningeal —*see* condition
Meningioma —*see also* Neoplasm, meninges,
    benign
  angioblastic —*see* Neoplasm, meninges,
    benign
  angiomatous —*see* Neoplasm, meninges,
    benign
▶ atypical —*see* Neoplasm, meninges, uncertain
    behavior
  endotheliomatous —*see* Neoplasm, meninges,
    benign
  fibroblastic —*see* Neoplasm, meninges,
    benign
  fibrous —*see* Neoplasm, meninges, benign
  hemangioblastic —*see* Neoplasm, meninges,
    benign
  hemangiopericytic —*see* Neoplasm,
    meninges, benign
  malignant —*see* Neoplasm, meninges,
    malignant
  meningiothelial —*see* Neoplasm, meninges,
    benign
  meningotheliomatous —*see* Neoplasm,
    meninges, benign
  mixed —*see* Neoplasm, meninges, benign
  multiple —*see* Neoplasm, meninges,
    uncertain behavior
  papillary —*see* Neoplasm, meninges,
    uncertain behavior
  psammomatous —*see* Neoplasm, meninges,
    benign
  syncytial —*see* Neoplasm, meninges, benign
  transitional —*see* Neoplasm, meninges,
    benign
Meningiomatosis (diffuse) —*see* Neoplasm,
    meninges, uncertain behavior
Meningism —*see* Meningismus
Meningismus (infectional) (pneumococcal) R29.1
  due to serum or vaccine R29.1
  influenzal —*see* Influenza, with,
    manifestations NEC

Meningitis (basal) (basic) (brain) (cerebral)
    (cervical) (congestive) (diffuse)
    (hemorrhagic) infantile) (membranous)
    (metastatic) (nonspecific) (pontine)
    (progressive) (simple) (spinal) (subacute)
    (sympathetic) (toxic) G03.9
  abacterial G03.0
  actinomycotic A42.81
  adenoviral A87.1
  arbovirus A87.8
  aseptic (acute) G03.0
  bacterial G00.9
    Escherichia coli (E. coli) G00.8
    Friedländer (bacillus) G00.8
    gram-negative G00.9
    H. influenzae G00.0
    Klebsiella G00.8
    pneumococcal G00.1
    specified organism NEC G00.8
    staphylococcal G00.3
    streptococcal (acute) G00.2
  benign recurrent (Mollaret) G03.2
  candidal B37.5
  caseous (tuberculous) A17.0
  cerebrospinal A39.0
  chronic NEC G03.1
  clear cerebrospinal fluid NEC G03.0
  coxsackievirus A87.0
  cryptococcal B45.1
  diplococcal (gram positive) A39.0
  echovirus A87.0
  enteroviral A87.0
  eosinophilic B83.2
  epidemic NEC A39.0
  Escherichia coli (E. coli) G00.8
  fibrinopurulent G00.9
    specified organism NEC G00.8
  Friedländer (bacillus) G00.8
  gonococcal A54.81
  gram-negative cocci G00.9
  gram-positive cocci G00.9
  Haemophilus (influenzae) G00.0
  H. influenzae G00.0
  in (due to)
    adenovirus A87.1
    African trypanosomiasis B56.9 *[G02]*
    anthrax A22.8
    bacterial disease NEC A48.8 *[G01]*
    Chagas' disease (chronic) B57.41
    chickenpox B01.0
    coccidioidomycosis B38.4
    Diplococcus pneumoniae G00.1
    enterovirus A87.0
    herpes (simplex) virus B00.3
      zoster B02.1
    infectious mononucleosis B27.92
    leptospirosis A27.81
    Listeria monocytogenes A32.11
    Lyme disease A69.21
    measles B05.1
    mumps (virus) B26.1
    neurosyphilis (late) A52.13
    parasitic disease NEC B89 *[G02]*
    poliovirus A80.9 *[G02]*
    preventive immunization, inoculation or
      vaccination G03.8
    rubella B06.02
    Salmonella infection A02.21
    specified cause NEC G03.8
    Streptococcal pneumoniae G00.1
    typhoid fever A01.01
    varicella B01.0
    viral disease NEC A87.8
    whooping cough A37.90
    zoster B02.1
  infectious G00.9
  influenzal (H. influenzae) G00.0
  Klebsiella G00.8
  leptospiral (aseptic) A27.81
  lymphocytic (acute) (benign) (serous) A87.2
  meningococcal A39.0

▶ New ⇒ Revised ~~deleted~~ Deleted ● Use Additional Character(s)

Meningitis *(Continued)*
    Mima polymorpha G00.8
    Mollaret (benign recurrent) G03.2
    monilial B37.5
    mycotic NEC B49 *[G02]*
    Neisseria A39.0
    nonbacterial G03.0
    nonpyogenic NEC G03.0
➡ ossificans G96.198
    pneumococcal streptococcus pneumoniae
        G00.1
    poliovirus A80.9 *[G02]*
    postmeasles B05.1
    purulent G00.9
        specified organism NEC G00.8
    pyogenic G00.9
        specified organism NEC G00.8
    Salmonella (arizonae) (Cholerae-Suis)
        (enteritidis) (typhimurium) A02.21
    septic G00.9
        specified organism NEC G00.8
    serosa circumscripta NEC G03.0
    serous NEC G93.2
    specified organism NEC G00.8
    sporotrichosis B42.81
    staphylococcal G00.3
    sterile G03.0
    Streptococcal (acute) G00.2
        pneumoniae G00.1
    suppurative G00.9
        specified organism NEC G00.8
    syphilitic (late) (tertiary) A52.13
        acute A51.41
        congenital A50.41
        secondary A51.41
    Torula histolytica (cryptococcal) B45.1
    traumatic (complication of injury) T79.8
    tuberculous A17.0
    typhoid A01.01
    viral NEC A87.9
    Yersinia pestis A20.3
Meningocele (spinal) —*see also* Spina bifida
    with hydrocephalus —*see* Spina bifida, by
        site, with hydrocephalus
➡ acquired (traumatic) G96.198
    cerebral —*see* Encephalocele
Meningocerebritis —*see* Meningoencephalitis
Meningococcemia A39.4
    acute A39.2
    chronic A39.3
Meningococcus, meningococcal —*see also*
        condition A39.9
    adrenalitis, hemorrhagic A39.1
    carrier (suspected) of Z22.31
    meningitis (cerebrospinal) A39.0
Meningoencephalitis —*see also* Encephalitis
        G04.90
    acute NEC —*see also* Encephalitis, viral A86
    bacterial NEC G04.2
    California A83.5
    diphasic A84.1
    eosinophilic B83.2
    epidemic A39.81
    herpesviral, herpetic B00.4
        due to herpesvirus 6 B10.01
        due to herpesvirus 7 B10.09
        specified NEC B10.09
    in (due to)
        blastomycosis NEC B40.81
        diseases classified elsewhere G05.3
        free-living ambeae B60.2
        Hemophilus influenzae (H. influenzae)
            G00.0
        herpes B00.4
            due to herpesvirus 6 B10.01
            due to herpesvirus 7 B10.09
            specified NEC B10.09
        H. influenzae G00.0
        Lyme disease A69.22
        mercury —*see* subcategory T56.1
        mumps B26.2

Meningoencephalitis *(Continued)*
    in (due to) *(Continued)*
        Naegleria (amebae) (organisms) (fowleri)
            B60.2
        Parastrongylus cantonensis B83.2
        toxoplasmosis (acquired) B58.2
            congenital P37.1
    infectious (acute) (viral) A86
    influenzal (H. influenzae) G00.0
    Listeria monocytogenes A32.12
    lymphocytic (serous) A87.2
    mumps B26.2
    parasitic NEC B89 *[G05.3]*
    pneumococcal G04.2
    primary amebic B60.2
    specific (syphilitic) A52.14
    specified organism NEC G04.81
    staphylococcal G04.2
    streptococcal G04.2
    syphilitic A52.14
    toxic NEC G92
        due to mercury —*see* subcategory T56.1
    tuberculous A17.82
    virus NEC A86
Meningoencephalocele —*see also*
        Encephalocele
    syphilitic A52.19
        congenital A50.49
Meningoencephalomyelitis —*see also*
        Meningoencephalitis
    acute NEC (viral) A86
        disseminated G04.00
            postimmunization or postvaccination
                G04.02
            postinfectious G04.01
    due to
        actinomycosis A42.82
        Torula B45.1
        Toxoplasma or toxoplasmosis (acquired)
            B58.2
            congenital P37.1
    postimmunization or postvaccination
        G04.02
Meningoencephalomyelopathy G96.9
Meningoencephalopathy G96.9
Meningomyelitis —*see also*
        Meningoencephalitis
    bacterial NEC G04.2
    blastomycotic NEC B40.81
    cryptococcal B45.1
    in diseases classified elsewhere G05.4
    meningococcal A39.81
    syphilitic A52.14
    tuberculous A17.82
Meningomyelocele —*see also* Spina bifida
    syphilitic A52.19
Meningomyeloneuritis —*see*
        Meningoencephalitis
Meningoradiculitis —*see* Meningitis
Meningovascular —*see* condition
Menkes' disease or syndrome E83.09
    meaning maple-syrup-urine disease E71.0
Menometrorrhagia N92.1
Menopause, menopausal (asymptomatic)
        (state) Z78.0
    arthritis (any site) NEC —*see* Arthritis,
        specified form NEC
    bleeding N92.4
    depression (single episode) F32.89
        agitated (single episode) F32.2
            recurrent episode F33.9
        psychotic (single episode) F32.89
            zrecurrent episode F33.8
        recurrent episode F33.9
    melancholia (single episode) F32.89
        recurrent episode F33.8
    paranoid state F22
    premature E28.319
        asymptomatic E28.319
            postirradiation E89.40
            postsurgical E89.40

Menopause, menopausal *(Continued)*
    premature *(Continued)*
        symptomatic E28.310
            postirradiation E89.41
            postsurgical E89.41
    psychosis NEC F28
    symptomatic N95.1
    toxic polyarthritis NEC —*see* Arthritis,
        specified form NEC
Menorrhagia (primary) N92.0
    climacteric N92.4
        menopausal N92.4
    menopausal N92.4
    perimenopausal N92.4
    postclimacteric N95.0
    postmenopausal N95.0
    preclimacteric or premenopausal N92.4
    pubertal (menses retained) N92.2
Menostaxis N92.0
Menses, retention N94.89
Menstrual —*see* Menstruation
Menstruation
    absent —*see* Amenorrhea
    anovulatory N97.0
    cycle, irregular N92.6
    delayed N91.0
    disorder N93.9
        psychogenic F45.8
    during pregnancy O20.8
    excessive (with regular cycle) N92.0
        with irregular cycle N92.1
        at puberty N92.2
    frequent N92.0
    infrequent —*see* Oligomenorrhea
    irregular N92.6
        specified NEC N92.5
    latent N92.5
    membranous N92.5
    painful —*see also* Dysmenorrhea N94.6
        primary N94.4
        psychogenic F45.8
        secondary N94.5
    passage of clots N92.0
    precocious E30.1
    protracted N92.5
    rare —*see* Oligomenorrhea
    retained N94.89
    retrograde N92.5
    scanty —*see* Oligomenorrhea
    suppression N94.89
    vicarious (nasal) N94.89
Mental —*see also* condition
    deficiency —*see* Disability, intellectual
    deterioration —*see* Psychosis
    disorder —*see* Disorder, mental
    exhaustion F48.8
    insufficiency (congenital) —*see* Disability,
        intellectual
    observation without need for further medical
        care Z03.89
    retardation —*see* Disability, intellectual
    subnormality —*see* Disability, intellectual
    upset —*see* Disorder, mental
Meralgia paresthetica G57.1-●
Mercurial —*see* condition
Mercurialism —*see* subcategory T56.1
MERRF syndrome (myoclonic epilepsy
        associated with ragged-red fiber) E88.42
Merkel cell tumor —*see* Carcinoma, Merkel cell
Merocele —*see* Hernia, femoral
Meromelia
    lower limb —*see* Defect, reduction, lower
        limb
        intercalary
            femur —*see* Defect, reduction, lower
                limb, specified type NEC
                tibiofibular (complete) (incomplete) —
                    see Defect, reduction, lower limb
    upper limb —*see* Defect, reduction, upper
        limb
        intercalary, humeral, radioulnar —*see*
            Agenesis, arm, with hand present

M

Merzbacher-Pelizaeus disease E75.29
Mesaortitis —see Aortitis
Mesarteritis —see Arteritis
Mesencephalitis —see Encephalitis
Mesenchymoma —see also Neoplasm,
    connective tissue, uncertain behavior
  benign —see Neoplasm, connective tissue,
    benign
  malignant —see Neoplasm, connective tissue,
    malignant
Mesenteritis
  retractile K65.4
  sclerosing K65.4
Mesentery, mesenteric —see condition
Mesiodens, mesiodentes K00.1
Mesio-occlusion M26.213
Mesocolon —see condition
Mesonephroma (malignant) —see Neoplasm,
    malignant, by site
  benign —see Neoplasm, benign, by site
Mesophlebitis —see Phlebitis
Mesostromal dysgenesia Q13.89
Mesothelioma (malignant) C45.9
  benign
    mesentery D19.1
    mesocolon D19.1
    omentum D19.1
    peritoneum D19.1
    pleura D19.0
    specified site NEC D19.7
    unspecified site D19.9
  biphasic C45.9
    benign
      mesentery D19.1
      mesocolon D19.1
      omentum D19.1
      peritoneum D19.1
      pleura D19.0
      specified site NEC D19.7
      unspecified site D19.9
  cystic D48.4
  epithelioid C45.9
    benign
      mesentery D19.1
      mesocolon D19.1
      omentum D19.1
      peritoneum D19.1
      pleura D19.0
      specified site NEC D19.7
      unspecified site D19.9
  fibrous C45.9
    benign
      mesentery D19.1
      mesocolon D19.1
      omentum D19.1
      peritoneum D19.1
      pleura D19.0
      specified site NEC D19.7
      unspecified site D19.9
  site classification
    liver C45.7
    lung C45.7
    mediastinum C45.7
    mesentery C45.1
    mesocolon C45.1
    omentum C45.1
    pericardium C45.2
    peritoneum C45.1
    pleura C45.0
      parietal C45.0
    retroperitoneum C45.7
    specified site NEC C45.7
    unspecified C45.9
Metabolic syndrome E88.81
Metagonimiasis B66.8
Metagonimus infestation (intestine)
    B66.8
Metal
  pigmentation L81.8
  polisher's disease J62.8
Metamorphopsia H53.15

Metaplasia
  apocrine (breast) —see Dysplasia, mammary,
    specified type NEC
  cervix (squamous) —see Dysplasia, cervix
  endometrium (squamous) (uterus) N85.8
  esophagus K22.7-●
  kidney (pelvis) (squamous) N28.89
  myelogenous D73.1
  myeloid (agnogenic) (megakaryocytic) D73.1
  spleen D73.1
  squamous cell, bladder N32.89
Metastasis, metastatic
  abscess —see Abscess
  calcification E83.59
  cancer
    from specified site —see Neoplasm,
      malignant, by site
    to specified site —see Neoplasm, secondary,
      by site
  deposits (in) —see Neoplasm, secondary, by
    site
  disease (see also Neoplasm, secondary, by site)
    C79.9
  spread (to) —see Neoplasm, secondary, by site
Metastrongyliasis B83.8
Metatarsalgia M77.4-●
  anterior G57.6-●
  Morton's G57.6-●
Metatarsus, metatarsal —see also condition
  adductus, congenital Q66.22-●
  valgus (abductus), congenital Q66.6
  varus (congenital) Q66.22-●
    primus Q66.21-●
Methadone use —see Use, opioid
Methemoglobinemia D74.9
  acquired (with sulfhemoglobinemia) D74.8
  congenital D74.0
  enzymatic (congenital) D74.0
  Hb M disease D74.0
  hereditary D74.0
  toxic D74.8
Methemoglobinuria —see Hemoglobinuria
Methioninemia E72.19
Methylmalonic acidemia E71.120
Metritis (catarrhal) (hemorrhagic) (septic)
    (suppurative) —see also Endometritis
  cervical —see Cervicitis
Metropathia hemorrhagica N93.8
Metroperitonitis —see Peritonitis, pelvic, female
Metrorrhagia N92.1
  climacteric N92.4
  menopausal N92.4
  perimenopausal N92.4
  postpartum NEC (atonic) (following delivery
    of placenta) O72.1
    delayed or secondary O72.2
  preclimacteric or premenopausal N92.4
  psychogenic F45.8
Metrorrhexis —see Rupture, uterus
Metrosalpingitis N70.91
Metrostaxis N93.8
Metrovaginitis —see Endometritis
Meyer-Schwickerath and Weyers syndrome
    Q87.0
Meynert's amentia (nonalcoholic) F04
  alcoholic F10.96
    with dependence F10.26
Mibelli's disease (porokeratosis) Q82.8
Mice, joint —see Loose, body, joint
  knee M23.4
Micrencephalon, micrencephaly Q02
Microalbuminuria R80.9
Microaneurysm, retinal —see also Disorder,
    retina, microaneurysms
  diabetic —see E08-E13 with .31
Microangiopathy (peripheral) I73.9
  thrombotic M31.1
Microcalcifications, breast R92.0
Microcephalus, microcephalic, microcephaly
    Q02
  due to toxoplasmosis (congenital) P37.1

Microcheilia Q18.7
Microcolon (congenital) Q43.8
Microcornea (congenital) Q13.4
Microcytic —see condition D57.40
Microdeletions NEC Q93.88
Microdontia K00.2
Microdrepanocytosis D57.40
▶ with
  ▶ acute chest syndrome D57.411
  ▶ cerebral vascular involvement D57.413
  ▶ crisis (painful) D57.419
    ▶ with specified complication NEC D57.418
  ▶ splenic sequestration D57.412
  ▶ vasoocclusive pain D57.419
  with crisis (vasoocclusive pain) D57.419
    with
      acute chest syndrome D57.411
      splenic sequestration D57.412
Microembolism
  atherothrombotic —see Atheroembolism
  retinal —see Occlusion, artery, retina
Microencephalon Q02
Microfilaria streptocerca infestation —see
    Onchocerciasis
Microgastria (congenital) Q40.2
Microgenia M26.06
Microgenitalia, congenital
  female Q52.8
  male Q55.8
Microglioma —see Lymphoma, non-Hodgkin,
    specified NEC
Microglossia (congenital) Q38.3
Micrognathia, micrognathism (congenital)
    (mandibular) (maxillary) M26.09
Microgyria (congenital) Q04.3
Microinfarct of heart —see Insufficiency,
    coronary
Microlentia (congenital) Q12.8
Microlithiasis, alveolar, pulmonary J84.02
Micromastia N64.82
Micromyelia (congenital) Q06.8
Micropenis Q55.62
Microphakia (congenital) Q12.8
Microphthalmos, microphthalmia (congenital)
    Q11.2
  due to toxoplasmosis P37.1
Micropsia H53.15
Microscopic polyangiitis (polyarteritis) M31.7
Microsporidiosis B60.8
  intestinal A07.8
Microsporon furfur infestation B36.0
Microsporosis —see also Dermatophytosis
  nigra B36.1
Microstomia (congenital) Q18.5
Microtia (congenital) (external ear) Q17.2
Microtropia H50.40
Microvillus inclusion disease (MVD) (MVID)
    Q43.8
Micturition
  disorder NEC —see also Difficulty, micturition
    R39.198
    psychogenic F45.8
  frequency R35.0
    psychogenic F45.8
  hesitancy R39.11
  incomplete emptying R39.14
  nocturnal R35.1
  painful R30.9
    dysuria R30.0
    psychogenic F45.8
    tenesmus R30.1
  poor stream R39.12
  position dependent R39.192
  split stream R39.13
  straining R39.16
  urgency R39.15
Mid plane —see condition
Middle
  ear —see condition
  lobe (right) syndrome J98.19
Miescher's elastoma L87.2

▶ New   ⟹ Revised   ~~deleted~~ Deleted   ● Use Additional Character(s)

Mietens' syndrome Q87.2
Migraine (idiopathic) G43.909
　with refractory migraine G43.919
　　with status migrainosus G43.911
　　without status migrainosus G43.919
　with aura (acute-onset) (prolonged) (typical)
　　　(without headache) G43.109
　　with refractory migraine G43.119
　　　with status migrainosus G43.111
　　　without status migrainosus G43.119
　　intractable G43.119
　　　with status migrainosus G43.111
　　　without status migrainosus G43.119
　　not intractable G43.109
　　　with status migrainosus G43.101
　　　without status migrainosus G43.109
　　persistent G43.509
　　　with cerebral infarction G43.609
　　　　with refractory migraine G43.619
　　　　　with status migrainosus G43.611
　　　　　without status migrainosus G43.619
　　　　intractable G43.619
　　　　　with status migrainosus G43.611
　　　　　without status migrainosus G43.619
　　　　not intractable G43.609
　　　　　with status migrainosus G43.601
　　　　　without status migrainosus G43.609
　　　　without refractory migraine G43.609
　　　　　with status migrainosus G43.601
　　　　　without status migrainosus G43.609
　　　without cerebral infarction G43.509
　　　　with refractory migraine G43.519
　　　　　with status migrainosus G43.511
　　　　　without status migrainosus G43.519
　　　　intractable G43.519
　　　　　with status migrainosus G43.511
　　　　　without status migrainosus G43.519
　　　　not intractable G43.509
　　　　　with status migrainosus G43.501
　　　　　without status migrainosus G43.509
　　　　without refractory migraine G43.509
　　　　　with status migrainosus G43.501
　　　　　without status migrainosus G43.509
　　without mention of refractory migraine
　　　　G43.109
　　　with status migrainosus G43.101
　　　without status migrainosus G43.109
　abdominal G43.D0
　　with refractory migraine G43.D1
　　intractable G43.D1
　　not intractable G43.D0
　　without refractory migraine G43.D0
　basilar —see Migraine, with aura
　classical —see Migraine, with aura
　common —see Migraine, without aura
　complicated G43.109
　equivalents —see Migraine, with aura
　familial —see Migraine, hemiplegic
　hemiplegic G43.409
　　with refractory migraine G43.419
　　　with status migrainosus G43.411
　　　without status migrainosus G43.419
　　intractable G43.419
　　　with status migrainosus G43.411
　　　without status migrainosus G43.419
　　not intractable G43.409
　　　with status migrainosus G43.401
　　　without status migrainosus G43.409
　　without refractory migraine G43.409
　　　with status migrainosus G43.401
　　　without status migrainosus G43.409
　intractable G43.919
　　with status migrainosus G43.911
　　without status migrainosus G43.919
　menstrual G43.829
　　with refractory migraine G43.839
　　　with status migrainosus G43.831
　　　without status migrainosus G43.839
　　intractable G43.839
　　　with status migrainosus G43.831
　　　without status migrainosus G43.839

Migraine (Continued)
　menstrual (Continued)
　　not intractable G43.829
　　　with status migrainosus G43.821
　　　without status migrainosus G43.829
　　without refractory migraine G43.829
　　　with status migrainosus G43.821
　　　without status migrainosus G43.829
　menstrually related —see Migraine,
　　　menstrual
　not intractable G43.909
　　with status migrainosus G43.901
　　without status migrainosus G43.919
　ophthalmoplegic G43.B0
　　with refractory migraine G43.B1
　　intractable G43.B1
　　not intractable G43.B0
　　　without refractory migraine
　　　　G43.B0
　persistent aura (with, without) cerebral
　　　infarction —see Migraine, with aura,
　　　persistent
　preceded or accompanied by transient focal
　　　neurological phenomena —see Migraine,
　　　with aura
　pre-menstrual —see Migraine, menstrual
　pure menstrual —see Migraine, menstrual
　retinal —see Migraine, with aura
　specified NEC G43.809
　　intractable G43.819
　　　with status migrainosus G43.811
　　　without status migrainosus G43.819
　　not intractable G43.809
　　　with status migrainosus G43.801
　　　without status migrainosus G43.809
　sporadic —see Migraine, hemiplegic
　transformed —see Migraine, without aura,
　　　chronic
　triggered seizures —see Migraine, with aura
　without aura G43.009
　　with refractory migraine G43.019
　　　with status migrainosus G43.011
　　　without status migrainosus G43.019
　　chronic G43.709
　　　with refractory migraine G43.719
　　　　with status migrainosus G43.711
　　　　without status migrainosus G43.719
　　　intractable
　　　　with status migrainosus G43.711
　　　　without status migrainosus G43.719
　　　not intractable
　　　　with status migrainosus G43.701
　　　　without status migrainosus G43.709
　　　without refractory migraine G43.709
　　　　with status migrainosus G43.701
　　　　without status migrainosus G43.709
　　intractable
　　　with status migrainosus G43.011
　　　without status migrainosus G43.019
　　not intractable
　　　with status migrainosus G43.001
　　　without status migrainosus G43.009
　　without mention of refractory migraine
　　　　G43.009
　　　with status migrainosus G43.001
　　　without status migrainosus G43.009
　　without refractory migraine G43.909
　　　with status migrainosus G43.901
　　　without status migrainosus G43.919
Migrant, social Z59.0
Migration, anxiety concerning Z60.3
Migratory, migrating —see also condition
　person Z59.0
　testis Q55.29
Mikity-Wilson disease or syndrome P27.0
Mikulicz' disease or syndrome K11.8
Miliaria L74.3
　alba L74.1
　apocrine L75.2
　crystallina L74.1
　profunda L74.2

Miliaria (Continued)
　rubra L74.0
　tropicalis L74.2
Miliary —see condition
Milium L72.0
　colloid L57.8
Milk
　crust L21.0
　excessive secretion O92.6
　poisoning —see Poisoning, food, noxious
　retention O92.79
　sickness —see Poisoning, food, noxious
　spots I31.0
Milk-alkali disease or syndrome E83.52
Milk-leg (deep vessels) (nonpuerperal) —see
　　　Embolism, vein, lower extremity
　complicating pregnancy O22.3-●
　puerperal, postpartum, childbirth O87.1
Milkman's disease or syndrome M83.8
Milky urine —see Chyluria
Millard-Gubler (-Foville) paralysis or
　　　syndrome G46.3
Millar's asthma J38.5
Miller-Fisher syndrome G61.0
Mills' disease —see Hemiplegia
Millstone maker's pneumoconiosis J62.8
Milroy's disease (chronic hereditary edema)
　　　Q82.0
Minamata disease T56.1-●
Miners' asthma or lung J60
Minkowski-Chauffard syndrome —see
　　　Spherocytosis
Minor —see condition
Minor's disease (hematomyelia) G95.19
Minot's disease (hemorrhagic disease),
　　　newborn P53
Minot-von Willebrand-Jurgens disease or
　　　syndrome (angiohemophilia) D68.0
Minus (and plus) hand (intrinsic) —see
　　　Deformity, limb, specified type NEC,
　　　forearm
Miosis (pupil) H57.03
Mirizzi's syndrome (hepatic duct stenosis) K83.1
Mirror writing F81.0
Misadventure (of) (prophylactic) (therapeutic) —
　　　see also Complications T88.9
　administration of insulin (by accident) —see
　　　subcategory T38.3
　infusion —see Complications, infusion
　local applications (of fomentations, plasters,
　　　etc.) T88.9
　　burn or scald —see Burn
　　specified NEC T88.8
　medical care (early) (late) T88.9
　　adverse effect of drugs or chemicals —see
　　　Table of Drugs and Chemicals
　medical care (early) (late)
　　burn or scald —see Burn
　　specified NEC T88.8
　specified NEC T88.8
　surgical procedure (early) (late) —see
　　　Complications, surgical procedure
　transfusion —see Complications, transfusion
　vaccination or other immunological
　　　procedure —see Complications,
　　　vaccination
Miscarriage O03.9
Misdirection, aqueous H40.83-●
Misperception, sleep state F51.02
Misplaced, misplacement
　ear Q17.4
　kidney (acquired) N28.89
　　congenital Q63.2
　organ or site, congenital NEC —see
　　　Malposition, congenital
Missed
　abortion O02.1
　delivery O36.4
Missing —see also Absence
　string of intrauterine contraceptive device
　　　T83.32

Misuse of drugs F19.99
Mitchell's disease (erythromelalgia) I73.81
Mite(s) (infestation) B88.9
  diarrhea B88.0
  grain (itch) B88.0
  hair follicle (itch) B88.0
  in sputum B88.0
Mitral —see condition
Mittelschmerz N94.0
Mixed —see condition
MMN (multifocal motor neuropathy) G61.82
MNGIE (Mitochondrial Neurogastrointestinal
    Encephalopathy) syndrome E88.49
Mobile, mobility
  cecum Q43.3
  excessive —see Hypermobility
  gallbladder, congenital Q44.1
  kidney N28.89
  organ or site, congenital NEC —see
    Malposition, congenital
Mobitz heart block (atrioventricular) I44.1
Moebius, Möbius
  disease (ophthalmoplegic migraine) —see
    Migraine, ophthalmoplegic
  syndrome Q87.0
    congenital oculofacial paralysis (with other
      anomalies) Q87.0
    ophthalmoplegic migraine —see Migraine,
      ophthalmoplegic
Moeller's glossitis K14.0
Mohr's syndrome (Types I and II) Q87.0
Mola destruens D39.2
Molar pregnancy O02.0
Molarization of premolars K00.2
Molding, head (during birth) - omit code
Mole (pigmented) —see also Nevus
  blood O02.0
  Breus' O02.0
  cancerous —see Melanoma
  carneous O02.0
  destructive D39.2
  fleshy O02.0
  hydatid, hydatidiform (benign) (complicating
    pregnancy) (delivered) (undelivered)
    O01.9
    classical O01.0
    complete O01.0
    incomplete O01.1
    invasive D39.2
    malignant D39.2
    partial O01.1
  intrauterine O02.0
  invasive (hydatidiform) D39.2
  malignant
    meaning
      malignant hydatidiform mole D39.2
      melanoma —see Melanoma
  nonhydatidiform O02.0
  nonpigmented —see Nevus
  pregnancy NEC O02.0
  skin —see Nevus
  tubal O00.10-
    with intrauterine pregnancy O00.11-
  vesicular —see Mole, hydatidiform
Molimen, molimina (menstrual) N94.3
Molluscum contagiosum (epitheliale) B08.1
Mönckeberg's arteriosclerosis, disease, or
    sclerosis —see Arteriosclerosis, extremities
Mondini's malformation (cochlea) Q16.5
Mondor's disease I80.8
Monge's disease T70.29
Monilethrix (congenital) Q84.1
Moniliasis —see also Candidiasis B37.9
  neonatal P37.5
Monitoring (encounter for)
  therapeutic drug level Z51.81
Monkey malaria B53.1
Monkeypox B04
Monoarthritis M13.10
  ankle M13.17-●
  elbow M13.12-●

Monoarthritis (Continued)
  foot joint M13.17-●
  hand joint M13.14-●
  hip M13.15-●
  knee M13.16-●
  shoulder M13.11-●
  wrist M13.13-●
Monoblastic —see condition
Monochromat (ism), monochromatopsia
    (acquired) (congenital) H53.51
Monocytic —see condition
Monocytopenia D72.818
Monocytosis (symptomatic) D72.821
Monomania —see Psychosis
Mononeuritis G58.9
  cranial nerve —see Disorder, nerve,
    cranial
  femoral nerve G57.2-●
  lateral
    cutaneous nerve of thigh G57.1-●
    popliteal nerve G57.3-●
  lower limb G57.9-●
    specified nerve NEC G57.8-●
  medial popliteal nerve G57.4-●
  median nerve G56.1-●
  multiplex G58.7
  plantar nerve G57.6-●
  posterior tibial nerve G57.5-●
  radial nerve G56.3-●
  sciatic nerve G57.0-●
  specified NEC G58.8
  tibial nerve G57.4-●
  ulnar nerve G56.2-●
  upper limb G56.9-●
    specified nerve NEC G56.8-●
  vestibular —see subcategory H93.3
Mononeuropathy G58.9
  carpal tunnel syndrome —see Syndrome,
    carpal tunnel
  diabetic NEC —see E08-E13 with .41
  femoral nerve —see Lesion, nerve, femoral
  ilioinguinal nerve G57.8-●
  in diseases classified elsewhere —see category
    G59
  intercostal G58.0
  lower limb G57.9-●
    causalgia —see Causalgia, lower limb
    femoral nerve —see Lesion, nerve,
      femoral
    meralgia paresthetica G57.1-●
    plantar nerve —see Lesion, nerve, plantar
    popliteal nerve —see Lesion, nerve,
      popliteal
    sciatic nerve —see Lesion, nerve, sciatic
    specified NEC G57.8-●
    tarsal tunnel syndrome —see Syndrome,
      tarsal tunnel
  median nerve —see Lesion, nerve, median
  multiplex G58.7
  obturator nerve G57.8-●
  popliteal nerve —see Lesion, nerve, popliteal
  radial nerve —see Lesion, nerve, radial
  saphenous nerve G57.8-●
  specified NEC G58.8
  tarsal tunnel syndrome —see Syndrome,
    tarsal tunnel
  tuberculous A17.83
  ulnar nerve —see Lesion, nerve, ulnar
  upper limb G56.9-●
    carpal tunnel syndrome —see Syndrome,
      carpal tunnel
    causalgia —see Causalgia
    median nerve —see Lesion, nerve, median
    radial nerve —see Lesion, nerve, radial
    specified site NEC G56.8-●
    ulnar nerve —see Lesion, nerve, ulnar
Mononucleosis, infectious B27.90
  with
    complication NEC B27.99
    meningitis B27.92
    polyneuropathy B27.91

Mononucleosis, infectious (Continued)
  cytomegaloviral B27.10
    with
      complication NEC B27.19
      meningitis B27.12
      polyneuropathy B27.11
  Epstein-Barr (virus) B27.00
    with
      complication NEC B27.09
      meningitis B27.02
      polyneuropathy B27.01
  gammaherpesviral B27.00
    with
      complication NEC B27.09
      meningitis B27.02
      polyneuropathy B27.01
  specified NEC B27.80
    with
      complication NEC B27.89
      meningitis B27.82
      polyneuropathy B27.81
Monoplegia G83.3-●
  congenital (cerebral) G80.8
    spastic G80.1
  embolic (current episode) I63.4-●
  following
    cerebrovascular disease
      cerebral infarction
        lower limb I69.34-●
        upper limb I69.33-●
      intracerebral hemorrhage
        lower limb I69.14-●
        upper limb I69.13-●
      lower limb I69.94-●
      nontraumatic intracranial hemorrhage
        NEC
        lower limb I69.24-●
        upper limb I69.23-●
      specified disease NEC
        lower limb I69.84-●
        upper limb I69.83-●
      stroke NOS
        lower limb I69.34-●
        upper limb I69.33-●
      subarachnoid hemorrhage
        lower limb I69.04-●
        upper limb I69.03-●
      upper limb I69.93-●
  hysterical (transient) F44.4
  lower limb G83.1-●
  psychogenic (conversion reaction) F44.4
  thrombotic (current episode) I63.3-●
  transient R29.818
  upper limb G83.2-●
Monorchism, monorchidism Q55.0
Monosomy —see also Deletion, chromosome
    Q93.9
  specified NEC Q93.89
  whole chromosome
    meiotic nondisjunction Q93.0
    mitotic nondisjunction Q93.1
    mosaicism Q93.1
  X Q96.9
Monster, monstrosity (single) Q89.7
  acephalic Q00.0
  twin Q89.4
Monteggia's fracture (-dislocation) S52.27-●
Mooren's ulcer (cornea) —see Ulcer, cornea,
    Mooren's
Moore's syndrome —see Epilepsy, specified
    NEC
Mooser-Neill reaction A75.2
Mooser's bodies A75.2
Morbidity not stated or unknown R69
Morbilli —see Measles
Morbus —see also Disease
  angelicus, anglorum E55.0
  Beigel B36.2
  caducus —see Epilepsy
  celiacus K90.0
  comitialis —see Epilepsy

Morbus *(Continued)*
  cordis —*see also* Disease, heart I51.9
    valvulorum —*see* Endocarditis
  coxae senilis M16.9
    tuberculous A18.02
  hemorrhagicus neonatorum P53
  maculosus neonatorum P54.5
Morel (-Stewart)(-Morgagni) syndrome M85.2
Morel-Kraepelin disease —*see* Schizophrenia
Morel-Moore syndrome M85.2
Morgagni's
  cyst, organ, hydatid, or appendage
    female Q50.5
      male (epididymal) Q55.4
        testicular Q55.29
  syndrome M85.2
Morgagni-Stewart-Morel syndrome M85.2
Morgagni-Stokes-Adams syndrome I45.9
Morgagni-Turner (-Albright) syndrome Q96.9
Moria F07.0
Moron (I.Q. 50-69) F70
Morphea L94.0
Morphinism (without remission) F11.20
  with remission F11.21
Morphinomania (without remission) F11.20
  with remission F11.21
Morquio (-Ullrich)(-Brailsford) disease or syndrome —*see* Mucopolysaccharidosis
Mortification (dry) (moist) —*see* Gangrene
Morton's metatarsalgia (neuralgia)(neuroma) (syndrome) G57.6
Morvan's disease or syndrome G60.8
Mosaicism, mosaic (autosomal) (chromosomal) 45,X/46,XX Q96.3
  45,X/other cell lines NEC with abnormal sex chromosome Q96.4
  sex chromosome
    female Q97.8
      lines with various numbers of X chromosomes Q97.2
    male Q98.7
  XY Q96.3
Moschowitz' disease M31.1
Mother yaw A66.0
Motion sickness (from travel, any vehicle) (from roundabouts or swings) T75.3
Mottled, mottling, teeth (enamel) (endemic) (nonendemic) K00.3
Mounier-Kuhn syndrome Q32.4
  with bronchiectasis J47.9
    exacerbation (acute) J47.1
    lower respiratory infection J47.0
  acquired J98.09
    with bronchiectasis J47.9
      with
        exacerbation (acute) J47.1
        lower respiratory infection J47.0
Mountain
  sickness T70.29
    with polycythemia , acquired (acute) D75.1
  tick fever A93.2
Mouse, joint —*see* Loose, body, joint
  knee M23.4-●
Mouth —*see* condition
Movable
  coccyx —*see* subcategory M53.2
  kidney N28.89
    congenital Q63.8
  spleen D73.89
Movements, dystonic R25.8
Moyamoya disease I67.5
MRSA (Methicillin resistant Staphylococcus aureus)
  infection A49.02
    as the cause of diseases classified elsewhere B95.62
  sepsis A41.02
MSD (multiple sulfatase deficiency) E75.26

MSSA (Methicillin susceptible Staphylococcus aureus)
  infection A49.01
    as the cause of diseases classified elsewhere B95.61
  sepsis A41.01
Mucha-Habermann disease L41.0
Mucinosis (cutaneous) (focal) (papular) (reticular erythematous) (skin) L98.5
  oral K13.79
Mucocele
  appendix K38.8
  buccal cavity K13.79
  gallbladder K82.1
  lacrimal sac, chronic H04.43-●
  nasal sinus J34.1
  nose J34.1
  salivary gland (any) K11.6
  sinus (accessory) (nasal) J34.1
  turbinate (bone) (middle) (nasal) J34.1
  uterus N85.8
Mucolipidosis
  I E77.1
  II, III E77.0
  IV E75.11
Mucopolysaccharidosis E76.3
  beta-gluduronidase deficiency E76.29
  cardiopathy E76.3 *[I52]*
  Hunter's syndrome E76.1
  Hurler's syndrome E76.01
  Hurler-Scheie syndrome E76.02
  Maroteaux-Lamy syndrome E76.29
  Morquio syndrome E76.219
    A E76.210
    B E76.211
    classic E76.210
  Sanfilippo syndrome E76.22
  Scheie's syndrome E76.03
  specified NEC E76.29
  type
    I
      Hurler's syndrome E76.01
      Hurler-Scheie syndrome E76.02
      Scheie's syndrome E76.03
    II E76.1
    III E76.22
    IV E76.219
    IVA E76.210
    IVB E76.211
    VI E76.29
    VII E76.29
Mucormycosis B46.5
  cutaneous B46.3
  disseminated B46.4
  gastrointestinal B46.2
  generalized B46.4
  pulmonary B46.0
  rhinocerebral B46.1
  skin B46.3
  subcutaneous B46.3
Mucositis (ulcerative) K12.30
  due to drugs NEC K12.32
  gastrointestinal K92.81
  mouth (oral) (oropharyngeal) K12.30
    due to antineoplastic therapy K12.31
    due to drugs NEC K12.32
    due to radiation K12.33
    specified NEC K12.39
    viral K12.39
  nasal J34.81
  oral cavity —*see* Mucositis, mouth
  oral soft tissues —*see* Mucositis, mouth
  vagina and vulva N76.81
Mucositis necroticans agranulocytica —*see* Agranulocytosis
Mucous —*see also* condition
  patches (syphilitic) A51.39
    congenital A50.07
Mucoviscidosis E84.9
  with meconium obstruction E84.11

Mucus
  asphyxia or suffocation —*see* Asphyxia, mucus
  in stool R19.5
  plug —*see* Asphyxia, mucus
Muguet B37.0
Mulberry molars (congenital syphilis) A50.52
Müllerian mixed tumor
  specified site —*see* Neoplasm, malignant, by site
  unspecified site C54.9
Multicystic kidney (development) Q61.4
Multiparity (grand) Z64.1
  affecting management of pregnancy, labor and delivery (supervision only) O09.4-●
  requiring contraceptive management —*see* Contraception
Multipartita placenta O43.19-●
Multiple, multiplex —*see also* condition
  digits (congenital) Q69.9
  endocrine neoplasia —*see* Neoplasia, endocrine, multiple [MEN]
  personality F44.81
Mumps B26.9
  arthritis B26.85
  complication NEC B26.89
  encephalitis B26.2
  hepatitis B26.81
  meningitis (aseptic) B26.1
  meningoencephalitis B26.2
  myocarditis B26.82
  oophoritis B26.89
  orchitis B26.0
  pancreatitis B26.3
  polyneuropathy B26.84
Mumu —*see also* Infestation, filarial B74.9 *[N51]*
Münchhausen's syndrome —*see* Disorder, factitious
Münchmeyer's syndrome —*see* Myositis, ossificans, progressiva
Mural —*see* condition
Murmur (cardiac) (heart) (organic) R01.1
  abdominal R19.15
  aortic (valve) —*see* Endocarditis, aortic
  benign R01.0
  diastolic —*see* Endocarditis
  Flint I35.1
  functional R01.0
  Graham Steell I37.1
  innocent R01.0
  mitral (valve) —*see* Insufficiency, mitral
  nonorganic R01.0
  presystolic, mitral —*see* Insufficiency, mitral
  pulmonic (valve) I37.8
  systolic R01.1
  tricuspid (valve) I07.9
  valvular —*see* Endocarditis
Murri's disease (intermittent hemoglobinuria) D59.6
Muscle, muscular —*see also* condition
  carnitine (palmityltransferase) deficiency E71.314
Musculoneuralgia —*see* Neuralgia
Mushroom-workers' (pickers') disease or lung J67.5
Mushrooming hip —*see* Derangement, joint, specified NEC, hip
Mutation(s)
  factor V Leiden D68.51
  surfactant, of lung J84.83
  prothrombin gene D68.52
Mutism —*see also* Aphasia
  deaf (acquired) (congenital) NEC H91.3
  elective (adjustment reaction) (childhood) F94.0
  hysterical F44.4
  selective (childhood) F94.0
MVD (microvillus inclusion disease) Q43.8
MVID (microvillus inclusion disease) Q43.8

M

Myalgia M79.1Ø
  auxiliary muscles, head and neck M79.12
  epidemic (cervical) B33.Ø
  mastication muscle M79.11
  site specified NEC M79.18
  traumatic NEC T14.8
Myasthenia G7Ø.9
  congenital G7Ø.2
  cordis —see Failure, heart
  developmental G7Ø.2
  gravis G7Ø.ØØ
    with exacerbation (acute) G7Ø.Ø1
    in crisis G7Ø.Ø1
    neonatal, transient P94.Ø
    pseudoparalytica G7Ø.ØØ
      with exacerbation (acute) G7Ø.Ø1
      in crisis G7Ø.Ø1
  stomach, psychogenic F45.8
  syndrome
    in
      diabetes mellitus —see EØ8-E13 with .44
      neoplastic disease —see also Neoplasm
        D49.9 [G73.3]
      pernicious anemia D51.Ø [G73.3]
      thyrotoxicosis EØ5.9Ø [G73.3]
        with thyroid storm EØ5.91 [G73.3]
Myasthenic M62.81
Mycelium infection B49
Mycetismus —see Poisoning, food, noxious,
    mushroom
Mycetoma B47.9
  actinomycotic B47.1
  bone (mycotic) B47.9 [M9Ø.8Ø]
  eumycotic B47.Ø
  foot B47.9
    actinomycotic B47.1
    mycotic B47.Ø
  madurae NEC B47.9
    mycotic B47.Ø
  maduromycotic B47.Ø
  mycotic B47.Ø
  nocardial B47.1
Mycobacteriosis —see Mycobacterium
Mycobacterium, mycobacterial (infection)
    A31.9
  anonymous A31.9
  atypical A31.9
    cutaneous A31.1
    pulmonary A31.Ø
      tuberculous —see Tuberculosis,
        pulmonary
    specified site NEC A31.8
  avium (intracellulare complex) A31.Ø
  balnei A31.1
  Battey A31.Ø
  chelonei A31.8
  cutaneous A31.1
  extrapulmonary systemic A31.8
  fortuitum A31.8
  intracellulare (Battey bacillus) A31.Ø
  kakaferifu A31.8
  kansasii (yellow bacillus) A31.Ø
  kasongo A31.8
  leprae —see also Leprosy A3Ø.9
  luciflavum A31.1
  marinum (M. balnei) A31.1
  nonspecific —see Mycobacterium, atypical
  pulmonary (atypical) A31.Ø
    tuberculous —see Tuberculosis, pulmonary
  scrofulaceum A31.8
  simiae A31.8
  systemic, extrapulmonary A31.8
  szulgai A31.8
  terrae A31.8
  triviale A31.8
  tuberculosis (human, bovine) —see
    Tuberculosis
  ulcerans A31.1
  xenopi A31.8
Mycoplasma (M.) pneumoniae, as cause of
    disease classified elsewhere B96.Ø

Mycosis, mycotic B49
  cutaneous NEC B36.9
  ear B36.9
    in
      aspergillosis B44.89
      candidiasis B37.84
      moniliasis B37.84
  fungoides (extranodal) (solid organ) C84.Ø-●
  mouth B37.Ø
  nails B35.1
  opportunistic B48.8
  skin NEC B36.9
  specified NEC B48.8
  stomatitis B37.Ø
  vagina, vaginitis (candidal) B37.3
Mydriasis (pupil) H57.Ø4
Myelatelia QØ6.1
Myelinolysis, pontine, central G37.2
Myelitis (acute) (ascending) (childhood)
    (chronic) (descending) (diffuse)
    (disseminated) (idiopathic) (pressure)
    (progressive) (spinal cord) (subacute) —see
    also Encephalitis GØ4.91
▶ flaccid GØ4.89
  herpes simplex BØØ.82
  herpes zoster BØ2.24
  in diseases classified elsewhere GØ5.4
  necrotizing, subacute G37.4
  optic neuritis in G36.Ø
  postchickenpox BØ1.12
  postherpetic BØ2.24
  postimmunization GØ4.Ø2
  postinfectious NEC GØ4.89
  postvaccinal GØ4.Ø2
  specified NEC GØ4.89
  syphilitic (transverse) A52.14
  toxic G92
  transverse (in demyelinating diseases of
    central nervous system) G37.3
  tuberculous A17.82
  varicella BØ1.12
Myeloblastic —see condition
Myeloblastoma
  granular cell —see also Neoplasm, connective
    tissue
    malignant —see Neoplasm, connective
      tissue, malignant
  tongue D1Ø.1
Myelocele —see Spina bifida
Myelocystocele —see Spina bifida
Myelocytic —see condition
Myelodysplasia D46.9
  specified NEC D46.Z
  spinal cord (congenital) QØ6.1
➠ Myelodysplastic syndrome (see also Syndrome,
    myelodysplastic) D46.9
  with
    5q deletion D46.C
    isolated del (5q) chromosomal abnormality
      C46.C
  specified NEC D46.Z
Myeloencephalitis —see Encephalitis
Myelofibrosis D75.81
  with myeloid metaplasia D47.4
  acute C94.4-●
  idiopathic (chronic) D47.4
  primary D47.1
  secondary D75.81
    in myeloproliferative disease
      D47.4
Myelogenous —see condition
Myeloid —see condition
Myelokathexis D7Ø.9
Myeloleukodystrophy E75.29
Myelolipoma —see Lipoma
Myeloma (multiple) C9Ø.Ø-●
  monostotic C9Ø.3
    plasma cell C9Ø.Ø-●
  plasma cell C9Ø.Ø-●
  solitary —see also Plasmacytoma, solitary
    C9Ø.3-●

Myelomalacia G95.89
Myelomatosis C9Ø.Ø-●
Myelomeningitis —see Meningoencephalitis
Myelomeningocele (spinal cord) —see Spina
    bifida
Myelo-osteo-musculodysplasia hereditaria
    Q79.8
Myelopathic
  anemia D64.89
  muscle atrophy —see Atrophy, muscle,
    spinal
  pain syndrome G89.Ø
Myelopathy (spinal cord) G95.9
  drug-induced G95.89
  in (due to)
    degeneration or displacement,
      intervertebral disc NEC —see
      Disorder, disc, with, myelopathy
    infection —see Encephalitis
    intervertebral disc disorder —see also
      Disorder, disc, with, myelopathy
    mercury —see subcategory T56.1
    neoplastic disease —see also Neoplasm
      D49.9 [G99.2]
    pernicious anemia D51.Ø [G99.2]
    spondylosis —see Spondylosis, with
      myelopathy NEC
  necrotic (subacute) (vascular) G95.19
  radiation-induced G95.89
  spondylogenic NEC —see Spondylosis, with
    myelopathy NEC
  toxic G95.89
  transverse, acute G37.3
  vascular G95.19
  vitamin B12 E53.8 [G32.Ø]
Myelophthisis D61.82
Myeloradiculitis GØ4.91
Myeloradiculodysplasia (spinal)
    QØ6.1
Myelosarcoma C92.3-●
Myelosclerosis D75.89
  with myeloid metaplasia D47.4
  disseminated, of nervous system
    G35
  megakaryocytic D47.4
    with myeloid metaplasia
      D47.4
Myelosis
  acute C92.Ø-●
  aleukemic C92.9-●
  chronic D47.1
  erythremic (acute) C94.Ø-●
  megakaryocytic C94.2-●
  nonleukemic D72.828
  subacute C92.9-●
Myiasis (cavernous) B87.9
  aural B87.4
  creeping B87.Ø
  cutaneous B87.Ø
  dermal B87.Ø
  ear (external) (middle) B87.4
  eye B87.2
  genitourinary B87.81
  intestinal B87.82
  laryngeal B87.3
  nasopharyngeal B87.3
  ocular B87.2
  orbit B87.2
  skin B87.Ø
  specified site NEC B87.89
  traumatic B87.1
  wound B87.1
Myoadenoma, prostate —see Hyperplasia,
    prostate
Myoblastoma
  granular cell —see also Neoplasm, connective
    tissue, benign
    malignant —see Neoplasm, connective
      tissue, malignant
  tongue D1Ø.1
Myocardial —see condition

▶ New   ➠ Revised   ~~deleted~~ Deleted   ● Use Additional Character(s)

M

Myocardiopathy (congestive) (constrictive) (familial) (hypertrophic nonobstructive) (idiopathic) (infiltrative) (obstructive) (primary) (restrictive) (sporadic) —see also Cardiomyopathy I42.9
  alcoholic I42.6
  cobalt-beer I42.6
  glycogen storage E74.02 [I43]
  hypertrophic obstructive I42.1
  in (due to)
    beriberi E51.12
    cardiac glycogenosis E74.02 [I43]
    Friedreich's ataxia G11.11 [I43]
    myotonia atrophica G71.11 [I43]
    progressive muscular dystrophy G71.03 [I43]
  obscure (African) I42.8
  secondary I42.9
  thyrotoxic E05.90 [I43]
    with storm E05.91 [I43]
  toxic NEC I42.7
Myocarditis (with arteriosclerosis) (chronic) (fibroid) (interstitial) (old) (progressive) (senile) I51.4
  with
    rheumatic fever (conditions in I00) I09.0
      active —see Myocarditis, acute, rheumatic
      inactive or quiescent (with chorea) I09.0
  active I40.9
    rheumatic I01.2
      with chorea (acute) (rheumatic) (Sydenham's) I02.0
  acute or subacute (interstitial) I40.9
    due to
      streptococcus (beta-hemolytic) I01.2
    idiopathic I40.1
    rheumatic I01.2
      with chorea (acute) (rheumatic) (Sydenham's) I02.0
    specified NEC I40.8
  aseptic of newborn B33.22
  bacterial (acute) I40.0
  Coxsackie (virus) B33.22
  diphtheritic A36.81
  eosinophilic I40.1
  epidemic of newborn (Coxsackie) B33.22
  Fiedler's (acute) (isolated) I40.1
  giant cell (acute) (subacute) I40.1
  gonococcal A54.83
  granulomatous (idiopathic) (isolated) (nonspecific) I40.1
  hypertensive —see Hypertension, heart
  idiopathic (granulomatous) I40.1
  in (due to)
    diphtheria A36.81
    epidemic louse-borne typhus A75.0 [I41]
    Lyme disease A69.29
    sarcoidosis D86.85
    scarlet fever A38.1
    toxoplasmosis (acquired) B58.81
    typhoid A01.02
    typhus NEC A75.9 [I41]
  infective I40.0
  influenzal —see Influenza, with, myocarditis
  isolated (acute) I40.1
  meningococcal A39.52
  mumps B26.82
  nonrheumatic, active I40.9
  parenchymatous I40.9
  pneumococcal I40.0
  rheumatic (chronic) (inactive) (with chorea) I09.0
    active or acute I01.2
      with chorea (acute) (rheumatic) (Sydenham's) I02.0
  rheumatoid —see Rheumatoid, carditis
  septic I40.0
  staphylococcal I40.0
  suppurative I40.0
  syphilitic (chronic) A52.06

Myocarditis (Continued)
  toxic I40.8
    rheumatic —see Myocarditis, acute, rheumatic
  tuberculous A18.84
  typhoid A01.02
  valvular —see Endocarditis
  virus, viral I40.0
    of newborn (Coxsackie) B33.22
Myocardium, myocardial —see condition
Myocardosis —see Cardiomyopathy
Myoclonus, myoclonic, myoclonia (familial) (essential) (multifocal) (simplex) G25.3
  drug-induced G25.3
  epilepsy —see also Epilepsy, generalized, specified NEC G40.4-●
    familial (progressive) G25.3
  epileptica G40.409
    with status epilepticus G40.401
  facial G51.3-●
  familial progressive G25.3
  Friedreich's G25.3
  jerks G25.3
  massive G25.3
  palatal G25.3
  pharyngeal G25.3
Myocytolysis I51.5
Myodiastasis —see Diastasis, muscle
Myoendocarditis —see Endocarditis
Myoepithelioma —see Neoplasm, benign, by site
Myofasciitis (acute) —see Myositis
Myofibroma —see also Neoplasm, connective tissue, benign
  uterus (cervix) (corpus) —see Leiomyoma
Myofibromatosis D48.1
  infantile Q89.8
Myofibrosis M62.89
  heart —see Myocarditis
  scapulohumeral —see Lesion, shoulder, specified NEC
Myofibrositis M79.7
  scapulohumeral —see Lesion, shoulder, specified NEC
Myoglobulinuria, myoglobinuria (primary) R82.1
Myokymia, facial G51.4
Myolipoma —see Lipoma
Myoma —see also Neoplasm, connective tissue, benign
  malignant —see Neoplasm, connective tissue, malignant
  prostate D29.1
  uterus (cervix) (corpus) —see Leiomyoma
Myomalacia M62.89
Myometritis —see Endometritis
Myometrium —see condition
Myonecrosis, clostridial A48.0
Myopathy G72.9
  acute
    necrotizing G72.81
    quadriplegic G72.81
  alcoholic G72.1
  benign congenital G71.20
  central core G71.29
  centronuclear G71.228
    autosomal (dominant) (recessive) G71.228
    other specified NEC G71.228
  congenital (benign) G71.20
  critical illness G72.81
  distal G71.09
  drug-induced G72.0
  endocrine NEC E34.9 [G73.7]
  extraocular muscles H05.82-●
  facioscapulohumeral G71.02
  hereditary G71.9
    specified NEC G71.8
  hyaline body G71.29
  myosin storage G71.29
  immune NEC G72.49

Myopathy (Continued)
  in (due to)
    Addison's disease E27.1 [G73.7]
    alcohol G72.1
    amyloidosis E85.0 [G73.7]
    cretinism E00.9 [G73.7]
    Cushing's syndrome E24.9 [G73.7]
    drugs G72.0
    endocrine disease NEC E34.9 [G73.7]
    giant cell arteritis M31.6 [G73.7]
    glycogen storage disease E74.00 [G73.7]
    hyperadrenocorticism E24.9 [G73.7]
    hyperparathyroidism NEC E21.3 [G73.7]
    hypoparathyroidism E20.9 [G73.7]
    hypopituitarism E23.0 [G73.7]
    hypothyroidism E03.9 [G73.7]
    infectious disease NEC B99 [G73.7]
    lipid storage disease E75.6 [G73.7]
    metabolic disease NEC E88.9 [G73.7]
    myxedema E03.9 [G73.7]
    parasitic disease NEC B89 [G73.7]
    polyarteritis nodosa M30.0 [G73.7]
    rheumatoid arthritis —see Rheumatoid, myopathy
    sarcoidosis D86.87
    scleroderma M34.82
    sicca syndrome M35.03
    Sjögren's syndrome M35.03
    systemic lupus erythematosus M32.19
    thyrotoxicosis (hyperthyroidism) E05.90 [G73.7]
      with thyroid storm E05.91 [G73.7]
    toxic agent NEC G72.2
  inflammatory NEC G72.49
  intensive care (ICU) G72.81
  limb-girdle G71.09
  mitochondrial NEC G71.3
  myosin storage G71.29
  mytonic, proximal (PROMM) G71.11
  myotubular (centronuclear) G71.220
    X-linked G71.220
  mytonic, proximal (PROMM) G71.11
  nemaline G71.21
  ocular G71.09
  oculopharyngeal G71.09
  of critical illness G72.81
  primary G71.9
    specified NEC G71.8
  progressive NEC G72.89
  proximal myotonic (PROMM) G71.11
  rod (body) G71.21
  scapulohumeral G71.02
  specified NEC G72.89
  toxic G72.2
Myopericarditis —see also Pericarditis
  chronic rheumatic I09.2
Myopia (axial) (congenital) H52.1-●
  degenerative (malignant) H44.20
    with
      choroidal neovascularization H44.2A-●
      foveoschisis H44.2D-●
      macular hole H44.2B-●
      retinal detachment H44.2C-●
      specified maculopathy NEC H44.2E-●
    bilateral H44.23
    left eye H44.22
    right eye H44.21
  malignant —see also Myopia, degenerative H44.2-●
  pernicious —see also Myopia, degenerative H44.2-●
  progressive high (degenerative) —see also Myopia, degenerative H44.2-●
Myosarcoma —see Neoplasm, connective tissue, malignant
Myosis (pupil) H57.03
  stromal (endolymphatic) D39.0
Myositis M60.9
  clostridial A48.0
  due to posture —see Myositis, specified type NEC

Myositis *(Continued)*
  epidemic B33.0
  fibrosa or fibrous (chronic), Volkmann's T79.6
  foreign body granuloma —*see* Granuloma,
    foreign body
  in (due to)
    bilharziasis B65.9 *[M63.8-●]*
    cysticercosis B69.81
    leprosy A30.9 *[M63.8-●]*
    mycosis B49 *[M63.8-●]*
    sarcoidosis D86.87
    schistosomiasis B65.9 *[M63.8-●]*
    syphilis
      late A52.78
      secondary A51.49
    toxoplasmosis (acquired) B58.82
    trichinellosis B75 *[M63.8-●]*
    tuberculosis A18.09
  inclusion body [IBM] G72.41
  infective M60.009
    arm M60.002
      left M60.001
      right M60.000
    leg M60.005
      left M60.004
      right M60.003
    lower limb M60.005
      ankle M60.07-●
      foot M60.07-●
      lower leg M60.06-●
      thigh M60.05-●
      toe M60.07-●
    multiple sites M60.09
    specified site NEC M60.08
    upper limb M60.002
      finger M60.04-●
      forearm M60.03-●
      hand M60.04-●
      shoulder region M60.01-●
      upper arm M60.02-●
  interstitial M60.10
    ankle M60.17-●
    foot M60.17-●
    forearm M60.13-●
    hand M60.14-●
    lower leg M60.16-●
    multiple sites M60.19
    shoulder region M60.11-●
    specified site NEC M60.18
    thigh M60.15-●
    upper arm M60.12-●
  mycotic B49 *[M63.8-●]*
  ossificans or ossifying (circumscripta) —*see*
    also Ossification, muscle, specified NEC
    in (due to)
      burns M61.30
        ankle M61.37-●
        foot M61.37-●
        forearm M61.33-●
        hand M61.34-●
        lower leg M61.36-●

Myositis *(Continued)*
  ossificans or ossifying *(Continued)*
    in (due to) *(Continued)*
      burns *(Continued)*
        multiple sites M61.39
        pelvic region M61.35-●
        shoulder region M61.31-●
        specified site NEC M61.38
        thigh M61.35-●
        upper arm M61.32-●
    quadriplegia or paraplegia M61.20
      ankle M61.27-●
      foot M61.27-●
      forearm M61.23-●
      hand M61.24-●
      lower leg M61.26-●
      multiple sites M61.29
      pelvic region M61.25-●
      shoulder region M61.21-●
      specified site NEC M61.28
      thigh M61.25-●
      upper arm M61.22-●
    progressiva M61.10
      ankle M61.17-●
      finger M61.14-●
      foot M61.17-●
      forearm M61.13-●
      hand M61.14-●
      lower leg M61.16-●
      multiple sites M61.19
      pelvic region M61.15-●
      shoulder region M61.11-●
      specified site NEC M61.18
      thigh M61.15-●
      toe M61.17-●
      upper arm M61.12-●
    traumatica M61.00
      ankle M61.07-●
      foot M61.07-●
      forearm M61.03-●
      hand M61.04-●
      lower leg M61.06-●
      multiple sites M61.09
      pelvic region M61.05-●
      shoulder region M61.01-●
      specified site NEC M61.08
      thigh M61.05-●
      upper arm M61.02-●
  purulent —*see* Myositis, infective
  specified type NEC M60.80
    ankle M60.87-●
    foot M60.87-●
    forearm M60.83-●
    hand M60.84-●
    lower leg M60.86-●
    multiple sites M60.89
    pelvic region M60.85-●
    shoulder region M60.81-●
    specified site NEC M60.88
    thigh M60.85-●
    upper arm M60.82-●

Myositis *(Continued)*
  suppurative —*see* Myositis, infective
  traumatic (old) —*see* Myositis, specified type
    NEC
Myospasia impulsiva F95.2
Myotonia (acquisita) (intermittens) M62.89
  atrophica G71.11
  chondrodystrophic G71.13
  congenita (acetazolamide responsive)
    (dominant) (recessive) G71.12
  drug-induced G71.14
  dystrophica G71.11
  fluctuans G71.19
  levior G71.12
  permanens G71.19
  symptomatic G71.19
Myotonic pupil —*see* Anomaly, pupil, function,
  tonic pupil
Myriapodiasis B88.2
Myringitis H73.2-●
  with otitis media —*see* Otitis, media
  acute H73.00-●
    bullous H73.01-●
    specified NEC H73.09-●
  bullous —*see* Myringitis, acute, bullous
  chronic H73.1-●
Mysophobia F40.228
Mytilotoxism —*see* Poisoning, fish
Myxadenitis labialis K13.0
Myxedema (adult) (idiocy) (infantile)
  (juvenile) —*see also* Hypothyroidism
  E03.9
  circumscribed E05.90
    with storm E05.91
  coma E03.5
  congenital E00.1
  cutis L98.5
  localized (pretibial) E05.90
    with storm E05.91
  papular L98.5
Myxochondrosarcoma —*see* Neoplasm,
  cartilage, malignant
Myxofibroma —*see* Neoplasm, connective
  tissue, benign
  odontogenic —*see* Cyst, calcifying
    odontogenic
Myxofibrosarcoma —*see* Neoplasm, connective
  tissue, malignant
Myxolipoma D17.9
Myxoliposarcoma —*see* Neoplasm, connective
  tissue, malignant
Myxoma —*see also* Neoplasm, connective tissue,
  benign
  nerve sheath —*see* Neoplasm, nerve,
    benign
  odontogenic —*see* Cyst, calcifying
    odontogenic
Myxosarcoma —*see* Neoplasm, connective
  tissue, malignant

M

▶ New   ⇒ Revised   ~~deleted~~ Deleted   ● Use Additional Character(s)

N

Naegeli's
  disease Q82.8
  leukemia, monocytic C93.1-●
Naegleriasis (with meningoencephalitis)
    B60.2
Naffziger's syndrome G54.0
Naga sore —see Ulcer, skin
Nägele's pelvis M95.5
  with disproportion (fetopelvic) O33.0
    causing obstructed labor O65.0
Nail —see also condition
  biting F98.8
  patella syndrome Q87.2
Nanism, nanosomia —see Dwarfism
Nanophyetiasis B66.8
Nanukayami A27.89
Napkin rash L22
Narcolepsy G47.419
  with cataplexy G47.411
  in conditions classified elsewhere G47.429
    with cataplexy G47.421
Narcosis R06.89
Narcotism —see Dependence
NARP (Neuropathy, Ataxia and Retinitis
    pigmentosa) syndrome E88.49
Narrow
  anterior chamber angle H40.03-●
  gingival width (of periodontal soft tissue)
      K05.5
  pelvis —see Contraction, pelvis
Narrowing —see also Stenosis
  artery I77.1
    auditory, internal I65.8
    basilar —see Occlusion, artery, basilar
    carotid —see Occlusion, artery, carotid
    cerebellar —see Occlusion, artery, cerebellar
    cerebral —see Occlusion artery, cerebral
    choroidal —see Occlusion, artery,
        precerebral, specified NEC
    communicating posterior —see
        Occlusion, artery, precerebral,
        specified NEC
    coronary —see also Disease, heart, ischemic,
        atherosclerotic
      congenital Q24.5
        syphilitic A50.54 [I52]
      due to syphilis NEC A52.06
    hypophyseal —see Occlusion, artery,
        precerebral, specified NEC
    pontine —see Occlusion, artery, precerebral,
        specified NEC
    precerebral —see Occlusion, artery,
        precerebral
    vertebral —see Occlusion, artery, vertebral
  auditory canal (external) —see Stenosis,
      external ear canal
  eustachian tube —see Obstruction, eustachian
      tube
  eyelid —see Disorder, eyelid function
  larynx J38.6
  mesenteric artery —see also Ischemia,
      intestine, acute K55.059
  palate M26.89
  palpebral fissure —see Disorder, eyelid
      function
  ureter N13.5
    with infection N13.6
  urethra —see Stricture, urethra
Narrowness, abnormal, eyelid Q10.3
Nasal —see condition
Nasolachrymal, nasolacrimal —see condition
Nasopharyngeal —see also condition
  pituitary gland Q89.2
  torticollis M43.6
Nasopharyngitis (acute) (infective)
    (streptococcal) (subacute) J00
  chronic (suppurative) (ulcerative) J31.1
Nasopharynx, nasopharyngeal —see condition
Natal tooth, teeth K00.6

Nausea (without vomiting) R11.0
  with vomiting R11.2
  gravidarum —see Hyperemesis, gravidarum
  marina T75.3
  navalis T75.3
Navel —see condition
Neapolitan fever —see Brucellosis
Near drowning T75.1
Nearsightedness —see Myopia
Near-syncope R55
Nebula, cornea —see Opacity, cornea
Necator americanus infestation B76.1
Necatoriasis B76.1
Neck —see condition
Necrobiosis R68.89
  lipoidica NEC L92.1
    with diabetes —see E08-E13 with .620
Necrolysis, toxic epidermal L51.2
  due to drug
    correct substance properly administered —
        see Table of Drugs and Chemicals, by
        drug, adverse effect
    overdose or wrong substance given
        or taken —see Table of Drugs and
        Chemicals, by drug, poisoning
Necrophilia F65.89
Necrosis, necrotic (ischemic) —see also
    Gangrene
  adrenal (capsule) (gland) E27.49
  amputation stump (surgical) (late) T87.50
    arm T87.5-●
    leg T87.5-●
  antrum J32.0
  aorta (hyaline) —see also Aneurysm, aorta
    cystic medial —see Dissection, aorta
  artery I77.5
  bladder (aseptic) (sphincter) N32.89
  bone —see also Osteonecrosis M87.9
    aseptic or avascular —see Osteonecrosis
      idiopathic M87.00
    ethmoid J32.2
    jaw M27.2
    tuberculous —see Tuberculosis, bone
  brain I67.89
  breast (aseptic) (fat) (segmental) N64.1
  bronchus J98.09
  central nervous system NEC I67.89
  cerebellar I67.89
  cerebral I67.89
  colon —see also Infarct, intestine K55.049
  cornea H18.89-●
  cortical (acute) (renal) N17.1
  cystic medial (aorta) —see Dissection, aorta
  dental pulp K04.1
  esophagus K22.8
  ethmoid (bone) J32.2
  eyelid —see Disorder, eyelid, degenerative
  fat, fatty (generalized) —see also Disorder, soft
      tissue, specified type NEC
    abdominal wall K65.4
    breast (aseptic) (segmental) N64.1
    localized —see Degeneration, by site, fatty
    mesentery K65.4
    omentum K65.4
    pancreas K86.89
    peritoneum K65.4
    skin (subcutaneous), newborn P83.0
    subcutaneous, due to birth injury P15.6
  gallbladder —see Cholecystitis, acute
  heart —see Infarct, myocardium
  hip, aseptic or avascular —see Osteonecrosis,
      by type, femur
  intestine (acute) (hemorrhagic) (massive) —
      see also Infarct, intestine K55.069
  jaw M27.2
  kidney (bilateral) N28.0
    acute N17.9
    cortical (acute) (bilateral) N17.1
      with ectopic or molar pregnancy O08.4
    medullary (bilateral) (in acute renal failure)
        (papillary) N17.2

Necrosis, necrotic (Continued)
  kidney (Continued)
    papillary (bilateral) (in acute renal
        failure) N17.2
    tubular N17.0
      with ectopic or molar pregnancy
          O08.4
      complicating
        abortion —see Abortion, by type,
            complicated by, tubular necrosis
        ectopic or molar pregnancy O08.4
        pregnancy —see Pregnancy,
            complicated by, diseases of,
            specified type or system NEC
      following ectopic or molar pregnancy
          O08.4
      traumatic T79.5
  larynx J38.7
  liver (with hepatic failure) (cell) —see Failure,
      hepatic
    hemorrhagic, central K76.2
  lung J85.0
  lymphatic gland —see Lymphadenitis, acute
  mammary gland (fat) (segmental) N64.1
  mastoid (chronic) —see Mastoiditis, chronic
  medullary (acute) (renal) N17.2
  mesentery —see also Infarct, intestine
      K55.069
    fat K65.4
  mitral valve —see Insufficiency, mitral
  myocardium, myocardial —see Infarct,
      myocardium
  nose J34.0
  omentum (with mesenteric infarction) —see
      also Infarct, intestine K55.069
    fat K65.4
  orbit, orbital —see Osteomyelitis, orbit
  ossicles, ear —see Abnormal, ear ossicles
  ovary N70.92
  pancreas (aseptic) (duct) (fat) K86.89
    acute (infective) —see Pancreatitis, acute
    infective —see Pancreatitis, acute
  papillary (acute) (renal) N17.2
  perineum N90.89
  peritoneum (with mesenteric infarction) —see
      also Infarct, intestine K55.069
    fat K65.4
  pharynx J02.9
    in granulocytopenia —see Neutropenia
    Vincent's A69.1
  phosphorus —see subcategory T54.2
  pituitary (gland) E23.0
    postpartum O99.285
    Sheehan O99.285
  pressure —see Ulcer, pressure, by site
  pulmonary J85.0
  pulp (dental) K04.1
  radiation —see Necrosis, by site
  radium —see Necrosis, by site
  renal —see Necrosis, kidney
  sclera H15.89
  scrotum N50.89
  skin or subcutaneous tissue NEC I96
  spine, spinal (column) —see also
      Osteonecrosis, by type, vertebra
    cord G95.19
  spleen D73.5
  stomach K31.89
  stomatitis (ulcerative) A69.0
  subcutaneous fat, newborn P83.88
  subendocardial (acute) I21.4
    chronic I25.89
  suprarenal (capsule) (gland) E27.49
  testis N50.89
  thymus (gland) E32.8
  tonsil J35.8
  trachea J39.8
  tuberculous NEC —see Tuberculosis
  tubular (acute) (anoxic) (renal) (toxic)
      N17.0
    postprocedural N99.0

Necrosis, necrotic *(Continued)*
  vagina N89.8
  vertebra —*see also* Osteonecrosis, by type,
    vertebra
    tuberculous A18.01
  vulva N90.89
  X-ray —*see* Necrosis, by site
Necrospermia —*see* Infertility, male
Need (for)
  care provider because of (of)
    assistance with personal care Z74.1
    continuous supervision required Z74.3
    impaired mobility Z74.09
    no other household member able to render
      care Z74.2
    specified reason NEC Z74.8
  immunization —*see* Vaccination
  vaccination —*see* Vaccination
Neglect
  adult
    confirmed T74.01
    history of Z91.412
    suspected T76.01
  child (childhood)
    confirmed T74.02
    history of Z62.812
    suspected T76.02
  emotional, in childhood Z62.898
  hemispatial R41.4
  left-sided R41.4
  sensory R41.4
  visuospatial R41.4
Neisserian infection NEC —*see* Gonococcus
Nelaton's syndrome G60.8
Nelson's syndrome E24.1
Nematodiasis (intestinal) B82.0
  Ancylostoma B76.0
Neonatal —*see also* Newborn
  acne L70.4
  bradycardia P29.12
  screening, abnormal findings on P09
  tachycardia P29.11
  tooth, teeth K00.6
Neonatorum —*see* condition
Neoplasia
  endocrine, multiple (MEN) E31.20
    type I E31.21
    type IIA E31.22
    type IIB E31.23
  intraepithelial (histologically confirmed)
    anal (AIN) (histologically confirmed)
      K62.82
      grade I K62.82
      grade II K62.82
      severe D01.3
    cervical glandular (histologically
      confirmed) D06.9
    cervix (uteri) (CIN) (histologically
      confirmed) N87.9
      glandular D06.9
      grade I N87.0
      grade II N87.1
      grade III (severe dysplasia) —*see also*
        Carcinoma, cervix uteri, in situ
        D06.9
    prostate (histologically confirmed) (PIN)
      N42.31
      grade I N42.31
      grade II N42.31
      grade III (severe dysplasia) D07.5
    vagina (histologically confirmed) (VAIN)
      N89.3
      grade I N89.0
      grade II N89.1
      grade III (severe dysplasia) D07.2
    vulva (histologically confirmed) (VIN)
      N90.3
      grade I N90.0
      grade II N90.1
      grade III (severe dysplasia)
        D07.1

Neoplasm, neoplastic —*see also* Table of
  Neoplasms
  lipomatous, benign —*see* Lipoma
  malignant mast cell C96.20
    specified type NEC C96.29
  mast cell, of uncertain behavior NEC D47.09
Neovascularization
  ciliary body —*see* Disorder, iris, vascular
  cornea H16.40-●
    deep H16.44-●
    ghost vessels —*see* Ghost, vessels
    localized H16.43-●
    pannus —*see* Pannus
  iris —*see* Disorder, iris, vascular
  retina H35.05-●
Nephralgia N23
Nephritis, nephritic (albuminuric) (azotemic)
  (congenital) (disseminated) (epithelial)
  (familial) (focal) (granulomatous)
  (hemorrhagic) (infantile) (nonsuppurative,
  excretory) (uremic) N05.9
  with
  ▶C3
    ▶glomerulonephritis N05.A
    ▶glomerulopathy N05.A
      ▶with dense deposit disease N05.6
    dense deposit disease N05.6
    diffuse
      crescentic glomerulonephritis N05.7
      endocapillary proliferative
        glomerulonephritis N05.4
      membranous glomerulonephritis N05.2
      mesangial proliferative
        glomerulonephritis N05.3
      mesangiocapillary glomerulonephritis
        N05.5
    edema —*see* Nephrosis
    focal and segmental glomerular lesions
      N05.1
    foot process disease N04.9
    glomerular lesion
      diffuse sclerosing N05.8
      hypocomplementemic —*see* Nephritis,
        membranoproliferative
      IgA —*see* Nephropathy, IgA
      lobular, lobulonodular —*see* Nephritis,
        membranoproliferative
      nodular —*see* Nephritis,
        membranoproliferative
    lesion of
      glomerulonephritis, proliferative N05.8
      renal necrosis N05.9
    minor glomerular abnormality N05.0
    specified morphological changes NEC
      N05.8
  acute N00.9
    with
    ▶C3
      ▶glomerulonephritis N00.A
      ▶glomerulopathy N00.A
        ▶with dense deposit disease N00.6
      dense deposit disease N00.6
      diffuse
        crescentic glomerulonephritis N00.7
        endocapillary proliferative
          glomerulonephritis N00.4
        membranous glomerulonephritis
          N00.2
        mesangial proliferative
          glomerulonephritis N00.3
        mesangiocapillary glomerulonephritis
          N00.5
      focal and segmental glomerular lesions
        N00.1
      minor glomerular abnormality N00.0
      specified morphological changes NEC
        N00.8
  amyloid E85.4 *[N08]*
  antiglomerular basement membrane (anti-
    GBM) antibody NEC
    in Goodpasture's syndrome M31.0

Nephritis, nephritic *(Continued)*
  antitubular basement membrane (tubulo-
    interstitial) NEC N12
    toxic —*see* Nephropathy, toxic
  arteriolar —*see* Hypertension, kidney
  arteriosclerotic —*see* Hypertension, kidney
  ascending —*see* Nephritis, tubulo-interstitial
  atrophic N03.9
  Balkan (endemic) N15.0
  calculous, calculus —*see* Calculus,
    kidney
  cardiac —*see* Hypertension, kidney
  cardiovascular —*see* Hypertension,
    kidney
  chronic N03.9
    with
    ▶C3
      ▶glomerulonephritis N03.A
      ▶glomerulopathy N03.A
        ▶with dense deposit disease N03.6
      dense deposit disease N03.6
      diffuse
        crescentic glomerulonephritis
          N03.7
        endocapillary proliferative
          glomerulonephritis N03.4
        membranous glomerulonephritis
          N03.2
        mesangial proliferative
          glomerulonephritis N03.3
        mesangiocapillary glomerulonephritis
          N03.5
      focal and segmental glomerular lesions
        N03.1
      minor glomerular abnormality
        N03.0
      specified morphological changes
        NEC N03.8
    arteriosclerotic —*see* Hypertension,
      kidney
  cirrhotic N26.9
  complicating pregnancy O26.83-●
  croupous N00.9
  degenerative —*see* Nephrosis
  diffuse sclerosing N05.8
  due to
    diabetes mellitus —*see* E08-E13 with .21
    subacute bacterial endocarditis I33.0
    systemic lupus erythematosus (chronic)
      M32.14
    typhoid fever A01.09
  gonococcal (acute) (chronic) A54.21
  hypocomplementemic —*see* Nephritis,
    membranoproliferative
  IgA —*see* Nephropathy, IgA
  immune complex (circulating) NEC N05.8
  infective —*see* Nephritis, tubulo-interstitial
  interstitial —*see* Nephritis, tubulo-interstitial
  lead N14.3
  membranoproliferative (diffuse) (type 1
    or 3) —*see also* N00-N07 with fourth
    character .5 N05.5
    type 2 —*see also* N00-N07 with fourth
      character .6 N05.6
  minimal change N05.0
  necrotic, necrotizing NEC —*see also* N00-N07
    with fourth character .8 N05.8
  nephrotic —*see* Nephrosis
  nodular —*see* Nephritis,
    membranoproliferative
  polycystic Q61.3
    adult type Q61.2
    autosomal
      dominant Q61.2
      recessive NEC Q61.19
    childhood type NEC Q61.19
    infantile type NEC Q61.19
  poststreptococcal N05.9
    acute N00.9
    chronic N03.9
  rapidly progressive N01.9

▶ New   ⇛ Revised   ~~deleted~~ Deleted   ● Use Additional Character(s)

Nephritis, nephritic *(Continued)*
  proliferative NEC —*see also* N00-N07 with
      fourth character .8 N05.8
  purulent —*see* Nephritis, tubulo-interstitial
  rapidly progressive N01.9
    with
      ►C3
        ►glomerulonephritis N01.A
        ►glomerulopathy N01.A
          ►with dense deposit disease N01.6
        dense deposit disease N01.6
        diffuse
          crescentic glomerulonephritis N01.7
          endocapillary proliferative
              glomerulonephritis N01.4
          membranous glomerulonephritis
              N01.2
          mesangial proliferative
              glomerulonephritis N01.3
          mesangiocapillary glomerulonephritis
              N01.5
        focal and segmental glomerular lesions
            N01.1
        minor glomerular abnormality N01.0
        specified morphological changes NEC
            N01.8
  salt losing or wasting NEC N28.89
  saturnine N14.3
  sclerosing, diffuse N05.8
  septic —*see* Nephritis, tubulo-interstitial
  specified pathology NEC —*see also* N00-N07
      with fourth character .8 N05.8
  subacute N01.9
  suppurative —*see* Nephritis,
      tubulo-interstitial
  syphilitic (late) A52.75
    congenital A50.59 *[N08]*
    early (secondary) A51.44
  toxic —*see* Nephropathy, toxic
  tubal, tubular —*see* Nephritis,
      tubulo-interstitial
  tuberculous A18.11
  tubulo-interstitial (in) N12
    acute (infectious) N10
    chronic (infectious) N11.9
      nonobstructive N11.8
        reflux-associated N11.0
      obstructive N11.1
      specified NEC N11.8
    due to
      brucellosis A23.9 *[N16]*
      cryoglobulinemia D89.1 *[N16]*
      glycogen storage disease E74.00 *[N16]*
      Sjögren's syndrome M35.04
  vascular —*see* Hypertension, kidney
  war N00.9
Nephroblastoma (epithelial) (mesenchymal)
    C64-•
Nephrocalcinosis E83.59 *[N29]*
Nephrocystitis, pustular —*see* Nephritis,
    tubulo-interstitial
Nephrolithiasis (congenital) (pelvis)
    (recurrent) —*see also* Calculus, kidney
Nephroma C64-•
  mesoblastic D41.0-•
Nephronephritis —*see* Nephrosis
Nephronophthisis Q61.5
Nephropathia epidemica A98.5
Nephropathy —*see also* Nephritis N28.9
  with
    edema —*see* Nephrosis
    glomerular lesion —*see*
        Glomerulonephritis
  amyloid, hereditary E85.0
  analgesic N14.0
    with medullary necrosis, acute N17.2
  Balkan (endemic) N15.0
  chemical —*see* Nephropathy, toxic
  diabetic —*see* E08-E13 with .21
  drug-induced N14.2
    specified NEC N14.1

Nephropathy *(Continued)*
  focal and segmental hyalinosis or sclerosis
      N02.1
  heavy metal-induced N14.3
  hereditary NEC N07.9
    with
      ►C3
        ►glomerulonephritis N07.A
        ►glomerulopathy N07.A
          ►with dense deposit disease N07.6
        dense deposit disease N07.6
        diffuse
          crescentic glomerulonephritis N07.7
          endocapillary proliferative
              glomerulonephritis N07.4
          membranous glomerulonephritis
              N07.2
          mesangial proliferative
              glomerulonephritis N07.3
          mesangiocapillary glomerulonephritis
              N07.5
        focal and segmental glomerular lesions
            N07.1
        minor glomerular abnormality N07.0
        specified morphological changes NEC
            N07.8
  hypercalcemic N25.89
  hypertensive —*see* Hypertension, kidney
  hypokalemic (vacuolar) N25.89
  IgA N02.8
    with glomerular lesion N02.9
      focal and segmental hyalinosis or
          sclerosis N02.1
      membranoproliferative (diffuse) N02.5
      membranous (diffuse) N02.2
      mesangial proliferative (diffuse) N02.3
      mesangiocapillary (diffuse) N02.5
      proliferative NEC N02.8
      specified pathology NEC N02.8
  lead N14.3
  membranoproliferative (diffuse) N02.5
  membranous (diffuse) N02.2
  mesangial (IgA/IgG) —*see* Nephropathy, IgA
    proliferative (diffuse) N02.3
  mesangiocapillary (diffuse) N02.5
  obstructive N13.8
  phenacetin N17.2
  phosphate-losing N25.0
  potassium depletion N25.89
  pregnancy-related O26.83-•
  proliferative NEC (*see also* N00-N07 with
      fourth character .8) N05.8
  protein-losing N25.89
  saturnine N14.3
  sickle-cell D57.-• *[N08]*
  toxic NEC N14.4
    due to
      drugs N14.2
        analgesic N14.0
        specified NEC N14.1
      heavy metals N14.3
  vasomotor N17.0
  water-losing N25.89
Nephroptosis N28.83
Nephropyosis —*see* Abscess, kidney
Nephrorrhagia N28.89
Nephrosclerosis (arteriolar) (arteriosclerotic)
    (chronic) (hyaline) —*see also* Hypertension,
    kidney
  hyperplastic —*see* Hypertension, kidney
  senile N26.9
Nephrosis, nephrotic (Epstein's) (syndrome)
    (congenital) N04.9
  with
    foot process disease N04.9
    glomerular lesion N04.1
    hypocomplementemic N04.5
  acute N04.9
  anoxic —*see* Nephrosis, tubular
  chemical —*see* Nephrosis, tubular
  cholemic K76.7

Nephrosis, nephrotic *(Continued)*
  diabetic —*see* E08-E13 with .21
  Finnish type (congenital) Q89.8
  hemoglobin N10
  hemoglobinuric —*see* Nephrosis, tubular
  in
    amyloidosis E85.4 *[N08]*
    diabetes mellitus —*see* E08-E13 with .21
    epidemic hemorrhagic fever A98.5
    malaria (malariae) B52.0
  ischemic —*see* Nephrosis, tubular
  lipoid N04.9
  lower nephron —*see* Nephrosis, tubular
  malarial (malariae) B52.0
  minimal change N04.0
  myoglobin N10
  necrotizing —*see* Nephrosis, tubular
  osmotic (sucrose) N25.89
  radiation N04.9
  syphilitic (late) A52.75
  toxic —*see* Nephrosis, tubular
  tubular (acute) N17.0
    postprocedural N99.0
    radiation N04.9
Nephrosonephritis, hemorrhagic (endemic)
    A98.5
Nephrostomy
  attention to Z43.6
  status Z93.6
Nerve —*see also* condition
  injury —*see* Injury, nerve, by body site
Nerves R45.0
Nervous —*see also* condition R45.0
  heart F45.8
  stomach F45.8
  tension R45.0
Nervousness R45.0
Nesidioblastoma
  pancreas D13.7
  specified site NEC —*see* Neoplasm, benign,
      by site
  unspecified site D13.7
Nettleship's syndrome —*see* Urticaria
    pigmentosa
Neumann's disease or syndrome L10.1
Neuralgia, neuralgic (acute) M79.2
  accessory (nerve) G52.8
  acoustic (nerve) —*see* subcategory H93.3
  auditory (nerve) —*see* subcategory H93.3
  ciliary G44.009
    intractable G44.001
    not intractable G44.009
  cranial
    nerve —*see also* Disorder, nerve, cranial
      fifth or trigeminal —*see* Neuralgia,
          trigeminal
      postherpetic, postzoster B02.29
  ear —*see* subcategory H92.0
  facialis vera G51.1
  Fothergill's —*see* Neuralgia, trigeminal
  glossopharyngeal (nerve) G52.1
  Horton's G44.099
    intractable G44.091
    not intractable G44.099
  Hunt's B02.21
  hypoglossal (nerve) G52.3
  infraorbital —*see* Neuralgia, trigeminal
  malarial —*see* Malaria
  migrainous G44.009
    intractable G44.001
    not intractable G44.009
  Morton's G57.6-•
  nerve, cranial —*see* Disorder, nerve, cranial
  nose G52.0
  occipital M54.81
  olfactory G52.0
  penis N48.9
  perineum R10.2
  postherpetic NEC B02.29
    trigeminal B02.22
  pubic region R10.2

Neuralgia, neuralgic (Continued)
  scrotum R10.2
  Sluder's G44.89
  specified nerve NEC G58.8
  spermatic cord R10.2
  sphenopalatine (ganglion) G90.09
  trifacial —see Neuralgia, trigeminal
  trigeminal G50.0
    postherpetic, postzoster B02.22
  vagus (nerve) G52.2
  writer's F48.8
    organic G25.89
Neurapraxia —see Injury, nerve
Neurasthenia F48.8
  cardiac F45.8
  gastric F45.8
  heart F45.8
Neurilemmoma —see also Neoplasm, nerve,
  benign
  acoustic (nerve) D33.3
  malignant —see also Neoplasm, nerve,
    malignant
    acoustic (nerve) C72.4
Neurilemmosarcoma —see Neoplasm, nerve,
  malignant
Neurinoma —see Neoplasm, nerve, benign
Neurinomatosis —see Neoplasm, nerve,
  uncertain behavior
Neuritis (rheumatoid) M79.2
  abducens (nerve) —see Strabismus, paralytic,
    sixth nerve
  accessory (nerve) G52.8
  acoustic (nerve) —see also subcategory H93.3
    in (due to)
      infectious disease NEC B99 [H94.0-●]
      parasitic disease NEC B89 [H94.0-●]
      syphilitic A52.15
  alcoholic G62.1
    with psychosis —see Psychosis, alcoholic
  amyloid, any site E85.4 [G63]
  auditory (nerve) —see subcategory H93.3
  brachial —see Radiculopathy
    due to displacement, intervertebral disc —
      see Disorder, disc, cervical, with neuritis
  cranial nerve
    due to Lyme disease A69.22
    eighth or acoustic or auditory —see
      subcategory H93.3
    eleventh or accessory G52.8
    fifth or trigeminal G51.0
    first or olfactory G52.0
    fourth or trochlear —see Strabismus,
      paralytic, fourth nerve
    second or optic —see Neuritis, optic
    seventh or facial G51.8
      newborn (birth injury) P11.3
    sixth or abducent —see Strabismus,
      paralytic, sixth nerve
    tenth or vagus G52.2
    third or oculomotor —see Strabismus,
      paralytic, third nerve
    twelfth or hypoglossal G52.3
  Déjérine-Sottas G60.0
  diabetic (mononeuropathy) —see E08-E13
    with .41
    polyneuropathy —see E08-E13 with .42
  due to
    beriberi E51.11
    displacement, prolapse or rupture,
      intervertebral disc —see Disorder, disc,
      with, radiculopathy
    herniation, nucleus pulposus M51.9 [G55]
  endemic E51.11
  facial G51.8
    newborn (birth injury) P11.3
  general —see Polyneuropathy
  geniculate ganglion G51.1
    due to herpes (zoster) B02.21
  gouty —see also Gout, by type M10.9 [G63]
  hypoglossal (nerve) G52.3
  ilioinguinal (nerve) G57.9-●
  infectious (multiple) NEC G61.0

Neuritis (Continued)
  interstitial hypertrophic progressive G60.0
  lumbar M54.16
  lumbosacral M54.17
  multiple —see also Polyneuropathy
    endemic E51.11
    infective, acute G61.0
  multiplex endemica E51.11
  nerve root —see Radiculopathy
  oculomotor (nerve) —see Strabismus,
    paralytic, third nerve
  olfactory nerve G52.0
  optic (nerve) (hereditary) (sympathetic) H46.9
    with demyelination G36.0
    in myelitis G36.0
    nutritional H46.2
    papillitis —see Papillitis, optic
    retrobulbar H46.1-●
    specified type NEC H46.8
    toxic H46.3
  peripheral (nerve) G62.9
    multiple —see Polyneuropathy
    single —see Mononeuritis
  pneumogastric (nerve) G52.2
  postherpetic, postzoster B02.29
  progressive hypertrophic interstitial G60.0
  retrobulbar —see also Neuritis, optic,
    retrobulbar
    in (due to)
      late syphilis A52.15
      meningococcal infection A39.82
    meningococcal A39.82
    syphilitic A52.15
  sciatic (nerve) —see also Sciatica
    due to displacement of intervertebral
      disc —see Disorder, disc, with,
      radiculopathy
  serum —see also Reaction, serum T80.69
  shoulder-girdle G54.5
  specified nerve NEC G58.8
  spinal (nerve) root —see Radiculopathy
  syphilitic A52.15
  thenar (median) G56.1-●
  thoracic M54.14
  toxic NEC G62.2
  trochlear (nerve) —see Strabismus, paralytic,
    fourth nerve
  vagus (nerve) G52.2
Neuroastrocytoma —see Neoplasm, uncertain
  behavior, by site
Neuroavitaminosis E56.9 [G99.8]
Neuroblastoma
  olfactory C30.0
  specified site —see Neoplasm, malignant, by
    site
  unspecified site C74.90
Neurochorioretinitis —see Chorioretinitis
Neurocirculatory asthenia F45.8
Neurocysticercosis B69.0
Neurocytoma —see Neoplasm, benign, by site
Neurodermatitis (circumscribed)
  (circumscripta) (local) L28.0
  atopic L20.81
  diffuse (Brocq) L20.81
  disseminated L20.81
Neuroencephalomyelopathy, optic G36.0
Neuroepithelioma —see also Neoplasm,
  malignant, by site
  olfactory C30.0
Neurofibroma —see also Neoplasm, nerve,
  benign
  melanotic —see Neoplasm, nerve, benign
  multiple —see Neurofibromatosis
  plexiform —see Neoplasm, nerve, benign
Neurofibromatosis (multiple) (nonmalignant)
  Q85.00
  acoustic Q85.02
  malignant —see Neoplasm, nerve, malignant
  specified NEC Q85.09
  type 1 (von Recklinghausen) Q85.01
  type 2 Q85.02

Neurofibrosarcoma —see Neoplasm, nerve,
  malignant
Neurogenic —see also condition
  bladder —see also Dysfunction, bladder,
    neuromuscular N31.9
    cauda equina syndrome G83.4
  bowel NEC K59.2
  heart F45.8
Neuroglioma —see Neoplasm, uncertain
  behavior, by site
Neurolabyrinthitis (of Dix and Hallpike) —see
  Neuronitis, vestibular
Neurolathyrism —see Poisoning, food, noxious,
  plant
Neuroleprosy A30.9
Neuroma —see also Neoplasm, nerve, benign
  acoustic (nerve) D33.3
  amputation (stump) (traumatic) (surgical
    complication) (late) T87.3-●
    arm T87.3-●
    leg T87.3-●
  digital (toe) G57.6-●
  interdigital G58.8
    lower limb toe G57.8-●
    upper limb G56.8-●
  intermetatarsal G57.8-●
  Morton's G57.6-●
  nonneoplastic
    arm G56.9-●
    leg G57.9-●
    lower extremity G57.9-●
    upper extremity G56.9-●
  optic (nerve) D33.3
  plantar G57.6-●
  plexiform —see Neoplasm, nerve,
    benign
  surgical (nonneoplastic)
    arm G56.9-●
    leg G57.9-●
    lower extremity G57.9-●
    upper extremity G56.9-●
Neuromyalgia —see Neuralgia
Neuromyasthenia (epidemic) (postinfectious)
  G93.3
Neuromyelitis G36.9
  ascending G61.0
  optica G36.0
Neuromyopathy G70.9
  paraneoplastic D49.9 [G13.0]
Neuromyotonia (Isaacs) G71.19
Neuronevus —see Nevus
Neuronitis G58.9
  ascending (acute) G57.2-●
  vestibular H81.2-●
Neuroparalytic —see condition
Neuropathy, neuropathic G62.9
  acute motor G62.81
  alcoholic G62.1
    with psychosis —see Psychosis,
      alcoholic
  arm G56.9-●
  autonomic, peripheral —see Neuropathy,
    peripheral, autonomic
  axillary G56.9-●
  bladder N31.9
    atonic (motor) (sensory) N31.2
    autonomous N31.2
    flaccid N31.2
    nonreflex N31.2
    reflex N31.1
    uninhibited N31.0
  brachial plexus G54.0
  cervical plexus G54.2
  chronic
    progressive segmentally demyelinating
      G62.89
    relapsing demyelinating G62.89
  Déjérine-Sottas G60.0
  diabetic —see E08-E13 with .40
    mononeuropathy —see E08-E13 with .41
    polyneuropathy —see E08-E13 with .42

▶ New   ⇒ Revised   ~~deleted~~ Deleted   ● Use Additional Character(s)

Neuropathy, neuropathic *(Continued)*
  entrapment G58.9
    iliohypogastric nerve G57.8-●
    ilioinguinal nerve G57.8-●
    lateral cutaneous nerve of thigh
        G57.1-●
    median nerve G56.0-●
    obturator nerve G57.8-●
    peroneal nerve G57.3-●
    posterior tibial nerve G57.5-●
    saphenous nerve G57.8-●
    ulnar nerve G56.2-●
  facial nerve G51.9
  hereditary G60.9
    motor and sensory (types I-IV) G60.0
    sensory G60.8
    specified NEC G60.8
  hypertrophic G60.0
    Charcot-Marie-Tooth G60.0
    Déjérine-Sottas G60.0
    interstitial progressive G60.0
    of infancy G60.0
    Refsum G60.1
  idiopathic G60.9
    progressive G60.3
    specified NEC G60.8
  in association with hereditary ataxia
      G60.2
  intercostal G58.0
  ischemic —*see* Disorder, nerve
  Jamaica (ginger) G62.2
  leg NEC G57.9-●
  lower extremity G57.9-●
  lumbar plexus G54.1
  median nerve G56.1-●
  motor and sensory —*see also* Polyneuropathy
    hereditary (types I-IV) G60.0
  multifocal motor (MMN) G61.82
  multiple (acute) (chronic) —*see*
      Polyneuropathy
  optic (nerve) —*see also* Neuritis, optic
    ischemic H47.01-●
  paraneoplastic (sensorial) (Denny Brown)
      D49.9 *[G13.0]*
  peripheral (nerve) —*see also* Polyneuropathy
      G62.9
    autonomic G90.9
      idiopathic G90.09
      in (due to)
        amyloidosis E85.4 *[G99.0]*
        diabetes mellitus —*see* E08-E13 with
            .43
        endocrine disease NEC E34.9 *[G99.0]*
        gout M10.00 *[G99.0]*
        hyperthyroidism E05.90 *[G99.0]*
          with thyroid storm E05.91 *[G99.0]*
        metabolic disease NEC E88.9 *[G99.0]*
    idiopathic G60.9
      progressive G60.3
    in (due to)
      antitetanus serum G62.0
      arsenic G62.2
      drugs NEC G62.0
      lead G62.2
      organophosphate compounds G62.2
      toxic agent NEC G62.2
  plantar nerves G57.6-●
  progressive
    hypertrophic interstitial G60.0
    inflammatory G62.81
  radicular NEC —*see* Radiculopathy
  sacral plexus G54.1
  sciatic G57.0-●
  serum G61.1
  toxic NEC G62.2
  trigeminal sensory G50.8
  ulnar nerve G56.2-●
  uremic N18.9 *[G63]*
  vitamin B12 E53.8 *[G63]*
    with anemia (pernicious) D51.0 *[G63]*
      due to dietary deficiency D51.3 *[G63]*

Neurophthisis —*see also* Disorder, nerve
  peripheral, diabetic —*see* E08-E13 with .42
Neuroretinitis —*see* Chorioretinitis
Neuroretinopathy, hereditary optic H47.22
Neurosarcoma —*see* Neoplasm, nerve, malignant
Neurosclerosis —*see* Disorder, nerve
Neurosis, neurotic F48.9
  anankastic F42.8
  anxiety (state) F41.1
    panic type F41.0
  asthenic F48.8
  bladder F45.8
  cardiac (reflex) F45.8
  cardiovascular F45.8
  character F60.9
  colon F45.8
  compensation F68.10
  compulsive, compulsion F42.8
  conversion F44.9
  craft F48.8
  cutaneous F45.8
  depersonalization F48.1
  depressive (reaction) (type) F34.1
  environmental F48.8
  excoriation L98.1
  fatigue F48.8
  functional —*see* Disorder, somatoform
  gastric F45.8
  gastrointestinal F45.8
  heart F45.8
  hypochondriacal F45.21
  hysterical F44.9
  incoordination F45.8
    larynx F45.8
    vocal cord F45.8
  intestine F45.8
  larynx (sensory) F45.8
    hysterical F44.4
  mixed NEC F48.8
  musculoskeletal F45.8
  obsessional F42.8
  obsessive-compulsive F42.8
  occupational F48.8
  ocular NEC F45.8
  organ —*see* Disorder, somatoform
  pharynx F45.8
  phobic F40.9
  posttraumatic (situational) F43.10
    acute F43.11
    chronic F43.12
  psychasthenic (type) F48.8
  railroad F48.8
  rectum F45.8
  respiratory F45.8
  rumination F45.8
  sexual F65.9
  situational F48.8
  social F40.10
    generalized F40.11
  specified type NEC F48.8
  state F48.9
    with depersonalization episode F48.1
  stomach F45.8
  traumatic F43.10
    acute F43.11
    chronic F43.12
  vasomotor F45.8
  visceral F45.8
  war F48.8
Neurospongioblastosis diffusa Q85.1
Neurosyphilis (arrested) (early) (gumma) (late)
    (latent) (recurrent) (relapse) A52.3
  with ataxia (cerebellar) (locomotor) (spastic)
      (spinal) A52.19
  aneurysm (cerebral) A52.05
  arachnoid (adhesive) A52.13
  arteritis (any artery) (cerebral) A52.04
  asymptomatic A52.2
  congenital A50.40
  dura (mater) A52.13
  general paresis A52.17

Neurosyphilis *(Continued)*
  hemorrhagic A52.05
  juvenile (asymptomatic) (meningeal)
      A50.40
  leptomeninges (aseptic) A52.13
  meningeal, meninges (adhesive) A52.13
  meningitis A52.13
  meningovascular (diffuse) A52.13
  optic atrophy A52.15
  parenchymatous (degenerative) A52.19
  paresis, paretic A52.17
    juvenile A50.45
  remission in (sustained) A52.3
  serological (without symptoms) A52.2
  specified nature or site NEC A52.19
  tabes, tabetic (dorsalis) A52.11
    juvenile A50.45
  taboparesis A52.17
    juvenile A50.45
  thrombosis (cerebral) A52.05
  vascular (cerebral) NEC A52.05
Neurothekeoma —*see* Neoplasm, nerve, benign
Neurotic —*see* Neurosis
Neurotoxemia —*see* Toxemia
Neutroclusion M26.211
Neutropenia, neutropenic (chronic) (genetic)
    (idiopathic) (immune) (infantile)
    (malignant) (pernicious) (splenic) D70.9
  congenital (primary) D70.0
  cyclic D70.4
  cytoreductive cancer chemotherapy sequela
      D70.1
  drug-induced D70.2
    due to cytoreductive cancer chemotherapy
        D70.1
  due to infection D70.3
  fever D70.9
  neonatal, transitory (isoimmune) (maternal
      transfer) P61.5
  periodic D70.4
  secondary (cyclic) (periodic) (splenic) D70.4
    drug-induced D70.2
      due to cytoreductive cancer
          chemotherapy D70.1
  toxic D70.8
Neutrophilia, hereditary giant D72.0
Nevocarcinoma —*see* Melanoma
Nevus D22.9
  achromic —*see* Neoplasm, skin, benign
  amelanotic —*see* Neoplasm, skin, benign
  angiomatous D18.00
    intra-abdominal D18.03
    intracranial D18.02
    skin D18.01
    specified site NEC D18.09
  araneus I78.1
  balloon cell —*see* Neoplasm, skin, benign
  bathing trunk D48.5
  blue —*see* Neoplasm, skin, benign
    cellular —*see* Neoplasm, skin, benign
    giant —*see* Neoplasm, skin, benign
    Jadassohn's —*see* Neoplasm, skin, benign
    malignant —*see* Melanoma
  capillary D18.00
    intra-abdominal D18.03
    intracranial D18.02
    skin D18.01
    specified site NEC D18.09
  cavernous D18.00
    intra-abdominal D18.03
    intracranial D18.02
    skin D18.01
    specified site NEC D18.09
  cellular —*see* Neoplasm, skin, benign
    blue —*see* Neoplasm, skin, benign
  choroid D31.3-●
  comedonicus Q82.5
  conjunctiva D31.0-●
  dermal —*see* Neoplasm, skin, benign
    with epidermal nevus —*see* Neoplasm,
        skin, benign

Nevus *(Continued)*
    dysplastic —*see* Neoplasm, skin, benign
    eye D31.9-•
    flammeus Q82.5
    hemangiomatous D18.00
        intra-abdominal D18.03
        intracranial D18.02
        skin D18.01
        specified site NEC D18.09
    iris D31.4-•
    lacrimal gland D31.5-•
    lymphatic D18.1
    magnocellular
        specified site —*see* Neoplasm, benign, by
            site
        unspecified site D31.40
    malignant —*see* Melanoma
    meaning hemangioma D18.00
        intra-abdominal D18.03
        intracranial D18.02
        skin D18.01
        specified site NEC D18.09
    mouth (mucosa) D10.30
        specified site NEC D10.39
        white sponge Q38.6
    multiplex Q85.1
    non-neoplastic I78.1
    oral mucosa D10.30
        specified site NEC D10.39
        white sponge Q38.6
    orbit D31.6-•
    pigmented
        giant —*see also* Neoplasm, skin, uncertain
            behavior D48.5
            malignant melanoma in —*see* Melanoma
    portwine Q82.5
    retina D31.2-•
    retrobulbar D31.6-•
    sanguineous Q82.5
    senile I78.1
    skin D22.9
        abdominal wall D22.5
        ala nasi D22.39
        ankle D22.7-•
        anus, anal D22.5
        arm D22.6-•
        auditory canal (external) D22.2-•
        auricle (ear) D22.2-•
        auricular canal (external) D22.2-•
        axilla, axillary fold D22.5
        back D22.5
        breast D22.5
        brow D22.39
        buttock D22.5
        canthus (eye) D22.1-•
        cheek (external) D22.39
        chest wall D22.5
        chin D22.39
        ear (external) D22.2-•
        external meatus (ear) D22.2-•
        eyebrow D22.39
        eyelid (lower) (upper) D22.1-•
        face D22.30
            specified NEC D22.39
        female genital organ (external) NEC D28.0
        finger D22.6-•
        flank D22.5
        foot D22.7-•
        forearm D22.6-•
        forehead D22.39
        foreskin D29.0
        genital organ (external) NEC
            female D28.0
            male D29.9
        gluteal region D22.5
        groin D22.5
        hand D22.6-•
        heel D22.7-•
        helix D22.2-•
        hip D22.7-•
        interscapular region D22.5

Nevus *(Continued)*
    skin *(Continued)*
        jaw D22.39
        knee D22.7-•
        labium (majus) (minus) D28.0
        leg D22.7-•
        lip (lower) (upper) D22.0
        lower limb D22.7-•
        male genital organ (external) D29.9
        nail D22.9
            finger D22.6-•
            toe D22.7-•
        nasolabial groove D22.39
        nates D22.5
        neck D22.4
        nose (external) D22.39
        palpebra D22.1-•
        penis D29.0
        perianal skin D22.5
        perineum D22.5
        pinna D22.2-•
        popliteal fossa or space D22.7-•
        prepuce D29.0
        pudendum D28.0
        scalp D22.4
        scrotum D29.4
        shoulder D22.6-•
        submammary fold D22.5
        temple D22.39
        thigh D22.7-•
        toe D22.7-•
        trunk NEC D22.5
        umbilicus D22.5
        upper limb D22.6-•
        vulva D28.0
    specified site NEC —*see* Neoplasm, benign,
        by site
    spider I78.1
    stellar I78.1
    strawberry Q82.5
    Sutton's benign D22.9
    unius lateris Q82.5
    Unna's Q82.5
    vascular Q82.5
    verrucous Q82.5
Newborn (infant) (liveborn) (singleton)
        Z38.2
    abstinence syndrome P96.1
    acne L70.4
    affected by
        abnormalities of membranes P02.9
            specified NEC P02.8
        abruptio placenta P02.1
        amino-acid metabolic disorder, transitory
            P74.8
        amniocentesis (while in utero) P00.6
        amnionitis P02.78
        apparent life threatening event (ALTE)
            R68.13
        bleeding (into)
            cerebral cortex P52.22
            germinal matrix P52.0
            ventricles P52.1
        breech delivery P03.0
        cardiac arrest P29.81
        cardiomyopathy I42.8
            congenital I42.4
        cerebral ischemia P91.0
        Cesarean delivery P03.4
        chemotherapy agents P04.11
        chorioamnionitis P02.78
        cocaine (crack) P04.41
        complications of labor and delivery P03.9
            specified NEC P03.89
        compression of umbilical cord NEC P02.5
        contracted pelvis P03.1
        cyanosis P28.2
        delivery P03.9
            Cesarean P03.4
            forceps P03.2
            vacuum extractor P03.3

Newborn *(Continued)*
    affected by *(Continued)*
        drugs of addiction P04.40
            cocaine P04.41
            hallucinogens P04.42
            specified drug NEC P04.49
        entanglement (knot) in umbilical cord P02.5
        environmental chemicals P04.6
        fetal (intrauterine)
            growth retardation P05.9
            inflammatory response syndrome (FIRS)
                P02.70
            malnutrition not light or small for
                gestational age P05.2
        FIRS (fetal inflammatory response
            syndrome) P02.70
        forceps delivery P03.2
        heart rate abnormalities
            bradycardia P29.12
            intrauterine P03.819
                before onset of labor P03.810
                during labor P03.811
            tachycardia P29.11
        hemorrhage (antepartum) P02.1
            cerebellar (nontraumatic) P52.6
            intracerebral (nontraumatic) P52.4
            intracranial (nontraumatic) P52.9
                specified NEC P52.8
            intraventricular (nontraumatic) P52.3
                grade 1 P52.0
                grade 2 P52.1
                grade 3 P52.21
                grade 4 P52.22
            posterior fossa (nontraumatic) P52.6
            subarachnoid (nontraumatic) P52.5
            subependymal P52.0
                with intracerebral extension P52.22
                with intraventricular extension P52.1
                    with enlargment of ventricles P52.21
                without intraventricular extension
                    P52.0
        hypoxic ischemic encephalopathy [HIE]
            P91.60
            mild P91.61
            moderate P91.62
            severe P91.63
        induction of labor P03.89
        intestinal perforation P78.0
        intrauterine (fetal) blood loss P50.9
            due to (from)
                cut end of co-twin cord P50.5
                hemorrhage into
                    co-twin P50.3
                    maternal circulation P50.4
                placenta P50.2
                ruptured cord blood P50.1
                vasa previa P50.0
            specified NEC P50.8
        intrauterine (fetal) hemorrhage P50.9
        intrauterine (in utero) procedure P96.5
        malpresentation (malposition) NEC P03.1
        maternal (complication of) (use of)
            alcohol P04.3
            amphetamines P04.16
            analgesia (maternal) P04.0
            anesthesia (maternal) P04.0
            anticonvulsants P04.13
            antidepressants P04.15
            antineoplastic chemotherapy P04.11
            anxiolytics P04.1A
            blood loss P02.1
            cannabis P04.81
            circulatory disease P00.3
            condition P00.9
                specified NEC P00.89
            cytotoxic drugs P04.12
            delivery P03.9
                Cesarean P03.4
                forceps P03.2
                vacuum extractor P03.3
            diabetes mellitus (pre-existing) P70.1

▶ New   ⇒ Revised   ~~deleted~~ Deleted   • Use Additional Character(s)

Newborn *(Continued)*
  affected by *(Continued)*
    maternal *(Continued)*
      disorder P00.9
        specified NEC P00.89
      drugs (addictive) (illegal) NEC P04.49
      ectopic pregnancy P01.4
      gestational diabetes P70.0
      hemorrhage P02.1
      hypertensive disorder P00.0
      incompetent cervix P01.0
      infectious disease P00.2
      injury P00.5
      labor and delivery P03.9
      malpresentation before labor P01.7
      maternal death P01.6
      medical procedure P00.7
      medication P04.19
        specified type NEC P04.18
      multiple pregnancy P01.5
      nutritional disorder P00.4
      oligohydramnios P01.2
      opiates P04.14
        administered for procedures during
            pregnancy or labor and delivery
            P04.0
      parasitic disease P00.2
      periodontal disease P00.81
      placenta previa P02.0
      polyhydramnios P01.3
      precipitate delivery P03.5
      pregnancy P01.9
        specified P01.8
      premature rupture of membranes P01.1
      renal disease P00.1
      respiratory disease P00.3
      sedative-hypnotics P04.17
      surgical procedure P00.6
      tranquilizers administered for
          procedures during pregnancy or
          labor and delivery P04.0
      urinary tract disease P00.1
      uterine contraction (abnormal) P03.6
    meconium peritonitis P78.0
    medication (legal) (maternal use)
        (prescribed) P04.19
    membrane abnormalities P02.9
      specified NEC P02.8
    membranitis P02.78
    methamphetamine(s) P04.49
    mixed metabolic and respiratory acidosis
        P84
    neonatal abstinence syndrome P96.1
    noxious substances transmitted via
        placenta or breast milk P04.9
      cannabis P04.81
      specified NEC P04.89
    nutritional supplements P04.5
    placenta previa P02.0
    placental
      abnormality (functional)
          (morphological) P02.20
        specified NEC P02.29
      dysfunction P02.29
      infarction P02.29
      insufficiency P02.29
      separation NEC P02.1
      transfusion syndromes P02.3
    placentitis P02.78
    precipitate delivery P03.5
    prolapsed cord P02.4
    respiratory arrest P28.81
    slow intrauterine growth P05.9
    tobacco P04.2
    twin to twin transplacental transfusion P02.3
    umbilical cord (tightly) around neck P02.5
    umbilical cord condition P02.60
      short cord P02.69
      specified NEC P02.69
    uterine contractions (abnormal) P03.6
    vasa previa P02.69
      from intrauterine blood loss P50.0

Newborn *(Continued)*
  apnea P28.4
    obstructive P28.4
    primary P28.3
    sleep (central) (obstructive) (primary)
        P28.3
  born in hospital Z38.00
    by cesarean Z38.01
  born outside hospital Z38.1
  breast buds P96.89
  breast engorgement P83.4
  check-up —*see* Newborn, examination
  convulsion P90
  dehydration P74.1
  examination
    8 to 28 days old Z00.111
    under 8 days old Z00.110
  fever P81.9
    environmentally-induced P81.0
  hyperbilirubinemia P59.9
    of prematurity P59.0
  hypernatremia P74.21
  hyponatremia P74.22
  infection P39.9
    candidal P37.5
    specified NEC P39.8
    urinary tract P39.3
  jaundice P59.9
    due to
      breast milk inhibitor P59.3
      hepatocellular damage P59.20
        specified NEC P59.29
      preterm delivery P59.0
    of prematurity P59.0
    specified NEC P59.8
  late metabolic acidosis P74.0
  mastitis P39.0
    infective P39.0
    noninfective P83.4
  multiple born NEC Z38.8
    born in hospital Z38.68
      by cesarean Z38.69
    born outside hospital Z38.7
  omphalitis P38.9
    with mild hemorrhage P38.1
    without hemorrhage P38.9
  post-term P08.21
  prolonged gestation (over 42 completed
      weeks) P08.22
  quadruplet Z38.8
    born in hospital Z38.63
      by cesarean Z38.64
    born outside hospital Z38.7
  quintuplet Z38.8
    born in hospital Z38.65
      by cesarean Z38.66
    born outside hospital Z38.7
  seizure P90
  sepsis (congenital) P36.9
    due to
      anaerobes NEC P36.5
      Escherichia coli P36.4
      Staphylococcus P36.30
        aureus P36.2
        specified NEC P36.39
      Streptococcus P36.10
        group B P36.0
        specified NEC P36.19
    specified NEC P36.8
  triplet Z38.8
    born in hospital Z38.61
      by cesarean Z38.62
    born outside hospital Z38.7
  twin Z38.5
    born in hospital Z38.30
      by cesarean Z38.31
    born outside hospital Z38.4
  vomiting P92.09
    bilious P92.01
  weight check Z00.111
Newcastle conjunctivitis or disease B30.8

Nezelof's syndrome (pure alymphocytosis)
    D81.4
Niacin (amide) deficiency E52
Nicolas (-Durand)-Favre disease A55
Nicotine —*see* Tobacco
Nicotinic acid deficiency E52
Niemann-Pick disease or syndrome E75.249
  specified NEC E75.248
  type
    A E75.240
    B E75.241
    C E75.242
    D E75.243
Night
  blindness —*see* Blindness, night
  sweats R61
  terrors (child) F51.4
Nightmares (REM sleep type) F51.5
NIHSS (National Institutes of Health Stroke
    Scale) score R29.7-●
Nipple —*see* condition
Nisbet's chancre A57
Nishimoto (-Takeuchi) disease I67.5
Nitritoid crisis or reaction —*see* Crisis,
    nitritoid
Nitrosohemoglobinemia D74.8
Njovera A65
Nocardiosis, nocardiasis A43.9
  cutaneous A43.1
  lung A43.0
  pneumonia A43.0
  pulmonary A43.0
  specified site NEC A43.8
Nocturia R35.1
  psychogenic F45.8
Nocturnal —*see* condition
Nodal rhythm I49.8
Node(s) —*see also* Nodule
  Bouchard's (with arthropathy) M15.2
  Haygarth's M15.8
  Heberden's (with arthropathy) M15.1
  larynx J38.7
  lymph —*see* condition
  milker's B08.03
  Osler's I33.0
  Schmorl's —*see* Schmorl's disease
  singer's J38.2
  teacher's J38.2
  tuberculous —*see* Tuberculosis, lymph
      gland
  vocal cord J38.2
Nodule(s), nodular
  actinomycotic —*see* Actinomycosis
  breast NEC —*see also* Lump, breast
      N63.0
  colloid (cystic), thyroid E04.1
  cutaneous —*see* Swelling, localized
  endometrial (stromal) D26.1
  Haygarth's M15.8
  inflammatory —*see* Inflammation
  juxta-articular
    syphilitic A52.77
    yaws A66.7
  larynx J38.7
  lung, solitary (subsegmental branch of the
      bronchial tree) R91.1
    multiple R91.8
  milker's B08.03
  prostate N40.2
    with lower urinary tract symptoms (LUTS)
        N40.3
    without lower urinary tract symptoms
        (LUTS) N40.2
  pulmonary, solitary (subsegmental branch of
      the bronchial tree) R91.1
  retrocardiac R09.89
  rheumatoid M06.30
    ankle M06.37-●
    elbow M06.32-●
    foot joint M06.37-●
    hand joint M06.34-●

Nodule(s), nodular (Continued)
  rheumatoid (Continued)
    hip M06.35-●
    knee M06.36-●
    multiple site M06.39
    shoulder M06.31-●
    vertebra M06.38
    wrist M06.33-●
  scrotum (inflammatory) N49.2
  singer's J38.2
  solitary, lung (subsegmental branch of the
      bronchial tree) R91.1
    multiple R91.8
  subcutaneous —see Swelling, localized
  teacher's J38.2
  thyroid (cold) (gland) (nontoxic) E04.1
    with thyrotoxicosis E05.20
      with thyroid storm E05.21
    toxic or with hyperthyroidism E05.20
      with thyroid storm E05.21
  vocal cord J38.2
Noma (gangrenous) (hospital) (infective)
    A69.0
  auricle I96
  mouth A69.0
  pudendi N76.89
  vulvae N76.89
Nomad, nomadism Z59.0
NOMID (neonatal onset multisystemic
    inflammatory disorder) M04.2
Nonadherence to medical treatment Z91.19
Nonautoimmune hemolytic anemia D59.4
  drug-induced D59.2
Nonclosure —see also Imperfect, closure
  ductus arteriosus (Botallo's) Q25.0
  foramen
    botalli Q21.1
    ovale Q21.1
Noncompliance Z91.19
  with
    dialysis Z91.15
    dietary regimen Z91.11
    medical treatment Z91.19
    medication regimen NEC Z91.14
      underdosing —see also Table of Drugs
          and Chemicals, categories T36-T50,
          with final character 6 Z91.14
        intentional NEC Z91.128
          due to financial hardship of patient
              Z91.120
        unintentional NEC Z91.138
          due to patient's age related debility
              Z91.130
    renal dialysis Z91.15
Nondescent (congenital) —see also Malposition,
    congenital
  cecum Q43.3
  colon Q43.3

Nondescent (Continued)
  testicle Q53.9
    bilateral Q53.20
      abdominal Q53.211
      perineal Q53.22
    unilateral Q53.10
      abdominal Q53.111
      perineal Q53.12
Nondevelopment
  brain Q02
    part of Q04.3
  heart Q24.8
  organ or site, congenital NEC —see
      Hypoplasia
Nonengagement
  head NEC O32.4
    in labor, causing obstructed labor
        O64.8
Nonexanthematous tick fever A93.2
Nonexpansion, lung (newborn) P28.0
Nonfunctioning
  cystic duct —see also Disease, gallbladder
      K82.8
  gallbladder —see also Disease, gallbladder
      K82.8
  kidney N28.9
  labyrinth —see subcategory H83.2
Non-Hodgkin lymphoma NEC —see
    Lymphoma, non-Hodgkin
Nonimplantation, ovum N97.2
Noninsufflation, fallopian tube N97.1
Non-ketotic hyperglycinemia E72.51
Nonne-Milroy syndrome Q82.0
Nonovulation N97.0
Non-palpable testicle(s)
  bilateral R39.84
  unilateral R39.83
Nonpatent fallopian tube N97.1
Nonpneumatization, lung NEC P28.0
Nonrotation —see Malrotation
Nonsecretion, urine —see Anuria
Nonunion
  fracture —see Fracture, by site
  joint, following fusion or arthrodesis
      M96.0
  organ or site, congenital NEC —see
      Imperfect, closure
  symphysis pubis, congenital Q74.2
Nonvisualization, gallbladder R93.2
Nonvital, nonvitalized tooth K04.99
Non-working side interference
    M26.56
Noonan's syndrome Q87.19
Normocytic anemia (infectional) due to
    blood loss (chronic) D50.0
  acute D62
Norrie's disease (congenital) Q15.8
North American blastomycosis B40.9

Norwegian itch B86
Nose, nasal —see condition
Nosebleed R04.0
Nose-picking F98.8
Nosomania F45.21
Nosophobia F45.22
Nostalgia F43.20
Notch of iris Q13.2
Notching nose, congenital (tip)
    Q30.2
Nothnagel's
  syndrome —see Strabismus, paralytic, third
      nerve
  vasomotor acroparesthesia I73.89
Novy's relapsing fever A68.9
  louse-borne A68.0
  tick-borne A68.1
Noxious
  foodstuffs, poisoning by —see Poisoning,
      food, noxious, plant
  substances transmitted through placenta or
      breast milk P04.9
Nucleus pulposus —see condition
Numbness R20.0
Nuns' knee —see Bursitis, prepatellar
Nursemaid's elbow S53.03-●
Nutcracker esophagus K22.4
Nutmeg liver K76.1
Nutrient element deficiency E61.9
  specified NEC E61.8
Nutrition deficient or insufficient —see also
    Malnutrition E46
  due to
    insufficient food T73.0
    lack of
      care (child) T76.02
        adult T76.01
      food T73.0
Nutritional stunting E45
Nyctalopia (night blindness) —see Blindness,
    night
Nycturia R35.1
  psychogenic F45.8
Nymphomania F52.8
Nystagmus H55.00
  benign paroxysmal —see Vertigo, benign
      paroxysmal
  central positional H81.4
  congenital H55.01
  dissociated H55.04
  latent H55.02
  miners' H55.09
  positional
    benign paroxysmal H81.4
    central H81.4
  specified form NEC H55.09
  visual deprivation H55.03

▶ New ➠ Revised ~~deleted~~ Deleted ● Use Additional Character(s)

O

Obermeyer's relapsing fever (European)
A68.0
Obesity E66.9
with alveolar hypoventilation E66.2
adrenal E27.8
complicating
childbirth O99.214
pregnancy O99.21-●
puerperium O99.215
constitutional E66.8
dietary counseling and surveillance Z71.3
drug-induced E66.1
due to
drug E66.1
excess calories E66.09
morbid E66.01
severe E66.01
endocrine E66.8
endogenous E66.8
exogenous E66.09
familial E66.8
glandular E66.8
hypothyroid —see Hypothyroidism
hypoventilation syndrome (OHS)
E66.2
morbid E66.01
with
alveolar hypoventilation E66.2
obesity hypoventilation syndrome
(OHS) E66.2
due to excess calories E66.01
nutritional E66.09
pituitary E23.6
severe E66.01
specified type NEC E66.8
Oblique —see condition
Obliteration
appendix (lumen) K38.8
artery I77.1
bile duct (noncalculous) K83.1
common duct (noncalculous) K83.1
cystic duct —see Obstruction, gallbladder
disease, arteriolar I77.1
endometrium N85.8
eye, anterior chamber —see Disorder, globe,
hypotony
fallopian tube N97.1
lymphatic vessel I89.0
due to mastectomy I97.2
organ or site, congenital NEC —see Atresia,
by site
ureter N13.5
with infection N13.6
urethra —see Stricture, urethra
vein I87.8
vestibule (oral) K08.89
Observation (following) (for) (without need for
further medical care) Z04.9
accident NEC Z04.3
at work Z04.2
transport Z04.1
adverse effect of drug Z03.6
alleged rape or sexual assault (victim),
ruled out
adult Z04.41
child Z04.42
criminal assault Z04.89
development state
adolescent Z00.3
period of rapid growth in childhood Z00.2
puberty Z00.3
disease, specified NEC Z03.89
following work accident Z04.2
forced sexual exploitation Z04.81
forced labor exploitation Z04.82
growth and development state —see
Observation, development state
injuries (accidental) NEC —see also
Observation, accident

Observation (Continued)
newborn (for)
suspected condition, related to exposure
from the mother or birth process —
see Newborn, affected by, maternal
ruled out Z05.9
cardiac Z05.0
connective tissue Z05.73
gastrointestinal Z05.5
genetic Z05.41
genitourinary Z05.6
immunologic Z05.43
infectious Z05.1
metabolic Z05.42
musculoskeletal Z05.72
neurological Z05.2
respiratory Z05.3
skin and subcutaneous tissue Z05.71
specified condition NEC Z05.8
postpartum
immediately after delivery Z39.0
routine follow-up Z39.2
pregnancy (normal) (without complication)
Z34.9-●
high risk O09.9-●
suicide attempt, alleged NEC Z03.89
self-poisoning Z03.6
suspected, ruled out —see also Suspected
condition, ruled out
abuse, physical
adult Z04.71
child Z04.72
accident at work Z04.2
adult battering victim Z04.71
child battering victim Z04.72
condition NEC Z03.89
newborn —see also Observation,
newborn (for), suspected condition,
ruled out Z05.9
drug poisoning or adverse effect Z03.6
exposure (to)
anthrax Z03.810
biological agent NEC Z03.818
▶foreign body
▶aspirated (inhaled) Z03.822
▶ingested Z03.821
▶inserted (injected), in (eye) (orifice)
(skin) Z03.823
inflicted injury NEC Z04.89
suicide attempt, alleged Z03.89
self-poisoning Z03.6
toxic effects from ingested substance (drug)
(poison) Z03.6
toxic effects from ingested substance (drug)
(poison) Z03.6
Obsession, obsessional state F42.8
mixed thoughts and acts F42.2
Obsessive-compulsive neurosis or reaction
F42.8
Obstetric embolism, septic —see Embolism,
obstetric, septic
Obstetrical trauma (complicating delivery)
O71.9
with or following ectopic or molar pregnancy
O08.6
specified type NEC O71.89
Obstipation —see Constipation
Obstruction, obstructed, obstructive
airway J98.8
with
allergic alveolitis J67.9
asthma J45.909
with
exacerbation (acute) J45.901
status asthmaticus J45.902
bronchiectasis J47.9
with
exacerbation (acute) J47.1
lower respiratory infection J47.0
bronchitis (chronic) J44.9
emphysema J43.9

Obstruction, obstructed, obstructive
(Continued)
airway (Continued)
chronic J44.9
with
allergic alveolitis —see Pneumonitis,
hypersensitivity
bronchiectasis J47.9
with
exacerbation (acute) J47.1
lower respiratory infection J47.0
due to
foreign body —see Foreign body, by site,
causing asphyxia
inhalation of fumes or vapors J68.9
laryngospasm J38.5
ampulla of Vater K83.1
aortic (heart) (valve) —see Stenosis, aortic
aortoiliac I74.09
aqueduct of Sylvius G91.1
congenital Q03.0
with spina bifida —see Spina bifida, by
site, with hydrocephalus
Arnold-Chiari —see Arnold-Chiari disease
artery (see also Atherosclerosis, artery) I70.9
basilar (complete) (partial) —see Occlusion,
artery, basilar
carotid (complete) (partial) —see Occlusion,
artery, carotid
cerebellar —see Occlusion, artery, cerebellar
cerebral (anterior) (middle) (posterior) —
see Occlusion, artery, cerebral
precerebral —see Occlusion, artery,
precerebral
renal N28.0
retinal NEC —see Occlusion, artery, retina
stent —see Restenosis, stent
vertebral (complete) (partial) —see
Occlusion, artery, vertebral
band (intestinal) —see also Obstruction,
intestine, specified NEC K56.699
bile duct or passage (common) (hepatic)
(noncalculous) K83.1
with calculus K80.51
congenital (causing jaundice) Q44.3
biliary (duct) (tract) K83.1
gallbladder K82.0
bladder-neck (acquired) N32.0
congenital Q64.31
due to hyperplasia (hypertrophy) of
prostate —see Hyperplasia, prostate
bowel —see Obstruction, intestine
bronchus J98.09
canal, ear —see Stenosis, external ear canal
cardia K22.2
caval veins (inferior) (superior) I87.1
cecum —see Obstruction, intestine
circulatory I99.8
colon —see Obstruction, intestine
common duct (noncalculous) K83.1
coronary (artery) —see Occlusion, coronary
cystic duct —see also Obstruction, gallbladder
with calculus K80.21
device, implant or graft —see also
Complications, by site and type,
mechanical T85.698
arterial graft NEC —see Complication,
cardiovascular device, mechanical,
vascular
catheter NEC T85.628
cystostomy T83.090
dialysis (renal) T82.49
intraperitoneal T85.691
Hopkins T83.098
ileostomy T83.098
infusion NEC T82.594
spinal (epidural) (subdural) T85.690
nephrostomy T83.092
urethral indwelling T83.091
urinary T83.098
urostomy T83.098

Obstruction, obstructed, obstructive
(Continued)
  device, implant or graft *(Continued)*
    due to infection T85.79
    gastrointestinal —*see* Complications,
      prosthetic device, mechanical,
      gastrointestinal device
    genital NEC T83.498
      intrauterine contraceptive device T83.39
      penile prosthesis (cylinder) (implanted)
        (pump) (resevoir) T83.490
      testicular prosthesis T83.491
    heart NEC —*see* Complication,
      cardiovascular device, mechanical
    joint prosthesis —*see* Complications, joint
      prosthesis, mechanical, specified NEC,
      by site
    orthopedic NEC —*see* Complication,
      orthopedic, device, mechanical
    specified NEC T85.628
    urinary NEC —*see also* Complication,
      genitourinary, device, urinary,
      mechanical
      graft T83.29
    vascular NEC —*see* Complication,
      cardiovascular device, mechanical
    ventricular intracranial shunt T85.09
  due to foreign body accidentally left in
    operative wound T81.529
  duodenum K31.5
  ejaculatory duct N50.89
  esophagus K22.2
  eustachian tube (complete) (partial) H68.10-●
    cartilagenous (extrinsic) H68.13-●
      intrinsic H68.12-●
    osseous H68.11-●
  fallopian tube (bilateral) N97.1
  fecal K56.41
    with hernia —*see* Hernia, by site, with
      obstruction
  foramen of Monro (congenital) Q03.8
    with spina bifida —*see* Spina bifida,
      by site, with hydrocephalus
  foreign body —*see* Foreign body
  gallbladder K82.0
    with calculus, stones K80.21
    congenital Q44.1
  gastric outlet K31.1
  gastrointestinal —*see* Obstruction, intestine
  hepatic K76.89
    duct (noncalculous) K83.1
  hepatobiliary K83.1
  ileum —*see* Obstruction, intestine
  iliofemoral (artery) I74.5
  intestine K56.609
    complete K56.601
    incomplete K56.600
    partial K56.600
    with
      adhesions (intestinal) (peritoneal) K56.50
        complete K56.52
        incomplete K56.51
        partial K56.51
    adynamic K56.0
    by gallstone K56.3
    congenital (small) Q41.9
      large Q42.9
        specified part NEC Q42.8
    neurogenic K56.0
      Hirschsprung's disease or megacolon
        Q43.1
    newborn P76.9
      due to
        fecaliths P76.8
        inspissated milk P76.2
        meconium (plug) P76.0
          in mucoviscidosis E84.11
      specified NEC P76.8
    postoperative K91.30
      complete K91.32
      incomplete K91.31
      partial K91.31

Obstruction, obstructed, obstructive
(Continued)
  intestine *(Continued)*
    reflex K56.0
    specified NEC K56.699
      complete K56.691
      incomplete K56.690
      partial K56.690
    volvulus K56.2
  intracardiac ball valve prosthesis T82.09
  jejunum —*see* Obstruction, intestine
  joint prosthesis —*see* Complications, joint
    prosthesis, mechanical, specified NEC,
    by site
  kidney (calices) N28.89
  labor —*see* Delivery
  lacrimal (passages) (duct)
    by
      dacryolith —*see* Dacryolith
      stenosis —*see* Stenosis, lacrimal
    congenital Q10.5
    neonatal H04.53-●
  lacrimonasal duct —*see* Obstruction, lacrimal
  lacteal, with steatorrhea K90.2
  laryngitis —*see* Laryngitis
  larynx NEC J38.6
    congenital Q31.8
  lung J98.4
    disease, chronic J44.9
  lymphatic I89.0
  meconium (plug)
    newborn P76.0
      due to fecaliths P76.0
      in mucoviscidosis E84.11
  mitral —*see* Stenosis, mitral
  nasal J34.89
  nasolacrimal duct —*see also* Obstruction,
    lacrimal
    congenital Q10.5
  nasopharynx J39.2
  nose J34.89
  organ or site, congenital NEC —*see* Atresia,
    by site
  pancreatic duct K86.89
  parotid duct or gland K11.8
  pelviureteral junction N13.5
    with hydronephrosis N13.0
    congenital Q62.39
  pharynx J39.2
  portal (circulation) (vein) I81
  prostate —*see also* Hyperplasia, prostate
    valve (urinary) N32.0
  pulmonary valve (heart) I37.0
  pyelonephritis (chronic) N11.1
  pylorus
    adult K31.1
    congenital or infantile Q40.0
  rectosigmoid —*see* Obstruction,
    intestine
  rectum K62.4
  renal N28.89
    outflow N13.8
    pelvis, congenital Q62.39
  respiratory J98.8
    chronic J44.9
  retinal (vessels) H34.9
  salivary duct (any) K11.8
    with calculus K11.5
  sigmoid —*see* Obstruction, intestine
  sinus (accessory) (nasal) J34.89
  Stensen's duct K11.8
  stomach NEC K31.89
    acute K31.0
    congenital Q40.2
    due to pylorospasm K31.3
  submandibular duct K11.8
  submaxillary gland K11.8
    with calculus K11.5
  thoracic duct I89.0
  thrombotic —*see* Thrombosis
  trachea J39.8

Obstruction, obstructed, obstructive
(Continued)
  tracheostomy airway J95.03
  tricuspid (valve) —*see* Stenosis, tricuspid
  upper respiratory, congenital Q34.8
  ureter (functional) (pelvic junction) NEC N13.5
    with
      hydronephrosis N13.1
        with infection N13.6
      pyelonephritis (chronic) N11.1
    congenital Q62.39
    due to calculus —*see* Calculus, ureter
  urethra NEC N36.8
    congenital Q64.39
  urinary (moderate) N13.9
    due to hyperplasia (hypertrophy) of
      prostate —*see* Hyperplasia, prostate
    organ or tract (lower) N13.9
    prostatic valve N32.0
    specified NEC N13.8
  uropathy N13.9
  uterus N85.8
  vagina N89.5
  valvular —*see* Endocarditis
  vein, venous I87.1
    caval (inferior) (superior) I87.1
    thrombotic —*see* Thrombosis
    vena cava (inferior) (superior) I87.1
  vesical NEC N32.0
  vesicourethral orifice N32.0
    congenital Q64.31
  vessel NEC I99.8
    stent —*see* Restenosis, stent
Obturator —*see* condition
Occlusal wear, teeth K03.0
Occlusio pupillae —*see* Membrane, pupillary
Occlusion, occluded
  anus K62.4
    congenital Q42.3
      with fistula Q42.2
  aortoiliac (chronic) I74.09
  aqueduct of Sylvius G91.1
    congenital Q03.0
      with spina bifida —*see* Spina bifida, by
        site, with hydrocephalus
  artery —*see also* Atherosclerosis, artery I70.9
    auditory, internal I65.8
    basilar I65.1
      with
        infarction I63.22
        due to
          embolism I63.12
          thrombosis I63.02
    brain or cerebral I66.9
      with infarction (due to) I63.5-●
        embolism I63.4-●
        thrombosis I63.3-●
    carotid I65.2-●
      with
        infarction I63.23-●
        due to
          embolism I63.13-●
          thrombosis I63.03-●
    cerebellar (anterior inferior) (posterior
      inferior) (superior) I66.3
      with infarction I63.54-●
        due to
          embolism I63.44-●
          thrombosis I63.34-●
    cerebral I66.9
      with infarction I63.50
        due to
          embolism I63.40
            specified NEC I63.49
          thrombosis I63.30
            specified NEC I63.39
      anterior I66.1-●
        with infarction I63.52-●
        due to
          embolism I63.42-●
          thrombosis I63.32-●

▶ New　➡ Revised　~~deleted~~ Deleted　● Use Additional Character(s)

Occlusion, occluded (Continued)
  artery (Continued)
    cerebral (Continued)
      middle I66.0-●
        with infarction I63.51-●
          due to
            embolism I63.41-●
            thrombosis I63.31-●
      posterior I66.2-●
        with infarction I63.53-●
          due to
            embolism I63.43-●
            thrombosis I63.33-●
      specified NEC I66.8
        with infarction I63.59
          due to
            embolism I63.4-●
            thrombosis I63.3-●
    choroidal (anterior) —see Occlusion,
        artery, cerebral, specified NEC
    communicating posterior —see Occlusion,
        artery, precerebral, specified NEC
    complete
      coronary I25.82
      extremities I70.92
    coronary (acute) (thrombotic) (without
        myocardial infarction) I24.0
      with myocardial infarction —see
          Infarction, myocardium
      chronic total I25.82
      complete I25.82
      healed or old I25.2
      total (chronic) I25.82
    hypophyseal —see Occlusion, artery,
        precerebral, specified NEC
    iliac I74.5
    lower extremities due to stenosis or
        stricture I77.1
    mesenteric (embolic) (thrombotic) —see also
        Infarct, intestine K55.069
    perforating —see Occlusion, artery,
        cerebral, specified NEC
    peripheral I77.9
      thrombotic or embolic I74.4
    pontine —see Occlusion, artery, precerebral,
        specified NEC
    precerebral I65.9
      with infarction I63.20
        due to
          embolism I63.10
            specified NEC I63.19
          thrombosis I63.00
            specified NEC I63.09
        specified NEC I63.29
      basilar —see Occlusion, artery, basilar
      carotid —see Occlusion, artery, carotid
      puerperal O88.23
      specified NEC I65.8
        with infarction I63.29
          due to
            embolism I63.19
            thrombosis I63.09
      vertebral —see Occlusion, artery,
          vertebral
    renal N28.0
    retinal
      branch H34.23-●
      central H34.1-●
      partial H34.21-●
      transient H34.0-●
    spinal —see Occlusion, artery, precerebral,
        vertebral
    total (chronic)
      coronary I25.82
      extremities I70.92
    vertebral I65.0-●
      with
        infarction I63.21-●
          due to
            embolism I63.11-●
            thrombosis I63.01-●

Occlusion, occluded (Continued)
  basilar artery —see Occlusion, artery, basilar
  bile duct (common) (hepatic) (noncalculous)
      K83.1
  bowel —see Obstruction, intestine
  carotid (artery) (common) (internal) —see
      Occlusion, artery, carotid
  centric (of teeth) M26.59
    maximum intercuspation discrepancy
        M26.55
  cerebellar (artery) —see Occlusion, artery,
      cerebellar
  cerebral (artery) —see Occlusion, artery,
      cerebral
  cerebrovascular —see also Occlusion, artery,
      cerebral
    with infarction I63.5-●
  cervical canal —see Stricture, cervix
  cervix (uteri) —see Stricture, cervix
  choanal Q30.0
  choroidal (artery) —see Occlusion, artery,
      precerebral, specified NEC
  colon —see Obstruction, intestine
  communicating posterior artery —see
      Occlusion, artery, precerebral, specified
      NEC
  coronary (artery) (vein) (thrombotic) —see
      also Infarct, myocardium
    chronic total I25.82
    healed or old I25.2
    not resulting in infarction I24.0
    total (chronic) I25.82
  cystic duct —see Obstruction, gallbladder
  embolic —see Embolism
  fallopian tube N97.1
    congenital Q50.6
  gallbladder —see also Obstruction,
      gallbladder
    congenital (causing jaundice) Q44.1
  gingiva, traumatic K06.2
  hymen N89.6
    congenital Q52.3
  hypophyseal (artery) —see Occlusion, artery,
      precerebral, specified NEC
  iliac artery I74.5
  intestine —see Obstruction, intestine
  lacrimal passages —see Obstruction, lacrimal
  lung J98.4
  lymph or lymphatic channel I89.0
  mammary duct N64.89
  mesenteric artery (embolic) (thrombotic) —
      see also Infarct, intestine K55.069
  nose J34.89
    congenital Q30.0
  organ or site, congenital NEC —see Atresia,
      by site
  oviduct N97.1
    congenital Q50.6
  peripheral arteries
    due to stricture or stenosis I77.1
    upper extremity I74.2
  pontine (artery) —see Occlusion, artery,
      precerebral, specified NEC
  posterior lingual, of mandibular teeth M26.29
  precerebral artery —see Occlusion, artery,
      precerebral
  punctum lacrimale —see Obstruction,
      lacrimal
  pupil —see Membrane, pupillary
  pylorus, adult —see also Stricture, pylorus
      K31.1
  renal artery N28.0
  retina, retinal
    artery —see Occlusion, artery, retinal
    vein (central) H34.81-●
      engorgement H34.82-●
      tributary H34.83-●
    vessels H34.9
  spinal artery —see Occlusion, artery,
      precerebral, vertebral
  teeth (mandibular) (posterior lingual) M26.29

Occlusion, occluded (Continued)
  thoracic duct I89.0
  thrombotic —see Thrombosis, artery
  traumatic
    edentulous (alveolar) ridge K06.2
    gingiva K06.2
    periodontal K05.5
  tubal N97.1
  ureter (complete) (partial) N13.5
    congenital Q62.10
  ureteropelvic junction N13.5
    congenital Q62.11
  ureterovesical orifice N13.5
    congenital Q62.12
  urethra —see Stricture, urethra
  uterus N85.8
  vagina N89.5
  vascular NEC I99.8
  vein —see Thrombosis
    retinal —see Occlusion, retinal, vein
  vena cava (inferior) (superior) —see
      Embolism, vena cava
  ventricle (brain) NEC G91.1
  vertebral (artery) —see Occlusion, artery,
      vertebral
  vessel (blood) I99.8
  vulva N90.5
Occult
  blood in feces (stools) R19.5
Occupational
  problems NEC Z56.89
Ochlophobia —see Agoraphobia
Ochronosis (endogenous) E70.29
Ocular muscle —see condition
Oculogyric crisis or disturbance H51.8
  psychogenic F45.8
Oculomotor syndrome H51.9
Oculopathy
  syphilitic NEC A52.71
    congenital
      early A50.01
      late A50.30
    early (secondary) A51.43
    late A52.71
Oddi's sphincter spasm K83.4
Odontalgia K08.89
Odontoameloblastoma —see Cyst, calcifying
    odontogenic
Odontoclasia K03.89
Odontodysplasia, regional K00.4
Odontogenesis imperfecta K00.5
Odontoma (ameloblastic) (complex)
    (compound) (fibroameloblastic) —see Cyst,
    calcifying odontogenic
Odontomyelitis (closed) (open) K04.01
  irreversible K04.02
  reversible K04.01
Odontorrhagia K08.89
Odontosarcoma, ameloblastic C41.1
  upper jaw (bone) C41.0
Oestriasis —see Myiasis
Oguchi's disease H53.63
Ohara's disease —see Tularemia
OHS (obesity hypoventilation syndrome) E66.2

Oidiomycosis —see Candidiasis
Oidium albicans infection —see Candidiasis
Old (previous) myocardial infarction
    I25.2
Old age (without mention of debility) R54-●
  dementia F03
Olfactory —see condition
Oligemia —see Anemia
Oligoastrocytoma
  specified site —see Neoplasm, malignant,
      by site
  unspecified site C71.9
Oligocythemia D64.9
Oligodendroblastoma
  specified site —see Neoplasm, malignant,
  unspecified site C71.9

Oligodendroglioma
  anaplastic type
    specified site —see Neoplasm, malignant,
        by site
    unspecified site C71.9
  specified site —see Neoplasm, malignant,
      by site
  unspecified site C71.9
Oligodontia —see Anodontia
Oligoencephalon Q02
Oligohidrosis L74.4
Oligohydramnios O41.0-●
Oligohydrosis L74.4
Oligomenorrhea N91.5
  primary N91.3
  secondary N91.4
Oligophrenia —see also Disability, intellectual
  phenylpyruvic E70.0
Oligospermia N46.11
  due to
    drug therapy N46.121
    efferent duct obstruction N46.123
    infection N46.122
    radiation N46.124
    specified cause NEC N46.129
    systemic disease N46.125
Oligotrichia —see Alopecia
Oliguria R34
  with, complicating or following ectopic or
      molar pregnancy O08.4
  postprocedural N99.0
Ollier's disease Q78.4
Omenotocele —see Hernia, abdomen, specified
      site NEC
Omentitis —see Peritonitis
Omentum, omental —see condition
Omphalitis (congenital) (newborn) P38.9
  with mild hemorrhage P38.1
  without hemorrhage P38.9
  not of newborn L08.82
  tetanus A33
Omphalocele Q79.2
Omphalomesenteric duct, persistent Q43.0
Omphalorrhagia, newborn P51.9
Omsk hemorrhagic fever A98.1
Onanism (excessive) F98.8
Onchocerciasis, onchocercosis B73.1
  with
    eye disease B73.00
      endophthalmitis B73.01
      eyelid B73.09
      glaucoma B73.02
      specified NEC B73.09
    eye NEC B73.00
    eyelid B73.09
Oncocytoma —see Neoplasm, benign, by site
Oncovirus, as cause of disease classified
    elsewhere B97.32
Ondine's curse —see Apnea, sleep
Oneirophrenia F23
Onychauxis L60.2
  congenital Q84.5
Onychia —see also Cellulitis, digit
  with lymphangitis —see Lymphangitis, acute,
      digit
  candidal B37.2
  dermatophytic B35.1
Onychitis —see also Cellulitis, digit
  with lymphangitis —see Lymphangitis, acute,
      digit
Onychocryptosis L60.0
Onychodystrophy L60.3
  congenital Q84.6
Onychogryphosis, onychogryposis L60.2
Onycholysis L60.1
Onychomadesis L60.8
Onychomalacia L60.3
Onychomycosis (finger) (toe) B35.1
Onycho-osteodysplasia Q87.2
Onychophagia F98.8
Onychophosis L60.8

Onychoptosis L60.8
Onychorrhexis L60.3
  congenital Q84.6
Onychoschizia L60.3
Onyxis (finger) (toe) L60.0
Onyxitis —see also Cellulitis, digit
  with lymphangitis —see Lymphangitis, acute,
      digit
Oophoritis (cystic) (infectional) (interstitial)
    N70.92
  with salpingitis N70.93
  acute N70.02
    with salpingitis N70.03
  chronic N70.12
    with salpingitis N70.13
  complicating abortion —see Abortion, by
      type, complicated by, oophoritis
Oophorocele N83.4-●
Opacity, opacities
  cornea H17.-●
    central H17.1-●
    congenital Q13.3
    degenerative —see Degeneration, cornea
    hereditary —see Dystrophy, cornea
    inflammatory —see Keratitis
    minor H17.81-●
    peripheral H17.82-●
    sequelae of trachoma (healed) B94.0
    specified NEC H17.89
  enamel (teeth) (fluoride) (nonfluoride) K00.3
  lens —see Cataract
  snowball —see Deposit, crystalline
  vitreous (humor) NEC H43.39-●
    congenital Q14.0
    membranes and strands H43.31-●
Opalescent dentin (hereditary) K00.5
Open, opening
  abnormal, organ or site, congenital —see
      Imperfect, closure
  angle with
    borderline
      findings
        high risk H40.02-●
        low risk H40.01-●
      intraocular pressure H40.00-●
    cupping of discs H40.01-●
    glaucoma (primary) —see Glaucoma, open
        angle
  bite
    anterior M26.220
    posterior M26.221
  false —see Imperfect, closure
  margin on tooth restoration K08.51
  restoration margins of tooth K08.51
  wound —see Wound, open
Operational fatigue F48.8
Operative —see condition
Operculitis —see Periodontitis
Operculum —see Break, retina
Ophiasis L63.2
Ophthalmia —see also Conjunctivitis H10.9
  actinic rays —see Photokeratitis
  allergic (acute) —see Conjunctivitis, acute,
      atopic
  blennorrhagic (gonococcal) (neonatorum)
      A54.31
  diphtheritic A36.86
  Egyptian A71.1
  electrica —see Photokeratitis
  gonococcal (neonatorum) A54.31
  metastatic —see Endophthalmitis, purulent
  migraine —see Migraine, ophthalmoplegic
  neonatorum, newborn P39.1
    gonococcal A54.31
  nodosa H16.24-●
  purulent —see Conjunctivitis, acute,
      mucopurulent
  spring —see Conjunctivitis, acute, atopic
  sympathetic —see Uveitis, sympathetic
Ophthalmitis —see Ophthalmia
Ophthalmocele (congenital) Q15.8

Ophthalmoneuromyelitis G36.0
Ophthalmoplegia —see also Strabismus, paralytic
  anterior internuclear —see Ophthalmoplegia,
      internuclear
  ataxia-areflexia G61.0
  diabetic —see E08-E13 with .39
  exophthalmic E05.00
    with thyroid storm E05.01
  external H49.88-●
    progressive H49.4-●
      with pigmentary retinopathy —see
          Kearns-Sayre syndrome
    total H49.3-●
  internal (complete) (total) H52.51-●
  internuclear H51.2-●
  migraine —see Migraine, ophthalmoplegic
  Parinaud's H49.88-●
  progressive external —see Ophthalmoplegia,
      external, progressive
  supranuclear, progressive G23.1
  total (external) —see Ophthalmoplegia,
      external, total
Opioid(s)
  abuse —see Abuse, drug, opioids
  dependence —see Dependence, drug, opioids
  induced, without use disorder
    anxiety disorder F11.988
    delirium F11.921
    depressive disorder F11.94
    sexual dysfunction F11.981
    sleep disorder F11.982
Opisthognathism M26.09
Opisthorchiasis (felineus) (viverrini) B66.0
Opitz' disease D73.2
Opiumism —see Dependence, drug, opioid
Oppenheim's disease G70.2
Oppenheim-Urbach disease (necrobiosis
    lipoidica diabeticorum) —see E08-E13 with
    .620
Optic nerve —see condition
Orbit —see condition
Orchioblastoma C62.9-●
Orchitis (gangrenous) (nonspecific) (septic)
    (suppurative) N45.2
  blennorrhagic (gonococcal) (acute) (chronic)
      A54.23
  chlamydial A56.19
  filarial —see also Infestation, filarial B74.9
      [N51]
  gonococcal (acute) (chronic) A54.23
  mumps B26.0
  syphilitic A52.76
  tuberculous A18.15
Orf (virus disease) B08.02
Organic —see also condition
  brain syndrome F09
  heart —see Disease, heart
  mental disorder F09
  psychosis F09
Orgasm
  anejaculatory N53.13
Oriental
  bilharziasis B65.2
  schistosomiasis B65.2
Orifice —see condition
Origin of both great vessels from right
    ventricle Q20.1
Ormond's disease (with ureteral obstruction)
    N13.5
  with infection N13.6
Ornithine metabolism disorder E72.4
Ornithinemia (Type I) (Type II) E72.4
Ornithosis A70
Orotaciduria, oroticaciduria (congenital)
    (hereditary) (pyrimidine deficiency) E79.8
  anemia D53.0
Orthodontics
  adjustment Z46.4
  fitting Z46.4
Orthopnea R06.01
Orthopoxvirus B08.09

▶ New   ➡ Revised   ~~deleted~~ Deleted   ● Use Additional Character(s)

Os, uterus —*see* condition
⮕Osgood-Schlatter disease or osteochondrosis M92.52-●
Osler (-Weber)-Rendu disease I78.0
Osler's nodes I33.0
Osmidrosis L75.0
Osseous —*see* condition
Ossification
  artery —*see* Arteriosclerosis
  auricle (ear) —*see* Disorder, pinna, specified type NEC
  bronchial J98.09
  cardiac —*see* Degeneration, myocardial
  cartilage (senile) —*see* Disorder, cartilage, specified type NEC
  coronary (artery) —*see* Disease, heart, ischemic, atherosclerotic
  diaphragm J98.6
  ear, middle —*see* Otosclerosis
⮕falx cerebri G96.198
  fontanel, premature Q75.0
  heart —*see also* Degeneration, myocardial
    valve —*see* Endocarditis
  larynx J38.7
  ligament —*see* Disorder, tendon, specified type NEC
    posterior longitudinal —*see* Spondylopathy, specified NEC
⮕meninges (cerebral) (spinal) G96.198
  multiple, eccentric centers —*see* Disorder, bone, development or growth
  muscle —*see also* Calcification, muscle
    due to burns —*see* Myositis, ossificans, in, burns
    paralytic —*see* Myositis, ossificans, in, quadriplegia
    progressive —*see* Myositis, ossificans, progressiva
    specified NEC M61.50
      ankle M61.57-●
      foot M61.57-●
      forearm M61.53-●
      hand M61.54-●
      lower leg M61.56-●
      multiple sites M61.59
      pelvic region M61.55-●
      shoulder region M61.51-●
      specified site NEC M61.58
      thigh M61.55-●
      upper arm M61.52-●
    traumatic —*see* Myositis, ossificans, traumatica
  myocardium, myocardial —*see* Degeneration, myocardial
  penis N48.89
  periarticular —*see* Disorder, joint, specified type NEC
  pinna —*see* Disorder, pinna, specified type NEC
  rider's bone —*see* Ossification, muscle, specified NEC
  sclera H15.89
  subperiosteal, post-traumatic M89.8X-●
  tendon —*see* Disorder, tendon, specified type NEC
  trachea J39.8
  tympanic membrane —*see* Disorder, tympanic membrane, specified NEC
  vitreous (humor) —*see* Deposit, crystalline
Osteitis —*see also* Osteomyelitis
  alveolar M27.3
  condensans M85.30
    ankle M85.37-●
    foot M85.37-●
    forearm M85.33-●
    hand M85.34-●
    lower leg M85.36-●
    multiple site M85.39
    neck M85.38
    rib M85.38
    shoulder M85.31-●

Osteitis *(Continued)*
  condensans *(Continued)*
    skull M85.38
    specified site NEC M85.38
    thigh M85.35-●
    toe M85.37-●
    upper arm M85.32-●
    vertebra M85.38
  deformans M88.9
    in (due to)
      malignant neoplasm of bone C41.9 [M90.60]
      neoplastic disease —*see also* Neoplasm D49.9 [M90.60]
        carpus D49.9 [M90.64-●]
        clavicle D49.9 [M90.61-●]
        femur D49.9 [M90.65-●]
        fibula D49.9 [M90.66-●]
        finger D49.9 [M90.64-●]
        humerus D49.9 [M90.62-●]
        ilium D49.9 [M90.65-●]
        ischium D49.9 [M90.65-●]
        metacarpus D49.9 [M90.64-●]
        metatarsus D49.9 [M90.67-●]
        multiple sites D49.9 [M90.69]
        neck D49.9 [M90.68]
        radius D49.9 [M90.63-●]
        rib D49.9 [M90.68]
        scapula D49.9 [M90.61-●]
        skull D49.9 [M90.68]
        tarsus D49.9 [M90.67-●]
        tibia D49.9 [M90.66-●]
        toe D49.9 [M90.67-●]
        ulna D49.9 [M90.63-●]
        vertebra D49.9 [M90.68]
    skull M88.0
    specified NEC —*see* Paget's disease, bone, by site
    vertebra M88.1
  due to yaws A66.6
  fibrosa NEC —*see* Cyst, bone, by site
    circumscripta —*see* Dysplasia, fibrous, bone NEC
    cystica (generalisata) E21.0
    disseminata Q78.1
    osteoplastica E21.0
  fragilitans Q78.0
  Garr's (sclerosing) —*see* Osteomyelitis, specified type NEC
  jaw (acute) (chronic) (lower) (suppurative) (upper) M27.2
  parathyroid E21.0
  petrous bone (acute) (chronic) —*see* Petrositis
  sclerotic, nonsuppurative —*see* Osteomyelitis, specified type NEC
  tuberculosa A18.09
    cystica D86.89
    multiplex cystoides D86.89
Osteoarthritis M19.90
  ankle M19.07-●
  elbow M19.02-●
  foot joint M19.07-●
  generalized M15.9
    erosive M15.4
    primary M15.0
    specified NEC M15.8
  hand joint M19.04-●
    first carpometacarpal joint M18.9-●
  hip M16.1-●
    bilateral M16.0
    due to hip dysplasia (unilateral) M16.3-●
      bilateral M16.2
  interphalangeal
    distal (Heberden) M15.1
    proximal (Bouchard) M15.2
  knee M17.1-●
    bilateral M17.0
  post-traumatic NEC M19.92
    ankle M19.17-●
    elbow M19.12-●
    foot joint M19.17-●

Osteoarthritis *(Continued)*
  post-traumatic NEC *(Continued)*
    hand joint M19.14-●
      first carpometacarpal joint M18.3-●
        bilateral M18.2
    hip M16.5-●
      bilateral M16.4
    knee M17.3-●
      bilateral M17.2
    shoulder M19.11-●
    ▶specified site NEC M19.19
    wrist M19.13-●
  primary M19.91
    ankle M19.07-●
    elbow M19.02-●
    foot joint M19.07-●
    hand joint M19.04-●
      first carpometacarpal joint M18.1-●
        bilateral M18.0
    hip M16.1-●
      bilateral M16.0
    knee M17.1-●
      bilateral M17.0
    multiple sites M89.49
    shoulder M19.01-●
    spine —*see* Spondylosis
    wrist M19.03-●
  secondary M19.93
    ankle M19.27-●
    elbow M19.22-●
    foot joint M19.27-●
    hand joint M19.24-●
      first carpometacarpal joint M18.5-●
        bilateral M18.4
    hip M16.7
      bilateral M16.6
    knee M17.5
      bilateral M17.4
    multiple M15.3
    shoulder M19.21-●
    ▶specified site NEC M19.29
    spine —*see* Spondylosis
    wrist M19.23-●
  shoulder M19.01-●
  ▶specified site NEC M19.09
  spine —*see* Spondylosis
  wrist M19.03-●
Osteoarthropathy (hypertrophic) M19.90
  ankle —*see* Osteoarthritis, primary, ankle
  elbow —*see* Osteoarthritis, primary, elbow
  foot joint —*see* Osteoarthritis, primary, foot
  hand joint —*see* Osteoarthritis, primary, hand joint
  knee joint —*see* Osteoarthritis, primary, knee
  multiple site —*see* Osteoarthritis, primary, multiple joint
  pulmonary —*see also* Osteoarthropathy, specified type NEC
    hypertrophic —*see* Osteoarthropathy, hypertrophic, specified type NEC
  secondary —*see* Osteoarthropathy, specified type NEC
  secondary hypertrophic —*see* Osteoarthropathy, specified type NEC
  shoulder —*see* Osteoarthritis, primary, shoulder
  specified joint NEC —*see* Osteoarthritis, primary, specified joint NEC
  specified type NEC M89.40
    carpus M89.44-●
    clavicle M89.41-●
    femur M89.45-●
    fibula M89.46-●
    finger M89.44-●
    humerus M89.42-●
    ilium M89.459
    ischium M89.459
    metacarpus M89.44-●
    metatarsus M89.47-●
    multiple sites M89.49
    neck M89.48
    radius M89.43-●

Osteoarthropathy (Continued)
   specified type NEC (Continued)
      rib M89.48
      scapula M89.41-●
      skull M89.48
      tarsus M89.47-●
      tibia M89.46-●
      toe M89.47-●
      ulna M89.43-●
      vertebra M89.48
   spine —see Spondylosis
   wrist —see Osteoarthritis, primary, wrist
Osteoarthrosis (degenerative) (hypertrophic)
   (joint) —see also Osteoarthritis
   deformans alkaptonurica E70.29 [M36.8]
   erosive M15.4
   generalized M15.9
      primary M15.0
   polyarticular M15.9
   spine —see Spondylosis
Osteoblastoma —see Neoplasm, bone, benign
   aggressive —see Neoplasm, bone, uncertain
      behavior
Osteochondroarthrosis deformans
   endemica —see Disease, Kaschin-Beck
Osteochondritis —see also Osteochondropathy,
   by site
   Brailsford's —see Osteochondrosis, juvenile,
      radius
   dissecans M93.20
      ankle M93.27-●
      elbow M93.22-●
      foot M93.27-●
      hand M93.24-●
      hip M93.25-●
      knee M93.26-●
      multiple sites M93.29
      shoulder joint M93.21-●
      specified site NEC M93.28
      wrist M93.23-●
   juvenile M92.9
      patellar —see Osteochondrosis, juvenile,
         patella
   syphilitic (congenital) (early) A50.02
      [M90.80]
      ankle A50.02 [M90.87-●]
      elbow A50.02 [M90.82-●]
      foot A50.02 [M90.87-●]
      forearm A50.02 [M90.83-●]
      hand A50.02 [M90.84-●]
      hip A50.02 [M90.85-●]
      knee A50.02 [M90.86-●-]
      multiple sites A50.02 [M90.89]
      shoulder joint A50.02 [M90.81-●]
      specified site NEC A50.02 [M90.88]
Osteochondrodysplasia Q78.9
   with defects of growth of tubular bones and
      spine Q77.9
   specified NEC Q77.8
   specified NEC Q78.8
Osteochondrodystrophy E78.9
Osteochondrolysis —see Osteochondritis,
   dissecans
Osteochondroma —see Neoplasm, bone, benign
Osteochondromatosis D48.0
   syndrome Q78.4
Osteochondromyxosarcoma —see Neoplasm,
   bone, malignant
Osteochondropathy M93.90
   ankle M93.97-●
   elbow M93.92-●
   foot M93.97-●
   hand M93.94-●
   hip M93.95-●
   Kienböck's disease of adults M93.1
   knee M93.96-●
   multiple joints M93.99
   osteochondritis dissecans —see
      Osteochondritis, dissecans
   osteochondrosis —see Osteochondrosis
   shoulder region M93.91-●

Osteochondropathy (Continued)
   slipped upper femoral epiphysis —see
      Slipped, epiphysis, upper femoral
   specified joint NEC M93.98
   specified type NEC M93.80
      ankle M93.87-●
      elbow M93.82-●
      foot M93.87-●
      hand M93.84-●
      hip M93.85-●
      knee M93.86-●
      multiple joints M93.89
      shoulder region M93.81-●
      specified joint NEC M93.88
      wrist M93.83-●
   syphilitic, congenital
      early A50.02 [M90.80]
      late A50.56 [M90.80]
   wrist M93.93-●
Osteochondrosarcoma —see Neoplasm, bone,
   malignant
Osteochondrosis —see also Osteochondropathy,
   by site
   acetabulum (juvenile) M91.0
   adult —see Osteochondropathy, specified
      type NEC, by site
   astragalus (juvenile) —see Osteochondrosis,
      juvenile, tarsus
   Blount's —see Osteochondrosis, juvenile, tibia
   ▶Blount M92.51-●
   Buchanan's M91.0
   Burns' —see Osteochondrosis, juvenile, ulna
   calcaneus (juvenile) —see Osteochondrosis,
      juvenile, tarsus
   capitular epiphysis (femur) (juvenile) —see
      Legg-Calvé-Perthes disease
   carpal (juvenile) (lunate) (scaphoid) —see
      Osteochondrosis, juvenile, hand, carpal
      lunate
      adult M93.1
   coxae juvenilis —see Legg-Calvé-Perthes
      disease
   deformans juvenilis, coxae —see Legg-Calvé-
      Perthes disease
   Diaz's —see Osteochondrosis, juvenile, tarsus
   dissecans (knee) (shoulder) —see
      Osteochondritis, dissecans
   femoral capital epiphysis (juvenile) —see
      Legg-Calvé-Perthes disease
   femur (head), juvenile —see Legg-Calvé-
      Perthes disease
   fibula (juvenile) —see Osteochondrosis,
      juvenile, fibula
   foot NEC (juvenile) M92.8
   Freiberg's —see Osteochondrosis, juvenile,
      metatarsus
   Haas' (juvenile) —see Osteochondrosis,
      juvenile, humerus
   Haglund's —see Osteochondrosis, juvenile,
      tarsus
   hip (juvenile) —see Legg-Calvé-Perthes disease
   humerus (capitulum) (head) (juvenile) —see
      Osteochondrosis, juvenile, humerus
   ilium, iliac crest (juvenile) M91.0
   ischiopubic synchondrosis M91.0
   Iselin's —see Osteochondrosis, juvenile,
      metatarsus
   juvenile, juvenilis M92.9
      after congenital dislocation of hip
         reduction —see Osteochondrosis,
         juvenile, hip, specified NEC
      arm —see Osteochondrosis, juvenile, upper
         limb NEC
      capitular epiphysis (femur) —see Legg-
         Calvé-Perthes disease
      clavicle, sternal epiphysis —see
         Osteochondrosis, juvenile, upper limb
         NEC
      coxae —see Legg-Calvé-Perthes disease
      deformans M92.9
   ⇒fibula M92.50-●

Osteochondrosis (Continued)
   juvenile, juvenilis (Continued)
      foot NEC M92.8
      hand M92.20-●
         carpal lunate M92.21-●
         metacarpal head M92.22-●
         specified site NEC M92.29-●
      head of femur —see Legg-Calvé-Perthes
         disease
      hip and pelvis M91.9-●
         coxa plana —see Coxa, plana
         femoral head —see Legg-Calvé-Perthes
           disease
         pelvis M91.0
         pseudocoxalgia —see Pseudocoxalgia
         specified NEC M91.8-●
      humerus M92.0-●
      limb
         lower NEC M92.8
         upper NEC —see Osteochondrosis,
           juvenile, upper limb NEC
      medial cuneiform bone —see
         Osteochondrosis, juvenile, tarsus
      metatarsus M92.7-●
      patella M92.4-●
      radius M92.1-●
      ▶specified
      ▶site NEC M92.8
      ▶type NEC M92.8
         ▶tibia and fibula M92.59-●
      specified site NEC M92.8
      spine M42.00
         cervical region M42.02
         cervicothoracic region M42.03
         lumbar region M42.06
         lumbosacral region M42.07
         multiple sites M42.09
         occipito-atlanto-axial region
           M42.01
         sacrococcygeal region M42.08
         thoracic region M42.04
         thoracolumbar region M42.05
      tarsus M92.6-●
      ⇒tibia M92.50-●
         ▶proximal M92.51-●
         ▶tubercle M92.52-●
      ulna M92.1-●
      upper limb NEC M92.3-●
      vertebra (body) (epiphyseal plates)
         (Calvé's) (Scheuermann's) —see
         Osteochondrosis, juvenile, spine
   Kienböck's —see Osteochondrosis, juvenile,
      hand, carpal lunate
      adult M93.1
   Köhler's
      patellar —see Osteochondrosis, juvenile,
         patella
      tarsal navicular —see Osteochondrosis,
         juvenile, tarsus
   Legg-Perthes (-Calvé's) (-Waldenström) —see
      Legg-Calvé-Perthes disease
   limb
      lower NEC (juvenile) M92.8
      ▶tibia and fibula M92.59-●
      upper NEC (juvenile) —see
         Osteochondrosis, juvenile, upper limb
         NEC
   lunate bone (carpal) (juvenile) —see also
      Osteochondrosis, juvenile, hand, carpal
      lunate
      adult M93.1
   Mauclaire's —see Osteochondrosis, juvenile,
      hand, metacarpal
   metacarpal (head) (juvenile) —see
      Osteochondrosis, juvenile, hand,
      metacarpal
   metatarsus (fifth) (head) (juvenile)
      (second) —see Osteochondrosis, juvenile,
      metatarsus
   navicular (juvenile) —see Osteochondrosis,
      juvenile, tarsus

▶ New   ⇒ Revised   ~~deleted~~ Deleted   ● Use Additional Character(s)

Osteochondrosis *(Continued)*
  os
    calcis (juvenile) —*see* Osteochondrosis,
        juvenile, tarsus
    tibiale externum (juvenile) —*see*
        Osteochondrosis, juvenile, tarsus
Osgood-Schlatter M92.52-●
Panner's —*see* Osteochondrosis, juvenile,
    humerus
patellar center (juvenile) (primary)
    (secondary) —*see* Osteochondrosis,
    juvenile, patella
pelvis (juvenile) M91.0
Pierson's M91.0
radius (head) (juvenile) —*see*
    Osteochondrosis, juvenile, radius
Scheuermann's —*see* Osteochondrosis,
    juvenile, spine
Sever's —*see* Osteochondrosis, juvenile, tarsus
Sinding-Larsen —*see* Osteochondrosis,
    juvenile, patella
spine M42.9
    adult M42.10
        cervical region M42.12
        cervicothoracic region M42.13
        lumbar region M42.16
        lumbosacral region M42.17
        multiple sites M42.19
        occipito-atlanto-axial region M42.11
        sacrococcygeal region M42.18
        thoracic region M42.14
        thoracolumbar region M42.15
    juvenile —*see* Osteochondrosis, juvenile,
        spine
symphysis pubis (juvenile) M91.0
syphilitic (congenital) A50.02
talus (juvenile) —*see* Osteochondrosis,
    juvenile, tarsus
tarsus (navicular) (juvenile) —*see*
    Osteochondrosis, juvenile, tarsus
tibia (proximal) (tubercle) (juvenile) —*see*
    Osteochondrosis, juvenile, tibia
tuberculous —*see* Tuberculosis, bone
ulna (lower) (juvenile) —*see* Osteochondrosis,
    juvenile, ulna
van Neck's M91.0
vertebral —*see* Osteochondrosis, spine
Osteoclastoma D48.0
    malignant —*see* Neoplasm, bone, malignant
Osteodynia —*see* Disorder, bone, specified type
    NEC
Osteodystrophy Q78.9
    azotemic N25.0
    congenital Q78.9
    parathyroid, secondary E21.1
    renal N25.0
Osteofibroma —*see* Neoplasm, bone, benign
Osteofibrosarcoma —*see* Neoplasm, bone,
    malignant
Osteogenesis imperfecta Q78.0
Osteogenic —*see* condition
Osteolysis M89.50
    carpus M89.54-●
    clavicle M89.51-●
    femur M89.55-●
    fibula M89.56-●
    finger M89.54-●
    humerus M89.52-●
    ilium M89.559
    ischium M89.559
    joint prosthesis (periprosthetic) —*see*
        Complications, joint prosthesis,
        mechanical, periprosthetic, osteolysis,
        by site
    metacarpus M89.54-●
    metatarsus M89.57-●
    multiple sites M89.59
    neck M89.58
    periprosthetic —*see* Complications, joint
        prosthesis, mechanical, periprosthetic,
        osteolysis, by site

Osteolysis *(Continued)*
    radius M89.53-●
    rib M89.58
    scapula M89.51-●
    skull M89.58
    tarsus M89.57-●
    tibia M89.56-●
    toe M89.57-●
    ulna M89.53-●
    vertebra M89.58
Osteoma —*see also* Neoplasm, bone, benign
    osteoid —*see also* Neoplasm, bone, benign
        giant —*see* Neoplasm, bone, benign
Osteomalacia M83.9
    adult M83.9
        drug-induced NEC M83.5
        due to
            malabsorption (postsurgical) M83.2
            malnutrition M83.3
        specified NEC M83.8
    aluminium-induced M83.4
    infantile —*see* Rickets
    juvenile —*see* Rickets
    oncogenic E83.89
    pelvis M83.8
    puerperal M83.0
    senile M83.1
    vitamin-D-resistant in adults E83.31 *[M90.8-●]*
        carpus E83.31 *[M90.84-●]*
        clavicle E83.31 *[M90.81-●]*
        femur E83.31 *[M90.85-●]*
        fibula E83.31 *[M90.86-●]*
        finger E83.31 *[M90.84-●]*
        humerus E83.31 *[M90.82-●]*
        ilium E83.31 *[M90.859]*
        ischium E83.31 *[M90.859]*
        metacarpus E83.31 *[M90.84-●]*
        metatarsus E83.31 *[M90.87-●]*
        multiple sites E83.31 *[M90.89]*
        neck E83.31 *[M90.88]*
        radius E83.31 *[M90.83-●]*
        rib E83.31 *[M90.88]*
        scapula E83.31 *[M90.819]*
        skull E83.31 *[M90.88]*
        tarsus E83.31 *[M90.879]*
        tibia E83.31 *[M90.869]*
        toe E83.31 *[M90.879]*
        ulna E83.31 *[M90.839]*
        vertebra E83.31 *[M90.88]*
Osteomyelitis (general) (infective)
    (localized) (neonatal) (purulent)
    (septic) (staphylococcal) (streptococcal)
    (suppurative) (with periostitis) M86.9
    acute M86.10
        carpus M86.14-●
        clavicle M86.11-●
        femur M86.15-●
        fibula M86.16-●
        finger M86.14-●
        hematogenous M86.00
            carpus M86.04-●
            clavicle M86.01-●
            femur M86.05-●
            fibula M86.06-●
            finger M86.04-●
            humerus M86.02-●
            ilium M86.059
            ischium M86.059
            mandible M27.2
            metacarpus M86.04-●
            metatarsus M86.07-●
            multiple sites M86.09
            neck M86.08
            orbit H05.02-●
            petrous bone —*see* Petrositis
            radius M86.03-●
            rib M86.08
            scapula M86.01-●
            skull M86.08
            tarsus M86.07-●
            tibia M86.06-●

Osteomyelitis *(Continued)*
    acute *(Continued)*
        hematogenous *(Continued)*
            toe M86.07-●
            ulna M86.03-●
            vertebra —*see* Osteomyelitis, vertebra
        humerus M86.12-●
        ilium M86.18
        ischium M86.18
        mandible M27.2
        metacarpus M86.14-●
        metatarsus M86.17-●
        multiple sites M86.19
        neck M86.18
        orbit H05.02-●
        petrous bone —*see* Petrositis
        radius M86.13-●
        rib M86.18
        scapula M86.11-●
        skull M86.18
        tarsus M86.17-●
        tibia M86.16-●
        toe M86.17-●
        ulna M86.13-●
        vertebra —*see* Osteomyelitis, vertebra
    chronic (or old) M86.60
        with draining sinus M86.40
            carpus M86.44-●
            clavicle M86.41-●
            femur M86.45-●
            fibula M86.46-●
            finger M86.44-●
            humerus M86.42-●
            ilium M86.459
            ischium M86.459
            mandible M27.2
            metacarpus M86.44-●
            metatarsus M86.47-●
            multiple sites M86.49
            neck M86.48
            orbit H05.02-●
            petrous bone —*see* Petrositis
            radius M86.43-●
            rib M86.48
            scapula M86.41-●
            skull M86.48
            tarsus M86.47-●
            tibia M86.46-●
            toe M86.47-●
            ulna M86.43-●
            vertebra —*see* Osteomyelitis, vertebra
        carpus M86.64-●
        clavicle M86.61-●
        femur M86.65-●
        fibula M86.66-●
        finger M86.64-●
        hematogenous NEC M86.50
            carpus M86.54-●
            clavicle M86.51-●
            femur M86.55-●
            fibula M86.56-●
            finger M86.54-●
            humerus M86.52-●
            ilium M86.559
            ischium M86.559
            mandible M27.2
            metacarpus M86.54-●
            metatarsus M86.57-●
            multifocal M86.30
                carpus M86.34-●
                clavicle M86.31-●
                femur M86.35-●
                fibula M86.36-●
                finger M86.34-●
                humerus M86.32-●
                ilium M86.359
                ischium M86.359
                metacarpus M86.34-●
                metatarsus M86.37-●
                multiple sites M86.39
                neck M86.38

Osteomyelitis (Continued)
  chronic (Continued)
    hematogenous NEC (Continued)
      multifocal (Continued)
        radius M86.33-●
        rib M86.38
        scapula M86.31-●
        skull M86.38
        tarsus M86.37-●
        tibia M86.36-●
        toe M86.37-●
        ulna M86.33-●
        vertebra —see Osteomyelitis, vertebra
      multiple sites M86.59
      neck M86.58
      orbit H05.02-●
      petrous bone —see Petrositis
      radius M86.53-●
      rib M86.58
      scapula M86.51-●
      skull M86.58
      tarsus M86.57-●
      tibia M86.56-●
      toe M86.57-●
      ulna M86.53-●
      vertebra —see Osteomyelitis, vertebra
    humerus M86.62-●
    ilium M86.659
    ischium M86.659
    mandible M27.2
    metacarpus M86.64-●
    metatarsus M86.67-●
    multifocal —see Osteomyelitis, chronic,
      hematogenous, multifocal
    multiple sites M86.69
    neck M86.68
    orbit H05.02-●
    petrous bone —see Petrositis
    radius M86.63-●
    rib M86.68
    scapula M86.61-●
    skull M86.68
    tarsus M86.67-●
    tibia M86.66-●
    toe M86.67-●
    ulna M86.63-●
    vertebra —see Osteomyelitis, vertebra
  echinococcal B67.2
  Garr's —see Osteomyelitis, specified type NEC
  in diabetes mellitus —see E08-E13 with .69
  jaw (acute) (chronic) (lower) (neonatal)
    (suppurative) (upper) M27.2
  nonsuppurating —see Osteomyelitis,
    specified type NEC
  orbit H05.02-●
  petrous bone —see Petrositis
  Salmonella (arizonae) (cholerae-suis)
    (enteritidis) (typhimurium) A02.24
  sclerosing, nonsuppurative —see
    Osteomyelitis, specified type NEC
  specified type NEC —see also subcategory
    M86.8X-●
    mandible M27.2
    orbit H05.02-●
    petrous bone —see Petrositis
    vertebra —see Osteomyelitis, vertebra
  subacute M86.20
    carpus M86.24-●
    clavicle M86.21-●
    femur M86.25-●
    fibula M86.26-●
    finger M86.24-●
    humerus M86.22-●
    mandible M27.2
    metacarpus M86.24-●
    metatarsus M86.27-●
    multiple sites M86.29
    neck M86.28
    orbit H05.02-●
    petrous bone —see Petrositis
    radius M86.23-●

Osteomyelitis (Continued)
  subacute (Continued)
    rib M86.28
    scapula M86.21-●
    skull M86.28
    tarsus M86.27-●
    tibia M86.26-●
    toe M86.27-●
    ulna M86.23-●
    vertebra —see Osteomyelitis, vertebra
  syphilitic A52.77
    congenital (early) A50.02 [M90.80]
  tuberculous —see Tuberculosis, bone
  typhoid A01.05
  vertebra M46.20
    cervical region M46.22
    cervicothoracic region M46.23
    lumbar region M46.26
    lumbosacral region M46.27
    occipito-atlanto-axial region M46.21
    sacrococcygeal region M46.28
    thoracic region M46.24
    thoracolumbar region M46.25
Osteomyelofibrosis D47.4
Osteomyelosclerosis D75.89
Osteonecrosis M87.9
  due to
    drugs —see Osteonecrosis, secondary, due
      to, drugs
    trauma —see Osteonecrosis, secondary, due
      to, trauma
  idiopathic aseptic M87.00
    ankle M87.07-●
    carpus M87.03-●
    clavicle M87.01-●
    femur M87.05-●
    fibula M87.06-●
    finger M87.04-●
    humerus M87.02-●
    ilium M87.050
    ischium M87.050
    metacarpus M87.04-●
    metatarsus M87.07-●
    multiple sites M87.09
    neck M87.08
    pelvis M87.050
    radius M87.03-●
    rib M87.08
    scapula M87.01-●
    skull M87.08
    tarsus M87.07-●
    tibia M87.06-●
    toe M87.07-●
    ulna M87.03-●
    vertebra M87.08
  secondary NEC M87.30
    carpus M87.33-●
    clavicle M87.31-●
    due to
      drugs M87.10
        carpus M87.13-●
        clavicle M87.11-●
        femur M87.15-●
        fibula M87.16-●
        finger M87.14-●
        humerus M87.12-●
        ilium M87.159
        ischium M87.159
        jaw M87.180
        metacarpus M87.14-●
        metatarsus M87.17-●
        multiple sites M87.19
        neck M87.18
        radius M87.13-●
        rib M87.18
        scapula M87.11-●
        skull M87.18
        tarsus M87.17-●
        tibia M87.16-●
        toe M87.17-●
        ulna M87.13-●
        vertebra M87.18

Osteonecrosis (Continued)
  secondary NEC (Continued)
    due to (Continued)
      hemoglobinopathy NEC D58.2
        [M90.50]
        carpus D58.2 [M90.54-●]
        clavicle D58.2 [M90.51-●]
        femur D58.2 [M90.55-●]
        fibula D58.2 [M90.56-●]
        finger D58.2 [M90.54-●]
        humerus D58.2 [M90.52-●]
        ilium D58.2 [M90.55-●]
        ischium D58.2 [M90.55-●]
        metacarpus D58.2 [M90.54-●]
        metatarsus D58.2 [M90.57-●]
        multiple sites D58.2 [M90.58]
        neck D58.2 [M90.58]
        radius D58.2 [M90.53-●]
        rib D58.2 [M90.58]
        scapula D58.2 [M90.51-●]
        skull D58.2 [M90.58]
        tarsus D58.2 [M90.57-●]
        tibia D58.2 [M90.56-●]
        toe D58.2 [M90.57-●]
        ulna D58.2 [M90.53-●]
        vertebra D58.2 [M90.58]
      trauma (previous) M87.20
        carpus M87.23-●
        clavicle M87.21-●
        femur M87.25-●
        fibula M87.26-●
        finger M87.24-●
        humerus M87.22-●
        ilium M87.25-●
        ischium M87.25-●
        metacarpus M87.24-●
        metatarsus M87.27-●
        multiple sites M87.29
        neck M87.28
        radius M87.23-●
        rib M87.28
        scapula M87.21-●
        skull M87.28
        tarsus M87.27-●
        tibia M87.26-●
        toe M87.27-●
        ulna M87.23-●
        vertebra M87.28
    femur M87.35-●
    fibula M87.36-●
    finger M87.34-●
    humerus M87.32
    ilium M87.350
    in
      caisson disease T70.3 [M90.50]
        carpus T70.3 [M90.54-●]
        clavicle T70.3 [M90.51-●]
        femur T70.3 [M90.55-●]
        fibula T70.3 [M90.56-●]
        finger T70.3 [M90.54-●]
        humerus T70.3 [M90.52-●]
        ilium T70.3 [M90.55-●]
        ischium T70.3 [M90.55-●]
        metacarpus T70.3 [M90.54-●]
        metatarsus T70.3 [M90.57-●]
        multiple sites T70.3 [M90.59]
        neck T70.3 [M90.58]
        radius T70.3 [M90.53-●]
        rib T70.3 [M90.58]
        scapula T70.3 [M90.51-●]
        skull T70.3 [M90.58]
        tarsus T70.3 [M90.57-●]
        tibia T70.3 [M90.56-●]
        toe T70.3 [M90.57-●]
        ulna T70.3 [M90.53-●]
        vertebra T70.3 [M90.58]
    ischium M87.350
    metacarpus M87.34-●
    metatarsus M87.37-●
    multiple site M87.39
    neck M87.38

▶ New   ⇒ Revised   ~~deleted~~ Deleted   ● Use Additional Character(s)

Osteonecrosis *(Continued)*
  secondary NEC *(Continued)*
    radius M87.33-●
    rib M87.38
    scapula M87.319
    skull M87.38
    tarsus M87.379
    tibia M87.366
    toe M87.379
    ulna M87.33-●
    vertebra M87.38
  specified type NEC M87.80
    carpus M87.83-●
    clavicle M87.81-●
    femur M87.85-●
    fibula M87.86-●
    finger M87.84-●
    humerus M87.82-●
    ilium M87.85-●
    ischium M87.85-●
    metacarpus M87.84-●
    metatarsus M87.87-●
    multiple sites M87.89
    neck M87.88
    radius M87.83-●
    rib M87.88-●
    scapula M87.81-●
    skull M87.88
    tarsus M87.87-●
    tibia M87.86-●
    toe M87.87-●
    ulna M87.83-●
    vertebra M87.88
Osteo-onycho-arthro-dysplasia Q87.2
Osteo-onychodysplasia, hereditary Q87.2
Osteopathia condensans disseminata Q78.8
Osteopathy —*see also* Osteomyelitis,
  Osteonecrosis, Osteoporosis
  after poliomyelitis M89.60
    carpus M89.64-●
    clavicle M89.61-●
    femur M89.65-●
    fibula M89.66-●
    finger M89.64-●
    humerus M89.62-●
    ilium M89.659
    ischium M89.659
    metacarpus M89.64-●
    metatarsus M89.67-●
    multiple sites M89.69
    neck M89.68
    radius M89.63-●
    rib M89.68
    scapula M89.61-●
    skull M89.68
    tarsus M89.67-●
    tibia M89.66-●
    toe M89.67-●
    ulna M89.63-●
    vertebra M89.68
  in (due to)
    renal osteodystrophy N25.0
    specified diseases classified elsewhere —
      see subcategory M90.8
Osteopenia M85.8-●
  borderline M85.8-●
Osteoperiostitis —*see* Osteomyelitis, specified
  type NEC
Osteopetrosis (familial) Q78.2
Osteophyte M25.70
  ankle M25.77-●
  elbow M25.72-●
  foot joint M25.77-●
  hand joint M25.74-●
  hip M25.75-●
  knee M25.76-●
  shoulder M25.71-●
  spine M25.78
  vertebrae M25.78
  wrist M25.73-●
Osteopoikilosis Q78.8

Osteoporosis (female) (male) M81.0
  with current pathological fracture M80.00
  age-related M81.0
    with current pathologic fracture M80.00
      carpus M80.04-●
      clavicle M80.01-●
      fibula M80.06-●
      finger M80.04-●
      humerus M80.02-●
      ilium M80.05-●
      ischium M80.05-●
      metacarpus M80.04-●
      metatarsus M80.07-●
      pelvis M80.05-●
      radius M80.03-●
      scapula M80.01-●
      ▶ site specified NEC M80.0A
      tarsus M80.07-●
      tibia M80.06-●
      toe M80.07-●
      ulna M80.03-●
      vertebra M80.08
  disuse M81.8
    with current pathological fracture M80.80
      carpus M80.84-●
      clavicle M80.81-●
      fibula M80.86-●
      finger M80.84-●
      humerus M80.82-●
      ilium M80.85-●
      ischium M80.85-●
      metacarpus M80.84-●
      metatarsus M80.87-●
      pelvis M80.85-●
      radius M80.83-●
      scapula M80.81-●
      ▶ site specified NEC M80.8A
      tarsus M80.87-●
      tibia M80.86-●
      toe M80.87-●
      ulna M80.83-●
      vertebra M80.88
  drug-induced —*see* Osteoporosis, specified
    type NEC
  idiopathic —*see* Osteoporosis, specified type
    NEC
  involutional —*see* Osteoporosis, age-related
  Lequesne M81.6
  localized M81.6
  postmenopausal M81.0
    with pathological fracture M80.00
      carpus M80.04-●
      clavicle M80.01-●
      fibula M80.06-●
      finger M80.04-●
      humerus M80.02-●
      ilium M80.05-●
      ischium M80.05-●
      metacarpus M80.04-●
      metatarsus M80.07-●
      pelvis M80.05-●
      radius M80.03-●
      scapula M80.01-●
      ▶ site specified NEC M80.0A
      tarsus M80.07-●
      tibia M80.06-●
      toe M80.07-●
      ulna M80.03-●
      vertebra M80.08
  postoophorectomy —*see* Osteoporosis,
    specified type NEC
  postsurgical malabsorption —*see*
    Osteoporosis, specified type NEC
  post-traumatic —*see* Osteoporosis, specified
    type NEC
  senile —*see* Osteoporosis, age-related
  specified type NEC M81.8
    with pathological fracture M80.80
      carpus M80.84-●
      clavicle M80.81-●
      fibula M80.86-●

Osteoporosis *(Continued)*
  specified type NEC *(Continued)*
    with pathological fracture *(Continued)*
      finger M80.84-●
      humerus M80.82-●
      ilium M80.85-●
      ischium M80.85-●
      metacarpus M80.84-●
      metatarsus M80.87-●
      pelvis M80.85-●
      radius M80.83-●
      scapula M80.81-●
      ▶ site specified NEC M80.8A
      tarsus M80.87-●
      tibia M80.86-●
      toe M80.87-●
      ulna M80.83-●
      vertebra M80.88
Osteopsathyrosis (idiopathica) Q78.0
Osteoradionecrosis, jaw (acute) (chronic)
  (lower) (suppurative) (upper) M27.2
Osteosarcoma (any form) —*see* Neoplasm,
  bone, malignant
Osteosclerosis Q78.2
  acquired M85.8-●
  congenita Q77.4
  fragilitas (generalisata) Q78.2
  myelofibrosis D75.81
Osteosclerotic anemia D64.89
Osteosis
  cutis L94.2
  renal fibrocystic N25.0
Österreicher-Turner syndrome Q87.2
Ostium
  atrioventriculare commune Q21.2
  primum (arteriosum) (defect) (persistent) Q21.2
  secundum (arteriosum) (defect) (patent)
    (persistent) Q21.1
Ostrum-Furst syndrome Q75.8
Otalgia —*see* subcategory H92.0
Otitis (acute) H66.90
  with effusion —*see also* Otitis, media,
    nonsuppurative
    purulent —*see* Otitis, media, suppurative
  adhesive —*see* subcategory H74.1
  chronic —*see also* Otitis, media, chronic
    with effusion —*see also* Otitis, media,
      nonsuppurative, chronic
  externa H60.9-●
    abscess —*see* Abscess, ear, external
    acute (noninfective) H60.50-●
      actinic H60.51-●
      chemical H60.52-●
      contact H60.53-●
      eczematoid H60.54-●
      infective —*see* Otitis, externa, infective
      reactive H60.55-●
      specified NEC H60.59-●
    cellulitis —*see* Cellulitis, ear
    chronic H60.6-●
    diffuse —*see* Otitis, externa, infective, diffuse
    hemorrhagic —*see* Otitis, externa, infective,
      hemorrhagic
    in (due to)
      aspergillosis B44.89
      candidiasis B37.84
      erysipelas A46 *[H62.40]*
      herpes (simplex) virus infection B00.1
        zoster B02.8
      impetigo L01.00 *[H62.40]*
      infectious disease NEC B99 *[H62.4-●]*
      mycosis NEC B36.9 *[H62.40]*
      parasitic disease NEC B89 *[H62.40]*
      viral disease NEC B34.9 *[H62.40]*
      zoster B02.8
    infective NEC H60.39-●
      abscess —*see* Abscess, ear, external
      cellulitis —*see* Cellulitis, ear
      diffuse H60.31-●
      hemorrhagic H60.32-●
      swimmer's ear —*see* Swimmer's, ear

Otitis *(Continued)*
  externa *(Continued)*
    malignant H60.2-●
    mycotic NEC B36.9 *[H62.40]*
      in
        aspergillosis B44.89
        candidiasis B37.84
        moniliasis B37.84
    necrotizing —*see* Otitis, externa,
      malignant
    Pseudomonas aeruginosa —*see* Otitis,
      externa, malignant
    reactive —*see* Otitis, externa, acute,
      reactive
    specified NEC —*see* subcategory
      H60.8
    tropical NEC B36.9 *[H62.40]*
      in
        aspergillosis B44.89
        candidiasis B37.84
        moniliasis B37.84
  insidiosa —*see* Otosclerosis
  interna —*see* subcategory H83.0
  media (hemorrhagic) (staphylococcal)
    (streptococcal) H66.9-●
    with effusion (nonpurulent) —*see* Otitis,
      media, nonsuppurative
    acute, subacute H66.90
      allergic —*see* Otitis, media,
        nonsuppurative, acute, allergic
      exudative —*see* Otitis, media,
        suppurative, acute
      mucoid —*see* Otitis, media,
        nonsuppurative, acute
      necrotizing —*see also* Otitis, media,
        suppurative, acute
        in
          measles B05.3
          scarlet fever A38.0
      nonsuppurative NEC —*see* Otitis, media,
        nonsuppurative, acute
      purulent —*see* Otitis, media,
        suppurative, acute
      sanguinous —*see* Otitis, media,
        nonsuppurative, acute
      secretory —*see* Otitis, media,
        nonsuppurative, acute, serous
      seromucinous —*see* Otitis, media,
        nonsuppurative, acute
      serous —*see* Otitis, media,
        nonsuppurative, acute, serous
      suppurative —*see* Otitis, media,
        suppurative, acute
    allergic —*see* Otitis, media, nonsuppurative
    catarrhal —*see* Otitis, media,
      nonsuppurative
    chronic H66.90
      with effusion (nonpurulent) —*see* Otitis,
        media, nonsuppurative, chronic
      allergic —*see* Otitis, media,
        nonsuppurative, chronic, allergic
      benign suppurative —*see* Otitis, media,
        suppurative, chronic, tubotympanic
      catarrhal —*see* Otitis, media,
        nonsuppurative, chronic, serous
      exudative —*see* Otitis, media,
        suppurative, chronic
      mucinous —*see* Otitis, media,
        nonsuppurative, chronic, mucoid
      mucoid —*see* Otitis, media,
        nonsuppurative, chronic, mucoid
      nonsuppurative NEC —*see* Otitis, media,
        nonsuppurative, chronic
      purulent —*see* Otitis, media,
        suppurative, chronic
      secretory —*see* Otitis, media,
        nonsuppurative, chronic, mucoid
      seromucinous —*see* Otitis, media,
        nonsuppurative, chronic
      serous —*see* Otitis, media,
        nonsuppurative, chronic, serous

Otitis *(Continued)*
  media *(Continued)*
    chronic *(Continued)*
      suppurative —*see* Otitis, media,
        suppurative, chronic
      transudative —*see* Otitis, media,
        nonsuppurative, chronic, mucoid
    exudative —*see* Otitis, media,
      nonsuppurative
    in (due to) (with)
      influenza —*see* Influenza, with, otitis
        media
      measles B05.3
      scarlet fever A38.0
      tuberculosis A18.6
      viral disease NEC B34.-● *[H67.-●]*
    mucoid —*see* Otitis, media,
      nonsuppurative
    nonsuppurative H65.9-●
      acute or subacute NEC H65.19-●
        allergic H65.11-●
          recurrent H65.11-●
        recurrent H65.19-●
        secretory —*see* Otitis, media,
          nonsuppurative, serous
        serous H65.0-●
          recurrent H65.0-●
      chronic H65.49-●
        allergic H65.41-●
        mucoid H65.3-●
        serous H65.2-●
      postmeasles B05.3
      purulent —*see* Otitis, media, suppurative
      secretory —*see* Otitis, media,
        nonsuppurative
      seromucinous —*see* Otitis, media,
        nonsuppurative
      serous —*see* Otitis, media, nonsuppurative
      suppurative H66.4-●
        acute H66.00-●
          with rupture of ear drum H66.01-●
          recurrent H66.00-●
            with rupture of ear drum H66.01-●
        chronic —*see also* subcategory H66.3
          atticoantral H66.2-●
          benign —*see* Otitis, media,
            suppurative, chronic,
            tubotympanic
          tubotympanic H66.1-●
      transudative —*see* Otitis, media,
        nonsuppurative
      tuberculous A18.6
Otocephaly Q18.2
Otolith syndrome —*see* subcategory H81.8
Otomycosis (diffuse) NEC B36.9 *[H62.40]*
  in
    aspergillosis B44.89
    candidiasis B37.84
    moniliasis B37.84
Otoporosis —*see* Otosclerosis
Otorrhagia (nontraumatic) H92.2-●
  traumatic - code by Type of injury
Otorrhea H92.1-●
  cerebrospinal (fluid) G96.01
    ▶postoperative G96.08
    ▶specified NEC G96.08
    ▶spontaneous G96.01
    ▶traumatic G96.08
Otosclerosis (general) H80.9-●
  cochlear (endosteal) H80.2-●
  involving
    otic capsule —*see* Otosclerosis, cochlear
    oval window
      nonobliterative H80.0-●
      obliterative H80.1-●
    round window —*see* Otosclerosis, cochlear
  nonobliterative —*see* Otosclerosis, involving,
    oval window, nonobliterative
  obliterative —*see* Otosclerosis, involving, oval
    window, obliterative
  specified NEC H80.8-●

Otospongiosis —*see* Otosclerosis
Otto's disease or pelvis M24.7
Outcome of delivery Z37.9
  multiple births Z37.9
    all liveborn Z37.50
      quadruplets Z37.52
      quintuplets Z37.53
      sextuplets Z37.54
      specified number NEC Z37.59
      triplets Z37.51
    all stillborn Z37.7
    some liveborn Z37.60
      quadruplets Z37.62
      quintuplets Z37.63
      sextuplets Z37.64
      specified number NEC Z37.69
      triplets Z37.61
  single NEC Z37.9
    liveborn Z37.0
    stillborn Z37.1
  twins NEC Z37.9
    both liveborn Z37.2
    both stillborn Z37.4
    one liveborn, one stillborn Z37.3
Outlet —*see* condition
Ovalocytosis (congenital) (hereditary) —*see*
  Elliptocytosis
Ovarian —*see* Condition
Ovariocele N83.4-●
Ovaritis (cystic) —*see* Oophoritis
Ovary, ovarian —*see also* condition
  resistant syndrome E28.39
  vein syndrome N13.8
Overactive —*see also* Hyperfunction
  adrenal cortex NEC E27.0
  bladder N32.81
  hypothalamus E23.3
  thyroid —*see* Hyperthyroidism
Overactivity R46.3
  child —*see* Disorder, attention-deficit
    hyperactivity
Overbite (deep) (excessive) (horizontal)
  (vertical) M26.29
Overbreathing —*see* Hyperventilation
Overconscientious personality F60.5
Overdevelopment —*see* Hypertrophy
Overdistension —*see* Distension
Overdose, overdosage (drug) —*see* Table of
  Drugs and Chemicals, by drug, poisoning
Overeating R63.2
  nonorganic origin F50.89
  psychogenic F50.89
Overexertion (effects) (exhaustion) T73.3
Overexposure (effects) T73.9
  exhaustion T73.2
Overfeeding —*see* Overeating
  newborn P92.4
Overfill, endodontic M27.52
Overgrowth, bone —*see* Hypertrophy, bone
Overhanging of dental restorative material
  (unrepairable) K08.52
Overheated (places) (effects) —*see* Heat
Overjet (excessive horizontal) M26.23
Overlaid, overlying (suffocation) —*see* Asphyxia,
  traumatic, due to mechanical threat
Overlap, excessive horizontal (teeth) M26.23
Overlapping toe (acquired) —*see also*
  Deformity, toe, specified NEC
  congenital (fifth toe) Q66.89
Overload
  circulatory, due to transfusion (blood) (blood
    components) (TACO) E87.71
  fluid E87.70
    due to transfusion (blood) (blood
      components) E87.71
    specified NEC E87.79
  iron, due to repeated red blood cell
    transfusions E83.111
  potassium (K) E87.5
  sodium (Na) E87.0
Overnutrition —*see* Hyperalimentation

▶ New   ⇒ Revised   ~~deleted~~ Deleted   ● Use Additional Character(s)

Overproduction —*see also* Hypersecretion
ACTH E27.0
catecholamine E27.5
growth hormone E22.0
Overprotection, child by parent Z62.1
Overriding
aorta Q25.49
finger (acquired) —*see* Deformity, finger
congenital Q68.1
toe (acquired) —*see also* Deformity, toe,
specified NEC
congenital Q66.89

Overstrained R53.83
heart —*see* Hypertrophy, cardiac
Overuse, muscle NEC
M70.8-●
Overweight E66.3
Overworked R53.83
Oviduct —*see* condition
Ovotestis Q56.0
Ovulation (cycle)
failure or lack of N97.0
pain N94.0

Ovum —*see* condition
Owren's disease or syndrome (parahemophilia)
D68.2
Ox heart —*see* Hypertrophy, cardiac
Oxalosis E72.53
Oxaluria E72.53
Oxycephaly, oxycephalic Q75.0
syphilitic, congenital A50.02
Oxyuriasis B80
Oxyuris vermicularis (infestation) B80
Ozena J31.0

P

Pachyderma, pachydermia L85.9
  larynx (verrucosa) J38.7
Pachydermatocele (congenital) Q82.8
Pachydermoperiostosis —see also
    Osteoarthropathy, hypertrophic, specified
      type NEC
  clubbed nail M89.40 [L62]
Pachygyria Q04.3
Pachymeningitis (adhesive) (basal) (brain)
    (cervical) (chronic) (circumscribed)
    (external) (fibrous) (hemorrhagic)
    (hypertrophic) (internal) (purulent) (spinal)
    (suppurative) —see Meningitis
Pachyonychia (congenital) Q84.5
Pacinian tumor —see Neoplasm, skin, benign
Pad, knuckle or Garrod's M72.1
Paget-Schroetter syndrome I82.890
Paget's disease
  with infiltrating duct carcinoma —see
      Neoplasm, breast, malignant
  bone M88.9
    carpus M88.84-●
    clavicle M88.81-●
    femur M88.85-●
    fibula M88.86-●
    finger M88.84-●
    humerus M88.82-●
    ilium M88.85-●
    in neoplastic disease —see Osteitis,
        deformans, in neoplastic disease
    ischium M88.85-●
    metacarpus M88.84-●
    metatarsus M88.87-●
    multiple sites M88.89
    neck M88.88
    radius M88.83-●
    rib M88.88
    scapula M88.81-●
    skull M88.0
    specified NEC M88.88
    tarsus M88.87-●
    tibia M88.86-●
    toe M88.87-●
    ulna M88.83-●
    vertebra M88.1
  breast (female) C50.01-●
    male C50.02-●
  extramammary —see also Neoplasm, skin,
      malignant
    anus C21.0
      margin C44.590
      skin C44.590
  intraductal carcinoma —see Neoplasm,
      breast, malignant
  malignant —see Neoplasm, skin, malignant
    breast (female) C50.01-●
      male C50.02-●
    unspecified site (female) C50.01-●
      male C50.02-●
  mammary —see Paget's disease, breast
  nipple —see Paget's disease, breast
  osteitis deformans —see Paget's disease, bone
Pain(s) —see also Painful R52
  abdominal R10.9
    colic R10.83
    generalized R10.84
      with acute abdomen R10.0
    lower R10.30
      left quadrant R10.32
      pelvic or perineal R10.2
      periumbilical R10.33
      right quadrant R10.31
    rebound —see Tenderness, abdominal,
        rebound
    severe with abdominal rigidity R10.0
    tenderness —see Tenderness, abdominal
    upper R10.10
      epigastric R10.13
      left quadrant R10.12
      right quadrant R10.11

Pain (Continued)
  acute R52
    due to trauma G89.11
    neoplasm related G89.3
    postprocedural NEC G89.18
    post-thoracotomy G89.12
    specified by site — code to Pain, by site
  adnexa (uteri) R10.2
  anginoid —see Pain, precordial
  anus K62.89
  arm —see Pain, limb, upper
  axillary (axilla) M79.62-●
  back (postural) M54.9
  bladder R39.89
    associated with micturition —see
        Micturition, painful
    chronic R39.82
  bone —see Disorder, bone, specified type
      NEC
  breast N64.4
  broad ligament R10.2
  cancer associated (acute) (chronic) G89.3
  cecum —see Pain, abdominal
  cervicobrachial M53.1
  chest (central) R07.9
    anterior wall R07.89
    atypical R07.89
    ischemic I20.9
    musculoskeletal R07.89
    non-cardiac R07.89
    on breathing R07.1
    pleurodynia R07.81
    precordial R07.2
    wall (anterior) R07.89
  chronic G89.29
    associated with significant psychosocial
        dysfunction G89.4
    due to trauma G89.21
    neoplasm related G89.3
    postoperative NEC G89.28
    postprocedural NEC G89.28
    post-thoracotomy G89.22
    specified NEC G89.29
  coccyx M53.3
  colon —see Pain, abdominal
  coronary —see Angina
  costochondral R07.1
  diaphragm R07.1
  due to cancer G89.3
  due to device, implant or graft —see also
      Complications, by site and type,
      specified NEC T85.848
    arterial graft NEC T82.848
    breast (implant) T85.848
    catheter NEC T85.848
      dialysis (renal) T82.848
        intraperitoneal T85.848
      infusion NEC T82.848
        spinal (epidural) (subdural) T85.840
      urinary (indwelling) T83.84
    electronic (electrode) (pulse generator)
        (stimulator)
      bone T84.84
      cardiac T82.847
      nervous system (brain) (peripheral
          nerve) (spinal) T85.840
      urinary T83.84
    fixation, internal (orthopedic) NEC T84.84
    gastrointestinal (bile duct) (esophagus)
        T85.848
    genital NEC T83.84
    heart NEC T82.847
    infusion NEC T85.848
    joint prosthesis T84.84
    ocular (corneal graft) (orbital implant)
        NEC T85.848
    orthopedic NEC T84.84
    specified NEC T85.848
    urinary NEC T83.84
    vascular NEC T82.848
    ventricular intracranial shunt T85.840

Pain (Continued)
  due to malignancy (primary) (secondary)
      G89.3
  ear —see subcategory H92.0
  epigastric, epigastrium R10.13
  eye —see Pain, ocular
⇒ face, facial R51.9
    atypical G50.1
  female genital organs NEC N94.89
  finger —see Pain, limb, upper
  flank —see Pain, abdominal
  foot —see Pain, limb, lower
  gallbladder K82.9
  gas (intestinal) R14.1
  gastric —see Pain, abdominal
  generalized NOS R52
  genital organ
    female N94.89
    male N50.89
  groin —see Pain, abdominal, lower
  hand —see Pain, limb, upper
  head —see Headache
  heart —see Pain, precordial
  infra-orbital —see Neuralgia, trigeminal
  intercostal R07.82
  intermenstrual N94.0
  jaw R68.84
  joint M25.50
    ankle M25.57-●
    elbow M25.52-●
    finger M25.54-●
    foot M25.57-●
    hand M25.54-●
    hip M25.55-●
    knee M25.56-●
    shoulder M25.51-●
    ▶ specified site NEC M25.59
    toe M25.57-●
    wrist M25.53-●
  kidney N23
  laryngeal R07.0
  leg —see Pain, limb, lower
  limb M79.609
    lower M79.60-●
      foot M79.67-●
      lower leg M79.66-●
      thigh M79.65-●
      toe M79.67-●
    upper M79.60-●
      axilla M79.62-●
      finger M79.64-●
      forearm M79.63-●
      hand M79.64-●
      upper arm M79.62-●
  loin M54.5
  low back M54.5
  lumbar region M54.5
  mandibular R68.84
  mastoid —see subcategory H92.0
  maxilla R68.84
  menstrual —see also Dysmenorrhea N94.6
  metacarpophalangeal (joint) —see Pain, joint,
      hand
  metatarsophalangeal (joint) —see Pain, joint,
      foot
  mouth K13.79
  muscle —see Myalgia
  musculoskeletal —see also Pain, by site M79.18
  myofascial M79.18
  nasal J34.89
  nasopharynx J39.2
  neck NEC M54.2
  nerve NEC —see Neuralgia
  neuromuscular —see Neuralgia
  nose J34.89
  ocular H57.1-●
  ophthalmic —see Pain, ocular
  orbital region —see Pain, ocular
  ovary N94.89
  over heart —see Pain, precordial
  ovulation N94.0

▶ New   ⇒ Revised   deleted Deleted   ● Use Additional Character(s)

Pain (*Continued*)
  pelvic (female) R10.2
  penis N48.89
  pericardial —*see* Pain, precordial
  perineal, perineum R10.2
  pharynx J39.2
  pleura, pleural, pleuritic R07.81
  postoperative NOS G89.18
  postprocedural NOS G89.18
  post-thoracotomy G89.12
  precordial (region) R07.2
  premenstrual N94.3
  psychogenic (persistent) (any site) F45.41
  radicular (spinal) —*see* Radiculopathy
  rectum K62.89
  respiration R07.1
  retrosternal R07.2
  rheumatoid, muscular —*see* Myalgia
  rib R07.81
  root (spinal) —*see* Radiculopathy
  round ligament (stretch) R10.2
  sacroiliac M53.3
  sciatic —*see* Sciatica
  scrotum N50.82
  seminal vesicle N50.89
  shoulder M25.51-●
  spermatic cord N50.89
  spinal root —*see* Radiculopathy
  spine M54.9
    cervical M54.2
    low back M54.5
      with sciatica M54.4-●
    thoracic M54.6
  stomach —*see* Pain, abdominal
  substernal R07.2
  temporomandibular (joint) M26.62-●
  testis N50.81-●
  thoracic spine M54.6
    with radicular and visceral pain M54.14
  throat R07.0
  tibia —*see* Pain, limb, lower
  toe —*see* Pain, limb, lower
  tongue K14.6
  tooth K08.89
  trigeminal —*see* Neuralgia, trigeminal
  tumor associated G89.3
  ureter N23
  urinary (organ) (system) N23
  uterus NEC N94.89
  vagina R10.2
  vertebrogenic (syndrome) M54.89
  vesical R39.89
    associated with micturition —*see*
      Micturition, painful
  vulva R10.2
Painful —*see also* Pain
  coitus
    female N94.10
    male N53.12
    psychogenic F52.6
  ejaculation (semen) N53.12
    psychogenic F52.6
  erection —*see* Priapism
  feet syndrome E53.8
  joint replacement (hip) (knee) T84.84
  menstruation —*see* Dysmenorrhea
    psychogenic F45.8
  micturition —*see* Micturition, painful
  respiration R07.1
  scar NEC L90.5
  wire sutures T81.89
Painter's colic —*see* subcategory T56.0
Palate —*see* condition
Palatoplegia K13.79
Palatoschisis —*see* Cleft, palate
Palilalia R48.8
Palliative care Z51.5
Pallor R23.1
  optic disc, temporal —*see* Atrophy, optic
Palmar —*see also* condition
  fascia —*see* condition

Palpable
  cecum K63.89
  kidney N28.89
  ovary N83.8
  prostate N42.9
  spleen —*see* Splenomegaly
Palpitations (heart) R00.2
  psychogenic F45.8
Palsy —*see also* Paralysis G83.9
  atrophic diffuse (progressive) G12.22
  Bell's —*see also* Palsy, facial
    newborn P11.3
  brachial plexus NEC G54.0
    newborn (birth injury) P14.3
  brain —*see* Palsy, cerebral
  bulbar (progressive) (chronic) G12.22
    of childhood (Fazio-Londe) G12.1
    pseudo NEC G12.29
    supranuclear (progressive) G23.1
  cerebral (congenital) G80.9
    ataxic G80.4
    athetoid G80.3
    choreathetoid G80.3
    diplegic G80.8
      spastic G80.1
    dyskinetic G80.3
      athetoid G80.3
      choreathetoid G80.3
      distonic G80.3
    dystonic G80.3
    hemiplegic G80.8
      spastic G80.2
    mixed G80.8
    monoplegic G80.8
      spastic G80.1
    paraplegic G80.8
      spastic G80.1
    quadriplegic G80.8
      spastic G80.0
    spastic G80.1
      diplegic G80.1
      hemiplegic G80.2
      monoplegic G80.1
      quadriplegic G80.0
      specified NEC G80.1
      tetrapelgic G80.0
    specified NEC G80.8
    syphilitic A52.12
      congenital A50.49
    tetraplegic G80.8
      spastic G80.0
  cranial nerve —*see also* Disorder, nerve,
    cranial
    multiple G52.7
      in
        infectious disease B99 [G53]
        neoplastic disease —*see also* Neoplasm
          D49.9 [G53]
        parasitic disease B89 [G53]
        sarcoidosis D86.82
  creeping G12.22
  diver's T70.3
  Erb's P14.0
  facial G51.0
    newborn (birth injury) P11.3
  glossopharyngeal G52.1
  Klumpke (-Déjérine) P14.1
  lead —*see* subcategory T56.0
  median nerve (tardy) G56.1-●
  nerve G58.9
    specified NEC G58.8
  peroneal nerve (acute) (tardy) G57.3-●
  progressive supranuclear G23.1
  pseudobulbar NEC G12.29
  radial nerve (acute) G56.3-●
  seventh nerve —*see also* Palsy, facial
    newborn P11.3
  shaking —*see* Parkinsonism
  spastic (cerebral) (spinal) G80.1
  ulnar nerve (tardy) G56.2-●
  wasting G12.29

Paludism —*see* Malaria
Panangiitis M30.0
Panaris, panaritium —*see also* Cellulitis, digit
  with lymphangitis —*see* Lymphangitis, acute,
    digit
Panarteritis nodosa M30.0
  brain or cerebral I67.7
Pancake heart R93.1
  with cor pulmonale (chronic) I27.81
Pancarditis (acute) (chronic) I51.89
  rheumatic I09.89
    active or acute I01.8
Pancoast's syndrome or tumor C34.1-●
Pancolitis, ulcerative (chronic) K51.00
  with
    abscess K51.014
    complication K51.019
    fistula K51.013
    obstruction K51.012
    rectal bleeding K51.011
    specified complication NEC K51.018
Pancreas, pancreatic —*see* condition
⟹Pancreatitis (annular) (apoplectic) (calcareous)
    (edematous) (hemorrhagic) (malignant)
    (subacute) (suppurative) K85.90
  with necrosis (uninfected) K85.91
    infected K85.92
  acute (without necrosis or infection)
    K85.90
    with necrosis (uninfected) K85.91
      infected K85.92
    alcohol induced (without necrosis or
      infection) K85.20
      with necrosis (uninfected) K85.21
        infected K85.22
    biliary (without necrosis or infection)
      K85.10
      with necrosis (uninfected) K85.11
        infected K85.12
    drug induced (without necrosis or
      infection) K85.30
      with necrosis (uninfected) K85.31
        infected K85.32
    gallstone (without necrosis or infection)
      K85.10
      with necrosis (uninfected) K85.11
        infected K85.12
    idiopathic (without necrosis or infection)
      K85.00
      with necrosis (uninfected) K85.01
        infected K85.02
    specified NEC (without necrosis or
      infection) K85.80
      with necrosis (uninfected)
        K85.81
        infected K85.82
  chronic (infectious) K86.1
    alcohol-induced K86.0
    recurrent K86.1
    relapsing K86.1
  cystic (chronic) K86.1
  cytomegaloviral B25.2
  fibrous (chronic) K86.1
  gallstone (without necrosis or infection)
    K85.10
    with necrosis (uninfected)
      K85.11
      infected K85.12
  gangrenous —*see* Pancreatitis, acute
  interstitial (chronic) K86.1
    acute —*see also* Pancreatitis, acute K85.80
  mumps B26.3
⟹recurrent
    ▶acute K85.50
    ▶chronic K86.1
  relapsing, chronic K86.1
  syphilitic A52.74
Pancreatoblastoma —*see* Neoplasm, pancreas,
  malignant
Pancreolithiasis K86.89
Pancytolysis D75.89

Pancytopenia (acquired) D61.818
　with
　　malformations D61.09
　　myelodysplastic syndrome —*see*
　　　Syndrome, myelodysplastic
　antineoplastic chemotherapy induced
　　D61.810
　congenital D61.09
　drug-induced NEC D61.811
PANDAS (pediatric autoimmune
　neuropsychiatric disorders associated with
　streptococcal infections syndrome) D89.89
Panencephalitis, subacute, sclerosing
　A81.1
Panhematopenia D61.9
　congenital D61.09
　constitutional D61.09
　splenic, primary D73.1
Panhemocytopenia D61.9
　congenital D61.09
　constitutional D61.09
Panhypogonadism E29.1
Panhypopituitarism E23.0
　prepubertal E23.0
Panic (attack) (state) F41.0
　reaction to exceptional stress (transient) F43.0
Panmyelopathy, familial, constitutional D61.09
Panmyelophthisis D61.82
　congenital D61.09
Panmyelosis (acute) (with myelofibrosis)
　　C94.4-●
Panner's disease —*see* Osteochondrosis,
　juvenile, humerus
Panneuritis endemica E51.11
Panniculitis (nodular) (nonsuppurative) M79.3
　back M54.00
　　cervical region M54.02
　　cervicothoracic region M54.03
　　lumbar region M54.06
　　lumbosacral region M54.07
　　multiple sites M54.09
　　occipito-atlanto-axial region M54.01
　　sacrococcygeal region M54.08
　　thoracic region M54.04
　　thoracolumbar region M54.05
　lupus L93.2
　mesenteric K65.4
　neck M54.02
　　cervicothoracic region M54.03
　　occipito-atlanto-axial region M54.01
　relapsing M35.6
Panniculus adiposus (abdominal) E65
Pannus (allergic) (cornea) (degenerativus)
　　(keratic) H16.42-●
　abdominal (symptomatic) E65
　trachomatosus, trachomatous (active) A71.1
Panophthalmitis H44.01-●
Pansinusitis (chronic) (hyperplastic)
　　(nonpurulent) (purulent) J32.4
　acute J01.40
　　recurrent J01.41
　tuberculous A15.8
Panuveitis (sympathetic) H44.11-●
Panvalvular disease I08.9
　specified NEC I08.8
PAPA (pyogenic arthritis, pyoderma
　gangrenosum, and acne syndrome) M04.8
Papanicolaou smear, cervix Z12.4
　as part of routine gynecological examination
　　Z01.419
　　with abnormal findings Z01.411
　for suspected neoplasm Z12.4
　nonspecific abnormal finding R87.619
　routine Z01.419
　　with abnormal findings Z01.411
Papilledema (choked disc) H47.10
　associated with
　　decreased ocular pressure H47.12
　　increased intracranial pressure H47.11
　　retinal disorder H47.13
　Foster-Kennedy syndrome H47.14-●

Papillitis H46.00
　anus K62.89
　chronic lingual K14.4
　necrotizing, kidney N17.2
　optic H46.0-●
　rectum K62.89
　renal, necrotizing N17.2
　tongue K14.0
Papilloma —*see also* Neoplasm, benign,
　by site
　acuminatum (female) (male) (anogenital)
　　A63.0
　basal cell L82.1
　　inflamed L82.0
　benign pinta (primary) A67.0
　bladder (urinary) (transitional cell) D41.4
　choroid plexus (lateral ventricle) (third
　　ventricle) D33.0
　　anaplastic C71.5
　　fourth ventricle D33.1
　　malignant C71.5
　renal pelvis (transitional cell) D41.1-●
　　benign D30.1-●
　Schneiderian
　　specified site —*see* Neoplasm, benign, by
　　　site
　　unspecified site D14.0
　serous surface
　　borderline malignancy
　　　specified site —*see* Neoplasm, uncertain
　　　　behavior, by site
　　　unspecified site D39.10
　　specified site —*see* Neoplasm, benign, by
　　　site
　　unspecified site D27.9
　transitional (cell)
　　bladder (urinary) D41.4
　　inverted type —*see* Neoplasm, uncertain
　　　behavior, by site
　　renal pelvis D41.1-●
　　ureter D41.2-●
　ureter (transitional cell) D41.2-●
　　benign D30.2-●
　urothelial —*see* Neoplasm, uncertain
　　behavior, by site
　villous —*see* Neoplasm, uncertain behavior,
　　by site
　　adenocarcinoma in —*see* Neoplasm,
　　　malignant, by site
　　in situ —*see* Neoplasm, in situ
　yaws, plantar or palmar A66.1
Papillomata, multiple, of yaws A66.1
Papillomatosis —*see also* Neoplasm, benign,
　by site
　confluent and reticulated L83
　cystic, breast —*see* Mastopathy, cystic
　ductal, breast —*see* Mastopathy, cystic
　intraductal (diffuse) —*see* Neoplasm, benign,
　　by site
　subareolar duct D24-●
Papillomavirus, as cause of disease classified
　elsewhere B97.7
Papillon-Léage and Psaume syndrome
　Q87.0
Papule(s) R23.8
　carate (primary) A67.0
　fibrous, of nose D22.39
　Gottron's L94.4
　pinta (primary) A67.0
Papulosis
　lymphomatoid C86.6
　malignant I77.89
Papyraceous fetus O31.0-●
Para-albuminemia E88.09
Paracephalus Q89.7
Parachute mitral valve Q23.2
Paracoccidioidomycosis B41.9
　disseminated B41.7
　generalized B41.7
　mucocutaneous-lymphangitic B41.8
　pulmonary B41.0

Paracoccidioidomycosis (*Continued*)
　specified NEC B41.8
　visceral B41.8
Paradentosis K05.4
Paraffinoma T88.8
Paraganglioma D44.7
　adrenal D35.0-●
　　malignant C74.1-●
　aortic body D44.7
　　malignant C75.5
　carotid body D44.6
　　malignant C75.4
　chromaffin —*see also* Neoplasm, benign, by
　　site
　　malignant —*see* Neoplasm, malignant, by
　　　site
　extra-adrenal D44.7
　　malignant C75.5
　　　specified site —*see* Neoplasm,
　　　　malignant, by site
　　　unspecified site C75.5
　　specified site —*see* Neoplasm, uncertain
　　　behavior, by site
　　unspecified site D44.7
　gangliocytic D13.2
　　specified site —*see* Neoplasm, benign, by
　　　site
　　unspecified site D13.2
　glomus jugulare D44.7
　　malignant C75.5
　jugular D44.7
　malignant C75.5
　　specified site —*see* Neoplasm, malignant,
　　　by site
　　unspecified site C75.5
　nonchromaffin D44.7
　　malignant C75.5
　　　specified site —*see* Neoplasm,
　　　　malignant, by site
　　　unspecified site C75.5
　　specified site —*see* Neoplasm, uncertain
　　　behavior, by site
　　unspecified site D44.7
　parasympathetic D44.7
　　specified site —*see* Neoplasm, uncertain
　　　behavior, by site
　　unspecified site D44.7
　specified site —*see* Neoplasm, uncertain
　　behavior, by site
　sympathetic D44.7
　　specified site —*see* Neoplasm, uncertain
　　　behavior, by site
　　unspecified site D44.7
　unspecified site D44.7
Parageusia R43.2
　psychogenic F45.8
Paragonimiasis B66.4
Paragranuloma, Hodgkin —*see* Lymphoma,
　Hodgkin, specified NEC
Parahemophilia —*see also* Defect, coagulation
　D68.2
Parakeratosis R23.4
　variegata L41.0
Paralysis, paralytic (complete) (incomplete)
　G83.9
　with
　　syphilis A52.17
　abducens, abducent (nerve) —*see* Strabismus,
　　paralytic, sixth nerve
　abductor, lower extremity G57.9-●
　accessory nerve G52.8
　accommodation —*see also* Paresis, of
　　accommodation
　　hysterical F44.89
　acoustic nerve (except Deafness) —*see*
　　subcategory H93.3
　agitans —*see also* Parkinsonism G20
　　arteriosclerotic G21.4
　alternating (oculomotor) G83.89
　amyotrophic G12.21

　▶ New　⇒ Revised　~~deleted~~ Deleted　● Use Additional Character(s)

Paralysis, paralytic *(Continued)*
  ankle G57.9-●
  anus (sphincter) K62.89
  arm —*see* Monoplegia, upper limb
  ascending (spinal), acute G61.0
  association G12.29
  asthenic bulbar G70.00
    with exacerbation (acute) G70.01
    in crisis G70.01
  ataxic (hereditary) G11.9
    general (syphilitic) A52.17
  atrophic G58.9
    infantile, acute —*see* Poliomyelitis, paralytic
    progressive G12.22
    spinal (acute) —*see* Poliomyelitis, paralytic
  axillary G54.0
  Babinski-Nageotte's G83.89
  Bell's G51.0
    newborn P11.3
  Benedikt's G46.3
  birth injury P14.9
    spinal cord P11.5
  bladder (neurogenic) (sphincter)
      N31.2
  bowel, colon or intestine K56.0
  brachial plexus G54.0
    birth injury P14.3
    newborn (birth injury) P14.3
  brain G83.9
    diplegia G83.0
    triplegia G83.89
  bronchial J98.09
  Brown-Séquard G83.81
  bulbar (chronic) (progressive) G12.22
    infantile —*see* Poliomyelitis, paralytic
    poliomyelitic —*see* Poliomyelitis, paralytic
    pseudo G12.29
  bulbospinal G70.00
    with exacerbation (acute) G70.01
    in crisis G70.01
  cardiac —*see also* Failure, heart I50.9
  cerebrocerebellar, diplegic G80.1
  cervical
    plexus G54.2
    sympathetic G90.09
  Céstan-Chenais G46.3
  Charcot-Marie-Tooth type G60.0
  Clark's G80.9
  colon K56.0
  compressed air T70.3
  compression
    arm G56.9-●
    leg G57.9-●
    lower extremity G57.9-●
    upper extremity G56.9-●
  congenital (cerebral) —*see* Palsy, cerebral
  conjugate movement (gaze) (of eye) H51.0
    cortical (nuclear) (supranuclear) H51.0
  cordis —*see* Failure, heart
  cranial or cerebral nerve G52.9
  creeping G12.22
  crossed leg G83.89
  crutch —*see* Injury, brachial plexus
  deglutition R13.0
    hysterical F44.4
  dementia A52.17
  descending (spinal) NEC G12.29
  diaphragm (flaccid) J98.6
    due to accidental dissection of phrenic
        nerve during procedure —*see*
        Puncture, accidental complicating
        surgery
  digestive organs NEC K59.89
  diplegic —*see* Diplegia
  divergence (nuclear) H51.8
  diver's T70.3
  Duchenne's
    birth injury P14.0
    due to or associated with
      motor neuron disease G12.22
      muscular dystrophy G71.01

Paralysis, paralytic *(Continued)*
  due to intracranial or spinal birth injury —*see*
      Palsy, cerebral
  embolic (current episode) I63.4-●
  Erb (-Duchenne) (birth) (newborn) P14.0
  Erb's syphilitic spastic spinal A52.17
  esophagus K22.8
  eye muscle (extrinsic) H49.9
    intrinsic —*see also* Paresis, of
        accommodation
  facial (nerve) G51.0
    birth injury P11.3
    congenital P11.3
    following operation NEC —*see* Puncture,
        accidental complicating surgery
    newborn (birth injury) P11.3
  familial (recurrent) (periodic) G72.3
    spastic G11.4
  fauces J39.2
  finger G56.9-●
  gait R26.1
  gastric nerve (nondiabetic) G52.2
  gaze, conjugate H51.0
  general (progressive) (syphilitic) A52.17
    juvenile A50.45
  glottis J38.00
    bilateral J38.02
    unilateral J38.01
  gluteal G54.1
  Gubler (-Millard) G46.3
  hand —*see* Monoplegia, upper limb
  heart —*see* Arrest, cardiac
  hemiplegic —*see* Hemiplegia
  hyperkalemic periodic (familial) G72.3
  hypoglossal (nerve) G52.3
  hypokalemic periodic G72.3
  hysterical F44.4
  ileus K56.0
  infantile —*see also* Poliomyelitis, paralytic
      A80.30
    bulbar —*see* Poliomyelitis, paralytic
    cerebral —*see* Palsy, cerebral
    spastic —*see* Palsy, cerebral, spastic
  infective —*see* Poliomyelitis, paralytic
  inferior nuclear G83.9
  internuclear —*see* Ophthalmoplegia,
      internuclear
  intestine K56.0
  iris H57.09
    due to diphtheria (toxin) A36.89
  ischemic, Volkmann's (complicating trauma)
      T79.6
  Jackson's G83.89
  jake —*see* Poisoning, food, noxious, plant
  Jamaica ginger (jake) G62.2
  juvenile general A50.45
  Klumpke (-Déjérine) (birth) (newborn) P14.1
  labioglossal (laryngeal) (pharyngeal) G12.29
  Landry's G61.0
  laryngeal nerve (recurrent) (superior)
      (unilateral) J38.00
    bilateral J38.02
    unilateral J38.01
  larynx J38.00
    bilateral J38.02
    due to diphtheria (toxin) A36.2
    unilateral J38.01
  lateral G12.23
  lead —*see* subcategory T56.0
  left side —*see* Hemiplegia
  leg G83.1-●
    both —*see* Paraplegia
    crossed G83.89
    hysterical F44.4
    psychogenic F44.4
    transient or transitory R29.818
      traumatic NEC —*see* Injury, nerve, leg
  levator palpebrae superioris —*see*
      Blepharoptosis, paralytic
  limb —*see* Monoplegia
  lip K13.0

Paralysis, paralytic *(Continued)*
  Lissauer's A52.17
  lower limb —*see* Monoplegia, lower limb
    both —*see* Paraplegia
  lung J98.4
  median nerve G56.1-●
  medullary (tegmental) G83.89
  mesencephalic NEC G83.89
    tegmental G83.89
  middle alternating G83.89
  Millard-Gubler-Foville G46.3
  monoplegic —*see* Monoplegia
  motor G83.9
  muscle, muscular NEC G72.89
    due to nerve lesion G58.9
    eye (extrinsic) H49.9
      intrinsic —*see* Paresis, of accommodation
      oblique —*see* Strabismus, paralytic,
          fourth nerve
    iris sphincter H21.9
    ischemic (Volkmann's) (complicating
        trauma) T79.6
    progressive G12.21
    progressive, spinal G12.25
    pseudohypertrophic G71.02
    spinal progressive G12.25
  musculocutaneous nerve G56.9-●
  musculospiral G56.9-●
  nerve —*see also* Disorder, nerve
    abducent —*see* Strabismus, paralytic, sixth
        nerve
    accessory G52.8
    auditory (except Deafness) —*see*
        subcategory H93.3
    birth injury P14.9
    cranial or cerebral G52.9
    facial G51.0
      birth injury P11.3
      congenital P11.3
      newborn (birth injury) P11.3
    fourth or trochlear —*see* Strabismus,
        paralytic, fourth nerve
    newborn (birth injury) P14.9
    oculomotor —*see* Strabismus, paralytic,
        third nerve
    phrenic (birth injury) P14.2
    radial G56.3-●
    seventh or facial G51.0
      newborn (birth injury) P11.3
    sixth or abducent —*see* Strabismus,
        paralytic, sixth nerve
    syphilitic A52.15
    third or oculomotor —*see* Strabismus,
        paralytic, third nerve
    trigeminal G50.9
    trochlear —*see* Strabismus, paralytic,
        fourth nerve
    ulnar G56.2-●
  normokalemic periodic G72.3
  ocular H49.9
    alternating G83.89
  oculofacial, congenital (Moebius) Q87.0
  oculomotor (external bilateral) (nerve) —*see*
      Strabismus, paralytic, third nerve
  palate (soft) K13.79
  paratrigeminal G50.9
  periodic (familial) (hyperkalemic)
      (hypokalemic) (myotonic)
      (normokalemic) (potassium sensitive)
      (secondary) G72.3
  peripheral autonomic nervous system —*see*
      Neuropathy, peripheral, autonomic
  peroneal (nerve) G57.3-●
  pharynx J39.2
  phrenic nerve G56.8-●
  plantar nerve(s) G57.6-●
  pneumogastric nerve G52.2
  poliomyelitis (current) —*see* Poliomyelitis,
      paralytic
  popliteal nerve G57.3-●
  postepileptic transitory G83.84

Paralysis, paralytic *(Continued)*
  progressive (atrophic) (bulbar) (spinal)
      G12.22
    general A52.17
    infantile acute —*see* Poliomyelitis, paralytic
    supranuclear G23.1
  pseudobulbar G12.29
  pseudohypertrophic (muscle) G71.09
  psychogenic F44.4
  quadriceps G57.9-●
  quadriplegic —*see* Tetraplegia
  radial nerve G56.3-●
  rectus muscle (eye) H49.9
  recurrent isolated sleep G47.53
  respiratory (muscle) (system) (tract) R06.81
    center NEC G93.89
    congenital P28.89
    newborn P28.89
  right side —*see* Hemiplegia
  saturnine —*see* subcategory T56.0
  sciatic nerve G57.0-●
  senile G83.9
  shaking —*see* Parkinsonism
  shoulder G56.9-●
  sleep, recurrent isolated G47.53
  spastic G83.9
    cerebral —*see* Palsy, cerebral, spastic
    congenital (cerebral) —*see* Palsy, cerebral,
        spastic
    familial G11.4
    hereditary G11.4
    quadriplegic G80.0
    syphilitic (spinal) A52.17
  sphincter, bladder —*see* Paralysis, bladder
  spinal (cord) G83.9
    accessory nerve G52.8
    acute —*see* Poliomyelitis, paralytic
    ascending acute G61.0
    atrophic (acute) —*see also* Poliomyelitis,
        paralytic
      spastic, syphilitic A52.17
    congenital NEC —*see* Palsy, cerebral
    hereditary G95.89
    infantile —*see* Poliomyelitis, paralytic
    progressive G12.21
    muscle G12.25
    sequelae NEC G83.89
  sternomastoid G52.8
  stomach K31.84
    diabetic —*see* Diabetes, by type, with
        gastroparesis
    nerve G52.2
      diabetic —*see* Diabetes, by type, with
          gastroparesis
  stroke —*see* Infarct, brain
  subcapsularis G56.8-●
  supranuclear (progressive) G23.1
  sympathetic G90.8
    cervical G90.09
    nervous system —*see* Neuropathy,
        peripheral, autonomic
  syndrome G83.9
    specified NEC G83.89
  syphilitic spastic spinal (Erb's) A52.17
  thigh G57.9-●
  throat J39.2
    diphtheritic A36.0
    muscle J39.2
  thrombotic (current episode) I63.3-●
  thumb G56.9-●
  tick —*see* Toxicity, venom, arthropod,
      specified NEC
  Todd's (postepileptic transitory paralysis)
      G83.84
  toe G57.6-●
  tongue K14.8
  transient R29.5
    arm or leg NEC R29.818
    traumatic NEC —*see* Injury, nerve
  trapezius G52.8
  traumatic, transient NEC —*see* Injury, nerve

Paralysis, paralytic *(Continued)*
  trembling —*see* Parkinsonism
  triceps brachii G56.9-●
  trigeminal nerve G50.9
  trochlear (nerve) —*see* Strabismus, paralytic,
      fourth nerve
  ulnar nerve G56.2-●
  upper limb —*see* Monoplegia, upper limb
  uremic N18.9 *[G99.8]*
  uveoparotitic D86.89
  uvula K13.79
    postdiphtheritic A36.0
  vagus nerve G52.2
  vasomotor NEC G90.8
  velum palati K13.79
  vesical —*see* Paralysis, bladder
  vestibular nerve (except Vertigo) —*see*
      subcategory H93.3
  vocal cords J38.00
    bilateral J38.02
    unilateral J38.01
  Volkmann's (complicating trauma)
      T79.6
  wasting G12.29
  Weber's G46.3
  wrist G56.9-●
Paramedial urethrovesical orifice
    Q64.79
Paramenia N92.6
Parametritis —*see also* Disease, pelvis,
    inflammatory N73.2
  acute N73.0
  complicating abortion —*see* Abortion, by
      type, complicated by, parametritis
Parametrium, parametric —*see* condition
Paramnesia —*see* Amnesia
Paramolar K00.1
Paramyloidosis E85.89
Paramyoclonus multiplex G25.3
Paramyotonia (congenita) G71.19
Parangi —*see* Yaws
Paranoia (querulans) F22
  senile F03
Paranoid
  dementia (senile) F03
    praecox —*see* Schizophrenia
  personality F60.0
  psychosis (climacteric) (involutional)
      (menopausal) F22
    psychogenic (acute) F23
    senile F03
  reaction (acute) F23
    chronic F22
  schizophrenia F20.0
  state (climacteric) (involutional)
      (menopausal) (simple) F22
    senile F03
  tendencies F60.0
  traits F60.0
  trends F60.0
  type, psychopathic personality F60.0
Paraparesis —*see* Paraplegia
Paraphasia R47.02
Paraphilia F65.9
Paraphimosis (congenital) N47.2
  chancroidal A57
Paraphrenia, paraphrenic (late) F22
  schizophrenia F20.0
Paraplegia (lower) G82.20
  ataxic —*see* Degeneration, combined, spinal
      cord
  complete G82.21
  congenital (cerebral) G80.8
    spastic G80.1
  familial spastic G11.4
  functional (hysterical) F44.4
  hereditary, spastic G11.4
  hysterical F44.4
  incomplete G82.22
  Pott's A18.01
  psychogenic F44.4

Paraplegia *(Continued)*
  spastic
    Erb's spinal, syphilitic A52.17
    hereditary G11.4
    tropical G04.1
  syphilitic (spastic) A52.17
  traumatic
    current injury - code to injury with seventh
        character A
      sequela of previous injury - code to
          injury with seventh character S
  tropical spastic G04.1
Parapoxvirus B08.60
  specified NEC B08.69
Paraproteinemia D89.2
  benign (familial) D89.2
  monoclonal D47.2
  secondary to malignant disease D47.2
Parapsoriasis L41.9
  en plaques L41.4
  guttata L41.1
  large plaque L41.4
  retiform, retiformis L41.5
  small plaque L41.3
  specified NEC L41.8
  varioliformis (acuta) L41.0
Parasitic —*see also* condition
  disease NEC B89
  stomatitis B37.0
  sycosis (beard) (scalp) B35.0
  twin Q89.4
Parasitism B89
  intestinal B82.9
  skin B88.9
  specified —*see* Infestation
Parasitophobia F40.218
Parasomnia G47.50
  due to
    alcohol
      abuse F10.182
      dependence F10.282
      use F10.982
    amphetamines
      abuse F15.182
      dependence F15.282
      use F15.982
    caffeine
      abuse F15.182
      dependence F15.282
      use F15.982
    cocaine
      abuse F14.182
      dependence F14.282
      use F14.982
    drug NEC
      abuse F19.182
      dependence F19.282
      use F19.982
    opioid
      abuse F11.182
      dependence F11.282
      use F11.982
    psychoactive substance NEC
      abuse F19.182
      dependence F19.282
      use F19.982
    sedative, hypnotic, or anxiolytic
      abuse F13.182
      dependence F13.282
      use F13.982
    stimulant NEC
      abuse F15.182
      dependence F15.282
      use F15.982
  in conditions classified elsewhere
      G47.54
  nonorganic origin F51.8
  organic G47.50
  specified NEC G47.59
Paraspadias Q54.9
Paraspasmus facialis G51.8

▶ New   ⇒ Revised   ~~deleted~~ Deleted   ● Use Additional Character(s)

Parasuicide (attempt)
history of (personal) Z91.5
in family Z81.8
Parathyroid gland —*see* condition
Parathyroid tetany E20.9
Paratrachoma A74.0
Paratyphilitis —*see* Appendicitis
Paratyphoid (fever) —*see* Fever, paratyphoid
Paratyphus —*see* Fever, paratyphoid
Paraurethral duct Q64.79
Paraurethritis —*see also* Urethritis
gonococcal (acute) (chronic) (with abscess)
A54.1
Paravaccinia NEC B08.04
Paravaginitis —*see* Vaginitis
Parencephalitis —*see also* Encephalitis
sequelae G09
Parent-child conflict —*see* Conflict, parent-child
estrangement NEC Z62.890
Paresis —*see also* Paralysis
accommodation —*see* Paresis, of
accommodation
Bernhardt's G57.1-●
bladder (sphincter) —*see also* Paralysis, bladder
tabetic A52.17
bowel, colon or intestine K56.0
extrinsic muscle, eye H49.9
general (progressive) (syphilitic) A52.17
juvenile A50.45
heart —*see* Failure, heart
insane (syphilitic) A52.17
juvenile (general) A50.45
of accommodation H52.52-●
peripheral progressive (idiopathic) G60.3
pseudohypertrophic G71.09
senile G83.9
syphilitic (general) A52.17
congenital A50.45
vesical NEC N31.2
Paresthesia —*see also* Disturbance, sensation,
skin R20.2
Bernhardt G57.1-●
Paretic —*see* condition
Parinaud's
conjunctivitis H10.89
oculoglandular syndrome H10.89
ophthalmoplegia H49.88
Parkinsonism (idiopathic) (primary) G20
with neurogenic orthostatic hypotension
(symptomatic) G90.3
arteriosclerotic G21.4
dementia G31.83 [F02.80]
with behavioral disturbance G31.83 [F02.81]
due to
drugs NEC G21.19
neuroleptic G21.11
medication-induced NEC G21.19
neuroleptic induced G21.11
postencephalitic G21.3
secondary G21.9
due to
arteriosclerosis G21.4
drugs NEC G21.19
neuroleptic G21.11
encephalitis G21.3
external agents NEC G21.2
syphilis A52.19
specified NEC G21.8
syphilitic A52.19
treatment-induced NEC G21.19
vascular G21.4
Parkinson's disease, syndrome or tremor —*see*
Parkinsonism
Parodontitis —*see* Periodontitis
Parodontosis K05.4
Paronychia —*see also* Cellulitis, digit
with lymphangitis —*see* Lymphangitis, acute,
digit
candidal (chronic) B37.2
tuberculous (primary) A18.4
Parorexia (psychogenic) F50.89

Parosmia R43.1
psychogenic F45.8
Parotid gland —*see* condition
Parotitis, parotiditis (allergic) (nonspecific
toxic) (purulent) (septic) (suppurative) —
see also Sialoadenitis
epidemic —*see* Mumps
infectious —*see* Mumps
postoperative K91.89
surgical K91.89
Parrot fever A70
Parrot's disease (early congenital syphilitic
pseudoparalysis) A50.02
Parry-Romberg syndrome G51.8
Parry's disease or syndrome E05.00
with thyroid storm E05.01
Pars planitis —*see* Cyclitis
Parsonage (-Aldren)-Turner syndrome G54.5
Parson's disease (exophthalmic goiter) E05.00
with thyroid storm E05.01
Particolored infant Q82.8
Parturition —*see* Delivery
Parulis K04.7
with sinus K04.6
Parvovirus, as cause of disease classified
elsewhere B97.6
Pasini and Pierini's atrophoderma L90.3
Passage
false, urethra N36.5
meconium (newborn) during delivery P03.82
of sounds or bougies —*see* Attention to,
artificial, opening
Passive —*see* condition
smoking Z77.22
Pasteurella septica A28.0
Pasteurellosis —*see* Infection, Pasteurella
PAT (paroxysmal atrial tachycardia) I47.1
Patau's syndrome —*see* Trisomy, 13
Patches
mucous (syphilitic) A51.39
congenital A50.07
smokers' (mouth) K13.24
Patellar —*see* condition
Patent —*see also* Imperfect, closure
canal of Nuck Q52.4
cervix N88.3
ductus arteriosus or Botallo's Q25.0
foramen
botalli Q21.1
ovale Q21.1
interauricular septum Q21.1
interventricular septum Q21.0
omphalomesenteric duct Q43.0
os (uteri) —*see* Patent, cervix
ostium secundum Q21.1
urachus Q64.4
vitelline duct Q43.0
Paterson (-Brown)(-Kelly) syndrome or web
D50.1
Pathologic, pathological —*see also* condition
asphyxia R09.01
fire-setting F63.1
gambling F63.0
ovum O02.0
resorption, tooth K03.3
stealing F63.2
Pathology (of) —*see* Disease
periradicular, associated with previous
endodontic treatment NEC M27.59
Pattern, sleep-wake, irregular G47.23
Patulous —*see also* Imperfect, closure
(congenital)
alimentary tract Q45.8
lower Q43.8
upper Q40.8
eustachian tube H69.0-●
Pause, sinoatrial I49.5
Paxton's disease B36.2
Pearl(s)
enamel K00.2
Epstein's K09.8

Pearl-worker's disease —*see* Osteomyelitis,
specified type NEC
Pectenosis K62.4
Pectoral —*see* condition
Pectus
carinatum (congenital) Q67.7
acquired M95.4
rachitic sequelae (late effect) E64.3
excavatum (congenital) Q67.6
acquired M95.4
rachitic sequelae (late effect) E64.3
recurvatum (congenital) Q67.6
Pedatrophia E41
Pederosis F65.4
Pediculosis (infestation) B85.2
capitis (head-louse) (any site) B85.0
corporis (body-louse) (any site) B85.1
eyelid B85.0
mixed (classifiable to more than one of the
titles B85.0-B85.3) B85.4
pubis (pubic louse) (any site) B85.3
vestimenti B85.1
vulvae B85.3
Pediculus (infestation) —*see* Pediculosis
Pedophilia F65.4
Peg-shaped teeth K00.2
Pelade —*see* Alopecia, areata
Pelger-Huët anomaly or syndrome D72.0
Peliosis (rheumatica) D69.0
hepatis K76.4
with toxic liver disease K71.8
Pelizaeus-Merzbacher disease E75.29
Pellagra (alcoholic) (with polyneuropathy) E52
Pellagra-cerebellar-ataxia-renal aminoaciduria
syndrome E72.02
Pellegrini (-Stieda) disease or syndrome —*see*
Bursitis, tibial collateral
Pellizzi's syndrome E34.8
Pel's crisis A52.11
Pelvic —*see also* condition
examination (periodic) (routine) Z01.419
with abnormal findings Z01.411
kidney, congenital Q63.2
Pelviolithiasis —*see* Calculus, kidney
Pelviperitonitis —*see also* Peritonitis, pelvic
gonococcal A54.24
puerperal O85
Pelvis —*see* condition or type
Pemphigoid L12.9
benign, mucous membrane L12.1
bullous L12.0
cicatricial L12.1
juvenile L12.2
ocular L12.1
specified NEC L12.8
Pemphigus L10.9
benign familial (chronic) Q82.8
Brazilian L10.3
circinatus L13.0
conjunctiva L12.1
drug-induced L10.5
erythematosus L10.4
foliaceous L10.2
gangrenous —*see* Gangrene
neonatorum L01.03
ocular L12.1
paraneoplastic L10.81
specified NEC L10.89
syphilitic (congenital) A50.06
vegetans L10.1
vulgaris L10.0
wildfire L10.3
Pendred's syndrome E07.1
Pendulous
abdomen, in pregnancy —*see* Pregnancy,
complicated by, abnormal, pelvic organs
or tissues NEC
breast N64.89
Penetrating wound —*see also* Puncture
with internal injury —*see* Injury, by site
eyeball —*see* Puncture, eyeball

Penetrating wound (*Continued*)
orbit (with or without foreign body) —*see*
Puncture, orbit
uterus by instrument with or following
ectopic or molar pregnancy O08.6
Penicillosis B48.4
Penis —*see* condition
Penitis N48.29
Pentalogy of Fallot Q21.8
Pentasomy X syndrome Q97.1
Pentosuria (essential) E74.89
Percreta placenta O43.23-●
Peregrinating patient —*see* Disorder, factitious
Perforation, perforated (nontraumatic) (of)
accidental during procedure (blood vessel)
(nerve) (organ) —*see* Complication,
accidental puncture or laceration
antrum —*see* Sinusitis, maxillary
appendix K35.22
with localized peritonitis K35.32
atrial septum, multiple Q21.1
attic, ear —*see* Perforation, tympanum, attic
bile duct (common) (hepatic) K83.2
cystic K82.2
bladder (urinary)
with or following ectopic or molar
pregnancy O08.6
obstetrical trauma O71.5
traumatic S37.29
at delivery O71.5
bowel K63.1
with or following ectopic or molar
pregnancy O08.6
newborn P78.0
obstetrical trauma O71.5
traumatic —*see* Laceration, intestine
broad ligament N83.8
with or following ectopic or molar
pregnancy O08.6
obstetrical trauma O71.6
by
device, implant or graft —*see also*
Complications, by site and type,
mechanical T85.628
arterial graft NEC —*see* Complication,
cardiovascular device, mechanical,
vascular
breast (implant) T85.49
catheter NEC T85.698
cystostomy T83.090
dialysis (renal) T82.49
intraperitoneal T85.691
infusion NEC T82.594
spinal (epidural) (subdural) T85.690
urinary —*see also* Complications,
catheter, urinary T83.098
electronic (electrode) (pulse generator)
(stimulator)
bone T84.390
cardiac T82.199
electrode T82.190
pulse generator T82.191
specified type NEC T82.198
nervous system —*see* Complication,
prosthetic device, mechanical,
electronic nervous system
stimulator
urinary —*see* Complication,
genitourinary, device, urinary,
mechanical
fixation, internal (orthopedic) NEC —
see Complication, fixation device,
mechanical
gastrointestinal —*see* Complications,
prosthetic device, mechanical,
gastrointestinal device
genital NEC T83.498
intrauterine contraceptive device
T83.39
penile prosthesis T83.490
heart NEC —*see* Complication,
cardiovascular device, mechanical

Perforation, perforated (*Continued*)
by (*Continued*)
urinary (*Continued*)
joint prosthesis —*see* Complications,
joint prosthesis, mechanical,
specified NEC, by site
ocular NEC —*see* Complications,
prosthetic device, mechanical,
ocular device
orthopedic NEC —*see* Complication,
orthopedic, device, mechanical
specified NEC T85.628
urinary NEC —*see also* Complication,
genitourinary, device, urinary,
mechanical
graft T83.29
vascular NEC —*see* Complication,
cardiovascular device, mechanical
ventricular intracranial shunt T85.09
foreign body left accidentally in
operative wound T81.539
instrument (any) during a procedure,
accidental —*see* Puncture, accidental
complicating surgery
cecum K35.22
with localized peritonitis K35.32
cervix (uteri) N88.8
with or following ectopic or molar
pregnancy O08.6
obstetrical trauma O71.3
colon K63.1
newborn P78.0
obstetrical trauma O71.5
traumatic —*see* Laceration, intestine, large
common duct (bile) K83.2
cornea (due to ulceration) —*see* Ulcer,
cornea, perforated
cystic duct K82.2
diverticulum (intestine) K57.80
with bleeding K57.81
large intestine K57.20
with
bleeding K57.21
small intestine K57.40
with bleeding K57.41
small intestine K57.00
with
bleeding K57.01
large intestine K57.40
with bleeding K57.41
ear drum —*see* Perforation, tympanum
esophagus K22.3
ethmoidal sinus —*see* Sinusitis, ethmoidal
frontal sinus —*see* Sinusitis, frontal
gallbladder K82.2
heart valve —*see* Endocarditis
ileum K63.1
newborn P78.0
obstetrical trauma O71.5
traumatic —*see* Laceration, intestine, small
instrumental, surgical (accidental) (blood
vessel) (nerve) (organ) —*see* Puncture,
accidental complicating surgery
intestine NEC K63.1
with ectopic or molar pregnancy O08.6
newborn P78.0
obstetrical trauma O71.5
traumatic —*see* Laceration, intestine
ulcerative NEC K63.1
newborn P78.0
jejunum, jejunal K63.1
obstetrical trauma O71.5
traumatic —*see* Laceration, intestine, small
ulcer —*see* Ulcer, gastrojejunal, with
perforation
joint prosthesis —*see* Complications, joint
prosthesis, mechanical, specified NEC,
by site
mastoid (antrum) (cell) —*see* Disorder,
mastoid, specified NEC
maxillary sinus —*see* Sinusitis, maxillary

Perforation, perforated (*Continued*)
membrana tympani —*see* Perforation,
tympanum
nasal
septum J34.89
congenital Q30.3
syphilitic A52.73
sinus J34.89
congenital Q30.8
due to sinusitis —*see* Sinusitis
palate —*see also* Cleft, palate Q35.9
syphilitic A52.79
palatine vault —*see also* Cleft, palate, hard Q35.1
syphilitic A52.79
congenital A50.59
pars flaccida (ear drum) —*see* Perforation,
tympanum, attic
pelvic
floor S31.030
with
ectopic or molar pregnancy O08.6
penetration into retroperitoneal space
S31.031
retained foreign body S31.040
with penetration into
retroperitoneal space S31.041
following ectopic or molar pregnancy
O08.6
obstetrical trauma O70.1
organ S37.99
adrenal gland S37.818
bladder —*see* Perforation, bladder
fallopian tube S37.599
bilateral S37.592
unilateral S37.591
kidney S37.09-●
obstetrical trauma O71.5
ovary S37.499
bilateral S37.492
unilateral S37.491
prostate S37.828
specified organ NEC S37.898
ureter —*see* Perforation, ureter
urethra —*see* Perforation, urethra
uterus —*see* Perforation, uterus
perineum —*see* Laceration, perineum
pharynx J39.2
rectum K63.1
newborn P78.0
obstetrical trauma O71.5
traumatic S36.63
root canal space due to endodontic treatment
M27.51
sigmoid K63.1
newborn P78.0
obstetrical trauma O71.5
traumatic S36.533
sinus (accessory) (chronic) (nasal) J34.89
sphenoidal sinus —*see* Sinusitis, sphenoidal
surgical (accidental) (by instrument) (blood
vessel) (nerve) (organ) —*see* Puncture,
accidental complicating surgery
traumatic
external —*see* Puncture
eye —*see* Puncture, eyeball
internal organ —*see* Injury, by site
tympanum, tympanic (membrane) (persistent
post-traumatic) (postinflammatory)
H72.9-●
attic H72.1-●
multiple —*see* Perforation, tympanum,
multiple
total —*see* Perforation, tympanum, total
central H72.0-●
multiple —*see* Perforation, tympanum,
multiple
total —*see* Perforation, tympanum, total
marginal NEC —*see* subcategory H72.2
multiple H72.81-●
pars flaccida —*see* Perforation, tympanum,
attic

▶ New   ⇨ Revised   ~~deleted~~ Deleted   ● Use Additional Character(s)

Perforation, perforated *(Continued)*
  tympanum, tympanic *(Continued)*
    total H72.82-●
    traumatic, current episode S09.2-●
  typhoid, gastrointestinal —*see* Typhoid
  ulcer —*see* Ulcer, by site, with perforation
  ureter N28.89
    traumatic S37.19
  urethra N36.8
    with ectopic or molar pregnancy O08.6
    following ectopic or molar pregnancy O08.6
    obstetrical trauma O71.5
    traumatic S37.39
      at delivery O71.5
  uterus
    with ectopic or molar pregnancy O08.6
    by intrauterine contraceptive device T83.39
    following ectopic or molar pregnancy
      O08.6
    obstetrical trauma O71.1
    traumatic S37.69
      obstetric O71.1
  uvula K13.79
    syphilitic A52.79
  vagina
    obstetrical trauma O71.4
    other trauma - *see* Puncture, vagina
Periadenitis mucosa necrotica recurrens K12.0
Periappendicitis (acute) —*see* Appendicitis
Periarteritis nodosa (disseminated) (infectious)
  (necrotizing) M30.0
Periarthritis (joint) —*see also* Enthesopathy
  Duplay's M75.0-●
  gonococcal A54.42
  humeroscapularis —*see* Capsulitis, adhesive
  scapulohumeral —*see* Capsulitis, adhesive
  shoulder —*see* Capsulitis, adhesive
  wrist M77.2-●
Periarthrosis (angioneural) —*see* Enthesopathy
Pericapsulitis, adhesive (shoulder) —*see*
  Capsulitis, adhesive
Pericarditis (with decompensation) (with
  effusion) I31.9
  with rheumatic fever (conditions in I00)
    active —*see* Pericarditis, rheumatic
    inactive or quiescent I09.2
  acute (hemorrhagic) (nonrheumatic) (Sicca)
    I30.9
    with chorea (acute) (rheumatic)
      (Sydenham's) I02.0
    benign I30.8
    nonspecific I30.0
    rheumatic I01.0
      with chorea (acute) (Sydenham's) I02.0
  adhesive or adherent (chronic) (external)
    (internal) I31.0
    acute —*see* Pericarditis, acute
    rheumatic I09.2
  bacterial (acute) (subacute) (with serous or
    seropurulent effusion) I30.1
  calcareous I31.1
  cholesterol (chronic) I31.8
    acute I30.9
  chronic (nonrheumatic) I31.9
    rheumatic I09.2
  constrictive (chronic) I31.1
  coxsackie B33.23
  fibrinocaseous (tuberculous) A18.84
  fibrinopurulent I30.1
  fibrinous I30.8
  fibrous I31.0
  gonococcal A54.83
  idiopathic I30.0
  in systemic lupus erythematosus M32.12
  infective I30.1
  meningococcal A39.53
  neoplastic (chronic) I31.8
    acute I30.9
  obliterans, obliterating I31.0
  plastic I31.0
  pneumococcal I30.1

Pericarditis *(Continued)*
  postinfarction I24.1
  purulent I30.1
  rheumatic (active) (acute) (with effusion)
    (with pneumonia) I01.0
    with chorea (acute) (rheumatic)
      (Sydenham's) I02.0
    chronic or inactive (with chorea) I09.2
  rheumatoid —*see* Rheumatoid, carditis
  septic I30.1
  serofibrinous I30.8
  staphylococcal I30.1
  streptococcal I30.1
  suppurative I30.1
  syphilitic A52.06
  tuberculous A18.84
  uremic N18.9 *[I32]*
  viral I30.1
Pericardium, pericardial —*see* condition
Pericellulitis —*see* Cellulitis
Pericementitis (chronic) (suppurative) —*see also*
  Periodontitis
  acute K05.20
    generalized —*see* Periodontitis, aggressive,
      generalized
    localized —*see* Periodontitis, aggressive,
      localized
Perichondritis
  auricle —*see* Perichondritis, ear
  bronchus J98.09
  ear (external) H61.00-●
    acute H61.01-●
    chronic H61.02-●
  external auditory canal —*see* Perichondritis,
    ear
  larynx J38.7
    syphilitic A52.73
    typhoid A01.09
  nose J34.89
  pinna —*see* Perichondritis, ear
  trachea J39.8
Periclasia K05.4
Pericoronitis —*see* Periodontitis
Pericystitis N30.90
  with hematuria N30.91
Peridiverticulitis (intestine) K57.92
  cecum —*see* Diverticulitis, intestine, large
  colon —*see* Diverticulitis, intestine, large
  duodenum —*see* Diverticulitis, intestine,
    small
  intestine —*see* Diverticulitis, intestine
  jejunum —*see* Diverticulitis, intestine, small
  rectosigmoid —*see* Diverticulitis, intestine,
    large
  rectum —*see* Diverticulitis, intestine, large
  sigmoid —*see* Diverticulitis, intestine, large
Periendocarditis —*see* Endocarditis
Periepididymitis N45.1
Perifolliculitis L01.02
  abscedens, caput, scalp L66.3
  capitis, abscedens (et suffodiens) L66.3
  superficial pustular L01.02
Perihepatitis K65.8
Perilabyrinthitis (acute) —*see* subcategory H83.0
Perimeningitis —*see* Meningitis
Perimetritis —*see* Endometritis
Perimetrosalpingitis —*see* Salpingo-oophoritis
Perineocele N81.81
Perinephric, perinephritic —*see* condition
Perinephritis —*see also* Infection, kidney
  purulent —*see* Abscess, kidney
Perineum, perineal —*see* condition
Perineuritis NEC —*see* Neuralgia
Periodic —*see* condition
Periodontitis (chronic) (complex) (compound)
  (local) (simplex) K05.30
  acute K05.20
    generalized K05.229
      moderate K05.222
      severe K05.223
      slight K05.221

Periodontitis *(Continued)*
  acute *(Continued)*
    localized K05.219
      moderate K05.212
      severe K05.213
      slight K05.211
  apical K04.5
    acute (pulpal origin) K04.4
  generalized K05.329
    moderate K05.322
    severe K05.323
    slight K05.321
  localized K05.319
    moderate K05.312
    severe K05.313
    slight K05.311
Periodontoclasia K05.4
Periodontosis (juvenile) K05.4
Periods —*see also* Menstruation
  heavy N92.0
  irregular N92.6
  shortened intervals (irregular) N92.1
Perionychia —*see also* Cellulitis, digit
  with lymphangitis —*see* Lymphangitis, acute,
    digit
Perioophoritis —*see* Salpingo-oophoritis
Periorchitis N45.2
Periosteum, periosteal —*see* condition
Periostitis (albuminosa) (circumscribed)
  (diffuse) (infective) (monomelic) —*see also*
  Osteomyelitis
  alveolar M27.3
  alveolodental M27.3
  dental M27.3
  gonorrheal A54.43
  jaw (lower) (upper) M27.2
  orbit H05.03-●
  syphilitic A52.77
    congenital (early) A50.02 *[M90.80]*
    secondary A51.46
  tuberculous —*see* Tuberculosis, bone
  yaws (hypertrophic) (early) (late) A66.6
    [M90.80]
Periostosis (hyperplastic) —*see also* Disorder,
  bone, specified type NEC
  with osteomyelitis —*see* Osteomyelitis,
    specified type NEC
Peripartum
  cardiomyopathy O90.3
Periphlebitis —*see* Phlebitis
Periproctitis K62.89
Periprostatitis —*see* Prostatitis
Perirectal —*see* condition
Perirenal —*see* condition
Perisalpingitis —*see* Salpingo-oophoritis
Perisplenitis (infectional) D73.89
Peristalsis, visible or reversed R19.2
Peritendinitis —*see* Enthesopathy
Peritoneum, peritoneal —*see* condition
Peritonitis (adhesive) (bacterial) (fibrinous)
  (hemorrhagic) (idiopathic) (localized)
  (perforative) (primary) (with adhesions)
  (with effusion) K65.9
  with or following
    abscess K65.1
    appendicitis
      with perforation or rupture K35.32
      generalized (*see also* Appendicitis) K35.20
      localized (*see also* Appendicitis) K35.30
    diverticular disease (intestine) K57.80
      with bleeding K57.81
    ectopic or molar pregnancy O08.0
    large intestine K57.20
      with
        bleeding K57.21
        small intestine K57.40
          with bleeding K57.41
    small intestine K57.00
      with
        bleeding K57.01
        large intestine K57.40
          with bleeding K57.41

Peritonitis *(Continued)*
  acute (generalized) K65.0
  aseptic T81.61
  bile, biliary K65.3
  chemical T81.61
  chlamydial A74.81
  chronic proliferative K65.8
  complicating abortion —*see* Abortion, by
      type, complicated by, pelvic peritonitis
  congenital P78.1
  diaphragmatic K65.0
  diffuse K65.0
  diphtheritic A36.89
  disseminated K65.0
  due to
    bile K65.3
    foreign
      body or object accidentally left during
          a procedure (instrument) (sponge)
          (swab) T81.599
      substance accidentally left during a
          procedure (chemical) (powder)
          (talc) T81.61
    talc T81.61
    urine K65.8
  eosinophilic K65.8
    acute K65.0
  fibrocaseous (tuberculous) A18.31
  fibropurulent K65.0
  following ectopic or molar pregnancy
      O08.0
  general (ized) K65.0
  gonococcal A54.85
  meconium (newborn) P78.0
  neonatal P78.1
    meconium P78.0
  pancreatic K65.0
  paroxysmal, familial E85.0
    benign E85.0
  pelvic
    female N73.5
      acute N73.3
      chronic N73.4
        with adhesions N73.6
    male K65.0
  periodic, familial E85.0
  proliferative, chronic K65.8
  puerperal, postpartum, childbirth O85
  purulent K65.0
  septic K65.0
  specified NEC K65.8
  spontaneous bacterial K65.2
  subdiaphragmatic K65.0
  subphrenic K65.0
  suppurative K65.0
  syphilitic A52.74
    congenital (early) A50.08 *[K67]*
  talc T81.61
  tuberculous A18.31
  urine K65.8
Peritonsillar —*see* condition
Peritonsillitis J36
Perityphlitis K37
Periureteritis N28.89
Periurethral —*see* condition
Periurethritis (gangrenous) —*see* Urethritis
Periuterine —*see* condition
Perivaginitis —*see* Vaginitis
Perivasculitis, retinal H35.06-●
Perivasitis (chronic) N49.1
Perivesiculitis (seminal) —*see* Vesiculitis
Perlèche NEC K13.0
  due to
    candidiasis B37.83
    moniliasis B37.83
    riboflavin deficiency E53.0
    vitamin B2 (riboflavin) deficiency E53.0
Pernicious —*see* condition
Pernio, perniosis T69.1
Perpetrator (of abuse) —*see* Index to External
    Causes of Injury, Perpetrator

Persecution
  delusion F22
  social Z60.5
Perseveration (tonic) R48.8
Persistence, persistent (congenital)
  anal membrane Q42.3
    with fistula Q42.2
  arteria stapedia Q16.3
  atrioventricular canal Q21.2
  branchial cleft NOS Q18.2
    cyst Q18.0
    fistula Q18.0
    sinus Q18.0
  bulbus cordis in left ventricle Q21.8
  canal of Cloquet Q14.0
  capsule (opaque) Q12.8
  cilioretinal artery or vein Q14.8
  cloaca Q43.7
  communication —*see* Fistula, congenital
  convolutions
    aortic arch Q25.46
    fallopian tube Q50.6
    oviduct Q50.6
    uterine tube Q50.6
  double aortic arch Q25.45
  ductus arteriosus (Botalli) Q25.0
  fetal
    circulation P29.38
    form of cervix (uteri) Q51.828
    hemoglobin, hereditary (HPFH) D56.4
  foramen
    Botalli Q21.1
    ovale Q21.1
  Gartner's duct Q52.4
  hemoglobin, fetal (hereditary) (HPFH)
      D56.4
  hyaloid
    artery (generally incomplete) Q14.0
    system Q14.8
  hymen, in pregnancy or childbirth —*see*
      Pregnancy, complicated by, abnormal,
      vulva
  lanugo Q84.2
  left
    posterior cardinal vein Q26.8
    root with right arch of aorta Q25.49
    superior vena cava Q26.1
  Meckel's diverticulum Q43.0
    malignant —*see* Table of Neoplasms, small
        intestine, malignant
  mucosal disease (middle ear) —*see*
      Otitis, media, suppurative, chronic,
      tubotympanic
  nail(s), anomalous Q84.6
  omphalomesenteric duct Q43.0
  organ or site not listed —*see* Anomaly, by site
  ostium
    atrioventriculare commune Q21.2
    primum Q21.2
    secundum Q21.1
  ovarian rests in fallopian tube Q50.6
  pancreatic tissue in intestinal tract Q43.8
  primary (deciduous)
    teeth K00.6
    vitreous hyperplasia Q14.0
  pupillary membrane Q13.89
  rhesus (Rh)titer —*see* Complication(s),
      transfusion, incompatibility reaction, Rh
      (factor)
  right aortic arch Q25.47
  sinus
    urogenitalis
      female Q52.8
      male Q55.8
    venosus with imperfect incorporation in
        right auricle Q26.8
  thymus (gland) (hyperplasia) E32.0
  thyroglossal duct Q89.2
  thyrolingual duct Q89.2
  truncus arteriosus or communis Q20.0
  tunica vasculosa lentis Q12.2

Persistence, persistent *(Continued)*
  umbilical sinus Q64.4
  urachus Q64.4
  vitelline duct Q43.0
Person (with)
  admitted for clinical research, as a
      control subject (normal comparison)
      (participant) Z00.6
  awaiting admission to adequate facility
      elsewhere Z75.1
  concern (normal) about sick person in family
      Z63.6
  consulting on behalf of another Z71.0
  feigning illness Z76.5
  living (in)
    without
      adequate housing (heating) (space) Z59.1
      housing (permanent) (temporary) Z59.0
      person able to render necessary care
          Z74.2
      shelter Z59.0
    alone Z60.2
    boarding school Z59.3
    residential institution Z59.3
  on waiting list Z75.1
  sick or handicapped in family Z63.6
Personality (disorder) F60.9
  accentuation of traits (type A pattern) Z73.1
  affective F34.0
  aggressive F60.3
  amoral F60.2
  anacastic, anankastic F60.5
  antisocial F60.2
  anxious F60.6
  asocial F60.2
  asthenic F60.7
  avoidant F60.6
  borderline F60.3
  change due to organic condition (enduring)
      F07.0
  compulsive F60.5
  cycloid F34.0
  cyclothymic F34.0
  dependent F60.7
  depressive F34.1
  dissocial F60.2
  dual F44.81
  eccentric F60.89
  emotionally unstable F60.3
  expansive paranoid F60.0
  explosive F60.3
  fanatic F60.0
  haltlose type F60.89
  histrionic F60.4
  hyperthymic F34.0
  hypothymic F34.1
  hysterical F60.4
  immature F60.89
  inadequate F60.7
  labile (emotional) F60.3
  mixed (nonspecific) F60.89
  morally defective F60.2
  multiple F44.81
  narcissistic F60.81
  obsessional F60.5
  obsessive (-compulsive) F60.5
  organic F07.0
  overconscientious F60.5
  paranoid F60.0
  passive (-dependent) F60.7
  passive-aggressive F60.89
  pathologic F60.9
  pattern defect or disturbance F60.9
  pseudopsychopathic (organic) F07.0
  pseudoretarded (organic) F07.0
  psychoinfantile F60.4
  psychoneurotic NEC F60.89
  psychopathic F60.2
  querulant F60.0
  sadistic F60.89
  schizoid F60.1

▶ New   ⇒ Revised   ~~deleted~~ Deleted   ● Use Additional Character(s)

Personality *(Continued)*
  self-defeating F60.89
  sensitive paranoid F60.0
  sociopathic (amoral) (antisocial) (asocial)
    (dissocial) F60.2
  specified NEC F60.89
  type A Z73.1
  unstable (emotional) F60.3
Perthes' disease —*see* Legg-Calvé-Perthes
  disease
Pertussis *(see also* Whooping cough) A37.90
Perversion, perverted
  appetite F50.89
    psychogenic F50.89
  function
    pituitary gland E23.2
      posterior lobe E22.2
  sense of smell and taste R43.8
    psychogenic F45.8
  sexual —*see* Deviation, sexual
Pervious, congenital —*see also* Imperfect, closure
  ductus arteriosus Q25.0
Pes (congenital) —*see also* Talipes
  acquired —*see also* Deformity, limb, foot,
    specified NEC
    planus —*see* Deformity, limb, flat foot
  adductus Q66.89
  cavus Q66.7-●
  deformity NEC, acquired —*see* Deformity,
    limb, foot, specified NEC
  planus (acquired) (any degree) —*see also*
    Deformity, limb, flat foot
    rachitic sequelae (late effect) E64.3
  valgus Q66.6
Pest, pestis —*see* Plague
Petechia, petechiae R23.3
  newborn P54.5
Petechial typhus A75.9
Peter's anomaly Q13.4
Petit mal seizure —*see* Epilepsy, childhood,
  absence
Petit's hernia —*see* Hernia, abdomen, specified
  site NEC
Petrellidosis B48.2
Petrositis H70.20-●
  acute H70.21-●
  chronic H70.22-●
Peutz-Jeghers disease or syndrome Q85.8
Peyronie's disease N48.6
PFAPA (periodic fever, aphthous stomatitis,
  pharyngitis, and adenopathy syndrome)
  M04.8
Pfeiffer's disease —*see* Mononucleosis,
  infectious
Phagedena (dry) (moist) (sloughing) —*see also*
  Gangrene
  geometric L88
  penis N48.29
  tropical —*see* Ulcer, skin
  vulva N76.6
Phagedenic —*see* condition
Phakoma H35.89
Phakomatosis —*see also* specific eponymous
  syndromes Q85.9
  Bourneville's Q85.1
  specified NEC Q85.8
Phantom limb syndrome (without pain) G54.7
  with pain G54.6
Pharyngeal pouch syndrome D82.1
Pharyngitis (acute) (catarrhal) (gangrenous)
  (infective) (malignant) (membranous)
  (phlegmonous) (pseudomembranous)
  (simple) (subacute) (suppurative)
  (ulcerative) (viral) J02.9
  with influenza, flu, or grippe —*see* Influenza,
    with, pharyngitis
  aphthous B08.5
  atrophic J31.2
  chlamydial A56.4
  chronic (atrophic) (granular) (hypertrophic)
    J31.2

Pharyngitis *(Continued)*
  coxsackievirus B08.5
  diphtheritic A36.0
  enteroviral vesicular B08.5
  follicular (chronic) J31.2
  fusospirochetal A69.1
  gonococcal A54.5
  granular (chronic) J31.2
  herpesviral B00.2
  hypertrophic J31.2
  infectional, chronic J31.2
  influenzal —*see* Influenza, with, respiratory
    manifestations NEC
  lymphonodular, acute (enteroviral) B08.8
  pneumococcal J02.8
  purulent J02.9
  putrid J02.9
  septic J02.0
  sicca J31.2
  specified organism NEC J02.8
  staphylococcal J02.8
  streptococcal J02.0
  syphilitic, congenital (early) A50.03
  tuberculous A15.8
  vesicular, enteroviral B08.5
  viral NEC J02.8
Pharyngoconjunctivitis, viral B30.2
Pharyngolaryngitis (acute) J06.0
  chronic J37.0
Pharyngoplegia J39.2
Pharyngotonsillitis, herpesviral B00.2
Pharyngotracheitis, chronic J42
Pharynx, pharyngeal —*see* condition
Phencyclidine-induced
  anxiety disorder F16.980
  bipolar and related disorder F16.94
  depressive disorder F16.94
  psychotic disorder F16.959
Phenomenon
  Arthus' —*see* Arthus' phenomenon
  jaw-winking Q07.8
  lupus erythematosus (LE) cell M32.9
  Raynaud's (secondary) I73.00
    with gangrene I73.01
  vasomotor R55
  vasospastic I73.9
  vasovagal R55
  Wenckebach's I44.1
Phenylketonuria E70.1
  classical E70.0
  maternal E70.1
Pheochromoblastoma
  specified site —*see* Neoplasm, malignant, by
    site
  unspecified site C74.10
Pheochromocytoma
  malignant
    specified site —*see* Neoplasm, malignant,
      by site
    unspecified site C74.10
  specified site —*see* Neoplasm, benign, by site
  unspecified site D35.00
Pheohyphomycosis —*see* Chromomycosis
Pheomycosis —*see* Chromomycosis
Phimosis (congenital) (due to infection) N47.1
  chancroidal A57
Phlebectasia —*see also* Varix
  congenital Q27.4
Phlebitis (infective) (pyemic) (septic)
  (suppurative) I80.9
  antepartum —*see* Thrombophlebitis,
    antepartum
  blue —*see* Phlebitis, leg, deep
  breast, superficial I80.8
  calf muscular vein (NOS) I80.25-●
  cavernous (venous) sinus —*see* Phlebitis,
    intracranial (venous) sinus
  cerebral (venous) sinus —*see* Phlebitis,
    intracranial (venous) sinus
  chest wall, superficial I80.8
  cranial (venous) sinus —*see* Phlebitis,
    intracranial (venous) sinus

Phlebitis *(Continued)*
  deep (vessels) —*see* Phlebitis, leg, deep
  due to implanted device —*see* Complications,
    by site and type, specified NEC
  during or resulting from a procedure T81.72
  femoral vein (superficial) I80.1-●
  femoropopliteal vein I80.0-●
  gastrocnemial vein I80.25-●
  gestational —*see* Phlebopathy, gestational
  hepatic veins I80.8
  iliac vein (common) (external) (internal)
    I80.21-●
  iliofemoral —*see* Phlebitis, femoral vein
  intracranial (venous) sinus (any) G08
    nonpyogenic I67.6
  intraspinal venous sinuses and veins G08
    nonpyogenic G95.19
  lateral (venous) sinus —*see* Phlebitis,
    intracranial (venous) sinus
  leg I80.3
    antepartum —*see* Thrombophlebitis,
      antepartum
    deep (vessels) NEC I80.20-●
      iliac I80.21-●
      popliteal vein I80.22-●
      specified vessel NEC I80.29-●
      tibial vein (anterior) (posterior) I80.23-●
    femoral vein (superficial) I80.1-●
    superficial (vessels) I80.0-●
  longitudinal sinus —*see* Phlebitis, intracranial
    (venous) sinus
  lower limb —*see* Phlebitis, leg
  migrans, migrating (superficial) I82.1
  pelvic
    with ectopic or molar pregnancy O08.0
    following ectopic or molar pregnancy O08.0
    puerperal, postpartum O87.1
  peroneal vein I80.24-●
  popliteal vein —*see* Phlebitis, leg, deep,
    popliteal
  portal (vein) K75.1
  postoperative T81.72
  pregnancy —*see* Thrombophlebitis,
    antepartum
  puerperal, postpartum, childbirth O87.0
    deep O87.1
    pelvic O87.1
    superficial O87.0
  retina —*see* Vasculitis, retina
  saphenous (accessory) (great) (long)
    (small) —*see* Phlebitis, leg, superficial
  sinus (meninges) —*see* Phlebitis, intracranial
    (venous) sinus
  soleal vein I80.25-●
  specified site NEC I80.8
  syphilitic A52.09
  tibial vein —*see* Phlebitis, leg, deep, tibial
  ulcerative I80.9
    leg —*see* Phlebitis, leg
  umbilicus I80.8
  uterus (septic) —*see* Endometritis
  varicose (leg) (lower limb) —*see* Varix, leg,
    with, inflammation
Phlebofibrosis I87.8
Phleboliths I87.8
Phlebopathy
  gestational O22.9-●
  puerperal O87.9
Phlebosclerosis I87.8
Phlebothrombosis —*see also* Thrombosis
  antepartum —*see* Thrombophlebitis,
    antepartum
  pregnancy —*see* Thrombophlebitis,
    antepartum
  puerperal —*see* Thrombophlebitis, puerperal
Phlebotomus fever A93.1
Phlegmasia
  alba dolens O87.1
    nonpuerperal —*see* Phlebitis, femoral vein
  cerulea dolens —*see* Phlebitis, leg, deep
Phlegmon —*see* Abscess
Phlegmonous —*see* condition

Phlyctenulosis (allergic) (keratoconjunctivitis) (nontuberculous) —see also Keratoconjunctivitis
  cornea —see Keratoconjunctivitis
  tuberculous A18.52
Phobia, phobic F40.9
  animal F40.218
    spiders F40.210
  examination F40.298
  reaction F40.9
  simple F40.298
  social F40.10
    generalized F40.11
  specific (isolated) F40.298
    animal F40.218
      spiders F40.210
    blood F40.230
    injection F40.231
    injury F40.233
    men F40.290
    natural environment F40.228
      thunderstorms F40.220
    situational F40.248
      bridges F40.242
      closed in spaces F40.240
      flying F40.243
      heights F40.241
    specified focus NEC F40.298
    transfusion F40.231
    women F40.291
  specified NEC F40.8
    medical care NEC F40.232
  state F40.9
Phocas' disease —see Mastopathy, cystic
Phocomelia Q73.1
  lower limb —see Agenesis, leg, with foot present
  upper limb —see Agenesis, arm, with hand present
Phoria H50.50
Phosphate-losing tubular disorder N25.0
Phosphatemia E83.39
Phosphaturia E83.39
Photodermatitis (sun) L56.8
  chronic L57.8
  due to drug L56.8
  light other than sun L59.8
Photokeratitis H16.13-•
Photophobia H53.14-•
Photophthalmia —see Photokeratitis
Photopsia H53.19
Photoretinitis —see Retinopathy, solar
Photosensitivity, photosensitization (sun) skin L56.8
  light other than sun L59.8
Phrenitis —see Encephalitis
Phrynoderma (vitamin A deficiency) E50.8
Phthiriasis (pubis) B85.3
  with any infestation classifiable to B85.0-B85.2 B85.4
Phthirus infestation —see Phthiriasis
Phthisis —see also Tuberculosis
  bulbi (infectional) —see Disorder, globe, degenerated condition, atrophy
  eyeball (due to infection) —see Disorder, globe, degenerated condition, atrophy
Phycomycosis —see Zygomycosis
Physalopteriasis B81.8
Physical restraint status Z78.1
Phytobezoar T18.9
  intestine T18.3
  stomach T18.2
Pian —see Yaws
Pianoma A66.1
Pica F50.89
  in adults F50.89
  infant or child F98.3
Picking, nose F98.8
Pick-Niemann disease —see Niemann-Pick disease or syndrome

Pick's
  cerebral atrophy G31.01 [F02.80]
    with behavioral disturbance G31.01 [F02.81]
  disease or syndrome (brain) G31.01 [F02.80]
    with behavioral disturbance G31.01 [F02.81]
    brain G31.01 [F02.80]
      with behavioral disturbance G31.01 [F02.81]
    pericardium (pericardial pseudocirrhosis of liver) I31.1
  syndrome
    brain G31.01 [F02.80]
      with behavioral disturbance G31.01 [F02.81]
    of heart (pericardial pseudocirrhosis of liver) I31.1
Pickwickian syndrome E66.2
Piebaldism E70.39
Piedra (beard) (scalp) B36.8
  black B36.3
  white B36.2
Pierre Robin deformity or syndrome Q87.0
Pierson's disease or osteochondrosis M91.0
Pig-bel A05.2
Pigeon
  breast or chest (acquired) M95.4
    congenital Q67.7
    rachitic sequelae (late effect) E64.3
  breeder's disease or lung J67.2
  fancier's disease or lung J67.2
  toe —see Deformity, toe, specified NEC
Pigmentation (abnormal) (anomaly) L81.9
  conjunctiva H11.13-•
  cornea (anterior) H18.01-•
    posterior H18.05-•
    stromal H18.06-•
  diminished melanin formation NEC L81.6
  iron L81.8
  lids, congenital Q82.8
  limbus corneae —see Pigmentation, cornea
  metals L81.8
  optic papilla, congenital Q14.2
  retina, congenital (grouped) (nevoid) Q14.1
  scrotum, congenital Q82.8
  tattoo L81.8
Piles —see also Hemorrhoids K64.9
Pili
  annulati or torti (congenital) Q84.1
  incarnati L73.1
Pill roller hand (intrinsic) —see Parkinsonism
Pilomatrixoma —see Neoplasm, skin, benign
  malignant —see Neoplasm, skin, malignant
Pilonidal —see condition
Pimple R23.8
PIN —see Neoplasia, intraepithelial, prostate
Pinched nerve —see Neuropathy, entrapment
Pindborg tumor —see Cyst, calcifying odontogenic
Pineal body or gland —see condition
Pinealoblastoma C75.3
Pinealoma D44.5
  malignant C75.3
Pineoblastoma C75.3
Pineocytoma D44.5
Pinguecula H11.15-•
Pingueculitis H10.81-•
Pinhole meatus —see also Stricture, urethra N35.919
Pink
  disease —see subcategory T56.1
  eye —see Conjunctivitis, acute, mucopurulent
Pinkus' disease (lichen nitidus) L44.1
Pinpoint
  meatus —see Stricture, urethra
  os (uteri) —see Stricture, cervix
Pins and needles R20.2
Pinta A67.9
  cardiovascular lesions A67.2
  chancre (primary) A67.0

Pinta (Continued)
  erythematous plaques A67.1
  hyperchromic lesions A67.1
  hyperkeratosis A67.1
  lesions A67.9
    cardiovascular A67.2
    hyperchromic A67.1
    intermediate A67.1
    late A67.2
    mixed A67.3
    primary A67.0
    skin (achromic) (cicatricial) (dyschromic) A67.2
      hyperchromic A67.1
      mixed (achromic and hyperchromic) A67.3
  papule (primary) A67.0
  skin lesions (achromic) (cicatricial) (dyschromic) A67.2
    hyperchromic A67.1
    mixed (achromic and hyperchromic) A67.3
  vitiligo A67.2
Pintids A67.1
Pinworm (disease) (infection) (infestation) B80
Piroplasmosis (see also Babesiosis) B60.00
  specified NEC B60.09
Pistol wound —see Gunshot wound
Pitchers' elbow —see Derangement, joint, specified type NEC, elbow
Pithecoid pelvis Q74.2
  with disproportion (fetopelvic) O33.0
    causing obstructed labor O65.0
Pithiatism F48.8
Pitted —see Pitting
Pitting —see also Edema R60.9
  lip R60.0
  nail L60.8
  teeth K00.4
Pituitary gland —see condition
Pituitary-snuff-taker's disease J67.8
Pityriasis (capitis) L21.0
  alba L30.5
  circinata (et maculata) L42
  furfuracea L21.0
  Hebra's L26
  lichenoides L41.0
    chronica L41.1
    et varioliformis (acuta) L41.0
  maculata (et circinata) L30.5
  nigra B36.1
  pilaris, Hebra's L44.0
  rosea L42
  rotunda L44.8
  rubra (Hebra) pilaris L44.0
  simplex L30.5
  specified type NEC L30.5
  streptogenes L30.5
  versicolor (scrotal) B36.0
Placenta, placental —see Pregnancy, complicated by (care of) (management affected by), specified condition
Placentitis O41.14-•
Plagiocephaly Q67.3
Plague A20.9
  abortive A20.8
  ambulatory A20.8
  asymptomatic A20.8
  bubonic A20.0
  cellulocutaneous A20.1
  cutaneobubonic A20.1
  lymphatic gland A20.0
  meningitis A20.3
  pharyngeal A20.8
  pneumonic (primary) (secondary) A20.2
  pulmonary, pulmonic A20.2
  septicemic A20.7
  tonsillar A20.8
    septicemic A20.7
Planning, family
  contraception Z30.9
  procreation Z31.69

Plaque(s)
artery, arterial —*see* Arteriosclerosis
calcareous —*see* Calcification
coronary, lipid rich I25.83
epicardial I31.8
erythematous, of pinta A67.1
Hollenhorst's —*see* Occlusion, artery, retina
lipid rich, coronary I25.83
pleural (without asbestos) J92.9
with asbestos J92.0
tongue K13.29
Plasmacytoma C90.3-●
extramedullary C90.2-●
medullary C90.0-●
solitary C90.3-●
Plasmacytopenia D72.818
Plasmacytosis D72.822
Plaster ulcer —*see* Ulcer, pressure, by site
Plateau iris syndrome (post-iridectomy)
(postprocedural) (without glaucoma)
H21.82
with glaucoma H40.22-●
Platybasia Q75.8
Platyonychia (congenital) Q84.6
acquired L60.8
Platypelloid pelvis M95.5
with disproportion (fetopelvic) O33.0
causing obstructed labor O65.0
congenital Q74.2
Platyspondylisis Q76.49
Plaut (-Vincent) disease —*see also* Vincent's
A69.1
Plethora R23.2
newborn P61.1
Pleura, pleural —*see* condition
Pleuralgia R07.81
Pleurisy (acute) (adhesive) (chronic) (costal)
(diaphragmatic) (double) (dry) (fibrinous)
(fibrous) (interlobar) (latent) (plastic)
(primary) (residual) (sicca) (sterile)
(subacute) (unresolved) R09.1
with
adherent pleura J86.0
effusion J90
chylous, chyliform J94.0
tuberculous (non primary) A15.6
primary (progressive) A15.7
tuberculosis —*see* Pleurisy, tuberculous
(non primary)
encysted —*see* Pleurisy, with effusion
exudative —*see* Pleurisy, with effusion
fibrinopurulent, fibropurulent —*see*
Pyothorax
hemorrhagic —*see* Hemothorax
pneumococcal J90
purulent —*see* Pyothorax
septic —*see* Pyothorax
serofibrinous —*see* Pleurisy, with effusion
seropurulent —*see* Pyothorax
serous —*see* Pleurisy, with effusion
staphylococcal J86.9
streptococcal J90
suppurative —*see* Pyothorax
traumatic (post) (current) —*see* Injury,
intrathoracic, pleura
tuberculous (with effusion) (non primary)
A15.6
primary (progressive) A15.7
Pleuritis sicca —*see* Pleurisy
Pleurobronchopneumonia —*see* Pneumonia,
broncho
Pleurodynia R07.81
epidemic B33.0
viral B33.0
Pleuropericarditis —*see also* Pericarditis
acute I30.9
Pleuropneumonia (acute) (bilateral) (double)
(septic) —*see also* Pneumonia J18.8
chronic —*see* Fibrosis, lung
Pleuro-pneumonia-like-organism (PPLO), as
cause of disease classified elsewhere B96.0

Pleurorrhea —*see* Pleurisy, with effusion
Plexitis, brachial G54.0
Plica
polonica B85.0
syndrome, knee M67.5
tonsil J35.8
Plicated tongue K14.5
Plug
bronchus NEC J98.09
meconium (newborn) NEC syndrome
P76.0
mucus —*see* Asphyxia, mucus
Plumbism —*see* subcategory T56.0
Plummer's disease E05.20
with thyroid storm E05.21
Plummer-Vinson syndrome D50.1
Pluricarential syndrome of infancy E40
Plus (and minus) hand (intrinsic) —*see*
Deformity, limb, specified type NEC,
forearm
► PMEI (polymorphic epilepsy in infancy)
G40.83-●
Pneumathemia —*see* Air, embolism
Pneumatic hammer (drill) syndrome T75.21
Pneumatocele (lung) J98.4
intracranial G93.89
tension J44.9
Pneumatosis
cystoides intestinalis K63.89
intestinalis K63.89
peritonei K66.8
Pneumaturia R39.89
Pneumoblastoma —*see* Neoplasm, lung,
malignant
Pneumocephalus G93.89
Pneumococcemia A40.3
Pneumococcus, pneumococcal —*see* condition
Pneumoconiosis (due to) (inhalation of) J64
with tuberculosis (any type in A15) J65
aluminum J63.0
asbestos J61
bagasse, bagassosis J67.1
bauxite J63.1
beryllium J63.2
coal miners' (simple) J60
coalworkers' (simple) J60
collier's J60
cotton dust J66.0
diatomite (diatomaceous earth) J62.8
dust
inorganic NEC J63.6
lime J62.8
marble J62.8
organic NEC J66.8
fumes or vapors (from silo) J68.9
graphite J63.3
grinder's J62.8
kaolin J62.8
mica J62.8
millstone maker's J62.8
mineral fibers NEC J61
miner's J60
moldy hay J67.0
potter's J62.8
rheumatoid —*see* Rheumatoid, lung
sandblaster's J62.8
silica, silicate NEC J62.8
with carbon J60
stonemason's J62.8
talc (dust) J62.0
Pneumocystis carinii pneumonia B59
Pneumocystis jiroveci (pneumonia) B59
Pneumocystosis (with pneumonia) B59
Pneumohemopericardium I31.2
Pneumohemothorax J94.2
traumatic S27.2
Pneumohydropericardium —*see* Pericarditis
Pneumohydrothorax —*see* Hydrothorax
Pneumomediastinum J98.2
congenital or perinatal P25.2
Pneumomycosis B49 [J99]

Pneumonia (acute) (double) (migratory)
(purulent) (septic) (unresolved) J18.9
with
influenza —*see* Influenza, with, pneumonia
lung abscess J85.1
due to specified organism —*see*
Pneumonia, in (due to)
adenoviral J12.0
adynamic J18.2
alba A50.04
► allergic (*see also* Pneumonitis,
hypersensitivity) J82.89
alveolar —*see* Pneumonia, lobar
anaerobes J15.8
anthrax A22.1
apex, apical —*see* Pneumonia, lobar
Ascaris B77.81
aspiration J69.0
due to
aspiration of microorganisms
bacterial J15.9
viral J12.9
food (regurgitated) J69.0
gastric secretions J69.0
milk (regurgitated) J69.0
oils, essences J69.1
solids, liquids NEC J69.8
vomitus J69.0
newborn P24.81
amniotic fluid (clear) P24.11
blood P24.21
food (regurgitated) P24.31
liquor (amnii) P24.11
meconium P24.01
milk P24.31
mucus P24.11
specified NEC P24.81
stomach contents P24.31
postprocedural J95.4
atypical NEC J18.9
bacillus J15.9
specified NEC J15.8
bacterial J15.9
specified NEC J15.8
Bacteroides (fragilis) (oralis)
(melaninogenicus) J15.8
basal, basic, basilar —*see* Pneumonia,
by type
bronchiolitis obliterans organized (BOOP)
J84.89
broncho-, bronchial (confluent) (croupous)
(diffuse) (disseminated) (hemorrhagic)
(involving lobes) (lobar) (terminal) J18.0
► allergic (*see also* Pneumonitis,
hypersensitivity) J82.89
aspiration —*see* Pneumonia, aspiration
bacterial J15.9
specified NEC J15.8
chronic —*see* Fibrosis, lung
diplococcal J13
Eaton's agent J15.7
Escherichia coli (E. coli) J15.5
Friedländer's bacillus J15.0
Hemophilus influenzae J14
hypostatic J18.2
inhalation —*see also* Pneumonia, aspiration
due to fumes or vapors (chemical) J68.0
of oils or essences J69.1
Klebsiella (pneumoniae) J15.0
lipid, lipoid J69.1
endogenous J84.89
Mycoplasma (pneumoniae) J15.7
pleuro-pneumonia-like-organisms (PPLO)
J15.7
pneumococcal J13
Proteus J15.6
Pseudomonas J15.1
Serratia marcescens J15.6
specified organism NEC J16.8
staphylococcal —*see* Pneumonia,
staphylococcal

Pneumonia *(Continued)*
  broncho-, bronchial *(Continued)*
    streptococcal NEC J15.4
      group B J15.3
      pneumoniae J13
    viral, virus —*see* Pneumonia, viral
  Butyrivibrio (fibriosolvens) J15.8
  Candida B37.1
  caseous —*see* Tuberculosis, pulmonary
  catarrhal —*see* Pneumonia, broncho
  chlamydial J16.0
    congenital P23.1
  cholesterol J84.89
  cirrhotic (chronic) —*see* Fibrosis, lung
  Clostridium (haemolyticum) (novyi) J15.8
  confluent —*see* Pneumonia, broncho
  congenital (infective) P23.9
    due to
      bacterium NEC P23.6
      Chlamydia P23.1
      Escherichia coli P23.4
      Haemophilus influenzae P23.6
      infective organism NEC P23.8
      Klebsiella pneumoniae P23.6
      Mycoplasma P23.6
      Pseudomonas P23.5
      Staphylococcus P23.2
      Streptococcus (except group B) P23.6
        group B P23.3
      viral agent P23.0
    specified NEC P23.8
  croupous —*see* Pneumonia, lobar
  cryptogenic organizing J84.116
  cytomegalic inclusion B25.0
  cytomegaloviral B25.0
  deglutition —*see* Pneumonia, aspiration
  desquamative interstitial J84.117
  diffuse —*see* Pneumonia, broncho
  diplococcal, diplococcus (broncho-) (lobar)
    J13
  disseminated (focal) —*see* Pneumonia,
    broncho
  Eaton's agent J15.7
  embolic, embolism —*see* Embolism,
    pulmonary
  Enterobacter J15.6
  eosinophilic J82.81
    acute J82.82
    chronic J82.81
  Escherichia coli (E. coli) J15.5
  Eubacterium J15.8
  fibrinous —*see* Pneumonia, lobar
  fibroid, fibrous (chronic) —*see* Fibrosis, lung
  Friedländer's bacillus J15.0
  Fusobacterium (nucleatum) J15.8
  gangrenous J85.0
  giant cell (measles) B05.2
  gonococcal A54.84
  gram-negative bacteria NEC J15.6
    anaerobic J15.8
  Hemophilus influenzae (broncho) (lobar) J14
  human metapneumovirus J12.3
  hypostatic (broncho) (lobar) J18.2
  in (due to)
    actinomycosis A42.0
    adenovirus J12.0
    anthrax A22.1
    ascariasis B77.81
    aspergillosis B44.9
    Bacillus anthracis A22.1
    Bacterium anitratum J15.6
    candidiasis B37.1
    chickenpox B01.2
    Chlamydia J16.0
      neonatal P23.1
    coccidioidomycosis B38.2
      acute B38.0
      chronic B38.1
    cytomegalovirus disease B25.0
    Diplococcus (pneumoniae) J13
    Eaton's agent J15.7

Pneumonia *(Continued)*
  in *(Continued)*
    Enterobacter J15.6
    Escherichia coli (E. coli) J15.5
    Friedländer's bacillus J15.0
    fumes and vapors (chemical) (inhalation)
      J68.0
    gonorrhea A54.84
    Hemophilus influenzae (H. influenzae) J14
    Herellea J15.6
    histoplasmosis B39.2
      acute B39.0
      chronic B39.1
    human metapneumovirus J12.3
    Klebsiella (pneumoniae) J15.0
    measles B05.2
    Mycoplasma (pneumoniae) J15.7
    nocardiosis, nocardiasis A43.0
    ornithosis A70
    parainfluenza virus J12.2
    pleuro-pneumonia-like-organism (PPLO)
      J15.7
    pneumococcus J13
    pneumocystosis (Pneumocystis carinii)
      (Pneumocystis jiroveci) B59
    Proteus J15.6
    Pseudomonas NEC J15.1
      pseudomallei A24.1
    psittacosis A70
    Q fever A78
    respiratory syncytial virus (RSV) J12.1
    rheumatic fever I00 *[J17]*
    rubella B06.81
    Salmonella (infection) A02.22
      typhi A01.03
    schistosomiasis B65.9 *[J17]*
    Serratia marcescens J15.6
    specified
      bacterium NEC J15.8
      organism NEC J16.8
    spirochetal NEC A69.8
    Staphylococcus J15.20
      aureus (methicillin susceptible) (MSSA)
        J15.211
        methicillin resistant (MRSA) J15.212
      specified NEC J15.29
    Streptococcus J15.4
      group B J15.3
      pneumoniae J13
      specified NEC J15.4
    toxoplasmosis B58.3
    tularemia A21.2
    typhoid (fever) A01.03
    varicella B01.2
    virus —*see* Pneumonia, viral
    whooping cough A37.91
      due to
        Bordetella parapertussis A37.11
        Bordetella pertussis A37.01
        specified NEC A37.81
    Yersinia pestis A20.2
  inhalation of food or vomit —*see* Pneumonia,
    aspiration
  interstitial J84.9
    chronic J84.111
    desquamative J84.117
    due to
      collagen vascular disease J84.178
      known underlying cause J84.178
    idiopathic NOS J84.111
    in disease classified elsewhere J84.178
    lymphocytic (due to collagen vascular
      disease) (in diseases classified
      elsewhere) J84.178
    lymphoid J84.2
    non-specific J84.89
      due to
        collagen vascular disease J84.178
        known underlying cause J84.178
      idiopathic J84.113
      in diseases classified elsewhere J84.178

Pneumonia *(Continued)*
  interstitial *(Continued)*
    plasma cell B59
    pseudomonas J15.1
    usual J84.112
      due to collagen vascular disease J84.178
      idiopathic J84.112
      in diseases classified elsewhere J84.178
  Klebsiella (pneumoniae) J15.0
  lipid, lipoid (exogenous) J69.1
    endogenous J84.89
  lobar (disseminated) (double) (interstitial)
    J18.1
    bacterial J15.9
      specified NEC J15.8
    chronic —*see* Fibrosis, lung
    Escherichia coli (E. coli) J15.5
    Friedländer's bacillus J15.0
    Hemophilus influenzae J14
    hypostatic J18.2
    Klebsiella (pneumoniae) J15.0
    pneumococcal J13
    Proteus J15.6
    Pseudomonas J15.1
    specified organism NEC J16.8
    staphylococcal —*see* Pneumonia,
      staphylococcal
    streptococcal NEC J15.4
    Streptococcus pneumoniae J13
    viral, virus —*see* Pneumonia, viral
  lobular —*see* Pneumonia, broncho
  Löffler's J82.89
  lymphoid interstitial J84.2
  massive —*see* Pneumonia, lobar
  meconium P24.01
  MRSA (Methicillin resistant Staphylococcus
    aureus) J15.212
  MSSA (methicillin susceptible Staphylococcus
    aureus) J15.211
  multilobar —*see* Pneumonia, by type
  Mycoplasma (pneumoniae) J15.7
  necrotic J85.0
  neonatal P23.9
    aspiration —*see* Aspiration, by substance,
      with pneumonia
  nitrogen dioxide J68.0
  organizing J84.89
    due to
      collagen vascular disease J84.178
      known underlying cause J84.178
    in diseases classified elsewhere J84.178
  orthostatic J18.2
  parainfluenza virus J12.2
  parenchymatous —*see* Fibrosis, lung
  passive J18.2
  patchy —*see* Pneumonia, broncho
  Peptococcus J15.8
  Peptostreptococcus J15.8
  plasma cell (of infants) B59
  pleurolobar —*see* Pneumonia, lobar
  pleuro-pneumonia-like organism (PPLO)
    J15.7
  pneumococcal (broncho) (lobar) J13
  Pneumocystis (carinii) (jiroveci) B59
  postinfectional NEC B99 *[J17]*
  postmeasles B05.2
  Proteus J15.6
  Pseudomonas J15.1
  psittacosis A70
  radiation J70.0
  respiratory syncytial virus (RSV) J12.1
  resulting from a procedure J95.89
  rheumatic I00 *[J17]*
  Salmonella (arizonae) (cholerae-suis)
    (enteritidis) (typhimurium) A02.22
    typhi A01.03
    typhoid fever A01.03
  SARS-associated coronavirus J12.81
  segmented, segmental —*see* Pneumonia,
    broncho-●
  Serratia marcescens J15.6

▶ New   ⟱ Revised   ~~deleted~~ Deleted   ● Use Additional Character(s)

Pneumonia *(Continued)*
  specified NEC J18.8
    bacterium NEC J15.8
    organism NEC J16.8
    virus NEC J12.89
  spirochetal NEC A69.8
  staphylococcal (broncho) (lobar) J15.20
    aureus (methicillin susceptible) (MSSA)
      J15.211
      methicillin resistant (MRSA) J15.212
    specified NEC J15.29
  static, stasis J18.2
  streptococcal NEC (broncho) (lobar) J15.4
    group
      A J15.4
      B J15.3
      specified NEC J15.4
  Streptococcus pneumoniae J13
  syphilitic, congenital (early) A50.04
  traumatic (complication) (early) (secondary)
    T79.8
  tuberculous (any) —*see* Tuberculosis,
    pulmonary
  tularemic A21.2
  varicella B01.2
  Veillonella J15.8
  ventilator associated J95.851
  viral, virus (broncho) (interstitial) (lobar) J12.9
    adenoviral J12.0
    congenital P23.0
    human metapneumovirus J12.3
    parainfluenza J12.2
    respiratory syncytial (RSV) J12.1
    SARS-associated coronavirus J12.81
    specified NEC J12.89
  white (congenital) A50.04
Pneumonic —*see* condition
Pneumonitis (acute) (primary) —*see also*
  Pneumonia
  air-conditioner J67.7
  allergic (due to) J67.9
    organic dust NEC J67.8
    red cedar dust J67.8
    sequoiosis J67.8
    wood dust J67.8
  aspiration J69.0
    due to
      anesthesia J95.4
        during
          labor and delivery O74.0
          pregnancy O29.01-●
          puerperium O89.01
      fumes or gases J68.0
      obstetric O74.0
  chemical (due to gases, fumes or vapors)
    (inhalation) J68.0
    due to anesthesia J95.4
  cholesterol J84.89
  chronic —*see* Fibrosis, lung
  congenital rubella P35.0
  crack (cocaine) J68.0
  due to
    beryllium J68.0
    cadmium J68.0
    crack (cocaine) J68.0
    detergent J69.8
    fluorocarbon-polymer J68.0
    food, vomit (aspiration) J69.0
    fumes or vapors J68.0
    gases, fumes or vapors (inhalation) J68.0
    inhalation
      blood J69.8
      essences J69.1
      food (regurgitated), milk, vomit J69.0
      oils, essences J69.1
      saliva J69.0
      solids, liquids NEC J69.8
    manganese J68.0
    nitrogen dioxide J68.0
    oils, essences J69.1
    solids, liquids NEC J69.8

Pneumonitis *(Continued)*
  due to *(Continued)*
    toxoplasmosis (acquired) B58.3
      congenital P37.1
    vanadium J68.0
    ventilator J95.851
  eosinophilic J82.81
    acute J82.82
    chronic J82.81
  hypersensitivity J67.9
    air conditioner lung J67.7
    bagassosis J67.1
    bird fancier's lung J67.2
    farmer's lung J67.0
    maltworker's lung J67.4
    maple bark-stripper's lung J67.6
    mushroom worker's lung J67.5
    specified organic dust NEC J67.8
    suberosis J67.3
  interstitial (chronic) J84.89
    acute J84.114
    lymphoid J84.2
    non-specific J84.89
      idiopathic J84.113
  lymphoid, interstitial J84.2
  meconium P24.01
  postanesthetic J95.4
    correct substance properly administered —
      see Table of Drugs and Chemcials, by
      drug, adverse effect
    in labor and delivery O74.0
    in pregnancy O29.01-●
    obstetric O74.0
    overdose or wrong substance given or taken
      (by accident) —*see* Table of Drugs and
      Chemicals, by drug, poisoning
    postpartum, puerperal O89.01
  postoperative J95.4
    obstetric O74.0
  radiation J70.0
  rubella, congenital P35.0
  ventilation (air-conditioning) J67.7
  ventilator associated J95.851
  wood-dust J67.8
Pneumonoconiosis —*see* Pneumoconiosis
Pneumoparotid K11.8
Pneumopathy NEC J98.4
  alveolar J84.09
  due to organic dust NEC J66.8
  parietoalveolar J84.09
Pneumopericarditis —*see also* Pericarditis
  acute I30.9
Pneumopericardium —*see also* Pericarditis
  congenital P25.3
  newborn P25.3
  traumatic (post) —*see* Injury, heart
Pneumophagia (psychogenic) F45.8
Pneumopleurisy, pneumopleuritis —*see also*
  Pneumonia J18.8
Pneumopyopericardium I30.1
Pneumopyothorax —*see* Pyopneumothorax
  with fistula J86.0
Pneumorrhagia —*see also* Hemorrhage, lung
  tuberculous —*see* Tuberculosis, pulmonary
Pneumothorax NOS J93.9
  acute J93.83
  chronic J93.81
  congenital P25.1
  perinatal period P25.1
  postprocedural J95.811
  specified NEC J93.83
  spontaneous NOS J93.83
    newborn P25.1
    primary J93.11
    secondary J93.12
    tension J93.0
  tense valvular, infectional J93.0
  tension (spontaneous) J93.0
  traumatic S27.0
    with hemothorax S27.2
  tuberculous —*see* Tuberculosis, pulmonary

Podagra —*see also* Gout M10.9
Podencephalus Q01.9
Poikilocytosis R71.8
Poikiloderma L81.6
  Civatte's L57.3
  congenital Q82.8
  vasculare atrophicans L94.5
Poikilodermatomyositis M33.10
  with
    myopathy M33.12
    respiratory involvement M33.11
    specified organ involvement NEC M33.19
Pointed ear (congenital) Q17.3
Poison ivy, oak, sumac or other plant
  dermatitis (allergic) (contact) L23.7
Poisoning (acute) —*see also* Table of Drugs and
  Chemicals
  algae and toxins T65.82-●
  Bacillus B (aertrycke) (cholerae (suis))
    (paratyphosus) (suipestifer) A02.9
    botulinus A05.1
  bacterial toxins A05.9
  berries, noxious —*see* Poisoning, food,
    noxious, berries
  botulism A05.1
  ciguatera fish T61.0-●
  Clostridium botulinum A05.1
  death-cap (Amanita phalloides) (Amanita
    verna) —*see* Poisoning, food, noxious,
    mushrooms
  drug —*see* Table of Drugs and Chemicals, by
    drug, poisoning
  epidemic, fish (noxious) —*see* Poisoning,
    seafood
    bacterial A05.9
  fava bean D55.0
  fish (noxious) T61.9-●
    bacterial —*see* Intoxication, foodborne, by
      agent
    ciguatera fish —*see* Poisoning, ciguatera
      fish
    scombroid fish —*see* Poisoning, scombroid
      fish
    specified type NEC T61.77-●
  food NEC A05.9
    bacterial —*see* Intoxication, foodborne, by
      agent
    due to
      Bacillus (aertrycke) (choleraesuis)
        (paratyphosus) (suipestifer) A02.9
      botulinus A05.1
      Clostridium (perfringens) (Welchii)
        A05.2
      salmonella (aertrycke) (callinarum)
        (choleraesuis) (enteritidis)
        (paratyphi) (suipestifer) A02.9
        with
          gastroenteritis A02.0
          sepsis A02.1
      staphylococcus A05.0
      Vibrio
        parahaemolyticus A05.3
        vulnificus A05.5
    noxious or naturally toxic T62.9-●
      berries —*see* subcategory T62.1-●
      fish —*see* Poisoning, seafood
      mushrooms —*see* subcategory T62.0X-●
      plants NEC —*see* subcategory T62.2X-●
      seafood —*see* Poisoning, seafood
      specified NEC —*see* subcategory
        T62.8X-●
  ichthyotoxism —*see* Poisoning, seafood
  kreotoxism, food A05.9
  latex T65.81-●
  lead T56.0-●
  mushroom —*see* Poisoning, food, noxious,
    mushroom
  mussels —*see also* Poisoning, shellfish
    bacterial —*see* Intoxication, foodborne, by
      agent
  nicotine (tobacco) T65.2-●

Poisoning (Continued)
  noxious foodstuffs —see Poisoning, food,
    noxious
  plants, noxious —see Poisoning, food,
    noxious, plants NEC
  ptomaine —see Poisoning, food
  radiation J70.0
  Salmonella (arizonae) (cholerae-suis)
    (enteritidis) (typhimurium) A02.9
  scombroid fish T61.1-●
  seafood (noxious) T61.9-●
    bacterial —see Intoxication, foodborne, by
      agent
    fish —see Poisoning, fish
    shellfish —see Poisoning, shellfish
    specified NEC —see subcategory T61.8X-●
  shellfish (amnesic) (azaspiracid) (diarrheic)
    (neurotoxic) (noxious) (paralytic)
    T61.78-●
    bacterial —see Intoxication, foodborne, by
      agent
    ciguatera mollusk —see Poisoning,
      ciguatera fish
  specified substance NEC T65.891
  Staphylococcus, food A05.0
  tobacco (nicotine) T65.2-●
  water E87.79
Poker spine —see Spondylitis, ankylosing
Poland syndrome Q79.8
Polioencephalitis (acute) (bulbar) A80.9
  inferior G12.22
  influenzal —see Influenza, with,
    encephalopathy
  superior hemorrhagic (acute) (Wernicke's)
    E51.2
  Wernicke's E51.2
Polioencephalomyelitis (acute) (anterior) A80.9
  with beriberi E51.2
Polioencephalopathy, superior hemorrhagic
    E51.2
  with
    beriberi E51.11
    pellagra E52
Poliomeningoencephalitis —see
  Meningoencephalitis
Poliomyelitis (acute) (anterior) (epidemic) A80.9
  with paralysis (bulbar) —see Poliomyelitis,
    paralytic
  abortive A80.4
  ascending (progressive) —see Poliomyelitis,
    paralytic
  bulbar (paralytic) —see Poliomyelitis,
    paralytic
  congenital P35.8
  nonepidemic A80.9
  nonparalytic A80.4
  paralytic A80.30
    specified NEC A80.39
    vaccine-associated A80.0
    wild virus
      imported A80.1
      indigenous A80.2
  spinal, acute A80.9
Poliosis (eyebrow) (eyelashes) L67.1
  circumscripta, acquired L67.1
Pollakiuria R35.0
  psychogenic F45.8
Pollinosis J30.1
Pollitzer's disease L73.2
Polyadenitis —see also Lymphadenitis
  malignant A20.0
Polyalgia M79.89
Polyangiitis M30.0
  microscopic M31.7
  overlap syndrome M30.8
Polyarteritis
  microscopic M31.7
  nodosa M30.0
    with lung involvement M30.1
    juvenile M30.2
    related condition NEC M30.8

Polyarthralgia —see Pain, joint
Polyarthritis, polyarthropathy —see also
    Arthritis M13.0
  due to or associated with other specified
    conditions —see Arthritis
  epidemic (Australian) (with exanthema) B33.1
  infective —see Arthritis, pyogenic or pyemic
  inflammatory M06.4
  juvenile (chronic) (seronegative) M08.3
  migratory M13.8-●
  rheumatic, acute —see Fever, rheumatic
Polyarthrosis M15.9
  post-traumatic M15.3
  primary M15.0
  specified NEC M15.8
Polycarential syndrome of infancy E40
Polychondritis (atrophic) (chronic) —see also
    Disorder, cartilage, specified type NEC
  relapsing M94.1
Polycoria Q13.2
Polycystic (disease)
  degeneration, kidney Q61.3
    autosomal dominant (adult type) Q61.2
    autosomal recessive (infantile type) NEC
      Q61.19
  kidney Q61.3
    autosomal
      dominant Q61.2
      recessive NEC Q61.19
    autosomal dominant (adult type) Q61.2
    autosomal recessive (childhood type) NEC
      Q61.19
    infantile type NEC Q61.19
  liver Q44.6
  lung J98.4
    congenital Q33.0
  ovary, ovaries E28.2
  spleen Q89.09
Polycythemia (secondary) D75.1
  acquired D75.1
  benign (familial) D75.0
  due to
    donor twin P61.1
    erythropoietin D75.1
    fall in plasma volume D75.1
    high altitude D75.1
    maternal-fetal transfusion P61.1
    stress D75.1
  emotional D75.1
  erythropoietin D75.1
  familial (benign) D75.0
  Gaisböck's (hypertonica) D75.1
  high altitude D75.1
  hypertonica D75.1
  hypoxemic D75.1
  neonatorum P61.1
  nephrogenous D75.1
  relative D75.1
  secondary D75.1
  spurious D75.1
  stress D75.1
  vera D45
Polycytosis cryptogenica D75.1
Polydactylism, polydactyly Q69.9
  toes Q69.2
Polydipsia R63.1
Polydystrophy, pseudo-Hurler E77.0
Polyembryoma —see Neoplasm, malignant,
    by site
Polyglandular
  deficiency E31.0
  dyscrasia E31.9
  dysfunction E31.9
  syndrome E31.8
Polyhydramnios O40.-●
Polymastia Q83.1
Polymenorrhea N92.0
Polymyalgia M35.3
  arteritica, giant cell M31.5
  rheumatica M35.3
    with giant cell arteritis M31.5

Polymyositis (acute) (chronic) (hemorrhagic)
    M33.20
  with
    myopathy M33.22
    respiratory involvement M33.21
    skin involvement —see
      Dermatopolymyositis
    specified organ involvement NEC M33.29
  ossificans (generalisata) (progressiva) —see
    Myositis, ossificans, progressiva
Polyneuritis, polyneuritic —see also
    Polyneuropathy
  acute (post-)infective G61.0
  alcoholic G62.1
  cranialis G52.7
  demyelinating, chronic inflammatory (CIDP)
    G61.81
  diabetic —see Diabetes, polyneuropathy
  diphtheritic A36.83
  due to lack of vitamin NEC E56.9 [G63]
  endemic E51.11
  erythredema —see subcategory T56.1
  febrile, acute G61.0
  hereditary ataxic G60.1
  idiopathic, acute G61.0
  infective (acute) G61.0
  inflammatory, chronic demyelinating (CIDP)
    G61.81
  nutritional E63.9 [G63]
  postinfective (acute) G61.0
  specified NEC G62.89
Polyneuropathy (peripheral) G62.9
  alcoholic G62.1
  amyloid (Portuguese) E85.1 [G63]
    transthyretin-related (ATTR) familial E85.1
  arsenical E85.1 [G63]
  critical illness G62.81
  demyelinating, chronic inflammatory (CIDP)
    G61.81
  diabetic —see Diabetes, polyneuropathy
  drug-induced G62.0
  hereditary G60.9
    specified NEC G60.8
  idiopathic G60.9
    progressive G60.3
  in (due to)
    alcohol G62.1
      sequelae G65.2
    amyloidosis, familial (Portuguese) E85.1
      [G63]
    antitetanus serum G61.1
    arsenic G62.2
      sequelae G65.2
    avitaminosis NEC E56.9 [G63]
    beriberi E51.11
    collagen vascular disease NEC M35.9 [G63]
    deficiency (of)
      B (-complex) vitamins E53.9 [G63]
      vitamin B6 E53.1 [G63]
    diabetes —see Diabetes, polyneuropathy
    diphtheria A36.83
    drug or medicament G62.0
      correct substance properly
        administered —see Table of Drugs
        and Chemicals, by drug, adverse
        effect
      overdose or wrong substance given
        or taken —see Table of Drugs and
        Chemicals, by drug, poisoning
    endocrine disease NEC E34.9 [G63]
    herpes zoster B02.23
    hypoglycemia E16.2 [G63]
    infectious
      disease NEC B99 [G63]
      mononucleosis B27.91
    lack of vitamin NEC E56.9 [G63]
    lead G62.2
      sequelae G65.2
    leprosy A30.9 [G63]
    Lyme disease A69.22
    metabolic disease NEC E88.9 [G63]

▶ New ⇨ Revised ~~deleted~~ Deleted ● Use Additional Character(s)

Polyneuropathy (Continued)
  in (Continued)
    microscopic polyangiitis M31.7 [G63]
    mumps B26.84
    neoplastic disease —see also Neoplasm
      D49.9 [G63]
    nutritional deficiency NEC E63.9 [G63]
    organophosphate compounds G62.2
      sequelae G65.2
    parasitic disease NEC B89 [G63]
    pellagra E52 [G63]
    polyarteritis nodosa M30.0
    porphyria E80.20 [G63]
    radiation G62.82
    rheumatoid arthritis —see Rheumatoid,
      polyneuropathy
    sarcoidosis D86.89
    serum G61.1
    syphilis (late) A52.15
      congenital A50.43
    systemic
      connective tissue disorder M35.9 [G63]
      lupus erythematosus M32.19
    toxic agent NEC G62.2
      sequelae G65.2
    transthyretin-related (ATTR) familial
      amyloid E85.1
    triorthocresyl phosphate G62.2
      sequelae G65.2
    tuberculosis A17.89
    uremia N18.9 [G63]
    vitamin B12 deficiency E53.8 [G63]
      with anemia (pernicious) D51.0
        [G63]
        due to dietary deficiency D51.3
          [G63]
    zoster B02.23
  inflammatory G61.9
    chronic demyelinating (CIDP) G61.81
      sequelae G65.1
    specified NEC G61.89
  lead G62.2
    sequelae G65.2
  nutritional NEC E63.9 [G63]
  postherpetic (zoster) B02.23
  progressive G60.3
  radiation-induced G62.82
  sensory (hereditary) (idiopathic) G60.8
  specified NEC G62.89
  syphilitic (late) A52.15
    congenital A50.43
Polyopia H53.8
Polyorchism, polyorchidism Q55.21
Polyosteoarthritis —see also Osteoarthritis,
  generalized M15.9-•
  post-traumatic M15.3
  specified NEC M15.8
Polyostotic fibrous dysplasia Q78.1
Polyotia Q17.0
Polyp, polypus
  accessory sinus J33.8
  adenocarcinoma in —see Neoplasm,
    malignant, by site
  adenocarcinoma in situ in —see Neoplasm, in
    situ, by site
  adenoid tissue J33.0
  adenomatous —see also Neoplasm, benign,
    by site
    adenocarcinoma in —see Neoplasm,
      malignant, by site
    adenocarcinoma in situ in —see Neoplasm,
      in situ, by site
    carcinoma in —see Neoplasm, malignant,
      by site
    carcinoma in situ in —see Neoplasm, in
      situ, by site
    multiple —see Neoplasm, benign
      adenocarcinoma in —see Neoplasm,
        malignant, by site
      adenocarcinoma in situ in —see
        Neoplasm, in situ, by site

Polyp, polypus (Continued)
  antrum J33.8
  anus, anal (canal) K62.0
  Bartholin's gland N84.3
  bladder D41.4
  carcinoma in —see Neoplasm, malignant, by
    site
  carcinoma in situ in —see Neoplasm, in situ,
    by site
  cecum D12.0
  cervix (uteri) N84.1
    in pregnancy or childbirth —see Pregnancy,
      complicated by, abnormal, cervix
    mucous N84.1
    nonneoplastic N84.1
  choanal J33.0
  cholesterol K82.4
  clitoris N84.3
  colon K63.5
    adenomatous D12.6
      ascending D12.6
      cecum D12.0
      descending D12.4
    inflammatory K51.40
      with
        abscess K51.414
        complication K51.419
          specified NEC K51.418
        fistula K51.413
        intestinal obstruction K51.412
        rectal bleeding K51.411
    sigmoid D12.5
    transverse D12.3
  corpus uteri N84.0
  dental K04.01
    irreversible K04.02
    reversible K04.01
  duodenum K31.7
  ear (middle) H74.4-•
  endometrium N84.0
  ethmoidal (sinus) J33.8
  fallopian tube N84.8
  female genital tract N84.9
    specified NEC N84.8
  frontal (sinus) J33.8
  gallbladder K82.4
  gingiva, gum K06.8
  hyperplastic, (any site) K63.5
  labia, labium (majus) (minus) N84.3
  larynx (mucous) J38.1
    adenomatous D14.1
  malignant —see Neoplasm, malignant,
    by site
  maxillary (sinus) J33.8
  middle ear —see Polyp, ear (middle)
  myometrium N84.0
  nares
    anterior J33.9
    posterior J33.0
  nasal (mucous) J33.9
    cavity J33.0
    septum J33.0
  nasopharyngeal J33.0
  nose (mucous) J33.9
  oviduct N84.8
  pharynx J39.2
  placenta O90.89
  prostate —see Enlargement, enlarged,
    prostate
  pudenda, pudendum N84.3
  pulpal (dental) K04.01
    irreversible K04.02
    reversible K04.01
  rectum (nonadenomatous) K62.1
    adenomatous —see Polyp, adenomatous
  septum (nasal) J33.0
  sinus (accessory) (ethmoidal) (frontal)
    (maxillary) (sphenoidal) J33.8
  sphenoidal (sinus) J33.8
  stomach K31.7
    adenomatous D13.1

Polyp, polypus (Continued)
  tube, fallopian N84.8
  turbinate, mucous membrane J33.8
  umbilical, newborn P83.6
  ureter N28.89
  urethra N36.2
  uterus (body) (corpus) (mucous) N84.0
    cervix N84.1
    in pregnancy or childbirth —see Pregnancy,
      complicated by, tumor, uterus
  vagina N84.2
  vocal cord (mucous) J38.1
  vulva N84.3
Polyphagia R63.2
Polyploidy Q92.7
Polypoid —see condition
Polyposis —see also Polyp
  coli (adenomatous) D12.6
    adenocarcinoma in C18.9
    adenocarcinoma in situ in —see Neoplasm,
      in situ, by site
    carcinoma in C18.9
  colon (adenomatous) D12.6
  familial D12.6
    adenocarcinoma in situ in —see Neoplasm,
      in situ, by site
  intestinal (adenomatous) D12.6
  malignant lymphomatous C83.1
  multiple, adenomatous —see also Neoplasm,
    benign D36.9
Polyradiculitis —see Polyneuropathy
Polyradiculoneuropathy (acute) (postinfective)
  (segmentally demyelinating) G61.0
Polyserositis
  due to pericarditis I31.1
  pericardial I31.1
  periodic, familial E85.0
  tuberculous A19.9
    acute A19.1
    chronic A19.8
Polysplenia syndrome Q89.09
Polysyndactyly —see also Syndactylism,
  syndactyly Q70.4
Polytrichia L68.3
Polyunguia Q84.6
Polyuria R35.8
  nocturnal R35.1
  psychogenic F45.8
Pompe's disease (glycogen storage) E74.02
Pompholyx L30.1
Poncet's disease (tuberculous rheumatism)
  A18.09
Pond fracture —see Fracture, skull
Ponos B55.0
Pons, pontine —see condition
Poor
  aesthetic of existing restoration of tooth
    K08.56
  contractions, labor O62.2
  gingival margin to tooth restoration K08.51
  personal hygiene R46.0
  prenatal care, affecting management of
    pregnancy —see Pregnancy, complicated
    by, insufficient, prenatal care
  sucking reflex (newborn) R29.2
  urinary stream R39.12
  vision NEC H54.7
Poradenitis, nostras inguinalis or venerea
  A55
Porencephaly (congenital) (developmental)
  (true) Q04.6
  acquired G93.0
  nondevelopmental G93.0
  traumatic (post) F07.89
Porocephaliasis B88.8
Porokeratosis Q82.8
Poroma, eccrine —see Neoplasm, skin, benign
Porphyria (South African) E80.20
  acquired E80.20
  acute intermittent (hepatic) (Swedish)
    E80.21

Porphyria (Continued)
- cutanea tarda (hereditary) (symptomatic) E80.1
- due to drugs E80.20
  - correct substance properly administered — see Table of Drugs and Chemicals, by drug, adverse effect
  - overdose or wrong substance given or taken — see Table of Drugs and Chemicals, by drug, poisoning
- erythropoietic (congenital) (hereditary) E80.0
- hepatocutaneous type E80.1
- secondary E80.20
- toxic NEC E80.20
- variegata E80.20

Porphyrinuria — see Porphyria
Porphyruria — see Porphyria
Portal — see condition
Port wine nevus, mark, or stain Q82.5
Posadas-Wernicke disease B38.9
Positive
- culture (nonspecific)
  - blood R78.81
  - bronchial washings R84.5
  - cerebrospinal fluid R83.5
  - cervix uteri R87.5
  - nasal secretions R84.5
  - nipple discharge R89.5
  - nose R84.5
    - staphylococcus (Methicillin susceptible) Z22.321
      - Methicillin resistant Z22.322
  - peritoneal fluid R85.5
  - pleural fluid R84.5
  - prostatic secretions R86.5
  - saliva R85.5
  - seminal fluid R86.5
  - sputum R84.5
  - synovial fluid R89.5
  - throat scrapings R84.5
  - urine R82.79
  - vagina R87.5
  - vulva R87.5
  - wound secretions R89.5
- PPD (skin test) R76.11
- serology for syphilis A53.0
  - with signs or symptoms - code as Syphilis, by site and stage
  - false R76.8
- skin test, tuberculin (without active tuberculosis) R76.11
- test, human immunodeficiency virus (HIV) R75
- VDRL A53.0
  - with signs or symptoms - code by site and stage under Syphilis A53.9
- Wassermann reaction A53.0
Postcardiotomy syndrome I97.0
Postcaval ureter Q62.62
Postcholecystectomy syndrome K91.5
Postclimacteric bleeding N95.0
Postcommissurotomy syndrome I97.0
Postconcussional syndrome F07.81
Postcontusional syndrome F07.81
Postcricoid region — see condition
Post-dates (40-42 weeks) (pregnancy) (mother) O48.0
- more than 42 weeks gestation O48.1
Postencephalitic syndrome F07.89
Posterior — see condition
Posterolateral sclerosis (spinal cord) — see Degeneration, combined
Postexanthematous — see condition
Postfebrile — see condition
Postgastrectomy dumping syndrome K91.1
Posthemiplegic chorea — see Monoplegia
Posthemorrhagic anemia (chronic) D50.0
- acute D62
- newborn P61.3
Postherpetic neuralgia (zoster) B02.29
- trigeminal B02.22
Posthitis N47.7

Postimmunization complication or reaction — see Complications, vaccination
Postinfectious — see condition
Postlaminectomy syndrome NEC M96.1
Postleukotomy syndrome F07.0
Postmastectomy lymphedema (syndrome) I97.2
Postmaturity, postmature (over 42 weeks)
- maternal (over 42 weeks gestation) O48.1
- newborn P08.22
Postmeasles complication NEC — see also condition B05.89
Postmenopausal
- endometrium (atrophic) N95.8
  - suppurative — see also Endometritis N71.9
- osteoporosis — see Osteoporosis, postmenopausal
Postnasal drip R09.82
- due to
  - allergic rhinitis — see Rhinitis, allergic
  - common cold J00
  - gastroesophageal reflux — see Reflux, gastroesophageal
  - nasopharyngitis — see Nasopharyngitis
  - other know condition — code to condition
  - sinusitis — see Sinusitis
Postnatal — see condition
Postoperative (postprocedural) — see Complication, postoperative
- pneumothorax, therapeutic Z98.3
- state NEC Z98.890
Postpancreatectomy hyperglycemia E89.1
Postpartum — see Puerperal
Postphlebitic syndrome — see Syndrome, postthrombotic
Postpolio (myelitic) syndrome G14
Postpoliomyelitic — see also condition
- osteopathy — see Osteopathy, after poliomyelitis
Postprocedural — see also Postoperative
- hypoinsulinemia E89.1
Postschizophrenic depression F32.89
Postsurgery status — see also Status (post)
- pneumothorax, therapeutic Z98.3
Post-term (40-42 weeks) (pregnancy) (mother) O48.0
- infant P08.21
- more than 42 weeks gestation (mother) O48.1
Post-traumatic brain syndrome, nonpsychotic F07.81
Post-typhoid abscess A01.09
Postures, hysterical F44.2
Postvaccinal reaction or complication — see Complications, vaccination
Postvalvulotomy syndrome I97.0
Potain's
- disease (pulmonary edema) — see Edema, lung
- syndrome (gastrectasis with dyspepsia) K31.0
Potter's
- asthma J62.8
- facies Q60.6
- lung J62.8
- syndrome (with renal agenesis) Q60.6
Pott's
- curvature (spinal) A18.01
- disease or paraplegia A18.01
- spinal curvature A18.01
- tumor, puffy — see Osteomyelitis, specified type NEC
Pouch
- bronchus Q32.4
- Douglas' — see condition
- esophagus, esophageal, congenital Q39.6
  - acquired K22.5
- gastric K31.4
- Hartmann's K82.8
- pharynx, pharyngeal (congenital) Q38.7
Pouchitis K91.850
Poultrymen's itch B88.0
Poverty NEC Z59.6
- extreme Z59.5
Poxvirus NEC B08.8

Prader-Willi syndrome Q87.11
Prader-Willi-like syndrome Q87.11
Preauricular appendage or tag Q17.0
Prebetalipoproteinemia (acquired) (essential) (familial) (hereditary) (primary) (secondary) E78.1
- with chylomicronemia E78.3
Precipitate labor or delivery O62.3
Preclimacteric bleeding (menorrhagia) N92.4
Precocious
- adrenarche E30.1
- menarche E30.1
- menstruation E30.1
- pubarche E30.1
- puberty E30.1
  - central E22.8
- sexual development NEC E30.1
- thelarche E30.8
Precocity, sexual (constitutional) (cryptogenic) (female) (idiopathic) (male) E30.1
- with adrenal hyperplasia E25.9
  - congenital E25.0
Precordial pain R07.2
Predeciduous teeth K00.2
Prediabetes, prediabetic R73.03
- complicating
  - pregnancy — see Pregnancy, complicated by, diseases of, specified type or system NEC
  - ➡ puerperium O99.893
Predislocation status of hip at birth Q65.6
Pre-eclampsia O14.9-●
- with pre-existing hypertension — see Hypertension, complicating pregnancy, pre-existing, with, pre-eclampsia
- complicating
  - childbirth O14.94
  - puerperium O14.95
- mild O14.0-●
  - complicating
    - childbirth O14.04
    - puerperium O14.05
- moderate O14.0-●
  - complicating
    - childbirth O14.04
    - puerperium O14.05
- severe O14.1-●
  - with hemolysis, elevated liver enzymes and low platelet count (HELLP) O14.2-●
  - complicating
    - childbirth O14.24
    - puerperium O14.25
  - complicating
    - childbirth O14.14
    - puerperium O14.15
Pre-eruptive color change, teeth, tooth K00.8
Pre-excitation atrioventricular conduction I45.6
Preglaucoma H40.00-●
➡ Pregnancy (single) (uterine) — see also Delivery and Puerperal Z33.1

Note: The Tabular must be reviewed for assignment of the appropriate character indicating the trimester of the pregnancy

Note: The Tabular must be reviewed for assignment of appropriate seventh character for multiple gestation codes in Chapter 15

- abdominal (ectopic) O00.00
  - with intrauterine pregnancy O00.01
  - with viable fetus O36.7-●
- ampullar O00.10-●
  - with intrauterine pregnancy O00.11-●
- biochemical O02.81
- broad ligament O00.80
  - with intrauterine pregnancy O00.81
- cervical O00.80
  - with intrauterine pregnancy O00.81

▶ New   ➡ Revised   ~~deleted~~ Deleted   ● Use Additional Character(s)

Pregnancy *(Continued)*
  chemical O02.81
  complicated NOS O26.9-●
  complicated by (care of) (management
    affected by)
    abnormal, abnormality
      cervix O34.4-●
        causing obstructed labor O65.5
      cord (umbilical) O69.9
      fetal heart rate or rhythm O36.83-●
      findings on antenatal screening of
        mother O28.9
        biochemical O28.1
        chromosomal O28.5
        cytological O28.2
        genetic O28.5
        hematological O28.0
        radiological O28.4
        specified NEC O28.8
        ultrasonic O28.3
      glucose (tolerance) NEC O99.810
      pelvic organs O34.9-●
        specified NEC O34.8-●
          causing obstructed labor O65.5
      pelvis (bony) (major) NEC O33.0
      perineum O34.7-●
      position
        placenta O44.0-●
          with hemorrhage O44.1-●
        uterus O34.59-●
      uterus O34.59-●
        causing obstructed labor O65.5
        congenital O34.0-●
      vagina O34.6-●
        causing obstructed labor O65.5
      vulva O34.7-●
        causing obstructed labor O65.5
    abruptio placentae —*see* Abruptio
      placentae
    abscess or cellulitis
      bladder O23.1-●
      breast O91.11-●
      genital organ or tract O23.9-●
    abuse
      physical O9A.31-●
      psychological O9A.51-●
      sexual O9A.41-●
    adverse effect anesthesia O29.9-●
      aspiration pneumonitis O29.01-●
      cardiac arrest O29.11-●
      cardiac complication NEC O29.19-●
      cardiac failure O29.12-●
      central nervous system complication
        NEC O29.29-●
      cerebral anoxia O29.21-●
      failed or difficult intubation O29.6-●
      inhalation of stomach contents or
        secretions NOS O29.01-●
      local, toxic reaction O29.3X
      Mendelson's syndrome O29.01-●
      pressure collapse of lung O29.02-●
      pulmonary complications NEC O29.09-●
      specified NEC O29.8X
      spinal and epidural type NEC O29.5X
        induced headache O29.4-●
    albuminuria —*see also* Proteinuria,
      gestational O12.1-●
    alcohol use O99.31-●
    amnionitis O41.12-●
    anaphylactoid syndrome of pregnancy
      O88.01-●
    anemia (conditions in D50-D64) (pre-
      existing) O99.01-●
      complicating the puerperium O99.03
    antepartum hemorrhage O46.9-●
      with coagulation defect —*see*
        Hemorrhage, antepartum, with
        coagulation defect
      specified NEC O46.8X-●
    appendicitis O99.61-●
    atrophy (yellow) (acute) liver (subacute)
      O26.61-●

Pregnancy *(Continued)*
  complicated by *(Continued)*
    bariatric surgery status O99.84-●
    bicornis or bicornuate uterus O34.0-●
    biliary tract problems O26.61-●
    breech presentation O32.1
    cardiovascular diseases (conditions in
      I00-I09, I20-I52, I70-I99) O99.41-●
    cerebrovascular disorders (conditions in
      I60-I69) O99.41-●
    cervical shortening O26.87-●
    cervicitis O23.51-●
  ▶ cesarean scar defect (isthmocele) O34.22
    chloasma (gravidarum) O26.89-●
    cholecystitis O99.61-●
    cholestasis (intrahepatic) O26.61-●
    chorioamnionitis O41.12-●
    circulatory system disorder (conditions in
      I00-I09, I20-I99, O99.41-●)
    compound presentation O32.6
    conjoined twins O30.02-●
  ➡ connective system disorders (conditions in
      M00-M99) O99.891
    contracted pelvis (general) O33.1
      inlet O33.2
      outlet O33.3
    convulsions (eclamptic) (uremic) —*see also*
      Eclampsia O15.9-●
    cracked nipple O92.11-●
    cystitis O23.1-●
    cystocele O34.8-●
    death of fetus (near term) O36.4
      early pregnancy O02.1
      of one fetus or more in multiple
        gestation O31.2-●
    deciduitis O41.14-●
    decreased fetal movement O36.81-●
    dental problems O99.61-●
    diabetes (mellitus) O24.91-●
      gestational (pregnancy induced) —*see*
        Diabetes, gestational
      pre-existing O24.31-●
        specified NEC O24.81-●
        type 1 O24.01-●
        type 2 O24.11-●
    digestive system disorders (conditions in
      K00-K93) O99.61-●
    diseases of —*see* Pregnancy, complicated
      by, specified body system disease
      biliary tract O26.61-●
      blood NEC (conditions in D65-D77)
        O99.11-●
      liver O26.61-●
  ➡ specified NEC O99.891
    disorders of —*see* Pregnancy, complicated
      by, specified body system disorder
      amniotic fluid and membranes
        O41.9-●
        specified NEC O41.8X-●
      biliary tract O26.61-●
  ➡ ear and mastoid process (conditions in
      H60-H95) O99.891
  ➡ eye and adnexa (conditions in H00-H59)
      O99.891
      liver O26.61-●
      skin (conditions in L00-L99) O99.71-●
  ➡ specified NEC O99.891
    displacement, uterus NEC O34.59-●
      causing obstructed labor O65.5
    disproportion (due to) O33.9
      fetal (ascites) (hydrops)
        (meningomyelocele) (sacral
        teratoma) (tumor) deformities NEC
        O33.7
      generally contracted pelvis O33.1
      hydrocephalic fetus O33.6
      inlet contraction of pelvis O33.2
      mixed maternal and fetal origin O33.4
      specified NEC O33.8
    double uterus O34.0-●
      causing obstructed labor O65.5
    drug use (conditions in F11-F19) O99.32-●

Pregnancy *(Continued)*
  complicated by *(Continued)*
    eclampsia, eclamptic (coma) (convulsions)
      (delirium) (nephritis) (uremia) (*see also*
      Eclampsia) O15-●
    ectopic pregnancy —*see* Pregnancy, ectopic
    edema O12.0-●
      with
        gestational hypertension, mild —*see*
          also Pre-eclampsia O14.0-●
        proteinuria O12.2-●
    effusion, amniotic fluid —*see* Pregnancy,
      complicated by, premature rupture of
      membranes
    elderly
      multigravida O09.52-●
      primigravida O09.51-●
    embolism —*see also* Embolism, obstetric,
      pregnancy O88.-●
    endocrine diseases NEC O99.28-●
    endometritis O86.12
    excessive weight gain O26.0-●
    exhaustion O26.81-●
      during labor and delivery O75.81
    face presentation O32.3
    failed induction of labor O61.9
    failed or difficult intubation for anesthesia
      O29.6-●
      instrumental O61.1
      mechanical O61.1
      medical O61.0
      specified NEC O61.8
      surgical O61.1
    false labor (pains) O47.9
      at or after 37 completed weeks of
        pregnancy O47.1
      before 37 completed weeks of pregnancy
        O47.0-●
    fatigue O26.81-●
      during labor and delivery O75.81
    fatty metamorphosis of liver O26.61-●
    female genital mutilation O34.8-● *[N90.81-●]*
    fetal (maternal care for)
      abnormality or damage O35.9
        acid-base balance O68
        specified type NEC O35.8
      acidemia O68
      acidosis O68
      alkalosis O68
      anemia and thrombocytopenia O36.82-●
      anencephaly O35.0
      bradycardia O36.83-●
      chromosomal abnormality (conditions in
        Q90-Q99) O35.1
      conjoined twins O30.02-●
      damage from
        amniocentesis O35.7
        biopsy procedures O35.7
        drug addiction O35.5
        hematological investigation O35.7
        intrauterine contraceptive device O35.7
        maternal
          alcohol addiction O35.4
          cytomegalovirus infection O35.3
          disease NEC O35.8
          drug addiction O35.5
          listeriosis O35.8
          rubella O35.3
          toxoplasmosis O35.8
          viral infection O35.3
        medical procedure NEC O35.7
        radiation O35.6
      death (near term) O36.4
        early pregnancy O02.1
      decreased movement O36.81-●
      depressed heart rate tones O36.83-●
      disproportion due to deformity (fetal)
        O33.7
      excessive growth (large for dates) O36.6-●
      growth retardation O36.59-●
        light for dates O36.59-●
        small for dates O36.59-●

Pregnancy (Continued)
  complicated by (Continued)
    fetal (Continued)
      heart rate irregularity (abnormal variability) (bradycardia) (decelerations) (tachycardia) O36.83-●
      hereditary disease O35.2
      hydrocephalus O35.0
      intrauterine death O36.4
      non-reassuring heart rate or rhythm O36.83-●
      poor growth O36.59-●
        light for dates O36.59-●
        small for dates O36.59-●
      problem O36.9-●
        specified NEC O36.89-●
      reduction (elective) O31.3-●
      selective termination O31.3-●
      spina bifida O35.0
      thrombocytopenia O36.82-●
    fibroid (tumor) (uterus) O34.1-●
    fissure of nipple O92.11-●
    gallstones O99.61-●
    gastric banding status O99.84-●
    gastric bypass status O99.84-●
    genital herpes (asymptomatic) (history of) (inactive) O98.3-●
    genital tract infection O23.9-●
    glomerular diseases (conditions in N00-N07) O26.83-●
      with hypertension, pre-existing —see Hypertension, complicating, pregnancy, pre-existing, with, renal disease
    gonorrhea O98.21-●
    grand multiparity O09.4
    habitual aborter —see Pregnancy, complicated by, recurrent pregnancy loss
    HELLP syndrome (hemolysis, elevated liver enzymes and low platelet count) O14.2-●
    hemorrhage
      antepartum —see Hemorrhage, antepartum
      before 20 completed weeks gestation O20.9
        specified NEC O20.8
      due to premature separation, placenta —see also Abruptio placentae O45.9-●
      early O20.9
        specified NEC O20.8
      threatened abortion O20.0
    hemorrhoids O22.4-●
    hepatitis (viral) O98.41-●
    herniation of uterus O34.59-●
    high
      head at term O32.4
      risk —see Supervision (of) (for), high-risk
    history of in utero procedure during previous pregnancy O09.82-●
    HIV O98.71-●
    human immunodeficiency virus (HIV) disease O98.71-●
    hydatidiform mole —see also Mole, hydatidiform O01.9-●
    hydramnios O40.-●
    hydrocephalic fetus (disproportion) O33.6
    hydrops
      amnii O40.-●
      fetalis O36.2-●
      associated with isoimmunization —see also Pregnancy, complicated by, isoimmunization O36.11-●
    hydrorrhea O42.90
    hyperemesis (gravidarum) (mild) —see also Hyperemesis, gravidarum O21.0-●
    hypertension —see Hypertension, complicating pregnancy

Pregnancy (Continued)
  complicated by (Continued)
    hypertensive
      heart and renal disease, pre-existing — see Hypertension, complicating, pregnancy, pre-existing, with, heart disease, with renal disease
      heart disease, pre-existing —see Hypertension, complicating, pregnancy, pre-existing, with, heart disease
      renal disease, pre-existing —see Hypertension, complicating, pregnancy, pre-existing, with, renal disease
    hypotension O26.5-●
    immune disorders NEC (conditions in D80-D89) O99.11-●
    incarceration, uterus O34.51-●
    incompetent cervix O34.3-●
    inconclusive fetal viability O36.80
    infection(s) O98.91-●
      amniotic fluid or sac O41.10-●
      bladder O23.1-●
      carrier state NEC O99.830
        streptococcus B O99.820
      genital organ or tract O23.9-●
        specified NEC O23.59-●
      genitourinary tract O23.9-●
      gonorrhea O98.21-●
      hepatitis (viral) O98.41-●
      HIV O98.71-●
      human immunodeficiency virus (HIV) O98.71-●
      kidney O23.0-●
      nipple O91.01-●
      parasitic disease O98.91-●
        specified NEC O98.81-●
      protozoal disease O98.61-●
      sexually transmitted NEC O98.31-●
      specified type NEC O98.81-●
      syphilis O98.11-●
      tuberculosis O98.01-●
      urethra O23.2-●
      urinary (tract) O23.4-●
        specified NEC O23.3-●
      viral disease O98.51-●
    injury or poisoning (conditions in S00-T88) O9A.21-●
      due to abuse
        physical O9A.31-●
        psychological O9A.51-●
        sexual O9A.41-●
    insufficient
      prenatal care O09.3-●
      weight gain O26.1-●
    insulin resistance O26.89
    intrauterine fetal death (near term) O36.4
      early pregnancy O02.1
      multiple gestation (one fetus or more) O31.2-●
    isoimmunization O36.11-●
      anti-A sensitization O36.11-●
      anti-B sensitization O36.19-●
      Rh O36.09-●
        anti-D antibody O36.01-●
      specified NEC O36.19-●
    laceration of uterus NEC O71.81
    malformation
      placenta, placental (vessel) O43.10-●
        specified NEC O43.19-●
      uterus (congenital) O34.0-●
    malnutrition (conditions in E40-E46) O25.1-●
    maternal hypotension syndrome O26.5-●
    ➡ mental disorders (conditions in F01-F09, F20-F52 and F54-F99) O99.34-●
      alcohol use O99.31-●
      drug use O99.32-●
      smoking O99.33-●
    mentum presentation O32.3

Pregnancy (Continued)
  complicated by (Continued)
    metabolic disorders O99.28-●
    missed
      abortion O02.1
      delivery O36.4
    multiple gestations O30.9-●
      conjoined twins O30.02-●
      quadruplet —see Pregnancy, quadruplet
      specified complication NEC O31.8X-●
      specified number of multiples NEC —see Pregnancy, multiple (gestation), specified NEC
      triplet —see Pregnancy, triplet
      twin —see Pregnancy, twin
    ➡ musculoskeletal condition (conditions is M00-M99) O99.891
    necrosis, liver (conditions in K72) O26.61-●
    neoplasm
      benign
        cervix O34.4-●
        corpus uteri O34.1-●
        uterus O34.1-●
      malignant O9A.11-●
    nephropathy NEC O26.83-●
    nervous system condition (conditions in G00-G99) O99.35-●
    nutritional diseases NEC O99.28-●
    obesity (pre-existing) O99.21-●
    obesity surgery status O99.84-●
    oblique lie or presentation O32.2
    older mother —see Pregnancy, complicated by, elderly
    oligohydramnios O41.0-●
      with premature rupture of membranes —see also Pregnancy, complicated by, premature rupture of membranes O42-●
    onset (spontaneous) of labor after 37 completed weeks of gestation but before 39 completed weeks gestation, with delivery by (planned) cesarean section O75.82
    oophoritis O23.52-●
    overdose, drug —see also Table of Drugs and Chemicals, by drug, poisoning O9A.21-●
    oversize fetus O33.5
    papyraceous fetus O31.0-●
    ➡ pelvic inflammatory disease O99.891
    periodontal disease O99.61-●
    peripheral neuritis O26.82-●
    ➡ peritoneal (pelvic) adhesions O99.891
    phlebitis O22.9-●
    phlebopathy O22.9-●
    phlebothrombosis (superficial) O22.2-●
      deep O22.3-●
    placenta accreta O43.21-●
    placenta increta O43.22-●
    placenta percreta O43.23-●
    placenta previa O44.0-●
      complete O44.0-●
        with hemorrhage O44.1-●
      marginal O44.2-●
        with hemorrhage O44.3-●
      partial O44.2-●
        with hemorrhage O44.3-●
    placental disorder O43.9-●
      specified NEC O43.89-●
    placental dysfunction O43.89-●
    placental infarction O43.81-●
    placental insufficiency O36.51-●
    placental transfusion syndromes
      fetomaternal O43.01-●
      fetus to fetus O43.02-●
      maternofetal O43.01-●
    placentitis O41.14-●
    pneumonia O99.51-●
    poisoning —see also Table of Drugs and Chemicals O9A.21-●
    polyhydramnios O40-●

▶ New   ➡ Revised   ~~deleted~~ Deleted   ● Use Additional Character(s)

Pregnancy *(Continued)*
complicated by *(Continued)*
polymorphic eruption of pregnancy O26.86
poor obstetric history NEC O09.29-●
postmaturity (post-term) (40 to 42 weeks) O48.0
more than 42 completed weeks gestation (prolonged) O48.1
pre-eclampsia O14.9-●
mild O14.0-●
moderate O14.0-●
severe O14.1-●
with hemolysis, elevated liver enzymes and low platelet count (HELLP) O14.2-●
premature labor —*see* Pregnancy, complicated by, preterm labor
premature rupture of membranes O42.90
full-term, unspecified as to length of time between rupture and onset of labor O42.92
with onset of labor
within 24 hours O42.00
at or after 37 weeks gestation, onset of labor within 24 hours of rupture O42.02
pre-term (before 37 completed weeks of gestation) O42.01-●
after 24 hours O42.10
at or after 37 weeks gestation, onset of labor more than 24 hours following rupture O42.12
pre-term (before 37 completed weeks of gestation) O42.11-●
at or after 37 weeks gestation, unspecified as to length of time between rupture and onset of labor O42.92
pre-term (before 37 completed weeks of gestation) O42.91-●
premature separation of placenta —*see also* Abruptio placentae O45.9-●
presentation, fetal —*see* Delivery, complicated by, malposition
preterm delivery O60.10
preterm labor
with delivery O60.10
preterm O60.10
term O60.20
second trimester
with preterm delivery
second trimester O60.12
third trimester O60.13
with term delivery O60.22
without delivery O60.02
third trimester
with term delivery O60.23
with third trimester preterm delivery O60.14
without delivery O60.03
without delivery O60.00
second trimester O60.02
third trimester O60.03
previous history of —*see* Pregnancy, supervision of, high-risk
prolapse, uterus O34.52-●
proteinuria (gestational) —*see also* Proteinuria, gestational O12.1-●
with edema O12.2-●
pruritic urticarial papules and plaques of pregnancy (PUPPP) O26.86
pruritus (neurogenic) O26.89-●
psychosis or psychoneurosis (puerperal) F53.1
ptyalism O26.89-●
PUPPP (pruritic urticarial papules and plaques of pregnancy) O26.86
pyelitis O23.0-●
recurrent pregnancy loss O26.2-●

Pregnancy *(Continued)*
complicated by *(Continued)*
renal disease or failure NEC O26.83-●
with secondary hypertension, pre-existing —*see* Hypertension, complicating, pregnancy, pre-existing, secondary
hypertensive, pre-existing —*see* Hypertension, complicating, pregnancy, pre-existing, with, renal disease
respiratory condition (conditions in J00-J99) O99.51-●
retained, retention
dead ovum O02.0
intrauterine contraceptive device O26.3-●
retroversion, uterus O34.53-●
Rh immunization, incompatibility or sensitization NEC O36.09-●
anti-D antibody O36.01-●
rupture
amnion (premature) —*see also* Pregnancy, complicated by, premature rupture of membranes O42-●
membranes (premature) —*see also* Pregnancy, complicated by, premature rupture of membranes O42-●
uterus (during labor) O71.1
before onset of labor O71.0-●
salivation (excessive) O26.89-●
salpingitis O23.52-●
salpingo-oophoritis O23.52-●
sepsis (conditions in A40, A41) O98.81-●
size date discrepancy (uterine) O26.84-●
skin condition (conditions in L00-L99) O99.71-●
smoking (tobacco) O99.33-●
social problem O09.7-●
specified condition NEC O26.89-●
spotting O26.85-●
streptococcus group B (GBS) carrier state O99.820
subluxation of symphysis (pubis) O26.71-●
syphilis (conditions in A50-A53) O98.11-●
threatened
abortion O20.0
labor O47.9
at or after 37 completed weeks of gestation O47.1
before 37 completed weeks of gestation O47.0-●
thrombophlebitis (superficial) O22.2-●
thrombosis O22.9-●
cerebral venous O22.5-●
cerebrovenous sinus O22.5-●
deep O22.3-●
tobacco use disorder (smoking) O99.33-●
torsion of uterus O34.59-●
toxemia O14.9-●
transverse lie or presentation O32.2
tuberculosis (conditions in A15-A19) O98.01-●
tumor (benign)
cervix O34.4-●
malignant O9A.11-●
uterus O34.1-●
unstable lie O32.0
upper respiratory infection O99.51-●
urethritis O23.2-●
uterine size date discrepancy O26.84-●
vaginitis or vulvitis O23.59-●
varicose veins (lower extremities) O22.0-●
genitals O22.1-●
legs O22.0-●
perineal O22.1-●
vaginal or vulval O22.1-●
venereal disease NEC (conditions in A63.8) O98.31-●

Pregnancy *(Continued)*
complicated by *(Continued)*
venous disorders O22.9-●
specified NEC O22.8X-●
very young mother —*see* Pregnancy, complicated by, young mother
viral diseases (conditions in A80-B09, B25-B34) O98.51-●
vomiting O21.9
due to diseases classified elsewhere O21.8
hyperemesis gravidarum (mild) —*see also* Hyperemesis, gravidarum O21.0-●
late (occurring after 20 weeks of gestation) O21.2
young mother
multigravida O09.62-●
primigravida O09.61-●
concealed O09.3-●
continuing following
elective fetal reduction of one or more fetus O31.3-●
intrauterine death of one or more fetus O31.2-●
spontaneous abortion of one or more fetus O31.1-●
cornual O00.80
with intrauterine pregnancy O00.81
ectopic (ruptured) O00.90
with intrauterine pregnancy O00.91
abdominal O00.00
with
intrauterine pregnancy O00.01
viable fetus O36.7-●
cervical O00.80
with intrauterine pregnancy O00.81
complicated (by) O08.9
afibrinogenemia O08.1
cardiac arrest O08.81
chemical damage of pelvic organ(s) O08.6
circulatory collapse O08.3
defibrination syndrome O08.1
electrolyte imbalance O08.5
embolism (amniotic fluid) (blood clot) (pulmonary) (septic) O08.2
endometritis O08.0
genital tract and pelvic infection O08.0
hemorrhage (delayed) (excessive) O08.1
infection
genital tract or pelvic O08.0
kidney 008.83
urinary tract O08.83
intravascular coagulation O08.1
laceration of pelvic organ(s) O08.6
metabolic disorder O08.5
oliguria O08.4
oophoritis O08.0
parametritis O08.0
pelvic peritonitis O08.0
perforation of pelvic organ(s) O08.6
renal failure or shutdown O08.4
salpingitis or salpingo-oophoritis O08.0
sepsis O08.82
shock O08.83
septic O08.82
specified condition NEC O08.89
tubular necrosis (renal) O08.4
uremia O08.4
urinary infection O08.83
venous complication NEC O08.7
embolism O08.2
cornual O00.80
with intrauterine pregnancy O00.81
intraligamentous O00.80
with intrauterine pregnancy O00.81

Pregnancy (Continued)

ectopic (Continued)
mural O00.80
with intrauterine pregnancy O00.81
ovarian O00.20-●
with intrauterine pregnancy O00.21-●
specified site NEC O00.80
with intrauterine pregnancy O00.81
tubal (ruptured) O00.10-●
with intrauterine pregnancy O00.11-●
examination (normal) Z34.9-●
first Z34.0-●
high-risk —see Pregnancy, supervision of, high-risk
specified Z34.8-●
extrauterine —see Pregnancy, ectopic
fallopian O00.10-●
with intrauterine pregnancy O00.11-●
false F45.8
gestational carrier Z33.3
heptachorionic, hepta-amniotic (septuplets) O30.83-●
hexachorionic, hexa-amniotic (sextuplets) O30.83-●
hidden O09.3-●
high-risk —see Pregnancy, supervision of, high-risk
incidental finding Z33.1
interstitial O00.80
with intrauterine pregnancy O00.81
intraligamentous O00.80
with intrauterine pregnancy O00.81
intramural O00.80
with intrauterine pregnancy O00.81
intraperitoneal O00.00
with intrauterine pregnancy O00.01
isthmian O00.10-●
with intrauterine pregnancy O00.11-●
mesometric (mural) O00.80
with intrauterine pregnancy O00.81
molar NEC O02.0
complicated (by) O08.9
afibrinogenemia O08.1
cardiac arrest O08.81
chemical damage of pelvic organ(s) O08.6
circulatory collapse O08.3
defibrination syndrome O08.1
electrolyte imbalance O08.5
embolism (amniotic fluid) (blood clot) (pulmonary) (septic) O08.2
endometritis O08.0
genital tract and pelvic infection O08.0
hemorrhage (delayed) (excessive) O08.1
infection
genital tract or pelvic O08.0
kidney O08.83
urinary tract O08.83
intravascular coagulation O08.1
laceration of pelvic organ(s) O08.6
metabolic disorder O08.5
oliguria O08.4
oophoritis O08.0
parametritis O08.0
pelvic peritonitis O08.0
perforation of pelvic organ(s) O08.6
renal failure or shutdown O08.4
salpingitis or salpingo-oophoritis O08.0
sepsis O08.82
shock O08.3
septic O08.82
specified condition NEC O08.89
tubular necrosis (renal) O08.4
uremia O08.4
urinary infection O08.83
venous complication NEC O08.7
embolism O08.2
hydatidiform —see also Mole, hydatidiform O01.9-●
multiple (gestation) O30.9-●
greater than quadruplets —see Pregnancy, multiple (gestation), specified NEC

Pregnancy (Continued)

multiple (gestation) (Continued)
specified NEC O30.80-●
with
two or more monoamniotic fetuses O30.82-●
two or more monochorionic fetuses O30.81-●
number of chorions and amnions are both equal to the number of fetuses O30.83-●
two or more monoamniotic fetuses O30.82-●
two or more monochorionic fetuses O30.81-●
unable to determine number of placenta and number of amniotic sacs O30.89-●
unspecified number of placenta and unspecified number of amniotic sacs O30.80-●
mural O00.80
with intrauterine pregnancy O00.81
normal (supervision of) Z34.9-●
first Z34.0-●
high-risk —see Pregnancy, supervision of, high-risk
specified Z34.8-●
ovarian O00.20-●
with intrauterine pregnancy O00.21-●
pentachorionic, penta-amniotic (quintuplets) O30.83-●
postmature (40 to 42 weeks) O48.0
more than 42 weeks gestation O48.1
post-term (40 to 42 weeks) O48.0
prenatal care only Z34.9-●
first Z34.0-●
high-risk —see Pregnancy, supervision of, high-risk
specified Z34.8-●
prolonged (more than 42 weeks gestation) O48.1
quadruplet O30.20-●
with
two or more monoamniotic fetuses O30.22-●
two or more monochorionic fetuses O30.21-●
quadrachorionic/quadra-amniotic O30.23-●
two or more monoamniotic fetuses O30.22-●
two or more monochorionic fetuses O30.21-●
unable to determine number of placenta and number of amniotic sacs O30.29-●
unspecified number of placenta and unspecified number of amniotic sacs O30.20-●
quintuplet —see Pregnancy, multiple (gestation), specified NEC
sextuplet —see Pregnancy, multiple (gestation), specified NEC
supervision of
concealed pregnancy O09.3-●
elderly mother
multigravida O09.52-●
primigravida O09.51-●
hidden pregnancy O09.3-●
high-risk O09.9-●
due to (history of)
ectopic pregnancy O09.1-●
elderly —see Pregnancy, supervision, elderly mother
grand multiparity O09.4
infertility O09.0-●
insufficient prenatal care O09.3-●
in utero procedure during previous pregnancy O09.82-●
in vitro fertilization O09.81-●
molar pregnancy O09.A-●
multiple previous pregnancies O09.4-●
older mother —see Pregnancy, supervision of, elderly mother

Pregnancy (Continued)

supervision of (Continued)
high-risk (Continued)
due to (Continued)
poor reproductive or obstetric history NEC O09.29-●
pre-term labor O09.21-●
previous
neonatal death O09.29-●
social problems O09.7-●
specified NEC O09.89-●
very young mother —see Pregnancy, supervision, young mother
resulting from in vitro fertilization O09.81-●
normal Z34.9-●
first Z34.0-●
specified NEC Z34.8-●
young mother
multigravida O09.62-●
primigravida O09.61-●
triplet O30.10-●
with
two or more monoamniotic fetuses O30.12-●
two or more monochorionic fetuses O30.11-●
trichorionic/triamniotic O30.13-●
two or more monoamniotic fetuses O30.12-●
two or more monochorionic fetuses O30.11-●
unable to determine number of placenta and number of amniotic sacs O30.19-●
unspecified number of placenta and unspecified number of amniotic sacs O30.10-●
tubal (with abortion) (with rupture) O00.10-●
with intrauterine pregnancy O00.11-●
twin O30.00-●
conjoined O30.02-●
dichorionic/diamniotic (two placenta, two amniotic sacs) O30.04-●
monochorionic/diamniotic (one placenta, two amniotic sacs) O30.03-●
monochorionic/monoamniotic (one placenta, one amniotic sac) O30.01-●
unable to determine number of placenta and number of amniotic sacs O30.09-●
unspecified number of placenta and unspecified number of amniotic sacs O30.00-●
unwanted Z64.0
weeks of gestation
8 weeks Z3A.08
9 weeks Z3A.09
10 weeks Z3A.10
11 weeks Z3A.11
12 weeks Z3A.12
13 weeks Z3A.13
14 weeks Z3A.14
15 weeks Z3A.15
16 weeks Z3A.16
17 weeks Z3A.17
18 weeks Z3A.18
19 weeks Z3A.19
20 weeks Z3A.20
21 weeks Z3A.21
22 weeks Z3A.22
23 weeks Z3A.23
24 weeks Z3A.24
25 weeks Z3A.25
26 weeks Z3A.26
27 weeks Z3A.27
28 weeks Z3A.28
29 weeks Z3A.29
30 weeks Z3A.30
31 weeks Z3A.31
32 weeks Z3A.32
33 weeks Z3A.33
34 weeks Z3A.34
35 weeks Z3A.35
36 weeks Z3A.36

▶ New　➡ Revised　~~deleted~~ Deleted　● Use Additional Character(s)

Pregnancy (Continued)
  weeks of gestation (Continued)
    37 weeks Z3A.37
    38 weeks Z3A.38
    39 weeks Z3A.39
    40 weeks Z3A.40
    41 weeks Z3A.41
    42 weeks Z3A.42
    greater than 42 weeks Z3A.49
    less than 8 weeks Z3A.01
    not specified Z3A.00
Preiser's disease —see Osteonecrosis,
    secondary, due to, trauma, metacarpus
Pre-kwashiorkor —see Malnutrition, severe
Preleukemia (syndrome) D46.9
Preluxation, hip, congenital Q65.6
Premature —see also condition
  adrenarche E27.0
  aging E34.8
  beats I49.40
    atrial I49.1
    auricular I49.1
    supraventricular I49.1
  birth NEC —see Preterm, newborn
  closure, foramen ovale Q21.8
  contraction
    atrial I49.1
    atrioventricular I49.49
    auricular I49.1
    auriculoventricular I49.2
    heart (extrasystole) I49.49
    junctional I49.2
    ventricular I49.3
  delivery —see also Pregnancy, complicated by,
    preterm labor O60.10
  ejaculation F52.4
  infant NEC —see Preterm, newborn
    light-for-dates —see Light for dates
  labor —see Pregnancy, complicated by,
    preterm labor
  lungs P28.0
  menopause E28.319
    asymptomatic E28.319
    symptomatic E28.310
  newborn
    extreme (less than 28 completed weeks) —
      see Immaturity, extreme
    less than 37 completed weeks —see
      Preterm, newborn
  puberty E30.1
  rupture membranes or amnion —see
    Pregnancy, complicated by, premature
    rupture of membranes
  senility E34.8
  thelarche E30.8
  ventricular systole I49.3
Prematurity NEC (less than 37 completed
    weeks) —see Preterm, newborn
  extreme (less than 28 completed weeks) —see
    Immaturity, extreme
Premenstrual
  dysphoric disorder (PMDD) F32.81
  tension (syndrome) N94.3
Premolarization, cuspids K00.2
Prenatal
  care, normal pregnancy —see Pregnancy,
    normal
  screening of mother —see also Encounter,
    antenatal Z36.9
  teeth K00.6
Preparatory care for subsequent treatment NEC
  for dialysis Z49.01
    peritoneal Z49.02
Prepartum —see condition
Preponderance, left or right ventricular I51.7
Prepuce —see condition
PRES (posterior reversible encephalopathy
    syndrome) I67.83
Presbycardia R54
Presbycusis, presbyacusia H91.1-●
Presbyesophagus K22.8

Presbyophrenia F03
Presbyopia H52.4
Prescription of contraceptives (initial) Z30.019
  barrier Z30.018
    diaphragm Z30.018
  emergency (postcoital) Z30.012
  implantable subdermal Z30.017
  injectable Z30.013
  intrauterine contraceptive device Z30.014
  pills Z30.011
  postcoital (emergency) Z30.012
  repeat Z30.40
    barrier Z30.49
    diaphragm Z30.49
    implantable subdermal Z30.46
    injectable Z30.42
    pills Z30.41
    specified type NEC Z30.49
    transdermal patch hormonal Z30.45
    vaginal ring hormonal Z30.44
  specified type NEC Z30.018
    transdermal patch hormonal Z30.016
    vaginal ring hormonal Z30.015
Presence (of)
  ankle-joint implant (functional) (prosthesis)
    Z96.66-●
  aortocoronary (bypass) graft Z95.1
  arterial-venous shunt (dialysis) Z99.2
  artificial
    eye (globe) Z97.0
    heart (fully implantable) (mechanical)
      Z95.812
    valve Z95.2
    larynx Z96.3
    lens (intraocular) Z96.1
    limb (complete) (partial) Z97.1-●
      arm Z97.1-●
        bilateral Z97.15
      leg Z97.1-●
        bilateral Z97.16
  audiological implant (functional) Z96.29
  bladder implant (functional) Z96.0
  bone
    conduction hearing device Z96.29
    implant (functional) NEC Z96.7
    joint (prosthesis) —see Presence, joint
      implant
  cardiac
    defibrillator (functional) (with synchronous
      cardiac pacemaker)Z95.810
    implant or graft Z95.9
      specified type NEC Z95.818
    pacemaker Z95.0
    resynchronization therapy
      defibrillator Z95.810
      pacemaker Z95.0
  cerebrospinal fluid drainage device Z98.2
  cochlear implant (functional) Z96.21
  contact lens (es) Z97.3
  coronary artery graft or prosthesis Z95.5
  CRT-D (cardiac resynchronization therapy
      defibrillator) Z95.810
  CRT-P (cardiac resynchronization therapy
      pacemaker) Z95.0
  cardioverter-defibrillator (ICD) Z95.810
  CSF shunt Z98.2
  dental prosthesis device Z97.2
  dentures Z97.2
  device (external) NEC Z97.8
    cardiac NEC Z95.818
    heart assist Z95.811
    implanted (functional) Z96.9
      specified NEC Z96.89
    prosthetic Z97.8
  ear implant Z96.20
    cochlear implant Z96.21
    myringotomy tube Z96.22
    specified type NEC Z96.29
  elbow-joint implant (functional) (prosthesis)
    Z96.62-●
  endocrine implant (functional) NEC Z96.49

Presence (Continued)
  eustachian tube stent or device (functional)
    Z96.29
  external hearing-aid or device Z97.4
  finger-joint implant (functional) (prosthetic)
    Z96.69-●
  functional implant Z96.9
    specified NEC Z96.89
  graft
    cardiac NEC Z95.818
    vascular NEC Z95.828
  hearing-aid or device (external) Z97.4
    implant (bone) (cochlear) (functional) Z96.21
  heart assist device Z95.811
  heart valve implant (functional) Z95.2
    prosthetic Z95.2
    specified type NEC Z95.4
    xenogenic Z95.3
  hip-joint implant (functional) (prosthesis)
    Z96.64-●
  ICD (cardioverter-defibrillator) Z95.810
  implanted device (artificial) (functional)
      (prosthetic) Z96.9
    automatic cardiac defibrillator (with
        synchronous cardiac pacemaker)
        Z95.810
    cardiac pacemaker Z95.0
    cochlear Z96.21
    dental Z96.5
    heart Z95.812
    heart valve Z95.2
      prosthetic Z95.2
      specified NEC Z95.4
      xenogenic Z95.3
    insulin pump Z96.41
    intraocular lens Z96.1
    joint Z96.60
      ankle Z96.66-●
      elbow Z96.62-●
      finger Z96.69-●
      hip Z96.64-●
      knee Z96.65-●
      shoulder Z96.61-●
      specified NEC Z96.698
      wrist Z96.63-●
    larynx Z96.3
    myringotomy tube Z96.22
    otological Z96.20
      cochlear Z96.21
      eustachian stent Z96.29
      myringotomy Z96.22
      specified NEC Z96.29
      stapes Z96.29
    skin Z96.81
    skull plate Z96.7
    specified NEC Z96.89
    urogenital Z96.0
  insulin pump (functional) Z96.41
  intestinal bypass or anastomosis Z98.0
  intraocular lens (functional) Z96.1
  intrauterine contraceptive device (IUD) Z97.5
  intravascular implant (functional) (prosthetic)
      NEC Z95.9
    coronary artery Z95.5
    defibrillator (with synchronous cardiac
        pacemaker) Z95.810
    peripheral vessel (with angioplasty) Z95.820
  joint implant (prosthetic) (any) Z96.60
    ankle —see Presence, ankle joint implant
    elbow —see Presence, elbow joint implant
    finger —see Presence, finger joint implant
    hip —see Presence, hip joint implant
    knee —see Presence, knee joint implant
    shoulder —see Presence, shoulder joint
        implant
    specified joint NEC Z96.698
    wrist —see Presence, wrist joint implant
  knee-joint implant (functional) (prosthesis)
    Z96.65-●
  laryngeal implant (functional) Z96.3
  mandibular implant (dental) Z96.5

Presence *(Continued)*
  myringotomy tube(s) Z96.22
  neurostimulator (brain) (gastric) (peripheral
    nerve) (sacral nerve) (spinal cord) (vagus
    nerve) Z96.82
  orthopedic-joint implant (prosthetic) (any) —
    see Presence, joint implant
  otological implant (functional) Z96.29
  shoulder-joint implant (functional)
    (prosthesis) Z96.61-●
  skull-plate implant Z96.7
  spectacles Z97.3
  stapes implant (functional) Z96.29
  systemic lupus erythematosus [SLE] inhibitor
    D68.62
  tendon implant (functional) (graft) Z96.7
  tooth root(s) implant Z96.5
  ureteral stent Z96.0
  urethral stent Z96.0
  urogenital implant (functional) Z96.0
  vascular implant or device Z95.9
    access port device Z95.828
    specified type NEC Z95.828
  wrist-joint implant (functional) (prosthesis)
    Z96.63-●
Presenile —*see also* condition
  dementia F03
  premature aging E34.8
Presentation, fetal —*see* Delivery, complicated
  by, malposition
Prespondylolisthesis (congenital) Q76.2
Pressure
  area, skin —*see* Ulcer, pressure, by site
  brachial plexus G54.0
  brain G93.5
    injury at birth NEC P11.1
  cerebral —*see* Pressure, brain
  chest R07.89
  cone, tentorial G93.5
  hyposystolic —*see also* Hypotension
    incidental reading, without diagnosis of
      hypotension R03.1
  increased
    intracranial, benign G93.2
      injury at birth P11.0
    intraocular H40.05-●
  injury —*see* Ulcer, pressure, by site
  lumbosacral plexus G54.1
  mediastinum J98.59
  necrosis (chronic) —*see* Ulcer, pressure,
    by site
  parental, inappropriate (excessive) Z62.6
  sore (chronic) —*see* Ulcer, pressure, by site
  spinal cord G95.20
  ulcer (chronic) —*see* Ulcer, pressure, by site
  venous, increased I87.8
Pre-syncope R55
Preterm
  delivery (*see also* Pregnancy, complicated by,
    preterm labor) O60.10
  labor —*see* Pregnancy, complicated by,
    preterm labor
  newborn (infant) P07.30
    gestational age
      28 completed weeks (28 weeks, 0 days
        through 28 weeks, 6 days) P07.31
      29 completed weeks (29 weeks, 0 days
        through 29 weeks, 6 days) P07.32
      30 completed weeks (30 weeks, 0 days
        through 30 weeks, 6 days) P07.33
      31 completed weeks (31 weeks, 0 days
        through 31 weeks, 6 days) P07.34
      32 completed weeks (32 weeks, 0 days
        through 32 weeks, 6 days) P07.35
      33 completed weeks (33 weeks, 0 days
        through 33 weeks, 6 days) P07.36
      34 completed weeks (34 weeks, 0 days
        through 34 weeks, 6 days) P07.37
      35 completed weeks (35 weeks, 0 days
        through 35 weeks, 6 days) P07.38
      36 completed weeks (36 weeks, 0 days
        through 36 weeks, 6 days) P07.39

Previa
  placenta (total) (without hemorrhage)
    O44.0-●
    with hemorrhage O44.1-●
    complete O44.0-●
      with hemorrhage O44.1-●
    low —*see also* Delivery, complicated, by,
      placenta, low O44.4-●
    with hemorrhage O44.5-●
    marginal O44.2-●
      with hemorrhage O44.3-●
    partial O44.2-●
      with hemorrhage O44.3-●
  vasa O69.4
Priapism N48.30
  due to
    disease classified elsewhere N48.32
    drug N48.33
    specified cause NEC N48.39
    trauma N48.31
Prickling sensation (skin) R20.2
Prickly heat L74.0
Primary —*see* condition
Primigravida
  elderly, affecting management of pregnancy,
    labor and delivery (supervision only) —
    see Pregnancy, complicated by, elderly,
    primigravida
  older, affecting management of pregnancy,
    labor and delivery (supervision only) —
    see Pregnancy, complicated by, elderly,
    primigravida
  very young, affecting management
    of pregnancy, labor and delivery
    (supervision only) —*see* Pregnancy,
    complicated by, young mother,
    primigravida
Primipara
  elderly, affecting management of pregnancy,
    labor and delivery (supervision only) —
    see Pregnancy, complicated by, elderly,
    primigravida
  older, affecting management of pregnancy,
    labor and delivery (supervision only) —
    see Pregnancy, complicated by, elderly,
    primigravida
  very young, affecting management
    of pregnancy, labor and delivery
    (supervision only) —*see* Pregnancy,
    complicated by, young mother,
    primigravida
Primus varus (bilateral) Q66.21-●
PRIND (Prolonged reversible ischemic
  neurologic deficit) I63.9
Pringle's disease (tuberous sclerosis) Q85.1
Prinzmetal angina I20.1
Prizefighter ear —*see* Cauliflower ear
Problem (with) (related to)
  academic Z55.8
  acculturation Z60.3
  adjustment (to)
    change of job Z56.1
    life-cycle transition Z60.0
    pension Z60.0
    retirement Z60.0
  adopted child Z62.821
  alcoholism in family Z63.72
  atypical parenting situation Z62.9
  bankruptcy Z59.8
  behavioral (adult) F69
    drug seeking Z76.5
  birth of sibling affecting child Z62.898
  care (of)
    provider dependency Z74.9
      specified NEC Z74.8
    sick or handicapped person in family or
      household Z63.6
  child
    abuse (affecting the child) —*see*
      Maltreatment, child
    custody or support proceedings Z65.3

Problem *(Continued)*
  child *(Continued)*
    in care of non-parental family member
      Z62.21
    in foster care Z62.21
    in welfare custody Z62.21
    living in orphanage or group home Z62.22
  child-rearing Z62.9
    specified NEC Z62.898
  communication (developmental) F80.9
  conflict or discord (with)
    boss Z56.4
    classmates Z55.4
    counselor Z64.4
    employer Z56.4
    family Z63.9
      specified NEC Z63.8
    probation officer Z64.4
    social worker Z64.4
    teachers Z55.4
    workmates Z56.4
  conviction in legal proceedings Z65.0
    with imprisonment Z65.1
  counselor Z64.4
  creditors Z59.8
  digestive K92.9
  drug addict in family Z63.72
  ear —*see* Disorder, ear
  economic Z59.9
    affecting care Z59.9
    specified NEC Z59.8
  education Z55.9
    specified NEC Z55.8
  employment Z56.9
    change of job Z56.1
    discord Z56.4
    environment Z56.5
    sexual harassment Z56.81
    specified NEC Z56.89
    stress NEC Z56.6
    stressful schedule Z56.3
    threat of job loss Z56.2
    unemployment Z56.0
  enuresis, child F98.0
  eye H57.9
  failed examinations (school) Z55.2
  falling Z91.81
  family —*see also* Disruption, family Z63.9-●
    specified NEC Z63.8
  feeding (elderly) (infant) R63.3
    newborn P92.9
      breast P92.5
      overfeeding P92.4
      slow P92.2
      specified NEC P92.8
      underfeeding P92.3
    nonorganic F50.89
  finance Z59.9
    specified NEC Z59.8
  foreclosure on loan Z59.8
  foster child Z62.822
  frightening experience(s) in childhood
    Z62.898
  genital NEC
    female N94.9
    male N50.9
  health care Z75.9
    specified NEC Z75.8
  hearing —*see* Deafness
  homelessness Z59.0
  housing Z59.9
    inadequate Z59.1
    isolated Z59.8
    specified NEC Z59.8
  identity (of childhood) F93.8
  illegitimate pregnancy (unwanted) Z64.0
  illiteracy Z55.0
  impaired mobility Z74.09
  imprisonment or incarceration Z65.1
  inadequate teaching affecting education
    Z55.8

▶ New   ➡ Revised   ~~deleted~~ Deleted   ● Use Additional Character(s)

Problem *(Continued)*
  inappropriate (excessive) parental pressure
    Z62.6
  influencing health status NEC Z78.9
  in-law Z63.1
  institutionalization, affecting child
    Z62.22
  intrafamilial communication Z63.8
  jealousy, child F93.8
  landlord Z59.2
  language (developmental) F80.9
  learning (developmental) F81.9
  legal Z65.3
    conviction without imprisonment Z65.0
    imprisonment Z65.1
    release from prison Z65.2
  life-management Z73.9
    specified NEC Z73.89
  life-style Z72.9
    gambling Z72.6
    high-risk sexual behavior (heterosexual)
      Z72.51
      bisexual Z72.53
      homosexual Z72.52
    inappropriate eating habits Z72.4
    self-damaging behavior NEC Z72.89
    specified NEC Z72.89
    tobacco use Z72.0
  literacy Z55.9
    low level Z55.0
    specified NEC Z55.8
  living alone Z60.2
  lodgers Z59.2
  loss of love relationship in childhood Z62.898
  marital Z63.0
    involving
      divorce Z63.5
      estrangement Z63.5
      gender identity F66
  mastication K08.89
  medical
    care, within family Z63.6
    facilities Z75.9
      specified NEC Z75.8
  mental F48.9
  multiparity Z64.1
  negative life events in childhood Z62.9
    altered pattern of family relationships
      Z62.898
    frightening experience Z62.898
    loss of
      love relationship Z62.898
      self-esteem Z62.898
    physical abuse (alleged) —*see*
      Maltreatment, child
    removal from home Z62.29
    specified event NEC Z62.898
  neighbor Z59.2
  neurological NEC R29.818
  new step-parent affecting child Z62.898
  none (feared complaint unfounded) Z71.1
  occupational NEC Z56.89
  parent-child —*see* Conflict, parent-child
  personal hygiene Z91.89
  personality F69
  phase-of-life transition, adjustment Z60.0
  presence of sick or disabled person
    in family or household Z63.79
    needing care Z63.6
  primary support group (family) Z63.9
    specified NEC Z63.8
  probation officer Z64.4
  psychiatric F99
  psychosexual (development) F66
  psychosocial Z65.9
    religious or spiritual Z65.8
    specified NEC Z65.8
  relationship Z63.9
    childhood F93.8
  release from prison Z65.2
    religious or spiritual Z65.8

Problem *(Continued)*
  removal from home affecting child
    Z62.29
  seeking and accepting known hazardous and
    harmful
    behavioral or psychological interventions
      Z65.8
    chemical, nutritional or physical
      interventions Z65.8
  sexual function (nonorganic) F52.9
  sight H54.7
  sleep disorder, child F51.9
  smell —*see* Disturbance, sensation, smell
  social
    environment Z60.9
      specified NEC Z60.8
    exclusion and rejection Z60.4
    worker Z64.4
  speech R47.9
    developmental F80.9
    specified NEC R47.89
  swallowing —*see* Dysphagia
  taste —*see* Disturbance, sensation, taste
  tic, child F95.0
  underachievement in school Z55.3
  unemployment Z56.0
    threatened Z56.2
  unwanted pregnancy Z64.0
  upbringing Z62.9
    specified NEC Z62.898
  urinary N39.9
  voice production R47.89
  work schedule (stressful) Z56.3
Procedure (surgical)
  converted
    arthroscopic to open Z53.33
    laparoscopic to open Z53.31
    specified procedure NEC to open
      Z53.39
    thoracoscopic to open Z53.32
  for purpose other than remedying health
    state Z41.9
    specified NEC Z41.8
  not done Z53.9
    because of
      administrative reasons Z53.8
      contraindication Z53.09
        smoking Z53.01
      patient's decision Z53.20
        for reasons of belief or group pressure
          Z53.1
        left against medical advice (AMA)
          Z53.21
        specified reason NEC Z53.29
      specified reason NEC Z53.8
Procidentia (uteri) N81.3
Proctalgia K62.89
  fugax K59.4
  spasmodic K59.4
Proctitis K62.89
  amebic (acute) A06.0
  chlamydial A56.3
  gonococcal A54.6
  granulomatous —*see* Enteritis, regional, large
    intestine
  herpetic A60.1
  radiation K62.7
  tuberculous A18.32
  ulcerative (chronic) K51.20
    with
      complication K51.219
        abscess K51.214
        fistula K51.213
        obstruction K51.212
        rectal bleeding K51.211
        specified NEC K51.218
Proctocele
  female (without uterine prolapse) N81.6
    with uterine prolapse N81.2
      complete N81.3
  male K62.3

Proctocolitis
  food-induced eosinophilic K52.82
  food protein-induced K52.82
  milk protein-induced K52.82
  mucosal —*see* Rectosigmoiditis, ulcerative
Proctoptosis K62.3
Proctorrhagia K62.5
Proctosigmoiditis K63.89
  ulcerative (chronic) —*see* Rectosigmoiditis,
    ulcerative
Proctospasm K59.4
  psychogenic F45.8
Profichet's disease —*see* Disorder, soft tissue,
  specified type NEC
Progeria E34.8
Prognathism (mandibular) (maxillary) M26.19
Progonoma (melanotic) —*see* Neoplasm,
  benign, by site
Progressive —*see* condition
Prolactinoma
  specified site —*see* Neoplasm, benign,
    by site
  unspecified site D35.2
Prolapse, prolapsed
  anus, anal (canal) (sphincter) K62.2
  arm or hand O32.2
    causing obstructed labor O64.4
  bladder (mucosa) (sphincter) (acquired)
    congenital Q79.4
    female —*see* Cystocele
    male N32.89
  breast implant (prosthetic) T85.49
  cecostomy K94.09
  cecum K63.4
  cervix, cervical (hypertrophied) N81.2
    anterior lip, obstructing labor O65.5
    congenital Q51.828
    postpartal, old N81.2
    stump N81.85
  ciliary body (traumatic) —*see* Laceration,
    eye(ball), with prolapse or loss of
    interocular tissue
  colon (pedunculated) K63.4
  colostomy K94.09
  disc (intervertebral) —*see* Displacement,
    intervertebral disc
  eye implant (orbital) T85.398
    lens (ocular) —*see* Complications,
      intraocular lens
  fallopian tube N83.4-•
  gastric (mucosa) K31.89
  genital, female N81.9
    specified NEC N81.89
  globe, nontraumatic —*see* Luxation, globe
  ileostomy bud K94.19
  intervertebral disc —*see* Displacement,
    intervertebral disc
  intestine (small) K63.4
  iris (traumatic) —*see* Laceration, eye(ball),
    with prolapse or loss of interocular
    tissue
    nontraumatic H21.89
  kidney N28.83
    congenital Q63.2
  laryngeal muscles or ventricle J38.7
  liver K76.89
  meatus urinarius N36.8
  mitral (valve) I34.1
  ocular lens implant —*see* Complications,
    intraocular lens
  organ or site, congenital NEC —*see*
    Malposition, congenital
  ovary N83.4-•
  pelvic floor, female N81.89
  perineum, female N81.89
  rectum (mucosa) (sphincter) K62.3
    due to trichuris trichuria B79
  spleen D73.89
  stomach K31.89
  umbilical cord
    complicating delivery O69.0

Prolapse, prolapsed *(Continued)*
  urachus, congenital Q64.4
  ureter N28.89
    with obstruction N13.5
      with infection N13.6
  ureterovesical orifice N28.89
  urethra (acquired) (infected) (mucosa)
    N36.8
    congenital Q64.71
  urinary meatus N36.8
    congenital Q64.72
  uterovaginal N81.4
    complete N81.3
    incomplete N81.2
  uterus (with prolapse of vagina) N81.4
    complete N81.3
    congenital Q51.818
    first degree N81.2
    in pregnancy or childbirth —*see*
      Pregnancy, complicated by,
      abnormal, uterus
    incomplete N81.2
    postpartal (old) N81.4
    second degree N81.2
    third degree N81.3
  uveal (traumatic) —*see* Laceration, eye(ball),
    with prolapse or loss of interocular
    tissue
  vagina (anterior) (wall) —*see* Cystocele
    with prolapse of uterus N81.4
      complete N81.3
      incomplete N81.2
    posterior wall N81.6
    posthysterectomy N99.3
  vitreous (humor) H43.0-●
    in wound —*see* Laceration, eye(ball), with
      prolapse or loss of interocular tissue
  womb —*see* Prolapse, uterus
Prolapsus, female N81.9
  specified NEC N81.89
Proliferation(s)
  primary cutaneous CD30-positive large T-cell
    C86.6
  prostate, atypical small acinar N42.32
Proliferative —*see* condition
Prolonged, prolongation (of)
  bleeding (time) (idiopathic) R79.1
  coagulation (time) R79.1
  gestation (over 42 completed weeks)
    mother O48.1
    newborn P08.22
  interval I44.0
  labor O63.9
    first stage O63.0
    second stage O63.1
  partial thromboplastin time (PTT) R79.1
  pregnancy (more than 42 weeks gestation)
    O48.1
  prothrombin time R79.1
  QT interval R94.31
  uterine contractions in labor O62.4
Prominence, prominent
▶ischial spine or sacral promontory with
    disproportion (fetopelvic) O33.0
   ▶causing obstructed labor O65.0
  with disproportion (fetopelvic) O33.0
    causing obstructed labor O65.0
  auricle (congenital) (ear) Q17.5
  ischial spine or sacral promontory
  nose (congenital) acquired M95.0
Promiscuity —*see* High, risk, sexual behavior
Pronation
  ankle —*see* Deformity, limb, foot, specified
    NEC
  foot —*see also* Deformity, limb, foot, specified
    NEC
    congenital Q74.2
Prophylactic
  administration of
    antibiotics, long-term Z79.2
      short-term use - omit code

Prophylactic *(Continued)*
  antibiotics, long-term *(Continued)*
    drug —*see also* Long-term (current) drug
      therapy (use of) Z79.899-●
  medication Z79.899
  organ removal (for neoplasia management)
    Z40.00
    breast Z40.01
    fallopian tube(s) Z40.03
      with ovary(s) Z40.02
    ovary(s) Z40.02
    specified site NEC Z40.09
  surgery Z40.9
    for risk factors related to malignant
      neoplasm —*see* Prophylactic, organ
      removal
    specified NEC Z40.8
  vaccination Z23
Propionic acidemia E71.121
Proptosis (ocular) —*see also* Exophthalmos
  thyroid —*see* Hyperthyroidism, with goiter
Prosecution, anxiety concerning Z65.3
Prosopagnosia R48.3
Prostadynia N42.81
Prostate, prostatic —*see* condition
Prostatism —*see* Hyperplasia, prostate
Prostatitis (congestive) (suppurative) (with
    cystitis) N41.9
  acute N41.0
  cavitary N41.8
  chronic N41.1
  diverticular N41.8
  due to Trichomonas (vaginalis) A59.02
  fibrous N41.1
  gonococcal (acute) (chronic) A54.22
  granulomatous N41.4
  hypertrophic N41.1
  subacute N41.1
  trichomonal A59.02
  tuberculous A18.14
Prostatocystitis N41.3
Prostatorrhea N42.89
Prostatosis N42.82
Prostration R53.83
  heat —*see also* Heat, exhaustion
    anhydrotic T67.3
    due to
      salt (and water) depletion T67.4
      water depletion T67.3
  nervous F48.8
  senile R54
Protanomaly (anomalous trichromat) H53.54
Protanopia (complete) (incomplete) H53.54
Protection (against) (from) —*see* Prophylactic
Protein
  deficiency NEC —*see* Malnutrition
  malnutrition —*see* Malnutrition
  sickness —*see also* Reaction, serum T80.69
Proteinemia R77.9
Proteinosis
  alveolar (pulmonary) J84.01
  lipid or lipoid (of Urbach) E78.89
Proteinuria R80.9
  Bence Jones R80.3
  complicating pregnancy —*see* Proteinuria,
    gestational
  gestational
    complicating
      childbirth O12.14
      pregnancy O12.1-●
        with edema O12.2-●
      puerperium O12.15
  idiopathic R80.0
  isolated R80.0
    with glomerular lesion N06.9
   ▶C3
     ▶glomerulonephritis N06.A
     ▶glomerulopathy N06.A
      ▶with dense deposit disease
        N06.6
     dense deposit disease N06.6

Proteinuria *(Continued)*
  isolated *(Continued)*
    with glomerular lesion *(Continued)*
      diffuse
        crescentic glomerulonephritis N06.7
        endocapillary proliferative
          glomerulonephritis N06.4
        mesangiocapillary glomerulonephritis
          N06.5
      focal and segmental hyalinosis or
        sclerosis N06.1
      membranous (diffuse) N06.2
      mesangial proliferative (diffuse) N06.3
      minimal change N06.0
      specified pathology NEC N06.8
  orthostatic R80.2
    with glomerular lesion —*see* Proteinuria,
      isolated, with glomerular lesion
  persistent R80.1
    with glomerular lesion —*see* Proteinuria,
      isolated, with glomerular lesion
  postural R80.2
    with glomerular lesion —*see* Proteinuria,
      isolated, with glomerular lesion
  pre-eclamptic —*see* Pre-eclampsia
  puerperal O12.15
  specified type NEC R80.8
Proteolysis, pathologic D65
Proteus (mirabilis) (morganii), as cause of
    disease classified elsewhere B96.4
Prothrombin gene mutation D68.52
Protoporphyria, erythropoietic E80.0
Protozoal —*see also* condition
  disease B64
    specified NEC B60.8
Protrusion, protrusio
  acetabuli M24.7
  acetabulum (into pelvis) M24.7
  device, implant or graft —*see also*
    Complications, by site and type,
    mechanical T85.698
    arterial graft NEC —*see* Complication,
      cardiovascular device, mechanical,
      vascular
    breast (implant) T85.49
    catheter NEC T85.698
      cystostomy T83.090
      dialysis (renal) T82.49
        intraperitoneal T85.691
      infusion NEC T82.594
        spinal (epidural) (subdural) T85.690
      urinary —*see also* Complications,
        catheter, urinary T83.098
    electronic (electrode) (pulse generator)
      (stimulator)
      bone T84.390
      nervous system —*see* Complication,
        prosthetic device, mechanical,
        electronic nervous system
        stimulator
    fixation, internal (orthopedic) NEC —
      see Complication, fixation device,
      mechanical
    gastrointestinal —*see* Complications,
      prosthetic device, mechanical,
      gastrointestinal device
    genital NEC T83.498
      intrauterine contraceptive device T83.39
      penile prosthesis (cylinder) (implanted)
        (pump) (resevoir) T83.490
      testicular prosthesis T83.491
    heart NEC —*see* Complication,
      cardiovascular device, mechanical
    joint prosthesis —*see* Complications, joint
      prosthesis, mechanical, specified NEC,
      by site
    ocular NEC —*see* Complications, prosthetic
      device, mechanical, ocular device
    orthopedic NEC —*see* Complication,
      orthopedic, device, mechanical
    specified NEC T85.628

▶ New   ⇒ Revised   ~~deleted~~ Deleted   ● Use Additional Character(s)

Protrusion, protrusio *(Continued)*
  device, implant or graft *(Continued)*
    urinary NEC —*see also* Complication,
      genitourinary, device, urinary,
      mechanical
      graft T83.29
    vascular NEC —*see* Complication,
      cardiovascular device, mechanical
    ventricular intracranial shunt T85.09
  intervertebral disc —*see* Displacement,
    intervertebral disc
  joint prosthesis —*see* Complications, joint
    prosthesis, mechanical, specified NEC,
    by site
  nucleus pulposus —*see* Displacement,
    intervertebral disc
Prune belly (syndrome) Q79.4
Prurigo (ferox) (gravis) (Hebrae) (Hebra's)
  (mitis) (simplex) L28.2
  Besnier's L20.0
  estivalis L56.4
  nodularis L28.1
  psychogenic F45.8
Pruritus, pruritic (essential) L29.9
  ani, anus L29.0
    psychogenic F45.8
  anogenital L29.3
    psychogenic F45.8
  due to onchocerca volvulus B73.1
  gravidarum —*see* Pregnancy, complicated by,
    specified pregnancy-related condition
    NEC
  hiemalis L29.8
  neurogenic (any site) F45.8
  perianal L29.0
  psychogenic (any site) F45.8
  scroti, scrotum L29.1
    psychogenic F45.8
  senile, senilis L29.8
  specified NEC L29.8
    psychogenic F45.8
  Trichomonas A59.9
  vulva, vulvae L29.2
    psychogenic F45.8
Pseudarthrosis, pseudoarthrosis (bone) —*see*
  Nonunion, fracture
  clavicle, congenital Q74.0
  joint, following fusion or arthrodesis M96.0
Pseudoaneurysm —*see* Aneurysm
Pseudoangina (pectoris) —*see* Angina
Pseudoangioma I81
Pseudoarteriosus Q28.8
Pseudoarthrosis —*see* Pseudarthrosis
Pseudobulbar affect (PBA) F48.2
Pseudochromhidrosis L67.8
Pseudocirrhosis, liver, pericardial I31.1
Pseudocowpox B08.03
Pseudocoxalgia M91.3-•
Pseudocroup J38.5
Pseudo-Cushing's syndrome, alcohol-induced
  E24.4
Pseudocyesis F45.8
Pseudocyst
  lung J98.4
  pancreas K86.3
  retina —*see* Cyst, retina
Pseudoelephantiasis neuroarthritica Q82.0
Pseudoexfoliation, capsule (lens) —*see*
  Cataract, specified NEC
Pseudofolliculitis barbae L73.1
Pseudoglioma H44.89
Pseudohemophilia (Bernuth's) (hereditary)
  (type B) D68.0
  Type A D69.8
  vascular D69.8
Pseudohermaphroditism Q56.3
  adrenal E25.8
  female Q56.2
    with adrenocortical disorder E25.8
    without adrenocortical disorder
      Q56.2

Pseudohermaphroditism *(Continued)*
  female *(Continued)*
    adrenal (congenital) E25.0
    unspecified E25.9
  male Q56.1
    with
      adrenocortical disorder E25.8
      androgen resistance E34.51
      cleft scrotum Q56.1
      feminizing testis E34.51
      5-alpha-reductase deficiency E29.1
    without gonadal disorder Q56.1
    adrenal E25.8
    unspecified E25.9
Pseudo-Hurler's polydystrophy E77.0
Pseudohydrocephalus G93.2
Pseudohypertrophic muscular dystrophy
  (Erb's) G71.02
Pseudohypertrophy, muscle G71.09
Pseudohypoparathyroidism E20.1
Pseudoinsomnia F51.03
Pseudoleukemia, infantile D64.89
Pseudomembranous —*see* condition
➡ Pseudomeningocele (cerebral) (infective)
  (post-traumatic) G96.198
  postprocedural (spinal) G97.82
Pseudomenses (newborn) P54.6
Pseudomenstruation (newborn) P54.6
Pseudomonas
  aeruginosa, as cause of disease classified
    elsewhere B96.5
  mallei infection A24.0
    as cause of disease classified elsewhere
      B96.5
  pseudomallei, as cause of disease classified
    elsewhere B96.5
Pseudomyotonia G71.19
Pseudomyxoma peritonei C78.6
Pseudoneuritis, optic (nerve) (disc) (papilla),
  congenital Q14.2
➡ Pseudo-obstruction intestine (acute) (chronic)
  (idiopathic) (intermittent secondary)
  (primary) K59.89
▶ colonic K59.81
Pseudopapilledema H47.33-•
  congenital Q14.2
Pseudoparalysis
  arm or leg R29.818
  atonic, congenital P94.2
Pseudopelade L66.0
Pseudophakia Z96.1
Pseudopolyarthritis, rhizomelic M35.3
Pseudopolycythemia D75.1
Pseudopseudohypoparathyroidism E20.1
Pseudopterygium H11.81-•
Pseudoptosis (eyelid) —*see* Blepharochalasis
Pseudopuberty, precocious
  female heterosexual E25.8
  male isosexual E25.8
Pseudorickets (renal) N25.0
Pseudorubella B08.20
Pseudosclerema, newborn P83.88
Pseudosclerosis (brain)
  Jakob's —*see* Creutzfeldt-Jakob disease or
    syndrome
  of Westphal (Strüümpell) E83.01
  spastic —*see* Creutzfeldt-Jakob disease or
    syndrome
Pseudotetanus —*see* Convulsions
Pseudotetany R29.0
  hysterical F44.5
Pseudotruncus arteriosus Q25.49
Pseudotuberculosis A28.2
  enterocolitis A04.8
  pasteurella (infection) A28.0
➡ Pseudotumor G93.2
  cerebri G93.2
  orbital H05.11-•
Pseudoxanthoma elasticum Q82.8
Psilosis (sprue) (tropical) K90.1
  nontropical K90.0

Psittacosis A70
Psoitis M60.88
Psoriasis L40.9
  arthropathic L40.50
    arthritis mutilans L40.52
    distal interphalangeal L40.51
    juvenile L40.54
    other specified L40.59
    spondylitis L40.53
  buccal K13.29
  flexural L40.8
  guttate L40.4
  mouth K13.29
  nummular L40.0
  plaque L40.0
  psychogenic F54
  pustular (generalized) L40.1
    palmaris et plantaris L40.3
  specified NEC L40.8
  vulgaris L40.0
Psychasthenia F48.8
Psychiatric disorder or problem F99
Psychogenic —*see also* condition
  factors associated with physical conditions
    F54
Psychological and behavioral factors affecting
  medical condition F59
Psychoneurosis, psychoneurotic —*see also*
  Neurosis
  anxiety (state) F41.1
  depersonalization F48.1
  hypochondriacal F45.21
  hysteria F44.9
  neurasthenic F48.8
  personality NEC F60.89
Psychopathy, psychopathic
  affectionless F94.2
  autistic F84.5
  constitution, post-traumatic F07.81
  personality —*see* Disorder, personality
  sexual —*see* Deviation, sexual
  state F60.2
Psychosexual identity disorder of childhood
  F64.2
Psychosis, psychotic F29
  acute (transient) F23
    hysterical F44.9
  affective —*see* Disorder, mood
  alcoholic F10.959
    with
      abuse F10.159
      anxiety disorder F10.980
        with
          abuse F10.180
          dependence F10.280
      delirium tremens F10.231
      delusions F10.950
        with
          abuse F10.150
          dependence F10.250
      dementia F10.97
        with dependence F10.27
      dependence F10.259
      hallucinosis F10.951
        with
          abuse F10.151
          dependence F10.251
      mood disorder F10.94
        with
          abuse F10.14
          dependence F10.24
      paranoia F10.950
        with
          abuse F10.150
          dependence F10.250
      persisting amnesia F10.96
        with dependence F10.26
    amnestic confabulatory F10.96
      with dependence F10.26
    delirium tremens F10.231
    Korsakoff's, Korsakov's, Korsakow's F10.26

Psychosis, psychotic (Continued)
  alcoholic (Continued)
    paranoid type F10.950
      with
        abuse F10.150
        dependence F10.250
  anergastic —see Psychosis, organic
  arteriosclerotic (simple type) (uncomplicated) F01.50
    with behavioral disturbance F01.51
  childhood F84.0
    atypical F84.8
  climacteric —see Psychosis, involutional
  confusional F29
    acute or subacute F05
    reactive F23
  cycloid F23
  depressive —see Disorder, depressive
  disintegrative (childhood) F84.3
  drug-induced —see F11-F19 with .x59
    paranoid and hallucinatory states —see F11-F19 with .x50 or .x51
  due to or associated with
    addiction, drug —see F11-F19 with .X59
    dependence
      alcohol F10.259
      drug —see F11-F19 with .x59
    epilepsy F06.8
    Huntington's chorea F06.8
    ischemia, cerebrovascular (generalized) F06.8
    multiple sclerosis F06.8
    physical disease F06.8
    presenile dementia F03
    senile dementia F03
    vascular disease (arteriosclerotic) (cerebral) F01.50
      with behavioral disturbance F01.51
  epileptic F06.8
  episode F23
    due to or associated with physical condition F06.8
  exhaustive F43.0
  hallucinatory, chronic F28
  hypomanic F30.8
  hysterical (acute) F44.9
  induced F24
  infantile F84.0
    atypical F84.8
  infective (acute) (subacute) F05
  involutional F28
    depressive —see Disorder, depressive
    melancholic —see Disorder, depressive
    paranoid (state) F22
  Korsakoff's, Korsakov's, Korsakow's (nonalcoholic) F04
    alcoholic F10.96
    in dependence F10.26
    induced by other psychoactive substance —see categories F11-F19 with .x5x
  mania, manic (single episode) F30.2
    recurrent type F31.89
  manic-depressive —see Disorder, bipolar
  menopausal —see Psychosis, involutional
  mixed schizophrenic and affective F25.8
  multi-infarct (cerebrovascular) F01.50
    with behavioral disturbance F01.51
  nonorganic F29
    specified NEC F28
  organic F09
    due to or associated with
      arteriosclerosis (cerebral) —see Psychosis, arteriosclerotic
      cerebrovascular disease, arteriosclerotic —see Psychosis, arteriosclerotic
      childbirth —see Psychosis, puerperal
      Creutzfeldt-Jakob disease or syndrome —see Creutzfeldt-Jakob disease or syndrome

Psychosis, psychotic (Continued)
  organic (Continued)
    due to or associated with (Continued)
      dependence, alcohol F10.259
      disease
        alcoholic liver F10.259
        brain, arteriosclerotic —see Psychosis, arteriosclerotic
        cerebrovascular F01.50
          with behavioral disturbance F01.51
        Creutzfeldt-Jakob —see Creutzfeldt-Jakob disease or syndrome
        endocrine or metabolic F06.8
          acute or subacute F05
        liver, alcoholic F10.259
      epilepsy transient (acute) F05
      infection
        brain (intracranial) F06.8
          acute or subacute F05
      intoxication
        alcoholic (acute) F10.259
        drug F11-F19 with .x59
      ischemia, cerebrovascular (generalized) —see Psychosis, arteriosclerotic
      puerperium —see Psychosis, puerperal
      trauma, brain (birth) (from electric current) (surgical) F06.8
        acute or subacute F05
    infective F06.8
      acute or subacute F05
    post-traumatic F06.8
      acute or subacute F05
  paranoiac F22
  paranoid (climacteric) (involutional) (menopausal) F22
    psychogenic (acute) F23
    schizophrenic F20.0
    senile F03
  postpartum F53.1
  presbyophrenic (type) F03
  presenile F03
  psychogenic (paranoid) F23
    depressive F32.3
  puerperal F53.1
    specified type —see Psychosis, by type
  reactive (brief) (transient) (emotional stress) (psychological trauma) F23
    depressive F32.3
      recurrent F33.3
    excitative type F30.8
  schizoaffective F25.9
    depressive type F25.1
    manic type F25.0
  schizophrenia, schizophrenic —see Schizophrenia
  schizophrenia-like, in epilepsy F06.2
  schizophreniform F20.81
    affective type F25.9
    brief F23
    confusional type F23
    mixed type F25.0
  senile NEC F03
    depressed or paranoid type F03
    simple deterioration F03
    specified type — code to condition
  shared F24
  situational (reactive) F23
  symbiotic (childhood) F84.3
  symptomatic F09
Psychosomatic —see Disorder, psychosomatic
Psychosyndrome, organic F07.9
Psychotic episode due to or associated with physical condition F06.8
Pterygium (eye) H11.00-●
  amyloid H11.01-●
  central H11.02-●
  colli Q18.3
  double H11.03-●

Psychosis, psychotic (Continued)
  peripheral
    progressive H11.05-●
    stationary H11.04-●
  recurrent H11.06-●
Ptilosis (eyelid) —see Madarosis
Ptomaine (poisoning) —see Poisoning, food
Ptosis —see also Blepharoptosis
  adiposa (false) —see Blepharoptosis
  breast N64.81
  brow H57.81-●
  cecum K63.4
  colon K63.4
  congenital (eyelid) Q10.0
    specified site NEC —see Anomaly, by site
  eyebrow H57.81-●
  eyelid —see Blepharoptosis
    congenital Q10.0
  gastric K31.89
  intestine K63.4
  kidney N28.83
  liver K76.89
  renal N28.83
  splanchnic K63.4
  spleen D73.89
  stomach K31.89
  viscera K63.4
PTP D69.51
Ptyalism (periodic) K11.7
  hysterical F45.8
  pregnancy —see Pregnancy, complicated by, specified pregnancy-related condition NEC
  psychogenic F45.8
Ptyalolithiasis K11.5
Pubarche, precocious E30.1
Pubertas praecox E30.1
Puberty (development state) Z00.3
  bleeding (excessive) N92.2
  delayed E30.0
  precocious (constitutional) (cryptogenic) (idiopathic) E30.1
    central E22.8
    due to
      ovarian hyperfunction E28.1
        estrogen E28.0
      testicular hyperfunction E29.0
  premature E30.1
    due to
      adrenal cortical hyperfunction E25.8
      pineal tumor E34.8
      pituitary (anterior) hyperfunction E22.8
Puckering, macula —see Degeneration, macula, puckering
Pudenda, pudendum —see condition
Puente's disease (simple glandular cheilitis) K13.0
Puerperal, puerperium (complicated by, complications)
  abnormal glucose (tolerance test) O99.815
  abscess
    areola O91.02
      associated with lactation O91.03
    Bartholin's gland O86.19
    breast O91.12
      associated with lactation O91.13
    cervix (uteri) O86.11
    genital organ NEC O86.19
    kidney O86.21
    mammary O91.12
      associated with lactation O91.13
    nipple O91.02
      associated with lactation O91.03
    peritoneum O85
    subareolar O91.12
      associated with lactation O91.13
    urinary tract —see Puerperal, infection, urinary
    uterus O86.12
    vagina (wall) O86.13
    vaginorectal O86.13
    vulvovaginal gland O86.13

▶ New   ⇒ Revised   ~~deleted~~ Deleted   ● Use Additional Character(s)

Puerperal, puerperium *(Continued)*
  adnexitis O86.19
  afibrinogenemia, or other coagulation defect
    O72.3
  albuminuria (acute) (subacute) —*see*
    Proteinuria, gestational
  alcohol use O99.315
  anemia O90.81
    pre-existing (pre-pregnancy) O99.03
  anesthetic death O89.8
  apoplexy O99.43
  bariatric surgery status O99.845
  blood disorder NEC O99.13
  blood dyscrasia O72.3
  cardiomyopathy O90.3
  cerebrovascular disorder (conditions in
    I60-I69) O99.43
  cervicitis O86.11
  circulatory system disorder O99.43
  coagulopathy (any) O99.13
    with hemorrhage O72.3
  complications O90.9
    specified NEC O90.89
  convulsions —*see* Eclampsia
  cystitis O86.22
  cystopyelitis O86.29
  delirium NEC F05
  diabetes O24.93
    gestational —*see* Puerperal, gestational
      diabetes
    pre-existing O24.33
      specified NEC O24.83
      type 1 O24.03
      type 2 O24.13
  digestive system disorder O99.63
  disease O90.9
    breast NEC O92.29
    cerebrovascular (acute) O99.43
    ⇒nonobstetric NEC O99.893
      tubo-ovarian O86.19
    Valsuani's O99.03
  disorder O90.9
    biliary tract O26.63
    lactation O92.70
    liver O26.63
    ⇒nonobstetric NEC O99.893
  disruption
    cesarean wound O90.0
    episiotomy wound O90.1
    perineal laceration wound O90.1
  drug use O99.325
  eclampsia (with pre-existing hypertension)
    O15.2
  embolism (pulmonary) (blood clot) —*see*
    Embolism, obstetric, puerperal
  endocrine, nutritional or metabolic disease
    NEC O99.285
  endophlebitis —*see* Puerperal, phlebitis
  endotrachelitis O86.11
  failure
    lactation (complete) O92.3
      partial O92.4
    renal, acute O90.4
  fever (of unknown origin) O86.4
    septic O85
  fissure, nipple O92.12
    associated with lactation O92.13
  fistula
    breast (due to mastitis) O91.12
      associated with lactation O91.13
    nipple O91.02
      associated with lactation O91.03
  galactophoritis O91.22
    associated with lactation O91.23
  galactorrhea O92.6
  gastric banding status O99.845
  gastric bypass status O99.845
  gastrointestinal disease NEC O99.63
  gestational
    diabetes O24.439
      diet controlled O24.430
      insulin (and diet) controlled O24.434

Puerperal, puerperium *(Continued)*
  gestational *(Continued)*
    diabetes *(Continued)*
      oral drug controlled (antidiabetic)
        (hypoglycemic) O24.435
    edema O12.05
      with proteinuria O12.25
    proteinuria O12.15
  gonorrhea O98.23
  hematoma, subdural O99.43
  hemiplegia, cerebral O99.355-●
    due to cerebrovascular disorder O99.43
  hemorrhage O72.1
    brain O99.43
    bulbar O99.43
    cerebellar O99.43
    cerebral O99.43
    cortical O99.43
    delayed or secondary O72.2
    extradural O99.43
    internal capsule O99.43
    intracranial O99.43
    intrapontine O99.43
    meningeal O99.43
    pontine O99.43
    retained placenta O72.0
    subarachnoid O99.43
    subcortical O99.43
    subdural O99.43
    third stage O72.0
    uterine, delayed O72.2
    ventricular O99.43
  hemorrhoids O87.2
  hepatorenal syndrome O90.4
  hypertension —*see* Hypertension,
    complicating, puerperium
  hypertrophy, breast O92.29
  induration breast (fibrous) O92.29
  infection O86.4
    cervix O86.11
    generalized O85
    genital tract NEC O86.19
      obstetric surgical wound O86.09
    kidney (bacillus coli) O86.21
    maternal O98.93
      carrier state NEC O99.835
      gonorrhea O98.23
      human immunodeficiency virus (HIV)
        O98.73
      protozoal O98.63
      sexually transmitted NEC O98.33
      specified NEC O98.83
      streptococcus group B (GBS) carrier state
        O99.825
      syphilis O98.13
      tuberculosis O98.03
      viral hepatitis O98.43
      viral NEC O98.53
    nipple O91.02
      associated with lactation O91.03
    peritoneum O85
    renal O86.21
    specified NEC O86.89
    urinary (asymptomatic) (tract) NEC O86.20
      bladder O86.22
      kidney O86.21
      specified site NEC O86.29
      urethra O86.22
    vagina O86.13
    vein —*see* Puerperal, phlebitis
  ischemia, cerebral O99.43
  lymphangitis O86.89
    breast O91.22
      associated with lactation O91.23
  malignancy O9A.13
  malnutrition O25.3
  mammillitis O91.02
    associated with lactation O91.03
  mammitis O91.22
    associated with lactation O91.23
  mania F30.8

Puerperal, puerperium *(Continued)*
  mastitis O91.22
    associated with lactation O91.23
    purulent O91.12
      associated with lactation O91.13
  melancholia —*see* Disorder, depressive
  mental disorder NEC O99.345
  metroperitonitis O85
  metrorrhagia —*see* Hemorrhage,
    postpartum
  metrosalpingitis O86.19
  metrovaginitis O86.13
  milk leg O87.1
  monoplegia, cerebral O99.43
  mood disturbance O90.6
  necrosis, liver (acute) (subacute)
    (conditions in subcategory K72.0) O26.63
    with renal failure O90.4
  nervous system disorder O99.355
  neuritis O90.89
  obesity (pre-existing prior to pregnancy)
    O99.215
  obesity surgery status O99.845
  occlusion, precerebral artery O99.43
  paralysis
    bladder (sphincter) O90.89
    cerebral O99.43
  paralytic stroke O99.43
  parametritis O85
  paravaginitis O86.13
  pelviperitonitis O85
  perimetritis O86.12
  perimetrosalpingitis O86.19
  perinephritis O86.21
  periphlebitis —*see* Puerperal phlebitis
  peritoneal infection O85
  peritonitis (pelvic) O85
  perivaginitis O86.13
  phlebitis O87.0
    deep O87.1
    pelvic O87.1
    superficial O87.0
  phlebothrombosis, deep O87.1
  phlegmasia alba dolens O87.1
  placental polyp O90.89
  pneumonia, embolic —*see* Embolism,
    obstetric, puerperal
  pre-eclampsia —*see* Pre-eclampsia
  psychosis F53.1
  pyelitis O86.21
  pyelocystitis O86.29
  pyelonephritis O86.21
  pyelonephrosis O86.21
  pyemia O85
  pyocystitis O86.29
  pyohemia O85
  pyometra O86.12
  pyonephritis O86.21
  pyosalpingitis O86.19
  pyrexia (of unknown origin) O86.4
  renal
    disease NEC O90.89
    failure O90.4
  respiratory disease NEC O99.53
  retention
    decidua —*see* Retention, decidua
    placenta O72.0
    secundines —*see* Retention,
      secundines
  retrated nipple O92.02
  salpingo-ovaritis O86.19
  salpingoperitonitis O85
  secondary perineal tear O90.1
  sepsis O85
  sepsis (pelvic) O85
  septic thrombophlebitis O86.81
  skin disorder NEC O99.73
  ⇒specified condition NEC O99.893
  stroke O99.43
  subinvolution (uterus) O90.89
  subluxation of symphysis (pubis) O26.73

Puerperal, puerperium (Continued)
  suppuration —see Puerperal, abscess
  tetanus A34
  thelitis O91.02
    associated with lactation O91.03
  thrombocytopenia O72.3
  thrombophlebitis (superficial) O87.0
    deep O87.1
    pelvic O87.1
    septic O86.81
  thrombosis (venous) —see Thrombosis,
      puerperal
  thyroiditis O90.5
  toxemia (eclamptic) (pre-eclamptic)
      (with convulsions) O15.2
  trauma, non-obstetric O9A.23
    caused by abuse (physical) (suspected)
        O9A.33
      confirmed O9A.33
      psychological (suspected) O9A.53
        confirmed O9A.53
      sexual (suspected) O9A.43
        confirmed O9A.43
  uremia (due to renal failure) O90.4
  urethritis O86.22
  vaginitis O86.13
  varicose veins (legs) O87.4
    vulva or perineum O87.8
  venous O87.9
  vulvitis O86.19
  vulvovaginitis O86.13
  white leg O87.1
Puerperium —see Puerperal
Pulmolithiasis J98.4
Pulmonary —see condition
Pulpitis (acute) (anachoretic) (chronic)
      (hyperplastic) (putrescent) (suppurative)
      (ulcerative) K04.01
  irreversible K04.02
  reversible K04.01
Pulpless tooth K04.99
Pulse
  alternating R00.8
  bigeminal R00.8
  fast R00.0
  feeble, rapid due to shock following injury
      T79.4
  rapid R00.0
  weak R09.89
Pulsus alternans or trigeminus R00.8
Punch drunk F07.81
Punctum lacrimale occlusion —see Obstruction,
      lacrimal
Puncture
  abdomen, abdominal
    wall S31.139
      with
        foreign body S31.149
        penetration into peritoneal cavity
            S31.639
          with foreign body S31.649
      epigastric region S31.132
        with
          foreign body S31.142
          penetration into peritoneal cavity
              S31.632
            with foreign body S31.642
      left
        lower quadrant S31.134
          with
            foreign body S31.144
            penetration into peritoneal cavity
                S31.634
              with foreign body S31.644
        upper quadrant S31.131
          with
            foreign body S31.141
            penetration into peritoneal cavity
                S31.631
              with foreign body S31.641

Puncture (Continued)
  abdomen, abdominal (Continued)
    wall (Continued)
      periumbilic region S31.135
        with
          foreign body S31.145
          penetration into peritoneal cavity
              S31.635
            with foreign body S31.645
      right
        lower quadrant S31.133
          with
            foreign body S31.143
            penetration into peritoneal cavity
                S31.633
              with foreign body S31.643
        upper quadrant S31.130
          with
            foreign body S31.140
            penetration into peritoneal cavity
                S31.630
              with foreign body S31.640
  accidental, complicating surgery —see
      Complication, accidental puncture or
      laceration
  alveolar (process) —see Puncture, oral cavity
  ankle S91.039
    with
      foreign body S91.049
    left S91.032
      with
        foreign body S91.042
    right S91.031
      with
        foreign body S91.041
  anus S31.833
    with foreign body S31.834
  arm (upper) S41.139
    with foreign body S41.149
    left S41.132
      with foreign body S41.142
    lower —see Puncture, forearm
    right S41.131
      with foreign body S41.141
  auditory canal (external) (meatus) —see
      Puncture, ear
  auricle, ear —see Puncture, ear
  axilla —see Puncture, arm
  back —see also Puncture, thorax, back
    lower S31.030
      with
        foreign body S31.040
          with penetration into
              retroperitoneal space S31.041
        penetration into retroperitoneal space
            S31.031
  bladder (traumatic) S37.29
    nontraumatic N32.89
  breast S21.039
    with foreign body S21.049
    left S21.032
      with foreign body S21.042
    right S21.031
      with foreign body S21.041
  buttock S31.803
    with foreign body S31.804
    left S31.823
      with foreign body S31.824
    right S31.813
      with foreign body S31.814
  by
    device, implant or graft —see
        Complications, by site and type,
        mechanical
    foreign body left accidentally in operative
        wound T81.539
    instrument (any) during a procedure,
        accidental —see Puncture, accidental
        complicating surgery
  calf —see Puncture, leg
  canaliculus lacrimalis —see Puncture, eyelid

Puncture (Continued)
  canthus, eye —see Puncture, eyelid
  cervical esophagus S11.23
    with foreign body S11.24
  cheek (external) S01.439
    with foreign body S01.449
    internal —see Puncture, oral cavity
    left S01.432
      with foreign body S01.442
    right S01.431
      with foreign body S01.441
  chest wall —see Puncture, thorax
  chin —see Puncture, head, specified site NEC
  clitoris —see Puncture, vulva
  costal region —see Puncture, thorax
  digit(s)
    foot —see Puncture, toe
    hand —see Puncture, finger
  ear (canal) (external) S01.339
    with foreign body S01.349
    drum S09.2-●
    left S01.332
      with foreign body S01.342
    right S01.331
      with foreign body S01.341
  elbow S51.039
    with
      foreign body S51.049
    left S51.032
      with
        foreign body S51.042
    right S51.031
      with
        foreign body S51.041
  epididymis —see Puncture, testis
  epigastric region —see Puncture, abdomen,
      wall, epigastric
  epiglottis S11.83
    with foreign body S11.84
  esophagus
    cervical S11.23
      with foreign body S11.24
    thoracic S27.818
  eyeball S05.6-●
    with foreign body S05.5-●
  eyebrow —see Puncture, eyelid
  eyelid S01.13-●
    with foreign body S01.14-●
    left S01.132
      with foreign body S01.142
    right S01.131
      with foreign body S01.141
  face NEC —see Puncture, head, specified site
      NEC
  finger(s) S61.239
    with
      damage to nail S61.339
        with
          foreign body S61.349
      foreign body S61.249
    index S61.238
      with
        damage to nail S61.338
          with
            foreign body S61.348
        foreign body S61.248
      left S61.231
        with
          damage to nail S61.331
            with
              foreign body S61.341
          foreign body S61.241
      right S61.230
        with
          damage to nail S61.330
            with
              foreign body S61.340
          foreign body S61.240
    little S61.238
      with
        damage to nail S61.338

▶ New ⇒ Revised ~~deleted~~ Deleted ● Use Additional Character(s)

Puncture (Continued)
  finger (Continued)
    with (Continued)
      with (Continued)
        damage to nail (Continued)
          with
            foreign body S61.348
          foreign body S61.248
        left S61.237
          with
            damage to nail S61.337
              with
                foreign body S61.347
            foreign body S61.247
        right S61.236
          with
            damage to nail S61.336
              with
                foreign body S61.346
            foreign body S61.246
    middle S61.238
      with
        damage to nail S61.338
          with
            foreign body S61.348
        foreign body S61.248
      left S61.233
        with
          damage to nail S61.333
            with
              foreign body S61.343
          foreign body S61.243
      right S61.232
        with
          damage to nail S61.332
            with
              foreign body S61.342
          foreign body S61.242
    ring S61.238
      with
        damage to nail S61.338
          with
            foreign body S61.348
        foreign body S61.248
      left S61.235
        with
          damage to nail S61.335
            with
              foreign body S61.345
          foreign body S61.245
      right S61.234
        with
          damage to nail S61.334
            with
              foreign body S61.344
          foreign body S61.244
  flank S31.139
    with foreign body S31.149
  foot (except toe(s) alone) S91.339
    with foreign body S91.349
    left S91.332
      with foreign body S91.342
    right S91.331
      with foreign body S91.341
    toe —see Puncture, toe
  forearm S51.839
    with
      foreign body S51.849
    elbow only —see Puncture, elbow
    left S51.832
      with
        foreign body S51.842
    right S51.831
      with
        foreign body S51.841
  forehead —see Puncture, head, specified site
    NEC
  genital organs, external
    female S31.532
      with foreign body S31.542
      vagina —see Puncture, vagina
      vulva —see Puncture, vulva

Puncture (Continued)
  genital organs, external (Continued)
    male S31.531
      with foreign body S31.541
      penis —see Puncture, penis
      scrotum —see Puncture, scrotum
      testis —see Puncture, testis
  groin —see Puncture, abdomen, wall
  gum —see Puncture, oral cavity
  hand S61.439
    with
      foreign body S61.449
    finger —see Puncture, finger
    left S61.432
      with
        foreign body S61.442
    right S61.431
      with
        foreign body S61.441
    thumb —see Puncture, thumb
  head S01.93
    with foreign body S01.94
    cheek —see Puncture, cheek
    ear —see Puncture, ear
    eyelid —see Puncture, eyelid
    lip —see Puncture, oral cavity
    nose —see Puncture, nose
    oral cavity —see Puncture, oral cavity
    scalp S01.03
      with foreign body S01.04
    specified site NEC S01.83
      with foreign body S01.84
    temporomandibular area —see Puncture,
      cheek
  heart S26.99
    with hemopericardium S26.09
    without hemopericardium S26.19
  heel —see Puncture, foot
  hip S71.039
    with foreign body S71.049
    left S71.032
      with foreign body S71.042
    right S71.031
      with foreign body S71.041
  hymen —see Puncture, vagina
  hypochondrium —see Puncture, abdomen,
    wall
  hypogastric region —see Puncture, abdomen,
    wall
  inguinal region —see Puncture, abdomen,
    wall
  instep —see Puncture, foot
  internal organs —see Injury, by site
  interscapular region —see Puncture, thorax,
    back
  intestine
    large
      colon S36.599
        ascending S36.590
        descending S36.592
        sigmoid S36.593
        specified site NEC S36.598
        transverse S36.591
      rectum S36.69
    small S36.499
      duodenum S36.490
      specified site NEC S36.498
  intra-abdominal organ S36.99
    gallbladder S36.128
    intestine —see Puncture, intestine
    liver S36.118
    pancreas —see Puncture, pancreas
    peritoneum S36.81
    specified site NEC S36.898
    spleen S36.09
    stomach S36.39
  jaw —see Puncture, head, specified site NEC
  knee S81.039
    with foreign body S81.049
    left S81.032
      with foreign body S81.042

Puncture (Continued)
  knee (Continued)
    right S81.031
      with foreign body S81.041
  labium (majus) (minus) —see Puncture,
    vulva
  lacrimal duct —see Puncture, eyelid
  larynx S11.013
    with foreign body S11.014
  leg (lower) S81.839
    with foreign body S81.849
    foot —see Puncture, foot
    knee —see Puncture, knee
    left S81.832
      with foreign body S81.842
    right S81.831
      with foreign body S81.841
    upper —see Puncture, thigh
  lip S01.531
    with foreign body S01.541
  loin —see Puncture, abdomen, wall
  lower back —see Puncture, back, lower
  lumbar region —see Puncture, back, lower
  malar region —see Puncture, head, specified
    site NEC
  mammary —see Puncture, breast
  mastoid region —see Puncture, head,
    specified site NEC
  mouth —see Puncture, oral cavity
  nail
    finger —see Puncture, finger, with damage
      to nail
    toe —see Puncture, toe, with damage to
      nail
  nasal (septum) (sinus) —see Puncture, nose
  nasopharynx —see Puncture, head, specified
    site NEC
  neck S11.93
    with foreign body S11.94
    involving
      cervical esophagus —see Puncture,
        cervical esophagus
      larynx —see Puncture, larynx
      pharynx —see Puncture, pharynx
      thyroid gland —see Puncture, thyroid
        gland
      trachea —see Puncture, trachea
    specified site NEC S11.83
      with foreign body S11.84
  nose (septum) (sinus) S01.23
    with foreign body S01.24
  ocular —see Puncture, eyeball - oral cavity
    S01.532
    with foreign body S01.542
  orbit S05.4- ●
  palate —see Puncture, oral cavity
  palm —see Puncture, hand
  pancreas S36.299
    body S36.291
    head S36.290
    tail S36.292
  pelvis —see Puncture, back, lower
  penis S31.23
    with foreign body S31.24
  perineum
    female S31.43
      with foreign body S31.44
    male S31.139
      with foreign body S31.149
  periocular area (with or without lacrimal
    passages) —see Puncture, eyelid
  phalanges
    finger —see Puncture, finger
    toe —see Puncture, toe
  pharynx S11.23
    with foreign body S11.24
  pinna —see Puncture, ear
  popliteal space —see Puncture, knee
  prepuce —see Puncture, penis
  pubic region S31.139
    with foreign body S31.149

Puncture *(Continued)*
  pudendum —*see* Puncture, genital organs,
    external
  rectovaginal septum —*see* Puncture,
    vagina
  sacral region —*see* Puncture, back,
    lower
  sacroiliac region —*see* Puncture, back,
    lower
  salivary gland —*see* Puncture, oral
    cavity
  scalp S01.03
    with foreign body S01.04
  scapular region —*see* Puncture,
    shoulder
  scrotum S31.33
    with foreign body S31.34
  shin —*see* Puncture, leg
  shoulder S41.039
    with foreign body S41.049
    left S41.032
      with foreign body S41.042
    right S41.031
      with foreign body S41.041
  spermatic cord —*see* Puncture, testis
  sternal region —*see* Puncture, thorax, front
  submaxillary region —*see* Puncture, head,
    specified site NEC
  submental region —*see* Puncture, head,
    specified site NEC
  subungual
    finger(s) —*see* Puncture, finger, with
      damage to nail
    toe —*see* Puncture, toe, with damage to
      nail
  supraclavicular fossa —*see* Puncture, neck,
    specified site NEC
  temple, temporal region —*see* Puncture, head,
    specified site NEC
  temporomandibular area —*see* Puncture,
    cheek
  testis S31.33
    with foreign body S31.34
  thigh S71.139
    with foreign body S71.149
    left S71.132
      with foreign body S71.142
    right S71.131
      with foreign body S71.141
  thorax, thoracic (wall) S21.93
    with foreign body S21.94
    back S21.23-●
      with
        foreign body S21.24-●
          with penetration S21.44
        penetration S21.43
    breast —*see* Puncture, breast
    front S21.13-●
      with
        foreign body S21.14-●
          with penetration S21.34
        penetration S21.33
  throat —*see* Puncture, neck
  thumb S61.039
    with
      damage to nail S61.139
        with
          foreign body S61.149
      foreign body S61.049
    left S61.032
      with
        damage to nail S61.132
          with
            foreign body S61.142
        foreign body S61.042
    right S61.031
      with
        damage to nail S61.131
          with
            foreign body S61.141
        foreign body S61.041

Puncture *(Continued)*
  thyroid gland S11.13
    with foreign body S11.14
  toe(s) S91.139
    with
      damage to nail S91.239
        with
          foreign body S91.249
      foreign body S91.149
    great S91.133
      with
        damage to nail S91.233
          with
            foreign body S91.243
        foreign body S91.143
    left S91.132
      with
        damage to nail S91.232
          with
            foreign body S91.242
        foreign body S91.142
    right S91.131
      with
        damage to nail S91.231
          with
            foreign body S91.241
        foreign body S91.141
    lesser S91.136
      with
        damage to nail S91.236
          with
            foreign body S91.246
        foreign body S91.146
    left S91.135
      with
        damage to nail S91.235
          with
            foreign body S91.245
        foreign body S91.145
    right S91.134
      with
        damage to nail S91.234
          with
            foreign body S91.244
        foreign body S91.144
  tongue —*see* Puncture, oral cavity
  trachea S11.023
    with foreign body S11.024
  tunica vaginalis —*see* Puncture, testis
  tympanum, tympanic membrane
    S09.2-●
  umbilical region S31.135
    with foreign body S31.145
  uvula —*see* Puncture, oral cavity
  vagina S31.43
    with foreign body S31.44
  vocal cords S11.033
    with foreign body S11.034
  vulva S31.43
    with foreign body S31.44
  wrist S61.539
    with
      foreign body S61.549
    left S61.532
      with
        foreign body S61.542
    right S61.531
      with
        foreign body S61.541
PUO (pyrexia of unknown origin) R50.9
Pupillary membrane (persistent) Q13.89
Pupillotonia —*see* Anomaly, pupil, function,
  tonic pupil
Purpura D69.2
  abdominal D69.0
  allergic D69.0
  anaphylactoid D69.0
  annularis telangiectodes L81.7
  arthritic D69.0
  autoerythrocyte sensitization D69.2
  autoimmune D69.0

Purpura *(Continued)*
  bacterial D69.0
  Bateman's (senile) D69.2
  capillary fragility (hereditary) (idiopathic)
    D69.8
  cryoglobulinemic D89.1
  Devil's pinches D69.2
  fibrinolytic —*see* Fibrinolysis
  fulminans, fulminous D65
  gangrenous D65
  hemorrhagic, hemorrhagica D69.3
    not due to thrombocytopenia D69.0
  Henoch (-Schönlein) (allergic) D69.0
  hypergammaglobulinemic (benign)
    (Waldenström's) D89.0
  idiopathic (thrombocytopenic) D69.3
    nonthrombocytopenic D69.0
  immune thrombocytopenic D69.3
  infectious D69.0
  malignant D69.0
  neonatorum P54.5
  nervosa D69.0
  newborn P54.5
  nonthrombocytopenic D69.2
    hemorrhagic D69.0
    idiopathic D69.0
  nonthrombopenic D69.2
  peliosis rheumatica D69.0
  posttransfusion (post-transfusion) (from
    (fresh) whole blood or blood products)
    D69.51
  primary D69.49
  red cell membrane sensitivity D69.2
  rheumatica D69.0
  Schönlein (-Henoch) (allergic) D69.0
  scorbutic E54 *[D77]*
  senile D69.2
  simplex D69.2
  symptomatica D69.0
  telangiectasia annularis L81.7
  thrombocytopenic D69.49
    congenital D69.42
    hemorrhagic D69.3
    hereditary D69.42
    idiopathic D69.3
    immune D69.3
    neonatal, transitory P61.0
    thrombotic M31.1
  thrombohemolytic —*see* Fibrinolysis
  thrombolytic —*see* Fibrinolysis
  thrombopenic D69.49
  thrombotic, thrombocytopenic
    M31.1
  toxic D69.0
  vascular D69.0
  visceral symptoms D69.0
Purpuric spots R23.3
Purulent —*see* condition
Pus
  in
    stool R19.5
    urine N39.0
  tube (rupture) —*see* Salpingo-oophoritis
Pustular rash L08.0
Pustule (nonmalignant) L08.9
  malignant A22.0
Pustulosis palmaris et plantaris
  L40.3
Putnam (-Dana) disease or syndrome —*see*
  Degeneration, combined
Putrescent pulp (dental) K04.1
Pyarthritis, pyarthrosis —*see* Arthritis,
  pyogenic or pyemic
  tuberculous —*see* Tuberculosis, joint
Pyelectasis —*see* Hydronephrosis
Pyelitis (congenital) (uremic) —*see also*
  Pyelonephritis
  with
    calculus —*see* category N20
      with hydronephrosis N13.6
    contracted kidney N11.9

▶ New   ⮕ Revised   ~~deleted~~ Deleted   ● Use Additional Character(s)

Pyelitis *(Continued)*
  acute N10
  chronic N11.9
    with calculus —*see* category N20
      with hydronephrosis N13.6
    cystica N28.84
    puerperal (postpartum) O86.21
    tuberculous A18.11
Pyelocystitis —*see* Pyelonephritis
Pyelonephritis —*see also* Nephritis,
    tubulo-interstitial
  with
    calculus —*see* category N20
      with hydronephrosis N13.6
    contracted kidney N11.9
  acute N10
  calculous —*see* category N20
    with hydronephrosis N13.6
  chronic N11.9
    with calculus —*see* category N20
      with hydronephrosis N13.6
    associated with ureteral obstruction or
      stricture N11.1
    nonobstructive N11.8
      with reflux (vesicoureteral) N11.0
    obstructive N11.1
    specified NEC N11.8
  in (due to)
    brucellosis A23.9 *[N16]*
    cryoglobulinemia (mixed) D89.1 *[N16]*
    cystinosis E72.04
    diphtheria A36.84
    glycogen storage disease E74.09 *[N16]*
    leukemia NEC C95.9-● *[N16]*
    lymphoma NEC C85.90 *[N16]*
    multiple myeloma C90.0-● *[N16]*
    obstruction N11.1
    Salmonella infection A02.25
    sarcoidosis D86.84
    sepsis A41.9 *[N16]*
    Sjögren's disease M35.04
    toxoplasmosis B58.83
    transplant rejection T86.91 *[N16]*
    Wilson's disease E83.01 *[N16]*
  nonobstructive N12
    with reflux (vesicoureteral) N11.0
    chronic N11.8
  syphilitic A52.75

Pyelonephrosis (obstructive) N11.1
  chronic N11.9
Pyelophlebitis I80.8
Pyeloureteritis cystica N28.85
Pyemia, pyemic (fever) (infection) (purulent) —
    see also Sepsis
  joint —*see* Arthritis, pyogenic or pyemic
  liver K75.1
  pneumococcal A40.3
  portal K75.1
  postvaccinal T88.0
  puerperal, postpartum, childbirth O85
  specified organism NEC A41.89
  tuberculous —*see* Tuberculosis, miliary
Pygopagus Q89.4
Pyknoepilepsy (idiopathic) —*see* Pyknolepsy
Pyknolepsy G40.A09
  intractable G40.A19
    with status epilepticus G40.A11
    without status epilepticus G40.A19
  not intractable G40.A09
    with status epilepticus G40.A01
    without status epilepticus G40.A09
Pylephlebitis K75.1
Pyle's syndrome Q78.5
Pylethrombophlebitis K75.1
Pylethrombosis K75.1
Pyloritis K29.90
  with bleeding K29.91
Pylorospasm (reflex) NEC K31.3
  congenital or infantile Q40.0
  neurotic F45.8
  newborn Q40.0
  psychogenic F45.8
Pylorus, pyloric —*see* condition
Pyoarthrosis —*see* Arthritis, pyogenic or
    pyemic
Pyocele
  mastoid —*see* Mastoiditis, acute
  sinus (accessory) —*see* Sinusitis
  turbinate (bone) J32.9
  urethra —*see also* Urethritis N34.0
Pyocolpos —*see* Vaginitis
Pyocystitis N30.80
  with hematuria N30.81
Pyoderma, pyodermia L08.0
  gangrenosum L88
  newborn P39.4

Pyoderma, pyodermia *(Continued)*
  phagedenic L88
  vegetans L08.81
Pyodermatitis L08.0
  vegetans L08.81
Pyogenic —*see* condition
Pyohydronephrosis N13.6
Pyometra, pyometrium, pyometritis —*see*
    Endometritis
Pyomyositis (tropical) —*see* Myositis,
    infective
Pyonephritis N12
Pyonephrosis N13.6
  tuberculous A18.11
Pyo-oophoritis —*see* Salpingo-oophoritis
Pyo-ovarium —*see* Salpingo-oophoritis
Pyopericarditis, pyopericardium
    I30.1
Pyophlebitis —*see* Phlebitis
Pyopneumopericardium I30.1
Pyopneumothorax (infective) J86.9
  with fistula J86.0
  tuberculous NEC A15.6
Pyosalpinx, pyosalpingitis —*see also*
    Salpingo-oophoritis
Pyothorax J86.9
  with fistula J86.0
  tuberculous NEC A15.6
Pyoureter N28.89
  tuberculous A18.11
Pyramidopallidonigral syndrome
    G20
Pyrexia (of unknown origin) R50.9
  atmospheric T67.01
  during labor NEC O75.2
  heat T67.01
  newborn P81.9
    environmentally-induced P81.0
  persistent R50.9
  puerperal O86.4
Pyroglobulinemia NEC E88.09
Pyromania F63.1
Pyrosis R12
Pyuria (bacterial) R82.81

Q

Q fever A78
  with pneumonia A78
Quadricuspid aortic valve Q23.8
Quadrilateral fever A78
Quadriparesis —*see* Quadriplegia
  meaning muscle weakness M62.81
Quadriplegia G82.50-●
  complete
    C1-C4 level G82.51
    C5-C7 level G82.53
  congenital (cerebral) (spinal) G80.8
    spastic G80.0

Quadriplegia (*Continued*)
  embolic (current episode) I63.4-●
  functional R53.2
  incomplete
    C1-C4 level G82.52
    C5-C7 level G82.54
  thrombotic (current episode) I63.3-●
  traumatic — code to injury with seventh
    character S
    current episode —*see* Injury, spinal (cord),
      cervical
Quadruplet, pregnancy —*see* Pregnancy,
  quadruplet
Quarrelsomeness F60.3

Queensland fever A77.3
Quervain's disease M65.4
  thyroid E06.1
Queyrat's erythroplasia D07.4
  penis D07.4
  specified site —*see* Neoplasm, skin,
    in situ
  unspecified site D07.4
Quincke's disease or edema T78.3
  hereditary D84.1
Quinsy (gangrenous) J36
Quintan fever A79.0
Quintuplet, pregnancy —*see* Pregnancy,
  quintuplet

▶ New   ⇒ Revised   ~~deleted~~ Deleted   ● Use Additional Character(s)

R

Rabbit fever —*see* Tularemia
Rabies A82.9
  contact Z20.3
  exposure to Z20.3
  inoculation reaction —*see* Complications,
    vaccination
  sylvatic A82.0
  urban A82.1
Rachischisis —*see* Spina bifida
Rachitic —*see also* condition
  deformities of spine (late effect) (sequelae)
    E64.3
  pelvis (late effect) (sequelae) E64.3
    with disproportion (fetopelvic) O33.0
      causing obstructed labor O65.0
Rachitis, rachitism (acute) (tarda) —*see also*
  Rickets
  renalis N25.0
  sequelae E64.3
Radial nerve —*see* condition
Radiation
  burn —*see* Burn
  effects NOS T66
  sickness NOS T66
  therapy, encounter for Z51.0
Radiculitis (pressure) (vertebrogenic) —*see*
  Radiculopathy
Radiculomyelitis —*see also* Encephalitis
  toxic, due to
    Clostridium tetani A35
    Corynebacterium diphtheriae A36.82
Radiculopathy M54.10
  cervical region M54.12
  cervicothoracic region M54.13
  due to
    disc disorder
      C3 M50.11
      C4 M50.11
      C5 M50.121
      C6 M50.122
      C7 M50.123
      C8 M50.13
    displacement of intervertebral disc —*see*
      Disorder, disc, with, radiculopathy
  leg M54.1-●
  lumbar region M54.16
  lumbosacral region M54.17
  occipito-atlanto-axial region M54.11
  postherpetic B02.29
  sacrococcygeal region M54.18
  syphilitic A52.11
  thoracic region (with visceral pain)
    M54.14
  thoracolumbar region M54.15
Radiodermal burns (acute, chronic, or
  occupational) —*see* Burn
Radiodermatitis L58.9
  acute L58.0
  chronic L58.1
Radiotherapy session Z51.0
RAEB (refractory anemia with excess blasts)
  D46.2-●
Rage, meaning rabies —*see* Rabies
Ragpicker's disease A22.1
Ragsorter's disease A22.1
Raillietiniasis B71.8
Railroad neurosis F48.8
Railway spine F48.8
Raised —*see also* Elevated
  antibody titer R76.0
Rake teeth, tooth M26.39
Rales R09.89
Ramifying renal pelvis Q63.8
Ramsay-Hunt disease or syndrome —*see also*
  Hunt's disease B02.21
  ➠meaning dyssynergia cerebellaris myoclonica
    G11.19
Ranula K11.6
  congenital Q38.4

Rape
  adult
    confirmed T74.21
    suspected T76.21
  alleged, observation or examination, ruled out
    adult Z04.41
    child Z04.42
  child
    confirmed T74.22
    suspected T76.22
Rapid
  feeble pulse, due to shock, following injury
    T79.4
  heart (beat) R00.0
    psychogenic F45.8
  second stage (delivery) O62.3
  time-zone change syndrome G47.25
Rarefaction, bone —*see* Disorder, bone, density
  and structure, specified NEC
Rash (toxic) R21
  canker A38.9
  diaper L22
  drug (internal use) L27.0
    contact —*see also* Dermatitis, due to, drugs,
      external L25.1
  following immunization T88.1
  food —*see* Dermatitis, due to, food
  heat L74.0
  napkin (psoriasiform) L22
  nettle —*see* Urticaria
  pustular L08.0
  rose R21
    epidemic B06.9
  scarlet A38.9
  serum —*see also* Reaction, serum T80.69
  wandering tongue K14.1
Rasmussen aneurysm —*see* Tuberculosis,
  pulmonary
Rasmussen encephalitis G04.81
Rat-bite fever A25.9
  due to Streptobacillus moniliformis A25.1
  spirochetal (morsus muris) A25.0
Rathke's pouch tumor D44.3
Raymond (-Céstan) syndrome I65.8
Raynaud's disease, phenomenon or syndrome
  (secondary) I73.00
  with gangrene (symmetric) I73.01
RDS (newborn) (type I) P22.0
  type II P22.1
Reaction —*see also* Disorder
  adaptation —*see* Disorder, adjustment
  adjustment (anxiety) (conduct disorder)
    (depressiveness) (distress) —*see*
    Disorder, adjustment
    with
      mutism, elective (child) (adolescent) F94.0
  adverse
    food (any) (ingested) NEC T78.1
      anaphylactic —*see* Shock, anaphylactic,
        due to food
  anaphylactoid —*see* Shock, anaphylactic
  affective —*see* Disorder, mood
  allergic —*see* Allergy
  anaphylactic —*see* Shock, anaphylactic
  anesthesia —*see* Anesthesia, complication
  antitoxin (prophylactic) (therapeutic) —*see*
    Complications, vaccination
  anxiety F41.1
  Arthus —*see* Arthus' phenomenon
  asthenic F48.8
  combat and operational stress F43.0
  compulsive F42.8
  conversion F44.9
  crisis, acute F43.0
  deoxyribonuclease (DNA) (DNase)
    hypersensitivity D69.2
  depressive (single episode) F32.9
    affective (single episode) F31.4
      recurrent episode F33.9
    neurotic F34.1
    psychoneurotic F34.1

Reaction (*Continued*)
  depressive (*Continued*)
    psychotic F32.3
    recurrent —*see* Disorder, depressive,
      recurrent
  dissociative F44.9
  drug NEC T88.7
    addictive —*see* Dependence, drug
      transmitted via placenta or breast
        milk —*see* Absorption, drug,
        addictive, through placenta
    allergic —*see* Allergy, drug
    lichenoid L43.2
    newborn P93.8
      gray baby syndrome P93.0
    overdose or poisoning (by accident) —*see*
      Table of Drugs and Chemicals, by
      drug, poisoning
    photoallergic L56.1
    phototoxic L56.0
    withdrawal —*see* Dependence, by drug,
      with, withdrawal
      infant of dependent mother P96.1
      newborn P96.1
    wrong substance given or taken (by
      accident) —*see* Table of Drugs and
      Chemicals, by drug, poisoning
  fear F40.9
    child (abnormal) F93.8
  febrile nonhemolytic transfusion (FNHTR)
    R50.84
  fluid loss, cerebrospinal G97.1
  foreign
    body NEC —*see* Granuloma, foreign body
      in operative wound (inadvertently
        left) —*see* Foreign body, accidentally
        left during a procedure
    substance accidentally left during a
      procedure (chemical) (powder) (talc)
      T81.60
      aseptic peritonitis T81.61
      body or object (instrument) (sponge)
        (swab) —*see* Foreign body,
        accidentally left during a
        procedure
      specified reaction NEC T81.69
  grief —*see* Disorder, adjustment
  Herxheimer's R68.89
  hyperkinetic —*see* Hyperkinesia
  hypochondriacal F45.20
  hypoglycemic, due to insulin E16.0
    with coma (diabetic) —*see* Diabetes, coma
      nondiabetic E15
    therapeutic misadventure —*see*
      subcategory T38.3
  hypomanic F30.8
  hysterical F44.9
  immunization —*see* Complications, vaccination
  incompatibility
    ABO blood group (infusion) (transfusion) —
      see Complication(s), transfusion,
      incompatibility reaction, ABO
    delayed serologic T80.39
    minor blood group (Duffy) (E) (K) (Kell)
      (Kidd) (Lewis) (M) (N) (P) (S)
      T80.89
    Rh (factor) (infusion) (transfusion) —
      see Complication(s), transfusion,
      incompatibility reaction, Rh (factor)
  inflammatory —*see* Infection
  infusion —*see* Complications, infusion
  inoculation (immune serum) —*see*
    Complications, vaccination
  insulin T38.3-●
  involutional psychotic —*see* Disorder,
    depressive
  leukemoid D72.823
    basophilic D72.823
    lymphocytic D72.823
    monocytic D72.823
    myelocytic D72.823
    neutrophilic D72.823

Reaction *(Continued)*
  LSD (acute)
    due to drug abuse —*see* Abuse, drug,
        hallucinogen
    due to drug dependence —*see* Dependence,
        drug, hallucinogen
  lumbar puncture G97.1
  manic-depressive —*see* Disorder, bipolar
  neurasthenic F48.8
  neurogenic —*see* Neurosis
  neurotic F48.9
  neurotic-depressive F34.1
  nitritoid —*see* Crisis, nitritoid - obsessive-
      compulsive F42
  nonspecific
    to
      cell mediated immunity measurement
          of gamma interferon antigen
          response without active
          tuberculosis R76.12
      QuantiFERON-TB test (QFT) without
          active tuberculosis R76.12
      tuberculin test —*see also* Reaction,
          tuberculin skin test R76.11
  obsessive-compulsive F42.8
  organic, acute or subacute —*see* Delirium
  paranoid (acute) F23
    chronic F22
    senile F03
  passive dependency F60.7
  phobic F40.9
  post-traumatic stress, uncomplicated Z73.3
  psychogenic F99
  psychoneurotic —*see also* Neurosis
    compulsive F42.8
    depersonalization F48.1
    depressive F34.1
    hypochondriacal F45.20
    neurasthenic F48.8
    obsessive F42.8
  psychophysiologic —*see* Disorder,
      somatoform
  psychosomatic —*see* Disorder, somatoform
  psychotic —*see* Psychosis
  scarlet fever toxin —*see* Complications,
      vaccination
  schizophrenic F23
    acute (brief) (undifferentiated) F23
    latent F21
    undifferentiated (acute) (brief) F23
  serological for syphilis —*see* Serology for
      syphilis
  serum T80.69
    anaphylactic (immediate) —*see also* Shock,
        anaphylactic T80.59
    specified reaction NEC
      due to
        administration of blood and blood
            products T80.61
        immunization T80.62
        serum specified NEC T80.69
        vaccination T80.62
  situational —*see* Disorder, adjustment
  somatization —*see* Disorder, somatoform
  spinal puncture G97.1
  ▶dural G97.1
  stress (severe) F43.9
    acute (agitation) ("daze") (disorientation)
        (disturbance of consciousness) (flight
        reaction) (fugue) F43.0
    specified NEC F43.8
  surgical procedure —*see* Complications,
      surgical procedure
  tetanus antitoxin —*see* Complications,
      vaccination
  toxic, to local anesthesia T81.59
    in labor and delivery O74.4
    in pregnancy O29.3X-●
    postpartum, puerperal O89.3
  toxin-antitoxin —*see* Complications,
      vaccination

Reaction *(Continued)*
  transfusion (blood) (bone marrow)
      (lymphocytes) (allergic) —*see*
      Complications, transfusion
  tuberculin skin test, abnormal R76.11
  vaccination (any) —*see* Complications,
      vaccination
  withdrawing, child or adolescent F93.8
Reactive airway disease —*see* Asthma
Reactive depression —*see* Reaction, depressive
Rearrangement
  chromosomal
    balanced (in) Q95.9
      abnormal individual (autosomal) Q95.2
        non-sex (autosomal) chromosomes
            Q95.2
        sex/non-sex chromosomes Q95.3
      specified NEC Q95.8
Recalcitrant patient —*see* Noncompliance
Recanalization, thrombus —*see* Thrombosis
Recession, receding
  chamber angle (eye) H21.55-●
  chin M26.09
  gingival (postinfective) (postoperative)
    generalized K06.020
      minimal K06.021
      moderate K06.022
      severe K06.023
    localized K06.010
      minimal K06.011
      moderate K06.012
      severe K06.013
Recklinghausen's disease Q85.01
  bones E21.0
Reclus' disease (cystic) —*see* Mastopathy, cystic
Recrudescent typhus (fever) A75.1
Recruitment, auditory H93.21-●
Rectalgia K62.89
Rectitis K62.89
Rectocele
  female (without uterine prolapse) N81.6
    with uterine prolapse N81.4
      incomplete N81.2
  in pregnancy —*see* Pregnancy, complicated
      by, abnormal, pelvic organs or tissues
      NEC
  male K62.3
Rectosigmoid junction —*see* condition
Rectosigmoiditis K63.89
  ulcerative (chronic) K51.30
    with
      complication K51.319
        abscess K51.314
        fistula K51.313
        obstruction K51.312
        rectal bleeding K51.311
        specified NEC K51.318
Rectourethral —*see* condition
Rectovaginal —*see* condition
Rectovesical —*see* condition
Rectum, rectal —*see* condition
Recurrent —*see* condition
  pregnancy loss —*see* Loss (of), pregnancy,
      recurrent
Red bugs B88.0
Red-cedar lung or pneumonitis J67.8
Red tide —*see also* Table of Drugs and
    Chemicals T65.82-●
Reduced
  mobility Z74.09
  ventilatory or vital capacity R94.2
Redundant, redundancy
  anus (congenital) Q43.8
  clitoris N90.89
  colon (congenital) Q43.8
  foreskin (congenital) N47.8
  intestine (congenital) Q43.8
  labia N90.69
  organ or site, congenital NEC —*see* Accessory
  panniculus (abdominal) E65
  prepuce (congenital) N47.8

Redundant, redundancy *(Continued)*
  pylorus K31.89
  rectum (congenital) Q43.8
  scrotum N50.89
  sigmoid (congenital) Q43.8
  skin L98.7
    and subcutaneous tissue L98.7
    of face L57.4
      eyelids —*see* Blepharochalasis
  stomach K31.89
Reduplication —*see* Duplication
Reflex R29.2
  hyperactive gag J39.2
  pupillary, abnormal —*see* Anomaly, pupil,
      function
  vasoconstriction I73.9
  vasovagal R55
Reflux K21.9
  acid K21.9
  esophageal K21.9
    ➠with esophagitis (without bleeding) K21.00
      ▶with bleeding K21.01
    newborn P78.83
  gastroesophageal K21.9
    ➠with esophagitis (without bleeding) K21.00
      ▶with bleeding K21.01
  mitral —*see* Insufficiency, mitral
  ureteral —*see* Reflux, vesicoureteral
  vesicoureteral (with scarring) N13.70
    with
      nephropathy N13.729
        with hydroureter N13.739
          bilateral N13.732
          unilateral N13.731
        without hydroureter N13.729
          bilateral N13.722
          unilateral N13.721
      bilateral N13.722
      unilateral N13.721
      pyelonephritis (chronic) N11.0
    without nephropathy N13.71
    congenital Q62.7
Reforming, artificial openings —*see* Attention
    to, artificial, opening
Refractive error —*see* Disorder, refraction
Refsum's disease or syndrome G60.1
Refusal of
  food, psychogenic F50.89
  treatment (because of) Z53.20
    left against medical advice (AMA) Z53.21
    patient's decision NEC Z53.29
    reasons of belief or group pressure Z53.1
Regional —*see* condition
Regurgitation R11.10
  aortic (valve) —*see* Insufficiency, aortic
  food —*see also* Vomiting
    with reswallowing —*see* Rumination
    newborn P92.1
  gastric contents —*see* Vomiting
  heart —*see* Endocarditis
  mitral (valve) —*see* Insufficiency, mitral
    congenital Q23.3
  myocardial —*see* Endocarditis
  pulmonary (valve) (heart) I37.1
    congenital Q22.2
    syphilitic A52.03
  tricuspid —*see* Insufficiency, tricuspid
  valve, valvular —*see* Endocarditis
    congenital Q24.8
  vesicoureteral —*see* Reflux, vesicoureteral
Reichmann's disease or syndrome K31.89
Reifenstein syndrome E34.52
Reinsertion
  implantable subdermal contraceptive Z30.46
  intrauterine contraceptive device Z30.433
Reiter's disease, syndrome, or urethritis
    M02.30
  ankle M02.37-●
  elbow M02.32-●
  foot joint M02.37-●
  hand joint M02.34-●

▶ New   ➠ Revised   ~~deleted~~ Deleted   ● Use Additional Character(s)

Reiter's disease, syndrome, or urethritis
    (Continued)
    hip M02.35-●
    knee M02.36-●
    multiple site M02.39
    shoulder M02.31-●
    vertebra M02.38
    wrist M02.33-●
Rejection
    food, psychogenic F50.89
    transplant T86.91
        bone T86.830
            marrow T86.01
    ➡ cornea T86.840-●
        heart T86.21
            with lung(s) T86.31
        intestine T86.850
        kidney T86.11
        liver T86.41
        lung(s) T86.810
            with heart T86.31
        organ (immune or nonimmune cause)
            T86.91
        pancreas T86.890
        skin (allograft) (autograft) T86.820
        specified NEC T86.890
        stem cell (peripheral blood) (umbilical
            cord) T86.5
Relapsing fever A68.9
    Carter's (Asiatic) A68.1
    Dutton's (West African) A68.1
    Koch's A68.9
    louse-borne (epidemic) A68.0
    Novy's (American) A68.1
    Obermeyers's (European) A68.0
    Spirillum A68.9
    tick-borne (endemic) A68.1
Relationship
    occlusal
        open anterior M26.220
        open posterior M26.221
Relaxation
    anus (sphincter) K62.89
        psychogenic F45.8
    arch (foot) —*see also* Deformity, limb, flat foot
    back ligaments —*see* Instability, joint, spine
    bladder (sphincter) N31.2
    cardioesophageal K21.9
    cervix —*see* Incompetency, cervix
    diaphragm J98.6
    joint (capsule) (ligament) (paralytic) —*see*
        Flail, joint
        congenital NEC Q74.8
    lumbosacral (joint) —*see* subcategory M53.2
    pelvic floor N81.89
    perineum N81.89
    posture R29.3
    rectum (sphincter) K62.89
    sacroiliac (joint) —*see* subcategory M53.2
    scrotum N50.89
    urethra (sphincter) N36.44
    vesical N31.2
Release from prison, anxiety concerning Z65.2
Remains
    canal of Cloquet Q14.0
    capsule (opaque) Q14.8
Remittent fever (malarial) B54
Remnant
    canal of Cloquet Q14.0
    capsule (opaque) Q14.8
    cervix, cervical stump (acquired)
        (postoperative) N88.8
    cystic duct, postcholecystectomy K91.5
    fingernail L60.8
        congenital Q84.6
    meniscus, knee —*see* Derangement, knee,
        meniscus, specified NEC
    thyroglossal duct Q89.2
    tonsil J35.8
        infected (chronic) J35.01
    urachus Q64.4

Removal (from) (of)
    artificial
        arm Z44.00-●
            complete Z44.01-●
            partial Z44.02-●
        eye Z44.2-●
        leg Z44.10-●
            complete Z44.11-●
            partial Z44.12-●
    breast implant Z45.81
    cardiac pulse generator (battery) (end-of-life)
        Z45.010
    catheter (urinary) (indwelling) Z46.6
        from artificial opening —*see* Attention to,
            artificial, opening
        non-vascular Z46.82
        vascular NEC Z45.2
    device Z46.9
        contraceptive Z30.432
            implantable subdermal Z30.46
        implanted NEC Z45.89
        specified NEC Z46.89
    drains Z48.03
    dressing (nonsurgical) Z48.00
        surgical Z48.01
    external
        fixation device — code to fracture with
            seventh character D
        prosthesis, prosthetic device Z44.9
            breast Z44.3-●
            specified NEC Z44.8
    home in childhood (to foster home or
        institution) Z62.29
    ileostomy Z43.2
    insulin pump Z46.81
    myringotomy device (stent) (tube) Z45.82
    nervous system device NEC Z46.2
        brain neuropacemaker Z46.2
        visual substitution device Z46.2
            implanted Z45.31
    non-vascular catheter Z46.82
    organ, prophylactic (for neoplasia
        management) —*see* Prophylactic, organ
        removal
    orthodontic device Z46.4
    staples Z48.02
    stent
        ureteral Z46.6
    suture Z48.02
    urinary device Z46.6
    vascular access device or catheter Z45.2
Ren
    arcuatus Q63.1
    mobile, mobilis N28.89
        congenital Q63.8
    unguliformis Q63.1
Renal —*see* condition
Rendu-Osler-Weber disease or syndrome I78.0
Reninoma D41.0-●
Renon-Delille syndrome E23.3
Reovirus, as cause of disease classified
        elsewhere B97.5
Repeated falls NEC R29.6
Replaced chromosome by dicentric ring Q93.2
Replacement by artificial or mechanical device
        or prosthesis of
    bladder Z96.0
    blood vessel NEC Z95.828
    bone NEC Z96.7
    cochlea Z96.21
    coronary artery Z95.5
    eustachian tube Z96.29
    eye globe Z97.0
    heart Z95.812
        valve Z95.2
            prosthetic Z95.2
            specified NEC Z95.4
            xenogenic Z95.3
    intestine Z96.89
    joint Z96.60
        hip —*see* Presence, hip joint implant
        knee —*see* Presence, knee joint implant
        specified site NEC Z96.698

Replacement by artificial or mechanical device
        or prosthesis of *(Continued)*
    larynx Z96.3
    lens Z96.1
    limb(s) —*see* Presence, artificial, limb
    mandible NEC (for tooth root implant(s)) Z96.5
    organ NEC Z96.89
    peripheral vessel NEC Z95.828
    stapes Z96.29
    teeth Z97.2
    tendon Z96.7
    tissue NEC Z96.89
    tooth root(s) Z96.5
    vessel NEC Z95.828
        coronary (artery) Z95.5
Request for expert evidence Z04.89
Reserve, decreased or low
    cardiac —*see* Disease, heart
    kidney N28.89
Residual —*see also* condition
    ovary syndrome N99.83
    state, schizophrenic F20.5
    urine R39.198
Resistance, resistant (to)
    activated protein C D68.51
    complicating pregnancy O26.89
    insulin E88.81
    organism(s)
        to
            drug Z16.30
                aminoglycosides Z16.29
                amoxicillin Z16.11
                ampicillin Z16.11
                antibiotic(s) Z16.20
                    multiple Z16.24
                    specified NEC Z16.29
                antifungal Z16.32
                antimicrobial (single) Z16.30
                    multiple Z16.35
                    specified NEC Z16.39
                antimycobacterial (single) Z16.341
                    multiple Z16.342
                antiparasitic Z16.31
                antiviral Z16.33
                beta lactam antibiotics Z16.10
                    specified NEC Z16.19
                cephalosporins Z16.19
                extended beta lactamase (ESBL) Z16.12
                fluoroquinolones Z16.23
                macrolides Z16.29
                methicillin —*see* MRSA
                multiple drugs (MDRO)
                    antibiotics Z16.24
                    antimicrobial Z16.35
                    antimycobacterials Z16.342
                penicillins Z16.11
                quinine (and related compounds)
                    Z16.31
                quinolones Z16.23
                sulfonamides Z16.29
                tetracyclines Z16.29
                tuberculostatics (single) Z16.341
                    multiple Z16.342
                vancomycin Z16.21
                    related antibiotics Z16.22
        thyroid hormone E07.89
Resorption
    dental (roots) K03.3
        alveoli M26.79
    teeth (external) (internal) (pathological)
        (roots) K03.3
Respiration
    Cheyne-Stokes R06.3
    decreased due to shock, following injury T79.4
    disorder of, psychogenic F45.8
    insufficient, or poor R06.89
        newborn P28.5
    painful R07.1
    sighing, psychogenic F45.8
Respiratory —*see also* condition
    distress syndrome (newborn) (type I) P22.0
        type II P22.1

Respiratory *(Continued)*
  syncytial virus, as cause of disease classified
      elsewhere *(see also* Virus, respiratory
      syncytial (RSV)) B97.4
Respite care Z75.5
Response (drug)
  photoallergic L56.1
  phototoxic L56.Ø
Restenosis
  stent
    vascular
      end stent
        adjacent to stent —*see* Arteriosclerosis

        within the stent
          coronary T82.855
          peripheral T82.856
      in stent
        coronary vessel T82.855
        peripheral vessel T82.856
Restless legs (syndrome) G25.81
Restlessness R45.1
Restoration (of)
  dental
    aesthetically inadequate or displeasing
      KØ8.56
    defective KØ8.5Ø
      specified NEC KØ8.59
    failure of marginal integrity KØ8.51
    failure of periodontal anatomical intergrity
      KØ8.54
    organ continuity from previous sterilization
      (tuboplasty) (vasoplasty) Z31.Ø
      aftercare Z31.42
    tooth (existing)
      contours biologically incompatible with
        oral health KØ8.54
      open margins KØ8.51
      overhanging KØ8.52
      poor aesthetic KØ8.56
      poor gingival margins KØ8.51
  unsatisfactory, of tooth KØ8.5Ø
    specified NEC KØ8.59
Restorative material (dental)
  allergy to KØ8.55
  fractured KØ8.539
    with loss of material KØ8.531
    without loss of material KØ8.53Ø
  unrepairable overhanging of KØ8.52
Restriction of housing space Z59.1
Rests, ovarian, in fallopian tube Q5Ø.6
Restzustand (schizophrenic) F2Ø.5
Retained —*see also* Retention
  cholelithiasis following cholecystectomy K91.86
  foreign body fragments (type of) Z18.9
    acrylics Z18.2
    animal quill(s) or spines Z18.31
    cement Z18.83
    concrete Z18.83
    crystalline Z18.83
    depleted isotope Z18.Ø9
    depleted uranium Z18.Ø1
    diethylhexyl phthalates Z18.2
    glass Z18.81
    isocyanate Z18.2
    magnetic metal Z18.11
    metal Z18.1Ø
    nonmagnetic metal Z18.12
    nontherapeutic radioactive Z18.Ø9
    organic NEC Z18.39
    plastic Z18.2
    quill(s) (animal) Z18.31
    radioactive (nontherapeutic) NEC Z18.Ø9
    specified NEC Z18.89
    spine(s) (animal) Z18.31
    stone Z18.83
    tooth (teeth) Z18.32
    wood Z18.33
  fragments (type of) Z18.9
    acrylics Z18.2
    animal quill(s) or spines Z18.31
    cement Z18.83

Retained *(Continued)*
  fragments (type of) *(Continued)*
    concrete Z18.83
    crystalline Z18.83
    depleted isotope Z18.Ø9
    depleted uranium Z18.Ø1
    diethylhexyl phthalates Z18.2
    glass Z18.81
    isocyanate Z18.2
    magnetic metal Z18.11
    metal Z18.1Ø
    nonmagnectic metal Z18.12
    nontherapeutic radioactive Z18.Ø9
    organic NEC Z18.39
    plastic Z18.2
    quill(s) (animal) Z18.31
    radioactive (nontherapeutic) NEC Z18.Ø9
    specified NEC Z18.89
    spine(s) (animal) Z18.31
    stone Z18.83
    tooth (teeth) Z18.32
    wood Z18.33
  gallstones, following cholecystectomy K91.86
Retardation
  development, developmental, specific —*see*
    Disorder, developmental
  endochondral bone growth —*see* Disorder,
    bone, development or growth
  growth R62.5Ø
    due to malnutrition E45
  mental —*see* Disability, intellectual
  motor function, specific F82
  physical (child) R62.52
    due to malnutrition E45
  reading (specific) F81.Ø
  spelling (specific) (without reading disorder)
    F81.81
Retching —*see* Vomiting
Retention —*see also* Retained
  bladder —*see* Retention, urine
  carbon dioxide E87.2
  cholelithiasis following cholecystectomy
    K91.86
  cyst —*see* Cyst
  dead
    fetus (at or near term) (mother) O36.4
      early fetal death OØ2.1
    ovum OØ2.Ø
  decidua (fragments) (following delivery)
    (with hemorrhage) O72.2
    without hemorrhage O73.1
  deciduous tooth KØØ.6
  dental root KØ8.3
  fecal —*see* Constipation
  fetus
    dead O36.4
    early OØ2.1
  fluid R6Ø.9
  foreign body —*see also* Foreign body,
    retained
    current trauma - code as Foreign body, by
      site or type
  gallstones, following cholecystectomy K91.86
  gastric K31.89
  intrauterine contraceptive device, in
    pregnancy —*see* Pregnancy, complicated
    by, retention, intrauterine device
  membranes (complicating delivery) (with
    hemorrhage) O72.2
    with abortion —*see* Abortion, by type
    without hemorrhage O73.1
  meniscus —*see* Derangement, meniscus
  menses N94.89
  milk (puerperal, postpartum) O92.79
  nitrogen, extrarenal R39.2
  ovary syndrome N99.83
  placenta (total) (with hemorrhage) O72.Ø
    without hemorrhage O73.Ø
    portions or fragments (with hemorrhage)
      O72.2
      without hemorrhage O73.1

Retention *(Continued)*
  products of conception
    early pregnancy (dead fetus) OØ2.1
    following
      delivery (with hemorrhage) O72.2
        without hemorrhage O73.1
    secundines (following delivery) (with
      hemorrhage) O72.Ø
    without hemorrhage O73.Ø
    complicating puerperium (delayed
      hemorrhage) O72.2
    partial O72.2
      without hemorrhage O73.1
  smegma, clitoris N9Ø.89
  urine R33.9
    drug-induced R33.Ø
    due to hyperplasia (hypertrophy) of
      prostate —*see* Hyperplasia, prostate
    organic R33.8
      drug-induced R33.Ø
    psychogenic F45.8
    specified NEC R33.8
  water (in tissues) —*see* Edema
Reticular erythematous mucinosis L98.5
Reticulation, dust —*see* Pneumoconiosis
Reticulocytosis R7Ø.1
Reticuloendotheliosis
  acute infantile C96.Ø
  leukemic C91.4-●
  nonlipid C96.Ø
Reticulohistiocytoma (giant-cell) D76.3
Reticuloid, actinic L57.1
Reticulosis (skin)
  acute of infancy C96.Ø
  hemophagocytic, familial D76.1
  histiocytic medullary C96.A
  lipomelanotic I89.8
  malignant (midline) C86.Ø
  polymorphic C86.Ø
  Sézary —*see* Sézary disease
Retina, retinal —*see also* condition
  dark area D49.81
Retinitis —*see also* Inflammation, chorioretinal
  albuminurica N18.9 *[H32]*
    diabetic —*see* Diabetes, retinitis
    disciformis —*see* Degeneration, macula
    focal —*see* Inflammation, chorioretinal, focal
    gravidarum —*see* Pregnancy, complicated by,
      specified pregnancy-related condition
      NEC
    juxtapapillaris —*see* Inflammation,
      chorioretinal, focal, juxtapapillary
    luetic —*see* Retinitis, syphilitic
    pigmentosa H35.52
    proliferans —*see* Disorder, globe,
      degenerative, specified type NEC
    proliferating —*see* Disorder, globe,
      degenerative, specified type NEC
    renal N18.9 *[H32]*
    syphilitic (early) (secondary) A51.43
      central, recurrent A52.71
      congenital (early) A5Ø.Ø1 *[H32]*
      late A52.71
    tuberculous A18.53
Retinoblastoma C69.2-●
  differentiated C69.2-●
  undifferentiated C69.2-●
Retinochoroiditis —*see also* Inflammation,
  chorioretinal
  disseminated —*see* Inflammation,
    chorioretinal, disseminated
    syphilitic A52.71
  focal —*see* Inflammation, chorioretinal
  juxtapapillaris —*see* Inflammation,
    chorioretinal, focal, juxtapapillary
Retinopathy (background) H35.ØØ
  arteriosclerotic I7Ø.8 *[H35.Ø-●]*
  atherosclerotic I7Ø.8 *[H35.Ø-●]*
  central serous —*see* Chorioretinopathy,
    central serous
  Coats H35.Ø2-●

▶ New   ⇒ Revised   ~~deleted~~ Deleted   ● Use Additional Character(s)

Retinopathy *(Continued)*
  diabetic —*see* Diabetes, retinopathy
  exudative H35.02-●
  hypertensive H35.03-●
  in (due to)
    diabetes —*see* Diabetes, retinopathy
  sickle-cell disorders D57.-● *[H36]*
  of prematurity H35.10-●
    stage 0 H35.11-●
    stage 1 H35.12-●
    stage 2 H35.13-●
    stage 3 H35.14-●
    stage 4 H35.15-●
    stage 5 H35.16-●
  pigmentary, congenital —*see* Dystrophy,
    retina
  proliferative NEC H35.2-●
    diabetic —*see* Diabetes, retinopathy,
      proliferative
    sickle-cell D57.-● *[H36]*
  solar H31.02-●
Retinoschisis H33.10-●
  congenital Q14.1
  specified type NEC H33.19-●
Retortamoniasis A07.8
Retractile testis Q55.22
Retraction
  cervix —*see* Retroversion, uterus
  drum (membrane) —*see* Disorder, tympanic
    membrane, specified NEC
  finger —*see* Deformity, finger
  lid H02.539
    left H02.536
      lower H02.535
      upper H02.534
    right H02.533
      lower H02.532
      upper H02.531
  lung J98.4
  mediastinum J98.59
  nipple N64.53
    associated with
      lactation O92.03
      pregnancy O92.01-●
      puerperium O92.02
    congenital Q83.8
  palmar fascia M72.0
  pleura —*see* Pleurisy
  ring, uterus (Bandl's) (pathological)
    O62.4
  sternum (congenital) Q76.7
    acquired M95.4
  uterus —*see* Retroversion, uterus
  valve (heart) —*see* Endocarditis
Retrobulbar —*see* condition
Retrocecal —*see* condition
Retrocession —*see* Retroversion
Retrodisplacement —*see* Retroversion
Retroflection, retroflexion —*see* Retroversion
Retrognathia, retrognathism (mandibular)
  (maxillary) M26.19
Retrograde menstruation N92.5
Retroperineal —*see* condition
Retroperitoneal —*see* condition
Retroperitonitis K68.9
Retropharyngeal —*see* condition
Retroplacental —*see* condition
Retroposition —*see* Retroversion
Retroprosthetic membrane T85.398
Retrosternal thyroid (congenital)
  Q89.2
Retroversion, retroverted
  cervix —*see* Retroversion, uterus
  female NEC —*see* Retroversion, uterus
  iris H21.89
  testis (congenital) Q55.29
  uterus (acquired) (acute) (any degree)
    (asymptomatic) (cervix) (postinfectional)
    (postpartal, old) N85.4
    congenital Q51.818
    in pregnancy O34.53-●

Retrovirus, as cause of disease classified
    elsewhere B97.30
  human
    immunodeficiency, type 2 (HIV 2) B97.35
    T-cell lymphotropic
      type I (HTLV-I) B97.33
      type II (HTLV-II) B97.34
  lentivirus B97.31
  oncovirus B97.32
  specified NEC B97.39
Retrusion, premaxilla (developmental) M26.09
Rett's disease or syndrome F84.2
Reverse peristalsis R19.2
Reye's syndrome G93.7
Rh (factor)
  hemolytic disease (newborn) P55.0
  incompatibility, immunization or sensitization
    affecting management of pregnancy NEC
      O36.09-●
    anti-D antibody O36.01-●
    newborn P55.0
    transfusion reaction —*see* Complication(s),
      transfusion, incompatibility reaction,
      Rh (factor)
  negative mother affecting newborn P55.0
  titer elevated —*see* Complication(s),
    transfusion, incompatibility reaction, Rh
    (factor)
  transfusion reaction —*see* Complication(s),
    transfusion, incompatibility reaction, Rh
    (factor)
Rhabdomyolysis (idiopathic) NEC M62.82
  traumatic T79.6
Rhabdomyoma —*see also* Neoplasm, connective
    tissue, benign
  adult —*see* Neoplasm, connective tissue, benign
  fetal —*see* Neoplasm, connective tissue, benign
  glycogenic —*see* Neoplasm, connective tissue,
    benign
Rhabdomyosarcoma (any type) —*see*
    Neoplasm, connective tissue, malignant
Rhabdosarcoma —*see* Rhabdomyosarcoma
Rhesus (factor) incompatibility —*see* Rh,
    incompatibility
Rheumatic (acute) (subacute)
  adherent pericardium I09.2
  chronic I09.89
  coronary arteritis I01.8
  degeneration, myocardium I09.0
  fever (acute) —*see* Fever, rheumatic
  heart —*see* Disease, heart, rheumatic
  myocardial degeneration —*see* Degeneration,
    myocardium
  myocarditis (chronic) (inactive) (with chorea)
    I09.0
    with chorea (acute) (rheumatic)
      (Sydenham's) I02.0
    active or acute I01.2
  pancarditis, acute I01.8
    with chorea (acute (rheumatic)
      Sydenham's) I02.0
  pericarditis (active) (acute) (with effusion)
    (with pneumonia) I01.0
    with chorea (acute) (rheumatic)
      (Sydenham's) I02.0
    chronic or inactive I09.2
  pneumonia I00 *[J17]*
  torticollis M43.6
  typhoid fever A01.09
Rheumatism (articular) (neuralgic)
    (nonarticular) M79.0
  gout —*see* Arthritis, rheumatoid
  intercostal, meaning Tietze's disease M94.0
  palindromic (any site) M12.30
    ankle M12.37-●
    elbow M12.32-●
    foot joint M12.37-●
    hand joint M12.34-●
    hip M12.35-●
    knee M12.36-●
    multiple site M12.39

Rheumatism *(Continued)*
  palindromic *(Continued)*
    shoulder M12.31-●
    specified joint NEC M12.38
    vertebrae M12.38
    wrist M12.33-●
  sciatic M54.4-●
Rheumatoid —*see also* condition
  arthritis —*see also* Arthritis, rheumatoid
    with involvement of organs NEC M05.60
      ankle M05.67-●
      elbow M05.62-●
      foot joint M05.67-●
      hand joint M05.64-●
      hip M05.65-●
      knee M05.66-●
      multiple site M05.69
      shoulder M05.61-●
      vertebra —*see* Spondylitis, ankylosing
      wrist M05.63-●
    seronegative —*see* Arthritis, rheumatoid,
      seronegative
    seropositive —*see* Arthritis, rheumatoid,
      seropositive
  carditis M05.30
    ankle M05.37-●
    elbow M05.32-●
    foot joint M05.37-●
    hand joint M05.34-●
    hip M05.35-●
    knee M05.36-●
    multiple site M05.39
    shoulder M05.31-●
    vertebra —*see* Spondylitis, ankylosing
    wrist M05.33-●
  endocarditis —*see* Rheumatoid, carditis
  lung (disease) M05.10
    ankle M05.17-●
    elbow M05.12-●
    foot joint M05.17-●
    hand joint M05.14-●
    hip M05.15-●
    knee M05.16-●
    multiple site M05.19
    shoulder M05.11-●
    vertebra —*see* Spondylitis, ankylosing
    wrist M05.13-●
  myocarditis —*see* Rheumatoid, carditis
  myopathy M05.40
    ankle M05.47-●
    elbow M05.42-●
    foot joint M05.47-●
    hand joint M05.44-●
    hip M05.45-●
    knee M05.46-●
    multiple site M05.49
    shoulder M05.41-●
    vertebra —*see* Spondylitis, ankylosing
    wrist M05.43-●
  pericarditis —*see* Rheumatoid, carditis
  polyarthritis —*see* Arthritis, rheumatoid
  polyneuropathy M05.50
    ankle M05.57-●
    elbow M05.52-●
    foot joint M05.57-●
    hand joint M05.54-●
    hip M05.55-●
    knee M05.56-●
    multiple site M05.59
    shoulder M05.51-●
    vertebra —*see* Spondylitis, ankylosing
    wrist M05.53-●
  vasculitis M05.20
    ankle M05.27-●
    elbow M05.22-●
    foot joint M05.27-●
    hand joint M05.24-●
    hip M05.25-●
    knee M05.26-●
    multiple site M05.29
    shoulder M05.21-●
    vertebra —*see* Spondylitis, ankylosing
    wrist M05.23-●

Rhinitis (atrophic) (catarrhal) (chronic)
    (croupous) (fibrinous) (granulomatous)
    (hyperplastic) (hypertrophic)
    (membranous) (obstructive) (purulent)
    (suppurative) (ulcerative) J31.0
  with
    sore throat —see Nasopharyngitis
  acute J00
  allergic J30.9
    with asthma J45.909
      with
        exacerbation (acute) J45.901
        status asthmaticus J45.902
    due to
      food J30.5
      pollen J30.1
    nonseasonal J30.89
    perennial J30.89
    seasonal NEC J30.2
    specified NEC J30.89
  infective J00
  pneumococcal J00
  syphilitic A52.73
    congenital A50.05 [J99]
  tuberculous A15.8
  vasomotor J30.0
Rhinoantritis (chronic) —see Sinusitis,
  maxillary
Rhinodacryolith —see Dacryolith
Rhinolith (nasal sinus) J34.89
Rhinomegaly J34.89
Rhinopharyngitis (acute) (subacute) —see also
  Nasopharyngitis
  chronic J31.1
  destructive ulcerating A66.5
  mutilans A66.5
Rhinophyma L71.1
Rhinorrhea J34.89
  cerebrospinal (fluid) G96.01
    postoperative G96.08
    specified NEC G96.08
    spontaneous G96.01
    traumatic G96.08
  paroxysmal —see Rhinitis, allergic
  spasmodic —see Rhinitis, allergic
Rhinosalpingitis —see Salpingitis, eustachian
Rhinoscleroma A48.8
Rhinosporidiosis B48.1
Rhinovirus infection NEC B34.8
Rhizomelic chondrodysplasia punctata E71.540
Rhythm
  atrioventricular nodal I49.8
  disorder I49.9
    coronary sinus I49.8
    ectopic I49.8
    nodal I49.8
  escape I49.9
  heart, abnormal I49.9
  idioventricular I44.2
  nodal I49.8
  sleep, inversion G47.2-●
    nonorganic origin —see Disorder, sleep,
      circadian rhythm, psychogenic
Rhytidosis facialis L98.8
Rib —see also condition
  cervical Q76.5
Riboflavin deficiency E53.0
Rice bodies —see also Loose, body, joint
  knee M23.4-●
Richter syndrome —see Leukemia, chronic
  lymphocytic, B-cell type
Richter's hernia —see Hernia, abdomen, with
  obstruction
Ricinism —see Poisoning, food, noxious, plant
Rickets (active) (acute) (adolescent) (chest wall)
  (congenital) (current) (infantile) (intestinal)
  E55.0
  adult —see Osteomalacia
  celiac K90.0
  hypophosphatemic with nephrotic-glycosuric
    dwarfism E72.09

Rickets (Continued)
  inactive E64.3
  kidney N25.0
  renal N25.0
  sequelae, any E64.3
  vitamin-D-resistant E83.31 [M90.80]
Rickettsia 364D/R. philipii (Pacific Coast tick
  fever) A77.8
Rickettsial disease A79.9
  specified type NEC A79.89
Rickettsialpox (Rickettsia akari) A79.1
Rickettsiosis A79.9
  due to
    Ehrlichia sennetsu A79.81
    Neorickettsia sennetsu A79.81
    Rickettsia akari (rickettsialpox) A79.1
  specified type NEC A79.89
  tick-borne A77.9
  vesicular A79.1
Rider's bone —see Ossification, muscle,
  specified NEC
Ridge, alveolus —see also condition
  flabby K06.8
Ridged ear, congenital Q17.3
Riedel's
  lobe, liver Q44.7
  struma, thyroiditis or disease E06.5
Rieger's anomaly or syndrome Q13.81
Riehl's melanosis L81.4
Rietti-Greppi-Micheli anemia D56.9
Rieux's hernia —see Hernia, abdomen, specified
  site NEC
Riga (-Fede) disease K14.0
Riggs' disease —see Periodontitis
Right aortic arch Q25.47
Right middle lobe syndrome J98.11
Rigid, rigidity —see also condition
  abdominal R19.30
    with severe abdominal pain R10.0
    epigastric R19.36
    generalized R19.37
    left lower quadrant R19.34
    left upper quadrant R19.32
    periumbilic R19.35
    right lower quadrant R19.33
    right upper quadrant R19.31
  articular, multiple, congenital Q68.8
  cervix (uteri) in pregnancy —see Pregnancy,
    complicated by, abnormal, cervix
  hymen (acquired) (congenital) N89.6
  nuchal R29.1
  pelvic floor in pregnancy —see Pregnancy,
    complicated by, abnormal, pelvic organs
    or tissues NEC
  perineum or vulva in pregnancy —see
    Pregnancy, complicated by, abnormal,
    vulva
  spine —see Dorsopathy, specified NEC
  vagina in pregnancy —see Pregnancy,
    complicated by, abnormal, vagina
Rigors R68.89
  with fever R50.9
Riley-Day syndrome G90.1
RIND (reversible ischemic neurologic deficit)
  I63.9
Ring(s)
  aorta (vascular) Q25.45
  Bandl's O62.4
  contraction, complicating delivery O62.4
  esophageal, lower (muscular) K22.2
  Fleischer's (cornea) H18.04-●
  hymenal, tight (acquired) (congenital)
    N89.6
  Kayser-Fleischer (cornea) H18.04-●
  retraction, uterus, pathological O62.4
  Schatzki's (esophagus) (lower) K22.2
    congenital Q39.3
  Soemmerring's —see Cataract, secondary
  vascular (congenital) Q25.8
    aorta Q25.45
Ringed hair (congenital) Q84.1

Ringworm B35.9
  beard B35.0
  black dot B35.0
  body B35.4
  Burmese B35.5
  corporeal B35.4
  foot B35.3
  groin B35.6
  hand B35.2
  honeycomb B35.0
  nails B35.1
  perianal (area) B35.6
  scalp B35.0
  specified NEC B35.8
  Tokelau B35.5
Rise, venous pressure I87.8
Rising, PSA following treatment for malignant
  neoplasm of prostate R97.21
Risk
  for
    dental caries Z91.849
      high Z91.843
      low Z91.841
      moderate Z91.842
  suicidal
    meaning personal history of attempted
      suicide Z91.5
    meaning suicidal ideation —see Ideation,
      suicidal
Ritter's disease L00
Rivalry, sibling Z62.891
Rivalta's disease A42.2
River blindness B73.01
Robert's pelvis Q74.2
  with disproportion (fetopelvic) O33.0
    causing obstructed labor O65.0
Robin (-Pierre) syndrome Q87.0
Robinow-Silvermann-Smith syndrome Q87.19
Robinson's (hidrotic) ectodermal dysplasia or
  syndrome Q82.4
Robles' disease B73.01
Rocky Mountain (spotted) fever A77.0
Roetheln —see Rubella
Roger's disease Q21.0
Rokitansky-Aschoff sinuses (gallbladder) K82.8
Rolando's fracture (displaced) S62.22-●
  nondisplaced S62.22-●
Romano-Ward (prolonged QT interval)
  syndrome I45.81
Romberg's disease or syndrome G51.8
Roof, mouth —see condition
Rosacea L71.9
  acne L71.9
  keratitis L71.8
  specified NEC L71.8
Rosary, rachitic E55.0
Rose
  cold J30.1
  fever J30.1
  rash R21
    epidemic B06.9
Rosenbach's erysipeloid A26.0
Rosenthal's disease or syndrome D68.1
Roseola B09
  infantum B08.20
    due to human herpesvirus 6 B08.21
    due to human herpesvirus 7 B08.22
Ross River disease or fever B33.1
Rossbach's disease K31.89
  psychogenic F45.8
Rostan's asthma (cardiac) —see Failure,
  ventricular, left
Rotation
  anomalous, incomplete or insufficient,
    intestine Q43.3
  cecum (congenital) Q43.3
  colon (congenital) Q43.3
  spine, incomplete or insufficient —see
    Dorsopathy, deforming, specified NEC
  tooth, teeth, fully erupted M26.35
  vertebra, incomplete or insufficient —see
    Dorsopathy, deforming, specified NEC

▶ New   ⇨ Revised   ~~deleted~~ Deleted   ● Use Additional Character(s)

Rotes Quérol disease or syndrome —*see*
Hyperostosis, ankylosing
Roth (-Bernhardt) disease or syndrome —*see*
Meralgia paraesthetica
Rothmund (-Thomson) syndrome Q82.8
Rotor's disease or syndrome E80.6
Round
back (with wedging of vertebrae) —*see*
Kyphosis
sequelae (late effect) of rickets E64.3
worms (large) (infestation) NEC B82.0
Ascariasis —*see also* Ascariasis B77.9
Roussy-Lévy syndrome G60.0
Rubella (German measles) B06.9
complication NEC B06.09
neurological B06.00
congenital P35.0
contact Z20.4
exposure to Z20.4
maternal
care for (suspected) damage to fetus O35.3
manifest rubella in infant P35.0
suspected damage to fetus affecting
management of pregnancy O35.3
specified complications NEC B06.89
Rubeola (meaning measles) —*see* Measles
meaning rubella —*see* Rubella
Rubeosis, iris —*see* Disorder, iris, vascular
Rubinstein-Taybi syndrome Q87.2
Rudimentary (congenital) —*see also* Agenesis
arm —*see* Defect, reduction, upper limb
bone Q79.9
cervix uteri Q51.828
eye Q11.2
lobule of ear Q17.3
patella Q74.1
respiratory organs in thoracopagus Q89.4
tracheal bronchus Q32.4
uterus Q51.818
in male Q56.1
vagina Q52.0
Ruled out condition —*see* Observation,
suspected
Rumination R11.10
with nausea R11.2
disorder of infancy F98.21
neurotic F42.8
newborn P92.1
obsessional F42.8
psychogenic F42.8
Runeberg's disease D51.0
Runny nose R09.89
Rupia (syphilitic) A51.39
congenital A50.06
tertiary A52.79
Rupture, ruptured
abscess (spontaneous) - code by site under
Abscess
aneurysm —*see* Aneurysm
anus (sphincter) —*see* Laceration, anus
aorta, aortic I71.8
abdominal I71.3
arch I71.1
ascending I71.1
descending I71.8
abdominal I71.3
thoracic I71.1
syphilitic A52.01
thoracoabdominal I71.5
thorax, thoracic I71.1
transverse I71.1
traumatic —*see* Injury, aorta, laceration,
major
valve or cusp —*see also* Endocarditis, aortic
I35.8
appendix (with peritonitis) (*see also*
Appendicitis) K35.32
with localized peritonitis (*see also*
Appendicitis) K35.32
arteriovenous fistula, brain —*see* Fistula,
arteriovenous, brain, ruptured

Rupture, ruptured (*Continued*)
artery I77.2
brain —*see* Hemorrhage, intracranial,
intracerebral
coronary —*see* Infarct, myocardium
heart —*see* Infarct, myocardium
pulmonary I28.8
traumatic (complication) —*see* Injury,
blood vessel
bile duct (common) (hepatic) K83.2
cystic K82.2
bladder (sphincter) (nontraumatic)
(spontaneous) N32.89
following ectopic or molar pregnancy
O08.6
obstetrical trauma O71.5
traumatic S37.29
blood vessel —*see also* Hemorrhage
brain —*see* Hemorrhage, intracranial,
intracerebral
heart —*see* Infarct, myocardium
traumatic (complication) —*see* Injury,
blood vessel, laceration, major, by site
bone —*see* Fracture
bowel (nontraumatic) K63.1
brain
aneurysm (congenital) —*see also*
Hemorrhage, intracranial,
subarachnoid
syphilitic A52.05
hemorrhagic —*see* Hemorrhage,
intracranial, intracerebral
capillaries I78.8
cardiac (auricle) (ventricle) (wall) I23.3
with hemopericardium I23.0
infectional I40.9
traumatic —*see* Injury, heart
cartilage (articular) (current) —*see also* Sprain
knee S83.3-●
semilunar —*see* Tear, meniscus
cecum (with peritonitis) K65.0
with peritoneal abscess K35.33
traumatic S36.598
celiac artery, traumatic —*see* Injury, blood
vessel, celiac artery, laceration, major
cerebral aneurysm (congenital) (*see*
Hemorrhage, intracranial, subarachnoid)
cervix (uteri)
with ectopic or molar pregnancy O08.6
following ectopic or molar pregnancy O08.6
obstetrical trauma O71.3
traumatic S37.69
chordae tendineae NEC I51.1
concurrent with acute myocardial
infarction —*see* Infarct, myocardium
following acute myocardial infarction
(current complication) I23.4
choroid (direct) (indirect) (traumatic) H31.32-●
circle of Willis I60.6
colon (nontraumatic) K63.1
traumatic —*see* Injury, intestine, large
cornea (traumatic) —*see* Injury, eye, laceration
coronary (artery) (thrombotic) —*see* Infarct,
myocardium
corpus luteum (infected) (ovary) N83.1-●
cyst —*see* Cyst
cystic duct K82.2
Descemet's membrane —*see* Change, corneal
membrane, Descemet's, rupture
traumatic —*see* Injury, eye, laceration
diaphragm, traumatic —*see* Injury,
intrathoracic, diaphragm
disc —*see* Rupture, intervertebral disc
diverticulum (intestine) K57.80
with bleeding K57.81
bladder N32.3
large intestine K57.20
with
bleeding K57.21
small intestine K57.40
with bleeding K57.41

Rupture, ruptured (*Continued*)
diverticulum (*Continued*)
small intestine K57.00
with
bleeding K57.01
large intestine K57.40
with bleeding K57.41
duodenal stump K31.89
ear drum (nontraumatic) —*see also*
Perforation, tympanum
traumatic S09.2-●
due to blast injury —*see* Injury, blast, ear
esophagus K22.3
eye (without prolapse or loss of intraocular
tissue) —*see* Injury, eye, laceration
fallopian tube NEC (nonobstetric)
(nontraumatic) N83.8
due to pregnancy O00.10-●
with intrauterine pregnancy O00.11-●
fontanel P13.1
gallbladder K82.2
traumatic S36.128
gastric —*see also* Rupture, stomach
vessel K92.2
globe (eye) (traumatic) —*see* Injury, eye,
laceration
graafian follicle (hematoma) N83.0-●
heart —*see* Rupture, cardiac
hymen (nontraumatic) (nonintentional) N89.8
internal organ, traumatic —*see* Injury, by site
intervertebral disc —*see* Displacement,
intervertebral disc
traumatic —*see* Rupture, traumatic,
intervertebral disc
intestine NEC (nontraumatic) K63.1
traumatic —*see* Injury, intestine
iris —*see also* Abnormality, pupillary
traumatic —*see* Injury, eye, laceration
joint capsule, traumatic —*see* Sprain
kidney (traumatic) S37.06-●
birth injury P15.8
nontraumatic N28.89
lacrimal duct (traumatic) —*see* Injury, eye,
specified site NEC
lens (cataract) (traumatic) —*see* Cataract,
traumatic
ligament, traumatic —*see* Rupture, traumatic,
ligament, by site
liver S36.116
birth injury P15.0
lymphatic vessel I89.8
marginal sinus (placental) (with
hemorrhage) —*see* Hemorrhage,
antepartum, specified cause NEC
membrana tympani (nontraumatic) —*see*
Perforation, tympanum
membranes (spontaneous)
artificial
delayed delivery following O75.5
delayed delivery following —*see*
Pregnancy, complicated by, premature
rupture of membranes
meningeal artery I60.8
meniscus (knee) —*see also* Tear, meniscus
old —*see* Derangement, meniscus
site other than knee - code as Sprain
mesenteric artery, traumatic —*see* Injury,
mesenteric, artery, laceration, major
mesentery (nontraumatic) K66.8
traumatic —*see* Injury, intra-abdominal,
specified, site NEC
mitral (valve) I34.8
muscle (traumatic) —*see also* Strain
diastasis —*see* Diastasis, muscle
nontraumatic M62.10
ankle M62.17-●
foot M62.17-●
forearm M62.13-●
hand M62.14-●
lower leg M62.16-●
pelvic region M62.15-●

Rupture, ruptured *(Continued)*
  muscle *(Continued)*
    nontraumatic *(Continued)*
      shoulder region M62.11-●
      specified site NEC M62.18
      thigh M62.15-●
      upper arm M62.12-●
    traumatic —*see* Strain, by site
  musculotendinous junction NEC,
    nontraumatic —*see* Rupture, tendon,
    spontaneous
  mycotic aneurysm causing cerebral
    hemorrhage —*see* Hemorrhage,
    intracranial, subarachnoid
  myocardium, myocardial —*see* Rupture,
    cardiac
    traumatic —*see* Injury, heart
  nontraumatic, meaning hernia —*see* Hernia
  obstructed —*see* Hernia, by site, obstructed
  operation wound —*see* Disruption, wound,
    operation
  ovary, ovarian N83.8
    corpus luteum cyst N83.1-●
    follicle (graafian) N83.0-●
  oviduct (nonobstetric) (nontraumatic)
    N83.8
    due to pregnancy O00.10-●
    with intrauterine pregnancy
      O00.11-●
  pancreas (nontraumatic) K86.89
    traumatic S36.299
  papillary muscle NEC I51.2
    following acute myocardial infarction
      (current complication) I23.5
  pelvic
    floor, complicating delivery O70.1
    organ NEC, obstetrical trauma O71.5
  perineum (nonobstetric) (nontraumatic)
    N90.89
    complicating delivery —*see* Delivery,
      complicated, by, laceration, anus
      (sphincter)
  postoperative wound —*see* Disruption,
    wound, operation
  prostate (traumatic) S37.828
  pulmonary
    artery I28.8
    valve (heart) I37.8
    vein I28.8
    vessel I28.8
  pus tube —*see* Salpingitis
  pyosalpinx —*see* Salpingitis
  rectum (nontraumatic) K63.1
    traumatic S36.69
  retina, retinal (traumatic) (without
    detachment) —*see also* Break, retina
    with detachment —*see* Detachment,
      retina, with retinal, break
  rotator cuff (nontraumatic) M75.10-●
    complete M75.12-●
    incomplete M75.11-●
  sclera —*see* Injury, eye, laceration
  sigmoid (nontraumatic) K63.1
    traumatic S36.593
  spinal cord —*see also* Injury, spinal cord, by
    region
    due to injury at birth P11.5
    newborn (birth injury) P11.5
  spleen (traumatic) S36.09
    birth injury P15.1
    congenital (birth injury) P15.1
    due to P. vivax malaria B51.0
    nontraumatic D73.5
    spontaneous D73.5
  splenic vein R58
    traumatic —*see* Injury, blood vessel,
      splenic vein
  stomach (nontraumatic) (spontaneous)
    K31.89
    traumatic S36.39

Rupture, ruptured *(Continued)*
  supraspinatus (complete) (incomplete)
    (nontraumatic) —*see* Tear, rotator cuff
  symphysis pubis
    obstetric O71.6
    traumatic S33.4
  synovium (cyst) M66.10
    ankle M66.17-●
    elbow M66.12-●
    finger M66.14-●
    foot M66.17-●
    forearm M66.13-●
    hand M66.14-●
    pelvic region M66.15-●
    shoulder region M66.11-●
    specified site NEC M66.18
    thigh M66.15-●
    toe M66.17-●
    upper arm M66.12-●
    wrist M66.13-●
  tendon (traumatic) —*see* Strain
    nontraumatic (spontaneous) M66.9
      ankle M66.87-●
      extensor M66.20
        ankle M66.27-●
        foot M66.27-●
        forearm M66.23-●
        hand M66.24-●
        lower leg M66.26-●
        multiple sites M66.29
        pelvic region M66.25-●
        shoulder region M66.21-●
        specified site NEC M66.28
        thigh M66.25-●
        upper arm M66.22-●
      flexor M66.30
        ankle M66.37-●
        foot M66.37-●
        forearm M66.33-●
        hand M66.34-●
        lower leg M66.36-●
        multiple sites M66.39
        pelvic region M66.35-●
        shoulder region M66.31-●
        specified site NEC M66.38
        thigh M66.35-●
        upper arm M66.32-●
      foot M66.87-●
      forearm M66.83-●
      hand M66.84-●
      lower leg M66.86-●
      multiple sites M66.89
      pelvic region M66.85-●
      shoulder region M66.81-●
      specified
        site NEC M66.88
        tendon M66.80
      thigh M66.85-●
      upper arm M66.82-●
  thoracic duct I89.8
  tonsil J35.8
  traumatic
    aorta —*see* Injury, aorta, laceration, major
    diaphragm —*see* Injury, intrathoracic,
      diaphragm
    external site —*see* Wound, open, by site
    eye —*see* Injury, eye, laceration
    internal organ —*see* Injury, by site
    intervertebral disc
      cervical S13.0
      lumbar S33.0
      thoracic S23.0
    kidney S37.06-●
    ligament —*see also* Sprain
      ankle —*see* Sprain, ankle
      carpus —*see* Rupture, traumatic,
        ligament, wrist
      collateral (hand) —*see* Rupture,
        traumatic, ligament, finger,
        collateral

Rupture, ruptured *(Continued)*
  traumatic *(Continued)*
    ligament *(Continued)*
      finger (metacarpophalangeal)
        (interphalangeal) S63.40-●
        collateral S63.41-●
          index S63.41-●
          little S63.41-●
          middle S63.41-●
          ring S63.41-●
        index S63.40-●
        little S63.40-●
        middle S63.40-●
        palmar S63.42-●
          index S63.42-●
          little S63.42-●
          middle S63.42-●
          ring S63.42-●
        ring S63.40-●
        specified site NEC S63.499
          index S63.49-●
          little S63.49-●
          middle S63.49-●
          ring S63.49-●
        volar plate S63.43-●
          index S63.43-●
          little S63.43-●
          middle S63.43-●
          ring S63.43-●
      foot —*see* Sprain, foot
      radial collateral S53.2-●
      radiocarpal —*see* Rupture, traumatic,
        ligament, wrist, radiocarpal
      ulnar collateral S53.3-●
      ulnocarpal —*see* Rupture, traumatic,
        ligament, wrist, ulnocarpal
      wrist S63.30-●
        collateral S63.31-●
        radiocarpal S63.32-●
        specified site NEC S63.39-●
        ulnocarpal (palmar) S63.33-●
    liver S36.116
    membrana tympani —*see* Rupture, ear
      drum, traumatic
    muscle or tendon —*see* Strain
    myocardium —*see* Injury, heart
    pancreas S36.299
    rectum S36.69
    sigmoid S36.593
    spleen S36.09
    stomach S36.39
    symphysis pubis S33.4
    tympanum, tympanic (membrane) —*see*
      Rupture, ear drum, traumatic
    ureter S37.19
    uterus S37.69
    vagina —*see* Injury, vagina
    vena cava —*see* Injury, vena cava,
      laceration, major
  tricuspid (heart) (valve) I07.8
  tube, tubal (nonobstetric) (nontraumatic)
    N83.8
    abscess —*see* Salpingitis
    due to pregnancy O00.10-●
    with intrauterine pregnancy O00.11-●
  tympanum, tympanic (membrane)
    (nontraumatic) —*see also* Perforation,
    tympanic membrane H72.9-●
    traumatic —*see* Rupture, ear drum,
      traumatic
  umbilical cord, complicating delivery
    O69.89
  ureter (traumatic) S37.19
    nontraumatic N28.89
  urethra (nontraumatic) N36.8
    with ectopic or molar pregnancy O08.6
    following ectopic or molar pregnancy
      O08.6
    obstetrical trauma O71.5
    traumatic S37.39

▶ New   ⇨ Revised   ~~deleted~~ Deleted   ● Use Additional Character(s)

Rupture, ruptured (Continued)
  uterosacral ligament (nonobstetric)
      (nontraumatic) N83.8
  uterus (traumatic) S37.69
    before labor O71.0-●
    during or after labor O71.1
    nonpuerperal, nontraumatic N85.8
    pregnant (during labor) O71.1
      before labor O71.0-●
  vagina —see Injury, vagina
  valve, valvular (heart) —see Endocarditis
  varicose vein —see Varix

Rupture, ruptured (Continued)
  varix —see Varix
  vena cava R58
    traumatic —see Injury, vena cava,
        laceration, major
  vesical (urinary) N32.89
  vessel (blood) R58
    pulmonary I28.8
    traumatic —see Injury, blood vessel
  viscus R19.8
  vulva complicating delivery O70.0

Russell-Silver syndrome Q87.19
Russian spring-summer type encephalitis
    A84.0
Rust's disease (tuberculous cervical spondylitis)
    A18.01
Ruvalcaba-Myhre-Smith syndrome E71.440
Rytand-Lipsitch syndrome I44.2

R

S

Saber, sabre shin or tibia (syphilitic) A50.56
   [M90.8-●]
Sac lacrimal —*see* condition
Saccharomyces infection B37.9
Saccharopinuria E72.3
Saccular —*see* condition
Sacculation
   aorta (nonsyphilitic) —*see* Aneurysm, aorta
   bladder N32.3
   intralaryngeal (congenital) (ventricular)
      Q31.3
   larynx (congenital) (ventricular) Q31.3
   organ or site, congenital —*see* Distortion
   pregnant uterus —*see* Pregnancy, complicated
      by, abnormal, uterus
   ureter N28.89
   urethra N36.1
   vesical N32.3
Sachs' amaurotic familial idiocy or disease
      E75.02
Sachs-Tay disease E75.02
Sacks-Libman disease M32.11
Sacralgia M53.3
Sacralization Q76.49
Sacrodynia M53.3
Sacroiliac joint —*see* condition
Sacroiliitis NEC M46.1
Sacrum —*see* condition
Saddle
   back —*see* Lordosis
   embolus
      abdominal aorta I74.01
      pulmonary artery I26.92
         with acute cor pulmonale I26.02
   injury — code to condition
   nose M95.0
      due to syphilis A50.57
Sadism (sexual) F65.52
Sadness, postpartal O90.6
Sadomasochism F65.50
Saemisch's ulcer (cornea) —*see* Ulcer, cornea,
      central
Sagging
   skin and subcutaneous tissue (following
      bariatric surgery weight loss) (following
      dietary weight loss) L98.7
Sahib disease B55.0
Sailors' skin L57.8
Saint
   Anthony's fire —*see* Erysipelas
   triad —*see* Hernia, diaphragm
   Vitus' dance —*see* Chorea, Sydenham's
Salaam
   attack(s) —*see* Epilepsy, spasms
   tic R25.8
Salicylism
   abuse F55.8
   overdose or wrong substance given —*see*
      Table of Drugs and Chemicals, by drug,
      poisoning
Salivary duct or gland —*see* condition
Salivation, excessive K11.7
Salmonella —*see* Infection, Salmonella
Salmonellosis A02.0
Salpingitis (catarrhal) (fallopian tube) (nodular)
      (pseudofollicular) (purulent) (septic)
      N70.91
   with oophoritis N70.93
   acute N70.01
      with oophoritis N70.03
   chlamydial A56.11
   chronic N70.11
      with oophoritis N70.13
   complicating abortion —*see* Abortion, by
      type, complicated by, salpingitis
   ear —*see* Salpingitis, eustachian
   eustachian (tube) H68.00-●
      acute H68.01-●
      chronic H68.02-●

Salpingitis (*Continued*)
   follicularis N70.11
      with oophoritis N70.13
   gonococcal (acute) (chronic) A54.24
   interstitial, chronic N70.11
      with oophoritis N70.13
   isthmica nodosa N70.11
      with oophoritis N70.13
   specific (gonococcal) (acute) (chronic) A54.24
   tuberculous (acute) (chronic) A18.17
   venereal (gonococcal) (acute) (chronic) A54.24
Salpingocele N83.4-●
Salpingo-oophoritis (catarrhal) (purulent)
      (ruptured) (septic) (suppurative) N70.93
   acute N70.03
      with ectopic or molar pregnancy O08.0
      following ectopic or molar pregnancy
         O08.0
      gonococcal A54.24
   chronic N70.13
   following ectopic or molar pregnancy O08.0
   gonococcal (acute) (chronic) A54.24
   puerperal O86.19
   specific (gonococcal) (acute) (chronic) A54.24
   subacute N70.03
   tuberculous (acute) (chronic) A18.17
   venereal (gonococcal) (acute) (chronic) A54.24
Salpingo-ovaritis —*see* Salpingo-oophoritis
Salpingoperitonitis —*see* Salpingo-oophoritis
Salzmann's nodular dystrophy —*see*
      Degeneration, cornea, nodular
Sampson's cyst or tumor N80.1
San Joaquin (Valley) fever B38.0
Sandblaster's asthma, lung or pneumoconiosis
      J62.8
Sander's disease (paranoia) F22
Sandfly fever A93.1
Sandhoff's disease E75.01
Sanfilippo (Type B) (Type C) (Type D)
      syndrome E76.22
Sanger-Brown ataxia G11.2
Sao Paulo fever or typhus A77.0
Saponification, mesenteric K65.8
Sarcocele (benign)
   syphilitic A52.76
      congenital A50.59
Sarcocystosis A07.8
Sarcoepiplocele —*see* Hernia
Sarcoepiplomphalocele Q79.2
Sarcoid —*see also* Sarcoidosis
   arthropathy D86.86
   Boeck's D86.9
   Darier-Roussy D86.3
   iridocyclitis D86.83
   meningitis D86.81
   myocarditis D86.85
   myositis D86.87
   pyelonephritis D86.84
   Spiegler-Fendt L08.89
Sarcoidosis D86.9
   with
      cranial nerve palsies D86.82
      hepatic granuloma D86.89
      polyarthritis D86.86
      tubulo-interstitial nephropathy D86.84
   combined sites NEC D86.89
   lung D86.0
      and lymph nodes D86.2
   lymph nodes D86.1
      and lung D86.2
   meninges D86.81
   skin D86.3
   specified type NEC D86.89
Sarcoma (of) —*see also* Neoplasm, connective
      tissue, malignant
   alveolar soft part —*see* Neoplasm, connective
      tissue, malignant
   ameloblastic C41.1
      upper jaw (bone) C41.0
   botryoid —*see* Neoplasm, connective tissue,
      malignant

Sarcoma (*Continued*)
   botryoides —*see* Neoplasm, connective tissue,
      malignant
   cerebellar C71.6
      circumscribed (arachnoidal) C71.6
   circumscribed (arachnoidal) cerebellar
      C71.6
   clear cell —*see also* Neoplasm, connective
      tissue, malignant
      kidney C64.-●
   dendritic cells (accessory cells) C96.4
   embryonal —*see* Neoplasm, connective tissue,
      malignant
   endometrial (stromal) C54.1
      isthmus C54.0
   epithelioid (cell) —*see* Neoplasm, connective
      tissue, malignant
   Ewing's —*see* Neoplasm, bone, malignant
   follicular dendritic cell C96.4
   germinoblastic (diffuse) —*see* Lymphoma,
      diffuse, large cell
      follicular —*see* Lymphoma, follicular,
         specified NEC
   giant cell (except of bone) —*see also*
      Neoplasm, connective tissue, malignant
      bone —*see* Neoplasm, bone, malignant
   glomoid —*see* Neoplasm, connective tissue,
      malignant
   granulocytic C92.3-●
   hemangioendothelial —*see* Neoplasm,
      connective tissue, malignant
   hemorrhagic, multiple —*see* Sarcoma,
      Kaposi's
   histiocytic C96.A
   Hodgkin —*see* Lymphoma, Hodgkin
   immunoblastic (diffuse) —*see* Lymphoma,
      diffuse large cell
   interdigitating dendritic cell C96.4
   Kaposi's
      colon C46.4
      connective tissue C46.1
      gastrointestinal organ C46.4
      lung C46.5-●
      lymph node(s) C46.3
      palate (hard) (soft) C46.2
      rectum C46.4
      skin C46.0
      specified site NEC C46.7
      stomach C46.4
      unspecified site C46.9
   Kupffer cell C22.3
   Langerhans cell C96.4
   leptomeningeal —*see* Neoplasm, meninges,
      malignant
   liver NEC C22.4
   lymphangioendothelial —*see* Neoplasm,
      connective tissue, malignant
   lymphoblastic —*see* Lymphoma,
      lymphoblastic (diffuse)
   lymphocytic —*see* Lymphoma, small cell
      B-cell
   mast cell C96.22
   melanotic —*see* Melanoma
   meningeal —*see* Neoplasm, meninges,
      malignant
   meningothelial —*see* Neoplasm, meninges,
      malignant
   mesenchymal —*see also* Neoplasm,
      connective tissue, malignant
      mixed —*see* Neoplasm, connective tissue,
         malignant
   mesothelial —*see* Mesothelioma
   monstrocellular
      specified site —*see* Neoplasm, malignant,
         by site
      unspecified site C71.9
   myeloid C92.3-●
   neurogenic —*see* Neoplasm, nerve,
      malignant
   odontogenic C41.1
      upper jaw (bone) C41.0

▶ New   ⇒ Revised   ~~deleted~~ Deleted   ● Use Additional Character(s)

Sarcoma *(Continued)*
  osteoblastic —*see* Neoplasm, bone, malignant
  osteogenic —*see also* Neoplasm, bone, malignant
    juxtacortical —*see* Neoplasm, bone, malignant
    periosteal —*see* Neoplasm, bone, malignant
  periosteal —*see also* Neoplasm, bone, malignant
    osteogenic —*see* Neoplasm, bone, malignant
  pleomorphic cell —*see* Neoplasm, connective tissue, malignant
  reticulum cell (diffuse) —*see* Lymphoma, diffuse large cell
    nodular —*see* Lymphoma, follicular
    pleomorphic cell type —*see* Lymphoma, diffuse large cell
  rhabdoid —*see* Neoplasm, malignant, by site
  round cell —*see* Neoplasm, connective tissue, malignant
  small cell —*see* Neoplasm, connective tissue, malignant
  soft tissue —*see* Neoplasm, connective tissue, malignant
  spindle cell —*see* Neoplasm, connective tissue, malignant
  stromal (endometrial) C54.1
    isthmus C54.0
  synovial —*see also* Neoplasm, connective tissue, malignant
    biphasic —*see* Neoplasm, connective tissue, malignant
    epithelioid cell —*see* Neoplasm, connective tissue, malignant
    spindle cell —*see* Neoplasm, connective tissue, malignant
Sarcomatosis
  meningeal —*see* Neoplasm, meninges, malignant
  specified site NEC —*see* Neoplasm, connective tissue, malignant
  unspecified site C80.1
Sarcopenia (age-related) M62.84
Sarcosinemia E72.59
Sarcosporidiosis (intestinal) A07.8
Satiety, early R68.81
Saturnine —*see* condition
Saturnism
  overdose or wrong substance given or taken —*see* Table of Drugs and Chemicals, by drug, poisoning
Satyriasis F52.8
Sauriasis —*see* Ichthyosis
SBE (subacute bacterial endocarditis) I33.0
Scabies (any site) B86
Scabs R23.4
Scaglietti-Dagnini syndrome E22.0
Scald —*see* Burn
Scalenus anticus (anterior) syndrome G54.0
Scales R23.4
Scaling, skin R23.4
Scalp —*see* condition
Scapegoating affecting child Z62.3
Scaphocephaly Q75.0
Scapulalgia M89.8X1
Scapulohumeral myopathy G71.02
Scar, scarring —*see also* Cicatrix L90.5
  adherent L90.5
  atrophic L90.5
  cervix
    in pregnancy or childbirth —*see* Pregnancy, complicated by, abnormal cervix
  cheloid L91.0
  chorioretinal H31.00-●
    posterior pole macula H31.01-●
    postsurgical H59.81-●
    solar retinopathy H31.02-●
    specified type NEC H31.09-●

Scar, scarring *(Continued)*
  choroid —*see* Scar, chorioretinal
  conjunctiva H11.24-●
  cornea H17.9
    xerophthalmic —*see also* Opacity, cornea vitamin A deficiency E50.6
▶ defect (isthmocele) O34.22
  duodenum, obstructive K31.5
  hypertrophic L91.0
  keloid L91.0
  labia N90.89
  lung (base) J98.4
  macula —*see* Scar, chorioretinal, posterior pole
  muscle M62.89
  myocardium, myocardial I25.2
  painful L90.5
  posterior pole (eye) —*see* Scar, chorioretinal, posterior pole
  retina —*see* Scar, chorioretinal
  trachea J39.8
  transmural uterine, in pregnancy O34.29
  uterus N85.8
    in pregnancy O34.29
  vagina N89.8
    postoperative N99.2
  vulva N90.89
Scarabiasis B88.2
Scarlatina (anginosa) (maligna) A38.9
  myocarditis (acute) A38.1
    old —*see* Myocarditis
  otitis media A38.0
  ulcerosa A38.8
Scarlet fever (albuminuria) (angina) A38.9
Schamberg's disease (progressive pigmentary dermatosis) L81.7
Schatzki's ring (acquired) (esophagus) (lower) K22.2
  congenital Q39.3
Schaufenster krankheit I20.8
Schaumann's
  benign lymphogranulomatosis D86.1
  disease or syndrome —*see* Sarcoidosis
Scheie's syndrome E76.03
Schenck's disease B42.1
Scheuermann's disease or osteochondrosis — *see* Osteochondrosis, juvenile, spine
Schilder (-Flatau) disease G37.0
Schilling-type monocytic leukemia C93.0-●
Schimmelbusch's disease, cystic mastitis, or hyperplasia —*see* Mastopathy, cystic
Schistosoma infestation —*see* Infestation, Schistosoma
Schistosomiasis B65.9
  with muscle disorder B65.9 [M63.80]
    ankle B65.9 [M63.87-●]
    foot B65.9 [M63.87-●]
    forearm B65.9 [M63.83-●]
    hand B65.9 [M63.84-●]
    lower leg B65.9 [M63.86-●]
    multiple sites B65.9 [M63.89]
    pelvic region B65.9 [M63.85-●]
    shoulder region B65.9 [M63.81-●]
    specified site NEC B65.9 [M63.88]
    thigh B65.9 [M63.85-●]
    upper arm B65.9 [M63.82-●]
  Asiatic B65.2
  bladder B65.0
  chestermani B65.8
  colon B65.1
  cutaneous B65.3
  due to
    S. haematobium B65.0
    S. japonicum B65.2
    S. mansoni B65.1
    S. mattheii B65.8
  Eastern B65.2
  genitourinary tract B65.0
  intestinal B65.1
  lung NEC B65.9 [J99]
    pneumonia B65.9 [J17]
  Manson's (intestinal) B65.1

Schistosomiasis *(Continued)*
  oriental B65.2
  pulmonary NEC B65.9 [J99]
    pneumonia B65.9
  Schistosoma
    haematobium B65.0
    japonicum B65.2
    mansoni B65.1
  specified type NEC B65.8
  urinary B65.0
  vesical B65.0
Schizencephaly Q04.6
Schizoaffective psychosis F25.9
Schizodontia K00.2
Schizoid personality F60.1
Schizophrenia, schizophrenic F20.9
  acute (brief) (undifferentiated) F23
  atypical (form) F20.3
  borderline F21
  catalepsy F20.2
  catatonic (type) (excited) (withdrawn) F20.2
  cenesthopathic, cenesthesiopathic F20.89
  childhood type F84.5
⟹ chronic undifferentiated F20.9
  cyclic F25.0
  disorganized (type) F20.1
  flexibilitas cerea F20.2
  hebephrenic (type) F20.1
  incipient F21
  latent F21
  negative type F20.5
  paranoid (type) F20.0
  paraphrenic F20.0
  post-psychotic depression F32.89
  prepsychotic F21
  prodromal F21
  pseudoneurotic F21
  pseudopsychopathic F21
  reaction F23
  residual (state) (type) F20.5
  restzustand F20.5
  schizoaffective (type) —*see* Psychosis, schizoaffective
  simple (type) F20.89
  simplex F20.89
  specified type NEC F20.89
  spectrum and other psychotic disorder F29
    specified NEC F28
  stupor F20.2
  syndrome of childhood F84.5
  undifferentiated (type) F20.3
    chronic F20.5
Schizothymia (persistent) F60.1
⟹ Schlatter-Osgood disease or osteochondrosis M92.52-●
Schlatter's tibia —*see* Osteochondrosis, juvenile, tibia
Schmidt's syndrome (polyglandular, autoimmune) E31.0
Schmincke's carcinoma or tumor —*see* Neoplasm, nasopharynx, malignant
Schmitz (-Stutzer) dysentery A03.0
Schmorl's disease or nodes
  lumbar region M51.46
  lumbosacral region M51.47
  sacrococcygeal region M53.3
  thoracic region M51.44
  thoracolumbar region M51.45
Schneiderian
  papilloma —*see* Neoplasm, nasopharynx benign
    specified site —*see* Neoplasm, benign, by site
    unspecified site D14.0
  specified site —*see* Neoplasm, malignant, by site
  unspecified site C30.0
Scholte's syndrome (malignant carcinoid) E34.0
Scholz (-Bielchowsky-Henneberg) disease or syndrome E75.25
Schönlein (-Henoch) disease or purpura (primary) (rheumatic) D69.0

Schottmuller's disease A01.4
Schroeder's syndrome (endocrine hypertensive) E27.0
Schüller-Christian disease or syndrome C96.5
Schultze's type acroparesthesia, simple I73.89
Schultz's disease or syndrome —see Agranulocytosis
Schwalbe-Ziehen-Oppenheim disease G24.1
Schwannoma —see also Neoplasm, nerve, benign
  malignant —see also Neoplasm, nerve, malignant
    with rhabdomyoblastic differentiation — see Neoplasm, nerve, malignant
  melanocytic —see Neoplasm, nerve, benign
  pigmented —see Neoplasm, nerve, benign
Schwannomatosis Q85.03
Schwartz (-Jampel) syndrome G71.13
Schwartz-Bartter syndrome E22.2
Schweniger-Buzzi anetoderma L90.1
Sciatic —see condition
Sciatica (infective)
  with lumbago M54.4-●
    due to intervertebral disc disorder —see Disorder, disc, with, radiculopathy
  due to displacement of intervertebral disc (with lumbago) —see Disorder, disc, with, radiculopathy
  wallet M54.3-●
Scimitar syndrome Q26.8
Sclera —see condition
Sclerectasia H15.84-●
Scleredema
  adultorum —see Sclerosis, systemic
  Buschke's —see Sclerosis, systemic
  newborn P83.0
Sclerema (adiposum) (edematosum) (neonatorum) (newborn) P83.0
  adultorum —see Sclerosis, systemic
Scleriasis —see Scleroderma
Scleritis H15.00-●
  with corneal involvement H15.04-●
  anterior H15.01-●
  brawny H15.02-●
  in (due to) zoster B02.34
  posterior H15.03-●
  specified type NEC H15.09-●
  syphilitic A52.71
  tuberculous (nodular) A18.51
Sclerochoroiditis H31.8
Scleroconjunctivitis —see Scleritis
Sclerocystic ovary syndrome E28.2
Sclerodactyly, sclerodactylia L94.3
Scleroderma, sclerodermia (acrosclerotic) (diffuse) (generalized) (progressive) (pulmonary) —see also Sclerosis, systemic M34.9-●
  circumscribed L94.0
  linear L94.1
  localized L94.0
  newborn P83.88
  systemic M34.9
Sclerokeratitis H16.8
  tuberculous A18.52
Scleroma nasi A48.8
Scleromalacia (perforans) H15.05-●
Scleromyxedema L98.5
Sclérose en plaques G35
Sclerosis, sclerotic
  adrenal (gland) E27.8
  Alzheimer's —see Disease, Alzheimer's
  amyotrophic (lateral) G12.21
  aorta, aortic I70.0
    valve —see Endocarditis, aortic
  artery, arterial, arteriolar, arteriovascular — see Arteriosclerosis
  ascending multiple G35
  brain (generalized) (lobular) G37.9
    artery, arterial I67.2
    diffuse G37.0
    disseminated G35

Sclerosis, sclerotic (Continued)
  brain (Continued)
    insular G35
    Krabbe's E75.23
    miliary G35
    multiple G35
    presenile (Alzheimer's) —see Disease, Alzheimer's, early onset
    senile (arteriosclerotic) I67.2
    stem, multiple G35
    tuberous Q85.1
  bulbar, multiple G35
  bundle of His I44.39
  cardiac —see Disease, heart, ischemic, atherosclerotic
  cardiorenal —see Hypertension, cardiorenal
  cardiovascular —see also Disease, cardiovascular
    renal —see Hypertension, cardiorenal
  cerebellar —see Sclerosis, brain
  cerebral —see Sclerosis, brain
  cerebrospinal (disseminated) (multiple) G35
  cerebrovascular I67.2
  choroid —see Degeneration, choroid
  combined (spinal cord) —see also Degeneration, combined
    multiple G35
  concentric (Balo) G37.5
  cornea —see Opacity, cornea
  coronary (artery) I25.10
    with angina pectoris —see Arteriosclerosis, coronary (artery),
  corpus cavernosum
    female N90.89
    male N48.6
  diffuse (brain) (spinal cord) G37.0
  disseminated G35
  dorsal G35
  dorsolateral (spinal cord) —see Degeneration, combined
  endometrium N85.5
  extrapyramidal G25.9
  eye, nuclear (senile) —see Cataract, senile, nuclear
  focal and segmental (glomerular) —see also N00-N07 with fourth character .1 N05.1
➡Friedreich's (spinal cord) G11.11
  funicular (spermatic cord) N50.89
  general (vascular) —see Arteriosclerosis
  gland (lymphatic) I89.8
  hepatic K74.1
    alcoholic K70.2
  hereditary
    cerebellar G11.9
➡   spinal (Friedreich's ataxia) G11.11
  hippocampal G93.81
  insular G35
  kidney —see Sclerosis, renal
  larynx J38.7
  lateral (amyotrophic) (descending) (spinal) G12.21
    primary G12.23
  lens, senile nuclear —see Cataract, senile, nuclear
  liver K74.1
    with fibrosis K74.2
      alcoholic K70.2
    alcoholic K70.2
    cardiac K76.1
  lung —see Fibrosis, lung
  mastoid —see Mastoiditis, chronic
  mesial temporal G93.81
  mitral I05.8
  Mönckeberg's (medial) —see Arteriosclerosis, extremities
  multiple (brain stem) (cerebral) (generalized) (spinal cord) G35
  myocardium, myocardial —see Disease, heart, ischemic, atherosclerotic
  nuclear (senile), eye —see Cataract, senile, nuclear

Sclerosis, sclerotic (Continued)
  ovary N83.8
  pancreas K86.89
  penis N48.6
  peripheral arteries —see Arteriosclerosis, extremities
  plaques G35
  pluriglandular E31.8
  polyglandular E31.8
  posterolateral (spinal cord) —see Degeneration, combined
  presenile (Alzheimer's) —see Disease, Alzheimer's, early onset
  primary, lateral G12.23
  progressive, systemic M34.0
  pulmonary —see Fibrosis, lung
    artery I27.0
    valve (heart) —see Endocarditis, pulmonary
  renal N26.9
    with
      cystine storage disease E72.09
      hypertensive heart disease (conditions in I11) —see Hypertension, cardiorenal
    arteriolar (hyaline) (hyperplastic) —see Hypertension, kidney
  retina (senile) (vascular) H35.00
  senile (vascular) —see Arteriosclerosis
  spinal (cord) (progressive) G95.89
    ascending G61.0
    combined —see also Degeneration, combined
      multiple G35
      syphilitic A52.11
    disseminated G35
    dorsolateral —see Degeneration, combined
➡   hereditary (Friedreich's) (mixed form) G11.11
    lateral (amyotrophic) G12.21
      progressive G12.23
    multiple G35
    posterior (syphilitic) A52.11
  stomach K31.89
  subendocardial, congenital I42.4
  systemic M34.9
    with
      lung involvement M34.81
      myopathy M34.82
      polyneuropathy M34.83
    drug-induced M34.2
    due to chemicals NEC M34.2
    progressive M34.0
    specified NEC M34.89
  temporal (mesial) G93.81
  tricuspid (heart) (valve) I07.8
  tuberous (brain) Q85.1
  tympanic membrane —see Disorder, tympanic membrane, specified NEC
  valve, valvular (heart) —see Endocarditis
  vascular —see Arteriosclerosis
  vein I87.8
Scoliosis (acquired) (postural) M41.9
  adolescent (idiopathic) —see Scoliosis, idiopathic, adolescent
  congenital Q67.5
    due to bony malformation Q76.3
    failure of segmentation (hemivertebra) Q76.3
    hemivertebra fusion Q76.3
    postural Q67.5
▶degenerative M41.8-●
  idiopathic M41.20
    adolescent M41.129
      cervical region M41.122
      cervicothoracic region M41.123
      lumbar region M41.126
      lumbosacral region M41.127
      thoracic region M41.124
      thoracolumbar region M41.125
    cervical region M41.22
    cervicothoracic region M41.23

▶ New   ➡ Revised   ~~deleted~~ Deleted   ● Use Additional Character(s)

Scoliosis *(Continued)*
  idiopathic *(Continued)*
    infantile M41.00
      cervical region M41.02
      cervicothoracic region M41.03
      lumbar region M41.06
      lumbosacral region M41.07
      sacrococcygeal region M41.08
      thoracic region M41.04
      thoracolumbar region M41.05
    juvenile M41.119
      cervical region M41.112
      cervicothoracic region M41.113
      lumbar region M41.116
      lumbosacral region M41.117
      thoracic region M41.114
      thoracolumbar region M41.115
    lumbar region M41.26
    lumbosacral region M41.27
    thoracic region M41.24
    thoracolumbar region M41.25
  infantile —*see* Scoliosis, idiopathic, infantile
  neuromuscular M41.40
    cervical region M41.42
    cervicothoracic region M41.43
    lumbar region M41.46
    lumbosacral region M41.47
    occipito-atlanto-axial region M41.41
    thoracic region M41.44
    thoracolumbar region M41.45
  paralytic —*see* Scoliosis, neuromuscular
  postradiation therapy M96.5
  rachitic (late effect or sequelae) E64.3 *[M49.80]*
    cervical region E64.3 *[M49.82]*
    cervicothoracic region E64.3 *[M49.83]*
    lumbar region E64.3 *[M49.86]*
    lumbosacral region E64.3 *[M49.87]*
    multiple sites E64.3 *[M49.89]*
    occipito-atlanto-axial region E64.3 *[M49.81]*
    sacrococcygeal region E64.3 *[M49.88]*
    thoracic region E64.3 *[M49.84]*
    thoracolumbar region E64.3 *[M49.85]*
  sciatic M54.4-●
  secondary (to) NEC M41.50
    cerebral palsy, Friedreich's ataxia, poliomyelitis, neuromuscular disorders —*see* Scoliosis, neuromuscular
    cervical region M41.52
    cervicothoracic region M41.53
    lumbar region M41.56
    lumbosacral region M41.57
    thoracic region M41.54
    thoracolumbar region M41.55
  specified form NEC M41.80
    cervical region M41.82
    cervicothoracic region M41.83
    lumbar region M41.86
    lumbosacral region M41.87
    thoracic region M41.84
    thoracolumbar region M41.85
  thoracogenic M41.30
    thoracic region M41.34
    thoracolumbar region M41.35
  tuberculous A18.01
Scoliotic pelvis
  with disproportion (fetopelvic) O33.0
    causing obstructed labor O65.0
Scorbutus, scorbutic —*see also* Scurvy
  anemia D53.2
Score, NIHSS (National Institutes of Health Stroke Scale) R29.7-●
Scotoma (arcuate) (Bjerrum) (central) (ring) — *see also* Defect, visual field, localized, scotoma
  scintillating H53.19
Scratch —*see* Abrasion

Scratchy throat R09.89
Screening (for) Z13.9
  alcoholism Z13.33
  anemia Z13.0
  anomaly, congenital Z13.89
  antenatal, of mother —*see also* Encounter, antenatal Z36.9
  arterial hypertension Z13.6
  arthropod-borne viral disease NEC Z11.59
  autism Z13.41
  bacteriuria, asymptomatic Z13.89
    specified NEC Z13.39
  behavioral disorder Z13.30
  brain injury, traumatic Z13.850
  bronchitis, chronic Z13.83
  brucellosis Z11.2
  cardiovascular disorder Z13.6
  cataract Z13.5
  chlamydial diseases Z11.8
  cholera Z11.0
  chromosomal abnormalities (nonprocreative) NEC Z13.79
  colonoscopy Z12.11
  congenital
    dislocation of hip Z13.89
    eye disorder Z13.5
    malformation or deformation Z13.89
  contamination NEC Z13.88
  cystic fibrosis Z13.228
  dengue fever Z11.59
  dental disorder Z13.84
  depression (adult) (adolescent) (child) Z13.31
    maternal Z13.32
    perinatal Z13.32
  developmental
    delays Z13.40
      global (milestones) Z13.42
      specified NEC Z13.49
    handicap Z13.42
      in early childhood Z13.42
  diabetes mellitus Z13.1
  diphtheria Z11.2
  disability, intellectual Z13.39
  disease or disorder Z13.9
    bacterial NEC Z11.2
      intestinal infectious Z11.0
      respiratory tuberculosis Z11.1
    behavioral Z13.30
      specified NEC Z13.39
    developmental delays Z13.40
      global (milestones) Z13.42
      specified NEC Z13.49
    mental health and behavioral Z13.30
      specified NEC Z13.39
    blood or blood-forming organ Z13.0
    cardiovascular Z13.6
    Chagas' Z11.6
    chlamydial Z11.8
    dental Z13.89
    digestive tract NEC Z13.818
      lower GI Z13.811
      upper GI Z13.810
    ear Z13.5
    endocrine Z13.29
    eye Z13.5
    genitourinary Z13.89
    heart Z13.6
    human immunodeficiency virus (HIV) infection Z11.4
    immunity Z13.0
    infection
      intestinal Z11.0
        specified NEC Z11.6
    infectious Z11.9
    metabolic Z13.228
    neurological Z13.89
    nutritional Z13.21
      metabolic Z13.228
        lipoid disorders Z13.220

Screening *(Continued)*
  disease or disorder *(Continued)*
    protozoal Z11.6
      intestinal Z11.0
    respiratory Z13.83
    rheumatic Z13.828
    rickettsial Z11.8
    sexually-transmitted NEC Z11.3
      human immunodeficiency virus (HIV) Z11.4
    sickle-cell (trait) Z13.0
    skin Z13.89
    specified NEC Z13.89
    spirochetal Z11.8
    thyroid Z13.29
    vascular Z13.6
    venereal Z11.3
    viral NEC Z11.59
      human immunodeficiency virus (HIV) Z11.4
      intestinal Z11.0
  elevated titer Z13.89
  emphysema Z13.83
  encephalitis, viral (mosquito- or tick-borne) Z11.59
  exposure to contaminants (toxic) Z13.88
  fever
    dengue Z11.59
    hemorrhagic Z11.59
    yellow Z11.59
  filariasis Z11.6
  galactosemia Z13.228
  gastrointestinal condition Z13.818
  genetic (nonprocreative)- for procreative management —*see* Testing, genetic, for procreative management
    disease carrier status (nonprocreative) Z13.71
    specified NEC (nonprocreative) Z13.79
  genitourinary condition Z13.89
  glaucoma Z13.5
  gonorrhea Z11.3
  gout Z13.89
  helminthiasis (intestinal) Z11.6
  hematopoietic malignancy Z12.89
  hemoglobinopathies NEC Z13.0
  hemorrhagic fever Z11.59
  Hodgkin disease Z12.89
  human immunodeficiency virus (HIV) Z11.4
  human papillomavirus Z11.51
  hypertension Z13.6
  infant or child (over 28 days old) Z00.129
    with abnormal findings Z00.121
  immunity disorders Z13.0
  infection
    mycotic Z11.8
    parasitic Z11.8
  ingestion of radioactive substance Z13.88
  intellectual disability Z13.39
  intestinal
    helminthiasis Z11.6
    infectious disease Z11.0
  leishmaniasis Z11.6
  leprosy Z11.2
  leptospirosis Z11.8
  leukemia Z12.89
  lymphoma Z12.89
  malaria Z11.6
  malnutrition Z13.29
    metabolic Z13.228
    nutritional Z13.21
  measles Z11.59
  mental health disorder Z13.30
    specified NEC Z13.39
  metabolic errors, inborn Z13.228
  multiphasic Z13.89
  musculoskeletal disorder Z13.828
    osteoporosis Z13.820
  mycoses Z11.8

S

Screening *(Continued)*
  myocardial infarction (acute) Z13.6
  neoplasm (malignant) (of) Z12.9
    bladder Z12.6
    blood Z12.89
    breast Z12.39
      routine mammogram Z12.31
    cervix Z12.4
    colon Z12.11
    genitourinary organs NEC Z12.79
      bladder Z12.6
      cervix Z12.4
      ovary Z12.73
      prostate Z12.5
      testis Z12.71
      vagina Z12.72
    hematopoietic system Z12.89
    intestinal tract Z12.10
      colon Z12.11
      rectum Z12.12
      small intestine Z12.13
    lung Z12.2
    lymph (glands) Z12.89
    nervous system Z12.82
    oral cavity Z12.81
    prostate Z12.5
    rectum Z12.12
    respiratory organs Z12.2
    skin Z12.83
    small intestine Z12.13
    specified site NEC Z12.89
    stomach Z12.0
  nephropathy Z13.89
  nervous system disorders NEC Z13.858
  neurological condition Z13.89
  osteoporosis Z13.820
  parasitic infestation Z11.9
    specified NEC Z11.8
  phenylketonuria Z13.228
  plague Z11.2
  poisoning (chemical) (heavy metal) Z13.88
  poliomyelitis Z11.59
  postnatal, chromosomal abnormalities Z13.89
  prenatal, of mother —*see also* Encounter,
    antenatal Z36.9
  protozoal disease Z11.6
    intestinal Z11.0
  pulmonary tuberculosis Z11.1
  radiation exposure Z13.88
  respiratory condition Z13.83
  respiratory tuberculosis Z11.1
  rheumatoid arthritis Z13.828
  rubella Z11.59
  schistosomiasis Z11.6
  sexually-transmitted disease NEC Z11.3
    human immunodeficiency virus (HIV) Z11.4
  sickle-cell disease or trait Z13.0
  skin condition Z13.89
  sleeping sickness Z11.6
  special Z13.9
    specified NEC Z13.89
  syphilis Z11.3
  tetanus Z11.2
  trachoma Z11.8
  traumatic brain injury Z13.850
  trypanosomiasis Z11.6
  tuberculosis, respiratory Z11.1
    active Z11.1
    latent Z11.7
  venereal disease Z11.3
  viral encephalitis (mosquito- or tick-borne)
    Z11.59
  whooping cough Z11.2
  worms, intestinal Z11.6
  yaws Z11.8
  yellow fever Z11.59
Scrofula, scrofulosis (tuberculosis of cervical
  lymph glands) A18.2
Scrofulide (primary) (tuberculous) A18.4
Scrofuloderma, scrofulodermia (any site)
  (primary) A18.4

Scrofulosus lichen (primary) (tuberculous) A18.4
Scrofulous —*see* condition
Scrotal tongue K14.5
Scrotum —*see* condition
Scurvy, scorbutic E54
  anemia D53.2
  gum E54
  infantile E54
  rickets E55.0 *[M90.80]*
Sealpox B08.62
Seasickness T75.3
Seatworm (infection) (infestation) B80
Sebaceous —*see also* condition
  cyst —*see* Cyst, sebaceous
Seborrhea, seborrheic L21.9
  capillitii R23.8
  capitis L21.0
  dermatitis L21.9
    infantile L21.1
  eczema L21.9
    infantile L21.1
  sicca L21.0
Seckel's syndrome Q87.19
Seclusion, pupil —*see* Membrane, pupillary
Second hand tobacco smoke exposure (acute)
  (chronic) Z77.22
  in the perinatal period P96.81
Secondary
  dentin (in pulp) K04.3
  neoplasm, secondaries —*see* Table of
    Neoplasms, secondary
Secretion
  antidiuretic hormone, inappropriate E22.2
  catecholamine, by pheochromocytoma E27.5
  hormone
    antidiuretic, inappropriate (syndrome) E22.2
    by
      carcinoid tumor E34.0
      pheochromocytoma E27.5
    ectopic NEC E34.2
  urinary
    excessive R35.8
    suppression R34
Section
  nerve, traumatic —*see* Injury, nerve
Sedative, hypnotic, or anxiolytic-induced
  anxiety disorder F13.980
  bipolar and related disorder F13.94
  delirium F13.921
  depressive disorder F13.94
  major neurocognitive disorder F13.97
  mild neurocognitive disorder F13.988
  psychotic disorder F13.959
  sexual dysfunction F13.981
  sleep disorder F13.982
Segmentation, incomplete (congenital) —*see
  also* Fusion
  bone NEC Q78.8
  lumbosacral (joint) (vertebra) Q76.49
Seitelberger's syndrome (infantile neuraxonal
  dystrophy) G31.89
Seizure(s) —*see also* Convulsions R56.9
  absence G40.A-•
  akinetic —*see* Epilepsy, generalized, specified
    NEC
  atonic —*see* Epilepsy, generalized, specified
    NEC
  autonomic (hysterical) F44.5
  convulsive —*see* Convulsions
  cortical (focal) (motor) —*see* Epilepsy,
    localization-related, symptomatic, with
    simple partial seizures
  disorder —*see also* Epilepsy G40.909
  due to stroke —*see* Sequelae (of), disease,
    cerebrovascular, by type, specified NEC
  epileptic —*see* Epilepsy
  febrile (simple) R56.00
    with status epilepticus G40.901
    complex (atypical) (complicated) R56.01
      with status epilepticus G40.901

Seizure *(Continued)*
  grand mal G40.409
    intractable G40.419
      with status epilepticus G40.411
      without status epilepticus G40.419
    not intractable G40.409
      with status epilepticus G40.401
      without status epilepticus G40.409
  heart —*see* Disease, heart
  hysterical F44.5
  intractable G40.919
    with status epilepticus G40.911
  Jacksonian (focal) (motor type) (sensory
    type) —*see* Epilepsy, localization-related,
    symptomatic, with simple partial seizures
  newborn P90
  nonspecific epileptic
    atonic —*see* Epilepsy, generalized, specified
      NEC
    clonic —*see* Epilepsy, generalized, specified
      NEC
    myoclonic —*see* Epilepsy, generalized,
      specified NEC
    tonic —*see* Epilepsy, generalized, specified
      NEC
    tonic-clonic —*see* Epilepsy, generalized,
      specified NEC
  partial, developing into secondarily
    generalized seizures
    complex —*see* Epilepsy, localization-
      related, symptomatic, with complex
      partial seizures
    simple —*see* Epilepsy, localization-related,
      symptomatic, with simple partial
      seizures
  petit mal G40.A-•
    intractable G40.419
      with status epilepticus G40.411
      without status epilepticus G40.419
    not intractable G40.409
      with status epilepticus G40.401
      without status epilepticus G40.409
  post traumatic R56.1
  recurrent G40.909
  specified NEC G40.89
  uncinate —*see* Epilepsy, localization-related,
    symptomatic, with complex partial
    seizures
Selenium deficiency, dietary E59
Self-damaging behavior (life-style) Z72.89
Self-harm (attempted)
  history (personal) Z91.5
    in family Z81.8
Self-mutilation (attempted)
  history (personal) Z91.5
    in family Z81.8
Self-poisoning
  history (personal) Z91.5
    in family Z81.8
  observation following (alleged) attempt Z03.6
Semicoma R40.1
Seminal vesiculitis N49.0
Seminoma C62.9-•
  specified site —*see* Neoplasm, malignant, by
    site
Senear-Usher disease or syndrome L10.4
Senectus R54
Senescence (without mention of psychosis) R54
Senile, senility —*see also* condition R41.81
  with
    acute confusional state F05
    mental changes NOS F03
    psychosis NEC —*see* Psychosis, senile
  asthenia R54
  cervix (atrophic) N88.8
  debility R54
  endometrium (atrophic) N85.8
  fallopian tube (atrophic) —*see* Atrophy,
    fallopian tube
  heart (failure) R54

Senile, senility *(Continued)*
  ovary (atrophic) —*see* Atrophy, ovary
  premature E34.8
  vagina, vaginitis (atrophic) N95.2
  wart L82.1
Sensation
  burning (skin) R20.8
    tongue K14.6
  loss of R20.8
  prickling (skin) R20.2
  tingling (skin) R20.2
Sense loss
  smell —*see* Disturbance, sensation, smell
  taste —*see* Disturbance, sensation, taste
  touch R20.8
Sensibility disturbance (cortical) (deep)
    (vibratory) R20.9
Sensitive, sensitivity —*see also* Allergy
  carotid sinus G90.01
  child (excessive) F93.8
  ➠ cold, autoimmune D59.12
  dentin K03.89
  gluten (non-celiac) K90.41
  latex Z91.040
  methemoglobin D74.8
  tuberculin, without clinical or radiological
    symptoms R76.11
  visual
    glare H53.71
    impaired contrast H53.72
Sensitiver Beziehungswahn F22
Sensitization, auto-erythrocytic D69.2
Separation
  anxiety, abnormal (of childhood) F93.0
  apophysis, traumatic - code as Fracture, by site
  choroid —*see* Detachment, choroid
  epiphysis, epiphyseal
    nontraumatic —*see also* Osteochondropathy,
      specified type NEC
      upper femoral —*see* Slipped, epiphysis,
        upper femoral
    traumatic - code as Fracture, by site
  fracture —*see* Fracture
  infundibulum cardiac from right ventricle by
    a partition Q24.3
  joint (traumatic) (current) - code by site under
    Dislocation
  muscle (nontraumatic) —*see* Diastasis, muscle
  pubic bone, obstetrical trauma O71.6
  retina, retinal —*see* Detachment, retina
  symphysis pubis, obstetrical trauma O71.6
  tracheal ring, incomplete, congenital Q32.1
Sepsis (generalized) (unspecified organism)
    A41.9
  with
    organ dysfunction (acute) (multiple) R65.20
      with septic shock R65.21
  actinomycotic A42.7
  adrenal hemorrhage syndrome
    (meningococcal) A39.1
  anaerobic A41.4
  Bacillus anthracis A22.7
  Brucella —*see also* Brucellosis A23.9
  candidal B37.7
  cryptogenic A41.9
  due to device, implant or graft T85.79
    arterial graft NEC T82.7
    breast (implant) T85.79
    catheter NEC T85.79
      dialysis (renal) T82.7
        intraperitoneal T85.71
      infusion NEC T82.7
        spinal (cranial) (epidural) (intrathecal)
          (spinal) (subarachnoid)
          (subdural) T85.735
      urethral indwelling T83.511
      urinary T83.518
    ectopic or molar pregnancy O08.82
    electronic (electrode) (pulse generator)
      (stimulator)
      bone T84.7

Sepsis *(Continued)*
  due to device, implant or graft *(Continued)*
    electronic *(Continued)*
      cardiac T82.7
      nervous system T85.738
        brain T85.731
        neurostimulator generator T85.734
        peripheral nerve T85.732
        spinal cord T85.733
      urinary T83.590
    fixation, internal (orthopedic) —*see*
      Complication, fixation device,
      infection
    gastrointestinal (bile duct) (esophagus)
      T85.79
    neurostimulator electrode (lead) T85.732
    genital T83.69
    heart NEC T82.7
      valve (prosthesis) T82.6
        graft T82.7
    joint prosthesis —*see* Complication, joint
      prosthesis, infection
    ocular (corneal graft) (orbital implant)
      T85.79
    orthopedic NEC T84.7
      fixation device, internal —*see*
        Complication, fixation device,
        infection
    specified NEC T85.79
    vascular T82.7
    ventricular intracranial (communicating)
      shunt T85.730
  during labor O75.3
  Enterococcus A41.81
  Erysipelothrix (rhusiopathiae) (erysipeloid)
    A26.7
  Escherichia coli (E. coli) A41.5
  extraintestinal yersiniosis A28.2
  following
    abortion (subsequent episode) O08.0
      current episode —*see* Abortion
    ectopic or molar pregnancy O08.82
    immunization T88.0
    infusion, therapeutic injection or
      transfusion NEC T80.29
    obstetrical procedure O86.04
  gangrenous A41.9
  gonococcal A54.86
  Gram-negative (organism) A41.5
    anaerobic A41.4
  Haemophilus influenzae A41.3
  herpesviral B00.7
  intra-abdominal K65.1
  intraocular —*see* Endophthalmitis, purulent
  Listeria monocytogenes A32.7
  localized — code to specific localized infection
    in operation wound T81.49
    skin —*see* Abscess
  malleus A24.0
  melioidosis A24.1
  meningeal —*see* Meningitis
  meningococcal A39.4
    acute A39.2
    chronic A39.3
  MSSA (Methicillin susceptible
    Staphylococcus aureus) A41.01
  newborn P36.9
    due to
      anaerobes NEC P36.5
      Escherichia coli P36.4
      Staphylococcus P36.30
        aureus P36.2
        specified NEC P36.39
      Streptococcus P36.10
        group B P36.0
        specified NEC P36.19
      specified NEC P36.8
  Pasteurella multocida A28.0
  pelvic, puerperal, postpartum, childbirth O85
  pneumococcal A40.3
  postprocedural T81.44

Sepsis *(Continued)*
  puerperal, postpartum, childbirth (pelvic) O85
  Salmonella (arizonae) (cholerae-suis)
    (enteritidis) (typhimurium) A02.1
  severe R65.20
    with septic shock R65.21
  Shigella (*see also* Dysentery, bacillary) A03.9
  skin, localized —*see* Abscess
  specified organism NEC A41.89
  Staphylococcus, staphylococcal A41.2
    aureus (methicillin susceptible) (MSSA)
      A41.01
      methicillin resistant (MRSA) A41.02
    coagulase-negative A41.1
    specified NEC A41.1
  Streptococcus, streptococcal A40.9
    agalactiae A40.1
    group
      A A40.0
      B A40.1
      D A41.81
    neonatal P36.10
      group B P36.0
      specified NEC P36.19
    pneumoniae A40.3
    pyogenes A40.0
    specified NEC A40.8
  tracheostomy stoma J95.02
  tularemic A21.7
  umbilical, umbilical cord (newborn) —*see*
    Sepsis, newborn
  Yersinia pestis A20.7
Septate —*see* Septum
Septic —*see* condition
  arm —*see* Cellulitis, upper limb
    with lymphangitis —*see* Lymphangitis,
      acute, upper limb
  embolus —*see* Embolism
  finger —*see* Cellulitis, digit
    with lymphangitis —*see* Lymphangitis,
      acute, digit
  foot —*see* Cellulitis, lower limb
    with lymphangitis —*see* Lymphangitis,
      acute, lower limb
  gallbladder (acute) K81.0
  hand —*see* Cellulitis, upper limb
    with lymphangitis —*see* Lymphangitis,
      acute, upper limb
  joint —*see* Arthritis, pyogenic or pyemic
  leg —*see* Cellulitis, lower limb
    with lymphangitis —*see* Lymphangitis,
      acute, lower limb
  nail —*see also* Cellulitis, digit
    with lymphangitis —*see* Lymphangitis,
      acute, digit
  sore —*see also* Abscess
    throat J02.0
      streptococcal J02.0
  spleen (acute) D73.89
  teeth, tooth (pulpal origin) K04.4
  throat —*see* Pharyngitis
  thrombus —*see* Thrombosis
  toe —*see* Cellulitis, digit
    with lymphangitis —*see* Lymphangitis,
      acute, digit
  tonsils, chronic J35.01
    with adenoiditis J35.03
  uterus —*see* Endometritis
Septicemia A41.9
  meaning sepsis —*see* Sepsis
Septum, septate (congenital) —*see also*
    Anomaly, by site
  anal Q42.3
    with fistula Q42.2
  aqueduct of Sylvius Q03.0
    with spina bifida —*see* Spina bifida, by site,
      with hydrocephalus
  ➠ uterus (complete) (partial) Q51.28
    complete Q51.21
    partial Q51.22
    specified NEC Q51.28

Septum, septate *(Continued)*
- vagina Q52.10
  - in pregnancy —*see* Pregnancy, complicated by, abnormal vagina
    - causing obstructed labor O65.5
  - longitudinal Q52.129
    - microperforate
      - left side Q52.124
      - right side Q52.123
    - nonobstruction Q52.120
    - obstructing Q52.129
      - left side Q52.122
      - right side Q52.121
  - transverse Q52.11

Sequelae (of) —*see also* condition
- abscess, intracranial or intraspinal (conditions in G06) G09
- amputation — code to injury with seventh character S
- burn and corrosion — code to injury with seventh character S
- calcium deficiency E64.8
- cerebrovascular disease —*see* Sequelae, disease, cerebrovascular
- childbirth O94
- contusion — code to injury with seventh character S
- corrosion —*see* Sequelae, burn and corrosion
- crushing injury — code to injury with seventh character S
- disease
  - cerebrovascular I69.90
    - alteration of sensation I69.998
    - aphasia I69.920
    - apraxia I69.990
    - ataxia I69.993
    - cognitive deficits I69.91
    - disturbance of vision I69.998
    - dysarthria I69.922
    - dysphagia I69.991
    - dysphasia I69.921
    - facial droop I69.992
    - facial weakness I69.992
    - fluency disorder I69.923
    - hemiplegia I69.95-●
    - hemorrhage
      - intracerebral —*see* Sequelae, hemorrhage, intracerebral
      - intracranial, nontraumatic NEC — *see* Sequelae, hemorrhage, intracranial, nontraumatic
      - subarachnoid —*see* Sequelae, hemorrhage, subarachnoid
    - language deficit I69.928
    - monoplegia
      - lower limb I69.94-●
      - upper limb I69.93-●
    - paralytic syndrome I69.96-●
    - specified effect NEC I69.998
    - specified type NEC I69.80
      - alteration of sensation I69.898
      - aphasia I69.820
      - apraxia I69.890
      - ataxia I69.893
      - cognitive deficits I69.81
      - disturbance of vision I69.898
      - dysarthria I69.822
      - dysphagia I69.891
      - dysphasia I69.821
      - facial droop I69.892
      - facial weakness I69.892
      - fluency disorder I69.823
      - hemiplegia I69.85-●
      - language deficit I69.828
      - monoplegia
        - lower limb I69.84-●
        - upper limb I69.83-●
      - paralytic syndrome I69.86-●
      - specified effect NEC I69.898
    - speech deficit I69.928
    - speech deficit I69.828
  - stroke NOS —*see* Sequelae, stroke NOS

Sequelae *(Continued)*
- dislocation — code to injury with seventh character S
- encephalitis or encephalomyelitis (conditions in G04) G09
  - in infectious disease NEC B94.8
  - viral B94.1
- external cause — code to injury with seventh character S
- foreign body entering natural orifice — code to injury with seventh character S
- fracture — code to injury with seventh character S
- frostbite — code to injury with seventh character S
- Hansen's disease B92
- hemorrhage
  - intracerebral I69.10
    - alteration of sensation I69.198
    - aphasia I69.120
    - apraxia I69.190
    - ataxia I69.193
    - cognitive deficits I69.11
    - disturbance of vision I69.198
    - dysarthria I69.122
    - dysphagia I69.191
    - dysphasia I69.121
    - facial droop I69.192
    - facial weakness I69.192
    - fluency disorder I69.123
    - hemiplegia I69.15-●
    - language deficit NEC I69.128
    - monoplegia
      - lower limb I69.14-●
      - upper limb I69.13-●
    - paralytic syndrome I69.16-●
    - specified effect NEC I69.198
    - speech deficit NEC I69.128
  - intracranial, nontraumatic NEC I69.20
    - alteration of sensation I69.298
    - aphasia I69.220
    - apraxia I69.290
    - ataxia I69.293
    - cognitive deficits I69.21
    - disturbance of vision I69.298
    - dysarthria I69.222
    - dysphagia I69.291
    - dysphasia I69.221
    - facial droop I69.292
    - facial weakness I69.292
    - fluency disorder I69.223
    - hemiplegia I69.25-●
    - language deficit NEC I69.228
    - monoplegia
      - lower limb I69.24-●
      - upper limb I69.23-●
    - paralytic syndrome I69.26-●
    - specified effect NEC I69.298
    - speech deficit NEC I69.228
  - subarachnoid I69.00
    - alteration of sensation I69.098
    - aphasia I69.020
    - apraxia I69.090
    - ataxia I69.093
    - cognitive deficits —*see* subcategory I69.01-●
    - disturbance of vision I69.098
    - dysarthria I69.022
    - dysphagia I69.091
    - dysphasia I69.021
    - facial droop I69.092
    - facial weakness I69.092
    - fluency disorder I69.023
    - hemiplegia I69.05-●
    - language deficit NEC I69.028
    - monoplegia
      - lower limb I69.04-●
      - upper limb I69.03-●
    - paralytic syndrome I69.06-●
    - specified effect NEC I69.098
    - speech deficit NEC I69.028

Sequelae *(Continued)*
- hepatitis, viral B94.2
- hyperalimentation E68
- infarction
  - cerebral I69.30
    - alteration of sensation I69.398
    - aphasia I69.320
    - apraxia I69.390
    - ataxia I69.393
    - cognitive deficits I69.31
    - disturbance of vision I69.398
    - dysarthria I69.322
    - dysphagia I69.391
    - dysphasia I69.321
    - facial droop I69.392
    - facial weakness I69.392
    - fluency disorder I69.323
    - hemiplegia I69.35-●
    - language deficit NEC I69.328
    - monoplegia
      - lower limb I69.34-●
      - upper limb I69.33-●
    - paralytic syndrome I69.36-●
    - specified effect NEC I69.398
    - speech deficit NEC I69.328
- infection, pyogenic, intracranial or intraspinal G09
- infectious disease B94.9
  - specified NEC B94.8
- injury — code to injury with seventh character S
- leprosy B92
- meningitis
  - bacterial (conditions in G00) G09
  - other or unspecified cause (conditions in G03) G09
- muscle (and tendon) injury — code to injury with seventh character S
- myelitis —*see* Sequelae, encephalitis
- niacin deficiency E64.8
- nutritional deficiency E64.9
  - specified NEC E64.8
- obstetrical condition O94
- parasitic disease B94.9
- phlebitis or thrombophlebitis of intracranial or intraspinal venous sinuses and veins (conditions in G08) G09
- poisoning — code to poisoning with seventh character S
  - nonmedicinal substance —*see* Sequelae, toxic effect, nonmedicinal substance
- poliomyelitis (acute) B91
- pregnancy O94
- protein-energy malnutrition E64.0
- puerperium O94
- rickets E64.3
- selenium deficiency E64.8
- sprain and strain — code to injury with seventh character S
- stroke NOS I69.30
  - alteration in sensation I69.398
  - aphasia I69.320
  - apraxia I69.390
  - ataxia I69.393
  - cognitive deficits I69.31
  - disturbance of vision I69.398
  - dysarthria I69.322
  - dysphagia I69.391
  - dysphasia I69.321
  - facial droop I69.392
  - facial weakness I69.392
  - hemiplegia I69.35-●
  - language deficit NEC I69.328
  - monoplegia
    - lower limb I69.34-●
    - upper limb I69.33-●
  - paralytic syndrome I69.36-●
  - specified effect NEC I69.398
  - speech deficit NEC I69.328
- tendon and muscle injury — code to injury with seventh character S

▶ New　　➡ Revised　　~~deleted~~ Deleted　　● Use Additional Character(s)

Sequelae *(Continued)*
  thiamine deficiency E64.8
  trachoma B94.0
  tuberculosis B90.9
    bones and joints B90.2
    central nervous system B90.0
    genitourinary B90.1
    pulmonary (respiratory) B90.9
    specified organs NEC B90.8
  viral
    encephalitis B94.1
    hepatitis B94.2
  vitamin deficiency NEC E64.8
    A E64.1
    B E64.8
    C E64.2
  wound, open — code to injury with seventh character S
Sequestration —*see also* Sequestrum
  disc —*see* Displacement, intervertebral disc
  lung, congenital Q33.2
Sequestrum
  bone —*see* Osteomyelitis, chronic
  dental M27.2
  jaw bone M27.2
  orbit —*see* Osteomyelitis, orbit
  sinus (accessory) (nasal) —*see* Sinusitis
Sequoiosis lung or pneumonitis J67.8
Serology for syphilis
  doubtful
    with signs or symptoms - code by site and stage under Syphilis
    follow-up of latent syphilis —*see* Syphilis, latent
  negative, with signs or symptoms — code by site and stage under Syphilis
  positive A53.0
    with signs or symptoms - code by site and stage under Syphilis
  reactivated A53.0
Seroma —*see also* Hematoma
  postprocedural —*see* Complication, postprocedural, seroma
  traumatic, secondary and recurrent T79.2
Seropurulent —*see* condition
Serositis, multiple K65.8
  pericardial I31.1
  peritoneal K65.8
Serous —*see* condition
Sertoli cell
  adenoma
    specified site —*see* Neoplasm, benign, by site
    unspecified site
      female D27.9
      male D29.20
  carcinoma
    specified site —*see* Neoplasm, malignant, by site
    unspecified site (male) C62.9-●
      female C56.9
  tumor
    with lipid storage
      specified site —*see* Neoplasm, benign, by site
      unspecified site
        female D27.9
        male D29.20
    specified site —*see* Neoplasm, benign, by site
    unspecified site
      female D27.9
      male D29.20
Sertoli-Leydig cell tumor —*see* Neoplasm, benign, by site
  specified site —*see* Neoplasm, benign, by site
  unspecified site
    female D27.9
    male D29.20

Serum
  allergy, allergic reaction —*see also* Reaction, serum T80.69
    shock —*see also* Shock, anaphylactic T80.59
  arthritis —*see also* Reaction, serum T80.69
  complication or reaction NEC —*see also* Reaction, serum T80.69
  disease NEC —*see also* Reaction, serum T80.69
  hepatitis —*see also* Hepatitis, viral, type B carrier (suspected) of B18.1
  intoxication —*see also* Reaction, serum T80.69
  neuritis —*see also* Reaction, serum T80.69
  neuropathy G61.1
  poisoning NEC —*see also* Reaction, serum T80.69
  rash NEC —*see also* Reaction, serum T80.69
  reaction NEC —*see also* Reaction, serum T80.69
  sickness NEC —*see also* Reaction, serum T80.69
  urticaria —*see also* Reaction, serum T80.69
Sesamoiditis M25.8-●
Sever's disease or osteochondrosis —*see* Osteochondrosis, juvenile, tarsus
Severe sepsis R65.20
  with septic shock R65.21
Sex
  chromosome mosaics Q97.8
    lines with various numbers of X chromosomes Q97.2
  education Z70.8
  reassignment surgery status Z87.890
Sextuplet pregnancy —*see* Pregnancy, sextuplet
Sexual
  function, disorder of (psychogenic) F52.9
  immaturity (female) (male) E30.0
  impotence (psychogenic) organic origin NEC —*see* Dysfunction, sexual, male
  precocity (constitutional) (cryptogenic) (female) (idiopathic) (male) E30.1
Sexuality, pathologic —*see* Deviation, sexual
Sézary disease C84.1-●
Shadow, lung R91.8
Shaking palsy or paralysis —*see* Parkinsonism
Shallowness, acetabulum —*see* Derangement, joint, specified type NEC, hip
Shaver's disease J63.1
Sheath (tendon) —*see* condition
Sheathing, retinal vessels H35.01-●
Shedding
  nail L60.8
  premature, primary (deciduous) teeth K00.6
Sheehan's disease or syndrome E23.0
Shelf, rectal K62.89
Shell teeth K00.5
Shellshock (current) F43.0
  lasting state —*see* Disorder, post-traumatic stress
Shield kidney Q63.1
Shift
  auditory threshold (temporary) H93.24-●
  mediastinal R93.89
Shifting sleep-work schedule (affecting sleep) G47.26
Shiga (-Kruse) dysentery A03.0
Shiga's bacillus A03.0
Shigella (dysentery) —*see* Dysentery, bacillary
Shigellosis A03.9
  Group A A03.0
  Group B A03.1
  Group C A03.2
  Group D A03.3
Shin splints S86.89
Shingles —*see* Herpes, zoster
Shipyard disease or eye B30.0
Shirodkar suture, in pregnancy —*see* Pregnancy, complicated by, incompetent cervix

Shock R57.9
  with ectopic or molar pregnancy O08.3
  adrenal (cortical) (Addisonian) E27.2
  adverse food reaction (anaphylactic) —*see* Shock, anaphylactic, due to food
  allergic —*see* Shock, anaphylactic
  anaphylactic T78.2
    chemical —*see* Table of Drugs and Chemicals
    due to drug or medicinal substance
      correct substance properly administered T88.6
      overdose or wrong substance given or taken (by accident) —*see* Table of Drugs and Chemicals, by drug, poisoning
    due to food (nonpoisonous) T78.00
      additives T78.06
      dairy products T78.07
      eggs T78.08
      fish T78.03
        shellfish T78.02
      fruit T78.04
      milk T78.07
      nuts T78.05
        multiple types T78.05
        peanuts T78.01
      peanuts T78.01
      seeds T78.05
      specified type NEC T78.09
      vegetable T78.04
    following sting(s) —*see* Venom
    immunization T80.52
    serum T80.59
      blood and blood products T80.51
      immunization T80.52
      specified NEC T80.59
      vaccination T80.52
  anaphylactoid —*see* Shock, anaphylactic
  anesthetic
    correct substance properly administered T88.2
    overdose or wrong substance given or taken —*see* Table of Drugs and Chemicals, by drug, poisoning
    specified anesthetic —*see* Table of Drugs and Chemicals, by drug, poisoning
  cardiogenic R57.0
  chemical substance —*see* Table of Drugs and Chemicals
  complicating ectopic or molar pregnancy O08.3
  culture —*see* Disorder, adjustment
  drug
    due to correct substance properly administered T88.6
    overdose or wrong substance given or taken (by accident) —*see* Table of Drugs and Chemicals, by drug, poisoning
  during or after labor and delivery O75.1
  electric T75.4
    (taser) T75.4
  endotoxic R65.21
    postprocedural (resulting from a procedure, not elsewhere classified) T81.12
  following
    ectopic or molar pregnancy O08.3
    injury (immediate) (delayed) T79.4
    labor and delivery O75.1
  food (anaphylactic) —*see* Shock, anaphylactic, due to food
  from electroshock gun (taser) T75.4
  gram-negative R65.21
    postprocedural (resulting from a procedure, not elsewhere classified) T81.12
  hematologic R57.8
  hemorrhagic R57.8
    surgery (intraoperative) (postoperative) T81.19
    trauma T79.4

Shock *(Continued)*
  hypovolemic R57.1
    surgical T81.19
    traumatic T79.4
  insulin E15
    therapeutic misadventure —*see*
      subcategory T38.3
  kidney N17.0
    traumatic (following crushing) T79.5
  lightning T75.01
  liver K72.00
  lung J80
  obstetric O75.1
    with ectopic or molar pregnancy O08.3
    following ectopic or molar pregnancy O08.3
  pleural (surgical) T81.19
    due to trauma T79.4
  postprocedural (postoperative) T81.10
    with ectopic or molar pregnancy O08.3
    cardiogenic T81.11
    endotoxic T81.12
    following ectopic or molar pregnancy O08.3
    gram-negative T81.12
    hypovolemic T81.19
    septic T81.12
    specified type NEC T81.19
  psychic F43.0
  septic (due to severe sepsis) R65.21
  specified NEC R57.8
  surgical T81.10
  taser gun (taser) T75.4
  therapeutic misadventure NEC T81.10
  thyroxin
    overdose or wrong substance given
      or taken —*see* Table of Drugs and
      Chemicals, by drug, poisoning
  toxic, syndrome A48.3
  transfusion —*see* Complications, transfusion
  traumatic (immediate) (delayed) T79.4
Shoemaker's chest M95.4
Short, shortening, shortness
  arm (acquired) —*see also* Deformity, limb,
    unequal length
    congenital Q71.81-•
    forearm —*see* Deformity, limb, unequal
      length
  bowel syndrome K91.2
  breath R06.02
  cervical (complicating pregnancy) O26.87-•
    non-gravid uterus N88.3
  common bile duct, congenital Q44.5
  cord (umbilical), complicating delivery O69.3
  cystic duct, congenital Q44.5
  esophagus (congenital) Q39.8
  femur (acquired) —*see* Deformity, limb,
    unequal length, femur
    congenital —*see* Defect, reduction, lower
      limb, longitudinal, femur
  frenum, frenulum, linguae (congenital) Q38.1
  hip (acquired) —*see also* Deformity, limb,
    unequal length
    congenital Q65.89
  leg (acquired) —*see also* Deformity, limb,
    unequal length
    congenital Q72.81-•
    lower leg —*see also* Deformity, limb,
      unequal length
  limbed stature, with immunodeficiency D82.2
  lower limb (acquired) —*see also* Deformity,
    limb, unequal length
    congenital Q72.81-•
  organ or site, congenital NEC —*see* Distortion
  palate, congenital Q38.5
  radius (acquired) —*see also* Deformity, limb,
    unequal length
    congenital —*see* Defect, reduction, upper
      limb, longitudinal, radius
  rib syndrome Q77.2
  stature (child) (hereditary) (idiopathic) NEC
    R62.52
    constitutional E34.3
    due to endocrine disorder E34.3
    Laron-type E34.3

Short, shortening, shortness *(Continued)*
  tendon —*see also* Contraction, tendon
    with contracture of joint —*see* Contraction,
      joint
    Achilles (acquired) M67.0-•
      congenital Q66.89
    congenital Q79.8
  thigh (acquired) —*see also* Deformity, limb,
    unequal length, femur
    congenital —*see* Defect, reduction, lower
      limb, longitudinal, femur
  tibialis anterior (tendon) —*see* Contraction,
    tendon
  umbilical cord
    complicating delivery O69.3
  upper limb, congenital —*see* Defect,
    reduction, upper limb, specified type
    NEC
  urethra N36.8
  uvula, congenital Q38.5
  vagina (congenital) Q52.4
Shortsightedness —*see* Myopia
Shoshin (acute fulminating beriberi) E51.11
Shoulder —*see* condition
Shovel-shaped incisors K00.2
Shower, thromboembolic —*see* Embolism
Shunt
  arterial-venous (dialysis) Z99.2
  arteriovenous, pulmonary (acquired) I28.0
    congenital Q25.72
  cerebral ventricle (communicating) in situ
    Z98.2
  surgical, prosthetic, with complications —*see*
    Complications, cardiovascular, device or
    implant Shutdown, renal N28.9
Shutdown, renal N28.9
Shy-Drager syndrome G90.3
Sialadenitis, sialadenosis (any gland) (chronic)
  (periodic) (suppurative) —*see* Sialoadenitis
Sialectasia K11.8
Sialidosis E77.1
Sialitis, silitis (any gland) (chronic)
  (suppurative) —*see* Sialoadenitis
Sialoadenitis (any gland) (periodic)
  (suppurative) K11.20
  acute K11.21
    recurrent K11.22
  chronic K11.23
Sialoadenopathy K11.9
Sialoangitis —*see* Sialoadenitis
Sialodochitis (fibrinosa) —*see* Sialoadenitis
Sialodocholithiasis K11.5
Sialolithiasis K11.5
Sialometaplasia, necrotizing K11.8
Sialorrhea —*see also* Ptyalism
  periodic —*see* Sialoadenitis
Sialosis K11.7
Siamese twin Q89.4
Sibling rivalry Z62.891
Sicard's syndrome G52.7
Sicca syndrome M35.00
  with
    keratoconjunctivitis M35.01
    lung involvement M35.02
    myopathy M35.03
    renal tubulo-interstitial disorders M35.04
  specified organ involvement NEC M35.09
Sick R69
  or handicapped person in family Z63.79
    needing care at home Z63.6
  sinus (syndrome) I49.5
Sick-euthyroid syndrome E07.81
Sickle-cell
  anemia —*see* Disease, sickle-cell
  ▶beta plus —*see* Disease, sickle-cell,
    thalassemia, beta plus
  ▶beta zero —*see* Disease, sickle-cell,
    thalassemia, beta zero
  trait D57.3
Sicklemia —*see also* Disease, sickle-cell
  trait D57.3

Sickness
  air (travel) T75.3
  airplane T75.3
  alpine T70.29
  altitude T70.20
  Andes T70.29
  aviator's T70.29
  balloon T70.29
  car T75.3
  compressed air T70.3
  decompression T70.3
  green D50.8
  milk —*see* Poisoning, food, noxious
  motion T75.3
  mountain T70.29
    acute D75.1
  protein —*see also* Reaction, serum T80.69
  radiation T66
  roundabout (motion) T75.3
  sea T75.3
  serum NEC —*see also* Reaction, serum T80.69
  sleeping (African) B56.9
    by Trypanosoma B56.9
      brucei
        gambiense B56.0
        rhodesiense B56.1
      East African B56.1
      Gambian B56.0
      Rhodesian B56.1
      West African B56.0
  swing (motion) T75.3
  train (railway) (travel) T75.3
  travel (any vehicle) T75.3
Sideropenia —*see* Anemia, iron deficiency
Siderosilicosis J62.8
Siderosis (lung) J63.4
  ▶brain G93.89
  eye (globe) —*see* Disorder, globe,
    degenerative, siderosis
Siemens' syndrome (ectodermal dysplasia) Q82.8
Sighing R06.89
  psychogenic F45.8
Sigmoid —*see also* condition
  flexure —*see* condition
  kidney Q63.1
Sigmoiditis —*see also* Enteritis K52.9
  infectious A09
  noninfectious K52.9
Silfversköld's syndrome Q78.9
Silicosiderosis J62.8
Silicosis, silicotic (simple) (complicated) J62.8
  with tuberculosis J65
Silicotuberculosis J65
Silo-fillers' disease J68.8
  bronchitis J68.0
  pneumonitis J68.0
  pulmonary edema J68.1
Silver's syndrome Q87.19
Simian malaria B53.1
Simmonds' cachexia or disease E23.0
Simons' disease or syndrome (progressive
  lipodystrophy) E88.1
Simple, simplex —*see* condition
Simulation, conscious (of illness) Z76.5
Simultanagnosia (asimultagnosia) R48.3
Sin Nombre virus disease (Hantavirus)
  (cardio)-pulmonary syndrome) B33.4
Sinding-Larsen disease or osteochondrosis —
  see Osteochondrosis, juvenile, patella
Singapore hemorrhagic fever A91
Singer's node or nodule J38.2
Single
  atrium Q21.2
  coronary artery Q24.5
  umbilical artery Q27.0
  ventricle Q20.4
Singultus R06.6
  epidemicus B33.0
Sinus —*see also* Fistula
  abdominal K63.89
  arrest I45.5

▶ New   ⇒ Revised   ~~deleted~~ Deleted   • Use Additional Character(s)

Sinus *(Continued)*
  arrhythmia I49.8
  bradycardia R00.1
  branchial cleft (internal) (external) Q18.0
  coccygeal —*see* Sinus, pilonidal
  dental K04.6
  dermal (congenital) Q06.8
    with abscess Q06.8
    coccygeal, pilonidal —*see* Sinus, coccygeal
  infected, skin NEC L08.89
  marginal, ruptured or bleeding —*see*
      Hemorrhage, antepartum, specified
      cause NEC
  medial, face and neck Q18.8
  pause I45.5
  pericranii Q01.9
  pilonidal (infected) (rectum) L05.92
    with abscess L05.02
  preauricular Q18.1
  rectovaginal N82.3
  Rokitansky-Aschoff (gallbladder) K82.8
  sacrococcygeal (dermoid) (infected) —*see*
      Sinus, pilonidal
  tachycardia R00.0
    paroxysmal I47.1
  tarsi syndrome M25.57-•
  testis N50.89
  tract (postinfective) —*see* Fistula
  urachus Q64.4
Sinusitis (accessory) (chronic) (hyperplastic)
    (nasal) (nonpurulent) (purulent) J32.9
  acute J01.90
    ethmoidal J01.20
      recurrent J01.21
    frontal J01.10
      recurrent J01.11
    involving more than one sinus, other than
        pansinusitis J01.80
      recurrent J01.81
    maxillary J01.00
      recurrent J01.01
    pansinusitis J01.40
      recurrent J01.41
    recurrent J01.91
    specified NEC J01.80
      recurrent J01.81
    sphenoidal J01.30
      recurrent J01.31
  allergic —*see* Rhinitis, allergic
  due to high altitude T70.1
  ethmoidal J32.2
    acute J01.20
      recurrent J01.21
  frontal J32.1
    acute J01.10
      recurrent J01.11
  influenzal —*see* Influenza, with, respiratory
      manifestations NEC
  involving more than one sinus but not
      pansinusitis J32.8
    acute J01.80
      recurrent J01.81
  maxillary J32.0
    acute J01.00
      recurrent J01.01
  sphenoidal J32.3
    acute J01.30
      recurrent J01.31
  tuberculous, any sinus A15.8
Sinusitis-bronchiectasis-situs inversus
    (syndrome) (triad) Q89.3
Sipple's syndrome E31.22
Sirenomelia (syndrome) Q87.2
Siriasis T67.01
Sirkari's disease B55.0
Siti A65
Situation, psychiatric F99
Situational
  disturbance (transient) —*see* Disorder,
      adjustment
    acute F43.0

Situational *(Continued)*
  maladjustment —*see* Disorder, adjustment
  reaction —*see* Disorder, adjustment
    acute F43.0
Situs inversus or transversus (abdominalis)
    (thoracis) Q89.3
Sixth disease B08.20
  due to human herpesvirus 6 B08.21
  due to human herpesvirus 7 B08.22
Sjögren-Larsson syndrome Q87.19
Sjögren's syndrome or disease —*see* Sicca
    syndrome
Skeletal —*see* condition
Skene's gland —*see* condition
Skenitis —*see* Urethritis
Skerljevo A65
Skevas-Zerfus disease —*see* Toxicity, venom,
    marine animal, sea anemone
Skin —*see also* condition
  clammy R23.1
  donor —*see* Donor, skin
  hidebound M35.9
Slate-dressers' or slate-miners' lung J62.8
Sleep
  apnea —*see* Apnea, sleep
  deprivation Z72.820
  disorder or disturbance G47.9
    child F51.9
    nonorganic origin F51.9
    specified NEC G47.8
  disturbance G47.9
    nonorganic origin F51.9
  drunkenness F51.9
  rhythm inversion G47.2-•
  terrors F51.4
  walking F51.3
    hysterical F44.89
Sleep hygiene
  abuse Z72.821
  inadequate Z72.821
  poor Z72.821
Sleeping sickness —*see* Sickness, sleeping
Sleeplessness —*see* Insomnia
  menopausal N95.11
Sleep-wake schedule disorder G47.20
Slim disease (in HIV infection) B20
Slipped, slipping
  epiphysis (traumatic) —*see also*
      Osteochondropathy, specified type
      NEC
    capital femoral (traumatic)
      acute (on chronic) S79.01-•
    current traumatic - code as Fracture,
        by site
    upper femoral (nontraumatic) M93.00-•
      acute M93.01-•
        on chronic M93.03-•
      chronic M93.02-•
  intervertebral disc —*see* Displacement,
      intervertebral disc
  ligature, umbilical P51.8
  patella —*see* Disorder, patella, derangement
      NEC
  rib M89.8X8
  sacroiliac joint —*see* subcategory M53.2
  tendon —*see* Disorder, tendon
  ulnar nerve, nontraumatic —*see* Lesion,
      nerve, ulnar
  vertebra NEC —*see* Spondylolisthesis
Slocumb's syndrome E27.0
Sloughing (multiple) (phagedena) (skin) —*see
    also* Gangrene
  abscess —*see* Abscess
  appendix K38.8
  fascia —*see* Disorder, soft tissue, specified
      type NEC
  scrotum N50.89
  tendon —*see* Disorder, tendon
  transplanted organ —*see* Rejection,
      transplant
  ulcer —*see* Ulcer, skin

Slow
  feeding, newborn P92.2
  flow syndrome, coronary I20.8
  heart(beat) R00.1
Slowing, urinary stream R39.198
Sluder's neuralgia (syndrome) G44.89
Slurred, slurring speech R47.81
Small (ness)
  for gestational age —*see* Small for dates
  introitus, vagina N89.6
  kidney (unknown cause) N27.9
    bilateral N27.1
    unilateral N27.0
  ovary (congenital) Q50.39
  pelvis
    with disproportion (fetopelvic) O33.1
      causing obstructed labor O65.1
  uterus N85.8
  white kidney N03.9
Small-and-light-for-dates —*see* Small for
    dates
Small-for-dates (infant) P05.10
  with weight of
    499 grams or less P05.11
    500-749 grams P05.12
    750-999 grams P05.13
    1000-1249 grams P05.14
    1250-1499 grams P05.15
    1500-1749 grams P05.16
    1750-1999 grams P05.17
    2000-2499 grams P05.18
    2500 grams and over P05.19
  specified NEC P05.19
Smallpox B03
Smearing, fecal R15.1
▶SMEI (severe myoclonic epilepsy in infancy)
    G40.83-•
Smith-Lemli-Opitz syndrome E78.72
Smith's fracture S52.54-•
Smoker —*see* Dependence, drug, nicotine
Smoker's
  bronchitis J41.0
  cough J41.0
  palate K13.24
  throat J31.2
  tongue K13.24
Smoking
  passive Z77.22
Smothering spells R06.81
Snaggle teeth, tooth M26.39
Snapping
  finger —*see* Trigger finger
  hip —*see* Derangement, joint, specified type
      NEC, hip
    involving the iliotiblial band M76.3-•
  knee —*see* Derangement, knee
    involving the iliotiblial band M76.3-•
Sneddon-Wilkinson disease or syndrome
    (sub-corneal pustular dermatosis)
    L13.1
Sneezing (intractable) R06.7
Sniffing
  cocaine
    abuse —*see* Abuse, drug, cocaine
    dependence —*see* Dependence, drug,
        cocaine
  gasoline
    abuse —*see* Abuse, drug, inhalant
    dependence —*see* Dependence, drug,
        inhalant
  glue (airplane)
    abuse —*see* Abuse, drug, inhalant
    drug dependence —*see* Dependence, drug,
        inhalant
Sniffles
  newborn P28.89
Snoring R06.83
Snow blindness —*see* Photokeratitis
Snuffles (non-syphilitic) R06.5
  newborn P28.89
  syphilitic (infant) A50.05 *[J99]*

Social
  exclusion Z60.4
    due to discrimination or persecution (perceived) Z60.5
  migrant Z59.0
    acculturation difficulty Z60.3
  rejection Z60.4
    due to discrimination or persecution Z60.5
  role conflict NEC Z73.5
  skills inadequacy NEC Z73.4
  transplantation Z60.3
Sodoku A25.0
Soemmerring's ring —see Cataract, secondary
Soft —see also condition
  nails L60.3
Softening
  bone —see Osteomalacia
  brain (necrotic) (progressive) G93.89
    congenital Q04.8
    embolic I63.4-●
    hemorrhagic —see Hemorrhage, intracranial, intracerebral
    occlusive I63.5-●
    thrombotic I63.3-●
  cartilage M94.2-●
    patella M22.4-●
  cerebellar —see Softening, brain
  cerebral —see Softening, brain
  cerebrospinal —see Softening, brain
  myocardial, heart —see Degeneration, myocardial
  spinal cord G95.89
  stomach K31.89
Soldier's
  heart F45.8
  patches I31.0
Solitary
  cyst, kidney N28.1
  kidney, congenital Q60.0
Solvent abuse —see Abuse, drug, inhalant
  dependence —see Dependence, drug, inhalant
Somatization reaction, somatic reaction —see Disorder, somatoform
Somnambulism F51.3
  hysterical F44.89
Somnolence R40.0
  nonorganic origin F51.11
Sonne dysentery A03.3
Soor B37.0
Sore
  bed —see Ulcer, pressure, by site
  chiclero B55.1
  Delhi B55.1
  desert —see Ulcer, skin
  eye H57.1-●
  Lahore B55.1
  mouth K13.79
    canker K12.0
  muscle M79.10
  Naga —see Ulcer, skin
  of skin —see Ulcer, skin - oriental B55.1
  pressure —see Ulcer, pressure, by site
  skin L98.9
  soft A57
  throat (acute) —see also Pharyngitis
    with influenza, flu, or grippe —see Influenza, with, respiratory manifestations NEC
    chronic J31.2
    coxsackie (virus) B08.5
    diphtheritic A36.0
    herpesviral B00.2
    influenzal —see Influenza, with, respiratory manifestations NEC
    septic J02.0
    streptococcal (ulcerative) J02.0
    viral NEC J02.8
      coxsackie B08.5
  tropical —see Ulcer, skin
  veldt —see Ulcer, skin

Soto's syndrome (cerebral gigantism) Q87.3
South African cardiomyopathy syndrome I42.8
Southeast Asian hemorrhagic fever A91
Spacing
  abnormal, tooth, teeth, fully erupted M26.30
  excessive, tooth, fully erupted M26.32
Spade-like hand (congenital) Q68.1
Spading nail L60.8
  congenital Q84.6
Spanish collar N47.1
Sparganosis B70.1
Spasm(s), spastic, spasticity —see also condition R25.2
  accommodation —see Spasm, of accommodation
  ampulla of Vater K83.4
  anus, ani (sphincter) (reflex) K59.4
    psychogenic F45.8
  artery I73.9
    cerebral G45.9
  Bell's G51.3-●
  bladder (sphincter, external or internal) N32.89
    psychogenic F45.8
  bronchus, bronchiole J98.01
  cardia K22.0
  cardiac I20.1
  carpopedal —see Tetany
  cerebral (arteries) (vascular) G45.9
  cervix, complicating delivery O62.4
  ciliary body (of accommodation) —see Spasm, of accommodation
  colon —see also Irritable, bowel K58.9
    with diarrhea K58.0
    psychogenic F45.8
  common duct K83.8
  compulsive —see Tic
  conjugate H51.8
  coronary (artery) I20.1
  diaphragm (reflex) R06.6
    epidemic B33.0
    psychogenic F45.8
  duodenum K59.89
  epidemic diaphragmatic (transient) B33.0
  esophagus (diffuse) K22.4
    psychogenic F45.8
  facial G51.3-●
  fallopian tube N83.8
  gastrointestinal (tract) K31.89
    psychogenic F45.8
  glottis J38.5
    hysterical F44.4
    psychogenic F45.8
      conversion reaction F44.4
    reflex through recurrent laryngeal nerve J38.5
  habit —see Tic
  heart I20.1
  hemifacial (clonic) G51.3-●
  hourglass —see Contraction, hourglass
  hysterical F44.4
  infantile —see Epilepsy, spasms
  inferior oblique, eye H51.8
  intestinal —see also Syndrome, irritable bowel K58.9
    psychogenic F45.8
  larynx, laryngeal J38.5
    hysterical F44.4
    psychogenic F45.8
      conversion reaction F44.4
  levator palpebrae superioris —see Disorder, eyelid function
  muscle NEC M62.838
    back M62.830
  nerve, trigeminal G51.0
  nervous F45.8
  nodding F98.4
  occupational F48.8
  oculogyric H51.8
    psychogenic F45.8
  of accommodation H52.53-●

Spasm(s), spastic, spasticity (Continued)
  ophthalmic artery —see Occlusion, artery, retina
  perineal, female N94.89
  peroneo-extensor —see also Deformity, limb, flat foot
  pharynx (reflex) J39.2
    hysterical F45.8
    psychogenic F45.8
  psychogenic F45.8
  pylorus NEC K31.3
    adult hypertrophic K31.89
    congenital or infantile Q40.0
    psychogenic F45.8
  rectum (sphincter) K59.4
    psychogenic F45.8
  retinal (artery) —see Occlusion, artery, retina
  sigmoid —see also Syndrome, irritable bowel K58.9
    psychogenic F45.8
  sphincter of Oddi K83.4
  stomach K31.89
    neurotic F45.8
  throat J39.2
    hysterical F45.8
    psychogenic F45.8
  tic F95.9
    chronic F95.1
    transient of childhood F95.0
  tongue K14.8
  torsion (progressive) G24.1
  trigeminal nerve —see Neuralgia, trigeminal
  ureter N13.5
  urethra (sphincter) N35.919
  uterus N85.8
    complicating labor O62.4
  vagina N94.2
    psychogenic F52.5
  vascular I73.9
  vasomotor I73.9
  vein NEC I87.8
  viscera —see Pain, abdominal
Spasmodic —see condition
Spasmophilia —see Tetany
Spasmus nutans F98.4
Spastic, spasticity —see also Spasm
  child (cerebral) (congenital) (paralysis) G80.1
Speaker's throat R49.8
Specific, specified —see condition
Speech
  defect, disorder, disturbance, impediment — see Disorder, speech R47.9
    psychogenic, in childhood and adolescence F98.8
    slurring R47.81
    specified NEC R47.89
Spencer's disease A08.19
Spens' syndrome (syncope with heart block) I45.9
Sperm counts (fertility testing) Z31.41
  postvasectomy Z30.8
  reversal Z31.42
Spermatic cord —see condition
Spermatocele N43.40
  congenital Q55.4
  multiple N43.42
  single N43.41
Spermatocystitis N49.0
Spermatocytoma C62.9-●
  specified site —see Neoplasm, malignant, by site
Spermatorrhea N50.89
Sphacelus —see Gangrene
Sphenoidal —see condition
Sphenoiditis (chronic) —see Sinusitis, sphenoidal
Sphenopalatine ganglion neuralgia G90.09
Sphericity, increased, lens (congenital) Q12.4

▶ New   ⇒ Revised   ~~deleted~~ Deleted   ● Use Additional Character(s)

Spherocytosis (congenital) (familial)
(hereditary) D58.0
 hemoglobin disease D58.0
 sickle-cell (disease) D57.8-•
Spherophakia Q12.4
Sphincter —see condition
Sphincteritis, sphincter of Oddi —see
 Cholangitis
Sphingolipidosis E75.3
 specified NEC E75.29
Sphingomyelinosis E75.3
Spicule tooth K00.2
Spider
 bite —see Toxicity, venom, spider
 ▶nonvenomous —see Bite, by site,
  superficial, insect
 fingers —see Syndrome, Marfan's
 nevus I78.1
 toes —see Syndrome, Marfan's
 vascular I78.1
Spiegler-Fendt
 benign lymphocytoma L98.8
 sarcoid L08.89
Spielmeyer-Vogt disease E75.4
Spina bifida (aperta) Q05.9
 with hydrocephalus NEC Q05.4
 cervical Q05.5
  with hydrocephalus Q05.0
 dorsal Q05.6
  with hydrocephalus Q05.1
 lumbar Q05.7
  with hydrocephalus Q05.2
 lumbosacral Q05.7
  with hydrocephalus Q05.2
 occulta Q76.0
 sacral Q05.8
  with hydrocephalus Q05.3
 thoracic Q05.6
  with hydrocephalus Q05.1
 thoracolumbar Q05.6
  with hydrocephalus Q05.1
Spindle, Krukenberg's —see Pigmentation,
 cornea, posterior
Spine, spinal —see condition
Spiradenoma (eccrine) —see Neoplasm, skin,
 benign
Spirillosis A25.0
Spirillum
 minus A25.0
 obermeieri infection A68.0
Spirochetal —see condition
Spirochetosis A69.9
 arthritic, arthritica A69.9
 bronchopulmonary A69.8
 icterohemorrhagic A27.0
 lung A69.8
Spirometrosis B70.1
Spitting blood —see Hemoptysis
Splanchnoptosis K63.4
Spleen, splenic —see condition
Splenectasis —see Splenomegaly
Splenitis (interstitial) (malignant) (nonspecific)
 D73.89
 malarial —see also Malaria B54 [D77]
 tuberculous A18.85
Splenocele D73.89
Splenomegaly, splenomegalia (Bengal)
 (cryptogenic) (idiopathic) (tropical) R16.1
 with hepatomegaly R16.2
 cirrhotic D73.2
 congenital Q89.09
 congestive, chronic D73.2
 Egyptian B65.1
 Gaucher's E75.22
 malarial —see also Malaria B54 [D77]
 neutropenic D73.81
 Niemann-Pick —see Niemann-Pick disease or
  syndrome
 siderotic D73.2
 syphilitic A52.79
  congenital (early) A50.08 [D77]

Splenopathy D73.9
Splenoptosis D73.89
Splenosis D73.89
Splinter —see Foreign body, superficial, by site
Split, splitting
 foot Q72.7-•
 hand Q71.6
 heart sounds R01.2
 lip, congenital —see Cleft, lip
 nails L60.3
 urinary stream R39.13
Spondylarthrosis —see Spondylosis
Spondylitis (chronic) —see also Spondylopathy,
 inflammatory
 ankylopoietica —see Spondylitis, ankylosing
 ankylosing (chronic) M45.9
  with lung involvement M45.9 [J99]
  cervical region M45.2
  cervicothoracic region M45.3
  juvenile M08.1
  lumbar region M45.6
  lumbosacral region M45.7
  multiple sites M45.0
  occipito-atlanto-axial region M45.1
  sacrococcygeal region M45.8
  thoracic region M45.4
  thoracolumbar region M45.5
 atrophic (ligamentous) —see Spondylitis,
  ankylosing
 deformans (chronic) —see Spondylosis
 gonococcal A54.41
 gouty —see also Gout, by type, vertebrae
  M10.08
 in (due to)
  brucellosis A23.9 [M49.80]
   cervical region A23.9 [M49.82]
   cervicothoracic region A23.9 [M49.83]
   lumbar region A23.9 [M49.86]
   lumbosacral region A23.9 [M49.87]
   multiple sites A23.9 [M49.89]
   occipito-atlanto-axial region A23.9
    [M49.81]
   sacrococcygeal region A23.9 [M49.88]
   thoracic region A23.9 [M49.84]
   thoracolumbar region A23.9 [M49.85]
  enterobacteria —see also subcategory M49.8
   A04.9
  tuberculosis A18.01
 infectious NEC —see Spondylopathy,
  infective
 juvenile ankylosing (chronic) M08.1
 Kümmell's —see Spondylopathy, traumatic
 Marie-Strümpell —see Spondylitis,
  ankylosing
 muscularis —see Spondylopathy, specified
  NEC
 psoriatic L40.53
 rheumatoid —see Spondylitis, ankylosing
 rhizomelica —see Spondylitis, ankylosing
 sacroiliac NEC M46.1
 senescent, senile —see Spondylosis
 traumatic (chronic) or post-traumatic —see
  Spondylopathy, traumatic
 tuberculous A18.01
 typhosa A01.05
▶Spondyloarthritis [new]
 ▶axial —see also Spondlyitis, ankylosing
  ▶non-radiographic M46.80
   ▶cervical M46.82
   ▶cervicothoracic M46.83
   ▶lumbar M46.84
   ▶lumbosacral M46.87
   ▶multiple sites M46.89
   ▶occipito-atlanto-axial region M46.81
   ▶sacral and sacrococcygeal M46.88
   ▶thoracic M46.84
   ▶thoracolumbar M46.85
Spondylolisthesis (acquired) (degenerative)
 M43.10
 with disproportion (fetopelvic) O33.0
  causing obstructed labor O65.0

Spondylolisthesis (Continued)
 cervical region M43.12
 cervicothoracic region M43.13
 congenital Q76.2
 lumbar region M43.16
 lumbosacral region M43.17
 multiple sites M43.19
 occipito-atlanto-axial region M43.11
 sacrococcygeal region M43.18
 thoracic region M43.14
 thoracolumbar region M43.15
 traumatic (old) M43.10
  acute
   fifth cervical (displaced) S12.430
    nondisplaced S12.431
    specified type NEC (displaced)
     S12.450
     nondisplaced S12.451
    type III S12.44
   fourth cervical (displaced) S12.330
    nondisplaced S12.331
    specified type NEC (displaced)
     S12.350
     nondisplaced S12.351
    type III S12.34
   second cervical (displaced) S12.130
    nondisplaced S12.131
    specified type NEC (displaced)
     S12.150
     nondisplaced S12.151
    type III S12.14
   seventh cervical (displaced) S12.630
    nondisplaced S12.631
    specified type NEC (displaced)
     S12.650
     nondisplaced S12.651
    type III S12.64
   sixth cervical (displaced) S12.530
    nondisplaced S12.531
    specified type NEC (displaced)
     S12.550
     nondisplaced S12.551
    type III S12.54
   third cervical (displaced) S12.230
    nondisplaced S12.231
    specified type NEC (displaced)
     S12.250
     nondisplaced S12.251
    type III S12.24
Spondylolysis (acquired) M43.00
 cervical region M43.02
 cervicothoracic region M43.03
 congenital Q76.2
 lumbar region M43.06
 lumbosacral region M43.07
  with disproportion (fetopelvic) O33.0
   causing obstructed labor O65.8
 multiple sites M43.09
 occipito-atlanto-axial region M43.01
 sacrococcygeal region M43.08
 thoracic region M43.04
 thoracolumbar region M43.05
Spondylopathy M48.9
 infective NEC M46.50
  cervical region M46.52
  cervicothoracic region M46.53
  lumbar region M46.56
  lumbosacral region M46.57
  multiple sites M46.59
  occipito-atlanto-axial region M46.51
  sacrococcygeal region M46.58
  thoracic region M46.54
  thoracolumbar region M46.55
 inflammatory M46.90
  cervical region M46.92
  cervicothoracic region M46.93
  lumbar region M46.96
  lumbosacral region M46.97
  multiple sites M46.99
  occipito-atlanto-axial region M46.91
  sacrococcygeal region M46.98

Spondylopathy *(Continued)*
  inflammatory *(Continued)*
    specified type NEC M46.80
      cervical region M46.82
      cervicothoracic region M46.83
      lumbar region M46.86
      lumbosacral region M46.87
      multiple sites M46.89
      occipito-atlanto-axial region M46.81
      sacrococcygeal region M46.88
      thoracic region M46.84
      thoracolumbar region M46.85
    thoracic region M46.94
    thoracolumbar region M46.95
  neuropathic, in
    syringomyelia and syringobulbia G95.0
    tabes dorsalis A52.11
  specified NEC —*see* subcategory M48.8
  traumatic M48.30
    cervical region M48.32
    cervicothoracic region M48.33
    lumbar region M48.36
    lumbosacral region M48.37
    occipito-atlanto-axial region M48.31
    sacrococcygeal region M48.38
    thoracic region M48.34
    thoracolumbar region M48.35
Spondylosis M47.9
  with
    disproportion (fetopelvic) O33.0
      causing obstructed labor O65.0
    myelopathy NEC M47.10
      cervical region M47.12
      cervicothoracic region M47.13
      lumbar region M47.16
      occipito-atlanto-axial region M47.11
      thoracic region M47.14
      thoracolumbar region M47.15
    radiculopathy M47.20
      cervical region M47.22
      cervicothoracic region M47.23
      lumbar region M47.26
      lumbosacral region M47.27
      occipito-atlanto-axial region M47.21
      sacrococcygeal region M47.28
      thoracic region M47.24
      thoracolumbar region M47.25
  without myelopathy or radiculopathy
    M47.819
    cervical region M47.812
    cervicothoracic region M47.813
    lumbar region M47.816
    lumbosacral region M47.817
    occipito-atlanto-axial region M47.811
    sacrococcygeal region M47.818
    thoracic region M47.814
    thoracolumbar region M47.815
  specified NEC M47.899
    cervical region M47.892
    cervicothoracic region M47.893
    lumbar region M47.896
    lumbosacral region M47.897
    occipito-atlanto-axial region M47.891
    sacrococcygeal region M47.898
    thoracic region M47.894
    thoracolumbar region M47.895
  traumatic —*see* Spondylopathy, traumatic
Sponge
  inadvertently left in operation wound —*see*
    Foreign body, accidentally left during a
    procedure
  kidney (medullary) Q61.5
Sponge-diver's disease —*see* Toxicity, venom,
  marine animal, sea anemone
Spongioblastoma (any type) —*see* Neoplasm,
  malignant, by site
  specified site —*see* Neoplasm, malignant, by
    site
  unspecified site C71.9
Spongioneuroblastoma —*see* Neoplasm,
  malignant, by site

Spontaneous —*see also* condition
  fracture (cause unknown) —*see* Fracture,
    pathological
Spoon nail L60.3
  congenital Q84.6
Sporadic —*see* condition
Sporothrix schenckii infection —*see*
  Sporotrichosis
Sporotrichosis B42.9
  arthritis B42.82
  disseminated B42.7
  generalized B42.7
  lymphocutaneous (fixed) (progressive)
    B42.1
  pulmonary B42.0
  specified NEC B42.89
Spots, spotting (in) (of)
  Bitot's —*see also* Pigmentation, conjunctiva
    in the young child E50.1
    vitamin A deficiency E50.1
  café, au lait L81.3
  Cayenne pepper I78.1
  cotton wool, retina —*see* Occlusion, artery,
    retina
  de Morgan's (senile angiomas) I78.1
  Fuchs' black (myopic) —*see also* Myopia,
    degenerative H44.2-●
  intermenstrual (regular) N92.0
    irregular N92.1
  Koplik's B05.9
  liver L81.4
  pregnancy O26.85-●
  purpuric R23.3
  ruby I78.1
Spotted fever —*see* Fever, spotted A77.9
Sprain (joint) (ligament)
  acromioclavicular joint or ligament S43.5-●
  ankle S93.40-●
    calcaneofibular ligament S93.41-●
    deltoid ligament S93.42-●
    internal collateral ligament —*see* Sprain,
      ankle, specified ligament NEC
    specified ligament NEC S93.49-●
    talofibular ligament —*see* Sprain, ankle,
      specified ligament NEC
    tibiofibular ligament S93.43-●
  anterior longitudinal, cervical S13.4
  atlas, atlanto-axial, atlanto-occipital S13.4
  breast bone —*see* Sprain, sternum
  calcaneofibular —*see* Sprain, ankle
  carpal —*see* Sprain, wrist
  carpometacarpal —*see* Sprain, hand, specified
    site NEC
  cartilage
    costal S23.41
    semilunar (knee) —*see* Sprain, knee,
      specified site NEC
      with current tear —*see* Tear, meniscus
    thyroid region S13.5
    xiphoid —*see* Sprain, sternum
  cervical, cervicodorsal, cervicothoracic S13.4
  chondrosternal S23.421
  coracoclavicular S43.8-●
  coracohumeral S43.41-●
  coronary, knee —*see* Sprain, knee, specified
    site NEC
  costal cartilage S23.41
  cricoarytenoid articulation or ligament S13.5
  cricothyroid articulation S13.5
  cruciate, knee —*see* Sprain, knee, cruciate
  deltoid, ankle —*see* Sprain, ankle
  dorsal (spine) S23.3
  elbow S53.40-●
    radial collateral ligament S53.43-●
    radiohumeral S53.41-●
    rupture
      radial collateral ligament —*see* Rupture,
        traumatic, ligament, radial
        collateral
      ulnar collateral ligament —*see* Rupture,
        traumatic, ligament, ulnar collateral

Sprain *(Continued)*
  elbow *(Continued)*
    specified type NEC S53.49-●
    ulnar collateral ligament S53.44-●
    ulnohumeral S53.42-●
  femur, head —*see* Sprain, hip
  fibular collateral, knee —*see* Sprain, knee,
    collateral
  fibulocalcaneal —*see* Sprain, ankle
  finger(s) S63.61-●
    index S63.61-●
    interphalangeal (joint) S63.63-●
      index S63.63-●
      little S63.63-●
      middle S63.63-●
      ring S63.63-●
    little S63.61-●
    metacarpophalangeal (joint) S63.65-●
    middle S63.61-●
    ring S63.61-●
    specified site NEC S63.69-●
      index S63.69-●
      little S63.69-●
      middle S63.69-●
      ring S63.69-●
  foot S93.60-●
    specified ligament NEC S93.69-●
    tarsal ligament S93.61-●
    tarsometatarsal ligament S93.62-●
    toe —*see* Sprain, toe
  hand S63.9-●
    finger —*see* Sprain, finger
    specified site NEC —*see* subcategory
      S63.8
    thumb —*see* Sprain, thumb
  head S03.9
  hip S73.10-●
    iliofemoral ligament S73.11-●
    ischiocapsular (ligament) S73.12-●
    specified NEC S73.19-●
  iliofemoral —*see* Sprain, hip
  innominate
    acetabulum —*see* Sprain, hip
    sacral junction S33.6
  internal
    collateral, ankle —*see* Sprain, ankle
    semilunar cartilage —*see* Sprain, knee,
      specified site NEC
  interphalangeal
    finger —*see* Sprain, finger, interphalangeal
      (joint)
    toe —*see* Sprain, toe, interphalangeal joint
  ischiocapsular —*see* Sprain, hip
  ischiofemoral —*see* Sprain, hip
  jaw (articular disc) (cartilage) (meniscus)
    S03.4-●
    old M26.69
  knee S83.9-●
    collateral ligament S83.40-●
      lateral (fibular) S83.42-●
      medial (tibial) S83.41-●
    cruciate ligament S83.50-●
      anterior S83.51-●
      posterior S83.52-●
    lateral (fibular) collateral ligament S83.42-●
    medial (tibial) collateral ligament S83.41-●
    patellar ligament S76.11-●
    specified site NEC S83.8X-●
    superior tibiofibular joint (ligament)
      S83.6-●
  lateral collateral, knee —*see* Sprain, knee,
    collateral
  lumbar (spine) S33.5
  lumbosacral S33.9
  mandible (articular disc) S03.4-●
    old M26.69
  medial collateral, knee —*see* Sprain, knee,
    collateral
  meniscus
    jaw S03.4-●
    old M26.69

▶ New   ⟹ Revised   ~~deleted~~ Deleted   ● Use Additional Character(s)

Sprain *(Continued)*
  meniscus *(Continued)*
    knee —*see* Sprain, knee, specified site NEC
      with current tear —*see* Tear, meniscus
        old —*see* Derangement, knee,
          meniscus, due to old tear
    mandible S03.4-•
      old M26.69
    metacarpal (distal) (proximal) —*see* Sprain,
      hand, specified site NEC
    metacarpophalangeal —*see* Sprain, finger,
      metacarpophalangeal (joint)
    metatarsophalangeal —*see* Sprain, toe,
      metatarsophalangeal joint
    midcarpal —*see* Sprain, hand, specified site
      NEC
    midtarsal —*see* Sprain, foot, specified site
      NEC
    neck S13.9
      anterior longitudinal cervical ligament
        S13.4
      atlanto-axial joint S13.4
      atlanto-occipital joint S13.4
      cervical spine S13.4
      cricoarytenoid ligament S13.5
      cricothyroid ligament S13.5
      specified site NEC S13.8
      thyroid region (cartilage) S13.5
    nose S03.8
    orbicular, hip —*see* Sprain, hip
    patella —*see* Sprain, knee, specified site
      NEC
    patellar ligament S76.11-•
    pelvis NEC S33.8
    phalanx
      finger —*see* Sprain, finger
      toe —*see* Sprain, toe
    pubofemoral —*see* Sprain, hip
    radiocarpal —*see* Sprain, wrist
    radiohumeral —*see* Sprain, elbow
    radius, collateral —*see* Rupture, traumatic,
      ligament, radial collateral
    rib (cage) S23.41
    rotator cuff (capsule) S43.42-•
    sacroiliac (region)
      chronic or old —*see* subcategory M53.2
      joint S33.6
    scaphoid (hand) —*see* Sprain, hand, specified
      site NEC
    scapula (r) —*see* Sprain, shoulder girdle,
      specified site NEC
    semilunar cartilage (knee) —*see* Sprain, knee,
      specified site NEC
      with current tear —*see* Tear, meniscus
        old —*see* Derangement, knee, meniscus,
          due to old tear
    shoulder joint S43.40-•
      acromioclavicular joint (ligament) —*see*
        Sprain, acromioclavicular joint
      blade —*see* Sprain, shoulder, girdle,
        specified site NEC
      coracoclavicular joint (ligament) —*see*
        Sprain, coracoclavicular joint
      coracohumeral ligament —*see* Sprain,
        coracohumeral joint
      girdle S43.9-•
        specified site NEC S43.8-•
      rotator cuff —*see* Sprain, rotator cuff
      specified site NEC S43.49-•
      sternoclavicular joint (ligament) —*see*
        Sprain, sternoclavicular joint
    spine
      cervical S13.4
      lumbar S33.5
      thoracic S23.3
    sternoclavicular joint S43.6-•
    sternum S23.429
      chondrosternal joint S23.421
      specified site NEC S23.428
      sternoclavicular (joint) (ligament)
        S23.420

Sprain *(Continued)*
  symphysis
    jaw S03.4-•
      old M26.69
    mandibular S03.4-•
      old M26.69
  talofibular —*see* Sprain, ankle
  tarsal —*see* Sprain, foot, specified site NEC
  tarsometatarsal —*see* Sprain, foot, specified
    site NEC
  temporomandibular S03.4-•
    old M26.69
  thorax S23.9
    ribs S23.41
    specified site NEC S23.8
    spine S23.3
    sternum —*see* Sprain, sternum
  thumb S63.60-•
    interphalangeal (joint) S63.62-•
    metacarpophalangeal (joint) S63.64-•
    specified site NEC S63.68-•
  thyroid cartilage or region S13.5
  tibia (proximal end) —*see* Sprain, knee,
    specified site NEC
  tibial collateral, knee —*see* Sprain, knee,
    collateral
  tibiofibular
    distal —*see* Sprain, ankle
    superior —*see* Sprain, knee, specified site
      NEC
  toe(s) S93.50-•
    great S93.50-•
    interphalangeal joint S93.51-•
      great S93.51-•
      lesser S93.51-•
    lesser S93.50-•
    metatarsophalangeal joint S93.52-•
      great S93.52-•
      lesser S93.52-•
  ulna, collateral —*see* Rupture, traumatic,
    ligament, ulnar collateral
  ulnohumeral —*see* Sprain, elbow
  wrist S63.50-•
    carpal S63.51-•
    radiocarpal S63.52-•
    specified site NEC S63.59-•
  xiphoid cartilage —*see* Sprain, sternum
Sprengel's deformity (congenital) Q74.0
Sprue (tropical) K90.1
  celiac K90.0
  idiopathic K90.49
  meaning thrush B37.0
  nontropical K90.0
Spur, bone —*see also* Enthesopathy
  calcaneal M77.3-•
  iliac crest M76.2-•
  nose (septum) J34.89
Spurway's syndrome Q78.0
Sputum
  abnormal (amount) (color) (odor) (purulent)
    R09.3
  blood-stained R04.2
  excessive (cause unknown) R09.3
Squamous —*see also* condition
  epithelium in
    cervical canal (congenital) Q51.828
    uterine mucosa (congenital) Q51.818
Squashed nose M95.0
  congenital Q67.4
Squeeze, diver's T70.3
Squint —*see also* Strabismus
  accommodative —*see* Strabismus, convergent
    concomitant
SSADHD (succinic semialdehyde
  dehydrogenase deficiency) E72.81
St. Hubert's disease A82.9
Stab —*see also* Laceration
  internal organs —*see* Injury, by site
Stafne's cyst or cavity M27.0
Staggering gait R26.0
  hysterical F44.4

Staghorn calculus —*see* Calculus, kidney
Stähli's line (cornea) (pigment) —*see*
  Pigmentation, cornea, anterior
Stain, staining
  meconium (newborn) P96.83
  port wine Q82.5
  tooth, teeth (hard tissues) (extrinsic) K03.6
    due to
      accretions K03.6
      deposits (betel) (black) (green) (materia
        alba) (orange) (soft) (tobacco) K03.6
      metals (copper) (silver) K03.7
      nicotine K03.6
      pulpal bleeding K03.7
      tobacco K03.6
    intrinsic K00.8
Stammering —*see also* Disorder, fluency
  F80.81
Standstill
  auricular I45.5
  cardiac —*see* Arrest, cardiac
  sinoatrial I45.5
  ventricular —*see* Arrest, cardiac
Stannosis J63.5
Stanton's disease —*see* Melioidosis
Staphylitis (acute) (catarrhal) (chronic)
  (gangrenous) (membranous) (suppurative)
  (ulcerative) K12.2
Staphylococcal scalded skin syndrome L00
Staphylococcemia A41.2
Staphylococcus, staphylococcal —*see also*
  condition
  as cause of disease classified elsewhere
    B95.8
    aureus (methicillin susceptible) (MSSA)
      B95.61
    methicillin resistant (MRSA) B95.62
  specified NEC, as cause of disease classified
    elsewhere B95.7
Staphyloma (sclera)
  cornea H18.72-•
  equatorial H15.81-•
  localized (anterior) H15.82-•
  posticum H15.83-•
  ring H15.85-•
Stargardt's disease —*see* Dystrophy, retina
Starvation (inanition) (due to lack of food)
  T73.0
  edema —*see* Malnutrition, severe
Stasis
  bile (noncalculous) K83.1
  bronchus J98.09
    with infection —*see* Bronchitis
  cardiac —*see* Failure, heart, congestive
⇒ cecum K59.89
⇒ colon K59.89
  dermatitis I87.2
    with
      varicose ulcer —*see* Varix, leg, with ulcer,
        with inflammation
      varicose veins —*see* Varix, leg, with,
        inflammation
    due to postthrombotic syndrome —*see*
      Syndrome, postthrombotic
  duodenal K31.5
  eczema —*see* Varix, leg, with, inflammation
  edema —*see* Hypertension, venous (chronic),
    idiopathic
  foot T69.0-•
⇒ ileocecal coil K59.89
⇒ ileum K59.89
⇒ intestinal K59.89
⇒ jejunum K59.89
  kidney N19
  liver (cirrhotic) K76.1
  lymphatic I89.8
  pneumonia J18.2
  pulmonary —*see* Edema, lung
⇒ rectal K59.89
  renal N19
    tubular N17.0

Stasis *(Continued)*
- ulcer —*see* Varix, leg, with, ulcer
  - without varicose veins I87.2
- urine —*see* Retention, urine
- venous I87.8

State *(of)*
- affective and paranoid, mixed, organic
  - psychotic F06.8
- agitated R45.1
  - acute reaction to stress F43.0
- anxiety (neurotic) F41.1
- apprehension F41.1
- burn-out Z73.0
- climacteric, female Z78.0
  - symptomatic N95.1
- compulsive F42.8
  - mixed with obsessional thoughts F42.2
- confusional (psychogenic) F44.89
  - acute —*see also* Delirium
    - with
      - arteriosclerotic dementia F01.50
        - with behavioral disturbance F01.51
      - senility or dementia F05
    - alcoholic F10.231
  - epileptic F05
  - reactive (from emotional stress,
    - psychological trauma) F44.89
  - subacute —*see* Delirium
- convulsive —*see* Convulsions
- crisis F43.0
- depressive F32.9
  - neurotic F34.1
- dissociative F44.9
- emotional shock (stress) R45.7
- hypercoagulation —*see* Hypercoagulable
- locked-in G83.5
- menopausal Z78.0
  - symptomatic N95.1
- neurotic F48.9
  - with depersonalization F48.1
- obsessional F42.8
- oneiroid (schizophrenia-like) F23
- organic
  - hallucinatory (nonalcoholic) F06.0
  - paranoid (-hallucinatory) F06.2
- panic F41.0
- paranoid F22
  - climacteric F22
  - involutional F22
  - menopausal F22
  - organic F06.2
  - senile F03
  - simple F22
- persistent vegetative R40.3
- phobic F40.9
- postleukotomy F07.0
- pregnant
  - gestational carrier Z33.3
  - incidental Z33.1
- psychogenic, twilight F44.89
- psychopathic (constitutional) F60.2
- psychotic, organic —*see also* Psychosis,
  - organic
  - mixed paranoid and affective F06.8
  - senile or presenile F03
  - transient NEC F06.8
    - with
      - depression F06.31
      - hallucinations F06.0
- residual schizophrenic F20.5
- restlessness R45.1
- stress (emotional) R45.7
- tension (mental) F48.9
  - specified NEC F48.8
- transient organic psychotic NEC F06.8
  - depressive type F06.31
  - hallucinatory type F06.0
- twilight
  - epileptic F05
  - psychogenic F44.89
- vegetative, persistent R40.3

State *(Continued)*
- vital exhaustion Z73.0
- withdrawal —*see* Withdrawal, state

Status (post) —*see also* Presence (of)
- absence, epileptic —*see* Epilepsy, by type,
  - with status epilepticus
- administration of tPA (rtPA) in a different
  - facility within the last 24 hours prior to
  - admission to the current facility
  - Z92.82
- adrenalectomy (unilateral) (bilateral)
  - E89.6
- anastomosis Z98.0
- anginosus I20.9
- angioplasty (peripheral) Z98.62
  - with implant Z95.820
  - coronary artery Z98.61
    - with implant Z95.5
- aortocoronary bypass Z95.1
- arthrodesis Z98.1
- artificial opening (of) Z93.9
  - gastrointestinal tract Z93.4
  - specified NEC Z93.8
  - urinary tract Z93.6
  - vagina Z93.8
- asthmaticus —*see* Asthma, by type, with
  - status asthmaticus
- awaiting organ transplant Z76.82
- bariatric surgery Z98.84
- bed confinement Z74.01
- bleb, filtering (vitreous), after glaucoma
  - surgery Z98.83
- breast implant Z98.82
  - removal Z98.86
- cataract extraction Z98.4-●
- cholecystectomy Z90.49
- clitorectomy N90.811
  - with excision of labia minora N90.812
- colectomy (complete) (partial) Z90.49
- colonization —*see* Carrier (suspected) of
- colostomy Z93.3
- convulsivus idiopathicus —*see* Epilepsy, by
  - type, with status epilepticus
- coronary artery angioplasty —*see* Status,
  - angioplasty, coronary artery
- coronary artery bypass graft Z95.1
- cystectomy (urinary bladder) Z90.6
- cystostomy Z93.50
  - appendico-vesicostomy Z93.52
  - cutaneous Z93.51
  - specified NEC Z93.59
- delinquent immunization Z28.3
- dental Z98.818
  - crown Z98.811
  - fillings Z98.811
  - restoration Z98.811
  - sealant Z98.810
  - specified NEC Z98.818
- deployment (current) (military) Z56.82
- dialysis (hemodialysis) (peritoneal) Z99.2
- do not resuscitate (DNR) Z66
- donor —*see* Donor
- embedded fragments —*see* Retained, foreign
  - body fragments (type of)
- embedded splinter —*see* Retained, foreign
  - body fragments (type of)
- enterostomy Z93.4
- epileptic, epilepticus —*see also* Epilepsy, by
  - type, with status epilepticus G40.901
- estrogen receptor
  - negative Z17.1
  - positive Z17.0
- female genital cutting —*see* Female genital
  - mutilation status
- female genital mutilation —*see* Female genital
  - mutilation status
- filtering (vitreous) bleb after glaucoma
  - surgery Z98.83
- gastrectomy (complete) (partial) Z90.3
- gastric banding Z98.84
- gastric bypass for obesity Z98.84

Status *(Continued)*
- gastrostomy Z93.1
- human immunodeficiency virus (HIV)
  - infection, asymptomatic Z21
- hysterectomy (complete) (total) Z90.710
  - partial (with remaining cervial stump)
    - Z90.711
- ileostomy Z93.2
- implant
  - breast Z98.82
- infibulation N90.813
- intestinal bypass Z98.0
- jejunostomy Z93.4
- lapsed immunization schedule Z28.3
- laryngectomy Z90.02
- lymphaticus E32.8
- malignancy
  - castrate resistant prostate Z19.2
  - hormone resistant Z19.2
  - hormone sensitive Z19.1
- marmoratus G80.3
- mastectomy (unilateral) (bilateral) Z90.1-●
- military deployment status (current) Z56.82
  - in theater or in support of military war,
    - peacekeeping and humanitarian
    - operations Z56.82
- nephrectomy (unilateral) (bilateral) Z90.5
- nephrostomy Z93.6
- obesity surgery Z98.84
- oophorectomy
  - bilateral Z90.722
  - unilateral Z90.721
- organ replacement
  - by artificial or mechanical device or
    - prosthesis of
    - artery Z95.828
    - bladder Z96.0
    - blood vessel Z95.828
    - breast Z97.8
    - eye globe Z97.0
    - heart Z95.812
      - valve Z95.2
    - intestine Z97.8
    - joint Z96.60
      - hip —*see* Presence, hip joint implant
      - knee —*see* Presence, knee joint
        - implant
      - specified site NEC Z96.698
    - kidney Z97.8
    - larynx Z96.3
    - lens Z96.1
    - limbs —*see* Presence, artificial, limb
    - liver Z97.8
    - lung Z97.8
    - pancreas Z97.8
  - by organ transplant (heterologous)
    - (homologous) —*see* Transplant
- pacemaker
  - brain Z96.89
  - cardiac Z95.0
  - specified NEC Z96.89
- pancreatectomy Z90.410
  - complete Z90.410
  - partial Z90.411
  - total Z90.410
- pneumonectomy (complete) (partial) Z90.2
- pneumothorax, therapeutic Z98.3
- postcommotio cerebri F07.81
- postoperative (postprocedural) NEC
  - Z98.890
  - breast implant Z98.82
  - dental Z98.818
    - crown Z98.811
    - fillings Z98.811
    - restoration Z98.811
    - sealant Z98.810
    - specified NEC Z98.818
  - pneumothorax, therapeutic Z98.3
  - uterine scar Z98.891
- postpartum (routine follow-up) Z39.2
  - care immediately after delivery Z39.0

▶ New   ⇒ Revised   ~~deleted~~ Deleted   ● Use Additional Character(s)

Status *(Continued)*
  postsurgical (postprocedural) NEC
      Z98.890
    pneumothorax, therapeutic Z98.3
  pregnancy, incidental Z33.1
  prosthesis coronary angioplasty Z95.5
  pseudophakia Z96.1
  renal dialysis (hemodialysis) (peritoneal)
      Z99.2
  retained foreign body —*see* Retained, foreign
      body fragments (type of)
  reversed jejunal transposition (for bypass
      Z98.0
  salpingo-oophorectomy
    bilateral Z90.722
    unilateral Z90.721
  sex reassignment surgery status Z87.890
  shunt
    arteriovenous (for dialysis) Z99.2
    cerebrospinal fluid Z98.2
    ventricular (communicating) (for drainage)
        Z98.2
  splenectomy Z90.81
  thymicolymphaticus E32.8
  thymicus E32.8
  thymolymphaticus E32.8
  thyroidectomy (hypothyroidism) E89.0
  tooth (teeth) extraction —*see also* Absence,
      teeth, acquired K08.409
  tPA (rtPA) administration in a different
      facility within the last 24 hours prior
      to admission to current facility
      Z92.82
  tracheostomy Z93.0
  transplant —*see* Transplant
    organ removed Z98.85
  tubal ligation Z98.51
  underimmunization Z28.3
  ureterostomy Z93.6
  urethrostomy Z93.6
  vagina, artificial Z93.8
  vasectomy Z98.52
  wheelchair confinement Z99.3
Stealing
  child problem F91.8
    in company with others Z72.810
  pathological (compulsive) F63.2
Steam burn —*see* Burn
Steatocystoma multiplex L72.2
Steatohepatitis (nonalcoholic) (NASH)
    K75.81
Steatoma L72.3
  eyelid (cystic) —*see* Dermatosis, eyelid
    infected —*see* Hordeolum
Steatorrhea (chronic) K90.9
  with lacteal obstruction K90.2
  idiopathic (adult) (infantile) K90.9
  pancreatic K90.3
  primary K90.0
  tropical K90.1
Steatosis E88.89
  heart —*see* Degeneration, myocardial
  kidney N28.89
  liver NEC K76.0
Steele-Richardson-Olszewski disease or
    syndrome G23.1
Steinbrocker's syndrome G90.8
Steinert's disease G71.11
Stein-Leventhal syndrome E28.2
Stein's syndrome E28.2
STEMI —*see also* Infarct, myocardium, ST
    elevation I21.3
Stenocardia I20.8
Stenocephaly Q75.8
Stenosis, stenotic (cicatricial) —*see also*
    Stricture
  ampulla of Vater K83.1
  anus, anal (canal) (sphincter) K62.4
    and rectum K62.4
    congenital Q42.3
      with fistula Q42.2

Stenosis, stenotic *(Continued)*
  aorta (ascending) (supraventricular)
      (congenital) Q25.1
    arteriosclerotic I70.0
    calcified I70.0
    supravalvular Q25.3
  aortic (valve) I35.0
    with insufficiency I35.2
    congenital Q23.0
    rheumatic I06.0
      with
        incompetency, insufficiency or
            regurgitation I06.2
          with mitral (valve) disease I08.0
            with tricuspid (valve) disease
                I08.3
        mitral (valve) disease I08.0
          with tricuspid (valve) disease
              I08.3
        tricuspid (valve) disease I08.2
          with mitral (valve) disease
              I08.3
    specified cause NEC I35.0
    syphilitic A52.03
  aqueduct of Sylvius (congenital) Q03.0
    with spina bifida —*see* Spina bifida,
        by site, with hydrocephalus
    acquired G91.1
  artery NEC —*see also* Arteriosclerosis
      I77.1
    celiac I77.4
    cerebral —*see* Occlusion, artery, cerebral
    extremities —*see* Arteriosclerosis,
        extremities
    precerebral —*see* Occlusion, artery,
        precerebral
    pulmonary (congenital) Q25.6
      acquired I28.8
    renal I70.1
    stent
      coronary T82.855
      peripheral T82.856
  bile duct (common) (hepatic) K83.1
    congenital Q44.3
  bladder-neck (acquired) N32.0
    congenital Q64.31
  brain G93.89
  bronchus J98.09
    congenital Q32.3
    syphilitic A52.72
  cardia (stomach) K22.2
    congenital Q39.3
  cardiovascular —*see* Disease, cardiovascular
  caudal M48.08
  cervix, cervical (canal) N88.2
    congenital Q51.828
    in pregnancy or childbirth —*see* Pregnancy,
        complicated by, abnormal cervix
  colon —*see also* Obstruction, intestine
    congenital Q42.9
      specified NEC Q42.8
  colostomy K94.03
  common (bile) duct K83.1
    congenital Q44.3
  coronary (artery) —*see* Disease, heart,
      ischemic, atherosclerotic
  cystic duct —*see* Obstruction, gallbladder
  due to presence of device, implant or
      graft —*see also* Complications, by site,
      and type, specified NEC T85.858
    arterial graft NEC T82.858
    breast (implant) T85.858
    catheter T85.858
      dialysis (renal) T82.858
        intraperitoneal T85.858
      infusion NEC T82.858
        spinal (epidural) (subdural)
            T85.850
      urinary (indwelling) T83.85
    fixation, internal (orthopedic) NEC
        T84.85

Stenosis, stenotic *(Continued)*
  due to presence of device, implant or graft
      (Continued)
    gastrointestinal (bile duct) (esophagus)
        T85.858
    genital NEC T83.85
    heart NEC T82.857
    joint prosthesis T84.85
    ocular (corneal graft) (orbital implant)
        NEC T85.858
    orthopedic NEC T84.85
    specified NEC T85.858
    urinary NEC T83.85
    vascular NEC T82.858
    ventricular intracranial shunt T85.850
  duodenum K31.5
    congenital Q41.0
  ejaculatory duct NEC N50.89
  endocervical os —*see* Stenosis, cervix
  enterostomy K94.13
  esophagus K22.2
    congenital Q39.3
    syphilitic A52.79
      congenital A50.59 *[K23]*
  eustachian tube —*see* Obstruction, eustachian
      tube
  external ear canal (acquired) H61.30-●
    congenital Q16.1
    due to
      inflammation H61.32-●
      trauma H61.31-●
    postprocedural H95.81-●
    specified cause NEC H61.39-●
  gallbladder —*see* Obstruction, gallbladder
  glottis J38.6
  heart valve (congenital) Q24.8
    aortic Q23.0
    mitral Q23.2
    pulmonary Q22.1
    tricuspid Q22.4
  hepatic duct K83.1
  hymen N89.6
  hypertrophic subaortic (idiopathic) I42.1
  ileum —*see also* Obstruction, intestine,
      specified NEC K56.699
    congenital Q41.2
  infundibulum cardia Q24.3
  intervertebral foramina —*see also* Lesion,
      biomechanical, specified NEC
    connective tissue M99.79
      abdomen M99.79
      cervical region M99.71
      cervicothoracic M99.71
      head region M99.70
      lumbar region M99.73
      lumbosacral M99.73
      occipitocervical M99.70
      sacral region M99.74
      sacrococcygeal M99.74
      sacroiliac M99.74
      specified NEC M99.79
      thoracic region M99.72
      thoracolumbar M99.72
    disc M99.79
      abdomen M99.79
      cervical region M99.71
      cervicothoracic M99.71
      head region M99.70
      lower extremity M99.76
      lumbar region M99.73
      lumbosacral M99.73
      occipitocervical M99.70
      pelvic M99.75
      rib cage M99.78
      sacral region M99.74
      sacrococcygeal M99.74
      sacroiliac M99.74
      specified NEC M99.79
      thoracic region M99.72
      thoracolumbar M99.72
      upper extremity M99.77

Stenosis, stenotic *(Continued)*
  intervertebral foramina *(Continued)*
    osseous M99.69
      abdomen M99.69
      cervical region M99.61
      cervicothoracic M99.61
      head region M99.60
      lower extremity M99.66
      lumbar region M99.63
      lumbosacral M99.63
      occipitocervical M99.60
      pelvic M99.65
      rib cage M99.68
      sacral region M99.64
      sacrococcygeal M99.64
      sacroiliac M99.64
      specified NEC M99.69
      thoracic region M99.62
      thoracolumbar M99.62
      upper extremity M99.67
    subluxation —*see* Stenosis, intervertebral
        foramina, osseous
  intestine —*see also* Obstruction, intestine
    congenital (small) Q41.9
      large Q42.9
        specified NEC Q42.8
      specified NEC Q41.8
  jejunum —*see also* Obstruction, intestine,
      specified NEC K56.699
    congenital Q41.1
  lacrimal (passage)
    canaliculi H04.54-●
    congenital Q10.5
    duct H04.55-●
    punctum H04.56-●
    sac H04.57-●
  lacrimonasal duct —*see* Stenosis, lacrimal,
      duct
    congenital Q10.5
  larynx J38.6
    congenital NEC Q31.8
      subglottic Q31.1
    syphilitic A52.73
      congenital A50.59 *[J99]*
  mitral (chronic) (inactive) (valve) I05.0
    with
      aortic valve disease I08.0
      incompetency, insufficiency or
          regurgitation I05.2
    active or acute I01.1
      with rheumatic or Sydenham's chorea
          I02.0
    congenital Q23.2
    specified cause, except rheumatic I34.2
    syphilitic A52.03
  myocardium, myocardial —*see also*
      Degeneration, myocardial
    hypertrophic subaortic (idiopathic) I42.1
  nares (anterior) (posterior) J34.89
    congenital Q30.0
  nasal duct —*see also* Stenosis, lacrimal, duct
    congenital Q10.5
  nasolacrimal duct —*see also* Stenosis, lacrimal,
      duct
    congenital Q10.5
  neural canal —*see also* Lesion, biomechanical,
      specified NEC
    connective tissue M99.49
      abdomen M99.49
      cervical region M99.41
      cervicothoracic M99.41
      head region M99.40
      lower extremity M99.46
      lumbar region M99.43
      lumbosacral M99.43
      occipitocervical M99.40
      pelvic M99.45
      rib cage M99.48
      sacral region M99.44
      sacrococcygeal M99.44
      sacroiliac M99.44

Stenosis, stenotic *(Continued)*
  neural canal *(Continued)*
    connective tissue *(Continued)*
      specified NEC M99.49
      thoracic region M99.42
      thoracolumbar M99.42
      upper extremity M99.47
    intervertebral disc M99.59
      abdomen M99.59
      cervical region M99.51
      cervicothoracic M99.51
      head region M99.50
      lower extremity M99.56
      lumbar region M99.53
      lumbosacral M99.53
      occipitocervical M99.50
      pelvic M99.55
      rib cage M99.58
      sacral region M99.54
      sacrococcygeal M99.54
      sacroiliac M99.54
      specified NEC M99.59
      thoracic region M99.52
      thoracolumbar M99.52
      upper extremity M99.57
    osseous M99.39
      abdomen M99.39
      cervical region M99.31
      cervicothoracic M99.31
      head region M99.30
      lower extremity M99.36
      lumbar region M99.33
      lumbosacral M99.33
      occipitocervical M99.30
      pelvic M99.35
      rib cage M99.38
      sacral region M99.34
      sacrococcygeal M99.34
      sacroiliac M99.34
      specified NEC M99.39
      thoracic region M99.32
      thoracolumbar M99.32
      upper extremity M99.37
    subluxation M99.29
      cervical region M99.21
      cervicothoracic M99.21
      head region M99.20
      lower extremity M99.26
      lumbar region M99.23
      lumbosacral M99.23
      occipitocervical M99.20
      pelvic M99.25
      rib cage M99.28
      sacral region M99.24
      sacrococcygeal M99.24
      sacroiliac M99.24
      specified NEC M99.29
      thoracic region M99.22
      thoracolumbar M99.22
      upper extremity M99.27
  organ or site, congenital NEC —*see* Atresia,
      by site
  papilla of Vater K83.1
  pulmonary (artery) (congenital) Q25.6
    with ventricular septal defect,
        transposition of aorta, and
        hypertrophy of right ventricle
        Q21.3
    acquired I28.8
    in tetralogy of Fallot Q21.3
    infundibular Q24.3
    subvalvular Q24.3
    supravalvular Q25.6
    valve I37.0
      with insufficiency I37.2
      congenital Q22.1
      rheumatic I09.89
        with aortic, mitral or tricuspid (valve)
            disease I08.8
    vein, acquired I28.8
    vessel NEC I28.8

Stenosis, stenotic *(Continued)*
  pulmonic (congenital) Q22.1
    infundibular Q24.3
    subvalvular Q24.3
  pylorus (hypertrophic) (acquired) K31.1
    adult K31.1
    congenital Q40.0
    infantile Q40.0
  rectum (sphincter) —*see* Stricture, rectum
  renal artery I70.1
    congenital Q27.1
  salivary duct (any) K11.8
  sphincter of Oddi K83.1
  spinal M48.00
    cervical region M48.02
    cervicothoracic region M48.03
    lumbar region (NOS) (without neurogenic
        claudication) M48.061
      with neurogenic claudication M48.062
    lumbosacral region M48.07
    occipito-atlanto-axial region M48.01
    sacrococcygeal region M48.08
    thoracic region M48.04
    thoracolumbar region M48.05
  stent
    vascular
      end stent
        adjacent to stent —*see* Arteriosclerosis
        within the stent
          coronary T82.855
          peripheral T82.856
      in stent
        coronary vessel T82.855
        peripheral vessel T82.856
  stomach, hourglass K31.2
  subaortic (congenital) Q24.4
    hypertrophic (idiopathic) I42.1
  subglottic J38.6
    congenital Q31.1
    postprocedural J95.5
  trachea J39.8
    congenital Q32.1
    syphilitic A52.73
    tuberculous NEC A15.5
  tracheostomy J95.03
  tricuspid (valve) I07.0
    with
      aortic (valve) disease I08.2
      incompetency, insufficiency or
          regurgitation I07.2
        with aortic (valve) disease I08.2
          with mitral (valve) disease I08.3
      mitral (valve) disease I08.1
        with aortic (valve) disease I08.3
    congenital Q22.4
    nonrheumatic I36.0
      with insufficiency I36.2
  tubal N97.1
  ureter —*see* Atresia, ureter
  ureteropelvic junction, congenital
      Q62.11
  ureterovesical orifice, congenital Q62.12
  urethra (valve) —*see also* Stricture, urethra
    congenital Q64.32
  urinary meatus, congenital Q64.33
  vagina N89.5
    congenital Q52.4
    in pregnancy —*see* Pregnancy, complicated
        by, abnormal vagina
      causing obstructed labor O65.5
  valve (cardiac) (heart) —*see also* Endocarditis
      I38
    congenital Q24.8
      aortic Q23.0
      mitral Q23.2
      pulmonary Q22.1
      tricuspid Q22.4
  vena cava (inferior) (superior) I87.1
    congenital Q26.0
  vesicourethral orifice Q64.31
  vulva N90.5

▶ New   ⇒ Revised   ~~deleted~~ Deleted   ● Use Additional Character(s)

Stent jail T82.897
Stercolith (impaction) K56.41
   appendix K38.1
Stercoraceous, stercoral ulcer K63.3
   anus or rectum K62.6
Stereotypies NEC F98.4
Sterility —*see* Infertility
Sterilization —*see* Encounter (for), sterilization
Sternalgia —*see* Angina
Sternopagus Q89.4
Sternum bifidum Q76.7
Steroid
   effects (adverse) (adrenocortical)
      (iatrogenic)
      cushingoid E24.2
        correct substance properly
           administered —*see* Table of Drugs
             and Chemicals, by drug, adverse
             effect
        overdose or wrong substance given
           or taken —*see* Table of Drugs and
             Chemicals, by drug, poisoning
      diabetes —*see* category E09
        correct substance properly
           administered —*see* Table of Drugs
             and Chemicals, by drug, adverse
             effect
        overdose or wrong substance given
           or taken —*see* Table of Drugs and
             Chemicals, by drug, poisoning
      fever R50.2
      insufficiency E27.3
        correct substance properly
           administered —*see* Table of Drugs
             and Chemicals, by drug, adverse
             effect
        overdose or wrong substance given
           or taken —*see* Table of Drugs and
             Chemicals, by drug, poisoning
   responder H40.04-●
Stevens-Johnson disease or syndrome L51.1
   toxic epidermal necrolysis overlap L51.3
Stewart-Morel syndrome M85.2
Sticker's disease B08.3
Sticky eye —*see* Conjunctivitis, acute,
   mucopurulent
Stieda's disease —*see* Bursitis, tibial collateral
Stiff neck —*see* Torticollis
Stiff-man syndrome G25.82
Stiffness, joint NEC M25.60-●
   ankle M25.67-●
   ankylosis —*see* Ankylosis, joint
   contracture —*see* Contraction, joint
   elbow M25.62-●
   foot M25.67-●
   hand M25.64-●
   hip M25.65-●
   knee M25.66-●
   shoulder M25.61-●
  ▶specified site NEC M25.69
   wrist M25.63-●
Stigmata congenital syphilis A50.59
Stillbirth P95
Still-Felty syndrome —*see* Felty's syndrome
Still's disease or syndrome (juvenile) M08.20
   adult-onset M06.1
   ankle M08.27-●
   elbow M08.22-●
   foot joint M08.27-●
   hand joint M08.24-●
   hip M08.25-●
   knee M08.26-●
   multiple site M08.29
   shoulder M08.21-●
  ▶specified site NEC M08.2A
   vertebra M08.28
   wrist M08.23-●
Stimulation, ovary E28.1
Sting (venomous) (with allergic or anaphylactic
   shock) —*see* Table of Drugs and Chemicals,
   by animal or substance, poisoning

Stippled epiphyses Q78.8
Stitch
   abscess T81.41
   burst (in operation wound) —*see* Disruption,
      wound, operation
Stokes-Adams disease or syndrome
   I45.9
Stokes' disease E05.00
   with thyroid storm E05.01
Stokvis (-Talma) disease D74.8
Stoma malfunction
   colostomy K94.03
   enterostomy K94.13
   gastrostomy K94.23
   ileostomy K94.13
   tracheostomy J95.03
Stomach —*see* condition
Stomatitis (denture) (ulcerative)
   K12.1
   angular K13.0
      due to dietary or vitamin deficiency
        E53.0
   aphthous K12.0
   bovine B08.61
   candidal B37.0
   catarrhal K12.1
   diphtheritic A36.89
   due to
      dietary deficiency E53.0
      thrush B37.0
      vitamin deficiency
        B group NEC E53.9
        B2 (riboflavin) E53.0
   epidemic B08.8
   epizootic B08.8
   follicular K12.1
   gangrenous A69.0
   Geotrichum B48.3
   herpesviral, herpetic B00.2
   herpetiformis K12.0
   malignant K12.1
   membranous acute K12.1
   monilial B37.0
   mycotic B37.0
   necrotizing ulcerative A69.0
   parasitic B37.0
   septic K12.1
   spirochetal A69.1
   suppurative (acute) K12.2
   ulceromembranous A69.1
   vesicular K12.1
      with exanthem (enteroviral)
        B08.4
      virus disease A93.8
   Vincent's A69.1
Stomatocytosis D58.8
Stomatomycosis B37.0
Stomatorrhagia K13.79
Stone(s) —*see also* Calculus
   bladder (diverticulum) N21.0
   cystine E72.09
   heart syndrome I50.1
   kidney N20.0
   prostate N42.0
   pulpal (dental) K04.2
   renal N20.0
   salivary gland or duct (any) K11.5
   urethra (impacted) N21.1
   urinary (duct) (impacted) (passage)
      N20.9
      bladder (diverticulum) N21.0
      lower tract N21.9
      specified NEC N21.8
      xanthine E79.8 *[N22]*
Stonecutter's lung J62.8
Stonemason's asthma, disease, lung or
   pneumoconiosis J62.8
Stoppage
   heart —*see* Arrest, cardiac
   urine —*see* Retention, urine
Storm, thyroid —*see* Thyrotoxicosis

Strabismus (congenital) (nonparalytic)
   H50.9
   concomitant H50.40
      convergent —*see* Strabismus, convergent
        concomitant
      divergent —*see* Strabismus, divergent
        concomitant
   convergent concomitant H50.00
      accommodative component H50.43
      alternating H50.05
        with
          A pattern H50.06
          specified nonconcomitances NEC
            H50.08
          V pattern H50.07
      monocular H50.01-●
        with
          A pattern H50.02-●
          specified nonconcomitances NEC
            H50.04-●
          V pattern H50.03-●
        intermittent H50.31-●
          alternating H50.32
   cyclotropia H50.41
   divergent concomitant H50.10
      alternating H50.15
        with
          A pattern H50.16
          specified noncomitances NEC
            H50.18
          V pattern H50.17
      monocular H50.11-●
        with
          A pattern H50.12-●
          specified noncomitances NEC
            H50.14-●
          V pattern H50.13-●
        intermittent H50.33-●
          alternating H50.34
   Duane's syndrome H50.81-●
   due to adhesions, scars H50.69
   heterophoria H50.50
      alternating H50.55
      cyclophoria H50.54
      esophoria H50.51
      exophoria H50.52
      vertical H50.53
   heterotropia H50.40
      intermittent H50.30
   hypertropia H50.2-●
   hypotropia —*see* Hypertropia
   latent H50.50
   mechanical H50.60
      Brown's sheath syndrome H50.61-●
      specified type NEC H50.69
   monofixation syndrome H50.42
   paralytic H49.9
      abducens nerve H49.2-●
      fourth nerve H49.1-●
      Kearns-Sayre syndrome H49.81-●
      ophthalmoplegia (external)
        progressive H49.4-●
          with pigmentary retinopathy H49.81-●
        total H49.3-●
      sixth nerve H49.2-●
      specified type NEC H49.88-●
      third nerve H49.0-●
      trochlear nerve H49.1-●
   specified type NEC H50.89
   vertical H50.2-●
Strain
   back S39.012
   cervical S16.1
   eye NEC —*see* Disturbance, vision, subjective
   heart —*see* Disease, heart
   low back S39.012
   mental NOS Z73.3
      work-related Z56.6
   muscle (tendon) —*see* Injury, muscle, by site,
      strain
   neck S16.1

Strain (Continued)
- physical NOS Z73.3
  - work-related Z56.6
- postural —see also Disorder, soft tissue, due
  - to use
- psychological NEC Z73.3
- tendon —see Injury, muscle, by site, strain

Straining, on urination R39.16
Strand, vitreous —see Opacity, vitreous,
  membranes and strands
Strangulation, strangulated —see also
  Asphyxia, traumatic
- appendix K38.8
- bladder-neck N32.0
- bowel or colon K56.2
- food or foreign body —see Foreign body, by
  site
- hemorrhoids —see Hemorrhoids, with
  complication
- hernia —see also Hernia, by site, with
  obstruction
  - with gangrene —see Hernia, by site, with
    gangrene
- intestine (large) (small) K56.2
  - with hernia —see also Hernia, by site, with
    obstruction
    - with gangrene —see Hernia, by site, with
      gangrene
- mesentery K56.2
- mucus —see Asphyxia, mucus
- omentum K56.2
- organ or site, congenital NEC —see Atresia,
  by site
- ovary —see Torsion, ovary
- penis N48.89
  - foreign body T19.4
- rupture —see Hernia, by site, with obstruction
- stomach due to hernia —see also Hernia, by
  site, with obstruction
  - with gangrene —see Hernia, by site, with
    gangrene
- vesicourethral orifice N32.0

Strangury R30.0
Straw itch B88.0
Strawberry
- gallbladder K82.4
- mark Q82.5
- tongue (red) (white) K14.3

Streak(s)
- macula, angioid H35.33
- ovarian Q50.32

Strephosymbolia F81.0
- secondary to organic lesion R48.8
Streptobacillary fever A25.1
Streptobacillosis A25.1
Streptobacillus moniliformis A25.1
Streptococcus, streptococcal —see also
  condition
- as cause of disease classified elsewhere B95.5
- group
  - A, as cause of disease classified elsewhere
    B95.0
  - B, as cause of disease classified elsewhere
    B95.1
  - D, as cause of disease classified elsewhere
    B95.2
- pneumoniae, as cause of disease classified
  elsewhere B95.3
- specified NEC, as cause of disease classified
  elsewhere B95.4

Streptomycosis B47.1
Streptotrichosis A48.8
Stress F43.9
- family —see Disruption, family
- fetal P84
  - complicating pregnancy O77.9
    - due to drug administration O77.1
- mental NEC Z73.3
  - work-related Z56.6
- physical NEC Z73.3
  - work-related Z56.6

Stress (Continued)
- polycythemia D75.1
- reaction —see also Reaction, stress F43.9
- work schedule Z56.3
Stretching, nerve —see Injury, nerve
Striae albicantes, atrophicae or distensae
  (cutis) L90.6
Stricture —see also Stenosis
- ampulla of Vater K83.1
- anus (sphincter) K62.4
  - congenital Q42.3
    - with fistula Q42.2
  - infantile Q42.3
    - with fistula Q42.2
- aorta (ascending) (congenital) Q25.1
  - arteriosclerotic I70.0
  - calcified I70.0
  - supravalvular, congenital Q25.3
- aortic (valve) —see Stenosis, aortic
- aqueduct of Sylvius (congenital) Q03.0
  - with spina bifida —see Spina bifida, by site,
    with hydrocephalus
  - acquired G91.1
- artery I77.1
  - basilar —see Occlusion, artery, basilar
  - carotid —see Occlusion, artery, carotid
  - celiac I77.4
  - congenital (peripheral) Q27.8
    - cerebral Q28.3
    - coronary Q24.5
    - digestive system Q27.8
    - lower limb Q27.8
    - retinal Q14.1
    - specified site NEC Q27.8
    - umbilical Q27.0
    - upper limb Q27.8
  - coronary —see Disease, heart, ischemic,
    atherosclerotic
    - congenital Q24.5
  - precerebral —see Occlusion, artery,
    precerebral
  - pulmonary (congenital) Q25.6
    - acquired I28.8
  - renal I70.1
  - vertebral —see Occlusion, artery, vertebral
- auditory canal (external) (congenital)
  - acquired —see Stenosis, external ear canal
- bile duct (common) (hepatic) K83.1
  - congenital Q44.3
  - postoperative K91.89
- bladder N32.89
  - neck N32.0
- bowel —see Obstruction, intestine
- brain G93.89
- bronchus J98.09
  - congenital Q32.3
  - syphilitic A52.72
- cardia (stomach) K22.2
  - congenital Q39.3
- cardiac —see also Disease, heart
  - orifice (stomach) K22.2
- cecum —see Obstruction, intestine
- cervix, cervical (canal) N88.2
  - congenital Q51.828
  - in pregnancy —see Pregnancy, complicated
    by, abnormal cervix
    - causing obstructed labor O65.5
- colon —see also Obstruction, intestine
  - congenital Q42.9
    - specified NEC Q42.8
- colostomy K94.03
- common (bile) duct K83.1
- coronary (artery) —see Disease, heart,
  ischemic, atherosclerotic
- cystic duct —see Obstruction, gallbladder
- digestive organs NEC, congenital Q45.8
- duodenum K31.5
  - congenital Q41.0
- ear canal (external) (congenital) Q16.1
  - acquired —see Stricture, auditory canal,
    acquired

Stricture (Continued)
- ejaculatory duct N50.89
- enterostomy K94.13
- esophagus K22.2
  - congenital Q39.3
  - syphilitic A52.79
    - congenital A50.59 [K23]
- eustachian tube —see also Obstruction,
  eustachian tube
  - congenital Q17.8
- fallopian tube N97.1
  - gonococcal A54.24
  - tuberculous A18.17
- gallbladder —see Obstruction, gallbladder
- glottis J38.6
- heart —see also Disease, heart
  - valve (see also Endocarditis) I38
    - aortic Q23.0
    - mitral Q23.2
    - pulmonary Q22.1
    - tricuspid Q22.4
- hepatic duct K83.1
- hourglass, of stomach K31.2
- hymen N89.6
- hypopharynx J39.2
- ileum —see also Obstruction, intestine,
  specified NEC K56.699
  - congenital Q41.2
- intestine —see also Obstruction, intestine
  - congenital (small) Q41.9
    - large Q42.9
      - specified NEC Q42.8
    - specified NEC Q41.8
  - ischemic K55.1
- jejunum —see also Obstruction, intestine,
  specified NEC K56.699
  - congenital Q41.1
- lacrimal passages —see also Stenosis, lacrimal
  - congenital Q10.5
- larynx J38.6
  - congenital NEC Q31.8
    - subglottic Q31.1
  - syphilitic A52.73
    - congenital A50.59 [J99]
- meatus
  - ear (congenital) Q16.1
    - acquired —see Stricture, auditory canal,
      acquired
  - osseous (ear) (congenital) Q16.1
    - acquired —see Stricture, auditory canal,
      acquired
  - urinarius —see also Stricture, urethra
    - congenital Q64.33
- mitral (valve) —see Stenosis, mitral
- myocardium, myocardial I51.5
  - hypertrophic subaortic (idiopathic) I42.1
- nares (anterior) (posterior) J34.89
  - congenital Q30.0
- nasal duct —see also Stenosis, lacrimal, duct
  - congenital Q10.5
- nasolacrimal duct —see also Stenosis, lacrimal,
  duct
  - congenital Q10.5
- nasopharynx J39.2
  - syphilitic A52.73
- nose J34.89
  - congenital Q30.0
- nostril (anterior) (posterior) J34.89
  - congenital Q30.0
  - syphilitic A52.73
    - congenital A50.59 [J99]
- organ or site, congenital NEC —see Atresia,
  by site
- os uteri —see Stricture, cervix
- osseous meatus (ear) (congenital) Q16.1
  - acquired —see Stricture, auditory canal,
    acquired
- oviduct —see Stricture, fallopian tube
- pelviureteric junction (congenital) Q62.11
  - acquired, with hydronephrosis N13.0
- penis, by foreign body T19.4

Stricture *(Continued)*
  pharynx J39.2
  prostate N42.89
  pulmonary, pulmonic
    artery (congenital) Q25.6
      acquired I28.8
      noncongenital I28.8
    infundibulum (congenital) Q24.3
    valve I37.0
      congenital Q22.1
    vein, acquired I28.8
    vessel NEC I28.8
  punctum lacrimale —*see also* Stenosis,
    lacrimal, punctum
    congenital Q10.5
  pylorus (hypertrophic) K31.1
    adult K31.1
    congenital Q40.0
    infantile Q40.0
  rectosigmoid —*see also* Obstruction, intestine,
    specified NEC K56.699
  rectum (sphincter) K62.4
    congenital Q42.1
      with fistula Q42.0
    due to
      chlamydial lymphogranuloma A55
      irradiation K91.89
      lymphogranuloma venereum A55
    gonococcal A54.6
    inflammatory (chlamydial) A55
    syphilitic A52.74
    tuberculous A18.32
  renal artery I70.1
    congenital Q27.1
  salivary duct or gland (any) K11.8
  sigmoid (flexure) —*see* Obstruction, intestine
  spermatic cord N50.89
  stoma (following) (of)
    colostomy K94.03
    enterostomy K94.13
    gastrostomy K94.23
    ileostomy K94.13
    tracheostomy J95.03
  stomach K31.89
    congenital Q40.2
    hourglass K31.2
  subaortic Q24.4
    hypertrophic (acquired) (idiopathic) I42.1
  subglottic J38.6
  syphilitic NEC A52.79
  trachea J39.8
    congenital Q32.1
    syphilitic A52.73
    tuberculous NEC A15.5
  tracheostomy J95.03
  tricuspid (valve) —*see* Stenosis, tricuspid
  tunica vaginalis N50.89
  ureter (postoperative) N13.5
    with
      hydronephrosis N13.1
        with infection N13.6
      pyelonephritis (chronic) N11.1
    congenital —*see* Atresia, ureter
    tuberculous A18.11
  ureteropelvic junction (congenital) Q62.11
    acquired, with hydronephrosis N13.0
  ureterovesical orifice N13.5
    with infection N13.6
  urethra (organic) (spasmodic) *(see also*
    Stricture, urethra, male N35.919
    associated with schistosomiasis
      B65.0 *[N37]*
    congenital Q64.39
      valvular (posterior) Q64.2
    due to
      infection —*see* Stricture, urethra,
        postinfective
      trauma —*see* Stricture, urethra,
        post-traumatic
    female N35.92
    gonococcal, gonorrheal A54.01

Stricture *(Continued)*
  urethra (organic) (spasmodic) *(Continued)*
    infective NEC —*see* Stricture, urethra,
      postinfective
    late effect (sequelae) of injury —*see*
      Stricture, urethra, post-traumatic
    male N35.919
      anterior urethra N35.914
      bulbous urethra N35.912
      meatal N35.911
      membranous urethra N35.913
      overlapping sites N35.916
    postcatheterization —*see* Stricture, urethra,
      postprocedural
    postinfective NEC
      female N35.12
      male N35.119
        anterior urethra N35.114
        bulbous urethra N35.112
        meatal N35.111
        membranous urethra N35.113
        overlapping sites N35.116
    postobstetric N35.021
    postoperative —*see* Stricture, urethra,
      postprocedural
    postprocedural
      female N99.12
      male N99.114
        anterior bulbous urethra N99.113
        bulbous urethra N99.111
        fossa navicularis N99.115
        meatal N99.110
        membranous urethra N99.112
        overlapping sites N35.116
    post-traumatic
      female N35.028
        due to childbirth N35.021
      male N35.014
        anterior urethra N35.013
        bulbous urethra N35.011
        meatal N35.010
        membranous urethra N35.012
        overlapping sites N35.016
    sequela (late effect) of
      childbirth N35.021
      injury —*see* Stricture, urethra,
        post-traumatic
    specified cause NEC
      female N35.82
      male N35.819
        anterior urethra N35.814
        bulbous urethra N35.812
        meatal N35.811
        membranous urethra N35.813
        overlapping sites N35.816
    syphilitic A52.76
    traumatic —*see* Stricture, urethra,
      post-traumatic
    valvular (posterior), congenital Q64.2
  urinary meatus —*see* Stricture, urethra
  uterus, uterine (synechiae) N85.6
    os (external) (internal) —*see* Stricture,
      cervix
  vagina (outlet) —*see* Stenosis, vagina
  valve (cardiac) (heart) —*see also* Endocarditis
    congenital
      aortic Q23.0
      mitral Q23.2
      pulmonary Q22.1
      tricuspid Q22.4
  vas deferens N50.89
    congenital Q55.4
  vein I87.1
  vena cava (inferior) (superior) NEC I87.1
    congenital Q26.0
  vesicourethral orifice N32.0
    congenital Q64.31
  vulva (acquired) N90.5
Stridor R06.1
  congenital (larynx) P28.89
Stridulous —*see* condition

Stroke (apoplectic) (brain) (embolic) (ischemic)
  (paralytic) (thrombotic) I63.9
▶cerebral, perinatal P91.82-●
  cryptogenic —*see also* infarction, cerebral
    I63.9
  epileptic —*see* Epilepsy
  heat T67.01
    exertional T67.02
    specified NEC T67.09
  in evolution I63.9
  intraoperative
    during cardiac surgery I97.810
    during other surgery I97.811
▶ischemic, perinatal arterial P91.82-●
  lightning —*see* Lightning
  meaning
    cerebral hemorrhage — code to
      Hemorrhage, intracranial
    cerebral infarction — code to Infarction,
      cerebral
▶neonatal P91.82-●
  postprocedural
    following cardiac surgery I97.820
    following other surgery I97.821
  sun T67.01
    specified NEC T67.09
  unspecified (NOS) I63.9
Stromatosis, endometrial D39.0
Strongyloidiasis, strongyloidosis B78.9
  cutaneous B78.1
  disseminated B78.7
  intestinal B78.0
Strophulus pruriginosus L28.2
Struck by lightning —*see* Lightning
Struma —*see also* Goiter
  Hashimoto E06.3
  lymphomatosa E06.3
  nodosa (simplex) E04.9
    endemic E01.2
      multinodular E01.1
    multinodular E04.2
      iodine-deficiency related E01.1
    toxic or with hyperthyroidism E05.20
      with thyroid storm E05.21
      multinodular E05.20
        with thyroid storm E05.21
      uninodular E05.10
        with thyroid storm E05.11
    toxicosa E05.20
      with thyroid storm E05.21
      multinodular E05.20
        with thyroid storm E05.21
      uninodular E05.10
        with thyroid storm E05.11
    uninodular E04.1
  ovarii D27.-●
  Riedel's E06.5
Strumipriva cachexia E03.4
Strümpell-Marie spine —*see* Spondylitis,
  ankylosing
Strümpell-Westphal pseudosclerosis E83.01
Stuart deficiency disease (factor X) D68.2
Stuart-Prower factor deficiency (factor X)
  D68.2
Student's elbow —*see* Bursitis, elbow,
  olecranon
Stump —*see* Amputation
Stunting, nutritional E45
Stupor (catatonic) R40.1
  depressive (single episode) F32.89
    recurrent episode F33.8
  dissociative F44.2
  manic F30.2
  manic-depressive F31.89
  psychogenic (anergic) F44.2
  reaction to exceptional stress (transient) F43.0
Sturge (-Weber) (-Dimitri) (-Kalischer) disease
  or syndrome Q85.8
Stuttering F80.81
  adult onset F98.5
  childhood onset F80.81

S

Stuttering (*Continued*)
  following cerebrovascular disease —
    see Disorder, fluency, following
    cerebrovascular disease
  in conditions classified elsewhere R47.82
Sty, stye (external) (internal) (meibomian)
  (zeisian) —*see* Hordeolum
Subacidity, gastric K31.89
  psychogenic F45.8
Subacute —*see* condition
Subarachnoid —*see* condition
Subcortical —*see* condition
Subcostal syndrome, nerve compression —*see*
  Mononeuropathy, upper limb, specified
  site NEC
Subcutaneous, subcuticular —*see* condition
Subdural —*see* condition
Subendocardium —*see* condition
Subependymoma
  specified site —*see* Neoplasm, uncertain
    behavior, by site
  unspecified site D43.2
Suberosis J67.3
Subglossitis —*see* Glossitis
Subhemophilia D66
Subinvolution
  breast (postlactational) (postpuerperal)
    N64.89
  puerperal O90.89
  uterus (chronic) (nonpuerperal) N85.3
    puerperal O90.89
Sublingual —*see* condition
Sublinguitis —*see* Sialoadenitis
Subluxatable hip Q65.6
Subluxation —*see also* Dislocation
  acromioclavicular S43.11-●
  ankle S93.0-●
  atlantoaxial, recurrent M43.4
    with myelopathy M43.3
  carpometacarpal (joint) NEC S63.05-●
    thumb S63.04-●
  complex, vertebral —*see* Complex,
    subluxation
  congenital —*see also* Malposition, congenital
    hip —*see* Dislocation, hip, congenital,
      partial
    joint (excluding hip)
      lower limb Q68.8
      shoulder Q68.8
      upper limb Q68.8
  elbow (traumatic) S53.10-●
    anterior S53.11-●
    lateral S53.14-●
    medial S53.13-●
    posterior S53.12-●
    specified type NEC S53.19-●
  finger S63.20-●
    index S63.20-●
    interphalangeal S63.22-●
      distal S63.24-●
        index S63.24-●
        little S63.24-●
        middle S63.24-●
        ring S63.24-●
      index S63.22-●
      little S63.22-●
      middle S63.22-●
      proximal S63.23-●
        index S63.23-●
        little S63.23-●
        middle S63.23-●
        ring S63.23-●
      ring S63.22-●
    little S63.20-●
    metacarpophalangeal S63.21-●
      index S63.21-●
      little S63.21-●
      middle S63.21-●
      ring S63.21-●
    middle S63.20-●
    ring S63.20-●

Subluxation (*Continued*)
  foot S93.30-●
    specified site NEC S93.33-●
    tarsal joint S93.31-●
    tarsometatarsal joint S93.32-●
    toe —*see* Subluxation, toe
  hip S73.00-●
    anterior S73.03-●
      obturator S73.02-●
    central S73.04-●
    posterior S73.01-●
  interphalangeal (joint)
    finger S63.22-●
      distal joint S63.24-●
        index S63.24-●
        little S63.24-●
        middle S63.24-●
        ring S63.24-●
      index S63.22-●
      little S63.22-●
      middle S63.22-●
      proximal joint S63.23-●
        index S63.23-●
        little S63.23-●
        middle S63.23-●
        ring S63.23-●
      ring S63.22-●
    thumb S63.12-●
    toe S93.13-●
      great S93.13-●
      lesser S93.13-●
  joint prosthesis —*see* Complications, joint
    prosthesis, mechanical, displacement,
    by site
  knee S83.10-●
    cap —*see* Subluxation, patella
    patella —*see* Subluxation, patella
    proximal tibia
      anteriorly S83.11-●
      laterally S83.14-●
      medially S83.13-●
      posteriorly S83.12-●
    specified type NEC S83.19-●
  lens —*see* Dislocation, lens, partial
  ligament, traumatic —*see* Sprain,
    by site
  metacarpal (bone)
    proximal end S63.06-●
  metacarpophalangeal (joint)
    finger S63.21-●
      index S63.21-●
      little S63.21-●
      middle S63.21-●
      ring S63.21-●
    thumb S63.11-●
  metatarsophalangeal joint S93.14-●
    great toe S93.14-●
    lesser toe S93.14-●
  midcarpal (joint) S63.03-●
  patella S83.00-●
    lateral S83.01-●
    recurrent (nontraumatic) —*see*
      Dislocation, patella, recurrent,
      incomplete
    specified type NEC S83.09-●
  pathological —*see* Dislocation,
    pathological
  radial head S53.00-●
    anterior S53.01-●
    nursemaid's elbow S53.03-●
    posterior S53.02-●
    specified type NEC S53.09-●
  radiocarpal (joint) S63.02-●
  radioulnar (joint)
    distal S63.01-●
    proximal —*see* Subluxation, elbow
  shoulder
    congenital Q68.8
    girdle S43.30-●
      scapula S43.31-●
      specified site NEC S43.39-●

Subluxation (*Continued*)
  shoulder (*Continued*)
    traumatic S43.00-●
      anterior S43.01-●
      inferior S43.03-●
      posterior S43.02-●
      specified type NEC S43.08-●
  sternoclavicular (joint) S43.20-●
    anterior S43.21-●
    posterior S43.22-●
  symphysis (pubis)
  thumb S63.103
    interphalangeal joint —*see* Subluxation,
      interphalangeal (joint), thumb
    metacarpophalangeal joint —*see*
      Subluxation, metacarpophalangeal
      (joint), thumb
  toe(s) S93.10-●
    great S93.10-●
      interphalangeal joint S93.13-●
      metatarsophalangeal joint S93.14-●
    interphalangeal joint S93.13-●
    lesser S93.10-●
      interphalangeal joint S93.13-●
      metatarsophalangeal joint S93.14-●
    metatarsophalangeal joint S93.149
  ulnohumeral joint —*see* Subluxation, elbow
  vertebral
    recurrent NEC —*see* subcategory M43.5
    traumatic
      cervical S13.100
        atlantoaxial joint S13.120
        atlantooccipital joint S13.110
        atloidooccipital joint S13.110
        joint between
          C0 and C1 S13.110
          C1 and C2 S13.120
          C2 and C3 S13.130
          C3 and C4 S13.140
          C4 and C5 S13.150
          C5 and C6 S13.160
          C6 and C7 S13.170
          C7 and T1 S13.180
        occipitoatloid joint S13.110
      lumbar S33.100
        joint between
          L1 and L2 S33.110
          L2 and L3 S33.120
          L3 and L4 S33.130
          L4 and L5 S33.140
      thoracic S23.100
        joint between
          T1 and T2 S23.110
          T2 and T3 S23.120
          T3 and T4 S23.122
          T4 and T5 S23.130
          T5 and T6 S23.132
          T6 and T7 S23.140
          T7 and T8 S23.142
          T8 and T9 S23.150
          T9 and T10 S23.152
          T10 and T11 S23.160
          T11 and T12 S23.162
          T12 and L1 S23.170
  ulna
    distal end S63.07-●
    proximal end —*see* Subluxation, elbow
  wrist (carpal bone) S63.00-●
    carpometacarpal joint —*see* Subluxation,
      carpometacarpal (joint)
    distal radioulnar joint —*see* Subluxation,
      radioulnar (joint), distal
    metacarpal bone, proximal —*see* Subluxation,
      metacarpal (bone), proximal end
    midcarpal —*see* Subluxation, midcarpal
      (joint)
    radiocarpal joint —*see* Subluxation,
      radiocarpal (joint)
    recurrent —*see* Dislocation, recurrent, wrist
    specified site NEC S63.09-●
    ulna —*see* Subluxation, ulna, distal end

▶ New   ⇒ Revised   ~~deleted~~ Deleted   ● Use Additional Character(s)

Submaxillary —*see* condition
Submersion (fatal) (nonfatal) T75.1
Submucous —*see* condition
Subnormal, subnormality
　accommodation (old age) H52.4
　mental —*see* Disability, intellectual
　temperature (accidental) T68
Subphrenic —*see* condition
Subscapular nerve —*see* condition
Subseptus uterus Q51.28
Subsiding appendicitis K36
Substance (other psychoactive) -induced
　anxiety disorder F19.980
　bipolar and related disorder F19.94
　delirium F19.921
　depressive disorder F19.94
　major neurocognitive disorder F19.97
　mild neurocognitive disorder F19.988
　obsessive-compulsive and related disorder
　　F19.988
　psychotic disorder F19.959
　sexual dysfunction F19.981
　sleep disorder F19.982
Substernal thyroid E04.9
　congenital Q89.2
Substitution disorder F44.9
Subtentorial —*see* condition
Subthyroidism (acquired) —*see also*
　Hypothyroidism
　congenital E03.1
Succenturiate placenta O43.19-●
Sucking thumb, child (excessive) F98.8
Sudamen, sudamina L74.1
Sudanese kala-azar B55.0
Sudden
　hearing loss —*see* Deafness, sudden
　heart failure —*see* Failure, heart
Sudeck's atrophy, disease, or syndrome —*see*
　Algoneurodystrophy
Suffocation —*see* Asphyxia, traumatic
Sugar
　blood
　　high (transient) R73.9
　　low (transient) E16.2
　in urine R81
Suicide, suicidal (attempted) T14.91
　by poisoning —*see* Table of Drugs and
　　Chemicals
　history of (personal) Z91.5
　　in family Z81.8
　ideation —*see* Ideation, suicidal
　risk
　　meaning personal history of attempted
　　　suicide Z91.5
　　meaning suicidal ideation —*see* Ideation,
　　　suicidal
　tendencies
　　meaning personal history of attempted
　　　suicide Z91.5
　　meaning suicidal ideation —*see* Ideation,
　　　suicidal
　trauma —*see* nature of injury by site
Suipestifer infection —*see* Infection, salmonella
Sulfhemoglobinemia, sulphemoglobinemia
　(acquired) (with methemoglobinemia) D74.8
Sumatran mite fever A75.3
Summer —*see* condition
Sunburn L55.9
　due to
　　tanning bed (acute) L56.8
　　　chronic L57.8
　　ultraviolet radiation (acute) L56.8
　　　chronic L57.8
　first degree L55.0
　second degree L55.1
　third degree L55.2
SUNCT (short lasting unilateral neuralgiform
　headache with conjunctival injection and
　tearing) G44.059
　intractable G44.051
　not intractable G44.059

Sundowning F05
Sunken acetabulum —*see* Derangement, joint,
　specified type NEC, hip
Sunstroke T67.01
　specified NEC T67.09
Superfecundation —*see* Pregnancy, multiple
Superfetation —*see* Pregnancy, multiple
Superinvolution (uterus) N85.8
Supernumerary (congenital)
　aortic cusps Q23.8
　auditory ossicles Q16.3
　bone Q79.8
　breast Q83.1
　carpal bones Q74.0
　cusps, heart valve NEC Q24.8
　　aortic Q23.8
　　mitral Q23.2
　　pulmonary Q22.3
　digit(s) Q69.9
　ear (lobule) Q17.0
　fallopian tube Q50.6
　finger Q69.0
　hymen Q52.4
　kidney Q63.0
　lacrimonasal duct Q10.6
　lobule (ear) Q17.0
　mitral cusps Q23.2
　muscle Q79.8
　nipple(s) Q83.3
　organ or site not listed —*see* Accessory
　ossicles, auditory Q16.3
　ovary Q50.31
　oviduct Q50.6
　pulmonary, pulmonic cusps Q22.3
　rib Q76.6
　　cervical or first (syndrome) Q76.5
　roots (of teeth) K00.2
　spleen Q89.09
　tarsal bones Q74.2
　teeth K00.1
　testis Q55.29
　thumb Q69.1
　toe Q69.2
　uterus Q51.28
　vagina Q52.1
　vertebra Q76.49
Supervision (of)
　contraceptive —*see* Prescription,
　　contraceptives
　dietary (for) Z71.3
　　allergy (food) Z71.3
　　colitis Z71.3
　　diabetes mellitus Z71.3
　　food allergy or intolerance Z71.3
　　gastritis Z71.3
　　hypercholesterolemia Z71.3
　　hypoglycemia Z71.3
　　intolerance (food) Z71.3
　　obesity Z71.3
　　specified NEC Z71.3
　healthy infant or child Z76.2
　　foundling Z76.1
　high-risk pregnancy —*see* Pregnancy,
　　complicated by, high, risk
　lactation Z39.1
　pregnancy —*see* Pregnancy, supervision of
Supplemental teeth K00.1
Suppression
　binocular vision H53.34
　lactation O92.5
　menstruation N94.89
　ovarian secretion E28.39
　renal N28.9
　urine, urinary secretion R34
Suppuration, suppurative —*see also* condition
　accessory sinus (chronic) —*see* Sinusitis
　adrenal gland
　antrum (chronic) —*see* Sinusitis, maxillary
　bladder —*see* Cystitis
　brain G06.0
　　sequelae G09

Suppuration, suppurative (Continued)
　breast N61.1
　　puerperal, postpartum or gestational —*see*
　　　Mastitis, obstetric, purulent
　dental periosteum M27.3
　ear (middle) —*see also* Otitis, media
　　external NEC —*see* Otitis, externa, infective
　　internal —*see* subcategory H83.0
　ethmoidal (chronic) (sinus) —*see* Sinusitis,
　　ethmoidal
　fallopian tube —*see* Salpingo-oophoritis
　frontal (chronic) (sinus) —*see* Sinusitis, frontal
　gallbladder (acute) K81.0
　gum K05.20
　　generalized —*see* Periodontitis, aggressive,
　　　generalized
　　localized —*see* Periodontitis, aggressive,
　　　localized
　intracranial G06.0
　joint —*see* Arthritis, pyogenic or pyemic
　labyrinthine —*see* subcategory H83.0
　lung —*see* Abscess, lung
　mammary gland N61.1
　　puerperal, postpartum O91.12
　　associated with lactation O91.13
　maxilla, maxillary M27.2
　　sinus (chronic) —*see* Sinusitis, maxillary
　muscle —*see* Myositis, infective
　nasal sinus (chronic) —*see* Sinusitis
　pancreas, acute —*see also* Pancreatitis, acute
　　K85.80
　parotid gland —*see* Sialoadenitis
　pelvis, pelvic
　　female —*see* Disease, pelvis, inflammatory
　　male K65.0
　pericranial —*see* Osteomyelitis
　salivary duct or gland (any) —*see*
　　Sialoadenitis
　sinus (accessory) (chronic) (nasal) —*see*
　　Sinusitis
　sphenoidal sinus (chronic) —*see* Sinusitis,
　　sphenoidal
　thymus (gland) E32.1
　thyroid (gland) E06.0
　tonsil —*see* Tonsillitis
　uterus —*see* Endometritis
Supraeruption of tooth (teeth) M26.34
Supraglottitis J04.30
　with obstruction J04.31
Suprarenal (gland) —*see* condition
Suprascapular nerve —*see* condition
Suprasellar —*see* condition
Surfer's knots or nodules S89.8-●
Surgical
　emphysema T81.82
　procedures, complication or misadventure —
　　see Complications, surgical procedures
　shock T81.10
Surveillance (of) (for) —*see also* Observation
　alcohol abuse Z71.41
　contraceptive —*see* Prescription, contraceptives
　dietary Z71.3
　drug abuse Z71.51
Susceptibility to disease, genetic Z15.89
　malignant neoplasm Z15.09
　　breast Z15.01
　　endometrium Z15.04
　　ovary Z15.02
　　prostate Z15.03
　　specified NEC Z15.09
　multiple endocrine neoplasia Z15.81
Suspected condition, ruled out —*see also*
　Observation, suspected
　amniotic cavity and membrane Z03.71
　cervical shortening Z03.75
　fetal anomaly Z03.73
　fetal growth Z03.74
　maternal and fetal conditions NEC Z03.79
　newborn —*see also* Observation, newborn,
　　suspected condition ruled out Z05.9
　oligohydramnios Z03.71

Suspected condition, ruled out (Continued)
- placental problem Z03.72
- polyhydramnios Z03.71

Suspended uterus
- in pregnancy or childbirth —see Pregnancy, complicated by, abnormal uterus

Sutton's nevus D22.9

Suture
- burst (in operation wound) T81.31
  - external operation wound T81.31
  - internal operation wound T81.32
- inadvertently left in operation wound —see Foreign body, accidentally left during a procedure
- removal Z48.02

Swab inadvertently left in operation wound —see Foreign body, accidentally left during a procedure

Swallowed, swallowing
- difficulty —see Dysphagia
- foreign body —see Foreign body, alimentary tract

Swan-neck deformity (finger) —see Deformity, finger, swan-neck

Swearing, compulsive F42.8
- in Gilles de la Tourette's syndrome F95.2

Sweat, sweats
- fetid L75.0
- night R61

Sweating, excessive R61

Sweeley-Klionsky disease E75.21

Sweet's disease or dermatosis L98.2

Swelling (of) R60.9
- abdomen, abdominal (not referable to any particular organ) —see Mass, abdominal
- ankle —see Effusion, joint, ankle
- arm M79.89
  - forearm M79.89
- breast —see also Lump, breast N63.0
- Calabar B74.3
- cervical gland R59.0
- chest, localized R22.2
- ear H93.8-●
- extremity (lower) (upper) —see Disorder, soft tissue, specified type NEC
- finger M79.89
- foot M79.89
- glands R59.9
  - generalized R59.1
  - localized R59.0
- hand M79.89
- head (localized) R22.0
- inflammatory —see Inflammation
- intra-abdominal —see Mass, abdominal
- joint —see Effusion, joint
- leg M79.89
  - lower M79.89
- limb —see Disorder, soft tissue, specified type NEC
- localized (skin) R22.9
  - chest R22.2
  - head R22.0
  - limb
    - lower —see Mass, localized, limb, lower
    - upper —see Mass, localized, limb, upper
  - neck R22.1
  - trunk R22.2
- neck (localized) R22.1
- pelvic —see Mass, abdominal
- scrotum N50.89
- splenic —see Splenomegaly
- testis N50.89
- toe M79.89
- umbilical R19.09
- wandering, due to Gnathostoma (spinigerum) B83.1
- white —see Tuberculosis, arthritis

Swift (-Feer) disease
- overdose or wrong substance given or taken —see Table of Drugs and Chemicals, by drug, poisoning

Swimmer's
- cramp T75.1
- ear H60.33-●
- itch B65.3

Swimming in the head R42

Swollen —see Swelling

Swyer syndrome Q99.1

Sycosis L73.8
- barbae (not parasitic) L73.8
- contagiosa (mycotic) B35.0
- lupoides L73.8
- mycotic B35.0
- parasitic B35.0
- vulgaris L73.8

Sydenham's chorea —see Chorea, Sydenham's

Sylvatic yellow fever A95.0

Sylvest's disease B33.0

Symblepharon H11.23-●
- congenital Q10.3

Symond's syndrome G93.2

Sympathetic —see condition

Sympatheticotonia G90.8

Sympathicoblastoma
- specified site —see Neoplasm, malignant, by site
- unspecified site C74.90

Sympathogonioma —see Sympathicoblastoma

Symphalangy (fingers) (toes) Q70.9

Symptoms NEC R68.89
- breast NEC N64.59
- cold J00
- development NEC R63.8
- factitious, self-induced —see Disorder, factitious
- genital organs, female R10.2
- involving
  - abdomen NEC R19.8
  - appearance NEC R46.89
  - awareness R41.9
    - altered mental status R41.82
    - amnesia —see Amnesia
    - borderline intellectual functioning R41.83
    - coma —see Coma
    - disorientation R41.0
    - neurologic neglect syndrome R41.4
    - senile cognitive decline R41.81
    - specified symptom NEC R41.89
  - behavior NEC R46.89
  - cardiovascular system NEC R09.89
  - chest NEC R09.89
  - circulatory system NEC R09.89
  - cognitive functions R41.9
    - altered mental status R41.82
    - amnesia —see Amnesia
    - borderline intellectual functioning R41.83
    - coma —see Coma
    - disorientation R41.0
    - neurologic neglect syndrome R41.4
    - senile cognitive decline R41.81
    - specified symptom NEC R41.89
  - development NEC R62.50
  - digestive system NEC R19.8
  - emotional state NEC R45.89
    - emotional lability R45.86
  - food and fluid intake R63.8
  - general perceptions and sensations R44.9
    - specified NEC R44.8
  - musculoskeletal system R29.91
    - specified NEC R29.898
  - nervous system R29.90
    - specified NEC R29.818
  - pelvis NEC R19.8
  - respiratory system NEC R09.89
  - skin and integument R23.9
  - urinary system R39.9
- menopausal N95.1
- metabolism NEC R63.8

Symptoms NEC (Continued)
- neurotic F48.8
- of infancy R68.19
- pelvis NEC, female R10.2
- skin and integument NEC R23.9
- subcutaneous tissue NEC R23.9
- viral cold J00

Sympus Q74.2

Syncephalus Q89.4

Synchondrosis
- abnormal (congenital) Q78.8
- ischiopubic M91.0

Synchysis (scintillans) (senile) (vitreous body) H43.89

Syncope (near) (pre-) R55
- anginosa I20.8
- bradycardia R00.1
- cardiac R55
- carotid sinus G90.01
- due to spinal (lumbar) puncture G97.1
- heart R55
- heat T67.1
- laryngeal R05
- psychogenic F48.8
- tussive R05
- vasoconstriction R55
- vasodepressor R55
- vasomotor R55
- vasovagal R55

Syndactylism, syndactyly Q70.9
- complex (with synostosis)
  - fingers Q70.0-●
  - toes Q70.2-●
- simple (without synostosis)
  - fingers Q70.1-●
  - toes Q70.3-●

Syndrome —see also Disease
- 5q minus NOS D46.C
- 48,XXXX Q97.1
- 49,XXXXX Q97.1
- abdominal
  - acute R10.0
  - muscle deficiency Q79.4
- abnormal innervation H02.519
  - left H02.516
    - lower H02.515
    - upper H02.514
  - right H02.513
    - lower H02.512
    - upper H02.511
- abstinence, neonatal P96.1
- acid pulmonary aspiration, obstetric O74.0
- acquired immunodeficiency —see Human, immunodeficiency virus (HIV) disease
- acute abdominal R10.0
- acute respiratory distress (adult) (child) J80
  - idiopathic J84.114
- Adair-Dighton Q78.0
- Adams-Stokes (-Morgagni) I45.9
- adiposogenital E23.6
- adrenal
  - hemorrhage (meningococcal) A39.1
  - meningococcic A39.1
- adrenocortical —see Cushing's, syndrome
- adrenogenital E25.9
  - congenital, associated with enzyme deficiency E25.0
- afferent loop NEC K91.89
- Alagille's Q44.7
- alcohol withdrawal (without convulsions) —see Dependence, alcohol, with, withdrawal
- Alder's D72.0
- Aldrich (-Wiskott) D82.0
- alien hand R41.4
- Alport Q87.81
- alveolar hypoventilation E66.2
- alveolocapillary block J84.10
- amnesic, amnestic (confabulatory) (due to) —see Disorder, amnesic
- amyostatic (Wilson's disease) E83.01

Syndrome *(Continued)*
  androgen insensitivity E34.50
    complete E34.51
    partial E34.52
  androgen resistance *(see also* Syndrome,
      androgen insensitivity) E34.50
  Angelman Q93.51
  anginal —*see* Angina
  ankyloglossia superior Q38.1
  anterior
    chest wall R07.89
    cord G83.82
    spinal artery G95.19
      compression M47.019
        cervical region M47.012
        cervicothoracic region M47.013
        lumbar region M47.016
        occipito-atlanto-axial region M47.011
        thoracic region M47.014
        thoracolumbar region M47.015
    tibial M76.81-●
  antibody deficiency D80.9
    agammaglobulinemic D80.1
      hereditary D80.0
    congenital D80.0
    hypogammaglobulinemic D80.1
      hereditary D80.0
  anticardiolipin (-antibody) D68.61
  antidepressant discontinuation T43.205
  antiphospholipid (-antibody) D68.61
  aortic
    arch M31.4
    bifurcation I74.09
  aortomesenteric duodenum occlusion K31.5
  apical ballooning (transient left ventricular)
      I51.81
  arcuate ligament I77.4
  argentaffin, argentaffinoma E34.0
  Arnold-Chiari —*see* Arnold-Chiari disease
  Arrillaga-Ayerza I27.0
  arterial tortuosity Q87.82
  arteriovenous steal T82.898-●
  Asherman's N85.6
  aspiration, of newborn —*see* Aspiration, by
      substance, with pneumonia
    meconium P24.01
  ataxia-telangiectasia G11.3
  auriculotemporal G50.8
  autoerythrocyte sensitization (Gardner-
      Diamond) D69.2
  autoimmune lymphoproliferative [ALPS]
      D89.82
  autoimmune polyglandular E31.0
  autoinflammatory M04.9
    specified type NEC M04.8
  autosomal —*see* Abnormal, autosomes
  Avellis' G46.8
  Ayerza (-Arrillaga) I27.0
  Babinski-Nageotte G83.89
  Bakwin-Krida Q78.5
  bare lymphocyte D81.6
  Barré-Guillain G61.0
  Barré-Liéou M53.0
  Barrett's —*see* Barrett's, esophagus
  Barsony-Polgar K22.4
  Barsony-Teschendorf K22.4
  Barth E78.71
  Bartter's E26.81
  basal cell nevus Q87.89
  Basedow's E05.00
    with thyroid storm E05.01
  basilar artery G45.0
  Batten-Steinert G71.11
  battered
    baby or child —*see* Maltreatment, child,
        physical abuse
    spouse —*see* Maltreatment, adult, physical
        abuse
  Beals Q87.40
  Beau's I51.5
  Beck's I65.8

Syndrome *(Continued)*
  Benedikt's G46.3
  Béquez César (-Steinbrinck-Chédiak-Higashi)
      D70.330
  Bernhardt-Roth —*see* Meralgia paresthetica
  Bernheim's —*see* Failure, heart, right
  big spleen D73.1
  bilateral polycystic ovarian E28.2
  Bing-Horton's —*see* Horton's headache
  Birt-Hogg-Dube syndrome Q87.89
  Björck (-Thorsen) E34.0
  black
    lung J60
    widow spider bite —*see* Toxicity, venom,
        spider, black widow
  Blackfan-Diamond D61.01
  Blau M04.8
  blind loop K90.2
    congenital Q43.8
    postsurgical K91.2
  blue sclera Q78.0
  blue toe I75.02-●
  Boder-Sedgewick G11.3
  Boerhaave's K22.3
  Borjeson Forssman Lehmann Q89.8
  Bouillaud's I01.9
  Bourneville (-Pringle) Q85.1
  Bouveret (-Hoffman) I47.9
  brachial plexus G54.0
  bradycardia-tachycardia I49.5
  brain (nonpsychotic) F09
    with psychosis, psychotic reaction F09
      acute or subacute —*see* Delirium
    congenital —*see* Disability, intellectual
    organic F09
      post-traumatic (nonpsychotic) F07.81
        psychotic F09
      personality change F07.0
      postcontusional F07.81
      post-traumatic, nonpsychotic F07.81
      psycho-organic F09
      psychotic F06.8
    brain stem stroke G46.3
  Brandt's (acrodermatitis enteropathica)
      E83.2
  broad ligament laceration N83.8
  Brock's J98.11
  bronze baby P83.88
  Brown-Sequard G83.81
  Brugada I49.8
  bubbly lung P27.0
  Buchem's M85.2
  Budd-Chiari I82.0
  bulbar (progressive) G12.22
  Bürger-Grütz E78.3
  Burke's K86.89
  Burnett's (milk-alkali) E83.52
  burning feet E53.9
  Bywaters' T79.5
  Call-Fleming I67.841
  carbohydrate-deficient glycoprotein (CDGS)
      E77.8
  carcinogenic thrombophlebitis I82.1
  carcinoid E34.0
  cardiac asthma I50.1
  cardiacos negros I27.0
  cardiofaciocutaneous Q87.89
  cardiopulmonary-obesity E66.2
  cardiorenal —*see* Hypertension, cardiorenal
  cardiorespiratory distress (idiopathic),
      newborn P22.0
  cardiovascular renal —*see* Hypertension,
      cardiorenal
  carotid
    artery (hemispheric) (internal)
        G45.1
    body G90.01
    sinus G90.01
  carpal tunnel G56.0-●
  Cassidy (-Scholte) E34.0
  cat-cry Q93.4

Syndrome *(Continued)*
  cat eye Q92.8
  cauda equina G83.4
  causalgia —*see* Causalgia
  celiac K90.0
    artery compression I77.4
    axis I77.4
  central pain G89.0
  cerebellar
    hereditary G11.9
    stroke G46.4
  cerebellomedullary malformation —*see* Spina
      bifida
  cerebral
    artery
      anterior G46.1
      middle G46.0
      posterior G46.2
    gigantism E22.0
  cervical (root) M53.1
    disc —*see* Disorder, disc, cervical, with
        neuritis
    fusion Q76.1
    posterior, sympathicus M53.0
    rib Q76.5
    sympathetic paralysis G90.2
  cervicobrachial (diffuse) M53.1
  cervicocranial M53.0
  cervicodorsal outlet G54.2
  cervicothoracic outlet G54.0
  Céstan (-Raymond) I65.8
  Charcot's (angina cruris) (intermittent
      claudication) I73.9
  Charcot-Weiss-Baker G90.09
  CHARGE Q89.8
  Chédiak-Higashi (-Steinbrinck) E70.330
  chest wall R07.1
  Chiari's (hepatic vein thrombosis) I82.0
  Chilaiditi's Q43.3
  child maltreatment —*see* Maltreatment,
      child
  chondrocostal junction M94.0
  chondroectodermal dysplasia Q77.6
  chromosome 4 short arm deletion Q93.3
  chromosome 5 short arm deletion Q93.4
  chronic
    infantile neurological, cutaneous and
        articular (CINCA) M04.2
    pain G89.4
      personality F68.8
  Churg-Strauss M30.1
  Clarke-Hadfield K86.89
  Clerambault's automatism G93.89
  Clouston's (hidrotic ectodermal dysplasia)
      Q82.4
  clumsiness, clumsy child F82
  cluster headache G44.009
    intractable G44.001
    not intractable G44.009
  Coffin-Lowry Q89.8
  cold injury (newborn) P80.0
  combined immunity deficiency D81.9
  compartment (deep) (posterior) (traumatic)
      T79.A0
    abdomen T79.A3
    lower extremity (hip, buttock, thigh, leg,
        foot, toes) T79.A2
    nontraumatic
      abdomen M79.A3
      lower extremity (hip, buttock, thigh, leg,
          foot, toes) M79.A2-●
      specified site NEC M79.A9
      upper extremity (shoulder, arm, forearm,
          wrist, hand, fingers) M79.A1-●
    postprocedural —*see* Syndrome
        compartment, nontraumatic
    specified site NEC T79.A9
    upper extremity (shoulder, arm, forearm,
        wrist, hand, fingers) T79.A1
  complex regional pain —*see* Syndrome, pain,
      complex regional

Syndrome *(Continued)*
  compression T79.5
    anterior spinal —*see* Syndrome, anterior,
      spinal artery, compression
    cauda equina G83.4
    celiac artery I77.4
    vertebral artery M47.029
      cervical region M47.022
      occipito-atlanto-axial region M47.021
  concussion F07.81
  congenital
    affecting multiple systems NEC Q87.89
    central alveolar hypoventilation G47.35
    facial diplegia Q87.0
    muscular hypertrophy-cerebral
      Q87.89
    oculo-auriculovertebral Q87.0
    oculofacial diplegia (Moebius)
      Q87.0
    rubella (manifest) P35.0
  congestion-fibrosis (pelvic), female
    N94.89
  congestive dysmenorrhea N94.6
  Conn's E26.01
  connective tissue M35.9
    overlap NEC M35.1
  conus medullaris G95.81
  cord
    anterior G83.82
    posterior G83.83
  coronary
    acute NEC I24.9
    insufficiency or intermediate I20.0
    slow flow I20.8
  Costen's (complex) M26.69
  costochondral junction M94.0
  costoclavicular G54.0
  costovertebral E22.0
  Cowden Q85.8
  craniovertebral M53.0
  Creutzfeldt-Jakob —*see* Creutzfeldt-Jakob
    disease or syndrome
  cri-du-chat Q93.4
  crib death R99
  cricopharyngeal —*see* Dysphagia
  croup J05.0
  CRPS I —*see* Syndrome, pain, complex
    regional I
  crush T79.5
  cubital tunnel —*see* Lesion, nerve, ulnar
  Curschmann (-Batten) (-Steinert) G71.11
  Cushing's E24.9
    alcohol-induced E24.4
    drug-induced E24.2
    due to
      alcohol
      drugs E24.2
      ectopic ACTH E24.3
      overproduction of pituitary ACTH
        E24.0
    overdose or wrong substance given
      or taken —*see* Table of Drugs and
      Chemicals, by drug, poisoning
    pituitary-dependent E24.0
    specified type NEC E24.8
  cryopyrin-associated periodic M04.2
  cryptophthalmos Q87.0
  cystic duct stump K91.5
▸ cytokine release D89.839
    ▸ grade 1 D89.831
    ▸ grade 2 D89.832
    ▸ grade 3 D89.833
    ▸ grade 4 D89.834
    ▸ grade 5 D89.835
  Dana-Putnam D51.0
  Danbolt (-Cross) (acrodermatitis
    enteropathica) E83.2
  Dandy-Walker Q03.1
    with spina bifida Q07.01
  Danlos' (*see also* Syndrome, Ehlers-Danlos)
    Q79.60

Syndrome *(Continued)*
  defibrination —*see also* Fibrinolysis
    with
      antepartum hemorrhage —*see*
        Hemorrhage, antepartum, with
        coagulation defect
      intrapartum hemorrhage —*see*
        Hemorrhage, complicating,
        delivery
    newborn P60
    postpartum O72.3
  Degos' I77.8
  Déjérine-Roussy G89.0
  delayed sleep phase G47.21
  demyelinating G37.9
  dependence —*see* F10-F19 with fourth
    character .2
  depersonalization (-derealization) F48.1
  De Quervain E34.51
  de Toni-Fanconi (-Debré) E72.09
    with cystinosis E72.04
▸ de Vivo syndrome E74.810
  diabetes mellitus-hypertension-nephrosis —
    see Diabetes, nephrosis
  diabetes mellitus in newborn infant P70.2
  diabetes-nephrosis —*see* Diabetes, nephrosis
  diabetic amyotrophy —*see* Diabetes,
    amyotrophy
  dialysis associated steal T82.898-●
  Diamond-Blackfan D61.01
  Diamond-Gardener D69.2
  DIC (diffuse or disseminated intravascular
    coagulopathy) D65
  di George's D82.1
  Dighton's Q78.0
  disequilibrium E87.8
  Döhle body-panmyelopathic D72.0
  dorsolateral medullary G46.4
  double athetosis G80.3
  Down (*see also* Down syndrome) Q90.9
▸ Dravet (intractable) G40.834
    ▸ with status epilepticus G40.833
    ▸ without status epilepticus G40.834
  Dresbach's (elliptocytosis) D58.1
▸ DRESS (drug rash with eosinophilia and
    systemic symptoms) D72.12
  Dressler's (postmyocardial infarction) I24.1
    postcardiotomy I97.0
▸ drug rash with eosinophilia and systemic
    symptoms (DRESS) D72.12
  drug withdrawal, infant of dependent mother
    P96.1
  dry eye H04.12-●
  due to abnormality
    chromosomal Q99.9
      sex
        female phenotype Q97.9
        male phenotype Q98.9
      specified NEC Q99.8
  dumping (postgastrectomy) K91.1
    nonsurgical K31.89
  Dupré's (meningism) R29.1
  dysmetabolic X E88.81
  dyspraxia, developmental F82
  Eagle-Barrett Q79.4
  Eaton-Lambert —*see* Syndrome, Lambert-Eaton
  Ebstein's Q22.5
  ectopic ACTH E24.3
  eczema-thrombocytopenia D82.0
  Eddowes' Q78.0
  effort (psychogenic) F45.8
  Ehlers-Danlos Q79.60
    classical (cEDS) (classical EDS) Q79.61
    hypermobile (hEDS) (hypermobile EDS)
      Q79.62
    specified NEC Q79.69
    vascular (vascular EDS) (vEDS) Q79.63
  Eisenmenger's I27.83
  Ekman's Q78.0
  electric feet E53.8
  Ellis-van Creveld Q77.6

Syndrome *(Continued)*
  empty nest Z60.0
  endocrine-hypertensive E27.0
  entrapment —*see* Neuropathy, entrapment
  eosinophilia-myalgia M35.8
  epileptic —*see also* Epilepsy, by type
    absence G40.A09
      intractable G40.A19
        with status epilepticus G40.A11
        without status epilepticus G40.A19
      not intractable G40.A09
        with status epilepticus G40.A01
        without status epilepticus G40.A09
  Erdheim-Chester (ECD) E88.89
  Erdheim's E22.0
  erythrocyte fragmentation D59.4
  Evans D69.41
  exhaustion F48.8
  extrapyramidal G25.9
    specified NEC G25.89
  eye retraction —*see* Strabismus
  eyelid-malar-mandible Q87.0
  Faber's D50.9
▸ facet M47.89-●
  facial pain, paroxysmal G50.0
  Fallot's Q21.3
  familial cold autoinflammatory M04.2
  familial eczema-thrombocytopenia (Wiskott-
    Aldrich) D82.0
  Fanconi (-de Toni) (-Debré) E72.09
    with cystinosis E72.04
  Fanconi's (anemia) (congenital pancytopenia)
    D61.09
  fatigue
    chronic R53.82
    psychogenic F48.8
  faulty bowel habit K59.39
  Feil-Klippel (brevicollis) Q76.1
  Felty's —*see* Felty's syndrome
  fertile eunuch E23.0
  fetal
    alcohol (dysmorphic) Q86.0
    hydantoin Q86.1
  Fiedler's I40.1
  first arch Q87.0
  fish odor E72.89
  Fisher's G61.0
  Fitzhugh-Curtis
    due to
      Chlamydia trachomatis A74.81
      Neisseria gonorrhorea (gonococcal
        peritonitis) A54.85
  Fitz's —*see also* Pancreatitis, acute K85.80
  Flajani (-Basedow) E05.00
    with thyroid storm E05.01
  flatback —*see* Flatback syndrome
  floppy
    baby P94.2
    iris (intraoeprative) (IFIS) H21.81
    mitral valve I34.1
  flush E34.0
  Foix-Alajouanine G95.19
  Fong's Q87.2
  food protein-induced enterocolitis (FPIES)
    K52.21
  foramen magnum G93.5
  Foster-Kennedy H47.14-●
  Foville's (peduncular) G46.3
  fragile X Q99.2
  Franceschetti Q75.4
  Frey's
    auriculotemporal G50.8
    hyperhidrosis L74.52
  Friderichsen-Waterhouse A39.1
  Froin's G95.89
  frontal lobe F07.0
  Fukuhara E88.49
  functional
    bowel K59.9
    prepubertal castrate E29.1
  Gaisböck's D75.1

▶ New   ⇒ Revised   ~~deleted~~ Deleted   ● Use Additional Character(s)

Syndrome *(Continued)*
- ganglion (basal ganglia brain) G25.9
  - geniculi G51.1
- Gardner-Diamond D69.2
- gastroesophageal
  - junction K22.0
  - laceration-hemorrhage K22.6
- gastrojejunal loop obstruction K91.89
- Gee-Herter-Heubner K90.0
- Gelineau's G47.419
  - with cataplexy G47.411
- genito-anorectal A55
- Gerstmann-Sträussler-Scheinker (GSS) A81.82
- Gianotti-Crosti L44.4
- giant platelet (Bernard-Soulier) D69.1
- Gilles de la Tourette's F95.2
- Glass Q87.89
- ▶ Gleich's D72.118
- goiter-deafness E07.1
- Goldberg Q89.8
- Goldberg-Maxwell E34.51
- Good's D83.8
- Gopalan' (burning feet) E53.8
- Gorlin's Q87.89
- Gougerot-Blum L81.7
- Gouley's I31.1
- Gower's R55
- gray or grey (newborn) P93.0
  - platelet D69.1
- Gubler-Millard G46.3
- Guillain-Barré (-Strohl) G61.0
- gustatory sweating G50.8
- Hadfield-Clarke K86.89
- hair tourniquet —*see* Constriction, external, by site
- Hamman's J98.19
- hand-foot L27.1
- hand-shoulder G90.8
- hantavirus (cardio)-pulmonary (HPS) (HCPS) B33.4
- happy puppet Q93.51
- Harada's H30.81-●
- Hayem-Faber D50.9
- headache NEC G44.89
  - complicated NEC G44.59
- Heberden's I20.8
- Hedinger's E34.0
- Hegglin's D72.0
- HELLP (hemolysis, elevated liver enzymes and low platelet count) O14.2-●
  - complicating
    - childbirth O14.24
      - puerperium O14.25
- hemolytic-uremic D59.3
- hemophagocytic, infection-associated D76.2
- Henoch-Schönlein D69.0
- ⇒ hepatic flexure K59.89
- hepatopulmonary K76.81
- hepatorenal K76.7
  - following delivery O90.4
  - postoperative or postprocedural K91.83
  - postpartum, puerperal O90.4
- hepatourologic K76.7
- Herter (-Gee) (nontropical sprue) K90.0
- Heubner-Herter K90.0
- Heyd's K76.7
- Hilger's G90.09
- histamine-like (fish poisoning) —*see* Poisoning, fish
- histiocytic D76.3
- histiocytosis NEC D76.3
- HIV infection, acute B20
- Hoffmann-Werdnig G12.0
- Hollander-Simons E88.1
- Hoppe-Goldflam G70.00
  - with exacerbation (acute) G70.01
  - in crisis G70.01
- Horner's G90.2
- hungry bone E83.81
- hunterian glossitis D51.0
- Hutchinson's triad A50.53

Syndrome *(Continued)*
- hyperabduction G54.0
- hyperammonemia-hyperornithinemia-homocitrullinemia E72.4
- ⇒ hypereosinophilic (HES) D72.119
  - ▶ idiopathic (IHES) D72.110
  - ▶ lymphocytic variant (LHES) D72.111
  - ▶ specified NEC D72.118
- hyperimmunoglobulin D M04.1
- hyperimmunoglobulin E (IgE) D82.4
- hyperkalemic E87.5
- hyperkinetic —*see* Hyperkinesia
- hypermobility M35.7
- hypernatremia E87.0
- hyperosmolarity E87.0
- hyperperfusion G97.82
- hypersplenic D73.1
- hypertransfusion, newborn P61.1
- hyperventilation F45.8
- hyperviscosity (of serum)
  - polycythemic D75.1
  - sclerothymic D58.8
- hypoglycemic (familial) (neonatal) E16.2
- hypokalemic E87.6
- hyponatremic E87.1
- hypopituitarism E23.0
- hypoplastic left-heart Q23.4
- hypopotassemia E87.6
- hyposmolality E87.1
- hypotension, maternal O26.5-●
- hypothenar hammer I73.89
- hypoventilation, obesity (OHS) E66.2
- ICF (intravascular coagulation-fibrinolysis) D65
- idiopathic
  - cardiorespiratory distress, newborn P22.0
  - nephrotic (infantile) N04.9
- iliotibial band M76.3-●
- immobility, immobilization (paraplegic) M62.3
- immune reconstitution D89.3
- immune reconstitution inflammatory [IRIS] D89.3
- immunity deficiency, combined D81.9
- immunodeficiency
  - acquired —*see* Human, immunodeficiency virus (HIV) disease
  - combined D81.9
- impending coronary I20.0
- impingement, shoulder M75.4-●
- inappropriate secretion of antidiuretic hormone E22.2
- infant
  - gestational diabetes P70.0
  - of diabetic mother P70.1
- infantilism (pituitary) E23.0
- inferior vena cava I87.1
- inspissated bile (newborn) P59.1
- institutional (childhood) F94.2
- insufficient sleep F51.12
- intermediate coronary (artery) I20.0
- interspinous ligament —*see* Spondylopathy, specified NEC
- intestinal
  - carcinoid E34.0
  - knot K56.2
- intravascular coagulation-fibrinolysis (ICF) D65
- iodine-deficiency, congenital E00.9
  - type
    - mixed E00.2
    - myxedematous E00.1
    - neurological E00.0
- IRDS (idiopathic respiratory distress, newborn) P22.0
- irritable
  - bowel K58.9
    - with
      - constipation K58.1
      - diarrhea K58.0
    - mixed K58.2
    - psychogenic F45.8
    - specified NEC K58.8

Syndrome *(Continued)*
- irritable *(Continued)*
  - heart (psychogenic) F45.8
  - weakness F48.8
- ischemic
  - bowel (transient) K55.9
    - chronic K55.1
    - due to mesenteric artery insufficiency K55.1
  - steal T82.898
- IVC (intravascular coagulopathy) D65
- Ivemark's Q89.01
- Jaccoud's —*see* Arthropathy, postrheumatic, chronic
- Jackson's G83.89
- Jakob-Creutzfeldt —*see* Creutzfeldt-Jakob disease or syndrome
- jaw-winking Q07.8
- Jervell-Lange-Nielsen I45.81
- jet lag G47.25
- Job's D71
- Joseph-Diamond-Blackfan D61.01
- jugular foramen G52.7
- Kabuki Q89.8
- Kanner's (autism) F84.0
- Kartagener's Q89.3
- Kelly's D50.1
- Kimmelstiel-Wilson —*see* Diabetes, specified type, with Kimmelstiel-Wilson disease
- Klein (e)-Levine G47.13
- Klippel-Feil (brevicollis) Q76.1
- Köhler-Pellegrini-Steida —*see* Bursitis, tibial collateral
- ⇒ König's K59.89
- Korsakoff (-Wernicke) (nonalcoholic) F04
  - alcoholic F10.26
- Kostmann's D70.0
- Krabbe's congenital muscle hypoplasia Q79.8
- labyrinthine —*see* subcategory H83.2
- lacunar NEC G46.7
- Lambert-Eaton G70.80
  - in
    - neoplastic disease G73.1
    - specified disease NEC G70.81
- Landau-Kleffner —*see* Epilepsy, specified NEC
- Larsen's Q74.8
- lateral
  - cutaneous nerve of thigh G57.1-●
  - medullary G46.4
- Launois' E22.0
- lazy
  - leukocyte D70.8
  - posture M62.3
- Lemiere I80.8
- Lennox-Gastaut G40.812
  - intractable G40.814
    - with status epilepticus G40.813
    - without status epilepticus G40.814
  - not intractable G40.812
    - with status epilepticus G40.811
    - without status epilepticus G40.812
- lenticular, progressive E83.01
- Leopold-Levi's E05.90
- Lev's I44.2
- Li-Fraumeni Z15.01
- Lichtheim's D51.0
- Lightwood's N25.89
- Lignac (de Toni) (-Fanconi) (-Debré) E72.09
  - with cystinosis E72.04
- Likoff's I20.8
- limbic epilepsy personality F07.0
- liver-kidney K76.7
- lobotomy F07.0
- ~~Loffler's J82~~
- ▶ Löffler's J82.89
- long arm 18 or 21 deletion Q93.89
- long QT I45.81
- Louis-Barré G11.3

Syndrome *(Continued)*
    plantar fascia M72.2
    plateau iris (post-iridectomy)
            (postprocedural) H21.82
    Plummer-Vinson D50.1
    pluricarential of infancy E40
    plurideficiency E40
    pluriglandular (compensatory) E31.8
        autoimmune E31.0
    pneumatic hammer T75.21
    polyangiitis overlap M30.8
    polycarential of infancy E40
    polyglandular E31.8
        autoimmune E31.0
    polysplenia Q89.09
    pontine NEC G93.89
    popliteal
        artery entrapment I77.89
        ~~post endometrial ablation N99.85~~
        web Q87.89
    postcardiac injury
        postcardiotomy I97.0
        postmyocardial infarction I24.1
    postcardiotomy I97.0
    post chemoembolization — code to
            associated conditions
    postcholecystectomy K91.5
    postcommissurotomy I97.0
    postconcussional F07.81
    postcontusional F07.81
    postencephalitic F07.89
    ▶ post endometrial ablation N99.85
    posterior
        cervical sympathetic M53.0
        cord G83.83
        fossa compression G93.5
        reversible encephalopathy (PRES)
                I67.83
    postgastrectomy (dumping) K91.1
    postgastric surgery K91.1
    postinfarction I24.1
    postlaminectomy NEC M96.1
    postleukotomy F07.0
    postmastectomy lymphedema I97.2
    postmyocardial infarction I24.1
    postoperative NEC T81.9
        blind loop K90.2
    postpartum panhypopituitary (Sheehan)
            E23.0
    postpolio (myelitic) G14
    postthrombotic I87.009
        with
            inflammation I87.02-•
                with ulcer I87.03-•
            specified complication NEC I87.09-•
            ulcer I87.01-•
                with inflammation I87.03-•
        asymptomatic I87.00-•
    postvagotomy K91.1
    postvalvulotomy I97.0
    postviral NEC G93.3
        fatigue G93.3
    Potain's K31.0
    potassium intoxication E87.5
    Prader-Willi Q87.11
    Prader-Willi-like Q87.19
    precerebral artery (multiple) (bilateral)
            G45.2
    preinfarction I20.0
    preleukemic D46.9
    premature senility E34.8
    premenstrual dysphoric F32.81
    premenstrual tension N94.3
    Prinzmetal-Massumi R07.1
    prune belly Q79.4
    pseudocarpal tunnel (sublimis) —*see*
            Syndrome, carpal tunnel
    pseudoparalytica G70.00
        with exacerbation (acute) G70.01
        in crisis G70.01
    pseudo-Turner's Q87.19

Syndrome *(Continued)*
    psycho-organic (nonpsychotic severity) F07.9
        acute or subacute F05
        depressive type F06.31
        hallucinatory type F06.0
        nonpsychotic severity F07.0
        specified NEC F07.89
    pulmonary
        arteriosclerosis I27.0
        dysmaturity (Wilson-Mikity) P27.0
        hypoperfusion (idiopathic) P22.0
        renal (hemorrhagic) (Goodpasture's) M31.0
    pure
        motor lacunar G46.5
        sensory lacunar G46.6
    Putnam-Dana D51.0
    pyogenic arthritis, pyoderma gangrenosum,
            and acne [PAPA] M04.8
    pyramidopallidonigral G20
    pyriformis —*see* Lesion, nerve, sciatic
    QT interval prolongation I45.81
    radicular NEC —*see* Radiculopathy
        upper limbs, newborn (birth injury) P14.3
    rapid time-zone change G47.25
    Rasmussen G04.81
    Raymond (-Céstan) I65.8
    Raynaud's I73.00
        with gangrene I73.01
    RDS (respiratory distress syndrome,
            newborn) P22.0
    reactive airways dysfunction J68.3
    Refsum's G60.1
    Reifenstein E34.52
    renal glomerulohyalinosis-diabetic —*see*
            Diabetes, nephrosis
    Rendu-Osler-Weber I78.0
    residual ovary N99.83
    resistant ovary E28.39
    respiratory
        distress
            acute J80
                adult J80
                child J80
                idiopathic J84.114
            newborn (idiopathic) (type I) P22.0
                type II P22.1
    restless legs G25.81
    retinoblastoma (familial) C69.2
    retroperitoneal fibrosis N13.5
    retroviral seroconversion (acute) Z21
    Reye's G93.7
    Richter —*see* Leukemia, chronic lymphocytic,
            B-cell type
    Ridley's I50.1
    right
        heart, hypoplastic Q22.6
        ventricular obstruction —*see* Failure, heart,
                right
    Romano-Ward (prolonged QT interval) I45.81
    rotator cuff, shoulder —*see also* Tear, rotator
            cuff M75.10-•
    Rotes Quérol —*see* Hyperostosis, ankylosing
    Roth —*see* Meralgia paresthetica
    rubella (congenital) P35.0
    Ruvalcaba-Myhre-Smith E71.440
    Rytand-Lipsitch I44.2
    salt
        depletion E87.1
            due to heat NEC T67.8
                causing heat exhaustion or prostration
                        T67.4
        low E87.1
    salt-losing N28.89
    SATB2-associated Q87.89
    Scaglietti-Dagnini E22.0
    scalenus anticus (anterior) G54.0
    scapulocostal —*see* Mononeuropathy, upper
            limb, specified site NEC
    scapuloperoneal G71.09
    schizophrenic, of childhood NEC F84.5
    Schnitzler D47.2

Syndrome *(Continued)*
    Scholte's E34.0
    Schroeder's E27.0
    Schüller-Christian C96.5
    Schwachman's —*see* Syndrome,
            Shwachman's
    Schwartz (-Jampel) G71.13
    Schwartz-Bartter E22.2
    scimitar Q26.8
    sclerocystic ovary E28.2
    Seitelberger's G31.89
    septicemic adrenal hemorrhage A39.1
    seroconversion, retroviral (acute) Z21
    serous meningitis G93.2
    severe acute respiratory (SARS) J12.81
    shaken infant T74.4
    shock (traumatic) T79.4
        kidney N17.0
            following crush injury T79.5
        toxic A48.3
    shock-lung J80
    Shone's — code to specific anomalies
    short
        bowel K91.2
        rib Q77.2
    shoulder-hand —*see* Algoneurodystrophy
    Shwachman's D70.4
    sicca —*see* Sicca syndrome
    sick
        cell E87.1
        sinus I49.5
    sick-euthyroid E07.81
    sideropenic D50.1
    Siemens' ectodermal dysplasia Q82.4
    Silfversköld's Q78.9
    Simons' E88.1
    sinus tarsi M25.57-•
    sinusitis-bronchiectasis-situs inversus Q89.3
    Sipple's E31.22
    sirenomelia Q87.2
    Slocumb's E27.0
    slow flow, coronary I20.8
    Sluder's G44.89
    Smith-Magenis Q93.88
    Sneddon-Wilkinson L13.1
    Sotos' Q87.3
    South African cardiomyopathy I42.8
    spasmodic
        upward movement, eyes H51.8
        winking F95.8
    Spen's I45.9
    splenic
        agenesis Q89.01
    ⇒ flexure K59.89
        neutropenia D73.81
    Spurway's Q78.0
    staphylococcal scalded skin L00
    steal
        arteriovenous T82.898-•
        ischemic T82.898-•
        subclavian G45.8
    Stein-Leventhal E28.2
    Stein's E28.2
    Stevens-Johnson syndrome L51.1
        toxic epidermal necrolysis overlap L51.3
    Stewart-Morel M85.2
    Stickler Q89.8
    stiff baby Q89.8
    stiff man G25.82
    Still-Felty —*see* Felty's syndrome
    Stokes (-Adams) I45.9
    stone heart I50.1
    straight back, congenital Q76.49
    subclavian steal G45.8
    subcoracoid-pectoralis minor G54.0
    subcostal nerve compression I77.89
    subphrenic interposition Q43.3
    superior
        cerebellar artery I63.89
        mesenteric artery K55.1
        semi-circular canal dehiscence H83.8X-•
        vena cava I87.1

S

Syndrome *(Continued)*
  supine hypotensive (maternal) —*see*
      Syndrome, hypotension, maternal
  suprarenal cortical E27.0
  supraspinatus —*see also* Tear, rotator cuff
      M75.10-●
  Susac G93.49
  swallowed blood P78.2
  sweat retention L74.0
  Swyer Q99.1
  Symond's G93.2
  sympathetic
      cervical paralysis G90.2
      pelvic, female N94.89
  systemic inflammatory response (SIRS), of
      non-infectious origin (without organ
      dysfunction) R65.10
      with acute organ dysfunction R65.11
  tachycardia-bradycardia I49.5
  takotsubo I51.81
  TAR (thrombocytopenia with absent radius)
      Q87.2
  tarsal tunnel G57.5-●
  teething K00.7
  tegmental G93.89
  telangiectasic-pigmentation-cataract Q82.8
  temporal pyramidal apex —*see* Otitis,
      media, suppurative, acute
  temporomandibular joint-pain-dysfunction
      M26.62-●
  Terry's —*see also* Myopia, degenerative
      H44.2-●
  testicular feminization —*see also* Syndrome,
      androgen insensitivity E34.51
  thalamic pain (hyperesthetic) G89.0
  thoracic outlet (compression) G54.0
  Thorson-Björck E34.0
  thrombocytopenia with absent radius (TAR)
      Q87.2
  thyroid-adrenocortical insufficiency E31.0
  tibial
      anterior M76.81-●
      posterior M76.82-●
  Tietze's M94.0
  time-zone (rapid) G47.25
  Toni-Fanconi E72.09
      with cystinosis E72.04
  Touraine's Q79.8
  tourniquet —*see* Constriction, external,
      by site
  toxic shock A48.3
  transient left ventricular apical ballooning
      I51.81
  traumatic vasospastic T75.22
  Treacher Collins Q75.4
  triple X, female Q97.0
  trisomy Q92.9
      13 Q91.7
          meiotic nondisjunction Q91.4
          mitotic nondisjunction Q91.5
          mosaicism Q91.5
          translocation Q91.6
      18 Q91.3
          meiotic nondisjunction Q91.0
          mitotic nondisjunction Q91.1
          mosaicism Q91.1
          translocation Q91.2
      20 (q)(p) Q92.8
      21 Q90.9
          meiotic nondisjunction Q90.0
          mitotic nondisjunction Q90.1
          mosaicism Q90.1
          translocation Q90.2
      22 Q92.8
  tropical wet feet T69.0-●
  Trousseau's I82.1
  tumor lysis (following antineoplastic
      chemotherapy) (spontaneous) NEC
      E88.3
  tumor necrosis factor receptor associated
      periodic (TRAPS) M04.1

Syndrome *(Continued)*
  Twiddler's (due to)
      automatic implantable defibrillator
          T82.198
      cardiac pacemaker T82.198
  Unverricht (-Lundborg) —*see* Epilepsy,
      generalized, idiopathic
  upward gaze H51.8
  uremia, chronic —*see also* Disease, kidney,
      chronic N18.9
  urethral N34.3
  urethro-oculo-articular —*see* Reiter's disease
  urohepatic K76.7
  vago-hypoglossal G52.7
  van Buchem's M85.2
  van der Hoeve's Q78.0
  vascular NEC in cerebrovascular disease
      G46.8
  vasoconstriction, reversible cerebrovascular
      I67.841
  vasomotor I73.9
  vasospastic (traumatic) T75.22
  vasovagal R55
  VATER Q87.2
  velo-cardio-facial Q93.81
  vena cava (inferior) (superior) (obstruction)
      I87.1
  vertebral
      artery G45.0
          compression —*see* Syndrome, anterior,
              spinal artery, compression
          steal G45.0
  vertebro-basilar artery G45.0
  vertebrogenic (pain) M54.89
  vertiginous —*see* Disorder, vestibular
      function
  Vinson-Plummer D50.1
  virus B34.9
  visceral larva migrans B83.0
  visual disorientation H53.8
  vitamin B6 deficiency E53.1
  vitreal corneal H59.01-●
  vitreous (touch) H59.01-●
  Vogt-Koyanagi H20.82-●
  Volkmann's T79.6
  von Schroetter's I82.890
  von Willebrand (-Jürgen) D68.0
  Waldenström-Kjellberg D50.1
  Wallenberg's G46.3
  water retention E87.79
  Waterhouse (-Friderichsen) A39.1
  Weber-Gubler G46.3
  Weber-Leyden G46.3
  Weber's G46.3
  Wegener's M31.30
      with
          kidney involvement M31.31
          lung involvement M31.30
              with kidney involvement M31.31
  ⇒Weingarten's (tropical eosinophilia)
      J82.89
  Weiss-Baker G90.09
  Werdnig-Hoffman G12.0
  Wermer's E31.21
  Werner's E34.8
  Wernicke-Korsakoff (nonalcoholic) F04
      alcoholic F10.26
  West's —*see* Epilepsy, spasms
  Westphal-Strümpell E83.01
  wet
      feet (maceration) (tropical) T69.0-●
      lung, newborn P22.1
  whiplash S13.4
  whistling face Q87.0
  Wilkie's K55.1
  Wilkinson-Sneddon L13.1
  Willebrand (-Jürgens) D68.0
  Williams Q93.82
  Wilson's (hepatolenticular degeneration)
      E83.01
  Wiskott-Aldrich D82.0

Syndrome *(Continued)*
  withdrawal —*see* Withdrawal, state
      drug
          infant of dependent mother P96.1
          therapeutic use, newborn P96.2
  Woakes' (ethmoiditis) J33.1
  Wright's (hyperabduction) G54.0
  X I20.9
  XXXX Q97.1
  XXXXX Q97.1
  XXXXY Q98.1
  XXY Q98.0
  Yao M04.8
  yellow nail L60.5
  Zahorsky's B08.5
  Zellweger syndrome E71.510
  Zellweger-like syndrome E71.541
Synechia (anterior) (iris) (posterior) (pupil) —
      see also Adhesions, iris
  intra-uterine (traumatic) N85.6
Synesthesia R20.8
Syngamiasis, syngamosis B83.3
Synodontia K00.2
Synorchidism, synorchism Q55.1
Synostosis (congenital) Q78.8
  astragalo-scaphoid Q74.2
  radioulnar Q74.0
Synovial sarcoma —*see* Neoplasm, connective
      tissue, malignant
Synovioma (malignant) —*see also* Neoplasm,
      connective tissue, malignant
  benign —*see* Neoplasm, connective tissue,
      benign
Synoviosarcoma —*see* Neoplasm, connective
      tissue, malignant
Synovitis —*see also* Tenosynovitis M65.9
  crepitant
      hand M70.0-●
      wrist M70.03-●
  gonococcal A54.49
  gouty —*see* Gout
  in (due to)
      crystals M65.8-●
      gonorrhea A54.49
      syphilis (late) A52.78
      use, overuse, pressure —*see* Disorder, soft
          tissue, due to use
  infective NEC —*see* Tenosynovitis, infective
      NEC
  specified NEC —*see* Tenosynovitis, specified
      type NEC
  syphilitic A52.78
      congenital (early) A50.02
  toxic —*see* Synovitis, transient
  transient M67.3-●
      ankle M67.37-●
      elbow M67.32-●
      foot joint M67.37-●
      hand M67.34-●
      hip M67.35-●
      knee M67.36-●
      multiple site M67.39
      pelvic region M67.35-●
      shoulder M67.31-●
      specified joint NEC M67.38
      wrist M67.33-●
  traumatic, current —*see* Sprain
  tuberculous —*see* Tuberculosis, synovitis
  villonodular (pigmented) M12.2-●
      ankle M12.27-●
      elbow M12.22-●
      foot joint M12.27-●
      hand joint M12.24-●
      hip M12.25-●
      knee M12.26-●
      multiple site M12.29
      pelvic region M12.25-●
      shoulder M12.21-●
      specified joint NEC M12.28
      vertebrae M12.28
      wrist M12.23-●

▶ New   ⇒ Revised   ~~deleted~~ Deleted   ● Use Additional Character(s)

Syphilid A51.39
  congenital A50.06
  newborn A50.06
  tubercular (late) A52.79
Syphilis, syphilitic (acquired) A53.9
  abdomen (late) A52.79
  acoustic nerve A52.15
  adenopathy (secondary) A51.49
  adrenal (gland) (with cortical hypofunction)
      A52.79
  age under 2 years NOS —see also Syphilis,
      congenital, early
    acquired A51.9
  alopecia (secondary) A51.32
  anemia (late) A52.79 [D63.8]
  aneurysm (aorta) (ruptured) A52.01
    central nervous system A52.05
    congenital A50.54 [I79.0]
  anus (late) A52.74
    primary A51.1
    secondary A51.39
  aorta (arch) (abdominal) (thoracic)
      A52.02
    aneurysm A52.01
  aortic (insufficiency) (regurgitation)
      (stenosis)A52.03
    aneurysm A52.01
  arachnoid (adhesive) (cerebral) (spinal)
      A52.13
  asymptomatic —see Syphilis, latent
  ataxia (locomotor) A52.11
  atrophoderma maculatum A51.39
  auricular fibrillation A52.06
  bladder (late) A52.76
  bone A52.77
    secondary A51.46
  brain A52.17
  breast (late) A52.79
  bronchus (late) A52.72
  bubo (primary) A51.0
  bulbar palsy A52.19
  bursa (late) A52.78
  cardiac decompensation A52.06
  cardiovascular A52.00
  central nervous system (late) (recurrent)
        (relapse) (tertiary) A52.3
    with
      ataxia A52.11
      general paralysis A52.17
        juvenile A50.45
      paresis (general) A52.17
        juvenile A50.45
      tabes (dorsalis) A52.11
        juvenile A50.45
      taboparesis A52.17
        juvenile A50.45
    aneurysm A52.05
    congenital A50.40
    juvenile A50.40
    remission in (sustained) A52.3
    serology doubtful, negative, or positive
        A52.3
    specified nature or site NEC A52.19
    vascular A52.05
  cerebral A52.17
    meningovascular A52.13
    nerves (multiple palsies) A52.15
    sclerosis A52.17
    thrombosis A52.05
  cerebrospinal (tabetic type) A52.12
  cerebrovascular A52.05
  cervix (late) A52.76
  chancre (multiple) A51.0
    extragenital A51.2
    Rollet's A51.0
  Charcot's joint A52.16
  chorioretinitis A51.43
    congenital A50.01
    late A52.71
    prenatal A50.01
  choroiditis —see Syphilitic chorioretinitis

Syphilis, syphilitic (Continued)
  choroidoretinitis —see Syphilitic
      chorioretinitis
  ciliary body (secondary) A51.43
    late A52.71
  colon (late) A52.74
  combined spinal sclerosis A52.11
  condyloma (latum) A51.31
  congenital A50.9
    with
      paresis (general) A50.45
      tabes (dorsalis) A50.45
      taboparesis A50.45
    chorioretinitis, choroiditis A50.01 [H32]
    early, or less than 2 years after birth NEC
        A50.2
      with manifestations —see Syphilis,
          congenital, early, symptomatic
      latent (without manifestations) A50.1
        negative spinal fluid test A50.1
        serology positive A50.1
      symptomatic A50.09
        cutaneous A50.06
        mucocutaneous A50.07
        oculopathy A50.01
        osteochondropathy A50.02
        pharyngitis A50.03
        pneumonia A50.04
        rhinitis A50.05
        visceral A50.08
    interstitial keratitis A50.31
    juvenile neurosyphilis A50.45
    late, or 2 years or more after birth NEC
        A50.7
      chorioretinitis, choroiditis A50.32
      interstitial keratitis A50.31
      juvenile neurosyphilis A50.45
      latent (without manifestations) A50.6
        negative spinal fluid test A50.6
        serology positive A50.6
      symptomatic or with manifestations
          NEC A50.59
        arthropathy A50.55
        cardiovascular A50.54
        Clutton's joints A50.51
        Hutchinson's teeth A50.52
        Hutchinson's triad A50.53
        osteochondropathy A50.56
        saddle nose A50.57
  conjugal A53.9
    tabes A52.11
  conjunctiva (late) A52.71
  contact Z20.2
  cord bladder A52.19
  cornea, late A52.71
  coronary (artery) (sclerosis) A52.06
  coryza, congenital A50.05
  cranial nerve A52.15
    multiple palsies A52.15
  cutaneous —see Syphilis, skin
  dacryocystitis (late) A52.71
  degeneration, spinal cord A52.12
  dementia paralytica A52.17
    juvenilis A50.45
  destruction of bone A52.77
  dilatation, aorta A52.01
  due to blood transfusion A53.9
  dura mater A52.13
  ear A52.79
    inner A52.79
      nerve (eighth) A52.15
      neurorecurrence A52.15
  early A51.9
    cardiovascular A52.00
    central nervous system A52.3
    latent (without manifestations) (less than 2
        years after infection) A51.5
      negative spinal fluid test A51.5
      serological relapse after treatment A51.5
      serology positive A51.5
    relapse (treated, untreated) A51.9

Syphilis, syphilitic (Continued)
  early (Continued)
    skin A51.39
    symptomatic A51.9
      extragenital chancre A51.2
      primary, except extragenital chancre
          A51.0
      secondary —see also Syphilis, secondary
          A51.39
        relapse (treated, untreated) A51.49
    ulcer A51.39
  eighth nerve (neuritis) A52.15
  endemic A65
  endocarditis A52.03
    aortic A52.03
    pulmonary A52.03
  epididymis (late) A52.76
  epiglottis (late) A52.73
  epiphysitis (congenital) (early) A50.02
  episcleritis (late) A52.71
  esophagus A52.79
  eustachian tube A52.73
  exposure to Z20.2
  eye A52.71
  eyelid (late) (with gumma) A52.71
  fallopian tube (late) A52.76
  fracture A52.77
  gallbladder (late) A52.74
  gastric (polyposis) (late) A52.74
  general A53.9
    paralysis A52.17
      juvenile A50.45
  genital (primary) A51.0
  glaucoma A52.71
  gumma NEC A52.79
    cardiovascular system A52.00
    central nervous system A52.3
    congenital A50.59
  heart (block) (decompensation) (disease)
      (failure) A52.06 [I52]
    valve NEC A52.03
  hemianesthesia A52.19
  hemianopsia A52.71
  hemiparesis A52.17
  hemiplegia A52.17
  hepatic artery A52.09
  hepatis A52.74
  hepatomegaly, congenital A50.08
  hereditaria tarda —see Syphilis, congenital,
      late
  hereditary —see Syphilis, congenital
  Hutchinson's teeth A50.52
  hyalitis A52.71
  inactive —see Syphilis, latent
  infantum —see Syphilis, congenital
  inherited —see Syphilis, congenital
  internal ear A52.79
  intestine (late) A52.74
  iris, iritis (secondary) A51.43
    late A52.71
  joint (late) A52.77
  keratitis (congenital) (interstitial) (late) A50.31
  kidney (late) A52.75
  lacrimal passages (late) A52.71
  larynx (late) A52.73
  late A52.9
    cardiovascular A52.00
    central nervous system A52.3
    kidney A52.75
    latent or 2 years or more after infection
        (without manifestations) A52.8
      negative spinal fluid test A52.8
      serology positive A52.8
    paresis A52.17
    specified site NEC A52.79
    symptomatic or with manifestations
        A52.79
    tabes A52.11
  latent A53.0
    with signs or symptoms - code by site and
        stage under Syphilis

Syphilis, syphilitic (Continued)
  latent (Continued)
    central nervous system A52.2
    date of infection unspecified A53.0
    early, or less than 2 years after infection
        A51.5
    follow-up of latent syphilis A53.0
      date of infection unspecified A53.0
      late, or 2 years or more after infection
          A52.8
    late, or 2 years or more after infection A52.8
    positive serology (only finding) A53.0
      date of infection unspecified A53.0
      early, or less than 2 years after infection
          A51.5
      late, or 2 years or more after infection
          A52.8
  lens (late) A52.71
  leukoderma A51.39
    late A52.79
  lienitis A52.79
  lip A51.39
    chancre (primary) A51.2
    late A52.79
  Lissauer's paralysis A52.17
  liver A52.74
  locomotor ataxia A52.11
  lung A52.72
  lymph gland (early) (secondary) A51.49
    late A52.79
  lymphadenitis (secondary) A51.49
  macular atrophy of skin A51.39
    striated A52.79
  mediastinum (late) A52.73
  meninges (adhesive) (brain) (spinal cord)
      A52.13
  meningitis A52.13
    acute (secondary) A51.41
    congenital A50.41
  meningoencephalitis A52.14
  meningovascular A52.13
    congenital A50.41
  mesarteritis A52.09
    brain A52.04
  middle ear A52.77
  mitral stenosis A52.03
  monoplegia A52.17
  mouth (secondary) A51.39
    late A52.79
  mucocutaneous (secondary) A51.39
    late A52.79
  mucous
    membrane (secondary) A51.39
      late A52.79
    patches A51.39
      congenital A50.07
  mulberry molars A50.52
  muscle A52.78
  myocardium A52.06
  nasal sinus (late) A52.73
  neonatorum —see Syphilis, congenital
  nephrotic syndrome (secondary) A51.44
  nerve palsy (any cranial nerve) A52.15
    multiple A52.15
  nervous system, central A52.3
  neuritis A52.15
    acoustic A52.15
  neurorecidive of retina A52.19
  neuroretinitis A52.19
  newborn —see Syphilis, congenital
  nodular superficial (late) A52.79
  nonvenereal A65
  nose (late) A52.73
    saddle back deformity A50.57
  occlusive arterial disease A52.09
  oculopathy A52.71
  ophthalmic (late) A52.71
  optic nerve (atrophy) (neuritis) (papilla)
      A52.15
  orbit (late) A52.71

Syphilis, syphilitic (Continued)
  organic A53.9
  osseous (late) A52.77
  osteochondritis (congenital) (early) A50.02
      [M90.80]
  osteoporosis A52.77
  ovary (late) A52.76
  oviduct (late) A52.76
  palate (late) A52.79
  pancreas (late) A52.74
  paralysis A52.17
    general A52.17
      juvenile A50.45
  paresis (general) A52.17
    juvenile A50.45
  paresthesia A52.19
  Parkinson's disease or syndrome A52.19
  paroxysmal tachycardia A52.06
  pemphigus (congenital) A50.06
  penis (chancre) A51.0
    late A52.76
  pericardium A52.06
  perichondritis, larynx (late) A52.73
  periosteum (late) A52.77
    congenital (early) A50.02 [M90.80]
    early (secondary) A51.46
  peripheral nerve A52.79
  petrous bone (late) A52.77
  pharynx (late) A52.73
    secondary A51.39
  pituitary (gland) A52.79
  pleura (late) A52.73
  pneumonia, white A50.04
  pontine lesion A52.17
  portal vein A52.09
  primary A51.0
    anal A51.1
    and secondary —see Syphilis, secondary
    central nervous system A52.3
    extragenital chancre NEC A51.2
    fingers A51.2
    genital A51.0
    lip A51.2
    specified site NEC A51.2
    tonsils A51.2
  prostate (late) A52.76
  ptosis (eyelid) A52.71
  pulmonary (late) A52.72
    artery A52.09
  pyelonephritis (late) A52.75
  recently acquired, symptomatic A51.9
  rectum (late) A52.74
  respiratory tract (late) A52.73
  retina, late A52.71
  retrobulbar neuritis A52.15
  salpingitis A52.76
  sclera (late) A52.71
  sclerosis
    cerebral A52.17
    coronary A52.06
    multiple A52.11
  scotoma (central) A52.71
  scrotum (late) A52.76
  secondary (and primary) A51.49
    adenopathy A51.49
    anus A51.39
    bone A51.46
    chorioretinitis, choroiditis A51.43
    hepatitis A51.45
    liver A51.45
    lymphadenitis A51.49
    meningitis (acute) A51.41
    mouth A51.39
    mucous membranes A51.39
    periosteum, periostitis A51.46
    pharynx A51.39
    relapse (treated, untreated) A51.49
    skin A51.39
    specified form NEC A51.49
    tonsil A51.39

Syphilis, syphilitic (Continued)
  secondary (Continued)
    ulcer A51.39
      viscera NEC A51.49
      vulva A51.39
  seminal vesicle (late) A52.76
  seronegative with signs or symptoms - code
      by site and stage under Syphilis
  seropositive
    with signs or symptoms - code by site and
        stage under Syphilis
    follow-up of latent syphilis —see Syphilis,
        latent
    only finding —see Syphilis, latent
  seventh nerve (paralysis) A52.15
  sinus, sinusitis (late) A52.73
  skeletal system A52.77
  skin (with ulceration) (early) (secondary)
      A51.39
    late or tertiary A52.79
  small intestine A52.74
  spastic spinal paralysis A52.17
  spermatic cord (late) A52.76
  spinal (cord) A52.12
  spleen A52.79
  splenomegaly A52.79
  spondylitis A52.77
  staphyloma A52.71
  stigmata (congenital) A50.59
  stomach A52.74
  synovium A52.78
  tabes dorsalis (late) A52.11
    juvenile A50.45
  tabetic type A52.11
    juvenile A50.45
  taboparesis A52.17
    juvenile A50.45
  tachycardia A52.06
  tendon (late) A52.78
  tertiary A52.9
    with symptoms NEC A52.79
    cardiovascular A52.00
    central nervous system A52.3
    multiple NEC A52.79
    specified site NEC A52.79
  testis A52.76
  thorax A52.73
  throat A52.73
  thymus (gland) (late) A52.79
  thyroid (late) A52.79
  tongue (late) A52.79
  tonsil (lingual) (late) A52.73
    primary A51.2
    secondary A51.39
  trachea (late) A52.73
  tunica vaginalis (late) A52.76
  ulcer (any site) (early) (secondary)
      A51.39
    late A52.79
    perforating A52.79
      foot A52.11
  urethra (late) A52.76
  urogenital (late) A52.76
  uterus (late) A52.76
  uveal tract (secondary) A51.43
    late A52.71
  uveitis (secondary) A51.43
    late A52.71
  uvula (late) (perforated) A52.79
  vagina A51.0
    late A52.76
  valvulitis NEC A52.03
  vascular A52.00
    brain (cerebral) A52.05
  ventriculi A52.74
  vesicae urinariae (late) A52.76
  viscera (abdominal) (late) A52.74
    secondary A51.49
  vitreous (opacities) (late) A52.71
    hemorrhage A52.71

▶ New   ⇒ Revised   ~~deleted~~ Deleted   ● Use Additional Character(s)

Syphilis, syphilitic *(Continued)*
  vulva A51.0
    late A52.76
    secondary A51.39
Syphiloma A52.79
  cardiovascular system A52.00
  central nervous system A52.3
  circulatory system A52.00
  congenital A50.59
Syphilophobia F45.29
Syringadenoma —*see also* Neoplasm, skin, benign
  papillary —*see* Neoplasm, skin, benign

Syringobulbia G95.0
Syringocystadenoma —*see* Neoplasm, skin, benign
  papillary —*see* Neoplasm, skin, benign
Syringoma —*see also* Neoplasm, skin, benign
  chondroid —*see* Neoplasm, skin, benign
Syringomyelia G95.0
Syringomyelitis —*see* Encephalitis
Syringomyelocele —*see* Spina bifida
Syringopontia G95.0

System, systemic —*see also* condition
  disease, combined —*see* Degeneration, combined
  inflammatory response syndrome (SIRS) of non-infectious origin (without organ dysfunction) R65.10
    with acute organ dysfunction R65.11
  lupus erythematosus M32.9
    inhibitor present D68.62

T

Tabacism, tabacosis, tabagism —see also
    Poisoning, tobacco
    meaning dependence (without remission)
      F17.200
      with
        disorder F17.299
          in remission F17.211
          specified disorder NEC F17.298
        withdrawal F17.203
Tabardillo A75.9
    flea-borne A75.2
    louse-borne A75.0
Tabes, tabetic A52.10
    with
      central nervous system syphilis A52.10
      Charcot's joint A52.16
      cord bladder A52.19
      crisis, viscera (any) A52.19
      paralysis, general A52.17
      paresis (general) A52.17
      perforating ulcer (foot) A52.19
    arthropathy (Charcot) A52.16
    bladder A52.19
    bone A52.11
    cerebrospinal A52.12
    congenital A50.45
    conjugal A52.10
    dorsalis A52.11
      juvenile A50.49
    juvenile A50.49
    latent A52.19
    mesenterica A18.39
    paralysis, insane, general A52.17
    spasmodic A52.17
    syphilis (cerebrospinal) A52.12
Taboparalysis A52.17
Taboparesis (remission) A52.17
    juvenile A50.45
TAC (trigeminal autonomic cephalgia) NEC
    G44.099
    intractable G44.091
    not intractable G44.099
Tache noir S60.22-•
Tachyalimentation K91.2
Tachyarrhythmia, tachyrhythmia —see
    Tachycardia
Tachycardia R00.0
    atrial (paroxysmal) I47.1
    auricular I47.1
    AV nodal re-entry (re-entrant) I47.1
    junctional (paroxysmal) I47.1
    newborn P29.11
    nodal (paroxysmal) I47.1
    non-paroxysmal AV nodal I45.89
    paroxysmal (sustained) (nonsustained)
      I47.9
      with sinus bradycardia I49.5
      atrial (PAT) I47.1
      atrioventricular (AV) (re-entrant) I47.1
        psychogenic F54
      junctional I47.1
        ectopic I47.1
      nodal I47.1
      psychogenic (atrial) (supraventricular)
        (ventricular) F54
      supraventricular (sustained) I47.1
        psychogenic F54
      ventricular I47.2
        psychogenic F54
    psychogenic F45.8
    sick sinus I49.5
    sinoauricular NOS R00.0
      paroxysmal I47.1
    sinus [sinusal] NOS R00.0
      paroxysmal I47.1
    supraventricular I47.1
    ventricular (paroxysmal) (sustained) I47.2
      psychogenic F54
Tachygastria K31.89

Tachypnea R06.82
    hysterical F45.8
    newborn (idiopathic) (transitory) P22.1
    psychogenic F45.8
    transitory, of newborn P22.1
TACO (transfusion associated circulatory
    overload) E87.71
Taenia (infection) (infestation) B68.9
    diminuta B71.0
    echinococcal infestation B67.90
    mediocanellata B68.1
    nana B71.0
    saginata B68.1
    solium (intestinal form) B68.0
      larval form —see Cysticercosis
Taeniasis (intestine) —see Taenia
Tag (hypertrophied skin) (infected) L91.8
    adenoid J35.8
    anus K64.4
    hemorrhoidal K64.4
    hymen N89.8
    perineal N90.89
    preauricular Q17.0
    sentinel K64.4
    skin L91.8
      accessory (congenital) Q82.8
      anus K64.4
      congenital Q82.8
      preauricular Q17.0
    tonsil J35.8
    urethra, urethral N36.8
    vulva N90.89
Tahyna fever B33.8
Takahara's disease E80.3
Takayasu's disease or syndrome M31.4
▶Talaromycosis B48.4
Talcosis (pulmonary) J62.0
Talipes (congenital) Q66.89
    acquired, planus —see Deformity, limb, flat foot
    asymmetric Q66.89
    calcaneovalgus Q66.4-•
    calcaneovarus Q66.1-•
    calcaneus Q66.89
    cavus Q66.7-•
    equinovalgus Q66.6
    equinovarus Q66.0-•
    equinus Q66.89
    percavus Q66.7-•
    planovalgus Q66.6
    planus (acquired) (any degree) —see also
      Deformity, limb, flat foot
      congenital Q66.5-•
      due to rickets (sequelae) E64.3
    valgus Q66.6
    varus Q66.3-•
Tall stature, constitutional E34.4
Talma's disease M62.89
Talon noir S90.3-•
    hand S60.22-•
    heel S90.3-•
    toe S90.1-•
Tamponade, heart I31.4
Tanapox (virus disease) B08.71
Tangier disease E78.6
Tantrum, child problem F91.8
Tapeworm (infection) (infestation) —see
    Infestation, tapeworm
Tapia's syndrome G52.7
TAR (thrombocytopenia with absent radius)
    syndrome Q87.2
Tarral-Besnier disease L44.0
Tarsal tunnel syndrome —see Syndrome, tarsal
    tunnel
Tarsalgia —see Pain, limb, lower
Tarsitis (eyelid) H01.8
    syphilitic A52.71
    tuberculous A18.4
Tartar (teeth) (dental calculus) K03.6
Tattoo (mark) L81.8
Tauri's disease E74.09
Taurodontism K00.2

Taussig-Bing syndrome Q20.1
Taybi's syndrome Q87.2
Tay-Sachs amaurotic familial idiocy or disease
    E75.02
TBI (traumatic brain injury) S06.9
Teacher's node or nodule J38.2
Tear, torn (traumatic) —see also Laceration
    with abortion —see Abortion
    annular fibrosis M51.35
    anus, anal (sphincter) S31.831
      complicating delivery
        with third degree perineal laceration —
          see also Delivery, complicated, by,
          laceration, perineum, third degree
          O70.20
          with mucosa O70.3
        without third degree perineal laceration
          O70.4
      nontraumatic (healed) (old) K62.81
    articular cartilage, old —see Derangement,
      joint, articular cartilage, by site
    bladder
      with ectopic or molar pregnancy O08.6
      following ectopic or molar pregnancy
        O08.6
      obstetrical O71.5
      traumatic —see Injury, bladder
    bowel
      with ectopic or molar pregnancy O08.6
      following ectopic or molar pregnancy
        O08.6
      obstetrical trauma O71.5
    broad ligament
      with ectopic or molar pregnancy O08.6
      following ectopic or molar pregnancy O08.6
      obstetrical trauma O71.6
    bucket handle (knee) (meniscus) —see Tear,
      meniscus
    capsule, joint —see Sprain
    cartilage —see also Sprain
      articular, old —see Derangement, joint,
        articular cartilage, by site
    cervix
      with ectopic or molar pregnancy O08.6
      following ectopic or molar pregnancy
        O08.6
      obstetrical trauma (current) O71.3
      old N88.1
      traumatic —see Injury, uterus
    dural G97.41
      nontraumatic G96.11
    internal organ —see Injury, by site
    knee cartilage
      articular (current) S83.3-•
      old —see Derangement, knee, meniscus,
        due to old tear
    ligament —see Sprain
    meniscus (knee) (current injury) S83.209
      bucket-handle S83.20-•
      lateral
        bucket-handle S83.25-•
        complex S83.27-•
        peripheral S83.26-•
        specified type NEC S83.28-•
      medial
        bucket-handle S83.21-•
        complex S83.23-•
        peripheral S83.22-•
        specified type NEC S83.24-•
      old —see Derangement, knee, meniscus,
        due to old tear
      site other than knee - code as Sprain
      specified type NEC S83.20-•
    muscle —see Strain
    pelvic
      floor, complicating delivery O70.1
      organ NEC, obstetrical trauma O71.5
        with ectopic or molar pregnancy O08.6
        following ectopic or molar pregnancy
          O08.6
    perineal, secondary O90.1

▶ New   ⇒ Revised   ~~deleted~~ Deleted   • Use Additional Character(s)

Tear, torn *(Continued)*
  periurethral tissue, obstetrical trauma O71.82
    with ectopic or molar pregnancy O08.6
    following ectopic or molar pregnancy
      O08.6
  rectovaginal septum —*see* Laceration, vagina
  retina, retinal (without detachment)
    (horseshoe) —*see also* Break, retina,
    horseshoe
    with detachment —*see* Detachment, retina,
      with retinal, break
  rotator cuff (nontraumatic) M75.10-●
    complete M75.12-●
    incomplete M75.11-●
    traumatic S46.01-●
      capsule S43.42-●
  semilunar cartilage, knee —*see* Tear, meniscus
  supraspinatus (complete) (incomplete)
    (nontraumatic) —*see also* Tear, rotator
    cuff M75.10-●
  tendon —*see* Strain
  tentorial, at birth P10.4
  umbilical cord
    complicating delivery O69.89
  urethra
    with ectopic or molar pregnancy O08.6
    following ectopic or molar pregnancy
      O08.6
    obstetrical trauma O71.5
  uterus —*see* Injury, uterus
  vagina —*see* Laceration, vagina
  vessel, from catheter —*see* Puncture,
    accidental complicating surgery
  vulva, complicating delivery O70.0
Tear-stone —*see* Dacryolith
Teeth —*see also* condition
  grinding
    psychogenic F45.8
    sleep related G47.63
Teething (syndrome) K00.7
Telangiectasia, telangiectasis (verrucous) I78.1
  ataxic (cerebellar) (Louis-Bar) G11.3
  familial I78.0
  hemorrhagic, hereditary (congenital) (senile)
    I78.0
  hereditary, hemorrhagic (congenital) (senile)
    I78.0
  juxtafoveal H35.07-●
  macular H35.07-●
  macularis eruptiva perstans D47.01
  parafoveal H35.07-●
  retinal (idiopathic) (juxtafoveal) (macular)
    (parafoveal) H35.07-●
  spider I78.1
Telephone scatologia F65.89
Telescoped bowel or intestine K56.1
  congenital Q43.8
Temperature
  body, high (of unknown origin) R50.9
  cold, trauma from T69.9
    newborn P80.0
    specified effect NEC T69.8
Temple —*see* condition
Temporal —*see* condition
Temporomandibular joint pain-dysfunction
  syndrome M26.62-●
Temporosphenoidal —*see* condition
Tendency
  bleeding —*see* Defect, coagulation
  suicide
    meaning personal history of attempted
      suicide Z91.5
    meaning suicidal ideation —*see* Ideation,
      suicidal
  to fall R29.6
Tenderness, abdominal R10.819
  epigastric R10.816
  generalized R10.817
  left lower quadrant R10.814
  left upper quadrant R10.812
  periumbilic R10.815

Tenderness, abdominal *(Continued)*
  rebound R10.829
    epigastric R10.826
    generalized R10.827
    left lower quadrant R10.824
    left upper quadrant R10.822
    periumbilic R10.825
    right lower quadrant R10.823
    right upper quadrant R10.821
  right lower quadrant R10.813
  right upper quadrant R10.811
Tendinitis, tendonitis —*see also* Enthesopathy
  Achilles M76.6-●
  adhesive —*see* Tenosynovitis, specified type
    NEC
    shoulder —*see* Capsulitis, adhesive
  bicipital M75.2-●
  calcific M65.2-●
    ankle M65.27-●
    foot M65.27-●
    forearm M65.23-●
    hand M65.24-●
    lower leg M65.26-●
    multiple sites M65.29
    pelvic region M65.25-●
    shoulder M75.3-●
    specified site NEC M65.28
    thigh M65.25-●
    upper arm M65.22-●
  due to use, overuse, pressure —*see also*
    Disorder, soft tissue, due to use
    specified NEC —*see* Disorder, soft tissue,
      due to use, specified NEC
  gluteal M76.0-●
  patellar M76.5-●
  peroneal M76.7-●
  psoas M76.1-●
  tibial (posterior) M76.82-●
    anterior M76.81-●
  trochanteric —*see* Bursitis, hip, trochanteric
Tendon —*see* condition
Tendosynovitis —*see* Tenosynovitis
Tenesmus (rectal) R19.8
  vesical R30.1
Tennis elbow —*see* Epicondylitis, lateral
Tenonitis —*see also* Tenosynovitis
  eye (capsule) H05.04-●
Tenontosynovitis —*see* Tenosynovitis
Tenontothecitis —*see* Tenosynovitis
Tenophyte —*see* Disorder, synovium, specified
  type NEC
Tenosynovitis —*see also* Synovitis M65.9
  adhesive —*see* Tenosynovitis, specified type
    NEC
    shoulder —*see* Capsulitis, adhesive
  bicipital (calcifying) —*see* Tendinitis,
    bicipital
  gonococcal A54.49
  in (due to)
    crystals M65.8-●
    gonorrhea A54.49
    syphilis (late) A52.78
    use, overuse, pressure —*see also* Disorder,
      soft tissue, due to use
      specified NEC —*see* Disorder, soft tissue,
        due to use, specified NEC
  infective NEC M65.1-●
    ankle M65.17-●
    foot M65.17-●
    forearm M65.13-●
    hand M65.14-●
    lower leg M65.16-●
    multiple sites M65.19
    pelvic region M65.15-●
    shoulder region M65.11-●
    specified site NEC M65.18
    thigh M65.15-●
    upper arm M65.12-●
  radial styloid M65.4
  shoulder region M65.81-●
    adhesive —*see* Capsulitis, adhesive

Tenosynovitis *(Continued)*
  specified type NEC M65.88-●
    ankle M65.87-●
    foot M65.87-●
    forearm M65.83-●
    hand M65.84-●
    lower leg M65.86-●
    multiple sites M65.89
    pelvic region M65.85-●
    shoulder region M65.81-●
    specified site NEC M65.88
    thigh M65.85-●
    upper arm M65.82-●
  tuberculous —*see* Tuberculosis, tenosynovitis
Tenovaginitis —*see* Tenosynovitis
Tension
  arterial, high —*see also* Hypertension
    without diagnosis of hypertension R03.0
  headache G44.209
    intractable G44.201
    not intractable G44.209
  nervous R45.0
  pneumothorax J93.0
  premenstrual N94.3
  state (mental) F48.9
Tentorium —*see* condition
Teratencephalus Q89.8
Teratism Q89.7
Teratoblastoma (malignant) —*see* Neoplasm,
  malignant, by site
Teratocarcinoma —*see also* Neoplasm,
  malignant, by site
  liver C22.7
Teratoma (solid) —*see also* Neoplasm, uncertain
  behavior, by site
  with embryonal carcinoma, mixed —*see*
    Neoplasm, malignant, by site
  with malignant transformation —*see*
    Neoplasm, malignant, by site
  adult (cystic) —*see* Neoplasm, benign, by site
  benign —*see* Neoplasm, benign, by site
  combined with choriocarcinoma —*see*
    Neoplasm, malignant, by site
  cystic (adult) —*see* Neoplasm, benign, by site
  differentiated —*see* Neoplasm, benign, by site
  embryonal —*see also* Neoplasm, malignant,
    by site
    liver C22.7
  immature —*see* Neoplasm, malignant, by site
  liver C22.7
    adult, benign, cystic, differentiated type or
      mature D13.4
  malignant —*see also* Neoplasm, malignant,
    by site
    anaplastic —*see* Neoplasm, malignant, by
      site
    intermediate —*see* Neoplasm, malignant,
      by site
    specified site —*see* Neoplasm,
      malignant, by site
    unspecified site C62.90
  undifferentiated —*see* Neoplasm,
    malignant, by site
  mature —*see* Neoplasm, uncertain behavior,
    by site
    malignant —*see* Neoplasm, by site,
      malignant, by site
  ovary D27.-●
    embryonal, immature or malignant C56-●
  solid —*see* Neoplasm, uncertain behavior,
    by site
  testis C62.9-●
    adult, benign, cystic, differentiated type or
      mature D29.2-●
    scrotal C62.1-●
    undescended C62.0-●
Termination
  anomalous —*see also* Malposition, congenital
    right pulmonary vein Q26.3
  pregnancy, elective Z33.2
Ternidens diminutus infestation B81.8
Ternidensiasis B81.8

Terror(s) night (child) F51.4
Terrorism, victim of Z65.4
Terry's syndrome —see also Myopia,
degenerative H44.2-•
Tertiary —see condition
Test, tests, testing (for)
adequacy (for dialysis)
hemodialysis Z49.31
peritoneal Z49.32
blood pressure Z01.30
abnormal reading —see Blood, pressure
blood typing Z01.83
Rh typing Z01.83
blood-alcohol Z04.89
positive —see Findings, abnormal, in blood
blood-drug Z04.89
positive —see Findings, abnormal, in blood
cardiac pulse generator (battery) Z45.010
fertility Z31.41
genetic
disease carrier status for procreative
management
female Z31.430
male Z31.440
male partner of patient with recurrent
pregnancy loss Z31.441
procreative management NEC
female Z31.438
male Z31.448
hearing Z01.10
with abnormal findings NEC Z01.118
infant or child (over 28 days old) Z00.129
with abnormal findings Z00.121
HIV (human immunodeficiency virus)
nonconclusive (in infants) R75
positive Z21
seropositive Z21
immunity status Z01.84
intelligence NEC Z01.89
laboratory (as part of a general medical
examination) Z00.00
with abnormal finding Z00.01
for medicolegal reason NEC Z04.89
male partner of patient with recurrent
pregnancy loss Z31.441
Mantoux (for tuberculosis) Z11.1
abnormal result R76.11
pregnancy, positive first pregnancy —see
Pregnancy, normal, first
procreative Z31.49
fertility Z31.41
skin, diagnostic
allergy Z01.82
special screening examination —see
Screening, by name of disease
Mantoux Z11.1
tuberculin Z11.1
specified NEC Z01.89
tuberculin Z11.1
abnormal result R76.11
vision Z01.00
with abnormal findings Z01.01
following failed vision screening Z01.020
with abnormal findings Z01.021
infant or child (over 28 days old) Z00.129
with abnormal findings Z00.121
Wassermann Z11.3
positive —see Serology for syphilis, positive
Testicle, testicular, testis —see also condition
feminization syndrome —see also Syndrome,
androgen insensitivity E34.51
migrans Q55.29
Tetanus, tetanic (cephalic) (convulsions) A35
with
abortion A34
ectopic or molar pregnancy O08.0
following ectopic or molar pregnancy O08.0
inoculation reaction (due to serum) —see
Complications, vaccination
neonatorum A33
obstetrical A34
puerperal, postpartum, childbirth A34

Tetany (due to) R29.0
alkalosis E87.3
associated with rickets E55.0
convulsions R29.0
hysterical F44.5
functional (hysterical) F44.5
hyperkinetic R29.0
hysterical F44.5
hyperpnea R06.4
hysterical F44.5
psychogenic F45.8
hyperventilation —see also Hyperventilation
R06.4
hysterical F44.5
neonatal (without calcium or magnesium
deficiency) P71.3
parathyroid (gland) E20.9
parathyroprival E89.2
post- (para)thyroidectomy E89.2
postoperative E89.2
pseudotetany R29.0
psychogenic (conversion reaction) F44.5
Tetralogy of Fallot Q21.3
Tetraplegia (chronic) —see also Quadriplegia
G82.50-•
Thailand hemorrhagic fever A91
Thalassanemia —see Thalassemia
Thalassemia (anemia) (disease) D56.9
with other hemoglobinopathy D56.8
alpha (major) (severe) (triple gene defect)
D56.0
minor D56.3
silent carrier D56.3
trait D56.3
beta (severe) D56.1
homozygous D56.1
major D56.1
minor D56.3
trait D56.3
delta-beta (homozygous) D56.2
minor D56.3
trait D56.3
dominant D56.8
hemoglobin
C D56.8
E-beta D56.5
intermedia D56.1
major D56.1
minor D56.3
mixed D56.8
sickle-cell —see Disease, sickle-cell,
thalassemia
specified type NEC D56.8
trait D56.3
variants D56.8
Thanatophoric dwarfism or short stature Q77.1
Thaysen-Gee disease (nontropical sprue) K90.0
Thaysen's disease K90.0
Thecoma D27-•
luteinized D27-•
malignant C56-•
Thelarche, premature E30.8
Thelaziasis B83.8
Thelitis N61.0
puerperal, postpartum or gestational —see
Infection, nipple
Therapeutic —see condition
Therapy
drug, long-term (current) (prophylactic)
agents affecting estrogen receptors and
estrogen levels NEC Z79.818
anastrozole (Arimidex) Z79.811
antibiotics Z79.2
short-term use - omit code
anticoagulants Z79.01
anti-inflammatory Z79.1
antiplatelet Z79.02
antithrombotics Z79.02
aromatase inhibitors Z79.811
aspirin Z79.82
birth control pill or patch Z79.3

Therapy (Continued)
drug, long-term (Continued)
bisphosphonates Z79.83
contraceptive, oral Z79.3
drug, specified NEC Z79.899
estrogen receptor downregulators
Z79.818
Evista Z79.810
exemestane (Aromasin) Z79.811
Fareston Z79.810
fulvestrant (Faslodex) Z79.818
gonadotropin-releasing hormone (GnRH)
agonist Z79.818
goserelin acetate (Zoladex) Z79.818
hormone replacement Z79.890
insulin Z79.4
letrozole (Femara) Z79.811
leuprolide acetate (leuprorelin) (Lupron)
Z79.818
megestrol acetate (Megace) Z79.818
methadone
for pain management Z79.891
maintenance therapy F11.20
Nolvadex Z79.810
opiate analgesic Z79.891
oral contraceptive Z79.3
raloxifene (Evista) Z79.810
selective estrogen receptor modulators
(SERMs) Z79.810
short term - omit code
steroids
inhaled Z79.51
systemic Z79.52
tamoxifen (Nolvadex) Z79.810
toremifene (Fareston) Z79.810
Thermic —see condition
Thermography (abnormal) —see also Abnormal,
diagnostic imaging R93.89
breast R92.8
Thermoplegia T67.01
Thesaurismosis, glycogen —see Disease,
glycogen storage
Thiamin deficiency E51.9
specified NEC E51.8
Thiaminic deficiency with beriberi E51.11
Thibierge-Weissenbach syndrome —see
Sclerosis, systemic
Thickening
bone —see Hypertrophy, bone
breast N64.59
endometrium R93.89
epidermal L85.9
specified NEC L85.8
hymen N89.6
larynx J38.7
nail L60.2
congenital Q84.5
periosteal —see Hypertrophy, bone
pleura J92.9
with asbestos J92.0
skin R23.4
subepiglottic J38.7
tongue K14.8
valve, heart —see Endocarditis
Thigh —see condition
Thinning vertebra —see Spondylopathy,
specified NEC
Thirst, excessive R63.1
due to deprivation of water T73.1
Thomsen disease G71.12
Thoracic —see also condition
kidney Q63.2
outlet syndrome G54.0
Thoracogastroschisis (congenital)
Q79.8
Thoracopagus Q89.4
Thorax —see condition
Thorn's syndrome N28.89
Thorson-Björck syndrome E34.0
Threadworm (infection) (infestation)
B80

▶ New   ⇒ Revised   ~~deleted~~ Deleted   • Use Additional Character(s)

Threatened
abortion O20.0
with subsequent abortion O03.9
job loss, anxiety concerning Z56.2
labor (without delivery) O47.9
at or after 37 completed weeks of gestation
O47.1
before 37 completed weeks of gestation
O47.0-●
loss of job, anxiety concerning Z56.2
miscarriage O20.0
unemployment, anxiety concerning Z56.2
Three-day fever A93.1
Threshers' lung J67.0
Thrix annulata (congenital) Q84.1
Throat —see condition
Thrombasthenia (Glanzmann) (hemorrhagic)
(hereditary) D69.1
Thromboangiitis I73.1
obliterans (general) I73.1
cerebral I67.89
vessels
brain I67.89
spinal cord I67.89
Thromboarteritis —see Arteritis
Thromboasthenia (Glanzmann) (hemorrhagic)
(hereditary) D69.1
Thrombocytasthenia (Glanzmann) D69.1
Thrombocythemia (essential) (hemorrhagic)
(idiopathic) (primary) D47.3
Thrombocytopathy (dystrophic) (granulopenic)
D69.1
Thrombocytopenia, thrombocytopenic D69.6
with absent radius (TAR) Q87.2
congenital D69.42
dilutional D69.59
due to
drugs D69.59
extracorporeal circulation of blood D69.59
(massive)blood transfusion D69.59
platelet alloimmunization D69.59
essential D69.3
heparin induced (HIT) D75.82
hereditary D69.42
idiopathic D69.3
neonatal, transitory P61.0
due to
exchange transfusion P61.0
idiopathic maternal thrombocytopenia
P61.0
isoimmunization P61.0
primary NEC D69.49
idiopathic D69.3
puerperal, postpartum O72.3
secondary D69.59
transient neonatal P61.0
Thrombocytosis, essential D47.3
primary D47.3
Thromboembolism —see Embolism
Thrombopathy (Bernard-Soulier) D69.1
constitutional D68.0
Willebrand-Jurgens D68.0
Thrombopenia —see Thrombocytopenia
Thrombophilia D68.59
primary NEC D68.59
secondary NEC D68.69
specified NEC D68.69
Thrombophlebitis I80.9
antepartum O22.2-●
deep O22.3-●
superficial O22.2-●
calf muscular vein (NOS) I80.25-●
cavernous (venous) sinus G08
complicating pregnancy O22.5-●
nonpyogenic I67.6
cerebral (sinus) (vein) G08
nonpyogenic I67.6
sequelae G09
due to implanted device —see Complications,
by site and type, specified NEC
during or resulting from a procedure NEC
T81.72

Thrombophlebitis (Continued)
femoral vein (superficial) I80.1-●
femoropopliteal vein I80.0-●
gastrocnemial vein I80.25-●
hepatic (vein) I80.8
idiopathic, recurrent I82.1
iliac vein (common) (external) (internal)
I80.21-●
iliofemoral I80.1-●
intracranial venous sinus (any) G08
nonpyogenic I67.6
sequelae G09
intraspinal venous sinuses and veins G08
nonpyogenic G95.19
lateral (venous) sinus G08
nonpyogenic I67.6
leg I80.3
superficial I80.0-●
longitudinal (venous) sinus G08
nonpyogenic I67.6
lower extremity I80.299
migrans, migrating I82.1
pelvic
with ectopic or molar pregnancy O08.0
following ectopic or molar pregnancy O08.0
puerperal O87.1
peroneal vein I80.24-●
popliteal vein —see Phlebitis, leg, deep,
popliteal
portal (vein) K75.1
postoperative T81.72
pregnancy —see Thrombophlebitis,
antepartum
puerperal, postpartum, childbirth O87.0
deep O87.1
pelvic O87.1
septic O86.81
superficial O87.0
saphenous (greater) (lesser) I80.0-●
sinus (intracranial) G08
nonpyogenic I67.6
soleal vein I80.25-●
specified site NEC I80.8
tibial vein (anterior) (posterior) I80.23-●
Thrombosis, thrombotic (bland) (multiple)
(progressive) (silent) (vessel) I82.90
anal K64.5
antepartum —see Thrombophlebitis,
antepartum
aorta, aortic I74.10
abdominal I74.09
saddle I74.01
bifurcation I74.09
saddle I74.01
specified site NEC I74.19
terminal I74.09
thoracic I74.11
valve —see Endocarditis, aortic
apoplexy I63.3-●
artery, arteries (postinfectional) I74.9
auditory, internal —see Occlusion, artery,
precerebral, specified NEC
basilar —see Occlusion, artery, basilar
carotid (common) (internal) —see
Occlusion, artery, carotid
cerebellar (anterior inferior) (posterior
inferior) (superior) —see Occlusion,
artery, cerebellar
cerebral —see Occlusion, artery, cerebral
choroidal (anterior) —see Occlusion, artery,
precerebral, specified NEC
communicating, posterior —see Occlusion,
artery, precerebral, specified NEC
coronary —see also Infarct, myocardium
not resulting in infarction I24.0
hepatic I74.8
hypophyseal —see Occlusion, artery,
precerebral, specified NEC
iliac I74.5
limb I74.4
lower I74.3
upper I74.2

Thrombosis, thrombotic (Continued)
artery, arteries (Continued)
meningeal, anterior or posterior —see
Occlusion, artery, cerebral, specified
NEC
mesenteric (with gangrene) —see also
Infarct, intestine K55.069
ophthalmic —see Occlusion, artery, retina
pontine —see Occlusion, artery, precerebral,
specified NEC
precerebral —see Occlusion, artery,
precerebral
pulmonary (iatrogenic) —see Embolism,
pulmonary
renal N28.0
retinal —see Occlusion, artery, retina
spinal, anterior or posterior G95.11
traumatic NEC T14.8
vertebral —see Occlusion, artery, vertebral
atrium, auricular —see also Infarct, myocardium
following acute myocardial infarction
(current complication) I23.6
not resulting in infarction I51.3
old I51.3
basilar (artery) —see Occlusion, artery, basilar
brain (artery) (stem) —see also Occlusion,
artery, cerebral
due to syphilis A52.05
puerperal O99.43
sinus —see Thrombosis, intracranial
venous sinus
capillary I78.8
cardiac —see also Infarct, myocardium
not resulting in infarction I51.3
valve —see Endocarditis
old I51.3
carotid (artery) (common) (internal) —see
Occlusion, artery, carotid
cavernous (venous) sinus —see Thrombosis,
intracranial venous sinus
cerebellar artery (anterior inferior) (posterior
inferior) (superior) I66.3
cerebral (artery) —see Occlusion, artery,
cerebral
cerebrovenous sinus —see also Thrombosis,
intracranial venous sinus
puerperium O87.3
chronic I82.91
coronary (artery) (vein) —see also Infarct,
myocardium
not resulting in infarction I24.0
corpus cavernosum N48.89
cortical I66.9
deep —see Embolism, vein, lower extremity
due to device, implant or graft —see also
Complications, by site and type,
specified NEC T85.868
arterial graft NEC T82.868
breast (implant) T85.868
catheter NEC T85.868
dialysis (renal) T82.868
intraperitoneal T85.868
infusion NEC T82.868
spinal (epidural) (subdural) T85.860
urinary (indwelling) T83.86
electronic (electrode) (pulse generator)
(stimulator)
bone T84.86
cardiac T82.867
nervous system (brain) (peripheral
nerve) (spinal) T85.860
urinary T83.86
fixation, internal (orthopedic) NEC T84.86
gastrointestinal (bile duct) (esophagus)
T85.868
genital NEC T83.86
heart T82.867
joint prosthesis T84.86
ocular (corneal graft) (orbital implant)
NEC T85.868
orthopedic NEC T84.86

Thrombosis, thrombotic *(Continued)*
  due to device, implant or graft *(Continued)*
    specified NEC T85.868
    urinary NEC T83.86
    vascular NEC T82.868
    ventricular intracranial shunt T85.860
  during the puerperium —*see* Thrombosis, puerperal
  endocardial —*see also* Infarct, myocardium
    not resulting in infarction I51.3
  eye —*see* Occlusion, retina
  genital organ
    female NEC N94.89
      pregnancy —*see* Thrombophlebitis, antepartum
    male N50.1
  gestational —*see* Phlebopathy, gestational
  heart (chamber) —*see also* Infarct, myocardium
    not resulting in infarction I51.3
    old I51.3
  hepatic (vein) I82.0
    artery I74.8
  history (of) Z86.718
  intestine (with gangrene) —*see also* Infarct, intestine K55.069
  intracardiac NEC (apical) (atrial) (auricular) (ventricular) (old) I51.3
  intracranial (arterial) I66.9
    venous sinus (any) G08
      nonpyogenic origin I67.6
      puerperium O87.3
  intramural —*see also* Infarct, myocardium
    not resulting in infarction I51.3
    old I51.3
  intraspinal venous sinuses and veins G08
    nonpyogenic G95.19
  kidney (artery) N28.0
  lateral (venous) sinus —*see* Thrombosis, intracranial venous sinus
  leg —*see* Thrombosis, vein, lower extremity
    arterial I74.3
  liver (venous) I82.0
    artery I74.8
    portal vein I81
  longitudinal (venous) sinus —*see* Thrombosis, intracranial venous sinus
  lower limb —*see* Thrombosis, vein, lower extremity
  lung (iatrogenic) (postoperative) —*see* Embolism, pulmonary
  meninges (brain) (arterial) I66.8
  mesenteric (artery) (with gangrene) —*see also* Infarct, intestine K55.069
    ⮕vein (inferior) (superior) K55.0-●
  mitral I34.8
  mural —*see also* Infarct, myocardium
    due to syphilis A52.06
    not resulting in infarction I51.3
    old I51.3
  omentum (with gangrene) —*see also* Infarct, intestine K55.069
  ophthalmic —*see* Occlusion, retina
  pampiniform plexus (male) N50.1
  parietal —*see also* Infarct, myocardium
    not resulting in infarction I24.0
  penis, superficial vein N48.81
  perianal venous K64.5
  peripheral arteries I74.4
    upper I74.2
  personal history (of) Z86.718
  portal I81
    due to syphilis A52.09
  precerebral artery —*see* Occlusion, artery, precerebral
  puerperal, postpartum O87.0
    brain (artery) O99.43
      venous (sinus) O87.3
    cardiac O99.43
    cerebral (artery) O99.43
      venous (sinus) O87.3
    superficial O87.0

Thrombosis, thrombotic *(Continued)*
  pulmonary (artery) (iatrogenic) (postoperative) (vein) —*see* Embolism, pulmonary
  renal (artery) N28.0
    vein I82.3
  resulting from presence of device, implant or graft —*see* Complications, by site and type, specified NEC
  retina, retinal —*see* Occlusion, retina
  scrotum N50.1
  seminal vesicle N50.1
  sigmoid (venous) sinus —*see* Thrombosis, intracranial venous sinus
  sinus, intracranial (any) —*see* Thrombosis, intracranial venous sinus
  specified site NEC I82.890
    chronic I82.891
  spermatic cord N50.1
  spinal cord (arterial) G95.11
    due to syphilis A52.09
    pyogenic origin G06.1
  spleen, splenic D73.5
    artery I74.8
  testis N50.1
  traumatic NEC T14.8
  tricuspid I07.8
  tumor —*see* Neoplasm, by site
  tunica vaginalis N50.1
  umbilical cord (vessels), complicating delivery O69.5
  vas deferens N50.1
  vein (acute) I82.90
    antecubital I82.61-●
      chronic I82.71-●
    axillary I82.A1-●
      chronic I82.A2-●
    basilic I82.61-●
      chronic I82.71-●
    brachial I82.62-●
      chronic I82.72-●
    brachiocephalic (innominate) I82.290
      chronic I82.291
    cerebral, nonpyogenic I67.6
    cephalic I82.61-●
      chronic I82.71-●
    chronic I82.91
    deep (DVT) I82.40-●
      calf I82.4Z-●
        chronic I82.5Z-●
      lower leg I82.4Z-●
        chronic I82.5Z-●
      thigh I82.4Y-●
        chronic I82.5Y-●
      upper leg I82.4Y
        chronic I82.5y-●
    femoral I82.41-●
      chronic I82.51-●
    iliac (iliofemoral) I82.42-●
      chronic I82.52-●
    innominate I82.290
      chronic I82.291
    internal jugular I82.C1-●
      chronic I82.C2-●
    lower extremity
      deep I82.40-●
        chronic I82.50-●
        specified NEC I82.49-●
          chronic NEC I82.59-●
      distal
        deep I82.4Z-●
      proximal
        deep I82.4Y-●
          chronic I82.5Y-●
      superficial I82.81-●
    perianal K64.5
    popliteal I82.43-●
      chronic I82.53-●
    radial I82.62-●
      chronic I82.72-●
    renal I82.3

Thrombosis, thrombotic *(Continued)*
  vein *(Continued)*
    saphenous (greater) (lesser) I82.81-●
    specified NEC I82.890
      chronic NEC I82.891
    subclavian I82.B1-●
      chronic I82.B2-●
    thoracic NEC I82.290
      chronic I82.291
    tibial I82.44-●
      chronic I82.54-●
    ulnar I82.62-●
      chronic I82.72-●
    upper extremity I82.60-●
      chronic I82.70-●
      deep I82.62-●
        chronic I82.72-●
      superficial I82.61-●
        chronic I82.71-●
  vena cava
    inferior I82.220
      chronic I82.221
    superior I82.210
      chronic I82.211
  venous, perianal K64.5
  ventricle —*see also* Infarct, myocardium
    following acute myocardial infarction (current complication) I23.6
    not resulting in infarction I24.0
    old I51.3
Thrombus —*see* Thrombosis
Thrush —*see also* Candidiasis
  newborn P37.5
  oral B37.0
  vaginal B37.3
Thumb —*see also* condition
  sucking (child problem) F98.8
Thymitis E32.8
⮕**Thymoma** —*see also* Neoplasm, thymus, by type
  malignant C37
  ▶metaplastic C37
  ▶microscopic D15.0
  ▶sclerosing C37
  ▶type A C37
  ▶type AB C37
  ▶type B1 C37
  ▶type B2 C37
  ▶type B3 C37
Thymus, thymic (gland) —*see* condition
Thyrocele —*see* Goiter
Thyroglossal —*see also* condition
  cyst Q89.2
  duct, persistent Q89.2
Thyroid (gland) (body) —*see also* condition
  hormone resistance E07.89
  lingual Q89.2
  nodule (cystic) (nontoxic) (single) E04.1
Thyroiditis E06.9
  acute (nonsuppurative) (pyogenic) (suppurative) E06.0
  autoimmune E06.3
  chronic (nonspecific) (sclerosing) E06.5
    with thyrotoxicosis, transient E06.2
    fibrous E06.5
    lymphadenoid E06.3
    lymphocytic E06.3
    lymphoid E06.3
  de Quervain's E06.1
  drug-induced E06.4
  fibrous (chronic) E06.5
  giant-cell (follicular) E06.1
  granulomatous (de Quervain) (subacute) E06.1
  Hashimoto's (struma lymphomatosa) E06.3
  iatrogenic E06.4
  ligneous E06.5
  lymphocytic (chronic) E06.3
  lymphoid E06.3
  lymphomatous E06.3
  nonsuppurative E06.1
  postpartum, puerperal O90.5
  pseudotuberculous E06.1

▶ New   ⮕ Revised   ~~deleted~~ Deleted   ● Use Additional Character(s)

Thyroiditis *(Continued)*
  pyogenic E06.0
  radiation E06.4
  Riedel's E06.5
  subacute (granulomatous) E06.1
  suppurative E06.0
  tuberculous A18.81
  viral E06.1
  woody E06.5
Thyrolingual duct, persistent Q89.2
Thyromegaly E01.0
Thyrotoxic
  crisis —*see* Thyrotoxicosis
  heart disease or failure —*see also*
      Thyrotoxicosis E05.90 *[I43]*
    with thyroid storm E05.91 *[I43]*
  storm —*see* Thyrotoxicosis
Thyrotoxicosis (recurrent) E05.90
  with
    goiter (diffuse) E05.00
      with thyroid storm E05.01
        adenomatous uninodular E05.10
          with thyroid storm E05.11
        multinodular E05.20
          with thyroid storm E05.21
        nodular E05.20
          with thyroid storm E05.21
        uninodular E05.10
          with thyroid storm E05.11
      infiltrative
        dermopathy E05.00
          with thyroid storm E05.01
        ophthalmopathy E05.00
          with thyroid storm E05.01
      single thyroid nodule E05.10
        with thyroid storm E05.11
      thyroid storm E05.91
  due to
    ectopic thyroid nodule or tissue E05.30
      with thyroid storm E05.31
    ingestion of (excessive) thyroid material
        E05.40
      with thyroid storm E05.41
    overproduction of thyroid-stimulating
        hormone E05.80
      with thyroid storm E05.81
    specified cause NEC E05.80
      with thyroid storm E05.81
  factitia E05.40
    with thyroid storm E05.41
  heart —*see also* Failure, heart, high-output
      E05.90 *[I43]*
    with thyroid storm —*see also* Failure, heart,
        high-output E05.91 *[I43]*
    failure —*see also* Failure, heart, high-output
        E05.90 *[I43]*
  neonatal (transient) P72.1
  transient with chronic thyroiditis E06.2
➡ Tibia vara M92.51-●
Tic (disorder) F95.9
  breathing F95.8
  child problem F95.0
  compulsive F95.1
  de la Tourette F95.2
  degenerative (generalized) (localized) G25.69
    facial G25.69
  disorder
    chronic
      motor F95.1
      vocal F95.1
    combined vocal and multiple motor F95.2
    transient F95.0
  douloureux G50.0
    atypical G50.1
    postherpetic, postzoster B02.22
  drug-induced G25.61
  eyelid F95.8
  habit F95.9
    chronic F95.1
    transient of childhood F95.0
  lid, transient of childhood F95.0

Tic *(Continued)*
  motor-verbal F95.2
  occupational F48.8
  orbicularis F95.8
    transient of childhood F95.0
  organic origin G25.69
  postchoreic G25.69
  provisional F95.0
  psychogenic, compulsive F95.1
  salaam R25.8
  spasm (motor or vocal) F95.9
    chronic F95.1
    transient of childhood F95.0
  specified NEC F95.8
Tick-borne —*see* condition
Tietze's disease or syndrome M94.0
Tight, tightness
  anus K62.89
  chest R07.89
  fascia (lata) M62.89
  foreskin (congenital) N47.1
  hymen, hymenal ring N89.6
  introitus (acquired) (congenital) N89.6
  rectal sphincter K62.89
  tendon —*see* Short, tendon
  urethral sphincter N35.919
Tilting vertebra —*see* Dorsopathy, deforming,
    specified NEC
Timidity, child F93.8
Tin-miner's lung J63.5
Tinea (intersecta) (tarsi) B35.9
  amiantacea L44.8
  asbestina B35.0
  barbae B35.0
  beard B35.0
  black dot B35.0
  blanca B36.2
  capitis B35.0
  corporis B35.4
  cruris B35.6
  flava B36.0
  foot B35.3
  furfuracea B36.0
  imbricata (Tokelau) B35.5
  kerion B35.0
  manuum B35.2
  microsporic —*see* Dermatophytosis
  nigra B36.1
  nodosa —*see* Piedra
  pedis B35.3
  scalp B35.0
  specified NEC B35.8
  sycosis B35.0
  tonsurans B35.0
  trichophytic —*see* Dermatophytosis
  unguium B35.1
  versicolor B36.0
Tingling sensation (skin) R20.2
Tinnitus NOS H93.1-●
  audible H93.1-●
  aurium H93.1-●
  pulsatile H93.A-●
  subjective H93.1-●
Tipped tooth (teeth) M26.33
Tipping
  pelvis M95.5
    with disproportion (fetopelvic) O33.0
      causing obstructed labor O65.0
  tooth (teeth), fully erupted M26.33
Tiredness R53.83
Tissue —*see* condition
Tobacco (nicotine)
  abuse —*see* Tobacco, use
  dependence —*see* Dependence, drug, nicotine
  harmful use Z72.0
  heart —*see* Tobacco, toxic effect
  maternal use, affecting newborn P04.2
  toxic effect —*see* Table of Drugs and
      Chemicals, by substance, poisoning
    chewing tobacco —*see* Table of Drugs
        and Chemicals, by substance, poisoning

Tobacco *(Continued)*
  toxic effect *(Continued)*
    cigarettes —*see* Table of Drugs and
        Chemicals, by substance, poisoning
  use Z72.0
    complicating
      childbirth O99.334
      pregnancy O99.33-●
      puerperium O99.335
    counseling and surveillance Z71.6
    history Z87.891
  withdrawal state —*see also* Dependence,
      drug, nicotine F17.203
Tocopherol deficiency E56.0
Todd's
  cirrhosis K74.3
  paralysis (postepileptic) (transitory) G83.84
Toe —*see* condition
Toilet, artificial opening —*see* Attention to,
    artificial, opening
Tokelau (ringworm) B35.5
Tollwut —*see* Rabies
Tommaselli's disease R31.9
  correct substance properly administered —*see*
      Table of Drugs and Chemicals, by drug,
      adverse effect
  overdose or wrong substance given
      or taken —*see* Table of Drugs and
      Chemicals, by drug, poisoning
Tongue —*see also* condition
  tie Q38.1
Tonic pupil —*see* Anomaly, pupil, function,
    tonic pupil
Toni-Fanconi syndrome (cystinosis)
    E72.09
  with cystinosis E72.04
Tonsil —*see* condition
Tonsillitis (acute) (catarrhal) (croupous)
    (follicular) (gangrenous) (infective)
    (lacunar) (lingual) (malignant)
    (membranous) (parenchymatous)
    (phlegmonous) (pseudomembranous)
    (purulent) (septic) (subacute) (suppurative)
    (toxic) (ulcerative) (vesicular) (viral) J03.90
  chronic J35.01
    with adenoiditis J35.03
  diphtheritic A36.0
  hypertrophic J35.01
    with adenoiditis J35.03
  recurrent J03.91
  specified organism NEC J03.80
    recurrent J03.81
  staphylococcal J03.80
    recurrent J03.81
  streptococcal J03.00
    recurrent J03.01
  tuberculous A15.8
  Vincent's A69.1
Tooth, teeth —*see* condition
Toothache K08.89
Topagnosis R20.8
Tophi —*see* Gout, chronic
TORCH infection —*see* Infection, congenital
    without active infection P00.2
Torn —*see* Tear
Tornwaldt's cyst or disease J39.2
Torsion
  accessory tube —*see* Torsion, fallopian tube
  adnexa (female) —*see* Torsion, fallopian tube
  aorta, acquired I77.1
  appendix epididymis N44.04
  appendix testis N44.03
  bile duct (common) (hepatic) K83.8
    congenital Q44.5
  bowel, colon or intestine K56.2
  cervix —*see* Malposition, uterus
  cystic duct K82.8
  dystonia —*see* Dystonia, torsion
  epididymis (appendix) N44.04
  fallopian tube N83.52-●
    with ovary N83.53

Transection *(Continued)*
pulmonary vessel (incomplete) —*see also* Injury, blood vessel, thoracic, pulmonary, laceration
  complete —*see* Injury, blood vessel, thoracic, pulmonary, laceration, major
subclavian —*see* Transection, innominate
vena cava (incomplete) —*see also* Injury, vena cava
  complete —*see* Injury, vena cava, laceration, major
vertebral artery (incomplete) —*see also* Injury, blood vessel, vertebral, laceration
  complete —*see* Injury, blood vessel, vertebral, laceration, major
Transfusion
associated (red blood cell) hemochromatosis E83.111
blood
  ABO incompatible —*see* Complication(s), transfusion, incompatibility reaction, ABO
  minor blood group (Duffy) (E) (K) (Kell) (Kidd) (Lewis) (M) (N) (P) (S) T80.89
  reaction or complication —*see* Complications, transfusion
fetomaternal (mother) —*see* Pregnancy, complicated by, placenta, transfusion syndrome
maternofetal (mother) —*see* Pregnancy, complicated by, placenta, transfusion syndrome
placental (syndrome) (mother) —*see* Pregnancy, complicated by, placenta, transfusion syndrome
reaction (adverse) —*see* Complications, transfusion
related acute lung injury (TRALI) J95.84
twin-to-twin —*see* Pregnancy, complicated by, placenta, transfusion syndrome, fetus to fetus
Transient (meaning homeless) —*see also* condition Z59.0
Translocation
balanced autosomal Q95.9
  in normal individual Q95.0
chromosomes NEC Q99.8
  balanced and insertion in normal individual Q95.0
Down's syndrome Q90.2
trisomy
  13 Q91.6
  18 Q91.2
  21 Q90.2
Translucency, iris —*see* Degeneration, iris
Transmission of chemical substances through the placenta —*see* Absorption, chemical, through placenta
Transparency, lung, unilateral J43.0
Transplant (ed) (status) Z94.9
awaiting organ Z76.82
bone Z94.6
  marrow Z94.81
candidate Z76.82
complication —*see* Complication, transplant
cornea Z94.7
heart Z94.1
  and lung(s) Z94.3
  valve Z95.2
    prosthetic Z95.2
    specified NEC Z95.4
    xenogenic Z95.3
intestine Z94.82
kidney Z94.0
liver Z94.4
lung(s) Z94.2
  and heart Z94.3
organ (failure) (infection) (rejection)Z94.9
  removal status Z98.85
pancreas Z94.83

Transplant *(Continued)*
skin Z94.5
social Z60.3
specified organ or tissue NEC Z94.89
stem cells Z94.84
tissue Z94.9
Transplants, ovarian, endometrial N80.1
Transposed —*see* Transposition
Transposition (congenital) —*see also* Malposition, congenital
abdominal viscera Q89.3
aorta (dextra) Q20.3
appendix Q43.8
colon Q43.8
corrected Q20.5
great vessels (complete) (partial) Q20.3
heart Q24.0
  with complete transposition of viscera Q89.3
intestine (large) (small) Q43.8
reversed jejunal (for bypass) (status) Z98.0
scrotum Q55.23
stomach Q40.2
  with general transposition of viscera Q89.3
tooth, teeth, fully erupted M26.30
vessels, great (complete) (partial) Q20.3
viscera (abdominal) (thoracic) Q89.3
Transsexualism F64.0
Transverse —*see also* condition
arrest (deep), in labor O64.0
lie (mother) O32.2
  causing obstructed labor O64.8
Transvestism, transvestitism (dual-role) F64.1
fetishistic F65.1
Trapped placenta (with hemorrhage) O72.0
without hemorrhage O73.0
TRAPS (tumor necrosis factor receptor associated periodic syndrome) M04.1
Trauma, traumatism —*see also* Injury
acoustic —*see* subcategory H83.3
birth —*see* Birth, injury
complicating ectopic or molar pregnancy O08.6
during delivery O71.9
following ectopic or molar pregnancy O08.6
obstetric O71.9
  specified NEC O71.89
occlusal
  primary K08.81
  secondary K08.82
Traumatic —*see also* condition
brain injury S06.9
Treacher Collins syndrome Q75.4
Treitz's hernia —*see* Hernia, abdomen, specified site NEC
Trematode infestation —*see* Infestation, fluke
Trematodiasis —*see* Infestation, fluke
Trembling paralysis —*see* Parkinsonism
Tremor(s) R25.1
drug induced G25.1
essential (benign) G25.0
familial G25.0
hereditary G25.0
hysterical F44.4
intention G25.2
medication induced postural G25.1
mercurial —*see* subcategory T56.1
Parkinson's —*see* Parkinsonism
psychogenic (conversion reaction) F44.4
senilis R54
specified type NEC G25.2
Trench
fever A79.0
foot —*see* Immersion, foot
mouth A69.1
Treponema pallidum infection —*see* Syphilis
Treponematosis
due to
  T. pallidum —*see* Syphilis
  T. pertenue —*see* Yaws

Triad
Hutchinson's (congenital syphilis) A50.53
Kartagener's Q89.3
Saint's —*see* Hernia, diaphragm
Trichiasis (eyelid) H02.059
with entropion —*see* Entropion
left H02.056
  lower H02.055
  upper H02.054
right H02.053
  lower H02.052
  upper H02.051
Trichinella spiralis (infection) (infestation) B75
Trichinellosis, trichiniasis, trichinelliasis, trichinosis B75
with muscle disorder B75 *[M63.80]*
  ankle B75 *[M63.87-●]*
  foot B75 *[M63.87-●]*
  forearm B75 *[M63.83-●]*
  hand B75 *[M63.84-●]*
  lower leg B75 *[M63.86-●]*
  multiple sites B75 *[M63.89]*
  pelvic region B75 *[M63.85-●]*
  shoulder region B75 *[M63.81-●]*
  specified site NEC B75 *[M63.88]*
  thigh B75 *[M63.85-●]*
  upper arm B75 *[M63.82-●]*
Trichobezoar T18.9
intestine T18.3
stomach T18.2
Trichocephaliasis, trichocephalosis B79
Trichocephalus infestation B79
Trichoclasis L67.8
Trichoepithelioma —*see also* Neoplasm, skin, benign
malignant —*see* Neoplasm, skin, malignant
Trichofolliculoma —*see* Neoplasm, skin, benign
Tricholemmoma —*see* Neoplasm, skin, benign
Trichomoniasis A59.9
bladder A59.03
cervix A59.09
intestinal A07.8
prostate A59.02
seminal vesicles A59.09
specified site NEC A59.8
urethra A59.03
urogenitalis A59.00
vagina A59.01
vulva A59.01
Trichomycosis
axillaris A48.8
nodosa, nodularis B36.8
Trichonodosis L67.8
Trichophytid, trichophyton infection —*see* Dermatophytosis
Trichophytobezoar T18.9
intestine T18.3
stomach T18.2
Trichophytosis —*see* Dermatophytosis
Trichoptilosis L67.8
Trichorrhexis (nodosa) (invaginata) L67.0
Trichosis axillaris A48.8
Trichosporosis nodosa B36.2
Trichostasis spinulosa (congenital) Q84.1
Trichostrongyliasis, trichostrongylosis (small intestine) B81.2
Trichostrongylus infection B81.2
Trichotillomania F63.3
Trichromat, trichromatopsia, anomalous (congenital) H53.55
Trichuriasis B79
Trichuris trichiura (infection) (infestation) (any site) B79
Tricuspid (valve) —*see* condition
Trifid —*see also* Accessory
kidney (pelvis) Q63.8
tongue Q38.3
Trigeminal neuralgia —*see* Neuralgia, trigeminal

Trigeminy R00.8
Trigger finger (acquired) M65.30
  congenital Q74.0
  index finger M65.32-●
  little finger M65.35-●
  middle finger M65.33-●
  ring finger M65.34-●
  thumb M65.31-●
Trigonitis (bladder) (chronic)
  (pseudomembranous) N30.30
  with hematuria N30.31
Trigonocephaly Q75.0
Trilocular heart —see Cor triloculare
Trimethylaminuria E72.52
Tripartite placenta O43.19-●
Triphalangeal thumb Q74.0
Triple —see also Accessory
  kidneys Q63.0
  uteri Q51.818
  X, female Q97.0
▶Triple I O41.12-●
Triplegia G83.89
  congenital G80.8
Triplet (newborn) —see also Newborn, triplet
  complicating pregnancy —see Pregnancy,
    triplet
Triplication —see Accessory
Triploidy Q92.7
Trismus R25.2
  neonatorum A33
  newborn A33
Trisomy (syndrome) Q92.9
  13 (partial) Q91.7
    meiotic nondisjunction Q91.4
    mitotic nondisjunction Q91.5
    mosaicism Q91.5
    translocation Q91.6
  18 (partial) Q91.3
    meiotic nondisjunction Q91.0
    mitotic nondisjunction Q91.1
    mosaicism Q91.1
    translocation Q91.2
  20 Q92.8
  21 (partial) Q90.9
    meiotic nondisjunction Q90.0
    mitotic nondisjunction Q90.1
    mosaicism Q90.1
    translocation Q90.2
  22 Q92.8
  autosomes Q92.9
  chromosome specified NEC Q92.8
    partial Q92.2
      due to unbalanced translocation Q92.5
    specified NEC Q92.8
    whole (nonsex chromosome)
      meiotic nondisjunction Q92.0
      mitotic nondisjunction Q92.1
      mosaicism Q92.1
  due to
    dicentrics —see Extra, marker
      chromosomes
    extra rings —see Extra, marker
      chromosomes
    isochromosomes —see Extra, marker
      chromosomes
  specified NEC Q92.8
  whole chromosome Q92.9
    meiotic nondisjunction Q92.0
    mitotic nondisjunction Q92.1
    mosaicism Q92.1
    partial Q92.9
    specified NEC Q92.8
Tritanomaly, tritanopia H53.55
Trombiculosis, trombiculiasis, trombidiosis
  B88.0
Trophedema (congenital) (hereditary) Q82.0
Trophoblastic disease —see also Mole,
  hydatidiform O01.9
Tropholymphedema Q82.0
➠Trophoneurosis NEC G96.89
  disseminated M34.9

Tropical —see condition
Trouble —see also Disease
  heart —see Disease, heart
  kidney —see Disease, renal
  nervous R45.0
  sinus —see Sinusitis
Trousseau's syndrome (thrombophlebitis
  migrans) I82.1
Truancy, childhood
  from school Z72.810
Truncus
  arteriosus (persistent) Q20.0
  communis Q20.0
Trunk —see condition
Trypanosomiasis
  African B56.9
    by Trypanosoma brucei
      gambiense B56.0
      rhodesiense B56.1
  American —see Chagas' disease
  Brazilian —see Chagas' disease
  by Trypanosoma
    brucei gambiense B56.0
    brucei rhodesiense B56.1
    cruzi —see Chagas' disease
  gambiensis, Gambian B56.0
  rhodesiensis, Rhodesian B56.1
  South American —see Chagas' disease
  where
    African trypanosomiasis is prevalent
      B56.9
    Chagas' disease is prevalent B57.2
T-shaped incisors K00.2
Tsutsugamushi (disease) (fever) A75.3
Tube, tubal, tubular —see condition
Tubercle —see also Tuberculosis
  brain, solitary A17.81
  Darwin's Q17.8
  Ghon, primary infection A15.7
Tuberculid, tuberculide (indurating,
  subcutaneous) (lichenoid) (miliary)
  (papulonecrotic) (primary) (skin) A18.4
Tuberculoma —see also Tuberculosis
  brain A17.81
  meninges (cerebral) (spinal) A17.1
  spinal cord A17.81
Tuberculosis, tubercular, tuberculous
  (calcification) (calcified) (caseous)
  (chromogenic acid-fast bacilli)
  (degeneration) (fibrocaseous) (fistula)
  (interstitial) (isolated circumscribed
  lesions) (necrosis) (parenchymatous)
  (ulcerative) A15.9
  with pneumoconiosis (any condition in
    J60-J64) J65
  abdomen (lymph gland) A18.39
  abscess (respiratory) A15.9
    bone A18.03
      hip A18.02
      knee A18.02
      sacrum A18.01
      specified site NEC A18.03
      spinal A18.01
      vertebra A18.01
    brain A17.81
    breast A18.89
    Cowper's gland A18.15
    dura (mater) (cerebral) (spinal) A17.81
    epidural (cerebral) (spinal) A17.81
    female pelvis A18.17
    frontal sinus A15.8
    genital organs NEC A18.10
    genitourinary A18.10
    gland (lymphatic) —see Tuberculosis,
      lymph gland
    hip A18.02
    intestine A18.32
    ischiorectal A18.32
    joint NEC A18.02
      hip A18.02
      knee A18.02

Tuberculosis, tubercular, tuberculous
  (Continued)
  abscess (Continued)
    joint NEC (Continued)
      specified NEC A18.02
      vertebral A18.01
    kidney A18.11
    knee A18.02
    latent Z22.7
    lumbar (spine) A18.01
    lung —see Tuberculosis, pulmonary
    meninges (cerebral) (spinal) A17.0
    muscle A18.09
    perianal (fistula) A18.32
    perinephritic A18.11
    perirectal A18.32
    rectum A18.32
    retropharyngeal A15.8
    sacrum A18.01
    scrofulous A18.2
    scrotum A18.15
    skin (primary) A18.4
    spinal cord A17.81
    spine or vertebra (column) A18.01
    subdiaphragmatic A18.31
    testis A18.15
    urinary A18.13
    uterus A18.17
  accessory sinus —see Tuberculosis, sinus
  Addison's disease A18.7
  adenitis —see Tuberculosis, lymph gland
  adenoids A15.8
  adenopathy —see Tuberculosis, lymph gland
  adherent pericardium A18.84
  adnexa (uteri) A18.17
  adrenal (capsule) (gland) A18.7
  alimentary canal A18.32
  anemia A18.89
  ankle (joint) (bone) A18.02
  anus A18.32
  apex, apical —see Tuberculosis, pulmonary
  appendicitis, appendix A18.32
  arachnoid A17.0
  artery, arteritis A18.89
    cerebral A18.89
  arthritis (chronic) (synovial) A18.02
    spine or vertebra (column) A18.01
  articular —see Tuberculosis, joint
  ascites A18.31
  asthma —see Tuberculosis, pulmonary
  axilla, axillary (gland) A18.2
  bladder A18.12
  bone A18.03
    hip A18.02
    knee A18.02
    limb NEC A18.03
    sacrum A18.01
    spine or vertebral column A18.01
  bowel (miliary) A18.32
  brain A17.81
  breast A18.89
  broad ligament A18.17
  bronchi, bronchial, bronchus A15.5
    ectasia, ectasis (bronchiectasis) —see
      Tuberculosis, pulmonary
    fistula A15.5
      primary (progressive) A15.7
    gland or node A15.4
      primary (progressive) A15.7
    lymph gland or node A15.4
      primary (progressive) A15.7
  bronchiectasis —see Tuberculosis, pulmonary
  bronchitis A15.5
  bronchopleural A15.6
  bronchopneumonia, bronchopneumonic —see
    Tuberculosis, pulmonary
  bronchorrhagia A15.5
  bronchotracheal A15.5
  bronze disease A18.7
  buccal cavity A18.83
  bulbourethral gland A18.15

Tuberculosis, tubercular, tuberculous
(Continued)
bursa A18.09
cachexia A15.9
cardiomyopathy A18.84
caries —*see* Tuberculosis, bone
cartilage A18.02
  intervertebral A18.01
catarrhal —*see* Tuberculosis, respiratory
cecum A18.32
cellulitis (primary) A18.4
cerebellum A17.81
cerebral, cerebrum A17.81
cerebrospinal A17.81
  meninges A17.0
cervical (lymph gland or node) A18.2
cervicitis, cervix (uteri) A18.16
chest —*see* Tuberculosis, respiratory
chorioretinitis A18.53
choroid, choroiditis A18.53
ciliary body A18.54
colitis A18.32
collier's J65
colliquativa (primary) A18.4
colon A18.32
complex, primary A15.7
congenital P37.0
conjunctiva A18.59
connective tissue (systemic) A18.89
contact Z20.1
cornea (ulcer) A18.52
Cowper's gland A18.15
coxae A18.02
coxalgia A18.02
cul-de-sac of Douglas A18.17
curvature, spine A18.01
cutis (colliquativa) (primary) A18.4
cyst, ovary A18.18
cystitis A18.12
dactylitis A18.03
diarrhea A18.32
diffuse —*see* Tuberculosis, miliary
digestive tract A18.32
disseminated —*see* Tuberculosis, miliary
duodenum A18.32
dura (mater) (cerebral) (spinal) A17.0
  abscess (cerebral) (spinal) A17.81
dysentery A18.32
ear (inner) (middle) A18.6
  bone A18.03
  external (primary) A18.4
  skin (primary) A18.4
elbow A18.02
emphysema —*see* Tuberculosis, pulmonary
empyema A15.6
encephalitis A17.82
endarteritis A18.89
endocarditis A18.84
  aortic A18.84
  mitral A18.84
  pulmonary A18.84
  tricuspid A18.84
endocrine glands NEC A18.82
endometrium A18.17
enteric, enterica, enteritis A18.32
enterocolitis A18.32
epididymis, epididymitis A18.15
epidural abscess (cerebral) (spinal) A17.81
epiglottis A15.5
episcleritis A18.51
erythema (induratum) (nodosum) (primary)
  A18.4
esophagus A18.83
eustachian tube A18.6
exposure (to) Z20.1
exudative —*see* Tuberculosis, pulmonary
eye A18.50
eyelid (primary) (lupus) A18.4
fallopian tube (acute) (chronic) A18.17
fascia A18.09
fauces A15.8

Tuberculosis, tubercular, tuberculous
(Continued)
female pelvic inflammatory disease
  A18.17
finger A18.03
first infection A15.7
gallbladder A18.83
ganglion A18.09
gastritis A18.83
gastrocolic fistula A18.32
gastroenteritis A18.32
gastrointestinal tract A18.32
general, generalized —*see* Tuberculosis,
  miliary
genital organs A18.10
genitourinary A18.10
genu A18.02
glandula suprarenalis A18.7
glandular, general A18.2
glottis A15.5
grinder's J65
gum A18.83
hand A18.03
heart A18.84
hematogenous —*see* Tuberculosis, miliary
hemoptysis —*see* Tuberculosis, pulmonary
hemorrhage NEC —*see* Tuberculosis,
  pulmonary
hemothorax A15.6
hepatitis A18.83
hilar lymph nodes A15.4
  primary (progressive) A15.7
hip (joint) (disease) (bone) A18.02
hydropneumothorax A15.6
hydrothorax A15.6
hypoadrenalism A18.7
hypopharynx A15.8
ileocecal (hyperplastic) A18.32
ileocolitis A18.32
ileum A18.32
iliac spine (superior) A18.03
immunological findings only A15.7
indurativa (primary) A18.4
infantile A15.7
infection A15.9
  without clinical manifestations A15.7
infraclavicular gland A18.2
inguinal gland A18.2
inguinalis A18.2
intestine (any part) A18.32
iridocyclitis A18.54
iris, iritis A18.54
ischiorectal A18.32
jaw A18.03
jejunum A18.32
joint A18.02
  vertebral A18.01
keratitis (interstitial) A18.52
keratoconjunctivitis A18.52
kidney A18.11
knee (joint) A18.02
kyphosis, kyphoscoliosis A18.01
laryngitis A15.5
larynx A15.5
latent Z22.7
leptomeninges, leptomeningitis (cerebral)
  (spinal) A17.0
lichenoides (primary) A18.4
linguae A18.83
lip A18.83
liver A18.83
lordosis A18.01
lung —*see* Tuberculosis, pulmonary
lupus vulgaris A18.4
lymph gland or node (peripheral) A18.2
  abdomen A18.39
  bronchial A15.4
    primary (progressive) A15.7
  cervical A18.2
  hilar A15.4
    primary (progressive) A15.7

Tuberculosis, tubercular, tuberculous
(Continued)
lymph gland or node *(Continued)*
  intrathoracic A15.4
    primary (progressive) A15.7
  mediastinal A15.4
    primary (progressive) A15.7
  mesenteric A18.39
  retroperitoneal A18.39
  tracheobronchial A15.4
    primary (progressive) A15.7
lymphadenitis —*see* Tuberculosis, lymph
  gland
lymphangitis —*see* Tuberculosis, lymph
  gland
lymphatic (gland) (vessel) —*see* Tuberculosis,
  lymph gland
mammary gland A18.89
marasmus A15.9
mastoiditis A18.03
mediastinal lymph gland or node
  A15.4
    primary (progressive) A15.7
mediastinitis A15.8
    primary (progressive) A15.7
mediastinum A15.8
    primary (progressive) A15.7
medulla A17.81
melanosis, Addisonian A18.7
meninges, meningitis (basilar) (cerebral)
    (cerebrospinal) (spinal) A17.0
meningoencephalitis A17.82
mesentery, mesenteric (gland or node)
    A18.39
miliary A19.9
  acute A19.2
    multiple sites A19.1
    single specified site A19.0
  chronic A19.8
  specified NEC A19.8
millstone makers' J65
miner's J65
molder's J65
mouth A18.83
multiple A19.9
  acute A19.1
  chronic A19.8
muscle A18.09
myelitis A17.82
myocardium, myocarditis A18.84
nasal (passage) (sinus) A15.8
nasopharynx A15.8
neck gland A18.2
nephritis A18.11
nerve (mononeuropathy) A17.83
nervous system A17.9
nose (septum) A15.8
ocular A18.50
omentum A18.31
oophoritis (acute) (chronic) A18.17
optic (nerve trunk) (papilla) A18.59
orbit A18.59
orchitis A18.15
organ, specified NEC A18.89
osseous —*see* Tuberculosis, bone
osteitis —*see* Tuberculosis, bone
osteomyelitis —*see* Tuberculosis, bone
otitis media A18.6
ovary, ovaritis (acute) (chronic) A18.17
oviduct (acute) (chronic) A18.17
pachymeningitis A17.0
palate (soft) A18.83
pancreas A18.83
papulonecrotic (a) (primary) A18.4
parathyroid glands A18.82
paronychia (primary) A18.4
parotid gland or region A18.83
pelvis (bony) A18.03
penis A18.15
peribronchitis A15.5
pericardium, pericarditis A18.84

Tuberculosis, tubercular, tuberculous
 (Continued)
  perichondritis, larynx A15.5
  periostitis —*see* Tuberculosis, bone
  perirectal fistula A18.32
  peritoneum NEC A18.31
  peritonitis A18.31
  pharynx, pharyngitis A15.8
  phlyctenulosis (keratoconjunctivitis) A18.52
  phthisis NEC —*see* Tuberculosis, pulmonary
  pituitary gland A18.82
  pleura, pleural, pleurisy, pleuritis (fibrinous)
    (obliterative) (purulent) (simple plastic)
    (with effusion) A15.6
    primary (progressive) A15.7
  pneumonia, pneumonic —*see* Tuberculosis,
    pulmonary
  pneumothorax (spontaneous) (tense
    valvular) —*see* Tuberculosis, pulmonary
  polyneuropathy A17.89
  polyserositis A19.9
    acute A19.1
    chronic A19.8
  potter's J65
  prepuce A18.15
  primary (complex) A15.7
  proctitis A18.32
  prostate, prostatitis A18.14
  pulmonalis —*see* Tuberculosis, pulmonary
  pulmonary (cavitated) (fibrotic) (infiltrative)
    (nodular) A15.0
    childhood type or first infection A15.7
    primary (complex) A15.7
  pyelitis A18.11
  pyelonephritis A18.11
  pyemia —*see* Tuberculosis, miliary
  pyonephrosis A18.11
  pyopneumothorax A15.6
  pyothorax A15.6
  rectum (fistula) (with abscess) A18.32
  reinfection stage —*see* Tuberculosis,
    pulmonary
  renal A18.11
  renis A18.11
  respiratory A15.9
    primary A15.7
    specified site NEC A15.8
  retina, retinitis A18.53
  retroperitoneal (lymph gland or node)
    A18.39
  rheumatism NEC A18.09
  rhinitis A15.8
  sacroiliac (joint) A18.01
  sacrum A18.01
  salivary gland A18.83
  salpingitis (acute) (chronic) A18.17
  sandblaster's J65
  sclera A18.51
  scoliosis A18.01
  scrofulous A18.2
  scrotum A18.15
  seminal tract or vesicle A18.15
  senile A15.9
  septic —*see* Tuberculosis, miliary
  shoulder (joint) A18.02
    blade A18.03
  sigmoid A18.32
  sinus (any nasal) A15.8
    bone A18.03
    epididymis A18.15
  skeletal NEC A18.03
  skin (any site) (primary) A18.4
  small intestine A18.32
  soft palate A18.83
  spermatic cord A18.15
  spine, spinal (column) A18.01
    cord A17.81
    medulla A17.81
    membrane A17.0
    meninges A17.0
  spleen, splenitis A18.85

Tuberculosis, tubercular, tuberculous
 (Continued)
  spondylitis A18.01
  sternoclavicular joint A18.02
  stomach A18.83
  stonemason's J65
  subcutaneous tissue (cellular) (primary)
    A18.4
  subcutis (primary) A18.4
  subdeltoid bursa A18.83
  submaxillary (region) A18.83
  supraclavicular gland A18.2
  suprarenal (capsule) (gland) A18.7
  swelling, joint —*see also* category M01 (*see also*
    Tuberculosis, joint) A18.02
  symphysis pubis A18.02
  synovitis A18.09
    articular A18.02
    spine or vertebra A18.01
  systemic —*see* Tuberculosis, miliary
  tarsitis A18.4
  tendon (sheath) —*see* Tuberculosis,
    tenosynovitis
  tenosynovitis A18.09
    spine or vertebra A18.01
  testis A18.15
  throat A15.8
  thymus gland A18.82
  thyroid gland A18.81
  tongue A18.83
  tonsil, tonsillitis A15.8
  trachea, tracheal A15.5
    lymph gland or node A15.4
      primary (progressive) A15.7
  tracheobronchial A15.5
    lymph gland or node A15.4
      primary (progressive) A15.7
  tubal (acute) (chronic) A18.17
  tunica vaginalis A18.15
  ulcer (skin) (primary) A18.4
    bowel or intestine A18.32
    specified NEC - code under Tuberculosis,
      by site
  unspecified site A15.9
  ureter A18.11
  urethra, urethral (gland) A18.13
  urinary organ or tract A18.13
  uterus A18.17
  uveal tract A18.54
  uvula A18.83
  vagina A18.18
  vas deferens A18.15
  verruca, verrucosa (cutis) (primary) A18.4
  vertebra (column) A18.01
  vesiculitis A18.15
  vulva A18.18
  wrist (joint) A18.02
Tuberculum
  Carabelli —*see* Note at K00.2
  occlusal —*see* Note at K00.2
  paramolare K00.2
Tuberosity, enitre maxillary M26.07
Tuberous sclerosis (brain) Q85.1
Tubo-ovarian —*see* condition
Tuboplasty, after previous sterilization
  Z31.0
  aftercare Z31.42
Tubotympanitis, catarrhal (chronic) —*see* Otitis,
  media, nonsuppurative, chronic, serous
Tularemia A21.9
  with
    conjunctivitis A21.1
    pneumonia A21.2
  abdominal A21.3
  bronchopneumonic A21.2
  conjunctivitis A21.1
  cryptogenic A21.3
  enteric A21.3
  gastrointestinal A21.3
  generalized A21.7
  ingestion A21.3

Tularemia *(Continued)*
  intestinal A21.3
  oculoglandular A21.1
  ophthalmic A21.1
  pneumonia (any), pneumonic A21.2
  pulmonary A21.2
  sepsis A21.7
  specified NEC A21.8
  typhoidal A21.7
  ulceroglandular A21.0
Tularensis conjunctivitis A21.1
Tumefaction —*see also* Swelling
  liver —*see* Hypertrophy, liver
Tumor —*see also* Neoplasm, unspecified
  behavior, by site
  acinar cell —*see* Neoplasm, uncertain
    behavior, by site
  acinic cell —*see* Neoplasm, uncertain
    behavior, by site
  adenocarcinoid —*see* Neoplasm, malignant,
    by site
  adenomatoid —*see also* Neoplasm, benign,
    by site
    odontogenic —*see* Cyst, calcifying
      odontogenic
  adnexal (skin) —*see* Neoplasm, skin, benign,
    by site
  adrenal
    cortical (benign) D35.0-●
      malignant C74.0-●
    rest —*see* Neoplasm, benign, by site
  alpha-cell
    malignant
      pancreas C25.4
      specified site NEC —*see* Neoplasm,
        malignant, by site
      unspecified site C25.4
    pancreas D13.7
    specified site NEC —*see* Neoplasm, benign,
      by site
    unspecified site D13.7
  aneurysmal —*see* Aneurysm
  aortic body D44.7
    malignant C75.5
  Askin's —*see* Neoplasm, connective tissue,
    malignant
  basal cell —*see also* Neoplasm, skin, uncertain
    behavior D48.5
  Bednar —*see* Neoplasm, skin, malignant
  benign (unclassified) —*see* Neoplasm, benign,
    by site
  beta-cell
    malignant
      pancreas C25.4
      specified site NEC —*see* Neoplasm,
        malignant, by site
      unspecified site C25.4
    pancreas D13.7
    specified site NEC —*see* Neoplasm, benign,
      by site
    unspecified site D13.7
  Brenner D27.9
    borderline malignancy D39.1-●
    malignant C56-●
    proliferating D39.1
  bronchial alveolar, intravascular D38.1
  Brooke's —*see* Neoplasm, skin, benign
  brown fat —*see* Lipoma
  Burkitt —*see* Lymphoma, Burkitt
  calcifying epithelial odontogenic —*see* Cyst,
    calcifying odontogenic
  carcinoid D3A.00
    benign D3A.00
      appendix D3A.020
      ascending colon D3A.022
      bronchus (lung) D3A.090
      cecum D3A.021
      colon D3A.029
      descending colon D3A.024
      duodenum D3A.010
      foregut NOS D3A.094

▶ New   ⇒ Revised   ~~deleted~~ Deleted   ● Use Additional Character(s)

Tumor *(Continued)*
  carcinoid *(Continued)*
    malignant *(Continued)*
      hindgut NOS D3A.096
      ileum D3A.012
      jejunum D3A.011
      kidney D3A.093
      large intestine D3A.029
      lung (bronchus) D3A.090
      midgut NOS D3A.095
      rectum D3A.026
      sigmoid colon D3A.025
      small intestine D3A.019
      specified NEC D3A.098
      stomach D3A.092
      thymus D3A.091
      transverse colon D3A.023
    malignant C7A.00
      appendix C7A.020
      ascending colon C7A.022
      bronchus (lung) C7A.090
      cecum C7A.021
      colon C7A.029
      descending colon C7A.024
      duodenum C7A.010
      foregut NOS C7A.094
      hindgut NOS C7A.096
      ileum C7A.012
      jejunum C7A.011
      kidney C7A.093
      large intestine C7A.029
      lung (bronchus) C7A.090
      midgut NOS C7A.095
      rectum C7A.026
      sigmoid colon C7A.025
      small intestine C7A.019
      specified NEC C7A.098
      stomach C7A.092
      thymus C7A.091
      transverse colon C7A.023
    mesentary metastasis C7B.04
    secondary C7B.00
      bone C7B.03
      distant lymph nodes C7B.01
      liver C7B.02
      peritoneum C7B.04
      specified NEC C7B.09
  carotid body D44.6
    malignant C75.4
  cells —*see also* Neoplasm, unspecified
    behavior, by site
    benign —*see* Neoplasm, benign,
      by site
    malignant —*see* Neoplasm, malignant,
      by site
    uncertain whether benign or malignant —
      see Neoplasm, uncertain behavior,
      by site
  cervix, in pregnancy or childbirth —*see*
    Pregnancy, complicated by, tumor,
    cervix
  chondromatous giant cell —*see* Neoplasm,
    bone, benign
  chromaffin —*see also* Neoplasm, benign, by
    site
    malignant —*see* Neoplasm, malignant, by
      site
  Cock's peculiar L72.3
  Codman's —*see* Neoplasm, bone, benign
  dentigerous, mixed —*see* Cyst, calcifying
    odontogenic
  dermoid —*see* Neoplasm, benign,
    by site
    with malignant transformation C56.-●
  desmoid (extra-abdominal) —*see also*
    Neoplasm, connective tissue, uncertain
    behavior
    abdominal —*see* Neoplasm, connective
      tissue, uncertain behavior
  embolus —*see* Neoplasm, secondary,
    by site

embryonal (mixed) —*see also* Neoplasm,
  uncertain behavior, by site
  liver C22.7
endodermal sinus
  specified site —*see* Neoplasm, malignant,
    by site
  unspecified site
    female C56.-●
    male C62.90
epithelial
  benign —*see* Neoplasm, benign,
    by site
  malignant —*see* Neoplasm, malignant,
    by site
Ewing's —*see* Neoplasm, bone, malignant,
  by site
fatty —*see* Lipoma
fibroid —*see* Leiomyoma
G cell
  malignant
    pancreas C25.4
    specified site NEC —*see* Neoplasm,
      malignant, by site
    unspecified site C25.4
  specified site —*see* Neoplasm, uncertain
    behavior, by site
  unspecified site D37.8
germ cell —*see also* Neoplasm, malignant,
  by site
  mixed —*see* Neoplasm, malignant,
    by site
ghost cell, odontogenic —*see* Cyst, calcifying
  odontogenic
giant cell —*see also* Neoplasm, uncertain
  behavior, by site
  bone D48.0
    malignant —*see* Neoplasm, bone,
      malignant
    chondromatous —*see* Neoplasm, bone,
      benign
    malignant —*see* Neoplasm, malignant,
      by site
    soft parts —*see* Neoplasm, connective
      tissue, uncertain behavior
      malignant —*see* Neoplasm, connective
        tissue, malignant
glomus D18.00
  intra-abdominal D18.03
  intracranial D18.02
  jugulare D44.7
    malignant C75.5
  skin D18.01
  specified site NEC D18.09
gonadal stromal —*see* Neoplasm, uncertain
  behavior, by site
granular cell —*see also* Neoplasm, connective
  tissue, benign
  malignant —*see* Neoplasm, connective
    tissue, malignant
granulosa cell D39.1-●
  juvenile D39.1-●
  malignant C56-●
granulosa cell-theca cell D39.1-●
  malignant C56-●
Grawitz's C64-●
hemorrhoidal —*see* Hemorrhoids
hilar cell D27-●
hilus cell D27-●
Hurthle cell (benign) D34
  malignant C73
hydatid —*see* Echinococcus
hypernephroid —*see also* Neoplasm,
  uncertain behavior, by site
interstitial cell —*see also* Neoplasm, uncertain
  behavior, by site
  benign —*see* Neoplasm, benign, by site
  malignant —*see* Neoplasm, malignant,
    by site
intravascular bronchial alveolar
  D38.1

islet cell —*see* Neoplasm, benign, by site
  malignant —*see* Neoplasm, malignant, by
    site
    pancreas C25.4
    specified site NEC —*see* Neoplasm,
      malignant, by site
    unspecified site C25.4
  pancreas D13.7
  specified site NEC —*see* Neoplasm, benign,
    by site
  unspecified site D13.7
juxtaglomerular D41.0-●
Klatskin's C24.0
Krukenberg's C79.6-●
Leydig cell —*see* Neoplasm, uncertain
  behavior, by site
  benign —*see* Neoplasm, benign, by site
    specified site —*see* Neoplasm, benign,
      by site
    unspecified site
      female D27.9
      male D29.20
  malignant —*see* Neoplasm, malignant, by
    site
    specified site —*see* Neoplasm,
      malignant, by site
    unspecified site
      female C56.9
      male C62.90
  specified site —*see* Neoplasm, uncertain
    behavior, by site
  unspecified site
    female D39.10
    male D40.10
lipid cell, ovary D27-●
lipoid cell, ovary D27-●
malignant —*see also* Neoplasm, malignant, by
  site C80.1
  fusiform cell (type) C80.1
  giant cell (type) C80.1
  localized, plasma cell —*see* Plasmacytoma,
    solitary
  mixed NEC C80.1
  small cell (type) C80.1
  spindle cell (type) C80.1
  unclassified C80.1
mast cell D47.09
melanotic, neuroectodermal —*see* Neoplasm,
  benign, by site
Merkel cell —*see* Carcinoma, Merkel cell
mesenchymal
  malignant —*see* Neoplasm, connective
    tissue, malignant
  mixed —*see* Neoplasm, connective tissue,
    uncertain behavior
mesodermal, mixed —*see also* Neoplasm,
  malignant, by site
  liver C22.4
mesonephric —*see also* Neoplasm, uncertain
  behavior, by site
  malignant —*see* Neoplasm, malignant, by
    site
metastatic
  from specified site —*see* Neoplasm,
    malignant, by site
  of specified site —*see* Neoplasm,
    malignant, by site
  to specified site —*see* Neoplasm, secondary,
    by site
mixed NEC —*see also* Neoplasm, benign, by
  site
  malignant —*see* Neoplasm, malignant, by
    site
mucinous of low malignant potential
  specified site —*see* Neoplasm, malignant,
    by site
  unspecified site C56.9
mucocarcinoid
  specified site —*see* Neoplasm, malignant,
    by site
  unspecified site C18.1

Tumor *(Continued)*
 mucoepidermoid —*see* Neoplasm, uncertain
   behavior, by site
 Müllerian, mixed
   specified site —*see* Neoplasm, malignant,
     by site
   unspecified site C54.9
 myoepithelial —*see* Neoplasm, benign,
   by site
 neuroectodermal (peripheral) —*see*
   Neoplasm, malignant, by site
   primitive
     specified site —*see* Neoplasm,
       malignant, by site
     unspecified site C71.9
 neuroendocrine D3A.8
   malignant poorly differentiated C7A.1
   secondary NEC C7B.8
   specified NEC C7A.8
 neurogenic olfactory C30.0
 nonencapsulated sclerosing C73
 odontogenic (adenomatoid) (benign)
   (calcifying epithelial) (keratocystic)
   (squamous) —*see* Cyst, calcifying
   odontogenic
   malignant C41.1
     upper jaw (bone) C41.0
 ovarian stromal D39.1-•
 ovary, in pregnancy —*see* Pregnancy,
   complicated by
 pacinian —*see* Neoplasm, skin, benign
 Pancoast's —*see* Pancoast's syndrome
 papillary —*see also* Papilloma
   cystic D37.9
   mucinous of low malignant potential
     C56-•
     specified site —*see* Neoplasm,
       malignant, by site
     unspecified site C56.9
   serous of low malignant potential
     specified site —*see* Neoplasm,
       malignant, by site
     unspecified site C56.9
 pelvic, in pregnancy or childbirth —*see*
   Pregnancy, complicated by
 phantom F45.8
 phyllodes D48.6-•
   benign D24-•
   malignant —*see* Neoplasm, breast,
     malignant
 Pindborg —*see* Cyst, calcifying odontogenic
 placental site trophoblastic D39.2
 plasma cell (malignant) (localized) —*see*
   Plasmacytoma, solitary
 polyvesicular vitelline
   specified site —*see* Neoplasm, malignant,
     by site
   unspecified site
     female C56.9
     male C62.90
 Pott's puffy —*see* Osteomyelitis, specified
   NEC
 Rathke's pouch D44.3
 retinal anlage —*see* Neoplasm, benign, by site
 salivary gland type, mixed —*see* Neoplasm,
   salivary gland, benign
   malignant —*see* Neoplasm, salivary gland,
     malignant
 Sampson's N80.1
 Schmincke's —*see* Neoplasm, nasopharynx,
   malignant
 sclerosing stromal D27-•
 sebaceous —*see* Cyst, sebaceous
 secondary —*see* Neoplasm, secondary, by site
   carcinoid C7B.00
     bone C7B.03
     distant lymph nodes C7B.01
     liver C7B.02
     peritoneum C7B.04
     specified NEC C7B.09
   neuroendocrine NEC C7B.8

Tumor *(Continued)*
 serous of low malignant potential
   specified site —*see* Neoplasm, malignant,
     by site
   unspecified site C56.9
 Sertoli cell —*see* Neoplasm, benign, by site
   with lipid storage
     specified site —*see* Neoplasm, benign,
       by site
     unspecified site
       female D27.9
       male D29.20
   specified site —*see* Neoplasm, benign, by
     site
   unspecified site
     female D27.9
     male D29.20
 Sertoli-Leydig cell —*see* Neoplasm, benign,
   by site
   specified site —*see* Neoplasm, benign, by
     site
   unspecified site
     female D27.9
     male D29.20
 sex cord(-stromal) —*see* Neoplasm, uncertain
   behavior, by site
   with annular tubules D39.1-•
 skin appendage —*see* Neoplasm, skin,
   benign
 smooth muscle —*see* Neoplasm, connective
   tissue, uncertain behavior
 soft tissue
   benign —*see* Neoplasm, connective tissue,
     benign
   malignant —*see* Neoplasm, connective
     tissue, malignant
 sternomastoid (congenital) Q68.0
 stromal
   endometrial D39.0
   gastric D48.1
     benign D21.4
     malignant C16.9
     uncertain behavior D48.1
   gastrointestinal C49.A-•
     benign D21.4
     esophagus C49.A1
     large intestine C49.A4
     malignant C49.A0
       colon C49.A4
       duodenum C49.A3
       esophagus C49.A1
       ileum C49.A3
       jejunum C49.A3
       Meckel diverticulum C49.A3
       large intestine C49.A4
       omentum C49.A9
       peritoneum C49.A9
       rectum C49.A5
       small intestine C49.A3
       specified site NEC C49.A9
       stomach C49.A2
     rectum C49.A5
     small intestine C49.A3
     specified site NEC C49.A9
     stomach C49.A2
     uncertain behavior D48.1
   intestine
     benign D21.4
     malignant
       large C49.A4
       small C49.A3
     uncertain behavior D48.1
   ovarian D39.1-•
   stomach C49.A2
     benign D21.4
     malignant C49.A2
     uncertain behavior D48.1
 sweat gland —*see also* Neoplasm, skin,
   uncertain behavior
   benign —*see* Neoplasm, skin, benign
   malignant —*see* Neoplasm, skin, malignant

Tumor *(Continued)*
 syphilitic, brain A52.17
 testicular D40.10
 testicular stromal D40.1-•
 theca cell D27.-•
 theca cell-granulosa cell D39.1-•
 Triton, malignant —*see* Neoplasm, nerve,
   malignant
 trophoblastic, placental site D39.2
 turban D23.4
 uterus (body), in pregnancy or childbirth —
   see Pregnancy, complicated by, tumor,
   uterus
 vagina, in pregnancy or childbirth —*see*
   Pregnancy, complicated by
 varicose —*see* Varix
 von Recklinghausen's —*see*
   Neurofibromatosis
 vulva or perineum, in pregnancy or
   childbirth —*see* Pregnancy,
   complicated by
   causing obstructed labor O65.5
 Warthin's —*see* Neoplasm, salivary gland,
   benign
 Wilms' C64-•
 yolk sac —*see* Neoplasm, malignant, by site
   specified site —*see* Neoplasm, malignant,
     by site
   unspecified site
     female C56.9
     male C62.90
Tumor lysis syndrome (following
 antineoplastic chemotherapy)
 (spontaneous) NEC E88.3
Tumorlet —*see* Neoplasm, uncertain behavior,
 by site
Tungiasis B88.1
Tunica vasculosa lentis Q12.2
Turban tumor D23.4
Türck's trachoma J37.0
Turner-Kieser syndrome Q87.2
Turner-like syndrome Q87.19
Turner's
 hypoplasia (tooth) K00.4
 syndrome Q96.9
   specified NEC Q96.8
 tooth K00.4
Turner-Ullrich syndrome Q96.9
Tussis convulsiva —*see* Whooping cough
Twiddler's syndrome (due to)
 automatic implantable defibrillator T82.198
 cardiac pacemaker T82.198
Twilight state
 epileptic F05
 psychogenic F44.89
Twin (newborn) —*see also* Newborn, twin
 conjoined Q89.4
 pregnancy —*see* Pregnancy, twin
Twinning, teeth K00.2
Twist, twisted
 bowel, colon or intestine K56.2
 hair (congenital) Q84.1
 mesentery K56.2
 omentum K56.2
 organ or site, congenital NEC —*see* Anomaly,
   by site
 ovarian pedicle —*see* Torsion, ovary
Twitching R25.3
Tylosis (acquired) L84
 buccalis K13.29
 linguae K13.29
 palmaris et plantaris (congenital) (inherited)
   Q82.8
   acquired L85.1
Tympanism R14.0
Tympanites (abdominal) (intestinal)
 R14.0
Tympanitis —*see* Myringitis
Tympanosclerosis —*see* subcategory
 H74.0
Tympanum —*see* condition

▶ New ➡ Revised ~~deleted~~ Deleted ● Use Additional Character(s)

Tympany
  abdomen R14.0
  chest R09.89
Type A behavior pattern Z73.1
Typhlitis —*see* Appendicitis
Typhoenteritis —*see* Typhoid
Typhoid (abortive) (ambulant) (any site)
      (clinical) (fever) (hemorrhagic) (infection)
      (intermittent) (malignant) (rheumatic)
      (Widal negative) A01.00
  with pneumonia A01.03
  abdominal A01.09
  arthritis A01.04
  carrier (suspected) of Z22.0
  cholecystitis (current) A01.09
  endocarditis A01.02
  heart involvement A01.02
  inoculation reaction —*see* Complications,
      vaccination
  meningitis A01.01
  mesenteric lymph nodes A01.09
  myocarditis A01.02
▶ Orientia Tsutsugamushi (scrub typhus) A75.3
  osteomyelitis A01.05
  perichondritis, larynx A01.09
  pneumonia A01.03

Typhoid (Continued)
  specified NEC A01.09
  spine A01.05
  ulcer (perforating) A01.09
Typhomalaria (fever) —*see* Malaria
Typhomania A01.00
Typhoperitonitis A01.09
Typhus (fever) A75.9
  abdominal, abdominalis —*see* Typhoid
  African tick A77.1
  amarillic A95.9
  brain A75.9 [G94]
  cerebral A75.9 [G94]
  classical A75.0
  due to Rickettsia
      prowazekii A75.0
          recrudescent A75.1
      tsutsugamushi A75.3
      typhi A75.2
  endemic (flea-borne) A75.2
  epidemic (louse-borne) A75.0
  exanthematic NEC A75.0
  exanthematicus SAI A75.0
      brillii SAI A75.1
      mexicanus SAI A75.2
      typhus murinus A75.2

Typhus (Continued)
  exanthematicus (Continued)
      flea-borne A75.2
      India tick A77.1
      Kenya (tick) A77.1
      louse-borne A75.0
      Mexican A75.2
      mite-borne A75.3
      murine A75.2
      North Asian tick-borne A77.2
      petechial A75.9
      Queensland tick A77.3
      rat A75.2
      recrudescent A75.1
      recurrens —*see* Fever, relapsing
      Sao Paulo A77.0
      scrub (China) (India) (Malaysia) (New
          Guinea) A75.3
      shop (of Malaysia) A75.2
      Siberian tick A77.2
      tick-borne A77.9
      tropical (mite-borne) A75.3
Tyrosinemia E70.21
  newborn, transitory P74.5
Tyrosinosis E70.21
Tyrosinuria E70.29

U

Uhl's anomaly or disease Q24.8
Ulcer, ulcerated, ulcerating, ulceration,
ulcerative
alveolar process M27.3
amebic (intestine) A06.1
skin A06.7
anastomotic —see Ulcer, gastrojejunal
anorectal K62.6
antral —see Ulcer, stomach
anus (sphincter) (solitary) K62.6
aorta —see Aneurysm
aphthous (oral) (recurrent) K12.0
genital organ(s)
female N76.6
male N50.89
artery I77.2
atrophic —see Ulcer, skin
decubitus —see Ulcer, pressure, by site
back L98.429
with
bone involvement without evidence of
necrosis L98.426
bone necrosis L98.424
exposed fat layer L98.422
muscle involvement without evidence of
necrosis L98.425
muscle necrosis L98.423
skin breakdown only L98.421
specified severity NEC L98.428
Barrett's (esophagus) K22.10
with bleeding K22.11
bile duct (common) (hepatic) K83.8
bladder (solitary) (sphincter) NEC N32.89
bilharzial B65.9 [N33]
in schistosomiasis (bilharzial) B65.9 [N33]
submucosal —see Cystitis, interstitial
tuberculous A18.12
bleeding K27.4
bone —see Osteomyelitis, specified type NEC
bowel —see Ulcer, intestine
breast N61.1
bronchus J98.09
buccal (cavity) (traumatic) K12.1
Buruli A31.1
buttock L98.419
with
bone involvement without evidence of
necrosis L98.416
bone necrosis L98.414
exposed fat layer L98.412
muscle involvement without evidence of
necrosis L98.415
muscle necrosis L98.413
skin breakdown only L98.411
specified severity NEC L98.418
cancerous —see Neoplasm, malignant, by site
cardia K22.10
with bleeding K22.11
cardioesophageal (peptic) K22.10
with bleeding K22.11
cecum —see Ulcer, intestine
cervix (uteri) (decubitus) (trophic) N86
with cervicitis N72
chancroidal A57
chiclero B55.1
chronic (cause unknown) —see Ulcer, skin
Cochin-China B55.1
colon —see Ulcer, intestine
conjunctiva H10.89
cornea H16.00-•
with hypopyon H16.03-•
central H16.01-•
dendritic (herpes simplex) B00.52
marginal H16.04-•
Mooren's H16.05-•
mycotic H16.06-•
perforated H16.07-•
ring H16.02-•
tuberculous (phlyctenular) A18.52

Ulcer, ulcerated, ulcerating, ulceration,
ulcerative (Continued)
corpus cavernosum (chronic) N48.5
crural —see Ulcer, lower limb
Curling's —see Ulcer, peptic, acute
Cushing's —see Ulcer, peptic, acute
cystic duct K82.8
cystitis (interstitial) —see Cystitis,
interstitial
decubitus —see Ulcer, pressure, by site
dendritic, cornea (herpes simplex) B00.52
diabetes, diabetic —see Diabetes, ulcer
Dieulafoy's K25.0
due to
infection NEC —see Ulcer, skin
radiation NEC L59.8
trophic disturbance (any region) —see
Ulcer, skin
X-ray L58.1
duodenum, duodenal (eroded) (peptic)
K26.9
with
hemorrhage K26.4
and perforation K26.6
perforation K26.5
acute K26.3
with
hemorrhage K26.0
and perforation K26.2
perforation K26.1
chronic K26.7
with
hemorrhage K26.4
and perforation K26.6
perforation K26.5
dysenteric A09
elusive —see Cystitis, interstitial
endocarditis (acute) (chronic) (subacute) I28.8
epiglottis J38.7
esophagus (peptic) K22.10
with bleeding K22.11
due to
aspirin K22.10
with bleeding K22.11
�megastrointestinal reflux disease (without
bleeding) K21.00
▶with bleeding K21.01
ingestion of chemical or medicament
K22.10
with bleeding K22.11
fungal K22.10
with bleeding K22.11
infective K22.10
with bleeding K22.11
varicose —see Varix, esophagus
eyelid (region) H01.8
fauces J39.2
Fenwick (-Hunner) (solitary) —see Cystitis,
interstitial
fistulous —see Ulcer, skin
foot (indolent) (trophic) —see Ulcer, lower
limb
frambesial, initial A66.0
frenum (tongue) K14.0
gallbladder or duct K82.8
gangrenous —see Gangrene
gastric —see Ulcer, stomach
gastrocolic —see Ulcer, gastrojejunal
gastroduodenal —see Ulcer, peptic
gastroesophageal —see Ulcer, stomach
gastrointestinal —see Ulcer, gastrojejunal
gastrojejunal (peptic) K28.9
with
hemorrhage K28.4
and perforation K28.6
perforation K28.5
acute K28.3
with
hemorrhage K28.0
and perforation K28.2
perforation K28.1

Ulcer, ulcerated, ulcerating, ulceration,
ulcerative (Continued)
gastrojejunal (Continued)
chronic K28.7
with
hemorrhage K28.4
and perforation K28.6
perforation K28.5
gastrojejunocolic —see Ulcer, gastrojejunal
gingiva K06.8
gingivitis K05.10
nonplaque induced K05.11
plaque induced K05.10
glottis J38.7
granuloma of pudenda A58
gum K06.8
gumma, due to yaws A66.4
heel —see Ulcer, lower limb
hemorrhoid —see also Hemorrhoids, by
degree K64.8
Hunner's —see Cystitis, interstitial
hypopharynx J39.2
hypopyon (chronic) (subacute) —see Ulcer,
cornea, with hypopyon
hypostaticum —see Ulcer, varicose
ileum —see Ulcer, intestine
intestine, intestinal K63.3
with perforation K63.1
amebic A06.1
duodenal —see Ulcer, duodenum
granulocytopenic (with hemorrhage) —see
Neutropenia
marginal —see Ulcer, gastrojejunal
perforating K63.1
newborn P78.0
primary, small intestine K63.3
rectum K62.6
stercoraceous, stercoral K63.3
tuberculous A18.32
typhoid (fever) —see Typhoid
varicose I86.8
jejunum, jejunal —see Ulcer, gastrojejunal
keratitis —see Ulcer, cornea
knee —see Ulcer, lower limb
labium (majus) (minus) N76.6
laryngitis —see Laryngitis
larynx (aphthous) (contact) J38.7
diphtheritic A36.2
leg —see Ulcer, lower limb
lip K13.0
Lipschütz's N76.6
lower limb (atrophic) (chronic) (neurogenic)
(perforating) (pyogenic) (trophic)
(tropical) L97.909
with
bone involvement without evidence of
necrosis L97.906
bone necrosis L97.904
exposed fat layer L97.902
muscle involvement without evidence of
necrosis L97.905
muscle necrosis L97.903
skin breakdown only L97.901
specified severity NEC L97.908
ankle L97.309
with
bone involvement without evidence of
necrosis L97.306
bone necrosis L97.304
exposed fat layer L97.302
muscle involvement without evidence
of necrosis L97.305
muscle necrosis L97.303
skin breakdown only L97.301
specified severity NEC L97.308
left L97.329
with
bone involvement without evidence
of necrosis L97.326
bone necrosis L97.324
exposed fat layer L97.322

Ulcer, ulcerated, ulcerating, ulceration, ulcerative *(Continued)*
lower limb *(Continued)*
ankle *(Continued)*
left *(Continued)*
with *(Continued)*
muscle involvement without evidence of necrosis L97.325
muscle necrosis L97.323
skin breakdown only L97.321
specified severity NEC L97.328
right L97.319
with
bone involvement without evidence of necrosis L97.316
bone necrosis L97.314
exposed fat layer L97.312
muscle involvement without evidence of necrosis L97.315
muscle necrosis L97.313
skin breakdown only L97.311
specified severity NEC L97.318
calf L97.209
with
bone involvement without evidence of necrosis L97.206
bone necrosis L97.204
exposed fat layer L97.202
muscle involvement without evidence of necrosis L97.205
muscle necrosis L97.203
skin breakdown only L97.201
specified severity NEC L97.208
left L97.229
with
bone involvement without evidence of necrosis L97.226
bone necrosis L97.224
exposed fat layer L97.222
muscle involvement without evidence of necrosis L97.225
muscle necrosis L97.223
skin breakdown only L97.221
specified severity NEC L97.228
right L97.219
with
bone involvement without evidence of necrosis L97.216
bone necrosis L97.214
exposed fat layer L97.212
muscle involvement without evidence of necrosis L97.215
muscle necrosis L97.213
skin breakdown only L97.211
specified severity NEC L97.218
decubitus —*see* Ulcer, pressure, by site
foot specified NEC L97.509
with
bone involvement without evidence of necrosis L97.506
bone necrosis L97.504
exposed fat layer L97.502
muscle involvement without evidence of necrosis L97.505
muscle necrosis L97.503
skin breakdown only L97.501
specified severity NEC L97.508
left L97.529
with
bone involvement without evidence of necrosis L97.526
bone necrosis L97.524
exposed fat layer L97.522
muscle involvement without evidence of necrosis L97.525
muscle necrosis L97.523
skin breakdown only L97.521
specified severity NEC L97.528

Ulcer, ulcerated, ulcerating, ulceration, ulcerative *(Continued)*
lower limb *(Continued)*
foot specified *(Continued)*
right L97.519
with
bone involvement without evidence of necrosis L97.516
bone necrosis L97.514
exposed fat layer L97.512
muscle involvement without evidence of necrosis L97.515
muscle necrosis L97.513
skin breakdown only L97.511
specified severity NEC L97.518
heel L97.409
with
bone involvement without evidence of necrosis L97.406
bone necrosis L97.404
exposed fat layer L97.402
muscle involvement without evidence of necrosis L97.405
muscle necrosis L97.403
skin breakdown only L97.401
specified severity NEC L97.408
left L97.429
with
bone involvement without evidence of necrosis L97.426
bone necrosis L97.424
exposed fat layer L97.422
muscle involvement without evidence of necrosis L97.425
muscle necrosis L97.423
skin breakdown only L97.421
specified severity NEC L97.428
right L97.419
with
bone involvement without evidence of necrosis L97.416
bone necrosis L97.414
exposed fat layer L97.412
muscle involvement without evidence of necrosis L97.415
muscle necrosis L97.413
skin breakdown only L97.411
specified severity NEC L97.418
left L97.929
with
bone involvement without evidence of necrosis L97.926
bone necrosis L97.924
exposed fat layer L97.922
muscle involvement without evidence of necrosis L97.925
muscle necrosis L97.923
skin breakdown only L97.921
specified severity NEC L97.928
lower leg NOS L97.909
with
bone involvement without evidence of necrosis L97.906
bone necrosis L97.904
exposed fat layer L97.902
muscle involvement without evidence of necrosis L97.905
muscle necrosis L97.903
skin breakdown only L97.901
specified severity NEC L97.908
left L97.929
with
bone involvement without evidence of necrosis L97.926
bone necrosis L97.924
exposed fat layer L97.922
muscle involvement without evidence of necrosis L97.925
muscle necrosis L97.923
skin breakdown only L97.921
specified severity NEC L97.928

Ulcer, ulcerated, ulcerating, ulceration, ulcerative *(Continued)*
lower limb *(Continued)*
lower leg NOS *(Continued)*
right L97.919
with
bone involvement without evidence of necrosis L97.916
bone necrosis L97.914
exposed fat layer L97.912
muscle involvement without evidence of necrosis L97.915
muscle necrosis L97.913
skin breakdown only L97.911
specified severity NEC L97.918
specified site NEC L97.809
with
bone involvement without evidence of necrosis L97.806
bone necrosis L97.804
exposed fat layer L97.802
muscle involvement without evidence of necrosis L97.805
muscle necrosis L97.803
skin breakdown only L97.801
specified severity NEC L97.808
left L97.829
with
bone involvement without evidence of necrosis L97.826
bone necrosis L97.824
exposed fat layer L97.822
muscle involvement without evidence of necrosis L97.825
muscle necrosis L97.823
skin breakdown only L97.821
specified severity NEC L97.828
right L97.819
with
bone involvement without evidence of necrosis L97.816
bone necrosis L97.814
exposed fat layer L97.812
muscle involvement without evidence of necrosis L97.815
muscle necrosis L97.813
skin breakdown only L97.811
specified severity NEC L97.818
midfoot L97.409
with
bone involvement without evidence of necrosis L97.406
bone necrosis L97.404
exposed fat layer L97.402
muscle involvement without evidence of necrosis L97.405
muscle necrosis L97.403
skin breakdown only L97.401
specified severity NEC L97.408
left L97.429
with
bone involvement without evidence of necrosis L97.426
bone necrosis L97.424
exposed fat layer L97.422
muscle involvement without evidence of necrosis L97.425
muscle necrosis L97.423
skin breakdown only L97.421
specified severity NEC L97.428
right L97.419
with
bone involvement without evidence of necrosis L97.416
bone necrosis L97.414
exposed fat layer L97.412
muscle involvement without evidence of necrosis L97.415
muscle necrosis L97.413
skin breakdown only L97.411
specified severity NEC L97.418

▶ New   ⇒ Revised   ~~deleted~~ Deleted   • Use Additional Character(s)

Ulcer, ulcerated, ulcerating, ulceration, ulcerative (Continued)
 lower limb (Continued)
  right L97.919
   with
    bone involvement without evidence of necrosis L97.916
    bone necrosis L97.914
    exposed fat layer L97.912
    muscle involvement without evidence of necrosis L97.915
    muscle necrosis L97.913
    skin breakdown only L97.911
    specified severity NEC L97.918
  thigh L97.109
   with
    bone involvement without evidence of necrosis L97.106
    bone necrosis L97.104
    exposed fat layer L97.102
    muscle involvement without evidence of necrosis L97.105
    muscle necrosis L97.103
    skin breakdown only L97.101
    specified severity NEC L97.108
   left L97.129
    with
     bone involvement without evidence of necrosis L97.126
     bone necrosis L97.124
     exposed fat layer L97.122
     muscle involvement without evidence of necrosis L97.125
     muscle necrosis L97.123
     skin breakdown only L97.121
     specified severity NEC L97.128
   right L97.119
    with
     bone involvement without evidence of necrosis L97.116
     bone necrosis L97.114
     exposed fat layer L97.112
     muscle involvement without evidence of necrosis L97.115
     muscle necrosis L97.113
     skin breakdown only L97.111
     specified severity NEC L97.118
  toe L97.509
   with
    bone involvement without evidence of necrosis L97.506
    bone necrosis L97.504
    exposed fat layer L97.502
    muscle involvement without evidence of necrosis L97.505
    muscle necrosis L97.503
    skin breakdown only L97.501
    specified severity NEC L97.508
   left L97.529
    with
     bone involvement without evidence of necrosis L97.526
     bone necrosis L97.524
     exposed fat layer L97.522
     muscle involvement without evidence of necrosis L97.525
     muscle necrosis L97.523
     skin breakdown only L97.521
     specified severity NEC L97.528
   right L97.519
    with
     bone involvement without evidence of necrosis L97.516
     bone necrosis L97.514
     exposed fat layer L97.512
     muscle involvement without evidence of necrosis L97.515
     muscle necrosis L97.513
     skin breakdown only L97.511
     specified severity NEC L97.518

Ulcer, ulcerated, ulcerating, ulceration, ulcerative (Continued)
 lower limb (Continued)
  leprous A30.1
  syphilitic A52.19
  varicose —see Varix, leg, with, ulcer
 luetic —see Ulcer, syphilitic
 lung J98.4
  tuberculous —see Tuberculosis, pulmonary
 malignant —see Neoplasm, malignant, by site
 marginal NEC —see Ulcer, gastrojejunal
 meatus (urinarius) N34.2
 Meckel's diverticulum Q43.0
  malignant —see Table of Neoplasms, small intestine, malignant
 Meleney's (chronic undermining) —see Ulcer, skin
 Mooren's (cornea) —see Ulcer, cornea, Mooren's
 mycobacterial (skin) A31.1
 nasopharynx J39.2
 neck, uterus N86
 neurogenic NEC —see Ulcer, skin
 nose, nasal (passage) (infective) (septum) J34.0
  skin —see Ulcer, skin
  spirochetal A69.8
  varicose (bleeding) I86.8
 oral mucosa (traumatic) K12.1
 palate (soft) K12.1
 penis (chronic) N48.5
 peptic (site unspecified) K27.9
  with
   hemorrhage K27.4
    and perforation K27.6
   perforation K27.5
  acute K27.3
   with
    hemorrhage K27.0
     and perforation K27.2
    perforation K27.1
  chronic K27.7
   with
    hemorrhage K27.4
     and perforation K27.6
    perforation K27.5
  esophagus K22.10
   with bleeding K22.11
  newborn P78.82
 perforating K27.5
  skin —see Ulcer, skin
 peritonsillar J35.8
 phagedenic (tropical) —see Ulcer, skin
 pharynx J39.2
 phlebitis —see Phlebitis
 plaster —see Ulcer, pressure, by site
 popliteal space —see Ulcer, lower limb
 postpyloric —see Ulcer, duodenum
 prepuce N47.7
 prepyloric —see Ulcer, stomach
 pressure (pressure area) L89.9-●
  ankle L89.5-●
  back L89.1-●
  buttock L89.3-●
  coccyx L89.15-●
  contiguous site of back, buttock, hip L89.4-●
  elbow L89.0-●
  face L89.81-●
  head L89.81-●
  heel L89.6-●
  hip L89.2-●
  sacral region (tailbone) L89.15-●
  specified site NEC L89.89-●
  stage 1 (healing) (pre-ulcer skin changes limited to persistent focal edema)
   ankle L89.5-●
   back L89.1-●
   buttock L89.3-●
   coccyx L89.15-●
   contiguous site of back, buttock, hip L89.4-●

Ulcer, ulcerated, ulcerating, ulceration, ulcerative (Continued)
 pressure (Continued)
  stage 1 (Continued)
   elbow L89.0-●
   face L89.81-●
   head L89.81-●
   heel L89.6-●
   hip L89.2-●
   sacral region (tailbone) L89.15-●
   specified site NEC L89.89-●
  stage 2 (healing) (abrasion, blister, partial thickness skin loss involving epidermis and/or dermis)
   ankle L89.5-●
   back L89.1-●
   buttock L89.3-●
   coccyx L89.15-●
   contiguous site of back, buttock, hip L89.4-●
   elbow L89.0-●
   face L89.81-●
   head L89.81-●
   heel L89.6-●
   hip L89.2-●
   sacral region (tailbone) L89.15-●
   specified site NEC L89.89-●
  stage 3 (healing) (full thickness skin loss involving damage or necrosis of subcutaneous tissue)
   ankle L89.5-●
   back L89.1-●
   buttock L89.3-●
   coccyx L89.15-●
   contiguous site of back, buttock, hip L89.4-●
   elbow L89.0-●
   face L89.81-●
   head L89.81-●
   heel L89.6-●
   hip L89.2-●
   sacral region (tailbone) L89.15-●
   specified site NEC L89.89-●
  stage 4 (healing) (necrosis of soft tissues through to underlying muscle, tendon, or bone)
   ankle L89.5-●
   back L89.1-●
   buttock L89.3-●
   coccyx L89.15-●
   contiguous site of back, buttock, hip L89.4-●
   elbow L89.0-●
   face L89.81-●
   head L89.81-●
   heel L89.6-●
   hip L89.2-●
   sacral region (tailbone) L89.15-●
   specified site NEC L89.89-●
  unspecified stage
   ankle L89.5-●
   back L89.1-●
   buttock L89.3-●
   coccyx L89.15-●
   contiguous site of back, buttock, hip L89.4-●
   elbow L89.0-●
   face L89.81-●
   head L89.81-●
   heel L89.6-●
   hip L89.2-●
   sacral region (tailbone) L89.15-●
   specified site NEC L89.89-●
  unstageable
   ankle L89.5-●
   back L89.1-●
   buttock L89.3-●
   coccyx L89.15-●
   contiguous site of back, buttock, hip L89.4-●
   elbow L89.0-●

▶ New   ⇨ Revised   ~~deleted~~ Deleted   ● Use Additional Character(s)

Ulcer, ulcerated, ulcerating, ulceration,
   ulcerative (Continued)
  pressure (Continued)
    unstageable (Continued)
      face L89.81-●
      head L89.81-●
      heel L89.6-●
      hip L89.2-●
      sacral region (tailbone) L89.15-●
      specified site NEC L89.89-●
  primary of intestine K63.3
    with perforation K63.1
  prostate N41.9
  pyloric —see Ulcer, stomach
  rectosigmoid K63.3
    with perforation K63.1
  rectum (sphincter) (solitary) K62.6
    stercoraceous, stercoral K62.6
  retina —see Inflammation, chorioretinal
  rodent —see also Neoplasm, skin,
    malignant
  sclera —see Scleritis
  scrofulous (tuberculous) A18.2
  scrotum N50.89
    tuberculous A18.15
    varicose I86.1
  seminal vesicle N50.89
  sigmoid —see Ulcer, intestine
  skin (atrophic) (chronic) (neurogenic)
    (non-healing) (perforating) (pyogenic)
    (trophic) (tropical) L98.499
    with gangrene —see Gangrene
    amebic A06.7
    back —see Ulcer, back
    buttock —see Ulcer, buttock
    decubitus —see Ulcer, pressure
    lower limb —see Ulcer, lower limb
    mycobacterial A31.1
    specified site NEC L98.499
      with
        bone involvement without evidence of
          necrosis L98.496
        bone necrosis L98.494
        exposed fat layer L98.492
        muscle involvement without evidence
          of necrosis L98.495
        muscle necrosis L98.493
        skin breakdown only L98.491
        specified severity NEC L98.498
    tuberculous (primary) A18.4
    varicose —see Ulcer, varicose
  sloughing —see Ulcer, skin
  solitary, anus or rectum (sphincter) K62.6
  sore throat J02.9
    streptococcal J02.0
  spermatic cord N50.89
  spine (tuberculous) A18.01
  stasis (venous) —see Varix, leg, with, ulcer
    without varicose veins I87.2
  stercoraceous, stercoral K63.3
    with perforation K63.1
    anus or rectum K62.6
  stoma, stomal —see Ulcer, gastrojejunal
  stomach (eroded) (peptic) (round) K25.9
    with
      hemorrhage K25.4
        and perforation K25.6
      perforation K25.5
    acute K25.3
      with
        hemorrhage K25.0
          and perforation K25.2
        perforation K25.1
    chronic K25.7
      with
        hemorrhage K25.4
          and perforation K25.6
        perforation K25.5
  stomal —see Ulcer, gastrojejunal
  stomatitis K12.1
  stress —see Ulcer, peptic

Ulcer, ulcerated, ulcerating, ulceration,
   ulcerative (Continued)
  strumous (tuberculous) A18.2
  submucosal, bladder —see Cystitis, interstitial
  syphilitic (any site) (early) (secondary)
    A51.39
    late A52.79
      perforating A52.79
        foot A52.11
  testis N50.89
  thigh —see Ulcer, lower limb
  throat J39.2
    diphtheritic A36.0
  toe —see Ulcer, lower limb
  tongue (traumatic) K14.0
  tonsil J35.8
    diphtheritic A36.0
  trachea J39.8
  trophic —see Ulcer, skin
  tropical —see Ulcer, skin
  tuberculous —see Tuberculosis, ulcer
  tunica vaginalis N50.89
  turbinate J34.89
  typhoid (perforating) —see Typhoid
  unspecified site —see Ulcer, skin
  urethra (meatus) —see Urethritis
  uterus N85.8
    cervix N86
      with cervicitis N72
    neck N86
      with cervicitis N72
  vagina N76.5
    in Behçet's disease M35.2 [N77.0]
    pessary N89.8
  valve, heart I33.0
  varicose (lower limb, any part) —see also
    Varix, leg, with, ulcer
    broad ligament I86.2
    esophagus —see Varix, esophagus
    inflamed or infected —see Varix, leg, with
      ulcer, with inflammation
    nasal septum I86.8
    perineum I86.3
    scrotum I86.1
    specified site NEC I86.8
    sublingual I86.0
    vulva I86.3
  vas deferens N50.89
  vulva (acute) (infectional) N76.6
    in (due to)
      Behçet's disease M35.2 [N77.0]
      herpesviral (herpes simplex) infection
        A60.04
      tuberculosis A18.18
  vulvobuccal, recurring N76.6
  X-ray L58.1
  yaws A66.4
Ulcerosa scarlatina A38.8
Ulcus —see also Ulcer
  cutis tuberculosum A18.4
  duodeni —see Ulcer, duodenum
  durum (syphilitic) A51.0
    extragenital A51.2
  gastrojejunale —see Ulcer, gastrojejunal
  hypostaticum —see Ulcer, varicose
  molle (cutis) (skin) A57
  serpens corneae —see Ulcer, cornea, central
  ventriculi —see Ulcer, stomach
Ulegyria Q04.8
Ulerythema
  ophryogenes, congenital Q84.2
  sycosiforme L73.8
Ullrich(-Bonnevie)(-Turner) syndrome —see
  also Turner's syndrome Q87.19
Ullrich-Feichtiger syndrome Q87.0
Ulnar —see condition
Ulorrhagia, ulorrhea K06.8
Umbilicus, umbilical —see condition
Unacceptable
  contours of tooth K08.54
  morphology of tooth K08.54

Unavailability (of)
  bed at medical facility Z75.1
  health service-related agencies Z75.4
  medical facilities (at) Z75.3
    due to
      investigation by social service agency
        Z75.2
      lack of services at home Z75.0
      remoteness from facility Z75.3
      waiting list Z75.1
    home Z75.0
    outpatient clinic Z75.3
  schooling Z55.1
  social service agencies Z75.4
Uncinaria americana infestation B76.1
Uncinariasis B76.9
Uncongenial work Z56.5
Unconscious (ness) —see Coma
Underachievement in school Z55.3
Underdevelopment —see also Undeveloped
  nose Q30.1
  sexual E30.0
Underdosing —see also Table of Drugs and
  Chemicals, categories T36-T50, with final
  character 6 Z91.14
  intentional NEC Z91.128
    due to financial hardship of patient Z91.120
  unintentional NEC Z91.138
    due to patient's age related debility Z91.130
Underfeeding, newborn P92.3
Underfill, endodontic M27.53
Underimmunization status Z28.3
Undernourishment —see Malnutrition
Undernutrition —see Malnutrition
Under observation —see Observation
Underweight R63.6
  for gestational age —see Light for dates
Underwood's disease P83.0
Undescended —see also Malposition, congenital
  cecum Q43.3
  colon Q43.3
  testicle —see Cryptorchid
Undeveloped, undevelopment —see also
  Hypoplasia
  brain (congenital) Q02
  cerebral (congenital) Q02
  heart Q24.8
  lung Q33.6
  testis E29.1
  uterus E30.0
Undiagnosed (disease) R69
Undulant fever —see Brucellosis
Unemployment, anxiety concerning Z56.0
  threatened Z56.2
Unequal length (acquired) (limb) —see also
  Deformity, limb, unequal length
  leg —see also Deformity, limb, unequal length
    congenital Q72.9-●
Unextracted dental root K08.3
Unguis incarnatus L60.0
Unhappiness R45.2
Unicornate uterus Q51.4
  in pregnancy or childbirth O34.00
Unilateral —see also condition
  development, breast N64.89
  organ or site, congenital NEC —see Agenesis,
    by site
Unilocular heart Q20.8
Union, abnormal —see also Fusion
  larynx and trachea Q34.8
Universal mesentery Q43.3
Unrepairable overhanging of dental
  restorative materials K08.52
Unsatisfactory
  restoration of tooth K08.50
    specified NEC K08.59
  sample of cytologic smear
    anus R85.615
    cervix R87.615
    vagina R87.625
  surroundings Z59.1
  work Z56.5

Unsoundness of mind —*see* Psychosis
Unstable
   back NEC —*see* Instability, joint, spine
   hip (congenital) Q65.6
      acquired —*see* Derangement, joint,
         specified type NEC, hip
   joint —*see* Instability, joint
      secondary to removal of joint prosthesis
         M96.89
   lie (mother) O32.0
   lumbosacral joint (congenital) —*see*
      subcategory M53.2
   sacroiliac —*see* subcategory M53.2
   spine NEC —*see* Instability, joint, spine
Unsteadiness on feet R26.81
Untruthfulness, child problem F91.8
Unverricht(-Lundborg) disease or epilepsy —
     see Epilepsy, generalized, idiopathic
Unwanted pregnancy Z64.0
Upbringing, institutional Z62.22
   away from parents NEC Z62.29
   in care of non-parental family member Z62.21
   in foster care Z62.21
   in orphanage or group home Z62.22
   in welfare custody Z62.21
Upper respiratory —*see* condition
Upset
   gastric K30
   gastrointestinal K30
      psychogenic F45.8
   intestinal (large) (small) K59.9
      psychogenic F45.8
   menstruation N93.9
   mental F48.9
   stomach K30
      psychogenic F45.8
Urachus —*see also* condition
   patent or persistent Q64.4
Urbach-Oppenheim disease (necrobiosis
      lipoidica diabeticorum) —*see* E08-E13 with
      .620
Urbach's lipoid proteinosis E78.89
Urbach-Wiethe disease E78.89
Urban yellow fever A95.1
Urea
   blood, high —*see* Uremia
   cycle metabolism disorder —*see* Disorder,
      urea cycle metabolism
Uremia, uremic N19
   with
      ectopic or molar pregnancy O08.4
      polyneuropathy N18.9 [G63]
   chronic NOS —*see also* Disease, kidney,
      chronic N18.9
      due to hypertension —*see* Hypertensive,
         kidney
   complicating
      ectopic or molar pregnancy O08.4
   congenital P96.0
   extrarenal R39.2
   following ectopic or molar pregnancy O08.4
   newborn P96.0
   prerenal R39.2
Ureter, ureteral —*see* condition
Ureteralgia N23
Ureterectasis —*see* Hydroureter
Ureteritis N28.89
   cystica N28.86
   due to calculus N20.1
      with calculus, kidney N20.2
         with hydronephrosis N13.2
   gonococcal (acute) (chronic) A54.21
   nonspecific N28.89
Ureterocele N28.89
   congenital (orthotopic) Q62.31
      ectopic Q62.32
Ureterolith, ureterolithiasis —*see* Calculus,
     ureter
Ureterostomy
   attention to Z43.6
   status Z93.6

Urethra, urethral —*see* condition
Urethralgia R39.89
Urethritis (anterior) (posterior) N34.2
   calculous N21.1
   candidal B37.41
   chlamydial A56.01
   diplococcal (gonococcal) A54.01
      with abscess (accessory gland)
         (periurethral) A54.1
   gonococcal A54.01
      with abscess (accessory gland)
         (periurethral) A54.1
   nongonococcal N34.1
      Reiter's —*see* Reiter's disease
   nonspecific N34.1
   nonvenereal N34.1
   postmenopausal N34.2
   puerperal O86.22
   Reiter's —*see* Reiter's disease
   specified NEC N34.2
   trichomonal or due to Trichomonas
      (vaginalis) A59.03
Urethrocele N81.0
   with
      cystocele —*see* Cystocele
      prolapse of uterus —*see* Prolapse, uterus
Urethrolithiasis (with colic or infection) N21.1
Urethrorectal —*see* condition
Urethrorrhagia N36.8
Urethrorrhea R36.9
Urethrostomy
   attention to Z43.6
   status Z93.6
Urethrotrigonitis —*see* Trigonitis
Urethrovaginal —*see* condition
Urgency
   fecal R15.2
   hypertensive —*see* Hypertension
   urinary N39.15
Urhidrosis, uridrosis L74.8
Uric acid in blood (increased) E79.0
Uricacidemia (asymptomatic) E79.0
Uricemia (asymptomatic) E79.0
Uricosuria R82.998
Urinary —*see* condition
Urination
   frequent R35.0
   painful R30.9
Urine
   blood in —*see* Hematuria
   discharge, excessive R35.8
   enuresis, nonorganic origin F98.0
   extravasation R39.0
   frequency R35.0
   incontinence R32
      nonorganic origin F98.0
   intermittent stream R39.198
   pus in N39.0
   retention or stasis R33.9
      organic R33.8
         drug-induced R33.0
      psychogenic F45.8
   secretion
      deficient R34
      excessive R35.8
      frequency R35.0
   stream
      intermittent R39.198
      slowing R39.198
      splitting R39.13
      weak R39.12
Urinemia —*see* Uremia
Urinoma, urethra N36.8
Uroarthritis, infectious (Reiter's) —*see* Reiter's
   disease
Urodialysis R34
Urolithiasis —*see* Calculus, urinary
Uronephrosis —*see* Hydronephrosis
Uropathy N39.9
   obstructive N13.9
      specified NEC N13.8

Uropathy (Continued)
   reflux N13.9
      specified NEC N13.8
   vesicoureteral reflux-associated —*see* Reflux,
      vesicoureteral
Urosepsis — code to condition
Urticaria L50.9
   with angioneurotic edema T78.3
      hereditary D84.1
   allergic L50.0
   cholinergic L50.5
   chronic L50.8
   cold, familial L50.2
   contact L50.6
   dermatographic L50.3
   due to
      cold or heat L50.2
      drugs L50.0
      food L50.0
      inhalants L50.0
      plants L50.6
      serum —*see also* Reaction, serum
         T80.69
   factitial L50.3
   familial cold M04.2
   giant T78.3
      hereditary D84.1
   gigantea T78.3
   idiopathic L50.1
   larynx T78.3
      hereditary D84.1
   neonatorum P83.88
   nonallergic L50.1
   papulosa (Hebra) L28.2
   pigmentosa D47.01
      congenital Q82.2
      of neonatal onset Q82.2
      of newborn onset Q82.2
   recurrent periodic L50.8
   serum —*see also* Reaction, serum T80.69
   solar L56.3
   specified type NEC L50.8
   thermal (cold) (heat) L50.2
   vibratory L50.4
   xanthelasmoidea —*see* Urticaria pigmentosa
Use (of)
   alcohol Z72.89
      with
         intoxication F10.929
         sleep disorder F10.982
       ▶ withdrawal F10.939
         ▶ with
          ▶ perceptual disturbance F10.932
         ▶ delirium F10.931
         ▶ uncomplicated F10.930
      harmful —*see* Abuse, alcohol
   amphetamines —*see* Use, stimulant NEC
   caffeine —*see* Use, stimulant NEC
   cannabis F12.90
      with
         anxiety disorder F12.980
         intoxication F12.929
           with
              delirium F12.921
              perceptual disturbance F12.922
           uncomplicated F12.920
         other specified disorder F12.988
         psychosis F12.959
           delusions F12.950
           hallucinations F12.951
         unspecified disorder F12.99
         withdrawal F12.93
   cocaine F14.90
      with
         anxiety disorder F14.980
         intoxication F14.929
           with
              delirium F14.921
              perceptual disturbance F14.922
           uncomplicated F14.920
         other specified disorder F14.988

▶ New   ⇉ Revised   ~~deleted~~ Deleted   ● Use Additional Character(s)

Use (Continued)
  cocaine (Continued)
    with (Continued)
      psychosis F14.959
        delusions F14.950
        hallucinations F14.951
      sexual dysfunction F14.981
      sleep disorder F14.982
      unspecified disorder F14.99
      ▶withdrawal F14.93
    harmful —see Abuse, drug, cocaine
  drug(s) NEC F19.90
    with sleep disorder F19.982
    harmful —see Abuse, drug, by type
  hallucinogen NEC F16.90
    with
      anxiety disorder F16.980
      intoxication F16.929
        with
          delirium F16.921
        uncomplicated F16.920
      mood disorder F16.94
      other specified disorder F16.988
      perception disorder (flashbacks) F16.983
      psychosis F16.959
        delusions F16.950
        hallucinations F16.951
      unspecified disorder F16.99
    harmful —see Abuse, drug, hallucinogen
      NEC
  inhalants F18.90
    with
      anxiety disorder F18.980
      intoxication F18.929
        with delirium F18.921
        uncomplicated F18.920
      mood disorder F18.94
      other specified disorder F18.988
      persisting dementia F18.97
      psychosis F18.959
        delusions F18.950
        hallucinations F18.951
      unspecified disorder F18.99
    harmful —see Abuse, drug, inhalant
  methadone —see Use, opioid
  nonprescribed drugs F19.90
    harmful —see Abuse, non-psychoactive
      substance
  opioid F11.90
    with
      disorder F11.99
        mood F11.94
        sleep F11.982
        specified type NEC F11.988
      intoxication F11.929
        with
          delirium F11.921
          perceptual disturbance F11.922
        uncomplicated F11.920
      withdrawal F11.93
    harmful —see Abuse, drug, opioid

Use (Continued)
  patent medicines F19.90
    harmful —see Abuse, non-psychoactive
      substance
  psychoactive drug NEC F19.90
    with
      anxiety disorder F19.980
      intoxication F19.929
        with
          delirium F19.921
          perceptual disturbance
            F19.922
        uncomplicated F19.920
      mood disorder F19.94
      other specified disorder F19.988
      persisting
        amnestic disorder F19.96
        dementia F19.97
      psychosis F19.959
        delusions F19.950
        hallucinations F19.951
      sexual dysfunction F19.981
      sleep disorder F19.982
      unspecified disorder F19.99
      withdrawal F19.939
        with
          delirium F19.931
          perceptual disturbance
            F19.932
        uncomplicated F19.930
    harmful —see Abuse, drug NEC,
      psychoactive NEC
  sedative, hypnotic, or anxiolytic
    F13.90
    with
      anxiety disorder F13.980
      intoxication F13.929
        with
          delirium F13.921
        uncomplicated F13.920
      other specified disorder F13.988
      persisting
        amnestic disorder F13.96
        dementia F13.97
      psychosis F13.959
        delusions F13.950
        hallucinations F13.951
      sexual dysfunction F13.981
      sleep disorder F13.982
      unspecified disorder F13.99
    harmful —see Abuse, drug, sedative,
      hypnotic, or anxiolytic
  stimulant NEC F15.90
    with
      anxiety disorder F15.980
      intoxication F15.929
        with
          delirium F15.921
          perceptual disturbance
            F15.922
        uncomplicated F15.920

Use (Continued)
  stimulant NEC (Continued)
    with (Continued)
      mood disorder F15.94
      other specified disorder F15.988
      psychosis F15.959
        delusions F15.950
        hallucinations F15.951
      sexual dysfunction F15.981
      sleep disorder F15.982
      unspecified disorder F15.99
      withdrawal F15.93
    harmful —see Abuse, drug, stimulant
      NEC
  tobacco Z72.0
    with dependence —see Dependence,
      drug, nicotine
  volatile solvents —see also Use, inhalant
    F18.90
    harmful —see Abuse, drug, inhalant
Usher-Senear disease or syndrome L10.4
Uta B55.1
Uteromegaly N85.2
Uterovaginal —see condition
Uterovesical —see condition
Uveal —see condition
Uveitis (anterior) —see also Iridocyclitis
  acute —see Iridocyclitis, acute
  chronic —see Iridocyclitis, chronic
  due to toxoplasmosis (acquired) B58.09
    congenital P37.1
  granulomatous —see Iridocyclitis,
    chronic
  heterochromic —see Cyclitis, Fuchs'
    heterochromic
  lens-induced —see Iridocyclitis,
    lens-induced
  posterior —see Chorioretinitis
  sympathetic H44.13-●
  syphilitic (secondary) A51.43
    congenital (early) A50.01
    late A52.71
  tuberculous A18.54
Uveoencephalitis —see Inflammation,
  chorioretinal
Uveokeratitis —see Iridocyclitis
Uveoparotitis D86.89
Uvula —see condition
Uvulitis (acute) (catarrhal) (chronic)
  (membranous) (suppurative) (ulcerative)
  K12.2

V

Vaccination (prophylactic)
  complication or reaction —*see* Complications, vaccination
  delayed Z28.9
  encounter for Z23
  not done —*see* Immunization, not done, because (of)
Vaccinia (generalized) (localized) T88.1
  without vaccination B08.011
  congenital P35.8
Vacuum, in sinus (accessory) (nasal) J34.89
Vagabond, vagabondage Z59.0
Vagabond's disease B85.1
Vagina, vaginal —*see* condition
Vaginalitis (tunica) (testis) N49.1
Vaginismus (reflex) N94.2
  functional F52.5
  nonorganic F52.5
  psychogenic F52.5
  secondary N94.2
Vaginitis (acute) (circumscribed) (diffuse) (emphysematous) (nonvenereal) (ulcerative) N76.0
  with ectopic or molar pregnancy O08.0
  amebic A06.82
  atrophic, postmenopausal N95.2
  bacterial N76.0
  blennorrhagic (gonococcal) A54.02
  candidal B37.3
  chlamydial A56.02
  chronic N76.1
  due to Trichomonas (vaginalis) A59.01
  following ectopic or molar pregnancy O08.0
  gonococcal A54.02
    with abscess (accessory gland) (periurethral) A54.1
  granuloma A58
  in (due to)
    candidiasis B37.3
    herpesviral (herpes simplex) infection A60.04
    pinworm infection B80 [N77.1]
  monilial B37.3
  mycotic (candidal) B37.3
  postmenopausal atrophic N95.2
  puerperal (postpartum) O86.13
  senile (atrophic) N95.2
  subacute or chronic N76.1
  syphilitic (early) A51.0
    late A52.76
  trichomonal A59.01
  tuberculous A18.18
Vaginosis —*see* Vaginitis
Vagotonia G52.2
Vagrancy Z59.0
VAIN —*see* Neoplasia, intraepithelial, vagina
Vallecula —*see* condition
Valley fever B38.0
Valsuani's disease —*see* Anemia, obstetric
Valve, valvular (formation) —*see also* condition
  cerebral ventricle (communicating) in situ Z98.2
  cervix, internal os Q51.828
  congenital NEC —*see* Atresia, by site
  ureter (pelvic junction) (vesical orifice) Q62.39
  urethra (congenital) (posterior) Q64.2
Valvulitis (chronic) —*see* Endocarditis
Valvulopathy —*see* Endocarditis
Van Bogaert's leukoencephalopathy (sclerosing) (subacute) A81.1
Van Bogaert-Scherer-Epstein disease or syndrome E75.5
Van Buchem's syndrome M85.2
Van Creveld-von Gierke disease E74.01
Van der Hoeve (-de Kleyn) syndrome Q78.0
Van der Woude's syndrome Q38.0
Van Neck's disease or osteochondrosis M91.0
Vanishing lung J44.9

Vapor asphyxia or suffocation T59.9
  specified agent —*see* Table of Drugs and Chemicals
Variance, lethal ball, prosthetic heart valve T82.09
Variants, thalassemic D56.8
Variations in hair color L67.1
Varicella B01.9
  with
    complications NEC B01.89
    encephalitis B01.11
    encephalomyelitis B01.11
    meningitis B01.0
    myelitis B01.12
    pneumonia B01.2
  congenital P35.8
Varices —*see* Varix
Varicocele (scrotum) (thrombosed) I86.1
  ovary I86.2
  perineum I86.3
  spermatic cord (ulcerated) I86.1
Varicose
  aneurysm (ruptured) I77.0
  dermatitis —*see* Varix, leg, with, inflammation
  eczema —*see* Varix, leg, with, inflammation
  phlebitis —*see* Varix, with, inflammation
  tumor —*see* Varix
  ulcer (lower limb, any part) —*see also* Varix, leg, with, ulcer
    anus —*see also* Hemorrhoids K64.8
    esophagus —*see* Varix, esophagus
    inflamed or infected —*see* Varix, leg, with ulcer, with inflammation
    nasal septum I86.8
    perineum I86.3
    scrotum I86.1
    specified site NEC I86.8
  vein —*see* Varix
  vessel —*see* Varix, leg
Varicosis, varicosities, varicosity —*see* Varix
Variola (major) (minor) B03
Varioloid B03
Varix (lower limb) I83.90
  with
    bleeding I83.899
    edema I83.899
    inflammation I83.10
      with ulcer (venous) I83.209
    pain I83.819
    rupture I83.899
    specified complication NEC I83.899
    stasis dermatitis I83.10
      with ulcer (venous) I83.209
    swelling I83.899
    ulcer I83.009
      with inflammation I83.209
  aneurysmal I77.0
  asymptomatic I83.9-●
  bladder I86.2
  broad ligament I86.2
  complicating
    childbirth (lower extremity) O87.4
      anus or rectum O87.2
      genital (vagina, vulva or perineum) O87.8
    pregnancy (lower extremity) O22.0-●
      anus or rectum O22.4-●
      genital (vagina, vulva or perineum) O22.1-●
    puerperium (lower extremity) O87.4
      anus or rectum O87.2
      genital (vagina, vulva, perineum) O87.8
  congenital (any site) Q27.8
  esophagus (idiopathic) (primary) (ulcerated) I85.00
    bleeding I85.01
    congenital Q27.8
    in (due to)
      alcoholic liver disease I85.10
        bleeding I85.11
      cirrhosis of liver I85.10
        bleeding I85.11

Varix (*Continued*)
  esophagus (*Continued*)
    in (*Continued*)
      portal hypertension I85.10
        bleeding I85.11
      schistosomiasis I85.10
        bleeding I85.11
      toxic liver disease I85.10
        bleeding I85.11
    secondary I85.10
      bleeding I85.11
  gastric I86.4
  inflamed or infected I83.10
    ulcerated I83.209
  labia (majora) I86.3
  leg (asymptomatic) I83.90
    with
      edema I83.899
      inflammation I83.10
        with ulcer —*see* Varix, leg, with, ulcer, with inflammation by site
      pain I83.819
      specified complication NEC I83.899
      swelling I83.899
      ulcer I83.009
        with inflammation I83.209
        ankle I83.003
          with inflammation I83.203
        calf I83.002
          with inflammation I83.202
        foot NEC I83.005
          with inflammation I83.205
        heel I83.004
          with inflammation I83.204
        lower leg NEC I83.008
          with inflammation I83.208
        midfoot I83.004
          with inflammation I83.204
        thigh I83.001
          with inflammation I83.201
    bilateral (asymptomatic) I83.93
      with
        edema I83.893
        pain I83.813
        specified complication NEC I83.893
        swelling I83.893
        ulcer I83.0-●
          with inflammation I83.209
    left (asymptomatic) I83.92
      with
        edema I83.892
        inflammation I83.12
          with ulcer —*see* Varix, leg, with, ulcer, with inflammation by site
        pain I83.812
        specified complication NEC I83.892
        swelling I83.892
        ulcer I83.029
          with inflammation I83.229
          ankle I83.023
            with inflammation I83.223
          calf I83.022
            with inflammation I83.222
          foot NEC I83.025
            with inflammation I83.225
          heel I83.024
            with inflammation I83.224
          lower leg NEC I83.028
            with inflammation I83.228
          midfoot I83.024
            with inflammation I83.224
          thigh I83.021
            with inflammation I83.221
    right (asymptomatic) I83.91
      with
        edema I83.891
        inflammation I83.11
          with ulcer —*see* Varix, leg, with, ulcer, with inflammation by site

▶ New   ⇒ Revised   ~~deleted~~ Deleted   ● Use Additional Character(s)

Virulent bubo A57
Virus, viral —*see also* condition
  as cause of disease classified elsewhere
    B97.89
    respiratory syncytial virus (RSV) —*see* Virus,
      infection, respiratory syncytial (RSV)
  cytomegalovirus B25.9
  human immunodeficiency (HIV) —*see*
    Human, immunodeficiency virus (HIV)
    disease
  infection —*see* Infection, virus
  respiratory syncytial (RSV)
    as cause of disease classified elsewhere
      B97.4
    bronchiolitis J21.0
    bronchitis J20.5
    bronchopneumonia J12.1
    otitis media H65-● [B97.4]
    pneumonia J12.1
    upper respiratory infection J06.9 [B97.4]
  specified NEC B34.8
  swine influenza (viruses that normally cause
    infections in pigs) —*see also* Influenza,
    due to, identified novel influenza A virus
    J09.X2
  West Nile (fever) A92.30
    with
      complications NEC A92.39
      cranial nerve disorders A92.32
      encephalitis A92.31
      encephalomyelitis A92.31
      neurologic manifestation NEC A92.32
      optic neuritis A92.32
      polyradiculitis A92.32
Viscera, visceral —*see* condition
Visceroptosis K63.4
Visible peristalsis R19.2
Vision, visual
  binocular, suppression H53.34
  blurred, blurring H53.8
    hysterical F44.6
  defect, defective NEC H54.7
  disorientation (syndrome) H53.8
  disturbance H53.9
    hysterical F44.6
  double H53.2
  examination Z01.00
    with abnormal findings Z01.01
    following failed vision screening Z01.020
      with abnormal findings Z01.021
  field, limitation (defect) —*see* Defect, visual
    field
  hallucinations R44.1
  halos H53.19
  loss —*see* Loss, vision
    sudden —*see* Disturbance, vision,
      subjective, loss, sudden
  low (both eyes) —*see* Low, vision
  perception, simultaneous without fusion
    H53.33
Vitality, lack or want of R53.83
  newborn P96.89
Vitamin deficiency —*see* Deficiency, vitamin

Vitelline duct, persistent Q43.0
Vitiligo L80
  eyelid H02.739
    left H02.736
      lower H02.735
      upper H02.734
    right H02.733
      lower H02.732
      upper H02.731
  pinta A67.2
  vulva N90.89
Vitreal corneal syndrome H59.01-●
Vitreoretinopathy, proliferative —*see also*
  Retinopathy, proliferative
  with retinal detachment —*see* Detachment,
    retina, traction
Vitreous —*see also* condition
  touch syndrome —*see* Complication,
    postprocedural, following cataract
    surgery
Vocal cord —*see* condition
Vogt-Koyanagi syndrome H20.82-●
Vogt's disease or syndrome G80.3
Vogt-Spielmeyer amaurotic idiocy or disease
  E75.4
Voice
  change R49.9
    specified NEC R49.8
  loss —*see* Aphonia
Volhynian fever A79.0
Volkmann's ischemic contracture or paralysis
  (complicating trauma) T79.6
Volvulus (bowel) (colon) (intestine) K56.2
  with perforation K56.2
  congenital Q43.8
  duodenum K31.5
  fallopian tube —*see* Torsion, fallopian tube
  oviduct —*see* Torsion, fallopian tube
  stomach (due to absence of gastrocolic
    ligament) K31.89
Vomiting R11.10
  with nausea R11.2
  without nausea R11.11
  asphyxia —*see* Foreign body, by site, causing
    asphyxia, gastric contents
  bilious (cause unknown) R11.14
    following gastro-intestinal surgery K91.0
    in newborn P92.01
  blood —*see* Hematemesis
  causing asphyxia, choking, or suffocation —
    see Foreign body, by site
  cyclical, in migraine G43.A0
    with refractory migraine G43.A1
    intractable G43.A1
    not intractable G43.A0
    psychogenic F50.89
    without refractory migraine G43.A0
  cyclical syndrome NOS (unrelated to
    migraine) R53.1
    persistent R11.15

Vomiting (*Continued*)
  fecal mater R11.13
  following gastrointestinal surgery K91.0
    psychogenic F50.89
  functional K31.89
  hysterical F50.89
  nervous F50.89
  neurotic F50.89
  newborn NEC P92.09
    bilious P92.01
  periodic R11.10
    psychogenic F50.89
  projectile R11.12
  psychogenic F50.89
  uremic —*see* Uremia
Vomito negro —*see* Fever, yellow
Von Bezold's abscess —*see* Mastoiditis, acute
Von Economo-Cruchet disease A85.8
Von Eulenburg's disease G71.19
Von Gierke's disease E74.01
Von Hippel (-Lindau) disease or syndrome
  Q85.8
Von Jaksch's anemia or disease D64.89
Von Recklinghausen
  disease (neurofibromatosis) Q85.01
  bones E21.0
Von Schroetter's syndrome I82.890
Von Willebrand (-Jurgens)(-Minot) disease or
  syndrome D68.0
Von Zumbusch's disease L40.1
Voyeurism F65.3
Vrolik's disease Q78.0
Vulva —*see* condition
Vulvismus N94.2
Vulvitis (acute) (allergic) (atrophic)
  (hypertrophic) (intertriginous) (senile)
  N76.2
  with ectopic or molar pregnancy O08.0
  adhesive, congenital Q52.79
  blennorrhagic (gonococcal) A54.02
  candidal B37.3
  chlamydial A56.02
  due to Haemophilus ducreyi A57
  following ectopic or molar pregnancy O08.0
  gonococcal A54.02
    with abscess (accessory gland)
      (periurethral) A54.1
  herpesviral A60.04
  leukoplakic N90.4
  monilial B37.3
  puerperal (postpartum) O86.19
  subacute or chronic N76.3
  syphilitic (early) A51.0
    late A52.76
  trichomonal A59.01
  tuberculous A18.18
Vulvodynia N94.819
  specified NEC N94.818
Vulvorectal —*see* condition
Vulvovaginitis (acute) —*see* Vaginitis

▶ New   ⇨ Revised   ~~deleted~~ Deleted   ● Use Additional Character(s)

W

Waiting list, person on Z75.1
for organ transplant Z76.82
undergoing social agency investigation Z75.2
Waldenström
hypergammaglobulinemia D89.0
syndrome or macroglobulinemia C88.0
Waldenström-Kjellberg syndrome D50.1
Walking
difficulty R26.2
psychogenic F44.4
sleep F51.3
hysterical F44.89
Wall, abdominal —see condition
Wallenberg's disease or syndrome G46.3
Wallgren's disease I87.8
Wandering
gallbladder, congenital Q44.1
in diseases classified elsewhere Z91.83
kidney, congenital Q63.8
organ or site, congenital NEC —see Malposition, congenital, by site
pacemaker (heart) I49.8
spleen D73.89
War neurosis F48.8
Wart (due to HPV) (filiform) (infectious) (viral) B07.9
anogenital region (venereal) A63.0
common B07.8
external genital organs (venereal) A63.0
flat B07.8
Hassal-Henle's (of cornea) H18.49
Peruvian A44.1
plantar B07.0
prosector (tuberculous) A18.4
seborrheic L82.1
inflamed L82.0
senile (seborrheic) L82.1
inflamed L82.0
tuberculous A18.4
venereal A63.0
Warthin's tumor —see Neoplasm, salivary gland, benign
Wassilieff's disease A27.0
Wasting
disease R64
due to malnutrition E41
extreme (due to malnutrition) E41
muscle NEC —see Atrophy, muscle
Water
clefts (senile cataract) —see Cataract, senile, incipient
deprivation of T73.1
intoxication E87.79
itch B76.9
lack of T73.1
loading E87.70
on
brain —see Hydrocephalus
chest J94.8
poisoning E87.79
Waterbrash R12
Waterhouse(-Friderichsen) syndrome or disease (meningococcal) A39.1
Water-losing nephritis N25.89
Watermelon stomach K31.819
with hemorrhage K31.811
without hemorrhage K31.819
Watsoniasis B66.8
Wax in ear —see Impaction, cerumen
Weak, weakening, weakness (generalized) R53.1
arches (acquired) —see also Deformity, limb, flat foot
bladder (sphincter) R32

Weak, weakening, weakness (Continued)
facial R29.810
following
cerebrovascular disease I69.992
cerebral infarction I69.392
intracerebral hemorrhage I69.192
nontraumatic intracranial hemorrhage NEC I69.292
specified disease NEC I69.892
stroke I69.392
subarachnoid hemorrhage I69.092
foot (double) —see also Weak, arches
heart, cardiac —see Failure, heart
mind F70
muscle M62.81
myocardium —see Failure, heart
newborn P96.89
pelvic fundus N81.89
pubocervical tissue N81.82
rectovaginal tissue N81.83
senile R54
urinary stream R39.12
valvular —see Endocarditis
Wear, worn (with normal or routine use)
articular bearing surface of internal joint prosthesis —see Complications, joint prosthesis, mechanical, wear of articular bearing surfaces, by site
device, implant or graft —see Complications, by site, mechanical complication
tooth, teeth (approximal) (hard tissues) (interproximal) (occlusal) K03.0
Weather, weathered
effects of
cold T69.9
specified effect NEC T69.8
hot —see Heat
skin L57.8
Weaver's syndrome Q87.3
Web, webbed (congenital)
duodenal Q43.8
esophagus Q39.4
fingers Q70.1
larynx (glottic) (subglottic) Q31.0
neck (pterygium colli) Q18.3
Paterson-Kelly D50.1
popliteal syndrome Q87.89
toes Q70.3
Weber-Christian disease M35.6
Weber-Cockayne syndrome (epidermolysis bullosa) Q81.8
Weber-Gubler syndrome G46.3
Weber-Leyden syndrome G46.3
Weber-Osler syndrome I78.0
Weber's paralysis or syndrome G46.3
Wedge-shaped or wedging vertebra —see Collapse, vertebra NEC
Wegener's granulomatosis or syndrome M31.30
with
kidney involvement M31.31
lung involvement M31.30
with kidney involvement M31.31
Wegner's disease A50.02
Weight
1000-2499 grams at birth (low) —see Low, birthweight
999 grams or less at birth (extremely low) — see Low, birthweight, extreme
and length below 10th percentile for gestational age P05.1-●
below but length above 10th percentile for gestational age P05.0-●
gain (abnormal) (excessive) R63.5
in pregnancy —see Pregnancy, complicated by, excessive weight gain
low —see Pregnancy, complicated by, insufficient, weight gain
loss (abnormal) (cause unknown) R63.4
Weightlessness (effect of) T75.82

Weil (l)-Marchesani syndrome Q87.19
Weil's disease A27.0
Weingarten's syndrome J82.89
Weir Mitchell's disease I73.81
Weiss-Baker syndrome G90.09
Wells' disease L98.3
Wen —see Cyst, sebaceous
Wenckebach's block or phenomenon I44.1
Werdnig-Hoffmann syndrome (muscular atrophy) G12.0
Werlhof's disease D69.3
Werner-His disease A79.0
Wermer's disease or syndrome E31.21
Werner's disease or syndrome E34.8
Wernicke-Korsakoff's syndrome or psychosis (alcoholic) F10.96
with dependence F10.26
drug-induced
due to drug abuse —see Abuse, drug, by type, with amnestic disorder
due to drug dependence —see Dependence, drug, by type, with amnestic disorder
nonalcoholic F04
Wernicke-Posadas disease B38.9
Wernicke's
developmental aphasia F80.2
disease or syndrome E51.2
encephalopathy E51.2
polioencephalitis, superior E51.2
West African fever B50.8
Westphal-Strümpell syndrome E83.01
West's syndrome —see Epilepsy, spasms
Wet
feet, tropical (maceration) (syndrome) —see Immersion, foot
lung (syndrome), newborn P22.1
Wharton's duct —see condition
Wheal —see Urticaria
Wheezing R06.2
Whiplash injury S13.4
Whipple's disease —see also subcategory M14.8-● K90.81
Whipworm (disease) (infection) (infestation) B79
Whistling face Q87.0
White —see also condition
kidney, small N03.9
leg, puerperal, postpartum, childbirth O87.1
mouth B37.0
patches of mouth K13.29
spot lesions, teeth
chewing surface K02.51
pit and fissure surface K02.51
smooth surface K02.61
Whitehead L70.0
Whitlow —see also Cellulitis, digit
with lymphangitis —see Lymphangitis, acute, digit
herpesviral B00.89
Whitmore's disease or fever —see Melioidosis
Whooping cough A37.90
with pneumonia A37.91
due to Bordetella
bronchiseptica A37.81
parapertussis A37.11
pertussis A37.01
specified organism NEC A37.81
due to
Bordetella
bronchiseptica A37.80
with pneumonia A37.81
parapertussis A37.10
with pneumonia A37.11
pertussis A37.00
with pneumonia A37.01
specified NEC A37.80
with pneumonia A37.81
Wichman's asthma J38.5
Wide cranial sutures, newborn P96.3

Widening aorta —*see* Ectasia, aorta
  with aneurysm —*see* Aneurysm, aorta
Wilkie's disease or syndrome K55.1
Wilkinson-Sneddon disease or syndrome
  L13.1
Willebrand (-Jürgens) thrombopathy D68.0
Williams syndrome Q93.82
Willige-Hunt disease or syndrome G23.1
Wilms' tumor C64-●
Wilson-Mikity syndrome P27.0
Wilson's
  disease or syndrome E83.01
  hepatolenticular degeneration E83.01
  lichen ruber L43.9
Window —*see also* Imperfect, closure
  aorticopulmonary Q21.4
Winter —*see* condition
Wiskott-Aldrich syndrome D82.0
Withdrawal state —*see also* Dependence, drug
  by type, with withdrawal
  alcohol
    with perceptual disturbances F10.232
    without perceptual disturbances F10.239
  caffeine F15.93
  cannabis F12.23
  newborn
    correct therapeutic substance properly
      administered P96.2
    infant of dependent mother P96.1
    therapeutic substance, neonatal P96.2
Witts' anemia D50.8
Witzelsucht F07.0
Woakes' ethmoiditis or syndrome J33.1
Wolff-Hirschorn syndrome Q93.3
Wolff-Parkinson-White syndrome I45.6
Wolhynian fever A79.0
Wolman's disease E75.5
Wood lung or pneumonitis J67.8
Woolly, wooly hair (congenital) (nevus) Q84.1
Woolsorter's disease A22.1
Word
  blindness (congenital) (developmental)
    F81.0
  deafness (congenital) (developmental)
    H93.25
Worm(s) (infection) (infestation) —*see also*
  Infestation, helminth
  guinea B72
  in intestine NEC B82.0
Worm-eaten soles A66.3
Worn out —*see* Exhaustion
  cardiac
    defibrillator (with synchronous cardiac
      pacemaker) Z45.02
    pacemaker
      battery Z45.010
      lead Z45.018
  device, implant or graft —*see* Complications,
    by site, mechanical
Worried well Z71.1
Worries R45.82
Wound check Z48.0-●
  due to injury - code to Injury, by site, using
    appropriate seventh character for
    subsequent encounter
Wound, open T14.8-●
  abdomen, abdominal
    wall S31.109
      with penetration into peritoneal cavity
        S31.609
      bite —*see* Bite, abdomen, wall
      epigastric region S31.102
        with penetration into peritoneal cavity
          S31.602
        bite —*see* Bite, abdomen, wall,
          epigastric region
        laceration —*see* Laceration, abdomen,
          wall, epigastric region
        puncture —*see* Puncture, abdomen,
          wall, epigastric region

Wound, open *(Continued)*
  abdomen, abdominal *(Continued)*
    wall *(Continued)*
      laceration —*see* Laceration, abdomen, wall
      left
        lower quadrant S31.104
          with penetration into peritoneal
            cavity S31.604
          bite —*see* Bite, abdomen, wall, left,
            lower quadrant
          laceration —*see* Laceration, abdomen,
            wall, left, lower quadrant
          puncture —*see* Puncture, abdomen,
            wall, left, lower quadrant
        upper quadrant S31.101
          with penetration into peritoneal
            cavity S31.601
          bite —*see* Bite, abdomen, wall, left,
            upper quadrant
          laceration —*see* Laceration,
            abdomen, wall, left, upper
            quadrant
          puncture —*see* Puncture, abdomen,
            wall, left, upper quadrant
      periumbilic region S31.105
        with penetration into peritoneal cavity
          S31.605
        bite —*see* Bite, abdomen, wall,
          periumbilic region
        laceration —*see* Laceration, abdomen,
          wall, periumbilic region
        puncture —*see* Puncture, abdomen,
          wall, periumbilic region
      puncture —*see* Puncture, abdomen,
        wall
      right
        lower quadrant S31.103
          with penetration into peritoneal
            cavity S31.603
          bite —*see* Bite, abdomen, wall, right,
            lower quadrant
          laceration —*see* Laceration,
            abdomen, wall, right, lower
            quadrant
          puncture —*see* Puncture, abdomen,
            wall, right, lower quadrant
        upper quadrant S31.100
          with penetration into peritoneal
            cavity S31.600
          bite —*see* Bite, abdomen, wall, right,
            upper quadrant
          laceration —*see* Laceration,
            abdomen, wall, right, upper
            quadrant
          puncture —*see* Puncture, abdomen,
            wall, right, upper quadrant
    alveolar (process) —*see* Wound, open, oral
      cavity
    ankle S91.00-●
      bite —*see* Bite, ankle
      laceration —*see* Laceration, ankle
      puncture —*see* Puncture, ankle
    antecubital space —*see* Wound, open, elbow
    anterior chamber, eye —*see* Wound, open,
      ocular
    anus S31.839
      bite S31.835
      laceration —*see* Laceration, anus
      puncture —*see* Puncture, anus
    arm (upper) S41.10-●
      with amputation —*see* Amputation,
        traumatic, arm
      bite —*see* Bite, arm
      forearm —*see* Wound, open, forearm
      laceration —*see* Laceration, arm
      puncture —*see* Puncture, arm
    auditory canal (external) (meatus) —*see*
      Wound, open, ear
    auricle, ear —*see* Wound, open, ear
    axilla —*see* Wound, open, arm

Wound, open *(Continued)*
  back —*see also* Wound, open, thorax, back
    lower S31.000
      with penetration into retroperitoneal
        space S31.001
      bite —*see* Bite, back, lower
      laceration —*see* Laceration, back, lower
      puncture —*see* Puncture, back, lower
  bite —*see* Bite
  blood vessel —*see* Injury, blood vessel
  breast S21.00-●
    with amputation —*see* Amputation,
      traumatic, breast
    bite —*see* Bite, breast
    laceration —*see* Laceration, breast
    puncture —*see* Puncture, breast
  buttock S31.809
    bite —*see* Bite, buttock
    laceration —*see* Laceration, buttock
    left S31.829
    puncture —*see* Puncture, buttock
    right S31.819
  calf —*see* Wound, open, leg
  canaliculus lacrimalis —*see* Wound, open,
    eyelid
  canthus, eye —*see* Wound, open, eyelid
  cervical esophagus S11.20
    bite S11.25
    laceration —*see* Laceration, esophagus,
      traumatic, cervical
    puncture —*see* Puncture, cervical
      esophagus
  cheek (external) S01.40-●
    bite —*see* Bite, cheek
    internal —*see* Wound, open, oral cavity
    laceration —*see* Laceration, cheek
    puncture —*see* Puncture, cheek
  chest wall —*see* Wound, open, thorax
  chin —*see* Wound, open, head, specified site
    NEC
  choroid —*see* Wound, open, ocular
  ciliary body (eye) —*see* Wound, open,
    ocular
  clitoris S31.40
    with amputation —*see* Amputation,
      traumatic, clitoris
    bite S31.45
    laceration —*see* Laceration, vulva
    puncture —*see* Puncture, vulva
  conjunctiva —*see* Wound, open, ocular
  cornea —*see* Wound, open, ocular
  costal region —*see* Wound, open, thorax
  Descemet's membrane —*see* Wound, open,
    ocular
  digit(s)
    foot —*see* Wound, open, toe
    hand —*see* Wound, open, finger
  ear (canal) (external) S01.30-●
    with amputation —*see* Amputation,
      traumatic, ear
    bite —*see* Bite, ear
    drum S09.2-●
    laceration —*see* Laceration, ear
    puncture —*see* Puncture, ear
  elbow S51.00-●
    bite —*see* Bite, elbow
    laceration —*see* Laceration, elbow
    puncture —*see* Puncture, elbow
  epididymis —*see* Wound, open, testis
  epigastric region S31.102
    with penetration into peritoneal cavity
      S31.602
    bite —*see* Bite, abdomen, wall, epigastric
      region
    laceration —*see* Laceration, abdomen, wall,
      epigastric region
    puncture —*see* Puncture, abdomen, wall,
      epigastric region
  epiglottis —*see* Wound, open, neck, specified
    site NEC

Wound, open *(Continued)*
  esophagus (thoracic) S27.819
    cervical —*see* Wound, open, cervical
      esophagus
    laceration S27.813
    specified type NEC S27.818
  eye —*see* Wound, open, ocular
  eyeball —*see* Wound, open, ocular
  eyebrow —*see* Wound, open, eyelid
  eyelid S01.10-●
    bite —*see* Bite, eyelid
    laceration —*see* Laceration, eyelid
    puncture —*see* Puncture, eyelid
  face NEC —*see* Wound, open, head, specified
    site NEC
  finger(s) S61.209
    with
      amputation —*see* Amputation,
        traumatic, finger
      damage to nail S61.309
    bite —*see* Bite, finger
    index S61.208
      with
        damage to nail S61.308
      left S61.201
        with
          damage to nail S61.301
      right S61.200
        with
          damage to nail S61.300
    laceration —*see* Laceration, finger
    little S61.208
      with
        damage to nail S61.308
      left S61.207
        with damage to nail S61.307
      right S61.206
        with damage to nail S61.306
    middle S61.208
      with
        damage to nail S61.308
      left S61.203
        with damage to nail S61.303
      right S61.202
        with damage to nail S61.302
    puncture —*see* Puncture, finger
    ring S61.208
      with
        damage to nail S61.308
      left S61.205
        with damage to nail S61.305
      right S61.204
        with damage to nail S61.304
  flank —*see* Wound, open, abdomen, wall
  foot (except toe(s) alone) S91.30-●
    with amputation —*see* Amputation,
      traumatic, foot
    bite —*see* Bite, foot
    laceration —*see* Laceration, foot
    puncture —*see* Puncture, foot
    toe —*see* Wound, open, toe
  forearm S51.80-●
    with
      amputation —*see* Amputation,
        traumatic, forearm
    bite —*see* Bite, forearm
    elbow only —*see* Wound, open, elbow
    laceration —*see* Laceration, forearm
    puncture —*see* Puncture, forearm
  forehead —*see* Wound, open, head, specified
    site NEC
  genital organs, external
    with amputation —*see* Amputation,
      traumatic, genital organs
    bite —*see* Bite, genital organ
    female S31.502
      vagina S31.40
      vulva S31.40
    laceration —*see* Laceration, genital
      organ

Wound, open *(Continued)*
  genital organs, external *(Continued)*
    male S31.501
      penis S31.20
      scrotum S31.30
      testes S31.30
    puncture —*see* Puncture, genital organ
  globe (eye) —*see* Wound, open, ocular
  groin —*see* Wound, open, abdomen, wall
  gum —*see* Wound, open, oral cavity
  hand S61.40-●
    with
      amputation —*see* Amputation,
        traumatic, hand
    bite —*see* Bite, hand
    finger(s) —*see* Wound, open, finger
    laceration —*see* Laceration, hand
    puncture —*see* Puncture, hand
    thumb —*see* Wound, open, thumb
  head S01.90
    bite —*see* Bite, head
    cheek —*see* Wound, open, cheek
    ear —*see* Wound, open, ear
    eyelid —*see* Wound, open, eyelid
    laceration —*see* Laceration, head
    lip —*see* Wound, open, lip
    nose S01.20
    oral cavity —*see* Wound, open, oral
      cavity
    puncture —*see* Puncture, head
    scalp —*see* Wound, open, scalp
    specified site NEC S01.80
    temporomandibular area —*see* Wound,
      open, cheek
  heel —*see* Wound, open, foot
  hip S71.00-●
    with amputation —*see* Amputation,
      traumatic, hip
    bite —*see* Bite, hip
    laceration —*see* Laceration, hip
    puncture —*see* Puncture, hip
  hymen S31.40
    bite —*see* Bite, vulva
    laceration —*see* Laceration, vagina
    puncture —*see* Puncture, vagina
  hypochondrium S31.109
    bite —*see* Bite, hypochondrium
    laceration —*see* Laceration,
      hypochondrium
    puncture —*see* Puncture, hypochondrium
  hypogastric region S31.109
    bite —*see* Bite, hypogastric region
    laceration —*see* Laceration, hypogastric
      region
    puncture —*see* Puncture, hypogastric
      region
  iliac (region) —*see* Wound, open, inguinal
    region
  inguinal region S31.109
    bite —*see* Bite, abdomen, wall, lower
      quadrant
    laceration —*see* Laceration, inguinal
      region
    puncture —*see* Puncture, inguinal
      region
  instep —*see* Wound, open, foot
  interscapular region —*see* Wound, open,
    thorax, back
  intraocular —*see* Wound, open, ocular
  iris —*see* Wound, open, ocular
  jaw —*see* Wound, open, head, specified site
    NEC
  knee S81.00-●
    bite —*see* Bite, knee
    laceration —*see* Laceration, knee
    puncture —*see* Puncture, knee
  labium (majus) (minus) —*see* Wound, open,
    vulva
  laceration —*see* Laceration, by site
  lacrimal duct —*see* Wound, open, eyelid

Wound, open *(Continued)*
  larynx S11.019
    bite —*see* Bite, larynx
    laceration —*see* Laceration, larynx
    puncture —*see* Puncture, larynx
  left
    lower quadrant S31.104
      with penetration into peritoneal cavity
        S31.604
      bite —*see* Bite, abdomen, wall, left, lower
        quadrant
      laceration —*see* Laceration, abdomen,
        wall, left, lower quadrant
      puncture —*see* Puncture, abdomen, wall,
        left, lower quadrant
    upper quadrant S31.101
      with penetration into peritoneal cavity
        S31.601
      bite —*see* Bite, abdomen, wall, left,
        upper quadrant
      laceration —*see* Laceration, abdomen,
        wall, left, upper quadrant
      puncture —*see* Puncture, abdomen, wall,
        left, upper quadrant
  leg (lower) S81.80-●
    with amputation —*see* Amputation,
      traumatic, leg
    ankle —*see* Wound, open, ankle
    bite —*see* Bite, leg
    foot —*see* Wound, open, foot
    knee —*see* Wound, open, knee
    laceration —*see* Laceration, leg
    puncture —*see* Puncture, leg
    toe —*see* Wound, open, toe
    upper —*see* Wound, open, thigh
  lip S01.501
    bite —*see* Bite, lip
    laceration —*see* Laceration, lip
    puncture —*see* Puncture, lip
  loin S31.109
    bite —*see* Bite, abdomen, wall
    laceration —*see* Laceration, loin
    puncture —*see* Puncture, loin
  lower back —*see* Wound, open, back,
    lower
  lumbar region —*see* Wound, open, back,
    lower
  malar region —*see* Wound, open, head,
    specified site NEC
  mammary —*see* Wound, open, breast
  mastoid region —*see* Wound, open, head,
    specified site NEC
  mouth —*see* Wound, open, oral cavity
  nail
    finger —*see* Wound, open, finger, with
      damage to nail
    toe —*see* Wound, open, toe, with damage
      to nail
  nape (neck) —*see* Wound, open, neck
  nasal (septum) (sinus) —*see* Wound, open,
    nose
  nasopharynx —*see* Wound, open, head,
    specified site NEC
  neck S11.90
    bite —*see* Bite, neck
    involving
      cervical esophagus S11.20
      larynx —*see* Wound, open, larynx
      pharynx S11.20
      thyroid S11.10
      trachea (cervical) S11.029
        bite —*see* Bite, trachea
        laceration S11.021
          with foreign body S11.022
        puncture S11.023
          with foreign body S11.024
    laceration —*see* Laceration, neck
    puncture —*see* Puncture, neck
    specified site NEC S11.80
      specified type NEC S11.89

Wound, open (*Continued*)
  nose (septum) (sinus) S01.20
    with amputation —*see* Amputation,
        traumatic, nose
    bite —*see* Bite, nose
    laceration —*see* Laceration, nose
    puncture —*see* Puncture, nose
  ocular S05.90
    avulsion (traumatic enucleation) S05.7-●
    eyeball S05.6-●
      with foreign body S05.5-●
    eyelid —*see* Wound, open, eyelid
    laceration and rupture S05.3-●
      with prolapse or loss of intraocular
          tissue S05.2-●
    orbit (penetrating) (with or without foreign
        body) S05.4-●
    periocular area —*see* Wound, open, eyelid
    specified NEC S05.8X-●
  oral cavity S01.502
    bite S01.552
    laceration —*see* Laceration, oral cavity
    puncture —*see* Puncture, oral cavity
  orbit —*see* Wound, open, ocular, orbit
  palate —*see* Wound, open, oral cavity
  palm —*see* Wound, open, hand
  pelvis, pelvic —*see also* Wound, open, back,
      lower
    girdle —*see* Wound, open, hip
  penetrating —*see* Puncture, by site
  penis S31.20
    with amputation —*see* Amputation,
        traumatic, penis
    bite S31.25
    laceration —*see* Laceration, penis
    puncture —*see* Puncture, penis
  perineum
    bite —*see* Bite, perineum
    female S31.502
    laceration —*see* Laceration, perineum
    male S31.501
    puncture —*see* Puncture, perineum
  periocular area (with or without lacrimal
      passages) —*see* Wound, open, eyelid
  periumbilic region S31.105
    with penetration into peritoneal cavity
        S31.605
    bite —*see* Bite, abdomen, wall, periumbilic
        region
    laceration —*see* Laceration, abdomen, wall,
        periumbilic region
    puncture —*see* Puncture, abdomen, wall,
        periumbilic region
  phalanges
    finger —*see* Wound, open, finger
    toe —*see* Wound, open, toe
  pharynx S11.20
  pinna —*see* Wound, open, ear
  popliteal space —*see* Wound, open, knee
  prepuce —*see* Wound, open, penis
  pubic region —*see* Wound, open, back, lower
  pudendum —*see* Wound, open, genital
      organs, external
  puncture wound —*see* Puncture
  rectovaginal septum —*see* Wound, open,
      vagina
  right
    lower quadrant S31.103
      with penetration into peritoneal cavity
          S31.603
      bite —*see* Bite, abdomen, wall, right,
          lower quadrant
      laceration —*see* Laceration, abdomen,
          wall, right, lower quadrant
      puncture —*see* Puncture, abdomen, wall,
          right, lower quadrant
    upper quadrant S31.100
      with penetration into peritoneal cavity
          S31.600

Wound, open (*Continued*)
  right (*Continued*)
    upper quadrant (*Continued*)
      bite —*see* Bite, abdomen, wall, right,
          upper quadrant
      laceration —*see* Laceration, abdomen,
          wall, right, upper quadrant
      puncture —*see* Puncture, abdomen, wall,
          right, upper quadrant
    sacral region —*see* Wound, open, back, lower
    sacroiliac region —*see* Wound, open, back,
        lower
    salivary gland —*see* Wound, open, oral cavity
    scalp S01.00
      bite S01.05
      laceration —*see* Laceration, scalp
      puncture —*see* Puncture, scalp
    scalpel, newborn (birth injury) P15.8
    scapular region —*see* Wound, open, shoulder
    sclera —*see* Wound, open, ocular
    scrotum S31.30
      with amputation —*see* Amputation,
          traumatic, scrotum
      bite S31.35
      laceration —*see* Laceration, scrotum
      puncture —*see* Puncture, scrotum
    shin —*see* Wound, open, leg
    shoulder S41.00-●
      with amputation —*see* Amputation,
          traumatic, arm
      bite —*see* Bite, shoulder
      laceration —*see* Laceration, shoulder
      puncture —*see* Puncture, shoulder
    skin NOS T14.8
    spermatic cord —*see* Wound, open, testis
    sternal region —*see* Wound, open, thorax,
        front wall
    submaxillary region —*see* Wound, open,
        head, specified site NEC
    submental region —*see* Wound, open, head,
        specified site NEC
    subungual
      finger(s) —*see* Wound, open, finger
      toe(s) —*see* Wound, open, toe
    supraclavicular region —*see* Wound, open,
        neck, specified site NEC
    temple, temporal region —*see* Wound, open,
        head, specified site NEC
    temporomandibular area —*see* Wound, open,
        cheek
    testis S31.30
      with amputation —*see* Amputation,
          traumatic, testes
      bite S31.35
      laceration —*see* Laceration, testis
      puncture —*see* Puncture, testis
    thigh S71.10-●
      with amputation —*see* Amputation,
          traumatic, hip
      bite —*see* Bite, thigh
      laceration —*see* Laceration, thigh
      puncture —*see* Puncture, thigh
    thorax, thoracic (wall) S21.90
      back S21.20-●
        with penetration S21.40
      bite —*see* Bite, thorax
      breast —*see* Wound, open, breast
      front S21.10-●
        with penetration S21.30
      laceration —*see* Laceration, thorax
      puncture —*see* Puncture, thorax
    throat —*see* Wound, open, neck
    thumb S61.009
      with
        amputation —*see* Amputation,
            traumatic, thumb
        damage to nail S61.109
      bite —*see* Bite, thumb
      laceration —*see* Laceration, thumb

Wound, open (*Continued*)
  thumb (*Continued*)
    left S61.002
      with
        damage to nail S61.102
      puncture —*see* Puncture, thumb
    right S61.001
      with
        damage to nail S61.101
    thyroid (gland) —*see* Wound, open, neck,
        thyroid
    toe(s) S91.109
      with
        amputation —*see* Amputation,
            traumatic, toe
        damage to nail S91.209
      bite —*see* Bite, toe
      great S91.103
        with
          damage to nail S91.203
        left S91.102
          with
            damage to nail S91.202
        right S91.101
          with
            damage to nail S91.201
        laceration —*see* Laceration, toe
      lesser S91.106
        with
          damage to nail S91.206
        left S91.105
          with
            damage to nail S91.205
        right S91.104
          with
            damage to nail S91.204
      puncture —*see* Puncture, toe
    tongue —*see* Wound, open, oral cavity
    trachea (cervical region) —*see* Wound, open,
        neck, trachea
    tunica vaginalis —*see* Wound, open, testis
    tympanum, tympanic membrane S09.2-●
      laceration —*see* Laceration, ear, drum
      puncture —*see* Puncture, tympanum
    umbilical region —*see* Wound, open,
        abdomen, wall, periumbilic region
    uvula —*see* Wound, open, oral cavity
    vagina S31.40
      bite S31.45
      laceration —*see* Laceration, vagina
      puncture —*see* Puncture, vagina
    vitreous (humor) —*see* Wound, open, ocular
    vocal cord S11.039
      bite —*see* Bite, vocal cord
      laceration S11.031
        with foreign body S11.032
      puncture S11.033
        with foreign body S11.034
    vulva S31.40
      with amputation —*see* Amputation,
          traumatic, vulva
      bite S31.45
      laceration —*see* Laceration, vulva
      puncture —*see* Puncture, vulva
    wrist S61.50-●
      bite —*see* Bite, wrist
      laceration —*see* Laceration, wrist
      puncture —*see* Puncture, wrist
Wound, superficial —*see* Injury (*see also*
    specified injury type)
Wright's syndrome G54.0
Wrist —*see* condition
Wrong drug (by accident) (given in error) —
    see Table of Drugs and Chemicals, by
    drug, poisoning
Wry neck —*see* Torticollis
Wuchereria (bancrofti) infestation B74.0
Wuchereriasis B74.0
Wuchernde Struma Langhans C73

▶ New   ⇒ Revised   ~~deleted~~ Deleted   ● Use Additional Character(s)

X

Xanthelasma (eyelid) (palpebrarum) H02.60
  left H02.66
    lower H02.65
    upper H02.64
  right H02.63
    lower H02.62
    upper H02.61
Xanthelasmatosis (essential) E78.2
Xanthinuria, hereditary E79.8
Xanthoastrocytoma
  specified site —*see* Neoplasm, malignant, by
      site
  unspecified site C71.9
Xanthofibroma —*see* Neoplasm, connective
      tissue, benign
Xanthogranuloma D76.3
Xanthoma(s), xanthomatosis (primary)
      (familial) (hereditary) E75.5
  with
    hyperlipoproteinemia
      Type I E78.3
      Type III E78.2
      Type IV E78.1
      Type V E78.3
  bone (generalisata) C96.5
  cerebrotendinous E75.5
  cutaneotendinous E75.5

Xanthoma(s), xanthomatosis (Continued)
  disseminatum (skin) E78.2
  eruptive E78.2
  hypercholesterinemic E78.00
  hypercholesterolemic E78.00
  hyperlipidemic E78.5
  joint E75.5
  multiple (skin) E78.2
  tendon (sheath) E75.5
  tuberosum E78.2
  tuberous E78.2
  tubo-eruptive E78.2
  verrucous, oral mucosa K13.4
Xanthosis R23.8
Xenophobia F40.10
Xeroderma —*see also* Ichthyosis
  acquired L85.0
  eyelid H01.149
    left H01.146
      lower H01.145
      upper H01.144
    right H01.143
      lower H01.142
      upper H01.141
  pigmentosum Q82.1
  vitamin A deficiency E50.8
Xerophthalmia (vitamin A deficiency) E50.7
  unrelated to vitamin A deficiency —*see*
      Keratoconjunctivitis

Xerosis
  conjunctiva H11.14-●
    with Bitot's spots —*see also* Pigmentation,
        conjunctiva
      vitamin A deficiency E50.1
    vitamin A deficiency E50.0
  cornea H18.89-●
    with ulceration —*see* Ulcer, cornea
      vitamin A deficiency E50.3
    vitamin A deficiency E50.2
  cutis L85.3
  skin L85.3
Xerostomia K11.7
Xiphopagus Q89.4
XO syndrome Q96.9
X-ray (of)
  abnormal findings —*see* Abnormal,
      diagnostic imaging
  breast (mammogram) (routine) Z12.31
  chest
    routine (as part of a general medical
        examination) Z00.00
    with abnormal findings Z00.01
  routine (as part of a general medical
      examination) Z00.00
    with abnormal findings Z00.01
XXXXY syndrome Q98.1
XXY syndrome Q98.0

Y

Yaba pox virus disease B08.72
Yatapoxvirus B08.70
  specified NEC B08.79
Yawning R06.89
  psychogenic F45.8
Yaws A66.9
  bone lesions A66.6
  butter A66.1
  chancre A66.0
  cutaneous, less than five years after infection
    A66.2
  early (cutaneous) (macular) (maculopapular)
    (micropapular) (papular) A66.2
    frambeside A66.2
    skin lesions NEC A66.2
  eyelid A66.2
  ganglion A66.6
  gangosis, gangosa A66.5
  gumma, gummata A66.4
    bone A66.6
  gummatous
    frambeside A66.4
    osteitis A66.6
    periostitis A66.6
  hydrarthrosis —*see also* subcategory
    M14.8-● A66.6
  hyperkeratosis (early) (late) A66.3

Yaws (*Continued*)
  initial lesions A66.0
  joint lesions —*see also* subcategory
    M14.8-● A66.6
  juxta-articular nodules A66.7
  late nodular (ulcerated) A66.4
  latent (without clinical manifestations) (with
    positive serology) A66.8
  mother A66.0
  mucosal A66.7
  multiple papillomata A66.1
  nodular, late (ulcerated) A66.4
  osteitis A66.6
  papilloma, plantar or palmar A66.1
  periostitis (hypertrophic) A66.6
  specified NEC A66.7
  ulcers A66.4
  wet crab A66.1
Yeast infection —*see also* Candidiasis B37.9
Yellow
  atrophy (liver) —*see* Failure, hepatic
  fever —*see* Fever, yellow
  jack —*see* Fever, yellow
  jaundice —*see* Jaundice
  nail syndrome L60.5
Yersiniosis —*see also* Infection, Yersinia
  extraintestinal A28.2
  intestinal A04.6

Z

Zahorsky's syndrome (herpangina) B08.5
Zellweger's syndrome E71.510
Zenker's diverticulum (esophagus) K22.5
Ziehen-Oppenheim disease G24.1
Zieve's syndrome K70.0
Zika NOS A92.5
  congenital P35.4
Zinc
  deficiency, dietary E60
  metabolism disorder E83.2
Zollinger-Ellison syndrome E16.4
Zona —*see* Herpes, zoster
Zoophobia F40.218
Zoster (herpes) —*see* Herpes, zoster
Zygomycosis B46.9
  specified NEC B46.8
Zymotic —*see* condition

▶ New   ⟾ Revised   ~~deleted~~ Deleted   ● Use Additional Character(s)

ICD-10-CM
Table of Neoplasms

ICD-10-CM
Table of Neoplasms

The list below gives the code numbers for neoplasms by anatomical site. For each site there are six possible code numbers according to whether the neoplasm in question is malignant, benign, in situ, of uncertain behavior, or of unspecified nature. The description of the neoplasm will often indicate which of the six columns is appropriate; e.g., malignant melanoma of skin, benign fibroadenoma of breast, carcinoma in situ of cervix uteri.

Where such descriptors are not present, the remainder of the Index should be consulted where guidance is given to the appropriate column for each morphological (histological) variety listed; e.g., Mesonephroma—see Neoplasm, malignant; Embryoma—see also Neoplasm, uncertain behavior; Disease, Bowen's—see Neoplasm, skin, in situ. However, the guidance in the Index can be overridden if one of the descriptors mentioned above is present; e.g., malignant adenoma of colon is coded to C18.9 and not to D12.6 as the adjective "Malignant" overrides the Index entry 'Adenoma—see also Neoplasm, benign.'

Codes listed with a dash -, following the code have a required additional character for laterality. The Tablular must be reviewed for the complete code.

	Malignant Primary	Malignant Secondary	Ca in situ	Benign	Uncertain Behavior	Unspecified Behavior
Neoplasm, neoplastic	C80.1	C79.9	D09.9	D36.9	D48.9	D49.9
abdomen, abdominal	C76.2	C79.8-●	D09.8	D36.7	D48.7	D49.89
cavity	C76.2	C79.8-●	D09.8	D36.7	D48.7	D49.89
organ	C76.2	C79.8-●	D09.8	D36.7	D48.7	D49.89
viscera	C76.2	C79.8-●	D09.8	D36.7	D48.7	D49.89
wall—see also Neoplasm, abdomen, wall, skin	C44.509	C79.2-●	D04.5	D23.5	D48.5	D49.2
connective tissue	C49.4	C79.8-●	—	D21.4	D48.1	D49.2
skin	C44.509					
basal cell carcinoma	C44.519	—	—	—	—	—
specified type NEC	C44.599	—	—	—	—	—
squamous cell carcinoma	C44.529	—	—	—	—	—
abdominopelvic	C76.8	C79.8-●	—	D36.7	D48.7	D49.89
accessory sinus—see Neoplasm, sinus						
acoustic nerve	C72.4-●	C79.49	—	D33.3	D43.3	D49.7
adenoid (pharynx) (tissue)	C11.1	C79.89	D00.08	D10.6	D37.05	D49.0
adipose tissue—see also Neoplasm, connective tissue	C49.4	C79.89	—	D21.9	D48.1	D49.2
adnexa (uterine)	C57.4	C79.89	D07.39	D28.7	D39.8	D49.59
adrenal	C74.9-●	C79.7-●	D09.3	D35.0-●	D44.1-●	D49.7
capsule	C74.9-●	C79.7-●	D09.3	D35.0-●	D44.1-●	D49.7
cortex	C74.0-●	C79.7-●	D09.3	D35.0-●	D44.1-●	D49.7
gland	C74.9-●	C79.7-●	D09.3	D35.0-●	D44.1-●	D49.7
medulla	C74.1-●	C79.7-●	D09.3	D35.0-●	D44.1-●	D49.7
ala nasi (external)—see also Neoplasm, skin, nose	C44.301	C79.2	D04.39	D23.39	D48.5	D49.2

	Malignant Primary	Malignant Secondary	Ca in situ	Benign	Uncertain Behavior	Unspecified Behavior
alimentary canal or tract NEC	C26.9	C78.80	D01.9	D13.9	D37.9	D49.0
alveolar	C03.9	C79.89	D00.03	D10.39	D37.09	D49.0
mucosa	C03.9	C79.89	D00.03	D10.39	D37.09	D49.0
lower	C03.1	C79.89	D00.03	D10.39	D37.09	D49.0
upper	C03.0	C79.89	D00.03	D10.39	D37.09	D49.0
ridge or process	C41.1	C79.51	—	D16.5-●	D48.0	D49.2
carcinoma	C03.9	C79.8-●	—	—	—	—
lower	C03.1	C79.8-●	—	—	—	—
upper	C03.0	C79.8-●	—	—	—	—
lower	C41.1	C79.51	—	D16.5-●	D48.0	D49.2
mucosa	C03.9	C79.89	D00.03	D10.39	D37.09	D49.0
lower	C03.1	C79.89	D00.03	D10.39	D37.09	D49.0
upper	C03.0	C79.89	D00.03	D10.39	D37.09	D49.0
upper	C41.0	C79.51	—	D16.4-●	D48.0	D49.2
sulcus	C06.1	C79.89	D00.02	D10.39	D37.09	D49.0
alveolus	C03.9	C79.89	D00.03	D10.39	D37.09	D49.0
lower	C03.1	C79.89	D00.03	D10.39	D37.09	D49.0
upper	C03.0	C79.89	D00.03	D10.39	D37.09	D49.0
ampulla of Vater	C24.1	C78.89	D01.5	D13.5	D37.6	D49.0
ankle NEC	C76.5-●	C79.89	D04.7-●	D36.7	D48.7	D49.89
anorectum, anorectal (junction)	C21.8	C78.5	D01.3	D12.9	D37.8	D49.0
antecubital fossa or space	C76.4-●	C79.89	D04.6-●	D36.7	D48.7	D49.89
antrum (Highmore) (maxillary)	C31.0	C78.39	D02.3	D14.0	D38.5	D49.1
pyloric	C16.3	C78.89	D00.2	D13.1	D37.1	D49.0
tympanicum	C30.1	C78.39	D02.3	D14.0	D38.5	D49.1
anus, anal	C21.0	C78.5	D01.3	D12.9	D37.8	D49.0
canal	C21.1	C78.5	D01.3	D12.9	D37.8	D49.0
cloacogenic zone	C21.2	C78.5	D01.3	D12.9	D37.8	D49.0
margin—see also Neoplasm, anus, skin	C44.500	C79.2	D04.5	D23.5	D48.5	D49.2
overlapping lesion with rectosigmoid junction or rectum	C21.8	—	—	—	—	—
skin	C44.500	C79.2	D04.5	D23.5	D48.5	D49.2
basal cell carcinoma	C44.510	—	—	—	—	—
specified type NEC	C44.590	—	—	—	—	—
squamous cell carcinoma	C44.520	—	—	—	—	—
sphincter	C21.1	C78.5	D01.3	D12.9	D37.8	D49.0
aorta (thoracic)	C49.3	C79.89	—	D21.3	D48.1	D49.2
abdominal	C49.4	C79.89	—	D21.4	D48.1	D49.2
aortic body	C75.5	C79.89	—	D35.6	D44.7	D49.7
aponeurosis	C49.9	C79.89	—	D21.9	D48.1	D49.2
palmar	C49.1-●	C79.89	—	D21.1-●	D48.1	D49.2
plantar	C49.2-●	C79.89	—	D21.2-●	D48.1	D49.2

TABLE OF NEOPLASMS

TABLE OF NEOPLASMS

	Malignant Primary	Malignant Secondary	Ca in situ	Benign	Uncertain Behavior	Unspecified Behavior
appendix	C18.1	C78.5	D01.0	D12.1	D37.3	D49.0
arachnoid	C70.9	C79.49	—	D32.9	D42.9	D49.7
cerebral	C70.0	C79.32	—	D32.0	D42.0	D49.7
spinal	C70.1	C79.49	—	D32.1	D42.1	D49.7
areola	C50.0-●	C79.81	D05.-●	D24.-●	D48.6-●	D49.3
arm NEC	C76.4-●	C79.89	D04.6-●	D36.7	D48.7	D49.89
artery — see Neoplasm, connective tissue						
aryepiglottic fold	C13.1	C79.89	D00.08	D10.7	D37.05	D49.0
hypopharyngeal aspect	C13.1	C79.89	D00.08	D10.7	D37.05	D49.0
laryngeal aspect	C32.1	C78.39	D02.0	D14.1	D38.0	D49.1
marginal zone	C13.1	C79.89	D00.08	D10.7	D37.05	D49.0
arytenoid (cartilage)	C32.3	C78.39	D02.0	D14.1	D38.0	D49.1
fold — see Neoplasm, aryepiglottic						
associated with transplanted organ	C80.2	—	—	—	—	—
atlas	C41.2	C79.51	—	D16.6	D48.0	D49.2
atrium, cardiac	C38.0	C79.89		D15.1	D48.7	D49.89
auditory						
canal (external) (skin)	C44.20-●	C79.2	D04.2-●	D23.2-●	D48.5	D49.2
internal	C30.1	C78.39	D02.3	D14.0	D38.5	D49.1
nerve	C72.4-●	C79.49	—	D33.3	D43.3	D49.7
tube	C30.1	C78.39	D02.3	D14.0	D38.5	D49.1
opening	C11.2	C79.89	D00.08	D10.6	D37.05	D49.0
auricle, ear — see also Neoplasm, skin, ear	C44.20-●	C79.2	D04.2-●	D23.2-●	D48.5	D49.2
auricular canal (external) — see also Neoplasm, skin, ear	C44.20-●	C79.2	D04.2-●	D23.2-●	D48.5	D49.2
internal	C30.1	C78.39	D02.3	D14.0	D38.5	D49.2
autonomic nerve or nervous system NEC (see Neoplasm, nerve, peripheral)						
axilla, axillary	C76.1	C79.89	D09.8	D36.7	D48.7	D49.89
fold — see also Neoplasm, skin, trunk	C44.509	C79.2	D04.5	D23.5	D48.5	D49.2
back NEC	C76.8	C79.89	D04.5	D36.7	D48.7	D49.89
Bartholin's gland	C51.0	C79.82	D07.1	D28.0	D39.8	D49.59
basal ganglia	C71.0	C79.31	—	D33.0	D43.0	D49.6
basis pedunculi	C71.7	C79.31	—	D33.1	D43.1	D49.6
bile or biliary (tract)	C24.9	C78.89	D01.5	D13.5	D37.6	D49.0
canaliculi (biliferi) (intrahepatic)	C22.1	C78.7	D01.5	D13.4	D37.6	D49.0
canals, interlobular	C22.1	C78.89	D01.5	D13.4	D37.6	D49.0

	Malignant Primary	Malignant Secondary	Ca in situ	Benign	Uncertain Behavior	Unspecified Behavior
bile or biliary (Continued)						
duct or passage (common) (cystic) (extrahepatic)	C24.0	C78.89	D01.5	D13.5	D37.6	D49.0
interlobular	C22.1	C78.89	D01.5	D13.4	D37.6	D49.0
intrahepatic	C22.1	C78.7	D01.5	D13.4	D37.6	D49.0
and extrahepatic	C24.8	C78.89	D01.5	D13.5	D37.6	D49.0
bladder (urinary)	C67.9	C79.11	D09.0	D30.3	D41.4	D49.4
dome	C67.1	C79.11	D09.0	D30.3	D41.4	D49.4
neck	C67.5	C79.11	D09.0	D30.3	D41.4	D49.4
orifice	C67.9	C79.11	D09.0	D30.3	D41.4	D49.4
ureteric	C67.6	C79.11	D09.0	D30.3	D41.4	D49.4
urethral	C67.5	C79.11	D09.0	D30.3	D41.4	D49.4
overlapping lesion	C67.8	—	—	—	—	—
sphincter	C67.8	C79.11	D09.0	D30.3	D41.4	D49.4
trigone	C67.0	C79.11	D09.0	D30.3	D41.4	D49.4
urachus	C67.7	C79.11	D09.0	D30.3	D41.4	D49.4
wall	C67.9	C79.11	D09.0	D30.3	D41.4	D49.4
anterior	C67.3	C79.11	D09.0	D30.3	D41.4	D49.4
lateral	C67.2	C79.11	D09.0	D30.3	D41.4	D49.4
posterior	C67.4	C79.11	D09.0	D30.3	D41.4	D49.4
blood vessel — see Neoplasm, connective tissue						
bone (periosteum)	C41.9	C79.51	—	D16.9-●	D48.0	D49.2
acetabulum	C41.4	C79.51	—	D16.8-●	D48.0	D49.2
ankle	C40.3-●	C79.51	—	D16.3-●	—	—
arm NEC	C40.0-●	C79.51	—	D16.0-●	—	—
astragalus	C40.3-●	C79.51	—	D16.3-●	—	—
atlas	C41.2	C79.51	—	D16.6-●	D48.0	D49.2
axis	C41.2	C79.51	—	D16.6-●	D48.0	D49.2
back NEC	C41.2	C79.51	—	D16.6-●	D48.0	D49.2
calcaneus	C40.3-●	C79.51	—	D16.3-●	—	—
calvarium	C41.0	C79.51	—	D16.4-●	D48.0	D49.2
carpus (any)	C40.1-●	C79.51	—	D16.1-●	—	—
cartilage NEC	C41.9	C79.51	—	D16.9-●	D48.0	D49.2
clavicle	C41.3	C79.51	—	D16.7-●	D48.0	D49.2
clivus	C41.0	C79.51	—	D16.4-●	D48.0	D49.2
coccygeal vertebra	C41.4	C79.51	—	D16.8-●	D48.0	D49.2
coccyx	C41.4	C79.51	—	D16.8-●	D48.0	D49.2
costal cartilage	C41.3	C79.51	—	D16.7-●	D48.0	D49.2
costovertebral joint	C41.3	C79.51	—	D16.7-●	D48.0	D49.2
cranial	C41.0	C79.51	—	D16.4-●	D48.0	D49.2
cuboid	C40.3-●	C79.51	—	D16.3-●	—	—
cuneiform	C41.9	C79.51	—	D16.9-●	D48.0	D49.2
elbow	C40.0-●	C79.51	—	D16.0-●	—	—

◀ New ◀ Revised ~~deleted~~ Deleted ● Use Additional Character(s)

bone *(Continued)*	Malignant Primary	Malignant Secondary	Ca in situ	Benign	Uncertain Behavior	Unspecified Behavior
ethmoid (labyrinth)	C41.0	C79.51	—	D16.4-●	D48.0	D49.2
face	C41.0	C79.51	—	D16.4-●	D48.0	D49.2
femur (any part)	C40.2-●	C79.51	—	D16.2-●	—	—
fibula (any part)	C40.2-●	C79.51	—	D16.2-●	—	—
finger (any)	C40.1-●	C79.51	—	D16.1-●	—	—
foot	C40.3-●	C79.51	—	D16.3-●	—	—
forearm	C40.0-●	C79.51	—	D16.0-●	—	—
frontal	C41.0	C79.51	—	D16.4-●	D48.0	D49.2
hand	C40.1-●	C79.51	—	D16.1-●	—	—
heel	C40.3-●	C79.51	—	D16.3-●	—	—
hip	C41.4	C79.51	—	D16.8-●	D48.0	D49.2
humerus (any part)	C40.0-●	C79.51	—	D16.0-●	—	—
hyoid	C41.0	C79.51	—	D16.4-●	D48.0	D49.2
ilium	C41.4	C79.51	—	D16.8-●	D48.0	D49.2
innominate	C41.4	C79.51	—	D16.8-●	D48.0	D49.2
intervertebral cartilage or disc	C41.2	C79.51	—	D16.6-●	D48.0	D49.2
ischium	C41.4	C79.51	—	D16.8-●	D48.0	D49.2
jaw (lower)	C41.1	C79.51	—	D16.5-●	D48.0	D49.2
knee	C40.2-●	C79.51	—	D16.2-●	—	—
leg NEC	C40.2-●	C79.51	—	D16.2-●	—	—
limb NEC	C40.9-●	C79.51	—	D16.9-●	—	—
lower (long bones)	C40.2-●	C79.51	—	D16.2-●	—	—
short bones	C40.3-●	C79.51	—	D16.3-●	—	—
upper (long bones)	C40.0-●	C79.51	—	D16.0-●	—	—
short bones	C40.1-●	C79.51	—	D16.1-●	—	—
malar	C41.0	C79.51	—	D16.4-●	D48.0	D49.2
mandible	C41.1	C79.51	—	D16.5-●	D48.0	D49.2
marrow NEC (any bone)	C96.9	C79.52	—	—	D47.9	D49.89
mastoid	C41.0	C79.51	—	D16.4-●	D48.0	D49.2
maxilla, maxillary (superior)	C41.0	C79.51	—	D16.4-●	D48.0	D49.2
inferior	C41.1	C79.51	—	D16.5-●	D48.0	D49.2
metacarpus (any)	C40.1-●	C79.51	—	D16.1-●	—	—
metatarsus (any)	C40.3-●	C79.51	—	D16.3-●	—	—
overlapping sites	C40.8-●	—	—	—	—	—
navicular						
ankle	C40.3-●	C79.51	—	—	—	—
hand	C40.1-●	C79.51	—	—	—	—
nose, nasal	C41.0	C79.51	—	D16.4-●	D48.0	D49.2
occipital	C41.0	C79.51	—	D16.4-●	D48.0	D49.2
orbit	C41.0	C79.51	—	D16.4-●	D48.0	D49.2
parietal	C41.0	C79.51	—	D16.4-●	D48.0	D49.2
patella	C40.2-●	C79.51	—	—	—	—
pelvic	C41.4	C79.51	—	D16.8	D48.0	D49.2

bone *(Continued)*	Malignant Primary	Malignant Secondary	Ca in situ	Benign	Uncertain Behavior	Unspecified Behavior
phalanges						
foot	C40.3-●	C79.51	—	—	—	—
hand	C40.1-●	C79.51	—	—	—	—
pubic	C41.4	C79.51	—	D16.8	D48.0	D49.2
radius (any part)	C40.0-●	C79.51	—	D16.0-●	—	—
rib	C41.3	C79.51	—	D16.7	D48.0	D49.2
sacral vertebra	C41.4	C79.51	—	D16.8	D48.0	D49.2
sacrum	C41.4	C79.51	—	D16.8	D48.0	D49.2
scaphoid	—	—	—	—	—	—
of ankle	C40.3-●	C79.51	—	—	—	—
of hand	C40.1-●	C79.51	—	—	—	—
scapula (any part)	C40.0-●	C79.51	—	D16.0-●	—	—
sella turcica	C41.0	C79.51	—	D16.4-●	D48.0	D49.2
shoulder	C40.0-●	C79.51	—	D16.0-●	—	—
skull	C41.0	C79.51	—	D16.4-●	D48.0	D49.2
sphenoid	C41.0	C79.51	—	D16.4-●	D48.0	D49.2
spine, spinal (column)	C41.2	C79.51	—	D16.6	D48.0	D49.2
coccyx	C41.4	C79.51	—	D16.8	D48.0	D49.2
sacrum	C41.4	C79.51	—	D16.8	D48.0	D49.2
sternum	C41.3	C79.51	—	D16.7	D48.0	D49.2
tarsus (any)	C40.3-●	C79.51	—	—	—	—
temporal	C41.0	C79.51	—	D16.4-●	D48.0	D49.2
thumb	C40.1-●	C79.51	—	—	—	—
tibia (any part)	C40.2-●	C79.51	—	—	—	—
toe (any)	C40.3-●	C79.51	—	—	—	—
trapezium	C40.1-●	C79.51	—	—	—	—
trapezoid	C40.1-●	C79.51	—	—	—	—
turbinate	C41.0	C79.51	—	D16.4-●	D48.0	D49.2
ulna (any part)	C40.0-●	C79.51	—	D16.0-●	—	—
unciform	C40.1-●	C79.51	—	—	—	—
vertebra (column)	C41.2	C79.51	—	D16.6	D48.0	D49.2
coccyx	C41.4	C79.51	—	D16.8	D48.0	D49.2
sacrum	C41.4	C79.51	—	D16.8	D48.0	D49.2
vomer	C41.0	C79.51	—	D16.4-●	D48.0	D49.2
wrist	C40.1-●	C79.51	—	—	—	—
xiphoid process	C41.3	C79.51	—	D16.7	D48.0	D49.2
zygomatic	C41.0	C79.51	—	D16.4-●	D48.0	D49.2
book-leaf (mouth)	C06.89	C79.89	D00.00	D10.39	D37.09	D49.0
bowel—*see Neoplasm, intestine*						
brachial plexus	C47.1-●	C79.89	—	D36.12	D48.2	D49.2
brain NEC	C71.9	C79.31	—	D33.2	D43.2	D49.6
basal ganglia	C71.0	C79.31	—	D33.0	D43.0	D49.6
cerebellopontine angle	C71.6	C79.31	—	D33.1	D43.1	D49.6

◀ New   ◀ Revised   ~~deleted~~ Deleted   ● Use Additional Character(s)

	Malignant Primary	Malignant Secondary	Ca in situ	Benign	Uncertain Behavior	Unspecified Behavior
brain NEC *(Continued)*						
cerebellum NOS	C71.6	C79.31	—	D33.1	D43.1	D49.6
cerebrum	C71.0	C79.31	—	D33.0	D43.0	D49.6
choroid plexus	C71.7	C79.31	—	D33.1	D43.1	D49.6
corpus callosum	C71.8	C79.31	—	D33.2	D43.2	D49.6
corpus striatum	C71.0	C79.31	—	D33.0	D43.0	D49.6
cortex (cerebral)	C71.0	C79.31	—	D33.0	D43.0	D49.6
frontal lobe	C71.1	C79.31	—	D33.0	D43.0	D49.6
globus pallidus	C71.0	C79.31	—	D33.0	D43.0	D49.6
hippocampus	C71.2	C79.31	—	D33.0	D43.0	D49.6
hypothalamus	C71.0	C79.31	—	D33.0	D43.0	D49.6
internal capsule	C71.0	C79.31	—	D33.0	D43.0	D49.6
medulla oblongata	C71.7	C79.31	—	D33.1	D43.1	D49.6
meninges	C70.0	C79.32	—	D32.0	D42.0	D49.7
midbrain	C71.7	C79.31	—	D33.1	D43.1	D49.6
occipital lobe	C71.4	C79.31	—	D33.0	D43.0	D49.6
overlapping lesion	C71.8	C79.31	—	—	—	—
parietal lobe	C71.3	C79.31	—	D33.0	D43.0	D49.6
peduncle	C71.7	C79.31	—	D33.1	D43.1	D49.6
pons	C71.7	C79.31	—	D33.1	D43.1	D49.6
stem	C71.7	C79.31	—	D33.1	D43.1	D49.6
tapetum	C71.8	C79.31	—	D33.2	D43.2	D49.6
temporal lobe	C71.2	C79.31	—	D33.0	D43.0	D49.6
thalamus	C71.0	C79.31	—	D33.0	D43.0	D49.6
uncus	C71.2	C79.31	—	D33.0	D43.0	D49.6
ventricle (floor)	C71.5	C79.31	—	D33.0	D43.0	D49.6
fourth	C71.7	C79.31	—	D33.1	D43.1	D49.6
branchial (cleft) (cyst) (vestiges)	C10.4	C79.89	D00.08	D10.5	D37.05	D49.0
breast (connective tissue) (glandular tissue) (soft parts)	C50.9-●	C79.81	D05.-●	D24.-●	D48.6-●	D49.3
areola	C50.0-●	C79.81	D05.-●	D24.-●	D48.6-●	D49.3
axillary tail	C50.6-●	C79.81	D05.-●	D24.-●	D48.6-●	D49.3
central portion	C50.1-●	C79.81	D05.-●	D24.-●	D48.6-●	D49.3
inner	C50.8-●	C79.81	D05.-●	D24.-●	D48.6-●	D49.3
lower	C50.8-●	C79.81	D05.-●	D24.-●	D48.6-●	D49.3
lower-inner quadrant	C50.3-●	C79.81	D05.-●	D24.-●	D48.6-●	D49.3
lower-outer quadrant	C50.5-●	C79.81	D05.-●	D24.-●	D48.6-●	D49.3
mastectomy site (skin) — *see also Neoplasm, breast, skin*	C44.501	C79.2	—	—	—	—
specified as breast tissue	C50.8-●	C79.81				
midline	C50.8-●	C79.81	D05.-●	D24.-●	D48.6-●	D49.3
nipple	C50.0-●	C79.81	D05.-●	D24.-●	D48.6-●	D49.3
outer	C50.8-●	C79.81	D05.-●	D24.-●	D48.6-●	D49.3
overlapping lesion	C50.8-●		—	—	—	—

	Malignant Primary	Malignant Secondary	Ca in situ	Benign	Uncertain Behavior	Unspecified Behavior
breast *(Continued)*						
skin	C44.501	C79.2	D04.5	D23.5	D48.5	D49.2
basal cell carcinoma	C44.511	—	—	—	—	—
specified type NEC	C44.591	—	—	—	—	—
squamous cell carcinoma	C44.521	—	—	—	—	—
tail (axillary)	C50.6-●	C79.81	D05.-●	D24.-●	D48.6-●	D49.3
upper	C50.8-●	C79.81	D05.-●	D24.-●	D48.6-●	D49.3
upper-inner quadrant	C50.2-●	C79.81	D05.-●	D24.-●	D48.6-●	D49.3
upper-outer quadrant	C50.4-●	C79.81	D05.-●	D24.-●	D48.6-●	D49.3
broad ligament	C57.1	C79.82	D07.39	D28.2	D39.8	D49.59
bronchiogenic, bronchogenic (lung)	C34.9-●	C78.0-●	D02.2-●	D14.3-●	D38.1	D49.1
bronchiole	C34.9-●	C78.0-●	D02.2-●	D14.3-●	D38.1	D49.1
bronchus	C34.9-●	C78.0-●	D02.2-●	D14.3-●	D38.1	D49.1
carina	C34.0-●	C78.0-●	D02.2-●	D14.3-●	D38.1	D49.1
lower lobe of lung	C34.3-●	C78.0-●	D02.2-●	D14.3-●	D38.1	D49.1
main	C34.0-●	C78.0-●	D02.2-●	D14.3-●	D38.1	D49.1
middle lobe of lung	C34.2	C78.0-●	D02.21	D14.31	D38.1	D49.1
overlapping lesion	C34.8-●	—	—	—	—	—
upper lobe of lung	C34.1-●	C78.0-●	D02.2-●	D14.3-●	D38.1	D49.1
brow	C44.309	C79.2	D04.39	D23.39	D48.5	D49.2
basal cell carcinoma	C44.319	—	—	—	—	—
specified type NEC	C44.399	—	—	—	—	—
squamous cell carcinoma	C44.329	—	—	—	—	—
buccal (cavity)	C06.9	C79.89	D00.00	D10.39	D37.09	D49.0
commissure	C06.0	C79.89	D00.02	D10.39	D37.09	D49.0
groove (lower) (upper)	C06.1	C79.89	D00.02	D10.39	D37.09	D49.0
mucosa	C06.0	C79.89	D00.02	D10.39	D37.09	D49.0
sulcus (lower) (upper)	C06.1	C79.89	D00.02	D10.39	D37.09	D49.0
bulbourethral gland	C68.0	C79.19	D09.19	D30.4	D41.3	D49.59
bursa — *see Neoplasm, connective tissue*						
buttock NEC	C76.3	C79.89	D04.5	D36.7	D48.7	D49.89
calf	C76.5-●	C79.89	D04.7-●	D36.7	D48.7	D49.89
calvarium	C41.0	C79.51	—	D16.4-●	D48.0	D49.2
calyx, renal	C65.-●	C79.0-●	D09.19	D30.1-●	D41.1-●	D49.51-●
canal						
anal	C21.1	C78.5	D01.3	D12.9	D37.8	D49.0
auditory (external) — *see also Neoplasm, skin, ear*	C44.20-●	C79.2	D04.2-●	D23.2-●	D48.5	D49.2
auricular (external) — *see also Neoplasm, skin, ear*	C44.20-●	C79.2	D04.2-●	D23.2-●	D48.5	D49.2
canaliculi, biliary (biliferi) (intrahepatic)	C22.1	C78.7	D01.5	D13.4	D37.6	D49.0

◀ New　◀ Revised　~~deleted~~ Deleted　● Use Additional Character(s)

	Malignant Primary	Malignant Secondary	Ca in situ	Benign	Uncertain Behavior	Unspecified Behavior
canthus (eye) (inner) (outer)	C44.10-●	C79.2	D04.1-●	D23.1-●	D48.5	D49.2
basal cell carcinoma	C44.11-●	—	—	—	—	—
sebaceous cell	C44.13-●	—	—	—	—	—
specified type NEC	C44.19-●	—	—	—	—	—
squamous cell carcinoma	C44.12-●	—	—	—	—	—
capillary — *see* Neoplasm, connective tissue						
caput coli	C18.0	C78.5	D01.0	D12.0	D37.4	D49.0
carcinoid — *see* Tumor, carcinoid						
cardia (gastric)	C16.0	C78.89	D00.2	D13.1	D37.1	D49.0
cardiac orifice (stomach)	C16.0	C78.89	D00.2	D13.1	D37.1	D49.0
cardio-esophageal junction	C16.0	C78.89	D00.2	D13.1	D37.1	D49.0
cardio-esophagus	C16.0	C78.89	D00.2	D13.1	D37.1	D49.0
carina (bronchus)	C34.0-●	C78.0-●	D02.2-●	D14.3-●	D38.1	D49.1
carotid (artery)	C49.0	C79.89	—	D21.0	D48.1	D49.2
body	C75.4	C79.89	—	D35.5	D44.6	D49.7
carpus (any bone)	C40.1-●	C79.51	—	D16.1-●	—	—
cartilage (articular) (joint) NEC — *see also* Neoplasm, bone	C41.9	C79.51	—	D16.9-●	D48.0	D49.2
arytenoid	C32.3	C78.39	D02.0	D14.1	D38.0	D49.1
auricular	C49.0	C79.89	—	D21.0	D48.1	D49.2
bronchi	C34.0-●	C78.39	—	D14.3-●	D38.1	D49.1
costal	C41.3	C79.51	—	D16.7	D48.0	D49.2
cricoid	C32.3	C78.39	D02.0	D14.1	D38.0	D49.1
cuneiform	C32.3	C78.39	D02.0	D14.1	D38.0	D49.1
ear (external)	C49.0	C79.89	—	D21.0	D48.1	D49.2
ensiform	C41.3	C79.51	—	D16.7	D48.0	D49.2
epiglottis	C32.1	C78.39	D02.0	D14.1	D38.0	D49.1
anterior surface	C10.1	C79.89	D00.08	D10.5	D37.05	D49.0
eyelid	C49.0	C79.89	—	D21.0	D48.1	D49.2
intervertebral	C41.2	C79.51	—	D16.6	D48.0	D49.2
larynx, laryngeal	C32.3	C78.39	D02.0	D14.1	D38.0	D49.1
nose, nasal	C30.0	C78.39	D02.3	D14.0	D38.5	D49.1
pinna	C49.0	C79.89	—	D21.0	D48.1	D49.2
rib	C41.3	C79.51	—	D16.7	D48.0	D49.2
semilunar (knee)	C40.2-●	C79.51	—	D16.2-●	D48.0	D49.2
thyroid	C32.3	C78.39	D02.0	D14.1	D38.0	D49.1
trachea	C33	C78.39	D02.1	D14.2	D38.1	D49.1
cauda equina	C72.1	C79.49	—	D33.4	D43.4	D49.7
cavity						
buccal	C06.9	C79.89	D00.00	D10.30	D37.09	D49.0
nasal	C30.0	C78.39	D02.3	D14.0	D38.5	D49.1
oral	C06.9	C79.89	D00.00	D10.30	D37.09	D49.0

	Malignant Primary	Malignant Secondary	Ca in situ	Benign	Uncertain Behavior	Unspecified Behavior
cavity *(Continued)*						
peritoneal	C48.2	C78.6	—	D20.1	D48.4	D49.0
tympanic	C30.1	C78.39	D02.3	D14.0	D38.5	D49.1
cecum	C18.0	C78.5	D01.0	D12.0	D37.4	D49.0
central nervous system	C72.9	C79.40	—	—	—	—
cerebellopontine (angle)	C71.6	C79.31	—	D33.1	D43.1	D49.6
cerebellum, cerebellar	C71.6	C79.31	—	D33.1	D43.1	D49.6
cerebrum, cerebra (cortex) (hemisphere) (white matter)	C71.0	C79.31	—	D33.0	D43.0	D49.6
meninges	C70.0	C79.32	—	D32.0	D42.0	D49.7
peduncle	C71.7	C79.31	—	D33.1	D43.1	D49.6
ventricle	C71.5	C79.31	—	D33.0	D43.0	D49.6
fourth	C71.7	C79.31	—	D33.1	D43.1	D49.6
cervical region	C76.0	C79.89	D09.8	D36.7	D48.7	D49.89
cervix (cervical) (uteri) (uterus)	C53.9	C79.82	D06.9	D26.0	D39.0	D49.59
canal	C53.0	C79.82	D06.0	D26.0	D39.0	D49.59
endocervix (canal) (gland)	C53.0	C79.82	D06.0	D26.0	D39.0	D49.59
exocervix	C53.1	C79.82	D06.1	D26.0	D39.0	D49.59
external os	C53.1	C79.82	D06.1	D26.0	D39.0	D49.59
internal os	C53.0	C79.82	D06.0	D26.0	D39.0	D49.59
nabothian gland	C53.0	C79.82	D06.0	D26.0	D39.0	D49.59
overlapping lesion	C53.8	—	—	—	—	—
squamocolumnar junction	C53.8	C79.82	D06.7	D26.0	D39.0	D49.59
stump	C53.8	C79.82	D06.7	D26.0	D39.0	D49.59
cheek	C76.0	C79.89	D09.8	D36.7	D48.7	D49.89
external	C44.309	C79.2	D04.39	D23.39	D48.5	D49.2
basal cell carcinoma	C44.319	—	—	—	—	—
specified type NEC	C44.399	—	—	—	—	—
squamous cell carcinoma	C44.329	—	—	—	—	—
inner aspect	C06.0	C79.89	D00.02	D10.39	D37.09	D49.0
internal	C06.0	C79.89	D00.02	D10.39	D37.09	D49.0
mucosa	C06.0	C79.89	D00.02	D10.39	D37.09	D49.0
chest (wall) NEC	C76.1	C79.89	D09.8	D36.7	D48.7	D49.89
chiasma opticum	C72.3-●	C79.49	—	D33.3	D43.3	D49.7
chin	C44.309	C79.2	D04.39	D23.39	D48.5	D49.2
basal cell carcinoma	C44.319	—	—	—	—	—
specified type NEC	C44.399	—	—	—	—	—
squamous cell carcinoma	C44.329	—	—	—	—	—
choana	C11.3	C79.89	D00.08	D10.6	D37.05	D49.0
cholangiole	C22.1	C78.89	D01.5	D13.4	D37.6	D49.0
choledochal duct	C24.0	C78.89	D01.5	D13.5	D37.6	D49.0
choroid	C69.3-●	C79.49	D09.2-●	D31.3-●	D48.7	D49.81
plexus	C71.5	C79.31	—	D33.0	D43.0	D49.6
ciliary body	C69.4-●	C79.49	D09.2-●	D31.4-●	D48.7	D49.89

◀ New　　◀ Revised　　~~deleted~~ Deleted　　● Use Additional Character(s)

TABLE OF NEOPLASMS

	Malignant Primary	Malignant Secondary	Ca in situ	Benign	Uncertain Behavior	Unspecified Behavior
clavicle	C41.3	C79.51	—	D16.7	D48.0	D49.2
clitoris	C51.2	C79.82	D07.1	D28.0	D39.8	D49.59
clivus	C41.0	C79.51	—	D16.4-●	D48.0	D49.2
cloacogenic zone	C21.2	C78.5	D01.3	D12.9	D37.8	D49.0
coccygeal						
body or glomus	C49.5	C79.89	—	D21.5	D48.1	D49.2
vertebra	C41.4	C79.51	—	D16.8	D48.0	D49.2
coccyx	C41.4	C79.51	—	D16.8	D48.0	D49.2
colon — see also Neoplasm, intestine, large	C18.9	C78.5	—	—	—	—
with rectum	C19	C78.5	D01.1	D12.7	D37.5	D49.0
column, spinal — see Neoplasm, spine						
columnella — see also Neoplasm, skin, face	C44.390	C79.2	D04.39	D23.39	D48.5	D49.2
commissure						
labial, lip	C00.6	C79.89	D00.01	D10.39	D37.01	D49.0
laryngeal	C32.0	C78.39	D02.0	D14.1	D38.0	D49.1
common (bile) duct	C24.0	C78.89	D01.5	D13.5	D37.6	D49.0
concha — see also Neoplasm, skin, ear	C44.20-●	C79.2	D04.2-●	D23.2-●	D48.5	D49.2
nose	C30.0	C78.39	D02.3	D14.0	D38.5	D49.1
conjunctiva	C69.0-●	C79.49	D09.2-●	D31.0-●	D48.7	D49.89
connective tissue NEC	C49.9	C79.89	—	D21.9	D48.1	D49.2

Note: For neoplasms of connective tissue (blood vessel, bursa, fascia, ligament, muscle, peripheral nerves, sympathetic and parasympathetic nerves and ganglia, synovia, tendon, etc.) or of morphological types that indicate connective tissue, code according to the list under "Neoplasm, connective tissue." For sites that do not appear in this list, code to neoplasm of that site; e.g., fibrosarcoma, pancreas (C25.9)

Note: Morphological types that indicate connective tissue appear in their proper place in the alphabetic index with the instruction "see Neoplasm, connective tissue ...."

	Malignant Primary	Malignant Secondary	Ca in situ	Benign	Uncertain Behavior	Unspecified Behavior
abdomen	C49.4	C79.89	—	D21.4	D48.1	D49.2
abdominal wall	C49.4	C79.89	—	D21.4	D48.1	D49.2
ankle	C49.2-●	C79.89	—	D21.2-●	D48.1	D49.2
antecubital fossa or space	C49.1-●	C79.89	—	D21.1-●	D48.1	D49.2
arm	C49.1-●	C79.89	—	D21.1-●	D48.1	D49.2
auricle (ear)	C49.0	C79.89	—	D21.0	D48.1	D49.2
axilla	C49.3	C79.89	—	D21.3	D48.1	D49.2
back	C49.6	C79.89	—	D21.6	D48.1	D49.2
breast — see Neoplasm, breast						
buttock	C49.5	C79.89	—	D21.5	D48.1	D49.2
calf	C49.2-●	C79.89	—	D21.2-●	D48.1	D49.2
cervical region	C49.0	C79.89	—	D21.0	D48.1	D49.2

	Malignant Primary	Malignant Secondary	Ca in situ	Benign	Uncertain Behavior	Unspecified Behavior
connective tissue NEC (Continued)						
cheek	C49.0	C79.89	—	D21.0	D48.1	D49.2
chest (wall)	C49.3	C79.89	—	D21.3	D48.1	D49.2
chin	C49.0	C79.89	—	D21.0	D48.1	D49.2
diaphragm	C49.3	C79.89	—	D21.3	D48.1	D49.2
ear (external)	C49.0	C79.89	—	D21.0	D48.1	D49.2
elbow	C49.1-●	C79.89	—	D21.1-●	D48.1	D49.2
extrarectal	C49.5	C79.89	—	D21.5	D48.1	D49.2
extremity	C49.9	C79.89	—	D21.9	D48.1	D49.2
lower	C49.2-●	C79.89	—	D21.2-●	D48.1	D49.2
upper	C49.1-●	C79.89	—	D21.1-●	D48.1	D49.2
eyelid	C49.0	C79.89	—	D21.0	D48.1	D49.2
face	C49.0	C79.89	—	D21.0	D48.1	D49.2
finger	C49.1-●	C79.89	—	D21.1-●	D48.1	D49.2
flank	C49.6	C79.89	—	D21.6	D48.1	D49.2
foot	C49.2-●	C79.89	—	D21.2-●	D48.1	D49.2
forearm	C49.1-●	C79.89	—	D21.1-●	D48.1	D49.2
forehead	C49.0	C79.89	—	D21.0	D48.1	D49.2
gastric	C49.4	C79.89	—	D21.4	D48.1	D49.2
gastrointestinal	C49.4	C79.89	—	D21.4	D48.1	D49.2
gluteal region	C49.5	C79.89	—	D21.5	D48.1	D49.2
great vessels NEC	C49.3	C79.89	—	D21.3	D48.1	D49.2
groin	C49.5	C79.89	—	D21.5	D48.1	D49.2
hand	C49.1-●	C79.89	—	D21.1-●	D48.1	D49.2
head	C49.0	C79.89	—	D21.0	D48.1	D49.2
heel	C49.2-●	C79.89	—	D21.2-●	D48.1	D49.2
hip	C49.2-●	C79.89	—	D21.2-●	D48.1	D49.2
hypochondrium	C49.4	C79.89	—	D21.4	D48.1	D49.2
iliopsoas muscle	C49.5	C79.89	—	D21.5	D48.1	D49.2
infraclavicular region	C49.3	C79.89	—	D21.3	D48.1	D49.2
inguinal (canal) (region)	C49.5	C79.89	—	D21.5	D48.1	D49.2
intestinal	C49.4	C79.89	—	D21.4	D48.1	D49.2
intrathoracic	C49.3	C79.89	—	D21.3	D48.1	D49.2
ischiorectal fossa	C49.5	C79.89	—	D21.5	D48.1	D49.2
jaw	C03.9	C79.89	D00.03	D10.39	D48.1	D49.0
knee	C49.2-●	C79.89	—	D21.2-●	D48.1	D49.2
leg	C49.2-●	C79.89	—	D21.2-●	D48.1	D49.2
limb NEC	C49.9	C79.89	—	D21.9	D48.1	D49.2
lower	C49.2-●	C79.89	—	D21.2-●	D48.1	D49.2
upper	C49.1-●	C79.89	—	D21.1-●	D48.1	D49.2
nates	C49.5	C79.89	—	D21.5	D48.1	D49.2
neck	C49.0	C79.89	—	D21.0	D48.1	D49.2
orbit	C69.6-●	C79.49	D09.2-●	D31.6-●	D48.1	D49.89
overlapping lesion	C49.8	—	—	—	—	—

◀ New   ◀ Revised   deleted Deleted   ● Use Additional Character(s)

	Malignant Primary	Malignant Secondary	Ca in situ	Benign	Uncertain Behavior	Unspecified Behavior
connective tissue NEC *(Continued)*						
pararectal	C49.5	C79.89	—	D21.5	D48.1	D49.2
para-urethral	C49.5	C79.89	—	D21.5	D48.1	D49.2
paravaginal	C49.5	C79.89	—	D21.5	D48.1	D49.2
pelvis (floor)	C49.5	C79.89	—	D21.5	D48.1	D49.2
pelvo-abdominal	C49.8	C79.89	—	D21.6	D48.1	D49.2
perineum	C49.5	C79.89	—	D21.5	D48.1	D49.2
perirectal (tissue)	C49.5	C79.89	—	D21.5	D48.1	D49.2
periurethral (tissue)	C49.5	C79.89	—	D21.5	D48.1	D49.2
popliteal fossa or space	C49.2-●	C79.89	—	D21.2-●	D48.1	D49.2
presacral	C49.5	C79.89	—	D21.5	D48.1	D49.2
psoas muscle	C49.4	C79.89	—	D21.4	D48.1	D49.2
pterygoid fossa	C49.0	C79.89	—	D21.0	D48.1	D49.2
rectovaginal septum or wall	C49.5	C79.89	—	D21.5	D48.1	D49.2
rectovesical	C49.5	C79.89	—	D21.5	D48.1	D49.2
retroperitoneum	C48.0	C78.6	—	D20.0	D48.3	D49.0
sacrococcygeal region	C49.5	C79.89	—	D21.5	D48.1	D49.2
scalp	C49.0	C79.89	—	D21.0	D48.1	D49.2
scapular region	C49.3	C79.89	—	D21.3	D48.1	D49.2
shoulder	C49.1-●	C79.89	—	D21.1-●	D48.1	D49.2
skin (dermis) NEC—*see also Neoplasm, skin, by site*	C44.90	C79.2	D04.9	D23.9	D48.5	D49.2
stomach	C49.4	C79.89	—	D21.4	D48.1	D49.2
submental	C49.0	C79.89	—	D21.0	D48.1	D49.2
supraclavicular region	C49.0	C79.89	—	D21.0	D48.1	D49.2
temple	C49.0	C79.89	—	D21.0	D48.1	D49.2
temporal region	C49.0	C79.89	—	D21.0	D48.1	D49.2
thigh	C49.2-●	C79.89	—	D21.2-●	D48.1	D49.2
thoracic (duct) (wall)	C49.3	C79.89	—	D21.3	D48.1	D49.2
thorax	C49.3	C79.89	—	D21.3	D48.1	D49.2
thumb	C49.1-●	C79.89	—	D21.1-●	D48.1	D49.2
toe	C49.2-●	C79.89	—	D21.2-●	D48.1	D49.2
trunk	C49.6	C79.89	—	D21.6	D48.1	D49.2
umbilicus	C49.4	C79.89	—	D21.4	D48.1	D49.2
vesicorectal	C49.5	C79.89	—	D21.5	D48.1	D49.2
wrist	C49.1-●	C79.89	—	D21.1-●	D48.1	D49.2
conus medullaris	C72.0	C79.49	—	D33.4	D43.4	D49.7
cord (true) (vocal)	C32.0	C78.39	D02.0	D14.1	D38.0	D49.1
false	C32.1	C78.39	D02.0	D14.1	D38.0	D49.1
spermatic	C63.1-●	C79.82	D07.69	D29.8	D40.8	D49.59
spinal (cervical) (lumbar) (thoracic)	C72.0	C79.49	—	D33.4	D43.4	D49.7
cornea (limbus)	C69.1-●	C79.49	D09.2-●	D31.1-●	D48.7	D49.89
corpus						

	Malignant Primary	Malignant Secondary	Ca in situ	Benign	Uncertain Behavior	Unspecified Behavior
corpus *(Continued)*						
albicans	C56.-●	C79.6-●	D07.39	D27.-●	D39.1-●	D49.59
callosum, brain	C71.0	C79.31	—	D33.2	D43.2	D49.6
cavernosum	C60.2	C79.82	D07.4	D29.0	D40.8	D49.59
gastric	C16.2	C78.89	D00.2	D13.1	D37.1	D49.0
overlapping sites	C54.8	—	—	—	—	—
penis	C60.2	C79.82	D07.4	D29.0	D40.8	D49.59
striatum, cerebrum	C71.0	C79.31	—	D33.0	D43.0	D49.6
uteri	C54.9	C79.82	D07.0	D26.1	D39.0	D49.59
isthmus	C54.0	C79.82	D07.0	D26.1	D39.0	D49.59
cortex						
adrenal	C74.0-●	C79.7-●	D09.3	D35.0-●	D44.1-●	D49.7
cerebral	C71.0	C79.31	—	D33.0	D43.0	D49.6
costal cartilage	C41.3	C79.51	—	D16.7	D48.0	D49.2
costovertebral joint	C41.3	C79.51	—	D16.7	D48.0	D49.2
Cowper's gland	C68.0	C79.19	D09.19	D30.4	D41.3	D49.59
cranial (fossa, any)	C71.9	C79.31	—	D33.2	D43.2	D49.6
meninges	C70.0	C79.32	—	D32.0	D42.0	D49.7
nerve	C72.50	C79.49	—	D33.3	D43.3	D49.7
specified NEC	C72.59	C79.49	—	D33.3	D43.3	D49.7
craniobuccal pouch	C75.2	C79.89	D09.3	D35.2	D44.3	D49.7
craniopharyngeal (duct) (pouch)	C75.2	C79.89	D09.3	D35.3	D44.4	D49.7
cricoid	C13.0	C79.89	D00.08	D10.7	D37.05	D49.0
cartilage	C32.3	C78.39	D02.0	D14.1	D38.0	D49.1
cricopharynx	C13.0	C79.89	D00.08	D10.7	D37.05	D49.0
crypt of Morgagni	C21.8	C78.5	D01.3	D12.9	D37.8	D49.0
crystalline lens	C69.4-●	C79.49	D09.2-●	D31.4-●	D48.7	D49.89
cul-de-sac (Douglas')	C48.1	C78.6	—	D20.1	D48.4	D49.0
cuneiform cartilage	C32.3	C78.39	D02.0	D14.1	D38.0	D49.1
cutaneous—*see Neoplasm, skin*						
cutis—*see Neoplasm, skin*						
cystic (bile) duct (common)	C24.0	C78.89	D01.5	D13.5	D37.6	D49.0
dermis—*see Neoplasm, skin*						
diaphragm	C49.3	C79.89	—	D21.3	D48.1	D49.2
digestive organs, system, tube, or tract NEC	C26.9	C78.89	D01.9	D13.9	D37.9	D49.0
disc, intervertebral	C41.2	C79.51	—	D16.6	D48.0	D49.2
disease, generalized	C80.0	—	—	—	—	—
disseminated	C80.0	—	—	—	—	—
Douglas' cul-de-sac or pouch	C48.1	C78.6	—	D20.1	D48.4	D49.0
duodenojejunal junction	C17.8	C78.4	D01.49	D13.39	D37.2	D49.0
duodenum	C17.0	C78.4	D01.49	D13.2	D37.2	D49.0

TABLE OF NEOPLASMS

TABLE OF NEOPLASMS

	Malignant Primary	Malignant Secondary	Ca in situ	Benign	Uncertain Behavior	Unspecified Behavior
dura (cranial) (mater)	C70.9	C79.49	—	D32.9	D42.9	D49.7
cerebral	C70.0	C79.32	—	D32.0	D42.0	D49.7
spinal	C70.1	C79.49	—	D32.1	D42.1	D49.7
ear (external) — see also Neoplasm, skin, ear	C44.20-●	C79.2	D04.2-●	D23.2-●	D48.5	D49.2
auricle or auris — see also Neoplasm, skin, ear	C44.20-●	C79.2	D04.2-●	D23.2-●	D48.5	D49.2
canal, external — see also Neoplasm, skin, ear	C44.20-●	C79.2	D04.2-●	D23.2-●	D48.5	D49.2
cartilage	C49.0	C79.89	—	D21.0	D48.1	D49.2
external meatus — see also Neoplasm, skin, ear	C44.20-●	C79.2	D04.2-●	D23.2-●	D48.5	D49.2
inner	C30.1	C78.39	D02.3	D14.0	D38.5	D49.1
lobule — see also Neoplasm, skin, ear	C44.20-●	C79.2	D04.2-●	D23.2-●	D48.5	D49.2
middle	C30.1	C78.39	D02.3	D14.0	D38.5	D49.1
overlapping lesion with accessory sinuses	C31.8	—	—	—	—	—
skin	C44.20-●	C79.2	D04.2-●	D23.2-●	D48.5	D49.2
basal cell carcinoma	C44.21-●	—	—	—	—	—
specified type NEC	C44.29-●	—	—	—	—	—
squamous cell carcinoma	C44.22-●	—	—	—	—	—
earlobe	C44.20-●	C79.2	D04.2-●	D23.2-●	D48.5	D49.2
basal cell carcinoma	C44.21-●	—	—	—	—	—
specified type NEC	C44.29-●	—	—	—	—	—
squamous cell carcinoma	C44.22-●	—	—	—	—	—
ejaculatory duct	C63.7	C79.82	D07.69	D29.8	D40.8	D49.59
elbow NEC	C76.4-●	C79.89	D04.6-●	D36.7	D48.7	D49.89
endocardium	C38.0	C79.89	—	D15.1	D48.7	D49.89
endocervix (canal) (gland)	C53.0	C79.82	D06.0	D26.0	D39.0	D49.59
endocrine gland NEC	C75.9	C79.89	D09.3	D35.9	D44.9	D49.7
pluriglandular	C75.8	C79.89	D09.3	D35.7	D44.9	D49.7
endometrium (gland) (stroma)	C54.1	C79.82	D07.0	D26.1	D39.0	D49.59
ensiform cartilage	C41.3	C79.51	—	D16.7	D48.0	D49.2
enteric — see Neoplasm, intestine						
ependyma (brain)	C71.5	C79.31	—	D33.0	D43.0	D49.6
fourth ventricle	C71.7	C79.31	—	D33.1	D43.1	D49.6
epicardium	C38.0	C79.89	—	D15.1	D48.7	D49.89
epididymis	C63.0-●	C79.82	D07.69	D29.3-●	D40.8	D49.59
epidural	C72.9	C79.49	—	D33.9	D43.9	D49.7
epiglottis	C32.1	C78.39	D02.0	D14.1	D38.0	D49.1
anterior aspect or surface	C10.1	C79.89	D00.08	D10.5	D37.05	D49.0
cartilage	C32.3	C78.39	D02.0	D14.1	D38.0	D49.1
free border (margin)	C10.1	C79.89	D00.08	D10.5	D37.05	D49.0
junctional region	C10.8	C79.89	D00.08	D10.5	D37.05	D49.0
posterior (laryngeal) surface	C32.1	C78.39	D02.0	D14.1	D38.0	D49.1
suprahyoid portion	C32.1	C78.39	D02.0	D14.1	D38.0	D49.1
esophagogastric junction	C16.0	C78.89	D00.2	D13.1	D37.1	D49.0
esophagus	C15.9	C78.89	D00.1	D13.0	D37.8	D49.0
abdominal	C15.5	C78.89	D00.1	D13.0	D37.8	D49.0
cervical	C15.3	C78.89	D00.1	D13.0	D37.8	D49.0
distal (third)	C15.5	C78.89	D00.1	D13.0	D37.8	D49.0
lower (third)	C15.5	C78.89	D00.1	D13.0	D37.8	D49.0
middle (third)	C15.4	C78.89	D00.1	D13.0	D37.8	D49.0
overlapping lesion	C15.8	—	—	—	—	—
proximal (third)	C15.3	C78.89	D00.1	D13.0	D37.8	D49.0
thoracic	C15.4	C78.89	D00.1	D13.0	D37.8	D49.0
upper (third)	C15.3	C78.89	D00.1	D13.0	D37.8	D49.0
ethmoid (sinus)	C31.1	C78.39	D02.3	D14.0	D38.5	D49.1
bone or labyrinth	C41.0	C79.51	—	D16.4-●	D48.0	D49.2
eustachian tube	C30.1	C78.39	D02.3	D14.0	D38.5	D49.1
exocervix	C53.1	C79.82	D06.1	D26.0	D39.0	D49.59
external						
meatus (ear) — see also Neoplasm, skin, ear	C44.20-●	C79.2	D04.2-●	D23.2-●	D48.5	D49.2
os, cervix uteri	C53.1	C79.82	D06.1	D26.0	D39.0	D49.59
extradural	C72.9	C79.49	—	D33.9	D43.9	D49.7
extrahepatic (bile) duct	C24.0	C78.89	D01.5	D13.5	D37.6	D49.0
overlapping lesion with gallbladder	C24.8	—	—	—	—	—
extraocular muscle	C69.6-●	C79.49	D09.2-●	D31.6-●	D48.7	D49.89
extrarectal	C76.3	C79.89	D09.8	D36.7	D48.7	D49.89
extremity	C76.8	C79.89	D04.8	D36.7	D48.7	D49.89
lower	C76.5-●	C79.89	D04.7-●	D36.7	D48.7	D49.89
upper	C76.4-●	C79.89	D04.6-●	D36.7	D48.7	D49.89
eye NEC	C69.9-●	C79.49	D09.2	D31.9	D48.7	D49.89
overlapping sites	C69.8	—	—	—	—	—
eyeball	C69.9-●	C79.49	D09.2-●	D31.9-●	D48.7	D49.89
eyebrow	C44.309	C79.2	D04.39	D23.39	D48.5	D49.2
basal cell carcinoma	C44.319	—	—	—	—	—
specified type NEC	C44.399	—	—	—	—	—
squamous cell carcinoma	C44.329	—	—	—	—	—
eyelid (lower) (skin) (upper)	C44.10-●	—	—	—	—	—
basal cell carcinoma	C44.11-●	—	—	—	—	—
cartilage	C49.0	C79.89	—	D21.0	D48.1	D49.2
sebaceous cell	C44.13-●	—	—	—	—	—
specified type NEC	C44.19-●	—	—	—	—	—
squamous cell carcinoma	C44.12-●	—	—	—	—	—

◀ New　◀ Revised　deleted Deleted　● Use Additional Character(s)

	Malignant Primary	Malignant Secondary	Ca in situ	Benign	Uncertain Behavior	Unspecified Behavior
face NEC	C76.0	C79.89	D04.39	D36.7	D48.7	D49.89
fallopian tube (accessory)	C57.0-●	C79.82	D07.39	D28.2	D39.8	D49.59
falx (cerebella) (cerebri)	C70.0	C79.32	—	D32.0	D42.0	D49.7
fascia — *see also Neoplasm, connective tissue*						
palmar	C49.1-●	C79.89	—	D21.1-●	D48.1	D49.2
plantar	C49.2-●	C79.89	—	D21.2-●	D48.1	D49.2
fatty tissue — *see Neoplasm, connective tissue*						
fauces, faucial NEC	C10.9	C79.89	D00.08	D10.5	D37.05	D49.0
pillars	C09.1	C79.89	D00.08	D10.5	D37.05	D49.0
tonsil	C09.9	C79.89	D00.08	D10.4	D37.05	D49.0
femur (any part)	C40.2-●	—	—	D16.2-●	—	—
fetal membrane	C58	C79.82	D07.0	D26.7	D39.2	D49.59
fibrous tissue — *see Neoplasm, connective tissue*						
fibula (any part)	C40.2-●	C79.51	—	D16.2-●	—	—
filum terminale	C72.0	C79.49	—	D33.4	D43.4	D49.7
finger NEC	C76.4-●	C79.89	D04.6-●	D36.7	D48.7	D49.89
flank NEC	C76.8	C79.89	D04.5	D36.7	D48.7	D49.89
follicle, nabothian	C53.0	C79.82	D06.0	D26.0	D39.0	D49.59
foot NEC	C76.5-●	C79.89	D04.7-●	D36.7	D48.7	D49.89
forearm NEC	C76.4-●	C79.89	D04.6-●	D36.7	D48.7	D49.89
forehead (skin)	C44.309	C79.2	D04.39	D23.39	D48.5	D49.2
basal cell carcinoma	C44.319	—	—	—	—	—
specified type NEC	C44.399	—	—	—	—	—
squamous cell carcinoma	C44.329	—	—	—	—	—
foreskin	C60.0	C79.82	D07.4	D29.0	D40.8	D49.59
fornix						
pharyngeal	C11.3	C79.89	D00.08	D10.6	D37.05	D49.0
vagina	C52	C79.82	D07.2	D28.1	D39.8	D49.59
fossa (of)						
anterior (cranial)	C71.9	C79.31	—	D33.2	D43.2	D49.6
cranial	C71.9	C79.31	—	D33.2	D43.2	D49.6
ischiorectal	C76.3	C79.89	D09.8	D36.7	D48.7	D49.89
middle (cranial)	C71.9	C79.31	—	D33.2	D43.2	D49.6
piriform	C12	C79.89	D00.08	D10.7	D37.05	D49.0
pituitary	C75.1	C79.89	D09.3	D35.2	D44.3	D49.7
posterior (cranial)	C71.9	C79.31	—	D33.2	D43.2	D49.6
pterygoid	C49.0	C79.89	—	D21.0	D48.1	D49.2
pyriform	C12	C79.89	D00.08	D10.7	D37.05	D49.0
Rosenmuller	C11.2	C79.89	D00.08	D10.6	D37.05	D49.0
tonsillar	C09.0	C79.89	D00.08	D10.5	D37.05	D49.0
fourchette	C51.9	C79.82	D07.1	D28.0	D39.8	D49.59

	Malignant Primary	Malignant Secondary	Ca in situ	Benign	Uncertain Behavior	Unspecified Behavior
frenulum						
labii — *see Neoplasm, lip, internal*						
linguae	C02.2	C79.89	D00.07	D10.1	D37.02	D49.0
frontal						
bone	C41.0	C79.51	—	D16.4-●	D48.0	D49.2
lobe, brain	C71.1	C79.31	—	D33.0	D43.0	D49.6
pole	C71.1	C79.31	—	D33.0	D43.0	D49.6
sinus	C31.2	C78.39	D02.3	D14.0	D38.5	D49.1
fundus						
stomach	C16.1	C78.89	D00.2	D13.1	D37.1	D49.0
uterus	C54.3	C79.82	D07.0	D26.1	D39.0	D49.59
gall duct (extrahepatic)	C24.0	C78.89	D01.5	D13.5	D37.6	D49.0
intrahepatic	C22.1	C78.7	D01.5	D13.4	D37.6	D49.0
gallbladder	C23	C78.89	D01.5	D13.5	D37.6	D49.0
overlapping lesion with extrahepatic bile ducts	C24.8					
ganglia — *see also Neoplasm, nerve, peripheral*	C47.9	C79.89	—	D36.10	D48.2	D49.2
basal	C71.0	C79.31	—	D33.0	D43.0	D49.6
cranial nerve	C72.50	C79.49	—	D33.3	D43.3	D49.7
Gartner's duct	C52	C79.82	D07.2	D28.1	D39.8	D49.59
gastric — *see Neoplasm, stomach*						
gastrocolic	C26.9	C78.89	D01.9	D13.9	D37.9	D49.0
gastroesophageal junction	C16.0	C78.89	D00.2	D13.1	D37.1	D49.0
gastrointestinal (tract) NEC	C26.9	C78.89	D01.9	D13.9	D37.9	D49.0
generalized	C80.0	—	—	—	—	—
genital organ or tract						
female NEC	C57.9	C79.82	D07.30	D28.9	D39.9	D49.59
overlapping lesion	C57.8	—	—	—	—	—
specified site NEC	C57.7	C79.82	D07.39	D28.7	D39.8	D49.59
male NEC	C63.9	C79.82	D07.60	D29.9	D40.9	D49.59
overlapping lesion	C63.8	—	—	—	—	—
specified site NEC	C63.7	C79.82	D07.69	D29.8	D40.8	D49.59
genitourinary tract						
female	C57.9	C79.82	D07.30	D28.9	D39.9	D49.59
male	C63.9	C79.82	D07.60	D29.9	D40.9	D49.59
gingiva (alveolar) (marginal)	C03.9	C79.89	D00.03	D10.39	D37.09	D49.0
lower	C03.1	C79.89	D00.03	D10.39	D37.09	D49.0
mandibular	C03.1	C79.89	D00.03	D10.39	D37.09	D49.0
maxillary	C03.0	C79.89	D00.03	D10.39	D37.09	D49.0
upper	C03.0	C79.89	D00.03	D10.39	D37.09	D49.0

	Malignant Primary	Malignant Secondary	Ca in situ	Benign	Uncertain Behavior	Unspecified Behavior
gland, glandular (lymphatic) (system) — see also Neoplasm, lymph gland						
endocrine NEC	C75.9	C79.89	D09.3	D35.9	D44.9	D49.7
salivary — see Neoplasm, salivary gland						
glans penis	C60.1	C79.82	D07.4	D29.0	D40.8	D49.59
globus pallidus	C71.0	C79.31	—	D33.0	D43.0	D49.6
glomus						
coccygeal	C49.5	C79.89	—	D21.5	D48.1	D49.2
jugularis	C75.5	C79.89	—	D35.6	D44.7	D49.7
glosso-epiglottic fold(s)	C10.1	C79.89	D00.08	D10.5	D37.05	D49.0
glossopalatine fold	C09.1	C79.89	D00.08	D10.5	D37.05	D49.0
glossopharyngeal sulcus	C09.0	C79.89	D00.08	D10.5	D37.05	D49.0
glottis	C32.0	C78.39	D02.0	D14.1	D38.0	D49.1
gluteal region	C76.3	C79.89	D04.5	D36.7	D48.7	D49.89
great vessels NEC	C49.3	C79.89	—	D21.3	D48.1	D49.2
groin NEC	C76.3	C79.89	D04.5	D36.7	D48.7	D49.89
gum	C03.9	C79.89	D00.03	D10.39	D37.09	D49.0
lower	C03.1	C79.89	D00.03	D10.39	D37.09	D49.0
upper	C03.0	C79.89	D00.03	D10.39	D37.09	D49.0
hand NEC	C76.4-●	C79.89	D04.6-●	D36.7	D48.7	D49.89
head NEC	C76.0	C79.89	D04.4	D36.7	D48.7	D49.89
heart	C38.0	C79.89	—	D15.1	D48.7	D49.89
heel NEC	C76.5-●	C79.89	D04.7-●	D36.7	D48.7	D49.89
helix — see also Neoplasm, skin, ear	C44.20-●	C79.2	D04.2-●	D23.2-●	D48.5	D49.2
hematopoietic, hemopoietic tissue NEC	C96.9	—	—	—	—	—
specified NEC	C96.Z	—	—	—	—	—
hemisphere, cerebral	C71.0	C79.31	—	D33.0	D43.0	D49.6
hemorrhoidal zone	C21.1	C78.5	D01.3	D12.9	D37.8	D49.0
hepatic — see also Index to disease, by histology	C22.9	C78.7	D01.5	D13.4	D37.6	D49.0
duct (bile)	C24.0	C78.89	D01.5	D13.5	D37.6	D49.0
flexure (colon)	C18.3	C78.5	D01.0	D12.3	D37.4	D49.0
primary	C22.8	C78.7	D01.5	D13.4	D37.6	D49.0
hepatobiliary	C24.9	C79.89	D01.5	D13.5	D37.6	D49.0
hepatoblastoma	C22.2	C78.7	D01.5	D13.4	D37.6	D49.0
hepatoma	C22.0	C78.7	D01.5	D13.4	D37.6	D49.0
hilus of lung	C34.0-●	C78.0-●	D02.2-●	D14.3-●	D38.1	D49.1
hip NEC	C76.5-●	C79.89	D04.7-●	D36.7	D48.7	D49.89
hippocampus, brain	C71.2	C79.31	—	D33.0	D43.0	D49.6
humerus (any part)	C40.0-●	C79.51	—	D16.0-●	—	—
hymen	C52	C79.82	D07.2	D28.1	D39.8	D49.59

	Malignant Primary	Malignant Secondary	Ca in situ	Benign	Uncertain Behavior	Unspecified Behavior
hypopharynx, hypopharyngeal NEC	C13.9	C79.89	D00.08	D10.7	D37.05	D49.0
overlapping lesion	C13.8	—	—	—	—	—
postcricoid region	C13.0	C79.89	D00.08	D10.7	D37.05	D49.0
posterior wall	C13.2	C79.89	D00.08	D10.7	D37.05	D49.0
pyriform fossa (sinus)	C12	C79.89	D00.08	D10.7	D37.05	D49.0
hypophysis	C75.1	C79.89	D09.3	D35.2	D44.3	D49.7
hypothalamus	C71.0	C79.31	—	D33.0	D43.0	D49.6
ileocecum, ileocecal (coil) (junction) (valve)	C18.0	C78.5	D01.0	D12.0	D37.4	D49.0
ileum	C17.2	C78.4	D01.49	D13.39	D37.2	D49.0
ilium	C41.4	C79.51	—	D16.8	D48.0	D49.2
immunoproliferative NEC	C88.9	—	—	—	—	—
infraclavicular (region)	C76.1	C79.89	D04.5	D36.7	D48.7	D49.89
inguinal (region)	C76.3	C79.89	D04.5	D36.7	D48.7	D49.89
insula	C71.0	C79.31	—	D33.0	D43.0	D49.6
insular tissue (pancreas)	C25.4	C78.89	D01.7	D13.7	D37.8	D49.0
brain	C71.0	C79.31	—	D33.0	D43.0	D49.6
interarytenoid fold	C13.1	C79.89	D00.08	D10.7	D37.05	D49.0
hypopharyngeal aspect	C13.1	C79.89	D00.08	D10.7	D37.05	D49.0
laryngeal aspect	C32.1	C78.39	D02.0	D14.1	D38.0	D49.1
marginal zone	C13.1	C79.89	D00.08	D10.7	D37.05	D49.0
interdental papillae	C03.9	C79.89	D00.03	D10.39	D37.09	D49.0
lower	C03.1	C79.89	D00.03	D10.39	D37.09	D49.0
upper	C03.0	C79.89	D00.03	D10.39	D37.09	D49.0
internal						
capsule	C71.0	C79.31	—	D33.0	D43.0	D49.6
os (cervix)	C53.0	C79.82	D06.0	D26.0	D39.0	D49.59
intervertebral cartilage or disc	C41.2	C79.51	—	D16.6	D48.0	D49.2
intestine, intestinal	C26.0	C78.80	D01.40	D13.9	D37.8	D49.0
large	C18.9	C78.5	D01.0	D12.6	D37.4	D49.0
appendix	C18.1	C78.5	D01.0	D12.1	D37.3	D49.0
caput coli	C18.0	C78.5	D01.0	D12.0	D37.4	D49.0
cecum	C18.0	C78.5	D01.0	D12.0	D37.4	D49.0
colon	C18.9	C78.5	D01.0	D12.6	D37.4	D49.0
and rectum	C19	C78.5	D01.1	D12.7	D37.5	D49.0
ascending	C18.2	C78.5	D01.0	D12.2	D37.4	D49.0
caput	C18.0	C78.5	D01.0	D12.0	D37.4	D49.0
descending	C18.6	C78.5	D01.0	D12.4	D37.4	D49.0
distal	C18.6	C78.5	D01.0	D12.4	D37.4	D49.0
left	C18.6	C78.5	D01.0	D12.4	D37.4	D49.0
overlapping lesion	C18.8	—	—	—	—	—
pelvic	C18.7	C78.5	D01.0	D12.5	D37.4	D49.0
right	C18.2	C78.5	D01.0	D12.2	D37.4	D49.0

◀ New   ◀ Revised   ~~deleted~~ Deleted   ● Use Additional Character(s)

	Malignant Primary	Malignant Secondary	Ca in situ	Benign	Uncertain Behavior	Unspecified Behavior
intestine, intestinal (Continued)						
large (Continued)						
colon (Continued)						
sigmoid (flexure)	C18.7	C78.5	D01.0	D12.5	D37.4	D49.0
transverse	C18.4	C78.5	D01.0	D12.3	D37.4	D49.0
hepatic flexure	C18.3	C78.5	D01.0	D12.3	D37.4	D49.0
ileocecum, ileocecal (coil) (valve)	C18.0	C78.5	D01.0	D12.0	D37.4	D49.0
overlapping lesion	C18.8	—	—	—	—	—
sigmoid flexure (lower) (upper)	C18.7	C78.5	D01.0	D12.5	D37.4	D49.0
splenic flexure	C18.5	C78.5	D01.0	D12.3	D37.4	D49.0
small	C17.9	C78.4	D01.40	D13.30	D37.2	D49.0
duodenum	C17.0	C78.4	D01.49	D13.2	D37.2	D49.0
ileum	C17.2	C78.4	D01.49	D13.39	D37.2	D49.0
jejunum	C17.1	C78.4	D01.49	D13.39	D37.2	D49.0
overlapping lesion	C17.8	—	—	—	—	—
tract NEC	C26.0	C78.89	D01.40	D13.9	D37.8	D49.0
intra-abdominal	C76.2	C79.89	D09.8	D36.7	D48.7	D49.89
intracranial NEC	C71.9	C79.31	—	D33.2	D43.2	D49.6
intrahepatic (bile) duct	C22.1	C78.7	D01.5	D13.4	D37.6	D49.0
intraocular	C69.9-●	C79.49	D09.2-●	D31.9-●	D48.7	D49.89
intraorbital	C69.6-●	C79.49	D09.2-●	D31.6-●	D48.7	D49.89
intrasellar	C75.1	C79.89	D09.3	D35.2	D44.3	D49.7
intrathoracic (cavity) (organs)	C76.1	C79.89	D09.8	D15.9	D48.7	D49.89
specified NEC	C76.1	C79.89	D09.8	D15.7	—	—
iris	C69.4-●	C79.49	D09.2-●	D31.4-●	D48.7	D49.89
ischiorectal (fossa)	C76.3	C79.89	D09.8	D36.7	D48.7	D49.89
ischium	C41.4	C79.51	—	D16.8	D48.0	D49.2
island of Reil	C71.0	C79.31	—	D33.0	D43.0	D49.6
islands or islets of Langerhans	C25.4	C78.89	D01.7	D13.7	D37.8	D49.0
isthmus uteri	C54.0	C79.82	D07.0	D26.1	D39.0	D49.59
jaw	C76.0	C79.89	D09.8	D36.7	D48.7	D49.89
bone	C41.1	C79.51	—	D16.5-●	D48.0	D49.2
lower	C41.1	C79.51	—	D16.5-●	—	—
upper	C41.0	C79.51	—	D16.4-●	—	—
carcinoma (any type) (lower) (upper)	C76.0	C79.89	—	—	—	—
skin — see also Neoplasm, skin, face	C44.309	C79.2	D04.39	D23.39	D48.5	D49.2
soft tissues	C03.9	C79.89	D00.03	D10.39	D37.09	D49.0
lower	C03.1	C79.89	D00.03	D10.39	D37.09	D49.0
upper	C03.0	C79.89	D00.03	D10.39	D37.09	D49.0
jejunum	C17.1	C78.4	D01.49	D13.39	D37.2	D49.0

	Malignant Primary	Malignant Secondary	Ca in situ	Benign	Uncertain Behavior	Unspecified Behavior
joint NEC — see also Neoplasm, bone	C41.9	C79.51	—	D16.9-●	D48.0	D49.2
acromioclavicular	C40.0-●	C79.51	—	D16.0-●	—	—
bursa or synovial membrane — see Neoplasm, connective tissue						
costovertebral	C41.3	C79.51	—	D16.7	D48.0	D49.2
sternocostal	C41.3	C79.51	—	D16.7	D48.0	D49.2
temporomandibular	C41.1	C79.51	—	D16.5-●	D48.0	D49.2
junction						
anorectal	C21.8	C78.5	D01.3	D12.9	D37.8	D49.0
cardioesophageal	C16.0	C78.89	D00.2	D13.1	D37.1	D49.0
esophagogastric	C16.0	C78.89	D00.2	D13.1	D37.1	D49.0
gastroesophageal	C16.0	C78.89	D00.2	D13.1	D37.1	D49.0
hard and soft palate	C05.9	C79.89	D00.00	D10.39	D37.09	D49.0
ileocecal	C18.0	C78.5	D01.0	D12.0	D37.4	D49.0
pelvirectal	C19	C78.5	D01.1	D12.7	D37.5	D49.0
pelviureteric	C65.-●	C79.0-●	D09.19	D30.1-●	D41.1-●	D49.59
rectosigmoid	C19	C78.5	D01.1	D12.7	D37.5	D49.0
squamocolumnar, of cervix	C53.8	C79.82	D06.7	D26.0	D39.0	D49.59
Kaposi's sarcoma — see Kaposi's, sarcoma						
kidney (parenchymal)	C64.-●	C79.0-●	D09.19	D30.0-●	D41.0-●	D49.51-●
calyx	C65.-●	C79.0-●	D09.19	D30.1-●	D41.1-●	D49.51-●
hilus	C65.-●	C79.0-●	D09.19	D30.1-●	D41.1-●	D49.51-●
pelvis	C65.-●	C79.0-●	D09.19	D30.1-●	D41.1-●	D49.51-●
knee NEC	C76.5-●	C79.89	D04.7-●	D36.7	D48.7	D49.89
labia (skin)	C51.9	C79.82	D07.1	D28.0	D39.8	D49.59
majora	C51.0	C79.82	D07.1	D28.0	D39.8	D49.59
minora	C51.1	C79.82	D07.1	D28.0	D39.8	D49.59
labial — see also Neoplasm, lip	C00.9	C79.89	D00.01	D10.0	D37.01	D49.0
sulcus (lower) (upper)	C06.1	C79.89	D00.02	D10.39	D37.09	D49.0
labium (skin)	C51.9	C79.82	D07.1	D28.0	D39.8	D49.59
majus	C51.0	C79.82	D07.1	D28.0	D39.8	D49.59
minus	C51.1	C79.82	D07.1	D28.0	D39.8	D49.59
lacrimal						
canaliculi	C69.5-●	C79.49	D09.2-●	D31.5-●	D48.7	D49.89
duct (nasal)	C69.5-●	C79.49	D09.2-●	D31.5-●	D48.7	D49.89
gland	C69.5-●	C79.49	D09.2-●	D31.5-●	D48.7	D49.89
punctum	C69.5-●	C79.49	D09.2-●	D31.5-●	D48.7	D49.89
sac	C69.5-●	C79.49	D09.2-●	D31.5-●	D48.7	D49.89
Langerhans, islands or islets	C25.4	C78.89	D01.7	D13.7	D37.8	D49.0
laryngopharynx	C13.9	C79.89	D00.08	D10.7	D37.05	D49.0

◄ New   ◄ Revised   ~~deleted~~ Deleted   ● Use Additional Character(s)

TABLE OF NEOPLASMS

	Malignant Primary	Malignant Secondary	Ca in situ	Benign	Uncertain Behavior	Unspecified Behavior
larynx, laryngeal NEC	C32.9	C78.39	D02.0	D14.1	D38.0	D49.1
aryepiglottic fold	C32.1	C78.39	D02.0	D14.1	D38.0	D49.1
cartilage (arytenoid) (cricoid) (cuneiform) (thyroid)	C32.3	C78.39	D02.0	D14.1	D38.0	D49.1
commissure (anterior) (posterior)	C32.0	C78.39	D02.0	D14.1	D38.0	D49.1
extrinsic NEC	C32.1	C78.39	D02.0	D14.1	D38.0	D49.1
meaning hypopharynx	C13.9	C79.89	D00.08	D10.7	D37.05	D49.0
interarytenoid fold	C32.1	C78.39	D02.0	D14.1	D38.0	D49.1
intrinsic	C32.0	C78.39	D02.0	D14.1	D38.0	D49.1
overlapping lesion	C32.8	—	—	—	—	—
ventricular band	C32.1	C78.39	D02.0	D14.1	D38.0	D49.1
leg NEC	C76.5-●	C79.89	D04.7-●	D36.7	D48.7	D49.89
lens, crystalline	C69.4-●	C79.49	D09.2-●	D31.4-●	D48.7	D49.89
lid (lower) (upper)	C44.10-●	C79.2	D04.1-●	D23.1-●	D48.5	D49.2
basal cell carcinoma	C44.11-●	—	—	—	—	—
sebaceous cell	C44.13-●	—	—	—	—	—
specified type NEC	C44.19-●	—	—	—	—	—
squamous cell carcinoma	C44.12-●	—	—	—	—	—
ligament — *see also Neoplasm, connective tissue*						
broad	C57.1	C79.82	D07.39	D28.2	D39.8	D49.59
Mackenrodt's	C57.7	C79.82	D07.39	D28.7	D39.8	D49.59
non-uterine — *see Neoplasm, connective tissue*						
round	C57.2	C79.82	—	D28.2	D39.8	D49.59
sacro-uterine	C57.3	C79.82	—	D28.2	D39.8	D49.59
uterine	C57.3	C79.82	—	D28.2	D39.8	D49.59
utero-ovarian	C57.7	C79.82	D07.39	D28.2	D39.8	D49.59
uterosacral	C57.3	C79.82	—	D28.2	D39.8	D49.59
limb	C76.8	C79.89	D04.8	D36.7	D48.7	D49.89
lower	C76.5-●	C79.89	D04.7-●	D36.7	D48.7	D49.89
upper	C76.4-●	C79.89	D04.6-●	D36.7	D48.7	D49.89
limbus of cornea	C69.1-●	C79.49	D09.2-●	D31.1-●	D48.7	D49.89
lingual NEC — *see also Neoplasm, tongue*	C02.9	C79.89	D00.07	D10.1	D37.02	D49.0
lingula, lung	C34.1-●	C78.0-●	D02.2-●	D14.3-●	D38.1	D49.1
lip	C00.9	C79.89	D00.01	D10.0	D37.01	D49.0
buccal aspect — *see Neoplasm, lip, internal*						
commissure	C00.6	C79.89	D00.01	D10.0	D37.01	D49.0
external	C00.2	C79.89	D00.01	D10.0	D37.01	D49.0
lower	C00.1	C79.89	D00.01	D10.0	D37.01	D49.0
upper	C00.0	C79.89	D00.01	D10.0	D37.01	D49.0
frenulum — *see Neoplasm, lip, internal*						

	Malignant Primary	Malignant Secondary	Ca in situ	Benign	Uncertain Behavior	Unspecified Behavior
lip *(Continued)*						
inner aspect — *see Neoplasm, lip, internal*						
internal	C00.5	C79.89	D00.01	D10.0	D37.01	D49.0
lower	C00.4	C79.89	D00.01	D10.0	D37.01	D49.0
upper	C00.3	C79.89	D00.01	D10.0	D37.01	D49.0
lipstick area	C00.2	C79.89	D00.01	D10.0	D37.01	D49.0
lower	C00.1	C79.89	D00.01	D10.0	D37.01	D49.0
upper	C00.0	C79.89	D00.01	D10.0	D37.01	D49.0
lower	C00.1	C79.89	D00.01	D10.0	D37.01	D49.0
internal	C00.4	C79.89	D00.01	D10.0	D37.01	D49.0
mucosa — *see Neoplasm, lip, internal*						
oral aspect — *see Neoplasm, lip, internal*						
overlapping lesion	C00.8	—	—	—	—	—
with oral cavity or pharynx	C14.8	—	—	—	—	—
skin (commissure) (lower) (upper)	C44.00	C79.2	D04.0	D23.0	D48.5	D49.2
basal cell carcinoma	C44.01	—	—	—	—	—
specified type NEC	C44.09	—	—	—	—	—
squamous cell carcinoma	C44.02	—	—	—	—	—
upper	C00.0	C79.89	D00.01	D10.0	D37.01	D49.0
internal	C00.3	C79.89	D00.01	D10.0	D37.01	D49.0
vermilion border	C00.2	C79.89	D00.01	D10.0	D37.01	D49.0
lower	C00.1	C79.89	D00.01	D10.0	D37.01	D49.0
upper	C00.0	C79.89	D00.01	D10.0	D37.01	D49.0
lipomatous — *see Lipoma, by site*						
liver — *see also Index to disease, by histology*	C22.9	C78.7	D01.5	D13.4	D37.6	D49.0
primary	C22.8	C78.7	D01.5	D13.4	D37.6	D49.0
lumbosacral plexus	C47.5	C79.89	—	D36.16	D48.2	D49.2
lung	C34.9-●	C78.0-●	D02.2-●	D14.3-●	D38.1	D49.1
azygos lobe	C34.1-●	C78.0-●	D02.2-●	D14.3-●	D38.1	D49.1
carina	C34.0-●	C78.0-●	D02.2-●	D14.3-●	D38.1	D49.1
hilus	C34.0-●	C78.0-●	D02.2-●	D14.3-●	D38.1	D49.1
lingula	C34.1-●	C78.0-●	D02.2-●	D14.3-●	D38.1	D49.1
lobe NEC	C34.9-●	C78.0-●	D02.2-●	D14.3-●	D38.1	D49.1
lower lobe	C34.3-●	C78.0-●	D02.2-●	D14.3-●	D38.1	D49.1
main bronchus	C34.0-●	C78.0-●	D02.2-●	D14.3-●	D38.1	D49.1
mesothelioma — *see Mesothelioma*						
middle lobe	C34.2	C78.0-●	D02.21	D14.31	D38.1	D49.1
overlapping lesion	C34.8-●	—	—	—	—	—
upper lobe	C34.1-●	C78.0-●	D02.2-●	D14.3-●	D38.1	D49.1

◀ New   ◀ Revised   ~~deleted~~ Deleted   ● Use Additional Character(s)

	Malignant Primary	Malignant Secondary	Ca in situ	Benign	Uncertain Behavior	Unspecified Behavior
lymph, lymphatic channel NEC	C49.9	C79.89	—	D21.9	D48.1	D49.2
gland (secondary)	—	C77.9	—	D36.0	D48.7	D49.89
abdominal	—	C77.2	—	D36.0	D48.7	D49.89
aortic	—	C77.2	—	D36.0	D48.7	D49.89
arm	—	C77.3	—	D36.0	D48.7	D49.89
auricular (anterior) (posterior)	—	C77.0	—	D36.0	D48.7	D49.89
axilla, axillary	—	C77.3	—	D36.0	D48.7	D49.89
brachial	—	C77.3	—	D36.0	D48.7	D49.89
bronchial	—	C77.1	—	D36.0	D48.7	D49.89
bronchopulmonary	—	C77.1	—	D36.0	D48.7	D49.89
celiac	—	C77.2	—	D36.0	D48.7	D49.89
cervical	—	C77.0	—	D36.0	D48.7	D49.89
cervicofacial	—	C77.0	—	D36.0	D48.7	D49.89
Cloquet	—	C77.4	—	D36.0	D48.7	D49.89
colic	—	C77.2	—	D36.0	D48.7	D49.89
common duct	—	C77.2	—	D36.0	D48.7	D49.89
cubital	—	C77.3	—	D36.0	D48.7	D49.89
diaphragmatic	—	C77.1	—	D36.0	D48.7	D49.89
epigastric, inferior	—	C77.1	—	D36.0	D48.7	D49.89
epitrochlear	—	C77.3	—	D36.0	D48.7	D49.89
esophageal	—	C77.1	—	D36.0	D48.7	D49.89
face	—	C77.0	—	D36.0	D48.7	D49.89
femoral	—	C77.4	—	D36.0	D48.7	D49.89
gastric	—	C77.2	—	D36.0	D48.7	D49.89
groin	—	C77.4	—	D36.0	D48.7	D49.89
head	—	C77.0	—	D36.0	D48.7	D49.89
hepatic	—	C77.2	—	D36.0	D48.7	D49.89
hilar (pulmonary)	—	C77.1	—	D36.0	D48.7	D49.89
splenic	—	C77.2	—	D36.0	D48.7	D49.89
hypogastric	—	C77.5	—	D36.0	D48.7	D49.89
ileocolic	—	C77.2	—	D36.0	D48.7	D49.89
iliac	—	C77.5	—	D36.0	D48.7	D49.89
infraclavicular	—	C77.3	—	D36.0	D48.7	D49.89
inguina, inguinal	—	C77.4	—	D36.0	D48.7	D49.89
innominate	—	C77.1	—	D36.0	D48.7	D49.89
intercostal	—	C77.1	—	D36.0	D48.7	D49.89
intestinal	—	C77.2	—	D36.0	D48.7	D49.89
intrabdominal	—	C77.2	—	D36.0	D48.7	D49.89
intrapelvic	—	C77.5	—	D36.0	D48.7	D49.89
intrathoracic	—	C77.1	—	D36.0	D48.7	D49.89
jugular	—	C77.0	—	D36.0	D48.7	D49.89
leg	—	C77.4	—	D36.0	D48.7	D49.89
limb						
lower	—	C77.4	—	D36.0	D48.7	D49.89
upper	—	C77.3	—	D36.0	D48.7	D49.89

	Malignant Primary	Malignant Secondary	Ca in situ	Benign	Uncertain Behavior	Unspecified Behavior
lymph, lymphatic channel NEC *(Continued)*						
gland *(Continued)*						
lower limb	—	C77.4	—	D36.0	D48.7	D49.89
lumbar	—	C77.2	—	D36.0	D48.7	D49.89
mandibular	—	C77.0	—	D36.0	D48.7	D49.89
mediastinal	—	C77.1	—	D36.0	D48.7	D49.89
mesenteric (inferior) (superior)	—	C77.2	—	D36.0	D48.7	D49.89
midcolic		C77.2	—	D36.0	D48.7	D49.89
multiple sites in categories C77.0 - C77.5	—	C77.8	—	D36.0	D48.7	D49.89
neck	—	C77.0	—	D36.0	D48.7	D49.89
obturator	—	C77.5	—	D36.0	D48.7	D49.89
occipital	—	C77.0	—	D36.0	D48.7	D49.89
pancreatic	—	C77.2	—	D36.0	D48.7	D49.89
para-aortic	—	C77.2	—	D36.0	D48.7	D49.89
paracervical	—	C77.5	—	D36.0	D48.7	D49.89
parametrial	—	C77.5	—	D36.0	D48.7	D49.89
parasternal	—	C77.1	—	D36.0	D48.7	D49.89
parotid	—	C77.0	—	D36.0	D48.7	D49.89
pectoral	—	C77.3	—	D36.0	D48.7	D49.89
pelvic	—	C77.5	—	D36.0	D48.7	D49.89
peri-aortic	—	C77.2	—	D36.0	D48.7	D49.89
peripancreatic	—	C77.2	—	D36.0	D48.7	D49.89
popliteal	—	C77.4	—	D36.0	D48.7	D49.89
porta hepatis	—	C77.2	—	D36.0	D48.7	D49.89
portal	—	C77.2	—	D36.0	D48.7	D49.89
preauricular	—	C77.0	—	D36.0	D48.7	D49.89
prelaryngeal	—	C77.0	—	D36.0	D48.7	D49.89
presymphysial	—	C77.5	—	D36.0	D48.7	D49.89
pretracheal	—	C77.0	—	D36.0	D48.7	D49.89
primary (any site) NEC	C96.9	—	—	—	—	—
pulmonary (hiler)	—	C77.1	—	D36.0	D48.7	D49.89
pyloric	—	C77.2	—	D36.0	D48.7	D49.89
retroperitoneal	—	C77.2	—	D36.0	D48.7	D49.89
retropharyngeal	—	C77.0	—	D36.0	D48.7	D49.89
Rosenmuller's	—	C77.4	—	D36.0	D48.7	D49.89
sacral	—	C77.5	—	D36.0	D48.7	D49.89
scalene	—	C77.0	—	D36.0	D48.7	D49.89
site NEC	—	C77.9	—	D36.0	D48.7	D49.89
splenic (hilar)	—	C77.2	—	D36.0	D48.7	D49.89
subclavicular	—	C77.3	—	D36.0	D48.7	D49.89
subinguinal	—	C77.4	—	D36.0	D48.7	D49.89

◀ New　◀ Revised　deleted Deleted　● Use Additional Character(s)

TABLE OF NEOPLASMS

	Malignant Primary	Malignant Secondary	Ca in situ	Benign	Uncertain Behavior	Unspecified Behavior
lymph, lymphatic channel NEC *(Continued)*						
gland *(Continued)*						
sublingual	—	C77.0	—	D36.0	D48.7	D49.89
submandibular	—	C77.0	—	D36.0	D48.7	D49.89
submaxillary	—	C77.0	—	D36.0	D48.7	D49.89
submental	—	C77.0	—	D36.0	D48.7	D49.89
subscapular	—	C77.3	—	D36.0	D48.7	D49.89
supraclavicular	—	C77.0	—	D36.0	D48.7	D49.89
thoracic	—	C77.1	—	D36.0	D48.7	D49.89
tibial	—	C77.4	—	D36.0	D48.7	D49.89
tracheal	—	C77.1	—	D36.0	D48.7	D49.89
tracheobronchial	—	C77.1	—	D36.0	D48.7	D49.89
upper limb	—	C77.3	—	D36.0	D48.7	D49.89
Virchow's	—	C77.0	—	D36.0	D48.7	D49.89
node — *see also* Neoplasm, lymph gland						
primary NEC	C96.9	—	—	—	—	—
vessel — *see also* Neoplasm, connective tissue	C49.9	C79.89	—	D21.9	D48.1	D49.2
Mackenrodt's ligament	C57.7	C79.82	D07.39	D28.7	D39.8	D49.59
malar	C41.0	C79.51	—	D16.4-●	D48.0	D49.2
region — *see Neoplasm, cheek*						
mammary gland — *see Neoplasm, breast*						
mandible	C41.1	C79.51	—	D16.5-●	D48.0	D49.2
alveolar						
mucosa (carcinoma)	C03.1	C79.89	D00.03	D10.39	D37.09	D49.0
ridge or process	C41.1	C79.51	—	D16.5-●	D48.0	D49.2
marrow (bone) NEC	C96.9	C79.52	—	—	D47.9	D49.89
mastectomy site (skin) — *see also* Neoplasm, breast, skin	C44.501	C79.2	—	—	—	—
specified as breast tissue	C50.8-●	C79.81	—	—	—	—
mastoid (air cells) (antrum) (cavity)	C30.1	C78.39	D02.3	D14.0	D38.5	D49.1
bone or process	C41.0	C79.51	—	D16.4-●	D48.0	D49.2
maxilla, maxillary (superior)	C41.0	C79.51	—	D16.4-●	D48.0	D49.2
alveolar						
mucosa	C03.0	C79.89	D00.03	D10.39	D37.09	D49.0
ridge or process (carcinoma)	C41.0	C79.51	—	D16.4-●	D48.0	D49.2
antrum	C31.0	C78.39	D02.3	D14.0	D38.5	D49.1
carcinoma	C03.0	C79.51	—	—	—	—
inferior — *see Neoplasm, mandible*						
sinus	C31.0	C78.39	D02.3	D14.0	D38.5	D49.1

	Malignant Primary	Malignant Secondary	Ca in situ	Benign	Uncertain Behavior	Unspecified Behavior
meatus external (ear) — *see also* Neoplasm, skin, ear	C44.20-●	C79.2	D04.2-●	D23.2-●	D48.5	D49.2
Meckel diverticulum, malignant	C17.3	C78.4	D01.49	D13.39	D37.2	D49.0
mediastinum, mediastinal	C38.3	C78.1	—	D15.2	D38.3	D49.89
anterior	C38.1	C78.1	—	D15.2	D38.3	D49.89
posterior	C38.2	C78.1	—	D15.2	D38.3	D49.89
medulla						
adrenal	C74.1-●	C79.7-●	D09.3	D35.0-●	D44.1-●	D49.7
oblongata	C71.7	C79.31	—	D33.1	D43.1	D49.6
meibomian gland	C44.10-●	C79.2	D04.1-●	D23.1-●	D48.5	D49.2
basal cell carcinoma	C44.11-●	—	—	—	—	—
sebaceous cell	C44.13-●	—	—	—	—	—
specified type NEC	C44.19-●	—	—	—	—	—
squamous cell carcinoma	C44.12-●	—	—	—	—	—
melanoma — *see Melanoma*						
meninges	C70.9	C79.49	—	D32.9	D42.9	D49.7
brain	C70.0	C79.32	—	D32.0	D42.0	D49.7
cerebral	C70.0	C79.32	—	D32.0	D42.0	D49.7
crainial	C70.0	C79.32	—	D32.0	D42.0	D49.7
intracranial	C70.0	C79.32	—	D32.0	D42.0	D49.7
spinal (cord)	C70.1	C79.49	—	D32.1	D42.1	D49.7
meniscus, knee joint (lateral) (medial)	C40.2-●	C79.51	—	D16.2-●	D48.0	D49.2
Merkel cell — *see Carcinoma, Merkel cell*						
mesentery, mesenteric	C48.1	C78.6	—	D20.1	D48.4	D49.0
mesoappendix	C48.1	C78.6	—	D20.1	D48.4	D49.0
mesocolon	C48.1	C78.6	—	D20.1	D48.4	D49.0
mesopharynx — *see Neoplasm, oropharynx*						
mesosalpinx	C57.1	C79.82	D07.39	D28.2	D39.8	D49.59
mesothelial tissue — *see Mesothelioma*						
mesothelioma — *see Mesothelioma*						
mesovarium	C57.1	C79.82	D07.39	D28.2	D39.8	D49.59
metacarpus (any bone)	C40.1-●	C79.51	—	D16.1-●	—	—
metastatic NEC — *see also* Neoplasm, by site, secondary	—	C79.9	—	—	—	—
metatarsus (any bone)	C40.3-●	C79.51	—	D16.3-●	—	—
midbrain	C71.7	C79.31	—	D33.1	D43.1	D49.6
milk duct — *see Neoplasm, breast*						
mons						
pubis	C51.9	C79.82	D07.1	D28.0	D39.8	D49.59
veneris	C51.9	C79.82	D07.1	D28.0	D39.8	D49.59

◀ New   ◀ Revised   ~~deleted~~ Deleted   ● Use Additional Character(s)

	Malignant Primary	Malignant Secondary	Ca in situ	Benign	Uncertain Behavior	Unspecified Behavior
motor tract	C72.9	C79.49	—	D33.9	D43.9	D49.7
brain	C71.9	C79.31	—	D33.2	D43.2	D49.6
cauda equina	C72.1	C79.49	—	D33.4	D43.4	D49.7
spinal	C72.0	C79.49	—	D33.4	D43.4	D49.7
mouth	C06.9	C79.89	D00.00	D10.30	D37.09	D49.0
book-leaf	C06.89	C79.89	—	—	—	—
floor	C04.9	C79.89	D00.06	D10.2	D37.09	D49.0
anterior portion	C04.0	C79.89	D00.06	D10.2	D37.09	D49.0
lateral portion	C04.1	C79.89	D00.06	D10.2	D37.09	D49.0
overlapping lesion	C04.8	—	—	—	—	—
overlapping NEC	C06.80	—	—	—	—	—
roof	C05.9	C79.89	D00.00	D10.39	D37.09	D49.0
specified part NEC	C06.89	C79.89	D00.00	D10.39	D37.09	D49.0
vestibule	C06.1	C79.89	D00.00	D10.39	D37.09	D49.0
mucosa						
alveolar (ridge or process)	C03.9	C79.89	D00.03	D10.39	D37.09	D49.0
lower	C03.1	C79.89	D00.03	D10.39	D37.09	D49.0
upper	C03.0	C79.89	D00.03	D10.39	D37.09	D49.0
buccal	C06.0	C79.89	D00.02	D10.39	D37.09	D49.0
cheek	C06.0	C79.89	D00.02	D10.39	D37.09	D49.0
lip — see Neoplasm, lip, internal						
nasal	C30.0	C78.39	D02.3	D14.0	D38.5	D49.1
oral	C06.0	C79.89	D00.02	D10.39	D37.09	D49.0
Mullerian duct						
female	C57.7	C79.82	D07.39	D28.7	D39.8	D49.59
male	C63.7	C79.82	D07.69	D29.8	D40.8	D49.59
muscle — see also Neoplasm, connective tissue						
extraocular	C69.6-●	C79.49	D09.2-●	D31.6-●	D48.7	D49.89
myocardium	C38.0	C79.89	—	D15.1	D48.7	D49.89
myometrium	C54.2	C79.82	D07.0	D26.1	D39.0	D49.59
myopericardium	C38.0	C79.89	—	D15.1	D48.7	D49.89
nabothian gland (follicle)	C53.0	C79.82	D06.0	D26.0	D39.0	D49.59
nail — see also Neoplasm, skin, limb	C44.90	C79.2	D04.9	D23.9	D48.5	D49.2
finger — see also Neoplasm, skin, limb, upper	C44.60-●	C79.2	D04.6-●	D23.6-●	D48.5	D49.2
toe — see also Neoplasm, skin, limb, lower	C44.70-●	C79.2	D04.7-●	D23.7-●	D48.5	D49.2
nares, naris (anterior) (posterior)	C30.0	C78.39	D02.3	D14.0	D38.5	D49.1
nasal — see Neoplasm, nose						
nasolabial groove — see also Neoplasm, skin, face	C44.309	C79.2	D04.39	D23.39	D48.5	D49.2
nasolacrimal duct	C69.5-●	C79.49	D09.2-●	D31.5-●	D48.7	D49.89

	Malignant Primary	Malignant Secondary	Ca in situ	Benign	Uncertain Behavior	Unspecified Behavior
nasopharynx, nasopharyngeal	C11.9	C79.89	D00.08	D10.6	D37.05	D49.0
floor	C11.3	C79.89	D00.08	D10.6	D37.05	D49.0
overlapping lesion	C11.8	—	—	—	—	—
roof	C11.0	C79.89	D00.08	D10.6	D37.05	D49.0
wall	C11.9	C79.89	D00.08	D10.6	D37.05	D49.0
anterior	C11.3	C79.89	D00.08	D10.6	D37.05	D49.0
lateral	C11.2	C79.89	D00.08	D10.6	D37.05	D49.0
posterior	C11.1	C79.89	D00.08	D10.6	D37.05	D49.0
superior	C11.0	C79.89	D00.08	D10.6	D37.05	D49.0
nates — see also Neoplasm, skin, trunk	C44.509	C79.2	D04.5	D23.5	D48.5	D49.2
neck NEC	C76.0	C79.89	D09.8	D36.7	D48.7	D49.89
skin	C44.40	—	—	—	—	—
basal cell carcinoma	C44.41	—	—	—	—	—
specified type NEC	C44.49	—	—	—	—	—
squamous cell carcinoma	C44.42	—	—	—	—	—
nerve (ganglion)	C47.9	C79.89	—	D36.10	D48.2	D49.2
abducens	C72.59	C79.49	—	D33.3	D43.3	D49.7
accessory (spinal)	C72.59	C79.49	—	D33.3	D43.3	D49.7
acoustic	C72.4-●	C79.49	—	D33.3	D43.3	D49.7
auditory	C72.4-●	C79.49	—	D33.3	D43.3	D49.7
autonomic NEC — see also Neoplasm, nerve, peripheral	C47.9	C79.89	—	D36.10	D48.2	D49.2
brachial	C47.1-●	C79.89	—	D36.12	D48.2	D49.2
cranial	C72.50	C79.49	—	D33.3	D43.3	D49.7
specified NEC	C72.59	C79.49	—	D33.3	D43.3	D49.7
facial	C72.59	C79.49	—	D33.3	D43.3	D49.7
femoral	C47.2-●	C79.89	—	D36.13	D48.2	D49.2
ganglion NEC — see also Neoplasm, nerve, peripheral	C47.9	C79.89	—	D36.10	D48.2	D49.2
glossopharyngeal	C72.59	C79.49	—	D33.3	D43.3	D49.7
hypoglossal	C72.59	C79.49	—	D33.3	D43.3	D49.7
intercostal	C47.3	C79.89	—	D36.14	D48.2	D49.2
lumbar	C47.6	C79.89	—	D36.17	D48.2	D49.2
median	C47.1-●	C79.89	—	D36.12	D48.2	D49.2
obturator	C47.2-●	C79.89	—	D36.13	D48.2	D49.2
oculomotor	C72.59	C79.49	—	D33.3	D43.3	D49.7
olfactory	C47.2-●	C79.49	—	D33.3	D43.3	D49.7
optic	C72.3-●	C79.49	—	D33.3	D43.3	D49.7
parasympathetic NEC	C47.9	C79.89	—	D36.10	D48.2	D49.2
peripheral NEC	C47.9	C79.89	—	D36.10	D48.2	D49.2
abdomen	C47.4	C79.89	—	D36.15	D48.2	D49.2
abdominal wall	C47.4	C79.89	—	D36.15	D48.2	D49.2

◄ New ◄ Revised ~~deleted~~ Deleted ● Use Additional Character(s)

nerve *(Continued)*	Malignant Primary	Malignant Secondary	Ca in situ	Benign	Uncertain Behavior	Unspecified Behavior
peripheral NEC *(Continued)*						
ankle	C47.2-●	C79.89	—	D36.13	D48.2	D49.2
antecubital fossa or space	C47.1-●	C79.89	—	D36.12	D48.2	D49.2
arm	C47.1-●	C79.89	—	D36.12	D48.2	D49.2
auricle (ear)	C47.0	C79.89	—	D36.11	D48.2	D49.2
axilla	C47.3	C79.89	—	D36.12	D48.2	D49.2
back	C47.6	C79.89	—	D36.17	D48.2	D49.2
buttock	C47.5	C79.89	—	D36.16	D48.2	D49.2
calf	C47.2-●	C79.89	—	D36.13	D48.2	D49.2
cervical region	C47.0	C79.89	—	D36.11	D48.2	D49.2
cheek	C47.0	C79.89	—	D36.11	D48.2	D49.2
chest (wall)	C47.3	C79.89	—	D36.14	D48.2	D49.2
chin	C47.0	C79.89	—	D36.11	D48.2	D49.2
ear (external)	C47.0	C79.89	—	D36.11	D48.2	D49.2
elbow	C47.1-●	C79.89	—	D36.12	D48.2	D49.2
extrarectal	C47.5	C79.89	—	D36.16	D48.2	D49.2
extremity	C47.9	C79.89	—	D36.10	D48.2	D49.2
lower	C47.2-●	C79.89	—	D36.13	D48.2	D49.2
upper	C47.1-●	C79.89	—	D36.12	D48.2	D49.2
eyelid	C47.0	C79.89	—	D36.11	D48.2	D49.2
face	C47.0	C79.89	—	D36.11	D48.2	D49.2
finger	C47.1-●	C79.89	—	D36.12	D48.2	D49.2
flank	C47.6	C79.89	—	D36.17	D48.2	D49.2
foot	C47.2-●	C79.89	—	D36.13	D48.2	D49.2
forearm	C47.1-●	C79.89	—	D36.12	D48.2	D49.2
forehead	C47.0	C79.89	—	D36.11	D48.2	D49.2
gluteal region	C47.5	C79.89	—	D36.16	D48.2	D49.2
groin	C47.5	C79.89	—	D36.16	D48.2	D49.2
hand	C47.1-●	C79.89	—	D36.12	D48.2	D49.2
head	C47.0	C79.89	—	D36.11	D48.2	D49.2
heel	C47.2-●	C79.89	—	D36.13	D48.2	D49.2
hip	C47.2-●	C79.89	—	D36.13	D48.2	D49.2
infraclavicular region	C47.3	C79.89	—	D36.14	D48.2	D49.2
inguinal (canal) (region)	C47.5	C79.89	—	D36.16	D48.2	D49.2
intrathoracic	C47.3	C79.89	—	D36.14	D48.2	D49.2
ischiorectal fossa	C47.5	C79.89	—	D36.16	D48.2	D49.2
knee	C47.2-●	C79.89	—	D36.13	D48.2	D49.2
leg	C47.2-●	C79.89	—	D36.13	D48.2	D49.2
limb NEC	C47.9	C79.89	—	D36.10	D48.2	D49.2
lower	C47.2-●	C79.89	—	D36.13	D48.2	D49.2
upper	C47.1-●	C79.89	—	D36.12	D48.2	D49.2
nates	C47.5	C79.89	—	D36.16	D48.2	D49.2
neck	C47.0	C79.89	—	D36.11	D48.2	D49.2

nerve *(Continued)*	Malignant Primary	Malignant Secondary	Ca in situ	Benign	Uncertain Behavior	Unspecified Behavior
peripheral NEC *(Continued)*						
orbit	C69.6-●	C79.49	—	D31.6-●	D48.7	D49.2
pararectal	C47.5	C79.89	—	D36.16	D48.2	D49.2
paraurethral	C47.5	C79.89	—	D36.16	D48.2	D49.2
paravaginal	C47.5	C79.89	—	D36.16	D48.2	D49.2
pelvis (floor)	C47.5	C79.89	—	D36.16	D48.2	D49.2
pelvoabdominal	C47.8	C79.89	—	D36.17	D48.2	D49.2
perineum	C47.5	C79.89	—	D36.16	D48.2	D49.2
perirectal (tissue)	C47.5	C79.89	—	D36.16	D48.2	D49.2
periurethral (tissue)	C47.5	C79.89	—	D36.16	D48.2	D49.2
popliteal fossa or space	C47.2-●	C79.89	—	D36.13	D48.2	D49.2
presacral	C47.5	C79.89	—	D36.16	D48.2	D49.2
pterygoid fossa	C47.0	C79.89	—	D36.11	D48.2	D49.2
rectovaginal septum or wall	C47.5	C79.89	—	D36.16	D48.2	D49.2
rectovesical	C47.5	C79.89	—	D36.16	D48.2	D49.2
sacrococcygeal region	C47.5	C79.89	—	D36.16	D48.2	D49.2
scalp	C47.0	C79.89	—	D36.11	D48.2	D49.2
scapular region	C47.3	C79.89	—	D36.14	D48.2	D49.2
shoulder	C47.1-●	C79.89	—	D36.12	D48.2	D49.2
submental	C47.0	C79.89	—	D36.11	D48.2	D49.2
supraclavicular region	C47.0	C79.89	—	D36.11	D48.2	D49.2
temple	C47.0	C79.89	—	D36.11	D48.2	D49.2
temporal region	C47.0	C79.89	—	D36.11	D48.2	D49.2
thigh	C47.2-●	C79.89	—	D36.13	D48.2	D49.2
thoracic (duct) (wall)	C47.3	C79.89	—	D36.14	D48.2	D49.2
thorax	C47.3	C79.89	—	D36.14	D48.2	D49.2
thumb	C47.1-●	C79.89	—	D36.12	D48.2	D49.2
toe	C47.2-●	C79.89	—	D36.13	D48.2	D49.2
trunk	C47.6	C79.89	—	D36.17	D48.2	D49.2
umbilicus	C47.4	C79.89	—	D36.15	D48.2	D49.2
vesicorectal	C47.5	C79.89	—	D36.16	D48.2	D49.2
wrist	C47.1-●	C79.89	—	D36.12	D48.2	D49.2
radial	C47.1-●	C79.89	—	D36.12	D48.2	D49.2
sacral	C47.5	C79.89	—	D36.16	D48.2	D49.2
sciatic	C47.2-●	C79.89	—	D36.13	D48.2	D49.2
spinal NEC	C47.9	C79.89	—	D36.10	D48.2	D49.2
accessory	C72.59	C79.49	—	D33.3	D43.3	D49.7
sympathetic NEC—*see also Neoplasm, nerve, peripheral*	C47.9	C79.89	—	D36.10	D48.2	D49.2
trigeminal	C72.59	C79.49	—	D33.3	D43.3	D49.7
trochlear	C72.59	C79.49	—	D33.3	D43.3	D49.7
ulnar	C47.1-●	C79.89	—	D36.12	D48.2	D49.2
vagus	C72.59	C79.49	—	D33.3	D43.3	D49.7

◀ New   ◀ Revised   deleted Deleted   ● Use Additional Character(s)

	Malignant Primary	Malignant Secondary	Ca in situ	Benign	Uncertain Behavior	Unspecified Behavior
nervous system (central)	C72.9	C79.40	—	D33.9	D43.9	D49.7
autonomic — *see Neoplasm, nerve, peripheral*						
parasympathetic — *see Neoplasm, nerve, peripheral*						
specified site NEC	—	C79.49	—	D33.7	D43.8	—
sympathetic — *see Neoplasm, nerve, peripheral*						
nevus — *see Nevus*						
nipple	C50.0-●	C79.81	D05.-●	D24.-●	—	—
nose, nasal	C76.0	C79.89	D09.8	D36.7	D48.7	D49.89
ala (external) (nasi) — *see also Neoplasm, nose, skin*	C44.301	C79.2	D04.39	D23.39	D48.5	D49.2
bone	C41.0	C79.51	—	D16.4-●	D48.0	D49.2
cartilage	C30.0	C78.39	D02.3	D14.0	D38.5	D49.1
cavity	C30.0	C78.39	D02.3	D14.0	D38.5	D49.1
choana	C11.3	C79.89	D00.08	D10.6	D37.05	D49.0
external (skin) — *see also Neoplasm, nose, skin*	C44.301	C79.2	D04.39	D23.39	D48.5	D49.2
fossa	C30.0	C78.39	D02.3	D14.0	D38.5	D49.1
internal	C30.0	C78.39	D02.3	D14.0	D38.5	D49.1
mucosa	C30.0	C78.39	D02.3	D14.0	D38.5	D49.1
septum	C30.0	C78.39	D02.3	D14.0	D38.5	D49.1
posterior margin	C11.3	C79.89	D00.08	D10.6	D37.05	D49.0
sinus — *see Neoplasm, sinus*						
skin	C44.301	C79.2	D04.39	D23.39	D48.5	D49.2
basal cell carcinoma	C44.311	—	—	—	—	—
specified type NEC	C44.391	—	—	—	—	—
squamous cell carcinoma	C44.321	—	—	—	—	—
turbinate (mucosa)	C30.0	C78.39	D02.3	D14.0	D38.5	D49.1
bone	C41.0	C79.51	—	D16.4-●	D48.0	D49.2
vestibule	C30.0	C78.39	D02.3	D14.0	D38.5	D49.1
nostril	C30.0	C78.39	D02.3	D14.0	D38.5	D49.1
nucleus pulposus	C41.2	C79.51	—	D16.6	D48.0	D49.2
occipital						
bone	C41.0	C79.51	—	D16.4-●	D48.0	D49.2
lobe or pole, brain	C71.4	C79.31	—	D33.0	D43.0	D49.6
odontogenic — *see Neoplasm, jaw bone*						
olfactory nerve or bulb	C72.2-●	C79.49	—	D33.3	D43.3	D49.7
olive (brain)	C71.7	C79.31	—	D33.1	D43.1	D49.6
omentum	C48.1	C78.6		D20.1	D48.4	D49.0
operculum (brain)	C71.0	C79.31	—	D33.0	D43.0	D49.6
optic nerve, chiasm, or tract	C72.3-●	C79.49	—	D33.3	D43.3	D49.7

	Malignant Primary	Malignant Secondary	Ca in situ	Benign	Uncertain Behavior	Unspecified Behavior
oral (cavity)	C06.9	C79.89	D00.00	D10.30	D37.09	D49.0
ill-defined	C14.8	C79.89	D00.00	D10.30	D37.09	D49.0
mucosa	C06.0	C79.89	D00.02	D10.39	D37.09	D49.0
orbit	C69.6-●	C79.49	D09.2-●	D31.6-●	D48.7	D49.89
autonomic nerve	C69.6-●	C79.49	—	D31.6-●	D48.7	D49.2
bone	C41.0	C79.51	—	D16.4-●	D48.0	D49.2
eye	C69.6-●	C79.49	D09.2-●	D31.6-●	D48.7	D49.89
peripheral nerves	C69.6-●	C79.49	—	D31.6-●	D48.7	D49.2
soft parts	C69.6-●	C79.49	D09.2-●	D31.6-●	D48.7	D49.89
organ of Zuckerkandl	C75.5	C79.89	—	D35.6	D44.7	D49.7
oropharynx	C10.9	C79.89	D00.08	D10.5	D37.05	D49.0
branchial cleft (vestige)	C10.4	C79.89	D00.08	D10.5	D37.05	D49.0
junctional region	C10.8	C79.89	D00.08	D10.5	D37.05	D49.0
lateral wall	C10.2	C79.89	D00.08	D10.5	D37.05	D49.0
overlapping lesion	C10.8	—	—	—	—	—
pillars or fauces	C09.1	C79.89	D00.08	D10.5	D37.05	D49.0
posterior wall	C10.3	C79.89	D00.08	D10.5	D37.05	D49.0
vallecula	C10.0	C79.89	D00.08	D10.5	D37.05	D49.0
os						
external	C53.1	C79.82	D06.1	D26.0	D39.0	D49.59
internal	C53.0	C79.82	D06.0	D26.0	D39.0	D49.59
ovary	C56.-●	C79.6-●	D07.39	D27.-●	D39.1-●	D49.59
oviduct	C57.0-●	C79.82	D07.39	D28.2	D39.8	D49.59
palate	C05.9	C79.89	D00.00	D10.39	D37.09	D49.0
hard	C05.0	C79.89	N00.05	D10.39	D37.09	D49.0
junction of hard and soft palate	C05.9	C79.89	D00.00	D10.39	D37.09	D49.0
overlapping lesions	C05.8	—	—	—	—	—
soft	C05.1	C79.89	D00.04	D10.39	D37.09	D49.0
nasopharyngeal surface	C11.3	C79.89	D00.08	D10.6	D37.05	D49.0
posterior surface	C11.3	C79.89	D00.08	D10.6	D37.05	D49.0
superior surface	C11.3	C79.89	D00.08	D10.6	D37.05	D49.0
palatoglossal arch	C09.1	C79.89	D00.08	D10.5	D37.09	D49.0
palatopharyngeal arch	C09.1	C79.89	D00.00	D10.5	D37.09	D49.0
pallium	C71.0	C79.31	—	D33.0	D43.0	D49.6
palpebra	C44.10-●	C79.2	D04.1-●	D23.1-●	D48.5	D49.2
basal cell carcinoma	C44.11-●	—	—	—	—	—
sebaceous cell	C44.13-●	—	—	—	—	—
specified type NEC	C44.19-●	—	—	—	—	—
squamous cell carcinoma	C44.12-●	—	—	—	—	—
pancreas	C25.9	C78.89	D01.7	D13.6	D37.8	D49.0
body	C25.1	C78.89	D01.7	D13.6	D37.8	D49.0
duct (of Santorini) (of Wirsung)	C25.3	C78.89	D01.7	D13.6	D37.8	D49.0
ectopic tissue	C25.7	C78.89	—	D13.6	D37.8	D49.0
head	C25.0	C78.89	D01.7	D13.6	D37.8	D49.0

◀ New ◀ Revised ~~deleted~~ Deleted ● Use Additional Character(s)

TABLE OF NEOPLASMS

	Malignant Primary	Malignant Secondary	Ca in situ	Benign	Uncertain Behavior	Unspecified Behavior
pancreas *(Continued)*						
islet cells	C25.4	C78.89	D01.7	D13.7	D37.8	D49.0
neck	C25.7	C78.89	D01.7	D13.6	D37.8	D49.0
overlapping lesion	C25.8	—	—	—	—	—
tail	C25.2	C78.89	D01.7	D13.6	D37.8	D49.0
para-aortic body	C75.5	C79.89	—	D35.6	D44.7	D49.7
paraganglion NEC	C75.5	C79.89	—	D35.6	D44.7	D49.7
parametrium	C57.3	C79.82	—	D28.2	D39.8	D49.59
paranephric	C48.0	C78.6	—	D20.0	D48.3	D49.0
pararectal	C76.3	C79.89	—	D36.7	D48.7	D49.89
parasagittal (region)	C76.0	C79.89	D09.8	D36.7	D48.7	D49.89
parasellar	C72.9	C79.49	—	D33.9	D43.8	D49.7
parathyroid (gland)	C75.0	C79.89	D09.3	D35.1	D44.2	D49.7
paraurethral	C76.3	C79.89	—	D36.7	D48.7	D49.89
gland	C68.1	C79.19	D09.19	D30.8	D41.8	D49.59
paravaginal	C76.3	C79.89	—	D36.7	D48.7	D49.89
parenchyma, kidney	C64.-●	C79.0-●	D09.19	D30.0-●	D41.0-●	D49.51-●
parietal						
bone	C41.0	C79.51	—	D16.4-●	D48.0	D49.2
lobe, brain	C71.3	C79.31	—	D33.0	D43.0	D49.6
paroophoron	C57.1	C79.82	D07.39	D28.2	D39.8	D49.59
parotid (duct) (gland)	C07	C79.89	D00.00	D11.0	D37.030	D49.0
parovarium	C57.1	C79.82	D07.39	D28.2	D39.8	D49.59
patella	C40.20	C79.51	—	—	—	—
peduncle, cerebral	C71.7	C79.31	—	D33.1	D43.1	D49.6
pelvirectal junction	C19	C78.5	D01.1	D12.7	D37.5	D49.0
pelvis, pelvic	C76.3	C79.89	D09.8	D36.7	D48.7	D49.89
bone	C41.4	C79.51	—	D16.8	D48.0	D49.2
floor	C76.3	C79.89	D09.8	D36.7	D48.7	D49.89
renal	C65.-●	C79.0-●	D09.19	D30.1-●	D41.1-●	D49.51-●
viscera	C76.3	C79.89	D09.8	D36.7	D48.7	D49.89
wall	C76.3	C79.89	D09.8	D36.7	D48.7	D49.89
pelvo-abdominal	C76.8	C79.89	D09.8	D36.7	D48.7	D49.89
penis	C60.9	C79.82	D07.4	D29.0	D40.8	D49.59
body	C60.2	C79.82	D07.4	D29.0	D40.8	D49.59
corpus (cavernosum)	C60.2	C79.82	D07.4	D29.0	D40.8	D49.59
glans	C60.1	C79.82	D07.4	D29.0	D40.8	D49.59
overlapping sites	C60.8	—	—	—	—	—
skin NEC	C60.9	C79.82	D07.4	D29.0	D40.8	D49.59
periadrenal (tissue)	C48.0	C78.6	—	D20.0	D48.3	D49.0
perianal (skin) — *see also* Neoplasm, anus, skin	C44.500	C79.2	D04.5	D23.5	D48.5	D49.2
pericardium	C38.0	C79.89	—	D15.1	D48.7	D49.89
perinephric	C48.0	C78.6	—	D20.0	D48.3	D49.0
perineum	C76.3	C79.89	D09.8	D36.7	D48.7	D49.89
periodontal tissue NEC	C03.9	C79.89	D00.03	D10.39	D37.09	D49.0
periosteum — *see Neoplasm, bone*						
peripancreatic	C48.0	C78.6	—	D20.0	D48.3	D49.0
peripheral nerve NEC	C47.9	C79.89	—	D36.10	D48.2	D49.2
perirectal (tissue)	C76.3	C79.89	—	D36.7	D48.7	D49.89
perirenal (tissue)	C48.0	C78.6	—	D20.0	D48.3	D49.0
peritoneum, peritoneal (cavity)	C48.2	C78.6	—	D20.1	D48.4	D49.0
benign mesothelial tissue — *see Mesothelioma, benign*						
overlapping lesion	C48.8	—	—	—	—	—
with digestive organs	C26.9	—	—	—	—	—
parietal	C48.1	C78.6	—	D20.1	D48.4	D49.0
pelvic	C48.1	C78.6	—	D20.1	D48.4	D49.0
specified part NEC	C48.1	C78.6	—	D20.1	D48.4	D49.0
peritonsillar (tissue)	C76.0	C79.89	D09.8	D36.7	D48.7	D49.89
periurethral tissue	C76.3	C79.89	—	D36.7	D48.7	D49.89
phalanges						
foot	C40.3-●	C79.51	—	D16.3-●	—	—
hand	C40.1-●	C79.51	—	D16.1-●	—	—
pharynx, pharyngeal	C14.0	C79.89	D00.08	D10.9	D37.05	D49.0
bursa	C11.1	C79.89	D00.08	D10.6	D37.05	D49.0
fornix	C11.3	C79.89	D00.08	D10.6	D37.05	D49.0
recess	C11.2	C79.89	D00.08	D10.6	D37.05	D49.0
region	C14.0	C79.89	D00.08	D10.9	D37.05	D49.0
tonsil	C11.1	C79.89	D00.08	D10.6	D37.05	D49.0
wall (lateral) (posterior)	C14.0	C79.89	D00.08	D10.9	D37.05	D49.0
pia mater	C70.9	C79.40	—	D32.9	D42.9	D49.7
cerebral	C70.0	C79.32	—	D32.0	D42.0	D49.7
cranial	C70.0	C79.32	—	D32.0	D42.0	D49.7
spinal	C70.1	C79.49	—	D32.1	D42.1	D49.7
pillars of fauces	C09.1	C79.89	D00.08	D10.5	D37.05	D49.0
pineal (body) (gland)	C75.3	C79.89	D09.3	D35.4	D44.5	D49.7
pinna (ear) NEC — *see also* Neoplasm, skin, ear	C44.20-●	C79.2	D04.2-●	D23.2-●	D48.5	D49.2
piriform fossa or sinus	C12	C79.89	D00.08	D10.7	D37.05	D49.0
pituitary (body) (fossa) (gland) (lobe)	C75.1	C79.89	D09.3	D35.2	D44.3	D49.7
placenta	C58	C79.82	D07.0	D26.7	D39.2	D49.59
pleura, pleural (cavity)	C38.4	C78.2	—	D19.0	D38.2	D49.1
overlapping lesion with heart or mediastinum	C38.8	—	—	—	—	—
parietal	C38.4	C78.2	—	D19.0	D38.2	D49.1
visceral	C38.4	C78.2	—	D19.0	D38.2	D49.1

◀ New　◀ Revised　deleted Deleted　● Use Additional Character(s)

	Malignant Primary	Malignant Secondary	Ca in situ	Benign	Uncertain Behavior	Unspecified Behavior
plexus						
brachial	C47.1-•	C79.89	—	D36.12	D48.2	D49.2
cervical	C47.0	C79.89	—	D36.11	D48.2	D49.2
choroid	C71.5	C79.31	—	D33.0	D43.0	D49.6
lumbosacral	C47.5	C79.89	—	D36.16	D48.2	D49.2
sacral	C47.5	C79.89	—	D36.16	D48.2	D49.2
pluriendocrine	C75.8	C79.89	D09.3	D35.7	D44.9	D49.7
pole						
frontal	C71.1	C79.31	—	D33.0	D43.0	D49.6
occipital	C71.4	C79.31	—	D33.0	D43.0	D49.6
pons (varolii)	C71.7	C79.31	—	D33.1	D43.1	D49.6
popliteal fossa or space	C76.5-•	C79.89	D04.7-•	D36.7	D48.7	D49.89
postcricoid (region)	C13.0	C79.89	D00.08	D10.7	D37.05	D49.0
posterior fossa (cranial)	C71.9	C79.31	—	D33.2	D43.2	D49.6
postnasal space	C11.9	C79.89	D00.08	D10.6	D37.05	D49.0
prepuce	C60.0	C79.82	D07.4	D29.0	D40.8	D49.59
prepylorus	C16.4	C78.89	D00.2	D13.1	D37.1	D49.0
presacral (region)	C76.3	C79.89	—	D36.7	D48.7	D49.89
prostate (gland)	C61	C79.82	D07.5	D29.1	D40.0	D49.59
utricle	C68.0	C79.19	D09.19	D30.4	D41.3	D49.59
pterygoid fossa	C49.0	C79.89	—	D21.0	D48.1	D49.2
pubic bone	C41.4	C79.51	—	D16.8	D48.0	D49.2
pudenda, pudendum (female)	C51.9	C79.82	D07.1	D28.0	D39.8	D49.59
pulmonary — see also Neoplasm, lung	C34.9-•	C78.0-•	D02.2-•	D14.3-•	D38.1	D49.1
putamen	C71.0	C79.31	—	D33.0	D43.0	D49.6
pyloric						
antrum	C16.3	C78.89	D00.2	D13.1	D37.1	D49.0
canal	C16.4	C78.89	D00.2	D13.1	D37.1	D49.0
pylorus	C16.4	C78.89	D00.2	D13.1	D37.1	D49.0
pyramid (brain)	C71.7	C79.31	—	D33.1	D43.1	D49.6
pyriform fossa or sinus	C12	C79.89	D00.08	D10.7	D37.05	D49.0
radius (any part)	C40.0-•	C79.51	—	D16.0-•	—	—
Rathke's pouch	C75.1	C79.89	D09.3	D35.2	D44.3	D49.7
rectosigmoid (junction)	C19	C78.5	D01.1	D12.7	D37.5	D49.0
overlapping lesion with anus or rectum	C21.8	—	—	—	—	—
rectouterine pouch	C48.1	C78.6	—	D20.1	D48.4	D49.0
rectovaginal septum or wall	C76.3	C79.89	D09.8	D36.7	D48.7	D49.89
rectovesical septum	C76.3	C79.89	D09.8	D36.7	D48.7	D49.89
rectum (ampulla)	C20	C78.5	D01.2	D12.8	D37.5	D49.0
and colon	C19	C78.5	D01.1	D12.7	D37.5	D49.0
overlapping lesion with anus or rectosigmoid junction	C21.8	—	—	—	—	—
renal	C64.-•	C79.0-•	D09.19	D30.0-•	D41.0-•	D49.51-•
calyx	C65.-•	C79.0-•	D09.19	D30.1-•	D41.1-•	D49.51-•
hilus	C65.-•	C79.0-•	D09.19	D30.1-•	D41.1-•	D49.51-•
parenchyma	C64.-•	C79.0-•	D09.19	D30.0-•	D41.0-•	D49.51-•
pelvis	C65.-•	C79.0-•	D09.19	D30.1-•	D41.1-•	D49.51-•
respiratory						
organs or system NEC	C39.9	C78.30	D02.4	D14.4	D38.6	D49.1
tract NEC	C39.9	C78.30	D02.4	D14.4	D38.5	D49.1
upper	C39.0	C78.30	D02.4	D14.4	D38.5	D49.1
retina	C69.2-•	C79.49	D09.2-•	D31.2-•	D48.7	D49.81
retrobulbar	C69.6-•	C79.49	—	D31.6-•	D48.7	D49.89
retrocecal	C48.0	C78.6	—	D20.0	D48.3	D49.0
retromolar (area) (triangle) (trigone)	C06.2	C79.89	D00.00	D10.39	D37.09	D49.0
retro-orbital	C76.0	C79.89	D09.8	D36.7	D48.7	D49.89
retroperitoneal (space) (tissue)	C48.0	C78.6	—	D20.0	D48.3	D49.0
retroperitoneum	C48.0	C78.6	—	D20.0	D48.3	D49.0
retropharyngeal	C14.0	C79.89	D00.08	D10.9	D37.05	D49.0
retrovesical (septum)	C76.3	C79.89	D09.8	D36.7	D48.7	D49.89
rhinencephalon	C71.0	C79.31	—	D33.0	D43.0	D49.6
rib	C41.3	C79.51	—	D16.7	D48.0	D49.2
Rosenmuller's fossa	C11.2	C79.89	D00.08	D10.6	D37.05	D49.0
round ligament	C57.2	C79.82	—	D28.2	D39.8	D49.59
sacrococcyx, sacrococcygeal	C41.4	C79.51	—	D16.8	D48.0	D49.2
region	C76.3	C79.89	D09.8	D36.7	D48.7	D49.89
sacrouterine ligament	C57.3	C79.82	—	D28.2	D39.8	D49.59
sacrum, sacral (vertebra)	C41.4	C79.51	—	D16.8	D48.0	D49.2
salivary gland or duct (major)	C08.9	C79.89	D00.00	D11.9	D37.039	D49.0
minor NEC	C06.9	C79.89	D00.00	D10.39	D37.04	D49.0
overlapping lesion	C08.9	—	—	—	—	—
parotid	C07	C79.89	D00.00	D11.0	D37.030	D49.0
pluriglandular	C08.9	C79.89	D00.00	D11.9	D37.039	D49.0
sublingual	C08.1	C79.89	D00.00	D11.7	D37.031	D49.0
submandibular	C08.0	C79.89	D00.00	D11.7	D37.032	D49.0
submaxillary	C08.0	C79.89	D00.00	D11.7	D37.032	D49.0
salpinx (uterine)	C57.0-•	C79.82	D07.39	D28.2	D39.8	D49.59
Santorini's duct	C25.3	C78.89	D01.7	D13.6	D37.8	D49.0
scalp	C44.40	C79.2	D04.4	D23.4	D48.5	D49.2
basal cell carcinoma	C44.41	—	—	—	—	—
specified type NEC	C44.49	—	—	—	—	—
squamous cell carcinoma	C44.42	—	—	—	—	—
scapula (any part)	C40.0-•	C79.51	—	D16.0-•	—	—
scapular region	C76.1	C79.89	D09.8	D36.7	D48.7	D49.89

◄ New ◄ Revised ~~deleted~~ Deleted • Use Additional Character(s)

	Malignant Primary	Malignant Secondary	Ca in situ	Benign	Uncertain Behavior	Unspecified Behavior
scar NEC—see also Neoplasm, skin, by site	C44.90	C79.2	D04.9	D23.9	D48.5	D49.2
sciatic nerve	C47.2-●	C79.89	—	D36.13	D48.2	D49.2
sclera	C69.4-●	C79.49	D09.2-●	D31.4-●	D48.7	D49.89
scrotum (skin)	C63.2	C79.82	D07.61	D29.4	D40.8	D49.59
sebaceous gland—see Neoplasm, skin						
sella turcica	C75.1	C79.89	D09.3	D35.2	D44.3	D49.7
bone	C41.0	C79.51	—	D16.4-●	D48.0	D49.2
semilunar cartilage (knee)	C40.2-●	C79.51	—	D16.2-●	D48.0	D49.2
seminal vesicle	C63.7	C79.82	D07.69	D29.8	D40.8	D49.59
septum						
nasal	C30.0	C78.39	D02.3	D14.0	D38.5	D49.1
posterior margin	C11.3	C79.89	D00.08	D10.6	D37.05	D49.0
rectovaginal	C76.3	C79.89	D09.8	D36.7	D48.7	D49.89
rectovesical	C76.3	C79.89	D09.8	D36.7	D48.7	D49.89
urethrovaginal	C57.9	C79.82	D07.30	D28.9	D39.9	D49.59
vesicovaginal	C57.9	C79.82	D07.30	D28.9	D39.9	D49.59
shoulder NEC	C76.4-●	C79.89	D04.6-●	D36.7	D48.7	D49.89
sigmoid flexure (lower) (upper)	C18.7	C78.5	D01.0	D12.5	D37.4	D49.0
sinus (accessory)	C31.9	C78.39	D02.3	D14.0	D38.5	D49.1
bone (any)	C41.0	C79.51	—	D16.4-●	D48.0	D49.2
ethmoidal	C31.1	C78.39	D02.3	D14.0	D38.5	D49.1
frontal	C31.2	C78.39	D02.3	D14.0	D38.5	D49.1
maxillary	C31.0	C78.39	D02.3	D14.0	D38.5	D49.1
nasal, paranasal NEC	C31.9	C78.39	D02.3	D14.0	D38.5	D49.1
overlapping lesion	C31.8	—	—	—	—	—
pyriform	C12	C79.89	D00.08	D10.7	D37.05	D49.0
sphenoid	C31.3	C78.39	D02.3	D14.0	D38.5	D49.1
skeleton, skeletal NEC	C41.9	C79.51	—	D16.9-●	D48.0	D49.2
Skene's gland	C68.1	C79.19	D09.19	D30.8	D41.8	D49.59
skin NOS	C44.90	C79.2	D04.9	D23.9	D48.5	D49.2
abdominal wall	C44.509	C79.2	D04.5	D23.5	D48.5	D49.2
basal cell carcinoma	C44.519	—	—	—	—	—
specified type NEC	C44.599	—	—	—	—	—
squamous cell carcinoma	C44.529	—	—	—	—	—
ala nasi—see also Neoplasm, nose, skin	C44.301	C79.2	D04.39	D23.39	D48.5	D49.2
ankle—see also Neoplasm, skin, limb, lower	C44.70-●	C79.2	D04.7-●	D23.7-●	D48.5	D49.2
antecubital space—see also Neoplasm, skin, limb, upper	C44.60-●	C79.2	D04.6-●	D23.6-●	D48.5	D49.2

	Malignant Primary	Malignant Secondary	Ca in situ	Benign	Uncertain Behavior	Unspecified Behavior
skin NOS (Continued)						
anus	C44.500	C79.2	D04.5	D23.5	D48.5	D49.2
basal cell carcinoma	C44.510	—	—	—	—	—
specified type NEC	C44.590	—	—	—	—	—
squamous cell carcinoma	C44.520	—	—	—	—	—
arm—see also Neoplasm, skin, limb, upper	C44.60-●	C79.2	D04.6-●	D23.6-●	D48.5	D49.2
auditory canal (external)—see also Neoplasm, skin, ear	C44.20-●	C79.2	D04.2-●	D23.2-●	D48.5	D49.2
auricle (ear)—see also Neoplasm, skin, ear	C44.20-●	C79.2	D04.2-●	D23.2-●	D48.5	D49.2
auricular canal (external)—see also Neoplasm, skin, ear	C44.20-●	C79.2	D04.2-●	D23.2-●	D48.5	D49.2
axilla, axillary fold—see also Neoplasm, skin, trunk	C44.509	C79.2	D04.5	D23.5	D48.5	D49.2
back—see also Neoplasm, skin, trunk	C44.509	C79.2	D04.5	D23.5	D48.5	D49.2
basal cell carcinoma	C44.91					
breast	C44.501	C79.2	D04.5	D23.5	D48.5	D49.2
basal cell carcinoma	C44.511	—	—	—	—	—
specified type NEC	C44.591	—	—	—	—	—
squamous cell carcinoma	C44.521	—	—	—	—	—
brow—see also Neoplasm, skin, face	C44.309	C79.2	D04.39	D23.39	D48.5	D49.2
buttock—see also Neoplasm, skin, trunk	C44.509	C79.2	D04.5	D23.5	D48.5	D49.2
calf—see also Neoplasm, skin, limb, lower	C44.70-●	C79.2	D04.7-●	D23.7-●	D48.5	D49.2
canthus (eye) (inner) (outer)	C44.10-●	C79.2	D04.1-●	D23.1-●	D48.5	D49.2
basal cell carcinoma	C44.11-●	—	—	—	—	—
sebaceous cell	C44.13-●	—	—	—	—	—
specified type NEC	C44.19-●	—	—	—	—	—
squamous cell carcinoma	C44.12-●	—	—	—	—	—
cervical region—see also Neoplasm, skin, neck	C44.40	C79.2	D04.4	D23.4	D48.5	D49.2
cheek (external)—see also Neoplasm, skin, face	C44.309	C79.2	D04.39	D23.39	D48.5	D49.2
chest (wall)—see also Neoplasm, skin, trunk	C44.509	C79.2	D04.5	D23.5	D48.5	D49.2
chin—see also Neoplasm, skin, face	C44.309	C79.2	D04.39	D23.39	D48.5	D49.2
clavicular area—see also Neoplasm, skin, trunk	C44.509	C79.2	D04.5	D23.5	D48.5	D49.2
clitoris	C51.2	C79.82	D07.1	D28.0	D39.8	D49.59

◄ New ◄ Revised ~~deleted~~ Deleted ● Use Additional Character(s)

skin NOS *(Continued)*

	Malignant Primary	Malignant Secondary	Ca in situ	Benign	Uncertain Behavior	Unspecified Behavior
columnella — *see also Neoplasm, skin, face*	C44.309	C79.2	D04.39	D23.39	D48.5	D49.2
concha — *see also skin, ear*	C44.20-•	C79.2	D04.2-•	D23.2-•	D48.5	D49.2
ear (external)	C44.20-•	C79.2	D04.2-•	D23.2-•	D48.5	D49.2
basal cell carcinoma	C44.21-•	—	—	—	—	—
specified type NEC	C44.29-•	—	—	—	—	—
squamous cell carcinoma	C44.22-•	—	—	—	—	—
elbow — *see also Neoplasm, skin, limb, upper*	C44.60-•	C79.2	D04.6-•	D23.6-•	D48.5	D49.2
eyebrow — *see also Neoplasm, skin, face*	C44.309	C79.2	D04.39	D23.39	D48.5	D49.2
eyelid	C44.10-•	C79.2	D04.1-•	D23.1-•	D48.5	D49.2
basal cell carcinoma	C44.11-•	—	—	—	—	—
sebaceous cell	C44.13-•	—	—	—	—	—
specified type NEC	C44.19-•	—	—	—	—	—
squamous cell carcinoma	C44.12-•	—	—	—	—	—
face NOS	C44.300	C79.2	D04.30	D23.30	D48.5	D49.2
basal cell carcinoma	C44.310	—	—	—	—	—
specified type NEC	C44.390	—	—	—	—	—
squamous cell carcinoma	C44.320	—	—	—	—	—
female genital organs (external)	C51.9	C79.82	D07.1	D28.0	D39.8	D49.59
clitoris	C51.2	C79.82	D07.1	D28.0	D39.8	D49.59
labium NEC	C51.9	C79.82	D07.1	D28.0	D39.8	D49.59
majus	C51.0	C79.82	D07.1	D28.0	D39.8	D49.59
minus	C51.1	C79.82	D07.1	D28.0	D39.8	D49.59
pudendum	C51.9	C79.82	D07.1	D28.0	D39.8	D49.59
vulva	C51.9	C79.82	D07.1	D28.0	D39.8	D49.59
finger — *see also Neoplasm, skin, limb, upper*	C44.60-•	C79.2	D04.6-•	D23.6-•	D48.5	D49.2
flank — *see also Neoplasm, skin, trunk*	C44.509	C79.2	D04.5	D23.5	D48.5	D49.2
foot — *see also Neoplasm, skin, limb, lower*	C44.70-•	C79.2	D04.7-•	D23.7-•	D48.5	D49.2
forearm — *see also Neoplasm, skin, limb, upper*	C44.60-•	C79.2	D04.6-•	D23.6-•	D48.5	D49.2
forehead — *see also Neoplasm, skin, face*	C44.309	C79.2	D04.39	D23.39	D48.5	D49.2
glabella — *see also Neoplasm, skin, face*	C44.309	C79.2	D04.39	D23.39	D48.5	D49.2
gluteal region — *see also Neoplasm, skin, trunk*	C44.509	C79.2	D04.5	D23.5	D48.5	D49.2
groin — *see also Neoplasm, skin, trunk*	C44.509	C79.2	D04.5	D23.5	D48.5	D49.2

skin NOS *(Continued)*

	Malignant Primary	Malignant Secondary	Ca in situ	Benign	Uncertain Behavior	Unspecified Behavior
hand — *see also Neoplasm, skin, limb, upper*	C44.60-•	C79.2	D04.6-•	D23.6-•	D48.5	D49.2
head NEC — *see also Neoplasm, skin, scalp*	C44.40	C79.2	D04.4	D23.4	D48.5	D49.2
heel — *see also Neoplasm, skin, limb, lower*	C44.70-•	C79.2	D04.7-•	D23.7-•	D48.5	D49.2
helix — *see also Neoplasm, skin, ear*	C44.20-•	C79.2	D04.2-•	D23.2-•	D48.5	D49.2
hip — *see also Neoplasm, skin, limb, lower*	C44.70-•	C79.2	D04.7-•	D23.7-•	D48.5	D49.2
infraclavicular region — *see also Neoplasm, skin, trunk*	C44.509	C79.2	D04.5	D23.5	D48.5	D49.2
inguinal region — *see also Neoplasm, skin, trunk*	C44.509	C79.2	D04.5	D23.5	D48.5	D49.2
jaw — *see also Neoplasm, skin, face*	C44.309	C79.2	D04.39	D23.39	D48.5	D49.2
Kaposi's sarcoma — *see Kaposi's, sarcoma, skin*						
knee — *see also Neoplasm, skin, limb, lower*	C44.70-•	C79.2	D04.7-•	D23.7-•	D48.5	D49.2
labia						
majora	C51.0	C79.82	D07.1	D28.0	D39.8	D49.59
minora	C51.1	C79.82	D07.1	D28.0	D39.8	D49.59
leg — *see also Neoplasm, skin, limb, lower*	C44.70-•	C79.2	D04.7-•	D23.7-•	D48.5	D49.2
lid (lower) (upper)	C44.10-•	C79.2	D04.1-•	D23.1-•	D48.5	D49.2
basal cell carcinoma	C44.11-•	—	—	—	—	—
sebaceous cell	C44.13-•	—	—	—	—	—
specified type NEC	C44.19-•	—	—	—	—	—
squamous cell carcinoma	C44.12-•	—	—	—	—	—
limb NEC	C44.90	C79.2	D04.9	D23.9	D48.5	D49.2
basal cell carcinoma	C44.91					
lower	C44.70-•	C79.2	D04.7-•	D23.7-•	D48.5	D49.2
basal cell carcinoma	C44.71-•	—	—	—	—	—
specified type NEC	C44.79-•	—	—	—	—	—
squamous cell carcinoma	C44.72-•	—	—	—	—	—
upper	C44.60-•	C79.2	D04.6-•	D23.6-•	D48.5	D49.2
basal cell carcinoma	C44.61-•	—	—	—	—	—
specified type NEC	C44.69-•	—	—	—	—	—
squamous cell carcinoma	C44.62-•	—	—	—	—	—
lip (lower) (upper)	C44.00	C79.2	D04.0	D23.0	D48.5	D49.2
basal cell carcinoma	C44.01	—	—	—	—	—
specified type NEC	C44.09	—	—	—	—	—
squamous cell carcinoma	C44.02	—	—	—	—	—

◄ New   ◄ Revised   ~~deleted~~ Deleted   • Use Additional Character(s)

TABLE OF NEOPLASMS

skin NOS (Continued)	Malignant Primary	Malignant Secondary	Ca in situ	Benign	Uncertain Behavior	Unspecified Behavior
male genital organs	C63.9	C79.82	D07.60	D29.9	D40.8	D49.59
penis	C60.9	C79.82	D07.4	D29.0	D40.8	D49.59
prepuce	C60.0	C79.82	D07.4	D29.0	D40.8	D49.59
scrotum	C63.2	C79.82	D07.61	D29.4	D40.8	D49.59
mastectomy site (skin) — see also Neoplasm, skin, breast	C44.501	C79.2	—	—	—	—
specified as breast tissue	C50.8-●	C79.81	—	—	—	—
meatus, acoustic (external) — see also Neoplasm, skin, ear	C44.20-●	C79.2	D04.2-●	D23.2-●	D48.5	D49.2
melanotic — see Melanoma						
Merkel cell — see Carcinoma, Merkel cell						
nates — see also Neoplasm, skin, trunk	C44.509	C79.2	D04.5	D23.5	D48.5	D49.2
neck	C44.40	C79.2	D04.4	D23.4	D48.5	D49.2
basal cell carcinoma	C44.41	—	—	—	—	—
specified type NEC	C44.49	—	—	—	—	—
squamous cell carcinoma	C44.42	—	—	—	—	—
nevus — see Nevus, skin						
nose (external) — see also Neoplasm, nose, skin	C44.301	C79.2	D04.39	D23.39	D48.5	D49.2
overlapping lesion	C44.80	—	—	—	—	—
basal cell carcinoma	C44.81	—	—	—	—	—
specified type NEC	C44.89	—	—	—	—	—
squamous cell carcinoma	C44.82	—	—	—	—	—
palm — see also Neoplasm, skin, limb, upper	C44.60-●	C79.2	D04.6-●	D23.6-●	D48.5	D49.2
palpebra	C44.10-●	C79.2	D04.1-●	D23.1-●	D48.5	D49.2
basal cell carcinoma	C44.11-●	—	—	—	—	—
sebaceous cell	C44.13-●	—	—	—	—	—
specified type NEC	C44.19-●	—	—	—	—	—
squamous cell carcinoma	C44.12-●	—	—	—	—	—
penis NEC	C60.9	C79.82	D07.4	D29.0	D40.8	D49.59
perianal — see also Neoplasm, skin, anus	C44.500	C79.2	D04.5	D23.5	D48.5	D49.2
perineum — see also Neoplasm, skin, anus	C44.500	C79.2	D04.5	D23.5	D48.5	D49.2
pinna — see also Neoplasm, skin, ear	C44.20-●	C79.2	D04.2-●	D23.2-●	D48.5	D49.2
plantar — see also Neoplasm, skin, limb, lower	C44.70-●	C79.2	D04.7-●	D23.7-●	D48.5	D49.2
popliteal fossa or space — see also Neoplasm, skin, limb, lower	C44.70-●	C79.2	D04.7-●	D23.7-●	D48.5	D49.2

skin NOS (Continued)	Malignant Primary	Malignant Secondary	Ca in situ	Benign	Uncertain Behavior	Unspecified Behavior
prepuce	C60.0	C79.82	D07.4	D29.0	D40.8	D49.59
pubes — see also Neoplasm, skin, trunk	C44.509	C79.2	D04.5	D23.5	D48.5	D49.2
sacrococcygeal region — see also Neoplasm, skin, trunk	C44.509	C79.2	D04.5	D23.5	D48.5	D49.2
scalp	C44.40	C79.2	D04.4	D23.4	D48.5	D49.2
basal cell carcinoma	C44.41	—	—	—	—	—
specified type NEC	C44.49	—	—	—	—	—
squamous cell carcinoma	C44.42	—	—	—	—	—
scapular region — see also Neoplasm, skin, trunk	C44.509	C79.2	D04.5	D23.5	D48.5	D49.2
scrotum	C63.2	C79.82	D07.61	D29.4	D40.8	D49.59
shoulder — see also Neoplasm, skin, limb, upper	C44.60-●	C79.2	D04.6-●	D23.6-●	D48.5	D49.2
sole (foot) — see also Neoplasm, skin, limb, lower	C44.70-●	C79.2	D04.7-●	D23.7-●	D48.5	D49.2
specified sites NEC	C44.80	C79.2	D04.8	D23.9	D48.5	D49.2
basal cell carcinoma	C44.81	—	—	—	—	—
specified type NEC	C44.89	—	—	—	—	—
squamous cell carcinoma	C44.82	—	—	—	—	—
specified type NEC	C44.99	—	—	—	—	—
squamous cell carcinoma	C44.92	—	—	—	—	—
submammary fold — see also Neoplasm, skin, trunk	C44.509	C79.2	D04.5	D23.5	D48.5	D49.2
supraclavicular region — see also Neoplasm, skin, neck	C44.40	C79.2	D04.4	D23.4	D48.5	D49.2
temple — see also Neoplasm, skin, face	C44.309	C79.2	D04.39	D23.39	D48.5	D49.2
thigh — see also Neoplasm, skin, limb, lower	C44.70-●	C79.2	D04.7-●	D23.7-●	D48.5	D49.2
thoracic wall — see also Neoplasm, skin, trunk	C44.509	C79.2	D04.5	D23.5	D48.5	D49.2
thumb — see also Neoplasm, skin, limb, upper	C44.60-●	C79.2	D04.6-●	D23.6-●	D48.5	D49.2
toe — see also Neoplasm, skin, limb, lower	C44.70-●	C79.2	D04.7-●	D23.7-●	D48.5	D49.2
tragus — see also Neoplasm, skin, ear	C44.20-●	C79.2	D04.2-●	D23.2-●	D48.5	D49.2
trunk	C44.509	C79.2	D04.5	D23.5	D48.5	D49.2
basal cell carcinoma	C44.519	—	—	—	—	—
specified type NEC	C44.599	—	—	—	—	—
squamous cell carcinoma	C44.529	—	—	—	—	—
umbilicus — see also Neoplasm, skin, trunk	C44.509	C79.2	D04.5	D23.5	D48.5	D49.2

◄ New   ◄ Revised   ~~deleted~~ Deleted   ● Use Additional Character(s)

	Malignant Primary	Malignant Secondary	Ca in situ	Benign	Uncertain Behavior	Unspecified Behavior
skin NOS *(Continued)*						
vulva	C51.9	C79.82	D07.1	D28.0	D39.8	D49.59
overlapping lesion	C51.8	—	—	—	—	—
wrist — *see also Neoplasm, skin, limb, upper*	C44.60-●	C79.2	D04.6-●	D23.6-●	D48.5	D49.2
skull	C41.0	C79.51	—	D16.4-●	D48.0	D49.2
soft parts or tissues — *see Neoplasm, connective tissue*						
specified site NEC	C76.8	C79.89	D09.8	D36.7	D48.7	D49.89
spermatic cord	C63.1-●	C79.82	D07.69	D29.8	D40.8	D49.59
sphenoid	C31.3	C78.39	D02.3	D14.0	D38.5	D49.1
bone	C41.0	C79.51	—	D16.4-●	D48.0	D49.2
sinus	C31.3	C78.39	D02.3	D14.0	D38.5	D49.1
sphincter						
anal	C21.1	C78.5	D01.3	D12.9	D37.8	D49.0
of Oddi	C24.0	C78.89	D01.5	D13.5	D37.6	D49.0
spine, spinal (column)	C41.2	C79.51	—	D16.6	D48.0	D49.2
bulb	C71.7	C79.31	—	D33.1	D43.1	D49.6
coccyx	C41.4	C79.51	—	D16.8	D48.0	D49.2
cord (cervical) (lumbar) (sacral) (thoracic)	C72.0	C79.49	—	D33.4	D43.4	D49.7
dura mater	C70.1	C79.49	—	D32.1	D42.1	D49.7
lumbosacral	C41.2	C79.51	—	D16.6	D48.0	D49.2
marrow NEC	C96.9	C79.52	—	—	D47.9	D49.89
membrane	C70.1	C79.49	—	D32.1	D42.1	D49.7
meninges	C70.1	C79.49	—	D32.1	D42.1	D49.7
nerve (root)	C47.9	C79.89	—	D36.10	D48.2	D49.2
pia mater	C70.1	C79.49	—	D32.1	D42.1	D49.7
root	C47.9	C79.89	—	D36.10	D48.2	D49.2
sacrum	C41.4	C79.51	—	D16.8	D48.0	D49.2
spleen, splenic NEC	C26.1	C78.89	D01.7	D13.9	D37.8	D49.0
flexure (colon)	C18.5	C78.5	D01.0	D12.3	D37.4	D49.0
stem, brain	C71.7	C79.31	—	D33.1	D43.1	D49.6
Stensen's duct	C07	C79.89	D00.00	D11.0	D37.030	D49.0
sternum	C41.3	C79.51	—	D16.7	D48.0	D49.2
stomach	C16.9	C78.89	D00.2	D13.1	D37.1	D49.0
antrum (pyloric)	C16.3	C78.89	D00.2	D13.1	D37.1	D49.0
body	C16.2	C78.89	D00.2	D13.1	D37.1	D49.0
cardia	C16.0	C78.89	D00.2	D13.1	D37.1	D49.0
cardiac orifice	C16.0	C78.89	D00.2	D13.1	D37.1	D49.0
corpus	C16.2	C78.89	D00.2	D13.1	D37.1	D49.0
fundus	C16.1	C78.89	D00.2	D13.1	D37.1	D49.0
greater curvature NEC	C16.6	C78.89	D00.2	D13.1	D37.1	D49.0
lesser curvature NEC	C16.5	C78.89	D00.2	D13.1	D37.1	D49.0

	Malignant Primary	Malignant Secondary	Ca in situ	Benign	Uncertain Behavior	Unspecified Behavior
stomach *(Continued)*						
overlapping lesion	C16.8	—	—	—	—	—
prepylorus	C16.4	C78.89	D00.2	D13.1	D37.1	D49.0
pylorus	C16.4	C78.89	D00.2	D13.1	D37.1	D49.0
wall NEC	C16.9	C78.89	D00.2	D13.1	D37.1	D49.0
anterior NEC	C16.8	C78.89	D00.2	D13.1	D37.1	D49.0
posterior NEC	C16.8	C78.89	D00.2	D13.1	D37.1	D49.0
stroma, endometrial	C54.1	C79.82	D07.0	D26.1	D39.0	D49.59
stump, cervical	C53.8	C79.82	D06.7	D26.0	D39.0	D49.59
subcutaneous (nodule) (tissue) NEC — *see Neoplasm, connective tissue*						
subdural	C70.9	C79.32	—	D32.9	D42.9	D49.7
subglottis, subglottic	C32.2	C78.39	D02.0	D14.1	D38.0	D49.1
sublingual	C04.9	C79.89	D00.06	D10.2	D37.09	D49.0
gland or duct	C08.1	C79.89	D00.00	D11.7	D37.031	D49.0
submandibular gland	C08.0	C79.89	D00.00	D11.7	D37.032	D49.0
submaxillary gland or duct	C08.0	C79.89	D00.00	D11.7	D37.032	D49.0
submental	C76.0	C79.89	D09.8	D36.7	D48.7	D49.89
subpleural	C34.9-●	C78.0-●	D02.2-●	D14.3-●	D38.1	D49.1
substernal	C38.1	C78.1	—	D15.2	D38.3	D49.89
sudoriferous, sudoriparous gland, site unspecified	C44.90	C79.2	D04.9	D23.9	D48.5	D49.2
specified site — *see Neoplasm, skin*						
supraclavicular region	C76.0	C79.89	D09.8	D36.7	D48.7	D49.89
supraglottis	C32.1	C78.39	D02.0	D14.1	D38.0	D49.1
suprarenal	C74.9-●	C79.7-●	D09.3	D35.0-●	D44.1-●	D49.7
capsule	C74.9-●	C79.7-●	D09.3	D35.0-●	D44.1-●	D49.7
cortex	C74.0-●	C79.7-●	D09.3	D35.0-●	D44.1-●	D49.7
gland	C74.9-●	C79.7-●	D09.3	D35.0-●	D44.1-●	D49.7
medulla	C74.1-●	C79.7-●	D09.3	D35.0-●	D44.1-●	D49.7
suprasellar (region)	C71.9	C79.31	—	D33.2	D43.2	D49.6
supratentorial (brain) NEC	C71.0	C79.31	—	D33.0	D43.0	D49.6
sweat gland (apocrine) (eccrine), site unspecified	C44.90	C79.2	D04.9	D23.9	D48.5	D49.2
specified site — *see Neoplasm, skin*						
sympathetic nerve or nervous system NEC	C47.9	C79.89	—	D36.10	D48.2	D49.2
symphysis pubis	C41.4	C79.51	—	D16.8	D48.0	D49.2
synovial membrane — *see Neoplasm, connective tissue*						
tapetum, brain	C71.8	C79.31	—	D33.2	D43.2	D49.6

◀ New　◀ Revised　~~deleted~~ Deleted　● Use Additional Character(s)

TABLE OF NEOPLASMS

	Malignant Primary	Malignant Secondary	Ca in situ	Benign	Uncertain Behavior	Unspecified Behavior
tarsus (any bone)	C40.3-●	C79.51	—	D16.3-●	—	—
temple (skin) — see also Neoplasm, skin, face	C44.309	C79.2	D04.39	D23.39	D48.5	D49.2
temporal						
bone	C41.0	C79.51	—	D16.4-●	D48.0	D49.2
lobe or pole	C71.2	C79.31	—	D33.0	D43.0	D49.6
region	C76.0	C79.89	D09.8	D36.7	D48.7	D49.89
skin — see also Neoplasm, skin, face	C44.309	C79.2	D04.39	D23.39	D48.5	D49.2
tendon (sheath) — see Neoplasm, connective tissue						
tentorium (cerebelli)	C70.0	C79.32	—	D32.0	D42.0	D49.7
testis, testes	C62.9-●	C79.82	D07.69	D29.2-●	D40.1-●	D49.59
descended	C62.1-●	C79.82	D07.69	D29.2-●	D40.1-●	D49.59
ectopic	C62.0-●	C79.82	D07.69	D29.2-●	D40.1-●	D49.59
retained	C62.0-●	C79.82	D07.69	D29.2-●	D40.1-●	D49.59
scrotal	C62.1-●	C79.82	D07.69	D29.2-●	D40.1-●	D49.59
undescended	C62.0-●	C79.82	D07.69	D29.2-●	D40.1-●	D49.59
unspecified whether descended or undescended	C62.9-●	C79.82	D07.69	D29.2-●	D40.1-●	D49.59
thalamus	C71.0	C79.31	—	D33.0	D43.0	D49.6
thigh NEC	C76.5-●	C79.89	D04.7-●	D36.7	D48.7	D49.89
thorax, thoracic (cavity) (organs NEC)	C76.1	C79.89	D09.8	D36.7	D48.7	D49.89
duct	C49.3	C79.89		D21.3	D48.1	D49.2
wall NEC	C76.1	C79.89	D09.8	D36.7	D48.7	D49.89
throat	C14.0	C79.89	D00.08	D10.9	D37.05	D49.0
thumb NEC	C76.4-●	C79.89	D04.6-●	D36.7	D48.7	D49.89
thymus (gland)	C37	C79.89	D09.3	D15.0	D38.4	D49.89
thyroglossal duct	C73	C79.89	D09.3	D34	D44.0	D49.7
thyroid (gland)	C73	C79.89	D09.3	D34	D44.0	D49.7
cartilage	C32.3	C78.39	D02.0	D14.1	D38.0	D49.1
tibia (any part)	C40.2-●	C79.51	—	D16.2-●	—	—
toe NEC	C76.5-●	C79.89	D04.7-●	D36.7	D48.7	D49.89
tongue	C02.9	C79.89	D00.07	D10.1	D37.02	D49.0
anterior (two-thirds) NEC	C02.3	C79.89	D00.07	D10.1	D37.02	D49.0
dorsal surface	C02.0	C79.89	D00.07	D10.1	D37.02	D49.0
ventral surface	C02.2	C79.89	D00.07	D10.1	D37.02	D49.0
base (dorsal surface)	C01	C79.89	D00.07	D10.1	D37.02	D49.0
border (lateral)	C02.1	C79.89	D00.07	D10.1	D37.02	D49.0
dorsal surface NEC	C02.0	C79.89	D00.07	D10.1	D37.02	D49.0
fixed part NEC	C01	C79.89	D00.07	D10.1	D37.02	D49.0
foreamen cecum	C02.0	C79.89	D00.07	D10.1	D37.02	D49.0
frenulum linguae	C02.2	C79.89	D00.07	D10.1	D37.02	D49.0

	Malignant Primary	Malignant Secondary	Ca in situ	Benign	Uncertain Behavior	Unspecified Behavior
tongue (Continued)						
junctional zone	C02.8	C79.89	D00.07	D10.1	D37.02	D49.0
margin (lateral)	C02.1	C79.89	D00.07	D10.1	D37.02	D49.0
midline NEC	C02.0	C79.89	D00.07	D10.1	D37.02	D49.0
mobile part NEC	C02.3	C79.89	D00.07	D10.1	D37.02	D49.0
overlapping lesion	C02.8	—	—	—	—	—
posterior (third)	C01	C79.89	D00.07	D10.1	D37.02	D49.0
root	C01	C79.89	D00.07	D10.1	D37.02	D49.0
surface (dorsal)	C02.0	C79.89	D00.07	D10.1	D37.02	D49.0
base	C01	C79.89	D00.07	D10.1	D37.02	D49.0
ventral	C02.2	C79.89	D00.07	D10.1	D37.02	D49.0
tip	C02.1	C79.89	D00.07	D10.1	D37.02	D49.0
tonsil	C02.4	C79.89	D00.07	D10.1	D37.02	D49.0
tonsil	C09.9	C79.89	D00.08	D10.4	D37.05	D49.0
fauces, faucial	C09.9	C79.89	D00.08	D10.4	D37.05	D49.0
lingual	C02.4	C79.89	D00.07	D10.1	D37.02	D49.0
overlapping sites	C09.8	—	—	—	—	—
palatine	C09.9	C79.89	D00.08	D10.4	D37.05	D49.0
pharyngeal	C11.1	C79.89	D00.08	D10.6	D37.05	D49.0
pillar (anterior) (posterior)	C09.1	C79.89	D00.08	D10.5	D37.05	D49.0
tonsillar fossa	C09.0	C79.89	D00.08	D10.5	D37.05	D49.0
tooth socket NEC	C03.9	C79.89	D00.03	D10.39	D37.09	D49.0
trachea (cartilage) (mucosa)	C33	C78.39	D02.1	D14.2	D38.1	D49.1
overlapping lesion with bronchus or lung	C34.8-●	—	—	—	—	—
tracheobronchial	C34.8-●	C78.39	D02.1	D14.2	D38.1	D49.1
overlapping lesion with lung	C34.8-●	—	—	—	—	—
tragus — see also Neoplasm, skin, ear	C44.20-●	C79.2	D04.2-●	D23.2-●	D48.5	D49.2
trunk NEC	C76.8	C79.89	D04.5	D36.7	D48.7	D49.89
tubo-ovarian	C57.8	C79.82	D07.39	D28.7	D39.8	D49.59
tunica vaginalis	C63.7	C79.82	D07.69	D29.8	D40.8	D49.59
turbinate (bone)	C41.0	C79.51	—	D16.4-●	D48.0	D49.2
nasal	C30.0	C78.39	D02.3	D14.0	D38.5	D49.1
tympanic cavity	C30.1	C78.39	D02.3	D14.0	D38.5	D49.1
ulna (any part)	C40.0-●	C79.51	—	D16.0-●	—	—
umbilicus, umbilical — see also Neoplasm, skin, trunk	C44.509	C79.2	D04.5	D23.5	D48.5	D49.2
uncus, brain	C71.2	C79.31	—	D33.0	D43.0	D49.6
unknown site or unspecified	C80.1	C79.9	D09.9	D36.9	D48.9	D49.9
urachus	C67.7	C79.11	D09.0	D30.3	D41.4	D49.4
ureter, ureteral	C66.-●	C79.19	D09.19	D30.2-●	D41.2-●	D49.59
orifice (bladder)	C67.6	C79.11	D09.0	D30.3	D41.4	D49.4
ureter-bladder (junction)	C67.6	C79.11	D09.0	D30.3	D41.4	D49.4

◀ New   ◀ Revised   ~~deleted~~ Deleted   ● Use Additional Character(s)

	Malignant Primary	Malignant Secondary	Ca in situ	Benign	Uncertain Behavior	Unspecified Behavior
urethra, urethral (gland)	C68.0	C79.19	D09.19	D30.4	D41.3	D49.59
orifice, internal	C67.5	C79.11	D09.0	D30.3	D41.4	D49.4
urethrovaginal (septum)	C57.9	C79.82	D07.30	D28.9	D39.8	D49.59
urinary organ or system	C68.9	C79.10	D09.10	D30.9	D41.9	D49.59
bladder — *see Neoplasm, bladder*						
overlapping lesion	C68.8	—	—	—	—	—
specified sites NEC	C68.8	C79.19	D09.19	D30.8	D41.8	D49.59
utero-ovarian	C57.8	C79.82	D07.39	D28.7	D39.8	D49.59
ligament	C57.1	C79.82	D07.39	D28.2	D39.8	D49.59
uterosacral ligament	C57.3	C79.82	—	D28.2	D39.8	D49.59
uterus, uteri, uterine	C55	C79.82	D07.0	D26.9	D39.0	D49.59
adnexa NEC	C57.4	C79.82	D07.39	D28.7	D39.8	D49.59
body	C54.9	C79.82	D07.0	D26.1	D39.0	D49.59
cervix	C53.9	C79.82	D06.9	D26.0	D39.0	D49.59
cornu	C54.9	C79.82	D07.0	D26.1	D39.0	D49.59
corpus	C54.9	C79.82	D07.0	D26.1	D39.0	D49.59
endocervix (canal) (gland)	C53.0	C79.82	D06.0	D26.0	D39.0	D49.59
endometrium	C54.1	C79.82	D07.0	D26.1	D39.0	D49.59
exocervix	C53.1	C79.82	D06.1	D26.0	D39.0	D49.59
external os	C53.1	C79.82	D06.1	D26.0	D39.0	D49.59
fundus	C54.3	C79.82	D07.0	D26.1	D39.0	D49.59
internal os	C53.0	C79.82	D06.0	D26.0	D39.0	D49.59
isthmus	C54.0	C79.82	D07.0	D26.1	D39.0	D49.59
ligament	C57.3	C79.82	—	D28.2	D39.8	D49.59
broad	C57.1	C79.82	D07.39	D28.2	D39.8	D49.59
round	C57.2	C79.82	—	D28.2	D39.8	D49.59
lower segment	C54.0	C79.82	D07.0	D26.1	D39.0	D49.59
myometrium	C54.2	C79.82	D07.0	D26.1	D39.0	D49.59
overlapping sites	C54.8	—	—	—	—	—
squamocolumnar junction	C53.8	C79.82	D06.7	D26.0	D39.0	D49.59
tube	C57.0-●	C79.82	D07.39	D28.2	D39.8	D49.59
utricle, prostatic	C68.0	C79.19	D09.19	D30.4	D41.3	D49.59
uveal tract	C69.4-●	C79.49	D09.2-●	D31.4-●	D48.7	D49.89
uvula	C05.2	C79.89	D00.04	D10.39	D37.09	D49.0
vagina, vaginal (fornix) (vault) (wall)	C52	C79.82	D07.2	D28.1	D39.8	D49.59
vaginovesical	C57.9	C79.82	D07.30	D28.9	D39.9	D49.59
septum	C57.9	C79.82	D07.30	D28.9	D39.9	D49.59
vallecula (epigiottis)	C10.0	C79.89	D00.08	D10.5	D37.05	D49.0
vas deferens	C63.1-●	C79.82	D07.69	D29.8	D40.8	D49.59
vascular — *see Neoplasm, connective tissue*						

	Malignant Primary	Malignant Secondary	Ca in situ	Benign	Uncertain Behavior	Unspecified Behavior
Vater's ampulla	C24.1	C78.89	D01.5	D13.5	D37.6	D49.0
vein, venous — *see Neoplasm, connective tissue*						
vena cava (abdominal) (inferior)	C49.4	C79.89	—	D21.4	D48.1	D49.2
superior	C49.3	C79.89	—	D21.3	D48.1	D49.2
ventricle (cerebral) (floor) (lateral) (third)	C71.5	C79.31	—	D33.0	D43.0	D49.6
cardiac (left) (right)	C38.0	C79.89	—	D15.1	D48.7	D49.89
fourth	C71.7	C79.31	—	D33.1	D43.1	D49.6
ventricular band of larynx	C32.1	C78.39	D02.0	D14.1	D38.0	D49.1
ventriculus — *see Neoplasm, stomach*						
vermillion border — *see Neoplasm, lip*						
vermis, cerebellum	C71.6	C79.31	—	D33.1	D43.1	D49.6
vertebra (column)	C41.2	C79.51	—	D16.6	D48.0	D49.2
coccyx	C41.4	C79.51	—	D16.8-●	D48.0	D49.2
marrow NEC	C96.9	C79.52	—	—	D47.9	D49.89
sacrum	C41.4	C79.51	—	D16.8-●	D48.0	D49.2
vesical — *see Neoplasm, bladder*						
vesicle, seminal	C63.7	C79.82	D07.69	D29.8	D40.8	D49.59
vesicocervical tissue	C57.9	C79.82	D07.30	D28.9	D39.9	D49.59
vesicorectal	C76.3	C79.82	D09.8	D36.7	D48.7	D49.89
vesicovaginal	C57.9	C79.82	D07.30	D28.9	D39.9	D49.59
septum	C57.9	C79.82	D07.30	D28.9	D39.8	D49.59
vessel (blood) — *see Neoplasm, connective tissue*						
vestibular gland, greater	C51.0	C79.82	D07.1	D28.0	D39.8	D49.59
vestibule						
mouth	C06.1	C79.89	D00.00	D10.39	D37.09	D49.0
nose	C30.0	C78.39	D02.3	D14.0	D38.5	D49.1
Virchow's gland	C77.0	C77.0	—	D36.0	D48.7	D49.89
viscera NEC	C76.8	C79.89	D09.8	D36.7	D48.7	D49.89
vocal cords (true)	C32.0	C78.39	D02.0	D14.1	D38.0	D49.1
false	C32.1	C78.39	D02.0	D14.1	D38.0	D49.1
vomer	C41.0	C79.51	—	D16.4-●	D48.0	D49.2
vulva	C51.9	C79.82	D07.1	D28.0	D39.8	D49.59
vulvovaginal gland	C51.0	C79.82	D07.1	D28.0	D39.8	D49.59
Waldeyer's ring	C14.2	C79.89	D00.08	D10.9	D37.05	D49.0
Wharton's duct	C08.0	C79.89	D00.00	D11.7	D37.032	D49.0
white matter (central) (cerebral)	C71.0	C79.31	—	D33.0	D43.0	D49.6
windpipe	C33	C78.39	D02.1	D14.2	D38.1	D49.1

◄ New   ◄ Revised   ~~deleted~~ Deleted   ● Use Additional Character(s)

TABLE OF NEOPLASMS

	Malignant Primary	Malignant Secondary	Ca in situ	Benign	Uncertain Behavior	Unspecified Behavior
Wirsung's duct	C25.3	C78.89	D01.7	D13.6	D37.8	D49.0
wolffian (body) (duct)						
female	C57.7	C79.82	D07.39	D28.7	D39.8	D49.59
male	C63.7	C79.82	D07.69	D29.8	D40.8	D49.59

	Malignant Primary	Malignant Secondary	Ca in situ	Benign	Uncertain Behavior	Unspecified Behavior
womb— *see Neoplasm, uterus*						
wrist NEC	C76.4-●	C79.89	D04.6-●	D36.7	D48.7	D49.89
xiphoid process	C41.3	C79.51	—	D16.7	D48.0	D49.2
Zuckerkandl organ	C75.5	C79.89	—	D35.6	D44.7	D49.7

◀ New   ◀ Revised   ~~deleted~~ Deleted   ● Use Additional Character(s)

ICD-10-CM
Table of Drugs and Chemicals

ICD-10-CM
Table of Drugs and Chemicals

Substance	Poisoning, Accidental (Unintentional)	Poisoning, Intentional Self-Harm	Poisoning, Assault	Poisoning, Undetermined	Adverse Effect	Underdosing
#						
1-propanol	T51.3X1	T51.3X2	T51.3X3	T51.3X4	—	—
2-propanol	T51.2X1	T51.2X2	T51.2X3	T51.2X4	—	—
2,4-D (dichlorophen-oxyacetic acid)	T60.3X1	T60.3X2	T60.3X3	T60.3X4	—	—
2,4-toluene diisocyanate	T65.0X1	T65.0X2	T65.0X3	T65.0X4	—	—
2,4,5-T (trichloro-phenoxyacetic acid)	T60.1X1	T60.1X2	T60.1X3	T60.1X4	—	—
3,4-methylenedioxy-methamphetamine	T43.641	T43.642	T43.643	T43.644		
14-hydroxydihydro-morphinone	T40.2X1	T40.2X2	T40.2X3	T40.2X4	T40.2X5	T40.2X6
A						
ABOB	T37.5X1	T37.5X2	T37.5X3	T37.5X4	T37.5X5	T37.5X6
Abrine	T62.2X1	T62.2X2	T62.2X3	T62.2X4	—	—
Abrus (seed)	T62.2X1	T62.2X2	T62.2X3	T62.2X4	—	—
Absinthe	T51.0X1	T51.0X2	T51.0X3	T51.0X4	—	—
beverage	T51.0X1	T51.0X2	T51.0X3	T51.0X4	—	—
Acaricide	T60.8X1	T60.8X2	T60.8X3	T60.8X4	—	—
Acebutolol	T44.7X1	T44.7X2	T44.7X3	T44.7X4	T44.7X5	T44.7X6
Acecarbromal	T42.6X1	T42.6X2	T42.6X3	T42.6X4	T42.6X5	T42.6X6
Aceclidine	T44.1X1	T44.1X2	T44.1X3	T44.1X4	T44.1X5	T44.1X6
Acedapsone	T37.0X1	T37.0X2	T37.0X3	T37.0X4	T37.0X5	T37.0X6
Acefylline piperazine	T48.6X1	T48.6X2	T48.6X3	T48.6X4	T48.6X5	T48.6X6
Acemorphan	T40.2X1	T40.2X2	T40.2X3	T40.2X4	T40.2X5	T40.2X6
Acenocoumarin	T45.511	T45.512	T45.513	T45.514	T45.515	T45.516
Acenocoumarol	T45.511	T45.512	T45.513	T45.514	T45.515	T45.516
Acepifylline	T48.6X1	T48.6X2	T48.6X3	T48.6X4	T48.6X5	T48.6X6
Acepromazine	T43.3X1	T43.3X2	T43.3X3	T43.3X4	T43.3X5	T43.3X6
Acesulfamethoxypyridazine	T37.0X1	T37.0X2	T37.0X3	T37.0X4	T37.0X5	T37.0X6
Acetal	T52.8X1	T52.8X2	T52.8X3	T52.8X4	—	—
Acetaldehyde (vapor)	T52.8X1	T52.8X2	T52.8X3	T52.8X4	—	—
liquid	T65.891	T65.892	T65.893	T65.894	—	—
P-Acetamidophenol	T39.1X1	T39.1X2	T39.1X3	T39.1X4	T39.1X5	T39.1X6
Acetaminophen	T39.1X1	T39.1X2	T39.1X3	T39.1X4	T39.1X5	T39.1X6
Acetaminosalol	T39.1X1	T39.1X2	T39.1X3	T39.1X4	T39.1X5	T39.1X6
Acetanilide	T39.1X1	T39.1X2	T39.1X3	T39.1X4	T39.1X5	T39.1X6
Acetarsol	T37.3X1	T37.3X2	T37.3X3	T37.3X4	T37.3X5	T37.3X6
Acetazolamide	T50.2X1	T50.2X2	T50.2X3	T50.2X4	T50.2X5	T50.2X6
Acetiamine	T45.2X1	T45.2X2	T45.2X3	T45.2X4	T45.2X5	T45.2X6
Acetic						
acid	T54.2X1	T54.2X2	T54.2X3	T54.2X4	—	—
with sodium acetate (ointment)	T49.3X1	T49.3X2	T49.3X3	T49.3X4	T49.3X5	T49.3X6

Substance	Poisoning, Accidental (Unintentional)	Poisoning, Intentional Self-Harm	Poisoning, Assault	Poisoning, Undetermined	Adverse Effect	Underdosing
Acetic (Continued)						
acid (Continued)						
ester (solvent) (vapor)	T52.8X1	T52.8X2	T52.8X3	T52.8X4	—	—
irrigating solution	T50.3X1	T50.3X2	T50.3X3	T50.3X4	T50.3X5	T50.3X6
medicinal (lotion)	T49.2X1	T49.2X2	T49.2X3	T49.2X4	T49.2X5	T49.2X6
anhydride	T65.891	T65.892	T65.893	T65.894		
ether (vapor)	T52.8X1	T52.8X2	T52.8X3	T52.8X4		
Acetohexamide	T38.3X1	T38.3X2	T38.3X3	T38.3X4	T38.3X5	T38.3X6
Acetohydroxamic acid	T50.991	T50.992	T50.993	T50.994	T50.995	T50.996
Acetomenaphthone	T45.7X1	T45.7X2	T45.7X3	T45.7X4	T45.7X5	T45.7X6
Acetomorphine	T40.1X1	T40.1X2	T40.1X3	T40.1X4	—	—
Acetone (oils)	T52.4X1	T52.4X2	T52.4X3	T52.4X4	—	—
chlorinated	T52.4X1	T52.4X2	T52.4X3	T52.4X4	—	—
vapor	T52.4X1	T52.4X2	T52.4X3	T52.4X4	—	—
Acetonitrile	T52.8X1	T52.8X2	T52.8X3	T52.8X4	—	—
Acetophenazine	T43.3X1	T43.3X2	T43.3X3	T43.3X4	T43.3X5	T43.3X6
Acetophenetedin	T39.1X1	T39.1X2	T39.1X3	T39.1X4	T39.1X5	T39.1X6
Acetophenone	T52.4X1	T52.4X2	T52.4X3	T52.4X4	—	—
Acetorphine	T40.2X1	T40.2X2	T40.2X3	T40.2X4	—	—
Acetosulfone (sodium)	T37.1X1	T37.1X2	T37.1X3	T37.1X4	T37.1X5	T37.1X6
Acetrizoate (sodium)	T50.8X1	T50.8X2	T50.8X3	T50.8X4	T50.8X5	T50.8X6
Acetylcarbromal	T42.6X1	T42.6X2	T42.6X3	T42.6X4	T42.6X5	T42.6X6
Acetrizoic acid	T50.8X1	T50.8X2	T50.8X3	T50.8X4	T50.8X5	T50.8X6
Acetyl						
bromide	T53.6X1	T53.6X2	T53.6X3	T53.6X4		
chloride	T53.6X1	T53.6X2	T53.6X3	T53.6X4	—	—
Acetylcholine						
chloride	T44.1X1	T44.1X2	T44.1X3	T44.1X4	T44.1X5	T44.1X6
derivative	T44.1X1	T44.1X2	T44.1X3	T44.1X4	T44.1X5	T44.1X6
Acetylcysteine	T48.4X1	T48.4X2	T48.4X3	T48.4X4	T48.4X5	T48.4X6
Acetyldigitoxin	T46.0X1	T46.0X2	T46.0X3	T46.0X4	T46.0X5	T46.0X6
Acetyldigoxin	T46.0X1	T46.0X2	T46.0X3	T46.0X4	T46.0X5	T46.0X6
Acetyldihydrocodeine	T40.2X1	T40.2X2	T40.2X3	T40.2X4	—	—
Acetyldihydrocodeinone	T40.2X1	T40.2X2	T40.2X3	T40.2X4	—	—
Acetylene (gas)	T59.891	T59.892	T59.893	T59.894	—	—
dichloride	T53.6X1	T53.6X2	T53.6X3	T53.6X4	—	—
incomplete combustion of	T58.11	T58.12	T58.13	T58.14		
industrial	T59.891	T59.892	T59.893	T59.894	—	—
tetrachloride	T53.6X1	T53.6X2	T53.6X3	T53.6X4	—	—
vapor	T53.6X1	T53.6X2	T53.6X3	T53.6X4	—	—
Acetylphenylhydrazine	T39.8X1	T39.8X2	T39.8X3	T39.8X4	T39.8X5	T39.8X6
Acetylpheneturide	T42.6X1	T42.6X2	T42.6X3	T42.6X4	T42.6X5	T42.6X6

◄ New   ◄ Revised   deleted Deleted

Substance	Poisoning, Accidental (Unintentional)	Poisoning, Intentional Self-Harm	Poisoning, Assault	Poisoning, Undetermined	Adverse Effect	Underdosing
Acetylsalicylic acid (salts)	T39.011	T39.012	T39.013	T39.014	T39.015	T39.016
enteric coated	T39.011	T39.012	T39.013	T39.014	T39.015	T39.016
Acetylsulfamethoxypyridazine	T37.0X1	T37.0X2	T37.0X3	T37.0X4	T37.0X5	T37.0X6
Achromycin	T36.4X1	T36.4X2	T36.4X3	T36.4X4	T36.4X5	T36.4X6
ophthalmic preparation	T49.5X1	T49.5X2	T49.5X3	T49.5X4	T49.5X5	T49.5X6
topical NEC	T49.0X1	T49.0X2	T49.0X3	T49.0X4	T49.0X5	T49.0X6
Aciclovir	T37.5X1	T37.5X2	T37.5X3	T37.5X4	T37.5X5	T37.5X6
Acid (corrosive) NEC	T54.2X1	T54.2X2	T54.2X3	T54.2X4	—	—
Acidifying agent NEC	T50.901	T50.902	T50.903	T50.904	T50.905	T50.906
Acipimox	T46.6X1	T46.6X2	T46.6X3	T46.6X4	T46.6X5	T46.6X6
Acitretin	T50.991	T50.992	T50.993	T50.994	T50.995	T50.996
Aclarubicin	T45.1X1	T45.1X2	T45.1X3	T45.1X4	T45.1X5	T45.1X6
Aclatonium napadisilate	T48.1X1	T48.1X2	T48.1X3	T48.1X4	T48.1X5	T48.1X6
Aconite (wild)	T46.991	T46.992	T46.993	T46.994	T46.995	T46.996
Aconitine	T46.991	T46.992	T46.993	T46.994	T46.995	T46.996
Aconitum ferox	T46.991	T46.992	T46.993	T46.994	T46.995	T46.996
Acridine	T65.6X1	T65.6X2	T65.6X3	T65.6X4	—	—
vapor	T59.891	T59.892	T59.893	T59.894	—	—
Acriflavine	T37.91	T37.92	T37.93	T37.94	T37.95	T37.96
Acriflavinium chloride	T49.0X1	T49.0X2	T49.0X3	T49.0X4	T49.0X5	T49.0X6
Acrinol	T49.0X1	T49.0X2	T49.0X3	T49.0X4	T49.0X5	T49.0X6
Acrisorcin	T49.0X1	T49.0X2	T49.0X3	T49.0X4	T49.0X5	T49.0X6
Acrivastine	T45.0X1	T45.0X2	T45.0X3	T45.0X4	T45.0X5	T45.0X6
Acrolein (gas)	T59.891	T59.892	T59.893	T59.894	—	—
liquid	T54.1X1	T54.1X2	T54.1X3	T54.1X4	—	—
Acrylamide	T65.891	T65.892	T65.893	T65.894	—	—
Acrylic resin	T49.3X1	T49.3X2	T49.3X3	T49.3X4	T49.3X5	T49.3X6
Acrylonitrile	T65.891	T65.892	T65.893	T65.894	—	—
Actaea spicata	T62.2X1	T62.2X2	T62.2X3	T62.2X4	—	—
berry	T62.1X1	T62.1X2	T62.1X3	T62.1X4	—	—
Acterol	T37.3X1	T37.3X2	T37.3X3	T37.3X4	T37.3X5	T37.3X6
ACTH	T38.811	T38.812	T38.813	T38.814	T38.815	T38.816
Actinomycin C	T45.1X1	T45.1X2	T45.1X3	T45.1X4	T45.1X5	T45.1X6
Actinomycin D	T45.1X1	T45.1X2	T45.1X3	T45.1X4	T45.1X5	T45.1X6
Activated charcoal — see also Charcoal, medicinal	T47.6X1	T47.6X2	T47.6X3	T47.6X4	T47.6X5	T47.6X6
Acyclovir	T37.5X1	T37.5X2	T37.5X3	T37.5X4	T37.5X5	T37.5X6
Adenine	T45.2X1	T45.2X2	T45.2X3	T45.2X4	T45.2X5	T45.2X6
arabinoside	T37.5X1	T37.5X2	T37.5X3	T37.5X4	T37.5X5	T37.5X6
Adenosine (phosphate)	T46.2X1	T46.2X2	T46.2X3	T46.2X4	T46.2X5	T46.2X6
ADH	T38.891	T38.892	T38.893	T38.894	T38.895	T38.896
Adhesive NEC	T65.891	T65.892	T65.893	T65.894	—	—

Substance	Poisoning, Accidental (Unintentional)	Poisoning, Intentional Self-Harm	Poisoning, Assault	Poisoning, Undetermined	Adverse Effect	Underdosing
Adicillin	T36.0X1	T36.0X2	T36.0X3	T36.0X4	T36.0X5	T36.0X6
Adiphenine	T44.3X1	T44.3X2	T44.3X3	T44.3X4	T44.3X5	T44.3X6
Adipiodone	T50.8X1	T50.8X2	T50.8X3	T50.8X4	T50.8X5	T50.8X6
Adjunct, pharmaceutical	T50.901	T50.902	T50.903	T50.904	T50.905	T50.906
Adrenal (extract, cortex or medulla) (glucocorticoids) (hormones) (mineralo corticoids)	T38.0X1	T38.0X2	T38.0X3	T38.0X4	T38.0X5	T38.0X6
ENT agent	T49.6X1	T49.6X2	T49.6X3	T49.6X4	T49.6X5	T49.6X6
ophthalmic preparation	T49.5X1	T49.5X2	T49.5X3	T49.5X4	T49.5X5	T49.5X6
topical NEC	T49.0X1	T49.0X2	T49.0X3	T49.0X4	T49.0X5	T49.0X6
Adrenaline	T44.5X1	T44.5X2	T44.5X3	T44.5X4	T44.5X5	T44.5X6
Adrenalin — see Adrenaline						
Adrenergic NEC	T44.901	T44.902	T44.903	T44.904	T44.905	T44.906
blocking agent NEC	T44.8X1	T44.8X2	T44.8X3	T44.8X4	T44.8X5	T44.8X6
beta, heart	T44.7X1	T44.7X2	T44.7X3	T44.7X4	T44.7X5	T44.7X6
specified NEC	T44.991	T44.992	T44.993	T44.994	T44.995	T44.996
Adrenochrome						
(mono) semicarbazone	T46.991	T46.992	T46.993	T46.994	T46.995	T46.996
derivative	T46.991	T46.992	T46.993	T46.994	T46.995	T46.996
Adrenocorticotrophic hormone	T38.811	T38.812	T38.813	T38.814	T38.815	T38.816
Adrenocorticotrophin	T38.811	T38.812	T38.813	T38.814	T38.815	T38.816
Adriamycin	T45.1X1	T45.1X2	T45.1X3	T45.1X4	T45.1X5	T45.1X6
Aerosol spray NEC	T65.91	T65.92	T65.93	T65.94	—	—
Aerosporin	T36.8X1	T36.8X2	T36.8X3	T36.8X4	T36.8X5	T36.8X6
ENT agent	T49.6X1	T49.6X2	T49.6X3	T49.6X4	T49.6X5	T49.6X6
ophthalmic preparation	T49.5X1	T49.5X2	T49.5X3	T49.5X4	T49.5X5	T49.5X6
topical NEC	T49.0X1	T49.0X2	T49.0X3	T49.0X4	T49.0X5	T49.0X6
Aethusa cynapium	T62.2X1	T62.2X2	T62.2X3	T62.2X4	—	—
Afghanistan black	T40.7X1	T40.7X2	T40.7X3	T40.7X4	T40.7X5	T40.7X6
Aflatoxin	T64.01	T64.02	T64.03	T64.04	—	—
Afloqualone	T42.8X1	T42.8X2	T42.8X3	T42.8X4	T42.8X5	T42.8X6
African boxwood	T62.2X1	T62.2X2	T62.2X3	T62.2X4	—	—
Agar	T47.4X1	T47.4X2	T47.4X3	T47.4X4	T47.4X5	T47.4X6
Agonist						
predominantly						
alpha-adrenoreceptor	T44.4X1	T44.4X2	T44.4X3	T44.4X4	T44.4X5	T44.4X6
beta-adrenoreceptor	T44.5X1	T44.5X2	T44.5X3	T44.5X4	T44.5X5	T44.5X6
Agricultural agent NEC	T65.91	T65.92	T65.93	T65.94	—	—
Agrypnal	T42.3X1	T42.3X2	T42.3X3	T42.3X4	T42.3X5	T42.3X6
AHLG	T50.Z11	T50.Z12	T50.Z13	T50.Z14	T50.Z15	T50.Z16
Air contaminant(s), source/type NOS	T65.91	T65.92	T65.93	T65.94	—	—

◀ New   ◀ Revised   ~~deleted~~ Deleted

Substance	External Cause (T-Code)					
	Poisoning, Accidental (Unintentional)	Poisoning, Intentional Self-Harm	Poisoning, Assault	Poisoning, Undetermined	Adverse Effect	Underdosing
Ajmaline	T46.2X1	T46.2X2	T46.2X3	T46.2X4	T46.2X5	T46.2X6
Akritoin	T37.8X1	T37.8X2	T37.8X3	T37.8X4	T37.8X5	T37.8X6
Akee	T62.1X1	T62.1X2	T62.1X3	T62.1X4	—	—
Akrinol	T49.0X1	T49.0X2	T49.0X3	T49.0X4	T49.0X5	T49.0X6
Alacepril	T46.4X1	T46.4X2	T46.4X3	T46.4X4	T46.4X5	T46.4X6
Alantolactone	T37.4X1	T37.4X2	T37.4X3	T37.4X4	T37.4X5	T37.4X6
Albamycin	T36.8X1	T36.8X2	T36.8X3	T36.8X4	T36.8X5	T36.8X6
Albendazole	T37.4X1	T37.4X2	T37.4X3	T37.4X4	T37.4X5	T37.4X6
Albumin						
bovine	T45.8X1	T45.8X2	T45.8X3	T45.8X4	T45.8X5	T45.8X6
human serum	T45.8X1	T45.8X2	T45.8X3	T45.8X4	T45.8X5	T45.8X6
salt-poor	T45.8X1	T45.8X2	T45.8X3	T45.8X4	T45.8X5	T45.8X6
normal human serum	T45.8X1	T45.8X2	T45.8X3	T45.8X4	T45.8X5	T45.8X6
Albuterol	T48.6X1	T48.6X2	T48.6X3	T48.6X4	T48.6X5	T48.6X6
Albutoin	T42.0X1	T42.0X2	T42.0X3	T42.0X4	T42.0X5	T42.0X6
Alclometasone	T49.0X1	T49.0X2	T49.0X3	T49.0X4	T49.0X5	T49.0X6
Alcohol	T51.91	T51.92	T51.93	T51.94	—	—
absolute	T51.0X1	T51.0X2	T51.0X3	T51.0X4	—	—
beverage	T51.0X1	T51.0X2	T51.0X3	T51.0X4	—	—
allyl	T51.8X1	T51.8X2	T51.8X3	T51.8X4	—	—
amyl	T51.3X1	T51.3X2	T51.3X3	T51.3X4	—	—
antifreeze	T51.1X1	T51.1X2	T51.1X3	T51.1X4	—	—
beverage	T51.0X1	T51.0X2	T51.0X3	T51.0X4	—	—
butyl	T51.3X1	T51.3X2	T51.3X3	T51.3X4	—	—
dehydrated	T51.0X1	T51.0X2	T51.0X3	T51.0X4	—	—
beverage	T51.0X1	T51.0X2	T51.0X3	T51.0X4	—	—
denatured	T51.0X1	T51.0X2	T51.0X3	T51.0X4	—	—
deterrent NEC	T50.6X1	T50.6X2	T50.6X3	T50.6X4	T50.6X5	T50.6X6
diagnostic (gastric function)	T50.8X1	T50.8X2	T50.8X3	T50.8X4	T50.8X5	T50.8X6
ethyl	T51.0X1	T51.0X2	T51.0X3	T51.0X4	—	—
beverage	T51.0X1	T51.0X2	T51.0X3	T51.0X4	—	—
grain	T51.0X1	T51.0X2	T51.0X3	T51.0X4	—	—
beverage	T51.0X1	T51.0X2	T51.0X3	T51.0X4	—	—
industrial	T51.0X1	T51.0X2	T51.0X3	T51.0X4	—	—
isopropyl	T51.2X1	T51.2X2	T51.2X3	T51.2X4	—	—
methyl	T51.1X1	T51.1X2	T51.1X3	T51.1X4	—	—
preparation for consumption	T51.0X1	T51.0X2	T51.0X3	T51.0X4	—	—
propyl	T51.3X1	T51.3X2	T51.3X3	T51.3X4	—	—
secondary	T51.2X1	T51.2X2	T51.2X3	T51.2X4	—	—
radiator	T51.1X1	T51.1X2	T51.1X3	T51.1X4	—	—
rubbing	T51.2X1	T51.2X2	T51.2X3	T51.2X4	—	—
specified type NEC	T51.8X1	T51.8X2	T51.8X3	T51.8X4	—	—

Substance	External Cause (T-Code)					
	Poisoning, Accidental (Unintentional)	Poisoning, Intentional Self-Harm	Poisoning, Assault	Poisoning, Undetermined	Adverse Effect	Underdosing
Alcohol *(Continued)*						
surgical	T51.0X1	T51.0X2	T51.0X3	T51.0X4	—	—
vapor (from any type of Alcohol)	T59.891	T59.892	T59.893	T59.894	—	—
wood	T51.1X1	T51.1X2	T51.1X3	T51.1X4	—	—
Alcuronium (chloride)	T48.1X1	T48.1X2	T48.1X3	T48.1X4	T48.1X5	T48.1X6
Aldactone	T50.0X1	T50.0X2	T50.0X3	T50.0X4	T50.0X5	T50.0X6
Aldesulfone sodium	T37.1X1	T37.1X2	T37.1X3	T37.1X4	T37.1X5	T37.1X6
Aldicarb	T60.0X1	T60.0X2	T60.0X3	T60.0X4	—	—
Aldomet	T46.5X1	T46.5X2	T46.5X3	T46.5X4	T46.5X5	T46.5X6
Aldosterone	T50.0X1	T50.0X2	T50.0X3	T50.0X4	T50.0X5	T50.0X6
Aldrin (dust)	T60.1X1	T60.1X2	T60.1X3	T60.1X4	—	—
Aleve — *see Naproxen*						
Alexitol sodium	T47.1X1	T47.1X2	T47.1X3	T47.1X4	T47.1X5	T47.1X6
Alfacalcidol	T45.2X1	T45.2X2	T45.2X3	T45.2X4	T45.2X5	T45.2X6
Alfadolone	T41.1X1	T41.1X2	T41.1X3	T41.1X4	T41.1X5	T41.1X6
Alfaxalone	T41.1X1	T41.1X2	T41.1X3	T41.1X4	T41.1X5	T41.1X6
Alfentanil	T40.411	T40.412	T40.413	T40.414	T40.415	T40.416 |◄
Alfuzosin (hydrochloride)	T44.8X1	T44.8X2	T44.8X3	T44.8X4	T44.8X5	T44.8X6
Algae (harmful) (toxin)	T65.821	T65.822	T65.823	T65.824	—	—
Algeldrate	T47.1X1	T47.1X2	T47.1X3	T47.1X4	T47.1X5	T47.1X6
Algin	T47.8X1	T47.8X2	T47.8X3	T47.8X4	T47.8X5	T47.8X6
Alglucerase	T45.3X1	T45.3X2	T45.3X3	T45.3X4	T45.3X5	T45.3X6
Alidase	T45.3X1	T45.3X2	T45.3X3	T45.3X4	T45.3X5	T45.3X6
Alimemazine	T43.3X1	T43.3X2	T43.3X3	T43.3X4	T43.3X5	T43.3X6
Aliphatic thiocyanates	T65.0X1	T65.0X2	T65.0X3	T65.0X4	—	—
Alizapride	T45.0X1	T45.0X2	T45.0X3	T45.0X4	T45.0X5	T45.0X6
Alkali (caustic)	T54.3X1	T54.3X2	T54.3X3	T54.3X4	—	—
Alkalizing agent NEC	T50.901	T50.902	T50.903	T50.904	T50.905	T50.906
Alkaline antiseptic solution (aromatic)	T49.6X1	T49.6X2	T49.6X3	T49.6X4	T49.6X5	T49.6X6
Alkalinizing agents (medicinal)	T50.901	T50.902	T50.903	T50.904	T50.905	T50.906
Alka-seltzer	T39.011	T39.012	T39.013	T39.014	T39.015	T39.016
Alkavervir	T46.5X1	T46.5X2	T46.5X3	T46.5X4	T46.5X5	T46.5X6
Alkonium (bromide)	T49.0X1	T49.0X2	T49.0X3	T49.0X4	T49.0X5	T49.0X6
Alkylating drug NEC	T45.1X1	T45.1X2	T45.1X3	T45.1X4	T45.1X5	T45.1X6
antimyeloproliferative	T45.1X1	T45.1X2	T45.1X3	T45.1X4	T45.1X5	T45.1X6
lymphatic	T45.1X1	T45.1X2	T45.1X3	T45.1X4	T45.1X5	T45.1X6
Alkylisocyanate	T65.0X1	T65.0X2	T65.0X3	T65.0X4	—	—
Allantoin	T49.411	T49.412	T49.413	T49.414	T49.415	T49.416
Allegron	T43.0X1	T43.0X2	T43.0X3	T43.0X4	T43.0X5	T43.0X6
Allethrin	T49.0X1	T49.0X2	T49.0X3	T49.0X4	T49.0X5	T49.0X6
Allobarbital	T42.3X1	T42.3X2	T42.3X3	T42.3X4	T42.3X5	T42.3X6

◄ New   ◄ Revised   ~~deleted~~ Deleted

Substance	Poisoning, Accidental (Unintentional)	Poisoning, Intentional Self-Harm	Poisoning, Assault	Poisoning, Undetermined	Adverse Effect	Underdosing
Allopurinol	T50.4X1	T50.4X2	T50.4X3	T50.4X4	T50.4X5	T50.4X6
Allyl						
alcohol	T51.8X1	T51.8X2	T51.8X3	T51.8X4	—	—
disulfide	T46.6X1	T46.6X2	T46.6X3	T46.6X4	T46.6X5	T46.6X6
Allylestrenol	T38.5X1	T38.5X2	T38.5X3	T38.5X4	T38.5X5	T38.5X6
Allylisopropylacetylurea	T42.6X1	T42.6X2	T42.6X3	T42.6X4	T42.6X5	T42.6X6
Allylisopropylmalonylurea	T42.3X1	T42.3X2	T42.3X3	T42.3X4	T42.3X5	T42.3X6
Allylthiourea	T49.3X1	T49.3X2	T49.3X3	T49.3X4	T49.3X5	T49.3X6
Allyltribromide	T42.6X1	T42.6X2	T42.6X3	T42.6X4	T42.6X5	T42.6X6
Allypropymal	T42.3X1	T42.3X2	T42.3X3	T42.3X4	T42.3X5	T42.3X6
Almagate	T47.1X1	T47.1X2	T47.1X3	T47.1X4	T47.1X5	T47.1X6
Almasilate	T47.1X1	T47.1X2	T47.1X3	T47.1X4	T47.1X5	T47.1X6
Almitrine	T50.7X1	T50.7X2	T50.7X3	T50.7X4	T50.7X5	T50.7X6
Aloes	T47.2X1	T47.2X2	T47.2X3	T47.2X4	T47.2X5	T47.2X6
Aloglutamol	T47.1X1	T47.1X2	T47.1X3	T47.1X4	T47.1X5	T47.1X6
Aloin	T47.2X1	T47.2X2	T47.2X3	T47.2X4	T47.2X5	T47.2X6
Aloxidone	T42.2X1	T42.2X2	T42.2X3	T42.2X4	T42.2X5	T42.2X6
Alpha						
acetyldigoxin	T46.0X1	T46.0X2	T46.0X3	T46.0X4	T46.0X5	T46.0X6
adrenergic blocking drug	T44.6X1	T44.6X2	T44.6X3	T44.6X4	T44.6X5	T44.6X6
amylase	T45.3X1	T45.3X2	T45.3X3	T45.3X4	T45.3X5	T45.3X6
tocoferol (acetate)	T45.2X1	T45.2X2	T45.2X3	T45.2X4	T45.2X5	T45.2X6
tocopherol	T45.2X1	T45.2X2	T45.2X3	T45.2X4	T45.2X5	T45.2X6
Alphadolone	T41.1X1	T41.1X2	T41.1X3	T41.1X4	T41.1X5	T41.1X6
Alphaprodine	T40.491	T40.492	T40.493	T40.494	T40.495	T40.496
Alphaxalone	T41.1X1	T41.1X2	T41.1X3	T41.1X4	T41.1X5	T41.1X6
Alprazolam	T42.4X1	T42.4X2	T42.4X3	T42.4X4	T42.4X5	T42.4X6
Alprenolol	T44.7X1	T44.7X2	T44.7X3	T44.7X4	T44.7X5	T44.7X6
Alprostadil	T46.7X1	T46.7X2	T46.7X3	T46.7X4	T46.7X5	T46.7X6
Alsactide	T38.811	T38.812	T38.813	T38.814	T38.815	T38.816
Alseroxylon	T46.5X1	T46.5X2	T46.5X3	T46.5X4	T46.5X5	T46.5X6
Alteplase	T45.611	T45.612	T45.613	T45.614	T45.615	T45.616
Altizide	T50.2X1	T50.2X2	T50.2X3	T50.2X4	T50.2X5	T50.2X6
Altretamine	T45.1X1	T45.1X2	T45.1X3	T45.1X4	T45.1X5	T45.1X6
Alum (medicinal)	T49.4X1	T49.4X2	T49.4X3	T49.4X4	T49.4X5	T49.4X6
nonmedicinal (ammonium) (potassium)	T56.891	T56.892	T56.893	T56.894	—	—
Aluminium, aluminum						
acetate	T49.2X1	T49.2X2	T49.2X3	T49.2X4	T49.2X5	T49.2X6
solution	T49.0X1	T49.0X2	T49.0X3	T49.0X4	T49.0X5	T49.0X6
aspirin	T39.011	T39.012	T39.013	T39.014	T39.015	T39.016
bis (acetylsalicylate)	T39.011	T39.012	T39.013	T39.014	T39.015	T39.016

Substance	Poisoning, Accidental (Unintentional)	Poisoning, Intentional Self-Harm	Poisoning, Assault	Poisoning, Undetermined	Adverse Effect	Underdosing
Aluminium, aluminum (Continued)						
carbonate (gel, basic)	T47.1X1	T47.1X2	T47.1X3	T47.1X4	T47.1X5	T47.1X6
chlorhydroxide-complex	T47.1X1	T47.1X2	T47.1X3	T47.1X4	T47.1X5	T47.1X6
chloride	T49.2X1	T49.2X2	T49.2X3	T49.2X4	T49.2X5	T49.2X6
clofibrate	T46.6X1	T46.6X2	T46.6X3	T46.6X4	T46.6X5	T46.6X6
diacetate	T49.2X1	T49.2X2	T49.2X3	T49.2X4	T49.2X5	T49.2X6
glycinate	T47.1X1	T47.1X2	T47.1X3	T47.1X4	T47.1X5	T47.1X6
hydroxide (gel)	T47.1X1	T47.1X2	T47.1X3	T47.1X4	T47.1X5	T47.1X6
hydroxide-magnesium carb. gel	T47.1X1	T47.1X2	T47.1X3	T47.1X4	T47.1X5	T47.1X6
magnesium silicate	T47.1X1	T47.1X2	T47.1X3	T47.1X4	T47.1X5	T47.1X6
nicotinate	T46.7X1	T46.7X2	T46.7X3	T46.7X4	T46.7X5	T46.7X6
ointment (surgical) (topical)	T49.3X1	T49.3X2	T49.3X3	T49.3X4	T49.3X5	T49.3X6
phosphate	T47.1X1	T47.1X2	T47.1X3	T47.1X4	T47.1X5	T47.1X6
salicylate	T39.091	T39.092	T39.093	T39.094	T39.095	T39.096
silicate	T47.1X1	T47.1X2	T47.1X3	T47.1X4	T47.1X5	T47.1X6
sodium silicate	T47.1X1	T47.1X2	T47.1X3	T47.1X4	T47.1X5	T47.1X6
subacetate	T49.2X1	T49.2X2	T49.2X3	T49.2X4	T49.2X5	T49.2X6
sulfate	T49.0X1	T49.0X2	T49.0X3	T49.0X4	T49.0X5	T49.0X6
tannate	T47.6X1	T47.6X2	T47.6X3	T47.6X4	T47.6X5	T47.6X6
topical NEC	T49.3X1	T49.3X2	T49.3X3	T49.3X4	T49.3X5	T49.3X6
Alurate	T42.3X1	T42.3X2	T42.3X3	T42.3X4	T42.3X5	T42.3X6
Alverine	T44.3X1	T44.3X2	T44.3X3	T44.3X4	T44.3X5	T44.3X6
Alvodine	T40.2X1	T40.2X2	T40.2X3	T40.2X4	T40.2X5	T40.2X6
Amanita phalloides	T62.0X1	T62.0X2	T62.0X3	T62.0X4	—	—
Amanitine	T62.0X1	T62.0X2	T62.0X3	T62.0X4	—	—
Amantadine	T42.8X1	T42.8X2	T42.8X3	T42.8X4	T42.8X5	T42.8X6
Ambazone	T49.6X1	T49.6X2	T49.6X3	T49.6X4	T49.6X5	T49.6X6
Ambenonium (chloride)	T44.0X1	T44.0X2	T44.0X3	T44.0X4	T44.0X5	T44.0X6
Ambroxol	T48.4X1	T48.4X2	T48.4X3	T48.4X4	T48.4X5	T48.4X6
Ambuphylline	T48.6X1	T48.6X2	T48.6X3	T48.6X4	T48.6X5	T48.6X6
Ambutonium bromide	T44.3X1	T44.3X2	T44.3X3	T44.3X4	T44.3X5	T44.3X6
Amcinonide	T49.0X1	T49.0X2	T49.0X3	T49.0X4	T49.0X5	T49.0X6
Amdinocilline	T36.0X1	T36.0X2	T36.0X3	T36.0X4	T36.0X5	T36.0X6
Ametazole	T50.8X1	T50.8X2	T50.8X3	T50.8X4	T50.8X5	T50.8X6
Amethocaine	T41.3X1	T41.3X2	T41.3X3	T41.3X4	T41.3X5	T41.3X6
regional	T41.3X1	T41.3X2	T41.3X3	T41.3X4	T41.3X5	T41.3X6
spinal	T41.3X1	T41.3X2	T41.3X3	T41.3X4	T41.3X5	T41.3X6
Amethopterin	T45.1X1	T45.1X2	T45.1X3	T45.1X4	T45.1X5	T45.1X6
Amezinium metilsulfate	T44.991	T44.992	T44.993	T44.994	T44.995	T44.996
Amfebutamone	T43.291	T43.292	T43.293	T43.294	T43.295	T43.296
Amfepramone	T50.5X1	T50.5X2	T50.5X3	T50.5X4	T50.5X5	T50.5X6

◀ New   ◀ Revised   ~~deleted~~ Deleted

Substance	Poisoning, Accidental (Unintentional)	Poisoning, Intentional Self-Harm	Poisoning, Assault	Poisoning, Undetermined	Adverse Effect	Underdosing
Amfetamine	T43.621	T43.622	T43.623	T43.624	T43.625	T43.626
Amfetaminil	T43.621	T43.622	T43.623	T43.624	T43.625	T43.626
Amfomycin	T36.8X1	T36.8X2	T36.8X3	T36.8X4	T36.8X5	T36.8X6
Amidefrine mesilate	T48.5X1	T48.5X2	T48.5X3	T48.5X4	T48.5X5	T48.5X6
Amidone	T40.3X1	T40.3X2	T40.3X3	T40.3X4	T40.3X5	T40.3X6
Amidopyrine	T39.2X1	T39.2X2	T39.2X3	T39.2X4	T39.2X5	T39.2X6
Amidotrizoate	T50.8X1	T50.8X2	T50.8X3	T50.8X4	T50.8X5	T50.8X6
Amiflamine	T43.1X1	T43.1X2	T43.1X3	T43.1X4	T43.1X5	T43.1X6
Amikacin	T36.5X1	T36.5X2	T36.5X3	T36.5X4	T36.5X5	T36.5X6
Amikhelline	T46.3X1	T46.3X2	T46.3X3	T46.3X4	T46.3X5	T46.3X6
Amiloride	T50.2X1	T50.2X2	T50.2X3	T50.2X4	T50.2X5	T50.2X6
Aminacrine	T49.0X1	T49.0X2	T49.0X3	T49.0X4	T49.0X5	T49.0X6
Amineptine	T43.011	T43.012	T43.013	T43.014	T43.015	T43.016
Aminitrozole	T37.3X1	T37.3X2	T37.3X3	T37.3X4	T37.3X5	T37.3X6
Aminoacetic acid (derivatives)	T50.3X1	T50.3X2	T50.3X3	T50.3X4	T50.3X5	T50.3X6
Amino acids	T50.3X1	T50.3X2	T50.3X3	T50.3X4	T50.3X5	T50.3X6
Aminoacridine	T49.0X1	T49.0X2	T49.0X3	T49.0X4	T49.0X5	T49.0X6
Aminobenzoic acid (-p)	T49.3X1	T49.3X2	T49.3X3	T49.3X4	T49.3X5	T49.3X6
4-Aminobutyric acid	T43.8X1	T43.8X2	T43.8X3	T43.8X4	T43.8X5	T43.8X6
Aminocaproic acid	T45.621	T45.622	T45.623	T45.624	T45.625	T45.626
Aminofenazone	T39.2X1	T39.2X2	T39.2X3	T39.2X4	T39.2X5	T39.2X6
Aminoethylisothiourium	T45.8X1	T45.8X2	T45.8X3	T45.8X4	T45.8X5	T45.8X6
Aminoglutethimide	T45.1X1	T45.1X2	T45.1X3	T45.1X4	T45.1X5	T45.1X6
Aminohippuric acid	T50.8X1	T50.8X2	T50.8X3	T50.8X4	T50.8X5	T50.8X6
Aminomethylbenzoic acid	T45.691	T45.692	T45.693	T45.694	T45.695	T45.696
Aminometradine	T50.2X1	T50.2X2	T50.2X3	T50.2X4	T50.2X5	T50.2X6
Aminopentamide	T44.3X1	T44.3X2	T44.3X3	T44.3X4	T44.3X5	T44.3X6
Aminophenazone	T39.2X1	T39.2X2	T39.2X3	T39.2X4	T39.2X5	T39.2X6
Aminophenol	T54.0X1	T54.0X2	T54.0X3	T54.0X4	—	—
4-Aminophenol derivatives	T39.1X1	T39.1X2	T39.1X3	T39.1X4	T39.1X5	T39.1X6
Aminophenylpyridone	T43.591	T43.592	T43.593	T43.594	T43.595	T43.596
Aminophylline	T48.6X1	T48.6X2	T48.6X3	T48.6X4	T48.6X5	T48.6X6
Aminopterin sodium	T45.1X1	T45.1X2	T45.1X3	T45.1X4	T45.1X5	T45.1X6
Aminopyrine	T39.2X1	T39.2X2	T39.2X3	T39.2X4	T39.2X5	T39.2X6
8-Aminoquinoline drugs	T37.2X1	T37.2X2	T37.2X3	T37.2X4	T37.2X5	T37.2X6
Aminorex	T50.5X1	T50.5X2	T50.5X3	T50.5X4	T50.5X5	T50.5X6
Aminosalicylic acid	T37.1X1	T37.1X2	T37.1X3	T37.1X4	T37.1X5	T37.1X6
Aminosalylum	T37.1X1	T37.1X2	T37.1X3	T37.1X4	T37.1X5	T37.1X6
Amiodarone	T46.2X1	T46.2X2	T46.2X3	T46.2X4	T46.2X5	T46.2X6
Amiphenazole	T50.7X1	T50.7X2	T50.7X3	T50.7X4	T50.7X5	T50.7X6
Amiquinsin	T46.5X1	T46.5X2	T46.5X3	T46.5X4	T46.5X5	T46.5X6
Amisometradine	T50.2X1	T50.2X2	T50.2X3	T50.2X4	T50.2X5	T50.2X6

Substance	Poisoning, Accidental (Unintentional)	Poisoning, Intentional Self-Harm	Poisoning, Assault	Poisoning, Undetermined	Adverse Effect	Underdosing
Amisulpride	T43.591	T43.592	T43.593	T43.594	T43.595	T43.596
Amitriptyline	T43.021	T43.022	T43.023	T43.024	T43.025	T43.026
Amitriptylinoxide	T43.021	T43.022	T43.023	T43.024	T43.025	T43.026
Amlexanox	T48.6X1	T48.6X2	T48.6X3	T48.6X4	T48.6X5	T48.6X6
Ammonia (fumes) (gas) (vapor)	T59.891	T59.892	T59.893	T59.894	—	—
aromatic spirit	T48.991	T48.992	T48.993	T48.994	T48.995	T48.996
liquid (household)	T54.3X1	T54.3X2	T54.3X3	T54.3X4	—	—
Ammoniated mercury	T49.0X1	T49.0X2	T49.0X3	T49.0X4	T49.0X5	T49.0X6
Ammonium						
acid tartrate	T49.5X1	T49.5X2	T49.5X3	T49.5X4	T49.5X5	T49.5X6
bromide	T42.6X1	T42.6X2	T42.6X3	T42.6X4	T42.6X5	T42.6X6
carbonate	T54.3X1	T54.3X2	T54.3X3	T54.3X4	—	—
chloride	T50.991	T50.992	T50.993	T50.994	T50.995	T50.996
expectorant	T48.4X1	T48.4X2	T48.4X3	T48.4X4	T48.4X5	T48.4X6
compounds (household) NEC	T54.3X1	T54.3X2	T54.3X3	T54.3X4	—	—
fumes (any usage)	T59.891	T59.892	T59.893	T59.894	—	—
industrial	T54.3X1	T54.3X2	T54.3X3	T54.3X4	—	—
ichthyosulronate	T49.4X1	T49.4X2	T49.4X3	T49.4X4	T49.4X5	T49.4X6
mandelate	T37.91	T37.92	T37.93	T37.94	T37.95	T37.96
sulfamate	T60.3X1	T60.3X2	T60.3X3	T60.3X4	—	—
sulfonate resin	T47.8X1	T47.8X2	T47.8X3	T47.8X4	T47.8X5	T47.8X6
Amobarbital (sodium)	T42.3X1	T42.3X2	T42.3X3	T42.3X4	T42.3X5	T42.3X6
Amodiaquine	T37.2X1	T37.2X2	T37.2X3	T37.2X4	T37.2X5	T37.2X6
Amopyroquin(e)	T37.2X1	T37.2X2	T37.2X3	T37.2X4	T37.2X5	T37.2X6
Amoxapine	T43.011	T43.012	T43.013	T43.014	T43.015	T43.016
Amoxicillin	T36.0X1	T36.0X2	T36.0X3	T36.0X4	T36.0X5	T36.0X6
Amperozide	T43.591	T43.592	T43.593	T43.594	T43.595	T43.596
Amphenidone	T43.591	T43.592	T43.593	T43.594	T43.595	T43.596
Amphetamine NEC	T43.621	T43.622	T43.623	T43.624	T43.625	T43.626
Amphomycin	T36.8X1	T36.8X2	T36.8X3	T36.8X4	T36.8X5	T36.8X6
Amphotalide	T37.4X1	T37.4X2	T37.4X3	T37.4X4	T37.4X5	T37.4X6
Amphotericin B	T36.7X1	T36.7X2	T36.7X3	T36.7X4	T36.7X5	T36.7X6
topical	T49.0X1	T49.0X2	T49.0X3	T49.0X4	T49.0X5	T49.0X6
Ampicillin	T36.0X1	T36.0X2	T36.0X3	T36.0X4	T36.0X5	T36.0X6
Amprotropine	T44.3X1	T44.3X2	T44.3X3	T44.3X4	T44.3X5	T44.3X6
Amsacrine	T45.1X1	T45.1X2	T45.1X3	T45.1X4	T45.1X5	T45.1X6
Amygdaline	T62.2X1	T62.2X2	T62.2X3	T62.2X4	—	—
Amyl						
acetate	T52.8X1	T52.8X2	T52.8X3	T52.8X4	—	—
vapor	T59.891	T59.892	T59.893	T59.894	—	—
alcohol	T51.3X1	T51.3X2	T51.3X3	T51.3X4	—	—
chloride	T53.6X1	T53.6X2	T53.6X3	T53.6X4	—	—

◀ New ◀ Revised ~~deleted~~ Deleted

Substance	External Cause (T-Code)					
	Poisoning, Accidental (Unintentional)	Poisoning, Intentional Self-Harm	Poisoning, Assault	Poisoning, Undetermined	Adverse Effect	Underdosing
Amyl (Continued)						
formate	T52.8X1	T52.8X2	T52.8X3	T52.8X4	—	—
nitrite	T46.3X1	T46.3X2	T46.3X3	T46.3X4	T46.3X5	T46.3X6
propionate	T65.891	T65.892	T65.893	T65.894	—	—
Amylase	T47.5X1	T47.5X2	T47.5X3	T47.5X4	T47.5X5	T47.5X6
Amyleine, regional	T41.3X1	T41.3X2	T41.3X3	T41.3X4	T41.3X5	T41.3X6
Amylene						
dichloride	T53.6X1	T53.6X2	T53.6X3	T53.6X4	—	—
hydrate	T51.3X1	T51.3X2	T51.3X3	T51.3X4	—	—
Amylmetacresol	T49.6X1	T49.6X2	T49.6X3	T49.6X4	T49.6X5	T49.6X6
Amylobarbitone	T42.3X1	T42.3X2	T42.3X3	T42.3X4	T42.3X5	T42.3X6
Amylocaine, regional	T41.3X1	T41.3X2	T41.3X3	T41.3X4	T41.3X5	T41.3X6
infiltration (subcutaneous)	T41.3X1	T41.3X2	T41.3X3	T41.3X4	T41.3X5	T41.3X6
nerve block (peripheral) (plexus)	T41.3X1	T41.3X2	T41.3X3	T41.3X4	T41.3X5	T41.3X6
spinal	T41.3X1	T41.3X2	T41.3X3	T41.3X4	T41.3X5	T41.3X6
topical (surface)	T41.3X1	T41.3X2	T41.3X3	T41.3X4	T41.3X5	T41.3X6
Amylopectin	T47.6X1	T47.6X2	T47.6X3	T47.6X4	T47.6X5	T47.6X6
Amytal (sodium)	T42.3X1	T42.3X2	T42.3X3	T42.3X4	T42.3X5	T42.3X6
Anabolic steroid	T38.7X1	T38.7X2	T38.7X3	T38.7X4	T38.7X5	T38.7X6
Analeptic NEC	T50.7X1	T50.7X2	T50.7X3	T50.7X4	T50.7X5	T50.7X6
Analgesic	T39.91	T39.92	T39.93	T39.94	T39.95	T39.96
anti-inflammatory NEC	T39.91	T39.92	T39.93	T39.94	T39.95	T39.96
propionic acid derivative	T39.311	T39.312	T39.313	T39.314	T39.315	T39.316
antirheumatic NEC	T39.4X1	T39.4X2	T39.4X3	T39.4X4	T39.4X5	T39.4X6
aromatic NEC	T39.1X1	T39.1X2	T39.1X3	T39.1X4	T39.1X5	T39.1X6
narcotic NEC	T40.601	T40.602	T40.603	T40.604	T40.605	T40.606
combination	T40.601	T40.602	T40.603	T40.604	T40.605	T40.606
obstetric	T40.601	T40.602	T40.603	T40.604	T40.605	T40.606
non-narcotic NEC	T39.91	T39.92	T39.93	T39.94	T39.95	T39.96
combination	T39.91	T39.92	T39.93	T39.94	T39.95	T39.96
pyrazole	T39.2X1	T39.2X2	T39.2X3	T39.2X4	T39.2X5	T39.2X6
specified NEC	T39.8X1	T39.8X2	T39.8X3	T39.8X4	T39.8X5	T39.8X6
Analgin	T39.2X1	T39.2X2	T39.2X3	T39.2X4	T39.2X5	T39.2X6
Anamirta cocculus	T62.1X1	T62.1X2	T62.1X3	T62.1X4	—	—
Ancillin	T36.0X1	T36.0X2	T36.0X3	T36.0X4	T36.0X5	T36.0X6
Ancrod	T45.691	T45.692	T45.693	T45.694	T45.695	T45.696
Androgen	T38.7X1	T38.7X2	T38.7X3	T38.7X4	T38.7X5	T38.7X6
Androgen-estrogen mixture	T38.7X1	T38.7X2	T38.7X3	T38.7X4	T38.7X5	T38.7X6
Androstalone	T38.7X1	T38.7X2	T38.7X3	T38.7X4	T38.7X5	T38.7X6
Androstanolone	T38.7X1	T38.7X2	T38.7X3	T38.7X4	T38.7X5	T38.7X6
Androsterone	T38.7X1	T38.7X2	T38.7X3	T38.7X4	T38.7X5	T38.7X6

Substance	External Cause (T-Code)					
	Poisoning, Accidental (Unintentional)	Poisoning, Intentional Self-Harm	Poisoning, Assault	Poisoning, Undetermined	Adverse Effect	Underdosing
Anemone pulsatilla	T62.2X1	T62.2X2	T62.2X3	T62.2X4	—	—
Anesthesia						
caudal	T41.3X1	T41.3X2	T41.3X3	T41.3X4	T41.3X5	T41.3X6
endotracheal	T41.0X1	T41.0X2	T41.0X3	T41.0X4	T41.0X5	T41.0X6
epidural	T41.3X1	T41.3X2	T41.3X3	T41.3X4	T41.3X5	T41.3X6
inhalation	T41.0X1	T41.0X2	T41.0X3	T41.0X4	T41.0X5	T41.0X6
local	T41.3X1	T41.3X2	T41.3X3	T41.3X4	T41.3X5	T41.3X6
mucosal	T41.3X1	T41.3X2	T41.3X3	T41.3X4	T41.3X5	T41.3X6
muscle relaxation	T48.1X1	T48.1X2	T48.1X3	T48.1X4	T48.1X5	T48.1X6
nerve blocking	T41.3X1	T41.3X2	T41.3X3	T41.3X4	T41.3X5	T41.3X6
plexus blocking	T41.3X1	T41.3X2	T41.3X3	T41.3X4	T41.3X5	T41.3X6
potentiated	T41.201	T41.202	T41.203	T41.204	T41.205	T41.206
rectal	T41.201	T41.202	T41.203	T41.204	T41.205	T41.206
general	T41.201	T41.202	T41.203	T41.204	T41.205	T41.206
local	T41.3X1	T41.3X2	T41.3X3	T41.3X4	T41.3X5	T41.3X6
regional	T41.3X1	T41.3X2	T41.3X3	T41.3X4	T41.3X5	T41.3X6
surface	T41.3X1	T41.3X2	T41.3X3	T41.3X4	T41.3X5	T41.3X6
Anesthetic NEC — see also Anesthesia	T41.41	T41.42	T41.43	T41.44	T41.45	T41.46
with muscle relaxant	T41.201	T41.202	T41.203	T41.204	T41.205	T41.206
general	T41.201	T41.202	T41.203	T41.204	T41.205	T41.206
local	T41.3X1	T41.3X2	T41.3X3	T41.3X4	T41.3X5	T41.3X6
gaseous NEC	T41.0X1	T41.0X2	T41.0X3	T41.0X4	T41.0X5	T41.0X6
general NEC	T41.201	T41.202	T41.203	T41.204	T41.205	T41.206
halogenated hydrocarbon derivatives NEC	T41.0X1	T41.0X2	T41.0X3	T41.0X4	T41.0X5	T41.0X6
infiltration NEC	T41.3X1	T41.3X2	T41.3X3	T41.3X4	T41.3X5	T41.3X6
intravenous NEC	T41.1X1	T41.1X2	T41.1X3	T41.1X4	T41.1X5	T41.1X6
local NEC	T41.3X1	T41.3X2	T41.3X3	T41.3X4	T41.3X5	T41.3X6
rectal	T41.201	T41.202	T41.203	T41.204	T41.205	T41.206
general	T41.201	T41.202	T41.203	T41.204	T41.205	T41.206
local	T41.3X1	T41.3X2	T41.3X3	T41.3X4	T41.3X5	T41.3X6
regional NEC	T41.3X1	T41.3X2	T41.3X3	T41.3X4	T41.3X5	T41.3X6
spinal NEC	T41.3X1	T41.3X2	T41.3X3	T41.3X4	T41.3X5	T41.3X6
thiobarbiturate	T41.1X1	T41.1X2	T41.1X3	T41.1X4	T41.1X5	T41.1X6
topical	T41.3X1	T41.3X2	T41.3X3	T41.3X4	T41.3X5	T41.3X6
Aneurine	T45.2X1	T45.2X2	T45.2X3	T45.2X4	T45.2X5	T45.2X6
Angio-Conray	T50.8X1	T50.8X2	T50.8X3	T50.8X4	T50.8X5	T50.8X6
Angiotensin	T44.5X1	T44.5X2	T44.5X3	T44.5X4	T44.5X5	T44.5X6
Angiotensinamide	T44.991	T44.992	T44.993	T44.994	T44.995	T44.996
Anhydrohydroxy-progesterone	T38.5X1	T38.5X2	T38.5X3	T38.5X4	T38.5X5	T38.5X6
Anhydron	T50.2X1	T50.2X2	T50.2X3	T50.2X4	T50.2X5	T50.2X6
Anileridine	T40.491	T40.492	T40.493	T40.494	T40.495	T40.496

◀ New ◀ Revised ~~deleted~~ Deleted

Substance	External Cause (T-Code) Poisoning, Accidental (Unintentional)	Poisoning, Intentional Self-Harm	Poisoning, Assault	Poisoning, Undetermined	Adverse Effect	Underdosing
Aniline (dye) (liquid)	T65.3X1	T65.3X2	T65.3X3	T65.3X4	—	—
analgesic	T39.1X1	T39.1X2	T39.1X3	T39.1X4	T39.1X5	T39.1X6
derivatives, therapeutic NEC	T39.1X1	T39.1X2	T39.1X3	T39.1X4	T39.1X5	T39.1X6
vapor	T65.3X1	T65.3X2	T65.3X3	T65.3X4	—	—
Anise oil	T47.5X1	T47.5X2	T47.5X3	T47.5X4	T47.5X5	T47.5X6
Aniscoropine	T44.3X1	T44.3X2	T44.3X3	T44.3X4	T44.3X5	T44.3X6
Anisidine	T65.3X1	T65.3X2	T65.3X3	T65.3X4	—	—
Anisindione	T45.511	T45.512	T45.513	T45.514	T45.515	T45.516
Anisotropine methyl-bromide	T44.3X1	T44.3X2	T44.3X3	T44.3X4	T44.3X5	T44.3X6
Anistreplase	T45.611	T45.612	T45.613	T45.614	T45.615	T45.616
Anorexiant (central)	T50.5X1	T50.5X2	T50.5X3	T50.5X4	T50.5X5	T50.5X6
Anorexic agents	T50.5X1	T50.5X2	T50.5X3	T50.5X4	T50.5X5	T50.5X6
Ansamycin	T36.6X1	T36.6X2	T36.6X3	T36.6X4	T36.6X5	T36.6X6
Ant (bite) (sting)	T63.421	T63.422	T63.423	T63.424	—	—
Antabuse	T50.6X1	T50.6X2	T50.6X3	T50.6X4	T50.6X5	T50.6X6
Ant poison — *see* Insecticide						
Antacid NEC	T47.1X1	T47.1X2	T47.1X3	T47.1X4	T47.1X5	T47.1X6
Antagonist						
Aldosterone	T50.0X1	T50.0X2	T50.0X3	T50.0X4	T50.0X5	T50.0X6
alpha-adrenoreceptor	T44.6X1	T44.6X2	T44.6X3	T44.6X4	T44.6X5	T44.6X6
anticoagulant	T45.7X1	T45.7X2	T45.7X3	T45.7X4	T45.7X5	T45.7X6
beta-adrenoreceptor	T44.7X1	T44.7X2	T44.7X3	T44.7X4	T44.7X5	T44.7X6
extrapyramidal NEC	T44.3X1	T44.3X2	T44.3X3	T44.3X4	T44.3X5	T44.3X6
folic acid	T45.1X1	T45.1X2	T45.1X3	T45.1X4	T45.1X5	T45.1X6
H2 receptor	T47.0X1	T47.0X2	T47.0X3	T47.0X4	T47.0X5	T47.0X6
heavy metal	T45.8X1	T45.8X2	T45.8X3	T45.8X4	T45.8X5	T45.8X6
narcotic analgesic	T50.7X1	T50.7X2	T50.7X3	T50.7X4	T50.7X5	T50.7X6
opiate	T50.7X1	T50.7X2	T50.7X3	T50.7X4	T50.7X5	T50.7X6
pyrimidine	T45.1X1	T45.1X2	T45.1X3	T45.1X4	T45.1X5	T45.1X6
serotonin	T46.5X1	T46.5X2	T46.5X3	T46.5X4	T46.5X5	T46.5X6
Antazolin(e)	T45.0X1	T45.0X2	T45.0X3	T45.0X4	T45.0X5	T45.0X6
Anterior pituitary hormone NEC	T38.811	T38.812	T38.813	T38.814	T38.815	T38.816
Anthelmintic NEC	T37.4X1	T37.4X2	T37.4X3	T37.4X4	T37.4X5	T37.4X6
Anthiolimine	T37.4X1	T37.4X2	T37.4X3	T37.4X4	T37.4X5	T37.4X6
Anthralin	T49.4X1	T49.4X2	T49.4X3	T49.4X4	T49.4X5	T49.4X6
Anthramycin	T45.1X1	T45.1X2	T45.1X3	T45.1X4	T45.1X5	T45.1X6
Antiadrenergic NEC	T44.8X1	T44.8X2	T44.8X3	T44.8X4	T44.8X5	T44.8X6
Antiallergic NEC	T45.0X1	T45.0X2	T45.0X3	T45.0X4	T45.0X5	T45.0X6
Anti-anemic (drug) (preparation)	T45.8X1	T45.8X2	T45.8X3	T45.8X4	T45.8X5	T45.8X6
Antiandrogen NEC	T38.6X1	T38.6X2	T38.6X3	T38.6X4	T38.6X5	T38.6X6
Antianxiety drug NEC	T43.501	T43.502	T43.503	T43.504	T43.505	T43.506
Antiaris toxicaria	T65.891	T65.892	T65.893	T65.894	—	—

Substance	External Cause (T-Code) Poisoning, Accidental (Unintentional)	Poisoning, Intentional Self-Harm	Poisoning, Assault	Poisoning, Undetermined	Adverse Effect	Underdosing
Antiarteriosclerotic drug	T46.6X1	T46.6X2	T46.6X3	T46.6X4	T46.6X5	T46.6X6
Antiasthmatic drug NEC	T48.6X1	T48.6X2	T48.6X3	T48.6X4	T48.6X5	T48.6X6
Antibiotic NEC	T36.91	T36.92	T36.93	T36.94	T36.95	T36.96
aminoglycoside	T36.5X1	T36.5X2	T36.5X3	T36.5X4	T36.5X5	T36.5X6
anticancer	T45.1X1	T45.1X2	T45.1X3	T45.1X4	T45.1X5	T45.1X6
antifungal	T36.7X1	T36.7X2	T36.7X3	T36.7X4	T36.7X5	T36.7X6
antimycobacterial	T36.5X1	T36.5X2	T36.5X3	T36.5X4	T36.5X5	T36.5X6
antineoplastic	T45.1X1	T45.1X2	T45.1X3	T45.1X4	T45.1X5	T45.1X6
cephalosporin (group)	T36.1X1	T36.1X2	T36.1X3	T36.1X4	T36.1X5	T36.1X6
chloramphenicol (group)	T36.2X1	T36.2X2	T36.2X3	T36.2X4	T36.2X5	T36.2X6
ENT	T49.6X1	T49.6X2	T49.6X3	T49.6X4	T49.6X5	T49.6X6
eye	T49.5X1	T49.5X2	T49.5X3	T49.5X4	T49.5X5	T49.5X6
fungicidal (local)	T49.0X1	T49.0X2	T49.0X3	T49.0X4	T49.0X5	T49.0X6
intestinal	T36.8X1	T36.8X2	T36.8X3	T36.8X4	T36.8X5	T36.8X6
b-lactam NEC	T36.1X1	T36.1X2	T36.1X3	T36.1X4	T36.1X5	T36.1X6
local	T49.0X1	T49.0X2	T49.0X3	T49.0X4	T49.0X5	T49.0X6
macrolides	T36.3X1	T36.3X2	T36.3X3	T36.3X4	T36.3X5	T36.3X6
polypeptide	T36.8X1	T36.8X2	T36.8X3	T36.8X4	T36.8X5	T36.8X6
specified NEC	T36.8X1	T36.8X2	T36.8X3	T36.8X4	T36.8X5	T36.8X6
tetracycline (group)	T36.4X1	T36.4X2	T36.4X3	T36.4X4	T36.4X5	T36.4X6
throat	T49.6X1	T49.6X2	T49.6X3	T49.6X4	T49.6X5	T49.6X6
Anticancer agents NEC	T45.1X1	T45.1X2	T45.1X3	T45.1X4	T45.1X5	T45.1X6
Anticholesterolemic drug NEC	T46.6X1	T46.6X2	T46.6X3	T46.6X4	T46.6X5	T46.6X6
Anticholinergic NEC	T44.3X1	T44.3X2	T44.3X3	T44.3X4	T44.3X5	T44.3X6
Anticholinesterase	T44.0X1	T44.0X2	T44.0X3	T44.0X4	T44.0X5	T44.0X6
organophosphorus	T44.0X1	T44.0X2	T44.0X3	T44.0X4	T44.0X5	T44.0X6
insecticide	T60.0X1	T60.0X2	T60.0X3	T60.0X4	—	—
nerve gas	T59.891	T59.892	T59.893	T59.894	—	—
reversible	T44.0X1	T44.0X2	T44.0X3	T44.0X4	T44.0X5	T44.0X6
ophthalmological	T49.5X1	T49.5X2	T49.5X3	T49.5X4	T49.5X5	T49.5X6
Anticoagulant NEC	T45.511	T45.512	T45.513	T45.514	T45.515	T45.516
Antagonist	T45.7X1	T45.7X2	T45.7X3	T45.7X4	T45.7X5	T45.7X6
Anti-common-cold drug NEC	T48.5X1	T48.5X2	T48.5X3	T48.5X4	T48.5X5	T48.5X6
Anticonvulsant	T42.71	T42.72	T42.73	T42.74	T42.75	T42.76
barbiturate	T42.3X1	T42.3X2	T42.3X3	T42.3X4	T42.3X5	T42.3X6
combination (with barbiturate)	T42.3X1	T42.3X2	T42.3X3	T42.3X4	T42.3X5	T42.3X6
hydantoin	T42.0X1	T42.0X2	T42.0X3	T42.0X4	T42.0X5	T42.0X6
hypnotic NEC	T42.6X1	T42.6X2	T42.6X3	T42.6X4	T42.6X5	T42.6X6
oxazolidinedione	T42.2X1	T42.2X2	T42.2X3	T42.2X4	T42.2X5	T42.2X6
pyrimidinedione	T42.6X1	T42.6X2	T42.6X3	T42.6X4	T42.6X5	T42.6X6
specified NEC	T42.6X1	T42.6X2	T42.6X3	T42.6X4	T42.6X5	T42.6X6
succinimide	T42.2X1	T42.2X2	T42.2X3	T42.2X4	T42.2X5	T42.2X6

◀ New　◀ Revised　deleted Deleted

TABLE OF DRUGS AND CHEMICALS

Substance	Poisoning, Accidental (Unintentional)	Poisoning, Intentional Self-Harm	Poisoning, Assault	Poisoning, Undetermined	Adverse Effect	Underdosing
External Cause (T-Code)						
Anti-D immunoglobulin (human)	T50.Z11	T50.Z12	T50.Z13	T50.Z14	T50.Z15	T50.Z16
Antidepressant NEC	T43.201	T43.202	T43.203	T43.204	T43.205	T43.206
monoamine oxidase inhibitor	T43.1X1	T43.1X2	T43.1X3	T43.1X4	T43.1X5	T43.1X6
selective serotonin norepinephrine reuptake inhibitor	T43.211	T43.212	T43.213	T43.214	T43.215	T43.216
selective serotonin reuptake inhibitor	T43.221	T43.222	T43.223	T43.224	T43.225	T43.226
specified NEC	T43.291	T43.292	T43.293	T43.294	T43.295	T43.296
tetracyclic	T43.021	T43.022	T43.023	T43.024	T43.025	T43.026
triazolopyridine	T43.221	T43.222	T43.223	T43.224	T43.225	T43.226
tricyclic	T43.011	T43.012	T43.013	T43.014	T43.015	T43.016
Antidiabetic NEC	T38.3X1	T38.3X2	T38.3X3	T38.3X4	T38.3X5	T38.3X6
biguanide	T38.3X1	T38.3X2	T38.3X3	T38.3X4	T38.3X5	T38.3X6
and sulfonyl combined	T38.3X1	T38.3X2	T38.3X3	T38.3X4	T38.3X5	T38.3X6
combined	T38.3X1	T38.3X2	T38.3X3	T38.3X4	T38.3X5	T38.3X6
sulfonylurea	T38.3X1	T38.3X2	T38.3X3	T38.3X4	T38.3X5	T38.3X6
Antidiarrheal drug NEC	T47.6X1	T47.6X2	T47.6X3	T47.6X4	T47.6X5	T47.6X6
absorbent	T47.6X1	T47.6X2	T47.6X3	T47.6X4	T47.6X5	T47.6X6
Antidiphtheria serum	T50.Z11	T50.Z12	T50.Z13	T50.Z14	T50.Z15	T50.Z16
Antidiuretic hormone	T38.891	T38.892	T38.893	T38.894	T38.895	T38.896
Antidote NEC	T50.6X1	T50.6X2	T50.6X3	T50.6X4	T50.6X5	T50.6X6
heavy metal	T45.8X1	T45.8X2	T45.8X3	T45.8X4	T45.8X5	T45.8X6
Antidysrhythmic NEC	T46.2X1	T46.2X2	T46.2X3	T46.2X4	T46.2X5	T46.2X6
Antiemetic drug	T45.0X1	T45.0X2	T45.0X3	T45.0X4	T45.0X5	T45.0X6
Antiepilepsy agent	T42.71	T42.72	T42.73	T42.74	T42.75	T42.76
combination	T42.5X1	T42.5X2	T42.5X3	T42.5X4	T42.5X5	T42.5X6
mixed	T42.5X1	T42.5X2	T42.5X3	T42.5X4	T42.5X5	T42.5X6
specified, NEC	T42.6X1	T42.6X2	T42.6X3	T42.6X4	T42.6X5	T42.6X6
Antiestrogen NEC	T38.6X1	T38.6X2	T38.6X3	T38.6X4	T38.6X5	T38.6X6
Antifertility pill	T38.4X1	T38.4X2	T38.4X3	T38.4X4	T38.4X5	T38.4X6
Antifibrinolytic drug	T45.621	T45.622	T45.623	T45.624	T45.625	T45.626
Antifilarial drug	T37.4X1	T37.4X2	T37.4X3	T37.4X4	T37.4X5	T37.4X6
Antiflatulent	T47.5X1	T47.5X2	T47.5X3	T47.5X4	T47.5X5	T47.5X6
Antifreeze	T65.91	T65.92	T65.93	T65.94	—	—
alcohol	T51.1X1	T51.1X2	T51.1X3	T51.1X4	—	—
ethylene glycol	T51.8X1	T51.8X2	T51.8X3	T51.8X4	—	—
Antifungal						
antibiotic (systemic)	T36.7X1	T36.7X2	T36.7X3	T36.7X4	T36.7X5	T36.7X6
anti-infective NEC	T37.91	T37.92	T37.93	T37.94	T37.95	T37.96
disinfectant, local	T49.0X1	T49.0X2	T49.0X3	T49.0X4	T49.0X5	T49.0X6
nonmedicinal (spray)	T60.3X1	T60.3X2	T60.3X3	T60.3X4	—	—
topical	T49.0X1	T49.0X2	T49.0X3	T49.0X4	T49.0X5	T49.0X6

Substance	Poisoning, Accidental (Unintentional)	Poisoning, Intentional Self-Harm	Poisoning, Assault	Poisoning, Undetermined	Adverse Effect	Underdosing
External Cause (T-Code)						
Anti-gastric-secretion drug NEC	T47.1X1	T47.1X2	T47.1X3	T47.1X4	T47.1X5	T47.1X6
Antigonadotrophin NEC	T38.6X1	T38.6X2	T38.6X3	T38.6X4	T38.6X5	T38.6X6
Antihallucinogen	T43.501	T43.502	T43.503	T43.504	T43.505	T43.506
Antihelmintics	T37.4X1	T37.4X2	T37.4X3	T37.4X4	T37.4X5	T37.4X6
Antihemophilic						
factor	T45.8X1	T45.8X2	T45.8X3	T45.8X4	T45.8X5	T45.8X6
fraction	T45.8X1	T45.8X2	T45.8X3	T45.8X4	T45.8X5	T45.8X6
globulin concentrate	T45.7X1	T45.7X2	T45.7X3	T45.7X4	T45.7X5	T45.7X6
human plasma	T45.8X1	T45.8X2	T45.8X3	T45.8X4	T45.8X5	T45.8X6
plasma, dried	T45.7X1	T45.7X2	T45.7X3	T45.7X4	T45.7X5	T45.7X6
Antihemorrhoidal preparation	T49.2X1	T49.2X2	T49.2X3	T49.2X4	T49.2X5	T49.2X6
Antiheparin drug	T45.7X1	T45.7X2	T45.7X3	T45.7X4	T45.7X5	T45.7X6
Antihistamine	T45.0X1	T45.0X2	T45.0X3	T45.0X4	T45.0X5	T45.0X6
Antihookworm drug	T37.4X1	T37.4X2	T37.4X3	T37.4X4	T37.4X5	T37.4X6
Anti-human lymphocytic globulin	T50.Z11	T50.Z12	T50.Z13	T50.Z14	T50.Z15	T50.Z16
Antihyperlipidemic drug	T46.6X1	T46.6X2	T46.6X3	T46.6X4	T46.6X5	T46.6X6
Antihypertensive drug NEC	T46.5X1	T46.5X2	T46.5X3	T46.5X4	T46.5X5	T46.5X6
Anti-infective NEC	T37.91	T37.92	T37.93	T37.94	T37.95	T37.96
anthelmintic	T37.4X1	T37.4X2	T37.4X3	T37.4X4	T37.4X5	T37.4X6
antibiotics	T36.91	T36.92	T36.93	T36.94	T36.95	T36.96
specified NEC	T36.8X1	T36.8X2	T36.8X3	T36.8X4	T36.8X5	T36.8X6
antimalarial	T37.2X1	T37.2X2	T37.2X3	T37.2X4	T37.2X5	T37.2X6
antimycobacterial NEC	T37.1X1	T37.1X2	T37.1X3	T37.1X4	T37.1X5	T37.1X6
antibiotics	T36.5X1	T36.5X2	T36.5X3	T36.5X4	T36.5X5	T36.5X6
antiprotozoal NEC	T37.3X1	T37.3X2	T37.3X3	T37.3X4	T37.3X5	T37.3X6
blood	T37.2X1	T37.2X2	T37.2X3	T37.2X4	T37.2X5	T37.2X6
antiviral	T37.5X1	T37.5X2	T37.5X3	T37.5X4	T37.5X5	T37.5X6
arsenical	T37.8X1	T37.8X2	T37.8X3	T37.8X4	T37.8X5	T37.8X6
bismuth, local	T49.0X1	T49.0X2	T49.0X3	T49.0X4	T49.0X5	T49.0X6
ENT	T49.6X1	T49.6X2	T49.6X3	T49.6X4	T49.6X5	T49.6X6
eye NEC	T49.5X1	T49.5X2	T49.5X3	T49.5X4	T49.5X5	T49.5X6
heavy metals NEC	T37.8X1	T37.8X2	T37.8X3	T37.8X4	T37.8X5	T37.8X6
local NEC	T49.0X1	T49.0X2	T49.0X3	T49.0X4	T49.0X5	T49.0X6
specified NEC	T49.0X1	T49.0X2	T49.0X3	T49.0X4	T49.0X5	T49.0X6
mixed	T37.91	T37.92	T37.93	T37.94	T37.95	T37.96
ophthalmic preparation	T49.5X1	T49.5X2	T49.5X3	T49.5X4	T49.5X5	T49.5X6
topical NEC	T49.0X1	T49.0X2	T49.0X3	T49.0X4	T49.0X5	T49.0X6
Anti-inflammatory drug NEC	T49.0X1	T49.0X2	T49.0X3	T49.0X4	T49.0X5	T49.0X6
local	T49.0X1	T49.0X2	T49.0X3	T49.0X4	T49.0X5	T49.0X6
nonsteroidal NEC	T39.391	T39.392	T39.393	T39.394	T39.395	T39.396
propionic acid derivative	T39.311	T39.312	T39.313	T39.314	T39.315	T39.316
specified NEC	T39.391	T39.392	T39.393	T39.394	T39.395	T39.396

◀ New ◀ Revised deleted Deleted

Substance	Poisoning, Accidental (Unintentional)	Poisoning, Intentional Self-Harm	Poisoning, Assault	Poisoning, Undetermined	Adverse Effect	Underdosing
Antikaluretic	T50.3X1	T50.3X2	T50.3X3	T50.3X4	T50.3X5	T50.3X6
Antiknock (tetraethyl lead)	T56.0X1	T56.0X2	T56.0X3	T56.0X4	—	—
Antilipemic drug NEC	T46.6X1	T46.6X2	T46.6X3	T46.6X4	T46.6X5	T46.6X6
Antimalarial	T37.2X1	T37.2X2	T37.2X3	T37.2X4	T37.2X5	T37.2X6
prophylactic NEC	T37.2X1	T37.2X2	T37.2X3	T37.2X4	T37.2X5	T37.2X6
pyrimidine derivative	T37.2X1	T37.2X2	T37.2X3	T37.2X4	T37.2X5	T37.2X6
Antimetabolite	T45.1X1	T45.1X2	T45.1X3	T45.1X4	T45.1X5	T45.1X6
Antimitotic agent	T45.1X1	T45.1X2	T45.1X3	T45.1X4	T45.1X5	T45.1X6
Antimony (compounds) (vapor) NEC	T56.891	T56.892	T56.893	T56.894	—	—
anti-infectives	T37.8X1	T37.8X2	T37.8X3	T37.8X4	T37.8X5	T37.8X6
dimercaptosuccinate	T37.3X1	T37.3X2	T37.3X3	T37.3X4	T37.3X5	T37.3X6
hydride	T56.891	T56.892	T56.893	T56.894		
pesticide (vapor)	T60.8X1	T60.8X2	T60.8X3	T60.8X4	—	—
potassium (sodium) tartrate	T37.8X1	T37.8X2	T37.8X3	T37.8X4	T37.8X5	T37.8X6
sodium dimercaptosuccinate	T37.3X1	T37.3X2	T37.3X3	T37.3X4	T37.3X5	T37.3X6
tartrated	T37.8X1	T37.8X2	T37.8X3	T37.8X4	T37.8X5	T37.8X6
Antimuscarinic NEC	T44.3X1	T44.3X2	T44.3X3	T44.3X4	T44.3X5	T44.3X6
Antimycobacterial drug NEC	T37.1X1	T37.1X2	T37.1X3	T37.1X4	T37.1X5	T37.1X6
antibiotics	T36.5X1	T36.5X2	T36.5X3	T36.5X4	T36.5X5	T36.5X6
combination	T37.1X1	T37.1X2	T37.1X3	T37.1X4	T37.1X5	T37.1X6
Antinausea drug	T45.0X1	T45.0X2	T45.0X3	T45.0X4	T45.0X5	T45.0X6
Antinematode drug	T37.4X1	T37.4X2	T37.4X3	T37.4X4	T37.4X5	T37.4X6
Antineoplastic NEC	T45.1X1	T45.1X2	T45.1X3	T45.1X4	T45.1X5	T45.1X6
alkaloidal	T45.1X1	T45.1X2	T45.1X3	T45.1X4	T45.1X5	T45.1X6
antibiotics	T45.1X1	T45.1X2	T45.1X3	T45.1X4	T45.1X5	T45.1X6
combination	T45.1X1	T45.1X2	T45.1X3	T45.1X4	T45.1X5	T45.1X6
estrogen	T38.5X1	T38.5X2	T38.5X3	T38.5X4	T38.5X5	T38.5X6
steroid	T38.7X1	T38.7X2	T38.7X3	T38.7X4	T38.7X5	T38.7X6
Antiparasitic drug (systemic)	T37.91	T37.92	T37.93	T37.94	T37.95	T37.96
local	T49.0X1	T49.0X2	T49.0X3	T49.0X4	T49.0X5	T49.0X6
specified NEC	T37.8X1	T37.8X2	T37.8X3	T37.8X4	T37.8X5	T37.8X6
Antiparkinsonism drug NEC	T42.8X1	T42.8X2	T42.8X3	T42.8X4	T42.8X5	T42.8X6
Antiperspirant NEC	T49.2X1	T49.2X2	T49.2X3	T49.2X4	T49.2X5	T49.2X6
Antiphlogistic NEC	T39.4X1	T39.4X2	T39.4X3	T39.4X4	T39.4X5	T39.4X6
Antiplatyhelmintic drug	T37.4X1	T37.4X2	T37.4X3	T37.4X4	T37.4X5	T37.4X6
Antiprotozoal drug NEC	T37.3X1	T37.3X2	T37.3X3	T37.3X4	T37.3X5	T37.3X6
blood	T37.2X1	T37.2X2	T37.2X3	T37.2X4	T37.2X5	T37.2X6
local	T49.0X1	T49.0X2	T49.0X3	T49.0X4	T49.0X5	T49.0X6
Antipruritic drug NEC	T49.1X1	T49.1X2	T49.1X3	T49.1X4	T49.1X5	T49.1X6
Antipsychotic drug	T43.501	T43.502	T43.503	T43.504	T43.505	T43.506
specified NEC	T43.591	T43.592	T43.593	T43.594	T43.595	T43.596

Substance	Poisoning, Accidental (Unintentional)	Poisoning, Intentional Self-Harm	Poisoning, Assault	Poisoning, Undetermined	Adverse Effect	Underdosing
Antipyretic	T39.91	T39.92	T39.93	T39.94	T39.95	T39.96
specified NEC	T39.8X1	T39.8X2	T39.8X3	T39.8X4	T39.8X5	T39.8X6
Antipyrine	T39.2X1	T39.2X2	T39.2X3	T39.2X4	T39.2X5	T39.2X6
Antirabies hyperimmune serum	T50.Z11	T50.Z12	T50.Z13	T50.Z14	T50.Z15	T50.Z16
Antirheumatic NEC	T39.4X1	T39.4X2	T39.4X3	T39.4X4	T39.4X5	T39.4X6
Antirigidity drug NEC	T42.8X1	T42.8X2	T42.8X3	T42.8X4	T42.8X5	T42.8X6
Antischistosomal drug	T37.4X1	T37.4X2	T37.4X3	T37.4X4	T37.4X5	T37.4X6
Antiscorpion sera	T50.Z11	T50.Z12	T50.Z13	T50.Z14	T50.Z15	T50.Z16
Antiseborrheics	T49.4X1	T49.4X2	T49.4X3	T49.4X4	T49.4X5	T49.4X6
Antiseptics (external) (medicinal)	T49.0X1	T49.0X2	T49.0X3	T49.0X4	T49.0X5	T49.0X6
Antistine	T45.0X1	T45.0X2	T45.0X3	T45.0X4	T45.0X5	T45.0X6
Antitapeworm drug	T37.4X1	T37.4X2	T37.4X3	T37.4X4	T37.4X5	T37.4X6
Antitetanus immunoglobulin	T50.Z11	T50.Z12	T50.Z13	T50.Z14	T50.Z15	T50.Z16
Antithrombotic	T45.521	T45.522	T45.523	T45.524	T45.525	T45.526
Antithyroid drug NEC	T38.2X1	T38.2X2	T38.2X3	T38.2X4	T38.2X5	T38.2X6
Antitoxin	T50.Z11	T50.Z12	T50.Z13	T50.Z14	T50.Z15	T50.Z16
diphtheria	T50.Z11	T50.Z12	T50.Z13	T50.Z14	T50.Z15	T50.Z16
gas gangrene	T50.Z11	T50.Z12	T50.Z13	T50.Z14	T50.Z15	T50.Z16
tetanus	T50.Z11	T50.Z12	T50.Z13	T50.Z14	T50.Z15	T50.Z16
Antitoxin, any	T50.901	T50.902	T50.903	T50.904	T50.905	T50.906
Antitrichomonal drug	T37.3X1	T37.3X2	T37.3X3	T37.3X4	T37.3X5	T37.3X6
Antituberculars	T37.1X1	T37.1X2	T37.1X3	T37.1X4	T37.1X5	T37.1X6
antibiotics	T36.5X1	T36.5X2	T36.5X3	T36.5X4	T36.5X5	T36.5X6
Antitussive NEC	T48.3X1	T48.3X2	T48.3X3	T48.3X4	T48.3X5	T48.3X6
codeine mixture	T40.2X1	T40.2X2	T40.2X3	T40.2X4	T40.2X5	T40.2X6
opiate	T40.2X1	T40.2X2	T40.2X3	T40.2X4	T40.2X5	T40.2X6
Antivaricose drug	T46.8X1	T46.8X2	T46.8X3	T46.8X4	T46.8X5	T46.8X6
Antivenin, antivenom (sera)	T50.Z11	T50.Z12	T50.Z13	T50.Z14	T50.Z15	T50.Z16
crotaline	T50.Z11	T50.Z12	T50.Z13	T50.Z14	T50.Z15	T50.Z16
spider bite	T50.Z11	T50.Z12	T50.Z13	T50.Z14	T50.Z15	T50.Z16
Antivertigo drug	T45.0X1	T45.0X2	T45.0X3	T45.0X4	T45.0X5	T45.0X6
Antiviral drug NEC	T37.5X1	T37.5X2	T37.5X3	T37.5X4	T37.5X5	T37.5X6
eye	T49.5X1	T49.5X2	T49.5X3	T49.5X4	T49.5X5	T49.5X6
Antiwhipworm drug	T37.4X1	T37.4X2	T37.4X3	T37.4X4	T37.4X5	T37.4X6
Ant poisons—see Pesticides						
Antrol—see also by specific chemical substance	T60.91	T60.92	T60.93	T60.94	—	—
fungicide	T60.91	T60.92	T60.93	T60.94	—	—
ANTU (alpha naphthylthiourea)	T60.4X1	T60.4X2	T60.4X3	T60.4X4	—	—
Apalcillin	T36.0X1	T36.0X2	T36.0X3	T36.0X4	T36.0X5	T36.0X6
APC	T48.5X1	T48.5X2	T48.5X3	T48.5X4	T48.5X5	T48.5X6
Aplonidine	T44.4X1	T44.4X2	T44.4X3	T44.4X4	T44.4X5	T44.4X6
Apomorphine	T47.7X1	T47.7X2	T47.7X3	T47.7X4	T47.7X5	T47.7X6

◀ New ◀ Revised ~~deleted~~ Deleted

TABLE OF DRUGS AND CHEMICALS

Substance	Poisoning, Accidental (Unintentional)	Poisoning, Intentional Self-Harm	Poisoning, Assault	Poisoning, Undetermined	Adverse Effect	Underdosing
Appetite depressants, central	T50.5X1	T50.5X2	T50.5X3	T50.5X4	T50.5X5	T50.5X6
Apraclonidine (hydrochloride)	T44.4X1	T44.4X2	T44.4X3	T44.4X4	T44.4X5	T44.4X6
Apresoline	T46.5X1	T46.5X2	T46.5X3	T46.5X4	T46.5X5	T46.5X6
Aprindine	T46.2X1	T46.2X2	T46.2X3	T46.2X4	T46.2X5	T46.2X6
Aprobarbital	T42.3X1	T42.3X2	T42.3X3	T42.3X4	T42.3X5	T42.3X6
Apronalide	T42.6X1	T42.6X2	T42.6X3	T42.6X4	T42.6X5	T42.6X6
Aprotinin	T45.621	T45.622	T45.623	T45.624	T45.625	T45.626
Aptocaine	T41.3X1	T41.3X2	T41.3X3	T41.3X4	T41.3X5	T41.3X6
Aqua fortis	T54.2X1	T54.2X2	T54.2X3	T54.2X4	—	—
Ara-A	T37.5X1	T37.5X2	T37.5X3	T37.5X4	T37.5X5	T37.5X6
Ara-C	T45.1X1	T45.1X2	T45.1X3	T45.1X4	T45.1X5	T45.1X6
Arachis oil	T49.3X1	T49.3X2	T49.3X3	T49.3X4	T49.3X5	T49.3X6
cathartic	T47.4X1	T47.4X2	T47.4X3	T47.4X4	T47.4X5	T47.4X6
Aralen	T37.2X1	T37.2X2	T37.2X3	T37.2X4	T37.2X5	T37.2X6
Arecoline	T44.1X1	T44.1X2	T44.1X3	T44.1X4	T44.1X5	T44.1X6
Arginine	T50.991	T50.992	T50.993	T50.994	T50.995	T50.996
glutamate	T50.991	T50.992	T50.993	T50.994	T50.995	T50.996
Argyrol	T49.0X1	T49.0X2	T49.0X3	T49.0X4	T49.0X5	T49.0X6
ENT agent	T49.6X1	T49.6X2	T49.6X3	T49.6X4	T49.6X5	T49.6X6
ophthalmic preparation	T49.5X1	T49.5X2	T49.5X3	T49.5X4	T49.5X5	T49.5X6
Aristocort	T38.0X1	T38.0X2	T38.0X3	T38.0X4	T38.0X5	T38.0X6
ENT agent	T49.6X1	T49.6X2	T49.6X3	T49.6X4	T49.6X5	T49.6X6
ophthalmic preparation	T49.5X1	T49.5X2	T49.5X3	T49.5X4	T49.5X5	T49.5X6
topical NEC	T49.0X1	T49.0X2	T49.0X3	T49.0X4	T49.0X5	T49.0X6
Aromatics, corrosive	T54.1X1	T54.1X2	T54.1X3	T54.1X4	—	—
disinfectants	T54.1X1	T54.1X2	T54.1X3	T54.1X4	—	—
Arsenate of lead	T57.0X1	T57.0X2	T57.0X3	T57.0X4	—	—
herbicide	T57.0X1	T57.0X2	T57.0X3	T57.0X4	—	—
Arsenic, arsenicals (compounds) (dust) (vapor) NEC	T57.0X1	T57.0X2	T57.0X3	T57.0X4	—	—
anti-infectives	T37.8X1	T37.8X2	T37.8X3	T37.8X4	T37.8X5	T37.8X6
pesticide (dust) (fumes)	T57.0X1	T57.0X2	T57.0X3	T57.0X4	—	—
Arsine (gas)	T57.0X1	T57.0X2	T57.0X3	T57.0X4	—	—
Arsphenamine (silver)	T37.8X1	T37.8X2	T37.8X3	T37.8X4	T37.8X5	T37.8X6
Arsthinol	T37.3X1	T37.3X2	T37.3X3	T37.3X4	T37.3X5	T37.3X6
Artane	T44.3X1	T44.3X2	T44.3X3	T44.3X4	T44.3X5	T44.3X6
Arthropod (venomous) NEC	T63.481	T63.482	T63.483	T63.484	—	—
Articaine	T41.3X1	T41.3X2	T41.3X3	T41.3X4	T41.3X5	T41.3X6
Asbestos	T57.8X1	T57.8X2	T57.8X3	T57.8X4	—	—
Ascaridole	T37.4X1	T37.4X2	T37.4X3	T37.4X4	T37.4X5	T37.4X6
Ascorbic acid	T45.2X1	T45.2X2	T45.2X3	T45.2X4	T45.2X5	T45.2X6
Asiaticoside	T49.0X1	T49.0X2	T49.0X3	T49.0X4	T49.0X5	T49.0X6

Substance	Poisoning, Accidental (Unintentional)	Poisoning, Intentional Self-Harm	Poisoning, Assault	Poisoning, Undetermined	Adverse Effect	Underdosing
Asparaginase	T45.1X1	T45.1X2	T45.1X3	T45.1X4	T45.1X5	T45.1X6
Aspidium (oleoresin)	T37.4X1	T37.4X2	T37.4X3	T37.4X4	T37.4X5	T37.4X6
Aspirin (aluminum) (soluble)	T39.011	T39.012	T39.013	T39.014	T39.015	T39.016
Aspoxicillin	T36.0X1	T36.0X2	T36.0X3	T36.0X4	T36.0X5	T36.0X6
Astemizole	T45.0X1	T45.0X2	T45.0X3	T45.0X4	T45.0X5	T45.0X6
Astringent (local)	T49.2X1	T49.2X2	T49.2X3	T49.2X4	T49.2X5	T49.2X6
specified NEC	T49.2X1	T49.2X2	T49.2X3	T49.2X4	T49.2X5	T49.2X6
Astromicin	T36.5X1	T36.5X2	T36.5X3	T36.5X4	T36.5X5	T36.5X6
Ataractic drug NEC	T43.501	T43.502	T43.503	T43.504	T43.505	T43.506
Atenolol	T44.7X1	T44.7X2	T44.7X3	T44.7X4	T44.7X5	T44.7X6
Atonia drug, intestinal	T47.4X1	T47.4X2	T47.4X3	T47.4X4	T47.4X5	T47.4X6
Atophan	T50.4X1	T50.4X2	T50.4X3	T50.4X4	T50.4X5	T50.4X6
Atracurium besilate	T48.1X1	T48.1X2	T48.1X3	T48.1X4	T48.1X5	T48.1X6
Atropine	T44.3X1	T44.3X2	T44.3X3	T44.3X4	T44.3X5	T44.3X6
derivative	T44.3X1	T44.3X2	T44.3X3	T44.3X4	T44.3X5	T44.3X6
methonitrate	T44.3X1	T44.3X2	T44.3X3	T44.3X4	T44.3X5	T44.3X6
Attapulgite	T47.6X1	T47.6X2	T47.6X3	T47.6X4	T47.6X5	T47.6X6
Attenuvax	T50.991	T50.992	T50.993	T50.994	T50.995	T50.996
Auramine	T65.891	T65.892	T65.893	T65.894	—	—
dye	T65.6X1	T65.6X2	T65.6X3	T65.6X4	—	—
fungicide	T60.3X1	T60.3X2	T60.3X3	T60.3X4	—	—
Auranofin	T39.4X1	T39.4X2	T39.4X3	T39.4X4	T39.4X5	T39.4X6
Aurantiin	T46.991	T46.992	T46.993	T46.994	T46.995	T46.996
Aureomycin	T36.4X1	T36.4X2	T36.4X3	T36.4X4	T36.4X5	T36.4X6
ophthalmic preparation	T49.5X1	T49.5X2	T49.5X3	T49.5X4	T49.5X5	T49.5X6
topical NEC	T49.0X1	T49.0X2	T49.0X3	T49.0X4	T49.0X5	T49.0X6
Aurothioglucose	T39.4X1	T39.4X2	T39.4X3	T39.4X4	T39.4X5	T39.4X6
Aurothioglycanide	T39.4X1	T39.4X2	T39.4X3	T39.4X4	T39.4X5	T39.4X6
Aurothiomalate sodium	T39.4X1	T39.4X2	T39.4X3	T39.4X4	T39.4X5	T39.4X6
Aurotioprol	T39.4X1	T39.4X2	T39.4X3	T39.4X4	T39.4X5	T39.4X6
Automobile fuel	T52.0X1	T52.0X2	T52.0X3	T52.0X4	—	—
Autonomic nervous system agent NEC	T44.901	T44.902	T44.903	T44.904	T44.905	T44.906
Avlosulfon	T37.1X1	T37.1X2	T37.1X3	T37.1X4	T37.1X5	T37.1X6
Avomine	T42.6X1	T42.6X2	T42.6X3	T42.6X4	T42.6X5	T42.6X6
Axerophthol	T45.2X1	T45.2X2	T45.2X3	T45.2X4	T45.2X5	T45.2X6
Azacitidine	T45.1X1	T45.1X2	T45.1X3	T45.1X4	T45.1X5	T45.1X6
Azacyclonol	T43.591	T43.592	T43.593	T43.594	T43.595	T43.596
Azadirachta	T60.2X1	T60.2X2	T60.2X3	T60.2X4	—	—
Azanidazole	T37.3X1	T37.3X2	T37.3X3	T37.3X4	T37.3X5	T37.3X6
Azapetine	T46.7X1	T46.7X2	T46.7X3	T46.7X4	T46.7X5	T46.7X6
Azapropazone	T39.2X1	T39.2X2	T39.2X3	T39.2X4	T39.2X5	T39.2X6

◀ New ◀ Revised ~~deleted~~ Deleted

Substance	Poisoning, Accidental (Unintentional)	Poisoning, Intentional Self-Harm	Poisoning, Assault	Poisoning, Undetermined	Adverse Effect	Underdosing
Azaribine	T45.1X1	T45.1X2	T45.1X3	T45.1X4	T45.1X5	T45.1X6
Azaserine	T45.1X1	T45.1X2	T45.1X3	T45.1X4	T45.1X5	T45.1X6
Azatadine	T45.0X1	T45.0X2	T45.0X3	T45.0X4	T45.0X5	T45.0X6
Azatepa	T45.1X1	T45.1X2	T45.1X3	T45.1X4	T45.1X5	T45.1X6
Azathioprine	T45.1X1	T45.1X2	T45.1X3	T45.1X4	T45.1X5	T45.1X6
Azelaic acid	T49.0X1	T49.0X2	T49.0X3	T49.0X4	T49.0X5	T49.0X6
Azelastine	T45.0X1	T45.0X2	T45.0X3	T45.0X4	T45.0X5	T45.0X6
Azidocillin	T36.0X1	T36.0X2	T36.0X3	T36.0X4	T36.0X5	T36.0X6
Azidothymidine	T37.5X1	T37.5X2	T37.5X3	T37.5X4	T37.5X5	T37.5X6
Azinphos (ethyl) (methyl)	T60.0X1	T60.0X2	T60.0X3	T60.0X4	—	—
Aziridine (chelating)	T54.1X1	T54.1X2	T54.1X3	T54.1X4	—	—
Azithromycin	T36.3X1	T36.3X2	T36.3X3	T36.3X4	T36.3X5	T36.3X6
Azlocillin	T36.01	T36.02	T36.03	T36.04	T36.05	T36.06
Azobenzene smoke	T65.3X1	T65.3X2	T65.3X3	T65.3X4	—	—
acaricide	T60.8X1	T60.8X2	T60.8X3	T60.8X4	—	—
Azosulfamide	T37.0X1	T37.0X2	T37.0X3	T37.0X4	T37.0X5	T37.0X6
AZT	T37.5X1	T37.5X2	T37.5X3	T37.5X4	T37.5X5	T37.5X6
Aztreonam	T36.1X1	T36.1X2	T36.1X3	T36.1X4	T36.1X5	T36.1X6
Azulfidine	T37.0X1	T37.0X2	T37.0X3	T37.0X4	T37.0X5	T37.0X6
Azuresin	T50.8X1	T50.8X2	T50.8X3	T50.8X4	T50.8X5	T50.8X6
B						
Bacampicillin	T36.0X1	T36.0X2	T36.0X3	T36.0X4	T36.0X5	T36.0X6
Bacillus						
lactobacillus	T47.8X1	T47.8X2	T47.8X3	T47.8X4	T47.8X5	T47.8X6
subtilis	T47.6X1	T47.6X2	T47.6X3	T47.6X4	T47.6X5	T47.6X6
Bacimycin	T49.0X1	T49.0X2	T49.0X3	T49.0X4	T49.0X5	T49.0X6
ophthalmic preparation	T49.5X1	T49.5X2	T49.5X3	T49.5X4	T49.5X5	T49.5X6
Bacitracin zinc	T49.0X1	T49.0X2	T49.0X3	T49.0X4	T49.0X5	T49.0X6
with neomycin	T49.0X1	T49.0X2	T49.0X3	T49.0X4	T49.0X5	T49.0X6
ENT agent	T49.6X1	T49.6X2	T49.6X3	T49.6X4	T49.6X5	T49.6X6
ophthalmic preparation	T49.5X1	T49.5X2	T49.5X3	T49.5X4	T49.5X5	T49.5X6
topical NEC	T49.0X1	T49.0X2	T49.0X3	T49.0X4	T49.0X5	T49.0X6
Baclofen	T42.8X1	T42.8X2	T42.8X3	T42.8X4	T42.8X5	T42.8X6
Baking soda	T50.991	T50.992	T50.993	T50.994	T50.995	T50.996
BAL	T45.8X1	T45.8X2	T45.8X3	T45.8X4	T45.8X5	T45.8X6
Bambuterol	T48.6X1	T48.6X2	T48.6X3	T48.6X4	T48.6X5	T48.6X6
Bamethan (sulfate)	T46.7X1	T46.7X2	T46.7X3	T46.7X4	T46.7X5	T46.7X6
Bamifylline	T48.6X1	T48.6X2	T48.6X3	T48.6X4	T48.6X5	T48.6X6
Bamipine	T45.0X1	T45.0X2	T45.0X3	T45.0X4	T45.0X5	T45.0X6
Baneberry — see Actaea spicata						
Banewort — see Belladonna						

Substance	Poisoning, Accidental (Unintentional)	Poisoning, Intentional Self-Harm	Poisoning, Assault	Poisoning, Undetermined	Adverse Effect	Underdosing
Barbenyl	T42.3X1	T42.3X2	T42.3X3	T42.3X4	T42.3X5	T42.3X6
Barbexaclone	T42.6X1	T42.6X2	T42.6X3	T42.6X4	T42.6X5	T42.6X6
Barbital	T42.3X1	T42.3X2	T42.3X3	T42.3X4	T42.3X5	T42.3X6
sodium	T42.3X1	T42.3X2	T42.3X3	T42.3X4	T42.3X5	T42.3X6
Barbitone	T42.3X1	T42.3X2	T42.3X3	T42.3X4	T42.3X5	T42.3X6
Barbiturate NEC	T42.3X1	T42.3X2	T42.3X3	T42.3X4	T42.3X5	T42.3X6
with tranquilizer	T42.3X1	T42.3X2	T42.3X3	T42.3X4	T42.3X5	T42.3X6
anesthetic (intravenous)	T41.1X1	T41.1X2	T41.1X3	T41.1X4	T41.1X5	T41.1X6
Barium (carbonate) (chloride) (sulfite)	T57.8X1	T57.8X2	T57.8X3	T57.8X4	—	—
diagnostic agent	T50.8X1	T50.8X2	T50.8X3	T50.8X4	T50.8X5	T50.8X6
pesticide	T60.4X1	T60.4X2	T60.4X3	T60.4X4	—	—
rodenticide	T60.4X1	T60.4X2	T60.4X3	T60.4X4	—	—
sulfate (medicinal)	T50.8X1	T50.8X2	T50.8X3	T50.8X4	T50.8X5	T50.8X6
Barrier cream	T49.3X1	T49.3X2	T49.3X3	T49.3X4	T49.3X5	T49.3X6
Basic fuchsin	T49.0X1	T49.0X2	T49.0X3	T49.0X4	T49.0X5	T49.0X6
Battery acid or fluid	T54.2X1	T54.2X2	T54.2X3	T54.2X4	—	—
Bay rum	T51.8X1	T51.8X2	T51.8X3	T51.8X4	—	—
BCG (vaccine)	T50.A91	T50.A92	T50.A93	T50.A94	T50.A95	T50.A96
BCNU	T45.1X1	T45.1X2	T45.1X3	T45.1X4	T45.1X5	T45.1X6
Bearsfoot	T62.2X1	T62.2X2	T62.2X3	T62.2X4	—	—
Beclamide	T42.6X1	T42.6X2	T42.6X3	T42.6X4	T42.6X5	T42.6X6
Beclomethasone	T44.5X1	T44.5X2	T44.5X3	T44.5X4	T44.5X5	T44.5X6
Bee (sting) (venom)	T63.441	T63.442	T63.443	T63.444	—	—
Befunolol	T49.5X1	T49.5X2	T49.5X3	T49.5X4	T49.5X5	T49.5X6
Bekanamycin	T36.5X1	T36.5X2	T36.5X3	T36.5X4	T36.5X5	T36.5X6
Belladonna — see also Nightshade						
alkaloids	T44.3X1	T44.3X2	T44.3X3	T44.3X4	T44.3X5	T44.3X6
extract	T44.3X1	T44.3X2	T44.3X3	T44.3X4	T44.3X5	T44.3X6
herb	T44.3X1	T44.3X2	T44.3X3	T44.3X4	T44.3X5	T44.3X6
Bemegride	T50.7X1	T50.7X2	T50.7X3	T50.7X4	T50.7X5	T50.7X6
Benactyzine	T44.3X1	T44.3X2	T44.3X3	T44.3X4	T44.3X5	T44.3X6
Benadryl	T45.0X1	T45.0X2	T45.0X3	T45.0X4	T45.0X5	T45.0X6
Benaprizine	T44.3X1	T44.3X2	T44.3X3	T44.3X4	T44.3X5	T44.3X6
Benazepril	T46.4X1	T46.4X2	T46.4X3	T46.4X4	T46.4X5	T46.4X6
Bencyclane	T46.7X1	T46.7X2	T46.7X3	T46.7X4	T46.7X5	T46.7X6
Bendazol	T46.3X1	T46.3X2	T46.3X3	T46.3X4	T46.3X5	T46.3X6
Bendrofluazide	T50.2X1	T50.2X2	T50.2X3	T50.2X4	T50.2X5	T50.2X6
Bendroflumethiazide	T50.2X1	T50.2X2	T50.2X3	T50.2X4	T50.2X5	T50.2X6
Benemid	T50.4X1	T50.4X2	T50.4X3	T50.4X4	T50.4X5	T50.4X6
Benethamine penicillin	T36.0X1	T36.0X2	T36.0X3	T36.0X4	T36.0X5	T36.0X6
Benisone	T49.0X1	T49.0X2	T49.0X3	T49.0X4	T49.0X5	T49.0X6

Substance	Poisoning, Accidental (Unintentional)	Poisoning, Intentional Self-Harm	Poisoning, Assault	Poisoning, Undetermined	Adverse Effect	Underdosing
Benexate	T47.1X1	T47.1X2	T47.1X3	T47.1X4	T47.1X5	T47.1X6
Benfluorex	T46.6X1	T46.6X2	T46.6X3	T46.6X4	T46.6X5	T46.6X6
Benfotiamine	T45.2X1	T45.2X2	T45.2X3	T45.2X4	T45.2X5	T45.2X6
Benomyl	T60.0X1	T60.0X2	T60.0X3	T60.0X4	—	—
Benoquin	T49.8X1	T49.8X2	T49.8X3	T49.8X4	T49.8X5	T49.8X6
Benoxinate	T41.3X1	T41.3X2	T41.3X3	T41.3X4	T41.3X5	T41.3X6
Benperidol	T43.4X1	T43.4X2	T43.4X3	T43.4X4	T43.4X5	T43.4X6
Benproperine	T48.3X1	T48.3X2	T48.3X3	T48.3X4	T48.3X5	T48.3X6
Benserazide	T42.8X1	T42.8X2	T42.8X3	T42.8X4	T42.8X5	T42.8X6
Bentazepam	T42.4X1	T42.4X2	T42.4X3	T42.4X4	T42.4X5	T42.4X6
Bentiromide	T50.8X1	T50.8X2	T50.8X3	T50.8X4	T50.8X5	T50.8X6
Bentonite	T49.3X1	T49.3X2	T49.3X3	T49.3X4	T49.3X5	T49.3X6
Benzalbutyramide	T46.6X1	T46.6X2	T46.6X3	T46.6X4	T46.6X5	T46.6X6
Benzalkonium (chloride)	T49.0X1	T49.0X2	T49.0X3	T49.0X4	T49.0X5	T49.0X6
ophthalmic preparation	T49.5X1	T49.5X2	T49.5X3	T49.5X4	T49.5X5	T49.5X6
Benzamine	T41.3X1	T41.3X2	T41.3X3	T41.3X4	T41.3X5	T41.3X6
lactate	T49.1X1	T49.1X2	T49.1X3	T49.1X4	T49.1X5	T49.1X6
Benzamidosalicylate (calcium)	T37.1X1	T37.1X2	T37.1X3	T37.1X4	T37.1X5	T37.1X6
Benzamphetamine	T50.5X1	T50.5X2	T50.5X3	T50.5X4	T50.5X5	T50.5X6
Benzapril hydrochloride	T46.5X1	T46.5X2	T46.5X3	T46.5X4	T46.5X5	T46.5X6
Benzathine benzylpenicillin	T36.0X1	T36.0X2	T36.0X3	T36.0X4	T36.0X5	T36.0X6
Benzathine penicillin	T36.0X1	T36.0X2	T36.0X3	T36.0X4	T36.0X5	T36.0X6
Benzatropine	T42.8X1	T42.8X2	T42.8X3	T42.8X4	T42.8X5	T42.8X6
Benzbromarone	T50.4X1	T50.4X2	T50.4X3	T50.4X4	T50.4X5	T50.4X6
Benzcarbimine	T45.1X1	T45.1X2	T45.1X3	T45.1X4	T45.1X5	T45.1X6
Benzedrex	T44.991	T44.992	T44.993	T44.994	T44.995	T44.996
Benzedrine (amphetamine)	T43.621	T43.622	T43.623	T43.624	T43.625	T43.626
Benzenamine	T65.3X1	T65.3X2	T65.3X3	T65.3X4	—	—
Benzene	T52.1X1	T52.1X2	T52.1X3	T52.1X4	—	—
homologues (acetyl) (dimethyl) (methyl) (solvent)	T52.2X1	T52.2X2	T52.2X3	T52.2X4	—	—
Benzethonium (chloride)	T49.0X1	T49.0X2	T49.0X3	T49.0X4	T49.0X5	T49.0X6
Benzfetamine	T50.5X1	T50.5X2	T50.5X3	T50.5X4	T50.5X5	T50.5X6
Benzhexol	T44.3X1	T44.3X2	T44.3X3	T44.3X4	T44.3X5	T44.3X6
Benzhydramine (chloride)	T45.0X1	T45.0X2	T45.0X3	T45.0X4	T45.0X5	T45.0X6
Benzidine	T65.891	T65.892	T65.893	T65.894	—	—
Benzilonium bromide	T44.3X1	T44.3X2	T44.3X3	T44.3X4	T44.3X5	T44.3X6
Benzimidazole	T60.3X1	T60.3X2	T60.3X3	T60.3X4	—	—
Benzin(e) — see Ligroin						
Benziodarone	T46.3X1	T46.3X2	T46.3X3	T46.3X4	T46.3X5	T46.3X6
Benznidazole	T37.3X1	T37.3X2	T37.3X3	T37.3X4	T37.3X5	T37.3X6
Benzocaine	T41.3X1	T41.3X2	T41.3X3	T41.3X4	T41.3X5	T41.3X6

Substance	Poisoning, Accidental (Unintentional)	Poisoning, Intentional Self-Harm	Poisoning, Assault	Poisoning, Undetermined	Adverse Effect	Underdosing
Benzoctamine	T43.0X1	T43.0X2	T43.0X3	T43.0X4	T43.0X5	T43.0X6
Benzodiapin	T42.4X1	T42.4X2	T42.4X3	T42.4X4	T42.4X5	T42.4X6
Benzodiazepine NEC	T42.4X1	T42.4X2	T42.4X3	T42.4X4	T42.4X5	T42.4X6
Benzoic acid	T49.0X1	T49.0X2	T49.0X3	T49.0X4	T49.0X5	T49.0X6
with salicylic acid	T49.0X1	T49.0X2	T49.0X3	T49.0X4	T49.0X5	T49.0X6
Benzoin (tincture)	T48.5X1	T48.5X2	T48.5X3	T48.5X4	T48.5X5	T48.5X6
Benzol (benzene)	T52.1X1	T52.1X2	T52.1X3	T52.1X4	—	—
vapor	T52.0X1	T52.0X2	T52.0X3	T52.0X4	—	—
Benzomorphan	T40.2X1	T40.2X2	T40.2X3	T40.2X4	T40.2X5	T40.2X6
Benzonatate	T48.3X1	T48.3X2	T48.3X3	T48.3X4	T48.3X5	T48.3X6
Benzophenones	T49.3X1	T49.3X2	T49.3X3	T49.3X4	T49.3X5	T49.3X6
Benzopyrone	T46.991	T46.992	T46.993	T46.994	T46.995	T46.996
Benzothiadiazides	T50.2X1	T50.2X2	T50.2X3	T50.2X4	T50.2X5	T50.2X6
Benzoxonium chloride	T49.0X1	T49.0X2	T49.0X3	T49.0X4	T49.0X5	T49.0X6
Benzoyl peroxide	T49.0X1	T49.0X2	T49.0X3	T49.0X4	T49.0X5	T49.0X6
Benzoylpas calcium	T37.1X1	T37.1X2	T37.1X3	T37.1X4	T37.1X5	T37.1X6
Benzperidin	T43.591	T43.592	T43.593	T43.594	T43.595	T43.596
Benzperidol	T43.591	T43.592	T43.593	T43.594	T43.595	T43.596
Benzphetamine	T50.5X1	T50.5X2	T50.5X3	T50.5X4	T50.5X5	T50.5X6
Benzpyrinium bromide	T44.1X1	T44.1X2	T44.1X3	T44.1X4	T44.1X5	T44.1X6
Benzquinamide	T45.0X1	T45.0X2	T45.0X3	T45.0X4	T45.0X5	T45.0X6
Benzthiazide	T50.2X1	T50.2X2	T50.2X3	T50.2X4	T50.2X5	T50.2X6
Benztropine						
anticholinergic	T44.3X1	T44.3X2	T44.3X3	T44.3X4	T44.3X5	T44.3X6
antiparkinson	T42.8X1	T42.8X2	T42.8X3	T42.8X4	T42.8X5	T42.8X6
Benzydamine	T49.0X1	T49.0X2	T49.0X3	T49.0X4	T49.0X5	T49.0X6
Benzyl						
acetate	T52.8X1	T52.8X2	T52.8X3	T52.8X4	—	—
alcohol	T49.0X1	T49.0X2	T49.0X3	T49.0X4	T49.0X5	T49.0X6
benzoate	T49.0X1	T49.0X2	T49.0X3	T49.0X4	T49.0X5	T49.0X6
Benzoic acid	T49.0X1	T49.0X2	T49.0X3	T49.0X4	T49.0X5	T49.0X6
morphine	T40.2X1	T40.2X2	T40.2X3	T40.2X4	—	—
nicotinate	T46.6X1	T46.6X2	T46.6X3	T46.6X4	T46.6X5	T46.6X6
penicillin	T36.0X1	T36.0X2	T36.0X3	T36.0X4	T36.0X5	T36.0X6
Benzylhydrochlorthia-zide	T50.2X1	T50.2X2	T50.2X3	T50.2X4	T50.2X5	T50.2X6
Benzylpenicillin	T36.0X1	T36.0X2	T36.0X3	T36.0X4	T36.0X5	T36.0X6
Benzylthiouracil	T38.2X1	T38.2X2	T38.2X3	T38.2X4	T38.2X5	T38.2X6
Bephenium hydroxy-naphthoate	T37.4X1	T37.4X2	T37.4X3	T37.4X4	T37.4X5	T37.4X6
Bepridil	T46.1X1	T46.1X2	T46.1X3	T46.1X4	T46.1X5	T46.1X6
Bergamot oil	T65.891	T65.892	T65.893	T65.894	—	—
Bergapten	T50.991	T50.992	T50.993	T50.994	T50.995	T50.996
Berries, poisonous	T62.1X1	T62.1X2	T62.1X3	T62.1X4	—	—

◀ New ◀ Revised deleted Deleted

Substance	External Cause (T-Code) Poisoning, Accidental (Unintentional)	Poisoning, Intentional Self-Harm	Poisoning, Assault	Poisoning, Undetermined	Adverse Effect	Underdosing
Beryllium (compounds)	T56.7X1	T56.7X2	T56.7X3	T56.7X4	—	—
b-acetyldigoxin	T46.0X1	T46.0X2	T46.0X3	T46.0X4	T46.0X5	T46.0X6
beta adrenergic blocking agent, heart	T44.7X1	T44.7X2	T44.7X3	T44.7X4	T44.7X5	T44.7X6
b-benzalbutyramide	T46.6X1	T46.6X2	T46.6X3	T46.6X4	T46.6X5	T46.6X6
Betacarotene	T45.2X1	T45.2X2	T45.2X3	T45.2X4	T45.2X5	T45.2X6
b-eucaine	T49.1X1	T49.1X2	T49.1X3	T49.1X4	T49.1X5	T49.1X6
Beta-Chlor	T42.6X1	T42.6X2	T42.6X3	T42.6X4	T42.6X5	T42.6X6
b-galactosidase	T47.5X1	T47.5X2	T47.5X3	T47.5X4	T47.5X5	T47.5X6
Betahistine	T46.7X1	T46.7X2	T46.7X3	T46.7X4	T46.7X5	T46.7X6
Betaine	T47.5X1	T47.5X2	T47.5X3	T47.5X4	T47.5X5	T47.5X6
Betamethasone	T49.0X1	T49.0X2	T49.0X3	T49.0X4	T49.0X5	T49.0X6
topical	T49.0X1	T49.0X2	T49.0X3	T49.0X4	T49.0X5	T49.0X6
Betamicin	T36.8X1	T36.8X2	T36.8X3	T36.8X4	T36.8X5	T36.8X6
Betanidine	T46.5X1	T46.5X2	T46.5X3	T46.5X4	T46.5X5	T46.5X6
b-sitosterol(s)	T46.6X1	T46.6X2	T46.6X3	T46.6X4	T46.6X5	T46.6X6
Betaxolol	T44.7X1	T44.7X2	T44.7X3	T44.7X4	T44.7X5	T44.7X6
Betazole	T50.8X1	T50.8X2	T50.8X3	T50.8X4	T50.8X5	T50.8X6
Bethanechol	T44.1X1	T44.1X2	T44.1X3	T44.1X4	T44.1X5	T44.1X6
chloride	T44.1X1	T44.1X2	T44.1X3	T44.1X4	T44.1X5	T44.1X6
Bethanidine	T46.5X1	T46.5X2	T46.5X3	T46.5X4	T46.5X5	T46.5X6
Betoxycaine	T41.3X1	T41.3X2	T41.3X3	T41.3X4	T41.3X5	T41.3X6
Betula oil	T49.3X1	T49.3X2	T49.3X3	T49.3X4	T49.3X5	T49.3X6
Bevantolol	T44.7X1	T44.7X2	T44.7X3	T44.7X4	T44.7X5	T44.7X6
Bevonium metilsulfate	T44.3X1	T44.3X2	T44.3X3	T44.3X4	T44.3X5	T44.3X6
Bezafibrate	T46.6X1	T46.6X2	T46.6X3	T46.6X4	T46.6X5	T46.6X6
Bezitramide	T40.491	T40.492	T40.493	T40.494	T40.495	T40.496
BHA	T50.991	T50.992	T50.993	T50.994	T50.995	T50.996
Bhang	T40.7X1	T40.7X2	T40.7X3	T40.7X4	T40.7X5	T40.7X6
BHC (medicinal)	T49.0X1	T49.0X2	T49.0X3	T49.0X4	T49.0X5	T49.0X6
nonmedicinal (vapor)	T53.6X1	T53.6X2	T53.6X3	T53.6X4	—	—
Bialamicol	T37.3X1	T37.3X2	T37.3X3	T37.3X4	T37.3X5	T37.3X6
Bibenzonium bromide	T48.3X1	T48.3X2	T48.3X3	T48.3X4	T48.3X5	T48.3X6
Bibrocathol	T49.5X1	T49.5X2	T49.5X3	T49.5X4	T49.5X5	T49.5X6
Bichloride of mercury — see Mercury, chloride						
Bichromates (calcium) (potassium) (sodium) (crystals)	T57.8X1	T57.8X2	T57.8X3	T57.8X4	—	—
fumes	T56.2X1	T56.2X2	T56.2X3	T56.2X4	—	—
Biclotymol	T49.6X1	T49.6X2	T49.6X3	T49.6X4	T49.6X5	T49.6X6
Bicucculine	T50.7X1	T50.7X2	T50.7X3	T50.7X4	T50.7X5	T50.7X6
Bifemelane	T43.291	T43.292	T43.293	T43.294	T43.295	T43.296
Biguanide derivatives, oral	T38.3X1	T38.3X2	T38.3X3	T38.3X4	T38.3X5	T38.3X6

Substance	External Cause (T-Code) Poisoning, Accidental (Unintentional)	Poisoning, Intentional Self-Harm	Poisoning, Assault	Poisoning, Undetermined	Adverse Effect	Underdosing
Biligrafin	T50.8X1	T50.8X2	T50.8X3	T50.8X4	T50.8X5	T50.8X6
Bile salts	T47.5X1	T47.5X2	T47.5X3	T47.5X4	T47.5X5	T47.5X6
Bilopaque	T50.8X1	T50.8X2	T50.8X3	T50.8X4	T50.8X5	T50.8X6
Binifibrate	T46.6X1	T46.6X2	T46.6X3	T46.6X4	T46.6X5	T46.6X6
Binitrobenzol	T65.3X1	T65.3X2	T65.3X3	T65.3X4	—	—
Bioflavonoid(s)	T46.991	T46.992	T46.993	T46.994	T46.995	T46.996
Biological substance NEC	T50.901	T50.902	T50.903	T50.904	T50.905	T50.906
Biotin	T45.2X1	T45.2X2	T45.2X3	T45.2X4	T45.2X5	T45.2X6
Biperiden	T44.3X1	T44.3X2	T44.3X3	T44.3X4	T44.3X5	T44.3X6
Bisacodyl	T47.2X1	T47.2X2	T47.2X3	T47.2X4	T47.2X5	T47.2X6
Bisbentiamine	T45.2X1	T45.2X2	T45.2X3	T45.2X4	T45.2X5	T45.2X6
Bisbutiamine	T45.2X1	T45.2X2	T45.2X3	T45.2X4	T45.2X5	T45.2X6
Bisdequalinium (salts) (diacetate)	T49.6X1	T49.6X2	T49.6X3	T49.6X4	T49.6X5	T49.6X6
Bishydroxycoumarin	T45.511	T45.512	T45.513	T45.514	T45.515	T45.516
Bismarsen	T37.8X1	T37.8X2	T37.8X3	T37.8X4	T37.8X5	T37.8X6
Bismuth salts	T47.6X1	T47.6X2	T47.6X3	T47.6X4	T47.6X5	T47.6X6
aluminate	T47.1X1	T47.1X2	T47.1X3	T47.1X4	T47.1X5	T47.1X6
anti-infectives	T37.8X1	T37.8X2	T37.8X3	T37.8X4	T37.8X5	T37.8X6
formic iodide	T49.0X1	T49.0X2	T49.0X3	T49.0X4	T49.0X5	T49.0X6
glycolylarsenate	T49.0X1	T49.0X2	T49.0X3	T49.0X4	T49.0X5	T49.0X6
nonmedicinal (compounds) NEC	T65.91	T65.92	T65.93	T65.94	—	—
subcarbonate	T47.6X1	T47.6X2	T47.6X3	T47.6X4	T47.6X5	T47.6X6
subsalicylate	T37.8X1	T37.8X2	T37.8X3	T37.8X4	T37.8X5	T37.8X6
sulfarsphenamine	T37.8X1	T37.8X2	T37.8X3	T37.8X4	T37.8X5	T37.8X6
Bisoprolol	T44.7X1	T44.7X2	T44.7X3	T44.7X4	T44.7X5	T44.7X6
Bisoxatin	T47.2X1	T47.2X2	T47.2X3	T47.2X4	T47.2X5	T47.2X6
Bisulepin (hydrochloride)	T45.0X1	T45.0X2	T45.0X3	T45.0X4	T45.0X5	T45.0X6
Bithionol	T37.8X1	T37.8X2	T37.8X3	T37.8X4	T37.8X5	T37.8X6
anthelminthic	T37.4X1	T37.4X2	T37.4X3	T37.4X4	T37.4X5	T37.4X6
Bitolterol	T48.6X1	T48.6X2	T48.6X3	T48.6X4	T48.6X5	T48.6X6
Bitoscanate	T37.4X1	T37.4X2	T37.4X3	T37.4X4	T37.4X5	T37.4X6
Bitter almond oil	T62.8X1	T62.8X2	T62.8X3	T62.8X4	—	—
Bittersweet	T62.2X1	T62.2X2	T62.2X3	T62.2X4	—	—
Black						
flag	T60.91	T60.92	T60.93	T60.94	—	—
henbane	T62.2X1	T62.2X2	T62.2X3	T62.2X4	—	—
leaf (40)	T60.91	T60.92	T60.93	T60.94	—	—
widow spider (bite)	T63.311	T63.312	T63.313	T63.314	—	—
antivenin	T50.Z11	T50.Z12	T50.Z13	T50.Z14	T50.Z15	T50.Z16
Blast furnace gas (carbon monoxide from)	T58.8X1	T58.8X2	T58.8X3	T58.8X4	—	—
Bleach	T54.91	T54.92	T54.93	T54.94		

◀ New   ◀ Revised   ~~deleted~~ Deleted

TABLE OF DRUGS AND CHEMICALS

Substance	External Cause (T-Code)					
	Poisoning, Accidental (Unintentional)	Poisoning, Intentional Self-Harm	Poisoning, Assault	Poisoning, Undetermined	Adverse Effect	Underdosing
Bleaching agent (medicinal)	T49.4X1	T49.4X2	T49.4X3	T49.4X4	T49.4X5	T49.4X6
Bleomycin	T45.1X1	T45.1X2	T45.1X3	T45.1X4	T45.1X5	T45.1X6
Blockain	T41.3X1	T41.3X2	T41.3X3	T41.3X4	T41.3X5	T41.3X6
infiltration (subcutaneous)	T41.3X1	T41.3X2	T41.3X3	T41.3X4	T41.3X5	T41.3X6
nerve block (peripheral) (plexus)	T41.3X1	T41.3X2	T41.3X3	T41.3X4	T41.3X5	T41.3X6
topical (surface)	T41.3X1	T41.3X2	T41.3X3	T41.3X4	T41.3X5	T41.3X6
Blockers, calcium channel	T46.1X1	T46.1X2	T46.1X3	T46.1X4	T46.1X5	T46.1X6
Blood (derivatives) (natural) (plasma) (whole)	T45.8X1	T45.8X2	T45.8X3	T45.8X4	T45.8X5	T45.8X6
dried	T45.8X1	T45.8X2	T45.8X3	T45.8X4	T45.8X5	T45.8X6
drug affecting NEC	T45.91	T45.92	T45.93	T45.94	T45.95	T45.96
expander NEC	T45.8X1	T45.8X2	T45.8X3	T45.8X4	T45.8X5	T45.8X6
fraction NEC	T45.8X1	T45.8X2	T45.8X3	T45.8X4	T45.8X5	T45.8X6
substitute (macromolecular)	T45.8X1	T45.8X2	T45.8X3	T45.8X4	T45.8X5	T45.8X6
Blue velvet	T40.2X1	T40.2X2	T40.2X3	T40.2X4	—	—
Bone meal	T62.8X1	T62.8X2	T62.8X3	T62.8X4	—	—
Bonine	T45.0X1	T45.0X2	T45.0X3	T45.0X4	T45.0X5	T45.0X6
Bopindolol	T44.7X1	T44.7X2	T44.7X3	T44.7X4	T44.7X5	T44.7X6
Boracic acid	T49.0X1	T49.0X2	T49.0X3	T49.0X4	T49.0X5	T49.0X6
ENT agent	T49.6X1	T49.6X2	T49.6X3	T49.6X4	T49.6X5	T49.6X6
ophthalmic preparation	T49.5X1	T49.5X2	T49.5X3	T49.5X4	T49.5X5	T49.5X6
Borane complex	T57.8X1	T57.8X2	T57.8X3	T57.8X4	—	—
Borate(s)	T57.8X1	T57.8X2	T57.8X3	T57.8X4	—	—
buffer	T50.991	T50.992	T50.993	T50.994	T50.995	T50.996
cleanser	T54.91	T54.92	T54.93	T54.94		
sodium	T57.8X1	T57.8X2	T57.8X3	T57.8X4	—	—
Borax (cleanser)	T54.91	T54.92	T54.93	T54.94		
Bordeaux mixture	T60.3X1	T60.3X2	T60.3X3	T60.3X4	—	—
Boric acid	T49.0X1	T49.0X2	T49.0X3	T49.0X4	T49.0X5	T49.0X6
ENT agent	T49.6X1	T49.6X2	T49.6X3	T49.6X4	T49.6X5	T49.6X6
ophthalmic preparation	T49.5X1	T49.5X2	T49.5X3	T49.5X4	T49.5X5	T49.5X6
Bornaprine	T44.3X1	T44.3X2	T44.3X3	T44.3X4	T44.3X5	T44.3X6
Boron	T57.8X1	T57.8X2	T57.8X3	T57.8X4	—	—
hydride NEC	T57.8X1	T57.8X2	T57.8X3	T57.8X4	—	—
fumes or gas	T57.8X1	T57.8X2	T57.8X3	T57.8X4	—	—
trifluoride	T59.891	T59.892	T59.893	T59.894	—	—
Botox	T48.291	T48.292	T48.293	T48.294	T48.295	T48.296
Botulinus anti-toxin (type A, B)	T50.Z11	T50.Z12	T50.Z13	T50.Z14	T50.Z15	T50.Z16
Brake fluid vapor	T59.891	T59.892	T59.893	T59.894		
Brallobarbital	T42.3X1	T42.3X2	T42.3X3	T42.3X4	T42.3X5	T42.3X6
Bran (wheat)	T47.4X1	T47.4X2	T47.4X3	T47.4X4	T47.4X5	T47.4X6
Brass (fumes)	T56.891	T56.892	T56.893	T56.894		

Substance	External Cause (T-Code)					
	Poisoning, Accidental (Unintentional)	Poisoning, Intentional Self-Harm	Poisoning, Assault	Poisoning, Undetermined	Adverse Effect	Underdosing
Brasso	T52.0X1	T52.0X2	T52.0X3	T52.0X4	—	—
Bretylium tosilate	T46.2X1	T46.2X2	T46.2X3	T46.2X4	T46.2X5	T46.2X6
Brevital (sodium)	T41.1X1	T41.1X2	T41.1X3	T41.1X4	T41.1X5	T41.1X6
Brinase	T45.3X1	T45.3X2	T45.3X3	T45.3X4	T45.3X5	T45.3X6
British antilewisite	T45.8X1	T45.8X2	T45.8X3	T45.8X4	T45.8X5	T45.8X6
Brodifacoum	T60.4X1	T60.4X2	T60.4X3	T60.4X4	—	—
Bromal (hydrate)	T42.6X1	T42.6X2	T42.6X3	T42.6X4	T42.6X5	T42.6X6
Bromazepam	T42.4X1	T42.4X2	T42.4X3	T42.4X4	T42.4X5	T42.4X6
Bromazine	T45.0X1	T45.0X2	T45.0X3	T45.0X4	T45.0X5	T45.0X6
Brombenzylcyanide	T59.3X1	T59.3X2	T59.3X3	T59.3X4	—	—
Bromelains	T45.3X1	T45.3X2	T45.3X3	T45.3X4	T45.3X5	T45.3X6
Bromethalin	T60.4X1	T60.4X2	T60.4X3	T60.4X4	—	—
Bromhexine	T48.4X1	T48.4X2	T48.4X3	T48.4X4	T48.4X5	T48.4X6
Bromide salts	T42.6X1	T42.6X2	T42.6X3	T42.6X4	T42.6X5	T42.6X6
Bromindione	T45.511	T45.512	T45.513	T45.514	T45.515	T45.516
Bromine						
compounds (medicinal)	T42.6X1	T42.6X2	T42.6X3	T42.6X4	T42.6X5	T42.6X6
sedative	T42.6X1	T42.6X2	T42.6X3	T42.6X4	T42.6X5	T42.6X6
vapor	T59.891	T59.892	T59.893	T59.894	—	—
Bromisovalum	T42.6X1	T42.6X2	T42.6X3	T42.6X4	T42.6X5	T42.6X6
Bromisoval	T42.6X1	T42.6X2	T42.6X3	T42.6X4	T42.6X5	T42.6X6
Bromobenzylcyanide	T59.3X1	T59.3X2	T59.3X3	T59.3X4	—	—
Bromochlorosalicylani-lide	T49.0X1	T49.0X2	T49.0X3	T49.0X4	T49.0X5	T49.0X6
Bromocriptine	T42.8X1	T42.8X2	T42.8X3	T42.8X4	T42.8X5	T42.8X6
Bromodiphenhydramine	T45.0X1	T45.0X2	T45.0X3	T45.0X4	T45.0X5	T45.0X6
Bromoform	T42.6X1	T42.6X2	T42.6X3	T42.6X4	T42.6X5	T42.6X6
Bromophenol blue reagent	T50.991	T50.992	T50.993	T50.994	T50.995	T50.996
Bromopride	T47.8X1	T47.8X2	T47.8X3	T47.8X4	T47.8X5	T47.8X6
Bromosalicylchloranitide	T49.0X1	T49.0X2	T49.0X3	T49.0X4	T49.0X5	T49.0X6
Bromosalicylhydroxamic acid	T37.1X1	T37.1X2	T37.1X3	T37.1X4	T37.1X5	T37.1X6
Bromo-seltzer	T39.1X1	T39.1X2	T39.1X3	T39.1X4	T39.1X5	T39.1X6
Bromoxynil	T60.3X1	T60.3X2	T60.3X3	T60.3X4	—	—
Bromperidol	T43.4X1	T43.4X2	T43.4X3	T43.4X4	T43.4X5	T43.4X6
Brompheniramine	T45.0X1	T45.0X2	T45.0X3	T45.0X4	T45.0X5	T45.0X6
Bromsulfophthalein	T50.8X1	T50.8X2	T50.8X3	T50.8X4	T50.8X5	T50.8X6
Bromural	T42.6X1	T42.6X2	T42.6X3	T42.6X4	T42.6X5	T42.6X6
Bromvaletone	T42.6X1	T42.6X2	T42.6X3	T42.6X4	T42.6X5	T42.6X6
Bronchodilator NEC	T48.6X1	T48.6X2	T48.6X3	T48.6X4	T48.6X5	T48.6X6
Brotizolam	T42.4X1	T42.4X2	T42.4X3	T42.4X4	T42.4X5	T42.4X6
Brovincamine	T46.7X1	T46.7X2	T46.7X3	T46.7X4	T46.7X5	T46.7X6
Brown spider (bite) (venom)	T63.391	T63.392	T63.393	T63.394	—	—

◀ New ◀ Revised ~~deleted~~ Deleted

Substance	Poisoning, Accidental (Unintentional)	Poisoning, Intentional Self-Harm	Poisoning, Assault	Poisoning, Undetermined	Adverse Effect	Underdosing
Brown recluse spider (bite) (venom)	T63.331	T63.332	T63.333	T63.334	—	—
Broxaterol	T48.6X1	T48.6X2	T48.6X3	T48.6X4	T48.6X5	T48.6X6
Broxuridine	T45.1X1	T45.1X2	T45.1X3	T45.1X4	T45.1X5	T45.1X6
Broxyquinoline	T37.8X1	T37.8X2	T37.8X3	T37.8X4	T37.8X5	T37.8X6
Bruceine	T48.291	T48.292	T48.293	T48.294	T48.295	T48.296
Brucia	T62.2X1	T62.2X2	T62.2X3	T62.2X4	—	—
Brucine	T65.1X1	T65.1X2	T65.1X3	T65.1X4	—	—
Brunswick green — *see* Copper						
Bruten — *see* Ibuprofen						
Bryonia	T47.2X1	T47.2X2	T47.2X3	T47.2X4	T47.2X5	T47.2X6
Buclizine	T45.0X1	T45.0X2	T45.0X3	T45.0X4	T45.0X5	T45.0X6
Buclosamide	T49.0X1	T49.0X2	T49.0X3	T49.0X4	T49.0X5	T49.0X6
Budesonide	T44.5X1	T44.5X2	T44.5X3	T44.5X4	T44.5X5	T44.5X6
Budralazine	T46.5X1	T46.5X2	T46.5X3	T46.5X4	T46.5X5	T46.5X6
Bufferin	T39.011	T39.012	T39.013	T39.014	T39.015	T39.016
Buflomedil	T46.7X1	T46.7X2	T46.7X3	T46.7X4	T46.7X5	T46.7X6
Buformin	T38.3X1	T38.3X2	T38.3X3	T38.3X4	T38.3X5	T38.3X6
Bufotenine	T40.991	T40.992	T40.993	T40.994	—	—
Bufrolin	T48.6X1	T48.6X2	T48.6X3	T48.6X4	T48.6X5	T48.6X6
Bufylline	T48.6X1	T48.6X2	T48.6X3	T48.6X4	T48.6X5	T48.6X6
Bulk filler	T50.5X1	T50.5X2	T50.5X3	T50.5X4	T50.5X5	T50.5X6
cathartic	T47.4X1	T47.4X2	T47.4X3	T47.4X4	T47.4X5	T47.4X6
Bumetanide	T50.1X1	T50.1X2	T50.1X3	T50.1X4	T50.1X5	T50.1X6
Bunaftine	T46.2X1	T46.2X2	T46.2X3	T46.2X4	T46.2X5	T46.2X6
Bunamiodyl	T50.8X1	T50.8X2	T50.8X3	T50.8X4	T50.8X5	T50.8X6
Bunazosin	T44.6X1	T44.6X2	T44.6X3	T44.6X4	T44.6X5	T44.6X6
Bunitrolol	T44.7X1	T44.7X2	T44.7X3	T44.7X4	T44.7X5	T44.7X6
Buphenine	T46.7X1	T46.7X2	T46.7X3	T46.7X4	T46.7X5	T46.7X6
Bupivacaine	T41.3X1	T41.3X2	T41.3X3	T41.3X4	T41.3X5	T41.3X6
infiltration (subcutaneous)	T41.3X1	T41.3X2	T41.3X3	T41.3X4	T41.3X5	T41.3X6
nerve block (peripheral) (plexus)	T41.3X1	T41.3X2	T41.3X3	T41.3X4	T41.3X5	T41.3X6
spinal	T41.3X1	T41.3X2	T41.3X3	T41.3X4	T41.3X5	T41.3X6
Bupranolol	T44.7X1	T44.7X2	T44.7X3	T44.7X4	T44.7X5	T44.7X6
Buprenorphine	T40.491	T40.492	T40.493	T40.494	T40.495	T40.496
Bupropion	T43.291	T43.292	T43.293	T43.294	T43.295	T43.296
Burimamide	T47.1X1	T47.1X2	T47.1X3	T47.1X4	T47.1X5	T47.1X6
Buserelin	T38.891	T38.892	T38.893	T38.894	T38.895	T38.896
Buspirone	T43.591	T43.592	T43.593	T43.594	T43.595	T43.596
Busulfan, busulphan	T45.1X1	T45.1X2	T45.1X3	T45.1X4	T45.1X5	T45.1X6
Butabarbital (sodium)	T42.3X1	T42.3X2	T42.3X3	T42.3X4	T42.3X5	T42.3X6
Butabarbitone	T42.3X1	T42.3X2	T42.3X3	T42.3X4	T42.3X5	T42.3X6

Substance	Poisoning, Accidental (Unintentional)	Poisoning, Intentional Self-Harm	Poisoning, Assault	Poisoning, Undetermined	Adverse Effect	Underdosing
Butabarpal	T42.3X1	T42.3X2	T42.3X3	T42.3X4	T42.3X5	T42.3X6
Butacaine	T41.3X1	T41.3X2	T41.3X3	T41.3X4	T41.3X5	T41.3X6
Butalamine	T46.7X1	T46.7X2	T46.7X3	T46.7X4	T46.7X5	T46.7X6
Butalbital	T42.3X1	T42.3X2	T42.3X3	T42.3X4	T42.3X5	T42.3X6
Butallylonal	T42.3X1	T42.3X2	T42.3X3	T42.3X4	T42.3X5	T42.3X6
Butamben	T41.3X1	T41.3X2	T41.3X3	T41.3X4	T41.3X5	T41.3X6
Butamirate	T48.3X1	T48.3X2	T48.3X3	T48.3X4	T48.3X5	T48.3X6
Butane (distributed in mobile container)	T59.891	T59.892	T59.893	T59.894	—	—
distributed through pipes	T59.891	T59.892	T59.893	T59.894	—	—
incomplete combustion	T58.11	T58.12	T58.13	T58.14	—	—
Butanilicaine	T41.3X1	T41.3X2	T41.3X3	T41.3X4	T41.3X5	T41.3X6
Butanol	T51.3X1	T51.3X2	T51.3X3	T51.3X4		
Butanone, 2-butanone	T52.4X1	T52.4X2	T52.4X3	T52.4X4	—	—
Butantrone	T49.4X1	T49.4X2	T49.4X3	T49.4X4	T49.4X5	T49.4X6
Butaperazine	T43.3X1	T43.3X2	T43.3X3	T43.3X4	T43.3X5	T43.3X6
Butazolidin	T39.2X1	T39.2X2	T39.2X3	T39.2X4	T39.2X5	T39.2X6
Butetamate	T48.6X1	T48.6X2	T48.6X3	T48.6X4	T48.6X5	T48.6X6
Butethal	T42.3X1	T42.3X2	T42.3X3	T42.3X4	T42.3X5	T42.3X6
Butethamate	T44.3X1	T44.3X2	T44.3X3	T44.3X4	T44.3X5	T44.3X6
Buthalitone (sodium)	T41.1X1	T41.1X2	T41.1X3	T41.1X4	T41.1X5	T41.1X6
Butisol (sodium)	T42.3X1	T42.3X2	T42.3X3	T42.3X4	T42.3X5	T42.3X6
Butizide	T50.2X1	T50.2X2	T50.2X3	T50.2X4	T50.2X5	T50.2X6
Butobarbital	T42.3X1	T42.3X2	T42.3X3	T42.3X4	T42.3X5	T42.3X6
sodium	T42.3X1	T42.3X2	T42.3X3	T42.3X4	T42.3X5	T42.3X6
Butobarbitone	T42.3X1	T42.3X2	T42.3X3	T42.3X4	T42.3X5	T42.3X6
Butoconazole (nitrate)	T49.0X1	T49.0X2	T49.0X3	T49.0X4	T49.0X5	T49.0X6
Butorphanol	T40.491	T40.492	T40.493	T40.494	T40.495	T40.496
Butriptyline	T43.011	T43.012	T43.013	T43.014	T43.015	T43.016
Butropium bromide	T44.3X1	T44.3X2	T44.3X3	T44.3X4	T44.3X5	T44.3X6
Buttercups	T62.2X1	T62.2X2	T62.2X3	T62.2X4	—	—
Butter of antimony — *see* Antimony						
Butyl						
acetate (secondary)	T52.8X1	T52.8X2	T52.8X3	T52.8X4	—	—
alcohol	T51.3X1	T51.3X2	T51.3X3	T51.3X4	—	—
aminobenzoate	T41.3X1	T41.3X2	T41.3X3	T41.3X4	T41.3X5	T41.3X6
butyrate	T52.8X1	T52.8X2	T52.8X3	T52.8X4	—	—
carbinol	T51.3X1	T51.3X2	T51.3X3	T51.3X4	—	—
carbitol	T52.3X1	T52.3X2	T52.3X3	T52.3X4	—	—
cellosolve	T52.3X1	T52.3X2	T52.3X3	T52.3X4	—	—
chloral (hydrate)	T42.6X1	T42.6X2	T42.6X3	T42.6X4	T42.6X5	T42.6X6
formate	T52.8X1	T52.8X2	T52.8X3	T52.8X4	—	—

Substance	External Cause (T-Code)					
	Poisoning, Accidental (Unintentional)	Poisoning, Intentional Self-Harm	Poisoning, Assault	Poisoning, Undetermined	Adverse Effect	Underdosing
Butyl (Continued)						
lactate	T52.8X1	T52.8X2	T52.8X3	T52.8X4	—	—
propionate	T52.8X1	T52.8X2	T52.8X3	T52.8X4	—	—
scopolamine bromide	T44.3X1	T44.3X2	T44.3X3	T44.3X4	T44.3X5	T44.3X6
thiobarbital sodium	T41.1X1	T41.1X2	T41.1X3	T41.1X4	T41.1X5	T41.1X6
Butylated hydroxy-anisole	T50.991	T50.992	T50.993	T50.994	T50.995	T50.996
Butylchloral hydrate	T42.6X1	T42.6X2	T42.6X3	T42.6X4	T42.6X5	T42.6X6
Butyltoluene	T52.2X1	T52.2X2	T52.2X3	T52.2X4	—	—
Butyn	T41.3X1	T41.3X2	T41.3X3	T41.3X4	T41.3X5	T41.3X6
Butyrophenone (-based tranquilizers)	T43.4X1	T43.4X2	T43.4X3	T43.4X4	T43.4X5	T43.4X6
C						
Cabergoline	T42.8X1	T42.8X2	T42.8X3	T42.8X4	T42.8X5	T42.8X6
Cacodyl, cacodylic acid	T57.0X1	T57.0X2	T57.0X3	T57.0X4	—	—
Cactinomycin	T45.1X1	T45.1X2	T45.1X3	T45.1X4	T45.1X5	T45.1X6
Cade oil	T49.4X1	T49.4X2	T49.4X3	T49.4X4	T49.4X5	T49.4X6
Cadexomer iodine	T49.0X1	T49.0X2	T49.0X3	T49.0X4	T49.0X5	T49.0X6
Cadmium (chloride) (fumes) (oxide)	T56.3X1	T56.3X2	T56.3X3	T56.3X4	—	—
sulfide (medicinal) NEC	T49.4X1	T49.4X2	T49.4X3	T49.4X4	T49.4X5	T49.4X6
Cadralazine	T46.5X1	T46.5X2	T46.5X3	T46.5X4	T46.5X5	T46.5X6
Caffeine	T43.611	T43.612	T43.613	T43.614	T43.615	T43.616
Calabar bean	T62.2X1	T62.2X2	T62.2X3	T62.2X4	—	—
Caladium seguinum	T62.2X1	T62.2X2	T62.2X3	T62.2X4	—	—
Calamine (lotion)	T49.3X1	T49.3X2	T49.3X3	T49.3X4	T49.3X5	T49.3X6
Calcifediol	T45.2X1	T45.2X2	T45.2X3	T45.2X4	T45.2X5	T45.2X6
Calciferol	T45.2X1	T45.2X2	T45.2X3	T45.2X4	T45.2X5	T45.2X6
Calcitonin	T50.991	T50.992	T50.993	T50.994	T50.995	T50.996
Calcitriol	T45.2X1	T45.2X2	T45.2X3	T45.2X4	T45.2X5	T45.2X6
Calcium	T50.3X1	T50.3X2	T50.3X3	T50.3X4	T50.3X5	T50.3X6
actylsalicylate	T39.011	T39.012	T39.013	T39.014	T39.015	T39.016
benzamidosalicylate	T37.1X1	T37.1X2	T37.1X3	T37.1X4	T37.1X5	T37.1X6
bromide	T42.6X1	T42.6X2	T42.6X3	T42.6X4	T42.6X5	T42.6X6
bromolactobionate	T42.6X1	T42.6X2	T42.6X3	T42.6X4	T42.6X5	T42.6X6
carbaspirin	T39.011	T39.012	T39.013	T39.014	T39.015	T39.016
carbimide	T50.6X1	T50.6X2	T50.6X3	T50.6X4	T50.6X5	T50.6X6
carbonate	T47.1X1	T47.1X2	T47.1X3	T47.1X4	T47.1X5	T47.1X6
chloride	T50.991	T50.992	T50.993	T50.994	T50.995	T50.996
anhydrous	T50.991	T50.992	T50.993	T50.994	T50.995	T50.996
cyanide	T57.8X1	T57.8X2	T57.8X3	T57.8X4	—	—
dioctyl sulfosuccinate	T47.4X1	T47.4X2	T47.4X3	T47.4X4	T47.4X5	T47.4X6
disodium edathamil	T45.8X1	T45.8X2	T45.8X3	T45.8X4	T45.8X5	T45.8X6

Substance	External Cause (T-Code)					
	Poisoning, Accidental (Unintentional)	Poisoning, Intentional Self-Harm	Poisoning, Assault	Poisoning, Undetermined	Adverse Effect	Underdosing
Calcium (Continued)						
disodium edetate	T45.8X1	T45.8X2	T45.8X3	T45.8X4	T45.8X5	T45.8X6
dobesilate	T46.991	T46.992	T46.993	T46.994	T46.995	T46.996
EDTA	T45.8X1	T45.8X2	T45.8X3	T45.8X4	T45.8X5	T45.8X6
ferrous citrate	T45.4X1	T45.4X2	T45.4X3	T45.4X4	T45.4X5	T45.4X6
folinate	T45.8X1	T45.8X2	T45.8X3	T45.8X4	T45.8X5	T45.8X6
glubionate	T50.3X1	T50.3X2	T50.3X3	T50.3X4	T50.3X5	T50.3X6
gluconate	T50.3X1	T50.3X2	T50.3X3	T50.3X4	T50.3X5	T50.3X6
gluconogalactogluconate	T50.3X1	T50.3X2	T50.3X3	T50.3X4	T50.3X5	T50.3X6
hydrate, hydroxide	T54.3X1	T54.3X2	T54.3X3	T54.3X4	—	—
hypochlorite	T54.3X1	T54.3X2	T54.3X3	T54.3X4	—	—
iodide	T48.4X1	T48.4X2	T48.4X3	T48.4X4	T48.4X5	T48.4X6
ipodate	T50.8X1	T50.8X2	T50.8X3	T50.8X4	T50.8X5	T50.8X6
lactate	T50.3X1	T50.3X2	T50.3X3	T50.3X4	T50.3X5	T50.3X6
leucovorin	T45.8X1	T45.8X2	T45.8X3	T45.8X4	T45.8X5	T45.8X6
mandelate	T37.91	T37.92	T37.93	T37.94	T37.95	T37.96
oxide	T54.3X1	T54.3X2	T54.3X3	T54.3X4	—	—
pantothenate	T45.2X1	T45.2X2	T45.2X3	T45.2X4	T45.2X5	T45.2X6
phosphate	T50.3X1	T50.3X2	T50.3X3	T50.3X4	T50.3X5	T50.3X6
salicylate	T39.091	T39.092	T39.093	T39.094	T39.095	T39.096
salts	T50.3X1	T50.3X2	T50.3X3	T50.3X4	T50.3X5	T50.3X6
Calculus-dissolving drug	T50.991	T50.992	T50.993	T50.994	T50.995	T50.996
Calomel	T49.0X1	T49.0X2	T49.0X3	T49.0X4	T49.0X5	T49.0X6
Caloric agent	T50.3X1	T50.3X2	T50.3X3	T50.3X4	T50.3X5	T50.3X6
Calusterone	T38.7X1	T38.7X2	T38.7X3	T38.7X4	T38.7X5	T38.7X6
Camazepam	T42.4X1	T42.4X2	T42.4X3	T42.4X4	T42.4X5	T42.4X6
Camomile	T49.0X1	T49.0X2	T49.0X3	T49.0X4	T49.0X5	T49.0X6
Camoquin	T37.2X1	T37.2X2	T37.2X3	T37.2X4	T37.2X5	T37.2X6
Camphor						
insecticide	T60.2X1	T60.2X2	T60.2X3	T60.2X4	—	—
medicinal	T49.8X1	T49.8X2	T49.8X3	T49.8X4	T49.8X5	T49.8X6
Camylofin	T44.3X1	T44.3X2	T44.3X3	T44.3X4	T44.3X5	T44.3X6
Cancer chemotherapy drug regimen	T45.1X1	T45.1X2	T45.1X3	T45.1X4	T45.1X5	T45.1X6
Candeptin	T49.0X1	T49.0X2	T49.0X3	T49.0X4	T49.0X5	T49.0X6
Candicidin	T49.0X1	T49.0X2	T49.0X3	T49.0X4	T49.0X5	T49.0X6
Cannabinol	T40.7X1	T40.7X2	T40.7X3	T40.7X4	T40.7X5	T40.7X6
Cannabis (derivatives)	T40.7X1	T40.7X2	T40.7X3	T40.7X4	T40.7X5	T40.7X6
Canned heat	T51.1X1	T51.1X2	T51.1X3	T51.1X4	—	—
Canrenoic acid	T50.0X1	T50.0X2	T50.0X3	T50.0X4	T50.0X5	T50.0X6
Canrenone	T50.0X1	T50.0X2	T50.0X3	T50.0X4	T50.0X5	T50.0X6
Cantharides, cantharidin, cantharis	T49.8X1	T49.8X2	T49.8X3	T49.8X4	T49.8X5	T49.8X6

◀ New ◀ Revised ~~deleted~~ Deleted

Substance	Poisoning, Accidental (Unintentional)	Poisoning, Intentional Self-Harm	Poisoning, Assault	Poisoning, Undetermined	Adverse Effect	Underdosing
Canthaxanthin	T50.991	T50.992	T50.993	T50.994	T50.995	T50.996
Capillary-active drug NEC	T46.901	T46.902	T46.903	T46.904	T46.905	T46.906
Capreomycin	T36.8X1	T36.8X2	T36.8X3	T36.8X4	T36.8X5	T36.8X6
Capsicum	T49.4X1	T49.4X2	T49.4X3	T49.4X4	T49.4X5	T49.4X6
Captafol	T60.3X1	T60.3X2	T60.3X3	T60.3X4	—	—
Captan	T60.3X1	T60.3X2	T60.3X3	T60.3X4	—	—
Captodiame, captodiamine	T43.591	T43.592	T43.593	T43.594	T43.595	T43.596
Captopril	T46.4X1	T46.4X2	T46.4X3	T46.4X4	T46.4X5	T46.4X6
Caramiphen	T44.3X1	T44.3X2	T44.3X3	T44.3X4	T44.3X5	T44.3X6
Carazolol	T44.7X1	T44.7X2	T44.7X3	T44.7X4	T44.7X5	T44.7X6
Carbachol	T44.1X1	T44.1X2	T44.1X3	T44.1X4	T44.1X5	T44.1X6
Carbacrylamine (resin)	T50.3X1	T50.3X2	T50.3X3	T50.3X4	T50.3X5	T50.3X6
Carbamate (insecticide)	T60.0X1	T60.0X2	T60.0X3	T60.0X4	—	—
Carbamate (sedative)	T42.6X1	T42.6X2	T42.6X3	T42.6X4	T42.6X5	T42.6X6
herbicide	T60.0X1	T60.0X2	T60.0X3	T60.0X4	—	—
insecticide	T60.0X1	T60.0X2	T60.0X3	T60.0X4	—	—
Carbamazepine	T42.1X1	T42.1X2	T42.1X3	T42.1X4	T42.1X5	T42.1X6
Carbamide	T47.3X1	T47.3X2	T47.3X3	T47.3X4	T47.3X5	T47.3X6
peroxide	T49.0X1	T49.0X2	T49.0X3	T49.0X4	T49.0X5	T49.0X6
topical	T49.8X1	T49.8X2	T49.8X3	T49.8X4	T49.8X5	T49.8X6
Carbamylcholine chloride	T44.1X1	T44.1X2	T44.1X3	T44.1X4	T44.1X5	T44.1X6
Carbaril	T60.0X1	T60.0X2	T60.0X3	T60.0X4	—	—
Carbarsone	T37.3X1	T37.3X2	T37.3X3	T37.3X4	T37.3X5	T37.3X6
Carbaryl	T60.0X1	T60.0X2	T60.0X3	T60.0X4	—	—
Carbaspirin	T39.011	T39.012	T39.013	T39.014	T39.015	T39.016
Carbazochrome (salicylate) (sodium sulfonate)	T49.4X1	T49.4X2	T49.4X3	T49.4X4	T49.4X5	T49.4X6
Carbenicillin	T36.0X1	T36.0X2	T36.0X3	T36.0X4	T36.0X5	T36.0X6
Carbenoxolone	T47.1X1	T47.1X2	T47.1X3	T47.1X4	T47.1X5	T47.1X6
Carbetapentane	T48.3X1	T48.3X2	T48.3X3	T48.3X4	T48.3X5	T48.3X6
Carbethyl salicylate	T39.091	T39.092	T39.093	T39.094	T39.095	T39.096
Carbidopa (with levodopa)	T42.8X1	T42.8X2	T42.8X3	T42.8X4	T42.8X5	T42.8X6
Carbimazole	T38.2X1	T38.2X2	T38.2X3	T38.2X4	T38.2X5	T38.2X6
Carbinol	T51.1X1	T51.1X2	T51.1X3	T51.1X4	—	—
Carbinoxamine	T45.0X1	T45.0X2	T45.0X3	T45.0X4	T45.0X5	T45.0X6
Carbiphene	T39.8X1	T39.8X2	T39.8X3	T39.8X4	T39.8X5	T39.8X6
Carbitol	T52.3X1	T52.3X2	T52.3X3	T52.3X4	—	—
Carbocaine	T41.3X1	T41.3X2	T41.3X3	T41.3X4	T41.3X5	T41.3X6
infiltration (subcutaneous)	T41.3X1	T41.3X2	T41.3X3	T41.3X4	T41.3X5	T41.3X6
nerve block (peripheral) (plexus)	T41.3X1	T41.3X2	T41.3X3	T41.3X4	T41.3X5	T41.3X6
topical (surface)	T41.3X1	T41.3X2	T41.3X3	T41.3X4	T41.3X5	T41.3X6
Carbo medicinalis	T47.6X1	T47.6X2	T47.6X3	T47.6X4	T47.6X5	T47.6X6

Substance	Poisoning, Accidental (Unintentional)	Poisoning, Intentional Self-Harm	Poisoning, Assault	Poisoning, Undetermined	Adverse Effect	Underdosing
Carbomycin	T36.8X1	T36.8X2	T36.8X3	T36.8X4	T36.8X5	T36.8X6
Carbocisteine	T48.4X1	T48.4X2	T48.4X3	T48.4X4	T48.4X5	T48.4X6
Carbocromen	T46.3X1	T46.3X2	T46.3X3	T46.3X4	T46.3X5	T46.3X6
Carbol fuchsin	T49.0X1	T49.0X2	T49.0X3	T49.0X4	T49.0X5	T49.0X6
Carbolic acid — see also Phenol	T54.0X1	T54.0X2	T54.0X3	T54.0X4	—	—
Carbolonium (bromide)	T48.1X1	T48.1X2	T48.1X3	T48.1X4	T48.1X5	T48.1X6
Carbon						
bisulfide (liquid)	T65.4X1	T65.4X2	T65.4X3	T65.4X4	—	—
vapor	T65.4X1	T65.4X2	T65.4X3	T65.4X4	—	—
dioxide (gas)	T59.7X1	T59.7X2	T59.7X3	T59.7X4	—	—
medicinal	T41.5X1	T41.5X2	T41.5X3	T41.5X4	T41.5X5	T41.5X6
nonmedicinal	T59.7X1	T59.7X2	T59.7X3	T59.7X4	—	—
snow	T49.4X1	T49.4X2	T49.4X3	T49.4X4	T49.4X5	T49.4X6
disulfide (liquid)	T65.4X1	T65.4X2	T65.4X3	T65.4X4	—	—
vapor	T65.4X1	T65.4X2	T65.4X3	T65.4X4	—	—
monoxide (from incomplete combustion)	T58.91	T58.92	T58.93	T58.94	—	—
blast furnace gas	T58.8X1	T58.8X2	T58.8X3	T58.8X4	—	—
butane (distributed in mobile container)	T58.11	T58.12	T58.13	T58.14		
distributed through pipes	T58.11	T58.12	T58.13	T58.14		
charcoal fumes	T58.2X1	T58.2X2	T58.2X3	T58.2X4	—	—
coal	T58.2X1	T58.2X2	T58.2X3	T58.2X4		
coke (in domestic stoves, fireplaces)	T58.2X1	T58.2X2	T58.2X3	T58.2X4		
gas (piped)	T58.11	T58.12	T58.13	T58.14		
solid (in domestic stoves, fireplaces)	T58.2X1	T58.2X2	T58.2X3	T58.2X4	—	—
exhaust gas (motor) not in transit	T58.01	T58.02	T58.03	T58.04	—	—
combustion engine, any not in watercraft	T58.01	T58.02	T58.03	T58.04	—	—
farm tractor, not in transit	T58.01	T58.02	T58.03	T58.04	—	—
gas engine	T58.01	T58.02	T58.03	T58.04	—	—
motor pump	T58.01	T58.02	T58.03	T58.04	—	—
motor vehicle, not in transit	T58.01	T58.02	T58.03	T58.04	—	—
fuel (in domestic use)	T58.2X1	T58.2X2	T58.2X3	T58.2X4	—	—
gas (piped)	T58.11	T58.12	T58.13	T58.14	—	—
in mobile container	T58.11	T58.12	T58.13	T58.14		
utility	T58.11	T58.12	T58.13	T58.14	—	—
in mobile container	T58.11	T58.12	T58.13	T58.14	—	—
piped (natural)	T58.11	T58.12	T58.13	T58.14	—	—

◀ New   ◀ Revised   ~~deleted~~ Deleted

Substance	External Cause (T-Code) Poisoning, Accidental (Unintentional)	Poisoning, Intentional Self-Harm	Poisoning, Assault	Poisoning, Undetermined	Adverse Effect	Underdosing
Carbon *(Continued)*						
monoxide *(Continued)*						
illuminating gas	T58.11	T58.12	T58.13	T58.14	—	—
industrial fuels or gases, any	T58.8X1	T58.8X2	T58.8X3	T58.8X4		
kerosene (in domestic stoves, fireplaces)	T58.2X1	T58.2X2	T58.2X3	T58.2X4	—	—
kiln gas or vapor	T58.8X1	T58.8X2	T58.8X3	T58.8X4	—	—
motor exhaust gas, not in transit	T58.01	T58.02	T58.03	T58.04		
piped gas (manufactured) (natural)	T58.11	T58.12	T58.13	T58.14		
producer gas	T58.8X1	T58.8X2	T58.8X3	T58.8X4	—	—
propane (distributed in mobile container)	T58.11	T58.12	T58.13	T58.14	—	—
distributed through pipes	T58.11	T58.12	T58.13	T58.14	—	—
specified source NEC	T58.8X1	T58.8X2	T58.8X3	T58.8X4		
stove gas	T58.11	T58.12	T58.13	T58.14	—	—
piped	T58.11	T58.12	T58.13	T58.14		
utility gas	T58.11	T58.12	T58.13	T58.14	—	—
piped	T58.11	T58.12	T58.13	T58.14		
water gas	T58.11	T58.12	T58.13	T58.14	—	—
wood (in domestic stoves, fireplaces)	T58.2X1	T58.2X2	T58.2X3	T58.2X4		
tetrachloride (vapor) NEC	T53.0X1	T53.0X2	T53.0X3	T53.0X4	—	—
liquid (cleansing agent) NEC	T53.0X1	T53.0X2	T53.0X3	T53.0X4	—	—
solvent	T53.0X1	T53.0X2	T53.0X3	T53.0X4	—	—
Carbonic acid gas	T59.7X1	T59.7X2	T59.7X3	T59.7X4	—	—
anhydrase inhibitor NEC	T50.2X1	T50.2X2	T50.2X3	T50.2X4	T50.2X5	T50.2X6
Carbophenothion	T60.0X1	T60.0X2	T60.0X3	T60.0X4		
Carboplatin	T45.1X1	T45.1X2	T45.1X3	T45.1X4	T45.1X5	T45.1X6
Carboprost	T48.0X1	T48.0X2	T48.0X3	T48.0X4	T48.0X5	T48.0X6
Carboquone	T45.1X1	T45.1X2	T45.1X3	T45.1X4	T45.1X5	T45.1X6
Carbowax	T49.3X1	T49.3X2	T49.3X3	T49.3X4	T49.3X5	T49.3X6
Carboxymethyl-cellulose	T47.4X1	T47.4X2	T47.4X3	T47.4X4	T47.4X5	T47.4X6
S-Carboxymethyl-cysteine	T48.4X1	T48.4X2	T48.4X3	T48.4X4	T48.4X5	T48.4X6
Carbrital	T42.3X1	T42.3X2	T42.3X3	T42.3X4	T42.3X5	T42.3X6
Carbromal	T42.6X1	T42.6X2	T42.6X3	T42.6X4	T42.6X5	T42.6X6
Carbutamide	T38.3X1	T38.3X2	T38.3X3	T38.3X4	T38.3X5	T38.3X6
Carbuterol	T48.6X1	T48.6X2	T48.6X3	T48.6X4	T48.6X5	T48.6X6
Cardiac						
depressants	T46.2X1	T46.2X2	T46.2X3	T46.2X4	T46.2X5	T46.2X6
rhythm regulator	T46.2X1	T46.2X2	T46.2X3	T46.2X4	T46.2X5	T46.2X6
specified NEC	T46.2X1	T46.2X2	T46.2X3	T46.2X4	T46.2X5	T46.2X6

Substance	External Cause (T-Code) Poisoning, Accidental (Unintentional)	Poisoning, Intentional Self-Harm	Poisoning, Assault	Poisoning, Undetermined	Adverse Effect	Underdosing
Cardiografin	T50.8X1	T50.8X2	T50.8X3	T50.8X4	T50.8X5	T50.8X6
Cardio-green	T50.8X1	T50.8X2	T50.8X3	T50.8X4	T50.8X5	T50.8X6
Cardiotonic (glycoside) NEC	T46.0X1	T46.0X2	T46.0X3	T46.0X4	T46.0X5	T46.0X6
Cardiovascular drug NEC	T46.901	T46.902	T46.903	T46.904	T46.905	T46.906
Cardrase	T50.2X1	T50.2X2	T50.2X3	T50.2X4	T50.2X5	T50.2X6
Carfusin	T49.0X1	T49.0X2	T49.0X3	T49.0X4	T49.0X5	T49.0X6
Carfecillin	T36.0X1	T36.0X2	T36.0X3	T36.0X4	T36.0X5	T36.0X6
Carfenazine	T43.3X1	T43.3X2	T43.3X3	T43.3X4	T43.3X5	T43.3X6
Carindacillin	T36.0X1	T36.0X2	T36.0X3	T36.0X4	T36.0X5	T36.0X6
Carisoprodol	T42.8X1	T42.8X2	T42.8X3	T42.8X4	T42.8X5	T42.8X6
Carmellose	T47.4X1	T47.4X2	T47.4X3	T47.4X4	T47.4X5	T47.4X6
Carminative	T47.5X1	T47.5X2	T47.5X3	T47.5X4	T47.5X5	T47.5X6
Carmofur	T45.1X1	T45.1X2	T45.1X3	T45.1X4	T45.1X5	T45.1X6
Carmustine	T45.1X1	T45.1X2	T45.1X3	T45.1X4	T45.1X5	T45.1X6
Carotene	T45.2X1	T45.2X2	T45.2X3	T45.2X4	T45.2X5	T45.2X6
Carphenazine	T43.3X1	T43.3X2	T43.3X3	T43.3X4	T43.3X5	T43.3X6
Carpipramine	T42.4X1	T42.4X2	T42.4X3	T42.4X4	T42.4X5	T42.4X6
Carprofen	T39.311	T39.312	T39.313	T39.314	T39.315	T39.316
Carpronium chloride	T44.3X1	T44.3X2	T44.3X3	T44.3X4	T44.3X5	T44.3X6
Carrageenan	T47.8X1	T47.8X2	T47.8X3	T47.8X4	T47.8X5	T47.8X6
Carteolol	T44.7X1	T44.7X2	T44.7X3	T44.7X4	T44.7X5	T44.7X6
Carter's Little Pills	T47.2X1	T47.2X2	T47.2X3	T47.2X4	T47.2X5	T47.2X6
Cascara (sagrada)	T47.2X1	T47.2X2	T47.2X3	T47.2X4	T47.2X5	T47.2X6
Cassava	T62.2X1	T62.2X2	T62.2X3	T62.2X4	—	—
Castellani's paint	T49.0X1	T49.0X2	T49.0X3	T49.0X4	T49.0X5	T49.0X6
Castor						
bean	T62.2X1	T62.2X2	T62.2X3	T62.2X4	—	—
oil	T47.2X1	T47.2X2	T47.2X3	T47.2X4	T47.2X5	T47.2X6
Catalase	T45.3X1	T45.3X2	T45.3X3	T45.3X4	T45.3X5	T45.3X6
Caterpillar (sting)	T63.431	T63.432	T63.433	T63.434	—	—
Catha (edulis) (tea)	T43.691	T43.692	T43.693	T43.694	—	—
Cathartic NEC	T47.4X1	T47.4X2	T47.4X3	T47.4X4	T47.4X5	T47.4X6
anthracene derivative	T47.2X1	T47.2X2	T47.2X3	T47.2X4	T47.2X5	T47.2X6
bulk	T47.4X1	T47.4X2	T47.4X3	T47.4X4	T47.4X5	T47.4X6
contact	T47.2X1	T47.2X2	T47.2X3	T47.2X4	T47.2X5	T47.2X6
emollient NEC	T47.4X1	T47.4X2	T47.4X3	T47.4X4	T47.4X5	T47.4X6
irritant NEC	T47.2X1	T47.2X2	T47.2X3	T47.2X4	T47.2X5	T47.2X6
mucilage	T47.4X1	T47.4X2	T47.4X3	T47.4X4	T47.4X5	T47.4X6
saline	T47.3X1	T47.3X2	T47.3X3	T47.3X4	T47.3X5	T47.3X6
vegetable	T47.2X1	T47.2X2	T47.2X3	T47.2X4	T47.2X5	T47.2X6
Cathine	T50.5X1	T50.5X2	T50.5X3	T50.5X4	T50.5X5	T50.5X6
Cathomycin	T36.8X1	T36.8X2	T36.8X3	T36.8X4	T36.8X5	T36.8X6

◀ New ◀ Revised ~~deleted~~ Deleted

	External Cause (T-Code)					
Substance	Poisoning, Accidental (Unintentional)	Poisoning, Intentional Self-Harm	Poisoning, Assault	Poisoning, Undetermined	Adverse Effect	Underdosing
Cation exchange resin	T50.3X1	T50.3X2	T50.3X3	T50.3X4	T50.3X5	T50.3X6
Caustic(s) NEC	T54.91	T54.92	T54.93	T54.94	—	—
alkali	T54.3X1	T54.3X2	T54.3X3	T54.3X4	—	—
hydroxide	T54.3X1	T54.3X2	T54.3X3	T54.3X4	—	—
potash	T54.3X1	T54.3X2	T54.3X3	T54.3X4	—	—
soda	T54.3X1	T54.3X2	T54.3X3	T54.3X4	—	—
specified NEC	T54.91	T54.92	T54.93	T54.94	—	—
Ceepryn	T49.0X1	T49.0X2	T49.0X3	T49.0X4	T49.0X5	T49.0X6
ENT agent	T49.6X1	T49.6X2	T49.6X3	T49.6X4	T49.6X5	T49.6X6
lozenges	T49.6X1	T49.6X2	T49.6X3	T49.6X4	T49.6X5	T49.6X6
Cefacetrile	T36.1X1	T36.1X2	T36.1X3	T36.1X4	T36.1X5	T36.1X6
Cefaclor	T36.1X1	T36.1X2	T36.1X3	T36.1X4	T36.1X5	T36.1X6
Cefadroxil	T36.1X1	T36.1X2	T36.1X3	T36.1X4	T36.1X5	T36.1X6
Cefalexin	T36.1X1	T36.1X2	T36.1X3	T36.1X4	T36.1X5	T36.1X6
Cefaloglycin	T36.1X1	T36.1X2	T36.1X3	T36.1X4	T36.1X5	T36.1X6
Cefaloridine	T36.1X1	T36.1X2	T36.1X3	T36.1X4	T36.1X5	T36.1X6
Cefalosporins	T36.1X1	T36.1X2	T36.1X3	T36.1X4	T36.1X5	T36.1X6
Cefalotin	T36.1X1	T36.1X2	T36.1X3	T36.1X4	T36.1X5	T36.1X6
Cefamandole	T36.1X1	T36.1X2	T36.1X3	T36.1X4	T36.1X5	T36.1X6
Cefamycin antibiotic	T36.1X1	T36.1X2	T36.1X3	T36.1X4	T36.1X5	T36.1X6
Cefapirin	T36.1X1	T36.1X2	T36.1X3	T36.1X4	T36.1X5	T36.1X6
Cefatrizine	T36.1X1	T36.1X2	T36.1X3	T36.1X4	T36.1X5	T36.1X6
Cefazedone	T36.1X1	T36.1X2	T36.1X3	T36.1X4	T36.1X5	T36.1X6
Cefazolin	T36.1X1	T36.1X2	T36.1X3	T36.1X4	T36.1X5	T36.1X6
Cefbuperazone	T36.1X1	T36.1X2	T36.1X3	T36.1X4	T36.1X5	T36.1X6
Cefetamet	T36.1X1	T36.1X2	T36.1X3	T36.1X4	T36.1X5	T36.1X6
Cefixime	T36.1X1	T36.1X2	T36.1X3	T36.1X4	T36.1X5	T36.1X6
Cefmenoxime	T36.1X1	T36.1X2	T36.1X3	T36.1X4	T36.1X5	T36.1X6
Cefmetazole	T36.1X1	T36.1X2	T36.1X3	T36.1X4	T36.1X5	T36.1X6
Cefminox	T36.1X1	T36.1X2	T36.1X3	T36.1X4	T36.1X5	T36.1X6
Cefonicid	T36.1X1	T36.1X2	T36.1X3	T36.1X4	T36.1X5	T36.1X6
Cefoperazone	T36.1X1	T36.1X2	T36.1X3	T36.1X4	T36.1X5	T36.1X6
Ceforanide	T36.1X1	T36.1X2	T36.1X3	T36.1X4	T36.1X5	T36.1X6
Cefotaxime	T36.1X1	T36.1X2	T36.1X3	T36.1X4	T36.1X5	T36.1X6
Cefotetan	T36.1X1	T36.1X2	T36.1X3	T36.1X4	T36.1X5	T36.1X6
Cefotiam	T36.1X1	T36.1X2	T36.1X3	T36.1X4	T36.1X5	T36.1X6
Cefoxitin	T36.1X1	T36.1X2	T36.1X3	T36.1X4	T36.1X5	T36.1X6
Cefpimizole	T36.1X1	T36.1X2	T36.1X3	T36.1X4	T36.1X5	T36.1X6
Cefpiramide	T36.1X1	T36.1X2	T36.1X3	T36.1X4	T36.1X5	T36.1X6
Cefradine	T36.1X1	T36.1X2	T36.1X3	T36.1X4	T36.1X5	T36.1X6
Cefroxadine	T36.1X1	T36.1X2	T36.1X3	T36.1X4	T36.1X5	T36.1X6
Cefsulodin	T36.1X1	T36.1X2	T36.1X3	T36.1X4	T36.1X5	T36.1X6

	External Cause (T-Code)					
Substance	Poisoning, Accidental (Unintentional)	Poisoning, Intentional Self-Harm	Poisoning, Assault	Poisoning, Undetermined	Adverse Effect	Underdosing
Ceftazidime	T36.1X1	T36.1X2	T36.1X3	T36.1X4	T36.1X5	T36.1X6
Cefteram	T36.1X1	T36.1X2	T36.1X3	T36.1X4	T36.1X5	T36.1X6
Ceftezole	T36.1X1	T36.1X2	T36.1X3	T36.1X4	T36.1X5	T36.1X6
Ceftizoxime	T36.1X1	T36.1X2	T36.1X3	T36.1X4	T36.1X5	T36.1X6
Ceftriaxone	T36.1X1	T36.1X2	T36.1X3	T36.1X4	T36.1X5	T36.1X6
Cefuroxime	T36.1X1	T36.1X2	T36.1X3	T36.1X4	T36.1X5	T36.1X6
Cefuzonam	T36.1X1	T36.1X2	T36.1X3	T36.1X4	T36.1X5	T36.1X6
Celestone	T38.0X1	T38.0X2	T38.0X3	T38.0X4	T38.0X5	T38.0X6
topical	T49.0X1	T49.0X2	T49.0X3	T49.0X4	T49.0X5	T49.0X6
Celiprolol	T44.7X1	T44.7X2	T44.7X3	T44.7X4	T44.7X5	T44.7X6
Cellosolve	T52.91	T52.92	T52.93	T52.94	—	—
Cell stimulants and proliferants	T49.8X1	T49.8X2	T49.8X3	T49.8X4	T49.8X5	T49.8X6
Cellulose						
cathartic	T47.4X1	T47.4X2	T47.4X3	T47.4X4	T47.4X5	T47.4X6
hydroxyethyl	T47.4X1	T47.4X2	T47.4X3	T47.4X4	T47.4X5	T47.4X6
nitrates (topical)	T49.3X1	T49.3X2	T49.3X3	T49.3X4	T49.3X5	T49.3X6
oxidized	T49.4X1	T49.4X2	T49.4X3	T49.4X4	T49.4X5	T49.4X6
Centipede (bite)	T63.411	T63.412	T63.413	T63.414	—	—
Central nervous system						
depressants	T42.71	T42.72	T42.73	T42.74	T42.75	T42.76
anesthetic (general) NEC	T41.201	T41.202	T41.203	T41.204	T41.205	T41.206
gases NEC	T41.0X1	T41.0X2	T41.0X3	T41.0X4	T41.0X5	T41.0X6
intravenous	T41.1X1	T41.1X2	T41.1X3	T41.1X4	T41.1X5	T41.1X6
barbiturates	T42.3X1	T42.3X2	T42.3X3	T42.3X4	T42.3X5	T42.3X6
benzodiazepines	T42.4X1	T42.4X2	T42.4X3	T42.4X4	T42.4X5	T42.4X6
bromides	T42.6X1	T42.6X2	T42.6X3	T42.6X4	T42.6X5	T42.6X6
cannabis sativa	T40.7X1	T40.7X2	T40.7X3	T40.7X4	T40.7X5	T40.7X6
chloral hydrate	T42.6X1	T42.6X2	T42.6X3	T42.6X4	T42.6X5	T42.6X6
ethanol	T51.0X1	T51.0X2	T51.0X3	T51.0X4	—	—
hallucinogenics	T40.901	T40.902	T40.903	T40.904	T40.905	T40.906
hypnotics	T42.71	T42.72	T42.73	T42.74	T42.75	T42.76
specified NEC	T42.6X1	T42.6X2	T42.6X3	T42.6X4	T42.6X5	T42.6X6
muscle relaxants	T42.8X1	T42.8X2	T42.8X3	T42.8X4	T42.8X5	T42.8X6
paraldehyde	T42.6X1	T42.6X2	T42.6X3	T42.6X4	T42.6X5	T42.6X6
sedatives; sedative-hypnotics	T42.71	T42.72	T42.73	T42.74	T42.75	T42.76
mixed NEC	T42.6X1	T42.6X2	T42.6X3	T42.6X4	T42.6X5	T42.6X6
specified NEC	T42.6X1	T42.6X2	T42.6X3	T42.6X4	T42.6X5	T42.6X6
muscle-tone depressants	T42.8X1	T42.8X2	T42.8X3	T42.8X4	T42.8X5	T42.8X6
stimulants	T43.601	T43.602	T43.603	T43.604	T43.605	T43.606
amphetamines	T43.621	T43.622	T43.623	T43.624	T43.625	T43.626
analeptics	T50.7X1	T50.7X2	T50.7X3	T50.7X4	T50.7X5	T50.7X6

TABLE OF DRUGS AND CHEMICALS

Substance	Poisoning, Accidental (Unintentional)	Poisoning, Intentional Self-Harm	Poisoning, Assault	Poisoning, Undetermined	Adverse Effect	Underdosing
Central nervous system *(Continued)*						
stimulants *(Continued)*						
antidepressants	T43.201	T43.202	T43.203	T43.204	T43.205	T43.206
opiate antagonists	T50.7X1	T50.7X2	T50.7X3	T50.7X4	T50.7X5	T50.7X6
specified NEC	T43.691	T43.692	T43.693	T43.694	T43.695	T43.696
Cephalexin	T36.1X1	T36.1X2	T36.1X3	T36.1X4	T36.1X5	T36.1X6
Cephaloglycin	T36.1X1	T36.1X2	T36.1X3	T36.1X4	T36.1X5	T36.1X6
Cephaloridine	T36.1X1	T36.1X2	T36.1X3	T36.1X4	T36.1X5	T36.1X6
Cephalosporins	T36.1X1	T36.1X2	T36.1X3	T36.1X4	T36.1X5	T36.1X6
N (adicillin)	T36.0X1	T36.0X2	T36.0X3	T36.0X4	T36.0X5	T36.0X6
Cephalothin	T36.1X1	T36.1X2	T36.1X3	T36.1X4	T36.1X5	T36.1X6
Cephalotin	T36.1X1	T36.1X2	T36.1X3	T36.1X4	T36.1X5	T36.1X6
Cephradine	T36.1X1	T36.1X2	T36.1X3	T36.1X4	T36.1X5	T36.1X6
Cerbera (odallam)	T62.2X1	T62.2X2	T62.2X3	T62.2X4	—	—
Cerberin	T46.0X1	T46.0X2	T46.0X3	T46.0X4	T46.0X5	T46.0X6
Cerebral stimulants	T43.601	T43.602	T43.603	T43.604	T43.605	T43.606
psychotherapeutic	T43.601	T43.602	T43.603	T43.604	T43.605	T43.606
specified NEC	T43.691	T43.692	T43.693	T43.694	T43.695	T43.696
Cerium oxalate	T45.0X1	T45.0X2	T45.0X3	T45.0X4	T45.0X5	T45.0X6
Cerous oxalate	T45.0X1	T45.0X2	T45.0X3	T45.0X4	T45.0X5	T45.0X6
Ceruletide	T50.8X1	T50.8X2	T50.8X3	T50.8X4	T50.8X5	T50.8X6
Cetalkonium (chloride)	T49.0X1	T49.0X2	T49.0X3	T49.0X4	T49.0X5	T49.0X6
Cethexonium chloride	T49.0X1	T49.0X2	T49.0X3	T49.0X4	T49.0X5	T49.0X6
Cetiedil	T46.7X1	T46.7X2	T46.7X3	T46.7X4	T46.7X5	T46.7X6
Cetirizine	T45.0X1	T45.0X2	T45.0X3	T45.0X4	T45.0X5	T45.0X6
Cetomacrogol	T50.991	T50.992	T50.993	T50.994	T50.995	T50.996
Cetotiamine	T45.2X1	T45.2X2	T45.2X3	T45.2X4	T45.2X5	T45.2X6
Cetoxime	T45.0X1	T45.0X2	T45.0X3	T45.0X4	T45.0X5	T45.0X6
Cetraxate	T47.1X1	T47.1X2	T47.1X3	T47.1X4	T47.1X5	T47.1X6
Cetrimide	T49.0X1	T49.0X2	T49.0X3	T49.0X4	T49.0X5	T49.0X6
Cetrimonium (bromide)	T49.0X1	T49.0X2	T49.0X3	T49.0X4	T49.0X5	T49.0X6
Cetylpyridinium chloride	T49.0X1	T49.0X2	T49.0X3	T49.0X4	T49.0X5	T49.0X6
ENT agent	T49.6X1	T49.6X2	T49.6X3	T49.6X4	T49.6X5	T49.6X6
lozenges	T49.6X1	T49.6X2	T49.6X3	T49.6X4	T49.6X5	T49.6X6
Cevadillasee Sabadilla						
Cevitamic acid	T45.2X1	T45.2X2	T45.2X3	T45.2X4	T45.2X5	T45.2X6
Chalk, precipitated	T47.1X1	T47.1X2	T47.1X3	T47.1X4	T47.1X5	T47.1X6
Chamomile	T49.0X1	T49.0X2	T49.0X3	T49.0X4	T49.0X5	T49.0X6
Ch'an su	T46.0X1	T46.0X2	T46.0X3	T46.0X4	T46.0X5	T46.0X6
Charcoal	T47.6X1	T47.6X2	T47.6X3	T47.6X4	T47.6X5	T47.6X6
activated — *see also Charcoal, medicinal*	T47.6X1	T47.6X2	T47.6X3	T47.6X4	T47.6X5	T47.6X6

Substance	Poisoning, Accidental (Unintentional)	Poisoning, Intentional Self-Harm	Poisoning, Assault	Poisoning, Undetermined	Adverse Effect	Underdosing
Charcoal *(Continued)*						
fumes (Carbon monoxide)	T58.2X1	T58.2X2	T58.2X3	T58.2X4	—	—
industrial	T58.8X1	T58.8X2	T58.8X3	T58.8X4	—	—
medicinal (activated)	T47.6X1	T47.6X2	T47.6X3	T47.6X4	T47.6X5	T47.6X6
antidiarrheal	T47.6X1	T47.6X2	T47.6X3	T47.6X4	T47.6X5	T47.6X6
poison control	T47.8X1	T47.8X2	T47.8X3	T47.8X4	T47.8X5	T47.8X6
specified use other than for diarrhea	T47.8X1	T47.8X2	T47.8X3	T47.8X4	T47.8X5	T47.8X6
topical	T49.8X1	T49.8X2	T49.8X3	T49.8X4	T49.8X5	T49.8X6
Chaulmosulfone	T37.1X1	T37.1X2	T37.1X3	T37.1X4	T37.1X5	T37.1X6
Chelating agent NEC	T50.6X1	T50.6X2	T50.6X3	T50.6X4	T50.6X5	T50.6X6
Chelidonium majus	T62.2X1	T62.2X2	T62.2X3	T62.2X4	—	—
Chemical substance NEC	T65.91	T65.92	T65.93	T65.94	—	—
Chenodeoxycholic acid	T47.5X1	T47.5X2	T47.5X3	T47.5X4	T47.5X5	T47.5X6
Chenodiol	T47.5X1	T47.5X2	T47.5X3	T47.5X4	T47.5X5	T47.5X6
Chenopodium	T37.4X1	T37.4X2	T37.4X3	T37.4X4	T37.4X5	T37.4X6
Cherry laurel	T62.2X1	T62.2X2	T62.2X3	T62.2X4	—	—
Chinidin(e)	T46.2X1	T46.2X2	T46.2X3	T46.2X4	T46.2X5	T46.2X6
Chiniofon	T37.8X1	T37.8X2	T37.8X3	T37.8X4	T37.8X5	T37.8X6
Chlophedianol	T48.3X1	T48.3X2	T48.3X3	T48.3X4	T48.3X5	T48.3X6
Chloral	T42.6X1	T42.6X2	T42.6X3	T42.6X4	T42.6X5	T42.6X6
derivative	T42.6X1	T42.6X2	T42.6X3	T42.6X4	T42.6X5	T42.6X6
hydrate	T42.6X1	T42.6X2	T42.6X3	T42.6X4	T42.6X5	T42.6X6
Chloralamide	T42.6X1	T42.6X2	T42.6X3	T42.6X4	T42.6X5	T42.6X6
Chloralodol	T42.6X1	T42.6X2	T42.6X3	T42.6X4	T42.6X5	T42.6X6
Chloralose	T60.4X1	T60.4X2	T60.4X3	T60.4X4	—	—
Chlorambucil	T45.1X1	T45.1X2	T45.1X3	T45.1X4	T45.1X5	T45.1X6
Chloramine	T57.8X1	T57.8X2	T57.8X3	T57.8X4	—	—
T	T49.0X1	T49.0X2	T49.0X3	T49.0X4	T49.0X5	T49.0X6
topical	T49.0X1	T49.0X2	T49.0X3	T49.0X4	T49.0X5	T49.0X6
Chloramphenicol	T36.2X1	T36.2X2	T36.2X3	T36.2X4	T36.2X5	T36.2X6
ENT agent	T49.6X1	T49.6X2	T49.6X3	T49.6X4	T49.6X5	T49.6X6
ophthalmic preparation	T49.5X1	T49.5X2	T49.5X3	T49.5X4	T49.5X5	T49.5X6
topical NEC	T49.0X1	T49.0X2	T49.0X3	T49.0X4	T49.0X5	T49.0X6
Chlorate (potassium) (sodium) NEC	T60.3X1	T60.3X2	T60.3X3	T60.3X4	—	—
herbicide	T60.3X1	T60.3X2	T60.3X3	T60.3X4	—	—
Chlorazanil	T50.2X1	T50.2X2	T50.2X3	T50.2X4	T50.2X5	T50.2X6
Chlorbenzene, chlorbenzol	T53.7X1	T53.7X2	T53.7X3	T53.7X4	—	—
Chlorbenzoxamine	T44.3X1	T44.3X2	T44.3X3	T44.3X4	T44.3X5	T44.3X6
Chlorbutol	T42.6X1	T42.6X2	T42.6X3	T42.6X4	T42.6X5	T42.6X6
Chlorcyclizine	T45.0X1	T45.0X2	T45.0X3	T45.0X4	T45.0X5	T45.0X6

◀ New   ◀ Revised   ~~deleted~~ Deleted

Substance	External Cause (T-Code)					
	Poisoning, Accidental (Unintentional)	Poisoning, Intentional Self-Harm	Poisoning, Assault	Poisoning, Undetermined	Adverse Effect	Underdosing
Chlordan(e) (dust)	T60.1X1	T60.1X2	T60.1X3	T60.1X4	—	—
Chlordantoin	T49.0X1	T49.0X2	T49.0X3	T49.0X4	T49.0X5	T49.0X6
Chlordiazepoxide	T42.4X1	T42.4X2	T42.4X3	T42.4X4	T42.4X5	T42.4X6
Chlordiethyl benzamide	T49.3X1	T49.3X2	T49.3X3	T49.3X4	T49.3X5	T49.3X6
Chloresium	T49.8X1	T49.8X2	T49.8X3	T49.8X4	T49.8X5	T49.8X6
Chlorethiazol	T42.6X1	T42.6X2	T42.6X3	T42.6X4	T42.6X5	T42.6X6
Chlorethyl — see Ethyl chloride						
Chloretone	T42.6X1	T42.6X2	T42.6X3	T42.6X4	T42.6X5	T42.6X6
Chlorex	T53.6X1	T53.6X2	T53.6X3	T53.6X4	—	—
insecticide	T60.1X1	T60.1X2	T60.1X3	T60.1X4	—	—
Chlorfenvinphos	T60.0X1	T60.0X2	T60.0X3	T60.0X4	—	—
Chlorhexadol	T42.6X1	T42.6X2	T42.6X3	T42.6X4	T42.6X5	T42.6X6
Chlorhexamide	T45.1X1	T45.1X2	T45.1X3	T45.1X4	T45.1X5	T45.1X6
Chlorhexidine	T49.0X1	T49.0X2	T49.0X3	T49.0X4	T49.0X5	T49.0X6
Chlorhydroxyquinolin	T49.0X1	T49.0X2	T49.0X3	T49.0X4	T49.0X5	T49.0X6
Chloride of lime (bleach)	T54.3X1	T54.3X2	T54.3X3	T54.3X4	—	—
Chlorimipramine	T43.011	T43.012	T43.013	T43.014	T43.015	T43.016
Chlorinated						
camphene	T53.6X1	T53.6X2	T53.6X3	T53.6X4	—	—
diphenyl	T53.7X1	T53.7X2	T53.7X3	T53.7X4	—	—
hydrocarbons NEC	T53.91	T53.92	T53.93	T53.94	—	—
solvents	T53.91	T53.92	T53.93	T53.94	—	—
lime (bleach)	T54.3X1	T54.3X2	T54.3X3	T54.3X4	—	—
and boric acid solution	T49.0X1	T49.0X2	T49.0X3	T49.0X4	T49.0X5	T49.0X6
naphthalene (insecticide)	T60.1X1	T60.1X2	T60.1X3	T60.1X4	—	—
industrial (non-pesticide)	T53.7X1	T53.7X2	T53.7X3	T53.7X4	—	—
pesticide NEC	T60.8X1	T60.8X2	T60.8X3	T60.8X4	—	—
soda — see also Sodium hypochlorite						
solution	T49.0X1	T49.0X2	T49.0X3	T49.0X4	T49.0X5	T49.0X6
Chlorine (fumes) (gas)	T59.4X1	T59.4X2	T59.4X3	T59.4X4	—	—
bleach	T54.3X1	T54.3X2	T54.3X3	T54.3X4	—	—
compound gas NEC	T59.4X1	T59.4X2	T59.4X3	T59.4X4	—	—
disinfectant	T59.4X1	T59.4X2	T59.4X3	T59.4X4	—	—
releasing agents NEC	T59.4X1	T59.4X2	T59.4X3	T59.4X4	—	—
Chlorisondamine chloride	T46.991	T46.992	T46.993	T46.994	T46.995	T46.996
Chlormadinone	T38.5X1	T38.5X2	T38.5X3	T38.5X4	T38.5X5	T38.5X6
Chlormephos	T60.0X1	T60.0X2	T60.0X3	T60.0X4	—	—
Chlormerodrin	T50.2X1	T50.2X2	T50.2X3	T50.2X4	T50.2X5	T50.2X6
Chlormethiazole	T42.6X1	T42.6X2	T42.6X3	T42.6X4	T42.6X5	T42.6X6
Chlormethine	T45.1X1	T45.1X2	T45.1X3	T45.1X4	T45.1X5	T45.1X6
Chlormethylenecycline	T36.4X1	T36.4X2	T36.4X3	T36.4X4	T36.4X5	T36.4X6

Substance	External Cause (T-Code)					
	Poisoning, Accidental (Unintentional)	Poisoning, Intentional Self-Harm	Poisoning, Assault	Poisoning, Undetermined	Adverse Effect	Underdosing
Chlormezanone	T42.6X1	T42.6X2	T42.6X3	T42.6X4	T42.6X5	T42.6X6
Chloroacetic acid	T60.3X1	T60.3X2	T60.3X3	T60.3X4	—	—
Chloroacetone	T59.3X1	T59.3X2	T59.3X3	T59.3X4	—	—
Chloroacetophenone	T59.3X1	T59.3X2	T59.3X3	T59.3X4	—	—
Chloroaniline	T53.7X1	T53.7X2	T53.7X3	T53.7X4	—	—
Chlorobenzene, chlorobenzol	T53.7X1	T53.7X2	T53.7X3	T53.7X4	—	—
Chlorobromomethane (fire extinguisher)	T53.6X1	T53.6X2	T53.6X3	T53.6X4	—	—
Chlorobutanol	T49.0X1	T49.0X2	T49.0X3	T49.0X4	T49.0X5	T49.0X6
Chlorocresol	T49.0X1	T49.0X2	T49.0X3	T49.0X4	T49.0X5	T49.0X6
Chlorodehydro-methyltestosterone	T38.7X1	T38.7X2	T38.7X3	T38.7X4	T38.7X5	T38.7X6
Chlorodinitrobenzene	T53.7X1	T53.7X2	T53.7X3	T53.7X4	—	—
dust or vapor	T53.7X1	T53.7X2	T53.7X3	T53.7X4	—	—
Chlorodiphenyl	T53.7X1	T53.7X2	T53.7X3	T53.7X4	—	—
Chloroethane — see Ethyl chloride						
Chloroethylene	T53.6X1	T53.6X2	T53.6X3	T53.6X4	—	—
Chlorofluorocarbons	T53.5X1	T53.5X2	T53.5X3	T53.5X4	—	—
Chloroform (fumes) (vapor)	T53.1X1	T53.1X2	T53.1X3	T53.1X4	—	—
anesthetic	T41.0X1	T41.0X2	T41.0X3	T41.0X4	T41.0X5	T41.0X6
solvent	T53.1X1	T53.1X2	T53.1X3	T53.1X4	—	—
water, concentrated	T41.0X1	T41.0X2	T41.0X3	T41.0X4	T41.0X5	T41.0X6
Chloroguanide	T37.2X1	T37.2X2	T37.2X3	T37.2X4	T37.2X5	T37.2X6
Chloromycetin	T36.2X1	T36.2X2	T36.2X3	T36.2X4	T36.2X5	T36.2X6
ENT agent	T49.6X1	T49.6X2	T49.6X3	T49.6X4	T49.6X5	T49.6X6
ophthalmic preparation	T49.5X1	T49.5X2	T49.5X3	T49.5X4	T49.5X5	T49.5X6
otic solution	T49.6X1	T49.6X2	T49.6X3	T49.6X4	T49.6X5	T49.6X6
topical NEC	T49.0X1	T49.0X2	T49.0X3	T49.0X4	T49.0X5	T49.0X6
Chloronitrobenzene	T53.7X1	T53.7X2	T53.7X3	T53.7X4	—	—
dust or vapor	T53.7X1	T53.7X2	T53.7X3	T53.7X4	—	—
Chlorophacinone	T60.4X1	T60.4X2	T60.4X3	T60.4X4	—	—
Chlorophenol	T53.7X1	T53.7X2	T53.7X3	T53.7X4	—	—
Chlorophenothane	T60.1X1	T60.1X2	T60.1X3	T60.1X4	—	—
Chlorophyll	T50.991	T50.992	T50.993	T50.994	T50.995	T50.996
Chloropicrin (fumes)	T53.6X1	T53.6X2	T53.6X3	T53.6X4	—	—
fumigant	T60.8X1	T60.8X2	T60.8X3	T60.8X4	—	—
fungicide	T60.3X1	T60.3X2	T60.3X3	T60.3X4	—	—
pesticide	T60.8X1	T60.8X2	T60.8X3	T60.8X4	—	—
Chloroprocaine	T41.3X1	T41.3X2	T41.3X3	T41.3X4	T41.3X5	T41.3X6
infiltration (subcutaneous)	T41.3X1	T41.3X2	T41.3X3	T41.3X4	T41.3X5	T41.3X6
nerve block (peripheral) (plexus)	T41.3X1	T41.3X2	T41.3X3	T41.3X4	T41.3X5	T41.3X6
spinal	T41.3X1	T41.3X2	T41.3X3	T41.3X4	T41.3X5	T41.3X6

Substance	Poisoning, Accidental (Unintentional)	Poisoning, Intentional Self-Harm	Poisoning, Assault	Poisoning, Undetermined	Adverse Effect	Underdosing
Chloroptic	T49.5X1	T49.5X2	T49.5X3	T49.5X4	T49.5X5	T49.5X6
Chloropurine	T45.1X1	T45.1X2	T45.1X3	T45.1X4	T45.1X5	T45.1X6
Chloropyramine	T45.0X1	T45.0X2	T45.0X3	T45.0X4	T45.0X5	T45.0X6
Chloropyrifos	T60.0X1	T60.0X2	T60.0X3	T60.0X4	—	—
Chloropyrilene	T45.0X1	T45.0X2	T45.0X3	T45.0X4	T45.0X5	T45.0X6
Chloroquine	T37.2X1	T37.2X2	T37.2X3	T37.2X4	T37.2X5	T37.2X6
Chlorothalonil	T60.3X1	T60.3X2	T60.3X3	T60.3X4	—	—
Chlorothen	T45.0X1	T45.0X2	T45.0X3	T45.0X4	T45.0X5	T45.0X6
Chlorothiazide	T50.2X1	T50.2X2	T50.2X3	T50.2X4	T50.2X5	T50.2X6
Chlorothymol	T49.4X1	T49.4X2	T49.4X3	T49.4X4	T49.4X5	T49.4X6
Chlorotrianisene	T38.5X1	T38.5X2	T38.5X3	T38.5X4	T38.5X5	T38.5X6
Chlorovinyldichloro-arsine, not in war	T57.0X1	T57.0X2	T57.0X3	T57.0X4	—	—
Chloroxine	T49.4X1	T49.4X2	T49.4X3	T49.4X4	T49.4X5	T49.4X6
Chloroxylenol	T49.0X1	T49.0X2	T49.0X3	T49.0X4	T49.0X5	T49.0X6
Chlorphenamine	T45.0X1	T45.0X2	T45.0X3	T45.0X4	T45.0X5	T45.0X6
Chlorphenesin	T42.8X1	T42.8X2	T42.8X3	T42.8X4	T42.8X5	T42.8X6
topical (antifungal)	T49.0X1	T49.0X2	T49.0X3	T49.0X4	T49.0X5	T49.0X6
Chlorpheniramine	T45.0X1	T45.0X2	T45.0X3	T45.0X4	T45.0X5	T45.0X6
Chlorphenoxamine	T45.0X1	T45.0X2	T45.0X3	T45.0X4	T45.0X5	T45.0X6
Chlorphentermine	T50.5X1	T50.5X2	T50.5X3	T50.5X4	T50.5X5	T50.5X6
Chlorprocaine — see Chloroprocaine						
Chlorproguanil	T37.2X1	T37.2X2	T37.2X3	T37.2X4	T37.2X5	T37.2X6
Chlorpromazine	T43.3X1	T43.3X2	T43.3X3	T43.3X4	T43.3X5	T43.3X6
Chlorpropamide	T38.3X1	T38.3X2	T38.3X3	T38.3X4	T38.3X5	T38.3X6
Chlorprothixene	T43.4X1	T43.4X2	T43.4X3	T43.4X4	T43.4X5	T43.4X6
Chlorquinaldol	T49.0X1	T49.0X2	T49.0X3	T49.0X4	T49.0X5	T49.0X6
Chlorquinol	T49.0X1	T49.0X2	T49.0X3	T49.0X4	T49.0X5	T49.0X6
Chlortalidone	T50.2X1	T50.2X2	T50.2X3	T50.2X4	T50.2X5	T50.2X6
Chlortetracycline	T36.4X1	T36.4X2	T36.4X3	T36.4X4	T36.4X5	T36.4X6
Chlorthalidone	T50.2X1	T50.2X2	T50.2X3	T50.2X4	T50.2X5	T50.2X6
Chlorthiophos	T60.0X1	T60.0X2	T60.0X3	T60.0X4	—	—
Chlorotrianisene	T38.5X1	T38.5X2	T38.5X3	T38.5X4	T38.5X5	T38.5X6
Chlor-Trimeton	T45.0X1	T45.0X2	T45.0X3	T45.0X4	T45.0X5	T45.0X6
Chlorthion	T60.0X1	T60.0X2	T60.0X3	T60.0X4	—	—
Chlorzoxazone	T42.8X1	T42.8X2	T42.8X3	T42.8X4	T42.8X5	T42.8X6
Choke damp	T59.7X1	T59.7X2	T59.7X3	T59.7X4	—	—
Cholagogues	T47.5X1	T47.5X2	T47.5X3	T47.5X4	T47.5X5	T47.5X6
Cholebrine	T50.8X1	T50.8X2	T50.8X3	T50.8X4	T50.8X5	T50.8X6
Cholecalciferol	T45.2X1	T45.2X2	T45.2X3	T45.2X4	T45.2X5	T45.2X6
Cholecystokinin	T50.8X1	T50.8X2	T50.8X3	T50.8X4	T50.8X5	T50.8X6
Cholera vaccine	T50.A91	T50.A92	T50.A93	T50.A94	T50.A95	T50.A96

Substance	Poisoning, Accidental (Unintentional)	Poisoning, Intentional Self-Harm	Poisoning, Assault	Poisoning, Undetermined	Adverse Effect	Underdosing
Choleretic	T47.5X1	T47.5X2	T47.5X3	T47.5X4	T47.5X5	T47.5X6
Cholesterol-lowering agents	T46.6X1	T46.6X2	T46.6X3	T46.6X4	T46.6X5	T46.6X6
Cholestyramine (resin)	T46.6X1	T46.6X2	T46.6X3	T46.6X4	T46.6X5	T46.6X6
Cholic acid	T47.5X1	T47.5X2	T47.5X3	T47.5X4	T47.5X5	T47.5X6
Choline	T48.6X1	T48.6X2	T48.6X3	T48.6X4	T48.6X5	T48.6X6
chloride	T50.991	T50.992	T50.993	T50.994	T50.995	T50.996
dihydrogen citrate	T50.991	T50.992	T50.993	T50.994	T50.995	T50.996
salicylate	T39.091	T39.092	T39.093	T39.094	T39.095	T39.096
theophyllinate	T48.6X1	T48.6X2	T48.6X3	T48.6X4	T48.6X5	T48.6X6
Cholinergic (drug) NEC	T44.1X1	T44.1X2	T44.1X3	T44.1X4	T44.1X5	T44.1X6
muscle tone enhancer	T44.1X1	T44.1X2	T44.1X3	T44.1X4	T44.1X5	T44.1X6
organophosphorus	T44.0X1	T44.0X2	T44.0X3	T44.0X4	T44.0X5	T44.0X6
insecticide	T60.0X1	T60.0X2	T60.0X3	T60.0X4	—	—
nerve gas	T59.891	T59.892	T59.893	T59.894	—	—
trimethyl ammonium propanediol	T44.1X1	T44.1X2	T44.1X3	T44.1X4	T44.1X5	T44.1X6
Cholinesterase reactivator	T50.6X1	T50.6X2	T50.6X3	T50.6X4	T50.6X5	T50.6X6
Cholografin	T50.8X1	T50.8X2	T50.8X3	T50.8X4	T50.8X5	T50.8X6
Chorionic gonadotropin	T38.891	T38.892	T38.893	T38.894	T38.895	T38.896
Chromate	T56.2X1	T56.2X2	T56.2X3	T56.2X4	—	—
dust or mist	T56.2X1	T56.2X2	T56.2X3	T56.2X4	—	—
lead — see also Lead	T56.0X1	T56.0X2	T56.0X3	T56.0X4	—	—
paint	T56.0X1	T56.0X2	T56.0X3	T56.0X4	—	—
Chromic						
acid	T56.2X1	T56.2X2	T56.2X3	T56.2X4	—	—
dust or mist	T56.2X1	T56.2X2	T56.2X3	T56.2X4	—	—
phosphate 32P	T45.1X1	T45.1X2	T45.1X3	T45.1X4	T45.1X5	T45.1X6
Chromium	T56.2X1	T56.2X2	T56.2X3	T56.2X4	—	—
compounds — see Chromate						
sesquioxide	T50.8X1	T50.8X2	T50.8X3	T50.8X4	T50.8X5	T50.8X6
Chromomycin A3	T45.1X1	T45.1X2	T45.1X3	T45.1X4	T45.1X5	T45.1X6
Chromonar	T46.3X1	T46.3X2	T46.3X3	T46.3X4	T46.3X5	T46.3X6
Chromyl chloride	T56.2X1	T56.2X2	T56.2X3	T56.2X4	—	—
Chrysarobin	T49.4X1	T49.4X2	T49.4X3	T49.4X4	T49.4X5	T49.4X6
Chrysazin	T47.2X1	T47.2X2	T47.2X3	T47.2X4	T47.2X5	T47.2X6
Chymar	T45.3X1	T45.3X2	T45.3X3	T45.3X4	T45.3X5	T45.3X6
ophthalmic preparation	T49.5X1	T49.5X2	T49.5X3	T49.5X4	T49.5X5	T49.5X6
Chymopapain	T45.3X1	T45.3X2	T45.3X3	T45.3X4	T45.3X5	T45.3X6
Chymotrypsin	T45.3X1	T45.3X2	T45.3X3	T45.3X4	T45.3X5	T45.3X6
ophthalmic preparation	T49.5X1	T49.5X2	T49.5X3	T49.5X4	T49.5X5	T49.5X6
Cianidanol	T50.991	T50.992	T50.993	T50.994	T50.995	T50.996
Cianopramine	T43.011	T43.012	T43.013	T43.014	T43.015	T43.016
Cibenzoline	T46.2X1	T46.2X2	T46.2X3	T46.2X4	T46.2X5	T46.2X6

◄ New   ◄ Revised   ~~deleted~~ Deleted

Substance	External Cause (T-Code)					
	Poisoning, Accidental (Unintentional)	Poisoning, Intentional Self-Harm	Poisoning, Assault	Poisoning, Undetermined	Adverse Effect	Underdosing
Ciclacillin	T36.0X1	T36.0X2	T36.0X3	T36.0X4	T36.0X5	T36.0X6
Ciclobarbital — *see Hexobarbital*						
Ciclonicate	T46.7X1	T46.7X2	T46.7X3	T46.7X4	T46.7X5	T46.7X6
Ciclopirox (olamine)	T49.0X1	T49.0X2	T49.0X3	T49.0X4	T49.0X5	T49.0X6
Ciclosporin	T45.1X1	T45.1X2	T45.1X3	T45.1X4	T45.1X5	T45.1X6
Cicuta maculata or virosa	T62.2X1	T62.2X2	T62.2X3	T62.2X4	—	—
Cicutoxin	T62.2X1	T62.2X2	T62.2X3	T62.2X4	—	—
Cigarette lighter fluid	T52.0X1	T52.0X2	T52.0X3	T52.0X4	—	—
Cigarettes (tobacco)	T65.221	T65.222	T65.223	T65.224	—	—
Ciguatoxin	T61.01	T61.02	T61.03	T61.04	—	—
Cilazapril	T46.4X1	T46.4X2	T46.4X3	T46.4X4	T46.4X5	T46.4X6
Cimetidine	T47.0X1	T47.0X2	T47.0X3	T47.0X4	T47.0X5	T47.0X6
Cimetropium bromide	T44.3X1	T44.3X2	T44.3X3	T44.3X4	T44.3X5	T44.3X6
Cinchocaine	T41.3X1	T41.3X2	T41.3X3	T41.3X4	T41.3X5	T41.3X6
topical (surface)	T41.3X1	T41.3X2	T41.3X3	T41.3X4	T41.3X5	T41.3X6
Cinchona	T37.2X1	T37.2X2	T37.2X3	T37.2X4	T37.2X5	T37.2X6
Cinchonine alkaloids	T37.2X1	T37.2X2	T37.2X3	T37.2X4	T37.2X5	T37.2X6
Cinchophen	T50.4X1	T50.4X2	T50.4X3	T50.4X4	T50.4X5	T50.4X6
Cinepazide	T46.7X1	T46.7X2	T46.7X3	T46.7X4	T46.7X5	T46.7X6
Cinnamedrine	T48.5X1	T48.5X2	T48.5X3	T48.5X4	T48.5X5	T48.5X6
Cinnarizine	T45.0X1	T45.0X2	T45.0X3	T45.0X4	T45.0X5	T45.0X6
Cinoxacin	T37.8X1	T37.8X2	T37.8X3	T37.8X4	T37.8X5	T37.8X6
Ciprofibrate	T46.6X1	T46.6X2	T46.6X3	T46.6X4	T46.6X5	T46.6X6
Ciprofloxacin	T36.8X1	T36.8X2	T36.8X3	T36.8X4	T36.8X5	T36.8X6
Cisapride	T47.8X1	T47.8X2	T47.8X3	T47.8X4	T47.8X5	T47.8X6
Cisplatin	T45.1X1	T45.1X2	T45.1X3	T45.1X4	T45.1X5	T45.1X6
Citalopram	T43.221	T43.222	T43.223	T43.224	T43.225	T43.226
Citanest	T41.3X1	T41.3X2	T41.3X3	T41.3X4	T41.3X5	T41.3X6
infiltration (subcutaneous)	T41.3X1	T41.3X2	T41.3X3	T41.3X4	T41.3X5	T41.3X6
nerve block (peripheral) (plexus)	T41.3X1	T41.3X2	T41.3X3	T41.3X4	T41.3X5	T41.3X6
Citric acid	T47.5X1	T47.5X2	T47.5X3	T47.5X4	T47.5X5	T47.5X6
Citrovorum (factor)	T45.8X1	T45.8X2	T45.8X3	T45.8X4	T45.8X5	T45.8X6
Claviceps purpurea	T62.2X1	T62.2X2	T62.2X3	T62.2X4	—	—
Clavulanic acid	T36.1X1	T36.1X2	T36.1X3	T36.1X4	T36.1X5	T36.1X6
Cleaner, cleansing agent, type not specified	T65.891	T65.892	T65.893	T65.894	—	—
of paint or varnish	T52.91	T52.92	T52.93	T52.94	—	—
specified type NEC	T65.891	T65.892	T65.893	T65.894	—	—
Clebopride	T47.8X1	T47.8X2	T47.8X3	T47.8X4	T47.8X5	T47.8X6
Clefamide	T37.3X1	T37.3X2	T37.3X3	T37.3X4	T37.3X5	T37.3X6
Clemastine	T45.0X1	T45.0X2	T45.0X3	T45.0X4	T45.0X5	T45.0X6
Clematis vitalba	T62.2X1	T62.2X2	T62.2X3	T62.2X4	—	—

Substance	External Cause (T-Code)					
	Poisoning, Accidental (Unintentional)	Poisoning, Intentional Self-Harm	Poisoning, Assault	Poisoning, Undetermined	Adverse Effect	Underdosing
Clemizole	T45.0X1	T45.0X2	T45.0X3	T45.0X4	T45.0X5	T45.0X6
penicillin	T36.0X1	T36.0X2	T36.0X3	T36.0X4	T36.0X5	T36.0X6
Clenbuterol	T48.6X1	T48.6X2	T48.6X3	T48.6X4	T48.6X5	T48.6X6
Clidinium bromide	T44.3X1	T44.3X2	T44.3X3	T44.3X4	T44.3X5	T44.3X6
Clindamycin	T36.8X1	T36.8X2	T36.8X3	T36.8X4	T36.8X5	T36.8X6
Clinofibrate	T46.6X1	T46.6X2	T46.6X3	T46.6X4	T46.6X5	T46.6X6
Clioquinol	T37.8X1	T37.8X2	T37.8X3	T37.8X4	T37.8X5	T37.8X6
Cliradon	T40.2X1	T40.2X2	T40.2X3	T40.2X4	—	—
Clobazam	T42.4X1	T42.4X2	T42.4X3	T42.4X4	T42.4X5	T42.4X6
Clobenzorex	T50.5X1	T50.5X2	T50.5X3	T50.5X4	T50.5X5	T50.5X6
Clobetasol	T49.0X1	T49.0X2	T49.0X3	T49.0X4	T49.0X5	T49.0X6
Clobetasone	T49.0X1	T49.0X2	T49.0X3	T49.0X4	T49.0X5	T49.0X6
Clobutinol	T48.3X1	T48.3X2	T48.3X3	T48.3X4	T48.3X5	T48.3X6
Clocapramine	T43.0X1	T43.0X2	T43.0X3	T43.0X4	T43.0X5	T43.0X6
Clocortolone	T38.0X1	T38.0X2	T38.0X3	T38.0X4	T38.0X5	T38.0X6
Clodantoin	T49.0X1	T49.0X2	T49.0X3	T49.0X4	T49.0X5	T49.0X6
Clodronic acid	T50.991	T50.992	T50.993	T50.994	T50.995	T50.996
Clofazimine	T37.1X1	T37.1X2	T37.1X3	T37.1X4	T37.1X5	T37.1X6
Clofedanol	T48.3X1	T48.3X2	T48.3X3	T48.3X4	T48.3X5	T48.3X6
Clofenamide	T50.2X1	T50.2X2	T50.2X3	T50.2X4	T50.2X5	T50.2X6
Clofenotane	T49.0X1	T49.0X2	T49.0X3	T49.0X4	T49.0X5	T49.0X6
Clofezone	T39.2X1	T39.2X2	T39.2X3	T39.2X4	T39.2X5	T39.2X6
Clofibrate	T46.6X1	T46.6X2	T46.6X3	T46.6X4	T46.6X5	T46.6X6
Clofibride	T46.6X1	T46.6X2	T46.6X3	T46.6X4	T46.6X5	T46.6X6
Cloforex	T50.5X1	T50.5X2	T50.5X3	T50.5X4	T50.5X5	T50.5X6
Clomacran	T43.0X1	T43.0X2	T43.0X3	T43.0X4	T43.0X5	T43.0X6
Clomethiazole	T42.6X1	T42.6X2	T42.6X3	T42.6X4	T42.6X5	T42.6X6
Clometocillin	T36.0X1	T36.0X2	T36.0X3	T36.0X4	T36.0X5	T36.0X6
Clomifene	T38.5X1	T38.5X2	T38.5X3	T38.5X4	T38.5X5	T38.5X6
Clomiphene	T38.5X1	T38.5X2	T38.5X3	T38.5X4	T38.5X5	T38.5X6
Clomipramine	T43.011	T43.012	T43.013	T43.014	T43.015	T43.016
Clomocycline	T36.4X1	T36.4X2	T36.4X3	T36.4X4	T36.4X5	T36.4X6
Clonazepam	T42.4X1	T42.4X2	T42.4X3	T42.4X4	T42.4X5	T42.4X6
Clonidine	T46.5X1	T46.5X2	T46.5X3	T46.5X4	T46.5X5	T46.5X6
Clonixin	T39.8X1	T39.8X2	T39.8X3	T39.8X4	T39.8X5	T39.8X6
Clopamide	T50.2X1	T50.2X2	T50.2X3	T50.2X4	T50.2X5	T50.2X6
Clopenthixol	T43.4X1	T43.4X2	T43.4X3	T43.4X4	T43.4X5	T43.4X6
Cloperastine	T48.3X1	T48.3X2	T48.3X3	T48.3X4	T48.3X5	T48.3X6
Clophedianol	T48.3X1	T48.3X2	T48.3X3	T48.3X4	T48.3X5	T48.3X6
Cloponone	T36.2X1	T36.2X2	T36.2X3	T36.2X4	T36.2X5	T36.2X6
Cloprednol	T38.0X1	T38.0X2	T38.0X3	T38.0X4	T38.0X5	T38.0X6
Cloral betaine	T42.6X1	T42.6X2	T42.6X3	T42.6X4	T42.6X5	T42.6X6

◀ New ◀◀ Revised ~~deleted~~ Deleted

Substance	External Cause (T-Code) Poisoning, Accidental (Unintentional)	Poisoning, Intentional Self-Harm	Poisoning, Assault	Poisoning, Undetermined	Adverse Effect	Underdosing
Cloramfenicol	T36.2X1	T36.2X2	T36.2X3	T36.2X4	T36.2X5	T36.2X6
Clorazepate (dipotassium)	T42.4X1	T42.4X2	T42.4X3	T42.4X4	T42.4X5	T42.4X6
Clorexolone	T50.2X1	T50.2X2	T50.2X3	T50.2X4	T50.2X5	T50.2X6
Clorox (bleach)	T54.91	T54.92	T54.93	T54.94	—	—
Clorfenamine	T45.0X1	T45.0X2	T45.0X3	T45.0X4	T45.0X5	T45.0X6
Clorgiline	T43.1X1	T43.1X2	T43.1X3	T43.1X4	T43.1X5	T43.1X6
Clorotepine	T44.3X1	T44.3X2	T44.3X3	T44.3X4	T44.3X5	T44.3X6
Clorprenaline	T48.6X1	T48.6X2	T48.6X3	T48.6X4	T48.6X5	T48.6X6
Clortermine	T50.5X1	T50.5X2	T50.5X3	T50.5X4	T50.5X5	T50.5X6
Clotiapine	T43.591	T43.592	T43.593	T43.594	T43.595	T43.596
Clotiazepam	T42.4X1	T42.4X2	T42.4X3	T42.4X4	T42.4X5	T42.4X6
Clotibric acid	T46.6X1	T46.6X2	T46.6X3	T46.6X4	T46.6X5	T46.6X6
Clotrimazole	T49.0X1	T49.0X2	T49.0X3	T49.0X4	T49.0X5	T49.0X6
Cloxacillin	T36.0X1	T36.0X2	T36.0X3	T36.0X4	T36.0X5	T36.0X6
Cloxazolam	T42.4X1	T42.4X2	T42.4X3	T42.4X4	T42.4X5	T42.4X6
Cloxiquine	T49.0X1	T49.0X2	T49.0X3	T49.0X4	T49.0X5	T49.0X6
Clozapine	T42.4X1	T42.4X2	T42.4X3	T42.4X4	T42.4X5	T42.4X6
Coagulant NEC	T45.7X1	T45.7X2	T45.7X3	T45.7X4	T45.7X5	T45.7X6
Coal (carbon monoxide from) — see also Carbon, monoxide, coal	T58.2X1	T58.2X2	T58.2X3	T58.2X4	—	—
oil — see Kerosene						
tar	T49.1X1	T49.1X2	T49.1X3	T49.1X4	T49.1X5	T49.1X6
fumes	T59.891	T59.892	T59.893	T59.894	—	—
medicinal (ointment)	T49.4X1	T49.4X2	T49.4X3	T49.4X4	T49.4X5	T49.4X6
analgesics NEC	T39.2X1	T39.2X2	T39.2X3	T39.2X4	T39.2X5	T39.2X6
naphtha (solvent)	T52.0X1	T52.0X2	T52.0X3	T52.0X4		
Cobalamine	T45.2X1	T45.2X2	T45.2X3	T45.2X4	T45.2X5	T45.2X6
Cobalt (nonmedicinal) (fumes) (industrial)	T56.891	T56.892	T56.893	T56.894		
medicinal (trace) (chloride)	T45.8X1	T45.8X2	T45.8X3	T45.8X4	T45.8X5	T45.8X6
Cobra (venom)	T63.041	T63.042	T63.043	T63.044		
Coca (leaf)	T40.5X1	T40.5X2	T40.5X3	T40.5X4	T40.5X5	T40.5X6
Cocaine	T40.5X1	T40.5X2	T40.5X3	T40.5X4	T40.5X5	T40.5X6
topical anesthetic	T41.3X1	T41.3X2	T41.3X3	T41.3X4	T41.3X5	T41.3X6
Cocarboxylase	T45.3X1	T45.3X2	T45.3X3	T45.3X4	T45.3X5	T45.3X6
Coccidioidin	T50.8X1	T50.8X2	T50.8X3	T50.8X4	T50.8X5	T50.8X6
Cocculus indicus	T62.1X1	T62.1X2	T62.1X3	T62.1X4		
Cochineal	T65.6X1	T65.6X2	T65.6X3	T65.6X4		
medicinal products	T50.991	T50.992	T50.993	T50.994	T50.995	T50.996
Codeine	T40.2X1	T40.2X2	T40.2X3	T40.2X4	T40.2X5	T40.2X6
Cod-liver oil	T45.2X1	T45.2X2	T45.2X3	T45.2X4	T45.2X5	T45.2X6

Substance	External Cause (T-Code) Poisoning, Accidental (Unintentional)	Poisoning, Intentional Self-Harm	Poisoning, Assault	Poisoning, Undetermined	Adverse Effect	Underdosing
Coenzyme A	T50.991	T50.992	T50.993	T50.994	T50.995	T50.996
Coffee	T62.8X1	T62.8X2	T62.8X3	T62.8X4	—	—
Cogalactoisomerase	T50.991	T50.992	T50.993	T50.994	T50.995	T50.996
Cogentin	T44.3X1	T44.3X2	T44.3X3	T44.3X4	T44.3X5	T44.3X6
Coke fumes or gas (carbon monoxide)	T58.2X1	T58.2X2	T58.2X3	T58.2X4	—	—
industrial use	T58.8X1	T58.8X2	T58.8X3	T58.8X4	—	—
Colace	T47.4X1	T47.4X2	T47.4X3	T47.4X4	T47.4X5	T47.4X6
Colaspase	T45.1X1	T45.1X2	T45.1X3	T45.1X4	T45.1X5	T45.1X6
Colchicine	T50.4X1	T50.4X2	T50.4X3	T50.4X4	T50.4X5	T50.4X6
Colchicum	T62.2X1	T62.2X2	T62.2X3	T62.2X4	—	—
Cold cream	T49.3X1	T49.3X2	T49.3X3	T49.3X4	T49.3X5	T49.3X6
Colecalciferol	T45.2X1	T45.2X2	T45.2X3	T45.2X4	T45.2X5	T45.2X6
Colestipol	T46.6X1	T46.6X2	T46.6X3	T46.6X4	T46.6X5	T46.6X6
Colestyramine	T46.6X1	T46.6X2	T46.6X3	T46.6X4	T46.6X5	T46.6X6
Colimycin	T36.8X1	T36.8X2	T36.8X3	T36.8X4	T36.8X5	T36.8X6
Colistimethate	T36.8X1	T36.8X2	T36.8X3	T36.8X4	T36.8X5	T36.8X6
Colistin	T36.8X1	T36.8X2	T36.8X3	T36.8X4	T36.8X5	T36.8X6
sulfate (eye preparation)	T49.5X1	T49.5X2	T49.5X3	T49.5X4	T49.5X5	T49.5X6
Collagen	T50.991	T50.992	T50.993	T50.994	T50.995	T50.996
Collagenase	T49.4X1	T49.4X2	T49.4X3	T49.4X4	T49.4X5	T49.4X6
Collodion	T49.3X1	T49.3X2	T49.3X3	T49.3X4	T49.3X5	T49.3X6
Colocynth	T47.2X1	T47.2X2	T47.2X3	T47.2X4	T47.2X5	T47.2X6
Colophony adhesive	T49.3X1	T49.3X2	T49.3X3	T49.3X4	T49.3X5	T49.3X6
Colorant — see also Dye	T50.991	T50.992	T50.993	T50.994	T50.995	T50.996
Coloring matter — see Dye(s)						
Combustion gas (after combustion) — see Carbon, monoxide						
prior to combustion	T59.891	T59.892	T59.893	T59.894	—	—
Compazine	T43.3X1	T43.3X2	T43.3X3	T43.3X4	T43.3X5	T43.3X6
Compound						
42 (warfarin)	T60.4X1	T60.4X2	T60.4X3	T60.4X4	—	—
269 (endrin)	T60.1X1	T60.1X2	T60.1X3	T60.1X4	—	—
497 (dieldrin)	T60.1X1	T60.1X2	T60.1X3	T60.1X4	—	—
1080 (sodium fluoroacetate)	T60.4X1	T60.4X2	T60.4X3	T60.4X4	—	—
3422 (parathion)	T60.0X1	T60.0X2	T60.0X3	T60.0X4	—	—
3911 (phorate)	T60.0X1	T60.0X2	T60.0X3	T60.0X4	—	—
3956 (toxaphene)	T60.1X1	T60.1X2	T60.1X3	T60.1X4	—	—
4049 (malathion)	T60.0X1	T60.0X2	T60.0X3	T60.0X4	—	—
4069 (malathion)	T60.0X1	T60.0X2	T60.0X3	T60.0X4	—	—
4124 (dicapthon)	T60.0X1	T60.0X2	T60.0X3	T60.0X4	—	—

◀ New ◀ Revised deleted Deleted

Substance	Poisoning, Accidental (Unintentional)	Poisoning, Intentional Self-Harm	Poisoning, Assault	Poisoning, Undetermined	Adverse Effect	Underdosing
External Cause (T-Code)						
Compound *(Continued)*						
E (cortisone)	T38.0X1	T38.0X2	T38.0X3	T38.0X4	T38.0X5	T38.0X6
F (hydrocortisone)	T38.0X1	T38.0X2	T38.0X3	T38.0X4	T38.0X5	T38.0X6
Congener, anabolic	T38.7X1	T38.7X2	T38.7X3	T38.7X4	T38.7X5	T38.7X6
Congo red	T50.8X1	T50.8X2	T50.8X3	T50.8X4	T50.8X5	T50.8X6
Coniine, conine	T62.2X1	T62.2X2	T62.2X3	T62.2X4	—	—
Conium (maculatum)	T62.2X1	T62.2X2	T62.2X3	T62.2X4	—	—
Conjugated estrogenic substances	T38.5X1	T38.5X2	T38.5X3	T38.5X4	T38.5X5	T38.5X6
Contac	T48.5X1	T48.5X2	T48.5X3	T48.5X4	T48.5X5	T48.5X6
Contact lens solution	T49.5X1	T49.5X2	T49.5X3	T49.5X4	T49.5X5	T49.5X6
Contraceptive (oral)	T38.4X1	T38.4X2	T38.4X3	T38.4X4	T38.4X5	T38.4X6
vaginal	T49.8X1	T49.8X2	T49.8X3	T49.8X4	T49.8X5	T49.8X6
Contrast medium, radiography	T50.8X1	T50.8X2	T50.8X3	T50.8X4	T50.8X5	T50.8X6
Convallaria glycosides	T46.0X1	T46.0X2	T46.0X3	T46.0X4	T46.0X5	T46.0X6
Convallaria majalis	T62.2X1	T62.2X2	T62.2X3	T62.2X4	—	—
berry	T62.1X1	T62.1X2	T62.1X3	T62.1X4	—	—
Copper (dust) (fumes) (nonmedicinal) NEC	T56.4X1	T56.4X2	T56.4X3	T56.4X4	—	—
arsenate, arsenite	T57.0X1	T57.0X2	T57.0X3	T57.0X4	—	—
insecticide	T60.2X1	T60.2X2	T60.2X3	T60.2X4	—	—
emetic	T47.7X1	T47.7X2	T47.7X3	T47.7X4	T47.7X5	T47.7X6
fungicide	T60.3X1	T60.3X2	T60.3X3	T60.3X4	—	—
gluconate	T49.0X1	T49.0X2	T49.0X3	T49.0X4	T49.0X5	T49.0X6
insecticide	T60.2X1	T60.2X2	T60.2X3	T60.2X4	—	—
medicinal (trace)	T45.8X1	T45.8X2	T45.8X3	T45.8X4	T45.8X5	T45.8X6
oleate	T49.0X1	T49.0X2	T49.0X3	T49.0X4	T49.0X5	T49.0X6
sulfate	T56.4X1	T56.4X2	T56.4X3	T56.4X4	—	—
cupric	T56.4X1	T56.4X2	T56.4X3	T56.4X4	—	—
fungicide	T60.3X1	T60.3X2	T60.3X3	T60.3X4	—	—
medicinal						
ear	T49.6X1	T49.6X2	T49.6X3	T49.6X4	T49.6X5	T49.6X6
emetic	T47.7X1	T47.7X2	T47.7X3	T47.7X4	T47.7X5	T47.7X6
eye	T49.5X1	T49.5X2	T49.5X3	T49.5X4	T49.5X5	T49.5X6
cuprous	T56.4X1	T56.4X2	T56.4X3	T56.4X4	—	—
fungicide	T60.3X1	T60.3X2	T60.3X3	T60.3X4	—	—
medicinal						
ear	T49.6X1	T49.6X2	T49.6X3	T49.6X4	T49.6X5	T49.6X6
emetic	T47.7X1	T47.7X2	T47.7X3	T47.7X4	T47.7X5	T47.7X6
eye	T49.5X1	T49.5X2	T49.5X3	T49.5X4	T49.5X5	T49.5X6
Copperhead snake (bite) (venom)	T63.061	T63.062	T63.063	T63.064	—	—
Coral (sting)	T63.691	T63.692	T63.693	T63.694	—	—
snake (bite) (venom)	T63.021	T63.022	T63.023	T63.024	—	—

Substance	Poisoning, Accidental (Unintentional)	Poisoning, Intentional Self-Harm	Poisoning, Assault	Poisoning, Undetermined	Adverse Effect	Underdosing
External Cause (T-Code)						
Corbadrine	T49.6X1	T49.6X2	T49.6X3	T49.6X4	T49.6X5	T49.6X6
Cordran	T49.0X1	T49.0X2	T49.0X3	T49.0X4	T49.0X5	T49.0X6
Cordite	T65.891	T65.892	T65.893	T65.894	—	—
vapor	T59.891	T59.892	T59.893	T59.894	—	—
Corn cures	T49.4X1	T49.4X2	T49.4X3	T49.4X4	T49.4X5	T49.4X6
Cornhusker's lotion	T49.3X1	T49.3X2	T49.3X3	T49.3X4	T49.3X5	T49.3X6
Corn starch	T49.3X1	T49.3X2	T49.3X3	T49.3X4	T49.3X5	T49.3X6
Coronary vasodilator NEC	T46.3X1	T46.3X2	T46.3X3	T46.3X4	T46.3X5	T46.3X6
Corrosive NEC	T54.91	T54.92	T54.93	T54.94	—	—
acid NEC	T54.2X1	T54.2X2	T54.2X3	T54.2X4	—	—
aromatics	T54.1X1	T54.1X2	T54.1X3	T54.1X4	—	—
disinfectant	T54.1X1	T54.1X2	T54.1X3	T54.1X4	—	—
fumes NEC	T54.91	T54.92	T54.93	T54.94	—	—
specified NEC	T54.91	T54.92	T54.93	T54.94	—	—
sublimate	T56.1X1	T56.1X2	T56.1X3	T56.1X4	—	—
Cortate	T38.0X1	T38.0X2	T38.0X3	T38.0X4	T38.0X5	T38.0X6
Cort-Dome	T38.0X1	T38.0X2	T38.0X3	T38.0X4	T38.0X5	T38.0X6
ENT agent	T49.6X1	T49.6X2	T49.6X3	T49.6X4	T49.6X5	T49.6X6
ophthalmic preparation	T49.5X1	T49.5X2	T49.5X3	T49.5X4	T49.5X5	T49.5X6
topical NEC	T49.0X1	T49.0X2	T49.0X3	T49.0X4	T49.0X5	T49.0X6
Cortef	T38.0X1	T38.0X2	T38.0X3	T38.0X4	T38.0X5	T38.0X6
ENT agent	T49.6X1	T49.6X2	T49.6X3	T49.6X4	T49.6X5	T49.6X6
ophthalmic preparation	T49.5X1	T49.5X2	T49.5X3	T49.5X4	T49.5X5	T49.5X6
topical NEC	T49.0X1	T49.0X2	T49.0X3	T49.0X4	T49.0X5	T49.0X6
Corticosteroid	T38.0X1	T38.0X2	T38.0X3	T38.0X4	T38.0X5	T38.0X6
ENT agent	T49.6X1	T49.6X2	T49.6X3	T49.6X4	T49.6X5	T49.6X6
mineral	T50.0X1	T50.0X2	T50.0X3	T50.0X4	T50.0X5	T50.0X6
ophthalmic	T49.5X1	T49.5X2	T49.5X3	T49.5X4	T49.5X5	T49.5X6
topical NEC	T49.0X1	T49.0X2	T49.0X3	T49.0X4	T49.0X5	T49.0X6
Corticotropin	T38.811	T38.812	T38.813	T38.814	T38.815	T38.816
Cortisol	T49.0X1	T49.0X2	T49.0X3	T49.0X4	T49.0X5	T49.0X6
ENT agent	T49.6X1	T49.6X2	T49.6X3	T49.6X4	T49.6X5	T49.6X6
ophthalmic preparation	T49.5X1	T49.5X2	T49.5X3	T49.5X4	T49.5X5	T49.5X6
topical NEC	T49.0X1	T49.0X2	T49.0X3	T49.0X4	T49.0X5	T49.0X6
Cortisone (acetate)	T38.0X1	T38.0X2	T38.0X3	T38.0X4	T38.0X5	T38.0X6
ENT agent	T49.6X1	T49.6X2	T49.6X3	T49.6X4	T49.6X5	T49.6X6
ophthalmic preparation	T49.5X1	T49.5X2	T49.5X3	T49.5X4	T49.5X5	T49.5X6
topical NEC	T49.0X1	T49.0X2	T49.0X3	T49.0X4	T49.0X5	T49.0X6
Cortivazol	T38.0X1	T38.0X2	T38.0X3	T38.0X4	T38.0X5	T38.0X6
Cortogen	T38.0X1	T38.0X2	T38.0X3	T38.0X4	T38.0X5	T38.0X6
ENT agent	T49.6X1	T49.6X2	T49.6X3	T49.6X4	T49.6X5	T49.6X6
ophthalmic preparation	T49.5X1	T49.5X2	T49.5X3	T49.5X4	T49.5X5	T49.5X6

◀ New   ◀ Revised   ~~deleted~~ Deleted

TABLE OF DRUGS AND CHEMICALS

Substance	Poisoning, Accidental (Unintentional)	Poisoning, Intentional Self-Harm	Poisoning, Assault	Poisoning, Undetermined	Adverse Effect	Underdosing
Cortone	T38.0X1	T38.0X2	T38.0X3	T38.0X4	T38.0X5	T38.0X6
ENT agent	T49.6X1	T49.6X2	T49.6X3	T49.6X4	T49.6X5	T49.6X6
ophthalmic preparation	T49.5X1	T49.5X2	T49.5X3	T49.5X4	T49.5X5	T49.5X6
Cortril	T38.0X1	T38.0X2	T38.0X3	T38.0X4	T38.0X5	T38.0X6
ENT agent	T49.6X1	T49.6X2	T49.6X3	T49.6X4	T49.6X5	T49.6X6
ophthalmic preparation	T49.5X1	T49.5X2	T49.5X3	T49.5X4	T49.5X5	T49.5X6
topical NEC	T49.0X1	T49.0X2	T49.0X3	T49.0X4	T49.0X5	T49.0X6
Corynebacterium parvum	T45.1X1	T45.1X2	T45.1X3	T45.1X4	T45.1X5	T45.1X6
Cosmetic preparation	T49.8X1	T49.8X2	T49.8X3	T49.8X4	T49.8X5	T49.8X6
Cosmetics	T49.8X1	T49.8X2	T49.8X3	T49.8X4	T49.8X5	T49.8X6
Cosyntropin	T38.811	T38.812	T38.813	T38.814	T38.815	T38.816
Cotarnine	T45.7X1	T45.7X2	T45.7X3	T45.7X4	T45.7X5	T45.7X6
Co-trimoxazole	T36.8X1	T36.8X2	T36.8X3	T36.8X4	T36.8X5	T36.8X6
Cottonseed oil	T49.3X1	T49.3X2	T49.3X3	T49.3X4	T49.3X5	T49.3X6
Cough mixture (syrup)	T48.4X1	T48.4X2	T48.4X3	T48.4X4	T48.4X5	T48.4X6
containing opiates	T40.2X1	T40.2X2	T40.2X3	T40.2X4	T40.2X5	T40.2X6
expectorants	T48.4X1	T48.4X2	T48.4X3	T48.4X4	T48.4X5	T48.4X6
Coumadin	T45.511	T45.512	T45.513	T45.514	T45.515	T45.516
rodenticide	T60.4X1	T60.4X2	T60.4X3	T60.4X4	—	—
Coumaphos	T60.0X1	T60.0X2	T60.0X3	T60.0X4	—	—
Coumarin	T45.511	T45.512	T45.513	T45.514	T45.515	T45.516
Coumetarol	T45.511	T45.512	T45.513	T45.514	T45.515	T45.516
Cowbane	T62.2X1	T62.2X2	T62.2X3	T62.2X4	—	—
Cozyme	T45.2X1	T45.2X2	T45.2X3	T45.2X4	T45.2X5	T45.2X6
Crack	T40.5X1	T40.5X2	T40.5X3	T40.5X4	—	—
Crataegus extract	T46.0X1	T46.0X2	T46.0X3	T46.0X4	T46.0X5	T46.0X6
Creolin	T54.1X1	T54.1X2	T54.1X3	T54.1X4	—	—
disinfectant	T54.1X1	T54.1X2	T54.1X3	T54.1X4	—	—
Creosol (compound)	T49.0X1	T49.0X2	T49.0X3	T49.0X4	T49.0X5	T49.0X6
Creosote (coal tar) (beechwood)	T49.0X1	T49.0X2	T49.0X3	T49.0X4	T49.0X5	T49.0X6
medicinal (expectorant)	T48.4X1	T48.4X2	T48.4X3	T48.4X4	T48.4X5	T48.4X6
syrup	T48.4X1	T48.4X2	T48.4X3	T48.4X4	T48.4X5	T48.4X6
Cresol(s)	T49.0X1	T49.0X2	T49.0X3	T49.0X4	T49.0X5	T49.0X6
and soap solution	T49.0X1	T49.0X2	T49.0X3	T49.0X4	T49.0X5	T49.0X6
Cresyl acetate	T49.0X1	T49.0X2	T49.0X3	T49.0X4	T49.0X5	T49.0X6
Cresylic acid	T49.0X1	T49.0X2	T49.0X3	T49.0X4	T49.0X5	T49.0X6
Crimidine	T60.4X1	T60.4X2	T60.4X3	T60.4X4	—	—
Croconazole	T37.8X1	T37.8X2	T37.8X3	T37.8X4	T37.8X5	T37.8X6
Cromoglicic acid	T48.6X1	T48.6X2	T48.6X3	T48.6X4	T48.6X5	T48.6X6
Cromolyn	T48.6X1	T48.6X2	T48.6X3	T48.6X4	T48.6X5	T48.6X6
Cromonar	T46.3X1	T46.3X2	T46.3X3	T46.3X4	T46.3X5	T46.3X6

Substance	Poisoning, Accidental (Unintentional)	Poisoning, Intentional Self-Harm	Poisoning, Assault	Poisoning, Undetermined	Adverse Effect	Underdosing
Cropropamide	T39.8X1	T39.8X2	T39.8X3	T39.8X4	T39.8X5	T39.8X6
with crotethamide	T50.7X1	T50.7X2	T50.7X3	T50.7X4	T50.7X5	T50.7X6
Crotamiton	T49.0X1	T49.0X2	T49.0X3	T49.0X4	T49.0X5	T49.0X6
Crotethamide	T39.8X1	T39.8X2	T39.8X3	T39.8X4	T39.8X5	T39.8X6
with cropropamide	T50.7X1	T50.7X2	T50.7X3	T50.7X4	T50.7X5	T50.7X6
Croton (oil)	T47.2X1	T47.2X2	T47.2X3	T47.2X4	T47.2X5	T47.2X6
chloral	T42.6X1	T42.6X2	T42.6X3	T42.6X4	T42.6X5	T42.6X6
Crude oil	T52.0X1	T52.0X2	T52.0X3	T52.0X4	—	—
Cryogenine	T39.8X1	T39.8X2	T39.8X3	T39.8X4	T39.8X5	T39.8X6
Cryolite (vapor)	T60.1X1	T60.1X2	T60.1X3	T60.1X4	—	—
insecticide	T60.1X1	T60.1X2	T60.1X3	T60.1X4	—	—
Cryptenamine (tannates)	T46.5X1	T46.5X2	T46.5X3	T46.5X4	T46.5X5	T46.5X6
Crystal violet	T49.0X1	T49.0X2	T49.0X3	T49.0X4	T49.0X5	T49.0X6
Cuckoopint	T62.2X1	T62.2X2	T62.2X3	T62.2X4	—	—
Cumetharol	T45.511	T45.512	T45.513	T45.514	T45.515	T45.516
Cupric						
acetate	T60.3X1	T60.3X2	T60.3X3	T60.3X4	—	—
acetoarsenite	T57.0X1	T57.0X2	T57.0X3	T57.0X4	—	—
arsenate	T57.0X1	T57.0X2	T57.0X3	T57.0X4	—	—
gluconate	T49.0X1	T49.0X2	T49.0X3	T49.0X4	T49.0X5	T49.0X6
oleate	T49.0X1	T49.0X2	T49.0X3	T49.0X4	T49.0X5	T49.0X6
sulfate	T56.4X1	T56.4X2	T56.4X3	T56.4X4	—	—
Cuprous sulfate — see also Copper sulfate	T56.4X1	T56.4X2	T56.4X3	T56.4X4	—	—
Curare, curarine	T48.1X1	T48.1X2	T48.1X3	T48.1X4	T48.1X5	T48.1X6
Cyamemazine	T43.3X1	T43.3X2	T43.3X3	T43.3X4	T43.3X5	T43.3X6
Cyamopsis tetragono-loba	T46.6X1	T46.6X2	T46.6X3	T46.6X4	T46.6X5	T46.6X6
Cyanacetyl hydrazide	T37.1X1	T37.1X2	T37.1X3	T37.1X4	T37.1X5	T37.1X6
Cyanic acid (gas)	T59.891	T59.892	T59.893	T59.894	—	—
Cyanide(s) (compounds) (potassium) (sodium) NEC	T65.0X1	T65.0X2	T65.0X3	T65.0X4	—	—
dust or gas (inhalation) NEC	T57.3X1	T57.3X2	T57.3X3	T57.3X4	—	—
fumigant	T65.0X1	T65.0X2	T65.0X3	T65.0X4	—	—
hydrogen	T57.3X1	T57.3X2	T57.3X3	T57.3X4	—	—
mercuric — see Mercury						
pesticide (dust) (fumes)	T65.0X1	T65.0X2	T65.0X3	T65.0X4	—	—
Cyanoacrylate adhesive	T49.3X1	T49.3X2	T49.3X3	T49.3X4	T49.3X5	T49.3X6
Cyanocobalamin	T45.8X1	T45.8X2	T45.8X3	T45.8X4	T45.8X5	T45.8X6
Cyanogen (chloride) (gas) NEC	T59.891	T59.892	T59.893	T59.894	—	—
Cyclacillin	T36.0X1	T36.0X2	T36.0X3	T36.0X4	T36.0X5	T36.0X6
Cyclaine	T41.3X1	T41.3X2	T41.3X3	T41.3X4	T41.3X5	T41.3X6
Cyclamate	T50.991	T50.992	T50.993	T50.994	T50.995	T50.996

◀ New ◀ Revised ~~deleted~~ Deleted

Substance	External Cause (T-Code) Poisoning, Accidental (Unintentional)	Poisoning, Intentional Self-Harm	Poisoning, Assault	Poisoning, Undetermined	Adverse Effect	Underdosing
Cyclamen europaeum	T62.2X1	T62.2X2	T62.2X3	T62.2X4	—	—
Cyclandelate	T46.7X1	T46.7X2	T46.7X3	T46.7X4	T46.7X5	T46.7X6
Cyclazocine	T50.7X1	T50.7X2	T50.7X3	T50.7X4	T50.7X5	T50.7X6
Cyclizine	T45.0X1	T45.0X2	T45.0X3	T45.0X4	T45.0X5	T45.0X6
Cyclobarbital	T42.3X1	T42.3X2	T42.3X3	T42.3X4	T42.3X5	T42.3X6
Cyclobarbitone	T42.3X1	T42.3X2	T42.3X3	T42.3X4	T42.3X5	T42.3X6
Cyclobenzaprine	T48.1X1	T48.1X2	T48.1X3	T48.1X4	T48.1X5	T48.1X6
Cyclodrine	T44.3X1	T44.3X2	T44.3X3	T44.3X4	T44.3X5	T44.3X6
Cycloguanil embonate	T37.2X1	T37.2X2	T37.2X3	T37.2X4	T37.2X5	T37.2X6
Cycloheptadiene	T43.291	T43.292	T43.293	T43.294	T43.295	T43.296
Cyclohexane	T52.8X1	T52.8X2	T52.8X3	T52.8X4	—	—
Cyclohexanol	T51.8X1	T51.8X2	T51.8X3	T51.8X4	—	—
Cyclohexanone	T52.4X1	T52.4X2	T52.4X3	T52.4X4	—	—
Cycloheximide	T60.3X1	T60.3X2	T60.3X3	T60.3X4	—	—
Cyclohexyl acetate	T52.8X1	T52.8X2	T52.8X3	T52.8X4	—	—
Cycloleucin	T45.1X1	T45.1X2	T45.1X3	T45.1X4	T45.1X5	T45.1X6
Cyclomethycaine	T41.3X1	T41.3X2	T41.3X3	T41.3X4	T41.3X5	T41.3X6
Cyclopentamine	T44.4X1	T44.4X2	T44.4X3	T44.4X4	T44.4X5	T44.4X6
Cyclopenthiazide	T50.2X1	T50.2X2	T50.2X3	T50.2X4	T50.2X5	T50.2X6
Cyclopentolate	T44.3X1	T44.3X2	T44.3X3	T44.3X4	T44.3X5	T44.3X6
Cyclophosphamide	T45.1X1	T45.1X2	T45.1X3	T45.1X4	T45.1X5	T45.1X6
Cycloplegic drug	T49.5X1	T49.5X2	T49.5X3	T49.5X4	T49.5X5	T49.5X6
Cyclopropane	T41.291	T41.292	T41.293	T41.294	T41.295	T41.296
Cyclopyrabital	T39.8X1	T39.8X2	T39.8X3	T39.8X4	T39.8X5	T39.8X6
Cycloserine	T37.1X1	T37.1X2	T37.1X3	T37.1X4	T37.1X5	T37.1X6
Cyclosporin	T45.1X1	T45.1X2	T45.1X3	T45.1X4	T45.1X5	T45.1X6
Cyclothiazide	T50.2X1	T50.2X2	T50.2X3	T50.2X4	T50.2X5	T50.2X6
Cycrimine	T44.3X1	T44.3X2	T44.3X3	T44.3X4	T44.3X5	T44.3X6
Cyhalothrin	T60.1X1	T60.1X2	T60.1X3	T60.1X4	—	—
Cymarin	T46.0X1	T46.0X2	T46.0X3	T46.0X4	T46.0X5	T46.0X6
Cypermethrin	T60.1X1	T60.1X2	T60.1X3	T60.1X4	—	—
Cyphenothrin	T60.2X1	T60.2X2	T60.2X3	T60.2X4	—	—
Cyproheptadine	T45.0X1	T45.0X2	T45.0X3	T45.0X4	T45.0X5	T45.0X6
Cyprolidol	T43.291	T43.292	T43.293	T43.294	T43.295	T43.296
Cyproterone	T38.6X1	T38.6X2	T38.6X3	T38.6X4	T38.6X5	T38.6X6
Cysteamine	T50.6X1	T50.6X2	T50.6X3	T50.6X4	T50.6X5	T50.6X6
Cytarabine	T45.1X1	T45.1X2	T45.1X3	T45.1X4	T45.1X5	T45.1X6
Cytisus						
laburnum	T62.2X1	T62.2X2	T62.2X3	T62.2X4	—	—
scoparius	T62.2X1	T62.2X2	T62.2X3	T62.2X4	—	—
Cytochrome C	T47.5X1	T47.5X2	T47.5X3	T47.5X4	T47.5X5	T47.5X6
Cytomel	T38.1X1	T38.1X2	T38.1X3	T38.1X4	T38.1X5	T38.1X6

Substance	External Cause (T-Code) Poisoning, Accidental (Unintentional)	Poisoning, Intentional Self-Harm	Poisoning, Assault	Poisoning, Undetermined	Adverse Effect	Underdosing
Cytosine arabinoside	T45.1X1	T45.1X2	T45.1X3	T45.1X4	T45.1X5	T45.1X6
Cytoxan	T45.1X1	T45.1X2	T45.1X3	T45.1X4	T45.1X5	T45.1X6
Cytozyme	T45.7X1	T45.7X2	T45.7X3	T45.7X4	T45.7X5	T45.7X6
2,4-D	T60.3X1	T60.3X2	T60.3X3	T60.3X4	—	—
D						
Dacarbazine	T45.1X1	T45.1X2	T45.1X3	T45.1X4	T45.1X5	T45.1X6
Dactinomycin	T45.1X1	T45.1X2	T45.1X3	T45.1X4	T45.1X5	T45.1X6
DADPS	T37.1X1	T37.1X2	T37.1X3	T37.1X4	T37.1X5	T37.1X6
Dakin's solution	T49.0X1	T49.0X2	T49.0X3	T49.0X4	T49.0X5	T49.0X6
Dalapon (sodium)	T60.3X1	T60.3X2	T60.3X3	T60.3X4	—	—
Dalmane	T42.4X1	T42.4X2	T42.4X3	T42.4X4	T42.4X5	T42.4X6
Danazol	T38.6X1	T38.6X2	T38.6X3	T38.6X4	T38.6X5	T38.6X6
Danilone	T45.511	T45.512	T45.513	T45.514	T45.515	T45.516
Danthron	T47.2X1	T47.2X2	T47.2X3	T47.2X4	T47.2X5	T47.2X6
Dantrolene	T42.8X1	T42.8X2	T42.8X3	T42.8X4	T42.8X5	T42.8X6
Dantron	T47.2X1	T47.2X2	T47.2X3	T47.2X4	T47.2X5	T47.2X6
Daphne (gnidium) (mezereum)	T62.2X1	T62.2X2	T62.2X3	T62.2X4	—	—
berry	T62.1X1	T62.1X2	T62.1X3	T62.1X4	—	—
Dapsone	T37.1X1	T37.1X2	T37.1X3	T37.1X4	T37.1X5	T37.1X6
Daraprim	T37.2X1	T37.2X2	T37.2X3	T37.2X4	T37.2X5	T37.2X6
Darnel	T62.2X1	T62.2X2	T62.2X3	T62.2X4	—	—
Darvon	T39.8X1	T39.8X2	T39.8X3	T39.8X4	T39.8X5	T39.8X6
Daunomycin	T45.1X1	T45.1X2	T45.1X3	T45.1X4	T45.1X5	T45.1X6
Daunorubicin	T45.1X1	T45.1X2	T45.1X3	T45.1X4	T45.1X5	T45.1X6
DBI	T38.3X1	T38.3X2	T38.3X3	T38.3X4	T38.3X5	T38.3X6
D-Con	T60.91	T60.92	T60.93	T60.94	—	—
insecticide	T60.2X1	T60.2X2	T60.2X3	T60.2X4	—	—
rodenticide	T60.4X1	T60.4X2	T60.4X3	T60.4X4	—	—
DDAVP	T38.891	T38.892	T38.893	T38.894	T38.895	T38.896
DDE (bis(chlorophenyl)-dichloroethylene)	T60.2X1	T60.2X2	T60.2X3	T60.2X4	—	—
DDS	T37.1X1	T37.1X2	T37.1X3	T37.1X4	T37.1X5	T37.1X6
DDT (dust)	T60.1X1	T60.1X2	T60.1X3	T60.1X4	—	—
Deadly nightshade — see also Belladonna	T62.2X1	T62.2X2	T62.2X3	T62.2X4	—	—
berry	T62.1X1	T62.1X2	T62.1X3	T62.1X4	—	—
Deamino-D-arginine vasopressin	T38.891	T38.892	T38.893	T38.894	T38.895	T38.896
Deanol (aceglumate)	T50.991	T50.992	T50.993	T50.994	T50.995	T50.996
Debrisoquine	T46.5X1	T46.5X2	T46.5X3	T46.5X4	T46.5X5	T46.5X6
Decaborane	T57.8X1	T57.8X2	T57.8X3	T57.8X4	—	—
fumes	T59.891	T59.892	T59.893	T59.894	—	—

◀ New   ◀ Revised   ~~deleted~~ Deleted

TABLE OF DRUGS AND CHEMICALS

Substance	Poisoning, Accidental (Unintentional)	Poisoning, Intentional Self-Harm	Poisoning, Assault	Poisoning, Undetermined	Adverse Effect	Underdosing
Decadron	T38.0X1	T38.0X2	T38.0X3	T38.0X4	T38.0X5	T38.0X6
ENT agent	T49.6X1	T49.6X2	T49.6X3	T49.6X4	T49.6X5	T49.6X6
ophthalmic preparation	T49.5X1	T49.5X2	T49.5X3	T49.5X4	T49.5X5	T49.5X6
topical NEC	T49.0X1	T49.0X2	T49.0X3	T49.0X4	T49.0X5	T49.0X6
Decahydronaphthalene	T52.8X1	T52.8X2	T52.8X3	T52.8X4	—	—
Decalin	T52.8X1	T52.8X2	T52.8X3	T52.8X4	—	—
Decamethonium (bromide)	T48.1X1	T48.1X2	T48.1X3	T48.1X4	T48.1X5	T48.1X6
Decholin	T47.5X1	T47.5X2	T47.5X3	T47.5X4	T47.5X5	T47.5X6
Declomycin	T36.4X1	T36.4X2	T36.4X3	T36.4X4	T36.4X5	T36.4X6
Decongestant, nasal (mucosa)	T48.5X1	T48.5X2	T48.5X3	T48.5X4	T48.5X5	T48.5X6
combination	T48.5X1	T48.5X2	T48.5X3	T48.5X4	T48.5X5	T48.5X6
Deet	T60.8X1	T60.8X2	T60.8X3	T60.8X4	—	—
Deferoxamine	T45.8X1	T45.8X2	T45.8X3	T45.8X4	T45.8X5	T45.8X6
Deflazacort	T38.0X1	T38.0X2	T38.0X3	T38.0X4	T38.0X5	T38.0X6
Deglycyrrhizinized extract of licorice	T48.4X1	T48.4X2	T48.4X3	T48.4X4	T48.4X5	T48.4X6
Dehydrocholic acid	T47.5X1	T47.5X2	T47.5X3	T47.5X4	T47.5X5	T47.5X6
Dehydroemetine	T37.3X1	T37.3X2	T37.3X3	T37.3X4	T37.3X5	T37.3X6
Dekalin	T52.8X1	T52.8X2	T52.8X3	T52.8X4	—	—
Delalutin	T38.5X1	T38.5X2	T38.5X3	T38.5X4	T38.5X5	T38.5X6
Delphinium	T62.2X1	T62.2X2	T62.2X3	T62.2X4	—	—
Deltasone	T38.0X1	T38.0X2	T38.0X3	T38.0X4	T38.0X5	T38.0X6
Deltra	T38.0X1	T38.0X2	T38.0X3	T38.0X4	T38.0X5	T38.0X6
Delvinal	T42.3X1	T42.3X2	T42.3X3	T42.3X4	T42.3X5	T42.3X6
Delorazepam	T42.4X1	T42.4X2	T42.4X3	T42.4X4	T42.4X5	T42.4X6
Deltamethrin	T60.1X1	T60.1X2	T60.1X3	T60.1X4	—	—
Demecarium (bromide)	T49.5X1	T49.5X2	T49.5X3	T49.5X4	T49.5X5	T49.5X6
Demeclocycline	T36.4X1	T36.4X2	T36.4X3	T36.4X4	T36.4X5	T36.4X6
Demecolcine	T45.1X1	T45.1X2	T45.1X3	T45.1X4	T45.1X5	T45.1X6
Demegestone	T38.5X1	T38.5X2	T38.5X3	T38.5X4	T38.5X5	T38.5X6
Demelanizing agents	T49.8X1	T49.8X2	T49.8X3	T49.8X4	T49.8X5	T49.8X6
Demephion -O and -S	T60.0X1	T60.0X2	T60.0X3	T60.0X4	—	—
Demerol	T40.2X1	T40.2X2	T40.2X3	T40.2X4	T40.2X5	T40.2X6
Demethylchlortetracycline	T36.4X1	T36.4X2	T36.4X3	T36.4X4	T36.4X5	T36.4X6
Demethyltetracycline	T36.4X1	T36.4X2	T36.4X3	T36.4X4	T36.4X5	T36.4X6
Demeton -O and -S	T60.0X1	T60.0X2	T60.0X3	T60.0X4	—	—
Demulcent (external)	T49.3X1	T49.3X2	T49.3X3	T49.3X4	T49.3X5	T49.3X6
specified NEC	T49.3X1	T49.3X2	T49.3X3	T49.3X4	T49.3X5	T49.3X6
Demulen	T38.4X1	T38.4X2	T38.4X3	T38.4X4	T38.4X5	T38.4X6
Denatured alcohol	T51.0X1	T51.0X2	T51.0X3	T51.0X4	—	—
Dendrid	T49.5X1	T49.5X2	T49.5X3	T49.5X4	T49.5X5	T49.5X6
Dental drug, topical application NEC	T49.7X1	T49.7X2	T49.7X3	T49.7X4	T49.7X5	T49.7X6

Substance	Poisoning, Accidental (Unintentional)	Poisoning, Intentional Self-Harm	Poisoning, Assault	Poisoning, Undetermined	Adverse Effect	Underdosing
Dentifrice	T49.7X1	T49.7X2	T49.7X3	T49.7X4	T49.7X5	T49.7X6
Deodorant spray (feminine hygiene)	T49.8X1	T49.8X2	T49.8X3	T49.8X4	T49.8X5	T49.8X6
Deoxycortone	T50.0X1	T50.0X2	T50.0X3	T50.0X4	T50.0X5	T50.0X6
2-Deoxy-5-fluorouridine	T45.1X1	T45.1X2	T45.1X3	T45.1X4	T45.1X5	T45.1X6
5-Deoxy-5-fluorouridine	T45.1X1	T45.1X2	T45.1X3	T45.1X4	T45.1X5	T45.1X6
Deoxyribonuclease (pancreatic)	T45.3X1	T45.3X2	T45.3X3	T45.3X4	T45.3X5	T45.3X6
Depilatory	T49.4X1	T49.4X2	T49.4X3	T49.4X4	T49.4X5	T49.4X6
Deprenalin	T42.8X1	T42.8X2	T42.8X3	T42.8X4	T42.8X5	T42.8X6
Deprenyl	T42.8X1	T42.8X2	T42.8X3	T42.8X4	T42.8X5	T42.8X6
Depressant, appetite	T50.5X1	T50.5X2	T50.5X3	T50.5X4	T50.5X5	T50.5X6
Depressant						
appetite, central	T50.5X1	T50.5X2	T50.5X3	T50.5X4	T50.5X5	T50.5X6
cardiac	T46.2X1	T46.2X2	T46.2X3	T46.2X4	T46.2X5	T46.2X6
central nervous system (anesthetic) — see also Central nervous system, depressants	T42.71	T42.72	T42.73	T42.74	T42.75	T42.76
general anesthetic	T41.201	T41.202	T41.203	T41.204	T41.205	T41.206
muscle tone	T42.8X1	T42.8X2	T42.8X3	T42.8X4	T42.8X5	T42.8X6
muscle tone, central	T42.8X1	T42.8X2	T42.8X3	T42.8X4	T42.8X5	T42.8X6
psychotherapeutic	T43.501	T43.502	T43.503	T43.504	T43.505	T43.506
Deptropine	T45.0X1	T45.0X2	T45.0X3	T45.0X4	T45.0X5	T45.0X6
Dequalinium (chloride)	T49.0X1	T49.0X2	T49.0X3	T49.0X4	T49.0X5	T49.0X6
Derris root	T60.2X1	T60.2X2	T60.2X3	T60.2X4	—	—
Deserpidine	T43.011	T43.012	T43.013	T43.014	T43.015	T43.016
Desferrioxamine	T45.8X1	T45.8X2	T45.8X3	T45.8X4	T45.8X5	T45.8X6
Desipramine	T43.0X1	T43.0X2	T43.0X3	T43.0X4	T43.0X5	T43.0X6
Deslanoside	T46.0X1	T46.0X2	T46.0X3	T46.0X4	T46.0X5	T46.0X6
Desloughing agent	T49.4X1	T49.4X2	T49.4X3	T49.4X4	T49.4X5	T49.4X6
Desmethylimipramine	T43.011	T43.012	T43.013	T43.014	T43.015	T43.016
Desmopressin	T38.891	T38.892	T38.893	T38.894	T38.895	T38.896
Desocodeine	T40.2X1	T40.2X2	T40.2X3	T40.2X4	T40.2X5	T40.2X6
Desogestrel	T38.5X1	T38.5X2	T38.5X3	T38.5X4	T38.5X5	T38.5X6
Desomorphine	T40.2X1	T40.2X2	T40.2X3	T40.2X4	—	—
Desonide	T49.0X1	T49.0X2	T49.0X3	T49.0X4	T49.0X5	T49.0X6
Desoximetasone	T49.0X1	T49.0X2	T49.0X3	T49.0X4	T49.0X5	T49.0X6
Desoxycorticosteroid	T50.0X1	T50.0X2	T50.0X3	T50.0X4	T50.0X5	T50.0X6
Desoxycortone	T50.0X1	T50.0X2	T50.0X3	T50.0X4	T50.0X5	T50.0X6
Desoxyephedrine	T43.621	T43.622	T43.623	T43.624	T43.625	T43.626
Detaxtran	T46.6X1	T46.6X2	T46.6X3	T46.6X4	T46.6X5	T46.6X6
Detergent	T49.2X1	T49.2X2	T49.2X3	T49.2X4	T49.2X5	T49.2X6
external medication	T49.2X1	T49.2X2	T49.2X3	T49.2X4	T49.2X5	T49.2X6
local	T49.2X1	T49.2X2	T49.2X3	T49.2X4	T49.2X5	T49.2X6

◀ New   ◀ Revised   ~~deleted~~ Deleted

Substance	Poisoning, Accidental (Unintentional)	Poisoning, Intentional Self-Harm	Poisoning, Assault	Poisoning, Undetermined	Adverse Effect	Underdosing
Detergent *(Continued)*						
medicinal	T49.2X1	T49.2X2	T49.2X3	T49.2X4	T49.2X5	T49.2X6
nonmedicinal	T55.1X1	T55.1X2	T55.1X3	T55.1X4	—	—
specified NEC	T55.1X1	T55.1X2	T55.1X3	T55.1X4	T55.1X5	T55.1X6
Deterrent, alcohol	T50.6X1	T50.6X2	T50.6X3	T50.6X4	T50.6X5	T50.6X6
Detoxifying agent	T50.6X1	T50.6X2	T50.6X3	T50.6X4	T50.6X5	T50.6X6
Detrothyronine	T38.1X1	T38.1X2	T38.1X3	T38.1X4	T38.1X5	T38.1X6
Dettol (external medication)	T49.0X1	T49.0X2	T49.0X3	T49.0X4	T49.0X5	T49.0X6
Dexamethasone	T38.0X1	T38.0X2	T38.0X3	T38.0X4	T38.0X5	T38.0X6
ENT agent	T49.6X1	T49.6X2	T49.6X3	T49.6X4	T49.6X5	T49.6X6
ophthalmic preparation	T49.5X1	T49.5X2	T49.5X3	T49.5X4	T49.5X5	T49.5X6
topical NEC	T49.0X1	T49.0X2	T49.0X3	T49.0X4	T49.0X5	T49.0X6
Dexamfetamine	T43.621	T43.622	T43.623	T43.624	T43.625	T43.626
Dexamphetamine	T43.621	T43.622	T43.623	T43.624	T43.625	T43.626
Dexbrompheniramine	T45.0X1	T45.0X2	T45.0X3	T45.0X4	T45.0X5	T45.0X6
Dexchlorpheniramine	T45.0X1	T45.0X2	T45.0X3	T45.0X4	T45.0X5	T45.0X6
Dexedrine	T43.621	T43.622	T43.623	T43.624	T43.625	T43.626
Dexetimide	T44.3X1	T44.3X2	T44.3X3	T44.3X4	T44.3X5	T44.3X6
Dexfenfluramine	T50.5X1	T50.5X2	T50.5X3	T50.5X4	T50.5X5	T50.5X6
Dexpanthenol	T45.2X1	T45.2X2	T45.2X3	T45.2X4	T45.2X5	T45.2X6
Dextran (40) (70) (150)	T45.8X1	T45.8X2	T45.8X3	T45.8X4	T45.8X5	T45.8X6
Dextriferron	T45.4X1	T45.4X2	T45.4X3	T45.4X4	T45.4X5	T45.4X6
Dextroamphetamine	T43.621	T43.622	T43.623	T43.624	T43.625	T43.626
Dextro calcium pantothenate	T45.2X1	T45.2X2	T45.2X3	T45.2X4	T45.2X5	T45.2X6
Dextromethorphan	T48.3X1	T48.3X2	T48.3X3	T48.3X4	T48.3X5	T48.3X6
Dextromoramide	T40.491	T40.492	T40.493	T40.494	—	—
topical	T49.8X1	T49.8X2	T49.8X3	T49.8X4	T49.8X5	T49.8X6
Dextro pantothenyl alcohol	T45.2X1	T45.2X2	T45.2X3	T45.2X4	T45.2X5	T45.2X6
Dextropropoxyphene	T40.491	T40.492	T40.493	T40.494	T40.495	T40.496
Dextrorphan	T40.2X1	T40.2X2	T40.2X3	T40.2X4	T40.2X5	T40.2X6
Dextrose	T50.3X1	T50.3X2	T50.3X3	T50.3X4	T50.3X5	T50.3X6
concentrated solution, intravenous	T46.8X1	T46.8X2	T46.8X3	T46.8X4	T46.8X5	T46.8X6
Dextrothyroxin	T38.1X1	T38.1X2	T38.1X3	T38.1X4	T38.1X5	T38.1X6
Dextrothyroxine sodium	T38.1X1	T38.1X2	T38.1X3	T38.1X4	T38.1X5	T38.1X6
DFP	T44.0X1	T44.0X2	T44.0X3	T44.0X4	T44.0X5	T44.0X6
DHE	T37.3X1	T37.3X2	T37.3X3	T37.3X4	T37.3X5	T37.3X6
45	T46.5X1	T46.5X2	T46.5X3	T46.5X4	T46.5X5	T46.5X6
Diabinese	T38.3X1	T38.3X2	T38.3X3	T38.3X4	T38.3X5	T38.3X6
Diacetone alcohol	T52.4X1	T52.4X2	T52.4X3	T52.4X4	—	—
Diacetyl monoxime	T50.991	T50.992	T50.993	T50.994	—	—
Diacetylmorphine	T40.1X1	T40.1X2	T40.1X3	T40.1X4	—	—

Substance	Poisoning, Accidental (Unintentional)	Poisoning, Intentional Self-Harm	Poisoning, Assault	Poisoning, Undetermined	Adverse Effect	Underdosing
Diachylon plaster	T49.4X1	T49.4X2	T49.4X3	T49.4X4	T49.4X5	T49.4X6
Diaethylstilboestrolum	T38.5X1	T38.5X2	T38.5X3	T38.5X4	T38.5X5	T38.5X6
Diagnostic agent NEC	T50.8X1	T50.8X2	T50.8X3	T50.8X4	T50.8X5	T50.8X6
Dial (soap)	T49.2X1	T49.2X2	T49.2X3	T49.2X4	T49.2X5	T49.2X6
sedative	T42.3X1	T42.3X2	T42.3X3	T42.3X4	T42.3X5	T42.3X6
Dialkyl carbonate	T52.91	T52.92	T52.93	T52.94	—	—
Diallylbarbituric acid	T42.3X1	T42.3X2	T42.3X3	T42.3X4	T42.3X5	T42.3X6
Diallymal	T42.3X1	T42.3X2	T42.3X3	T42.3X4	T42.3X5	T42.3X6
Dialysis solution (intraperitoneal)	T50.3X1	T50.3X2	T50.3X3	T50.3X4	T50.3X5	T50.3X6
Diaminodiphenylsulfone	T37.1X1	T37.1X2	T37.1X3	T37.1X4	T37.1X5	T37.1X6
Diamorphine	T40.1X1	T40.1X2	T40.1X3	T40.1X4	—	—
Diamox	T50.2X1	T50.2X2	T50.2X3	T50.2X4	T50.2X5	T50.2X6
Diamthazole	T49.0X1	T49.0X2	T49.0X3	T49.0X4	T49.0X5	T49.0X6
Dianthone	T47.2X1	T47.2X2	T47.2X3	T47.2X4	T47.2X5	T47.2X6
Diaphenylsulfone	T37.0X1	T37.0X2	T37.0X3	T37.0X4	T37.0X5	T37.0X6
Diasone (sodium)	T37.1X1	T37.1X2	T37.1X3	T37.1X4	T37.1X5	T37.1X6
Diastase	T47.5X1	T47.5X2	T47.5X3	T47.5X4	T47.5X5	T47.5X6
Diatrizoate	T50.8X1	T50.8X2	T50.8X3	T50.8X4	T50.8X5	T50.8X6
Diazepam	T42.4X1	T42.4X2	T42.4X3	T42.4X4	T42.4X5	T42.4X6
Diazinon	T60.0X1	T60.0X2	T60.0X3	T60.0X4	—	—
Diazomethane (gas)	T59.891	T59.892	T59.893	T59.894	—	—
Diazoxide	T46.5X1	T46.5X2	T46.5X3	T46.5X4	T46.5X5	T46.5X6
Dibekacin	T36.5X1	T36.5X2	T36.5X3	T36.5X4	T36.5X5	T36.5X6
Dibenamine	T44.6X1	T44.6X2	T44.6X3	T44.6X4	T44.6X5	T44.6X6
Dibenzepin	T43.011	T43.012	T43.013	T43.014	T43.015	T43.016
Dibenzheptropine	T45.0X1	T45.0X2	T45.0X3	T45.0X4	T45.0X5	T45.0X6
Dibenzyline	T44.6X1	T44.6X2	T44.6X3	T44.6X4	T44.6X5	T44.6X6
Diborane (gas)	T59.891	T59.892	T59.893	T59.894	—	—
Dibromochloropropane	T60.8X1	T60.8X2	T60.8X3	T60.8X4	—	—
Dibromodulcitol	T45.1X1	T45.1X2	T45.1X3	T45.1X4	T45.1X5	T45.1X6
Dibromoethane	T53.6X1	T53.6X2	T53.6X3	T53.6X4	—	—
Dibromomannitol	T45.1X1	T45.1X2	T45.1X3	T45.1X4	T45.1X5	T45.1X6
Dibromopropamidine isethionate	T49.0X1	T49.0X2	T49.0X3	T49.0X4	T49.0X5	T49.0X6
Dibrompropamidine	T49.0X1	T49.0X2	T49.0X3	T49.0X4	T49.0X5	T49.0X6
Dibucaine	T41.3X1	T41.3X2	T41.3X3	T41.3X4	T41.3X5	T41.3X6
topical (surface)	T41.3X1	T41.3X2	T41.3X3	T41.3X4	T41.3X5	T41.3X6
Dibunate sodium	T48.3X1	T48.3X2	T48.3X3	T48.3X4	T48.3X5	T48.3X6
Dibutoline sulfate	T44.3X1	T44.3X2	T44.3X3	T44.3X4	T44.3X5	T44.3X6
Dicamba	T60.3X1	T60.3X2	T60.3X3	T60.3X4	—	—
Dicapthon	T60.0X1	T60.0X2	T60.0X3	T60.0X4	—	—
Dichlobenil	T60.3X1	T60.3X2	T60.3X3	T60.3X4	—	—
Dichlone	T60.3X1	T60.3X2	T60.3X3	T60.3X4	—	—

◀ New   ◀ Revised   deleted Deleted

Substance	External Cause (T-Code)					
	Poisoning, Accidental (Unintentional)	Poisoning, Intentional Self-Harm	Poisoning, Assault	Poisoning, Undetermined	Adverse Effect	Underdosing
Dichloralphenozone	T42.6X1	T42.6X2	T42.6X3	T42.6X4	T42.6X5	T42.6X6
Dichlorbenzidine	T65.3X1	T65.3X2	T65.3X3	T65.3X4	—	—
Dichlorhydrin	T52.8X1	T52.8X2	T52.8X3	T52.8X4	—	—
Dichlorhydroxyquinoline	T37.8X1	T37.8X2	T37.8X3	T37.8X4	T37.8X5	T37.8X6
Dichlorobenzene	T53.7X1	T53.7X2	T53.7X3	T53.7X4	—	—
Dichlorobenzyl alcohol	T49.6X1	T49.6X2	T49.6X3	T49.6X4	T49.6X5	T49.6X6
Dichlorodifluoromethane	T53.5X1	T53.5X2	T53.5X3	T53.5X4	—	—
Dichloroethane	T52.8X1	T52.8X2	T52.8X3	T52.8X4	—	—
Sym-Dichloroethyl ether	T53.6X1	T53.6X2	T53.6X3	T53.6X4	—	—
Dichloroethyl sulfide, not in war	T59.891	T59.892	T59.893	T59.894	—	—
Dichloroethylene	T53.6X1	T53.6X2	T53.6X3	T53.6X4	—	—
Dichloroformoxine, not in war	T59.891	T59.892	T59.893	T59.894	—	—
Dichlorohydrin, alpha-dichlorohydrin	T52.8X1	T52.8X2	T52.8X3	T52.8X4	—	—
Dichloromethane (solvent)	T53.4X1	T53.4X2	T53.4X3	T53.4X4	—	—
vapor	T53.4X1	T53.4X2	T53.4X3	T53.4X4	—	—
Dichloronaphthoquinone	T60.3X1	T60.3X2	T60.3X3	T60.3X4	—	—
Dichlorophen	T37.4X1	T37.4X2	T37.4X3	T37.4X4	T37.4X5	T37.4X6
2,4-Dichlorophenoxy-acetic acid	T60.3X1	T60.3X2	T60.3X3	T60.3X4	—	—
Dichloropropene	T60.3X1	T60.3X2	T60.3X3	T60.3X4	—	—
Dichloropropionic acid	T60.3X1	T60.3X2	T60.3X3	T60.3X4	—	—
Dichlorphenamide	T50.2X1	T50.2X2	T50.2X3	T50.2X4	T50.2X5	T50.2X6
Dichlorvos	T60.0X1	T60.0X2	T60.0X3	T60.0X4	—	—
Diclofenac	T39.391	T39.392	T39.393	T39.394	T39.395	T39.396
Diclofenamide	T50.2X1	T50.2X2	T50.2X3	T50.2X4	T50.2X5	T50.2X6
Diclofensine	T43.291	T43.292	T43.293	T43.294	T43.295	T43.296
Diclonixine	T39.8X1	T39.8X2	T39.8X3	T39.8X4	T39.8X5	T39.8X6
Dicloxacillin	T36.0X1	T36.0X2	T36.0X3	T36.0X4	T36.0X5	T36.0X6
Dicophane	T49.0X1	T49.0X2	T49.0X3	T49.0X4	T49.0X5	T49.0X6
Dicoumarol, dicoumarin, dicumarol	T45.511	T45.512	T45.513	T45.514	T45.515	T45.516
Dicrotophos	T60.0X1	T60.0X2	T60.0X3	T60.0X4	—	—
Dicyanogen (gas)	T65.0X1	T65.0X2	T65.0X3	T65.0X4	—	—
Dicyclomine	T44.3X1	T44.3X2	T44.3X3	T44.3X4	T44.3X5	T44.3X6
Dicycloverine	T44.3X1	T44.3X2	T44.3X3	T44.3X4	T44.3X5	T44.3X6
Dideoxycytidine	T37.5X1	T37.5X2	T37.5X3	T37.5X4	T37.5X5	T37.5X6
Dideoxyinosine	T37.5X1	T37.5X2	T37.5X3	T37.5X4	T37.5X5	T37.5X6
Dieldrin (vapor)	T60.1X1	T60.1X2	T60.1X3	T60.1X4	—	—
Diemal	T42.3X1	T42.3X2	T42.3X3	T42.3X4	T42.3X5	T42.3X6
Dienestrol	T38.5X1	T38.5X2	T38.5X3	T38.5X4	T38.5X5	T38.5X6
Dienoestrol	T38.5X1	T38.5X2	T38.5X3	T38.5X4	T38.5X5	T38.5X6
Dietetic drug NEC	T50.901	T50.902	T50.903	T50.904	T50.905	T50.906
Diethazine	T42.8X1	T42.8X2	T42.8X3	T42.8X4	T42.8X5	T42.8X6

Substance	External Cause (T-Code)					
	Poisoning, Accidental (Unintentional)	Poisoning, Intentional Self-Harm	Poisoning, Assault	Poisoning, Undetermined	Adverse Effect	Underdosing
Diethyl						
barbituric acid	T42.3X1	T42.3X2	T42.3X3	T42.3X4	T42.3X5	T42.3X6
carbamazine	T37.4X1	T37.4X2	T37.4X3	T37.4X4	T37.4X5	T37.4X6
carbinol	T51.3X1	T51.3X2	T51.3X3	T51.3X4	—	—
carbonate	T52.8X1	T52.8X2	T52.8X3	T52.8X4	—	—
ether (vapor) — see also Ether	T41.0X1	T41.0X2	T41.0X3	T41.0X4	T41.0X5	T41.0X6
oxide	T52.8X1	T52.8X2	T52.8X3	T52.8X4	—	—
propion	T50.5X1	T50.5X2	T50.5X3	T50.5X4	T50.5X5	T50.5X6
stilbestrol	T38.5X1	T38.5X2	T38.5X3	T38.5X4	T38.5X5	T38.5X6
toluamide (nonmedicinal)	T60.8X1	T60.8X2	T60.8X3	T60.8X4	—	—
medicinal	T49.3X1	T49.3X2	T49.3X3	T49.3X4	T49.3X5	T49.3X6
Diethylcarbamazine	T37.4X1	T37.4X2	T37.4X3	T37.4X4	T37.4X5	T37.4X6
Diethylene						
dioxide	T52.8X1	T52.8X2	T52.8X3	T52.8X4	—	—
glycol (monoacetate) (monobutyl ether) (monoethyl ether)	T52.3X1	T52.3X2	T52.3X3	T52.3X4	—	—
Diethylhexylphthalate	T65.891	T65.892	T65.893	T65.894	—	—
Diethylpropion	T50.5X1	T50.5X2	T50.5X3	T50.5X4	T50.5X5	T50.5X6
Diethylstilbestrol	T38.5X1	T38.5X2	T38.5X3	T38.5X4	T38.5X5	T38.5X6
Diethylstilboestrol	T38.5X1	T38.5X2	T38.5X3	T38.5X4	T38.5X5	T38.5X6
Diethylsulfone-diethylmethane	T42.6X1	T42.6X2	T42.6X3	T42.6X4	T42.6X5	T42.6X6
Diethyltoluamide	T49.0X1	T49.0X2	T49.0X3	T49.0X4	T49.0X5	T49.0X6
Diethyltryptamine (DET)	T40.991	T40.992	T40.993	T40.994	—	—
Difebarbamate	T42.3X1	T42.3X2	T42.3X3	T42.3X4	T42.3X5	T42.3X6
Difencloxazine	T40.2X1	T40.2X2	T40.2X3	T40.2X4	T40.2X5	T40.2X6
Difenidol	T45.0X1	T45.0X2	T45.0X3	T45.0X4	T45.0X5	T45.0X6
Difenoxin	T47.6X1	T47.6X2	T47.6X3	T47.6X4	T47.6X5	T47.6X6
Difetarsone	T37.3X1	T37.3X2	T37.3X3	T37.3X4	T37.3X5	T37.3X6
Diffusin	T45.3X1	T45.3X2	T45.3X3	T45.3X4	T45.3X5	T45.3X6
Diflorasone	T49.0X1	T49.0X2	T49.0X3	T49.0X4	T49.0X5	T49.0X6
Diflubenzuron	T60.1X1	T60.1X2	T60.1X3	T60.1X4	—	—
Diflos	T44.0X1	T44.0X2	T44.0X3	T44.0X4	T44.0X5	T44.0X6
Diflucortolone	T49.0X1	T49.0X2	T49.0X3	T49.0X4	T49.0X5	T49.0X6
Diflunisal	T39.091	T39.092	T39.093	T39.094	T39.095	T39.096
Difluoromethyldopa	T42.8X1	T42.8X2	T42.8X3	T42.8X4	T42.8X5	T42.8X6
Difluorophate	T44.0X1	T44.0X2	T44.0X3	T44.0X4	T44.0X5	T44.0X6
Digestant NEC	T47.5X1	T47.5X2	T47.5X3	T47.5X4	T47.5X5	T47.5X6
Digitalin(e)	T46.0X1	T46.0X2	T46.0X3	T46.0X4	T46.0X5	T46.0X6
Digitalis (leaf) (glycoside)	T46.0X1	T46.0X2	T46.0X3	T46.0X4	T46.0X5	T46.0X6
lanata	T46.0X1	T46.0X2	T46.0X3	T46.0X4	T46.0X5	T46.0X6
purpurea	T46.0X1	T46.0X2	T46.0X3	T46.0X4	T46.0X5	T46.0X6
Digitoxin	T46.0X1	T46.0X2	T46.0X3	T46.0X4	T46.0X5	T46.0X6

◀ New ◀ Revised deleted Deleted

Substance	Poisoning, Accidental (Unintentional)	Poisoning, Intentional Self-Harm	Poisoning, Assault	Poisoning, Undetermined	Adverse Effect	Underdosing
Digitoxose	T46.0X1	T46.0X2	T46.0X3	T46.0X4	T46.0X5	T46.0X6
Digoxin	T46.0X1	T46.0X2	T46.0X3	T46.0X4	T46.0X5	T46.0X6
Digoxine	T46.0X1	T46.0X2	T46.0X3	T46.0X4	T46.0X5	T46.0X6
Dihydralazine	T46.5X1	T46.5X2	T46.5X3	T46.5X4	T46.5X5	T46.5X6
Dihydrazine	T46.5X1	T46.5X2	T46.5X3	T46.5X4	T46.5X5	T46.5X6
Dihydrocodeinone	T40.2X1	T40.2X2	T40.2X3	T40.2X4	T40.2X5	T40.2X6
Dihydroergocornine	T46.7X1	T46.7X2	T46.7X3	T46.7X4	T46.7X5	T46.7X6
Dihydroergocristine (mesilate)	T46.7X1	T46.7X2	T46.7X3	T46.7X4	T46.7X5	T46.7X6
Dihydroergokryptine	T46.7X1	T46.7X2	T46.7X3	T46.7X4	T46.7X5	T46.7X6
Dihydroergotamine	T46.5X1	T46.5X2	T46.5X3	T46.5X4	T46.5X5	T46.5X6
Dihydroergotoxine	T46.7X1	T46.7X2	T46.7X3	T46.7X4	T46.7X5	T46.7X6
mesilate	T46.7X1	T46.7X2	T46.7X3	T46.7X4	T46.7X5	T46.7X6
Dihydrohydroxycodein-one	T40.2X1	T40.2X2	T40.2X3	T40.2X4	T40.2X5	T40.2X6
Dihydrohydroxymorphinone	T40.2X1	T40.2X2	T40.2X3	T40.2X4	T40.2X5	T40.2X6
Dihydroisocodeine	T40.2X1	T40.2X2	T40.2X3	T40.2X4	T40.2X5	T40.2X6
Dihydromorphine	T40.2X1	T40.2X2	T40.2X3	T40.2X4	—	—
Dihydromorphinone	T40.2X1	T40.2X2	T40.2X3	T40.2X4	T40.2X5	T40.2X6
Dihydrostreptomycin	T36.5X1	T36.5X2	T36.5X3	T36.5X4	T36.5X5	T36.5X6
Dihydrotachysterol	T45.2X1	T45.2X2	T45.2X3	T45.2X4	T45.2X5	T45.2X6
Dihydroxyaluminum aminoacetate	T47.1X1	T47.1X2	T47.1X3	T47.1X4	T47.1X5	T47.1X6
Dihydroxyaluminum sodium carbonate	T47.1X1	T47.1X2	T47.1X3	T47.1X4	T47.1X5	T47.1X6
Dihydroxyanthraquinone	T47.2X1	T47.2X2	T47.2X3	T47.2X4	T47.2X5	T47.2X6
Dihydroxycodeinone	T40.2X1	T40.2X2	T40.2X3	T40.2X4	T40.2X5	T40.2X6
Dihydroxypropyl theophylline	T50.2X1	T50.2X2	T50.2X3	T50.2X4	T50.2X5	T50.2X6
Diiodohydroxyquin	T37.8X1	T37.8X2	T37.8X3	T37.8X4	T37.8X5	T37.8X6
topical	T49.0X1	T49.0X2	T49.0X3	T49.0X4	T49.0X5	T49.0X6
Diiodohydroxyquinoline	T37.8X1	T37.8X2	T37.8X3	T37.8X4	T37.8X5	T37.8X6
Diiodotyrosine	T38.2X1	T38.2X2	T38.2X3	T38.2X4	T38.2X5	T38.2X6
Diisopromine	T44.3X1	T44.3X2	T44.3X3	T44.3X4	T44.3X5	T44.3X6
Diisopropylamine	T46.3X1	T46.3X2	T46.3X3	T46.3X4	T46.3X5	T46.3X6
Diisopropylfluorophosphonate	T44.0X1	T44.0X2	T44.0X3	T44.0X4	T44.0X5	T44.0X6
Dilantin	T42.0X1	T42.0X2	T42.0X3	T42.0X4	T42.0X5	T42.0X6
Dilaudid	T40.2X1	T40.2X2	T40.2X3	T40.2X4	T40.2X5	T40.2X6
Dilazep	T46.3X1	T46.3X2	T46.3X3	T46.3X4	T46.3X5	T46.3X6
Dill	T47.5X1	T47.5X2	T47.5X3	T47.5X4	T47.5X5	T47.5X6
Diloxanide	T37.3X1	T37.3X2	T37.3X3	T37.3X4	T37.3X5	T37.3X6
Diltiazem	T46.1X1	T46.1X2	T46.1X3	T46.1X4	T46.1X5	T46.1X6
Dimazole	T49.0X1	T49.0X2	T49.0X3	T49.0X4	T49.0X5	T49.0X6
Dimefline	T50.7X1	T50.7X2	T50.7X3	T50.7X4	T50.7X5	T50.7X6
Dimefox	T60.0X1	T60.0X2	T60.0X3	T60.0X4	—	—

Substance	Poisoning, Accidental (Unintentional)	Poisoning, Intentional Self-Harm	Poisoning, Assault	Poisoning, Undetermined	Adverse Effect	Underdosing
Dimemorfan	T48.3X1	T48.3X2	T48.3X3	T48.3X4	T48.3X5	T48.3X6
Dimenhydrinate	T45.0X1	T45.0X2	T45.0X3	T45.0X4	T45.0X5	T45.0X6
Dimercaprol (British anti-lewisite)	T45.8X1	T45.8X2	T45.8X3	T45.8X4	T45.8X5	T45.8X6
Dimercaptopropanol	T45.8X1	T45.8X2	T45.8X3	T45.8X4	T45.8X5	T45.8X6
Dimestrol	T38.5X1	T38.5X2	T38.5X3	T38.5X4	T38.5X5	T38.5X6
Dimetane	T45.0X1	T45.0X2	T45.0X3	T45.0X4	T45.0X5	T45.0X6
Dimethicone	T47.1X1	T47.1X2	T47.1X3	T47.1X4	T47.1X5	T47.1X6
Dimethindene	T45.0X1	T45.0X2	T45.0X3	T45.0X4	T45.0X5	T45.0X6
Dimethisoquin	T49.1X1	T49.1X2	T49.1X3	T49.1X4	T49.1X5	T49.1X6
Dimethisterone	T38.5X1	T38.5X2	T38.5X3	T38.5X4	T38.5X5	T38.5X6
Dimethoate	T60.0X1	T60.0X2	T60.0X3	T60.0X4	—	—
Dimethocaine	T41.3X1	T41.3X2	T41.3X3	T41.3X4	T41.3X5	T41.3X6
Dimethoxanate	T48.3X1	T48.3X2	T48.3X3	T48.3X4	T48.3X5	T48.3X6
Dimethyl						
arsine, arsinic acid	T57.0X1	T57.0X2	T57.0X3	T57.0X4	—	—
carbinol	T51.2X1	T51.2X2	T51.2X3	T51.2X4	—	—
carbonate	T52.8X1	T52.8X2	T52.8X3	T52.8X4	—	—
diguanide	T38.3X1	T38.3X2	T38.3X3	T38.3X4	T38.3X5	T38.3X6
ketone	T52.4X1	T52.4X2	T52.4X3	T52.4X4	—	—
vapor	T52.4X1	T52.4X2	T52.4X3	T52.4X4	—	—
meperidine	T40.2X1	T40.2X2	T40.2X3	T40.2X4	T40.2X5	T40.2X6
parathion	T60.0X1	T60.0X2	T60.0X3	T60.0X4	—	—
phthlate	T49.3X1	T49.3X2	T49.3X3	T49.3X4	T49.3X5	T49.3X6
polysiloxane	T47.8X1	T47.8X2	T47.8X3	T47.8X4	T47.8X5	T47.8X6
sulfate (fumes)	T59.891	T59.892	T59.893	T59.894	—	—
liquid	T65.891	T65.892	T65.893	T65.894	—	—
sulfoxide (nonmedicinal)	T52.8X1	T52.8X2	T52.8X3	T52.8X4	—	—
medicinal	T49.4X1	T49.4X2	T49.4X3	T49.4X4	T49.4X5	T49.4X6
tryptamine	T40.991	T40.992	T40.993	T40.994	—	—
tubocurarine	T48.1X1	T48.1X2	T48.1X3	T48.1X4	T48.1X5	T48.1X6
Dimethylamine sulfate	T49.4X1	T49.4X2	T49.4X3	T49.4X4	T49.4X5	T49.4X6
Dimethylformamide	T52.8X1	T52.8X2	T52.8X3	T52.8X4	—	—
Dimethyltubocurarinium chloride	T48.1X1	T48.1X2	T48.1X3	T48.1X4	T48.1X5	T48.1X6
Dimeticone	T47.1X1	T47.1X2	T47.1X3	T47.1X4	T47.1X5	T47.1X6
Dimetilan	T60.0X1	T60.0X2	T60.0X3	T60.0X4	—	—
Dimetindene	T45.0X1	T45.0X2	T45.0X3	T45.0X4	T45.0X5	T45.0X6
Dimetotiazine	T43.3X1	T43.3X2	T43.3X3	T43.3X4	T43.3X5	T43.3X6
Dimorpholamine	T50.7X1	T50.7X2	T50.7X3	T50.7X4	T50.7X5	T50.7X6
Dimoxyline	T46.3X1	T46.3X2	T46.3X3	T46.3X4	T46.3X5	T46.3X6
Dinitrobenzene	T65.3X1	T65.3X2	T65.3X3	T65.3X4	—	—
vapor	T59.891	T59.892	T59.893	T59.894	—	—

TABLE OF DRUGS AND CHEMICALS

TABLE OF DRUGS AND CHEMICALS

Substance	External Cause (T-Code) Poisoning, Accidental (Unintentional)	Poisoning, Intentional Self-Harm	Poisoning, Assault	Poisoning, Undetermined	Adverse Effect	Underdosing
Dinitrobenzol	T65.3X1	T65.3X2	T65.3X3	T65.3X4	—	—
vapor	T59.891	T59.892	T59.893	T59.894	—	—
Dinitrobutylphenol	T65.3X1	T65.3X2	T65.3X3	T65.3X4	—	—
Dinitro (-ortho-)cresol (pesticide) (spray)	T65.3X1	T65.3X2	T65.3X3	T65.3X4	—	—
Dinitrocyclohexylphenol	T65.3X1	T65.3X2	T65.3X3	T65.3X4	—	—
Dinitrophenol	T65.3X1	T65.3X2	T65.3X3	T65.3X4	—	—
Dinoprost	T48.0X1	T48.0X2	T48.0X3	T48.0X4	T48.0X5	T48.0X6
Dinoprostone	T48.0X1	T48.0X2	T48.0X3	T48.0X4	T48.0X5	T48.0X6
Dinoseb	T60.3X1	T60.3X2	T60.3X3	T60.3X4	—	—
Dioctyl sulfosuccinate (calcium) (sodium)	T47.4X1	T47.4X2	T47.4X3	T47.4X4	T47.4X5	T47.4X6
Diodone	T50.8X1	T50.8X2	T50.8X3	T50.8X4	T50.8X5	T50.8X6
Diodoquin	T37.8X1	T37.8X2	T37.8X3	T37.8X4	T37.8X5	T37.8X6
Dionin	T40.2X1	T40.2X2	T40.2X3	T40.2X4	T40.2X5	T40.2X6
Diosmin	T46.991	T46.992	T46.993	T46.994	T46.995	T46.996
Dioxane	T52.8X1	T52.8X2	T52.8X3	T52.8X4	—	—
Dioxathion	T60.0X1	T60.0X2	T60.0X3	T60.0X4	—	—
Dioxin	T53.7X1	T53.7X2	T53.7X3	T53.7X4	—	—
Dioxopromethazine	T43.3X1	T43.3X2	T43.3X3	T43.3X4	T43.3X5	T43.3X6
Dioxyline	T46.3X1	T46.3X2	T46.3X3	T46.3X4	T46.3X5	T46.3X6
Dipentene	T52.8X1	T52.8X2	T52.8X3	T52.8X4	—	—
Diperodon	T41.3X1	T41.3X2	T41.3X3	T41.3X4	T41.3X5	T41.3X6
Diphacinone	T60.4X1	T60.4X2	T60.4X3	T60.4X4	—	—
Diphemanil	T44.3X1	T44.3X2	T44.3X3	T44.3X4	T44.3X5	T44.3X6
metilsulfate	T44.3X1	T44.3X2	T44.3X3	T44.3X4	T44.3X5	T44.3X6
Diphenadione	T45.511	T45.512	T45.513	T45.514	T45.515	T45.516
rodenticide	T60.4X1	T60.4X2	T60.4X3	T60.4X4	—	—
Diphenhydramine	T45.0X1	T45.0X2	T45.0X3	T45.0X4	T45.0X5	T45.0X6
Diphenidol	T45.0X1	T45.0X2	T45.0X3	T45.0X4	T45.0X5	T45.0X6
Diphenoxylate	T47.6X1	T47.6X2	T47.6X3	T47.6X4	T47.6X5	T47.6X6
Diphenylamine	T65.3X1	T65.3X2	T65.3X3	T65.3X4	—	—
Diphenylbutazone	T39.2X1	T39.2X2	T39.2X3	T39.2X4	T39.2X5	T39.2X6
Diphenylchloroarsine, not in war	T57.0X1	T57.0X2	T57.0X3	T57.0X4	—	—
Diphenylhydantoin	T42.0X1	T42.0X2	T42.0X3	T42.0X4	T42.0X5	T42.0X6
Diphenylmethane dye	T52.1X1	T52.1X2	T52.1X3	T52.1X4	—	—
Diphenylpyraline	T45.0X1	T45.0X2	T45.0X3	T45.0X4	T45.0X5	T45.0X6
Diphtheria						
antitoxin	T50.Z11	T50.Z12	T50.Z13	T50.Z14	T50.Z15	T50.Z16
toxoid	T50.A91	T50.A92	T50.A93	T50.A94	T50.A95	T50.A96
with tetanus toxoid	T50.A21	T50.A22	T50.A23	T50.A24	T50.A25	T50.A26
with pertussis component	T50.A11	T50.A12	T50.A13	T50.A14	T50.A15	T50.A16

Substance	External Cause (T-Code) Poisoning, Accidental (Unintentional)	Poisoning, Intentional Self-Harm	Poisoning, Assault	Poisoning, Undetermined	Adverse Effect	Underdosing
Diphtheria (Continued)						
vaccine (combination)	T50.A91	T50.A92	T50.A93	T50.A94	T50.A95	T50.A96
combination						
including pertussis	T50.A11	T50.A12	T50.A13	T50.A14	T50.A15	T50.A16
without pertussis	T50.A21	T50.A22	T50.A23	T50.A24	T50.A25	T50.A26
Diphylline	T50.2X1	T50.2X2	T50.2X3	T50.2X4	T50.2X5	T50.2X6
Dipipanone	T40.491	T40.492	T40.493	T40.494	—	—
Dipivefrine	T49.5X1	T49.5X2	T49.5X3	T49.5X4	T49.5X5	T49.5X6
Diplovax	T50.B91	T50.B92	T50.B93	T50.B94	T50.B95	T50.B96
Diprophylline	T50.2X1	T50.2X2	T50.2X3	T50.2X4	T50.2X5	T50.2X6
Dipropyline	T48.291	T48.292	T48.293	T48.294	T48.295	T48.296
Dipyridamole	T46.3X1	T46.3X2	T46.3X3	T46.3X4	T46.3X5	T46.3X6
Dipyrone	T39.2X1	T39.2X2	T39.2X3	T39.2X4	T39.2X5	T39.2X6
Diquat (dibromide)	T60.3X1	T60.3X2	T60.3X3	T60.3X4	—	—
Disinfectant	T65.891	T65.892	T65.893	T65.894	—	—
alkaline	T54.3X1	T54.3X2	T54.3X3	T54.3X4	—	—
aromatic	T54.1X1	T54.1X2	T54.1X3	T54.1X4	—	—
intestinal	T37.8X1	T37.8X2	T37.8X3	T37.8X4	T37.8X5	T37.8X6
Disipal	T42.8X1	T42.8X2	T42.8X3	T42.8X4	T42.8X5	T42.8X6
Disodium edetate	T50.6X1	T50.6X2	T50.6X3	T50.6X4	T50.6X5	T50.6X6
Disoprofol	T41.291	T41.292	T41.293	T41.294	T41.295	T41.296
Disopyramide	T46.2X1	T46.2X2	T46.2X3	T46.2X4	T46.2X5	T46.2X6
Distigmine (bromide)	T44.0X1	T44.0X2	T44.0X3	T44.0X4	T44.0X5	T44.0X6
Disulfamide	T50.2X1	T50.2X2	T50.2X3	T50.2X4	T50.2X5	T50.2X6
Disulfanilamide	T37.0X1	T37.0X2	T37.0X3	T37.0X4	T37.0X5	T37.0X6
Disulfiram	T50.6X1	T50.6X2	T50.6X3	T50.6X4	T50.6X5	T50.6X6
Disulfoton	T60.0X1	T60.0X2	T60.0X3	T60.0X4	—	—
Dithiazanine iodide	T37.4X1	T37.4X2	T37.4X3	T37.4X4	T37.4X5	T37.4X6
Dithiocarbamate	T60.0X1	T60.0X2	T60.0X3	T60.0X4	—	—
Dithranol	T49.4X1	T49.4X2	T49.4X3	T49.4X4	T49.4X5	T49.4X6
Diucardin	T50.2X1	T50.2X2	T50.2X3	T50.2X4	T50.2X5	T50.2X6
Diupres	T50.2X1	T50.2X2	T50.2X3	T50.2X4	T50.2X5	T50.2X6
Diuretic NEC	T50.2X1	T50.2X2	T50.2X3	T50.2X4	T50.2X5	T50.2X6
benzothiadiazine	T50.2X1	T50.2X2	T50.2X3	T50.2X4	T50.2X5	T50.2X6
carbonic acid anhydrase inhibitors	T50.2X1	T50.2X2	T50.2X3	T50.2X4	T50.2X5	T50.2X6
furfuryl NEC	T50.2X1	T50.2X2	T50.2X3	T50.2X4	T50.2X5	T50.2X6
loop (high-ceiling)	T50.1X1	T50.1X2	T50.1X3	T50.1X4	T50.1X5	T50.1X6
mercurial NEC	T50.2X1	T50.2X2	T50.2X3	T50.2X4	T50.2X5	T50.2X6
osmotic	T50.2X1	T50.2X2	T50.2X3	T50.2X4	T50.2X5	T50.2X6
purine NEC	T50.2X1	T50.2X2	T50.2X3	T50.2X4	T50.2X5	T50.2X6
saluretic NEC	T50.2X1	T50.2X2	T50.2X3	T50.2X4	T50.2X5	T50.2X6

◀ New ◀ Revised ~~deleted~~ Deleted

Substance	External Cause (T-Code) Poisoning, Accidental (Unintentional)	Poisoning, Intentional Self-Harm	Poisoning, Assault	Poisoning, Undetermined	Adverse Effect	Underdosing
Diuretic NEC *(Continued)*						
sulfonamide	T50.2X1	T50.2X2	T50.2X3	T50.2X4	T50.2X5	T50.2X6
thiazide NEC	T50.2X1	T50.2X2	T50.2X3	T50.2X4	T50.2X5	T50.2X6
xanthine	T50.2X1	T50.2X2	T50.2X3	T50.2X4	T50.2X5	T50.2X6
Diurgin	T50.2X1	T50.2X2	T50.2X3	T50.2X4	T50.2X5	T50.2X6
Diuril	T50.2X1	T50.2X2	T50.2X3	T50.2X4	T50.2X5	T50.2X6
Diuron	T60.3X1	T60.3X2	T60.3X3	T60.3X4	—	—
Divalproex	T42.6X1	T42.6X2	T42.6X3	T42.6X4	T42.6X5	T42.6X6
Divinyl ether	T41.0X1	T41.0X2	T41.0X3	T41.0X4	T41.0X5	T41.0X6
Dixanthogen	T49.0X1	T49.0X2	T49.0X3	T49.0X4	T49.0X5	T49.0X6
Dixyrazine	T43.3X1	T43.3X2	T43.3X3	T43.3X4	T43.3X5	T43.3X6
D-lysergic acid diethylamide	T40.8X1	T40.8X2	T40.8X3	T40.8X4	—	—
DMCT	T36.4X1	T36.4X2	T36.4X3	T36.4X4	T36.4X5	T36.4X6
DMSO — *see Dimethyl sulfoxide*						
DNBP	T60.3X1	T60.3X2	T60.3X3	T60.3X4		
DNOC	T65.3X1	T65.3X2	T65.3X3	T65.3X4	—	—
DOCA	T38.0X1	T38.0X2	T38.0X3	T38.0X4	T38.0X5	T38.0X6
Dobutamine	T44.5X1	T44.5X2	T44.5X3	T44.5X4	T44.5X5	T44.5X6
Docusate sodium	T47.4X1	T47.4X2	T47.4X3	T47.4X4	T47.4X5	T47.4X6
Dodicin	T49.0X1	T49.0X2	T49.0X3	T49.0X4	T49.0X5	T49.0X6
Dofamium chloride	T49.0X1	T49.0X2	T49.0X3	T49.0X4	T49.0X5	T49.0X6
Dolophine	T40.3X1	T40.3X2	T40.3X3	T40.3X4	T40.3X5	T40.3X6
Doloxene	T39.8X1	T39.8X2	T39.8X3	T39.8X4	T39.8X5	T39.8X6
Domestic gas (after combustion) — *see Gas, utility*						
prior to combustion	T59.891	T59.892	T59.893	T59.894	—	—
Domiodol	T48.4X1	T48.4X2	T48.4X3	T48.4X4	T48.4X5	T48.4X6
Domiphen (bromide)	T49.0X1	T49.0X2	T49.0X3	T49.0X4	T49.0X5	T49.0X6
Domperidone	T45.0X1	T45.0X2	T45.0X3	T45.0X4	T45.0X5	T45.0X6
Dopa	T42.8X1	T42.8X2	T42.8X3	T42.8X4	T42.8X5	T42.8X6
Dopamine	T44.991	T44.992	T44.993	T44.994	T44.995	T44.996
Doriden	T42.6X1	T42.6X2	T42.6X3	T42.6X4	T42.6X5	T42.6X6
Dormiral	T42.3X1	T42.3X2	T42.3X3	T42.3X4	T42.3X5	T42.3X6
Dormison	T42.6X1	T42.6X2	T42.6X3	T42.6X4	T42.6X5	T42.6X6
Dornase	T48.4X1	T48.4X2	T48.4X3	T48.4X4	T48.4X5	T48.4X6
Dorsacaine	T41.3X1	T41.3X2	T41.3X3	T41.3X4	T41.3X5	T41.3X6
Dosulepin	T43.011	T43.012	T43.013	T43.014	T43.015	T43.016
Dothiepin	T43.011	T43.012	T43.013	T43.014	T43.015	T43.016
Doxantrazole	T48.6X1	T48.6X2	T48.6X3	T48.6X4	T48.6X5	T48.6X6
Doxapram	T50.7X1	T50.7X2	T50.7X3	T50.7X4	T50.7X5	T50.7X6
Doxazosin	T44.6X1	T44.6X2	T44.6X3	T44.6X4	T44.6X5	T44.6X6
Doxepin	T43.011	T43.012	T43.013	T43.014	T43.015	T43.016

Substance	External Cause (T-Code) Poisoning, Accidental (Unintentional)	Poisoning, Intentional Self-Harm	Poisoning, Assault	Poisoning, Undetermined	Adverse Effect	Underdosing
Doxifluridine	T45.1X1	T45.1X2	T45.1X3	T45.1X4	T45.1X5	T45.1X6
Doxorubicin	T45.1X1	T45.1X2	T45.1X3	T45.1X4	T45.1X5	T45.1X6
Doxycycline	T36.4X1	T36.4X2	T36.4X3	T36.4X4	T36.4X5	T36.4X6
Doxylamine	T45.0X1	T45.0X2	T45.0X3	T45.0X4	T45.0X5	T45.0X6
Dramamine	T45.0X1	T45.0X2	T45.0X3	T45.0X4	T45.0X5	T45.0X6
Drano (drain cleaner)	T54.3X1	T54.3X2	T54.3X3	T54.3X4	—	—
Dressing, live pulp	T49.7X1	T49.7X2	T49.7X3	T49.7X4	T49.7X5	T49.7X6
Drocode	T40.2X1	T40.2X2	T40.2X3	T40.2X4	T40.2X5	T40.2X6
Dromoran	T40.2X1	T40.2X2	T40.2X3	T40.2X4	T40.2X5	T40.2X6
Dromostanolone	T38.7X1	T38.7X2	T38.7X3	T38.7X4	T38.7X5	T38.7X6
Dronabinol	T40.7X1	T40.7X2	T40.7X3	T40.7X4	T40.7X5	T40.7X6
Droperidol	T43.591	T43.592	T43.593	T43.594	T43.595	T43.596
Dropropizine	T48.3X1	T48.3X2	T48.3X3	T48.3X4	T48.3X5	T48.3X6
Drostanolone	T38.7X1	T38.7X2	T38.7X3	T38.7X4	T38.7X5	T38.7X6
Drotaverine	T44.3X1	T44.3X2	T44.3X3	T44.3X4	T44.3X5	T44.3X6
Drotrecogin alfa	T45.511	T45.512	T45.513	T45.514	T45.515	T45.516
Drug NEC	T50.901	T50.902	T50.903	T50.904	T50.905	T50.906
specified NEC	T50.991	T50.992	T50.993	T50.994	T50.995	T50.996
DTIC	T45.1X1	T45.1X2	T45.1X3	T45.1X4	T45.1X5	T45.1X6
Duboisine	T44.3X1	T44.3X2	T44.3X3	T44.3X4	T44.3X5	T44.3X6
Dulcolax	T47.2X1	T47.2X2	T47.2X3	T47.2X4	T47.2X5	T47.2X6
Duponol (C) (EP)	T49.2X1	T49.2X2	T49.2X3	T49.2X4	T49.2X5	T49.2X6
Durabolin	T38.7X1	T38.7X2	T38.7X3	T38.7X4	T38.7X5	T38.7X6
Dyclone	T41.3X1	T41.3X2	T41.3X3	T41.3X4	T41.3X5	T41.3X6
Dyclonine	T41.3X1	T41.3X2	T41.3X3	T41.3X4	T41.3X5	T41.3X6
Dydrogesterone	T38.5X1	T38.5X2	T38.5X3	T38.5X4	T38.5X5	T38.5X6
Dye NEC	T65.6X1	T65.6X2	T65.6X3	T65.6X4	—	—
antiseptic	T49.0X1	T49.0X2	T49.0X3	T49.0X4	T49.0X5	T49.0X6
diagnostic agents	T50.8X1	T50.8X2	T50.8X3	T50.8X4	T50.8X5	T50.8X6
pharmaceutical NEC	T50.901	T50.902	T50.903	T50.904	T50.905	T50.906
Dyflos	T44.0X1	T44.0X2	T44.0X3	T44.0X4	T44.0X5	T44.0X6
Dymelor	T38.3X1	T38.3X2	T38.3X3	T38.3X4	T38.3X5	T38.3X6
Dynamite	T65.3X1	T65.3X2	T65.3X3	T65.3X4	—	—
fumes	T59.891	T59.892	T59.893	T59.894	—	—
Dyphylline	T44.3X1	T44.3X2	T44.3X3	T44.3X4	T44.3X5	T44.3X6
E						
Ear drug NEC	T49.6X1	T49.6X2	T49.6X3	T49.6X4	T49.6X5	T49.6X6
Ear preparations	T49.6X1	T49.6X2	T49.6X3	T49.6X4	T49.6X5	T49.6X6
Econazole	T49.0X1	T49.0X2	T49.0X3	T49.0X4	T49.0X5	T49.0X6
Ecothiopate iodide	T49.5X1	T49.5X2	T49.5X3	T49.5X4	T49.5X5	T49.5X6
Echothiophate, echothiopate, ecothiopate	T49.5X1	T49.5X2	T49.5X3	T49.5X4	T49.5X5	T49.5X6

Substance	External Cause (T-Code)					
	Poisoning, Accidental (Unintentional)	Poisoning, Intentional Self-Harm	Poisoning, Assault	Poisoning, Undetermined	Adverse Effect	Underdosing
Ecstasy	T43.641	T43.642	T43.643	T43.644	—	—
Ectylurea	T42.6X1	T42.6X2	T42.6X3	T42.6X4	T42.6X5	T42.6X6
Edathamil disodium	T45.8X1	T45.8X2	T45.8X3	T45.8X4	T45.8X5	T45.8X6
Edecrin	T50.1X1	T50.1X2	T50.1X3	T50.1X4	T50.1X5	T50.1X6
Edetate, disodium (calcium)	T45.8X1	T45.8X2	T45.8X3	T45.8X4	T45.8X5	T45.8X6
Edoxudine	T49.5X1	T49.5X2	T49.5X3	T49.5X4	T49.5X5	T49.5X6
Edrophonium	T44.0X1	T44.0X2	T44.0X3	T44.0X4	T44.0X5	T44.0X6
chloride	T44.0X1	T44.0X2	T44.0X3	T44.0X4	T44.0X5	T44.0X6
EDTA	T50.6X1	T50.6X2	T50.6X3	T50.6X4	T50.6X5	T50.6X6
Eflornithine	T37.2X1	T37.2X2	T37.2X3	T37.2X4	T37.2X5	T37.2X6
Efloxate	T46.3X1	T46.3X2	T46.3X3	T46.3X4	T46.3X5	T46.3X6
Elase	T49.8X1	T49.8X2	T49.8X3	T49.8X4	T49.8X5	T49.8X6
Elastase	T47.5X1	T47.5X2	T47.5X3	T47.5X4	T47.5X5	T47.5X6
Elaterium	T47.2X1	T47.2X2	T47.2X3	T47.2X4	T47.2X5	T47.2X6
Elcatonin	T50.991	T50.992	T50.993	T50.994	T50.995	T50.996
Elder	T62.2X1	T62.2X2	T62.2X3	T62.2X4	—	—
berry (unripe)	T62.1X1	T62.1X2	T62.1X3	T62.1X4	—	—
Electrolyte balance drug	T50.3X1	T50.3X2	T50.3X3	T50.3X4	T50.3X5	T50.3X6
Electrolytes NEC	T50.3X1	T50.3X2	T50.3X3	T50.3X4	T50.3X5	T50.3X6
Electrolytic agent NEC	T50.3X1	T50.3X2	T50.3X3	T50.3X4	T50.3X5	T50.3X6
Elemental diet	T50.901	T50.902	T50.903	T50.904	T50.905	T50.906
Elliptinium acetate	T45.1X1	T45.1X2	T45.1X3	T45.1X4	T45.1X5	T45.1X6
Embramine	T45.0X1	T45.0X2	T45.0X3	T45.0X4	T45.0X5	T45.0X6
Emepronium (salts)	T44.3X1	T44.3X2	T44.3X3	T44.3X4	T44.3X5	T44.3X6
bromide	T44.3X1	T44.3X2	T44.3X3	T44.3X4	T44.3X5	T44.3X6
Emetic NEC	T47.7X1	T47.7X2	T47.7X3	T47.7X4	T47.7X5	T47.7X6
Emetine	T37.3X1	T37.3X2	T37.3X3	T37.3X4	T37.3X5	T37.3X6
Emollient NEC	T49.3X1	T49.3X2	T49.3X3	T49.3X4	T49.3X5	T49.3X6
Emorfazone	T39.8X1	T39.8X2	T39.8X3	T39.8X4	T39.8X5	T39.8X6
Emylcamate	T43.591	T43.592	T43.593	T43.594	T43.595	T43.596
Enalapril	T46.4X1	T46.4X2	T46.4X3	T46.4X4	T46.4X5	T46.4X6
Enalaprilat	T46.4X1	T46.4X2	T46.4X3	T46.4X4	T46.4X5	T46.4X6
Encainide	T46.2X1	T46.2X2	T46.2X3	T46.2X4	T46.2X5	T46.2X6
Endocaine	T41.3X1	T41.3X2	T41.3X3	T41.3X4	T41.3X5	T41.3X6
Endosulfan	T60.2X1	T60.2X2	T60.2X3	T60.2X4	—	—
Endothall	T60.3X1	T60.3X2	T60.3X3	T60.3X4	—	—
Endralazine	T46.5X1	T46.5X2	T46.5X3	T46.5X4	T46.5X5	T46.5X6
Endrin	T60.1X1	T60.1X2	T60.1X3	T60.1X4	—	—
Enflurane	T41.0X1	T41.0X2	T41.0X3	T41.0X4	T41.0X5	T41.0X6
Enhexymal	T42.3X1	T42.3X2	T42.3X3	T42.3X4	T42.3X5	T42.3X6
Enocitabine	T45.1X1	T45.1X2	T45.1X3	T45.1X4	T45.1X5	T45.1X6
Enovid	T38.4X1	T38.4X2	T38.4X3	T38.4X4	T38.4X5	T38.4X6

Substance	External Cause (T-Code)					
	Poisoning, Accidental (Unintentional)	Poisoning, Intentional Self-Harm	Poisoning, Assault	Poisoning, Undetermined	Adverse Effect	Underdosing
Enoxacin	T36.8X1	T36.8X2	T36.8X3	T36.8X4	T36.8X5	T36.8X6
Enoxaparin (sodium)	T45.511	T45.512	T45.513	T45.514	T45.515	T45.516
Enpiprazole	T43.591	T43.592	T43.593	T43.594	T43.595	T43.596
Enprofylline	T48.6X1	T48.6X2	T48.6X3	T48.6X4	T48.6X5	T48.6X6
Enprostil	T47.1X1	T47.1X2	T47.1X3	T47.1X4	T47.1X5	T47.1X6
ENT preparations (anti-infectives)	T49.6X1	T49.6X2	T49.6X3	T49.6X4	T49.6X5	T49.6X6
Enviomycin	T36.8X1	T36.8X2	T36.8X3	T36.8X4	T36.8X5	T36.8X6
Enzodase	T45.3X1	T45.3X2	T45.3X3	T45.3X4	T45.3X5	T45.3X6
Enzyme NEC	T45.3X1	T45.3X2	T45.3X3	T45.3X4	T45.3X5	T45.3X6
depolymerizing	T49.8X1	T49.8X2	T49.8X3	T49.8X4	T49.8X5	T49.8X6
fibrolytic	T45.3X1	T45.3X2	T45.3X3	T45.3X4	T45.3X5	T45.3X6
gastric	T47.5X1	T47.5X2	T47.5X3	T47.5X4	T47.5X5	T47.5X6
intestinal	T47.5X1	T47.5X2	T47.5X3	T47.5X4	T47.5X5	T47.5X6
local action	T49.4X1	T49.4X2	T49.4X3	T49.4X4	T49.4X5	T49.4X6
proteolytic	T49.4X1	T49.4X2	T49.4X3	T49.4X4	T49.4X5	T49.4X6
thrombolytic	T45.3X1	T45.3X2	T45.3X3	T45.3X4	T45.3X5	T45.3X6
EPAB	T41.3X1	T41.3X2	T41.3X3	T41.3X4	T41.3X5	T41.3X6
Epanutin	T42.0X1	T42.0X2	T42.0X3	T42.0X4	T42.0X5	T42.0X6
Ephedra	T44.991	T44.992	T44.993	T44.994	T44.995	T44.996
Ephedrine	T44.991	T44.992	T44.993	T44.994	T44.995	T44.996
Epichlorhydrin, epichlorohydrin	T52.8X1	T52.8X2	T52.8X3	T52.8X4	—	—
Epicillin	T36.0X1	T36.0X2	T36.0X3	T36.0X4	T36.0X5	T36.0X6
Epiestriol	T38.5X1	T38.5X2	T38.5X3	T38.5X4	T38.5X5	T38.5X6
Epilim — see Sodium valproate						
Epimestrol	T38.5X1	T38.5X2	T38.5X3	T38.5X4	T38.5X5	T38.5X6
Epinephrine	T44.5X1	T44.5X2	T44.5X3	T44.5X4	T44.5X5	T44.5X6
Epirubicin	T45.1X1	T45.1X2	T45.1X3	T45.1X4	T45.1X5	T45.1X6
Epitiostanol	T38.7X1	T38.7X2	T38.7X3	T38.7X4	T38.7X5	T38.7X6
Epitizide	T50.2X1	T50.2X2	T50.2X3	T50.2X4	T50.2X5	T50.2X6
EPN	T60.0X1	T60.0X2	T60.0X3	T60.0X4	—	—
EPO	T45.8X1	T45.8X2	T45.8X3	T45.8X4	T45.8X5	T45.8X6
Epoetin alpha	T45.8X1	T45.8X2	T45.8X3	T45.8X4	T45.8X5	T45.8X6
Epomediol	T50.991	T50.992	T50.993	T50.994	T50.995	T50.996
Epoprostenol	T45.521	T45.522	T45.523	T45.524	T45.525	T45.526
Epoxy resin	T65.891	T65.892	T65.893	T65.894	—	—
Eprazinone	T48.4X1	T48.4X2	T48.4X3	T48.4X4	T48.4X5	T48.4X6
Epsilon amino-caproic acid	T45.621	T45.622	T45.623	T45.624	T45.625	T45.626
Epsom salt	T47.3X1	T47.3X2	T47.3X3	T47.3X4	T47.3X5	T47.3X6
Eptazocine	T40.491	T40.492	T40.493	T40.494	T40.495	T40.496
Equanil	T43.591	T43.592	T43.593	T43.594	T43.595	T43.596
Equisetum	T62.2X1	T62.2X2	T62.2X3	T62.2X4	—	—
diuretic	T50.2X1	T50.2X2	T50.2X3	T50.2X4	T50.2X5	T50.2X6

◀ New   ◀ Revised   ~~deleted~~ Deleted

Substance	Poisoning, Accidental (Unintentional)	Poisoning, Intentional Self-Harm	Poisoning, Assault	Poisoning, Undetermined	Adverse Effect	Underdosing
Ergobasine	T48.0X1	T48.0X2	T48.0X3	T48.0X4	T48.0X5	T48.0X6
Ergocalciferol	T45.2X1	T45.2X2	T45.2X3	T45.2X4	T45.2X5	T45.2X6
Ergoloid mesylates	T46.7X1	T46.7X2	T46.7X3	T46.7X4	T46.7X5	T46.7X6
Ergometrine	T48.0X1	T48.0X2	T48.0X3	T48.0X4	T48.0X5	T48.0X6
Ergonovine	T48.0X1	T48.0X2	T48.0X3	T48.0X4	T48.0X5	T48.0X6
Ergot NEC	T64.81	T64.82	T64.83	T64.84	—	—
derivative	T48.0X1	T48.0X2	T48.0X3	T48.0X4	T48.0X5	T48.0X6
medicinal (alkaloids)	T48.0X1	T48.0X2	T48.0X3	T48.0X4	T48.0X5	T48.0X6
prepared	T48.0X1	T48.0X2	T48.0X3	T48.0X4	T48.0X5	T48.0X6
Ergotamine	T46.5X1	T46.5X2	T46.5X3	T46.5X4	T46.5X5	T46.5X6
Ergotocine	T48.0X1	T48.0X2	T48.0X3	T48.0X4	T48.0X5	T48.0X6
Ergotrate	T48.0X1	T48.0X2	T48.0X3	T48.0X4	T48.0X5	T48.0X6
Eritrityl tetranitrate	T46.3X1	T46.3X2	T46.3X3	T46.3X4	T46.3X5	T46.3X6
Erythrityl tetranitrate	T46.3X1	T46.3X2	T46.3X3	T46.3X4	T46.3X5	T46.3X6
Erythrol tetranitrate	T46.3X1	T46.3X2	T46.3X3	T46.3X4	T46.3X5	T46.3X6
Erythromycin (salts)	T36.3X1	T36.3X2	T36.3X3	T36.3X4	T36.3X5	T36.3X6
ophthalmic preparation	T49.5X1	T49.5X2	T49.5X3	T49.5X4	T49.5X5	T49.5X6
topical NEC	T49.0X1	T49.0X2	T49.0X3	T49.0X4	T49.0X5	T49.0X6
Erythropoietin	T45.8X1	T45.8X2	T45.8X3	T45.8X4	T45.8X5	T45.8X6
human	T45.8X1	T45.8X2	T45.8X3	T45.8X4	T45.8X5	T45.8X6
Escin	T46.991	T46.992	T46.993	T46.994	T46.995	T46.996
Esculin	T45.2X1	T45.2X2	T45.2X3	T45.2X4	T45.2X5	T45.2X6
Esculoside	T45.2X1	T45.2X2	T45.2X3	T45.2X4	T45.2X5	T45.2X6
ESDT (ether-soluble tar distillate)	T49.1X1	T49.1X2	T49.1X3	T49.1X4	T49.1X5	T49.1X6
Eserine	T49.5X1	T49.5X2	T49.5X3	T49.5X4	T49.5X5	T49.5X6
Esflurbiprofen	T39.311	T39.312	T39.313	T39.314	T39.315	T39.316
Eskabarb	T42.3X1	T42.3X2	T42.3X3	T42.3X4	T42.3X5	T42.3X6
Eskalith	T43.8X1	T43.8X2	T43.8X3	T43.8X4	T43.8X5	T43.8X6
Esmolol	T44.7X1	T44.7X2	T44.7X3	T44.7X4	T44.7X5	T44.7X6
Estanozolol	T38.7X1	T38.7X2	T38.7X3	T38.7X4	T38.7X5	T38.7X6
Estazolam	T42.4X1	T42.4X2	T42.4X3	T42.4X4	T42.4X5	T42.4X6
Estradiol	T38.5X1	T38.5X2	T38.5X3	T38.5X4	T38.5X5	T38.5X6
with testosterone	T38.7X1	T38.7X2	T38.7X3	T38.7X4	T38.7X5	T38.7X6
benzoate	T38.5X1	T38.5X2	T38.5X3	T38.5X4	T38.5X5	T38.5X6
Estramustine	T45.1X1	T45.1X2	T45.1X3	T45.1X4	T45.1X5	T45.1X6
Estriol	T38.5X1	T38.5X2	T38.5X3	T38.5X4	T38.5X5	T38.5X6
Estrogen	T38.5X1	T38.5X2	T38.5X3	T38.5X4	T38.5X5	T38.5X6
with progesterone	T38.5X1	T38.5X2	T38.5X3	T38.5X4	T38.5X5	T38.5X6
conjugated	T38.5X1	T38.5X2	T38.5X3	T38.5X4	T38.5X5	T38.5X6
Estrone	T38.5X1	T38.5X2	T38.5X3	T38.5X4	T38.5X5	T38.5X6
Estropipate	T38.5X1	T38.5X2	T38.5X3	T38.5X4	T38.5X5	T38.5X6

Substance	Poisoning, Accidental (Unintentional)	Poisoning, Intentional Self-Harm	Poisoning, Assault	Poisoning, Undetermined	Adverse Effect	Underdosing
Etacrynate sodium	T50.1X1	T50.1X2	T50.1X3	T50.1X4	T50.1X5	T50.1X6
Etacrynic acid	T50.1X1	T50.1X2	T50.1X3	T50.1X4	T50.1X5	T50.1X6
Etafedrine	T48.6X1	T48.6X2	T48.6X3	T48.6X4	T48.6X5	T48.6X6
Etafenone	T46.3X1	T46.3X2	T46.3X3	T46.3X4	T46.3X5	T46.3X6
Etambutol	T37.1X1	T37.1X2	T37.1X3	T37.1X4	T37.1X5	T37.1X6
Etamiphyllin	T48.6X1	T48.6X2	T48.6X3	T48.6X4	T48.6X5	T48.6X6
Etamivan	T50.7X1	T50.7X2	T50.7X3	T50.7X4	T50.7X5	T50.7X6
Etamsylate	T45.7X1	T45.7X2	T45.7X3	T45.7X4	T45.7X5	T45.7X6
Etebenecid	T50.4X1	T50.4X2	T50.4X3	T50.4X4	T50.4X5	T50.4X6
Ethacridine	T49.0X1	T49.0X2	T49.0X3	T49.0X4	T49.0X5	T49.0X6
Ethacrynic acid	T50.1X1	T50.1X2	T50.1X3	T50.1X4	T50.1X5	T50.1X6
Ethadione	T42.2X1	T42.2X2	T42.2X3	T42.2X4	T42.2X5	T42.2X6
Ethambutol	T37.1X1	T37.1X2	T37.1X3	T37.1X4	T37.1X5	T37.1X6
Ethamide	T50.2X1	T50.2X2	T50.2X3	T50.2X4	T50.2X5	T50.2X6
Ethamivan	T50.7X1	T50.7X2	T50.7X3	T50.7X4	T50.7X5	T50.7X6
Ethamsylate	T45.7X1	T45.7X2	T45.7X3	T45.7X4	T45.7X5	T45.7X6
Ethanol	T51.0X1	T51.0X2	T51.0X3	T51.0X4	—	—
beverage	T51.0X1	T51.0X2	T51.0X3	T51.0X4	—	—
Ethanolamine oleate	T46.8X1	T46.8X2	T46.8X3	T46.8X4	T46.8X5	T46.8X6
Ethaverine	T44.3X1	T44.3X2	T44.3X3	T44.3X4	T44.3X5	T44.3X6
Ethchlorvynol	T42.6X1	T42.6X2	T42.6X3	T42.6X4	T42.6X5	T42.6X6
Ethebenecid	T50.4X1	T50.4X2	T50.4X3	T50.4X4	T50.4X5	T50.4X6
Ether (vapor)	T41.0X1	T41.0X2	T41.0X3	T41.0X4	T41.0X5	T41.0X6
anesthetic	T41.0X1	T41.0X2	T41.0X3	T41.0X4	T41.0X5	T41.0X6
divinyl	T41.0X1	T41.0X2	T41.0X3	T41.0X4	T41.0X5	T41.0X6
ethyl (medicinal)	T41.0X1	T41.0X2	T41.0X3	T41.0X4	T41.0X5	T41.0X6
nonmedicinal	T52.8X1	T52.8X2	T52.8X3	T52.8X4	—	—
petroleum — see Ligroin						
solvent	T52.8X1	T52.8X2	T52.8X3	T52.8X4	—	—
Ethiazide	T50.2X1	T50.2X2	T50.2X3	T50.2X4	T50.2X5	T50.2X6
Ethidium chloride (vapor)	T59.891	T59.892	T59.893	T59.894	—	—
Ethinamate	T42.6X1	T42.6X2	T42.6X3	T42.6X4	T42.6X5	T42.6X6
Ethinylestradiol, ethinyloestradiol	T38.5X1	T38.5X2	T38.5X3	T38.5X4	T38.5X5	T38.5X6
with						
levonorgestrel	T38.4X1	T38.4X2	T38.4X3	T38.4X4	T38.4X5	T38.4X6
norethisterone	T38.4X1	T38.4X2	T38.4X3	T38.4X4	T38.4X5	T38.4X6
Ethiodized oil (131 I)	T50.8X1	T50.8X2	T50.8X3	T50.8X4	T50.8X5	T50.8X6
Ethion	T60.0X1	T60.0X2	T60.0X3	T60.0X4	—	—
Ethionamide	T37.1X1	T37.1X2	T37.1X3	T37.1X4	T37.1X5	T37.1X6
Ethioniamide	T37.1X1	T37.1X2	T37.1X3	T37.1X4	T37.1X5	T37.1X6
Ethisterone	T38.5X1	T38.5X2	T38.5X3	T38.5X4	T38.5X5	T38.5X6
Ethobral	T42.3X1	T42.3X2	T42.3X3	T42.3X4	T42.3X5	T42.3X6

◄ New ◄ Revised deleted Deleted

Substance	Poisoning, Accidental (Unintentional)	Poisoning, Intentional Self-Harm	Poisoning, Assault	Poisoning, Undetermined	Adverse Effect	Underdosing
Ethocaine (infiltration) (topical)	T41.3X1	T41.3X2	T41.3X3	T41.3X4	T41.3X5	T41.3X6
nerve block (peripheral) (plexus)	T41.3X1	T41.3X2	T41.3X3	T41.3X4	T41.3X5	T41.3X6
spinal	T41.3X1	T41.3X2	T41.3X3	T41.3X4	T41.3X5	T41.3X6
Ethoheptazine	T40.491	T40.492	T40.493	T40.494	T40.495	T40.496
Ethopropazine	T44.3X1	T44.3X2	T44.3X3	T44.3X4	T44.3X5	T44.3X6
Ethosuximide	T42.2X1	T42.2X2	T42.2X3	T42.2X4	T42.2X5	T42.2X6
Ethotoin	T42.0X1	T42.0X2	T42.0X3	T42.0X4	T42.0X5	T42.0X6
Ethoxazene	T37.91	T37.92	T37.93	T37.94	T37.95	T37.96
Ethoxazorutoside	T46.991	T46.992	T46.993	T46.994	T46.995	T46.996
2-Ethoxyethanol	T52.3X1	T52.3X2	T52.3X3	T52.3X4	—	—
Ethoxzolamide	T50.2X1	T50.2X2	T50.2X3	T50.2X4	T50.2X5	T50.2X6
Ethyl						
acetate	T52.8X1	T52.8X2	T52.8X3	T52.8X4	—	—
alcohol	T51.0X1	T51.0X2	T51.0X3	T51.0X4	—	—
beverage	T51.0X1	T51.0X2	T51.0X3	T51.0X4	—	—
aldehyde (vapor)	T59.891	T59.892	T59.893	T59.894	—	—
liquid	T52.8X1	T52.8X2	T52.8X3	T52.8X4	—	—
aminobenzoate	T41.3X1	T41.3X2	T41.3X3	T41.3X4	T41.3X5	T41.3X6
aminophenothiazine	T43.3X1	T43.3X2	T43.3X3	T43.3X4	T43.3X5	T43.3X6
benzoate	T52.8X1	T52.8X2	T52.8X3	T52.8X4	—	—
biscoumacetate	T45.511	T45.512	T45.513	T45.514	T45.515	T45.516
bromide (anesthetic)	T41.0X1	T41.0X2	T41.0X3	T41.0X4	T41.0X5	T41.0X6
carbamate	T45.1X1	T45.1X2	T45.1X3	T45.1X4	T45.1X5	T45.1X6
carbinol	T51.3X1	T51.3X2	T51.3X3	T51.3X4	—	—
carbonate	T52.8X1	T52.8X2	T52.8X3	T52.8X4	—	—
chaulmoograte	T37.1X1	T37.1X2	T37.1X3	T37.1X4	T37.1X5	T37.1X6
chloride (anesthetic)	T41.0X1	T41.0X2	T41.0X3	T41.0X4	T41.0X5	T41.0X6
anesthetic (local)	T41.3X1	T41.3X2	T41.3X3	T41.3X4	T41.3X5	T41.3X6
inhaled	T41.0X1	T41.0X2	T41.0X3	T41.0X4	T41.0X5	T41.0X6
local	T49.4X1	T49.4X2	T49.4X3	T49.4X4	T49.4X5	T49.4X6
solvent	T53.6X1	T53.6X2	T53.6X3	T53.6X4	—	—
dibunate	T48.3X1	T48.3X2	T48.3X3	T48.3X4	T48.3X5	T48.3X6
dichloroarsine (vapor)	T57.0X1	T57.0X2	T57.0X3	T57.0X4	—	—
estranol	T38.7X1	T38.7X2	T38.7X3	T38.7X4	T38.7X5	T38.7X6
ether — see also Ether	T52.8X1	T52.8X2	T52.8X3	T52.8X4	—	—
formate NEC (solvent)	T52.0X1	T52.0X2	T52.0X3	T52.0X4	—	—
fumarate	T49.4X1	T49.4X2	T49.4X3	T49.4X4	T49.4X5	T49.4X6
hydroxyisobutyrate NEC (solvent)	T52.8X1	T52.8X2	T52.8X3	T52.8X4	—	—
iodoacetate	T59.3X1	T59.3X2	T59.3X3	T59.3X4	—	—
lactate NEC (solvent)	T52.8X1	T52.8X2	T52.8X3	T52.8X4	—	—
loflazepate	T42.4X1	T42.4X2	T42.4X3	T42.4X4	T42.4X5	T42.4X6

Substance	Poisoning, Accidental (Unintentional)	Poisoning, Intentional Self-Harm	Poisoning, Assault	Poisoning, Undetermined	Adverse Effect	Underdosing
Ethyl (Continued)						
mercuric chloride	T56.1X1	T56.1X2	T56.1X3	T56.1X4	—	—
methylcarbinol	T51.8X1	T51.8X2	T51.8X3	T51.8X4	—	—
morphine	T40.2X1	T40.2X2	T40.2X3	T40.2X4	T40.2X5	T40.2X6
noradrenaline	T48.6X1	T48.6X2	T48.6X3	T48.6X4	T48.6X5	T48.6X6
oxybutyrate NEC (solvent)	T52.8X1	T52.8X2	T52.8X3	T52.8X4	—	—
Ethylene (gas)	T59.891	T59.892	T59.893	T59.894	—	—
anesthetic (general)	T41.0X1	T41.0X2	T41.0X3	T41.0X4	T41.0X5	T41.0X6
chlorohydrin	T52.8X1	T52.8X2	T52.8X3	T52.8X4	—	—
vapor	T53.6X1	T53.6X2	T53.6X3	T53.6X4	—	—
dichloride	T52.8X1	T52.8X2	T52.8X3	T52.8X4	—	—
vapor	T53.6X1	T53.6X2	T53.6X3	T53.6X4	—	—
dinitrate	T52.3X1	T52.3X2	T52.3X3	T52.3X4	—	—
glycol(s)	T52.8X1	T52.8X2	T52.8X3	T52.8X4	—	—
dinitrate	T52.3X1	T52.3X2	T52.3X3	T52.3X4	—	—
monobutyl ether	T52.3X1	T52.3X2	T52.3X3	T52.3X4	—	—
imine	T54.1X1	T54.1X2	T54.1X3	T54.1X4	—	—
oxide (fumigant) (nonmedicinal)	T59.891	T59.892	T59.893	T59.894	—	—
medicinal	T49.0X1	T49.0X2	T49.0X3	T49.0X4	T49.0X5	T49.0X6
Ethylenediamine theophylline	T48.6X1	T48.6X2	T48.6X3	T48.6X4	T48.6X5	T48.6X6
Ethylenediaminetetra-acetic acid	T50.6X1	T50.6X2	T50.6X3	T50.6X4	T50.6X5	T50.6X6
Ethylenedinitrilotetra-acetate	T50.6X1	T50.6X2	T50.6X3	T50.6X4	T50.6X5	T50.6X6
Ethylestrenol	T38.7X1	T38.7X2	T38.7X3	T38.7X4	T38.7X5	T38.7X6
Ethylhydroxycellulose	T47.4X1	T47.4X2	T47.4X3	T47.4X4	T47.4X5	T47.4X6
Ethylidene						
chloride NEC	T53.6X1	T53.6X2	T53.6X3	T53.6X4	—	—
diacetate	T60.3X1	T60.3X2	T60.3X3	T60.3X4	—	—
dicoumarin	T45.511	T45.512	T45.513	T45.514	T45.515	T45.516
dicoumarol	T45.511	T45.512	T45.513	T45.514	T45.515	T45.516
diethyl ether	T52.0X1	T52.0X2	T52.0X3	T52.0X4	—	—
Ethylmorphine	T40.2X1	T40.2X2	T40.2X3	T40.2X4	T40.2X5	T40.2X6
Ethylnorepinephrine	T48.6X1	T48.6X2	T48.6X3	T48.6X4	T48.6X5	T48.6X6
Ethylparachlorophen-oxyisobutyrate	T46.6X1	T46.6X2	T46.6X3	T46.6X4	T46.6X5	T46.6X6
Ethynodiol	T38.4X1	T38.4X2	T38.4X3	T38.4X4	T38.4X5	T38.4X6
with mestranol diacetate	T38.4X1	T38.4X2	T38.4X3	T38.4X4	T38.4X5	T38.4X6
Etidocaine	T41.3X1	T41.3X2	T41.3X3	T41.3X4	T41.3X5	T41.3X6
infiltration (subcutaneous)	T41.3X1	T41.3X2	T41.3X3	T41.3X4	T41.3X5	T41.3X6
nerve (peripheral) (plexus)	T41.3X1	T41.3X2	T41.3X3	T41.3X4	T41.3X5	T41.3X6
Etidronate	T50.991	T50.992	T50.993	T50.994	T50.995	T50.996
Etidronic acid (disodium salt)	T50.991	T50.992	T50.993	T50.994	T50.995	T50.996
Etifoxine	T42.6X1	T42.6X2	T42.6X3	T42.6X4	T42.6X5	T42.6X6

◀ New　◀ Revised　deleted Deleted

Substance	Poisoning, Accidental (Unintentional)	Poisoning, Intentional Self-Harm	Poisoning, Assault	Poisoning, Undetermined	Adverse Effect	Underdosing
Etilefrine	T44.4X1	T44.4X2	T44.4X3	T44.4X4	T44.4X5	T44.4X6
Etilfen	T42.3X1	T42.3X2	T42.3X3	T42.3X4	T42.3X5	T42.3X6
Etinodiol	T38.4X1	T38.4X2	T38.4X3	T38.4X4	T38.4X5	T38.4X6
Etiroxate	T46.6X1	T46.6X2	T46.6X3	T46.6X4	T46.6X5	T46.6X6
Etizolam	T42.4X1	T42.4X2	T42.4X3	T42.4X4	T42.4X5	T42.4X6
Etodolac	T39.391	T39.392	T39.393	T39.394	T39.395	T39.396
Etofamide	T37.3X1	T37.3X2	T37.3X3	T37.3X4	T37.3X5	T37.3X6
Etofibrate	T46.6X1	T46.6X2	T46.6X3	T46.6X4	T46.6X5	T46.6X6
Etofylline	T46.7X1	T46.7X2	T46.7X3	T46.7X4	T46.7X5	T46.7X6
clofibrate	T46.6X1	T46.6X2	T46.6X3	T46.6X4	T46.6X5	T46.6X6
Etoglucid	T45.1X1	T45.1X2	T45.1X3	T45.1X4	T45.1X5	T45.1X6
Etomidate	T41.1X1	T41.1X2	T41.1X3	T41.1X4	T41.1X5	T41.1X6
Etomide	T39.8X1	T39.8X2	T39.8X3	T39.8X4	T39.8X5	T39.8X6
Etomidoline	T44.3X1	T44.3X2	T44.3X3	T44.3X4	T44.3X5	T44.3X6
Etoposide	T45.1X1	T45.1X2	T45.1X3	T45.1X4	T45.1X5	T45.1X6
Etorphine	T40.2X1	T40.2X2	T40.2X3	T40.2X4	T40.2X5	T40.2X6
Etoval	T42.3X1	T42.3X2	T42.3X3	T42.3X4	T42.3X5	T42.3X6
Etozolin	T50.1X1	T50.1X2	T50.1X3	T50.1X4	T50.1X5	T50.1X6
Etretinate	T50.991	T50.992	T50.993	T50.994	T50.995	T50.996
Etryptamine	T43.691	T43.692	T43.693	T43.694	T43.695	T43.696
Etybenzatropine	T44.3X1	T44.3X2	T44.3X3	T44.3X4	T44.3X5	T44.3X6
Etynodiol	T38.4X1	T38.4X2	T38.4X3	T38.4X4	T38.4X5	T38.4X6
Eucaine	T41.3X1	T41.3X2	T41.3X3	T41.3X4	T41.3X5	T41.3X6
Eucalyptus oil	T49.7X1	T49.7X2	T49.7X3	T49.7X4	T49.7X5	T49.7X6
Eucatropine	T49.5X1	T49.5X2	T49.5X3	T49.5X4	T49.5X5	T49.5X6
Eucodal	T40.2X1	T40.2X2	T40.2X3	T40.2X4	T40.2X5	T40.2X6
Euneryl	T42.3X1	T42.3X2	T42.3X3	T42.3X4	T42.3X5	T42.3X6
Euphthalmine	T44.3X1	T44.3X2	T44.3X3	T44.3X4	T44.3X5	T44.3X6
Eurax	T49.0X1	T49.0X2	T49.0X3	T49.0X4	T49.0X5	T49.0X6
Euresol	T49.4X1	T49.4X2	T49.4X3	T49.4X4	T49.4X5	T49.4X6
Euthroid	T38.1X1	T38.1X2	T38.1X3	T38.1X4	T38.1X5	T38.1X6
Evans blue	T50.8X1	T50.8X2	T50.8X3	T50.8X4	T50.8X5	T50.8X6
Evipal	T42.3X1	T42.3X2	T42.3X3	T42.3X4	T42.3X5	T42.3X6
sodium	T41.1X1	T41.1X2	T41.1X3	T41.1X4	T41.1X5	T41.1X6
Evipan	T42.3X1	T42.3X2	T42.3X3	T42.3X4	T42.3X5	T42.3X6
sodium	T41.1X1	T41.1X2	T41.1X3	T41.1X4	T41.1X5	T41.1X6
Exalamide	T49.0X1	T49.0X2	T49.0X3	T49.0X4	T49.0X5	T49.0X6
Exalgin	T39.1X1	T39.1X2	T39.1X3	T39.1X4	T39.1X5	T39.1X6
Excipients, pharmaceutical	T50.901	T50.902	T50.903	T50.904	T50.905	T50.906
Exhaust gas (engine) (motor vehicle)	T58.01	T58.02	T58.03	T58.04	—	—
Ex-Lax (phenolphthalein)	T47.2X1	T47.2X2	T47.2X3	T47.2X4	T47.2X5	T47.2X6
Expectorant NEC	T48.4X1	T48.4X2	T48.4X3	T48.4X4	T48.4X5	T48.4X6

Substance	Poisoning, Accidental (Unintentional)	Poisoning, Intentional Self-Harm	Poisoning, Assault	Poisoning, Undetermined	Adverse Effect	Underdosing
Extended insulin zinc suspension	T38.3X1	T38.3X2	T38.3X3	T38.3X4	T38.3X5	T38.3X6
External medications (skin) (mucous membrane)	T49.91	T49.92	T49.93	T49.94	T49.95	T49.96
dental agent	T49.7X1	T49.7X2	T49.7X3	T49.7X4	T49.7X5	T49.7X6
ENT agent	T49.6X1	T49.6X2	T49.6X3	T49.6X4	T49.6X5	T49.6X6
ophthalmic preparation	T49.5X1	T49.5X2	T49.5X3	T49.5X4	T49.5X5	T49.5X6
specified NEC	T49.8X1	T49.8X2	T49.8X3	T49.8X4	T49.8X5	T49.8X6
Extrapyramidal antagonist NEC	T44.3X1	T44.3X2	T44.3X3	T44.3X4	T44.3X5	T44.3X6
Eye agents (anti-infective)	T49.5X1	T49.5X2	T49.5X3	T49.5X4	T49.5X5	T49.5X6
Eye drug NEC	T49.5X1	T49.5X2	T49.5X3	T49.5X4	T49.5X5	T49.5X6
F						
FAC (fluorouracil + doxorubicin + cyclophosphamide)	T45.1X1	T45.1X2	T45.1X3	T45.1X4	T45.1X5	T45.1X6
Factor						
I (fibrinogen)	T45.8X1	T45.8X2	T45.8X3	T45.8X4	T45.8X5	T45.8X6
III (thromboplastin)	T45.8X1	T45.8X2	T45.8X3	T45.8X4	T45.8X5	T45.8X6
VIII (antihemophilic Factor) (Concentrate)	T45.8X1	T45.8X2	T45.8X3	T45.8X4	T45.8X5	T45.8X6
IX complex	T45.7X1	T45.7X2	T45.7X3	T45.7X4	T45.7X5	T45.7X6
human	T45.8X1	T45.8X2	T45.8X3	T45.8X4	T45.8X5	T45.8X6
Famotidine	T47.0X1	T47.0X2	T47.0X3	T47.0X4	T47.0X5	T47.0X6
Fat suspension, intravenous	T50.991	T50.992	T50.993	T50.994	T50.995	T50.996
Fazadinium bromide	T48.1X1	T48.1X2	T48.1X3	T48.1X4	T48.1X5	T48.1X6
Febarbamate	T42.3X1	T42.3X2	T42.3X3	T42.3X4	T42.3X5	T42.3X6
Fecal softener	T47.4X1	T47.4X2	T47.4X3	T47.4X4	T47.4X5	T47.4X6
Fedrilate	T48.3X1	T48.3X2	T48.3X3	T48.3X4	T48.3X5	T48.3X6
Felodipine	T46.1X1	T46.1X2	T46.1X3	T46.1X4	T46.1X5	T46.1X6
Felypressin	T38.891	T38.892	T38.893	T38.894	T38.895	T38.896
Femoxetine	T43.221	T43.222	T43.223	T43.224	T43.225	T43.226
Fenalcomine	T46.3X1	T46.3X2	T46.3X3	T46.3X4	T46.3X5	T46.3X6
Fenamisal	T37.1X1	T37.1X2	T37.1X3	T37.1X4	T37.1X5	T37.1X6
Fenazone	T39.2X1	T39.2X2	T39.2X3	T39.2X4	T39.2X5	T39.2X6
Fenbendazole	T37.4X1	T37.4X2	T37.4X3	T37.4X4	T37.4X5	T37.4X6
Fenbutrazate	T50.5X1	T50.5X2	T50.5X3	T50.5X4	T50.5X5	T50.5X6
Fencamfamine	T43.691	T43.692	T43.693	T43.694	T43.695	T43.696
Fendiline	T46.1X1	T46.1X2	T46.1X3	T46.1X4	T46.1X5	T46.1X6
Fenetylline	T43.691	T43.692	T43.693	T43.694	T43.695	T43.696
Fenflumizole	T39.391	T39.392	T39.393	T39.394	T39.395	T39.396
Fenfluramine	T50.5X1	T50.5X2	T50.5X3	T50.5X4	T50.5X5	T50.5X6
Fenobarbital	T42.3X1	T42.3X2	T42.3X3	T42.3X4	T42.3X5	T42.3X6
Fenofibrate	T46.6X1	T46.6X2	T46.6X3	T46.6X4	T46.6X5	T46.6X6
Fenoprofen	T39.311	T39.312	T39.313	T39.314	T39.315	T39.316
Fenoterol	T48.6X1	T48.6X2	T48.6X3	T48.6X4	T48.6X5	T48.6X6

◀ New   ◀ Revised   ~~deleted~~ Deleted

	External Cause (T-Code)					
Substance	Poisoning, Accidental (Unintentional)	Poisoning, Intentional Self-Harm	Poisoning, Assault	Poisoning, Undetermined	Adverse Effect	Underdosing
Fenoverine	T44.3X1	T44.3X2	T44.3X3	T44.3X4	T44.3X5	T44.3X6
Fenoxazoline	T48.5X1	T48.5X2	T48.5X3	T48.5X4	T48.5X5	T48.5X6
Fenproporex	T50.5X1	T50.5X2	T50.5X3	T50.5X4	T50.5X5	T50.5X6
Fenquizone	T50.2X1	T50.2X2	T50.2X3	T50.2X4	T50.2X5	T50.2X6
Fentanyl (analogs)	T40.411	T40.412	T40.413	T40.414	T40.415	T40.416
Fentazin	T43.3X1	T43.3X2	T43.3X3	T43.3X4	T43.3X5	T43.3X6
Fenthion	T60.0X1	T60.0X2	T60.0X3	T60.0X4	—	—
Fenticlor	T49.0X1	T49.0X2	T49.0X3	T49.0X4	T49.0X5	T49.0X6
Fenylbutazone	T39.2X1	T39.2X2	T39.2X3	T39.2X4	T39.2X5	T39.2X6
Feprazone	T39.2X1	T39.2X2	T39.2X3	T39.2X4	T39.2X5	T39.2X6
Fer de lance (bite) (venom)	T63.061	T63.062	T63.063	T63.064	—	—
Ferric — see also Iron						
chloride	T45.4X1	T45.4X2	T45.4X3	T45.4X4	T45.4X5	T45.4X6
citrate	T45.4X1	T45.4X2	T45.4X3	T45.4X4	T45.4X5	T45.4X6
hydroxide						
colloidal	T45.4X1	T45.4X2	T45.4X3	T45.4X4	T45.4X5	T45.4X6
polymaltose	T45.4X1	T45.4X2	T45.4X3	T45.4X4	T45.4X5	T45.4X6
pyrophosphate	T45.4X1	T45.4X2	T45.4X3	T45.4X4	T45.4X5	T45.4X6
Ferritin	T45.4X1	T45.4X2	T45.4X3	T45.4X4	T45.4X5	T45.4X6
Ferrocholinate	T45.4X1	T45.4X2	T45.4X3	T45.4X4	T45.4X5	T45.4X6
Ferrodextrane	T45.4X1	T45.4X2	T45.4X3	T45.4X4	T45.4X5	T45.4X6
Ferropolimaler	T45.4X1	T45.4X2	T45.4X3	T45.4X4	T45.4X5	T45.4X6
Ferrous — see also Iron						
phosphate	T45.4X1	T45.4X2	T45.4X3	T45.4X4	T45.4X5	T45.4X6
salt	T45.4X1	T45.4X2	T45.4X3	T45.4X4	T45.4X5	T45.4X6
with folic acid	T45.4X1	T45.4X2	T45.4X3	T45.4X4	T45.4X5	T45.4X6
Ferrous fumarate, gluconate, lactate, salt NEC, sulfate (medicinal)	T45.4X1	T45.4X2	T45.4X3	T45.4X4	T45.4X5	T45.4X6
Ferrovanadium (fumes)	T59.891	T59.892	T59.893	T59.894	—	—
Ferrum — see Iron						
Fertilizers NEC	T65.891	T65.892	T65.893	T65.894	—	—
with herbicide mixture	T60.3X1	T60.3X2	T60.3X3	T60.3X4	—	—
Fetoxilate	T47.6X1	T47.6X2	T47.6X3	T47.6X4	T47.6X5	T47.6X6
Fiber, dietary	T47.4X1	T47.4X2	T47.4X3	T47.4X4	T47.4X5	T47.4X6
Fibrinogen (human)	T45.8X1	T45.8X2	T45.8X3	T45.8X4	T45.8X5	T45.8X6
Fibrinolysin (human)	T45.691	T45.692	T45.693	T45.694	T45.695	T45.696
Fibrinolysis						
affecting drug	T45.601	T45.602	T45.603	T45.604	T45.605	T45.606
inhibitor NEC	T45.621	T45.622	T45.623	T45.624	T45.625	T45.626
Fibrinolytic drug	T45.611	T45.612	T45.613	T45.614	T45.615	T45.616
Filix mas	T37.4X1	T37.4X2	T37.4X3	T37.4X4	T37.4X5	T37.4X6
Filtering cream	T49.3X1	T49.3X2	T49.3X3	T49.3X4	T49.3X5	T49.3X6

	External Cause (T-Code)					
Substance	Poisoning, Accidental (Unintentional)	Poisoning, Intentional Self-Harm	Poisoning, Assault	Poisoning, Undetermined	Adverse Effect	Underdosing
Fiorinal	T39.011	T39.012	T39.013	T39.014	T39.015	T39.016
Firedamp	T59.891	T59.892	T59.893	T59.894	—	—
Fish, noxious, nonbacterial	T61.91	T61.92	T61.93	T61.94	—	—
ciguatera	T61.01	T61.02	T61.03	T61.04	—	—
scombroid	T61.11	T61.12	T61.13	T61.14	—	—
shell	T61.781	T61.782	T61.783	T61.784	—	—
specified NEC	T61.771	T61.772	T61.773	T61.774	—	—
Flagyl	T37.3X1	T37.3X2	T37.3X3	T37.3X4	T37.3X5	T37.3X6
Flavine adenine dinucleotide	T45.2X1	T45.2X2	T45.2X3	T45.2X4	T45.2X5	T45.2X6
Flavodic acid	T46.991	T46.992	T46.993	T46.994	T46.995	T46.996
Flavoxate	T44.3X1	T44.3X2	T44.3X3	T44.3X4	T44.3X5	T44.3X6
Flaxedil	T48.1X1	T48.1X2	T48.1X3	T48.1X4	T48.1X5	T48.1X6
Flaxseed (medicinal)	T49.3X1	T49.3X2	T49.3X3	T49.3X4	T49.3X5	T49.3X6
Flecainide	T46.2X1	T46.2X2	T46.2X3	T46.2X4	T46.2X5	T46.2X6
Fleroxacin	T36.8X1	T36.8X2	T36.8X3	T36.8X4	T36.8X5	T36.8X6
Floctafenine	T39.8X1	T39.8X2	T39.8X3	T39.8X4	T39.8X5	T39.8X6
Flomax	T44.6X1	T44.6X2	T44.6X3	T44.6X4	T44.6X5	T44.6X6
Flomoxef	T36.1X1	T36.1X2	T36.1X3	T36.1X4	T36.1X5	T36.1X6
Flopropione	T44.3X1	T44.3X2	T44.3X3	T44.3X4	T44.3X5	T44.3X6
Florantyrone	T47.5X1	T47.5X2	T47.5X3	T47.5X4	T47.5X5	T47.5X6
Floraquin	T37.8X1	T37.8X2	T37.8X3	T37.8X4	T37.8X5	T37.8X6
Florinef	T38.0X1	T38.0X2	T38.0X3	T38.0X4	T38.0X5	T38.0X6
ENT agent	T49.6X1	T49.6X2	T49.6X3	T49.6X4	T49.6X5	T49.6X6
ophthalmic preparation	T49.5X1	T49.5X2	T49.5X3	T49.5X4	T49.5X5	T49.5X6
topical NEC	T49.0X1	T49.0X2	T49.0X3	T49.0X4	T49.0X5	T49.0X6
Flowers of sulfur	T49.4X1	T49.4X2	T49.4X3	T49.4X4	T49.4X5	T49.4X6
Floxuridine	T45.1X1	T45.1X2	T45.1X3	T45.1X4	T45.1X5	T45.1X6
Fluanisone	T43.4X1	T43.4X2	T43.4X3	T43.4X4	T43.4X5	T43.4X6
Flubendazole	T37.4X1	T37.4X2	T37.4X3	T37.4X4	T37.4X5	T37.4X6
Fluclorolone acetonide	T49.0X1	T49.0X2	T49.0X3	T49.0X4	T49.0X5	T49.0X6
Flucloxacillin	T36.0X1	T36.0X2	T36.0X3	T36.0X4	T36.0X5	T36.0X6
Fluconazole	T37.8X1	T37.8X2	T37.8X3	T37.8X4	T37.8X5	T37.8X6
Flucytosine	T37.8X1	T37.8X2	T37.8X3	T37.8X4	T37.8X5	T37.8X6
Fludeoxyglucose (18F)	T50.8X1	T50.8X2	T50.8X3	T50.8X4	T50.8X5	T50.8X6
Fludiazepam	T42.4X1	T42.4X2	T42.4X3	T42.4X4	T42.4X5	T42.4X6
Fludrocortisone	T50.0X1	T50.0X2	T50.0X3	T50.0X4	T50.0X5	T50.0X6
ENT agent	T49.6X1	T49.6X2	T49.6X3	T49.6X4	T49.6X5	T49.6X6
ophthalmic preparation	T49.5X1	T49.5X2	T49.5X3	T49.5X4	T49.5X5	T49.5X6
topical NEC	T49.0X1	T49.0X2	T49.0X3	T49.0X4	T49.0X5	T49.0X6
Fludroxycortide	T49.0X1	T49.0X2	T49.0X3	T49.0X4	T49.0X5	T49.0X6
Flufenamic acid	T39.391	T39.392	T39.393	T39.394	T39.395	T39.396
Fluindione	T45.511	T45.512	T45.513	T45.514	T45.515	T45.516

◀ New ◀ Revised ~~deleted~~ Deleted

Substance	Poisoning, Accidental (Unintentional)	Poisoning, Intentional Self-Harm	Poisoning, Assault	Poisoning, Undetermined	Adverse Effect	Underdosing
Flumequine	T37.8X1	T37.8X2	T37.8X3	T37.8X4	T37.8X5	T37.8X6
Flumethasone	T49.0X1	T49.0X2	T49.0X3	T49.0X4	T49.0X5	T49.0X6
Flumethiazide	T50.2X1	T50.2X2	T50.2X3	T50.2X4	T50.2X5	T50.2X6
Flumidin	T37.5X1	T37.5X2	T37.5X3	T37.5X4	T37.5X5	T37.5X6
Flunarizine	T46.7X1	T46.7X2	T46.7X3	T46.7X4	T46.7X5	T46.7X6
Flunidazole	T37.8X1	T37.8X2	T37.8X3	T37.8X4	T37.8X5	T37.8X6
Flunisolide	T48.6X1	T48.6X2	T48.6X3	T48.6X4	T48.6X5	T48.6X6
Flunitrazepam	T42.4X1	T42.4X2	T42.4X3	T42.4X4	T42.4X5	T42.4X6
Fluocinolone (acetonide)	T49.0X1	T49.0X2	T49.0X3	T49.0X4	T49.0X5	T49.0X6
Fluocinonide	T49.0X1	T49.0X2	T49.0X3	T49.0X4	T49.0X5	T49.0X6
Fluocortin (butyl)	T49.0X1	T49.0X2	T49.0X3	T49.0X4	T49.0X5	T49.0X6
Fluocortolone	T49.0X1	T49.0X2	T49.0X3	T49.0X4	T49.0X5	T49.0X6
Fluohydrocortisone	T38.0X1	T38.0X2	T38.0X3	T38.0X4	T38.0X5	T38.0X6
ENT agent	T49.6X1	T49.6X2	T49.6X3	T49.6X4	T49.6X5	T49.6X6
ophthalmic preparation	T49.5X1	T49.5X2	T49.5X3	T49.5X4	T49.5X5	T49.5X6
topical NEC	T49.0X1	T49.0X2	T49.0X3	T49.0X4	T49.0X5	T49.0X6
Fluonid	T49.0X1	T49.0X2	T49.0X3	T49.0X4	T49.0X5	T49.0X6
Fluopromazine	T43.3X1	T43.3X2	T43.3X3	T43.3X4	T43.3X5	T43.3X6
Fluoroacetate	T60.8X1	T60.8X2	T60.8X3	T60.8X4	—	—
Fluorescein	T50.8X1	T50.8X2	T50.8X3	T50.8X4	T50.8X5	T50.8X6
Fluorhydrocortisone	T50.0X1	T50.0X2	T50.0X3	T50.0X4	T50.0X5	T50.0X6
Fluoride (nonmedicinal) (pesticide) (sodium) NEC	T60.8X1	T60.8X2	T60.8X3	T60.8X4	—	—
hydrogen — see Hydrofluoric acid						
medicinal NEC	T50.991	T50.992	T50.993	T50.994	T50.995	T50.996
dental use	T49.7X1	T49.7X2	T49.7X3	T49.7X4	T49.7X5	T49.7X6
not pesticide NEC	T54.91	T54.92	T54.93	T54.94	—	—
stannous	T49.7X1	T49.7X2	T49.7X3	T49.7X4	T49.7X5	T49.7X6
Fluorinated corticosteroids	T38.0X1	T38.0X2	T38.0X3	T38.0X4	T38.0X5	T38.0X6
Fluorine (gas)	T59.5X1	T59.5X2	T59.5X3	T59.5X4	—	—
salt — see Fluoride(s)						
Fluoristan	T49.7X1	T49.7X2	T49.7X3	T49.7X4	T49.7X5	T49.7X6
Fluormetholone	T49.0X1	T49.0X2	T49.0X3	T49.0X4	T49.0X5	T49.0X6
Fluoroacetate	T60.8X1	T60.8X2	T60.8X3	T60.8X4	—	—
Fluorocarbon monomer	T53.6X1	T53.6X2	T53.6X3	T53.6X4	—	—
Fluorocytosine	T37.8X1	T37.8X2	T37.8X3	T37.8X4	T37.8X5	T37.8X6
Fluorodeoxyuridine	T45.1X1	T45.1X2	T45.1X3	T45.1X4	T45.1X5	T45.1X6
Fluorometholone	T49.0X1	T49.0X2	T49.0X3	T49.0X4	T49.0X5	T49.0X6
ophthalmic preparation	T49.5X1	T49.5X2	T49.5X3	T49.5X4	T49.5X5	T49.5X6
Fluorophosphate insecticide	T60.0X1	T60.0X2	T60.0X3	T60.0X4	—	—
Fluorosol	T46.3X1	T46.3X2	T46.3X3	T46.3X4	T46.3X5	T46.3X6
Fluorouracil	T45.1X1	T45.1X2	T45.1X3	T45.1X4	T45.1X5	T45.1X6

Substance	Poisoning, Accidental (Unintentional)	Poisoning, Intentional Self-Harm	Poisoning, Assault	Poisoning, Undetermined	Adverse Effect	Underdosing
Fluorphenylalanine	T49.5X1	T49.5X2	T49.5X3	T49.5X4	T49.5X5	T49.5X6
Fluothane	T41.0X1	T41.0X2	T41.0X3	T41.0X4	T41.0X5	T41.0X6
Fluoxetine	T43.221	T43.222	T43.223	T43.224	T43.225	T43.226
Fluoxymesterone	T38.7X1	T38.7X2	T38.7X3	T38.7X4	T38.7X5	T38.7X6
Flupenthixol	T43.4X1	T43.4X2	T43.4X3	T43.4X4	T43.4X5	T43.4X6
Flupentixol	T43.4X1	T43.4X2	T43.4X3	T43.4X4	T43.4X5	T43.4X6
Fluphenazine	T43.3X1	T43.3X2	T43.3X3	T43.3X4	T43.3X5	T43.3X6
Fluprednidene	T49.0X1	T49.0X2	T49.0X3	T49.0X4	T49.0X5	T49.0X6
Fluprednisolone	T38.0X1	T38.0X2	T38.0X3	T38.0X4	T38.0X5	T38.0X6
Fluradoline	T39.8X1	T39.8X2	T39.8X3	T39.8X4	T39.8X5	T39.8X6
Flurandrenolide	T49.0X1	T49.0X2	T49.0X3	T49.0X4	T49.0X5	T49.0X6
Flurandrenolone	T49.0X1	T49.0X2	T49.0X3	T49.0X4	T49.0X5	T49.0X6
Flurazepam	T42.4X1	T42.4X2	T42.4X3	T42.4X4	T42.4X5	T42.4X6
Flurbiprofen	T39.311	T39.312	T39.313	T39.314	T39.315	T39.316
Flurobate	T49.0X1	T49.0X2	T49.0X3	T49.0X4	T49.0X5	T49.0X6
Flurotyl	T43.291	T43.292	T43.293	T43.294	T43.295	T43.296
Fluroxene	T41.0X1	T41.0X2	T41.0X3	T41.0X4	T41.0X5	T41.0X6
Fluspirilene	T43.591	T43.592	T43.593	T43.594	T43.595	T43.596
Flutamide	T38.6X1	T38.6X2	T38.6X3	T38.6X4	T38.6X5	T38.6X6
Flutazolam	T42.4X1	T42.4X2	T42.4X3	T42.4X4	T42.4X5	T42.4X6
Fluticasone propionate	T38.0X1	T38.0X2	T38.0X3	T38.0X4	T38.0X5	T38.0X6
Flutoprazepam	T42.4X1	T42.4X2	T42.4X3	T42.4X4	T42.4X5	T42.4X6
Flutropium bromide	T48.6X1	T48.6X2	T48.6X3	T48.6X4	T48.6X5	T48.6X6
Fluvoxamine	T43.221	T43.222	T43.223	T43.224	T43.225	T43.226
Folacin	T45.8X1	T45.8X2	T45.8X3	T45.8X4	T45.8X5	T45.8X6
Folic acid	T45.8X1	T45.8X2	T45.8X3	T45.8X4	T45.8X5	T45.8X6
with ferrous salt	T45.2X1	T45.2X2	T45.2X3	T45.2X4	T45.2X5	T45.2X6
antagonist	T45.1X1	T45.1X2	T45.1X3	T45.1X4	T45.1X5	T45.1X6
Folinic acid	T45.8X1	T45.8X2	T45.8X3	T45.8X4	T45.8X5	T45.8X6
Folium stramoniae	T48.6X1	T48.6X2	T48.6X3	T48.6X4	T48.6X5	T48.6X6
Follicle-stimulating hormone, human	T38.811	T38.812	T38.813	T38.814	T38.815	T38.816
Folpet	T60.3X1	T60.3X2	T60.3X3	T60.3X4	—	—
Fominoben	T48.3X1	T48.3X2	T48.3X3	T48.3X4	T48.3X5	T48.3X6
Food, foodstuffs, noxious, nonbacterial, NEC	T62.91	T62.92	T62.93	T62.94	—	—
berries	T62.1X1	T62.1X2	T62.1X3	T62.1X4	—	—
fish — see also Fish	T61.91	T61.92	T61.93	T61.94	—	—
mushrooms	T62.0X1	T62.0X2	T62.0X3	T62.0X4	—	—
plants	T62.2X1	T62.2X2	T62.2X3	T62.2X4	—	—
seafood	T61.91	T61.92	T61.93	T61.94	—	—
specified NEC	T61.8X1	T61.8X2	T61.8X3	T61.8X4	—	—
seeds	T62.2X1	T62.2X2	T62.2X3	T62.2X4	—	—

◄ New ◄ Revised deleted Deleted

Substance	External Cause (T-Code)					
	Poisoning, Accidental (Unintentional)	Poisoning, Intentional Self-Harm	Poisoning, Assault	Poisoning, Undetermined	Adverse Effect	Underdosing
Food, foodstuffs, noxious, nonbacterial, NEC (Continued)						
shellfish	T61.781	T61.782	T61.783	T61.784	—	—
specified NEC	T62.8X1	T62.8X2	T62.8X3	T62.8X4	—	—
Fool's parsley	T62.2X1	T62.2X2	T62.2X3	T62.2X4	—	—
Formaldehyde (solution), gas or vapor	T59.2X1	T59.2X2	T59.2X3	T59.2X4	—	—
fungicide	T60.3X1	T60.3X2	T60.3X3	T60.3X4	—	—
Formalin	T59.2X1	T59.2X2	T59.2X3	T59.2X4	—	—
fungicide	T60.3X1	T60.3X2	T60.3X3	T60.3X4	—	—
vapor	T59.2X1	T59.2X2	T59.2X3	T59.2X4	—	—
Formic acid	T54.2X1	T54.2X2	T54.2X3	T54.2X4	—	—
vapor	T59.891	T59.892	T59.893	T59.894	—	—
Foscarnet sodium	T37.5X1	T37.5X2	T37.5X3	T37.5X4	T37.5X5	T37.5X6
Fosfestrol	T38.5X1	T38.5X2	T38.5X3	T38.5X4	T38.5X5	T38.5X6
Fosfomycin	T36.8X1	T36.8X2	T36.8X3	T36.8X4	T36.8X5	T36.8X6
Fosfonet sodium	T37.5X1	T37.5X2	T37.5X3	T37.5X4	T37.5X5	T37.5X6
Fosinopril	T46.4X1	T46.4X2	T46.4X3	T46.4X4	T46.4X5	T46.4X6
sodium	T46.4X1	T46.4X2	T46.4X3	T46.4X4	T46.4X5	T46.4X6
Fowler's solution	T57.0X1	T57.0X2	T57.0X3	T57.0X4	—	—
Foxglove	T62.2X1	T62.2X2	T62.2X3	T62.2X4	—	—
Framycetin	T36.5X1	T36.5X2	T36.5X3	T36.5X4	T36.5X5	T36.5X6
Frangula	T47.2X1	T47.2X2	T47.2X3	T47.2X4	T47.2X5	T47.2X6
extract	T47.2X1	T47.2X2	T47.2X3	T47.2X4	T47.2X5	T47.2X6
Frei antigen	T50.8X1	T50.8X2	T50.8X3	T50.8X4	T50.8X5	T50.8X6
Freon	T53.5X1	T53.5X2	T53.5X3	T53.5X4	—	—
Fructose	T50.3X1	T50.3X2	T50.3X3	T50.3X4	T50.3X5	T50.3X6
Frusemide	T50.1X1	T50.1X2	T50.1X3	T50.1X4	T50.1X5	T50.1X6
FSH	T38.811	T38.812	T38.813	T38.814	T38.815	T38.816
Ftorafur	T45.1X1	T45.1X2	T45.1X3	T45.1X4	T45.1X5	T45.1X6
Fuel						
automobile	T52.0X1	T52.0X2	T52.0X3	T52.0X4	—	—
exhaust gas, not in transit	T58.01	T58.02	T58.03	T58.04	—	—
vapor NEC	T52.0X1	T52.0X2	T52.0X3	T52.0X4	—	—
gas (domestic use) — see also Carbon, monoxide, fuel, utility	T59.891	T59.892	T59.893	T59.894	—	—
utility	T59.891	T59.892	T59.893	T59.894	—	—
in mobile container	T59.891	T59.892	T59.893	T59.894	—	—
incomplete combustion of — see Carbon, monoxide, fuel, utility						
piped (natural)	T59.891	T59.892	T59.893	T59.894	—	—
industrial, incomplete combustion	T58.8X1	T58.8X2	T58.8X3	T58.8X4	—	—

Substance	External Cause (T-Code)					
	Poisoning, Accidental (Unintentional)	Poisoning, Intentional Self-Harm	Poisoning, Assault	Poisoning, Undetermined	Adverse Effect	Underdosing
Fugillin	T36.8X1	T36.8X2	T36.8X3	T36.8X4	T36.8X5	T36.8X6
Fulminate of mercury	T56.1X1	T56.1X2	T56.1X3	T56.1X4	—	—
Fulvicin	T36.7X1	T36.7X2	T36.7X3	T36.7X4	T36.7X5	T36.7X6
Fumadil	T36.8X1	T36.8X2	T36.8X3	T36.8X4	T36.8X5	T36.8X6
Fumagillin	T36.8X1	T36.8X2	T36.8X3	T36.8X4	T36.8X5	T36.8X6
Fumaric acid	T49.4X1	T49.4X2	T49.4X3	T49.4X4	T49.4X5	T49.4X6
Fumes (from)	T59.91	T59.92	T59.93	T59.94	—	—
carbon monoxide — see Carbon, monoxide						
charcoal (domestic use) — see Charcoal, fumes						
chloroform — see Chloroform						
coke (in domestic stoves, fireplaces) — see Coke, fumes						
corrosive NEC	T54.91	T54.92	T54.93	T54.94	—	—
ether — see Ether						
freons	T53.5X1	T53.5X2	T53.5X3	T53.5X4	—	—
hydrocarbons	T59.891	T59.892	T59.893	T59.894	—	—
petroleum (liquefied)	T59.891	T59.892	T59.893	T59.894	—	—
distributed through pipes (pure or mixed with air)	T59.891	T59.892	T59.893	T59.894	—	—
lead — see Lead						
metal — see Metals, or the specified metal						
nitrogen dioxide	T59.0X1	T59.0X2	T59.0X3	T59.0X4	—	—
pesticides — see Pesticides						
petroleum (liquefied)	T59.891	T59.892	T59.893	T59.894	—	—
distributed through pipes (pure or mixed with air)	T59.891	T59.892	T59.893	T59.894	—	—
polyester	T59.891	T59.892	T59.893	T59.894	—	—
specified source NEC — see also substance specified	T59.891	T59.892	T59.893	T59.894	—	—
sulfur dioxide	T59.1X1	T59.1X2	T59.1X3	T59.1X4	—	—
Fumigant NEC	T60.91	T60.92	T60.93	T60.94	—	—
Fungi, noxious, used as food	T62.0X1	T62.0X2	T62.0X3	T62.0X4	—	—
Fungicide NEC (nonmedicinal)	T60.3X1	T60.3X2	T60.3X3	T60.3X4	—	—
Fungizone	T36.7X1	T36.7X2	T36.7X3	T36.7X4	T36.7X5	T36.7X6
topical	T49.0X1	T49.0X2	T49.0X3	T49.0X4	T49.0X5	T49.0X6
Furacin	T49.0X1	T49.0X2	T49.0X3	T49.0X4	T49.0X5	T49.0X6
Furadantin	T37.91	T37.92	T37.93	T37.94	T37.95	T37.96
Furazolidone	T37.8X1	T37.8X2	T37.8X3	T37.8X4	T37.8X5	T37.8X6
Furazolium chloride	T49.0X1	T49.0X2	T49.0X3	T49.0X4	T49.0X5	T49.0X6
Furfural	T52.8X1	T52.8X2	T52.8X3	T52.8X4	—	—

◀ New ◀ Revised deleted Deleted

Substance	Poisoning, Accidental (Unintentional)	Poisoning, Intentional Self-Harm	Poisoning, Assault	Poisoning, Undetermined	Adverse Effect	Underdosing
Furnace (coal burning) (domestic), gas from industrial	T58.2X1	T58.2X2	T58.2X3	T58.2X4	—	—
industrial	T58.8X1	T58.8X2	T58.8X3	T58.8X4	—	—
Furniture polish	T65.891	T65.892	T65.893	T65.894	—	—
Furosemide	T50.1X1	T50.1X2	T50.1X3	T50.1X4	T50.1X5	T50.1X6
Furoxone	T37.91	T37.92	T37.93	T37.94	T37.95	T37.96
Fursultiamine	T45.2X1	T45.2X2	T45.2X3	T45.2X4	T45.2X5	T45.2X6
Fusafungine	T36.8X1	T36.8X2	T36.8X3	T36.8X4	T36.8X5	T36.8X6
Fusel oil (any) (amyl) (butyl) (propyl), vapor	T51.3X1	T51.3X2	T51.3X3	T51.3X4	—	—
Fusidate (ethanolamine) (sodium)	T36.8X1	T36.8X2	T36.8X3	T36.8X4	T36.8X5	T36.8X6
Fusidic acid	T36.8X1	T36.8X2	T36.8X3	T36.8X4	T36.8X5	T36.8X6
Fytic acid, nonasodium	T50.6X1	T50.6X2	T50.6X3	T50.6X4	T50.6X5	T50.6X6
G						
GABA	T43.8X1	T43.8X2	T43.8X3	T43.8X4	T43.8X5	T43.8X6
Gadopentetic acid	T50.8X1	T50.8X2	T50.8X3	T50.8X4	T50.8X5	T50.8X6
Galactose	T50.3X1	T50.3X2	T50.3X3	T50.3X4	T50.3X5	T50.3X6
b-Galactosidase	T47.5X1	T47.5X2	T47.5X3	T47.5X4	T47.5X5	T47.5X6
Galantamine	T44.0X1	T44.0X2	T44.0X3	T44.0X4	T44.0X5	T44.0X6
Gallamine (triethiodide)	T48.1X1	T48.1X2	T48.1X3	T48.1X4	T48.1X5	T48.1X6
Gallium citrate	T50.991	T50.992	T50.993	T50.994	T50.995	T50.996
Gallopamil	T46.1X1	T46.1X2	T46.1X3	T46.1X4	T46.1X5	T46.1X6
Gamboge	T47.2X1	T47.2X2	T47.2X3	T47.2X4	T47.2X5	T47.2X6
Gamimune	T50.Z11	T50.Z12	T50.Z13	T50.Z14	T50.Z15	T50.Z16
Gamma-aminobutyric acid	T43.8X1	T43.8X2	T43.8X3	T43.8X4	T43.8X5	T43.8X6
Gamma-benzene hexachloride (medicinal)	T49.0X1	T49.0X2	T49.0X3	T49.0X4	T49.0X5	T49.0X6
nonmedicinal, vapor	T53.6X1	T53.6X2	T53.6X3	T53.6X4	—	—
Gamma-BHC (medicinal) — see also Gamma-benzene hexachloride	T49.0X1	T49.0X2	T49.0X3	T49.0X4	T49.0X5	T49.0X6
Gamma globulin	T50.Z11	T50.Z12	T50.Z13	T50.Z14	T50.Z15	T50.Z16
Gamulin	T50.Z11	T50.Z12	T50.Z13	T50.Z14	T50.Z15	T50.Z16
Ganciclovir (sodium)	T37.5X1	T37.5X2	T37.5X3	T37.5X4	T37.5X5	T37.5X6
Ganglionic blocking drug NEC	T44.2X1	T44.2X2	T44.2X3	T44.2X4	T44.2X5	T44.2X6
specified NEC	T44.2X1	T44.2X2	T44.2X3	T44.2X4	T44.2X5	T44.2X6
Ganja	T40.7X1	T40.7X2	T40.7X3	T40.7X4	T40.7X5	T40.7X6
Garamycin	T36.5X1	T36.5X2	T36.5X3	T36.5X4	T36.5X5	T36.5X6
ophthalmic preparation	T49.5X1	T49.5X2	T49.5X3	T49.5X4	T49.5X5	T49.5X6
topical NEC	T49.0X1	T49.0X2	T49.0X3	T49.0X4	T49.0X5	T49.0X6
Gardenal	T42.3X1	T42.3X2	T42.3X3	T42.3X4	T42.3X5	T42.3X6
Gardepanyl	T42.3X1	T42.3X2	T42.3X3	T42.3X4	T42.3X5	T42.3X6

Substance	Poisoning, Accidental (Unintentional)	Poisoning, Intentional Self-Harm	Poisoning, Assault	Poisoning, Undetermined	Adverse Effect	Underdosing
Gas NEC	T59.91	T59.92	T59.93	T59.94	—	—
acetylene	T59.891	T59.892	T59.893	T59.894	—	—
incomplete combustion of	T58.11	T58.12	T58.13	T58.14	—	—
air contaminants, source or type not specified	T59.91	T59.92	T59.93	T59.94	—	—
anesthetic	T41.0X1	T41.0X2	T41.0X3	T41.0X4	T41.0X5	T41.0X6
blast furnace	T58.8X1	T58.8X2	T58.8X3	T58.8X4	—	—
butane — see Butane						
carbon monoxide — see Carbon, monoxide						
chlorine	T59.4X1	T59.4X2	T59.4X3	T59.4X4	—	—
coal	T58.2X1	T58.2X2	T58.2X3	T58.2X4	—	—
cyanide	T57.3X1	T57.3X2	T57.3X3	T57.3X4	—	—
dicyanogen	T65.0X1	T65.0X2	T65.0X3	T65.0X4	—	—
domestic — see Domestic gas	T57.91	T57.92	T57.93	T57.94	—	—
exhaust	T57.91	T57.92	T57.93	T57.94	—	—
from utility (for cooking, heating, or lighting) (after combustion) — see Carbon, monoxide, fuel, utility						
prior to combustion	T59.891	T59.892	T59.893	T59.894	—	—
from wood or coal-burning stove or fireplace	T57.91	T57.92	T57.93	T57.94	—	—
fuel (domestic use) (after combustion) — see also Carbon, monoxide, fuel	T57.91	T57.92	T57.93	T57.94	—	—
industrial use	T58.8X1	T58.8X2	T58.8X3	T58.8X4	—	—
prior to combustion	T59.891	T59.892	T59.893	T59.894	—	—
utility	T59.891	T59.892	T59.893	T59.894	—	—
in mobile container	T59.891	T59.892	T59.893	T59.894	—	—
incomplete combustion of — see Carbon, monoxide, fuel, utility						
piped (natural)	T59.891	T59.892	T59.893	T59.894	—	—
garage	T58.01	T58.02	T58.03	T58.04	—	—
hydrocarbon NEC	T59.891	T59.892	T59.893	T59.894	—	—
incomplete combustion of — see Carbon, monoxide, fuel, utility						
liquefied — see Butane						
piped	T59.891	T59.892	T59.893	T59.894	—	—
hydrocyanic acid	T65.0X1	T65.0X2	T65.0X3	T65.0X4	—	—

◀ New　◀ Revised　deleted Deleted

Substance	Poisoning, Accidental (Unintentional)	Poisoning, Intentional Self-Harm	Poisoning, Assault	Poisoning, Undetermined	Adverse Effect	Underdosing
Gas NEC (Continued)						
illuminating (after combustion)	T58.11	T58.12	T58.13	T58.14	—	—
prior to combustion	T59.891	T59.892	T59.893	T59.894	—	—
incomplete combustion, any — see Carbon, monoxide						
kiln	T58.8X1	T58.8X2	T58.8X3	T58.8X4	—	—
lacrimogenic	T59.3X1	T59.3X2	T59.3X3	T59.3X4	—	—
liquefied petroleum — see Butane						
marsh	T59.891	T59.892	T59.893	T59.894	—	—
motor exhaust, not in transit	T58.01	T58.02	T58.03	T58.04	—	—
mustard, not in war	T59.891	T59.892	T59.893	T59.894	—	—
natural	T59.891	T59.892	T59.893	T59.894	—	—
nerve, not in war	T59.91	T59.92	T59.93	T59.94	—	—
oil	T52.0X1	T52.0X2	T52.0X3	T52.0X4	—	—
petroleum (liquefied) (distributed in mobile containers)	T59.891	T59.892	T59.893	T59.894	—	—
piped (pure or mixed with air)	T59.891	T59.892	T59.893	T59.894	—	—
piped (manufactured) (natural) NEC	T59.891	T59.892	T59.893	T59.894	—	—
producer	T58.8X1	T58.8X2	T58.8X3	T58.8X4	—	—
propane — see Propane						
refrigerant (chlorofluoro-carbon)	T53.5X1	T53.5X2	T53.5X3	T53.5X4	—	—
not chlorofluoro-carbon	T59.891	T59.892	T59.893	T59.894	—	—
sewer	T59.91	T59.92	T59.93	T59.94	—	—
specified source NEC	T59.91	T59.92	T59.93	T59.94	—	—
stove (after combustion)	T58.11	T58.12	T58.13	T58.14	—	—
tear	T59.3X1	T59.3X2	T59.3X3	T59.3X4	—	—
therapeutic	T41.5X1	T41.5X2	T41.5X3	T41.5X4	T41.5X5	T41.5X6
utility (for cooking, heating, or lighting) (piped) NEC	T59.891	T59.892	T59.893	T59.894	—	—
in mobile container	T59.891	T59.892	T59.893	T59.894	—	—
incomplete combustion of — see Carbon, monoxide, fuel, utilty						
piped (natural)	T59.891	T59.892	T59.893	T59.894	—	—
water	T58.11	T58.12	T58.13	T58.14	—	—
incomplete combustion of — see Carbon, monoxide, fuel, utility						

Substance	Poisoning, Accidental (Unintentional)	Poisoning, Intentional Self-Harm	Poisoning, Assault	Poisoning, Undetermined	Adverse Effect	Underdosing
Gaseous substance — see Gas						
Gasoline	T52.0X1	T52.0X2	T52.0X3	T52.0X4	—	—
vapor	T52.0X1	T52.0X2	T52.0X3	T52.0X4	—	—
Gastric enzymes	T47.5X1	T47.5X2	T47.5X3	T47.5X4	T47.5X5	T47.5X6
Gastrografin	T50.8X1	T50.8X2	T50.8X3	T50.8X4	T50.8X5	T50.8X6
Gastrointestinal drug	T47.91	T47.92	T47.93	T47.94	T47.95	T47.96
biological	T47.8X1	T47.8X2	T47.8X3	T47.8X4	T47.8X5	T47.8X6
specified NEC	T47.8X1	T47.8X2	T47.8X3	T47.8X4	T47.8X5	T47.8X6
Gaultheria procumbens	T62.2X1	T62.2X2	T62.2X3	T62.2X4	—	—
Gelatin (intravenous)	T45.8X1	T45.8X2	T45.8X3	T45.8X4	T45.8X5	T45.8X6
absorbable (sponge)	T45.7X1	T45.7X2	T45.7X3	T45.7X4	T45.7X5	T45.7X6
Gefarnate	T44.3X1	T44.3X2	T44.3X3	T44.3X4	T44.3X5	T44.3X6
Gelfilm	T49.8X1	T49.8X2	T49.8X3	T49.8X4	T49.8X5	T49.8X6
Gelfoam	T45.7X1	T45.7X2	T45.7X3	T45.7X4	T45.7X5	T45.7X6
Gelsemine	T50.991	T50.992	T50.993	T50.994	T50.995	T50.996
Gelsemium (sempervirens)	T62.2X1	T62.2X2	T62.2X3	T62.2X4	—	—
Gemeprost	T48.0X1	T48.0X2	T48.0X3	T48.0X4	T48.0X5	T48.0X6
Gemfibrozil	T46.6X1	T46.6X2	T46.6X3	T46.6X4	T46.6X5	T46.6X6
Gemonil	T42.3X1	T42.3X2	T42.3X3	T42.3X4	T42.3X5	T42.3X6
Gentamicin	T36.5X1	T36.5X2	T36.5X3	T36.5X4	T36.5X5	T36.5X6
ophthalmic preparation	T49.5X1	T49.5X2	T49.5X3	T49.5X4	T49.5X5	T49.5X6
topical NEC	T49.0X1	T49.0X2	T49.0X3	T49.0X4	T49.0X5	T49.0X6
Gentian	T47.5X1	T47.5X2	T47.5X3	T47.5X4	T47.5X5	T47.5X6
violet	T49.0X1	T49.0X2	T49.0X3	T49.0X4	T49.0X5	T49.0X6
Gepefrine	T44.4X1	T44.4X2	T44.4X3	T44.4X4	T44.4X5	T44.4X6
Gestonorone caproate	T38.5X1	T38.5X2	T38.5X3	T38.5X4	T38.5X5	T38.5X6
Gexane	T49.0X1	T49.0X2	T49.0X3	T49.0X4	T49.0X5	T49.0X6
Gila monster (venom)	T63.111	T63.112	T63.113	T63.114	—	—
Ginger	T47.5X1	T47.5X2	T47.5X3	T47.5X4	T47.5X5	T47.5X6
Jamaica — see Jamaica, ginger						
Gitalin	T46.0X1	T46.0X2	T46.0X3	T46.0X4	T46.0X5	T46.0X6
amorphous	T46.0X1	T46.0X2	T46.0X3	T46.0X4	T46.0X5	T46.0X6
Gitaloxin	T46.0X1	T46.0X2	T46.0X3	T46.0X4	T46.0X5	T46.0X6
Gitoxin	T46.0X1	T46.0X2	T46.0X3	T46.0X4	T46.0X5	T46.0X6
Glafenine	T39.8X1	T39.8X2	T39.8X3	T39.8X4	T39.8X5	T39.8X6
Glandular extract (medicinal) NEC	T50.Z91	T50.Z92	T50.Z93	T50.Z94	T50.Z95	T50.Z96
Glaucarubin	T37.3X1	T37.3X2	T37.3X3	T37.3X4	T37.3X5	T37.3X6
Glibenclamide	T38.3X1	T38.3X2	T38.3X3	T38.3X4	T38.3X5	T38.3X6
Glibornuride	T38.3X1	T38.3X2	T38.3X3	T38.3X4	T38.3X5	T38.3X6
Gliclazide	T38.3X1	T38.3X2	T38.3X3	T38.3X4	T38.3X5	T38.3X6
Glimidine	T38.3X1	T38.3X2	T38.3X3	T38.3X4	T38.3X5	T38.3X6

◀ New   ◀ Revised   ~~deleted~~ Deleted

Substance	Poisoning, Accidental (Unintentional)	Poisoning, Intentional Self-Harm	Poisoning, Assault	Poisoning, Undetermined	Adverse Effect	Underdosing
Glipizide	T38.3X1	T38.3X2	T38.3X3	T38.3X4	T38.3X5	T38.3X6
Gliquidone	T38.3X1	T38.3X2	T38.3X3	T38.3X4	T38.3X5	T38.3X6
Glisolamide	T38.3X1	T38.3X2	T38.3X3	T38.3X4	T38.3X5	T38.3X6
Glisoxepide	T38.3X1	T38.3X2	T38.3X3	T38.3X4	T38.3X5	T38.3X6
Globin zinc insulin	T38.3X1	T38.3X2	T38.3X3	T38.3X4	T38.3X5	T38.3X6
Globulin						
antilymphocytic	T50.Z11	T50.Z12	T50.Z13	T50.Z14	T50.Z15	T50.Z16
antirhesus	T50.Z11	T50.Z12	T50.Z13	T50.Z14	T50.Z15	T50.Z16
antivenin	T50.Z11	T50.Z12	T50.Z13	T50.Z14	T50.Z15	T50.Z16
antiviral	T50.Z11	T50.Z12	T50.Z13	T50.Z14	T50.Z15	T50.Z16
Glucagon	T38.3X1	T38.3X2	T38.3X3	T38.3X4	T38.3X5	T38.3X6
Glucocorticoids	T38.0X1	T38.0X2	T38.0X3	T38.0X4	T38.0X5	T38.0X6
Glucocorticosteroid	T38.0X1	T38.0X2	T38.0X3	T38.0X4	T38.0X5	T38.0X6
Gluconic acid	T50.991	T50.992	T50.993	T50.994	T50.995	T50.996
Glucosamine sulfate	T39.4X1	T39.4X2	T39.4X3	T39.4X4	T39.4X5	T39.4X6
Glucose	T50.3X1	T50.3X2	T50.3X3	T50.3X4	T50.3X5	T50.3X6
with sodium chloride	T50.3X1	T50.3X2	T50.3X3	T50.3X4	T50.3X5	T50.3X6
Glucosulfone sodium	T37.1X1	T37.1X2	T37.1X3	T37.1X4	T37.1X5	T37.1X6
Glucurolactone	T47.8X1	T47.8X2	T47.8X3	T47.8X4	T47.8X5	T47.8X6
Glue NEC	T52.8X1	T52.8X2	T52.8X3	T52.8X4	—	—
Glutamic acid	T47.5X1	T47.5X2	T47.5X3	T47.5X4	T47.5X5	T47.5X6
Glutaral (medicinal)	T49.0X1	T49.0X2	T49.0X3	T49.0X4	T49.0X5	T49.0X6
nonmedicinal	T65.891	T65.892	T65.893	T65.894	—	—
Glutaraldehyde (nonmedicinal)	T65.891	T65.892	T65.893	T65.894	—	—
medicinal	T49.0X1	T49.0X2	T49.0X3	T49.0X4	T49.0X5	T49.0X6
Glutathione	T50.6X1	T50.6X2	T50.6X3	T50.6X4	T50.6X5	T50.6X6
Glutethimide	T42.6X1	T42.6X2	T42.6X3	T42.6X4	T42.6X5	T42.6X6
Glyburide	T38.3X1	T38.3X2	T38.3X3	T38.3X4	T38.3X5	T38.3X6
Glycerin	T47.4X1	T47.4X2	T47.4X3	T47.4X4	T47.4X5	T47.4X6
Glycerol	T47.4X1	T47.4X2	T47.4X3	T47.4X4	T47.4X5	T47.4X6
borax	T49.6X1	T49.6X2	T49.6X3	T49.6X4	T49.6X5	T49.6X6
intravenous	T50.3X1	T50.3X2	T50.3X3	T50.3X4	T50.3X5	T50.3X6
iodinated	T48.4X1	T48.4X2	T48.4X3	T48.4X4	T48.4X5	T48.4X6
Glycerophosphate	T50.991	T50.992	T50.993	T50.994	T50.995	T50.996
Glyceryl						
gualacolate	T48.4X1	T48.4X2	T48.4X3	T48.4X4	T48.4X5	T48.4X6
nitrate	T46.3X1	T46.3X2	T46.3X3	T46.3X4	T46.3X5	T46.3X6
triacetate (topical)	T49.0X1	T49.0X2	T49.0X3	T49.0X4	T49.0X5	T49.0X6
trinitrate	T46.3X1	T46.3X2	T46.3X3	T46.3X4	T46.3X5	T46.3X6
Glycine	T50.3X1	T50.3X2	T50.3X3	T50.3X4	T50.3X5	T50.3X6
Glyclopyramide	T38.3X1	T38.3X2	T38.3X3	T38.3X4	T38.3X5	T38.3X6
Glycobiarsol	T37.3X1	T37.3X2	T37.3X3	T37.3X4	T37.3X5	T37.3X6

Substance	Poisoning, Accidental (Unintentional)	Poisoning, Intentional Self-Harm	Poisoning, Assault	Poisoning, Undetermined	Adverse Effect	Underdosing
Glycols (ether)	T52.3X1	T52.3X2	T52.3X3	T52.3X4	—	—
Glyconiazide	T37.1X1	T37.1X2	T37.1X3	T37.1X4	T37.1X5	T37.1X6
Glycopyrrolate	T44.3X1	T44.3X2	T44.3X3	T44.3X4	T44.3X5	T44.3X6
Glycopyrronium	T44.3X1	T44.3X2	T44.3X3	T44.3X4	T44.3X5	T44.3X6
bromide	T44.3X1	T44.3X2	T44.3X3	T44.3X4	T44.3X5	T44.3X6
Glycoside, cardiac (stimulant)	T46.0X1	T46.0X2	T46.0X3	T46.0X4	T46.0X5	T46.0X6
Glycyclamide	T38.3X1	T38.3X2	T38.3X3	T38.3X4	T38.3X5	T38.3X6
Glycyrrhiza extract	T48.4X1	T48.4X2	T48.4X3	T48.4X4	T48.4X5	T48.4X6
Glycyrrhizic acid	T48.4X1	T48.4X2	T48.4X3	T48.4X4	T48.4X5	T48.4X6
Glycyrrhizinate potassium	T48.4X1	T48.4X2	T48.4X3	T48.4X4	T48.4X5	T48.4X6
Glymidine sodium	T38.3X1	T38.3X2	T38.3X3	T38.3X4	T38.3X5	T38.3X6
Glyphosate	T60.3X1	T60.3X2	T60.3X3	T60.3X4	—	—
Glyphylline	T48.6X1	T48.6X2	T48.6X3	T48.6X4	T48.6X5	T48.6X6
Gold						
colloidal (l98Au)	T45.1X1	T45.1X2	T45.1X3	T45.1X4	T45.1X5	T45.1X6
salts	T39.4X1	T39.4X2	T39.4X3	T39.4X4	T39.4X5	T39.4X6
Golden sulfide of antimony	T56.891	T56.892	T56.893	T56.894	—	—
Goldylocks	T62.2X1	T62.2X2	T62.2X3	T62.2X4	—	—
Gonadal tissue extract	T38.901	T38.902	T38.903	T38.904	T38.905	T38.906
female	T38.5X1	T38.5X2	T38.5X3	T38.5X4	T38.5X5	T38.5X6
male	T38.7X1	T38.7X2	T38.7X3	T38.7X4	T38.7X5	T38.7X6
Gonadorelin	T38.891	T38.892	T38.893	T38.894	T38.895	T38.896
Gonadotropin	T38.891	T38.892	T38.893	T38.894	T38.895	T38.896
chorionic	T38.891	T38.892	T38.893	T38.894	T38.895	T38.896
pituitary	T38.811	T38.812	T38.813	T38.814	T38.815	T38.816
Goserelin	T45.1X1	T45.1X2	T45.1X3	T45.1X4	T45.1X5	T45.1X6
Grain alcohol	T51.0X1	T51.0X2	T51.0X3	T51.0X4	—	—
Gramicidin	T49.0X1	T49.0X2	T49.0X3	T49.0X4	T49.0X5	T49.0X6
Granisetron	T45.0X1	T45.0X2	T45.0X3	T45.0X4	T45.0X5	T45.0X6
Gratiola officinalis	T62.2X1	T62.2X2	T62.2X3	T62.2X4	—	—
Grease	T65.891	T65.892	T65.893	T65.894	—	—
Green hellebore	T62.2X1	T62.2X2	T62.2X3	T62.2X4	—	—
Green soap	T49.2X1	T49.2X2	T49.2X3	T49.2X4	T49.2X5	T49.2X6
Grifulvin	T36.7X1	T36.7X2	T36.7X3	T36.7X4	T36.7X5	T36.7X6
Griseofulvin	T36.7X1	T36.7X2	T36.7X3	T36.7X4	T36.7X5	T36.7X6
Growth hormone	T38.811	T38.812	T38.813	T38.814	T38.815	T38.816
Guaiacol derivatives	T48.4X1	T48.4X2	T48.4X3	T48.4X4	T48.4X5	T48.4X6
Guaiac reagent	T50.991	T50.992	T50.993	T50.994	T50.995	T50.996
Guaifenesin	T48.4X1	T48.4X2	T48.4X3	T48.4X4	T48.4X5	T48.4X6
Guaimesal	T48.4X1	T48.4X2	T48.4X3	T48.4X4	T48.4X5	T48.4X6
Guaiphenesin	T48.4X1	T48.4X2	T48.4X3	T48.4X4	T48.4X5	T48.4X6
Guamecycline	T36.4X1	T36.4X2	T36.4X3	T36.4X4	T36.4X5	T36.4X6

◀ New ◀ Revised ~~deleted~~ Deleted

Substance	External Cause (T-Code) Poisoning, Accidental (Unintentional)	Poisoning, Intentional Self-Harm	Poisoning, Assault	Poisoning, Undetermined	Adverse Effect	Underdosing
Guanabenz	T46.5X1	T46.5X2	T46.5X3	T46.5X4	T46.5X5	T46.5X6
Guanacline	T46.5X1	T46.5X2	T46.5X3	T46.5X4	T46.5X5	T46.5X6
Guanadrel	T46.5X1	T46.5X2	T46.5X3	T46.5X4	T46.5X5	T46.5X6
Guanatol	T37.2X1	T37.2X2	T37.2X3	T37.2X4	T37.2X5	T37.2X6
Guanethidine	T46.5X1	T46.5X2	T46.5X3	T46.5X4	T46.5X5	T46.5X6
Guanfacine	T46.5X1	T46.5X2	T46.5X3	T46.5X4	T46.5X5	T46.5X6
Guano	T65.891	T65.892	T65.893	T65.894	—	—
Guanochlor	T46.5X1	T46.5X2	T46.5X3	T46.5X4	T46.5X5	T46.5X6
Guanoclor	T46.5X1	T46.5X2	T46.5X3	T46.5X4	T46.5X5	T46.5X6
Guanoctine	T46.5X1	T46.5X2	T46.5X3	T46.5X4	T46.5X5	T46.5X6
Guanoxabenz	T46.5X1	T46.5X2	T46.5X3	T46.5X4	T46.5X5	T46.5X6
Guanoxan	T46.5X1	T46.5X2	T46.5X3	T46.5X4	T46.5X5	T46.5X6
Guar gum (medicinal)	T46.6X1	T46.6X2	T46.6X3	T46.6X4	T46.6X5	T46.6X6
H						
Hachimycin	T36.7X1	T36.7X2	T36.7X3	T36.7X4	T36.7X5	T36.7X6
Hair						
dye	T49.4X1	T49.4X2	T49.4X3	T49.4X4	T49.4X5	T49.4X6
preparation NEC	T49.4X1	T49.4X2	T49.4X3	T49.4X4	T49.4X5	T49.4X6
Halazepam	T42.4X1	T42.4X2	T42.4X3	T42.4X4	T42.4X5	T42.4X6
Halcinolone	T49.0X1	T49.0X2	T49.0X3	T49.0X4	T49.0X5	T49.0X6
Halcinonide	T49.0X1	T49.0X2	T49.0X3	T49.0X4	T49.0X5	T49.0X6
Halethazole	T49.0X1	T49.0X2	T49.0X3	T49.0X4	T49.0X5	T49.0X6
Hallucinogen NOS	T40.901	T40.902	T40.903	T40.904	T40.905	T40.906
specified NEC	T40.991	T40.992	T40.993	T40.994	T40.995	T40.996
Halofantrine	T37.2X1	T37.2X2	T37.2X3	T37.2X4	T37.2X5	T37.2X6
Halofenate	T46.6X1	T46.6X2	T46.6X3	T46.6X4	T46.6X5	T46.6X6
Halometasone	T49.0X1	T49.0X2	T49.0X3	T49.0X4	T49.0X5	T49.0X6
Haloperidol	T43.4X1	T43.4X2	T43.4X3	T43.4X4	T43.4X5	T43.4X6
Haloprogin	T49.0X1	T49.0X2	T49.0X3	T49.0X4	T49.0X5	T49.0X6
Halotex	T49.0X1	T49.0X2	T49.0X3	T49.0X4	T49.0X5	T49.0X6
Halothane	T41.0X1	T41.0X2	T41.0X3	T41.0X4	T41.0X5	T41.0X6
Haloxazolam	T42.4X1	T42.4X2	T42.4X3	T42.4X4	T42.4X5	T42.4X6
Halquinols	T49.0X1	T49.0X2	T49.0X3	T49.0X4	T49.0X5	T49.0X6
Hamamelis	T49.2X1	T49.2X2	T49.2X3	T49.2X4	T49.2X5	T49.2X6
Haptendextran	T45.8X1	T45.8X2	T45.8X3	T45.8X4	T45.8X5	T45.8X6
Harmonyl	T46.5X1	T46.5X2	T46.5X3	T46.5X4	T46.5X5	T46.5X6
Hartmann's solution	T50.3X1	T50.3X2	T50.3X3	T50.3X4	T50.3X5	T50.3X6
Hashish	T40.7X1	T40.7X2	T40.7X3	T40.7X4	T40.7X5	T40.7X6
Hawaiian Woodrose seeds	T40.991	T40.992	T40.993	T40.994	—	—
HCB	T60.3X1	T60.3X2	T60.3X3	T60.3X4	—	—
HCH	T53.6X1	T53.6X2	T53.6X3	T53.6X4	—	—
medicinal	T49.0X1	T49.0X2	T49.0X3	T49.0X4	T49.0X5	T49.0X6

Substance	External Cause (T-Code) Poisoning, Accidental (Unintentional)	Poisoning, Intentional Self-Harm	Poisoning, Assault	Poisoning, Undetermined	Adverse Effect	Underdosing
HCN	T57.3X1	T57.3X2	T57.3X3	T57.3X4	—	—
Headache cures, drugs, powders NEC	T50.901	T50.902	T50.903	T50.904	T50.905	T50.906
Heavenly Blue (morning glory)	T40.991	T40.992	T40.993	T40.994	—	—
Heavy metal antidote	T45.8X1	T45.8X2	T45.8X3	T45.8X4	T45.8X5	T45.8X6
Hedaquinium	T49.0X1	T49.0X2	T49.0X3	T49.0X4	T49.0X5	T49.0X6
Hedge hyssop	T62.2X1	T62.2X2	T62.2X3	T62.2X4		
Heet	T49.8X1	T49.8X2	T49.8X3	T49.8X4	T49.8X5	T49.8X6
Helium	T48.991	T48.992	T48.993	T48.994	T48.995	T48.996
Helenin	T37.4X1	T37.4X2	T37.4X3	T37.4X4	T37.4X5	T37.4X6
Hellebore (black) (green) (white)	T62.2X1	T62.2X2	T62.2X3	T62.2X4		
Helium (nonmedicinal) NEC	T59.891	T59.892	T59.893	T59.894	—	—
medicinal	T48.991	T48.992	T48.993	T48.994	T48.995	T48.996
Hematin	T45.8X1	T45.8X2	T45.8X3	T45.8X4	T45.8X5	T45.8X6
Hematinic preparation	T45.8X1	T45.8X2	T45.8X3	T45.8X4	T45.8X5	T45.8X6
Hemlock	T62.2X1	T62.2X2	T62.2X3	T62.2X4	—	—
Hemostatic	T45.621	T45.622	T45.623	T45.624	T45.625	T45.626
drug, systemic	T45.621	T45.622	T45.623	T45.624	T45.625	T45.626
Hemostyptic	T49.4X1	T49.4X2	T49.4X3	T49.4X4	T49.4X5	T49.4X6
Henbane	T62.2X1	T62.2X2	T62.2X3	T62.2X4	—	—
Heparin (sodium)	T45.511	T45.512	T45.513	T45.514	T45.515	T45.516
action reverser	T45.7X1	T45.7X2	T45.7X3	T45.7X4	T45.7X5	T45.7X6
Heparin-fraction	T45.511	T45.512	T45.513	T45.514	T45.515	T45.516
Heparinoid (systemic)	T45.511	T45.512	T45.513	T45.514	T45.515	T45.516
Hepatic secretion stimulant	T47.8X1	T47.8X2	T47.8X3	T47.8X4	T47.8X5	T47.8X6
Hepatitis B						
immune globulin	T50.Z11	T50.Z12	T50.Z13	T50.Z14	T50.Z15	T50.Z16
vaccine	T50.B91	T50.B92	T50.B93	T50.B94	T50.B95	T50.B96
Hepronicate	T46.7X1	T46.7X2	T46.7X3	T46.7X4	T46.7X5	T46.7X6
Heptabarb	T42.3X1	T42.3X2	T42.3X3	T42.3X4	T42.3X5	T42.3X6
Heptabarbitone	T42.3X1	T42.3X2	T42.3X3	T42.3X4	T42.3X5	T42.3X6
Heptabarbital	T42.3X1	T42.3X2	T42.3X3	T42.3X4	T42.3X5	T42.3X6
Heptachlor	T60.1X1	T60.1X2	T60.1X3	T60.1X4	—	—
Heptalgin	T40.2X1	T40.2X2	T40.2X3	T40.2X4	T40.2X5	T40.2X6
Heptaminol	T46.3X1	T46.3X2	T46.3X3	T46.3X4	T46.3X5	T46.3X6
Herbicide NEC	T60.3X1	T60.3X2	T60.3X3	T60.3X4	—	—
Heroin	T40.1X1	T40.1X2	T40.1X3	T40.1X4		
Herplex	T49.5X1	T49.5X2	T49.5X3	T49.5X4	T49.5X5	T49.5X6
HES	T45.8X1	T45.8X2	T45.8X3	T45.8X4	T45.8X5	T45.8X6
Hesperidin	T46.991	T46.992	T46.993	T46.994	T46.995	T46.996
Hetacillin	T36.0X1	T36.0X2	T36.0X3	T36.0X4	T36.0X5	T36.0X6

◀ New　◀ Revised　~~deleted~~ Deleted

Substance	Poisoning, Accidental (Unintentional)	Poisoning, Intentional Self-Harm	Poisoning, Assault	Poisoning, Undetermined	Adverse Effect	Underdosing
Hetastarch	T45.8X1	T45.8X2	T45.8X3	T45.8X4	T45.8X5	T45.8X6
HETP	T60.0X1	T60.0X2	T60.0X3	T60.0X4	—	—
Hexachlorobenzene (vapor)	T60.3X1	T60.3X2	T60.3X3	T60.3X4	—	—
Hexachlorocyclohexane	T53.6X1	T53.6X2	T53.6X3	T53.6X4	—	—
Hexachlorophene	T49.0X1	T49.0X2	T49.0X3	T49.0X4	T49.0X5	T49.0X6
Hexadiline	T46.3X1	T46.3X2	T46.3X3	T46.3X4	T46.3X5	T46.3X6
Hexadimethrine (bromide)	T45.7X1	T45.7X2	T45.7X3	T45.7X4	T45.7X5	T45.7X6
Hexadylamine	T46.3X1	T46.3X2	T46.3X3	T46.3X4	T46.3X5	T46.3X6
Hexaethyl tetraphosphate	T60.0X1	T60.0X2	T60.0X3	T60.0X4	—	—
Hexafluorenium bromide	T48.1X1	T48.1X2	T48.1X3	T48.1X4	T48.1X5	T48.1X6
Hexafluorodiethyl ether	T43.291	T43.292	T43.293	T43.294	T43.295	T43.296
Hexafluronium (bromide)	T48.1X1	T48.1X2	T48.1X3	T48.1X4	T48.1X5	T48.1X6
Hexahydrobenzol	T52.8X1	T52.8X2	T52.8X3	T52.8X4	—	—
Hexahydrocresol(s)	T51.8X1	T51.8X2	T51.8X3	T51.8X4	—	—
arsenide	T57.0X1	T57.0X2	T57.0X3	T57.0X4	—	—
arseniurated	T57.0X1	T57.0X2	T57.0X3	T57.0X4	—	—
cyanide	T57.3X1	T57.3X2	T57.3X3	T57.3X4	—	—
gas	T59.891	T59.892	T59.893	T59.894	—	—
Fluoride (liquid)	T57.8X1	T57.8X2	T57.8X3	T57.8X4	—	—
vapor	T59.891	T59.892	T59.893	T59.894	—	—
phophorated	T60.0X1	T60.0X2	T60.0X3	T60.0X4	—	—
sulfate	T57.8X1	T57.8X2	T57.8X3	T57.8X4	—	—
sulfide (gas)	T59.6X1	T59.6X2	T59.6X3	T59.6X4	—	—
arseniurated	T57.0X1	T57.0X2	T57.0X3	T57.0X4	—	—
sulfurated	T57.8X1	T57.8X2	T57.8X3	T57.8X4	—	—
Hexahydrophenol	T51.8X1	T51.8X2	T51.8X3	T51.8X4	—	—
Hexa-germ	T49.2X1	T49.2X2	T49.2X3	T49.2X4	T49.2X5	T49.2X6
Hexalen	T51.8X1	T51.8X2	T51.8X3	T51.8X4	—	—
Hexamethonium bromide	T44.2X1	T44.2X2	T44.2X3	T44.2X4	T44.2X5	T44.2X6
Hexamethylene	T52.8X1	T52.8X2	T52.8X3	T52.8X4	—	—
Hexamethylmelamine	T45.1X1	T45.1X2	T45.1X3	T45.1X4	T45.1X5	T45.1X6
Hexamidine	T49.0X1	T49.0X2	T49.0X3	T49.0X4	T49.0X5	T49.0X6
Hexamine (mandelate)	T37.8X1	T37.8X2	T37.8X3	T37.8X4	T37.8X5	T37.8X6
Hexanone, 2-hexanone	T52.4X1	T52.4X2	T52.4X3	T52.4X4	—	—
Hexanuorenium	T48.1X1	T48.1X2	T48.1X3	T48.1X4	T48.1X5	T48.1X6
Hexapropymate	T42.6X1	T42.6X2	T42.6X3	T42.6X4	T42.6X5	T42.6X6
Hexasonium iodide	T44.3X1	T44.3X2	T44.3X3	T44.3X4	T44.3X5	T44.3X6
Hexcarbacholine bromide	T48.1X1	T48.1X2	T48.1X3	T48.1X4	T48.1X5	T48.1X6
Hexemal	T42.3X1	T42.3X2	T42.3X3	T42.3X4	T42.3X5	T42.3X6
Hexestrol	T38.5X1	T38.5X2	T38.5X3	T38.5X4	T38.5X5	T38.5X6
Hexethal (sodium)	T42.3X1	T42.3X2	T42.3X3	T42.3X4	T42.3X5	T42.3X6
Hexetidine	T37.8X1	T37.8X2	T37.8X3	T37.8X4	T37.8X5	T37.8X6

Substance	Poisoning, Accidental (Unintentional)	Poisoning, Intentional Self-Harm	Poisoning, Assault	Poisoning, Undetermined	Adverse Effect	Underdosing
Hexobarbital	T42.3X1	T42.3X2	T42.3X3	T42.3X4	T42.3X5	T42.3X6
rectal	T41.291	T41.292	T41.293	T41.294	T41.295	T41.296
sodium	T41.1X1	T41.1X2	T41.1X3	T41.1X4	T41.1X5	T41.1X6
Hexobendine	T46.3X1	T46.3X2	T46.3X3	T46.3X4	T46.3X5	T46.3X6
Hexocyclium	T44.3X1	T44.3X2	T44.3X3	T44.3X4	T44.3X5	T44.3X6
metilsulfate	T44.3X1	T44.3X2	T44.3X3	T44.3X4	T44.3X5	T44.3X6
Hexoestrol	T38.5X1	T38.5X2	T38.5X3	T38.5X4	T38.5X5	T38.5X6
Hexone	T52.4X1	T52.4X2	T52.4X3	T52.4X4	—	—
Hexoprenaline	T48.6X1	T48.6X2	T48.6X3	T48.6X4	T48.6X5	T48.6X6
Hexylcaine	T41.3X1	T41.3X2	T41.3X3	T41.3X4	T41.3X5	T41.3X6
Hexylresorcinol	T52.2X1	T52.2X2	T52.2X3	T52.2X4	—	—
HGH (human growth hormone)	T38.811	T38.812	T38.813	T38.814	T38.815	T38.816
Hinkle's pills	T47.2X1	T47.2X2	T47.2X3	T47.2X4	T47.2X5	T47.2X6
Histalog	T50.8X1	T50.8X2	T50.8X3	T50.8X4	T50.8X5	T50.8X6
Histamine (phosphate)	T50.8X1	T50.8X2	T50.8X3	T50.8X4	T50.8X5	T50.8X6
Histoplasmin	T50.8X1	T50.8X2	T50.8X3	T50.8X4	T50.8X5	T50.8X6
Holly berries	T62.2X1	T62.2X2	T62.2X3	T62.2X4	—	—
Homatropine	T44.3X1	T44.3X2	T44.3X3	T44.3X4	T44.3X5	T44.3X6
methylbromide	T44.3X1	T44.3X2	T44.3X3	T44.3X4	T44.3X5	T44.3X6
Homochlorcyclizine	T45.0X1	T45.0X2	T45.0X3	T45.0X4	T45.0X5	T45.0X6
Homosalate	T49.3X1	T49.3X2	T49.3X3	T49.3X4	T49.3X5	T49.3X6
Homo-tet	T50.Z11	T50.Z12	T50.Z13	T50.Z14	T50.Z15	T50.Z16
Hormone	T38.801	T38.802	T38.803	T38.804	T38.805	T38.806
adrenal cortical steroids	T38.0X1	T38.0X2	T38.0X3	T38.0X4	T38.0X5	T38.0X6
androgenic	T38.7X1	T38.7X2	T38.7X3	T38.7X4	T38.7X5	T38.7X6
anterior pituitary NEC	T38.811	T38.812	T38.813	T38.814	T38.815	T38.816
antidiabetic agents	T38.3X1	T38.3X2	T38.3X3	T38.3X4	T38.3X5	T38.3X6
antidiuretic	T38.891	T38.892	T38.893	T38.894	T38.895	T38.896
cancer therapy	T45.1X1	T45.1X2	T45.1X3	T45.1X4	T45.1X5	T45.1X6
follicle stimulating	T38.811	T38.812	T38.813	T38.814	T38.815	T38.816
gonadotropic	T38.891	T38.892	T38.893	T38.894	T38.895	T38.896
pituitary	T38.811	T38.812	T38.813	T38.814	T38.815	T38.816
growth	T38.811	T38.812	T38.813	T38.814	T38.815	T38.816
luteinizing	T38.811	T38.812	T38.813	T38.814	T38.815	T38.816
ovarian	T38.5X1	T38.5X2	T38.5X3	T38.5X4	T38.5X5	T38.5X6
oxytocic	T48.0X1	T48.0X2	T48.0X3	T48.0X4	T48.0X5	T48.0X6
parathyroid (derivatives)	T50.991	T50.992	T50.993	T50.994	T50.995	T50.996
pituitary (posterior) NEC	T38.891	T38.892	T38.893	T38.894	T38.895	T38.896
anterior	T38.811	T38.812	T38.813	T38.814	T38.815	T38.816
specified, NEC	T38.891	T38.892	T38.893	T38.894	T38.895	T38.896
thyroid	T38.1X1	T38.1X2	T38.1X3	T38.1X4	T38.1X5	T38.1X6
Hornet (sting)	T63.451	T63.452	T63.453	T63.454	—	—

◀ New　◀ Revised　deleted Deleted

Substance	Poisoning, Accidental (Unintentional)	Poisoning, Intentional Self-Harm	Poisoning, Assault	Poisoning, Undetermined	Adverse Effect	Underdosing
Horse anti-human lymphocytic serum	T50.Z11	T50.Z12	T50.Z13	T50.Z14	T50.Z15	T50.Z16
Horticulture agent NEC	T65.91	T65.92	T65.93	T65.94	—	—
with pesticide	T60.91	T60.92	T60.93	T60.94	—	—
Human						
albumin	T45.8X1	T45.8X2	T45.8X3	T45.8X4	T45.8X5	T45.8X6
growth hormone (HGH)	T38.811	T38.812	T38.813	T38.814	T38.815	T38.816
immune serum	T50.Z11	T50.Z12	T50.Z13	T50.Z14	T50.Z15	T50.Z16
Hyaluronidase	T45.3X1	T45.3X2	T45.3X3	T45.3X4	T45.3X5	T45.3X6
Hyazyme	T45.3X1	T45.3X2	T45.3X3	T45.3X4	T45.3X5	T45.3X6
Hycodan	T40.2X1	T40.2X2	T40.2X3	T40.2X4	T40.2X5	T40.2X6
Hydantoin derivative NEC	T42.0X1	T42.0X2	T42.0X3	T42.0X4	T42.0X5	T42.0X6
Hydeltra	T38.0X1	T38.0X2	T38.0X3	T38.0X4	T38.0X5	T38.0X6
Hydergine	T44.6X1	T44.6X2	T44.6X3	T44.6X4	T44.6X5	T44.6X6
Hydrabamine penicillin	T36.0X1	T36.0X2	T36.0X3	T36.0X4	T36.0X5	T36.0X6
Hydralazine	T46.5X1	T46.5X2	T46.5X3	T46.5X4	T46.5X5	T46.5X6
Hydrargaphen	T49.0X1	T49.0X2	T49.0X3	T49.0X4	T49.0X5	T49.0X6
Hydrargyri amino-chloridum	T49.0X1	T49.0X2	T49.0X3	T49.0X4	T49.0X5	T49.0X6
Hydrastine	T48.291	T48.292	T48.293	T48.294	T48.295	T48.296
Hydrazine	T54.1X1	T54.1X2	T54.1X3	T54.1X4	—	—
monoamine oxidase inhibitors	T43.1X1	T43.1X2	T43.1X3	T43.1X4	T43.1X5	T43.1X6
Hydrazoic acid, azides	T54.2X1	T54.2X2	T54.2X3	T54.2X4	—	—
Hydriodic acid	T48.4X1	T48.4X2	T48.4X3	T48.4X4	T48.4X5	T48.4X6
Hydrocarbon gas	T59.891	T59.892	T59.893	T59.894	—	—
incomplete combustion of— see Carbon, monoxide, fuel, utility						
liquefied (mobile container)	T59.891	T59.892	T59.893	T59.894	—	—
piped (natural)	T59.891	T59.892	T59.893	T59.894	—	—
Hydrochloric acid (liquid)	T54.2X1	T54.2X2	T54.2X3	T54.2X4	—	—
medicinal (digestant)	T47.5X1	T47.5X2	T47.5X3	T47.5X4	T47.5X5	T47.5X6
vapor	T59.891	T59.892	T59.893	T59.894	—	—
Hydrochlorothiazide	T50.2X1	T50.2X2	T50.2X3	T50.2X4	T50.2X5	T50.2X6
Hydrocodone	T40.2X1	T40.2X2	T40.2X3	T40.2X4	T40.2X5	T40.2X6
Hydrocortisone (derivatives)	T38.0X1	T38.0X2	T38.0X3	T38.0X4	T38.0X5	T38.0X6
aceponate	T49.0X1	T49.0X2	T49.0X3	T49.0X4	T49.0X5	T49.0X6
ENT agent	T49.6X1	T49.6X2	T49.6X3	T49.6X4	T49.6X5	T49.6X6
ophthalmic preparation	T49.5X1	T49.5X2	T49.5X3	T49.5X4	T49.5X5	T49.5X6
topical NEC	T49.0X1	T49.0X2	T49.0X3	T49.0X4	T49.0X5	T49.0X6
Hydrocortone	T38.0X1	T38.0X2	T38.0X3	T38.0X4	T38.0X5	T38.0X6
ENT agent	T49.6X1	T49.6X2	T49.6X3	T49.6X4	T49.6X5	T49.6X6
ophthalmic preparation	T49.5X1	T49.5X2	T49.5X3	T49.5X4	T49.5X5	T49.5X6
topical NEC	T49.0X1	T49.0X2	T49.0X3	T49.0X4	T49.0X5	T49.0X6

Substance	Poisoning, Accidental (Unintentional)	Poisoning, Intentional Self-Harm	Poisoning, Assault	Poisoning, Undetermined	Adverse Effect	Underdosing
Hydrocyanic acid (liquid)	T57.3X1	T57.3X2	T57.3X3	T57.3X4	—	—
gas	T65.0X1	T65.0X2	T65.0X3	T65.0X4	—	—
Hydroflumethiazide	T50.2X1	T50.2X2	T50.2X3	T50.2X4	T50.2X5	T50.2X6
Hydrofluoric acid (liquid)	T54.2X1	T54.2X2	T54.2X3	T54.2X4	—	—
vapor	T59.891	T59.892	T59.893	T59.894	—	—
Hydrogen	T59.891	T59.892	T59.893	T59.894	—	—
arsenide	T57.0X1	T57.0X2	T57.0X3	T57.0X4	—	—
arseniureted	T57.0X1	T57.0X2	T57.0X3	T57.0X4	—	—
chloride	T57.8X1	T57.8X2	T57.8X3	T57.8X4	—	—
cyanide (salts)	T57.3X1	T57.3X2	T57.3X3	T57.3X4	—	—
gas	T57.3X1	T57.3X2	T57.3X3	T57.3X4	—	—
Fluoride	T59.5X1	T59.5X2	T59.5X3	T59.5X4	—	—
vapor	T59.5X1	T59.5X2	T59.5X3	T59.5X4	—	—
peroxide	T49.0X1	T49.0X2	T49.0X3	T49.0X4	T49.0X5	T49.0X6
phosphureted	T57.1X1	T57.1X2	T57.1X3	T57.1X4	—	—
sulfide	T59.6X1	T59.6X2	T59.6X3	T59.6X4	—	—
arseniureted	T57.0X1	T57.0X2	T57.0X3	T57.0X4	—	—
sulfureted	T59.6X1	T59.6X2	T59.6X3	T59.6X4	—	—
Hydromethylpyridine	T46.7X1	T46.7X2	T46.7X3	T46.7X4	T46.7X5	T46.7X6
Hydromorphinol	T40.2X1	T40.2X2	T40.2X3	T40.2X4	—	—
Hydromorphinone	T40.2X1	T40.2X2	T40.2X3	T40.2X4	T40.2X5	T40.2X6
Hydromorphone	T40.2X1	T40.2X2	T40.2X3	T40.2X4	T40.2X5	T40.2X6
Hydromox	T50.2X1	T50.2X2	T50.2X3	T50.2X4	T50.2X5	T50.2X6
Hydrophilic lotion	T49.3X1	T49.3X2	T49.3X3	T49.3X4	T49.3X5	T49.3X6
Hydroquinidine	T46.2X1	T46.2X2	T46.2X3	T46.2X4	T46.2X5	T46.2X6
Hydroquinone	T52.2X1	T52.2X2	T52.2X3	T52.2X4	—	—
vapor	T59.891	T59.892	T59.893	T59.894	—	—
Hydrosulfuric acid (gas)	T59.6X1	T59.6X2	T59.6X3	T59.6X4	—	—
Hydrotalcite	T47.1X1	T47.1X2	T47.1X3	T47.1X4	T47.1X5	T47.1X6
Hydrous wool fat	T49.3X1	T49.3X2	T49.3X3	T49.3X4	T49.3X5	T49.3X6
Hydroxide, caustic	T54.3X1	T54.3X2	T54.3X3	T54.3X4	—	—
Hydroxocobalamin	T45.8X1	T45.8X2	T45.8X3	T45.8X4	T45.8X5	T45.8X6
Hydroxyamphetamine	T49.5X1	T49.5X2	T49.5X3	T49.5X4	T49.5X5	T49.5X6
Hydroxycarbamide	T45.1X1	T45.1X2	T45.1X3	T45.1X4	T45.1X5	T45.1X6
Hydroxychloroquine	T37.8X1	T37.8X2	T37.8X3	T37.8X4	T37.8X5	T37.8X6
Hydroxydihydrocodeinone	T40.2X1	T40.2X2	T40.2X3	T40.2X4	T40.2X5	T40.2X6
Hydroxyestrone	T38.5X1	T38.5X2	T38.5X3	T38.5X4	T38.5X5	T38.5X6
Hydroxyethyl starch	T45.8X1	T45.8X2	T45.8X3	T45.8X4	T45.8X5	T45.8X6
Hydroxymethylpentanone	T52.4X1	T52.4X2	T52.4X3	T52.4X4	—	—
Hydroxyphenamate	T43.591	T43.592	T43.593	T43.594	T43.595	T43.596
Hydroxyphenylbutazone	T39.2X1	T39.2X2	T39.2X3	T39.2X4	T39.2X5	T39.2X6

◀ New　◀ Revised　deleted Deleted

Substance	Poisoning, Accidental (Unintentional)	Poisoning, Intentional Self-Harm	Poisoning, Assault	Poisoning, Undetermined	Adverse Effect	Underdosing
Hydroxyprogesterone	T38.5X1	T38.5X2	T38.5X3	T38.5X4	T38.5X5	T38.5X6
caproate	T38.5X1	T38.5X2	T38.5X3	T38.5X4	T38.5X5	T38.5X6
Hydroxyquinoline (derivatives) NEC	T37.8X1	T37.8X2	T37.8X3	T37.8X4	T37.8X5	T37.8X6
Hydroxystilbamidine	T37.3X1	T37.3X2	T37.3X3	T37.3X4	T37.3X5	T37.3X6
Hydroxytoluene (nonmedicinal)	T54.0X1	T54.0X2	T54.0X3	T54.0X4	—	—
medicinal	T49.0X1	T49.0X2	T49.0X3	T49.0X4	T49.0X5	T49.0X6
Hydroxyurea	T45.1X1	T45.1X2	T45.1X3	T45.1X4	T45.1X5	T45.1X6
Hydroxyzine	T43.591	T43.592	T43.593	T43.594	T43.595	T43.596
Hyoscine	T44.3X1	T44.3X2	T44.3X3	T44.3X4	T44.3X5	T44.3X6
Hyoscyamine	T44.3X1	T44.3X2	T44.3X3	T44.3X4	T44.3X5	T44.3X6
Hyoscyamus	T44.3X1	T44.3X2	T44.3X3	T44.3X4	T44.3X5	T44.3X6
dry extract	T44.3X1	T44.3X2	T44.3X3	T44.3X4	T44.3X5	T44.3X6
Hypaque	T50.8X1	T50.8X2	T50.8X3	T50.8X4	T50.8X5	T50.8X6
Hypertussis	T50.Z11	T50.Z12	T50.Z13	T50.Z14	T50.Z15	T50.Z16
Hypnotic	T42.71	T42.72	T42.73	T42.74	T42.75	T42.76
anticonvulsant	T42.71	T42.72	T42.73	T42.74	T42.75	T42.76
specified NEC	T42.6X1	T42.6X2	T42.6X3	T42.6X4	T42.6X5	T42.6X6
Hypochlorite	T49.0X1	T49.0X2	T49.0X3	T49.0X4	T49.0X5	T49.0X6
Hypophysis, posterior	T38.891	T38.892	T38.893	T38.894	T38.895	T38.896
Hypotensive NEC	T46.5X1	T46.5X2	T46.5X3	T46.5X4	T46.5X5	T46.5X6
Hypromellose	T49.5X1	T49.5X2	T49.5X3	T49.5X4	T49.5X5	T49.5X6

I

Substance	Poisoning, Accidental (Unintentional)	Poisoning, Intentional Self-Harm	Poisoning, Assault	Poisoning, Undetermined	Adverse Effect	Underdosing
Ibacitabine	T37.5X1	T37.5X2	T37.5X3	T37.5X4	T37.5X5	T37.5X6
Ibopamine	T44.991	T44.992	T44.993	T44.994	T44.995	T44.996
Ibufenac	T39.311	T39.312	T39.313	T39.314	T39.315	T39.316
Ibuprofen	T39.311	T39.312	T39.313	T39.314	T39.315	T39.316
Ibuproxam	T39.311	T39.312	T39.313	T39.314	T39.315	T39.316
Ibuterol	T48.6X1	T48.6X2	T48.6X3	T48.6X4	T48.6X5	T48.6X6
Ichthammol	T49.0X1	T49.0X2	T49.0X3	T49.0X4	T49.0X5	T49.0X6
Ichthyol	T49.4X1	T49.4X2	T49.4X3	T49.4X4	T49.4X5	T49.4X6
Idarubicin	T45.1X1	T45.1X2	T45.1X3	T45.1X4	T45.1X5	T45.1X6
Idrocilamide	T42.8X1	T42.8X2	T42.8X3	T42.8X4	T42.8X5	T42.8X6
Ifenprodil	T46.7X1	T46.7X2	T46.7X3	T46.7X4	T46.7X5	T46.7X6
Ifosfamide	T45.1X1	T45.1X2	T45.1X3	T45.1X4	T45.1X5	T45.1X6
Iletin	T38.3X1	T38.3X2	T38.3X3	T38.3X4	T38.3X5	T38.3X6
Ilex	T62.2X1	T62.2X2	T62.2X3	T62.2X4	—	—
Illuminating gas (after combustion)	T58.11	T58.12	T58.13	T58.14	—	—
prior to combustion	T59.891	T59.892	T59.893	T59.894	—	—
Ilopan	T45.2X1	T45.2X2	T45.2X3	T45.2X4	T45.2X5	T45.2X6
Iloprost	T46.7X1	T46.7X2	T46.7X3	T46.7X4	T46.7X5	T46.7X6

Substance	Poisoning, Accidental (Unintentional)	Poisoning, Intentional Self-Harm	Poisoning, Assault	Poisoning, Undetermined	Adverse Effect	Underdosing
Ilotycin	T36.3X1	T36.3X2	T36.3X3	T36.3X4	T36.3X5	T36.3X6
ophthalmic preparation	T49.5X1	T49.5X2	T49.5X3	T49.5X4	T49.5X5	T49.5X6
topical NEC	T49.0X1	T49.0X2	T49.0X3	T49.0X4	T49.0X5	T49.0X6
Imidazole-4-carboxamide	T45.1X1	T45.1X2	T45.1X3	T45.1X4	T45.1X5	T45.1X6
Imipenem	T36.0X1	T36.0X2	T36.0X3	T36.0X4	T36.0X5	T36.0X6
Imipramine	T43.011	T43.012	T43.013	T43.014	T43.015	T43.016
Iminostilbene	T42.1X1	T42.1X2	T42.1X3	T42.1X4	T42.1X5	T42.1X6
Immu-G	T50.Z11	T50.Z12	T50.Z13	T50.Z14	T50.Z15	T50.Z16
Immuglobin	T50.Z11	T50.Z12	T50.Z13	T50.Z14	T50.Z15	T50.Z16
Immune						
globulin	T50.Z11	T50.Z12	T50.Z13	T50.Z14	T50.Z15	T50.Z16
serum globulin	T50.Z11	T50.Z12	T50.Z13	T50.Z14	T50.Z15	T50.Z16
Immunoglobin human (intravenous) (normal)	T50.Z11	T50.Z12	T50.Z13	T50.Z14	T50.Z15	T50.Z16
unmodified	T50.Z11	T50.Z12	T50.Z13	T50.Z14	T50.Z15	T50.Z16
Immunosuppressive drug	T45.1X1	T45.1X2	T45.1X3	T45.1X4	T45.1X5	T45.1X6
Immu-tetanus	T50.Z11	T50.Z12	T50.Z13	T50.Z14	T50.Z15	T50.Z16
Indalpine	T43.221	T43.222	T43.223	T43.224	T43.225	T43.226
Indanazoline	T48.5X1	T48.5X2	T48.5X3	T48.5X4	T48.5X5	T48.5X6
Indandione (derivatives)	T45.511	T45.512	T45.513	T45.514	T45.515	T45.516
Indapamide	T46.5X1	T46.5X2	T46.5X3	T46.5X4	T46.5X5	T46.5X6
Indendione (derivatives)	T45.511	T45.512	T45.513	T45.514	T45.515	T45.516
Indenolol	T44.7X1	T44.7X2	T44.7X3	T44.7X4	T44.7X5	T44.7X6
Inderal	T44.7X1	T44.7X2	T44.7X3	T44.7X4	T44.7X5	T44.7X6
Indian						
hemp	T40.7X1	T40.7X2	T40.7X3	T40.7X4	T40.7X5	T40.7X6
tobacco	T62.2X1	T62.2X2	T62.2X3	T62.2X4	—	—
Indigo carmine	T50.8X1	T50.8X2	T50.8X3	T50.8X4	T50.8X5	T50.8X6
Indobufen	T45.521	T45.522	T45.523	T45.524	T45.525	T45.526
Indocin	T39.2X1	T39.2X2	T39.2X3	T39.2X4	T39.2X5	T39.2X6
Indocyanine green	T50.8X1	T50.8X2	T50.8X3	T50.8X4	T50.8X5	T50.8X6
Indometacin	T39.391	T39.392	T39.393	T39.394	T39.395	T39.396
Indomethacin	T39.391	T39.392	T39.393	T39.394	T39.395	T39.396
farnesil	T39.4X1	T39.4X2	T39.4X3	T39.4X4	T39.4X5	T39.4X6
Indoramin	T44.6X1	T44.6X2	T44.6X3	T44.6X4	T44.6X5	T44.6X6
Industrial						
alcohol	T51.0X1	T51.0X2	T51.0X3	T51.0X4	—	—
fumes	T59.891	T59.892	T59.893	T59.894	—	—
solvents (fumes) (vapors)	T52.91	T52.92	T52.93	T52.94	—	—
Influenza vaccine	T50.B91	T50.B92	T50.B93	T50.B94	T50.B95	T50.B96
Ingested substance NEC	T65.91	T65.92	T65.93	T65.94	—	—
INH	T37.1X1	T37.1X2	T37.1X3	T37.1X4	T37.1X5	T37.1X6

◀ New　◀ Revised　deleted Deleted

Substance	Poisoning, Accidental (Unintentional)	Poisoning, Intentional Self-Harm	Poisoning, Assault	Poisoning, Undetermined	Adverse Effect	Underdosing
Inhalation, gas (noxious) — see Gas						
Inhibitor						
angiotensin-converting enzyme	T46.4X1	T46.4X2	T46.4X3	T46.4X4	T46.4X5	T46.4X6
carbonic anhydrase	T50.2X1	T50.2X2	T50.2X3	T50.2X4	T50.2X5	T50.2X6
fibrinolysis	T45.621	T45.622	T45.623	T45.624	T45.625	T45.626
monoamine oxidase NEC	T43.1X1	T43.1X2	T43.1X3	T43.1X4	T43.1X5	T43.1X6
hydrazine	T43.1X1	T43.1X2	T43.1X3	T43.1X4	T43.1X5	T43.1X6
postsynaptic	T43.8X1	T43.8X2	T43.8X3	T43.8X4	T43.8X5	T43.8X6
prothrombin synthesis	T45.511	T45.512	T45.513	T45.514	T45.515	T45.516
Ink	T65.891	T65.892	T65.893	T65.894	—	—
Inorganic substance NEC	T57.91	T57.92	T57.93	T57.94	—	—
Inosine pranobex	T37.5X1	T37.5X2	T37.5X3	T37.5X4	T37.5X5	T37.5X6
Inositol	T50.991	T50.992	T50.993	T50.994	T50.995	T50.996
nicotinate	T46.7X1	T46.7X2	T46.7X3	T46.7X4	T46.7X5	T46.7X6
Inproquone	T45.1X1	T45.1X2	T45.1X3	T45.1X4	T45.1X5	T45.1X6
Insect (sting), venomous	T63.481	T63.482	T63.483	T63.484	—	—
ant	T63.421	T63.422	T63.423	T63.424	—	—
bee	T63.441	T63.442	T63.443	T63.444	—	—
caterpillar	T63.431	T63.432	T63.433	T63.434	—	—
hornet	T63.451	T63.452	T63.453	T63.454	—	—
wasp	T63.461	T63.462	T63.463	T63.464	—	—
Insecticide NEC	T60.91	T60.92	T60.93	T60.94	—	—
carbamate	T60.0X1	T60.0X2	T60.0X3	T60.0X4	—	—
chlorinated	T60.1X1	T60.1X2	T60.1X3	T60.1X4	—	—
mixed	T60.91	T60.92	T60.93	T60.94	—	—
organochlorine	T60.1X1	T60.1X2	T60.1X3	T60.1X4	—	—
organophosphorus	T60.0X1	T60.0X2	T60.0X3	T60.0X4	—	—
Insular tissue extract	T38.3X1	T38.3X2	T38.3X3	T38.3X4	T38.3X5	T38.3X6
Insulin (amorphous) (globin) (isophane) (Lente) (NPH) (Semilente) (Ultralente)	T38.3X1	T38.3X2	T38.3X3	T38.3X4	T38.3X5	T38.3X6
defalan	T38.3X1	T38.3X2	T38.3X3	T38.3X4	T38.3X5	T38.3X6
human	T38.3X1	T38.3X2	T38.3X3	T38.3X4	T38.3X5	T38.3X6
injection, soluble	T38.3X1	T38.3X2	T38.3X3	T38.3X4	T38.3X5	T38.3X6
biphasic	T38.3X1	T38.3X2	T38.3X3	T38.3X4	T38.3X5	T38.3X6
intermediate acting	T38.3X1	T38.3X2	T38.3X3	T38.3X4	T38.3X5	T38.3X6
protamine zinc	T38.3X1	T38.3X2	T38.3X3	T38.3X4	T38.3X5	T38.3X6
slow acting	T38.3X1	T38.3X2	T38.3X3	T38.3X4	T38.3X5	T38.3X6
zinc						
protamine injection	T38.3X1	T38.3X2	T38.3X3	T38.3X4	T38.3X5	T38.3X6
suspension (amorphous) (crystalline)	T38.3X1	T38.3X2	T38.3X3	T38.3X4	T38.3X5	T38.3X6

Substance	Poisoning, Accidental (Unintentional)	Poisoning, Intentional Self-Harm	Poisoning, Assault	Poisoning, Undetermined	Adverse Effect	Underdosing
Interferon (alpha) (beta) (gamma)	T37.5X1	T37.5X2	T37.5X3	T37.5X4	T37.5X5	T37.5X6
Intestinal motility control drug	T47.6X1	T47.6X2	T47.6X3	T47.6X4	T47.6X5	T47.6X6
biological	T47.8X1	T47.8X2	T47.8X3	T47.8X4	T47.8X5	T47.8X6
Intranarcon	T41.1X1	T41.1X2	T41.1X3	T41.1X4	T41.1X5	T41.1X6
Intravenous						
amino acids	T50.991	T50.992	T50.993	T50.994	T50.995	T50.996
fat suspension	T50.991	T50.992	T50.993	T50.994	T50.995	T50.996
Inulin	T50.8X1	T50.8X2	T50.8X3	T50.8X4	T50.8X5	T50.8X6
Invert sugar	T50.3X1	T50.3X2	T50.3X3	T50.3X4	T50.3X5	T50.3X6
Inza — see Naproxen						
Iobenzamic acid	T50.8X1	T50.8X2	T50.8X3	T50.8X4	T50.8X5	T50.8X6
Iocarmic acid	T50.8X1	T50.8X2	T50.8X3	T50.8X4	T50.8X5	T50.8X6
Iocetamic acid	T50.8X1	T50.8X2	T50.8X3	T50.8X4	T50.8X5	T50.8X6
Iodamide	T50.8X1	T50.8X2	T50.8X3	T50.8X4	T50.8X5	T50.8X6
Iodide NEC — see also Iodine	T49.0X1	T49.0X2	T49.0X3	T49.0X4	T49.0X5	T49.0X6
mercury (ointment)	T49.0X1	T49.0X2	T49.0X3	T49.0X4	T49.0X5	T49.0X6
methylate	T49.0X1	T49.0X2	T49.0X3	T49.0X4	T49.0X5	T49.0X6
potassium (expectorant) NEC	T48.4X1	T48.4X2	T48.4X3	T48.4X4	T48.4X5	T48.4X6
Iodinated						
contrast medium	T50.8X1	T50.8X2	T50.8X3	T50.8X4	T50.8X5	T50.8X6
glycerol	T48.4X1	T48.4X2	T48.4X3	T48.4X4	T48.4X5	T48.4X6
human serum albumin (131I)	T50.8X1	T50.8X2	T50.8X3	T50.8X4	T50.8X5	T50.8X6
Iodine (antiseptic, external) (tincture) NEC	T49.0X1	T49.0X2	T49.0X3	T49.0X4	T49.0X5	T49.0X6
125 — see also Radiation sickness, and Exposure to radioactivce isotopes	T50.8X1	T50.8X2	T50.8X3	T50.8X4	T50.8X5	T50.8X6
therapeutic	T50.991	T50.992	T50.993	T50.994	T50.995	T50.996
131 — see also Radiation sickness, and Exposure to radioactivce isotopes	T50.8X1	T50.8X2	T50.8X3	T50.8X4	T50.8X5	T50.8X6
therapeutic	T38.2X1	T38.2X2	T38.2X3	T38.2X4	T38.2X5	T38.2X6
diagnostic	T50.8X1	T50.8X2	T50.8X3	T50.8X4	T50.8X5	T50.8X6
for thyroid conditions (antithyroid)	T38.2X1	T38.2X2	T38.2X3	T38.2X4	T38.2X5	T38.2X6
solution	T49.0X1	T49.0X2	T49.0X3	T49.0X4	T49.0X5	T49.0X6
vapor	T59.891	T59.892	T59.893	T59.894	—	—
Iodipamide	T50.8X1	T50.8X2	T50.8X3	T50.8X4	T50.8X5	T50.8X6
Iodized (poppy seed) oil	T50.8X1	T50.8X2	T50.8X3	T50.8X4	T50.8X5	T50.8X6
Iodobismitol	T37.8X1	T37.8X2	T37.8X3	T37.8X4	T37.8X5	T37.8X6
Iodochlorhydroxyquin	T37.8X1	T37.8X2	T37.8X3	T37.8X4	T37.8X5	T37.8X6
topical	T49.0X1	T49.0X2	T49.0X3	T49.0X4	T49.0X5	T49.0X6
Iodochlorhydroxyquino-line	T37.8X1	T37.8X2	T37.8X3	T37.8X4	T37.8X5	T37.8X6
Iodocholesterol (131I)	T50.8X1	T50.8X2	T50.8X3	T50.8X4	T50.8X5	T50.8X6

◀ New   ◀ Revised   deleted Deleted

Substance	Poisoning, Accidental (Unintentional)	Poisoning, Intentional Self-Harm	Poisoning, Assault	Poisoning, Undetermined	Adverse Effect	Underdosing
Iodoform	T49.0X1	T49.0X2	T49.0X3	T49.0X4	T49.0X5	T49.0X6
Iodohippuric acid	T50.8X1	T50.8X2	T50.8X3	T50.8X4	T50.8X5	T50.8X6
Iodopanoic acid	T50.8X1	T50.8X2	T50.8X3	T50.8X4	T50.8X5	T50.8X6
Iodophthalein (sodium)	T50.8X1	T50.8X2	T50.8X3	T50.8X4	T50.8X5	T50.8X6
Iodopyracet	T50.8X1	T50.8X2	T50.8X3	T50.8X4	T50.8X5	T50.8X6
Iodoquinol	T37.8X1	T37.8X2	T37.8X3	T37.8X4	T37.8X5	T37.8X6
Iodoxamic acid	T50.8X1	T50.8X2	T50.8X3	T50.8X4	T50.8X5	T50.8X6
Iofendylate	T50.8X1	T50.8X2	T50.8X3	T50.8X4	T50.8X5	T50.8X6
Ioglycamic acid	T50.8X1	T50.8X2	T50.8X3	T50.8X4	T50.8X5	T50.8X6
Iohexol	T50.8X1	T50.8X2	T50.8X3	T50.8X4	T50.8X5	T50.8X6
Ion exchange resin						
anion	T47.8X1	T47.8X2	T47.8X3	T47.8X4	T47.8X5	T47.8X6
cation	T50.3X1	T50.3X2	T50.3X3	T50.3X4	T50.3X5	T50.3X6
cholestyramine	T46.6X1	T46.6X2	T46.6X3	T46.6X4	T46.6X5	T46.6X6
intestinal	T47.8X1	T47.8X2	T47.8X3	T47.8X4	T47.8X5	T47.8X6
Iopamidol	T50.8X1	T50.8X2	T50.8X3	T50.8X4	T50.8X5	T50.8X6
Iopanoic acid	T50.8X1	T50.8X2	T50.8X3	T50.8X4	T50.8X5	T50.8X6
Iophenoic acid	T50.8X1	T50.8X2	T50.8X3	T50.8X4	T50.8X5	T50.8X6
Iopodate, sodium	T50.8X1	T50.8X2	T50.8X3	T50.8X4	T50.8X5	T50.8X6
Iopodic acid	T50.8X1	T50.8X2	T50.8X3	T50.8X4	T50.8X5	T50.8X6
Iopromide	T50.8X1	T50.8X2	T50.8X3	T50.8X4	T50.8X5	T50.8X6
Iopydol	T50.8X1	T50.8X2	T50.8X3	T50.8X4	T50.8X5	T50.8X6
Iotalamic acid	T50.8X1	T50.8X2	T50.8X3	T50.8X4	T50.8X5	T50.8X6
Iothalamate	T50.8X1	T50.8X2	T50.8X3	T50.8X4	T50.8X5	T50.8X6
Iothiouracil	T38.2X1	T38.2X2	T38.2X3	T38.2X4	T38.2X5	T38.2X6
Iotrol	T50.8X1	T50.8X2	T50.8X3	T50.8X4	T50.8X5	T50.8X6
Iotrolan	T50.8X1	T50.8X2	T50.8X3	T50.8X4	T50.8X5	T50.8X6
Iotroxate	T50.8X1	T50.8X2	T50.8X3	T50.8X4	T50.8X5	T50.8X6
Iotroxic acid	T50.8X1	T50.8X2	T50.8X3	T50.8X4	T50.8X5	T50.8X6
Ioversol	T50.8X1	T50.8X2	T50.8X3	T50.8X4	T50.8X5	T50.8X6
Ioxaglate	T50.8X1	T50.8X2	T50.8X3	T50.8X4	T50.8X5	T50.8X6
Ioxaglic acid	T50.8X1	T50.8X2	T50.8X3	T50.8X4	T50.8X5	T50.8X6
Ioxitalamic acid	T50.8X1	T50.8X2	T50.8X3	T50.8X4	T50.8X5	T50.8X6
Ipecac	T47.7X1	T47.7X2	T47.7X3	T47.7X4	T47.7X5	T47.7X6
Ipecacuanha	T48.4X1	T48.4X2	T48.4X3	T48.4X4	T48.4X5	T48.4X6
Ipodate, calcium	T50.8X1	T50.8X2	T50.8X3	T50.8X4	T50.8X5	T50.8X6
Ipral	T42.3X1	T42.3X2	T42.3X3	T42.3X4	T42.3X5	T42.3X6
Ipratropium (bromide)	T48.6X1	T48.6X2	T48.6X3	T48.6X4	T48.6X5	T48.6X6
Ipriflavone	T46.3X1	T46.3X2	T46.3X3	T46.3X4	T46.3X5	T46.3X6
Iprindole	T43.011	T43.012	T43.013	T43.014	T43.015	T43.016
Iproclozide	T43.1X1	T43.1X2	T43.1X3	T43.1X4	T43.1X5	T43.1X6
Iprofenin	T50.8X1	T50.8X2	T50.8X3	T50.8X4	T50.8X5	T50.8X6

Substance	Poisoning, Accidental (Unintentional)	Poisoning, Intentional Self-Harm	Poisoning, Assault	Poisoning, Undetermined	Adverse Effect	Underdosing
Iproheptine	T49.2X1	T49.2X2	T49.2X3	T49.2X4	T49.2X5	T49.2X6
Iproniazid	T43.1X1	T43.1X2	T43.1X3	T43.1X4	T43.1X5	T43.1X6
Iproplatin	T45.1X1	T45.1X2	T45.1X3	T45.1X4	T45.1X5	T45.1X6
Iproveratril	T46.1X1	T46.1X2	T46.1X3	T46.1X4	T46.1X5	T46.1X6
Iron (compounds) (medicinal) NEC	T45.4X1	T45.4X2	T45.4X3	T45.4X4	T45.4X5	T45.4X6
ammonium	T45.4X1	T45.4X2	T45.4X3	T45.4X4	T45.4X5	T45.4X6
dextran injection	T45.4X1	T45.4X2	T45.4X3	T45.4X4	T45.4X5	T45.4X6
nonmedicinal	T56.891	T56.892	T56.893	T56.894	—	—
salts	T45.4X1	T45.4X2	T45.4X3	T45.4X4	T45.4X5	T45.4X6
sorbitex	T45.4X1	T45.4X2	T45.4X3	T45.4X4	T45.4X5	T45.4X6
sorbitol citric acid complex	T45.4X1	T45.4X2	T45.4X3	T45.4X4	T45.4X5	T45.4X6
Irrigating fluid (vaginal)	T49.8X1	T49.8X2	T49.8X3	T49.8X4	T49.8X5	T49.8X6
eye	T49.5X1	T49.5X2	T49.5X3	T49.5X4	T49.5X5	T49.5X6
Isepamicin	T36.5X1	T36.5X2	T36.5X3	T36.5X4	T36.5X5	T36.5X6
Isoaminile (citrate)	T48.3X1	T48.3X2	T48.3X3	T48.3X4	T48.3X5	T48.3X6
Isoamyl nitrite	T46.3X1	T46.3X2	T46.3X3	T46.3X4	T46.3X5	T46.3X6
Isobenzan	T60.1X1	T60.1X2	T60.1X3	T60.1X4	—	—
Isobutyl acetate	T52.8X1	T52.8X2	T52.8X3	T52.8X4	—	—
Isocarboxazid	T43.1X1	T43.1X2	T43.1X3	T43.1X4	T43.1X5	T43.1X6
Isoconazole	T49.0X1	T49.0X2	T49.0X3	T49.0X4	T49.0X5	T49.0X6
Isocyanate	T65.0X1	T65.0X2	T65.0X3	T65.0X4	—	—
Isoephedrine	T44.991	T44.992	T44.993	T44.994	T44.995	T44.996
Isoetarine	T48.6X1	T48.6X2	T48.6X3	T48.6X4	T48.6X5	T48.6X6
Isoethadione	T42.2X1	T42.2X2	T42.2X3	T42.2X4	T42.2X5	T42.2X6
Isoetharine	T44.5X1	T44.5X2	T44.5X3	T44.5X4	T44.5X5	T44.5X6
Isoflurane	T41.0X1	T41.0X2	T41.0X3	T41.0X4	T41.0X5	T41.0X6
Isoflurophate	T44.0X1	T44.0X2	T44.0X3	T44.0X4	T44.0X5	T44.0X6
Isomaltose, ferric complex	T45.4X1	T45.4X2	T45.4X3	T45.4X4	T45.4X5	T45.4X6
Isometheptene	T44.3X1	T44.3X2	T44.3X3	T44.3X4	T44.3X5	T44.3X6
Isoniazid	T37.1X1	T37.1X2	T37.1X3	T37.1X4	T37.1X5	T37.1X6
with						
rifampicin	T36.6X1	T36.6X2	T36.6X3	T36.6X4	T36.6X5	T36.6X6
thioacetazone	T37.1X1	T37.1X2	T37.1X3	T37.1X4	T37.1X5	T37.1X6
Isonicotinic acid hydrazide	T37.1X1	T37.1X2	T37.1X3	T37.1X4	T37.1X5	T37.1X6
Isonipecaine	T40.491	T40.492	T40.493	T40.494	T40.495	T40.496
Isopentaquine	T37.2X1	T37.2X2	T37.2X3	T37.2X4	T37.2X5	T37.2X6
Isophane insulin	T38.3X1	T38.3X2	T38.3X3	T38.3X4	T38.3X5	T38.3X6
Isophorone	T65.891	T65.892	T65.893	T65.894	—	—
Isophosphamide	T45.1X1	T45.1X2	T45.1X3	T45.1X4	T45.1X5	T45.1X6
Isopregnenone	T38.5X1	T38.5X2	T38.5X3	T38.5X4	T38.5X5	T38.5X6
Isoprenaline	T48.6X1	T48.6X2	T48.6X3	T48.6X4	T48.6X5	T48.6X6
Isopromethazine	T43.3X1	T43.3X2	T43.3X3	T43.3X4	T43.3X5	T43.3X6

◀ New   ◀ Revised   ~~deleted~~ Deleted

Substance	Poisoning, Accidental (Unintentional)	Poisoning, Intentional Self-Harm	Poisoning, Assault	Poisoning, Undetermined	Adverse Effect	Underdosing
Isopropamide	T44.3X1	T44.3X2	T44.3X3	T44.3X4	T44.3X5	T44.3X6
iodide	T44.3X1	T44.3X2	T44.3X3	T44.3X4	T44.3X5	T44.3X6
Isopropanol	T51.2X1	T51.2X2	T51.2X3	T51.2X4	—	—
Isopropyl						
acetate	T52.8X1	T52.8X2	T52.8X3	T52.8X4	—	—
alcohol	T51.2X1	T51.2X2	T51.2X3	T51.2X4	—	—
medicinal	T49.4X1	T49.4X2	T49.4X3	T49.4X4	T49.4X5	T49.4X6
ether	T52.8X1	T52.8X2	T52.8X3	T52.8X4	—	—
Isopropylaminophena-zone	T39.2X1	T39.2X2	T39.2X3	T39.2X4	T39.2X5	T39.2X6
Isoproterenol	T48.6X1	T48.6X2	T48.6X3	T48.6X4	T48.6X5	T48.6X6
Isosorbide dinitrate	T46.3X1	T46.3X2	T46.3X3	T46.3X4	T46.3X5	T46.3X6
Isothipendyl	T45.0X1	T45.0X2	T45.0X3	T45.0X4	T45.0X5	T45.0X6
Isotretinoin	T50.991	T50.992	T50.993	T50.994	T50.995	T50.996
Isoxazolyl penicillin	T36.0X1	T36.0X2	T36.0X3	T36.0X4	T36.0X5	T36.0X6
Isoxicam	T39.391	T39.392	T39.393	T39.394	T39.395	T39.396
Isoxsuprine	T46.7X1	T46.7X2	T46.7X3	T46.7X4	T46.7X5	T46.7X6
Ispagula	T47.4X1	T47.4X2	T47.4X3	T47.4X4	T47.4X5	T47.4X6
husk	T47.4X1	T47.4X2	T47.4X3	T47.4X4	T47.4X5	T47.4X6
Isradipine	T46.1X1	T46.1X2	T46.1X3	T46.1X4	T46.1X5	T46.1X6
I-thyroxine sodium	T38.1X1	T38.1X2	T38.1X3	T38.1X4	T38.1X5	T38.1X6
Itraconazole	T37.8X1	T37.8X2	T37.8X3	T37.8X4	T37.8X5	T37.8X6
Itramin tosilate	T46.3X1	T46.3X2	T46.3X3	T46.3X4	T46.3X5	T46.3X6
Ivermectin	T37.4X1	T37.4X2	T37.4X3	T37.4X4	T37.4X5	T37.4X6
Izoniazid	T37.1X1	T37.1X2	T37.1X3	T37.1X4	T37.1X5	T37.1X6
with thioacetazone	T37.1X1	T37.1X2	T37.1X3	T37.1X4	T37.1X5	T37.1X6
J						
Jalap	T47.2X1	T47.2X2	T47.2X3	T47.2X4	T47.2X5	T47.2X6
Jamaica						
dogwood (bark)	T39.8X1	T39.8X2	T39.8X3	T39.8X4	T39.8X5	T39.8X6
ginger	T65.891	T65.892	T65.893	T65.894	—	—
root	T62.2X1	T62.2X2	T62.2X3	T62.2X4	—	—
Jatropha	T62.2X1	T62.2X2	T62.2X3	T62.2X4	—	—
curcas	T62.2X1	T62.2X2	T62.2X3	T62.2X4	—	—
Jectofer	T45.4X1	T45.4X2	T45.4X3	T45.4X4	T45.4X5	T45.4X6
Jellyfish (sting)	T63.621	T63.622	T63.623	T63.624	—	—
Jequirity (bean)	T62.2X1	T62.2X2	T62.2X3	T62.2X4	—	—
Jimson weed (stramonium)	T62.2X1	T62.2X2	T62.2X3	T62.2X4	—	—
seeds	T62.2X1	T62.2X2	T62.2X3	T62.2X4	—	—
Josamycin	T36.3X1	T36.3X2	T36.3X3	T36.3X4	T36.3X5	T36.3X6
Juniper tar	T49.1X1	T49.1X2	T49.1X3	T49.1X4	T49.1X5	T49.1X6

Substance	Poisoning, Accidental (Unintentional)	Poisoning, Intentional Self-Harm	Poisoning, Assault	Poisoning, Undetermined	Adverse Effect	Underdosing
K						
Kallidinogenase	T46.7X1	T46.7X2	T46.7X3	T46.7X4	T46.7X5	T46.7X6
Kallikrein	T46.7X1	T46.7X2	T46.7X3	T46.7X4	T46.7X5	T46.7X6
Kanamycin	T36.5X1	T36.5X2	T36.5X3	T36.5X4	T36.5X5	T36.5X6
Kantrex	T36.5X1	T36.5X2	T36.5X3	T36.5X4	T36.5X5	T36.5X6
Kaolin	T47.6X1	T47.6X2	T47.6X3	T47.6X4	T47.6X5	T47.6X6
light	T47.6X1	T47.6X2	T47.6X3	T47.6X4	T47.6X5	T47.6X6
Karaya (gum)	T47.4X1	T47.4X2	T47.4X3	T47.4X4	T47.4X5	T47.4X6
Kebuzone	T39.2X1	T39.2X2	T39.2X3	T39.2X4	T39.2X5	T39.2X6
Kelevan	T60.1X1	T60.1X2	T60.1X3	T60.1X4	—	—
Kemithal	T41.1X1	T41.1X2	T41.1X3	T41.1X4	T41.1X5	T41.1X6
Kenacort	T38.0X1	T38.0X2	T38.0X3	T38.0X4	T38.0X5	T38.0X6
Keratolytic drug NEC	T49.4X1	T49.4X2	T49.4X3	T49.4X4	T49.4X5	T49.4X6
anthracene	T49.4X1	T49.4X2	T49.4X3	T49.4X4	T49.4X5	T49.4X6
Keratoplastic NEC	T49.4X1	T49.4X2	T49.4X3	T49.4X4	T49.4X5	T49.4X6
Kerosene, kerosine (fuel) (solvent) NEC	T52.0X1	T52.0X2	T52.0X3	T52.0X4	—	—
insecticide	T52.0X1	T52.0X2	T52.0X3	T52.0X4	—	—
vapor	T52.0X1	T52.0X2	T52.0X3	T52.0X4	—	—
Ketamine	T41.291	T41.292	T41.293	T41.294	T41.295	T41.296
Ketazolam	T42.4X1	T42.4X2	T42.4X3	T42.4X4	T42.4X5	T42.4X6
Ketazon	T39.2X1	T39.2X2	T39.2X3	T39.2X4	T39.2X5	T39.2X6
Ketobemidone	T40.491	T40.492	T40.493	T40.494	—	—
Ketoconazole	T49.0X1	T49.0X2	T49.0X3	T49.0X4	T49.0X5	T49.0X6
Ketols	T52.4X1	T52.4X2	T52.4X3	T52.4X4	—	—
Ketone oils	T52.4X1	T52.4X2	T52.4X3	T52.4X4	—	—
Ketoprofen	T39.311	T39.312	T39.313	T39.314	T39.315	T39.316
Ketorolac	T39.8X1	T39.8X2	T39.8X3	T39.8X4	T39.8X5	T39.8X6
Ketotifen	T45.0X1	T45.0X2	T45.0X3	T45.0X4	T45.0X5	T45.0X6
Khat	T43.691	T43.692	T43.693	T43.694	—	—
Khellin	T46.3X1	T46.3X2	T46.3X3	T46.3X4	T46.3X5	T46.3X6
Khelloside	T46.3X1	T46.3X2	T46.3X3	T46.3X4	T46.3X5	T46.3X6
Kiln gas or vapor (carbon monoxide)	T58.8X1	T58.8X2	T58.8X3	T58.8X4		
Kitasamycin	T36.3X1	T36.3X2	T36.3X3	T36.3X4	T36.3X5	T36.3X6
Konsyl	T47.4X1	T47.4X2	T47.4X3	T47.4X4	T47.4X5	T47.4X6
Kosam seed	T62.2X1	T62.2X2	T62.2X3	T62.2X4	—	—
Krait (venom)	T63.091	T63.092	T63.093	T63.094	—	—
Kwell (insecticide)	T60.1X1	T60.1X2	T60.1X3	T60.1X4	—	—
anti-infective (topical)	T49.0X1	T49.0X2	T49.0X3	T49.0X4	T49.0X5	T49.0X6

◀ New   ◀ Revised   ~~deleted~~ Deleted

Substance	Poisoning, Accidental (Unintentional)	Poisoning, Intentional Self-Harm	Poisoning, Assault	Poisoning, Undetermined	Adverse Effect	Underdosing
L						
Labetalol	T44.8X1	T44.8X2	T44.8X3	T44.8X4	T44.8X5	T44.8X6
Laburnum (seeds)	T62.2X1	T62.2X2	T62.2X3	T62.2X4	—	—
leaves	T62.2X1	T62.2X2	T62.2X3	T62.2X4	—	—
Lachesine	T49.5X1	T49.5X2	T49.5X3	T49.5X4	T49.5X5	T49.5X6
Lacidipine	T46.5X1	T46.5X2	T46.5X3	T46.5X4	T46.5X5	T46.5X6
Lacquer	T65.6X1	T65.6X2	T65.6X3	T65.6X4	—	—
Lacrimogenic gas	T59.3X1	T59.3X2	T59.3X3	T59.3X4	—	—
Lactated potassic saline	T50.3X1	T50.3X2	T50.3X3	T50.3X4	T50.3X5	T50.3X6
Lactic acid	T49.8X1	T49.8X2	T49.8X3	T49.8X4	T49.8X5	T49.8X6
Lactobacillus						
acidophilus	T47.6X1	T47.6X2	T47.6X3	T47.6X4	T47.6X5	T47.6X6
compound	T47.6X1	T47.6X2	T47.6X3	T47.6X4	T47.6X5	T47.6X6
bifidus, lyophilized	T47.6X1	T47.6X2	T47.6X3	T47.6X4	T47.6X5	T47.6X6
bulgaricus	T47.6X1	T47.6X2	T47.6X3	T47.6X4	T47.6X5	T47.6X6
sporogenes	T47.6X1	T47.6X2	T47.6X3	T47.6X4	T47.6X5	T47.6X6
Lactoflavin	T45.2X1	T45.2X2	T45.2X3	T45.2X4	T45.2X5	T45.2X6
Lactose (as excipient)	T50.901	T50.902	T50.903	T50.904	T50.905	T50.906
Lactuca (virosa) (extract)	T42.6X1	T42.6X2	T42.6X3	T42.6X4	T42.6X5	T42.6X6
Lactucarium	T42.6X1	T42.6X2	T42.6X3	T42.6X4	T42.6X5	T42.6X6
Lactulose	T47.3X1	T47.3X2	T47.3X3	T47.3X4	T47.3X5	T47.3X6
Laevo — *see* Levo-						
Lanatosides	T46.0X1	T46.0X2	T46.0X3	T46.0X4	T46.0X5	T46.0X6
Lanolin	T49.3X1	T49.3X2	T49.3X3	T49.3X4	T49.3X5	T49.3X6
Largactil	T43.3X1	T43.3X2	T43.3X3	T43.3X4	T43.3X5	T43.3X6
Larkspur	T62.2X1	T62.2X2	T62.2X3	T62.2X4	—	—
Laroxyl	T43.011	T43.012	T43.013	T43.014	T43.015	T43.016
Lassar's paste	T49.4X1	T49.4X2	T49.4X3	T49.4X4	T49.4X5	T49.4X6
Lasix	T50.1X1	T50.1X2	T50.1X3	T50.1X4	T50.1X5	T50.1X6
Latamoxef	T36.1X1	T36.1X2	T36.1X3	T36.1X4	T36.1X5	T36.1X6
Latex	T65.811	T65.812	T65.813	T65.814	—	—
Lathyrus (seed)	T62.2X1	T62.2X2	T62.2X3	T62.2X4	—	—
Laudanum	T40.0X1	T40.0X2	T40.0X3	T40.0X4	T40.0X5	T40.0X6
Laudexium	T48.1X1	T48.1X2	T48.1X3	T48.1X4	T48.1X5	T48.1X6
Laughing gas	T41.0X1	T41.0X2	T41.0X3	T41.0X4	T41.0X5	T41.0X6
Laurel, black or cherry	T62.2X1	T62.2X2	T62.2X3	T62.2X4	—	—
Laurolinium	T49.0X1	T49.0X2	T49.0X3	T49.0X4	T49.0X5	T49.0X6
Lauryl sulfoacetate	T49.2X1	T49.2X2	T49.2X3	T49.2X4	T49.2X5	T49.2X6

Substance	Poisoning, Accidental (Unintentional)	Poisoning, Intentional Self-Harm	Poisoning, Assault	Poisoning, Undetermined	Adverse Effect	Underdosing
Laxative NEC	T47.4X1	T47.4X2	T47.4X3	T47.4X4	T47.4X5	T47.4X6
osmotic	T47.3X1	T47.3X2	T47.3X3	T47.3X4	T47.3X5	T47.3X6
saline	T47.3X1	T47.3X2	T47.3X3	T47.3X4	T47.3X5	T47.3X6
stimulant	T47.2X1	T47.2X2	T47.2X3	T47.2X4	T47.2X5	T47.2X6
L-dopa	T42.8X1	T42.8X2	T42.8X3	T42.8X4	T42.8X5	T42.8X6
Lead (dust) (fumes) (vapor) NEC	T56.0X1	T56.0X2	T56.0X3	T56.0X4	—	—
acetate	T49.2X1	T49.2X2	T49.2X3	T49.2X4	T49.2X5	T49.2X6
alkyl (fuel additive)	T56.0X1	T56.0X2	T56.0X3	T56.0X4	—	—
anti-infectives	T37.8X1	T37.8X2	T37.8X3	T37.8X4	T37.8X5	T37.8X6
antiknock compound (tetraethyl)	T56.0X1	T56.0X2	T56.0X3	T56.0X4		
arsenate, arsenite (dust) (herbicide) (insecticide) (vapor)	T57.0X1	T57.0X2	T57.0X3	T57.0X4	—	—
carbonate	T56.0X1	T56.0X2	T56.0X3	T56.0X4	—	—
paint	T56.0X1	T56.0X2	T56.0X3	T56.0X4	—	—
chromate	T56.0X1	T56.0X2	T56.0X3	T56.0X4	—	—
paint	T56.0X1	T56.0X2	T56.0X3	T56.0X4	—	—
dioxide	T56.0X1	T56.0X2	T56.0X3	T56.0X4	—	—
inorganic	T56.0X1	T56.0X2	T56.0X3	T56.0X4	—	—
iodide	T56.0X1	T56.0X2	T56.0X3	T56.0X4	—	—
pigment (paint)	T56.0X1	T56.0X2	T56.0X3	T56.0X4	—	—
monoxide (dust)	T56.0X1	T56.0X2	T56.0X3	T56.0X4	—	—
paint	T56.0X1	T56.0X2	T56.0X3	T56.0X4	—	—
organic	T56.0X1	T56.0X2	T56.0X3	T56.0X4	—	—
oxide	T56.0X1	T56.0X2	T56.0X3	T56.0X4	—	—
paint	T56.0X1	T56.0X2	T56.0X3	T56.0X4	—	—
paint	T56.0X1	T56.0X2	T56.0X3	T56.0X4	—	—
salts	T56.0X1	T56.0X2	T56.0X3	T56.0X4	—	—
specified compound NEC	T56.0X1	T56.0X2	T56.0X3	T56.0X4	—	—
tetra-ethyl	T56.0X1	T56.0X2	T56.0X3	T56.0X4	—	—
Lebanese red	T40.7X1	T40.7X2	T40.7X3	T40.7X4	T40.7X5	T40.7X6
Lefetamine	T39.8X1	T39.8X2	T39.8X3	T39.8X4	T39.8X5	T39.8X6
Lenperone	T43.4X1	T43.4X2	T43.4X3	T43.4X4	T43.4X5	T43.4X6
Lente lietin (insulin)	T38.3X1	T38.3X2	T38.3X3	T38.3X4	T38.3X5	T38.3X6
Leptazol	T50.7X1	T50.7X2	T50.7X3	T50.7X4	T50.7X5	T50.7X6
Leptophos	T60.0X1	T60.0X2	T60.0X3	T60.0X4	—	—
Leritine	T40.2X1	T40.2X2	T40.2X3	T40.2X4	T40.2X5	T40.2X6
Letosteine	T48.4X1	T48.4X2	T48.4X3	T48.4X4	T48.4X5	T48.4X6
Letter	T38.1X1	T38.1X2	T38.1X3	T38.1X4	T38.1X5	T38.1X6
Lettuce opium	T42.6X1	T42.6X2	T42.6X3	T42.6X4	T42.6X5	T42.6X6
Leucinocaine	T41.3X1	T41.3X2	T41.3X3	T41.3X4	T41.3X5	T41.3X6

◄ New ◄ Revised ~~deleted~~ Deleted

Substance	Poisoning, Accidental (Unintentional)	Poisoning, Intentional Self-Harm	Poisoning, Assault	Poisoning, Undetermined	Adverse Effect	Underdosing
Leucocianidol	T46.991	T46.992	T46.993	T46.994	T46.995	T46.996
Leucovorin (factor)	T45.8X1	T45.8X2	T45.8X3	T45.8X4	T45.8X5	T45.8X6
Leukeran	T45.1X1	T45.1X2	T45.1X3	T45.1X4	T45.1X5	T45.1X6
Leuprolide	T38.891	T38.892	T38.893	T38.894	T38.895	T38.896
Levalbuterol	T48.6X1	T48.6X2	T48.6X3	T48.6X4	T48.6X5	T48.6X6
Levallorphan	T50.7X1	T50.7X2	T50.7X3	T50.7X4	T50.7X5	T50.7X6
Levamisole	T37.4X1	T37.4X2	T37.4X3	T37.4X4	T37.4X5	T37.4X6
Levanil	T42.6X1	T42.6X2	T42.6X3	T42.6X4	T42.6X5	T42.6X6
Levarterenol	T44.4X1	T44.4X2	T44.4X3	T44.4X4	T44.4X5	T44.4X6
Levdropropizine	T48.3X1	T48.3X2	T48.3X3	T48.3X4	T48.3X5	T48.3X6
Levobunolol	T49.5X1	T49.5X2	T49.5X3	T49.5X4	T49.5X5	T49.5X6
Levocabastine (hydrochloride)	T45.0X1	T45.0X2	T45.0X3	T45.0X4	T45.0X5	T45.0X6
Levocarnitine	T50.991	T50.992	T50.993	T50.994	T50.995	T50.996
Levodopa	T42.8X1	T42.8X2	T42.8X3	T42.8X4	T42.8X5	T42.8X6
with carbidopa	T42.8X1	T42.8X2	T42.8X3	T42.8X4	T42.8X5	T42.8X6
Levo-dromoran	T40.2X1	T40.2X2	T40.2X3	T40.2X4	T40.2X5	T40.2X6
Levoglutamide	T50.991	T50.992	T50.993	T50.994	T50.995	T50.996
Levoid	T38.1X1	T38.1X2	T38.1X3	T38.1X4	T38.1X5	T38.1X6
Levo-iso-methadone	T40.3X1	T40.3X2	T40.3X3	T40.3X4	T40.3X5	T40.3X6
Levomepromazine	T43.3X1	T43.3X2	T43.3X3	T43.3X4	T43.3X5	T43.3X6
Levonordefrin	T49.6X1	T49.6X2	T49.6X3	T49.6X4	T49.6X5	T49.6X6
Levonorgestrel	T38.4X1	T38.4X2	T38.4X3	T38.4X4	T38.4X5	T38.4X6
with ethinylestradiol	T38.5X1	T38.5X2	T38.5X3	T38.5X4	T38.5X5	T38.5X6
Levopromazine	T43.3X1	T43.3X2	T43.3X3	T43.3X4	T43.3X5	T43.3X6
Levoprome	T42.6X1	T42.6X2	T42.6X3	T42.6X4	T42.6X5	T42.6X6
Levopropoxyphene	T40.491	T40.492	T40.493	T40.494	T40.495	T40.496 ◄
Levopropylhexedrine	T50.5X1	T50.5X2	T50.5X3	T50.5X4	T50.5X5	T50.5X6
Levoproxyphylline	T48.6X1	T48.6X2	T48.6X3	T48.6X4	T48.6X5	T48.6X6
Levorphanol	T40.491	T40.492	T40.493	T40.494	T40.495	T40.496 ◄
Levothyroxine	T38.1X1	T38.1X2	T38.1X3	T38.1X4	T38.1X5	T38.1X6
sodium	T38.1X1	T38.1X2	T38.1X3	T38.1X4	T38.1X5	T38.1X6
Levsin	T44.3X1	T44.3X2	T44.3X3	T44.3X4	T44.3X5	T44.3X6
Levulose	T50.3X1	T50.3X2	T50.3X3	T50.3X4	T50.3X5	T50.3X6
Lewisite (gas), not in war	T57.0X1	T57.0X2	T57.0X3	T57.0X4	—	—
Librium	T42.4X1	T42.4X2	T42.4X3	T42.4X4	T42.4X5	T42.4X6
Lidex	T49.0X1	T49.0X2	T49.0X3	T49.0X4	T49.0X5	T49.0X6
Lidocaine	T41.3X1	T41.3X2	T41.3X3	T41.3X4	T41.3X5	T41.3X6
regional	T41.3X1	T41.3X2	T41.3X3	T41.3X4	T41.3X5	T41.3X6
spinal	T41.3X1	T41.3X2	T41.3X3	T41.3X4	T41.3X5	T41.3X6
Lidofenin	T50.8X1	T50.8X2	T50.8X3	T50.8X4	T50.8X5	T50.8X6
Lidoflazine	T46.1X1	T46.1X2	T46.1X3	T46.1X4	T46.1X5	T46.1X6
Lighter fluid	T52.0X1	T52.0X2	T52.0X3	T52.0X4	—	—

Substance	Poisoning, Accidental (Unintentional)	Poisoning, Intentional Self-Harm	Poisoning, Assault	Poisoning, Undetermined	Adverse Effect	Underdosing
Lignin hemicellulose	T47.6X1	T47.6X2	T47.6X3	T47.6X4	T47.6X5	T47.6X6
Lignocaine	T41.3X1	T41.3X2	T41.3X3	T41.3X4	T41.3X5	T41.3X6
regional	T41.3X1	T41.3X2	T41.3X3	T41.3X4	T41.3X5	T41.3X6
spinal	T41.3X1	T41.3X2	T41.3X3	T41.3X4	T41.3X5	T41.3X6
Ligroin(e) (solvent)	T52.0X1	T52.0X2	T52.0X3	T52.0X4	—	—
vapor	T59.891	T59.892	T59.893	T59.894	—	—
Ligustrum vulgare	T62.2X1	T62.2X2	T62.2X3	T62.2X4	—	—
Lily of the valley	T62.2X1	T62.2X2	T62.2X3	T62.2X4	—	—
Lime (chloride)	T54.3X1	T54.3X2	T54.3X3	T54.3X4	—	—
Limonene	T52.8X1	T52.8X2	T52.8X3	T52.8X4	—	—
Lincomycin	T36.8X1	T36.8X2	T36.8X3	T36.8X4	T36.8X5	T36.8X6
Lindane (insecticide) (nonmedicinal) (vapor)	T53.6X1	T53.6X2	T53.6X3	T53.6X4	—	—
medicinal	T49.0X1	T49.0X2	T49.0X3	T49.0X4	T49.0X5	T49.0X6
Liniments NEC	T49.91	T49.92	T49.93	T49.94	T49.95	T49.96
Linoleic acid	T46.6X1	T46.6X2	T46.6X3	T46.6X4	T46.6X5	T46.6X6
Linolenic acid	T46.6X1	T46.6X2	T46.6X3	T46.6X4	T46.6X5	T46.6X6
Linseed	T47.4X1	T47.4X2	T47.4X3	T47.4X4	T47.4X5	T47.4X6
Liothyronine	T38.1X1	T38.1X2	T38.1X3	T38.1X4	T38.1X5	T38.1X6
Liotrix	T38.1X1	T38.1X2	T38.1X3	T38.1X4	T38.1X5	T38.1X6
Lipancreatin	T47.5X1	T47.5X2	T47.5X3	T47.5X4	T47.5X5	T47.5X6
Lipo-alprostadil	T46.7X1	T46.7X2	T46.7X3	T46.7X4	T46.7X5	T46.7X6
Lipo-Lutin	T38.5X1	T38.5X2	T38.5X3	T38.5X4	T38.5X5	T38.5X6
Lipotropic drug NEC	T50.901	T50.902	T50.903	T50.904	T50.905	T50.906
Liquefied petroleum gases	T59.891	T59.892	T59.893	T59.894	—	—
piped (pure or mixed with air)	T59.891	T59.892	T59.893	T59.894	—	—
Liquid						
paraffin	T47.4X1	T47.4X2	T47.4X3	T47.4X4	T47.4X5	T47.4X6
petrolatum	T47.4X1	T47.4X2	T47.4X3	T47.4X4	T47.4X5	T47.4X6
topical	T49.3X1	T49.3X2	T49.3X3	T49.3X4	T49.3X5	T49.3X6
specified NEC	T65.891	T65.892	T65.893	T65.894	—	—
substance	T65.91	T65.92	T65.93	T65.94	—	—
Liquor creosolis compositus	T65.891	T65.892	T65.893	T65.894	—	—
Liquorice	T48.4X1	T48.4X2	T48.4X3	T48.4X4	T48.4X5	T48.4X6
extract	T47.8X1	T47.8X2	T47.8X3	T47.8X4	T47.8X5	T47.8X6
Lirugen	T50.991	T50.992	T50.993	T50.994	T50.995	T50.996
Lisinopril	T46.4X1	T46.4X2	T46.4X3	T46.4X4	T46.4X5	T46.4X6
Lisuride	T42.8X1	T42.8X2	T42.8X3	T42.8X4	T42.8X5	T42.8X6
Lithane	T43.8X1	T43.8X2	T43.8X3	T43.8X4	T43.8X5	T43.8X6
Lithium	T56.891	T56.892	T56.893	T56.894	—	—
gluconate	T43.591	T43.592	T43.593	T43.594	T43.595	T43.596
salts (carbonate)	T43.591	T43.592	T43.593	T43.594	T43.595	T43.596

◄ New ◄ Revised ~~deleted~~ Deleted

Substance	External Cause (T-Code)					
	Poisoning, Accidental (Unintentional)	Poisoning, Intentional Self-Harm	Poisoning, Assault	Poisoning, Undetermined	Adverse Effect	Underdosing
Lithonate	T43.8X1	T43.8X2	T43.8X3	T43.8X4	T43.8X5	T43.8X6
Liver						
extract	T45.8X1	T45.8X2	T45.8X3	T45.8X4	T45.8X5	T45.8X6
for parenteral use	T45.8X1	T45.8X2	T45.8X3	T45.8X4	T45.8X5	T45.8X6
fraction 1	T45.8X1	T45.8X2	T45.8X3	T45.8X4	T45.8X5	T45.8X6
hydrolysate	T45.8X1	T45.8X2	T45.8X3	T45.8X4	T45.8X5	T45.8X6
Lizard (bite) (venom)	T63.121	T63.122	T63.123	T63.124	—	—
LMD	T45.8X1	T45.8X2	T45.8X3	T45.8X4	T45.8X5	T45.8X6
Lobelia	T62.2X1	T62.2X2	T62.2X3	T62.2X4	—	—
Lobeline	T50.7X1	T50.7X2	T50.7X3	T50.7X4	T50.7X5	T50.7X6
Local action drug NEC	T49.8X1	T49.8X2	T49.8X3	T49.8X4	T49.8X5	T49.8X6
Locorten	T49.0X1	T49.0X2	T49.0X3	T49.0X4	T49.0X5	T49.0X6
Lofepramine	T43.011	T43.012	T43.013	T43.014	T43.015	T43.016
Lolium temulentum	T62.2X1	T62.2X2	T62.2X3	T62.2X4	—	—
Lomotil	T47.6X1	T47.6X2	T47.6X3	T47.6X4	T47.6X5	T47.6X6
Lomustine	T45.1X1	T45.1X2	T45.1X3	T45.1X4	T45.1X5	T45.1X6
Lonidamine	T45.1X1	T45.1X2	T45.1X3	T45.1X4	T45.1X5	T45.1X6
Loperamide	T47.6X1	T47.6X2	T47.6X3	T47.6X4	T47.6X5	T47.6X6
Loprazolam	T42.4X1	T42.4X2	T42.4X3	T42.4X4	T42.4X5	T42.4X6
Lorajmine	T46.2X1	T46.2X2	T46.2X3	T46.2X4	T46.2X5	T46.2X6
Loratidine	T45.0X1	T45.0X2	T45.0X3	T45.0X4	T45.0X5	T45.0X6
Lorazepam	T42.4X1	T42.4X2	T42.4X3	T42.4X4	T42.4X5	T42.4X6
Lorcainide	T46.2X1	T46.2X2	T46.2X3	T46.2X4	T46.2X5	T46.2X6
Lormetazepam	T42.4X1	T42.4X2	T42.4X3	T42.4X4	T42.4X5	T42.4X6
Lotions NEC	T49.91	T49.92	T49.93	T49.94	T49.95	T49.96
Lotusate	T42.3X1	T42.3X2	T42.3X3	T42.3X4	T42.3X5	T42.3X6
Lovastatin	T46.6X1	T46.6X2	T46.6X3	T46.6X4	T46.6X5	T46.6X6
Loxapine	T43.591	T43.592	T43.593	T43.594	T43.595	T43.596
Lowila	T49.2X1	T49.2X2	T49.2X3	T49.2X4	T49.2X5	T49.2X6
Lozenges (throat)	T49.6X1	T49.6X2	T49.6X3	T49.6X4	T49.6X5	T49.6X6
LSD	T40.8X1	T40.8X2	T40.8X3	T40.8X4	—	—
L-Tryptophan — see Amino acid						
Lubricant, eye	T49.5X1	T49.5X2	T49.5X3	T49.5X4	T49.5X5	T49.5X6
Lubricating oil NEC	T52.0X1	T52.0X2	T52.0X3	T52.0X4	—	—
Lucanthone	T37.4X1	T37.4X2	T37.4X3	T37.4X4	T37.4X5	T37.4X6
Luminal	T42.3X1	T42.3X2	T42.3X3	T42.3X4	T42.3X5	T42.3X6
Lung irritant (gas) NEC	T59.91	T59.92	T59.93	T59.94	—	—
Luteinizing hormone	T38.811	T38.812	T38.813	T38.814	T38.815	T38.816
Lutocylol	T38.5X1	T38.5X2	T38.5X3	T38.5X4	T38.5X5	T38.5X6
Lutromone	T38.5X1	T38.5X2	T38.5X3	T38.5X4	T38.5X5	T38.5X6
Lututrin	T48.291	T48.292	T48.293	T48.294	T48.295	T48.296
Lye (Concentrated)	T54.3X1	T54.3X2	T54.3X3	T54.3X4	—	—

Substance	External Cause (T-Code)					
	Poisoning, Accidental (Unintentional)	Poisoning, Intentional Self-Harm	Poisoning, Assault	Poisoning, Undetermined	Adverse Effect	Underdosing
Lygranum (skin test)	T50.8X1	T50.8X2	T50.8X3	T50.8X4	T50.8X5	T50.8X6
Lymecycline	T36.4X1	T36.4X2	T36.4X3	T36.4X4	T36.4X5	T36.4X6
Lymphogranuloma venereum antigen	T50.8X1	T50.8X2	T50.8X3	T50.8X4	T50.8X5	T50.8X6
Lynestrenol	T38.4X1	T38.4X2	T38.4X3	T38.4X4	T38.4X5	T38.4X6
Lypressin	T38.891	T38.892	T38.893	T38.894	T38.895	T38.896
Lyovac Sodium Edecrin	T50.1X1	T50.1X2	T50.1X3	T50.1X4	T50.1X5	T50.1X6
Lysergic acid diethylamide	T40.8X1	T40.8X2	T40.8X3	T40.8X4	—	—
Lysergide	T40.8X1	T40.8X2	T40.8X3	T40.8X4	—	—
Lysine vasopressin	T38.891	T38.892	T38.893	T38.894	T38.895	T38.896
Lysol	T54.1X1	T54.1X2	T54.1X3	T54.1X4	—	—
Lysozyme	T49.0X1	T49.0X2	T49.0X3	T49.0X4	T49.0X5	T49.0X6
Lytta (vitatta)	T49.8X1	T49.8X2	T49.8X3	T49.8X4	T49.8X5	T49.8X6
M						
Mace	T59.3X1	T59.3X2	T59.3X3	T59.3X4	—	—
Macrogol	T50.991	T50.992	T50.993	T50.994	T50.995	T50.996
Macrolide						
anabolic drug	T38.7X1	T38.7X2	T38.7X3	T38.7X4	T38.7X5	T38.7X6
antibiotic	T36.3X1	T36.3X2	T36.3X3	T36.3X4	T36.3X5	T36.3X6
Mafenide	T49.0X1	T49.0X2	T49.0X3	T49.0X4	T49.0X5	T49.0X6
Magaldrate	T47.1X1	T47.1X2	T47.1X3	T47.1X4	T47.1X5	T47.1X6
Magic mushroom	T40.991	T40.992	T40.993	T40.994	—	—
Magnamycin	T36.8X1	T36.8X2	T36.8X3	T36.8X4	T36.8X5	T36.8X6
Magnesia magma	T47.1X1	T47.1X2	T47.1X3	T47.1X4	T47.1X5	T47.1X6
Magnesium NEC	T56.891	T56.892	T56.893	T56.894	—	—
carbonate	T47.1X1	T47.1X2	T47.1X3	T47.1X4	T47.1X5	T47.1X6
citrate	T47.4X1	T47.4X2	T47.4X3	T47.4X4	T47.4X5	T47.4X6
hydroxide	T47.1X1	T47.1X2	T47.1X3	T47.1X4	T47.1X5	T47.1X6
oxide	T47.1X1	T47.1X2	T47.1X3	T47.1X4	T47.1X5	T47.1X6
peroxide	T49.0X1	T49.0X2	T49.0X3	T49.0X4	T49.0X5	T49.0X6
salicylate	T39.091	T39.092	T39.093	T39.094	T39.095	T39.096
silicofluoride	T50.3X1	T50.3X2	T50.3X3	T50.3X4	T50.3X5	T50.3X6
sulfate	T47.4X1	T47.4X2	T47.4X3	T47.4X4	T47.4X5	T47.4X6
thiosulfate	T45.0X1	T45.0X2	T45.0X3	T45.0X4	T45.0X5	T45.0X6
trisilicate	T47.1X1	T47.1X2	T47.1X3	T47.1X4	T47.1X5	T47.1X6
Malathion (medicinal)	T49.0X1	T49.0X2	T49.0X3	T49.0X4	T49.0X5	T49.0X6
insecticide	T60.0X1	T60.0X2	T60.0X3	T60.0X4	—	—
Male fern extract	T37.4X1	T37.4X2	T37.4X3	T37.4X4	T37.4X5	T37.4X6
M-AMSA	T45.1X1	T45.1X2	T45.1X3	T45.1X4	T45.1X5	T45.1X6
Mandelic acid	T37.8X1	T37.8X2	T37.8X3	T37.8X4	T37.8X5	T37.8X6
Manganese (dioxide) (salts)	T57.2X1	T57.2X2	T57.2X3	T57.2X4	—	—
medicinal	T50.991	T50.992	T50.993	T50.994	T50.995	T50.996

◀ New   ◀ Revised   ~~deleted~~ Deleted

Substance	External Cause (T-Code)					
	Poisoning, Accidental (Unintentional)	Poisoning, Intentional Self-Harm	Poisoning, Assault	Poisoning, Undetermined	Adverse Effect	Underdosing
Mannitol	T47.3X1	T47.3X2	T47.3X3	T47.3X4	T47.3X5	T47.3X6
hexanitrate	T46.3X1	T46.3X2	T46.3X3	T46.3X4	T46.3X5	T46.3X6
Mannomustine	T45.1X1	T45.1X2	T45.1X3	T45.1X4	T45.1X5	T45.1X6
MAO inhibitors	T43.1X1	T43.1X2	T43.1X3	T43.1X4	T43.1X5	T43.1X6
Mapharsen	T37.8X1	T37.8X2	T37.8X3	T37.8X4	T37.8X5	T37.8X6
Maphenide	T49.0X1	T49.0X2	T49.0X3	T49.0X4	T49.0X5	T49.0X6
Maprotiline	T43.021	T43.022	T43.023	T43.024	T43.025	T43.026
Marcaine	T41.3X1	T41.3X2	T41.3X3	T41.3X4	T41.3X5	T41.3X6
infiltration (subcutaneous)	T41.3X1	T41.3X2	T41.3X3	T41.3X4	T41.3X5	T41.3X6
nerve block (peripheral) (plexus)	T41.3X1	T41.3X2	T41.3X3	T41.3X4	T41.3X5	T41.3X6
Marezine	T45.0X1	T45.0X2	T45.0X3	T45.0X4	T45.0X5	T45.0X6
Marihuana	T40.7X1	T40.7X2	T40.7X3	T40.7X4	T40.7X5	T40.7X6
Marijuana	T40.7X1	T40.7X2	T40.7X3	T40.7X4	T40.7X5	T40.7X6
Marine (sting)	T63.691	T63.692	T63.693	T63.694	—	—
animals (sting)	T63.691	T63.692	T63.693	T63.694	—	—
plants (sting)	T63.711	T63.712	T63.713	T63.714	—	—
Marplan	T43.1X1	T43.1X2	T43.1X3	T43.1X4	T43.1X5	T43.1X6
Marsh gas	T59.891	T59.892	T59.893	T59.894	—	—
Marsilid	T43.1X1	T43.1X2	T43.1X3	T43.1X4	T43.1X5	T43.1X6
Matulane	T45.1X1	T45.1X2	T45.1X3	T45.1X4	T45.1X5	T45.1X6
Mazindol	T50.5X1	T50.5X2	T50.5X3	T50.5X4	T50.5X5	T50.5X6
MCPA	T60.3X1	T60.3X2	T60.3X3	T60.3X4	—	—
MDMA	T43.641	T43.642	T43.643	T43.644	—	—
Meadow saffron	T62.2X1	T62.2X2	T62.2X3	T62.2X4	—	—
Measles virus vaccine (attenuated)	T50.B91	T50.B92	T50.B93	T50.B94	T50.B95	T50.B96
Meat, noxious	T62.8X1	T62.8X2	T62.8X3	T62.8X4	—	—
Meballymal	T42.3X1	T42.3X2	T42.3X3	T42.3X4	T42.3X5	T42.3X6
Mebanazine	T43.1X1	T43.1X2	T43.1X3	T43.1X4	T43.1X5	T43.1X6
Mebaral	T42.3X1	T42.3X2	T42.3X3	T42.3X4	T42.3X5	T42.3X6
Mebendazole	T37.4X1	T37.4X2	T37.4X3	T37.4X4	T37.4X5	T37.4X6
Mebeverine	T44.3X1	T44.3X2	T44.3X3	T44.3X4	T44.3X5	T44.3X6
Mebhydrolin	T45.0X1	T45.0X2	T45.0X3	T45.0X4	T45.0X5	T45.0X6
Mebumal	T42.3X1	T42.3X2	T42.3X3	T42.3X4	T42.3X5	T42.3X6
Mebutamate	T43.591	T43.592	T43.593	T43.594	T43.595	T43.596
Mecamylamine	T44.2X1	T44.2X2	T44.2X3	T44.2X4	T44.2X5	T44.2X6
Mechlorethamine	T45.1X1	T45.1X2	T45.1X3	T45.1X4	T45.1X5	T45.1X6
Mecillinam	T36.0X1	T36.0X2	T36.0X3	T36.0X4	T36.0X5	T36.0X6
Meclizine (hydrochloride)	T45.0X1	T45.0X2	T45.0X3	T45.0X4	T45.0X5	T45.0X6
Meclocycline	T36.4X1	T36.4X2	T36.4X3	T36.4X4	T36.4X5	T36.4X6
Meclofenamate	T39.391	T39.392	T39.393	T39.394	T39.395	T39.396
Meclofenamic acid	T39.391	T39.392	T39.393	T39.394	T39.395	T39.396

Substance	External Cause (T-Code)					
	Poisoning, Accidental (Unintentional)	Poisoning, Intentional Self-Harm	Poisoning, Assault	Poisoning, Undetermined	Adverse Effect	Underdosing
Meclofenoxate	T43.691	T43.692	T43.693	T43.694	T43.695	T43.696
Meclozine	T45.0X1	T45.0X2	T45.0X3	T45.0X4	T45.0X5	T45.0X6
Mecobalamin	T45.8X1	T45.8X2	T45.8X3	T45.8X4	T45.8X5	T45.8X6
Mecoprop	T60.3X1	T60.3X2	T60.3X3	T60.3X4	—	—
Mecrilate	T49.3X1	T49.3X2	T49.3X3	T49.3X4	T49.3X5	T49.3X6
Mecysteine	T48.4X1	T48.4X2	T48.4X3	T48.4X4	T48.4X5	T48.4X6
Medazepam	T42.4X1	T42.4X2	T42.4X3	T42.4X4	T42.4X5	T42.4X6
Medicament NEC	T50.901	T50.902	T50.903	T50.904	T50.905	T50.906
Medinal	T42.3X1	T42.3X2	T42.3X3	T42.3X4	T42.3X5	T42.3X6
Medomin	T42.3X1	T42.3X2	T42.3X3	T42.3X4	T42.3X5	T42.3X6
Medrogestone	T38.5X1	T38.5X2	T38.5X3	T38.5X4	T38.5X5	T38.5X6
Medroxalol	T44.8X1	T44.8X2	T44.8X3	T44.8X4	T44.8X5	T44.8X6
Medroxyprogesterone acetate (depot)	T38.5X1	T38.5X2	T38.5X3	T38.5X4	T38.5X5	T38.5X6
Medrysone	T49.0X1	T49.0X2	T49.0X3	T49.0X4	T49.0X5	T49.0X6
Mefenamic acid	T39.391	T39.392	T39.393	T39.394	T39.395	T39.396
Mefenorex	T50.5X1	T50.5X2	T50.5X3	T50.5X4	T50.5X5	T50.5X6
Mefloquine	T37.2X1	T37.2X2	T37.2X3	T37.2X4	T37.2X5	T37.2X6
Mefruside	T50.2X1	T50.2X2	T50.2X3	T50.2X4	T50.2X5	T50.2X6
Megahallucinogen	T40.901	T40.902	T40.903	T40.904	T40.905	T40.906
Megestrol	T38.5X1	T38.5X2	T38.5X3	T38.5X4	T38.5X5	T38.5X6
Meglumine						
antimoniate	T37.8X1	T37.8X2	T37.8X3	T37.8X4	T37.8X5	T37.8X6
diatrizoate	T50.8X1	T50.8X2	T50.8X3	T50.8X4	T50.8X5	T50.8X6
iodipamide	T50.8X1	T50.8X2	T50.8X3	T50.8X4	T50.8X5	T50.8X6
iotroxate	T50.8X1	T50.8X2	T50.8X3	T50.8X4	T50.8X5	T50.8X6
MEK (methyl ethyl ketone)	T52.4X1	T52.4X2	T52.4X3	T52.4X4	—	—
Meladrazine	T44.3X1	T44.3X2	T44.3X3	T44.3X4	T44.3X5	T44.3X6
Meladinin	T49.3X1	T49.3X2	T49.3X3	T49.3X4	T49.3X5	T49.3X6
Melaleuca alternifolia oil	T49.0X1	T49.0X2	T49.0X3	T49.0X4	T49.0X5	T49.0X6
Melanizing agents	T49.3X1	T49.3X2	T49.3X3	T49.3X4	T49.3X5	T49.3X6
Melanocyte-stimulating hormone	T38.891	T38.892	T38.893	T38.894	T38.895	T38.896
Melarsonyl potassium	T37.3X1	T37.3X2	T37.3X3	T37.3X4	T37.3X5	T37.3X6
Melarsoprol	T37.3X1	T37.3X2	T37.3X3	T37.3X4	T37.3X5	T37.3X6
Melia azedarach	T62.2X1	T62.2X2	T62.2X3	T62.2X4	—	—
Melitracen	T43.011	T43.012	T43.013	T43.014	T43.015	T43.016
Mellaril	T43.3X1	T43.3X2	T43.3X3	T43.3X4	T43.3X5	T43.3X6
Meloxine	T49.3X1	T49.3X2	T49.3X3	T49.3X4	T49.3X5	T49.3X6
Melperone	T43.4X1	T43.4X2	T43.4X3	T43.4X4	T43.4X5	T43.4X6
Melphalan	T45.1X1	T45.1X2	T45.1X3	T45.1X4	T45.1X5	T45.1X6
Memantine	T43.8X1	T43.8X2	T43.8X3	T43.8X4	T43.8X5	T43.8X6

◀ New ◀ Revised ~~deleted~~ Deleted

Substance	External Cause (T-Code) Poisoning, Accidental (Unintentional)	Poisoning, Intentional Self-Harm	Poisoning, Assault	Poisoning, Undetermined	Adverse Effect	Underdosing
Menadiol	T45.7X1	T45.7X2	T45.7X3	T45.7X4	T45.7X5	T45.7X6
sodium sulfate	T45.7X1	T45.7X2	T45.7X3	T45.7X4	T45.7X5	T45.7X6
Menadione	T45.7X1	T45.7X2	T45.7X3	T45.7X4	T45.7X5	T45.7X6
sodium bisulfite	T45.7X1	T45.7X2	T45.7X3	T45.7X4	T45.7X5	T45.7X6
Menaphthone	T45.7X1	T45.7X2	T45.7X3	T45.7X4	T45.7X5	T45.7X6
Menaquinone	T45.7X1	T45.7X2	T45.7X3	T45.7X4	T45.7X5	T45.7X6
Menatetrenone	T45.7X1	T45.7X2	T45.7X3	T45.7X4	T45.7X5	T45.7X6
Meningococcal vaccine	T50.A91	T50.A92	T50.A93	T50.A94	T50.A95	T50.A96
Menningovax (-AC) (-C)	T50.A91	T50.A92	T50.A93	T50.A94	T50.A95	T50.A96
Menotropins	T38.811	T38.812	T38.813	T38.814	T38.815	T38.816
Menthol	T48.5X1	T48.5X2	T48.5X3	T48.5X4	T48.5X5	T48.5X6
Mepacrine	T37.2X1	T37.2X2	T37.2X3	T37.2X4	T37.2X5	T37.2X6
Meparfynol	T42.6X1	T42.6X2	T42.6X3	T42.6X4	T42.6X5	T42.6X6
Mepartricin	T36.7X1	T36.7X2	T36.7X3	T36.7X4	T36.7X5	T36.7X6
Mepazine	T43.3X1	T43.3X2	T43.3X3	T43.3X4	T43.3X5	T43.3X6
Mepenzolate	T44.3X1	T44.3X2	T44.3X3	T44.3X4	T44.3X5	T44.3X6
bromide	T44.3X1	T44.3X2	T44.3X3	T44.3X4	T44.3X5	T44.3X6
Meperidine	T40.491	T40.492	T40.493	T40.494	T40.495	T40.496
Mephebarbital	T42.3X1	T42.3X2	T42.3X3	T42.3X4	T42.3X5	T42.3X6
Mephenamin(e)	T42.8X1	T42.8X2	T42.8X3	T42.8X4	T42.8X5	T42.8X6
Mephenesin	T42.8X1	T42.8X2	T42.8X3	T42.8X4	T42.8X5	T42.8X6
Mephenhydramine	T45.0X1	T45.0X2	T45.0X3	T45.0X4	T45.0X5	T45.0X6
Mephenoxalone	T42.8X1	T42.8X2	T42.8X3	T42.8X4	T42.8X5	T42.8X6
Mephentermine	T44.991	T44.992	T44.993	T44.994	T44.995	T44.996
Mephenytoin	T42.0X1	T42.0X2	T42.0X3	T42.0X4	T42.0X5	T42.0X6
with phenobarbital	T42.3X1	T42.3X2	T42.3X3	T42.3X4	T42.3X5	T42.3X6
Mephobarbital	T42.3X1	T42.3X2	T42.3X3	T42.3X4	T42.3X5	T42.3X6
Mephosfolan	T60.0X1	T60.0X2	T60.0X3	T60.0X4	—	—
Mepindolol	T44.7X1	T44.7X2	T44.7X3	T44.7X4	T44.7X5	T44.7X6
Mepiperphenidol	T44.3X1	T44.3X2	T44.3X3	T44.3X4	T44.3X5	T44.3X6
Mepitiostane	T38.7X1	T38.7X2	T38.7X3	T38.7X4	T38.7X5	T38.7X6
Mepivacaine	T41.3X1	T41.3X2	T41.3X3	T41.3X4	T41.3X5	T41.3X6
epidural	T41.3X1	T41.3X2	T41.3X3	T41.3X4	T41.3X5	T41.3X6
Meprednisone	T38.0X1	T38.0X2	T38.0X3	T38.0X4	T38.0X5	T38.0X6
Meprobam	T43.591	T43.592	T43.593	T43.594	T43.595	T43.596
Meprobamate	T43.591	T43.592	T43.593	T43.594	T43.595	T43.596
Meproscillarin	T46.0X1	T46.0X2	T46.0X3	T46.0X4	T46.0X5	T46.0X6
Meprylcaine	T41.3X1	T41.3X2	T41.3X3	T41.3X4	T41.3X5	T41.3X6
Meptazinol	T39.8X1	T39.8X2	T39.8X3	T39.8X4	T39.8X5	T39.8X6
Mepyramine	T45.0X1	T45.0X2	T45.0X3	T45.0X4	T45.0X5	T45.0X6
Mequitazine	T43.3X1	T43.3X2	T43.3X3	T43.3X4	T43.3X5	T43.3X6
Meralluride	T50.2X1	T50.2X2	T50.2X3	T50.2X4	T50.2X5	T50.2X6

Substance	External Cause (T-Code) Poisoning, Accidental (Unintentional)	Poisoning, Intentional Self-Harm	Poisoning, Assault	Poisoning, Undetermined	Adverse Effect	Underdosing
Merbaphen	T50.2X1	T50.2X2	T50.2X3	T50.2X4	T50.2X5	T50.2X6
Merbromin	T49.0X1	T49.0X2	T49.0X3	T49.0X4	T49.0X5	T49.0X6
Mercaptobenzothiazole salts	T49.0X1	T49.0X2	T49.0X3	T49.0X4	T49.0X5	T49.0X6
Mercaptomerin	T50.2X1	T50.2X2	T50.2X3	T50.2X4	T50.2X5	T50.2X6
Mercaptopurine	T45.1X1	T45.1X2	T45.1X3	T45.1X4	T45.1X5	T45.1X6
Mercumatilin	T50.2X1	T50.2X2	T50.2X3	T50.2X4	T50.2X5	T50.2X6
Mercuramide	T50.2X1	T50.2X2	T50.2X3	T50.2X4	T50.2X5	T50.2X6
Mercurochrome	T49.0X1	T49.0X2	T49.0X3	T49.0X4	T49.0X5	T49.0X6
Mercurophylline	T50.2X1	T50.2X2	T50.2X3	T50.2X4	T50.2X5	T50.2X6
Mercury, mercurial, mercuric, mercurous (compounds) (cyanide) (fumes) (nonmedicinal) (vapor) NEC	T56.1X1	T56.1X2	T56.1X3	T56.1X4	—	—
ammoniated	T49.0X1	T49.0X2	T49.0X3	T49.0X4	T49.0X5	T49.0X6
anti-infective						
local	T49.0X1	T49.0X2	T49.0X3	T49.0X4	T49.0X5	T49.0X6
systemic	T37.8X1	T37.8X2	T37.8X3	T37.8X4	T37.8X5	T37.8X6
topical	T49.0X1	T49.0X2	T49.0X3	T49.0X4	T49.0X5	T49.0X6
chloride (ammoniated)	T49.0X1	T49.0X2	T49.0X3	T49.0X4	T49.0X5	T49.0X6
fungicide	T56.1X1	T56.1X2	T56.1X3	T56.1X4	—	—
diuretic NEC	T50.2X1	T50.2X2	T50.2X3	T50.2X4	T50.2X5	T50.2X6
fungicide	T56.1X1	T56.1X2	T56.1X3	T56.1X4		
organic (fungicide)	T56.1X1	T56.1X2	T56.1X3	T56.1X4		
oxide, yellow	T49.0X1	T49.0X2	T49.0X3	T49.0X4	T49.0X5	T49.0X6
Mersalyl	T50.2X1	T50.2X2	T50.2X3	T50.2X4	T50.2X5	T50.2X6
Merthiolate	T49.0X1	T49.0X2	T49.0X3	T49.0X4	T49.0X5	T49.0X6
ophthalmic preparation	T49.5X1	T49.5X2	T49.5X3	T49.5X4	T49.5X5	T49.5X6
Meruvax	T50.B91	T50.B92	T50.B93	T50.B94	T50.B95	T50.B96
Mesalazine	T47.8X1	T47.8X2	T47.8X3	T47.8X4	T47.8X5	T47.8X6
Mescal buttons	T40.991	T40.992	T40.993	T40.994	—	—
Mescaline	T40.991	T40.992	T40.993	T40.994	—	—
Mesna	T48.4X1	T48.4X2	T48.4X3	T48.4X4	T48.4X5	T48.4X6
Mesoglycan	T46.6X1	T46.6X2	T46.6X3	T46.6X4	T46.6X5	T46.6X6
Mesoridazine	T43.3X1	T43.3X2	T43.3X3	T43.3X4	T43.3X5	T43.3X6
Mestanolone	T38.7X1	T38.7X2	T38.7X3	T38.7X4	T38.7X5	T38.7X6
Mesterolone	T38.7X1	T38.7X2	T38.7X3	T38.7X4	T38.7X5	T38.7X6
Mestranol	T38.5X1	T38.5X2	T38.5X3	T38.5X4	T38.5X5	T38.5X6
Mesulergine	T42.8X1	T42.8X2	T42.8X3	T42.8X4	T42.8X5	T42.8X6
Mesulfen	T49.0X1	T49.0X2	T49.0X3	T49.0X4	T49.0X5	T49.0X6
Mesuximide	T42.2X1	T42.2X2	T42.2X3	T42.2X4	T42.2X5	T42.2X6
Metabutethamine	T41.3X1	T41.3X2	T41.3X3	T41.3X4	T41.3X5	T41.3X6
Metactesylacetate	T49.0X1	T49.0X2	T49.0X3	T49.0X4	T49.0X5	T49.0X6

◀ New   ◀ Revised   ~~deleted~~ Deleted

Substance	External Cause (T-Code)					
	Poisoning, Accidental (Unintentional)	Poisoning, Intentional Self-Harm	Poisoning, Assault	Poisoning, Undetermined	Adverse Effect	Underdosing
Metacycline	T36.4X1	T36.4X2	T36.4X3	T36.4X4	T36.4X5	T36.4X6
Metaldehyde (snail killer) NEC	T60.8X1	T60.8X2	T60.8X3	T60.8X4	—	—
Metals (heavy) (nonmedicinal)	T56.91	T56.92	T56.93	T56.94	—	—
dust, fumes, or vapor NEC	T56.91	T56.92	T56.93	T56.94	—	—
light NEC	T56.91	T56.92	T56.93	T56.94	—	—
dust, fumes, or vapor NEC	T56.91	T56.92	T56.93	T56.94	—	—
specified NEC	T56.891	T56.892	T56.893	T56.894	—	—
thallium	T56.811	T56.812	T56.813	T56.814	—	—
Metamfetamine	T43.621	T43.622	T43.623	T43.624	T43.625	T43.626
Metamizole sodium	T39.2X1	T39.2X2	T39.2X3	T39.2X4	T39.2X5	T39.2X6
Metampicillin	T36.0X1	T36.0X2	T36.0X3	T36.0X4	T36.0X5	T36.0X6
Metamucil	T47.4X1	T47.4X2	T47.4X3	T47.4X4	T47.4X5	T47.4X6
Metaphen	T49.0X1	T49.0X2	T49.0X3	T49.0X4	T49.0X5	T49.0X6
Metandienone	T38.7X1	T38.7X2	T38.7X3	T38.7X4	T38.7X5	T38.7X6
Metandrostenolone	T38.7X1	T38.7X2	T38.7X3	T38.7X4	T38.7X5	T38.7X6
Metaphos	T60.0X1	T60.0X2	T60.0X3	T60.0X4	—	—
Metapramine	T43.011	T43.012	T43.013	T43.014	T43.015	T43.016
Metaproterenol	T48.291	T48.292	T48.293	T48.294	T48.295	T48.296
Metaraminol	T44.4X1	T44.4X2	T44.4X3	T44.4X4	T44.4X5	T44.4X6
Metaxalone	T42.8X1	T42.8X2	T42.8X3	T42.8X4	T42.8X5	T42.8X6
Metenolone	T38.7X1	T38.7X2	T38.7X3	T38.7X4	T38.7X5	T38.7X6
Metergoline	T42.8X1	T42.8X2	T42.8X3	T42.8X4	T42.8X5	T42.8X6
Metescufylline	T46.991	T46.992	T46.993	T46.994	T46.995	T46.996
Metetoin	T42.0X1	T42.0X2	T42.0X3	T42.0X4	T42.0X5	T42.0X6
Metformin	T38.3X1	T38.3X2	T38.3X3	T38.3X4	T38.3X5	T38.3X6
Methacholine	T44.1X1	T44.1X2	T44.1X3	T44.1X4	T44.1X5	T44.1X6
Methacycline	T36.4X1	T36.4X2	T36.4X3	T36.4X4	T36.4X5	T36.4X6
Methadone	T40.3X1	T40.3X2	T40.3X3	T40.3X4	T40.3X5	T40.3X6
Methallenestril	T38.5X1	T38.5X2	T38.5X3	T38.5X4	T38.5X5	T38.5X6
Methallenoestril	T38.5X1	T38.5X2	T38.5X3	T38.5X4	T38.5X5	T38.5X6
Methamphetamine	T43.621	T43.622	T43.623	T43.624	T43.625	T43.626
Methampyrone	T39.2X1	T39.2X2	T39.2X3	T39.2X4	T39.2X5	T39.2X6
Methandienone	T38.7X1	T38.7X2	T38.7X3	T38.7X4	T38.7X5	T38.7X6
Methandriol	T38.7X1	T38.7X2	T38.7X3	T38.7X4	T38.7X5	T38.7X6
Methandrostenolone	T38.7X1	T38.7X2	T38.7X3	T38.7X4	T38.7X5	T38.7X6
Methane	T59.891	T59.892	T59.893	T59.894	—	—
Methanethiol	T59.891	T59.892	T59.893	T59.894	—	—
Methaniazide	T37.1X1	T37.1X2	T37.1X3	T37.1X4	T37.1X5	T37.1X6
Methanol (vapor)	T51.1X1	T51.1X2	T51.1X3	T51.1X4	—	—
Methantheline	T44.3X1	T44.3X2	T44.3X3	T44.3X4	T44.3X5	T44.3X6
Methanthelinium bromide	T44.3X1	T44.3X2	T44.3X3	T44.3X4	T44.3X5	T44.3X6
Methaphenilene	T45.0X1	T45.0X2	T45.0X3	T45.0X4	T45.0X5	T45.0X6

Substance	External Cause (T-Code)					
	Poisoning, Accidental (Unintentional)	Poisoning, Intentional Self-Harm	Poisoning, Assault	Poisoning, Undetermined	Adverse Effect	Underdosing
Methapyrilene	T45.0X1	T45.0X2	T45.0X3	T45.0X4	T45.0X5	T45.0X6
Methaqualone (compound)	T42.6X1	T42.6X2	T42.6X3	T42.6X4	T42.6X5	T42.6X6
Metharbital	T42.3X1	T42.3X2	T42.3X3	T42.3X4	T42.3X5	T42.3X6
Methazolamide	T50.2X1	T50.2X2	T50.2X3	T50.2X4	T50.2X5	T50.2X6
Methdilazine	T43.3X1	T43.3X2	T43.3X3	T43.3X4	T43.3X5	T43.3X6
Methedrine	T43.621	T43.622	T43.623	T43.624	T43.625	T43.626
Methenamine (mandelate)	T37.8X1	T37.8X2	T37.8X3	T37.8X4	T37.8X5	T37.8X6
Methenolone	T38.7X1	T38.7X2	T38.7X3	T38.7X4	T38.7X5	T38.7X6
Methergine	T48.0X1	T48.0X2	T48.0X3	T48.0X4	T48.0X5	T48.0X6
Methetoin	T42.0X1	T42.0X2	T42.0X3	T42.0X4	T42.0X5	T42.0X6
Methiacil	T38.2X1	T38.2X2	T38.2X3	T38.2X4	T38.2X5	T38.2X6
Methicillin	T36.0X1	T36.0X2	T36.0X3	T36.0X4	T36.0X5	T36.0X6
Methimazole	T38.2X1	T38.2X2	T38.2X3	T38.2X4	T38.2X5	T38.2X6
Methiodal sodium	T50.8X1	T50.8X2	T50.8X3	T50.8X4	T50.8X5	T50.8X6
Methionine	T50.991	T50.992	T50.993	T50.994	T50.995	T50.996
Methisazone	T37.5X1	T37.5X2	T37.5X3	T37.5X4	T37.5X5	T37.5X6
Methisoprinol	T37.5X1	T37.5X2	T37.5X3	T37.5X4	T37.5X5	T37.5X6
Methitural	T42.3X1	T42.3X2	T42.3X3	T42.3X4	T42.3X5	T42.3X6
Methixene	T44.3X1	T44.3X2	T44.3X3	T44.3X4	T44.3X5	T44.3X6
Methobarbital, methobarbitone	T42.3X1	T42.3X2	T42.3X3	T42.3X4	T42.3X5	T42.3X6
Methocarbamol	T42.8X1	T42.8X2	T42.8X3	T42.8X4	T42.8X5	T42.8X6
skeletal muscle relaxant	T48.1X1	T48.1X2	T48.1X3	T48.1X4	T48.1X5	T48.1X6
Methohexital	T41.1X1	T41.1X2	T41.1X3	T41.1X4	T41.1X5	T41.1X6
Methohexitone	T41.1X1	T41.1X2	T41.1X3	T41.1X4	T41.1X5	T41.1X6
Methoin	T42.0X1	T42.0X2	T42.0X3	T42.0X4	T42.0X5	T42.0X6
Methopholine	T39.8X1	T39.8X2	T39.8X3	T39.8X4	T39.8X5	T39.8X6
Methopromazine	T43.3X1	T43.3X2	T43.3X3	T43.3X4	T43.3X5	T43.3X6
Methorate	T48.3X1	T48.3X2	T48.3X3	T48.3X4	T48.3X5	T48.3X6
Methoserpidine	T46.5X1	T46.5X2	T46.5X3	T46.5X4	T46.5X5	T46.5X6
Methotrexate	T45.1X1	T45.1X2	T45.1X3	T45.1X4	T45.1X5	T45.1X6
Methotrimeprazine	T43.3X1	T43.3X2	T43.3X3	T43.3X4	T43.3X5	T43.3X6
Methoxa-Dome	T49.3X1	T49.3X2	T49.3X3	T49.3X4	T49.3X5	T49.3X6
Methoxamine	T44.4X1	T44.4X2	T44.4X3	T44.4X4	T44.4X5	T44.4X6
Methoxsalen	T50.991	T50.992	T50.993	T50.994	T50.995	T50.996
Methoxyaniline	T65.3X1	T65.3X2	T65.3X3	T65.3X4	—	—
Methoxybenzyl penicillin	T36.0X1	T36.0X2	T36.0X3	T36.0X4	T36.0X5	T36.0X6
Methoxychlor	T53.7X1	T53.7X2	T53.7X3	T53.7X4	—	—
Methoxy-DDT	T53.7X1	T53.7X2	T53.7X3	T53.7X4	—	—
2-Methoxyethanol	T52.3X1	T52.3X2	T52.3X3	T52.3X4	—	—
Methoxyflurane	T41.0X1	T41.0X2	T41.0X3	T41.0X4	T41.0X5	T41.0X6
Methoxyphenamine	T48.6X1	T48.6X2	T48.6X3	T48.6X4	T48.6X5	T48.6X6
Methoxypromazine	T43.3X1	T43.3X2	T43.3X3	T43.3X4	T43.3X5	T43.3X6

◀ New   ◀ Revised   ~~deleted~~ Deleted

Substance	Poisoning, Accidental (Unintentional)	Poisoning, Intentional Self-Harm	Poisoning, Assault	Poisoning, Undetermined	Adverse Effect	Underdosing
5-Methoxypsoralen (5-MOP)	T50.991	T50.992	T50.993	T50.994	T50.995	T50.996
8-Methoxypsoralen (8-MOP)	T50.991	T50.992	T50.993	T50.994	T50.995	T50.996
Methscopolamine bromide	T44.3X1	T44.3X2	T44.3X3	T44.3X4	T44.3X5	T44.3X6
Methsuximide	T42.2X1	T42.2X2	T42.2X3	T42.2X4	T42.2X5	T42.2X6
Methyclothiazide	T50.2X1	T50.2X2	T50.2X3	T50.2X4	T50.2X5	T50.2X6
Methyl						
acetate	T52.4X1	T52.4X2	T52.4X3	T52.4X4	—	—
acetone	T52.4X1	T52.4X2	T52.4X3	T52.4X4	—	—
acrylate	T65.891	T65.892	T65.893	T65.894	—	—
alcohol	T51.1X1	T51.1X2	T51.1X3	T51.1X4	—	—
aminophenol	T65.3X1	T65.3X2	T65.3X3	T65.3X4	—	—
amphetamine	T43.621	T43.622	T43.623	T43.624	T43.625	T43.626
androstanolone	T38.7X1	T38.7X2	T38.7X3	T38.7X4	T38.7X5	T38.7X6
atropine	T44.3X1	T44.3X2	T44.3X3	T44.3X4	T44.3X5	T44.3X6
benzene	T52.2X1	T52.2X2	T52.2X3	T52.2X4	—	—
benzoate	T52.8X1	T52.8X2	T52.8X3	T52.8X4	—	—
benzol	T52.2X1	T52.2X2	T52.2X3	T52.2X4	—	—
bromide (gas)	T59.891	T59.892	T59.893	T59.894	—	—
fumigant	T60.8X1	T60.8X2	T60.8X3	T60.8X4	—	—
butanol	T51.3X1	T51.3X2	T51.3X3	T51.3X4	—	—
carbinol	T51.1X1	T51.1X2	T51.1X3	T51.1X4	—	—
carbonate	T52.8X1	T52.8X2	T52.8X3	T52.8X4	—	—
CCNU	T45.1X1	T45.1X2	T45.1X3	T45.1X4	T45.1X5	T45.1X6
cellosolve	T52.91	T52.92	T52.93	T52.94	—	—
cellulose	T47.4X1	T47.4X2	T47.4X3	T47.4X4	T47.4X5	T47.4X6
chloride (gas)	T59.891	T59.892	T59.893	T59.894	—	—
chloroformate	T59.3X1	T59.3X2	T59.3X3	T59.3X4	—	—
cyclohexane	T52.8X1	T52.8X2	T52.8X3	T52.8X4	—	—
cyclohexanol	T51.8X1	T51.8X2	T51.8X3	T51.8X4	—	—
cyclohexanone	T52.8X1	T52.8X2	T52.8X3	T52.8X4	—	—
cyclohexyl acetate	T52.8X1	T52.8X2	T52.8X3	T52.8X4	—	—
demeton	T60.0X1	T60.0X2	T60.0X3	T60.0X4	—	—
dihydromorphinone	T40.2X1	T40.2X2	T40.2X3	T40.2X4	T40.2X5	T40.2X6
ergometrine	T48.0X1	T48.0X2	T48.0X3	T48.0X4	T48.0X5	T48.0X6
ergonovine	T48.0X1	T48.0X2	T48.0X3	T48.0X4	T48.0X5	T48.0X6
ethyl ketone	T52.4X1	T52.4X2	T52.4X3	T52.4X4	—	—
glucamine antimonate	T37.8X1	T37.8X2	T37.8X3	T37.8X4	T37.8X5	T37.8X6
hydrazine	T65.891	T65.892	T65.893	T65.894	—	—
iodide	T65.891	T65.892	T65.893	T65.894	—	—
isobutyl ketone	T52.4X1	T52.4X2	T52.4X3	T52.4X4	—	—
isothiocyanate	T60.3X1	T60.3X2	T60.3X3	T60.3X4	—	—
mercaptan	T59.891	T59.892	T59.893	T59.894	—	—

Substance	Poisoning, Accidental (Unintentional)	Poisoning, Intentional Self-Harm	Poisoning, Assault	Poisoning, Undetermined	Adverse Effect	Underdosing
Methyl *(Continued)*						
morphine NEC	T40.2X1	T40.2X2	T40.2X3	T40.2X4	T40.2X5	T40.2X6
nicotinate	T49.4X1	T49.4X2	T49.4X3	T49.4X4	T49.4X5	T49.4X6
paraben	T49.0X1	T49.0X2	T49.0X3	T49.0X4	T49.0X5	T49.0X6
parafynol	T42.6X1	T42.6X2	T42.6X3	T42.6X4	T42.6X5	T42.6X6
parathion	T60.0X1	T60.0X2	T60.0X3	T60.0X4	—	—
peridol	T43.4X1	T43.4X2	T43.4X3	T43.4X4	T43.4X5	T43.4X6
phenidate	T43.631	T43.632	T43.633	T43.634	T43.635	T43.636
prednisolone	T38.0X1	T38.0X2	T38.0X3	T38.0X4	T38.0X5	T38.0X6
ENT agent	T49.6X1	T49.6X2	T49.6X3	T49.6X4	T49.6X5	T49.6X6
ophthalmic preparation	T49.5X1	T49.5X2	T49.5X3	T49.5X4	T49.5X5	T49.5X6
topical NEC	T49.0X1	T49.0X2	T49.0X3	T49.0X4	T49.0X5	T49.0X6
propylcarbinol	T51.3X1	T51.3X2	T51.3X3	T51.3X4	—	—
rosaniline NEC	T49.0X1	T49.0X2	T49.0X3	T49.0X4	T49.0X5	T49.0X6
salicylate	T49.2X1	T49.2X2	T49.2X3	T49.2X4	T49.2X5	T49.2X6
sulfate (fumes)	T59.891	T59.892	T59.893	T59.894	—	—
liquid	T52.8X1	T52.8X2	T52.8X3	T52.8X4	—	—
sulfonal	T42.6X1	T42.6X2	T42.6X3	T42.6X4	T42.6X5	T42.6X6
testosterone	T38.7X1	T38.7X2	T38.7X3	T38.7X4	T38.7X5	T38.7X6
thiouracil	T38.2X1	T38.2X2	T38.2X3	T38.2X4	T38.2X5	T38.2X6
Methylamphetamine	T43.621	T43.622	T43.623	T43.624	T43.625	T43.626
Methylated spirit	T51.1X1	T51.1X2	T51.1X3	T51.1X4	—	—
Methylatropine nitrate	T44.3X1	T44.3X2	T44.3X3	T44.3X4	T44.3X5	T44.3X6
Methylbenactyzium bromide	T44.3X1	T44.3X2	T44.3X3	T44.3X4	T44.3X5	T44.3X6
Methylbenzethonium chloride	T49.0X1	T49.0X2	T49.0X3	T49.0X4	T49.0X5	T49.0X6
Methylcellulose	T47.4X1	T47.4X2	T47.4X3	T47.4X4	T47.4X5	T47.4X6
laxative	T47.4X1	T47.4X2	T47.4X3	T47.4X4	T47.4X5	T47.4X6
Methylchlorophenoxy-acetic acid	T60.3X1	T60.3X2	T60.3X3	T60.3X4	—	—
Methyldopa	T46.5X1	T46.5X2	T46.5X3	T46.5X4	T46.5X5	T46.5X6
Methyldopate	T46.5X1	T46.5X2	T46.5X3	T46.5X4	T46.5X5	T46.5X6
Methylene						
blue	T50.6X1	T50.6X2	T50.6X3	T50.6X4	T50.6X5	T50.6X6
chloride or dichloride (solvent) NEC	T53.4X1	T53.4X2	T53.4X3	T53.4X4	—	—
Methylenedioxyamphet-amine	T43.621	T43.622	T43.623	T43.624	T43.625	T43.626
Methylenedioxymethamphetamine	T43.641	T43.642	T43.643	T43.644	—	—
Methylergometrine	T48.0X1	T48.0X2	T48.0X3	T48.0X4	T48.0X5	T48.0X6
Methylergonovine	T48.0X1	T48.0X2	T48.0X3	T48.0X4	T48.0X5	T48.0X6
Methylestrenolone	T38.5X1	T38.5X2	T38.5X3	T38.5X4	T38.5X5	T38.5X6
Methylethyl cellulose	T50.991	T50.992	T50.993	T50.994	T50.995	T50.996
Methylhexabital	T42.3X1	T42.3X2	T42.3X3	T42.3X4	T42.3X5	T42.3X6
Methylmorphine	T40.2X1	T40.2X2	T40.2X3	T40.2X4	T40.2X5	T40.2X6

◄ New   ◄ Revised   ~~deleted~~ Deleted

Substance	External Cause (T-Code)					
	Poisoning, Accidental (Unintentional)	Poisoning, Intentional Self-Harm	Poisoning, Assault	Poisoning, Undetermined	Adverse Effect	Underdosing
Methylparaben (ophthalmic)	T49.5X1	T49.5X2	T49.5X3	T49.5X4	T49.5X5	T49.5X6
Methylparafynol	T42.6X1	T42.6X2	T42.6X3	T42.6X4	T42.6X5	T42.6X6
Methylpentynol, methylpenthynol	T42.6X1	T42.6X2	T42.6X3	T42.6X4	T42.6X5	T42.6X6
Methylphenidate	T43.631	T43.632	T43.633	T43.634	T43.635	T43.636
Methylphenobarbital	T42.3X1	T42.3X2	T42.3X3	T42.3X4	T42.3X5	T42.3X6
Methylpolysiloxane	T47.1X1	T47.1X2	T47.1X3	T47.1X4	T47.1X5	T47.1X6
Methylprednisolone — see Methyl, prednisolone						
Methylrosaniline	T49.0X1	T49.0X2	T49.0X3	T49.0X4	T49.0X5	T49.0X6
Methylrosanilinium chloride	T49.0X1	T49.0X2	T49.0X3	T49.0X4	T49.0X5	T49.0X6
Methyltestosterone	T38.7X1	T38.7X2	T38.7X3	T38.7X4	T38.7X5	T38.7X6
Methylthionine chloride	T50.6X1	T50.6X2	T50.6X3	T50.6X4	T50.6X5	T50.6X6
Methylthioninium chloride	T50.6X1	T50.6X2	T50.6X3	T50.6X4	T50.6X5	T50.6X6
Methylthiouracil	T38.2X1	T38.2X2	T38.2X3	T38.2X4	T38.2X5	T38.2X6
Methyprylon	T42.6X1	T42.6X2	T42.6X3	T42.6X4	T42.6X5	T42.6X6
Methysergide	T46.5X1	T46.5X2	T46.5X3	T46.5X4	T46.5X5	T46.5X6
Metiamide	T47.1X1	T47.1X2	T47.1X3	T47.1X4	T47.1X5	T47.1X6
Meticillin	T36.0X1	T36.0X2	T36.0X3	T36.0X4	T36.0X5	T36.0X6
Meticrane	T50.2X1	T50.2X2	T50.2X3	T50.2X4	T50.2X5	T50.2X6
Metildigoxin	T46.0X1	T46.0X2	T46.0X3	T46.0X4	T46.0X5	T46.0X6
Metipranolol	T49.5X1	T49.5X2	T49.5X3	T49.5X4	T49.5X5	T49.5X6
Metirosine	T46.5X1	T46.5X2	T46.5X3	T46.5X4	T46.5X5	T46.5X6
Metisazone	T37.5X1	T37.5X2	T37.5X3	T37.5X4	T37.5X5	T37.5X6
Metixene	T44.3X1	T44.3X2	T44.3X3	T44.3X4	T44.3X5	T44.3X6
Metizoline	T48.5X1	T48.5X2	T48.5X3	T48.5X4	T48.5X5	T48.5X6
Metoclopramide	T45.0X1	T45.0X2	T45.0X3	T45.0X4	T45.0X5	T45.0X6
Metofenazate	T43.3X1	T43.3X2	T43.3X3	T43.3X4	T43.3X5	T43.3X6
Metofoline	T39.8X1	T39.8X2	T39.8X3	T39.8X4	T39.8X5	T39.8X6
Metolazone	T50.2X1	T50.2X2	T50.2X3	T50.2X4	T50.2X5	T50.2X6
Metopon	T40.2X1	T40.2X2	T40.2X3	T40.2X4	T40.2X5	T40.2X6
Metoprine	T45.1X1	T45.1X2	T45.1X3	T45.1X4	T45.1X5	T45.1X6
Metoprolol	T44.7X1	T44.7X2	T44.7X3	T44.7X4	T44.7X5	T44.7X6
Metrifonate	T60.0X1	T60.0X2	T60.0X3	T60.0X4	—	—
Metrizamide	T50.8X1	T50.8X2	T50.8X3	T50.8X4	T50.8X5	T50.8X6
Metrizoic acid	T50.8X1	T50.8X2	T50.8X3	T50.8X4	T50.8X5	T50.8X6
Metronidazole	T37.8X1	T37.8X2	T37.8X3	T37.8X4	T37.8X5	T37.8X6
Metycaine	T41.3X1	T41.3X2	T41.3X3	T41.3X4	T41.3X5	T41.3X6
infiltration (subcutaneous)	T41.3X1	T41.3X2	T41.3X3	T41.3X4	T41.3X5	T41.3X6
nerve block (peripheral) (plexus)	T41.3X1	T41.3X2	T41.3X3	T41.3X4	T41.3X5	T41.3X6
topical (surface)	T41.3X1	T41.3X2	T41.3X3	T41.3X4	T41.3X5	T41.3X6
Metyrapone	T50.8X1	T50.8X2	T50.8X3	T50.8X4	T50.8X5	T50.8X6
Mevinphos	T60.0X1	T60.0X2	T60.0X3	T60.0X4	—	—

Substance	External Cause (T-Code)					
	Poisoning, Accidental (Unintentional)	Poisoning, Intentional Self-Harm	Poisoning, Assault	Poisoning, Undetermined	Adverse Effect	Underdosing
Mexazolam	T42.4X1	T42.4X2	T42.4X3	T42.4X4	T42.4X5	T42.4X6
Mexenone	T49.3X1	T49.3X2	T49.3X3	T49.3X4	T49.3X5	T49.3X6
Mexiletine	T46.2X1	T46.2X2	T46.2X3	T46.2X4	T46.2X5	T46.2X6
Mezereon	T62.2X1	T62.2X2	T62.2X3	T62.2X4	—	—
berries	T62.1X1	T62.1X2	T62.1X3	T62.1X4	—	—
Mezlocillin	T36.0X1	T36.0X2	T36.0X3	T36.0X4	T36.0X5	T36.0X6
Mianserin	T43.021	T43.022	T43.023	T43.024	T43.025	T43.026
Micatin	T49.0X1	T49.0X2	T49.0X3	T49.0X4	T49.0X5	T49.0X6
Miconazole	T49.0X1	T49.0X2	T49.0X3	T49.0X4	T49.0X5	T49.0X6
Micronomicin	T36.5X1	T36.5X2	T36.5X3	T36.5X4	T36.5X5	T36.5X6
Midazolam	T42.4X1	T42.4X2	T42.4X3	T42.4X4	T42.4X5	T42.4X6
Midecamycin	T36.3X1	T36.3X2	T36.3X3	T36.3X4	T36.3X5	T36.3X6
Mifepristone	T38.6X1	T38.6X2	T38.6X3	T38.6X4	T38.6X5	T38.6X6
Milk of magnesia	T47.1X1	T47.1X2	T47.1X3	T47.1X4	T47.1X5	T47.1X6
Millipede (tropical) (venomous)	T63.411	T63.412	T63.413	T63.414	—	—
Miltown	T43.591	T43.592	T43.593	T43.594	T43.595	T43.596
Milverine	T44.3X1	T44.3X2	T44.3X3	T44.3X4	T44.3X5	T44.3X6
Minaprine	T43.291	T43.292	T43.293	T43.294	T43.295	T43.296
Minaxolone	T41.291	T41.292	T41.293	T41.294	T41.295	T41.296
Mineral						
acids	T54.2X1	T54.2X2	T54.2X3	T54.2X4	—	—
oil (laxative) (medicinal)	T47.4X1	T47.4X2	T47.4X3	T47.4X4	T47.4X5	T47.4X6
emulsion	T47.2X1	T47.2X2	T47.2X3	T47.2X4	T47.2X5	T47.2X6
nonmedicinal	T52.0X1	T52.0X2	T52.0X3	T52.0X4	—	—
topical	T49.3X1	T49.3X2	T49.3X3	T49.3X4	T49.3X5	T49.3X6
salt NEC	T50.3X1	T50.3X2	T50.3X3	T50.3X4	T50.3X5	T50.3X6
spirits	T52.0X1	T52.0X2	T52.0X3	T52.0X4	—	—
Mineralocorticosteroid	T50.0X1	T50.0X2	T50.0X3	T50.0X4	T50.0X5	T50.0X6
Minocycline	T36.4X1	T36.4X2	T36.4X3	T36.4X4	T36.4X5	T36.4X6
Minoxidil	T46.7X1	T46.7X2	T46.7X3	T46.7X4	T46.7X5	T46.7X6
Miokamycin	T36.3X1	T36.3X2	T36.3X3	T36.3X4	T36.3X5	T36.3X6
Miotic drug	T49.5X1	T49.5X2	T49.5X3	T49.5X4	T49.5X5	T49.5X6
Mipafox	T60.0X1	T60.0X2	T60.0X3	T60.0X4	—	—
Mirex	T60.1X1	T60.1X2	T60.1X3	T60.1X4	—	—
Mirtazapine	T43.021	T43.022	T43.023	T43.024	T43.025	T43.026
Misonidazole	T37.3X1	T37.3X2	T37.3X3	T37.3X4	T37.3X5	T37.3X6
Misoprostol	T47.1X1	T47.1X2	T47.1X3	T47.1X4	T47.1X5	T47.1X6
Mithramycin	T45.1X1	T45.1X2	T45.1X3	T45.1X4	T45.1X5	T45.1X6
Mitobronitol	T45.1X1	T45.1X2	T45.1X3	T45.1X4	T45.1X5	T45.1X6
Mitoguazone	T45.1X1	T45.1X2	T45.1X3	T45.1X4	T45.1X5	T45.1X6
Mitolactol	T45.1X1	T45.1X2	T45.1X3	T45.1X4	T45.1X5	T45.1X6
Mitomycin	T45.1X1	T45.1X2	T45.1X3	T45.1X4	T45.1X5	T45.1X6

◀ New ◀ Revised ~~deleted~~ Deleted

Substance	External Cause (T-Code)					
	Poisoning, Accidental (Unintentional)	Poisoning, Intentional Self-Harm	Poisoning, Assault	Poisoning, Undetermined	Adverse Effect	Underdosing
Mitopodozide	T45.1X1	T45.1X2	T45.1X3	T45.1X4	T45.1X5	T45.1X6
Mitotane	T45.1X1	T45.1X2	T45.1X3	T45.1X4	T45.1X5	T45.1X6
Mitoxantrone	T45.1X1	T45.1X2	T45.1X3	T45.1X4	T45.1X5	T45.1X6
Mivacurium chloride	T48.1X1	T48.1X2	T48.1X3	T48.1X4	T48.1X5	T48.1X6
Miyari bacteria	T47.6X1	T47.6X2	T47.6X3	T47.6X4	T47.6X5	T47.6X6
Moclobemide	T43.1X1	T43.1X2	T43.1X3	T43.1X4	T43.1X5	T43.1X6
Moderil	T46.5X1	T46.5X2	T46.5X3	T46.5X4	T46.5X5	T46.5X6
Mofebutazone	T39.2X1	T39.2X2	T39.2X3	T39.2X4	T39.2X5	T39.2X6
Mogadon — see Nitrazepam						
Molindone	T43.591	T43.592	T43.593	T43.594	T43.595	T43.596
Molsidomine	T46.3X1	T46.3X2	T46.3X3	T46.3X4	T46.3X5	T46.3X6
Mometasone	T49.0X1	T49.0X2	T49.0X3	T49.0X4	T49.0X5	T49.0X6
Monistat	T49.0X1	T49.0X2	T49.0X3	T49.0X4	T49.0X5	T49.0X6
Monkshood	T62.2X1	T62.2X2	T62.2X3	T62.2X4	—	—
Monoamine oxidase inhibitor NEC	T43.1X1	T43.1X2	T43.1X3	T43.1X4	T43.1X5	T43.1X6
hydrazine	T43.1X1	T43.1X2	T43.1X3	T43.1X4	T43.1X5	T43.1X6
Monobenzone	T49.4X1	T49.4X2	T49.4X3	T49.4X4	T49.4X5	T49.4X6
Monochloroacetic acid	T60.3X1	T60.3X2	T60.3X3	T60.3X4	—	—
Monochlorobenzene	T53.7X1	T53.7X2	T53.7X3	T53.7X4	—	—
Monoethanolamine	T46.8X1	T46.8X2	T46.8X3	T46.8X4	T46.8X5	T46.8X6
oleate	T46.8X1	T46.8X2	T46.8X3	T46.8X4	T46.8X5	T46.8X6
Monooctanoin	T50.991	T50.992	T50.993	T50.994	T50.995	T50.996
Monophenylbutazone	T39.2X1	T39.2X2	T39.2X3	T39.2X4	T39.2X5	T39.2X6
Monosodium glutamate	T65.891	T65.892	T65.893	T65.894	—	—
Monosulfiram	T49.0X1	T49.0X2	T49.0X3	T49.0X4	T49.0X5	T49.0X6
Monoxide, carbon — see Carbon, monoxide	T57.91	T57.92	T57.93	T57.94	—	—
Monoxidine hydrochloride	T46.1X1	T46.1X2	T46.1X3	T46.1X4	T46.1X5	T46.1X6
Monuron	T60.3X1	T60.3X2	T60.3X3	T60.3X4	—	—
Moperone	T43.4X1	T43.4X2	T43.4X3	T43.4X4	T43.4X5	T43.4X6
Mopidamol	T45.1X1	T45.1X2	T45.1X3	T45.1X4	T45.1X5	T45.1X6
MOPP (mechlorethamine + vincristine + prednisone + procarbazine)	T45.1X1	T45.1X2	T45.1X3	T45.1X4	T45.1X5	T45.1X6
Morfin	T40.2X1	T40.2X2	T40.2X3	T40.2X4	T40.2X5	T40.2X6
Morinamide	T37.1X1	T37.1X2	T37.1X3	T37.1X4	T37.1X5	T37.1X6
Morning glory seeds	T40.991	T40.992	T40.993	T40.994	—	—
Moroxydine	T37.5X1	T37.5X2	T37.5X3	T37.5X4	T37.5X5	T37.5X6
Morphazinamide	T37.1X1	T37.1X2	T37.1X3	T37.1X4	T37.1X5	T37.1X6
Morphine	T40.2X1	T40.2X2	T40.2X3	T40.2X4	T40.2X5	T40.2X6
antagonist	T50.7X1	T50.7X2	T50.7X3	T50.7X4	T50.7X5	T50.7X6
Morpholinylethylmorphine	T40.2X1	T40.2X2	T40.2X3	T40.2X4	—	—
Morsuximide	T42.2X1	T42.2X2	T42.2X3	T42.2X4	T42.2X5	T42.2X6

Substance	External Cause (T-Code)					
	Poisoning, Accidental (Unintentional)	Poisoning, Intentional Self-Harm	Poisoning, Assault	Poisoning, Undetermined	Adverse Effect	Underdosing
Mosapramine	T43.591	T43.592	T43.593	T43.594	T43.595	T43.596
Moth balls — see also Pesticides	T60.2X1	T60.2X2	T60.2X3	T60.2X4	—	—
naphthalene	T60.2X1	T60.2X2	T60.2X3	T60.2X4	—	—
paradichlorobenzene	T60.1X1	T60.1X2	T60.1X3	T60.1X4	—	—
Motor exhaust gas	T58.01	T58.02	T58.03	T58.04		
Mouthwash (antiseptic) (zinc chloride)	T49.6X1	T49.6X2	T49.6X3	T49.6X4	T49.6X5	T49.6X6
Moxastine	T45.0X1	T45.0X2	T45.0X3	T45.0X4	T45.0X5	T45.0X6
Moxaverine	T44.3X1	T44.3X2	T44.3X3	T44.3X4	T44.3X5	T44.3X6
Moxifensine	T43.291	T43.292	T43.293	T43.294	T43.295	T43.296
Moxisylyte	T46.7X1	T46.7X2	T46.7X3	T46.7X4	T46.7X5	T46.7X6
Mucilage, plant	T47.4X1	T47.4X2	T47.4X3	T47.4X4	T47.4X5	T47.4X6
Mucolytic drug	T48.4X1	T48.4X2	T48.4X3	T48.4X4	T48.4X5	T48.4X6
Mucomyst	T48.4X1	T48.4X2	T48.4X3	T48.4X4	T48.4X5	T48.4X6
Mucous membrane agents (external)	T49.91	T49.92	T49.93	T49.94	T49.95	T49.96
specified NEC	T49.8X1	T49.8X2	T49.8X3	T49.8X4	T49.8X5	T49.8X6
Multiple unspecified drugs, medicaments and biological substances	T50.911	T50.912	T50.913	T50.914	T50.915	T50.916
Mumps						
immune globulin (human)	T50.Z11	T50.Z12	T50.Z13	T50.Z14	T50.Z15	T50.Z16
skin test antigen	T50.8X1	T50.8X2	T50.8X3	T50.8X4	T50.8X5	T50.8X6
vaccine	T50.B91	T50.B92	T50.B93	T50.B94	T50.B95	T50.B96
Mumpsvax	T50.B91	T50.B92	T50.B93	T50.B94	T50.B95	T50.B96
Mupirocin	T49.0X1	T49.0X2	T49.0X3	T49.0X4	T49.0X5	T49.0X6
Muriatic acid — see Hydrochloric acid						
Muromonab-CD3	T45.1X1	T45.1X2	T45.1X3	T45.1X4	T45.1X5	T45.1X6
Muscle relaxant — see Relaxant, muscle						
Muscle-action drug NEC	T48.201	T48.202	T48.203	T48.204	T48.205	T48.206
Muscle affecting agents NEC	T48.201	T48.202	T48.203	T48.204	T48.205	T48.206
oxytocic	T48.0X1	T48.0X2	T48.0X3	T48.0X4	T48.0X5	T48.0X6
relaxants	T48.201	T48.202	T48.203	T48.204	T48.205	T48.206
central nervous system	T42.8X1	T42.8X2	T42.8X3	T42.8X4	T42.8X5	T42.8X6
skeletal	T48.1X1	T48.1X2	T48.1X3	T48.1X4	T48.1X5	T48.1X6
smooth	T44.3X1	T44.3X2	T44.3X3	T44.3X4	T44.3X5	T44.3X6
Muscle-tone depressant, central NEC	T42.8X1	T42.8X2	T42.8X3	T42.8X4	T42.8X5	T42.8X6
specified NEC	T42.8X1	T42.8X2	T42.8X3	T42.8X4	T42.8X5	T42.8X6
Mushroom, noxious	T62.0X1	T62.0X2	T62.0X3	T62.0X4	—	—
Mussel, noxious	T61.781	T61.782	T61.783	T61.784	—	—

TABLE OF DRUGS AND CHEMICALS

Substance	External Cause (T-Code) Poisoning, Accidental (Unintentional)	Poisoning, Intentional Self-Harm	Poisoning, Assault	Poisoning, Undetermined	Adverse Effect	Underdosing
Mustard (emetic)	T47.7X1	T47.7X2	T47.7X3	T47.7X4	T47.7X5	T47.7X6
black	T47.7X1	T47.7X2	T47.7X3	T47.7X4	T47.7X5	T47.7X6
gas, not in war	T59.91	T59.92	T59.93	T59.94	—	—
nitrogen	T45.1X1	T45.1X2	T45.1X3	T45.1X4	T45.1X5	T45.1X6
Mustine	T45.1X1	T45.1X2	T45.1X3	T45.1X4	T45.1X5	T45.1X6
M-vac	T45.1X1	T45.1X2	T45.1X3	T45.1X4	T45.1X5	T45.1X6
Mycifradin	T36.5X1	T36.5X2	T36.5X3	T36.5X4	T36.5X5	T36.5X6
topical	T49.0X1	T49.0X2	T49.0X3	T49.0X4	T49.0X5	T49.0X6
Mycitracin	T36.8X1	T36.8X2	T36.8X3	T36.8X4	T36.8X5	T36.8X6
ophthalmic preparation	T49.5X1	T49.5X2	T49.5X3	T49.5X4	T49.5X5	T49.5X6
Mycostatin	T36.7X1	T36.7X2	T36.7X3	T36.7X4	T36.7X5	T36.7X6
topical	T49.0X1	T49.0X2	T49.0X3	T49.0X4	T49.0X5	T49.0X6
Mycotoxins	T64.81	T64.82	T64.83	T64.84	—	—
aflatoxin	T64.01	T64.02	T64.03	T64.04	—	—
specified NEC	T64.81	T64.82	T64.83	T64.84	—	—
Mydriacyl	T44.3X1	T44.3X2	T44.3X3	T44.3X4	T44.3X5	T44.3X6
Mydriatic drug	T49.5X1	T49.5X2	T49.5X3	T49.5X4	T49.5X5	T49.5X6
Myelobromal	T45.1X1	T45.1X2	T45.1X3	T45.1X4	T45.1X5	T45.1X6
Myleran	T45.1X1	T45.1X2	T45.1X3	T45.1X4	T45.1X5	T45.1X6
Myochrysin(e)	T39.2X1	T39.2X2	T39.2X3	T39.2X4	T39.2X5	T39.2X6
Myoneural blocking agents	T48.1X1	T48.1X2	T48.1X3	T48.1X4	T48.1X5	T48.1X6
Myralact	T49.0X1	T49.0X2	T49.0X3	T49.0X4	T49.0X5	T49.0X6
Myristica fragrans	T62.2X1	T62.2X2	T62.2X3	T62.2X4	—	—
Myristicin	T65.891	T65.892	T65.893	T65.894	—	—
Mysoline	T42.3X1	T42.3X2	T42.3X3	T42.3X4	T42.3X5	T42.3X6
N						
Nabilone	T40.7X1	T40.7X2	T40.7X3	T40.7X4	T40.7X5	T40.7X6
Nabumetone	T39.391	T39.392	T39.393	T39.394	T39.395	T39.396
Nadolol	T44.7X1	T44.7X2	T44.7X3	T44.7X4	T44.7X5	T44.7X6
Nafcillin	T36.0X1	T36.0X2	T36.0X3	T36.0X4	T36.0X5	T36.0X6
Nafoxidine	T38.6X1	T38.6X2	T38.6X3	T38.6X4	T38.6X5	T38.6X6
Naftazone	T46.991	T46.992	T46.993	T46.994	T46.995	T46.996
Naftidrofuryl (oxalate)	T46.7X1	T46.7X2	T46.7X3	T46.7X4	T46.7X5	T46.7X6
Naftifine	T49.0X1	T49.0X2	T49.0X3	T49.0X4	T49.0X5	T49.0X6
Nail polish remover	T52.91	T52.92	T52.93	T52.94	—	—
Nalbuphine	T40.491	T40.492	T40.493	T40.494	T40.495	T40.496
Naled	T60.0X1	T60.0X2	T60.0X3	T60.0X4	—	—
Nalidixic acid	T37.8X1	T37.8X2	T37.8X3	T37.8X4	T37.8X5	T37.8X6
Nalorphine	T50.7X1	T50.7X2	T50.7X3	T50.7X4	T50.7X5	T50.7X6
Naloxone	T50.7X1	T50.7X2	T50.7X3	T50.7X4	T50.7X5	T50.7X6
Naltrexone	T50.7X1	T50.7X2	T50.7X3	T50.7X4	T50.7X5	T50.7X6
Namenda	T43.8X1	T43.8X2	T43.8X3	T43.8X4	T43.8X5	T43.8X6

Substance	External Cause (T-Code) Poisoning, Accidental (Unintentional)	Poisoning, Intentional Self-Harm	Poisoning, Assault	Poisoning, Undetermined	Adverse Effect	Underdosing
Nandrolone	T38.7X1	T38.7X2	T38.7X3	T38.7X4	T38.7X5	T38.7X6
Naphazoline	T48.5X1	T48.5X2	T48.5X3	T48.5X4	T48.5X5	T48.5X6
Naphtha (painters') (petroleum)	T52.0X1	T52.0X2	T52.0X3	T52.0X4	—	—
solvent	T52.0X1	T52.0X2	T52.0X3	T52.0X4	—	—
vapor	T52.0X1	T52.0X2	T52.0X3	T52.0X4	—	—
Naphthalene (non-chlorinated)	T60.2X1	T60.2X2	T60.2X3	T60.2X4	—	—
chlorinated	T60.1X1	T60.1X2	T60.1X3	T60.1X4	—	—
vapor	T60.1X1	T60.1X2	T60.1X3	T60.1X4	—	—
insecticide or moth repellent	T60.2X1	T60.2X2	T60.2X3	T60.2X4	—	—
chlorinated	T60.1X1	T60.1X2	T60.1X3	T60.1X4	—	—
vapor	T60.2X1	T60.2X2	T60.2X3	T60.2X4	—	—
chlorinated	T60.1X1	T60.1X2	T60.1X3	T60.1X4	—	—
Naphthol	T65.891	T65.892	T65.893	T65.894	—	—
Naphthylamine	T65.891	T65.892	T65.893	T65.894	—	—
Naphthylthiourea (ANTU)	T60.4X1	T60.4X2	T60.4X3	T60.4X4	—	—
Naprosyn — see Naproxen						
Naproxen	T39.311	T39.312	T39.313	T39.314	T39.315	T39.316
Narcotic (drug)	T40.601	T40.602	T40.603	T40.604	T40.605	T40.606
analgesic NEC	T40.601	T40.602	T40.603	T40.604	T40.605	T40.606
antagonist	T50.7X1	T50.7X2	T50.7X3	T50.7X4	T50.7X5	T50.7X6
specified NEC	T40.691	T40.692	T40.693	T40.694	T40.695	T40.696
synthetic	T40.491	T40.492	T40.493	T40.494	T40.495	T40.496
Narcotine	T48.3X1	T48.3X2	T48.3X3	T48.3X4	T48.3X5	T48.3X6
Nardil	T43.1X1	T43.1X2	T43.1X3	T43.1X4	T43.1X5	T43.1X6
Nasal drug NEC	T49.6X1	T49.6X2	T49.6X3	T49.6X4	T49.6X5	T49.6X6
Natamycin	T49.0X1	T49.0X2	T49.0X3	T49.0X4	T49.0X5	T49.0X6
Natrium cyanide — see Cyanide(s)						
Natural gas	T59.891	T59.892	T59.893	T59.894	—	—
incomplete combustion	T57.91	T57.92	T57.93	T57.94	—	—
Natural						
blood (product)	T45.8X1	T45.8X2	T45.8X3	T45.8X4	T45.8X5	T45.8X6
gas (piped)	T59.891	T59.892	T59.893	T59.894	—	—
incomplete combustion	T58.11	T58.12	T58.13	T58.14	—	—
Nealbarbital	T42.3X1	T42.3X2	T42.3X3	T42.3X4	T42.3X5	T42.3X6
Nectadon	T48.3X1	T48.3X2	T48.3X3	T48.3X4	T48.3X5	T48.3X6
Nedocromil	T48.6X1	T48.6X2	T48.6X3	T48.6X4	T48.6X5	T48.6X6
Nefopam	T39.8X1	T39.8X2	T39.8X3	T39.8X4	T39.8X5	T39.8X6
Nematocyst (sting)	T63.691	T63.692	T63.693	T63.694	—	—
Nembutal	T42.3X1	T42.3X2	T42.3X3	T42.3X4	T42.3X5	T42.3X6
Nemonapride	T43.591	T43.592	T43.593	T43.594	T43.595	T43.596
Neoarsphenamine	T37.8X1	T37.8X2	T37.8X3	T37.8X4	T37.8X5	T37.8X6

◀ New   ◀ Revised   ~~deleted~~ Deleted

Substance	Poisoning, Accidental (Unintentional)	Poisoning, Intentional Self-Harm	Poisoning, Assault	Poisoning, Undetermined	Adverse Effect	Underdosing
External Cause (T-Code)						
Neocinchophen	T50.4X1	T50.4X2	T50.4X3	T50.4X4	T50.4X5	T50.4X6
Neomycin (derivatives)	T36.5X1	T36.5X2	T36.5X3	T36.5X4	T36.5X5	T36.5X6
with						
bacitracin	T49.0X1	T49.0X2	T49.0X3	T49.0X4	T49.0X5	T49.0X6
neostigmine	T44.0X1	T44.0X2	T44.0X3	T44.0X4	T44.0X5	T44.0X6
ENT agent	T49.6X1	T49.6X2	T49.6X3	T49.6X4	T49.6X5	T49.6X6
ophthalmic preparation	T49.5X1	T49.5X2	T49.5X3	T49.5X4	T49.5X5	T49.5X6
topical NEC	T49.0X1	T49.0X2	T49.0X3	T49.0X4	T49.0X5	T49.0X6
Neonal	T42.3X1	T42.3X2	T42.3X3	T42.3X4	T42.3X5	T42.3X6
Neoprontosil	T37.0X1	T37.0X2	T37.0X3	T37.0X4	T37.0X5	T37.0X6
Neosalvarsan	T37.8X1	T37.8X2	T37.8X3	T37.8X4	T37.8X5	T37.8X6
Neosilversalvarsan	T37.8X1	T37.8X2	T37.8X3	T37.8X4	T37.8X5	T37.8X6
Neosporin	T36.8X1	T36.8X2	T36.8X3	T36.8X4	T36.8X5	T36.8X6
ENT agent	T49.6X1	T49.6X2	T49.6X3	T49.6X4	T49.6X5	T49.6X6
opthalmic preparation	T49.5X1	T49.5X2	T49.5X3	T49.5X4	T49.5X5	T49.5X6
topical NEC	T49.0X1	T49.0X2	T49.0X3	T49.0X4	T49.0X5	T49.0X6
Neostigmine bromide	T44.0X1	T44.0X2	T44.0X3	T44.0X4	T44.0X5	T44.0X6
Neraval	T42.3X1	T42.3X2	T42.3X3	T42.3X4	T42.3X5	T42.3X6
Neravan	T42.3X1	T42.3X2	T42.3X3	T42.3X4	T42.3X5	T42.3X6
Nerium oleander	T62.2X1	T62.2X2	T62.2X3	T62.2X4	—	—
Nerve gas, not in war	T59.91	T59.92	T59.93	T59.94	—	—
Nesacaine	T41.3X1	T41.3X2	T41.3X3	T41.3X4	T41.3X5	T41.3X6
infiltration (subcutaneous)	T41.3X1	T41.3X2	T41.3X3	T41.3X4	T41.3X5	T41.3X6
nerve block (peripheral) (plexus)	T41.3X1	T41.3X2	T41.3X3	T41.3X4	T41.3X5	T41.3X6
Netilmicin	T36.5X1	T36.5X2	T36.5X3	T36.5X4	T36.5X5	T36.5X6
Neurobarb	T42.3X1	T42.3X2	T42.3X3	T42.3X4	T42.3X5	T42.3X6
Neuroleptic drug NEC	T43.501	T43.502	T43.503	T43.504	T43.505	T43.506
Neuromuscular blocking drug	T48.1X1	T48.1X2	T48.1X3	T48.1X4	T48.1X5	T48.1X6
Neutral insulin injection	T38.3X1	T38.3X2	T38.3X3	T38.3X4	T38.3X5	T38.3X6
Neutral spirits	T51.0X1	T51.0X2	T51.0X3	T51.0X4	—	—
beverage	T51.0X1	T51.0X2	T51.0X3	T51.0X4	—	—
Niacin	T46.7X1	T46.7X2	T46.7X3	T46.7X4	T46.7X5	T46.7X6
Niacinamide	T45.2X1	T45.2X2	T45.2X3	T45.2X4	T45.2X5	T45.2X6
Nialamide	T43.1X1	T43.1X2	T43.1X3	T43.1X4	T43.1X5	T43.1X6
Niaprazine	T42.6X1	T42.6X2	T42.6X3	T42.6X4	T42.6X5	T42.6X6
Nicametate	T46.7X1	T46.7X2	T46.7X3	T46.7X4	T46.7X5	T46.7X6
Nicardipine	T46.1X1	T46.1X2	T46.1X3	T46.1X4	T46.1X5	T46.1X6
Nicergoline	T46.7X1	T46.7X2	T46.7X3	T46.7X4	T46.7X5	T46.7X6
Nickel (carbonyl) (tetra-carbonyl) (fumes) (vapor)	T56.891	T56.892	T56.893	T56.894	—	—

Substance	Poisoning, Accidental (Unintentional)	Poisoning, Intentional Self-Harm	Poisoning, Assault	Poisoning, Undetermined	Adverse Effect	Underdosing
External Cause (T-Code)						
Nickelocene	T56.891	T56.892	T56.893	T56.894	—	—
Niclosamide	T37.4X1	T37.4X2	T37.4X3	T37.4X4	T37.4X5	T37.4X6
Nicofuranose	T46.7X1	T46.7X2	T46.7X3	T46.7X4	T46.7X5	T46.7X6
Nicomorphine	T40.2X1	T40.2X2	T40.2X3	T40.2X4		
Nicorandil	T46.3X1	T46.3X2	T46.3X3	T46.3X4	T46.3X5	T46.3X6
Nicotiana (plant)	T62.2X1	T62.2X2	T62.2X3	T62.2X4	—	—
Nicotinamide	T45.2X1	T45.2X2	T45.2X3	T45.2X4	T45.2X5	T45.2X6
Nicotine (insecticide) (spray) (sulfate) NEC	T60.2X1	T60.2X2	T60.2X3	T60.2X4		
from tobacco	T65.291	T65.292	T65.293	T65.294	—	—
cigarettes	T65.221	T65.222	T65.223	T65.224	—	—
not insecticide	T65.291	T65.292	T65.293	T65.294		
Nicotinic acid	T46.7X1	T46.7X2	T46.7X3	T46.7X4	T46.7X5	T46.7X6
Nicotinyl alcohol	T46.7X1	T46.7X2	T46.7X3	T46.7X4	T46.7X5	T46.7X6
Nicoumalone	T45.511	T45.512	T45.513	T45.514	T45.515	T45.516
Nifedipine	T46.1X1	T46.1X2	T46.1X3	T46.1X4	T46.1X5	T46.1X6
Nifenazone	T39.2X1	T39.2X2	T39.2X3	T39.2X4	T39.2X5	T39.2X6
Nifuraldezone	T37.91	T37.92	T37.93	T37.94	T37.95	T37.96
Nifuratel	T37.8X1	T37.8X2	T37.8X3	T37.8X4	T37.8X5	T37.8X6
Nifurtimox	T37.3X1	T37.3X2	T37.3X3	T37.3X4	T37.3X5	T37.3X6
Nifurtoinol	T37.8X1	T37.8X2	T37.8X3	T37.8X4	T37.8X5	T37.8X6
Nightshade, deadly (solanum)— see also Belladonna	T62.2X1	T62.2X2	T62.2X3	T62.2X4	—	—
berry	T62.1X1	T62.1X2	T62.1X3	T62.1X4	—	—
Nikethamide	T50.7X1	T50.7X2	T50.7X3	T50.7X4	T50.7X5	T50.7X6
Nilstat	T36.7X1	T36.7X2	T36.7X3	T36.7X4	T36.7X5	T36.7X6
topical	T49.0X1	T49.0X2	T49.0X3	T49.0X4	T49.0X5	T49.0X6
Nilutamide	T38.6X1	T38.6X2	T38.6X3	T38.6X4	T38.6X5	T38.6X6
Nimesulide	T39.391	T39.392	T39.393	T39.394	T39.395	T39.396
Nimetazepam	T42.4X1	T42.4X2	T42.4X3	T42.4X4	T42.4X5	T42.4X6
Nimodipine	T46.1X1	T46.1X2	T46.1X3	T46.1X4	T46.1X5	T46.1X6
Nimorazole	T37.3X1	T37.3X2	T37.3X3	T37.3X4	T37.3X5	T37.3X6
Nimustine	T45.1X1	T45.1X2	T45.1X3	T45.1X4	T45.1X5	T45.1X6
Niridazole	T37.4X1	T37.4X2	T37.4X3	T37.4X4	T37.4X5	T37.4X6
Nisentil	T40.2X1	T40.2X2	T40.2X3	T40.2X4	T40.2X5	T40.2X6
Nisoldipine	T46.1X1	T46.1X2	T46.1X3	T46.1X4	T46.1X5	T46.1X6
Nitramine	T65.3X1	T65.3X2	T65.3X3	T65.3X4	—	—
Nitrate, organic	T46.3X1	T46.3X2	T46.3X3	T46.3X4	T46.3X5	T46.3X6
Nitrazepam	T42.4X1	T42.4X2	T42.4X3	T42.4X4	T42.4X5	T42.4X6
Nitrefazole	T50.6X1	T50.6X2	T50.6X3	T50.6X4	T50.6X5	T50.6X6
Nitrendipine	T46.1X1	T46.1X2	T46.1X3	T46.1X4	T46.1X5	T46.1X6

◀ New ◀ Revised ~~deleted~~ Deleted

Substance	External Cause (T-Code) Poisoning, Accidental (Unintentional)	Poisoning, Intentional Self-Harm	Poisoning, Assault	Poisoning, Undetermined	Adverse Effect	Underdosing
Nitric						
acid (liquid)	T54.2X1	T54.2X2	T54.2X3	T54.2X4	—	—
vapor	T59.891	T59.892	T59.893	T59.894	—	—
oxide (gas)	T59.0X1	T59.0X2	T59.0X3	T59.0X4	—	—
Nitrimidazine	T37.3X1	T37.3X2	T37.3X3	T37.3X4	T37.3X5	T37.3X6
Nitrite, amyl (medicinal) (vapor)	T46.3X1	T46.3X2	T46.3X3	T46.3X4	T46.3X5	T46.3X6
Nitroaniline	T65.3X1	T65.3X2	T65.3X3	T65.3X4	—	—
vapor	T59.891	T59.892	T59.893	T59.894	—	—
Nitrobenzene, nitrobenzol	T65.3X1	T65.3X2	T65.3X3	T65.3X4	—	—
vapor	T65.3X1	T65.3X2	T65.3X3	T65.3X4	—	—
Nitrocellulose	T65.891	T65.892	T65.893	T65.894	—	—
lacquer	T65.891	T65.892	T65.893	T65.894	—	—
Nitrodiphenyl	T65.3X1	T65.3X2	T65.3X3	T65.3X4	—	—
Nitrofural	T49.0X1	T49.0X2	T49.0X3	T49.0X4	T49.0X5	T49.0X6
Nitrofurantoin	T37.8X1	T37.8X2	T37.8X3	T37.8X4	T37.8X5	T37.8X6
Nitrofurazone	T49.0X1	T49.0X2	T49.0X3	T49.0X4	T49.0X5	T49.0X6
Nitrogen	T59.0X1	T59.0X2	T59.0X3	T59.0X4	—	—
mustard	T45.1X1	T45.1X2	T45.1X3	T45.1X4	T45.1X5	T45.1X6
Nitroglycerin, nitro-glycerol (medicinal)	T46.3X1	T46.3X2	T46.3X3	T46.3X4	T46.3X5	T46.3X6
nonmedicinal	T65.5X1	T65.5X2	T65.5X3	T65.5X4	—	—
fumes	T65.5X1	T65.5X2	T65.5X3	T65.5X4	—	—
Nitroglycol	T52.3X1	T52.3X2	T52.3X3	T52.3X4	—	—
Nitrohydrochloric acid	T54.2X1	T54.2X2	T54.2X3	T54.2X4	—	—
Nitromersol	T49.0X1	T49.0X2	T49.0X3	T49.0X4	T49.0X5	T49.0X6
Nitronaphthalene	T65.891	T65.892	T65.893	T65.894	—	—
Nitrophenol	T54.0X1	T54.0X2	T54.0X3	T54.0X4	—	—
Nitropropane	T52.8X1	T52.8X2	T52.8X3	T52.8X4	—	—
Nitroprusside	T46.5X1	T46.5X2	T46.5X3	T46.5X4	T46.5X5	T46.5X6
Nitrosodimethylamine	T65.3X1	T65.3X2	T65.3X3	T65.3X4	—	—
Nitrothiazol	T37.4X1	T37.4X2	T37.4X3	T37.4X4	T37.4X5	T37.4X6
Nitrotoluene, nitrotoluol	T65.3X1	T65.3X2	T65.3X3	T65.3X4	—	—
vapor	T65.3X1	T65.3X2	T65.3X3	T65.3X4	—	—
Nitrous						
acid (liquid)	T54.2X1	T54.2X2	T54.2X3	T54.2X4	—	—
fumes	T59.891	T59.892	T59.893	T59.894	—	—
ether spirit	T46.3X1	T46.3X2	T46.3X3	T46.3X4	T46.3X5	T46.3X6
oxide	T41.0X1	T41.0X2	T41.0X3	T41.0X4	T41.0X5	T41.0X6
Nitroxoline	T37.8X1	T37.8X2	T37.8X3	T37.8X4	T37.8X5	T37.8X6
Nitrozone	T49.0X1	T49.0X2	T49.0X3	T49.0X4	T49.0X5	T49.0X6
Nizatidine	T47.0X1	T47.0X2	T47.0X3	T47.0X4	T47.0X5	T47.0X6

Substance	External Cause (T-Code) Poisoning, Accidental (Unintentional)	Poisoning, Intentional Self-Harm	Poisoning, Assault	Poisoning, Undetermined	Adverse Effect	Underdosing
Nizofenone	T43.8X1	T43.8X2	T43.8X3	T43.8X4	T43.8X5	T43.8X6
Noctec	T42.6X1	T42.6X2	T42.6X3	T42.6X4	T42.6X5	T42.6X6
Noludar	T42.6X1	T42.6X2	T42.6X3	T42.6X4	T42.6X5	T42.6X6
Noptil	T42.3X1	T42.3X2	T42.3X3	T42.3X4	T42.3X5	T42.3X6
Nomegestrol	T38.5X1	T38.5X2	T38.5X3	T38.5X4	T38.5X5	T38.5X6
Nomifensine	T43.291	T43.292	T43.293	T43.294	T43.295	T43.296
Nonoxinol	T49.8X1	T49.8X2	T49.8X3	T49.8X4	T49.8X5	T49.8X6
Nonylphenoxy (polyethoxy-ethanol)	T49.8X1	T49.8X2	T49.8X3	T49.8X4	T49.8X5	T49.8X6
Noptil	T42.3X1	T42.3X2	T42.3X3	T42.3X4	T42.3X5	T42.3X6
Noradrenaline	T44.4X1	T44.4X2	T44.4X3	T44.4X4	T44.4X5	T44.4X6
Noramidopyrine	T39.2X1	T39.2X2	T39.2X3	T39.2X4	T39.2X5	T39.2X6
methanesulfonate sodium	T39.2X1	T39.2X2	T39.2X3	T39.2X4	T39.2X5	T39.2X6
Norbormide	T60.4X1	T60.4X2	T60.4X3	T60.4X4	—	—
Nordazepam	T42.4X1	T42.4X2	T42.4X3	T42.4X4	T42.4X5	T42.4X6
Norepinephrine	T44.4X1	T44.4X2	T44.4X3	T44.4X4	T44.4X5	T44.4X6
Norethandrolone	T38.7X1	T38.7X2	T38.7X3	T38.7X4	T38.7X5	T38.7X6
Norethindrone	T38.4X1	T38.4X2	T38.4X3	T38.4X4	T38.4X5	T38.4X6
Norethisterone (acetate) (enantate)	T38.4X1	T38.4X2	T38.4X3	T38.4X4	T38.4X5	T38.4X6
with ethinylestradiol	T38.5X1	T38.5X2	T38.5X3	T38.5X4	T38.5X5	T38.5X6
Noretynodrel	T38.5X1	T38.5X2	T38.5X3	T38.5X4	T38.5X5	T38.5X6
Norfenefrine	T44.4X1	T44.4X2	T44.4X3	T44.4X4	T44.4X5	T44.4X6
Norfloxacin	T36.8X1	T36.8X2	T36.8X3	T36.8X4	T36.8X5	T36.8X6
Norgestrel	T38.4X1	T38.4X2	T38.4X3	T38.4X4	T38.4X5	T38.4X6
Norgestrienone	T38.4X1	T38.4X2	T38.4X3	T38.4X4	T38.4X5	T38.4X6
Norlestrin	T38.4X1	T38.4X2	T38.4X3	T38.4X4	T38.4X5	T38.4X6
Norlutin	T38.4X1	T38.4X2	T38.4X3	T38.4X4	T38.4X5	T38.4X6
Normal serum albumin (human), salt-poor	T45.8X1	T45.8X2	T45.8X3	T45.8X4	T45.8X5	T45.8X6
Normethandrone	T38.5X1	T38.5X2	T38.5X3	T38.5X4	T38.5X5	T38.5X6
Normison—see Benzodiazepines						
Normorphine	T40.2X1	T40.2X2	T40.2X3	T40.2X4	—	—
Norpseudoephedrine	T50.5X1	T50.5X2	T50.5X3	T50.5X4	T50.5X5	T50.5X6
Nortestosterone (furanpropionate)	T38.7X1	T38.7X2	T38.7X3	T39.7X4	T38.7X5	T38.7X6
Nortriptyline	T43.011	T43.012	T43.013	T43.014	T43.015	T43.016
Noscapine	T48.3X1	T48.3X2	T48.3X3	T48.3X4	T48.3X5	T48.3X6
Nose preparations	T49.6X1	T49.6X2	T49.6X3	T49.6X4	T49.6X5	T49.6X6
Novobiocin	T36.5X1	T36.5X2	T36.5X3	T36.5X4	T36.5X5	T36.5X6
Novocain (infiltration) (topical)	T41.3X1	T41.3X2	T41.3X3	T41.3X4	T41.3X5	T41.3X6
nerve block (peripheral) (plexus)	T41.3X1	T41.3X2	T41.3X3	T41.3X4	T41.3X5	T41.3X6
spinal	T41.3X1	T41.3X2	T41.3X3	T41.3X4	T41.3X5	T41.3X6

◀ New ◀ Revised ~~deleted~~ Deleted

Substance	Poisoning, Accidental (Unintentional)	Poisoning, Intentional Self-Harm	Poisoning, Assault	Poisoning, Undetermined	Adverse Effect	Underdosing
Noxious foodstuff	T62.91	T62.92	T62.93	T62.94	—	—
specified NEC	T62.8X1	T62.8X2	T62.8X3	T62.8X4	—	—
Noxiptiline	T43.011	T43.012	T43.013	T43.014	T43.015	T43.016
Noxytiolin	T49.0X1	T49.0X2	T49.0X3	T49.0X4	T49.0X5	T49.0X6
NPH Iletin (insulin)	T38.3X1	T38.3X2	T38.3X3	T38.3X4	T38.3X5	T38.3X6
Numorphan	T40.2X1	T40.2X2	T40.2X3	T40.2X4	T40.2X5	T40.2X6
Nunol	T42.3X1	T42.3X2	T42.3X3	T42.3X4	T42.3X5	T42.3X6
Nupercaine (spinal anesthetic)	T41.3X1	T41.3X2	T41.3X3	T41.3X4	T41.3X5	T41.3X6
topical (surface)	T41.3X1	T41.3X2	T41.3X3	T41.3X4	T41.3X5	T41.3X6
Nutmeg oil (liniment)	T49.3X1	T49.3X2	T49.3X3	T49.3X4	T49.3X5	T49.3X6
Nutritional supplement	T50.901	T50.902	T50.903	T50.904	T50.905	T50.906
Nux vomica	T65.1X1	T65.1X2	T65.1X3	T65.1X4	—	—
Nydrazid	T37.1X1	T37.1X2	T37.1X3	T37.1X4	T37.1X5	T37.1X6
Nylidrin	T46.7X1	T46.7X2	T46.7X3	T46.7X4	T46.7X5	T46.7X6
Nystatin	T36.7X1	T36.7X2	T36.7X3	T36.7X4	T36.7X5	T36.7X6
topical	T49.0X1	T49.0X2	T49.0X3	T49.0X4	T49.0X5	T49.0X6
Nytol	T45.0X1	T45.0X2	T45.0X3	T45.0X4	T45.0X5	T45.0X6

○

Substance	Poisoning, Accidental (Unintentional)	Poisoning, Intentional Self-Harm	Poisoning, Assault	Poisoning, Undetermined	Adverse Effect	Underdosing
Obidoxime chloride	T50.6X1	T50.6X2	T50.6X3	T50.6X4	T50.6X5	T50.6X6
Octafonium (chloride)	T49.3X1	T49.3X2	T49.3X3	T49.3X4	T49.3X5	T49.3X6
Octamethyl pyrophos- phoramide	T60.0X1	T60.0X2	T60.0X3	T60.0X4	—	—
Octanoin	T50.991	T50.992	T50.993	T50.994	T50.995	T50.996
Octatropine methyl- bromide	T44.3X1	T44.3X2	T44.3X3	T44.3X4	T44.3X5	T44.3X6
Octotiamine	T45.2X1	T45.2X2	T45.2X3	T45.2X4	T45.2X5	T45.2X6
Octoxinol (9)	T49.8X1	T49.8X2	T49.8X3	T49.8X4	T49.8X5	T49.8X6
Octreotide	T38.991	T38.992	T38.993	T38.994	T38.995	T38.996
Octyl nitrite	T46.3X1	T46.3X2	T46.3X3	T46.3X4	T46.3X5	T46.3X6
Oestradiol	T38.5X1	T38.5X2	T38.5X3	T38.5X4	T38.5X5	T38.5X6
Oestriol	T38.5X1	T38.5X2	T38.5X3	T38.5X4	T38.5X5	T38.5X6
Oestrogen	T38.5X1	T38.5X2	T38.5X3	T38.5X4	T38.5X5	T38.5X6
Oestrone	T38.5X1	T38.5X2	T38.5X3	T38.5X4	T38.5X5	T38.5X6
Ofloxacin	T36.8X1	T36.8X2	T36.8X3	T36.8X4	T36.8X5	T36.8X6
Oil (of)	T65.891	T65.892	T65.893	T65.894		
bitter almond	T62.8X1	T62.8X2	T62.8X3	T62.8X4	—	—
cloves	T49.7X1	T49.7X2	T49.7X3	T49.7X4	T49.7X5	T49.7X6
colors	T65.6X1	T65.6X2	T65.6X3	T65.6X4	—	—
fumes	T59.891	T59.892	T59.893	T59.894	—	—
lubricating	T52.0X1	T52.0X2	T52.0X3	T52.0X4	—	—
Niobe	T52.8X1	T52.8X2	T52.8X3	T52.8X4	—	—

Substance	Poisoning, Accidental (Unintentional)	Poisoning, Intentional Self-Harm	Poisoning, Assault	Poisoning, Undetermined	Adverse Effect	Underdosing
Oil (of) (Continued)						
vitriol (liquid)	T54.2X1	T54.2X2	T54.2X3	T54.2X4	—	—
fumes	T54.2X1	T54.2X2	T54.2X3	T54.2X4	—	—
wintergreen (bitter) NEC	T49.3X1	T49.3X2	T49.3X3	T49.3X4	T49.3X5	T49.3X6
Oily preparation (for skin)	T49.3X1	T49.3X2	T49.3X3	T49.3X4	T49.3X5	T49.3X6
Ointment NEC	T49.3X1	T49.3X2	T49.3X3	T49.3X4	T49.3X5	T49.3X6
Olanzapine	T43.591	T43.592	T43.593	T43.594	T43.595	T43.596
Oleander	T62.2X1	T62.2X2	T62.2X3	T62.2X4	—	—
Oleandomycin	T36.3X1	T36.3X2	T36.3X3	T36.3X4	T36.3X5	T36.3X6
Oleandrin	T46.0X1	T46.0X2	T46.0X3	T46.0X4	T46.0X5	T46.0X6
Oleic acid	T46.6X1	T46.6X2	T46.6X3	T46.6X4	T46.6X5	T46.6X6
Oleovitamin A	T45.2X1	T45.2X2	T45.2X3	T45.2X4	T45.2X5	T45.2X6
Oleum ricini	T47.2X1	T47.2X2	T47.2X3	T47.2X4	T47.2X5	T47.2X6
Olive oil (medicinal) NEC	T47.4X1	T47.4X2	T47.4X3	T47.4X4	T47.4X5	T47.4X6
Olivomycin	T45.1X1	T45.1X2	T45.1X3	T45.1X4	T45.1X5	T45.1X6
Olsalazine	T47.8X1	T47.8X2	T47.8X3	T47.8X4	T47.8X5	T47.8X6
Omeprazole	T47.1X1	T47.1X2	T47.1X3	T47.1X4	T47.1X5	T47.1X6
OMPA	T60.0X1	T60.0X2	T60.0X3	T60.0X4	—	—
Ondansetron	T45.0X1	T45.0X2	T45.0X3	T45.0X4	T45.0X5	T45.0X6
Oncovin	T45.1X1	T45.1X2	T45.1X3	T45.1X4	T45.1X5	T45.1X6
Ophthaine	T41.3X1	T41.3X2	T41.3X3	T41.3X4	T41.3X5	T41.3X6
Ophthetic	T41.3X1	T41.3X2	T41.3X3	T41.3X4	T41.3X5	T41.3X6
Opiate NEC	T40.601	T40.602	T40.603	T40.604	T40.605	T40.606
antagonists	T50.7X1	T50.7X2	T50.7X3	T50.7X4	T50.7X5	T50.7X6
Opioid NEC	T40.2X1	T40.2X2	T40.2X3	T40.2X4	T40.2X5	T40.2X6
Opipramol	T43.011	T43.012	T43.013	T43.014	T43.015	T43.016
Opium alkaloids (total)	T40.0X1	T40.0X2	T40.0X3	T40.0X4	T40.0X5	T40.0X6
standardized powdered	T40.0X1	T40.0X2	T40.0X3	T40.0X4	T40.0X5	T40.0X6
tincture (camphorated)	T40.0X1	T40.0X2	T40.0X3	T40.0X4	T40.0X5	T40.0X6
Oracon	T38.4X1	T38.4X2	T38.4X3	T38.4X4	T38.4X5	T38.4X6
Oragrafin	T50.8X1	T50.8X2	T50.8X3	T50.8X4	T50.8X5	T50.8X6
Oral contraceptives	T38.4X1	T38.4X2	T38.4X3	T38.4X4	T38.4X5	T38.4X6
Oral rehydration salts	T50.3X1	T50.3X2	T50.3X3	T50.3X4	T50.3X5	T50.3X6
Orazamide	T50.991	T50.992	T50.993	T50.994	T50.995	T50.996
Orciprenaline	T48.291	T48.292	T48.293	T48.294	T48.295	T48.296
Organidin	T48.4X1	T48.4X2	T48.4X3	T48.4X4	T48.4X5	T48.4X6
Organonitrate NEC	T46.3X1	T46.3X2	T46.3X3	T46.3X4	T46.3X5	T46.3X6
Organophosphates	T60.0X1	T60.0X2	T60.0X3	T60.0X4	—	—
Orimune	T50.B91	T50.B92	T50.B93	T50.B94	T50.B95	T50.B96
Orinase	T38.3X1	T38.3X2	T38.3X3	T38.3X4	T38.3X5	T38.3X6
Ormeloxifene	T38.6X1	T38.6X2	T38.6X3	T38.6X4	T38.6X5	T38.6X6

◀ New ◀ Revised deleted Deleted

Substance	External Cause (T-Code) Poisoning, Accidental (Unintentional)	Poisoning, Intentional Self-Harm	Poisoning, Assault	Poisoning, Undetermined	Adverse Effect	Underdosing
Ornidazole	T37.3X1	T37.3X2	T37.3X3	T37.3X4	T37.3X5	T37.3X6
Ornithine aspartate	T50.991	T50.992	T50.993	T50.994	T50.995	T50.996
Ornoprostil	T47.1X1	T47.1X2	T47.1X3	T47.1X4	T47.1X5	T47.1X6
Orphenadrine (hydrochloride)	T42.8X1	T42.8X2	T42.8X3	T42.8X4	T42.8X5	T42.8X6
Ortal (sodium)	T42.3X1	T42.3X2	T42.3X3	T42.3X4	T42.3X5	T42.3X6
Orthoboric acid	T49.0X1	T49.0X2	T49.0X3	T49.0X4	T49.0X5	T49.0X6
ENT agent	T49.6X1	T49.6X2	T49.6X3	T49.6X4	T49.6X5	T49.6X6
ophthalmic preparation	T49.5X1	T49.5X2	T49.5X3	T49.5X4	T49.5X5	T49.5X6
Orthocaine	T41.3X1	T41.3X2	T41.3X3	T41.3X4	T41.3X5	T41.3X6
Orthodichlorobenzene	T53.7X1	T53.7X2	T53.7X3	T53.7X4	—	—
Ortho-Novum	T38.4X1	T38.4X2	T38.4X3	T38.4X4	T38.4X5	T38.4X6
Orthotolidine (reagent)	T54.2X1	T54.2X2	T54.2X3	T54.2X4	—	—
Osmic acid (liquid)	T54.2X1	T54.2X2	T54.2X3	T54.2X4	—	—
fumes	T54.2X1	T54.2X2	T54.2X3	T54.2X4	—	—
Osmotic diuretics	T50.2X1	T50.2X2	T50.2X3	T50.2X4	T50.2X5	T50.2X6
Otilonium bromide	T44.3X1	T44.3X2	T44.3X3	T44.3X4	T44.3X5	T44.3X6
Otorhinolaryngological drug NEC	T49.6X1	T49.6X2	T49.6X3	T49.6X4	T49.6X5	T49.6X6
Ouabain(e)	T46.0X1	T46.0X2	T46.0X3	T46.0X4	T46.0X5	T46.0X6
Ovarian						
hormone	T38.5X1	T38.5X2	T38.5X3	T38.5X4	T38.5X5	T38.5X6
stimulant	T38.5X1	T38.5X2	T38.5X3	T38.5X4	T38.5X5	T38.5X6
Ovral	T38.4X1	T38.4X2	T38.4X3	T38.4X4	T38.4X5	T38.4X6
Ovulen	T38.4X1	T38.4X2	T38.4X3	T38.4X4	T38.4X5	T38.4X6
Oxacillin	T36.0X1	T36.0X2	T36.0X3	T36.0X4	T36.0X5	T36.0X6
Oxalic acid	T54.2X1	T54.2X2	T54.2X3	T54.2X4	—	—
ammonium salt	T50.991	T50.992	T50.993	T50.994	T50.995	T50.996
Oxamniquine	T37.4X1	T37.4X2	T37.4X3	T37.4X4	T37.4X5	T37.4X6
Oxanamide	T43.591	T43.592	T43.593	T43.594	T43.595	T43.596
Oxandrolone	T38.7X1	T38.7X2	T38.7X3	T38.7X4	T38.7X5	T38.7X6
Oxantel	T37.4X1	T37.4X2	T37.4X3	T37.4X4	T37.4X5	T37.4X6
Oxapium iodide	T44.3X1	T44.3X2	T44.3X3	T44.3X4	T44.3X5	T44.3X6
Oxaprotiline	T43.021	T43.022	T43.023	T43.024	T43.025	T43.026
Oxaprozin	T39.311	T39.312	T39.313	T39.314	T39.315	T39.316
Oxatomide	T45.0X1	T45.0X2	T45.0X3	T45.0X4	T45.0X5	T45.0X6
Oxazepam	T42.4X1	T42.4X2	T42.4X3	T42.4X4	T42.4X5	T42.4X6
Oxazimedrine	T50.5X1	T50.5X2	T50.5X3	T50.5X4	T50.5X5	T50.5X6
Oxazolam	T42.4X1	T42.4X2	T42.4X3	T42.4X4	T42.4X5	T42.4X6
Oxazolidine derivatives	T42.2X1	T42.2X2	T42.2X3	T42.2X4	T42.2X5	T42.2X6
Oxazolidinedione (derivative)	T42.2X1	T42.2X2	T42.2X3	T42.2X4	T42.2X5	T42.2X6
Ox bile extract	T47.5X1	T47.5X2	T47.5X3	T47.5X4	T47.5X5	T47.5X6
Oxcarbazepine	T42.1X1	T42.1X2	T42.1X3	T42.1X4	T42.1X5	T42.1X6
Oxedrine	T44.4X1	T44.4X2	T44.4X3	T44.4X4	T44.4X5	T44.4X6

Substance	External Cause (T-Code) Poisoning, Accidental (Unintentional)	Poisoning, Intentional Self-Harm	Poisoning, Assault	Poisoning, Undetermined	Adverse Effect	Underdosing
Oxeladin (citrate)	T48.3X1	T48.3X2	T48.3X3	T48.3X4	T48.3X5	T48.3X6
Oxendolone	T38.5X1	T38.5X2	T38.5X3	T38.5X4	T38.5X5	T38.5X6
Oxetacaine	T41.3X1	T41.3X2	T41.3X3	T41.3X4	T41.3X5	T41.3X6
Oxethazine	T41.3X1	T41.3X2	T41.3X3	T41.3X4	T41.3X5	T41.3X6
Oxetorone	T39.8X1	T39.8X2	T39.8X3	T39.8X4	T39.8X5	T39.8X6
Oxiconazole	T49.0X1	T49.0X2	T49.0X3	T49.0X4	T49.0X5	T49.0X6
Oxidizing agent NEC	T54.91	T54.92	T54.93	T54.94	—	—
Oxipurinol	T50.4X1	T50.4X2	T50.4X3	T50.4X4	T50.4X5	T50.4X6
Oxitriptan	T43.291	T43.292	T43.293	T43.294	T43.295	T43.296
Oxitropium bromide	T48.6X1	T48.6X2	T48.6X3	T48.6X4	T48.6X5	T48.6X6
Oxodipine	T46.1X1	T46.1X2	T46.1X3	T46.1X4	T46.1X5	T46.1X6
Oxolamine	T48.3X1	T48.3X2	T48.3X3	T48.3X4	T48.3X5	T48.3X6
Oxolinic acid	T37.8X1	T37.8X2	T37.8X3	T37.8X4	T37.8X5	T37.8X6
Oxomemazine	T43.3X1	T43.3X2	T43.3X3	T43.3X4	T43.3X5	T43.3X6
Oxophenarsine	T37.3X1	T37.3X2	T37.3X3	T37.3X4	T37.3X5	T37.3X6
Oxprenolol	T44.7X1	T44.7X2	T44.7X3	T44.7X4	T44.7X5	T44.7X6
Oxsoralen	T49.3X1	T49.3X2	T49.3X3	T49.3X4	T49.3X5	T49.3X6
Oxtriphylline	T48.6X1	T48.6X2	T48.6X3	T48.6X4	T48.6X5	T48.6X6
Oxybate sodium	T41.291	T41.292	T41.293	T41.294	T41.295	T41.296
Oxybuprocaine	T41.3X1	T41.3X2	T41.3X3	T41.3X4	T41.3X5	T41.3X6
Oxybutynin	T44.3X1	T44.3X2	T44.3X3	T44.3X4	T44.3X5	T44.3X6
Oxychlorosene	T49.0X1	T49.0X2	T49.0X3	T49.0X4	T49.0X5	T49.0X6
Oxycodone	T40.2X1	T40.2X2	T40.2X3	T40.2X4	T40.2X5	T40.2X6
Oxyfedrine	T46.3X1	T46.3X2	T46.3X3	T46.3X4	T46.3X5	T46.3X6
Oxygen	T41.5X1	T41.5X2	T41.5X3	T41.5X4	T41.5X5	T41.5X6
Oxylone	T49.0X1	T49.0X2	T49.0X3	T49.0X4	T49.0X5	T49.0X6
ophthalmic preparation	T49.5X1	T49.5X2	T49.5X3	T49.5X4	T49.5X5	T49.5X6
Oxymesterone	T38.7X1	T38.7X2	T38.7X3	T38.7X4	T38.7X5	T38.7X6
Oxymetazoline	T48.5X1	T48.5X2	T48.5X3	T48.5X4	T48.5X5	T48.5X6
Oxymetholone	T38.7X1	T38.7X2	T38.7X3	T38.7X4	T38.7X5	T38.7X6
Oxymorphone	T40.2X1	T40.2X2	T40.2X3	T40.2X4	T40.2X5	T40.2X6
Oxypertine	T43.591	T43.592	T43.593	T43.594	T43.595	T43.596
Oxyphenbutazone	T39.2X1	T39.2X2	T39.2X3	T39.2X4	T39.2X5	T39.2X6
Oxyphencyclimine	T44.3X1	T44.3X2	T44.3X3	T44.3X4	T44.3X5	T44.3X6
Oxyphenisatine	T47.2X1	T47.2X2	T47.2X3	T47.2X4	T47.2X5	T47.2X6
Oxyphenonium bromide	T44.3X1	T44.3X2	T44.3X3	T44.3X4	T44.3X5	T44.3X6
Oxypolygelatin	T45.8X1	T45.8X2	T45.8X3	T45.8X4	T45.8X5	T45.8X6
Oxyquinoline (derivatives)	T37.8X1	T37.8X2	T37.8X3	T37.8X4	T37.8X5	T37.8X6
Oxytetracycline	T36.4X1	T36.4X2	T36.4X3	T36.4X4	T36.4X5	T36.4X6
Oxytocic drug NEC	T48.0X1	T48.0X2	T48.0X3	T48.0X4	T48.0X5	T48.0X6
Oxytocin (synthetic)	T48.0X1	T48.0X2	T48.0X3	T48.0X4	T48.0X5	T48.0X6
Ozone	T59.891	T59.892	T59.893	T59.894	—	—

◀ New ◀ Revised ~~deleted~~ Deleted

Substance	External Cause (T-Code)					
	Poisoning, Accidental (Unintentional)	Poisoning, Intentional Self-Harm	Poisoning, Assault	Poisoning, Undetermined	Adverse Effect	Underdosing
P						
PABA	T49.3X1	T49.3X2	T49.3X3	T49.3X4	T49.3X5	T49.3X6
Packed red cells	T45.8X1	T45.8X2	T45.8X3	T45.8X4	T45.8X5	T45.8X6
Padimate	T49.3X1	T49.3X2	T49.3X3	T49.3X4	T49.3X5	T49.3X6
Paint NEC	T65.6X1	T65.6X2	T65.6X3	T65.6X4	—	—
cleaner	T52.91	T52.92	T52.93	T52.94	—	—
fumes NEC	T59.891	T59.892	T59.893	T59.894	—	—
lead (fumes)	T56.0X1	T56.0X2	T56.0X3	T56.0X4	—	—
solvent NEC	T52.8X1	T52.8X2	T52.8X3	T52.8X4	—	—
stripper	T52.8X1	T52.8X2	T52.8X3	T52.8X4	—	—
Palfium	T40.2X1	T40.2X2	T40.2X3	T40.2X4	—	—
Palm kernel oil	T50.991	T50.992	T50.993	T50.994	T50.995	T50.996
Paludrine	T37.2X1	T37.2X2	T37.2X3	T37.2X4	T37.2X5	T37.2X6
PAM (pralidoxime)	T50.6X1	T50.6X2	T50.6X3	T50.6X4	T50.6X5	T50.6X6
Pamaquine (naphthoute)	T37.2X1	T37.2X2	T37.2X3	T37.2X4	T37.2X5	T37.2X6
Panadol	T39.1X1	T39.1X2	T39.1X3	T39.1X4	T39.1X5	T39.1X6
Pancreatic						
digestive secretion stimulant	T47.8X1	T47.8X2	T47.8X3	T47.8X4	T47.8X5	T47.8X6
dornase	T45.3X1	T45.3X2	T45.3X3	T45.3X4	T45.3X5	T45.3X6
Pancreatin	T47.5X1	T47.5X2	T47.5X3	T47.5X4	T47.5X5	T47.5X6
Pancrelipase	T47.5X1	T47.5X2	T47.5X3	T47.5X4	T47.5X5	T47.5X6
Pancuronium (bromide)	T48.1X1	T48.1X2	T48.1X3	T48.1X4	T48.1X5	T48.1X6
Pangamic acid	T45.2X1	T45.2X2	T45.2X3	T45.2X4	T45.2X5	T45.2X6
Panthenol	T45.2X1	T45.2X2	T45.2X3	T45.2X4	T45.2X5	T45.2X6
topical	T49.8X1	T49.8X2	T49.8X3	T49.8X4	T49.8X5	T49.8X6
Pantopon	T40.0X1	T40.0X2	T40.0X3	T40.0X4	T40.0X5	T40.0X6
Pantothenic acid	T45.2X1	T45.2X2	T45.2X3	T45.2X4	T45.2X5	T45.2X6
Panwarfin	T45.511	T45.512	T45.513	T45.514	T45.515	T45.516
Papain	T47.5X1	T47.5X2	T47.5X3	T47.5X4	T47.5X5	T47.5X6
digestant	T47.5X1	T47.5X2	T47.5X3	T47.5X4	T47.5X5	T47.5X6
Papaveretum	T40.0X1	T40.0X2	T40.0X3	T40.0X4	T40.0X5	T40.0X6
Papaverine	T44.3X1	T44.3X2	T44.3X3	T44.3X4	T44.3X5	T44.3X6
Para-acetamidophenol	T39.1X1	T39.1X2	T39.1X3	T39.1X4	T39.1X5	T39.1X6
Para-aminobenzoic acid	T49.3X1	T49.3X2	T49.3X3	T49.3X4	T49.3X5	T49.3X6
Para-aminophenol derivatives	T39.1X1	T39.1X2	T39.1X3	T39.1X4	T39.1X5	T39.1X6
Para-aminosalicylic acid	T37.1X1	T37.1X2	T37.1X3	T37.1X4	T37.1X5	T37.1X6
Paracetaldehyde	T42.6X1	T42.6X2	T42.6X3	T42.6X4	T42.6X5	T42.6X6
Paracetamol	T39.1X1	T39.1X2	T39.1X3	T39.1X4	T39.1X5	T39.1X6
Parachlorophenol (camphorated)	T49.0X1	T49.0X2	T49.0X3	T49.0X4	T49.0X5	T49.0X6
Paracodin	T40.2X1	T40.2X2	T40.2X3	T40.2X4	T40.2X5	T40.2X6
Paradione	T42.2X1	T42.2X2	T42.2X3	T42.2X4	T42.2X5	T42.2X6

Substance	External Cause (T-Code)					
	Poisoning, Accidental (Unintentional)	Poisoning, Intentional Self-Harm	Poisoning, Assault	Poisoning, Undetermined	Adverse Effect	Underdosing
Paraffin(s) (wax)	T52.0X1	T52.0X2	T52.0X3	T52.0X4	—	—
liquid (medicinal)	T47.4X1	T47.4X2	T47.4X3	T47.4X4	T47.4X5	T47.4X6
nonmedicinal	T52.0X1	T52.0X2	T52.0X3	T52.0X4	—	—
Paraformaldehyde	T60.3X1	T60.3X2	T60.3X3	T60.3X4	—	—
Paraldehyde	T42.6X1	T42.6X2	T42.6X3	T42.6X4	T42.6X5	T42.6X6
Paramethadione	T42.2X1	T42.2X2	T42.2X3	T42.2X4	T42.2X5	T42.2X6
Paramethasone	T38.0X1	T38.0X2	T38.0X3	T38.0X4	T38.0X5	T38.0X6
acetate	T49.0X1	T49.0X2	T49.0X3	T49.0X4	T49.0X5	T49.0X6
Paraoxon	T60.0X1	T60.0X2	T60.0X3	T60.0X4	—	—
Paraquat	T60.3X1	T60.3X2	T60.3X3	T60.3X4	—	—
Parasympatholytic NEC	T44.3X1	T44.3X2	T44.3X3	T44.3X4	T44.3X5	T44.3X6
Parasympathomimetic drug NEC	T44.1X1	T44.1X2	T44.1X3	T44.1X4	T44.1X5	T44.1X6
Parathion	T60.0X1	T60.0X2	T60.0X3	T60.0X4	—	—
Parathormone	T50.991	T50.992	T50.993	T50.994	T50.995	T50.996
Parathyroid extract	T50.991	T50.992	T50.993	T50.994	T50.995	T50.996
Paratyphoid vaccine	T50.A91	T50.A92	T50.A93	T50.A94	T50.A95	T50.A96
Paredrine	T44.4X1	T44.4X2	T44.4X3	T44.4X4	T44.4X5	T44.4X6
Paregoric	T40.0X1	T40.0X2	T40.0X3	T40.0X4	T40.0X5	T40.0X6
Pargyline	T46.5X1	T46.5X2	T46.5X3	T46.5X4	T46.5X5	T46.5X6
Paris green	T57.0X1	T57.0X2	T57.0X3	T57.0X4	—	—
insecticide	T57.0X1	T57.0X2	T57.0X3	T57.0X4	—	—
Parnate	T43.1X1	T43.1X2	T43.1X3	T43.1X4	T43.1X5	T43.1X6
Paromomycin	T36.5X1	T36.5X2	T36.5X3	T36.5X4	T36.5X5	T36.5X6
Paroxypropione	T45.1X1	T45.1X2	T45.1X3	T45.1X4	T45.1X5	T45.1X6
Parzone	T40.2X1	T40.2X2	T40.2X3	T40.2X4	T40.2X5	T40.2X6
PAS	T37.1X1	T37.1X2	T37.1X3	T37.1X4	T37.1X5	T37.1X6
Pasiniazid	T37.1X1	T37.1X2	T37.1X3	T37.1X4	T37.1X5	T37.1X6
PBB (polybrominated biphenyls)	T65.891	T65.892	T65.893	T65.894	—	—
PCB	T65.891	T65.892	T65.893	T65.894	—	—
PCP						
meaning pentachlorophenol	T60.1X1	T60.1X2	T60.1X3	T60.1X4	—	—
fungicide	T60.3X1	T60.3X2	T60.3X3	T60.3X4	—	—
herbicide	T60.3X1	T60.3X2	T60.3X3	T60.3X4	—	—
insecticide	T60.1X1	T60.1X2	T60.1X3	T60.1X4	—	—
meaning phencyclidine	T40.991	T40.992	T40.993	T40.994		
Peach kernel oil (emulsion)	T47.4X1	T47.4X2	T47.4X3	T47.4X4	T47.4X5	T47.4X6
Peanut oil (emulsion) NEC	T47.4X1	T47.4X2	T47.4X3	T47.4X4	T47.4X5	T47.4X6
topical	T49.3X1	T49.3X2	T49.3X3	T49.3X4	T49.3X5	T49.3X6
Pearly Gates (morning glory seeds)	T40.991	T40.992	T40.993	T40.994	—	—
Pecazine	T43.3X1	T43.3X2	T43.3X3	T43.3X4	T43.3X5	T43.3X6
Pectin	T47.6X1	T47.6X2	T47.6X3	T47.6X4	T47.6X5	T47.6X6

◀ New   ◀ Revised   ~~deleted~~ Deleted

TABLE OF DRUGS AND CHEMICALS

Substance	Poisoning, Accidental (Unintentional)	Poisoning, Intentional Self-Harm	Poisoning, Assault	Poisoning, Undetermined	Adverse Effect	Underdosing
Pefloxacin	T37.8X1	T37.8X2	T37.8X3	T37.8X4	T37.8X5	T37.8X6
Pegademase, bovine	T50.Z91	T50.Z92	T50.Z93	T50.Z94	T50.Z95	T50.Z96
Pelletierine tannate	T37.4X1	T37.4X2	T37.4X3	T37.4X4	T37.4X5	T37.4X6
Pemirolast (potassium)	T48.6X1	T48.6X2	T48.6X3	T48.6X4	T48.6X5	T48.6X6
Pemoline	T50.7X1	T50.7X2	T50.7X3	T50.7X4	T50.7X5	T50.7X6
Pempidine	T44.2X1	T44.2X2	T44.2X3	T44.2X4	T44.2X5	T44.2X6
Penamecillin	T36.0X1	T36.0X2	T36.0X3	T36.0X4	T36.0X5	T36.0X6
Penbutolol	T44.7X1	T44.7X2	T44.7X3	T44.7X4	T44.7X5	T44.7X6
Penethamate	T36.0X1	T36.0X2	T36.0X3	T36.0X4	T36.0X5	T36.0X6
Penfluridol	T43.591	T43.592	T43.593	T43.594	T43.595	T43.596
Penflutizide	T50.2X1	T50.2X2	T50.2X3	T50.2X4	T50.2X5	T50.2X6
Pengitoxin	T46.0X1	T46.0X2	T46.0X3	T46.0X4	T46.0X5	T46.0X6
Penicillamine	T50.6X1	T50.6X2	T50.6X3	T50.6X4	T50.6X5	T50.6X6
Penicillin (any)	T36.0X1	T36.0X2	T36.0X3	T36.0X4	T36.0X5	T36.0X6
Penicillinase	T45.3X1	T45.3X2	T45.3X3	T45.3X4	T45.3X5	T45.3X6
Penicilloyl polylysine	T50.8X1	T50.8X2	T50.8X3	T50.8X4	T50.8X5	T50.8X6
Penimepicycline	T36.4X1	T36.4X2	T36.4X3	T36.4X4	T36.4X5	T36.4X6
Pentachloroethane	T53.6X1	T53.6X2	T53.6X3	T53.6X4	—	—
Pentachloronaphthalene	T53.7X1	T53.7X2	T53.7X3	T53.7X4	—	—
Pentachlorophenol (pesticide)	T60.1X1	T60.1X2	T60.1X3	T60.1X4	—	—
fungicide	T60.3X1	T60.3X2	T60.3X3	T60.3X4	—	—
herbicide	T60.3X1	T60.3X2	T60.3X3	T60.3X4	—	—
insecticide	T60.1X1	T60.1X2	T60.1X3	T60.1X4	—	—
Pentaerythritol tetranitrate	T46.3X1	T46.3X2	T46.3X3	T46.3X4	T46.3X5	T46.3X6
Pentaerythritol	T46.3X1	T46.3X2	T46.3X3	T46.3X4	T46.3X5	T46.3X6
chloral	T42.6X1	T42.6X2	T42.6X3	T42.6X4	T42.6X5	T42.6X6
tetranitrate NEC	T46.3X1	T46.3X2	T46.3X3	T46.3X4	T46.3X5	T46.3X6
Pentagastrin	T50.8X1	T50.8X2	T50.8X3	T50.8X4	T50.8X5	T50.8X6
Pentalin	T53.6X1	T53.6X2	T53.6X3	T53.6X4	—	—
Pentamethonium bromide	T44.2X1	T44.2X2	T44.2X3	T44.2X4	T44.2X5	T44.2X6
Pentamidine	T37.3X1	T37.3X2	T37.3X3	T37.3X4	T37.3X5	T37.3X6
Pentanol	T51.3X1	T51.3X2	T51.3X3	T51.3X4	—	—
Pentapyrrolinium (bitartrate)	T44.2X1	T44.2X2	T44.2X3	T44.2X4	T44.2X5	T44.2X6
Pentaquine	T37.2X1	T37.2X2	T37.2X3	T37.2X4	T37.2X5	T37.2X6
Pentazocine	T40.491	T40.492	T40.493	T40.494	T40.495	T40.496
Pentetrazole	T50.7X1	T50.7X2	T50.7X3	T50.7X4	T50.7X5	T50.7X6
Penthienate bromide	T44.3X1	T44.3X2	T44.3X3	T44.3X4	T44.3X5	T44.3X6
Pentifylline	T46.7X1	T46.7X2	T46.7X3	T46.7X4	T46.7X5	T46.7X6
Pentobarbital	T42.3X1	T42.3X2	T42.3X3	T42.3X4	T42.3X5	T42.3X6
sodium	T42.3X1	T42.3X2	T42.3X3	T42.3X4	T42.3X5	T42.3X6
Pentobarbitone	T42.3X1	T42.3X2	T42.3X3	T42.3X4	T42.3X5	T42.3X6
Pentolonium tartrate	T44.2X1	T44.2X2	T44.2X3	T44.2X4	T44.2X5	T44.2X6

Substance	Poisoning, Accidental (Unintentional)	Poisoning, Intentional Self-Harm	Poisoning, Assault	Poisoning, Undetermined	Adverse Effect	Underdosing
Pentosan polysulfate (sodium)	T39.8X1	T39.8X2	T39.8X3	T39.8X4	T39.8X5	T39.8X6
Pentostatin	T45.1X1	T45.1X2	T45.1X3	T45.1X4	T45.1X5	T45.1X6
Pentothal	T41.1X1	T41.1X2	T41.1X3	T41.1X4	T41.1X5	T41.1X6
Pentoxifylline	T46.7X1	T46.7X2	T46.7X3	T46.7X4	T46.7X5	T46.7X6
Pentoxyverine	T48.3X1	T48.3X2	T48.3X3	T48.3X4	T48.3X5	T48.3X6
Pentrinat	T46.3X1	T46.3X2	T46.3X3	T46.3X4	T46.3X5	T46.3X6
Pentylenetetrazole	T50.7X1	T50.7X2	T50.7X3	T50.7X4	T50.7X5	T50.7X6
Pentylsalicylamide	T37.1X1	T37.1X2	T37.1X3	T37.1X4	T37.1X5	T37.1X6
Pentymal	T42.3X1	T42.3X2	T42.3X3	T42.3X4	T42.3X5	T42.3X6
Peplomycin	T45.1X1	T45.1X2	T45.1X3	T45.1X4	T45.1X5	T45.1X6
Peppermint (oil)	T47.5X1	T47.5X2	T47.5X3	T47.5X4	T47.5X5	T47.5X6
Pepsin	T47.5X1	T47.5X2	T47.5X3	T47.5X4	T47.5X5	T47.5X6
digestant	T47.5X1	T47.5X2	T47.5X3	T47.5X4	T47.5X5	T47.5X6
Pepstatin	T47.1X1	T47.1X2	T47.1X3	T47.1X4	T47.1X5	T47.1X6
Peptavlon	T50.8X1	T50.8X2	T50.8X3	T50.8X4	T50.8X5	T50.8X6
Perazine	T43.3X1	T43.3X2	T43.3X3	T43.3X4	T43.3X5	T43.3X6
Percaine (spinal)	T41.3X1	T41.3X2	T41.3X3	T41.3X4	T41.3X5	T41.3X6
topical (surface)	T41.3X1	T41.3X2	T41.3X3	T41.3X4	T41.3X5	T41.3X6
Perchloroethylene	T53.3X1	T53.3X2	T53.3X3	T53.3X4	—	—
medicinal	T37.4X1	T37.4X2	T37.4X3	T37.4X4	T37.4X5	T37.4X6
vapor	T53.3X1	T53.3X2	T53.3X3	T53.3X4	—	—
Percodan	T40.2X1	T40.2X2	T40.2X3	T40.2X4	T40.2X5	T40.2X6
Percogesic — see also Acetaminophen	T45.0X1	T45.0X2	T45.0X3	T45.0X4	T45.0X5	T45.0X6
Percorten	T38.0X1	T38.0X2	T38.0X3	T38.0X4	T38.0X5	T38.0X6
Pergolide	T42.8X1	T42.8X2	T42.8X3	T42.8X4	T42.8X5	T42.8X6
Pergonal	T38.811	T38.812	T38.813	T38.814	T38.815	T38.816
Perhexilene	T46.3X1	T46.3X2	T46.3X3	T46.3X4	T46.3X5	T46.3X6
Perhexiline (maleate)	T46.3X1	T46.3X2	T46.3X3	T46.3X4	T46.3X5	T46.3X6
Periactin	T45.0X1	T45.0X2	T45.0X3	T45.0X4	T45.0X5	T45.0X6
Periciazine	T43.3X1	T43.3X2	T43.3X3	T43.3X4	T43.3X5	T43.3X6
Periclor	T42.6X1	T42.6X2	T42.6X3	T42.6X4	T42.6X5	T42.6X6
Perindopril	T46.4X1	T46.4X2	T46.4X3	T46.4X4	T46.4X5	T46.4X6
Perisoxal	T39.8X1	T39.8X2	T39.8X3	T39.8X4	T39.8X5	T39.8X6
Peritrate	T46.3X1	T46.3X2	T46.3X3	T46.3X4	T46.3X5	T46.3X6
Peritoneal dialysis solution	T50.3X1	T50.3X2	T50.3X3	T50.3X4	T50.3X5	T50.3X6
Perlapine	T42.4X1	T42.4X2	T42.4X3	T42.4X4	T42.4X5	T42.4X6
Permanganate	T65.891	T65.892	T65.893	T65.894	—	—
Permethrin	T60.1X1	T60.1X2	T60.1X3	T60.1X4	—	—
Pernocton	T42.3X1	T42.3X2	T42.3X3	T42.3X4	T42.3X5	T42.3X6
Pernoston	T42.3X1	T42.3X2	T42.3X3	T42.3X4	T42.3X5	T42.3X6
Peronine	T40.2X1	T40.2X2	T40.2X3	T40.2X4	—	—
Perphenazine	T43.3X1	T43.3X2	T43.3X3	T43.3X4	T43.3X5	T43.3X6

◀ New　◀ Revised　deleted Deleted

Substance	Poisoning, Accidental (Unintentional)	Poisoning, Intentional Self-Harm	Poisoning, Assault	Poisoning, Undetermined	Adverse Effect	Underdosing
Pertofrane	T43.011	T43.012	T43.013	T43.014	T43.015	T43.016
Pertussis						
immune serum (human)	T50.Z11	T50.Z12	T50.Z13	T50.Z14	T50.Z15	T50.Z16
vaccine (with diphtheria toxoid) (with tetanus toxoid)	T50.A11	T50.A12	T50.A13	T50.A14	T50.A15	T50.A16
Peruvian balsam	T49.0X1	T49.0X2	T49.0X3	T49.0X4	T49.0X5	T49.0X6
Peruvoside	T46.0X1	T46.0X2	T46.0X3	T46.0X4	T46.0X5	T46.0X6
Pesticide (dust) (fumes) (vapor) NEC	T60.91	T60.92	T60.93	T60.94	—	—
arsenic	T57.0X1	T57.0X2	T57.0X3	T57.0X4	—	—
chlorinated	T60.1X1	T60.1X2	T60.1X3	T60.1X4	—	—
cyanide	T65.0X1	T65.0X2	T65.0X3	T65.0X4	—	—
kerosene	T52.0X1	T52.0X2	T52.0X3	T52.0X4	—	—
mixture (of compounds)	T60.91	T60.92	T60.93	T60.94	—	—
naphthalene	T60.2X1	T60.2X2	T60.2X3	T60.2X4	—	—
organochlorine (compounds)	T60.1X1	T60.1X2	T60.1X3	T60.1X4	—	—
petroleum (distillate) (products) NEC	T60.8X1	T60.8X2	T60.8X3	T60.8X4	—	—
specified ingredient NEC	T60.8X1	T60.8X2	T60.8X3	T60.8X4	—	—
strychnine	T65.1X1	T65.1X2	T65.1X3	T65.1X4	—	—
thallium	T60.4X1	T60.4X2	T60.4X3	T60.4X4	—	—
Pethidine	T40.491	T40.492	T40.493	T40.494	T40.495	T40.496
Petrichloral	T42.6X1	T42.6X2	T42.6X3	T42.6X4	T42.6X5	T42.6X6
Petrol	T52.0X1	T52.0X2	T52.0X3	T52.0X4	—	—
vapor	T52.0X1	T52.0X2	T52.0X3	T52.0X4	—	—
Petrolatum	T49.3X1	T49.3X2	T49.3X3	T49.3X4	T49.3X5	T49.3X6
hydrophilic	T49.3X1	T49.3X2	T49.3X3	T49.3X4	T49.3X5	T49.3X6
liquid	T47.4X1	T47.4X2	T47.4X3	T47.4X4	T47.4X5	T47.4X6
topical	T49.3X1	T49.3X2	T49.3X3	T49.3X4	T49.3X5	T49.3X6
nonmedicinal	T52.0X1	T52.0X2	T52.0X3	T52.0X4	—	—
red veterinary	T49.3X1	T49.3X2	T49.3X3	T49.3X4	T49.3X5	T49.3X6
white	T49.3X1	T49.3X2	T49.3X3	T49.3X4	T49.3X5	T49.3X6
Petroleum (products) NEC	T52.0X1	T52.0X2	T52.0X3	T52.0X4	—	—
benzine(s) — see Ligroin						
ether — see Ligroin						
jelly — see Petrolatum						
naphtha — see Ligroin						
pesticide	T60.8X1	T60.8X2	T60.8X3	T60.8X4	—	—
solids	T52.0X1	T52.0X2	T52.0X3	T52.0X4	—	—
solvents	T52.0X1	T52.0X2	T52.0X3	T52.0X4	—	—
vapor	T52.0X1	T52.0X2	T52.0X3	T52.0X4	—	—
Peyote	T40.991	T40.992	T40.993	T40.994	—	—
Phanodorm, phanodorn	T42.3X1	T42.3X2	T42.3X3	T42.3X4	T42.3X5	T42.3X6

Substance	Poisoning, Accidental (Unintentional)	Poisoning, Intentional Self-Harm	Poisoning, Assault	Poisoning, Undetermined	Adverse Effect	Underdosing
Phanquinone	T37.3X1	T37.3X2	T37.3X3	T37.3X4	T37.3X5	T37.3X6
Phanquone	T37.3X1	T37.3X2	T37.3X3	T37.3X4	T37.3X5	T37.3X6
Pharmaceutical						
adjunct NEC	T50.901	T50.902	T50.903	T50.904	T50.905	T50.906
excipient NEC	T50.901	T50.902	T50.903	T50.904	T50.905	T50.906
sweetener	T50.901	T50.902	T50.903	T50.904	T50.905	T50.906
viscous agent	T50.901	T50.902	T50.903	T50.904	T50.905	T50.906
Phemitone	T42.3X1	T42.3X2	T42.3X3	T42.3X4	T42.3X5	T42.3X6
Phenacaine	T41.3X1	T41.3X2	T41.3X3	T41.3X4	T41.3X5	T41.3X6
Phenacemide	T42.6X1	T42.6X2	T42.6X3	T42.6X4	T42.6X5	T42.6X6
Phenacetin	T39.1X1	T39.1X2	T39.1X3	T39.1X4	T39.1X5	T39.1X6
Phenadoxone	T40.2X1	T40.2X2	T40.2X3	T40.2X4	—	—
Phenaglycodol	T43.591	T43.592	T43.593	T43.594	T43.595	T43.596
Phenantoin	T42.0X1	T42.0X2	T42.0X3	T42.0X4	T42.0X5	T42.0X6
Phenaphthazine reagent	T50.991	T50.992	T50.993	T50.994	T50.995	T50.996
Phenazocine	T40.491	T40.492	T40.493	T40.494	T40.495	T40.496
Phenazone	T39.2X1	T39.2X2	T39.2X3	T39.2X4	T39.2X5	T39.2X6
Phenazopyridine	T39.8X1	T39.8X2	T39.8X3	T39.8X4	T39.8X5	T39.8X6
Phenbenicillin	T36.0X1	T36.0X2	T36.0X3	T36.0X4	T36.0X5	T36.0X6
Phenbutrazate	T50.5X1	T50.5X2	T50.5X3	T50.5X4	T50.5X5	T50.5X6
Phencyclidine	T40.991	T40.992	T40.993	T40.994	T40.995	T40.996
Phendimetrazine	T50.5X1	T50.5X2	T50.5X3	T50.5X4	T50.5X5	T50.5X6
Phenelzine	T43.1X1	T43.1X2	T43.1X3	T43.1X4	T43.1X5	T43.1X6
Phenemal	T42.3X1	T42.3X2	T42.3X3	T42.3X4	T42.3X5	T42.3X6
Phenergan	T42.6X1	T42.6X2	T42.6X3	T42.6X4	T42.6X5	T42.6X6
Pheneticillin	T36.0X1	T36.0X2	T36.0X3	T36.0X4	T36.0X5	T36.0X6
Pheneturide	T42.6X1	T42.6X2	T42.6X3	T42.6X4	T42.6X5	T42.6X6
Phenformin	T38.3X1	T38.3X2	T38.3X3	T38.3X4	T38.3X5	T38.3X6
Phenglutarimide	T44.3X1	T44.3X2	T44.3X3	T44.3X4	T44.3X5	T44.3X6
Phenicarbazide	T39.8X1	T39.8X2	T39.8X3	T39.8X4	T39.8X5	T39.8X6
Phenindamine	T45.0X1	T45.0X2	T45.0X3	T45.0X4	T45.0X5	T45.0X6
Phenindione	T45.511	T45.512	T45.513	T45.514	T45.515	T45.516
Pheniprazine	T43.1X1	T43.1X2	T43.1X3	T43.1X4	T43.1X5	T43.1X6
Pheniramine	T45.0X1	T45.0X2	T45.0X3	T45.0X4	T45.0X5	T45.0X6
Phenisatin	T47.2X1	T47.2X2	T47.2X3	T47.2X4	T47.2X5	T47.2X6
Phenmetrazine	T50.5X1	T50.5X2	T50.5X3	T50.5X4	T50.5X5	T50.5X6
Phenobal	T42.3X1	T42.3X2	T42.3X3	T42.3X4	T42.3X5	T42.3X6
Phenobarbital	T42.3X1	T42.3X2	T42.3X3	T42.3X4	T42.3X5	T42.3X6
with						
mephenytoin	T42.3X1	T42.3X2	T42.3X3	T42.3X4	T42.3X5	T42.3X6
phenytoin	T42.3X1	T42.3X2	T42.3X3	T42.3X4	T42.3X5	T42.3X6
sodium	T42.3X1	T42.3X2	T42.3X3	T42.3X4	T42.3X5	T42.3X6

Substance	External Cause (T-Code) Poisoning, Accidental (Unintentional)	Poisoning, Intentional Self-Harm	Poisoning, Assault	Poisoning, Undetermined	Adverse Effect	Underdosing
Phenobarbitone	T42.3X1	T42.3X2	T42.3X3	T42.3X4	T42.3X5	T42.3X6
Phenobutiodil	T50.8X1	T50.8X2	T50.8X3	T50.8X4	T50.8X5	T50.8X6
Phenoctide	T49.0X1	T49.0X2	T49.0X3	T49.0X4	T49.0X5	T49.0X6
Phenol	T49.0X1	T49.0X2	T49.0X3	T49.0X4	T49.0X5	T49.0X6
disinfectant	T54.0X1	T54.0X2	T54.0X3	T54.0X4	—	—
in oil injection	T46.8X1	T46.8X2	T46.8X3	T46.8X4	T46.8X5	T46.8X6
medicinal	T49.1X1	T49.1X2	T49.1X3	T49.1X4	T49.1X5	T49.1X6
nonmedicinal NEC	T54.0X1	T54.0X2	T54.0X3	T54.0X4	—	—
pesticide	T60.8X1	T60.8X2	T60.8X3	T60.8X4	—	—
red	T50.8X1	T50.8X2	T50.8X3	T50.8X4	T50.8X5	T50.8X6
Phenolic preparation	T49.1X1	T49.1X2	T49.1X3	T49.1X4	T49.1X5	T49.1X6
Phenolphthalein	T47.2X1	T47.2X2	T47.2X3	T47.2X4	T47.2X5	T47.2X6
Phenolsulfonphthalein	T50.8X1	T50.8X2	T50.8X3	T50.8X4	T50.8X5	T50.8X6
Phenomorphan	T40.2X1	T40.2X2	T40.2X3	T40.2X4	—	—
Phenonyl	T42.3X1	T42.3X2	T42.3X3	T42.3X4	T42.3X5	T42.3X6
Phenoperidine	T40.491	T40.492	T40.493	T40.494	—	—
Phenopyrazone	T46.991	T46.992	T46.993	T46.994	T46.995	T46.996
Phenoquin	T50.4X1	T50.4X2	T50.4X3	T50.4X4	T50.4X5	T50.4X6
Phenothiazine (psychotropic) NEC	T43.3X1	T43.3X2	T43.3X3	T43.3X4	T43.3X5	T43.3X6
insecticide	T60.2X1	T60.2X2	T60.2X3	T60.2X4	—	—
Phenothrin	T49.0X1	T49.0X2	T49.0X3	T49.0X4	T49.0X5	T49.0X6
Phenoxybenzamine	T46.7X1	T46.7X2	T46.7X3	T46.7X4	T46.7X5	T46.7X6
Phenoxyethanol	T49.0X1	T49.0X2	T49.0X3	T49.0X4	T49.0X5	T49.0X6
Phenoxymethyl penicillin	T36.0X1	T36.0X2	T36.0X3	T36.0X4	T36.0X5	T36.0X6
Phenprobamate	T42.8X1	T42.8X2	T42.8X3	T42.8X4	T42.8X5	T42.8X6
Phenprocoumon	T45.511	T45.512	T45.513	T45.514	T45.515	T45.516
Phensuximide	T42.2X1	T42.2X2	T42.2X3	T42.2X4	T42.2X5	T42.2X6
Phentermine	T50.5X1	T50.5X2	T50.5X3	T50.5X4	T50.5X5	T50.5X6
Phenthicillin	T36.0X1	T36.0X2	T36.0X3	T36.0X4	T36.0X5	T36.0X6
Phentolamine	T46.7X1	T46.7X2	T46.7X3	T46.7X4	T46.7X5	T46.7X6
Phenyl						
butazone	T39.2X1	T39.2X2	T39.2X3	T39.2X4	T39.2X5	T39.2X6
enediamine	T65.3X1	T65.3X2	T65.3X3	T65.3X4	—	—
hydrazine	T65.3X1	T65.3X2	T65.3X3	T65.3X4	—	—
antineoplastic	T45.1X1	T45.1X2	T45.1X3	T45.1X4	T45.1X5	T45.1X6
mercuric compounds — see Mercury						
salicylate	T49.3X1	T49.3X2	T49.3X3	T49.3X4	T49.3X5	T49.3X6
Phenylalanine mustard	T45.1X1	T45.1X2	T45.1X3	T45.1X4	T45.1X5	T45.1X6
Phenylbutazone	T39.2X1	T39.2X2	T39.2X3	T39.2X4	T39.2X5	T39.2X6
Phenylenediamine	T65.3X1	T65.3X2	T65.3X3	T65.3X4	—	—
Phenylephrine	T44.4X1	T44.4X2	T44.4X3	T44.4X4	T44.4X5	T44.4X6

Substance	External Cause (T-Code) Poisoning, Accidental (Unintentional)	Poisoning, Intentional Self-Harm	Poisoning, Assault	Poisoning, Undetermined	Adverse Effect	Underdosing
Phenylethylbiguanide	T38.3X1	T38.3X2	T38.3X3	T38.3X4	T38.3X5	T38.3X6
Phenylmercuric						
acetate	T49.0X1	T49.0X2	T49.0X3	T49.0X4	T49.0X5	T49.0X6
borate	T49.0X1	T49.0X2	T49.0X3	T49.0X4	T49.0X5	T49.0X6
nitrate	T49.0X1	T49.0X2	T49.0X3	T49.0X4	T49.0X5	T49.0X6
Phenylmethylbarbitone	T42.3X1	T42.3X2	T42.3X3	T42.3X4	T42.3X5	T42.3X6
Phenylpropanol	T47.5X1	T47.5X2	T47.5X3	T47.5X4	T47.5X5	T47.5X6
Phenylpropanolamine	T44.991	T44.992	T44.993	T44.994	T44.995	T44.996
Phenylsulfthion	T60.0X1	T60.0X2	T60.0X3	T60.0X4	—	—
Phenyltoloxamine	T45.0X1	T45.0X2	T45.0X3	T45.0X4	T45.0X5	T45.0X6
Phenyramidol, phenyramidon	T39.8X1	T39.8X2	T39.8X3	T39.8X4	T39.8X5	T39.8X6
Phenytoin	T42.0X1	T42.0X2	T42.0X3	T42.0X4	T42.0X5	T42.0X6
with Phenobarbital	T42.3X1	T42.3X2	T42.3X3	T42.3X4	T42.3X5	T42.3X6
pHisoHex	T49.2X1	T49.2X2	T49.2X3	T49.2X4	T49.2X5	T49.2X6
Pholcodine	T48.3X1	T48.3X2	T48.3X3	T48.3X4	T48.3X5	T48.3X6
Pholedrine	T46.991	T46.992	T46.993	T46.994	T46.995	T46.996
Phorate	T60.0X1	T60.0X2	T60.0X3	T60.0X4	—	—
Phosdrin	T60.0X1	T60.0X2	T60.0X3	T60.0X4	—	—
Phosfolan	T60.0X1	T60.0X2	T60.0X3	T60.0X4	—	—
Phosgene (gas)	T59.891	T59.892	T59.893	T59.894		
Phosphamidon	T60.0X1	T60.0X2	T60.0X3	T60.0X4	—	—
Phosphate	T65.891	T65.892	T65.893	T65.894		
laxative	T47.4X1	T47.4X2	T47.4X3	T47.4X4	T47.4X5	T47.4X6
organic	T60.0X1	T60.0X2	T60.0X3	T60.0X4	—	—
solvent	T52.91	T52.92	T52.93	T52.94	—	—
tricresyl	T65.891	T65.892	T65.893	T65.894	—	—
Phosphine	T57.1X1	T57.1X2	T57.1X3	T57.1X4		
fumigant	T57.1X1	T57.1X2	T57.1X3	T57.1X4		
Phospholine	T49.5X1	T49.5X2	T49.5X3	T49.5X4	T49.5X5	T49.5X6
Phosphoric acid	T54.2X1	T54.2X2	T54.2X3	T54.2X4	—	—
Phosphorus (compound) NEC	T57.1X1	T57.1X2	T57.1X3	T57.1X4		
pesticide	T60.0X1	T60.0X2	T60.0X3	T60.0X4	—	—
Phthalates	T65.891	T65.892	T65.893	T65.894		
Phthalic anhydride	T65.891	T65.892	T65.893	T65.894		
Phthalimidoglutarimide	T42.6X1	T42.6X2	T42.6X3	T42.6X4	T42.6X5	T42.6X6
Phthalylsulfathiazole	T37.0X1	T37.0X2	T37.0X3	T37.0X4	T37.0X5	T37.0X6
Phylloquinone	T45.7X1	T45.7X2	T45.7X3	T45.7X4	T45.7X5	T45.7X6
Physeptone	T40.3X1	T40.3X2	T40.3X3	T40.3X4	T40.3X5	T40.3X6
Physostigma venenosum	T62.2X1	T62.2X2	T62.2X3	T62.2X4	—	—
Physostigmine	T49.5X1	T49.5X2	T49.5X3	T49.5X4	T49.5X5	T49.5X6
Phytolacca decandra	T62.2X1	T62.2X2	T62.2X3	T62.2X4	—	—
berries	T62.1X1	T62.1X2	T62.1X3	T62.1X4	—	—

◀ New ◀ Revised ~~deleted~~ Deleted

Substance	External Cause (T-Code) Poisoning, Accidental (Unintentional)	Poisoning, Intentional Self-Harm	Poisoning, Assault	Poisoning, Undetermined	Adverse Effect	Underdosing
Phytomenadione	T45.7X1	T45.7X2	T45.7X3	T45.7X4	T45.7X5	T45.7X6
Phytonadione	T45.7X1	T45.7X2	T45.7X3	T45.7X4	T45.7X5	T45.7X6
Picoperine	T48.3X1	T48.3X2	T48.3X3	T48.3X4	T48.3X5	T48.3X6
Picosulfate (sodium)	T47.2X1	T47.2X2	T47.2X3	T47.2X4	T47.2X5	T47.2X6
Picric (acid)	T54.2X1	T54.2X2	T54.2X3	T54.2X4	—	—
Picrotoxin	T50.7X1	T50.7X2	T50.7X3	T50.7X4	T50.7X5	T50.7X6
Piketoprofen	T49.0X1	T49.0X2	T49.0X3	T49.0X4	T49.0X5	T49.0X6
Pilocarpine	T44.1X1	T44.1X2	T44.1X3	T44.1X4	T44.1X5	T44.1X6
Pilocarpus (jaborandi) extract	T44.1X1	T44.1X2	T44.1X3	T44.1X4	T44.1X5	T44.1X6
Pilsicainide (hydrochloride)	T46.2X1	T46.2X2	T46.2X3	T46.2X4	T46.2X5	T46.2X6
Pimaricin	T36.7X1	T36.7X2	T36.7X3	T36.7X4	T36.7X5	T36.7X6
Pimeclone	T50.7X1	T50.7X2	T50.7X3	T50.7X4	T50.7X5	T50.7X6
Pimelic ketone	T52.8X1	T52.8X2	T52.8X3	T52.8X4	—	—
Pimethixene	T45.0X1	T45.0X2	T45.0X3	T45.0X4	T45.0X5	T45.0X6
Piminodine	T40.2X1	T40.2X2	T40.2X3	T40.2X4	T40.2X5	T40.2X6
Pimozide	T43.591	T43.592	T43.593	T43.594	T43.595	T43.596
Pinacidil	T46.5X1	T46.5X2	T46.5X3	T46.5X4	T46.5X5	T46.5X6
Pinaverium bromide	T44.3X1	T44.3X2	T44.3X3	T44.3X4	T44.3X5	T44.3X6
Pinazepam	T42.4X1	T42.4X2	T42.4X3	T42.4X4	T42.4X5	T42.4X6
Pindolol	T44.7X1	T44.7X2	T44.7X3	T44.7X4	T44.7X5	T44.7X6
Pindone	T60.4X1	T60.4X2	T60.4X3	T60.4X4	—	—
Pine oil (disinfectant)	T65.891	T65.892	T65.893	T65.894	—	—
Pinkroot	T37.4X1	T37.4X2	T37.4X3	T37.4X4	T37.4X5	T37.4X6
Pipadone	T40.2X1	T40.2X2	T40.2X3	T40.2X4	—	—
Pipamazine	T45.0X1	T45.0X2	T45.0X3	T45.0X4	T45.0X5	T45.0X6
Pipamperone	T43.4X1	T43.4X2	T43.4X3	T43.4X4	T43.4X5	T43.4X6
Pipazetate	T48.3X1	T48.3X2	T48.3X3	T48.3X4	T48.3X5	T48.3X6
Pipemidic acid	T37.8X1	T37.8X2	T37.8X3	T37.8X4	T37.8X5	T37.8X6
Pipenzolate bromide	T44.3X1	T44.3X2	T44.3X3	T44.3X4	T44.3X5	T44.3X6
Piperacetazine	T43.3X1	T43.3X2	T43.3X3	T43.3X4	T43.3X5	T43.3X6
Piperacillin	T36.0X1	T36.0X2	T36.0X3	T36.0X4	T36.0X5	T36.0X6
Piperazine	T37.4X1	T37.4X2	T37.4X3	T37.4X4	T37.4X5	T37.4X6
estrone sulfate	T38.5X1	T38.5X2	T38.5X3	T38.5X4	T38.5X5	T38.5X6
Piper cubeba	T62.2X1	T62.2X2	T62.2X3	T62.2X4	—	—
Piperidione	T48.3X1	T48.3X2	T48.3X3	T48.3X4	—	—
Piperidolate	T44.3X1	T44.3X2	T44.3X3	T44.3X4	T44.3X5	T44.3X6
Piperocaine	T41.3X1	T41.3X2	T41.3X3	T41.3X4	T41.3X5	T41.3X6
infiltration (subcutaneous)	T41.3X1	T41.3X2	T41.3X3	T41.3X4	T41.3X5	T41.3X6
nerve block (peripheral) (plexus)	T41.3X1	T41.3X2	T41.3X3	T41.3X4	T41.3X5	T41.3X6
topical (surface)	T41.3X1	T41.3X2	T41.3X3	T41.3X4	T41.3X5	T41.3X6
Piperonyl butoxide	T60.8X1	T60.8X2	T60.8X3	T60.8X4	—	—
Pipethanate	T44.3X1	T44.3X2	T44.3X3	T44.3X4	T44.3X5	T44.3X6

Substance	External Cause (T-Code) Poisoning, Accidental (Unintentional)	Poisoning, Intentional Self-Harm	Poisoning, Assault	Poisoning, Undetermined	Adverse Effect	Underdosing
Pipobroman	T45.1X1	T45.1X2	T45.1X3	T45.1X4	T45.1X5	T45.1X6
Pipofezine	T43.0X1	T43.0X2	T43.0X3	T43.0X4	T43.0X5	T43.0X6
Pipotiazine	T43.3X1	T43.3X2	T43.3X3	T43.3X4	T43.3X5	T43.3X6
Pipoxizine	T45.0X1	T45.0X2	T45.0X3	T45.0X4	T45.0X5	T45.0X6
Pipradrol	T43.691	T43.692	T43.693	T43.694	T43.695	T43.696
Piprinhydrinate	T45.0X1	T45.0X2	T45.0X3	T45.0X4	T45.0X5	T45.0X6
Pirarubicin	T45.1X1	T45.1X2	T45.1X3	T45.1X4	T45.1X5	T45.1X6
Pirazinamide	T37.1X1	T37.1X2	T37.1X3	T37.1X4	T37.1X5	T37.1X6
Pirbuterol	T48.6X1	T48.6X2	T48.6X3	T48.6X4	T48.6X5	T48.6X6
Pirenzepine	T47.1X1	T47.1X2	T47.1X3	T47.1X4	T47.1X5	T47.1X6
Piretanide	T50.1X1	T50.1X2	T50.1X3	T50.1X4	T50.1X5	T50.1X6
Piribedil	T42.8X1	T42.8X2	T42.8X3	T42.8X4	T42.8X5	T42.8X6
Piridoxilate	T46.3X1	T46.3X2	T46.3X3	T46.3X4	T46.3X5	T46.3X6
Piritramide	T40.491	T40.492	T40.493	T40.494	—	—
Pirlindole	T43.0X1	T43.0X2	T43.0X3	T43.0X4	T43.0X5	T43.0X6
Piromidic acid	T37.8X1	T37.8X2	T37.8X3	T37.8X4	T37.8X5	T37.8X6
Piroxicam	T39.391	T39.392	T39.393	T39.394	T39.395	T39.396
beta-cyclodextrin complex	T39.8X1	T39.8X2	T39.8X3	T39.8X4	T39.8X5	T39.8X6
Pirozadil	T46.6X1	T46.6X2	T46.6X3	T46.6X4	T46.6X5	T46.6X6
Piscidia (bark) (erythrina)	T39.8X1	T39.8X2	T39.8X3	T39.8X4	T39.8X5	T39.8X6
Pitch	T65.891	T65.892	T65.893	T65.894	—	—
Pitkin's solution	T41.3X1	T41.3X2	T41.3X3	T41.3X4	T41.3X5	T41.3X6
Pitocin	T48.0X1	T48.0X2	T48.0X3	T48.0X4	T48.0X5	T48.0X6
Pitressin (tannate)	T38.891	T38.892	T38.893	T38.894	T38.895	T38.896
Pituitary extracts (posterior)	T38.891	T38.892	T38.893	T38.894	T38.895	T38.896
anterior	T38.811	T38.812	T38.813	T38.814	T38.815	T38.816
Pituitrin	T38.891	T38.892	T38.893	T38.894	T38.895	T38.896
Pivampicillin	T36.0X1	T36.0X2	T36.0X3	T36.0X4	T36.0X5	T36.0X6
Pivmecillinam	T36.0X1	T36.0X2	T36.0X3	T36.0X4	T36.0X5	T36.0X6
Placental hormone	T38.891	T38.892	T38.893	T38.894	T38.895	T38.896
Placidyl	T42.6X1	T42.6X2	T42.6X3	T42.6X4	T42.6X5	T42.6X6
Plague vaccine	T50.A91	T50.A92	T50.A93	T50.A94	T50.A95	T50.A96
Plant						
food or fertilizer NEC	T65.891	T65.892	T65.893	T65.894	—	—
containing herbicide	T60.3X1	T60.3X2	T60.3X3	T60.3X4	—	—
noxious, used as food	T62.2X1	T62.2X2	T62.2X3	T62.2X4	—	—
berries	T62.1X1	T62.1X2	T62.1X3	T62.1X4	—	—
seeds	T62.2X1	T62.2X2	T62.2X3	T62.2X4	—	—
specified type NEC	T62.2X1	T62.2X2	T62.2X3	T62.2X4	—	—
Plasma	T45.8X1	T45.8X2	T45.8X3	T45.8X4	T45.8X5	T45.8X6
expander NEC	T45.8X1	T45.8X2	T45.8X3	T45.8X4	T45.8X5	T45.8X6
protein fraction (human)	T45.8X1	T45.8X2	T45.8X3	T45.8X4	T45.8X5	T45.8X6

◀ New   ◀ Revised   ~~deleted~~ Deleted

Substance	Poisoning, Accidental (Unintentional)	Poisoning, Intentional Self-Harm	Poisoning, Assault	Poisoning, Undetermined	Adverse Effect	Underdosing
Plasmanate	T45.8X1	T45.8X2	T45.8X3	T45.8X4	T45.8X5	T45.8X6
Plasminogen (tissue) activator	T45.611	T45.612	T45.613	T45.614	T45.615	T45.616
Plaster dressing	T49.3X1	T49.3X2	T49.3X3	T49.3X4	T49.3X5	T49.3X6
Plastic dressing	T49.3X1	T49.3X2	T49.3X3	T49.3X4	T49.3X5	T49.3X6
Plegicil	T43.3X1	T43.3X2	T43.3X3	T43.3X4	T43.3X5	T43.3X6
Plicamycin	T45.1X1	T45.1X2	T45.1X3	T45.1X4	T45.1X5	T45.1X6
Podophyllotoxin	T49.8X1	T49.8X2	T49.8X3	T49.8X4	T49.8X5	T49.8X6
Podophyllum (resin)	T49.4X1	T49.4X2	T49.4X3	T49.4X4	T49.4X5	T49.4X6
Poison NEC	T65.91	T65.92	T65.93	T65.94	—	—
Poisonous berries	T62.1X1	T62.1X2	T62.1X3	T62.1X4	—	—
Pokeweed (any part)	T62.2X1	T62.2X2	T62.2X3	T62.2X4	—	—
Poldine metilsulfate	T44.3X1	T44.3X2	T44.3X3	T44.3X4	T44.3X5	T44.3X6
Polidexide (sulfate)	T46.6X1	T46.6X2	T46.6X3	T46.6X4	T46.6X5	T46.6X6
Polidocanol	T46.8X1	T46.8X2	T46.8X3	T46.8X4	T46.8X5	T46.8X6
Poliomyelitis vaccine	T50.B91	T50.B92	T50.B93	T50.B94	T50.B95	T50.B96
Polish (car) (floor) (furniture) (metal) (porcelain) (silver)	T65.891	T65.892	T65.893	T65.894	—	—
abrasive	T65.891	T65.892	T65.893	T65.894	—	—
porcelain	T65.891	T65.892	T65.893	T65.894	—	—
Poloxalkol	T47.4X1	T47.4X2	T47.4X3	T47.4X4	T47.4X5	T47.4X6
Poloxamer	T47.4X1	T47.4X2	T47.4X3	T47.4X4	T47.4X5	T47.4X6
Polyaminostyrene resins	T50.3X1	T50.3X2	T50.3X3	T50.3X4	T50.3X5	T50.3X6
Polycarbophil	T47.4X1	T47.4X2	T47.4X3	T47.4X4	T47.4X5	T47.4X6
Polychlorinated biphenyl	T65.891	T65.892	T65.893	T65.894	—	—
Polycycline	T36.4X1	T36.4X2	T36.4X3	T36.4X4	T36.4X5	T36.4X6
Polyester fumes	T59.891	T59.892	T59.893	T59.894	—	—
Polyester resin hardener	T52.91	T52.92	T52.93	T52.94	—	—
fumes	T59.891	T59.892	T59.893	T59.894	—	—
Polyestradiol phosphate	T38.5X1	T38.5X2	T38.5X3	T38.5X4	T38.5X5	T38.5X6
Polyethanolamine alkyl sulfate	T49.2X1	T49.2X2	T49.2X3	T49.2X4	T49.2X5	T49.2X6
Polyethylene adhesive	T49.3X1	T49.3X2	T49.3X3	T49.3X4	T49.3X5	T49.3X6
Polyferose	T45.4X1	T45.4X2	T45.4X3	T45.4X4	T45.4X5	T45.4X6
Polygeline	T45.8X1	T45.8X2	T45.8X3	T45.8X4	T45.8X5	T45.8X6
Polymyxin	T36.8X1	T36.8X2	T36.8X3	T36.8X4	T36.8X5	T36.8X6
B	T36.8X1	T36.8X2	T36.8X3	T36.8X4	T36.8X5	T36.8X6
ENT agent	T49.6X1	T49.6X2	T49.6X3	T49.6X4	T49.6X5	T49.6X6
ophthalmic preparation	T49.5X1	T49.5X2	T49.5X3	T49.5X4	T49.5X5	T49.5X6
topical NEC	T49.0X1	T49.0X2	T49.0X3	T49.0X4	T49.0X5	T49.0X6
E sulfate (eye preparation)	T49.5X1	T49.5X2	T49.5X3	T49.5X4	T49.5X5	T49.5X6
Polynoxylin	T49.0X1	T49.0X2	T49.0X3	T49.0X4	T49.0X5	T49.0X6
Polyoestradiol phosphate	T38.5X1	T38.5X2	T38.5X3	T38.5X4	T38.5X5	T38.5X6
Polyoxymethyleneurea	T49.0X1	T49.0X2	T49.0X3	T49.0X4	T49.0X5	T49.0X6

Substance	Poisoning, Accidental (Unintentional)	Poisoning, Intentional Self-Harm	Poisoning, Assault	Poisoning, Undetermined	Adverse Effect	Underdosing
Polysilane	T47.8X1	T47.8X2	T47.8X3	T47.8X4	T47.8X5	T47.8X6
Polytetrafluoroethylene (inhaled)	T59.891	T59.892	T59.893	T59.894	—	—
Polythiazide	T50.2X1	T50.2X2	T50.2X3	T50.2X4	T50.2X5	T50.2X6
Polyvidone	T45.8X1	T45.8X2	T45.8X3	T45.8X4	T45.8X5	T45.8X6
Polyvinylpyrrolidone	T45.8X1	T45.8X2	T45.8X3	T45.8X4	T45.8X5	T45.8X6
Pontocaine (hydrochloride) (infiltration) (topical)	T41.3X1	T41.3X2	T41.3X3	T41.3X4	T41.3X5	T41.3X6
nerve block (peripheral) (plexus)	T41.3X1	T41.3X2	T41.3X3	T41.3X4	T41.3X5	T41.3X6
spinal	T41.3X1	T41.3X2	T41.3X3	T41.3X4	T41.3X5	T41.3X6
Porfiromycin	T45.1X1	T45.1X2	T45.1X3	T45.1X4	T45.1X5	T45.1X6
Posterior pituitary hormone NEC	T38.891	T38.892	T38.893	T38.894	T38.895	T38.896
Pot	T40.7X1	T40.7X2	T40.7X3	T40.7X4	T40.7X5	T40.7X6
Potash (caustic)	T54.3X1	T54.3X2	T54.3X3	T54.3X4	—	—
Potassic saline injection (lactated)	T50.3X1	T50.3X2	T50.3X3	T50.3X4	T50.3X5	T50.3X6
Potassium (salts) NEC	T50.3X1	T50.3X2	T50.3X3	T50.3X4	T50.3X5	T50.3X6
aminobenzoate	T45.8X1	T45.8X2	T45.8X3	T45.8X4	T45.8X5	T45.8X6
aminosalicylate	T37.1X1	T37.1X2	T37.1X3	T37.1X4	T37.1X5	T37.1X6
antimony 'tartrate'	T37.8X1	T37.8X2	T37.8X3	T37.8X4	T37.8X5	T37.8X6
arsenite (solution)	T57.0X1	T57.0X2	T57.0X3	T57.0X4	—	—
bichromate	T56.2X1	T56.2X2	T56.2X3	T56.2X4	—	—
bisulfate	T47.3X1	T47.3X2	T47.3X3	T47.3X4	T47.3X5	T47.3X6
bromide	T42.6X1	T42.6X2	T42.6X4	T42.6X4	T42.6X5	T42.6X6
canrenoate	T50.0X1	T50.0X2	T50.0X3	T50.0X4	T50.0X5	T50.0X6
carbonate	T54.3X1	T54.3X2	T54.3X3	T54.3X4	—	—
chlorate NEC	T65.891	T65.892	T65.893	T65.894	—	—
chloride	T50.3X1	T50.3X2	T50.3X3	T50.3X4	T50.3X5	T50.3X6
citrate	T50.991	T50.992	T50.993	T50.994	T50.995	T50.996
cyanide	T65.0X1	T65.0X2	T65.0X3	T65.0X4	—	—
ferric hexacyanoferrate (medicinal)	T50.6X1	T50.6X2	T50.6X3	T50.6X4	T50.6X5	T50.6X6
nonmedicinal	T65.891	T65.892	T65.893	T65.894	—	—
Fluoride	T57.8X1	T57.8X2	T57.8X3	T57.8X4	—	—
glucaldrate	T47.1X1	T47.1X2	T47.1X3	T47.1X4	T47.1X5	T47.1X6
hydroxide	T54.3X1	T54.3X2	T54.3X3	T54.3X4	—	—
iodate	T49.0X1	T49.0X2	T49.0X3	T49.0X4	T49.0X5	T49.0X6
iodide	T48.4X1	T48.4X2	T48.4X3	T48.4X4	T48.4X5	T48.4X6
nitrate	T57.8X1	T57.8X2	T57.8X3	T57.8X4	—	—
oxalate	T65.891	T65.892	T65.893	T65.894	—	—
perchlorate (nonmedicinal) NEC	T65.891	T65.892	T65.893	T65.894	—	—
antithyroid	T38.2X1	T38.2X2	T38.2X3	T38.2X4	T38.2X5	T38.2X6
medicinal	T38.2X1	T38.2X2	T38.2X3	T38.2X4	T38.2X5	T38.2X6

◀ New　◀◀ Revised　~~deleted~~ Deleted

Substance	External Cause (T-Code)					
	Poisoning, Accidental (Unintentional)	Poisoning, Intentional Self-Harm	Poisoning, Assault	Poisoning, Undetermined	Adverse Effect	Underdosing
Permanganate (nonmedicinal)	T65.891	T65.892	T65.893	T65.894	—	—
medicinal	T49.0X1	T49.0X2	T49.0X3	T49.0X4	T49.0X5	T49.0X6
sulfate	T47.2X1	T47.2X2	T47.2X3	T47.2X4	T47.2X5	T47.2X6
Potassium-removing resin	T50.3X1	T50.3X2	T50.3X3	T50.3X4	T50.3X5	T50.3X6
Potassium-retaining drug	T50.3X1	T50.3X2	T50.3X3	T50.3X4	T50.3X5	T50.3X6
Povidone	T45.8X1	T45.8X2	T45.8X3	T45.8X4	T45.8X5	T45.8X6
iodine	T49.0X1	T49.0X2	T49.0X3	T49.0X4	T49.0X5	T49.0X6
Practolol	T44.7X1	T44.7X2	T44.7X3	T44.7X4	T44.7X5	T44.7X6
Prajmalium bitartrate	T46.2X1	T46.2X2	T46.2X3	T46.2X4	T46.2X5	T46.2X6
Pralidoxime (iodide)	T50.6X1	T50.6X2	T50.6X3	T50.6X4	T50.6X5	T50.6X6
chloride	T50.6X1	T50.6X2	T50.6X3	T50.6X4	T50.6X5	T50.6X6
Pramiverine	T44.3X1	T44.3X2	T44.3X3	T44.3X4	T44.3X5	T44.3X6
Pramocaine	T49.1X1	T49.1X2	T49.1X3	T49.1X4	T49.1X5	T49.1X6
Pramoxine	T49.1X1	T49.1X2	T49.1X3	T49.1X4	T49.1X5	T49.1X6
Prasterone	T38.7X1	T38.7X2	T38.7X3	T38.7X4	T38.7X5	T38.7X6
Pravastatin	T46.6X1	T46.6X2	T46.6X3	T46.6X4	T46.6X5	T46.6X6
Prazepam	T42.4X1	T42.4X2	T42.4X3	T42.4X4	T42.4X5	T42.4X6
Praziquantel	T37.4X1	T37.4X2	T37.4X3	T37.4X4	T37.4X5	T37.4X6
Prazitone	T43.291	T43.292	T43.293	T43.294	T43.295	T43.296
Prazosin	T44.6X1	T44.6X2	T44.6X3	T44.6X4	T44.6X5	T44.6X6
Prednicarbate	T49.0X1	T49.0X2	T49.0X3	T49.0X4	T49.0X5	T49.0X6
Prednimustine	T45.1X1	T45.1X2	T45.1X3	T45.1X4	T45.1X5	T45.1X6
Prednisolone	T38.0X1	T38.0X2	T38.0X3	T38.0X4	T38.0X5	T38.0X6
ENT agent	T49.6X1	T49.6X2	T49.6X3	T49.6X4	T49.6X5	T49.6X6
ophthalmic preparation	T49.5X1	T49.5X2	T49.5X3	T49.5X4	T49.5X5	T49.5X6
steaglate	T49.0X1	T49.0X2	T49.0X3	T49.0X4	T49.0X5	T49.0X6
topical NEC	T49.0X1	T49.0X2	T49.0X3	T49.0X4	T49.0X5	T49.0X6
Prednisone	T38.0X1	T38.0X2	T38.0X3	T38.0X4	T38.0X5	T38.0X6
Prednylidene	T38.0X1	T38.0X2	T38.0X3	T38.0X4	T38.0X5	T38.0X6
Pregnandiol	T38.5X1	T38.5X2	T38.5X3	T38.5X4	T38.5X5	T38.5X6
Pregneninolone	T38.5X1	T38.5X2	T38.5X3	T38.5X4	T38.5X5	T38.5X6
Preludin	T43.691	T43.692	T43.693	T43.694	T43.695	T43.696
Premarin	T38.5X1	T38.5X2	T38.5X3	T38.5X4	T38.5X5	T38.5X6
Premedication anesthetic	T41.201	T41.202	T41.203	T41.204	T41.205	T41.206
Prenalterol	T44.5X1	T44.5X2	T44.5X3	T44.5X4	T44.5X5	T44.5X6
Prenoxdiazine	T48.3X1	T48.3X2	T48.3X3	T48.3X4	T48.3X5	T48.3X6
Prenylamine	T46.3X1	T46.3X2	T46.3X3	T46.3X4	T46.3X5	T46.3X6
Preparation, local	T49.4X1	T49.4X2	T49.4X3	T49.4X4	T49.4X5	T49.4X6
Preparation H	T49.8X1	T49.8X2	T49.8X3	T49.8X4	T49.8X5	T49.8X6
Preservative (nonmedicinal)	T65.891	T65.892	T65.893	T65.894	—	—
medicinal	T50.901	T50.902	T50.903	T50.904	T50.905	T50.906
wood	T60.91	T60.92	T60.93	T60.94	—	—

Substance	External Cause (T-Code)					
	Poisoning, Accidental (Unintentional)	Poisoning, Intentional Self-Harm	Poisoning, Assault	Poisoning, Undetermined	Adverse Effect	Underdosing
Prethcamide	T50.7X1	T50.7X2	T50.7X3	T50.7X4	T50.7X5	T50.7X6
Pride of China	T62.2X1	T62.2X2	T62.2X3	T62.2X4	—	—
Pridinol	T44.3X1	T44.3X2	T44.3X3	T44.3X4	T44.3X5	T44.3X6
Prifinium bromide	T44.3X1	T44.3X2	T44.3X3	T44.3X4	T44.3X5	T44.3X6
Prilocaine	T41.3X1	T41.3X2	T41.3X3	T41.3X4	T41.3X5	T41.3X6
infiltration (subcutaneous)	T41.3X1	T41.3X2	T41.3X3	T41.3X4	T41.3X5	T41.3X6
nerve block (peripheral) (plexus)	T41.3X1	T41.3X2	T41.3X3	T41.3X4	T41.3X5	T41.3X6
regional	T41.3X1	T41.3X2	T41.3X3	T41.3X4	T41.3X5	T41.3X6
Primaquine	T37.2X1	T37.2X2	T37.2X3	T37.2X4	T37.2X5	T37.2X6
Primidone	T42.6X1	T42.6X2	T42.6X3	T42.6X4	T42.6X5	T42.6X6
Primula (veris)	T62.2X1	T62.2X2	T62.2X3	T62.2X4	—	—
Prinadol	T40.2X1	T40.2X2	T40.2X3	T40.2X4	T40.2X5	T40.2X6
Priscol, Priscoline	T44.6X1	T44.6X2	T44.6X3	T44.6X4	T44.6X5	T44.6X6
Pristinamycin	T36.3X1	T36.3X2	T36.3X3	T36.3X4	T36.3X5	T36.3X6
Privet	T62.2X1	T62.2X2	T62.2X3	T62.2X4	—	—
berries	T62.1X1	T62.1X2	T62.1X3	T62.1X4	—	—
Privine	T44.4X1	T44.4X2	T44.4X3	T44.4X4	T44.4X5	T44.4X6
Pro-Banthine	T44.3X1	T44.3X2	T44.3X3	T44.3X4	T44.3X5	T44.3X6
Probarbital	T42.3X1	T42.3X2	T42.3X3	T42.3X4	T42.3X5	T42.3X6
Probenecid	T50.4X1	T50.4X2	T50.4X3	T50.4X4	T50.4X5	T50.4X6
Probucol	T46.6X1	T46.6X2	T46.6X3	T46.6X4	T46.6X5	T46.6X6
Procainamide	T46.2X1	T46.2X2	T46.2X3	T46.2X4	T46.2X5	T46.2X6
Procaine	T41.3X1	T41.3X2	T41.3X3	T41.3X4	T41.3X5	T41.3X6
benzylpenicillin	T36.0X1	T36.0X2	T36.0X3	T36.0X4	T36.0X5	T36.0X6
nerve block (periphreal) (plexus)	T41.3X1	T41.3X2	T41.3X3	T41.3X4	T41.3X5	T41.3X6
penicillin G	T36.0X1	T36.0X2	T36.0X3	T36.0X4	T36.0X5	T36.0X6
regional	T41.3X1	T41.3X2	T41.3X3	T41.3X4	T41.3X5	T41.3X6
spinal	T41.3X1	T41.3X2	T41.3X3	T41.3X4	T41.3X5	T41.3X6
Procalmidol	T43.591	T43.592	T43.593	T43.594	T43.595	T43.596
Procarbazine	T45.1X1	T45.1X2	T45.1X3	T45.1X4	T45.1X5	T45.1X6
Procaterol	T44.5X1	T44.5X2	T44.5X3	T44.5X4	T44.5X5	T44.5X6
Prochlorperazine	T43.3X1	T43.3X2	T43.3X3	T43.3X4	T43.3X5	T43.3X6
Procyclidine	T44.3X1	T44.3X2	T44.3X3	T44.3X4	T44.3X5	T44.3X6
Producer gas	T58.8X1	T58.8X2	T58.8X3	T58.8X4	—	—
Profadol	T40.491	T40.492	T40.493	T40.494	T40.495	T40.496
Profenamine	T44.3X1	T44.3X2	T44.3X3	T44.3X4	T44.3X5	T44.3X6
Profenil	T44.3X1	T44.3X2	T44.3X3	T44.3X4	T44.3X5	T44.3X6
Proflavine	T49.0X1	T49.0X2	T49.0X3	T49.0X4	T49.0X5	T49.0X6
Progabide	T42.6X1	T42.6X2	T42.6X3	T42.6X4	T42.6X5	T42.6X6
Progestin	T38.5X1	T38.5X2	T38.5X3	T38.5X4	T38.5X5	T38.5X6
oral contraceptive	T38.4X1	T38.4X2	T38.4X3	T38.4X4	T38.4X5	T38.4X6

◄ New ◄ Revised ~~deleted~~ Deleted

	External Cause (T-Code)					
Substance	Poisoning, Accidental (Unintentional)	Poisoning, Intentional Self-Harm	Poisoning, Assault	Poisoning, Undetermined	Adverse Effect	Underdosing
Progesterone	T38.5X1	T38.5X2	T38.5X3	T38.5X4	T38.5X5	T38.5X6
Progestogen NEC	T38.5X1	T38.5X2	T38.5X3	T38.5X4	T38.5X5	T38.5X6
Progestone	T38.5X1	T38.5X2	T38.5X3	T38.5X4	T38.5X5	T38.5X6
Proglumide	T47.1X1	T47.1X2	T47.1X3	T47.1X4	T47.1X5	T47.1X6
Proguanil	T37.2X1	T37.2X2	T37.2X3	T37.2X4	T37.2X5	T37.2X6
Prolactin	T38.811	T38.812	T38.813	T38.814	T38.815	T38.816
Prolintane	T43.691	T43.692	T43.693	T43.694	T43.695	T43.696
Proloid	T38.1X1	T38.1X2	T38.1X3	T38.1X4	T38.1X5	T38.1X6
Proluton	T38.5X1	T38.5X2	T38.5X3	T38.5X4	T38.5X5	T38.5X6
Promacetin	T37.1X1	T37.1X2	T37.1X3	T37.1X4	T37.1X5	T37.1X6
Promazine	T43.3X1	T43.3X2	T43.3X3	T43.3X4	T43.3X5	T43.3X6
Promedol	T40.2X1	T40.2X2	T40.2X3	T40.2X4	—	—
Promegestone	T38.5X1	T38.5X2	T38.5X3	T38.5X4	T38.5X5	T38.5X6
Promethazine (teoclate)	T43.3X1	T43.3X2	T43.3X3	T43.3X4	T43.3X5	T43.3X6
Promin	T37.1X1	T37.1X2	T37.1X3	T37.1X4	T37.1X5	T37.1X6
Pronase	T45.3X1	T45.3X2	T45.3X3	T45.3X4	T45.3X5	T45.3X6
Pronestyl (hydrochloride)	T46.2X1	T46.2X2	T46.2X3	T46.2X4	T46.2X5	T46.2X6
Pronetalol	T44.7X1	T44.7X2	T44.7X3	T44.7X4	T44.7X5	T44.7X6
Prontosil	T37.0X1	T37.0X2	T37.0X3	T37.0X4	T37.0X5	T37.0X6
Propachlor	T60.3X1	T60.3X2	T60.3X3	T60.3X4	—	—
Propafenone	T46.2X1	T46.2X2	T46.2X3	T46.2X4	T46.2X5	T46.2X6
Propallylonal	T42.3X1	T42.3X2	T42.3X3	T42.3X4	T42.3X5	T42.3X6
Propamidine	T49.0X1	T49.0X2	T49.0X3	T49.0X4	T49.0X5	T49.0X6
Propane (distributed in mobile container)	T59.891	T59.892	T59.893	T59.894	—	—
distributed through pipes	T59.891	T59.892	T59.893	T59.894	—	—
incomplete combustion	T57.11	T57.12	T57.13	T57.14	—	—
Propanidid	T41.291	T41.292	T41.293	T41.294	T41.295	T41.296
Propanil	T60.3X1	T60.3X2	T60.3X3	T60.3X4	—	—
1-Propanol	T51.3X1	T51.3X2	T51.3X3	T51.3X4	—	—
2-Propanol	T51.2X1	T51.2X2	T51.2X3	T51.2X4	—	—
Propantheline	T44.3X1	T44.3X2	T44.3X3	T44.3X4	T44.3X5	T44.3X6
bromide	T44.3X1	T44.3X2	T44.3X3	T44.3X4	T44.3X5	T44.3X6
Proparacaine	T41.3X1	T41.3X2	T41.3X3	T41.3X4	T41.3X5	T41.3X6
Propatylnitrate	T46.3X1	T46.3X2	T46.3X3	T46.3X4	T46.3X5	T46.3X6
Propicillin	T36.0X1	T36.0X2	T36.0X3	T36.0X4	T36.0X5	T36.0X6
Propiolactone	T49.0X1	T49.0X2	T49.0X3	T49.0X4	T49.0X5	T49.0X6
Propiomazine	T45.0X1	T45.0X2	T45.0X3	T45.0X4	T45.0X5	T45.0X6
Propionaldehyde (medicinal)	T42.6X1	T42.6X2	T42.6X3	T42.6X4	T42.6X5	T42.6X6
Propionate (calcium) (sodium)	T49.0X1	T49.0X2	T49.0X3	T49.0X4	T49.0X5	T49.0X6
Propion gel	T49.0X1	T49.0X2	T49.0X3	T49.0X4	T49.0X5	T49.0X6

	External Cause (T-Code)					
Substance	Poisoning, Accidental (Unintentional)	Poisoning, Intentional Self-Harm	Poisoning, Assault	Poisoning, Undetermined	Adverse Effect	Underdosing
Propitocaine	T41.3X1	T41.3X2	T41.3X3	T41.3X4	T41.3X5	T41.3X6
infiltration (subcutaneous)	T41.3X1	T41.3X2	T41.3X3	T41.3X4	T41.3X5	T41.3X6
nerve block (peripheral) (plexus)	T41.3X1	T41.3X2	T41.3X3	T41.3X4	T41.3X5	T41.3X6
Propofol	T41.291	T41.292	T41.293	T41.294	T41.295	T41.296
Propoxur	T60.0X1	T60.0X2	T60.0X3	T60.0X4	—	—
Propoxycaine	T41.3X1	T41.3X2	T41.3X3	T41.3X4	T41.3X5	T41.3X6
infiltration (subcutaneous)	T41.3X1	T41.3X2	T41.3X3	T41.3X4	T41.3X5	T41.3X6
nerve block (peripheral) (plexus)	T41.3X1	T41.3X2	T41.3X3	T41.3X4	T41.3X5	T41.3X6
topical (surface)	T41.3X1	T41.3X2	T41.3X3	T41.3X4	T41.3X5	T41.3X6
Propoxyphene	T40.491	T40.492	T40.493	T40.494	T40.495	T40.496
Propranolol	T44.7X1	T44.7X2	T44.7X3	T44.7X4	T44.7X5	T44.7X6
Propyl						
alcohol	T51.3X1	T51.3X2	T51.3X3	T51.3X4	—	—
carbinol	T51.3X1	T51.3X2	T51.3X3	T51.3X4	—	—
hexadrine	T44.4X1	T44.4X2	T44.4X3	T44.4X4	T44.4X5	T44.4X6
iodone	T50.8X1	T50.8X2	T50.8X3	T50.8X4	T50.8X5	T50.8X6
thiouracil	T38.2X1	T38.2X2	T38.2X3	T38.2X4	T38.2X5	T38.2X6
Propylaminophenothiazine	T43.3X1	T43.3X2	T43.3X3	T43.3X4	T43.3X5	T43.3X6
Propylene	T59.891	T59.892	T59.893	T59.894	—	—
Propylhexedrine	T48.5X1	T48.5X2	T48.5X3	T48.5X4	T48.5X5	T48.5X6
Propyliodone	T50.8X1	T50.8X2	T50.8X3	T50.8X4	T50.8X5	T50.8X6
Propylthiouracil	T38.2X1	T38.2X2	T38.2X3	T38.2X4	T38.2X5	T38.2X6
Propylparaben (ophthalmic)	T49.5X1	T49.5X2	T49.5X3	T49.5X4	T49.5X5	T49.5X6
Propyphenazone	T39.2X1	T39.2X2	T39.2X3	T39.2X4	T39.2X5	T39.2X6
Proquazone	T39.391	T39.392	T39.393	T39.394	T39.395	T39.396
Proscillaridin	T46.0X1	T46.0X2	T46.0X3	T46.0X4	T46.0X5	T46.0X6
Prostacyclin	T45.521	T45.522	T45.523	T45.524	T45.525	T45.526
Prostaglandin (I2)	T45.521	T45.522	T45.523	T45.524	T45.525	T45.526
E1	T46.7X1	T46.7X2	T46.7X3	T46.7X4	T46.7X5	T46.7X6
E2	T48.0X1	T48.0X2	T48.0X3	T48.0X4	T48.0X5	T48.0X6
F2 alpha	T48.0X1	T48.0X2	T48.0X3	T48.0X4	T48.0X5	T48.0X6
Prostigmin	T44.0X1	T44.0X2	T44.0X3	T44.0X4	T44.0X5	T44.0X6
Prosultiamine	T45.2X1	T45.2X2	T45.2X3	T45.2X4	T45.2X5	T45.2X6
Protamine sulfate	T45.7X1	T45.7X2	T45.7X3	T45.7X4	T45.7X5	T45.7X6
zinc insulin	T38.3X1	T38.3X2	T38.3X3	T38.3X4	T38.3X5	T38.3X6
Protease	T47.5X1	T47.5X2	T47.5X3	T47.5X4	T47.5X5	T47.5X6
Protectant, skin NEC	T49.3X1	T49.3X2	T49.3X3	T49.3X4	T49.3X5	T49.3X6
Protein hydrolysate	T50.991	T50.992	T50.993	T50.994	T50.995	T50.996
Prothiaden — see Dothiepin hydrochloride						
Prothionamide	T37.1X1	T37.1X2	T37.1X3	T37.1X4	T37.1X5	T37.1X6

◀ New ◀ Revised deleted Deleted

Substance	Poisoning, Accidental (Unintentional)	Poisoning, Intentional Self-Harm	Poisoning, Assault	Poisoning, Undetermined	Adverse Effect	Underdosing
			External Cause (T-Code)			
Prothipendyl	T43.591	T43.592	T43.593	T43.594	T43.595	T43.596
Prothoate	T60.0X1	T60.0X2	T60.0X3	T60.0X4	—	—
Prothrombin						
activator	T45.7X1	T45.7X2	T45.7X3	T45.7X4	T45.7X5	T45.7X6
synthesis inhibitor	T45.511	T45.512	T45.513	T45.514	T45.515	T45.516
Protionamide	T37.1X1	T37.1X2	T37.1X3	T37.1X4	T37.1X5	T37.1X6
Protirelin	T38.891	T38.892	T38.893	T38.894	T38.895	T38.896
Protokylol	T48.6X1	T48.6X2	T48.6X3	T48.6X4	T48.6X5	T48.6X6
Protopam	T50.6X1	T50.6X2	T50.6X3	T50.6X4	T50.6X5	T50.6X6
Protoveratrine(s) (A) (B)	T46.5X1	T46.5X2	T46.5X3	T46.5X4	T46.5X5	T46.5X6
Protriptyline	T43.011	T43.012	T43.013	T43.014	T43.015	T43.016
Provera	T38.5X1	T38.5X2	T38.5X3	T38.5X4	T38.5X5	T38.5X6
Provitamin A	T45.2X1	T45.2X2	T45.2X3	T45.2X4	T45.2X5	T45.2X6
Proxibarbal	T42.3X1	T42.3X2	T42.3X3	T42.3X4	T42.3X5	T42.3X6
Proxymetacaine	T41.3X1	T41.3X2	T41.3X3	T41.3X4	T41.3X5	T41.3X6
Proxyphylline	T48.6X1	T48.6X2	T48.6X3	T48.6X4	T48.6X5	T48.6X6
Prozac — *see Fluoxetine hydrochloride*						
Prunus						
laurocerasus	T62.2X1	T62.2X2	T62.2X3	T62.2X4	—	—
virginiana	T62.2X1	T62.2X2	T62.2X3	T62.2X4	—	—
Prussian blue						
commercial	T65.891	T65.892	T65.893	T65.894	—	—
therapeutic	T50.6X1	T50.6X2	T50.6X3	T50.6X4	T50.6X5	T50.6X6
Prussic acid	T65.0X1	T65.0X2	T65.0X3	T65.0X4	—	—
vapor	T57.3X1	T57.3X2	T57.3X3	T57.3X4	—	—
Pseudoephedrine	T44.991	T44.992	T44.993	T44.994	T44.995	T44.996
Psilocin	T40.991	T40.992	T40.993	T40.994		
Psilocybin	T40.991	T40.992	T40.993	T40.994	—	—
Psilocybine	T40.991	T40.992	T40.993	T40.994	—	—
Psoralene (nonmedicinal)	T65.891	T65.892	T65.893	T65.894	—	—
Psoralens (medicinal)	T50.991	T50.992	T50.993	T50.994	T50.995	T50.996
PSP (phenolsulfonphthalein)	T50.8X1	T50.8X2	T50.8X3	T50.8X4	T50.8X5	T50.8X6
Psychodysleptic drug NOS	T40.901	T40.902	T40.903	T40.904	T40.905	T40.906
specified NEC	T40.991	T40.992	T40.993	T40.994	T40.995	T40.996
Psychostimulant	T43.601	T43.602	T43.603	T43.604	T43.605	T43.606
amphetamine	T43.621	T43.622	T43.623	T43.624	T43.625	T43.626
caffeine	T43.611	T43.612	T43.613	T43.614	T43.615	T43.616
methylphenidate	T43.631	T43.632	T43.633	T43.634	T43.635	T43.636
specified NEC	T43.691	T43.692	T43.693	T43.694	T43.695	T43.696
Psychotherapeutic drug NEC	T43.91	T43.92	T43.93	T43.94	T43.95	T43.96
antidepressants — *see also Antidepressant*	T43.201	T43.202	T43.203	T43.204	T43.205	T43.206

Substance	Poisoning, Accidental (Unintentional)	Poisoning, Intentional Self-Harm	Poisoning, Assault	Poisoning, Undetermined	Adverse Effect	Underdosing
			External Cause (T-Code)			
Psychotherapeutic drug NEC *(Continued)*						
specified NEC	T43.8X1	T43.8X2	T43.8X3	T43.8X4	T43.8X5	T43.8X6
tranquilizers NEC	T43.501	T43.502	T43.503	T43.504	T43.505	T43.506
Psychotomimetic agents	T40.901	T40.902	T40.903	T40.904	T40.905	T40.906
Psychotropic drug NEC	T43.91	T43.92	T43.93	T43.94	T43.95	T43.96
specified NEC	T43.8X1	T43.8X2	T43.8X3	T43.8X4	T43.8X5	T43.8X6
Psyllium hydrophilic mucilloid	T47.4X1	T47.4X2	T47.4X3	T47.4X4	T47.4X5	T47.4X6
Pteroylglutamic acid	T45.8X1	T45.8X2	T45.8X3	T45.8X4	T45.8X5	T45.8X6
Pteroyltriglutamate	T45.1X1	T45.1X2	T45.1X3	T45.1X4	T45.1X5	T45.1X6
PTFE — *see Polytetrafluoroethylene*						
Pulp						
devitalizing paste	T49.7X1	T49.7X2	T49.7X3	T49.7X4	T49.7X5	T49.7X6
dressing	T49.7X1	T49.7X2	T49.7X3	T49.7X4	T49.7X5	T49.7X6
Pulsatilla	T62.2X1	T62.2X2	T62.2X3	T62.2X4	—	—
Pumpkin seed extract	T37.4X1	T37.4X2	T37.4X3	T37.4X4	T37.4X5	T37.4X6
Purex (bleach)	T54.91	T54.92	T54.93	T54.94	—	—
Purgative NEC — *see also Cathartic*	T47.4X1	T47.4X2	T47.4X3	T47.4X4	T47.4X5	T47.4X6
Purine analogue (antineoplastic)	T45.1X1	T45.1X2	T45.1X3	T45.1X4	T45.1X5	T45.1X6
Purine diuretics	T50.2X1	T50.2X2	T50.2X3	T50.2X4	T50.2X5	T50.2X6
Purinethol	T45.1X1	T45.1X2	T45.1X3	T45.1X4	T45.1X5	T45.1X6
PVP	T45.8X1	T45.8X2	T45.8X3	T45.8X4	T45.8X5	T45.8X6
Pyrabital	T39.8X1	T39.8X2	T39.8X3	T39.8X4	T39.8X5	T39.8X6
Pyramidon	T39.2X1	T39.2X2	T39.2X3	T39.2X4	T39.2X5	T39.2X6
Pyrantel	T37.4X1	T37.4X2	T37.4X3	T37.4X4	T37.4X5	T37.4X6
Pyrathiazine	T45.0X1	T45.0X2	T45.0X3	T45.0X4	T45.0X5	T45.0X6
Pyrazinamide	T37.1X1	T37.1X2	T37.1X3	T37.1X4	T37.1X5	T37.1X6
Pyrazinoic acid (amide)	T37.1X1	T37.1X2	T37.1X3	T37.1X4	T37.1X5	T37.1X6
Pyrazole (derivatives)	T39.2X1	T39.2X2	T39.2X3	T39.2X4	T39.2X5	T39.2X6
Pyrazolone analgesic NEC	T39.2X1	T39.2X2	T39.2X3	T39.2X4	T39.2X5	T39.2X6
Pyrethrin, pyrethrum (nonmedicinal)	T60.2X1	T60.2X2	T60.2X3	T60.2X4	—	—
Pyrethrum extract	T49.0X1	T49.0X2	T49.0X3	T49.0X4	T49.0X5	T49.0X6
Pyribenzamine	T45.0X1	T45.0X2	T45.0X3	T45.0X4	T45.0X5	T45.0X6
Pyridine	T52.8X1	T52.8X2	T52.8X3	T52.8X4	—	—
aldoxime methiodide	T50.6X1	T50.6X2	T50.6X3	T50.6X4	T50.6X5	T50.6X6
aldoxime methyl chloride	T50.6X1	T50.6X2	T50.6X3	T50.6X4	T50.6X5	T50.6X6
vapor	T59.891	T59.892	T59.893	T59.894	—	—
Pyridium	T39.8X1	T39.8X2	T39.8X3	T39.8X4	T39.8X5	T39.8X6
Pyridostigmine bromide	T44.0X1	T44.0X2	T44.0X3	T44.0X4	T44.0X5	T44.0X6
Pyridoxal phosphate	T45.2X1	T45.2X2	T45.2X3	T45.2X4	T45.2X5	T45.2X6

Substance	Poisoning, Accidental (Unintentional)	Poisoning, Intentional Self-Harm	Poisoning, Assault	Poisoning, Undetermined	Adverse Effect	Underdosing
Pyridoxine	T45.2X1	T45.2X2	T45.2X3	T45.2X4	T45.2X5	T45.2X6
Pyrilamine	T45.0X1	T45.0X2	T45.0X3	T45.0X4	T45.0X5	T45.0X6
Pyrimethamine	T37.2X1	T37.2X2	T37.2X3	T37.2X4	T37.2X5	T37.2X6
with sulfadoxine	T37.2X1	T37.2X2	T37.2X3	T37.2X4	T37.2X5	T37.2X6
Pyrimidine antagonist	T45.1X1	T45.1X2	T45.1X3	T45.1X4	T45.1X5	T45.1X6
Pyriminil	T60.4X1	T60.4X2	T60.4X3	T60.4X4	—	—
Pyrithione zinc	T49.4X1	T49.4X2	T49.4X3	T49.4X4	T49.4X5	T49.4X6
Pyrithyldione	T42.6X1	T42.6X2	T42.6X3	T42.6X4	T42.6X5	T42.6X6
Pyrogallic acid	T49.0X1	T49.0X2	T49.0X3	T49.0X4	T49.0X5	T49.0X6
Pyrogallol	T49.0X1	T49.0X2	T49.0X3	T49.0X4	T49.0X5	T49.0X6
Pyroxylin	T49.3X1	T49.3X2	T49.3X3	T49.3X4	T49.3X5	T49.3X6
Pyrrobutamine	T45.0X1	T45.0X2	T45.0X3	T45.0X4	T45.0X5	T45.0X6
Pyrrolizidine alkaloids	T62.8X1	T62.8X2	T62.8X3	T62.8X4	—	—
Pyrvinium chloride	T37.4X1	T37.4X2	T37.4X3	T37.4X4	T37.4X5	T37.4X6
PZI	T38.3X1	T38.3X2	T38.3X3	T38.3X4	T38.3X5	T38.3X6
Q						
Quaalude	T42.6X1	T42.6X2	T42.6X3	T42.6X4	T42.6X5	T42.6X6
Quarternary ammonium						
anti-infective	T49.0X1	T49.0X2	T49.0X3	T49.0X4	T49.0X5	T49.0X6
ganglion blocking	T44.2X1	T44.2X2	T44.2X3	T44.2X4	T44.2X5	T44.2X6
parasympatholytic	T44.3X1	T44.3X2	T44.3X3	T44.3X4	T44.3X5	T44.3X6
Quazepam	T42.4X1	T42.4X2	T42.4X3	T42.4X4	T42.4X5	T42.4X6
Quicklime	T54.3X1	T54.3X2	T54.3X3	T54.3X4	—	—
Quillaja extract	T48.4X1	T48.4X2	T48.4X3	T48.4X4	T48.4X5	T48.4X6
Quinacrine	T37.2X1	T37.2X2	T37.2X3	T37.2X4	T37.2X5	T37.2X6
Quinaglute	T46.2X1	T46.2X2	T46.2X3	T46.2X4	T46.2X5	T46.2X6
Quinalbarbital	T42.3X1	T42.3X2	T42.3X3	T42.3X4	T42.3X5	T42.3X6
Quinalbarbitone sodium	T42.3X1	T42.3X2	T42.3X3	T42.3X4	T42.3X5	T42.3X6
Quinalphos	T60.0X1	T60.0X2	T60.0X3	T60.0X4	—	—
Quinapril	T46.4X1	T46.4X2	T46.4X3	T46.4X4	T46.4X5	T46.4X6
Quinestradiol	T38.5X1	T38.5X2	T38.5X3	T38.5X4	T38.5X5	T38.5X6
Quinestradol	T38.5X1	T38.5X2	T38.5X3	T38.5X4	T38.5X5	T38.5X6
Quinestrol	T38.5X1	T38.5X2	T38.5X3	T38.5X4	T38.5X5	T38.5X6
Quinethazone	T50.2X1	T50.2X2	T50.2X3	T50.2X4	T50.2X5	T50.2X6
Quingestanol	T38.4X1	T38.4X2	T38.4X3	T38.4X4	T38.4X5	T38.4X6
Quinidine	T46.2X1	T46.2X2	T46.2X3	T46.2X4	T46.2X5	T46.2X6
Quinine	T37.2X1	T37.2X2	T37.2X3	T37.2X4	T37.2X5	T37.2X6
Quiniobine	T37.8X1	T37.8X2	T37.8X3	T37.8X4	T37.8X5	T37.8X6
Quinisocaine	T49.1X1	T49.1X2	T49.1X3	T49.1X4	T49.1X5	T49.1X6
Quinocide	T37.2X1	T37.2X2	T37.2X3	T37.2X4	T37.2X5	T37.2X6
Quinoline (derivatives) NEC	T37.8X1	T37.8X2	T37.8X3	T37.8X4	T37.8X5	T37.8X6

Substance	Poisoning, Accidental (Unintentional)	Poisoning, Intentional Self-Harm	Poisoning, Assault	Poisoning, Undetermined	Adverse Effect	Underdosing
Quinupramine	T43.011	T43.012	T43.013	T43.014	T43.015	T43.016
Quotane	T41.3X1	T41.3X2	T41.3X3	T41.3X4	T41.3X5	T41.3X6
R						
Rabies						
immune globulin (human)	T50.Z11	T50.Z12	T50.Z13	T50.Z14	T50.Z15	T50.Z16
vaccine	T50.B91	T50.B92	T50.B93	T50.B94	T50.B95	T50.B96
Racemoramide	T40.2X1	T40.2X2	T40.2X3	T40.2X4	—	—
Racemorphan	T40.2X1	T40.2X2	T40.2X3	T40.2X4	T40.2X5	T40.2X6
Racepinefrin	T44.5X1	T44.5X2	T44.5X3	T44.5X4	T44.5X5	T44.5X6
Raclopride	T43.591	T43.592	T43.593	T43.594	T43.595	T43.596
Radiator alcohol	T51.1X1	T51.1X2	T51.1X3	T51.1X4	—	—
Radioactive drug NEC	T50.8X1	T50.8X2	T50.8X3	T50.8X4	T50.8X5	T50.8X6
Radio-opaque (drugs) (materials)	T50.8X1	T50.8X2	T50.8X3	T50.8X4	T50.8X5	T50.8X6
Ramifenazone	T39.2X1	T39.2X2	T39.2X3	T39.2X4	T39.2X5	T39.2X6
Ramipril	T46.4X1	T46.4X2	T46.4X3	T46.4X4	T46.4X5	T46.4X6
Ranitidine	T47.0X1	T47.0X2	T47.0X3	T47.0X4	T47.0X5	T47.0X6
Ranunculus	T62.2X1	T62.2X2	T62.2X3	T62.2X4	—	—
Rat poison NEC	T60.4X1	T60.4X2	T60.4X3	T60.4X4	—	—
Rattlesnake (venom)	T63.011	T63.012	T63.013	T63.014	—	—
Raubasine	T46.7X1	T46.7X2	T46.7X3	T46.7X4	T46.7X5	T46.7X6
Raudixin	T46.5X1	T46.5X2	T46.5X3	T46.5X4	T46.5X5	T46.5X6
Rautensin	T46.5X1	T46.5X2	T46.5X3	T46.5X4	T46.5X5	T46.5X6
Rautina	T46.5X1	T46.5X2	T46.5X3	T46.5X4	T46.5X5	T46.5X6
Rautotal	T46.5X1	T46.5X2	T46.5X3	T46.5X4	T46.5X5	T46.5X6
Rauwiloid	T46.5X1	T46.5X2	T46.5X3	T46.5X4	T46.5X5	T46.5X6
Rauwoldin	T46.5X1	T46.5X2	T46.5X3	T46.5X4	T46.5X5	T46.5X6
Rauwolfia (alkaloids)	T46.5X1	T46.5X2	T46.5X3	T46.5X4	T46.5X5	T46.5X6
Razoxane	T45.1X1	T45.1X2	T45.1X3	T45.1X4	T45.1X5	T45.1X6
Realgar	T57.0X1	T57.0X2	T57.0X3	T57.0X4	—	—
Recombinant (R) — see specific protein						
Red blood cells, packed	T45.8X1	T45.8X2	T45.8X3	T45.8X4	T45.8X5	T45.8X6
Red squill (scilliroside)	T60.4X1	T60.4X2	T60.4X3	T60.4X4	—	—
Reducing agent, industrial NEC	T65.891	T65.892	T65.893	T65.894	—	—
Refrigerant gas (chlorofluoro-carbon)	T53.5X1	T53.5X2	T53.5X3	T53.5X4	—	—
not chlorofluoro-carbon	T59.891	T59.892	T59.893	T59.894	—	—
Regroton	T50.2X1	T50.2X2	T50.2X3	T50.2X4	T50.2X5	T50.2X6
Rehydration salts (oral)	T50.3X1	T50.3X2	T50.3X3	T50.3X4	T50.3X5	T50.3X6
Rela	T42.8X1	T42.8X2	T42.8X3	T42.8X4	T42.8X5	T42.8X6

◀ New   ◀ Revised   deleted Deleted

	External Cause (T-Code)					
Substance	Poisoning, Accidental (Unintentional)	Poisoning, Intentional Self-Harm	Poisoning, Assault	Poisoning, Undetermined	Adverse Effect	Underdosing
Relaxant, muscle						
anesthetic	T48.1X1	T48.1X2	T48.1X3	T48.1X4	T48.1X5	T48.1X6
central nervous system	T42.8X1	T42.8X2	T42.8X3	T42.8X4	T42.8X5	T42.8X6
skeletal NEC	T48.1X1	T48.1X2	T48.1X3	T48.1X4	T48.1X5	T48.1X6
smooth NEC	T44.3X1	T44.3X2	T44.3X3	T44.3X4	T44.3X5	T44.3X6
Remoxipride	T43.591	T43.592	T43.593	T43.594	T43.595	T43.596
Renese	T50.2X1	T50.2X2	T50.2X3	T50.2X4	T50.2X5	T50.2X6
Renografin	T50.8X1	T50.8X2	T50.8X3	T50.8X4	T50.8X5	T50.8X6
Replacement solution	T50.3X1	T50.3X2	T50.3X3	T50.3X4	T50.3X5	T50.3X6
Reproterol	T48.6X1	T48.6X2	T48.6X3	T48.6X4	T48.6X5	T48.6X6
Rescinnamine	T46.5X1	T46.5X2	T46.5X3	T46.5X4	T46.5X5	T46.5X6
Reserpin(e)	T46.5X1	T46.5X2	T46.5X3	T46.5X4	T46.5X5	T46.5X6
Resorcin, resorcinol (nonmedicinal)	T65.891	T65.892	T65.893	T65.894	—	—
medicinal	T49.4X1	T49.4X2	T49.4X3	T49.4X4	T49.4X5	T49.4X6
Respaire	T48.4X1	T48.4X2	T48.4X3	T48.4X4	T48.4X5	T48.4X6
Respiratory drug NEC	T48.901	T48.902	T48.903	T48.904	T48.905	T48.906
antiasthmatic NEC	T48.6X1	T48.6X2	T48.6X3	T48.6X4	T48.6X5	T48.6X6
anti-common-cold NEC	T48.5X1	T48.5X2	T48.5X3	T48.5X4	T48.5X5	T48.5X6
expectorant NEC	T48.4X1	T48.4X2	T48.4X3	T48.4X4	T48.4X5	T48.4X6
stimulant	T48.901	T48.902	T48.903	T48.904	T48.905	T48.906
Retinoic acid	T49.0X1	T49.0X2	T49.0X3	T49.0X4	T49.0X5	T49.0X6
Retinol	T45.2X1	T45.2X2	T45.2X3	T45.2X4	T45.2X5	T45.2X6
Rh (D) immune globulin (human)	T50.Z11	T50.Z12	T50.Z13	T50.Z14	T50.Z15	T50.Z16
Rhodine	T39.011	T39.012	T39.013	T39.014	T39.015	T39.016
RhoGAM	T50.Z11	T50.Z12	T50.Z13	T50.Z14	T50.Z15	T50.Z16
Rhubarb						
dry extract	T47.2X1	T47.2X2	T47.2X3	T47.2X4	T47.2X5	T47.2X6
tincture, compound	T47.2X1	T47.2X2	T47.2X3	T47.2X4	T47.2X5	T47.2X6
Ribavirin	T37.5X1	T37.5X2	T37.5X3	T37.5X4	T37.5X5	T37.5X6
Riboflavin	T45.2X1	T45.2X2	T45.2X3	T45.2X4	T45.2X5	T45.2X6
Ribostamycin	T36.5X1	T36.5X2	T36.5X3	T36.5X4	T36.5X5	T36.5X6
Ricin	T62.2X1	T62.2X2	T62.2X3	T62.2X4	—	—
Ricinus communis	T62.2X1	T62.2X2	T62.2X3	T62.2X4	—	—
Rickettsial vaccine NEC	T50.A91	T50.A92	T50.A93	T50.A94	T50.A95	T50.A96
Rifabutin	T36.6X1	T36.6X2	T36.6X3	T36.6X4	T36.6X5	T36.6X6
Rifamide	T36.6X1	T36.6X2	T36.6X3	T36.6X4	T36.6X5	T36.6X6
Rifampicin	T36.6X1	T36.6X2	T36.6X3	T36.6X4	T36.6X5	T36.6X6
with isoniazid	T37.1X1	T37.1X2	T37.1X3	T37.1X4	T37.1X5	T37.1X6
Rifampin	T36.6X1	T36.6X2	T36.6X3	T36.6X4	T36.6X5	T36.6X6
Rifamycin	T36.6X1	T36.6X2	T36.6X3	T36.6X4	T36.6X5	T36.6X6
Rifaximin	T36.6X1	T36.6X2	T36.6X3	T36.6X4	T36.6X5	T36.6X6

	External Cause (T-Code)					
Substance	Poisoning, Accidental (Unintentional)	Poisoning, Intentional Self-Harm	Poisoning, Assault	Poisoning, Undetermined	Adverse Effect	Underdosing
Rimantadine	T37.5X1	T37.5X2	T37.5X3	T37.5X4	T37.5X5	T37.5X6
Rimazolium metilsulfate	T39.8X1	T39.8X2	T39.8X3	T39.8X4	T39.8X5	T39.8X6
Rimifon	T37.1X1	T37.1X2	T37.1X3	T37.1X4	T37.1X5	T37.1X6
Rimiterol	T48.6X1	T48.6X2	T48.6X3	T48.6X4	T48.6X5	T48.6X6
Ringer (lactate) solution	T50.3X1	T50.3X2	T50.3X3	T50.3X4	T50.3X5	T50.3X6
Ristocetin	T36.8X1	T36.8X2	T36.8X3	T36.8X4	T36.8X5	T36.8X6
Ritalin	T43.631	T43.632	T43.633	T43.634	T43.635	T43.636
Ritodrine	T44.5X1	T44.5X2	T44.5X3	T44.5X4	T44.5X5	T44.5X6
Roach killer — see Insecticide						
Rociverine	T44.3X1	T44.3X2	T44.3X3	T44.3X4	T44.3X5	T44.3X6
Rocky Mountain spotted fever vaccine	T50.A91	T50.A92	T50.A93	T50.A94	T50.A95	T50.A96
Rodenticide NEC	T60.4X1	T60.4X2	T60.4X3	T60.4X4	—	—
Rohypnol	T42.4X1	T42.4X2	T42.4X3	T42.4X4	T42.4X5	T42.4X6
Rokitamycin	T36.3X1	T36.3X2	T36.3X3	T36.3X4	T36.3X5	T36.3X6
Rolaids	T47.1X1	T47.1X2	T47.1X3	T47.1X4	T47.1X5	T47.1X6
Rolitetracycline	T36.4X1	T36.4X2	T36.4X3	T36.4X4	T36.4X5	T36.4X6
Romilar	T48.3X1	T48.3X2	T48.3X3	T48.3X4	T48.3X5	T48.3X6
Ronifibrate	T46.6X1	T46.6X2	T46.6X3	T46.6X4	T46.6X5	T46.6X6
Rosaprostol	T47.1X1	T47.1X2	T47.1X3	T47.1X4	T47.1X5	T47.1X6
Rose bengal sodium (131I)	T50.8X1	T50.8X2	T50.8X3	T50.8X4	T50.8X5	T50.8X6
Rose water ointment	T49.3X1	T49.3X2	T49.3X3	T49.3X4	T49.3X5	T49.3X6
Rosoxacin	T37.8X1	T37.8X2	T37.8X3	T37.8X4	T37.8X5	T37.8X6
Rotenone	T60.2X1	T60.2X2	T60.2X3	T60.2X4	—	—
Rotoxamine	T45.0X1	T45.0X2	T45.0X3	T45.0X4	T45.0X5	T45.0X6
Rough-on-rats	T60.4X1	T60.4X2	T60.4X3	T60.4X4	—	—
Roxatidine	T47.0X1	T47.0X2	T47.0X3	T47.0X4	T47.0X5	T47.0X6
Roxithromycin	T36.3X1	T36.3X2	T36.3X3	T36.3X4	T36.3X5	T36.3X6
Rt-PA	T45.611	T45.612	T45.613	T45.614	T45.615	T45.616
Rubbing alcohol	T51.2X1	T51.2X2	T51.2X3	T51.2X4	—	—
Rubefacient	T49.4X1	T49.4X2	T49.4X3	T49.4X4	T49.4X5	T49.4X6
Rubella vaccine	T50.B91	T50.B92	T50.B93	T50.B94	T50.B95	T50.B96
Rubelogen	T50.B91	T50.B92	T50.B93	T50.B94	T50.B95	T50.B96
Rubeovax	T50.991	T50.992	T50.993	T50.994	T50.995	T50.996
Rubidium chloride Rb82	T50.8X1	T50.8X2	T50.8X3	T50.8X4	T50.8X5	T50.8X6
Rubidomycin	T45.1X1	T45.1X2	T45.1X3	T45.1X4	T45.1X5	T45.1X6
Rue	T62.2X1	T62.2X2	T62.2X3	T62.2X4	—	—
Rufocromomycin	T45.1X1	T45.1X2	T45.1X3	T45.1X4	T45.1X5	T45.1X6
Russel's viper venin	T45.7X1	T45.7X2	T45.7X3	T45.7X4	T45.7X5	T45.7X6
Ruta (graveolens)	T62.2X1	T62.2X2	T62.2X3	T62.2X4	—	—
Rutinum	T46.991	T46.992	T46.993	T46.994	T46.995	T46.996
Rutoside	T46.991	T46.992	T46.993	T46.994	T46.995	T46.996

◀ New   ◀ Revised   deleted Deleted

Substance	Poisoning, Accidental (Unintentional)	Poisoning, Intentional Self-Harm	Poisoning, Assault	Poisoning, Undetermined	Adverse Effect	Underdosing
S						
Sabadilla (plant)	T62.2X1	T62.2X2	T62.2X3	T62.2X4	—	—
pesticide	T60.2X1	T60.2X2	T60.2X3	T60.2X4	—	—
Saccharated iron oxide	T45.8X1	T45.8X2	T45.8X3	T45.8X4	T45.8X5	T45.8X6
Saccharin	T50.901	T50.902	T50.903	T50.904	T50.905	T50.906
Saccharomyces boulardii	T47.6X1	T47.6X2	T47.6X3	T47.6X4	T47.6X5	T47.6X6
Safflower oil	T46.6X1	T46.6X2	T46.6X3	T46.6X4	T46.6X5	T46.6X6
Safrazine	T43.1X1	T43.1X2	T43.1X3	T43.1X4	T43.1X5	T43.1X6
Salazosulfapyridine	T37.0X1	T37.0X2	T37.0X3	T37.0X4	T37.0X5	T37.0X6
Salbutamol	T48.6X1	T48.6X2	T48.6X3	T48.6X4	T48.6X5	T48.6X6
Salicylamide	T39.091	T39.092	T39.093	T39.094	T39.095	T39.096
Salicylate NEC	T39.091	T39.092	T39.093	T39.094	T39.095	T39.096
methyl	T49.3X1	T49.3X2	T49.3X3	T49.3X4	T49.3X5	T49.3X6
theobromine calcium	T50.2X1	T50.2X2	T50.2X3	T50.2X4	T50.2X5	T50.2X6
Salicylazosulfapyridine	T37.0X1	T37.0X2	T37.0X3	T37.0X4	T37.0X5	T37.0X6
Salicylhydroxamic acid	T49.0X1	T49.0X2	T49.0X3	T49.0X4	T49.0X5	T49.0X6
Salicylic acid	T49.4X1	T49.4X2	T49.4X3	T49.4X4	T49.4X5	T49.4X6
with benzoic acid	T49.4X1	T49.4X2	T49.4X3	T49.4X4	T49.4X5	T49.4X6
congeners	T39.091	T39.092	T39.093	T39.094	T39.095	T39.096
derivative	T39.091	T39.092	T39.093	T39.094	T39.095	T39.096
salts	T39.091	T39.092	T39.093	T39.094	T39.095	T39.096
Salinazid	T37.1X1	T37.1X2	T37.1X3	T37.1X4	T37.1X5	T37.1X6
Salmeterol	T48.6X1	T48.6X2	T48.6X3	T48.6X4	T48.6X5	T48.6X6
Salol	T49.3X1	T49.3X2	T49.3X3	T49.3X4	T49.3X5	T49.3X6
Salsalate	T39.091	T39.092	T39.093	T39.094	T39.095	T39.096
Salt substitute	T50.901	T50.902	T50.903	T50.904	T50.905	T50.906
Salt-replacing drug	T50.901	T50.902	T50.903	T50.904	T50.905	T50.906
Salt-retaining mineralocorticoid	T50.0X1	T50.0X2	T50.0X3	T50.0X4	T50.0X5	T50.0X6
Saluretic NEC	T50.2X1	T50.2X2	T50.2X3	T50.2X4	T50.2X5	T50.2X6
Saluron	T50.2X1	T50.2X2	T50.2X3	T50.2X4	T50.2X5	T50.2X6
Salvarsan 606 (neosilver) (silver)	T37.8X1	T37.8X2	T37.8X3	T37.8X4	T37.8X5	T37.8X6
Sambucus canadensis	T62.2X1	T62.2X2	T62.2X3	T62.2X4	—	—
berry	T62.1X1	T62.1X2	T62.1X3	T62.1X4	—	—
Sandril	T46.5X1	T46.5X2	T46.5X3	T46.5X4	T46.5X5	T46.5X6
Sanguinaria canadensis	T62.2X1	T62.2X2	T62.2X3	T62.2X4	—	—
Saniflush (cleaner)	T54.2X1	T54.2X2	T54.2X3	T54.2X4		
Santonin	T37.4X1	T37.4X2	T37.4X3	T37.4X4	T37.4X5	T37.4X6
Santyl	T49.8X1	T49.8X2	T49.8X3	T49.8X4	T49.8X5	T49.8X6
Saralasin	T46.5X1	T46.5X2	T46.5X3	T46.5X4	T46.5X5	T46.5X6
Sarcolysin	T45.1X1	T45.1X2	T45.1X3	T45.1X4	T45.1X5	T45.1X6
Sarkomycin	T45.1X1	T45.1X2	T45.1X3	T45.1X4	T45.1X5	T45.1X6
Saroten	T43.011	T43.012	T43.013	T43.014	T43.015	T43.016

Substance	Poisoning, Accidental (Unintentional)	Poisoning, Intentional Self-Harm	Poisoning, Assault	Poisoning, Undetermined	Adverse Effect	Underdosing
Saturnine—see Lead						
Savin (oil)	T49.4X1	T49.4X2	T49.4X3	T49.4X4	T49.4X5	T49.4X6
Scammony	T47.2X1	T47.2X2	T47.2X3	T47.2X4	T47.2X5	T47.2X6
Scarlet red	T49.8X1	T49.8X2	T49.8X3	T49.8X4	T49.8X5	T49.8X6
Scheele's green	T57.0X1	T57.0X2	T57.0X3	T57.0X4	—	—
insecticide	T57.0X1	T57.0X2	T57.0X3	T57.0X4		
Schizontozide (blood) (tissue)	T37.2X1	T37.2X2	T37.2X3	T37.2X4	T37.2X5	T37.2X6
Schradan	T60.0X1	T60.0X2	T60.0X3	T60.0X4	—	—
Schweinfurth green	T57.0X1	T57.0X2	T57.0X3	T57.0X4	—	—
insecticide	T57.0X1	T57.0X2	T57.0X3	T57.0X4		
Scilla, rat poison	T60.4X1	T60.4X2	T60.4X3	T60.4X4	—	—
Scillaren	T60.4X1	T60.4X2	T60.4X3	T60.4X4		
Sclerosing agent	T46.8X1	T46.8X2	T46.8X3	T46.8X4	T46.8X5	T46.8X6
Scombrotoxin	T61.11	T61.12	T61.13	T61.14	—	—
Scopolamine	T44.3X1	T44.3X2	T44.3X3	T44.3X4	T44.3X5	T44.3X6
Scopolia extract	T44.3X1	T44.3X2	T44.3X3	T44.3X4	T44.3X5	T44.3X6
Scouring powder	T65.891	T65.892	T65.893	T65.894	—	—
Sea						
anemone (sting)	T63.631	T63.632	T63.633	T63.634	—	—
cucumber (sting)	T63.691	T63.692	T63.693	T63.694	—	—
snake (bite) (venom)	T63.091	T63.092	T63.093	T63.094	—	—
urchin spine (puncture)	T63.691	T63.692	T63.693	T63.694	—	—
Seafood	T61.91	T61.92	T61.93	T61.94	—	—
specified NEC	T61.8X1	T61.8X2	T61.8X3	T61.8X4		
Secbutabarbital	T42.3X1	T42.3X2	T42.3X3	T42.3X4	T42.3X5	T42.3X6
Secbutabarbitone	T42.3X1	T42.3X2	T42.3X3	T42.3X4	T42.3X5	T42.3X6
Secnidazole	T37.3X1	T37.3X2	T37.3X3	T37.3X4	T37.3X5	T37.3X6
Secobarbital	T42.3X1	T42.3X2	T42.3X3	T42.3X4	T42.3X5	T42.3X6
Seconal	T42.3X1	T42.3X2	T42.3X3	T42.3X4	T42.3X5	T42.3X6
Secretin	T50.8X1	T50.8X2	T50.8X3	T50.8X4	T50.8X5	T50.8X6
Sedative NEC	T42.71	T42.72	T42.73	T42.74	T42.75	T42.76
mixed NEC	T42.6X1	T42.6X2	T42.6X3	T42.6X4	T42.6X5	T42.6X6
Sedormid	T42.6X1	T42.6X2	T42.6X3	T42.6X4	T42.6X5	T42.6X6
Seed disinfectant or dressing	T60.8X1	T60.8X2	T60.8X3	T60.8X4	—	—
Seeds (poisonous)	T62.2X1	T62.2X2	T62.2X3	T62.2X4	—	—
Selegiline	T42.8X1	T42.8X2	T42.8X3	T42.8X4	T42.8X5	T42.8X6
Selenium NEC	T56.891	T56.892	T56.893	T56.894		
disulfide or sulfide	T49.4X1	T49.4X2	T49.4X3	T49.4X4	T49.4X5	T49.4X6
fumes	T59.891	T59.892	T59.893	T59.894	—	—
sulfide	T49.4X1	T49.4X2	T49.4X3	T49.4X4	T49.4X5	T49.4X6
Selenomethionine (75Se)	T50.8X1	T50.8X2	T50.8X3	T50.8X4	T50.8X5	T50.8X6
Selsun	T49.4X1	T49.4X2	T49.4X3	T49.4X4	T49.4X5	T49.4X6

◀ New ◀ Revised ~~deleted~~ Deleted

Substance	External Cause (T-Code) Poisoning, Accidental (Unintentional)	Poisoning, Intentional Self-Harm	Poisoning, Assault	Poisoning, Undetermined	Adverse Effect	Underdosing
Semustine	T45.1X1	T45.1X2	T45.1X3	T45.1X4	T45.1X5	T45.1X6
Senega syrup	T48.4X1	T48.4X2	T48.4X3	T48.4X4	T48.4X5	T48.4X6
Senna	T47.2X1	T47.2X2	T47.2X3	T47.2X4	T47.2X5	T47.2X6
Sennoside A+B	T47.2X1	T47.2X2	T47.2X3	T47.2X4	T47.2X5	T47.2X6
Septisol	T49.2X1	T49.2X2	T49.2X3	T49.2X4	T49.2X5	T49.2X6
Seractide	T38.811	T38.812	T38.813	T38.814	T38.815	T38.816
Serax	T42.4X1	T42.4X2	T42.4X3	T42.4X4	T42.4X5	T42.4X6
Serenesil	T42.6X1	T42.6X2	T42.6X3	T42.6X4	T42.6X5	T42.6X6
Serenium (hydrochloride)	T37.91	T37.92	T37.93	T37.94	T37.95	T37.96
Serepax — see Oxazepam						
Sermorelin	T38.891	T38.892	T38.893	T38.894	T38.895	T38.896
Sernyl	T41.1X1	T41.1X2	T41.1X3	T41.1X4	T41.1X5	T41.1X6
Serotonin	T50.991	T50.992	T50.993	T50.994	T50.995	T50.996
Serpasil	T46.5X1	T46.5X2	T46.5X3	T46.5X4	T46.5X5	T46.5X6
Serrapeptase	T45.3X1	T45.3X2	T45.3X3	T45.3X4	T45.3X5	T45.3X6
Serum						
antibotulinus	T50.Z11	T50.Z12	T50.Z13	T50.Z14	T50.Z15	T50.Z16
anticytotoxic	T50.Z11	T50.Z12	T50.Z13	T50.Z14	T50.Z15	T50.Z16
antidiphtheria	T50.Z11	T50.Z12	T50.Z13	T50.Z14	T50.Z15	T50.Z16
antimeningococcus	T50.Z11	T50.Z12	T50.Z13	T50.Z14	T50.Z15	T50.Z16
anti-Rh	T50.Z11	T50.Z12	T50.Z13	T50.Z14	T50.Z15	T50.Z16
anti-snake-bite	T50.Z11	T50.Z12	T50.Z13	T50.Z14	T50.Z15	T50.Z16
antitetanic	T50.Z11	T50.Z12	T50.Z13	T50.Z14	T50.Z15	T50.Z16
antitoxic	T50.Z11	T50.Z12	T50.Z13	T50.Z14	T50.Z15	T50.Z16
complement (inhibitor)	T45.8X1	T45.8X2	T45.8X3	T45.8X4	T45.8X5	T45.8X6
convalescent	T50.Z11	T50.Z12	T50.Z13	T50.Z14	T50.Z15	T50.Z16
hemolytic complement	T45.8X1	T45.8X2	T45.8X3	T45.8X4	T45.8X5	T45.8X6
immune (human)	T50.Z11	T50.Z12	T50.Z13	T50.Z14	T50.Z15	T50.Z16
protective NEC	T50.Z11	T50.Z12	T50.Z13	T50.Z14	T50.Z15	T50.Z16
Setastine	T45.0X1	T45.0X2	T45.0X3	T45.0X4	T45.0X5	T45.0X6
Setoperone	T43.591	T43.592	T43.593	T43.594	T43.595	T43.596
Sewer gas	T59.91	T59.92	T59.93	T59.94	—	—
Shampoo	T55.0X1	T55.0X2	T55.0X3	T55.0X4	—	—
Shellfish, noxious, nonbacterial	T61.781	T61.782	T61.783	T61.784	—	—
Sildenafil	T46.7X1	T46.7X2	T46.7X3	T46.7X4	T46.7X5	T46.7X6
Silibinin	T50.991	T50.992	T50.993	T50.994	T50.995	T50.996
Silicone NEC	T65.891	T65.892	T65.893	T65.894	—	—
medicinal	T49.3X1	T49.3X2	T49.3X3	T49.3X4	T49.3X5	T49.3X6
Silvadene	T49.0X1	T49.0X2	T49.0X3	T49.0X4	T49.0X5	T49.0X6
Silver	T49.0X1	T49.0X2	T49.0X3	T49.0X4	T49.0X5	T49.0X6
anti-infectives	T49.0X1	T49.0X2	T49.0X3	T49.0X4	T49.0X5	T49.0X6
arsphenamine	T37.8X1	T37.8X2	T37.8X3	T37.8X4	T37.8X5	T37.8X6

Substance	External Cause (T-Code) Poisoning, Accidental (Unintentional)	Poisoning, Intentional Self-Harm	Poisoning, Assault	Poisoning, Undetermined	Adverse Effect	Underdosing
Silver (Continued)						
colloidal	T49.0X1	T49.0X2	T49.0X3	T49.0X4	T49.0X5	T49.0X6
nitrate	T49.0X1	T49.0X2	T49.0X3	T49.0X4	T49.0X5	T49.0X6
ophthalmic preparation	T49.5X1	T49.5X2	T49.5X3	T49.5X4	T49.5X5	T49.5X6
toughened (keratolytic)	T49.4X1	T49.4X2	T49.4X3	T49.4X4	T49.4X5	T49.4X6
nonmedicinal (dust)	T56.891	T56.892	T56.893	T56.894	—	—
protein	T49.5X1	T49.5X2	T49.5X3	T49.5X4	T49.5X5	T49.5X6
salvarsan	T37.8X1	T37.8X2	T37.8X3	T37.8X4	T37.8X5	T37.8X6
sulfadiazine	T49.4X1	T49.4X2	T49.4X3	T49.4X4	T49.4X5	T49.4X6
Silymarin	T50.991	T50.992	T50.993	T50.994	T50.995	T50.996
Simaldrate	T47.1X1	T47.1X2	T47.1X3	T47.1X4	T47.1X5	T47.1X6
Simazine	T60.3X1	T60.3X2	T60.3X3	T60.3X4	—	—
Simethicone	T47.1X1	T47.1X2	T47.1X3	T47.1X4	T47.1X5	T47.1X6
Simfibrate	T46.6X1	T46.6X2	T46.6X3	T46.6X4	T46.6X5	T46.6X6
Simvastatin	T46.6X1	T46.6X2	T46.6X3	T46.6X4	T46.6X5	T46.6X6
Sincalide	T50.8X1	T50.8X2	T50.8X3	T50.8X4	T50.8X5	T50.8X6
Sinequan	T43.011	T43.012	T43.013	T43.014	T43.015	T43.016
Singoserp	T46.5X1	T46.5X2	T46.5X3	T46.5X4	T46.5X5	T46.5X6
Sintrom	T45.511	T45.512	T45.513	T45.514	T45.515	T45.516
Sisomicin	T36.5X1	T36.5X2	T36.5X3	T36.5X4	T36.5X5	T36.5X6
Sitosterols	T46.6X1	T46.6X2	T46.6X3	T46.6X4	T46.6X5	T46.6X6
Skeletal muscle relaxants	T48.1X1	T48.1X2	T48.1X3	T48.1X4	T48.1X5	T48.1X6
Skin						
agents (external)	T49.91	T49.92	T49.93	T49.94	T49.95	T49.96
specified NEC	T49.8X1	T49.8X2	T49.8X3	T49.8X4	T49.8X5	T49.8X6
test antigen	T50.8X1	T50.8X2	T50.8X3	T50.8X4	T50.8X5	T50.8X6
Sleep-eze	T45.0X1	T45.0X2	T45.0X3	T45.0X4	T45.0X5	T45.0X6
Sleeping draught, pill	T42.71	T42.72	T42.73	T42.74	T42.75	T42.76
Smallpox vaccine	T50.B11	T50.B12	T50.B13	T50.B14	T50.B15	T50.B16
Smelter fumes NEC	T56.91	T56.92	T56.93	T56.94	—	—
Smog	T59.1X1	T59.1X2	T59.1X3	T59.1X4	—	—
Smoke NEC	T59.811	T59.812	T59.813	T59.814	—	—
Smooth muscle relaxant	T44.3X1	T44.3X2	T44.3X3	T44.3X4	T44.3X5	T44.3X6
Snail killer NEC	T60.8X1	T60.8X2	T60.8X3	T60.8X4	—	—
Snake venom or bite	T63.001	T63.002	T63.003	T63.004	—	—
hemocoagulase	T45.7X1	T45.7X2	T45.7X3	T45.7X4	T45.7X5	T45.7X6
Snuff	T65.211	T65.212	T65.213	T65.214	—	—
Soap (powder) (product)	T55.0X1	T55.0X2	T55.0X3	T55.0X4	—	—
enema	T47.4X1	T47.4X2	T47.4X3	T47.4X4	T47.4X5	T47.4X6
medicinal, soft	T49.2X1	T49.2X2	T49.2X3	T49.2X4	T49.2X5	T49.2X6
superfatted	T49.2X1	T49.2X2	T49.2X3	T49.2X4	T49.2X5	T49.2X6
Sobrerol	T48.4X1	T48.4X2	T48.4X3	T48.4X4	T48.4X5	T48.4X6

◀ New   ◀ Revised   ~~deleted~~ Deleted

Substance	Poisoning, Accidental (Unintentional)	Poisoning, Intentional Self-Harm	Poisoning, Assault	Poisoning, Undetermined	Adverse Effect	Underdosing
Soda (caustic)	T54.3X1	T54.3X2	T54.3X3	T54.3X4	—	—
bicarb	T47.1X1	T47.1X2	T47.1X3	T47.1X4	T47.1X5	T47.1X6
chlorinated — *see Sodium, hypochlorite*						
Sodium						
acetosulfone	T37.1X1	T37.1X2	T37.1X3	T37.1X4	T37.1X5	T37.1X6
acetrizoate	T50.8X1	T50.8X2	T50.8X3	T50.8X4	T50.8X5	T50.8X6
acid phosphate	T50.3X1	T50.3X2	T50.3X3	T50.3X4	T50.3X5	T50.3X6
alginate	T47.8X1	T47.8X2	T47.8X3	T47.8X4	T47.8X5	T47.8X6
amidotrizoate	T50.8X1	T50.8X2	T50.8X3	T50.8X4	T50.8X5	T50.8X6
aminopterin	T45.1X1	T45.1X2	T45.1X3	T45.1X4	T45.1X5	T45.1X6
amylosulfate	T47.8X1	T47.8X2	T47.8X3	T47.8X4	T47.8X5	T47.8X6
amytal	T42.3X1	T42.3X2	T42.3X3	T42.3X4	T42.3X5	T42.3X6
antimony gluconate	T37.3X1	T37.3X2	T37.3X3	T37.3X4	T37.3X5	T37.3X6
arsenate	T57.0X1	T57.0X2	T57.0X3	T57.0X4	—	—
aurothiomalate	T39.4X1	T39.4X2	T39.4X3	T39.4X4	T39.4X5	T39.4X6
aurothiosulfate	T39.4X1	T39.4X2	T39.4X3	T39.4X4	T39.4X5	T39.4X6
barbiturate	T42.3X1	T42.3X2	T42.3X3	T42.3X4	T42.3X5	T42.3X6
basic phosphate	T47.4X1	T47.4X2	T47.4X3	T47.4X4	T47.4X5	T47.4X6
bicarbonate	T47.1X1	T47.1X2	T47.1X3	T47.1X4	T47.1X5	T47.1X6
bichromate	T57.8X1	T57.8X2	T57.8X3	T57.8X4	—	—
biphosphate	T50.3X1	T50.3X2	T50.3X3	T50.3X4	T50.3X5	T50.3X6
bisulfate	T65.891	T65.892	T65.893	T65.894	—	—
borate						
cleanser	T57.8X1	T57.8X2	T57.8X3	T57.8X4	—	—
eye	T49.5X1	T49.5X2	T49.5X3	T49.5X4	T49.5X5	T49.5X6
therapeutic	T49.8X1	T49.8X2	T49.8X3	T49.8X4	T49.8X5	T49.8X6
bromide	T42.6X1	T42.6X2	T42.6X3	T42.6X4	T42.6X5	T42.6X6
cacodylate (nonmedicinal) NEC	T50.8X1	T50.8X2	T50.8X3	T50.8X4	T50.8X5	T50.8X6
anti-infective	T37.8X1	T37.8X2	T37.8X3	T37.8X4	T37.8X5	T37.8X6
herbicide	T60.3X1	T60.3X2	T60.3X3	T60.3X4	—	—
calcium edetate	T45.8X1	T45.8X2	T45.8X3	T45.8X4	T45.8X5	T45.8X6
carbonate NEC	T54.3X1	T54.3X2	T54.3X3	T54.3X4	—	—
chlorate NEC	T65.891	T65.892	T65.893	T65.894	—	—
herbicide	T54.91	T54.92	T54.93	T54.94	—	—
chloride	T50.3X1	T50.3X2	T50.3X3	T50.3X4	T50.3X5	T50.3X6
with glucose	T50.3X1	T50.3X2	T50.3X3	T50.3X4	T50.3X5	T50.3X6
chromate	T65.891	T65.892	T65.893	T65.894	—	—
citrate	T50.991	T50.992	T50.993	T50.994	T50.995	T50.996
cromoglicate	T48.6X1	T48.6X2	T48.6X3	T48.6X4	T48.6X5	T48.6X6
cyanide	T65.0X1	T65.0X2	T65.0X3	T65.0X4	—	—
cyclamate	T50.3X1	T50.3X2	T50.3X3	T50.3X4	T50.3X5	T50.3X6

Substance	Poisoning, Accidental (Unintentional)	Poisoning, Intentional Self-Harm	Poisoning, Assault	Poisoning, Undetermined	Adverse Effect	Underdosing
Sodium *(Continued)*						
dehydrocholate	T45.8X1	T45.8X2	T45.8X3	T45.8X4	T45.8X5	T45.8X6
diatrizoate	T50.8X1	T50.8X2	T50.8X3	T50.8X4	T50.8X5	T50.8X6
dibunate	T48.4X1	T48.4X2	T48.4X3	T48.4X4	T48.4X5	T48.4X6
dioctyl sulfosuccinate	T47.4X1	T47.4X2	T47.4X3	T47.4X4	T47.4X5	T47.4X6
dipantoyl ferrate	T45.8X1	T45.8X2	T45.8X3	T45.8X4	T45.8X5	T45.8X6
edetate	T45.8X1	T45.8X2	T45.8X3	T45.8X4	T45.8X5	T45.8X6
ethacrynate	T50.1X1	T50.1X2	T50.1X3	T50.1X4	T50.1X5	T50.1X6
feredetate	T45.8X1	T45.8X2	T45.8X3	T45.8X4	T45.8X5	T45.8X6
Fluoride — *see Fluoride*						
fluoroacetate (dust) (pesticide)	T60.4X1	T60.4X2	T60.4X3	T60.4X4	—	—
free salt	T50.3X1	T50.3X2	T50.3X3	T50.3X4	T50.3X5	T50.3X6
fusidate	T36.8X1	T36.8X2	T36.8X3	T36.8X4	T36.8X5	T36.8X6
glucaldrate	T47.1X1	T47.1X2	T47.1X3	T47.1X4	T47.1X5	T47.1X6
glucosulfone	T37.1X1	T37.1X2	T37.1X3	T37.1X4	T37.1X5	T37.1X6
glutamate	T45.8X1	T45.8X2	T45.8X3	T45.8X4	T45.8X5	T45.8X6
hydrogen carbonate	T50.3X1	T50.3X2	T50.3X3	T50.3X4	T50.3X5	T50.3X6
hydroxide	T54.3X1	T54.3X2	T54.3X3	T54.3X4	—	—
hypochlorite (bleach) NEC	T54.3X1	T54.3X2	T54.3X3	T54.3X4	—	—
disinfectant	T54.3X1	T54.3X2	T54.3X3	T54.3X4	—	—
medicinal (anti-infective) (external)	T49.0X1	T49.0X2	T49.0X3	T49.0X4	T49.0X5	T49.0X6
vapor	T54.3X1	T54.3X2	T54.3X3	T54.3X4	—	—
hyposulfite	T49.0X1	T49.0X2	T49.0X3	T49.0X4	T49.0X5	T49.0X6
indigotin disulfonate	T50.8X1	T50.8X2	T50.8X3	T50.8X4	T50.8X5	T50.8X6
iodide	T50.991	T50.992	T50.993	T50.994	T50.995	T50.996
I-131	T50.8X1	T50.8X2	T50.8X3	T50.8X4	T50.8X5	T50.8X6
therapeutic	T38.2X1	T38.2X2	T38.2X3	T38.2X4	T38.2X5	T38.2X6
iodohippurate (131I)	T50.8X1	T50.8X2	T50.8X3	T50.8X4	T50.8X5	T50.8X6
iopodate	T50.8X1	T50.8X2	T50.8X3	T50.8X4	T50.8X5	T50.8X6
iothalamate	T50.8X1	T50.8X2	T50.8X3	T50.8X4	T50.8X5	T50.8X6
iron edetate	T45.4X1	T45.4X2	T45.4X3	T45.4X4	T45.4X5	T45.4X6
lactate (compound solution)	T45.8X1	T45.8X2	T45.8X3	T45.8X4	T45.8X5	T45.8X6
lauryl (sulfate)	T49.2X1	T49.2X2	T49.2X3	T49.2X4	T49.2X5	T49.2X6
(L)-triiodothyronine	T38.1X1	T38.1X2	T38.1X3	T38.1X4	T38.1X5	T38.1X6
magnesium citrate	T50.991	T50.992	T50.993	T50.994	T50.995	T50.996
mersalate	T50.2X1	T50.2X2	T50.2X3	T50.2X4	T50.2X5	T50.2X6
metasilicate	T65.891	T65.892	T65.893	T65.894	—	—
metrizoate	T50.8X1	T50.8X2	T50.8X3	T50.8X4	T50.8X5	T50.8X6
monofluoroacetate (pesticide)	T60.1X1	T60.1X2	T60.1X3	T60.1X4	—	—
morrhuate	T46.8X1	T46.8X2	T46.8X3	T46.8X4	T46.8X5	T46.8X6
nafcillin	T36.0X1	T36.0X2	T36.0X3	T36.0X4	T36.0X5	T36.0X6

◄ New ◄ Revised ~~deleted~~ Deleted

Substance	External Cause (T-Code) Poisoning, Accidental (Unintentional)	Poisoning, Intentional Self-Harm	Poisoning, Assault	Poisoning, Undetermined	Adverse Effect	Underdosing
Sodium *(Continued)*						
nitrate (oxidizing agent)	T65.891	T65.892	T65.893	T65.894	—	—
nitrite	T50.6X1	T50.6X2	T50.6X3	T50.6X4	T50.6X5	T50.6X6
nitroferricyanide	T46.5X1	T46.5X2	T46.5X3	T46.5X4	T46.5X5	T46.5X6
nitroprusside	T46.5X1	T46.5X2	T46.5X3	T46.5X4	T46.5X5	T46.5X6
oxalate	T65.891	T65.892	T65.893	T65.894	—	—
oxide/peroxide	T65.891	T65.892	T65.893	T65.894	—	—
oxybate	T41.291	T41.292	T41.293	T41.294	T41.295	T41.296
para-aminohippurate	T50.8X1	T50.8X2	T50.8X3	T50.8X4	T50.8X5	T50.8X6
perborate (nonmedicinal) NEC	T65.891	T65.892	T65.893	T65.894	—	—
medicinal	T49.0X1	T49.0X2	T49.0X3	T49.0X4	T49.0X5	T49.0X6
soap	T55.0X1	T55.0X2	T55.0X3	T55.0X4	—	—
percarbonate — *see Sodium, perborate*						
pertechnetate Tc99m	T50.8X1	T50.8X2	T50.8X3	T50.8X4	T50.8X5	T50.8X6
phosphate						
cellulose	T45.8X1	T45.8X2	T45.8X3	T45.8X4	T45.8X5	T45.8X6
dibasic	T47.2X1	T47.2X2	T47.2X3	T47.2X4	T47.2X5	T47.2X6
monobasic	T47.2X1	T47.2X2	T47.2X3	T47.2X4	T47.2X5	T47.2X6
phytate	T50.6X1	T50.6X2	T50.6X3	T50.6X4	T50.6X5	T50.6X6
picosulfate	T47.2X1	T47.2X2	T47.2X3	T47.2X4	T47.2X5	T47.2X6
polyhydroxyaluminium monocarbonate	T47.1X1	T47.1X2	T47.1X3	T47.1X4	T47.1X5	T47.1X6
polystyrene sulfonate	T50.3X1	T50.3X2	T50.3X3	T50.3X4	T50.3X5	T50.3X6
propionate	T49.0X1	T49.0X2	T49.0X3	T49.0X4	T49.0X5	T49.0X6
propyl hydroxybenzoate	T50.991	T50.992	T50.993	T50.994	T50.995	T50.996
psylliate	T46.8X1	T46.8X2	T46.8X3	T46.8X4	T46.8X5	T46.8X6
removing resins	T50.3X1	T50.3X2	T50.3X3	T50.3X4	T50.3X5	T50.3X6
salicylate	T39.091	T39.092	T39.093	T39.094	T39.095	T39.096
salt NEC	T50.3X1	T50.3X2	T50.3X3	T50.3X4	T50.3X5	T50.3X6
selenate	T60.2X1	T60.2X2	T60.2X3	T60.2X4	—	—
stibogluconate	T37.3X1	T37.3X2	T37.3X3	T37.3X4	T37.3X5	T37.3X6
sulfate	T47.4X1	T47.4X2	T47.4X3	T47.4X4	T47.4X5	T47.4X6
sulfoxone	T37.1X1	T37.1X2	T37.1X3	T37.1X4	T37.1X5	T37.1X6
tetradecyl sulfate	T46.8X1	T46.8X2	T46.8X3	T46.8X4	T46.8X5	T46.8X6
thiopental	T41.1X1	T41.1X2	T41.1X3	T41.1X4	T41.1X5	T41.1X6
thiosalicylate	T39.091	T39.092	T39.093	T39.094	T39.095	T39.096
thiosulfate	T50.6X1	T50.6X2	T50.6X3	T50.6X4	T50.6X5	T50.6X6
tolbutamide	T38.3X1	T38.3X2	T38.3X3	T38.3X4	T38.3X5	T38.3X6
l-triiodothyronine	T38.1X1	T38.1X2	T38.1X3	T38.1X4	T38.1X5	T38.1X6
tyropanoate	T50.8X1	T50.8X2	T50.8X3	T50.8X4	T50.8X5	T50.8X6
valproate	T42.6X1	T42.6X2	T42.6X3	T42.6X4	T42.6X5	T42.6X6
versenate	T50.6X1	T50.6X2	T50.6X3	T50.6X4	T50.6X5	T50.6X6

Substance	External Cause (T-Code) Poisoning, Accidental (Unintentional)	Poisoning, Intentional Self-Harm	Poisoning, Assault	Poisoning, Undetermined	Adverse Effect	Underdosing
Sodium-free salt	T50.901	T50.902	T50.903	T50.904	T50.905	T50.906
Sodium-removing resin	T50.3X1	T50.3X2	T50.3X3	T50.3X4	T50.3X5	T50.3X6
Soft soap	T55.0X1	T55.0X2	T55.0X3	T55.0X4	—	—
Solanine	T62.2X1	T62.2X2	T62.2X3	T62.2X4	—	—
berries	T62.1X1	T62.1X2	T62.1X3	T62.1X4	—	—
Solanum dulcamara	T62.2X1	T62.2X2	T62.2X3	T62.2X4	—	—
berries	T62.1X1	T62.1X2	T62.1X3	T62.1X4	—	—
Solapsone	T37.1X1	T37.1X2	T37.1X3	T37.1X4	T37.1X5	T37.1X6
Solar lotion	T49.3X1	T49.3X2	T49.3X3	T49.3X4	T49.3X5	T49.3X6
Solasulfone	T37.1X1	T37.1X2	T37.1X3	T37.1X4	T37.1X5	T37.1X6
Soldering fluid	T65.891	T65.892	T65.893	T65.894	—	—
Solid substance	T65.91	T65.92	T65.93	T65.94	—	—
specified NEC	T65.891	T65.892	T65.893	T65.894	—	—
Solvent, industrial NEC	T52.91	T52.92	T52.93	T52.94	—	—
naphtha	T52.0X1	T52.0X2	T52.0X3	T52.0X4	—	—
petroleum	T52.0X1	T52.0X2	T52.0X3	T52.0X4	—	—
specified NEC	T52.8X1	T52.8X2	T52.8X3	T52.8X4	—	—
Soma	T42.8X1	T42.8X2	T42.8X3	T42.8X4	T42.8X5	T42.8X6
Somatorelin	T38.891	T38.892	T38.893	T38.894	T38.895	T38.896
Somatostatin	T38.991	T38.992	T38.993	T38.994	T38.995	T38.996
Somatotropin	T38.811	T38.812	T38.813	T38.814	T38.815	T38.816
Somatrem	T38.811	T38.812	T38.813	T38.814	T38.815	T38.816
Somatropin	T38.811	T38.812	T38.813	T38.814	T38.815	T38.816
Sominex	T45.0X1	T45.0X2	T45.0X3	T45.0X4	T45.0X5	T45.0X6
Somnos	T42.6X1	T42.6X2	T42.6X3	T42.6X4	T42.6X5	T42.6X6
Somonal	T42.3X1	T42.3X2	T42.3X3	T42.3X4	T42.3X5	T42.3X6
Soneryl	T42.3X1	T42.3X2	T42.3X3	T42.3X4	T42.3X5	T42.3X6
Soothing syrup	T50.901	T50.902	T50.903	T50.904	T50.905	T50.906
Sopor	T42.6X1	T42.6X2	T42.6X3	T42.6X4	T42.6X5	T42.6X6
Soporific	T42.71	T42.72	T42.73	T42.74	T42.75	T42.76
Soporific drug	T42.71	T42.72	T42.73	T42.74	T42.75	T42.76
specified type NEC	T42.6X1	T42.6X2	T42.6X3	T42.6X4	T42.6X5	T42.6X6
Sorbide nitrate	T46.3X1	T46.3X2	T46.3X3	T46.3X4	T46.3X5	T46.3X6
Sorbitol	T47.4X1	T47.4X2	T47.4X3	T47.4X4	T47.4X5	T47.4X6
Sotalol	T44.7X1	T44.7X2	T44.7X3	T44.7X4	T44.7X5	T44.7X6
Sotradecol	T46.8X1	T46.8X2	T46.8X3	T46.8X4	T46.8X5	T46.8X6
Soysterol	T46.6X1	T46.6X2	T46.6X3	T46.6X4	T46.6X5	T46.6X6
Spacoline	T44.3X1	T44.3X2	T44.3X3	T44.3X4	T44.3X5	T44.3X6
Spanish fly	T49.8X1	T49.8X2	T49.8X3	T49.8X4	T49.8X5	T49.8X6
Sparine	T43.3X1	T43.3X2	T43.3X3	T43.3X4	T43.3X5	T43.3X6
Sparteine	T48.0X1	T48.0X2	T48.0X3	T48.0X4	T48.0X5	T48.0X6

◀ New   ◀ Revised   ~~deleted~~ Deleted

Substance	Poisoning, Accidental (Unintentional)	Poisoning, Intentional Self-Harm	Poisoning, Assault	Poisoning, Undetermined	Adverse Effect	Underdosing
Spasmolytic						
anticholinergics	T44.3X1	T44.3X2	T44.3X3	T44.3X4	T44.3X5	T44.3X6
autonomic	T44.3X1	T44.3X2	T44.3X3	T44.3X4	T44.3X5	T44.3X6
bronchial NEC	T48.6X1	T48.6X2	T48.6X3	T48.6X4	T48.6X5	T48.6X6
quaternary ammonium	T44.3X1	T44.3X2	T44.3X3	T44.3X4	T44.3X5	T44.3X6
skeletal muscle NEC	T48.1X1	T48.1X2	T48.1X3	T48.1X4	T48.1X5	T48.1X6
Spectinomycin	T36.5X1	T36.5X2	T36.5X3	T36.5X4	T36.5X5	T36.5X6
Speed	T43.621	T43.622	T43.623	T43.624	T43.625	T43.626
Spermicide	T49.8X1	T49.8X2	T49.8X3	T49.8X4	T49.8X5	T49.8X6
Spider (bite) (venom)	T63.391	T63.392	T63.393	T63.394	—	—
antivenin	T50.Z11	T50.Z12	T50.Z13	T50.Z14	T50.Z15	T50.Z16
Spigelia (root)	T37.4X1	T37.4X2	T37.4X3	T37.4X4	T37.4X5	T37.4X6
Spindle inactivator	T50.4X1	T50.4X2	T50.4X3	T50.4X4	T50.4X5	T50.4X6
Spiperone	T43.4X1	T43.4X2	T43.4X3	T43.4X4	T43.4X5	T43.4X6
Spiramycin	T36.3X1	T36.3X2	T36.3X3	T36.3X4	T36.3X5	T36.3X6
Spirapril	T46.4X1	T46.4X2	T46.4X3	T46.4X4	T46.4X5	T46.4X6
Spirilene	T43.591	T43.592	T43.593	T43.594	T43.595	T43.596
Spirit(s) (neutral) NEC	T51.0X1	T51.0X2	T51.0X3	T51.0X4	—	—
beverage	T51.0X1	T51.0X2	T51.0X3	T51.0X4	—	—
industrial	T51.0X1	T51.0X2	T51.0X3	T51.0X4	—	—
mineral	T52.0X1	T52.0X2	T52.0X3	T52.0X4	—	—
of salt — see Hydrochloric acid						
surgical	T51.0X1	T51.0X2	T51.0X3	T51.0X4	—	—
Spironolactone	T50.0X1	T50.0X2	T50.0X3	T50.0X4	T50.0X5	T50.0X6
Spiroperidol	T43.4X1	T43.4X2	T43.4X3	T43.4X4	T43.4X5	T43.4X6
Sponge, absorbable (gelatin)	T45.7X1	T45.7X2	T45.7X3	T45.7X4	T45.7X5	T45.7X6
Sporostacin	T49.0X1	T49.0X2	T49.0X3	T49.0X4	T49.0X5	T49.0X6
Spray (aerosol)	T65.91	T65.92	T65.93	T65.94	—	—
cosmetic	T65.891	T65.892	T65.893	T65.894	—	—
medicinal NEC	T50.901	T50.902	T50.903	T50.904	T50.905	T50.906
pesticides — see Pesticides						
specified content — see specific substance						
Spurge flax	T62.2X1	T62.2X2	T62.2X3	T62.2X4	—	—
Spurges	T62.2X1	T62.2X2	T62.2X3	T62.2X4	—	—
Sputum viscosity-lowering drug	T48.4X1	T48.4X2	T48.4X3	T48.4X4	T48.4X5	T48.4X6
Squill	T46.0X1	T46.0X2	T46.0X3	T46.0X4	T46.0X5	T46.0X6
rat poison	T60.4X1	T60.4X2	T60.4X3	T60.4X4	—	—
Squirting cucumber (cathartic)	T47.2X1	T47.2X2	T47.2X3	T47.2X4	T47.2X5	T47.2X6
Stains	T65.6X1	T65.6X2	T65.6X3	T65.6X4	—	—
Stannous fluoride	T49.7X1	T49.7X2	T49.7X3	T49.7X4	T49.7X5	T49.7X6
Stanolone	T38.7X1	T38.7X2	T38.7X3	T38.7X4	T38.7X5	T38.7X6

Substance	Poisoning, Accidental (Unintentional)	Poisoning, Intentional Self-Harm	Poisoning, Assault	Poisoning, Undetermined	Adverse Effect	Underdosing
Stanozolol	T38.7X1	T38.7X2	T38.7X3	T38.7X4	T38.7X5	T38.7X6
Staphisagria or stavesacre (pediculicide)	T49.0X1	T49.0X2	T49.0X3	T49.0X4	T49.0X5	T49.0X6
Starch	T50.901	T50.902	T50.903	T50.904	T50.905	T50.906
Stelazine	T43.3X1	T43.3X2	T43.3X3	T43.3X4	T43.3X5	T43.3X6
Stemetil	T43.3X1	T43.3X2	T43.3X3	T43.3X4	T43.3X5	T43.3X6
Stepronin	T48.4X1	T48.4X2	T48.4X3	T48.4X4	T48.4X5	T48.4X6
Sterculia	T47.4X1	T47.4X2	T47.4X3	T47.4X4	T47.4X5	T47.4X6
Sternutator gas	T59.891	T59.892	T59.893	T59.894	—	—
Steroid	T38.0X1	T38.0X2	T38.0X3	T38.0X4	T38.0X5	T38.0X6
anabolic	T38.7X1	T38.7X2	T38.7X3	T38.7X4	T38.7X5	T38.7X6
androgenic	T38.7X1	T38.7X2	T38.7X3	T38.7X4	T38.7X5	T38.7X6
antineoplastic, hormone	T38.7X1	T38.7X2	T38.7X3	T38.7X4	T38.7X5	T38.7X6
estrogen	T38.5X1	T38.5X2	T38.5X3	T38.5X4	T38.5X5	T38.5X6
ENT agent	T49.6X1	T49.6X2	T49.6X3	T49.6X4	T49.6X5	T49.6X6
ophthalmic preparation	T49.5X1	T49.5X2	T49.5X3	T49.5X4	T49.5X5	T49.5X6
topical NEC	T49.0X1	T49.0X2	T49.0X3	T49.0X4	T49.0X5	T49.0X6
Stibine	T56.891	T56.892	T56.893	T56.894	—	—
Stibogluconate	T37.3X1	T37.3X2	T37.3X3	T37.3X4	T37.3X5	T37.3X6
Stibophen	T37.4X1	T37.4X2	T37.4X3	T37.4X4	T37.4X5	T37.4X6
Stilbamidine (isetionate)	T37.3X1	T37.3X2	T37.3X3	T37.3X4	T37.3X5	T37.3X6
Stilbestrol	T38.5X1	T38.5X2	T38.5X3	T38.5X4	T38.5X5	T38.5X6
Stilboestrol	T38.5X1	T38.5X2	T38.5X3	T38.5X4	T38.5X5	T38.5X6
Stimulant						
central nervous system — see also Psychostimulant	T43.601	T43.602	T43.603	T43.604	T43.605	T43.606
analeptics	T50.7X1	T50.7X2	T50.7X3	T50.7X4	T50.7X5	T50.7X6
opiate antagonist	T50.7X1	T50.7X2	T50.7X3	T50.7X4	T50.7X5	T50.7X6
psychotherapeutic NEC — see also Psychotherapeutic drug	T43.601	T43.602	T43.603	T43.604	T43.605	T43.606
specified NEC	T43.691	T43.692	T43.693	T43.694	T43.695	T43.696
respiratory	T48.901	T48.902	T48.903	T48.904	T48.905	T48.906
Stone-dissolving drug	T50.901	T50.902	T50.903	T50.904	T50.905	T50.906
Storage battery (cells) (acid)	T54.2X1	T54.2X2	T54.2X3	T54.2X4	—	—
Stovaine	T41.3X1	T41.3X2	T41.3X3	T41.3X4	T41.3X5	T41.3X6
infiltration (subcutaneous)	T41.3X1	T41.3X2	T41.3X3	T41.3X4	T41.3X5	T41.3X6
nerve block (peripheral) (plexus)	T41.3X1	T41.3X2	T41.3X3	T41.3X4	T41.3X5	T41.3X6
spinal	T41.3X1	T41.3X2	T41.3X3	T41.3X4	T41.3X5	T41.3X6
topical (surface)	T41.3X1	T41.3X2	T41.3X3	T41.3X4	T41.3X5	T41.3X6
Stovarsal	T37.8X1	T37.8X2	T37.8X3	T37.8X4	T37.8X5	T37.8X6
Stove gas — see Gas, stove	T57.91	T57.92	T57.93	T57.94	—	—

◀ New   ◀ Revised   ~~deleted~~ Deleted

Substance	External Cause (T-Code)					
	Poisoning, Accidental (Unintentional)	Poisoning, Intentional Self-Harm	Poisoning, Assault	Poisoning, Undetermined	Adverse Effect	Underdosing
Stoxil	T49.5X1	T49.5X2	T49.5X3	T49.5X4	T49.5X5	T49.5X6
Stramonium	T48.6X1	T48.6X2	T48.6X3	T48.6X4	T48.6X5	T48.6X6
natural state	T62.2X1	T62.2X2	T62.2X3	T62.2X4	—	—
Streptodornase	T45.3X1	T45.3X2	T45.3X3	T45.3X4	T45.3X5	T45.3X6
Streptoduocin	T36.5X1	T36.5X2	T36.5X3	T36.5X4	T36.5X5	T36.5X6
Streptokinase	T45.611	T45.612	T45.613	T45.614	T45.615	T45.616
Streptomycin (derivative)	T36.5X1	T36.5X2	T36.5X3	T36.5X4	T36.5X5	T36.5X6
Streptonivicin	T36.5X1	T36.5X2	T36.5X3	T36.5X4	T36.5X5	T36.5X6
Streptovarycin	T36.5X1	T36.5X2	T36.5X3	T36.5X4	T36.5X5	T36.5X6
Streptozocin	T45.1X1	T45.1X2	T45.1X3	T45.1X4	T45.1X5	T45.1X6
Streptozotocin	T45.1X1	T45.1X2	T45.1X3	T45.1X4	T45.1X5	T45.1X6
Stripper (paint) (solvent)	T52.8X1	T52.8X2	T52.8X3	T52.8X4	—	—
Strobane	T60.1X1	T60.1X2	T60.1X3	T60.1X4	—	—
Strofantina	T46.0X1	T46.0X2	T46.0X3	T46.0X4	T46.0X5	T46.0X6
Strophanthin (g) (k)	T46.0X1	T46.0X2	T46.0X3	T46.0X4	T46.0X5	T46.0X6
Strophanthus	T46.0X1	T46.0X2	T46.0X3	T46.0X4	T46.0X5	T46.0X6
Strophantin	T46.0X1	T46.0X2	T46.0X3	T46.0X4	T46.0X5	T46.0X6
Strophantin-g	T46.0X1	T46.0X2	T46.0X3	T46.0X4	T46.0X5	T46.0X6
Strychnine (nonmedicinal) (pesticide) (salts)	T65.1X1	T65.1X2	T65.1X3	T65.1X4	—	—
medicinal	T48.291	T48.292	T48.293	T48.294	T48.295	T48.296
Strychnos (ignatii) — see Strychnine						
Styramate	T42.8X1	T42.8X2	T42.8X3	T42.8X4	T42.8X5	T42.8X6
Styrene	T65.891	T65.892	T65.893	T65.894	—	—
Succinimide, antiepileptic or anticonvulsant	T42.2X1	T42.2X2	T42.2X3	T42.2X4	T42.2X5	T42.2X6
mercuric — see Mercury						
Succinylcholine	T48.1X1	T48.1X2	T48.1X3	T48.1X4	T48.1X5	T48.1X6
Succinylsulfathiazole	T37.0X1	T37.0X2	T37.0X3	T37.0X4	T37.0X5	T37.0X6
Sucralfate	T47.1X1	T47.1X2	T47.1X3	T47.1X4	T47.1X5	T47.1X6
Sucrose	T50.3X1	T50.3X2	T50.3X3	T50.3X4	T50.3X5	T50.3X6
Sufentanil	T40.411	T40.412	T40.413	T40.414	T40.415	T40.416 ◄
Sulbactam	T36.0X1	T36.0X2	T36.0X3	T36.0X4	T36.0X5	T36.0X6
Sulbenicillin	T36.0X1	T36.0X2	T36.0X3	T36.0X4	T36.0X5	T36.0X6
Sulbentine	T49.0X1	T49.0X2	T49.0X3	T49.0X4	T49.0X5	T49.0X6
Sulfacetamide	T49.0X1	T49.0X2	T49.0X3	T49.0X4	T49.0X5	T49.0X6
ophthalmic preparation	T49.5X1	T49.5X2	T49.5X3	T49.5X4	T49.5X5	T49.5X6
Sulfachlorpyridazine	T37.0X1	T37.0X2	T37.0X3	T37.0X4	T37.0X5	T37.0X6
Sulfacitine	T37.0X1	T37.0X2	T37.0X3	T37.0X4	T37.0X5	T37.0X6
Sulfadiasulfone sodium	T37.0X1	T37.0X2	T37.0X3	T37.0X4	T37.0X5	T37.0X6
Sulfadiazine	T37.0X1	T37.0X2	T37.0X3	T37.0X4	T37.0X5	T37.0X6
silver (topical)	T49.0X1	T49.0X2	T49.0X3	T49.0X4	T49.0X5	T49.0X6

Substance	External Cause (T-Code)					
	Poisoning, Accidental (Unintentional)	Poisoning, Intentional Self-Harm	Poisoning, Assault	Poisoning, Undetermined	Adverse Effect	Underdosing
Sulfadimethoxine	T37.0X1	T37.0X2	T37.0X3	T37.0X4	T37.0X5	T37.0X6
Sulfadimidine	T37.0X1	T37.0X2	T37.0X3	T37.0X4	T37.0X5	T37.0X6
Sulfadoxine	T37.0X1	T37.0X2	T37.0X3	T37.0X4	T37.0X5	T37.0X6
with pyrimethamine	T37.2X1	T37.2X2	T37.2X3	T37.2X4	T37.2X5	T37.2X6
Sulfaethidole	T37.0X1	T37.0X2	T37.0X3	T37.0X4	T37.0X5	T37.0X6
Sulfafurazole	T37.0X1	T37.0X2	T37.0X3	T37.0X4	T37.0X5	T37.0X6
Sulfaguanidine	T37.0X1	T37.0X2	T37.0X3	T37.0X4	T37.0X5	T37.0X6
Sulfalene	T37.0X1	T37.0X2	T37.0X3	T37.0X4	T37.0X5	T37.0X6
Sulfaloxate	T37.0X1	T37.0X2	T37.0X3	T37.0X4	T37.0X5	T37.0X6
Sulfaloxic acid	T37.0X1	T37.0X2	T37.0X3	T37.0X4	T37.0X5	T37.0X6
Sulfamazone	T39.2X1	T39.2X2	T39.2X3	T39.2X4	T39.2X5	T39.2X6
Sulfamerazine	T37.0X1	T37.0X2	T37.0X3	T37.0X4	T37.0X5	T37.0X6
Sulfameter	T37.0X1	T37.0X2	T37.0X3	T37.0X4	T37.0X5	T37.0X6
Sulfamethazine	T37.0X1	T37.0X2	T37.0X3	T37.0X4	T37.0X5	T37.0X6
Sulfamethizole	T37.0X1	T37.0X2	T37.0X3	T37.0X4	T37.0X5	T37.0X6
Sulfamethoxazole	T37.0X1	T37.0X2	T37.0X3	T37.0X4	T37.0X5	T37.0X6
with trimethoprim	T36.8X1	T36.8X2	T36.8X3	T36.8X4	T36.8X5	T36.8X6
Sulfamethoxydiazine	T37.0X1	T37.0X2	T37.0X3	T37.0X4	T37.0X5	T37.0X6
Sulfamethoxypyridazine	T37.0X1	T37.0X2	T37.0X3	T37.0X4	T37.0X5	T37.0X6
Sulfamethylthiazole	T37.0X1	T37.0X2	T37.0X3	T37.0X4	T37.0X5	T37.0X6
Sulfametoxydiazine	T37.0X1	T37.0X2	T37.0X3	T37.0X4	T37.0X5	T37.0X6
Sulfamidopyrine	T39.2X1	T39.2X2	T39.2X3	T39.2X4	T39.2X5	T39.2X6
Sulfamonomethoxine	T37.0X1	T37.0X2	T37.0X3	T37.0X4	T37.0X5	T37.0X6
Sulfamoxole	T37.0X1	T37.0X2	T37.0X3	T37.0X4	T37.0X5	T37.0X6
Sulfamylon	T49.0X1	T49.0X2	T49.0X3	T49.0X4	T49.0X5	T49.0X6
Sulfan blue (diagnostic dye)	T50.8X1	T50.8X2	T50.8X3	T50.8X4	T50.8X5	T50.8X6
Sulfanilamide	T37.0X1	T37.0X2	T37.0X3	T37.0X4	T37.0X5	T37.0X6
Sulfanilylguanidine	T37.0X1	T37.0X2	T37.0X3	T37.0X4	T37.0X5	T37.0X6
Sulfaperin	T37.0X1	T37.0X2	T37.0X3	T37.0X4	T37.0X5	T37.0X6
Sulfaphenazole	T37.0X1	T37.0X2	T37.0X3	T37.0X4	T37.0X5	T37.0X6
Sulfaphenylthiazole	T37.0X1	T37.0X2	T37.0X3	T37.0X4	T37.0X5	T37.0X6
Sulfaproxyline	T37.0X1	T37.0X2	T37.0X3	T37.0X4	T37.0X5	T37.0X6
Sulfapyridine	T37.0X1	T37.0X2	T37.0X3	T37.0X4	T37.0X5	T37.0X6
Sulfapyrimidine	T37.0X1	T37.0X2	T37.0X3	T37.0X4	T37.0X5	T37.0X6
Sulfarsphenamine	T37.8X1	T37.8X2	T37.8X3	T37.8X4	T37.8X5	T37.8X6
Sulfasalazine	T37.0X1	T37.0X2	T37.0X3	T37.0X4	T37.0X5	T37.0X6
Sulfasuxidine	T37.0X1	T37.0X2	T37.0X3	T37.0X4	T37.0X5	T37.0X6
Sulfasymazine	T37.0X1	T37.0X2	T37.0X3	T37.0X4	T37.0X5	T37.0X6
Sulfated amylopectin	T47.8X1	T47.8X2	T47.8X3	T47.8X4	T47.8X5	T47.8X6
Sulfathiazole	T37.0X1	T37.0X2	T37.0X3	T37.0X4	T37.0X5	T37.0X6
Sulfatostearate	T49.2X1	T49.2X2	T49.2X3	T49.2X4	T49.2X5	T49.2X6
Sulfinpyrazone	T50.4X1	T50.4X2	T50.4X3	T50.4X4	T50.4X5	T50.4X6

◄ New   ◄ Revised   ~~deleted~~ Deleted

	External Cause (T-Code)					
Substance	Poisoning, Accidental (Unintentional)	Poisoning, Intentional Self-Harm	Poisoning, Assault	Poisoning, Undetermined	Adverse Effect	Underdosing
Sulfiram	T49.0X1	T49.0X2	T49.0X3	T49.0X4	T49.0X5	T49.0X6
Sulfisomidine	T37.0X1	T37.0X2	T37.0X3	T37.0X4	T37.0X5	T37.0X6
Sulfisoxazole	T37.0X1	T37.0X2	T37.0X3	T37.0X4	T37.0X5	T37.0X6
ophthalmic preparation	T49.5X1	T49.5X2	T49.5X3	T49.5X4	T49.5X5	T49.5X6
Sulfobromophthalein (sodium)	T50.8X1	T50.8X2	T50.8X3	T50.8X4	T50.8X5	T50.8X6
Sulfobromphthalein	T50.8X1	T50.8X2	T50.8X3	T50.8X4	T50.8X5	T50.8X6
Sulfogaiacol	T48.4X1	T48.4X2	T48.4X3	T48.4X4	T48.4X5	T48.4X6
Sulfomyxin	T36.8X1	T36.8X2	T36.8X3	T36.8X4	T36.8X5	T36.8X6
Sulfonal	T42.6X1	T42.6X2	T42.6X3	T42.6X4	T42.6X5	T42.6X6
Sulfonamide NEC	T37.0X1	T37.0X2	T37.0X3	T37.0X4	T37.0X5	T37.0X6
eye	T49.5X1	T49.5X2	T49.5X3	T49.5X4	T49.5X5	T49.5X6
Sulfonazide	T37.1X1	T37.1X2	T37.1X3	T37.1X4	T37.1X5	T37.1X6
Sulfones	T37.1X1	T37.1X2	T37.1X3	T37.1X4	T37.1X5	T37.1X6
Sulfonethylmethane	T42.6X1	T42.6X2	T42.6X3	T42.6X4	T42.6X5	T42.6X6
Sulfonmethane	T42.6X1	T42.6X2	T42.6X3	T42.6X4	T42.6X5	T42.6X6
Sulfonphthal, sulfonphthol	T50.8X1	T50.8X2	T50.8X3	T50.8X4	T50.8X5	T50.8X6
Sulfonylurea derivatives, oral	T38.3X1	T38.3X2	T38.3X3	T38.3X4	T38.3X5	T38.3X6
Sulforidazine	T43.3X1	T43.3X2	T43.3X3	T43.3X4	T43.3X5	T43.3X6
Sulfoxone	T37.1X1	T37.1X2	T37.1X3	T37.1X4	T37.1X5	T37.1X6
Sulfur, sulfurated, sulfuric, sulfurous, sulfuryl (compounds NEC) (medicinal)	T49.4X1	T49.4X2	T49.4X3	T49.4X4	T49.4X5	T49.4X6
acid	T54.2X1	T54.2X2	T54.2X3	T54.2X4	—	—
dioxide (gas)	T59.1X1	T59.1X2	T59.1X3	T59.1X4	—	—
ether — see Ether(s)						
hydrogen	T59.6X1	T59.6X2	T59.6X3	T59.6X4	—	—
medicinal (keratolytic) (ointment) NEC	T49.4X1	T49.4X2	T49.4X3	T49.4X4	T49.4X5	T49.4X6
ointment	T49.0X1	T49.0X2	T49.0X3	T49.0X4	T49.0X5	T49.0X6
pesticide (vapor)	T60.91	T60.92	T60.93	T60.94	—	—
vapor NEC	T59.891	T59.892	T59.893	T59.894	—	—
Sulfuric acid	T54.2X1	T54.2X2	T54.2X3	T54.2X4	—	—
Sulglicotide	T47.1X1	T47.1X2	T47.1X3	T47.1X4	T47.1X5	T47.1X6
Sulindac	T39.391	T39.392	T39.393	T39.394	T39.395	T39.396
Sulisatin	T47.2X1	T47.2X2	T47.2X3	T47.2X4	T47.2X5	T47.2X6
Sulisobenzone	T49.3X1	T49.3X2	T49.3X3	T49.3X4	T49.3X5	T49.3X6
Sulkowitch's reagent	T50.8X1	T50.8X2	T50.8X3	T50.8X4	T50.8X5	T50.8X6
Sulmetozine	T44.3X1	T44.3X2	T44.3X3	T44.3X4	T44.3X5	T44.3X6
Suloctidil	T46.7X1	T46.7X2	T46.7X3	T46.7X4	T46.7X5	T46.7X6
Sulph — see also Sulf-						
Sulphadiazine	T37.0X1	T37.0X2	T37.0X3	T37.0X4	T37.0X5	T37.0X6

	External Cause (T-Code)					
Substance	Poisoning, Accidental (Unintentional)	Poisoning, Intentional Self-Harm	Poisoning, Assault	Poisoning, Undetermined	Adverse Effect	Underdosing
Sulphadimethoxine	T37.0X1	T37.0X2	T37.0X3	T37.0X4	T37.0X5	T37.0X6
Sulphadimidine	T37.0X1	T37.0X2	T37.0X3	T37.0X4	T37.0X5	T37.0X6
Sulphadione	T37.1X1	T37.1X2	T37.1X3	T37.1X4	T37.1X5	T37.1X6
Sulphafurazole	T37.0X1	T37.0X2	T37.0X3	T37.0X4	T37.0X5	T37.0X6
Sulphamethizole	T37.0X1	T37.0X2	T37.0X3	T37.0X4	T37.0X5	T37.0X6
Sulphamethoxazole	T37.0X1	T37.0X2	T37.0X3	T37.0X4	T37.0X5	T37.0X6
Sulphan blue	T50.8X1	T50.8X2	T50.8X3	T50.8X4	T50.8X5	T50.8X6
Sulphaphenazole	T37.0X1	T37.0X2	T37.0X3	T37.0X4	T37.0X5	T37.0X6
Sulphapyridine	T37.0X1	T37.0X2	T37.0X3	T37.0X4	T37.0X5	T37.0X6
Sulphasalazine	T37.0X1	T37.0X2	T37.0X3	T37.0X4	T37.0X5	T37.0X6
Sulphinpyrazone	T50.4X1	T50.4X2	T50.4X3	T50.4X4	T50.4X5	T50.4X6
Sulpiride	T43.591	T43.592	T43.593	T43.594	T43.595	T43.596
Sulprostone	T48.0X1	T48.0X2	T48.0X3	T48.0X4	T48.0X5	T48.0X6
Sulpyrine	T39.2X1	T39.2X2	T39.2X3	T39.2X4	T39.2X5	T39.2X6
Sultamicillin	T36.0X1	T36.0X2	T36.0X3	T36.0X4	T36.0X5	T36.0X6
Sulthiame	T42.6X1	T42.6X2	T42.6X3	T42.6X4	T42.6X5	T42.6X6
Sultiame	T42.6X1	T42.6X2	T42.6X3	T42.6X4	T42.6X5	T42.6X6
Sultopride	T43.591	T43.592	T43.593	T43.594	T43.595	T43.596
Sumatriptan	T39.8X1	T39.8X2	T39.8X3	T39.8X4	T39.8X5	T39.8X6
Sunflower seed oil	T46.6X1	T46.6X2	T46.6X3	T46.6X4	T46.6X5	T46.6X6
Superinone	T48.4X1	T48.4X2	T48.4X3	T48.4X4	T48.4X5	T48.4X6
Suprofen	T39.311	T39.312	T39.313	T39.314	T39.315	T39.316
Suramin (sodium)	T37.4X1	T37.4X2	T37.4X3	T37.4X4	T37.4X5	T37.4X6
Surfacaine	T41.3X1	T41.3X2	T41.3X3	T41.3X4	T41.3X5	T41.3X6
Surital	T41.1X1	T41.1X2	T41.1X3	T41.1X4	T41.1X5	T41.1X6
Sutilains	T45.3X1	T45.3X2	T45.3X3	T45.3X4	T45.3X5	T45.3X6
Suxamethonium (chloride)	T48.1X1	T48.1X2	T48.1X3	T48.1X4	T48.1X5	T48.1X6
Suxethonium (chloride)	T48.1X1	T48.1X2	T48.1X3	T48.1X4	T48.1X5	T48.1X6
Suxibuzone	T39.2X1	T39.2X2	T39.2X3	T39.2X4	T39.2X5	T39.2X6
Sweet oil (birch)	T49.3X1	T49.3X2	T49.3X3	T49.3X4	T49.3X5	T49.3X6
Sweet niter spirit	T46.3X1	T46.3X2	T46.3X3	T46.3X4	T46.3X5	T46.3X6
Sweetener	T50.901	T50.902	T50.903	T50.904	T50.905	T50.906
Sym-dichloroethyl ether	T53.6X1	T53.6X2	T53.6X3	T53.6X4	—	—
Sympatholytic NEC	T44.8X1	T44.8X2	T44.8X3	T44.8X4	T44.8X5	T44.8X6
haloalkylamine	T44.8X1	T44.8X2	T44.8X3	T44.8X4	T44.8X5	T44.8X6
Sympathomimetic NEC	T44.901	T44.902	T44.903	T44.904	T44.905	T44.906
anti-common-cold	T48.5X1	T48.5X2	T48.5X3	T48.5X4	T48.5X5	T48.5X6
bronchodilator	T48.6X1	T48.6X2	T48.6X3	T48.6X4	T48.6X5	T48.6X6
specified NEC	T44.991	T44.992	T44.993	T44.994	T44.995	T44.996
Synagis	T50.B91	T50.B92	T50.B93	T50.B94	T50.B95	T50.B96
Synalar	T49.0X1	T49.0X2	T49.0X3	T49.0X4	T49.0X5	T49.0X6
Synthroid	T38.1X1	T38.1X2	T38.1X3	T38.1X4	T38.1X5	T38.1X6

◀ New　◀ Revised　deleted Deleted

Substance	Poisoning, Accidental (Unintentional)	Poisoning, Intentional Self-Harm	Poisoning, Assault	Poisoning, Undetermined	Adverse Effect	Underdosing
Syntocinon	T48.0X1	T48.0X2	T48.0X3	T48.0X4	T48.0X5	T48.0X6
Syrosingopine	T46.5X1	T46.5X2	T46.5X3	T46.5X4	T46.5X5	T46.5X6
Systemic drug	T45.91	T45.92	T45.93	T45.94	T45.95	T45.96
specified NEC	T45.8X1	T45.8X2	T45.8X3	T45.8X4	T45.8X5	T45.8X6
2,4,5-T	T60.3X1	T60.3X2	T60.3X3	T60.3X4	—	—

T

Substance	Poisoning, Accidental (Unintentional)	Poisoning, Intentional Self-Harm	Poisoning, Assault	Poisoning, Undetermined	Adverse Effect	Underdosing
Tablets — *see also specified substance*	T50.901	T50.902	T50.903	T50.904	T50.905	T50.906
Tace	T38.5X1	T38.5X2	T38.5X3	T38.5X4	T38.5X5	T38.5X6
Tacrine	T44.0X1	T44.0X2	T44.0X3	T44.0X4	T44.0X5	T44.0X6
Tadalafil	T46.7X1	T46.7X2	T46.7X3	T46.7X4	T46.7X5	T46.7X6
Talampicillin	T36.0X1	T36.0X2	T36.0X3	T36.0X4	T36.0X5	T36.0X6
Talbutal	T42.3X1	T42.3X2	T42.3X3	T42.3X4	T42.3X5	T42.3X6
Talc powder	T49.3X1	T49.3X2	T49.3X3	T49.3X4	T49.3X5	T49.3X6
Talcum	T49.3X1	T49.3X2	T49.3X3	T49.3X4	T49.3X5	T49.3X6
Taleranol	T38.6X1	T38.6X2	T38.6X3	T38.6X4	T38.6X5	T38.6X6
Tamoxifen	T38.6X1	T38.6X2	T38.6X3	T38.6X4	T38.6X5	T38.6X6
Tamsulosin	T44.6X1	T44.6X2	T44.6X3	T44.6X4	T44.6X5	T44.6X6
Tandearil, tanderil	T39.2X1	T39.2X2	T39.2X3	T39.2X4	T39.2X5	T39.2X6
Tannic acid	T49.2X1	T49.2X2	T49.2X3	T49.2X4	T49.2X5	T49.2X6
medicinal (astringent)	T49.2X1	T49.2X2	T49.2X3	T49.2X4	T49.2X5	T49.2X6
Tannin — *see Tannic acid*						
Tansy	T62.2X1	T62.2X2	T62.2X3	T62.2X4	—	—
TAO	T36.3X1	T36.3X2	T36.3X3	T36.3X4	T36.3X5	T36.3X6
Tapazole	T38.2X1	T38.2X2	T38.2X3	T38.2X4	T38.2X5	T38.2X6
Tar NEC	T52.0X1	T52.0X2	T52.0X3	T52.0X4	—	—
camphor	T60.1X1	T60.1X2	T60.1X3	T60.1X4	—	—
distillate	T49.1X1	T49.1X2	T49.1X3	T49.1X4	T49.1X5	T49.1X6
fumes	T59.891	T59.892	T59.893	T59.894	—	—
medicinal	T49.1X1	T49.1X2	T49.1X3	T49.1X4	T49.1X5	T49.1X6
ointment	T49.1X1	T49.1X2	T49.1X3	T49.1X4	T49.1X5	T49.1X6
Taractan	T43.591	T43.592	T43.593	T43.594	T43.595	T43.596
Tarantula (venomous)	T63.321	T63.322	T63.323	T63.324	—	—
Tartar emetic	T37.8X1	T37.8X2	T37.8X3	T37.8X4	T37.8X5	T37.8X6
Tartaric acid	T65.891	T65.892	T65.893	T65.894	—	—
Tartrated antimony (anti-infective)	T37.8X1	T37.8X2	T37.8X3	T37.8X4	T37.8X5	T37.8X6
Tartrate, laxative	T47.4X1	T47.4X2	T47.4X3	T47.4X4	T47.4X5	T47.4X6
Tauromustine	T45.1X1	T45.1X2	T45.1X3	T45.1X4	T45.1X5	T45.1X6
TCA — *see Trichloroacetic acid*						
TCDD	T53.7X1	T53.7X2	T53.7X3	T53.7X4	—	—
TDI (vapor)	T65.0X1	T65.0X2	T65.0X3	T65.0X4	—	—

Substance	Poisoning, Accidental (Unintentional)	Poisoning, Intentional Self-Harm	Poisoning, Assault	Poisoning, Undetermined	Adverse Effect	Underdosing
Tear						
gas	T59.3X1	T59.3X2	T59.3X3	T59.3X4	—	—
solution	T49.5X1	T49.5X2	T49.5X3	T49.5X4	T49.5X5	T49.5X6
Teclothiazide	T50.2X1	T50.2X2	T50.2X3	T50.2X4	T50.2X5	T50.2X6
Teclozan	T37.3X1	T37.3X2	T37.3X3	T37.3X4	T37.3X5	T37.3X6
Tegafur	T45.1X1	T45.1X2	T45.1X3	T45.1X4	T45.1X5	T45.1X6
Tegretol	T42.1X1	T42.1X2	T42.1X3	T42.1X4	T42.1X5	T42.1X6
Teicoplanin	T36.8X1	T36.8X2	T36.8X3	T36.8X4	T36.8X5	T36.8X6
Telepaque	T50.8X1	T50.8X2	T50.8X3	T50.8X4	T50.8X5	T50.8X6
Tellurium	T56.891	T56.892	T56.893	T56.894	—	—
fumes	T56.891	T56.892	T56.893	T56.894	—	—
TEM	T45.1X1	T45.1X2	T45.1X3	T45.1X4	T45.1X5	T45.1X6
Temazepam	T42.4X1	T42.4X2	T42.4X3	T42.4X4	T42.4X5	T42.4X6
Temocillin	T36.0X1	T36.0X2	T36.0X3	T36.0X4	T36.0X5	T36.0X6
Tenamfetamine	T43.621	T43.622	T43.623	T43.624	T43.625	T43.626
Teniposide	T45.1X1	T45.1X2	T45.1X3	T45.1X4	T45.1X5	T45.1X6
Tenitramine	T46.3X1	T46.3X2	T46.3X3	T46.3X4	T46.3X5	T46.3X6
Tenoglicin	T48.4X1	T48.4X2	T48.4X3	T48.4X4	T48.4X5	T48.4X6
Tenonitrozole	T37.3X1	T37.3X2	T37.3X3	T37.3X4	T37.3X5	T37.3X6
Tenoxicam	T39.391	T39.392	T39.393	T39.394	T39.395	T39.396
TEPA	T45.1X1	T45.1X2	T45.1X3	T45.1X4	T45.1X5	T45.1X6
TEPP	T60.0X1	T60.0X2	T60.0X3	T60.0X4	—	—
Teprotide	T46.5X1	T46.5X2	T46.5X3	T46.5X4	T46.5X5	T46.5X6
Terazosin	T44.6X1	T44.6X2	T44.6X3	T44.6X4	T44.6X5	T44.6X6
Terbufos	T60.0X1	T60.0X2	T60.0X3	T60.0X4	—	—
Terbutaline	T48.6X1	T48.6X2	T48.6X3	T48.6X4	T48.6X5	T48.6X6
Terconazole	T49.0X1	T49.0X2	T49.0X3	T49.0X4	T49.0X5	T49.0X6
Terfenadine	T45.0X1	T45.0X2	T45.0X3	T45.0X4	T45.0X5	T45.0X6
Teriparatide (acetate)	T50.991	T50.992	T50.993	T50.994	T50.995	T50.996
Terizidone	T37.1X1	T37.1X2	T37.1X3	T37.1X4	T37.1X5	T37.1X6
Terlipressin	T38.891	T38.892	T38.893	T38.894	T38.895	T38.896
Terodiline	T46.3X1	T46.3X2	T46.3X3	T46.3X4	T46.3X5	T46.3X6
Teroxalene	T37.4X1	T37.4X2	T37.4X3	T37.4X4	T37.4X5	T37.4X6
Terpin(cis) hydrate	T48.4X1	T48.4X2	T48.4X3	T48.4X4	T48.4X5	T48.4X6
Terramycin	T36.4X1	T36.4X2	T36.4X3	T36.4X4	T36.4X5	T36.4X6
Tertatolol	T44.7X1	T44.7X2	T44.7X3	T44.7X4	T44.7X5	T44.7X6
Tessalon	T48.3X1	T48.3X2	T48.3X3	T48.3X4	T48.3X5	T48.3X6
Testolactone	T38.7X1	T38.7X2	T38.7X3	T38.7X4	T38.7X5	T38.7X6
Testosterone	T38.7X1	T38.7X2	T38.7X3	T38.7X4	T38.7X5	T38.7X6
Tetanus toxoid or vaccine	T50.A91	T50.A92	T50.A93	T50.A94	T50.A95	T50.A96
antitoxin	T50.Z11	T50.Z12	T50.Z13	T50.Z14	T50.Z15	T50.Z16
immune globulin (human)	T50.Z11	T50.Z12	T50.Z13	T50.Z14	T50.Z15	T50.Z16

◀ New ◀ Revised ~~deleted~~ Deleted

Substance	External Cause (T-Code) Poisoning, Accidental (Unintentional)	Poisoning, Intentional Self-Harm	Poisoning, Assault	Poisoning, Undetermined	Adverse Effect	Underdosing
Tetanus toxoid or vaccine (Continued)						
toxoid	T50.A91	T50.A92	T50.A93	T50.A94	T50.A95	T50.A96
with diphtheria toxoid	T50.A21	T50.A22	T50.A23	T50.A24	T50.A25	T50.A26
with pertussis	T50.A11	T50.A12	T50.A13	T50.A14	T50.A15	T50.A16
Tetrabenazine	T43.591	T43.592	T43.593	T43.594	T43.595	T43.596
Tetracaine	T41.3X1	T41.3X2	T41.3X3	T41.3X4	T41.3X5	T41.3X6
nerve block (peripheral) (plexus)	T41.3X1	T41.3X2	T41.3X3	T41.3X4	T41.3X5	T41.3X6
regional	T41.3X1	T41.3X2	T41.3X3	T41.3X4	T41.3X5	T41.3X6
spinal	T41.3X1	T41.3X2	T41.3X3	T41.3X4	T41.3X5	T41.3X6
Tetrachlorethylene — see Tetrachloroethylene						
Tetrachlormethiazide	T50.2X1	T50.2X2	T50.2X3	T50.2X4	T50.2X5	T50.2X6
2,3,7,8-Tetrachlorodibenzo-p-dioxin	T53.7X1	T53.7X2	T53.7X3	T53.7X4	—	—
Tetrachloroethane	T53.6X1	T53.6X2	T53.6X3	T53.6X4	—	—
vapor	T53.6X1	T53.6X2	T53.6X3	T53.6X4	—	—
paint or varnish	T53.6X1	T53.6X2	T53.6X3	T53.6X4	—	—
Tetrachloroethylene (liquid)	T53.3X1	T53.3X2	T53.3X3	T53.3X4	—	—
medicinal	T37.4X1	T37.4X2	T37.4X3	T37.4X4	T37.4X5	T37.4X6
vapor	T53.3X1	T53.3X2	T53.3X3	T53.3X4	—	—
Tetrachloromethane — see Carbon tetrachloride						
Tetracosactide	T38.811	T38.812	T38.813	T38.814	T38.815	T38.816
Tetracosactrin	T38.811	T38.812	T38.813	T38.814	T38.815	T38.816
Tetracycline	T36.4X1	T36.4X2	T36.4X3	T36.4X4	T36.4X5	T36.4X6
ophthalmic preparation	T49.5X1	T49.5X2	T49.5X3	T49.5X4	T49.5X5	T49.5X6
topical NEC	T49.0X1	T49.0X2	T49.0X3	T49.0X4	T49.0X5	T49.0X6
Tetradifon	T60.8X1	T60.8X2	T60.8X3	T60.8X4	—	—
Tetradotoxin	T61.771	T61.772	T61.773	T61.774	—	—
Tetraethyl						
lead	T56.0X1	T56.0X2	T56.0X3	T56.0X4	—	—
pyrophosphate	T60.0X1	T60.0X2	T60.0X3	T60.0X4	—	—
Tetraethylammonium chloride	T44.2X1	T44.2X2	T44.2X3	T44.2X4	T44.2X5	T44.2X6
Tetraethylthiuram disulfide	T50.6X1	T50.6X2	T50.6X3	T50.6X4	T50.6X5	T50.6X6
Tetrahydroaminoacridine	T44.0X1	T44.0X2	T44.0X3	T44.0X4	T44.0X5	T44.0X6
Tetrahydrocannabinol	T40.7X1	T40.7X2	T40.7X3	T40.7X4	T40.7X5	T40.7X6
Tetrahydrofuran	T52.8X1	T52.8X2	T52.8X3	T52.8X4	—	—
Tetrahydronaphthalene	T52.8X1	T52.8X2	T52.8X3	T52.8X4	—	—
Tetrahydrozoline	T49.5X1	T49.5X2	T49.5X3	T49.5X4	T49.5X5	T49.5X6
Tetralin	T52.8X1	T52.8X2	T52.8X3	T52.8X4	—	—
Tetramethrin	T60.2X1	T60.2X2	T60.2X3	T60.2X4	—	—

Substance	External Cause (T-Code) Poisoning, Accidental (Unintentional)	Poisoning, Intentional Self-Harm	Poisoning, Assault	Poisoning, Undetermined	Adverse Effect	Underdosing
Tetramethylthiuram (disulfide) NEC	T60.3X1	T60.3X2	T60.3X3	T60.3X4	—	—
medicinal	T49.0X1	T49.0X2	T49.0X3	T49.0X4	T49.0X5	T49.0X6
Tetramisole	T37.4X1	T37.4X2	T37.4X3	T37.4X4	T37.4X5	T37.4X6
Tetranicotinoyl fructose	T46.7X1	T46.7X2	T46.7X3	T46.7X4	T46.7X5	T46.7X6
Tetronal	T42.6X1	T42.6X2	T42.6X3	T42.6X4	T42.6X5	T42.6X6
Tetrazepam	T42.4X1	T42.4X2	T42.4X3	T42.4X4	T42.4X5	T42.4X6
Tetryl	T65.3X1	T65.3X2	T65.3X3	T65.3X4	—	—
Tetrylammonium chloride	T44.2X1	T44.2X2	T44.2X3	T44.2X4	T44.2X5	T44.2X6
Tetryzoline	T49.5X1	T49.5X2	T49.5X3	T49.5X4	T49.5X5	T49.5X6
Thalidomide	T45.1X1	T45.1X2	T45.1X3	T45.1X4	T45.1X5	T45.1X6
Thallium (compounds) (dust) NEC	T56.811	T56.812	T56.813	T56.814	—	—
pesticide	T60.4X1	T60.4X2	T60.4X3	T60.4X4	—	—
THC	T40.7X1	T40.7X2	T40.7X3	T40.7X4	T40.7X5	T40.7X6
Thebacon	T48.3X1	T48.3X2	T48.3X3	T48.3X4	T48.3X5	T48.3X6
Thebaine	T40.2X1	T40.2X2	T40.2X3	T40.2X4	T40.2X5	T40.2X6
Thenoic acid	T49.6X1	T49.6X2	T49.6X3	T49.6X4	T49.6X5	T49.6X6
Thenyldiamine	T45.0X1	T45.0X2	T45.0X3	T45.0X4	T45.0X5	T45.0X6
Theobromine (calcium salicylate)	T48.6X1	T48.6X2	T48.6X3	T48.6X4	T48.6X5	T48.6X6
sodium salicylate	T48.6X1	T48.6X2	T48.6X3	T48.6X4	T48.6X5	T48.6X6
Theophyllamine	T48.6X1	T48.6X2	T48.6X3	T48.6X4	T48.6X5	T48.6X6
Theophylline	T48.6X1	T48.6X2	T48.6X3	T48.6X4	T48.6X5	T48.6X6
aminobenzoic acid	T48.6X1	T48.6X2	T48.6X3	T48.6X4	T48.6X5	T48.6X6
ethylenediamine	T48.6X1	T48.6X2	T48.6X3	T48.6X4	T48.6X5	T48.6X6
piperazine p-amino-benzoate	T48.6X1	T48.6X2	T48.6X3	T48.6X4	T48.6X5	T48.6X6
Thiabendazole	T37.4X1	T37.4X2	T37.4X3	T37.4X4	T37.4X5	T37.4X6
Thialbarbital	T41.1X1	T41.1X2	T41.1X3	T41.1X4	T41.1X5	T41.1X6
Thiamazole	T38.2X1	T38.2X2	T38.2X3	T38.2X4	T38.2X5	T38.2X6
Thiambutosine	T37.1X1	T37.1X2	T37.1X3	T37.1X4	T37.1X5	T37.1X6
Thiamine	T45.2X1	T45.2X2	T45.2X3	T45.2X4	T45.2X5	T45.2X6
Thiamphenicol	T36.2X1	T36.2X2	T36.2X3	T36.2X4	T36.2X5	T36.2X6
Thiamylal	T41.1X1	T41.1X2	T41.1X3	T41.1X4	T41.1X5	T41.1X6
sodium	T41.1X1	T41.1X2	T41.1X3	T41.1X4	T41.1X5	T41.1X6
Thiazesim	T43.291	T43.292	T43.293	T43.294	T43.295	T43.296
Thiazides (diuretics)	T50.2X1	T50.2X2	T50.2X3	T50.2X4	T50.2X5	T50.2X6
Thiazinamium metilsulfate	T43.3X1	T43.3X2	T43.3X3	T43.3X4	T43.3X5	T43.3X6
Thiethylperazine	T43.3X1	T43.3X2	T43.3X3	T43.3X4	T43.3X5	T43.3X6
Thimerosal	T49.0X1	T49.0X2	T49.0X3	T49.0X4	T49.0X5	T49.0X6
ophthalmic preparation	T49.5X1	T49.5X2	T49.5X3	T49.5X4	T49.5X5	T49.5X6
Thioacetazone	T37.1X1	T37.1X2	T37.1X3	T37.1X4	T37.1X5	T37.1X6
with isoniazid	T37.1X1	T37.1X2	T37.1X3	T37.1X4	T37.1X5	T37.1X6
Thiobarbital sodium	T41.1X1	T41.1X2	T41.1X3	T41.1X4	T41.1X5	T41.1X6

◀ New ◀ Revised ~~deleted~~ Deleted

Substance	External Cause (T-Code)					
	Poisoning, Accidental (Unintentional)	Poisoning, Intentional Self-Harm	Poisoning, Assault	Poisoning, Undetermined	Adverse Effect	Underdosing
Thiobarbiturate anesthetic	T41.1X1	T41.1X2	T41.1X3	T41.1X4	T41.1X5	T41.1X6
Thiobismol	T37.8X1	T37.8X2	T37.8X3	T37.8X4	T37.8X5	T37.8X6
Thiobutabarbital sodium	T41.1X1	T41.1X2	T41.1X3	T41.1X4	T41.1X5	T41.1X6
Thiocarbamate (insecticide)	T60.0X1	T60.0X2	T60.0X3	T60.0X4	—	—
Thiocarbamide	T38.2X1	T38.2X2	T38.2X3	T38.2X4	T38.2X5	T38.2X6
Thiocarbarsone	T37.8X1	T37.8X2	T37.8X3	T37.8X4	T37.8X5	T37.8X6
Thiocarlide	T37.1X1	T37.1X2	T37.1X3	T37.1X4	T37.1X5	T37.1X6
Thioctamide	T50.991	T50.992	T50.993	T50.994	T50.995	T50.996
Thioctic acid	T50.991	T50.992	T50.993	T50.994	T50.995	T50.996
Thiofos	T60.0X1	T60.0X2	T60.0X3	T60.0X4	—	—
Thioglycolate	T49.4X1	T49.4X2	T49.4X3	T49.4X4	T49.4X5	T49.4X6
Thioglycolic acid	T65.891	T65.892	T65.893	T65.894		
Thioguanine	T45.1X1	T45.1X2	T45.1X3	T45.1X4	T45.1X5	T45.1X6
Thiomercaptomerin	T50.2X1	T50.2X2	T50.2X3	T50.2X4	T50.2X5	T50.2X6
Thiomerin	T50.2X1	T50.2X2	T50.2X3	T50.2X4	T50.2X5	T50.2X6
Thiomersal	T49.0X1	T49.0X2	T49.0X3	T49.0X4	T49.0X5	T49.0X6
Thionazin	T60.0X1	T60.0X2	T60.0X3	T60.0X4	—	—
Thiopental (sodium)	T41.1X1	T41.1X2	T41.1X3	T41.1X4	T41.1X5	T41.1X6
Thiopentone (sodium)	T41.1X1	T41.1X2	T41.1X3	T41.1X4	T41.1X5	T41.1X6
Thiopropazate	T43.3X1	T43.3X2	T43.3X3	T43.3X4	T43.3X5	T43.3X6
Thioproperazine	T43.3X1	T43.3X2	T43.3X3	T43.3X4	T43.3X5	T43.3X6
Thioridazine	T43.3X1	T43.3X2	T43.3X3	T43.3X4	T43.3X5	T43.3X6
Thiosinamine	T49.3X1	T49.3X2	T49.3X3	T49.3X4	T49.3X5	T49.3X6
Thiotepa	T45.1X1	T45.1X2	T45.1X3	T45.1X4	T45.1X5	T45.1X6
Thiothixene	T43.4X1	T43.4X2	T43.4X3	T43.4X4	T43.4X5	T43.4X6
Thiouracil (benzyl) (methyl) (propyl)	T38.2X1	T38.2X2	T38.2X3	T38.2X4	T38.2X5	T38.2X6
Thiourea	T38.2X1	T38.2X2	T38.2X3	T38.2X4	T38.2X5	T38.2X6
Thiphenamil	T44.3X1	T44.3X2	T44.3X3	T44.3X4	T44.3X5	T44.3X6
Thiram	T60.3X1	T60.3X2	T60.3X3	T60.3X4	—	—
medicinal	T49.2X1	T49.2X2	T49.2X3	T49.2X4	T49.2X5	T49.2X6
Thonzylamine (systemic)	T45.0X1	T45.0X2	T45.0X3	T45.0X4	T45.0X5	T45.0X6
mucosal decongestant	T48.5X1	T48.5X2	T48.5X3	T48.5X4	T48.5X5	T48.5X6
Thorazine	T43.3X1	T43.3X2	T43.3X3	T43.3X4	T43.3X5	T43.3X6
Thorium dioxide suspension	T50.8X1	T50.8X2	T50.8X3	T50.8X4	T50.8X5	T50.8X6
Thornapple	T62.2X1	T62.2X2	T62.2X3	T62.2X4	—	—
Throat drug NEC	T49.6X1	T49.6X2	T49.6X3	T49.6X4	T49.6X5	T49.6X6
Thrombin	T45.7X1	T45.7X2	T45.7X3	T45.7X4	T45.7X5	T45.7X6
Thrombolysin	T45.611	T45.612	T45.613	T45.614	T45.615	T45.616
Thromboplastin	T45.7X1	T45.7X2	T45.7X3	T45.7X4	T45.7X5	T45.7X6
Thurfyl nicotinate	T46.7X1	T46.7X2	T46.7X3	T46.7X4	T46.7X5	T46.7X6
Thymol	T49.0X1	T49.0X2	T49.0X3	T49.0X4	T49.0X5	T49.0X6

Substance	External Cause (T-Code)					
	Poisoning, Accidental (Unintentional)	Poisoning, Intentional Self-Harm	Poisoning, Assault	Poisoning, Undetermined	Adverse Effect	Underdosing
Thymopentin	T37.5X1	T37.5X2	T37.5X3	T37.5X4	T37.5X5	T37.5X6
Thymoxamine	T46.7X1	T46.7X2	T46.7X3	T46.7X4	T46.7X5	T46.7X6
Thymus extract	T38.891	T38.892	T38.893	T38.894	T38.895	T38.896
Thyreotrophic hormone	T38.811	T38.812	T38.813	T38.814	T38.815	T38.816
Thyroglobulin	T38.1X1	T38.1X2	T38.1X3	T38.1X4	T38.1X5	T38.1X6
Thyroid (hormone)	T38.1X1	T38.1X2	T38.1X3	T38.1X4	T38.1X5	T38.1X6
Thyrolar	T38.1X1	T38.1X2	T38.1X3	T38.1X4	T38.1X5	T38.1X6
Thyrotrophin	T38.811	T38.812	T38.813	T38.814	T38.815	T38.816
Thyrotropic hormone	T38.811	T38.812	T38.813	T38.814	T38.815	T38.816
Thyroxine	T38.1X1	T38.1X2	T38.1X3	T38.1X4	T38.1X5	T38.1X6
Tiabendazole	T37.4X1	T37.4X2	T37.4X3	T37.4X4	T37.4X5	T37.4X6
Tiamizide	T50.2X1	T50.2X2	T50.2X3	T50.2X4	T50.2X5	T50.2X6
Tianeptine	T43.291	T43.292	T43.293	T43.294	T43.295	T43.296
Tiapamil	T46.1X1	T46.1X2	T46.1X3	T46.1X4	T46.1X5	T46.1X6
Tiapride	T43.591	T43.592	T43.593	T43.594	T43.595	T43.596
Tiaprofenic acid	T39.311	T39.312	T39.313	T39.314	T39.315	T39.316
Tiaramide	T39.8X1	T39.8X2	T39.8X3	T39.8X4	T39.8X5	T39.8X6
Ticarcillin	T36.0X1	T36.0X2	T36.0X3	T36.0X4	T36.0X5	T36.0X6
Ticlatone	T49.0X1	T49.0X2	T49.0X3	T49.0X4	T49.0X5	T49.0X6
Ticlopidine	T45.521	T45.522	T45.523	T45.524	T45.525	T45.526
Ticrynafen	T50.1X1	T50.1X2	T50.1X3	T50.1X4	T50.1X5	T50.1X6
Tidiacic	T50.991	T50.992	T50.993	T50.994	T50.995	T50.996
Tiemonium	T44.3X1	T44.3X2	T44.3X3	T44.3X4	T44.3X5	T44.3X6
iodide	T44.3X1	T44.3X2	T44.3X3	T44.3X4	T44.3X5	T44.3X6
Tienilic acid	T50.1X1	T50.1X2	T50.1X3	T50.1X4	T50.1X5	T50.1X6
Tifenamil	T44.3X1	T44.3X2	T44.3X3	T44.3X4	T44.3X5	T44.3X6
Tigan	T45.0X1	T45.0X2	T45.0X3	T45.0X4	T45.0X5	T45.0X6
Tigloidine	T44.3X1	T44.3X2	T44.3X3	T44.3X4	T44.3X5	T44.3X6
Tilactase	T47.5X1	T47.5X2	T47.5X3	T47.5X4	T47.5X5	T47.5X6
Tiletamine	T41.291	T41.292	T41.293	T41.294	T41.295	T41.296
Tilidine	T40.441	T40.442	T40.443	T40.444	—	—
Timepidium bromide	T44.3X1	T44.3X2	T44.3X3	T44.3X4	T44.3X5	T44.3X6
Timiperone	T43.4X1	T43.4X2	T43.4X3	T43.4X4	T43.4X5	T43.4X6
Timolol	T44.7X1	T44.7X2	T44.7X3	T44.7X4	T44.7X5	T44.7X6
Tin (chloride) (dust) (oxide) NEC	T56.6X1	T56.6X2	T56.6X3	T56.6X4	—	—
anti-infectives	T37.8X1	T37.8X2	T37.8X3	T37.8X4	T37.8X5	T37.8X6
Tincture, iodine—see Iodine						
Tindal	T43.3X1	T43.3X2	T43.3X3	T43.3X4	T43.3X5	T43.3X6
Tinidazole	T37.3X1	T37.3X2	T37.3X3	T37.3X4	T37.3X5	T37.3X6
Tinoridine	T39.8X1	T39.8X2	T39.8X3	T39.8X4	T39.8X5	T39.8X6
Tiocarlide	T37.1X1	T37.1X2	T37.1X3	T37.1X4	T37.1X5	T37.1X6
Tioclomarol	T45.511	T45.512	T45.513	T45.514	T45.515	T45.516

◀ New   ◀ Revised   ~~deleted~~ Deleted

Substance	Poisoning, Accidental (Unintentional)	Poisoning, Intentional Self-Harm	Poisoning, Assault	Poisoning, Undetermined	Adverse Effect	Underdosing
Tioconazole	T49.0X1	T49.0X2	T49.0X3	T49.0X4	T49.0X5	T49.0X6
Tioguanine	T45.1X1	T45.1X2	T45.1X3	T45.1X4	T45.1X5	T45.1X6
Tiopronin	T50.991	T50.992	T50.993	T50.994	T50.995	T50.996
Tiotixene	T43.4X1	T43.4X2	T43.4X3	T43.4X4	T43.4X5	T43.4X6
Tioxolone	T49.4X1	T49.4X2	T49.4X3	T49.4X4	T49.4X5	T49.4X6
Tipepidine	T48.3X1	T48.3X2	T48.3X3	T48.3X4	T48.3X5	T48.3X6
Tiquizium bromide	T44.3X1	T44.3X2	T44.3X3	T44.3X4	T44.3X5	T44.3X6
Tiratricol	T38.1X1	T38.1X2	T38.1X3	T38.1X4	T38.1X5	T38.1X6
Tisopurine	T50.4X1	T50.4X2	T50.4X3	T50.4X4	T50.4X5	T50.4X6
Titanium (compounds) (vapor)	T56.891	T56.892	T56.893	T56.894	—	—
dioxide	T49.3X1	T49.3X2	T49.3X3	T49.3X4	T49.3X5	T49.3X6
ointment	T49.3X1	T49.3X2	T49.3X3	T49.3X4	T49.3X5	T49.3X6
oxide	T49.3X1	T49.3X2	T49.3X3	T49.3X4	T49.3X5	T49.3X6
tetrachloride	T56.891	T56.892	T56.893	T56.894	—	—
Titanocene	T56.891	T56.892	T56.893	T56.894	—	—
Titroid	T38.1X1	T38.1X2	T38.1X3	T38.1X4	T38.1X5	T38.1X6
Tizanidine	T42.8X1	T42.8X2	T42.8X3	T42.8X4	T42.8X5	T42.8X6
TMTD	T60.3X1	T60.3X2	T60.3X3	T60.3X4	—	—
TNT (fumes)	T65.3X1	T65.3X2	T65.3X3	T65.3X4	—	—
Toadstool	T62.0X1	T62.0X2	T62.0X3	T62.0X4	—	—
Tobacco NEC	T65.291	T65.292	T65.293	T65.294	—	—
cigarettes	T65.221	T65.222	T65.223	T65.224	—	—
Indian	T62.2X1	T62.2X2	T62.2X3	T62.2X4	—	—
smoke, second-hand	T65.221	T65.222	T65.223	T65.224	—	—
Tobramycin	T36.5X1	T36.5X2	T36.5X3	T36.5X4	T36.5X5	T36.5X6
Tocainide	T46.2X1	T46.2X2	T46.2X3	T46.2X4	T46.2X5	T46.2X6
Tocoferol	T45.2X1	T45.2X2	T45.2X3	T45.2X4	T45.2X5	T45.2X6
Tocopherol	T45.2X1	T45.2X2	T45.2X3	T45.2X4	T45.2X5	T45.2X6
acetate	T45.2X1	T45.2X2	T45.2X3	T45.2X4	T45.2X5	T45.2X6
Tocosamine	T48.0X1	T48.0X2	T48.0X3	T48.0X4	T48.0X5	T48.0X6
Todralazine	T46.5X1	T46.5X2	T46.5X3	T46.5X4	T46.5X5	T46.5X6
Tofisopam	T42.4X1	T42.4X2	T42.4X3	T42.4X4	T42.4X5	T42.4X6
Tofranil	T43.011	T43.012	T43.013	T43.014	T43.015	T43.016
Toilet deodorizer	T65.891	T65.892	T65.893	T65.894	—	—
Tolamolol	T44.7X1	T44.7X2	T44.7X3	T44.7X4	T44.7X5	T44.7X6
Tolazamide	T38.3X1	T38.3X2	T38.3X3	T38.3X4	T38.3X5	T38.3X6
Tolazoline	T46.7X1	T46.7X2	T46.7X3	T46.7X4	T46.7X5	T46.7X6
Tolbutamide (sodium)	T38.3X1	T38.3X2	T38.3X3	T38.3X4	T38.3X5	T38.3X6
Tolciclate	T49.0X1	T49.0X2	T49.0X3	T49.0X4	T49.0X5	T49.0X6
Tolmetin	T39.391	T39.392	T39.393	T39.394	T39.395	T39.396
Tolnaftate	T49.0X1	T49.0X2	T49.0X3	T49.0X4	T49.0X5	T49.0X6
Tolonidine	T46.5X1	T46.5X2	T46.5X3	T46.5X4	T46.5X5	T46.5X6

Substance	Poisoning, Accidental (Unintentional)	Poisoning, Intentional Self-Harm	Poisoning, Assault	Poisoning, Undetermined	Adverse Effect	Underdosing
Toloxatone	T42.6X1	T42.6X2	T42.6X3	T42.6X4	T42.6X5	T42.6X6
Tolperisone	T44.3X1	T44.3X2	T44.3X3	T44.3X4	T44.3X5	T44.3X6
Tolserol	T42.8X1	T42.8X2	T42.8X3	T42.8X4	T42.8X5	T42.8X6
Toluene (liquid)	T52.2X1	T52.2X2	T52.2X3	T52.2X4	—	—
diisocyanate	T65.0X1	T65.0X2	T65.0X3	T65.0X4	—	—
Toluidine	T65.891	T65.892	T65.893	T65.894	—	—
vapor	T59.891	T59.892	T59.893	T59.894	—	—
Toluol (liquid)	T52.2X1	T52.2X2	T52.2X3	T52.2X4	—	—
vapor	T52.2X1	T52.2X2	T52.2X3	T52.2X4	—	—
Toluylenediamine	T65.3X1	T65.3X2	T65.3X3	T65.3X4	—	—
Tolylene-2,4-diisocyanate	T65.0X1	T65.0X2	T65.0X3	T65.0X4	—	—
Tonic NEC	T50.901	T50.902	T50.903	T50.904	T50.905	T50.906
Topical action drug NEC	T49.91	T49.92	T49.93	T49.94	T49.95	T49.96
ear, nose or throat	T49.6X1	T49.6X2	T49.6X3	T49.6X4	T49.6X5	T49.6X6
eye	T49.5X1	T49.5X2	T49.5X3	T49.5X4	T49.5X5	T49.5X6
skin	T49.91	T49.92	T49.93	T49.94	T49.95	T49.96
specified NEC	T49.8X1	T49.8X2	T49.8X3	T49.8X4	T49.8X5	T49.8X6
Toquizine	T44.3X1	T44.3X2	T44.3X3	T44.3X4	T44.3X5	T44.3X6
Toremifene	T38.6X1	T38.6X2	T38.6X3	T38.6X4	T38.6X5	T38.6X6
Tosylchloramide sodium	T49.8X1	T49.8X2	T49.8X3	T49.8X4	T49.8X5	T49.8X6
Toxaphene (dust) (spray)	T60.1X1	T60.1X2	T60.1X3	T60.1X4	—	—
Toxin, diphtheria (Schick Test)	T50.8X1	T50.8X2	T50.8X3	T50.8X4	T50.8X5	T50.8X6
Toxoid						
combined	T50.A21	T50.A22	T50.A23	T50.A24	T50.A25	T50.A26
diphtheria	T50.A91	T50.A92	T50.A93	T50.A94	T50.A95	T50.A96
tetanus	T50.A91	T50.A92	T50.A93	T50.A94	T50.A95	T50.A96
Trace element NEC	T45.8X1	T45.8X2	T45.8X3	T45.8X4	T45.8X5	T45.8X6
Tractor fuel NEC	T52.0X1	T52.0X2	T52.0X3	T52.0X4	—	—
Tragacanth	T50.991	T50.992	T50.993	T50.994	T50.995	T50.996
Tramadol	T40.421	T40.422	T40.423	T40.424	T40.425	T40.426 ◀
Tramazoline	T48.5X1	T48.5X2	T48.5X3	T48.5X4	T48.5X5	T48.5X6
Tranexamic acid	T45.621	T45.622	T45.623	T45.624	T45.625	T45.626
Tranilast	T45.0X1	T45.0X2	T45.0X3	T45.0X4	T45.0X5	T45.0X6
Tranquilizer NEC	T43.501	T43.502	T43.503	T43.504	T43.505	T43.506
with hypnotic or sedative	T42.6X1	T42.6X2	T42.6X3	T42.6X4	T42.6X5	T42.6X6
benzodiazepine NEC	T42.4X1	T42.4X2	T42.4X3	T42.4X4	T42.4X5	T42.4X6
butyrophenone NEC	T43.4X1	T43.4X2	T43.4X3	T43.4X4	T43.4X5	T43.4X6
carbamate	T43.591	T43.592	T43.593	T43.594	T43.595	T43.596
dimethylamine	T43.3X1	T43.3X2	T43.3X3	T43.3X4	T43.3X5	T43.3X6
ethylamine	T43.3X1	T43.3X2	T43.3X3	T43.3X4	T43.3X5	T43.3X6
hydroxyzine	T43.591	T43.592	T43.593	T43.594	T43.595	T43.596
major NEC	T43.501	T43.502	T43.503	T43.504	T43.505	T43.506

◀ New   ◀ Revised   ~~deleted~~ Deleted

Substance	Poisoning, Accidental (Unintentional)	Poisoning, Intentional Self-Harm	Poisoning, Assault	Poisoning, Undetermined	Adverse Effect	Underdosing
Tranquilizer NEC *(Continued)*						
penothiazine NEC	T43.3X1	T43.3X2	T43.3X3	T43.3X4	T43.3X5	T43.3X6
phenothiazine-based	T43.3X1	T43.3X2	T43.3X3	T43.3X4	T43.3X5	T43.3X6
piperazine NEC	T43.3X1	T43.3X2	T43.3X3	T43.3X4	T43.3X5	T43.3X6
piperidine	T43.3X1	T43.3X2	T43.3X3	T43.3X4	T43.3X5	T43.3X6
propylamine	T43.3X1	T43.3X2	T43.3X3	T43.3X4	T43.3X5	T43.3X6
specified NEC	T43.591	T43.592	T43.593	T43.594	T43.595	T43.596
thioxanthene NEC	T43.591	T43.592	T43.593	T43.594	T43.595	T43.596
Tranxene	T42.4X1	T42.4X2	T42.4X3	T42.4X4	T42.4X5	T42.4X6
Tranylcypromine	T43.1X1	T43.1X2	T43.1X3	T43.1X4	T43.1X5	T43.1X6
Trapidil	T46.3X1	T46.3X2	T46.3X3	T46.3X4	T46.3X5	T46.3X6
Trasentine	T44.3X1	T44.3X2	T44.3X3	T44.3X4	T44.3X5	T44.3X6
Travert	T50.3X1	T50.3X2	T50.3X3	T50.3X4	T50.3X5	T50.3X6
Trazodone	T43.211	T43.212	T43.213	T43.214	T43.215	T43.216
Trecator	T37.1X1	T37.1X2	T37.1X3	T37.1X4	T37.1X5	T37.1X6
Treosulfan	T45.1X1	T45.1X2	T45.1X3	T45.1X4	T45.1X5	T45.1X6
Tretamine	T45.1X1	T45.1X2	T45.1X3	T45.1X4	T45.1X5	T45.1X6
Tretinoin	T49.0X1	T49.0X2	T49.0X3	T49.0X4	T49.0X5	T49.0X6
Tretoquinol	T48.6X1	T48.6X2	T48.6X3	T48.6X4	T48.6X5	T48.6X6
Triacetin	T49.0X1	T49.0X2	T49.0X3	T49.0X4	T49.0X5	T49.0X6
Triacetoxyanthracene	T49.4X1	T49.4X2	T49.4X3	T49.4X4	T49.4X5	T49.4X6
Triacetyloleandomycin	T36.3X1	T36.3X2	T36.3X3	T36.3X4	T36.3X5	T36.3X6
Triamcinolone	T38.0X1	T38.0X2	T38.0X3	T38.0X4	T38.0X5	T38.0X6
ENT agent	T49.6X1	T49.6X2	T49.6X3	T49.6X4	T49.6X5	T49.6X6
hexacetonide	T49.0X1	T49.0X2	T49.0X3	T49.0X4	T49.0X5	T49.0X6
ophthalmic preparation	T49.5X1	T49.5X2	T49.5X3	T49.5X4	T49.5X5	T49.5X6
topical NEC	T49.0X1	T49.0X2	T49.0X3	T49.0X4	T49.0X5	T49.0X6
Triampyzine	T44.3X1	T44.3X2	T44.3X3	T44.3X4	T44.3X5	T44.3X6
Triamterene	T50.2X1	T50.2X2	T50.2X3	T50.2X4	T50.2X5	T50.2X6
Triazine (herbicide)	T60.3X1	T60.3X2	T60.3X3	T60.3X4	—	—
Triaziquone	T45.1X1	T45.1X2	T45.1X3	T45.1X4	T45.1X5	T45.1X6
Triazolam	T42.4X1	T42.4X2	T42.4X3	T42.4X4	T42.4X5	T42.4X6
Triazole (herbicide)	T60.3X1	T60.3X2	T60.3X3	T60.3X4	—	—
Tribenoside	T46.991	T46.992	T46.993	T46.994	T46.995	T46.996
Tribromacetaldehyde	T42.6X1	T42.6X2	T42.6X3	T42.6X4	T42.6X5	T42.6X6
Tribromoethanol, rectal	T41.291	T41.292	T41.293	T41.294	T41.295	T41.296
Tribromomethane	T42.6X1	T42.6X2	T42.6X3	T42.6X4	T42.6X5	T42.6X6
Trichlorethane	T53.2X1	T53.2X2	T53.2X3	T53.2X4	—	—
Trichlorethylene	T53.2X1	T53.2X2	T53.2X3	T53.2X4	—	—
Trichlorfon	T60.0X1	T60.0X2	T60.0X3	T60.0X4	—	—
Trichlormethiazide	T50.2X1	T50.2X2	T50.2X3	T50.2X4	T50.2X5	T50.2X6
Trichlormethine	T45.1X1	T45.1X2	T45.1X3	T45.1X4	T45.1X5	T45.1X6

Substance	Poisoning, Accidental (Unintentional)	Poisoning, Intentional Self-Harm	Poisoning, Assault	Poisoning, Undetermined	Adverse Effect	Underdosing
Trichloroacetic acid, Trichloracetic acid	T54.2X1	T54.2X2	T54.2X3	T54.2X4	—	—
medicinal	T49.4X1	T49.4X2	T49.4X3	T49.4X4	T49.4X5	T49.4X6
Trichloroethane	T53.2X1	T53.2X2	T53.2X3	T53.2X4	—	—
Trichloroethanol	T42.6X1	T42.6X2	T42.6X3	T42.6X4	T42.6X5	T42.6X6
Trichloroethylene (liquid) (vapor)	T53.2X1	T53.2X2	T53.2X3	T53.2X4	—	—
anesthetic (gas)	T41.0X1	T41.0X2	T41.0X3	T41.0X4	T41.0X5	T41.0X6
vapor NEC	T53.2X1	T53.2X2	T53.2X3	T53.2X4	—	—
Trichloroethyl phosphate	T42.6X1	T42.6X2	T42.6X3	T42.6X4	T42.6X5	T42.6X6
Trichlorofluoromethane NEC	T53.5X1	T53.5X2	T53.5X3	T53.5X4	—	—
Trichloronate	T60.0X1	T60.0X2	T60.0X3	T60.0X4	—	—
2,4,5-Trichlorophen-oxyacetic acid	T60.3X1	T60.3X2	T60.3X3	T60.3X4	—	—
Trichloropropane	T53.6X1	T53.6X2	T53.6X3	T53.6X4	—	—
Trichlorotriethylamine	T45.1X1	T45.1X2	T45.1X3	T45.1X4	T45.1X5	T45.1X6
Trichomonacides NEC	T37.3X1	T37.3X2	T37.3X3	T37.3X4	T37.3X5	T37.3X6
Trichomycin	T36.7X1	T36.7X2	T36.7X3	T36.7X4	T36.7X5	T36.7X6
Triclobisonium chloride	T49.0X1	T49.0X2	T49.0X3	T49.0X4	T49.0X5	T49.0X6
Triclocarban	T49.0X1	T49.0X2	T49.0X3	T49.0X4	T49.0X5	T49.0X6
Triclofos	T42.6X1	T42.6X2	T42.6X3	T42.6X4	T42.6X5	T42.6X6
Triclosan	T49.0X1	T49.0X2	T49.0X3	T49.0X4	T49.0X5	T49.0X6
Tricresyl phosphate	T65.891	T65.892	T65.893	T65.894	—	—
solvent	T52.91	T52.92	T52.93	T52.94	—	—
Tricyclamol chloride	T44.3X1	T44.3X2	T44.3X3	T44.3X4	T44.3X5	T44.3X6
Tridesilon	T49.0X1	T49.0X2	T49.0X3	T49.0X4	T49.0X5	T49.0X6
Tridihexethyl iodide	T44.3X1	T44.3X2	T44.3X3	T44.3X4	T44.3X5	T44.3X6
Tridione	T42.2X1	T42.2X2	T42.2X3	T42.2X4	T42.2X5	T42.2X6
Trientine	T45.8X1	T45.8X2	T45.8X3	T45.8X4	T45.8X5	T45.8X6
Triethanolamine NEC	T54.3X1	T54.3X2	T54.3X3	T54.3X4	—	—
detergent	T54.3X1	T54.3X2	T54.3X3	T54.3X4	—	—
trinitrate (biphosphate)	T46.3X1	T46.3X2	T46.3X3	T46.3X4	T46.3X5	T46.3X6
Triethanomelamine	T45.1X1	T45.1X2	T45.1X3	T45.1X4	T45.1X5	T45.1X6
Triethylenemelamine	T45.1X1	T45.1X2	T45.1X3	T45.1X4	T45.1X5	T45.1X6
Triethylenephosphoramide	T45.1X1	T45.1X2	T45.1X3	T45.1X4	T45.1X5	T45.1X6
Triethylenethiophosphoramide	T45.1X1	T45.1X2	T45.1X3	T45.1X4	T45.1X5	T45.1X6
Trifluoperazine	T43.3X1	T43.3X2	T43.3X3	T43.3X4	T43.3X5	T43.3X6
Trifluoroethyl vinyl ether	T41.0X1	T41.0X2	T41.0X3	T41.0X4	T41.0X5	T41.0X6
Trifluperidol	T43.4X1	T43.4X2	T43.4X3	T43.4X4	T43.4X5	T43.4X6
Triflupromazine	T43.3X1	T43.3X2	T43.3X3	T43.3X4	T43.3X5	T43.3X6
Trifluridine	T37.5X1	T37.5X2	T37.5X3	T37.5X4	T37.5X5	T37.5X6
Triflusal	T45.521	T45.522	T45.523	T45.524	T45.525	T45.526
Trihexyphenidyl	T44.3X1	T44.3X2	T44.3X3	T44.3X4	T44.3X5	T44.3X6
Triiodothyronine	T38.1X1	T38.1X2	T38.1X3	T38.1X4	T38.1X5	T38.1X6

◀ New ◀ Revised ~~deleted~~ Deleted

Substance	Poisoning, Accidental (Unintentional)	Poisoning, Intentional Self-Harm	Poisoning, Assault	Poisoning, Undetermined	Adverse Effect	Underdosing
Trilene	T41.0X1	T41.0X2	T41.0X3	T41.0X4	T41.0X5	T41.0X6
Trilostane	T38.991	T38.992	T38.993	T38.994	T38.995	T38.996
Trimebutine	T44.3X1	T44.3X2	T44.3X3	T44.3X4	T44.3X5	T44.3X6
Trimecaine	T41.3X1	T41.3X2	T41.3X3	T41.3X4	T41.3X5	T41.3X6
Trimeprazine (tartrate)	T44.3X1	T44.3X2	T44.3X3	T44.3X4	T44.3X5	T44.3X6
Trimetaphan camsilate	T44.2X1	T44.2X2	T44.2X3	T44.2X4	T44.2X5	T44.2X6
Trimetazidine	T46.7X1	T46.7X2	T46.7X3	T46.7X4	T46.7X5	T46.7X6
Trimethadione	T42.2X1	T42.2X2	T42.2X3	T42.2X4	T42.2X5	T42.2X6
Trimethaphan	T44.2X1	T44.2X2	T44.2X3	T44.2X4	T44.2X5	T44.2X6
Trimethidinium	T44.2X1	T44.2X2	T44.2X3	T44.2X4	T44.2X5	T44.2X6
Trimethobenzamide	T45.0X1	T45.0X2	T45.0X3	T45.0X4	T45.0X5	T45.0X6
Trimethoprim	T37.8X1	T37.8X2	T37.8X3	T37.8X4	T37.8X5	T37.8X6
with sulfamethoxazole	T36.8X1	T36.8X2	T36.8X3	T36.8X4	T36.8X5	T36.8X6
Trimethylcarbinol	T51.3X1	T51.3X2	T51.3X3	T51.3X4	—	—
Trimethylpsoralen	T49.3X1	T49.3X2	T49.3X3	T49.3X4	T49.3X5	T49.3X6
Trimeton	T45.0X1	T45.0X2	T45.0X3	T45.0X4	T45.0X5	T45.0X6
Trimetrexate	T45.1X1	T45.1X2	T45.1X3	T45.1X4	T45.1X5	T45.1X6
Trimipramine	T43.011	T43.012	T43.013	T43.014	T43.015	T43.016
Trimustine	T45.1X1	T45.1X2	T45.1X3	T45.1X4	T45.1X5	T45.1X6
Trinitrine	T46.3X1	T46.3X2	T46.3X3	T46.3X4	T46.3X5	T46.3X6
Trinitrobenzol	T65.3X1	T65.3X2	T65.3X3	T65.3X4	—	—
Trinitrophenol	T65.3X1	T65.3X2	T65.3X3	T65.3X4	—	—
Trinitrotoluene (fumes)	T65.3X1	T65.3X2	T65.3X3	T65.3X4	—	—
Trional	T42.6X1	T42.6X2	T42.6X3	T42.6X4	T42.6X5	T42.6X6
Triorthocresyl phosphate	T65.891	T65.892	T65.893	T65.894	—	—
Trioxide of arsenic	T57.0X1	T57.0X2	T57.0X3	T57.0X4	—	—
Trioxysalen	T49.4X1	T49.4X2	T49.4X3	T49.4X4	T49.4X5	T49.4X6
Tripamide	T50.2X1	T50.2X2	T50.2X3	T50.2X4	T50.2X5	T50.2X6
Triparanol	T46.6X1	T46.6X2	T46.6X3	T46.6X4	T46.6X5	T46.6X6
Tripelennamine	T45.0X1	T45.0X2	T45.0X3	T45.0X4	T45.0X5	T45.0X6
Triperiden	T44.3X1	T44.3X2	T44.3X3	T44.3X4	T44.3X5	T44.3X6
Triperidol	T43.4X1	T43.4X2	T43.4X3	T43.4X4	T43.4X5	T43.4X6
Triphenylphosphate	T65.891	T65.892	T65.893	T65.894	—	—
Triple						
bromides	T42.6X1	T42.6X2	T42.6X3	T42.6X4	T42.6X5	T42.6X6
carbonate	T47.1X1	T47.1X2	T47.1X3	T47.1X4	T47.1X5	T47.1X6
vaccine						
DPT	T50.A11	T50.A12	T50.A13	T50.A14	T50.A15	T50.A16
including pertussis	T50.A11	T50.A12	T50.A13	T50.A14	T50.A15	T50.A16
MMR	T50.B91	T50.B92	—	—	—	—
Triprolidine	T45.0X1	T45.0X2	T45.0X3	T45.0X4	T45.0X5	T45.0X6
Trisodium hydrogen edetate	T50.6X1	T50.6X2	T50.6X3	T50.6X4	T50.6X5	T50.6X6

Substance	Poisoning, Accidental (Unintentional)	Poisoning, Intentional Self-Harm	Poisoning, Assault	Poisoning, Undetermined	Adverse Effect	Underdosing
Trisoralen	T49.3X1	T49.3X2	T49.3X3	T49.3X4	T49.3X5	T49.3X6
Trisulfapyrimidines	T37.0X1	T37.0X2	T37.0X3	T37.0X4	T37.0X5	T37.0X6
Trithiozine	T44.3X1	T44.3X2	T44.3X3	T44.3X4	T44.3X5	T44.3X6
Tritiozine	T44.3X1	T44.3X2	T44.3X3	T44.3X4	T44.3X5	T44.3X6
Tritoqualine	T45.0X1	T45.0X2	T45.0X3	T45.0X4	T45.0X5	T45.0X6
Trofosfamide	T45.1X1	T45.1X2	T45.1X3	T45.1X4	T45.1X5	T45.1X6
Troleandomycin	T36.3X1	T36.3X2	T36.3X3	T36.3X4	T36.3X5	T36.3X6
Trolnitrate (phosphate)	T46.3X1	T46.3X2	T46.3X3	T46.3X4	T46.3X5	T46.3X6
Tromantadine	T37.5X1	T37.5X2	T37.5X3	T37.5X4	T37.5X5	T37.5X6
Trometamol	T50.2X1	T50.2X2	T50.2X3	T50.2X4	T50.2X5	T50.2X6
Tromethamine	T50.2X1	T50.2X2	T50.2X3	T50.2X4	T50.2X5	T50.2X6
Tronothane	T41.3X1	T41.3X2	T41.3X3	T41.3X4	T41.3X5	T41.3X6
Tropacine	T44.3X1	T44.3X2	T44.3X3	T44.3X4	T44.3X5	T44.3X6
Tropatepine	T44.3X1	T44.3X2	T44.3X3	T44.3X4	T44.3X5	T44.3X6
Tropicamide	T44.3X1	T44.3X2	T44.3X3	T44.3X4	T44.3X5	T44.3X6
Trospium chloride	T44.3X1	T44.3X2	T44.3X3	T44.3X4	T44.3X5	T44.3X6
Troxerutin	T46.991	T46.992	T46.993	T46.994	T46.995	T46.996
Troxidone	T42.2X1	T42.2X2	T42.2X3	T42.2X4	T42.2X5	T42.2X6
Tryparsamide	T37.3X1	T37.3X2	T37.3X3	T37.3X4	T37.3X5	T37.3X6
Trypsin	T45.3X1	T45.3X2	T45.3X3	T45.3X4	T45.3X5	T45.3X6
Tryptizol	T43.011	T43.012	T43.013	T43.014	T43.015	T43.016
TSH	T38.811	T38.812	T38.813	T38.814	T38.815	T38.816
Tuaminoheptane	T48.5X1	T48.5X2	T48.5X3	T48.5X4	T48.5X5	T48.5X6
Tuberculin, purified protein derivative (PPD)	T50.8X1	T50.8X2	T50.8X3	T50.8X4	T50.8X5	T50.8X6
Tubocurare	T48.1X1	T48.1X2	T48.1X3	T48.1X4	T48.1X5	T48.1X6
Tubocurarine (chloride)	T48.1X1	T48.1X2	T48.1X3	T48.1X4	T48.1X5	T48.1X6
Tulobuterol	T48.6X1	T48.6X2	T48.6X3	T48.6X4	T48.6X5	T48.6X6
Turpentine (spirits of)	T52.8X1	T52.8X2	T52.8X3	T52.8X4	—	—
vapor	T52.8X1	T52.8X2	T52.8X3	T52.8X4	—	—
Tybamate	T43.591	T43.592	T43.593	T43.594	T43.595	T43.596
Tyloxapol	T48.4X1	T48.4X2	T48.4X3	T48.4X4	T48.4X5	T48.4X6
Tymazoline	T48.5X1	T48.5X2	T48.5X3	T48.5X4	T48.5X5	T48.5X6
Typhoid-paratyphoid vaccine	T50.A91	T50.A92	T50.A93	T50.A94	T50.A95	T50.A96
Typhus vaccine	T50.A91	T50.A92	T50.A93	T50.A94	T50.A95	T50.A96
Tyropanoate	T50.8X1	T50.8X2	T50.8X3	T50.8X4	T50.8X5	T50.8X6
Tyrothricin	T49.6X1	T49.6X2	T49.6X3	T49.6X4	T49.6X5	T49.6X6
ENT agent	T49.6X1	T49.6X2	T49.6X3	T49.6X4	T49.6X5	T49.6X6
ophthalmic preparation	T49.5X1	T49.5X2	T49.5X3	T49.5X4	T49.5X5	T49.5X6
U						
Ufenamate	T39.391	T39.392	T39.393	T39.394	T39.395	T39.396
Ultraviolet light protectant	T49.3X1	T49.3X2	T49.3X3	T49.3X4	T49.3X5	T49.3X6

◀ New ◀ Revised deleted Deleted

Substance	External Cause (T-Code)					
	Poisoning, Accidental (Unintentional)	Poisoning, Intentional Self-Harm	Poisoning, Assault	Poisoning, Undetermined	Adverse Effect	Underdosing
Undecenoic acid	T49.0X1	T49.0X2	T49.0X3	T49.0X4	T49.0X5	T49.0X6
Undecoylium	T49.0X1	T49.0X2	T49.0X3	T49.0X4	T49.0X5	T49.0X6
Undecylenic acid (derivatives)	T49.0X1	T49.0X2	T49.0X3	T49.0X4	T49.0X5	T49.0X6
Unna's boot	T49.3X1	T49.3X2	T49.3X3	T49.3X4	T49.3X5	T49.3X6
Unsaturated fatty acid	T46.6X1	T46.6X2	T46.6X3	T46.6X4	T46.6X5	T46.6X6
Uracil mustard	T45.1X1	T45.1X2	T45.1X3	T45.1X4	T45.1X5	T45.1X6
Uramustine	T45.1X1	T45.1X2	T45.1X3	T45.1X4	T45.1X5	T45.1X6
Urapidil	T46.5X1	T46.5X2	T46.5X3	T46.5X4	T46.5X5	T46.5X6
Urari	T48.1X1	T48.1X2	T48.1X3	T48.1X4	T48.1X5	T48.1X6
Urate oxidase	T50.4X1	T50.4X2	T50.4X3	T50.4X4	T50.4X5	T50.4X6
Urea	T47.3X1	T47.3X2	T47.3X3	T47.3X4	T47.3X5	T47.3X6
peroxide	T49.0X1	T49.0X2	T49.0X3	T49.0X4	T49.0X5	T49.0X6
stibamine	T37.4X1	T37.4X2	T37.4X3	T37.4X4	T37.4X5	T37.4X6
topical	T49.8X1	T49.8X2	T49.8X3	T49.8X4	T49.8X5	T49.8X6
Urethane	T45.1X1	T45.1X2	T45.1X3	T45.1X4	T45.1X5	T45.1X6
Urginea (maritima) (scilla) — see Squill						
Uric acid metabolism drug NEC	T50.4X1	T50.4X2	T50.4X3	T50.4X4	T50.4X5	T50.4X6
Uricosuric agent	T50.4X1	T50.4X2	T50.4X3	T50.4X4	T50.4X5	T50.4X6
Urinary anti-infective	T37.8X1	T37.8X2	T37.8X3	T37.8X4	T37.8X5	T37.8X6
Urofollitropin	T38.811	T38.812	T38.813	T38.814	T38.815	T38.816
Urokinase	T45.611	T45.612	T45.613	T45.614	T45.615	T45.616
Urokon	T50.8X1	T50.8X2	T50.8X3	T50.8X4	T50.8X5	T50.8X6
Ursodeoxycholic acid	T50.991	T50.992	T50.993	T50.994	T50.995	T50.996
Ursodiol	T50.991	T50.992	T50.993	T50.994	T50.995	T50.996
Urtica	T62.2X1	T62.2X2	T62.2X3	T62.2X4	—	—
Utility gas — see Gas, utility						
V						
Vaccine NEC	T50.Z91	T50.Z92	T50.Z93	T50.Z94	T50.Z95	T50.Z96
antineoplastic	T50.Z91	T50.Z92	T50.Z93	T50.Z94	T50.Z95	T50.Z96
bacterial NEC	T50.A91	T50.A92	T50.A93	T50.A94	T50.A95	T50.A96
with						
other bacterial component	T50.A91	T50.A92	T50.A93	T50.A94	T50.A95	T50.A96
pertussis component	T50.A91	T50.A92	T50.A93	T50.A94	T50.A95	T50.A96
viral-rickettsial component	T50.A91	T50.A92	T50.A93	T50.A94	T50.A95	T50.A96
mixed NEC	T50.A91	T50.A92	T50.A93	T50.A94	T50.A95	T50.A96
BCG	T50.A91	T50.A92	T50.A93	T50.A94	T50.A95	T50.A96
cholera	T50.A91	T50.A92	T50.A93	T50.A94	T50.A95	T50.A96
diphtheria	T50.A91	T50.A92	T50.A93	T50.A94	T50.A95	T50.A96
with tetanus	T50.A21	T50.A22	T50.A23	T50.A24	T50.A25	T50.A26
and pertussis	T50.A11	T50.A12	T50.A13	T50.A14	T50.A15	T50.A16

Substance	External Cause (T-Code)					
	Poisoning, Accidental (Unintentional)	Poisoning, Intentional Self-Harm	Poisoning, Assault	Poisoning, Undetermined	Adverse Effect	Underdosing
Vaccine NEC *(Continued)*						
influenza	T50.B91	T50.B92	T50.B93	T50.B94	T50.B95	T50.B96
measles	T50.B91	T50.B92	T50.B93	T50.B94	T50.B95	T50.B96
with mumps and rubella	T50.B91	T50.B92	T50.B93	T50.B94	T50.B95	T50.B96
meningococcal	T50.A91	T50.A92	T50.A93	T50.A94	T50.A95	T50.A96
mumps	T50.B91	T50.B92	T50.B93	T50.B94	T50.B95	T50.B96
paratyphoid	T50.A91	T50.A92	T50.A93	T50.A94	T50.A95	T50.A96
pertussis	T50.A11	T50.A12	T50.A13	T50.A14	T50.A15	T50.A16
with diphtheria	T50.A11	T50.A12	T50.A13	T50.A14	T50.A15	T50.A16
and tetanus	T50.A11	T50.A12	T50.A13	T50.A14	T50.A15	T50.A16
plague	T50.A91	T50.A92	T50.A93	T50.A94	T50.A95	T50.A96
poliomyelitis	T50.B91	T50.B92	T50.B93	T50.B94	T50.B95	T50.B96
poliovirus	T50.B91	T50.B92	T50.B93	T50.B94	T50.B95	T50.B96
rabies	T50.B91	T50.B92	T50.B93	T50.B94	T50.B95	T50.B96
respiratory syncytial virus	T50.B91	T50.B92	T50.B93	T50.B94	T50.B95	T50.B96
rickettsial NEC	T50.A91	T50.A92	T50.A93	T50.A94	T50.A95	T50.A96
with						
bacterial component	T50.A21	T50.A22	T50.A23	T50.A24	T50.A25	T50.A26
Rocky Mountain spotted fever	T50.A91	T50.A92	T50.A93	T50.A94	T50.A95	T50.A96
rubella	T50.B91	T50.B92	T50.B93	T50.B94	T50.B95	T50.B96
sabin oral	T50.B91	T50.B92	T50.B93	T50.B94	T50.B95	T50.B96
smallpox	T50.B11	T50.B12	T50.B13	T50.B14	T50.B15	T50.B16
TAB	T50.A91	T50.A92	T50.A93	T50.A94	T50.A95	T50.A96
tetanus	T50.A91	T50.A92	T50.A93	T50.A94	T50.A95	T50.A96
typhoid	T50.A91	T50.A92	T50.A93	T50.A94	T50.A95	T50.A96
typhus	T50.A91	T50.A92	T50.A93	T50.A94	T50.A95	T50.A96
viral NEC	T50.B91	T50.B92	T50.B93	T50.B94	T50.B95	T50.B96
yellow fever	T50.B91	T50.B92	T50.B93	T50.B94	T50.B95	T50.B96
Vaccinia immune globulin	T50.Z11	T50.Z12	T50.Z13	T50.Z14	T50.Z15	T50.Z16
Vaginal contraceptives	T49.8X1	T49.8X2	T49.8X3	T49.8X4	T49.8X5	T49.8X6
Valerian						
root	T42.6X1	T42.6X2	T42.6X3	T42.6X4	T42.6X5	T42.6X6
tincture	T42.6X1	T42.6X2	T42.6X3	T42.6X4	T42.6X5	T42.6X6
Valethamate bromide	T44.3X1	T44.3X2	T44.3X3	T44.3X4	T44.3X5	T44.3X6
Valisone	T49.0X1	T49.0X2	T49.0X3	T49.0X4	T49.0X5	T49.0X6
Valium	T42.4X1	T42.4X2	T42.4X3	T42.4X4	T42.4X5	T42.4X6
Valmid	T42.6X1	T42.6X2	T42.6X3	T42.6X4	T42.6X5	T42.6X6
Valnoctamide	T42.6X1	T42.6X2	T42.6X3	T42.6X4	T42.6X5	T42.6X6
Valproate (sodium)	T42.6X1	T42.6X2	T42.6X3	T42.6X4	T42.6X5	T42.6X6
Valproic acid	T42.6X1	T42.6X2	T42.6X3	T42.6X4	T42.6X5	T42.6X6
Valpromide	T42.6X1	T42.6X2	T42.6X3	T42.6X4	T42.6X5	T42.6X6
Vanadium	T56.891	T56.892	T56.893	T56.894	—	—

◀ New   ◀ Revised   ~~deleted~~ Deleted

Substance	External Cause (T-Code) Poisoning, Accidental (Unintentional)	Poisoning, Intentional Self-Harm	Poisoning, Assault	Poisoning, Undetermined	Adverse Effect	Underdosing
Vancomycin	T36.8X1	T36.8X2	T36.8X3	T36.8X4	T36.8X5	T36.8X6
Vapor—*see also Gas*	T59.91	T59.92	T59.93	T59.94	—	—
kiln (carbon monoxide)	T58.8X1	T58.8X2	T58.8X3	T58.8X4	—	—
lead—*see Lead*						
specified source NEC	T59.891	T59.892	T59.893	T59.894	—	—
Vardenafil	T46.7X1	T46.7X2	T46.7X3	T46.7X4	T46.7X5	T46.7X6
Varicose reduction drug	T46.8X1	T46.8X2	T46.8X3	T46.8X4	T46.8X5	T46.8X6
Varnish	T65.4X1	T65.4X2	T65.4X3	T65.4X4	—	—
cleaner	T52.91	T52.92	T52.93	T52.94	—	—
Vaseline	T49.3X1	T49.3X2	T49.3X3	T49.3X4	T49.3X5	T49.3X6
Vasodilan	T46.7X1	T46.7X2	T46.7X3	T46.7X4	T46.7X5	T46.7X6
Vasodilator						
coronary NEC	T46.3X1	T46.3X2	T46.3X3	T46.3X4	T46.3X5	T46.3X6
peripheral NEC	T46.7X1	T46.7X2	T46.7X3	T46.7X4	T46.7X5	T46.7X6
Vasopressin	T38.891	T38.892	T38.893	T38.894	T38.895	T38.896
Vasopressor drugs	T38.891	T38.892	T38.893	T38.894	T38.895	T38.896
Vecuronium bromide	T48.1X1	T48.1X2	T48.1X3	T48.1X4	T48.1X5	T48.1X6
Vegetable extract, astringent	T49.2X1	T49.2X2	T49.2X3	T49.2X4	T49.2X5	T49.2X6
Venlafaxine	T43.211	T43.212	T43.213	T43.214	T43.215	T43.216
Venom, venomous (bite) (sting)	T63.91	T63.92	T63.93	T63.94	—	—
amphibian NEC	T63.831	T63.832	T63.833	T63.834	—	—
animal NEC	T63.891	T63.892	T63.893	T63.894	—	—
ant	T63.421	T63.422	T63.423	T63.424	—	—
arthropod NEC	T63.481	T63.482	T63.483	T63.484	—	—
bee	T63.441	T63.442	T63.443	T63.444	—	—
centipede	T63.411	T63.412	T63.413	T63.414	—	—
fish	T63.591	T63.592	T63.593	T63.594	—	—
frog	T63.811	T63.812	T63.813	T63.814	—	—
hornet	T63.451	T63.452	T63.453	T63.454	—	—
insect NEC	T63.481	T63.482	T63.483	T63.484	—	—
lizard	T63.121	T63.122	T63.123	T63.124	—	—
marine						
animals	T63.691	T63.692	T63.693	T63.694	—	—
bluebottle	T63.611	T63.612	T63.613	T63.614	—	—
jellyfish NEC	T63.621	T63.622	T63.623	T63.624	—	—
Portugese Man-o-war	T63.611	T63.612	T63.613	T63.614	—	—
sea anemone	T63.631	T63.632	T63.633	T63.634	—	—
specified NEC	T63.691	T63.692	T63.693	T63.694	—	—
fish	T63.591	T63.592	T63.593	T63.594	—	—
plants	T63.711	T63.712	T63.713	T63.714	—	—
sting ray	T63.511	T63.512	T63.513	T63.514	—	—

Substance	External Cause (T-Code) Poisoning, Accidental (Unintentional)	Poisoning, Intentional Self-Harm	Poisoning, Assault	Poisoning, Undetermined	Adverse Effect	Underdosing
Venom, venomous *(Continued)*						
millipede (tropical)	T63.411	T63.412	T63.413	T63.414	—	—
plant NEC	T63.791	T63.792	T63.793	T63.794	—	—
marine	T63.711	T63.712	T63.713	T63.714	—	—
reptile	T63.191	T63.192	T63.193	T63.194	—	—
gila monster	T63.111	T63.112	T63.113	T63.114	—	—
lizard NEC	T63.121	T63.122	T63.123	T63.124	—	—
scorpion	T63.2X1	T63.2X2	T63.2X3	T63.2X4	—	—
snake	T63.001	T63.002	T63.003	T63.004	—	—
African NEC	T63.081	T63.082	T63.083	T63.084	—	—
American (North) (South) NEC	T63.061	T63.062	T63.063	T63.064	—	—
Asian	T63.081	T63.082	T63.083	T63.084	—	—
Australian	T63.071	T63.072	T63.073	T63.074	—	—
cobra	T63.041	T63.042	T63.043	T63.044	—	—
coral snake	T63.021	T63.022	T63.023	T63.024	—	—
rattlesnake	T63.011	T63.012	T63.013	T63.014	—	—
specified NEC	T63.091	T63.092	T63.093	T63.094	—	—
taipan	T63.031	T63.032	T63.033	T63.034	—	—
specified NEC	T63.891	T63.892	T63.893	T63.894	—	—
spider	T63.301	T63.302	T63.303	T63.304	—	—
black widow	T63.311	T63.312	T63.313	T63.314	—	—
brown recluse	T63.331	T63.332	T63.333	T63.334	—	—
specified NEC	T63.391	T63.392	T63.393	T63.394	—	—
tarantula	T63.321	T63.322	T63.323	T63.324	—	—
sting ray	T63.511	T63.512	T63.513	T63.514	—	—
toad	T63.821	T63.822	T63.823	T63.824	—	—
wasp	T63.461	T63.462	T63.463	T63.464	—	—
Venous sclerosing drug NEC	T46.8X1	T46.8X2	T46.8X3	T46.8X4	T46.8X5	T46.8X6
Ventolin—*see Albuterol*						
Verapamil	T46.1X1	T46.1X2	T46.1X3	T46.1X4	T46.1X5	T46.1X6
Veramon	T42.3X1	T42.3X2	T42.3X3	T42.3X4	T42.3X5	T42.3X6
Veratrine	T46.5X1	T46.5X2	T46.5X3	T46.5X4	T46.5X5	T46.5X6
Veratrum						
album	T62.2X1	T62.2X2	T62.2X3	T62.2X4	—	—
alkaloids	T46.5X1	T46.5X2	T46.5X3	T46.5X4	T46.5X5	T46.5X6
viride	T62.2X1	T62.2X2	T62.2X3	T62.2X4	—	—
Verdigris	T60.3X1	T60.3X2	T60.3X3	T60.3X4	—	—
Veronal	T42.3X1	T42.3X2	T42.3X3	T42.3X4	T42.3X5	T42.3X6
Veroxil	T37.4X1	T37.4X2	T37.4X3	T37.4X4	T37.4X5	T37.4X6
Versenate	T50.6X1	T50.6X2	T50.6X3	T50.6X4	T50.6X5	T50.6X6

◀ New ◀ Revised ~~deleted~~ Deleted

Substance	Poisoning, Accidental (Unintentional)	Poisoning, Intentional Self-Harm	Poisoning, Assault	Poisoning, Undetermined	Adverse Effect	Underdosing
Versidyne	T39.8X1	T39.8X2	T39.8X3	T39.8X4	T39.8X5	T39.8X6
Vetrabutine	T48.0X1	T48.0X2	T48.0X3	T48.0X4	T48.0X5	T48.0X6
Vidarabine	T37.5X1	T37.5X2	T37.5X3	T37.5X4	T37.5X5	T37.5X6
Vienna						
green	T57.0X1	T57.0X2	T57.0X3	T57.0X4	—	—
insecticide	T60.2X1	T60.2X2	T60.2X3	T60.2X4	—	—
red	T57.0X1	T57.0X2	T57.0X3	T57.0X4	—	—
pharmaceutical dye	T50.991	T50.992	T50.993	T50.994	T50.995	T50.996
Vigabatrin	T42.6X1	T42.6X2	T42.6X3	T42.6X4	T42.6X5	T42.6X6
Viloxazine	T43.291	T43.292	T43.293	T43.294	T43.295	T43.296
Viminol	T39.8X1	T39.8X2	T39.8X3	T39.8X4	T39.8X5	T39.8X6
Vinbarbital, vinbarbitone	T42.3X1	T42.3X2	T42.3X3	T42.3X4	T42.3X5	T42.3X6
Vinblastine	T45.1X1	T45.1X2	T45.1X3	T45.1X4	T45.1X5	T45.1X6
Vinburnine	T46.7X1	T46.7X2	T46.7X3	T46.7X4	T46.7X5	T46.7X6
Vincamine	T45.1X1	T45.1X2	T45.1X3	T45.1X4	T45.1X5	T45.1X6
Vincristine	T45.1X1	T45.1X2	T45.1X3	T45.1X4	T45.1X5	T45.1X6
Vindesine	T45.1X1	T45.1X2	T45.1X3	T45.1X4	T45.1X5	T45.1X6
Vinesthene, vinethene	T41.0X1	T41.0X2	T41.0X3	T41.0X4	T41.0X5	T41.0X6
Vinorelbine tartrate	T45.1X1	T45.1X2	T45.1X3	T45.1X4	T45.1X5	T45.1X6
Vinpocetine	T46.7X1	T46.7X2	T46.7X3	T46.7X4	T46.7X5	T46.7X6
Vinyl						
acetate	T65.891	T65.892	T65.893	T65.894	—	—
bital	T42.3X1	T42.3X2	T42.3X3	T42.3X4	T42.3X5	T42.3X6
bromide	T65.891	T65.892	T65.893	T65.894	—	—
chloride	T59.891	T59.892	T59.893	T59.894	—	—
ether	T41.0X1	T41.0X2	T41.0X3	T41.0X4	T41.0X5	T41.0X6
Vinylbital	T42.3X1	T42.3X2	T42.3X3	T42.3X4	T42.3X5	T42.3X6
Vinylidene chloride	T65.891	T65.892	T65.893	T65.894	—	—
Vioform	T37.8X1	T37.8X2	T37.8X3	T37.8X4	T37.8X5	T37.8X6
topical	T49.0X1	T49.0X2	T49.0X3	T49.0X4	T49.0X5	T49.0X6
Viomycin	T36.8X1	T36.8X2	T36.8X3	T36.8X4	T36.8X5	T36.8X6
Viosterol	T45.2X1	T45.2X2	T45.2X3	T45.2X4	T45.2X5	T45.2X6
Viper (venom)	T63.091	T63.092	T63.093	T63.094	—	—
Viprynium	T37.4X1	T37.4X2	T37.4X3	T37.4X4	T37.4X5	T37.4X6
Viquidil	T46.7X1	T46.7X2	T46.7X3	T46.7X4	T46.7X5	T46.7X6
Viral vaccine NEC	T50.B91	T50.B92	T50.B93	T50.B94	T50.B95	T50.B96
Virginiamycin	T36.8X1	T36.8X2	T36.8X3	T36.8X4	T36.8X5	T36.8X6
Virugon	T37.5X1	T37.5X2	T37.5X3	T37.5X4	T37.5X5	T37.5X6
Viscous agent	T50.901	T50.902	T50.903	T50.904	T50.905	T50.906
Visine	T49.5X1	T49.5X2	T49.5X3	T49.5X4	T49.5X5	T49.5X6
Visnadine	T46.3X1	T46.3X2	T46.3X3	T46.3X4	T46.3X5	T46.3X6

Substance	Poisoning, Accidental (Unintentional)	Poisoning, Intentional Self-Harm	Poisoning, Assault	Poisoning, Undetermined	Adverse Effect	Underdosing
Vitamin NEC	T45.2X1	T45.2X2	T45.2X3	T45.2X4	T45.2X5	T45.2X6
A	T45.2X1	T45.2X2	T45.2X3	T45.2X4	T45.2X5	T45.2X6
B NEC	T45.2X1	T45.2X2	T45.2X3	T45.2X4	T45.2X5	T45.2X6
nicotinic acid	T46.7X1	T46.7X2	T46.7X3	T46.7X4	T46.7X5	T46.7X6
B1	T45.2X1	T45.2X2	T45.2X3	T45.2X4	T45.2X5	T45.2X6
B2	T45.2X1	T45.2X2	T45.2X3	T45.2X4	T45.2X5	T45.2X6
B6	T45.2X1	T45.2X2	T45.2X3	T45.2X4	T45.2X5	T45.2X6
B12	T45.2X1	T45.2X2	T45.2X3	T45.2X4	T45.2X5	T45.2X6
B15	T45.2X1	T45.2X2	T45.2X3	T45.2X4	T45.2X5	T45.2X6
C	T45.2X1	T45.2X2	T45.2X3	T45.2X4	T45.2X5	T45.2X6
D	T45.2X1	T45.2X2	T45.2X3	T45.2X4	T45.2X5	T45.2X6
D2	T45.2X1	T45.2X2	T45.2X3	T45.2X4	T45.2X5	T45.2X6
D3	T45.2X1	T45.2X2	T45.2X3	T45.2X4	T45.2X5	T45.2X6
E	T45.2X1	T45.2X2	T45.2X3	T45.2X4	T45.2X5	T45.2X6
E acetate	T45.2X1	T45.2X2	T45.2X3	T45.2X4	T45.2X5	T45.2X6
hematopoietic	T45.8X1	T45.8X2	T45.8X3	T45.8X4	T45.8X5	T45.8X6
K NEC	T45.7X1	T45.7X2	T45.7X3	T45.7X4	T45.7X5	T45.7X6
K1	T45.7X1	T45.7X2	T45.7X3	T45.7X4	T45.7X5	T45.7X6
K2	T45.7X1	T45.7X2	T45.7X3	T45.7X4	T45.7X5	T45.7X6
PP	T45.2X1	T45.2X2	T45.2X3	T45.2X4	T45.2X5	T45.2X6
ulceroprotectant	T47.1X1	T47.1X2	T47.1X3	T47.1X4	T47.1X5	T47.1X6
Vleminckx's solution	T49.4X1	T49.4X2	T49.4X3	T49.4X4	T49.4X5	T49.4X6
Voltaren — see Diclofenac sodium						
W						
Warfarin	T45.511	T45.512	T45.513	T45.514	T45.515	T45.516
rodenticide	T60.4X1	T60.4X2	T60.4X3	T60.4X4	—	—
sodium	T45.511	T45.512	T45.513	T45.514	T45.515	T45.516
Wasp (sting)	T63.461	T63.462	T63.463	T63.464	—	—
Water						
balance drug	T50.3X1	T50.3X2	T50.3X3	T50.3X4	T50.3X5	T50.3X6
distilled	T50.3X1	T50.3X2	T50.3X3	T50.3X4	T50.3X5	T50.3X6
gas — see Gas, water						
incomplete combustion of — see Carbon, monoxide, fuel, utility						
hemlock	T62.2X1	T62.2X2	T62.2X3	T62.2X4	—	—
moccasin (venom)	T63.061	T63.062	T63.063	T63.064	—	—
purified	T50.3X1	T50.3X2	T50.3X3	T50.3X4	T50.3X5	T50.3X6
Wax (paraffin) (petroleum)	T52.0X1	T52.0X2	T52.0X3	T52.0X4	—	—
automobile	T65.891	T65.892	T65.893	T65.894	—	—
floor	T52.0X1	T52.0X2	T52.0X3	T52.0X4	—	—

◄ New   ◄ Revised   ~~deleted~~ Deleted

Substance	Poisoning, Accidental (Unintentional)	Poisoning, Intentional Self-Harm	Poisoning, Assault	Poisoning, Undetermined	Adverse Effect	Underdosing
Weed killers NEC	T60.3X1	T60.3X2	T60.3X3	T60.3X4	—	—
Welldorm	T42.6X1	T42.6X2	T42.6X3	T42.6X4	T42.6X5	T42.6X6
White						
arsenic	T57.0X1	T57.0X2	T57.0X3	T57.0X4	—	—
hellebore	T62.2X1	T62.2X2	T62.2X3	T62.2X4	—	—
lotion (keratolytic)	T49.4X1	T49.4X2	T49.4X3	T49.4X4	T49.4X5	T49.4X6
spirit	T52.0X1	T52.0X2	T52.0X3	T52.0X4	—	—
Whitewash	T65.891	T65.892	T65.893	T65.894	—	—
Whole blood (human)	T45.8X1	T45.8X2	T45.8X3	T45.8X4	T45.8X5	T45.8X6
Wild						
black cherry	T62.2X1	T62.2X2	T62.2X3	T62.2X4	—	—
poisonous plants NEC	T62.2X1	T62.2X2	T62.2X3	T62.2X4	—	—
Window cleaning fluid	T65.891	T65.892	T65.893	T65.894	—	—
Wintergreen (oil)	T49.3X1	T49.3X2	T49.3X3	T49.3X4	T49.3X5	T49.3X6
Wisterine	T62.2X1	T62.2X2	T62.2X3	T62.2X4	—	—
Witch hazel	T49.2X1	T49.2X2	T49.2X3	T49.2X4	T49.2X5	T49.2X6
Wood alcohol or spirit	T51.1X1	T51.1X2	T51.1X3	T51.1X4	—	—
Wool fat (hydrous)	T49.3X1	T49.3X2	T49.3X3	T49.3X4	T49.3X5	T49.3X6
Woorali	T48.1X1	T48.1X2	T48.1X3	T48.1X4	T48.1X5	T48.1X6
Wormseed, American	T37.4X1	T37.4X2	T37.4X3	T37.4X4	T37.4X5	T37.4X6

X

Substance	Poisoning, Accidental (Unintentional)	Poisoning, Intentional Self-Harm	Poisoning, Assault	Poisoning, Undetermined	Adverse Effect	Underdosing
Xamoterol	T44.5X1	T44.5X2	T44.5X3	T44.5X4	T44.5X5	T44.5X6
Xanthine diuretics	T50.2X1	T50.2X2	T50.2X3	T50.2X4	T50.2X5	T50.2X6
Xanthinol nicotinate	T46.7X1	T46.7X2	T46.7X3	T46.7X4	T46.7X5	T46.7X6
Xanthotoxin	T49.3X1	T49.3X2	T49.3X3	T49.3X4	T49.3X5	T49.3X6
Xantinol nicotinate	T46.7X1	T46.7X2	T46.7X3	T46.7X4	T46.7X5	T46.7X6
Xantocillin	T36.0X1	T36.0X2	T36.0X3	T36.0X4	T36.0X5	T36.0X6
Xenon (127Xe) (133Xe)	T50.8X1	T50.8X2	T50.8X3	T50.8X4	T50.8X5	T50.8X6
Xenysalate	T49.4X1	T49.4X2	T49.4X3	T49.4X4	T49.4X5	T49.4X6
Xibornol	T37.8X1	T37.8X2	T37.8X3	T37.8X4	T37.8X5	T37.8X6
Xigris	T45.511	T45.512	T45.513	T45.514	T45.515	T45.516
Xipamide	T50.2X1	T50.2X2	T50.2X3	T50.2X4	T50.2X5	T50.2X6
Xylene (vapor)	T52.2X1	T52.2X2	T52.2X3	T52.2X4	—	—
Xylocaine (infiltration) (topical)	T41.3X1	T41.3X2	T41.3X3	T41.3X4	T41.3X5	T41.3X6
nerve block (peripheral) (plexus)	T41.3X1	T41.3X2	T41.3X3	T41.3X4	T41.3X5	T41.3X6
spinal	T41.3X1	T41.3X2	T41.3X3	T41.3X4	T41.3X5	T41.3X6
Xylol (vapor)	T52.2X1	T52.2X2	T52.2X3	T52.2X4	—	—
Xylometazoline	T48.5X1	T48.5X2	T48.5X3	T48.5X4	T48.5X5	T48.5X6

Y

Substance	Poisoning, Accidental (Unintentional)	Poisoning, Intentional Self-Harm	Poisoning, Assault	Poisoning, Undetermined	Adverse Effect	Underdosing
Yeast	T45.2X1	T45.2X2	T45.2X3	T45.2X4	T45.2X5	T45.2X6
dried	T45.2X1	T45.2X2	T45.2X3	T45.2X4	T45.2X5	T45.2X6
Yellow						
fever vaccine	T50.B91	T50.B92	T50.B93	T50.B94	T50.B95	T50.B96
jasmine	T62.2X1	T62.2X2	T62.2X3	T62.2X4	—	—
phenolphthalein	T47.2X1	T47.2X2	T47.2X3	T47.2X4	T47.2X5	T47.2X6
Yew	T62.2X1	T62.2X2	T62.2X3	T62.2X4	—	—
Yohimbic acid	T40.991	T40.992	T40.993	T40.994	T40.995	T40.996

Z

Substance	Poisoning, Accidental (Unintentional)	Poisoning, Intentional Self-Harm	Poisoning, Assault	Poisoning, Undetermined	Adverse Effect	Underdosing
Zactane	T39.8X1	T39.8X2	T39.8X3	T39.8X4	T39.8X5	T39.8X6
Zalcitabine	T37.5X1	T37.5X2	T37.5X3	T37.5X4	T37.5X5	T37.5X6
Zaroxolyn	T50.2X1	T50.2X2	T50.2X3	T50.2X4	T50.2X5	T50.2X6
Zephiran (topical)	T49.0X1	T49.0X2	T49.0X3	T49.0X4	T49.0X5	T49.0X6
ophthalmic preparation	T49.5X1	T49.5X2	T49.5X3	T49.5X4	T49.5X5	T49.5X6
Zeranol	T38.7X1	T38.7X2	T38.7X3	T38.7X4	T38.7X5	T38.7X6
Zerone	T51.1X1	T51.1X2	T51.1X3	T51.1X4	—	—
Zidovudine	T37.5X1	T37.5X2	T37.5X3	T37.5X4	T37.5X5	T37.5X6
Zimeldine	T43.221	T43.222	T43.223	T43.224	T43.225	T43.226
Zinc (compounds) (fumes) (vapor) NEC	T56.5X1	T56.5X2	T56.5X3	T56.5X4	—	—
anti-infectives	T49.0X1	T49.0X2	T49.0X3	T49.0X4	T49.0X5	T49.0X6
antivaricose	T46.8X1	T46.8X2	T46.8X3	T46.8X4	T46.8X5	T46.8X6
bacitracin	T49.0X1	T49.0X2	T49.0X3	T49.0X4	T49.0X5	T49.0X6
chloride (mouthwash)	T49.6X1	T49.6X2	T49.6X3	T49.6X4	T49.6X5	T49.6X6
chromate	T56.5X1	T56.5X2	T56.5X3	T56.5X4	—	—
gelatin	T49.3X1	T49.3X2	T49.3X3	T49.3X4	T49.3X5	T49.3X6
oxide	T49.3X1	T49.3X2	T49.3X3	T49.3X4	T49.3X5	T49.3X6
plaster	T49.3X1	T49.3X2	T49.3X3	T49.3X4	T49.3X5	T49.3X6
peroxide	T49.0X1	T49.0X2	T49.0X3	T49.0X4	T49.0X5	T49.0X6
pesticides	T56.5X1	T56.5X2	T56.5X3	T56.5X4	—	—
phosphide	T60.4X1	T60.4X2	T60.4X3	T60.4X4	—	—
pyrithionate	T49.4X1	T49.4X2	T49.4X3	T49.4X4	T49.4X5	T49.4X6
stearate	T49.3X1	T49.3X2	T49.3X3	T49.3X4	T49.3X5	T49.3X6
sulfate	T49.5X1	T49.5X2	T49.5X3	T49.5X4	T49.5X5	T49.5X6
ENT agent	T49.6X1	T49.6X2	T49.6X3	T49.6X4	T49.6X5	T49.6X6
ophthalmic solution	T49.5X1	T49.5X2	T49.5X3	T49.5X4	T49.5X5	T49.5X6
topical NEC	T49.0X1	T49.0X2	T49.0X3	T49.0X4	T49.0X5	T49.0X6
undecylenate	T49.0X1	T49.0X2	T49.0X3	T49.0X4	T49.0X5	T49.0X6

◀ New   ◀ Revised   ~~deleted~~ Deleted

Substance	External Cause (T-Code)					
	Poisoning, Accidental (Unintentional)	Poisoning, Intentional Self-Harm	Poisoning, Assault	Poisoning, Undetermined	Adverse Effect	Underdosing
Zineb	T60.0X1	T60.0X2	T60.0X3	T60.0X4	—	—
Zinostatin	T45.1X1	T45.1X2	T45.1X3	T45.1X4	T45.1X5	T45.1X6
Zipeprol	T48.3X1	T48.3X2	T48.3X3	T48.3X4	T48.3X5	T48.3X6
Zofenopril	T46.4X1	T46.4X2	T46.4X3	T46.4X4	T46.4X5	T46.4X6
Zolpidem	T42.6X1	T42.6X2	T42.6X3	T42.6X4	T42.6X5	T42.6X6
Zomepirac	T39.391	T39.392	T39.393	T39.394	T39.395	T39.396
Zopiclone	T42.6X1	T42.6X2	T42.6X3	T42.6X4	T42.6X5	T42.6X6

Substance	External Cause (T-Code)					
	Poisoning, Accidental (Unintentional)	Poisoning, Intentional Self-Harm	Poisoning, Assault	Poisoning, Undetermined	Adverse Effect	Underdosing
Zorubicin	T45.1X1	T45.1X2	T45.1X3	T45.1X4	T45.1X5	T45.1X6
Zotepine	T43.591	T43.592	T43.593	T43.594	T43.595	T43.596
Zovant	T45.511	T45.512	T45.513	T45.514	T45.515	T45.516
Zoxazolamine	T42.8X1	T42.8X2	T42.8X3	T42.8X4	T42.8X5	T42.8X6
Zuclopenthixol	T43.4X1	T43.4X2	T43.4X3	T43.4X4	T43.4X5	T43.4X6
Zygadenus (venenosus)	T62.2X1	T62.2X2	T62.2X3	T62.2X4	—	—
Zyprexa	T43.591	T43.592	T43.593	T43.594	T43.595	T43.596

◀ New   ◀ Revised   ~~deleted~~ Deleted

External Cause
of Injuries Index

A

Abandonment (causing exposure to weather conditions) (with intent to injure or kill) NEC X58

Abuse (adult) (child) (mental) (physical) (sexual) X58

Accident (to) X58
  aircraft (in transit) (powered) —see also Accident, transport, aircraft
    due to, caused by cataclysm —see Forces of nature, by type
  animal-drawn vehicle —see Accident, transport, animal-drawn vehicle occupant
  animal-rider —see Accident, transport, animal-rider
  automobile —see Accident, transport, car occupant
  bare foot water skiier V94.4
  boat, boating —see also Accident, watercraft
    striking swimmer
      powered V94.11
      unpowered V94.12
  bus —see Accident, transport, bus occupant
  cable car, not on rails V98.0
    on rails —see Accident, transport, streetcar occupant
  car —see Accident, transport, car occupant
  caused by, due to
    animal NEC W64
    chain hoist W24.0
    cold (excessive) —see Exposure, cold
    corrosive liquid, substance —see Table of Drugs and Chemicals
    cutting or piercing instrument —see Contact, with, by type of instrument
    drive belt W24.0
    electric
      current —see Exposure, electric current
      motor —see also Contact, with, by type of machine W31.3
        current (of) W86.8
    environmental factor NEC X58
    explosive material —see Explosion
    fire, flames —see Exposure, fire
    firearm missile —see Discharge, firearm by type
    heat (excessive) —see Heat
    hot —see Contact, with, hot
    ignition —see Ignition
    lifting device W24.0
    lightning —see subcategory T75.0
      causing fire —see Exposure, fire
    machine, machinery —see Contact, with, by type of machine
    natural factor NEC X58
    pulley (block) W24.0
    radiation —see Radiation
    steam X13.1
      inhalation X13.0
      pipe X16
    thunderbolt —see subcategory T75.0
      causing fire —see Exposure, fire
    transmission device W24.1
  coach —see Accident, transport, bus occupant
  coal car —see Accident, transport, industrial vehicle occupant
  diving —see also Fall, into, water
    with
      drowning or submersion —see Drowning
  forklift —see Accident, transport, industrial vehicle occupant
  heavy transport vehicle NOS —see Accident, transport, truck occupant
  ice yacht V98.2

Accident (Continued)
  in
    medical, surgical procedure
      as, or due to misadventure —see Misadventure
      causing an abnormal reaction or later complication without mention of misadventure —see also Complication of or following, by type of procedure Y84.9
  land yacht V98.1
  late effect of —see W00-X58 with 7th character S
  logging car —see Accident, transport, industrial vehicle occupant
  machine, machinery —see also Contact, with, by type of machine
    on board watercraft V93.69
      explosion —see Explosion, in, watercraft
      fire —see Burn, on board watercraft
      powered craft V93.63
        ferry boat V93.61
        fishing boat V93.62
        jet ski V93.63
        liner V93.61
        merchant ship V93.60
        passenger ship V93.61
        sailboat V93.64
  mine tram —see Accident, transport, industrial vehicle occupant
  mobility scooter (motorized) —see Accident, transport, pedestrian, conveyance, specified type NEC
  motor scooter —see Accident, transport, motorcyclist
  motor vehicle NOS (traffic) —see also Accident, transport V89.2
    nontraffic V89.0
    three-wheeled NOS —see Accident, transport, three-wheeled motor vehicle occupant
  motorcycle NOS —see Accident, transport, motorcyclist
  nonmotor vehicle NOS (nontraffic) —see also Accident, transport V89.1
    traffic NOS V89.3
  nontraffic (victim's mode of transport NOS) V88.9
    collision (between) V88.7
      bus and truck V88.5
      car and:
        bus V88.3
        pickup V88.2
        three-wheeled motor vehicle V88.0
        train V88.6
        truck V88.4
        two-wheeled motor vehicle V88.0
        van V88.2
      specified vehicle NEC and:
        three-wheeled motor vehicle V88.1
        two-wheeled motor vehicle V88.1
    known mode of transport —see Accident, transport, by type of vehicle
    noncollision V88.8
  on board watercraft V93.89
    powered craft V93.83
      ferry boat V93.81
      fishing boat V93.82
      jet ski V93.83
      liner V93.81
      merchant ship V93.80
      passenger ship V93.81
    unpowered craft V93.88
      canoe V93.85
      inflatable V93.86
        in tow
          recreational V94.31
          specified NEC V94.32
      kayak V93.85

Accident (Continued)
  on board watercraft (Continued)
    unpowered craft (Continued)
      sailboat V93.84
      surf-board V93.88
      water skis V93.87
      windsurfer V93.88
  parachutist V97.29
    entangled in object V97.21
    injured on landing V97.22
  pedal cycle —see Accident, transport, pedal cyclist
  pedestrian (on foot)
    with
      another pedestrian W51
        with fall W03
          due to ice or snow W00.0
          on pedestrian conveyance NEC V00.09
  ▶rider of
      ▶hoverboard V00.038
      ▶Segway V00.038
      ▶standing
        ▶electric scooter V00.031
        ▶micro-mobility pedestrian conveyance NEC V00.038
    roller skater (in-line) V00.01
    skate boarder V00.02
    transport vehicle —see Accident, transport
  on pedestrian conveyance —see Accident, transport, pedestrian, conveyance
  pick-up truck or van —see Accident, transport, pickup truck occupant
  quarry truck —see Accident, transport, industrial vehicle occupant
  railway vehicle (any) (in motion) —see Accident, transport, railway vehicle occupant
    due to cataclysm —see Forces of nature, by type
  scooter (non-motorized) —see Accident, transport, pedestrian, conveyance, scooter
  sequelae of —see W00-X58 with 7th character S
  skateboard —see Accident, transport, pedestrian, conveyance, skateboard
  ski (ing) —see Accident, transport, pedestrian, conveyance
    lift V98.3
  specified cause NEC X58
  streetcar —see Accident, transport, streetcar occupant
  traffic (victim's mode of transport NOS) V87.9
    collision (between) V87.7
      bus and truck V87.5
      car and:
        bus V87.3
        pickup V87.2
        three-wheeled motor vehicle V87.0
        train V87.6
        truck V87.4
        two-wheeled motor vehicle V87.0
        van V87.2
      specified vehicle NEC V86.39
        and
          three-wheeled motor vehicle V87.1
          two-wheeled motor vehicle V87.1
        driver V86.09
        person on outside V86.29
        passenger V86.19
        while boarding or alighting V86.49
    known mode of transport —see Accident, transport, by type of vehicle
    noncollision V87.8

▶ New   ⟹ Revised   ~~deleted~~ Deleted   ● Use Additional Character(s)

Accident (*Continued*)
  transport (involving injury to) V99
    18 wheeler —*see* Accident, transport, truck
      occupant
    agricultural vehicle occupant (nontraffic)
      V84.9
      driver V84.5
      hanger-on V84.7
      passenger V84.6
      traffic V84.3
        driver V84.0
        hanger-on V84.2
        passenger V84.1
      while boarding or alighting
        V84.4
    aircraft NEC V97.89
      military NEC V97.818
        with civilian aircraft V97.810
        civilian injured by V97.811
      occupant injured (in)
        nonpowered craft accident V96.9
          balloon V96.00
            collision V96.03
            crash V96.01
            explosion V96.05
            fire V96.04
            forced landing V96.02
            specified type NEC V96.09
          glider V96.20
            collision V96.23
            crash V96.21
            explosion V96.25
            fire V96.24
            forced landing V96.22
            specified type NEC V96.29
          hang glider V96.10
            collision V96.13
            crash V96.11
            explosion V96.15
            fire V96.14
            forced landing V96.12
            specified type NEC V96.19
          specified craft NEC V96.8
        powered craft accident V95.9
          fixed wing NEC
            commercial V95.30
              collision V95.33
              crash V95.31
              explosion V95.35
              fire V95.34
              forced landing V95.32
              specified type NEC V95.39
            private V95.20
              collision V95.23
              crash V95.21
              explosion V95.25
              fire V95.24
              forced landing V95.22
              specified type NEC V95.29
           glider V95.10
            collision V95.13
            crash V95.11
            explosion V95.15
            fire V95.14
            forced landing V95.12
            specified type NEC V95.19
          helicopter V95.00
            collision V95.03
            crash V95.01
            explosion V95.05
            fire V95.04
            forced landing V95.02
            specified type NEC V95.09
          spacecraft V95.40
            collision V95.43
            crash V95.41
            explosion V95.45
            fire V95.44
            forced landing V95.42
            specified type NEC V95.49
          specified craft NEC V95.8

Accident (*Continued*)
  transport (*Continued*)
    aircraft NEC (*Continued*)
      occupant injured (*Continued*)
        powered craft accident (*Continued*)
          ultralight V95.10
            collision V95.13
            crash V95.11
            explosion V95.15
            fire V95.14
            forced landing V95.12
            specified type NEC V95.19
        specified accident NEC V97.0
        while boarding or alighting V97.1
      person (injured by)
        falling from, in or on aircraft V97.0
        machinery on aircraft V97.89
        on ground with aircraft involvement
          V97.39
        rotating propeller V97.32
        struck by object falling from aircraft
          V97.31
        sucked into aircraft jet V97.33
        while boarding or alighting aircraft
          V97.1
    airport (battery-powered) passenger
      vehicle —*see* Accident, transport,
      industrial vehicle occupant
    all-terrain vehicle occupant (nontraffic)
      V86.95
      driver V86.55
      dune buggy —*see* Accident, transport,
        dune buggy occupant
      hanger-on V86.75
      passenger V86.65
      snowmobile —*see* Accident, transport,
        snowmobile occupant
      specified type NEC V86.99
        driver V86.59
        passenger V86.69
        person on outside V86.79
      traffic V86.35
        driver V86.05
        hanger-on V86.25
        passenger V86.15
      while boarding or alighting V86.45
    ambulance occupant (traffic) V86.31
      driver V86.01
      hanger-on V86.21
      nontraffic V86.91
        driver V86.51
        hanger-on V86.71
        passenger V86.61
      passenger V86.11
      while boarding or alighting V86.41
    animal-drawn vehicle occupant (in) V80.929
      collision (with)
        animal V80.12
          being ridden V80.711
        animal-drawn vehicle V80.721
        bus V80.42
        car V80.42
        fixed or stationary object V80.82
        military vehicle V80.920
        nonmotor vehicle V80.791
        pedal cycle V80.22
        pedestrian V80.12
        pickup V80.42
        railway train or vehicle V80.62
        specified motor vehicle NEC V80.52
        streetcar V80.731
        truck V80.42
        two-or three-wheeled motor vehicle
          V80.32
        van V80.42
      noncollision V80.02
      specified circumstance NEC V80. 928
    animal-rider V80.919
      collision (with)
        animal V80.11
          being ridden V80.710

Accident (*Continued*)
  transport (*Continued*)
    animal-rider (*Continued*)
      collision (*Continued*)
        animal-drawn vehicle V80.720
        bus V80.41
        car V80.41
        fixed or stationary object V80.81
        military vehicle V80.910
        nonmotor vehicle V80.790
        pedal cycle V80.21
        pedestrian V80.11
        pickup V80.41
        railway train or vehicle V80.61
        specified motor vehicle NEC V80.51
        streetcar V80.730
        truck V80.41
        two- or three-wheeled motor vehicle
          V80.31
        van V80.41
      noncollision V80.018
        specified as horse rider V80.010
      specified circumstance NEC V80.918
    armored car —*see* Accident, transport,
      truck occupant
    battery-powered truck (baggage) (mail) —
      see Accident, transport, industrial
      vehicle occupant
    bus occupant V79.9
      collision (with)
        animal (traffic) V70.9
          being ridden (traffic) V76.9
            nontraffic V76.3
            while boarding or alighting V76.4
          nontraffic V70.3
          while boarding or alighting V70.4
        animal-drawn vehicle (traffic) V76.9
          nontraffic V76.3
          while boarding or alighting V76.4
        bus (traffic) V74.9
          nontraffic V74.3
          while boarding or alighting V74.4
        car (traffic) V73.9
          nontraffic V73.3
          while boarding or alighting V73.4
        motor vehicle NOS (traffic) V79.60
          nontraffic V79.20
          specified type NEC (traffic) V79.69
            nontraffic V79.29
        pedal cycle (traffic) V71.9
          nontraffic V71.3
          while boarding or alighting V71.4
        pickup truck (traffic) V73.9
          nontraffic V73.3
          while boarding or alighting V73.4
        railway vehicle (traffic) V75.9
          nontraffic V75.3
          while boarding or alighting V75.4
        specified vehicle NEC (traffic) V76.9
          nontraffic V76.3
          while boarding or alighting V76.4
        stationary object (traffic) V77.9
          nontraffic V77.3
          while boarding or alighting V77.4
        streetcar (traffic) V76.9
          nontraffic V76.3
          while boarding or alighting V76.4
        three wheeled motor vehicle (traffic)
          V72.9
          nontraffic V72.3
          while boarding or alighting V72.4
        truck (traffic) V74.9
          nontraffic V74.3
          while boarding or alighting V74.4
        two wheeled motor vehicle (traffic)
          V72.9
          nontraffic V72.3
          while boarding or alighting V72.4
        van (traffic) V73.9
          nontraffic V73.3
          while boarding or alighting V73.4

Accident *(Continued)*
  transport *(Continued)*
    bus occupant *(Continued)*
      driver
        collision (with)
          animal (traffic) V70.5
            being ridden (traffic) V76.5
              nontraffic V76.0
            nontraffic V70.0
          animal-drawn vehicle (traffic)
            V76.5
            nontraffic V76.0
          bus (traffic) V74.5
            nontraffic V74.0
          car (traffic) V73.5
            nontraffic V73.0
          motor vehicle NOS (traffic) V79.40
            nontraffic V79.00
            specified type NEC (traffic)
              V79.49
              nontraffic V79.09
          pedal cycle (traffic) V71.5
            nontraffic V71.0
          pickup truck (traffic) V73.5
            nontraffic V73.0
          railway vehicle (traffic) V75.5
            nontraffic V75.0
          specified vehicle NEC (traffic) V76.5
            nontraffic V76.0
          stationary object (traffic) V77.5
            nontraffic V77.0
          streetcar (traffic) V76.5
            nontraffic V76.0
          three wheeled motor vehicle
            (traffic) V72.5
            nontraffic V72.0
          truck (traffic) V74.5
            nontraffic V74.0
          two wheeled motor vehicle (traffic)
            V72.5
            nontraffic V72.0
          van (traffic) V73.5
            nontraffic V73.0
        noncollision accident (traffic) V78.5
          nontraffic V78.0
      hanger-on
        collision (with)
          animal (traffic) V70.7
            being ridden (traffic) V76.7
              nontraffic V76.2
            nontraffic V70.2
          animal-drawn vehicle (traffic) V76.7
            nontraffic V76.2
          bus (traffic) V74.7
            nontraffic V74.2
          car (traffic) V73.7
            nontraffic V73.2
          pedal cycle (traffic) V71.7
            nontraffic V71.2
          pickup truck (traffic) V73.7
            nontraffic V73.2
          railway vehicle (traffic) V75.7
            nontraffic V75.2
          specified vehicle NEC (traffic) V76.7
            nontraffic V76.2
          stationary object (traffic) V77.7
            nontraffic V77.2
          streetcar (traffic) V76.7
            nontraffic V76.2
          three wheeled motor vehicle
            (traffic) V72.7
            nontraffic V72.2
          truck (traffic) V74.7
            nontraffic V74.2
          two wheeled motor vehicle (traffic)
            V72.7
            nontraffic V72.2
          van (traffic) V73.7
            nontraffic V73.2
        noncollision accident (traffic) V78.7
          nontraffic V78.2

Accident *(Continued)*
  transport *(Continued)*
    bus occupant *(Continued)*
      noncollision accident (traffic) V78.9
        nontraffic V78.3
        while boarding or alighting V78.4
      nontraffic V79.3
      passenger
        collision (with)
          animal (traffic) V70.6
            being ridden (traffic) V76.6
              nontraffic V76.1
            nontraffic V70.1
          animal-drawn vehicle (traffic)
            V76.6
            nontraffic V76.1
          bus (traffic) V74.6
            nontraffic V74.1
          car (traffic) V73.6
            nontraffic V73.1
          motor vehicle NOS (traffic) V79.50
            nontraffic V79.10
            specified type NEC (traffic)
              V79.59
              nontraffic V79.19
          pedal cycle (traffic) V71.6
            nontraffic V71.1
          pickup truck (traffic) V73.6
            nontraffic V73.1
          railway vehicle (traffic) V75.6
            nontraffic V75.1
          specified vehicle NEC (traffic) V76.6
            nontraffic V76.1
          stationary object (traffic) V77.6
            nontraffic V77.1
          streetcar (traffic) V76.6
            nontraffic V76.1
          three wheeled motor vehicle
            (traffic) V72.6
            nontraffic V72.1
          truck (traffic) V74.6
            nontraffic V74.1
          two wheeled motor vehicle (traffic)
            V72.6
            nontraffic V72.1
          van (traffic) V73.6
            nontraffic V73.1
        noncollision accident (traffic) V78.6
          nontraffic V78.1
      specified type NEC V79.88
        military vehicle V79.81
    cable car, not on rails V98.0
    on rails —*see* Accident, transport,
      streetcar occupant
    car occupant V49.9
      ambulance occupant —*see* Accident,
        transport, ambulance occupant
      collision (with)
        animal (traffic) V40.9
          being ridden (traffic) V46.9
            nontraffic V46.3
            while boarding or alighting
              V46.4
          nontraffic V40.3
          while boarding or alighting V40.4
        animal-drawn vehicle (traffic) V46.9
          nontraffic V46.3
          while boarding or alighting V46.4
        bus (traffic) V44.9
          nontraffic V44.3
          while boarding or alighting V44.4
        car (traffic) V43.92
          nontraffic V43.32
          while boarding or alighting V43.42
        motor vehicle NOS (traffic) V49.60
          nontraffic V49.20
          specified type NEC (traffic) V49.69
           nontraffic V49.29
        pedal cycle (traffic) V41.9
          nontraffic V41.3
          while boarding or alighting V41.4

Accident *(Continued)*
  transport *(Continued)*
    car occupant *(Continued)*
      collision *(Continued)*
        pickup truck (traffic) V43.93
          nontraffic V43.33
          while boarding or alighting
            V43.43
        railway vehicle (traffic) V45.9
          nontraffic V45.3
          while boarding or alighting V45.4
        specified vehicle NEC (traffic) V46.9
          nontraffic V46.3
          while boarding or alighting V46.4
        sport utility vehicle (traffic) V43.91
          nontraffic V43.31
          while boarding or alighting V43.41
        stationary object (traffic) V47.9
          nontraffic V47.3
          while boarding or alighting V47.4
        streetcar (traffic) V46.9
          nontraffic V46.3
          while boarding or alighting V46.4
        three wheeled motor vehicle (traffic)
          V42.9
          nontraffic V42.3
          while boarding or alighting V42.4
        truck (traffic) V44.9
          nontraffic V44.3
          while boarding or alighting V44.4
        two wheeled motor vehicle (traffic)
          V42.9
          nontraffic V42.3
          while boarding or alighting V42.4
        van (traffic) V43.94
          nontraffic V43.34
          while boarding or alighting V43.44
      driver
        collision (with)
          animal (traffic) V40.5
           being ridden (traffic) V46.5
            nontraffic V46.0
           nontraffic V40.0
          animal-drawn vehicle (traffic) V46.5
           nontraffic V46.0
          bus (traffic) V44.5
           nontraffic V44.0
          car (traffic) V43.52
           nontraffic V43.02
          motor vehicle NOS (traffic) V49.40
           nontraffic V49.00
           specified type NEC (traffic)
            V49.49
            nontraffic V49.09
          pedal cycle (traffic) V41.5
           nontraffic V41.0
          pickup truck (traffic) V43.53
           nontraffic V43.03
          railway vehicle (traffic) V45.5
           nontraffic V45.0
          specified vehicle NEC (traffic)
            V46.5
           nontraffic V46.0
          sport utility vehicle (traffic) V43.51
           nontraffic V43.01
          stationary object (traffic) V47.5
           nontraffic V47.0
          streetcar (traffic) V46.5
           nontraffic V46.0
          three wheeled motor vehicle
            (traffic) V42.5
           nontraffic V42.0
          truck (traffic) V44.5
           nontraffic V44.0
          two wheeled motor vehicle (traffic)
            V42.5
           nontraffic V42.0
          van (traffic) V43.54
           nontraffic V43.04
        noncollision accident (traffic) V48.5
          nontraffic V48.0

▶ New   ⮞ Revised   ~~deleted~~ Deleted   ● Use Additional Character(s)

Accident *(Continued)*
  transport *(Continued)*
    car occupant *(Continued)*
      hanger-on
        collision (with)
          animal (traffic) V40.7
            being ridden (traffic) V46.7
              nontraffic V46.2
            nontraffic V40.2
          animal-drawn vehicle (traffic) V46.7
            nontraffic V46.2
          bus (traffic) V44.7
            nontraffic V44.2
          car (traffic) V43.72
            nontraffic V43.22
          pedal cycle (traffic) V41.7
            nontraffic V41.2
          pickup truck (traffic) V43.73
            nontraffic V43.23
          railway vehicle (traffic) V45.7
            nontraffic V45.2
          specified vehicle NEC (traffic) V46.7
            nontraffic V46.2
          sport utility vehicle (traffic) V43.71
            nontraffic V43.21
          stationary object (traffic) V47.7
            nontraffic V47.2
          streetcar (traffic) V46.7
            nontraffic V46.2
          three wheeled motor vehicle (traffic) V42.7
            nontraffic V42.2
          truck (traffic) V44.7
            nontraffic V44.2
          two wheeled motor vehicle (traffic) V42.7
            nontraffic V42.2
          van (traffic) V43.74
            nontraffic V43.24
        noncollision accident (traffic) V48.7
         nontraffic V48.2
      noncollision accident (traffic) V48.9
        nontraffic V48.3
        while boarding or alighting V48.4
      nontraffic V49.3
      passenger
        collision (with)
          animal (traffic) V40.6
            being ridden (traffic) V46.6
              nontraffic V46.1
            nontraffic V40.1
          animal-drawn vehicle (traffic) V46.6
            nontraffic V46.1
          bus (traffic) V44.6
            nontraffic V44.1
          car (traffic) V43.62
            nontraffic V43.12
          motor vehicle NOS (traffic) V49.50
            nontraffic V49.10
            specified type NEC (traffic) V49.59
              nontraffic V49.19
          pedal cycle (traffic) V41.6
            nontraffic V41.1
          pickup truck (traffic) V43.63
            nontraffic V43.13
          railway vehicle (traffic) V45.6
            nontraffic V45.1
          specified vehicle NEC (traffic) V46.6
            nontraffic V46.1
          sport utility vehicle (traffic) V43.61
            nontraffic V43.11
          stationary object (traffic) V47.6
            nontraffic V47.1
          streetcar (traffic) V46.6
            nontraffic V46.1
          three wheeled motor vehicle (traffic) V42.6
            nontraffic V42.1
          truck (traffic) V44.6
            nontraffic V44.1

Accident *(Continued)*
  transport *(Continued)*
    car occupant *(Continued)*
      passenger *(Continued)*
        collision *(Continued)*
          two wheeled motor vehicle (traffic) V42.6
            nontraffic V42.1
          van (traffic) V43.64
            nontraffic V43.14
        noncollision accident (traffic) V48.6
         nontraffic V48.1
        specified type NEC V49.88
        military vehicle V49.81
    coal car —*see* Accident, transport, industrial vehicle occupant
    construction vehicle occupant (nontraffic) V85.9
      driver V85.5
      hanger-on V85.7
      passenger V85.6
      traffic V85.3
        driver V85.0
        hanger-on V85.2
        passenger V85.1
      while boarding or alighting V85.4
    dirt bike rider (nontraffic) V86.96
      driver V86.56
      hanger-on V86.76
      passenger V86.66
      traffic V86.36
        driver V86.06
        hanger-on V86.26
        passenger V86.16
      while boarding or alighting V86.46
    due to cataclysm —*see* Forces of nature, by type
    dune buggy occupant (nontraffic) V86.93
      driver V86.53
      hanger-on V86.73
      passenger V86.63
      traffic V86.33
        driver V86.03
        hanger-on V86.23
        passenger V86.13
      while boarding or alighting V86.43
    forklift —*see* Accident, transport, industrial vehicle occupant
    go cart —*see* Accident, transport, all-terrain vehicle occupant
    golf cart —*see* Accident, transport, all-terrain vehicle occupant
    heavy transport vehicle occupant — *see* Accident, transport, truck occupant
    ▶hoverboard V00.848
    ice yacht V98.2
    industrial vehicle occupant (nontraffic) V83.9
      driver V83.5
      hanger-on V83.7
      passenger V83.6
      traffic V83.3
        driver V83.0
        hanger-on V83.2
        passenger V83.1
      while boarding or alighting V83.4
    interurban electric car —*see* Accident, transport, streetcar
    land yacht V98.1
    logging car —*see* Accident, transport, industrial vehicle occupant
    military vehicle occupant (traffic) V86.34
      driver V86.04
      hanger-on V86.24
      nontraffic V86.94
        driver V86.54
        hanger-on V86.74
        passenger V86.64
      passenger V86.14
      while boarding or alighting V86.44

Accident *(Continued)*
  transport *(Continued)*
    mine tram —*see* Accident, transport, industrial vehicle occupant
    motor vehicle NEC occupant (traffic) V89.2
    motorcoach —*see* Accident, transport, bus occupant
    motor/cross bike rider —*see also* Accident, transport, dirt bike rider V86.96
    motorcyclist V29.9
      collision (with)
        animal (traffic) V20.9
          being ridden (traffic) V26.9
            nontraffic V26.2
            while boarding or alighting V26.3
          nontraffic V20.2
          while boarding or alighting V20.3
        animal-drawn vehicle (traffic) V26.9
          nontraffic V26.2
          while boarding or alighting V26.3
        bus (traffic) V24.9
          nontraffic V24.2
          while boarding or alighting V24.3
        car (traffic) V23.9
          nontraffic V23.2
          while boarding or alighting V23.3
        motor vehicle NOS (traffic) V29.60
          nontraffic V29.20
          specified type NEC (traffic) V29.69
            nontraffic V29.29
        pedal cycle (traffic) V21.9
          nontraffic V21.2
          while boarding or alighting V21.3
        pickup truck (traffic) V23.9
          nontraffic V23.2
          while boarding or alighting V23.3
        railway vehicle (traffic) V25.9
          nontraffic V25.2
          while boarding or alighting V25.3
        specified vehicle NEC (traffic) V26.9
          nontraffic V26.2
          while boarding or alighting V26.3
        stationary object (traffic) V27.9
          nontraffic V27.2
          while boarding or alighting V27.3
        streetcar (traffic) V26.9
          nontraffic V26.2
          while boarding or alighting V26.3
        three wheeled motor vehicle (traffic) V22.9
          nontraffic V22.2
          while boarding or alighting V22.3
        truck (traffic) V24.9
          nontraffic V24.2
          while boarding or alighting V24.3
        two wheeled motor vehicle (traffic) V22.9
          nontraffic V22.2
          while boarding or alighting V22.3
        van (traffic) V23.9
          nontraffic V23.2
          while boarding or alighting V23.3
      driver
        collision (with)
          animal (traffic) V20.4
            being ridden (traffic) V26.4
              nontraffic V26.0
            nontraffic V20.0
          animal-drawn vehicle (traffic) V26.4
            nontraffic V26.0
          bus (traffic) V24.4
            nontraffic V24.0
          car (traffic) V23.4
            nontraffic V23.0
          motor vehicle NOS (traffic) V29.40
            nontraffic V29.00
            specified type NEC (traffic) V29.49
              nontraffic V29.09
          pedal cycle (traffic) V21.4
            nontraffic V21.0

Accident (Continued)
 transport (Continued)
  motorcyclist (Continued)
   driver (Continued)
    collision (Continued)
     pickup truck (traffic) V23.4
      nontraffic V23.0
     railway vehicle (traffic) V25.4
      nontraffic V25.0
     specified vehicle NEC (traffic) V26.4
      nontraffic V26.0
     stationary object (traffic) V27.4
      nontraffic V27.0
     streetcar (traffic) V26.4
      nontraffic V26.0
     three wheeled motor vehicle
       (traffic) V22.4
      nontraffic V22.0
     truck (traffic) V24.4
      nontraffic V24.0
     two wheeled motor vehicle (traffic)
       V22.4
      nontraffic V22.0
     van (traffic) V23.4
      nontraffic V23.0
    noncollision accident (traffic) V28.4
      nontraffic V28.0
   noncollision accident (traffic) V28.9
    nontraffic V28.2
    while boarding or alighting V28.3
   nontraffic V29.3
   passenger
    collision (with)
     animal (traffic) V20.5
      being ridden (traffic) V26.5
       nontraffic V26.1
      nontraffic V20.1
     animal-drawn vehicle (traffic) V26.5
      nontraffic V26.1
     bus (traffic) V24.5
      nontraffic V24.1
     car (traffic) V23.5
      nontraffic V23.1
     motor vehicle NOS (traffic) V29.50
      nontraffic V29.10
      specified type NEC (traffic)
        V29.59
       nontraffic V29.19
     pedal cycle (traffic) V21.5
      nontraffic V21.1
     pickup truck (traffic) V23.5
      nontraffic V23.1
     railway vehicle (traffic) V25.5
      nontraffic V25.1
     specified vehicle NEC (traffic) V26.5
      nontraffic V26.1
     stationary object (traffic) V27.5
      nontraffic V27.1
     streetcar (traffic) V26.5
      nontraffic V26.1
     three wheeled motor vehicle
       (traffic) V22.5
      nontraffic V22.1
     truck (traffic) V24.5
      nontraffic V24.1
     two wheeled motor vehicle (traffic)
       V22.5
      nontraffic V22.1
     van (traffic) V23.5
      nontraffic V23.1
    noncollision accident (traffic) V28.5
      nontraffic V28.1
    specified type NEC V29.88
    military vehicle V29.81
  occupant (of)
   aircraft (powered) V95.9
    fixed wing
     commercial —see Accident,
       transport, aircraft, occupant,
       powered, fixed wing,
       commercial

Accident (Continued)
 transport (Continued)
  occupant (Continued)
   aircraft (Continued)
    fixed wing (Continued)
     private —see Accident, transport,
       aircraft, occupant, powered,
       fixed wing, private
    nonpowered V96.9
    specified NEC V95.8
   airport battery-powered vehicle —see
     Accident, transport, industrial
     vehicle occupant
   all-terrain vehicle (ATV) —see Accident,
     transport, all-terrain vehicle
     occupant
   animal-drawn vehicle —see Accident,
     transport, animal-drawn vehicle
     occupant
   automobile —see Accident, transport, car
     occupant
   balloon V96.00
   battery-powered vehicle —see Accident,
     transport, industrial vehicle
     occupant
   bicycle —see Accident, transport, pedal
     cyclist
    motorized —see Accident, transport,
      motorcycle rider
   boat NEC —see Accident, watercraft
   bulldozer —see Accident, transport,
     construction vehicle occupant
   bus —see Accident, transport, bus
     occupant
   cable car (on rails) —see also Accident,
     transport, streetcar occupant
    not on rails V98.0
   car —see also Accident, transport, car
     occupant
    cable (on rails) —see also Accident,
      transport, streetcar occupant
     not on rails V98.0
   coach —see Accident, transport, bus
     occupant
   coal-car —see Accident, transport,
     industrial vehicle occupant
   digger —see Accident, transport,
     construction vehicle occupant
   dump truck —see Accident, transport,
     construction vehicle occupant
   earth-leveler —see Accident, transport,
     construction vehicle occupant
   farm machinery (self-propelled) —see
     Accident, transport, agricultural
     vehicle occupant
   forklift —see Accident, transport,
     industrial vehicle occupant
   glider (unpowered) V96.20
    hang V96.10
    powered (microlight) (ultralight) —see
      Accident, transport, aircraft,
      occupant, powered, glider
   glider (unpowered) NEC V96.20
   hang-glider V96.10
   harvester —see Accident, transport,
     agricultural vehicle occupant
   heavy (transport) vehicle —see Accident,
     transport, truck occupant
   helicopter —see Accident, transport,
     aircraft, occupant, helicopter
   ice-yacht V98.2
   kite (carrying person) V96.8
   land-yacht V98.1
   logging car —see Accident, transport,
     industrial vehicle occupant
   mechanical shovel —see Accident,
     transport, construction vehicle
     occupant
   microlight —see Accident, transport,
     aircraft, occupant, powered,
     glider

Accident (Continued)
 transport (Continued)
  occupant (Continued)
   minibus —see Accident, transport,
     pickup truck occupant
   minivan —see Accident, transport,
     pickup truck occupant
   moped —see Accident, transport,
     motorcycle
   motor scooter —see Accident, transport,
     motorcycle
   motorcycle (with sidecar) —see Accident,
     transport, motorcycle
   off-road motor-vehicle —see also
     Accident, transport, all-terrain
     vehicle occupant V86.99
   pedal cycle —see also Accident,
     transport, pedal cyclist
   pick-up (truck) —see Accident, transport,
     pickup truck occupant
   railway (train) (vehicle) (subterranean)
     (elevated) —see Accident, transport,
     railway vehicle occupant
   rickshaw —see Accident, transport,
     pedal cycle
    pedal driven —see Accident, transport,
      pedal cyclist
   road-roller —see Accident, transport,
     construction vehicle occupant
   ship NOS V94.9
   ski-lift (chair) (gondola) V98.3
   snowmobile —see Accident, transport,
     snowmobile occupant
   spacecraft, spaceship —see Accident,
     transport, aircraft, occupant,
     spacecraft
   sport utility vehicle —see Accident,
     transport, pickup truck occupant
   streetcar (interurban) (operating on
     public street or highway) —see
     Accident, transport, streetcar
     occupant
   SUV —see Accident, transport, pickup
     truck occupant
   téléférique V98.0
   three-wheeled vehicle (motorized) —see
     also Accident, transport, three-
     wheeled motor vehicle occupant
    nonmotorized —see Accident,
      transport, pedal cycle
   tractor (farm) (and trailer) —see
     Accident, transport, agricultural
     vehicle occupant
   train —see Accident, transport, railway
     vehicle occupant
   tram —see Accident, transport, streetcar
     occupant
    in mine or quarry —see Accident,
      transport, industrial vehicle
      occupant
   tricycle —see Accident, transport, pedal
     cycle
    motorized —see Accident, transport,
      three-wheeled motor vehicle
   trolley —see Accident, transport,
     streetcar occupant
    in mine or quarry —see Accident,
      transport, industrial vehicle
      occupant
   tub, in mine or quarry —see Accident,
     transport, industrial vehicle
     occupant
   ultralight —see Accident, transport,
     aircraft, occupant, powered, glider
   van —see Accident, transport, van
     occupant
   vehicle NEC V89.9
    heavy transport —see Accident,
      transport, truck occupant
    motor (traffic) NEC V89.2
     nontraffic NEC V89.0

▶ New   ⇒ Revised   ~~deleted~~ Deleted   ● Use Additional Character(s)

Accident *(Continued)*
  transport *(Continued)*
    occupant *(Continued)*
      watercraft NOS V94.9
        causing drowning —*see* Drowning,
          resulting from accident to boat
      off-road motor-vehicle —*see also* Accident,
        transport, all-terrain vehicle occupant
        V86.99
    parachutist V97.29
      after accident to aircraft —*see* Accident,
        transport, aircraft
      entangled in object V97.21
      injured on landing V97.22
    pedal cyclist V19.9
      collision (with)
        animal (traffic) V10.9
          being ridden (traffic) V16.9
            nontraffic V16.2
              while boarding or alighting
                V16.3
          nontraffic V10.2
          while boarding or alighting V10.3
        animal-drawn vehicle (traffic) V16.9
          nontraffic V16.2
          while boarding or alighting V16.3
        bus (traffic) V14.9
          nontraffic V14.2
          while boarding or alighting V14.3
        car (traffic) V13.9
          nontraffic V13.2
          while boarding or alighting V13.3
        motor vehicle NOS (traffic) V19.60
          nontraffic V19.20
          specified type NEC (traffic) V19.69
            nontraffic V19.29
        pedal cycle (traffic) V11.9
          nontraffic V11.2
          while boarding or alighting V11.3
        pickup truck (traffic) V13.9
          nontraffic V13.2
          while boarding or alighting V13.3
        railway vehicle (traffic) V15.9
          nontraffic V15.2
          while boarding or alighting V15.3
        specified vehicle NEC (traffic) V16.9
          nontraffic V16.2
          while boarding or alighting V16.3
        stationary object (traffic) V17.9
          nontraffic V17.2
          while boarding or alighting V17.3
        streetcar (traffic) V16.9
          nontraffic V16.2
          while boarding or alighting V16.3
        three wheeled motor vehicle (traffic)
          V12.9
          nontraffic V12.2
          while boarding or alighting V12.3
        truck (traffic) V14.9
          nontraffic V14.2
          while boarding or alighting V14.3
        two wheeled motor vehicle (traffic)
          V12.9
          nontraffic V12.2
          while boarding or alighting V12.3
        van (traffic) V13.9
          nontraffic V13.2
          while boarding or alighting V13.3
      driver
        collision (with)
          animal (traffic) V10.4
            being ridden (traffic) V16.4
              nontraffic V16.0
            nontraffic V10.0
          animal-drawn vehicle (traffic)
            V16.4
            nontraffic V16.0
          bus (traffic) V14.4
            nontraffic V14.0
          car (traffic) V13.4
            nontraffic V13.0

Accident *(Continued)*
  transport *(Continued)*
    pedal cyclist *(Continued)*
      driver *(Continued)*
        collision *(Continued)*
          motor vehicle NOS (traffic) V19.40
            nontraffic V19.00
            specified type NEC (traffic) V19.49
              nontraffic V19.09
          pedal cycle (traffic) V11.4
            nontraffic V11.0
          pickup truck (traffic) V13.4
            nontraffic V13.0
          railway vehicle (traffic) V15.4
            nontraffic V15.0
          specified vehicle NEC (traffic) V16.4
            nontraffic V16.0
          stationary object (traffic) V17.4
            nontraffic V17.0
          streetcar (traffic) V16.4
            nontraffic V16.0
          three wheeled motor vehicle
            (traffic) V12.4
            nontraffic V12.0
          truck (traffic) V14.4
            nontraffic V14.0
          two wheeled motor vehicle (traffic)
            V12.4
            nontraffic V12.0
          van (traffic) V13.4
            nontraffic V13.0
        noncollision accident (traffic) V18.4
          nontraffic V18.0
      noncollision accident (traffic) V18.9
        nontraffic V18.2
        while boarding or alighting V18.3
      nontraffic V19.3
      passenger
        collision (with)
          animal (traffic) V10.5
            being ridden (traffic) V16.5
              nontraffic V16.1
            nontraffic V10.1
          animal-drawn vehicle (traffic) V16.5
            nontraffic V16.1
          bus (traffic) V14.5
            nontraffic V14.1
          car (traffic) V13.5
            nontraffic V13.1
          motor vehicle NOS (traffic) V19.50
            nontraffic V19.10
            specified type NEC (traffic)
              V19.59
              nontraffic V19.19
          pedal cycle (traffic) V11.5
            nontraffic V11.1
          pickup truck (traffic) V13.5
            nontraffic V13.1
          railway vehicle (traffic) V15.5
            nontraffic V15.1
          specified vehicle NEC (traffic) V16.5
            nontraffic V16.1
          stationary object (traffic) V17.5
            nontraffic V17.1
          streetcar (traffic) V16.5
            nontraffic V16.1
          three wheeled motor vehicle
            (traffic) V12.5
            nontraffic V12.1
          truck (traffic) V14.5
            nontraffic V14.1
          two wheeled motor vehicle (traffic)
            V12.5
            nontraffic V12.1
          van (traffic) V13.5
            nontraffic V13.1
        noncollision accident (traffic) V18.5
          nontraffic V18.1
      specified type NEC V19.88
        military vehicle V19.81
    pedestrian

Accident *(Continued)*
  transport *(Continued)*
    pedestrian *(Continued)*
      conveyance (occupant) V09.9
        baby stroller V00.828
          collision (with) V09.9
            animal being ridden or animal
              drawn vehicle V06.99
              nontraffic V06.09
              traffic V06.19
            bus or heavy transport V04.99
              nontraffic V04.09
              traffic V04.19
            car V03.99
              nontraffic V03.09
              traffic V03.19
            pedal cycle V01.99
              nontraffic V01.09
              traffic V01.19
            pick-up truck or van V03.99
              nontraffic V03.09
              traffic V03.19
            railway (train) (vehicle)
              V05.99
              nontraffic V05.09
              traffic V05.19
            stationary object V00.822
            streetcar V06.99
              nontraffic V06.09
              traffic V06.19
            two- or three-wheeled motor
              vehicle V02.99
              nontraffic V02.09
              traffic V02.19
            vehicle V09.9
              animal-drawn V06.99
                nontraffic V06.09
                traffic V06.19
              motor
                nontraffic V09.00
                traffic V09.20
        fall V00.821
        nontraffic V09.1
          involving motor vehicle NEC
            V09.00
        traffic V09.3
          involving motor vehicle NEC
            V09.20
        flat-bottomed NEC V00.388
          collision (with) V09.9
            animal being ridden or animal
              drawn vehicle V06.99
              nontraffic V06.09
              traffic V06.19
            bus or heavy transport V04.99
              nontraffic V04.09
              traffic V04.19
            car V03.99
              nontraffic V03.09
              traffic V03.19
            pedal cycle V01.99
              nontraffic V01.09
              traffic V01.19
            pick-up truck or van V03.99
              nontraffic V03.09
              traffic V03.19
            railway (train) (vehicle) V05.99
              nontraffic V05.09
              traffic V05.19
            stationary object V00.382
            streetcar V06.99
              nontraffic V06.09
              traffic V06.19
            two-or three-wheeled motor
              vehicle V02.99
              nontraffic V02.09
              traffic V02.19
            vehicle V09.9
              animal-drawn V06.99
                nontraffic V06.09
                traffic V06.19

A

Accident *(Continued)*
  transport *(Continued)*
    pedestrian *(Continued)*
      conveyance *(Continued)*
        flat-bottomed NEC *(Continued)*
          collision *(Continued)*
            vehicle *(Continued)*
              motor
                nontraffic V09.00
                traffic V09.20
            fall V00.381
            nontraffic V09.1
              involving motor vehicle NEC
                V09.00
            snow
              board —*see* Accident, transport,
                pedestrian, conveyance,
                snow board
              ski —*see* Accident, transport,
                pedestrian, conveyance, skis
                (snow)
            traffic V09.3
              involving motor vehicle NEC
                V09.20
        gliding type NEC V00.288
          collision (with) V09.9
            animal being ridden or animal
              drawn vehicle V06.99
              nontraffic V06.09
              traffic V06.19
            bus or heavy transport
              V04.99
              nontraffic V04.09
              traffic V04.19
            car V03.99
              nontraffic V03.09
              traffic V03.19
            pedal cycle V01.99
              nontraffic V01.09
              traffic V01.19
            pick-up truck or van V03.99
              nontraffic V03.09
              traffic V03.19
            railway (train) (vehicle) V05.99
              nontraffic V05.09
              traffic V05.19
            stationary object V00.282
            streetcar V06.99
              nontraffic V06.09
              traffic V06.19
            two- or three-wheeled motor
              vehicle V02.99
              nontraffic V02.09
              traffic V02.19
            vehicle V09.9
              animal-drawn V06.99
                nontraffic V06.09
                traffic V06.19
              motor
                nontraffic V09.00
                traffic V09.20
          fall V00.281
          heelies —*see* Accident, transport,
            pedestrian, conveyance,
            heelies
        ▶hoverboard
          ▶collision with
            ▶animal being ridden or animal
                drawn vehicle V06.938
              ▶nontraffic V06.038
              ▶traffic V06.138
            ▶bus or heavy transport
                V04.938
              ▶nontraffic V04.038
              ▶traffic V04.138
            ▶car V03.938
              ▶nontraffic V03.038
              ▶traffic V03.138
            ▶pedal cycle V01.938
              ▶nontraffic V01.038
              ▶traffic V01.138

Accident *(Continued)*
  transport *(Continued)*
    pedestrian *(Continued)*
      conveyance *(Continued)*
        gliding type NEC *(Continued)*
          hoverboard *(Continued)*
            collision with *(Continued)*
              ▶pick-up or van V03.938
                ▶nontraffic V03.038
                ▶traffic V03.138
              ▶railway (train) (vehicle) V05.938
                ▶nontraffic V05.038
                ▶traffic V05.138
              ▶streetcar V06.938
                ▶nontraffic V06.038
                ▶traffic V06.138
              ▶three-wheeled motor vehicle
                  V02.938
                ▶nontraffic V02.038
                ▶traffic V02.138
              ▶two-wheeled motor vehicle
                  V02.938
                ▶nontraffic V02.038
                ▶traffic V02.138
              ▶vehicle, nonmotor, specified
                  NEC V06.938
                ▶nontraffic V06.038
                ▶traffic V06.138
            ▶fall V00.848
          ice skate —*see* Accident, transport,
            pedestrian, conveyance, ice
            skate
          nontraffic V09.1
            involving motor vehicle NEC
              V09.00
        ▶Segway
          ▶collision with
            ▶animal being ridden or animal
                drawn vehicle V06.938
              ▶nontraffic V06.038
              ▶traffic V06.138
            ▶bus or heavy transport V04.938
              ▶nontraffic V04.038
              ▶traffic V04.138
            ▶car V03.938
              ▶nontraffic V03.038
              ▶traffic V03.138
            ▶pedal cycle V01.938
              ▶nontraffic V01.038
              ▶traffic V01.138
            ▶pick-up or van V03.038
              ▶nontraffic V01.038
              ▶traffic V03.138
            ▶railway (train) (vehicle) V05.938
              ▶nontraffic V05.038
              ▶traffic V05.138
            ▶streetcar V06.938
              ▶nontraffic V06.038
              ▶traffic V06.138
            ▶three-wheeled motor vehicle
                V02.938
              ▶nontraffic V02.038
              ▶traffic V02.138
            ▶two-wheeled motor vehicle
                V02.938
              ▶nontraffic V02.038
              ▶traffic V02.138
            ▶vehicle, nonmotor, specified
                NEC V06.938
              ▶nontraffic V06.038
              ▶traffic V06.138
          ▶fall V00.848
          sled —*see* Accident, transport,
            pedestrian, conveyance, sled
        ▶standing
          ▶electric scooter
            ▶collision with
              ▶animal being ridden or
                  animal drawn vehicle
                  V06.931
                ▶nontraffic V06.031
                ▶traffic V06.131

Accident *(Continued)*
  transport *(Continued)*
    pedestrian *(Continued)*
      conveyance *(Continued)*
        gliding type NEC *(Continued)*
          standing *(Continued)*
            electric scooter *(Continued)*
              collision with *(Continued)*
                ▶bus or heavy transport
                    V04.931
                  ▶nontraffic V04.031
                  ▶traffic V04.131
                ▶car V03.931
                  ▶nontraffic V03.031
                  ▶traffic V03.131
                ▶pedal cycle V01.931
                  ▶nontraffic V01.031
                  ▶traffic V01.131
                ▶pick-up or van V03.931
                  ▶nontraffic V03.031
                  ▶traffic V03.131
                ▶railway (train) (vehicle)
                    V05.931
                  ▶nontraffic V05.031
                  ▶traffic V05.131
                ▶streetcar V06.931
                  ▶nontraffic V06.031
                  ▶traffic V06.131
                ▶three-wheeled motor vehicle
                    V02.931
                  ▶nontraffic V02.031
                  ▶traffic V02.131
                ▶two-wheeled motor vehicle
                    V02.931
                  ▶nontraffic V02.031
                  ▶traffic V02.131
                ▶vehicle, nonmotor, specified
                    NEC V06.931
                  ▶nontraffic V06.031
                  ▶traffic V06.131
              ▶fall V00.841
          ▶micro-mobility pedestrian
              conveyance
            ▶collision with
              ▶animal being ridden or
                  animal drawn vehicle
                  V06.938
                ▶nontraffic V06.038
                ▶traffic V06.138
              ▶bus or heavy transport
                  V04.938
                ▶nontraffic V04.038
                ▶traffic V04.138
              ▶car V03.938
                ▶nontraffic V03.038
                ▶traffic V03.138
              ▶pedal cycle V01.938
                ▶nontraffic V01.038
                ▶traffic V01.138
              ▶pick-up or van V03.938
                ▶nontraffic V03.038
                ▶traffic V03.138
              ▶railway (train) (vehicle)
                  V05.938
                ▶nontraffic V05.038
                ▶traffic V05.138
              ▶stationary object V00.842
              ▶streetcar V06.938
                ▶nontraffic V06.038
                ▶traffic V06.138
              ▶three-wheeled motor vehicle
                  V02.938
                ▶nontraffic V02.038
                ▶traffic V02.138
              ▶two-wheeled motor vehicle
                  V02.938
                ▶nontraffic V02.038
                ▶traffic V02.138
              ▶vehicle, nonmotor, specified
                  NEC V06.938
                ▶nontraffic V06.038
                ▶traffic V06.138
            ▶fall V00.848

▶ New   ⇒ Revised   ~~deleted~~ Deleted   ● Use Additional Character(s)

Accident *(Continued)*
  transport *(Continued)*
    pedestrian *(Continued)*
      conveyance *(Continued)*
        gliding type NEC *(Continued)*
          traffic V09.3
            involving motor vehicle NEC
              V09.20
            wheelies —*see* Accident,
              transport, pedestrian,
              conveyance, heelies
        heelies V00.158
          colliding with stationary object
            V00.152
          fall V00.151
        ice skates V00.218
          collision (with) V09.9
            animal being ridden or animal
              drawn vehicle V06.99
              nontraffic V06.09
              traffic V06.19
            bus or heavy transport V04.99
              nontraffic V04.09
              traffic V04.19
            car V03.99
              nontraffic V03.09
              traffic V03.19
            pedal cycle V01.99
              nontraffic V01.09
              traffic V01.19
            pick-up truck or van V03.99
              nontraffic V03.09
              traffic V03.19
            railway (train) (vehicle)
              V05.99
              nontraffic V05.09
              traffic V05.19
            stationary object V00.212
            streetcar V06.99
              nontraffic V06.09
              traffic V06.19
            two- or three-wheeled motor
              vehicle V02.99
              nontraffic V02.09
              traffic V02.19
            vehicle V09.9
              animal-drawn V06.99
                nontraffic V06.09
                traffic V06.19
              motor
                nontraffic V09.00
                traffic V09.20
          fall V00.211
          nontraffic V09.1
            involving motor vehicle NEC
              V09.00
          traffic V09.3
            involving motor vehicle NEC
              V09.20
        motorized mobility scooter
          V00.838
          collision with stationary object
            V00.832
          fall from V00.831
          nontraffic V09.1
            involving motor vehicle
              V09.00
            military V09.01
            specified type NEC V09.09
        roller skates (non in-line) V00.128
          collision (with) V09.9
            animal being ridden or animal
              drawn vehicle V06.91
              nontraffic V06.01
              traffic V06.11
            bus or heavy transport V04.91
              nontraffic V04.01
              traffic V04.11
            car V03.91
              nontraffic V03.01
              traffic V03.11

Accident *(Continued)*
  transport *(Continued)*
    pedestrian *(Continued)*
      conveyance *(Continued)*
        roller skates *(Continued)*
          collision *(Continued)*
            pedal cycle V01.91
              nontraffic V01.01
              traffic V01.11
            pick-up truck or van
              V03.91
              nontraffic V03.01
              traffic V03.11
            railway (train) (vehicle)
              V05.91
              nontraffic V05.01
              traffic V05.11
            stationary object V00.122
            streetcar V06.91
              nontraffic V06.01
              traffic V06.11
            two- or three-wheeled motor
              vehicle V02.91
              nontraffic V02.01
              traffic V02.11
            vehicle V09.9
              animal-drawn V06.91
                nontraffic V06.01
                traffic V06.11
              motor
                nontraffic V09.00
                traffic V09.20
          fall V00.121
          in-line V00.118
            collision —*see also* Accident,
              transport, pedestrian,
              conveyance occupant, roller
              skates, collision
              with stationary object
                V00.112
            fall V00.111
            nontraffic V09.1
              involving motor vehicle NEC
                V09.00
            traffic V09.3
              involving motor vehicle NEC
                V09.20
        rolling shoes V00.158
          colliding with stationary object
            V00.152
          fall V00.151
        rolling type NEC V00.188
          collision (with) V09.9
            animal being ridden or animal
              drawn vehicle V06.99
              nontraffic V06.09
              traffic V06.19
            bus or heavy transport V04.99
              nontraffic V04.09
              traffic V04.19
            car V03.99
              nontraffic V03.09
              traffic V03.19
            pedal cycle V01.99
              nontraffic V01.09
              traffic V01.19
            pick-up truck or van V03.99
              nontraffic V03.09
              traffic V03.19
            railway (train) (vehicle)
              V05.99
              nontraffic V05.09
              traffic V05.19
            stationary object V00.182
            streetcar V06.99
              nontraffic V06.09
              traffic V06.19
            two- or three-wheeled motor
              vehicle V02.99
              nontraffic V02.09
              traffic V02.19

Accident *(Continued)*
  transport *(Continued)*
    pedestrian *(Continued)*
      conveyance *(Continued)*
        rolling type NEC *(Continued)*
          collision *(Continued)*
            vehicle V09.9
              animal-drawn V06.99
                nontraffic V06.09
                traffic V06.19
              motor
                nontraffic V09.00
                traffic V09.20
          fall V00.181
        in-line roller skate —*see* Accident,
          transport, pedestrian,
          conveyance, roller skate,
          in-line
        nontraffic V09.1
          involving motor vehicle NEC
            V09.00
        roller skate —*see* Accident,
          transport, pedestrian,
          conveyance, roller skate
        scooter (non-motorized) —
          see Accident, transport,
          pedestrian, conveyance,
          scooter
        skateboard —*see* Accident,
          transport, pedestrian,
          conveyance, skateboard
        traffic V09.3
          involving motor vehicle NEC
            V09.20
        scooter (non-motorized) V00.148
          collision (with) V09.9
            animal being ridden or
              animal drawn vehicle
              V06.99
              nontraffic V06.09
              traffic V06.19
            bus or heavy transport
              V04.99
              nontraffic V04.09
              traffic V04.19
            car V03.99
              nontraffic V03.09
              traffic V03.19
            pedal cycle V01.99
              nontraffic V01.09
              traffic V01.19
            pick-up truck or van
              V03.99
              nontraffic V03.09
              traffic V03.19
            railway (train) (vehicle)
              V05.99
              nontraffic V05.09
              traffic V05.19
            stationary object V00.142
            streetcar V06.99
              nontraffic V06.09
              traffic V06.19
            two- or three-wheeled motor
              vehicle V02.99
              nontraffic V02.09
              traffic V02.19
            vehicle V09.9
              animal-drawn V06.99
                nontraffic V06.09
                traffic V06.19
              motor
                nontraffic V09.00
                traffic V09.20
          fall V00.141
          nontraffic V09.1
            involving motor vehicle NEC
              V09.00
          traffic V09.3
            involving motor vehicle NEC
              V09.20

A

Accident *(Continued)*
transport *(Continued)*
pedestrian *(Continued)*
conveyance *(Continued)*
skate board V00.138
collision (with) V09.9
animal being ridden or animal
drawn vehicle V06.92
nontraffic V06.02
traffic V06.12
bus or heavy transport
V04.92
nontraffic V04.02
traffic V04.12
car V03.92
nontraffic V03.02
traffic V03.12
pedal cycle V01.92
nontraffic V01.02
traffic V01.12
pick-up truck or van V03.92
nontraffic V03.02
traffic V03.12
railway (train) (vehicle) V05.92
nontraffic V05.02
traffic V05.12
stationary object V00.132
streetcar V06.92
nontraffic V06.02
traffic V06.12
two- or three-wheeled motor
vehicle V02.92
nontraffic V02.02
traffic V02.12
vehicle V09.9
animal-drawn V06.92
nontraffic V06.02
traffic V06.12
motor
nontraffic V09.00
traffic V09.20
fall V00.131
nontraffic V09.1
involving motor vehicle NEC
V09.00
traffic V09.3
involving motor vehicle NEC
V09.20
skis (snow) V00.328
collision (with) V09.9
animal being ridden or animal
drawn vehicle V06.99
nontraffic V06.09
traffic V06.19
bus or heavy transport V04.99
nontraffic V04.09
traffic V04.19
car V03.99
nontraffic V03.09
traffic V03.19
pedal cycle V01.99
nontraffic V01.09
traffic V01.19
pick-up truck or van V03.99
nontraffic V03.09
traffic V03.19
railway (train) (vehicle) V05.99
nontraffic V05.09
traffic V05.19
stationary object V00.322
streetcar V06.99
nontraffic V06.09
traffic V06.19
two- or three-wheeled motor
vehicle V02.99
nontraffic V02.09
traffic V02.19
vehicle V09.9
animal-drawn V06.99
nontraffic V06.09
traffic V06.19

Accident *(Continued)*
transport *(Continued)*
pedestrian *(Continued)*
conveyance *(Continued)*
sled *(Continued)*
collision *(Continued)*
vehicle *(Continued)*
motor
nontraffic V09.00
traffic V09.20
fall V00.321
nontraffic V09.1
involving motor vehicle NEC
V09.00
traffic V09.3
involving motor vehicle NEC
V09.20
sled V00.228
collision (with) V09.9
animal being ridden or animal
drawn vehicle V06.99
nontraffic V06.09
traffic V06.19
bus or heavy transport V04.99
nontraffic V04.09
traffic V04.19
car V03.99
nontraffic V03.09
traffic V03.19
pedal cycle V01.99
nontraffic V01.09
traffic V01.19
pick-up truck or van V03.99
nontraffic V03.09
traffic V03.19
railway (train) (vehicle) V05.99
nontraffic V05.09
traffic V05.19
stationary object V00.222
streetcar V06.99
nontraffic V06.09
traffic V06.19
two- or three-wheeled motor
vehicle V02.99
nontraffic V02.09
traffic V02.19
vehicle V09.9
animal-drawn V06.99
nontraffic V06.09
traffic V06.19
motor
nontraffic V09.00
traffic V09.20
fall V00.221
nontraffic V09.1
involving motor vehicle NEC
V09.00
traffic V09.3
involving motor vehicle NEC
V09.20
snow board V00.318
collision (with) V09.9
animal being ridden or animal
drawn vehicle V06.99
nontraffic V06.09
traffic V06.19
bus or heavy transport V04.99
nontraffic V04.09
traffic V04.19
car V03.99
nontraffic V03.09
traffic V03.19
pedal cycle V01.99
nontraffic V01.09
traffic V01.19
pick-up truck or van V03.99
nontraffic V03.09
traffic V03.19
railway (train) (vehicle) V05.99
nontraffic V05.09
traffic V05.19

Accident *(Continued)*
transport *(Continued)*
pedestrian *(Continued)*
conveyance *(Continued)*
snow board *(Continued)*
collision *(Continued)*
stationary object V00.312
streetcar V06.99
nontraffic V06.09
traffic V06.19
two- or three-wheeled motor
vehicle V02.99
nontraffic V02.09
traffic V02.19
vehicle V09.9
animal-drawn V06.99
nontraffic V06.09
traffic V06.19
motor
nontraffic V09.00
traffic V09.20
fall V00.311
nontraffic V09.1
involving motor vehicle NEC
V09.00
traffic V09.3
involving motor vehicle NEC
V09.20
specified type NEC V00.898
collision (with) V09.9
animal being ridden or animal
drawn vehicle V06.99
nontraffic V06.09
traffic V06.19
bus or heavy transport V04.99
nontraffic V04.09
traffic V04.19
car V03.99
nontraffic V03.09
traffic V03.19
pedal cycle V01.99
nontraffic V01.09
traffic V01.19
pick-up truck or van V03.99
nontraffic V03.09
traffic V03.19
railway (train) (vehicle) V05.99
nontraffic V05.09
traffic V05.19
stationary object V00.892
streetcar V06.99
nontraffic V06.09
traffic V06.19
two- or three-wheeled motor
vehicle V02.99
nontraffic V02.09
traffic V02.19
vehicle V09.9
animal-drawn V06.99
nontraffic V06.09
traffic V06.19
motor
nontraffic V09.00
traffic V09.20
fall V00.891
nontraffic V09.1
involving motor vehicle NEC
V09.00
traffic V09.3
involving motor vehicle NEC
V09.20
traffic V09.3
involving motor vehicle V09.20
military V09.21
specified type NEC V09.29
wheelchair (powered) V00.818
collision (with) V09.9
animal being ridden or animal
drawn vehicle V06.99
nontraffic V06.09
traffic V06.19

▶ New   ⇒ Revised   ~~deleted~~ Deleted   ● Use Additional Character(s)

Accident *(Continued)*
  transport *(Continued)*
    pedestrian *(Continued)*
      conveyance *(Continued)*
        wheelchair *(Continued)*
          collision *(Continued)*
            bus or heavy transport V04.99
              nontraffic V04.09
              traffic V04.19
            car V03.99
              nontraffic V03.09
              traffic V03.19
            pedal cycle V01.99
              nontraffic V01.09
              traffic V01.19
            pick-up truck or van V03.99
              nontraffic V03.09
              traffic V03.19
            railway (train) (vehicle) V05.99
              nontraffic V05.09
              traffic V05.19
            stationary object V00.812
            streetcar V06.99
              nontraffic V06.09
              traffic V06.19
            two- or three-wheeled motor
              vehicle V02.99
              nontraffic V02.09
              traffic V02.19
            vehicle V09.9
              animal-drawn V06.99
                nontraffic V06.09
                traffic V06.19
              motor
                nontraffic V09.00
                traffic V09.20
          fall V00.811
          nontraffic V09.1
            involving motor vehicle NEC
              V09.00
          traffic V09.3
            involving motor vehicle NEC
              V09.20
        wheeled shoe V00.158
          colliding with stationary object
            V00.152
          fall V00.151
      on foot —*see also* Accident, pedestrian
        collision (with)
          animal being ridden or animal
            drawn vehicle V06.90
            nontraffic V06.00
            traffic V06.10
          bus or heavy transport V04.90
            nontraffic V04.00
            traffic V04.10
          car V03.90
            nontraffic V03.00
            traffic V03.10
          pedal cycle V01.90
            nontraffic V01.00
            traffic V01.10
          pick-up truck or van V03.90
            nontraffic V03.00
            traffic V03.10
          railway (train) (vehicle) V05.90
            nontraffic V05.00
            traffic V05.10
          streetcar V06.90
            nontraffic V06.00
            traffic V06.10
          two- or three-wheeled motor
            vehicle V02.90
            nontraffic V02.00
            traffic V02.10
          vehicle V09.9
           animal-drawn V06.90
            nontraffic V06.00
            traffic V06.10
           motor
            nontraffic V09.00
            traffic V09.20

Accident *(Continued)*
  transport *(Continued)*
    pedestrian *(Continued)*
      on foot *(Continued)*
        nontraffic V09.1
          involving motor vehicle V09.00
            military V09.01
            specified type NEC V09.09
        traffic V09.3
          involving motor vehicle V09.20
            military V09.21
            specified type NEC V09.29
      person NEC (unknown way or
        transportation) V99
      collision (between)
        bus (with)
          heavy transport vehicle (traffic)
            V87.5
            nontraffic V88.5
        car (with)
          nontraffic V88.5
          bus (traffic) V87.3
            nontraffic V88.3
          heavy transport vehicle (traffic)
            V87.4
            nontraffic V88.4
          pick-up truck or van (traffic)
            V87.2
            nontraffic V88.2
          train or railway vehicle (traffic)
            V87.6
            nontraffic V88.6
          two- or three-wheeled motor
            vehicle (traffic) V87.0
            nontraffic V88.0
          motor vehicle (traffic) NEC V87.7
            nontraffic V88.7
          two- or three-wheeled vehicle (with)
          (traffic)
            motor vehicle NEC V87.1
            nontraffic V88.1
        nonmotor vehicle (collision)
          (noncollision) (traffic) V87.9
          nontraffic V88.9
      pickup truck occupant V59.9
        collision (with)
          animal (traffic) V50.9
            being ridden (traffic) V56.9
              nontraffic V56.3
              while boarding or alighting
                V56.4
            nontraffic V50.3
            while boarding or alighting V50.4
          animal-drawn vehicle (traffic) V56.9
            nontraffic V56.3
            while boarding or alighting V56.4
          bus (traffic) V54.9
            nontraffic V54.3
            while boarding or alighting V54.4
          car (traffic) V53.9
            nontraffic V53.3
            while boarding or alighting V53.4
          motor vehicle NOS (traffic) V59.60
           nontraffic V59.20
           specified type NEC (traffic) V59.69
            nontraffic V59.29
          pedal cycle (traffic) V51.9
            nontraffic V51.3
            while boarding or alighting V51.4
          pickup truck (traffic) V53.9
            nontraffic V53.3
            while boarding or alighting V53.4
          railway vehicle (traffic) V55.9
            nontraffic V55.3
            while boarding or alighting V55.4
          specified vehicle NEC (traffic) V56.9
           nontraffic V56.3
            while boarding or alighting V56.4
          stationary object (traffic) V57.9
           nontraffic V57.3
            while boarding or alighting V57.4

Accident *(Continued)*
  transport *(Continued)*
    pickup truck occupant *(Continued)*
      Accident *(Continued)*
        streetcar (traffic) V56.9
          nontraffic V56.3
          while boarding or alighting V56.4
        three wheeled motor vehicle (traffic)
          V52.9
          nontraffic V52.3
          while boarding or alighting V52.4
        truck (traffic) V54.9
          nontraffic V54.3
          while boarding or alighting V54.4
        two wheeled motor vehicle (traffic)
          V52.9
          nontraffic V52.3
          while boarding or alighting V52.4
        van (traffic) V53.9
          nontraffic V53.3
          while boarding or alighting V53.4
    driver
      collision (with)
        animal (traffic) V50.5
          being ridden (traffic) V56.5
           nontraffic V56.0
          nontraffic V50.0
        animal-drawn vehicle (traffic)
          V56.5
          nontraffic V56.0
        bus (traffic) V54.5
          nontraffic V54.0
        car (traffic) V53.5
          nontraffic V53.0
        motor vehicle NOS (traffic) V59.40
          nontraffic V59.00
          specified type NEC (traffic)
           V59.49
           nontraffic V59.09
        pedal cycle (traffic) V51.5
          nontraffic V51.0
        pickup truck (traffic) V53.5
          nontraffic V53.0
        railway vehicle (traffic) V55.5
          nontraffic V55.0
        specified vehicle NEC (traffic) V56.5
          nontraffic V56.0
        stationary object (traffic) V57.5
          nontraffic V57.0
        streetcar (traffic) V56.5
          nontraffic V56.0
        three wheeled motor vehicle
          (traffic) V52.5
          nontraffic V52.0
        truck (traffic) V54.5
          nontraffic V54.0
        two wheeled motor vehicle (traffic)
          V52.5
          nontraffic V52.0
        van (traffic) V53.5
          nontraffic V53.0
      noncollision accident (traffic) V58.5
        nontraffic V58.0
    hanger-on
      collision (with)
        animal (traffic) V50.7
          being ridden (traffic) V56.7
           nontraffic V56.2
          nontraffic V50.2
        animal-drawn vehicle (traffic) V56.7
          nontraffic V56.2
        bus (traffic) V54.7
          nontraffic V54.2
        car (traffic) V53.7
          nontraffic V53.2
        pedal cycle (traffic) V51.7
          nontraffic V51.2
        pickup truck (traffic) V53.7
          nontraffic V53.2
        railway vehicle (traffic) V55.7
          nontraffic V55.2

Accident (Continued)
  transport (Continued)
    pickup truck occupant (Continued)
      hanger-on (Continued)
        collision (Continued)
          specified vehicle NEC (traffic) V56.7
            nontraffic V56.2
          stationary object (traffic) V57.7
            nontraffic V57.2
          streetcar (traffic) V56.7
            nontraffic V56.2
          three wheeled motor vehicle
            (traffic) V52.7
            nontraffic V52.2
          truck (traffic) V54.7
            nontraffic V54.2
          two wheeled motor vehicle (traffic)
            V52.7
            nontraffic V52.2
          van (traffic) V53.7
            nontraffic V53.2
        noncollision accident (traffic) V58.7
          nontraffic V58.2
        noncollision accident (traffic) V58.9
          nontraffic V58.3
        while boarding or alighting V58.4
      nontraffic V59.3
      passenger
        collision (with)
          animal (traffic) V50.6
            being ridden (traffic) V56.6
              nontraffic V56.1
            nontraffic V50.1
          animal-drawn vehicle (traffic) V56.6
            nontraffic V56.1
          bus (traffic) V54.6
            nontraffic V54.1
          car (traffic) V53.6
            nontraffic V53.1
          motor vehicle NOS (traffic) V59.50
            nontraffic V59.10
            specified type NEC (traffic) V59.59
              nontraffic V59.19
          pedal cycle (traffic) V51.6
            nontraffic V51.1
          pickup truck (traffic) V53.6
            nontraffic V53.1
          railway vehicle (traffic) V55.6
            nontraffic V55.1
          specified vehicle NEC (traffic) V56.6
            nontraffic V56.1
          stationary object (traffic) V57.6
            nontraffic V57.1
          streetcar (traffic) V56.6
            nontraffic V56.1
          three wheeled motor vehicle
            (traffic) V52.6
            nontraffic V52.1
          truck (traffic) V54.6
            nontraffic V54.1
          two wheeled motor vehicle (traffic)
            V52.6
            nontraffic V52.1
          van (traffic) V53.6
            nontraffic V53.1
        noncollision accident (traffic) V58.6
          nontraffic V58.1
      specified type NEC V59.88
        military vehicle V59.81
    quarry truck —see Accident, transport,
      industrial vehicle occupant
    race car —see Accident, transport, motor
      vehicle NEC occupant
    railway vehicle occupant V81.9
      collision (with) V81.3
        motor vehicle (non-military) (traffic)
          V81.1
          military V81.83
          nontraffic V81.0
        rolling stock V81.2
        specified object NEC V81.3

Accident (Continued)
  transport (Continued)
    railway vehicle occupant (Continued)
      during derailment V81.7
        with antecedent collision —see
          Accident, transport, railway
          vehicle occupant, collision
      explosion V81.81
      fall (in railway vehicle) V81.5
        during derailment V81.7
          with antecedent collision —see
            Accident, transport, railway
            vehicle occupant, collision
        from railway vehicle V81.6
          during derailment V81.7
            with antecedent collision —see
              Accident, transport,
              railway vehicle occupant,
              collision
        while boarding or alighting V81.4
      fire V81.81
      object falling onto train V81.82
      specified type NEC V81.89
      while boarding or alighting V81.4
    ▶Segway V00.848
    ski lift V98.3
    snowmobile occupant (nontraffic) V86.92
      driver V86.52
      hanger-on V86.72
      passenger V86.62
      traffic V86.32
        driver V86.02
        hanger-on V86.22
        passenger V86.12
      while boarding or alighting V86.42
    specified NEC V98.8
    sport utility vehicle occupant —see also
      Accident, transport, pickup truck
      occupant
    streetcar occupant V82.9
      collision (with) V82.3
        motor vehicle (traffic) V82.1
          nontraffic V82.0
        rolling stock V82.2
      during derailment V82.7
        with antecedent collision —see
          Accident, transport, streetcar
          occupant, collision
      fall (in streetcar) V82.5
        during derailment V82.7
          with antecedent collision —see
           Accident, transport, streetcar
           occupant, collision
        from streetcar V82.6
          during derailment V82.7
           with antecedent collision —see
            Accident, transport, streetcar
            occupant, collision
        while boarding or alighting
          V82.4
      while boarding or alighting V82.4
      specified type NEC V82.8
      while boarding or alighting V82.4
    three-wheeled motor vehicle occupant
      V39.9
      collision (with)
        animal (traffic) V30.9
          being ridden (traffic) V36.9
            nontraffic V36.3
            while boarding or alighting V36.4
          nontraffic V30.3
          while boarding or alighting V30.4
        animal-drawn vehicle (traffic) V36.9
          nontraffic V36.3
          while boarding or alighting V36.4
        bus (traffic) V34.9
          nontraffic V34.3
          while boarding or alighting V34.4
        car (traffic) V33.9
          nontraffic V33.3
          while boarding or alighting V33.4

Accident (Continued)
  transport (Continued)
    three-wheeled motor vehicle occupant
      (Continued)
      collision (Continued)
        motor vehicle NOS (traffic) V39.60
          nontraffic V39.20
          specified type NEC (traffic)
           V39.69
           nontraffic V39.29
        pedal cycle (traffic) V31.9
          nontraffic V31.3
          while boarding or alighting
           V31.4
        pickup truck (traffic) V33.9
          nontraffic V33.3
          while boarding or alighting
           V33.4
        railway vehicle (traffic) V35.9
          nontraffic V35.3
          while boarding or alighting
           V35.4
        specified vehicle NEC (traffic) V36.9
          nontraffic V36.3
          while boarding or alighting V36.4
        stationary object (traffic) V37.9
          nontraffic V37.3
          while boarding or alighting V37.4
        streetcar (traffic) V36.9
          nontraffic V36.3
          while boarding or alighting V36.4
        three wheeled motor vehicle (traffic)
          V32.9
          nontraffic V32.3
          while boarding or alighting V32.4
        truck (traffic) V34.9
          nontraffic V34.3
          while boarding or alighting V34.4
        two wheeled motor vehicle (traffic)
          V32.9
          nontraffic V32.3
          while boarding or alighting V32.4
        van (traffic) V33.9
          nontraffic V33.3
          while boarding or alighting V33.4
      driver
        collision (with)
          animal (traffic) V30.5
            being ridden (traffic) V36.5
              nontraffic V36.0
            nontraffic V30.0
          animal-drawn vehicle (traffic) V36.5
            nontraffic V36.0
          bus (traffic) V34.5
            nontraffic V34.0
          car (traffic) V33.5
            nontraffic V33.0
          motor vehicle NOS (traffic)
            V39.40
            nontraffic V39.00
            specified type NEC (traffic)
             V39.49
             nontraffic V39.09
          pedal cycle (traffic) V31.5
            nontraffic V31.0
          pickup truck (traffic) V33.5
            nontraffic V33.0
          railway vehicle (traffic) V35.5
            nontraffic V35.0
          specified vehicle NEC (traffic)
            V36.5
            nontraffic V36.0
          stationary object (traffic) V37.5
            nontraffic V37.0
          streetcar (traffic) V36.5
            nontraffic V36.0
          three wheeled motor vehicle
            (traffic) V32.5
            nontraffic V32.0
          truck (traffic) V34.5
            nontraffic V34.0

▶ New   ⇒ Revised   ~~deleted~~ Deleted   ● Use Additional Character(s)

A

Accident *(Continued)*
  transport *(Continued)*
    three-wheeled motor vehicle occupant
        (Continued)
      driver *(Continued)*
        collision *(Continued)*
          two wheeled motor vehicle (traffic)
              V32.5
            nontraffic V32.0
          van (traffic) V33.5
            nontraffic V33.0
          noncollision accident (traffic) V38.5
            nontraffic V38.0
      hanger-on
        collision (with)
          animal (traffic) V30.7
            being ridden (traffic) V36.7
              nontraffic V36.2
            nontraffic V30.2
          animal-drawn vehicle (traffic) V36.7
            nontraffic V36.2
          bus (traffic) V34.7
            nontraffic V34.2
          car (traffic) V33.7
            nontraffic V33.2
          pedal cycle (traffic) V31.7
            nontraffic V31.2
          pickup truck (traffic) V33.7
            nontraffic V33.2
          railway vehicle (traffic) V35.7
            nontraffic V35.2
          specified vehicle NEC (traffic) V36.7
            nontraffic V36.2
          stationary object (traffic) V37.7
            nontraffic V37.2
          streetcar (traffic) V36.7
            nontraffic V36.2
          three wheeled motor vehicle
              (traffic) V32.7
            nontraffic V32.2
          truck (traffic) V34.7
            nontraffic V34.2
          two wheeled motor vehicle (traffic)
              V32.7
            nontraffic V32.2
          van (traffic) V33.7
            nontraffic V33.2
        noncollision accident (traffic) V38.7
          nontraffic V38.2
      noncollision accident (traffic) V38.9
        nontraffic V38.3
        while boarding or alighting V38.4
      nontraffic V39.3
      passenger
        collision (with)
          animal (traffic) V30.6
            being ridden (traffic) V36.6
              nontraffic V36.1
            nontraffic V30.1
          animal-drawn vehicle (traffic) V36.6
            nontraffic V36.1
          bus (traffic) V34.6
            nontraffic V34.1
          car (traffic) V33.6
            nontraffic V33.1
          motor vehicle NOS (traffic) V39.50
            nontraffic V39.10
            specified type NEC (traffic)
                V39.59
              nontraffic V39.19
          pedal cycle (traffic) V31.6
            nontraffic V31.1
          pickup truck (traffic) V33.6
            nontraffic V33.1
          railway vehicle (traffic) V35.6
            nontraffic V35.1
          specified vehicle NEC (traffic)
              V36.6
            nontraffic V36.1
          stationary object (traffic) V37.6
            nontraffic V37.1

Accident *(Continued)*
  transport *(Continued)*
    three-wheeled motor vehicle occupant
        (Continued)
      passenger *(Continued)*
        collision *(Continued)*
          streetcar (traffic) V36.6
            nontraffic V36.1
          three wheeled motor vehicle
              (traffic) V32.6
            nontraffic V32.1
          truck (traffic) V34.6
            nontraffic V34.1
          two wheeled motor vehicle (traffic)
              V32.6
            nontraffic V32.1
          van (traffic) V33.6
            nontraffic V33.1
        noncollision accident (traffic)
            V38.6
          nontraffic V38.1
      specified type NEC V39.89
      military vehicle V39.81
    tractor (farm) (and trailer) —*see* Accident,
        transport, agricultural vehicle
        occupant
    tram —*see* Accident, transport, streetcar
    in mine or quarry —*see* Accident,
        transport, industrial vehicle
        occupant
    trolley —*see* Accident, transport, streetcar
    in mine or quarry —*see* Accident,
        transport, industrial vehicle
        occupant
    truck (heavy) occupant V69.9
      collision (with)
        animal (traffic) V60.9
          being ridden (traffic) V66.9
            nontraffic V66.3
            while boarding or alighting
                V66.4
          nontraffic V60.3
          while boarding or alighting V60.4
        animal-drawn vehicle (traffic) V66.9
          nontraffic V66.3
          while boarding or alighting V66.4
        bus (traffic) V64.9
          nontraffic V64.3
          while boarding or alighting V64.4
        car (traffic) V63.9
          nontraffic V63.3
          while boarding or alighting V63.4
        motor vehicle NOS (traffic) V69.60
          nontraffic V69.20
          specified type NEC (traffic) V69.69
            nontraffic V69.29
        pedal cycle (traffic) V61.9
          nontraffic V61.3
          while boarding or alighting V61.4
        pickup truck (traffic) V63.9
          nontraffic V63.3
          while boarding or alighting V63.4
        railway vehicle (traffic) V65.9
          nontraffic V65.3
          while boarding or alighting V65.4
        specified vehicle NEC (traffic) V66.9
          nontraffic V66.3
          while boarding or alighting V66.4
        stationary object (traffic) V67.9
          nontraffic V67.3
          while boarding or alighting V67.4
        streetcar (traffic) V66.9
          nontraffic V66.3
          while boarding or alighting V66.4
        three wheeled motor vehicle (traffic)
            V62.9
          nontraffic V62.3
          while boarding or alighting V62.4
        truck (traffic) V64.9
          nontraffic V64.3
          while boarding or alighting V64.4

Accident *(Continued)*
  transport *(Continued)*
    truck occupant *(Continued)*
      collision *(Continued)*
        two wheeled motor vehicle (traffic)
            V62.9
          nontraffic V62.3
          while boarding or alighting V62.4
        van (traffic) V63.9
          nontraffic V63.3
          while boarding or alighting V63.4
      driver
        collision (with)
          animal (traffic) V60.5
            being ridden (traffic) V66.5
              nontraffic V66.0
            nontraffic V60.0
          animal-drawn vehicle (traffic) V66.5
            nontraffic V66.0
          bus (traffic) V64.5
            nontraffic V64.0
          car (traffic) V63.5
            nontraffic V63.0
          motor vehicle NOS (traffic) V69.40
            nontraffic V69.00
            specified type NEC (traffic)
                V69.49
              nontraffic V69.09
          pedal cycle (traffic) V61.5
            nontraffic V61.0
          pickup truck (traffic) V63.5
            nontraffic V63.0
          railway vehicle (traffic) V65.5
            nontraffic V65.0
          specified vehicle NEC (traffic) V66.5
            nontraffic V66.0
          stationary object (traffic) V67.5
            nontraffic V67.0
          streetcar (traffic) V66.5
            nontraffic V66.0
          three wheeled motor vehicle
              (traffic) V62.5
            nontraffic V62.0
          truck (traffic) V64.5
            nontraffic V64.0
          two wheeled motor vehicle (traffic)
              V62.5
            nontraffic V62.0
          van (traffic) V63.5
            nontraffic V63.0
        noncollision accident (traffic) V68.5
          nontraffic V68.0
      dump —*see* Accident, transport,
          construction vehicle occupant
      hanger-on
        collision (with)
          animal (traffic) V60.7
            being ridden (traffic) V66.7
              nontraffic V66.2
            nontraffic V60.2
          animal-drawn vehicle (traffic) V66.7
            nontraffic V66.2
          bus (traffic) V64.7
            nontraffic V64.2
          car (traffic) V63.7
            nontraffic V63.2
          pedal cycle (traffic) V61.7
            nontraffic V61.2
          pickup truck (traffic) V63.7
            nontraffic V63.2
          railway vehicle (traffic) V65.7
            nontraffic V65.2
          specified vehicle NEC (traffic) V66.7
            nontraffic V66.2
          stationary object (traffic) V67.7
            nontraffic V67.2
          streetcar (traffic) V66.7
            nontraffic V66.2
          three wheeled motor vehicle
              (traffic) V62.7
            nontraffic V62.2

A

Accident *(Continued)*
  transport *(Continued)*
    truck occupant *(Continued)*
      hanger-on *(Continued)*
        collision *(Continued)*
          truck (traffic) V64.7
            nontraffic V64.2
          two wheeled motor vehicle (traffic) V62.7
            nontraffic V62.2
          van (traffic) V63.7
            nontraffic V63.2
        noncollision accident (traffic) V68.7
          nontraffic V68.2
      noncollision accident (traffic) V68.9
        nontraffic V68.3
        while boarding or alighting V68.4
      nontraffic V69.3
      passenger
        collision (with)
          animal (traffic) V60.6
            being ridden (traffic) V66.6
              nontraffic V66.1
            nontraffic V60.1
          animal-drawn vehicle (traffic) V66.6
            nontraffic V66.1
          bus (traffic) V64.6
            nontraffic V64.1
          car (traffic) V63.6
            nontraffic V63.1
          motor vehicle NOS (traffic) V69.50
            nontraffic V69.10
            specified type NEC (traffic) V69.59
              nontraffic V69.19
          pedal cycle (traffic) V61.6
            nontraffic V61.1
          pickup truck (traffic) V63.6
            nontraffic V63.1
          railway vehicle (traffic) V65.6
            nontraffic V65.1
          specified vehicle NEC (traffic) V66.6
            nontraffic V66.1
          stationary object (traffic) V67.6
            nontraffic V67.1
          streetcar (traffic) V66.6
            nontraffic V66.1
          three wheeled motor vehicle (traffic) V62.6
            nontraffic V62.1
          truck (traffic) V64.6
            nontraffic V64.1
          two wheeled motor vehicle (traffic) V62.6
            nontraffic V62.1
          van (traffic) V63.6
            nontraffic V63.1
        noncollision accident (traffic) V68.6
          nontraffic V68.1
      pickup —*see* Accident, transport, pickup truck occupant
      specified type NEC V69.88
      military vehicle V69.81
    van occupant V59.9
      collision (with)
        animal (traffic) V50.9
          being ridden (traffic) V56.9
            nontraffic V56.3
            while boarding or alighting V56.4
          nontraffic V50.3
          while boarding or alighting V50.4
        animal-drawn vehicle (traffic) V56.9
          nontraffic V56.3
          while boarding or alighting V56.4
        bus (traffic) V54.9
          nontraffic V54.3
          while boarding or alighting V54.4
        car (traffic) V53.9
          nontraffic V53.3
          while boarding or alighting V53.4

Accident *(Continued)*
  transport *(Continued)*
    van occupant *(Continued)*
      collision *(Continued)*
        motor vehicle NOS (traffic) V59.60
          nontraffic V59.20
          specified type NEC (traffic) V59.69
            nontraffic V59.29
        pedal cycle (traffic) V51.9
          nontraffic V51.3
          while boarding or alighting V51.4
        pickup truck (traffic) V53.9
          nontraffic V53.3
          while boarding or alighting V53.4
        railway vehicle (traffic) V55.9
          nontraffic V55.3
          while boarding or alighting V55.4
        specified vehicle NEC (traffic) V56.9
          nontraffic V56.3
          while boarding or alighting V56.4
        stationary object (traffic) V57.9
          nontraffic V57.3
          while boarding or alighting V57.4
        streetcar (traffic) V56.9
          nontraffic V56.3
          while boarding or alighting V56.4
        three wheeled motor vehicle (traffic) V52.9
          nontraffic V52.3
          while boarding or alighting V52.4
        truck (traffic) V54.9
          nontraffic V54.3
          while boarding or alighting V54.4
        two wheeled motor vehicle (traffic) V52.9
          nontraffic V52.3
          while boarding or alighting V52.4
        van (traffic) V53.9
          nontraffic V53.3
          while boarding or alighting V53.4
      driver
        collision (with)
          animal (traffic) V50.5
            being ridden (traffic) V56.5
              nontraffic V56.0
            nontraffic V50.0
          animal-drawn vehicle (traffic) V56.5
            nontraffic V56.0
          bus (traffic) V54.5
            nontraffic V54.0
          car (traffic) V53.5
            nontraffic V53.0
          motor vehicle NOS (traffic) V59.40
            nontraffic V59.00
            specified type NEC (traffic) V59.49
              nontraffic V59.09
          pedal cycle (traffic) V51.5
            nontraffic V51.0
          pickup truck (traffic) V53.5
            nontraffic V53.0
          railway vehicle (traffic) V55.5
            nontraffic V55.0
          specified vehicle NEC (traffic) V56.5
            nontraffic V56.0
          stationary object (traffic) V57.5
            nontraffic V57.0
          streetcar (traffic) V56.5
            nontraffic V56.0
          three wheeled motor vehicle (traffic) V52.5
            nontraffic V52.0
          truck (traffic) V54.5
            nontraffic V54.0
          two wheeled motor vehicle (traffic) V52.5
            nontraffic V52.0
          van (traffic) V53.5
            nontraffic V53.0
        noncollision accident (traffic) V58.5
          nontraffic V58.0

Accident *(Continued)*
  transport *(Continued)*
    van occupant *(Continued)*
      hanger-on
        collision (with)
          animal (traffic) V50.7
            being ridden (traffic) V56.7
              nontraffic V56.2
            nontraffic V50.2
          animal-drawn vehicle (traffic) V56.7
            nontraffic V56.2
          bus (traffic) V54.7
            nontraffic V54.2
          car (traffic) V53.7
            nontraffic V53.2
          pedal cycle (traffic) V51.7
            nontraffic V51.2
          pickup truck (traffic) V53.7
            nontraffic V53.2
          railway vehicle (traffic) V55.7
            nontraffic V55.2
          specified vehicle NEC (traffic) V56.7
            nontraffic V56.2
          stationary object (traffic) V57.7
            nontraffic V57.2
          streetcar (traffic) V56.7
            nontraffic V56.2
          three wheeled motor vehicle (traffic) V52.7
            nontraffic V52.2
          truck (traffic) V54.7
            nontraffic V54.2
          two wheeled motor vehicle (traffic) V52.7
            nontraffic V52.2
          van (traffic) V53.7
            nontraffic V53.2
        noncollision accident (traffic) V58.7
          nontraffic V58.2
      noncollision accident (traffic) V58.9
        nontraffic V58.3
        while boarding or alighting V58.4
      nontraffic V59.3
      passenger
        collision (with)
          animal (traffic) V50.6
            being ridden (traffic) V56.6
              nontraffic V56.1
            nontraffic V50.1
          animal-drawn vehicle (traffic) V56.6
            nontraffic V56.1
          bus (traffic) V54.6
            nontraffic V54.1
          car (traffic) V53.6
            nontraffic V53.1
          motor vehicle NOS (traffic) V59.50
            nontraffic V59.10
            specified type NEC (traffic) V59.59
              nontraffic V59.19
          pedal cycle (traffic) V51.6
            nontraffic V51.1
          pickup truck (traffic) V53.6
            nontraffic V53.1
          railway vehicle (traffic) V55.6
            nontraffic V55.1
          specified vehicle NEC (traffic) V56.6
            nontraffic V56.1
          stationary object (traffic) V57.6
            nontraffic V57.1
          streetcar (traffic) V56.6
            nontraffic V56.1
          three wheeled motor vehicle (traffic) V52.6
            nontraffic V52.1
          truck (traffic) V54.6
            nontraffic V54.1
          two wheeled motor vehicle (traffic) V52.6
            nontraffic V52.1
          van (traffic) V53.6
            nontraffic V53.1

▶ New   ⇒ Revised   ~~deleted~~ Deleted   ● Use Additional Character(s)

Accident *(Continued)*
  transport *(Continued)*
    van occupant *(Continued)*
      passenger *(Continued)*
        noncollision accident (traffic) V58.6
        nontraffic V58.1
      specified type NEC V59.88
      military vehicle V59.81
    watercraft occupant —*see* Accident,
      watercraft
  vehicle NEC V89.9
    animal-drawn NEC —*see* Accident,
      transport, animal-drawn vehicle
      occupant
    special
      agricultural —*see* Accident, transport,
        agricultural vehicle occupant
      construction —*see* Accident, transport,
        construction vehicle occupant
      industrial —*see* Accident, transport,
        industrial vehicle occupant
      three-wheeled NEC (motorized) —*see*
        Accident, transport, three-wheeled
        motor vehicle occupant
  watercraft V94.9
    causing
      drowning —*see* Drowning, due to,
        accident to, watercraft
      injury NEC V91.89
        crushed between craft and object
          V91.19
          powered craft V91.13
            ferry boat V91.11
            fishing boat V91.12
            jet ski V91.13
            liner V91.11
            merchant ship V91.10
            passenger ship V91.11
          unpowered craft V91.18
            canoe V91.15
            inflatable V91.16
            kayak V91.15
            sailboat V91.14
            surf-board V91.18
            windsurfer V91.18
        fall on board V91.29
          powered craft V91.23
            ferry boat V91.21
            fishing boat V91.22
            jet ski V91.23
            liner V91.21
            merchant ship V91.20
            passenger ship V91.21
          unpowered craft
            canoe V91.25
            inflatable V91.26
            kayak V91.25
            sailboat V91.24
        fire on board causing burn V91.09
          powered craft V91.03
            ferry boat V91.01
            fishing boat V91.02
            jet ski V91.03
            liner V91.01
            merchant ship V91.00
            passenger ship V91.01
          unpowered craft V91.08
            canoe V91.05
            inflatable V91.06
            kayak V91.05
            sailboat V91.04
            surf-board V91.08
            water skis V91.07
            windsurfer V91.08
        hit by falling object V91.39
          powered craft V91.33
            ferry boat V91.31
            fishing boat V91.32
            jet skis V91.33
            liner V91.31
            merchant ship V91.30
            passenger ship V91.31

Accident *(Continued)*
  watercraft *(Continued)*
    causing *(Continued)*
      injury NEC *(Continued)*
        hit by falling object *(Continued)*
          unpowered craft V91.38
            canoe V91.35
            inflatable V91.36
            kayak V91.35
            sailboat V91.34
            surf-board V91.38
            water skis V91.37
            windsurfer V91.38
        specified type NEC V91.89
          powered craft V91.83
            ferry boat V91.81
            fishing boat V91.82
            jet ski V91.83
            liner V91.81
            merchant ship V91.80
            passenger ship V91.81
          unpowered craft V91.88
            canoe V91.85
            inflatable V91.86
            kayak V91.85
            sailboat V91.84
            surf-board V91.88
            water skis V91.87
            windsurfer V91.88
      due to, caused by cataclysm —*see* Forces of
        nature, by type
      military NEC V94.818
        with civilian watercraft V94.810
        civilian in water injured by V94.811
      nonpowered, struck by
        nonpowered vessel V94.22
        powered vessel V94.21
      specified type NEC V94.89
      striking swimmer
        powered V94.11
        unpowered V94.12
Acid throwing (assault) Y08.89
Activity (involving) (of victim at time of event)
  Y93.9
aerobic and step exercise (class) Y93.A3
alpine skiing Y93.23
animal care NEC Y93.K9
arts and handcrafts NEC Y93.D9
athletics NEC Y93.79
athletics played as a team or group NEC
  Y93.69
athletics played individually NEC Y93.59
baking Y93.G3
ballet Y93.41
barbells Y93.B3
BASE (Building, Antenna, Span, Earth)
  jumping Y93.33
baseball Y93.64
basketball Y93.67
bathing (personal) Y93.E1
beach volleyball Y93.68
bike riding Y93.55
blackout game Y93.85
boogie boarding Y93.18
bowling Y93.54
boxing Y93.71
brass instrument playing Y93.J4
building construction Y93.H3
bungee jumping Y93.34
calisthenics Y93.A2
canoeing (in calm and turbulent water) Y93.16
capture the flag Y93.6A
cardiorespiratory exercise NEC Y93.A9
caregiving (providing) NEC Y93.F9
  bathing Y93.F1
  lifting Y93.F2
cellular
  communication device Y93.C2
  telephone Y93.C2
challenge course Y93.A5
cheerleading Y93.45

Activity *(Continued)*
choking game Y93.85
circuit training Y93.A4
cleaning
  floor Y93.E5
climbing NEC Y93.39
  mountain Y93.31
  rock Y93.31
  wall Y93.31
clothing care and maintenance NEC Y93.E9
combatives Y93.75
computer
  keyboarding Y93.C1
  technology NEC Y93.C9
confidence course Y93.A5
construction (building) Y93.H3
cooking and baking Y93.G3
cool down exercises Y93.A2
cricket Y93.69
crocheting Y93.D1
cross country skiing Y93.24
dancing (all types) Y93.41
digging
  dirt Y93.H1
dirt digging Y93.H1
dishwashing Y93.G1
diving (platform) (springboard) Y93.12
  underwater Y93.15
dodge ball Y93.6A
downhill skiing Y93.23
drum playing Y93.J2
dumbbells Y93.B3
electronic
  devices NEC Y93.C9
    hand held interactive Y93.C2
  game playing (using) (with)
    interactive device Y93.C2
    keyboard or other stationary device
      Y93.C1
elliptical machine Y93.A1
exercise(s)
  machines ((primarily) for)
    cardiorespiratory conditioning Y93.A1
    muscle strengthening Y93.B1
  muscle strengthening (non-machine) NEC
    Y93.B9
external motion NEC Y93.I9
  rollercoaster Y93.I1
fainting game Y93.85
field hockey Y93.65
figure skating (pairs) (singles) Y93.21
flag football Y93.62
floor mopping and cleaning Y93.E5
food preparation and clean up Y93.G1
football (American) NOS Y93.61
  flag Y93.62
  tackle Y93.61
  touch Y93.62
four square Y93.6A
free weights Y93.B3
frisbee (ultimate) Y93.74
furniture
  building Y93.D3
  finishing Y93.D3
  repair Y93.D3
game playing (electronic)
  using interactive device Y93.C2
  using keyboard or other stationary device
    Y93.C1
gardening Y93.H2
golf Y93.53
grass drills Y93.A6
grilling and smoking food Y93.G2
grooming and shearing an animal Y93.K3
guerilla drills Y93.A6
gymnastics (rhythmic) Y93.43
hand held interactive electronic device Y93.C2
handball Y93.73
handcrafts NEC Y93.D9
hang gliding Y93.35
hiking (on level or elevated terrain) Y93.01

▶ New   ⇒ Revised   ~~deleted~~ Deleted   ● Use Additional Character(s)

Activity (Continued)
hockey (ice) Y93.22
field Y93.65
horseback riding Y93.52
household (interior) maintenance NEC Y93.
E9
ice NEC Y93.29
dancing Y93.21
hockey Y93.22
skating Y93.21
inline roller skating Y93.51
ironing Y93.E4
judo Y93.75
jumping (off) NEC Y93.39
BASE (Building, Antenna, Span, Earth)
Y93.33
bungee Y93.34
jacks Y93.A2
rope Y93.56
jumping jacks Y93.A2
jumping rope Y93.56
karate Y93.75
kayaking (in calm and turbulent water) Y93.16
keyboarding (computer) Y93.C1
kickball Y93.6A
knitting Y93.D1
lacrosse Y93.65
land maintenance NEC Y93.H9
landscaping Y93.H2
laundry Y93.E2
machines (exercise)
primarily for cardiorespiratory
conditioning Y93.A1
primarily for muscle strengthening Y93.B1
maintenance
exterior building NEC Y93.H9
household (interior) NEC Y93.E9
land Y93.H9
property Y93.H9
marching (on level or elevated terrain) Y93.Ø1
martial arts Y93.75
microwave oven Y93.G3
milking an animal Y93.K2
mopping (floor) Y93.E5
mountain climbing Y93.31
muscle strengthening
exercises (non-machine) NEC Y93.B9
machines Y93.B1
musical keyboard (electronic) playing Y93.J1
nordic skiing Y93.24
obstacle course Y93.A5
oven (microwave) Y93.G3
packing up and unpacking in moving to a
new residence Y93.E6
parasailing Y93.19
pass out game Y93.85
percussion instrument playing NEC Y93.J2
personal
bathing and showering Y93.E1
hygiene NEC Y93.E8
showering Y93.E1
physical games generally associated with
school recess, summer camp and
children Y93.6A
physical training NEC Y93.A9
piano playing Y93.J1
pilates Y93.B4
platform diving Y93.12
playing musical instrument
brass instrument Y93.J4
drum Y93.J2
musical keyboard (electronic) Y93.J1
percussion instrument NEC Y93.J2
piano Y93.J1
string instrument Y93.J3
winds instrument Y93.J4
property maintenance
exterior NEC Y93.H9
interior NEC Y93.E9
pruning (garden and lawn) Y93.H2

Activity (Continued)
pull-ups Y93.B2
push-ups Y93.B2
racquetball Y93.73
rafting (in calm and turbulent water) Y93.16
raking (leaves) Y93.H1
rappelling Y93.32
refereeing a sports activity Y93.81
residential relocation Y93.E6
rhythmic gymnastics Y93.43
rhythmic movement NEC Y93.49
riding
horseback Y93.52
rollercoaster Y93.I1
rock climbing Y93.31
roller skating (inline) Y93.51
rollercoaster riding Y93.I1
rough housing and horseplay Y93.83
rowing (in calm and turbulent water)
Y93.16
rugby Y93.63
SCUBA diving Y93.15
sewing Y93.D2
shoveling Y93.H1
dirt Y93.H1
snow Y93.H1
showering (personal) Y93.E1
sit-ups Y93.B2
skateboarding Y93.51
skating (ice) Y93.21
roller Y93.51
skiing (alpine) (downhill) Y93.23
cross country Y93.24
nordic Y93.24
water Y93.17
sledding (snow) Y93.23
sleeping (sleep) Y93.84
smoking and grilling food Y93.G2
snorkeling Y93.15
snow NEC Y93.29
boarding Y93.23
shoveling Y93.H1
sledding Y93.23
tubing Y93.23
soccer Y93.66
softball Y93.64
specified NEC Y93.89
spectator at an event Y93.82
sports NEC Y93.79
sports played as a team or group NEC
Y93.69
sports played individually NEC Y93.59
springboard diving Y93.12
squash Y93.73
stationary bike Y93.A1
step (stepping) exercise (class) Y93.A3
stepper machine Y93.A1
stove Y93.G3
string instrument playing Y93.J3
surfing Y93.18
wind Y93.18
swimming Y93.11
tackle football Y93.61
tap dancing Y93.41
tennis Y93.73
tobogganing Y93.23
touch football Y93.62
track and field events (non-running) Y93.57
running Y93.Ø2
trampoline Y93.44
treadmill Y93.A1
trimming shrubs Y93.H2
tubing (in calm and turbulent water) Y93.16
snow Y93.H1
ultimate frisbee Y93.74
underwater diving Y93.15
unpacking in moving to a new residence
Y93.E6
use of stove, oven and microwave oven Y93.
G3

Activity (Continued)
vacuuming Y93.E3
volleyball (beach) (court) Y93.68
wake boarding Y93.17
walking (on level or elevated terrain)
Y93.Ø1
an animal Y93.K1
walking an animal Y93.K1
wall climbing Y93.31
warm up and cool down exercises Y93.A2
water NEC Y93.19
aerobics Y93.14
craft NEC Y93.19
exercise Y93.14
polo Y93.13
skiing Y93.17
sliding Y93.18
survival training and testing Y93.19
weeding (garden and lawn) Y93.H2
wind instrument playing Y93.J4
windsurfing Y93.18
wrestling Y93.72
yoga Y93.42
Adverse effect of drugs —see Table of Drugs
and Chemicals
Aerosinusitis —see Air, pressure
After-effect, late —see Sequelae
Air
blast in war operations —see War operations,
air blast
pressure
change, rapid
during
ascent W94.29
while (in) (surfacing from)
aircraft W94.23
deep water diving W94.21
underground W94.22
descent W94.39
in
aircraft W94.31
water W94.32
high, prolonged W94.Ø
low, prolonged W94.12
due to residence or long visit at high
altitude W94.11
Alpine sickness W94.11
Altitude sickness W94.11
Anaphylactic shock, anaphylaxis —see Table of
Drugs and Chemicals
Andes disease W94.11
Arachnidism, arachnoidism X58
Arson (with intent to injure or kill) X97
Asphyxia, asphyxiation
by
food (bone) (seed) —see categories T17
and T18
gas —see also Table of Drugs and
Chemicals
legal
execution —see Legal, intervention,
gas
intervention —see Legal, intervention,
gas
from
fire —see also Exposure, fire
in war operations —see War operations,
fire
ignition —see Ignition
vomitus T17.81
in war operations —see War operations,
restriction of airway
Aspiration
food (any type) (into respiratory tract) (with
asphyxia, obstruction respiratory tract,
suffocation) —see categories T17 and T18
foreign body —see Foreign body, aspiration
vomitus (with asphyxia, obstruction
respiratory tract, suffocation) T17.81
Assassination (attempt) —see Assault

▶ New   ⇒ Revised   ~~deleted~~ Deleted   ● Use Additional Character(s)

Assault (homicidal) (by) (in) Y09
 arson X97
 bite (of human being) Y04.1
 bodily force Y04.8
  bite Y04.1
  bumping into Y04.2
  sexual —*see* subcategories T74.0, T76.0
  unarmed fight Y04.0
 bomb X96.9
  antipersonnel X96.0
  fertilizer X96.3
  gasoline X96.1
  letter X96.2
  petrol X96.1
  pipe X96.3
  specified NEC X96.8
 brawl (hand) (fists) (foot) (unarmed)
  Y04.0
 burning, burns (by fire) NEC X97
  acid Y08.89
  caustic, corrosive substance Y08.89
  chemical from swallowing caustic,
   corrosive substance —*see* Table of
   Drugs and Chemicals
  cigarette(s) X97
  hot object X98.9
   fluid NEC X98.2
   household appliance X98.3
   specified NEC X98.8
   steam X98.0
   tap water X98.1
   vapors X98.0
  scalding —*see* Assault, burning
  steam X98.0
  vitriol Y08.89
 caustic, corrosive substance (gas) Y08.89
 crashing of
  aircraft Y08.81
  motor vehicle Y03.8
   pushed in front of Y02.0
   run over Y03.0
   specified NEC Y03.8
 cutting or piercing instrument X99.9
  dagger X99.2
  glass X99.0

Assault *(Continued)*
 cutting or piercing instrument *(Continued)*
  knife X99.1
  specified NEC X99.8
  sword X99.2
 dagger X99.2
 drowning (in) X92.9
  bathtub X92.0
  natural water X92.3
  specified NEC X92.8
  swimming pool X92.1
   following fall X92.2
 dynamite X96.8
 explosive(s) (material) X96.9
 fight (hand) (fists) (foot) (unarmed)
  Y04.0
  with weapon —*see* Assault, by type of
   weapon
 fire X97
 firearm X95.9
  airgun X95.01
  handgun X93
  hunting rifle X94.1
  larger X94.9
   specified NEC X94.8
  machine gun X94.2
  shotgun X94.0
  specified NEC X95.8
 from high place Y01
 gunshot (wound) NEC —*see* Assault, firearm,
  by type
 incendiary device X97
 injury Y09
  to child due to criminal abortion attempt
   NEC Y08.89
 knife X99.1
 late effect of —*see* X92-Y08 with 7th
  character S
 placing before moving object NEC
  Y02.8
  motor vehicle Y02.0
 poisoning —*see* categories T36-T65 with 7th
  character S
 puncture, any part of body —*see* Assault,
  cutting or piercing instrument

Assault *(Continued)*
 pushing
  before moving object NEC Y02.8
   motor vehicle Y02.0
   subway train Y02.1
   train Y02.1
 rape T74.2-●
 scalding —*see* Assault, burning
 sequelae of —*see* X92-Y08 with 7th character S
 sexual (by bodily force) T74.2-●
 shooting —*see* Assault, firearm
 specified means NEC Y08.89
 stab, any part of body —*see* Assault, cutting
  or piercing instrument
 steam X98.0
 striking against
  other person Y04.2
  sports equipment Y08.09
   baseball bat Y08.02
   hockey stick Y08.01
 struck by
  sports equipment Y08.09
   baseball bat Y08.02
   hockey stick Y08.01
 submersion —*see* Assault, drowning
 violence Y09
 weapon Y09
  blunt Y00
  cutting or piercing —*see* Assault, cutting or
   piercing instrument
  firearm —*see* Assault, firearm
 wound Y09
  cutting —*see* Assault, cutting or piercing
   instrument
  gunshot —*see* Assault, firearm
  knife X99.1
  piercing —*see* Assault, cutting or piercing
   instrument
  puncture —*see* Assault, cutting or piercing
   instrument
  stab —*see* Assault, cutting or piercing
   instrument
Attack by mammals NEC W55.89
Avalanche —*see* Landslide
Aviator's disease —*see* Air, pressure

A

B

Barotitis, barodontalgia, barosinusitis, barotrauma (otitic) (sinus) —see Air, pressure
Battered (baby) (child) (person) (syndrome) X58
Bayonet wound W26.1
  in
    legal intervention —see Legal, intervention, sharp object, bayonet
    war operations —see War operations, combat
  stated as undetermined whether accidental or intentional Y28.8
  suicide (attempt) X78.2
Bean in nose —see categories T17 and T18
Bed set on fire NEC —see Exposure, fire, uncontrolled, building, bed
Beheading (by guillotine)
  homicide X99.9
  legal execution —see Legal, intervention
Bending, injury in (prolonged) (static) X50.1
Bends —see Air, pressure, change
Bite, bitten by
  alligator W58.01
  arthropod (nonvenomous) NEC W57
  bull W55.21
  cat W55.01
  cow W55.21
  crocodile W58.11
  dog W54.0
  goat W55.31
  hoof stock NEC W55.31
  horse W55.11
  human being (accidentally) W50.3
    with intent to injure or kill Y04.1
    as, or caused by, a crowd or human stampede (with fall) W52
    assault Y04.1
    homicide (attempt) Y04.1
    in
      fight Y04.1
  insect (nonvenomous) W57
  lizard (nonvenomous) W59.01
  mammal NEC W55.81
    marine W56.31
  marine animal (nonvenomous) W56.81
  millipede W57
  moray eel W56.51
  mouse W53.01
  person(s) (accidentally) W50.3
    with intent to injure or kill Y04.1
    as, or caused by, a crowd or human stampede (with fall) W52
    assault Y04.1
    homicide (attempt) Y04.1
    in
      fight Y04.1
  pig W55.41
  raccoon W55.51
  rat W53.11
  reptile W59.81
    lizard W59.01
    snake W59.11
    turtle W59.21
      terrestrial W59.81
  rodent W53.81
    mouse W53.01
    rat W53.11
    specified NEC W53.81
    squirrel W53.21
  shark W56.41
  sheep W55.31
  snake (nonvenomous) W59.11
  spider (nonvenomous) W57
  squirrel W53.21
Blast (air) in war operations —see War operations, blast
Blizzard X37.2

Blood alcohol level Y90.9
  20-39mg/100ml Y90.1
  40-59mg/100ml Y90.2
  60-79mg/100ml Y90.3
  80-99mg/100ml Y90.4
  100-119mg/100ml Y90.5
  120-199mg/100ml Y90.6
  200-239mg/100ml Y90.7
  less than 20mg/100ml Y90.0
  presence in blood, level not specified Y90.9
Blow X58
  by law-enforcing agent, police (on duty) —see Legal, intervention, manhandling
    blunt object —see Legal, intervention, blunt object
Blowing up —see Explosion
Brawl (hand) (fists) (foot) Y04.0
Breakage (accidental) (part of)
  ladder (causing fall) W11
  scaffolding (causing fall) W12
Broken
  glass, contact with —see Contact, with, glass
  power line (causing electric shock) W85
Bumping against, into (accidentally)
  object NEC W22.8
    with fall —see Fall, due to, bumping against, object
    caused by crowd or human stampede (with fall) W52
    sports equipment W21.9
  person(s) W51
    with fall W03
      due to ice or snow W00.0
    assault Y04.2
    caused by, a crowd or human stampede (with fall) W52
    homicide (attempt) Y04.2
  sports equipment W21.9
Burn, burned, burning (accidental) (by) (from) (on)
  acid NEC —see Table of Drugs and Chemicals
  bed linen —see Exposure, fire, uncontrolled, in building, bed
  blowtorch X08.8
    with ignition of clothing NEC X06.2
    nightwear X05
  bonfire, campfire (controlled) —see also Exposure, fire, controlled, not in building
    uncontrolled —see Exposure, fire, uncontrolled, not in building
  candle X08.8
    with ignition of clothing NEC X06.2
    nightwear X05
  caustic liquid, substance (external) (internal) NEC —see Table of Drugs and Chemicals
  chemical (external) (internal) —see also Table of Drugs and Chemicals
    in war operations —see War operations, fire
  cigar(s) or cigarette(s) X08.8
    with ignition of clothing NEC X06.2
    nightwear X05
  clothes, clothing NEC (from controlled fire) X06.2
    with conflagration —see Exposure, fire, uncontrolled, building
    not in building or structure —see Exposure, fire, uncontrolled, not in building
  cooker (hot) X15.8
    stated as undetermined whether accidental or intentional Y27.3
    suicide (attempt) X77.3
  electric blanket X16
  engine (hot) X17
  fire, flames —see Exposure, fire
  flare, Very pistol —see Discharge, firearm NEC

Burn, burned, burning (Continued)
  heat
    from appliance (electrical) (household) X15.8
      cooker X15.8
      hotplate X15.2
      kettle X15.8
      light bulb X15.8
      saucepan X15.3
      skillet X15.3
      stated as undetermined whether accidental or intentional Y27.3
      stove X15.0
      suicide (attempt) X77.3
      toaster X15.1
    in local application or packing during medical or surgical procedure Y63.5
  heating
    appliance, radiator or pipe X16
  homicide (attempt) —see Assault, burning
  hot
    air X14.1
    cooker X15.8
    drink X10.0
    engine X17
    fat X10.2
    fluid NEC X12
    food X10.1
    gases X14.1
    heating appliance X16
    household appliance NEC X15.8
    kettle X15.8
    liquid NEC X12
    machinery X17
    metal (molten) (liquid) NEC X18
    object (not producing fire or flames) NEC X19
    oil (cooking) X10.2
    pipe(s) X16
    radiator X16
    saucepan (glass) (metal) X15.3
    stove (kitchen) X15.0
    substance NEC X19
      caustic or corrosive NEC —see Table of Drugs and Chemicals
    toaster X15.1
    tool X17
    vapor X13.1
    water (tap) —see Contact, with, hot, tap water
  hotplate X15.2
    suicide (attempt) X77.3
  ignition —see Ignition
  in war operations —see War operations, fire
  inflicted by other person X97
    by hot objects, hot vapor, and steam —see Assault, burning, hot object
  internal, from swallowed caustic, corrosive liquid, substance —see Table of Drugs and Chemicals
  iron (hot) X15.8
    stated as undetermined whether accidental or intentional Y27.3
    suicide (attempt) X77.3
  kettle (hot) X15.8
    stated as undetermined whether accidental or intentional Y27.3
    suicide (attempt) X77.3
  lamp (flame) X08.8
    with ignition of clothing NEC X06.2
    nightwear X05
  lighter (cigar) (cigarette) X08.8
    with ignition of clothing NEC X06.2
    nightwear X05
  lightning —see subcategory T75.0
    causing fire —see Exposure, fire
  liquid (boiling) (hot) NEC X12
    stated as undetermined whether accidental or intentional Y27.2
    suicide (attempt) X77.2

▶ New   ⟹ Revised   ~~deleted~~ Deleted   ● Use Additional Character(s)

Burn, burned, burning (*Continued*)
  local application of externally applied
      substance in medical or surgical care
      Y63.5
  machinery (hot) X17
  matches X08.8
    with ignition of clothing NEC X06.2
      nightwear X05
  mattress —*see* Exposure, fire, uncontrolled,
    building, bed
  medicament, externally applied Y63.5
  metal (hot) (liquid) (molten) NEC X18
  nightwear (nightclothes, nightdress, gown,
    pajamas, robe) X05
  object (hot) NEC X19
  on board watercraft
    due to
      accident to watercraft V91.09
        powered craft V91.03
          ferry boat V91.01
          fishing boat V91.02
          jet ski V91.03
          liner V91.01
          merchant ship V91.00
          passenger ship V91.01
        unpowered craft V91.08
          canoe V91.05
          inflatable V91.06
          kayak V91.05
          sailboat V91.04
          surf-board V91.08
          water skis V91.07
          windsurfer V91.08
      fire on board V93.09
        ferry boat V93.01
        fishing boat V93.02
        jet ski V93.03
        liner V93.01
        merchant ship V93.00
        passenger ship V93.01
        powered craft NEC V93.03
        sailboat V93.04

Burn, burned, burning (*Continued*)
  on board watercraft (*Continued*)
    due to (*Continued*)
      specified heat source NEC on board
        V93.19
        ferry boat V93.11
        fishing boat V93.12
        jet ski V93.13
        liner V93.11
        merchant ship V93.10
        passenger ship V93.11
        powered craft NEC V93.13
        sailboat V93.14
  pipe (hot) X16
    smoking X08.8
      with ignition of clothing NEC X06.2
        nightwear X05
  powder —*see* Powder burn
  radiator (hot) X16
  saucepan (hot) (glass) (metal) X15.3
    stated as undetermined whether
      accidental or intentional
      Y27.3
    suicide (attempt) X77.3
  self-inflicted X76
    stated as undetermined whether
      accidental or intentional
      Y26
  stated as undetermined whether
    accidental or intentional Y27.0
  steam X13.1
    pipe X16
      stated as undetermined whether
        accidental or intentional
        Y27.8
    stated as undetermined whether
      accidental or intentional Y27.0
    suicide (attempt) X77.0
  stove (hot) (kitchen) X15.0
    stated as undetermined whether
      accidental or intentional Y27.3
    suicide (attempt) X77.3

Burn, burned, burning (*Continued*)
  substance (hot) NEC X19
    boiling X12
      stated as undetermined whether
        accidental or intentional Y27.2
      suicide (attempt) X77.2
    molten (metal) X18
  suicide (attempt) NEC X76
    hot
      household appliance X77.3
      object X77.9
  stated as undetermined whether accidental or
    intentional Y27.0
  therapeutic misadventure
    heat in local application or packing during
      medical or surgical procedure Y63.5
    overdose of radiation Y63.2
  toaster (hot) X15.1
    stated as undetermined whether accidental
      or intentional Y27.3
    suicide (attempt) X77.3
  tool (hot) X17
  torch, welding X08.8
    with ignition of clothing NEC X06.2
      nightwear X05
  trash fire (controlled) —*see* Exposure, fire,
    controlled, not in building
    uncontrolled —*see* Exposure, fire,
      uncontrolled, not in building
  vapor (hot) X13.1
    stated as undetermined whether accidental
      or intentional Y27.0
    suicide (attempt) X77.0
  Very pistol —*see* Discharge, firearm NEC
Butted by animal W55.82
  bull W55.22
  cow W55.22
  goat W55.32
  horse W55.12
  pig W55.42
  sheep W55.32

C

Caisson disease —see Air, pressure, change
Campfire (exposure to) (controlled) —see also Exposure, fire, controlled, not in building
  uncontrolled —see Exposure, fire, uncontrolled, not in building
Capital punishment (any means) —see Legal, intervention
Car sickness T75.3
Casualty (not due to war) NEC X58
  war —see War operations
Cat
  bite W55.01
  scratch W55.03
Cataclysm, cataclysmic (any injury) NEC —see Forces of nature
Catching fire —see Exposure, fire
Caught
  between
    folding object W23.0
    objects (moving) (stationary and moving) W23.0
      and machinery —see Contact, with, by type of machine
      stationary W23.1
    sliding door and door frame W23.0
  by, in
    machinery (moving parts of) —see Contact, with, by type of machine
    washing-machine wringer W23.0
  under packing crate (due to losing grip) W23.1
Cave-in caused by cataclysmic earth surface movement or eruption —see Landslide
Change(s) in air pressure —see Air, pressure, change
Choked, choking (on) (any object except food or vomitus)
  food (bone) (seed) —see categories T17 and T18
  vomitus T17.81-●
Civil insurrection —see War operations
Cloudburst (any injury) X37.8
Cold, exposure to (accidental) (excessive) (extreme) (natural) (place) NEC —see Exposure, cold
Collapse
  building W20.1
    burning (uncontrolled fire) X00.2
  dam or man-made structure (causing earth movement) X36.0
  machinery —see Contact, with, by type of machine
  structure W20.1
    burning (uncontrolled fire) X00.2
Collision (accidental) NEC —see also Accident, transport V89.9
  pedestrian W51
    with fall W03
      due to ice or snow W00.0
      involving pedestrian conveyance —see Accident, transport, pedestrian, conveyance
    and
      crowd or human stampede (with fall) W52
      object W22.8
        with fall —see Fall, due to, bumping against, object
  person(s) —see Collision, pedestrian
  transport vehicle NEC V89.9
    and
      avalanche, fallen or not moving —see Accident, transport
      falling or moving —see Landslide
      landslide, fallen or not moving —see Accident, transport
      falling or moving —see Landslide

Collision NEC (Continued)
  transport vehicle NEC (Continued)
    due to cataclysm —see Forces of nature, by type
    intentional, purposeful suicide (attempt) —see Suicide, collision
Combustion, spontaneous —see Ignition
Complication (delayed) of or following (medical or surgical procedure) Y84.9
  with misadventure —see Misadventure
  amputation of limb(s) Y83.5
  anastomosis (arteriovenous) (blood vessel) (gastrojejunal) (tendon) (natural or artificial material) Y83.2
  aspiration (of fluid) Y84.4
    tissue Y84.8
  biopsy Y84.8
  blood
    sampling Y84.7
    transfusion
      procedure Y84.8
  bypass Y83.2
  catheterization (urinary) Y84.6
    cardiac Y84.0
  colostomy Y83.3
  cystostomy Y83.3
  dialysis (kidney) Y84.1
  drug —see Table of Drugs and Chemicals
  due to misadventure —see Misadventure
  duodenostomy Y83.3
  electroshock therapy Y84.3
  external stoma, creation of Y83.3
  formation of external stoma Y83.3
  gastrostomy Y83.3
  graft Y83.2
  hypothermia (medically-induced) Y84.8
  implant, implantation (of)
    artificial
      internal device (cardiac pacemaker) (electrodes in brain) (heart valve prosthesis) (orthopedic) Y83.1
      material or tissue (for anastomosis or bypass) Y83.2
        with creation of external stoma Y83.3
    natural tissues (for anastomosis or bypass) Y83.2
      with creation of external stoma Y83.3
  infusion
    procedure Y84.8
  injection —see Table of Drugs and Chemicals
    procedure Y84.8
  insertion of gastric or duodenal sound Y84.5
  insulin-shock therapy Y84.3
  paracentesis (abdominal) (thoracic) (aspirative) Y84.4
  procedures other than surgical operation —see Complication of or following, by type of procedure
  radiological procedure or therapy Y84.2
  removal of organ (partial) (total) NEC Y83.6
  sampling
    blood Y84.7
    fluid NEC Y84.4
    tissue Y84.8
  shock therapy Y84.3
  surgical operation NEC —see also Complication of or following, by type of operation Y83.9
    reconstructive NEC Y83.4
      with
        anastomosis, bypass or graft Y83.2
        formation of external stoma Y83.3
    specified NEC Y83.8
  transfusion —see also Table of Drugs and Chemicals
    procedure Y84.8
  transplant, transplantation (heart) (kidney) (liver) (whole organ, any) Y83.0
    partial organ Y83.4
  ureterostomy Y83.3

Complication of or following (Continued)
  vaccination —see also Table of Drugs and Chemicals
    procedure Y84.8
Compression
  divers' squeeze —see Air, pressure, change
  trachea by
    food (lodged in esophagus) —see categories T17 and T18
    vomitus (lodged in esophagus) T17.81-●
Conflagration —see Exposure, fire, uncontrolled
Constriction (external)
  hair W49.01
  jewelry W49.04
  ring W49.04
  rubber band W49.03
  specified item NEC W49.09
  string W49.02
  thread W49.02
Contact (accidental)
  with
    abrasive wheel (metalworking) W31.1
    alligator W58.09
      bite W58.01
      crushing W58.03
      strike W58.02
    amphibian W62.9
      frog W62.0
      toad W62.1
    animal (nonvenomous) NEC W64
      marine W56.89
        bite W56.81
        dolphin —see Contact, with, dolphin
        fish NEC —see Contact, with, fish
        mammal —see Contact, with, mammal, marine
        orca —see Contact, with, orca
        sea lion —see Contact, with, sea lion
        shark —see Contact, with, shark
        strike W56.82
    animate mechanical force NEC W64
    arrow W21.89
      not thrown, projected or falling W45.8
    arthropods (nonvenomous) W57
    axe W27.0
    band-saw (industrial) W31.2
    bayonet —see Bayonet wound
    bee(s) X58
    bench-saw (industrial) W31.2
    bird W61.99
      bite W61.91
      chicken —see Contact, with, chicken
      duck —see Contact, with, duck
      goose —see Contact, with, goose
      macaw —see Contact, with, macaw
      parrot —see Contact, with, parrot
      psittacine —see Contact, with, psittacine
      strike W61.92
      turkey —see Contact, with, turkey
    blender W29.0
    boiling water X12
      stated as undetermined whether accidental or intentional Y27.2
      suicide (attempt) X77.2
    bore, earth-drilling or mining (land) (seabed) W31.0
    buffalo —see Contact, with, hoof stock NEC
    bull W55.29
      bite W55.21
      gored W55.22
      strike W55.22
    bumper cars W31.81
    camel —see Contact, with, hoof stock NEC
    can
      lid W26.8
      opener W27.4
        powered W29.0
    cat W55.09
      bite W55.01
      scratch W55.03
    caterpillar (venomous) X58

▶ New   ⇒ Revised   ~~deleted~~ Deleted   ● Use Additional Character(s)

Contact (Continued)
 with (Continued)
  centipede (venomous) X58
  chain
   hoist W24.0
    agricultural operations W30.89
   saw W29.3
  chicken W61.39
   peck W61.33
   strike W61.32
  chisel W27.0
  circular saw W31.2
  cobra X58
  combine (harvester) W30.0
  conveyer belt W24.1
  cooker (hot) X15.8
   stated as undetermined whether
    accidental or intentional Y27.3
   suicide (attempt) X77.3
  coral X58
  cotton gin W31.82
  cow W55.29
   bite W55.21
   strike W55.22
  crane W24.0
   agricultural operations W30.89
  crocodile W58.19
   bite W58.11
   crushing W58.13
   strike W58.12
  dagger W26.1
   stated as undetermined whether
    accidental or intentional Y28.2
   suicide (attempt) X78.2
  dairy equipment W31.82
  dart W21.89
   not thrown, projected or falling W45.8
  deer —see Contact, with, hoof stock
    NEC
  derrick W24.0
   agricultural operations W30.89
    hay W30.2
  dog W54.8
   bite W54.0
   strike W54.1
  dolphin W56.09
   bite W56.01
   strike W56.02
  donkey —see Contact, with, hoof stock
    NEC
  drill (powered) W29.8
   earth (land) (seabed) W31.0
   nonpowered W27.8
  drive belt W24.0
   agricultural operations W30.89
  dry ice —see Exposure, cold, man-made
  dryer (clothes) (powered) (spin) W29.2
  duck W61.69
   bite W61.61
   strike W61.62
  earth(-)
   drilling machine (industrial) W31.0
   scraping machine in stationary use
    W31.83
  edge of stiff paper W26.2
  electric
   beater W29.0
   blanket X16
   fan W29.2
    commercial W31.82
   knife W29.1
   mixer W29.0
  elevator (building) W24.0
   agricultural operations W30.89
    grain W30.3
  engine(s), hot NEC X17
  excavating machine W31.0
  farm machine W30.9
  feces —see Contact, with, by type of
    animal
  fer de lance X58

Contact (Continued)
 with (Continued)
  fish W56.59
   bite W56.51
   shark —see Contact, with, shark
   strike W56.52
  flying horses W31.81
  forging (metalworking) machine
    W31.1
  fork W27.4
  forklift (truck) W24.0
   agricultural operations W30.89
  frog W62.0
  garden
   cultivator (powered) W29.3
    riding W30.89
   fork W27.1
  gas turbine W31.3
  Gila monster X58
  giraffe —see Contact, with, hoof stock
    NEC
  glass (sharp) (broken) W25
   with subsequent fall W18.02
   assault X99.0
   due to fall —see Fall, by type
   stated as undetermined whether
    accidental or intentional Y28. 0
   suicide (attempt) X78.0
  goat W55.39
   bite W55.31
   strike W55.32
  goose W61.59
   bite W61.51
   strike W61.52
  hand
   saw W27.0
   tool (not powered) NEC W27.8
    powered W29.8
  harvester W30.0
  hay-derrick W30.2
  heat NEC X19
   from appliance (electrical)
    (household) —see Contact, with,
    hot, household appliance
   heating appliance X16
  heating
   appliance (hot) X16
   pad (electric) X16
  hedge-trimmer (powered) W29.3
  hoe W27.1
  hoist (chain) (shaft) NEC W24.0
   agricultural W30.89
  hoof stock NEC W55.39
   bite W55.31
   strike W55.32
  hornet(s) X58
  horse W55.19
   bite W55.11
   strike W55.12
  hot
   air X14.1
    inhalation X14.0
   cooker X15.8
   drinks X10.0
   engine X17
   fats X10.2
   fluids NEC X12
    assault X98.2
    suicide (attempt) X77.2
    undetermined whether accidental or
     intentional Y27.2
   food X10.1
   gases X14.1
    inhalation X14.0
   heating appliance X16
   household appliance X15.8
    assault X98.3
    cooker X15.8
    hotplate X15.2
    kettle X15.8
    light bulb X15.8

Contact (Continued)
 with (Continued)
  hot (Continued)
   household appliance (Continued)
    object NEC X19
     assault X98.8
     stated as undetermined whether
      accidental or intentional Y27.9
     suicide (attempt) X77.8
    saucepan X15.3
    skillet X15.3
    stated as undetermined whether
     accidental or intentional Y27.3
    stove X15.0
     suicide (attempt) X77.3
    toaster X15.1
   kettle X15.8
   light bulb X15.8
   liquid NEC —see also Burn X12
    drinks X10.0
    stated as undetermined whether
     accidental or intentional Y27.2
    suicide (attempt) X77.2
    tap water X11.8
     stated as undetermined whether
      accidental or intentional Y27.1
     suicide (attempt) X77.1
   machinery X17
   metal (molten) (liquid) NEC X18
   object (not producing fire or flames)
     NEC X19
   oil (cooking) X10.2
   pipe X16
   plate X15.2
   radiator X16
   saucepan (glass) (metal) X15.3
   skillet X15.3
   stove (kitchen) X15.0
   substance NEC X19
   tap-water X11.8
    assault X98.1
    heated on stove X12
     stated as undetermined whether
      accidental or intentional Y27.2
     suicide (attempt) X77.2
    in bathtub X11.0
    running X11.1
     stated as undetermined whether
      accidental or intentional Y27.1
     suicide (attempt) X77.1
   toaster X15.1
   tool X17
   vapors X13.1
    inhalation X13.0
   water (tap) X11.8
    boiling X12
     stated as undetermined whether
      accidental or intentional Y27.2
     suicide (attempt) X77.2
    heated on stove X12
     stated as undetermined whether
      accidental or intentional Y27.2
     suicide (attempt) X77.2
    in bathtub X11.0
    running X11.1
     stated as undetermined whether
      accidental or intentional Y27.1
     suicide (attempt) X77.1
  hotplate X15.2
  ice-pick W27.4
  insect (nonvenomous) NEC W57
  kettle (hot) X15.8
  knife W26.0
   assault X99.1
   electric W29.1
   stated as undetermined whether
    accidental or intentional Y28.1
   suicide (attempt) X78.1
  lathe (metalworking) W31.1
   turnings W45.8
   woodworking W31.2

▶ New   ⇒ Revised   ~~deleted~~ Deleted   ● Use Additional Character(s)

Contact *(Continued)*
  with *(Continued)*
    lawnmower (powered) (ridden) W28
      causing electrocution W86.8
        suicide (attempt) X83.1
      unpowered W27.1
    lift, lifting (devices) W24.0
      agricultural operations W30.89
      shaft W24.0
    liquefied gas —*see* Exposure, cold,
        man-made
    liquid air, hydrogen, nitrogen —*see*
        Exposure, cold, man-made
    lizard (nonvenomous) W59.09
      bite W59.01
      strike W59.02
    llama —*see* Contact, with, hoof stock NEC
    macaw W61.19
      bite W61.11
      strike W61.12
    machine, machinery W31.9
      abrasive wheel W31.1
      agricultural including animal-powered
          W30.9
        combine harvester W30.0
        grain storage elevator W30.3
        hay derrick W30.2
        power take-off device W30.1
        reaper W30.0
        specified NEC W30.89
        thresher W30.0
        transport vehicle, stationary W30.81
      band saw W31.2
      bench saw W31.2
      circular saw W31.2
      commercial NEC W31.82
      drilling, metal (industrial) W31.1
      earth-drilling W31.0
      earthmoving or scraping W31.89
      excavating W31.89
      forging machine W31.1
      gas turbine W31.3
      hot X17
      internal combustion engine W31.3
      land drill W31.0
      lathe W31.1
      lifting (devices) W24.0
      metal drill W31.1
      metalworking (industrial) W31.1
      milling, metal W31.1
      mining W31.0
      molding W31.2
      overhead plane W31.2
      power press, metal W31.1
      prime mover W31.3
      printing W31.89
      radial saw W31.2
      recreational W31.81
      roller-coaster W31.81
      rolling mill, metal W31.1
      sander W31.2
      seabed drill W31.0
      shaft
        hoist W31.0
        lift W31.0
      specified NEC W31.89
      spinning W31.89
      steam engine W31.3
      transmission W24.1
      undercutter W31.0
      water driven turbine W31.3
      weaving W31.89
      woodworking or forming (industrial)
          W31.2
    mammal (feces) (urine) W55.89
      bull —*see* Contact, with, bull
      cat —*see* Contact, with, cat
      cow —*see* Contact, with, cow
      goat —*see* Contact, with, goat
      hoof stock —*see* Contact, with, hoof
          stock

Contact *(Continued)*
  with *(Continued)*
    mammal *(Continued)*
      horse —*see* Contact, with, horse
      marine W56.39
        dolphin —*see* Contact, with, dolphin
        orca —*see* Contact, with, orca
        sea lion —*see* Contact, with, sea lion
        specified NEC W56.39
          bite W56.31
          strike W56.32
      pig —*see* Contact, with, pig
      raccoon —*see* Contact, with, raccoon
      rodent —*see* Contact, with, rodent
      sheep —*see* Contact, with, sheep
      specified NEC W55.89
        bite W55.81
        strike W55.82
    marine
      animal W56.89
        bite W56.81
        dolphin —*see* Contact, with, dolphin
        fish NEC —*see* Contact, with, fish
        mammal —*see* Contact, with,
            mammal, marine
        orca —*see* Contact, with, orca
        sea lion —*see* Contact, with, sea lion
        shark —*see* Contact, with, shark
        strike W56.82
    meat
      grinder (domestic) W29.0
        industrial W31.82
        nonpowered W27.4
      slicer (domestic) W29.0
        industrial W31.82
    merry go round W31.81
    metal, (hot) (liquid) (molten) NEC X18
    millipede W57
    nail W45.0
      gun W29.4
    needle (sewing) W27.3
      hypodermic W46.0
        contaminated W46.1
    object (blunt) NEC
      hot NEC X19
      legal intervention —*see* Legal,
          intervention, blunt object
      sharp NEC W45.8
        inflicted by other person NEC W45.8
          stated as
            intentional homicide (attempt) —
                see Assault, cutting or
                piercing instrument
        legal intervention —*see* Legal,
            intervention, sharp object
        self-inflicted X78.9
    orca W56.29
      bite W56.21
      strike W56.22
    overhead plane W31.2
    paper (as sharp object) W26.2
    paper-cutter W27.5
    parrot W61.09
      bite W61.01
      strike W61.02
    pig W55.49
      bite W55.41
      strike W55.42
    pipe, hot X16
    pitchfork W27.1
    plane (metal) (wood) W27.0
      overhead W31.2
    plant thorns, spines, sharp leaves or other
        mechanisms W60
    powered
      garden cultivator W29.3
      household appliance, implement, or
          machine W29.8
      saw (industrial) W31.2
        hand W29.8
    printing machine W31.89

Contact *(Continued)*
  with *(Continued)*
    psittacine bird W61.29
      bite W61.21
      macaw —*see* Contact, with, macaw
      parrot —*see* Contact, with, parrot
      strike W61.22
    pulley (block) (transmission) W24.0
      agricultural operations W30.89
    raccoon W55.59
      bite W55.51
      strike W55.52
    radial-saw (industrial) W31.2
    radiator (hot) X16
    rake W27.1
    rattlesnake X58
    reaper W30.0
    reptile W59.89
      lizard —*see* Contact, with, lizard
      snake —*see* Contact, with, snake
      specified NEC W59.89
        bite W59.81
        crushing W59.83
        strike W59.82
      turtle —*see* Contact, with, turtle
    rivet gun (powered) W29.4
    road scraper —*see* Accident, transport,
        construction vehicle
    rodent (feces) (urine) W53.89
      bite W53.81
      mouse W53.09
        bite W53.01
      rat W53.19
        bite W53.11
      specified NEC W53.89
        bite W53.81
      squirrel W53.29
        bite W53.21
    roller coaster W31.81
    rope NEC W24.0
      agricultural operations W30.89
    saliva —*see* Contact, with, by type of
        animal
    sander W29.8
      industrial W31.2
    saucepan (hot) (glass) (metal) X15.3
    saw W27.0
      band (industrial) W31.2
      bench (industrial) W31.2
      chain W29.3
      hand W27.0
    sawing machine, metal W31.1
    scissors W27.2
    scorpion X58
    screwdriver W27.0
      powered W29.8
    sea
      anemone, cucumber or urchin (spine)
          X58
      lion W56.19
        bite W56.11
        strike W56.12
    serpent —*see* Contact, with, snake, by type
    sewing-machine (electric) (powered) W29.2
      not powered W27.8
    shaft (hoist) (lift) (transmission) NEC W24.0
      agricultural W30.89
    shark W56.49
      bite W56.41
      strike W56.42
    sharp object(s) W26.9
      specified NEC W26.8
    shears (hand) W27.2
      powered (industrial) W31.1
        domestic W29.2
    sheep W55.39
      bite W55.31
      strike W55.32
    shovel W27.8
      steam —*see* Accident, transport,
          construction vehicle

Contact *(Continued)*
  with *(Continued)*
    snake (nonvenomous) W59.19
      bite W59.11
      crushing W59.13
      strike W59.12
    spade W27.1
    spider (venomous) X58
    spin-drier W29.2
    spinning machine W31.89
    splinter W45.8
    sports equipment W21.9
    staple gun (powered) W29.8
    steam X13.1
      engine W31.3
      inhalation X13.0
      pipe X16
      shovel W31.89
    stove (hot) (kitchen) X15.0
    substance, hot NEC X19
      molten (metal) X18
    sword W26.1
      assault X99.2
      stated as undetermined whether
          accidental or intentional
          Y28.2
      suicide (attempt) X78.2
    tarantula X58
    thresher W30.0
    tin can lid W26.8
    toad W62.1
    toaster (hot) X15.1
    tool W27.8
      hand (not powered) W27.8
        auger W27.0
        axe W27.0
        can opener W27.4
        chisel W27.0
        fork W27.4
        garden W27.1
        handsaw W27.0
        hoe W27.1
        ice-pick W27.4
        kitchen utensil W27.4
        manual
          lawn mower W27.1
            sewing machine W27.8
        meat grinder W27.4
        needle (sewing) W27.3
          hypodermic W46.0
            contaminated W46.1
        paper cutter W27.5
        pitchfork W27.1
        rake W27.1
        scissors W27.2
        screwdriver W27.0
        specified NEC W27.8
        workbench W27.0
      hot X17
      powered W29.8
        blender W29.0
          commercial W31.82
        can opener W29.0
          commercial W31.82
        chainsaw W29.3
        clothes dryer W29.2
          commercial W31.82
        dishwasher W29.2
          commercial W31.82
        edger W29.3
        electric fan W29.2
          commercial W31.82
        electric knife W29.1
        food processor W29.0
          commercial W31.82
        garbage disposal W29.0
          commercial W31.82

Contact *(Continued)*
  with *(Continued)*
    tool *(Continued)*
      powered *(Continued)*
        garden tool W29.3
        hedge trimmer W29.3
        ice maker W29.0
          commercial W31.82
        kitchen appliance W29.0
          commercial W31.82
        lawn mower W28
        meat grinder W29.0
          commercial W31.82
        mixer W29.0
          commercial W31.82
        rototiller W29.3
        sewing machine W29.2
          commercial W31.82
        washing machine W29.2
          commercial W31.82
    transmission device (belt, cable, chain,
        gear, pinion, shaft) W24.1
      agricultural operations W30.89
    turbine (gas) (water-driven) W31.3
    turkey W61.49
      peck W61.43
      strike W61.42
    turtle (nonvenomous) W59.29
      bite W59.21
      strike W59.22
      terrestrial W59.89
        bite W59.81
        crushing W59.83
        strike W59.82
    under-cutter W31.0
    urine —*see* Contact, with, by type of animal
    vehicle
      agricultural use (transport) —*see*
          Accident, transport, agricultural
          vehicle
        not on public highway W30.81
      industrial use (transport) —*see*
          Accident, transport, industrial
          vehicle
        not on public highway W31.83
      off-road use (transport) —*see* Accident,
          transport, all-terrain or off-road
          vehicle
        not on public highway W31.83
      special construction use (transport) —*see*
          Accident, transport, construction
          vehicle
        not on public highway W31.83
    venomous
      animal X58
      arthropods X58
      lizard X58
      marine animal NEC X58
      marine plant NEC X58
      millipedes (tropical) X58
      plant(s) X58
      snake X58
      spider X58
      viper X58
    washing-machine (powered) W29.2
    wasp X58
    weaving-machine W31.89
    winch W24.0
      agricultural operations W30.89
    wire NEC W24.0
      agricultural operations W30.89
    wood slivers W45.8
    yellow jacket X58
    zebra —*see* Contact, with, hoof stock NEC
  pressure X50.9
  stress X50.9
Coup de soleil X32

Crash
  aircraft (in transit) (powered) V95.9
    balloon V96.01
    fixed wing NEC (private) V95.21
      commercial V95.31
    glider V96.21
      hang V96.11
      powered V95.11
    helicopter V95.01
    in war operations —*see* War operations,
        destruction of aircraft
    microlight V95.11
    nonpowered V96.9
      specified NEC V96.8
    powered NEC V95.8
    stated as
      homicide (attempt) Y08.81
      suicide (attempt) X83.0
    ultralight V95.11
  spacecraft V95.41
  transport vehicle NEC —*see also* Accident,
      transport V89.9
    homicide (attempt) Y03.8
    motor NEC (traffic) V89.2
      homicide (attempt) Y03.8
      suicide (attempt) —*see* Suicide, collision
Cruelty (mental) (physical) (sexual) X58
Crushed (accidentally) X58
  between objects (moving) (stationary and
      moving) W23.0
    stationary W23.1
  by
    alligator W58.03
    avalanche NEC —*see* Landslide
    cave-in W20.0
      caused by cataclysmic earth surface
          movement —*see* Landslide
    crocodile W58.13
    crowd or human stampede W52
    falling
      aircraft V97.39
        in war operations —*see* War
            operations, destruction of aircraft
      earth, material W20.0
        caused by cataclysmic earth surface
            movement —*see* Landslide
      object NEC W20.8
    landslide NEC —*see* Landslide
    lizard (nonvenomous) W59.09
    machinery —*see* Contact, with, by type of
        machine
    reptile NEC W59.89
    snake (nonvenomous) W59.13
  in
    machinery —*see* Contact, with, by type of
        machine
Cut, cutting (any part of body) (accidental) —
    see also Contact, with, by object or machine
  during medical or surgical treatment as
      misadventure —*see* Index to Diseases
      and Injuries, Complications
  homicide (attempt) —*see* Assault, cutting or
      piercing instrument
  inflicted by other person —*see* Assault,
      cutting or piercing instrument
  legal
    execution —*see* Legal, intervention
    intervention —*see* Legal, intervention,
        sharp object
  machine NEC —*see also* Contact, with, by
      type of machine W31.9
  self-inflicted —*see* Suicide, cutting or piercing
      instrument
  suicide (attempt) —*see* Suicide, cutting or
      piercing instrument
Cyclone (any injury) X37.1

D

Decapitation (accidental circumstances)
   NEC X58
   homicide X99.9
   legal execution —*see* Legal, intervention
Dehydration from lack of water X58
Deprivation X58
Derailment (accidental)
   railway (rolling stock) (train) (vehicle)
      (without antecedent collision) V81.7
      with antecedent collision —*see* Accident,
         transport, railway vehicle occupant
   streetcar (without antecedent collision) V82.7
      with antecedent collision —*see* Accident,
         transport, streetcar occupant
Descent
   parachute (voluntary) (without accident to
      aircraft) V97.29
      due to accident to aircraft —*see* Accident,
         transport, aircraft
Desertion X58
Destitution X58
Disability, late effect or sequela of injury —*see*
   Sequelae
Discharge (accidental)
   airgun W34.010
      assault X95.01
      homicide (attempt) X95.01
      stated as undetermined whether accidental
         or intentional Y24.0
      suicide (attempt) X74.01
   BB gun —*see* Discharge, airgun
   firearm (accidental) W34.00
      assault X95.9
      handgun (pistol) (revolver) W32.0
         assault X93
         homicide (attempt) X93
         legal intervention —*see* Legal,
            intervention, firearm, handgun
         stated as undetermined whether
            accidental or intentional Y22
         suicide (attempt) X72
      homicide (attempt) X95.9
      hunting rifle W33.02
         assault X94.1
         homicide (attempt) X94.1
         legal intervention
            injuring
               bystander Y35.032
               law enforcement personnel Y35.031
               suspect Y35.033
               unspecified person Y35.039
            stated as undetermined whether
               accidental or intentional Y23.1
            suicide (attempt) X73.1
      larger W33.00
         assault X94.9
         homicide (attempt) X94.9
         hunting rifle —*see* Discharge, firearm,
            hunting rifle
         legal intervention —*see* Legal,
            intervention, firearm by type of
            firearm
         machine gun —*see* Discharge, firearm,
            machine gun
         shotgun —*see* Discharge, firearm,
            shotgun
         specified NEC W33.09
            assault X94.8
            homicide (attempt) X94.8
            legal intervention
               injuring
                  bystander Y35.092
                  law enforcement personnel
                     Y35.091
                  suspect Y35.093
                  unspecified person Y35.099
            stated as undetermined whether
               accidental or intentional Y23.8
            suicide (attempt) X73.8

Discharge (Continued)
   firearm (Continued)
      larger (Continued)
         stated as undetermined whether
            accidental or intentional Y23.9
         suicide (attempt) X73.9
      legal intervention
         injuring
            bystander Y35.002
            law enforcement personnel Y35.001
            suspect Y35.03
            unspecified person Y35.009
         using rubber bullet
            injuring
               bystander Y35.042
               law enforcement personnel Y35.041
               suspect Y35.043
               unspecified person Y35.049
      machine gun W33.03
         assault X94.2
         homicide (attempt) X94.2
         legal intervention —*see* Legal,
            intervention, firearm, machine gun
         stated as undetermined whether
            accidental or intentional Y23.3
         suicide (attempt) X73.2
      pellet gun —*see* Discharge, airgun
      shotgun W33.01
         assault X94.0
         homicide (attempt) X94.0
         legal intervention —*see* Legal,
            intervention, firearm, specified NEC
         stated as undetermined whether
            accidental or intentional Y23.0
         suicide (attempt) X73.0
      specified NEC W34.09
         assault X95.8
         homicide (attempt) X95.8
         legal intervention —*see* Legal,
            intervention, firearm, specified NEC
         stated as undetermined whether
            accidental or intentional Y24.8
         suicide (attempt) X74.8
      stated as undetermined whether accidental
         or intentional Y24.9
      suicide (attempt) X74.9
      Very pistol W34.09
         assault X95.8
         homicide (attempt) X95.8
         stated as undetermined whether
            accidental or intentional Y24.8
         suicide (attempt) X74.8
   firework(s) W39
      stated as undetermined whether accidental
         or intentional Y25
   gas-operated gun NEC W34.018
      airgun —*see* Discharge, airgun
      assault X95.09
      homicide (attempt) X95.09
      paintball gun —*see* Discharge, paintball gun
      stated as undetermined whether accidental
         or intentional Y24.8
      suicide (attempt) X74.09
   gun NEC —*see also* Discharge, firearm NEC
      air —*see* Discharge, airgun
      BB —*see* Discharge, airgun
      for single hand use —*see* Discharge,
         firearm, handgun
      hand —*see* Discharge, firearm, handgun
      machine —*see* Discharge, firearm, machine
         gun
      other specified —*see* Discharge, firearm
         NEC
      paintball —*see* Discharge, paintball gun
      pellet —*see* Discharge, airgun
   handgun —*see* Discharge, firearm, handgun
   machine gun —*see* Discharge, firearm,
      machine gun
   paintball gun W34.011
      assault X95.02
      homicide (attempt) X95.02

Discharge (Continued)
   paintball gun (Continued)
      stated as undetermined whether accidental
         or intentional Y24.8
      suicide (attempt) X74.02
   pistol —*see* Discharge, firearm, handgun
      flare —*see* Discharge, firearm, Very pistol
      pellet —*see* Discharge, airgun
      Very —*see* Discharge, firearm, Very pistol
   revolver —*see* Discharge, firearm, handgun
   rifle (hunting) —*see* Discharge, firearm,
      hunting rifle
   shotgun —*see* Discharge, firearm, shotgun
   spring-operated gun NEC W34.018
      assault X95.09
      homicide (attempt) X95.09
      stated as undetermined whether accidental
         or intentional Y24.8
      suicide (attempt) X74.09
Disease
   Andes W94.11
   aviator's —*see* Air, pressure
   range W94.11
Diver's disease, palsy, paralysis, squeeze —*see*
   Air, pressure
Diving (into water) —*see* Accident, diving
Dog bite W54.0
Dragged by transport vehicle NEC —*see also*
   Accident, transport V09.9
Drinking poison (accidental) —*see* Table of
   Drugs and Chemicals
Dropped (accidentally) **while being carried or**
   supported by other person W04
Drowning (accidental) W74
   assault X92.9
   due to
      accident (to)
         machinery —*see* Contact, with, by type
            of machine
         watercraft V90.89
            burning V90.29
               powered V90.23
                  fishing boat V90.22
                  jet ski V90.23
                  merchant ship V90.20
                  passenger ship V90.21
               unpowered V90.28
                  canoe V90.25
                  inflatable V90.26
                  kayak V90.25
                  sailboat V90.24
                  water skis V90.27
            crushed V90.39
               powered V90.33
                  fishing boat V90.32
                  jet ski V90.33
                  merchant ship V90.30
                  passenger ship V90.31
               unpowered V90.38
                  canoe V90.35
                  inflatable V90.36
                  kayak V90.35
                  sailboat V90.34
                  water skis V90.37
            overturning V90.09
               powered V90.03
                  fishing boat V90.02
                  jet ski V90.03
                  merchant ship V90.00
                  passenger ship V90.01
               unpowered V90.08
                  canoe V90.05
                  inflatable V90.06
                  kayak V90.05
                  sailboat V90.04
            sinking V90.19
               powered V90.13
                  fishing boat V90.12
                  jet ski V90.13
                  merchant ship V90.10
                  passenger ship V90.11

▶ New   ⇒ Revised   ~~deleted~~ Deleted   ● Use Additional Character(s)

Drowning (Continued)
  due to (Continued)
    accident (Continued)
      watercraft (Continued)
        sinking (Continued)
          unpowered V90.18
            canoe V90.15
            inflatable V90.16
            kayak V90.15
            sailboat V90.14
          specified type NEC V90.89
        powered V90.83
          fishing boat V90.82
          jet ski V90.83
          merchant ship V90.80
          passenger ship V90.81
        unpowered V90.88
          canoe V90.85
          inflatable V90.86
          kayak V90.85
          sailboat V90.84
          water skis V90.87
    avalanche —see Landslide
    cataclysmic
      earth surface movement NEC —see
        Forces of nature, earth movement
      storm —see Forces of nature, cataclysmic
        storm
    cloudburst X37.8
    cyclone X37.1
    fall overboard (from) V92.09
      powered craft V92.03
        ferry boat V92.01
        fishing boat V92.02
        jet ski V92.03
        liner V92.01
        merchant ship V92.00
        passenger ship V92.01
      resulting from
        accident to watercraft —see Drowning,
          due to, accident to, watercraft
        being washed overboard (from)
          V92.29
          powered craft V92.23
            ferry boat V92.21
            fishing boat V92.22
            jet ski V92.23
            liner V92.21
            merchant ship V92.20
            passenger ship V92.21
          unpowered craft V92.28
            canoe V92.25
            inflatable V92.26
            kayak V92.25
            sailboat V92.24
            surf-board V92.28
            water skis V92.27
            windsurfer V92.28
        motion of watercraft V92.19
          powered craft V92.13
            ferry boat V92.11
            fishing boat V92.12
            jet ski V92.13
            liner V92.11
            merchant ship V92.10
            passenger ship V92.11
          unpowered craft
            canoe V92.15
            inflatable V92.16
            kayak V92.15
            sailboat V92.14
      unpowered craft V92.08
        canoe V92.05
        inflatable V92.06
        kayak V92.05

Drowning (Continued)
  due to (Continued)
    fall overboard (Continued)
      unpowered craft (Continued)
        sailboat V92.04
        surf-board V92.08
        water skis V92.07
        windsurfer V92.08
    hurricane X37.0
    jumping into water from watercraft
      (involved in accident) —see also
      Drowning, due to, accident to,
      watercraft
      without accident to or on watercraft
        W16.711
    tidal wave NEC —see Forces of nature,
      tidal wave
    torrential rain X37.8
  following
    fall
      into
        bathtub W16.211
        bucket W16.221
        fountain —see Drowning, following,
          fall, into, water, specified NEC
        quarry —see Drowning, following,
          fall, into, water, specified NEC
        reservoir —see Drowning, following,
          fall, into, water, specified NEC
        swimming-pool W16.011
          stated as undetermined whether
            accidental or intentional
            Y21.3
          striking
            bottom W16.021
            wall W16.031
          suicide (attempt) X71.2
        water NOS W16.41
          natural (lake) (open sea) (river)
            (stream) (pond) W16.111
            striking
              bottom W16.121
              side W16.131
          specified NEC W16.311
            striking
              bottom W16.321
              wall W16.331
      overboard NEC —see Drowning, due to,
        fall overboard
    jump or dive
      from boat W16.711
        striking bottom W16.721
      into
        fountain —see Drowning, following,
          jump or dive, into, water,
          specified NEC
        quarry —see Drowning, following,
          jump or dive, into, water,
          specified NEC
        reservoir —see Drowning, following,
          jump or dive, into, water,
          specified NEC
        swimming-pool W16.511
          striking
            bottom W16.521
            wall W16.531
          suicide (attempt) X71.2
        water NOS W16.91
          natural (lake) (open sea) (river)
            (stream) (pond) W16.611
          specified NEC W16.811
            striking
              bottom W16.821
              wall W16.831
            striking bottom W16.621

Drowning (Continued)
  homicide (attempt) X92.9
  in
    bathtub (accidental) W65
      assault X92.0
      following fall W16.211
        stated as undetermined whether
          accidental or intentional
          Y21.1
      stated as undetermined whether
        accidental or intentional Y21.0
      suicide (attempt) X71.0
    lake —see Drowning, in, natural water
    natural water (lake) (open sea) (river)
      (stream) (pond) W69
      assault X92.3
      following
        dive or jump W16.611
          striking bottom W16.621
        fall W16.111
          striking
            bottom W16.121
            side W16.131
      stated as undetermined whether
        accidental or intentional Y21.4
      suicide (attempt) X71.3
    quarry —see Drowning, in, specified place
      NEC
    quenching tank —see Drowning, in,
      specified place NEC
    reservoir —see Drowning, in, specified
      place NEC
    river —see Drowning, in, natural water
    sea —see Drowning, in, natural water
    specified place NEC W73
      assault X92.8
      following
        dive or jump W16.811
          striking
            bottom W16.821
            wall W16.831
        fall W16.311
          striking
            bottom W16.321
            wall W16.331
      stated as undetermined whether
        accidental or intentional Y21.8
      suicide (attempt) X71.8
    stream —see Drowning, in, natural water
    swimming-pool W67
      assault X92.1
        following fall X92.2
      following
        dive or jump W16.511
          striking
            bottom W16.521
            wall W16.531
        fall W16.011
          striking
            bottom W16.021
            wall W16.031
      stated as undetermined whether
        accidental or intentional Y21.2
        following fall Y21.3
      suicide (attempt) X71.1
        following fall X71.2
    war operations —see War operations,
      restriction of airway
  resulting from accident to watercraft —see
    Drowning, due to, accident, watercraft
  self-inflicted X71.9
  stated as undetermined whether accidental or
    intentional Y21.9
  suicide (attempt) X71.9

E

Earth (surface) movement NEC —*see* Forces of nature, earth movement
Earth falling (on) W20.0
  caused by cataclysmic earth surface movement or eruption —*see* Landslide
Earthquake (any injury) X34
Effect(s) (adverse) of
  air pressure (any) —*see* Air, pressure
  cold, excessive (exposure to) —*see* Exposure, cold
  heat (excessive) —*see* Heat
  hot place (weather) —*see* Heat
  insolation X30
  late —*see* Sequelae
  motion —*see* Motion
  nuclear explosion or weapon in war operations —*see* War operations, nuclear weapon
  radiation —*see* Radiation
  travel —*see* Travel
Electric shock (accidental) (by) (in) —*see* Exposure, electric current
Electrocution (accidental) —*see* Exposure, electric current
Endotracheal tube wrongly placed during anesthetic procedure Y65.3
Entanglement
  in
    bed linen, causing suffocation —*see* category T71
    wheel of pedal cycle V19.88
Entry of foreign body or material —*see* Foreign body
Environmental pollution related condition — *see* Z57
Execution, legal (any method) —*see* Legal, intervention
Exhaustion
  cold —*see* Exposure, cold
  due to excessive exertion —*see also* Overexertion X50.9
  heat —*see* Heat
Explosion (accidental) (of) (with secondary fire) W40.9
  acetylene W40.1
  aerosol can W36.1
  air tank (compressed) (in machinery) W36.2
  aircraft (in transit) (powered) NEC V95.9
    balloon V96.05
    fixed wing NEC (private) V95.25
      commercial V95.35
    glider V96.25
      hang V96.15
      powered V95.15
    helicopter V95.05
    in war operations —*see* War operations, destruction of aircraft
    microlight V95.15
    nonpowered V96.9
      specified NEC V96.8
    powered NEC V95.8
    stated as
      homicide (attempt) Y03.8
      suicide (attempt) X83.0
    ultralight V95.15
  anesthetic gas in operating room W40.1
  antipersonnel bomb W40.8
    assault X96.0
    homicide (attempt) X96.0
    suicide (attempt) X75
  assault X96.9
  bicycle tire W37.0
  blasting (cap) (materials) W40.0
  boiler (machinery), not on transport vehicle W35
    on watercraft —*see* Explosion, in, watercraft
  butane W40.1
  caused by other person X96.9
  coal gas W40.1

Explosion (*Continued*)
  detonator W40.0
  dump (munitions) W40.8
  dynamite W40.0
    in
      assault X96.8
      homicide (attempt) X96.8
      legal intervention
        injuring
          bystander Y35.112
          law enforcement personnel Y35.111
          suspect Y35.113
          unspecified person Y35.119
      suicide (attempt) X75
  explosive (material) W40.9
    gas W40.1
    in blasting operation W40.0
    specified NEC W40.8
      in
        assault X96.8
        homicide (attempt) X96.8
        legal intervention
          injuring
            bystander Y35.192
            law enforcement personnel Y35.191
            suspect Y35.193
            unspecified person Y35.199
        suicide (attempt) X75
  factory (munitions) W40.8
  fertilizer bomb W40.8
    assault X96.3
    homicide (attempt) X96.3
    suicide (attempt) X75
  fire-damp W40.1
  firearm (parts) NEC W34.19
    airgun W34.110
    BB gun W34.110
    gas, air or spring-operated gun NEC W34.118
    handgun W32.1
    hunting rifle W33.12
    larger firearm W33.10
      specified NEC W33.19
    machine gun W33.13
    paintball gun W34.111
    pellet gun W34.110
    shotgun W33.11
    Very pistol [flare] W34.19
  fireworks W39
  gas (coal) (explosive) W40.1
    cylinder W36.9
      aerosol can W36.1
      air tank W36.2
      pressurized W36.3
      specified NEC W36.8
  gasoline (fumes) (tank) not in moving motor vehicle W40.1
    bomb W40.8
      assault X96.1
      homicide (attempt) X96.1
      suicide (attempt) X75
    in motor vehicle —*see* Accident, transport, by type of vehicle
  grain store W40.8
  grenade W40.8
    in
      assault X96.8
      homicide (attempt) X96.8
      legal intervention
        injuring
          bystander Y35.192
          law enforcement personnel Y35.191
          suspect Y35.193
          unspecified person Y35.199
      suicide (attempt) X75
  handgun (parts) —*see* Explosion, firearm, handgun (parts)
  homicide (attempt) X96.9
    antipersonnel bomb —*see* Explosion, antipersonnel bomb
    fertilizer bomb —*see* Explosion, fertilizer bomb

Explosion (*Continued*)
  homicide (*Continued*)
    gasoline bomb —*see* Explosion, gasoline bomb
    letter bomb —*see* Explosion, letter bomb
    pipe bomb —*see* Explosion, pipe bomb
    specified NEC X96.8
  hose, pressurized W37.8
  hot water heater, tank (in machinery) W35
    on watercraft —*see* Explosion, in, watercraft
  in, on
    dump W40.8
    factory W40.8
    mine (of explosive gases) NEC W40.1
    watercraft V93.59
      powered craft V93.53
        ferry boat V93.51
        fishing boat V93.52
        jet ski V93.53
        liner V93.51
        merchant ship V93.50
        passenger ship V93.51
        sailboat V93.54
  letter bomb W40.8
    assault X96.2
    homicide (attempt) X96.2
    suicide (attempt) X75
  machinery —*see also* Contact, with, by type of machine
    on board watercraft —*see* Explosion, in, watercraft
    pressure vessel —*see* Explosion, by type of vessel
  methane W40.1
  mine W40.1
  missile NEC W40.8
  mortar bomb W40.8
    in
      assault X96.8
      homicide (attempt) X96.8
      legal intervention
        injuring
          bystander Y35.192
          law enforcement personnel Y35.191
          suspect Y35.193
          unspecified person Y35.199
      suicide (attempt) X75
  munitions (dump) (factory) W40.8
  pipe, pressurized W37.8
    bomb W40.8
      assault X96.4
      homicide (attempt) X96.4
      suicide (attempt) X75
  pressure, pressurized
    cooker W38
    gas tank (in machinery) W36.3
    hose W37.8
    pipe W37.8
    specified device NEC W38
    tire W37.8
      bicycle W37.0
    vessel (in machinery) W38
  propane W40.1
  self-inflicted X75
  shell (artillery) NEC W40.8
    during war operations —*see* War operations, explosion
    in
      legal intervention
        injuring
          bystander Y35.122
          law enforcement personnel Y35.121
          suspect Y35.123
          unspecified person Y35.129
    war —*see* War operations, explosion
  spacecraft V95.45
  stated as undetermined whether accidental or intentional Y25
  steam or water lines (in machinery) W37.8
  stove W40.9
  suicide (attempt) X75

▶ New ⟹ Revised ~~deleted~~ Deleted ● Use Additional Character(s)

Explosion (Continued)
tire, pressurized W37.8
  bicycle W37.0
undetermined whether accidental or
  intentional Y25
vehicle tire NEC W37.8
  bicycle W37.0
war operations —see War operations,
  explosion
Exposure (to) X58
air pressure change —see Air, pressure
cold (accidental) (excessive) (extreme)
  (natural) (place) X31
  assault Y08.89
  due to
    man-made conditions W93.8
      dry ice (contact) W93.01
        inhalation W93.02
      liquid air (contact) (hydrogen)
        (nitrogen) W93.11
        inhalation W93.12
      refrigeration unit (deep freeze)
        W93.2
    suicide (attempt) X83.2
    weather (conditions) X31
  homicide (attempt) Y08.89
  self-inflicted X83.2
due to abandonment or neglect X58
electric current W86.8
  appliance (faulty) W86.8
    domestic W86.0
  caused by other person Y08.89
  conductor (faulty) W86.1
  control apparatus (faulty) W86.1
  electric power generating plant,
    distribution station W86.1
  electroshock gun —see Exposure, electric
    current, taser
  high-voltage cable W85
  homicide (attempt) Y08.89
  legal execution —see Legal, intervention,
    specified means NEC
  lightning —see subcategory T75.0
  live rail W86.8
  misadventure in medical or surgical
    procedure in electroshock therapy
    Y63.4
  motor (electric) (faulty) W86.8
    domestic W86.0
  self-inflicted X83.1
  specified NEC W86.8
    domestic W86.0
  stun gun —see Exposure, electric current,
    taser
  suicide (attempt) X83.1
  taser W86.8
    assault Y08.89
    legal intervention —see category Y35
    self-harm (intentional) X83.8
    undetermined intent Y33
  third rail W86.8
  transformer (faulty) W86.1
  transmission lines W85
environmental tobacco smoke X58
excessive
  cold —see Exposure, cold
  heat (natural) NEC X30
    man-made W92
factor(s) NOS X58
  environmental NEC X58
    man-made NEC W99
    natural NEC —see Forces of nature
  specified NEC X58
fire, flames (accidental) X08.8
  assault X97
  campfire —see Exposure, fire, controlled,
    not in building
  controlled (in)
    with ignition (of) clothing —see also
      Ignition, clothes X06.2
      nightwear X05

Exposure (Continued)
fire, flames (Continued)
  controlled (Continued)
    bonfire —see Exposure, fire, controlled,
      not in building
    brazier (in building or structure) —see
      also Exposure, fire, controlled,
      building
      not in building or structure —see
        Exposure, fire, controlled, not in
        building
    building or structure X02.0
      with
        fall from building X02.3
        from building X02.5
        injury due to building collapse
          X02.2
        smoke inhalation X02.1
      hit by object from building X02.4
      specified mode of injury NEC X02.8
    fireplace, furnace or stove —see
      Exposure, fire, controlled, building
    not in building or structure X03.0
      with
        fall X03.3
        smoke inhalation X03.1
      hit by object X03.4
      specified mode of injury NEC X03.8
    trash —see Exposure, fire, controlled, not
      in building
  fireplace —see Exposure, fire, controlled,
    building
  fittings or furniture (in building or
    structure) (uncontrolled) —see
    Exposure, fire, uncontrolled, building
  forest (uncontrolled) —see Exposure, fire,
    uncontrolled, not in building
  grass (uncontrolled) —see Exposure, fire,
    uncontrolled, not in building
  hay (uncontrolled) —see Exposure, fire,
    uncontrolled, not in building
  homicide (attempt) X97
  ignition of highly flammable material X04
  in, of, on, starting in
    machinery —see Contact, with, by type
      of machine
    motor vehicle (in motion) —see also
      Accident, transport, occupant by
      type of vehicle V87.8
      with collision —see Collision
    railway rolling stock, train, vehicle
      V81.81
      with collision —see Accident,
        transport, railway vehicle
        occupant
    street car (in motion) V82.8
      with collision —see Accident,
        transport, streetcar occupant
    transport vehicle NEC —see also
      Accident, transport
      with collision —see Collision
    war operations —see also War operations,
      fire
      from nuclear explosion —see War
        operations, nuclear weapons
    watercraft (in transit) (not in transit)
      V91.09
      localized —see Burn, on board
        watercraft, due to, fire on board
      powered craft V91.03
        ferry boat V91.01
        fishing boat V91.02
        jet skis V91.03
        liner V91.01
        merchant ship V91.00
        passenger ship V91.01
      unpowered craft V91.08
        canoe V91.05
        inflatable V91.06
        kayak V91.05
        sailboat V91.04

Exposure (Continued)
fire, flames (Continued)
  in, of, on, starting in (Continued)
    watercraft (Continued)
      unpowered craft (Continued)
        surf-board V91.08
        waterskis V91.07
        windsurfer V91.08
  lumber (uncontrolled) —see Exposure, fire,
    uncontrolled, not in building
  mine (uncontrolled) —see Exposure, fire,
    uncontrolled, not in building
  prairie (uncontrolled) —see Exposure, fire,
    uncontrolled, not in building
  resulting from
    explosion —see Explosion
    lightning X08.8
  self-inflicted X76
  specified NEC X08.8
  started by other person X97
  stated as undetermined whether accidental
    or intentional Y26
  stove —see Exposure, fire, controlled,
    building
  suicide (attempt) X76
  tunnel (uncontrolled) —see Exposure, fire,
    uncontrolled, not in building
  uncontrolled
    in building or structure X00.0
      with
        fall from building X00.3
        injury due to building collapse
          X00.2
        jump from building X00.5
        smoke inhalation X00.1
      bed X08.00
        due to
          cigarette X08.01
          specified material NEC X08.09
      furniture NEC X08.20
        due to
          cigarette X08.21
          specified material NEC X08.29
      hit by object from building X00.4
      sofa X08.10
        due to
          cigarette X08.11
          specified material NEC
            X08.19
      specified mode of injury NEC
        X00.8
    not in building or structure (any)
      X01.0
      with
        fall X01.3
        smoke inhalation X01.1
      hit by object X01.4
      specified mode of injury NEC
        X01.8
  undetermined whether accidental or
    intentional Y26
forces of nature NEC —see Forces of nature
G-forces (abnormal) W49.9
gravitational forces (abnormal) W49.9
heat (natural) NEC —see Heat
high-pressure jet (hydraulic) (pneumatic)
  W49.9
hydraulic jet W49.9
inanimate mechanical force W49.9
jet, high-pressure (hydraulic) (pneumatic)
  W49.9
lightning —see subcategory T75.0
  causing fire —see Exposure, fire
mechanical forces NEC W49.9
  animate NEC W64
  inanimate NEC W49.9
noise W42.9
  supersonic W42.0
noxious substance —see Table of Drugs and
  Chemicals
pneumatic jet W49.9

Exposure (*Continued*)
  prolonged in deep-freeze unit or refrigerator
    W93.2
  radiation —*see* Radiation
  smoke —*see also* Exposure, fire
    tobacco, second hand Z77.22
  specified factors NEC X58
  sunlight X32
    man-made (sun lamp) W89.8
      tanning bed W89.1
  supersonic waves W42.0
  transmission line(s), electric W85
  vibration W49.9

Exposure (*Continued*)
  waves
    infrasound W49.9
    sound W42.9
    supersonic W42.0
  weather NEC —*see* Forces of nature
External cause status Y99.9
  child assisting in compensated work for
    family Y99.8
  civilian activity done for financial or other
    compensation Y99.0
  civilian activity done for income or pay
    Y99.0

External cause status (*Continued*)
  family member assisting in compensated
    work for other family member Y99.8
  hobby not done for income Y99.8
  leisure activity Y99.8
  military activity Y99.1
  off-duty activity of military personnel Y99.8
  recreation or sport not for income or while a
    student Y99.8
  specified NEC Y99.8
  student activity Y99.8
  volunteer activity Y99.2

▶ New   ⇒ Revised   ~~deleted~~ Deleted   ● Use Additional Character(s)

F

Factors, supplemental
  alcohol
    blood level
      less than 20mg/100ml Y90.0
      presence in blood, level not specified
        Y90.9
      20-39mg/100ml Y90.1
      40-59mg/100ml Y90.2
      60-79mg/100ml Y90.3
      80-99mg/100ml Y90.4
      100-119mg/100ml Y90.5
      120-199mg/100ml Y90.6
      200-239mg/100ml Y90.7
      240mg/100ml or more Y90.8
      presence in blood, but level not specified
        Y90.9
  environmental-pollution-related condition —
    see Z57
  nosocomial condition Y95
  work-related condition Y99.0
Failure
  in suture or ligature during surgical
    procedure Y65.2
  mechanical, of instrument or apparatus
    (any) (during any medical or surgical
    procedure) Y65.8
  sterile precautions (during medical and
    surgical care) —see Misadventure,
    failure, sterile precautions, by type of
    procedure
  to
    introduce tube or instrument Y65.4
      endotracheal tube during anesthesia Y65.3
    make curve (transport vehicle) NEC —see
      Accident, transport
    remove tube or instrument Y65.4
Fall, falling (accidental) W19
  building W20.1
    burning (uncontrolled fire) X00.3
  down
    embankment W17.81
    escalator W10.0
    hill W17.81
    ladder W11
    ramp W10.2
    stairs, steps W10.9
  due to
    bumping against
      object W18.00
        sharp glass W18.02
        specified NEC W18.09
        sports equipment W18.01
      person W03
        due to ice or snow W00.0
        on pedestrian conveyance —see
          Accident, transport, pedestrian,
          conveyance
    collision with another person W03
      due to ice or snow W00.0
      involving pedestrian conveyance —see
        Accident, transport, pedestrian,
        conveyance
    grocery cart tipping over W17.82
    ice or snow W00.9
      from one level to another W00.2
        on stairs or steps W00.1
      involving pedestrian conveyance —see
        Accident, transport, pedestrian,
        conveyance
      on same level W00.0
    slipping (on moving sidewalk) W01.0
      with subsequent striking against object
        W01.10
        furniture W01.190
        sharp object W01.119
          glass W01.110
          power tool or machine W01.111
          specified NEC W01.118
        specified NEC W01.198

Fall, falling (Continued)
  due to (Continued)
    striking against
      object W18.00
        sharp glass W18.02
        specified NEC W18.09
        sports equipment W18.01
      person W03
        due to ice or snow W00.0
        on pedestrian conveyance —see
          Accident, transport, pedestrian,
          conveyance
  earth (with asphyxia or suffocation (by
    pressure)) —see Earth, falling
  from, off, out of
    aircraft NEC (with accident to aircraft
      NEC) V97.0
      while boarding or alighting V97.1
    balcony W13.0
    bed W06
    boat, ship, watercraft NEC (with drowning
      or submersion) —see Drowning, due
      to, fall overboard
      with hitting bottom or object V94.0
    bridge W13.1
    building W13.9
      burning (uncontrolled fire) X00.3
    cavity W17.2
    chair W07
    cherry picker W17.89
    cliff W15
    dock W17.4
    embankment W17.81
    escalator W10.0
    flagpole W13.8
    furniture NEC W08
    grocery cart W17.82
    haystack W17.89
    high place NEC W17.89
      stated as undetermined whether
        accidental or intentional Y30
    hole W17.2
    incline W10.2
    ladder W11
    lifting device W17.89
    machine, machinery —see also Contact,
      with, by type of machine
      not in operation W17.89
    manhole W17.1
    mobile elevated work platform [MEWP]
      W17.89
    motorized mobility scooter W05.2
    one level to another NEC W17.89
      intentional, purposeful, suicide
        (attempt) X80
      stated as undetermined whether
        accidental or intentional Y30
    pit W17.2
    playground equipment W09.8
      jungle gym W09.2
      slide W09.0
      swing W09.1
    quarry W17.89
    railing W13.9
    ramp W10.2
    roof W13.2
    scaffolding W12
    scooter (nonmotorized) W05.1
      motorized mobility W05.2
    sky lift W17.89
    stairs, steps W10.9
      curb W10.1
      due to ice or snow W00.1
      escalator W10.0
      incline W10.2
      ramp W10.2
      sidewalk curb W10.1
      specified NEC W10.8
  ▶Standing
    ▶electric scooter V00.841
    ▶micro-mobility pedestrian conveyance
      V00.848

Fall, falling (Continued)
  from, off, out of (Continued)
    stepladder W11
    storm drain W17.1
    streetcar NEC V82.6
      with antecedent collision —see
        Accident, transport, streetcar
        occupant
      while boarding or alighting V82.4
    structure NEC W13.8
      burning (uncontrolled fire) X00.3
    table W08
    toilet W18.11
      with subsequent striking against object
        W18.12
    train NEC V81.6
      during derailment (without antecedent
        collision) V81.7
      with antecedent collision —see
        Accident, transport, railway
        vehicle occupant
      while boarding or alighting V81.4
    transport vehicle after collision —see
      Accident, transport, by type of
      vehicle, collision
    tree W14
    vehicle (in motion) NEC —see also
      Accident, transport V89.9
      motor NEC —see also Accident,
        transport, occupant, by type of
        vehicle V87.8
      stationary W17.89
        while boarding or alighting —see
          Accident, transport, by type of
          vehicle, while boarding or
          alighting
    viaduct W13.8
    wall W13.8
    watercraft —see also Drowning, due to, fall
      overboard
      with hitting bottom or object V94.0
    well W17.0
    wheelchair, non-moving W05.0
      powered —see Accident, transport,
        pedestrian, conveyance occupant,
        specified type NEC
    window W13.4
  in, on
    aircraft NEC V97.0
      with accident to aircraft V97.0
      while boarding or alighting V97.1
    bathtub (empty) W18.2
      filled W16.212
        causing drowning W16.211
    escalator W10.0
    incline W10.2
    ladder W11
    machine, machinery —see Contact, with,
      by type of machine
    object, edged, pointed or sharp (with
      cut) —see Fall, by type
    playground equipment W09.8
      jungle gym W09.2
      slide W09.0
      swing W09.1
    ramp W10.2
    scaffolding W12
    shower W18.2
      causing drowning W16.211
    staircase, stairs, steps W10.9
      curb W10.1
      due to ice or snow W00.1
      escalator W10.0
      incline W10.2
      specified NEC W10.8
    streetcar (without antecedent collision)
      V82.5
      with antecedent collision —see
        Accident, transport, streetcar
        occupant
      while boarding or alighting V82.4

▶ New   ⇒ Revised   ~~deleted~~ Deleted   ● Use Additional Character(s)

Fall, falling *(Continued)*
  in, on *(Continued)*
    train (without antecedent collision) V81.5
      with antecedent collision —*see* Accident,
        transport, railway vehicle occupant
      during derailment (without antecedent
        collision) V81.7
        with antecedent collision —*see*
          Accident, transport, railway
          vehicle occupant
      while boarding or alighting V81.4
    transport vehicle after collision —*see*
      Accident, transport, by type of
      vehicle, collision
    watercraft V93.39
      due to
        accident to craft V91.29
          powered craft V91.23
            ferry boat V91.21
            fishing boat V91.22
            jet ski V91.23
            liner V91.21
            merchant ship V91.20
            passenger ship V91.21
          unpowered craft
            canoe V91.25
            inflatable V91.26
            kayak V91.25
            sailboat V91.24
        powered craft V93.33
          ferry boat V93.31
          fishing boat V93.32
          jet ski V93.33
          liner V93.31
          merchant ship V93.30
          passenger ship V93.31
        unpowered craft V93.38
          canoe V93.35
          inflatable V93.36
          kayak V93.35
          sailboat V93.34
          surf-board V93.38
          windsurfer V93.38
  into
    cavity W17.2
    dock W17.4
    fire —*see* Exposure, fire, by type
    haystack W17.89
    hole W17.2
    manhole W17.1
    moving part of machinery —*see* Contact,
      with, by type of machine
    ocean —*see* Fall, into, water
    opening in surface NEC W17.89
    pit W17.2
    pond —*see* Fall, into, water
    quarry W17.89
    river —*see* Fall, into, water
    shaft W17.89
    storm drain W17.1
    stream —*see* Fall, into, water
    swimming pool —*see also* Fall, into, water,
      in, swimming pool
      empty W17.3
    tank W17.89
    water W16.42
      causing drowning W16.41
      from watercraft —*see* Drowning, due to,
        fall overboard
      hitting diving board W21.4
      in
        bathtub W16.212
          causing drowning W16.211
        bucket W16.222
          causing drowning W16.221
        natural body of water W16.112
          causing drowning W16.111
          striking
            bottom W16.122
              causing drowning
                W16.121

Fall, falling *(Continued)*
  into *(Continued)*
    water *(Continued)*
      in *(Continued)*
        natural body of water *(Continued)*
          striking *(Continued)*
            side W16.132
              causing drowning W16.131
        specified water NEC W16.312
          causing drowning W16.311
          striking
            bottom W16.322
              causing drowning W16.321
            wall W16.332
              causing drowning W16.331
        swimming pool W16.012
          causing drowning W16.011
          striking
            bottom W16.022
              causing drowning W16.021
            wall W16.032
              causing drowning W16.031
        utility bucket W16.222
          causing drowning W16.221
    well W17.0
  involving
    bed W06
    chair W07
    furniture NEC W08
    glass —*see* Fall, by type
    playground equipment W09.8
      jungle gym W09.2
      slide W09.0
      swing W09.1
    roller blades —*see* Accident, transport,
      pedestrian, conveyance
    skateboard(s) —*see* Accident, transport,
      pedestrian, conveyance
    skates (ice) (in line) (roller) —*see*
      Accident, transport, pedestrian,
      conveyance
    skis —*see* Accident, transport, pedestrian,
      conveyance
    table W08
    wheelchair, non-moving W05.0
      powered —*see* Accident, transport,
        pedestrian, conveyance, specified
        type NEC
  object —*see* Struck by, object, falling
  off
    toilet W18.11
      with subsequent striking against object
        W18.12
  on same level W18.30
    due to
      specified NEC W18.39
      stepping on an object W18.31
  out of
    bed W06
    building NEC W13.8
    chair W07
    furniture NEC W08
    wheelchair, non-moving W05.0
      powered —*see* Accident, transport,
        pedestrian, conveyance, specified
        type NEC
    window W13.4
  over
    animal W01.0
    cliff W15
    embankment W17.81
    small object W01.0
  rock W20.8
  same level W18.30
    from
      being crushed, pushed, or stepped on
        by a crowd or human stampede
        W52
      collision, pushing, shoving, by or with
        other person W03
      slipping, stumbling, tripping W01.0

Fall, falling *(Continued)*
  same level *(Continued)*
    involving ice or snow W00.0
      involving skates (ice) (roller),
        skateboard, skis —*see* Accident,
        transport, pedestrian, conveyance
    snowslide (avalanche) —*see* Landslide
    stone W20.8
    structure W20.1
      burning (uncontrolled fire) X00.3
    through
      bridge W13.1
      floor W13.3
      roof W13.2
      wall W13.8
      window W13.4
    timber W20.8
    tree (caused by lightning) W20.8
    while being carried or supported by other
      person(s) W04
Fallen on by
  animal (not being ridden) NEC W55.89
Felo-de-se —*see* Suicide
Fight (hand) (fists) (foot) —*see* Assault, fight
Fire (accidental) —*see* Exposure, fire
Firearm discharge —*see* Discharge, firearm
Fireball effects from nuclear explosion in war
  operations —*see* War operations, nuclear
  weapons
Fireworks (explosion) W39
Flash burns from explosion —*see* Explosion
Flood (any injury) (caused by) X38
  collapse of man-made structure causing earth
    movement X36.0
  tidal wave —*see* Forces of nature, tidal wave
Food (any type) in
  air passages (with asphyxia, obstruction, or
    suffocation) —*see* categories T17 and T18
  alimentary tract causing asphyxia (due to
    compression of trachea) —*see* categories
    T17 and T18
Forces of nature X39.8
  avalanche X36.1
    causing transport accident —*see* Accident,
      transport, by type of vehicle
  blizzard X37.2
  cataclysmic storm X37.9
    with flood X38
    blizzard X37.2
    cloudburst X37.8
    cyclone X37.1
    dust storm X37.3
    hurricane X37.0
    specified storm NEC X37.8
    storm surge X37.0
    tornado X37.1
    twister X37.1
    typhoon X37.0
  cloudburst X37.8
  cold (natural) X31
  cyclone X37.1
  dam collapse causing earth movement X36.0
  dust storm X37.3
  earth movement X36.1
    caused by dam or structure collapse X36.0
    earthquake X34
  earthquake X34
  flood (caused by) X38
    dam collapse X36.0
    tidal wave —*see* Forces of nature, tidal
      wave
  heat (natural) X30
  hurricane X37.0
  landslide X36.1
    causing transport accident —*see* Accident,
      transport, by type of vehicle
  lightning —*see* subcategory T75.0
    causing fire —*see* Exposure, fire
  mudslide X36.1
    causing transport accident —*see* Accident,
      transport, by type of vehicle

Forces of nature *(Continued)*
  radiation (natural) X39.08
    radon X39.01
  radon X39.01
  specified force NEC X39.8
  storm surge X37.0
  structure collapse causing
      earth movement
      X36.0
  sunlight X32
  tidal wave X37.41
    due to
        earthquake X37.41
        landslide X37.43
        storm X37.42
        volcanic eruption X37.41
  tornado X37.1

Forces of nature *(Continued)*
  tsunami X37.41
  twister X37.1
  typhoon X37.0
  volcanic eruption X35
Foreign body
  aspiration —*see* Index to Diseases and
      Injuries, Foreign body, respitory
      tract
  embedded in skin W45
  entering through skin W45.8
    can lid W26.2
    nail W45.0
    paper W26.2
    specified NEC 45.8
    splinter W45.8

Forest fire (exposure to) —*see* Exposure, fire,
    uncontrolled, not in building
Found injured X58
  from exposure (to) —*see* Exposure
  on
      highway, road(way), street V89.9
      railway right of way V81.9
Fracture (circumstances unknown or
    unspecified) X58
  due to specified cause NEC X58
Freezing —*see* Exposure, cold
Frostbite X31
  due to man-made conditions —*see* Exposure,
      cold, man-made
Frozen —*see* Exposure, cold

G

Gored by bull W55.22
Gunshot wound W34.00

H

Hailstones, injured by X39.8
Hanged herself or himself —*see* Hanging,
    self-inflicted
Hanging (accidental) —*see also* category T71
  legal execution —*see* Legal, intervention,
      specified means NEC
Heat (effects of) (excessive) X30
  due to
      man-made conditions W92
        on board watercraft V93.29
          fishing boat V93.22
          merchant ship V93.20
          passenger ship V93.21
          sailboat V93.24
          specified powered craft NEC V93.23
      weather (conditions) X30

Heat *(Continued)*
  from
      electric heating apparatus causing
          burning X16
      nuclear explosion in war operations —
          see War operations, nuclear
          weapons
      inappropriate in local application or
          packing in medical or surgical
          procedure Y63.5
Hemorrhage
  delayed following medical or surgical
      treatment without mention of
      misadventure —*see* Index to Diseases
      and Injuries, Complication(s)
  during medical or surgical treatment as
      misadventure —*see* Index to Diseases
      and Injuries, Complication(s)

High
  altitude (effects) —*see* Air, pressure, low
  level of radioactivity, effects —*see* Radiation
  pressure (effects) —*see* Air, pressure, high
  temperature, effects —*see* Heat
Hit, hitting (accidental) by —*see* Struck by
Hitting against —*see* Striking against
Homicide (attempt) (justifiable) —*see* Assault
Hot
  place, effects —*see also* Heat
  weather, effects X30
House fire (uncontrolled) —*see* Exposure, fire,
    uncontrolled, building
Humidity, causing problem X39.8
Hunger X58
Hurricane (any injury) X37.0
Hypobarism, hypobaropathy —*see* Air,
    pressure, low

I

Ictus
  caloris —*see also* Heat
  solaris X30
Ignition (accidental) —*see also* Exposure, fire
    X08.8
  anesthetic gas in operating room W40.1
  apparel X06.2
    from highly flammable material X04
    nightwear X05
  bed linen (sheets) (spreads) (pillows)
      (mattress) —*see* Exposure, fire,
      uncontrolled, building, bed
  benzine X04
  clothes, clothing NEC (from controlled fire)
      X06.2
    from
      highly flammable material X04
  ether X04
    in operating room W40.1
  explosive material —*see* Explosion
  gasoline X04
  jewelry (plastic) (any) X06.0
  kerosene X04
  material
    explosive —*see* Explosion
    highly flammable with secondary
        explosion X04
  nightwear X05
  paraffin X04
  petrol X04
Immersion (accidental) —*see also* Drowning
  hand or foot due to cold (excessive) X31
Implantation of quills of porcupine W55.89
Inanition (from) (hunger) X58
  thirst X58.8
Inappropriate operation performed
  correct operation on wrong side or body part
      (wrong side) (wrong site) Y65.53
  operation intended for another patient done
      on wrong patient Y65.52
  wrong operation performed on correct
      patient Y65.51
Inattention after, at birth (homicidal intent)
    (infanticidal intent) X58
Incident, adverse
  device
    anesthesiology Y70.8
      accessory Y70.2
      diagnostic Y70.0
      miscellaneous Y70.8
      monitoring Y70.0
      prosthetic Y70.2
      rehabilitative Y70.1
      surgical Y70.3
      therapeutic Y70.1
    cardiovascular Y71.8
      accessory Y71.2
      diagnostic Y71.0
      miscellaneous Y71.8
      monitoring Y71.0
      prosthetic Y71.2
      rehabilitative Y71.1
      surgical Y71.3
      therapeutic Y71.1
    gastroenterology Y73.8
      accessory Y73.2
      diagnostic Y73.0
      miscellaneous Y73.8
      monitoring Y73.0
      prosthetic Y73.2
      rehabilitative Y73.1
      surgical Y73.3
      therapeutic Y73.1
    general
      hospital Y74.8
        accessory Y74.2
        diagnostic Y74.0
        miscellaneous Y74.8
        monitoring Y74.0

Incident, adverse (Continued)
  device (Continued)
    general (Continued)
      hospital (Continued)
        prosthetic Y74.2
        rehabilitative Y74.1
        surgical Y74.3
        therapeutic Y74.1
      surgical Y81.8
        accessory Y81.2
        diagnostic Y81.0
        miscellaneous Y81.8
        monitoring Y81.0
        prosthetic Y81.2
        rehabilitative Y81.1
        surgical Y81.3
        therapeutic Y81.1
    gynecological Y76.8
      accessory Y76.2
      diagnostic Y76.0
      miscellaneous Y76.8
      monitoring Y76.0
      prosthetic Y76.2
      rehabilitative Y76.1
      surgical Y76.3
      therapeutic Y76.1
    medical Y82.9
      specified type NEC Y82.8
    neurological Y75.8
      accessory Y75.2
      diagnostic Y75.0
      miscellaneous Y75.8
      monitoring Y75.0
      prosthetic Y75.2
      rehabilitative Y75.1
      surgical Y75.3
      therapeutic Y75.1
    obstetrical Y76.8
      accessory Y76.2
      diagnostic Y76.0
      miscellaneous Y76.8
      monitoring Y76.0
      prosthetic Y76.2
      rehabilitative Y76.1
      surgical Y76.3
      therapeutic Y76.1
    ophthalmic Y77.8
      accessory Y77.2
    ▶contact lens (rigid gas permeable)
        (soft) (hydrophilic)) Y77.11
      diagnostic Y77.0
      miscellaneous Y77.8
      monitoring Y77.0
      prosthetic Y77.2
    ⇒rehabilitative Y77.19
      surgical Y77.3
    ⇒therapeutic Y77.19
    orthopedic Y79.8
      accessory Y79.2
      diagnostic Y79.0
      miscellaneous Y79.8
      monitoring Y79.0
      prosthetic Y79.2
      rehabilitative Y79.1
      surgical Y79.3
      therapeutic Y79.1
    otorhinolaryngological Y72.8
      accessory Y72.2
      diagnostic Y72.0
      miscellaneous Y72.8
      monitoring Y72.0
      prosthetic Y72.2
      rehabilitative Y72.1
      surgical Y72.3
      therapeutic Y72.1
    personal use Y74.8
      accessory Y74.2
      diagnostic Y74.0
      miscellaneous Y74.8
      monitoring Y74.0
      prosthetic Y74.2

Incident, adverse (Continued)
  device (Continued)
    personal use (Continued)
      rehabilitative Y74.1
      surgical Y74.3
      therapeutic Y74.1
    physical medicine Y80.8
      accessory Y80.2
      diagnostic Y80.0
      miscellaneous Y80.8
      monitoring Y80.0
      prosthetic Y80.2
      rehabilitative Y80.1
      surgical Y80.3
      therapeutic Y80.1
    plastic surgical Y81.8
      accessory Y81.2
      diagnostic Y81.0
      miscellaneous Y81.8
      monitoring Y81.0
      prosthetic Y81.2
      rehabilitative Y81.1
      surgical Y81.3
      therapeutic Y81.1
    radiological Y78.8
      accessory Y78.2
      diagnostic Y78.0
      miscellaneous Y78.8
      monitoring Y78.0
      prosthetic Y78.2
      rehabilitative Y78.1
      surgical Y78.3
      therapeutic Y78.1
    urology Y73.8
      accessory Y73.2
      diagnostic Y73.0
      miscellaneous Y73.8
      monitoring Y73.0
      prosthetic Y73.2
      rehabilitative Y73.1
      surgical Y73.3
      therapeutic Y73.1
Incineration (accidental) —*see* Exposure, fire
Infanticide —*see* Assault
Infrasound waves (causing injury) W49.9
Ingestion
  foreign body (causing injury) (with
      obstruction) —*see* Foreign body,
      alimentary canal
  poisonous
    plant(s) X58
    substance NEC —*see* Table of Drugs and
        Chemicals
Inhalation
  excessively cold substance, man-made —*see*
      Exposure, cold, man-made
  food (any type) (into respiratory tract) (with
      asphyxia, obstruction respiratory tract,
      suffocation) —*see* categories T17 and T18
  foreign body —*see* Foreign body, aspiration
  gastric contents (with asphyxia, obstruction
      respiratory passage, suffocation) T17.81-●
  hot air or gases X14.0
  liquid air, hydrogen, nitrogen W93.12
    suicide (attempt) X83.2
  steam X13.0
    assault X98.0
    stated as undetermined whether accidental
        or intentional Y27.0
    suicide (attempt) X77.0
  toxic gas —*see* Table of Drugs and
      Chemicals
  vomitus (with asphyxia, obstruction
      respiratory passage, suffocation) T17.81-●
Injury, injured (accidental(ly)) NOS X58
  by, caused by, from
    assault —*see* Assault
    law-enforcing agent, police, in course
        of legal intervention —*see* Legal
        intervention
    suicide (attempt) X83.8

▶ New   ⇒ Revised   ~~deleted~~ Deleted   ● Use Additional Character(s)

Injury, injured NOS *(Continued)*
  due to, in
    civil insurrection —*see* War
      operations
    fight —*see also* Assault, fight
      Y04.0
    war operations —*see* War
      operations
  homicide —*see also* Assault Y09
  inflicted (by)
    in course of arrest (attempted), suppression
      of disturbance, maintenance of order,
      by law-enforcing agents —*see* Legal
      intervention

Injury, injured NOS *(Continued)*
  inflicted *(Continued)*
    other person
      stated as
        accidental X58
        intentional, homicide (attempt) —*see*
          Assault
        undetermined whether accidental or
          intentional Y33
    purposely (inflicted) by other person(s) —*see*
      Assault
    self-inflicted X83.8
      stated as accidental X58
    specified cause NEC X58

Injury, injured NOS *(Continued)*
  undetermined whether accidental or
    intentional Y33
Insolation, effects X30
Insufficient nourishment X58
Interruption of respiration (by)
  food (lodged in esophagus) —*see* categories
    T17 and T18
  vomitus (lodged in esophagus) T17.81-●
Intervention, legal —*see* Legal intervention
Intoxication
  drug —*see* Table of Drugs and Chemicals
  poison —*see* Table of Drugs and
    Chemicals

J

Jammed (accidentally)
  between objects (moving) (stationary and
    moving) W23.0
    stationary W23.1
Jumped, jumping
  before moving object NEC X81.8
    motor vehicle X81.0
    subway train X81.1
    train X81.1
    undetermined whether accidental or
      intentional Y31
  from
    boat (into water) voluntarily,
      without accident (to or on boat)
      W16.712
      with
        accident to or on boat —*see* Accident,
          watercraft
        drowning or submersion W16.711
          suicide (attempt) X71.3

Jumped, jumping *(Continued)*
  from *(Continued)*
    boat voluntarily, without accident
      (Continued)
      striking bottom W16.722
        causing drowning W16.721
    building —*see also* Jumped, from,
      high place W13.9
      burning (uncontrolled fire)
        X00.5
    high place NEC W17.89
      suicide (attempt) X80
      undetermined whether accidental or
        intentional Y30
    structure —*see also* Jumped, from, high
      place W13.9
      burning (uncontrolled fire)
        X00.5
  into water W16.92
    causing drowning W16.91
    from, off watercraft —*see* Jumped, from,
      boat

Jumped, jumping *(Continued)*
  into water *(Continued)*
    in
      natural body W16.612
        causing drowning W16.611
        striking bottom W16.622
          causing drowning W16.621
      specified place NEC W16.812
        causing drowning W16.811
        striking
          bottom W16.822
            causing drowning W16.821
          wall W16.832
            causing drowning W16.831
      swimming pool W16.512
        causing drowning W16.511
        striking
          bottom W16.522
            causing drowning W16.521
          wall W16.532
            causing drowning W16.531
    suicide (attempt) X71.3

K

Kicked by
  animal NEC W55.82
  person(s) (accidentally) W50.1
    with intent to injure or kill Y04.0
    as, or caused by, a crowd or human
      stampede (with fall) W52
    assault Y04.0
    homicide (attempt) Y04.0
    in
      fight Y04.0
      legal intervention
        injuring
          bystander Y35.812
          law enforcement personnel
            Y35.811
          suspect Y35.813
          unspecified person Y35.819

Kicking
  against
    object W22.8
      sports equipment W21.9
      stationary W22.09
        sports equipment W21.89
    person —*see* Striking against, person
    sports equipment W21.9
  carpet stretcher with knee X50.3
Killed, killing (accidentally) NOS —*see also*
    Injury X58
  in
    action —*see* War operations
    brawl, fight (hand) (fists) (foot) Y04.0
      by weapon —*see also* Assault
        cutting, piercing —*see* Assault, cutting
          or piercing instrument
        firearm —*see* Discharge, firearm, by
          type, homicide

Killed, killing NOS *(Continued)*
  self
    stated as
      accident NOS X58
      suicide —*see* Suicide
      undetermined whether accidental or
        intentional Y33
Kneeling (prolonged) (static) X50.1
Knocked down (accidentally) (by) NOS X58
  animal (not being ridden) NEC —*see also*
    Struck by, by type of animal
  crowd or human stampede W52
  person W51
    in brawl, fight Y04.0
  transport vehicle NEC —*see also* Accident,
    transport V09.9

I, J, & K

L

Laceration NEC —see Injury
Lack of
  care (helpless person) (infant) (newborn) X58
  food except as result of abandonment or neglect X58
    due to abandonment or neglect X58
  water except as result of transport accident X58
    due to transport accident —see Accident, transport, by type
  helpless person, infant, newborn X58
Landslide (falling on transport vehicle) X36.1
  caused by collapse of man-made structure X36.0
Late effect —see Sequelae
Legal
  execution (any method) —see Legal, intervention
  intervention (by)
    baton —see Legal, intervention, blunt object, baton
    bayonet —see Legal, intervention, sharp object, bayonet
    blow —see Legal, intervention, manhandling
    blunt object
      baton
        injuring
          bystander Y35.312
          law enforcement personnel Y35.311
          suspect Y35.313
          unspecified person Y35.319
      injuring
        bystander Y35.302
        law enforcement personnel Y35.301
        suspect Y35.303
        unspecified person Y35.309
      specified NEC
        injuring
          bystander Y35.392
          law enforcement personnel Y35.391
          suspect Y35.393
          unspecified person Y35.399
      stave
        injuring
          bystander Y35.392
          law enforcement personnel Y35.391
          suspect Y35.393
          unspecified person Y35.399
    bomb —see Legal, intervention, explosive
    conducted energy device
      injuring
        bystander Y35.832
        law enforcement personnel Y35.831
        suspect Y35.833
        unspecified person Y35.839
    cutting or piercing instrument —see Legal, intervention, sharp object
    dynamite —see Legal, intervention, explosive, dynamite
    electroshock device (taser)
      injuring
        bystander Y35.832
        law enforcement personnel Y35.831
        suspect Y35.833
        unspecified person Y35.839
    explosive(s)
      dynamite
        injuring
          bystander Y35.112
          law enforcement personnel Y35.111
          suspect Y35.113
          unspecified person Y35.119
      grenade
        injuring
          bystander Y35.192
          law enforcement personnel Y35.191
          suspect Y35.193
          unspecified person Y35.199

Legal *(Continued)*
  intervention *(Continued)*
    explosive *(Continued)*
      injuring
        bystander Y35.102
        law enforcement personnel Y35.101
        suspect Y35.103
        unspecified person Y35.109
      mortar bomb
        injuring
          bystander Y35.192
          law enforcement personnel Y35.191
          suspect Y35.193
          unspecified person Y35.199
      shell
        injuring
          bystander Y35.122
          law enforcement personnel Y35.121
          suspect Y35.123
          unspecified person Y35.129
      specified NEC
        injuring
          bystander Y35.192
          law enforcement personnel Y35.191
          suspect Y35.193
          unspecified person Y35.199
    firearm(s) (discharge)
      handgun
        injuring
          bystander Y35.022
          law enforcement personnel Y35.021
          suspect Y35.023
          unspecified person Y35.029
      injuring
        bystander Y35.002
        law enforcement personnel Y35.001
        suspect Y35.003
        unspecified person Y35.009
      machine gun
        injuring
          bystander Y35.012
          law enforcement personnel Y35.011
          suspect Y35.013
          unspecified person Y35.019
      rifle pellet
        injuring
          bystander Y35.032
          law enforcement personnel Y35.031
          suspect Y35.033
          unspecified person Y35.039
      rubber bullet
        injuring
          bystander Y35.042
          law enforcement personnel Y35.041
          suspect Y35.043
          unspecified person Y35.049
      shotgun —see Legal, intervention, firearm, specified NEC
      specified NEC
        injuring
          bystander Y35.092
          law enforcement personnel Y35.091
          suspect Y35.093
          unspecified person Y35.099
    gas (asphyxiation) (poisoning)
      injuring
        bystander Y35.202
        law enforcement personnel Y35.201
        suspect Y35.203
        unspecified person Y35.209
      specified NEC
        injuring
          bystander Y35.292
          law enforcement personnel Y35.291
          suspect Y35.293
          unspecified person Y35.299
      tear gas
        injuring
          bystander Y35.212
          law enforcement personnel Y35.211
          suspect Y35.213
          unspecified person Y35.219

Legal *(Continued)*
  intervention *(Continued)*
    grenade —see Legal, intervention, explosive, grenade
    injuring
      bystander Y35.92
      law enforcement personnel Y35.91
      suspect Y35.93
      unspecified person Y35.99
    late effect (of) —see with 7th character S Y35
    manhandling
      injuring
        bystander Y35.812
        law enforcement personnel Y35.811
        suspect Y35.813
        unspecified person Y35.819
    sequelae (of) —see with 7th character S Y35
    sharp objects
      bayonet
        injuring
          bystander Y35.412
          law enforcement personnel Y35.411
          suspect Y35.413
          unspecified person Y35.419
      injuring
        bystander Y35.402
        law enforcement personnel Y35.401
        suspect Y35.403
        unspecified person Y35.409
      specified NEC
        injuring
          bystander Y35.492
          law enforcement personnel Y35.491
          suspect Y35.493
          unspecified person Y35.499
    specified means NEC
      injuring
        bystander Y35.892
        law enforcement personnel Y35.891
        suspect Y35.893
    stabbing —see Legal, intervention, sharp object
    stave —see Legal, intervention, blunt object, stave
    stun gun
      injuring
        bystander Y35.832
        law enforcement personnel Y35.831
        suspect Y35.833
        unspecified person Y35.839
    taser
      injuring
        bystander Y35.832
        law enforcement personnel Y35.831
        suspect Y35.833
        unspecified person Y35.839
    tear gas —see Legal, intervention, gas, tear gas
    truncheon —see Legal, intervention, blunt object, stave
Lifting —see also Overexertion
  heavy objects X50.0
  weights X50.0
Lightning (shock) (stroke) (struck by) —see subcategory T75.0
  causing fire —see Exposure, fire
Loss of control (transport vehicle) NEC —see Accident, transport
Lost at sea NOS —see Drowning, due to, fall overboard
Low
  pressure (effects) —see Air, pressure, low
  temperature (effects) —see Exposure, cold
Lying before train, vehicle or other moving object X81.8
  subway train X81.1
  train X81.1
  undetermined whether accidental or intentional Y31
Lynching —see Assault

▶ New   ⟶ Revised   ~~deleted~~ Deleted   ● Use Additional Character(s)

M

Malfunction (mechanism or component) (of)
  firearm
    airgun W34.10
    BB gun W34.110
    gas, air or spring-operated gun NEC
      W34.118
    handgun W32.1
    hunting rifle W33.12
    larger firearm W33.10
      specified NEC W33.19
    machine gun W33.13
    paintball gun W34.111
    pellet gun W34.110
    shotgun W33.11
    specified NEC W34.19
    Very pistol [flare] W34.19
  handgun —see Malfunction, firearm,
    handgun
Maltreatment —see Perpetrator
Mangled (accidentally) NOS X58
Manhandling (in brawl, fight) Y04.0
  legal intervention —see Legal, intervention,
    manhandling
Manslaughter (nonaccidental) —see Assault
Mauled by animal NEC W55.89
Medical procedure, complication of
  (delayed or as an abnormal reaction
    without mention of misadventure) —see
    Complication of or following, by specified
    type of procedure
  due to or as a result of misadventure —see
    Misadventure
Melting (due to fire) —see also Exposure, fire
  apparel NEC X06.3
  clothes, clothing NEC X06.3
    nightwear X05
  fittings or furniture (burning building)
    (uncontrolled fire) X00.8
  nightwear X05
  plastic jewelry X06.1
Mental cruelty X58
Military operations (injuries to military and
  civilians occuring during peacetime on
  military property and during routine
  military exercises and operations) (by)
  (from) (involving) Y37.90-●
  air blast Y37.20-●
  aircraft
    destruction —see Military operations,
      destruction of aircraft
    airway restriction —see Military operations,
      restriction of airways
    asphyxiation —see Military operations,
      restriction of airways
  biological weapons Y37.6X-●
  blast Y37.20-●
  blast fragments Y37.20-●
  blast wave Y37.20-●
  blast wind Y37.20-●
  bomb Y37.20-●
    dirty Y37.50-●
    gasoline Y37.31-●
    incendiary Y37.31-●
    petrol Y37.31-●
  bullet Y37.43-●
    incendiary Y37.32-●
    rubber Y37.41-●
  chemical weapons Y37.7X-●
  combat
    hand to hand (unarmed) combat
      Y37.44-●
    using blunt or piercing object Y37.45-●
  conflagration —see Military operations, fire
  conventional warfare NEC Y37.49-●
  depth-charge Y37.01-●
  destruction of aircraft Y37.10-●
    due to
      air to air missile Y37.11-●
      collision with other aircraft Y37.12-●

Military operations (Continued)
  destruction of aircraft (Continued)
    due to (Continued)
      detonation (accidental) of onboard
        munitions and explosives Y37.14-●
      enemy fire or explosives Y37.11-●
      explosive placed on aircraft Y37.11-●
      onboard fire Y37.13-●
      rocket propelled grenade [RPG] Y37.11-●
      small arms fire Y37.11-●
      surface to air missile Y37.11-●
    specified NEC Y37.19-●
  detonation (accidental) of
    onboard marine weapons Y37.05-●
    own munitions or munitions launch device
      Y37.24-●
  dirty bomb Y37.50-●
  explosion (of) Y37.20-●
    aerial bomb Y37.21-●
    bomb NOS —see also Military operations,
      bomb(s) Y37.20-●
    fragments Y37.20-●
    grenade Y37.29-●
    guided missile Y37.22-●
    improvised explosive device [IED]
      (person-borne) (roadside) (vehicle-
      borne) Y37.23-●
    land mine Y37.29-●
    marine mine (at sea) (in harbor) Y37.02-●
    marine weapon Y37.00-●
      specified NEC Y37.09-●
    own munitions or munitions launch device
      (accidental) Y37.24-●
    sea-based artillery shell Y37.03-●
    specified NEC Y37.29-●
    torpedo Y37.04-●
  fire Y37.30-●
    specified NEC Y37.39-●
  firearms
    discharge Y37.43-●
    pellets Y37.42-●
  flamethrower Y37.33-●
  fragments (from) (of)
    improvised explosive device [IED]
      (person-borne) (roadside) (vehicle-
      borne) Y37.26-●
    munitions Y37.25-●
    specified NEC Y37.29-●
    weapons Y37.27-●
  friendly fire Y37.92-●
  hand to hand (unarmed) combat Y37.44-●
  hot substances —see Military operations, fire
  incendiary bullet Y37.32-●
  nuclear weapon (effects of) Y37.50-●
    acute radiation exposure Y37.54-●
    blast pressure Y37.51-●
    direct blast Y37.51-●
    direct heat Y37.53-●
    fallout exposure Y37.54-●
    fireball Y37.53-●
    indirect blast (struck or crushed by blast
      debris) (being thrown by blast)
      Y37.52-●
    ionizing radiation (immediate exposure)
      Y37.54-●
    nuclear radiation Y37.54-●
    radiation
      ionizing (immediate exposure) Y37.54-●
      nuclear Y37.54-●
      thermal Y37.53-●
    secondary effects Y37.54-●
    specified NEC Y37.59-●
    thermal radiation Y37.53-●
  restriction of air (airway)
    intentional Y37.46-●
    unintentional Y37.47-●
  rubber bullets Y37.41-●
  shrapnel NOS Y37.29-●
  suffocation —see Military operations,
    restriction of airways
  unconventional warfare NEC Y37.7X-●

Military operations (Continued)
  underwater blast NOS Y37.00-●
  warfare
    conventional NEC Y37.49-●
    unconventional NEC Y37.7X-●
  weapon of mass destruction [WMD]
    Y37.91-●
  weapons
    biological weapons Y37.6X-●
    chemical Y37.7X-●
    nuclear (effects of) Y37.50-●
      acute radiation exposure Y37.54-●
      blast pressure Y37.51-●
      direct blast Y37.51-●
      direct heat Y37.53-●
      fallout exposure Y37.54-●
      fireball Y37.53-●
      radiation
        ionizing (immediate exposure)
          Y37.54-●
        nuclear Y37.54-●
        thermal Y37.53-●
      secondary effects Y37.54-●
      specified NEC Y37.59-●
    of mass destruction [WMD] Y37.91-●
Misadventure(s) to patient(s) during surgical
  or medical care Y69
  contaminated medical or biological substance
    (blood, drug, fluid) Y64.9
    administered (by) NEC Y64.9
      immunization Y64.1
      infusion Y64.0
      injection Y64.1
      specified means NEC Y64.8
      transfusion Y64.0
      vaccination Y64.1
  excessive amount of blood or other fluid
    during transfusion or infusion Y63.0
  failure
    in dosage Y63.9
      electroshock therapy Y63.4
      inappropriate temperature (too hot or
        too cold) in local application and
        packing Y63.5
      infusion
        excessive amount of fluid Y63.0
        incorrect dilution of fluid Y63.1
      insulin-shock therapy Y63.4
      nonadministration of necessary drug or
        biological substance Y63.6
      overdose —see Table of Drugs and
        Chemicals
      radiation, in therapy Y63.2
      radiation
        overdose Y63.2
      specified procedure NEC Y63.8
      transfusion
        excessive amount of blood Y63.0
    mechanical, of instrument or apparatus
      (any) (during any procedure) Y65.8
    sterile precautions (during procedure)
      Y62.9
      aspiration of fluid or tissue (by puncture
        or catheterization, except heart)
        Y62.6
      biopsy (except needle aspiration)
        Y62.8
        needle (aspirating) Y62.6
      blood sampling Y62.6
      catheterization Y62.6
        heart Y62.5
      dialysis (kidney) Y62.2
      endoscopic examination Y62.4
      enema Y62.8
      immunization Y62.3
      infusion Y62.1
      injection Y62.3
      needle biopsy Y62.6
      paracentesis (abdominal) (thoracic)
        Y62.6
      perfusion Y62.2

Misadventure(s) to patient(s) during surgical or medical care *(Continued)*
  failure *(Continued)*
    sterile precautions *(Continued)*
      puncture (lumbar) Y62.6
      removal of catheter or packing Y62.8
      specified procedure NEC Y62.8
      surgical operation Y62.0
      transfusion Y62.1
      vaccination Y62.3
    suture or ligature during surgical procedure Y65.2
    to introduce or to remove tube or instrument —*see* Failure, to
  hemorrhage —*see* Index to Diseases and Injuries, Complication(s)
  inadvertent exposure of patient to radiation Y63.3
  inappropriate
    operation performed —*see* Inappropriate operation performed
    temperature (too hot or too cold) in local application or packing Y63.5

infusion —*see also* Misadventure, by type, infusion Y69
  excessive amount of fluid Y63.0
  incorrect dilution of fluid Y63.1
  wrong fluid Y65.1
mismatched blood in transfusion Y65.0
nonadministration of necessary drug or biological substance Y63.6
overdose —*see* Table of Drugs and Chemicals
  radiation (in therapy) Y63.2
perforation —*see* Index to Diseases and Injuries, Complication(s)
performance of inappropriate operation —*see* Inappropriate operation performed
puncture —*see* Index to Diseases and Injuries, Complication(s)
specified type NEC Y65.8
  failure
    suture or ligature during surgical operation Y65.2
    to introduce or to remove tube or instrument —*see* Failure, to
  infusion of wrong fluid Y65.1

specified type NEC *(Continued)*
  performance of inappropriate operation —*see* Inappropriate operation performed
  transfusion of mismatched blood Y65.0
  wrong
    fluid in infusion Y65.1
    placement of endotracheal tube during anesthetic procedure Y65.3
transfusion —*see* Misadventure, by type, transfusion
  excessive amount of blood Y63.0
  mismatched blood Y65.0
wrong
  drug given in error —*see* Table of Drugs and Chemicals
  fluid in infusion Y65.1
  placement of endotracheal tube during anesthetic procedure Y65.3
Mismatched blood in transfusion Y65.0
Motion sickness T75.3
Mountain sickness W94.11
Mudslide (of cataclysmic nature) —*see* Landslide
Murder (attempt) —*see* Assault

N

Nail
  contact with W45.0
  gun W29.4
  embedded in skin W45.0
Neglect (criminal) (homicidal intent) X58

Noise (causing injury) (pollution) W42.9
  supersonic W42.0
Nonadministration (of)
  drug or biological substance (necessary) Y63.6
  surgical and medical care Y66
Nosocomial condition Y95

O

Object
  falling
    from, in, on, hitting
      machinery —*see* Contact, with, by type of machine
    set in motion by
      accidental explosion or rupture of pressure vessel W38
      firearm —*see* Discharge, firearm, by type
      machine (ry) —*see* Contact, with, by type of machine
Overdose (drug) —*see* Table of Drugs and Chemicals
  radiation Y63.2

Overexertion X50.9
  from
    prolonged static or awkward postures X50.1
    repetitive movements X50.3
    specified strenuous movements or postures NEC X50.9
    strenuous movement or load X50.0
Overexposure (accidental) (to)
  cold —*see also* Exposure, cold X31
    due to man-made conditions —*see* Exposure, cold, man-made
  heat —*see also* Heat X30
  radiation —*see* Radiation
  radioactivity W88.0
  sun (sunburn) X32

Overexposure *(Continued)*
  weather NEC —*see* Forces of nature
  wind NEC —*see* Forces of nature
Overheated —*see* Heat
Overturning (accidental)
  machinery —*see* Contact, with, by type of machine
  transport vehicle NEC —*see also* Accident, transport V89.9
  watercraft (causing drowning, submersion) —*see also* Drowning, due to, accident to, watercraft, overturning
    causing injury except drowning or submersion —*see* Accident, watercraft, causing, injury NEC

▶ New   ⇒ Revised   ~~deleted~~ Deleted   • Use Additional Character(s)

M, N, & O

P

Parachute descent (voluntary) (without accident to aircraft) V97.29
    due to accident to aircraft —*see* Accident, transport, aircraft
Pecked by bird W61.99
Perforation during medical or surgical treatment as misadventure —*see* Index to Diseases and Injuries, Complication(s)
Perpetrator, perpetration, of assault, maltreatment and neglect (by) Y07.9
    boyfriend Y07.03
    brother Y07.410
        stepbrother Y07.435
    coach Y07.53
    cousin
        female Y07.491
        male Y07.490
    daycare provider Y07.519
        at-home
            adult care Y07.512
            childcare Y07.510
        care center
            adult care Y07.513
            childcare Y07.511
    family member NEC Y07.499
    father Y07.11
        adoptive Y07.13
        foster Y07.420
        stepfather Y07.430
    foster father Y07.420
    foster mother Y07.421
    girl friend Y07.04
    healthcare provider Y07.529
        mental health Y07.521
        specified NEC Y07.528
    husband Y07.01
    instructor Y07.53
    mother Y07.12
        adoptive Y07.14
        foster Y07.421
        stepmother Y07.433
    nonfamily member Y07.50
        specified NEC Y07.59
    nurse Y07.528
    occupational therapist Y07.528
    partner of parent
        female Y07.434
        male Y07.432
    physical therapist Y07.528
    sister Y07.411
    speech therapist Y07.528
    stepbrother Y07.435
    stepfather Y07.430
    stepmother Y07.433
    stepsister Y07.436
    teacher Y07.53
    wife Y07.02
Piercing —*see* Contact, with, by type of object or machine
Pinched
    between objects (moving) (stationary and moving) W23.0
        stationary W23.1
Pinned under machine (ry) —*see* Contact, with, by type of machine
Place of occurrence Y92.9
    abandoned house Y92.89
    airplane Y92.813
    airport Y92.520
    ambulatory health services establishment NEC Y92.538
    ambulatory surgery center Y92.530
    amusement park Y92.831
    apartment (co-op) —*see* Place of occurrence, residence, apartment
    assembly hall Y92.29
    bank Y92.510
    barn Y92.71
    baseball field Y92.320

Place of occurrence (*Continued*)
    basketball court Y92.310
    beach Y92.832
    boarding house —*see* Place of occurrence, residence, boarding house
    boat Y92.814
    bowling alley Y92.39
    bridge Y92.89
    building under construction Y92.61
    bus Y92.811
        station Y92.521
    cafe Y92.511
    campsite Y92.833
    campus —*see* Place of occurrence, school
    canal Y92.89
    car Y92.810
    casino Y92.59
    children's home —*see* Place of occurrence, residence, institutional, orphanage
    church Y92.22
    cinema Y92.26
    clubhouse Y92.29
    coal pit Y92.64
    college (community) Y92.214
    condominium —*see* Place of occurrence, residence, apartment
    construction area —*see* Place of occurrence, industrial and construction area
    convalescent home —*see* Place of occurrence, residence, institutional, nursing home
    court-house Y92.240
    cricket ground Y92.328
    cultural building Y92.258
        art gallery Y92.250
        museum Y92.251
        music hall Y92.252
        opera house Y92.253
        specified NEC Y92.258
        theater Y92.254
    dancehall Y92.252
    day nursery Y92.210
    dentist office Y92.531
    derelict house Y92.89
    desert Y92.820
    dock NOS Y92.89
    dockyard Y92.62
    doctor's office Y92.531
    dormitory —*see* Place of occurrence, residence, institutional, school dormitory
    dry dock Y92.62
    factory (building) (premises) Y92.63
    farm (land under cultivation) (outbuildings) Y92.79
        barn Y92.71
        chicken coop Y92.72
        field Y92.73
        hen house Y92.72
        house —*see* Place of occurrence, residence, house
        orchard Y92.74
        specified NEC Y92.79
    football field Y92.321
    forest Y92.821
    freeway Y92.411
    gallery Y92.250
    garage (commercial) Y92.59
        boarding house Y92.044
        military base Y92.135
        mobile home Y92.025
        nursing home Y92.124
        orphanage Y92.114
        private house Y92.015
        reform school Y92.155
    gas station Y92.524
    gasworks Y92.69
    golf course Y92.39
    gravel pit Y92.64
    grocery Y92.512
    gymnasium Y92.39
    handball court Y92.318
    harbor Y92.89

Place of occurrence (*Continued*)
    harness racing course Y92.39
    healthcare provider office Y92.531
    highway (interstate) Y92.411
    hill Y92.828
    hockey rink Y92.330
    home —*see* Place of occurrence, residence
    hospice —*see* Place of occurrence, residence, institutional, nursing home
    hospital Y92.239
        cafeteria Y92.233
        corridor Y92.232
        operating room Y92.234
        patient
            bathroom Y92.231
            room Y92.230
        specified NEC Y92.238
    hotel Y92.59
    house —*see also* Place of occurrence, residence
        abandoned Y92.89
        under construction Y92.61
    industrial and construction area (yard) Y92.69
        building under construction Y92.61
        dock Y92.62
        dry dock Y92.62
        factory Y92.63
        gasworks Y92.69
        mine Y92.64
        oil rig Y92.65
        pit Y92.64
        power station Y92.69
        shipyard Y92.62
        specified NEC Y92.69
        tunnel under construction Y92.69
        workshop Y92.69
    kindergarten Y92.211
    lacrosse field Y92.328
    lake Y92.828
    library Y92.241
    mall Y92.59
    market Y92.512
    marsh Y92.828
    military
        base —*see* Place of occurrence, residence, institutional, military base
        training ground Y92.84
    mine Y92.64
    mosque Y92.22
    motel Y92.59
    motorway (interstate) Y92.411
    mountain Y92.828
    movie-house Y92.26
    museum Y92.251
    music-hall Y92.252
    not applicable Y92.9
    nuclear power station Y92.69
    nursing home —*see* Place of occurrence, residence, institutional, nursing home
    office building Y92.59
    offshore installation Y92.65
    oil rig Y92.65
    old people's home —*see* Place of occurrence, residence, institutional, specified NEC
    opera-house Y92.253
    orphanage —*see* Place of occurrence, residence, institutional, orphanage
    outpatient surgery center Y92.530
    park (public) Y92.830
        amusement Y92.831
    parking garage Y92.89
        lot Y92.481
    pavement Y92.480
    physician office Y92.531
    polo field Y92.328
    pond Y92.828
    post office Y92.242
    power station Y92.69
    prairie Y92.828
    prison —*see* Place of occurrence, residence, institutional, prison

P

▶ New   ⇒ Revised   ~~deleted~~ Deleted   ● Use Additional Character(s)   637

Place of occurrence (Continued)
  public
    administration building Y92.248
      city hall Y92.243
      courthouse Y92.240
      library Y92.241
      post office Y92.242
      specified NEC Y92.248
    building NEC Y92.29
    hall Y92.29
    place NOS Y92.89
  race course Y92.39
  radio station Y92.59
  railway line (bridge) Y92.85
  ranch (outbuildings) —see Place of
    occurrence, farm
  recreation area Y92.838
    amusement park Y92.831
    beach Y92.832
    campsite Y92.833
    park (public) Y92.830
    seashore Y92.832
    specified NEC Y92.838
  reform school —see Place of occurrence,
    residence, institutional, reform school
  religious institution Y92.22
  residence (non-institutional) (private) Y92.009
    apartment Y92.039
      bathroom Y92.031
      bedroom Y92.032
      kitchen Y92.030
      specified NEC Y92.038
    bathroom Y92.002
    bedroom Y92.003
    boarding house Y92.049
      bathroom Y92.041
      bedroom Y92.042
      driveway Y92.043
      garage Y92.044
      garden Y92.046
      kitchen Y92.040
      specified NEC Y92.048
      swimming pool Y92.045
      yard Y92.046
    dining room Y92.001
    garden Y92.007
    home Y92.009
    house, single family Y92.019
      bathroom Y92.012
      bedroom Y92.013
      dining room Y92.011
      driveway Y92.014
      garage Y92.015
      garden Y92.017
      kitchen Y92.010
      specified NEC Y92.018
      swimming pool Y92.016
      yard Y92.017
    institutional Y92.10
      children's home —see Place of
        occurrence, residence, institutional,
        orphanage
      hospice —see Place of occurrence,
        residence, institutional, nursing
        home
      military base Y92.139
        barracks Y92.133
        garage Y92.135
        garden Y92.137
        kitchen Y92.130
        mess hall Y92.131
        specified NEC Y92.138
        swimming pool Y92.136
        yard Y92.137
      nursing home Y92.129
        bathroom Y92.121
        bedroom Y92.122
        driveway Y92.123
        garage Y92.124
        garden Y92.126
        kitchen Y92.120

Place of occurrence (Continued)
  residence (Continued)
    institutional (Continued)
      nursing home (Continued)
        specified NEC Y92.128
        swimming pool Y92.125
        yard Y92.126
      orphanage Y92.119
        bathroom Y92.111
        bedroom Y92.112
        driveway Y92.113
        garage Y92.114
        garden Y92.116
        kitchen Y92.110
        specified NEC Y92.118
        swimming pool Y92.115
        yard Y92.116
      prison Y92.149
        bathroom Y92.142
        cell Y92.143
        courtyard Y92.147
        dining room Y92.141
        kitchen Y92.140
        specified NEC Y92.148
        swimming pool Y92.146
      reform school Y92.159
        bathroom Y92.152
        bedroom Y92.153
        dining room Y92.151
        driveway Y92.154
        garage Y92.155
        garden Y92.157
        kitchen Y92.150
        specified NEC Y92.158
        swimming pool Y92.156
        yard Y92.157
      school dormitory Y92.169
        bathroom Y92.162
        bedroom Y92.163
        dining room Y92.161
        kitchen Y92.160
        specified NEC Y92.168
      specified NEC Y92.199
        bathroom Y92.192
        bedroom Y92.193
        dining room Y92.191
        driveway Y92.194
        garage Y92.195
        garden Y92.197
        kitchen Y92.190
        specified NEC Y92.198
        swimming pool Y92.196
        yard Y92.197
    kitchen Y92.000
    mobile home Y92.029
      bathroom Y92.022
      bedroom Y92.023
      dining room Y92.021
      driveway Y92.024
      garage Y92.025
      garden Y92.027
      kitchen Y92.020
      specified NEC Y92.028
      swimming pool Y92.026
      yard Y92.027
    specified place in residence NEC Y92.008
    specified residence type NEC Y92.099
      bathroom Y92.091
      bedroom Y92.092
      driveway Y92.093
      garage Y92.094
      garden Y92.096
      kitchen Y92.090
      specified NEC Y92.098
      swimming pool Y92.095
      yard Y92.096
  restaurant Y92.511
  riding school Y92.39
  river Y92.828
  road Y92.410
  rodeo ring Y92.39

Place of occurrence (Continued)
  rugby field Y92.328
  same day surgery center Y92.530
  sand pit Y92.64
  school (private) (public) (state) Y92.219
    college Y92.214
    daycare center Y92.210
    elementary school Y92.211
    high school Y92.213
    kindergarten Y92.211
    middle school Y92.212
    specified NEC Y92.218
    trace school Y92.215
    university Y92.214
    vocational school Y92.215
  sea (shore) Y92.832
  senior citizen center Y92.29
  service area
    airport Y92.520
    bus station Y92.521
    gas station Y92.524
    highway rest stop Y92.523
    railway station Y92.522
  shipyard Y92.62
  shop(commercial) Y92.513
  sidewalk Y92.480
  silo Y92.79
  skating rink (roller) Y92.331
    ice Y92.330
  slaughter house Y92.86
  soccer field Y92.322
  specified place NEC Y92.89
  sports area Y92.39
    athletic
      court Y92.318
        basketball Y92.310
        specified NEC Y92.318
        squash Y92.311
        tennis Y92.312
      field Y92.328
        baseball Y92.320
        cricket ground Y92.328
        football Y92.321
        hockey Y92.328
        soccer Y92.322
        specified NEC Y92.328
    golf course Y92.39
    gymnasium Y92.39
    riding school Y92.39
    skating rink (roller) Y92.331
      ice Y92.330
    stadium Y92.39
    swimming pool Y92.34
  squash court Y92.311
  stadium Y92.39
  steeplechasing course Y92.39
  store Y92.512
  stream Y92.828
  street and highway Y92.410
    bike path Y92.482
    freeway Y92.411
    highway ramp Y92.415
    interstate highway Y92.411
    local residential or business street
      Y92.414
    motorway Y92.411
    parking lot Y92.481
    parkway Y92.412
    sidewalk Y92.480
    specified NEC Y92.488
    state road Y92.413
  subway car Y92.816
  supermarket Y92.512
  swamp Y92.828
  swimming pool (public) Y92.34
    private (at) Y92.095
      boarding house Y92.045
      military base Y92.136
      mobile home Y92.026
      nursing home Y92.125
      orphanage Y92.115

▶ New   ⇛ Revised   ~~deleted~~ Deleted   ● Use Additional Character(s)

Place of occurrence (Continued)
  swimming pool (Continued)
    private (Continued)
      prison Y92.146
      reform school Y92.156
      single family residence Y92.016
  synagogue Y92.22
  television station Y92.59
  tennis court Y92.312
  theater Y92.254
  trade area Y92.59
    bank Y92.510
    cafe Y92.511
    casino Y92.59
    garage Y92.59
    hotel Y92.59
    market Y92.512
    office building Y92.59
    radio station Y92.59
    restaurant Y92.511
    shop Y92.513
    shopping mall Y92.59
    store Y92.512
    supermarket Y92.512
    television station Y92.59
    warehouse Y92.59
  trailer park, residential —see Place of occurrence, residence, mobile home
  trailer site NOS Y92.89
  train Y92.815
    station Y92.522
  truck Y92.812
  tunnel under construction Y92. 69
  university Y92.214
  urgent (health) care center Y92.532
  vehicle (transport) Y92.818
    airplane Y92.813
    boat Y92.814
    bus Y92.811
    car Y92.810
    specified NEC Y92.818
    subway car Y92.816
    train Y92.815
    truck Y92.812
  warehouse Y92.59
  water reservoir Y92.89
  wilderness area Y92.828
    desert Y92.820
    forest Y92.821
    marsh Y92.828
    mountain Y92.828
    prairie Y92.828
    specified NEC Y92.828
    swamp Y92.828
  workshop Y92.69
  yard, private Y92.096
    boarding house Y92.046
    mobile home Y92.027
    single family house Y92.017

Place of occurrence (Continued)
  youth center Y92.29
  zoo (zoological garden) Y92.834
Plumbism —see Table of Drugs and Chemicals, lead
Poisoning (accidental) (by) —see also Table of Drugs and Chemicals
  by plant, thorns, spines, sharp leaves or other mechanisms NEC X58
  carbon monoxide
    generated by
      motor vehicle —see Accident, transport
      watercraft (in transit) (not in transit) V93.89
        ferry boat V93.81
        fishing boat V93.82
        jet skis V93.83
        liner V93.81
        merchant ship V93.80
        passenger ship V93.81
        powered craft NEC V93.83
  caused by injection of poisons into skin by plant thorns, spines, sharp leaves X58
    marine or sea plants (venomous) X58
  exhaust gas
    generated by
      motor vehicle —see Accident, transport
      watercraft (in transit) (not in transit) V93.89
        ferry boat V93.81
        fishing boat V93.82
        jet skis V93.83
        liner V93.81
        merchant ship V93.80
        passenger ship V93.81
        powered craft NEC V93.83
  fumes or smoke due to
    explosion —see also Explosion W40.9
    fire —see Exposure, fire
    ignition —see Ignition
  gas
    in legal intervention —see Legal, intervention, gas
    legal execution —see Legal, intervention, gas
  in war operations —see War operations
  legal
    execution —see Legal, intervention, gas
    intervention
      by gas —see Legal, intervention, gas
      other specified means —see Legal, intervention, specified means NEC
Powder burn (by) (from)
  airgun W34.110
  BB gun W34.110
  firearm NEC W34.19
  gas, air or spring-operated gun NEC W34.118
  handgun W32.1
  hunting rifle W33.12

Powder burn (Continued)
  larger firearm W33.10
    specified NEC W33.19
  machine gun W33.13
  paintball gun W34.111
  pellet gun W34.110
  shotgun W33.11
  Very pistol [flare] W34.19
Premature cessation (of) surgical and medical care Y66
Privation (food) (water) X58
Procedure (operation)
  correct, on wrong side or body part (wrong side) (wrong site) Y65.53
  intended for another patient done on wrong patient Y65.52
  performed on patient not scheduled for surgery Y65.52
  performed on wrong patient Y65.52
  wrong, performed on correct patient Y65.51
Prolonged
  sitting in transport vehicle —see Travel, by type of vehicle
  stay in
    high altitude as cause of anoxia, barodontalgia, barotitis or hypoxia W94.11
    weightless environment X52
Pulling, excessive —see also Overexertion X50.9
Puncture, puncturing —see also Contact, with, by type of object or machine
  by
    plant thorns, spines, sharp leaves or other mechanisms NEC W60
  during medical or surgical treatment as misadventure —see Index to Diseases and Injuries, Complication(s)
Pushed, pushing (accidental) (injury in)
  by other person(s) (accidental) W51
    with fall W03
      due to ice or snow W00.0
    as, or caused by, a crowd or human stampede (with fall) W52
    before moving object NEC Y02.8
      motor vehicle Y02.0
      subway train Y02.1
      train Y02.1
  from
    high place NEC
      in accidental circumstances W17.89
      stated as
        intentional, homicide (attempt) Y01
        undetermined whether accidental or intentional Y30
    transport vehicle NEC —see also Accident, transport V89.9
      stated as
        intentional, homicide (attempt) Y08.89
  overexertion X50.9

P

R

Radiation (exposure to)
  arc lamps W89.Ø
  atomic power plant (malfunction) NEC
    W88.1
  complication of or abnormal reaction to
    medical radiotherapy Y84.2
  electromagnetic, ionizing W88.Ø
  gamma rays W88.1
  in
    war operations (from or following
      nuclear explosion) —see also War
      operations
  inadvertent exposure of patient (receiving
    test or therapy) Y63.3
  infrared (heaters and lamps) W90.1
    excessive heat from W92
  ionized, ionizing (particles, artificially
    accelerated)
    radioisotopes W88.1
    specified NEC W88.8
    x-rays W88.Ø
  isotopes, radioactive —see Radiation,
    radioactive isotopes
  laser(s) W90.2
    in war operations —see War operations
    misadventure in medical care Y63.2
  light sources (man-made visible and
    ultraviolet) W89.9
    natural X32
    specified NEC W89.8
    tanning bed W89.1
    welding light W89.Ø
  man-made visible light W89.9
    specified NEC W89.8
    tanning bed W89.1
    welding light W89.Ø
  microwave W90.8
  misadventure in medical or surgical
    procedure Y63.2

Radiation (Continued)
  natural NEC X39.Ø8
    radon X39.Ø1
  overdose (in medical or surgical procedure)
    Y63.2
  radar W90.Ø
  radioactive isotopes (any) W88.1
    atomic power plant malfunction W88.1
    misadventure in medical or surgical
      treatment Y63.2
  radiofrequency W90.Ø
  radium NEC W88.1
  sun X32
  ultraviolet (light) (man-made) W89.9
    natural X32
    specified NEC W89.8
    tanning bed W89.1
    welding light W89.Ø
  welding arc, torch, or light W89.Ø
    excessive heat from W92
  x-rays (hard) (soft) W88.Ø
Range disease W94.11
Rape (attempted) T74.2-●
Rat bite W53.11
Reaching (prolonged) (static) X5Ø.1
Reaction, abnormal to medical procedure —see
  also Complication of or following, by type
  of procedure Y84.9
  with misadventure —see Misadventure
  biologicals —see Table of Drugs and
    Chemicals
  drugs —see Table of Drugs and Chemicals
  vaccine —see Table of Drugs and
    Chemicals
Recoil
  airgun W34.11Ø
  BB gun W34.11Ø
  firearm NEC W34.19
  gas, air or spring-operated gun NEC W34.118

Recoil (Continued)
  handgun W32.1
  hunting rifle W33.12
  larger firearm W33.1Ø
    specified NEC W33.19
  machine gun W33.13
  paintball gun W34.111
  pellet W34.11Ø
  shotgun W33.11
  Very pistol [flare] W34.19
Reduction in
  atmospheric pressure —see Air, pressure,
    change
Rock falling on or hitting (accidentally)
    (person) W2Ø.8
  in cave-in W2Ø.Ø
Run over (accidentally) (by)
  animal (not being ridden) NEC W55.89
  machinery —see Contact, with, by specified
    type of machine
  transport vehicle NEC —see also Accident,
    transport V09.9
    intentional homicide (attempt) Y03.0
    motor NEC V09.20
      intentional homicide (attempt) Y03.0
Running
  before moving object X81.8
    motor vehicle X81.Ø
Running off, away
  animal (being ridden) —see also Accident,
    transport V8Ø.918
    not being ridden W55.89
  animal-drawn vehicle NEC —see also
    Accident, transport V8Ø.928
  highway, road(way), street
    transport vehicle NEC —see also Accident,
      transport V89.9
Rupture pressurized devices —see Explosion,
  by type of device

▶ New   ⇒ Revised   ~~deleted~~ Deleted   ● Use Additional Character(s)

S

Saturnism —see Table of Drugs and Chemicals, lead
Scald, scalding (accidental) (by) (from) (in) X19
air (hot) X14.1
gases (hot) X14.1
homicide (attempt) —see Assault, burning, hot object
inflicted by other person
stated as intentional, homicide (attempt) — see Assault, burning, hot object
liquid (boiling) (hot) NEC X12
stated as undetermined whether accidental or intentional Y27.2
suicide (attempt) X77.2
local application of externally applied substance in medical or surgical care Y63.5
metal (molten) (liquid) (hot) NEC X18
self-inflicted X77.9
stated as undetermined whether accidental or intentional Y27.8
steam X13.1
assault X98.0
stated as undetermined whether accidental or intentional Y27.0
suicide (attempt) X77.0
suicide (attempt) X77.9
vapor (hot) X13.1
assault X98.0
stated as undetermined whether accidental or intentional Y27.0
suicide (attempt) X77.0
Scratched by
cat W55.03
person(s) (accidentally) W50.4
with intent to injure or kill Y04.0
as, or caused by, a crowd or human stampede (with fall) W52
assault Y04.0
homicide (attempt) Y04.0
in
fight Y04.0
legal intervention
injuring
bystander Y35.892
law enforcement personnel Y35.891
suspect Y35.893
Seasickness T75.3
Self-harm NEC —see also External cause by type, undetermined whether accidental or intentional
intentional —see Suicide
poisoning NEC —see Table of drugs and biologicals, accident
Self-inflicted (injury) NEC —see also External cause by type, undetermined whether accidental or intentional
intentional —see Suicide
poisoning NEC —see Table of drugs and biologicals, accident
Sequelae (of)
accident NEC —see W00-X58 with 7th character S
assault (homicidal) (any means) —see X92-Y08 with 7th character S
homicide, attempt (any means) —see X92-Y08 with 7th character S
injury undetermined whether accidentally or purposely inflicted —see Y21-Y33 with 7th character S
intentional self-harm (classifiable to X71-X83) —see X71-X83 with 7th character S
legal intervention (see with 7th character S Y35)
motor vehicle accident —see V00-V99 with 7th character S
suicide, attempt (any means) —see X71-X83 with 7th character S

Sequelae (Continued)
transport accident —see V00-V99 with 7th character S
war operations —see War operations
Shock
electric —see Exposure, electric current
from electric appliance (any) (faulty) W86.8
domestic W86.0
suicide (attempt) X83.1
Shooting, shot (accidental (ly)) —see also Discharge, firearm, by type
herself or himself —see Discharge, firearm by type, self-inflicted
homicide (attempt) —see Discharge, firearm by type, homicide
in war operations —see War operations
inflicted by other person —see Discharge, firearm by type, homicide
accidental —see Discharge, firearm, by type of firearm
legal
execution —see Legal, intervention, firearm
intervention —see Legal, intervention, firearm
self-inflicted —see Discharge, firearm by type, suicide
accidental —see Discharge, firearm, by type of firearm
suicide (attempt) —see Discharge, firearm by type, suicide
Shoving (accidentally) by other person —see Pushed, by other person
Sickness
alpine W94.11
motion —see Motion
mountain W94.11
Sinking (accidental)
watercraft (causing drowning, submersion) —see also Drowning, due to, accident to, watercraft, sinking
causing injury except drowning or submersion —see Accident, watercraft, causing, injury NEC
Siriasis X32
Sitting (prolonged) (static) X50.1
Slashed wrists —see Cut, self-inflicted
Slipping (accidental) (on same level) (with fall) W01.0
without fall W18.40
due to
specified NEC W18.49
stepping from one level to another W18.43
stepping into hole or opening W18.42
stepping on object W18.41
on
ice W00.0
with skates —see Accident, transport, pedestrian, conveyance
mud W01.0
oil W01.0
snow W00.0
with skis —see Accident, transport, pedestrian, conveyance
surface (slippery) (wet) NEC W01.0
Sliver, wood, contact with W45.8
Smoldering (due to fire) —see Exposure, fire
Sodomy (attempted) by force T74.2-●
Sound waves (causing injury) W42.9
supersonic W42.0
Splinter, contact with W45.8
Stab, stabbing —see Cut
Standing (prolonged) (static) X50.1
Starvation X58
Status of external cause Y99.9
child assisting in compensated work for family Y99.8
civilian activity done for financial or other compensation Y99.0
civilian activity done for income or pay Y99.0

Status of external cause (Continued)
family member assisting in compensated work for other family member Y99.8
hobby not done for income Y99.8
leisure activity Y99.8
military activity Y99.1
off-duty activity of military personnel Y99.8
recreation or sport not for income or while a student Y99.8
specified NEC Y99.8
student activity Y99.8
volunteer activity Y99.2
Stepped on
by
animal (not being ridden) NEC W55.89
crowd or human stampede W52
person W50.0
Stepping on
object W22.8
with fall W18.31
sports equipment W21.9
stationary W22.09
sports equipment W21.89
person W51
by crowd or human stampede W52
sports equipment W21.9
Sting
arthropod, nonvenomous W57
insect, nonvenomous W57
Storm (cataclysmic) —see Forces of nature, cataclysmic storm
Straining, excessive —see also Overexertion X50.9
Strangling —see Strangulation
Strangulation (accidental) —see category T71
Strenuous movements —see also Overexertion X50.9
Striking against
airbag (automobile) W22.10
driver side W22.11
front passenger side W22.12
specified NEC W22.19
bottom when
diving or jumping into water (in) W16.822
causing drowning W16.821
from boat W16.722
causing drowning W16.721
natural body W16.622
causing drowning W16.821
swimming pool W16.522
causing drowning W16.521
falling into water (in) W16.322
causing drowning W16.321
fountain —see Striking against, bottom when, falling into water, specified NEC
natural body W16.122
causing drowning W16.121
reservoir —see Striking against, bottom when, falling into water, specified NEC
specified NEC W16.322
causing drowning W16.321
swimming pool W16.022
causing drowning W16.021
diving board (swimming-pool) W21.4
object W22.8
with
drowning or submersion —see Drowning
fall —see Fall, due to, bumping against, object
caused by crowd or human stampede (with fall) W52
furniture W22.03
lamppost W22.02
sports equipment W21.9
stationary W22.09
sports equipment W21.89
wall W22.01

Striking against (*Continued*)
  person(s) W51
    with fall W03
      due to ice or snow W00.0
    as, or caused by, a crowd or human
      stampede (with fall) W52
    assault Y04.2
    homicide (attempt) Y04.2
  sports equipment W21.9
  wall (when) W22.01
    diving or jumping into water (in) W16.832
      causing drowning W16.831
      swimming pool W16.532
        causing drowning W16.531
    falling into water (in) W16.332
      causing drowning W16.331
      fountain —*see* Striking against, wall
        when, falling into water, specified
        NEC
      natural body W16.132
        causing drowning W16.131
      reservoir —*see* Striking against, wall
        when, falling into water, specified
        NEC
      specified NEC W16.332
        causing drowning W16.331
      swimming pool W16.032
        causing drowning W16.031
    swimming pool (when) W22.042
      causing drowning W22.041
      diving or jumping into water W16.532
        causing drowning W16.531
      falling into water W16.032
        causing drowning W16.031

Struck (accidentally) **by**
  airbag (automobile) W22.10
    driver side W22.11
    front passenger side W22.12
    specified NEC W22.19
  alligator W58.02
  animal (not being ridden) NEC W55.89
  avalanche —*see* Landslide
  ball (hit) (thrown) W21.00
    assault Y08.09
    baseball W21.03
    basketball W21.05
    football W21.01
    golf ball W21.04
    football W21.01
    soccer W21.02
    softball W21.07
    specified NEC W21.09
    volleyball W21.06
  bat or racquet
    baseball bat W21.11
      assault Y08.02
    golf club W21.13
      assault Y08.09
    specified NEC W21.19
      assault Y08.09
    tennis racquet W21.12
      assault Y08.09
  bullet —*see also* Discharge, firearm by type
    in war operations —*see* War operations
  crocodile W58.12
  dog W54.1
  flare, Very pistol —*see* Discharge, firearm
    NEC
  hailstones X39.8
  hockey (ice)
    field
      puck W21.221
      stick W21.211
    puck W21.220
    stick W21.210
      assault Y08.01
  landslide —*see* Landslide
  law-enforcement agent (on duty) —*see* Legal,
    intervention, manhandling
    with blunt object —*see* Legal, intervention,
      blunt object

Struck by (*Continued*)
  lightning —*see* subcategory T75.0
    causing fire —*see* Exposure, fire
  machine —*see* Contact, with, by type of
    machine
  mammal NEC W55.89
    marine W56.32
  marine animal W56.82
  missile
    firearm —*see* Discharge, firearm by type
    in war operations —*see* War operations,
      missile
  object W22.8
    blunt W22.8
      assault Y00
      suicide (attempt) X79
      undetermined whether accidental or
        intentional Y29
    falling W20.8
      from, in, on
        building W20.1
          burning (uncontrolled fire) X00.4
        cataclysmic
          earth surface movement NEC —*see*
            Landslide
          storm —*see* Forces of nature,
            cataclysmic storm
        cave-in W20.0
        earthquake X34
        machine (in operation) —*see* Contact,
          with, by type of machine
        structure W20.1
          burning X00.4
        transport vehicle (in motion) —*see*
          Accident, transport, by type of
          vehicle
        watercraft V93.49
          due to
            accident to craft V91.39
              powered craft V91.33
                ferry boat V91.31
                fishing boat V91.32
                jet ski V91.33
                liner V91.31
                merchant ship V91.30
                passenger ship V91.31
             unpowered craft V91.38
                canoe V91.35
                inflatable V91.36
                kayak V91.35
                sailboat V91.34
                surf-board V91.38
                windsurfer V91.38
            powered craft V93.43
              ferry boat V93.41
              fishing boat V93.42
              jet ski V93.43
              liner V93.41
              merchant ship V93.40
              passenger ship V93.41
            unpowered craft V93.48
              sailboat V93.44
              surf-board V93.48
              windsurfer V93.48
    moving NEC W20.8
    projected W20.8
      assault Y00
      in sports W21.9
        assault Y08.09
        ball W21.00
          baseball W21.03
          basketball W21.05
          football W21.01
          golf ball W21.04
          soccer W21.02
          softball W21.07
          specified NEC W21.09
          volleyball W21.06
        bat or racquet
          baseball bat W21.11
            assault Y08.02

Struck by (*Continued*)
  object (*Continued*)
    projected (*Continued*)
      in sports (*Continued*)
        bat or racquet (*Continued*)
          golf club W21.13
            assault Y08.09-●
          specified NEC W21.19
            assault Y08.09
          tennis racquet W21.12
            assault Y08.09
        hockey (ice)
          field
            puck W21.221
            stick W21.211
          puck W21.220
          stick W21.210
            assault Y08.01
        specified NEC W21.89
    set in motion by explosion —*see* Explosion
    thrown W20.8
      assault Y00
      in sports W21.9
        assault Y08.09
        ball W21.00
          baseball W21.03
          basketball W21.05
          football W21.01
          golf ball W21.04
          soccer W21.02
          soft ball W21.07
          specified NEC W21.09
          volleyball W21.06
        bat or racquet
          baseball bat W21.11
            assault Y08.02
          golf club W21.13
            assault Y08.09
          specified NEC W21.19
            assault Y08.09
          tennis racquet W21.12
            assault Y08.09
        hockey (ice)
          field
            puck W21.221
            stick W21.211
          puck W21.220
          stick W21.210
            assault Y08.01
        specified NEC W21.89
  other person(s) W50.0
    with
      blunt object W22.8
        intentional, homicide (attempt) Y00
        sports equipment W21.9
        undetermined whether accidental or
          intentional Y29
      fall W03
        due to ice or snow W00.0
      as, or caused by, a crowd or human
        stampede (with fall) W52
      assault Y04.2
      homicide (attempt) Y04.2
      in legal intervention
        injuring
          bystander Y35.812
          law enforcement personnel Y35.811
          suspect Y35.813
          unspecified person Y35.819
      sports equipment W21.9
  police (on duty) —*see* Legal, intervention,
    manhandling
    with blunt object —*see* Legal, intervention,
      blunt object
  sports equipment W21.9
    assault Y08.09
    ball W21.00
      baseball W21.03
      basketball W21.05
      football W21.01
      golf ball W21.04
      soccer W21.02

▶ New   ⟹ Revised   ~~deleted~~ Deleted   ● Use Additional Character(s)

Struck by *(Continued)*
  sports equipment *(Continued)*
    ball *(Continued)*
      soft ball W21.07
      specified NEC W21.09
      volleyball W21.06
    bat or racquet
      baseball bat W21.11
        assault Y08.02
      golf club W21.13
        assault Y08.09
      specified NEC W21.19
      tennis racquet W21.12
        assault Y08.09
    cleats (shoe) W21.31
    foot wear NEC W21.39
    football helmet W21.81
    hockey (ice)
      field
        puck W21.221
        stick W21.211
      puck W21.220
      stick W21.210
        assault Y08.01
    skate blades W21.32
    specified NEC W21.89
      assault Y08.09
  thunderbolt —*see* subcategory
    T75.0
    causing fire —*see* Exposure, fire
  transport vehicle NEC —*see also* Accident,
    transport V09.9
    intentional, homicide (attempt) Y03.0
    motor NEC —*see also* Accident, transport
      V09.20
      homicide Y03.0
  vehicle (transport) NEC —*see* Accident,
    transport, by type of vehicle
    stationary (falling from jack,
      hydraulic lift, ramp)
      W20.8
Stumbling
  without fall W18.40
    due to
      specified NEC W18.49
      stepping from one level to another
        W18.43
      stepping into hole or opening W18.42
      stepping on object W18.41
  over
    animal NEC W01.0
      with fall W18.09
    carpet, rug or (small) object W22.8
      with fall W18.09
    person W51
      with fall W03
        due to ice or snow W00.0

Submersion (accidental) —*see* Drowning
Suffocation (accidental) (by external means)
  (by pressure) (mechanical) —*see also*
    category T71
  due to, by
    avalanche —*see* Landslide
    explosion —*see* Explosion
    fire —*see* Exposure, fire
    food, any type (aspiration) (ingestion)
      (inhalation) —*see* categories T17 and
      T18
    ignition —*see* Ignition
    landslide —*see* Landslide
    machine (ry) —*see* Contact, with, by type
      of machine
    vomitus (aspiration) (inhalation)
      T17.81-●
  in
    burning building X00.8
Suicide, suicidal (attempted) (by) X83.8
  blunt object X79
  burning, burns X76
    hot object X77.9
      fluid NEC X77.2
      household appliance X77.3
      specified NEC X77.8
      steam X77.0
      tap water X77.1
      vapors X77.0
  caustic substance —*see* Table of Drugs and
    Chemicals
  cold, extreme X83.2
  collision of motor vehicle with
    motor vehicle X82.0
    specified NEC X82.8
    train X82.1
    tree X82.2
  crashing of aircraft X83.0
  cut (any part of body) X78.9
  cutting or piercing instrument X78.9
    dagger X78.2
    glass X78.0
    knife X78.1
    specified NEC X78.8
    sword X78.2
  drowning (in) X71.9
    bathtub X71.0
    natural water X71.3
    specified NEC X71.8
    swimming pool X71.1
      following fall X71.2
  electrocution X83.1
  explosive(s) (material) X75
  fire, flames X76
  firearm X74.9
    airgun X74.01
    handgun X72

Suicide, suicidal *(Continued)*
  firearm *(Continued)*
    hunting rifle X73.1
    larger X73.9
      specified NEC X73.8
    machine gun X73.2
    shotgun X73.0
    specified NEC X74.8
  hanging X83.8
  hot object —*see* Suicide, burning, hot object
  jumping
    before moving object X81.8
      motor vehicle X81.0
      subway train X81.1
      train X81.1
    from high place X80
  late effect of attempt —*see* X71-X83 with 7th
    character S
  lying before moving object, train, vehicle X81.8
  poisoning —*see* Table of Drugs and
    Chemicals
  puncture (any part of body) —*see* Suicide,
    cutting or piercing instrument
  scald —*see* Suicide, burning, hot object
  sequelae of attempt —*see* X71-X83 with 7th
    character S
  sharp object (any) —*see* Suicide, cutting or
    piercing instrument
  shooting —*see* Suicide, firearm
  specified means NEC X83.8
  stab (any part of body) —*see* Suicide, cutting
    or piercing instrument
  steam, hot vapors X77.0
  strangulation X83.8
  submersion —*see* Suicide, drowning
  suffocation X83.8
  wound NEC X83.8
Sunstroke X32
Supersonic waves (causing injury) W42.0
Surgical procedure, complication of (delayed
  or as an abnormal reaction without
  mention of misadventure) —*see also*
  Complication of or following, by type of
  procedure
  due to or as a result of misadventure —*see*
    Misadventure
Swallowed, swallowing
  foreign body —*see* Foreign body, alimentary
    canal
  poison —*see* Table of Drugs and Chemicals
  substance
    caustic or corrosive —*see* Table of Drugs
      and Chemicals
    poisonous —*see* Table of Drugs and
      Chemicals

T

Tackle in sport W03
Terrorism (involving) Y38.80
  biological weapons Y38.6X-•
  chemical weapons Y38.7X-•
  conflagration Y38.3X-•
  drowning and submersion Y38.89-•
  explosion Y38.2X-•
    destruction of aircraft Y38.1X-•
    marine weapons Y38.0X-•
  fire Y38.3X-•
  firearms Y38.4X-•
  hot substances Y38.3X-•
  lasers Y38.89-•
  nuclear weapons Y38.5X-•
  piercing or stabbing instruments
    Y38.89-•
  secondary effects Y38.9X-•
  specified method NEC Y38.89-•
  suicide bomber Y38.81-•
Thirst X58
Threat to breathing
  aspiration —*see* Aspiration
  due to cave-in, falling earth or substance
    NEC —*see* category T71
Thrown (accidentally)
  against part (any) of or object in transport
    vehicle (in motion) NEC —*see also*
    Accident, transport

Thrown (*Continued*)
  from
    high place, homicide (attempt) Y01
    machinery —*see* Contact, with, by type of
      machine
    transport vehicle NEC —*see also* Accident,
      transport V89.9
  off —*see* Thrown, from
Thunderbolt —*see* subcategory T75.0
  causing fire —*see* Exposure, fire
Tidal wave (any injury) NEC —*see* Forces of
  nature, tidal wave
Took
  overdose (drug) —*see* Table of Drugs and
    Chemicals
  poison —*see* Table of Drugs and
    Chemicals
Tornado (any injury) X37.1
Torrential rain (any injury) X37.8
Torture X58
Trampled by animal NEC W55.89
Trapped (accidentally)
  between objects (moving) (stationary and
    moving) —*see* Caught
  by part (any) of
    motorcycle V29.88
    pedal cycle V19.88
    transport vehicle NEC —*see also* Accident,
      transport V89.9
Travel (effects) (sickness) T75.3

Tree falling on or hitting (accidentally)
  (person) W20.8
Tripping
  without fall W18.40
    due to
      specified NEC W18.49
      stepping from one level to another
        W18.43
      stepping into hole or opening
        W18.42
      stepping on object W18.41
  over
    animal W01.0
      with fall W01.0
    carpet, rug or (small) object W22.8
      with fall W18.09
    person W51
      with fall W03
        due to ice or snow W00.0
Twisted by person(s) (accidentally) W50.2
  with intent to injure or kill Y04.0
  as, or caused by, a crowd or human stampede
    (with fall) W52
  assault Y04.0
  homicide (attempt) Y04.0
  in
    fight Y04.0
    legal intervention —*see* Legal, intervention,
      manhandling
Twisting (prolonged) (static) X50.1

U

Underdosing of necessary drugs, medicaments
  or biological substances Y63.6
Undetermined intent (contact)
  (exposure)
  automobile collision Y32
  blunt object Y29
  drowning (submersion) (in) Y21.9
    bathtub Y21.0
      after fall Y21.1
    natural water (lake) (ocean) (pond) (river)
      (stream) Y21.4
    specified place NEC Y21.8
    swimming pool Y21.2
      after fall Y21.3
  explosive material Y25
  fall, jump or push from high place Y30
  falling, lying or running before moving object
    Y31
  fire Y26

Undetermined intent (*Continued*)
  firearm discharge Y24.9
    airgun (BB) (pellet) Y24.0
    handgun (pistol) (revolver)
      Y22
    hunting rifle Y23.1
    larger Y23.9
      hunting rifle Y23.1
      machine gun Y23.3
      military Y23.2
      shotgun Y23.0
      specified type NEC Y23.8
    machine gun Y23.3
    military Y23.2
    shotgun Y23.0
    specified type NEC Y24.8
    Very pistol Y24.8
  hot object Y27.9
    fluid NEC Y27.2
    household appliance Y27.3
    specified object NEC Y27.8

Undetermined intent (*Continued*)
  hot object (*Continued*)
    steam Y27.0
    tap water Y27.1
    vapor Y27.0
  jump, fall or push from high place Y30
  lying, falling or running before moving object
    Y31
  motor vehicle crash Y32
  push, fall or jump from high place Y30
  running, falling or lying before moving object
    Y31
  sharp object Y28.9
    dagger Y28.2
    glass Y28.0
    knife Y28.1
    specified object NEC Y28.8
    sword Y28.2
  smoke Y26
  specified event NEC Y33
Use of hand as hammer X50.3

V

Vibration (causing injury) W49.9
Victim (of)
  avalanche —*see* Landslide
  earth movements NEC —*see* Forces of nature,
    earth movement
  earthquake X34

Victim (*Continued*)
  flood —*see* Flood
  landslide —*see* Landslide
  lightning —*see* subcategory T75.0
    causing fire —*see* Exposure, fire
  storm (cataclysmic) NEC —*see* Forces of
    nature, cataclysmic storm
  volcanic eruption X35

Volcanic eruption (any injury) X35
Vomitus, gastric contents in air passages (with
  asphyxia, obstruction or
  suffocation) T17.81-•

▶ New   ⇒ Revised   ~~deleted~~ Deleted   • Use Additional Character(s)

T, U, & V

W

Walked into stationary object (any) W22.09
  furniture W22.03
  lamppost W22.02
  wall W22.01
War operations (injuries to military personnel and civilians during war, civil insurrection and peacekeeping missions) (by) (from) (involving) Y36.90-●
  after cessation of hostilities Y36.89-●
    explosion (of)
      bomb placed during war operations Y36.82-●
      mine placed during war operations Y36.81-●
    specified NEC Y36.88-●
  air blast Y36.20-●
  aircraft
    destruction —see War operations, destruction of aircraft
  airway restriction —see War operations, restriction of airways
  asphyxiation —see War operations, restriction of airways
  biological weapons Y36.6X-●
  blast Y36.20-●
  blast fragments Y36.20-●
  blast wave Y36.20-●
  blast wind Y36.20-●
  bomb Y36.20-●
    dirty Y36.50-●
    gasoline Y36.31-●
    incendiary Y36.31-●
    petrol Y36.31-●
  bullet Y36.43-●
    incendiary Y36.32-●
    rubber Y36.41-●
  chemical weapons Y36.7X-●
  combat
    hand to hand (unarmed) combat Y36.44-●
    using blunt or piercing object Y36.45-●
  conflagration —see War operations, fire
  conventional warfare NEC Y36.49-●
  depth-charge Y36.01-●
  destruction of aircraft Y36.10-●
    due to
      air to air missile Y36.11-●
      collision with other aircraft Y36.12-●
      detonation (accidental) of onboard munitions and explosives Y36.14-●
      enemy fire or explosives Y36.11-●
      explosive placed on aircraft Y36.11-●
      onboard fire Y36.13-●
      rocket propelled grenade [RPG] Y36.11-●
      small arms fire Y36.11-●
      surface to air missile Y36.11-●
    specified NEC Y36.19-●
  detonation (accidental) of
    onboard marine weapons Y36.05-●
    own munitions or munitions launch device Y36.24-●

War operations (Continued)
  dirty bomb Y36.50-●
  explosion (of) Y36.20-●
    aerial bomb Y36.21-●
    after cessation of hostilities
      bomb placed during war operations Y36.82-●
      mine placed during war operations Y36.81-●
    bomb NOS —see also War operations, bomb(s) Y36.20-●
    fragments Y36.20-●
    grenade Y36.29-●
    guided missile Y36.22-●
    improvised explosive device [IED] (person-borne) (roadside) (vehicle-borne) Y36.23-●
    land mine Y36.29-●
    marine mine (at sea) (in harbor) Y36.02-●
    marine weapon Y36.00-●
      specified NEC Y36.09-●
    own munitions or munitions launch device (accidental) Y36.24-●
    sea-based artillery shell Y36.03-●
    specified NEC Y36.29-●
    torpedo Y36.04-●
  fire Y36.30-●
    specified NEC Y36.39-●
  firearms
    discharge Y36.43-●
    pellets Y36.42-●
  flamethrower Y36.33-●
  fragments (from) (of)
    improvised explosive device [IED] (person-borne) (roadside) (vehicle-borne) Y36.26-●
    munitions Y36.25-●
    specified NEC Y36.29-●
    weapons Y36.27-●
  friendly fire Y36.92
  hand to hand (unarmed) combat Y36.44-●
  hot substances —see War operations, fire
  incendiary bullet Y36.32-●
  nuclear weapon (effects of) Y36.50-●
    acute radiation exposure Y36.54-●
    blast pressure Y36.51-●
    direct blast Y36.51-●
    direct heat Y36.53-●
    fallout exposure Y36.54-●
    fireball Y36.53-●
    indirect blast (struck or crushed by blast debris) (being thrown by blast) Y36.52-●
    ionizing radiation (immediate exposure) Y36.54-●
    nuclear radiation Y36.54-●
    radiation
      ionizing (immediate exposure) Y36.54-●

War operations (Continued)
  nuclear weapon (Continued)
    radiation (Continued)
      nuclear Y36.54-●
      thermal Y36.53-●
    secondary effects Y36.54-●
    specified NEC Y36.59-●
    thermal radiation Y36.53-●
  restriction of air (airway)
    intentional Y36.46-●
    unintentional Y36.47-●
  rubber bullets Y36.41-●
  shrapnel NOS Y36.29-●
  suffocation —see War operations, restriction of airways
  unconventional warfare NEC Y36.7X-●
  underwater blast NOS Y36.00-●
  warfare
    conventional NEC Y36.49-●
    unconventional NEC Y36.7X-●
  weapon of mass destruction [WMD] Y36.91
  weapons
    biological weapons Y36.6X-●
    chemical Y36.7X-●
    nuclear (effects of) Y36.50-●
      acute radiation exposure Y36.54-●
      blast pressure Y36.51-●
      direct blast Y36.51-●
      direct heat Y36.53-●
      fallout exposure Y36.54-●
      fireball Y36.53-●
      radiation
        ionizing (immediate exposure) Y36.54-●
        nuclear Y36.54-●
        thermal Y36.53-●
      secondary effects Y36.54-●
      specified NEC Y36.59-●
    of mass destruction [WMD] Y36.91-●
Washed
  away by flood —see Flood
  off road by storm (transport vehicle) —see Forces of nature, cataclysmic storm
Weather exposure NEC —see Forces of nature
Weightlessness (causing injury) (effects of) (in spacecraft, real or simulated) X52
Work related condition Y99.0
Wound (accidental) NEC —see also Injury X58
  battle —see also War operations Y36.90
  gunshot —see Discharge, firearm by type
Wreck transport vehicle NEC —see also Accident, transport V89.9
Wrong
  device implanted into correct surgical site Y65.51
  fluid in infusion Y65.1
  patient, procedure performed on Y65.52
  procedure (operation) on correct patient Y65.51

W

PART III

ICD-10-CM Tabular List of Diseases and Injuries

CHAPTER 1

CERTAIN INFECTIOUS AND PARASITIC DISEASES (A00-B99)

OGCR Chapter-Specific Coding Guidelines

1. Chapter 1: Certain Infectious and Parasitic Diseases (A00-B99)

   a. **Human Immunodeficiency Virus (HIV) Infections**

      1) **Code only confirmed cases**

      Code only confirmed cases of HIV infection/illness. This is an exception to the hospital inpatient guideline Section II, H.

      In this context, "confirmation" does not require documentation of positive serology or culture for HIV; the provider's diagnostic statement that the patient is HIV positive, or has an HIV-related illness is sufficient.

      2) **Selection and sequencing of HIV codes**

         (a) **Patient admitted for HIV-related condition**

         If a patient is admitted for an HIV-related condition, the principal diagnosis should be B20, Human immunodeficiency virus [HIV] disease followed by additional diagnosis codes for all reported HIV-related conditions.

         (b) **Patient with HIV disease admitted for unrelated condition**

         If a patient with HIV disease is admitted for an unrelated condition (such as a traumatic injury), the code for the unrelated condition (e.g., the nature of injury code) should be the principal diagnosis. Other diagnoses would be B20 followed by additional diagnosis codes for all reported HIV-related conditions.

         (c) **Whether the patient is newly diagnosed**

         Whether the patient is newly diagnosed or has had previous admissions/encounters for HIV conditions is irrelevant to the sequencing decision.

         (d) **Asymptomatic human immunodeficiency virus**

         Z21, Asymptomatic human immunodeficiency virus [HIV] infection status, is to be applied when the patient without any documentation of symptoms is listed as being "HIV positive," "known HIV," "HIV test positive," or similar terminology. Do not use this code if the term "AIDS" is used or if the patient is treated for any HIV-related illness or is described as having any condition(s) resulting from his/her HIV positive status; use B20 in these cases.

         (e) **Patients with inconclusive HIV serology**

         Patients with inconclusive HIV serology, but no definitive diagnosis or manifestations of the illness, may be assigned code R75, Inconclusive laboratory evidence of human immunodeficiency virus [HIV].

         (f) **Previously diagnosed HIV-related illness**

         Patients with any known prior diagnosis of an HIV-related illness should be coded to B20. Once a patient has developed an HIV-related illness, the patient should always be assigned code B20 on every subsequent admission/encounter. Patients previously diagnosed with any HIV illness (B20) should never be assigned to R75 or Z21, Asymptomatic human immunodeficiency virus [HIV] infection status.

         (g) **HIV Infection in Pregnancy, Childbirth and the Puerperium**

         During pregnancy, childbirth or the puerperium, a patient admitted (or presenting for a health care encounter) because of an HIV-related illness should receive a principal diagnosis code of O98.7-, Human immunodeficiency [HIV] disease complicating pregnancy, childbirth and the puerperium, followed by B20 and the code(s) for the HIV-related illness(es). Codes from Chapter 15 always take sequencing priority.

         Patients with asymptomatic HIV infection status admitted (or presenting for a health care encounter) during pregnancy, childbirth, or the puerperium should receive codes of O98.7- and Z21.

         (h) **Encounters for testing for HIV**

         If a patient is being seen to determine his/her HIV status, use code Z11.4, Encounter for screening for human immunodeficiency virus [HIV]. Use additional codes for any associated high-risk behavior.

         If a patient with signs or symptoms is being seen for HIV testing, code the signs and symptoms. An additional counseling code Z71.7, Human immunodeficiency virus [HIV] counseling, may be used if counseling is provided during the encounter for the test.

         When a patient returns to be informed of his/her HIV test results and the test result is negative, use code Z71.7, Human immunodeficiency virus [HIV] counseling.

If the results are positive, see previous guidelines and assign codes as appropriate.

   b. **Infectious agents as the cause of diseases classified to other chapters**

   Certain infections are classified in chapters other than Chapter 1 and no organism is identified as part of the infection code. In these instances, it is necessary to use an additional code from Chapter 1 to identify the organism. A code from category B95, Streptococcus, Staphylococcus, and Enterococcus as the cause of diseases classified to other chapters, B96, Other bacterial agents as the cause of diseases classified to other chapters, or B97, Viral agents as the cause of diseases classified to other chapters, is to be used as an additional code to identify the organism. An instructional note will be found at the infection code advising that an additional organism code is required.

   c. **Infections resistant to antibiotics**

   Many bacterial infections are resistant to current antibiotics. It is necessary to identify all infections documented as antibiotic resistant. Assign a code from category Z16, Resistance to antimicrobial drugs, following the infection code only if the infection code does not identify drug resistance.

   d. **Sepsis, Severe Sepsis, and Septic Shock**

      1) **Coding of Sepsis and Severe Sepsis**

         (a) **Sepsis**

         For a diagnosis of sepsis, assign the appropriate code for the underlying systemic infection. If the type of infection or causal organism is not further specified, assign code A41.9, Sepsis, unspecified organism.

         A code from subcategory R65.2, Severe sepsis, should not be assigned unless severe sepsis or an associated acute organ dysfunction is documented.

            (i) Negative or inconclusive blood cultures and sepsis

            Negative or inconclusive blood cultures do not preclude a diagnosis of sepsis in patients with clinical evidence of the condition, however, the provider should be queried.

            (ii) Urosepsis

            The term urosepsis is a nonspecific term. It is not to be considered synonymous with sepsis. It has no default code in the Alphabetic Index. Should a provider use this term, he/she must be queried for clarification.

            (iii) Sepsis with organ dysfunction

            If a patient has sepsis and associated acute organ dysfunction or multiple organ dysfunction (MOD), follow the instructions for coding severe sepsis.

            (iv) Acute organ dysfunction that is not clearly associated with the sepsis

            If a patient has sepsis and an acute organ dysfunction, but the medical record documentation indicates that the acute organ dysfunction is related to a medical condition other than the sepsis, do not assign a code from subcategory R65.2, Severe sepsis. An acute organ dysfunction must be associated with the sepsis in order to assign the severe sepsis code. If the documentation is not clear as to whether an acute organ dysfunction is related to the sepsis or another medical condition, query the provider.

         (b) **Severe sepsis**

         The coding of severe sepsis requires a minimum of 2 codes: first a code for the underlying systemic infection, followed by a code from subcategory R65.2, Severe sepsis. If the causal organism is not documented, assign code A41.9, Sepsis, unspecified organism, for the infection. Additional code(s) for the associated acute organ dysfunction are also required.

         Due to the complex nature of severe sepsis, some cases may require querying the provider prior to assignment of the codes.

      2) **Septic shock**

         (a) Septic shock generally refers to circulatory failure associated with severe sepsis, and therefore, it represents a type of acute organ dysfunction.

         For all cases of septic shock, the code for the systemic infection should be sequenced first, followed by code R65.21, Severe sepsis with septic shock or code T81.12, Postprocedural septic shock.

648

Any additional codes for the other acute organ dysfunctions should also be assigned. As noted in the sequencing instructions in the Tabular List, the code for septic shock cannot be assigned as a principal diagnosis.

3) Sequencing of severe sepsis

If severe sepsis is present on admission, and meets the definition of principal diagnosis, the underlying systemic infection should be assigned as principal diagnosis followed by the appropriate code from subcategory R65.2 as required by the sequencing rules in the Tabular List. A code from subcategory R65.2 can never be assigned as a principal diagnosis.

When severe sepsis develops during an encounter (it was not present on admission) the underlying systemic infection and the appropriate code from subcategory R65.2 should be assigned as secondary diagnoses.

Severe sepsis may be present on admission but the diagnosis may not be confirmed until sometime after admission. If the documentation is not clear whether severe sepsis was present on admission, the provider should be queried.

4) Sepsis and severe sepsis with a localized infection

If the reason for admission is both sepsis or severe sepsis and a localized infection, such as pneumonia or cellulitis, a code(s) for the underlying systemic infection should be assigned first and the code for the localized infection should be assigned as a secondary diagnosis. If the patient has severe sepsis, a code from subcategory R65.2 should also be assigned as a secondary diagnosis. If the patient is admitted with a localized infection, such as pneumonia, and sepsis/severe sepsis doesn't develop until after admission, the localized infection should be assigned first, followed by the appropriate sepsis/severe sepsis codes.

5) Sepsis due to a postprocedural infection

(a) Documentation of causal relationship

As with all postprocedural complications, code assignment is based on the provider's documentation of the relationship between the infection and the procedure.

(b) Sepsis due to a postprocedural infection

For infections following a procedure, a code from T81.40, to T81.43. Infection following a procedure, or O86.00 to O86.03, Infection of obstetric surgical wound, that identifies the site of the infection should be coded first, if known. Assign an additional code for sepsis following a procedure (T81.44) or sepsis following an obstetrical procedure (O86.04). Use an additional code to identify the infectious agent. If the patient has severe sepsis the appropriate code from subcategory R65.2 should also be assigned with the additional code(s) for any acute organ dysfunction.

For infections following infusion, transfusion, therapeutic injection, or immunization, a code from subcategory T80.2, Infections following infusion, transfusion, and therapeutic injection, or code T88.0-, Infection following immunization, should be coded first, followed by the code for the specific infection. If the patient has severe sepsis, the appropriate code from subcategory R65.2 should also be assigned, with the additional codes(s) for any acute organ dysfunction.

(c) Postprocedural infection and postprocedural septic shock

If a postprocedural infection has resulted in postprocedural septic shock, assign the codes indicated above for sepsis due to a postprocedural infection, followed by code T81.12-, Postprocedural septic shock. Do not assign code R65.21, Severe sepsis with septic shock. Additional code(s) should be assigned for any acute organ dysfunction.

6) Sepsis and severe sepsis associated with a noninfectious process (condition)

In some cases a noninfectious process (condition), such as trauma, may lead to an infection which can result in sepsis or severe sepsis. If sepsis or severe sepsis is documented as associated with a noninfectious condition, such as a burn or serious injury, and this condition meets the definition for principal diagnosis, the code for the noninfectious condition should be sequenced first, followed by the code for the resulting infection. If severe sepsis is present, a code from subcategory R65.2 should also be assigned with any associated organ dysfunction(s) codes. It is not necessary to assign a code from subcategory R65.1, Systemic inflammatory response syndrome (SIRS) of noninfectious origin, for these cases.

If the infection meets the definition of principal diagnosis it should be sequenced before the noninfectious condition. When both the associated noninfectious condition and the infection meet the definition of principal diagnosis either may be assigned as principal diagnosis.

Only one code from category R65, Symptoms and signs specifically associated with systemic inflammation and infection, should be assigned. Therefore, when a noninfectious condition leads to an infection resulting in severe sepsis, assign the appropriate code from subcategory R65.2, Severe sepsis. Do not additionally assign a code from subcategory R65.1, Systemic inflammatory response syndrome (SIRS) of noninfectious origin.
See Section I.C.18. SIRS due to non-infectious process

7) Sepsis and septic shock complicating abortion, pregnancy, childbirth, and the puerperium

See Section I.C.15. Sepsis and septic shock complicating abortion, pregnancy, childbirth and the puerperium

8) Newborn sepsis

See Section I.C.16. f. Bacterial sepsis of Newborn

e. Methicillin Resistant Staphylococcus aureus (MRSA) Conditions

1) Selection and sequencing of MRSA codes

(a) Combination codes for MRSA infection

When a patient is diagnosed with an infection that is due to methicillin resistant *Staphylococcus aureus* (MRSA), and that infection has a combination code that includes the causal organism (e.g., sepsis, pneumonia) assign the appropriate combination code for the condition (e.g., code A41.02, Sepsis due to Methicillin resistant Staphylococcus aureus or code J15.212, Pneumonia due to Methicillin resistant Staphylococcus aureus). Do not assign code B95.62, Methicillin resistant Staphylococcus aureus infection as the cause of diseases classified elsewhere, as an additional code because the combination code includes the type of infection and the MRSA organism. Do not assign a code from subcategory Z16.11, Resistance to penicillins, as an additional diagnosis.
See Section C.1. for instructions on coding and sequencing of sepsis and severe sepsis.

(b) Other codes for MRSA infection

When there is documentation of a current infection (e.g., wound infection, stitch abscess, urinary tract infection) due to MRSA, and that infection does not have a combination code that includes the causal organism, assign the appropriate code to identify the condition along with code B95.62, Methicillin resistant Staphylococcus aureus infection as the cause of diseases classified elsewhere for the MRSA infection. Do not assign a code from subcategory Z16.11, Resistance to penicillins.

(c) Methicillin susceptible Staphylococcus aureus (MSSA) and MRSA colonization

The condition or state of being colonized or carrying MSSA or MRSA is called colonization or carriage, while an individual person is described as being colonized or being a carrier. Colonization means that MSSA or MSRA is present on or in the body without necessarily causing illness. A positive MRSA colonization test might be documented by the provider as "MRSA screen positive" or "MRSA nasal swab positive".

Assign code Z22.322, Carrier or suspected carrier of Methicillin resistant Staphylococcus aureus, for patients documented as having MRSA colonization. Assign code Z22.321, Carrier or suspected carrier of Methicillin susceptible Staphylococcus aureus, for patient documented as having MSSA colonization. Colonization is not necessarily indicative of a disease process or as the cause of a specific condition the patient may have unless documented as such by the provider.

(d) MRSA colonization and infection

If a patient is documented as having both MRSA colonization and infection during a hospital admission, code Z22.322, Carrier or suspected carrier of Methicillin resistant Staphylococcus aureus, and a code for the MRSA infection may both be assigned.

f. Zika virus infections

1) Code only confirmed cases

Code only a confirmed diagnosis of Zika virus (A92.5, Zika virus disease) as documented by the provider. This is an exception to the hospital inpatient guideline Section II, H.

In this context, "confirmation" does not require documentation of the type of test performed; the physician's diagnostic statement that the condition is confirmed is sufficient. This code should be assigned regardless of the stated mode of transmission.

If the provider documents "suspected", "possible" or "probable" Zika, do not assign code A92.5. Assign a code(s) explaining the reason for encounter (such as fever, rash, or joint pain) or Z20.821, Contact with and (suspected) exposure to Zika virus.

CHAPTER 1

CERTAIN INFECTIOUS AND PARASITIC DISEASES (A00-B99)

Includes   diseases generally recognized as communicable or transmissible

Use additional code to identify resistance to antimicrobial drugs (Z16.-)

Excludes1   certain localized infections - see body system-related chapters

Excludes2   carrier or suspected carrier of infectious disease (Z22.-)

infectious and parasitic diseases complicating pregnancy, childbirth and the puerperium (O98.-)

infectious and parasitic diseases specific to the perinatal period (P35-P39)

influenza and other acute respiratory infections (J00-J22)

This chapter contains the following blocks:

A00-A09	Intestinal infectious diseases
A15-A19	Tuberculosis
A20-A28	Certain zoonotic bacterial diseases
A30-A49	Other bacterial diseases
A50-A64	Infections with a predominantly sexual mode of transmission
A65-A69	Other spirochetal diseases
A70-A74	Other diseases caused by chlamydiae
A75-A79	Rickettsioses
A80-A89	Viral and prion infections of the central nervous system
A90-A99	Arthropod-borne viral fevers and viral hemorrhagic fevers
B00-B09	Viral infections characterized by skin and mucous membrane lesions
B10	Other human herpesviruses
B15-B19	Viral hepatitis
B20	Human immunodeficiency virus [HIV] disease
B25-B34	Other viral diseases
B35-B49	Mycoses
B50-B64	Protozoal diseases
B65-B83	Helminthiases
B85-B89	Pediculosis, acariasis and other infestations
B90-B94	Sequelae of infectious and parasitic diseases
B95-B97	Bacterial and viral infectious agents
B99	Other infectious diseases

INTESTINAL INFECTIOUS DISEASES (A00-A09)

● **A00   Cholera**
A serious, often deadly, infectious disease of the small intestine

A00.0   Cholera due to Vibrio cholerae 01, biovar cholerae
Classical cholera

A00.1   Cholera due to Vibrio cholerae 01, biovar eltor
Cholera eltor

A00.9   Cholera, unspecified

● **A01   Typhoid and paratyphoid fevers**
Caused by Salmonella typhi and Salmonella paratyphi A, B, and C bacteria

● **A01.0   Typhoid fever**
Infection due to Salmonella typhi

A01.00   Typhoid fever, unspecified

A01.01   Typhoid meningitis

A01.02   Typhoid fever with heart involvement
Typhoid endocarditis
Typhoid myocarditis

A01.03   Typhoid pneumonia 🦠

A01.04   Typhoid arthritis 🦠

A01.05   Typhoid osteomyelitis 🦠

A01.09   Typhoid fever with other complications

A01.1   Paratyphoid fever A

A01.2   Paratyphoid fever B

A01.3   Paratyphoid fever C

A01.4   Paratyphoid fever, unspecified
Infection due to Salmonella paratyphi NOS

● **A02   Other salmonella infections**
Includes   infection or foodborne intoxication due to any Salmonella species other than S. typhi and S. paratyphi

A02.0   Salmonella enteritis
Salmonellosis

A02.1   Salmonella sepsis 🦠

● **A02.2   Localized salmonella infections**

A02.20   Localized salmonella infection, unspecified
Specified in the documentation as localized, but unspecified as to type

A02.21   Salmonella meningitis
Specified as localized in the meninges

A02.22   Salmonella pneumonia 🦠
Specified as localized in the lungs

A02.23   Salmonella arthritis 🦠
Specified as localized in the joints

A02.24   Salmonella osteomyelitis 🦠
Specified as localized in bone

A02.25   Salmonella pyelonephritis
Salmonella tubulo-interstitial nephropathy

A02.29   Salmonella with other localized infection
Specified as localized (because it is still under localized heading) but does not assign into any of the above codes

A02.8   Other specified salmonella infections
Any specified salmonella infection which does NOT assign into any of the above codes (not specified as localized)

A02.9   Salmonella infection, unspecified
Unspecified in the documentation as to specific type of salmonella

● **A03   Shigellosis**
An infectious disease caused by bacteria (Shigella)

A03.0   Shigellosis due to Shigella dysenteriae
Group A shigellosis [Shiga-Kruse dysentery]

A03.1   Shigellosis due to Shigella flexneri
Group B shigellosis

A03.2   Shigellosis due to Shigella boydii
Group C shigellosis

A03.3   Shigellosis due to Shigella sonnei
Group D shigellosis

A03.8   Other shigellosis

A03.9   Shigellosis, unspecified
Bacillary dysentery NOS

Item 1-1   Salmonella is a bacterium that lives in the intestines of fowl and mammals and can spread to humans through improper food preparation and cooking. Salmonellosis is an infection with the bacterium. Symptoms include diarrhea, fever, and abdominal cramps 12 to 72 hours after infection. The illness usually lasts 4 to 7 days, and most persons recover without treatment. The diarrhea may be so severe that the patient needs to be hospitalized. Patients with immunocompromised systems in chronic, ill health are more likely to have the infection invade their bloodstream with life-threatening results. For example, patients with sickle cell disease are more prone to salmonella osteomyelitis than others.

▶ New   ⧫ Revised   ~~deleted~~ Deleted   Excludes 1   Excludes 2   Includes   Use additional   Code first   Code also   Key words

OGCR Official Guidelines   X Assign placeholder X   ● Use Additional Character(s)   ▶ Manifestation Code   🦠 Hierarchical Condition Category   **Coding Clinic**

Figure 1-1 Electron micrograph of escherichia coli (E. coli) expressing P fimbriae. (Getty Image)

Item 1-2 *Escherichia coli [E. coli]* is a Gram-negative bacterium found in the intestinal tracts of humans and animals and is usually nonpathogenic. Pathogenic strains can cause diarrhea or pyogenic (pus-producing) infections. Can be a threat to food safety.

● **A04** **Other bacterial intestinal infections**

> **Excludes1** bacterial foodborne intoxications, NEC (A05.-)
> tuberculous enteritis (A18.32)

A04.0 **Enteropathogenic Escherichia coli infection**
Pertaining to or producing intestinal disease

A04.1 **Enterotoxigenic Escherichia coli infection**
Producing or containing intestinal toxin

A04.2 **Enteroinvasive Escherichia coli infection**
Capable of penetrating and spreading through intestinal mucosal epithelium

A04.3 **Enterohemorrhagic Escherichia coli infection**
Causing bloody diarrhea, resulting from microorganisms

A04.4 **Other intestinal Escherichia coli infections**
Escherichia coli enteritis NOS

A04.5 **Campylobacter enteritis**
Spiral shaped bacterium

A04.6 **Enteritis due to Yersinia enterocolitica**
> **Excludes1** extraintestinal yersiniosis (A28.2)
Transmitted by infected food/water and person-to-person contact, affecting intestinal tract

● **A04.7** **Enterocolitis due to Clostridium difficile**
Foodborne intoxication by Clostridium difficile
Pseudomembraneous colitis
Marked by fibrinous deposit (false membrane) with enmeshed necrotic cells

A04.71 **Enterocolitis due to Clostridium difficile, recurrent**
Coding Clinic: 2020, Q1, P18

A04.72 **Enterocolitis due to Clostridium difficile, not specified as recurrent**

A04.8 **Other specified bacterial intestinal infections**

A04.9 **Bacterial intestinal infection, unspecified**
Bacterial enteritis NOS

● **A05** **Other bacterial foodborne intoxications, not elsewhere classified**

> **Excludes1** Clostridium difficile foodborne intoxication and infection (A04.7-)
> Escherichia coli infection (A04.0-A04.4)
> listeriosis (A32.-)
> salmonella foodborne intoxication and infection (A02.-)
> toxic effect of noxious foodstuffs (T61-T62)

A05.0 **Foodborne staphylococcal intoxication**

A05.1 **Botulism food poisoning**
Botulism NOS
Classical foodborne intoxication due to Clostridium botulinum
> **Excludes1** infant botulism (A48.51)
> wound botulism (A48.52)

A05.2 **Foodborne Clostridium perfringens [Clostridium welchii] intoxication**
Type A causes gas gangrene and necrotizing colitis; major cause of food poisoning in humans
Enteritis necroticans
Pig-bel

A05.3 **Foodborne Vibrio parahaemolyticus intoxication**
Organism that survives only in high salt environment (halophilic), major cause of gastroenteritis due to consumption of raw or improperly cooked fish/seafood

A05.4 **Foodborne Bacillus cereus intoxication**
Spore-forming species commonly found in soil, causes food poisoning from formation of intestinal toxins in contaminated foods

A05.5 **Foodborne Vibrio vulnificus intoxication**
Species that survives in high salt environment (halophilic) with infection by eating raw seafood causes septicemia and cellulitis

A05.8 **Other specified bacterial foodborne intoxications**

A05.9 **Bacterial foodborne intoxication, unspecified**

● **A06** **Amebiasis**
An intestinal illness caused by the microscopic parasite Entamoeba histolytica

> **Includes** infection due to Entamoeba histolytica
> **Excludes1** other protozoal intestinal diseases (A07.-)
> **Excludes2** acanthamebiasis (B60.1-)
> Naegleriasis (B60.2)

A06.0 **Acute amebic dysentery**
Acute amebiasis
Intestinal amebiasis NOS

A06.1 **Chronic intestinal amebiasis**

A06.2 **Amebic nondysenteric colitis**
Pertaining to single cell microorganism

A06.3 **Ameboma of intestine**
Tumorlike mass produced by localized inflammation often in intestine
Ameboma NOS

A06.4 **Amebic liver abscess**
Hepatic amebiasis

A06.5 **Amebic lung abscess** 🔖
Amebic abscess of lung (and liver)

A06.6 **Amebic brain abscess**
Amebic abscess of brain (and liver) (and lung)

A06.7 **Cutaneous amebiasis**

● **A06.8** **Amebic infection of other sites**

A06.81 **Amebic cystitis**

A06.82 **Other amebic genitourinary infections**
Amebic balanitis
Amebic vesiculitis
Amebic vulvovaginitis

A06.89 **Other amebic infections**
Amebic appendicitis
Amebic splenic abscess

A06.9 **Amebiasis, unspecified**

A07 Other protozoal intestinal diseases

    A07.0 **Balantidiasis**
        Balantidial dysentery
        Infection by protozoa that may cause diarrhea and dysentery,
        with ulceration of colonic mucous membranes

    A07.1 **Giardiasis [lambliasis]**
        Common infection in small intestine spread by contaminated
        food, water, or direct person-to-person contact

    A07.2 **Cryptosporidiosis** 🏷
        Human infection with protozoa usually seen as self-limited
        diarrhea in those who work with cattle

    A07.3 **Isosporiasis**
        Human intestinal disease caused by protozoa
        Infection due to Isospora belli and Isospora hominis
        Intestinal coccidiosis
        Isosporosis

    A07.4 **Cyclosporiasis**
        Infection by protozoa with most common species infecting
        humans being C cayetanensis

    A07.8 **Other specified protozoal intestinal diseases**
        Intestinal microsporidiosis
        Intestinal trichomoniasis
        Sarcocystosis
        Sarcosporidiosis

    A07.9 **Protozoal intestinal disease, unspecified**
        Flagellate diarrhea
        Protozoal colitis
        Protozoal diarrhea
        Protozoal dysentery

A08 Viral and other specified intestinal infections

    Excludes1 influenza with involvement of gastrointestinal
        tract (J09.X3, J10.2, J11.2)

    A08.0 **Rotaviral enteritis**

    A08.1 **Acute gastroenteropathy due to Norwalk agent and**
        other small round viruses

        A08.11 **Acute gastroenteropathy due to Norwalk agent**
            Acute gastroenteropathy due to Norovirus
            Acute gastroenteropathy due to Norwalk-like
            agent

        A08.19 **Acute gastroenteropathy due to other small**
            round viruses
            Acute gastroenteropathy due to small round
            virus [SRV] NOS

    A08.2 **Adenoviral enteritis**

    A08.3 **Other viral enteritis**

        A08.31 **Calicivirus enteritis**

        A08.32 **Astrovirus enteritis**

        A08.39 **Other viral enteritis**
            Coxsackie virus enteritis
            Echovirus enteritis
            Enterovirus enteritis NEC
            Torovirus enteritis

    A08.4 **Viral intestinal infection, unspecified**
        Viral enteritis NOS
        Viral gastroenteritis NOS
        Viral gastroenteropathy NOS
        Coding Clinic: 2016, Q3, P12

    A08.8 **Other specified intestinal infections**

A09 Infectious gastroenteritis and colitis, unspecified
    Infectious colitis NOS
    Infectious enteritis NOS
    Infectious gastroenteritis NOS

    Excludes1 colitis NOS (K52.9)
        diarrhea NOS (R19.7)
        enteritis NOS (K52.9)
        gastroenteritis NOS (K52.9)
        noninfective gastroenteritis and colitis,
        unspecified (K52.9)

Figure 1-2 Far advanced bilateral pulmonary tuberculosis before and after 8 months of treatment with streptomycin, PAS, and isoniazid. (Getty Image)

Item 1-3 Tuberculosis is a common and deadly infectious disease caused by the *Mycobacterium tuberculosis* organism. The first tuberculosis infection is called the **primary infection** and most commonly attacks the lungs but can affect the central nervous system, lymphatic system, circulatory system, genitourinary system, bones, joints, and even the skin. A **Ghon** lesion is the **initial lesion.** A **secondary lesion** occurs when the tubercle bacilli are carried to other areas.

Item 1-4 Although it primarily affects the lungs, the bacteria ***Mycobacterium tuberculosis*** can travel from the pulmonary circulation to virtually any organ in the body, much as a cancer metastasizes to a secondary site. If the immune system becomes compromised by age or disease, what would otherwise be a self-limiting primary tuberculosis in the lungs will develop in other organs. These are known as extrapulmonary sites.

TUBERCULOSIS (A15-A19)

    Includes infections due to Mycobacterium tuberculosis
        and Mycobacterium bovis

    Excludes1 congenital tuberculosis (P37.0)
        nonspecific reaction to test for tuberculosis
        without active tuberculosis (R76.1-)
        pneumoconiosis associated with tuberculosis, any
        type in A15 (J65)
        positive PPD (R76.11)
        positive tuberculin skin test without active
        tuberculosis (R76.11)
        sequelae of tuberculosis (B90.-)
        silicotuberculosis (J65)

A15 Respiratory tuberculosis

    A15.0 **Tuberculosis of lung**
        Tuberculous bronchiectasis
        Chronic dilatation of bronchi
        Tuberculous fibrosis of lung
        Tuberculous pneumonia
        Tuberculous pneumothorax

    A15.4 **Tuberculosis of intrathoracic lymph nodes**
        Tuberculosis of hilar lymph nodes
        Tuberculosis of mediastinal lymph nodes
        Tuberculosis of tracheobronchial lymph nodes

        Excludes1 tuberculosis specified as primary (A15.7)

    A15.5 **Tuberculosis of larynx, trachea and bronchus**
        Tuberculosis of bronchus
        Tuberculosis of glottis
        Tuberculosis of larynx
        Tuberculosis of trachea

    A15.6 **Tuberculous pleurisy**
        Tuberculosis of pleura
        Tuberculous empyema

        Excludes1 primary respiratory tuberculosis (A15.7)

    A15.7 **Primary respiratory tuberculosis**

    A15.8 **Other respiratory tuberculosis**
        Mediastinal tuberculosis
        Nasopharyngeal tuberculosis
        Tuberculosis of nose
        Tuberculosis of sinus [any nasal]

    A15.9 **Respiratory tuberculosis unspecified**

▶ New   ➡ Revised   ~~deleted~~ Deleted   Excludes 1   Excludes 2   Includes   Use additional   Code first   Code also   Key words

OGCR Official Guidelines   X Assign placeholder X   ● Use Additional Character(s)   ▷ Manifestation Code   🏷 Hierarchical Condition Category   **Coding Clinic**

● **A17 Tuberculosis of nervous system**

    A17.0 Tuberculous meningitis
        Tuberculosis of meninges (cerebral) (spinal)
        Tuberculous leptomeningitis

        Excludes1   tuberculous meningoencephalitis
                    (A17.82)

    A17.1 Meningeal tuberculoma
        Tuberculoma of meninges (cerebral) (spinal)

        Excludes2   tuberculoma of brain and spinal cord
                    (A17.81)

  ● **A17.8 Other tuberculosis of nervous system**

      A17.81 Tuberculoma of brain and spinal cord
          Tuberculous abscess of brain and spinal cord

      A17.82 Tuberculous meningoencephalitis
          Inflammation of brain and meninges; AKA
             cerebromeningitis and encephalomeningitis
          Tuberculous myelitis

      A17.83 Tuberculous neuritis
          Tuberculous mononeuropathy

      A17.89 Other tuberculosis of nervous system
          Tuberculous polyneuropathy

    A17.9 Tuberculosis of nervous system, unspecified

● **A18 Tuberculosis of other organs**

  ● **A18.0 Tuberculosis of bones and joints**

      A18.01 Tuberculosis of spine
          Pott's disease or curvature of spine
          Tuberculous arthritis
          Tuberculous osteomyelitis of spine
          Tuberculous spondylitis

      A18.02 Tuberculous arthritis of other joints
          Tuberculosis of hip (joint)
          Tuberculosis of knee (joint)

      A18.03 Tuberculosis of other bones
          Tuberculous mastoiditis
          Tuberculous osteomyelitis

      A18.09 Other musculoskeletal tuberculosis
          Tuberculous myositis
          Tuberculous synovitis
          Tuberculous tenosynovitis

  ● **A18.1 Tuberculosis of genitourinary system**

      A18.10 Tuberculosis of genitourinary system, unspecified

      A18.11 Tuberculosis of kidney and ureter

      A18.12 Tuberculosis of bladder

      A18.13 Tuberculosis of other urinary organs
          Tuberculous urethritis

      A18.14 Tuberculosis of prostate ♂   **A**

      A18.15 Tuberculosis of other male genital organs ♂

      A18.16 Tuberculosis of cervix ♀

      A18.17 Tuberculous female pelvic inflammatory disease ♀
          Tuberculous endometritis
          Tuberculous oophoritis and salpingitis
          Oophoritis = inflammation of ovary
          Salpingitis = inflammation of fallopian tube

      A18.18 Tuberculosis of other female genital organs ♀
          Tuberculous ulceration of vulva

    A18.2 Tuberculous peripheral lymphadenopathy
        Tuberculous adenitis

        Excludes2   tuberculosis of bronchial and mediastinal
                    lymph nodes (A15.4)
                    tuberculosis of mesenteric and
                    retroperitoneal lymph nodes
                    (A18.39)
                    tuberculous tracheobronchial adenopathy
                    (A15.4)

● **A18.3 Tuberculosis of intestines, peritoneum and mesenteric glands**

    A18.31 Tuberculous peritonitis
        Tuberculous ascites

    A18.32 Tuberculous enteritis
        Tuberculosis of anus and rectum
        Tuberculosis of intestine (large) (small)

    A18.39 Retroperitoneal tuberculosis
        Tuberculosis of mesenteric glands
        Tuberculosis of retroperitoneal (lymph glands)

  A18.4 Tuberculosis of skin and subcutaneous tissue
      Erythema induratum, tuberculous
      Lupus excedens
      Lupus vulgaris NOS
      Lupus vulgaris of eyelid
        Cutaneous tuberculosis characterized by reddish brown
          plaque on skin surrounded by papules and nodules
      Scrofuloderma
        Type of cutaneous tuberculosis, with direct extension of
          tuberculosis into skin from underlying structures;
          AKA tuberculosis colliquativa
      Tuberculosis of external ear

      Excludes2   lupus erythematosus (L93.-)
                  systemic lupus erythematosus (M32.-)

● **A18.5 Tuberculosis of eye**

    Excludes2   lupus vulgaris of eyelid (A18.4)

    A18.50 Tuberculosis of eye, unspecified

    A18.51 Tuberculous episcleritis
        Inflammation of episclera and adjacent tissues

    A18.52 Tuberculous keratitis
        Tuberculous interstitial keratitis
        Tuberculous keratoconjunctivitis (interstitial)
          (phlyctenular)
        Inflammation of cornea and conjunctiva

    A18.53 Tuberculous chorioretinitis
        Inflammation of choroid and retina;
          retinochoroiditis

    A18.54 Tuberculous iridocyclitis
        Inflammation of iris and ciliary body

    A18.59 Other tuberculosis of eye
        Tuberculous conjunctivitis

  A18.6 Tuberculosis of (inner) (middle) ear
      Tuberculous otitis media

      Excludes2   tuberculosis of external ear (A18.4)
                  tuberculous mastoiditis (A18.03)

  A18.7 Tuberculosis of adrenal glands
      Tuberculous Addison's disease

● **A18.8 Tuberculosis of other specified organs**

    A18.81 Tuberculosis of thyroid gland

    A18.82 Tuberculosis of other endocrine glands
        Tuberculosis of pituitary gland
        Tuberculosis of thymus gland

    A18.83 Tuberculosis of digestive tract organs, not elsewhere classified

      Excludes1   tuberculosis of intestine (A18.32)

    A18.84 Tuberculosis of heart
        Tuberculous cardiomyopathy
        Tuberculous endocarditis
        Tuberculous myocarditis
        Tuberculous pericarditis

    A18.85 Tuberculosis of spleen

    A18.89 Tuberculosis of other sites
        Tuberculosis of muscle
        Tuberculous cerebral arteritis

CHAPTER 1 (A00-B99)

Item 1–5 Miliary tuberculosis can be a life-threatening condition. If a tuberculous lesion enters a blood vessel, immense dissemination of tuberculous organisms can occur if the immune system is weak. High-risk populations—children under 4 years of age, the elderly, or the immunocompromised—are particularly prone to this type of infection. The lesions will have a millet seedlike appearance on chest x-ray. Bronchial washings and biopsy may aid in diagnosis.

● **A19**　**Miliary tuberculosis**
　　Includes　disseminated tuberculosis
　　　　　　　　generalized tuberculosis
　　　　　　　　tuberculous polyserositis
　　A19.0　Acute miliary tuberculosis of a single specified site
　　A19.1　Acute miliary tuberculosis of multiple sites
　　A19.2　Acute miliary tuberculosis, unspecified
　　A19.8　Other miliary tuberculosis
　　A19.9　Miliary tuberculosis, unspecified

CERTAIN ZOONOTIC BACTERIAL DISEASES (A20–A28)

● **A20**　**Plague**
　　Infectious disease caused by a Yersinia pestis bacterium, transmitted by a rodent flea bite or handling of infected animal
　　Includes　infection due to Yersinia pestis
　　A20.0　**Bubonic plague**
　　A20.1　**Cellulocutaneous plague**
　　　　　　Skin and subcutaneous tissue plague
　　A20.2　**Pneumonic plague** 🅒
　　A20.3　**Plague meningitis**
　　A20.7　**Septicemic plague** 🅒
　　A20.8　**Other forms of plague**
　　　　　　Abortive plague
　　　　　　Asymptomatic plague
　　　　　　Pestis minor
　　　　　　　Systemic bacterial disease
　　A20.9　**Plague, unspecified**

● **A21**　**Tularemia**
　　Caused by Francisella tularensis bacterium found in rodents, rabbits, and hares and transmitted to humans by contact with infected animal tissues or by ticks, biting flies, or mosquitoes
　　Includes　deer-fly fever
　　　　　　　　infection due to Francisella tularensis
　　　　　　　　rabbit fever
　　Coding Clinic: 2016, Q4, P25
　　A21.0　**Ulceroglandular tularemia**
　　　　　　Most common form of tularemia in humans is painful, swollen, erythematous papule at point of inoculation that ruptures to form shallow ulcer
　　A21.1　**Oculoglandular tularemia**
　　　　　　Primary site of entry is conjunctival sac, results in granulomatous corneal lesions
　　　　　　Ophthalmic tularemia
　　A21.2　**Pulmonary tularemia** 🅒
　　A21.3　**Gastrointestinal tularemia**
　　　　　　Abdominal tularemia
　　A21.7　**Generalized tularemia**
　　A21.8　**Other forms of tularemia**
　　A21.9　**Tularemia, unspecified**

● **A22**　**Anthrax**
　　An acute infectious disease caused by the spore-forming Bacillus anthracis; occurs in humans exposed to infected animals or tissue from infected animals
　　Includes　infection due to Bacillus anthracis
　　A22.0　**Cutaneous anthrax**
　　　　　　Malignant carbuncle
　　　　　　Malignant pustule
　　A22.1　**Pulmonary anthrax** 🅒
　　　　　　Inhalation anthrax
　　　　　　Ragpicker's disease
　　　　　　Woolsorter's disease
　　A22.2　**Gastrointestinal anthrax**
　　A22.7　**Anthrax sepsis** 🅒
　　　　　　Infectious bacterial disease
　　A22.8　**Other forms of anthrax**
　　　　　　Anthrax meningitis
　　A22.9　**Anthrax, unspecified**

● **A23**　**Brucellosis**
　　Includes　Malta fever
　　　　　　　　Mediterranean fever
　　　　　　　　undulant fever
　　A23.0　**Brucellosis due to Brucella melitensis**
　　　　　　Resulting in flu-like symptoms that may lead to chronic symptoms that include recurrent fevers, joint pain, and fatigue
　　A23.1　**Brucellosis due to Brucella abortus**
　　　　　　Most common cause of brucellosis in humans; AKA Bang bacillus
　　A23.2　**Brucellosis due to Brucella suis**
　　　　　　Species found primarily in pigs, rabbits, and reindeer
　　A23.3　**Brucellosis due to Brucella canis**
　　　　　　Species that causes respiratory tract infection in humans
　　A23.8　**Other brucellosis**
　　A23.9　**Brucellosis, unspecified**

● **A24**　**Glanders and melioidosis**
　　Infection, usually of rodents, which spreads to other animals and humans, caused by Burkholderia pseudomallei through break in skin contaminated with infested soil or water
　　A24.0　**Glanders**
　　　　　　Infection due to Pseudomonas mallei
　　　　　　Malleus
　　A24.1　**Acute and fulminating melioidosis**
　　　　　　Melioidosis pneumonia
　　　　　　Melioidosis sepsis
　　A24.2　**Subacute and chronic melioidosis**
　　A24.3　**Other melioidosis**
　　A24.9　**Melioidosis, unspecified**
　　　　　　Infection due to Pseudomonas pseudomallei NOS
　　　　　　Whitmore's disease

Item 1-6 Brucellosis: An infectious disease caused by the bacterium Brucella. Humans are infected by contact with contaminated animals or animal products. In humans brucellosis symptoms that are similar to the flu include fever, sweats, headaches, back pains, and physical weakness. Severe infections of the central nervous system or lining of the heart may occur. Brucellosis can also cause chronic symptoms that include recurrent fevers, joint pain, and fatigue.

▶ New　⇒ Revised　~~deleted~~ Deleted　| Excludes 1 |　| Excludes 2 |　| Includes |　| Use additional |　| Code first |　| Code also |　| Key words |
OGCR Official Guidelines　X Assign placeholder X　● Use Additional Character(s)　▶ Manifestation Code　🅒 Hierarchical Condition Category　**Coding Clinic**

● **A25   Rat-bite fevers**
RBF, infectious disease caused by Streptobacillus moniliformis or Spirillum minus.

  A25.0   Spirillosis
Any disease condition caused by spirilla
Sodoku

  A25.1   Streptobacillosis
Acute, febrile human illness caused by bacteria transmitted by rats in most cases, passed from rodent to human via rodent's urine or mucous secretions; AKA rat fever
Epidemic arthritic erythema
Haverhill fever
Streptobacillary rat-bite fever

  A25.9   Rat-bite fever, unspecified

● **A26   Erysipeloid**
Infection with Erysipelothrix rhusiopathiae, occurring often as occupational disease resulting from handling infected fish, shellfish, meat, or poultry

  A26.0   Cutaneous erysipeloid
Erythema migrans

  A26.7   Erysipelothrix sepsis 🔗

  A26.8   Other forms of erysipeloid

  A26.9   Erysipeloid, unspecified

● **A27   Leptospirosis**
Occurs most commonly in the tropics

  A27.0   Leptospirosis icterohemorrhagica
Leptospiral or spirochetal jaundice (hemorrhagic)
Weil's disease

 ● **A27.8   Other forms of leptospirosis**

    A27.81   Aseptic meningitis in leptospirosis

    A27.89   Other forms of leptospirosis

  A27.9   Leptospirosis, unspecified

● **A28   Other zoonotic bacterial diseases, not elsewhere classified**

  A28.0   Pasteurellosis
Infection of humans or other animals by species of Pasteurella

  A28.1   Cat-scratch disease
Cat-scratch fever

  A28.2   Extraintestinal yersiniosis
Infection from Yersinia enterocolitica; AKA enteric yersiniosis, intestinal yersiniosis, Yersinia enteritis

    Excludes1   enteritis due to Yersinia enterocolitica (A04.6)
plague (A20.-)

  A28.8   Other specified zoonotic bacterial diseases, not elsewhere classified

  A28.9   Zoonotic bacterial disease, unspecified

OTHER BACTERIAL DISEASES (A30-A49)

● **A30   Leprosy [Hansen's disease]**
Chronic infectious disease attacking the skin, peripheral nerves, and mucous membranes

    Includes   infection due to Mycobacterium leprae
    Excludes1   sequelae of leprosy (B92)

  A30.0   Indeterminate leprosy
I leprosy

  A30.1   Tuberculoid leprosy
TT leprosy

  A30.2   Borderline tuberculoid leprosy
BT leprosy

  A30.3   Borderline leprosy
BB leprosy

  A30.4   Borderline lepromatous leprosy
BL leprosy

  A30.5   Lepromatous leprosy
LL leprosy

  A30.8   Other forms of leprosy

  A30.9   Leprosy, unspecified

● **A31   Infection due to other mycobacteria**

    Excludes2   leprosy (A30.-)
tuberculosis (A15-A19)

  A31.0   Pulmonary mycobacterial infection 🔗
Infection due to Mycobacterium avium
Infection due to Mycobacterium intracellulare [Battey bacillus]
Infection due to Mycobacterium kansasii

  A31.1   Cutaneous mycobacterial infection
Buruli ulcer
Infection due to Mycobacterium marinum
Infection due to Mycobacterium ulcerans

  A31.2   Disseminated mycobacterium avium-intracellulare complex (DMAC) 🔗
MAC sepsis

  A31.8   Other mycobacterial infections

  A31.9   Mycobacterial infection, unspecified
Atypical mycobacterial infection NOS
Mycobacteriosis NOS

● **A32   Listeriosis**
Infection caused by Listeria monocytogenes

    Includes   listerial foodborne infection
    Excludes1   neonatal (disseminated) listeriosis (P37.2)

  A32.0   Cutaneous listeriosis

 ● **A32.1   Listerial meningitis and meningoencephalitis**

    A32.11   Listerial meningitis

    A32.12   Listerial meningoencephalitis

  A32.7   Listerial sepsis 🔗

 ● **A32.8   Other forms of listeriosis**

    A32.81   Oculoglandular listeriosis
Primary infection site is conjunctival sac, which if untreated may result in perforation of cornea and optic atrophy

    A32.82   Listerial endocarditis
Exudative and proliferative inflammatory condition of endocardium caused by listeria bacteria

    A32.89   Other forms of listeriosis
Listerial cerebral arteritis

  A32.9   Listeriosis, unspecified

 A33   Tetanus neonatorum   N
Neonate = newborn

 A34   Obstetrical tetanus ♀   M

 A35   Other tetanus
Tetanus NOS

    Excludes1   tetanus neonatorum (A33)
obstetrical tetanus (A34)

● **A36   Diphtheria**

  A36.0   Pharyngeal diphtheria
Diphtheritic membranous angina
Tonsillar diphtheria

  A36.1   Nasopharyngeal diphtheria

  A36.2   Laryngeal diphtheria
Diphtheritic laryngotracheitis

  A36.3   Cutaneous diphtheria

    Excludes2   erythrasma (L08.1)

Item 1-7 Diphtheria: A highly contagious bacterial disease that results in the formation of an adherent membrane in the throat that may lead to suffocation. In its most poisonous form, it attacks the heart and lungs. It is spread by direct physical contact or breathing the aerosolized secretions of infected individuals. The exact location is specified in the codes.

● **A36.8**   **Other diphtheria**

    A36.81   Diphtheritic **cardiomyopathy** 🅒
          Diphtheritic myocarditis

    A36.82   Diphtheritic **radiculomyelitis**

    A36.83   Diphtheritic **polyneuritis**

    A36.84   Diphtheritic **tubulo-interstitial nephropathy**

    A36.85   Diphtheritic **cystitis**

    A36.86   Diphtheritic **conjunctivitis**

    A36.89   **Other** diphtheritic **complications**
          Diphtheritic peritonitis

   A36.9   **Diphtheria, unspecified**

● **A37**   **Whooping cough**
    Pertussis is a highly contagious disease caused by the bacterium
    Bordetella pertussis and results in a whooping sounding cough.

● **A37.0**   **Whooping cough due to Bordetella pertussis**

    A37.00   **Whooping cough due to Bordetella pertussis without pneumonia**

    A37.01   **Whooping cough due to Bordetella pertussis with pneumonia**

● **A37.1**   **Whooping cough due to Bordetella parapertussis**

    A37.10   **Whooping cough due to Bordetella parapertussis without pneumonia**

    A37.11   **Whooping cough due to Bordetella parapertussis with pneumonia**

● **A37.8**   **Whooping cough due to other Bordetella species**

    A37.80   **Whooping cough due to other Bordetella species without pneumonia**

    A37.81   **Whooping cough due to other Bordetella species with pneumonia**

● **A37.9**   **Whooping cough, unspecified species**

    A37.90   **Whooping cough, unspecified species without pneumonia**

    A37.91   **Whooping cough, unspecified species with pneumonia**

● **A38**   **Scarlet fever**
    Most commonly caused by the bacteria Streptococcus pneumoniae and
    Neisseria meningitides

    Includes   scarlatina

    Excludes2   streptococcal sore throat (J02.0)

   A38.0   **Scarlet fever with otitis media**

   A38.1   **Scarlet fever with myocarditis**

   A38.8   **Scarlet fever with other complications**

   A38.9   **Scarlet fever, uncomplicated**
       Scarlet fever, NOS

● **A39**   **Meningococcal infection**
    Most commonly caused by the bacteria Streptococcus pneumoniae and
    Neisseria meningitides

   A39.0   **Meningococcal meningitis**

   A39.1   **Waterhouse-Friderichsen syndrome** 🅒
       Fulminating complication of meningococcemia
       Meningococcal hemorrhagic adrenalitis
       Meningococcic adrenal syndrome

   A39.2   **Acute meningococcemia** 🅒

   A39.3   **Chronic meningococcemia** 🅒

   A39.4   **Meningococcemia, unspecified** 🅒

● **A39.5**   **Meningococcal heart disease**

    A39.50   **Meningococcal carditis, unspecified**

    A39.51   **Meningococcal endocarditis**

    A39.52   **Meningococcal myocarditis**

    A39.53   **Meningococcal pericarditis**

● **A39.8**   **Other meningococcal infections**

    A39.81   **Meningococcal encephalitis**

    A39.82   **Meningococcal retrobulbar neuritis**
       Optic neuritis in portion of optic nerve posterior to
       eyeball; AKA postocular optic neuritis

    A39.83   **Meningococcal arthritis** 🅒

    A39.84   **Postmeningococcal arthritis** 🅒

    A39.89   **Other meningococcal infections**
       Meningococcal conjunctivitis

   A39.9   **Meningococcal infection, unspecified**
       Meningococcal disease NOS

● **A40**   **Streptococcal sepsis**
    Code first
      postprocedural streptococcal sepsis (T81.44)
      streptococcal sepsis during labor (O75.3)
      streptococcal sepsis following abortion or ectopic or molar
        pregnancy (O03-O07, O08.0)
      streptococcal sepsis following immunization (T88.0)
      streptococcal sepsis following infusion, transfusion or
        therapeutic injection (T80.2-)

    Excludes1   neonatal (P36.0-P36.1)
             puerperal sepsis (O85)
             sepsis due to Streptococcus, group D (A41.81)

   A40.0   **Sepsis due to streptococcus, group A** 🅒

   A40.1   **Sepsis due to streptococcus, group B** 🅒
       Coding Clinic: 2019, Q1, P14

   A40.3   **Sepsis due to Streptococcus pneumoniae** 🅒
       Pneumococcal sepsis

   A40.8   **Other streptococcal sepsis** 🅒

   A40.9   **Streptococcal sepsis, unspecified** 🅒

● **A41**   **Other sepsis**
    Code first
      postprocedural sepsis (T81.44)
      sepsis during labor (O75.3)
      sepsis following abortion, ectopic or molar pregnancy
        (O03-O07, O08.0)
      sepsis following immunization (T88.0)
      sepsis following infusion, transfusion or therapeutic injection
        (T80.2-)

    Excludes1   bacteremia NOS (R78.81)
             neonatal (P36.-)
             puerperal sepsis (O85)
             streptococcal sepsis (A40.-)

    Excludes2   sepsis (due to) (in) actinomycotic (A42.7)
             sepsis (due to) (in) anthrax (A22.7)
             sepsis (due to) (in) candidal (B37.7)
             sepsis (due to) (in) Erysipelothrix (A26.7)
             sepsis (due to) (in) extraintestinal yersiniosis
               (A28.2)
             sepsis (due to) (in) gonococcal (A54.86)
             sepsis (due to) (in) herpesviral (B00.7)
             sepsis (due to) (in) listerial (A32.7)
             sepsis (due to) (in) melioidosis (A24.1)
             sepsis (due to) (in) meningococcal (A39.2-A39.4)
             sepsis (due to) (in) plague (A20.7)
             sepsis (due to) (in) tularemia (A21.7)
             toxic shock syndrome (A48.3)
    Coding Clinic: 2016, Q1, P39

● **A41.0**   **Sepsis due to Staphylococcus aureus**

    A41.01   **Sepsis due to Methicillin susceptible Staphylococcus aureus** 🅒
       MSSA sepsis
       Staphylococcus aureus sepsis NOS

    A41.02   **Sepsis due to Methicillin resistant Staphylococcus aureus** 🅒

▶ New   ⇒ Revised   ~~deleted~~ Deleted   Excludes 1   Excludes 2   Includes   Use additional   Code first   Code also   Key words

OGCR Official Guidelines   X Assign placeholder X   ● Use Additional Character(s)   ▶ Manifestation Code   🅒 Hierarchical Condition Category   **Coding Clinic**

Item 1–8   **Gas gangrene** is a necrotizing subcutaneous infection that will cause tissue death. Patients with poor circulation (e.g., diabetes, peripheral nephropathy) will have low oxygen content in their tissues (hypoxia), which allows the Clostridium bacteria to flourish. Gas gangrene often occurs at the site of a surgical wound or trauma. Onset is sudden and dramatic. Treatment can include debridement, amputation, and/or hyperbaric oxygen treatments.

A41.1   **Sepsis due to other specified staphylococcus** 🦠
        Coagulase negative staphylococcus sepsis

A41.2   **Sepsis due to unspecified staphylococcus** 🦠

A41.3   **Sepsis due to Hemophilus influenzae** 🦠

A41.4   **Sepsis due to anaerobes** 🦠
       Excludes1   gas gangrene (A48.0)

● A41.5   **Sepsis due to other Gram-negative organisms**
     A41.50   **Gram-negative sepsis, unspecified** 🦠
         Gram-negative sepsis NOS
     A41.51   **Sepsis due to Escherichia coli [E. coli]** 🦠
         Coding Clinic: 2018, Q1, P16
     A41.52   **Sepsis due to Pseudomonas** 🦠
         Pseudomonas aeroginosa
     A41.53   **Sepsis due to Serratia** 🦠
     A41.59   **Other Gram-negative sepsis** 🦠
         Coding Clinic: 2019, Q1, P13

● A41.8   **Other specified sepsis**
     A41.81   **Sepsis due to Enterococcus** 🦠
     A41.89   **Other specified sepsis** 🦠
         Coding Clinic: 2016, Q3, P8-14

A41.9   **Sepsis, unspecified organism** 🦠
       Septicemia NOS
       Coding Clinic: 2018, Q4, P18

● A42   **Actinomycosis**
    Excludes1   actinomycetoma (B47.1)
   A42.0   **Pulmonary actinomycosis** 🦠
   A42.1   **Abdominal actinomycosis**
   A42.2   **Cervicofacial actinomycosis**
   A42.7   **Actinomycotic sepsis** 🦠
 ● A42.8   **Other forms of actinomycosis**
     A42.81   **Actinomycotic meningitis**
     A42.82   **Actinomycotic encephalitis**
     A42.89   **Other forms of actinomycosis**
   A42.9   **Actinomycosis, unspecified**

● A43   **Nocardiosis**
   A43.0   **Pulmonary nocardiosis** 🦠
   A43.1   **Cutaneous nocardiosis**
   A43.8   **Other forms of nocardiosis**
   A43.9   **Nocardiosis, unspecified**

● A44   **Bartonellosis**
   A44.0   **Systemic bartonellosis**
       Oroya fever
   A44.1   **Cutaneous and mucocutaneous bartonellosis**
       Verruga peruana
   A44.8   **Other forms of bartonellosis**
   A44.9   **Bartonellosis, unspecified**

 A46   **Erysipelas**
    Excludes1   postpartum or puerperal erysipelas (O86.89)

● A48   **Other bacterial diseases, not elsewhere classified**
    Excludes1   actinomycetoma (B47.1)
   A48.0   **Gas gangrene** 🦠
       Clostridial cellulitis
       Clostridial myonecrosis
       Coding Clinic: 2017, Q4, P102

A48.1   **Legionnaires' disease** 🦠
A48.2   **Nonpneumonic Legionnaires' disease [Pontiac fever]**
A48.3   **Toxic shock syndrome** 🦠
       Use additional code to identify the organism (B95, B96)
      Excludes1   endotoxic shock NOS (R57.8)
                sepsis NOS (A41.9)
A48.4   **Brazilian purpuric fever**
       Systemic Hemophilus aegyptius infection
● A48.5   **Other specified botulism**
       Non-foodborne intoxication due to toxins of
          Clostridium botulinum [C. botulinum]
      Excludes1   food poisoning due to toxins of
                Clostridium botulinum (A05.1)
   A48.51   **Infant botulism**   P
   A48.52   **Wound botulism**
         Non-foodborne botulism NOS
         Use additional code for associated wound

A48.8   **Other specified bacterial diseases**

● A49   **Bacterial infection of unspecified site**
    Excludes1   bacterial agents as the cause of diseases classified
             elsewhere (B95-B96)
             chlamydial infection NOS (A74.9)
             meningococcal infection NOS (A39.9)
             rickettsial infection NOS (A79.9)
             spirochetal infection NOS (A69.9)
● A49.0   **Staphylococcal infection, unspecified site**
   A49.01   **Methicillin susceptible Staphylococcus aureus infection, unspecified site**
         Methicillin susceptible Staphylococcus aureus (MSSA) infection
         Staphylococcus aureus infection NOS
   A49.02   **Methicillin resistant Staphylococcus aureus infection, unspecified site**
         Methicillin resistant Staphylococcus aureus (MRSA) infection
A49.1   **Streptococcal infection, unspecified site**
A49.2   **Hemophilus influenzae infection, unspecified site**
       Any of seven bacterium of genus Haemophilus
A49.3   **Mycoplasma infection, unspecified site**
       Bacterium of class Mollicutes, unusual group of bacteria distinguished by absence of cell wall
A49.8   **Other bacterial infections of unspecified site**
A49.9   **Bacterial infection, unspecified**
    Excludes1   bacteremia NOS (R78.81)

INFECTIONS WITH A PREDOMINANTLY SEXUAL MODE OF TRANSMISSION (A50-A64)

    Excludes1   human immunodeficiency virus [HIV] disease (B20)
             nonspecific and nongonococcal urethritis (N34.1)
             Reiter's disease (M02.3-)

● A50   **Congenital syphilis**
 ● A50.0   **Early congenital syphilis, symptomatic**
       Any congenital syphilitic condition specified as early or manifest less than two years after birth
   A50.01   **Early congenital syphilitic oculopathy**
   A50.02   **Early congenital syphilitic osteochondropathy**
   A50.03   **Early congenital syphilitic pharyngitis**
         Early congenital syphilitic laryngitis
   A50.04   **Early congenital syphilitic pneumonia**
   A50.05   **Early congenital syphilitic rhinitis**
   A50.06   **Early cutaneous congenital syphilis**
   A50.07   **Early mucocutaneous congenital syphilis**
   A50.08   **Early visceral congenital syphilis**
   A50.09   **Other early congenital syphilis, symptomatic**

CHAPTER 1 (A00-B99)

Figure 1-3 Chancre of primary syphilis. (From James WD, Berger TG, Elston DM: Andrews' Diseases of the Skin: Clinical Dermatology, Philadelphia, Saunders Elsevier, 2006)

Item 1–9 Syphilis, also known as lues, is the most serious of the venereal diseases caused by *Treponema pallidum*. The **primary** stage is characterized by an ulceration known as **chancre,** which usually appears on the genitals but can also develop on the anus, lips, tonsils, breasts, or fingers. Syphilis is easy to cure in its early stages. A single intramuscular injection of penicillin will usually cure a person who has had syphilis for less than a year.

The **secondary** stage is characterized by a rash that can affect any area of the body. **Latent** syphilis is divided into **early,** which is diagnosed within two years of infection, and **late,** which is diagnosed two years or more after infection. Additional doses of penicillin or another antibiotic are needed to treat someone who has had syphilis for longer than a year. For those allergic to penicillin, there are other antibiotic treatments. **Congenital** syphilis is also labeled **early** or **late** based on the time of diagnosis.

A50.1　Early congenital syphilis, latent
　　　　Congenital syphilis without clinical manifestations, with positive serological reaction and negative spinal fluid test, less than two years after birth

A50.2　Early congenital syphilis, unspecified
　　　　Congenital syphilis NOS less than two years after birth

● **A50.3　Late congenital syphilitic oculopathy**
　　　　Excludes1　Hutchinson's triad (A50.53)

　　A50.30　Late congenital syphilitic oculopathy, unspecified

　　A50.31　Late congenital syphilitic interstitial keratitis

　　A50.32　Late congenital syphilitic chorioretinitis

　　A50.39　Other late congenital syphilitic oculopathy

● **A50.4　Late congenital neurosyphilis [juvenile neurosyphilis]**
　　　　Use additional code to identify any associated mental disorder

　　　　Excludes1　Hutchinson's triad (A50.53)

　　A50.40　Late congenital neurosyphilis, unspecified
　　　　　Juvenile neurosyphilis NOS

　　A50.41　Late congenital syphilitic meningitis

　　A50.42　Late congenital syphilitic encephalitis

　　A50.43　Late congenital syphilitic polyneuropathy

　　A50.44　Late congenital syphilitic optic nerve atrophy

　　A50.45　Juvenile general paresis
　　　　　Dementia paralytica juvenilis
　　　　　Juvenile tabetoparetic neurosyphilis

　　A50.49　Other late congenital neurosyphilis
　　　　　Juvenile tabes dorsalis

● **A50.5　Other late congenital syphilis, symptomatic**
　　　　Any congenital syphilitic condition specified as late or manifest two years or more after birth

　　A50.51　Clutton's joints

　　A50.52　Hutchinson's teeth

　　A50.53　Hutchinson's triad

　　A50.54　Late congenital cardiovascular syphilis

　　A50.55　Late congenital syphilitic arthropathy

　　A50.56　Late congenital syphilitic osteochondropathy

　　A50.57　Syphilitic saddle nose

　　A50.59　Other late congenital syphilis, symptomatic

A50.6　Late congenital syphilis, latent
　　　　Congenital syphilis without clinical manifestations, with positive serological reaction and negative spinal fluid test, two years or more after birth.

A50.7　Late congenital syphilis, unspecified
　　　　Congenital syphilis NOS two years or more after birth.

A50.9　Congenital syphilis, unspecified

● **A51　Early syphilis**

A51.0　Primary genital syphilis
　　　　Syphilitic chancre NOS

A51.1　Primary anal syphilis

A51.2　Primary syphilis of other sites

● **A51.3　Secondary syphilis of skin and mucous membranes**

　　A51.31　Condyloma latum

　　A51.32　Syphilitic alopecia

　　A51.39　Other secondary syphilis of skin
　　　　　Syphilitic leukoderma
　　　　　Syphilitic mucous patch
　　　　　Excludes1　late syphilitic leukoderma (A52.79)

● **A51.4　Other secondary syphilis**

　　A51.41　Secondary syphilitic meningitis

　　A51.42　Secondary syphilitic female pelvic disease ♀

　　A51.43　Secondary syphilitic oculopathy
　　　　　Secondary syphilitic chorioretinitis
　　　　　Secondary syphilitic iridocyclitis, iritis
　　　　　Secondary syphilitic uveitis

　　A51.44　Secondary syphilitic nephritis

　　A51.45　Secondary syphilitic hepatitis

　　A51.46　Secondary syphilitic osteopathy

　　A51.49　Other secondary syphilitic conditions
　　　　　Secondary syphilitic lymphadenopathy
　　　　　Secondary syphilitic myositis

A51.5　Early syphilis, latent
　　　　Syphilis (acquired) without clinical manifestations, with positive serological reaction and negative spinal fluid test, less than two years after infection.

A51.9　Early syphilis, unspecified

● **A52　Late syphilis**

● **A52.0　Cardiovascular and cerebrovascular syphilis**

　　A52.00　Cardiovascular syphilis, unspecified

　　A52.01　Syphilitic aneurysm of aorta

　　A52.02　Syphilitic aortitis

　　A52.03　Syphilitic endocarditis
　　　　　Syphilitic aortic valve incompetence or stenosis
　　　　　Syphilitic mitral valve stenosis
　　　　　Syphilitic pulmonary valve regurgitation

　　A52.04　Syphilitic cerebral arteritis

　　A52.05　Other cerebrovascular syphilis
　　　　　Syphilitic cerebral aneurysm (ruptured) (non-ruptured)
　　　　　Syphilitic cerebral thrombosis

　　A52.06　Other syphilitic heart involvement
　　　　　Syphilitic coronary artery disease
　　　　　Syphilitic myocarditis
　　　　　Syphilitic pericarditis

　　A52.09　Other cardiovascular syphilis

● **A52.1　Symptomatic neurosyphilis**

　　A52.10　Symptomatic neurosyphilis, unspecified

　　A52.11　Tabes dorsalis
　　　　　Cognitive decline with progressive degeneration of posterior columns, roots, and ganglia of spinal cord, occur 15-20 years after initial infection of syphilis; AKA Duchenne disease
　　　　　Locomotor ataxia (progressive)
　　　　　Tabetic neurosyphilis

　　A52.12　Other cerebrospinal syphilis

　　A52.13　Late syphilitic meningitis

　　A52.14　Late syphilitic encephalitis

　　A52.15　Late syphilitic neuropathy
　　　　　Late syphilitic acoustic neuritis
　　　　　Late syphilitic optic (nerve) atrophy
　　　　　Late syphilitic polyneuropathy
　　　　　Late syphilitic retrobulbar neuritis

▶ New　⟹ Revised　~~deleted~~ Deleted　Excludes 1　Excludes 2　Includes　Use additional　Code first　Code also　Key words

658　OGCR Official Guidelines　X Assign placeholder X　● Use Additional Character(s)　▸ Manifestation Code　🐾 Hierarchical Condition Category　**Coding Clinic**

CHAPTER 1 (A00-B99)

A52.16 **Charcôt's arthropathy (tabetic)**
Progressive musculoskeletal condition characterized by joint dislocation, fractures, and deformities, results in progressive destruction of bone and soft tissue of weight-bearing joints

A52.17 **General paresis**
Chronic meningoencephalitis results in loss of cortical function, or progressive dementia and generalized paralysis, occurring 10-20 years after initial infection of syphilis; AKA Bayle disease, dementia paralytica, paralytic dementiaparetic neurosyphilis, syphilitic meningoencephalitis
Dementia paralytica

A52.19 **Other symptomatic neurosyphilis**
Syphilitic parkinsonism

A52.2 **Asymptomatic neurosyphilis**

A52.3 **Neurosyphilis, unspecified**
Gumma (syphilitic)
Destructive lesions of syphilis
Syphilis (late)
Syphiloma

● **A52.7** **Other symptomatic late syphilis**

A52.71 **Late syphilitic oculopathy**
Late syphilitic chorioretinitis
Late syphilitic episcleritis

A52.72 **Syphilis of lung and bronchus**

A52.73 **Symptomatic late syphilis of other respiratory organs**

A52.74 **Syphilis of liver and other viscera**
Late syphilitic peritonitis

A52.75 **Syphilis of kidney and ureter**
Syphilitic glomerular disease

A52.76 **Other genitourinary symptomatic late syphilis ♀**
Late syphilitic female pelvic inflammatory disease

A52.77 **Syphilis of bone and joint**

A52.78 **Syphilis of other musculoskeletal tissue**
Late syphilitic bursitis
Syphilis [stage unspecified] of bursa
Syphilis [stage unspecified] of muscle
Syphilis [stage unspecified] of synovium
Syphilis [stage unspecified] of tendon

A52.79 **Other symptomatic late syphilis**
Late syphilitic leukoderma
Syphilis of adrenal gland
Syphilis of pituitary gland
Syphilis of thyroid gland
Syphilitic splenomegaly
Excludes1 syphilitic leukoderma (secondary) (A51.39)

A52.8 **Late syphilis, latent**
Syphilis (acquired) without clinical manifestations, with positive serological reaction and negative spinal fluid test, two years or more after infection

A52.9 **Late syphilis, unspecified**

● **A53** **Other and unspecified syphilis**

A53.0 **Latent syphilis, unspecified as early or late**
Latent syphilis NOS
Positive serological reaction for syphilis

A53.9 **Syphilis, unspecified**
Infection due to Treponema pallidum NOS
Syphilis (acquired) NOS
Excludes1 syphilis NOS under two years of age (A50.2)

Item 1-10 An STD (sexually transmitted disease) caused by **Neisseria gonorrhoeae** that flourishes in the warm, moist areas of the reproductive tract. Untreated gonorrhea spreads to other parts of the body, causing inflammation of the testes or prostate or pelvic inflammatory disease (PID).

● **A54** **Gonococcal infection**
● **A54.0** **Gonococcal infection of lower genitourinary tract without periurethral or accessory gland abscess**
Excludes1 gonococcal infection with genitourinary gland abscess (A54.1)
gonococcal infection with periurethral abscess (A54.1)

A54.00 **Gonococcal infection of lower genitourinary tract, unspecified**

A54.01 **Gonococcal cystitis and urethritis, unspecified**

A54.02 **Gonococcal vulvovaginitis, unspecified ♀**

A54.03 **Gonococcal cervicitis, unspecified ♀**

A54.09 **Other gonococcal infection of lower genitourinary tract**

A54.1 **Gonococcal infection of lower genitourinary tract with periurethral and accessory gland abscess**
Gonococcal Bartholin's gland abscess

● **A54.2** **Gonococcal pelviperitonitis and other gonococcal genitourinary infection**

A54.21 **Gonococcal infection of kidney and ureter**

A54.22 **Gonococcal prostatitis ♂**

A54.23 **Gonococcal infection of other male genital organs ♂**
Gonococcal epididymitis
Gonococcal orchitis

A54.24 **Gonococcal female pelvic inflammatory disease ♀**
Gonococcal pelviperitonitis
Excludes1 gonococcal peritonitis (A54.85)

A54.29 **Other gonococcal genitourinary infections**

● **A54.3** **Gonococcal infection of eye**

A54.30 **Gonococcal infection of eye, unspecified**

A54.31 **Gonococcal conjunctivitis**
Form of bacterial conjunctivitis contracted by newborns during delivery; AKA neonatal conjunctivitis
Ophthalmia neonatorum due to gonococcus

A54.32 **Gonococcal iridocyclitis**
Inflammation of iris and of ciliary body due to gonococcal infection

A54.33 **Gonococcal keratitis**
Inflammation of cornea due to gonococcal infection; AKA keratoconjunctivitis, keratopathy

A54.39 **Other gonococcal eye infection**
Gonococcal endophthalmia

● **A54.4** **Gonococcal infection of musculoskeletal system**

A54.40 **Gonococcal infection of musculoskeletal system, unspecified** ✹

A54.41 **Gonococcal spondylopathy** ✹
Disorder of vertebrae due to gonococcal infection; AKA rachiopathy

A54.42 **Gonococcal arthritis** ✹
Excludes2 gonococcal infection of spine (A54.41)

A54.43 **Gonococcal osteomyelitis** ✹
Excludes2 gonococcal infection of spine (A54.41)

A54.49 **Gonococcal infection of other musculoskeletal tissue** ✹
Gonococcal bursitis
Gonococcal myositis
Gonococcal synovitis
Gonococcal tenosynovitis

A54.5   Gonococcal pharyngitis

A54.6   Gonococcal infection of anus and rectum

● **A54.8**   Other gonococcal infections

     A54.81   Gonococcal meningitis

     A54.82   Gonococcal brain abscess

     A54.83   Gonococcal heart infection
           Gonococcal endocarditis
           Gonococcal myocarditis
           Gonococcal pericarditis

     A54.84   Gonococcal pneumonia 🅀

     A54.85   Gonococcal peritonitis 🅀

          Excludes1   gonococcal pelviperitonitis (A54.24)

     A54.86   Gonococcal sepsis 🅀

     A54.89   Other gonococcal infections
           Gonococcal keratoderma
           Gonococcal lymphadenitis

A54.9   Gonococcal infection, unspecified

A55   Chlamydial lymphogranuloma (venereum)
     Climatic or tropical bubo
     Durand-Nicolas-Favre disease
     Esthiomene
     Lymphogranuloma inguinale

● **A56**   Other sexually transmitted chlamydial diseases

     Includes   sexually transmitted diseases due to Chlamydia trachomatis

     Excludes1   neonatal chlamydial conjunctivitis (P39.1)
          neonatal chlamydial pneumonia (P23.1)

     Excludes2   chlamydial lymphogranuloma (A55)
          conditions classified to A74.-

   ● **A56.0**   Chlamydial infection of lower genitourinary tract

     A56.00   Chlamydial infection of lower genitourinary tract, unspecified

     A56.01   Chlamydial cystitis and urethritis

     A56.02   Chlamydial vulvovaginitis ♀

     A56.09   Other chlamydial infection of lower genitourinary tract
           Chlamydial cervicitis

   ● **A56.1**   Chlamydial infection of pelviperitoneum and other genitourinary organs

     A56.11   Chlamydial female pelvic inflammatory disease ♀

     A56.19   Other chlamydial genitourinary infection
           Chlamydial epididymitis
           Chlamydial orchitis

   A56.2   Chlamydial infection of genitourinary tract, unspecified

   A56.3   Chlamydial infection of anus and rectum

   A56.4   Chlamydial infection of pharynx

   A56.8   Sexually transmitted chlamydial infection of other sites

A57   Chancroid
     Ulcus molle
     Sexually transmitted infection caused by bacteria, Haemophilus ducreyi

A58   Granuloma inguinale
     Chronic, progressive, ulcerative granulomatous disease
     Donovanosis

● **A59**   Trichomoniasis

     Excludes2   intestinal trichomoniasis (A07.8)

     A common STD caused by a parasite, Trichomonas vaginalis

   ● **A59.0**   Urogenital trichomoniasis

     A59.00   Urogenital trichomoniasis, unspecified
           Fluor (vaginalis) due to Trichomonas
           Leukorrhea (vaginalis) due to Trichomonas

     A59.01   Trichomonal vulvovaginitis ♀

     A59.02   Trichomonal prostatitis ♂

     A59.03   Trichomonal cystitis and urethritis

     A59.09   Other urogenital trichomoniasis
          Common sexually transmitted disease (STD) caused by single-celled protozoan parasite; AKA trich
          Trichomonas cervicitis

   A59.8   Trichomoniasis of other sites

   A59.9   Trichomoniasis, unspecified

● **A60**   Anogenital herpesviral [herpes simplex] infections

   ● **A60.0**   Herpesviral infection of genitalia and urogenital tract

     A60.00   Herpesviral infection of urogenital system, unspecified

     A60.01   Herpesviral infection of penis ♂

     A60.02   Herpesviral infection of other male genital organs ♂

     A60.03   Herpesviral cervicitis ♀

     A60.04   Herpesviral vulvovaginitis ♀
          Herpesviral [herpes simplex] ulceration
          Herpesviral [herpes simplex] vaginitis
          Herpesviral [herpes simplex] vulvitis

     A60.09   Herpesviral infection of other urogenital tract
          Coding Clinic: 2020, Q1, P20

   A60.1   Herpesviral infection of perianal skin and rectum

   A60.9   Anogenital herpesviral infection, unspecified

● **A63**   Other predominantly sexually transmitted diseases, not elsewhere classified

     Excludes2   molluscum contagiosum (B08.1)
          papilloma of cervix (D26.0)

   A63.0   Anogenital (venereal) warts
       Anogenital warts due to (human) papillomavirus [HPV]
       Condyloma acuminatum

   A63.8   Other specified predominantly sexually transmitted diseases

A64   Unspecified sexually transmitted disease

OTHER SPIROCHETAL DISEASES (A65-A69)

     Excludes2   leptospirosis (A27.-)
          syphilis (A50-A53)

A65   Nonvenereal syphilis
     Bejel
     Endemic syphilis
     Njovera

● **A66**   Yaws
     Endemic, infectious, tropical disease caused by spirochete, spread by direct contact; AKA frambesia, framboesia, frambesia tropica

     Includes   bouba
          frambesia (tropica)
          pian

   A66.0   Initial lesions of yaws
       Chancre of yaws
       Frambesia, initial or primary
       Initial frambesial ulcer
       Mother yaw

   A66.1   Multiple papillomata and wet crab yaws
       Frambesioma
       Pianoma
       Plantar or palmar papilloma of yaws

   A66.2   Other early skin lesions of yaws
       Cutaneous yaws, less than five years after infection
       Early yaws (cutaneous)(macular)(maculopapular) (micropapular)(papular)
       Frambeside of early yaws

▶ New   ⇒ Revised   ~~deleted~~ Deleted   Excludes 1   Excludes 2   Includes   Use additional   Code first   Code also   Key words

OGCR Official Guidelines   X Assign placeholder X   ● Use Additional Character(s)   ▶ Manifestation Code   🅀 Hierarchical Condition Category   Coding Clinic

A66.3 Hyperkeratosis of yaws
Hypertrophy of stratum corneum of skin in which there are small, hard, verrucous scales
Ghoul hand
Hyperkeratosis, palmar or plantar (early) (late) due to yaws
Worm-eaten soles

A66.4 Gummata and ulcers of yaws
Small, rubbery granuloma with necrotic center and inflamed characteristic of advanced stage of syphilis; AKA syphiloma
Gummatous frambeside
Nodular late yaws (ulcerated)

A66.5 Gangosa
Manifestation of yaws that develops in the soft palate and spreads eroding bone, cartilage, and soft tissue
Rhinopharyngitis mutilans

A66.6 Bone and joint lesions of yaws 🔧
Yaws ganglion
Yaws goundou
Yaws gumma, bone
Yaws gummatous osteitis or periostitis
Yaws hydrarthrosis
Yaws osteitis
Yaws periostitis (hypertrophic)

A66.7 Other manifestations of yaws
Juxta-articular nodules of yaws
Mucosal yaws

A66.8 Latent yaws
Yaws without clinical manifestations, with positive serology

A66.9 Yaws, unspecified

⬤ **A67 Pinta [carate]**
Group of nonvenereal diseases caused by Treponema species

A67.0 Primary lesions of pinta
Chancre (primary) of pinta
Papule (primary) of pinta

A67.1 Intermediate lesions of pinta
Erythematous plaques of pinta
Hyperchromic lesions of pinta
Hyperkeratosis of pinta
Pintids

A67.2 Late lesions of pinta
Achromic skin lesions of pinta
Cicatricial skin lesions of pinta
Dyschromic skin lesions of pinta

A67.3 Mixed lesions of pinta
Achromic with hyperchromic skin lesions of pinta [carate]

A67.9 Pinta, unspecified

⬤ **A68 Relapsing fevers**
Includes recurrent fever
Excludes2 Lyme disease (A69.2-)

A68.0 Louse-borne relapsing fever
Relapsing fever due to Borrelia recurrentis

A68.1 Tick-borne relapsing fever
Relapsing fever due to any Borrelia species other than Borrelia recurrentis

A68.9 Relapsing fever, unspecified

Item 1-11 Cancrum oris, also known as **noma** or **gangrenous stomatitis,** begins as an ulcer of the gingiva and results in a progressive gangrenous process.

⬤ **A69 Other spirochetal infections**

A69.0 Necrotizing ulcerative stomatitis
Cancrum oris
Fusospirochetal gangrene
Noma
Stomatitis gangrenosa

A69.1 Other Vincent's infections
Fusospirochetal pharyngitis
Necrotizing ulcerative (acute) gingivitis
Necrotizing ulcerative (acute) gingivostomatitis
Spirochetal stomatitis
Trench mouth
Vincent's angina
Vincent's gingivitis

⬤ **A69.2 Lyme disease**
Erythema chronicum migrans due to Borrelia burgdorferi

A69.20 Lyme disease, unspecified

A69.21 Meningitis due to Lyme disease

A69.22 Other neurologic disorders in Lyme disease
Cranial neuritis
Meningoencephalitis
Polyneuropathy

A69.23 Arthritis due to Lyme disease 🔧

A69.29 Other conditions associated with Lyme disease
Myopericarditis due to Lyme disease
Coding Clinic: 2016, Q3, P12

A69.8 Other specified spirochetal infections

A69.9 Spirochetal infection, unspecified

OTHER DISEASES CAUSED BY CHLAMYDIAE (A70-A74)

Excludes1 sexually transmitted chlamydial diseases (A55-A56)

A70 Chlamydia psittaci infections
Ornithosis
Parrot fever
Psittacosis

⬤ **A71 Trachoma**
Excludes1 sequelae of trachoma (B94.0)

A71.0 Initial stage of trachoma
Trachoma dubium

A71.1 Active stage of trachoma
Granular conjunctivitis (trachomatous)
Trachomatous follicular conjunctivitis
Trachomatous pannus

A71.9 Trachoma, unspecified

⬤ **A74 Other diseases caused by chlamydiae**
Excludes1 neonatal chlamydial conjunctivitis (P39.1)
neonatal chlamydial pneumonia (P23.1)
Reiter's disease (M02.3-)
sexually transmitted chlamydial diseases (A55-A56)

Excludes2 chlamydial pneumonia (J16.0)

A74.0 Chlamydial conjunctivitis
Paratrachoma

⬤ **A74.8 Other chlamydial diseases**

A74.81 Chlamydial peritonitis

A74.89 Other chlamydial diseases

A74.9 Chlamydial infection, unspecified
Chlamydiosis NOS

CHAPTER 1 (A00-B99)

Item 1–12   **Rickettsioses** are diseases spread from ticks, lice, fleas, or mites to humans.

     Typhus is spread to humans chiefly by the fleas of rats.

     Endemic identifies a disease as being present in low numbers of humans at all times, whereas **epidemic** identifies a disease as being present in high numbers of humans at a specific time. Morbidity (death) is higher in epidemic diseases.

     Brill's disease, also known as **Brill-Zinsser disease,** is spread from human to human by body lice and also from the lice of flying squirrels. **Scrub typhus** is spread in the same ways as Brill's disease.

     Malaria is spread to humans by mosquitoes.

RICKETTSIOSES (A75-A79)

● **A75   Typhus fever**
     Excludes1   rickettsiosis due to Ehrlichia sennetsu (A79.81)

     A75.0   Epidemic louse-borne typhus fever due to Rickettsia prowazekii
         Organisms transmitted between humans via louse
         Classical typhus (fever)
         Epidemic (louse-borne) typhus

     A75.1   Recrudescent typhus [Brill's disease]
         Brill-Zinsser disease

     A75.2   Typhus fever due to Rickettsia typhi
         Murine (flea-borne) typhus

     A75.3   Typhus fever due to Rickettsia tsutsugamushi
         Scrub (mite-borne) typhus
         Tsutsugamushi fever
         ▶ Typhus fever due to Orientia Tsutsugamushi (scrub typhus)

     A75.9   Typhus fever, unspecified
         Typhus (fever) NOS

● **A77   Spotted fever [tick-borne rickettsioses]**

     A77.0   Spotted fever due to Rickettsia rickettsii
         Rocky Mountain spotted fever
         Sao Paulo fever

     A77.1   Spotted fever due to Rickettsia conorii
         African tick typhus
         Boutonneuse fever
         India tick typhus
         Kenya tick typhus
         Marseilles fever
         Mediterranean tick fever

     A77.2   Spotted fever due to Rickettsia siberica
         North Asian tick fever
         Siberian tick typhus

     A77.3   Spotted fever due to Rickettsia australis
         Queensland tick typhus

     ● **A77.4   Ehrlichiosis**
         Type of tick-borne fever caused by bacteria infection
         Excludes1   Rickettsiosis due to Ehrlichia sennetsu (A79.81)

         A77.40   Ehrlichiosis, unspecified
         A77.41   Ehrlichiosis chafeensis [E. chafeensis]
         A77.49   Other ehrlichiosis
            ▶ Ehrlichiosis due to E. ewingii
            ▶ Ehrlichiosis due to E. muris euclairensis

     A77.8   Other spotted fevers
         ▶ Rickettsia 364D/R. philipii (Pacific Coast tick fever)
         ▶ Spotted fever due to Rickettsia africae (African tick bite fever)
         ▶ Spotted fever due to Rickettsia parkeri]

     A77.9   Spotted fever, unspecified
         Tick-borne typhus NOS

A78   Q fever
     Infection due to Coxiella burnetii
     Nine Mile fever
     Quadrilateral fever

● **A79   Other rickettsioses**

     A79.0   Trench fever
         Quintan fever
         Wolhynian fever

     A79.1   Rickettsialpox due to Rickettsia akari
         Kew Garden fever
         Vesicular rickettsiosis

     ● **A79.8   Other specified rickettsioses**

         A79.81   Rickettsiosis due to Ehrlichia sennetsu
            ▶ Rickettsiosis due to Neorickettsia sennetsu

         A79.89   Other specified rickettsioses

     A79.9   Rickettsiosis, unspecified
         Rickettsial infection NOS

VIRAL AND PRION INFECTIONS OF THE CENTRAL NERVOUS SYSTEM (A80-A89)

     Excludes1   postpolio syndrome (G14)
                  sequelae of poliomyelitis (B91)
                  sequelae of viral encephalitis (B94.1)

● **A80   Acute poliomyelitis**

     A80.0   Acute paralytic poliomyelitis, vaccine-associated
     A80.1   Acute paralytic poliomyelitis, wild virus, imported
     A80.2   Acute paralytic poliomyelitis, wild virus, indigenous
     ● **A80.3   Acute paralytic poliomyelitis, other and unspecified**

         A80.30   Acute paralytic poliomyelitis, unspecified
         A80.39   Other acute paralytic poliomyelitis

     A80.4   Acute nonparalytic poliomyelitis
     A80.9   Acute poliomyelitis, unspecified

● **A81   Atypical virus infections of central nervous system**
     Includes   diseases of the central nervous system caused by prions
     Use additional code to identify:
     dementia with behavioral disturbance (F02.81)
     dementia without behavioral disturbance (F02.80)

     ● **A81.0   Creutzfeldt-Jakob disease**

         A81.00   Creutzfeldt-Jakob disease, unspecified
            Jakob-Creutzfeldt disease, unspecified

         A81.01   Variant Creutzfeldt-Jakob disease
            vCJD

         A81.09   Other Creutzfeldt-Jakob disease
            CJD
            Familial Creutzfeldt-Jakob disease
            Iatrogenic Creutzfeldt-Jakob disease
            Sporadic Creutzfeldt-Jakob disease
            Subacute spongiform encephalopathy (with dementia)

     A81.1   Subacute sclerosing panencephalitis
         Type of viral encephalitis that causes parenchymatous lesions in gray and white matter of brain
         Dawson's inclusion body encephalitis
         Van Bogaert's sclerosing leukoencephalopathy

     A81.2   Progressive multifocal leukoencephalopathy
         Group of diseases affecting white matter of brain
         Multifocal leukoencephalopathy NOS

     ● **A81.8   Other atypical virus infections of central nervous system**

         A81.81   Kuru
         A81.82   Gerstmann-Sträussler-Scheinker syndrome
            GSS syndrome

         A81.83   Fatal familial insomnia
            FFI

         A81.89   Other atypical virus infections of central nervous system

     A81.9   Atypical virus infection of central nervous system, unspecified
         Prion diseases of the central nervous system NOS

Item 1-13   **Acute Poliomyelitis:** Also called infantile paralysis and is caused by the poliovirus, which enters the body orally and infects the intestinal wall and then enters the blood stream and central nervous system, causing muscle weakness and paralysis. This disease has been nearly eradicated with the polio vaccine.

▶ New   ⇒ Revised   ~~deleted~~ Deleted   Excludes 1   Excludes 2   Includes   Use additional   Code first   Code also   Key words

OGCR Official Guidelines   X Assign placeholder X   ● Use Additional Character(s)   ▶ Manifestation Code   🝔 Hierarchical Condition Category   **Coding Clinic**

Item 1-14 **Encephalitis** is an inflammation of the brain most often caused by a virus but may also be caused by a bacteria and most commonly transmitted by a mosquito. **Myelitis** is an inflammation of the spinal cord that may disrupt CNS function. Untreated myelitis may rapidly lead to permanent damage to the spinal cord. **Encephalomyelitis** is a general term for an inflammation of the brain and spinal cord.

● **A82   Rabies**
Viral disease affecting the central nervous system and transmitted from infected mammals to man

A82.0   Sylvatic rabies

A82.1   Urban rabies

A82.9   Rabies, unspecified

● **A83   Mosquito-borne viral encephalitis**
Inflammation of the brain caused most commonly by Herpes Simplex virus

> **Includes**   mosquito-borne viral meningoencephalitis
> **Excludes2**   Venezuelan equine encephalitis (A92.2)
>   West Nile fever (A92.3-)
>   West Nile virus (A92.3-)

A83.0   Japanese encephalitis

A83.1   Western equine encephalitis

A83.2   Eastern equine encephalitis

A83.3   St. Louis encephalitis

A83.4   Australian encephalitis
Kunjin virus disease

A83.5   California encephalitis
California meningoencephalitis
La Crosse encephalitis

A83.6   Rocio virus disease
Mosquito-borne virus

A83.8   Other mosquito-borne viral encephalitis

A83.9   Mosquito-borne viral encephalitis, unspecified

● **A84   Tick-borne viral encephalitis**
> **Includes**   tick-borne viral meningoencephalitis

A84.0   Far Eastern tick-borne encephalitis [Russian spring-summer encephalitis]

A84.1   Central European tick-borne encephalitis

A84.8   Other tick-borne viral encephalitis
▶ **A84.81   Powassan virus disease**
▶ **A84.89   Other tick-borne viral encephalitis**
    ▶Louping ill

▶ *Code first, if applicable, transfusion related infection (T80.22-)*
    ~~Louping ill~~
    ~~Powassan virus disease~~

A84.9   Tick-borne viral encephalitis, unspecified

● **A85   Other viral encephalitis, not elsewhere classified**
> **Includes**   specified viral encephalomyelitis NEC
>   specified viral meningoencephalitis NEC
> **Excludes1**   benign myalgic encephalomyelitis (G93.3)
>   encephalitis due to cytomegalovirus (B25.8)
>   encephalitis due to herpesvirus NEC (B10.0-)
>   encephalitis due to herpesvirus [herpes simplex] (B00.4)
>   encephalitis due to measles virus (B05.0)
>   encephalitis due to mumps virus (B26.2)
>   encephalitis due to poliomyelitis virus (A80.-)
>   encephalitis due to zoster (B02.0)
>   lymphocytic choriomeningitis (A87.2)

A85.0   Enteroviral encephalitis
Enteroviral encephalomyelitis

A85.1   Adenoviral encephalitis
Adenoviral meningoencephalitis

A85.2   Arthropod-borne viral encephalitis, unspecified
> **Excludes1**   West nile virus with encephalitis (A92.31)

A85.8   Other specified viral encephalitis
Encephalitis lethargica
Von Economo-Cruchet disease

A86   Unspecified viral encephalitis
Viral encephalomyelitis NOS
Viral meningoencephalitis NOS

● **A87   Viral meningitis**
> **Excludes1**   meningitis due to herpesvirus [herpes simplex] (B00.3)
>   meningitis due to measles virus (B05.1)
>   meningitis due to mumps virus (B26.1)
>   meningitis due to poliomyelitis virus (A80.-)
>   meningitis due to zoster (B02.1)

A87.0   Enteroviral meningitis
Group of common viruses responsible for the majority of viral meningitis
Coxsackievirus meningitis
Echovirus meningitis

A87.1   Adenoviral meningitis

A87.2   Lymphocytic choriomeningitis
Lymphocytic meningoencephalitis

A87.8   Other viral meningitis

A87.9   Viral meningitis, unspecified

● **A88   Other viral infections of central nervous system, not elsewhere classified**
> **Excludes1**   viral encephalitis NOS (A86)
>   viral meningitis NOS (A87.9)

A88.0   Enteroviral exanthematous fever [Boston exanthem]
Infectious skin eruption

A88.1   Epidemic vertigo

A88.8   Other specified viral infections of central nervous system

A89   Unspecified viral infection of central nervous system

OGCR Section I. C.1.f.

Certain Infectious and Parasitic Diseases (A00-B99)

Zika virus infections

Code only confirmed cases

Code only a confirmed diagnosis of Zika virus (A92.5, Zika virus disease) as documented by the provider. This is an exception to the hospital inpatient guideline Section II, H.

In this context, "confirmation" does not require documentation of the type of test performed; the physician's diagnostic statement that the condition is confirmed is sufficient. This code should be assigned regardless of the stated mode of transmission.

If the provider documents "suspected", "possible" or "probable" Zika, do not assign code A92.5. Assign a code(s) explaining the reason for encounter (such as fever, rash, or joint pain) or Z20.828, Contact with and (suspected) exposure to other viral communicable diseases.

ARTHROPOD-BORNE VIRAL FEVERS AND VIRAL HEMORRHAGIC FEVERS (A90-A99)

A90   Dengue fever [classical dengue]
Acute, self-limited disease, characterized by fever, prostration, severe muscle pains, headache, rash, lymphadenopathy, and leukopenia, caused by dengue virus; AKA breakbone, dandy
> **Excludes1**   dengue hemorrhagic fever (A91)
> **Coding Clinic: 2016, Q3, P13**

A91   Dengue hemorrhagic fever
Serious follow-up to regular dengue, with symptoms of hemorrhage

● **A92   Other mosquito-borne viral fevers**
> **Excludes1**   Ross River disease (B33.1)

A92.0   Chikungunya virus disease
Transmitted by mosquitoes
Chikungunya (hemorrhagic) fever

A92.1   O'nyong-nyong fever
Acute, nonfatal febrile disease transmitted by mosquitoes, which clinically resembles dengue and chikungunya

A92.2 Venezuelan equine fever
Venezuelan equine encephalitis
Venezuelan equine encephalomyelitis virus disease

● **A92.3 West Nile virus infection**
West Nile fever

  A92.30 West Nile virus infection, unspecified
West Nile fever NOS
West Nile fever without complications
West Nile virus NOS

  A92.31 West Nile virus infection with encephalitis
West Nile encephalitis
West Nile encephalomyelitis
Coding Clinic: 2016, Q3, P13

  A92.32 West Nile virus infection with other neurologic manifestation
Use additional code to specify the neurologic manifestation

  A92.39 West Nile virus infection with other complications
Use additional code to specify the other conditions

A92.4 Rift Valley fever

A92.5 Zika virus disease
Zika virus fever
Zika virus infection
Zika NOS
  Excludes1 congenital Zika virus disease (P35.4)
Coding Clinic: 2016, Q4, P4-7, 121

A92.8 Other specified mosquito-borne viral fevers

A92.9 Mosquito-borne viral fever, unspecified

● **A93 Other arthropod-borne viral fevers, not elsewhere classified**

A93.0 Oropouche virus disease
Tropical viral infection
Oropouche fever

A93.1 Sandfly fever
Pappataci fever
Phlebotomus fever

A93.2 Colorado tick fever

A93.8 Other specified arthropod-borne viral fevers
Piry virus disease
Vesicular stomatitis virus disease [Indiana fever]

A94 Unspecified arthropod-borne viral fever
Arboviral fever NOS
Arbovirus infection NOS

● **A95 Yellow fever**
Acute infectious disease transmitted by mosquitoes

A95.0 Sylvatic yellow fever
Jungle yellow fever

A95.1 Urban yellow fever

A95.9 Yellow fever, unspecified

● **A96 Arenaviral hemorrhagic fever**
Virus that causes various hemorrhagic fevers

A96.0 Junin hemorrhagic fever
Argentinian hemorrhagic fever

A96.1 Machupo hemorrhagic fever
Transmitted by contact with infected rodents
Bolivian hemorrhagic fever

A96.2 Lassa fever
Acute type of hemorrhagic fever caused by contact with disease carrying mouse or person

A96.8 Other arenaviral hemorrhagic fevers

A96.9 Arenaviral hemorrhagic fever, unspecified

● **A98 Other viral hemorrhagic fevers, not elsewhere classified**
  Excludes1 chikungunya hemorrhagic fever (A92.0)
dengue hemorrhagic fever (A91)

A98.0 Crimean-Congo hemorrhagic fever
Virus transmitted by ticks and contact with blood, secretions, or fluids from infected humans or animals
Central Asian hemorrhagic fever

A98.1 Omsk hemorrhagic fever
Transmitted to humans by bites of infected ticks or contact with infected muskrats

A98.2 Kyasanur Forest disease
Transmitted via infected monkeys, voles, ticks

A98.3 Marburg virus disease
Rare, acute, often fatal type of hemorrhagic fever

A98.4 Ebola virus disease

A98.5 Hemorrhagic fever with renal syndrome
Epidemic hemorrhagic fever
Korean hemorrhagic fever
Russian hemorrhagic fever
Hantaan virus disease
Hantavirus disease with renal manifestations
Nephropathia epidemica
Songo fever
  Excludes1 hantavirus (cardio)-pulmonary syndrome (B33.4)

A98.8 Other specified viral hemorrhagic fevers

A99 Unspecified viral hemorrhagic fever

VIRAL INFECTIONS CHARACTERIZED BY SKIN AND MUCOUS MEMBRANE LESIONS (B00-B09)

● **B00 Herpesviral [herpes simplex] infections**
  Excludes1 congenital herpesviral infections (P35.2)
  Excludes2 anogenital herpesviral infection (A60.-)
gammaherpesviral mononucleosis (B27.0-)
herpangina (B08.5)

B00.0 Eczema herpeticum
Cutaneous eruption caused by herpes simplex virus (HSV) type 1, HSV-2, coxsackievirus A16, or vaccinia virus
Kaposi's varicelliform eruption

B00.1 Herpesviral vesicular dermatitis
Vesicle formation; characteristics include formation of blisters and scabs on feet and legs
Herpes simplex facialis
Herpes simplex labialis
Herpes simplex otitis externa
Vesicular dermatitis of ear
Vesicular dermatitis of lip

B00.2 Herpesviral gingivostomatitis and pharyngotonsillitis
Inflammation involving both gingivae and oral mucosa
Herpesviral pharyngitis
Inflammation of pharynx and tonsils; AKA tonsillopharyngitis

B00.3 Herpesviral meningitis

B00.4 Herpesviral encephalitis
Herpesviral meningoencephalitis
Simian B disease
  Excludes1 herpesviral encephalitis due to herpesvirus 6 and 7 (B10.01, B10.09)
non-simplex herpesviral encephalitis (B10.0-)

Figure 1-4 Primary herpes simplex in and around the mouth. The infection is usually acquired from siblings or parents and is readily transmitted to other direct contacts. (Getty Image)

Item 1-15 Herpes is a viral disease for which there is no cure. There are two types of the herpes simplex virus: **Type I** causes **cold sores** or **fever blisters,** and **Type II** causes **genital herpes.** The virus can be spread from a sore on the lips to the genitals or from the genitals to the lips.

▶ New   ⇒ Revised   ~~deleted~~ Deleted   Excludes 1   Excludes 2   Includes   Use additional   Code first   Code also   Key words

664

OGCR Official Guidelines   X Assign placeholder X   ● Use Additional Character(s)   ▶ Manifestation Code   🏷 Hierarchical Condition Category   **Coding Clinic**

● **B00.5   Herpesviral ocular disease**
    B00.50   **Herpesviral ocular disease, unspecified**
    B00.51   **Herpesviral iridocyclitis**
        Herpesviral iritis
        Herpesviral uveitis, anterior
    B00.52   **Herpesviral keratitis**
        Herpesviral keratoconjunctivitis
    B00.53   **Herpesviral conjunctivitis**
    B00.59   **Other herpesviral disease of eye**
        Herpesviral dermatitis of eyelid
● **B00.7   Disseminated herpesviral disease** 🔎
    Herpesviral sepsis
● **B00.8   Other forms of herpesviral infections**
    B00.81   **Herpesviral hepatitis**
    B00.82   **Herpes simplex myelitis** 🔎
    B00.89   **Other herpesviral infection**
        Herpesviral whitlow
    B00.9   **Herpesviral infection, unspecified**
        Herpes simplex infection NOS

● **B01   Varicella [chickenpox]**
    Very contagious disease caused by the varicella zoster virus that results in an itchy outbreak of skin blisters (varicella). The same virus causes shingles (zoster).
    B01.0   Varicella meningitis
●   **B01.1   Varicella encephalitis, myelitis and encephalomyelitis**
        Postchickenpox encephalitis, myelitis and encephalomyelitis
    B01.11   **Varicella encephalitis and encephalomyelitis**
        Postchickenpox encephalitis and encephalomyelitis
    B01.12   **Varicella myelitis** 🔎
        Postchickenpox myelitis
    B01.2   Varicella pneumonia
●   **B01.8   Varicella with other complications**
    B01.81   **Varicella keratitis**
    B01.89   **Other varicella complications**
    B01.9   Varicella without complication
        Varicella NOS

● **B02   Zoster [herpes zoster]**
    Includes   shingles
        zona
    B02.0   Zoster encephalitis
        Zoster meningoencephalitis
    B02.1   Zoster meningitis
●   **B02.2   Zoster with other nervous system involvement**
        Coding Clinic: 2019, Q1, P18
    B02.21   **Postherpetic geniculate ganglionitis**
    B02.22   **Postherpetic trigeminal neuralgia**
    B02.23   **Postherpetic polyneuropathy**
    B02.24   **Postherpetic myelitis** 🔎
        Herpes zoster myelitis
    B02.29   **Other postherpetic nervous system involvement**
        Postherpetic radiculopathy

Figure 1-5 Photograph of eyelids with marginal blepharitis. (From Hoyt CS, Taylor D: Pediatric Ophthalmology and Strabismus, London, Elsevier Saunders, 2005)

Item 1-17 Blepharitis is a common condition in which the eyelid is swollen and yellow scaling and conjunctivitis develop. Usually the hair on the scalp and brow is involved.

● **B02.3   Zoster ocular disease**
    B02.30   **Zoster ocular disease, unspecified**
    B02.31   **Zoster conjunctivitis**
    B02.32   **Zoster iridocyclitis**
    B02.33   **Zoster keratitis**
        Herpes zoster keratoconjunctivitis
    B02.34   **Zoster scleritis**
    B02.39   **Other herpes zoster eye disease**
        Zoster blepharitis
  B02.7   Disseminated zoster
  B02.8   Zoster with other complications
    Herpes zoster otitis externa
  B02.9   Zoster without complications
    Zoster NOS

B03   Smallpox
    Note: In 1980 the 33rd World Health Assembly declared that smallpox had been eradicated. The classification is maintained for surveillance purposes.

B04   Monkeypox
    Disease occurring in captive monkeys and other mammals that may be transmitted to humans, clinically similar to smallpox

● **B05   Measles**
    Includes   morbilli
    Excludes1   subacute sclerosing panencephalitis (A81.1)
    B05.0   Measles complicated by encephalitis
        Postmeasles encephalitis
    B05.1   Measles complicated by meningitis
        Postmeasles meningitis
    B05.2   Measles complicated by pneumonia
        Postmeasles pneumonia
    B05.3   Measles complicated by otitis media
        Postmeasles otitis media
    B05.4   Measles with intestinal complications
●   **B05.8   Measles with other complications**
    B05.81   **Measles keratitis and keratoconjunctivitis**
    B05.89   **Other measles complications**
    B05.9   Measles without complication
        Measles NOS

● **B06   Rubella [German measles]**
    Excludes1   congenital rubella (P35.0)
●   **B06.0   Rubella with neurological complications**
    B06.00   **Rubella with neurological complication, unspecified**
    B06.01   **Rubella encephalitis**
        Rubella meningoencephalitis
    B06.02   **Rubella meningitis**
    B06.09   **Other neurological complications of rubella**
●   **B06.8   Rubella with other complications**
    B06.81   **Rubella pneumonia**
    B06.82   **Rubella arthritis** 🔎
    B06.89   **Other rubella complications**
    B06.9   Rubella without complication
        Rubella NOS

Item 1-16 Zoster: Also known as ***shingles*** and is caused by the same virus as chickenpox. After exposure, the virus lies dormant in nerve tissue and is activated by factors including aging, stress, suppression of the immune system, and certain medication. It begins as a unilateral rash that leads to blisters and sores on the skin. It may involve the nerve pathways of the eye, forehead, nose, and eyelids and may be very painful with long-term systemic effects.

CHAPTER 1 (A00-B99)

N Newborn Age: 0   **P** Pediatric Age: 0–17   **M** Maternity DX: 12–55   **A** Adult Age: 15–124   ♀ Females Only   ♂ Males Only

CHAPTER 1 (A00–B99)

● **B07**   **Viral warts**

> **Includes**   verruca simplex
> verruca vulgaris
> viral warts due to human papillomavirus

> **Excludes2**   anogenital (venereal) warts (A63.0)
> papilloma of bladder (D41.4)
> papilloma of cervix (D26.0)
> papilloma larynx (D14.1)

   B07.0   **Plantar wart**
       Verruca plantaris

   B07.8   **Other viral warts**
       Common wart
       Flat wart
       Verruca plana

   B07.9   **Viral wart, unspecified**

● **B08**   **Other viral infections characterized by skin and mucous membrane lesions, not elsewhere classified**

> **Excludes1**   vesicular stomatitis virus disease (A93.8)

●   **B08.0**   **Other orthopoxvirus infections**

> **Excludes2**   monkeypox (B04)

   ● **B08.01**   **Cowpox and vaccinia not from vaccine**

       B08.010   **Cowpox**

       B08.011   **Vaccinia not from vaccine**

> **Excludes1**   vaccinia (from vaccination) (generalized) (T88.1)

   B08.02   **Orf virus disease**
       Contagious pustular dermatitis
       Ecthyma contagiosum

   B08.03   **Pseudocowpox [milker's node]**

   B08.04   **Paravaccinia, unspecified**

   B08.09   **Other orthopoxvirus infections**
       Orthopoxvirus infection NOS

   B08.1   **Molluscum contagiosum**
       Various skin diseases characterized by soft, rounded, cutaneous lesions

●   **B08.2**   **Exanthema subitum [sixth disease] Roseola infantum**
       Acute, short-lived high fever in infants and young children followed by a rash mainly on the trunk, caused by human herpesvirus 6

     B08.20   **Exanthema subitum [sixth disease], unspecified Roseola infantum, unspecified**   P

     B08.21   **Exanthema subitum [sixth disease] due to human herpesvirus 6 Roseola infantum due to human herpesvirus 6**   P
       Virus results in sudden rash; infection results in lifelong persistence

     B08.22   **Exanthema subitum [sixth disease] due to human herpesvirus 7 Roseola infantum due to human herpesvirus 7**   P

   B08.3   **Erythema infectiosum [fifth disease]**
       Moderately contagious, epidemic disease in children caused by B19 virus; onset of rash that begins as redness of cheeks, later there is rash on trunk and limbs; when this fades, there may be central clearing that leaves lacelike pattern

   B08.4   **Enteroviral vesicular stomatitis with exanthem**
       Hand, foot and mouth disease
       Check your documentation—this code is HAND, foot, and mouth disease. Code B08.8 is foot and mouth disease.

   B08.5   **Enteroviral vesicular pharyngitis**
       Herpangina

●   **B08.6**   **Parapoxvirus infections**

     B08.60   **Parapoxvirus infection, unspecified**

     B08.61   **Bovine stomatitis**

     B08.62   **Sealpox**

     B08.69   **Other parapoxvirus infections**

   B08.7   **Yatapoxvirus infections**

     B08.70   **Yatapoxvirus infection, unspecified**

     B08.71   **Tanapox virus disease**

     B08.72   **Yaba pox virus disease**
       Yaba monkey tumor disease

     B08.79   **Other yatapoxvirus infections**

   B08.8   **Other specified viral infections characterized by skin and mucous membrane lesions**
       Enteroviral lymphonodular pharyngitis
       Foot-and-mouth disease
       Check your documentation. Code B08.4 is for HAND, foot, and mouth disease.
       Poxvirus NEC

B09   **Unspecified viral infection characterized by skin and mucous membrane lesions**
       Viral enanthema NOS
       Viral exanthema NOS

OTHER HUMAN HERPESVIRUSES (B10)

● **B10**   **Other human herpesviruses**

> **Excludes2**   cytomegalovirus (B25.9)
> Epstein-Barr virus (B27.0-)
> herpes NOS (B00.9)
> herpes simplex (B00.-)
> herpes zoster (B02.-)
> human herpesvirus NOS (B00.-)
> human herpesvirus 1 and 2 (B00.-)
> human herpesvirus 3 (B01.-, B02.-)
> human herpesvirus 4 (B27.0-)
> human herpesvirus 5 (B25.-)
> varicella (B01.-)
> zoster (B02.-)

●   **B10.0**   **Other human herpesvirus encephalitis**

> **Excludes2**   herpes encephalitis NOS (B00.4)
> herpes simplex encephalitis (B00.4)
> human herpesvirus encephalitis (B00.4)
> simian B herpes virus encephalitis (B00.4)

     B10.01   **Human herpesvirus 6 encephalitis**
       Sudden rash or roseola

     B10.09   **Other human herpesvirus encephalitis**
       Human herpesvirus 7 encephalitis
       Virus closely related to human herpesvirus 6, but not known to cause any disease

●   **B10.8**   **Other human herpesvirus infection**

     B10.81   **Human herpesvirus 6 infection**
       Causative agent of exanthema subitum that results in sudden rash

     B10.82   **Human herpesvirus 7 infection**
       Closely related to human herpesvirus 6, but not known cause any disease

     B10.89   **Other human herpesvirus infection**
       Human herpesvirus 8 infection
       May be the cause of Kaposi sarcoma, a malignant tumor
       Kaposi's sarcoma-associated herpesvirus infection

Figure 1-6   Hepatitis B viral infection. **A.** Liver parenchyma showing hepatocytes with diffuse granular cytoplasm, so-called ground glass hepatocytes (H&E). **B.** Immunoperoxidase stains from the same case, showing cytoplasmic inclusions of viral particles. (From Kumar: Robbins and Cotran: Pathologic Basis of Disease, ed 8, Saunders, An Imprint of Elsevier, 2009)

▶ New   ⇒ Revised   ~~deleted~~ Deleted   Excludes 1   Excludes 2   Includes   Use additional   Code first   Code also   Key words

OGCR Official Guidelines   X Assign placeholder X   ● Use Additional Character(s)   ▶ Manifestation Code   Hierarchical Condition Category   **Coding Clinic**

Item 1–18 Hepatitis A (HAV) was formerly called epidemic, infectious, short-incubation, or acute catarrhal jaundice hepatitis. The primary transmission mode is the oral–fecal route. **Hepatitis B (HBV)** was formerly called long-incubation period, serum, or homologous serum hepatitis. Transmission modes are through blood from infected persons and from body fluids of infected mother to neonate. **Hepatitis C (HCV),** caused by the hepatitis C virus, is primarily transfusion associated. **Hepatitis D (HDV),** also called delta hepatitis, is caused by the hepatitis D virus in patients formerly or currently infected with hepatitis B. **Hepatitis E (HEV)** is also called enterically transmitted non-A, non-B hepatitis. The primary transmission mode is the oral–fecal route, usually through contaminated water.

VIRAL HEPATITIS (B15-B19)

Excludes1	sequelae of viral hepatitis (B94.2)
Excludes2	cytomegaloviral hepatitis (B25.1)
	herpesviral [herpes simplex] hepatitis (B00.81)

- **B15 Acute hepatitis A**
  - **B15.0 Hepatitis A with hepatic coma**
  - **B15.9 Hepatitis A without hepatic coma**
    Hepatitis A (acute) (viral) NOS

- **B16 Acute hepatitis B**
  - **B16.0 Acute hepatitis B with delta-agent with hepatic coma**
  - **B16.1 Acute hepatitis B with delta-agent without hepatic coma**
  - **B16.2 Acute hepatitis B without delta-agent with hepatic coma**
  - **B16.9 Acute hepatitis B without delta-agent and without hepatic coma**
    Hepatitis B (acute) (viral) NOS
    Coding Clinic: 2016, Q3, P13

- **B17 Other acute viral hepatitis**
  - **B17.0 Acute delta-(super) infection of hepatitis B carrier**
  - **B17.1 Acute hepatitis C**
    - **B17.10 Acute hepatitis C without hepatic coma**
      Acute hepatitis C NOS
    - **B17.11 Acute hepatitis C with hepatic coma**
  - **B17.2 Acute hepatitis E**
  - **B17.8 Other specified acute viral hepatitis**
    Hepatitis non-A non-B (acute) (viral) NEC
  - **B17.9 Acute viral hepatitis, unspecified**
    Acute hepatitis NOS
    Acute infectious hepatitis NOS

- **B18 Chronic viral hepatitis**
  - **Includes** Carrier of viral hepatitis
  - **B18.0 Chronic viral hepatitis B with delta-agent** 🐾
  - **B18.1 Chronic viral hepatitis B without delta-agent** 🐾
    Carrier of viral hepatitis B
    Chronic (viral) hepatitis B
  - **B18.2 Chronic viral hepatitis C** 🐾
    Carrier of viral hepatitis C
    Coding Clinic: 2018, Q1, P4; 2017, Q1, P41
  - **B18.8 Other chronic viral hepatitis** 🐾
    Carrier of other viral hepatitis
  - **B18.9 Chronic viral hepatitis, unspecified** 🐾
    Carrier of unspecified viral hepatitis

- **B19 Unspecified viral hepatitis**
  - **B19.0 Unspecified viral hepatitis with hepatic coma**
  - **B19.1 Unspecified viral hepatitis B**
    - **B19.10 Unspecified viral hepatitis B without hepatic coma**
      Unspecified viral hepatitis B NOS
    - **B19.11 Unspecified viral hepatitis B with hepatic coma**
  - **B19.2 Unspecified viral hepatitis C**
    - **B19.20 Unspecified viral hepatitis C without hepatic coma**
      Viral hepatitis C NOS
    - **B19.21 Unspecified viral hepatitis C with hepatic coma**
  - **B19.9 Unspecified viral hepatitis without hepatic coma**
    Viral hepatitis NOS

Figure 1-7 Kaposi's sarcoma. There are large confluent hyperpigmented patch-stage lesions with lymphedema. (From Kanski, JJ: Clinical Diagnosis in Ophthalmology, London, Elsevier Mosby, 2006)

Item 1–19 AIDS (acquired immune deficiency syndrome) is caused by **HIV** (human immunodeficiency virus). HIV affects certain white blood cells (T-4 lymphocytes) and destroys the ability of the cells to fight infections, making patients susceptible to a host of infectious diseases (e.g., **Pneumocystis carinii pneumonia [PCP], Kaposi's sarcoma,** and **lymphoma**). **AIDS-related complex (ARC)** is an early stage of AIDS in which tests for HIV are positive but the symptoms are mild.

OGCR Section I. C.1.a.

Certain Infectious and Parasitic Diseases (A00-B99)

a. Human Immunodeficiency Virus (HIV) Infections

  1) Code only confirmed cases

    Code only confirmed cases of HIV infection illness. This is an exception to the hospital inpatient guideline Section II, H.

    In this context, "confirmation" does not require documentation of positive serology or culture for HIV; the provider's diagnostic statement that the patient is HIV positive or has an HIV-related illness is sufficient.

HUMAN IMMUNODEFICIENCY VIRUS [HIV] DISEASE (B20)

- **B20 Human immunodeficiency virus [HIV] disease** 🐾
  - **Includes** acquired immune deficiency syndrome [AIDS]
    AIDS-related complex [ARC]
    HIV infection, symptomatic
  - *Code first* Human immunodeficiency virus [HIV] disease complicating pregnancy, childbirth and the puerperium, if applicable (O98.7-)
  - Use additional code(s) to identify all manifestations of HIV infection
  - **Excludes1** asymptomatic human immunodeficiency virus [HIV] infection status (Z21)
    exposure to HIV virus (Z20.6)
    inconclusive serologic evidence of HIV (R75)
  - **Coding Clinic: 2019, Q1, P9-11**

OTHER VIRAL DISEASES (B25-B34)

- **B25 Cytomegaloviral disease**
  AKA: HCMV or Human Herpesvirus 5 (HHV-5)
  - **Excludes1** congenital cytomegalovirus infection (P35.1)
    cytomegaloviral mononucleosis (B27.1-)
  - **B25.0 Cytomegaloviral pneumonitis** 🐾
  - **B25.1 Cytomegaloviral hepatitis** 🐾
  - **B25.2 Cytomegaloviral pancreatitis** 🐾
  - **B25.8 Other cytomegaloviral diseases** 🐾
    Cytomegaloviral encephalitis
  - **B25.9 Cytomegaloviral disease, unspecified** 🐾

- **B26 Mumps**
  - **Includes** epidemic parotitis
    infectious parotitis
    Acute, contagious, viral disease
  - **B26.0 Mumps orchitis** ♂
  - **B26.1 Mumps meningitis**
  - **B26.2 Mumps encephalitis**
  - **B26.3 Mumps pancreatitis**

CHAPTER 1 (A00-B99)

● **B26.8**   **Mumps with other complications**

     B26.81   **Mumps hepatitis**

     B26.82   **Mumps myocarditis**

     B26.83   **Mumps nephritis**

     B26.84   **Mumps polyneuropathy**

     B26.85   **Mumps arthritis** 🅗

     B26.89   **Other mumps complications**

   B26.9   **Mumps without complication**
        Mumps NOS
        Mumps parotitis NOS

● **B27**   **Infectious mononucleosis**

     Includes   glandular fever
              monocytic angina
              Pfeiffer's disease

● **B27.0**   **Gammaherpesviral mononucleosis**
      AKA: Pfeiffer's disease, infective mononucleosis
      Mononucleosis due to Epstein-Barr virus

     B27.00   **Gammaherpesviral mononucleosis without complication**
           Infective mononucleosis

     B27.01   **Gammaherpesviral mononucleosis with polyneuropathy**

     B27.02   **Gammaherpesviral mononucleosis with meningitis**

     B27.09   **Gammaherpesviral mononucleosis with other complications**
           Hepatomegaly in gammaherpesviral mononucleosis

● **B27.1**   **Cytomegaloviral mononucleosis**
      Infectious disease resembling infectious mononucleosis

     B27.10   **Cytomegaloviral mononucleosis without complications**

     B27.11   **Cytomegaloviral mononucleosis with polyneuropathy**

     B27.12   **Cytomegaloviral mononucleosis with meningitis**

     B27.19   **Cytomegaloviral mononucleosis with other complication**
           Hepatomegaly in cytomegaloviral mononucleosis

● **B27.8**   **Other infectious mononucleosis**

     B27.80   **Other infectious mononucleosis without complication**

     B27.81   **Other infectious mononucleosis with polyneuropathy**

     B27.82   **Other infectious mononucleosis with meningitis**

     B27.89   **Other infectious mononucleosis with other complication**
           Hepatomegaly in other infectious mononucleosis

● **B27.9**   **Infectious mononucleosis, unspecified**

     B27.90   **Infectious mononucleosis, unspecified without complication**

     B27.91   **Infectious mononucleosis, unspecified with polyneuropathy**

     B27.92   **Infectious mononucleosis, unspecified with meningitis**

     B27.99   **Infectious mononucleosis, unspecified with other complication**
           Hepatomegaly in unspecified infectious mononucleosis

● **B30**   **Viral conjunctivitis**

     Excludes1   herpesviral [herpes simplex] ocular disease (B00.5)
                 ocular zoster (B02.3)

   B30.0   **Keratoconjunctivitis due to adenovirus**
        Epidemic keratoconjunctivitis
        Shipyard eye

   B30.1   **Conjunctivitis due to adenovirus**
        Acute adenoviral follicular conjunctivitis
        Swimming-pool conjunctivitis

   B30.2   **Viral pharyngoconjunctivitis**

   B30.3   **Acute epidemic hemorrhagic conjunctivitis (enteroviral)**
        Conjunctivitis due to coxsackievirus 24
        Conjunctivitis due to enterovirus 70
        Hemorrhagic conjunctivitis (acute)(epidemic)

   B30.8   **Other viral conjunctivitis**
        Newcastle conjunctivitis

   B30.9   **Viral conjunctivitis, unspecified**

● **B33**   **Other viral diseases, not elsewhere classified**

   B33.0   **Epidemic myalgia**
        Acute infectious disease, caused by group A coxsackie viruses or other enteroviruses with symptoms that include sudden pain in chest or upper abdomen with fever
        Bornholm disease

   B33.1   **Ross River disease**
        Epidemic polyarthritis and exanthema
        Ross River fever

● **B33.2**   **Viral carditis**
        Coxsackie (virus) carditis

     B33.20   **Viral carditis, unspecified**

     B33.21   **Viral endocarditis**

     B33.22   **Viral myocarditis**

     B33.23   **Viral pericarditis**

     B33.24   **Viral cardiomyopathy** 🅗

   B33.3   **Retrovirus infections, not elsewhere classified**
        Retrovirus infection NOS

   B33.4   **Hantavirus (cardio)-pulmonary syndrome [HPS] [HCPS]**
        Hantavirus disease with pulmonary manifestations
        Sin nombre virus disease

        Use additional code to identify any associated acute kidney failure (N17.9)

     Excludes1   hantavirus disease with renal manifestations (A98.5)
                 hemorrhagic fever with renal manifestations (A98.5)

   B33.8   **Other specified viral diseases**

     Excludes1   anogenital human papillomavirus infection (A63.0)
                 viral warts due to human papillomavirus infection (B07)

● **B34**   **Viral infection of unspecified site**

     Excludes1   anogenital human papillomavirus infection (A63.0)
                 cytomegaloviral disease NOS (B25.9)
                 herpesvirus [herpes simplex] infection NOS (B00.9)
                 retrovirus infection NOS (B33.3)
                 viral agents as the cause of diseases classified elsewhere (B97.-)
                 viral warts due to human papillomavirus infection (B07)

   B34.0   **Adenovirus infection, unspecified**

   B34.1   **Enterovirus infection, unspecified**
        Intestinal tract infection
        Coxsackievirus infection NOS
        Echovirus infection NOS

   B34.2   **Coronavirus infection, unspecified**

     Excludes1 ▶ COVID-19 (U07.1)
                 pneumonia due to SARS-associated coronavirus (J12.81)

▶ New   ⇒ Revised   ~~deleted~~ Deleted   Excludes 1   Excludes 2   Includes   Use additional   Code first   Code also   Key words

OGCR Official Guidelines   **X** Assign placeholder X   ● Use Additional Character(s)   ▌ Manifestation Code   🅗 Hierarchical Condition Category   **Coding Clinic**

B34.3   **Parvovirus infection, unspecified**

B34.4   **Papovavirus infection, unspecified**

B34.8   **Other viral infections of unspecified site**

B34.9   **Viral infection, unspecified**
Viremia NOS
Coding Clinic: 2016, Q3, P10

MYCOSES (B35-B49)

Excludes2   hypersensitivity pneumonitis due to organic dust (J67.-)
mycosis fungoides (C84.0-)

● **B35**   **Dermatophytosis**
AKA tinea or ringworm

   Includes   favus
infections due to species of Epidermophyton, Micro-sporum and Trichophyton
tinea, any type except those in B36.-

B35.0   **Tinea barbae and tinea capitis**
Beard ringworm
Kerion
Scalp ringworm
Sycosis, mycotic

B35.1   **Tinea unguium**
White patches or pits on surface or edges of nails, followed by infection under nail plate
Dermatophytic onychia
Dermatophytosis of nail
Onychomycosis
Ringworm of nails

B35.2   **Tinea manuum**
Tinea of hands
Dermatophytosis of hand
Hand ringworm

B35.3   **Tinea pedis**
Tinea affecting feet
Athlete's foot
Dermatophytosis of foot
Foot ringworm

B35.4   **Tinea corporis**
Infecting skin areas other than hands
Ringworm of the body

B35.5   **Tinea imbricata**
Chronic tropical tinea corporis; AKA Oriental ringworm, tinea inguinalis, tinea cruris
Tokelau

B35.6   **Tinea cruris**
In groin or perineal area, spreading to adjacent regions; AKA jock itch, eczema marginatum, ringworm of groin, or tinea inguinalis
Dhobi itch
Groin ringworm
Jock itch

B35.8   **Other dermatophytoses**
Disseminated dermatophytosis
Granulomatous dermatophytosis

B35.9   **Dermatophytosis, unspecified**
Ringworm NOS

● **B36**   **Other superficial mycoses**

B36.0   **Pityriasis versicolor**
Common, chronic, symptomless disorder that includes macular patches of various sizes and shapes; AKA liver spots
Tinea flava
Tinea versicolor

B36.1   **Tinea nigra**
Minor fungal infection, with dark lesions, usually on skin of hands
Keratomycosis nigricans palmaris
Microsporosis nigra
Pityriasis nigra

Figure 1-8   Oral candidiasis (thrush). (From James WD, Berger T, Elston D: Andrews' Diseases of the Skin: Clinical Dermatology, 11e, Saunders, 2011)

Item 1–20 Candidiasis, also called oidiomycosis or moniliasis, is a fungal infection. It most often appears on moist cutaneous areas of the body but can also be responsible for a variety of systemic infections such as endocarditis, meningitis, arthritis, and myositis. Antifungal medications cure most yeast infections.

B36.2   **White piedra**
White to light brown nodules on hair of beard, axilla, or groin; AKA trichosporosis
Tinea blanca

B36.3   **Black piedra**
Characterized by small black or brown nodules on shafts of scalp hair

B36.8   **Other specified superficial mycoses**

B36.9   **Superficial mycosis, unspecified**

● **B37**   **Candidiasis**

   Includes   candidosis
moniliasis

   Excludes1   neonatal candidiasis (P37.5)

B37.0   **Candidal stomatitis**
Oral thrush

B37.1   **Pulmonary candidiasis** 🔖
Candidal bronchitis
Candidal pneumonia

B37.2   **Candidiasis of skin and nail**
Candidal onychia
Candidal paronychia

   Excludes2   diaper dermatitis (L22)

B37.3   **Candidiasis of vulva and vagina** ♀
Candidal vulvovaginitis
Monilial vulvovaginitis
Vaginal thrush

● **B37.4**   **Candidiasis of other urogenital sites**

   B37.41   **Candidal cystitis and urethritis**

   B37.42   **Candidal balanitis** ♂
Male condition only

   B37.49   **Other urogenital candidiasis**
Candidal pyelonephritis

B37.5   **Candidal meningitis**

B37.6   **Candidal endocarditis**

B37.7   **Candidal sepsis** 🔖
Disseminated candidiasis systemic candidiasis

● **B37.8**   **Candidiasis of other sites**

   B37.81   **Candidal esophagitis** 🔖

   B37.82   **Candidal enteritis**
Candidal proctitis

   B37.83   **Candidal cheilitis**
Inflammation affecting lip

   B37.84   **Candidal otitis externa**
Inflammation of external auditory canal

   B37.89   **Other sites of candidiasis**
Infection manifested by invasive candidiasis
Candidal osteomyelitis

B37.9   **Candidiasis, unspecified**
Thrush NOS

CHAPTER 1 (A00-B99)

Item 1–21 Bird and bat droppings that fall into the soil give rise to a fungus that can spread airborne spores. When inhaled into the lungs, these spores divide and multiply into lesions. Histoplasmosis capsulatum takes three forms: primary (lodged in the lungs only), chronic (resembles TB), and disseminated (infection has moved to other organs). This is an opportunistic infection in immunosuppressed patients.

● **B38   Coccidioidomycosis**
Fungal disease; AKA coccidioidosis, coccidioidal granuloma, Posadas, or Posadas-Wernicke disease

    B38.0   Acute pulmonary coccidioidomycosis 🦠

    B38.1   Chronic pulmonary coccidioidomycosis 🦠

    B38.2   Pulmonary coccidioidomycosis, unspecified 🦠

    B38.3   Cutaneous coccidioidomycosis

    B38.4   Coccidioidomycosis meningitis

    B38.7   Disseminated coccidioidomycosis
        Generalized coccidioidomycosis

  ● **B38.8   Other forms of coccidioidomycosis**

        B38.81   Prostatic coccidioidomycosis ♂

        B38.89   Other forms of coccidioidomycosis

    B38.9   Coccidioidomycosis, unspecified

● **B39   Histoplasmosis**
Infection resulting from inhalation or ingestion of spores; AKA Darling disease

    Code first associated AIDS (B20)

    Use additional code for any associated manifestations, such as:
      endocarditis (I39)
      meningitis (G02)
      pericarditis (I32)
      retinitis (H32)

    B39.0   Acute pulmonary histoplasmosis capsulati 🦠

    B39.1   Chronic pulmonary histoplasmosis capsulati 🦠

    B39.2   Pulmonary histoplasmosis capsulati, unspecified 🦠

    B39.3   Disseminated histoplasmosis capsulati
        Generalized histoplasmosis capsulati

    B39.4   Histoplasmosis capsulati, unspecified
        American histoplasmosis

    B39.5   Histoplasmosis duboisii
        African histoplasmosis

    B39.9   Histoplasmosis, unspecified

● **B40   Blastomycosis**
Rare and potentially fatal infection caused by inhaling fungus found in moist soil in temperate climates.

    Excludes1   Brazilian blastomycosis (B41.-)
                keloidal blastomycosis (B48.0)

    B40.0   Acute pulmonary blastomycosis 🦠

    B40.1   Chronic pulmonary blastomycosis 🦠

    B40.2   Pulmonary blastomycosis, unspecified 🦠

    B40.3   Cutaneous blastomycosis

    B40.7   Disseminated blastomycosis
        Generalized blastomycosis

  ● **B40.8   Other forms of blastomycosis**

        B40.81   Blastomycotic meningoencephalitis
             Meningomyelitis due to blastomycosis

        B40.89   Other forms of blastomycosis

    B40.9   Blastomycosis, unspecified

● **B41   Paracoccidioidomycosis**
Fungal infection usually chronic that begins in lungs, spreads to mucocutaneous areas which may extend to skin, tonsils, gastrointestinal lymphatics, liver, and spleen; AKA Almeida or Lutz-Splendore-Almeida disease, Brazilian or South American blastomycosis, or paracoccidioidal granuloma

    Includes   Brazilian blastomycosis
             Lutz' disease

    B41.0   Pulmonary paracoccidioidomycosis 🦠

    B41.7   Disseminated paracoccidioidomycosis
        Generalized paracoccidioidomycosis

    B41.8   Other forms of paracoccidioidomycosis

    B41.9   Paracoccidioidomycosis, unspecified

● **B42   Sporotrichosis**
Chronic fungal infection with nodular lesions

    B42.0   Pulmonary sporotrichosis

    B42.1   Lymphocutaneous sporotrichosis

    B42.7   Disseminated sporotrichosis
        Generalized sporotrichosis

  ● **B42.8   Other forms of sporotrichosis**

        B42.81   Cerebral sporotrichosis
             Meningitis due to sporotrichosis

        B42.82   Sporotrichosis arthritis 🦠

        B42.89   Other forms of sporotrichosis

    B42.9   Sporotrichosis, unspecified

● **B43   Chromomycosis and pheomycotic abscess**
Chronic fungal infection of skin, initiated at site of puncture affecting lower limb or foot (mossy foot)

    B43.0   Cutaneous chromomycosis
        Dermatitis verrucosa

    B43.1   Pheomycotic brain abscess
        Cerebral chromomycosis

    B43.2   Subcutaneous pheomycotic abscess and cyst

    B43.8   Other forms of chromomycosis

    B43.9   Chromomycosis, unspecified

● **B44   Aspergillosis**
Infection marked by inflammatory lesions in skin, ear, orbit, nasal sinuses, lungs, and occasionally bones and meninges

    Includes   aspergilloma

    B44.0   Invasive pulmonary aspergillosis 🦠

    B44.1   Other pulmonary aspergillosis 🦠

    B44.2   Tonsillar aspergillosis 🦠

    B44.7   Disseminated aspergillosis 🦠
        Generalized aspergillosis

  ● **B44.8   Other forms of aspergillosis**

        B44.81   Allergic bronchopulmonary aspergillosis 🦠

        B44.89   Other forms of aspergillosis

    B44.9   Aspergillosis, unspecified 🦠

● **B45   Cryptococcosis**
Infection in the immunocompromised and fatal if left untreated; AKA torulosis, Buschke, or Busse-Buschke disease

    B45.0   Pulmonary cryptococcosis 🦠

    B45.1   Cerebral cryptococcosis 🦠
        Cryptococcal meningitis
        Cryptococcosis meningocerebralis

    B45.2   Cutaneous cryptococcosis 🦠

    B45.3   Osseous cryptococcosis 🦠

    B45.7   Disseminated cryptococcosis 🦠
        Generalized cryptococcosis

    B45.8   Other forms of cryptococcosis 🦠

    B45.9   Cryptococcosis, unspecified 🦠

● **B46   Zygomycosis**
Fungal infections including subcutaneous lesions and infection of sinuses, brain, or lungs

    B46.0   Pulmonary mucormycosis 🦠
        Fungal infection affecting lung

    B46.1   Rhinocerebral mucormycosis 🦠

    B46.2   Gastrointestinal mucormycosis 🦠

    B46.3   Cutaneous mucormycosis 🦠
        Subcutaneous mucormycosis

    B46.4   Disseminated mucormycosis 🦠
        Generalized mucormycosis

    B46.5   Mucormycosis, unspecified 🦠

    B46.8   Other zygomycoses 🦠
        Entomophthoromycosis

    B46.9   Zygomycosis, unspecified 🦠
        Phycomycosis NOS

▶ New   ⇛ Revised   ~~deleted~~ Deleted   Excludes 1   Excludes 2   Includes   Use additional   Code first   Code also   Key words
OGCR Official Guidelines   X Assign placeholder X   ● Use Additional Character(s)   ▌ Manifestation Code   🦠 Hierarchical Condition Category   **Coding Clinic**

● **B47   Mycetoma**
  *Slow progressive, destructive fungal infection of cutaneous and
  subcutaneous tissues, fascia, and bone, primarily seen in foot
  (Madura foot) or leg*

   B47.0   Eumycetoma
          Madura foot, mycotic Maduromycosis

   B47.1   Actinomycetoma

   B47.9   Mycetoma, unspecified
          Madura foot NOS

● **B48   Other mycoses, not elsewhere classified**

   B48.0   Lobomycosis
          *Infection with symptoms of red, smooth, hard cutaneous
          nodules resembling keloids*
          Keloidal blastomycosis
          Lobo's disease

   B48.1   Rhinosporidiosis
          *Chronic, localized granulomatous fungal infection, affecting
          mucocutaneous tissues, usually of nose characterized by
          polyps, papillomas, and wartlike lesions*

   B48.2   Allescheriasis
          Fungal infection
          Infection due to Pseudallescheria boydii
          | **Excludes1**   eumycetoma (B47.0) |

   B48.3   Geotrichosis
          *Fungal infection usually of bronchi, lungs, mouth, or
          intestinal tract*
          Geotrichum stomatitis

   B48.4   Penicillosis 🦠
          Fungal infection
          ▶Talaromycosis

   B48.8   Other specified mycoses 🦠
          Adiaspiromycosis
          Infection of tissue and organs by Alternaria
          Infection of tissue and organs by Drechslera
          Infection of tissue and organs by Fusarium
          Infection of tissue and organs by saprophytic fungi
          NEC

 B49   Unspecified mycosis
       Fungemia NOS

PROTOZOAL DISEASES (B50-B64)

| **Excludes1**   amebiasis (A06.-)
            other protozoal intestinal diseases (A07.-) |

● **B50   Plasmodium falciparum malaria**
  Severe form of malaria that can be fatal
  | **Includes**   mixed infections of Plasmodium falciparum with
            any other Plasmodium species |

   **B50.0   Plasmodium falciparum malaria with cerebral
          complications**
          Cerebral malaria NOS

   **B50.8   Other severe and complicated Plasmodium falciparum
          malaria**
          Severe or complicated Plasmodium falciparum malaria
          NOS

   B50.9   Plasmodium falciparum malaria, unspecified

● **B51   Plasmodium vivax malaria**
  | **Includes**   mixed infections of Plasmodium vivax with other
            Plasmodium species, except Plasmodium
            falciparum |
  | **Excludes1**   plasmodium vivax with Plasmodium falciparum
            (B50.-) |

   B51.0   Plasmodium vivax malaria with rupture of spleen

   B51.8   Plasmodium vivax malaria with other complications

   B51.9   Plasmodium vivax malaria without complication
          Plasmodium vivax malaria NOS

● **B52   Plasmodium malariae malaria**
  *Causes fever that recurs at approximately three-day intervals (quartan
  fever), longer than two-day (tertian) intervals of other malarial
  parasites*
  | **Includes**   mixed infections of Plasmodium malariae
            with other Plasmodium species, except
            Plasmodium falciparum and Plasmodium
            vivax |
  | **Excludes1**   plasmodium falciparum (B50.-)
            plasmodium vivax (B51.-) |

   B52.0   Plasmodium malariae malaria with nephropathy

   B52.8   Plasmodium malariae malaria with other complications

   B52.9   Plasmodium malariae malaria without complication
          Plasmodium malariae malaria NOS

● **B53   Other specified malaria**

   B53.0   Plasmodium ovale malaria
          *Least diagnosed type of malaria spread by female mosquitoes
          of rare species*
          | **Excludes1**   plasmodium ovale with Plasmodium
                    falciparum (B50.-)
                    plasmodium ovale with Plasmodium
                    malariae (B52.-)
                    plasmodium ovale with Plasmodium
                    vivax (B51.-) |

   B53.1   Malaria due to simian plasmodia
          Malaria-like disease (parasite infection)
          | **Excludes1**   malaria due to simian plasmodia with
                    Plasmodium falciparum (B50.-)
                    malaria due to simian plasmodia with
                    Plasmodium malariae (B52.-)
                    malaria due to simian plasmodia with
                    Plasmodium ovale (B53.0)
                    malaria due to simian plasmodia with
                    Plasmodium vivax (B51.-) |

   B53.8   Other malaria, not elsewhere classified

 B54   Unspecified malaria

● **B55   Leishmaniasis**
  Protozoal infection

   B55.0   Visceral leishmaniasis
          Kala-azar
          Post-kala-azar dermal leishmaniasis

   B55.1   Cutaneous leishmaniasis

   B55.2   Mucocutaneous leishmaniasis

   B55.9   Leishmaniasis, unspecified

● **B56   African trypanosomiasis**
  Human African trypanosomiasis (HAT) is transmitted by fly bites

   B56.0   Gambiense trypanosomiasis
          Infection due to Trypanosoma brucei gambiense
          West African sleeping sickness

   B56.1   Rhodesiense trypanosomiasis
          East African sleeping sickness
          Infection due to Trypanosoma brucei rhodesiense

   B56.9   African trypanosomiasis, unspecified
          Sleeping sickness NOS

● **B57   Chagas' disease**
  Tropical parasitic disease
  | **Includes**   American trypanosomiasis
            infection due to Trypanosoma cruzi |

   B57.0   Acute Chagas' disease with heart involvement
          Acute Chagas' disease with myocarditis

   B57.1   Acute Chagas' disease without heart involvement
          Acute Chagas' disease NOS

   B57.2   Chagas' disease (chronic) with heart involvement
          American trypanosomiasis NOS
          Chagas' disease (chronic) NOS
          Chagas' disease (chronic) with myocarditis
          Trypanosomiasis NOS

● **B57.3**   Chagas' disease (chronic) with digestive system involvement

     B57.30   Chagas' disease with digestive system involvement, unspecified

     B57.31   Megaesophagus in Chagas' disease

     B57.32   Megacolon in Chagas' disease

     B57.39   Other digestive system involvement in Chagas' disease

● **B57.4**   Chagas' disease (chronic) with nervous system involvement

     B57.40   Chagas' disease with nervous system involvement, unspecified

     B57.41   Meningitis in Chagas' disease

     B57.42   Meningoencephalitis in Chagas' disease

     B57.49   Other nervous system involvement in Chagas' disease

   B57.5   Chagas' disease (chronic) with other organ involvement

● **B58**   **Toxoplasmosis**

Infection by protozoon transmitted in cysts in feces of cats

     Includes   infection due to Toxoplasma gondii

     Excludes1   congenital toxoplasmosis (P37.1)

● **B58.0**   Toxoplasma oculopathy

     B58.00   Toxoplasma oculopathy, unspecified

     B58.01   Toxoplasma chorioretinitis

     B58.09   Other toxoplasma oculopathy
              Toxoplasma uveitis

   B58.1   Toxoplasma hepatitis

   B58.2   Toxoplasma meningoencephalitis 🦠

   B58.3   Pulmonary toxoplasmosis 🦠

● **B58.8**   Toxoplasmosis with other organ involvement

     B58.81   Toxoplasma myocarditis

     B58.82   Toxoplasma myositis

     B58.83   Toxoplasma tubulo-interstitial nephropathy
              Toxoplasma pyelonephritis

     B58.89   Toxoplasmosis with other organ involvement

   B58.9   Toxoplasmosis, unspecified

   B59   **Pneumocystosis** 🦠

Caused by fungus

Pneumonia due to Pneumocystis carinii

Pneumonia due to Pneumocystis jiroveci

● **B60**   **Other protozoal diseases, not elsewhere classified**

     Excludes1   cryptosporidiosis (A07.2)
               intestinal microsporidiosis (A07.8)
               isosporiasis (A07.3)

   B60.0   Babesiosis

Tickborne disease caused by microscopic organisms

~~Piroplasmosis~~

▶   B60.00   Babesiosis, unspecified
         ▶Babesiosis due to unspecified Babesia species
         ▶Piroplasmosis, unspecified

▶   B60.01   Babesiosis due to Babesia microti
         ▶Infection due to B. microti

▶   B60.02   Babesiosis due to Babesia duncani
         ▶Infection due to B. duncani and B. duncani-type species

▶   B60.03   Babesiosis due to Babesia divergens
         ▶Babesiosis due to Babesia MO-1
         ▶Infection due to B. divergens and B. divergens-like strains

▶   B60.09   Other babesiosis
         ▶Babesiosis due to Babesia KO-1
         ▶Babesiosis due to Babesia venatorum
         ▶Infection due to other Babesia species
         ▶Infection due to other protozoa of the order Piroplasmida
         ▶Other piroplasmosis

Item 1–22 Toxoplasmosis is caused by the protozoa **Toxoplasma gondii**, of which the house cat can be a host. Human infection occurs when contact is made with materials containing the pathogen, such as feces, contaminated soil, or ingestion of infected lamb, goat, or pork. Of the infected, very few have symptoms because a healthy person's immune system keeps the parasite from causing illness. When the immune system is compromised, symptoms may occur. Clinical symptoms include flu-like symptoms, but the disease progresses to include the eyes and the brain in babies.

● **B60.1**   Acanthamebiasis

     B60.10   Acanthamebiasis, unspecified

     B60.11   Meningoencephalitis due to Acanthamoeba (culbertsoni)

     B60.12   Conjunctivitis due to Acanthamoeba

     B60.13   Keratoconjunctivitis due to Acanthamoeba

     B60.19   Other acanthamebic disease

   B60.2   Naegleriasis
         Infection with microscopic organisms
         Primary amebic meningoencephalitis

   B60.8   Other specified protozoal diseases
         Microsporidiosis

   B64   **Unspecified protozoal disease**

HELMINTHIASES (B65-B83)

Diseases or infestations caused by parasitic worms

● **B65**   **Schistosomiasis [bilharziasis]**

Infection with flukes (flat parasitic worms)

     Includes   snail fever

   B65.0   Schistosomiasis due to Schistosoma haematobium [urinary schistosomiasis]

   B65.1   Schistosomiasis due to Schistosoma mansoni [intestinal schistosomiasis]

   B65.2   Schistosomiasis due to Schistosoma japonicum
         Asiatic schistosomiasis

   B65.3   Cercarial dermatitis
         Swimmer's itch

   B65.8   Other schistosomiasis
         Infection due to Schistosoma intercalatum
         Infection due to Schistosoma mattheei
         Infection due to Schistosoma mekongi

   B65.9   Schistosomiasis, unspecified

● **B66**   **Other fluke infections**

Trematode (parasitic worms)

   B66.0   Opisthorchiasis
         Infection due to cat liver fluke
         Infection due to Opisthorchis (felineus)(viverrini)

   B66.1   Clonorchiasis
         Chinese liver fluke disease
         Infection due to Clonorchis sinensis
         Oriental liver fluke disease

   B66.2   Dicroceliasis
         Liver fluke
         Infection due to Dicrocoelium dendriticum
         Lancet fluke infection

   B66.3   Fascioliasis
         Infection due to Fasciola gigantica
         Infection due to Fasciola hepatica
         Infection due to Fasciola indica
         Sheep liver fluke disease

   B66.4   Paragonimiasis 🦠
         Infection due to Paragonimus species
         Lung fluke disease
         Pulmonary distomiasis

   B66.5   Fasciolopsiasis
         Largest intestinal fluke in humans
         Infection due to Fasciolopsis buski
         Intestinal distomiasis

▶ New   ⟹ Revised   ~~deleted~~ Deleted   Excludes 1   Excludes 2   Includes   Use additional   Code first   Code also   Key words

OGCR Official Guidelines   X Assign placeholder X   ● Use Additional Character(s)   ▶ Manifestation Code   🦠 Hierarchical Condition Category   **Coding Clinic**

Item 1-23 Echinococcosis: Also known as hydatid disease; is caused by Echinococcus granulosus, E. multilocularis, and E. vogeli tapeworms; and is contracted from infected food. Found in southern South America, the Mediterranean, the Middle East, central Asia, and Africa and uncommon in the United States but has been reported in California, New Mexico, Arizona and Utah. The disease is treated with medication over a long course, as it is resistive.

B66.8   Other specified fluke infections
Echinostomiasis
Heterophyiasis
Metagonimiasis
Nanophyetiasis
Watsoniasis

B66.9   Fluke infection, unspecified

● **B67   Echinococcosis**
Larval forms of tapeworms usually of liver or lungs
Includes   hydatidosis

B67.0   Echinococcus granulosus infection of liver

B67.1   Echinococcus granulosus infection of lung 🔍

B67.2   Echinococcus granulosus infection of bone

● **B67.3   Echinococcus granulosus infection, other and multiple sites**

    B67.31   Echinococcus granulosus infection, thyroid gland

    B67.32   Echinococcus granulosus infection, multiple sites

    B67.39   Echinococcus granulosus infection, other sites

B67.4   Echinococcus granulosus infection, unspecified
Dog tapeworm (infection)

B67.5   Echinococcus multilocularis infection of liver

● **B67.6   Echinococcus multilocularis infection, other and multiple sites**

    B67.61   Echinococcus multilocularis infection, multiple sites

    B67.69   Echinococcus multilocularis infection, other sites

B67.7   Echinococcus multilocularis infection, unspecified

B67.8   Echinococcosis, unspecified, of liver

● **B67.9   Echinococcosis, other and unspecified**

    B67.90   Echinococcosis, unspecified
        Echinococcosis NOS

    B67.99   Other echinococcosis

● **B68   Taeniasis**
Intestinal tapeworm (cestode) infection from raw or undercooked meat of infected animal
Excludes1   cysticercosis (B69.-)

B68.0   Taenia solium taeniasis
Pork tapeworm (infection)

B68.1   Taenia saginata taeniasis
Beef tapeworm (infection)
Infection due to adult tapeworm Taenia saginata

B68.9   Taeniasis, unspecified

● **B69   Cysticercosis**
Systemic illness caused by the larvae of pork tapeworm
Includes   cysticerciasis infection due to larval form of Taenia solium

B69.0   Cysticercosis of central nervous system

B69.1   Cysticercosis of eye

● **B69.8   Cysticercosis of other sites**

    B69.81   Myositis in cysticercosis

    B69.89   Cysticercosis of other sites

B69.9   Cysticercosis, unspecified

● **B70   Diphyllobothriasis and sparganosis**
Infection with tapeworms seen most often from inadequately cooked fish

B70.0   Diphyllobothriasis
Diphyllobothrium (adult) (latum) (pacificum) infection
Fish tapeworm (infection)
Excludes2   larval diphyllobothriasis (B70.1)

B70.1   Sparganosis
Infection with migrating tapeworm larvae, which invade subcutaneous tissues, causing inflammation and fibrosis that resembles cellulitis
Infection due to Sparganum (mansoni) (proliferum)
Infection due to Spirometra larva
Larval diphyllobothriasis
Spirometrosis

● **B71   Other cestode infections**

B71.0   Hymenolepiasis
Intestinal infestation with tapeworms
Dwarf tapeworm infection
Rat tapeworm (infection)

B71.1   Dipylidiasis
Infection with tapeworm common to dogs and cats and seen in children having close contact with infected pets

B71.8   Other specified cestode infections
Infection by the larval stage of a tapeworm, usually through fruit or vegetables
Coenurosis

B71.9   Cestode infection, unspecified
Tapeworm (infection) NOS

B72   Dracunculiasis
Infection with roundworms
Includes   guinea worm infection
infection due to Dracunculus medinensis

● **B73   Onchocerciasis**
Infection with parasitic worm
Includes   onchocerca volvulus infection
onchocercosis
river blindness

● **B73.0   Onchocerciasis with eye disease**

    B73.00   Onchocerciasis with eye involvement, unspecified

    B73.01   Onchocerciasis with endophthalmitis

    B73.02   Onchocerciasis with glaucoma

    B73.09   Onchocerciasis with other eye involvement
        Infestation of eyelid due to onchocerciasis

B73.1   Onchocerciasis without eye disease

● **B74   Filariasis**
Infestation with slender threadlike worms
Excludes2   onchocerciasis (B73)
tropical (pulmonary) eosinophilia NOS (J82)

B74.0   Filariasis due to Wuchereria bancrofti
Bancroftian elephantiasis
Bancroftian filariasis

B74.1   Filariasis due to Brugia malayi

B74.2   Filariasis due to Brugia timori

B74.3   Loiasis
Infection with round worms growing in subcutaneous connective tissue
Calabar swelling
Eyeworm disease of Africa
Loa loa infection

B74.4   Mansonelliasis
Infection with filarial parasite
Infection due to Mansonella ozzardi
Infection due to Mansonella perstans
Infection due to Mansonella streptocerca

B74.8   Other filariases
Dirofilariasis

B74.9   Filariasis, unspecified

B75 Trichinellosis
Infestation with parasitic roundworms ingested in undercooked contaminated meat
> **Includes**   infection due to Trichinella species trichiniasis

● **B76 Hookworm diseases**
Occurs in hot, humid parts of world where larvae are soil borne, enter digestive tract through skin of feet/legs or in contaminated food/water; AKA ground itch
> **Includes**   uncinariasis

     B76.0 Ancylostomiasis
        Infection due to Ancylostoma species

     B76.1 Necatoriasis
        Infection due to Necator americanus

     B76.8 Other hookworm diseases

     B76.9 Hookworm disease, unspecified
        Cutaneous larva migrans NOS

● **B77 Ascariasis**
Infection by roundworm in small intestine
> **Includes**   ascaridiasis
>   roundworm infection

     B77.0 Ascariasis with intestinal complications
   ● **B77.8 Ascariasis with other complications**
        B77.81 Ascariasis pneumonia
        B77.89 Ascariasis with other complications
     B77.9 Ascariasis, unspecified

● **B78 Strongyloidiasis**
Infection with adult female roundworms
> **Excludes1**   trichostrongyliasis (B81.2)

     B78.0 Intestinal strongyloidiasis
     B78.1 Cutaneous strongyloidiasis
     B78.7 Disseminated strongyloidiasis
     B78.9 Strongyloidiasis, unspecified

 B79 Trichuriasis
Intestinal infection with roundworms
> **Includes**   trichocephaliasis
>   whipworm (disease)(infection)

 B80 Enterobiasis
Intestinal infection with pinworms
> **Includes**   oxyuriasis
>   pinworm infection
>   threadworm infection

● **B81 Other intestinal helminthiases, not elsewhere classified**
Diseases or infestations caused by parasitic worms
> **Excludes1**   angiostrongyliasis due to:
>   Angiostrongylus cantonensis (B83.2)
>   Parastrongylus cantonensis (B83.2)

     B81.0 Anisakiasis
        Roundworm infection via contaminated undercooked infected fish or marine mammals
        Infection due to Anisakis larva

     B81.1 Intestinal capillariasis
        Infestation with of parasites (nematodes)
        Capillariasis NOS
        Infection due to Capillaria philippinensis
>   **Excludes2**   hepatic capillariasis (B83.8)

     B81.2 Trichostrongyliasis

     B81.3 Intestinal angiostrongyliasis
        Angiostrongyliasis due to:
           Angiostrongylus costaricensis (B83.2)
           Parastrongylus costaricensis (B83.2)

     B81.4 Mixed intestinal helminthiases
        Infection due to intestinal helminths classified to more than one of the categories B65.0-B81.3 and B81.8
        Mixed helminthiasis NOS

     B81.8 Other specified intestinal helminthiases
        Infection due to Oesophagostomum species [esophagostomiasis]
        Infection due to Ternidens diminutus [ternidensiasis]

● **B82 Unspecified intestinal parasitism**
     B82.0 Intestinal helminthiasis, unspecified
        Infected with worms
     B82.9 Intestinal parasitism, unspecified

● **B83 Other helminthiases**
Caused by parasitic worms
> **Excludes1**   capillariasis NOS (B81.1)
> **Excludes2**   intestinal capillariasis (B81.1)

     B83.0 Visceral larva migrans
        Prolonged migration of nematode larvae
        Toxocariasis

     B83.1 Gnathostomiasis
        Infection with nematode occurring from ingested undercooked fish contaminated with larvae; larvae migrate to subcutaneous tissue or deeper tissues, results are abscesses
        Wandering swelling

     B83.2 Angiostrongyliasis due to Parastrongylus cantonensis
        Nematode infection caused by eating contaminated raw snails, slugs, or paratenic hosts such as prawns or crabs; larval worms migrate to central nervous system resulting in eosinophilic meningitis
        Eosinophilic meningoencephalitis due to Parastrongylus cantonensis
>   **Excludes2**   intestinal angiostrongyliasis (B81.3)

     B83.3 Syngamiasis
        Infestation with gapeworm from turkey, pheasant, guinea fowl, goose, and wild birds
        Syngamosis

     B83.4 Internal hirudiniasis
        Infestation by leeches
>   **Excludes2**   external hirudiniasis (B88.3)

     B83.8 Other specified helminthiases
        Parasitic worm infestation
        Acanthocephaliasis
        Gongylonemiasis
        Hepatic capillariasis
        Metastrongyliasis
        Thelaziasis

     B83.9 Helminthiasis, unspecified
        Worms NOS
>   **Excludes1**   intestinal helminthiasis NOS (B82.0)

PEDICULOSIS, ACARIASIS AND OTHER INFESTATIONS (B85-B89)

● **B85 Pediculosis and phthiriasis**
Infestation of lice

     B85.0 Pediculosis due to Pediculus humanus capitis
        Head-louse infestation

     B85.1 Pediculosis due to Pediculus humanus corporis
        Body-louse infestation

     B85.2 Pediculosis, unspecified

     B85.3 Phthiriasis
        Crab or pubic lice
        Infestation by crab-louse
        Infestation by Phthirus pubis

     B85.4 Mixed pediculosis and phthiriasis
        Infestation classifiable to more than one of the categories B85.0-B85.3

 B86 Scabies
Contagious dermatitis caused by mites
Sarcoptic itch

▶ New   ➡ Revised   ~~deleted~~ Deleted   Excludes 1   Excludes 2   Includes   Use additional   Code first   Code also   Key words

OGCR Official Guidelines   X Assign placeholder X   ● Use Additional Character(s)   ▌ Manifestation Code   ✿ Hierarchical Condition Category   **Coding Clinic**

● **B87   Myiasis**
    Infestation by fly maggots
    Includes   infestation by larva of flies
    B87.0   Cutaneous myiasis
        Creeping myiasis
    B87.1   Wound myiasis
        Traumatic myiasis
    B87.2   Ocular myiasis
    B87.3   Nasopharyngeal myiasis
        Laryngeal myiasis
    B87.4   Aural myiasis
  ● **B87.8   Myiasis of other sites**
        B87.81   Genitourinary myiasis
        B87.82   Intestinal myiasis
        B87.89   Myiasis of other sites
    B87.9   Myiasis, unspecified

● **B88   Other infestations**
    B88.0   Other acariasis
        Acarine dermatitis
        Dermatitis due to Demodex species
        Dermatitis due to Dermanyssus gallinae
        Dermatitis due to Liponyssoides sanguineus
        Trombiculosis
        Excludes2   scabies (B86)
    B88.1   Tungiasis [sandflea infestation]
        Inflammatory skin disease caused by infestation of fleas
    B88.2   Other arthropod infestations
        Scarabiasis
    B88.3   External hirudiniasis
        Leech infestation NOS
        Excludes2   internal hirudiniasis (B83.4)
    B88.8   Other specified infestations
        Infection of topical fresh water fish parasite
        Ichthyoparasitism due to Vandellia cirrhosa
        Linguatulosis
        Porocephaliasis
    B88.9   Infestation, unspecified
        Infestation (skin) NOS
        Infestation by mites NOS
        Skin parasites NOS

  B89   Unspecified parasitic disease

SEQUELAE OF INFECTIOUS AND PARASITIC DISEASES (B90-B94)

Note: Categories B90-B94 are to be used to indicate conditions in categories A00-B89 as the cause of sequelae, which are themselves classified elsewhere. The 'sequelae' include conditions specified as such; they also include residuals of diseases classifiable to the above categories if there is evidence that the disease itself is no longer present. Codes from these categories are not to be used for chronic infections. Code chronic current infections to active infectious disease as appropriate.

Code first condition resulting from (sequela) the infectious or parasitic disease

● **B90   Sequelae of tuberculosis**
    Condition resulting from tuberculosis
    B90.0   Sequelae of central nervous system tuberculosis
    B90.1   Sequelae of genitourinary tuberculosis
    B90.2   Sequelae of tuberculosis of bones and joints
    B90.8   Sequelae of tuberculosis of other organs
        Excludes2   sequelae of respiratory tuberculosis
                 (B90.9)
    B90.9   Sequelae of respiratory and unspecified tuberculosis
        Sequelae of tuberculosis NOS

  B91   Sequelae of poliomyelitis
    Excludes1   postpolio syndrome (G14)

  B92   Sequelae of leprosy

● **B94   Sequelae of other and unspecified infectious and parasitic diseases**
    B94.0   Sequelae of trachoma
    B94.1   Sequelae of viral encephalitis
    B94.2   Sequelae of viral hepatitis
    B94.8   Sequelae of other specified infectious and parasitic diseases
    B94.9   Sequelae of unspecified infectious and parasitic disease
        Coding Clinic: 2017, Q4, P109

OGCR   Section I.C.1.b.

Certain infectious and parasitic diseases
Infectious agents as the cause of diseases classified to other chapters
Certain infections are classified in chapters other than Chapter 1 and no organism is identified as part of the infection code. In these instances, it is necessary to use an additional code from Chapter 1 to identify the organism. A code from category B95, Streptococcus, Staphylococcus, and Enterococcus as the cause of diseases classified to other chapters, B96, Other bacterial agents as the cause of diseases classified to other chapters, or B97, Viral agents as the cause of diseases classified to other chapters, is to be used as an additional code to identify the organism. An instructional note will be found at the infection code advising that an additional organism code is required.

BACTERIAL AND VIRAL INFECTIOUS AGENTS (B95-B97)

Note: These categories are provided for use as supplementary or additional codes to identify the infectious agent(s) in diseases classified elsewhere.
Code the disease first, then the bacterium. Do not report codes from B95-B97 for sepsis.

● **B95   Streptococcus, Staphylococcus, and Enterococcus as the cause of diseases classified elsewhere**
    B95.0   Streptococcus, group A, as the cause of diseases classified elsewhere
    B95.1   Streptococcus, group B, as the cause of diseases classified elsewhere
        Coding Clinic: 2020, Q1, P10; 2019, Q2, P9-10; 2018, Q4, P23
    B95.2   Enterococcus as the cause of diseases classified elsewhere
    B95.3   Streptococcus pneumoniae as the cause of diseases classified elsewhere
    B95.4   Other streptococcus as the cause of diseases classified elsewhere
    B95.5   Unspecified streptococcus as the cause of diseases classified elsewhere
  ● **B95.6   Staphylococcus aureus as the cause of diseases classified elsewhere**
        B95.61   Methicillin susceptible Staphylococcus aureus infection as the cause of diseases classified elsewhere
            Methicillin susceptible Staphylococcus aureus (MSSA) infection as the cause of diseases classified elsewhere
            Staphylococcus aureus infection NOS as the cause of diseases classified elsewhere
        B95.62   Methicillin resistant Staphylococcus aureus infection as the cause of diseases classified elsewhere
            Methicillin resistant staphylococcus aureus (MRSA) infection as the cause of diseases classified elsewhere
            Coding Clinic: 2016, Q1, P13
    B95.7   Other staphylococcus as the cause of diseases classified elsewhere
    B95.8   Unspecified staphylococcus as the cause of diseases classified elsewhere

CHAPTER 1 (A00-B99)

N Newborn Age: 0   **P** Pediatric Age: 0–17   **M** Maternity DX: 12–55   **A** Adult Age: 15–124   ♀ Females Only   ♂ Males Only

675

● **B96**   **Other bacterial agents as the cause of diseases classified elsewhere**

    B96.0   **Mycoplasma pneumoniae [M. pneumoniae] as the cause of diseases classified elsewhere**
        Pleuro-pneumonia-like-organism [PPLO]

    B96.1   **Klebsiella pneumoniae [K. pneumoniae] as the cause of diseases classified elsewhere**

●   **B96.2**   **Escherichia coli [E. coli] as the cause of diseases classified elsewhere**

        B96.20   **Unspecified Escherichia coli [E. coli] as the cause of diseases classified elsewhere**
            Escherichia coli [E. coli] NOS
            Coding Clinic: 2018, Q4, P34; 2018, Q1, P16

        B96.21   **Shiga toxin-producing Escherichia coli [E. coli] [STEC] O157 as the cause of diseases classified elsewhere**
            E. coli O157:H- (nonmotile) with confirmation of Shiga toxin
            E. coli O157 with confirmation of Shiga toxin when H antigen is unknown, or is not H7
            O157:H7 Escherichia coli [E.coli] with or without confirmation of Shiga toxin-production
            Shiga toxin-producing Escherichia coli [E.coli] O157:H7 with or without confirmation of Shiga toxin-production
            STEC O157:H7 with or without confirmation of Shiga toxin-production

        B96.22   **Other specified Shiga toxin-producing Escherichia coli [E. coli] [STEC] as the cause of diseases classified elsewhere**
            Non-O157 Shiga toxin-producing Escherichia coli [E.coli]
            Non-O157 Shiga toxin-producing Escherichia coli [E.coli] with known O group

        B96.23   **Unspecified Shiga toxin-producing Escherichia coli [E. coli] [STEC] as the cause of diseases classified elsewhere**
            Shiga toxin-producing Escherichia coli [E. coli] with unspecified O group
            STEC NOS

        B96.29   **Other Escherichia coli [E. coli] as the cause of diseases classified elsewhere**
            Non-Shiga toxin-producing E. coli

    B96.3   **Hemophilus influenzae [H. influenzae] as the cause of diseases classified elsewhere**

    B96.4   **Proteus (mirabilis) (morganii) as the cause of diseases classified elsewhere**

    B96.5   **Pseudomonas (aeruginosa) (mallei) (pseudomallei) as the cause of diseases classified elsewhere**
        Coding Clinic: 2015, Q1, P18

    B96.6   **Bacteroides fragilis [B. fragilis] as the cause of diseases classified elsewhere**

    B96.7   **Clostridium perfringens [C. perfringens] as the cause of diseases classified elsewhere**

●   **B96.8**   **Other specified bacterial agents as the cause of diseases classified elsewhere**

        B96.81   **Helicobacter pylori [H. pylori] as the cause of diseases classified elsewhere**

        B96.82   **Vibrio vulnificus as the cause of diseases classified elsewhere**

        B96.89   **Other specified bacterial agents as the cause of diseases classified elsewhere**

● **B97**   **Viral agents as the cause of diseases classified elsewhere**

    B97.0   **Adenovirus as the cause of diseases classified elsewhere**

●   **B97.1**   **Enterovirus as the cause of diseases classified elsewhere**

        B97.10   **Unspecified enterovirus as the cause of diseases classified elsewhere**

        B97.11   **Coxsackievirus as the cause of diseases classified elsewhere**

        B97.12   **Echovirus as the cause of diseases classified elsewhere**

        B97.19   **Other enterovirus as the cause of diseases classified elsewhere**

Item 1–24   **Retrovirus** develops by copying its RNA, genetic materials, into the DNA, which then produces new virus particles. It is from the Retroviridae virus family. **Human T-cell lymphotropic virus, Type I (HTLV-I),** is also called human T-cell leukemia virus, Type I, and is a retrovirus thought to cause T-cell leukemia/lymphoma. **Human T-cell lymphotropic virus, Type II (HTLV-II),** is also called human T-cell leukemia virus, Type II, and is a retrovirus associated with hematologic disorders.

    HIV-2 is one of the serotypes of HIV and is usually confined to West Africa, whereas **HIV-1** is found worldwide.

● **B97.2**   **Coronavirus as the cause of diseases classified elsewhere**

    B97.21   **SARS-associated coronavirus as the cause of diseases classified elsewhere**
        Excludes1   pneumonia due to SARS-associated coronavirus (J12.81)

    B97.29   **Other coronavirus as the cause of diseases classified elsewhere**

● **B97.3**   **Retrovirus as the cause of diseases classified elsewhere**
    Excludes1   human immunodeficiency virus [HIV] disease (B20)

    B97.30   **Unspecified retrovirus as the cause of diseases classified elsewhere**

    B97.31   **Lentivirus as the cause of diseases classified elsewhere**

    B97.32   **Oncovirus as the cause of diseases classified elsewhere**

    B97.33   **Human T-cell lymphotrophic virus, type I [HTLV-I] as the cause of diseases classified elsewhere**

    B97.34   **Human T-cell lymphotrophic virus, type II [HTLV-II] as the cause of diseases classified elsewhere**

    B97.35   **Human immunodeficiency virus, type 2 [HIV 2] as the cause of diseases classified elsewhere** 🐾

    B97.39   **Other retrovirus as the cause of diseases classified elsewhere**

  B97.4   **Respiratory syncytial virus as the cause of diseases classified elsewhere**
    RSV as the cause of diseases classified elsewhere
    Code first related disorders, such as:
      otitis media (H65.-)
      upper respiratory infection (J06.9)
    Excludes2   acute bronchiolitis due to respiratory syncytial virus (RSV) (J21.0)
          acute bronchitis due to respiratory syncytial virus (RSV) (J20.5)
          respiratory syncytial virus (RSV) pneumonia (J12.1)

  B97.5   **Reovirus as the cause of diseases classified elsewhere**

  B97.6   **Parvovirus as the cause of diseases classified elsewhere**

  B97.7   **Papillomavirus as the cause of diseases classified elsewhere**

●   **B97.8**   **Other viral agents as the cause of diseases classified elsewhere**

    B97.81   **Human metapneumovirus as the cause of diseases classified elsewhere**

    B97.89   **Other viral agents as the cause of diseases classified elsewhere**
        Coding Clinic: 2016, Q3, P8-10, 14

OTHER INFECTIOUS DISEASES (B99)

● **B99**   **Other and unspecified infectious diseases**

    B99.8   **Other infectious disease**

    B99.9   **Unspecified infectious disease**

▶ New   ⇒ Revised   ~~deleted~~ Deleted   Excludes 1   Excludes 2   Includes   Use additional   Code first   Code also   Key words

OGCR Official Guidelines   X Assign placeholder X   ● Use Additional Character(s)   ▶ Manifestation Code   🐾 Hierarchical Condition Category   **Coding Clinic**

CHAPTER 2

NEOPLASMS (C00-D49)

OGCR Chapter-Specific Coding Guidelines

2. **Chapter 2: Neoplasms (C00-D49)**
General guidelines
Chapter 2 of the ICD-10-CM contains the codes for most benign and all malignant neoplasms. Certain benign neoplasms, such as prostatic adenomas, may be found in the specific body system chapters. To properly code a neoplasm it is necessary to determine from the record if the neoplasm is benign, in-situ, malignant, or of uncertain histologic behavior. If malignant, any secondary (metastatic) sites should also be determined.

Primary malignant neoplasms overlapping site boundaries
    A primary malignant neoplasm that overlaps two or more contiguous (next to each other) sites should be classified to the subcategory/code .8 ('overlapping lesion'), unless the combination is specifically indexed elsewhere. For multiple neoplasms of the same site that are not contiguous such as tumors in different quadrants of the same breast, codes for each site should be assigned.

Malignant neoplasm of ectopic tissue
    Malignant neoplasms of ectopic tissue are to be coded to the site of origin mentioned, e.g., ectopic pancreatic malignant neoplasms involving the stomach are coded to malignant neoplasm of pancreas, unspecified (C25.9).
    The neoplasm table in the Alphabetic Index should be referenced first. However, if the histological term is documented, that term should be referenced first, rather than going immediately to the Neoplasm Table, in order to determine which column in the Neoplasm Table is appropriate. For example, if the documentation indicates "adenoma," refer to the term in the Alphabetic Index to review the entries under this term and the instructional note to "see also neoplasm, by site, benign." The table provides the proper code based on the type of neoplasm and the site. It is important to select the proper column in the table that corresponds to the type of neoplasm. The Tabular List should then be referenced to verify that the correct code has been selected from the table and that a more specific site code does not exist.
    See Section I.C.21. Factors influencing health status and contact with health services, Status, for information regarding Z15.0, codes for genetic susceptibility to cancer.

a. **Treatment directed at the malignancy**
If the treatment is directed at the malignancy, designate the malignancy as the principal diagnosis.
    The only exception to this guideline is if a patient admission/encounter is solely for the administration of chemotherapy, immunotherapy or external beam radiation therapy, assign the appropriate Z51.— code as the first-listed or principal diagnosis, and the diagnosis or problem for which the service is being performed as a secondary diagnosis.

b. **Treatment of secondary site**
When a patient is admitted because of a primary neoplasm with metastasis and treatment is directed toward the secondary site only, the secondary neoplasm is designated as the principal diagnosis even though the primary malignancy is still present.

c. **Coding and sequencing of complications**
Coding and sequencing of complications associated with the malignancies or with the therapy thereof are subject to the following guidelines:

1) **Anemia associated with malignancy**
When admission/encounter is for management of an anemia associated with the malignancy, and the treatment is only for anemia, the appropriate code for the malignancy is sequenced as the principal or first-listed diagnosis followed by the appropriate code for the anemia (such as code D63.0, Anemia in neoplastic disease).

2) **Anemia associated with chemotherapy, immunotherapy and radiation therapy**
When the admission/encounter is for management of an anemia associated with an adverse effect of the administration of chemotherapy or immunotherapy and the only treatment is for the anemia, the anemia code is sequenced first followed by the appropriate codes for the neoplasm and the adverse effect (T45.1X5, Adverse effect of antineoplastic and immunosuppressive drugs).
    When the admission/encounter is for management of an anemia associated with an adverse effect of radiotherapy, the anemia code should be sequenced first, followed by the appropriate neoplasm code and code Y84.2, Radiological procedure and radiotherapy as the cause of abnormal reaction of the patient, or of later complication, without mention of misadventure at the time of the procedure.

3) **Management of dehydration due to the malignancy**
When the admission/encounter is for management of dehydration due to the malignancy and only the dehydration is being treated (intravenous rehydration), the dehydration is sequenced first, followed by the code(s) for the malignancy.

4) **Treatment of a complication resulting from a surgical procedure**
When the admission/encounter is for treatment of a complication resulting from a surgical procedure, designate the complication as the principal or first-listed diagnosis if treatment is directed at resolving the complication.

d. **Primary malignancy previously excised**
When a primary malignancy has been previously excised or eradicated from its site and there is no further treatment directed to that site and there is no evidence of any existing primary malignancy at that site, a code from category Z85, Personal history of malignant neoplasm, should be used to indicate the former site of the malignancy. Any mention of extension, invasion, or metastasis to another site is coded as a secondary malignant neoplasm to that site. The secondary site may be the principal or first-listed with the Z85 code used as a secondary code.

e. **Admissions/Encounters involving chemotherapy, immunotherapy and radiation therapy**

1) **Episode of care involves surgical removal of neoplasm**
When an episode of care involves the surgical removal of a neoplasm, primary or secondary site, followed by adjunct chemotherapy or radiation treatment during the same episode of care, the code for the neoplasm should be assigned as principal or first-listed diagnosis.

2) **Patient admission/encounter solely for administration of chemotherapy, immunotherapy and radiation therapy**
If a patient admission/encounter is solely for the administration of chemotherapy, immunotherapy or external beam radiation therapy assign code Z51.0, Encounter for antineoplastic radiation therapy, or Z51.11, Encounter for antineoplastic chemotherapy, or Z51.12, Encounter for antineoplastic immunotherapy as the first-listed or principal diagnosis. If a patient receives more than one of these therapies during the same admission more than one of these codes may be assigned, in any sequence.
    The malignancy for which the therapy is being administered should be assigned as a secondary diagnosis.
    If a patient admission/encounter is for the insertion or implantation of radioactive elements (e.g., brachytherapy) the appropriate code for the malignancy is sequenced as the principal or first-listed diagnosis. Code Z51.0 should not be assigned.

3) **Patient admitted for radiation therapy, chemotherapy or immunotherapy and develops complications**
When a patient is admitted for the purpose of external beam radiotherapy, immunotherapy or chemotherapy and develops complications such as uncontrolled nausea and vomiting or dehydration, the principal or first-listed diagnosis is Z51.0, Encounter for antineoplastic radiation therapy, or Z51.11, Encounter for antineoplastic chemotherapy, or Z51.12, Encounter for antineoplastic immunotherapy followed by any codes for the complications.
    When a patient is admitted for the purpose of insertion or implantation of radioactive elements (e.g., brachytherapy) and develops complications such as uncontrolled nausea and vomiting or dehydration, the principal or first-listed diagnosis is the appropriate code for the malignancy followed by any codes for the complications.

f. **Admission/encounter to determine extent of malignancy**
When the reason for admission/encounter is to determine the extent of the malignancy, or for a procedure such as paracentesis

or thoracentesis, the primary malignancy or appropriate metastatic site is designated as the principal or first-listed diagnosis, even though chemotherapy or radiotherapy is administered.

g. Symptoms, signs, and abnormal findings listed in Chapter 18 associated with neoplasms

Symptoms, signs, and ill-defined conditions listed in Chapter 18 characteristic of, or associated with, an existing primary or secondary site malignancy cannot be used to replace the malignancy as principal or first-listed diagnosis, regardless of the number of admissions or encounters for treatment and care of the neoplasm.

See Section I.C.21. Factors influencing health status and contact with health services, Encounter for prophylactic organ removal.

h. Admission/encounter for pain control/management
See Section I.C.6. for information on coding admission/encounter for pain control/management.

i. Malignancy in two or more noncontiguous sites
A patient may have more than one malignant tumor in the same organ. These tumors may represent different primaries or metastatic disease, depending on the site. Should the documentation be unclear, the provider should be queried as to the status of each tumor so that the correct codes can be assigned.

j. Disseminated malignant neoplasm, unspecified
Code C80.0, Disseminated malignant neoplasm, unspecified, is for use only in those cases where the patient has advanced metastatic disease and no known primary or secondary sites are specified. It should not be used in place of assigning codes for the primary site and all known secondary sites.

k. Malignant neoplasm without specification of site
Code C80.1, Malignant (primary) neoplasm, unspecified, equates to Cancer, unspecified. This code should only be used when no determination can be made as to the primary site of a malignancy. This code should rarely be used in the inpatient setting.

l. Sequencing of neoplasm codes

1) Encounter for treatment of primary malignancy
If the reason for the encounter is for treatment of a primary malignancy, assign the malignancy as the principal/first-listed diagnosis. The primary site is to be sequenced first, followed by any metastatic sites.

2) Encounter for treatment of secondary malignancy
When an encounter is for a primary malignancy with metastasis and treatment is directed toward the metastatic (secondary) site(s) only, the metastatic site(s) is designated as the principal/first-listed diagnosis. The primary malignancy is coded as an additional code.

3) Malignant neoplasm in a pregnant patient
When a pregnant woman has a malignant neoplasm, a code from subcategory O9A.1-, Malignant neoplasm complicating pregnancy, childbirth, and the puerperium, should be sequenced first, followed by the appropriate code from Chapter 2 to indicate the type of neoplasm.

4) Encounter for complication associated with a neoplasm
When an encounter is for management of a complication associated with a neoplasm, such as dehydration, and the treatment is only for the complication, the complication is coded first, followed by the appropriate code(s) for the neoplasm.

The exception to this guideline is anemia. When the admission/encounter is for management of an anemia associated with the malignancy, and the treatment is only for anemia, the appropriate code for the malignancy is sequenced as the principal or first-listed diagnosis followed by code D63.0, Anemia in neoplastic disease.

5) Complication from surgical procedure for treatment of a neoplasm
When an encounter is for treatment of a complication resulting from a surgical procedure performed for the treatment of the neoplasm, designate the complication as the principal/first-listed diagnosis. See guideline regarding the coding of a current malignancy versus personal history to determine if the code for the neoplasm should also be assigned.

6) Pathologic fracture due to a neoplasm
When an encounter is for a pathological fracture due to a neoplasm, and the focus of treatment is the fracture, a code from subcategory M84.5, Pathological fracture in neoplastic disease, should be sequenced first, followed by the code for the neoplasm.

If the focus of treatment is the neoplasm with an associated pathological fracture, the neoplasm code should be sequenced first, followed by a code from M84.5 for the pathological fracture.

m. Current malignancy versus personal history of malignancy
When a primary malignancy has been excised but further treatment, such as an additional surgery for the malignancy, radiation therapy or chemotherapy is directed to that site, the primary malignancy code should be used until treatment is completed.

When a primary malignancy has been previously excised or eradicated from its site, there is no further treatment (of the malignancy) directed to that site, and there is no evidence of any existing primary malignancy at that site, a code from category Z85, Personal history of malignant neoplasm, should be used to indicate the former site of the malignancy.

Subcategories Z85.0–Z85.7 should only be assigned for the former site of a primary malignancy, not the site of a secondary malignancy. Codes from subcategory Z85.8-, may be assigned for the former site(s) of either a primary or secondary malignancy included in this subcategory.

See Section I.C.21. Factors influencing health status and contact with health services, History (of)

n. Leukemia, Multiple Myeloma, and Malignant Plasma Cell Neoplasms in remission versus personal history
The categories for leukemia, and category C90, Multiple myeloma and malignant plasma cell neoplasms, have codes indicating whether or not the leukemia has achieved remission. There are also codes Z85.6, Personal history of leukemia, and Z85.79, Personal history of other malignant neoplasms of lymphoid, hematopoietic and related tissues. If the documentation is unclear, as to whether the leukemia has achieved remission, the provider should be queried.

See Section I.C.21. Factors influencing health status and contact with health services, History (of)

o. Aftercare following surgery for neoplasm
See Section I.C.21. Factors influencing health status and contact with health services, Aftercare

p. Follow-up care for completed treatment of a malignancy
See Section I.C.21. Factors influencing health status and contact with health services, Follow-up

q. Prophylactic organ removal for prevention of malignancy
See Section I.C. 21, Factors influencing health status and contact with health services, Prophylactic organ removal

r. Malignant neoplasm associated with transplanted organ
A malignant neoplasm of a transplanted organ should be coded as a transplant complication. Assign first the appropriate code from category T86.-, Complications of transplanted organs and tissue, followed by code C80.2, Malignant neoplasm associated with transplanted organ. Use an additional code for the specific malignancy.

Item 2–1 Neoplasm: Neo = new, plasm = growth, development, formation. This new growth (mass, tumor) can be malignant or benign, which is confirmed by the pathology report. Do not assign a code to a neoplasm until you review the pathology report. Certain CPT codes will specify benign or malignant lesion, so be certain the diagnosis code supports the procedure code.

CHAPTER 2

NEOPLASMS (C00-D49)

This chapter contains the following blocks:

C00-C14	Malignant neoplasms of lip, oral cavity and pharynx
C15-C26	Malignant neoplasms of digestive organs
C30-C39	Malignant neoplasms of respiratory and intrathoracic organs
C40-C41	Malignant neoplasms of bone and articular cartilage
C43-C44	Melanoma and other malignant neoplasms of skin
C45-C49	Malignant neoplasms of mesothelial and soft tissue
C50	Malignant neoplasms of breast
C51-C58	Malignant neoplasms of female genital organs
C60-C63	Malignant neoplasms of male genital organs
C64-C68	Malignant neoplasms of urinary tract
C69-C72	Malignant neoplasms of eye, brain and other parts of central nervous system
C73-C75	Malignant neoplasms of thyroid and other endocrine glands
C7A	Malignant neuroendocrine tumors
C7B	Secondary neuroendocrine tumors
C76-C80	Malignant neoplasms of ill-defined, other secondary and unspecified sites
C81-C96	Malignant neoplasms of lymphoid, hematopoietic and related tissue
D00-D09	In situ neoplasms
D10-D36	Benign neoplasms, except benign neuroendocrine tumors
D3A	Benign neuroendocrine tumors
D37-D48	Neoplasms of uncertain behavior, polycythemia vera and myelodysplastic syndromes
D49	Neoplasms of unspecified behavior

Notes: Functional activity

All neoplasms are classified in this chapter, whether they are functionally active or not. An additional code from Chapter 4 may be used, to identify functional activity associated with any neoplasm.

Morphology [Histology]

Chapter 2 classifies neoplasms primarily by site (topography), with broad groupings for behavior, malignant, in situ, benign, etc. The Table of Neoplasms should be used to identify the correct topography code. In a few cases, such as for malignant melanoma and certain neuroendocrine tumors, the morphology (histologic type) is included in the category and codes.

Primary malignant neoplasms overlapping site boundaries

A primary malignant neoplasm that overlaps two or more contiguous (next to each other) sites should be classified to the subcategory/code .8 ("overlapping lesion"), unless the combination is specifically indexed elsewhere. For multiple neoplasms of the same site that are not contiguous, such as tumors in different quadrants of the same breast, codes for each site should be assigned.

Malignant neoplasm of ectopic tissue

Malignant neoplasms of ectopic tissue are to be coded to the site mentioned, e.g., ectopic pancreatic malignant neoplasms are coded to pancreas, unspecified (C25.9).

MALIGNANT NEOPLASMS (C00-C96)

MALIGNANT NEOPLASMS, STATED OR PRESUMED TO BE PRIMARY (OF SPECIFIED SITES), AND CERTAIN SPECIFIED HISTOLOGIES, EXCEPT NEUROENDOCRINE, AND OF LYMPHOID, HEMATOPOIETIC AND RELATED TISSUE (C00-C75)

MALIGNANT NEOPLASMS OF LIP, ORAL CAVITY AND PHARYNX (C00-C14)

● **C00**   **Malignant neoplasm of lip**
Use additional code to identify:
  alcohol abuse and dependence (F10.-)
  history of tobacco dependence (Z87.891)
  tobacco dependence (F17.-)
  tobacco use (Z72.0)

  Excludes1   malignant melanoma of lip (C43.0)
  Merkel cell carcinoma of lip (C4A.0)
  other and unspecified malignant neoplasm of skin of lip (C44.0-)

C00.0   **Malignant neoplasm of external upper lip**
  Malignant neoplasm of lipstick area of upper lip
  Malignant neoplasm of upper lip NOS
  Malignant neoplasm of vermilion border of upper lip

C00.1   **Malignant neoplasm of external lower lip**
  Malignant neoplasm of lower lip NOS
  Malignant neoplasm of lipstick area of lower lip
  Malignant neoplasm of vermilion border of lower lip

C00.2   **Malignant neoplasm of external lip, unspecified**
  Malignant neoplasm of vermilion border of lip NOS

C00.3   **Malignant neoplasm of upper lip, inner aspect**
  Malignant neoplasm of buccal aspect of upper lip
  Malignant neoplasm of frenulum of upper lip
  Malignant neoplasm of mucosa of upper lip
  Malignant neoplasm of oral aspect of upper lip

C00.4   **Malignant neoplasm of lower lip, inner aspect**
  Malignant neoplasm of buccal aspect of lower lip
  Malignant neoplasm of frenulum of lower lip
  Malignant neoplasm of mucosa of lower lip
  Malignant neoplasm of oral aspect of lower lip

C00.5   **Malignant neoplasm of lip, unspecified, inner aspect**
  Malignant neoplasm of buccal aspect of lip, unspecified
  Malignant neoplasm of frenulum of lip, unspecified
  Malignant neoplasm of mucosa of lip, unspecified
  Malignant neoplasm of oral aspect of lip, unspecified

C00.6   **Malignant neoplasm of commissure of lip, unspecified**
  Commissure: Site of union of corresponding parts

C00.8   **Malignant neoplasm of overlapping sites of lip**

C00.9   **Malignant neoplasm of lip, unspecified**

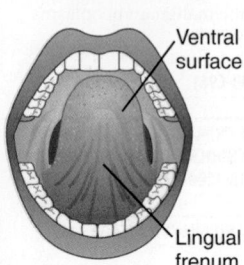

Transitional or vermilion surfaces

Lips are connected to the gums by frenulum
A

Hard palate
Soft palate
Vestibule
Uvula
Tonsil
Dorsal surface (anterior two-thirds of tongue)
B

Ventral surface
Lingual frenum
C

Figure 2-1 Anatomical structures of the mouth and lips. **A.** Transitional or vermilion borders. Lips are connected to the gums by frenulum. **B.** Dorsal surface. **C.** Ventral surface.

C01 Malignant neoplasm of base of tongue 🐾
  Malignant neoplasm of dorsal surface of base of tongue
  Malignant neoplasm of fixed part of tongue NOS
  Malignant neoplasm of posterior third of tongue

  Use additional code to identify:
    alcohol abuse and dependence (F10.-)
    history of tobacco dependence (Z87.891)
    tobacco dependence (F17.-)
    tobacco use (Z72.0)

● **C02** Malignant neoplasm of other and unspecified parts of tongue
  Use additional code to identify:
    alcohol abuse and dependence (F10.-)
    history of tobacco dependence (Z87.891)
    tobacco dependence (F17.-)
    tobacco use (Z72.0)

  C02.0 Malignant neoplasm of dorsal surface of tongue 🐾
    Malignant neoplasm of anterior two-thirds of tongue, dorsal surface
    Excludes2 malignant neoplasm of dorsal surface of base of tongue (C01)

  C02.1 Malignant neoplasm of border of tongue 🐾
    Malignant neoplasm of tip of tongue

  C02.2 Malignant neoplasm of ventral surface of tongue 🐾
    Malignant neoplasm of anterior two-thirds of tongue, ventral surface
    Malignant neoplasm of frenulum linguae

  C02.3 Malignant neoplasm of anterior two-thirds of tongue, part unspecified 🐾
    Malignant neoplasm of middle third of tongue NOS
    Malignant neoplasm of mobile part of tongue NOS

  C02.4 Malignant neoplasm of lingual tonsil 🐾
    Lingual tonsil: Aggregation of lymph follicles at root of tongue
    Excludes2 malignant neoplasm of tonsil NOS (C09.9)

  C02.8 Malignant neoplasm of overlapping sites of tongue 🐾
    Malignant neoplasm of two or more contiguous sites of tongue

  C02.9 Malignant neoplasm of tongue, unspecified 🐾

● **C03** Malignant neoplasm of gum
  Includes   malignant neoplasm of alveolar (ridge) mucosa
            malignant neoplasm of gingiva
  Use additional code to identify:
    alcohol abuse and dependence (F10.-)
    history of tobacco dependence (Z87.891)
    tobacco dependence (F17.-)
    tobacco use (Z72.0)
  Excludes2 malignant odontogenic neoplasms (C41.0-C41.1)

  C03.0 Malignant neoplasm of upper gum 🐾
  C03.1 Malignant neoplasm of lower gum 🐾
  C03.9 Malignant neoplasm of gum, unspecified 🐾

● **C04** Malignant neoplasm of floor of mouth
  Use additional code to identify:
    alcohol abuse and dependence (F10.-)
    history of tobacco dependence (Z87.891)
    tobacco dependence (F17.-)
    tobacco use (Z72.0)

  C04.0 Malignant neoplasm of anterior floor of mouth 🐾
    Malignant neoplasm of anterior to the premolar-canine junction
  C04.1 Malignant neoplasm of lateral floor of mouth 🐾
  C04.8 Malignant neoplasm of overlapping sites of floor of mouth 🐾
  C04.9 Malignant neoplasm of floor of mouth, unspecified 🐾

● **C05** Malignant neoplasm of palate
  Use additional code to identify:
    alcohol abuse and dependence (F10.-)
    history of tobacco dependence (Z87.891)
    tobacco dependence (F17.-)
    tobacco use (Z72.0)
  Excludes1   Kaposi's sarcoma of palate (C46.2)

  C05.0 Malignant neoplasm of hard palate 🐾
  C05.1 Malignant neoplasm of soft palate 🐾
    Excludes2   malignant neoplasm of nasopharyngeal surface of soft palate (C11.3)
  C05.2 Malignant neoplasm of uvula 🐾
  C05.8 Malignant neoplasm of overlapping sites of palate 🐾
  C05.9 Malignant neoplasm of palate, unspecified 🐾
    Malignant neoplasm of roof of mouth

● **C06** Malignant neoplasm of other and unspecified parts of mouth
  Use additional code to identify:
    alcohol abuse and dependence (F10.-)
    history of tobacco dependence (Z87.891)
    tobacco dependence (F17.-)
    tobacco use (Z72.0)

  C06.0 Malignant neoplasm of cheek mucosa 🐾
    Malignant neoplasm of buccal mucosa NOS
    Malignant neoplasm of internal cheek
  C06.1 Malignant neoplasm of vestibule of mouth 🐾
    Malignant neoplasm of buccal sulcus (upper) (lower)
    Malignant neoplasm of labial sulcus (upper) (lower)
  C06.2 Malignant neoplasm of retromolar area 🐾
● **C06.8** Malignant neoplasm of overlapping sites of other and unspecified parts of mouth
    C06.80 Malignant neoplasm of overlapping sites of unspecified parts of mouth 🐾
    C06.89 Malignant neoplasm of overlapping sites of other parts of mouth 🐾
      'book leaf' neoplasm [ventral surface of tongue and floor of mouth]
  C06.9 Malignant neoplasm of mouth, unspecified 🐾
    Malignant neoplasm of minor salivary gland, unspecified site
    Malignant neoplasm of oral cavity NOS

▶ New   ⇒ Revised   ~~deleted~~ Deleted   Excludes 1   Excludes 2   Includes   Use additional   Code first   Code also   Key words
OGCR Official Guidelines   X Assign placeholder X   ● Use Additional Character(s)   ▶ Manifestation Code   🐾 Hierarchical Condition Category   Coding Clinic

CHAPTER 2 (C00-D49)

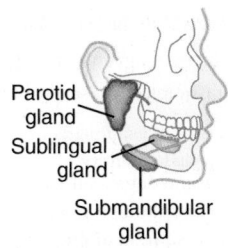

Parotid
gland
Sublingual
gland
Submandibular
gland

Figure 2-2 Major salivary glands.

C07 Malignant neoplasm of parotid gland 🔍
Use additional code to identify:
alcohol abuse and dependence (F10.-)
exposure to environmental tobacco smoke (Z77.22)
exposure to tobacco smoke in the perinatal period (P96.81)
history of tobacco dependence (Z87.891)
occupational exposure to environmental tobacco smoke (Z57.31)
tobacco dependence (F17.-)
tobacco use (Z72.0)

●**C08 Malignant neoplasm of other and unspecified major salivary glands**
Includes malignant neoplasm of salivary ducts
Use additional code to identify:
alcohol abuse and dependence (F10.-)
exposure to environmental tobacco smoke (Z77.22)
exposure to tobacco smoke in the perinatal period (P96.81)
history of tobacco dependence (Z87.891)
occupational exposure to environmental tobacco smoke (Z57.31)
tobacco dependence (F17.-)
tobacco use (Z72.0)
Excludes1 malignant neoplasms of specified minor salivary glands which are classified according to their anatomical location
Excludes2 malignant neoplasms of minor salivary glands NOS (C06.9)
malignant neoplasm of parotid gland (C07)
C08.0 Malignant neoplasm of submandibular gland 🔍
Malignant neoplasm of submaxillary gland
C08.1 Malignant neoplasm of sublingual gland 🔍
C08.9 Malignant neoplasm of major salivary gland, unspecified 🔍
Malignant neoplasm of salivary gland (major) NOS

★**(See Plate 28 of the Anatomy Illustrations.)**

●**C09 Malignant neoplasm of tonsil**
Use additional code to identify:
alcohol abuse and dependence (F10.-)
exposure to environmental tobacco smoke (Z77.22)
exposure to tobacco smoke in the perinatal period (P96.81)
history of tobacco dependence (Z87.891)
occupational exposure to environmental tobacco smoke (Z57.31)
tobacco dependence (F17.-)
tobacco use (Z72.0)
Excludes2 malignant neoplasm of lingual tonsil (C02.4)
malignant neoplasm of pharyngeal tonsil (C11.1)
C09.0 Malignant neoplasm of tonsillar fossa 🔍
Surface of palatine (two masses of lymphatic tissue on sides of throat) tonsils
C09.1 Malignant neoplasm of tonsillar pillar (anterior) (posterior) 🔍
Extension from palatine (two masses of lymphatic tissue on sides of throat) tonsils
C09.8 Malignant neoplasm of overlapping sites of tonsil 🔍
C09.9 Malignant neoplasm of tonsil, unspecified 🔍
Malignant neoplasm of tonsil NOS
Malignant neoplasm of faucial tonsils
Malignant neoplasm of palatine tonsils

●**C10 Malignant neoplasm of oropharynx**
Area of throat at back of mouth
Use additional code to identify:
alcohol abuse and dependence (F10.-)
exposure to environmental tobacco smoke (Z77.22)
exposure to tobacco smoke in the perinatal period (P96.81)
history of tobacco dependence (Z87.891)
occupational exposure to environmental tobacco smoke (Z57.31)
tobacco dependence (F17.-)
tobacco use (Z72.0)
Excludes2 malignant neoplasm of tonsil (C09.-)
C10.0 Malignant neoplasm of vallecula 🔍
Vallecula, depression or furrow
C10.1 Malignant neoplasm of anterior surface of epiglottis 🔍
Malignant neoplasm of epiglottis, free border [margin]
Malignant neoplasm of glossoepiglottic fold(s)
Excludes2 malignant neoplasm of epiglottis (suprahyoid portion) NOS (C32.1)
C10.2 Malignant neoplasm of lateral wall of oropharynx 🔍
C10.3 Malignant neoplasm of posterior wall of oropharynx 🔍
C10.4 Malignant neoplasm of branchial cleft 🔍
Congenital slitlike openings formed between branchial arches pharyngeal groove
Malignant neoplasm of branchial cyst [site of neoplasm]
C10.8 Malignant neoplasm of overlapping sites of oropharynx 🔍
Malignant neoplasm of junctional region of oropharynx
C10.9 Malignant neoplasm of oropharynx, unspecified 🔍

●**C11 Malignant neoplasm of nasopharynx**
Use additional code to identify:
exposure to environmental tobacco smoke (Z77.22)
exposure to tobacco smoke in the perinatal period (P96.81)
history of tobacco dependence (Z87.891)
occupational exposure to environmental tobacco smoke (Z57.31)
tobacco dependence (F17.-)
tobacco use (Z72.0)
C11.0 Malignant neoplasm of superior wall of nasopharynx 🔍
Part of pharynx that lies above soft palate
Malignant neoplasm of roof of nasopharynx
C11.1 Malignant neoplasm of posterior wall of nasopharynx 🔍
Malignant neoplasm of adenoid
Malignant neoplasm of pharyngeal tonsil
C11.2 Malignant neoplasm of lateral wall of nasopharynx 🔍
Malignant neoplasm of fossa of Rosenmüller
Malignant neoplasm of opening of auditory tube
Malignant neoplasm of pharyngeal recess
C11.3 Malignant neoplasm of anterior wall of nasopharynx 🔍
Malignant neoplasm of floor of nasopharynx
Malignant neoplasm of nasopharyngeal (anterior) (posterior) surface of soft palate
Malignant neoplasm of posterior margin of nasal choana
Malignant neoplasm of posterior margin of nasal septum
C11.8 Malignant neoplasm of overlapping sites of nasopharynx 🔍
C11.9 Malignant neoplasm of nasopharynx, unspecified 🔍
Malignant neoplasm of nasopharyngeal wall NOS

C12 Malignant neoplasm of pyriform sinus 🔍
Malignant neoplasm of pyriform fossa
Use additional code to identify:
exposure to environmental tobacco smoke (Z77.22)
exposure to tobacco smoke in the perinatal period (P96.81)
history of tobacco dependence (Z87.891)
occupational exposure to environmental tobacco smoke (Z57.31)
tobacco dependence (F17.-)
tobacco use (Z72.0)

CHAPTER 2 (C00-D49)

CHAPTER 2 (C00-D49)

● **C13   Malignant neoplasm of hypopharynx**

Use additional code to identify:
exposure to environmental tobacco smoke (Z77.22)
exposure to tobacco smoke in the perinatal period (P96.81)
history of tobacco dependence (Z87.891)
occupational exposure to environmental tobacco smoke (Z57.31)
tobacco dependence (F17.-)
tobacco use (Z72.0)

Excludes2   malignant neoplasm of pyriform sinus (C12)

C13.0   Malignant neoplasm of postcricoid region 🏷
Behind the cricoid cartilage of neck

C13.1   Malignant neoplasm of aryepiglottic fold, hypopharyngeal aspect 🏷
Arytenoepiglottic fold, triangular opening between side of epiglottis and apex of arytenoid cartilage
Malignant neoplasm of aryepiglottic fold, marginal zone
Malignant neoplasm of aryepiglottic fold NOS
Malignant neoplasm of interarytenoid fold, marginal zone
Malignant neoplasm of interarytenoid fold NOS

Excludes2   malignant neoplasm of aryepiglottic fold or interarytenoid fold, laryngeal aspect (C32.1)

C13.2   Malignant neoplasm of posterior wall of hypopharynx 🏷

C13.8   Malignant neoplasm of overlapping sites of hypopharynx 🏷

C13.9   Malignant neoplasm of hypopharynx, unspecified 🏷
Malignant neoplasm of hypopharyngeal wall NOS

● **C14   Malignant neoplasm of other and ill-defined sites in the lip, oral cavity and pharynx**

Use additional code to identify:
alcohol abuse and dependence (F10.-)
exposure to environmental tobacco smoke (Z77.22)
exposure to tobacco smoke in the perinatal period (P96.81)
history of tobacco dependence (Z87.891)
occupational exposure to environmental tobacco smoke (Z57.31)
tobacco dependence (F17.-)
tobacco use (Z72.0)

Excludes1   malignant neoplasm of oral cavity NOS (C06.9)

C14.0   Malignant neoplasm of pharynx, unspecified 🏷

C14.2   Malignant neoplasm of Waldeyer's ring 🏷

C14.8   Malignant neoplasm of overlapping sites of lip, oral cavity and pharynx 🏷
Primary malignant neoplasm of two or more contiguous sites of lip, oral cavity and pharynx

Excludes1   'book leaf' neoplasm [ventral surface of tongue and floor of mouth] (C06.89)

MALIGNANT NEOPLASM OF DIGESTIVE ORGANS (C15-C26)

Excludes1   Kaposi's sarcoma of gastrointestinal sites (C46.4)

Excludes2   gastrointestinal stromal tumors (C49.A-)

● **C15   Malignant neoplasms of esophagus**

Use additional code to identify:
alcohol abuse and dependence (F10.-)

C15.3   Malignant neoplasm of upper third of esophagus 🏷

C15.4   Malignant neoplasm of middle third of esophagus 🏷

C15.5   Malignant neoplasm of lower third of esophagus 🏷

Excludes1   malignant neoplasm of cardio-esophageal junction (C16.0)

C15.8   Malignant neoplasm of overlapping sites of esophagus 🏷

C15.9   Malignant neoplasm of esophagus, unspecified 🏷

● **C16   Malignant neoplasm of stomach**

Use additional code to identify:
alcohol abuse and dependence (F10.-)

Excludes2   malignant carcinoid tumor of the stomach (C7A.092)

C16.0   Malignant neoplasm of cardia 🏷
Malignant neoplasm of cardiac orifice
Malignant neoplasm of cardio-esophageal junction
Malignant neoplasm of esophagus and stomach
Malignant neoplasm of gastro-esophageal junction

C16.1   Malignant neoplasm of fundus of stomach 🏷

C16.2   Malignant neoplasm of body of stomach 🏷

C16.3   Malignant neoplasm of pyloric antrum 🏷
Malignant neoplasm of gastric antrum

C16.4   Malignant neoplasm of pylorus 🏷
Malignant neoplasm of prepylorus
Malignant neoplasm of pyloric canal

C16.5   Malignant neoplasm of lesser curvature of stomach, unspecified 🏷
Malignant neoplasm of lesser curvature of stomach, not classifiable to C16.1-C16.4

C16.6   Malignant neoplasm of greater curvature of stomach, unspecified 🏷
Malignant neoplasm of greater curvature of stomach, not classifiable to C16.0-C16.4

C16.8   Malignant neoplasm of overlapping sites of stomach 🏷

C16.9   Malignant neoplasm of stomach, unspecified 🏷
Gastric cancer NOS

Figure 2-3   The esophagus is the muscular tube that connects the pharynx and the stomach. The 10 inch (25 cm) long esophagus is divided into three parts: **cervical, thoracic,** and **abdominal.**

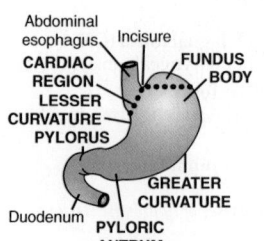

Figure 2-4   Parts of the stomach.

Item 2-2   The esophagus opens into the stomach through the **cardiac orifice,** also called the **cardioesophageal junction.** The **cardia** is adjacent to the cardiac orifice. The stomach widens into the **greater** and **lesser curvatures.** The **pyloric antrum** precedes the **pylorus,** which opens to the duodenum.

▶ New   ⇒ Revised   ~~deleted~~ Deleted   Excludes 1   Excludes 2   Includes   Use additional   Code first   Code also   Key words
OGCR Official Guidelines   X Assign placeholder X   ● Use Additional Character(s)   ▶ Manifestation Code   🏷 Hierarchical Condition Category   **Coding Clinic**

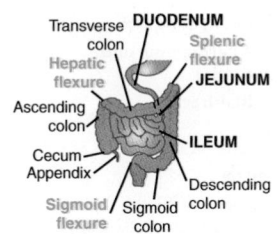

Figure 2-5 Small intestine and colon.

● **C17   Malignant neoplasm of small intestine**

> **Excludes 1**   malignant carcinoid tumor of the small intestine (C7A.Ø1)

C17.Ø   Malignant neoplasm of duodenum 🔎
> *First or proximal portion of small intestine, extending from pylorus to jejunum*

C17.1   Malignant neoplasm of jejunum 🔎
> *Second section of small intestine, extending from duodenum to ileum*

C17.2   Malignant neoplasm of ileum 🔎
> *Distal and longest portion of small intestine, extending from jejunum to cecum*
> **Excludes 1**   malignant neoplasm of ileocecal valve (C18.Ø)

C17.3   Meckel's diverticulum, malignant 🔎
> *Appendage of ileum*
> **Excludes 1**   Meckel's diverticulum, congenital (Q43.Ø)

C17.8   Malignant neoplasm of overlapping sites of small intestine 🔎

C17.9   Malignant neoplasm of small intestine, unspecified 🔎

● **C18   Malignant neoplasm of colon**

> **Excludes 1**   malignant carcinoid tumors of the colon (C7A.Ø2)

C18.Ø   Malignant neoplasm of cecum 🔎
> *First section of large intestine*
> Malignant neoplasm of ileocecal valve

C18.1   Malignant neoplasm of appendix 🔎
> *Blind ended tube connected to the cecum; AKA vermiform appendix*

C18.2   Malignant neoplasm of ascending colon 🔎
> *Ascending colon is between cecum and right colic flexure*

C18.3   Malignant neoplasm of hepatic flexure 🔎
> *A flexure is a bending in a structure or organ. Note the three flexures illustrated in Figure 2–5.*

C18.4   Malignant neoplasm of transverse colon 🔎
> *Portion of colon that runs transversely across upper part of abdomen, between right and left colic flexures*

C18.5   Malignant neoplasm of splenic flexure 🔎
> *Bend at junction of transverse and descending colon*

C18.6   Malignant neoplasm of descending colon 🔎
> *Portion between left colic flexure and sigmoid colon at pelvic brim; AKA iliac colon*

C18.7   Malignant neoplasm of sigmoid colon 🔎
> *S-shaped part of colon extending from pelvic brim to third segment of sacrum*
> Malignant neoplasm of sigmoid (flexure)
> **Excludes 1**   malignant neoplasm of rectosigmoid junction (C19)

C18.8   Malignant neoplasm of overlapping sites of colon 🔎

C18.9   Malignant neoplasm of colon, unspecified 🔎
> Malignant neoplasm of large intestine NOS

C19   Malignant neoplasm of rectosigmoid junction 🔎
> Malignant neoplasm of colon with rectum
> Malignant neoplasm of rectosigmoid (colon)
> **Excludes 1**   malignant carcinoid tumors of the colon (C7A.Ø2-)

C20   Malignant neoplasm of rectum 🔎
> Malignant neoplasm of rectal ampulla
> **Excludes 1**   malignant carcinoid tumor of the rectum (C7A.Ø26)

● **C21   Malignant neoplasm of anus and anal canal**

> **Excludes 2**   malignant carcinoid tumors of the colon (C7A.Ø2-)
> malignant melanoma of anal margin (C43.51)
> malignant melanoma of anal skin (C43.51)
> malignant melanoma of perianal skin (C43.51)
> other and unspecified malignant neoplasm of anal margin (C44.5ØØ, C44.51Ø, C44.52Ø, C44.59Ø)
> other and unspecified malignant neoplasm of anal skin (C44.5ØØ, C44.51Ø, C44.52Ø, C44.59Ø)
> other and unspecified malignant neoplasm of perianal skin (C44.5ØØ, C44.51Ø, C44.52Ø, C44.59Ø)

C21.Ø   Malignant neoplasm of anus, unspecified 🔎

C21.1   Malignant neoplasm of anal canal 🔎
> *Terminal part of large intestine*
> Malignant neoplasm of anal sphincter

C21.2   Malignant neoplasm of cloacogenic zone 🔎

C21.8   Malignant neoplasm of overlapping sites of rectum, anus and anal canal 🔎
> Malignant neoplasm of anorectal junction
> Malignant neoplasm of anorectum
> Primary malignant neoplasm of two or more contiguous sites of rectum, anus and anal canal

● **C22   Malignant neoplasm of liver and intrahepatic bile ducts**
> *Intrahepatic: Within liver*
> Use additional code to identify:
> alcohol abuse and dependence (F1Ø.-)
> hepatitis B (B16.-, B18.Ø-B18.1) hepatitis C (B17.1-, B18.2)
> **Excludes 1**   malignant neoplasm of biliary tract NOS (C24.9)
> secondary malignant neoplasm of liver and intrahepatic bile duct (C78.7)

C22.Ø   Liver cell carcinoma 🔎
> Hepatocellular carcinoma
> Hepatoma

C22.1   Intrahepatic bile duct carcinoma 🔎
> Cholangiocarcinoma
> *Adenocarcinoma (cancer that originates in glandular tissue) arising from epithelium of intrahepatic bile ducts*
> **Excludes 1**   malignant neoplasm of hepatic duct (C24.Ø)

C22.2   Hepatoblastoma 🔎
> *Malignant intrahepatic tumor*

C22.3   Angiosarcoma of liver 🔎
> Kupffer cell sarcoma

C22.4   Other sarcomas of liver 🔎

C22.7   Other specified carcinomas of liver 🔎

C22.8   Malignant neoplasm of liver, primary, unspecified as to type 🔎

C22.9   Malignant neoplasm of liver, not specified as primary or secondary 🔎

CHAPTER 2 (CØØ-D49)

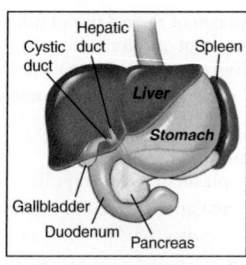

Figure 2-6 Diagram of liver, gallbladder, hepatic duct, pancreas, and spleen. (From Thibodeau and Patton: Anatomy and Physiology, ed 7, Mosby, 2010)

C23   Malignant neoplasm of gallbladder 🦠

● **C24   Malignant neoplasm of other and unspecified parts of biliary tract**

> **Excludes1**   malignant neoplasm of intrahepatic bile duct (C22.1)

C24.0   Malignant neoplasm of extrahepatic bile duct 🦠
Extrahepatic = outside the liver
Malignant neoplasm of biliary duct or passage NOS
Malignant neoplasm of common bile duct
Malignant neoplasm of cystic duct
Malignant neoplasm of hepatic duct

C24.1   Malignant neoplasm of ampulla of Vater 🦠
Union of pancreatic duct and common bile duct

C24.8   Malignant neoplasm of overlapping sites of biliary tract 🦠
Malignant neoplasm involving both intrahepatic and extrahepatic bile ducts
Primary malignant neoplasm of two or more contiguous sites of biliary tract

C24.9   Malignant neoplasm of biliary tract, unspecified 🦠

● **C25   Malignant neoplasm of pancreas**
Check documentation for specific site.
Code also exocrine pancreatic insufficiency (K86.81)
Use additional code to identify:
alcohol abuse and dependence (F10.-)

C25.0   Malignant neoplasm of head of pancreas 🦠
C25.1   Malignant neoplasm of body of pancreas 🦠
    Coding Clinic: 2018, Q4, P40
C25.2   Malignant neoplasm of tail of pancreas 🦠
C25.3   Malignant neoplasm of pancreatic duct 🦠
C25.4   Malignant neoplasm of endocrine pancreas 🦠
Malignant neoplasm of islets of Langerhans
That part of the pancreas that acts as endocrine gland and consists of islets of Langerhans
Use additional code to identify any functional activity.
C25.7   Malignant neoplasm of other parts of pancreas 🦠
Malignant neoplasm of neck of pancreas
C25.8   Malignant neoplasm of overlapping sites of pancreas 🦠
C25.9   Malignant neoplasm of pancreas, unspecified 🦠

Item 2–3   Islets of Langerhans (endocrine producing cells comprising 1% to 2% of the pancreatic mass) make and secrete hormones that regulate the body's production of insulin, glucagon, and stomach acid. Breakdown of the insulin-producing cells can cause diabetes mellitus. Islet cell tumors can be benign or malignant and include glucagonomas, insulinomas, gastrinomas, and neuroendocrine tumor. The neoplasm table must be consulted for the correct neoplasm code.

Figure 2-7 Paranasal sinuses. (From Buck CJ: Step-by-Step Medical Coding, ed 2016, St. Louis, Elsevier, 2016)

● **C26   Malignant neoplasm of other and ill-defined digestive organs**

> **Excludes1**   malignant neoplasm of peritoneum and retroperitoneum (C48.-)

C26.0   Malignant neoplasm of intestinal tract, part unspecified 🦠
Malignant neoplasm of intestine NOS

C26.1   Malignant neoplasm of spleen 🦠

> **Excludes1**   Hodgkin lymphoma (C81.-)
> non-Hodgkin lymphoma (C82-C85)

C26.9   Malignant neoplasm of ill-defined sites within the digestive system 🦠
Malignant neoplasm of alimentary canal or tract NOS
Malignant neoplasm of gastrointestinal tract NOS

> **Excludes1**   malignant neoplasm of abdominal NOS (C76.2)
> malignant neoplasm of intra-abdominal NOS (C76.2)

MALIGNANT NEOPLASMS OF RESPIRATORY AND INTRATHORACIC ORGANS (C30-C39)

> **Includes**   malignant neoplasm of middle ear
> **Excludes1**   mesothelioma (C45.-)

● **C30   Malignant neoplasm of nasal cavity and middle ear**

C30.0   Malignant neoplasm of nasal cavity 🦠
Malignant neoplasm of cartilage of nose
Malignant neoplasm of nasal concha
Malignant neoplasm of internal nose
Malignant neoplasm of septum of nose
Malignant neoplasm of vestibule of nose
Anterior part of nasal cavity

> **Excludes1**   malignant neoplasm of nasal bone (C41.0)
> malignant neoplasm of nose NOS (C76.0)
> malignant neoplasm of olfactory bulb (C72.2-)
> malignant neoplasm of posterior margin of nasal septum and choana (C11.3)
> malignant melanoma of skin of nose (C43.31)
> malignant neoplasm of turbinates (C41.0)
> other and unspecified malignant neoplasm of skin of nose C44.301, C44.321, C44.391

C30.1   Malignant neoplasm of middle ear 🦠
Malignant neoplasm of antrum tympanicum
Boney cavity or chamber
Malignant neoplasm of auditory tube
Malignant neoplasm of eustachian tube
Malignant neoplasm of inner ear
Malignant neoplasm of mastoid air cells
Malignant neoplasm of tympanic cavity

> **Excludes1**   malignant neoplasm of auricular canal (external) (C43.2-, C44.2-)
> malignant neoplasm of bone of ear (meatus) (C41.0)
> malignant neoplasm of cartilage of ear (C49.0)
> malignant melanoma of skin of (external) ear (C43.2-)
> other and unspecified malignant neoplasm of skin of (external) ear (C44.2-)

● **C31   Malignant neoplasm of accessory sinuses**
Paired sinuses in bones of face

C31.0   Malignant neoplasm of maxillary sinus 🦠
Malignant neoplasm of antrum (Highmore) (maxillary)
C31.1   Malignant neoplasm of ethmoidal sinus 🦠
C31.2   Malignant neoplasm of frontal sinus 🦠
C31.3   Malignant neoplasm of sphenoid sinus 🦠
C31.8   Malignant neoplasm of overlapping sites of accessory sinuses 🦠
C31.9   Malignant neoplasm of accessory sinus, unspecified 🦠

▶ New   ⇒ Revised   ~~deleted~~ Deleted   Excludes 1   Excludes 2   Includes   Use additional   Code first   Code also   Key words
OGCR Official Guidelines   X Assign placeholder X   ● Use Additional Character(s)   ▶ Manifestation Code   🦠 Hierarchical Condition Category   Coding Clinic

CHAPTER 2 (C00-D49)

● **C32**   **Malignant neoplasm of larynx**

    Use additional code to identify:
        alcohol abuse and dependence (F10.-)
        exposure to environmental tobacco smoke (Z77.22)
        exposure to tobacco smoke in the perinatal period (P96.81)
        history of tobacco dependence (Z87.891)
        occupational exposure to environmental tobacco smoke
           (Z57.31)
        tobacco dependence (F17.-)
        tobacco use (Z72.0)

  C32.0   **Malignant neoplasm of glottis** 🔍

      Vocal apparatus of larynx, consisting of true vocal cords (plicae vocales) and opening between them (rima glottidis)
      Malignant neoplasm of intrinsic larynx
      Malignant neoplasm of laryngeal commissure (anterior) (posterior)
      Malignant neoplasm of vocal cord (true) NOS
        *True vocal cords ("lower vocal folds") produce vocalization when air from the lungs passes between them. Check your documentation. Code C32.1 is for malignant neoplasm of the **false** vocal cords.*

  C32.1   **Malignant neoplasm of supraglottis** 🔍

      Area of pharynx above glottis
      Malignant neoplasm of aryepiglottic fold or interarytenoid fold, laryngeal aspect
      Malignant neoplasm of epiglottis (suprahyoid portion) NOS
      Malignant neoplasm of extrinsic larynx
      Malignant neoplasm of false vocal cord
        False vocal cords ("upper vocal folds") are not involved in vocalization. Check your documentation. Code C32.0 is for true vocal cords.
      Malignant neoplasm of posterior (laryngeal) surface of epiglottis
      Malignant neoplasm of ventricular bands

      Excludes2   malignant neoplasm of anterior surface of epiglottis (C10.1)
                malignant neoplasm of aryepiglottic fold or interarytenoid fold, hypopharyngeal aspect (C13.1)
                malignant neoplasm of aryepiglottic fold or interarytenoid fold, marginal zone (C13.1)
                malignant neoplasm of aryepiglottic fold or interarytenoid fold NOS (C13.1)

  C32.2   **Malignant neoplasm of subglottis** 🔍

      Lowest part of larynx from just below vocal cords down to top of trachea

  C32.3   **Malignant neoplasm of laryngeal cartilage** 🔍

      Cartilages of larynx, including cricoid, thyroid, and epiglottic, and two each of arytenoid, corniculate, and cuneiform

  C32.8   **Malignant neoplasm of overlapping sites of larynx** 🔍

  C32.9   **Malignant neoplasm of larynx, unspecified** 🔍

C33   **Malignant neoplasm of trachea** 🔍

    Use additional code to identify:
        exposure to environmental tobacco smoke (Z77.22)
        exposure to tobacco smoke in the perinatal period (P96.81)
        history of tobacco dependence (Z87.891)
        occupational exposure to environmental tobacco smoke
           (Z57.31)
        tobacco dependence (F17.-)
        tobacco use (Z72.0)

● **C34**   **Malignant neoplasm of bronchus and lung**

    Use additional code to identify:
        exposure to environmental tobacco smoke (Z77.22)
        exposure to tobacco smoke in the perinatal period (P96.81)
        history of tobacco dependence (Z87.891)
        occupational exposure to environmental tobacco smoke
           (Z57.31)
        tobacco dependence (F17.-)
        tobacco use (Z72.0)

    Excludes1   Kaposi's sarcoma of lung (C46.5-)
            malignant carcinoid tumor of the bronchus and lung (C7A.090)

● **C34.0**   **Malignant neoplasm of main bronchus**

      Malignant neoplasm of carina
        Ridgelike structure
      Malignant neoplasm of hilus (of lung)
        Anatomic depression or pit

    C34.00   **Malignant neoplasm of unspecified main bronchus** 🔍

    C34.01   **Malignant neoplasm of right main bronchus** 🔍

    C34.02   **Malignant neoplasm of left main bronchus** 🔍

● **C34.1**   **Malignant neoplasm of upper lobe, bronchus or lung**

    C34.10   **Malignant neoplasm of unspecified bronchus or lung** 🔍

    C34.11   **Malignant neoplasm of upper lobe, right bronchus or lung** 🔍

    C34.12   **Malignant neoplasm of upper lobe, left bronchus or lung** 🔍

  C34.2   **Malignant neoplasm of middle lobe, bronchus or lung** 🔍

● **C34.3**   **Malignant neoplasm of lower lobe, bronchus or lung**

    C34.30   **Malignant neoplasm of lower lobe, unspecified bronchus or lung** 🔍

    C34.31   **Malignant neoplasm of lower lobe, right bronchus or lung** 🔍

    C34.32   **Malignant neoplasm of lower lobe, left bronchus or lung** 🔍

● **C34.8**   **Malignant neoplasm of overlapping sites of bronchus and lung**

    C34.80   **Malignant neoplasm of overlapping sites of unspecified bronchus and lung** 🔍

    C34.81   **Malignant neoplasm of overlapping sites of right bronchus and lung** 🔍

    C34.82   **Malignant neoplasm of overlapping sites of left bronchus and lung** 🔍

● **C34.9**   **Malignant neoplasm of unspecified part of bronchus or lung**

    C34.90   **Malignant neoplasm of unspecified part of unspecified bronchus or lung** 🔍
        Lung cancer NOS

    C34.91   **Malignant neoplasm of unspecified part of right bronchus or lung** 🔍

    C34.92   **Malignant neoplasm of unspecified part of left bronchus or lung** 🔍

C37   **Malignant neoplasm of thymus** 🔍

    Excludes1   malignant carcinoid tumor of the thymus (C7A.091)

CHAPTER 2 (C00-D49)

● **C38** **Malignant neoplasm of heart, mediastinum and pleura**

> **Excludes1** mesothelioma (C45.-)

C38.0 **Malignant neoplasm of heart** 🅦
Malignant neoplasm of pericardium

> **Excludes1** malignant neoplasm of great vessels (C49.3)

C38.1 **Malignant neoplasm of anterior mediastinum** 🅦

C38.2 **Malignant neoplasm of posterior mediastinum** 🅦

C38.3 **Malignant neoplasm of mediastinum, part unspecified** 🅦

C38.4 **Malignant neoplasm of pleura** 🅦

C38.8 **Malignant neoplasm of overlapping sites of heart, mediastinum and pleura**
Pleura are comprised of serous membrane that lines the thoracic cavity (parietal) and covers the lungs (visceral).

● **C39** **Malignant neoplasm of other and ill-defined sites in the respiratory system and intrathoracic organs**
Intrathoracic: within thorax/chest
Use additional code to identify:
exposure to environmental tobacco smoke (Z77.22)
exposure to tobacco smoke in the perinatal period (P96.81)
history of tobacco dependence (Z87.891)
occupational exposure to environmental tobacco smoke (Z57.31)
tobacco dependence (F17.-)
tobacco use (Z72.0)

> **Excludes1** intrathoracic malignant neoplasm NOS (C76.1)
> thoracic malignant neoplasm NOS (C76.1)

C39.0 **Malignant neoplasm of upper respiratory tract, part unspecified** 🅦

C39.9 **Malignant neoplasm of lower respiratory tract, part unspecified** 🅦
Malignant neoplasm of respiratory tract NOS

MALIGNANT NEOPLASMS OF BONE AND ARTICULAR CARTILAGE (C40-C41)

> **Includes** malignant neoplasm of cartilage (articular) (joint)
> malignant neoplasm of periosteum
> **Excludes1** malignant neoplasm of bone marrow NOS (C96.9)
> malignant neoplasm of synovia (C49.-)

● **C40** **Malignant neoplasm of bone and articular cartilage of limbs**
Use additional code to identify major osseous defect, if applicable (M89.7-)

● **C40.0** **Malignant neoplasm of scapula and long bones of upper limb**

C40.00 **Malignant neoplasm of scapula and long bones of unspecified upper limb** 🅦

C40.01 **Malignant neoplasm of scapula and long bones of right upper limb** 🅦

C40.02 **Malignant neoplasm of scapula and long bones of left upper limb** 🅦

● **C40.1** **Malignant neoplasm of short bones of upper limb**

C40.10 **Malignant neoplasm of short bones of unspecified upper limb** 🅦

C40.11 **Malignant neoplasm of short bones of right upper limb** 🅦

C40.12 **Malignant neoplasm of short bones of left upper limb** 🅦

● **C40.2** **Malignant neoplasm of long bones of lower limb**

C40.20 **Malignant neoplasm of long bones of unspecified lower limb** 🅦

C40.21 **Malignant neoplasm of long bones of right lower limb** 🅦

C40.22 **Malignant neoplasm of long bones of left lower limb** 🅦

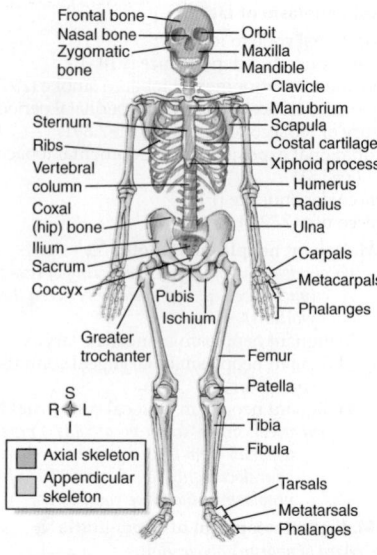

Figure 2-8 Diagram of skeleton of trunk and limbs with bones labeled. (From Thibodeau and Patton: Anatomy and Physiology, ed 7, Mosby, 2010)

● **C40.3** **Malignant neoplasm of short bones of lower limb**

C40.30 **Malignant neoplasm of short bones of unspecified lower limb** 🅦

C40.31 **Malignant neoplasm of short bones of right lower limb** 🅦

C40.32 **Malignant neoplasm of short bones of left lower limb** 🅦

● **C40.8** **Malignant neoplasm of overlapping sites of bone and articular cartilage of limb**

C40.80 **Malignant neoplasm of overlapping sites of bone and articular cartilage of unspecified limb** 🅦

C40.81 **Malignant neoplasm of overlapping sites of bone and articular cartilage of right limb** 🅦

C40.82 **Malignant neoplasm of overlapping sites of bone and articular cartilage of left limb** 🅦

● **C40.9** **Malignant neoplasm of unspecified bones and articular cartilage of limb**

C40.90 **Malignant neoplasm of unspecified bones and articular cartilage of unspecified limb** 🅦

C40.91 **Malignant neoplasm of unspecified bones and articular cartilage of right limb** 🅦

C40.92 **Malignant neoplasm of unspecified bones and articular cartilage of left limb** 🅦

● **C41** **Malignant neoplasm of bone and articular cartilage of other and unspecified sites**

> **Excludes1** malignant neoplasm of bones of limbs (C40.-)
> malignant neoplasm of cartilage of ear (C49.0)
> malignant neoplasm of cartilage of eyelid (C49.0)
> malignant neoplasm of cartilage of larynx (C32.3)
> malignant neoplasm of cartilage of limbs (C40.-)
> malignant neoplasm of cartilage of nose (C30.0)

C41.0 **Malignant neoplasm of bones of skull and face** 🅦
Malignant neoplasm of maxilla (superior)
Malignant neoplasm of orbital bone

> **Excludes2** carcinoma, any type except intraosseous or odontogenic of:
> maxillary sinus (C31.0)
> upper jaw (C03.0)
> malignant neoplasm of jaw bone (lower) (C41.1)

▶ New ⇒ Revised ~~deleted~~ Deleted Excludes 1 Excludes 2 Includes Use additional Code first Code also Key words
OGCR Official Guidelines X Assign placeholder X ● Use Additional Character(s) ⟩ Manifestation Code 🅦 Hierarchical Condition Category **Coding Clinic**

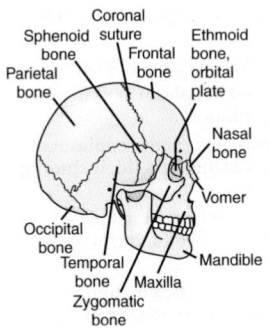

Figure 2-9 Bones of the skull.

Coronal suture, Sphenoid bone, Frontal bone, Parietal bone, Ethmoid bone, orbital plate, Nasal bone, Vomer, Occipital bone, Temporal bone, Maxilla, Zygomatic bone, Mandible

C41.1   Malignant neoplasm of mandible 🔖
    Malignant neoplasm of inferior maxilla
    Malignant neoplasm of lower jaw bone
    Excludes2   carcinoma, any type except intraosseous or odontogenic of:
       jaw NOS (C03.9)
       lower (C03.1)
      malignant neoplasm of upper jaw bone (C41.0)

C41.2   Malignant neoplasm of vertebral column 🔖
    Excludes1   malignant neoplasm of sacrum and coccyx (C41.4)

C41.3   Malignant neoplasm of ribs, sternum and clavicle 🔖

C41.4   Malignant neoplasm of pelvic bones, sacrum and coccyx 🔖

C41.9   Malignant neoplasm of bone and articular cartilage, unspecified 🔖

MELANOMA AND OTHER MALIGNANT NEOPLASMS OF SKIN (C43-C44)

● **C43**   Malignant melanoma of skin
    Excludes1   melanoma in situ (D03.-)
    Excludes2   malignant melanoma of skin of genital organs (C51-C52, C60.-, C63.-)
       Merkel cell carcinoma (C4A.-)
       sites other than skin-code to malignant neoplasm of the site

C43.0   Malignant melanoma of lip 🔖
    Excludes1   malignant neoplasm of vermilion border of lip (C00.0-C00.2)

● **C43.1**   Malignant melanoma of eyelid, including canthus
    Canthus: Either corner of eye where upper and lower eyelids meet
    C43.10   Malignant melanoma of unspecified eyelid, including canthus 🔖
    ● **C43.11**   Malignant melanoma of right eyelid, including canthus 🔖
       C43.111   Malignant melanoma of right upper eyelid, including canthus 🔖
       C43.112   Malignant melanoma of right lower eyelid, including canthus 🔖
    ● **C43.12**   Malignant melanoma of left eyelid, including canthus 🔖
       C43.121   Malignant melanoma of left upper eyelid, including canthus 🔖
       C43.122   Malignant melanoma of left lower eyelid, including canthus 🔖

● **C43.2**   Malignant melanoma of ear and external auricular canal
    C43.20   Malignant melanoma of unspecified ear and external auricular canal 🔖
    C43.21   Malignant melanoma of right ear and external auricular canal 🔖
    C43.22   Malignant melanoma of left ear and external auricular canal 🔖

Figure 2-10 Malignant melanoma of skin. (Getty Image)

Item 2–4   **Malignant melanoma** is a serious form of skin cancer that affects the melanocytes (pigment-forming cells) and is caused by ultraviolet (UV) rays from the sun that damage skin. It is most commonly seen in the 40- to 60-year-olds with fair skin, blue or green eyes, and red or blond hair who sunburn easily.

    Melanoma can spread very rapidly and is the most deadly form of skin cancer. It is less common than other types of skin cancer. The rate of melanoma is increasing and currently is the leading cause of death from skin disease.

● **C43.3**   Malignant melanoma of other and unspecified parts of face
    C43.30   Malignant melanoma of unspecified part of face 🔖
    C43.31   Malignant melanoma of nose 🔖
    C43.39   Malignant melanoma of other parts of face 🔖

C43.4   Malignant melanoma of scalp and neck 🔖

● **C43.5**   Malignant melanoma of trunk
    Excludes2   malignant neoplasm of anus NOS (C21.0)
       malignant neoplasm of scrotum (C63.2)
    C43.51   Malignant melanoma of anal skin 🔖
      Malignant melanoma of anal margin
      Malignant melanoma of perianal skin
    C43.52   Malignant melanoma of skin of breast 🔖
    C43.59   Malignant melanoma of other part of trunk 🔖

● **C43.6**   Malignant melanoma of upper limb, including shoulder
    C43.60   Malignant melanoma of upper limb, including shoulder, unspecified side 🔖
    C43.61   Malignant melanoma of right upper limb, including shoulder 🔖
    C43.62   Malignant melanoma of left upper limb, including shoulder 🔖

● **C43.7**   Malignant melanoma of lower limb, including hip
    C43.70   Malignant melanoma of unspecified lower limb, including hip 🔖
    C43.71   Malignant melanoma of right lower limb, including hip 🔖
    C43.72   Malignant melanoma of left lower limb, including hip 🔖

C43.8   Malignant melanoma of overlapping sites of skin 🔖

C43.9   Malignant melanoma of skin, unspecified 🔖
    Malignant melanoma of unspecified site of skin
    Melanoma (malignant) NOS

● **C4A**   Merkel cell carcinoma
    C4A.0   Merkel cell carcinoma of lip 🔖
      Excludes1   malignant neoplasm of vermilion border of lip (C00.0-C00.2)

● **C4A.1**   Merkel cell carcinoma of eyelid, including canthus
    C4A.10   Merkel cell carcinoma of unspecified eyelid, including canthus 🔖
    ● **C4A.11**   Merkel cell carcinoma of right eyelid, including canthus 🔖
       C4A.111   Merkel cell carcinoma of right upper eyelid, including canthus 🔖
       C4A.112   Merkel cell carcinoma of right lower eyelid, including canthus 🔖
    ● **C4A.12**   Merkel cell carcinoma of left eyelid, including canthus 🔖
       C4A.121   Merkel cell carcinoma of left upper eyelid, including canthus 🔖
       C4A.122   Merkel cell carcinoma of left lower eyelid, including canthus 🔖

CHAPTER 2 (C00-D49)

● C4A.2 Merkel cell carcinoma of ear and external auricular canal
  C4A.20 Merkel cell carcinoma of unspecified ear and external auricular canal 🅗
  C4A.21 Merkel cell carcinoma of right ear and external auricular canal 🅗
  C4A.22 Merkel cell carcinoma of left ear and external auricular canal 🅗
● C4A.3 Merkel cell carcinoma of other and unspecified parts of face
  C4A.30 Merkel cell carcinoma of unspecified part of face 🅗
  C4A.31 Merkel cell carcinoma of nose 🅗
  C4A.39 Merkel cell carcinoma of other parts of face 🅗
  C4A.4 Merkel cell carcinoma of scalp and neck 🅗
● C4A.5 Merkel cell carcinoma of trunk
    Excludes2   malignant neoplasm of anus NOS (C21.0)
                     malignant neoplasm of scrotum (C63.2)
  C4A.51 Merkel cell carcinoma of anal skin 🅗
          Merkel cell carcinoma of anal margin
          Merkel cell carcinoma of perianal skin
  C4A.52 Merkel cell carcinoma of skin of breast 🅗
  C4A.59 Merkel cell carcinoma of other part of trunk 🅗
● C4A.6 Merkel cell carcinoma of upper limb, including shoulder
  C4A.60 Merkel cell carcinoma of unspecified upper limb, including shoulder 🅗
  C4A.61 Merkel cell carcinoma of right upper limb, including shoulder 🅗
  C4A.62 Merkel cell carcinoma of left upper limb, including shoulder 🅗
● C4A.7 Merkel cell carcinoma of lower limb, including hip
  C4A.70 Merkel cell carcinoma of unspecified lower limb, including hip 🅗
  C4A.71 Merkel cell carcinoma of right lower limb, including hip 🅗
  C4A.72 Merkel cell carcinoma of left lower limb, including hip 🅗
  C4A.8 Merkel cell carcinoma of overlapping sites 🅗
  C4A.9 Merkel cell carcinoma, unspecified 🅗
          Merkel cell carcinoma of unspecified site
          Merkel cell carcinoma NOS

● C44 Other and unspecified malignant neoplasm of skin
    Includes   malignant neoplasm of sebaceous glands
                     malignant neoplasm of sweat glands
    Excludes1   Kaposi's sarcoma of skin (C46.0)
                     malignant melanoma of skin (C43.-)
                     malignant neoplasm of skin of genital organs
                        (C51-C52, C60.-, C63.2)
                     Merkel cell carcinoma (C4A.-)
● C44.0 Other and unspecified malignant neoplasm of skin of lip
    Excludes1   malignant neoplasm of lip (C00.-)
  C44.00 Unspecified malignant neoplasm of skin of lip
  C44.01 Basal cell carcinoma of skin of lip
  C44.02 Squamous cell carcinoma of skin of lip
  C44.09 Other specified malignant neoplasm of skin of lip

● C44.1 Other and unspecified malignant neoplasm of skin of eyelid, including canthus
    Excludes1   connective tissue of eyelid (C49.0)
● C44.10 Unspecified malignant neoplasm of skin of eyelid, including canthus
  C44.101 Unspecified malignant neoplasm of skin of unspecified eyelid, including canthus
● C44.102 Unspecified malignant neoplasm of skin of right eyelid, including canthus
    C44.1021 Unspecified malignant neoplasm of skin of right upper eyelid, including canthus
    C44.1022 Unspecified malignant neoplasm of skin of right lower eyelid, including canthus
● C44.109 Unspecified malignant neoplasm of skin of left eyelid, including canthus
    C44.1091 Unspecified malignant neoplasm of skin of left upper eyelid, including canthus
    C44.1092 Unspecified malignant neoplasm of skin of left lower eyelid, including canthus
● C44.11 Basal cell carcinoma of skin of eyelid, including canthus
  C44.111 Basal cell carcinoma of skin of unspecified eyelid, including canthus
● C44.112 Basal cell carcinoma of skin of right eyelid, including canthus
    C44.1121 Basal cell carcinoma of skin of right upper eyelid, including canthus
    C44.1122 Basal cell carcinoma of skin of right lower eyelid, including canthus
● C44.119 Basal cell carcinoma of skin of left eyelid, including canthus
    C44.1191 Basal cell carcinoma of skin of left upper eyelid, including canthus
    C44.1192 Basal cell carcinoma of skin of left lower eyelid, including canthus
● C44.12 Squamous cell carcinoma of skin of eyelid, including canthus
  C44.121 Squamous cell carcinoma of skin of unspecified eyelid, including canthus
● C44.122 Squamous cell carcinoma of skin of right eyelid, including canthus
    C44.1221 Squamous cell carcinoma of skin of right upper eyelid, including canthus
    C44.1222 Squamous cell carcinoma of skin of right lower eyelid, including canthus
● C44.129 Squamous cell carcinoma of skin of left eyelid, including canthus
    C44.1291 Squamous cell carcinoma of skin of left upper eyelid, including canthus
    C44.1292 Squamous cell carcinoma of skin of left lower eyelid, including canthus

▶ New   ⇒ Revised   ~~deleted~~ Deleted   Excludes 1   Excludes 2   Includes   Use additional   Code first   Code also   Key words
OGCR Official Guidelines   X Assign placeholder X   ● Use Additional Character(s)   ▶ Manifestation Code   🅗 Hierarchical Condition Category   Coding Clinic

● **C44.13**   Sebaceous cell carcinoma of skin of eyelid, including canthus

    C44.131   Sebaceous cell carcinoma of skin of unspecified eyelid, including canthus

●   **C44.132**   Sebaceous cell carcinoma of skin of right eyelid, including canthus

      C44.1321   Sebaceous cell carcinoma of skin of right upper eyelid, including canthus

      C44.1322   Sebaceous cell carcinoma of skin of right lower eyelid, including canthus

●   **C44.139**   Sebaceous cell carcinoma of skin of left eyelid, including canthus

      C44.1391   Sebaceous cell carcinoma of skin of left upper eyelid, including canthus

      C44.1392   Sebaceous cell carcinoma of skin of left lower eyelid, including canthus

● **C44.19**   Other specified malignant neoplasm of skin of eyelid, including canthus

    C44.191   Other specified malignant neoplasm of skin of unspecified eyelid, including canthus

●   **C44.192**   Other specified malignant neoplasm of skin of right eyelid, including canthus

      C44.1921   Other specified malignant neoplasm of skin of right upper eyelid, including canthus

      C44.1922   Other specified malignant neoplasm of skin of right lower eyelid, including canthus

●   **C44.199**   Other specified malignant neoplasm of skin of left eyelid, including canthus

      C44.1991   Other specified malignant neoplasm of skin of left upper eyelid, including canthus

      C44.1992   Other specified malignant neoplasm of skin of left lower eyelid, including canthus

● **C44.2**   Other and unspecified malignant neoplasm of skin of ear and external auricular canal

    Excludes1   connective tissue of ear (C49.0)

●   **C44.20**   Unspecified malignant neoplasm of skin of ear and external auricular canal

    C44.201   Unspecified malignant neoplasm of skin of unspecified ear and external auricular canal

    C44.202   Unspecified malignant neoplasm of skin of right ear and external auricular canal

    C44.209   Unspecified malignant neoplasm of skin of left ear and external auricular canal

●   **C44.21**   Basal cell carcinoma of skin of ear and external auricular canal

    C44.211   Basal cell carcinoma of skin of unspecified ear and external auricular canal

    C44.212   Basal cell carcinoma of skin of right ear and external auricular canal

    C44.219   Basal cell carcinoma of skin of left ear and external auricular canal

● **C44.22**   Squamous cell carcinoma of skin of ear and external auricular canal

    C44.221   Squamous cell carcinoma of skin of unspecified ear and external auricular canal

    C44.222   Squamous cell carcinoma of skin of right ear and external auricular canal

    C44.229   Squamous cell carcinoma of skin of left ear and external auricular canal

● **C44.29**   Other specified malignant neoplasm of skin of ear and external auricular canal

    C44.291   Other specified malignant neoplasm of skin of unspecified ear and external auricular canal

    C44.292   Other specified malignant neoplasm of skin of right ear and external auricular canal

    C44.299   Other specified malignant neoplasm of skin of left ear and external auricular canal

● **C44.3**   Other and unspecified malignant neoplasm of skin of other and unspecified parts of face

●   **C44.30**   Unspecified malignant neoplasm of skin of other and unspecified parts of face

    C44.300   Unspecified malignant neoplasm of skin of unspecified part of face

    C44.301   Unspecified malignant neoplasm of skin of nose

    C44.309   Unspecified malignant neoplasm of skin of other parts of face

●   **C44.31**   Basal cell carcinoma of skin of other and unspecified parts of face

    C44.310   Basal cell carcinoma of skin of unspecified parts of face

    C44.311   Basal cell carcinoma of skin of nose

    C44.319   Basal cell carcinoma of skin of other parts of face
       Coding Clinic: 2017, Q1, P4

●   **C44.32**   Squamous cell carcinoma of skin of other and unspecified parts of face

    C44.320   Squamous cell carcinoma of skin of unspecified parts of face

    C44.321   Squamous cell carcinoma of skin of nose

    C44.329   Squamous cell carcinoma of skin of other parts of face

●   **C44.39**   Other specified malignant neoplasm of skin of other and unspecified parts of face

    C44.390   Other specified malignant neoplasm of skin of unspecified parts of face

    C44.391   Other specified malignant neoplasm of skin of nose

    C44.399   Other specified malignant neoplasm of skin of other parts of face

● **C44.4**   Other and unspecified malignant neoplasm of skin of scalp and neck

    C44.40   Unspecified malignant neoplasm of skin of scalp and neck

    C44.41   Basal cell carcinoma of skin of scalp and neck

    C44.42   Squamous cell carcinoma of skin of scalp and neck

    C44.49   Other specified malignant neoplasm of skin of scalp and neck

CHAPTER 2 (C00–D49)

● **C44.5**   **Other and unspecified malignant neoplasm of skin of trunk**

     Excludes1   anus NOS (C21.0)
                  scrotum (C63.2)

   ● **C44.50**   **Unspecified malignant neoplasm of skin of trunk**

     C44.500   **Unspecified malignant neoplasm of anal skin**
          Unspecified malignant neoplasm of anal margin
          Unspecified malignant neoplasm of perianal skin

     C44.501   **Unspecified malignant neoplasm of skin of breast**

     C44.509   **Unspecified malignant neoplasm of skin of other part of trunk**

   ● **C44.51**   **Basal cell carcinoma of skin of trunk**

     C44.510   **Basal cell carcinoma of anal skin**
          Basal cell carcinoma of anal margin
          Basal cell carcinoma of perianal skin

     C44.511   **Basal cell carcinoma of skin of breast**

     C44.519   **Basal cell carcinoma of skin of other part of trunk**

   ● **C44.52**   **Squamous cell carcinoma of skin of trunk**

     C44.520   **Squamous cell carcinoma of anal skin**
          Squamous cell carcinoma of anal margin
          Squamous cell carcinoma of perianal skin

     C44.521   **Squamous cell carcinoma of skin of breast**

     C44.529   **Squamous cell carcinoma of skin of other part of trunk**

   ● **C44.59**   **Other specified malignant neoplasm of skin of trunk**

     C44.590   **Other specified malignant neoplasm of anal skin**
          Other specified malignant neoplasm of anal margin
          Other specified malignant neoplasm of perianal skin

     C44.591   **Other specified malignant neoplasm of skin of breast**

     C44.599   **Other specified malignant neoplasm of skin of other part of trunk**

● **C44.6**   **Other and unspecified malignant neoplasm of skin of upper limb, including shoulder**

   ● **C44.60**   **Unspecified malignant neoplasm of skin of upper limb, including shoulder**

     C44.601   **Unspecified malignant neoplasm of skin of unspecified upper limb, including shoulder**

     C44.602   **Unspecified malignant neoplasm of skin of right upper limb, including shoulder**

     C44.609   **Unspecified malignant neoplasm of skin of left upper limb, including shoulder**

   ● **C44.61**   **Basal cell carcinoma of skin of upper limb, including shoulder**

     C44.611   **Basal cell carcinoma of skin of unspecified upper limb, including shoulder**

     C44.612   **Basal cell carcinoma of skin of right upper limb, including shoulder**

     C44.619   **Basal cell carcinoma of skin of left upper limb, including shoulder**

● **C44.62**   **Squamous cell carcinoma of skin of upper limb, including shoulder**

     C44.621   **Squamous cell carcinoma of skin of unspecified upper limb, including shoulder**

     C44.622   **Squamous cell carcinoma of skin of right upper limb, including shoulder**

     C44.629   **Squamous cell carcinoma of skin of left upper limb, including shoulder**

   ● **C44.69**   **Other specified malignant neoplasm of skin of upper limb, including shoulder**

     C44.691   **Other specified malignant neoplasm of skin of unspecified upper limb, including shoulder**

     C44.692   **Other specified malignant neoplasm of skin of right upper limb, including shoulder**

     C44.699   **Other specified malignant neoplasm of skin of left upper limb, including shoulder**

● **C44.7**   **Other and unspecified malignant neoplasm of skin of lower limb, including hip**

   ● **C44.70**   **Unspecified malignant neoplasm of skin of lower limb, including hip**

     C44.701   **Unspecified malignant neoplasm of skin of unspecified lower limb, including hip**

     C44.702   **Unspecified malignant neoplasm of skin of right lower limb, including hip**

     C44.709   **Unspecified malignant neoplasm of skin of left lower limb, including hip**

   ● **C44.71**   **Basal cell carcinoma of skin of lower limb, including hip**

     C44.711   **Basal cell carcinoma of skin of unspecified lower limb, including hip**

     C44.712   **Basal cell carcinoma of skin of right lower limb, including hip**

     C44.719   **Basal cell carcinoma of skin of left lower limb, including hip**

   ● **C44.72**   **Squamous cell carcinoma of skin of lower limb, including hip**

     C44.721   **Squamous cell carcinoma of skin of unspecified lower limb, including hip**

     C44.722   **Squamous cell carcinoma of skin of right lower limb, including hip**

     C44.729   **Squamous cell carcinoma of skin of left lower limb, including hip**

   ● **C44.79**   **Other specified malignant neoplasm of skin of lower limb, including hip**

     C44.791   **Other specified malignant neoplasm of skin of unspecified lower limb, including hip**

     C44.792   **Other specified malignant neoplasm of skin of right lower limb, including hip**

     C44.799   **Other specified malignant neoplasm of skin of left lower limb, including hip**

● **C44.8**   **Other and unspecified malignant neoplasm of overlapping sites of skin**

     C44.80   **Unspecified malignant neoplasm of overlapping sites of skin**

     C44.81   **Basal cell carcinoma of overlapping sites of skin**

     C44.82   **Squamous cell carcinoma of overlapping sites of skin**

     C44.89   **Other specified malignant neoplasm of overlapping sites of skin**

▶ New   ⇒ Revised   ~~deleted~~ Deleted   Excludes 1   Excludes 2   Includes   Use additional   Code first   Code also   Key words

OGCR Official Guidelines   X Assign placeholder X   ● Use Additional Character(s)   ▶ Manifestation Code   🅠 Hierarchical Condition Category   **Coding Clinic**

● **C44.9**   **Other and unspecified malignant neoplasm of skin, unspecified**

     C44.90   **Unspecified malignant neoplasm of skin, unspecified**
         Malignant neoplasm of unspecified site of skin

     C44.91   **Basal cell carcinoma of skin, unspecified**

     C44.92   **Squamous cell carcinoma of skin, unspecified**

     C44.99   **Other specified malignant neoplasm of skin, unspecified**

MALIGNANT NEOPLASMS OF MESOTHELIAL AND SOFT TISSUE (C45-C49)

● **C45**   **Mesothelioma**
Malignant cells develop in protective lining that covers internal organs (mesothelium) caused by exposure to asbestos

     C45.0   **Mesothelioma of pleura** 🔊
         Excludes1   other malignant neoplasm of pleura (C38.4)
         Coding Clinic: 2017, Q2, P11

     C45.1   **Mesothelioma of peritoneum** 🔊
         Mesothelioma of cul-de-sac
         Mesothelioma of mesentery
         Mesothelioma of mesocolon
         Mesothelioma of omentum
         Mesothelioma of peritoneum (parietal) (pelvic)
         Excludes1   other malignant neoplasm of soft tissue of peritoneum (C48.-)

     C45.2   **Mesothelioma of pericardium** 🔊
         Excludes1   other malignant neoplasm of pericardium (C38.0)

     C45.7   **Mesothelioma of other sites** 🔊

     C45.9   **Mesothelioma, unspecified** 🔊

● **C46**   **Kaposi's sarcoma**
Code first any human immunodeficiency virus [HIV] disease (B20)

     C46.0   **Kaposi's sarcoma of skin** 🔊

     C46.1   **Kaposi's sarcoma of soft tissue** 🔊
         Kaposi's sarcoma of blood vessel
         Kaposi's sarcoma of connective tissue
         Kaposi's sarcoma of fascia
         Kaposi's sarcoma of ligament
         Kaposi's sarcoma of lymphatic(s) NEC
         Kaposi's sarcoma of muscle
         Excludes2   Kaposi's sarcoma of lymph glands and nodes (C46.3)

     C46.2   **Kaposi's sarcoma of palate** 🔊

     C46.3   **Kaposi's sarcoma of lymph nodes** 🔊

     C46.4   **Kaposi's sarcoma of gastrointestinal sites** 🔊

●   **C46.5**   **Kaposi's sarcoma of lung**
         C46.50   **Kaposi's sarcoma of unspecified lung** 🔊
         C46.51   **Kaposi's sarcoma of right lung** 🔊
         C46.52   **Kaposi's sarcoma of left lung** 🔊

     C46.7   **Kaposi's sarcoma of other sites** 🔊

     C46.9   **Kaposi's sarcoma, unspecified** 🔊
         Kaposi's sarcoma of unspecified site

Figure 2-11   Kaposi's sarcoma. There are large confluent hyperpigmented patch-stage lesions with lymphedema. (From Goldman L, Ausiello D, Arend W, Armitage J, Clemmons D, Drazen J, Griggs R, et al: Cecil Medicine: Expert Consult, 23e, Saunders, 2007)

● **C47**   **Malignant neoplasm of peripheral nerves and autonomic nervous system**
     Includes   malignant neoplasm of sympathetic and parasympathetic nerves and ganglia
     Excludes1   Kaposi's sarcoma of soft tissue (C46.1)

     C47.0   **Malignant neoplasm of peripheral nerves of head, face and neck** 🔊
         Excludes1   malignant neoplasm of peripheral nerves of orbit (C69.6-)

●   **C47.1**   **Malignant neoplasm of peripheral nerves of upper limb, including shoulder**
         C47.10   **Malignant neoplasm of peripheral nerves of unspecified upper limb, including shoulder** 🔊
         C47.11   **Malignant neoplasm of peripheral nerves of right upper limb, including shoulder** 🔊
         C47.12   **Malignant neoplasm of peripheral nerves of left upper limb, including shoulder** 🔊

●   **C47.2**   **Malignant neoplasm of peripheral nerves of lower limb, including hip**
         C47.20   **Malignant neoplasm of peripheral nerves of unspecified lower limb, including hip** 🔊
         C47.21   **Malignant neoplasm of peripheral nerves of right lower limb, including hip** 🔊
         C47.22   **Malignant neoplasm of peripheral nerves of left lower limb, including hip** 🔊

     C47.3   **Malignant neoplasm of peripheral nerves of thorax** 🔊

     C47.4   **Malignant neoplasm of peripheral nerves of abdomen** 🔊

     C47.5   **Malignant neoplasm of peripheral nerves of pelvis** 🔊

     C47.6   **Malignant neoplasm of peripheral nerves of trunk, unspecified** 🔊
         Malignant neoplasm of peripheral nerves of unspecified part of trunk

     C47.8   **Malignant neoplasm of overlapping sites of peripheral nerves and autonomic nervous system** 🔊

     C47.9   **Malignant neoplasm of peripheral nerves and autonomic nervous system, unspecified** 🔊
         Malignant neoplasm of unspecified site of peripheral nerves and autonomic nervous system

● **C48**   **Malignant neoplasm of retroperitoneum and peritoneum**
     Excludes1   Kaposi's sarcoma of connective tissue (C46.1)
         mesothelioma (C45.-)

     C48.0   **Malignant neoplasm of retroperitoneum** 🔊
         Behind/outside of peritoneum

     C48.1   **Malignant neoplasm of specified parts of peritoneum** 🔊
         Serous membrane lining abdominopelvic walls and covering viscera
         Malignant neoplasm of cul-de-sac
         Malignant neoplasm of mesentery
         Malignant neoplasm of mesocolon
         Malignant neoplasm of omentum
         Malignant neoplasm of parietal peritoneum
         Malignant neoplasm of pelvic peritoneum

     C48.2   **Malignant neoplasm of peritoneum, unspecified** 🔊

     C48.8   **Malignant neoplasm of overlapping sites of retroperitoneum and peritoneum** 🔊

Item 2-5   **Kaposi's sarcoma** is a cancer that causes patches of abnormal tissue to grow under the skin; in the lining of the mouth, nose, and throat; or in other organs, often beginning and spreading to other organs. Patients who have had organ transplants or patients with AIDS are at high risk for this malignancy.

● **C49**   **Malignant neoplasm of other connective and soft tissue**

     Includes   malignant neoplasm of blood vessel
                malignant neoplasm of bursa
                malignant neoplasm of cartilage
                malignant neoplasm of fascia
                malignant neoplasm of fat
                malignant neoplasm of ligament, except uterine
                malignant neoplasm of lymphatic vessel
                malignant neoplasm of muscle
                malignant neoplasm of synovia
                malignant neoplasm of tendon (sheath)

(Transcription truncated for brevity — full content continues.)

AXILLARY TAIL
UPPER-INNER
UPPER-OUTER
Nipple and areola
Central portion of
LOWER-OUTER
LOWER-INNER

Figure 2-12 Female breast quadrants and axillary tail.

● C50.2   Malignant neoplasm of upper-inner quadrant of breast
   ● C50.21   Malignant neoplasm of upper-inner quadrant of breast, female
      C50.211   Malignant neoplasm of upper-inner quadrant of right female breast ♀ 🦟
      C50.212   Malignant neoplasm of upper-inner quadrant of left female breast ♀ 🦟
      C50.219   Malignant neoplasm of upper-inner quadrant of unspecified female breast ♀ 🦟
   ● C50.22   Malignant neoplasm of upper-inner quadrant of breast, male
      C50.221   Malignant neoplasm of upper-inner quadrant of right male breast ♂ 🦟
      C50.222   Malignant neoplasm of upper-inner quadrant of left male breast ♂ 🦟
      C50.229   Malignant neoplasm of upper-inner quadrant of unspecified male breast ♂ 🦟

● C50.3   Malignant neoplasm of lower-inner quadrant of breast
   ● C50.31   Malignant neoplasm of lower-inner quadrant of breast, female
      C50.311   Malignant neoplasm of lower-inner quadrant of right female breast ♀ 🦟
      C50.312   Malignant neoplasm of lower-inner quadrant of left female breast ♀ 🦟
      C50.319   Malignant neoplasm of lower-inner quadrant of unspecified female breast ♀ 🦟
   ● C50.32   Malignant neoplasm of lower-inner quadrant of breast, male
      C50.321   Malignant neoplasm of lower-inner quadrant of right male breast ♂ 🦟
      C50.322   Malignant neoplasm of lower-inner quadrant of left male breast ♂ 🦟
      C50.329   Malignant neoplasm of lower-inner quadrant of unspecified male breast ♂ 🦟

● C50.4   Malignant neoplasm of upper-outer quadrant of breast
   ● C50.41   Malignant neoplasm of upper-outer quadrant of breast, female
      C50.411   Malignant neoplasm of upper-outer quadrant of right female breast ♀ 🦟
      C50.412   Malignant neoplasm of upper-outer quadrant of left female breast ♀ 🦟
      C50.419   Malignant neoplasm of upper-outer quadrant of unspecified female breast ♀ 🦟
   ● C50.42   Malignant neoplasm of upper-outer quadrant of breast, male
      C50.421   Malignant neoplasm of upper-outer quadrant of right male breast ♂ 🦟
      C50.422   Malignant neoplasm of upper-outer quadrant of left male breast ♂ 🦟
      C50.429   Malignant neoplasm of upper-outer quadrant of unspecified male breast ♂ 🦟

● C50.5   Malignant neoplasm of lower-outer quadrant of breast
   ● C50.51   Malignant neoplasm of lower-outer quadrant of breast, female
      C50.511   Malignant neoplasm of lower-outer quadrant of right female breast ♀ 🦟
      C50.512   Malignant neoplasm of lower-outer quadrant of left female breast ♀ 🦟
      C50.519   Malignant neoplasm of lower-outer quadrant of unspecified female breast ♀ 🦟
   ● C50.52   Malignant neoplasm of lower-outer quadrant of breast, male
      C50.521   Malignant neoplasm of lower-outer quadrant of right male breast ♂ 🦟
      C50.522   Malignant neoplasm of lower-outer quadrant of left male breast ♂ 🦟
      C50.529   Malignant neoplasm of lower-outer quadrant of unspecified male breast ♂ 🦟

● C50.6   Malignant neoplasm of axillary tail of breast
   ● C50.61   Malignant neoplasm of axillary tail of breast, female
      C50.611   Malignant neoplasm of axillary tail of right female breast ♀ 🦟
      C50.612   Malignant neoplasm of axillary tail of left female breast ♀ 🦟
      C50.619   Malignant neoplasm of axillary tail of unspecified female breast ♀ 🦟
   ● C50.62   Malignant neoplasm of axillary tail of breast, male
      C50.621   Malignant neoplasm of axillary tail of right male breast ♂ 🦟
      C50.622   Malignant neoplasm of axillary tail of left male breast ♂ 🦟
      C50.629   Malignant neoplasm of axillary tail of unspecified male breast ♂ 🦟

● C50.8   Malignant neoplasm of overlapping sites of breast
   ● C50.81   Malignant neoplasm of overlapping sites of breast, female
      C50.811   Malignant neoplasm of overlapping sites of right female breast ♀ 🦟
      C50.812   Malignant neoplasm of overlapping sites of left female breast ♀ 🦟
      C50.819   Malignant neoplasm of overlapping sites of unspecified female breast ♀ 🦟
   ● C50.82   Malignant neoplasm of overlapping sites of breast, male
      C50.821   Malignant neoplasm of overlapping sites of right male breast ♂ 🦟
      C50.822   Malignant neoplasm of overlapping sites of left male breast ♂ 🦟
      C50.829   Malignant neoplasm of overlapping sites of unspecified male breast ♂ 🦟

● C50.9   Malignant neoplasm of breast of unspecified site
   ● C50.91   Malignant neoplasm of breast of unspecified site, female
      C50.911   Malignant neoplasm of unspecified site of right female breast ♀ 🦟
      C50.912   Malignant neoplasm of unspecified site of left female breast ♀ 🦟
      C50.919   Malignant neoplasm of unspecified site of unspecified female breast ♀ 🦟
   ● C50.92   Malignant neoplasm of breast of unspecified site, male
      C50.921   Malignant neoplasm of unspecified site of right male breast ♂ 🦟
      C50.922   Malignant neoplasm of unspecified site of left male breast ♂ 🦟
      C50.929   Malignant neoplasm of unspecified site of unspecified male breast ♂ 🦟

CHAPTER 2 (C00-D49)

CHAPTER 2 (C00-D49)

MALIGNANT NEOPLASMS OF FEMALE GENITAL ORGANS (C51-C58)

Includes   malignant neoplasm of skin of female genital organs

● **C51   Malignant neoplasm of vulva**

    Excludes1   carcinoma in situ of vulva (D07.1)

  C51.0   Malignant neoplasm of labium majus ♀ 🐾
    Outer folds of skin external female genitalia
    Malignant neoplasm of Bartholin's [greater vestibular] gland

  C51.1   Malignant neoplasm of labium minus ♀ 🐾
    Two inner folds surrounding vulva in female genitalia

  C51.2   Malignant neoplasm of clitoris ♀ 🐾

  C51.8   Malignant neoplasm of overlapping sites of vulva ♀ 🐾

  C51.9   Malignant neoplasm of vulva, unspecified ♀ 🐾
    Malignant neoplasm of external female genitalia NOS
    Malignant neoplasm of pudendum

C52   Malignant neoplasm of vagina ♀ 🐾

  Excludes1   carcinoma in situ of vagina (D07.2)

● **C53   Malignant neoplasm of cervix uteri**

  Excludes1   carcinoma in situ of cervix uteri (D06.-)

  C53.0   Malignant neoplasm of endocervix ♀ 🐾
    Inside the cervix

  C53.1   Malignant neoplasm of exocervix ♀ 🐾
    Outside the cervix

  C53.8   Malignant neoplasm of overlapping sites of cervix uteri ♀ 🐾

  C53.9   Malignant neoplasm of cervix uteri, unspecified ♀ 🐾
    Coding Clinic: 2017, Q4, P103

● **C54   Malignant neoplasm of corpus uteri**

  C54.0   Malignant neoplasm of isthmus uteri ♀ 🐾
    Constricted part of uterus between cervix and body
    Malignant neoplasm of lower uterine segment

  C54.1   Malignant neoplasm of endometrium ♀ 🐾
    Lining of uterus

  C54.2   Malignant neoplasm of myometrium ♀ 🐾
    Middle layer of uterine wall consisting of smooth muscle supporting stromal and vascular tissue

  C54.3   Malignant neoplasm of fundus uteri ♀ 🐾
    Top rounded portion of uterus

  C54.8   Malignant neoplasm of overlapping sites of corpus uteri ♀ 🐾
    Main body of uterus

  C54.9   Malignant neoplasm of corpus uteri, unspecified ♀ 🐾

C55   Malignant neoplasm of uterus, part unspecified ♀ 🐾

● **C56   Malignant neoplasm of ovary**
    Use additional code to identify any functional activity

  C56.1   Malignant neoplasm of right ovary ♀ 🐾

  C56.2   Malignant neoplasm of left ovary ♀ 🐾

  C56.9   Malignant neoplasm of unspecified ovary ♀ 🐾

● **C57   Malignant neoplasm of other and unspecified female genital organs**

  ● **C57.0   Malignant neoplasm of fallopian tube**
    Malignant neoplasm of oviduct
    Malignant neoplasm of uterine tube

    C57.00   Malignant neoplasm of unspecified fallopian tube ♀ 🐾

    C57.01   Malignant neoplasm of right fallopian tube ♀ 🐾

    C57.02   Malignant neoplasm of left fallopian tube ♀ 🐾

  ● **C57.1   Malignant neoplasm of broad ligament**

    C57.10   Malignant neoplasm of unspecified broad ligament ♀ 🐾

    C57.11   Malignant neoplasm of right broad ligament ♀ 🐾

    C57.12   Malignant neoplasm of left broad ligament ♀ 🐾

  ● **C57.2   Malignant neoplasm of round ligament**

    C57.20   Malignant neoplasm of unspecified round ligament ♀ 🐾

    C57.21   Malignant neoplasm of right round ligament ♀ 🐾

    C57.22   Malignant neoplasm of left round ligament ♀ 🐾

  C57.3   Malignant neoplasm of parametrium ♀ 🐾
    Malignant neoplasm of uterine ligament NOS

  C57.4   Malignant neoplasm of uterine adnexa, unspecified ♀ 🐾

  C57.7   Malignant neoplasm of other specified female genital organs ♀ 🐾
    Malignant neoplasm of wolffian body or duct

  C57.8   Malignant neoplasm of overlapping sites of female genital organs ♀ 🐾
    Primary malignant neoplasm of two or more contiguous sites of the female genital organs whose point of origin cannot be determined
    Primary tubo-ovarian malignant neoplasm whose point of origin cannot be determined
    Primary utero-ovarian malignant neoplasm whose point of origin cannot be determined

  C57.9   Malignant neoplasm of female genital organ, unspecified ♀ 🐾
    Malignant neoplasm of female genitourinary tract NOS

C58   Malignant neoplasm of placenta ♀ 🐾   M

  Includes   choriocarcinoma NOS
           chorionepithelioma NOS

  Excludes1   chorioadenoma (destruens) (D39.2)
    hydatidiform mole NOS (O01.9)
    invasive hydatidiform mole (D39.2)
    male choriocarcinoma NOS (C62.9-)
    malignant hydatidiform mole (D39.2)

MALIGNANT NEOPLASMS OF MALE GENITAL ORGANS (C60-C63)

Includes   malignant neoplasm of skin of male genital organs

● **C60   Malignant neoplasm of penis**

  C60.0   Malignant neoplasm of prepuce ♂ 🐾
    Malignant neoplasm of foreskin

  C60.1   Malignant neoplasm of glans penis ♂ 🐾

  C60.2   Malignant neoplasm of body of penis ♂ 🐾
    Malignant neoplasm of corpus cavernosum

  C60.8   Malignant neoplasm of overlapping sites of penis ♂ 🐾

  C60.9   Malignant neoplasm of penis, unspecified ♂ 🐾
    Malignant neoplasm of skin of penis NOS

C61   Malignant neoplasm of prostate ♂ 🐾

  Use additional code to identify:
    hormone sensitivity status (Z19.1-Z19.2)
    rising PSA following treatment for malignant neoplasm of prostate (R97.21)

  Excludes1   malignant neoplasm of seminal vesicle (C63.7)

Figure 2-13   Cervix uteri.

▶ New   ⇒ Revised   ~~deleted~~ Deleted   Excludes 1   Excludes 2   Includes   Use additional   Code first   Code also   Key words

OGCR Official Guidelines   X Assign placeholder X   ● Use Additional Character(s)   ▶ Manifestation Code   🐾 Hierarchical Condition Category   Coding Clinic

Figure 2-14   Penis and other male genital organs.

● **C62**   **Malignant neoplasm of testis**
    Use additional code to identify any functional activity.
   ● **C62.0**   **Malignant neoplasm of undescended testis**
      Malignant neoplasm of ectopic testis
      Malignant neoplasm of retained testis
     C62.00   **Malignant neoplasm of unspecified undescended testis** ♂ 🔏
     C62.01   **Malignant neoplasm of undescended right testis** ♂ 🔏
     C62.02   **Malignant neoplasm of undescended left testis** ♂ 🔏
   ● **C62.1**   **Malignant neoplasm of descended testis**
      Malignant neoplasm of scrotal testis
     C62.10   **Malignant neoplasm of unspecified descended testis, unspecified side** ♂ 🔏
     C62.11   **Malignant neoplasm of descended right testis** ♂ 🔏
     C62.12   **Malignant neoplasm of descended left testis** ♂ 🔏
   ● **C62.9**   **Malignant neoplasm of testis, unspecified whether descended or undescended**
     C62.90   **Malignant neoplasm of unspecified testis, unspecified whether descended or undescended** ♂ 🔏
       Malignant neoplasm of testis NOS
     C62.91   **Malignant neoplasm of right testis, unspecified whether descended or undescended** ♂ 🔏
     C62.92   **Malignant neoplasm of left testis, unspecified whether descended or undescended** ♂ 🔏

● **C63**   **Malignant neoplasm of other and unspecified male genital organs**
   ● **C63.0**   **Malignant neoplasm of epididymis**
     C63.00   **Malignant neoplasm of unspecified epididymis** ♂ 🔏
     C63.01   **Malignant neoplasm of right epididymis** ♂ 🔏
     C63.02   **Malignant neoplasm of left epididymis** ♂ 🔏
   ● **C63.1**   **Malignant neoplasm of spermatic cord**
     C63.10   **Malignant neoplasm of unspecified spermatic cord** ♂ 🔏
     C63.11   **Malignant neoplasm of right spermatic cord** ♂ 🔏
     C63.12   **Malignant neoplasm of left spermatic cord** ♂ 🔏
    C63.2   **Malignant neoplasm of scrotum** ♂ 🔏
      Malignant neoplasm of skin of scrotum
    C63.7   **Malignant neoplasm of other specified male genital organs** ♂ 🔏
      Malignant neoplasm of seminal vesicle
      Malignant neoplasm of tunica vaginalis
    C63.8   **Malignant neoplasm of overlapping sites of male genital organs** ♂ 🔏
      Primary malignant neoplasm of two or more contiguous sites of male genital organs whose point of origin cannot be determined
    C63.9   **Malignant neoplasm of male genital organ, unspecified** ♂ 🔏
      Malignant neoplasm of male genitourinary tract NOS

MALIGNANT NEOPLASMS OF URINARY TRACT (C64-C68)

● **C64**   **Malignant neoplasm of kidney, except renal pelvis**
    Excludes1   malignant carcinoid tumor of the kidney (C7A.093)
      malignant neoplasm of renal calyces (C65.-)
      malignant neoplasm of renal pelvis (C65.-)
    C64.1   **Malignant neoplasm of right kidney, except renal pelvis** 🔏
    C64.2   **Malignant neoplasm of left kidney, except renal pelvis** 🔏
    C64.9   **Malignant neoplasm of unspecified kidney, except renal pelvis** 🔏

● **C65**   **Malignant neoplasm of renal pelvis**
    Includes   malignant neoplasm of pelviureteric junction
      malignant neoplasm of renal calyces
    C65.1   **Malignant neoplasm of right renal pelvis** 🔏
    C65.2   **Malignant neoplasm of left renal pelvis** 🔏
    C65.9   **Malignant neoplasm of unspecified renal pelvis** 🔏

● **C66**   **Malignant neoplasm of ureter**
    Excludes1   malignant neoplasm of ureteric orifice of bladder (C67.6)
    C66.1   **Malignant neoplasm of right ureter** 🔏
    C66.2   **Malignant neoplasm of left ureter** 🔏
    C66.9   **Malignant neoplasm of unspecified ureter** 🔏

● **C67**   **Malignant neoplasm of bladder**
    C67.0   **Malignant neoplasm of trigone of bladder** 🔏
      Triangular area formed by three openings in the floor of urinary bladder
    C67.1   **Malignant neoplasm of dome of bladder** 🔏
      Vaulted roof
    C67.2   **Malignant neoplasm of lateral wall of bladder** 🔏
      Side walls
    C67.3   **Malignant neoplasm of anterior wall of bladder** 🔏
      Front wall
    C67.4   **Malignant neoplasm of posterior wall of bladder** 🔏
      Back wall
    C67.5   **Malignant neoplasm of bladder neck** 🔏
      Joining of bladder and urethra
      Malignant neoplasm of internal urethral orifice
    C67.6   **Malignant neoplasm of ureteric orifice** 🔏
      Opening from bladder to ureters
    C67.7   **Malignant neoplasm of urachus** 🔏
      Embryonic canal that connects the urinary bladder with the structure that forms the umbilical cord (allantois)
    C67.8   **Malignant neoplasm of overlapping sites of bladder** 🔏
    C67.9   **Malignant neoplasm of bladder, unspecified** 🔏
      Coding Clinic: 2017, Q1, P6; 2016, Q1, P19

● **C68**   **Malignant neoplasm of other and unspecified urinary organs**
    Excludes1   malignant neoplasm of female genitourinary tract NOS (C57.9)
      malignant neoplasm of male genitourinary tract NOS (C63.9)
    C68.0   **Malignant neoplasm of urethra** 🔏
      Excludes1   malignant neoplasm of urethral orifice of bladder (C67.5)
    C68.1   **Malignant neoplasm of paraurethral glands** 🔏
      Group of glands of female urethra drained by paraurethral ducts; AKA Skene glands, female prostate
    C68.8   **Malignant neoplasm of overlapping sites of urinary organs** 🔏
      Primary malignant neoplasm of two or more contiguous sites of urinary organs whose point of origin cannot be determined
    C68.9   **Malignant neoplasm of urinary organ, unspecified** 🔏
      Malignant neoplasm of urinary system NOS

CHAPTER 2 (C00-D49)

MALIGNANT NEOPLASMS OF EYE, BRAIN AND OTHER PARTS OF CENTRAL NERVOUS SYSTEM (C69-C72)

● **C69**   **Malignant neoplasm of eye and adnexa**

     Excludes1   malignant neoplasm of connective tissue of eyelid (C49.0)
           malignant neoplasm of eyelid (skin) (C43.1-, C44.1-)
           malignant neoplasm of optic nerve (C72.3-)

  ● **C69.0**   **Malignant neoplasm of conjunctiva**

     C69.00   Malignant neoplasm of **unspecified conjunctiva** 🅢

     C69.01   Malignant neoplasm of **right** conjunctiva 🅢

     C69.02   Malignant neoplasm of **left** conjunctiva 🅢

  ● **C69.1**   **Malignant neoplasm of cornea**

     C69.10   Malignant neoplasm of **unspecified** cornea 🅢

     C69.11   Malignant neoplasm of **right** cornea 🅢

     C69.12   Malignant neoplasm of **left** cornea 🅢

  ● **C69.2**   **Malignant neoplasm of retina**

     Excludes1   dark area on retina (D49.81)
           neoplasm of unspecified behavior of retina and choroid (D49.81)
           retinal freckle (D49.81)

     C69.20   Malignant neoplasm of **unspecified** retina 🅢

     C69.21   Malignant neoplasm of **right** retina 🅢

     C69.22   Malignant neoplasm of **left** retina 🅢

  ● **C69.3**   **Malignant neoplasm of choroid**

     C69.30   Malignant neoplasm of **unspecified** choroid 🅢

     C69.31   Malignant neoplasm of **right** choroid 🅢

     C69.32   Malignant neoplasm of **left** choroid 🅢

  ● **C69.4**   **Malignant neoplasm of ciliary body**

     C69.40   Malignant neoplasm of **unspecified ciliary body** 🅢

     C69.41   Malignant neoplasm of **right ciliary body** 🅢

     C69.42   Malignant neoplasm of **left ciliary body** 🅢

  ● **C69.5**   **Malignant neoplasm of lacrimal gland and duct**
        Malignant neoplasm of lacrimal sac
        Malignant neoplasm of nasolacrimal duct

     C69.50   Malignant neoplasm of **unspecified lacrimal gland and duct** 🅢

     C69.51   Malignant neoplasm of **right lacrimal gland and duct** 🅢

     C69.52   Malignant neoplasm of **left lacrimal gland and duct** 🅢

  ● **C69.6**   **Malignant neoplasm of orbit**
        Malignant neoplasm of connective tissue of orbit
        Malignant neoplasm of extraocular muscle
        Malignant neoplasm of peripheral nerves of orbit
        Malignant neoplasm of retrobulbar tissue
        Malignant neoplasm of retro-ocular tissue

     Excludes1   malignant neoplasm of orbital bone (C41.0)

     C69.60   Malignant neoplasm of **unspecified** orbit 🅢

     C69.61   Malignant neoplasm of **right** orbit 🅢

     C69.62   Malignant neoplasm of **left** orbit 🅢

  ● **C69.8**   **Malignant neoplasm of overlapping sites of eye and adnexa**

     C69.80   Malignant neoplasm of overlapping sites of **unspecified eye and adnexa** 🅢

     C69.81   Malignant neoplasm of overlapping sites of **right eye and adnexa** 🅢

     C69.82   Malignant neoplasm of overlapping sites of **left eye and adnexa** 🅢

  ● **C69.9**   **Malignant neoplasm of unspecified site of eye**
        Malignant neoplasm of eyeball

     C69.90   Malignant neoplasm of unspecified site of **unspecified eye** 🅢

     C69.91   Malignant neoplasm of unspecified site of **right eye** 🅢

     C69.92   Malignant neoplasm of unspecified site of **left eye** 🅢

Figure 2-15   The brain.

● **C70**   **Malignant neoplasm of meninges**

     C70.0   Malignant neoplasm of **cerebral meninges** 🅢

     C70.1   Malignant neoplasm of **spinal meninges** 🅢

     C70.9   Malignant neoplasm of meninges, **unspecified** 🅢

● **C71**   **Malignant neoplasm of brain**

     Excludes1   malignant neoplasm of cranial nerves (C72.2-C72.5)
           retrobulbar malignant neoplasm (C69.6-)

     C71.0   **Malignant neoplasm of cerebrum, except lobes and ventricles** 🅢
        Malignant neoplasm of supratentorial NOS

     C71.1   Malignant neoplasm of **frontal lobe** 🅢

     C71.2   Malignant neoplasm of **temporal lobe** 🅢

     C71.3   Malignant neoplasm of **parietal lobe** 🅢

     C71.4   Malignant neoplasm of **occipital lobe** 🅢

     C71.5   Malignant neoplasm of **cerebral ventricle** 🅢

       Excludes1   malignant neoplasm of fourth cerebral ventricle (C71.7)

     C71.6   Malignant neoplasm of **cerebellum** 🅢

     C71.7   Malignant neoplasm of **brain stem** 🅢
        Malignant neoplasm of fourth cerebral ventricle
        Infratentorial malignant neoplasm NOS

     C71.8   Malignant neoplasm of **overlapping sites** of brain 🅢

     C71.9   Malignant neoplasm of brain, **unspecified** 🅢

● **C72**   **Malignant neoplasm of spinal cord, cranial nerves and other parts of central nervous system**

     Excludes1   malignant neoplasm of meninges (C70.-)
           malignant neoplasm of peripheral nerves and autonomic nervous system (C47.-)

     C72.0   Malignant neoplasm of **spinal cord** 🅢

     C72.1   Malignant neoplasm of **cauda equina** 🅢
        Lower end of spinal column

  ● **C72.2**   **Malignant neoplasm of olfactory nerve**
        Malignant neoplasm of olfactory bulb

     C72.20   Malignant neoplasm of **unspecified olfactory nerve** 🅢

     C72.21   Malignant neoplasm of **right olfactory nerve** 🅢

     C72.22   Malignant neoplasm of **left olfactory nerve** 🅢

  ● **C72.3**   **Malignant neoplasm of optic nerve**

     C72.30   Malignant neoplasm of **unspecified optic nerve** 🅢

     C72.31   Malignant neoplasm of **right optic nerve** 🅢

     C72.32   Malignant neoplasm of **left optic nerve** 🅢

  ● **C72.4**   **Malignant neoplasm of acoustic nerve**

     C72.40   Malignant neoplasm of **unspecified acoustic nerve** 🅢

     C72.41   Malignant neoplasm of **right acoustic nerve** 🅢

     C72.42   Malignant neoplasm of **left acoustic nerve** 🅢

CHAPTER 2 (C00-D49)

▶ New   ⟹ Revised   ~~deleted~~ Deleted   Excludes 1   Excludes 2   Includes   Use additional   Code first   Code also   Key words

OGCR Official Guidelines   X Assign placeholder X   ● Use Additional Character(s)   ▷ Manifestation Code   🅢 Hierarchical Condition Category   **Coding Clinic**

● C72.5 Malignant neoplasm of other and unspecified cranial nerves

C72.50 Malignant neoplasm of unspecified cranial nerve 🗣
Malignant neoplasm of cranial nerve NOS

C72.59 Malignant neoplasm of other cranial nerves 🗣

C72.9 Malignant neoplasm of central nervous system, unspecified 🗣
Malignant neoplasm of unspecified site of central nervous system
Malignant neoplasm of nervous system NOS

MALIGNANT NEOPLASMS OF THYROID AND OTHER ENDOCRINE GLANDS (C73-C75)

C73 Malignant neoplasm of thyroid gland 🗣
Use additional code to identify any functional activity

● C74 Malignant neoplasm of adrenal gland

● C74.0 Malignant neoplasm of cortex of adrenal gland

C74.00 Malignant neoplasm of cortex of unspecified adrenal gland 🗣

C74.01 Malignant neoplasm of cortex of right adrenal gland 🗣

C74.02 Malignant neoplasm of cortex of left adrenal gland 🗣

● C74.1 Malignant neoplasm of medulla of adrenal gland
Pair of glands situated on top of or above each kidney ("suprarenal")

C74.10 Malignant neoplasm of medulla of unspecified adrenal gland 🗣

C74.11 Malignant neoplasm of medulla of right adrenal gland 🗣

C74.12 Malignant neoplasm of medulla of left adrenal gland 🗣

● C74.9 Malignant neoplasm of unspecified part of adrenal gland

C74.90 Malignant neoplasm of unspecified part of unspecified adrenal gland 🗣

C74.91 Malignant neoplasm of unspecified part of right adrenal gland 🗣

C74.92 Malignant neoplasm of unspecified part of left adrenal gland 🗣

● C75 Malignant neoplasm of other endocrine glands and related structures

Excludes1 malignant carcinoid tumors (C7A.0-)
malignant neoplasm of adrenal gland (C74.-)
malignant neoplasm of endocrine pancreas (C25.4)
malignant neoplasm of islets of Langerhans (C25.4)
malignant neoplasm of ovary (C56.-)
malignant neoplasm of testis (C62.-)
malignant neoplasm of thymus (C37)
malignant neoplasm of thyroid gland (C73)
malignant neuroendocrine tumors (C7A.-)

C75.0 Malignant neoplasm of parathyroid gland 🗣

C75.1 Malignant neoplasm of pituitary gland 🗣

C75.2 Malignant neoplasm of craniopharyngeal duct 🗣

C75.3 Malignant neoplasm of pineal gland 🗣

C75.4 Malignant neoplasm of carotid body 🗣

C75.5 Malignant neoplasm of aortic body and other paraganglia 🗣

C75.8 Malignant neoplasm with pluriglandular involvement, unspecified 🗣

C75.9 Malignant neoplasm of endocrine gland, unspecified 🗣

MALIGNANT NEUROENDOCRINE TUMORS (C7A)

● C7A Malignant neuroendocrine tumors
Code also any associated multiple endocrine neoplasia [MEN] syndromes (E31.2-)
Use additional code to identify any associated endocrine syndrome, such as:
carcinoid syndrome (E34.0)

Excludes2 malignant pancreatic islet cell tumors (C25.4)
Merkel cell carcinoma (C4A.-)

● C7A.0 Malignant carcinoid tumors

C7A.00 Malignant carcinoid tumor of unspecified site 🗣

● C7A.01 Malignant carcinoid tumors of the small intestine

C7A.010 Malignant carcinoid tumor of the duodenum 🗣

C7A.011 Malignant carcinoid tumor of the jejunum 🗣

C7A.012 Malignant carcinoid tumor of the ileum 🗣

C7A.019 Malignant carcinoid tumor of the small intestine, unspecified portion 🗣

● C7A.02 Malignant carcinoid tumors of the appendix, large intestine, and rectum

C7A.020 Malignant carcinoid tumor of the appendix 🗣

C7A.021 Malignant carcinoid tumor of the cecum 🗣

C7A.022 Malignant carcinoid tumor of the ascending colon 🗣

C7A.023 Malignant carcinoid tumor of the transverse colon 🗣

C7A.024 Malignant carcinoid tumor of the descending colon 🗣

C7A.025 Malignant carcinoid tumor of the sigmoid colon 🗣

C7A.026 Malignant carcinoid tumor of the rectum 🗣

C7A.029 Malignant carcinoid tumor of the large intestine, unspecified portion 🗣
Malignant carcinoid tumor of the colon NOS

● C7A.09 Malignant carcinoid tumors of other sites

C7A.090 Malignant carcinoid tumor of the bronchus and lung 🗣

C7A.091 Malignant carcinoid tumor of the thymus 🗣

C7A.092 Malignant carcinoid tumor of the stomach 🗣

C7A.093 Malignant carcinoid tumor of the kidney 🗣

C7A.094 Malignant carcinoid tumor of the foregut, unspecified 🗣

C7A.095 Malignant carcinoid tumor of the midgut, unspecified 🗣

C7A.096 Malignant carcinoid tumor of the hindgut, unspecified 🗣

C7A.098 Malignant carcinoid tumors of other sites 🗣

C7A.1 Malignant poorly differentiated neuroendocrine tumors 🗣
Malignant poorly differentiated neuroendocrine tumor NOS
Malignant poorly differentiated neuroendocrine carcinoma, any site
High grade neuroendocrine carcinoma, any site

C7A.8 Other malignant neuroendocrine tumors 🗣
Secondary neuroendocrine tumors (C7B)
Coding Clinic: 2019, Q3, P7

N Newborn Age: 0   **P** Pediatric Age: 0–17   **M** Maternity DX: 12–55   **A** Adult Age: 15–124   ♀ Females Only   ♂ Males Only

SECONDARY NEUROENDOCRINE TUMORS (C7B)

● **C7B   Secondary neuroendocrine tumors**
Use additional code to identify any functional activity

  ● **C7B.0   Secondary carcinoid tumors**
     C7B.00   Secondary carcinoid tumors, unspecified site 🐾
     C7B.01   Secondary carcinoid tumors of distant lymph nodes 🐾
     C7B.02   Secondary carcinoid tumors of liver 🐾
     C7B.03   Secondary carcinoid tumors of bone 🐾
     C7B.04   Secondary carcinoid tumors of peritoneum 🐾
        Mesentary metastasis of carcinoid tumor
     C7B.09   Secondary carcinoid tumors of other sites 🐾

   C7B.1   Secondary Merkel cell carcinoma 🐾
     Merkel cell carcinoma nodal presentation
     Merkel cell carcinoma visceral metastatic presentation

   C7B.8   Other secondary neuroendocrine tumors 🐾
     Coding Clinic: 2019, Q3, P7

MALIGNANT NEOPLASMS OF ILL-DEFINED, OTHER SECONDARY AND UNSPECIFIED SITES (C76-C80)

● **C76   Malignant neoplasm of other and ill-defined sites**
   Excludes1   malignant neoplasm of female genitourinary tract NOS (C57.9)
        malignant neoplasm of male genitourinary tract NOS (C63.9)
        malignant neoplasm of lymphoid, hematopoietic and related tissue (C81-C96)
        malignant neoplasm of skin (C44.-)
        malignant neoplasm of unspecified site NOS (C80.1)

   C76.0   Malignant neoplasm of head, face and neck 🐾
     Malignant neoplasm of cheek NOS
     Malignant neoplasm of nose NOS

   C76.1   Malignant neoplasm of thorax 🐾
     Intrathoracic malignant neoplasm NOS
     Malignant neoplasm of axilla NOS
     Thoracic malignant neoplasm NOS

   C76.2   Malignant neoplasm of abdomen 🐾

   C76.3   Malignant neoplasm of pelvis 🐾
     Malignant neoplasm of groin NOS
     Malignant neoplasm of sites overlapping systems within the pelvis
     Rectovaginal (septum) malignant neoplasm
       Between rectum and vagina
     Rectovesical (septum) malignant neoplasm
       Between rectum and urinary bladder; AKA vesicorectal

  ● **C76.4   Malignant neoplasm of upper limb**
     C76.40   Malignant neoplasm of unspecified upper limb 🐾
     C76.41   Malignant neoplasm of right upper limb 🐾
     C76.42   Malignant neoplasm of left upper limb 🐾

  ● **C76.5   Malignant neoplasm of lower limb**
     C76.50   Malignant neoplasm of unspecified lower limb 🐾
     C76.51   Malignant neoplasm of right lower limb 🐾
     C76.52   Malignant neoplasm of left lower limb 🐾

   C76.8   Malignant neoplasm of other specified ill-defined sites 🐾
     Malignant neoplasm of overlapping ill-defined sites

● **C77   Secondary and unspecified malignant neoplasm of lymph nodes**
   Excludes1   malignant neoplasm of lymph nodes, specified as primary (C81-C86, C88, C96.-)
        mesentary metastasis of carcinoid tumor (C7B.04)
        secondary carcinoid tumors of distant lymph nodes (C7B.01)

   C77.0   Secondary and unspecified malignant neoplasm of lymph nodes of head, face and neck 🐾
     Secondary and unspecified malignant neoplasm of supraclavicular lymph nodes

   C77.1   Secondary and unspecified malignant neoplasm of intrathoracic lymph nodes 🐾

   C77.2   Secondary and unspecified malignant neoplasm of intra-abdominal lymph nodes 🐾

   C77.3   Secondary and unspecified malignant neoplasm of axilla and upper limb lymph nodes 🐾
     Secondary and unspecified malignant neoplasm of pectoral lymph nodes

   C77.4   Secondary and unspecified malignant neoplasm of inguinal and lower limb lymph nodes 🐾

   C77.5   Secondary and unspecified malignant neoplasm of intrapelvic lymph nodes 🐾

   C77.8   Secondary and unspecified malignant neoplasm of lymph nodes of multiple regions 🐾

   C77.9   Secondary and unspecified malignant neoplasm of lymph node, unspecified 🐾

● **C78   Secondary malignant neoplasm of respiratory and digestive organs**
   Excludes1   secondary carcinoid tumors of liver (C7B.02)
        secondary carcinoid tumors of peritoneum (C7B.04)
   Excludes2   lymph node metastases (C77.0)

  ● **C78.0   Secondary malignant neoplasm of lung**
     C78.00   Secondary malignant neoplasm of unspecified lung 🐾
     C78.01   Secondary malignant neoplasm of right lung 🐾
     C78.02   Secondary malignant neoplasm of left lung 🐾

   C78.1   Secondary malignant neoplasm of mediastinum 🐾
     Thoracic cavity between pleural cavities

   C78.2   Secondary malignant neoplasm of pleura 🐾
     Serous membrane covering lungs and lining thoracic cavity

  ● **C78.3   Secondary malignant neoplasm of other and unspecified respiratory organs**
     C78.30   Secondary malignant neoplasm of unspecified respiratory organ 🐾
     C78.39   Secondary malignant neoplasm of other respiratory organs 🐾

   C78.4   Secondary malignant neoplasm of small intestine 🐾

   C78.5   Secondary malignant neoplasm of large intestine and rectum 🐾

   C78.6   Secondary malignant neoplasm of retroperitoneum and peritoneum 🐾
     Coding Clinic: 2017, Q2, P12

   C78.7   Secondary malignant neoplasm of liver and intrahepatic bile duct 🐾

  ● **C78.8   Secondary malignant neoplasm of other and unspecified digestive organs**
     C78.80   Secondary malignant neoplasm of unspecified digestive organ 🐾
     C78.89   Secondary malignant neoplasm of other digestive organs 🐾
        Code also exocrine pancreatic insufficiency (K86.81)

● **C79   Secondary malignant neoplasm of other and unspecified sites**
   Excludes1   secondary carcinoid tumors (C7B.-)
        secondary neuroendocrine tumors (C7B.-)

  ● **C79.0   Secondary malignant neoplasm of kidney and renal pelvis**
     C79.00   Secondary malignant neoplasm of unspecified kidney and renal pelvis 🐾
     C79.01   Secondary malignant neoplasm of right kidney and renal pelvis 🐾
     C79.02   Secondary malignant neoplasm of left kidney and renal pelvis 🐾

Item 2–6 The adrenal glands are a pair of glands situated on top of or above each kidney ("suprarenal") and chiefly responsible for regulating the stress response through the synthesis of corticosteroids and catecholamines, including cortisol and adrenaline.

▶ New   ⇥ Revised   ~~deleted~~ Deleted   Excludes 1   Excludes 2   Includes   Use additional   Code first   Code also   Key words

OGCR Official Guidelines   X Assign placeholder X   ● Use Additional Character(s)   ▌ Manifestation Code   🐾 Hierarchical Condition Category   Coding Clinic

● **C79.1** Secondary malignant neoplasm of bladder and other and unspecified urinary organs

　　C79.10 Secondary malignant neoplasm of unspecified urinary organs 🦠

　　C79.11 Secondary malignant neoplasm of bladder 🦠

　　　　Excludes2 lymph node metastases (C77.0)

　　C79.19 Secondary malignant neoplasm of other urinary organs 🦠

　C79.2 Secondary malignant neoplasm of skin 🦠

　　　Excludes1 secondary Merkel cell carcinoma (C7B.1)

● **C79.3** Secondary malignant neoplasm of brain and cerebral meninges

　　C79.31 Secondary malignant neoplasm of brain 🦠

　　C79.32 Secondary malignant neoplasm of cerebral meninges 🦠
　　　　Coding Clinic: 2020, Q1, P13

● **C79.4** Secondary malignant neoplasm of other and unspecified parts of nervous system

　　C79.40 Secondary malignant neoplasm of unspecified part of nervous system 🦠

　　C79.49 Secondary malignant neoplasm of other parts of nervous system 🦠

● **C79.5** Secondary malignant neoplasm of bone and bone marrow

　　　Excludes1 secondary carcinoid tumors of bone (C7B.03)

　　C79.51 Secondary malignant neoplasm of bone 🦠

　　C79.52 Secondary malignant neoplasm of bone marrow 🦠

● **C79.6** Secondary malignant neoplasm of ovary

　　C79.60 Secondary malignant neoplasm of unspecified ovary ♀ 🦠

　　C79.61 Secondary malignant neoplasm of right ovary ♀ 🦠

　　C79.62 Secondary malignant neoplasm of left ovary ♀ 🦠

● **C79.7** Secondary malignant neoplasm of adrenal gland

　　C79.70 Secondary malignant neoplasm of unspecified adrenal gland 🦠

　　C79.71 Secondary malignant neoplasm of right adrenal gland 🦠

　　C79.72 Secondary malignant neoplasm of left adrenal gland 🦠

● **C79.8** Secondary malignant neoplasm of other specified sites

　　C79.81 Secondary malignant neoplasm of breast 🦠

　　C79.82 Secondary malignant neoplasm of genital organs 🦠

　　C79.89 Secondary malignant neoplasm of other specified sites 🦠
　　　　Coding Clinic: 2017, Q2, P11

　C79.9 Secondary malignant neoplasm of unspecified site 🦠
　　　Metastatic cancer NOS
　　　Metastatic disease NOS

　　　Excludes1 carcinomatosis NOS (C80.0)
　　　　　　generalized cancer NOS (C80.0)
　　　　　　malignant (primary) neoplasm of unspecified site (C80.1)

OGCR Section I.C.2.j and k

Disseminated malignant neoplasm, unspecified

j. Code C80.0, Disseminated malignant neoplasm, unspecified, is for use only in those cases where the patient has advanced metastatic disease and no known primary or secondary sites are specified. It should not be used in place of assigning codes for the primary site and all known secondary sites.

Malignant neoplasm without specification of site

k. Code C80.1, Malignant (primary) neoplasm, unspecified, equates to Cancer, unspecified. This code should only be used when no determination can be made as to the primary site of a malignancy. This code should rarely be used in the inpatient setting.

● **C80** Malignant neoplasm without specification of site

　　Excludes1 malignant carcinoid tumor of unspecified site (C7A.00)
　　　　malignant neoplasm of specified multiple sites-code to each site

　C80.0 Disseminated malignant neoplasm, unspecified 🦠
　　　Carcinomatosis NOS
　　　Generalized cancer, unspecified site (primary) (secondary)
　　　Generalized malignancy, unspecified site (primary) (secondary)

　C80.1 Malignant (primary) neoplasm, unspecified 🦠
　　　Cancer NOS
　　　Cancer unspecified site (primary)
　　　Carcinoma unspecified site (primary)
　　　Malignancy unspecified site (primary)

　　　Excludes1 secondary malignant neoplasm of unspecified site (C79.9)

　C80.2 Malignant neoplasm associated with transplanted organ 🦠

　　　Code first complication of transplanted organ (T86.-)
　　　Use additional code to identify the specific malignancy

★**(See Plate 1 of the Anatomy Illustrations.)**

MALIGNANT NEOPLASMS OF LYMPHOID, HEMATOPOIETIC AND RELATED TISSUE (C81-C96)

　　Excludes2 Kaposi's sarcoma of lymph nodes (C46.3)
　　　　secondary and unspecified neoplasm of lymph nodes (C77.-)
　　　　secondary neoplasm of bone marrow (C79.52)
　　　　secondary neoplasm of spleen (C78.89)

● **C81** Hodgkin lymphoma
　　Form of malignant lymphoma with four types, nodular sclerosis, mixed cellularity, lymphocyte depleted, and lymphocyte predominant

　　Excludes1 personal history of Hodgkin lymphoma (Z85.71)

● **C81.0** Nodular lymphocyte predominant Hodgkin lymphoma
　　Least aggressive, least common, typically no symptoms
　　Lymphocytic-histiocytic predominance Hodgkin's disease

　　C81.00 Nodular lymphocyte predominant Hodgkin lymphoma, unspecified site 🦠

　　C81.01 Nodular lymphocyte predominant Hodgkin lymphoma, lymph nodes of head, face, and neck 🦠

　　C81.02 Nodular lymphocyte predominant Hodgkin lymphoma, intrathoracic lymph nodes 🦠

　　C81.03 Nodular lymphocyte predominant Hodgkin lymphoma, intra-abdominal lymph nodes 🦠

　　C81.04 Nodular lymphocyte predominant Hodgkin lymphoma, lymph nodes of axilla and upper limb 🦠

　　C81.05 Nodular lymphocyte predominant Hodgkin lymphoma, lymph nodes of inguinal region and lower limb 🦠

　　C81.06 Nodular lymphocyte predominant Hodgkin lymphoma, intrapelvic lymph nodes 🦠

　　C81.07 Nodular lymphocyte predominant Hodgkin lymphoma, spleen 🦠

　　C81.08 Nodular lymphocyte predominant Hodgkin lymphoma, lymph nodes of multiple sites 🦠

　　C81.09 Nodular lymphocyte predominant Hodgkin lymphoma, extranodal and solid organ sites 🦠

CHAPTER 2 (C00-D49)

● **C81.1**   **Nodular sclerosis Hodgkin lymphoma**
Nodular sclerosis classical Hodgkin lymphoma
Moderately aggressive; most common in young adults

     C81.10   **Nodular sclerosis Hodgkin lymphoma, unspecified site** 🦠

     C81.11   **Nodular sclerosis Hodgkin lymphoma, lymph nodes of head, face, and neck** 🦠

     C81.12   **Nodular sclerosis Hodgkin lymphoma, intrathoracic lymph nodes** 🦠

     C81.13   **Nodular sclerosis Hodgkin lymphoma, intra-abdominal lymph nodes** 🦠

     C81.14   **Nodular sclerosis Hodgkin lymphoma, lymph nodes of axilla and upper limb** 🦠

     C81.15   **Nodular sclerosis Hodgkin lymphoma, lymph nodes of inguinal region and lower limb** 🦠

     C81.16   **Nodular sclerosis Hodgkin lymphoma, intrapelvic lymph nodes** 🦠

     C81.17   **Nodular sclerosis Hodgkin lymphoma, spleen** 🦠

     C81.18   **Nodular sclerosis Hodgkin lymphoma, lymph nodes of multiple sites** 🦠

     C81.19   **Nodular sclerosis Hodgkin lymphoma, extranodal and solid organ sites** 🦠

● **C81.2**   **Mixed cellularity Hodgkin lymphoma**
Mixed cellularity classical Hodgkin lymphoma
A type of Hodgkin's that is moderately aggressive with mixed cell types

     C81.20   **Mixed cellularity Hodgkin lymphoma, unspecified site** 🦠

     C81.21   **Mixed cellularity Hodgkin lymphoma, lymph nodes of head, face, and neck** 🦠

     C81.22   **Mixed cellularity Hodgkin lymphoma, intrathoracic lymph nodes** 🦠

     C81.23   **Mixed cellularity Hodgkin lymphoma, intra-abdominal lymph nodes** 🦠

     C81.24   **Mixed cellularity Hodgkin lymphoma, lymph nodes of axilla and upper limb** 🦠

     C81.25   **Mixed cellularity Hodgkin lymphoma, lymph nodes of inguinal region and lower limb** 🦠

     C81.26   **Mixed cellularity Hodgkin lymphoma, intrapelvic lymph nodes** 🦠

     C81.27   **Mixed cellularity Hodgkin lymphoma, spleen** 🦠

     C81.28   **Mixed cellularity Hodgkin lymphoma, lymph nodes of multiple sites** 🦠

     C81.29   **Mixed cellularity Hodgkin lymphoma, extranodal and solid organ sites** 🦠

● **C81.3**   **Lymphocyte depleted Hodgkin lymphoma**
Lymphocyte depleted classical Hodgkin lymphoma
Most aggressive type with poor prognosis

     C81.30   **Lymphocyte depleted Hodgkin lymphoma, unspecified site** 🦠

     C81.31   **Lymphocyte depleted Hodgkin lymphoma, lymph nodes of head, face, and neck** 🦠

     C81.32   **Lymphocyte depleted Hodgkin lymphoma, intrathoracic lymph nodes** 🦠

     C81.33   **Lymphocyte depleted Hodgkin lymphoma, intra-abdominal lymph nodes** 🦠

     C81.34   **Lymphocyte depleted Hodgkin lymphoma, lymph nodes of axilla and upper limb** 🦠

     C81.35   **Lymphocyte depleted Hodgkin lymphoma, lymph nodes of inguinal region and lower limb** 🦠

     C81.36   **Lymphocyte depleted Hodgkin lymphoma, intrapelvic lymph nodes** 🦠

     C81.37   **Lymphocyte depleted Hodgkin lymphoma, spleen** 🦠

     C81.38   **Lymphocyte depleted Hodgkin lymphoma, lymph nodes of multiple sites** 🦠

     C81.39   **Lymphocyte depleted Hodgkin lymphoma, extranodal and solid organ sites** 🦠

● **C81.4**   **Lymphocyte-rich Hodgkin lymphoma**
Lymphocyte-rich classical Hodgkin lymphoma

     Excludes1   nodular lymphocyte predominant Hodgkin lymphoma (C81.0-)

     C81.40   **Lymphocyte-rich Hodgkin lymphoma, unspecified site** 🦠

     C81.41   **Lymphocyte-rich Hodgkin lymphoma, lymph nodes of head, face, and neck** 🦠

     C81.42   **Lymphocyte-rich Hodgkin lymphoma, intrathoracic lymph nodes** 🦠

     C81.43   **Lymphocyte-rich Hodgkin lymphoma, intra-abdominal lymph nodes** 🦠

     C81.44   **Lymphocyte-rich Hodgkin lymphoma, lymph nodes of axilla and upper limb** 🦠

     C81.45   **Lymphocyte-rich Hodgkin lymphoma, lymph nodes of inguinal region and lower limb** 🦠

     C81.46   **Lymphocyte-rich Hodgkin lymphoma, intrapelvic lymph nodes** 🦠

     C81.47   **Lymphocyte-rich Hodgkin lymphoma, spleen** 🦠

     C81.48   **Lymphocyte-rich Hodgkin lymphoma, lymph nodes of multiple sites** 🦠

     C81.49   **Lymphocyte-rich Hodgkin lymphoma, extranodal and solid organ sites** 🦠

● **C81.7**   **Other Hodgkin lymphoma**
Classical Hodgkin lymphoma NOS
Other classical Hodgkin lymphoma

     C81.70   **Other Hodgkin lymphoma, unspecified site** 🦠

     C81.71   **Other Hodgkin lymphoma, lymph nodes of head, face, and neck** 🦠

     C81.72   **Other Hodgkin lymphoma, intrathoracic lymph nodes** 🦠

     C81.73   **Other Hodgkin lymphoma, intra-abdominal lymph nodes** 🦠

     C81.74   **Other Hodgkin lymphoma, lymph nodes of axilla and upper limb** 🦠

     C81.75   **Other Hodgkin lymphoma, lymph nodes of inguinal region and lower limb** 🦠

     C81.76   **Other Hodgkin lymphoma, intrapelvic lymph nodes** 🦠

     C81.77   **Other Hodgkin lymphoma, spleen** 🦠

     C81.78   **Other Hodgkin lymphoma, lymph nodes of multiple sites** 🦠

     C81.79   **Other Hodgkin lymphoma, extranodal and solid organ sites** 🦠

● **C81.9**   **Hodgkin lymphoma, unspecified**

     C81.90   **Hodgkin lymphoma, unspecified, unspecified site** 🦠

     C81.91   **Hodgkin lymphoma, unspecified, lymph nodes of head, face, and neck** 🦠

     C81.92   **Hodgkin lymphoma, unspecified, intrathoracic lymph nodes** 🦠

     C81.93   **Hodgkin lymphoma, unspecified, intra-abdominal lymph nodes** 🦠

     C81.94   **Hodgkin lymphoma, unspecified, lymph nodes of axilla and upper limb** 🦠

     C81.95   **Hodgkin lymphoma, unspecified, lymph nodes of inguinal region and lower limb** 🦠

     C81.96   **Hodgkin lymphoma, unspecified, intrapelvic lymph nodes** 🦠

     C81.97   **Hodgkin lymphoma, unspecified, spleen** 🦠

     C81.98   **Hodgkin lymphoma, unspecified, lymph nodes of multiple sites** 🦠

     C81.99   **Hodgkin lymphoma, unspecified, extranodal and solid organ sites** 🦠

▶ New   ⇒ Revised   ~~deleted~~ Deleted   Excludes 1   Excludes 2   Includes   Use additional   Code first   Code also   Key words
OGCR Official Guidelines   X Assign placeholder X   ● Use Additional Character(s)   ) Manifestation Code   🦠 Hierarchical Condition Category   **Coding Clinic**

● **C82**   **Follicular lymphoma**
     Group of malignant lymphomas
     Includes   follicular lymphoma with or without diffuse areas
     Excludes1   mature T/NK-cell lymphomas (C84.-)
           personal history of non-Hodgkin lymphoma (Z85.72)

   ● **C82.0**   Follicular lymphoma grade I
     C82.00   Follicular lymphoma grade I, unspecified site 🐾
     C82.01   Follicular lymphoma grade I, lymph nodes of head, face, and neck 🐾
     C82.02   Follicular lymphoma grade I, intrathoracic lymph nodes 🐾
     C82.03   Follicular lymphoma grade I, intra-abdominal lymph nodes 🐾
     C82.04   Follicular lymphoma grade I, lymph nodes of axilla and upper limb 🐾
     C82.05   Follicular lymphoma grade I, lymph nodes of inguinal region and lower limb 🐾
     C82.06   Follicular lymphoma grade I, intrapelvic lymph nodes 🐾
     C82.07   Follicular lymphoma grade I, spleen 🐾
     C82.08   Follicular lymphoma grade I, lymph nodes of multiple sites 🐾
     C82.09   Follicular lymphoma grade I, extranodal and solid organ sites 🐾

   ● **C82.1**   Follicular lymphoma grade II
     C82.10   Follicular lymphoma grade II, unspecified site 🐾
     C82.11   Follicular lymphoma grade II, lymph nodes of head, face, and neck 🐾
     C82.12   Follicular lymphoma grade II, intrathoracic lymph nodes 🐾
     C82.13   Follicular lymphoma grade II, intra-abdominal lymph nodes 🐾
     C82.14   Follicular lymphoma grade II, lymph nodes of axilla and upper limb 🐾
     C82.15   Follicular lymphoma grade II, lymph nodes of inguinal region and lower limb 🐾
     C82.16   Follicular lymphoma grade II, intrapelvic lymph nodes 🐾
     C82.17   Follicular lymphoma grade II, spleen 🐾
     C82.18   Follicular lymphoma grade II, lymph nodes of multiple sites 🐾
     C82.19   Follicular lymphoma grade II, extranodal and solid organ sites 🐾

   ● **C82.2**   Follicular lymphoma grade III, unspecified
     C82.20   Follicular lymphoma grade III, unspecified, unspecified site 🐾
     C82.21   Follicular lymphoma grade III, unspecified, lymph nodes of head, face, and neck 🐾
     C82.22   Follicular lymphoma grade III, unspecified, intrathoracic lymph nodes 🐾
     C82.23   Follicular lymphoma grade III, unspecified, intra-abdominal lymph nodes 🐾
     C82.24   Follicular lymphoma grade III, unspecified, lymph nodes of axilla and upper limb 🐾
     C82.25   Follicular lymphoma grade III, unspecified, lymph nodes of inguinal region and lower limb 🐾
     C82.26   Follicular lymphoma grade III, unspecified, intrapelvic lymph nodes 🐾
     C82.27   Follicular lymphoma grade III, unspecified, spleen 🐾
     C82.28   Follicular lymphoma grade III, unspecified, lymph nodes of multiple sites 🐾
     C82.29   Follicular lymphoma grade III, unspecified, extranodal and solid organ sites 🐾

   ● **C82.3**   Follicular lymphoma grade IIIa
     C82.30   Follicular lymphoma grade IIIa, unspecified site 🐾
     C82.31   Follicular lymphoma grade IIIa, lymph nodes of head, face, and neck 🐾
     C82.32   Follicular lymphoma grade IIIa, intrathoracic lymph nodes 🐾
     C82.33   Follicular lymphoma grade IIIa, intra-abdominal lymph nodes 🐾
     C82.34   Follicular lymphoma grade IIIa, lymph nodes of axilla and upper limb 🐾
     C82.35   Follicular lymphoma grade IIIa, lymph nodes of inguinal region and lower limb 🐾
     C82.36   Follicular lymphoma grade IIIa, intrapelvic lymph nodes 🐾
     C82.37   Follicular lymphoma grade IIIa, spleen 🐾
     C82.38   Follicular lymphoma grade IIIa, lymph nodes of multiple sites 🐾
     C82.39   Follicular lymphoma grade IIIa, extranodal and solid organ sites 🐾

   ● **C82.4**   Follicular lymphoma grade IIIb
     C82.40   Follicular lymphoma grade IIIb, unspecified site 🐾
     C82.41   Follicular lymphoma grade IIIb, lymph nodes of head, face, and neck 🐾
     C82.42   Follicular lymphoma grade IIIb, intrathoracic lymph nodes 🐾
     C82.43   Follicular lymphoma grade IIIb, intra-abdominal lymph nodes 🐾
     C82.44   Follicular lymphoma grade IIIb, lymph nodes of axilla and upper limb 🐾
     C82.45   Follicular lymphoma grade IIIb, lymph nodes of inguinal region and lower limb 🐾
     C82.46   Follicular lymphoma grade IIIb, intrapelvic lymph nodes 🐾
     C82.47   Follicular lymphoma grade IIIb, spleen 🐾
     C82.48   Follicular lymphoma grade IIIb, lymph nodes of multiple sites 🐾
     C82.49   Follicular lymphoma grade IIIb, extranodal and solid organ sites 🐾

   ● **C82.5**   Diffuse follicle center lymphoma
     C82.50   Diffuse follicle center lymphoma, unspecified site 🐾
     C82.51   Diffuse follicle center lymphoma, lymph nodes of head, face, and neck 🐾
     C82.52   Diffuse follicle center lymphoma, intrathoracic lymph nodes 🐾
     C82.53   Diffuse follicle center lymphoma, intra-abdominal lymph nodes 🐾
     C82.54   Diffuse follicle center lymphoma, lymph nodes of axilla and upper limb 🐾
     C82.55   Diffuse follicle center lymphoma, lymph nodes of inguinal region and lower limb 🐾
     C82.56   Diffuse follicle center lymphoma, intrapelvic lymph nodes 🐾
     C82.57   Diffuse follicle center lymphoma, spleen 🐾
     C82.58   Diffuse follicle center lymphoma, lymph nodes of multiple sites 🐾
     C82.59   Diffuse follicle center lymphoma, extranodal and solid organ sites 🐾

   ● **C82.6**   Cutaneous follicle center lymphoma
     C82.60   Cutaneous follicle center lymphoma, unspecified site 🐾
     C82.61   Cutaneous follicle center lymphoma, lymph nodes of head, face, and neck 🐾
     C82.62   Cutaneous follicle center lymphoma, intrathoracic lymph nodes 🐾
     C82.63   Cutaneous follicle center lymphoma, intra-abdominal lymph nodes 🐾

CHAPTER 2 (C00-D49)

C82.64 Cutaneous follicle center lymphoma, lymph nodes of axilla and upper limb 🦠

C82.65 Cutaneous follicle center lymphoma, lymph nodes of inguinal region and lower limb 🦠

C82.66 Cutaneous follicle center lymphoma, intrapelvic lymph nodes 🦠

C82.67 Cutaneous follicle center lymphoma, spleen 🦠

C82.68 Cutaneous follicle center lymphoma, lymph nodes of multiple sites 🦠

C82.69 Cutaneous follicle center lymphoma, extranodal and solid organ sites 🦠

● C82.8 Other types of follicular lymphoma

C82.80 Other types of follicular lymphoma, unspecified site 🦠

C82.81 Other types of follicular lymphoma, lymph nodes of head, face, and neck 🦠

C82.82 Other types of follicular lymphoma, intrathoracic lymph nodes 🦠

C82.83 Other types of follicular lymphoma, intra-abdominal lymph nodes 🦠

C82.84 Other types of follicular lymphoma, lymph nodes of axilla and upper limb 🦠

C82.85 Other types of follicular lymphoma, lymph nodes of inguinal region and lower limb 🦠

C82.86 Other types of follicular lymphoma, intrapelvic lymph nodes 🦠

C82.87 Other types of follicular lymphoma, spleen 🦠

C82.88 Other types of follicular lymphoma, lymph nodes of multiple sites 🦠

C82.89 Other types of follicular lymphoma, extranodal and solid organ sites 🦠

● C82.9 Follicular lymphoma, unspecified

C82.90 Follicular lymphoma, unspecified, unspecified site 🦠

C82.91 Follicular lymphoma, unspecified, lymph nodes of head, face, and neck 🦠

C82.92 Follicular lymphoma, unspecified, intrathoracic lymph nodes 🦠

C82.93 Follicular lymphoma, unspecified, intra-abdominal lymph nodes 🦠

C82.94 Follicular lymphoma, unspecified, lymph nodes of axilla and upper limb 🦠

C82.95 Follicular lymphoma, unspecified, lymph nodes of inguinal region and lower limb 🦠

C82.96 Follicular lymphoma, unspecified, intrapelvic lymph nodes 🦠

C82.97 Follicular lymphoma, unspecified, spleen 🦠

C82.98 Follicular lymphoma, unspecified, lymph nodes of multiple sites 🦠

C82.99 Follicular lymphoma, unspecified, extranodal and solid organ sites 🦠

● C83 Non-follicular lymphoma

Excludes1 personal history of non-Hodgkin lymphoma (Z85.72)

● C83.0 Small cell B-cell lymphoma

Lymphoplasmacytic lymphoma
Nodal marginal zone lymphoma
Non-leukemic variant of B-CLL
Splenic marginal zone lymphoma

Excludes1 chronic lymphocytic leukemia (C91.1)
mature T/NK-cell lymphomas (C84.-)
Waldenström macroglobulinemia (C88.0)

C83.00 Small cell B-cell lymphoma, unspecified site 🦠

C83.01 Small cell B-cell lymphoma, lymph nodes of head, face, and neck 🦠

C83.02 Small cell B-cell lymphoma, intrathoracic lymph nodes 🦠

C83.03 Small cell B-cell lymphoma, intra-abdominal lymph nodes 🦠

C83.04 Small cell B-cell lymphoma, lymph nodes of axilla and upper limb 🦠

C83.05 Small cell B-cell lymphoma, lymph nodes of inguinal region and lower limb 🦠

C83.06 Small cell B-cell lymphoma, intrapelvic lymph nodes 🦠

C83.07 Small cell B-cell lymphoma, spleen 🦠

C83.08 Small cell B-cell lymphoma, lymph nodes of multiple sites 🦠

C83.09 Small cell B-cell lymphoma, extranodal and solid organ sites 🦠

● C83.1 Mantle cell lymphoma

Centrocytic lymphoma
Malignant lymphomatous polyposis

C83.10 Mantle cell lymphoma, unspecified site 🦠

C83.11 Mantle cell lymphoma, lymph nodes of head, face, and neck 🦠

C83.12 Mantle cell lymphoma, intrathoracic lymph nodes 🦠

C83.13 Mantle cell lymphoma, intra-abdominal lymph nodes 🦠

C83.14 Mantle cell lymphoma, lymph nodes of axilla and upper limb 🦠

C83.15 Mantle cell lymphoma, lymph nodes of inguinal region and lower limb 🦠

C83.16 Mantle cell lymphoma, intrapelvic lymph nodes 🦠

C83.17 Mantle cell lymphoma, spleen 🦠

C83.18 Mantle cell lymphoma, lymph nodes of multiple sites 🦠

C83.19 Mantle cell lymphoma, extranodal and solid organ sites 🦠

● C83.3 Diffuse large B-cell lymphoma

Anaplastic diffuse large B-cell lymphoma
CD30-positive diffuse large B-cell lymphoma
Centroblastic diffuse large B-cell lymphoma
Diffuse large B-cell lymphoma, subtype not specified
Immunoblastic diffuse large B-cell lymphoma
Plasmablastic diffuse large B-cell lymphoma
Diffuse large B-cell lymphoma, subtype not specified
T-cell rich diffuse large B-cell lymphoma

Excludes1 mediastinal (thymic) large B-cell lymphoma (C85.2-)
mature T/NK-cell lymphomas (C84.-)

C83.30 Diffuse large B-cell lymphoma, unspecified site 🦠

C83.31 Diffuse large B-cell lymphoma, lymph nodes of head, face, and neck 🦠

C83.32 Diffuse large B-cell lymphoma, intrathoracic lymph nodes 🦠

C83.33 Diffuse large B-cell lymphoma, intra-abdominal lymph nodes 🦠

C83.34 Diffuse large B-cell lymphoma, lymph nodes of axilla and upper limb 🦠

C83.35 Diffuse large B-cell lymphoma, lymph nodes of inguinal region and lower limb 🦠

C83.36 Diffuse large B-cell lymphoma, intrapelvic lymph nodes 🦠

C83.37 Diffuse large B-cell lymphoma, spleen 🦠

C83.38 Diffuse large B-cell lymphoma, lymph nodes of multiple sites 🦠

C83.39 Diffuse large B-cell lymphoma, extranodal and solid organ sites 🦠

▶ New   ⇒ Revised   deleted Deleted   Excludes 1   Excludes 2   Includes   Use additional   Code first   Code also   Key words
OGCR Official Guidelines   X Assign placeholder X   ● Use Additional Character(s)   ▸ Manifestation Code   🦠 Hierarchical Condition Category   **Coding Clinic**

● **C83.5**   **Lymphoblastic (diffuse) lymphoma**
*Highly malignant type of non-Hodgkin lymphoma with
diffuse infiltration*
B-precursor lymphoma
Lymphoblastic B-cell lymphoma
Lymphoblastic lymphoma NOS
Lymphoblastic T-cell lymphoma
T-precursor lymphoma

C83.50   Lymphoblastic (diffuse) lymphoma, unspecified site 🐾

C83.51   Lymphoblastic (diffuse) lymphoma, lymph nodes of head, face, and neck 🐾

C83.52   Lymphoblastic (diffuse) lymphoma, intrathoracic lymph nodes 🐾

C83.53   Lymphoblastic (diffuse) lymphoma, intra-abdominal lymph nodes 🐾

C83.54   Lymphoblastic (diffuse) lymphoma, lymph nodes of axilla and upper limb 🐾

C83.55   Lymphoblastic (diffuse) lymphoma, lymph nodes of inguinal region and lower limb 🐾

C83.56   Lymphoblastic (diffuse) lymphoma, intrapelvic lymph nodes 🐾

C83.57   Lymphoblastic (diffuse) lymphoma, spleen 🐾

C83.58   Lymphoblastic (diffuse) lymphoma, lymph nodes of multiple sites 🐾

C83.59   Lymphoblastic (diffuse) lymphoma, extranodal and solid organ sites 🐾

● **C83.7**   **Burkitt lymphoma**
Form of small cell lymphoma
Atypical Burkitt lymphoma
Burkitt-like lymphoma

Excludes1   mature B-cell leukemia Burkitt type (C91.A-)

C83.70   Burkitt lymphoma, unspecified site 🐾

C83.71   Burkitt lymphoma, lymph nodes of head, face, and neck 🐾

C83.72   Burkitt lymphoma, intrathoracic lymph nodes 🐾

C83.73   Burkitt lymphoma, intra-abdominal lymph nodes 🐾

C83.74   Burkitt lymphoma, lymph nodes of axilla and upper limb 🐾

C83.75   Burkitt lymphoma, lymph nodes of inguinal region and lower limb 🐾

C83.76   Burkitt lymphoma, intrapelvic lymph nodes 🐾

C83.77   Burkitt lymphoma, spleen 🐾

C83.78   Burkitt lymphoma, lymph nodes of multiple sites 🐾

C83.79   Burkitt lymphoma, extranodal and solid organ sites 🐾

● **C83.8**   **Other non-follicular lymphoma**
Intravascular large B-cell lymphoma
Lymphoid granulomatosis
Primary effusion B-cell lymphoma

Excludes1   mediastinal (thymic) large B-cell lymphoma (C85.2-)
T-cell rich B-cell lymphoma (C83.3-)

C83.80   Other non-follicular lymphoma, unspecified site 🐾

C83.81   Other non-follicular lymphoma, lymph nodes of head, face, and neck 🐾

C83.82   Other non-follicular lymphoma, intrathoracic lymph nodes 🐾

C83.83   Other non-follicular lymphoma, intra-abdominal lymph nodes 🐾

C83.84   Other non-follicular lymphoma, lymph nodes of axilla and upper limb 🐾

C83.85   Other non-follicular lymphoma, lymph nodes of inguinal region and lower limb 🐾

C83.86   Other non-follicular lymphoma, intrapelvic lymph nodes 🐾

C83.87   Other non-follicular lymphoma, spleen 🐾

C83.88   Other non-follicular lymphoma, lymph nodes of multiple sites 🐾

C83.89   Other non-follicular lymphoma, extranodal and solid organ sites 🐾

● **C83.9**   **Non-follicular (diffuse) lymphoma, unspecified**

C83.90   Non-follicular (diffuse) lymphoma, unspecified, unspecified site 🐾

C83.91   Non-follicular (diffuse) lymphoma, unspecified, lymph nodes of head, face, and neck 🐾

C83.92   Non-follicular (diffuse) lymphoma, unspecified, intrathoracic lymph nodes 🐾

C83.93   Non-follicular (diffuse) lymphoma, unspecified, intra-abdominal lymph nodes 🐾

C83.94   Non-follicular (diffuse) lymphoma, unspecified, lymph nodes of axilla and upper limb 🐾

C83.95   Non-follicular (diffuse) lymphoma, unspecified, lymph nodes of inguinal region and lower limb 🐾

C83.96   Non-follicular (diffuse) lymphoma, unspecified, intrapelvic lymph nodes 🐾

C83.97   Non-follicular (diffuse) lymphoma, unspecified, spleen 🐾

C83.98   Non-follicular (diffuse) lymphoma, unspecified, lymph nodes of multiple sites 🐾

C83.99   Non-follicular (diffuse) lymphoma, unspecified, extranodal and solid organ sites 🐾

● **C84**   **Mature T/NK-cell lymphomas**
Excludes1   personal history of non-Hodgkin lymphoma (Z85.72)

● **C84.0**   **Mycosis fungoides**
*Chronic or rapidly progressive form of cutaneous T-cell
lymphoma; AKA granuloma fungoides*

Excludes1   peripheral T-cell lymphoma, not classified (C84.4-)

C84.00   Mycosis fungoides, unspecified site 🐾

C84.01   Mycosis fungoides, lymph nodes of head, face, and neck 🐾

C84.02   Mycosis fungoides, intrathoracic lymph nodes 🐾

C84.03   Mycosis fungoides, intra-abdominal lymph nodes 🐾

C84.04   Mycosis fungoides, lymph nodes of axilla and upper limb 🐾

C84.05   Mycosis fungoides, lymph nodes of inguinal region and lower limb 🐾

C84.06   Mycosis fungoides, intrapelvic lymph nodes 🐾

C84.07   Mycosis fungoides, spleen 🐾

C84.08   Mycosis fungoides, lymph nodes of multiple sites 🐾

C84.09   Mycosis fungoides, extranodal and solid organ sites 🐾

● **C84.1**   **Sézary disease**
Type of cutaneous lymphoma affecting T-cells

C84.10   Sézary disease, unspecified site 🐾

C84.11   Sézary disease, lymph nodes of head, face, and neck 🐾

C84.12   Sézary disease, intrathoracic lymph nodes 🐾

C84.13   Sézary disease, intra-abdominal lymph nodes 🐾

C84.14   Sézary disease, lymph nodes of axilla and upper limb 🐾

C84.15   Sézary disease, lymph nodes of inguinal region and lower limb 🐾

C84.16   Sézary disease, intrapelvic lymph nodes 🐾

C84.17   Sézary disease, spleen 🐾

C84.18   Sézary disease, lymph nodes of multiple sites 🐾

C84.19   Sézary disease, extranodal and solid organ sites 🐾

● **C84.4 Peripheral T-cell lymphoma, not classified**
*Diverse group of blood carcinomas originating from T-cells,
requiring aggressive chemotherapy*
Lennert's lymphoma
Lymphoepithelioid lymphoma
Mature T-cell lymphoma, not elsewhere classified

C84.40 Peripheral T-cell lymphoma, not classified, unspecified site 🦠

C84.41 Peripheral T-cell lymphoma, not classified, lymph nodes of head, face, and neck 🦠

C84.42 Peripheral T-cell lymphoma, not classified, intrathoracic lymph nodes 🦠

C84.43 Peripheral T-cell lymphoma, not classified, intra-abdominal lymph nodes 🦠

C84.44 Peripheral T-cell lymphoma, not classified, lymph nodes of axilla and upper limb 🦠

C84.45 Peripheral T-cell lymphoma, not classified, lymph nodes of inguinal region and lower limb 🦠

C84.46 Peripheral T-cell lymphoma, not classified, intrapelvic lymph nodes 🦠

C84.47 Peripheral T-cell lymphoma, not classified, spleen 🦠

C84.48 Peripheral T-cell lymphoma, not classified, lymph nodes of multiple sites 🦠

C84.49 Peripheral T-cell lymphoma, not classified, extranodal and solid organ sites 🦠

● **C84.6 Anaplastic large cell lymphoma, ALK-positive**
Anaplastic large cell lymphoma, CD30-positive

C84.60 Anaplastic large cell lymphoma, ALK-positive, unspecified site 🦠

C84.61 Anaplastic large cell lymphoma, ALK-positive, lymph nodes of head, face, and neck 🦠

C84.62 Anaplastic large cell lymphoma, ALK-positive, intrathoracic lymph nodes 🦠

C84.63 Anaplastic large cell lymphoma, ALK-positive, intra-abdominal lymph nodes 🦠

C84.64 Anaplastic large cell lymphoma, ALK-positive, lymph nodes of axilla and upper limb 🦠

C84.65 Anaplastic large cell lymphoma, ALK-positive, lymph nodes of inguinal region and lower limb 🦠

C84.66 Anaplastic large cell lymphoma, ALK-positive, intrapelvic lymph nodes 🦠

C84.67 Anaplastic large cell lymphoma, ALK-positive, spleen 🦠

C84.68 Anaplastic large cell lymphoma, ALK-positive, lymph nodes of multiple sites 🦠

C84.69 Anaplastic large cell lymphoma, ALK-positive, extranodal and solid organ sites 🦠

● **C84.7 Anaplastic large cell lymphoma, ALK-negative**
Excludes1   primary cutaneous CD30-positive T-cell proliferations (C86.6-)

C84.70 Anaplastic large cell lymphoma, ALK-negative, unspecified site 🦠

C84.71 Anaplastic large cell lymphoma, ALK-negative, lymph nodes of head, face, and neck 🦠

C84.72 Anaplastic large cell lymphoma, ALK-negative, intrathoracic lymph nodes 🦠

C84.73 Anaplastic large cell lymphoma, ALK-negative, intra-abdominal lymph nodes 🦠

C84.74 Anaplastic large cell lymphoma, ALK-negative, lymph nodes of axilla and upper limb 🦠

C84.75 Anaplastic large cell lymphoma, ALK-negative, lymph nodes of inguinal region and lower limb 🦠

C84.76 Anaplastic large cell lymphoma, ALK-negative, intrapelvic lymph nodes 🦠

C84.77 Anaplastic large cell lymphoma, ALK-negative, spleen 🦠

Item 2-7 Lymphosarcoma, also known as malignant lymphoma, is a cancer of the lymph system exhibiting abnormal cells encompassing an entire lymph node creating a diffuse pattern without any definite organization. Diffuse pattern lymphoma has a more unfavorable survival outlook than those with a follicular or nodular pattern. Reticulosarcoma is the most common aggressive form of non-Hodgkin lymphoma.

C84.78 Anaplastic large cell lymphoma, ALK-negative, lymph nodes of multiple sites 🦠

C84.79 Anaplastic large cell lymphoma, ALK-negative, extranodal and solid organ sites 🦠

● **C84.A Cutaneous T-cell lymphoma, unspecified**

C84.A0 Cutaneous T-cell lymphoma, unspecified, unspecified site 🦠

C84.A1 Cutaneous T-cell lymphoma, unspecified lymph nodes of head, face, and neck 🦠

C84.A2 Cutaneous T-cell lymphoma, unspecified, intrathoracic lymph nodes 🦠

C84.A3 Cutaneous T-cell lymphoma, unspecified, intra-abdominal lymph nodes 🦠

C84.A4 Cutaneous T-cell lymphoma, unspecified, lymph nodes of axilla and upper limb 🦠

C84.A5 Cutaneous T-cell lymphoma, unspecified, lymph nodes of inguinal region and lower limb 🦠

C84.A6 Cutaneous T-cell lymphoma, unspecified, intrapelvic lymph nodes 🦠

C84.A7 Cutaneous T-cell lymphoma, unspecified, spleen 🦠

C84.A8 Cutaneous T-cell lymphoma, unspecified, lymph nodes of multiple sites 🦠

C84.A9 Cutaneous T-cell lymphoma, unspecified, extranodal and solid organ sites 🦠

● **C84.Z Other mature T/NK-cell lymphomas**
Note: If T-cell lineage or involvement is mentioned in conjunction with a specific lymphoma, code to the more specific description.

Excludes1   angioimmunoblastic T-cell lymphoma (C86.5)
blastic NK-cell lymphoma (C86.4)
enteropathy-type T-cell lymphoma (C86.2)
extranodal NK-cell lymphoma, nasal type (C86.0)
hepatosplenic T-cell lymphoma (C86.1)
primary cutaneous CD30-positive T-cell proliferations (C86.6)
subcutaneous panniculitis-like T-cell lymphoma (C86.3)
T-cell leukemia (C91.1-)

C84.Z0 Other mature T/NK-cell lymphomas, unspecified site 🦠

C84.Z1 Other mature T/NK-cell lymphomas, lymph nodes of head, face, and neck 🦠

C84.Z2 Other mature T/NK-cell lymphomas, intrathoracic lymph nodes 🦠

C84.Z3 Other mature T/NK-cell lymphomas, intra-abdominal lymph nodes 🦠

C84.Z4 Other mature T/NK-cell lymphomas, lymph nodes of axilla and upper limb 🦠

C84.Z5 Other mature T/NK-cell lymphomas, lymph nodes of inguinal region and lower limb 🦠

C84.Z6 Other mature T/NK-cell lymphomas, intrapelvic lymph nodes 🦠

C84.Z7 Other mature T/NK-cell lymphomas, spleen 🦠

C84.Z8 Other mature T/NK-cell lymphomas, lymph nodes of multiple sites 🦠

C84.Z9 Other mature T/NK-cell lymphomas, extranodal and solid organ sites 🦠

▶ New 　 Revised 　 ~~deleted~~ Deleted 　 Excludes 1 　 Excludes 2 　 Includes 　 Use additional 　 Code first 　 Code also 　 Key words
OGCR Official Guidelines 　 X Assign placeholder X 　 ● Use Additional Character(s) 　 ▶ Manifestation Code 　 🦠 Hierarchical Condition Category 　 Coding Clinic

● **C84.9**   **Mature T/NK-cell lymphomas, unspecified**
NK/T cell lymphoma NOS

> **Excludes1**   mature T-cell lymphoma, not elsewhere
> classified (C84.4-)

C84.90   Mature T/NK-cell lymphomas, unspecified, unspecified site 🦠

C84.91   Mature T/NK-cell lymphomas, unspecified, lymph nodes of head, face, and neck 🦠

C84.92   Mature T/NK-cell lymphomas, unspecified, intrathoracic lymph nodes 🦠

C84.93   Mature T/NK-cell lymphomas, unspecified, intra-abdominal lymph nodes 🦠

C84.94   Mature T/NK-cell lymphomas, unspecified, lymph nodes of axilla and upper limb 🦠

C84.95   Mature T/NK-cell lymphomas, unspecified, lymph nodes of inguinal region and lower limb 🦠

C84.96   Mature T/NK-cell lymphomas, unspecified, intrapelvic lymph nodes 🦠

C84.97   Mature T/NK-cell lymphomas, unspecified, spleen 🦠

C84.98   Mature T/NK-cell lymphomas, unspecified, lymph nodes of multiple sites 🦠

C84.99   Mature T/NK-cell lymphomas, unspecified, extranodal and solid organ sites 🦠

● **C85**   **Other specified and unspecified types of non-Hodgkin lymphoma**

> **Excludes1**   other specified types of T/NK-cell lymphoma (C86.-)
> personal history of non-Hodgkin lymphoma (Z85.72)

● **C85.1**   **Unspecified B-cell lymphoma**

> **Note:** If B-cell lineage or involvement is mentioned in conjunction with a specific lymphoma, code to the more specific description.

C85.10   Unspecified B-cell lymphoma, unspecified site 🦠

C85.11   Unspecified B-cell lymphoma, lymph nodes of head, face, and neck 🦠

C85.12   Unspecified B-cell lymphoma, intrathoracic lymph nodes 🦠

C85.13   Unspecified B-cell lymphoma, intra-abdominal lymph nodes 🦠

C85.14   Unspecified B-cell lymphoma, lymph nodes of axilla and upper limb 🦠

C85.15   Unspecified B-cell lymphoma, lymph nodes of inguinal region and lower limb 🦠

C85.16   Unspecified B-cell lymphoma, intrapelvic lymph nodes 🦠

C85.17   Unspecified B-cell lymphoma, spleen 🦠

C85.18   Unspecified B-cell lymphoma, lymph nodes of multiple sites 🦠

C85.19   Unspecified B-cell lymphoma, extranodal and solid organ sites 🦠

● **C85.2**   **Mediastinal (thymic) large B-cell lymphoma**

C85.20   Mediastinal (thymic) large B-cell lymphoma, unspecified site 🦠

C85.21   Mediastinal (thymic) large B-cell lymphoma, lymph nodes of head, face, and neck 🦠

C85.22   Mediastinal (thymic) large B-cell lymphoma, intrathoracic lymph nodes 🦠

C85.23   Mediastinal (thymic) large B-cell lymphoma, intra-abdominal lymph nodes 🦠

C85.24   Mediastinal (thymic) large B-cell lymphoma, lymph nodes of axilla and upper limb 🦠

C85.25   Mediastinal (thymic) large B-cell lymphoma, lymph nodes of inguinal region and lower limb 🦠

C85.26   Mediastinal (thymic) large B-cell lymphoma, intrapelvic lymph nodes 🦠

C85.27   Mediastinal (thymic) large B-cell lymphoma, spleen 🦠

C85.28   Mediastinal (thymic) large B-cell lymphoma, lymph nodes of multiple sites 🦠

C85.29   Mediastinal (thymic) large B-cell lymphoma, extranodal and solid organ sites 🦠

● **C85.8**   **Other specified types of non-Hodgkin lymphoma**

C85.80   Other specified types of non-Hodgkin lymphoma, unspecified site 🦠

C85.81   Other specified types of non-Hodgkin lymphoma, lymph nodes of head, face, and neck 🦠

C85.82   Other specified types of non-Hodgkin lymphoma, intrathoracic lymph nodes 🦠

C85.83   Other specified types of non-Hodgkin lymphoma, intra-abdominal lymph nodes 🦠

C85.84   Other specified types of non-Hodgkin lymphoma, lymph nodes of axilla and upper limb 🦠

C85.85   Other specified types of non-Hodgkin lymphoma, lymph nodes of inguinal region and lower limb 🦠

C85.86   Other specified types of non-Hodgkin lymphoma, intrapelvic lymph nodes 🦠

C85.87   Other specified types of non-Hodgkin lymphoma, spleen 🦠

C85.88   Other specified types of non-Hodgkin lymphoma, lymph nodes of multiple sites 🦠

C85.89   Other specified types of non-Hodgkin lymphoma, extranodal and solid organ sites 🦠

● **C85.9**   **Non-Hodgkin lymphoma, unspecified**
Lymphoma NOS
Malignant lymphoma NOS
Non-Hodgkin lymphoma NOS

C85.90   Non-Hodgkin lymphoma, unspecified, unspecified site 🦠

C85.91   Non-Hodgkin lymphoma, unspecified, lymph nodes of head, face, and neck 🦠

C85.92   Non-Hodgkin lymphoma, unspecified, intrathoracic lymph nodes 🦠

C85.93   Non-Hodgkin lymphoma, unspecified, intra-abdominal lymph nodes 🦠

C85.94   Non-Hodgkin lymphoma, unspecified, lymph nodes of axilla and upper limb 🦠

C85.95   Non-Hodgkin lymphoma, unspecified, lymph nodes of inguinal region and lower limb 🦠

C85.96   Non-Hodgkin lymphoma, unspecified, intrapelvic lymph nodes 🦠

C85.97   Non-Hodgkin lymphoma, unspecified, spleen 🦠

C85.98   Non-Hodgkin lymphoma, unspecified, lymph nodes of multiple sites 🦠

C85.99   Non-Hodgkin lymphoma, unspecified, extranodal and solid organ sites 🦠

CHAPTER 2 (C00-D49)

C86 Other specified types of T/NK-cell lymphoma

> Excludes1 anaplastic large cell lymphoma, ALK negative (C84.7-)
> anaplastic large cell lymphoma, ALK positive (C84.6-)
> mature T/NK-cell lymphomas (C84.-)
> other specified types of non-Hodgkin lymphoma (C85.8-)

C86.0 Extranodal NK/T-cell lymphoma, nasal type

C86.1 Hepatosplenic T-cell lymphoma
 Alpha-beta and gamma delta types

C86.2 Enteropathy-type (intestinal) T-cell lymphoma
 Enteropathy associated T-cell lymphoma

C86.3 Subcutaneous panniculitis-like T-cell lymphoma

C86.4 Blastic NK-cell lymphoma
 Blastic plasmacytoid dendritic cell neoplasm (BPDCN)

C86.5 Angioimmunoblastic T-cell lymphoma
 Angioimmunoblastic lymphadenopathy with dysproteinemia (AILD)

C86.6 Primary cutaneous CD30-positive T-cell proliferations
 Lymphomatoid papulosis
 Primary cutaneous anaplastic large cell lymphoma
 Primary cutaneous CD30-positive large T-cell lymphoma

C88 Malignant immunoproliferative diseases and certain other B-cell lymphomas
 Diseases involving immune system

> Excludes1 B-cell lymphoma, unspecified (C85.1-)
> personal history of other malignant neoplasms of lymphoid, hematopoietic and related tissues (Z85.79)

C88.0 Waldenström's macroglobulinemia
 Lymphoplasmacytic lymphoma with IgM-production
 Macroglobulinemia (idiopathic) (primary)
> Excludes1 small cell B-cell lymphoma (C83.0)

C88.2 Heavy chain disease
 Franklin disease
 Gamma heavy chain disease
 Mu heavy chain disease

C88.3 Immunoproliferative small intestinal disease
 Alpha heavy chain disease
 Mediterranean lymphoma

C88.4 Extranodal marginal zone B-cell lymphoma of mucosa-associated lymphoid tissue [MALT-lymphoma]
 Lymphoma of skin-associated lymphoid tissue [SALT-lymphoma]
 Lymphoma of bronchial-associated lymphoid tissue [BALT-lymphoma]
> Excludes1 high malignant (diffuse large B-cell) lymphoma (C83.3-)

C88.8 Other malignant immunoproliferative diseases

C88.9 Malignant immunoproliferative disease, unspecified
 Immunoproliferative disease NOS

C90 Multiple myeloma and malignant plasma cell neoplasms
> Excludes1 personal history of other malignant neoplasms of lymphoid, hematopoietic and related tissues (Z85.79)

C90.0 Multiple myeloma
 Kahler's disease
 Medullary plasmacytoma
 Myelomatosis
 Plasma cell myeloma
> Excludes1 solitary myeloma (C90.3-)
> solitary plasmacytoma (C90.3-)

C90.00 Multiple myeloma not having achieved remission
 Multiple myeloma with failed remission
 Multiple myeloma NOS

C90.01 Multiple myeloma in remission

C90.02 Multiple myeloma in relapse

Item 2–8 Multiple myeloma is a cancer of a plasma cell (a type of white blood cell) and is an incurable but treatable disease. Immunoproliferative neoplasm is a term for diseases (mostly cancers) in which the immune system cells proliferate.

C90.1 Plasma cell leukemia
 Rare type of acute leukemia
 Plasmacytic leukemia
 Coding Clinic: 2019, Q2, P30

C90.10 Plasma cell leukemia not having achieved remission
 Plasma cell leukemia with failed remission
 Plasma cell leukemia NOS
 Coding Clinic: 2019, Q2, P30

C90.11 Plasma cell leukemia in remission

C90.12 Plasma cell leukemia in relapse

C90.2 Extramedullary plasmacytoma
 Malignant monoclonal plasma cell tumor growing in soft tissue; AKA plasma cell dyscrasias

C90.20 Extramedullary plasmacytoma not having achieved remission
 Extramedullary plasmacytoma with failed remission
 Extramedullary plasmacytoma NOS

C90.21 Extramedullary plasmacytoma in remission

C90.22 Extramedullary plasmacytoma in relapse

C90.3 Solitary plasmacytoma
 Localized malignant plasma cell tumor NOS
 Plasmacytoma NOS
 Solitary myeloma

C90.30 Solitary plasmacytoma not having achieved remission
 Solitary plasmacytoma with failed remission
 Solitary plasmacytoma NOS

C90.31 Solitary plasmacytoma in remission

C90.32 Solitary plasmacytoma in relapse

C91 Lymphoid leukemia
 Type of leukemia affecting circulating cells of lymphoid origin
> Excludes1 personal history of leukemia (Z85.6)

C91.0 Acute lymphoblastic leukemia [ALL]
> Note: Codes in subcategory C91.0 should only be used for T-cell and B-cell precursor leukemia

C91.00 Acute lymphoblastic leukemia not having achieved remission
 Acute lymphoblastic leukemia with failed remission
 Acute lymphoblastic leukemia NOS

C91.01 Acute lymphoblastic leukemia, in remission

C91.02 Acute lymphoblastic leukemia, in relapse

C91.1 Chronic lymphocytic leukemia of B-cell type
 Lymphoplasmacytic leukemia
 Richter syndrome
> Excludes1 lymphoplasmacytic lymphoma (C83.0-)

C91.10 Chronic lymphocytic leukemia of B-cell type not having achieved remission
 Chronic lymphocytic leukemia of B-cell type with failed remission
 Chronic lymphocytic leukemia of B-cell type NOS

C91.11 Chronic lymphocytic leukemia of B-cell type in remission

C91.12 Chronic lymphocytic leukemia of B-cell type in relapse

Item 2–9 Leukemia is a cancer (acute or chronic) of the blood-forming tissues of the bone marrow. Blood cells all start out as stem cells. They mature and become red cells, white cells, or platelets. There are three main types of leukocytes (white cells that fight infection): monocytes, lymphocytes, and granulocytes. **Acute monocytic leukemia** (AML) affects monocytes. **Acute lymphoid leukemia** (ALL) affects lymphocytes, and **acute myeloid leukemia** (AML) affects cells that typically develop into white blood cells (not lymphocytes), though it may develop in other blood cells.

New ▸ Revised ⇒ deleted Deleted Excludes 1 Excludes 2 Includes Use additional Code first Code also Key words
OGCR Official Guidelines X Assign placeholder X ● Use Additional Character(s) ▸ Manifestation Code Hierarchical Condition Category Coding Clinic

● **C91.3**   **Prolymphocytic leukemia of B-cell type**
Chronic leukemia with symptoms of large number of circulating lymphocytes

     C91.30   **Prolymphocytic leukemia of B-cell type not having achieved remission** 🔗
         Prolymphocytic leukemia of B-cell type with failed remission
         Prolymphocytic leukemia of B-cell type NOS

     C91.31   **Prolymphocytic leukemia of B-cell type, in remission** 🔗

     C91.32   **Prolymphocytic leukemia of B-cell type, in relapse** 🔗

● **C91.4**   **Hairy cell leukemia**
Chronic leukemia with splenomegaly and excessive number of abnormal large mononuclear cells covered by hairlike villi
Leukemic reticuloendotheliosis

     C91.40   **Hairy cell leukemia not having achieved remission** 🔗
         Hairy cell leukemia with failed remission
         Hairy cell leukemia NOS

     C91.41   **Hairy cell leukemia, in remission** 🔗

     C91.42   **Hairy cell leukemia, in relapse** 🔗

● **C91.5**   **Adult T-cell lymphoma/leukemia (HTLV-1-associated)**
Acute variant of adult T-cell lymphoma/leukemia (HTLV-1-associated)
Chronic variant of adult T-cell lymphoma/leukemia (HTLV-1-associated)
Lymphomatoid variant of adult T-cell lymphoma/leukemia (HTLV-1-associated)
Smouldering variant of adult T-cell lymphoma/leukemia (HTLV-1-associated)

     C91.50   **Adult T-cell lymphoma/leukemia (HTLV-1-associated) not having achieved remission** 🔗   A
         Adult T-cell lymphoma/leukemia (HTLV-1-associated) with failed remission
         Adult T-cell lymphoma/leukemia (HTLV-1-associated) NOS

     C91.51   **Adult T-cell lymphoma/leukemia (HTLV-1-associated), in remission** 🔗   A

     C91.52   **Adult T-cell lymphoma/leukemia (HTLV-1-associated), in relapse** 🔗   A

● **C91.6**   **Prolymphocytic leukemia of T-cell type**

     C91.60   **Prolymphocytic leukemia of T-cell type not having achieved remission** 🔗
         Prolymphocytic leukemia of T-cell type with failed remission
         Prolymphocytic leukemia of T-cell type NOS

     C91.61   **Prolymphocytic leukemia of T-cell type, in remission** 🔗

     C91.62   **Prolymphocytic leukemia of T-cell type, in relapse** 🔗

● **C91.A**   **Mature B-cell leukemia Burkitt-type**

     Excludes1   Burkitt lymphoma (C83.7-)

     C91.A0   **Mature B-cell leukemia Burkitt-type not having achieved remission** 🔗
         Mature B-cell leukemia Burkitt-type with failed remission
         Mature B-cell leukemia Burkitt-type NOS

     C91.A1   **Mature B-cell leukemia Burkitt-type, in remission** 🔗

     C91.A2   **Mature B-cell leukemia Burkitt-type, in relapse** 🔗

● **C91.Z**   **Other lymphoid leukemia**
T-cell large granular lymphocytic leukemia (associated with rheumatoid arthritis)

     C91.Z0   **Other lymphoid leukemia not having achieved remission** 🔗
         Other lymphoid leukemia with failed remission
         Other lymphoid leukemia NOS
         Coding Clinic: 2019, Q2, P25

     C91.Z1   **Other lymphoid leukemia, in remission** 🔗

     C91.Z2   **Other lymphoid leukemia, in relapse** 🔗

● **C91.9**   **Lymphoid leukemia, unspecified**

     C91.90   **Lymphoid leukemia, unspecified not having achieved remission** 🔗
         Lymphoid leukemia with failed remission
         Lymphoid leukemia NOS

     C91.91   **Lymphoid leukemia, unspecified, in remission** 🔗

     C91.92   **Lymphoid leukemia, unspecified, in relapse** 🔗

● **C92**   **Myeloid leukemia**

     Includes   granulocytic leukemia
                 myelogenous leukemia

     Excludes1   personal history of leukemia (Z85.6)

     Coding Clinic: 2019, Q1, P16

● **C92.0**   **Acute myeloblastic leukemia**
Acute myeloblastic leukemia, minimal differentiation
Acute myeloblastic leukemia (with maturation)
Acute myeloblastic leukemia 1/ETO
Acute myeloblastic leukemia M0
Acute myeloblastic leukemia M1
Acute myeloblastic leukemia M2
Acute myeloblastic leukemia with t(8;21)
Acute myeloblastic leukemia (without a FAB classification) NOS
Refractory anemia with excess blasts in transformation [RAEB T]

     Excludes1   acute exacerbation of chronic myeloid leukemia (C92.10)
                 refractory anemia with excess of blasts not in transformation (D46.2-)

     Coding Clinic: 2018, Q4, P87

     C92.00   **Acute myeloblastic leukemia, not having achieved remission** 🔗
         Acute myeloblastic leukemia with failed remission
         Acute myeloblastic leukemia NOS

     C92.01   **Acute myeloblastic leukemia, in remission** 🔗

     C92.02   **Acute myeloblastic leukemia, in relapse** 🔗

● **C92.1**   **Chronic myeloid leukemia, BCR/ABL-positive**
Chronic myelogenous leukemia, Philadelphia chromosome (Ph1) positive
Chronic myelogenous leukemia, t(9;22) (q34;q11)
Chronic myelogenous leukemia with crisis of blast cells

     Excludes1   atypical chronic myeloid leukemia BCR/ABL-negative (C92.2-)
                 chronic myelomonocytic leukemia (C93.1-)
                 chronic myeloproliferative disease (D47.1)

     C92.10   **Chronic myeloid leukemia, BCR/ABL-positive, not having achieved remission** 🔗
         Chronic myeloid leukemia, BCR/ABL-positive with failed remission
         Chronic myeloid leukemia, BCR/ABL-positive NOS
         Coding Clinic: 2017, Q1, P7

     C92.11   **Chronic myeloid leukemia, BCR/ABL-positive, in remission** 🔗

     C92.12   **Chronic myeloid leukemia, BCR/ABL-positive, in relapse** 🔗

● **C92.2**   **Atypical chronic myeloid leukemia, BCR/ABL-negative**

     C92.20   **Atypical chronic myeloid leukemia, BCR/ABL-negative, not having achieved remission** 🔗
         Atypical chronic myeloid leukemia, BCR/ABL-negative with failed remission
         Atypical chronic myeloid leukemia, BCR/ABL-negative NOS

     C92.21   **Atypical chronic myeloid leukemia, BCR/ABL-negative, in remission** 🔗

     C92.22   **Atypical chronic myeloid leukemia, BCR/ABL-negative, in relapse** 🔗

CHAPTER 2 (C00-D49)

● **C92.3**   **Myeloid sarcoma**
     A malignant tumor of immature myeloid cells
     Chloroma
     Granulocytic sarcoma

     C92.30   **Myeloid sarcoma, not having achieved remission** 🦠
         Myeloid sarcoma with failed remission
         Myeloid sarcoma NOS

     C92.31   **Myeloid sarcoma, in remission** 🦠

     C92.32   **Myeloid sarcoma, in relapse** 🦠

● **C92.4**   **Acute promyelocytic leukemia**
     AML M3
     AML Me with t(15;17) and variants

     C92.40   **Acute promyelocytic leukemia, not having achieved remission** 🦠
         Acute promyelocytic leukemia with failed remission
         Acute promyelocytic leukemia NOS

     C92.41   **Acute promyelocytic leukemia, in remission** 🦠

     C92.42   **Acute promyelocytic leukemia, in relapse** 🦠

● **C92.5**   **Acute myelomonocytic leukemia**
     AML M4
     AML M4 Eo with inv(16) or t(16;16)

     C92.50   **Acute myelomonocytic leukemia, not having achieved remission** 🦠
         Acute myelomonocytic leukemia with failed remission
         Acute myelomonocytic leukemia NOS

     C92.51   **Acute myelomonocytic leukemia, in remission** 🦠

     C92.52   **Acute myelomonocytic leukemia, in relapse** 🦠

● **C92.6**   **Acute myeloid leukemia with 11q23-abnormality**
     Acute myeloid leukemia with variation of MLL-gene

     C92.60   **Acute myeloid leukemia with 11q23-abnormality not having achieved remission** 🦠
         Acute myeloid leukemia with 11q23-abnormality with failed remission
         Acute myeloid leukemia with 11q23-abnormality NOS

     C92.61   **Acute myeloid leukemia with 11q23-abnormality in remission** 🦠

     C92.62   **Acute myeloid leukemia with 11q23-abnormality in relapse** 🦠

● **C92.A**   **Acute myeloid leukemia with multilineage dysplasia**
     Acute myeloid leukemia with dysplasia of remaining hematopoesis and/or myelodysplastic disease in its history

     C92.A0   **Acute myeloid leukemia with multilineage dysplasia, not having achieved remission** 🦠
         Acute myeloid leukemia with multilineage dysplasia with failed remission
         Acute myeloid leukemia with multilineage dysplasia NOS

     C92.A1   **Acute myeloid leukemia with multilineage dysplasia, in remission** 🦠

     C92.A2   **Acute myeloid leukemia with multilineage dysplasia, in relapse** 🦠

● **C92.Z**   **Other myeloid leukemia**

     C92.Z0   **Other myeloid leukemia not having achieved remission** 🦠
         Myeloid leukemia NEC with failed remission
         Myeloid leukemia NEC

     C92.Z1   **Other myeloid leukemia, in remission** 🦠

     C92.Z2   **Other myeloid leukemia, in relapse** 🦠

● **C92.9**   **Myeloid leukemia, unspecified**

     C92.90   **Myeloid leukemia, unspecified, not having achieved remission** 🦠
         Myeloid leukemia, unspecified with failed remission
         Myeloid leukemia, unspecified NOS

     C92.91   **Myeloid leukemia, unspecified in remission** 🦠

     C92.92   **Myeloid leukemia, unspecified in relapse** 🦠

● **C93**   **Monocytic leukemia**
     Includes   monocytoid leukemia
     Excludes1   personal history of leukemia (Z85.6)

     ● **C93.0**   **Acute monoblastic/monocytic leukemia**
         AML M5
         AML M5a
         AML M5b

         C93.00   **Acute monoblastic/monocytic leukemia, not having achieved remission** 🦠
             Acute monoblastic/monocytic leukemia with failed remission
             Acute monoblastic/monocytic leukemia NOS

         C93.01   **Acute monoblastic/monocytic leukemia, in remission** 🦠

         C93.02   **Acute monoblastic/monocytic leukemia, in relapse** 🦠

     ● **C93.1**   **Chronic myelomonocytic leukemia**
         Chronic monocytic leukemia
         CMML-1
         CMML-2
         CMML with eosinophilia
         ▶ Code also, if applicable, eosinophilia (D72.18)

         C93.10   **Chronic myelomonocytic leukemia not having achieved remission** 🦠
             Chronic myelomonocytic leukemia with failed remission
             Chronic myelomonocytic leukemia NOS

         C93.11   **Chronic myelomonocytic leukemia, in remission** 🦠

         C93.12   **Chronic myelomonocytic leukemia, in relapse** 🦠

     ● **C93.3**   **Juvenile myelomonocytic leukemia**

         C93.30   **Juvenile myelomonocytic leukemia, not having achieved remission** 🦠   P
             Juvenile myelomonocytic leukemia with failed remission
             Juvenile myelomonocytic leukemia NOS

         C93.31   **Juvenile myelomonocytic leukemia, in remission** 🦠   P

         C93.32   **Juvenile myelomonocytic leukemia, in relapse** 🦠   P

     ● **C93.Z**   **Other monocytic leukemia**

         C93.Z0   **Other monocytic leukemia, not having achieved remission** 🦠
             Other monocytic leukemia NOS

         C93.Z1   **Other monocytic leukemia, in remission** 🦠

         C93.Z2   **Other monocytic leukemia, in relapse** 🦠

     ● **C93.9**   **Monocytic leukemia, unspecified**

         C93.90   **Monocytic leukemia, unspecified, not having achieved remission** 🦠
             Monocytic leukemia, unspecified with failed remission
             Monocytic leukemia, unspecified NOS

         C93.91   **Monocytic leukemia, unspecified in remission** 🦠

         C93.92   **Monocytic leukemia, unspecified in relapse** 🦠

● **C94**   **Other leukemias of specified cell type**
     Excludes1   leukemic reticuloendotheliosis (C91.4-)
             myelodysplastic syndromes (D46.-)
             personal history of leukemia (Z85.6)
             plasma cell leukemia (C90.1-)

     ● **C94.0**   **Acute erythroid leukemia**
         Acute myeloid leukemia M6(a)(b)
         Erythroleukemia

         C94.00   **Acute erythroid leukemia, not having achieved remission** 🦠
             Acute erythroid leukemia with failed remission
             Acute erythroid leukemia NOS

         C94.01   **Acute erythroid leukemia, in remission** 🦠

         C94.02   **Acute erythroid leukemia, in relapse** 🦠

▶ New   ⇒ Revised   ~~deleted~~ Deleted   **Excludes 1**   Excludes 2   **Includes**   Use additional   **Code first**   Code also   **Key words**

OGCR Official Guidelines   X Assign placeholder X   ● Use Additional Character(s)   ▶ Manifestation Code   🦠 Hierarchical Condition Category   **Coding Clinic**

● **C94.2 Acute megakaryoblastic leukemia**
Acute myeloid leukemia M7
Acute megakaryocytic leukemia

  C94.20 Acute megakaryoblastic leukemia not having achieved remission 🔗
Acute megakaryoblastic leukemia with failed remission
Acute megakaryoblastic leukemia NOS

  C94.21 Acute megakaryoblastic leukemia, in remission 🔗

  C94.22 Acute megakaryoblastic leukemia, in relapse 🔗

● **C94.3 Mast cell leukemia**

  C94.30 Mast cell leukemia not having achieved remission 🔗
Mast cell leukemia with failed remission
Mast cell leukemia NOS

  C94.31 Mast cell leukemia, in remission 🔗

  C94.32 Mast cell leukemia, in relapse 🔗

● **C94.4 Acute panmyelosis with myelofibrosis**
Acute myelofibrosis

  Excludes1   myelofibrosis NOS (D75.81)
secondary myelofibrosis NOS (D75.81)

  C94.40 Acute panmyelosis with myelofibrosis not having achieved remission 🔗
Acute myelofibrosis NOS
Acute panmyelosis with myelofibrosis with failed remission
Acute panmyelosis NOS

  C94.41 Acute panmyelosis with myelofibrosis, in remission 🔗

  C94.42 Acute panmyelosis with myelofibrosis, in relapse 🔗

  C94.6 Myelodysplastic disease, not classified 🔗
Myeloproliferative disease, not classified

● **C94.8 Other specified leukemias**
Aggressive NK-cell leukemia
Acute basophilic leukemia

  C94.80 Other specified leukemias not having achieved remission 🔗
Other specified leukemia with failed remission
Other specified leukemias NOS

  C94.81 Other specified leukemias, in remission 🔗

  C94.82 Other specified leukemias, in relapse 🔗

● **C95 Leukemia of unspecified cell type**

  Excludes1   personal history of leukemia (Z85.6)

● **C95.0 Acute leukemia of unspecified cell type**
Acute bilineal leukemia
Acute mixed lineage leukemia
Biphenotypic acute leukemia
Stem cell leukemia of unclear lineage

  Excludes1   acute exacerbation of unspecified chronic leukemia (C95.10)

  C95.00 Acute leukemia of unspecified cell type not having achieved remission 🔗
Acute leukemia of unspecified cell type with failed remission
Acute leukemia NOS

  C95.01 Acute leukemia of unspecified cell type, in remission 🔗

  C95.02 Acute leukemia of unspecified cell type, in relapse 🔗

● **C95.1 Chronic leukemia of unspecified cell type**

  C95.10 Chronic leukemia of unspecified cell type not having achieved remission 🔗
Chronic leukemia of unspecified cell type with failed remission
Chronic leukemia NOS

  C95.11 Chronic leukemia of unspecified cell type, in remission 🔗

  C95.12 Chronic leukemia of unspecified cell type, in relapse 🔗

● **C95.9 Leukemia, unspecified** 🔗

  C95.90 Leukemia, unspecified not having achieved remission 🔗
Leukemia, unspecified with failed remission
Leukemia NOS

  C95.91 Leukemia, unspecified, in remission 🔗

  C95.92 Leukemia, unspecified, in relapse 🔗

● **C96 Other and unspecified malignant neoplasms of lymphoid, hematopoietic and related tissue**

  Excludes1   personal history of other malignant neoplasms of lymphoid, hematopoietic and related tissues (Z85.79)

  C96.0 Multifocal and multisystemic (disseminated) Langerhans-cell histiocytosis 🔗
Histiocytosis X, multisystemic
Letterer-Siwe disease

  Excludes1   adult pulmonary Langerhans cell histiocytosis (J84.82)
multifocal and unisystemic Langerhans-cell histiocytosis (C96.5)
unifocal Langerhans-cell histiocytosis (C96.6)

● **C96.2 Malignant mast cell neoplasm**

  Excludes1   indolent mastocytosis (D47.02)
mast cell leukemia (C94.30)
mastocytosis (congenital) (cutaneous) (Q82.2)

  C96.20 Malignant mast cell neoplasm, unspecified 🔗

  C96.21 Aggressive systemic mastocytosis 🔗

  C96.22 Mast cell sarcoma 🔗

  C96.29 Other malignant mast cell neoplasm 🔗

  C96.4 Sarcoma of dendritic cells (accessory cells) 🔗
Follicular dendritic cell sarcoma
Interdigitating dendritic cell sarcoma
Langerhans cell sarcoma

  C96.5 Multifocal and unisystemic Langerhans-cell histiocytosis 🔗
Hand-Schüller-Christian disease
Histiocytosis X, multifocal

  Excludes1   multifocal and multisystemic (disseminated) Langerhans-cell histiocytosis (C96.0)
unifocal Langerhans-cell histiocytosis (C96.6)

  C96.6 Unifocal Langerhans-cell histiocytosis 🔗
Eosinophilic granuloma
Histiocytosis X, unifocal
Histiocytosis X NOS
Langerhans-cell histiocytosis NOS

  Excludes1   multifocal and multisysemic (disseminated) Langerhans-cell histiocytosis (C96.0)
multifocal and unisystemic Langerhans-cell histiocytosis (C96.5)

  C96.A Histiocytic sarcoma 🔗
Malignant histiocytosis

  C96.Z Other specified malignant neoplasms of lymphoid, hematopoietic and related tissue 🔗

  C96.9 Malignant neoplasm of lymphoid, hematopoietic and related tissue, unspecified 🔗

CHAPTER 2 (C00–D49)

N Newborn Age: 0   **P** Pediatric Age: 0–17   **M** Maternity DX: 12–55   **A** Adult Age: 15–124   ♀ Females Only   ♂ Males Only

709

IN SITU NEOPLASMS (D00-D09)

In situ is carcinoma involving cells in localized tissues that has not spread to nearby tissues

Includes	Bowen's disease
	erythroplasia
	grade III intraepithelial neoplasia
	Queyrat's erythroplasia

● **D00   Carcinoma in situ of oral cavity, esophagus and stomach**

Excludes1   melanoma in situ (D03.-)

● **D00.0   Carcinoma in situ of lip, oral cavity and pharynx**

Use additional code to identify:
exposure to environmental tobacco smoke (Z77.22)
exposure to tobacco smoke in the perinatal period (P96.81)
history of tobacco dependence (Z87.891)
occupational exposure to environmental tobacco smoke (Z57.31)
tobacco dependence (F17.-)
tobacco use (Z72.0)

Excludes1   carcinoma in situ of aryepiglottic fold or interarytenoid fold, laryngeal aspect (D02.0)
carcinoma in situ of epiglottis NOS (D02.0)
carcinoma in situ of epiglottis suprahyoid portion (D02.0)
carcinoma in situ of skin of lip (D03.0, D04.0)

D00.00   Carcinoma in situ of oral cavity, unspecified site

D00.01   Carcinoma in situ of labial mucosa and vermilion border

D00.02   Carcinoma in situ of buccal mucosa

D00.03   Carcinoma in situ of gingiva and edentulous alveolar ridge

D00.04   Carcinoma in situ of soft palate

D00.05   Carcinoma in situ of hard palate

D00.06   Carcinoma in situ of floor of mouth

D00.07   Carcinoma in situ of tongue

D00.08   Carcinoma in situ of pharynx
Carcinoma in situ of aryepiglottic fold NOS
Carcinoma in situ of hypopharyngeal aspect of aryepiglottic fold
Carcinoma in situ of marginal zone of aryepiglottic fold

D00.1   Carcinoma in situ of esophagus

D00.2   Carcinoma in situ of stomach

● **D01   Carcinoma in situ of other and unspecified digestive organs**

Excludes1   melanoma in situ (D03.-)

D01.0   Carcinoma in situ of colon

Excludes1   carcinoma in situ of rectosigmoid junction (D01.1)

D01.1   Carcinoma in situ of rectosigmoid junction

D01.2   Carcinoma in situ of rectum

D01.3   Carcinoma in situ of anus and anal canal
Anal intraepithelial neoplasia III [AIN III]
Severe dysplasia of anus

Excludes1   anal intraepithelial neoplasia I and II [AIN I and AIN II] (K62.82)
carcinoma in situ of anal margin (D04.5)
carcinoma in situ of anal skin (D04.5)
carcinoma in situ of perianal skin (D04.5)

● **D01.4   Carcinoma in situ of other and unspecified parts of intestine**

Excludes1   carcinoma in situ of ampulla of Vater (D01.5)

D01.40   Carcinoma in situ of unspecified part of intestine

D01.49   Carcinoma in situ of other parts of intestine

D01.5   Carcinoma in situ of liver, gallbladder and bile ducts
Carcinoma in situ of ampulla of Vater

D01.7   Carcinoma in situ of other specified digestive organs
Carcinoma in situ of pancreas

D01.9   Carcinoma in situ of digestive organ, unspecified

● **D02   Carcinoma in situ of middle ear and respiratory system**

Use additional code to identify:
exposure to environmental tobacco smoke (Z77.22)
exposure to tobacco smoke in the perinatal period (P96.81)
history of tobacco dependence (Z87.891)
occupational exposure to environmental tobacco smoke (Z57.31)
tobacco dependence (F17.-)
tobacco use (Z72.0)

Excludes1   melanoma in situ (D03.-)

D02.0   Carcinoma in situ of larynx
Carcinoma in situ of aryepiglottic fold or interarytenoid fold, laryngeal aspect
Carcinoma in situ of epiglottis (suprahyoid portion)

Excludes1   carcinoma in situ of aryepiglottic fold or interarytenoid fold NOS (D00.08)
carcinoma in situ of hypopharyngeal aspect (D00.08)
carcinoma in situ of marginal zone (D00.08)

D02.1   Carcinoma in situ of trachea

● **D02.2   Carcinoma in situ of bronchus and lung**

D02.20   Carcinoma in situ of unspecified bronchus and lung

D02.21   Carcinoma in situ of right bronchus and lung

D02.22   Carcinoma in situ of left bronchus and lung

D02.3   Carcinoma in situ of other parts of respiratory system
Carcinoma in situ of accessory sinuses
Carcinoma in situ of middle ear
Carcinoma in situ of nasal cavities

Excludes1   carcinoma in situ of ear (external) (skin) (D04.2-)
carcinoma in situ of nose NOS (D09.8)
carcinoma in situ of skin of nose (D04.3)

D02.4   Carcinoma in situ of respiratory system, unspecified

● **D03   Melanoma in situ**

D03.0   Melanoma in situ of lip 🅗

● **D03.1   Melanoma in situ of eyelid, including canthus**

D03.10   Melanoma in situ of unspecified eyelid, including canthus 🅗

● **D03.11   Melanoma in situ of right eyelid, including canthus** 🅗

D03.111   Melanoma in situ of right upper eyelid, including canthus 🅗

D03.112   Melanoma in situ of right lower eyelid, including canthus 🅗

● **D03.12   Melanoma in situ of left eyelid, including canthus** 🅗

D03.121   Melanoma in situ of left upper eyelid, including canthus 🅗

D03.122   Melanoma in situ of left lower eyelid, including canthus 🅗

● **D03.2   Melanoma in situ of ear and external auricular canal**

D03.20   Melanoma in situ of unspecified ear and external auricular canal 🅗

D03.21   Melanoma in situ of right ear and external auricular canal 🅗

D03.22   Melanoma in situ of left ear and external auricular canal 🅗

● **D03.3   Melanoma in situ of other and unspecified parts of face**

D03.30   Melanoma in situ of unspecified part of face 🅗

D03.39   Melanoma in situ of other parts of face 🅗

D03.4   Melanoma in situ of scalp and neck 🅗

▶ New   ⇒ Revised   ~~deleted~~ Deleted   Excludes 1   Excludes 2   Includes   Use additional   Code first   Code also   Key words

OGCR Official Guidelines   X Assign placeholder X   ● Use Additional Character(s)   ⟩ Manifestation Code   🅗 Hierarchical Condition Category   **Coding Clinic**

● **D03.5** Melanoma in situ of trunk

    D03.51 Melanoma in situ of anal skin 🔲
        Melanoma in situ of anal margin
        Melanoma in situ of perianal skin

    D03.52 Melanoma in situ of breast (skin) (soft tissue) 🔲

    D03.59 Melanoma in situ of other part of trunk 🔲

● **D03.6** Melanoma in situ of upper limb, including shoulder

    D03.60 Melanoma in situ of unspecified upper limb, including shoulder 🔲

    D03.61 Melanoma in situ of right upper limb, including shoulder 🔲

    D03.62 Melanoma in situ of left upper limb, including shoulder 🔲

● **D03.7** Melanoma in situ of lower limb, including hip

    D03.70 Melanoma in situ of unspecified lower limb, including hip 🔲

    D03.71 Melanoma in situ of right lower limb, including hip 🔲

    D03.72 Melanoma in situ of left lower limb, including hip 🔲

  D03.8 Melanoma in situ of other sites 🔲
    Melanoma in situ of scrotum

    Excludes1 carcinoma in situ of scrotum (D07.61)

  D03.9 Melanoma in situ, unspecified 🔲

● **D04** Carcinoma in situ of skin

  Excludes1 erythroplasia of Queyrat (penis) NOS (D07.4)
      melanoma in situ (D03.-)

  D04.0 Carcinoma in situ of skin of lip

  Excludes2 carcinoma in situ of vermilion border of lip
      (D00.01)

● **D04.1** Carcinoma in situ of skin of eyelid, including canthus

    D04.10 Carcinoma in situ of skin of unspecified eyelid, including canthus

  ● **D04.11** Carcinoma in situ of skin of right eyelid, including canthus

      D04.111 Carcinoma in situ of skin of right upper eyelid, including canthus

      D04.112 Carcinoma in situ of skin of right lower eyelid, including canthus

  ● **D04.12** Carcinoma in situ of skin of left eyelid, including canthus

      D04.121 Carcinoma in situ of skin of left upper eyelid, including canthus

      D04.122 Carcinoma in situ of skin of left lower eyelid, including canthus

● **D04.2** Carcinoma in situ of skin of ear and external auricular canal

    D04.20 Carcinoma in situ of skin of unspecified ear and external auricular canal

    D04.21 Carcinoma in situ of skin of right ear and external auricular canal

    D04.22 Carcinoma in situ of skin of left ear and external auricular canal

● **D04.3** Carcinoma in situ of skin of other and unspecified parts of face

    D04.30 Carcinoma in situ of skin of unspecified part of face

    D04.39 Carcinoma in situ of skin of other parts of face

  D04.4 Carcinoma in situ of skin of scalp and neck

  D04.5 Carcinoma in situ of skin of trunk
    Carcinoma in situ of anal margin
    Carcinoma in situ of anal skin
    Carcinoma in situ of perianal skin
    Carcinoma in situ of skin of breast

    Excludes1 carcinoma in situ of anus NOS (D01.3)
      carcinoma in situ of scrotum (D07.61)
      carcinoma in situ of skin of genital organs
      (D07.-)

● **D04.6** Carcinoma in situ of skin of upper limb, including shoulder

    D04.60 Carcinoma in situ of skin of unspecified upper limb, including shoulder

    D04.61 Carcinoma in situ of skin of right upper limb, including shoulder

    D04.62 Carcinoma in situ of skin of left upper limb, including shoulder

● **D04.7** Carcinoma in situ of skin of lower limb, including hip

    D04.70 Carcinoma in situ of skin of unspecified lower limb, including hip

    D04.71 Carcinoma in situ of skin of right lower limb, including hip

    D04.72 Carcinoma in situ of skin of left lower limb, including hip

  D04.8 Carcinoma in situ of skin of other sites

  D04.9 Carcinoma in situ of skin, unspecified

● **D05** Carcinoma in situ of breast

  Excludes1 carcinoma in situ of skin of breast (D04.5)
      melanoma in situ of breast (skin) (D03.5)
      Paget's disease of breast or nipple (C50.-)

● **D05.0** Lobular carcinoma in situ of breast

    D05.00 Lobular carcinoma in situ of unspecified breast

    D05.01 Lobular carcinoma in situ of right breast

    D05.02 Lobular carcinoma in situ of left breast

● **D05.1** Intraductal carcinoma in situ of breast

    D05.10 Intraductal carcinoma in situ of unspecified breast

    D05.11 Intraductal carcinoma in situ of right breast

    D05.12 Intraductal carcinoma in situ of left breast

● **D05.8** Other specified type of carcinoma in situ of breast

    D05.80 Other specified type of carcinoma in situ of unspecified breast

    D05.81 Other specified type of carcinoma in situ of right breast

    D05.82 Other specified type of carcinoma in situ of left breast

● **D05.9** Unspecified type of carcinoma in situ of breast

    D05.90 Unspecified type of carcinoma in situ of unspecified breast

    D05.91 Unspecified type of carcinoma in situ of right breast

    D05.92 Unspecified type of carcinoma in situ of left breast

● **D06** Carcinoma in situ of cervix uteri

  Includes cervical adenocarcinoma in situ
      cervical intraepithelial glandular neoplasia
      cervical intraepithelial neoplasia III [CIN III]
      severe dysplasia of cervix uteri

  Excludes1 cervical intraepithelial neoplasia II [CIN II]
      (N87.1)
      cytologic evidence of malignancy of cervix without
        histologic confirmation (R87.614)
      high grade squamous intraepithelial lesion
        (HGSIL) of cervix (R87.613)
      melanoma in situ of cervix (D03.5)
      moderate cervical dysplasia (N87.1)

  D06.0 Carcinoma in situ of endocervix ♀

  D06.1 Carcinoma in situ of exocervix ♀

  D06.7 Carcinoma in situ of other parts of cervix ♀

  D06.9 Carcinoma in situ of cervix, unspecified ♀

CHAPTER 2 (C00-D49)

● **D07 Carcinoma in situ of other and unspecified genital organs**

    Excludes1   melanoma in situ of trunk (D03.5)

    D07.0 Carcinoma in situ of endometrium ♀

    D07.1 Carcinoma in situ of vulva ♀

        Severe dysplasia of vulva

        Vulvar intraepithelial neoplasia III [VIN III]

        Excludes1   moderate dysplasia of vulva (N90.1)

                vulvar intraepithelial neoplasia II [VIN II] (N90.1)

    D07.2 Carcinoma in situ of vagina ♀

        Severe dysplasia of vagina

        Vaginal intraepithelial neoplasia III [VIN III]

        Excludes1   moderate dysplasia of vagina (N89.1)

                vaginal intraepithelial neoplasia II [VIN II] (N89.1)

● **D07.3 Carcinoma in situ of other and unspecified female genital organs**

        D07.30 Carcinoma in situ of unspecified female genital organs ♀

        D07.39 Carcinoma in situ of other female genital organs ♀

    D07.4 Carcinoma in situ of penis ♂

        Erythroplasia of Queyrat NOS

    D07.5 Carcinoma in situ of prostate ♂

        Prostatic intraepithelial neoplasia III (PIN III)

        Severe dysplasia of prostate

        Excludes1   dysplasia (mild) (moderate) of prostate (N42.3-)

                prostatic intraepithelial neoplasia II [PIN II] (N42.3-)

● **D07.6 Carcinoma in situ of other and unspecified male genital organs**

        D07.60 Carcinoma in situ of unspecified male genital organs ♂

        D07.61 Carcinoma in situ of scrotum ♂

        D07.69 Carcinoma in situ of other male genital organs ♂

● **D09 Carcinoma in situ of other and unspecified sites**

    Excludes1   melanoma in situ (D03.-)

    D09.0 Carcinoma in situ of bladder

● **D09.1 Carcinoma in situ of other and unspecified urinary organs**

        D09.10 Carcinoma in situ of unspecified urinary organ

        D09.19 Carcinoma in situ of other urinary organs

● **D09.2 Carcinoma in situ of eye**

    Excludes1   carcinoma in situ of skin of eyelid (D04.1-)

        D09.20 Carcinoma in situ of unspecified eye

        D09.21 Carcinoma in situ of right eye

        D09.22 Carcinoma in situ of left eye

    D09.3 Carcinoma in situ of thyroid and other endocrine glands

        Excludes1   carcinoma in situ of endocrine pancreas (D01.7)

                carcinoma in situ of ovary (D07.39)

                carcinoma in situ of testis (D07.69)

    D09.8 Carcinoma in situ of other specified sites

    D09.9 Carcinoma in situ, unspecified

Figure 2-16 The esophagus is the muscular tube that connects the pharynx and the stomach. The 10 inch (25 cm) long esophagus is divided into three parts: **cervical, thoracic,** and **abdominal.**

BENIGN NEOPLASMS, EXCEPT BENIGN NEUROENDOCRINE TUMORS (D10-D36)

● **D10 Benign neoplasm of mouth and pharynx**

    D10.0 Benign neoplasm of lip

        Benign neoplasm of lip (frenulum) (inner aspect) (mucosa) (vermilion border)

        Excludes1   benign neoplasm of skin of lip (D22.0, D23.0)

    D10.1 Benign neoplasm of tongue

        Benign neoplasm of lingual tonsil

    D10.2 Benign neoplasm of floor of mouth

● **D10.3 Benign neoplasm of other and unspecified parts of mouth**

        D10.30 Benign neoplasm of unspecified part of mouth

        D10.39 Benign neoplasm of other parts of mouth

            Benign neoplasm of minor salivary gland NOS

            Excludes1   benign odontogenic neoplasms (D16.4-D16.5)

                benign neoplasm of mucosa of lip (D10.0)

                benign neoplasm of nasopharyngeal surface of soft palate (D10.6)

    D10.4 Benign neoplasm of tonsil

        Benign neoplasm of tonsil (faucial) (palatine)

        Excludes1   benign neoplasm of lingual tonsil (D10.1)

                benign neoplasm of pharyngeal tonsil (D10.6)

                benign neoplasm of tonsillar fossa (D10.5)

                benign neoplasm of tonsillar pillars (D10.5)

    D10.5 Benign neoplasm of other parts of oropharynx

        Division of pharynx lying between soft palate and upper edge of epiglottis

        Benign neoplasm of epiglottis, anterior aspect

        Benign neoplasm of tonsillar fossa

        Benign neoplasm of tonsillar pillars

        Benign neoplasm of vallecula

        Excludes1   benign neoplasm of epiglottis NOS (D14.1)

                benign neoplasm of epiglottis, suprahyoid portion (D14.1)

    D10.6 Benign neoplasm of nasopharynx

        Segment of pharynx that lies above soft palate

        Benign neoplasm of pharyngeal tonsil

        Benign neoplasm of posterior margin of septum and choanae

    D10.7 Benign neoplasm of hypopharynx

        Segment of pharynx that lies below upper edge of epiglottis and opens into larynx and esophagus

    D10.9 Benign neoplasm of pharynx, unspecified

    ▶ New   ⇒ Revised   ~~deleted~~ Deleted   Excludes 1   Excludes 2   Includes   Use additional   Code first   Code also   Key words

    OGCR Official Guidelines   X Assign placeholder X   ● Use Additional Character(s)   ▮ Manifestation Code   ◖ Hierarchical Condition Category   Coding Clinic

● **D11** **Benign neoplasm of major salivary glands**

    Excludes1   benign neoplasms of specified minor salivary glands which are classified according to their anatomical location

          benign neoplasms of minor salivary glands NOS (D10.39)

   D11.0   **Benign neoplasm of parotid gland**

   D11.7   **Benign neoplasm of other major salivary glands**
      Benign neoplasm of sublingual salivary gland
      Benign neoplasm of submandibular salivary gland

   D11.9   **Benign neoplasm of major salivary gland, unspecified**

● **D12** **Benign neoplasm of colon, rectum, anus and anal canal**

    Excludes1   benign carcinoid tumors of the large intestine, and rectum (D3A.02-)
          polyp of colon NOS (K63.5)
   Coding Clinic: 2017, Q1, P15; 2015, Q2, P14

   D12.0   **Benign neoplasm of cecum**
      Benign neoplasm of ileocecal valve

   D12.1   **Benign neoplasm of appendix**
      Excludes1   benign carcinoid tumor of the appendix (D3A.020)

   D12.2   **Benign neoplasm of ascending colon**
      Coding Clinic: 2018, Q2, P14; 2017, Q1, P15

   D12.3   **Benign neoplasm of transverse colon**
      Benign neoplasm of hepatic flexure
      Benign neoplasm of splenic flexure
         Flexure is a bending in a structure or organ. Note the three flexures illustrated in Figure 2–17. Hepatic = liver, sigmoid = colon, splenic = spleen.
      Coding Clinic: 2017, Q1, P16

   D12.4   **Benign neoplasm of descending colon**
      Coding Clinic: 2015, Q2, P14

   D12.5   **Benign neoplasm of sigmoid colon**

   D12.6   **Benign neoplasm of colon, unspecified**
      Adenomatosis of colon
      Benign neoplasm of large intestine NOS
      Polyposis (hereditary) of colon
      Excludes1   inflammatory polyp of colon (K51.4-)
      Coding Clinic: 2017, Q1, P8-9

   D12.7   **Benign neoplasm of rectosigmoid junction**
      Angle where sigmoid colon becomes rectum

   D12.8   **Benign neoplasm of rectum**
      Excludes1   benign carcinoid tumor of the rectum (D3A.026)
      Coding Clinic: 2018, Q1, P7

   D12.9   **Benign neoplasm of anus and anal canal**
      Benign neoplasm of anus NOS
      Excludes1   benign neoplasm of anal margin (D22.5, D23.5)
          benign neoplasm of anal skin (D22.5, D23.5)
          benign neoplasm of perianal skin (D22.5, D23.5)

● **D13** **Benign neoplasm of other and ill-defined parts of digestive system**

    Excludes1   benign stromal tumors of digestive system (D21.4)

   D13.0   **Benign neoplasm of esophagus**

   D13.1   **Benign neoplasm of stomach**
      Excludes1   benign carcinoid tumor of the stomach (D3A.092)

   D13.2   **Benign neoplasm of duodenum**
      Excludes1   benign carcinoid tumor of the duodenum (D3A.010)

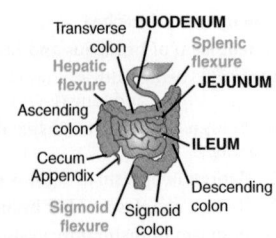

Figure 2-17   Small intestine and colon.

● **D13.3** **Benign neoplasm of other and unspecified parts of small intestine**

    Excludes1   benign carcinoid tumors of the small intestine (D3A.01-)
          benign neoplasm of ileocecal valve (D12.0)

   D13.30   **Benign neoplasm of unspecified part of small intestine**

   D13.39   **Benign neoplasm of other parts of small intestine**

   D13.4   **Benign neoplasm of liver**
      Benign neoplasm of intrahepatic bile ducts

   D13.5   **Benign neoplasm of extrahepatic bile ducts**
      Extensions of common hepatic bile duct (tube that collects bile from liver)

   D13.6   **Benign neoplasm of pancreas**
      Excludes1   benign neoplasm of endocrine pancreas (D13.7)

   D13.7   **Benign neoplasm of endocrine pancreas**
      Pancreatic islets: Cells scattered throughout pancreas
      Islet cell tumor
      Benign neoplasm of islets of Langerhans
      Use additional code to identify any functional activity.

   D13.9   **Benign neoplasm of ill-defined sites within the digestive system**
      Benign neoplasm of digestive system NOS
      Benign neoplasm of intestine NOS
      Benign neoplasm of spleen

● **D14** **Benign neoplasm of middle ear and respiratory system**

   D14.0   **Benign neoplasm of middle ear, nasal cavity and accessory sinuses**
      Benign neoplasm of cartilage of nose
      Excludes1   benign neoplasm of auricular canal (external) (D22.2-, D23.2-)
          benign neoplasm of bone of ear (D16.4)
          benign neoplasm of bone of nose (D16.4)
          benign neoplasm of cartilage of ear (D21.0)
          benign neoplasm of ear (external) (skin) (D22.2-, D23.2-)
          benign neoplasm of nose NOS (D36.7)
          benign neoplasm of skin of nose (D22.39, D23.39)
          benign neoplasm of olfactory bulb (D33.3)
          benign neoplasm of posterior margin of septum and choanae (D10.6)
          polyp of accessory sinus (J33.8)
          polyp of ear (middle) (H74.4)
          polyp of nasal (cavity) (J33.-)

   D14.1   **Benign neoplasm of larynx**
      Adenomatous polyp of larynx
      Benign neoplasm of epiglottis (suprahyoid portion)
      Horseshoe-shaped bone in anterior midline of neck between chin and thyroid cartilage
      Excludes1   benign neoplasm of epiglottis, anterior aspect (D10.5)
          polyp (nonadenomatous) of vocal cord or larynx (J38.1)

CHAPTER 2 (C00-D49)

CHAPTER 2 (C00-D49)

D14.2   Benign neoplasm of trachea

● D14.3   Benign neoplasm of bronchus and lung

> **Excludes1**   benign carcinoid tumor of the bronchus and lung (D3A.090)

     D14.30   Benign neoplasm of unspecified bronchus and lung

     D14.31   Benign neoplasm of right bronchus and lung

     D14.32   Benign neoplasm of left bronchus and lung

D14.4   Benign neoplasm of respiratory system, unspecified

● D15   Benign neoplasm of other and unspecified intrathoracic organs

> **Excludes1**   benign neoplasm of mesothelial tissue (D19.-)

D15.0   Benign neoplasm of thymus

> **Excludes1**   benign carcinoid tumor of the thymus (D3A.091)

D15.1   Benign neoplasm of heart

> **Excludes1**   benign neoplasm of great vessels (D21.3)

D15.2   Benign neoplasm of mediastinum

D15.7   Benign neoplasm of other specified intrathoracic organs

D15.9   Benign neoplasm of intrathoracic organ, unspecified

● D16   Benign neoplasm of bone and articular cartilage

> **Excludes1**   benign neoplasm of connective tissue of ear (D21.0)
> benign neoplasm of connective tissue of eyelid (D21.0)
> benign neoplasm of connective tissue of larynx (D14.1)
> benign neoplasm of connective tissue of nose (D14.0)
> benign neoplasm of synovia (D21.-)

● D16.0   Benign neoplasm of scapula and long bones of upper limb

     D16.00   Benign neoplasm of scapula and long bones of unspecified upper limb

     D16.01   Benign neoplasm of scapula and long bones of right upper limb

     D16.02   Benign neoplasm of scapula and long bones of left upper limb

● D16.1   Benign neoplasm of short bones of upper limb

     D16.10   Benign neoplasm of short bones of unspecified upper limb

     D16.11   Benign neoplasm of short bones of right upper limb

     D16.12   Benign neoplasm of short bones of left upper limb

● D16.2   Benign neoplasm of long bones of lower limb

     D16.20   Benign neoplasm of long bones of unspecified lower limb

     D16.21   Benign neoplasm of long bones of right lower limb

     D16.22   Benign neoplasm of long bones of left lower limb

● D16.3   Benign neoplasm of short bones of lower limb

     D16.30   Benign neoplasm of short bones of unspecified lower limb

     D16.31   Benign neoplasm of short bones of right lower limb

     D16.32   Benign neoplasm of short bones of left lower limb

D16.4   Benign neoplasm of bones of skull and face
Benign neoplasm of maxilla (superior)
Benign neoplasm of orbital bone
Cavity or socket of skull in which eye and its appendages are located
Keratocyst of maxilla
Keratocystic odontogenic tumor of maxilla

> **Excludes2**   benign neoplasm of lower jaw bone (D16.5)

D16.5   Benign neoplasm of lower jaw bone
Keratocyst of mandible
Keratocystic odontogenic tumor of mandible

D16.6   Benign neoplasm of vertebral column

> **Excludes1**   benign neoplasm of sacrum and coccyx (D16.8)

D16.7   Benign neoplasm of ribs, sternum and clavicle

D16.8   Benign neoplasm of pelvic bones, sacrum and coccyx

D16.9   Benign neoplasm of bone and articular cartilage, unspecified

● D17   Benign lipomatous neoplasm
Slow-growing benign tumors (rubbery masses) of mature fat cells enclosed in a thin fibrous capsule

D17.0   Benign lipomatous neoplasm of skin and subcutaneous tissue of head, face and neck

D17.1   Benign lipomatous neoplasm of skin and subcutaneous tissue of trunk

● D17.2   Benign lipomatous neoplasm of skin and subcutaneous tissue of limb

     D17.20   Benign lipomatous neoplasm of skin and subcutaneous tissue of unspecified limb

     D17.21   Benign lipomatous neoplasm of skin and subcutaneous tissue of right arm

     D17.22   Benign lipomatous neoplasm of skin and subcutaneous tissue of left arm

     D17.23   Benign lipomatous neoplasm of skin and subcutaneous tissue of right leg

     D17.24   Benign lipomatous neoplasm of skin and subcutaneous tissue of left leg

● D17.3   Benign lipomatous neoplasm of skin and subcutaneous tissue of other and unspecified sites

     D17.30   Benign lipomatous neoplasm of skin and subcutaneous tissue of unspecified sites

     D17.39   Benign lipomatous neoplasm of skin and subcutaneous tissue of other sites

D17.4   Benign lipomatous neoplasm of intrathoracic organs

D17.5   Benign lipomatous neoplasm of intra-abdominal organs

> **Excludes1**   benign lipomatous neoplasm of peritoneum and retroperitoneum (D17.79)

D17.6   Benign lipomatous neoplasm of spermatic cord ♂

● D17.7   Benign lipomatous neoplasm of other sites

     D17.71   Benign lipomatous neoplasm of kidney

     D17.72   Benign lipomatous neoplasm of other genitourinary organ

     D17.79   Benign lipomatous neoplasm of other sites
Benign lipomatous neoplasm of peritoneum
Benign lipomatous neoplasm of retroperitoneum

D17.9   Benign lipomatous neoplasm, unspecified
Lipoma NOS

● D18   Hemangioma and lymphangioma, any site

> **Excludes1**   benign neoplasm of glomus jugulare (D35.6)
> blue or pigmented nevus (D22.-)
> nevus NOS (D22.-)
> vascular nevus (Q82.5)

● D18.0   Hemangioma
Common type of vascular malformation
Angioma NOS
Cavernous nevus

     D18.00   Hemangioma unspecified site

     D18.01   Hemangioma of skin and subcutaneous tissue

     D18.02   Hemangioma of intracranial structures 🅗

     D18.03   Hemangioma of intra-abdominal structures

     D18.09   Hemangioma of other sites

D18.1   Lymphangioma, any site
Coding Clinic: 2018, Q2, P13

▶ New   ⇒ Revised   ~~deleted~~ Deleted   Excludes 1   Excludes 2   Includes   Use additional   Code first   Code also   Key words

OGCR Official Guidelines   X Assign placeholder X   ● Use Additional Character(s)   ⟩ Manifestation Code   🅗 Hierarchical Condition Category   Coding Clinic

Figure 2-18 Hemangioma of skin and subcutaneous tissue. (Getty Image)

Item 2–10 **Hemangiomas** are abnormally dense collections of dilated capillaries that occur on the skin or in internal organs. Hemangiomas are both deep and superficial and undergo a rapid growth phase when the size increases rapidly, followed by a rest phase, in which the tumor changes very little, followed by an involutional phase in which the tumor begins to and can disappear altogether. **Lymphangiomas** or cystic hygroma are benign collections of overgrown lymph vessels and, although rare, may occur anywhere but most commonly on the head and neck of children and infants. Visceral organs, lungs, and gastrointestinal tract may also be involved.

● **D19** **Benign neoplasm of mesothelial tissue**
    Mesothelial tissue is the membrane lining several body cavities

    D19.0 **Benign neoplasm of mesothelial tissue of pleura**

    D19.1 **Benign neoplasm of mesothelial tissue of peritoneum**

    D19.7 **Benign neoplasm of mesothelial tissue of other sites**

    D19.9 **Benign neoplasm of mesothelial tissue, unspecified**
        Benign mesothelioma NOS

● **D20** **Benign neoplasm of soft tissue of retroperitoneum and peritoneum**
    Excludes1 benign lipomatous neoplasm of peritoneum and retroperitoneum (D17.79)
            benign neoplasm of mesothelial tissue (D19.-)

    D20.0 **Benign neoplasm of soft tissue of retroperitoneum**

    D20.1 **Benign neoplasm of soft tissue of peritoneum**

● **D21** **Other benign neoplasms of connective and other soft tissue**
    Includes benign neoplasm of blood vessel
            benign neoplasm of bursa
            benign neoplasm of cartilage
            benign neoplasm of fascia
            benign neoplasm of fat
            benign neoplasm of ligament, except uterine
            benign neoplasm of lymphatic channel
            benign neoplasm of muscle
            benign neoplasm of synovia
            benign neoplasm of tendon (sheath)
            benign stromal tumors

    Excludes1 benign neoplasm of articular cartilage (D16.-)
            benign neoplasm of cartilage of larynx (D14.1)
            benign neoplasm of cartilage of nose (D14.0)
            benign neoplasm of connective tissue of breast (D24.-)
            benign neoplasm of peripheral nerves and autonomic nervous system (D36.1-)
            benign neoplasm of peritoneum (D20.1)
            benign neoplasm of retroperitoneum (D20.0)
            benign neoplasm of uterine ligament, any (D28.2)
            benign neoplasm of vascular tissue (D18.-)
            hemangioma (D18.0-)
            lipomatous neoplasm (D17.-)
            lymphangioma (D18.1)
            uterine leiomyoma (D25.-)

    D21.0 **Benign neoplasm of connective and other soft tissue of head, face and neck**
        Benign neoplasm of connective tissue of ear
        Benign neoplasm of connective tissue of eyelid
        Excludes1 benign neoplasm of connective tissue of orbit (D31.6-)

● **D21.1** **Benign neoplasm of connective and other soft tissue of upper limb, including shoulder**

    D21.10 **Benign neoplasm of connective and other soft tissue of unspecified upper limb, including shoulder**

    D21.11 **Benign neoplasm of connective and other soft tissue of right upper limb, including shoulder**

    D21.12 **Benign neoplasm of connective and other soft tissue of left upper limb, including shoulder**

● **D21.2** **Benign neoplasm of connective and other soft tissue of lower limb, including hip**

    D21.20 **Benign neoplasm of connective and other soft tissue of unspecified lower limb, including hip**

    D21.21 **Benign neoplasm of connective and other soft tissue of right lower limb, including hip**

    D21.22 **Benign neoplasm of connective and other soft tissue of left lower limb, including hip**

    D21.3 **Benign neoplasm of connective and other soft tissue of thorax**
        Benign neoplasm of axilla
        Benign neoplasm of diaphragm
        Benign neoplasm of great vessels
        Excludes1 benign neoplasm of heart (D15.1)
            benign neoplasm of mediastinum (D15.2)
            benign neoplasm of thymus (D15.0)

    D21.4 **Benign neoplasm of connective and other soft tissue of abdomen**
        Benign stromal tumors of abdomen

    D21.5 **Benign neoplasm of connective and other soft tissue of pelvis**
        Excludes1 benign neoplasm of any uterine ligament (D28.2)
            uterine leiomyoma (D25.-)

    D21.6 **Benign neoplasm of connective and other soft tissue of trunk, unspecified**
      ➠Benign neoplasm of connective and other soft tissue of back NOS

    D21.9 **Benign neoplasm of connective and other soft tissue, unspecified**

● **D22** **Melanocytic nevi**
    Includes atypical nevus
            blue hairy pigmented nevus
            nevus NOS

    D22.0 **Melanocytic nevi of lip**
        Skin lesions composed of nests of nevus cells with macules/ papules

● **D22.1** **Melanocytic nevi of eyelid, including canthus**

    D22.10 **Melanocytic nevi of unspecified eyelid, including canthus**

●   **D22.11** **Melanocytic nevi of right eyelid, including canthus**

        D22.111 **Melanocytic nevi of right upper eyelid, including canthus**

        D22.112 **Melanocytic nevi of right lower eyelid, including canthus**

●   **D22.12** **Melanocytic nevi of left eyelid, including canthus**

        D22.121 **Melanocytic nevi of left upper eyelid, including canthus**

        D22.122 **Melanocytic nevi of left lower eyelid, including canthus**

● **D22.2** **Melanocytic nevi of ear and external auricular canal**

    D22.20 **Melanocytic nevi of unspecified ear and external auricular canal**

    D22.21 **Melanocytic nevi of right ear and external auricular canal**

    D22.22 **Melanocytic nevi of left ear and external auricular canal**

N Newborn Age: 0   **P** Pediatric Age: 0–17   **M** Maternity DX: 12–55   **A** Adult Age: 15–124   ♀ Females Only   ♂ Males Only

715

CHAPTER 2 (C00-D49)

● **D22.3 Melanocytic nevi of other and unspecified parts of face**
     D22.30 Melanocytic nevi of unspecified part of face
     D22.39 Melanocytic nevi of other parts of face
  D22.4 Melanocytic nevi of scalp and neck
  D22.5 Melanocytic nevi of trunk
     Melanocytic nevi of anal margin
     Melanocytic nevi of anal skin
     Melanocytic nevi of perianal skin
     Melanocytic nevi of skin of breast
● **D22.6 Melanocytic nevi of upper limb, including shoulder**
     D22.60 Melanocytic nevi of unspecified upper limb, including shoulder
     D22.61 Melanocytic nevi of right upper limb, including shoulder
     D22.62 Melanocytic nevi of left upper limb, including shoulder
● **D22.7 Melanocytic nevi of lower limb, including hip**
     D22.70 Melanocytic nevi of unspecified lower limb, including hip
     D22.71 Melanocytic nevi of right lower limb, including hip
     D22.72 Melanocytic nevi of left lower limb, including hip
  D22.9 Melanocytic nevi, unspecified

● **D23 Other benign neoplasms of skin**
     Includes   benign neoplasm of hair follicles
                  benign neoplasm of sebaceous glands
                  benign neoplasm of sweat glands
     Excludes1   benign lipomatous neoplasms of skin (D17.0-D17.3)
     Excludes2   melanocytic nevi (D22.-)
  D23.0 Other benign neoplasm of skin of lip
     Excludes1   benign neoplasm of vermilion border of lip (D10.0)
● **D23.1 Other benign neoplasm of skin of eyelid, including canthus**
     D23.10 Other benign neoplasm of skin unspecified of eyelid, including canthus
     ● D23.11 Other benign neoplasm of skin of right eyelid, including canthus
         D23.111 Other benign neoplasm of skin of right upper eyelid, including canthus
         D23.112 Other benign neoplasm of skin of right lower eyelid, including canthus
     ● D23.12 Other benign neoplasm of skin of left eyelid, including canthus
         D23.121 Other benign neoplasm of skin of left upper eyelid, including canthus
         D23.122 Other benign neoplasm of skin of left lower eyelid, including canthus
● **D23.2 Other benign neoplasm of skin of ear and external auricular canal**
     D23.20 Other benign neoplasm of skin of unspecified ear and external auricular canal
     D23.21 Other benign neoplasm of skin of right ear and external auricular canal
     D23.22 Other benign neoplasm of skin of left ear and external auricular canal
● **D23.3 Other benign neoplasm of skin of other and unspecified parts of face**
     D23.30 Other benign neoplasm of skin of unspecified part of face
     D23.39 Other benign neoplasm of skin of other parts of face
  D23.4 Other benign neoplasm of skin of scalp and neck

  D23.5 Other benign neoplasm of skin of trunk
     Other benign neoplasm of anal margin
     Other benign neoplasm of anal skin
     Other benign neoplasm of perianal skin
     Other benign neoplasm of skin of breast
     Excludes1   benign neoplasm of anus NOS (D12.9)
● **D23.6 Other benign neoplasm of skin of upper limb, including shoulder**
     D23.60 Other benign neoplasm of skin of unspecified upper limb, including shoulder
     D23.61 Other benign neoplasm of skin of right upper limb, including shoulder
     D23.62 Other benign neoplasm of skin of left upper limb, including shoulder
● **D23.7 Other benign neoplasm of skin of lower limb, including hip**
     D23.70 Other benign neoplasm of skin of unspecified lower limb, including hip
     D23.71 Other benign neoplasm of skin of right lower limb, including hip
     D23.72 Other benign neoplasm of skin of left lower limb, including hip
  D23.9 Other benign neoplasm of skin, unspecified

● **D24 Benign neoplasm of breast**
     Includes   benign neoplasm of connective tissue of breast
                  benign neoplasm of soft parts of breast
                  fibroadenoma of breast
     Excludes2   adenofibrosis of breast (N60.2)
                   benign cyst of breast (N60.-)
                   benign mammary dysplasia (N60.-)
                   benign neoplasm of skin of breast (D22.5, D23.5)
                   fibrocystic disease of breast (N60.-)
  D24.1 Benign neoplasm of right breast
     Coding Clinic: 2017, Q1, P5
  D24.2 Benign neoplasm of left breast
  D24.9 Benign neoplasm of unspecified breast

● **D25 Leiomyoma of uterus**
     Benign tumors or nodules of the uterine wall
     Includes   uterine fibroid
                  uterine fibromyoma
                  uterine myoma
  D25.0 Submucous leiomyoma of uterus ♀
  D25.1 Intramural leiomyoma of uterus ♀
     Interstitial leiomyoma of uterus
  D25.2 Subserosal leiomyoma of uterus ♀
     Subperitoneal leiomyoma of uterus
  D25.9 Leiomyoma of uterus, unspecified ♀

● **D26 Other benign neoplasms of uterus**
  D26.0 Other benign neoplasm of cervix uteri ♀
  D26.1 Other benign neoplasm of corpus uteri ♀
  D26.7 Other benign neoplasm of other parts of uterus ♀
  D26.9 Other benign neoplasm of uterus, unspecified ♀

● **D27 Benign neoplasm of ovary**
     Use additional code to identify any functional activity.
     Excludes2   corpus albicans cyst (N83.2-)
                   corpus luteum cyst (N83.1-)
                   endometrial cyst (N80.1)
                   follicular (atretic) cyst (N83.0-)
                   graafian follicle cyst (N83.0-)
                   ovarian cyst NEC (N83.2-)
                   ovarian retention cyst (N83.2-)
  D27.0 Benign neoplasm of right ovary ♀
  D27.1 Benign neoplasm of left ovary ♀
  D27.9 Benign neoplasm of unspecified ovary ♀
     Ovarian teratoma

▶ New   ⇒ Revised   ~~deleted~~ Deleted   Excludes 1   Excludes 2   Includes   Use additional   Code first   Code also   Key words
OGCR Official Guidelines   X Assign placeholder X   ● Use Additional Character(s)   ▸ Manifestation Code   🐾 Hierarchical Condition Category   Coding Clinic

Item 2–11 Teratoma: terat = monster, oma = mass, tumor. Alternate terms: dermoid cyst of the ovary, ovarian teratoma. Teratomas are neoplasms and arise from germ cells (ovaries in female and testes in male) and can be benign or malignant. Teratomas have been known to contain hair, nails, and teeth, giving them a bizarre ("monster") appearance.

● **D28 Benign neoplasm of other and unspecified female genital organs**

     Includes   adenomatous polyp
                   benign neoplasm of skin of female genital organs
                   benign teratoma

     Excludes1   epoophoron cyst (Q50.5)
                   fimbrial cyst (Q50.4)
                   Gartner's duct cyst (Q52.4)
                   parovarian cyst (Q50.5)

   D28.0 Benign neoplasm of vulva ♀

   D28.1 Benign neoplasm of vagina ♀

   D28.2 Benign neoplasm of uterine tubes and ligaments ♀
       Benign neoplasm of fallopian tube
       Benign neoplasm of uterine ligament (broad) (round)

   D28.7 Benign neoplasm of other specified female genital organs ♀

   D28.9 Benign neoplasm of female genital organ, unspecified ♀

● **D29 Benign neoplasm of male genital organs**
     Includes   benign neoplasm of skin of male genital organs

   D29.0 Benign neoplasm of penis ♂

   D29.1 Benign neoplasm of prostate ♂
     Excludes1   enlarged prostate (N40.-)

●   **D29.2 Benign neoplasm of testis**
     Use additional code to identify any functional activity.
     D29.20 Benign neoplasm of unspecified testis ♂
     D29.21 Benign neoplasm of right testis ♂
     D29.22 Benign neoplasm of left testis ♂

●   **D29.3 Benign neoplasm of epididymis**
     D29.30 Benign neoplasm of unspecified epididymis ♂
     D29.31 Benign neoplasm of right epididymis ♂
     D29.32 Benign neoplasm of left epididymis ♂

   D29.4 Benign neoplasm of scrotum ♂
       Benign neoplasm of skin of scrotum

   D29.8 Benign neoplasm of other specified male genital organs ♂
       Benign neoplasm of seminal vesicle
       Benign neoplasm of spermatic cord
       Benign neoplasm of tunica vaginalis

   D29.9 Benign neoplasm of male genital organ, unspecified ♂

● **D30 Benign neoplasm of urinary organs**
●   **D30.0 Benign neoplasm of kidney**
     Excludes1   benign carcinoid tumor of the kidney (D3A.093)
                   benign neoplasm of renal calyces (D30.1-)
                   benign neoplasm of renal pelvis (D30.1-)

     D30.00 Benign neoplasm of unspecified kidney
     D30.01 Benign neoplasm of right kidney
     D30.02 Benign neoplasm of left kidney

●   **D30.1 Benign neoplasm of renal pelvis**
     D30.10 Benign neoplasm of unspecified renal pelvis
     D30.11 Benign neoplasm of right renal pelvis
     D30.12 Benign neoplasm of left renal pelvis

●   **D30.2 Benign neoplasm of ureter**
     Excludes1   benign neoplasm of ureteric orifice of bladder (D30.3)
     D30.20 Benign neoplasm of unspecified ureter
     D30.21 Benign neoplasm of right ureter
     D30.22 Benign neoplasm of left ureter

   D30.3 Benign neoplasm of bladder
       Benign neoplasm of ureteric orifice of bladder
       Benign neoplasm of urethral orifice of bladder

   D30.4 Benign neoplasm of urethra
     Excludes1   benign neoplasm of urethral orifice of bladder (D30.3)

   D30.8 Benign neoplasm of other specified urinary organs
       Benign neoplasm of paraurethral glands

   D30.9 Benign neoplasm of urinary organ, unspecified
       Benign neoplasm of urinary system NOS

● **D31 Benign neoplasm of eye and adnexa**
     Excludes1   benign neoplasm of connective tissue of eyelid (D21.0)
                   benign neoplasm of optic nerve (D33.3)
                   benign neoplasm of skin of eyelid (D22.1-, D23.1-)

●   **D31.0 Benign neoplasm of conjunctiva**
     D31.00 Benign neoplasm of unspecified conjunctiva
     D31.01 Benign neoplasm of right conjunctiva
     D31.02 Benign neoplasm of left conjunctiva

●   **D31.1 Benign neoplasm of cornea**
     D31.10 Benign neoplasm of unspecified cornea
     D31.11 Benign neoplasm of right cornea
     D31.12 Benign neoplasm of left cornea

●   **D31.2 Benign neoplasm of retina**
     Excludes1   dark area on retina (D49.81)
                   hemangioma of retina (D49.81)
                   neoplasm of unspecified behavior of retina and choroid (D49.81)
                   retinal freckle (D49.81)

     D31.20 Benign neoplasm of unspecified retina
     D31.21 Benign neoplasm of right retina
     D31.22 Benign neoplasm of left retina

●   **D31.3 Benign neoplasm of choroid**
     D31.30 Benign neoplasm of unspecified choroid
     D31.31 Benign neoplasm of right choroid
     D31.32 Benign neoplasm of left choroid

●   **D31.4 Benign neoplasm of ciliary body**
     D31.40 Benign neoplasm of unspecified ciliary body
     D31.41 Benign neoplasm of right ciliary body
     D31.42 Benign neoplasm of left ciliary body

●   **D31.5 Benign neoplasm of lacrimal gland and duct**
       Benign neoplasm of lacrimal sac
       Benign neoplasm of nasolacrimal duct
     D31.50 Benign neoplasm of unspecified lacrimal gland and duct
     D31.51 Benign neoplasm of right lacrimal gland and duct
     D31.52 Benign neoplasm of left lacrimal gland and duct

●   **D31.6 Benign neoplasm of unspecified site of orbit**
       Benign neoplasm of connective tissue of orbit
       Benign neoplasm of extraocular muscle
       Benign neoplasm of peripheral nerves of orbit
       Benign neoplasm of retrobulbar tissue
       Benign neoplasm of retro-ocular tissue
     Excludes1   benign neoplasm of orbital bone (D16.4)
     D31.60 Benign neoplasm of unspecified site of unspecified orbit
     D31.61 Benign neoplasm of unspecified site of right orbit
     D31.62 Benign neoplasm of unspecified site of left orbit

●   **D31.9 Benign neoplasm of unspecified part of eye**
       Benign neoplasm of eyeball
     D31.90 Benign neoplasm of unspecified part of unspecified eye
     D31.91 Benign neoplasm of unspecified part of right eye
     D31.92 Benign neoplasm of unspecified part of left eye

CHAPTER 2 (C00–D49)

● **D32 Benign neoplasm of meninges**

D32.0 Benign neoplasm of cerebral meninges 🐾

D32.1 Benign neoplasm of spinal meninges 🐾

D32.9 Benign neoplasm of meninges, unspecified 🐾
Meningioma NOS

● **D33 Benign neoplasm of brain and other parts of central nervous system**

Excludes1   angioma (D18.0-)
benign neoplasm of meninges (D32.-)
benign neoplasm of peripheral nerves and autonomic nervous system (D36.1-)
hemangioma (D18.0-)
neurofibromatosis (Q85.0-)
retro-ocular benign neoplasm (D31.6-)

D33.0 Benign neoplasm of brain, supratentorial 🐾
Benign neoplasm of cerebral ventricle
Benign neoplasm of cerebrum
Benign neoplasm of frontal lobe
Benign neoplasm of occipital lobe
Benign neoplasm of parietal lobe
Benign neoplasm of temporal lobe

Excludes1   benign neoplasm of fourth ventricle (D33.1)

D33.1 Benign neoplasm of brain, infratentorial 🐾
Benign neoplasm of brain stem
Benign neoplasm of cerebellum
Benign neoplasm of fourth ventricle

D33.2 Benign neoplasm of brain, unspecified 🐾

D33.3 Benign neoplasm of cranial nerves 🐾
Benign neoplasm of olfactory bulb

D33.4 Benign neoplasm of spinal cord 🐾

D33.7 Benign neoplasm of other specified parts of central nervous system 🐾

D33.9 Benign neoplasm of central nervous system, unspecified 🐾
Benign neoplasm of nervous system (central) NOS

D34 Benign neoplasm of thyroid gland
Use additional code to identify any functional activity.

● **D35 Benign neoplasm of other and unspecified endocrine glands**
Use additional code to identify any functional activity.

Excludes1   benign neoplasm of endocrine pancreas (D13.7)
benign neoplasm of ovary (D27.-)
benign neoplasm of testis (D29.2.-)
benign neoplasm of thymus (D15.0)

● **D35.0 Benign neoplasm of adrenal gland**

D35.00 Benign neoplasm of unspecified adrenal gland

D35.01 Benign neoplasm of right adrenal gland

D35.02 Benign neoplasm of left adrenal gland

D35.1 Benign neoplasm of parathyroid gland

D35.2 Benign neoplasm of pituitary gland 🐾

D35.3 Benign neoplasm of craniopharyngeal duct 🐾

D35.4 Benign neoplasm of pineal gland 🐾

D35.5 Benign neoplasm of carotid body

D35.6 Benign neoplasm of aortic body and other paraganglia
Benign tumor of glomus jugulare

D35.7 Benign neoplasm of other specified endocrine glands

D35.9 Benign neoplasm of endocrine gland, unspecified
Benign neoplasm of unspecified endocrine gland

● **D36 Benign neoplasm of other and unspecified sites**

D36.0 Benign neoplasm of lymph nodes

Excludes1   lymphangioma (D18.1)

● **D36.1 Benign neoplasm of peripheral nerves and autonomic nervous system**

Excludes1   benign neoplasm of peripheral nerves of orbit (D31.6-)
neurofibromatosis (Q85.0-)

D36.10 Benign neoplasm of peripheral nerves and autonomic nervous system, unspecified

D36.11 Benign neoplasm of peripheral nerves and autonomic nervous system of face, head, and neck

D36.12 Benign neoplasm of peripheral nerves and autonomic nervous system, upper limb, including shoulder

D36.13 Benign neoplasm of peripheral nerves and autonomic nervous system of lower limb, including hip

D36.14 Benign neoplasm of peripheral nerves and autonomic nervous system of thorax

D36.15 Benign neoplasm of peripheral nerves and autonomic nervous system of abdomen

D36.16 Benign neoplasm of peripheral nerves and autonomic nervous system of pelvis

D36.17 Benign neoplasm of peripheral nerves and autonomic nervous system of trunk, unspecified

D36.7 Benign neoplasm of other specified sites
Benign neoplasm of nose NOS
Benign neoplasm of back NOS

D36.9 Benign neoplasm, unspecified site

BENIGN NEUROENDOCRINE TUMORS (D3A)

● **D3A Benign neuroendocrine tumors**
Code also any associated multiple endocrine neoplasia [MEN] syndromes (E31.2-)
Use additional code to identify any associated endocrine syndrome, such as:
carcinoid syndrome (E34.0)

Excludes2   benign pancreatic islet cell tumors (D13.7)

● **D3A.0 Benign carcinoid tumors**

D3A.00 Benign carcinoid tumor of unspecified site
Carcinoid tumor NOS

● **D3A.01 Benign carcinoid tumors of the small intestine**

D3A.010 Benign carcinoid tumor of the duodenum

D3A.011 Benign carcinoid tumor of the jejunum

D3A.012 Benign carcinoid tumor of the ileum

D3A.019 Benign carcinoid tumor of the small intestine, unspecified portion

● **D3A.02 Benign carcinoid tumors of the appendix, large intestine, and rectum**

D3A.020 Benign carcinoid tumor of the appendix

D3A.021 Benign carcinoid tumor of the cecum

D3A.022 Benign carcinoid tumor of the ascending colon

D3A.023 Benign carcinoid tumor of the transverse colon

D3A.024 Benign carcinoid tumor of the descending colon

D3A.025 Benign carcinoid tumor of the sigmoid colon

D3A.026 Benign carcinoid tumor of the rectum

D3A.029 Benign carcinoid tumor of the large intestine, unspecified portion
Benign carcinoid tumor of the colon NOS

● **D3A.09 Benign carcinoid tumors of other sites**
    D3A.090   **Benign carcinoid tumor of the bronchus and lung**
    D3A.091   **Benign carcinoid tumor of the thymus**
    D3A.092   **Benign carcinoid tumor of the stomach**
    D3A.093   **Benign carcinoid tumor of the kidney**
    D3A.094   **Benign carcinoid tumor of the foregut, unspecified**
    D3A.095   **Benign carcinoid tumor of the midgut, unspecified**
    D3A.096   **Benign carcinoid tumor of the hindgut, unspecified**
    D3A.098   **Benign carcinoid tumors of other sites**

D3A.8 Other benign neuroendocrine tumors
    Neuroendocrine tumor NOS

NEOPLASMS OF UNCERTAIN BEHAVIOR, POLYCYTHEMIA VERA AND MYELODYSPLASTIC SYNDROMES (D37-D48)

Note: Categories D37-D44, and D48 classify by site neoplasms of uncertain behavior, i.e., histologic confirmation whether the neoplasm is malignant or benign cannot be made.

    Excludes1   neoplasms of unspecified behavior (D49.-)

● **D37 Neoplasm of uncertain behavior of oral cavity and digestive organs**

    Excludes1   stromal tumors of uncertain behavior of digestive system (D48.1)

● **D37.0   Neoplasm of uncertain behavior of lip, oral cavity and pharynx**

    Excludes1   neoplasm of uncertain behavior of aryepiglottic fold or interarytenoid fold, laryngeal aspect (D38.0)
      neoplasm of uncertain behavior of epiglottis NOS (D38.0)
      neoplasm of uncertain behavior of skin of lip (D48.5)
      neoplasm of uncertain behavior of suprahyoid portion of epiglottis (D38.0)

    D37.01   **Neoplasm of uncertain behavior of lip**
      Neoplasm of uncertain behavior of vermilion border of lip

    D37.02   **Neoplasm of uncertain behavior of tongue**

●   D37.03   **Neoplasm of uncertain behavior of the major salivary glands**
      D37.030   **Neoplasm of uncertain behavior of the parotid salivary glands**
      D37.031   **Neoplasm of uncertain behavior of the sublingual salivary glands**
      D37.032   **Neoplasm of uncertain behavior of the submandibular salivary glands**
      D37.039   **Neoplasm of uncertain behavior of the major salivary glands, unspecified**

D37.04   Neoplasm of uncertain behavior of the minor salivary glands
    Neoplasm of uncertain behavior of submucosal salivary glands of lip
    Neoplasm of uncertain behavior of submucosal salivary glands of cheek
    Neoplasm of uncertain behavior of submucosal salivary glands of hard palate
    Neoplasm of uncertain behavior of submucosal salivary glands of soft palate

D37.05   Neoplasm of uncertain behavior of pharynx
    Neoplasm of uncertain behavior of aryepiglottic fold of pharynx NOS
    Neoplasm of uncertain behavior of hypopharyngeal aspect of aryepiglottic fold of pharynx
    Neoplasm of uncertain behavior of marginal zone of aryepiglottic fold of pharynx

D37.09   Neoplasm of uncertain behavior of other specified sites of the oral cavity

D37.1   Neoplasm of uncertain behavior of stomach

D37.2   Neoplasm of uncertain behavior of small intestine

D37.3   Neoplasm of uncertain behavior of appendix

D37.4   Neoplasm of uncertain behavior of colon

D37.5   Neoplasm of uncertain behavior of rectum
    Neoplasm of uncertain behavior of rectosigmoid junction
    Rectosigmoid junction: Angle where sigmoid colon becomes rectum

D37.6   Neoplasm of uncertain behavior of liver, gallbladder and bile ducts
    Neoplasm of uncertain behavior of ampulla of Vater
    Ampulla of Vater: Enlarged segment of ducts from liver and pancreas at entry point to small intestine

D37.8   Neoplasm of uncertain behavior of other specified digestive organs
    Neoplasm of uncertain behavior of anal canal
    Neoplasm of uncertain behavior of anal sphincter
    Neoplasm of uncertain behavior of anus NOS
    Neoplasm of uncertain behavior of esophagus
    Neoplasm of uncertain behavior of intestine NOS
    Neoplasm of uncertain behavior of pancreas

    Excludes1   neoplasm of uncertain behavior of anal margin (D48.5)
      neoplasm of uncertain behavior of anal skin (D48.5)
      neoplasm of uncertain behavior of perianal skin (D48.5)

D37.9   Neoplasm of uncertain behavior of digestive organ, unspecified

Figure 2-19   Major salivary glands.

Parotid gland
Sublingual gland
Submandibular gland

CHAPTER 2 (C00-D49)

● **D38**   **Neoplasm of uncertain behavior of middle ear and respiratory and intrathoracic organs**

     Excludes1   neoplasm of uncertain behavior of heart (D48.7)

     D38.0   **Neoplasm of uncertain behavior of larynx**

       Neoplasm of uncertain behavior of aryepiglottic fold or interarytenoid fold, laryngeal aspect

       Neoplasm of uncertain behavior of epiglottis (suprahyoid portion)

       Excludes1   neoplasm of uncertain behavior of aryepiglottic fold or interarytenoid fold NOS (D37.05)

           neoplasm of uncertain behavior of hypopharyngeal aspect of aryepiglottic fold (D37.05)

           neoplasm of uncertain behavior of marginal zone of aryepiglottic fold (D37.05)

     D38.1   **Neoplasm of uncertain behavior of trachea, bronchus and lung**

     D38.2   **Neoplasm of uncertain behavior of pleura**

     D38.3   **Neoplasm of uncertain behavior of mediastinum**

     D38.4   **Neoplasm of uncertain behavior of thymus**

     D38.5   **Neoplasm of uncertain behavior of other respiratory organs**

       Neoplasm of uncertain behavior of accessory sinuses

       Neoplasm of uncertain behavior of cartilage of nose

       Neoplasm of uncertain behavior of middle ear

       Neoplasm of uncertain behavior of nasal cavities

       Excludes1   neoplasm of uncertain behavior of ear (external) (skin) (D48.5)

           neoplasm of uncertain behavior of nose NOS (D48.7)

           neoplasm of uncertain behavior of skin of nose (D48.5)

     D38.6   **Neoplasm of uncertain behavior of respiratory organ, unspecified**

● **D39**   **Neoplasm of uncertain behavior of female genital organs**

     D39.0   **Neoplasm of uncertain behavior of uterus ♀**

     ● **D39.1**   **Neoplasm of uncertain behavior of ovary**

       Use additional code to identify any functional activity.

       D39.10   **Neoplasm of uncertain behavior of unspecified ovary ♀**

       D39.11   **Neoplasm of uncertain behavior of right ovary ♀**

       D39.12   **Neoplasm of uncertain behavior of left ovary ♀**

     D39.2   **Neoplasm of uncertain behavior of placenta ♀M**

       Chorioadenoma destruens

       Invasive hydatidiform mole

       Malignant hydatidiform mole

       Excludes1   hydatidiform mole NOS (O01.9)

     D39.8   **Neoplasm of uncertain behavior of other specified female genital organs ♀**

       Neoplasm of uncertain behavior of skin of female genital organs

     D39.9   **Neoplasm of uncertain behavior of female genital organ, unspecified ♀**

● **D40**   **Neoplasm of uncertain behavior of male genital organs**

     D40.0   **Neoplasm of uncertain behavior of prostate ♂**

     ● **D40.1**   **Neoplasm of uncertain behavior of testis**

       D40.10   **Neoplasm of uncertain behavior of unspecified testis ♂**

       D40.11   **Neoplasm of uncertain behavior of right testis ♂**

       D40.12   **Neoplasm of uncertain behavior of left testis ♂**

     D40.8   **Neoplasm of uncertain behavior of other specified male genital organs ♂**

       Neoplasm of uncertain behavior of skin of male genital organs

     D40.9   **Neoplasm of uncertain behavior of male genital organ, unspecified ♂**

● **D41**   **Neoplasm of uncertain behavior of urinary organs**

     ● **D41.0**   **Neoplasm of uncertain behavior of kidney**

       Excludes1   neoplasm of uncertain behavior of renal pelvis (D41.1-)

       D41.00   **Neoplasm of uncertain behavior of unspecified kidney**

       D41.01   **Neoplasm of uncertain behavior of right kidney**

       D41.02   **Neoplasm of uncertain behavior of left kidney**

     ● **D41.1**   **Neoplasm of uncertain behavior of renal pelvis**

       D41.10   **Neoplasm of uncertain behavior of unspecified renal pelvis**

       D41.11   **Neoplasm of uncertain behavior of right renal pelvis**

       D41.12   **Neoplasm of uncertain behavior of left renal pelvis**

     ● **D41.2**   **Neoplasm of uncertain behavior of ureter**

       D41.20   **Neoplasm of uncertain behavior of unspecified ureter**

       D41.21   **Neoplasm of uncertain behavior of right ureter**

       D41.22   **Neoplasm of uncertain behavior of left ureter**

     D41.3   **Neoplasm of uncertain behavior of urethra**

     D41.4   **Neoplasm of uncertain behavior of bladder**

     D41.8   **Neoplasm of uncertain behavior of other specified urinary organs**

     D41.9   **Neoplasm of uncertain behavior of unspecified urinary organ**

● **D42**   **Neoplasm of uncertain behavior of meninges**

     D42.0   **Neoplasm of uncertain behavior of cerebral meninges** 🐾

     D42.1   **Neoplasm of uncertain behavior of spinal meninges** 🐾

     D42.9   **Neoplasm of uncertain behavior of meninges, unspecified** 🐾

● **D43**   **Neoplasm of uncertain behavior of brain and central nervous system**

     Excludes1   neoplasm of uncertain behavior of peripheral nerves and autonomic nervous system (D48.2)

     D43.0   **Neoplasm of uncertain behavior of brain, supratentorial** 🐾

       Superior to tentorium of cerebellum

       Neoplasm of uncertain behavior of cerebral ventricle

       Neoplasm of uncertain behavior of cerebrum

       Neoplasm of uncertain behavior of frontal lobe

       Neoplasm of uncertain behavior of occipital lobe

       Neoplasm of uncertain behavior of parietal lobe

       Neoplasm of uncertain behavior of temporal lobe

       Excludes1   neoplasm of uncertain behavior of fourth ventricle (D43.1)

     D43.1   **Neoplasm of uncertain behavior of brain, infratentorial** 🐾

       Beneath the tentorium of cerebellum

       Neoplasm of uncertain behavior of brain stem

       Neoplasm of uncertain behavior of cerebellum

       Neoplasm of uncertain behavior of fourth ventricle

     D43.2   **Neoplasm of uncertain behavior of brain, unspecified** 🐾

     D43.3   **Neoplasm of uncertain behavior of cranial nerves** 🐾

     D43.4   **Neoplasm of uncertain behavior of spinal cord** 🐾

     D43.8   **Neoplasm of uncertain behavior of other specified parts of central nervous system** 🐾

     D43.9   **Neoplasm of uncertain behavior of central nervous system, unspecified** 🐾

       Neoplasm of uncertain behavior of nervous system (central) NOS

▶ New   ⇒ Revised   ~~deleted~~ Deleted   Excludes 1   Excludes 2   Includes   Use additional   Code first   Code also   Key words

OGCR Official Guidelines   X Assign placeholder X   ● Use Additional Character(s)   ▶ Manifestation Code   🐾 Hierarchical Condition Category   **Coding Clinic**

● **D44**   **Neoplasm of uncertain behavior of endocrine glands**
> **Excludes1**   multiple endocrine adenomatosis (E31.2-)
> multiple endocrine neoplasia (E31.2-)
> neoplasm of uncertain behavior of endocrine pancreas (D37.8)
> neoplasm of uncertain behavior of ovary (D39.1-)
> neoplasm of uncertain behavior of testis (D40.1-)
> neoplasm of uncertain behavior of thymus (D38.4)

   D44.0   **Neoplasm of uncertain behavior of thyroid gland**

● **D44.1**   **Neoplasm of uncertain behavior of adrenal gland**
> Use additional code to identify any functional activity.

     D44.10   **Neoplasm of uncertain behavior of unspecified adrenal gland**

     D44.11   **Neoplasm of uncertain behavior of right adrenal gland**

     D44.12   **Neoplasm of uncertain behavior of left adrenal gland**

   D44.2   **Neoplasm of uncertain behavior of parathyroid gland**

   D44.3   **Neoplasm of uncertain behavior of pituitary gland** 🔖
> Use additional code to identify any functional activity.

   D44.4   **Neoplasm of uncertain behavior of craniopharyngeal duct** 🔖

   D44.5   **Neoplasm of uncertain behavior of pineal gland** 🔖

   D44.6   **Neoplasm of uncertain behavior of carotid body** 🔖

   D44.7   **Neoplasm of uncertain behavior of aortic body and other paraganglia** 🔖
> **Coding Clinic: 2016, Q4, P26**

   D44.9   **Neoplasm of uncertain behavior of unspecified endocrine gland**

D45   **Polycythemia vera** 🔖
> **Excludes1**   familial polycythemia (D75.0)
> secondary polycythemia (D75.1)
>
> *Primary polycythemia. Secondary polycythemia is D75.1. Check your documentation. Polycythemia is caused by too many red blood cells, which increase the thickness of blood (viscosity). This can cause engorgement of the spleen (splenomegaly) with extra RBCs and potential clot formation.*

● **D46**   **Myelodysplastic syndromes**
> Use additional code for adverse effect, if applicable, to identify drug (T36-T50 with fifth or sixth character 5)
>
> **Excludes2**   drug-induced aplastic anemia (D61.1)

   D46.0   **Refractory anemia without ring sideroblasts, so stated** 🔖
> Refractory anemia without sideroblasts, without excess of blasts

   D46.1   **Refractory anemia with ring sideroblasts RARS** 🔖

● **D46.2**   **Refractory anemia with excess of blasts [RAEB]**
> *Form of myelodysplasia with increased immature white blood cells (blasts) in bone marrow*

     D46.20   **Refractory anemia with excess of blasts, unspecified RAEB NOS** 🔖

     D46.21   **Refractory anemia with excess of blasts 1 RAEB 1** 🔖
> *Bone marrow disease which results in insufficient RBCs (anemia) in which level of blasts is less than 10%*

     D46.22   **Refractory anemia with excess of blasts 2 RAEB 2** 🔖
> *Bone marrow disease manifested by insufficient numbers of RBCs (anemia) with level of blasts 10-20%*

   D46.A   **Refractory cytopenia with multilineage dysplasia** 🔖

   D46.B   **Refractory cytopenia with multilineage dysplasia and ring sideroblasts** 🔖
> RCMD RS

   D46.C   **Myelodysplastic syndrome with isolated del(5q) chromosomal abnormality** 🔖
> Myelodysplastic syndrome with 5q deletion
> 5q minus syndrome NOS

   D46.4   **Refractory anemia, unspecified** 🔖

   D46.Z   **Other myelodysplastic syndromes** 🔖
> **Excludes1**   chronic myelomonocytic leukemia (C93.1-)

   D46.9   **Myelodysplastic syndrome, unspecified** 🔖
> Myelodysplasia NOS

● **D47**   **Other neoplasms of uncertain behavior of lymphoid, hematopoietic and related tissue**

● **D47.0**   **Mast cell neoplasms of uncertain behavior**
> **Excludes1**   congenital cutaneous mastocytosis (Q82.2)
> histiocytic neoplasms of uncertain behavior (D47.Z9)
> malignant mast cell neoplasm (C96.2-)

   D47.01   **Cutaneous mastocytosis**
> Diffuse cutaneous mastocytosis
> Maculopapular cutaneous mastocytosis
> Solitary mastocytoma
> Telangiectasia macularis eruptiva perstans
> Urticaria pigmentosa
>
> **Excludes1**   congenital (diffuse) (maculopapular) cutaneous mastocytosis (Q82.2)
> congenital urticaria pigmentosa (Q82.2)
> extracutaneous mastocytoma (D47.09)

   D47.02   **Systemic mastocytosis**
> Indolent systemic mastocytosis
> Isolated bone marrow mastocytosis
> Smoldering systemic mastocytosis
> Systemic mastocytosis, with an associated hematological non-mast cell lineage disease (SM-AHNMD)
>
> Code also if applicable, any associated hematological non-mast cell lineage disease, such as:
> acute myeloid leukemia (C92.6-, C92.A-)
> chronic myelomonocytic leukemia (C93.1-)
> essential thrombocytosis (D47.3)
> hypereosinophilic syndrome (D72.1)
> myelodysplastic syndrome (D46.9)
> myeloproliferative syndrome (D47.1)
> non-Hodgkin lymphoma (C82-C85)
> plasma cell myeloma (C90.0-)
> polycythemia vera (D45)
>
> **Excludes1**   aggressive systemic mastocytosis (C96.21)
> mast cell leukemia (C94.3-)

   D47.09   **Other mast cell neoplasms of uncertain behavior**
> Extracutaneous mastocytoma
> Mast cell tumor NOS
> Mastocytoma NOS
> Mastocytosis NOS

   D47.1   **Chronic myeloproliferative disease** 🔖
> Chronic neutrophilic leukemia
> Myeloproliferative disease, unspecified
>
> **Excludes1**   atypical chronic myeloid leukemia BCR/ABL-negative (C92.2-)
> chronic myeloid leukemia BCR/ABL-positive (C92.1-)
> myelofibrosis NOS (D75.81)
> myelophthisic anemia (D61.82)
> myelophthisis (D61.82)
> secondary myelofibrosis NOS (D75.81)

D47.2   Monoclonal gammopathy
Monoclonal gammopathy of undetermined significance [MGUS]

D47.3   Essential (hemorrhagic) thrombocythemia 🐾
Essential thrombocytosis
Idiopathic hemorrhagic thrombocythemia

D47.4   Osteomyelofibrosis 🐾
Chronic idiopathic myelofibrosis
Myelofibrosis (idiopathic) (with myeloid metaplasia)
Myelosclerosis (megakaryocytic) with myeloid metaplasia
Secondary myelofibrosis in myeloproliferative disease

> **Excludes1**   acute myelofibrosis (C94.4-)

● **D47.Z   Other specified neoplasms of uncertain behavior of lymphoid, hematopoietic and related tissue**

D47.Z1   Post-transplant lymphoproliferative disorder (PTLD) 🐾

> *Code first complications of transplanted organs and tissue (T86.-)*

D47.Z2   Castleman disease 🐾

> Code also if applicable human herpesvirus 8 infection (B10.89)

> ➠ **Excludes2**   Kaposi's sarcoma (C46.-)

> **Coding Clinic: 2016, Q4, P8**

D47.Z9   Other specified neoplasms of uncertain behavior of lymphoid, hematopoietic and related tissue 🐾
Histiocytic tumors of uncertain behavior

D47.9   Neoplasm of uncertain behavior of lymphoid, hematopoietic and related tissue, unspecified 🐾
Lymphoproliferative disease NOS

● **D48   Neoplasm of uncertain behavior of other and unspecified sites**

> **Excludes1**   neurofibromatosis (nonmalignant) (Q85.0-)

D48.0   Neoplasm of uncertain behavior of bone and articular cartilage

> **Excludes1**   neoplasm of uncertain behavior of cartilage of ear (D48.1)
> neoplasm of uncertain behavior of cartilage of larynx (D38.0)
> neoplasm of uncertain behavior of cartilage of nose (D38.5)
> neoplasm of uncertain behavior of connective tissue of eyelid (D48.1)
> neoplasm of uncertain behavior of synovia (D48.1)

D48.1   Neoplasm of uncertain behavior of connective and other soft tissue
Neoplasm of uncertain behavior of connective tissue of ear
Neoplasm of uncertain behavior of connective tissue of eyelid
Stromal tumors of uncertain behavior of digestive system

> **Excludes1**   neoplasm of uncertain behavior of articular cartilage (D48.0)
> neoplasm of uncertain behavior of cartilage of larynx (D38.0)
> neoplasm of uncertain behavior of cartilage of nose (D38.5)
> neoplasm of uncertain behavior of connective tissue of breast (D48.6-)

D48.2   Neoplasm of uncertain behavior of peripheral nerves and autonomic nervous system

> **Excludes1**   neoplasm of uncertain behavior of peripheral nerves of orbit (D48.7)

D48.3   Neoplasm of uncertain behavior of retroperitoneum

D48.4   Neoplasm of uncertain behavior of peritoneum

D48.5   Neoplasm of uncertain behavior of skin
Neoplasm of uncertain behavior of anal margin
Neoplasm of uncertain behavior of anal skin
Neoplasm of uncertain behavior of perianal skin
Neoplasm of uncertain behavior of skin of breast

> **Excludes1**   neoplasm of uncertain behavior of anus NOS (D37.8)
> neoplasm of uncertain behavior of skin of genital organs (D39.8, D40.8)
> neoplasm of uncertain behavior of vermilion border of lip (D37.0)

● **D48.6   Neoplasm of uncertain behavior of breast**
Neoplasm of uncertain behavior of connective tissue of breast
Cystosarcoma phyllodes

> **Excludes1**   neoplasm of uncertain behavior of skin of breast (D48.5)

D48.60   Neoplasm of uncertain behavior of unspecified breast

D48.61   Neoplasm of uncertain behavior of right breast

D48.62   Neoplasm of uncertain behavior of left breast

D48.7   Neoplasm of uncertain behavior of other specified sites
Neoplasm of uncertain behavior of eye
Neoplasm of uncertain behavior of heart
Neoplasm of uncertain behavior of peripheral nerves of orbit

> **Excludes1**   neoplasm of uncertain behavior of connective tissue (D48.1)
> neoplasm of uncertain behavior of skin of eyelid (D48.5)

D48.9   Neoplasm of uncertain behavior, unspecified

● **D49   Neoplasms of unspecified behavior**

Note: Category D49 classifies by site neoplasms of unspecified morphology and behavior. The term "mass," unless otherwise stated, is not to be regarded as a neoplastic growth.

> **Includes**   'growth' NOS
> neoplasm NOS
> new growth NOS
> tumor NOS

> **Excludes1**   neoplasms of uncertain behavior (D37-D44, D48)

D49.0   Neoplasm of unspecified behavior of digestive system

> **Excludes1**   neoplasm of unspecified behavior of margin of anus (D49.2)
> neoplasm of unspecified behavior of perianal skin (D49.2)
> neoplasm of unspecified behavior of skin of anus (D49.2)

D49.1   Neoplasm of unspecified behavior of respiratory system

D49.2   Neoplasm of unspecified behavior of bone, soft tissue, and skin

> **Excludes1**   neoplasm of unspecified behavior of anal canal (D49.0)
> neoplasm of unspecified behavior of anus NOS (D49.0)
> neoplasm of unspecified behavior of bone marrow (D49.89)
> neoplasm of unspecified behavior of cartilage of larynx (D49.1)
> neoplasm of unspecified behavior of cartilage of nose (D49.1)
> neoplasm of unspecified behavior of connective tissue of breast (D49.3)
> neoplasm of unspecified behavior of skin of genital organs (D49.59)
> neoplasm of unspecified behavior of vermilion border of lip (D49.0)

▶ New   ➠ Revised   ~~deleted~~ Deleted   Excludes 1   Excludes 2   Includes   Use additional   Code first   Code also   Key words
OGCR Official Guidelines   X Assign placeholder X   ● Use Additional Character(s)   ❱ Manifestation Code   🐾 Hierarchical Condition Category   **Coding Clinic**

D49.3   Neoplasm of unspecified behavior of breast
    Excludes1   neoplasm of unspecified behavior of skin
              of breast (D49.2)

D49.4   Neoplasm of unspecified behavior of bladder

● D49.5   Neoplasm of unspecified behavior of other
    genitourinary organs

    ● D49.51   Neoplasm of unspecified behavior of kidney

        D49.511   Neoplasm of unspecified behavior of
              right kidney
              Coding Clinic: 2016, Q4, P9

        D49.512   Neoplasm of unspecified behavior of
              left kidney
              Coding Clinic: 2016, Q4, P9

        D49.519   Neoplasm of unspecified behavior of
              unspecified kidney
              Coding Clinic: 2016, Q4, P9

    D49.59   Neoplasm of unspecified behavior of other
        genitourinary organ
        Coding Clinic: 2016, Q4, P9

D49.6   Neoplasm of unspecified behavior of brain 🔊
    Excludes1   neoplasm of unspecified behavior of
              cerebral meninges (D49.7)
           neoplasm of unspecified behavior of
              cranial nerves (D49.7)

D49.7   Neoplasm of unspecified behavior of endocrine glands
    and other parts of nervous system
    Excludes1   neoplasm of unspecified behavior
              of peripheral, sympathetic, and
              parasympathetic nerves and ganglia
              (D49.2)

● D49.8   Neoplasm of unspecified behavior of other specified
    sites
    Excludes1   neoplasm of unspecified behavior of
              eyelid (skin) (D49.2)
           neoplasm of unspecified behavior of
              eyelid cartilage (D49.2)
           neoplasm of unspecified behavior of great
              vessels (D49.2)
           neoplasm of unspecified behavior of optic
              nerve (D49.7)

    D49.81   Neoplasm of unspecified behavior of retina and
        choroid
        Dark area on retina
        Retinal freckle

    D49.89   Neoplasm of unspecified behavior of other
        specified sites

D49.9   Neoplasm of unspecified behavior of unspecified site

CHAPTER 2 (C00–D49)

OGCR Chapter-Specific Coding Guidelines

3. Chapter 3: Disease of the blood and blood-forming organs and certain disorders involving the immune mechanism (D50-D89)
Reserved for future guideline expansion

CHAPTER 3

DISEASES OF THE BLOOD AND BLOOD-FORMING ORGANS AND CERTAIN DISORDERS INVOLVING THE IMMUNE MECHANISM (D50-D89)

Excludes2   autoimmune disease (systemic) NOS (M35.9)
certain conditions originating in the perinatal period (P00-P96)
complications of pregnancy, childbirth and the puerperium (O00-O9A)
congenital malformations, deformations and chromosomal abnormalities (Q00-Q99)
endocrine, nutritional and metabolic diseases (E00-E88)
human immunodeficiency virus [HIV] disease (B20)
injury, poisoning and certain other consequences of external causes (S00-T88)
neoplasms (C00-D49)
symptoms, signs and abnormal clinical and laboratory findings, not elsewhere classified (R00-R94)

This chapter contains the following blocks:

D50-D53	Nutritional anemias
D55-D59	Hemolytic anemias
D60-D64	Aplastic and other anemias and other bone marrow failure syndromes
D65-D69	Coagulation defects, purpura and other hemorrhagic conditions
D70-D77	Other disorders of blood and blood-forming organs
D78	Intraoperative and postprocedural complications of the spleen
D80-D89	Certain disorders involving the immune mechanism

NUTRITIONAL ANEMIAS (D50-D53)

● **D50   Iron deficiency anemia**
A disease characterized by a decrease in the number of red cells (hemoglobin) in the blood.

     Includes   asiderotic anemia
hypochromic anemia

   D50.0   Iron deficiency anemia secondary to blood loss (chronic)
Posthemorrhagic anemia (chronic)

     Excludes1   acute posthemorrhagic anemia (D62)
congenital anemia from fetal blood loss (P61.3)

     Coding Clinic: 2019, Q3, P17

   D50.1   Sideropenic dysphagia
Weblike growth of membranes in throat that makes swallowing difficult
Kelly-Paterson syndrome
Plummer-Vinson syndrome

   D50.8   Other iron deficiency anemias
Iron deficiency anemia due to inadequate dietary iron intake

   D50.9   Iron deficiency anemia, unspecified

● **D51   Vitamin B12 deficiency anemia**

     Excludes1   vitamin B12 deficiency (E53.8)

   D51.0   Vitamin B12 deficiency anemia due to intrinsic factor deficiency
Addison anemia
Biermer anemia
Pernicious (congenital) anemia
Congenital intrinsic factor deficiency

   D51.1   Vitamin B12 deficiency anemia due to selective vitamin B12 malabsorption with proteinuria
Imerslund (Gräsbeck) syndrome
Megaloblastic hereditary anemia

   D51.2   Transcobalamin II deficiency

   D51.3   Other dietary vitamin B12 deficiency anemia
Vegan anemia

   D51.8   Other vitamin B12 deficiency anemias

   D51.9   Vitamin B12 deficiency anemia, unspecified

● **D52   Folate deficiency anemia**

     Excludes1   folate deficiency without anemia (E53.8)

   D52.0   Dietary folate deficiency anemia
Nutritional megaloblastic anemia

   D52.1   Drug-induced folate deficiency anemia
Use additional code for adverse effect, if applicable, to identify drug (T36-T50 with fifth or sixth character 5)

   D52.8   Other folate deficiency anemias

   D52.9   Folate deficiency anemia, unspecified
Folic acid deficiency anemia NOS

● **D53   Other nutritional anemias**

     Includes   megaloblastic anemia unresponsive to vitamin B12 or folate therapy

   D53.0   Protein deficiency anemia
Amino-acid deficiency anemia
Orotaciduric anemia

     Excludes1   Lesch-Nyhan syndrome (E79.1)

   D53.1   Other megaloblastic anemias, not elsewhere classified
Megaloblastic anemia NOS

     Excludes1   Di Guglielmo's disease (C94.0)

   D53.2   Scorbutic anemia
Anemia resulting from deficiency of ascorbic acid (vitamin C)

     Excludes1   scurvy (E54)

   D53.8   Other specified nutritional anemias
Anemia associated with deficiency of copper
Anemia associated with deficiency of molybdenum
Anemia associated with deficiency of zinc

     Excludes1   nutritional deficiencies without anemia, such as:
copper deficiency NOS (E61.0)
molybdenum deficiency NOS (E61.5)
zinc deficiency NOS (E60)

   D53.9   Nutritional anemia, unspecified
Simple chronic anemia

     Excludes1   anemia NOS (D64.9)

     Coding Clinic: 2018, Q4, P88

HEMOLYTIC ANEMIAS (D55-D59)

● **D55   Anemia due to enzyme disorders**

     Excludes1   drug-induced enzyme deficiency anemia (D59.2)

   D55.0   Anemia due to glucose-6-phosphate dehydrogenase [G6PD] deficiency 🔖
Favism
G6PD deficiency anemia

     Excludes1   glucose-6-phosphate dehydrogenase (G6PD) deficiency without anemia (D75.A)

   D55.1   Anemia due to other disorders of glutathione metabolism 🔖
Anemia (due to) enzyme deficiencies, except G6PD, related to the hexose monophosphate [HMP] shunt pathway
Anemia (due to) hemolytic nonspherocytic (hereditary), type I

▶ New   ⇒ Revised   ~~deleted~~ Deleted   Excludes 1   Excludes 2   Includes   Use additional   Code first   Code also   Key words

OGCR Official Guidelines   X Assign placeholder X   ● Use Additional Character(s)   ▶ Manifestation Code   🔖 Hierarchical Condition Category   **Coding Clinic**

D55.2   Anemia due to disorders of glycolytic enzymes 🦠
    Hemolytic nonspherocytic (hereditary) anemia, type II
    Hexokinase deficiency anemia
    Pyruvate kinase [PK] deficiency anemia
    Triose-phosphate isomerase deficiency anemia
      Excludes1   disorders of glycolysis not associated
               with anemia (E74.81-)

D55.3   Anemia due to disorders of nucleotide metabolism 🦠

D55.8   Other anemias due to enzyme disorders 🦠

D55.9   Anemia due to enzyme disorder, unspecified 🦠

● **D56   Thalassemia**
    Hereditary disorders characterized by low production of hemoglobin
    or excessive destruction of red blood cells
     Excludes1   sickle-cell thalassemia (D57.4-)

D56.0   Alpha thalassemia 🦠
    Alpha thalassemia major
    Hemoglobin H Constant Spring
    Hemoglobin H disease
    Hydrops fetalis due to alpha thalassemia
    Severe alpha thalassemia
    Triple gene defect alpha thalassemia
    Use additional code, if applicable, for hydrops fetalis
       due to alpha thalassemia (P56.99)
      Excludes1   alpha thalassemia trait or minor (D56.3)
              asymptomatic alpha thalassemia (D56.3)
              hydrops fetalis due to isoimmunization
                 (P56.0)
              hydrops fetalis not due to immune
                 hemolysis (P83.2)

D56.1   Beta thalassemia 🦠
    Beta thalassemia major
    Cooley's anemia
    Homozygous beta thalassemia
    Severe beta thalassemia
    Thalassemia intermedia
    Thalassemia major
      Excludes1   beta thalassemia minor (D56.3)
              beta thalassemia trait (D56.3)
              delta-beta thalassemia (D56.2)
              hemoglobin E-beta thalassemia (D56.5)
              sickle-cell beta thalassemia (D57.4-)

D56.2   Delta-beta thalassemia 🦠
    Homozygous delta-beta thalassemia
      Excludes1   delta-beta thalassemia minor (D56.3)
              delta-beta thalassemia trait (D56.3)

D56.3   Thalassemia minor
    Genetic disorders that have in common defective production
       of hemoglobin
    Alpha thalassemia minor
    Alpha thalassemia silent carrier
    Alpha thalassemia trait
    Beta thalassemia minor
    Beta thalassemia trait
    Delta-beta thalassemia minor
    Delta-beta thalassemia trait
    Thalassemia trait NOS
      Excludes1   alpha thalassemia (D56.0)
              beta thalassemia (D56.1)
              delta-beta thalassemia (D56.2)
              hemoglobin E-beta thalassemia (D56.5)
              sickle-cell trait (D57.3)

D56.4   Hereditary persistence of fetal hemoglobin [HPFH] 🦠
    Persistent production of hemoglobin

D56.5   Hemoglobin E-beta thalassemia 🦠
      Excludes1   beta thalassemia (D56.1)
              beta thalassemia minor (D56.3)
              beta thalassemia trait (D56.3)
              delta-beta thalassemia (D56.2)
              delta-beta thalassemia trait (D56.3)
              hemoglobin E disease (D58.2)
              other hemoglobinopathies (D58.2)
              sickle-cell beta thalassemia (D57.4-)

D56.8   Other thalassemias 🦠
    Dominant thalassemia
    Hemoglobin C thalassemia
    Mixed thalassemia
    Thalassemia with other hemoglobinopathy
      Excludes1   hemoglobin C disease (D58.2)
              hemoglobin E disease (D58.2)
              other hemoglobinopathies (D58.2)
              sickle cell anemia (D57.-)
              sickle-cell thalassemia (D57.4)

D56.9   Thalassemia, unspecified
    Mediterranean anemia (with other hemoglobinopathy)

● **D57   Sickle-cell disorders**
    Inherited disease in which red blood cells, normally disc-shaped,
      become crescent shaped
    Use additional code for any associated fever (R50.81)
     Excludes1   other hemoglobinopathies (D58.-)

● **D57.0   Hb-SS disease with crisis**
    Sickle-cell disease with crisis
    Hb-SS disease with vasoocclusive pain

    D57.00   Hb-SS disease with crisis, unspecified 🦠
      ▸ Hb-SS disease with (painful) crisis NOS
      ▸ Hb-SS disease with vasoocclusive pain NOS

    D57.01   Hb-SS disease with acute chest syndrome 🦠

    D57.02   Hb-SS disease with splenic sequestration 🦠

    ▸ **D57.03   Hb-SS disease with cerebral vascular**
       involvement
       ▸ Code also, if applicable, cerebral infarction
          (I63.-)

    ▸ **D57.09   Hb-SS disease with crisis with other specified**
       complication
      ▸ Use additional code to identify complications, such as:
       ▸ cholelithiasis (K80.-)
       ▸ priapism (N48.32)

**D57.1   Sickle-cell disease without crisis Hb-SS disease without
crisis** 🦠
    Sickle-cell anemia NOS
    Sickle-cell disease NOS
    Sickle-cell disorder NOS

● **D57.2   Sickle-cell/Hb-C disease**
    Hb-SC disease
    Hb-S/Hb-C disease

    D57.20   Sickle-cell/Hb-C disease without crisis 🦠

    ● **D57.21   Sickle-cell/Hb-C disease with crisis**

      **D57.211   Sickle-cell/Hb-C disease with acute
             chest syndrome** 🦠

      **D57.212   Sickle-cell/Hb-C disease with splenic
             sequestration** 🦠

      ▸ **D57.213   Sickle-cell/Hb-C disease with cerebral
             vascular involvement**
         ▸ Code also, if applicable, cerebral
            infarction (I63.-)

      ▸ **D57.218   Sickle-cell/Hb-C disease with crisis
             with other specified complication**
         ▸ Use additional code to identify
            complications, such as:
            ▸ cholelithiasis (K80.-)
            ▸ priapism (N48.32)

      **D57.219   Sickle-cell/Hb-C disease with
             crisis, unspecified** 🦠
         Sickle-cell/Hb-C disease with crisis
           NOS
         ▸ Sickle-cell/Hb-C disease with
           vasoocclusive pain NOS

D57.3   Sickle-cell trait 🦠
    Hb-S trait
    Heterozygous hemoglobin S

● **D57.4   Sickle-cell thalassemia**
          Sickle-cell beta thalassemia
          Thalassemia Hb-S disease

   D57.40   Sickle-cell thalassemia without crisis 🅗🅒
              Microdrepanocytosis
              Sickle-cell thalassemia NOS

➡● **D57.41   Sickle-cell thalassemia, unspecified, with crisis**
              *Sickle-cell "crisis" is precipitated when abnormally
              crescent-shaped red blood cells form clots and
              interrupt blood flow to major organs, causing
              severe pain and organ damage.*
              ▶Sickle-cell thalassemia with (painful) crisis
                 NOS
              ➡Sickle-cell thalassemia with vasoocclusive pain
                 NOS

      ➡ **D57.411   Sickle-cell thalassemia, unspecified,
                    with acute chest syndrome** 🅗🅒

      ➡ **D57.412   Sickle-cell thalassemia with,
                    unspecified, splenic sequestration** 🅗🅒

      ▶ **D57.413   Sickle-cell thalassemia, unspecified,
                    with cerebral vascular involvement**
                    ▶ Code also, if applicable cerebral
                       infarction (I63.-)

      ▶ **D57.418   Sickle-cell thalassemia, unspecified,
                    with crisis with other specified
                    complication**
                    ▶ Use additional code to identify
                       complications, such as:
                       ▶cholelithiasis (K80.-)
                       ▶priapism (N48.32)

      ➡ **D57.419   Sickle-cell thalassemia with,
                    unspecified, crisis, ~~unspecified~~** 🅗🅒
                    ➡Sickle-cell thalassemia with (painful)
                       crisis NOS
                    ▶Sickle-cell thalassemia with
                       vasoocclusive pain

   ▶ **D57.42   Sickle-cell thalassemia beta zero without crisis**
              ▶HbS-beta zero without crisis
              ▶Sickle-cell beta zero without crisis

➡● **D57.43   Sickle-cell thalassemia beta zero with crisis**
              ▶HbS-beta zero with crisis
              ▶Sickle-cell beta zero with crisis

      ▶ **D57.431   Sickle-cell thalassemia beta zero with
                    acute chest syndrome**
                    ▶HbS-beta zero with acute chest
                       syndrome
                    ▶Sickle-cell beta zero with acute chest
                       syndrome

      ▶ **D57.432   Sickle-cell thalassemia beta zero with
                    splenic sequestration**
                    ▶HbS-beta zero with splenic
                       sequestration
                    ▶Sickle-cell beta zero with splenic
                       sequestration

      ▶ **D57.433   Sickle-cell thalassemia beta zero with
                    cerebral vascular involvement**
                    ▶HbS-beta zero with cerebral vascular
                       involvement
                    ▶Sickle-cell beta zero with cerebral
                       vascular involvement
                    ▶Code also, if applicable cerebral
                       infarction (I63.-)

      ➡ **D57.438   Sickle-cell thalassemia beta zero with
                    crisis with other specified
                    complication**
                    ▶HbS-beta zero with other specified
                       complication
                    ▶Sickle-cell beta zero with other
                       specified complication
                    ▶Use additional code to identify
                       complications, such as:
                       ▶cholelithiasis (K80.-)
                       ▶priapism (N48.32)

▶ **D57.439   Sickle-cell thalassemia beta zero with
              crisis, unspecified**
              ▶HbS-beta zero with other specified
                 complication
              ▶Sickle-cell beta zero with crisis
                 unspecified
              ▶Sickle-cell thalassemia beta zero
                 with (painful) crisis NOS
              ▶Sickle-cell thalassemia beta zero
                 with vasoocclusive pain

▶ **D57.44   Sickle-cell thalassemia beta plus without crisis**
              ▶HbS-beta plus without crisis
              ▶Sickle-cell beta plus without crisis

▶● **D57.45   Sickle-cell thalassemia beta plus with crisis**
              ▶HbS-beta plus with crisis
              ▶Sickle-cell beta plus with crisis

      ▶ **D57.451   Sickle-cell thalassemia beta plus with
                    acute chest syndrome**
                    ▶HbS-beta plus with acute chest
                       syndrome
                    ▶Sickle-cell beta plus with acute chest
                       syndrome

      ▶ **D57.452   Sickle-cell thalassemia beta plus with
                    splenic sequestration**
                    ▶HbS-beta plus with splenic
                       sequestration
                    ▶Sickle-cell beta plus with splenic
                       sequestration

      ▶ **D57.453   Sickle-cell thalassemia beta plus with
                    cerebral vascular involvement**
                    ▶HbS-beta plus with cerebral vascular
                       involvement
                    ▶Sickle-cell beta plus with cerebral
                       vascular involvement
                    ▶Code also, if applicable cerebral
                       infarction (I63.-)

      ▶ **D57.458   Sickle-cell thalassemia beta plus with
                    crisis with other specified
                    complication**
                    ▶HbS-beta plus with crisis with other
                       specified complication
                    ▶Sickle-cell beta plus with crisis with
                       other specified complication
                    ▶Use additional code to identify
                       complications, such as:
                       ▶cholelithiasis (K80.-)
                       ▶priapism (N48.32)

      ▶ **D57.459   Sickle-cell thalassemia beta plus with
                    crisis, unspecified**
              ▶HbS-beta plus with crisis with unspecified
                 complication
              ▶Sickle-cell beta plus with crisis with
                 unspecified complication
              ▶Sickle-cell thalassemia beta plus with (painful)
                 crisis NOS
              ▶Sickle-cell thalassemia beta plus with
                 vasoocclusive pain

● **D57.8   Other sickle-cell disorders**
          Hb-SD disease
          Hb-SE disease

   D57.80   Other sickle-cell disorders without crisis 🅗🅒

● **D57.81   Other sickle-cell disorders with crisis**

      **D57.811   Other sickle-cell disorders with acute
                 chest syndrome** 🅗🅒

      **D57.812   Other sickle-cell disorders with
                 splenic sequestration** 🅗🅒

      ▶ **D57.813   Other sickle-cell disorders with
                    cerebral vascular involvement**
                    ▶Code also, if applicable: cerebral
                       infarction (I63.-)

▶ New   ➡ Revised   ~~deleted~~ Deleted   Excludes 1   Excludes 2   Includes   Use additional   Code first   Code also   Key words

OGCR Official Guidelines   X Assign placeholder X   ● Use Additional Character(s)   ▷ Manifestation Code   🅗🅒 Hierarchical Condition Category   **Coding Clinic**

CHAPTER 3 (D50-D89)

▶ **D57.818   Other sickle-cell disorders with crisis with other specified complication**
  ▶Use additional code to identify complications, such as:
    ▶cholelithiasis (K80.-)
    ▶priapism (N48.32)

D57.819   Other sickle-cell disorders with crisis, unspecified 🔖
    Other sickle-cell disorders with crisis NOS
    ▶Other sickle-cell disorders with vasooclusive pain NOS

● **D58   Other hereditary hemolytic anemias**
    Genetic condition in which bone marrow is unable to compensate for premature destruction of red blood cells
    Excludes1   hemolytic anemia of the newborn (P55.-)

D58.0   Hereditary spherocytosis
    Presence of spherocytes (spherically shaped red blood cells)
    Acholuric (familial) jaundice
    Congenital (spherocytic) hemolytic icterus
    Minkowski-Chauffard syndrome

D58.1   Hereditary elliptocytosis 🔖
    Presence of large numbers of elliptocytes in blood
    Elliptocytosis (congenital)
    Ovalocytosis (congenital) (hereditary)

D58.2   Other hemoglobinopathies 🔖
    Abnormal hemoglobin NOS
    Congenital Heinz body anemia
    Hb-C disease
    Hb-D disease
    Hb-E disease
    Hemoglobinopathy NOS
    Unstable hemoglobin hemolytic disease
    Excludes1   familial polycythemia (D75.0)
                Hb-M disease (D74.0)
                hemoglobin E-beta thalassemia (D56.5)
                hereditary persistence of fetal hemoglobin [HPFH] (D56.4)
                high-altitude polycythemia (D75.1)
                methemoglobinemia (D74.-)
                other hemoglobinopathies with thalassemia (D56.8)

D58.8   Other specified hereditary hemolytic anemias 🔖
    Stomatocytosis

D58.9   Hereditary hemolytic anemia, unspecified 🔖

● **D59   Acquired hemolytic anemia**

D59.0   Drug-induced autoimmune hemolytic anemia 🔖
    Use additional code for adverse effect, if applicable, to identify drug (T36-T50 with fifth or sixth character 5)

D59.1   Other autoimmune hemolytic anemias 🔖
    ▶ **Excludes2**   Evans syndrome (D69.41)
                ▶hemolytic disease of newborn (P55.-)
                ▶paroxysmal cold hemoglobinuria (D59.6)

▶ **D59.10   Autoimmune hemolytic anemia, unspecified**

▶ **D59.11   Warm autoimmune hemolytic anemia**
    ▶Warm type (primary) (secondary) (symptomatic) autoimmune hemolytic anemia
    ▶Warm type autoimmune hemolytic disease

▶ **D59.12   Cold autoimmune hemolytic anemia**
    ▶Chronic cold hemagglutinin disease
    ▶Cold agglutinin disease
    ▶Cold agglutinin hemoglobinuria
    ▶Cold type (primary) (secondary) (symptomatic) autoimmune hemolytic anemia
    ▶Cold type autoimmune hemolytic disease

▶ **D59.13   Mixed type autoimmune hemolytic anemia**
    ▶Mixed type autoimmune hemolytic disease
    ▶Mixed type, cold and warm, (primary) (secondary) (symptomatic) autoimmune hemolyticanemia

▶ **D59.19   Other autoimmune hemolytic anemia**
    Autoimmune hemolytic disease (cold type) (warm type)
    Chronic cold hemagglutinin disease
    Cold agglutinin disease
    Cold agglutinin hemoglobinuria
    Cold type (secondary) (symptomatic) hemolytic anemia
    Warm type (secondary) (symptomatic) hemolytic anemia
    Excludes1   Evans syndrome (D69.41)
                hemolytic disease of newborn (P55.-)
                paroxysmal cold hemoglobinuria (D59.6)

D59.2   Drug-induced nonautoimmune hemolytic anemia 🔖
    Drug-induced enzyme deficiency anemia
    Use additional code for adverse effect, if applicable, to identify drug (T36-T50 with fifth or sixth character 5)

D59.3   Hemolytic-uremic syndrome 🔖
    Use additional code to identify associated:
        E. coli infection (B96.2-)
        Pneumococcal pneumonia (J13)
        Shigella dysenteriae (A03.9)

D59.4   Other nonautoimmune hemolytic anemias 🔖
    Mechanical hemolytic anemia
    Microangiopathic hemolytic anemia
    Toxic hemolytic anemia

D59.5   Paroxysmal nocturnal hemoglobinuria [Marchiafava-Micheli] 🔖
    Excludes1   hemoglobinuria NOS (R82.3)

D59.6   Hemoglobinuria due to hemolysis from other external causes 🔖
    Hemoglobinuria from exertion
    March hemoglobinuria
    Paroxysmal cold hemoglobinuria
    Use additional code (Chapter 20) to identify external cause
    Excludes1   hemoglobinuria NOS (R82.3)

D59.8   Other acquired hemolytic anemias 🔖

D59.9   Acquired hemolytic anemia, unspecified 🔖
    Idiopathic hemolytic anemia, chronic

APLASTIC AND OTHER ANEMIAS AND OTHER BONE MARROW FAILURE SYNDROMES (D60-D64)

● **D60   Acquired pure red cell aplasia [erythroblastopenia]**
    Deficiency of erythroblasts
    Includes   red cell aplasia (acquired) (adult) (with thymoma)
    Excludes1   congenital red cell aplasia (D61.01)

D60.0   Chronic acquired pure red cell aplasia 🔖
    Lack of development of blood cell

D60.1   Transient acquired pure red cell aplasia 🔖

D60.8   Other acquired pure red cell aplasias 🔖

D60.9   Acquired pure red cell aplasia, unspecified 🔖

● **D61   Other aplastic anemias and other bone marrow failure syndromes**
    Excludes1   neutropenia (D70.-)
    ⇒ **Excludes2**   neutropenia (D70.-)

● **D61.0   Constitutional aplastic anemia**
    Condition where bone marrow is unable to produce blood cells

    D61.01   Constitutional (pure) red blood cell aplasia 🔖
        Blackfan-Diamond syndrome
        Congenital (pure) red cell aplasia
        Familial hypoplastic anemia
        Primary (pure) red cell aplasia
        Red cell (pure) aplasia of infants
        Excludes1   acquired red cell aplasia (D60.9)

    D61.09   Other constitutional aplastic anemia 🔖
        Fanconi's anemia
        Pancytopenia with malformations

N Newborn Age: 0   **P** Pediatric Age: 0–17   **M** Maternity DX: 12–55   **A** Adult Age: 15–124   ♀ Females Only   ♂ Males Only

D61.1 **Drug-induced aplastic anemia** 🦠

Use additional code for adverse effect, if applicable, to identify drug (T36-T50 with fifth or sixth character 5)

D61.2 **Aplastic anemia due to other external agents** 🦠

Code first, if applicable, toxic effects of substances chiefly nonmedicinal as to source (T51-T65)

D61.3 **Idiopathic aplastic anemia** 🦠

● **D61.8** **Other specified aplastic anemias and other bone marrow failure syndromes**

● **D61.81** **Pancytopenia**

Marked deficiency of all the blood elements: Red blood cells (erythrocytes), white blood cells (leukocytes), and platelets (thrombocytes). Check laboratory results.

Excludes1   pancytopenia (due to) (with) aplastic anemia (D61.9)

pancytopenia (due to) (with) bone marrow infiltration (D61.82)

pancytopenia (due to) (with) congenital (pure) red cell aplasia (D61.01)

pancytopenia (due to) (with) hairy cell leukemia (C91.4-)

pancytopenia (due to) (with) human immunodeficiency virus disease (B20.-)

pancytopenia (due to) (with) leukoerythroblastic anemia (D61.82)

pancytopenia (due to) (with) myeloproliferative disease (D47.1)

Excludes2   pancytopenia (due to) (with) myelodysplastic syndromes (D46.-)

D61.810 **Antineoplastic chemotherapy induced pancytopenia** 🦠

Excludes2   aplastic anemia due to antineoplastic chemotherapy (D61.1)

D61.811 **Other drug-induced pancytopenia** 🦠

Excludes2   aplastic anemia due to drugs (D61.1)

D61.818 **Other pancytopenia** 🦠
Coding Clinic: 2019, Q1, P16

D61.82 **Myelophthisis** 🦠
Leukoerythroblastic anemia
Myelophthisic anemia
Panmyelophthisis

Code also the underlying disorder, such as:
malignant neoplasm of breast (C50.-)
tuberculosis (A15.-)

Excludes1   idiopathic myelofibrosis (D47.1)
myelofibrosis NOS (D75.81)

myelofibrosis with myeloid metaplasia (D47.4)

primary myelofibrosis (D47.1)

secondary myelofibrosis (D75.81)

D61.89 **Other specified aplastic anemias and other bone marrow failure syndromes** 🦠

D61.9 **Aplastic anemia, unspecified** 🦠
Hypoplastic anemia NOS
Medullary hypoplasia

D62 **Acute posthemorrhagic anemia**

Excludes1   anemia due to chronic blood loss (D50.0)
blood loss anemia NOS (D50.0)
congenital anemia from fetal blood loss (P61.3)
Coding Clinic: 2019, Q3, P13,17

● **D63** **Anemia in chronic diseases classified elsewhere**

▷ **D63.0** *Anemia in neoplastic disease*
Code first neoplasm (C00-D49)

Excludes1   aplastic anemia due to antineoplastic chemotherapy (D61.1)

Excludes2   anemia due to antineoplastic chemotherapy (D64.81)

OGCR Section I.C.2.e.2.

2) Anemia associated with chemotherapy, immunotherapy and radiation therapy

When the admission/encounter is for management of an anemia associated with an adverse effect of the administration of chemotherapy or immunotherapy and the only treatment is for the anemia, the anemia code is sequenced first followed by the appropriate codes for the neoplasm and the adverse effect (T45.1X5, Adverse effect of antineoplastic and immunosuppressive drugs).

▷ **D63.1** *Anemia in chronic kidney disease*
Erythropoietin resistant anemia (EPO resistant anemia)
Code first underlying chronic kidney disease (CKD) (N18.-)

▷ **D63.8** *Anemia in other chronic diseases classified elsewhere*
Code first underlying disease, such as:
diphyllobothriasis (B70.0)
hookworm disease (B76.0-B76.9)
hypothyroidism (E00.0-E03.9)
malaria (B50.0-B54)
symptomatic late syphilis (A52.79)
tuberculosis (A18.89)

● **D64** **Other anemias**

Excludes1   refractory anemia (D46.-)
refractory anemia with excess blasts in transformation [RAEB T] (C92.0-)

D64.0 **Hereditary sideroblastic anemia** 🦠
Abnormal production RBCs (erythrocytes)
Sex-linked hypochromic sideroblastic anemia

▷ **D64.1** *Secondary sideroblastic anemia due to disease* 🦠
Code first underlying disease

D64.2 **Secondary sideroblastic anemia due to drugs and toxins** 🦠

Code first poisoning due to drug or toxin, if applicable (T36-T65 with fifth or sixth character 1-4 or 6)

Use additional code for adverse effect, if applicable, to identify drug (T36-T50 with fifth or sixth character 5)

D64.3 **Other sideroblastic anemias** 🦠
Sideroblastic anemia NOS
Pyridoxine-responsive sideroblastic anemia NEC

D64.4 **Congenital dyserythropoietic anemia**
Any of several rare hereditary anemias, mostly types of macrocytic anemia
Dyshematopoietic anemia (congenital)

Excludes1   Blackfan-Diamond syndrome (D61.01)
Di Guglielmo's disease (C94.0)

● **D64.8**   **Other specified anemias**

    D64.81   **Anemia due to antineoplastic chemotherapy**
       Antineoplastic chemotherapy induced anemia

       Excludes1   aplastic anemia due to antineoplastic chemotherapy (D61.1)

       Excludes2   anemia in neoplastic disease (D63.0)

    D64.89   **Other specified anemias**
       Infantile pseudoleukemia

   D64.9   **Anemia, unspecified**
     Coding Clinic: 2018, Q4, P88; 2017, Q1, P7

COAGULATION DEFECTS, PURPURA AND OTHER HEMORRHAGIC CONDITIONS (D65-D69)

D65   **Disseminated intravascular coagulation [defibrination syndrome]** 🔖

   Blood clots form and consume all coagulation proteins and platelets and disrupt normal coagulation, resulting in abnormal bleeding
   Afibrinogenemia, acquired
   Consumption coagulopathy
   Diffuse or disseminated intravascular coagulation [DIC]
   Fibrinolytic hemorrhage, acquired
   Fibrinolytic purpura
   Purpura fulminans

   Excludes1   disseminated intravascular coagulation (complicating):
      abortion or ectopic or molar pregnancy (O00-O07, O08.1)
      in newborn (P60)
      pregnancy, childbirth and the puerperium (O45.0, O46.0, O67.0, O72.3)

D66   **Hereditary factor VIII deficiency** 🔖

   Inherited coagulation disorder carried by females but most often affecting males
   Classical hemophilia
   Deficiency factor VIII (with functional defect)
   Hemophilia NOS
   Hemophilia A

   Excludes1   factor VIII deficiency with vascular defect (D68.0)

D67   **Hereditary factor IX deficiency** 🔖

   Christmas disease
   Factor IX deficiency (with functional defect)
   Hemophilia B
   Plasma thromboplastin component [PTC] deficiency

● **D68**   **Other coagulation defects**

   Excludes1   abnormal coagulation profile (R79.1)
     coagulation defects complicating abortion or ectopic or molar pregnancy (O00-O07, O08.1)
     coagulation defects complicating pregnancy, childbirth and the puerperium (O45.0, O46.0, O67.0, O72.3)

   Coding Clinic: 2016, Q1, P14

   D68.0   **Von Willebrand's disease** 🔖
     Congenital bleeding disorder
     Angiohemophilia
     Factor VIII deficiency with vascular defect
     Vascular hemophilia

     Excludes1   capillary fragility (hereditary) (D69.8)
       factor VIII deficiency NOS (D66)
       factor VIII deficiency with functional defect (D66)

   D68.1   **Hereditary factor XI deficiency** 🔖
     Deficiency of blood coagulation resulting in systemic blood-clotting defect
     Hemophilia C
     Plasma thromboplastin antecedent [PTA] deficiency
     Rosenthal's disease

● **D68.2**   **Hereditary deficiency of other clotting factors** 🔖
   Blood clotting disorders caused by hereditary deficiencies of one or more clotting factors
   AC globulin deficiency
   Congenital afibrinogenemia
   Deficiency of factor I [fibrinogen]
   Deficiency of factor II [prothrombin]
   Deficiency of factor V [labile]
   Deficiency of factor VII [stable]
   Deficiency of factor X [Stuart-Prower]
   Deficiency of factor XII [Hageman]
   Deficiency of factor XIII [fibrin stabilizing]
   Dysfibrinogenemia (congenital)
   Hypoproconvertinemia
   Owren's disease
   Proaccelerin deficiency

● **D68.3**   **Hemorrhagic disorder due to circulating anticoagulants**
   Blood clotting disorders caused by anticoagulants (warfarin and heparin)

● **D68.31**   **Hemorrhagic disorder due to intrinsic circulating anticoagulants, antibodies, or inhibitors**

     D68.311   **Acquired hemophilia** 🔖
       Autoimmune hemophilia
       Autoimmune inhibitors to clotting factors
       Secondary hemophilia

     D68.312   **Antiphospholipid antibody with hemorrhagic disorder** 🔖
       Lupus anticoagulant (LAC) with hemorrhagic disorder
       Systemic lupus erythematosus [SLE] inhibitor with hemorrhagic disorder

       Excludes1   antiphospholipid antibody, finding without diagnosis (R76.0)
         antiphospholipid antibody syndrome (D68.61)
         antiphospholipid antibody with hypercoagulable state (D68.61)
         lupus anticoagulant (LAC) finding without diagnosis (R76.0)
         lupus anticoagulant (LAC) with hypercoagulable state (D68.62)
         systemic lupus erythematosus [SLE] inhibitor finding without diagnosis (R76.0)
         systemic lupus erythematosus [SLE] inhibitor with hypercoagulable state (D68.62)

D68.318   Other hemorrhagic disorder due to intrinsic circulating anticoagulants, antibodies, or inhibitors 🐾

     Antithromboplastinemia
     Antithromboplastinogenemia
     Hemorrhagic disorder due to intrinsic increase in antithrombin
     Hemorrhagic disorder due to intrinsic increase in anti-VIIIa
     Hemorrhagic disorder due to intrinsic increase in anti-IXa
     Hemorrhagic disorder due to intrinsic increase in anti-XIa

D68.32   Hemorrhagic disorder due to extrinsic circulating anticoagulants 🐾

     Drug-induced hemorrhagic disorder
     Hemorrhagic disorder due to increase in anti-IIa
     Hemorrhagic disorder due to increase in anti-Xa
     Hyperheparinemia

     Use additional code for adverse effect, if applicable, to identify drug (T45.515, T45.525)

     Coding Clinic: 2016, Q1, P14-15

D68.4   Acquired coagulation factor deficiency 🐾

     Deficiency of coagulation factor due to liver disease
     Deficiency of coagulation factor due to vitamin K deficiency

     Excludes1   vitamin K deficiency of newborn (P53)

● **D68.5   Primary thrombophilia**

     AKA idiopathic thrombocytopenia, may be acquired or congenital and is a common cause of coagulation disorders.

     Primary hypercoagulable states

     Excludes1   antiphospholipid syndrome (D68.61)
               lupus anticoagulant (D68.62)
               secondary activated protein C resistance (D68.69)
               secondary antiphospholipid antibody syndrome (D68.69)
               secondary lupus anticoagulant with hypercoagulable state (D68.69)
               secondary systemic lupus erythematosus [SLE] inhibitor with hypercoagulable state (D68.69)
               systemic lupus erythematosus [SLE] inhibitor finding without diagnosis (R76.0)
               systemic lupus erythematosus [SLE] inhibitor with hemorrhagic disorder (D68.312)
               thrombotic thrombocytopenic purpura (M31.1)

D68.51   Activated protein C resistance 🐾
     Factor V Leiden mutation

D68.52   Prothrombin gene mutation 🐾

D68.59   Other primary thrombophilia 🐾
     Antithrombin III deficiency
     Hypercoagulable state NOS
     Primary hypercoagulable state NEC
     Primary thrombophilia NEC
     Protein C deficiency
     Protein S deficiency
     Thrombophilia NOS

● **D68.6   Other thrombophilia**
     Other hypercoagulable states

     Excludes1   diffuse or disseminated intravascular coagulation [DIC] (D65)
               heparin induced thrombocytopenia (HIT) (D75.82)
               hyperhomocysteinemia (E72.11)

D68.61   Antiphospholipid syndrome 🐾
     Anticardiolipin syndrome
     Antiphospholipid antibody syndrome

     Excludes1   anti-phospholipid antibody, finding without diagnosis (R76.0)
               anti-phospholipid antibody with hemorrhagic disorder (D68.312)
               lupus anticoagulant syndrome (D68.62)

D68.62   Lupus anticoagulant syndrome 🐾
     Lupus anticoagulant
     Presence of systemic lupus erythematosus [SLE] inhibitor

     Excludes1   anticardiolipin syndrome (D68.61)
               antiphospholipid syndrome (D68.61)
               lupus anticoagulant (LAC) finding without diagnosis (R76.0)
               lupus anticoagulant (LAC) with hemorrhagic disorder (D68.312)

D68.69   Other thrombophilia 🐾
     Hypercoagulable states NEC
     Secondary hypercoagulable state NOS

D68.8   Other specified coagulation defects 🐾
     Excludes1   hemorrhagic disease of newborn (P53)

D68.9   Coagulation defect, unspecified 🐾

● **D69   Purpura and other hemorrhagic conditions**
     Group of conditions characterized by small hemorrhages in skin, mucous membranes, or serosal surfaces

     Excludes1   benign hypergammaglobulinemic purpura (D89.0)
               cryoglobulinemic purpura (D89.1)
               essential (hemorrhagic) thrombocythemia (D47.3)
               hemorrhagic thrombocythemia (D47.3)
               purpura fulminans (D65)
               thrombotic thrombocytopenic purpura (M31.1)
               Waldenström hypergammaglobulinemic purpura (D89.0)

D69.0   Allergic purpura 🐾
     Allergic vasculitis
     Nonthrombocytopenic hemorrhagic purpura
     Nonthrombocytopenic idiopathic purpura
     Purpura anaphylactoid
     Purpura Henoch(-Schönlein)
     Purpura rheumatica
     Vascular purpura

     Excludes1   thrombocytopenic hemorrhagic purpura (D69.3)

D69.1   Qualitative platelet defects 🐾
     Bernard-Soulier [giant platelet] syndrome
     Glanzmann's disease
     Grey platelet syndrome
     Thromboasthenia (hemorrhagic) (hereditary)
     Thrombocytopathy

     Excludes1   von Willebrand's disease (D68.0)

D69.2   Other nonthrombocytopenic purpura 🐾
     Purpura NOS
     Purpura simplex
     Senile purpura

▶ New   ⇒ Revised   ~~deleted~~ Deleted   Excludes 1   Excludes 2   Includes   Use additional   Code first   Code also   Key words
OGCR Official Guidelines   X Assign placeholder X   ● Use Additional Character(s)   ] Manifestation Code   🐾 Hierarchical Condition Category   **Coding Clinic**

D69.3   **Immune thrombocytopenic purpura** 🔵
> Hemorrhagic (thrombocytopenic) purpura
> Idiopathic thrombocytopenic purpura
> Tidal platelet dysgenesis

● **D69.4**   **Other primary thrombocytopenia**
> **Excludes1**   transient neonatal thrombocytopenia (P61.0)
> > Wiskott-Aldrich syndrome (D82.0)

> **D69.41**   **Evans syndrome** 🔵
> > *Acquired hemolytic anemia and thrombocytopenia*

> **D69.42**   **Congenital and hereditary thrombocytopenia purpura** 🔵
> > Congenital thrombocytopenia
> > Hereditary thrombocytopenia
> > *Code first congential or hereditary disorder, such as:*
> > > thrombocytopenia with absent radius (TAR syndrome) (Q87.2)

> **D69.49**   **Other primary thrombocytopenia** 🔵
> > Megakaryocytic hypoplasia
> > Primary thrombocytopenia NOS

● **D69.5**   **Secondary thrombocytopenia**
> *Acquired reduction of number of platelets required for blood clotting*
> **Excludes1**   heparin induced thrombocytopenia (HIT) (D75.82)
> > transient thrombocytopenia of newborn (P61.0)

> **D69.51**   **Posttransfusion purpura**
> > Posttransfusion purpura from whole blood (fresh) or blood products PTP

> **D69.59**   **Other secondary thrombocytopenia**

D69.6   **Thrombocytopenia, unspecified** 🔵

D69.8   **Other specified hemorrhagic conditions** 🔵
> Capillary fragility (hereditary)
> Vascular pseudohemophilia

D69.9   **Hemorrhagic condition, unspecified** 🔵

OTHER DISORDERS OF BLOOD AND BLOOD-FORMING ORGANS (D70-D77)

● **D70**   **Neutropenia**
> *Decrease in number of neutrophils (type of white blood cell)*
> **Includes**   agranulocytosis
> > decreased absolute neurophile count (ANC)
> Use additional code for any associated:
> > fever (R50.81)
> > mucositis (J34.81, K12.3-, K92.81, N76.81)
> **Excludes1**   neutropenic splenomegaly (D73.81)
> > transient neonatal neutropenia (P61.5)

D70.0   **Congenital agranulocytosis** 🔵
> *Reduced numbers of neutrophils (type of white blood cell)*
> Congenital neutropenia
> Infantile genetic agranulocytosis
> Kostmann's disease

D70.1   **Agranulocytosis secondary to cancer chemotherapy** 🔵
> *Decreased numbers of granulocytes (type of white blood cell)*
> Code also *underlying neoplasm*
> Use additional code for adverse effect, if applicable, to identify drug (T45.1X5)

D70.2   **Other drug-induced agranulocytosis** 🔵
> Use additional code for adverse effect, if applicable, to identify drug (T36-T50 with fifth or sixth character 5)

D70.3   **Neutropenia due to infection** 🔵

D70.4   **Cyclic neutropenia** 🔵
> *Chronic neutropenia (low number of type of white blood cell)*
> Cyclic hematopoiesis
> Periodic neutropenia

D70.8   **Other neutropenia** 🔵

D70.9   **Neutropenia, unspecified** 🔵
> **Coding Clinic: 2019, Q2, P25**

D71   **Functional disorders of polymorphonuclear neutrophils** 🔵
> *Polymorphonuclear: varying shapes of nucleus; AKA PMNs*
> Cell membrane receptor complex [CR3] defect
> Chronic (childhood) granulomatous disease
> Congenital dysphagocytosis
> Progressive septic granulomatosis

● **D72**   **Other disorders of white blood cells**
> **Excludes1**   basophilia (D72.824)
> > immunity disorders (D80-D89)
> > neutropenia (D70)
> > preleukemia (syndrome) (D46.9)

> **D72.0**   **Genetic anomalies of leukocytes** 🔵
> > Alder (granulation) (granulocyte) anomaly
> > Alder syndrome
> > Hereditary leukocytic hypersegmentation
> > Hereditary leukocytic hyposegmentation
> > Hereditary leukomelanopathy
> > May-Hegglin (granulation) (granulocyte) anomaly
> > May-Hegglin syndrome
> > Pelger-Huët (granulation) (granulocyte) anomaly
> > Pelger-Huët syndrome
> > **Excludes1**   Chédiak (-Steinbrinck)-Higashi syndrome (E70.330)

● **D72.1**   **Eosinophilia**
> *Formation and accumulation of high number of white cells in blood/tissue*
> ▶ **Excludes2**   Löffler's syndrome (J82)
> > ▶ pulmonary eosinophilia (J82)
> ~~Allergic eosinophilia~~
> ~~Hereditary eosinophilia~~
> **Excludes1**   ~~Löffler's syndrome (J82)~~
> > ~~pulmonary eosinophilia (J82)~~

> ▶ **D72.10**   **Eosinophilia, unspecified**
> ▶● **D72.11**   **Hypereosinophilic syndrome [HES]**
> > ▶ **D72.110**   **Idiopathic hypereosinophilic syndrome [IHES]**
> > ▶ **D72.111**   **Lymphocytic Variant Hypereosinophilic Syndrome [LHES]**
> > > ▶Lymphocyte variant hypereosinophilia
> > > ▶Code also, if applicable, any associated lymphocytic neoplastic disorder
> > ▶ **D72.118**   **Other hypereosinophilic syndrome**
> > > ▶Episodic angioedema with eosinophilia
> > > ▶Gleich's syndrome
> > ▶ **D72.119**   **Hypereosinophilic syndrome [HES], unspecified**
> ▶ **D72.12**   **Drug rash with eosinophilia and systemic symptoms syndrome**
> > ▶DRESS syndrome
> > ▶Use additional code for adverse effect, if applicable, to identify drug (T36-T50 with fifth or sixth character 5)
> ▶ **D72.18**   **Eosinophilia in diseases classified elsewhere**
> > ▶*Code first underlying disease, such as:*
> > > ▶chronic myelomonocytic leukemia (C93.1-)
> ▶ **D72.19**   **Other eosinophilia**
> > ▶Familial eosinophilia
> > ▶Hereditary eosinophilia

N Newborn Age: 0   **P** Pediatric Age: 0–17   **M** Maternity DX: 12–55   **A** Adult Age: 15–124   ♀ Females Only   ♂ Males Only

731

CHAPTER 3 (D50-D89)

● D72.8   Other specified disorders of white blood cells
   Excludes1   leukemia (C91-C95)
   ● D72.81   Decreased white blood cell count
      Excludes1   neutropenia (D70.-)
      D72.810   Lymphocytopenia
         Decreased lymphocytes
         Reduction in number of lympho cytes in blood
      D72.818   Other decreased white blood cell count
         Basophilic leukopenia
         Eosinophilic leukopenia
         Monocytopenia
         Other decreased leukocytes
         Plasmacytopenia
      D72.819   Decreased white blood cell count, unspecified
         Decreased leukocytes, unspecified
         Leukocytopenia, unspecified
         Leukopenia
         Excludes1   malignant leukopenia (D70.9)
   ● D72.82   Elevated white blood cell count
      Excludes1   eosinophilia (D72.1)
      D72.820   Lymphocytosis (symptomatic)
         Elevated lymphocytes
         Excess of normal lymphocytes
      D72.821   Monocytosis (symptomatic)
         Excludes1   infectious mononucleosis (B27.-)
      D72.822   Plasmacytosis
         Presence of excess plasma cells
      D72.823   Leukemoid reaction
         Basophilic leukemoid reaction
         Leukemoid reaction NOS
         Lymphocytic leukemoid reaction
         Monocytic leukemoid reaction
         Myelocytic leukemoid reaction
         Neutrophilic leukemoid reaction
      D72.824   Basophilia
         Increase of basophils in blood
      D72.825   Bandemia
         Bandemia without diagnosis of specific infection
         Excess number of band cells (immature white blood cells) released by bone marrow
         Excludes1   confirmed infection -code to infection
                     leukemia (C91.-, C92.-, C93.-, C94.-, C95.-)
      D72.828   Other elevated white blood cell count
      D72.829   Elevated white blood cell count, unspecified
         Elevated leukocytes, unspecified
         Leukocytosis, unspecified
   D72.89   Other specified disorders of white blood cells
      Abnormality of white blood cells NEC
   D72.9   Disorder of white blood cells, unspecified
      Abnormal leukocyte differential NOS

● D73   Diseases of spleen
   D73.Ø   Hyposplenism
      Diminished functioning of spleen
      Atrophy of spleen
      Excludes1   asplenia (congenital) (Q89.Ø1)
                  postsurgical absence of spleen (Z90.81)
   D73.1   Hypersplenism
      Accelerated function of spleen
      Excludes1   neutropenic splenomegaly (D73.81)
                  primary splenic neutropenia (D73.81)
                  splenitis, splenomegaly in late syphilis (A52.79)
                  splenitis, splenomegaly in tuberculosis (A18.85)
                  splenomegaly NOS (R16.1)
                  splenomegaly congenital (Q89.Ø)
   D73.2   Chronic congestive splenomegaly
      Enlargement of spleen
   D73.3   Abscess of spleen
   D73.4   Cyst of spleen
   D73.5   Infarction of spleen
      Splenic rupture, nontraumatic
      Torsion of spleen
      Excludes1   rupture of spleen due to Plasmodium vivax malaria (B51.Ø)
                  traumatic rupture of spleen (S36.Ø3-)
   ● D73.8   Other diseases of spleen
      D73.81   Neutropenic splenomegaly
         Werner-Schultz disease
         Enlarged spleen responding to inadequate number of neutrophils
      D73.89   Other diseases of spleen
         Fibrosis of spleen NOS
         Perisplenitis
         Splenitis NOS
   D73.9   Disease of spleen, unspecified

● D74   Methemoglobinemia
      Excessive methemoglobin (form of hemoglobin)
   D74.Ø   Congenital methemoglobinemia
         Congenital NADH-methemoglobin reductase deficiency
         Hemoglobin-M [Hb-M] disease
         Methemoglobinemia, hereditary
   D74.8   Other methemoglobinemias
         Acquired methemoglobinemia (with sulfhemoglobinemia)
         Toxic methemoglobinemia
   D74.9   Methemoglobinemia, unspecified

● D75   Other and unspecified diseases of blood and blood-forming organs
      Excludes2   acute lymphadenitis (LØ4.-)
                  chronic lymphadenitis (I88.1)
                  enlarged lymph nodes (R59.-)
                  hypergammaglobulinemia NOS (D89.2)
                  lymphadenitis NOS (I88.9)
                  mesenteric lymphadenitis (acute) (chronic) (I88.Ø)
   D75.A   Glucose-6-phosphate dehydrogenase (G6PD) deficiency without anemia
      Excludes1   glucose-6-phosphate dehydrogenase (G6PD) deficiency with anemia (D55.Ø)
   D75.Ø   Familial erythrocytosis
      Genetic mutation of gene that results in increased circulating RBCs
      Benign polycythemia
      Familial polycythemia
      Excludes1   hereditary ovalocytosis (D58.1)

▶ New   ⇒ Revised   ~~deleted~~ Deleted   Excludes 1   Excludes 2   Includes   Use additional   Code first   Code also   Key words

OGCR Official Guidelines   X Assign placeholder X   ● Use Additional Character(s)   ▶ Manifestation Code   ✎ Hierarchical Condition Category   Coding Clinic

CHAPTER 3 (D5Ø-D89)

D75.1 Secondary polycythemia
Increase in total red cell mass
Acquired polycythemia
Emotional polycythemia
Erythrocytosis NOS
Hypoxemic polycythemia
Nephrogenous polycythemia
Polycythemia due to erythropoietin
Polycythemia due to fall in plasma volume
Polycythemia due to high altitude
Polycythemia due to stress
Polycythemia NOS
Relative polycythemia

> **Excludes1**   polycythemia neonatorum (P61.1)
> polycythemia vera (D45)

D75.8 Other specified diseases of blood and blood-forming organs

D75.81   Myelofibrosis 🔵
Replacing bone marrow by fibrous tissue
Myelofibrosis NOS
Secondary myelofibrosis NOS

Code first the underlying disorder, such as:
malignant neoplasm of breast (C50.-)

Use additional code, if applicable,
for associated therapy-related
myelodysplastic syndrome (D46.-)

Use additional code for adverse effect, if
applicable, to identify drug (T45.1X5)

> **Excludes1**   acute myelofibrosis (C94.4-)
> idiopathic myelofibrosis (D47.1)
> leukoerythroblastic anemia
> (D61.82)
> myelofibrosis with myeloid
> metaplasia (D47.4)
> myelophthisic anemia (D61.82)
> myelophthisis (D61.82)
> primary myelofibrosis (D47.1)

D75.82   Heparin induced thrombocytopenia (HIT) 🔵

D75.89   Other specified diseases of blood and blood-forming organs

D75.9 Disease of blood and blood-forming organs, unspecified

D76 Other specified diseases with participation of lymphoreticular and reticulohistiocytic tissue

> **Excludes1**   (Abt-) Letterer-Siwe disease (C96.0)
> eosinophilic granuloma (C96.6)
> Hand-Schüller-Christian disease (C96.5)
> histiocytic medullary reticulosis (C96.9)
> histiocytic sarcoma (C96.A)
> histiocytosis X, multifocal (C96.5)
> histiocytosis X, unifocal (C96.6)
> Langerhans-cell histiocytosis, multifocal (C96.5)
> Langerhans-cell histiocytosis NOS (C96.6)
> Langerhans-cell histiocytosis, unifocal (C96.6)
> leukemic reticuloendotheliosis (C91.4-)
> lipomelanotic reticulosis (I89.8)
> malignant histiocytosis (C96.A)
> malignant reticulosis (C86.0)
> nonlipid reticuloendotheliosis (C96.0)

D76.1 Hemophagocytic lymphohistiocytosis 🔵
Familial hemophagocytic reticulosis
Histiocytoses of mononuclear phagocytes

D76.2 Hemophagocytic syndrome, infection-associated 🔵
Use additional code to identify infectious agent or disease.

D76.3 Other histiocytosis syndromes 🔵
Reticulohistiocytoma (giant-cell)
Sinus histiocytosis with massive lymphadenopathy
Xanthogranuloma

D77 Other disorders of blood and blood-forming organs in diseases classified elsewhere

Code first underlying disease, such as:
amyloidosis (E85.-)
congenital early syphilis (A50.0)
echinococcosis (B67.0-B67.9)
malaria (B50.0-B54)
schistosomiasis [bilharziasis] (B65.0-B65.9)
vitamin C deficiency (E54)

> **Excludes1**   rupture of spleen due to Plasmodium vivax
> malaria (B51.0)
> splenitis, splenomegaly in late syphilis (A52.79)
> splenitis, splenomegaly in tuberculosis (A18.85)

INTRAOPERATIVE AND POSTPROCEDURAL COMPLICATIONS OF THE SPLEEN (D78)

D78 Intraoperative and postprocedural complications of the spleen
Coding Clinic: 2016, Q4, P9

D78.0 Intraoperative hemorrhage and hematoma of the spleen complicating a procedure

> **Excludes1**   intraoperative hemorrhage and
> hematoma of the spleen due to
> accidental puncture or laceration
> during a procedure (D78.1-)

D78.01   Intraoperative hemorrhage and hematoma of the spleen complicating a procedure on the spleen

D78.02   Intraoperative hemorrhage and hematoma of the spleen complicating other procedure

D78.1 Accidental puncture and laceration of the spleen during a procedure

D78.11   Accidental puncture and laceration of the spleen during a procedure on the spleen

D78.12   Accidental puncture and laceration of the spleen during other procedure

D78.2 Postprocedural hemorrhage of the spleen following a procedure

D78.21   Postprocedural hemorrhage of the spleen following a procedure on the spleen

D78.22   Postprocedural hemorrhage of the spleen following other procedure

D78.3 Postprocedural hematoma and seroma of the spleen following a procedure

D78.31   Postprocedural hematoma of the spleen following a procedure on the spleen

D78.32   Postprocedural hematoma of the spleen following other procedure

D78.33   Postprocedural seroma of the spleen following a procedure on the spleen

D78.34   Postprocedural seroma of the spleen following other procedure

D78.8 Other intraoperative and postprocedural complications of the spleen

Use additional code, if applicable, to further specify disorder

D78.81   Other intraoperative complications of the spleen

D78.89   Other postprocedural complications of the spleen

CERTAIN DISORDERS INVOLVING THE IMMUNE MECHANISM (D80-D89)

Includes   defects in the complement system
immunodeficiency disorders, except human
     immunodeficiency virus [HIV] disease
sarcoidosis

Excludes1   autoimmune disease (systemic) NOS (M35.9)
functional disorders of polymorphonuclear
     neutrophils (D71)
human immunodeficiency virus [HIV] disease (B20)

● **D80**   **Immunodeficiency with predominantly antibody defects**

D80.0   **Hereditary hypogammaglobulinemia** 🐾
Autosomal recessive agammaglobulinemia (Swiss type)
X-linked agammaglobulinemia [Bruton] (with growth
     hormone deficiency)

D80.1   **Nonfamilial hypogammaglobulinemia** 🐾
Abnormally low levels of all classes of immunoglobulins
Agammaglobulinemia with immunoglobulin-bearing
     B-lymphocytes
Common variable agammaglobulinemia [CVAgamma]
Hypogammaglobulinemia NOS

D80.2   **Selective deficiency of immunoglobulin A [IgA]** 🐾

D80.3   **Selective deficiency of immunoglobulin G [IgG]
subclasses** 🐾

D80.4   **Selective deficiency of immunoglobulin M [IgM]** 🐾

D80.5   **Immunodeficiency with increased immunoglobulin M
[IgM]** 🐾

D80.6   **Antibody deficiency with near-normal immunoglobulins
or with hyperimmunoglobulinemia** 🐾
Abnormally high levels of immunoglobulins in serum

D80.7   **Transient hypogammaglobulinemia of infancy** 🐾

D80.8   **Other immunodeficiencies with predominantly antibody
defects** 🐾
Kappa light chain deficiency

D80.9   **Immunodeficiency with predominantly antibody
defects, unspecified** 🐾

● **D81**   **Combined immunodeficiencies**

Excludes1   autosomal recessive agammaglobulinemia
     (Swiss type) (D80.0)

D81.0   **Severe combined immunodeficiency [SCID] with
reticular dysgenesis** 🐾

D81.1   **Severe combined immunodeficiency [SCID] with low
T- and B-cell numbers** 🐾

D81.2   **Severe combined immunodeficiency [SCID] with low or
normal B-cell numbers** 🐾

● **D81.3**   **Adenosine deaminase [ADA] deficiency** 🐾

D81.30   **Adenosine deaminase deficiency, unspecified**
ADA deficiency NOS

D81.31   **Severe combined immunodeficiency due to
adenosine deaminase deficiency**
ADA deficiency with SCID
Adenosine deaminase [ADA] deficiency with
     severe combined immunodeficiency

D81.32   **Adenosine deaminase 2 deficiency**
ADA2 deficiency
Adenosine deaminase deficiency type 2
*Code also, if applicable, any associated
     manifestations, such as:*
polyarteritis nodosa (M30.0)
stroke (I63.-)

D81.39   **Other adenosine deaminase deficiency**
Adenosine deaminase [ADA] deficiency
     type 1, NOS
Adenosine deaminase [ADA] deficiency
     type 1, without SCID
Adenosine deaminase [ADA] deficiency
     type 1, without severe combined
     immunodeficiency
Partial ADA deficiency (type 1)
Partial adenosine deaminase deficiency (type 1)

D81.4   **Nezelof's syndrome** 🐾

D81.5   **Purine nucleoside phosphorylase [PNP] deficiency** 🐾

D81.6   **Major histocompatibility complex class I deficiency** 🐾
Bare lymphocyte syndrome

D81.7   **Major histocompatibility complex class II deficiency** 🐾

● **D81.8**   **Other combined immunodeficiencies**

● **D81.81**   **Biotin-dependent carboxylase deficiency**
Multiple carboxylase deficiency

Excludes1   biotin-dependent carboxylase
     deficiency due to dietary
     deficiency of biotin (E53.8)

D81.810   **Biotinidase deficiency**

D81.818   **Other biotin-dependent carboxylase
deficiency**
Holocarboxylase synthetase
     deficiency
Other multiple carboxylase
     deficiency

D81.819   **Biotin-dependent carboxylase
deficiency, unspecified**
Multiple carboxylase deficiency,
     unspecified

D81.89   **Other combined immunodeficiencies** 🐾

D81.9   **Combined immunodeficiency, unspecified** 🐾
Severe combined immunodeficiency disorder [SCID]
     NOS

● **D82**   **Immunodeficiency associated with other major defects**

Excludes1   ataxia telangiectasia [Louis-Bar] (G11.3)

D82.0   **Wiskott-Aldrich syndrome** 🐾
X-linked immunodeficiency
Immunodeficiency with thrombocytopenia and eczema

D82.1   **Di George's syndrome** 🐾
*Congenital disorder with defective development of third and
     fourth pharyngeal pouches*
Pharyngeal pouch syndrome
Thymic alymphoplasia
Thymic aplasia or hypoplasia with immunodeficiency
Coding Clinic: 2019, Q3, P14

D82.2   **Immunodeficiency with short-limbed stature** 🐾

D82.3   **Immunodeficiency following hereditary defective
response to Epstein-Barr virus** 🐾
X-linked lymphoproliferative disease

D82.4   **Hyperimmunoglobulin E [IgE] syndrome** 🐾
*Suspected genetic defect that produces high levels of antibody
     immunoglobulin (IgE) that causes skin and lung
     infections and eczema*

D82.8   **Immunodeficiency associated with other specified major
defects** 🐾

D82.9   **Immunodeficiency associated with major
defect, unspecified** 🐾

● **D83**   **Common variable immunodeficiency**

D83.0   **Common variable immunodeficiency with predominant
abnormalities of B-cell numbers and function** 🐾

D83.1   **Common variable immunodeficiency with predominant
immunoregulatory T-cell disorders** 🐾

D83.2   **Common variable immunodeficiency with
autoantibodies to B- or T-cells** 🐾

D83.8   **Other common variable immunodeficiencies** 🐾

D83.9   **Common variable immunodeficiency, unspecified** 🐾

● **D84**   **Other immunodeficiencies**

D84.0   **Lymphocyte function antigen-1 [LFA-1] defect** 🐾

● **D84.1**   **Defects in the complement system** 🐾
C1 esterase inhibitor [C1-INH] deficiency

▶ New   ⮕ Revised   ~~deleted~~ Deleted   Excludes 1   Excludes 2   Includes   Use additional   Code first   Code also   Key words

OGCR Official Guidelines   X Assign placeholder X   ● Use Additional Character(s)   ▷ Manifestation Code   🐾 Hierarchical Condition Category   Coding Clinic

D84.8 Other specified immunodeficiencies 🔗

▷ **D84.81 Immunodeficiency due to conditions classified elsewhere**

▷Code first underlying condition, such as:
 ▷chromosomal abnormalities (Q90-Q99)
 ▷diabetes mellitus (E08-E13)
 ▷malignant neoplasms (C00-C96)

▷ **Excludes1** certain disorders involving the immune mechanism (D80-D83, D84.0, D84.1, D84.9)
 ▷human immunodeficiency virus [HIV] disease (B20)

▷● **D84.82 Immunodeficiency due to drugs and external causes**

▷ **D84.821 Immunodeficiency due to drugs**
 ▷Immunodeficiency due to (current or past) medication
 ▷Use additional code for adverse effect if applicable, to identify adverse effect of drug (T36-T50 with fifth or six character 5)
 ▷Use additional code, if applicable, for associated long term (current) drug therapy drug or medication such as:
  ▷long term (current) drug therapy systemic steroids (Z79.52)
  ▷other long term (current) drug therapy (Z79.899)

▷ **D84.822 Immunodeficiency due to external causes**
 ▷Code also, if applicable, radiological procedure and radiotherapy (Y84.2)
 ▷Use additional code for external cause such as:
  ▷exposure to ionizing radiation (W88)

▷ **D84.89 Other immunodeficiencies**

D84.9 Immunodeficiency, unspecified 🔗
 ▷Immunocompromised NOS
 ▷Immunodeficient NOS
 ▷Immunosuppressed NOS]

● **D86 Sarcoidosis**

D86.0 Sarcoidosis of lung 🔗

D86.1 Sarcoidosis of lymph nodes

D86.2 Sarcoidosis of lung with sarcoidosis of lymph nodes 🔗

D86.3 Sarcoidosis of skin

● **D86.8 Sarcoidosis of other sites**

D86.81 Sarcoid meningitis

D86.82 Multiple cranial nerve palsies in sarcoidosis 🔗

D86.83 Sarcoid iridocyclitis
 Rare large tumor with irregular surface of iris

D86.84 Sarcoid pyelonephritis
 Systemic disease of unknown etiology characterized by chronic granulomatous inflammation with tissue destruction of pelvis kidney
 Tubulo-interstitial nephropathy in sarcoidosis

D86.85 Sarcoid myocarditis

D86.86 Sarcoid arthropathy
 Polyarthritis in sarcoidosis

D86.87 Sarcoid myositis
 Granumloma of muscle

D86.89 Sarcoidosis of other sites
 Hepatic granuloma
 Uveoparotid fever [Heerfordt]

D86.9 Sarcoidosis, unspecified

Item 3-1 Sarcoidosis: A symptom of an inflammation producing tiny lumps of cells (granulomas) in various organs, most commonly the lungs and lymph nodes, that affect organ function. Cause is unknown occurring primarily in 20- to 40-year-olds, African-American, especially women, and those of Asian, German, Irish, Scandinavian, and Puerto Rican heritage.

● **D89 Other disorders involving the immune mechanism, not elsewhere classified**

Excludes1 hyperglobulinemia NOS (R77.1)
 monoclonal gammopathy (of undetermined significance) (D47.2)

Excludes2 transplant failure and rejection (T86.-)

D89.0 Polyclonal hypergammaglobulinemia
 Benign hypergammaglobulinemic purpura
 Polyclonal gammopathy NOS

D89.1 Cryoglobulinemia 🔗
 Cryoglobulin (proteins) in blood that precipitate temperatures below 98.6° F; usually symptomatic of underlying disease
 Cryoglobulinemic purpura
 Cryoglobulinemic vasculitis
 Essential cryoglobulinemia
 Idiopathic cryoglobulinemia
 Mixed cryoglobulinemia
 Primary cryoglobulinemia
 Secondary cryoglobulinemia

D89.2 Hypergammaglobulinemia, unspecified

D89.3 Immune reconstitution syndrome 🔗
 Immune reconstitution inflammatory syndrome [IRIS]
 Use additional code for adverse effect, if applicable, to identify drug (T36-T50 with fifth or sixth character 5)

● **D89.4 Mast cell activation syndrome and related disorders**

Excludes1 aggressive systemic mastocytosis (C96.21)
 congenital cutaneous mastocytosis (Q82.2)
 (non-congenital) cutaneous mastocytosis (D47.01)
 (indolent) systemic mastocytosis (D47.02)
 malignant mast cell neoplasm (C96.2-)
 malignant mastocytoma (C96.29)
 mast cell leukemia (C94.3-)
 mast cell sarcoma (C96.22)
 mastocytoma NOS (D47.09)
 other mast cell neoplasms of uncertain behavior (D47.09)
 systemic mastocytosis associated with a clonal hematologic non-mast cell lineage disease (SM-AHNMD) (D47.02)

Coding Clinic: 2016, Q4, P11

D89.40 Mast cell activation, unspecified 🔗
 Mast cell activation disorder, unspecified
 Mast cell activation syndrome, NOS

D89.41 Monoclonal mast cell activation syndrome 🔗
 Coding Clinic: 2016, Q4, P11

D89.42 Idiopathic mast cell activation syndrome 🔗
 Coding Clinic: 2016, Q4, P11

D89.43 Secondary mast cell activation 🔗
 Secondary mast cell activation syndrome
 Code also underlying etiology, if known
 Coding Clinic: 2016, Q4, P11

D89.49 Other mast cell activation disorder 🔗
 Other mast cell activation syndrome
 Coding Clinic: 2016, Q4, P11

CHAPTER 3 (D50-D89)

● **D89.8** **Other specified disorders involving the immune mechanism, not elsewhere classified**

● **D89.81** **Graft-versus-host disease**

Code first underlying cause, such as:
complications of transplanted organs and tissue (T86.-)
complications of blood transfusion (T80.89)

Use additional code to identify associated manifestations, such as:
desquamative dermatitis (L30.8)
diarrhea (R19.7)
elevated bilirubin (R17)
hair loss (L65.9)

D89.810 **Acute graft-versus-host disease** 🦠

D89.811 **Chronic graft-versus-host disease** 🦠

D89.812 **Acute on chronic graft-versus-host disease** 🦠

D89.813 **Graft-versus-host disease, unspecified** 🦠

D89.82 **Autoimmune lymphoproliferative syndrome [ALPS]** 🦠

▶● **D89.83** **Cytokine release syndrome**

▶*Code first* underlying cause, such as:
▶complications following infusion, transfusion and therapeutic injection (T80.89-)
▶complications of transplanted organs and tissue (T86.-)

▶Use additional code to identify associated manifestations

▶ **D89.831** **Cytokine release syndrome, grade 1**

▶ **D89.832** **Cytokine release syndrome, grade 2**

▶ **D89.833** **Cytokine release syndrome, grade 3**

▶ **D89.834** **Cytokine release syndrome, grade 4**

▶ **D89.835** **Cytokine release syndrome, grade 5**

▶ **D89.839** **Cytokine release syndrome, grade unspecified**

D89.89 **Other specified disorders involving the immune mechanism, not elsewhere classified** 🦠

Excludes1 human immunodeficiency virus disease (B20)

Coding Clinic: 2017, Q4, P109

D89.9 **Disorder involving the immune mechanism, unspecified** 🦠
Immune disease NOS
Coding Clinic: 2015, Q3, P22

CHAPTER 4

ENDOCRINE, NUTRITIONAL AND METABOLIC DISEASES (E00-E89)

OGCR Chapter-Specific Coding Guidelines

4. **Chapter 4: Endocrine, Nutritional, and Metabolic Diseases (E00-E89)**

   a. **Diabetes mellitus**
   The diabetes mellitus codes are combination codes that include the type of diabetes mellitus, the body system affected, and the complications affecting that body system. As many codes within a particular category as are necessary to describe all of the complications of the disease may be used. They should be sequenced based on the reason for a particular encounter. Assign as many codes from categories E08 – E13 as needed to identify all of the associated conditions that the patient has.

   1) **Type of diabetes**
   The age of a patient is not the sole determining factor, though most type 1 diabetics develop the condition before reaching puberty. For this reason type 1 diabetes mellitus is also referred to as juvenile diabetes.

   2) **Type of diabetes mellitus not documented**
   If the type of diabetes mellitus is not documented in the medical record the default is E11.-, Type 2 diabetes mellitus.

   3) **Diabetes mellitus and the use of insulin oral hypoglycemics**
   If the documentation in a medical record does not indicate the type of diabetes but does indicate that the patient uses insulin, code E11, Type 2 diabetes mellitus, should be assigned. An additional code should be assigned from category Z79 to identify the long-term (current) use of insulin or oral hypoglycemic drugs. If the patient is treated with both oral medications and insulin, only the code for long-term (current) use of insulin should be assigned. Code Z79.4 should not be assigned if insulin is given temporarily to bring a type 2 patient's blood sugar under control during an encounter.

   4) **Diabetes mellitus in pregnancy and gestational diabetes**
   See Section I.C.15. Diabetes mellitus in pregnancy.
   See Section I.C.15. Gestational (pregnancy induced) diabetes

   5) **Complications due to insulin pump malfunction**

   (a) **Underdose of insulin due to insulin pump failure**
   An underdose of insulin due to an insulin pump failure should be assigned to a code from subcategory T85.6, Mechanical complication of other specified internal and external prosthetic devices, implants and grafts, that specifies the type of pump malfunction, as the principal or first-listed code, followed by code T38.3X6-, Underdosing of insulin and oral hypoglycemic [antidiabetic] drugs. Additional codes for the type of diabetes mellitus and any associated complications due to the underdosing should also be assigned.

   (b) **Overdose of insulin due to insulin pump failure**
   The principal or first-listed code for an encounter due to an insulin pump malfunction resulting in an overdose of insulin, should also be T85.6-, Mechanical complication of other specified internal and external prosthetic devices, implants and grafts, followed by code T38.3X1-, Poisoning by insulin and oral hypoglycemic [antidiabetic] drugs, accidental (unintentional).

   6) **Secondary diabetes mellitus**
   Codes under categories E08, Diabetes mellitus due to underlying condition, E09, Drug or chemical induced diabetes mellitus and E13, Other specified diabetes mellitus, identify complications/manifestations associated with secondary diabetes mellitus. Secondary diabetes is always caused by another condition or event (e.g., cystic fibrosis, malignant neoplasm of pancreas, pancreatectomy, adverse effect of drug, or poisoning).

   (a) **Secondary diabetes mellitus and the use of insulin or hypoglycemic drugs**
   For patients with secondary diabetes mellitus who routinely use insulin or oral hypoglycemic drugs, an additional code from category Z79 should be assigned to identify the long-term (current) use of insulin or oral hypoglycemic drugs. If the patient is treated with both oral medications and insulin, only the code for long-term (current) use of insulin should be assigned. Code Z79.4 should not be assigned if insulin is given temporarily to bring a type 2 patient's blood sugar under control during an encounter.

   (b) **Assigning and sequencing secondary diabetes codes and its causes**
   The sequencing of the secondary diabetes codes in relationship to codes for the cause of the diabetes is based on the Tabular List instructions for categories E08, E09 and E13.

   (i) **Secondary diabetes mellitus due to pancreatectomy** For postpancreatectomy diabetes mellitus (lack of insulin due to the surgical removal of all or part of the pancreas), assign code E89.1, Postprocedural hypoinsulinemia. Assign a code from category E13 and a code from subcategory Z90.41-, Acquired absence of pancreas, as additional codes.

   (ii) **Secondary diabetes due to drugs** Secondary diabetes may be caused by an adverse effect of correctly administered medications, poisoning or sequela of poisoning.
   See Section I.C.19.e for coding of adverse effects and poisoning, and Section I.C.20 for external cause code reporting.

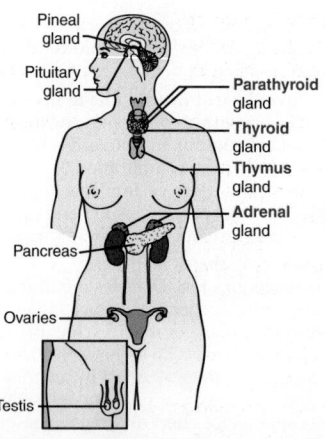

Figure 4-1 The endocrine system. (From Buck CJ: Step-by-Step Medical Coding, ed 2016, St. Louis, Elsevier, 2016)

CHAPTER 4

ENDOCRINE, NUTRITIONAL AND METABOLIC DISEASES (E00-E89)

All neoplasms, whether functionally active or not, are classified in Chapter 2. Appropriate codes in this chapter (i.e., E05.8, E07.0, E16-E31, E34.-) may be used as additional codes to indicate either functional activity by neoplasms and ectopic endocrine tissue or hyperfunction and hypofunction of endocrine glands associated with neoplasms and other conditions classified elsewhere.

Excludes1   transitory endocrine and metabolic disorders specific to newborn (P70-P74)

This chapter contains the following blocks:

E00-E07	Disorders of thyroid gland
E08-E13	Diabetes mellitus
E15-E16	Other disorders of glucose regulation and pancreatic internal secretion
E20-E35	Disorders of other endocrine glands
E36	Intraoperative complications of endocrine system
E40-E46	Malnutrition
E50-E64	Other nutritional deficiencies
E65-E68	Overweight, obesity and other hyperalimentation
E70-E88	Metabolic disorders
E89	Postprocedural endocrine and metabolic complications and disorders, not elsewhere classified

DISORDERS OF THYROID GLAND (E00-E07)

● **E00**   **Congenital iodine-deficiency syndrome**

Use additional code (F70-F79) to identify associated intellectual disabilities.

Excludes1   subclinical iodine-deficiency hypothyroidism (E02)

E00.0   **Congenital iodine-deficiency syndrome, neurological type**
Endemic cretinism, neurological type

E00.1   **Congenital iodine-deficiency syndrome, myxedematous type**
Dry, waxy type of swelling (nonpitting edema) with abnormal deposits of mucin in skin (mucinosis) and other tissues
Endemic hypothyroid cretinism
Endemic cretinism, myxedematous type

E00.2   **Congenital iodine-deficiency syndrome, mixed type**
Endemic cretinism, mixed type

E00.9   **Congenital iodine-deficiency syndrome, unspecified**
Congenital iodine-deficiency hypothyroidism NOS
Endemic cretinism NOS

Figure 4-2   Goiter is an enlargement of the thyroid gland.

Item 4-1   Simple goiter indicates no nodules are present. The most common type of goiter is a **diffuse colloidal,** also called a **nontoxic** or **endemic** goiter.

● **E01**   **Iodine-deficiency related thyroid disorders and allied conditions**

Excludes1   congenital iodine-deficiency syndrome (E00.-)
subclinical iodine-deficiency hypothyroidism (E02)

E01.0   **Iodine-deficiency related diffuse (endemic) goiter**
Thyroid gland is enlarged

E01.1   **Iodine-deficiency related multinodular (endemic) goiter**
Iodine-deficiency related nodular goiter

E01.2   **Iodine-deficiency related (endemic) goiter, unspecified**
Endemic goiter NOS

E01.8   **Other iodine-deficiency related thyroid disorders and allied conditions**
Acquired iodine-deficiency hypothyroidism NOS

E02   **Subclinical iodine-deficiency hypothyroidism**

● **E03**   **Other hypothyroidism**

Excludes1   iodine-deficiency related hypothyroidism (E00-E02)
postprocedural hypothyroidism (E89.0)

E03.0   **Congenital hypothyroidism with diffuse goiter**
Congenital parenchymatous goiter (nontoxic)
Congenital goiter (nontoxic) NOS

Excludes1   transitory congenital goiter with normal function (P72.0)

E03.1   **Congenital hypothyroidism without goiter**
Aplasia of thyroid (with myxedema)
Congenital atrophy of thyroid
Congenital hypothyroidism NOS

E03.2   **Hypothyroidism due to medicaments and other exogenous substances**
Code first poisoning due to drug or toxin, if applicable (T36-T65 with fifth or sixth character 1-4 or 6)
Use additional code for adverse effect, if applicable, to identify drug (T36-T50 with fifth or sixth character 5)

E03.3   **Postinfectious hypothyroidism**

E03.4   **Atrophy of thyroid (acquired)**

Excludes1   congenital atrophy of thyroid (E03.1)

E03.5   **Myxedema coma** 🔖
Often fatal complication of long-term hypothyroidism

E03.8   **Other specified hypothyroidism**

E03.9   **Hypothyroidism, unspecified**
Myxedema NOS

Item 4-2   Hypothyroidism is a condition in which there are insufficient levels of thyroxine. **Cretinism** is congenital hypothyroidism, which can result in mental and physical retardation.

▶ New   ⇒ Revised   ~~deleted~~ Deleted   Excludes 1   Excludes 2   Includes   Use additional   Code first   Code also   Key words
OGCR Official Guidelines   X Assign placeholder X   ● Use Additional Character(s)   ▌ Manifestation Code   🔖 Hierarchical Condition Category   Coding Clinic

● **E04 Other nontoxic goiter**

> **Excludes1** congenital goiter (NOS) (diffuse)
> (parenchymatous) (E03.0)
> iodine-deficiency related goiter (E00-E02)

E04.0 Nontoxic diffuse goiter
Thyroid gland is enlarged
Diffuse (colloid) nontoxic goiter
Simple nontoxic goiter

E04.1 Nontoxic single thyroid nodule
Colloid nodule (cystic) (thyroid)
Nontoxic uninodular goiter
Thyroid (cystic) nodule NOS

E04.2 Nontoxic multinodular goiter
Enlarged thyroid gland with multiple nodules
Cystic goiter NOS
Multinodular (cystic) goiter NOS

E04.8 Other specified nontoxic goiter

E04.9 Nontoxic goiter, unspecified
Goiter NOS
Nodular goiter (nontoxic) NOS

● **E05 Thyrotoxicosis [hyperthyroidism]**
Enlarged thyroid gland with multiple nodules

> **Excludes1** chronic thyroiditis with transient thyrotoxicosis
> (E06.2)
> neonatal thyrotoxicosis (P72.1)

● **E05.0 Thyrotoxicosis with diffuse goiter**
Exophthalmic or toxic goiter NOS
Graves' disease
Toxic diffuse goiter

E05.00 Thyrotoxicosis with diffuse goiter without thyrotoxic crisis or storm

E05.01 Thyrotoxicosis with diffuse goiter with thyrotoxic crisis or storm

● **E05.1 Thyrotoxicosis with toxic single thyroid nodule**
Thyrotoxicosis with toxic uninodular goiter

E05.10 Thyrotoxicosis with toxic single thyroid nodule without thyrotoxic crisis or storm

E05.11 Thyrotoxicosis with toxic single thyroid nodule with thyrotoxic crisis or storm

● **E05.2 Thyrotoxicosis with toxic multinodular goiter**
Toxic nodular goiter NOS

E05.20 Thyrotoxicosis with toxic multinodular goiter without thyrotoxic crisis or storm

E05.21 Thyrotoxicosis with toxic multinodular goiter with thyrotoxic crisis or storm

● **E05.3 Thyrotoxicosis from ectopic thyroid tissue**

E05.30 Thyrotoxicosis from ectopic thyroid tissue without thyrotoxic crisis or storm

E05.31 Thyrotoxicosis from ectopic thyroid tissue with thyrotoxic crisis or storm

● **E05.4 Thyrotoxicosis factitia**

E05.40 Thyrotoxicosis factitia without thyrotoxic crisis or storm

E05.41 Thyrotoxicosis factitia with thyrotoxic crisis or storm

Figure 4-3 Graves' disease. In Graves' disease, exophthalmos often looks more pronounced than it actually is because of the extreme lid retraction that may occur. This patient, for instance, had minimal proptosis of the left eye but marked lid retraction. (From Lissauer T, Clayden G, and Craft A: Illustrated Textbook of Paediatrics, Edinburgh, Mosby, 2015)

Item 4–3 Thyrotoxicosis is a condition caused by excessive amounts of the thyroid hormone thyroxine production or hyperthyroidism. **Graves' disease is associated with hyperthyroidism** (known as **Basedow's disease** in Europe).

● **E05.8 Other thyrotoxicosis**
Overproduction of thyroid-stimulating hormone

E05.80 Other thyrotoxicosis without thyrotoxic crisis or storm

E05.81 Other thyrotoxicosis with thyrotoxic crisis or storm

● **E05.9 Thyrotoxicosis, unspecified**
Hyperthyroidism NOS

E05.90 Thyrotoxicosis, unspecified without thyrotoxic crisis or storm

E05.91 Thyrotoxicosis, unspecified with thyrotoxic crisis or storm

● **E06 Thyroiditis**
An inflammation of the thyroid gland which results in an inability to convert iodine into thyroid hormone

> **Excludes1** postpartum thyroiditis (O90.5)

E06.0 Acute thyroiditis
Abscess of thyroid
Pyogenic thyroiditis
Suppurative thyroiditis

Use additional code (B95-B97) to identify infectious agent.

E06.1 Subacute thyroiditis
Inflammation of thyroid gland following viral upper respiratory infection
de Quervain thyroiditis
Giant-cell thyroiditis
Granulomatous thyroiditis
Nonsuppurative thyroiditis
Viral thyroiditis

> **Excludes1** autoimmune thyroiditis (E06.3)

E06.2 Chronic thyroiditis with transient thyrotoxicosis
Chronic inflammation of thyroid gland with intermittent overproduction of thyroid hormone

> **Excludes1** autoimmune thyroiditis (E06.3)

E06.3 Autoimmune thyroiditis
Hashimoto's thyroiditis
Hashitoxicosis (transient)
Lymphadenoid goiter
Lymphocytic thyroiditis
Struma lymphomatosa

E06.4 Drug-induced thyroiditis
Use additional code for adverse effect, if applicable, to identify drug (T36-T50 with fifth or sixth character 5)

E06.5 Other chronic thyroiditis
Chronic fibrous thyroiditis
Chronic thyroiditis NOS
Ligneous thyroiditis
Riedel thyroiditis

E06.9 Thyroiditis, unspecified

● **E07 Other disorders of thyroid**

E07.0 Hypersecretion of calcitonin
C-cell hyperplasia of thyroid
Hypersecretion of thyrocalcitonin

E07.1 Dyshormogenetic goiter
Group of several types of goiter resulting from enzyme defects in hormone synthesis
Familial dyshormogenetic goiter
Pendred's syndrome

> **Excludes1** transitory congenital goiter with normal function (P72.0)

● **E07.8 Other specified disorders of thyroid**

E07.81 Sick-euthyroid syndrome
Euthyroid sick-syndrome

E07.89 Other specified disorders of thyroid
Abnormality of thyroid-binding globulin
Hemorrhage of thyroid
Infarction of thyroid

E07.9 Disorder of thyroid, unspecified

N Newborn Age: 0   **P** Pediatric Age: 0–17   **M** Maternity DX: 12–55   **A** Adult Age: 15–124   ♀ Females Only   ♂ Males Only

OGCR Section I.C.4.a.

> Diabetes mellitus
>
> The diabetes mellitus codes are combination codes that include the type of diabetes mellitus, body system affected, and the complications affecting that body system. As many codes within a particular category as are necessary to describe all of the complications of the disease may be used. They should be sequenced based on the reason for a particular visit. Assign as many codes from categories E08–E13 as needed to identify all of the associated conditions that the patient has.

DIABETES MELLITUS (E08-E13)

A metabolic disease that results in persistent hyperglycemia
Coding Clinic: 2016, Q4, P142

- **E08**   **Diabetes mellitus due to underlying condition**

    Code first the underlying condition, such as:
    congenital rubella (P35.0)
    Cushing's syndrome (E24.-)
    cystic fibrosis (E84.-)
    malignant neoplasm (C00-C96)
    malnutrition (E40-E46)
    pancreatitis and other diseases of the pancreas (K85-K86.-)

    Use additional code to identify control using:
    insulin (Z79.4)
    oral antidiabetic drugs (Z79.84)
    oral hypoglycemic drugs (Z79.84)

    Excludes1   drug or chemical induced diabetes mellitus
    (E09.-)
    gestational diabetes (O24.4-)
    neonatal diabetes mellitus (P70.2)
    postpancreatectomy diabetes mellitus (E13.-)
    postprocedural diabetes mellitus (E13.-)
    secondary diabetes mellitus NEC (E13.-)
    type 1 diabetes mellitus (E10.-)
    type 2 diabetes mellitus (E11.-)

- **E08.0**   **Diabetes mellitus due to underlying condition with hyperosmolarity**

    - *E08.00*   *Diabetes mellitus due to underlying condition with hyperosmolarity without nonketotic hyperglycemic-hyperosmolar coma (NKHHC)* 🅗

    - *E08.01*   *Diabetes mellitus due to underlying condition with hyperosmolarity with coma* 🅗

- **E08.1**   **Diabetes mellitus due to underlying condition with ketoacidosis**

    - *E08.10*   *Diabetes mellitus due to underlying condition with ketoacidosis without coma* 🅗

    - *E08.11*   *Diabetes mellitus due to underlying condition with ketoacidosis with coma* 🅗

- **E08.2**   **Diabetes mellitus due to underlying condition with kidney complications**

    - *E08.21*   *Diabetes mellitus due to underlying condition with diabetic nephropathy* 🅗
        Diabetes mellitus due to underlying condition with intercapillary glomerulosclerosis
        Diabetes mellitus due to underlying condition with intracapillary glomerulonephrosis
        Diabetes mellitus due to underlying condition with Kimmelstiel-Wilson disease

    - *E08.22*   *Diabetes mellitus due to underlying condition with diabetic chronic kidney disease* 🅗
        Use additional code to identify stage of chronic kidney disease (N18.1-N18.6)

    - *E08.29*   *Diabetes mellitus due to underlying condition with other diabetic kidney complication* 🅗
        Renal tubular degeneration in diabetes mellitus due to underlying condition

- **E08.3**   **Diabetes mellitus due to underlying condition with ophthalmic complications**
    Changes in blood vessels of retina in which blood vessels swell and leak fluid into retinal surface.
    Coding Clinic: 2016, Q4, P11

    - **E08.31**   **Diabetes mellitus due to underlying condition with unspecified diabetic retinopathy**

        - *E08.311*   *Diabetes mellitus due to underlying condition with unspecified diabetic retinopathy with macular edema* 🅗

        - *E08.319*   *Diabetes mellitus due to underlying condition with unspecified diabetic retinopathy without macular edema* 🅗

    - **E08.32**   **Diabetes mellitus due to underlying condition with mild nonproliferative diabetic retinopathy**
        Diabetes mellitus due to underlying condition with nonproliferative diabetic retinopathy NOS

        One of the following 7th characters is to be assigned to codes in subcategory E08.32 to designate laterality of the disease:

1	right eye
2	left eye
3	bilateral
9	unspecified eye

        - *E08.321*   *Diabetes mellitus due to underlying condition with mild nonproliferative diabetic retinopathy with macular edema* 🅗

        - *E08.329*   *Diabetes mellitus due to underlying condition with mild nonproliferative diabetic retinopathy without macular edema* 🅗

    - **E08.33**   **Diabetes mellitus due to underlying condition with moderate nonproliferative diabetic retinopathy**

        One of the following 7th characters is to be assigned to codes in subcategory E08.33 to designate laterality of the disease:

1	right eye
2	left eye
3	bilateral
9	unspecified eye

        - *E08.331*   *Diabetes mellitus due to underlying condition with moderate nonproliferative diabetic retinopathy with macular edema* 🅗

        - *E08.339*   *Diabetes mellitus due to underlying condition with moderate nonproliferative diabetic retinopathy without macular edema* 🅗

    - **E08.34**   **Diabetes mellitus due to underlying condition with severe nonproliferative diabetic retinopathy**

        One of the following 7th characters is to be assigned to codes in subcategory E08.34 to designate laterality of the disease:

1	right eye
2	left eye
3	bilateral
9	unspecified eye

        - *E08.341*   *Diabetes mellitus due to underlying condition with severe nonproliferative diabetic retinopathy with macular edema* 🅗

        - *E08.349*   *Diabetes mellitus due to underlying condition with severe nonproliferative diabetic retinopathy without macular edema* 🅗

▶ New   ⇒ Revised   ~~deleted~~ Deleted   Excludes 1   Excludes 2   Includes   Use additional   Code first   Code also   Key words

OGCR Official Guidelines   X Assign placeholder X   ● Use Additional Character(s)   ▶ Manifestation Code   🅗 Hierarchical Condition Category   **Coding Clinic**

● E08.35 **Diabetes mellitus due to underlying condition with proliferative diabetic retinopathy**

One of the following 7th characters is to be assigned to codes in subcategory E08.35 to designate laterality of the disease:

1	right eye
2	left eye
3	bilateral
9	unspecified eye

● ▶ *E08.351 Diabetes mellitus due to underlying condition with proliferative diabetic retinopathy with macular edema* ✇

● ▶ *E08.352 Diabetes mellitus due to underlying condition with proliferative diabetic retinopathy with traction retinal detachment involving the macula* ✇

● ▶ *E08.353 Diabetes mellitus due to underlying condition with proliferative diabetic retinopathy with traction retinal detachment not involving the macula* ✇

● ▶ *E08.354 Diabetes mellitus due to underlying condition with proliferative diabetic retinopathy with combined traction retinal detachment and rhegmatogenous retinal detachment* ✇

● ▶ *E08.355 Diabetes mellitus due to underlying condition with stable proliferative diabetic retinopathy* ✇

● ▶ *E08.359 Diabetes mellitus due to underlying condition with proliferative diabetic retinopathy without macular edema* ✇

▶ *E08.36 Diabetes mellitus due to underlying condition with diabetic cataract* ✇

X ● ▶ *E08.37 Diabetes mellitus due to underlying condition with diabetic macular edema, resolved following treatment* ✇

One of the following 7th characters is to be assigned to code E08.37 to designate laterality of the disease:

1	right eye
2	left eye
3	bilateral
9	unspecified eye

▶ *E08.39 Diabetes mellitus due to underlying condition with other diabetic ophthalmic complication* ✇

Use additional code to identify manifestation, such as:
diabetic glaucoma (H40-H42)

● E08.4 **Diabetes mellitus due to underlying condition with neurological complications**

▶ *E08.40 Diabetes mellitus due to underlying condition with diabetic neuropathy, unspecified* ✇

▶ *E08.41 Diabetes mellitus due to underlying condition with diabetic mononeuropathy* ✇

▶ *E08.42 Diabetes mellitus due to underlying condition with diabetic polyneuropathy* ✇
Diabetes mellitus due to underlying condition with diabetic neuralgia

▶ *E08.43 Diabetes mellitus due to underlying condition with diabetic autonomic (poly)neuropathy* ✇
Diabetes mellitus due to underlying condition with diabetic gastroparesis

▶ *E08.44 Diabetes mellitus due to underlying condition with diabetic amyotrophy* ✇

▶ *E08.49 Diabetes mellitus due to underlying condition with other diabetic neurological complication* ✇

● E08.5 **Diabetes mellitus due to underlying condition with circulatory complications**

▶ *E08.51 Diabetes mellitus due to underlying condition with diabetic peripheral angiopathy without gangrene* ✇

▶ *E08.52 Diabetes mellitus due to underlying condition with diabetic peripheral angiopathy with gangrene* ✇
Diabetes mellitus due to underlying condition with diabetic gangrene

▶ *E08.59 Diabetes mellitus due to underlying condition with other circulatory complications* ✇

● E08.6 **Diabetes mellitus due to underlying condition with other specified complications**

● E08.61 **Diabetes mellitus due to underlying condition with diabetic arthropathy**

▶ *E08.610 Diabetes mellitus due to underlying condition with diabetic neuropathic arthropathy* ✇
Diabetes mellitus due to underlying condition with Charcôt's joints

▶ *E08.618 Diabetes mellitus due to underlying condition with other diabetic arthropathy* ✇

● E08.62 **Diabetes mellitus due to underlying condition with skin complications**

▶ *E08.620 Diabetes mellitus due to underlying condition with diabetic dermatitis* ✇
Diabetes mellitus due to underlying condition with diabetic necrobiosis lipoidica

▶ *E08.621 Diabetes mellitus due to underlying condition with foot ulcer* ✇
Use additional code to identify site of ulcer (L97.4-, L97.5-)

▶ *E08.622 Diabetes mellitus due to underlying condition with other skin ulcer* ✇
Use additional code to identify site of ulcer (L97.1-L97.9, L98.41-L98.49)

▶ *E08.628 Diabetes mellitus due to underlying condition with other skin complications* ✇

● E08.63 **Diabetes mellitus due to underlying condition with oral complications**

▶ *E08.630 Diabetes mellitus due to underlying condition with periodontal disease* ✇

▶ *E08.638 Diabetes mellitus due to underlying condition with other oral complications* ✇

● E08.64 **Diabetes mellitus due to underlying condition with hypoglycemia**

▶ *E08.641 Diabetes mellitus due to underlying condition with hypoglycemia with coma* ✇

▶ *E08.649 Diabetes mellitus due to underlying condition with hypoglycemia without coma* ✇

▶ *E08.65 Diabetes mellitus due to underlying condition with hyperglycemia* ✇

▶ *E08.69 Diabetes mellitus due to underlying condition with other specified complication* ✇
Use additional code to identify complication

▶ *E08.8 Diabetes mellitus due to underlying condition with unspecified complications* ✇

▶ *E08.9 Diabetes mellitus due to underlying condition without complications* ✇

● **E09**   **Drug or chemical induced diabetes mellitus**

Code first poisoning due to drug or toxin, if applicable (T36-T65 with fifth or sixth character 1-4 or 6)

Use additional code for adverse effect, if applicable, to identify drug (T36-T50 with fifth or sixth character 5)

Use additional code to identify control using:
insulin (Z79.4)
oral antidiabetic drugs (Z79.84)
oral hypoglycemic drugs (Z79.84)

Excludes1   diabetes mellitus due to underlying condition (E08.-)
gestational diabetes (O24.4-)
neonatal diabetes mellitus (P70.2)
postpancreatectomy diabetes mellitus (E13.-)
postprocedural diabetes mellitus (E13.-)
secondary diabetes mellitus NEC (E13.-)
type 1 diabetes mellitus (E10.-)
type 2 diabetes mellitus (E11.-)

● **E09.0**   **Drug or chemical induced diabetes mellitus with hyperosmolarity**

   E09.00   **Drug or chemical induced diabetes mellitus with hyperosmolarity without nonketotic hyperglycemic-hyperosmolar coma (NKHHC)** 🐾

   E09.01   **Drug or chemical induced diabetes mellitus with hyperosmolarity with coma** 🐾

● **E09.1**   **Drug or chemical induced diabetes mellitus with ketoacidosis**

   E09.10   **Drug or chemical induced diabetes mellitus with ketoacidosis without coma** 🐾

   E09.11   **Drug or chemical induced diabetes mellitus with ketoacidosis with coma** 🐾

● **E09.2**   **Drug or chemical induced diabetes mellitus with kidney complications**

   E09.21   **Drug or chemical induced diabetes mellitus with diabetic nephropathy** 🐾
   Drug or chemical induced diabetes mellitus with intercapillary glomerulosclerosis
   Drug or chemical induced diabetes mellitus with intracapillary glomerulonephrosis
   Drug or chemical induced diabetes mellitus with Kimmelstiel-Wilson disease

   E09.22   **Drug or chemical induced diabetes mellitus with diabetic chronic kidney disease** 🐾
   Use additional code to identify stage of chronic kidney disease (N18.1-N18.6)

   E09.29   **Drug or chemical induced diabetes mellitus with other diabetic kidney complication** 🐾
   Drug or chemical induced diabetes mellitus with renal tubular degeneration

● **E09.3**   **Drug or chemical induced diabetes mellitus with ophthalmic complications**
   Coding Clinic: 2016, Q4, P11

   E09.31   **Drug or chemical induced diabetes mellitus with unspecified diabetic retinopathy**

      E09.311   **Drug or chemical induced diabetes mellitus with unspecified diabetic retinopathy with macular edema** 🐾

      E09.319   **Drug or chemical induced diabetes mellitus with unspecified diabetic retinopathy without macular edema** 🐾

● **E09.32**   **Drug or chemical induced diabetes mellitus with mild nonproliferative diabetic retinopathy**
   Drug or chemical induced diabetes mellitus with nonproliferative diabetic retinopathy NOS

   One of the following 7th characters is to be assigned to codes in subcategory E09.32 to designate laterality of the disease:

1	right eye
2	left eye
3	bilateral
9	unspecified eye

   ● **E09.321**   **Drug or chemical induced diabetes mellitus with mild nonproliferative diabetic retinopathy with macular edema** 🐾

   ● **E09.329**   **Drug or chemical induced diabetes mellitus with mild nonproliferative diabetic retinopathy without macular edema** 🐾

● **E09.33**   **Drug or chemical induced diabetes mellitus with moderate nonproliferative diabetic retinopathy**

   One of the following 7th characters is to be assigned to codes in subcategory E09.33 to designate laterality of the disease:

1	right eye
2	left eye
3	bilateral
9	unspecified eye

   ● **E09.331**   **Drug or chemical induced diabetes mellitus with moderate nonproliferative diabetic retinopathy with macular edema** 🐾

   ● **E09.339**   **Drug or chemical induced diabetes mellitus with moderate nonproliferative diabetic retinopathy without macular edema** 🐾

● **E09.34**   **Drug or chemical induced diabetes mellitus with severe nonproliferative diabetic retinopathy**

   One of the following 7th characters is to be assigned to codes in subcategory E09.34 to designate laterality of the disease:

1	right eye
2	left eye
3	bilateral
9	unspecified eye

   ● **E09.341**   **Drug or chemical induced diabetes mellitus with severe nonproliferative diabetic retinopathy with macular edema** 🐾

   ● **E09.349**   **Drug or chemical induced diabetes mellitus with severe nonproliferative diabetic retinopathy without macular edema** 🐾

▶ New   ⇒ Revised   ~~deleted~~ Deleted   Excludes 1   Excludes 2   Includes   Use additional   Code first   Code also   Key words
OGCR Official Guidelines   X Assign placeholder X   ● Use Additional Character(s)   ▷ Manifestation Code   🐾 Hierarchical Condition Category   Coding Clinic

● **E09.35** **Drug or chemical induced diabetes mellitus with proliferative diabetic retinopathy**

One of the following 7th characters is to be assigned to codes in subcategory E09.35 to designate laterality of the disease:

1	right eye
2	left eye
3	bilateral
9	unspecified eye

● **E09.351** **Drug or chemical induced diabetes mellitus with proliferative diabetic retinopathy with macular edema** ✎

● **E09.352** **Drug or chemical induced diabetes mellitus with proliferative diabetic retinopathy with traction retinal detachment involving the macula** ✎

● **E09.353** **Drug or chemical induced diabetes mellitus with proliferative diabetic retinopathy with traction retinal detachment not involving the macula** ✎

● **E09.354** **Drug or chemical induced diabetes mellitus with proliferative diabetic retinopathy with combined traction retinal detachment and rhegmatogenous retinal detachment** ✎

● **E09.355** **Drug or chemical induced diabetes mellitus with stable proliferative diabetic retinopathy** ✎

● **E09.359** **Drug or chemical induced diabetes mellitus with proliferative diabetic retinopathy without macular edema** ✎

E09.36 **Drug or chemical induced diabetes mellitus with diabetic cataract** ✎

X ● **E09.37** **Drug or chemical induced diabetes mellitus with diabetic macular edema, resolved following treatment** ✎

One of the following 7th characters is to be assigned to code E09.37 to designate laterality of the disease:

1	right eye
2	left eye
3	bilateral
9	unspecified eye

E09.39 **Drug or chemical induced diabetes mellitus with other diabetic ophthalmic complication** ✎

Use additional code to identify manifestation, such as:
diabetic glaucoma (H40-H42)

● **E09.4** **Drug or chemical induced diabetes mellitus with neurological complications**

E09.40 **Drug or chemical induced diabetes mellitus with neurological complications with diabetic neuropathy, unspecified** ✎

E09.41 **Drug or chemical induced diabetes mellitus with neurological complications with diabetic mononeuropathy** ✎

E09.42 **Drug or chemical induced diabetes mellitus with neurological complications with diabetic polyneuropathy** ✎
Drug or chemical induced diabetes mellitus with diabetic neuralgia

E09.43 **Drug or chemical induced diabetes mellitus with neurological complications with diabetic autonomic (poly)neuropathy** ✎
Drug or chemical induced diabetes mellitus with diabetic gastroparesis

E09.44 **Drug or chemical induced diabetes mellitus with neurological complications with diabetic amyotrophy** ✎

E09.49 **Drug or chemical induced diabetes mellitus with neurological complications with other diabetic neurological complication** ✎

● **E09.5** **Drug or chemical induced diabetes mellitus with circulatory complications**

E09.51 **Drug or chemical induced diabetes mellitus with diabetic peripheral angiopathy without gangrene** ✎

E09.52 **Drug or chemical induced diabetes mellitus with diabetic peripheral angiopathy with gangrene** ✎
Drug or chemical induced diabetes mellitus with diabetic gangrene

E09.59 **Drug or chemical induced diabetes mellitus with other circulatory complications** ✎

● **E09.6** **Drug or chemical induced diabetes mellitus with other specified complications**

● **E09.61** **Drug or chemical induced diabetes mellitus with diabetic arthropathy**

E09.610 **Drug or chemical induced diabetes mellitus with diabetic neuropathic arthropathy** ✎
Drug or chemical induced diabetes mellitus with Charcôt's joints
Progressive degeneration of weight-bearing joint

E09.618 **Drug or chemical induced diabetes mellitus with other diabetic arthropathy** ✎

● **E09.62** **Drug or chemical induced diabetes mellitus with skin complications**

E09.620 **Drug or chemical induced diabetes mellitus with diabetic dermatitis** ✎
Drug or chemical induced diabetes mellitus with diabetic necrobiosis lipoidica
Necrotizing skin condition

E09.621 **Drug or chemical induced diabetes mellitus with foot ulcer** ✎
Use additional code to identify site of ulcer (L97.4-, L97.5-)

E09.622 **Drug or chemical induced diabetes mellitus with other skin ulcer** ✎
Use additional code to identify site of ulcer (L97.1-L97.9, L98.41-L98.49)

E09.628 **Drug or chemical induced diabetes mellitus with other skin complications** ✎

● **E09.63** **Drug or chemical induced diabetes mellitus with oral complications**

E09.630 **Drug or chemical induced diabetes mellitus with periodontal disease** ✎

E09.638 **Drug or chemical induced diabetes mellitus with other oral complications** ✎

● **E09.64** **Drug or chemical induced diabetes mellitus with hypoglycemia**

E09.641 **Drug or chemical induced diabetes mellitus with hypoglycemia with coma** ✎

E09.649 **Drug or chemical induced diabetes mellitus with hypoglycemia without coma** ✎

E09.65 **Drug or chemical induced diabetes mellitus with hyperglycemia** ✎

E09.69 **Drug or chemical induced diabetes mellitus with other specified complication** ✎
Use additional code to identify complication

E09.8 **Drug or chemical induced diabetes mellitus with unspecified complications** ✎

E09.9 **Drug or chemical induced diabetes mellitus without complications** ✎

CHAPTER 4 (E00-E90)

CHAPTER 4 (E00-E90)

● **E10**   **Type 1 diabetes mellitus**

     Includes   brittle diabetes (mellitus)
                  diabetes (mellitus) due to autoimmune process
                  diabetes (mellitus) due to immune mediated
                      pancreatic islet beta-cell destruction
                  idiopathic diabetes (mellitus)
                  juvenile onset diabetes (mellitus)
                  ketosis-prone diabetes (mellitus)

     Excludes1   diabetes mellitus due to underlying condition
                     (E08.-)
                  drug or chemical induced diabetes mellitus
                     (E09.-)
                  gestational diabetes (O24.4-)
                  hyperglycemia NOS (R73.9)
                  neonatal diabetes mellitus (P70.2)
                  postpancreatectomy diabetes mellitus (E13.-)
                  postprocedural diabetes mellitus (E13.-)
                  secondary diabetes mellitus NEC (E13.-)
                  type 2 diabetes mellitus (E11.-)

● **E10.1**   **Type 1 diabetes mellitus with ketoacidosis**
       Acidosis accompanied by accumulation of ketone bodies
       (ketosis) in body tissues and fluids

     E10.10   **Type 1 diabetes mellitus with ketoacidosis without coma** 🐾
              Coding Clinic: 2013, Q3, P20

     E10.11   **Type 1 diabetes mellitus with ketoacidosis with coma** 🐾

● **E10.2**   **Type 1 diabetes mellitus with kidney complications**

     E10.21   **Type 1 diabetes mellitus with diabetic nephropathy** 🐾
              Type 1 diabetes mellitus with intercapillary
                 glomerulosclerosis
              Type 1 diabetes mellitus with intracapillary
                 glomerulonephrosis
              Type 1 diabetes mellitus with Kimmelstiel-
                 Wilson disease

     E10.22   **Type 1 diabetes mellitus with diabetic chronic kidney disease** 🐾
              Use additional code to identify stage of chronic
                 kidney disease (N18.1-N18.6)

     E10.29   **Type 1 diabetes mellitus with other diabetic kidney complication** 🐾
              Type 1 diabetes mellitus with renal tubular
                 degeneration
              Coding Clinic: 2016, Q1, P13

● **E10.3**   **Type 1 diabetes mellitus with ophthalmic complications**
       Coding Clinic: 2016, Q4, P11

   ● **E10.31**   **Type 1 diabetes mellitus with unspecified diabetic retinopathy**

       E10.311   **Type 1 diabetes mellitus with unspecified diabetic retinopathy with macular edema** 🐾

       E10.319   **Type 1 diabetes mellitus with unspecified diabetic retinopathy without macular edema** 🐾

   ● **E10.32**   **Type 1 diabetes mellitus with mild nonproliferative diabetic retinopathy**
              Type 1 diabetes mellitus with nonproliferative
                 diabetic retinopathy NOS

              One of the following 7th characters is to be
                 assigned to codes in subcategory E10.32 to
                 designate laterality of the disease:

1	right eye
2	left eye
3	bilateral
9	unspecified eye

     ● **E10.321**   **Type 1 diabetes mellitus with mild nonproliferative diabetic retinopathy with macular edema** 🐾

     ● **E10.329**   **Type 1 diabetes mellitus with mild nonproliferative diabetic retinopathy without macular edema** 🐾

● **E10.33**   **Type 1 diabetes mellitus with moderate nonproliferative diabetic retinopathy**
       One of the following 7th characters is to be
           assigned to codes in subcategory E10.33 to
           designate laterality of the disease:

1	right eye
2	left eye
3	bilateral
9	unspecified eye

   ● **E10.331**   **Type 1 diabetes mellitus with moderate nonproliferative diabetic retinopathy with macular edema** 🐾

   ● **E10.339**   **Type 1 diabetes mellitus with moderate nonproliferative diabetic retinopathy without macular edema** 🐾

● **E10.34**   **Type 1 diabetes mellitus with severe nonproliferative diabetic retinopathy**
       One of the following 7th characters is to be
           assigned to codes in subcategory E10.34 to
           designate laterality of the disease:

1	right eye
2	left eye
3	bilateral
9	unspecified eye

   ● **E10.341**   **Type 1 diabetes mellitus with severe nonproliferative diabetic retinopathy with macular edema** 🐾

   ● **E10.349**   **Type 1 diabetes mellitus with severe nonproliferative diabetic retinopathy without macular edema** 🐾

● **E10.35**   **Type 1 diabetes mellitus with proliferative diabetic retinopathy**
       One of the following 7th characters is to be
           assigned to codes in subcategory E10.35 to
           designate laterality of the disease:

1	right eye
2	left eye
3	bilateral
9	unspecified eye

   ● **E10.351**   **Type 1 diabetes mellitus with proliferative diabetic retinopathy with macular edema** 🐾

   ● **E10.352**   **Type 1 diabetes mellitus with proliferative diabetic retinopathy with traction retinal detachment involving the macula** 🐾

   ● **E10.353**   **Type 1 diabetes mellitus with proliferative diabetic retinopathy with traction retinal detachment not involving the macula** 🐾

   ● **E10.354**   **Type 1 diabetes mellitus with proliferative diabetic retinopathy with combined traction retinal detachment and rhegmatogenous retinal detachment** 🐾

   ● **E10.355**   **Type 1 diabetes mellitus with stable proliferative diabetic retinopathy** 🐾

   ● **E10.359**   **Type 1 diabetes mellitus with proliferative diabetic retinopathy without macular edema** 🐾

▶ New   ⇒ Revised   ~~deleted~~ Deleted   Excludes 1   Excludes 2   Includes   Use additional   Code first   Code also   Key words

OGCR Official Guidelines   X Assign placeholder X   ● Use Additional Character(s)   ▶ Manifestation Code   🐾 Hierarchical Condition Category   **Coding Clinic**

E10.36   Type 1 diabetes mellitus with diabetic cataract 🔍

X● E10.37   Type 1 diabetes mellitus with diabetic macular edema, resolved following treatment 🔍

One of the following 7th characters is to be assigned to code E10.37 to designate laterality of the disease:

> 1   right eye
> 2   left eye
> 3   bilateral
> 9   unspecified eye

E10.39   Type 1 diabetes mellitus with other diabetic ophthalmic complication 🔍

Use additional code to identify manifestation, such as:
diabetic glaucoma (H40-H42)

● E10.4   Type 1 diabetes mellitus with neurological complications

E10.40   Type 1 diabetes mellitus with diabetic neuropathy, unspecified 🔍

E10.41   Type 1 diabetes mellitus with diabetic mononeuropathy 🔍

E10.42   Type 1 diabetes mellitus with diabetic polyneuropathy 🔍
Type 1 diabetes mellitus with diabetic neuralgia

E10.43   Type 1 diabetes mellitus with diabetic autonomic (poly)neuropathy 🔍
Type 1 diabetes mellitus with diabetic gastroparesis

E10.44   Type 1 diabetes mellitus with diabetic amyotrophy 🔍

E10.49   Type 1 diabetes mellitus with other diabetic neurological complication 🔍

● E10.5   Type 1 diabetes mellitus with circulatory complications

E10.51   Type 1 diabetes mellitus with diabetic peripheral angiopathy without gangrene 🔍

E10.52   Type 1 diabetes mellitus with diabetic peripheral angiopathy with gangrene 🔍
Type 1 diabetes mellitus with diabetic gangrene

E10.59   Type 1 diabetes mellitus with other circulatory complications 🔍

● E10.6   Type 1 diabetes mellitus with other specified complications

● E10.61   Type 1 diabetes mellitus with diabetic arthropathy

E10.610   Type 1 diabetes mellitus with diabetic neuropathic arthropathy 🔍
Type 1 diabetes mellitus with Charcôt's joints

E10.618   Type 1 diabetes mellitus with other diabetic arthropathy 🔍

● E10.62   Type 1 diabetes mellitus with skin complications

E10.620   Type 1 diabetes mellitus with diabetic dermatitis 🔍
Type 1 diabetes mellitus with diabetic necrobiosis lipoidica

E10.621   Type 1 diabetes mellitus with foot ulcer 🔍
Use additional code to identify site of ulcer (L97.4-, L97.5-)

E10.622   Type 1 diabetes mellitus with other skin ulcer 🔍
Use additional code to identify site of ulcer (L97.1-L97.9, L98.41-L98.49)

E10.628   Type 1 diabetes mellitus with other skin complications 🔍

● E10.63   Type 1 diabetes mellitus with oral complications

E10.630   Type 1 diabetes mellitus with periodontal disease 🔍

E10.638   Type 1 diabetes mellitus with other oral complications 🔍

● E10.64   Type 1 diabetes mellitus with hypoglycemia

E10.641   Type 1 diabetes mellitus with hypoglycemia with coma 🔍

E10.649   Type 1 diabetes mellitus with hypoglycemia without coma 🔍
Coding Clinic: 2016, Q1, P13

E10.65   Type 1 diabetes mellitus with hyperglycemia 🔍
Coding Clinic: 2013, Q3, P20

E10.69   Type 1 diabetes mellitus with other specified complication 🔍
Use additional code to identify complication

E10.8   Type 1 diabetes mellitus with unspecified complications 🔍

E10.9   Type 1 diabetes mellitus without complications 🔍

● E11   Type 2 diabetes mellitus

Includes   diabetes (mellitus) due to insulin secretory defect
diabetes NOS
insulin resistant diabetes (mellitus)

Use additional code to identify control using:
insulin (Z79.4)
oral antidiabetic drugs (Z79.84)
oral hypoglycemic drugs (Z79.84)

Excludes1   diabetes mellitus due to underlying condition (E08.-)
drug or chemical induced diabetes mellitus (E09.-)
gestational diabetes (O24.4-)
neonatal diabetes mellitus (P70.2)
postpancreatectomy diabetes mellitus (E13.-)
postprocedural diabetes mellitus (E13.-)
secondary diabetes mellitus NEC (E13.-)
type 1 diabetes mellitus (E10.-)
Coding Clinic: 2020, Q1, P12; 2016, Q4, P121, Q2, P10

● E11.0   Type 2 diabetes mellitus with hyperosmolarity

E11.00   Type 2 diabetes mellitus with hyperosmolarity without nonketotic hyperglycemic-hyperosmolar coma (NKHHC) 🔍

E11.01   Type 2 diabetes mellitus with hyperosmolarity with coma 🔍

● E11.1   Type 2 diabetes mellitus with ketoacidosis

E11.10   Type 2 diabetes mellitus with ketoacidosis without coma 🔍
Coding Clinic: 2017, Q4, P6

E11.11   Type 2 diabetes mellitus with ketoacidosis with coma 🔍

● E11.2   Type 2 diabetes mellitus with kidney complications

E11.21   Type 2 diabetes mellitus with diabetic nephropathy 🔍
Type 2 diabetes mellitus with intercapillary glomerulosclerosis
Type 2 diabetes mellitus with intracapillary glomerulonephrosis
Type 2 diabetes mellitus with Kimmelstiel-Wilson disease
Coding Clinic: 2019, Q3, P3

E11.22   Type 2 diabetes mellitus with diabetic chronic kidney disease 🔍
Use additional code to identify stage of chronic kidney disease (N18.1-N18.6)
Coding Clinic: 2019, Q3, P3; 2018, Q4, P88; 2016, Q2, P36, Q1, P13

E11.29   Type 2 diabetes mellitus with other diabetic kidney complication 🔍
Type 2 diabetes mellitus with renal tubular degeneration

CHAPTER 4 (E00-E90)

● **E11.3**   **Type 2 diabetes mellitus with ophthalmic complications**
Coding Clinic: 2016, Q4, P11

● **E11.31**   **Type 2 diabetes mellitus with unspecified diabetic retinopathy**

     E11.311   **Type 2 diabetes mellitus with unspecified diabetic retinopathy with macular edema** 🐾

     E11.319   **Type 2 diabetes mellitus with unspecified diabetic retinopathy without macular edema** 🐾
Coding Clinic: 2013, Q3, P20

● **E11.32**   **Type 2 diabetes mellitus with mild nonproliferative diabetic retinopathy**
Type 2 diabetes mellitus with nonproliferative diabetic retinopathy NOS

One of the following 7th characters is to be assigned to codes in subcategory E11.32 to designate laterality of the disease:

1	right eye
2	left eye
3	bilateral
9	unspecified eye

   ● **E11.321**   **Type 2 diabetes mellitus with mild nonproliferative diabetic retinopathy with macular edema** 🐾

   ● **E11.329**   **Type 2 diabetes mellitus with mild nonproliferative diabetic retinopathy without macular edema** 🐾

● **E11.33**   **Type 2 diabetes mellitus with moderate nonproliferative diabetic retinopathy**

One of the following 7th characters is to be assigned to codes in subcategory E11.33 to designate laterality of the disease:

1	right eye
2	left eye
3	bilateral
9	unspecified eye

   ● **E11.331**   **Type 2 diabetes mellitus with moderate nonproliferative diabetic retinopathy with macular edema** 🐾

   ● **E11.339**   **Type 2 diabetes mellitus with moderate nonproliferative diabetic retinopathy without macular edema** 🐾

● **E11.34**   **Type 2 diabetes mellitus with severe nonproliferative diabetic retinopathy**

One of the following 7th characters is to be assigned to codes in subcategory E11.34 to designate laterality of the disease:

1	right eye
2	left eye
3	bilateral
9	unspecified eye

   ● **E11.341**   **Type 2 diabetes mellitus with severe nonproliferative diabetic retinopathy with macular edema** 🐾

   ● **E11.349**   **Type 2 diabetes mellitus with severe nonproliferative diabetic retinopathy without macular edema** 🐾

● **E11.35**   **Type 2 diabetes mellitus with proliferative diabetic retinopathy**

One of the following 7th characters is to be assigned to codes in subcategory E11.35 to designate laterality of the disease:

1	right eye
2	left eye
3	bilateral
9	unspecified eye

   ● **E11.351**   **Type 2 diabetes mellitus with proliferative diabetic retinopathy with macular edema** 🐾

   ● **E11.352**   **Type 2 diabetes mellitus with proliferative diabetic retinopathy with traction retinal detachment involving the macula** 🐾

   ● **E11.353**   **Type 2 diabetes mellitus with proliferative diabetic retinopathy with traction retinal detachment not involving the macula** 🐾

   ● **E11.354**   **Type 2 diabetes mellitus with proliferative diabetic retinopathy with combined traction retinal detachment and rhegmatogenous retinal detachment** 🐾

   ● **E11.355**   **Type 2 diabetes mellitus with stable proliferative diabetic retinopathy** 🐾

   ● **E11.359**   **Type 2 diabetes mellitus with proliferative diabetic retinopathy without macular edema** 🐾

E11.36   **Type 2 diabetes mellitus with diabetic cataract** 🐾
Coding Clinic: 2019, Q2, P30-31; 2016, Q2, P36

X ● **E11.37**   **Type 2 diabetes mellitus with diabetic macular edema, resolved following treatment** 🐾

One of the following 7th characters is to be assigned to code E11.37 to designate laterality of the disease:

1	right eye
2	left eye
3	bilateral
9	unspecified eye

E11.39   **Type 2 diabetes mellitus with other diabetic ophthalmic complication** 🐾
Use additional code to identify manifestation, such as:
diabetic glaucoma (H40-H42)

● **E11.4**   **Type 2 diabetes mellitus with neurological complications**

E11.40   **Type 2 diabetes mellitus with diabetic neuropathy, unspecified** 🐾

E11.41   **Type 2 diabetes mellitus with diabetic mononeuropathy** 🐾

E11.42   **Type 2 diabetes mellitus with diabetic polyneuropathy** 🐾
Type 2 diabetes mellitus with diabetic neuralgia
Coding Clinic: 2020, Q1, P12; 2016, Q1, P13

E11.43   **Type 2 diabetes mellitus with diabetic autonomic (poly)neuropathy** 🐾
Type 2 diabetes mellitus with diabetic gastroparesis
Coding Clinic: 2016, Q2, P36

E11.44   **Type 2 diabetes mellitus with diabetic amyotrophy** 🐾
Coding Clinic: 2016, Q2, P36

E11.49   **Type 2 diabetes mellitus with other diabetic neurological complication** 🐾

746

▶ New   ⇒ Revised   ~~deleted~~ Deleted   Excludes 1   Excludes 2   Includes   Use additional   Code first   Code also   Key words

OGCR Official Guidelines   X Assign placeholder X   ● Use Additional Character(s)   ▶ Manifestation Code   🐾 Hierarchical Condition Category   Coding Clinic

● **E11.5**   **Type 2 diabetes mellitus with circulatory complications**

    E11.51   **Type 2 diabetes mellitus with diabetic peripheral angiopathy without gangrene** ℞

    E11.52   **Type 2 diabetes mellitus with diabetic peripheral angiopathy with gangrene** ℞
       Type 2 diabetes mellitus with diabetic gangrene
       Coding Clinic: 2017, Q4, P102

    E11.59   **Type 2 diabetes mellitus with other circulatory complications** ℞

● **E11.6**   **Type 2 diabetes mellitus with other specified complications**

   ● **E11.61**   **Type 2 diabetes mellitus with diabetic arthropathy**

      E11.610   **Type 2 diabetes mellitus with diabetic neuropathic arthropathy** ℞
         Type 2 diabetes mellitus with Charcôt's joints
         Coding Clinic: 2016, Q2, P36

      E11.618   **Type 2 diabetes mellitus with other diabetic arthropathy** ℞
         Coding Clinic: 2018, Q2, P7; 2016, Q2, P36

   ● **E11.62**   **Type 2 diabetes mellitus with skin complications**

      E11.620   **Type 2 diabetes mellitus with diabetic dermatitis** ℞
         Type 2 diabetes mellitus with diabetic necrobiosis lipoidica

      E11.621   **Type 2 diabetes mellitus with foot ulcer** ℞
         Use additional code to identify site of ulcer (L97.4-, L97.5-)
         Coding Clinic: 2020, Q1, P12; 2016, Q1, P12

      E11.622   **Type 2 diabetes mellitus with other skin ulcer** ℞
         Use additional code to identify site of ulcer (L97.1-L97.9, L98.41-L98.49)
         Coding Clinic: 2017, Q4, P17

      E11.628   **Type 2 diabetes mellitus with other skin complications** ℞

   ● **E11.63**   **Type 2 diabetes mellitus with oral complications**

      E11.630   **Type 2 diabetes mellitus with periodontal disease** ℞

      E11.638   **Type 2 diabetes mellitus with other oral complications** ℞

   ● **E11.64**   **Type 2 diabetes mellitus with hypoglycemia**

      E11.641   **Type 2 diabetes mellitus with hypoglycemia with coma** ℞

      E11.649   **Type 2 diabetes mellitus with hypoglycemia without coma** ℞
         Coding Clinic: 2016, Q3, P42; 2015, Q3, P21

    E11.65   **Type 2 diabetes mellitus with hyperglycemia** ℞
       Coding Clinic: 2013, Q3, P20

    E11.69   **Type 2 diabetes mellitus with other specified complication** ℞
       Use additional code to identify complication
       Coding Clinic: 2020, Q1, P12; 2016, Q4, P142

   E11.8   **Type 2 diabetes mellitus with unspecified complications** ℞

   E11.9   **Type 2 diabetes mellitus without complications** ℞
      Coding Clinic: 2016, Q4, P142, Q2, P36

● **E13**   **Other specified diabetes mellitus**

   Includes   diabetes mellitus due to genetic defects of beta-cell function
       diabetes mellitus due to genetic defects in insulin action
       postpancreatectomy diabetes mellitus
       postprocedural diabetes mellitus
       secondary diabetes mellitus NEC

  Use additional code to identify control using:
    insulin (Z79.4)
    oral antidiabetic drugs (Z79.84)
    oral hypoglycemic drugs (Z79.84)

   Excludes1   diabetes (mellitus) due to autoimmune process (E10.-)
       diabetes (mellitus) due to immune mediated pancreatic islet beta-cell destruction (E10.-)
       diabetes mellitus due to underlying condition (E08.-)
       drug or chemical induced diabetes mellitus (E09.-)
       gestational diabetes (O24.4-)
       neonatal diabetes mellitus (P70.2)
       type 1 diabetes mellitus (E10.-)

   ● **E13.0**   **Other specified diabetes mellitus with hyperosmolarity**

      E13.00   **Other specified diabetes mellitus with hyperosmolarity without nonketotic hyperglycemic-hyperosmolar coma (NKHHC)** ℞
         Excludes2   type 2 diabetes mellitus (E11.-)

      E13.01   **Other specified diabetes mellitus with hyperosmolarity with coma** ℞

   ● **E13.1**   **Other specified diabetes mellitus with ketoacidosis**

      E13.10   **Other specified diabetes mellitus with ketoacidosis without coma** ℞
         Coding Clinic: 2016, Q2, P10; 2013, Q1, P26

      E13.11   **Other specified diabetes mellitus with ketoacidosis with coma** ℞

   ● **E13.2**   **Other specified diabetes mellitus with kidney complications**

      E13.21   **Other specified diabetes mellitus with diabetic nephropathy** ℞
         Other specified diabetes mellitus with intercapillary glomerulosclerosis
         Other specified diabetes mellitus with intracapillary glomerulonephrosis
         Other specified diabetes mellitus with Kimmelstiel-Wilson disease

      E13.22   **Other specified diabetes mellitus with diabetic chronic kidney disease** ℞
         Use additional code to identify stage of chronic kidney disease (N18.1-N18.6)

      E13.29   **Other specified diabetes mellitus with other diabetic kidney complication** ℞
         Other specified diabetes mellitus with renal tubular degeneration

   ● **E13.3**   **Other specified diabetes mellitus with ophthalmic complications**
      Coding Clinic: 2016, Q4, P11

     ● **E13.31**   **Other specified diabetes mellitus with unspecified diabetic retinopathy**

       E13.311   **Other specified diabetes mellitus with unspecified diabetic retinopathy with macular edema** ℞

       E13.319   **Other specified diabetes mellitus with unspecified diabetic retinopathy without macular edema** ℞

CHAPTER 4 (E00-E90)

● **E13.32** **Other specified diabetes mellitus with mild nonproliferative diabetic retinopathy**
  Other specified diabetes mellitus with nonproliferative diabetic retinopathy NOS
  One of the following 7th characters is to be assigned to codes in subcategory E13.32 to designate laterality of the disease:

1	right eye
2	left eye
3	bilateral
9	unspecified eye

  ● **E13.321** **Other specified diabetes mellitus with mild nonproliferative diabetic retinopathy with macular edema** %
  ● **E13.329** **Other specified diabetes mellitus with mild nonproliferative diabetic retinopathy without macular edema** %

● **E13.33** **Other specified diabetes mellitus with moderate nonproliferative diabetic retinopathy**
  One of the following 7th characters is to be assigned to codes in subcategory E13.33 to designate laterality of the disease:

1	right eye
2	left eye
3	bilateral
9	unspecified eye

  ● **E13.331** **Other specified diabetes mellitus with moderate nonproliferative diabetic retinopathy with macular edema** %
  ● **E13.339** **Other specified diabetes mellitus with moderate nonproliferative diabetic retinopathy without macular edema** %

● **E13.34** **Other specified diabetes mellitus with severe nonproliferative diabetic retinopathy**
  One of the following 7th characters is to be assigned to codes in subcategory E13.34 to designate laterality of the disease:

1	right eye
2	left eye
3	bilateral
9	unspecified eye

  ● **E13.341** **Other specified diabetes mellitus with severe nonproliferative diabetic retinopathy with macular edema** %
  ● **E13.349** **Other specified diabetes mellitus with severe nonproliferative diabetic retinopathy without macular edema** %

● **E13.35** **Other specified diabetes mellitus with proliferative diabetic retinopathy**
  One of the following 7th characters is to be assigned to codes in subcategory E13.35 to designate laterality of the disease:

1	right eye
2	left eye
3	bilateral
9	unspecified eye

  ● **E13.351** **Other specified diabetes mellitus with proliferative diabetic retinopathy with macular edema** %
  ● **E13.352** **Other specified diabetes mellitus with proliferative diabetic retinopathy with traction retinal detachment involving the macula** %

  ● **E13.353** **Other specified diabetes mellitus with proliferative diabetic retinopathy with traction retinal detachment not involving the macula** %
  ● **E13.354** **Other specified diabetes mellitus with proliferative diabetic retinopathy with combined traction retinal detachment and rhegmatogenous retinal detachment** %
  ● **E13.355** **Other specified diabetes mellitus with stable proliferative diabetic retinopathy** %
  ● **E13.359** **Other specified diabetes mellitus with proliferative diabetic retinopathy without macular edema** %

E13.36 **Other specified diabetes mellitus with diabetic cataract** %

X ● **E13.37** **Other specified diabetes mellitus with diabetic macular edema, resolved following treatment** %
  One of the following 7th characters is to be assigned to code E13.37 to designate laterality of the disease:

1	right eye
2	left eye
3	bilateral
9	unspecified eye

E13.39 **Other specified diabetes mellitus with other diabetic ophthalmic complication** %
  Use additional code to identify manifestation, such as:
  diabetic glaucoma (H40-H42)

● **E13.4** **Other specified diabetes mellitus with neurological complications**
  E13.40 **Other specified diabetes mellitus with diabetic neuropathy, unspecified** %
  E13.41 **Other specified diabetes mellitus with diabetic mononeuropathy** %
  E13.42 **Other specified diabetes mellitus with diabetic polyneuropathy** %
    Other specified diabetes mellitus with diabetic neuralgia
  E13.43 **Other specified diabetes mellitus with diabetic autonomic (poly)neuropathy** %
    Other specified diabetes mellitus with diabetic gastroparesis
  E13.44 **Other specified diabetes mellitus with diabetic amyotrophy** %
  E13.49 **Other specified diabetes mellitus with other diabetic neurological complication** %

● **E13.5** **Other specified diabetes mellitus with circulatory complications**
  E13.51 **Other specified diabetes mellitus with diabetic peripheral angiopathy without gangrene** %
  E13.52 **Other specified diabetes mellitus with diabetic peripheral angiopathy with gangrene** %
    Other specified diabetes mellitus with diabetic gangrene
  E13.59 **Other specified diabetes mellitus with other circulatory complications** %

● **E13.6** **Other specified diabetes mellitus with other specified complications**
  ● **E13.61** **Other specified diabetes mellitus with diabetic arthropathy**
    E13.610 **Other specified diabetes mellitus with diabetic neuropathic arthropathy** %
      Other specified diabetes mellitus with Charcôt's joints
    E13.618 **Other specified diabetes mellitus with other diabetic arthropathy** %

▶ New   ⇒ Revised   ~~deleted~~ Deleted   Excludes 1   Excludes 2   Includes   Use additional   Code first   Code also   Key words
OGCR Official Guidelines   X Assign placeholder X   ● Use Additional Character(s)   ▶ Manifestation Code   % Hierarchical Condition Category   **Coding Clinic**

● **E13.62** **Other specified diabetes mellitus with skin complications**

     E13.620 **Other specified diabetes mellitus with diabetic dermatitis** ℞

         Other specified diabetes mellitus with diabetic necrobiosis lipoidica

     E13.621 **Other specified diabetes mellitus with foot ulcer** ℞

         Use additional code to identify site of ulcer (L97.4-, L97.5-)

     E13.622 **Other specified diabetes mellitus with other skin ulcer** ℞

         Use additional code to identify site of ulcer (L97.1-L97.9, L98.41-L98.49)

     E13.628 **Other specified diabetes mellitus with other skin complications** ℞

● **E13.63** **Other specified diabetes mellitus with oral complications**

     E13.630 **Other specified diabetes mellitus with periodontal disease** ℞

     E13.638 **Other specified diabetes mellitus with other oral complications** ℞

● **E13.64** **Other specified diabetes mellitus with hypoglycemia**

     E13.641 **Other specified diabetes mellitus with hypoglycemia with coma** ℞

     E13.649 **Other specified diabetes mellitus with hypoglycemia without coma** ℞

E13.65 **Other specified diabetes mellitus with hyperglycemia** ℞

E13.69 **Other specified diabetes mellitus with other specified complication** ℞

     Use additional code to identify complication

E13.8 **Other specified diabetes mellitus with unspecified complications** ℞

E13.9 **Other specified diabetes mellitus without complications** ℞

OTHER DISORDERS OF GLUCOSE REGULATION AND PANCREATIC INTERNAL SECRETION (E15-E16)

E15 **Nondiabetic hypoglycemic coma** ℞

     Includes   drug-induced insulin coma in nondiabetic hyperinsulinism with hypoglycemic coma hypoglycemic coma NOS

● **E16** **Other disorders of pancreatic internal secretion**

E16.0 **Drug-induced hypoglycemia without coma**

     Excludes1   diabetes with hypoglycemia without coma (E09.649)

     Use additional code for adverse effect, if applicable, to identify drug (T36-T50 with fifth or sixth character 5)

E16.1 **Other hypoglycemia**

     Functional hyperinsulinism

     Functional nonhyperinsulinemic hypoglycemia

     Hyperinsulinism NOS

     Hyperplasia of pancreatic islet beta cells NOS

     Excludes1   diabetes with hypoglycemia (E08.649, E10.649, E11.649, E13.649)

         hypoglycemia in infant of diabetic mother (P70.1)

         neonatal hypoglycemia (P70.4)

E16.2 **Hypoglycemia, unspecified**

     Excludes1   diabetes with hypoglycemia (E08.649, E10.649, E11.649, E13.649)

     Coding Clinic: 2016, Q3, P42

E16.3 **Increased secretion of glucagon**

     Hyperplasia of pancreatic endocrine cells with glucagon excess

---

E16.4 **Increased secretion of gastrin**

     Hypergastrinemia

     Hyperplasia of pancreatic endocrine cells with gastrin excess

     Zollinger-Ellison syndrome

E16.8 **Other specified disorders of pancreatic internal secretion**

     Increased secretion from endocrine pancreas of growth hormone-releasing hormone

     Increased secretion from endocrine pancreas of pancreatic polypeptide

     Increased secretion from endocrine pancreas of somatostatin

     Increased secretion from endocrine pancreas of vasoactive-intestinal polypeptide

E16.9 **Disorder of pancreatic internal secretion, unspecified**

     Islet-cell hyperplasia NOS

     Pancreatic endocrine cell hyperplasia NOS

DISORDERS OF OTHER ENDOCRINE GLANDS (E20-E35)

     Excludes1   galactorrhea (N64.3)

         gynecomastia (N62)

● **E20** **Hypoparathyroidism**

Greatly reduced function of parathyroid glands; AKA parathyroid insufficiency

     Excludes1   Di George's syndrome (D82.1)

         postprocedural hypoparathyroidism (E89.2)

         tetany NOS (R29.0)

         transitory neonatal hypoparathyroidism (P71.4)

E20.0 **Idiopathic hypoparathyroidism** ℞

Rare condition, unknown cause; short dwarf-like with round face

E20.1 **Pseudohypoparathyroidism**

Hereditary condition resembling hypoparathyroidism, but caused by inability to respond to parathyroid hormone

E20.8 **Other hypoparathyroidism** ℞

E20.9 **Hypoparathyroidism, unspecified** ℞

     Parathyroid tetany

● **E21** **Hyperparathyroidism and other disorders of parathyroid gland**

     Excludes1   adult osteomalacia (M83.-)

         ectopic hyperparathyroidism (E34.2)

         familial hypocalciuric hypercalcemia (E83.52)

         hungry bone syndrome (E83.81)

         infantile and juvenile osteomalacia (E55.0)

E21.0 **Primary hyperparathyroidism** ℞

     Hyperplasia of parathyroid

     Osteitis fibrosa cystica generalisata [von Recklinghausen's disease of bone]

E21.1 **Secondary hyperparathyroidism, not elsewhere classified** ℞

     Excludes1   secondary hyperparathyroidism of renal origin (N25.81)

E21.2 **Other hyperparathyroidism** ℞

     Tertiary hyperparathyroidism

     Excludes1   familial hypocalciuric hypercalcemia (E83.52)

E21.3 **Hyperparathyroidism, unspecified** ℞

E21.4 **Other specified disorders of parathyroid gland** ℞

E21.5 **Disorder of parathyroid gland, unspecified** ℞

Item 4–4 **Hyperparathyroidism** is an overactive parathyroid gland that secretes excessive parathormone, causing increased levels of circulating calcium. This results in a loss of calcium in the bone (osteoporosis).

     Hypoparathyroidism is an underactive parathyroid gland that results in decreased levels of circulating calcium. The primary manifestation is **tetany,** a continuous muscle spasm.

Figure 4-4 **Tetany** caused by hypoparathyroidism.

N   Newborn Age: 0   **P**   Pediatric Age: 0–17   **M**   Maternity DX: 12–55   **A**   Adult Age: 15–124   ♀   Females Only   ♂   Males Only

Item 4–5 **Hyperadrenalism** is overactivity of the adrenal cortex, which secretes corticosteroid hormones. Excessive glucocorticoid hormone results in hyperglycemia **(Cushing's syndrome),** and excessive aldosterone results in **Conn's syndrome. Adrenogenital syndrome** is the result of excessive secretion of androgens, male hormones, which stimulates premature sexual development. **Hypoadrenalism, Addison's disease,** is a condition in which the adrenal glands atrophy.

Figure 4-5 Centripetal and generalized obesity and dorsal kyphosis in a woman with Cushing's disease. (From Salvo SG: Mosby's Pathology for Massage Therapists, St. Louis, MO: Mosby/Elsevier, 2009)

● **E22** **Hyperfunction of pituitary gland**

> **Excludes1** Cushing's syndrome (E24.-)
> Nelson's syndrome (E24.1)
> overproduction of ACTH not associated with Cushing's disease (E27.0)
> overproduction of pituitary ACTH (E24.0)
> overproduction of thyroid-stimulating hormone (E05.8-)

E22.0 **Acromegaly and pituitary gigantism** 🦠
> *Chronic disease caused by hypersecretion of growth hormone*
> Overproduction of growth hormone
>
> **Excludes1** constitutional gigantism (E34.4)
> constitutional tall stature (E34.4)
> increased secretion from endocrine pancreas of growth hormone-releasing hormone (E16.8)

E22.1 **Hyperprolactinemia** 🦠
> *Increased levels of prolactin*
>
> Use additional code for adverse effect, if applicable, to identify drug (T36-T50 with fifth or sixth character 5)

E22.2 **Syndrome of inappropriate secretion of antidiuretic hormone** 🦠

E22.8 **Other hyperfunction of pituitary gland** 🦠
> Central precocious puberty

E22.9 **Hyperfunction of pituitary gland, unspecified** 🦠

● **E23** **Hypofunction and other disorders of the pituitary gland**

> **Includes** the listed conditions whether the disorder is in the pituitary or the hypothalamus
>
> **Excludes1** postprocedural hypopituitarism (E89.3)

E23.0 **Hypopituitarism** 🦠
> Fertile eunuch syndrome
> Hypogonadotropic hypogonadism
> Idiopathic growth hormone deficiency
> Isolated deficiency of gonadotropin
> Isolated deficiency of growth hormone
> Isolated deficiency of pituitary hormone
> Kallmann's syndrome
> Lorain-Levi short stature
> Necrosis of pituitary gland (postpartum)
> Panhypopituitarism
> Pituitary cachexia
> Pituitary insufficiency NOS
> Pituitary short stature
> Sheehan's syndrome
> Simmonds' disease

E23.1 **Drug-induced hypopituitarism** 🦠
> Use additional code for adverse effect, if applicable, to identify drug (T36-T50 with fifth or sixth character 5)

E23.2 **Diabetes insipidus** 🦠
> **Excludes1** nephrogenic diabetes insipidus (N25.1)

E23.3 **Hypothalamic dysfunction, not elsewhere classified** 🦠
> **Excludes1** Prader-Willi syndrome (Q87.11)
> Russell-Silver syndrome (Q87.19)

E23.6 **Other disorders of pituitary gland** 🦠
> Abscess of pituitary
> Adiposogenital dystrophy

E23.7 **Disorder of pituitary gland, unspecified** 🦠

● **E24** **Cushing's syndrome**

> **Excludes1** congenital adrenal hyperplasia (E25.0)

E24.0 **Pituitary-dependent Cushing's disease** 🦠
> Overproduction of pituitary ACTH
> Pituitary-dependent hypercorticalism

E24.1 **Nelson's syndrome** 🦠

E24.2 **Drug-induced Cushing's syndrome** 🦠
> Use additional code for adverse effect, if applicable, to identify drug (T36-T50 with fifth or sixth character 5)

E24.3 **Ectopic ACTH syndrome** 🦠

E24.4 **Alcohol-induced pseudo-Cushing's syndrome** 🦠

E24.8 **Other Cushing's syndrome** 🦠

E24.9 **Cushing's syndrome, unspecified** 🦠

● **E25** **Adrenogenital disorders**
> *Disorder of production of steroid hormone in adrenal gland*
>
> **Includes** adrenogenital syndromes, virilizing or feminizing, whether acquired or due to adrenal hyperplasia consequent on inborn enzyme defects in hormone synthesis
> female adrenal pseudohermaphroditism
> female heterosexual precocious pseudopuberty
> male isosexual precocious pseudopuberty
> male macrogenitosomia praecox
> male sexual precocity with adrenal hyperplasia
> male virilization (female)
>
> **Excludes1** indeterminate sex and pseudohermaphroditism (Q56)
> chromosomal abnormalities (Q90-Q99)

E25.0 **Congenital adrenogenital disorders associated with enzyme deficiency** 🦠
> Congenital adrenal hyperplasia
> 21-Hydroxylase deficiency
> Salt-losing congenital adrenal hyperplasia

E25.8 **Other adrenogenital disorders** 🦠
> Idiopathic adrenogenital disorder
>
> Use additional code for adverse effect, if applicable, to identify drug (T36-T50 with fifth or sixth character 5)

E25.9 **Adrenogenital disorder, unspecified** 🦠
> Adrenogenital syndrome NOS

● **E26** **Hyperaldosteronism**
> *Abnormality of electrolyte metabolism caused by excessive secretion of aldosterone*

● **E26.0** **Primary hyperaldosteronism**

E26.01 **Conn's syndrome** 🦠
> Code also adrenal adenoma (D35.0-)

E26.02 **Glucocorticoid-remediable aldosteronism** 🦠
> Familial aldosteronism type I

E26.09 **Other primary hyperaldosteronism** 🦠
> Primary aldosteronism due to adrenal hyperplasia (bilateral)

E26.1 **Secondary hyperaldosteronism** 🦠

● **E26.8** **Other hyperaldosteronism**

E26.81 **Bartter's syndrome** 🦠

E26.89 **Other hyperaldosteronism** 🦠

E26.9 **Hyperaldosteronism, unspecified** 🦠
> Aldosteronism NOS
> Hyperaldosteronism NOS

▶ New ⇒ Revised d̶e̶l̶e̶t̶e̶d̶ Deleted Excludes 1 Excludes 2 Includes Use additional Code first Code also Key words

OGCR Official Guidelines **X** Assign placeholder X ● Use Additional Character(s) ▶ Manifestation Code 🦠 Hierarchical Condition Category **Coding Clinic**

● **E27   Other disorders of adrenal gland**
   E27.0   Other adrenocortical overactivity 🔃
      Overproduction of ACTH, not associated with
         Cushing's disease
      Premature adrenarche
       Excludes1   Cushing's syndrome (E24.-)

   E27.1   Primary adrenocortical insufficiency 🔃
      Addison's disease
      Autoimmune adrenalitis
       Excludes1   Addison only phenotype
              adrenoleukodystrophy (E71.528)
             amyloidosis (E85.-)
             tuberculous Addison's disease (A18.7)
             Waterhouse-Friderichsen syndrome
                (A39.1)

   E27.2   Addisonian crisis 🔃
      Acute onset of adrenocortical insufficiency
      Adrenal crisis
      Adrenocortical crisis

   E27.3   Drug-induced adrenocortical insufficiency 🔃
      Use additional code for adverse effect, if applicable,
         to identify drug (T36-T50 with fifth or sixth
         character 5)

● **E27.4   Other and unspecified adrenocortical insufficiency**
       Excludes1   adrenoleukodystrophy [Addison-
              Schilder] (E71.528)
             Waterhouse-Friderichsen syndrome
                (A39.1)

     E27.40   Unspecified adrenocortical insufficiency 🔃
         Adrenocortical insufficiency NOS
         Hypoaldosteronism

     E27.49   Other adrenocortical insufficiency 🔃
         Adrenal hemorrhage
         Adrenal infarction

   E27.5   Adrenomedullary hyperfunction 🔃
      Adrenomedullary hyperplasia
      Catecholamine hypersecretion

   E27.8   Other specified disorders of adrenal gland 🔃
      Abnormality of cortisol-binding globulin

   E27.9   Disorder of adrenal gland, unspecified 🔃

● **E28   Ovarian dysfunction**
     Excludes1   isolated gonadotropin deficiency (E23.0)
            postprocedural ovarian failure (E89.4-)

   E28.0   Estrogen excess ♀
      Use additional code for adverse effect, if applicable,
         to identify drug (T36-T50 with fifth or sixth
         character 5)

   E28.1   Androgen excess ♀
      Hypersecretion of ovarian androgens
      Use additional code for adverse effect, if applicable,
         to identify drug (T36-T50 with fifth or sixth
         character 5)

   E28.2   Polycystic ovarian syndrome ♀
      Sclerocystic ovary syndrome
      Stein-Leventhal syndrome

● **E28.3   Primary ovarian failure**
       Excludes1   pure gonadal dysgenesis (Q99.1)
            Turner's syndrome (Q96.-)

    ● **E28.31   Premature menopause**
      **E28.310   Symptomatic premature
           menopause** ♀   A
             Symptoms such as flushing,
                sleeplessness, headache, lack of
                concentration, associated with
                premature menopause

      **E28.319   Asymptomatic premature
           menopause** ♀   A
             Premature menopause NOS

     E28.39   Other primary ovarian failure ♀
         Decreased estrogen
         Resistant ovary syndrome

   E28.8   Other ovarian dysfunction ♀
      Ovarian hyperfunction NOS
       Excludes1   postprocedural ovarian failure (E89.4-)

   E28.9   Ovarian dysfunction, unspecified ♀

● **E29   Testicular dysfunction**
     Excludes1   androgen insensitivity syndrome (E34.5-)
            azoospermia or oligospermia NOS (N46.0-N46.1)
            isolated gonadotropin deficiency (E23.0)
            Klinefelter's syndrome (Q98.0-Q98.1, Q98.4)

   E29.0   Testicular hyperfunction ♂
      Hypersecretion of testicular hormones

   E29.1   Testicular hypofunction ♂
      Defective biosynthesis of testicular androgen NOS
      5-delta-Reductase deficiency (with male
         pseudohermaphroditism)
      Testicular hypogonadism NOS
      Use additional code for adverse effect, if applicable,
         to identify drug (T36-T50 with fifth or sixth
         character 5)
       Excludes1   postprocedural testicular hypofunction
            (E89.5)

   E29.8   Other testicular dysfunction ♂

   E29.9   Testicular dysfunction, unspecified ♂

● **E30   Disorders of puberty, not elsewhere classified**
   E30.0   Delayed puberty
      Constitutional delay of puberty
      Delayed sexual development

   E30.1   Precocious puberty   P
      Sexual maturation at earlier age than normal, or before age
       8 in girls and 9 in boys, usually hormonal; AKA sexual
       precocity or pubertas praecox
      Precocious menstruation
       Excludes1   Albright (-McCune) (-Sternberg)
               syndrome (Q78.1)
            central precocious puberty (E22.8)
            congenital adrenal hyperplasia (E25.0)
            female heterosexual precocious
               pseudopuberty (E25.-)
            male isosexual precocious pseudopuberty
               (E25.-)

   E30.8   Other disorders of puberty   P
      Premature thelarche

   E30.9   Disorder of puberty, unspecified

● **E31   Polyglandular dysfunction**
     Excludes1   ataxia telangiectasia [Louis-Bar] (G11.3)
            dystrophia myotonica [Steinert] (G71.11)
            pseudohypoparathyroidism (E20.1)

   E31.0   Autoimmune polyglandular failure 🔃
      Schmidt's syndrome

   E31.1   Polyglandular hyperfunction 🔃
       Excludes1   multiple endocrine adenomatosis (E31.2-)
            multiple endocrine neoplasia (E31.2-)

● **E31.2   Multiple endocrine neoplasia [MEN] syndromes**
      Adenomatous hyperplasia and malignant tumors in
       endocrine glands
      Multiple endocrine adenomatosis
      Code also any associated malignancies and other
         conditions associated with the syndromes

     **E31.20   Multiple endocrine neoplasia [MEN]
           syndrome, unspecified** 🔃
         Multiple endocrine adenomatosis NOS
         Multiple endocrine neoplasia [MEN]
            syndrome NOS

     E31.21   Multiple endocrine neoplasia [MEN] type I 🔃
         Wermer's syndrome

     E31.22   Multiple endocrine neoplasia [MEN] type IIA 🔃
         Sipple's syndrome

     E31.23   Multiple endocrine neoplasia [MEN] type IIB 🔃

   E31.8   Other polyglandular dysfunction 🔃

   E31.9   Polyglandular dysfunction, unspecified 🔃

N Newborn Age: 0   **P** Pediatric Age: 0–17   **M** Maternity DX: 12–55   **A** Adult Age: 15–124   ♀ Females Only   ♂ Males Only

751

CHAPTER 4 (E00-E90)

● **E32 Diseases of thymus**

> **Excludes1**   aplasia or hypoplasia of thymus with
>   immunodeficiency (D82.1)
>   myasthenia gravis (G70.0)

E32.0 Persistent hyperplasia of thymus 🦌
      Hypertrophy of thymus

E32.1 Abscess of thymus 🦌

E32.8 Other diseases of thymus 🦌

> **Excludes1**   aplasia or hypoplasia with
>   immunodeficiency (D82.1)
>   thymoma (D15.0)

E32.9 Disease of thymus, unspecified 🦌

● **E34 Other endocrine disorders**

> **Excludes1**   pseudohypoparathyroidism (E20.1)

E34.0 Carcinoid syndrome 🦌

      Note: May be used as an additional code to identify
            functional activity associated with a carcinoid
            tumor.

E34.1 Other hypersecretion of intestinal hormones

E34.2 Ectopic hormone secretion, not elsewhere classified

> **Excludes1**   ectopic ACTH syndrome (E24.3)

E34.3 Short stature due to endocrine disorder
      Constitutional short stature
      Laron-type short stature

> **Excludes1**   achondroplastic short stature (Q77.4)
>   hypochondroplastic short stature (Q77.4)
>   nutritional short stature (E45)
>   pituitary short stature (E23.0)
>   progeria (E34.8)
>   renal short stature (N25.0)
>   Russell-Silver syndrome (Q87.19)
>   short-limbed stature with
>   immunodeficiency (D82.2)
>   short stature in specific dysmorphic
>   syndromes - code to syndrome - see
>   Alphabetical Index
>   short stature NOS (R62.52)

E34.4 Constitutional tall stature 🦌
      Constitutional gigantism

● **E34.5 Androgen insensitivity syndrome**

E34.50 Androgen insensitivity syndrome, unspecified
           Androgen insensitivity NOS

E34.51 Complete androgen insensitivity syndrome
           Complete androgen insensitivity
           de Quervain syndrome
           Goldberg-Maxwell syndrome

E34.52 Partial androgen insensitivity syndrome
           Partial androgen insensitivity
           Reifenstein syndrome

E34.8 Other specified endocrine disorders
      Pineal gland dysfunction
      Progeria

> **Excludes2**   pseudohypoparathyroidism (E20.1)

E34.9 Endocrine disorder, unspecified
      Endocrine disturbance NOS
      Hormone disturbance NOS

▷ **E35 *Disorders of endocrine glands in diseases classified elsewhere***

      Code first underlying disease, such as:
      late congenital syphilis of thymus gland [Dubois disease]
         (A50.5)

      Use additional code, if applicable, to identify:
      sequelae of tuberculosis of other organs (B90.8)

> **Excludes1**   Echinococcus granulosus infection of thyroid
>   gland (B67.3)
>   meningococcal hemorrhagic adrenalitis (A39.1)
>   syphilis of endocrine gland (A52.79)
>   tuberculosis of adrenal gland, except calcification
>   (A18.7)
>   tuberculosis of endocrine gland NEC (A18.82)
>   tuberculosis of thyroid gland (A18.81)
>   Waterhouse-Friderichsen syndrome (A39.1)

INTRAOPERATIVE COMPLICATIONS OF ENDOCRINE SYSTEM (E36)

● **E36 Intraoperative complications of endocrine system**

> **Excludes2**   postprocedural endocrine and metabolic
>   complications and disorders, not elsewhere
>   classified (E89.-)

● **E36.0 Intraoperative hemorrhage and hematoma of an
endocrine system organ or structure complicating a
procedure**

> **Excludes1**   intraoperative hemorrhage and
>   hematoma of an endocrine system
>   organ or structure due to accidental
>   puncture or laceration during a
>   procedure (E36.1-)

**E36.01 Intraoperative hemorrhage and hematoma
of an endocrine system organ or structure
complicating an endocrine system procedure**
           Coding Clinic: 2020, Q1, P19

**E36.02 Intraoperative hemorrhage and hematoma
of an endocrine system organ or structure
complicating other procedure**

● **E36.1 Accidental puncture and laceration of an endocrine
system organ or structure during a procedure**

**E36.11 Accidental puncture and laceration of an
endocrine system organ or structure during an
endocrine system procedure**

**E36.12 Accidental puncture and laceration of an
endocrine system organ or structure during
other procedure**

E36.8 Other intraoperative complications of endocrine system
      Use additional code, if applicable, to further specify
         disorder

MALNUTRITION (E40-E46)

> **Excludes1**   intestinal malabsorption (K90.-)
>   sequelae of protein-calorie malnutrition (E64.0)
>
> **Excludes2**   nutritional anemias (D50-D53)
>   starvation (T73.0)

E40 Kwashiorkor 🦌
      Malnutrition produced by severe protein deficiency
      Severe malnutrition with nutritional edema with
         dyspigmentation of skin and hair

> **Excludes1**   marasmic kwashiorkor (E42)

      Coding Clinic: 22017, Q3, P25

E41 Nutritional marasmus 🦌
      Severe malnutrition with marasmus

> **Excludes1**   marasmic kwashiorkor (E42)

      Coding Clinic: 2017, Q3, P24-25

E42 Marasmic kwashiorkor 🦌
      Severe protein malnutrition
      Intermediate form severe protein-calorie malnutrition
      Severe protein-calorie malnutrition with signs of both
         kwashiorkor and marasmus
      Coding Clinic: 2017, Q3, P25

E43 Unspecified severe protein-calorie malnutrition 🦌
      Starvation edema
      Coding Clinic: 2020, Q1, P5-6; 2017, Q4, P108-109; 2017, Q3, P25

● **E44 Protein-calorie malnutrition of moderate and mild degree**

E44.0 Moderate protein-calorie malnutrition 🦌

E44.1 Mild protein-calorie malnutrition 🦌

**E45 Retarded development following protein-calorie
malnutrition** 🦌
      Nutritional short stature
      Nutritional stunting
      Physical retardation due to malnutrition

E46   **Unspecified protein-calorie malnutrition**
           Malnutrition NOS
           Protein-calorie imbalance NOS
           Excludes1   nutritional deficiency NOS (E63.9)
           Coding Clinic: 2017, Q3, P25

OTHER NUTRITIONAL DEFICIENCIES (E50-E64)

           Excludes2   nutritional anemias (D50-D53)

● **E50**   **Vitamin A deficiency**
           Excludes1   sequelae of vitamin A deficiency (E64.1)
   E50.0   **Vitamin A deficiency with** conjunctival xerosis
   E50.1   **Vitamin A deficiency with** Bitot's spot and conjunctival
                xerosis
                Bitot's spot in the young child
   E50.2   **Vitamin A deficiency with** corneal xerosis
   E50.3   **Vitamin A deficiency with** corneal ulceration and xerosis
   E50.4   **Vitamin A deficiency with** keratomalacia
                Eye disorder that results in dry cornea caused by vitamin A
                deficiency
   E50.5   **Vitamin A deficiency with** night blindness
   E50.6   **Vitamin A deficiency with** xerophthalmic scars of cornea
                Abnormal dryness and thickening of conjunctiva and cornea
                due to vitamin A deficiency
   E50.7   **Other ocular manifestations of vitamin A deficiency**
                Xerophthalmia NOS
   E50.8   **Other manifestations of vitamin A deficiency**
                Follicular keratosis
                Xeroderma
   E50.9   **Vitamin A deficiency,** unspecified
                Hypovitaminosis A NOS

● **E51**   **Thiamine deficiency**
           Excludes1   sequelae of thiamine deficiency (E64.8)
   ● **E51.1**   **Beriberi**
      E51.11   **Dry beriberi**
                    Thiamine deficiency with nervous system
                    manifestation most often caused by excessive
                    alcohol consumption
                    Beriberi NOS
                    Beriberi with polyneuropathy
      E51.12   **Wet beriberi**
                    Thiamine deficiency with cardiovascular
                    manifestation most often caused by excessive
                    alcohol consumption
                    Beriberi with cardiovascular manifestations
                    Cardiovascular beriberi
                    Shoshin disease
   E51.2   **Wernicke's encephalopathy**
                Acute disease of brain due to thiamine deficiency most often
                associated with excessive alcohol consumption
   E51.8   **Other manifestations of thiamine deficiency**
   E51.9   **Thiamine deficiency,** unspecified

  E52   **Niacin deficiency [pellagra]**
             Niacin (-tryptophan) deficiency
             Nicotinamide deficiency
             Pellagra (alcoholic)
             Excludes1   sequelae of niacin deficiency (E64.8)

Item 4–6 Bitot's spots are the result of a buildup of keratin debris found
on the superficial surface the conjunctiva; oval, triangular, or irregular in
shape; and a sign of vitamin A deficiency and associated with night blindness.
The disease may progress to **keratomalacia,** which can result in eventual
prolapse of the iris and loss of the lens.

Figure 4-6   Bitot's spot on the conjunctiva.

Figure 4-7   The sharply demarcated,
characteristic scaling dermatitis of
pellagra. (From James WD, Berger TG,
Elston DM: Andrews' Diseases of the
Skin: Clinical Dermatology, Philadelphia,
Saunders Elsevier, 2006)

Item 4–7 Pellagra is associated with a deficiency of niacin and its
precursor, **tryptophan.** Characteristics of the condition include diarrhea,
dermatitis on exposed skin surfaces, dementia, and death. It is prevalent in
developing countries where nutrition is inadequate. **Beriberi** is associated with
thiamine deficiency.

● **E53**   **Deficiency of other B group vitamins**
           Excludes1   sequelae of vitamin B deficiency (E64.8)
   E53.0   **Riboflavin deficiency**
                Ariboflavinosis
                Vitamin B2 deficiency
   E53.1   **Pyridoxine deficiency**
                Vitamin B6 deficiency
                Excludes1   pyridoxine-responsive sideroblastic
                                 anemia (D64.3)
   E53.8   **Deficiency of other specified B group vitamins**
                Biotin deficiency
                Cyanocobalamin deficiency
                Folate deficiency
                Folic acid deficiency
                Pantothenic acid deficiency
                Vitamin B12 deficiency
                Excludes1   folate deficiency anemia (D52.-)
                                 vitamin B12 deficiency anemia (D51.-)
   E53.9   **Vitamin B deficiency,** unspecified

  E54   **Ascorbic acid deficiency**
             Deficiency of vitamin C
             Scurvy
             Excludes1   scorbutic anemia (D53.2)
                              sequelae of vitamin C deficiency (E64.2)

● **E55**   **Vitamin D deficiency**
           Excludes1   adult osteomalacia (M83.-)
                            osteoporosis (M80.-)
                            sequelae of rickets (E64.3)
   E55.0   **Rickets, active**
                Infantile osteomalacia
                Juvenile osteomalacia
                Softening of bone
                Excludes1   celiac rickets (K90.0)
                                 Crohn's rickets (K50.-)
                                 hereditary vitamin D-dependent rickets
                                 (E83.32)
                                 inactive rickets (E64.3)
                                 renal rickets (N25.0)
                                 sequelae of rickets (E64.3)
                                 vitamin D-resistant rickets (E83.31)
   E55.9   **Vitamin D deficiency,** unspecified
                Avitaminosis D

● **E56**   **Other vitamin deficiencies**
           Excludes1   sequelae of other vitamin deficiencies (E64.8)
   E56.0   **Deficiency of** vitamin E
   E56.1   **Deficiency of** vitamin K
                Excludes1   deficiency of coagulation factor due to
                                 vitamin K deficiency (D68.4)
                                 vitamin K deficiency of newborn (P53)
   E56.8   **Deficiency of other vitamins**
   E56.9   **Vitamin deficiency,** unspecified

CHAPTER 4 (E00-E90)

E58   **Dietary calcium deficiency**

     Excludes1   disorders of calcium metabolism (E83.5-)
                     sequelae of calcium deficiency (E64.8)

E59   **Dietary selenium deficiency**

     Keshan disease

     Excludes1   sequelae of selenium deficiency (E64.8)

E60   **Dietary zinc deficiency**

● **E61**   **Deficiency of other nutrient elements**

     Use additional code for adverse effect, if applicable, to identify drug (T36-T50 with fifth or sixth character 5)

     Excludes1   disorders of mineral metabolism (E83.-)
                     iodine deficiency related thyroid disorders (E00-E02)
                     sequelae of malnutrition and other nutritional deficiencies (E64.-)

     E61.0   **Copper deficiency**

     E61.1   **Iron deficiency**

         Excludes1   iron deficiency anemia (D50.-)

     E61.2   **Magnesium deficiency**

     E61.3   **Manganese deficiency**

     E61.4   **Chromium deficiency**

     E61.5   **Molybdenum deficiency**

     E61.6   **Vanadium deficiency**

     E61.7   **Deficiency of multiple nutrient elements**

     E61.8   **Deficiency of other specified nutrient elements**

     E61.9   **Deficiency of nutrient element, unspecified**

● **E63**   **Other nutritional deficiencies**

     Excludes1   dehydration (E86.0)
                     failure to thrive, adult (R62.7)
                     failure to thrive, child (R62.51)
                     feeding problems in newborn (P92.-)
                     sequelae of malnutrition and other nutritional deficiencies (E64.-)

     E63.0   **Essential fatty acid [EFA] deficiency**

     E63.1   **Imbalance of constituents of food intake**

     E63.8   **Other specified nutritional deficiencies**

     E63.9   **Nutritional deficiency, unspecified**

● **E64**   **Sequelae of malnutrition and other nutritional deficiencies**

     Pathological condition resulting from disease, injury, or other trauma

     Note: This category is to be used to indicate conditions in categories E43, E44, E46, E50-E63 as the cause of sequelae, which are themselves classified elsewhere. The "sequelae" include conditions specified as such; they also include the late effects of diseases classifiable to the above categories if the disease itself is no longer present

     Code first condition resulting from (sequela) of malnutrition and other nutritional deficiencies

     E64.0   **Sequelae of protein-calorie malnutrition** 🅱

         Excludes2   retarded development following protein-calorie malnutrition (E45)

     E64.1   **Sequelae of vitamin A deficiency**

     E64.2   **Sequelae of vitamin C deficiency**

     E64.3   **Sequelae of rickets**

     E64.8   **Sequelae of other nutritional deficiencies**

     E64.9   **Sequelae of unspecified nutritional deficiency**

OVERWEIGHT, OBESITY AND OTHER HYPERALIMENTATION (E65-E68)

E65   **Localized adiposity**

     Fat pad

● **E66**   **Overweight and obesity**

     Code first obesity complicating pregnancy, childbirth and the puerperium, if applicable (O99.21-)

     Use additional code to identify body mass index (BMI), if known (Z68.-)

     Excludes1   adiposogenital dystrophy (E23.6)
                     lipomatosis NOS (E88.2)
                     lipomatosis dolorosa [Dercum] (E88.2)
                     Prader-Willi syndrome (Q87.11)

     Coding Clinic: 2018, Q4, P80

   ● **E66.0**   **Obesity due to excess calories**

         E66.01   **Morbid (severe) obesity due to excess calories** 🅱

                 Excludes1   morbid (severe) obesity with alveolar hypoventilation (E66.2)

                 Coding Clinic: 2018, Q4, P79

         E66.09   **Other obesity due to excess calories**

     E66.1   **Drug-induced obesity**

         Use additional code for adverse effect, if applicable, to identify drug (T36-T50 with fifth or sixth character 5)

     E66.2   **Morbid (severe) obesity with alveolar hypoventilation** 🅱

         Uncommon condition of unknown cause leading to inadequate ventilation in lungs, even though lungs and airways are normal

         Obesity hypoventilation syndrome (OHS)

         Pickwickian syndrome

     E66.3   **Overweight**

     E66.8   **Other obesity**

     E66.9   **Obesity, unspecified**

         Obesity NOS

● **E67**   **Other hyperalimentation**

     Ingestion of more than optimal amount of nutrients

     Excludes1   hyperalimentation NOS (R63.2)
                     sequelae of hyperalimentation (E68)

     E67.0   **Hypervitaminosis A**

     E67.1   **Hypercarotenemia**

     E67.2   **Megavitamin-B6 syndrome**

     E67.3   **Hypervitaminosis D**

     E67.8   **Other specified hyperalimentation**

E68   **Sequelae of hyperalimentation**

     Code first condition resulting from (sequela) of hyperalimentation

---

METABOLIC DISORDERS (E70-E88)

     Excludes1   androgen insensitivity syndrome (E34.5-)
                     congenital adrenal hyperplasia (E25.0)
                ➠Ehlers-Danlos syndromes (Q79.6-)
                     hemolytic anemias attributable to enzyme disorders (D55.-)
                     Marfan's syndrome (Q87.4)
                     5-alpha-reductase deficiency (E29.1)

● **E70**   **Disorders of aromatic amino-acid metabolism**

     E70.0   **Classical phenylketonuria** 🅱

         Inherited disorder that increases to harmful levels amino acid phenylalanine

     E70.1   **Other hyperphenylalaninemias** 🅱

▶ New   ➠ Revised   ~~deleted~~ Deleted   Excludes 1   Excludes 2   Includes   Use additional   Code first   Code also   Key words

OGCR Official Guidelines   **X** Assign placeholder X   ● Use Additional Character(s)   ▶ Manifestation Code   🅱 Hierarchical Condition Category   **Coding Clinic**

● **E70.2**   **Disorders of tyrosine metabolism**
> **Excludes1**   transitory tyrosinemia of newborn (P74.5)

E70.20   **Disorder of tyrosine metabolism, unspecified** 🔖
> *Tyrosine: Nonessential amino acid occurring in most proteins*

E70.21   **Tyrosinemia** 🔖
> *Congenital amino acid metabolism*
> Hypertyrosinemia

E70.29   **Other disorders of tyrosine metabolism** 🔖
> Alkaptonuria
> Ochronosis

● **E70.3**   **Albinism**
> *Congenital condition of reduced or absent pigment in eyes, skin, and hair*

E70.30   **Albinism, unspecified** 🔖

● **E70.31**   **Ocular albinism**

E70.310   **X-linked ocular albinism** 🔖

E70.311   **Autosomal recessive ocular albinism** 🔖

E70.318   **Other ocular albinism** 🔖

E70.319   **Ocular albinism, unspecified** 🔖

● **E70.32**   **Oculocutaneous albinism**
> *Partial or total lack of melanin pigment in eyes*
> **Excludes1**   Chediak-Higashi syndrome (E70.330)
> Hermansky-Pudlak syndrome (E70.331)

E70.320   **Tyrosinase negative oculocutaneous albinism** 🔖
> Albinism I
> Oculocutaneous albinism ty-neg

E70.321   **Tyrosinase positive oculocutaneous albinism** 🔖
> Albinism II
> Oculocutaneous albinism ty-pos

E70.328   **Other oculocutaneous albinism** 🔖
> Cross syndrome

E70.329   **Oculocutaneous albinism, unspecified** 🔖

● **E70.33**   **Albinism with hematologic abnormality**

E70.330   **Chediak-Higashi syndrome** 🔖

E70.331   **Hermansky-Pudlak syndrome** 🔖

E70.338   **Other albinism with hematologic abnormality** 🔖

E70.339   **Albinism with hematologic abnormality, unspecified** 🔖

E70.39   **Other specified albinism** 🔖
> Piebaldism

● **E70.4**   **Disorders of histidine metabolism**

E70.40   **Disorders of histidine metabolism, unspecified** 🔖

E70.41   **Histidinemia** 🔖

E70.49   **Other disorders of histidine metabolism** 🔖

E70.5   **Disorders of tryptophan metabolism** 🔖

● **E70.8**   **Other disorders of aromatic amino-acid metabolism** 🔖

▶ **E70.81**   **Aromatic L-amino acid decarboxylase deficiency**
> ▶AADC deficiency

▶ **E70.89**   **Other disorders of aromatic amino-acid metabolism**

E70.9   **Disorder of aromatic amino-acid metabolism, unspecified** 🔖

● **E71**   **Disorders of branched-chain amino-acid metabolism and fatty-acid metabolism**

E71.0   **Maple-syrup-urine disease** 🔖
> *Due to defect in amino acid catabolism, causing severe ketoacidosis with smell of maple syrup in urine and on body*

● **E71.1**   **Other disorders of branched-chain amino-acid metabolism**

● **E71.11**   **Branched-chain organic acidurias**

E71.110   **Isovaleric acidemia** 🔖

E71.111   **3-methylglutaconic aciduria** 🔖

E71.118   **Other branched-chain organic acidurias** 🔖

● **E71.12**   **Disorders of propionate metabolism**

E71.120   **Methylmalonic acidemia** 🔖

E71.121   **Propionic acidemia** 🔖

E71.128   **Other disorders of propionate metabolism** 🔖

E71.19   **Other disorders of branched-chain amino-acid metabolism** 🔖
> Hyperleucine-isoleucinemia
> Hypervalinemia

E71.2   **Disorder of branched-chain amino-acid metabolism, unspecified** 🔖

● **E71.3**   **Disorders of fatty-acid metabolism**
> **Excludes1**   peroxisomal disorders (E71.5)
> Refsum's disease (G60.1)
> Schilder's disease (G37.0)
> **Excludes2**   carnitine deficiency due to inborn error of metabolism (E71.42)

E71.30   **Disorder of fatty-acid metabolism, unspecified**

● **E71.31**   **Disorders of fatty-acid oxidation**

E71.310   **Long chain/very long chain acyl CoA dehydrogenase deficiency** 🔖
> LCAD
> VLCAD

E71.311   **Medium chain acyl CoA dehydrogenase deficiency** 🔖
> MCAD

E71.312   **Short chain acyl CoA dehydrogenase deficiency** 🔖
> SCAD

E71.313   **Glutaric aciduria type II** 🔖
> Glutaric aciduria type II A
> Glutaric aciduria type II B
> Glutaric aciduria type II C
> **Excludes1**   glutaric aciduria (type 1) NOS (E72.3)

E71.314   **Muscle carnitine palmitoyltransferase deficiency** 🔖

E71.318   **Other disorders of fatty-acid oxidation** 🔖

E71.32   **Disorders of ketone metabolism** 🔖

E71.39   **Other disorders of fatty-acid metabolism** 🔖

● **E71.4**   **Disorders of carnitine metabolism**
> **Excludes1**   muscle carnitine palmitoyltransferase deficiency (E71.314)

E71.40   **Disorder of carnitine metabolism, unspecified** 🔖

E71.41   **Primary carnitine deficiency** 🔖

E71.42   **Carnitine deficiency due to inborn errors of metabolism** 🔖
> Code also associated inborn error or metabolism

E71.43   **Iatrogenic carnitine deficiency** 🔖
> *Iatrogenic: Outcomes from activity of physicians*
> Carnitine deficiency due to hemodialysis
> Carnitine deficiency due to Valproic acid therapy

CHAPTER 4 (E00–E90)

● E71.44   **Other secondary carnitine deficiency**
   E71.440   **Ruvalcaba-Myhre-Smith syndrome** 🦠
   E71.448   **Other secondary carnitine deficiency** 🦠

● E71.5   **Peroxisomal disorders**
   Class of conditions which lead to disorders of lipid metabolism
   Excludes1   Schilder's disease (G37.0)

   E71.50   **Peroxisomal disorder, unspecified** 🦠
● E71.51   **Disorders of peroxisome biogenesis**
   Group 1 peroxisomal disorders
   Excludes1   Refsum's disease (G60.1)
   E71.510   **Zellweger syndrome** 🦠
   E71.511   **Neonatal adrenoleukodystrophy** 🦠
      Excludes1   X-linked adrenoleuko-
                        dystrophy
                        (E71.42-)
   E71.518   **Other disorders of peroxisome biogenesis** 🦠

● E71.52   **X-linked adrenoleukodystrophy**
   E71.520   **Childhood cerebral X-linked adrenoleukodystrophy** 🦠
   E71.521   **Adolescent X-linked adrenoleukodystrophy** 🦠
   E71.522   **Adrenomyeloneuropathy** 🦠
   E71.528   **Other X-linked adrenoleukodystrophy** 🦠
      Addison only phenotype adrenoleukodystrophy
      Addison-Schilder adrenoleukodystrophy
   E71.529   **X-linked adrenoleukodystrophy, unspecified type** 🦠
   E71.53   **Other group 2 peroxisomal disorders** 🦠
● E71.54   **Other peroxisomal disorders**
   E71.540   **Rhizomelic chondrodysplasia punctata** 🦠
      Rare, severe, inherited disorder with limb shortening, bone and cartilage abnormalities, abnormal facial appearance, severe mental retardation, psychomotor retardation, and cataracts
      Excludes1   chondrodysplasia
                        punctata NOS
                        (Q77.3)
   E71.541   **Zellweger-like syndrome** 🦠
   E71.542   **Other group 3 peroxisomal disorders** 🦠
   E71.548   **Other peroxisomal disorders** 🦠

● E72   **Other disorders of amino-acid metabolism**
   Excludes1   disorders of:
      aromatic amino-acid metabolism (E70.-)
      branched-chain amino-acid metabolism (E71.0-E71.2)
      fatty-acid metabolism (E71.3)
      purine and pyrimidine metabolism (E79.-)
      gout (M1A.-, M10.-)
● E72.0   **Disorders of amino-acid transport**
   Excludes1   disorders of tryptophan metabolism (E70.5)
   E72.00   **Disorders of amino-acid transport, unspecified** 🦠
   E72.01   **Cystinuria** 🦠
      Hereditary aminoaciduria due to impairment of renal transport with predominant symptom of urinary cystine calculi
   E72.02   **Hartnup's disease** 🦠
      Inborn error of metabolism

   E72.03   **Lowe's syndrome** 🦠
      X-linked disorder with rickets, hydrophthalmia, congenital glaucoma, cataracts, mental retardation, and renal tubule dysfunction
      Use additional code for associated glaucoma (H42)
   E72.04   **Cystinosis** 🦠
      Genetic disease with excessive depostits of amino acid cystine in cells
      Fanconi (-de Toni) (-Debré) syndrome with cystinosis
      Excludes1   Fanconi (-de Toni) (-Debré)
                        syndrome without
                        cystinosis (E72.09)
   E72.09   **Other disorders of amino-acid transport** 🦠
      Fanconi (-de Toni) (-Debré) syndrome, unspecified
● E72.1   **Disorders of sulfur-bearing amino-acid metabolism**
   Excludes1   cystinosis (E72.04)
                     cystinuria (E72.01)
                     transcobalamin II deficiency (D51.2)
   E72.10   **Disorders of sulfur-bearing amino-acid metabolism, unspecified** 🦠
   E72.11   **Homocystinuria** 🦠
      Cystathionine synthase deficiency
   E72.12   **Methylenetetrahydrofolate reductase deficiency** 🦠
   E72.19   **Other disorders of sulfur-bearing amino-acid metabolism** 🦠
      Cystathioninuria
      Methioninemia
      Sulfite oxidase deficiency
● E72.2   **Disorders of urea cycle metabolism**
   Excludes1   disorders of ornithine metabolism (E72.4)
   E72.20   **Disorder of urea cycle metabolism, unspecified** 🦠
      Hyperammonemia
      Elevated levels of ammonia
      Excludes1   hyperammonemia-
                        hyperornithinemia-
                        homocitrullinemia
                        syndrome E72.4
                        transient hyperammonemia of
                        newborn (P74.6)
   E72.21   **Argininemia** 🦠
      Disorder in which deficiency of enzyme arginase causes build-up of arginine and ammonia in blood
   E72.22   **Arginosuccinic aciduria** 🦠
      Gene disorder of urea cycle resulting accumulation of ammonia
   E72.23   **Citrullinemia** 🦠
      Urea cycle disorder that causes ammonia and other toxic substances to accumulate in blood
   E72.29   **Other disorders of urea cycle metabolism** 🦠
   E72.3   **Disorders of lysine and hydroxylysine metabolism** 🦠
      Glutaric aciduria NOS
      Glutaric aciduria (type I)
      Hydroxylysinemia
      Hyperlysinemia
      Excludes1   glutaric aciduria type II (E71.313)
                        Refsum's disease (G60.1)
                        Zellweger syndrome (E71.510)
   E72.4   **Disorders of ornithine metabolism** 🦠
      Hyperammonemia-Hyperornithinemia-
         Homocitrullinemia syndrome
      Ornithinemia (types I, II)
      Ornithine transcarbamylase deficiency
      Excludes1   hereditary choroidal dystrophy (H31.2-)

▶ New   ⇒ Revised   ~~deleted~~ Deleted   Excludes 1   Excludes 2   Includes   Use additional   Code first   Code also   Key words
OGCR Official Guidelines   X Assign placeholder X   ● Use Additional Character(s)   ▶ Manifestation Code   🦠 Hierarchical Condition Category   Coding Clinic

● **E72.5　Disorders of glycine metabolism**

　E72.50　**Disorder of glycine metabolism, unspecified** 🐾

　E72.51　**Non-ketotic hyperglycinemia** 🐾

　E72.52　**Trimethylaminuria** 🐾

　E72.53　**Primary hyperoxaluria** 🐾
　　　　　Oxalosis
　　　　　Oxaluria

　E72.59　**Other disorders of glycine metabolism** 🐾
　　　　　D-glycericacidemia
　　　　　Hyperhydroxyprolinemia
　　　　　Hyperprolinemia (types I, II)
　　　　　Sarcosinemia

● **E72.8　Other specified disorders of amino-acid metabolism** 🐾

　E72.81　**Disorders of gamma aminobutyric acid metabolism** 🐾
　　　　　4-hydroxybutyric aciduria
　　　　　Disorders of GABA metabolism
　　　　　GABA metabolic defect
　　　　　GABA transaminase deficiency
　　　　　GABA-T deficiency
　　　　　Gamma-hydroxybutyric aciduria
　　　　　SSADHD
　　　　　Succinic semialdehyde dehydrogenase deficiency

　E72.89　**Other specified disorders of amino-acid metabolism** 🐾
　　　　　Disorders of beta-amino-acid metabolism
　　　　　Disorders of gamma-glutamyl cycle

　E72.9　**Disorder of amino-acid metabolism, unspecified** 🐾

● **E73　Lactose intolerance**
　　Intolerance for lactose, due to inherited deficiency of lactase activity in intestinal mucosa

　E73.0　**Congenital lactase deficiency**

　E73.1　**Secondary lactase deficiency**

　E73.8　**Other lactose intolerance**

　E73.9　**Lactose intolerance, unspecified**

● **E74　Other disorders of carbohydrate metabolism**
　　Excludes1　diabetes mellitus (E08-E13)
　　　　　　　　hypoglycemia NOS (E16.2)
　　　　　　　　increased secretion of glucagon (E16.3)
　　　　　　　　mucopolysaccharidosis (E76.0-E76.3)

● **E74.0　Glycogen storage disease**

　E74.00　**Glycogen storage disease, unspecified** 🐾

　E74.01　**von Gierke's disease** 🐾
　　　　　Type I glycogen storage disease

　E74.02　**Pompe disease** 🐾
　　　　　Cardiac glycogenosis
　　　　　Type II glycogen storage disease

　E74.03　**Cori disease** 🐾
　　　　　Forbes' disease
　　　　　Type III glycogen storage disease

　E74.04　**McArdle disease** 🐾
　　　　　Type V glycogen storage disease

　E74.09　**Other glycogen storage disease** 🐾
　　　　　Andersen disease
　　　　　Hers disease
　　　　　Tauri disease
　　　　　Glycogen storage disease, types 0, IV, VI-XI
　　　　　Liver phosphorylase deficiency
　　　　　Muscle phosfructokinase deficiency

● **E74.1　Disorders of fructose metabolism**
　　Excludes1　muscle phosphofructokinase deficiency (E74.09)

　E74.10　**Disorder of fructose metabolism, unspecified**

　E74.11　**Essential fructosuria**
　　　　　Fructokinase deficiency

　E74.12　**Hereditary fructose intolerance**
　　　　　Fructosemia

　E74.19　**Other disorders of fructose metabolism**
　　　　　Fructose-1, 6-diphosphatase deficiency

● **E74.2　Disorders of galactose metabolism**

　E74.20　**Disorders of galactose metabolism, unspecified** 🐾

　E74.21　**Galactosemia** 🐾
　　　　　Genetic disorders resulting from defective simple sugar (galactose) metabolism

　E74.29　**Other disorders of galactose metabolism** 🐾
　　　　　Galactokinase deficiency

● **E74.3　Other disorders of intestinal carbohydrate absorption**
　　Excludes2　lactose intolerance (E73.-)

　E74.31　**Sucrase-isomaltase deficiency**
　　　　　Deficiency in metabolism in intestinal mucosa results in malabsorption of sucrose and starch

　E74.39　**Other disorders of intestinal carbohydrate absorption**
　　　　　Disorder of intestinal carbohydrate absorption NOS
　　　　　Glucose-galactose malabsorption
　　　　　Sucrase deficiency

● **E74.4　Disorders of pyruvate metabolism and gluconeogenesis** 🐾
　　　　Deficiency of phosphoenolpyruvate carboxykinase
　　　　Deficiency of pyruvate carboxylase
　　　　Deficiency of pyruvate dehydrogenase
　　Excludes1　disorders of pyruvate metabolism and gluconeogenesis with anemia (D55.-)
　　　　　　　　Leigh's syndrome (G31.82)

● **E74.8　Other specified disorders of carbohydrate metabolism** 🐾
　　~~Essential pentosuria~~
　　~~Renal glycosuria~~

▶ ● **E74.81　Disorders of glucose transport, not elsewhere classified**

　▶ E74.810　**Glucose transporter protein type 1 deficiency**
　　　　　▶ De Vivo syndrome
　　　　　▶ Glucose transport defect, blood-brain barrier
　　　　　▶ GLUT1 deficiency
　　　　　▶ GLUT1 deficiency syndrome 1, infantile onset
　　　　　▶ GLUT1 deficiency syndrome 2, childhood onset

　▶ E74.818　**Other disorders of glucose transport**
　　　　　▶ (Familial) renal glycosuria

　▶ E74.819　**Disorders of glucose transport, unspecified**

　▶ E74.89　**Other specified disorders of carbohydrate metabolism**
　　　　　▶ Essential pentosuria

　E74.9　**Disorder of carbohydrate metabolism, unspecified** 🐾

● **E75　Disorders of sphingolipid metabolism and other lipid storage disorders**
　　Excludes1　mucolipidosis, types I-III (E77.0-E77.1)
　　　　　　　　Refsum's disease (G60.1)

● **E75.0　GM2 gangliosidosis**
　　Rare metabolic disorder that causes destruction of nerve cells of brain and spinal cord

　E75.00　**GM2 gangliosidosis, unspecified**

　E75.01　**Sandhoff disease**

　E75.02　**Tay-Sachs disease**

　E75.09　**Other GM2 gangliosidosis**
　　　　　Adult GM2 gangliosidosis
　　　　　Juvenile GM2 gangliosidosis

● **E75.1　Other and unspecified gangliosidosis**

　E75.10　**Unspecified gangliosidosis**
　　　　　Gangliosidosis NOS

　E75.11　**Mucolipidosis IV**
　　　　　Disorder with symptoms of psychomotor retardation and severe visual impairment

　E75.19　**Other gangliosidosis**
　　　　　GM1 gangliosidosis
　　　　　GM3 gangliosidosis

Item 4–8 Leukodystrophy is characterized by degeneration and/or failure of the myelin formation of the central nervous system and sometimes of the peripheral nervous system. The disease is inherited and progressive.

● **E75.2 Other sphingolipidosis**
Lysosomal (a particle in a cytoplasm cell that contains digestive enzymes) storage diseases with symptoms of abnormal storage of amino acids

> **Excludes1**   adrenoleukodystrophy [Addison-Schilder] (E71.528)

     E75.21 Fabry (-Anderson) disease 🏷
     E75.22 Gaucher disease 🏷
     E75.23 Krabbe disease
     ● **E75.24 Niemann-Pick disease**
         E75.240 Niemann-Pick disease type A 🏷
         E75.241 Niemann-Pick disease type B 🏷
         E75.242 Niemann-Pick disease type C 🏷
         E75.243 Niemann-Pick disease type D 🏷
         E75.248 Other Niemann-Pick disease 🏷
         E75.249 Niemann-Pick disease, unspecified 🏷
     E75.25 Metachromatic leukodystrophy
     E75.26 Sulfatase deficiency
         Multiple sulfatase deficiency (MSD)
     E75.29 Other sphingolipidosis
         Farber's syndrome
         Sulfatide lipidosis

E75.3 Sphingolipidosis, unspecified 🏷

E75.4 Neuronal ceroid lipofuscinosis
     Batten disease
     Bielschowsky-Jansky disease
     Kufs disease
     Spielmeyer-Vogt disease

E75.5 Other lipid storage disorders
     Cerebrotendinous cholesterosis [van Bogaert-Scherer-Epstein]
     Wolman's disease

E75.6 Lipid storage disorder, unspecified

● **E76 Disorders of glycosaminoglycan metabolism**
   ● **E76.0 Mucopolysaccharidosis, type I**
Inborn metabolic disorder of enzymes that break down carbohydrates

     E76.01 Hurler's syndrome 🏷
     E76.02 Hurler-Scheie syndrome 🏷
     E76.03 Scheie's syndrome 🏷
   E76.1 Mucopolysaccharidosis, type II 🏷
Inborn metabolic disorder of enzymes that break down carbohydrates occurs in 2-4 year old males
     Hunter's syndrome
   ● **E76.2 Other mucopolysaccharidoses**
     ● **E76.21 Morquio mucopolysaccharidoses**
         E76.210 Morquio A mucopolysaccharidoses 🏷
           Classic Morquio syndrome
           Morquio syndrome A
           Mucopolysaccharidosis, type IVA
         E76.211 Morquio B mucopolysaccharidoses 🏷
           Morquio-like mucopolysaccharidoses
           Morquio-like syndrome
           Morquio syndrome B
           Mucopolysaccharidosis, type IVB
         E76.219 Morquio mucopolysaccharidoses, unspecified 🏷
           Morquio syndrome
           Mucopolysaccharidosis, type IV
     E76.22 Sanfilippo mucopolysaccharidoses 🏷
         Mucopolysaccharidosis, type III (A) (B) (C) (D)
         Sanfilippo A syndrome
         Sanfilippo B syndrome
         Sanfilippo C syndrome
         Sanfilippo D syndrome

     E76.29 Other mucopolysaccharidoses 🏷
         beta-Glucuronidase deficiency
         Maroteaux-Lamy (mild) (severe) syndrome
         Mucopolysaccharidosis, types VI, VII

E76.3 Mucopolysaccharidosis, unspecified 🏷
E76.8 Other disorders of glucosaminoglycan metabolism 🏷
E76.9 Glucosaminoglycan metabolism disorder, unspecified 🏷

● **E77 Disorders of glycoprotein metabolism**
   E77.0 Defects in post-translational modification of lysosomal enzymes 🏷
     Mucolipidosis II [I-cell disease]
     Mucolipidosis III [pseudo-Hurler polydystrophy]

   E77.1 Defects in glycoprotein degradation 🏷
     Aspartylglucosaminuria
     Fucosidosis
     Mannosidosis
     Sialidosis [mucolipidosis I]

   E77.8 Other disorders of glycoprotein metabolism 🏷
   E77.9 Disorder of glycoprotein metabolism, unspecified 🏷

● **E78 Disorders of lipoprotein metabolism and other lipidemias**

> **Excludes1**   sphingolipidosis (E75.0-E75.3)

   ● **E78.0 Pure hypercholesterolemia**
     Coding Clinic: 2016, Q4, P13

     E78.00 Pure hypercholesterolemia, unspecified
         Fredrickson's hyperlipoproteinemia, type IIa
         Hyperbetalipoproteinemia
         Low-density-lipoprotein-type [LDL] hyperlipoproteinemia
         (Pure) hypercholesterolemia NOS
         Coding Clinic: 2016, Q4, P13

     E78.01 Familial hypercholesterolemia
         Coding Clinic: 2016, Q4, P13

   E78.1 Pure hyperglyceridemia
     Elevated fasting triglycerides
     Endogenous hyperglyceridemia
     Fredrickson's hyperlipoproteinemia, type IV
     Hyperlipidemia, group B
     Hyperprebetalipoproteinemia
     Very-low-density-lipoprotein-type [VLDL] hyperlipoproteinemia

   E78.2 Mixed hyperlipidemia
     Broad- or floating-betalipoproteinemia
     Combined hyperlipidemia NOS
     Elevated cholesterol with elevated triglycerides NEC
     Fredrickson's hyperlipoproteinemia, type IIb or III
     Hyperbetalipoproteinemia with prebetalipoproteinemia
     Hypercholesteremia with endogenous hyperglyceridemia
     Hyperlipidemia, group C
     Tubo-eruptive xanthoma
     Xanthoma tuberosum

> **Excludes1**   cerebrotendinous cholesterosis [van Bogaert-Scherer-Epstein] (E75.5)
>   familial combined hyperlipidemia (E78.49)

   E78.3 Hyperchylomicronemia
     Chylomicron retention disease
     Fredrickson's hyperlipoproteinemia, type I or V
     Hyperlipidemia, group D
     Mixed hyperglyceridemia

   ● **E78.4 Other hyperlipidemia**
     E78.41 Elevated Lipoprotein(a)
         Elevated Lp(a)

     E78.49 Other hyperlipidemia
         Familial combined hyperlipidemia

   E78.5 Hyperlipidemia, unspecified

   E78.6 Lipoprotein deficiency
     Abetalipoproteinemia
     Depressed HDL cholesterol
     High-density lipoprotein deficiency
     Hypoalphalipoproteinemia
     Hypobetalipoproteinemia (familial)
     Lecithin cholesterol acyltransferase deficiency
     Tangier disease

▶ New   ⇒ Revised   ~~deleted~~ Deleted   Excludes 1   Excludes 2   Includes   Use additional   Code first   Code also   Key words

OGCR Official Guidelines   X Assign placeholder X   ● Use Additional Character(s)   ▶ Manifestation Code   🏷 Hierarchical Condition Category   Coding Clinic

E78.7 Disorders of bile acid and cholesterol metabolism
> Excludes1   Niemann-Pick disease type C (E75.242)

  E78.70   **Disorder of bile acid and cholesterol metabolism, unspecified**

  E78.71   **Barth syndrome**

  E78.72   **Smith-Lemli-Opitz syndrome**

  E78.79   **Other disorders of bile acid and cholesterol metabolism**

E78.8 Other disorders of lipoprotein metabolism

  E78.81   **Lipoid dermatoarthritis**

  E78.89   **Other lipoprotein metabolism disorders**

E78.9 Disorder of lipoprotein metabolism, unspecified

E79 Disorders of purine and pyrimidine metabolism
> *Purines, along with pyrimidines, signal RNA and DNA production*
>
> Excludes1   Ataxia-telangiectasia (Q87.19)
> Bloom's syndrome (Q82.8)
> Cockayne's syndrome (Q87.19)
> calculus of kidney (N20.0)
> combined immunodeficiency disorders (D81.-)
> Fanconi's anemia (D61.09)
> gout (M1A.-, M10.-)
> orotaciduric anemia (D53.0)
> progeria (E34.8)
> Werner's syndrome (E34.8)
> xeroderma pigmentosum (Q82.1)

E79.0 Hyperuricemia without signs of inflammatory arthritis and tophaceous disease
> Asymptomatic hyperuricemia

E79.1 Lesch-Nyhan syndrome
> HGPRT deficiency

E79.2 Myoadenylate deaminase deficiency

E79.8 Other disorders of purine and pyrimidine metabolism
> Hereditary xanthinuria

E79.9 Disorder of purine and pyrimidine metabolism, unspecified

E80 Disorders of porphyrin and bilirubin metabolism
> *Group of chemical compounds in RBCs that combine with iron to form heme*
>
> Includes   defects of catalase and peroxidase

E80.0 Hereditary erythropoietic porphyria
> Congenital erythropoietic porphyria
> Erythropoietic protoporphyria

E80.1 Porphyria cutanea tarda

E80.2 Other and unspecified porphyria

  E80.20   **Unspecified porphyria**
> Porphyria NOS

  E80.21   **Acute intermittent (hepatic) porphyria**

  E80.29   **Other porphyria**
> Hereditary coproporphyria

E80.3 Defects of catalase and peroxidase
> Acatalasia [Takahara]

E80.4 Gilbert syndrome

E80.5 Crigler-Najjar syndrome

E80.6 Other disorders of bilirubin metabolism
> Dubin-Johnson syndrome
> Rotor's syndrome

E80.7 Disorder of bilirubin metabolism, unspecified

E83 Disorders of mineral metabolism
> Excludes1   dietary mineral deficiency (E58-E61)
> parathyroid disorders (E20-E21)
> vitamin D deficiency (E55.-)

E83.0 Disorders of copper metabolism

  E83.00   **Disorder of copper metabolism, unspecified**

  E83.01   **Wilson's disease**
> Code also associated Kayser Fleischer ring (H18.04-)

  E83.09   **Other disorders of copper metabolism**
> Menkes' (kinky hair) (steely hair) disease

E83.1 Disorders of iron metabolism
> Excludes1   iron deficiency anemia (D50.-)
> sideroblastic anemia (D64.0-D64.3)

  E83.10   **Disorder of iron metabolism, unspecified**

  E83.11   **Hemochromatosis**
> Excludes1   GALD (P78.84)
> Gestational alloimmune liver disease (P78.84)
> Neonatal hemochromatosis (P78.84)

    E83.110   **Hereditary hemochromatosis**
> Bronzed diabetes
> Pigmentary cirrhosis (of liver)
> Primary (hereditary) hemochromatosis

    E83.111   **Hemochromatosis due to repeated red blood cell transfusions**
> Iron overload due to repeated red blood cell transfusions
> Transfusion (red blood cell) associated hemochromatosis

    E83.118   **Other hemochromatosis**

    E83.119   **Hemochromatosis, unspecified**

  E83.19   **Other disorders of iron metabolism**
> Use additional code, if applicable, for idiopathic pulmonary hemosiderosis (J84.03)

E83.2 Disorders of zinc metabolism
> Acrodermatitis enteropathica

E83.3 Disorders of phosphorus metabolism and phosphatases
> Excludes1   adult osteomalacia (M83.-)
> osteoporosis (M80.-)

  E83.30   **Disorder of phosphorus metabolism, unspecified**

  E83.31   **Familial hypophosphatemia**
> Vitamin D-resistant osteomalacia
> Vitamin D-resistant rickets
>
> Excludes1   vitamin D-deficiency rickets (E55.0)

  E83.32   **Hereditary vitamin D-dependent rickets (type 1) (type 2)**
> 25-hydroxyvitamin D 1-alpha-hydroxylase deficiency
> Pseudovitamin D deficiency
> Vitamin D receptor defect

  E83.39   **Other disorders of phosphorus metabolism**
> Acid phosphatase deficiency
> Hypophosphatasia

E83.4 Disorders of magnesium metabolism

  E83.40   **Disorders of magnesium metabolism, unspecified**

  E83.41   **Hypermagnesemia**
> Coding Clinic: 2016, Q4, P55

  E83.42   **Hypomagnesemia**

  E83.49   **Other disorders of magnesium metabolism**

CHAPTER 4 (E00-E90)

N Newborn Age: 0   **P** Pediatric Age: 0–17   **M** Maternity DX: 12–55   **A** Adult Age: 15–124   ♀ Females Only   ♂ Males Only

759

● **E83.5** **Disorders of calcium metabolism**
    Excludes1   chondrocalcinosis (M11.1-M11.2)
                hungry bone syndrome (E83.81)
                hyperparathyroidism (E21.0-E21.3)
    E83.50   **Unspecified disorder of calcium metabolism**
    E83.51   **Hypocalcemia**
    E83.52   **Hypercalcemia**
            Familial hypocalciuric hypercalcemia
    E83.59   **Other disorders of calcium metabolism**
            Idiopathic hypercalciuria

● **E83.8** **Other disorders of mineral metabolism**
    E83.81   **Hungry bone syndrome**
    E83.89   **Other disorders of mineral metabolism**
    E83.9   **Disorder of mineral metabolism, unspecified**

● **E84** **Cystic fibrosis**
    Includes   mucoviscidosis

    Code also exocrine pancreatic insufficiency (K86.81)

    E84.0   **Cystic fibrosis with pulmonary manifestations** 🅒
            Use additional code to identify any infectious organism
                present, such as:
                Pseudomonas (B96.5)

    E84.1   **Cystic fibrosis with intestinal manifestations**
        E84.11   **Meconium ileus in cystic fibrosis** 🅒   **N**
              Excludes1   meconium ileus not due to cystic
                        fibrosis (P76.0)
        E84.19   **Cystic fibrosis with other intestinal**
                 manifestations
                 Distal intestinal obstruction syndrome

    E84.8   **Cystic fibrosis with other manifestations** 🅒
    E84.9   **Cystic fibrosis, unspecified** 🅒

● **E85** **Amyloidosis**
    A disorder resulting from the abnormal deposition of a particular
    protein (amyloid) into tissues of the body
    Excludes2   Alzheimer's disease (G30.0-)

    E85.0   **Non-neuropathic heredofamilial amyloidosis** 🅒
            Hereditary amyloid nephropathy
            Code also associated disorders, such as:
                autoinflammatory syndromes (M04.-)
             Excludes2   Transthyretin-related (ATTR) familial
                        amyloid cardiomyopathy (E85.4)

    E85.1   **Neuropathic heredofamilial amyloidosis** 🅒
            Amyloid polyneuropathy (Portuguese)
            Transthyretin-related (ATTR) familial amyloid
                polyneuropathy
            Coding Clinic: 2012, Q4, P100

    E85.2   **Heredofamilial amyloidosis, unspecified** 🅒
    E85.3   **Secondary systemic amyloidosis** 🅒
            Hemodialysis-associated amyloidosis

    E85.4   **Organ-limited amyloidosis** 🅒
            Localized amyloidosis
            Transthyretin-related (ATTR) familial amyloid
               cardiomyopathy

● **E85.8** **Other amyloidosis**
    E85.81   **Light chain (AL) amyloidosis** 🅒
    E85.82   **Wild-type transthyretin-related (ATTR)**
              amyloidosis 🅒
                Senile systemic amyloidosis (SSA)
    E85.89   **Other amyloidosis** 🅒

    E85.9   **Amyloidosis, unspecified** 🅒

Item 4–9   Circulating fluid volume is regulated by the amount of water and sodium ingested, excreted by the kidneys into the urine, and lost through the gastrointestinal tract, lungs, and skin. To maintain blood volume within a normal range, the kidneys regulate the amount of water and sodium lost into the urine. Too much **(fluid overload)** or too little fluid volume **(volume depletion)** will affect blood pressure. Severe cases of vomiting, diarrhea, bleeding, and burns (fluid loss through exposed burn surface area) can contribute to fluid loss. Internal body environment must maintain a precise balance (homeostasis) between too much fluid and too little fluid. This complex balancing mechanism is critical to good health.

● **E86** **Volume depletion**
    Excludes1   dehydration of newborn (P74.1)
                ~~hypovolemic shock NOS (R57.1)~~
                postprocedural hypovolemic shock (T81.19)
                traumatic hypovolemic shock (T79.4)
   ▶ **Excludes2**   hypovolemic shock NOS (R57.1)

    Use additional code(s) for any associated disorders of
        electrolyte and acid-base balance (E87.-)
    Coding Clinic: 2019, Q2, P7

    E86.0   **Dehydration**
            Excessive loss of body water
            Coding Clinic: 2019, Q2, P7-8

    E86.1   **Hypovolemia**
            Diminished volume of circulating blood
            Depletion of volume of plasma

    E86.9   **Volume depletion, unspecified**
            Coding Clinic: 2019, Q2, P7-8

● **E87** **Other disorders of fluid, electrolyte and acid-base balance**
    Excludes1   diabetes insipidus (E23.2)
                electrolyte imbalance associated with
                    hyperemesis gravidarum (O21.1)
                electrolyte imbalance following ectopic or molar
                    pregnancy (O08.5)
                familial periodic paralysis (G72.3)

    E87.0   **Hyperosmolality and hypernatremia**
            Sodium [Na] excess
            Sodium [Na] overload
            Coding Clinic: 2018, Q2, P6

    E87.1   **Hypo-osmolality and hyponatremia**
            Sodium [Na] deficiency
             Excludes1   syndrome of inappropriate secretion of
                        antidiuretic hormone (E22.2)
            Coding Clinic: 2018, Q2, P6

    E87.2   **Acidosis**
            Acidosis NOS
            Lactic acidosis
            Metabolic acidosis
            Respiratory acidosis
             Excludes1   diabetic acidosis - see categories E08-E10,
                        E13 with ketoacidosis

    E87.3   **Alkalosis**
            Alkalosis NOS
            Metabolic alkalosis
            Respiratory alkalosis

    E87.4   **Mixed disorder of acid-base balance**
    E87.5   **Hyperkalemia**
            Potassium [K] excess
            Potassium [K] overload

    E87.6   **Hypokalemia**
            Potassium [K] deficiency

▶ New   ⇛ Revised   ~~deleted~~ Deleted   Excludes 1   Excludes 2   Includes   Use additional   Code first   Code also   Key words
OGCR Official Guidelines   X Assign placeholder X   ● Use Additional Character(s)   ▷ Manifestation Code   🅒 Hierarchical Condition Category   **Coding Clinic**

● **E87.7**   **Fluid overload**
     Excludes1   edema NOS (R60.9)
                  fluid retention (R60.9)
     E87.70   **Fluid overload, unspecified**
     E87.71   **Transfusion associated circulatory overload**
           Fluid overload due to transfusion (blood)
                (blood components) TACO
     E87.79   **Other fluid overload**

E87.8   **Other disorders of electrolyte and fluid balance, not elsewhere classified**
     Electrolyte imbalance NOS
     Hyperchloremia
     Hypochloremia

● **E88**   **Other and unspecified metabolic disorders**
     Use additional codes for associated conditions
     Excludes1   histiocytosis X (chronic) (C96.6)

● **E88.0**   **Disorders of plasma-protein metabolism, not elsewhere classified**
     Excludes1   ~~disorder of lipoprotein metabolism (E78.-)~~
                monoclonal gammopathy (of
                   undetermined significance) (D47.2)
                polyclonal hypergammaglobulinemia
                   (D89.0)
                Waldenström macroglobulinemia (C88.0)
  ▶ **Excludes2**   disorder of lipoprotein metabolism (E78.-)
     E88.01   **Alpha-1-antitrypsin deficiency AAT deficiency** 🔍
     E88.02   **Plasminogen deficiency**
           Dysplasminogenemia
           Hypoplasminogenemia
           Type 1 plasminogen deficiency
           Type 2 plasminogen deficiency
           Code also, if applicable, ligneous conjunctivitis
              (H10.51)
           Use additional code for associated findings,
              such as:
              hydrocephalus (G91.4)
              otitis media (H67.-)
              respiratory disorder related to plasminogen
                deficiency (J99)
     E88.09   **Other disorders of plasma-protein metabolism, not elsewhere classified**
           Bisalbuminemia

E88.1   **Lipodystrophy, not elsewhere classified**
     Defective fat metabolism resulting in absence of subcutaneous fat
     Lipodystrophy NOS
     Excludes1   Whipple's disease (K90.81)

E88.2   **Lipomatosis, not elsewhere classified**
     Abnormal tumorlike accumulations of fat in tissue
     Lipomatosis NOS
     Lipomatosis (Check) dolorosa [Dercum]

E88.3   **Tumor lysis syndrome**
     Tumor lysis syndrome (spontaneous)
     Tumor lysis syndrome following antineoplastic drug
           chemotherapy
     Use additional code for adverse effect, if applicable, to
           identify drug (T45.1X5)
     Coding Clinic: 2019, Q2, P25

● **E88.4**   **Mitochondrial metabolism disorders**
     Congenital disorder of metabolism
     Excludes1   disorders of pyruvate metabolism (E74.4)
                Kearns-Sayre syndrome (H49.81)
                Leber's disease (H47.22)
                Leigh's encephalopathy (G31.82)
                Mitochondrial myopathy, NEC (G71.3)
                Reye's syndrome (G93.7)
     E88.40   **Mitochondrial metabolism disorder, unspecified** 🔍
     E88.41   **MELAS syndrome** 🔍
           Mitochondrial myopathy, encephalopathy,
              lactic acidosis and stroke-like episodes
     E88.42   **MERRF syndrome** 🔍
           Myoclonic epilepsy associated with ragged-red
              fibers
           Code also progressive myoclonic epilepsy
              (G40.3-)
     E88.49   **Other mitochondrial metabolism disorders** 🔍

● **E88.8**   **Other specified metabolic disorders**
     E88.81   **Metabolic syndrome**
           Dysmetabolic syndrome X
           Use additional codes for associated
              manifestations, such as:
              obesity (E66.-)
     E88.89   **Other specified metabolic disorders** 🔍
           Launois-Bensaude adenolipomatosis
        Excludes1   adult pulmonary Langerhans cell
                  histiocytosis (J84.82)

E88.9   **Metabolic disorder, unspecified**

POSTPROCEDURAL ENDOCRINE AND METABOLIC COMPLICATIONS AND DISORDERS, NOT ELSEWHERE CLASSIFIED (E89)

● **E89**   **Postprocedural endocrine and metabolic complications and disorders, not elsewhere classified**
     Excludes2   intraoperative complications of endocrine system
                organ or structure (E36.0-, E36.1-, E36.8)

E89.0   **Postprocedural hypothyroidism**
     Postirradiation hypothyroidism
     Postsurgical hypothyroidism

E89.1   **Postprocedural hypoinsulinemia**
     Postpancreatectomy hyperglycemia
     Postsurgical hypoinsulinemia
     Use additional code, if applicable, to identify:
           acquired absence of pancreas (Z90.41-)
           diabetes mellitus (postpancreatectomy)
              (postprocedural) (E13.-)
           insulin use (Z79.4)
     Excludes1   transient postprocedural hyperglycemia
                (R73.9)
                transient postprocedural hypoglycemia
                (E16.2)

E89.2   **Postprocedural hypoparathyroidism** 🔍
     Parathyroprival tetany

E89.3   **Postprocedural hypopituitarism** 🔍
     Postirradiation hypopituitarism

● **E89.4**   **Postprocedural ovarian failure**
     E89.40   **Asymptomatic postprocedural ovarian failure** ♀
           Postprocedural ovarian failure NOS
     E89.41   **Symptomatic postprocedural ovarian failure** ♀
           Symptoms such as flushing, sleeplessness,
              headache, lack of concentration,
              associated with postprocedural
              menopause

CHAPTER 4 (E00-E90)

E89.5   Postprocedural testicular hypofunction ♂

E89.6   Postprocedural adrenocortical (-medullary) hypofunction ⓗⓒⓒ

● E89.8   Other postprocedural endocrine and metabolic complications and disorders
Coding Clinic: 2016, Q4, P9

  ● E89.81   Postprocedural hemorrhage of an endocrine system organ or structure following a procedure

    E89.810   Postprocedural hemorrhage of an endocrine system organ or structure following an endocrine system procedure

    E89.811   Postprocedural hemorrhage of an endocrine system organ or structure following other procedure

● E89.82   Postprocedural hematoma and seroma of an endocrine system organ or structure

    E89.820   Postprocedural hematoma of an endocrine system organ or structure following an endocrine system procedure

    E89.821   Postprocedural hematoma of an endocrine system organ or structure following other procedure

    E89.822   Postprocedural seroma of an endocrine system organ or structure following an endocrine system procedure

    E89.823   Postprocedural seroma of an endocrine system organ or structure following other procedure

E89.89   Other postprocedural endocrine and metabolic complications and disorders

  Use additional code, if applicable, to further specify disorder

CHAPTER 5

MENTAL, BEHAVIORAL AND NEURODEVELOPMENTAL DISORDERS (F01-F99)

OGCR Chapter-Specific Coding Guidelines

5. Chapter 5: Mental, Behavioral and Neurodevelopmental disorders (F01 – F99)

a. Pain disorders related to psychological factors
Assign code F45.41, for pain that is exclusively related to psychological disorders. As indicated by the Excludes 1 note under category G89, a code from category G89 should not be assigned with code F45.41

Code F45.42, Pain disorders with related psychological factors, should be used with a code from category G89, Pain, not elsewhere classified, if there is documentation of a psychological component for a patient with acute or chronic pain.

See Section I.C.6. Pain

b. Mental and behavioral disorders due to psychoactive substance use

1) In Remission
Selection of codes for "in remission" for categories F10-F19, Mental and behavioral disorders due to psychoactive substance use (categories F10-F19 with -11, -.21) requires the provider's clinical judgment. The appropriate codes for "in remission" are assigned only on the basis of provider documentation (as defined in the Official Guidelines for Coding and Reporting), unless otherwise instructed by the classification.

Mild substance use disorders in early or sustained remission are classified to the appropriate codes for substance abuse in remission, and moderate or severe substance use disorders in early or sustained remission are classified to the appropriate codes for substance dependence in remission.

2) Psychoactive Substance Use, Abuse and Dependence
When the provider documentation refers to use, abuse and dependence of the same substance (e.g., alcohol, opioid, cannabis, etc.), only one code should be assigned to identify the pattern of use based on the following hierarchy:
- If both use and abuse are documented, assign only the code for abuse
- If both abuse and dependence are documented, assign only the code for dependence
- If use, abuse and dependence are all documented, assign only the code for dependence
- If both use and dependence are documented, assign only the code for dependence

3) Psychoactive Substance Use, Unspecified
As with all other unspecified diagnoses, the codes for unspecified psychoactive substance use disorders (F10.9-, F11.9-, F12.9-, F13.9-, F14.9-, F15.9-, F16.9-, F19.9-, F19.9-) should only be assigned based on provider documentation and when they meet the definition of a reportable diagnosis (see Section III, Reporting Additional Diagnoses). These codes are to be used only when the psychoactive substance use is associated with a physical, mental or behavioral disorder, and such a relationship is documented by the provider.

c. Factitious Disorder
Factitious disorder imposed on self or Munchausen's syndrome is a disorder in which a person falsely reports or causes his or her own physical or psychological signs or symptoms. For patients with documented factitious disorder on self or Munchausen's syndrome, assign the appropriate code from subcategory F68.1-, Factitious disorder imposed on self.

Munchausen's syndrome by proxy (MSBP) is a disorder in which a caregiver (perpetrator) falsely reports or causes an illness or injury in another person (victim) under his or her care, such as a child, an elderly adult, or a person who has a disability. The condition is also referred to as "factitious disorder imposed on another" or "factitious disorder by proxy." The perpetrator, not the victim, receives this diagnosis. Assign code F68.A, Factitious disorder imposed on another, to the perpetrator's record. For the victim of a patient suffering from MSBP, assign the appropriate code from categories T74, Adult and child abuse, neglect and other maltreatment, confirmed, or T76, Adult and child abuse, neglect and other maltreatment, suspected.

See Section I.C.19.f. Adult and child abuse, neglect and other maltreatment

CHAPTER 5

MENTAL, BEHAVIORAL AND NEURODEVELOPMENTAL DISORDERS (F01-F99)

Includes disorders of psychological development

Excludes2 symptoms, signs and abnormal clinical laboratory findings, not elsewhere classified (R00-R99)

This chapter contains the following blocks:

F01-F09	Mental disorders due to known physiological conditions
F10-F19	Mental and behavioral disorders due to psychoactive substance use
F20-F29	Schizophrenia, schizotypal, delusional, and other non-mood psychotic disorders
F30-F39	Mood [affective] disorders
F40-F48	Anxiety, dissociative, stress-related, somatoform and other nonpsychotic mental disorders
F50-F59	Behavioral syndromes associated with physiological disturbances and physical factors
F60-F69	Disorders of adult personality and behavior
F70-F79	Intellectual disabilities
F80-F89	Pervasive and specific developmental disorders
F90-F98	Behavioral and emotional disorders with onset usually occurring in childhood and adolescence
F99	Unspecified mental disorder

MENTAL DISORDERS DUE TO KNOWN PHYSIOLOGICAL CONDITIONS (F01-F09)

This block comprises a range of mental disorders grouped together on the basis of their having in common a demonstrable etiology in cerebral disease, brain injury, or other insult leading to cerebral dysfunction. The dysfunction may be primary, as in diseases, injuries, and insults that affect the brain directly and selectively; or secondary, as in systemic diseases and disorders that attack the brain only as one of the multiple organs or systems of the body that are involved.

● **F01   Vascular dementia**
Vascular dementia as a result of infarction of the brain due to vascular disease, including hypertensive cerebrovascular disease.

Includes arteriosclerotic dementia

Code first the underlying physiological condition or sequelae of cerebrovascular disease.

● **F01.5   Vascular dementia**

F01.50   Vascular dementia without behavioral disturbance   A
Major neurocognitive disorder without behavioral disturbance

F01.51   Vascular dementia with behavioral disturbance   A
Major neurocognitive disorder due to vascular disease, with behavioral disturbance
Major neurocognitive disorder with aggressive behavior
Major neurocognitive disorder with combative behavior
Major neurocognitive disorder with violent behavior
Vascular dementia with aggressive behavior
Vascular dementia with combative behavior
Vascular dementia with violent behavior
Use additional code, if applicable, to identify wandering in vascular dementia (Z91.83)

● **F02   Dementia in other diseases classified elsewhere**

Code first the underlying physiological condition, such as:
Alzheimer's (G30.-)
cerebral lipidosis (E75.4)
Creutzfeldt-Jakob disease (A81.0-)
dementia with Lewy bodies (G31.83)
dementia with Parkinsonism (G31.83)
epilepsy and recurrent seizures (G40.-)
frontotemporal dementia (G31.09)
hepatolenticular degeneration (E83.0)
human immunodeficiency virus [HIV] disease (B20)
Huntington's disease (G10)
hypercalcemia (E83.52)
hypothyroidism, acquired (E00-E03.-)
intoxications (T36-T65)
Jakob-Creutzfeldt disease (A81.0-)
multiple sclerosis (G35)
neurosyphilis (A52.17)
niacin deficiency [pellagra] (E52)
Parkinson's disease (G20)
Pick's disease (G31.01)
polyarteritis nodosa (M30.0)
prion disease (A81.9)
systemic lupus erythematosus (M32.-)
traumatic brain injury (S06.-)
trypanosomiasis (B56.-, B57.-)
vitamin B deficiency (E53.8)

Includes   Major neurocognitive disorder in other diseases classified elsewhere

Excludes2   dementia in alcohol and psychoactive substance disorders (F10-F19, with .17, .27, .97)
vascular dementia (F01.5-)

Coding Clinic: 2016, Q4, P141

● **F02.8   Dementia in other diseases classified elsewhere**

▶ *F02.80   Dementia in other diseases classified elsewhere without behavioral disturbance*
Dementia in other diseases classified elsewhere NOS
Major neurocognitive disorder in other diseases classified elsewhere
Coding Clinic: 2017, Q1, P43; 2016, Q2, P6

▶ *F02.81   Dementia in other diseases classified elsewhere with behavioral disturbance*
Dementia in other diseases classified elsewhere with aggressive behavior
Dementia in other diseases classified elsewhere with combative behavior
Dementia in other diseases classified elsewhere with violent behavior
Major neurocognitive disorder in other diseases classified elsewhere with aggressive behavior
Major neurocognitive disorder in other diseases classified elsewhere with combative behavior
Major neurocognitive disorder in other diseases classified elsewhere with violent behavior

Use additional code, if applicable, to identify wandering in dementia in conditions classified elsewhere (Z91.83)
Coding Clinic: 2017, Q2, P8, Q1, P43

Item 5-1 Psychosis was a term formerly applied to any mental disorder but is now restricted to disturbances of a great magnitude in which there is a personality disintegration and loss of contact with reality.

● **F03   Unspecified dementia**
Presenile dementia NOS
Presenile psychosis NOS
Primary degenerative dementia NOS
Senile dementia NOS
Senile dementia depressed or paranoid type
Senile psychosis NOS

Excludes1   senility NOS (R41.81)

Excludes2   mild memory disturbance due to known physiological condition (F06.8)
senile dementia with delirium or acute confusional state (F05)

● **F03.9   Unspecified dementia**

F03.90   Unspecified dementia without behavioral disturbance   A
Dementia NOS
Coding Clinic: 2012, Q4, P92

F03.91   Unspecified dementia with behavioral disturbance   A
Unspecified dementia with aggressive behavior
Unspecified dementia with combative behavior
Unspecified dementia with violent behavior

Use additional code, if applicable, to identify wandering in unspecified dementia (Z91.83)

F04   Amnestic disorder due to known physiological condition
Korsakov's psychosis or syndrome, nonalcoholic

Code first the underlying physiological condition

Excludes1   amnesia NOS (R41.3)
anterograde amnesia (R41.1)
dissociative amnesia (F44.0)
retrograde amnesia (R41.2)

Excludes2   alcohol-induced or unspecified Korsakov's syndrome (F10.26, F10.96)
Korsakov's syndrome induced by other psychoactive substances (F13.26, F13.96, F19.16, F19.26, F19.96)

F05   Delirium due to known physiological condition
Acute or subacute brain syndrome
Acute or subacute confusional state (nonalcoholic)
Acute or subacute infective psychosis
Acute or subacute organic reaction
Acute or subacute psycho-organic syndrome
Delirium of mixed etiology
Delirium superimposed on dementia
Sundowning

Code first the underlying physiological condition

Excludes1   delirium NOS (R41.0)

Excludes2   delirium tremens alcohol-induced or unspecified (F10.231, F10.921)

Coding Clinic: 2019, Q2, P34

● **F06   Other mental disorders due to known physiological condition**

Includes   mental disorders due to endocrine disorder
mental disorders due to exogenous hormone
mental disorders due to exogenous toxic substance
mental disorders due to primary cerebral disease
mental disorders due to somatic illness
mental disorders due to systemic disease affecting the brain

Code first the underlying physiological condition

Excludes1   unspecified dementia (F03)

Excludes2   delirium due to known physiological condition (F05)
dementia as classified in F01-F02
other mental disorders associated with alcohol and other psychoactive substances (F10-F19)

▶ New   ⇒ Revised   ~~deleted~~ Deleted   Excludes 1   Excludes 2   Includes   Use additional   Code first   Code also   Key words
OGCR Official Guidelines   X Assign placeholder X   ● Use Additional Character(s)   ▶ Manifestation Code   🗨 Hierarchical Condition Category   Coding Clinic

F06.0   **Psychotic disorder with hallucinations due to known physiological condition**
     Organic hallucinatory state (nonalcoholic)
> **Excludes2**   hallucinations and perceptual disturbance induced by alcohol and other psychoactive substances (F10-F19 with .151, .251, .951)
>   schizophrenia (F20.-)

F06.1   **Catatonic disorder due to known physiological condition**
     Catatonia associated with another mental disorder
     Catatonia NOS
> **Excludes1**   catatonic stupor (R40.1)
>   stupor NOS (R40.1)
>
> **Excludes2**   catatonic schizophrenia (F20.2)
>   dissociative stupor (F44.2)

F06.2   **Psychotic disorder with delusions due to known physiological condition**
     Paranoid and paranoid-hallucinatory organic states
     Schizophrenia-like psychosis in epilepsy
> **Excludes2**   alcohol and drug-induced psychotic disorder (F10-F19 with .150, .250, .950)
>   brief psychotic disorder (F23)
>   delusional disorder (F22)
>   schizophrenia (F20.-)

● **F06.3**   **Mood disorder due to known physiological condition**
> **Excludes2**   mood disorders due to alcohol and other psychoactive substances (F10-F19 with .14, .24, .94)
>   mood disorders, not due to known physiological condition or unspecified (F30-F39)

   F06.30   **Mood disorder due to known physiological condition, unspecified**

   F06.31   **Mood disorder due to known physiological condition with depressive features**
     Depressive disorder due to known physiological condition, with depressive features

   F06.32   **Mood disorder due to known physiological condition with major depressive-like episode**
     Depressive disorder due to known physiological condition, with major depressive-like episode

   F06.33   **Mood disorder due to known physiological condition with manic features**
     Bipolar and related disorder due to a known physiological condition, with manic features
     Bipolar and related disorder due to known physiological condition, with manic- or hypomanic-like episodes

   F06.34   **Mood disorder due to known physiological condition with mixed features**
     Bipolar and related disorder due to known physiological condition, with mixed features
     Depressive disorder due to known physiological condition, with mixed features

F06.4   **Anxiety disorder due to known physiological condition**
> **Excludes2**   anxiety disorders due to alcohol and other psychoactive substances (F10-F19 with .180, .280, .980)
>   anxiety disorders, not due to known physiological condition or unspecified (F40.-, F41.-)

F06.8   **Other specified mental disorders due to known physiological condition**
     Epileptic psychosis NOS
     Obsessive-compulsive and related disorder due to a known physiological condition
     Organic dissociative disorder
     Organic emotionally labile [asthenic] disorder

● **F07**   **Personality and behavioral disorders due to known physiological condition**
     Code first the underlying physiological condition

   F07.0   **Personality change due to known physiological condition**
     Frontal lobe syndrome
     Limbic epilepsy personality syndrome
     Lobotomy syndrome
     Organic personality disorder
     Organic pseudopsychopathic personality
     Organic pseudoretarded personality
     Postleucotomy syndrome
     Code first underlying physiological condition
> **Excludes1**   mild cognitive impairment (G31.84)
>   postconcussional syndrome (F07.81)
>   postencephalitic syndrome (F07.89)
>   signs and symptoms involving emotional state (R45.-)
>
> **Excludes2**   specific personality disorder (F60.-)

● **F07.8**   **Other personality and behavioral disorders due to known physiological condition**

   F07.81   **Postconcussional syndrome**
     Postcontusional syndrome (encephalopathy)
     Post-traumatic brain syndrome, nonpsychotic
     Use additional code to identify associated post-traumatic headache, if applicable (G44.3-)
> **Excludes1**   current concussion (brain) (S06.0-)
>   postencephalitic syndrome (F07.89)

   F07.89   **Other personality and behavioral disorders due to known physiological condition**
     Postencephalitic syndrome
     Damage to temporal brain lobes with memory loss and abnormal behavior
     Right hemispheric organic affective disorder

   F07.9   **Unspecified personality and behavioral disorder due to known physiological condition**
     Organic psychosyndrome
     Due to exposure to organic solvents

F09   **Unspecified mental disorder due to known physiological condition**
     Mental disorder NOS due to known physiological condition
     Organic brain syndrome NOS
     Organic mental disorder NOS
     Organic psychosis NOS
     Symptomatic psychosis NOS
     Code first the underlying physiological condition
> **Excludes1**   psychosis NOS (F29)

MENTAL AND BEHAVIORAL DISORDERS DUE TO PSYCHOACTIVE SUBSTANCE USE (F10-F19)

● **F10**   **Alcohol related disorders**
     Use additional code for blood alcohol level, if applicable (Y90.-)
     Coding Clinic: 2019, Q3, P8

● **F10.1**   **Alcohol abuse**
> **Excludes1**   alcohol dependence (F10.2-)
>   alcohol use, unspecified (F10.9-)

   F10.10   **Alcohol abuse, uncomplicated**
     Alcohol use disorder, mild

   F10.11   **Alcohol abuse, in remission**
     Alcohol use disorder, mild, in early remission
     Alcohol use disorder, mild, in sustained remission

● **F10.12**   **Alcohol abuse with intoxication**

     F10.120   **Alcohol abuse with intoxication, uncomplicated** ✇

     F10.121   **Alcohol abuse with intoxication, delirium** ✇

     F10.129   **Alcohol abuse with intoxication, unspecified** ✇

▶● **F10.13** Alcohol abuse, with withdrawal
  ▶ F10.130 Alcohol abuse with withdrawal, uncomplicated
  ▶ F10.131 Alcohol abuse with withdrawal delirium
  ▶ F10.132 Alcohol abuse with withdrawal with perceptual disturbance
  ▶ F10.139 Alcohol abuse with withdrawal, unspecified

F10.14 Alcohol abuse with alcohol-induced mood disorder 🐾
  Alcohol use disorder, mild, with alcohol-induced bipolar or related disorder
  Alcohol use disorder, mild, with alcohol-induced depressive disorder

● **F10.15** Alcohol abuse with alcohol-induced psychotic disorder
  F10.150 Alcohol abuse with alcohol-induced psychotic disorder with delusions 🐾
  F10.151 Alcohol abuse with alcohol-induced psychotic disorder with hallucinations 🐾
  F10.159 Alcohol abuse with alcohol-induced psychotic disorder, unspecified 🐾

● **F10.18** Alcohol abuse with other alcohol-induced disorders
  F10.180 Alcohol abuse with alcohol-induced anxiety disorder 🐾
  F10.181 Alcohol abuse with alcohol-induced sexual dysfunction 🐾
  F10.182 Alcohol abuse with alcohol-induced sleep disorder 🐾
  F10.188 Alcohol abuse with other alcohol-induced disorder 🐾

F10.19 Alcohol abuse with unspecified alcohol-induced disorder 🐾

● **F10.2** Alcohol dependence
  Excludes1 alcohol abuse (F10.1-)
               alcohol use, unspecified (F10.9-)
  Excludes2 toxic effect of alcohol (T51.0-)
  Coding Clinic: 2019, Q3, P8

F10.20 Alcohol dependence, uncomplicated 🐾
  Alcohol use disorder, moderate
  Alcohol use disorder, severe
  Coding Clinic: 2020, Q1, P9

F10.21 Alcohol dependence, in remission 🐾
  Alcohol use disorder, moderate, in early remission
  Alcohol use disorder, moderate, in sustained remission
  Alcohol use disorder, severe, in early remission
  Alcohol use disorder, severe, in sustained remission

● **F10.22** Alcohol dependence with intoxication
  Acute drunkenness (in alcoholism)
  Excludes2 alcohol dependence with withdrawal (F10.23-)
  F10.220 Alcohol dependence with intoxication, uncomplicated 🐾
  F10.221 Alcohol dependence with intoxication delirium 🐾
  F10.229 Alcohol dependence with intoxication, unspecified 🐾

● **F10.23** Alcohol dependence with withdrawal
  Excludes2 alcohol dependence with intoxication (F10.22-)
  F10.230 Alcohol dependence with withdrawal, uncomplicated 🐾
  F10.231 Alcohol dependence with withdrawal delirium 🐾

F10.232 Alcohol dependence with withdrawal with perceptual disturbance 🐾
F10.239 Alcohol dependence with withdrawal, unspecified 🐾
  Coding Clinic: 2015, Q2, P15

F10.24 Alcohol dependence with alcohol-induced mood disorder 🐾
  Alcohol use disorder, moderate, with alcohol-induced bipolar or related disorder
  Alcohol use disorder, moderate, with alcohol-induced depressive disorder
  Alcohol use disorder, severe, with alcohol-induced bipolar or related disorder
  Alcohol use disorder, severe, with alcohol-induced depressive disorder

● **F10.25** Alcohol dependence with alcohol-induced psychotic disorder
  F10.250 Alcohol dependence with alcohol-induced psychotic disorder with delusions 🐾
  F10.251 Alcohol dependence with alcohol-induced psychotic disorder with hallucinations 🐾
  F10.259 Alcohol dependence with alcohol-induced psychotic disorder, unspecified 🐾

F10.26 Alcohol dependence with alcohol-induced persisting amnestic disorder 🐾
  Alcohol use disorder, moderate, with alcohol-induced major neurocognitive disorder, amnestic-confabulatory type
  Alcohol use disorder, severe, with alcohol-induced major neurocognitive disorder, amnestic-confabulatory type

F10.27 Alcohol dependence with alcohol-induced persisting dementia 🐾
  Alcohol use disorder, moderate, with alcohol-induced major neurocognitive disorder, nonamnestic-confabulatory type
  Alcohol use disorder, severe, with alcohol-induced major neurocognitive disorder, nonamnestic-confabulatory type

● **F10.28** Alcohol dependence with other alcohol-induced disorders
  F10.280 Alcohol dependence with alcohol-induced anxiety disorder 🐾
  F10.281 Alcohol dependence with alcohol-induced sexual dysfunction 🐾
  F10.282 Alcohol dependence with alcohol-induced sleep disorder 🐾
  F10.288 Alcohol dependence with other alcohol-induced disorder 🐾
    Alcohol use disorder, moderate, with alcohol-induced mild neurocognitive disorder
    Alcohol use disorder, severe, with alcohol-induced mild neurocognitive disorder
    Coding Clinic: 2020, Q1, P9

F10.29 Alcohol dependence with unspecified alcohol-induced disorder 🐾

● **F10.9** Alcohol use, unspecified
  Excludes1 alcohol abuse (F10.1-)
               alcohol dependence (F10.2-)

● **F10.92** Alcohol use, unspecified with intoxication
  F10.920 Alcohol use, unspecified with intoxication, uncomplicated 🐾
  F10.921 Alcohol use, unspecified with intoxication delirium 🐾
  F10.929 Alcohol use, unspecified with intoxication, unspecified 🐾

▶ New   ⇒ Revised   ~~deleted~~ Deleted   Excludes 1   Excludes 2   Includes   Use additional   Code first   Code also   Key words
OGCR Official Guidelines   X Assign placeholder X   ● Use Additional Character(s)   ▷ Manifestation Code   🐾 Hierarchical Condition Category   Coding Clinic

▶● **F10.93**   **Alcohol use, unspecified with withdrawal**

    ▶ **F10.930**   **Alcohol use, unspecified with withdrawal, uncomplicated**

    ▶ **F10.931**   **Alcohol use, unspecified with withdrawal delirium**

    ▶ **F10.932**   **Alcohol use, unspecified with withdrawal with perceptual disturbance**

    ▶ **F10.939**   **Alcohol use, unspecified with withdrawal, unspecified**

F10.94   **Alcohol use, unspecified with alcohol-induced mood disorder** 🔎
     Alcohol-induced bipolar or related disorder, without use disorder
     Alcohol-induced depressive disorder, without use disorder

● **F10.95**   **Alcohol use, unspecified with alcohol-induced psychotic disorder**

     F10.950   **Alcohol use, unspecified with alcohol-induced psychotic disorder with delusions** 🔎

     F10.951   **Alcohol use, unspecified with alcohol-induced psychotic disorder with hallucinations** 🔎

     F10.959   **Alcohol use, unspecified with alcohol-induced psychotic disorder, unspecified** 🔎
       Alcohol-induced psychotic disorder without use disorder

F10.96   **Alcohol use, unspecified with alcohol-induced persisting amnestic disorder** 🔎
     Alcohol-induced major neurocognitive disorder, amnestic-confabulatory type, without use disorder

F10.97   **Alcohol use, unspecified with alcohol-induced persisting dementia** 🔎
     Alcohol-induced major neurocognitive disorder, nonamnestic-confabulatory type, without use disorder

● **F10.98**   **Alcohol use, unspecified with other alcohol-induced disorders**

     F10.980   **Alcohol use, unspecified with alcohol-induced anxiety disorder** 🔎
       Alcohol-induced anxiety disorder, without use disorder

     F10.981   **Alcohol use, unspecified with alcohol-induced sexual dysfunction** 🔎
       Alcohol-induced sexual dysfunction, without use disorder

     F10.982   **Alcohol use, unspecified with alcohol-induced sleep disorder** 🔎
       Alcohol-induced sleep disorder, without use disorder

     F10.988   **Alcohol use, unspecified with other alcohol-induced disorder** 🔎
       Alcohol-induced mild neurocognitive disorder, without use disorder
       Coding Clinic: 2019, Q3, P8

F10.99   **Alcohol use, unspecified with unspecified alcohol-induced disorder** 🔎

● **F11**   **Opioid related disorders**

● **F11.1**   **Opioid abuse**

     Excludes1   opioid dependence (F11.2-)
                opioid use, unspecified (F11.9-)

     F11.10   **Opioid abuse, uncomplicated**
       Opioid use disorder, mild

     F11.11   **Opioid abuse, in remission**
       Opioid use disorder, mild, in early remission
       Opioid use disorder, mild, in sustained remission

● **F11.12**   **Opioid abuse with intoxication**

     F11.120   **Opioid abuse with intoxication, uncomplicated** 🔎

     F11.121   **Opioid abuse with intoxication delirium** 🔎

     F11.122   **Opioid abuse with intoxication with perceptual disturbance** 🔎

     F11.129   **Opioid abuse with intoxication, unspecified** 🔎

▶ **F11.13**   **Opioid abuse with withdrawal**

F11.14   **Opioid abuse with opioid-induced mood disorder** 🔎
     Opioid use disorder, mild, with opioid-induced depressive disorder

● **F11.15**   **Opioid abuse with opioid-induced psychotic disorder**

     F11.150   **Opioid abuse with opioid-induced psychotic disorder with delusions** 🔎

     F11.151   **Opioid abuse with opioid-induced psychotic disorder with hallucinations** 🔎

     F11.159   **Opioid abuse with opioid-induced psychotic disorder, unspecified** 🔎

● **F11.18**   **Opioid abuse with other opioid-induced disorder**

     F11.181   **Opioid abuse with opioid-induced sexual dysfunction** 🔎

     F11.182   **Opioid abuse with opioid-induced sleep disorder** 🔎

     F11.188   **Opioid abuse with other opioid-induced disorder** 🔎

F11.19   **Opioid abuse with unspecified opioid-induced disorder** 🔎

● **F11.2**   **Opioid dependence**

     Excludes1   opioid abuse (F11.1-)
                opioid use, unspecified (F11.9-)

     Excludes2   opioid poisoning (T40.0—T40.2-)

F11.20   **Opioid dependence, uncomplicated** 🔎
     Opioid use disorder, moderate
     Opioid use disorder, severe

F11.21   **Opioid dependence, in remission** 🔎
     Opioid use disorder, moderate, in early remission
     Opioid use disorder, moderate, in sustained remission
     Opioid use disorder, severe, in early remission
     Opioid use disorder, severe, in sustained remission

● **F11.22**   **Opioid dependence with intoxication**

     Excludes1   opioid dependence with withdrawal (F11.23)

     F11.220   **Opioid dependence with intoxication, uncomplicated** 🔎

     F11.221   **Opioid dependence with intoxication delirium** 🔎

     F11.222   **Opioid dependence with intoxication with perceptual disturbance** 🔎

     F11.229   **Opioid dependence with intoxication, unspecified** 🔎

F11.23   **Opioid dependence with withdrawal** 🔎

     Excludes1   opioid dependence with intoxication (F11.22-)

F11.24   **Opioid dependence with opioid-induced mood disorder** 🔎
     Opioid use disorder, moderate, with opioid-induced depressive disorder

● **F11.25 Opioid dependence with opioid-induced psychotic disorder**

     F11.250 Opioid dependence with opioid-induced psychotic disorder with delusions 🦠

     F11.251 Opioid dependence with opioid-induced psychotic disorder with hallucinations 🦠

     F11.259 Opioid dependence with opioid-induced psychotic disorder, unspecified 🦠

● **F11.28 Opioid dependence with other opioid-induced disorder**

     F11.281 Opioid dependence with opioid-induced sexual dysfunction 🦠

     F11.282 Opioid dependence with opioid-induced sleep disorder 🦠

     F11.288 Opioid dependence with other opioid-induced disorder 🦠

     F11.29 Opioid dependence with unspecified opioid-induced disorder 🦠

● **F11.9 Opioid use, unspecified**

     Excludes1   opioid abuse (F11.1-)
               opioid dependence (F11.2-)

     F11.90 Opioid use, unspecified, uncomplicated

●   **F11.92 Opioid use, unspecified with intoxication**

     Excludes1   opioid use, unspecified with withdrawal (F11.93)

     F11.920 Opioid use, unspecified with intoxication, uncomplicated 🦠

     F11.921 Opioid use, unspecified with intoxication delirium 🦠
          Opioid-induced delirium

     F11.922 Opioid use, unspecified with intoxication with perceptual disturbance 🦠

     F11.929 Opioid use, unspecified with intoxication, unspecified 🦠

     F11.93 Opioid use, unspecified with withdrawal 🦠

     Excludes1   opioid use, unspecified with intoxication (F11.92-)

     F11.94 Opioid use, unspecified with opioid-induced mood disorder 🦠
          Opioid-induced depressive disorder, without use disorder

●   **F11.95 Opioid use, unspecified with opioid-induced psychotic disorder**

     F11.950 Opioid use, unspecified with opioid-induced psychotic disorder with delusions 🦠

     F11.951 Opioid use, unspecified with opioid-induced psychotic disorder with hallucinations 🦠

     F11.959 Opioid use, unspecified with opioid-induced psychotic disorder, unspecified 🦠

●   **F11.98 Opioid use, unspecified with other specified opioid-induced disorder**

     F11.981 Opioid use, unspecified with opioid-induced sexual dysfunction 🦠
          Opioid-induced sexual dysfunction, without use disorder

     F11.982 Opioid use, unspecified with opioid-induced sleep disorder 🦠
          Opioid-induced sleep disorder, without use disorder

     F11.988 Opioid use, unspecified with other opioid-induced disorder 🦠
          Opioid-induced anxiety disorder, without use disorder

     F11.99 Opioid use, unspecified with unspecified opioid-induced disorder 🦠

● **F12 Cannabis related disorders**

     Includes   marijuana

     Coding Clinic: 2020, Q1, P8

●   **F12.1 Cannabis abuse**

     Excludes1   cannabis dependence (F12.2-)
               cannabis use, unspecified (F12.9-)

     F12.10 Cannabis abuse, uncomplicated
          Cannabis use disorder, mild

     F12.11 Cannabis abuse, in remission
          Cannabis use disorder, mild, in early remission
          Cannabis use disorder, mild, in sustained remission

●   **F12.12 Cannabis abuse with intoxication**

     F12.120 Cannabis abuse with intoxication, uncomplicated 🦠

     F12.121 Cannabis abuse with intoxication delirium 🦠

     F12.122 Cannabis abuse with intoxication with perceptual disturbance 🦠

     F12.129 Cannabis abuse with intoxication, unspecified 🦠

▶   **F12.13 Cannabis abuse with withdrawal**

●   **F12.15 Cannabis abuse with psychotic disorder**

     F12.150 Cannabis abuse with psychotic disorder with delusions 🦠

     F12.151 Cannabis abuse with psychotic disorder with hallucinations 🦠

     F12.159 Cannabis abuse with psychotic disorder, unspecified 🦠

●   **F12.18 Cannabis abuse with other cannabis-induced disorder**

     F12.180 Cannabis abuse with cannabis-induced anxiety disorder 🦠

     F12.188 Cannabis abuse with other cannabis-induced disorder 🦠
          Cannabis use disorder, mild, with cannabis-induced sleep disorder

     F12.19 Cannabis abuse with unspecified cannabis-induced disorder 🦠

●   **F12.2 Cannabis dependence**

     Excludes1   cannabis abuse (F12.1-)
               cannabis use, unspecified (F12.9-)

     Excludes2   cannabis poisoning (T40.7-)

     F12.20 Cannabis dependence, uncomplicated 🦠
          Cannabis use disorder, moderate
          Cannabis use disorder, severe

     F12.21 Cannabis dependence, in remission 🦠
          Cannabis use disorder, moderate, in early remission
          Cannabis use disorder, moderate, in sustained remission
          Cannabis use disorder, severe, in early remission
          Cannabis use disorder, severe, in sustained remission

●   **F12.22 Cannabis dependence with intoxication**

     F12.220 Cannabis dependence with intoxication, uncomplicated 🦠

     F12.221 Cannabis dependence with intoxication delirium 🦠

     F12.222 Cannabis dependence with intoxication with perceptual disturbance 🦠

     F12.229 Cannabis dependence with intoxication, unspecified 🦠

     F12.23 Cannabis dependence with withdrawal 🦠

▶ New   ⇒ Revised   ~~deleted~~ Deleted   Excludes 1   Excludes 2   Includes   Use additional   Code first   Code also   Key words

OGCR Official Guidelines   **X** Assign placeholder X   ● Use Additional Character(s)   ❱ Manifestation Code   🦠 Hierarchical Condition Category   **Coding Clinic**

● F12.25   Cannabis dependence with psychotic disorder
    F12.250   Cannabis dependence with psychotic disorder with delusions 🔖
    F12.251   Cannabis dependence with psychotic disorder with hallucinations 🔖
    F12.259   Cannabis dependence with psychotic disorder, unspecified 🔖
● F12.28   Cannabis dependence with other cannabis-induced disorder
    F12.280   Cannabis dependence with cannabis-induced anxiety disorder 🔖
    F12.288   Cannabis dependence with other cannabis-induced disorder 🔖
       Cannabis use disorder, moderate, with cannabis-induced sleep disorder
       Cannabis use disorder, severe, with cannabis-induced sleep disorder
   F12.29   Cannabis dependence with unspecified cannabis-induced disorder 🔖
● F12.9   Cannabis use, unspecified
    Excludes1   cannabis abuse (F12.1-)
           cannabis dependence (F12.2-)
   F12.90   Cannabis use, unspecified, uncomplicated
● F12.92   Cannabis use, unspecified with intoxication
    F12.920   Cannabis use, unspecified with intoxication, uncomplicated 🔖
    F12.921   Cannabis use, unspecified with intoxication delirium 🔖
    F12.922   Cannabis use, unspecified with intoxication with perceptual disturbance 🔖
    F12.929   Cannabis use, unspecified with intoxication, unspecified 🔖
   F12.93   Cannabis use, unspecified with withdrawal 🔖
● F12.95   Cannabis use, unspecified with psychotic disorder
    F12.950   Cannabis use, unspecified with psychotic disorder with delusions 🔖
    F12.951   Cannabis use, unspecified with psychotic disorder with hallucinations 🔖
    F12.959   Cannabis use, unspecified with psychotic disorder, unspecified 🔖
       Cannabis-induced psychotic disorder, without use disorder
● F12.98   Cannabis use, unspecified with other cannabis-induced disorder
    F12.980   Cannabis use, unspecified with anxiety disorder 🔖
       Cannabis-induced anxiety disorder, without use disorder
    F12.988   Cannabis use, unspecified with other cannabis-induced disorder 🔖
       Cannabis-induced sleep disorder, without use disorder
   F12.99   Cannabis use, unspecified with unspecified cannabis-induced disorder 🔖
● F13   Sedative, hypnotic, or anxiolytic related disorders
● F13.1   Sedative, hypnotic or anxiolytic-related abuse
    Excludes1   sedative, hypnotic or anxiolytic-related dependence (F13.2-)
           sedative, hypnotic, or anxiolytic use, unspecified (F13.9-)
   F13.10   Sedative, hypnotic or anxiolytic abuse, uncomplicated
       Sedative, hypnotic, or anxiolytic use disorder, mild

F13.11   Sedative, hypnotic or anxiolytic abuse, in remission
       Sedative, hypnotic or anxiolytic use disorder, mild, in early remission
       Sedative, hypnotic or anxiolytic use disorder, mild, in sustained remission
● F13.12   Sedative, hypnotic or anxiolytic abuse with intoxication
    F13.120   Sedative, hypnotic or anxiolytic abuse with intoxication, uncomplicated 🔖
    F13.121   Sedative, hypnotic or anxiolytic abuse with intoxication delirium 🔖
    F13.129   Sedative, hypnotic or anxiolytic abuse with intoxication, unspecified 🔖
▶● F13.13   Sedative, hypnotic or anxiolytic abuse with withdrawal
 ▶ F13.130   Sedative, hypnotic or anxiolytic abuse with withdrawal, uncomplicated
 ▶ F13.131   Sedative, hypnotic or anxiolytic abuse with withdrawal delirium
 ▶ F13.132   Sedative, hypnotic or anxiolytic abuse with withdrawal with perceptual disturbance
 ▶ F13.139   Sedative, hypnotic or anxiolytic abuse with withdrawal, unspecified
F13.14   Sedative, hypnotic or anxiolytic abuse with sedative, hypnotic or anxiolytic-induced mood disorder 🔖
       Sedative, hypnotic, or anxiolytic use disorder, mild, with sedative, hypnotic, or anxiolytic-induced bipolar or related disorder
       Sedative, hypnotic, or anxiolytic use disorder, mild, with sedative, hypnotic, or anxiolytic-induced depressive disorder
● F13.15   Sedative, hypnotic or anxiolytic abuse with sedative, hypnotic or anxiolytic-induced psychotic disorder
    F13.150   Sedative, hypnotic or anxiolytic abuse with sedative, hypnotic or anxiolytic-induced psychotic disorder with delusions 🔖
    F13.151   Sedative, hypnotic or anxiolytic abuse with sedative, hypnotic or anxiolytic-induced psychotic disorder with hallucinations 🔖
    F13.159   Sedative, hypnotic or anxiolytic abuse with sedative, hypnotic or anxiolytic-induced psychotic disorder, unspecified 🔖
● F13.18   Sedative, hypnotic or anxiolytic abuse with other sedative, hypnotic or anxiolytic-induced disorders
    F13.180   Sedative, hypnotic or anxiolytic abuse with sedative, hypnotic or anxiolytic-induced anxiety disorder 🔖
    F13.181   Sedative, hypnotic or anxiolytic abuse with sedative, hypnotic or anxiolytic-induced sexual dysfunction 🔖
    F13.182   Sedative, hypnotic or anxiolytic abuse with sedative, hypnotic or anxiolytic-induced sleep disorder 🔖
    F13.188   Sedative, hypnotic or anxiolytic abuse with other sedative, hypnotic or anxiolytic-induced disorder 🔖
   F13.19   Sedative, hypnotic or anxiolytic abuse with unspecified sedative, hypnotic or anxiolytic-induced disorder 🔖

● **F13.2 Sedative, hypnotic or anxiolytic-related dependence**

    Excludes1   sedative, hypnotic or anxiolytic-related abuse (F13.1-)

               sedative, hypnotic, or anxiolytic use, unspecified (F13.9-)

    Excludes2   sedative, hypnotic, or anxiolytic poisoning (T42.-)

F13.20 Sedative, hypnotic or anxiolytic dependence, uncomplicated 🗫

F13.21 Sedative, hypnotic or anxiolytic dependence, in remission 🗫

     Sedative, hypnotic or anxiolytic use disorder, moderate, in early remission

     Sedative, hypnotic or anxiolytic use disorder, moderate, in sustained remission

     Sedative, hypnotic or anxiolytic use disorder, severe, in early remission

     Sedative, hypnotic or anxiolytic use disorder, severe, in sustained remission

● **F13.22 Sedative, hypnotic or anxiolytic dependence with intoxication**

    Excludes1   sedative, hypnotic or anxiolytic dependence with withdrawal (F13.23-)

F13.220 Sedative, hypnotic or anxiolytic dependence with intoxication, uncomplicated 🗫

F13.221 Sedative, hypnotic or anxiolytic dependence with intoxication delirium 🗫

F13.229 Sedative, hypnotic or anxiolytic dependence with intoxication, unspecified 🗫

● **F13.23 Sedative, hypnotic or anxiolytic dependence with withdrawal**

     Sedative, hypnotic, or anxiolytic use disorder, moderate

     Sedative, hypnotic, or anxiolytic use disorder, severe

    Excludes1   sedative, hypnotic or anxiolytic dependence with intoxication (F13.22-)

F13.230 Sedative, hypnotic or anxiolytic dependence with withdrawal, uncomplicated 🗫

F13.231 Sedative, hypnotic or anxiolytic dependence with withdrawal delirium 🗫

F13.232 Sedative, hypnotic or anxiolytic dependence with withdrawal with perceptual disturbance 🗫

     Sedative, hypnotic, or anxiolytic withdrawal with perceptual disturbances

F13.239 Sedative, hypnotic or anxiolytic dependence with withdrawal, unspecified 🗫

     Sedative, hypnotic, or anxiolytic withdrawal without perceptual disturbances

F13.24 Sedative, hypnotic or anxiolytic dependence with sedative, hypnotic or anxiolytic-induced mood disorder 🗫

     Sedative, hypnotic, or anxiolytic use disorder, moderate, with sedative, hypnotic, or anxiolytic-induced bipolar or related disorder

     Sedative, hypnotic, or anxiolytic use disorder, moderate, with sedative, hypnotic, or anxiolytic-induced depressive disorder

     Sedative, hypnotic, or anxiolytic use disorder, severe, with sedative, hypnotic, or anxiolytic-induced bipolar or related disorder

     Sedative, hypnotic, or anxiolytic use disorder, severe, with sedative, hypnotic, or anxiolytic-induced depressive disorder

● **F13.25 Sedative, hypnotic or anxiolytic dependence with sedative, hypnotic or anxiolytic-induced psychotic disorder**

F13.250 Sedative, hypnotic or anxiolytic dependence with sedative, hypnotic or anxiolytic-induced psychotic disorder with delusions 🗫

F13.251 Sedative, hypnotic or anxiolytic dependence with sedative, hypnotic or anxiolytic-induced psychotic disorder with hallucinations 🗫

F13.259 Sedative, hypnotic or anxiolytic dependence with sedative, hypnotic or anxiolytic-induced psychotic disorder, unspecified 🗫

F13.26 Sedative, hypnotic or anxiolytic dependence with sedative, hypnotic or anxiolytic-induced persisting amnestic disorder 🗫

F13.27 Sedative, hypnotic or anxiolytic dependence with sedative, hypnotic or anxiolytic-induced persisting dementia 🗫

     Sedative, hypnotic, or anxiolytic use disorder, moderate, with sedative, hypnotic, or anxiolytic-induced major neurocognitive disorder

     Sedative, hypnotic, or anxiolytic use disorder, severe, with sedative, hypnotic, or anxiolytic-induced major neurocognitive disorder

● **F13.28 Sedative, hypnotic or anxiolytic dependence with other sedative, hypnotic or anxiolytic-induced disorders**

F13.280 Sedative, hypnotic or anxiolytic dependence with sedative, hypnotic or anxiolytic-induced anxiety disorder 🗫

F13.281 Sedative, hypnotic or anxiolytic dependence with sedative, hypnotic or anxiolytic-induced sexual dysfunction 🗫

F13.282 Sedative, hypnotic or anxiolytic dependence with sedative, hypnotic or anxiolytic-induced sleep disorder 🗫

F13.288 Sedative, hypnotic or anxiolytic dependence with other sedative, hypnotic or anxiolytic-induced disorder 🦠

Sedative, hypnotic, or anxiolytic use disorder, moderate, with sedative, hypnotic, or anxiolytic-induced mild neurocognitive disorder

Sedative, hypnotic, or anxiolytic use disorder, severe, with sedative, hypnotic, or anxiolytic-induced mild neurocognitive disorder

F13.29 Sedative, hypnotic or anxiolytic dependence with unspecified sedative, hypnotic or anxiolytic-induced disorder 🦠

● **F13.9** Sedative, hypnotic or anxiolytic-related use, unspecified

Excludes1 sedative, hypnotic or anxiolytic-related abuse (F13.1-)
sedative, hypnotic or anxiolytic-related dependence (F13.2-)

F13.90 Sedative, hypnotic, or anxiolytic use, unspecified, uncomplicated

● **F13.92** Sedative, hypnotic or anxiolytic use, unspecified with intoxication

Excludes1 sedative, hypnotic or anxiolytic use, unspecified with withdrawal (F13.93-)

F13.920 Sedative, hypnotic or anxiolytic use, unspecified with intoxication, uncomplicated 🦠

F13.921 Sedative, hypnotic or anxiolytic use, unspecified with intoxication delirium 🦠

Sedative, hypnotic, or anxiolytic-induced delirium

F13.929 Sedative, hypnotic or anxiolytic use, unspecified with intoxication, unspecified 🦠

● **F13.93** Sedative, hypnotic or anxiolytic use, unspecified with withdrawal

Excludes1 sedative, hypnotic or anxiolytic use, unspecified with intoxication (F13.92-)

F13.930 Sedative, hypnotic or anxiolytic use, unspecified with withdrawal, uncomplicated 🦠

F13.931 Sedative, hypnotic or anxiolytic use, unspecified with withdrawal delirium 🦠

F13.932 Sedative, hypnotic or anxiolytic use, unspecified with withdrawal with perceptual disturbances 🦠

F13.939 Sedative, hypnotic or anxiolytic use, unspecified with withdrawal, unspecified 🦠

F13.94 Sedative, hypnotic or anxiolytic use, unspecified with sedative, hypnotic or anxiolytic-induced mood disorder 🦠

Sedative, hypnotic, or anxiolytic-induced bipolar or related disorder, without use disorder

Sedative, hypnotic, or anxiolytic-induced depressive disorder, without use disorder

● **F13.95** Sedative, hypnotic or anxiolytic use, unspecified with sedative, hypnotic or anxiolytic-induced psychotic disorder

F13.950 Sedative, hypnotic or anxiolytic use, unspecified with sedative, hypnotic or anxiolytic-induced psychotic disorder with delusions 🦠

F13.951 Sedative, hypnotic or anxiolytic use, unspecified with sedative, hypnotic or anxiolytic-induced psychotic disorder with hallucinations 🦠

F13.959 Sedative, hypnotic or anxiolytic use, unspecified with sedative, hypnotic or anxiolytic-induced psychotic disorder, unspecified 🦠

Sedative, hypnotic, or anxiolytic-induced psychotic disorder, without use disorder

F13.96 Sedative, hypnotic or anxiolytic use, unspecified with sedative, hypnotic or anxiolytic-induced persisting amnestic disorder 🦠

F13.97 Sedative, hypnotic or anxiolytic use, unspecified with sedative, hypnotic or anxiolytic-induced persisting dementia 🦠

Sedative, hypnotic, or anxiolytic-induced major neurocognitive disorder, without use disorder

● **F13.98** Sedative, hypnotic or anxiolytic use, unspecified with other sedative, hypnotic or anxiolytic-induced disorders

F13.980 Sedative, hypnotic or anxiolytic use, unspecified with sedative, hypnotic or anxiolytic-induced anxiety disorder 🦠

Sedative, hypnotic, or anxiolytic-induced anxiety disorder, without use disorder

F13.981 Sedative, hypnotic or anxiolytic use, unspecified with sedative, hypnotic or anxiolytic-induced sexual dysfunction 🦠

Sedative, hypnotic, or anxiolytic-induced sexual dysfunction disorder, without use disorder

F13.982 Sedative, hypnotic or anxiolytic use, unspecified with sedative, hypnotic or anxiolytic-induced sleep disorder 🦠

Sedative, hypnotic, or anxiolytic-induced sleep disorder, without use disorder

F13.988 Sedative, hypnotic or anxiolytic use, unspecified with other sedative, hypnotic or anxiolytic-induced disorder 🦠

Sedative, hypnotic, or anxiolytic-induced mild neurocognitive disorder

F13.99 Sedative, hypnotic or anxiolytic use, unspecified with unspecified sedative, hypnotic or anxiolytic-induced disorder 🦠

CHAPTER 5 (F01-F99)

● **F14   Cocaine related disorders**

     Excludes2   other stimulant-related disorders (F15.-)

● **F14.1   Cocaine abuse**

     Excludes1   cocaine dependence (F14.2-)
                       cocaine use, unspecified (F14.9-)

     F14.10   Cocaine abuse, uncomplicated
                Cocaine use disorder, mild

     F14.11   Cocaine abuse, in remission
                Cocaine use disorder, mild, in early remission
                Cocaine use disorder, mild, in sustained remission

● **F14.12   Cocaine abuse with intoxication**

         F14.120   Cocaine abuse with intoxication, uncomplicated 🐾

         F14.121   Cocaine abuse with intoxication with delirium 🐾

         F14.122   Cocaine abuse with intoxication with perceptual disturbance 🐾

         F14.129   Cocaine abuse with intoxication, unspecified 🐾

▶ **F14.13   Cocaine abuse, unspecified with withdrawal**

     F14.14   Cocaine abuse with cocaine-induced mood disorder 🐾
                Cocaine use disorder, mild, with cocaine-induced bipolar or related disorder
                Cocaine use disorder, mild, with cocaine-induced depressive disorder

● **F14.15   Cocaine abuse with cocaine-induced psychotic disorder**

         F14.150   Cocaine abuse with cocaine-induced psychotic disorder with delusions 🐾

         F14.151   Cocaine abuse with cocaine-induced psychotic disorder with hallucinations 🐾

         F14.159   Cocaine abuse with cocaine-induced psychotic disorder, unspecified 🐾

● **F14.18   Cocaine abuse with other cocaine-induced disorder**

         F14.180   Cocaine abuse with cocaine-induced anxiety disorder 🐾

         F14.181   Cocaine abuse with cocaine-induced sexual dysfunction 🐾

         F14.182   Cocaine abuse with cocaine-induced sleep disorder 🐾

         F14.188   Cocaine abuse with other cocaine-induced disorder 🐾
                    Cocaine use disorder, mild, with cocaine-induced obsessive-compulsive or related disorder

     F14.19   Cocaine abuse with unspecified cocaine-induced disorder 🐾

● **F14.2   Cocaine dependence**

     Excludes1   cocaine abuse (F14.1-)
                       cocaine use, unspecified (F14.9-)

     Excludes2   cocaine poisoning (T40.5-)

     F14.20   Cocaine dependence, uncomplicated 🐾
                Cocaine use disorder, moderate
                Cocaine use disorder, severe

     F14.21   Cocaine dependence, in remission 🐾
                Cocaine use disorder, moderate, in early remission
                Cocaine use disorder, moderate, in sustained remission
                Cocaine use disorder, severe, in early remission
                Cocaine use disorder, severe, in sustained remission
                Coding Clinic: 2017, Q2, P27

● **F14.22   Cocaine dependence with intoxication**

     Excludes1   cocaine dependence with withdrawal (F14.23)

     F14.220   Cocaine dependence with intoxication, uncomplicated

     F14.221   Cocaine dependence with intoxication delirium 🐾

     F14.222   Cocaine dependence with intoxication with perceptual disturbance 🐾

     F14.229   Cocaine dependence with intoxication, unspecified 🐾

     F14.23   Cocaine dependence with withdrawal

     Excludes1   cocaine dependence with intoxication (F14.22-)

     F14.24   Cocaine dependence with cocaine-induced mood disorder 🐾
                Cocaine use disorder, moderate, with cocaine-induced bipolar or related disorder
                Cocaine use disorder, moderate, with cocaine-induced depressive disorder
                Cocaine use disorder, severe, with cocaine-induced bipolar or related disorder
                Cocaine use disorder, severe, with cocaine-induced depressive disorder

● **F14.25   Cocaine dependence with cocaine-induced psychotic disorder**

     F14.250   Cocaine dependence with cocaine-induced psychotic disorder with delusions 🐾

     F14.251   Cocaine dependence with cocaine-induced psychotic disorder with hallucinations 🐾

     F14.259   Cocaine dependence with cocaine-induced psychotic disorder, unspecified 🐾

● **F14.28   Cocaine dependence with other cocaine-induced disorder**

     F14.280   Cocaine dependence with cocaine-induced anxiety disorder 🐾

     F14.281   Cocaine dependence with cocaine-induced sexual dysfunction 🐾

     F14.282   Cocaine dependence with cocaine-induced sleep disorder 🐾

     F14.288   Cocaine dependence with other cocaine-induced disorder 🐾
                Cocaine use disorder, moderate, with cocaine-induced obsessive-compulsive or related disorder
                Cocaine use disorder, severe, with cocaine-induced obsessive-compulsive or related disorder

     F14.29   Cocaine dependence with unspecified cocaine-induced disorder 🐾

● **F14.9   Cocaine use, unspecified**

     Excludes1   cocaine abuse (F14.1-)
                       cocaine dependence (F14.2-)

     F14.90   Cocaine use, unspecified, uncomplicated
                Coding Clinic: 2018, Q2, P11

● **F14.92   Cocaine use, unspecified with intoxication**

     F14.920   Cocaine use, unspecified with intoxication, uncomplicated 🐾

     F14.921   Cocaine use, unspecified with intoxication delirium 🐾

     F14.922   Cocaine use, unspecified with intoxication with perceptual disturbance 🐾

     F14.929   Cocaine use, unspecified with intoxication, unspecified 🐾

▶ New   ⇒ Revised   ~~deleted~~ Deleted   Excludes 1   Excludes 2   Includes   Use additional   Code first   Code also   Key words

OGCR Official Guidelines   X Assign placeholder X   ● Use Additional Character(s)   ❱ Manifestation Code   🐾 Hierarchical Condition Category   **Coding Clinic**

▶ F14.93 Cocaine use, unspecified with withdrawal

F14.94 Cocaine use, unspecified with cocaine-induced mood disorder 🦠
  Cocaine-induced bipolar or related disorder, without use disorder
  Cocaine-induced depressive disorder, without use disorder

● F14.95 Cocaine use, unspecified with cocaine-induced psychotic disorder

  F14.950 Cocaine use, unspecified with cocaine-induced psychotic disorder with delusions 🦠

  F14.951 Cocaine use, unspecified with cocaine-induced psychotic disorder with hallucinations 🦠

  F14.959 Cocaine use, unspecified with cocaine-induced psychotic disorder, unspecified 🦠
    Cocaine-induced psychotic disorder, without use disorder

● F14.98 Cocaine use, unspecified with other specified cocaine-induced disorder

  F14.980 Cocaine use, unspecified with cocaine-induced anxiety disorder 🦠
    Cocaine-induced anxiety disorder, without use disorder

  F14.981 Cocaine use, unspecified with cocaine-induced sexual dysfunction 🦠
    Cocaine-induced sexual dysfunction, without use disorder

  F14.982 Cocaine use, unspecified with cocaine-induced sleep disorder 🦠
    Cocaine-induced sleep disorder, without use disorder

  F14.988 Cocaine use, unspecified with other cocaine-induced disorder 🦠
    Cocaine-induced obsessive-compulsive or related disorder

F14.99 Cocaine use, unspecified with unspecified cocaine-induced disorder 🦠

● F15 Other stimulant related disorders

  Includes amphetamine-related disorders
    caffeine

  Excludes2 cocaine-related disorders (F14.-)

● F15.1 Other stimulant abuse

  Excludes1 other stimulant dependence (F15.2-)
    other stimulant use, unspecified (F15.9-)

  F15.10 Other stimulant abuse, uncomplicated
    Amphetamine type substance use disorder, mild
    Other or unspecified stimulant use disorder, mild

  F15.11 Other stimulant abuse, in remission
    Amphetamine type substance use disorder, mild, in early remission
    Amphetamine type substance use disorder, mild, in sustained remission
    Other or unspecified stimulant use disorder, mild, in early remission
    Other or unspecified stimulant use disorder, mild, in sustained remission

● F15.12 Other stimulant abuse with intoxication

  F15.120 Other stimulant abuse with intoxication, uncomplicated 🦠

  F15.121 Other stimulant abuse with intoxication delirium 🦠

  F15.122 Other stimulant abuse with intoxication with perceptual disturbance 🦠
    Amphetamine or other stimulant use disorder, mild, with amphetamine or other stimulant intoxication, with perceptual disturbances

  F15.129 Other stimulant abuse with intoxication, unspecified 🦠
    Amphetamine or other stimulant use disorder, mild, with amphetamine or other stimulant intoxication, without perceptual disturbances

▶ F15.13 Other stimulant abuse with withdrawal

F15.14 Other stimulant abuse with stimulant-induced mood disorder 🦠
  Amphetamine or other stimulant use disorder, mild, with amphetamine or other stimulant-induced bipolar or related disorder
  Amphetamine or other stimulant use disorder, mild, with amphetamine or other stimulant-induced depressive disorder

● F15.15 Other stimulant abuse with stimulant-induced psychotic disorder

  F15.150 Other stimulant abuse with stimulant-induced psychotic disorder with delusions 🦠

  F15.151 Other stimulant abuse with stimulant-induced psychotic disorder with hallucinations 🦠

  F15.159 Other stimulant abuse with stimulant-induced psychotic disorder, unspecified 🦠

● F15.18 Other stimulant abuse with other stimulant-induced disorder

  F15.180 Other stimulant abuse with stimulant-induced anxiety disorder 🦠

  F15.181 Other stimulant abuse with stimulant-induced sexual dysfunction 🦠

  F15.182 Other stimulant abuse with stimulant-induced sleep disorder 🦠

  F15.188 Other stimulant abuse with other stimulant-induced disorder 🦠
    Amphetamine or other stimulant use disorder, mild, with amphetamine or other stimulant-induced obsessive-compulsive or related disorder

F15.19 Other stimulant abuse with unspecified stimulant-induced disorder 🦠

● F15.2 Other stimulant dependence

  Excludes1 other stimulant abuse (F15.1-)
    other stimulant use, unspecified (F15.9-)

  F15.20 Other stimulant dependence, uncomplicated 🦠
    Amphetamine type substance use disorder, moderate
    Amphetamine type substance use disorder, severe
    Other or unspecified stimulant use disorder, moderate
    Other or unspecified stimulant use disorder, severe

N Newborn Age: 0   **P** Pediatric Age: 0–17   **M** Maternity DX: 12–55   **A** Adult Age: 15–124   ♀ Females Only   ♂ Males Only

773

F15.21   **Other stimulant dependence, in remission** 🦠
Amphetamine type substance use disorder, moderate, in early remission
Amphetamine type substance use disorder, moderate, in sustained remission
Amphetamine type substance use disorder, severe, in early remission
Amphetamine type substance use disorder, severe, in sustained remission
Other or unspecified stimulant use disorder, moderate, in early remission
Other or unspecified stimulant use disorder, moderate, in sustained remission
Other or unspecified stimulant use disorder, severe, in early remission
Other or unspecified stimulant use disorder, severe, in sustained remission

● F15.22   **Other stimulant dependence with intoxication**
Excludes1   other stimulant dependence with withdrawal (F15.23)

F15.220   **Other stimulant dependence with intoxication, uncomplicated** 🦠

F15.221   **Other stimulant dependence with intoxication delirium** 🦠

F15.222   **Other stimulant dependence with intoxication with perceptual disturbance** 🦠
Amphetamine or other stimulant use disorder, moderate, with amphetamine or other stimulant intoxication, with perceptual disturbances
Amphetamine or other stimulant use disorder, severe, with amphetamine or other stimulant intoxication, with perceptual disturbances

F15.229   **Other stimulant dependence with intoxication, unspecified** 🦠
Amphetamine or other stimulant use disorder, moderate, with amphetamine or other stimulant intoxication, without perceptual disturbances
Amphetamine or other stimulant use disorder, severe, with amphetamine or other stimulant intoxication, without perceptual disturbances

F15.23   **Other stimulant dependence with withdrawal** 🦠
Amphetamine or other stimulant withdrawal
Excludes1   other stimulant dependence with intoxication (F15.22-)

F15.24   **Other stimulant dependence with stimulant-induced mood disorder** 🦠
Amphetamine or other stimulant use disorder, moderate, with amphetamine or other stimulant-induced bipolar or related disorder
Amphetamine or other stimulant use disorder, moderate, with amphetamine or other stimulant-induced depressive disorder
Amphetamine or other stimulant use disorder, severe, with amphetamine or other stimulant-induced bipolar or related disorder
Amphetamine or other stimulant use disorder, severe, with amphetamine or other stimulant-induced depressive disorder

● F15.25   **Other stimulant dependence with stimulant-induced psychotic disorder**

F15.250   **Other stimulant dependence with stimulant-induced psychotic disorder with delusions** 🦠

F15.251   **Other stimulant dependence with stimulant-induced psychotic disorder with hallucinations** 🦠

F15.259   **Other stimulant dependence with stimulant-induced psychotic disorder, unspecified** 🦠

● F15.28   **Other stimulant dependence with other stimulant-induced disorder**

F15.280   **Other stimulant dependence with stimulant-induced anxiety disorder** 🦠

F15.281   **Other stimulant dependence with stimulant-induced sexual dysfunction** 🦠

F15.282   **Other stimulant dependence with stimulant-induced sleep disorder** 🦠

F15.288   **Other stimulant dependence with other stimulant-induced disorder** 🦠
Amphetamine or other stimulant use disorder, moderate, with amphetamine or other stimulant-induced obsessive-compulsive or related disorder
Amphetamine or other stimulant use disorder, severe, with amphetamine or other stimulant-induced obsessive-compulsive or related disorder

F15.29   **Other stimulant dependence with unspecified stimulant-induced disorder** 🦠

● F15.9   **Other stimulant use, unspecified**
Excludes1   other stimulant abuse (F15.1-)
other stimulant dependence (F15.2-)

F15.90   **Other stimulant use, unspecified, uncomplicated**

● F15.92   **Other stimulant use, unspecified with intoxication**
Excludes1   other stimulant use, unspecified with withdrawal (F15.93)

F15.920   **Other stimulant use, unspecified with intoxication, uncomplicated** 🦠

F15.921   **Other stimulant use, unspecified with intoxication delirium** 🦠
Amphetamine or other stimulant-induced delirium

F15.922   **Other stimulant use, unspecified with intoxication with perceptual disturbance** 🦠

F15.929   **Other stimulant use, unspecified with intoxication, unspecified** 🦠
Caffeine intoxication

F15.93   **Other stimulant use, unspecified with withdrawal** 🦠
Caffeine withdrawal
Excludes1   other stimulant use, unspecified with intoxication (F15.92-)

F15.94   **Other stimulant use, unspecified with stimulant-induced mood disorder** 🦠
Amphetamine or other stimulant-induced bipolar or related disorder, without use disorder
Amphetamine or other stimulant-induced depressive disorder, without use disorder

▶ New   ➡ Revised   ~~deleted~~ Deleted   Excludes 1   Excludes 2   Includes   Use additional   Code first   Code also   Key words
OGCR Official Guidelines   X Assign placeholder X   ● Use Additional Character(s)   ▶ Manifestation Code   🦠 Hierarchical Condition Category   **Coding Clinic**

● **F15.95** **Other stimulant use, unspecified with stimulant-induced psychotic disorder**

     F15.950 **Other stimulant use, unspecified with stimulant-induced psychotic disorder with delusions** 🔎

     F15.951 **Other stimulant use, unspecified with stimulant-induced psychotic disorder with hallucinations** 🔎

     F15.959 **Other stimulant use, unspecified with stimulant-induced psychotic disorder, unspecified** 🔎
       Amphetamine or other stimulant-induced psychotic disorder, without use disorder

● **F15.98** **Other stimulant use, unspecified with other stimulant-induced disorder**

     F15.980 **Other stimulant use, unspecified with stimulant-induced anxiety disorder** 🔎
       Amphetamine or other stimulant-induced anxiety disorder, without use disorder
       Caffeine-induced anxiety disorder, without use disorder

     F15.981 **Other stimulant use, unspecified with stimulant-induced sexual dysfunction** 🔎
       Amphetamine or other stimulant-induced sexual dysfunction, without use disorder

     F15.982 **Other stimulant use, unspecified with stimulant-induced sleep disorder** 🔎
       Amphetamine or other stimulant-induced sleep disorder, without use disorder
       Caffeine-induced sleep disorder, without use disorder

     F15.988 **Other stimulant use, unspecified with other stimulant-induced disorder** 🔎
       Amphetamine or other stimulant-induced obsessive-compulsive or related disorder, without use disorder

     F15.99 **Other stimulant use, unspecified with unspecified stimulant-induced disorder** 🔎

● **F16** **Hallucinogen related disorders**
     Includes   ecstasy
               PCP
               phencyclidine

● **F16.1** **Hallucinogen abuse**
     Excludes1   hallucinogen dependence (F16.2-)
                 hallucinogen use, unspecified (F16.9-)

     F16.10 **Hallucinogen abuse, uncomplicated**
       Other hallucinogen use disorder, mild
       Phencyclidine use disorder, mild
       Coding Clinic: 2018, Q4, P31

     F16.11 **Hallucinogen abuse, in remission**
       Other hallucinogen use disorder, mild, in early remission
       Other hallucinogen use disorder, mild, in sustained remission
       Phencyclidine use disorder, mild, in early remission
       Phencyclidine use disorder, mild, in sustained remission

● **F16.12** **Hallucinogen abuse with intoxication**

     F16.120 **Hallucinogen abuse with intoxication, uncomplicated** 🔎

     F16.121 **Hallucinogen abuse with intoxication with delirium** 🔎

     F16.122 **Hallucinogen abuse with intoxication with perceptual disturbance** 🔎

     F16.129 **Hallucinogen abuse with intoxication, unspecified** 🔎

F16.14 **Hallucinogen abuse with hallucinogen-induced mood disorder** 🔎
     Other hallucinogen use disorder, mild, with other hallucinogen-induced bipolar or related disorder
     Other hallucinogen use disorder, mild, with other hallucinogen-induced depressive disorder
     Phencyclidine use disorder, mild, with phencyclidine-induced bipolar or related disorder
     Phencyclidine use disorder, mild, with phencyclidine-induced depressive disorder

● **F16.15** **Hallucinogen abuse with hallucinogen-induced psychotic disorder**

     F16.150 **Hallucinogen abuse with hallucinogen-induced psychotic disorder with delusions** 🔎

     F16.151 **Hallucinogen abuse with hallucinogen-induced psychotic disorder with hallucinations** 🔎

     F16.159 **Hallucinogen abuse with hallucinogen-induced psychotic disorder, unspecified** 🔎

● **F16.18** **Hallucinogen abuse with other hallucinogen-induced disorder**

     F16.180 **Hallucinogen abuse with hallucinogen-induced anxiety disorder** 🔎

     F16.183 **Hallucinogen abuse with hallucinogen persisting perception disorder (flashbacks)** 🔎

     F16.188 **Hallucinogen abuse with other hallucinogen-induced disorder** 🔎

     F16.19 **Hallucinogen abuse with unspecified hallucinogen-induced disorder** 🔎

● **F16.2** **Hallucinogen dependence**
     Excludes1   hallucinogen abuse (F16.1-)
                 hallucinogen use, unspecified (F16.9-)

     F16.20 **Hallucinogen dependence, uncomplicated** 🔎
       Other hallucinogen use disorder, moderate
       Other hallucinogen use disorder, severe
       Phencyclidine use disorder, moderate
       Phencyclidine use disorder, severe

     F16.21 **Hallucinogen dependence, in remission** 🔎
       Other hallucinogen use disorder, moderate, in early remission
       Other hallucinogen use disorder, moderate, in sustained remission
       Other hallucinogen use disorder, severe, in early remission
       Other hallucinogen use disorder, severe, in sustained remission
       Phencyclidine use disorder, moderate, in early remission
       Phencyclidine use disorder, moderate, in sustained remission
       Phencyclidine use disorder, severe, in early remission
       Phencyclidine use disorder, severe, in sustained remission

● **F16.22** **Hallucinogen dependence with intoxication**

     F16.220 **Hallucinogen dependence with intoxication, uncomplicated** 🔎

     F16.221 **Hallucinogen dependence with intoxication with delirium** 🔎

     F16.229 **Hallucinogen dependence with intoxication, unspecified** 🔎

CHAPTER 5 (F01-F99)

F16.24   **Hallucinogen dependence with hallucinogen-induced mood disorder** 🐾
Other hallucinogen use disorder, moderate, with other hallucinogen-induced bipolar or related disorder
Other hallucinogen use disorder, moderate, with other hallucinogen-induced depressive disorder
Other hallucinogen use disorder, severe, with other hallucinogen-induced bipolar or related disorder
Other hallucinogen use disorder, severe, with other hallucinogen-induced depressive disorder
Phencyclidine use disorder, moderate, with phencyclidine-induced bipolar or related disorder
Phencyclidine use disorder, moderate, with phencyclidine-induced depressive disorder
Phencyclidine use disorder, severe, with phencyclidine-induced bipolar or related disorder
Phencyclidine use disorder, severe, with phencyclidine-induced depressive disorder

● **F16.25**   **Hallucinogen dependence with hallucinogen-induced psychotic disorder**

    F16.250   **Hallucinogen dependence with hallucinogen-induced psychotic disorder with delusions** 🐾

    F16.251   **Hallucinogen dependence with hallucinogen-induced psychotic disorder with hallucinations** 🐾

    F16.259   **Hallucinogen dependence with hallucinogen-induced psychotic disorder, unspecified** 🐾

● **F16.28**   **Hallucinogen dependence with other hallucinogen-induced disorder**

    F16.280   **Hallucinogen dependence with hallucinogen-induced anxiety disorder** 🐾

    F16.283   **Hallucinogen dependence with hallucinogen persisting perception disorder (flashbacks)** 🐾

    F16.288   **Hallucinogen dependence with other hallucinogen-induced disorder** 🐾

    F16.29   **Hallucinogen dependence with unspecified hallucinogen-induced disorder** 🐾

● **F16.9**   **Hallucinogen use, unspecified**

   Excludes1   hallucinogen abuse (F16.1-)
               hallucinogen dependence (F16.2-)

   F16.90   **Hallucinogen use, unspecified, uncomplicated**

● **F16.92**   **Hallucinogen use, unspecified with intoxication**

    F16.920   **Hallucinogen use, unspecified with intoxication, uncomplicated** 🐾

    F16.921   **Hallucinogen use, unspecified with intoxication with delirium** 🐾
Other hallucinogen intoxication delirium

    F16.929   **Hallucinogen use, unspecified with intoxication, unspecified** 🐾

   F16.94   **Hallucinogen use, unspecified with hallucinogen-induced mood disorder** 🐾
Other hallucinogen-induced bipolar or related disorder, without use disorder
Other hallucinogen-induced depressive disorder, without use disorder
Phencyclidine-induced bipolar or related disorder, without use disorder
Phencyclidine-induced depressive disorder, without use disorder

● **F16.95**   **Hallucinogen use, unspecified with hallucinogen-induced psychotic disorder**

    F16.950   **Hallucinogen use, unspecified with hallucinogen-induced psychotic disorder with delusions** 🐾

    F16.951   **Hallucinogen use, unspecified with hallucinogen-induced psychotic disorder with hallucinations** 🐾

    F16.959   **Hallucinogen use, unspecified with hallucinogen-induced psychotic disorder, unspecified** 🐾
Other hallucinogen-induced psychotic disorder, without use disorder
Phencyclidine-induced psychotic disorder, without use disorder

● **F16.98**   **Hallucinogen use, unspecified with other specified hallucinogen-induced disorder**

    F16.980   **Hallucinogen use, unspecified with hallucinogen-induced anxiety disorder** 🐾
Other hallucinogen-induced anxiety disorder, without use disorder
Phencyclidine-induced anxiety disorder, without use disorder

    F16.983   **Hallucinogen use, unspecified with hallucinogen persisting perception disorder (flashbacks)** 🐾

    F16.988   **Hallucinogen use, unspecified with other hallucinogen-induced disorder** 🐾

   F16.99   **Hallucinogen use, unspecified with unspecified hallucinogen-induced disorder** 🐾

● **F17**   **Nicotine dependence**

   Excludes1   history of tobacco dependence (Z87.891)
              tobacco use NOS (Z72.0)

   Excludes2   tobacco use (smoking) during pregnancy, childbirth and the puerperium (O99.33-)
              toxic effect of nicotine (T65.2-)

● **F17.2**   **Nicotine dependence**

● **F17.20**   **Nicotine dependence, unspecified**

    F17.200   **Nicotine dependence, unspecified, uncomplicated**
Tobacco use disorder, mild
Tobacco use disorder, moderate
Tobacco use disorder, severe
Coding Clinic: 2016, Q1, P37

    F17.201   **Nicotine dependence, unspecified, in remission**
Tobacco use disorder, mild, in early remission
Tobacco use disorder, mild, in sustained remission
Tobacco use disorder, moderate, in early remission
Tobacco use disorder, moderate, in sustained remission
Tobacco use disorder, severe, in early remission
Tobacco use disorder, severe, in sustained remission

    F17.203   **Nicotine dependence unspecified, with withdrawal**
Tobacco withdrawal

    F17.208   **Nicotine dependence, unspecified, with other nicotine-induced disorders**

    F17.209   **Nicotine dependence, unspecified, with unspecified nicotine-induced disorders**

● **F17.21**   **Nicotine dependence, cigarettes**

    F17.210   **Nicotine dependence, cigarettes, uncomplicated**
Coding Clinic: 2017, Q2, P28-29

▶ New   ⟾ Revised   ~~deleted~~ Deleted   Excludes 1   Excludes 2   Includes   Use additional   Code first   Code also   Key words
OGCR Official Guidelines   **X** Assign placeholder X   ● Use Additional Character(s)   ▶ Manifestation Code   🐾 Hierarchical Condition Category   **Coding Clinic**

F17.211 **Nicotine dependence, cigarettes, in remission**
　Tobacco use disorder, cigarettes, mild, in early remission
　Tobacco use disorder, cigarettes, mild, in sustained remission
　Tobacco use disorder, cigarettes, moderate, in early remission
　Tobacco use disorder, cigarettes, moderate, in sustained remission
　Tobacco use disorder, cigarettes, severe, in early remission
　Tobacco use disorder, cigarettes, severe, in sustained remission

F17.213 **Nicotine dependence, cigarettes, with withdrawal**

F17.218 **Nicotine dependence, cigarettes, with other nicotine-induced disorders**

F17.219 **Nicotine dependence, cigarettes, with unspecified nicotine-induced disorders**

● **F17.22** **Nicotine dependence, chewing tobacco**

F17.220 **Nicotine dependence, chewing tobacco, uncomplicated**

F17.221 **Nicotine dependence, chewing tobacco, in remission**
　Tobacco use disorder, chewing tobacco, mild, in early remission
　Tobacco use disorder, chewing tobacco, mild, in sustained remission
　Tobacco use disorder, chewing tobacco, moderate, in early remission
　Tobacco use disorder, chewing tobacco, moderate, in sustained remission
　Tobacco use disorder, chewing tobacco, severe, in early remission
　Tobacco use disorder, chewing tobacco, severe, in sustained remission

F17.223 **Nicotine dependence, chewing tobacco, with withdrawal**

F17.228 **Nicotine dependence, chewing tobacco, with other nicotine-induced disorders**

F17.229 **Nicotine dependence, chewing tobacco, with unspecified nicotine-induced disorders**

● **F17.29** **Nicotine dependence, other tobacco product**

F17.290 **Nicotine dependence, other tobacco product, uncomplicated**
　Coding Clinic: 2017, Q2, P28-29

F17.291 **Nicotine dependence, other tobacco product, in remission**
　Tobacco use disorder, other tobacco product, mild, in early remission
　Tobacco use disorder, other tobacco product, mild, in sustained remission
　Tobacco use disorder, other tobacco product, moderate, in early remission
　Tobacco use disorder, other tobacco product, moderate, in sustained remission
　Tobacco use disorder, other tobacco product, severe, in early remission
　Tobacco use disorder, other tobacco product, severe, in sustained remission

F17.293 **Nicotine dependence, other tobacco product, with withdrawal**

F17.298 **Nicotine dependence, other tobacco product, with other nicotine-induced disorders**

F17.299 **Nicotine dependence, other tobacco product, with unspecified nicotine-induced disorders**

● **F18** **Inhalant related disorders**
　Includes volatile solvents

● **F18.1** **Inhalant abuse**
　Excludes1 inhalant dependence (F18.2-)
　　inhalant use, unspecified (F18.9-)

F18.10 **Inhalant abuse, uncomplicated**
　Inhalant use disorder, mild

F18.11 **Inhalant abuse, in remission**
　Inhalant use disorder, mild, in early remission
　Inhalant use disorder, mild, in sustained remission

● **F18.12** **Inhalant abuse with intoxication**

F18.120 **Inhalant abuse with intoxication, uncomplicated** ✎

F18.121 **Inhalant abuse with intoxication delirium** ✎

F18.129 **Inhalant abuse with intoxication, unspecified** ✎

F18.14 **Inhalant abuse with inhalant-induced mood disorder** ✎
　Inhalant use disorder, mild, with inhalant-induced depressive disorder

● **F18.15** **Inhalant abuse with inhalant-induced psychotic disorder**

F18.150 **Inhalant abuse with inhalant-induced psychotic disorder with delusions** ✎

F18.151 **Inhalant abuse with inhalant-induced psychotic disorder with hallucinations** ✎

F18.159 **Inhalant abuse with inhalant-induced psychotic disorder, unspecified** ✎

F18.17 **Inhalant abuse with inhalant-induced dementia** ✎
　Inhalant use disorder, mild, with inhalant-induced major neurocognitive disorder

● **F18.18** **Inhalant abuse with other inhalant-induced disorders**

F18.180 **Inhalant abuse with inhalant-induced anxiety disorder** ✎

F18.188 **Inhalant abuse with other inhalant-induced disorder** ✎
　Inhalant use disorder, mild, with inhalant-induced mild neurocognitive disorder

F18.19 **Inhalant abuse with unspecified inhalant-induced disorder** ✎

● **F18.2** **Inhalant dependence**
　Excludes1 inhalant abuse (F18.1-)
　　inhalant use, unspecified (F18.9-)

F18.20 **Inhalant dependence, uncomplicated** ✎
　Inhalant use disorder, moderate
　Inhalant use disorder, severe

F18.21 **Inhalant dependence, in remission** ✎
　Inhalant use disorder, moderate, in early remission
　Inhalant use disorder, moderate, in sustained remission
　Inhalant use disorder, severe, in early remission
　Inhalant use disorder, severe, in sustained remission

● F18.22   Inhalant dependence with intoxication
      F18.220   Inhalant dependence with
                intoxication, uncomplicated 🅀
      F18.221   Inhalant dependence with
                intoxication delirium 🅀
      F18.229   Inhalant dependence with
                intoxication, unspecified 🅀
  F18.24   Inhalant dependence with inhalant-induced
           mood disorder 🅀
                Inhalant use disorder, moderate, with inhalant-
                   induced depressive disorder
                Inhalant use disorder, severe, with inhalant-
                   induced depressive disorder
● F18.25   Inhalant dependence with inhalant-induced
           psychotic disorder
      F18.250   Inhalant dependence with inhalant-
                induced psychotic disorder with
                delusions 🅀
      F18.251   Inhalant dependence with inhalant-
                induced psychotic disorder with
                hallucinations 🅀
      F18.259   Inhalant dependence with inhalant-
                induced psychotic disorder,
                unspecified 🅀
  F18.27   Inhalant dependence with inhalant-induced
           dementia 🅀
                Inhalant use disorder, moderate, with inhalant-
                   induced major neurocognitive disorder
                Inhalant use disorder, severe, with inhalant-
                   induced major neurocognitive disorder
● F18.28   Inhalant dependence with other inhalant-
           induced disorders
      F18.280   Inhalant dependence with inhalant-
                induced anxiety disorder 🅀
      F18.288   Inhalant dependence with other
                inhalant-induced disorder 🅀
                Inhalant use disorder, moderate,
                   with inhalant-induced mild
                   neurocognitive disorder
                Inhalant use disorder, severe,
                   with inhalant-induced mild
                   neurocognitive disorder
  F18.29   Inhalant dependence with unspecified inhalant-
           induced disorder 🅀
● F18.9   Inhalant use, unspecified
      Excludes1   inhalant abuse (F18.1-)
                  inhalant dependence (F18.2-)
  F18.90   Inhalant use, unspecified, uncomplicated
● F18.92   Inhalant use, unspecified with intoxication
      F18.920   Inhalant use, unspecified with
                intoxication, uncomplicated 🅀
      F18.921   Inhalant use, unspecified with
                intoxication with delirium 🅀
      F18.929   Inhalant use, unspecified with
                intoxication, unspecified 🅀
  F18.94   Inhalant use, unspecified with inhalant-
           induced mood disorder 🅀
                Inhalant-induced depressive disorder
● F18.95   Inhalant use, unspecified with inhalant-
           induced psychotic disorder
      F18.950   Inhalant use, unspecified with
                inhalant-induced psychotic disorder
                with delusions 🅀
      F18.951   Inhalant use, unspecified with
                inhalant-induced psychotic disorder
                with hallucinations 🅀
      F18.959   Inhalant use, unspecified with
                inhalant-induced psychotic disorder,
                unspecified 🅀
  F18.97   Inhalant use, unspecified with inhalant-
           induced persisting dementia 🅀
                Inhalant-induced major neurocognitive
                   disorder

● F18.98   Inhalant use, unspecified with other inhalant-
           induced disorders
      F18.980   Inhalant use, unspecified with
                inhalant-induced anxiety disorder 🅀
      F18.988   Inhalant use, unspecified with other
                inhalant-induced disorder 🅀
                Inhalant-induced mild
                   neurocognitive disorder
  F18.99   Inhalant use, unspecified with unspecified
           inhalant-induced disorder 🅀
● F19   Other psychoactive substance related disorders
      Includes   polysubstance drug use (indiscriminate drug use)
● F19.1   Other psychoactive substance abuse
      Excludes1   other psychoactive substance dependence
                     (F19.2-)
                  other psychoactive substance use,
                     unspecified (F19.9-)
  F19.10   Other psychoactive substance abuse,
           uncomplicated
                Other (or unknown) substance use disorder,
                   mild
  F19.11   Other psychoactive substance abuse,
           in remission
                Other (or unknown) substance use disorder,
                   mild, in early remission
                Other (or unknown) substance use disorder,
                   mild, in sustained remission
● F19.12   Other psychoactive substance abuse with
           intoxication
      F19.120   Other psychoactive substance abuse
                with intoxication, uncomplicated 🅀
      F19.121   Other psychoactive substance abuse
                with intoxication delirium 🅀
      F19.122   Other psychoactive substance abuse
                with intoxication with perceptual
                disturbances 🅀
      F19.129   Other psychoactive substance abuse
                with intoxication, unspecified 🅀
▶● F19.13   Other psychoactive substance abuse with
           withdrawal
    ▶ F19.130   Other psychoactive substance abuse
                with withdrawal, uncomplicated
    ▶ F19.131   Other psychoactive substance abuse
                with withdrawal delirium
    ▶ F19.132   Other psychoactive substance abuse
                with withdrawal with perceptual
                disturbance
    ▶ F19.139   Other psychoactive substance abuse
                with withdrawal, unspecified
  F19.14   Other psychoactive substance abuse with
           psychoactive substance-induced mood
           disorder 🅀
                Other (or unknown) substance use disorder,
                   mild, with other (or unknown) substance-
                   induced bipolar or related disorder
                Other (or unknown) substance use disorder,
                   mild, with other (or unknown) substance-
                   induced depressive disorder
● F19.15   Other psychoactive substance abuse with
           psychoactive substance-induced psychotic
           disorder
      F19.150   Other psychoactive substance abuse
                with psychoactive substance-induced
                psychotic disorder with delusions 🅀
      F19.151   Other psychoactive substance abuse
                with psychoactive substance-induced
                psychotic disorder with
                hallucinations 🅀
      F19.159   Other psychoactive substance abuse
                with psychoactive substance-induced
                psychotic disorder, unspecified 🅀

▶ New   ▶ Revised   d̶e̶l̶e̶t̶e̶d̶ Deleted   Excludes 1   Excludes 2   Includes   Use additional   Code first   Code also   Key words
OGCR Official Guidelines   X Assign placeholder X   ● Use Additional Character(s)   ▶ Manifestation Code   🅀 Hierarchical Condition Category   Coding Clinic

F19.16 Other psychoactive substance abuse with psychoactive substance-induced persisting amnestic disorder 🔍

F19.17 Other psychoactive substance abuse with psychoactive substance-induced persisting dementia 🔍
   Other (or unknown) substance use disorder, mild, with other (or unknown) substance-induced major neurocognitive disorder

● F19.18 Other psychoactive substance abuse with other psychoactive substance-induced disorders

   F19.180 Other psychoactive substance abuse with psychoactive substance-induced anxiety disorder 🔍

   F19.181 Other psychoactive substance abuse with psychoactive substance-induced sexual dysfunction 🔍

   F19.182 Other psychoactive substance abuse with psychoactive substance-induced sleep disorder 🔍

   F19.188 Other psychoactive substance abuse with other psychoactive substance-induced disorder 🔍
      Other (or unknown) substance use disorder, mild, with other (or unknown) substance-induced mild neurocognitive disorder
      Other (or unknown) substance use disorder, mild, with other (or unknown) substance-induced obsessive-compulsive or related disorder

   F19.19 Other psychoactive substance abuse with unspecified psychoactive substance-induced disorder 🔍

● F19.2 Other psychoactive substance dependence
   Excludes1 other psychoactive substance abuse (F19.1-)
      other psychoactive substance use, unspecified (F19.9-)

   F19.20 Other psychoactive substance dependence, uncomplicated 🔍
      Other (or unknown) substance use disorder, moderate
      Other (or unknown) substance use disorder, severe

   F19.21 Other psychoactive substance dependence, in remission 🔍
      Other (or unknown) substance use disorder, moderate, in early remission
      Other (or unknown) substance use disorder, moderate, in sustained remission
      Other (or unknown) substance use disorder, severe, in early remission
      Other (or unknown) substance use disorder, severe, in sustained remission

● F19.22 Other psychoactive substance dependence with intoxication
   Excludes1 other psychoactive substance dependence with withdrawal (F19.23-)

   F19.220 Other psychoactive substance dependence with intoxication, uncomplicated 🔍

   F19.221 Other psychoactive substance dependence with intoxication delirium 🔍

   F19.222 Other psychoactive substance dependence with intoxication with perceptual disturbance 🔍

   F19.229 Other psychoactive substance dependence with intoxication, unspecified 🔍

● F19.23 Other psychoactive substance dependence with withdrawal
   Excludes1 other psychoactive substance dependence with intoxication (F19.22-)

   F19.230 Other psychoactive substance dependence with withdrawal, uncomplicated 🔍

   F19.231 Other psychoactive substance dependence with withdrawal delirium 🔍

   F19.232 Other psychoactive substance dependence with withdrawal with perceptual disturbance 🔍

   F19.239 Other psychoactive substance dependence with withdrawal, unspecified 🔍

F19.24 Other psychoactive substance dependence with psychoactive substance-induced mood disorder 🔍
   Other (or unknown) substance use disorder, moderate, with other (or unknown) substance-induced bipolar or related disorder
   Other (or unknown) substance use disorder, moderate, with other (or unknown) substance-induced depressive disorder
   Other (or unknown) substance use disorder, severe, with other (or unknown) substance-induced bipolar or related disorder
   Other (or unknown) substance use disorder, severe, with other (or unknown) substance-induced depressive disorder

● F19.25 Other psychoactive substance dependence with psychoactive substance-induced psychotic disorder

   F19.250 Other psychoactive substance dependence with psychoactive substance-induced psychotic disorder with delusions 🔍

   F19.251 Other psychoactive substance dependence with psychoactive substance-induced psychotic disorder with hallucinations 🔍

   F19.259 Other psychoactive substance dependence with psychoactive substance-induced psychotic disorder, unspecified 🔍

F19.26 Other psychoactive substance dependence with psychoactive substance-induced persisting amnestic disorder 🔍

F19.27 Other psychoactive substance dependence with psychoactive substance-induced persisting dementia 🔍
   Other (or unknown) substance use disorder, moderate, with other (or unknown) substance-induced major neurocognitive disorder
   Other (or unknown) substance use disorder, severe, with other (or unknown) substance-induced major neurocognitive disorder

● F19.28 Other psychoactive substance dependence with other psychoactive substance-induced disorders

   F19.280 Other psychoactive substance dependence with psychoactive substance-induced anxiety disorder 🔍

   F19.281 Other psychoactive substance dependence with psychoactive substance-induced sexual dysfunction 🔍

   F19.282 Other psychoactive substance dependence with psychoactive substance-induced sleep disorder 🔍

F19.288   Other psychoactive substance dependence with other psychoactive substance-induced disorder 🦠
> Other (or unknown) substance use disorder, moderate, with other (or unknown) substance-induced mild neurocognitive disorder
> Other (or unknown) substance use disorder, severe, with other (or unknown) substance-induced mild neurocognitive disorder
> Other (or unknown) substance use disorder, moderate, with other (or unknown) substance-induced obsessive-compulsive or related disorder
> Other (or unknown) substance use disorder, severe, with other (or unknown) substance-induced obsessive-compulsive or related disorder

F19.29   Other psychoactive substance dependence with unspecified psychoactive substance-induced disorder 🦠

● **F19.9**   Other psychoactive substance use, unspecified
> **Excludes1**   other psychoactive substance abuse (F19.1-)
> other psychoactive substance dependence (F19.2-)

F19.90   Other psychoactive substance use, unspecified, uncomplicated

● **F19.92**   Other psychoactive substance use, unspecified with intoxication
> **Excludes1**   other psychoactive substance use, unspecified with withdrawal (F19.93)

F19.920   Other psychoactive substance use, unspecified with intoxication, uncomplicated 🦠

F19.921   Other psychoactive substance use, unspecified with intoxication with delirium 🦠
> Other (or unknown) substance-induced delirium

F19.922   Other psychoactive substance use, unspecified with intoxication with perceptual disturbance 🦠

F19.929   Other psychoactive substance use, unspecified with intoxication, unspecified 🦠

● **F19.93**   Other psychoactive substance use, unspecified with withdrawal
> **Excludes1**   other psychoactive substance use, unspecified with intoxication (F19.92-)

F19.930   Other psychoactive substance use, unspecified with withdrawal, uncomplicated 🦠

F19.931   Other psychoactive substance use, unspecified with withdrawal delirium 🦠

F19.932   Other psychoactive substance use, unspecified with withdrawal with perceptual disturbance 🦠

F19.939   Other psychoactive substance use, unspecified with withdrawal, unspecified 🦠

F19.94   Other psychoactive substance use, unspecified with psychoactive substance-induced mood disorder 🦠
> Other (or unknown) substance-induced bipolar or related disorder, without use disorder
> Other (or unknown) substance-induced depressive disorder, without use disorder

● **F19.95**   Other psychoactive substance use, unspecified with psychoactive substance-induced psychotic disorder

F19.950   Other psychoactive substance use, unspecified with psychoactive substance-induced psychotic disorder with delusions 🦠

F19.951   Other psychoactive substance use, unspecified with psychoactive substance-induced psychotic disorder with hallucinations 🦠

F19.959   Other psychoactive substance use, unspecified with psychoactive substance-induced psychotic disorder, unspecified 🦠
> Other or unknown substance-induced psychotic disorder, without use disorder

F19.96   Other psychoactive substance use, unspecified with psychoactive substance-induced persisting amnestic disorder 🦠

F19.97   Other psychoactive substance use, unspecified with psychoactive substance-induced persisting dementia 🦠
> Other (or unknown) substance-induced major neurocognitive disorder, without use disorder

● **F19.98**   Other psychoactive substance use, unspecified with other psychoactive substance-induced disorders

F19.980   Other psychoactive substance use, unspecified with psychoactive substance-induced anxiety disorder 🦠
> Other (or unknown) substance-induced anxiety disorder, without use disorder

F19.981   Other psychoactive substance use, unspecified with psychoactive substance-induced sexual dysfunction 🦠
> Other (or unknown) substance-induced sexual dysfunction, without use disorder

F19.982   Other psychoactive substance use, unspecified with psychoactive substance-induced sleep disorder 🦠
> Other (or unknown) substance-induced sleep disorder, without use disorder

F19.988   Other psychoactive substance use, unspecified with other psychoactive substance-induced disorder 🦠
> Other (or unknown) substance-induced mild neurocognitive disorder, without use disorder
> Other (or unknown) substance-induced obsessive-compulsive or related disorder, without use disorder

F19.99   Other psychoactive substance use, unspecified with unspecified psychoactive substance-induced disorder 🦠

▶ New   ⇒ Revised   ~~deleted~~ Deleted   Excludes 1   Excludes 2   Includes   Use additional   Code first   Code also   Key words

OGCR Official Guidelines   X Assign placeholder X   ● Use Additional Character(s)   ▶ Manifestation Code   🦠 Hierarchical Condition Category   **Coding Clinic**

SCHIZOPHRENIA, SCHIZOTYPAL, DELUSIONAL, AND OTHER NON-MOOD PSYCHOTIC DISORDERS (F20-F29)

● **F20**   **Schizophrenia**

Personality disorders characterized by multiple mental and behavioral irregularities (may exhibit disorganized thinking, delusions, and auditory hallucinations)

Excludes1   brief psychotic disorder (F23)
cyclic schizophrenia (F25.0)
mood [affective] disorders with psychotic symptoms (F30.2, F31.2, F31.5, F31.64, F32.3, F33.3)
schizoaffective disorder (F25.-)
schizophrenic reaction NOS (F23)

Excludes2   schizophrenic reaction in:
alcoholism (F10.15-, F10.25-, F10.95-)
brain disease (F06.2)
epilepsy (F06.2)
psychoactive drug use (F11-F19 with .15, .25, .95)
schizotypal disorder (F21)

Coding Clinic: 2019, Q2, P32

F20.0   **Paranoid schizophrenia** 🔍
Paraphrenic schizophrenia

    Excludes1   involutional paranoid state (F22)
paranoia (F22)

F20.1   **Disorganized schizophrenia** 🔍
Hebephrenic schizophrenia
Hebephrenia

F20.2   **Catatonic schizophrenia** 🔍
Schizophrenic catalepsy
Schizophrenic catatonia
Schizophrenic flexibilitas cerea

    Excludes1   catatonic stupor (R40.1)

F20.3   **Undifferentiated schizophrenia** 🔍
Atypical schizophrenia

    Excludes1   acute schizophrenia-like psychotic disorder (F23)

    Excludes2   post-schizophrenic depression (F32.89)

F20.5   **Residual schizophrenia** 🔍
Restzustand (schizophrenic)
Schizophrenic residual state

● **F20.8**   **Other schizophrenia**

F20.81   **Schizophreniform disorder** 🔍
Schizophreniform psychosis NOS

F20.89   **Other schizophrenia** 🔍
Cenesthopathic schizophrenia
Simple schizophrenia

F20.9   **Schizophrenia, unspecified** 🔍
Coding Clinic: 2019, Q2, P32

F21   **Schizotypal disorder**

Personality disorder characterized by need for social isolation, odd behavior and thinking, and often unconventional beliefs

Borderline schizophrenia
Latent schizophrenia
Latent schizophrenic reaction
Prepsychotic schizophrenia
Prodromal schizophrenia
Pseudoneurotic schizophrenia
Pseudopsychopathic schizophrenia
Schizotypal personality disorder

    Excludes2   Asperger's syndrome (F84.5)
schizoid personality disorder (F60.1)

F22   **Delusional disorders** 🔍
Delusional dysmorphophobia
Involutional paranoid state
Paranoia
Paranoia querulans
Paranoid psychosis
Paranoid state
Paraphrenia (late)
Sensitiver Beziehungswahn

    Excludes1   mood [affective] disorders with psychotic symptoms (F30.2, F31.2, F31.5, F31.64, F32.3, F33.3)
paranoid schizophrenia (F20.0)

    Excludes2   paranoid personality disorder (F60.0)
paranoid psychosis, psychogenic (F23)
paranoid reaction (F23)

F23   **Brief psychotic disorder**
Paranoid reaction
Psychogenic paranoid psychosis

    Excludes2   mood [affective] disorders with psychotic symptoms (F30.2, F31.2, F31.5, F31.64, F32.3, F33.3)

Coding Clinic: 2019, Q2, P32

F24   **Shared psychotic disorder** 🔍
Folie à deux
Induced paranoid disorder
Induced psychotic disorder

● **F25**   **Schizoaffective disorders**

Mental disorder exhibiting major depressive episode, manic episode, or mixed episode occurs with symptoms of schizophrenia, and mood disorder

    Excludes1   mood [affective] disorders with psychotic symptoms (F30.2, F31.2, F31.5, F31.64, F32.3, F33.3)
schizophrenia (F20.-)

F25.0   **Schizoaffective disorder, bipolar type** 🔍
Cyclic schizophrenia
Schizoaffective disorder, manic type
Schizoaffective disorder, mixed type
Schizoaffective psychosis, bipolar type

F25.1   **Schizoaffective disorder, depressive type** 🔍
Schizoaffective psychosis, depressive type

F25.8   **Other schizoaffective disorders** 🔍

F25.9   **Schizoaffective disorder, unspecified** 🔍
Schizoaffective psychosis NOS

F28   **Other psychotic disorder not due to a substance or known physiological condition**
Chronic hallucinatory psychosis
Other specified schizophrenia spectrum and other psychotic disorder

F29   **Unspecified psychosis not due to a substance or known physiological condition**
Psychosis NOS
Unspecified schizophrenia spectrum and other psychotic disorder

    Excludes1   mental disorder NOS (F99)
unspecified mental disorder due to known physiological condition (F09)

CHAPTER 5 (F01-F99)

MOOD [AFFECTIVE] DISORDERS (F30-F39)

● **F30** **Manic episode**
Elevated, expansive, or irritable mood

> **Includes**   bipolar disorder, single manic episode
> mixed affective episode

> **Excludes1**   bipolar disorder (F31.-)
> major depressive disorder, single episode (F32.-)
> major depressive disorder, recurrent (F33.-)

  ● **F30.1** **Manic episode without psychotic symptoms**

    F30.10 **Manic episode without psychotic symptoms, unspecified** 🐾

    F30.11 **Manic episode without psychotic symptoms, mild** 🐾

    F30.12 **Manic episode without psychotic symptoms, moderate** 🐾

    F30.13 **Manic episode, severe, without psychotic symptoms** 🐾

  F30.2 **Manic episode, severe with psychotic symptoms** 🐾
> Manic stupor
> Mania with mood-congruent psychotic symptoms
> Mania with mood-incongruent psychotic symptoms

  F30.3 **Manic episode in partial remission** 🐾
  F30.4 **Manic episode in full remission** 🐾
  F30.8 **Other manic episodes** 🐾
> *Abnormality of mood resembling mania but less intense*
> Hypomania

  F30.9 **Manic episode, unspecified** 🐾
> Mania NOS

● **F31** **Bipolar disorder**
Mood disorders with history of manic, mixed, or hypomanic episodes

> **Includes**   bipolar I disorder
> bipolar type I disorder
> manic-depressive illness
> manic-depressive psychosis
> manic-depressive reaction

> **Excludes1**   bipolar disorder, single manic episode (F30.-)
> major depressive disorder, single episode (F32.-)
> major depressive disorder, recurrent (F33.-)

> **Excludes2**   cyclothymia (F34.0)

> **Coding Clinic: 2020, Q1, P23**

  F31.0 **Bipolar disorder, current episode hypomanic** 🐾
  ● **F31.1** **Bipolar disorder, current episode manic without psychotic features**

    F31.10 **Bipolar disorder, current episode manic without psychotic features, unspecified** 🐾

    F31.11 **Bipolar disorder, current episode manic without psychotic features, mild** 🐾

    F31.12 **Bipolar disorder, current episode manic without psychotic features, moderate** 🐾

    F31.13 **Bipolar disorder, current episode manic without psychotic features, severe** 🐾

  F31.2 **Bipolar disorder, current episode manic severe with psychotic features** 🐾
> Bipolar disorder, current episode manic with mood-congruent psychotic symptoms
> Bipolar disorder, current episode manic with mood-incongruent psychotic symptoms
> Bipolar I disorder, current or most recent episode manic with psychotic features

  ● **F31.3** **Bipolar disorder, current episode depressed, mild or moderate severity**

    F31.30 **Bipolar disorder, current episode depressed, mild or moderate severity, unspecified** 🐾

    F31.31 **Bipolar disorder, current episode depressed, mild** 🐾

    F31.32 **Bipolar disorder, current episode depressed, moderate** 🐾

  F31.4 **Bipolar disorder, current episode depressed, severe, without psychotic features** 🐾

  F31.5 **Bipolar disorder, current episode depressed, severe, with psychotic features** 🐾
> Bipolar disorder, current episode depressed with mood-incongruent psychotic symptoms
> Bipolar disorder, current episode depressed with mood-congruent psychotic symptoms
> Bipolar I disorder, current or most recent episode depressed, with psychotic features

  ● **F31.6** **Bipolar disorder, current episode mixed**

    F31.60 **Bipolar disorder, current episode mixed, unspecified** 🐾

    F31.61 **Bipolar disorder, current episode mixed, mild** 🐾

    F31.62 **Bipolar disorder, current episode mixed, moderate** 🐾

    F31.63 **Bipolar disorder, current episode mixed, severe, without psychotic features** 🐾

    F31.64 **Bipolar disorder, current episode mixed, severe, with psychotic features** 🐾
> Bipolar disorder, current episode mixed with mood-congruent psychotic symptoms
> Bipolar disorder, current episode mixed with mood-incongruent psychotic symptoms

  ● **F31.7** **Bipolar disorder, currently in remission**

    F31.70 **Bipolar disorder, currently in remission, most recent episode unspecified** 🐾

    F31.71 **Bipolar disorder, in partial remission, most recent episode hypomanic** 🐾

    F31.72 **Bipolar disorder, in full remission, most recent episode hypomanic** 🐾

    F31.73 **Bipolar disorder, in partial remission, most recent episode manic** 🐾

    F31.74 **Bipolar disorder, in full remission, most recent episode manic** 🐾

    F31.75 **Bipolar disorder, in partial remission, most recent episode depressed** 🐾

    F31.76 **Bipolar disorder, in full remission, most recent episode depressed** 🐾

    F31.77 **Bipolar disorder, in partial remission, most recent episode mixed** 🐾

    F31.78 **Bipolar disorder, in full remission, most recent episode mixed** 🐾

  ● **F31.8** **Other bipolar disorders**

    F31.81 **Bipolar II disorder** 🐾
> Bipolar disorder, type 2

    F31.89 **Other bipolar disorder** 🐾
> Recurrent manic episodes NOS

  F31.9 **Bipolar disorder, unspecified** 🐾
> Manic depression
> **Coding Clinic: 2020, Q1, P23**

● **F32** **Major depressive disorder, single episode**

> **Includes**   single episode of agitated depression
> single episode of depressive reaction
> single episode of major depression
> single episode of psychogenic depression
> single episode of reactive depression
> single episode of vital depression

> **Excludes1**   bipolar disorder (F31.-)
> manic episode (F30.-)
> recurrent depressive disorder (F33.-)

> **Excludes2**   adjustment disorder (F43.2)

  F32.0 **Major depressive disorder, single episode, mild** 🐾
  F32.1 **Major depressive disorder, single episode, moderate** 🐾
  F32.2 **Major depressive disorder, single episode, severe without psychotic features** 🐾

▶ New   ⟹ Revised   ~~deleted~~ Deleted   Excludes 1   Excludes 2   Includes   Use additional   Code first   Code also   Key words

OGCR Official Guidelines   X Assign placeholder X   ● Use Additional Character(s)   ⟩ Manifestation Code   🐾 Hierarchical Condition Category   **Coding Clinic**

F32.3   **Major depressive disorder, single episode, severe with psychotic features** 🔖
  Single episode of major depression with mood-congruent psychotic symptoms
  Single episode of major depression with mood-incongruent psychotic symptoms
  Single episode of major depression with psychotic symptoms
  Single episode of psychogenic depressive psychosis
  Single episode of psychotic depression
  Single episode of reactive depressive psychosis

F32.4   **Major depressive disorder, single episode, in partial remission** 🔖

F32.5   **Major depressive disorder, single episode, in full remission** 🔖

●**F32.8**   **Other depressive episodes**

      F32.81   **Premenstrual dysphoric disorder** ♀
           Excludes1   premenstrual tension syndrome (N94.3)
           Coding Clinic: 2016, Q4, P14

      F32.89   **Other specified depressive episodes**
           Atypical depression
           Post-schizophrenic depression
           Single episode of 'masked' depression NOS
           Coding Clinic: 2016, Q4, P14

F32.9   **Major depressive disorder, single episode, unspecified**
  Depression NOS
  Depressive disorder NOS
  Major depression NOS

●**F33**   **Major depressive disorder, recurrent**
      Includes   recurrent episodes of depressive reaction
           recurrent episodes of endogenous depression
           recurrent episodes of major depression
           recurrent episodes of psychogenic depression
           recurrent episodes of reactive depression
           recurrent episodes of seasonal depressive disorder
           recurrent episodes of vital depression

      Excludes1   bipolar disorder (F31.-)
           manic episode (F30.-)
      Coding Clinic: 2020, Q1, P23

F33.0   **Major depressive disorder, recurrent, mild** 🔖

F33.1   **Major depressive disorder, recurrent, moderate** 🔖

F33.2   **Major depressive disorder, recurrent severe without psychotic features** 🔖

F33.3   **Major depressive disorder, recurrent, severe with psychotic symptoms** 🔖
  Endogenous depression with psychotic symptoms
  Major depressive disorder, recurrent, with psychotic features
  Recurrent severe episodes of major depression with mood-congruent psychotic symptoms
  Recurrent severe episodes of major depression with mood-incongruent psychotic symptoms
  Recurrent severe episodes of major depression with psychotic symptoms
  Recurrent severe episodes of psychogenic depressive psychosis
  Recurrent severe episodes of psychotic depression
  Recurrent severe episodes of reactive depressive psychosis

●**F33.4**   **Major depressive disorder, recurrent, in remission**

      F33.40   **Major depressive disorder, recurrent, in remission, unspecified** 🔖

      F33.41   **Major depressive disorder, recurrent, in partial remission** 🔖

      F33.42   **Major depressive disorder, recurrent, in full remission** 🔖

F33.8   **Other recurrent depressive disorders** 🔖
  Recurrent brief depressive episodes

F33.9   **Major depressive disorder, recurrent, unspecified** 🔖
  Monopolar depression NOS

Figure 5-1   PET scan of depressed individual's brain before and after recovery. (From Fortinash KM: Psychiatric Mental Health Nursing, ed 4, St. Louis, Mosby, 2008)

●**F34**   **Persistent mood [affective] disorders**

      F34.0   **Cyclothymic disorder**
           Affective personality disorder
           Cycloid personality
           Cyclothymia
           Cyclothymic personality

      F34.1   **Dysthymic disorder**
           Depressive neurosis
           Depressive personality disorder
           Dysthymia
           Neurotic depression
           Persistent anxiety depression
           Persistent depressive disorder
           Excludes2   anxiety depression (mild or not persistent) (F41.8)

●**F34.8**   **Other persistent mood [affective] disorders**

      F34.81   **Disruptive mood dysregulation disorder** 🔖
           Coding Clinic: 2016, Q4, P14

      F34.89   **Other specified persistent mood disorders** 🔖
           Coding Clinic: 2016, Q4, P14

      F34.9   **Persistent mood [affective] disorder, unspecified** 🔖

F39   **Unspecified mood [affective] disorder** 🔖
  Affective psychosis NOS

ANXIETY, DISSOCIATIVE, STRESS-RELATED, SOMATOFORM AND OTHER NONPSYCHOTIC MENTAL DISORDERS (F40-F48)

●**F40**   **Phobic anxiety disorders**
      Irrational fear with avoidance of the feared subject, activity, or situation even though the individual knows that the reaction is excessive

●**F40.0**   **Agoraphobia**
      Intense, irrational fear of open spaces

      F40.00   **Agoraphobia, unspecified**

      F40.01   **Agoraphobia with panic disorder**
           Panic disorder with agoraphobia
           Excludes1   panic disorder without agoraphobia (F41.0)

      F40.02   **Agoraphobia without panic disorder**

●**F40.1**   **Social phobias**
      Anthropophobia
      Social anxiety disorder
      Social anxiety disorder of childhood
      Social neurosis

      F40.10   **Social phobia, unspecified**

      F40.11   **Social phobia, generalized**

● **F40.2**   **Specific (isolated) phobias**
     Excludes2   dysmorphophobia (nondelusional) (F45.22)
                  nosophobia (F45.22)
   ● **F40.21**   **Animal type phobia**
       F40.210   **Arachnophobia**
             Fear of spiders
       F40.218   **Other animal type phobia**
   ● **F40.22**   **Natural environment type phobia**
       F40.220   **Fear of thunderstorms**
       F40.228   **Other natural environment type phobia**
   ● **F40.23**   **Blood, injection, injury type phobia**
       F40.230   **Fear of blood**
       F40.231   **Fear of injections and transfusions**
       F40.232   **Fear of other medical care**
       F40.233   **Fear of injury**
   ● **F40.24**   **Situational type phobia**
       F40.240   **Claustrophobia**
             Fear of closed spaces
       F40.241   **Acrophobia**
             Fear of heights
       F40.242   **Fear of bridges**
       F40.243   **Fear of flying**
       F40.248   **Other situational type phobia**
   ● **F40.29**   **Other specified phobia**
       F40.290   **Androphobia**
             Fear of men
       F40.291   **Gynephobia**
             Fear of women
       F40.298   **Other specified phobia**
   F40.8   **Other phobic anxiety disorders**
       Phobic anxiety disorder of childhood
   F40.9   **Phobic anxiety disorder, unspecified**
       Phobia NOS
       Phobic state NOS

● **F41**   **Other anxiety disorders**
     Excludes2   anxiety in:
                  acute stress reaction (F43.0)
                  transient adjustment reaction (F43.2)
                  neurasthenia (F48.8)
                  psychophysiologic disorders (F45.-)
                  separation anxiety (F93.0)
   F41.0   **Panic disorder [episodic paroxysmal anxiety]**
       Panic attack
       Panic state
       Excludes1   panic disorder with agoraphobia (F40.01)
   F41.1   **Generalized anxiety disorder**
       Anxiety neurosis
       Anxiety reaction
       Anxiety state
       Overanxious disorder
       Excludes2   neurasthenia (F48.8)
   F41.3   **Other mixed anxiety disorders**
   F41.8   **Other specified anxiety disorders**
       Anxiety depression (mild or not persistent)
       Anxiety hysteria
       Mixed anxiety and depressive disorder
   F41.9   **Anxiety disorder, unspecified**
       Anxiety NOS

● **F42**   **Obsessive-compulsive disorder**
     Anxiety disorder with recurrent obsessions or compulsions
     Excludes2   obsessive-compulsive personality (disorder) (F60.5)
                  obsessive-compulsive symptoms occurring in depression (F32-F33)
                  obsessive-compulsive symptoms occurring in schizophrenia (F20.-)
   F42.2   **Mixed obsessional thoughts and acts**
       Coding Clinic: 2016, Q4, P15
   F42.3   **Hoarding disorder**
       Coding Clinic: 2016, Q4, P14-15
   F42.4   **Excoriation (skin-picking) disorder**
       Excludes1   factitial dermatitis (L98.1)
                  other specified behavioral and emotional disorders with onset usually occurring in early childhood and adolescence (F98.8)
       Coding Clinic: 2016, Q4, P14-15
   F42.8   **Other obsessive-compulsive disorder**
       Anancastic neurosis
       Obsessive-compulsive neurosis
       Coding Clinic: 2016, Q4, P15
   F42.9   **Obsessive-compulsive disorder, unspecified**
       Coding Clinic: 2016, Q4, P15

● **F43**   **Reaction to severe stress and adjustment disorders**
   F43.0   **Acute stress reaction**
       Acute crisis reaction
       Acute reaction to stress
       Combat and operational stress reaction
       Combat fatigue
       Crisis state
       Psychic shock
   ● **F43.1**   **Post-traumatic stress disorder (PTSD)**
       Traumatic neurosis
       F43.10   **Post-traumatic stress disorder, unspecified**
       F43.11   **Post-traumatic stress disorder, acute**
       F43.12   **Post-traumatic stress disorder, chronic**
   ● **F43.2**   **Adjustment disorders**
       Culture shock
       Grief reaction
       Hospitalism in children
       Excludes2   separation anxiety disorder of childhood (F93.0)
       F43.20   **Adjustment disorder, unspecified**
       F43.21   **Adjustment disorder with depressed mood**
       F43.22   **Adjustment disorder with anxiety**
       F43.23   **Adjustment disorder with mixed anxiety and depressed mood**
       F43.24   **Adjustment disorder with disturbance of conduct**
       F43.25   **Adjustment disorder with mixed disturbance of emotions and conduct**
       F43.29   **Adjustment disorder with other symptoms**
   F43.8   **Other reactions to severe stress**
       Other specified trauma and stressor-related disorder
   F43.9   **Reaction to severe stress, unspecified**
       Trauma and stressor-related disorder, NOS

▶ New   ⇒ Revised   ~~deleted~~ Deleted   Excludes 1   Excludes 2   Includes   Use additional   Code first   Code also   Key words
OGCR Official Guidelines   X Assign placeholder X   ● Use Additional Character(s)   ▶ Manifestation Code   🏷 Hierarchical Condition Category   **Coding Clinic**

● **F44   Dissociative and conversion disorders**

> **Includes**   conversion hysteria
> conversion reaction
> hysteria
> hysterical psychosis

> **Excludes2**   malingering [conscious simulation] (Z76.5)

F44.0   Dissociative amnesia
Sudden loss of memory for personal information

> **Excludes1**   amnesia NOS (R41.3)
> anterograde amnesia (R41.1)
> dissociative amnesia with dissociative fugue (F44.1)
> retrograde amnesia (R41.2)

> **Excludes2**   alcohol or other psychoactive substance-induced amnestic disorder (F10, F13, F19 with .26, .96)
> amnestic disorder due to known physiological condition (F04)
> postictal amnesia in epilepsy (G40.-)

F44.1   Dissociative fugue
Characterized by episode of sudden, unexpected travel with amnesia for past and partial to total confusion about identity or assumption of new identity
Dissociative amnesia with dissociative fugue

> **Excludes2**   postictal fugue in epilepsy (G40.-)

F44.2   Dissociative stupor
Profound diminution or absence of voluntary movement and responsiveness to external stimuli

> **Excludes1**   catatonic stupor (R40.1)
> stupor NOS (R40.1)

> **Excludes2**   catatonic disorder due to known physiological condition (F06.1)
> depressive stupor (F32, F33)
> manic stupor (F30, F31)

F44.4   Conversion disorder with motor symptom or deficit
Conversion disorder with abnormal movement
Conversion disorder with speech symptoms
Conversion disorder with swallowing symptoms
Conversion disorder with weakness/paralysis
Dissociative motor disorders
Psychogenic aphonia
Psychogenic dysphonia

F44.5   Conversion disorder with seizures or convulsions
Conversion disorder with attacks or seizures
Dissociative convulsions
Coding Clinic: 2019, Q1, P19

F44.6   Conversion disorder with sensory symptom or deficit
Conversion disorder with anesthesia or sensory loss
Conversion disorder with special sensory symptoms
Dissociative anesthesia and sensory loss
Psychogenic deafness

F44.7   Conversion disorder with mixed symptom presentation

● **F44.8   Other dissociative and conversion disorders**

F44.81   Dissociative identity disorder
Multiple personality disorder

F44.89   Other dissociative and conversion disorders
Ganser's syndrome
Psychogenic confusion
Psychogenic twilight state
Trance and possession disorders

F44.9   Dissociative and conversion disorder, unspecified
Dissociative disorder NOS

OGCR Section I.C.5.a.

Pain disorders related to psychological factors
Assign code F45.41, for pain that is exclusively related to psychological disorders. As indicated by the Excludes 1 note under category G89, a code from category G89 should not be assigned with code F45.41 Code F45.42, Pain disorders with related psychological factors, should be used with a code from category G89, Pain, not elsewhere classified, if there is documentation of a psychological component for a patient with acute or chronic pain.
See Section I.C.6. Pain

● **F45   Somatoform disorders**
Mental disorders characterized by symptoms suggesting general medical condition

> **Excludes2**   dissociative and conversion disorders (F44.-)
> factitious disorders (F68.1-, F68.A)
> hair-plucking (F63.3)
> lalling (F80.0)
> lisping (F80.0)
> malingering [conscious simulation] (Z76.5)
> nail-biting (F98.8)
> psychological or behavioral factors associated with disorders or diseases classified elsewhere (F54)
> sexual dysfunction, not due to a substance or known physiological condition (F52.-)
> thumb-sucking (F98.8)
> tic disorders (in childhood and adolescence) (F95.-)
> Tourette's syndrome (F95.2)
> trichotillomania (F63.3)

F45.0   Somatization disorder
Briquet's disorder
Multiple psychosomatic disorder

F45.1   Undifferentiated somatoform disorder
Somatic symptom disorder
Undifferentiated psychosomatic disorder

● **F45.2   Hypochondriacal disorders**
Persistent, unrealistic preoccupation with possibility of having serious disease

> **Excludes2**   delusional dysmorphophobia (F22)
> fixed delusions about bodily functions or shape (F22)

F45.20   Hypochondriacal disorder, unspecified

F45.21   Hypochondriasis
Hypochondriacal neurosis
Illness anxiety disorder

F45.22   Body dysmorphic disorder
Dysmorphophobia (nondelusional)
Nosophobia

F45.29   Other hypochondriacal disorders

● **F45.4   Pain disorders related to psychological factors**

> **Excludes1**   pain NOS (R52)

F45.41   Pain disorder exclusively related to psychological factors
Somatoform pain disorder (persistent)

F45.42   Pain disorder with related psychological factors
Code also associated acute or chronic pain (G89.-)

F45.8   Other somatoform disorders
Psychogenic dysmenorrhea
Psychogenic dysphagia, including 'globus hystericus'
Psychogenic pruritus
Psychogenic torticollis
Somatoform autonomic dysfunction
Teeth grinding

> **Excludes1**   sleep related teeth grinding (G47.63)
> **Coding Clinic: 2016, Q4, P118**

F45.9   Somatoform disorder, unspecified
Psychosomatic disorder NOS

● **F48   Other nonpsychotic mental disorders**

F48.1   Depersonalization-derealization syndrome

F48.2   Pseudobulbar affect
Involuntary emotional expression disorder
Code first underlying cause, if known, such as:
amyotrophic lateral sclerosis (G12.21)
multiple sclerosis (G35)
sequelae of cerebrovascular disease (I69.-)
sequelae of traumatic intracranial injury (S06.-)

CHAPTER 5 (F01-F99)

F48.8   **Other specified nonpsychotic mental disorders**
     Dhat syndrome
     Neurasthenia
     Occupational neurosis, including writer's cramp
     Psychasthenia
     Psychasthenic neurosis
     Psychogenic syncope

F48.9   **Nonpsychotic mental disorder, unspecified**
     Neurosis NOS

BEHAVIORAL SYNDROMES ASSOCIATED WITH PHYSIOLOGICAL DISTURBANCES AND PHYSICAL FACTORS (F50-F59)

● **F50**   **Eating disorders**
     Excludes1   anorexia NOS (R63.0)
          feeding difficulties (R63.3)
          feeding problems of newborn (P92.-)
          polyphagia (R63.2)
     Excludes2   feeding disorder in infancy or childhood (F98.2-)

● **F50.0**   **Anorexia nervosa**
       Excludes1   loss of appetite (R63.0)
            psychogenic loss of appetite (F50.89)

       F50.00   **Anorexia nervosa, unspecified**

       F50.01   **Anorexia nervosa, restricting type**

       F50.02   **Anorexia nervosa, binge eating/purging type**
           Excludes1   bulimia nervosa (F50.2)

   F50.2   **Bulimia nervosa**
       Bulimia NOS
       Hyperorexia nervosa
       Excludes1   anorexia nervosa, binge eating/purging type (F50.02)

● **F50.8**   **Other eating disorders**
       Excludes2   pica of infancy and childhood (F98.3)

       F50.81   **Binge eating disorder**
          Coding Clinic: 2016, Q4, P15

       F50.82   **Avoidant/restrictive food intake disorder**

       F50.89   **Other specified eating disorder**
          Pica in adults
          Psychogenic loss of appetite
          Coding Clinic: 2016, Q4, P16

   F50.9   **Eating disorder, unspecified**
       Atypical anorexia nervosa
       Atypical bulimia nervosa
       Feeding or eating disorder, unspecified
       Other specified feeding disorder

● **F51**   **Sleep disorders not due to a substance or known physiological condition**
     Excludes2   organic sleep disorders (G47.-)

● **F51.0**   **Insomnia not due to a substance or known physiological condition**
       Excludes2   alcohol related insomnia (F10.182, F10.282, F10.982)
           drug-related insomnia (F11.182, F11.282, F11.982, F13.182, F13.282, F13.982, F14.182, F14.282, F14.982, F15.182, F15.282, F15.982, F19.182, F19.282, F19.982)
           insomnia NOS (G47.0-)
           insomnia due to known physiological condition (G47.0-)
           organic insomnia (G47.0-)
           sleep deprivation (Z72.820)

       F51.01   **Primary insomnia**
          Idiopathic insomnia

       F51.02   **Adjustment insomnia**

       F51.03   **Paradoxical insomnia**

       F51.04   **Psychophysiologic insomnia**

       F51.05   **Insomnia due to other mental disorder**
          Code also associated mental disorder

       F51.09   **Other insomnia not due to a substance or known physiological condition**

● **F51.1**   **Hypersomnia not due to a substance or known physiological condition**
       Hypersomnia: Excessive sleeping/sleepiness
       Excludes2   alcohol related hypersomnia (F10.182, F10.282, F10.982)
           drug-related hypersomnia (F11.182, F11.282, F11.982, F13.182, F13.282, F13.982, F14.182, F14.282, F14.982, F15.182, F15.282, F15.982, F19.182, F19.282, F19.982)
           hypersomnia NOS (G47.10)
           hypersomnia due to known physiological condition (G47.10)
           idiopathic hypersomnia (G47.11, G47.12)
           narcolepsy (G47.4-)

       F51.11   **Primary hypersomnia**

       F51.12   **Insufficient sleep syndrome**
          Excludes1   sleep deprivation (Z72.820)

       F51.13   **Hypersomnia due to other mental disorder**
          Code also associated mental disorder

       F51.19   **Other hypersomnia not due to a substance or known physiological condition**

   F51.3   **Sleepwalking [somnambulism]**
       Non-rapid eye movement sleep arousal disorders, sleepwalking type

   F51.4   **Sleep terrors [night terrors]**
       Non-rapid eye movement sleep arousal disorders, sleep terror type

   F51.5   **Nightmare disorder**
       Dream anxiety disorder

   F51.8   **Other sleep disorders not due to a substance or known physiological condition**

   F51.9   **Sleep disorder not due to a substance or known physiological condition, unspecified**
       Emotional sleep disorder NOS

● **F52**   **Sexual dysfunction not due to a substance or known physiological condition**
     Excludes2   Dhat syndrome (F48.8)

   F52.0   **Hypoactive sexual desire disorder**
       Total loss of feeling of sexual pleasure
       Lack or loss of sexual desire
       Male hypoactive sexual desire disorder
       Sexual anhedonia
       Excludes1   decreased libido (R68.82)

   F52.1   **Sexual aversion disorder**
       Sexual aversion and lack of sexual enjoyment

● **F52.2**   **Sexual arousal disorders**
       Failure of genital response

       F52.21   **Male erectile disorder ♂**
          Erectile disorder
          Psychogenic impotence
          Excludes1   impotence of organic origin (N52.-)
              impotence NOS (N52.-)

       F52.22   **Female sexual arousal disorder ♀**
          Female sexual interest/arousal disorder

● **F52.3**   **Orgasmic disorder**
       Inhibited orgasm
       Psychogenic anorgasmy

       F52.31   **Female orgasmic disorder ♀**

       F52.32   **Male orgasmic disorder ♂**
          Delayed ejaculation

   F52.4   **Premature ejaculation ♂**

▶ New   ⇒ Revised   ~~deleted~~ Deleted   Excludes 1   Excludes 2   Includes   Use additional   Code first   Code also   Key words

786   OGCR Official Guidelines   X Assign placeholder X   ● Use Additional Character(s)   ▶ Manifestation Code   Ⓗⓒ Hierarchical Condition Category   **Coding Clinic**

F52.5   **Vaginismus not due to a substance or known physiological condition ♀**
Psychogenic vaginismus

> **Excludes2**   vaginismus (due to a known physiological condition) (N94.2)

F52.6   **Dyspareunia not due to a substance or known physiological condition**
Dyspareunia: Difficult or painful sexual intercourse
Genito-pelvic pain penetration disorder
Psychogenic dyspareunia

> **Excludes2**   dyspareunia (due to a known physiological condition) (N94.1-)

F52.8   **Other sexual dysfunction not due to a substance or known physiological condition**
Excessive sexual drive
Nymphomania
Satyriasis

F52.9   **Unspecified sexual dysfunction not due to a substance or known physiological condition**
Sexual dysfunction NOS

● **F53**   **Mental and behavioral disorders associated with the puerperium, not elsewhere classified**
Acute mental illness with sudden onset following childbirth with symptoms of affective psychosis, disorientation, and confusion are prevalent

> **Excludes1**   mood disorders with psychotic features (F30.2, F31.2, F31.5, F31.64, F32.3, F33.3)
> postpartum dysphoria (O90.6)
> psychosis in schizophrenia, schizotypal, delusional, and other psychotic disorders (F20-F29)

F53.0   **Postpartum depression ♀**   **M**
Postnatal depression, NOS
Postpartum depression, NOS
Coding Clinic: 2018, Q4, P8

F53.1   **Puerperal psychosis ♀**   **M**
Postpartum psychosis
Puerperal psychosis, NOS
Coding Clinic: 2018, Q4, P9

▷ *F54*   *Psychological and behavioral factors associated with disorders or diseases classified elsewhere*
Psychological factors affecting physical conditions

> *Code first the associated physical disorder, such as:*
> asthma (J45.-)
> dermatitis (L23-L25)
> gastric ulcer (K25.-)
> mucous colitis (K58.-)
> ulcerative colitis (K51.-)
> urticaria (L50.-)

> **Excludes2**   tension-type headache (G44.2)

● **F55**   **Abuse of non-psychoactive substances**

> **Excludes2**   abuse of psychoactive substances (F10-F19)

F55.0   **Abuse of antacids**

F55.1   **Abuse of herbal or folk remedies**

F55.2   **Abuse of laxatives**

F55.3   **Abuse of steroids or hormones**

F55.4   **Abuse of vitamins**

F55.8   **Abuse of other non-psychoactive substances**

F59   **Unspecified behavioral syndromes associated with physiological disturbances and physical factors**
Psychogenic physiological dysfunction NOS

DISORDERS OF ADULT PERSONALITY AND BEHAVIOR (F60-F69)

● **F60**   **Specific personality disorders**
Long-term patterns of thoughts and behaviors causing serious problems with relationships and work

F60.0   **Paranoid personality disorder**
Hostile, devious, and combative response to disappointments
Expansive paranoid personality (disorder)
Fanatic personality (disorder)
Querulant personality (disorder)
Paranoid personality (disorder)
Sensitive paranoid personality (disorder)

> **Excludes2**   paranoia (F22)
> paranoia querulans (F22)
> paranoid psychosis (F22)
> paranoid schizophrenia (F20.0)
> paranoid state (F22)

F60.1   **Schizoid personality disorder**
Detachment from social relationships with minimal emotional experiences and expressions

> **Excludes2**   Asperger's syndrome (F84.5)
> delusional disorder (F22)
> schizoid disorder of childhood (F84.5)
> schizophrenia (F20.-)
> schizotypal disorder (F21)

F60.2   **Antisocial personality disorder**
Continuous and chronic antisocial behavior
Amoral personality (disorder)
Asocial personality (disorder)
Dissocial personality disorder
Psychopathic personality (disorder)
Sociopathic personality (disorder)

> **Excludes1**   conduct disorders (F91.-)
> **Excludes2**   borderline personality disorder (F60.3)

F60.3   **Borderline personality disorder**
Instability of mood, self-image or sense of self, and interpersonal relationships
Aggressive personality (disorder)
Emotionally unstable personality disorder
Explosive personality (disorder)

> **Excludes2**   antisocial personality disorder (F60.2)

F60.4   **Histrionic personality disorder**
Personality disorder with excessive emotional and attention-seeking behavior
Hysterical personality (disorder)
Psychoinfantile personality (disorder)

F60.5   **Obsessive-compulsive personality disorder**
Anankastic personality (disorder)
Compulsive personality (disorder)
Obsessional personality (disorder)

> ➡ **Excludes2**   obsessive-compulsive disorder (F42.-)

F60.6   **Avoidant personality disorder**
Anxious personality disorder

F60.7   **Dependent personality disorder**
Asthenic personality (disorder)
Inadequate personality (disorder)
Passive personality (disorder)

● **F60.8**   **Other specific personality disorders**

F60.81   **Narcissistic personality disorder**
Vanity, conceit, egotism or indifference to plight of others

F60.89   **Other specific personality disorders**
Eccentric personality disorder
'Haltlose' type personality disorder
Immature personality disorder
Passive-aggressive personality disorder
Psychoneurotic personality disorder
Self-defeating personality disorder

F60.9   **Personality disorder, unspecified**
Character disorder NOS
Character neurosis NOS
Pathological personality NOS

● **F63   Impulse disorders**

     Excludes2   habitual excessive use of alcohol or psychoactive
                 substances (F10-F19)
                 impulse disorders involving sexual behavior (F65.-)

     F63.0   Pathological gambling
           Compulsive gambling
           Gambling disorder

           Excludes1   gambling and betting NOS (Z72.6)

           Excludes2   excessive gambling by manic patients
                       (F30, F31)
                       gambling in antisocial personality
                       disorder (F60.2)

     F63.1   Pyromania
           Pathological fire-setting

           Excludes2   fire-setting (by) (in):
                       adult with antisocial personality
                          disorder (F60.2)
                       alcohol or psychoactive substance
                          intoxication (F10-F19)
                       conduct disorders (F91.-)
                       mental disorders due to known
                          physiological condition (F01-F09)
                       schizophrenia (F20.-)

     F63.2   Kleptomania
           Pathological stealing

           Excludes1   shoplifting as the reason for observation
                       for suspected mental disorder
                       (Z03.8)

           Excludes2   depressive disorder with stealing
                       (F31-F33)
                       stealing due to underlying mental
                       condition-code to mental condition
                       stealing in mental disorders due to known
                       physiological condition (F01-F09)

     F63.3   Trichotillomania
           Hair plucking

           Excludes2   other stereotyped movement disorder
                       (F98.4)

● **F63.8   Other impulse disorders**

         F63.81   Intermittent explosive disorder

         F63.89   Other impulse disorders

     F63.9   Impulse disorder, unspecified
           Impulse control disorder NOS

● **F64   Gender identity disorders**

     F64.0   Transsexualism
           Gender identity disorder in adolescence and adulthood
           Gender dysphoria in adolescents and adults
           Coding Clinic: 2016, Q4, P16

     F64.1   Dual role transvestism
           Use additional code to identify sex reassignment status
           (Z87.890)

           Excludes1   gender identity disorder in childhood
                       (F64.2)

           Excludes2   fetishistic transvestism (F65.1)
           Coding Clinic: 2016, Q4, P16

     F64.2   Gender identity disorder of childhood   P
           Gender dysphoria in children

           Excludes1   gender identity disorder in adolescence
                       and adulthood (F64.0)

           Excludes2   sexual maturation disorder (F66)

     F64.8   Other gender identity disorders
           Other specified gender dysphoria

     F64.9   Gender identity disorder, unspecified
           Gender dysphoria, unspecified
           Gender-role disorder NOS

● **F65   Paraphilias**

     F65.0   Fetishism
           Intense sexual urges and arousing fantasies using inanimate
           objects
           Fetishistic disorder

     F65.1   Transvestic fetishism
           Intense sexual urges, arousal, or orgasm associated with
           fantasized/actual cross-dressing
           Fetishistic transvestism
           Transvestic disorder

     F65.2   Exhibitionism
           Exhibitionistic disorder

     F65.3   Voyeurism
           Sexual urges or arousal involving real or fantasized
           observation of unsuspecting people who are naked,
           disrobing, or engaging in sexual activity
           Voyeuristic disorder

     F65.4   Pedophilia
           Pedophilic disorder

● **F65.5   Sadomasochism**

         F65.50   Sadomasochism, unspecified

         F65.51   Sexual masochism
                   Sexual masochism disorder

         F65.52   Sexual sadism
                   Sexual sadism disorder

● **F65.8   Other paraphilias**

         F65.81   Frotteurism
                   Sexual arousal or orgasm is achieved by rubbing
                   up against another person (or fantasies of), in
                   crowded place with unsuspecting victim
                   Frotteuristic disorder

         F65.89   Other paraphilias
                   Necrophilia
                   Other specified paraphilic disorder

     F65.9   Paraphilia, unspecified
           Paraphilic disorder, unspecified
           Sexual deviation NOS

   F66   Other sexual disorders
           Sexual maturation disorder
           Sexual relationship disorder

● **F68   Other disorders of adult personality and behavior**

● **F68.1   Factitious disorder imposed on self**
           Compensation neurosis
           Elaboration of physical symptoms for psychological
           reasons
           Hospital hopper syndrome
           Münchhausen's syndrome
           Peregrinating patient

           Excludes2   factitial dermatitis (L98.1)
                       person feigning illness (with obvious
                       motivation) (Z76.5)

         F68.10   Factitious disorder imposed on self,
                   unspecified

         F68.11   Factitious disorder imposed on self with
                   predominantly psychological signs and
                   symptoms

         F68.12   Factitious disorder imposed on self with
                   predominantly physical signs and symptoms

         F68.13   Factitious disorder imposed on self with
                   combined psychological and physical signs and
                   symptoms

     F68.8   Other specified disorders of adult personality and behavior

     F68.A   Factitious disorder imposed on another
           Factitious disorder by proxy
           Münchausen's by proxy

   F69   Unspecified disorder of adult personality and behavior   A

▶ New   ⏩ Revised   ~~deleted~~ Deleted   Excludes 1   Excludes 2   Includes   Use additional   Code first   Code also   Key words

OGCR Official Guidelines   X Assign placeholder X   ● Use Additional Character(s)   ▶ Manifestation Code   🔖 Hierarchical Condition Category   Coding Clinic

INTELLECTUAL DISABILITIES (F70-F79)

Code first any associated physical or developmental disorders

Excludes1   borderline intellectual functioning, IQ above 70 to 84 (R41.83)

F70   Mild intellectual disabilities
IQ level 50-55 to approximately 70
Mild mental subnormality

F71   Moderate intellectual disabilities
IQ level 35-40 to 50-55
Moderate mental subnormality

F72   Severe intellectual disabilities
IQ 20-25 to 35-40
Severe mental subnormality

F73   Profound intellectual disabilities
IQ level below 20-25
Profound mental subnormality

F78   Other intellectual disabilities

F79   Unspecified intellectual disabilities
Mental deficiency NOS
Mental subnormality NOS

PERVASIVE AND SPECIFIC DEVELOPMENTAL DISORDERS (F80-F89)

● **F80   Specific developmental disorders of speech and language**

F80.0   Phonological disorder
Communication disorder of unknown cause, characterized by failure to use age-appropriate sounds
Dyslalia
Functional speech articulation disorder
Lalling
Lisping
Phonological developmental disorder
Speech articulation developmental disorder
Speech-sound disorder

Excludes1   speech articulation impairment due to aphasia NOS (R47.01)
speech articulation impairment due to apraxia (R48.2)

Excludes2   speech articulation impairment due to hearing loss (F80.4)
speech articulation impairment due to intellectual disabilities (F70-F79)
speech articulation impairment with expressive language developmental disorder (F80.1)
speech articulation impairment with mixed receptive expressive language developmental disorder (F80.2)

F80.1   Expressive language disorder
Developmental dysphasia or aphasia, expressive type

Excludes1   mixed receptive-expressive language disorder (F80.2)
dysphasia and aphasia NOS (R47.-)

Excludes2   acquired aphasia with epilepsy [Landau-Kleffner] (G40.80-)
intellectual disabilities (F70-F79)
pervasive developmental disorders (F84.-)
selective mutism (F94.0)

F80.2   Mixed receptive-expressive language disorder
Developmental dysphasia or aphasia, receptive type
Developmental Wernicke's aphasia

Excludes1   central auditory processing disorder (H93.25)
dysphasia or aphasia NOS (R47.-)
expressive language disorder (F80.1)
expressive type dysphasia or aphasia (F80.1)
word deafness (H93.25)

Excludes2   acquired aphasia with epilepsy [Landau-Kleffner] (G40.80-)
intellectual disabilities (F70-F79)
pervasive developmental disorders (F84.-)
selective mutism (F94.0)

F80.4   Speech and language development delay due to hearing loss
Code also type of hearing loss (H90.-, H91.-)

● **F80.8   Other developmental disorders of speech or language**

F80.81   Childhood onset fluency disorder
Cluttering NOS
Stuttering NOS

Excludes1   adult onset fluency disorder (F98.5)
fluency disorder in conditions classified elsewhere (R47.82)
fluency disorder (stuttering) following cerebrovascular disease (I69. with final characters -23)

F80.82   Social pragmatic communication disorder

Excludes1   Asperger's syndrome (F84.5)
autistic disorder (F84.0)

Coding Clinic: 2016, Q4, P16

F80.89   Other developmental disorders of speech and language

Coding Clinic: 2017, Q1, P27

F80.9   Developmental disorder of speech and language, unspecified
Communication disorder NOS
Language disorder NOS

● **F81   Specific developmental disorders of scholastic skills**

F81.0   Specific reading disorder
'Backward reading'
Developmental dyslexia
Specific learning disorder, with impairment in reading
Specific reading retardation

Excludes1   alexia NOS (R48.0)
dyslexia NOS (R48.0)

F81.2   Mathematics disorder
Developmental acalculia
Developmental arithmetical disorder
Developmental Gerstmann's syndrome
Specific learning disorder, with impairment in mathematics

Excludes1   acalculia NOS (R48.8)

Excludes2   arithmetical difficulties associated with a reading disorder (F81.0)
arithmetical difficulties associated with a spelling disorder (F81.81)
arithmetical difficulties due to inadequate teaching (Z55.8)

● **F81.8   Other developmental disorders of scholastic skills**

F81.81   Disorder of written expression
Specific learning disorder, with impairment in written expression
Specific spelling disorder

F81.89   Other developmental disorders of scholastic skills

F81.9   Developmental disorder of scholastic skills, unspecified
Knowledge acquisition disability NOS
Learning disability NOS
Learning disorder NOS

F82   Specific developmental disorder of motor function
Clumsy child syndrome
Developmental coordination disorder
Developmental dyspraxia

Excludes1   abnormalities of gait and mobility (R26.-)
lack of coordination (R27.-)

Excludes2   lack of coordination secondary to intellectual disabilities (F70-F79)

CHAPTER 5 (F01-F99)

● **F84   Pervasive developmental disorders**

     Use additional code to identify any associated medical condition and intellectual disabilities.

     F84.0   Autistic disorder
         Autism spectrum disorder
         Infantile autism
         Infantile psychosis
         Kanner's syndrome
         Excludes1   Asperger's syndrome (F84.5)
         Coding Clinic: 2017, Q1, P27

     F84.2   Rett's syndrome
         Neurodevelopmental disorder
         Excludes1   Asperger's syndrome (F84.5)
                    Autistic disorder (F84.0)
                    other childhood disintegrative disorder (F84.3)

     F84.3   Other childhood disintegrative disorder   P
         Dementia infantilis
         At least two years of normal development followed by significant loss of language abilities, social skills, bowel/bladder control, motor skills
         Disintegrative psychosis
         Heller's syndrome
         At least two years of normal development followed by significant loss of language abilities, social skills, bowel/bladder control, motor skills
         Symbiotic psychosis
         Abnormal relationship to mothering figure, characterized by intense separation anxiety, severe regression, giving up of useful speech, and autism
         Use additional code to identify any associated neurological condition.
         Excludes1   Asperger's syndrome (F84.5)
                    Autistic disorder (F84.0)
                    Rett's syndrome (F84.2)

     F84.5   Asperger's syndrome
         Developmental disorder
         Asperger's disorder
         Autistic psychopathy
         Schizoid disorder of childhood

     F84.8   Other pervasive developmental disorders
         Overactive disorder associated with intellectual disabilities and stereotyped movements

     F84.9   Pervasive developmental disorder, unspecified
         Atypical autism

F88   Other disorders of psychological development
     Developmental agnosia
     Global developmental delay
     Other specified neurodevelopmental disorder

F89   Unspecified disorder of psychological development
     Developmental disorder NOS
     Neurodevelopmental disorder NOS

BEHAVIORAL AND EMOTIONAL DISORDERS WITH ONSET USUALLY OCCURRING IN CHILDHOOD AND ADOLESCENCE (F90-F98)

Note: Codes within categories F90-F98 may be used regardless of the age of a patient. These disorders generally have onset within the childhood or adolescent years, but may continue throughout life or not be diagnosed until adulthood.

● **F90   Attention-deficit hyperactivity disorders**
     Attention deficit disorder with hyperactivity=ADHD
     Includes   attention deficit disorder with hyperactivity
                 attention deficit syndrome with hyperactivity
     Excludes2   anxiety disorders (F40.-, F41.-)
                 mood [affective] disorders (F30-F39)
                 pervasive developmental disorders (F84.-)
                 schizophrenia (F20.-)

     F90.0   Attention-deficit hyperactivity disorder, predominantly inattentive type
         Attention-deficit/hyperactivity disorder, predominantly inattentive presentation

     F90.1   Attention-deficit hyperactivity disorder, predominantly hyperactive type
         Attention-deficit/hyperactivity disorder, predominantly hyperactive impulsive presentation

     F90.2   Attention-deficit hyperactivity disorder, combined type
         Attention-deficit/hyperactivity disorder, combined presentation

     F90.8   Attention-deficit hyperactivity disorder, other type

     F90.9   Attention-deficit hyperactivity disorder, unspecified type
         Attention-deficit hyperactivity disorder of childhood or adolescence NOS
         Attention-deficit hyperactivity disorder NOS

● **F91   Conduct disorders**
     Childhood/adolescence disruptive behavior disorder
     Excludes1   antisocial behavior (Z72.81-)
                 antisocial personality disorder (F60.2)
     Excludes2   conduct problems associated with attention-deficit hyperactivity disorder (F90.-)
                 mood [affective] disorders (F30-F39)
                 pervasive developmental disorders (F84.-)
                 schizophrenia (F20.-)

     F91.0   Conduct disorder confined to family context

     F91.1   Conduct disorder, childhood-onset type
         Unsocialized conduct disorder
         Conduct disorder, solitary aggressive type
         Unsocialized aggressive disorder

     F91.2   Conduct disorder, adolescent-onset type
         Socialized conduct disorder
         Conduct disorder, group type

     F91.3   Oppositional defiant disorder

     F91.8   Other conduct disorders
         Other specified conduct disorder
         Other specified disruptive disorder

     F91.9   Conduct disorder, unspecified
         Behavioral disorder NOS
         Conduct disorder NOS
         Disruptive behavior disorder NOS
         Disruptive disorder NOS

● **F93   Emotional disorders with onset specific to childhood**

     F93.0   Separation anxiety disorder of childhood
         Excludes2   mood [affective] disorders (F30-F39)
                    nonpsychotic mental disorders (F40-F48)
                    phobic anxiety disorder of childhood (F40.8)
                    social phobia (F40.1)

     F93.8   Other childhood emotional disorders
         Identity disorder
         Excludes2   gender identity disorder of childhood (F64.2)

     F93.9   Childhood emotional disorder, unspecified

● **F94   Disorders of social functioning with onset specific to childhood and adolescence**

     F94.0   Selective mutism
         Elective mutism
         Excludes2   pervasive developmental disorders (F84.-)
                    schizophrenia (F20.-)
                    specific developmental disorders of speech and language (F80.-)
                    transient mutism as part of separation anxiety in young children (F93.0)

     F94.1   Reactive attachment disorder of childhood
         Use additional code to identify any associated failure to thrive or growth retardation
         Excludes1   disinhibited attachment disorder of childhood (F94.2)
                    normal variation in pattern of selective attachment
         Excludes2   Asperger's syndrome (F84.5)
                    maltreatment syndromes (T74.-)
                    sexual or physical abuse in childhood, resulting in psychosocial problems (Z62.81-)

     ▶ New   ⇒ Revised   ~~deleted~~ Deleted   Excludes 1   Excludes 2   Includes   Use additional   Code first   Code also   Key words

     OGCR Official Guidelines   X Assign placeholder X   ● Use Additional Character(s)   ▌ Manifestation Code   🏷 Hierarchical Condition Category   Coding Clinic

F94.2   Disinhibited attachment disorder of childhood
Affectionless psychopathy
Institutional syndrome

> **Excludes1**   reactive attachment disorder of childhood (F94.1)

> **Excludes2**   Asperger's syndrome (F84.5)
> attention-deficit hyperactivity disorders (F90.-)
> hospitalism in children (F43.2-)

F94.8   Other childhood disorders of social functioning

F94.9   Childhood disorder of social functioning, unspecified

● **F95   Tic disorder**
Involuntary twitch

F95.0   Transient tic disorder
Provisional tic disorder

F95.1   Chronic motor or vocal tic disorder

F95.2   Tourette's disorder
Combined vocal and multiple motor tic disorder [de la Tourette]
Tourette's syndrome

F95.8   Other tic disorders

F95.9   Tic disorder, unspecified
Tic NOS

● **F98   Other behavioral and emotional disorders with onset usually occurring in childhood and adolescence**

> **Excludes2**   breath-holding spells (R06.89)
> gender identity disorder of childhood (F64.2)
> Kleine-Levin syndrome (G47.13)
> ➡ obsessive-compulsive disorder (42.3-)
> sleep disorders not due to a substance or known physiological condition (F51.-)

F98.0   Enuresis not due to a substance or known physiological condition
Enuresis: Urinary incontinence
Enuresis (primary) (secondary) of nonorganic origin
Functional enuresis
Psychogenic enuresis
Urinary incontinence of nonorganic origin

> **Excludes1**   enuresis NOS (R32)

F98.1   Encopresis not due to a substance or known physiological condition
Encopresis: Fecal incontinence
Functional encopresis
Incontinence of feces of nonorganic origin
Psychogenic encopresis

Use additional code to identify the cause of any coexisting constipation.

> **Excludes1**   encopresis NOS (R15.-)

● **F98.2   Other feeding disorders of infancy and childhood**

> **Excludes1**   feeding difficulties (R63.3)

> **Excludes2**   anorexia nervosa and other eating disorders (F50.-)
> feeding problems of newborn (P92.-)
> pica of infancy or childhood (F98.3)

F98.21   Rumination disorder of infancy

F98.29   Other feeding disorders of infancy and early childhood

F98.3   Pica of infancy and childhood
Craving and eating substances such as paint, clay, or dirt to replace a nutritional deficit in the body.

F98.4   Stereotyped movement disorders
Stereotype/habit disorder

> **Excludes1**   abnormal involuntary movements (R25.-)

> **Excludes2** ➡ compulsions in obsessive-compulsive disorder (F42.-)
> hair plucking (F63.3)
> movement disorders of organic origin (G20-G25)
> nail-biting (F98.8)
> nose-picking (F98.8)
> stereotypies that are part of a broader psychiatric condition (F01-F95)
> thumb-sucking (F98.8)
> tic disorders (F95.-)
> trichotillomania (F63.3)

F98.5   Adult onset fluency disorder

> **Excludes1**   childhood onset fluency disorder (F80.81)
> dysphasia (R47.02)
> fluency disorder in conditions classified elsewhere (R47.82)
> fluency disorder (stuttering) following cerebrovascular disease (I69. with final characters -23)
> tic disorders (F95.-)

F98.8   Other specified behavioral and emotional disorders with onset usually occurring in childhood and adolescence
Excessive masturbation
Nail-biting
Nose-picking
Thumb-sucking

F98.9   Unspecified behavioral and emotional disorders with onset usually occurring in childhood and adolescence

UNSPECIFIED MENTAL DISORDER (F99)

F99   Mental disorder, not otherwise specified
Mental illness NOS

> **Excludes1**   unspecified mental disorder due to known physiological condition (F09)

Item 5–2 Enuresis: Bed wetting by children at night. Causes can be either psychological or medical (diabetes, urinary tract infections, or abnormalities). **Encopresis:** Overflow incontinence of bowels sometimes resulting from chronic constipation or fecal impaction. Check the documentation for additional diagnoses.

CHAPTER 6

DISEASES OF THE NERVOUS SYSTEM (G00-G99)

OGCR Chapter-Specific Coding Guidelines

6. Chapter 6: Diseases of the Nervous System (G00-G99)

a. Dominant/nondominant side

Codes from category G81, Hemiplegia and hemiparesis, and subcategories, G83.1, Monoplegia of lower limb, G83.2, Monoplegia of upper limb, and G83.3, Monoplegia, unspecified, identify whether the dominant or nondominant side is affected. Should the affected side be documented, but not specified as dominant or nondominant, and the classification system does not indicate a default, code selection is as follows:

- For ambidextrous patients, the default should be dominant.
- If the left side is affected, the default is nondominant.
- If the right side is affected, the default is dominant.

b. Pain - Category G89

1) General coding information

Codes in category G89, Pain, not elsewhere classified, may be used in conjunction with codes from other categories and chapters to provide more detail about acute or chronic pain and neoplasm-related pain, unless otherwise indicated below.

If the pain is not specified as acute or chronic, post-thoracotomy, postprocedural, or neoplasm-related, do not assign codes from category G89.

A code from category G89 should not be assigned if the underlying (definitive) diagnosis is known, unless the reason for the encounter is pain control/management and not management of the underlying condition.

When an admission or encounter is for a procedure aimed at treating the underlying condition (e.g., spinal fusion, kyphoplasty), a code for the underlying condition (e.g., vertebral fracture, spinal stenosis) should be assigned as the principal diagnosis. No code from category G89 should be assigned.

(a) Category G89 Codes as Principal or First-Listed Diagnosis

Category G89 codes are acceptable as principal diagnosis or the first-listed code:

- When pain control or pain management is the reason for the admission/encounter (e.g., a patient with displaced intervertebral disc, nerve impingement and severe back pain presents for injection of steroid into the spinal canal). The underlying cause of the pain should be reported as an additional diagnosis, if known.
- When a patient is admitted for the insertion of a neurostimulator for pain control, assign the appropriate pain code as the principal or first-listed diagnosis. When an admission or encounter is for a procedure aimed at treating the underlying condition and a neurostimulator is inserted for pain control during the same admission/encounter, a code for the underlying condition should be assigned as the principal diagnosis and the appropriate pain code should be assigned as a secondary diagnosis.

(b) Use of Category G89 Codes in Conjunction with Site Specific Pain Codes

(i) Assigning Category G89 and Site-Specific Pain Codes

Codes from category G89 may be used in conjunction with codes that identify the site of pain (including codes from Chapter 18) if the category G89 code provides additional information. For example, if the code describes the site of the pain, but does not fully describe whether the pain is acute or chronic, then both codes should be assigned.

(ii) Sequencing of Category G89 Codes with Site-Specific Pain Codes

The sequencing of category G89 codes with site-specific pain codes (including Chapter 18 codes), is dependent on the circumstances of the encounter/admission as follows:

- If the encounter is for pain control or pain management, assign the code from category G89 followed by the code identifying the specific site of pain (e.g., encounter for pain management for acute neck pain from trauma is assigned code G89.11, Acute pain due to trauma, followed by code M54.2, Cervicalgia, to identify the site of pain).
- If the encounter is for any other reason except pain control or pain management, and a related definitive diagnosis has not been established (confirmed) by the provider, assign the code for the specific site of pain first, followed by the appropriate code from category G89.

2) Pain due to devices, implants and grafts

See Section I.C.19. Pain due to medical devices

3) Postoperative Pain

The provider's documentation should be used to guide the coding of postoperative pain, as well as *Section III. Reporting Additional Diagnoses* and *Section IV. Diagnostic Coding and Reporting in the Outpatient Setting.*

The default for post-thoracotomy and other postoperative pain not specified as acute or chronic is the code for the acute form.

Routine or expected postoperative pain immediately after surgery should not be coded.

(a) Postoperative pain not associated with specific postoperative complication

Postoperative pain not associated with a specific postoperative complication is assigned to the appropriate postoperative pain code in category G89.

(b) Postoperative pain associated with specific postoperative complication

Postoperative pain associated with a specific postoperative complication (such as painful wire sutures) is assigned to the appropriate code(s) found in Chapter 19, Injury, poisoning, and certain other consequences of external causes. If appropriate, use additional code(s) from category G89 to identify acute or chronic pain (G89.18 or G89.28).

4) Chronic pain

Chronic pain is classified to subcategory G89.2. There is no time frame defining when pain becomes chronic pain. The provider's documentation should be used to guide use of these codes.

5) Neoplasm Related Pain

Code G89.3 is assigned to pain documented as being related, associated or due to cancer, primary or secondary malignancy, or tumor. This code is assigned regardless of whether the pain is acute or chronic.

This code may be assigned as the principal or first-listed code when the stated reason for the admission/encounter is documented as pain control/pain management. The underlying neoplasm should be reported as an additional diagnosis.

When the reason for the admission/encounter is management of the neoplasm and the pain associated with the neoplasm is also documented, code G89.3 may be assigned as an additional diagnosis. It is not necessary to assign an additional code for the site of the pain.

See Section I.C.2 for instructions on the sequencing of neoplasms for all other stated reasons for the admission/encounter (except for pain control/pain management).

6) Chronic pain syndrome

Central pain syndrome (G89.0) and chronic pain syndrome (G89.4) are different than the term "chronic pain," and therefore codes should only be used when the provider has specifically documented this condition.

See Section I.C.5. Pain disorders related to psychological factors

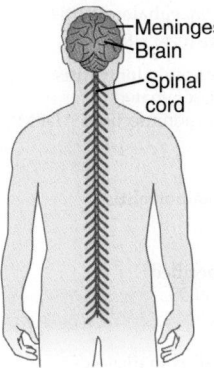

Figure 6-1 The brain and spinal cord make up the central nervous system.

Meninges
Brain
Spinal cord

Item 6-1 The two major classifications of the nervous system are the peripheral nervous system and the central nervous system (CNS). The central nervous system is composed of the brain and the spinal cord. The peripheral nervous system is composed of the parasympathetic and sympathetic systems. **Encephalitis** is the swelling of the brain. **Meningitis** is swelling of the covering of the brain, the meninges. Types and causes of brain infections are:

Type	Cause
purulent	bacterial
aseptic/abacterial	viral
chronic meningitis	mycobacterial and fungal

CHAPTER 6

DISEASES OF THE NERVOUS SYSTEM (G00-G99)

Excludes2   certain conditions originating in the perinatal period (P04-P96)
certain infectious and parasitic diseases (A00-B99)
complications of pregnancy, childbirth and the puerperium (O00-O9A)
congenital malformations, deformations, and chromosomal abnormalities (Q00-Q99)
endocrine, nutritional and metabolic diseases (E00-E88)
injury, poisoning and certain other consequences of external causes (S00-T88)
neoplasms (C00-D49)
symptoms, signs and abnormal clinical and laboratory findings, not elsewhere classified (R00-R94)

This chapter contains the following blocks:

G00-G09	Inflammatory diseases of the central nervous system
G10-G14	Systemic atrophies primarily affecting the central nervous system
G20-G26	Extrapyramidal and movement disorders
G30-G32	Other degenerative diseases of the nervous system
G35-G37	Demyelinating diseases of the central nervous system
G40-G47	Episodic and paroxysmal disorders
G50-G59	Nerve, nerve root and plexus disorders
G60-G65	Polyneuropathies and other disorders of the peripheral nervous system
G70-G73	Diseases of myoneural junction and muscle
G80-G83	Cerebral palsy and other paralytic syndromes
G89-G99	Other disorders of the nervous system

INFLAMMATORY DISEASES OF THE CENTRAL NERVOUS SYSTEM (G00-G09)

● **G00**   **Bacterial meningitis, not elsewhere classified**
An infection of the cerebrospinal fluid surrounding the spinal cord and brain.

Includes   bacterial arachnoiditis
bacterial leptomeningitis
bacterial meningitis
bacterial pachymeningitis

Excludes1   bacterial meningoencephalitis (G04.2)
bacterial meningomyelitis (G04.2)

G00.0   **Hemophilus meningitis**
Meningitis due to Hemophilus influenzae

G00.1   **Pneumococcal meningitis**
Meningitis due to Streptococcal pneumoniae

G00.2   **Streptococcal meningitis**
Use additional code to further identify organism (B95.0-B95.5)

G00.3   **Staphylococcal meningitis**
Use additional code to further identify organism (B95.61-B95.8)

G00.8   **Other bacterial meningitis**
Meningitis due to Escherichia coli
Meningitis due to Friedländer bacillus
Meningitis due to Klebsiella
Use additional code to further identify organism (B96.-)

G00.9   **Bacterial meningitis, unspecified**
Meningitis due to gram-negative bacteria, unspecified
Purulent meningitis NOS
Pyogenic meningitis NOS
Suppurative meningitis NOS

▷ **G01**   *Meningitis in bacterial diseases classified elsewhere*
Code first underlying disease
Excludes1   meningitis (in):
gonococcal (A54.81)
leptospirosis (A27.81)
listeriosis (A32.11)
Lyme disease (A69.21)
meningococcal (A39.0)
neurosyphilis (A52.13)
tuberculosis (A17.0)
meningoencephalitis and meningomyelitis in bacterial diseases classified elsewhere (G05)

▷ **G02**   *Meningitis in other infectious and parasitic diseases classified elsewhere*
Code first underlying disease, such as:
African trypanosomiasis (B56.-)
poliovirus infection (A80.-)
Excludes1   candidal meningitis (B37.5)
coccidioidomycosis meningitis (B38.4)
cryptococcal meningitis (B45.1)
herpesviral [herpes simplex] meningitis (B00.3)
infectious mononucleosis complicated by meningitis (B27.- with fourth character 2)
measles complicated by meningitis (B05.1)
meningoencephalitis and meningomyelitis in other infectious and parasitic diseases classified elsewhere (G05)
mumps meningitis (B26.1)
rubella meningitis (B06.02)
varicella [chickenpox] meningitis (B01.0)
zoster meningitis (B02.1)

● **G03**   **Meningitis due to other and unspecified causes**

> **Includes**   arachnoiditis NOS
> leptomeningitis NOS
> meningitis NOS
> pachymeningitis NOS

> **Excludes1**   meningoencephalitis (G04.-)
> meningomyelitis (G04.-)

G03.0   **Nonpyogenic meningitis**
> Aseptic meningitis
> Nonbacterial meningitis

G03.1   **Chronic meningitis**

G03.2   **Benign recurrent meningitis [Mollaret]**

G03.8   **Meningitis due to other specified causes**

G03.9   **Meningitis, unspecified**
> Arachnoiditis (spinal) NOS

● **G04**   **Encephalitis, myelitis and encephalomyelitis**

> **Includes**   acute ascending myelitis
> meningoencephalitis
> meningomyelitis

> **Excludes1**   encephalopathy NOS (G93.40)
> other noninfectious acute disseminated
> encephalomyelitis (noninfectious ADEM)
> (G04.81)

> **Excludes2**   acute transverse myelitis (G37.3-)
> alcoholic encephalopathy (G31.2)
> benign myalgic encephalomyelitis (G93.3)
> multiple sclerosis (G35)
> subacute necrotizing myelitis (G37.4)
> toxic encephalitis (G92)
> toxic encephalopathy (G92)

● **G04.0**   **Acute disseminated encephalitis and encephalomyelitis (ADEM)**

> **Excludes1**   acute necrotizing hemorrhagic
> encephalopathy (G04.3-)

G04.00   **Acute disseminated encephalitis and encephalomyelitis, unspecified**

▷ *G04.01*   *Postinfectious acute disseminated encephalitis and encephalomyelitis (postinfectious ADEM)*

> **Excludes1**   post chickenpox encephalitis
> (B01.1)
> post measles encephalitis (B05.0)
> post measles myelitis (B05.1)

G04.02   **Postimmunization acute disseminated encephalitis, myelitis and encephalomyelitis**
> Encephalitis, post immunization
> Encephalomyelitis, post immunization
> Use additional code to identify the vaccine
> (T50.A-, T50.B-, T50.Z-)

G04.1   **Tropical spastic paraplegia** 🐾

G04.2   **Bacterial meningoencephalitis and meningomyelitis, not elsewhere classified**

● **G04.3**   **Acute necrotizing hemorrhagic encephalopathy**
> *Sudden and severe CNS disease with pathology of hemorrhages and necrosis of white matter*

> **Excludes1**   acute disseminated encephalitis and
> encephalomyelitis (G04.0-)

G04.30   **Acute necrotizing hemorrhagic encephalopathy, unspecified**

G04.31   **Postinfectious acute necrotizing hemorrhagic encephalopathy**

G04.32   **Postimmunization acute necrotizing hemorrhagic encephalopathy**
> Use additional code to identify vaccine
> (T50.A-, T50.B-, T50.Z-)

G04.39   **Other acute necrotizing hemorrhagic encephalopathy**
> Code also underlying etiology, if applicable

● **G04.8**   **Other encephalitis, myelitis and encephalomyelitis**
> Code also any associated seizure (G40.-, R56.9)

G04.81   **Other encephalitis and encephalomyelitis**
> Noninfectious acute disseminated
> encephalomyelitis (noninfectious ADEM)

G04.89   **Other myelitis** 🐾
> Coding Clinic: 2020, Q1, P14

● **G04.9**   **Encephalitis, myelitis and encephalomyelitis, unspecified**

G04.90   **Encephalitis and encephalomyelitis, unspecified**
> Ventriculitis (cerebral) NOS

G04.91   **Myelitis, unspecified** 🐾

● **G05**   **Encephalitis, myelitis and encephalomyelitis in diseases classified elsewhere**

> *Code first underlying disease, such as:*
> human immunodeficiency virus [HIV] disease (B20)
> poliovirus (A80.-)
> suppurative otitis media (H66.01-H66.4)
> trichinellosis (B75)

> **Excludes1**   adenoviral encephalitis, myelitis and
> encephalomyelitis (A85.1)
> congenital toxoplasmosis encephalitis, myelitis
> and encephalomyelitis (P37.1)
> cytomegaloviral encephalitis, myelitis and
> encephalomyelitis (B25.8)
> encephalitis, myelitis and encephalomyelitis (in)
> measles (B05.0)
> encephalitis, myelitis and encephalomyelitis (in)
> systemic lupus erythematosus (M32.19)
> enteroviral encephalitis, myelitis and
> encephalomyelitis (A85.0)
> eosinophilic meningoencephalitis (B83.2)
> herpesviral [herpes simplex] encephalitis,
> myelitis and encephalomyelitis (B00.4)
> listerial encephalitis, myelitis and
> encephalomyelitis (A32.12)
> meningococcal encephalitis, myelitis and
> encephalomyelitis (A39.81)
> mumps encephalitis, myelitis and
> encephalomyelitis (B26.2)
> postchickenpox encephalitis, myelitis and
> encephalomyelitis (B01.1-)
> rubella encephalitis, myelitis and
> encephalomyelitis (B06.01)
> toxoplasmosis encephalitis, myelitis and
> encephalomyelitis (B58.2)
> zoster encephalitis, myelitis and
> encephalomyelitis (B02.0)

▷ *G05.3*   *Encephalitis and encephalomyelitis in diseases classified elsewhere*
> Meningoencephalitis in diseases classified elsewhere

▷ *G05.4*   *Myelitis in diseases classified elsewhere* 🐾
> Meningomyelitis in diseases classified elsewhere

● **G06**   **Intracranial and intraspinal abscess and granuloma**
> *An accumulation of pus in either the brain or spinal cord*
> Use additional code (B95-B97) to identify infectious agent.

G06.0   **Intracranial abscess and granuloma**
> Brain [any part] abscess (embolic)
> Cerebellar abscess (embolic)
> Cerebral abscess (embolic)
> Intracranial epidural abscess or granuloma
> Intracranial extradural abscess or granuloma
> Intracranial subdural abscess or granuloma
> Otogenic abscess (embolic)

> **Excludes1**   tuberculous intracranial abscess and
> granuloma (A17.81)

▶ New   ⇒ Revised   ~~deleted~~ Deleted   Excludes 1   Excludes 2   Includes   Use additional   Code first   Code also   Key words

OGCR Official Guidelines   X Assign placeholder X   ● Use Additional Character(s)   ▷ Manifestation Code   🐾 Hierarchical Condition Category   Coding Clinic

G06.1   Intraspinal abscess and granuloma
Abscess (embolic) of spinal cord [any part]
Intraspinal epidural abscess or granuloma
Intraspinal extradural abscess or granuloma
Intraspinal subdural abscess or granuloma

     Excludes1   tuberculous intraspinal abscess and granuloma (A17.81)

G06.2   Extradural and subdural abscess, unspecified

▶ *G07   Intracranial and intraspinal abscess and granuloma in diseases classified elsewhere*

     Code first underlying disease, such as:
schistosomiasis granuloma of brain (B65.-)

     Excludes1   abscess of brain:
         amebic (A06.6)
         chromomycotic (B43.1)
         gonococcal (A54.82)
         tuberculous (A17.81)
         tuberculoma of meninges (A17.1)

G08   Intracranial and intraspinal phlebitis and thrombophlebitis
Septic embolism of intracranial or intraspinal venous sinuses and veins
Septic endophlebitis of intracranial or intraspinal venous sinuses and veins
Septic phlebitis of intracranial or intraspinal venous sinuses and veins
Septic thrombophlebitis of intracranial or intraspinal venous sinuses and veins
Septic thrombosis of intracranial or intraspinal venous sinuses and veins

     Excludes1   intracranial phlebitis and thrombophlebitis complicating:
         abortion, ectopic or molar pregnancy (O00-O07, O08.7)
         pregnancy, childbirth and the puerperium (O22.5, O87.3)
         nonpyogenic intracranial phlebitis and thrombophlebitis (I67.6)

     Excludes2   intracranial phlebitis and thrombophlebitis complicating nonpyogenic intraspinal phlebitis and thrombophlebitis (G95.1)

G09   Sequelae of inflammatory diseases of central nervous system

     Note: Category G09 is to be used to indicate conditions whose primary classification is to G00-G08 as the cause of sequelae, themselves classifiable elsewhere. The 'sequelae' include conditions specified as residuals.

     Code first condition resulting from (sequela) of inflammatory diseases of central nervous system

SYSTEMIC ATROPHIES PRIMARILY AFFECTING THE CENTRAL NERVOUS SYSTEM (G10-G14)

G10   Huntington's disease 🔗
Genetic disease with degeneration of cells of the nervous system, including brain
Huntington's chorea
Huntington's dementia
Code also dementia in other diseases classified elsewhere without behavioral disturbance (F02.80)

● **G11   Hereditary ataxia**
Genetic neurological disorder affecting coordination
     Excludes2   cerebral palsy (G80.-)
         hereditary and idiopathic neuropathy (G60.-)
         metabolic disorders (E70-E88)

   G11.0   Congenital nonprogressive ataxia 🔗

● **G11.1   Early-onset cerebellar ataxia** 🔗

▶ G11.10 Early-onset cerebellar ataxia, unspecified
▶ G11.11 Friedreich ataxia
     ▶ Autosomal recessive Friedreich ataxia
     ▶ Friedreich ataxia with retained reflexes

▶ G11.19 Other early-onset cerebellar ataxia
     ▶ Early-onset cerebellar ataxia with essential tremor
     ▶ Early-onset cerebellar ataxia with myoclonus [Hunt's ataxia]
     ▶ Early-onset cerebellar ataxia with retained tendon reflexes
     ▶ X-linked recessive spinocerebellar ataxia
~~Early-onset cerebellar ataxia with essential tremor~~
~~Early-onset cerebellar ataxia with myoclonus [Hunt's ataxia]~~
~~Early-onset cerebellar ataxia with retained tendon reflexes~~
~~Friedreich's ataxia (autosomal recessive)~~
~~X-linked recessive spinocerebellar ataxia~~

G11.2   Late-onset cerebellar ataxia 🔗   A

G11.3   Cerebellar ataxia with defective DNA repair 🔗
Ataxia telangiectasia [Louis-Bar]
     Excludes2   Cockayne's syndrome (Q87.19)
         other disorders of purine and pyrimidine metabolism (E79.-)
         xeroderma pigmentosum (Q82.1)

G11.4   Hereditary spastic paraplegia 🔗

G11.8   Other hereditary ataxias 🔗

G11.9   Hereditary ataxia, unspecified 🔗
Hereditary cerebellar ataxia NOS
Hereditary cerebellar degeneration
Hereditary cerebellar disease
Hereditary cerebellar syndrome

● **G12   Spinal muscular atrophy and related syndromes**

   G12.0   Infantile spinal muscular atrophy, type I [Werdnig-Hoffman] 🔗

   G12.1   Other inherited spinal muscular atrophy 🔗
Adult form spinal muscular atrophy
Childhood form, type II spinal muscular atrophy
Distal spinal muscular atrophy
Juvenile form, type III spinal muscular atrophy [Kugelberg-Welander]
Progressive bulbar palsy of childhood [Fazio-Londe]
Scapuloperoneal form spinal muscular atrophy

● **G12.2   Motor neuron disease**
Progressive disease of motor neurons that carry impulses to muscles to move

     G12.20   Motor neuron disease, unspecified 🔗

     G12.21   Amyotrophic lateral sclerosis 🔗   A
Lou Gehrig's disease (ALS)

     G12.22   Progressive bulbar palsy 🔗

     G12.23   Primary lateral sclerosis 🔗

     G12.24   Familial motor neuron disease 🔗

     G12.25   Progressive spinal muscle atrophy 🔗

     G12.29   Other motor neuron disease 🔗

   G12.8   Other spinal muscular atrophies and related syndromes 🔗

   G12.9   Spinal muscular atrophy, unspecified 🔗

● **G13   Systemic atrophies primarily affecting central nervous system in diseases classified elsewhere**

▶ *G13.0   Paraneoplastic neuromyopathy and neuropathy* 🔗
Carcinomatous neuromyopathy
Sensorial paraneoplastic neuropathy [Denny Brown]
Code first underlying neoplasm (C00-D49)

▶ *G13.1   Other systemic atrophy primarily affecting central nervous system in neoplastic disease* 🔗
Paraneoplastic limbic encephalopathy
Code first underlying neoplasm (C00-D49)

▶ *G13.2   Systemic atrophy primarily affecting the central nervous system in myxedema*
Code first underlying disease, such as:
hypothyroidism (E03.-)
myxedematous congenital iodine deficiency (E00.1)

▶ *G13.8   Systemic atrophy primarily affecting central nervous system in other diseases classified elsewhere*
Code first underlying disease

Item 6-2 Huntington's chorea is an inherited degenerative disorder of the central nervous system and is characterized by ceaseless, jerky movements and progressive cognitive and behavioral deterioration.

CHAPTER 6 (G00-G99)

G14   Postpolio syndrome
> **Includes**   Postpolio myelitic syndrome
> **Excludes1**   sequelae of poliomyelitis (B91)

EXTRAPYRAMIDAL AND MOVEMENT DISORDERS (G20-G26)

G20   Parkinson's disease 🐾
Progressive disease of the nervous system that affects muscle coordination
Hemiparkinsonism
Idiopathic Parkinsonism or Parkinson's disease
Paralysis agitans
Parkinsonism or Parkinson's disease NOS
Primary Parkinsonism or Parkinson's disease
▶ Use additional code to identify:
  ▶ dementia with behavioral disturbance (F02.81)
  ▶ dementia without behavioral disturbance (F02.80)
> **Excludes1**   dementia with Parkinsonism (G31.83)

Coding Clinic: 2017, Q2, P7-8; 2016, Q2, P7

G21   Secondary parkinsonism
Symptoms of Parkinson's caused by medicines, illness, or other nervous system disorder
> **Excludes1**   dementia with Parkinsonism (G31.83)
>   Huntington's disease (G10)
>   Shy-Drager syndrome (G90.3)
>   syphilitic Parkinsonism (A52.19)

G21.0   Malignant neuroleptic syndrome
Use additional code for adverse effect, if applicable, to identify drug (T43.3X5, T43.4X5, T43.505, T43.595)
> **Excludes1**   neuroleptic induced parkinsonism (G21.11)

G21.1   Other drug-induced secondary parkinsonism
> **G21.11   Neuroleptic induced parkinsonism** 🐾
> Use additional code for adverse effect, if applicable, to identify drug (T43.3X5, T43.4X5, T43.505, T43.595)
> > **Excludes1**   malignant neuroleptic syndrome (G21.0)
>
> **G21.19   Other drug induced secondary parkinsonism** 🐾
> Other medication-induced parkinsonism
> Use additional code for adverse effect, if applicable, to identify drug (T36-T50 with fifth or sixth character 5)

G21.2   Secondary parkinsonism due to other external agents 🐾
Code first (T51-T65) to identify external agent
G21.3   Postencephalitic parkinsonism 🐾
G21.4   Vascular parkinsonism 🐾
G21.8   Other secondary parkinsonism 🐾
G21.9   Secondary parkinsonism, unspecified 🐾

G23   Other degenerative diseases of basal ganglia
> **Excludes2**   multi-system degeneration of the autonomic nervous system (G90.3)

G23.0   Hallervorden-Spatz disease 🐾
Pigmentary pallidal degeneration
G23.1   Progressive supranuclear ophthalmoplegia [Steele-Richardson-Olszewski] 🐾
Progressive supranuclear palsy
G23.2   Striatonigral degeneration 🐾
G23.8   Other specified degenerative diseases of basal ganglia 🐾
Calcification of basal ganglia
G23.9   Degenerative disease of basal ganglia, unspecified 🐾

G24   Dystonia
Involuntary movements
> **Includes**   dyskinesia
> **Excludes2**   athetoid cerebral palsy (G80.3)

G24.0   Drug induced dystonia
Use additional code for adverse effect, if applicable, to identify drug (T36-T50 with fifth or sixth character 5)
> **G24.01   Drug induced subacute dyskinesia**
> Drug induced blepharospasm
> Drug induced orofacial dyskinesia
> Neuroleptic induced tardive dyskinesia
> Tardive dyskinesia
>
> **G24.02   Drug induced acute dystonia**
> Acute dystonic reaction to drugs
> Neuroleptic induced acute dystonia
>
> **G24.09   Other drug induced dystonia**

G24.1   Genetic torsion dystonia
Dystonia deformans progressiva
Dystonia musculorum deformans
Familial torsion dystonia
Idiopathic familial dystonia
Idiopathic (torsion) dystonia NOS
(Schwalbe-) Ziehen-Oppenheim disease

G24.2   Idiopathic nonfamilial dystonia
G24.3   Spasmodic torticollis
Head tilts toward one side and chin is elevated and turned toward opposite side (wry neck)
> **Excludes1**   congenital torticollis (Q68.0)
>   hysterical torticollis (F44.4)
>   ocular torticollis (R29.891)
>   psychogenic torticollis (F45.8)
>   torticollis NOS (M43.6)
>   traumatic recurrent torticollis (S13.4)

G24.4   Idiopathic orofacial dystonia
Orofacial dyskinesia
> **Excludes1**   drug induced orofacial dyskinesia (G24.01)

G24.5   Blepharospasm
Tonic spasm of orbicularis oculi muscle, producing closure of eyelids
> **Excludes1**   drug induced blepharospasm (G24.01)

G24.8   Other dystonia
Acquired torsion dystonia NOS
G24.9   Dystonia, unspecified
Dyskinesia NOS

G25   Other extrapyramidal and movement disorders
Extrapyramidal: Other than pyramidal tracts
> **Excludes2**   sleep related movement disorders (G47.6-)

G25.0   Essential tremor
Familial tremor
> **Excludes1**   tremor NOS (R25.1)

G25.1   Drug-induced tremor
Use additional code for adverse effect, if applicable, to identify drug (T36-T50 with fifth or sixth character 5)

G25.2   Other specified forms of tremor
Intention tremor

G25.3   Myoclonus
Shocklike contractions muscle(s)
Drug-induced myoclonus
Palatal myoclonus
Use additional code for adverse effect, if applicable, to identify drug (T36-T50 with fifth or sixth character 5)
> **Excludes1**   facial myokymia (G51.4)
>   myoclonic epilepsy (G40.-)

▶ New   ⟹ Revised   ~~deleted~~ Deleted   Excludes 1   Excludes 2   Includes   Use additional   Code first   Code also   Key words
OGCR Official Guidelines   X Assign placeholder X   ● Use Additional Character(s)   ▶ Manifestation Code   🐾 Hierarchical Condition Category   Coding Clinic

G25.4 Drug-induced chorea
Use additional code for adverse effect, if applicable, to identify drug (T36-T50 with fifth or sixth character 5)

G25.5 Other chorea
Continual, involuntary, jerky, movements
Chorea NOS
> **Excludes1**   chorea NOS with heart involvement (I02.0)
> Huntington's chorea (G10)
> rheumatic chorea (I02.-)
> Sydenham's chorea (I02.-)

● **G25.6 Drug induced tics and other tics of organic origin**
     G25.61 Drug induced tics
Use additional code for adverse effect, if applicable, to identify drug (T36-T50 with fifth or sixth character 5)

     G25.69 Other tics of organic origin
> **Excludes1**   habit spasm (F95.9)
> tic NOS (F95.9)
> Tourette's syndrome (F95.2)

● **G25.7 Other and unspecified drug induced movement disorders**
Use additional code for adverse effect, if applicable, to identify drug (T36-T50 with fifth or sixth character 5)

     G25.70 Drug induced movement disorder, unspecified
     G25.71 Drug induced akathisia
Drug induced acathisia
Neuroleptic induced acute akathisia
Tardive akathisia

     G25.79 Other drug induced movement disorders

● **G25.8 Other specified extrapyramidal and movement disorders**
     G25.81 Restless legs syndrome
     G25.82 Stiff-man syndrome
     G25.83 Benign shuddering attacks
     G25.89 Other specified extrapyramidal and movement disorders

G25.9 Extrapyramidal and movement disorder, unspecified

▷ *G26 Extrapyramidal and movement disorders in diseases classified elsewhere*
Code first underlying disease

OTHER DEGENERATIVE DISEASES OF THE NERVOUS SYSTEM (G30-G32)

● **G30 Alzheimer's disease**
Progressive central neurodegenerative disorder
> **Includes**   Alzheimer's dementia senile and presenile forms

Use additional code to identify:
    delirium, if applicable (F05)
    dementia with behavioral disturbance (F02.81)
    dementia without behavioral disturbance (F02.80)
> **Excludes1**   senile degeneration of brain NEC (G31.1)
> senile dementia NOS (F03)
> senility NOS (R41.81)

G30.0 Alzheimer's disease with early onset
G30.1 Alzheimer's disease with late onset   A
G30.8 Other Alzheimer's disease
G30.9 Alzheimer's disease, unspecified
    Coding Clinic: 2017, Q1, P43; 2016, Q2, P6; 2012, Q4, P95

● **G31 Other degenerative diseases of nervous system, not elsewhere classified**
For codes G31.0-G31.83, G31.85-G31.9, use additional code to identify:
    dementia with behavioral disturbance (F02.81)
    dementia without behavioral disturbance (F02.80)
> **Excludes2**   Reye's syndrome (G93.7)

● **G31.0 Frontotemporal dementia**
     G31.01 Pick's disease
Primary progressive aphasia
Progressive isolated aphasia

     G31.09 Other frontotemporal dementia
Frontal dementia

G31.1 Senile degeneration of brain, not elsewhere classified
> **Excludes1**   Alzheimer's disease (G30.-)
> senility NOS (R41.81)

G31.2 Degeneration of nervous system due to alcohol
Alcoholic cerebellar ataxia
Alcoholic cerebellar degeneration
Alcoholic cerebral degeneration
Alcoholic encephalopathy
Dysfunction of the autonomic nervous system due to alcohol
Code also associated alcoholism (F10.-)

● **G31.8 Other specified degenerative diseases of nervous system**
     G31.81 Alpers' disease
Rare neuronal degeneration of cerebral cortex disease of young children
Grey-matter degeneration
    Coding Clinic: 2017, Q2, P7

     G31.82 Leigh's disease
Rare neurometabolic disorder that affects central nervous system
Subacute necrotizing encephalopathy

     G31.83 Dementia with Lewy bodies
Closely allied to Parkinson's Disease
Dementia with Parkinsonism
Lewy body dementia
Lewy body disease
    Coding Clinic: 2017, Q2, P7; 2016, Q4, P141

     G31.84 Mild cognitive impairment, so stated
Mild neurocognitive disorder
> **Excludes1**   age related cognitive decline (R41.81)
> altered mental status (R41.82)
> cerebral degeneration (G31.9)
> change in mental status (R41.82)
> cognitive deficits following (sequelae of) cerebral hemorrhage or infarction (I69.01-, I69.11-, I69.21-, I69.31-, I69.81-, I69.91-)
> cognitive impairment due to intracranial or head injury (S06.-)
> dementia (F01.-, F02.-, F03)
> mild memory disturbance (F06.8)
> neurologic neglect syndrome (R41.4)
> personality change, nonpsychotic (F68.8)

     G31.85 Corticobasal degeneration
     G31.89 Other specified degenerative diseases of nervous system

G31.9 Degenerative disease of nervous system, unspecified

● **G32**   **Other degenerative disorders of nervous system in diseases classified elsewhere**

▶ **G32.0**   *Subacute combined degeneration of spinal cord in diseases classified elsewhere* 🔖

     Dana-Putnam syndrome

     Sclerosis of spinal cord (combined) (dorsolateral) (posterolateral)

     Code first underlying disease, such as:

       anemia (D51.9)

       dietary (D51.3)

       pernicious (D51.0)

       vitamin B12 deficiency (E53.8)

     Excludes1   syphilitic combined degeneration of spinal cord (A52.11)

● **G32.8**   **Other specified degenerative disorders of nervous system in diseases classified elsewhere**

     Code first underlying disease, such as:

       amyloidosis cerebral degeneration (E85.-)

       cerebral degeneration (due to) hypothyroidism (E00.0-E03.9)

       cerebral degeneration (due to) neoplasm (C00-D49)

       cerebral degeneration (due to) vitamin B deficiency, except thiamine (E52-E53.-)

     Excludes1   superior hemorrhagic polioencephalitis [Wernicke's encephalopathy] (E51.2)

▶ **G32.81**   *Cerebellar ataxia in diseases classified elsewhere* 🔖

     Code first underlying disease, such as:

       celiac disease (with gluten ataxia) (K90.0)

       cerebellar ataxia (in) neoplastic disease (paraneoplastic cerebellar degeneration) (C00-D49)

       non-celiac gluten ataxia (M35.9)

     Excludes1   systemic atrophy primarily affecting the central nervous system in alcoholic cerebellar ataxia (G31.2)

         systemic atrophy primarily affecting the central nervous system in myxedema (G13.2)

▶ **G32.89**   *Other specified degenerative disorders of nervous system in diseases classified elsewhere*

     Degenerative encephalopathy in diseases classified elsewhere

DEMYELINATING DISEASES OF THE CENTRAL NERVOUS SYSTEM (G35-G37)

G35   **Multiple sclerosis** 🔖

     Destruction of central nervous system; four types: relapsing remitting, secondary progressive, primary progressive, and progressive relapsing

     Disseminated multiple sclerosis

     Generalized multiple sclerosis

     Multiple sclerosis NOS

     Multiple sclerosis of brain stem

     Multiple sclerosis of cord

● **G36**   **Other acute disseminated demyelination**

     Excludes1   postinfectious encephalitis and encephalomyelitis NOS (G04.01)

G36.0   **Neuromyelitis optica [Devic]** 🔖

     Inflammatory disorder in which immune system attacks optic nerves and spinal cord producing inflammation of optic nerve (optic neuritis) and spinal cord (myelitis)

     Demyelination in optic neuritis

     Excludes1   optic neuritis NOS (H46)

G36.1   **Acute and subacute hemorrhagic leukoencephalitis [Hurst]** 🔖

G36.8   **Other specified acute disseminated demyelination** 🔖

G36.9   **Acute disseminated demyelination, unspecified** 🔖

Item 6–3   **Multiple sclerosis** (MS) is a nervous system disease affecting the brain and spinal cord by damaging the myelin sheath surrounding and protecting nerve cells. The damage slows down/blocks messages between the brain and body. Symptoms are visual disturbances, muscle weakness, coordination and balance issues, numbness, prickling, thinking and memory problems. The cause is unknown, though it is thought that it may be an autoimmune disease. It affects women more than men, between 20 and 40 years of age. MS can be mild, but it may cause the loss of ability to write, walk, and speak. There is no cure, but medication may slow or control symptoms.

● **G37**   **Other demyelinating diseases of central nervous system**

     Destruction of central nervous system

G37.0   **Diffuse sclerosis of central nervous system** 🔖

     Periaxial encephalitis

     Schilder's disease

     Excludes1   X linked adrenoleukodystrophy (E71.52-)

G37.1   **Central demyelination of corpus callosum** 🔖

G37.2   **Central pontine myelinolysis** 🔖

G37.3   **Acute transverse myelitis in demyelinating disease of central nervous system** 🔖

     Acute transverse myelitis NOS

     Acute transverse myelopathy

     Excludes1   multiple sclerosis (G35)

         neuromyelitis optica [Devic] (G36.0)

G37.4   **Subacute necrotizing myelitis of central nervous system** 🔖

G37.5   **Concentric sclerosis [Baló] of central nervous system** 🔖

G37.8   **Other specified demyelinating diseases of central nervous system** 🔖

G37.9   **Demyelinating disease of central nervous system, unspecified** 🔖

EPISODIC AND PAROXYSMAL DISORDERS (G40-G47)

● **G40**   **Epilepsy and recurrent seizures**

     Note: The following terms are to be considered equivalent to intractable: pharmacoresistant (pharmacologically resistant), treatment resistant, refractory (medically) and poorly controlled

     Excludes1   conversion disorder with seizures (F44.5)

         convulsions NOS (R56.9)

         post traumatic seizures (R56.1)

         seizure (convulsive) NOS (R56.9)

         seizure of newborn (P90)

     Excludes2   hippocampal sclerosis (G93.81)

         mesial temporal sclerosis (G93.81)

         temporal sclerosis (G93.81)

         Todd's paralysis (G83.84)

● **G40.0**   **Localization-related (focal) (partial) idiopathic epilepsy and epileptic syndromes with seizures of localized onset**

     Benign childhood epilepsy with centrotemporal EEG spikes

     Childhood epilepsy with occipital EEG paroxysms

     Excludes1   adult onset localization-related epilepsy (G40.1-, G40.2-)

● **G40.00**   **Localization-related (focal) (partial) idiopathic epilepsy and epileptic syndromes with seizures of localized onset, not intractable**

     Localization-related (focal) (partial) idiopathic epilepsy and epileptic syndromes with seizures of localized onset without intractability

     G40.001   **Localization-related (focal) (partial) idiopathic epilepsy and epileptic syndromes with seizures of localized onset, not intractable, with status epilepticus** 🔖

▶ New   ⟹ Revised   ~~deleted~~ Deleted   Excludes 1   Excludes 2   Includes   Use additional   Code first   Code also   Key words

OGCR Official Guidelines   X Assign placeholder X   ● Use Additional Character(s)   ▶ Manifestation Code   🔖 Hierarchical Condition Category   **Coding Clinic**

G40.009 Localization-related (focal) (partial) idiopathic epilepsy and epileptic syndromes with seizures of localized onset, not intractable, without status epilepticus 🔍

Localization-related (focal) (partial) idiopathic epilepsy and epileptic syndromes with seizures of localized onset NOS

● G40.01 Localization-related (focal) (partial) idiopathic epilepsy and epileptic syndromes with seizures of localized onset, intractable

G40.011 Localization-related (focal) (partial) idiopathic epilepsy and epileptic syndromes with seizures of localized onset, intractable, with status epilepticus 🔍

G40.019 Localization-related (focal) (partial) idiopathic epilepsy and epileptic syndromes with seizures of localized onset, intractable, without status epilepticus 🔍

● G40.1 Localization-related (focal) (partial) symptomatic epilepsy and epileptic syndromes with simple partial seizures

Attacks without alteration of consciousness
Epilepsia partialis continua [Kozhevnikof]
Simple partial seizures developing into secondarily generalized seizures

● G40.10 Localization-related (focal) (partial) symptomatic epilepsy and epileptic syndromes with simple partial seizures, not intractable

Localization-related (focal) (partial) symptomatic epilepsy and epileptic syndromes with simple partial seizures without intractability

G40.101 Localization-related (focal) (partial) symptomatic epilepsy and epileptic syndromes with simple partial seizures, not intractable, with status epilepticus 🔍

G40.109 Localization-related (focal) (partial) symptomatic epilepsy and epileptic syndromes with simple partial seizures, not intractable, without status epilepticus 🔍

Localization-related (focal) (partial) symptomatic epilepsy and epileptic syndromes with simple partial seizures NOS

● G40.11 Localization-related (focal) (partial) symptomatic epilepsy and epileptic syndromes with simple partial seizures, intractable

G40.111 Localization-related (focal) (partial) symptomatic epilepsy and epileptic syndromes with simple partial seizures, intractable, with status epilepticus 🔍

G40.119 Localization-related (focal) (partial) symptomatic epilepsy and epileptic syndromes with simple partial seizures, intractable, without status epilepticus 🔍

● G40.2 Localization-related (focal) (partial) symptomatic epilepsy and epileptic syndromes with complex partial seizures

Attacks with alteration of consciousness, often with automatisms
Complex partial seizures developing into secondarily generalized seizures

● G40.20 Localization-related (focal) (partial) symptomatic epilepsy and epileptic syndromes with complex partial seizures, not intractable

Localization-related (focal) (partial) symptomatic epilepsy and epileptic syndromes with complex partial seizures without intractability

G40.201 Localization-related (focal) (partial) symptomatic epilepsy and epileptic syndromes with complex partial seizures, not intractable, with status epilepticus 🔍

G40.209 Localization-related (focal) (partial) symptomatic epilepsy and epileptic syndromes with complex partial seizures, not intractable, without status epilepticus 🔍

Localization-related (focal) (partial) symptomatic epilepsy and epileptic syndromes with complex partial seizures NOS

● G40.21 Localization-related (focal) (partial) symptomatic epilepsy and epileptic syndromes with complex partial seizures, intractable

G40.211 Localization-related (focal) (partial) symptomatic epilepsy and epileptic syndromes with complex partial seizures, intractable, with status epilepticus 🔍

G40.219 Localization-related (focal) (partial) symptomatic epilepsy and epileptic syndromes with complex partial seizures, intractable, without status epilepticus 🔍

● G40.3 Generalized idiopathic epilepsy and epileptic syndromes

Code also MERRF syndrome, if applicable (E88.42)

● G40.30 Generalized idiopathic epilepsy and epileptic syndromes, not intractable

Generalized idiopathic epilepsy and epileptic syndromes without intractability

G40.301 Generalized idiopathic epilepsy and epileptic syndromes, not intractable, with status epilepticus 🔍

G40.309 Generalized idiopathic epilepsy and epileptic syndromes, not intractable, without status epilepticus 🔍

Generalized idiopathic epilepsy and epileptic syndromes NOS

● G40.31 Generalized idiopathic epilepsy and epileptic syndromes, intractable

G40.311 Generalized idiopathic epilepsy and epileptic syndromes, intractable, with status epilepticus 🔍

G40.319 Generalized idiopathic epilepsy and epileptic syndromes, intractable, without status epilepticus 🔍

CHAPTER 6 (G00-G99)

CHAPTER 6 (G00-G99)

● **G40.4   Other generalized epilepsy and epileptic syndromes**
     Epilepsy with grand mal seizures on awakening
     Epilepsy with myoclonic absences
     Epilepsy with myoclonic-astatic seizures
     Grand mal seizure NOS
     Nonspecific atonic epileptic seizures
     Nonspecific clonic epileptic seizures
     Nonspecific myoclonic epileptic seizures
     Nonspecific tonic epileptic seizures
     Nonspecific tonic-clonic epileptic seizures
     Symptomatic early myoclonic encephalopathy

    ● **G40.40   Other generalized epilepsy and epileptic syndromes, not intractable**
        Other generalized epilepsy and epileptic syndromes without intractability
        Other generalized epilepsy and epileptic syndromes NOS

        G40.401   Other generalized epilepsy and epileptic syndromes, not intractable, with status epilepticus 🅢

        G40.409   Other generalized epilepsy and epileptic syndromes, not intractable, without status epilepticus 🅢

    ● **G40.41   Other generalized epilepsy and epileptic syndromes, intractable**

        G40.411   Other generalized epilepsy and epileptic syndromes, intractable, with status epilepticus 🅢

        G40.419   Other generalized epilepsy and epileptic syndromes, intractable, without status epilepticus 🅢

    ▶ **G40.42   Cyclin-Dependent Kinase-Like 5 Deficiency Disorder**
        CDKL5
        ▶ Use additional code, if known, to identify associated manifestations, such as:
          ▶ cortical blindness (H47.61-)
          ▶ global developmental delay (F88)

● **G40.5   Epileptic seizures related to external causes**
     Epileptic seizures related to alcohol
     Epileptic seizures related to drugs
     Epileptic seizures related to hormonal changes
     Epileptic seizures related to sleep deprivation
     Epileptic seizures related to stress
     Code also, if applicable, associated epilepsy and recurrent seizures (G40.-)
     Use additional code for adverse effect, if applicable, to identify drug (T36-T50 with fifth or sixth character 5)

    ● **G40.50   Epileptic seizures related to external causes, not intractable**

        G40.501   Epileptic seizures related to external causes, not intractable, with status epilepticus 🅢

        G40.509   Epileptic seizures related to external causes, not intractable, without status epilepticus 🅢
          Epileptic seizures related to external causes, NOS

● **G40.8   Other epilepsy and recurrent seizures**
     Epilepsies and epileptic syndromes undetermined as to whether they are focal or generalized
     Landau-Kleffner syndrome

    ● **G40.80   Other epilepsy**

        G40.801   Other epilepsy, not intractable, with status epilepticus 🅢
          Other epilepsy without intractability with status epilepticus

        G40.802   Other epilepsy, not intractable, without status epilepticus 🅢
          Other epilepsy NOS
          Other epilepsy without intractability without status epilepticus

        G40.803   Other epilepsy, intractable, with status epilepticus 🅢

        G40.804   Other epilepsy, intractable, without status epilepticus 🅢

    ● **G40.81   Lennox-Gastaut syndrome**

        G40.811   Lennox-Gastaut syndrome, not intractable, with status epilepticus 🅢

        G40.812   Lennox-Gastaut syndrome, not intractable, without status epilepticus 🅢

        G40.813   Lennox-Gastaut syndrome, intractable, with status epilepticus 🅢

        G40.814   Lennox-Gastaut syndrome, intractable, without status epilepticus 🅢

    ● **G40.82   Epileptic spasms**
        Infantile spasms
        Salaam attacks
        West's syndrome

        G40.821   Epileptic spasms, not intractable, with status epilepticus 🅢

        G40.822   Epileptic spasms, not intractable, without status epilepticus 🅢

        G40.823   Epileptic spasms, intractable, with status epilepticus 🅢

        G40.824   Epileptic spasms, intractable, without status epilepticus 🅢

    ▶ ● **G40.83   Dravet syndrome**
        ▶ Polymorphic epilepsy in infancy (PMEI)
        ▶ Severe myoclonic epilepsy in infancy (SMEI)

        ▶ **G40.833   Dravet syndrome, intractable, with status epilepticus**

        ▶ **G40.834   Dravet syndrome, intractable, without status epilepticus**
          ▶ Dravet syndrome NOS

    G40.89   Other seizures 🅢

        Excludes1   post traumatic seizures (R56.1)
                  recurrent seizures NOS (G40.909)
                  seizure NOS (R56.9)

● **G40.9   Epilepsy, unspecified**

    ● **G40.90   Epilepsy, unspecified, not intractable**
        Epilepsy, unspecified, without intractability

        G40.901   Epilepsy, unspecified, not intractable, with status epilepticus 🅢

        G40.909   Epilepsy, unspecified, not intractable, without status epilepticus 🅢
          Epilepsy NOS
          Epileptic convulsions NOS
          Epileptic fits NOS
          Epileptic seizures NOS
          Recurrent seizures NOS
          Seizure disorder NOS

    ● **G40.91   Epilepsy, unspecified, intractable**
        Intractable seizure disorder NOS

        G40.911   Epilepsy, unspecified, intractable, with status epilepticus 🅢

        G40.919   Epilepsy, unspecified, intractable, without status epilepticus 🅢

● **G40.A   Absence epileptic syndrome**
     Childhood absence epilepsy [pyknolepsy]
     Juvenile absence epilepsy
     Absence epileptic syndrome, NOS

    ● **G40.A0   Absence epileptic syndrome, not intractable**

        G40.A01   Absence epileptic syndrome, not intractable, with status epilepticus 🅢

        G40.A09   Absence epileptic syndrome, not intractable, without status epilepticus 🅢

    ● **G40.A1   Absence epileptic syndrome, intractable**

        G40.A11   Absence epileptic syndrome, intractable, with status epilepticus 🅢

        G40.A19   Absence epileptic syndrome, intractable, without status epilepticus 🅢

▶ New   ⇒ Revised   ~~deleted~~ Deleted   Excludes 1   Excludes 2   Includes   Use additional   Code first   Code also   Key words

OGCR Official Guidelines   **X** Assign placeholder X   ● Use Additional Character(s)   ▶ Manifestation Code   🅢 Hierarchical Condition Category   **Coding Clinic**

● **G40.B**   Juvenile myoclonic epilepsy [impulsive petit mal]

    ● **G40.B0**   Juvenile myoclonic epilepsy, not intractable

       G40.B01   Juvenile myoclonic epilepsy, not intractable, with status epilepticus 🕮

       G40.B09   Juvenile myoclonic epilepsy, not intractable, without status epilepticus 🕮

    ● **G40.B1**   Juvenile myoclonic epilepsy, intractable

       G40.B11   Juvenile myoclonic epilepsy, intractable, with status epilepticus 🕮

       G40.B19   Juvenile myoclonic epilepsy, intractable, without status epilepticus 🕮

● **G43**   **Migraine**

    Note: The following terms are to be considered equivalent to intractable: pharmacoresistant (pharmacologically resistant), treatment resistant, refractory (medically) and poorly controlled

    Use additional code for adverse effect, if applicable, to identify drug (T36-T50 with fifth or sixth character 5)

    ⮕ **Excludes1**   headache NOS (R51.9)
                 lower half migraine (G44.00)

    Excludes2   headache syndromes (G44.-)

   ● **G43.0**   **Migraine** without aura

      Neurological disorder, generally recurring headaches without early symptom (aura)

      Common migraine

      Excludes1   chronic migraine without aura (G43.7-)

    ● **G43.00**   Migraine without aura, not intractable

       Neurological disorder, generally recurring headaches without early symptom (aura); resistant to cure, relief, or control

       Migraine without aura without mention of refractory migraine

       G43.001   Migraine without aura, not intractable, with status migrainosus

       G43.009   Migraine without aura, not intractable, without status migrainosus
                 Migraine without aura NOS

    ● **G43.01**   Migraine without aura, intractable

       Intractable migraine: Not easily cured or managed; relentless pain from a migraine

       Migraine without aura with refractory migraine

       G43.011   Migraine without aura, intractable, with status migrainosus

       G43.019   Migraine without aura, intractable, without status migrainosus

   ● **G43.1**   Migraine with aura

      Basilar migraine
      Classical migraine
      Migraine equivalents
      Migraine preceded or accompanied by transient focal neurological phenomena
      Migraine triggered seizures
      Migraine with acute-onset aura
      Migraine with aura without headache (migraine equivalents)
      Migraine with prolonged aura
      Migraine with typical aura
      Retinal migraine

      Code also any associated seizure (G40.-, R56.9)

      Excludes1   persistent migraine aura (G43.5-, G43.6-)

    ● **G43.10**   Migraine with aura, not intractable

       Migraine with aura without mention of refractory migraine

       G43.101   Migraine with aura, not intractable, with status migrainosus

       G43.109   Migraine with aura, not intractable, without status migrainosus
                 Migraine with aura NOS

Item 6-4   Migraine headache is described as an intense pulsing or throbbing pain in one area of the head. It can be accompanied by extreme sensitivity to light (photophobic) and sound and is three times more common in women than in men. Symptoms include nausea and vomiting. Research indicates migraine headaches are caused by inherited abnormalities in genes that control the activities of certain cell populations in the brain.

    ● **G43.11**   Migraine with aura, intractable

       Migraine with aura with refractory migraine

       G43.111   Migraine with aura, intractable, with status migrainosus

       G43.119   Migraine with aura, intractable, without status migrainosus

   ● **G43.4**   Hemiplegic migraine

      Inherited migraine disorder causing temporary paralysis of one side of body followed by severe headache and nausea

      Familial migraine
      Sporadic migraine

    ● **G43.40**   Hemiplegic migraine, not intractable

       Hemiplegic migraine without refractory migraine

       G43.401   Hemiplegic migraine, not intractable, with status migrainosus

       G43.409   Hemiplegic migraine, not intractable, without status migrainosus
                 Hemiplegic migraine NOS

    ● **G43.41**   Hemiplegic migraine, intractable

       Hemiplegic migraine with refractory migraine

       G43.411   Hemiplegic migraine, intractable, with status migrainosus

       G43.419   Hemiplegic migraine, intractable, without status migrainosus

   ● **G43.5**   Persistent migraine aura without cerebral infarction

    ● **G43.50**   Persistent migraine aura without cerebral infarction, not intractable

       Persistent migraine aura without cerebral infarction, without refractory migraine

       G43.501   Persistent migraine aura without cerebral infarction, not intractable, with status migrainosus

       G43.509   Persistent migraine aura without cerebral infarction, not intractable, without status migrainosus
                 Persistent migraine aura NOS

    ● **G43.51**   Persistent migraine aura without cerebral infarction, intractable

       Persistent migraine aura without cerebral infarction, with refractory migraine

       G43.511   Persistent migraine aura without cerebral infarction, intractable, with status migrainosus

       G43.519   Persistent migraine aura without cerebral infarction, intractable, without status migrainosus

   ● **G43.6**   Persistent migraine aura with cerebral infarction

      Visual, motor, or psychic disturbances, paresthesias, and related neurologic abnormalities accompanying migraine

      Code also the type of cerebral infarction (I63.-)

    ● **G43.60**   Persistent migraine aura with cerebral infarction, not intractable

       Persistent migraine aura with cerebral infarction, without refractory migraine

       G43.601   Persistent migraine aura with cerebral infarction, not intractable, with status migrainosus

       G43.609   Persistent migraine aura with cerebral infarction, not intractable, without status migrainosus

CHAPTER 6 (G00-G99)

● **G43.61**   **Persistent migraine aura with cerebral infarction, intractable**
     Persistent migraine aura with cerebral infarction, with refractory migraine

     G43.611   **Persistent migraine aura with cerebral infarction, intractable, with status migrainosus**

     G43.619   **Persistent migraine aura with cerebral infarction, intractable, without status migrainosus**

● **G43.7**   **Chronic migraine without aura**
     Transformed migraine

     Excludes1   migraine without aura (G43.0-)

● **G43.70**   **Chronic migraine without aura, not intractable**
     Chronic migraine without aura, without refractory migraine

     G43.701   **Chronic migraine without aura, not intractable, with status migrainosus**

     G43.709   **Chronic migraine without aura, not intractable, without status migrainosus**
       Chronic migraine without aura NOS

● **G43.71**   **Chronic migraine without aura, intractable**
     Chronic migraine without aura, with refractory migraine

     G43.711   **Chronic migraine without aura, intractable, with status migrainosus**

     G43.719   **Chronic migraine without aura, intractable, without status migrainosus**

● **G43.A**   **Cyclical vomiting**

     Excludes1   cyclical vomiting syndrome unrelated to migraine (R11.15)

     G43.A0   **Cyclical vomiting, in migraine, not intractable**
       Cyclical vomiting, without refractory migraine

     G43.A1   **Cyclical vomiting, in migraine, intractable**
       Cyclical vomiting, with refractory migraine

● **G43.B**   **Ophthalmoplegic migraine**

     G43.B0   **Ophthalmoplegic migraine, not intractable**
       Ophthalmoplegic migraine, without refractory migraine

     G43.B1   **Ophthalmoplegic migraine, intractable**
       Ophthalmoplegic migraine, with refractory migraine

● **G43.C**   **Periodic headache syndromes in child or adult**

     G43.C0   **Periodic headache syndromes in child or adult, not intractable**
       Periodic headache syndromes in child or adult, without refractory migraine

     G43.C1   **Periodic headache syndromes in child or adult, intractable**
       Periodic headache syndromes in child or adult, with refractory migraine

● **G43.D**   **Abdominal migraine**

     G43.D0   **Abdominal migraine, not intractable**
       Abdominal migraine, without refractory migraine

     G43.D1   **Abdominal migraine, intractable**
       Abdominal migraine, with refractory migraine

● **G43.8**   **Other migraine**

● **G43.80**   **Other migraine, not intractable**
     Other migraine, without refractory migraine

     G43.801   **Other migraine, not intractable, with status migrainosus**

     G43.809   **Other migraine, not intractable, without status migrainosus**

● **G43.81**   **Other migraine, intractable**
     Other migraine, with refractory migraine

     G43.811   **Other migraine, intractable, with status migrainosus**

     G43.819   **Other migraine, intractable, without status migrainosus**

● **G43.82**   **Menstrual migraine, not intractable**
     Menstrual headache, not intractable
     Menstrual migraine, without refractory migraine
     Menstrually related migraine, not intractable
     Pre-menstrual headache, not intractable
     Pre-menstrual migraine, not intractable
     Pure menstrual migraine, not intractable

     Code also associated premenstrual tension syndrome (N94.3)

     G43.821   **Menstrual migraine, not intractable, with status migrainosus** ♀

     G43.829   **Menstrual migraine, not intractable, without status migrainosus** ♀
       Menstrual migraine NOS

● **G43.83**   **Menstrual migraine, intractable**
     Menstrual headache, intractable
     Menstrual migraine, with refractory migraine
     Menstrually related migraine, intractable
     Pre-menstrual headache, intractable
     Pre-menstrual migraine, intractable
     Pure menstrual migraine, intractable

     Code also associated premenstrual tension syndrome (N94.3)

     G43.831   **Menstrual migraine, intractable, with status migrainosus** ♀

     G43.839   **Menstrual migraine, intractable, without status migrainosus** ♀

● **G43.9**   **Migraine, unspecified**

● **G43.90**   **Migraine, unspecified, not intractable**
     Migraine, unspecified, without refractory migraine

     G43.901   **Migraine, unspecified, not intractable, with status migrainosus**
       Status migrainosus NOS

     G43.909   **Migraine, unspecified, not intractable, without status migrainosus**
       Migraine NOS

● **G43.91**   **Migraine, unspecified, intractable**
     Migraine, unspecified, with refractory migraine

     G43.911   **Migraine, unspecified, intractable, with status migrainosus**

     G43.919   **Migraine, unspecified, intractable, without status migrainosus**

● **G44**   **Other headache syndromes**

     ⟹ **Excludes1**   headache NOS (R51.9)

     Excludes2   atypical facial pain (G50.1)
       headache due to lumbar puncture (G97.1)
       migraines (G43.-)
       trigeminal neuralgia (G50.0)

● **G44.0**   **Cluster headaches and other trigeminal autonomic cephalgias (TAC)**

● **G44.00**   **Cluster headache syndrome, unspecified**
     Ciliary neuralgia
     Cluster headache NOS
     Histamine cephalgia
     Lower half migraine
     Migrainous neuralgia

     G44.001   **Cluster headache syndrome, unspecified, intractable**

     G44.009   **Cluster headache syndrome, unspecified, not intractable**
       Cluster headache syndrome NOS

● **G44.01**   **Episodic cluster headache**

     G44.011   **Episodic cluster headache, intractable**

     G44.019   **Episodic cluster headache, not intractable**
       Episodic cluster headache NOS

▶ New   ⟹ Revised   ~~deleted~~ Deleted   Excludes 1   Excludes 2   Includes   Use additional   Code first   Code also   Key words

OGCR Official Guidelines   X Assign placeholder X   ● Use Additional Character(s)   ▶ Manifestation Code   🅗🅒 Hierarchical Condition Category   **Coding Clinic**

802

● **G44.02 Chronic cluster headache**

G44.021 Chronic cluster headache, intractable

G44.029 Chronic cluster headache, not intractable

    Chronic cluster headache NOS

● **G44.03 Episodic paroxysmal hemicrania**

    Paroxysmal hemicrania NOS

G44.031 Episodic paroxysmal hemicrania, intractable

G44.039 Episodic paroxysmal hemicrania, not intractable

    Episodic paroxysmal hemicrania NOS

● **G44.04 Chronic paroxysmal hemicrania**

    Unilateral headache

G44.041 Chronic paroxysmal hemicrania, intractable

G44.049 Chronic paroxysmal hemicrania, not intractable

    Chronic paroxysmal hemicrania NOS

● **G44.05 Short lasting unilateral neuralgiform headache with conjunctival injection and tearing (SUNCT)**

G44.051 Short lasting unilateral neuralgiform headache with conjunctival injection and tearing (SUNCT), intractable

G44.059 Short lasting unilateral neuralgiform headache with conjunctival injection and tearing (SUNCT), not intractable

    Short lasting unilateral neuralgiform headache with conjunctival injection and tearing (SUNCT) NOS

● **G44.09 Other trigeminal autonomic cephalgias (TAC)**

    Cluster headaches

G44.091 Other trigeminal autonomic cephalgias (TAC), intractable

G44.099 Other trigeminal autonomic cephalgias (TAC), not intractable

G44.1 Vascular headache, not elsewhere classified

    Excludes2 cluster headache (G44.0)

        complicated headache syndromes (G44.5-)

        drug-induced headache (G44.4-)

        migraine (G43.-)

        other specified headache syndromes (G44.8-)

        post-traumatic headache (G44.3-)

        tension-type headache (G44.2-)

● **G44.2 Tension-type headache**

● **G44.20 Tension-type headache, unspecified**

G44.201 Tension-type headache, unspecified, intractable

G44.209 Tension-type headache, unspecified, not intractable

    Tension headache NOS

● **G44.21 Episodic tension-type headache**

G44.211 Episodic tension-type headache, intractable

G44.219 Episodic tension-type headache, not intractable

    Episodic tension-type headache NOS

● **G44.22 Chronic tension-type headache**

G44.221 Chronic tension-type headache, intractable

G44.229 Chronic tension-type headache, not intractable

    Chronic tension-type headache NOS

● **G44.3 Post-traumatic headache**

● **G44.30 Post-traumatic headache, unspecified**

G44.301 Post-traumatic headache, unspecified, intractable

G44.309 Post-traumatic headache, unspecified, not intractable

    Post-traumatic headache NOS

● **G44.31 Acute post-traumatic headache**

G44.311 Acute post-traumatic headache, intractable

G44.319 Acute post-traumatic headache, not intractable

    Acute post-traumatic headache NOS

● **G44.32 Chronic post-traumatic headache**

G44.321 Chronic post-traumatic headache, intractable

G44.329 Chronic post-traumatic headache, not intractable

    Chronic post-traumatic headache NOS

● **G44.4 Drug-induced headache, not elsewhere classified**

    Medication overuse headache

    Use additional code for adverse effect, if applicable, to identify drug (T36-T50 with fifth or sixth character 5)

G44.40 Drug-induced headache, not elsewhere classified, not intractable

G44.41 Drug-induced headache, not elsewhere classified, intractable

● **G44.5 Complicated headache syndromes**

G44.51 Hemicrania continua

    Persistent unilateral headache

G44.52 New daily persistent headache (NDPH)

G44.53 Primary thunderclap headache

G44.59 Other complicated headache syndrome

● **G44.8 Other specified headache syndromes**

    ▶ **Excludes2** headache with orthostatic or positional component, not elsewhere classified (R51.0)

G44.81 Hypnic headache

    Benign primary headaches

G44.82 Headache associated with sexual activity

    Orgasmic headache

    Preorgasmic headache

G44.83 Primary cough headache

G44.84 Primary exertional headache

G44.85 Primary stabbing headache

G44.89 Other headache syndrome

● **G45 Transient cerebral ischemic attacks and related syndromes**

    Excludes1 neonatal cerebral ischemia (P91.0)

        transient retinal artery occlusion (H34.0-)

    Coding Clinic: 2018, Q2, P9

G45.0 Vertebro-basilar artery syndrome

G45.1 Carotid artery syndrome (hemispheric)

G45.2 Multiple and bilateral precerebral artery syndromes

G45.3 Amaurosis fugax

    Transient visual loss in one eye

G45.4 Transient global amnesia

    Episode of short-term memory loss, nonrecurrent, lasting few hours

    Excludes1 amnesia NOS (R41.3)

G45.8 Other transient cerebral ischemic attacks and related syndromes

G45.9 Transient cerebral ischemic attack, unspecified

    Spasm of cerebral artery

    TIA

    Transient cerebral ischemia NOS

CHAPTER 6 (G00-G99)

CHAPTER 6 (G00-G99)

● **G46   Vascular syndromes of brain in cerebrovascular diseases**

Code first underlying cerebrovascular disease (I60-I69)

G46.0   Middle cerebral artery syndrome

G46.1   Anterior cerebral artery syndrome

G46.2   Posterior cerebral artery syndrome

G46.3   Brain stem stroke syndrome
Benedikt syndrome
Claude syndrome
Foville syndrome
Millard-Gubler syndrome
Wallenberg syndrome
Weber syndrome

G46.4   Cerebellar stroke syndrome

G46.5   Pure motor lacunar syndrome
Occlusion of single deep penetrating artery

G46.6   Pure sensory lacunar syndrome

G46.7   Other lacunar syndromes

G46.8   Other vascular syndromes of brain in cerebrovascular diseases

● **G47   Sleep disorders**

    Excludes2   nightmares (F51.5)
nonorganic sleep disorders (F51.-)
sleep terrors (F51.4)
sleepwalking (F51.3)

● **G47.0   Insomnia**

    Excludes2   alcohol related insomnia (F10.182, F10.282, F10.982)
drug-related insomnia (F11.182, F11.282, F11.982, F13.182, F13.282, F13.982, F14.182, F14.282, F14.982, F15.182, F15.282, F15.982, F19.182, F19.282, F19.982)
idiopathic insomnia (F51.01)
insomnia due to a mental disorder (F51.05)
insomnia not due to a substance or known physiological condition (F51.0-)
nonorganic insomnia (F51.0-)
primary insomnia (F51.01)
sleep apnea (G47.3-)

G47.00   Insomnia, unspecified
Insomnia NOS

G47.01   Insomnia due to medical condition
Code also associated medical condition

G47.09   Other insomnia

● **G47.1   Hypersomnia**

    Excludes2   alcohol-related hypersomnia (F10.182, F10.282, F10.982)
drug-related hypersomnia (F11.182, F11.282, F11.982, F13.182, F13.282, F13.982, F14.182, F14.282, F14.982, F15.182, F15.282, F15.982, F19.182, F19.282, F19.982)
hypersomnia due to a mental disorder (F51.13)
hypersomnia not due to a substance or known physiological condition (F51.1-)
primary hypersomnia (F51.11)
sleep apnea (G47.3-)

G47.10   Hypersomnia, unspecified
Hypersomnia NOS

G47.11   Idiopathic hypersomnia with long sleep time
Idiopathic hypersomnia NOS

G47.12   Idiopathic hypersomnia without long sleep time

G47.13   Recurrent hypersomnia
Kleine-Levin syndrome
Menstrual related hypersomnia

G47.14   Hypersomnia due to medical condition
Code also associated medical condition

G47.19   Other hypersomnia

● **G47.2   Circadian rhythm sleep disorders**
Disorders of the sleep wake schedule
Inversion of nyctohemeral rhythm
Inversion of sleep rhythm

G47.20   Circadian rhythm sleep disorder, unspecified type
Sleep wake schedule disorder NOS

G47.21   Circadian rhythm sleep disorder, delayed sleep phase type
Delayed sleep phase syndrome

G47.22   Circadian rhythm sleep disorder, advanced sleep phase type

G47.23   Circadian rhythm sleep disorder, irregular sleep wake type
Irregular sleep-wake pattern

G47.24   Circadian rhythm sleep disorder, free running type
Circadian rhythm sleep disorder, non-24-hour sleep-wake type

G47.25   Circadian rhythm sleep disorder, jet lag type

G47.26   Circadian rhythm sleep disorder, shift work type

▌ *G47.27   Circadian rhythm sleep disorder in conditions classified elsewhere*
Code first underlying condition

G47.29   Other circadian rhythm sleep disorder

● **G47.3   Sleep apnea**
Characterized by episodes in which breathing stops during sleep
Code also any associated underlying condition

    Excludes1   apnea NOS (R06.81)
Cheyne-Stokes breathing (R06.3)
pickwickian syndrome (E66.2)
sleep apnea of newborn (P28.3)

G47.30   Sleep apnea, unspecified
Sleep apnea NOS

G47.31   Primary central sleep apnea
Idiopathic central sleep apnea

G47.32   High altitude periodic breathing

G47.33   Obstructive sleep apnea (adult) (pediatric)
Obstructive sleep apnea hypopnea

    Excludes1   obstructive sleep apnea of newborn (P28.3)

G47.34   Idiopathic sleep related nonobstructive alveolar hypoventilation
Sleep related hypoxia

G47.35   Congenital central alveolar hypoventilation syndrome

▌ *G47.36   Sleep related hypoventilation in conditions classified elsewhere*
Sleep related hypoxemia in conditions classified elsewhere
Code first underlying condition

▌ *G47.37   Central sleep apnea in conditions classified elsewhere*
Code first underlying condition

G47.39   Other sleep apnea

● **G47.4   Narcolepsy and cataplexy**
Cataplexy is a disorder evidenced by seizures including minor slacking of the facial muscles to complete collapse and often affects people who have narcolepsy, a disorder in which there is great difficulty remaining awake during the daytime.

● **G47.41   Narcolepsy**

G47.411   Narcolepsy with cataplexy

G47.419   Narcolepsy without cataplexy
Narcolepsy NOS

▶ New   ⇒ Revised   ~~deleted~~ Deleted   Excludes 1   Excludes 2   Includes   Use additional   Code first   Code also   Key words

OGCR Official Guidelines   X Assign placeholder X   ● Use Additional Character(s)   ▌ Manifestation Code   🅚 Hierarchical Condition Category   **Coding Clinic**

● **G47.42 Narcolepsy in conditions classified elsewhere**
Code first underlying condition
▸ *G47.421 Narcolepsy in conditions classified elsewhere with cataplexy*
▸ *G47.429 Narcolepsy in conditions classified elsewhere without cataplexy*

● **G47.5 Parasomnia**
Excludes1   alcohol induced parasomnia (F10.182, F10.282, F10.982)
drug induced parasomnia (F11.182, F11.282, F11.982, F13.182, F13.282, F13.982, F14.182, F14.282, F14.982, F15.182, F15.282, F15.982, F19.182, F19.282, F19.982)
parasomnia not due to a substance or known physiological condition (F51.8)
G47.50 Parasomnia, unspecified
Parasomnia NOS
G47.51 Confusional arousals
G47.52 REM sleep behavior disorder
G47.53 Recurrent isolated sleep paralysis
▸ *G47.54 Parasomnia in conditions classified elsewhere*
Code first underlying condition
G47.59 Other parasomnia

● **G47.6 Sleep related movement disorders**
Excludes2   restless legs syndrome (G25.81)
G47.61 Periodic limb movement disorder
G47.62 Sleep related leg cramps
G47.63 Sleep related bruxism
Excludes1   psychogenic bruxism (F45.8)
Coding Clinic: 2016, Q4, P118
G47.69 Other sleep related movement disorders
G47.8 Other sleep disorders
Other specified sleep-wake disorder
G47.9 Sleep disorder, unspecified
Sleep disorder NOS
Unspecified sleep-wake disorder

★**(See Plate 6 of the Anatomy Illustrations.)**

NERVE, NERVE ROOT AND PLEXUS DISORDERS (G50-G59)

Excludes1   current traumatic nerve, nerve root and plexus disorders - see Injury, nerve by body region
neuralgia NOS (M79.2)
neuritis NOS (M79.2)
peripheral neuritis in pregnancy (O26.82-)
radiculitis NOS (M54.1-)

● **G50 Disorders of trigeminal nerve**
Includes   disorders of 5th cranial nerve
G50.0 Trigeminal neuralgia
Syndrome of paroxysmal facial pain
Tic douloureux
G50.1 Atypical facial pain
G50.8 Other disorders of trigeminal nerve
G50.9 Disorder of trigeminal nerve, unspecified

Item 6-5 Trigeminal neuralgia, tic douloureux, is a pain syndrome diagnosed from the patient's history alone. The condition is characterized by pain and a brief facial spasm or tic. Pain is unilateral and follows the sensory distribution of cranial nerve V, typically radiating to the maxillary (V2) or mandibular (V3) area.

Item 6-6   The most common facial nerve disorder is **Bell's Palsy,** which occurs suddenly and results in facial drooping unilaterally. This disorder is the result of a reaction to a virus that causes the facial nerve in the ear to swell, resulting in pressure in the bony canal.

● **G51 Facial nerve disorders**
Includes   disorders of 7th cranial nerve
G51.0 Bell's palsy
Facial palsy
G51.1 Geniculate ganglionitis
Rare disorder with symptoms of severe pain deep in ear, spreading to ear canal, outer ear, mastoid or eye regions
Excludes1   postherpetic geniculate ganglionitis (B02.21)
G51.2 Melkersson's syndrome
Melkersson-Rosenthal syndrome
● **G51.3 Clonic hemifacial spasm**
G51.31 Clonic hemifacial spasm, right
G51.32 Clonic hemifacial spasm, left
Coding Clinic: 2018, Q4, P10
G51.33 Clonic hemifacial spasm, bilateral
G51.39 Clonic hemifacial spasm, unspecified
G51.4 Facial myokymia
Involuntary facial muscle movement
G51.8 Other disorders of facial nerve
G51.9 Disorder of facial nerve, unspecified

● **G52 Disorders of other cranial nerves**
Excludes2   disorders of acoustic [8th] nerve (H93.3)
disorders of optic [2nd] nerve (H46, H47.0)
paralytic strabismus due to nerve palsy (H49.0-H49.2)
G52.0 Disorders of olfactory nerve
Disorders of 1st cranial nerve
G52.1 Disorders of glossopharyngeal nerve
Disorder of 9th cranial nerve
Glossopharyngeal neuralgia
G52.2 Disorders of vagus nerve
Disorders of pneumogastric [10th] nerve
G52.3 Disorders of hypoglossal nerve
Disorders of 12th cranial nerve
G52.7 Disorders of multiple cranial nerves
Polyneuritis cranialis
G52.8 Disorders of other specified cranial nerves
G52.9 Cranial nerve disorder, unspecified

▸ *G53 Cranial nerve disorders in diseases classified elsewhere*
Code first underlying disease, such as:
neoplasm (C00-D49)
Excludes1   multiple cranial nerve palsy in sarcoidosis (D86.82)
multiple cranial nerve palsy in syphilis (A52.15)
postherpetic geniculate ganglionitis (B02.21)
postherpetic trigeminal neuralgia (B02.22)

● **G54 Nerve root and plexus disorders**
Raiculopathy (nerve root disorder) caused by pressure on nerve root, most common cause is herniation of intervertebral disk. Plexus disorders (plexopathies) are due to compression or injury.
Excludes1   current traumatic nerve root and plexus disorders - see nerve injury by body region
intervertebral disc disorders (M50-M51)
neuralgia or neuritis NOS (M79.2)
neuritis or radiculitis brachial NOS (M54.13)
neuritis or radiculitis lumbar NOS (M54.16)
neuritis or radiculitis lumbosacral NOS (M54.17)
neuritis or radiculitis thoracic NOS (M54.14)
radiculitis NOS (M54.10)
radiculopathy NOS (M54.10)
spondylosis (M47.-)
G54.0 Brachial plexus disorders
Thoracic outlet syndrome
G54.1 Lumbosacral plexus disorders
G54.2 Cervical root disorders, not elsewhere classified
G54.3 Thoracic root disorders, not elsewhere classified
G54.4 Lumbosacral root disorders, not elsewhere classified

CHAPTER 6 (G00-G99)

G54.5 Neuralgic amyotrophy
Parsonage-Aldren-Turner syndrome
Shoulder-girdle neuritis
> **Excludes1** neuralgic amyotrophy in diabetes mellitus (E08-E13 with .44)

G54.6 Phantom limb syndrome with pain 🐾
Sensations (cramping, itching) in a limb that no longer exists

G54.7 Phantom limb syndrome without pain 🐾
Phantom limb syndrome NOS

G54.8 Other nerve root and plexus disorders

G54.9 Nerve root and plexus disorder, unspecified

▷ **G55 *Nerve root and plexus compressions in diseases classified elsewhere***
Code first underlying disease, such as:
neoplasm (C00-D49)
> **Excludes1** nerve root compression (due to) (in) ankylosing spondylitis (M45.-)
> nerve root compression (due to) (in)dorsopathies (M53.-, M54.-)
> nerve root compression (due to) (in)intervertebral disc disorders (M50.1.-, M51.1.-)
> nerve root compression (due to) (in) spondylopathies (M46.-, M48.-)

★ **(See Plates 472 and 473 on pages 56 and 57.)**

● **G56 Mononeuropathies of upper limb**
> **Excludes1** current traumatic nerve disorder - see nerve injury by body region

● **G56.0 Carpal tunnel syndrome**
    G56.00 Carpal tunnel syndrome, unspecified upper limb
    G56.01 Carpal tunnel syndrome, right upper limb
    G56.02 Carpal tunnel syndrome, left upper limb
    G56.03 Carpal tunnel syndrome, bilateral upper limbs
      Coding Clinic: 2016, Q4, P17

● **G56.1 Other lesions of median nerve**
    G56.10 Other lesions of median nerve, unspecified side
    G56.11 Other lesions of median nerve, right upper limb
    G56.12 Other lesions of median nerve, left upper limb
    G56.13 Other lesions of median nerve, bilateral upper limbs
      Coding Clinic: 2016, Q4, P17

● **G56.2 Lesion of ulnar nerve**
Tardy ulnar nerve palsy
    G56.20 Lesion of ulnar nerve, unspecified upper limb
    G56.21 Lesion of ulnar nerve, right upper limb
    G56.22 Lesion of ulnar nerve, left upper limb
    G56.23 Lesion of ulnar nerve, bilateral upper limbs
      Coding Clinic: 2016, Q4, P17

● **G56.3 Lesion of radial nerve**
    G56.30 Lesion of radial nerve, unspecified upper limb
    G56.31 Lesion of radial nerve, right upper limb
    G56.32 Lesion of radial nerve, left upper limb
    G56.33 Lesion of radial nerve, bilateral upper limbs
      Coding Clinic: 2016, Q4, P17

● **G56.4 Causalgia of upper limb**
Intense burning pain and sensitivity to slight touch
Complex regional pain syndrome II of upper limb
> **Excludes1** complex regional pain syndrome I of lower limb (G90.52-)
> complex regional pain syndrome I of upper limb (G90.51-)
> complex regional pain syndrome II of lower limb (G57.7-)
> reflex sympathetic dystrophy of lower limb (G90.52-)
> reflex sympathetic dystrophy (G90.51-)

    G56.40 Causalgia of unspecified upper limb
    G56.41 Causalgia of right upper limb
    G56.42 Causalgia of left upper limb
    G56.43 Causalgia of bilateral upper limbs
      Coding Clinic: 2016, Q4, P17

● **G56.8 Other specified mononeuropathies of upper limb**
Disease of a single nerve
Interdigital neuroma of upper limb
    G56.80 Other specified mononeuropathies of unspecified upper limb
    G56.81 Other specified mononeuropathies of right upper limb
    G56.82 Other specified mononeuropathies of left upper limb
    G56.83 Other specified mononeuropathies of bilateral upper limbs
      Coding Clinic: 2016, Q4, P17

● **G56.9 Unspecified mononeuropathy of upper limb**
Disease of a single nerve
    G56.90 Unspecified mononeuropathy of unspecified upper limb
    G56.91 Unspecified mononeuropathy of right upper limb
    G56.92 Unspecified mononeuropathy of left upper limb
    G56.93 Unspecified mononeuropathy of bilateral upper limbs
      Coding Clinic: 2016, Q4, P17

● **G57 Mononeuropathies of lower limb**
> **Excludes1** current traumatic nerve disorder - see nerve injury by body region

★ **(See Plates 544 and 545 on pages 58 and 59.)**

● **G57.0 Lesion of sciatic nerve**
> **Excludes1** sciatica NOS (M54.3-)
> **Excludes2** sciatica attributed to intervertebral disc disorder (M51.1.-)

    G57.00 Lesion of sciatic nerve, unspecified lower limb
    G57.01 Lesion of sciatic nerve, right lower limb
    G57.02 Lesion of sciatic nerve, left lower limb
    G57.03 Lesion of sciatic nerve, bilateral lower limbs
      Coding Clinic: 2016, Q4, P1

● **G57.1 Meralgia paresthetica**
Numbness or pain in outer thigh caused by injury to nerve
Lateral cutaneous nerve of thigh syndrome
    G57.10 Meralgia paresthetica, unspecified lower limb
    G57.11 Meralgia paresthetica, right lower limb
    G57.12 Meralgia paresthetica, left lower limb
    G57.13 Meralgia paresthetica, bilateral lower limbs
      Coding Clinic: 2016, Q4, P1

● **G57.2 Lesion of femoral nerve**
    G57.20 Lesion of femoral nerve, unspecified lower limb
    G57.21 Lesion of femoral nerve, right lower limb
    G57.22 Lesion of femoral nerve, left lower limb
    G57.23 Lesion of femoral nerve, bilateral lower limbs
      Coding Clinic: 2016, Q4, P1

▶ New   ⇒ Revised   ~~deleted~~ Deleted   Excludes 1   Excludes 2   Includes   Use additional   Code first   Code also   Key words
OGCR Official Guidelines   X Assign placeholder X   ● Use Additional Character(s)   ▷ Manifestation Code   🐾 Hierarchical Condition Category   **Coding Clinic**

● **G57.3   Lesion of lateral popliteal nerve**
     Peroneal nerve palsy

     G57.30   Lesion of lateral popliteal nerve, unspecified lower limb

     G57.31   Lesion of lateral popliteal nerve, right lower limb

     G57.32   Lesion of lateral popliteal nerve, left lower limb

     G57.33   Lesion of lateral popliteal nerve, bilateral lower limbs
         Coding Clinic: 2016, Q4, P1

● **G57.4   Lesion of medial popliteal nerve**

     G57.40   Lesion of medial popliteal nerve, unspecified lower limb

     G57.41   Lesion of medial popliteal nerve, right lower limb

     G57.42   Lesion of medial popliteal nerve, left lower limb

     G57.43   Lesion of medial popliteal nerve, bilateral lower limbs
         Coding Clinic: 2016, Q4, P1

● **G57.5   Tarsal tunnel syndrome**

     G57.50   Tarsal tunnel syndrome, unspecified lower limb

     G57.51   Tarsal tunnel syndrome, right lower limb

     G57.52   Tarsal tunnel syndrome, left lower limb

     G57.53   Tarsal tunnel syndrome, bilateral lower limbs
         Coding Clinic: 2016, Q4, P1

● **G57.6   Lesion of plantar nerve**
     Morton's metatarsalgia

     G57.60   Lesion of plantar nerve, unspecified lower limb

     G57.61   Lesion of plantar nerve, right lower limb

     G57.62   Lesion of plantar nerve, left lower limb

     G57.63   Lesion of plantar nerve, bilateral lower limbs
         Coding Clinic: 2016, Q4, P1

● **G57.7   Causalgia of lower limb**
     Complex regional pain syndrome II of lower limb

     Excludes1   complex regional pain syndrome I of lower limb (G90.52-)
           complex regional pain syndrome I of upper limb (G90.51-)
           complex regional pain syndrome II of upper limb (G56.4-)
           reflex sympathetic dystrophy of lower limb (G90.52-)
           reflex sympathetic dystrophy of upper limb (G90.51-)

     G57.70   Causalgia of unspecified lower limb

     G57.71   Causalgia of right lower limb

     G57.72   Causalgia of left lower limb

     G57.73   Causalgia of bilateral lower limbs
         Coding Clinic: 2016, Q4, P1

● **G57.8   Other specified mononeuropathies of lower limb**
     Interdigital neuroma of lower limb

     G57.80   Other specified mononeuropathies of unspecified lower limb

     G57.81   Other specified mononeuropathies of right lower limb

     G57.82   Other specified mononeuropathies of left lower limb

     G57.83   Other specified mononeuropathies of bilateral lower limbs
         Coding Clinic: 2016, Q4, P17

● **G57.9   Unspecified mononeuropathy of lower limb**

     G57.90   Unspecified mononeuropathy of unspecified lower limb

     G57.91   Unspecified mononeuropathy of right lower limb

     G57.92   Unspecified mononeuropathy of left lower limb

     G57.93   Unspecified mononeuropathy of bilateral lower limbs
         Coding Clinic: 2016, Q4, P17

● **G58   Other mononeuropathies**

     G58.0   Intercostal neuropathy

     G58.7   Mononeuritis multiplex

     G58.8   Other specified mononeuropathies

     G58.9   Mononeuropathy, unspecified

▶ **G59   *Mononeuropathy in diseases classified elsewhere***
     Code first underlying disease

     Excludes1   diabetic mononeuropathy (E08-E13 with .41)
           syphilitic nerve paralysis (A52.19)
           syphilitic neuritis (A52.15)
           tuberculous mononeuropathy (A17.83)

POLYNEUROPATHIES AND OTHER DISORDERS OF THE PERIPHERAL NERVOUS SYSTEM (G60-G65)

     Excludes1   neuralgia NOS (M79.2)
           neuritis NOS (M79.2)
           peripheral neuritis in pregnancy (O26.82-)
           radiculitis NOS (M54.10)

● **G60   Hereditary and idiopathic neuropathy**

     G60.0   Hereditary motor and sensory neuropathy
         Charcot-Marie-Tooth disease
         Déjerine-Sottas disease
         Hereditary motor and sensory neuropathy, types I-IV
         Hypertrophic neuropathy of infancy
         Peroneal muscular atrophy (axonal type) (hypertrophic type)
         Roussy-Lévy syndrome

     G60.1   Refsum's disease
         Genetic disorder affecting fatty acid metabolism
         Infantile Refsum disease

     G60.2   Neuropathy in association with hereditary ataxia

     G60.3   Idiopathic progressive neuropathy

Figure 6-2   Actions of parasympathetic and sympathetic nerves. (From Chabner: The Language of Medicine, ed 9, St. Louis, Saunders, 2011)

Item 6–7   The **peripheral nervous system** consists of 31 pairs of spinal nerves, 12 pairs of cranial nerves, and the autonomic nerves, which are divided into the parasympathetic and sympathetic nerves. The cranial nerves are: olfactory (I), optic (II), oculomotor (III), trochlear (IV), trigeminal (V), abducens (VI), facial (VII), vestibulocochlear (VIII), glossopharyngeal (IX), vagus (X), accessory (XI), and hypoglossal (XII).

CHAPTER 6 (G00-G99)

G60.8   Other hereditary and idiopathic neuropathies
Dominantly inherited sensory neuropathy
Morvan's disease
Nelaton's syndrome
Recessively inherited sensory neuropathy

G60.9   Hereditary and idiopathic neuropathy, unspecified

● **G61   Inflammatory polyneuropathy**

G61.0   Guillain-Barré syndrome 🐾
Autoimmune disease affecting peripheral nervous system
Acute (post-)infective polyneuritis
Miller Fisher Syndrome

G61.1   Serum neuropathy
Use additional code for adverse effect, if applicable, to identify serum (T50.-)

● **G61.8   Other inflammatory polyneuropathies**

G61.81   Chronic inflammatory demyelinating polyneuritis 🐾

G61.82   Multifocal motor neuropathy 🐾
MMN

G61.89   Other inflammatory polyneuropathies 🐾

G61.9   Inflammatory polyneuropathy, unspecified 🐾

● **G62   Other and unspecified polyneuropathies**

G62.0   Drug-induced polyneuropathy 🐾
Use additional code for adverse effect, if applicable, to identify drug (T36-T50 with fifth or sixth character 5)

G62.1   Alcoholic polyneuropathy 🐾
Malfunction of many peripheral nerves throughout the body
Coding Clinic: 2019, Q3, P8

G62.2   Polyneuropathy due to other toxic agents 🐾
Code first (T51-T65) to identify toxic agent

● **G62.8   Other specified polyneuropathies**

G62.81   Critical illness polyneuropathy 🐾
Acute motor neuropathy

G62.82   Radiation-induced polyneuropathy 🐾
Use additional external cause code (W88-W90, X39.0-) to identify cause
Coding Clinic: 2016, Q4, P18

G62.89   Other specified polyneuropathies
Coding Clinic: 2016, Q2, P11

G62.9   Polyneuropathy, unspecified
Neuropathy NOS

▷ *G63   Polyneuropathy in diseases classified elsewhere* 🐾
Code first underlying disease, such as:
amyloidosis (E85.-)
endocrine disease, except diabetes (E00-E07, E15-E16, E20-E34)
metabolic diseases (E70-E88)
neoplasm (C00-D49)
nutritional deficiency (E40-E64)

Excludes1   polyneuropathy (in):
diabetes mellitus (E08-E13 with .42)
diphtheria (A36.83)
infectious mononucleosis (B27.0-B27.9 with 1)
Lyme disease (A69.22)
mumps (B26.84)
postherpetic (B02.23)
rheumatoid arthritis (M05.5-)
scleroderma (M34.83)
systemic lupus erythematosus (M32.19)
Coding Clinic: 2012, Q4, P100

G64   Other disorders of peripheral nervous system
Disorder of peripheral nervous system NOS

● **G65   Sequelae of inflammatory and toxic polyneuropathies**
Code first condition resulting from (sequela) of inflammatory and toxic polyneuropathies

G65.0   Sequelae of Guillain-Barré syndrome 🐾

G65.1   Sequelae of other inflammatory polyneuropathy 🐾

G65.2   Sequelae of toxic polyneuropathy 🐾

DISEASES OF MYONEURAL JUNCTION AND MUSCLE (G70-G73)

● **G70   Myasthenia gravis and other myoneural disorders**
Excludes1   botulism (A05.1, A48.51-A48.52)
transient neonatal myasthenia gravis (P94.0)

● **G70.0   Myasthenia gravis**
Acquired and results in fatigable muscle weakness exacerbated by activity and improved with rest

G70.00   Myasthenia gravis without (acute) exacerbation 🐾
Myasthenia gravis NOS

G70.01   Myasthenia gravis with (acute) exacerbation 🐾
Myasthenia gravis in crisis

G70.1   Toxic myoneural disorders 🐾
Dysfunction at junction of muscle and motor nerve (myoneural junction)
Code first (T51-T65) to identify toxic agent

G70.2   Congenital and developmental myasthenia 🐾

● **G70.8   Other specified myoneural disorders**

G70.80   Lambert-Eaton syndrome, unspecified 🐾
Lambert-Eaton syndrome NOS

▷ *G70.81   Lambert-Eaton syndrome in disease classified elsewhere* 🐾
Code first underlying disease
Excludes1   Lambert-Eaton syndrome in neoplastic disease (G73.1)

G70.89   Other specified myoneural disorders 🐾

G70.9   Myoneural disorder, unspecified 🐾

● **G71   Primary disorders of muscles**
Excludes2   arthrogryposis multiplex congenita (Q74.3)
metabolic disorders (E70-E88)
myositis (M60.-)

● **G71.0   Muscular dystrophy**

G71.00   Muscular dystrophy, unspecified 🐾

G71.01   Duchenne or Becker muscular dystrophy 🐾
Autosomal recessive, childhood type, muscular dystrophy resembling Duchenne or Becker muscular dystrophy
Benign [Becker] muscular dystrophy
Severe [Duchenne] muscular dystrophy

G71.02   Facioscapulohumeral muscular dystrophy 🐾
Scapulohumeral muscular dystrophy
Coding Clinic: 2018, Q4, P12

G71.09   Other specified muscular dystrophies 🐾
Benign scapuloperoneal muscular dystrophy with early contractures [Emery-Dreifuss]
Congenital muscular dystrophy NOS
Congenital muscular dystrophy with specific morphological abnormalities of the muscle fiber
Distal muscular dystrophy
Limb-girdle muscular dystrophy
Ocular muscular dystrophy
Oculopharyngeal muscular dystrophy
Scapuloperoneal muscular dystrophy

Item 6-8   Muscular dystrophies (MD) are a group of rare inherited muscle diseases. Voluntary muscles become progressively weaker. In the late stages of MD, fat and connective tissue replace muscle fibers. In some types of muscular dystrophy, heart muscles, other involuntary muscles, and other organs are affected. **Myopathies** is a general term for neuromuscular diseases in which the muscle fibers dysfunction for any one of many reasons, resulting in muscular weakness.

▶ New   ⇒ Revised   ~~deleted~~ Deleted   Excludes 1   Excludes 2   Includes   Use additional   Code first   Code also   Key words
OGCR Official Guidelines   X Assign placeholder X   ● Use Additional Character(s)   ▷ Manifestation Code   🐾 Hierarchical Condition Category   **Coding Clinic**

● **G71.1** **Myotonic disorders**
Inherited disorder that affects muscles tone

  G71.11 **Myotonic muscular dystrophy** 🔖
    Dystrophia myotonica [Steinert]
    Myotonia atrophica
    Myotonic dystrophy
    Proximal myotonic myopathy (PROMM)
    Steinert disease

  G71.12 **Myotonia congenita**
    Acetazolamide responsive myotonia congenita
    Dominant myotonia congenita [Thomsen disease]
    Myotonia levior
    Recessive myotonia congenita [Becker disease]

  G71.13 **Myotonic chondrodystrophy**
    Chondrodystrophic myotonia
    Congenital myotonic chondrodystrophy
    Schwartz-Jampel disease

  G71.14 **Drug induced myotonia**
    Use additional code for adverse effect, if applicable, to identify drug (T36-T50 with fifth or sixth character 5)

  G71.19 **Other specified myotonic disorders**
    Myotonia fluctuans
    Myotonia permanens
    Neuromyotonia [Isaacs]
    Paramyotonia congenita (of von Eulenburg)
    Pseudomyotonia
    Symptomatic myotonia

● **G71.2** **Congenital myopathies** 🔖

  ▷ **Excludes2**   arthrogryposis multiplex congenita (Q74.3)

  ▷ **G71.20** **Congenital myopathy, unspecifed**

  ▷ **G71.21** **Nemaline myopathy**

 ▷● **G71.22** **Centronuclear myopathy**

    ▷ **G71.220** **X-linked myotubular myopathy**
      ▷ Myotubular (centronuclear) myopathy

    ▷ **G71.228** **Other centronuclear myopathy**
      ▷ Autosomal centronuclear myopathy
      ▷ Autosomal dominant centronuclear myopathy
      ▷ Autosomal recessive centronuclear myopathy
      ▷ Centronuclear myopathy, NOS

  ▷ **G71.29** **Other congenital myopathy**
    ▷ Central core disease
    ▷ Minicore disease
    ▷ Multicore disease
    ▷ Multiminicore disease

~~Central core disease~~
~~Fiber-type disproportion~~
~~Minicore disease~~
~~Multicore disease~~
~~Myotubular (centronuclear) myopathy~~
~~Nemaline myopathy~~
  ~~**Excludes1**   arthrogryposis multiplex congenita (Q74.3)~~

G71.3 **Mitochondrial myopathy, not elsewhere classified**
Myopathies associated with increased number of enlarged, often abnormal, mitochondria in muscle fibers

  Excludes1   Kearns-Sayre syndrome (H49.81)
    Leber's disease (H47.21)
    Leigh's encephalopathy (G31.82)
    mitochondrial metabolism disorders (E88.4.-)
    Reye's syndrome (G93.7)

G71.8 **Other primary disorders of muscles**

G71.9 **Primary disorder of muscle, unspecified**
  Hereditary myopathy NOS

● **G72** **Other and unspecified myopathies**

  Excludes1   arthrogryposis multiplex congenita (Q74.3)
    dermatopolymyositis (M33.-)
    ischemic infarction of muscle (M62.2-)
    myositis (M60.-)
    polymyositis (M33.2.-)

G72.0 **Drug-induced myopathy**
  Use additional code for adverse effect, if applicable, to identify drug (T36-T50 with fifth or sixth character 5)

G72.1 **Alcoholic myopathy**
  Use additional code to identify alcoholism (F10.-)

G72.2 **Myopathy due to other toxic agents**
Code first (T51-T65) to identify toxic agent

G72.3 **Periodic paralysis**
  Familial periodic paralysis
  Hyperkalemic periodic paralysis (familial)
  Hypokalemic periodic paralysis (familial)
  Myotonic periodic paralysis (familial)
  Normokalemic paralysis (familial)
  Potassium sensitive periodic paralysis

  Excludes1   paramyotonia congenita (of von Eulenburg) (G71.19)

● **G72.4** **Inflammatory and immune myopathies, not elsewhere classified**

  G72.41 **Inclusion body myositis [IBM]**

  G72.49 **Other inflammatory and immune myopathies, not elsewhere classified**
    Inflammatory myopathy NOS

● **G72.8** **Other specified myopathies**

  G72.81 **Critical illness myopathy**
    Acute necrotizing myopathy
    Acute quadriplegic myopathy
    Intensive care (ICU) myopathy
    Myopathy of critical illness

  G72.89 **Other specified myopathies**

G72.9 **Myopathy, unspecified**

● **G73** **Disorders of myoneural junction and muscle in diseases classified elsewhere**

 ▷ *G73.1*   *Lambert-Eaton syndrome in neoplastic disease* 🔖
Rare autoimmune disorder affecting calcium channels of nerve-muscle (neuromuscular) junction

  Code first underlying neoplasm (C00-D49)

  Excludes1   Lambert-Eaton syndrome not associated with neoplasm (G70.80-G70.81)

 ▷ *G73.3*   *Myasthenic syndromes in other diseases classified elsewhere* 🔖
Code first underlying disease, such as:
  neoplasm (C00-D49)
  thyrotoxicosis (E05.-)

 ▷ *G73.7*   *Myopathy in diseases classified elsewhere*
Code first underlying disease, such as:
  hyperparathyroidism (E21.0, E21.3)
  hypoparathyroidism (E20.-)
  glycogen storage disease (E74.0)
  lipid storage disorders (E75.-)

  Excludes1   myopathy in:
    rheumatoid arthritis (M05.32)
    sarcoidosis (D86.87)
    scleroderma (M34.82)
    sicca syndrome [Sjögren] (M35.03)
    systemic lupus erythematosus (M32.19)

CHAPTER 6 (G00-G99)

CEREBRAL PALSY AND OTHER PARALYTIC SYNDROMES (G80-G83)

● **G80   Cerebral palsy**

     Excludes1   hereditary spastic paraplegia (G11.4)

     G80.0   Spastic quadriplegic cerebral palsy 🅦
         Congenital spastic paralysis (cerebral)

     G80.1   Spastic diplegic cerebral palsy 🅦
         Spastic cerebral palsy NOS

     G80.2   Spastic hemiplegic cerebral palsy 🅦

     G80.3   Athetoid cerebral palsy 🅦
         Result of damage to cerebellum or basal ganglia responsible
         for processing neuromuscular signals
         Double athetosis (syndrome)
         Dyskinetic cerebral palsy
         Dystonic cerebral palsy
         Vogt disease

     G80.4   Ataxic cerebral palsy 🅦
         Poor muscle tone and coordination

     G80.8   Other cerebral palsy 🅦
         Mixed cerebral palsy syndromes

     G80.9   Cerebral palsy, unspecified 🅦
         Cerebral palsy NOS

OGCR Section I.C.6.a.

Dominant/nondominant side

Codes from category G81, Hemiplegia and hemiparesis, and subcategories, G83.1, Monoplegia of lower limb, G83.2, Monoplegia of upper limb, and G83.3, Monoplegia, unspecified, identify whether the dominant and nondominant side is affected. Should the affected side be documented, but not specified as dominant or nondominant, and the classification system does not indicate a default, code selection is as follows:

- For ambidextrous patients, the default should be dominant.
- If the left side is affected, the default is nondominant.
- If the right side is affected, the default is dominant.

● **G81   Hemiplegia and hemiparesis**

     Note: This category is to be used only when hemiplegia (complete)(incomplete) is reported without further specification, or is stated to be old or longstanding but of unspecified cause. The category is also for use in multiple coding to identify these types of hemiplegia resulting from any cause.

     Excludes1   congenital cerebral palsy (G80.-)
           hemiplegia and hemiparesis due to sequela of
             cerebrovascular disease (I69.05-, I69.15-,
             I69.25-, I69.35-, I69.85-, I69.95-)

     Coding Clinic: 2012, Q4, P106

●   **G81.0   Flaccid hemiplegia**
         Paralysis of half of body with loss of tone of muscles of
         paralyzed part and absence of tendon reflexes

     G81.00   Flaccid hemiplegia affecting unspecified side 🅦

     G81.01   Flaccid hemiplegia affecting right dominant side 🅦

     G81.02   Flaccid hemiplegia affecting left dominant side 🅦

     G81.03   Flaccid hemiplegia affecting right nondominant side 🅦

     G81.04   Flaccid hemiplegia affecting left nondominant side 🅦

●   **G81.1   Spastic hemiplegia**
         Paralysis of half of body with spasticity of muscles of
         paralyzed part and increased tendon reflexes

     G81.10   Spastic hemiplegia affecting unspecified side 🅦

     G81.11   Spastic hemiplegia affecting right dominant side 🅦

     G81.12   Spastic hemiplegia affecting left dominant side 🅦

     G81.13   Spastic hemiplegia affecting right nondominant side 🅦

     G81.14   Spastic hemiplegia affecting left nondominant side 🅦

●   **G81.9   Hemiplegia, unspecified**

     G81.90   Hemiplegia, unspecified affecting unspecified side 🅦

     G81.91   Hemiplegia, unspecified affecting right dominant side 🅦

     G81.92   Hemiplegia, unspecified affecting left dominant side 🅦

     G81.93   Hemiplegia, unspecified affecting right nondominant side 🅦

     G81.94   Hemiplegia, unspecified affecting left nondominant side 🅦
         Coding Clinic: 2015, Q1, P26

● **G82   Paraplegia (paraparesis) and quadriplegia (quadriparesis)**

     Note: This category is to be used only when the listed conditions are reported without further specification, or are stated to be old or longstanding but of unspecified cause. The category is also for use in multiple coding to identify these conditions resulting from any cause.

     Excludes1   congenital cerebral palsy (G80.-)
           functional quadriplegia (R53.2)
           hysterical paralysis (F44.4)

●   **G82.2   Paraplegia**
         Paralysis of both lower limbs NOS
         Paraparesis (lower) NOS
         Paraplegia (lower) NOS

     G82.20   Paraplegia, unspecified 🅦
         Coding Clinic: 2017, Q3, P3

     G82.21   Paraplegia, complete 🅦

     G82.22   Paraplegia, incomplete 🅦

●   **G82.5   Quadriplegia**
         Paralysis of all limbs; AKA tetraplegia

     G82.50   Quadriplegia, unspecified 🅦

     G82.51   Quadriplegia, C1-C4 complete 🅦

     G82.52   Quadriplegia, C1-C4 incomplete 🅦

     G82.53   Quadriplegia, C5-C7 complete 🅦

     G82.54   Quadriplegia, C5-C7 incomplete 🅦

● **G83   Other paralytic syndromes**

     Note: This category is to be used only when the listed conditions are reported without further specification, or are stated to be old or longstanding but of unspecified cause. The category is also for use in multiple coding to identify these conditions resulting from any cause.

     Includes   paralysis (complete) (incomplete), except as in
           G80-G82

     G83.0   Diplegia of upper limbs 🅦
         Paralysis affecting limbs on both sides; AKA bilateral
         paralysis
         Diplegia (upper)
         Paralysis of both upper limbs

Item 6–9   Hemiplegia is complete paralysis of one side of the body—arm, leg, and trunk. **Hemiparesis** is a generalized weakness or incomplete paralysis of one side of the body. If most activities (eating, writing) are performed with the right hand, the right is the dominant side, and the left is the nondominant side. **Quadriplegia,** also called tetraplegia, is the complete paralysis of all four limbs. **Quadriparesis** is the incomplete paralysis of all four limbs. Nerve damage in C1–C4 is associated with lower limb paralysis, and C5–C7 damage is associated with upper limb paralysis. **Diplegia** is the paralysis of the upper limbs. **Monoplegia** is the complete paralysis of one limb.

▶ New   ⇒ Revised   ~~deleted~~ Deleted   Excludes 1   Excludes 2   Includes   Use additional   Code first   Code also   Key words

OGCR Official Guidelines   X Assign placeholder X   ● Use Additional Character(s)   ▷ Manifestation Code   🅦 Hierarchical Condition Category   **Coding Clinic**

● **G83.1 Monoplegia of lower limb**
Paralysis of limb on one side
Paralysis of lower limb

> **Excludes1** monoplegia of lower limbs due to sequela of cerebrovascular disease (I69.04-, I69.14-, I69.24-, I69.34-, I69.84-, I69.94-)

Coding Clinic: 2012, Q4, P106

G83.10 **Monoplegia of lower limb affecting unspecified side** 🔲

G83.11 **Monoplegia of lower limb affecting right dominant side** 🔲

G83.12 **Monoplegia of lower limb affecting left dominant side** 🔲

G83.13 **Monoplegia of lower limb affecting right nondominant side** 🔲

G83.14 **Monoplegia of lower limb affecting left nondominant side** 🔲

● **G83.2 Monoplegia of upper limb**
Paralysis of upper limb

> **Excludes1** monoplegia of upper limbs due to sequela of cerebrovascular disease (I69.03-, I69.13-, I69.23-, I69.33-, I69.83-, I69.93-)

Coding Clinic: 2012, Q4, P106

G83.20 **Monoplegia of upper limb affecting unspecified side** 🔲

G83.21 **Monoplegia of upper limb affecting right dominant side** 🔲

G83.22 **Monoplegia of upper limb affecting left dominant side** 🔲

G83.23 **Monoplegia of upper limb affecting right nondominant side** 🔲

G83.24 **Monoplegia of upper limb affecting left nondominant side** 🔲

● **G83.3 Monoplegia, unspecified**
Coding Clinic: 2012, Q4, P106

G83.30 **Monoplegia, unspecified affecting unspecified side** 🔲

G83.31 **Monoplegia, unspecified affecting right dominant side** 🔲

G83.32 **Monoplegia, unspecified affecting left dominant side** 🔲

G83.33 **Monoplegia, unspecified affecting right nondominant side** 🔲

G83.34 **Monoplegia, unspecified affecting left nondominant side** 🔲

G83.4 Cauda equina syndrome 🔲
Aching pain due to compression of spinal nerve roots
Neurogenic bladder due to cauda equina syndrome

> **Excludes1** cord bladder NOS (G95.89)
> neurogenic bladder NOS (N31.9)

G83.5 Locked-in state 🔲

● **G83.8 Other specified paralytic syndromes**

> **Excludes1** paralytic syndromes due to current spinal cord injury-code to spinal cord injury (S14, S24, S34)

G83.81 **Brown-Séquard syndrome** 🔲

G83.82 **Anterior cord syndrome** 🔲

G83.83 **Posterior cord syndrome** 🔲

G83.84 **Todd's paralysis (postepileptic)** 🔲

G83.89 **Other specified paralytic syndromes** 🔲

G83.9 Paralytic syndrome, unspecified 🔲

OTHER DISORDERS OF THE NERVOUS SYSTEM (G89-G99)

● **G89 Pain, not elsewhere classified**
Code also related psychological factors associated with pain (F45.42)

> **Excludes1** generalized pain NOS (R52)
> pain disorders exclusively related to psychological factors (F45.41)
> pain NOS (R52)

> **Excludes2** atypical face pain (G50.1)
> headache syndromes (G44.-)
> localized pain, unspecified type - code to pain by site, such as:
>   abdomen pain (R10.-)
>   back pain (M54.9)
>   breast pain (N64.4)
>   chest pain (R07.1-R07.9)
>   ear pain (H92.0-)
>   eye pain (H57.1)
> ➡ headache (R51.9)
>   joint pain (M25.5-)
>   limb pain (M79.6-)
>   lumbar region pain (M54.5)
>   painful urination (R30.9)
>   pelvic and perineal pain (R10.2)
>   shoulder pain (M25.51-)
>   spine pain (M54.-)
>   throat pain (R07.0)
>   tongue pain (K14.6)
>   tooth pain (K08.8)
> renal colic (N23)
> migraines (G43.-)
> myalgia (M79.1-)
> pain from prosthetic devices, implants, and grafts (T82.84, T83.84, T84.84, T85.84-)
> phantom limb syndrome with pain (G54.6)
> vulvar vestibulitis (N94.810)
> vulvodynia (N94.81-)

G89.0 Central pain syndrome
Neurological condition causing intractable pain resulting from damage to CNS
Déjérine-Roussy syndrome
Myelopathic pain syndrome
Thalamic pain syndrome (hyperesthetic)

● **G89.1 Acute pain, not elsewhere classified**

G89.11 **Acute pain due to trauma**

G89.12 **Acute post-thoracotomy pain**
Post-thoracotomy pain NOS

G89.18 **Other acute postprocedural pain**
Postoperative pain NOS
Postprocedural pain NOS

● **G89.2 Chronic pain, not elsewhere classified**

> **Excludes1** causalgia, lower limb (G57.7-)
> causalgia, upper limb (G56.4-)
> central pain syndrome (G89.0)
> chronic pain syndrome (G89.4)
> complex regional pain syndrome II, lower limb (G57.7-)
> complex regional pain syndrome II, upper limb (G56.4-)
> neoplasm related chronic pain (G89.3)
> reflex sympathetic dystrophy (G90.5-)

G89.21 **Chronic pain due to trauma**

G89.22 **Chronic post-thoracotomy pain**

G89.28 **Other chronic postprocedural pain**
Other chronic postoperative pain

G89.29 **Other chronic pain**

G89.3 Neoplasm related pain (acute) (chronic)
Cancer associated pain
Pain due to malignancy (primary) (secondary)
Tumor associated pain

G89.4 Chronic pain syndrome
Chronic pain associated with significant psychosocial dysfunction

CHAPTER 6 (G00-G99)

● G90   Disorders of autonomic nervous system

> **Excludes1**   dysfunction of the autonomic nervous system due to alcohol (G31.2)

● G90.0   Idiopathic peripheral autonomic neuropathy

    G90.01   Carotid sinus syncope
       Carotid sinus syndrome

    G90.09   Other idiopathic peripheral autonomic neuropathy
       Idiopathic peripheral autonomic neuropathy NOS

G90.1   Familial dysautonomia [Riley-Day] ⓗ
   Inherited disorder that affects nerve function

G90.2   Horner's syndrome
   Due to damage of the sympathetic nervous system
   Bernard(-Horner) syndrome
   Cervical sympathetic dystrophy or paralysis

G90.3   Multi-system degeneration of the autonomic nervous system ⓗ
   Neurogenic orthostatic hypotension [Shy-Drager]

> **Excludes1**   orthostatic hypotension NOS (I95.1)

G90.4   Autonomic dysreflexia
   Syndrome resulting from lesions of spinal cord
   Use additional code to identify the cause, such as:
     fecal impaction (K56.41)
     pressure ulcer (pressure area) (L89.-)
     urinary tract infection (N39.0)

● G90.5   Complex regional pain syndrome I (CRPS I)
   Reflex sympathetic dystrophy

> **Excludes1**   causalgia of lower limb (G57.7-)
>   causalgia of upper limb (G56.4-)
>   complex regional pain syndrome II of lower limb (G57.7-)
>   complex regional pain syndrome II of upper limb (G56.4-)

    G90.50   Complex regional pain syndrome I, unspecified

    ● G90.51   Complex regional pain syndrome I of upper limb

       G90.511   Complex regional pain syndrome I of right upper limb

       G90.512   Complex regional pain syndrome I of left upper limb

       G90.513   Complex regional pain syndrome I of upper limb, bilateral

       G90.519   Complex regional pain syndrome I of unspecified upper limb

    ● G90.52   Complex regional pain syndrome I of lower limb

       G90.521   Complex regional pain syndrome I of right lower limb

       G90.522   Complex regional pain syndrome I of left lower limb

       G90.523   Complex regional pain syndrome I of lower limb, bilateral

       G90.529   Complex regional pain syndrome I of unspecified lower limb

    G90.59   Complex regional pain syndrome I of other specified site

G90.8   Other disorders of autonomic nervous system

G90.9   Disorder of the autonomic nervous system, unspecified

● G91   Hydrocephalus
Dilatation of cerebral ventricles, accompanied by accumulation of cerebrospinal fluid

> **Includes**   acquired hydrocephalus
> **Excludes1**   Arnold-Chiari syndrome with hydrocephalus (Q07.-)
>   congenital hydrocephalus (Q03.-)
>   spina bifida with hydrocephalus (Q05.-)

G91.0   Communicating hydrocephalus
   Secondary normal pressure hydrocephalus

G91.1   Obstructive hydrocephalus

G91.2   (Idiopathic) normal pressure hydrocephalus
   Normal pressure hydrocephalus NOS

G91.3   Post-traumatic hydrocephalus, unspecified

▸ **G91.4   Hydrocephalus in diseases classified elsewhere**
   Code first underlying condition, such as:
     congenital syphilis (A50.4-)
     neoplasm (C00-D49)
     plasminogen deficiency (E88.02)

> **Excludes1**   hydrocephalus due to congenital toxoplasmosis (P37.1)

G91.8   Other hydrocephalus

G91.9   Hydrocephalus, unspecified

G92   Toxic encephalopathy
Disorder or disease of brain caused by chemicals
Toxic encephalitis
Toxic metabolic encephalopathy

⇒ *Code first if applicable, drug induced (T36-T50) or use (T51-T65) to identify toxic agent*
Coding Clinic: 2017, Q1, P39-40

● G93   Other disorders of brain

G93.0   Cerebral cysts
   Arachnoid cyst
   Porencephalic cyst, acquired

> **Excludes1**   acquired periventricular cysts of newborn (P91.1)
>   congenital cerebral cysts (Q04.6)

G93.1   Anoxic brain damage, not elsewhere classified ⓗ
   Permanent brain damage by lack of oxygen perfusion through brain tissues.

> **Excludes1**   cerebral anoxia due to anesthesia during labor and delivery (O74.3)
>   cerebral anoxia due to anesthesia during the puerperium (O89.2)
>   neonatal anoxia (P84)

G93.2   Benign intracranial hypertension
▸ Pseudotumor

> **Excludes1**   hypertensive encephalopathy (I67.4)
>   ▸ obstructive hydrocephalus (G91.1)

G93.3   Postviral fatigue syndrome
   Benign myalgic encephalomyelitis

> **Excludes1**   chronic fatigue syndrome NOS (R53.82)

● G93.4   Other and unspecified encephalopathy

> **Excludes1**   alcoholic encephalopathy (G31.2)
>   encephalopathy in diseases classified elsewhere (G94)
>   hypertensive encephalopathy (I67.4)
>   ~~toxic (metabolic) encephalopathy (G92)~~

▸ **Excludes2**   toxic (metabolic) encephalopathy (G92)
Coding Clinic: 2017, Q2, P9

    G93.40   Encephalopathy, unspecified

    G93.41   Metabolic encephalopathy
       Septic encephalopathy
       Coding Clinic: 2017, Q2, P8; 2016, Q3, P42; 2015, Q3, P21

    G93.49   Other encephalopathy
       Encephalopathy NEC
       Coding Clinic: 2018, Q4, P16; 2018, Q2, P22; 2017, Q2, P9

▸ New   ⇒ Revised   ~~deleted~~ Deleted   Excludes 1   Excludes 2   Includes   Use additional   Code first   Code also   Key words

812   OGCR Official Guidelines   X Assign placeholder X   ● Use Additional Character(s)   ▸ Manifestation Code   ⓗ Hierarchical Condition Category   Coding Clinic

CHAPTER 6 (G00-G99)

G93.5   Compression of brain 🔾
Arnold-Chiari type 1 compression of brain
Compression of brain (stem)
Herniation of brain (stem)
    Excludes1   diffuse traumatic compression of brain
                 (S06.2-)
                   focal traumatic compression of brain
                   (S06.3-)

G93.6   Cerebral edema 🔾
    Excludes1   cerebral edema due to birth injury (P11.0)
                   traumatic cerebral edema (S06.1-)

G93.7   Reye's syndrome   **P**
Life-threatening neurological condition, usually follows viral illness
Code first (poisoning due to salicylates, if applicable (T39.0-, with sixth character 1-4)
Use additional code for adverse effect due to salicylates, if applicable (T39.0-, with sixth character 5)

● **G93.8   Other specified disorders of brain**
   G93.81   Temporal sclerosis
         Hippocampal sclerosis
         Mesial temporal sclerosis
   G93.82   Brain death
   G93.89   Other specified disorders of brain
         Postradiation encephalopathy
         Coding Clinic: 2019, Q3, P9; 2016, Q4, P7

G93.9   Disorder of brain, unspecified

◗ *G94   Other disorders of brain in diseases classified elsewhere*
    Code first underlying disease
    Excludes1   encephalopathy in congenital syphilis (A50.49)
                  encephalopathy in influenza (J09.X9, J10.81, J11.81)
                  encephalopathy in syphilis (A52.19)
                  hydrocephalus in diseases classified elsewhere (G91.4)
    Coding Clinic: 2018, Q2, P22; 2017, Q2, P8

● **G95   Other and unspecified diseases of spinal cord**
    Excludes2   myelitis (G04.-)
   G95.0   Syringomyelia and syringobulbia 🔾
● **G95.1   Vascular myelopathies**
    Excludes2   intraspinal phlebitis and thrombophlebitis, except non-pyogenic (G08)
   G95.11   Acute infarction of spinal cord (embolic) (nonembolic) 🔾
         Anoxia of spinal cord
         Arterial thrombosis of spinal cord
   G95.19   Other vascular myelopathies 🔾
         Edema of spinal cord
         Hematomyelia
         Nonpyogenic intraspinal phlebitis and thrombophlebitis
         Subacute necrotic myelopathy
● **G95.2   Other and unspecified cord compression**
   G95.20   Unspecified cord compression 🔾
   G95.29   Other cord compression 🔾
● **G95.8   Other specified diseases of spinal cord**
    Excludes1   neurogenic bladder NOS (N31.9)
                  neurogenic bladder due to cauda equina syndrome (G83.4)
                  neuromuscular dysfunction of bladder without spinal cord lesion (N31.-)
   G95.81   Conus medullaris syndrome 🔾
         Damage to gray matter and/or nerve roots in lower end of spinal cord
   G95.89   Other specified diseases of spinal cord 🔾
         Cord bladder NOS
         Drug-induced myelopathy
         Radiation-induced myelopathy
      Excludes1   myelopathy NOS (G95.9)
G95.9   Disease of spinal cord, unspecified 🔾
    Myelopathy NOS

● **G96   Other disorders of central nervous system**
● **G96.0   Cerebrospinal fluid leak**
    ▸Code also if applicable:
      ▸intracranial hypotension (G96.81-)
    Excludes1   cerebrospinal fluid leak from spinal puncture (G97.0)
    Coding Clinic: 2018, Q2, P13
   ▸ **G96.00   Cerebrospinal fluid leak, unspecified**
      ▸Code also if applicable:
        ▸head injury (S00.- to S09.-)
   ▸ **G96.01   Cranial cerebrospinal fluid leak, spontaneous**
      ▸Otorrhea due to spontaneous cerebrospinal fluid CSF leak
      ▸Rhinorrhea due to spontaneous cerebrospinal fluid CSF leak
      ▸Spontaneous cerebrospinal fluid leak from skull base
   ▸ **G96.02   Spinal cerebrospinal fluid leak, spontaneous**
      ▸Spontaneous cerebrospinal fluid leak from spine
   ▸ **G96.08   Other cranial cerebrospinal fluid leak**
      ▸Postoperative cranial cerebrospinal fluid leak
      ▸Traumatic cranial cerebrospinal fluid leak
      ▸Code also if applicable:
        ▸head injury (S00.- to S09.-)
   ▸ **G96.09   Other spinal cerebrospinal fluid leak**
      ▸Other spinal CSF leak
      ▸Postoperative spinal cerebrospinal fluid leak
      ▸Traumatic spinal cerebrospinal fluid leak
      ▸Code also if applicable:
        ▸head injury (S00.- to S09.-)
● **G96.1   Disorders of meninges, not elsewhere classified**
   G96.11   Dural tear
      ▸Code also intracranial hypotension, if applicable (G96.81-)
      Excludes1   accidental puncture or laceration of dura during a procedure (G97.41)
   G96.12   Meningeal adhesions (cerebral) (spinal)
● **G96.19   Other disorders of meninges, not elsewhere classified**
   ▸ **G96.191   Perineural cyst**
      ▸Cervical nerve root cyst
      ▸Lumbar nerve root cyst
      ▸Sacral nerve root cyst
      ▸Tarlov cyst
      ▸Thoracic nerve root cyst
   ▸ **G96.198   Other disorders of meninges, not elsewhere classified**
● **G96.8   Other specified disorders of central nervous system**
 ▸● **G96.81   Intracranial hypotension**
      ▸Code also any associated diagnoses, such as:
      ▸Brachial amyotrophy (G54.5)
      ▸Cerebrospinal fluid leak from spine (G96.02)
      ▸Cranial nerve disorders in diseases classified elsewhere (G53)
      ▸Nerve root and compressions in diseases classified elsewhere (G55)
      ▸Nonpyogenic thrombosis of intracranial venous system (I67.6)
      ▸Nontraumatic intracerebral hemorrhage (I61.-)
      ▸Nontraumatic subdural hemorrhage (I62.0-)
      ▸Other and unspecified cord compression (G95.2-)
      ▸Other secondary parkinsonism (G21.8)
      ▸Reversible cerebrovascular vasoconstriction syndrome (I67.841)
      ▸Spinal cord herniation (G95.89)
      ▸Stroke (I63.-)
      ▸Syringomyelia (G95.0)
   ▸ **G96.810   Intracranial hypotension, unspecified**
   ▸ **G96.811   Intracranial hypotension, spontaneous**
   ▸ **G96.819   Other intracranial hypotension**
   ▸ **G96.89   Other specified disorders of central nervous system**
G96.9   Disorder of central nervous system, unspecified

CHAPTER 6 (G00-G99)

● **G97   Intraoperative and postprocedural complications and disorders of nervous system, not elsewhere classified**

> **Excludes2**   intraoperative and postprocedural cerebrovascular infarction (I97.81-, I97.82-)

> Coding Clinic: 2016, Q4, P9

G97.0   Cerebrospinal fluid leak from spinal puncture
> ▶Code also any associated diagnoses or complications, such as:
>> ▶intracranial hypotension following a procedure (G97.83-G97.84)

G97.1   Other reaction to spinal and lumbar puncture
> Headache due to lumbar puncture
> ▶Other reaction to spinal dural puncture
> ▶Code also, if applicable, any associated headache with orthostatic component (R51.0)

G97.2   Intracranial hypotension following ventricular shunting
> ▶Code also any associated diagnoses or complications

● **G97.3   Intraoperative hemorrhage and hematoma of a nervous system organ or structure complicating a procedure**
> **Excludes1**   intraoperative hemorrhage and hematoma of a nervous system organ or structure due to accidental puncture and laceration during a procedure (G97.4-)

G97.31   Intraoperative hemorrhage and hematoma of a nervous system organ or structure complicating a nervous system procedure

G97.32   Intraoperative hemorrhage and hematoma of a nervous system organ or structure complicating other procedure

● **G97.4   Accidental puncture and laceration of a nervous system organ or structure during a procedure**

G97.41   Accidental puncture or laceration of dura during a procedure
> Incidental (inadvertent) durotomy
> ▶Code also any associated diagnoses or complications

G97.48   Accidental puncture and laceration of other nervous system organ or structure during a nervous system procedure

G97.49   Accidental puncture and laceration of other nervous system organ or structure during other procedure

● **G97.5   Postprocedural hemorrhage of a nervous system organ or structure following a procedure**

G97.51   Postprocedural hemorrhage of a nervous system organ or structure following a nervous system procedure

G97.52   Postprocedural hemorrhage of a nervous system organ or structure following other procedure

● **G97.6   Postprocedural hematoma and seroma of a nervous system organ or structure following a procedure**

G97.61   Postprocedural hematoma of a nervous system organ or structure following a nervous system procedure

G97.62   Postprocedural hematoma of a nervous system organ or structure following other procedure

G97.63   Postprocedural seroma of a nervous system organ or structure following a nervous system procedure

G97.64   Postprocedural seroma of a nervous system organ or structure following other procedure

● **G97.8   Other intraoperative and postprocedural complications and disorders of nervous system**
> Use additional code to further specify disorder

G97.81   Other intraoperative complications of nervous system

G97.82   Other postprocedural complications and disorders of nervous system

▶ **G97.83   Intracranial hypotension following lumbar cerebrospinal fluid shunting**
> ▶Code also any associated diagnoses or complications

▶ **G97.84   Intracranial hypotension following other procedure**
> ▶Code also, if applicable:
>> ▶accidental puncture or laceration of dura during a procedure (G97.41)
>> ▶cerebrospinal fluid leak from spinal puncture (G97.0)

● **G98   Other disorders of nervous system not elsewhere classified**
> **Includes**   nervous system disorder NOS

G98.0   Neurogenic arthritis, not elsewhere classified
> Nonsyphilitic neurogenic arthropathy NEC
> Nonsyphilitic neurogenic spondylopathy NEC
> **Excludes1**   spondylopathy (in):
>> syringomyelia and syringobulbia (G95.0)
>> tabes dorsalis (A52.11)

G98.8   Other disorders of nervous system
> Nervous system disorder NOS

● **G99   Other disorders of nervous system in diseases classified elsewhere**

▷ *G99.0   Autonomic neuropathy in diseases classified elsewhere*
> *Code first underlying disease, such as:*
>> amyloidosis (E85.-)
>> gout (M1A.-, M10.-)
>> hyperthyroidism (E05.-)
> **Excludes1**   diabetic autonomic neuropathy (E08-E13 with .43)

▷ *G99.2   Myelopathy in diseases classified elsewhere* 🅷
> *Code first underlying disease, such as:*
>> neoplasm (C00-D49)
> **Excludes1**   myelopathy in:
>> intervertebral disease (M50.0-, M51.0-)
>> spondylosis (M47.0-, M47.1-)

▷ *G99.8   Other specified disorders of nervous system in diseases classified elsewhere*
> *Code first underlying disorder, such as:*
>> amyloidosis (E85.-)
>> avitaminosis (E56.9)
> **Excludes1**   nervous system involvement in:
>> cysticercosis (B69.0)
>> rubella (B06.0-)
>> syphilis (A52.1-)

▶ New   ⇒ Revised   ~~deleted~~ Deleted   Excludes 1   Excludes 2   Includes   Use additional   Code first   Code also   Key words

OGCR Official Guidelines   X Assign placeholder X   ● Use Additional Character(s)   ▷ Manifestation Code   🅷 Hierarchical Condition Category   Coding Clinic

CHAPTER 7

DISEASES OF THE EYE AND ADNEXA
(H00-H59)

OGCR Chapter-Specific Coding Guidelines

7. Chapter 7: Diseases of the Eye and Adnexa (H00-H59)

a. Glaucoma

1) Assigning Glaucoma Codes

Assign as many codes from category H40, Glaucoma, as needed to identify the type of glaucoma, the affected eye, and the glaucoma stage.

2) Bilateral glaucoma with same type and stage

When a patient has bilateral glaucoma and both eyes are documented as being the same type and stage, and there is a code for bilateral glaucoma, report only the code for the type of glaucoma, bilateral, with the seventh character for the stage.

When a patient has bilateral glaucoma and both eyes are documented as being the same type and stage, and the classification does not provide a code for bilateral glaucoma (i.e., subcategories H40.10, H40.11, and H40.20) report only one code for the type of glaucoma with the appropriate seventh character for the stage.

3) Bilateral glaucoma stage with different types or stages

When a patient has bilateral glaucoma and each eye is documented as having a different type or stage, and the classification distinguishes laterality, assign the appropriate code for each eye rather than the code for bilateral glaucoma.

When a patient has bilateral glaucoma and each eye is documented as having a different type, and the classification does not distinguish laterality (i.e., subcategories H40.10, H40.11 and H40.20), assign one code for each type of glaucoma with the appropriate seventh character for the stage.

When a patient has bilateral glaucoma and each eye is documented as having the same type, but different stage, and the classification does not distinguish laterality (i.e., subcategories H40.10, H40.11, and H40.20), assign a code for the type of glaucoma for each eye with the seventh character for the specific glaucoma stage documented for each eye.

4) Patient admitted with glaucoma and stage evolves during the admission

If a patient is admitted with glaucoma and the stage progresses during the admission, assign the code for highest stage documented.

5) Indeterminate stage glaucoma

Assignment of the seventh character "4" for "indeterminate stage" should be based on the clinical documentation. The seventh character "4" is used for glaucomas whose stage cannot be clinically determined. This seventh character should not be confused with the seventh character "0", unspecified, which should be assigned when there is no documentation regarding the stage of the glaucoma.

b. Blindness

If "blindness" or "low vision" of both eyes is documented but the visual impairment category is not documented, assign code H54.3, Unqualified visual loss, both eyes. If "blindness" or "low vision" in one eye is documented but the visual impairment category is not documented, assign a code from H54.6-, Unqualified visual loss, one eye. If "blindness" or "visual loss" is documented without any information about whether one or both eyes are affected, assign code H54.7, Unspecified visual loss.

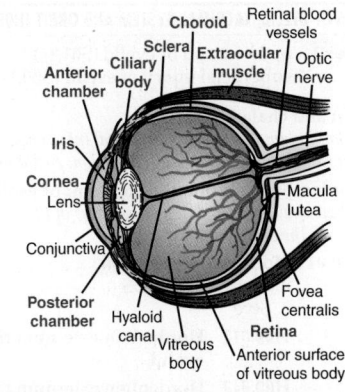

Figure 7–1 Eye and ocular adnexa. (From Buck CJ: Step-by-Step Medical Coding, ed 2016, St. Louis, Elsevier, 2016)

★**(See Plate 15 of the Anatomy Illustrations.)**

CHAPTER 7

DISEASES OF THE EYE AND ADNEXA
(H00-H59)

Note: Use an external cause code following the code for the eye condition, if applicable, to identify the cause of the eye condition

Excludes2 certain conditions originating in the perinatal period (P04-P96)

certain infectious and parasitic diseases (A00-B99)

complications of pregnancy, childbirth and the puerperium (O00-O9A)

congenital malformations, deformations, and chromosomal abnormalities (Q00-Q99)

diabetes mellitus related eye conditions (E09.3-, E10.3-, E11.3-, E13.3-)

endocrine, nutritional and metabolic diseases (E00-E88)

injury (trauma) of eye and orbit (S05.-)

injury, poisoning and certain other consequences of external causes (S00-T88)

neoplasms (C00-D49)

symptoms, signs and abnormal clinical and laboratory findings, not elsewhere classified (R00-R94)

syphilis related eye disorders (A50.01, A50.3-, A51.43, A52.71)

This chapter contains the following blocks:

H00-H05	Disorders of eyelid, lacrimal system and orbit
H10-H11	Disorders of conjunctiva
H15-H22	Disorders of sclera, cornea, iris and ciliary body
H25-H28	Disorders of lens
H30-H36	Disorders of choroid and retina
H40-H42	Glaucoma
H43-H44	Disorders of vitreous body and globe
H46-H47	Disorders of optic nerve and visual pathways
H49-H52	Disorders of ocular muscles, binocular movement, accommodation and refraction
H53-H54	Visual disturbances and blindness
H55-H57	Other disorders of eye and adnexa
H59	Intraoperative and postprocedural complications and disorders of eye and adnexa, not elsewhere classified

DISORDERS OF EYELID, LACRIMAL SYSTEM AND ORBIT (H00-H05)

Excludes2   open wound of eyelid (S01.1-)
              superficial injury of eyelid (S00.1-, S00.2-)

● H00   **Hordeolum and chalazion**
        Hordeolum: inflammatory staphylococcal infection of sebaceous
        glands of eyelids; AKA stye. Chalazion: eyelid mass

  ● H00.0   **Hordeolum (externum) (internum) of eyelid**
            Bacterial infection (staphylococcus) of the sebaceous gland of
            the eyelid (stye)

    ● H00.01   **Hordeolum externum**
               Hordeolum NOS
               Stye
               H00.011   Hordeolum externum **right upper**
                         eyelid
               H00.012   Hordeolum externum **right lower**
                         eyelid
               H00.013   Hordeolum externum **right eye,**
                         unspecified eyelid
               H00.014   Hordeolum externum **left upper**
                         eyelid
               H00.015   Hordeolum externum **left lower**
                         eyelid
               H00.016   Hordeolum externum **left eye,**
                         unspecified eyelid
               H00.019   Hordeolum externum **unspecified eye,**
                         unspecified eyelid

    ● H00.02   **Hordeolum internum**
               Infection of meibomian gland
               H00.021   Hordeolum internum **right upper**
                         eyelid
               H00.022   Hordeolum internum **right lower**
                         eyelid
               H00.023   Hordeolum internum **right eye,**
                         unspecified eyelid
               H00.024   Hordeolum internum **left upper**
                         eyelid
               H00.025   Hordeolum internum **left lower**
                         eyelid
               H00.026   Hordeolum internum **left eye,**
                         unspecified eyelid
               H00.029   Hordeolum internum **unspecified eye,**
                         unspecified eyelid

    ● H00.03   **Abscess of eyelid**
               Furuncle of eyelid
               H00.031   Abscess of **right upper** eyelid
               H00.032   Abscess of **right lower** eyelid
               H00.033   Abscess of eyelid **right eye,**
                         unspecified eyelid
               H00.034   Abscess of **left upper** eyelid
               H00.035   Abscess of **left lower** eyelid
               H00.036   Abscess of eyelid **left eye, unspecified**
                         eyelid
               H00.039   Abscess of eyelid **unspecified eye,**
                         unspecified eyelid

  ● H00.1   **Chalazion**
            Often caused by accumulation of meibomian gland secretions
            resulting from a blockage of duct.
            Meibomian (gland) cyst
            Excludes2   infected meibomian gland (H00.02-)
            H00.11   Chalazion **right upper eyelid**
            H00.12   Chalazion **right lower eyelid**
            H00.13   Chalazion **right eye, unspecified eyelid**
            H00.14   Chalazion **left upper eyelid**
            H00.15   Chalazion **left lower eyelid**
            H00.16   Chalazion **left eye, unspecified** eyelid
            H00.19   Chalazion **unspecified eye, unspecified eyelid**

● H01   **Other inflammation of eyelid**
  ● H01.0   **Blepharitis**
            Inflammation of eyelids
            Excludes1   blepharoconjunctivitis (H10.5-)

    ● H01.00   **Unspecified blepharitis**
               H01.001   Unspecified blepharitis **right upper**
                         eyelid
               H01.002   Unspecified blepharitis **right lower**
                         eyelid
               H01.003   Unspecified blepharitis **right eye,**
                         unspecified eyelid
               H01.004   Unspecified blepharitis **left upper**
                         eyelid
               H01.005   Unspecified blepharitis **left lower**
                         eyelid
               H01.006   Unspecified blepharitis **left eye,**
                         unspecified eyelid
               H01.009   Unspecified blepharitis **unspecified**
                         eye, unspecified eyelid
               H01.00A   Unspecified blepharitis right eye,
                         upper and lower eyelids
               H01.00B   Unspecified blepharitis left eye,
                         upper and lower eyelids

    ● H01.01   **Ulcerative blepharitis**
               H01.011   Ulcerative blepharitis **right upper**
                         eyelid
               H01.012   Ulcerative blepharitis **right lower**
                         eyelid
               H01.013   Ulcerative blepharitis **right eye,**
                         unspecified eyelid
               H01.014   Ulcerative blepharitis **left upper**
                         eyelid
               H01.015   Ulcerative blepharitis **left lower**
                         eyelid
               H01.016   Ulcerative blepharitis **left eye,**
                         unspecified eyelid
               H01.019   Ulcerative blepharitis **unspecified**
                         eye, unspecified eyelid
               H01.01A   Ulcerative blepharitis right eye, upper
                         and lower eyelids
               H01.01B   Ulcerative blepharitis left eye, upper
                         and lower eyelids

    ● H01.02   **Squamous blepharitis**
               H01.021   Squamous blepharitis **right upper**
                         eyelid
               H01.022   Squamous blepharitis **right lower**
                         eyelid
               H01.023   Squamous blepharitis **right eye,**
                         unspecified eyelid
               H01.024   Squamous blepharitis **left upper**
                         eyelid
               H01.025   Squamous blepharitis **left lower**
                         eyelid
               H01.026   Squamous blepharitis **left eye,**
                         unspecified eyelid
               H01.029   Squamous blepharitis **unspecified**
                         eye, unspecified eyelid
               H01.02A   Squamous blepharitis right eye,
                         upper and lower eyelids
               H01.02B   Squamous blepharitis left eye, upper
                         and lower eyelids

  ● H01.1   **Noninfectious dermatoses of eyelid**
    ● H01.11   **Allergic dermatitis of eyelid**
               Contact dermatitis of eyelid
               H01.111   Allergic dermatitis of **right upper**
                         eyelid
               H01.112   Allergic dermatitis of **right lower**
                         eyelid
               H01.113   Allergic dermatitis of **right eye,**
                         unspecified eyelid

▶ New   ⇒ Revised   ~~deleted~~ Deleted   Excludes 1   Excludes 2   Includes   Use additional   Code first   Code also   Key words

OGCR Official Guidelines   X Assign placeholder X   ● Use Additional Character(s)   ▶ Manifestation Code   🅗 Hierarchical Condition Category   Coding Clinic

H01.114   Allergic dermatitis of left upper eyelid

H01.115   Allergic dermatitis of left lower eyelid

H01.116   Allergic dermatitis of left eye, unspecified eyelid

H01.119   Allergic dermatitis of unspecified eye, unspecified eyelid

● H01.12   Discoid lupus erythematosus of eyelid

H01.121   Discoid lupus erythematosus of right upper eyelid

H01.122   Discoid lupus erythematosus of right lower eyelid

H01.123   Discoid lupus erythematosus of right eye, unspecified eyelid

H01.124   Discoid lupus erythematosus of left upper eyelid

H01.125   Discoid lupus erythematosus of left lower eyelid

H01.126   Discoid lupus erythematosus of left eye, unspecified eyelid

H01.129   Discoid lupus erythematosus of unspecified eye, unspecified eyelid

● H01.13   Eczematous dermatitis of eyelid

H01.131   Eczematous dermatitis of right upper eyelid

H01.132   Eczematous dermatitis of right lower eyelid

H01.133   Eczematous dermatitis of right eye, unspecified eyelid

H01.134   Eczematous dermatitis of left upper eyelid

H01.135   Eczematous dermatitis of left lower eyelid

H01.136   Eczematous dermatitis of left eye, unspecified eyelid

H01.139   Eczematous dermatitis of unspecified eye, unspecified eyelid

● H01.14   Xeroderma of eyelid
          Abnormally dry

H01.141   Xeroderma of right upper eyelid

H01.142   Xeroderma of right lower eyelid

H01.143   Xeroderma of right eye, unspecified eyelid

H01.144   Xeroderma of left upper eyelid

H01.145   Xeroderma of left lower eyelid

H01.146   Xeroderma of left eye, unspecified eyelid

H01.149   Xeroderma of unspecified eye, unspecified eyelid

H01.8   Other specified inflammations of eyelid

H01.9   Unspecified inflammation of eyelid
        Inflammation of eyelid NOS

● H02   Other disorders of eyelid
       Turning inward (inversion) of eyelid margin and ingrowing eyelashes

       Excludes1   congenital malformations of eyelid (Q10.0-Q10.3)

● H02.0   Entropion and trichiasis of eyelid

● H02.00   Unspecified entropion of eyelid

H02.001   Unspecified entropion of right upper eyelid

H02.002   Unspecified entropion of right lower eyelid

H02.003   Unspecified entropion of right eye, unspecified eyelid

H02.004   Unspecified entropion of left upper eyelid

H02.005   Unspecified entropion of left lower eyelid

Figure 7-2   Right lower eyelid entropion. Note the inward rotation of the tarsal plate about the horizontal axis and the resultant contact between the mucocutaneous junction and ocular surface. (From Glynn M, Drake WM, Hutchison R: Hutchison's Clinical Methods: An Integrated Approach to Clinical Practice, Edinburgh, Saunders/Elsevier, 2012)

H02.006   Unspecified entropion of left eye, unspecified eyelid

H02.009   Unspecified entropion of unspecified eye, unspecified eyelid

● H02.01   Cicatricial entropion of eyelid
          Scar

H02.011   Cicatricial entropion of right upper eyelid

H02.012   Cicatricial entropion of right lower eyelid

H02.013   Cicatricial entropion of right eye, unspecified eyelid

H02.014   Cicatricial entropion of left upper eyelid

H02.015   Cicatricial entropion of left lower eyelid

H02.016   Cicatricial entropion of left eye, unspecified eyelid

H02.019   Cicatricial entropion of unspecified eye, unspecified eyelid

● H02.02   Mechanical entropion of eyelid
          Turning inward (inversion) of eyelid margin due to lack of support

H02.021   Mechanical entropion of right upper eyelid

H02.022   Mechanical entropion of right lower eyelid

H02.023   Mechanical entropion of right eye, unspecified eyelid

H02.024   Mechanical entropion of left upper eyelid

H02.025   Mechanical entropion of left lower eyelid

H02.026   Mechanical entropion of left eye, unspecified eyelid

H02.029   Mechanical entropion of unspecified eye, unspecified eyelid

● H02.03   Senile entropion of eyelid
          Turning inward (inversion) of eyelid margin due to aging

H02.031   Senile entropion of right upper eyelid   A

H02.032   Senile entropion of right lower eyelid   A

H02.033   Senile entropion of right eye, unspecified eyelid   A

H02.034   Senile entropion of left upper eyelid   A

H02.035   Senile entropion of left lower eyelid   A

H02.036   Senile entropion of left eye, unspecified eyelid   A

H02.039   Senile entropion of unspecified eye, unspecified eyelid   A

● H02.04   Spastic entropion of eyelid
          Turning inward (inversion) of eyelid margin caused by spasm of muscle

H02.041   Spastic entropion of right upper eyelid

H02.042   Spastic entropion of right lower eyelid

H02.043   Spastic entropion of right eye, unspecified eyelid

H02.044   Spastic entropion of left upper eyelid

H02.045   Spastic entropion of left lower eyelid

H02.046   Spastic entropion of left eye, unspecified eyelid

H02.049   Spastic entropion of unspecified eye, unspecified eyelid

● H02.05   Trichiasis without entropion
Ingrowing hairs of eyelashes

H02.051   Trichiasis without entropion right upper eyelid

H02.052   Trichiasis without entropion right lower eyelid

H02.053   Trichiasis without entropion right eye, unspecified eyelid

H02.054   Trichiasis without entropion left upper eyelid

H02.055   Trichiasis without entropion left lower eyelid

H02.056   Trichiasis without entropion left eye, unspecified eyelid

H02.059   Trichiasis without entropion unspecified eye, unspecified eyelid

● H02.1   Ectropion of eyelid
Eversion (pulling away) of eyelid

● H02.10   Unspecified ectropion of eyelid

H02.101   Unspecified ectropion of right upper eyelid

H02.102   Unspecified ectropion of right lower eyelid

H02.103   Unspecified ectropion of right eye, unspecified eyelid

H02.104   Unspecified ectropion of left upper eyelid

H02.105   Unspecified ectropion of left lower eyelid

H02.106   Unspecified ectropion of left eye, unspecified eyelid

H02.109   Unspecified ectropion of unspecified eye, unspecified eyelid

● H02.11   Cicatricial ectropion of eyelid
Pulling of eyelid down and away from eye due to scar or tightening

H02.111   Cicatricial ectropion of right upper eyelid

H02.112   Cicatricial ectropion of right lower eyelid

H02.113   Cicatricial ectropion of right eye, unspecified eyelid

H02.114   Cicatricial ectropion of left upper eyelid

H02.115   Cicatricial ectropion of left lower eyelid

H02.116   Cicatricial ectropion of left eye, unspecified eyelid

H02.119   Cicatricial ectropion of unspecified eye, unspecified eyelid

● H02.12   Mechanical ectropion of eyelid
Eversion (pulling away) of eyelid due to lack of support

H02.121   Mechanical ectropion of right upper eyelid

H02.122   Mechanical ectropion of right lower eyelid

H02.123   Mechanical ectropion of right eye, unspecified eyelid

H02.124   Mechanical ectropion of left upper eyelid

H02.125   Mechanical ectropion of left lower eyelid

H02.126   Mechanical ectropion of left eye, unspecified eyelid

H02.129   Mechanical ectropion of unspecified eye, unspecified eyelid

● H02.13   Senile ectropion of eyelid
Eversion (pulling away) of eyelid due to age

H02.131   Senile ectropion of right upper eyelid   A

H02.132   Senile ectropion of right lower eyelid   A

H02.133   Senile ectropion of right eye, unspecified eyelid   A

H02.134   Senile ectropion of left upper eyelid   A

H02.135   Senile ectropion of left lower eyelid   A

H02.136   Senile ectropion of left eye, unspecified eyelid   A

H02.139   Senile ectropion of unspecified eye, unspecified eyelid   A

● H02.14   Spastic ectropion of eyelid
Eversion (pulling away) of eyelid due to tonic muscle spasm

H02.141   Spastic ectropion of right upper eyelid

H02.142   Spastic ectropion of right lower eyelid

H02.143   Spastic ectropion of right eye, unspecified eyelid

H02.144   Spastic ectropion of left upper eyelid

H02.145   Spastic ectropion of left lower eyelid

H02.146   Spastic ectropion of left eye, unspecified eyelid

H02.149   Spastic ectropion of unspecified eye, unspecified eyelid

● H02.15   Paralytic ectropion of eyelid

H02.151   Paralytic ectropion of right upper eyelid

H02.152   Paralytic ectropion of right lower eyelid

H02.153   Paralytic ectropion of right eye, unspecified eyelid

H02.154   Paralytic ectropion of left upper eyelid

H02.155   Paralytic ectropion of left lower eyelid

H02.156   Paralytic ectropion of left eye, unspecified eyelid

H02.159   Paralytic ectropion of unspecified eye, unspecified eyelid

● H02.2   Lagophthalmos
Condition in which eye cannot completely close

● H02.20   Unspecified lagophthalmos

H02.201   Unspecified lagophthalmos right upper eyelid

H02.202   Unspecified lagophthalmos right lower eyelid

H02.203   Unspecified lagophthalmos right eye, unspecified eyelid

H02.204   Unspecified lagophthalmos left upper eyelid

H02.205   Unspecified lagophthalmos left lower eyelid

H02.206   Unspecified lagophthalmos left eye, unspecified eyelid

H02.209   Unspecified lagophthalmos unspecified eye, unspecified eyelid

H02.20A   Unspecified lagophthalmos right eye, upper and lower eyelids

H02.20B   Unspecified lagophthalmos left eye, upper and lower eyelids

H02.20C   Unspecified lagophthalmos, bilateral, upper and lower eyelids

▶ New   ⇛ Revised   ~~deleted~~ Deleted   Excludes 1   Excludes 2   Includes   Use additional   Code first   Code also   Key words

OGCR Official Guidelines   X Assign placeholder X   ● Use Additional Character(s)   ▷ Manifestation Code   🅠 Hierarchical Condition Category   Coding Clinic

H02.21 Cicatricial lagophthalmos
Upper or lower eyelid does not close due to scar or tightening

H02.211   Cicatricial lagophthalmos right upper eyelid

H02.212   Cicatricial lagophthalmos right lower eyelid

H02.213   Cicatricial lagophthalmos right eye, unspecified eyelid

H02.214   Cicatricial lagophthalmos left upper eyelid

H02.215   Cicatricial lagophthalmos left lower eyelid

H02.216   Cicatricial lagophthalmos left eye, unspecified eyelid

H02.219   Cicatricial lagophthalmos unspecified eye, unspecified eyelid

H02.21A   Cicatricial lagophthalmos right eye, upper and lower eyelids

H02.21B   Cicatricial lagophthalmos left eye, upper and lower eyelids

H02.21C   Cicatricial lagophthalmos, bilateral, upper and lower eyelids

H02.22 Mechanical lagophthalmos
Inability to close lids due to structural disorder

H02.221   Mechanical lagophthalmos right upper eyelid

H02.222   Mechanical lagophthalmos right lower eyelid

H02.223   Mechanical lagophthalmos right eye, unspecified eyelid

H02.224   Mechanical lagophthalmos left upper eyelid

H02.225   Mechanical lagophthalmos left lower eyelid

H02.226   Mechanical lagophthalmos left eye, unspecified eyelid

H02.229   Mechanical lagophthalmos unspecified eye, unspecified eyelid

H02.22A   Mechanical lagophthalmos right eye, upper and lower eyelids

H02.22B   Mechanical lagophthalmos left eye, upper and lower eyelids

H02.22C   Mechanical lagophthalmos, bilateral, upper and lower eyelids

H02.23 Paralytic lagophthalmos
Eyelids do not close due to paralysis

H02.231   Paralytic lagophthalmos right upper eyelid

H02.232   Paralytic lagophthalmos right lower eyelid

H02.233   Paralytic lagophthalmos right eye, unspecified eyelid

H02.234   Paralytic lagophthalmos left upper eyelid

H02.235   Paralytic lagophthalmos left lower eyelid

H02.236   Paralytic lagophthalmos left eye, unspecified eyelid

H02.239   Paralytic lagophthalmos unspecified eye, unspecified eyelid

H02.23A   Paralytic lagophthalmos right eye, upper and lower eyelids

H02.23B   Paralytic lagophthalmos left eye, upper and lower eyelids

H02.23C   Paralytic lagophthalmos, bilateral, upper and lower eyelids

Figure 7-3 Ptosis of eyelid. (From Kanski JJ: Clinical Diagnosis in Ophthalmology, London, Elsevier Mosby, 2006)

Item 7-1 Ptosis of eyelid is drooping of the upper eyelid over the pupil when the eyes are fully opened resulting from nerve or muscle damage, which may require surgical correction.

★ **(See Plate 17 of the Anatomy Illustrations.)**

H02.3 Blepharochalasis
Relaxation of skin of eyelid, due to atrophy of intercellular tissue
Pseudoptosis

H02.30   Blepharochalasis unspecified eye, unspecified eyelid

H02.31   Blepharochalasis right upper eyelid

H02.32   Blepharochalasis right lower eyelid

H02.33   Blepharochalasis right eye, unspecified eyelid

H02.34   Blepharochalasis left upper eyelid

H02.35   Blepharochalasis left lower eyelid

H02.36   Blepharochalasis left eye, unspecified eyelid

H02.4 Ptosis of eyelid
Falling forward, drooping, sagging of eyelid

H02.40 Unspecified ptosis of eyelid

H02.401   Unspecified ptosis of right eyelid

H02.402   Unspecified ptosis of left eyelid

H02.403   Unspecified ptosis of bilateral eyelids

H02.409   Unspecified ptosis of unspecified eyelid

H02.41 Mechanical ptosis of eyelid

H02.411   Mechanical ptosis of right eyelid

H02.412   Mechanical ptosis of left eyelid

H02.413   Mechanical ptosis of bilateral eyelids

H02.419   Mechanical ptosis of unspecified eyelid

H02.42 Myogenic ptosis of eyelid

H02.421   Myogenic ptosis of right eyelid

H02.422   Myogenic ptosis of left eyelid

H02.423   Myogenic ptosis of bilateral eyelids

H02.429   Myogenic ptosis of unspecified eyelid

H02.43 Paralytic ptosis of eyelid
Neurogenic ptosis of eyelid

H02.431   Paralytic ptosis of right eyelid

H02.432   Paralytic ptosis of left eyelid

H02.433   Paralytic ptosis of bilateral eyelids

H02.439   Paralytic ptosis unspecified eyelid

H02.5 Other disorders affecting eyelid function

Excludes2   blepharospasm (G24.5)
          organic tic (G25.69)
          psychogenic tic (F95.-)

H02.51 Abnormal innervation syndrome

H02.511   Abnormal innervation syndrome right upper eyelid

H02.512   Abnormal innervation syndrome right lower eyelid

H02.513   Abnormal innervation syndrome right eye, unspecified eyelid

H02.514   Abnormal innervation syndrome left upper eyelid

H02.515   Abnormal innervation syndrome left lower eyelid

H02.516   Abnormal innervation syndrome left eye, unspecified eyelid

H02.519   Abnormal innervation syndrome unspecified eye, unspecified eyelid

● **H02.52 Blepharophimosis**
Drooping of eyelid with reduced lid size
Ankyloblepharon

   H02.521 Blepharophimosis right upper eyelid

   H02.522 Blepharophimosis right lower eyelid

   H02.523 Blepharophimosis right eye, unspecified eyelid

   H02.524 Blepharophimosis left upper eyelid

   H02.525 Blepharophimosis left lower eyelid

   H02.526 Blepharophimosis left eye, unspecified eyelid

   H02.529 Blepharophimosis unspecified eye, unspecified lid

● **H02.53 Eyelid retraction**
Eyelid lag

   H02.531 Eyelid retraction right upper eyelid

   H02.532 Eyelid retraction right lower eyelid

   H02.533 Eyelid retraction right eye, unspecified eyelid

   H02.534 Eyelid retraction left upper eyelid

   H02.535 Eyelid retraction left lower eyelid

   H02.536 Eyelid retraction left eye, unspecified eyelid

   H02.539 Eyelid retraction unspecified eye, unspecified lid

 H02.59 Other disorders affecting eyelid function
Deficient blink reflex
Sensory disorders

● **H02.6 Xanthelasma of eyelid**
Yellow-to-orange patches or pimples clustered together on eyelid

   H02.60 Xanthelasma of unspecified eye, unspecified eyelid

   H02.61 Xanthelasma of right upper eyelid

   H02.62 Xanthelasma of right lower eyelid

   H02.63 Xanthelasma of right eye, unspecified eyelid

   H02.64 Xanthelasma of left upper eyelid

   H02.65 Xanthelasma of left lower eyelid

   H02.66 Xanthelasma of left eye, unspecified eyelid

● **H02.7 Other and unspecified degenerative disorders of eyelid and periocular area**

   H02.70 Unspecified degenerative disorders of eyelid and periocular area

● **H02.71 Chloasma of eyelid and periocular area**
Dyspigmentation of eyelid
Hyperpigmentation of eyelid

   H02.711 Chloasma of right upper eyelid and periocular area

   H02.712 Chloasma of right lower eyelid and periocular area

   H02.713 Chloasma of right eye, unspecified eyelid and periocular area

   H02.714 Chloasma of left upper eyelid and periocular area

   H02.715 Chloasma of left lower eyelid and periocular area

   H02.716 Chloasma of left eye, unspecified eyelid and periocular area

   H02.719 Chloasma of unspecified eye, unspecified eyelid and periocular area

● **H02.72 Madarosis of eyelid and periocular area**
Loss of eyelashes and/or eyebrows
Hypotrichosis of eyelid

   H02.721 Madarosis of right upper eyelid and periocular area

   H02.722 Madarosis of right lower eyelid and periocular area

   H02.723 Madarosis of right eye, unspecified eyelid and periocular area

   H02.724 Madarosis of left upper eyelid and periocular area

   H02.725 Madarosis of left lower eyelid and periocular area

   H02.726 Madarosis of left eye, unspecified eyelid and periocular area

   H02.729 Madarosis of unspecified eye, unspecified eyelid and periocular area

● **H02.73 Vitiligo of eyelid and periocular area**
Skin pigmentation disease characterized by white patches
Hypopigmentation of eyelid

   H02.731 Vitiligo of right upper eyelid and periocular area

   H02.732 Vitiligo of right lower eyelid and periocular area

   H02.733 Vitiligo of right eye, unspecified eyelid and periocular area

   H02.734 Vitiligo of left upper eyelid and periocular area

   H02.735 Vitiligo of left lower eyelid and periocular area

   H02.736 Vitiligo of left eye, unspecified eyelid and periocular area

   H02.739 Vitiligo of unspecified eye, unspecified eyelid and periocular area

 H02.79 Other degenerative disorders of eyelid and periocular area

● **H02.8 Other specified disorders of eyelid**

● **H02.81 Retained foreign body in eyelid**
Use additional code to identify the type of retained foreign body (Z18.-)

   Excludes1 laceration of eyelid with foreign body (S01.12-)
retained intraocular foreign body (H44.6-, H44.7-)
superficial foreign body of eyelid and periocular area (S00.25-)

   H02.811 Retained foreign body in right upper eyelid

   H02.812 Retained foreign body in right lower eyelid

   H02.813 Retained foreign body in right eye, unspecified eyelid

   H02.814 Retained foreign body in left upper eyelid

   H02.815 Retained foreign body in left lower eyelid

   H02.816 Retained foreign body in left eye, unspecified eyelid

   H02.819 Retained foreign body in unspecified eye, unspecified eyelid

● **H02.82 Cysts of eyelid**
Sebaceous cyst of eyelid

   H02.821 Cysts of right upper eyelid

   H02.822 Cysts of right lower eyelid

   H02.823 Cysts of right eye, unspecified eyelid

   H02.824 Cysts of left upper eyelid

   H02.825 Cysts of left lower eyelid

   H02.826 Cysts of left eye, unspecified eyelid

   H02.829 Cysts of unspecified eye, unspecified eyelid

● **H02.83 Dermatochalasis of eyelid**
Skin is inelastic and hangs loosely in folds

   H02.831 Dermatochalasis of right upper eyelid

   H02.832 Dermatochalasis of right lower eyelid

   H02.833 Dermatochalasis of right eye, unspecified eyelid

   H02.834 Dermatochalasis of left upper eyelid

▶ New   ⇒ Revised   ~~deleted~~ Deleted   Excludes 1   Excludes 2   Includes   Use additional   Code first   Code also   Key words

OGCR Official Guidelines   X Assign placeholder X   ● Use Additional Character(s)   ▷ Manifestation Code   🝆 Hierarchical Condition Category   Coding Clinic

H02.835　Dermatochalasis of left lower eyelid

H02.836　Dermatochalasis of left eye, unspecified eyelid

H02.839　Dermatochalasis of unspecified eye, unspecified eyelid

● H02.84　Edema of eyelid
Hyperemia of eyelid

H02.841　Edema of right upper eyelid

H02.842　Edema of right lower eyelid

H02.843　Edema of right eye, unspecified eyelid

H02.844　Edema of left upper eyelid

H02.845　Edema of left lower eyelid

H02.846　Edema of left eye, unspecified eyelid

H02.849　Edema of unspecified eye, unspecified eyelid

● H02.85　Elephantiasis of eyelid
Massive secondary lymphedema with hypertrophy of skin and subcutaneous tissues (pachyderma)

H02.851　Elephantiasis of right upper eyelid

H02.852　Elephantiasis of right lower eyelid

H02.853　Elephantiasis of right eye, unspecified eyelid

H02.854　Elephantiasis of left upper eyelid

H02.855　Elephantiasis of left lower eyelid

H02.856　Elephantiasis of left eye, unspecified eyelid

H02.859　Elephantiasis of unspecified eye, unspecified eyelid

● H02.86　Hypertrichosis of eyelid
Excessive growth of hair

H02.861　Hypertrichosis of right upper eyelid

H02.862　Hypertrichosis of right lower eyelid

H02.863　Hypertrichosis of right eye, unspecified eyelid

H02.864　Hypertrichosis of left upper eyelid

H02.865　Hypertrichosis of left lower eyelid

H02.866　Hypertrichosis of left eye, unspecified eyelid

H02.869　Hypertrichosis of unspecified eye, unspecified eyelid

● H02.87　Vascular anomalies of eyelid

H02.871　Vascular anomalies of right upper eyelid

H02.872　Vascular anomalies of right lower eyelid

H02.873　Vascular anomalies of right eye, unspecified eyelid

H02.874　Vascular anomalies of left upper eyelid

H02.875　Vascular anomalies of left lower eyelid

H02.876　Vascular anomalies of left eye, unspecified eyelid

H02.879　Vascular anomalies of unspecified eye, unspecified eyelid

● H02.88　Meibomian gland dysfunction of eyelid

H02.881　Meibomian gland dysfunction right upper eyelid

H02.882　Meibomian gland dysfunction right lower eyelid

H02.883　Meibomian gland dysfunction of right eye, unspecified eyelid

H02.884　Meibomian gland dysfunction left upper eyelid

H02.885　Meibomian gland dysfunction left lower eyelid

H02.886　Meibomian gland dysfunction of left eye, unspecified eyelid

H02.889　Meibomian gland dysfunction of unspecified eye, unspecified eyelid

H02.88A　Meibomian gland dysfunction right eye, upper and lower eyelids

H02.88B　Meibomian gland dysfunction left eye, upper and lower eyelids

H02.89　Other specified disorders of eyelid
Hemorrhage of eyelid

H02.9　Unspecified disorder of eyelid
Disorder of eyelid NOS

● H04　Disorders of lacrimal system

Excludes1　congenital malformations of lacrimal system (Q10.4-Q10.6)

● H04.0　Dacryoadenitis
Inflammation of lacrimal gland

● H04.00　Unspecified dacryoadenitis

H04.001　Unspecified dacryoadenitis, right lacrimal gland

H04.002　Unspecified dacryoadenitis, left lacrimal gland

H04.003　Unspecified dacryoadenitis, bilateral lacrimal glands

H04.009　Unspecified dacryoadenitis, unspecified lacrimal gland

● H04.01　Acute dacryoadenitis

H04.011　Acute dacryoadenitis, right lacrimal gland

H04.012　Acute dacryoadenitis, left lacrimal gland

H04.013　Acute dacryoadenitis, bilateral lacrimal glands

H04.019　Acute dacryoadenitis, unspecified lacrimal gland

★ **(See Plate 19 of the Anatomy Illustrations.)**

● H04.02　Chronic dacryoadenitis

H04.021　Chronic dacryoadenitis, right lacrimal gland

H04.022　Chronic dacryoadenitis, left lacrimal gland

H04.023　Chronic dacryoadenitis, bilateral lacrimal gland

H04.029　Chronic dacryoadenitis, unspecified lacrimal gland

● H04.03　Chronic enlargement of lacrimal gland

H04.031　Chronic enlargement of right lacrimal gland

H04.032　Chronic enlargement of left lacrimal gland

H04.033　Chronic enlargement of bilateral lacrimal glands

H04.039　Chronic enlargement of unspecified lacrimal gland

● H04.1　Other disorders of lacrimal gland

● H04.11　Dacryops
Watery eye or distention of lacrimal duct due to fluid

H04.111　Dacryops of right lacrimal gland

H04.112　Dacryops of left lacrimal gland

H04.113　Dacryops of bilateral lacrimal glands

H04.119　Dacryops of unspecified lacrimal gland

Figure 7-4 Lacrimal apparatus. (From Buck CJ: Step-by-Step Medical Coding, 2016, St. Louis, Elsevier, 2016)

● **H04.12**   **Dry eye syndrome**
     Tear film insufficiency, NOS
     H04.121   Dry eye syndrome of right lacrimal gland
     H04.122   Dry eye syndrome of left lacrimal gland
     H04.123   Dry eye syndrome of bilateral lacrimal glands
     H04.129   Dry eye syndrome of unspecified lacrimal gland

● **H04.13**   **Lacrimal cyst**
     Lacrimal cystic degeneration
     H04.131   Lacrimal cyst right lacrimal gland
     H04.132   Lacrimal cyst left lacrimal gland
     H04.133   Lacrimal cyst bilateral lacrimal glands
     H04.139   Lacrimal cyst unspecified lacrimal gland

● **H04.14**   **Primary lacrimal gland atrophy**
     H04.141   Primary lacrimal gland atrophy, right lacrimal gland
     H04.142   Primary lacrimal gland atrophy, left lacrimal gland
     H04.143   Primary lacrimal gland atrophy, bilateral lacrimal glands
     H04.149   Primary lacrimal gland atrophy, unspecified lacrimal gland

● **H04.15**   **Secondary lacrimal gland atrophy**
     H04.151   Secondary lacrimal gland atrophy, right lacrimal gland
     H04.152   Secondary lacrimal gland atrophy, left lacrimal gland
     H04.153   Secondary lacrimal gland atrophy, bilateral lacrimal glands
     H04.159   Secondary lacrimal gland atrophy, unspecified lacrimal gland

● **H04.16**   **Lacrimal gland dislocation**
     H04.161   Lacrimal gland dislocation, right lacrimal gland
     H04.162   Lacrimal gland dislocation, left lacrimal gland
     H04.163   Lacrimal gland dislocation, bilateral lacrimal glands
     H04.169   Lacrimal gland dislocation, unspecified lacrimal gland

     H04.19   Other specified disorders of lacrimal gland

● **H04.2**   **Epiphora**
     Overflow of tears due to stricture of lacrimal passages; AKA lacrimation

● **H04.20**   **Unspecified epiphora**
     H04.201   Unspecified epiphora, right side
     H04.202   Unspecified epiphora, left side
     H04.203   Unspecified epiphora, bilateral
     H04.209   Unspecified epiphora, unspecified side

● **H04.21**   **Epiphora due to excess lacrimation**
     H04.211   Epiphora due to excess lacrimation, right lacrimal gland
     H04.212   Epiphora due to excess lacrimation, left lacrimal gland
     H04.213   Epiphora due to excess lacrimation, bilateral lacrimal glands
     H04.219   Epiphora due to excess lacrimation, unspecified lacrimal gland

● **H04.22**   **Epiphora due to insufficient drainage**
     H04.221   Epiphora due to insufficient drainage, right side
     H04.222   Epiphora due to insufficient drainage, left side
     H04.223   Epiphora due to insufficient drainage, bilateral
     H04.229   Epiphora due to insufficient drainage, unspecified side

● **H04.3**   **Acute and unspecified inflammation of lacrimal passages**
     Excludes1   neonatal dacryocystitis (P39.1)

● **H04.30**   **Unspecified dacryocystitis**
     H04.301   Unspecified dacryocystitis of right lacrimal passage
     H04.302   Unspecified dacryocystitis of left lacrimal passage
     H04.303   Unspecified dacryocystitis of bilateral lacrimal passages
     H04.309   Unspecified dacryocystitis of unspecified lacrimal passage

● **H04.31**   **Phlegmonous dacryocystitis**
     Cellulitis of lacrimal sac
     H04.311   Phlegmonous dacryocystitis of right lacrimal passage
     H04.312   Phlegmonous dacryocystitis of left lacrimal passage
     H04.313   Phlegmonous dacryocystitis of bilateral lacrimal passages
     H04.319   Phlegmonous dacryocystitis of unspecified lacrimal passage

● **H04.32**   **Acute dacryocystitis**
     Acute dacryopericystitis
     H04.321   Acute dacryocystitis of right lacrimal passage
     H04.322   Acute dacryocystitis of left lacrimal passage
     H04.323   Acute dacryocystitis of bilateral lacrimal passages
     H04.329   Acute dacryocystitis of unspecified lacrimal passage

● **H04.33**   **Acute lacrimal canaliculitis**
     H04.331   Acute lacrimal canaliculitis of right lacrimal passage
     H04.332   Acute lacrimal canaliculitis of left lacrimal passage
     H04.333   Acute lacrimal canaliculitis of bilateral lacrimal passages
     H04.339   Acute lacrimal canaliculitis of unspecified lacrimal passage

● **H04.4**   **Chronic inflammation of lacrimal passages**

● **H04.41**   **Chronic dacryocystitis**
     Inflammation of lacrimal sac
     H04.411   Chronic dacryocystitis of right lacrimal passage
     H04.412   Chronic dacryocystitis of left lacrimal passage
     H04.413   Chronic dacryocystitis of bilateral lacrimal passages
     H04.419   Chronic dacryocystitis of unspecified lacrimal passage

● **H04.42**   **Chronic lacrimal canaliculitis**
     Inflammation of lacrimal ducts
     H04.421   Chronic lacrimal canaliculitis of right lacrimal passage
     H04.422   Chronic lacrimal canaliculitis of left lacrimal passage
     H04.423   Chronic lacrimal canaliculitis of bilateral lacrimal passages
     H04.429   Chronic lacrimal canaliculitis of unspecified lacrimal passage

● **H04.43**   **Chronic lacrimal mucocele**
     Accumulation of mucous secretion
     H04.431   Chronic lacrimal mucocele of right lacrimal passage
     H04.432   Chronic lacrimal mucocele of left lacrimal passage
     H04.433   Chronic lacrimal mucocele of bilateral lacrimal passages
     H04.439   Chronic lacrimal mucocele of unspecified lacrimal passage

▶ New   ⇒ Revised   ~~deleted~~ Deleted   Excludes 1   Excludes 2   Includes   Use additional   Code first   Code also   Key words

OGCR Official Guidelines   X Assign placeholder X   ● Use Additional Character(s)   ⟩ Manifestation Code   🏷 Hierarchical Condition Category   **Coding Clinic**

● **H04.5   Stenosis and insufficiency of lacrimal passages**
   ● **H04.51   Dacryolith**
      Concretion in lacrimal sac/duct; AKA lacrimal calculus
      H04.511   Dacryolith of right lacrimal passage
      H04.512   Dacryolith of left lacrimal passage
      H04.513   Dacryolith of bilateral lacrimal passages
      H04.519   Dacryolith of unspecified lacrimal passage
   ● **H04.52   Eversion of lacrimal punctum**
      Turning out of lacrimal drainage opening
      H04.521   Eversion of right lacrimal punctum
      H04.522   Eversion of left lacrimal punctum
      H04.523   Eversion of bilateral lacrimal punctum
      H04.529   Eversion of unspecified lacrimal punctum
   ● **H04.53   Neonatal obstruction of nasolacrimal duct**
      Excludes1   congenital stenosis and stricture of lacrimal duct (Q10.5)
      H04.531   Neonatal obstruction of right nasolacrimal duct   **N**
      H04.532   Neonatal obstruction of left nasolacrimal duct   **N**
      H04.533   Neonatal obstruction of bilateral nasolacrimal duct   **N**
      H04.539   Neonatal obstruction of unspecified nasolacrimal duct   **N**
   ● **H04.54   Stenosis of lacrimal canaliculi**
      H04.541   Stenosis of right lacrimal canaliculi
      H04.542   Stenosis of left lacrimal canaliculi
      H04.543   Stenosis of bilateral lacrimal canaliculi
      H04.549   Stenosis of unspecified lacrimal canaliculi
   ● **H04.55   Acquired stenosis of nasolacrimal duct**
      H04.551   Acquired stenosis of right nasolacrimal duct
      H04.552   Acquired stenosis of left nasolacrimal duct
      H04.553   Acquired stenosis of bilateral nasolacrimal duct
      H04.559   Acquired stenosis of unspecified nasolacrimal duct
   ● **H04.56   Stenosis of lacrimal punctum**
      H04.561   Stenosis of right lacrimal punctum
      H04.562   Stenosis of left lacrimal punctum
      H04.563   Stenosis of bilateral lacrimal punctum
      H04.569   Stenosis of unspecified lacrimal punctum
   ● **H04.57   Stenosis of lacrimal sac**
      H04.571   Stenosis of right lacrimal sac
      H04.572   Stenosis of left lacrimal sac
      H04.573   Stenosis of bilateral lacrimal sac
      H04.579   Stenosis of unspecified lacrimal sac
● **H04.6   Other changes of lacrimal passages**
   ● **H04.61   Lacrimal fistula**
      H04.611   Lacrimal fistula right lacrimal passage
      H04.612   Lacrimal fistula left lacrimal passage
      H04.613   Lacrimal fistula bilateral lacrimal passages
      H04.619   Lacrimal fistula unspecified lacrimal passage
   H04.69   Other changes of lacrimal passages

● **H04.8   Other disorders of lacrimal system**
   ● **H04.81   Granuloma of lacrimal passages**
      Inflammatory response due to infectious or noninfectious agents
      H04.811   Granuloma of right lacrimal passage
      H04.812   Granuloma of left lacrimal passage
      H04.813   Granuloma of bilateral lacrimal passages
      H04.819   Granuloma of unspecified lacrimal passage
   H04.89   Other disorders of lacrimal system
   H04.9   Disorder of lacrimal system, unspecified
● **H05   Disorders of orbit**
      Excludes1   congenital malformation of orbit (Q10.7)
   ● **H05.0   Acute inflammation of orbit**
      H05.00   Unspecified acute inflammation of orbit
   ● **H05.01   Cellulitis of orbit**
      Infection of soft tissue of orbit
      Abscess of orbit
      H05.011   Cellulitis of right orbit
      H05.012   Cellulitis of left orbit
      H05.013   Cellulitis of bilateral orbits
      H05.019   Cellulitis of unspecified orbit
   ● **H05.02   Osteomyelitis of orbit**
      Infection of bony orbit of eye
      H05.021   Osteomyelitis of right orbit
      H05.022   Osteomyelitis of left orbit
      H05.023   Osteomyelitis of bilateral orbits
      H05.029   Osteomyelitis of unspecified orbit
   ● **H05.03   Periostitis of orbit**
      Inflammation of periosteum (membrane covering bone surface)
      H05.031   Periostitis of right orbit
      H05.032   Periostitis of left orbit
      H05.033   Periostitis of bilateral orbits
      H05.039   Periostitis of unspecified orbit
   ● **H05.04   Tenonitis of orbit**
      Inflammation of tenon capsule (space enclosing fascia of Tenon between eyeball and fat of orbit)
      H05.041   Tenonitis of right orbit
      H05.042   Tenonitis of left orbit
      H05.043   Tenonitis of bilateral orbits
      H05.049   Tenonitis of unspecified orbit
   ● **H05.1   Chronic inflammatory disorders of orbit**
      H05.10   Unspecified chronic inflammatory disorders of orbit
   ● **H05.11   Granuloma of orbit**
      Pseudotumor (inflammatory) of orbit
      H05.111   Granuloma of right orbit
      H05.112   Granuloma of left orbit
      H05.113   Granuloma of bilateral orbits
      H05.119   Granuloma of unspecified orbit
   ● **H05.12   Orbital myositis**
      Inflammation of extraocular muscles of orbit
      H05.121   Orbital myositis, right orbit
      H05.122   Orbital myositis, left orbit
      H05.123   Orbital myositis, bilateral
      H05.129   Orbital myositis, unspecified orbit

Figure 7-5 Exophthalmos. (From Black JM, Hokanson JH: Medical-Surgical Nursing: Clinical Management for Positive Outcomes, St. Louis, Saunders Elsevier, 2009)

● H05.2   **Exophthalmic conditions**
          Bulging eyes
    H05.20   Unspecified exophthalmos
    ● H05.21   Displacement (lateral) of globe
        H05.211   Displacement (lateral) of globe, right eye
        H05.212   Displacement (lateral) of globe, left eye
        H05.213   Displacement (lateral) of globe, bilateral
        H05.219   Displacement (lateral) of globe, unspecified eye
    ● H05.22   Edema of orbit
              Orbital congestion
        H05.221   Edema of right orbit
        H05.222   Edema of left orbit
        H05.223   Edema of bilateral orbit
        H05.229   Edema of unspecified orbit
    ● H05.23   Hemorrhage of orbit
        H05.231   Hemorrhage of right orbit
        H05.232   Hemorrhage of left orbit
        H05.233   Hemorrhage of bilateral orbit
        H05.239   Hemorrhage of unspecified orbit
    ● H05.24   Constant exophthalmos
              Constant bulging eyes, often symptom of Graves disease
        H05.241   Constant exophthalmos, right eye
        H05.242   Constant exophthalmos, left eye
        H05.243   Constant exophthalmos, bilateral
        H05.249   Constant exophthalmos, unspecified eye
    ● H05.25   Intermittent exophthalmos
              Intermittent bulging eye occurring with bending forward or sharp turning of head
        H05.251   Intermittent exophthalmos, right eye
        H05.252   Intermittent exophthalmos, left eye
        H05.253   Intermittent exophthalmos, bilateral
        H05.259   Intermittent exophthalmos, unspecified eye
    ● H05.26   Pulsating exophthalmos
              Bulging eyes with pulsation and bruit, often due to aneurysm pushing eye forward
        H05.261   Pulsating exophthalmos, right eye
        H05.262   Pulsating exophthalmos, left eye
        H05.263   Pulsating exophthalmos, bilateral
        H05.269   Pulsating exophthalmos, unspecified eye

● H05.3   **Deformity of orbit**
          Excludes1   congenital deformity of orbit (Q10.7)
                          hypertelorism (Q75.2)
    H05.30   Unspecified deformity of orbit
    ● H05.31   Atrophy of orbit
        H05.311   Atrophy of right orbit
        H05.312   Atrophy of left orbit
        H05.313   Atrophy of bilateral orbit
        H05.319   Atrophy of unspecified orbit
    ● H05.32   Deformity of orbit due to bone disease
              Code also associated bone disease
        H05.321   Deformity of right orbit due to bone disease
        H05.322   Deformity of left orbit due to bone disease
        H05.323   Deformity of bilateral orbits due to bone disease
        H05.329   Deformity of unspecified orbit due to bone disease
    ● H05.33   Deformity of orbit due to trauma or surgery
        H05.331   Deformity of right orbit due to trauma or surgery
        H05.332   Deformity of left orbit due to trauma or surgery
        H05.333   Deformity of bilateral orbits due to trauma or surgery
        H05.339   Deformity of unspecified orbit due to trauma or surgery
    ● H05.34   Enlargement of orbit
        H05.341   Enlargement of right orbit
        H05.342   Enlargement of left orbit
        H05.343   Enlargement of bilateral orbits
        H05.349   Enlargement of unspecified orbit
    ● H05.35   Exostosis of orbit
        H05.351   Exostosis of right orbit
        H05.352   Exostosis of left orbit
        H05.353   Exostosis of bilateral orbits
        H05.359   Exostosis of unspecified orbit
● H05.4   **Enophthalmos**
          Recessed eyeball into orbit
    ● H05.40   Unspecified enophthalmos
        H05.401   Unspecified enophthalmos, right eye
        H05.402   Unspecified enophthalmos, left eye
        H05.403   Unspecified enophthalmos, bilateral
        H05.409   Unspecified enophthalmos, unspecified eye
    ● H05.41   Enophthalmos due to atrophy of orbital tissue
        H05.411   Enophthalmos due to atrophy of orbital tissue, right eye
        H05.412   Enophthalmos due to atrophy of orbital tissue, left eye
        H05.413   Enophthalmos due to atrophy of orbital tissue, bilateral
        H05.419   Enophthalmos due to atrophy of orbital tissue, unspecified eye
    ● H05.42   Enophthalmos due to trauma or surgery
        H05.421   Enophthalmos due to trauma or surgery, right eye
        H05.422   Enophthalmos due to trauma or surgery, left eye
        H05.423   Enophthalmos due to trauma or surgery, bilateral
        H05.429   Enophthalmos due to trauma or surgery, unspecified eye

▶ New   ⇒ Revised   ~~deleted~~ Deleted   Excludes 1   Excludes 2   Includes   Use additional   Code first   Code also   Key words
OGCR Official Guidelines   X Assign placeholder X   ● Use Additional Character(s)   ▶ Manifestation Code   ⊘ Hierarchical Condition Category   Coding Clinic

● **H05.5**   **Retained (old) foreign body following penetrating wound of orbit**
Retrobulbar foreign body
Use additional code to identify the type of retained foreign body (Z18.-)

   Excludes1   current penetrating wound of orbit (S05.4-)

   Excludes2   retained foreign body of eyelid (H02.81-)
retained intraocular foreign body (H44.6-, H44.7-)

   H05.50   Retained (old) foreign body following penetrating wound of unspecified orbit

   H05.51   Retained (old) foreign body following penetrating wound of right orbit

   H05.52   Retained (old) foreign body following penetrating wound of left orbit

   H05.53   Retained (old) foreign body following penetrating wound of bilateral orbits

● **H05.8**   Other disorders of orbit

   ● **H05.81**   Cyst of orbit
Encephalocele of orbit

     H05.811   Cyst of right orbit

     H05.812   Cyst of left orbit

     H05.813   Cyst of bilateral orbits

     H05.819   Cyst of unspecified orbit

   ● **H05.82**   Myopathy of extraocular muscles
Weakness of muscles of eye

     H05.821   Myopathy of extraocular muscles, right orbit

     H05.822   Myopathy of extraocular muscles, left orbit

     H05.823   Myopathy of extraocular muscles, bilateral

     H05.829   Myopathy of extraocular muscles, unspecified orbit

   H05.89   Other disorders of orbit

● **H05.9**   Unspecified disorder of orbit

DISORDERS OF CONJUNCTIVA (H10-H11)

★ **(See Plate 18 of the Anatomy Illustrations.)**

● **H10**   Conjunctivitis
Inflammation of membrane of the inside of the eyelid or on surface of eye (conjunctiva)

   Excludes1   keratoconjunctivitis (H16.2-)

   ● **H10.0**   Mucopurulent conjunctivitis

     ● **H10.01**   Acute follicular conjunctivitis

       H10.011   Acute follicular conjunctivitis, right eye

       H10.012   Acute follicular conjunctivitis, left eye

       H10.013   Acute follicular conjunctivitis, bilateral

       H10.019   Acute follicular conjunctivitis, unspecified eye

     ● **H10.02**   Other mucopurulent conjunctivitis

       H10.021   Other mucopurulent conjunctivitis, right eye

       H10.022   Other mucopurulent conjunctivitis, left eye

       H10.023   Other mucopurulent conjunctivitis, bilateral

       H10.029   Other mucopurulent conjunctivitis, unspecified eye

   ● **H10.1**   Acute atopic conjunctivitis
Acute papillary conjunctivitis

     H10.10   Acute atopic conjunctivitis, unspecified eye

     H10.11   Acute atopic conjunctivitis, right eye

     H10.12   Acute atopic conjunctivitis, left eye

     H10.13   Acute atopic conjunctivitis, bilateral

● **H10.2**   Other acute conjunctivitis

   ● **H10.21**   Acute toxic conjunctivitis
Acute chemical conjunctivitis
Code first (T51-T65) to identify chemical and intent

     Excludes1   burn and corrosion of eye and adnexa (T26.-)

     H10.211   Acute toxic conjunctivitis, right eye

     H10.212   Acute toxic conjunctivitis, left eye

     H10.213   Acute toxic conjunctivitis, bilateral

     H10.219   Acute toxic conjunctivitis, unspecified eye

   ● **H10.22**   Pseudomembranous conjunctivitis

     H10.221   Pseudomembranous conjunctivitis, right eye

     H10.222   Pseudomembranous conjunctivitis, left eye

     H10.223   Pseudomembranous conjunctivitis, bilateral

     H10.229   Pseudomembranous conjunctivitis, unspecified eye

   ● **H10.23**   Serous conjunctivitis, except viral

     Excludes1   viral conjunctivitis (B30.-)

     H10.231   Serous conjunctivitis, except viral, right eye

     H10.232   Serous conjunctivitis, except viral, left eye

     H10.233   Serous conjunctivitis, except viral, bilateral

     H10.239   Serous conjunctivitis, except viral, unspecified eye

● **H10.3**   Unspecified acute conjunctivitis

   Excludes1   ophthalmia neonatorum NOS (P39.1)

   H10.30   Unspecified acute conjunctivitis, unspecified eye

   H10.31   Unspecified acute conjunctivitis, right eye

   H10.32   Unspecified acute conjunctivitis, left eye

   H10.33   Unspecified acute conjunctivitis, bilateral

● **H10.4**   Chronic conjunctivitis

   ● **H10.40**   Unspecified chronic conjunctivitis

     H10.401   Unspecified chronic conjunctivitis, right eye

     H10.402   Unspecified chronic conjunctivitis, left eye

     H10.403   Unspecified chronic conjunctivitis, bilateral

     H10.409   Unspecified chronic conjunctivitis, unspecified eye

   ● **H10.41**   Chronic giant papillary conjunctivitis
Inflammation of membrane of the inside of the eyelid or on surface of eye often associated with contact lens wear

     H10.411   Chronic giant papillary conjunctivitis, right eye

     H10.412   Chronic giant papillary conjunctivitis, left eye

     H10.413   Chronic giant papillary conjunctivitis, bilateral

     H10.419   Chronic giant papillary conjunctivitis, unspecified eye

   ● **H10.42**   Simple chronic conjunctivitis

     H10.421   Simple chronic conjunctivitis, right eye

     H10.422   Simple chronic conjunctivitis, left eye

     H10.423   Simple chronic conjunctivitis, bilateral

     H10.429   Simple chronic conjunctivitis, unspecified eye

● **H10.43   Chronic follicular conjunctivitis**
> *Inflammation of membrane of the inside of the eyelid or on surface of eye due to topical medications or infection*

    H10.431   Chronic follicular conjunctivitis, right eye

    H10.432   Chronic follicular conjunctivitis, left eye

    H10.433   Chronic follicular conjunctivitis, bilateral

    H10.439   Chronic follicular conjunctivitis, unspecified eye

H10.44   Vernal conjunctivitis
> *Affecting children, especially boys in which there are flattened papules with thick, gelatinous exudate on conjunctivae on inside of upper lid*

> **Excludes1**   vernal keratoconjunctivitis with limbar and corneal involvement (H16.26-)

H10.45   Other chronic allergic conjunctivitis

● **H10.5   Blepharoconjunctivitis**
> *Inflammation of eyelids and conjunctiva*

 ● **H10.50   Unspecified blepharoconjunctivitis**

    H10.501   Unspecified blepharoconjunctivitis, right eye

    H10.502   Unspecified blepharoconjunctivitis, left eye

    H10.503   Unspecified blepharoconjunctivitis, bilateral

    H10.509   Unspecified blepharoconjunctivitis, unspecified eye

 ● **H10.51   Ligneous conjunctivitis**
> Code also underlying condition if known, such as:
> plasminogen deficiency (E88.02)

    H10.511   Ligneous conjunctivitis, right eye
    H10.512   Ligneous conjunctivitis, left eye
    H10.513   Ligneous conjunctivitis, bilateral
    H10.519   Ligneous conjunctivitis, unspecified eye

 ● **H10.52   Angular blepharoconjunctivitis**

    H10.521   Angular blepharoconjunctivitis, right eye

    H10.522   Angular blepharoconjunctivitis, left eye

    H10.523   Angular blepharoconjunctivitis, bilateral

    H10.529   Angular blepharoconjunctivitis, unspecified eye

 ● **H10.53   Contact blepharoconjunctivitis**

    H10.531   Contact blepharoconjunctivitis, right eye

    H10.532   Contact blepharoconjunctivitis, left eye

    H10.533   Contact blepharoconjunctivitis, bilateral

    H10.539   Contact blepharoconjunctivitis, unspecified eye

● **H10.8   Other conjunctivitis**

 ● **H10.81   Pingueculitis**
> *Inflammation of a yellow, raised thickening on the white of the eye associated with chronic dry eyes*

> **Excludes1**   pinguecula (H11.15-)

    H10.811   Pingueculitis, right eye
    H10.812   Pingueculitis, left eye
    H10.813   Pingueculitis, bilateral
    H10.819   Pingueculitis, unspecified eye

● **H10.82   Rosacea conjunctivitis**
> *Code first underlying rosacea dermatitis (L71.-)*

    H10.821   Rosacea conjunctivitis, right eye
    H10.822   Rosacea conjunctivitis, left eye
    H10.823   Rosacea conjunctivitis, bilateral
>   Coding Clinic: 2018, Q4, P15
    H10.829   Rosacea conjunctivitis, unspecified eye

H10.89   Other conjunctivitis

H10.9   Unspecified conjunctivitis

● **H11   Other disorders of conjunctiva**
> **Excludes1**   keratoconjunctivitis (H16.2-)

 ● **H11.0   Pterygium of eye**
> **Excludes1**   pseudopterygium (H11.81-)

 ● **H11.00   Unspecified pterygium of eye**

    H11.001   Unspecified pterygium of right eye
    H11.002   Unspecified pterygium of left eye
    H11.003   Unspecified pterygium of eye, bilateral
    H11.009   Unspecified pterygium of unspecified eye

 ● **H11.01   Amyloid pterygium**

    H11.011   Amyloid pterygium of right eye
    H11.012   Amyloid pterygium of left eye
    H11.013   Amyloid pterygium of eye, bilateral
    H11.019   Amyloid pterygium of unspecified eye

 ● **H11.02   Central pterygium of eye**

    H11.021   Central pterygium of right eye
    H11.022   Central pterygium of left eye
    H11.023   Central pterygium of eye, bilateral
    H11.029   Central pterygium of unspecified eye

 ● **H11.03   Double pterygium of eye**

    H11.031   Double pterygium of right eye
    H11.032   Double pterygium of left eye
    H11.033   Double pterygium of eye, bilateral
    H11.039   Double pterygium of unspecified eye

 ● **H11.04   Peripheral pterygium of eye, stationary**

    H11.041   Peripheral pterygium, stationary, right eye

    H11.042   Peripheral pterygium, stationary, left eye

    H11.043   Peripheral pterygium, stationary, bilateral

    H11.049   Peripheral pterygium, stationary, unspecified eye

 ● **H11.05   Peripheral pterygium of eye, progressive**

    H11.051   Peripheral pterygium, progressive, right eye

    H11.052   Peripheral pterygium, progressive, left eye

    H11.053   Peripheral pterygium, progressive, bilateral

    H11.059   Peripheral pterygium, progressive, unspecified eye

 ● **H11.06   Recurrent pterygium of eye**

    H11.061   Recurrent pterygium of right eye
    H11.062   Recurrent pterygium of left eye
    H11.063   Recurrent pterygium of eye, bilateral
    H11.069   Recurrent pterygium of unspecified eye

Figure 7-6   Double pterygium. Note both nasal and temporal pterygia in a 57-year-old farmer. (From Brightbill FS, McDonnell PJ: Corneal Surgery: Theory, Technique and Tissue, S.l., Mosby Elsevier, 2009)

Item 7-2   Pterygium is Greek for batlike. The condition is characterized by a membrane that extends from the limbus to the center of the cornea and resembles a wing.

▶ New   ⇒ Revised   ~~deleted~~ Deleted   Excludes 1   Excludes 2   Includes   Use additional   Code first   Code also   Key words

OGCR Official Guidelines   X Assign placeholder X   ● Use Additional Character(s)   ▌ Manifestation Code   🅗 Hierarchical Condition Category   **Coding Clinic**

● **H11.1** Conjunctival degenerations and deposits
 Excludes2 pseudopterygium (H11.81)
 H11.10 Unspecified conjunctival degenerations
● **H11.11** Conjunctival deposits
 H11.111 Conjunctival deposits, right eye
 H11.112 Conjunctival deposits, left eye
 H11.113 Conjunctival deposits, bilateral
 H11.119 Conjunctival deposits, unspecified eye
● **H11.12** Conjunctival concretions
 White to yellow nodules within or beneath conjunctiva
 H11.121 Conjunctival concretions, right eye
 H11.122 Conjunctival concretions, left eye
 H11.123 Conjunctival concretions, bilateral
 H11.129 Conjunctival concretions, unspecified eye
● **H11.13** Conjunctival pigmentations
 Conjunctival argyrosis [argyria]
 H11.131 Conjunctival pigmentations, right eye
 H11.132 Conjunctival pigmentations, left eye
 H11.133 Conjunctival pigmentations, bilateral
 H11.139 Conjunctival pigmentations, unspecified eye
● **H11.14** Conjunctival xerosis, unspecified
 Excludes1 xerosis of conjunctiva due to vitamin A deficiency (E50.0, E50.1)
 H11.141 Conjunctival xerosis, unspecified, right eye
 H11.142 Conjunctival xerosis, unspecified, left eye
 H11.143 Conjunctival xerosis, unspecified, bilateral
 H11.149 Conjunctival xerosis, unspecified, unspecified eye
● **H11.15** Pinguecula
 Yellowish spot near sclerocorneal junction, usually on nasal side; associated with aging
 Excludes1 pingueculitis (H10.81-)
 H11.151 Pinguecula, right eye
 H11.152 Pinguecula, left eye
 H11.153 Pinguecula, bilateral
 H11.159 Pinguecula, unspecified eye
● **H11.2** Conjunctival scars
● **H11.21** Conjunctival adhesions and strands (localized)
 H11.211 Conjunctival adhesions and strands (localized), right eye
 H11.212 Conjunctival adhesions and strands (localized), left eye
 H11.213 Conjunctival adhesions and strands (localized), bilateral
 H11.219 Conjunctival adhesions and strands (localized), unspecified eye
● **H11.22** Conjunctival granuloma
 H11.221 Conjunctival granuloma, right eye
 H11.222 Conjunctival granuloma, left eye
 H11.223 Conjunctival granuloma, bilateral
 H11.229 Conjunctival granuloma, unspecified
● **H11.23** Symblepharon
 Adhesion between tarsal conjunctiva and bulbar conjunctiva
 H11.231 Symblepharon, right eye
 H11.232 Symblepharon, left eye
 H11.233 Symblepharon, bilateral
 H11.239 Symblepharon, unspecified eye

● **H11.24** Scarring of conjunctiva
 H11.241 Scarring of conjunctiva, right eye
 H11.242 Scarring of conjunctiva, left eye
 H11.243 Scarring of conjunctiva, bilateral
 H11.249 Scarring of conjunctiva, unspecified eye
● **H11.3** Conjunctival hemorrhage
 Subconjunctival hemorrhage
 H11.30 Conjunctival hemorrhage, unspecified eye
 H11.31 Conjunctival hemorrhage, right eye
 H11.32 Conjunctival hemorrhage, left eye
 H11.33 Conjunctival hemorrhage, bilateral
● **H11.4** Other conjunctival vascular disorders and cysts
● **H11.41** Vascular abnormalities of conjunctiva
 Conjunctival aneurysm
 H11.411 Vascular abnormalities of conjunctiva, right eye
 H11.412 Vascular abnormalities of conjunctiva, left eye
 H11.413 Vascular abnormalities of conjunctiva, bilateral
 H11.419 Vascular abnormalities of conjunctiva, unspecified eye
● **H11.42** Conjunctival edema
 H11.421 Conjunctival edema, right eye
 H11.422 Conjunctival edema, left eye
 H11.423 Conjunctival edema, bilateral
 H11.429 Conjunctival edema, unspecified eye
● **H11.43** Conjunctival hyperemia
 H11.431 Conjunctival hyperemia, right eye
 H11.432 Conjunctival hyperemia, left eye
 H11.433 Conjunctival hyperemia, bilateral
 H11.439 Conjunctival hyperemia, unspecified eye
● **H11.44** Conjunctival cysts
 H11.441 Conjunctival cysts, right eye
 H11.442 Conjunctival cysts, left eye
 H11.443 Conjunctival cysts, bilateral
 H11.449 Conjunctival cysts, unspecified eye
● **H11.8** Other specified disorders of conjunctiva
● **H11.81** Pseudopterygium of conjunctiva
 Conjunctival scar attached to cornea
 H11.811 Pseudopterygium of conjunctiva, right eye
 H11.812 Pseudopterygium of conjunctiva, left eye
 H11.813 Pseudopterygium of conjunctiva, bilateral
 H11.819 Pseudopterygium of conjunctiva, unspecified eye
● **H11.82** Conjunctivochalasis
 Conjunctiva bulges over eyelid margin or covers lower punctum
 H11.821 Conjunctivochalasis, right eye
 H11.822 Conjunctivochalasis, left eye
 H11.823 Conjunctivochalasis, bilateral
 H11.829 Conjunctivochalasis, unspecified eye
 H11.89 Other specified disorders of conjunctiva
 H11.9 Unspecified disorder of conjunctiva

DISORDERS OF SCLERA, CORNEA, IRIS AND CILIARY BODY (H15-H22)

● H15 Disorders of sclera
  ● H15.0 Scleritis
    Inflammation of the white (sclera and episclera) of the eye.
    ● H15.00 Unspecified scleritis
      H15.001 Unspecified scleritis, right eye
      H15.002 Unspecified scleritis, left eye
      H15.003 Unspecified scleritis, bilateral
      H15.009 Unspecified scleritis, unspecified eye
    ● H15.01 Anterior scleritis
      H15.011 Anterior scleritis, right eye
      H15.012 Anterior scleritis, left eye
      H15.013 Anterior scleritis, bilateral
      H15.019 Anterior scleritis, unspecified eye
    ● H15.02 Brawny scleritis
      Swelling around the cornea that is gelantinous in appearance
      H15.021 Brawny scleritis, right eye
      H15.022 Brawny scleritis, left eye
      H15.023 Brawny scleritis, bilateral
      H15.029 Brawny scleritis, unspecified eye
    ● H15.03 Posterior scleritis
      Sclerotenonitis
      H15.031 Posterior scleritis, right eye
      H15.032 Posterior scleritis, left eye
      H15.033 Posterior scleritis, bilateral
      H15.039 Posterior scleritis, unspecified eye
    ● H15.04 Scleritis with corneal involvement
      H15.041 Scleritis with corneal involvement, right eye
      H15.042 Scleritis with corneal involvement, left eye
      H15.043 Scleritis with corneal involvement, bilateral
      H15.049 Scleritis with corneal involvement, unspecified eye
    ● H15.05 Scleromalacia perforans
      Necrotic without inflammation; usually associated with rheumatoid arthritis
      H15.051 Scleromalacia perforans, right eye
      H15.052 Scleromalacia perforans, left eye
      H15.053 Scleromalacia perforans, bilateral
      H15.059 Scleromalacia perforans, unspecified eye
    ● H15.09 Other scleritis
      Scleral abscess
      H15.091 Other scleritis, right eye
      H15.092 Other scleritis, left eye
      H15.093 Other scleritis, bilateral
      H15.099 Other scleritis, unspecified eye
  ● H15.1 Episcleritis
    Inflammation of the white (sclera and episclera) of the eye.
    ● H15.10 Unspecified episcleritis
      H15.101 Unspecified episcleritis, right eye
      H15.102 Unspecified episcleritis, left eye
      H15.103 Unspecified episcleritis, bilateral
      H15.109 Unspecified episcleritis, unspecified eye
    ● H15.11 Episcleritis periodica fugax
      Transient, recurrent inflammation of portion of episclera (connective tissue on the surface of the sclera)
      H15.111 Episcleritis periodica fugax, right eye
      H15.112 Episcleritis periodica fugax, left eye
      H15.113 Episcleritis periodica fugax, bilateral
      H15.119 Episcleritis periodica fugax, unspecified eye

    ● H15.12 Nodular episcleritis
      Characterized by tender, localized, moveable nodule within inflamed area
      H15.121 Nodular episcleritis, right eye
      H15.122 Nodular episcleritis, left eye
      H15.123 Nodular episcleritis, bilateral
      H15.129 Nodular episcleritis, unspecified eye
  ● H15.8 Other disorders of sclera
    Excludes2 blue sclera (Q13.5)
          degenerative myopia (H44.2-)
    ● H15.81 Equatorial staphyloma
      H15.811 Equatorial staphyloma, right eye
      H15.812 Equatorial staphyloma, left eye
      H15.813 Equatorial staphyloma, bilateral
      H15.819 Equatorial staphyloma, unspecified eye
    ● H15.82 Localized anterior staphyloma
      H15.821 Localized anterior staphyloma, right eye
      H15.822 Localized anterior staphyloma, left eye
      H15.823 Localized anterior staphyloma, bilateral
      H15.829 Localized anterior staphyloma, unspecified eye
    ● H15.83 Staphyloma posticum
      H15.831 Staphyloma posticum, right eye
      H15.832 Staphyloma posticum, left eye
      H15.833 Staphyloma posticum, bilateral
      H15.839 Staphyloma posticum, unspecified eye
    ● H15.84 Scleral ectasia
      H15.841 Scleral ectasia, right eye
      H15.842 Scleral ectasia, left eye
      H15.843 Scleral ectasia, bilateral
      H15.849 Scleral ectasia, unspecified eye
    ● H15.85 Ring staphyloma
      H15.851 Ring staphyloma, right eye
      H15.852 Ring staphyloma, left eye
      H15.853 Ring staphyloma, bilateral
      H15.859 Ring staphyloma, unspecified eye
    H15.89 Other disorders of sclera
    H15.9 Unspecified disorder of sclera
● H16 Keratitis
  ● H16.0 Corneal ulcer
    ● H16.00 Unspecified corneal ulcer
      H16.001 Unspecified corneal ulcer, right eye
      H16.002 Unspecified corneal ulcer, left eye
      H16.003 Unspecified corneal ulcer, bilateral
      H16.009 Unspecified corneal ulcer, unspecified eye
    ● H16.01 Central corneal ulcer
      H16.011 Central corneal ulcer, right eye
      H16.012 Central corneal ulcer, left eye
      H16.013 Central corneal ulcer, bilateral
      H16.019 Central corneal ulcer, unspecified eye
    ● H16.02 Ring corneal ulcer
      H16.021 Ring corneal ulcer, right eye
      H16.022 Ring corneal ulcer, left eye
      H16.023 Ring corneal ulcer, bilateral
      H16.029 Ring corneal ulcer, unspecified eye
    ● H16.03 Corneal ulcer with hypopyon
      H16.031 Corneal ulcer with hypopyon, right eye
      H16.032 Corneal ulcer with hypopyon, left eye
      H16.033 Corneal ulcer with hypopyon, bilateral
      H16.039 Corneal ulcer with hypopyon, unspecified eye

▶ New   ⇒ Revised   ~~deleted~~ Deleted   Excludes 1   Excludes 2   Includes   Use additional   Code first   Code also   Key words

OGCR Official Guidelines   X Assign placeholder X   ● Use Additional Character(s)   ▶ Manifestation Code   🅗 Hierarchical Condition Category   Coding Clinic

Marginal (catarrhal) ulcer   Ring ulcer   Central corneal ulcer   Rosacea ulcer   Mooren's (rodent) ulcer

Figure 7-7 Corneal ulcers: marginal, ring, central corneal, rosacea, and Mooren's.

Item 7-3 An infected ulcer is usually called a **serpiginous** or **hypopyon** ulcer, which is a pus sac in the anterior chamber of the eye. **Marginal** ulcers are usually asymptomatic, not primary, and are often superficial and simple. More severe marginal ulcers spread to form a ring ulcer. **Ring** ulcers can extend around the entire corneal periphery. **Central corneal** ulcers develop when there is an abrasion to the epithelium and an infection develops in the eroded area. The **pyocyaneal** ulcer is the most serious corneal infection, which, if left untreated, can lead to loss of the eye.

● **H16.04** Marginal corneal ulcer
   H16.041 Marginal corneal ulcer, right eye
   H16.042 Marginal corneal ulcer, left eye
   H16.043 Marginal corneal ulcer, bilateral
   H16.049 Marginal corneal ulcer, unspecified eye

● **H16.05** Mooren's corneal ulcer
   H16.051 Mooren's corneal ulcer, right eye
   H16.052 Mooren's corneal ulcer, left eye
   H16.053 Mooren's corneal ulcer, bilateral
   H16.059 Mooren's corneal ulcer, unspecified eye

● **H16.06** Mycotic corneal ulcer
   H16.061 Mycotic corneal ulcer, right eye
   H16.062 Mycotic corneal ulcer, left eye
   H16.063 Mycotic corneal ulcer, bilateral
   H16.069 Mycotic corneal ulcer, unspecified eye

● **H16.07** Perforated corneal ulcer
   H16.071 Perforated corneal ulcer, right eye
   H16.072 Perforated corneal ulcer, left eye
   H16.073 Perforated corneal ulcer, bilateral
   H16.079 Perforated corneal ulcer, unspecified eye

● **H16.1** Other and unspecified superficial keratitis without conjunctivitis

● **H16.10** Unspecified superficial keratitis
   H16.101 Unspecified superficial keratitis, right eye
   H16.102 Unspecified superficial keratitis, left eye
   H16.103 Unspecified superficial keratitis, bilateral
   H16.109 Unspecified superficial keratitis, unspecified eye

● **H16.11** Macular keratitis
   Areolar keratitis
   Nummular keratitis
   Stellate keratitis
   Striate keratitis
   H16.111 Macular keratitis, right eye
   H16.112 Macular keratitis, left eye
   H16.113 Macular keratitis, bilateral
   H16.119 Macular keratitis, unspecified eye

● **H16.12** Filamentary keratitis
   H16.121 Filamentary keratitis, right eye
   H16.122 Filamentary keratitis, left eye
   H16.123 Filamentary keratitis, bilateral
   H16.129 Filamentary keratitis, unspecified eye

● **H16.13** Photokeratitis
   Snow blindness
   Welders' keratitis
   H16.131 Photokeratitis, right eye
   H16.132 Photokeratitis, left eye
   H16.133 Photokeratitis, bilateral
   H16.139 Photokeratitis, unspecified eye

● **H16.14** Punctate keratitis
   H16.141 Punctate keratitis, right eye
   H16.142 Punctate keratitis, left eye
   H16.143 Punctate keratitis, bilateral
   H16.149 Punctate keratitis, unspecified eye

● **H16.2** Keratoconjunctivitis

● **H16.20** Unspecified keratoconjunctivitis
   Superficial keratitis with conjunctivitis NOS
   H16.201 Unspecified keratoconjunctivitis, right eye
   H16.202 Unspecified keratoconjunctivitis, left eye
   H16.203 Unspecified keratoconjunctivitis, bilateral
   H16.209 Unspecified keratoconjunctivitis, unspecified eye

● **H16.21** Exposure keratoconjunctivitis
   H16.211 Exposure keratoconjunctivitis, right eye
   H16.212 Exposure keratoconjunctivitis, left eye
   H16.213 Exposure keratoconjunctivitis, bilateral
   H16.219 Exposure keratoconjunctivitis, unspecified eye

● **H16.22** Keratoconjunctivitis sicca, not specified as Sjögren's
   Excludes1 Sjogren's syndrome (M35.01)
   H16.221 Keratoconjunctivitis sicca, not specified as Sjögren's, right eye
   H16.222 Keratoconjunctivitis sicca, not specified as Sjögren's, left eye
   H16.223 Keratoconjunctivitis sicca, not specified as Sjögren's, bilateral
   H16.229 Keratoconjunctivitis sicca, not specified as Sjögren's, unspecified eye

● **H16.23** Neurotrophic keratoconjunctivitis
   H16.231 Neurotrophic keratoconjunctivitis, right eye
   H16.232 Neurotrophic keratoconjunctivitis, left eye
   H16.233 Neurotrophic keratoconjunctivitis, bilateral
   H16.239 Neurotrophic keratoconjunctivitis, unspecified eye

● **H16.24** Ophthalmia nodosa
   H16.241 Ophthalmia nodosa, right eye
   H16.242 Ophthalmia nodosa, left eye
   H16.243 Ophthalmia nodosa, bilateral
   H16.249 Ophthalmia nodosa, unspecified eye

● **H16.25** Phlyctenular keratoconjunctivitis
   H16.251 Phlyctenular keratoconjunctivitis, right eye
   H16.252 Phlyctenular keratoconjunctivitis, left eye
   H16.253 Phlyctenular keratoconjunctivitis, bilateral
   H16.259 Phlyctenular keratoconjunctivitis, unspecified eye

● **H16.26** **Vernal keratoconjunctivitis, with limbar and corneal involvement**

    Excludes1   vernal conjunctivitis without limbar and corneal involvement (H10.44)

    H16.261 Vernal keratoconjunctivitis, with limbar and corneal involvement, right eye

    H16.262 Vernal keratoconjunctivitis, with limbar and corneal involvement, left eye

    H16.263 Vernal keratoconjunctivitis, with limbar and corneal involvement, bilateral

    H16.269 Vernal keratoconjunctivitis, with limbar and corneal involvement, unspecified eye

● **H16.29** **Other keratoconjunctivitis**

    H16.291 Other keratoconjunctivitis, right eye

    H16.292 Other keratoconjunctivitis, left eye

    H16.293 Other keratoconjunctivitis, bilateral

    H16.299 Other keratoconjunctivitis, unspecified eye

● **H16.3** **Interstitial and deep keratitis**

● **H16.30** **Unspecified interstitial keratitis**

    H16.301 Unspecified interstitial keratitis, right eye

    H16.302 Unspecified interstitial keratitis, left eye

    H16.303 Unspecified interstitial keratitis, bilateral

    H16.309 Unspecified interstitial keratitis, unspecified eye

● **H16.31** **Corneal abscess**

    H16.311 Corneal abscess, right eye

    H16.312 Corneal abscess, left eye

    H16.313 Corneal abscess, bilateral

    H16.319 Corneal abscess, unspecified eye

● **H16.32** **Diffuse interstitial keratitis**

    Cogan's syndrome

    H16.321 Diffuse interstitial keratitis, right eye

    H16.322 Diffuse interstitial keratitis, left eye

    H16.323 Diffuse interstitial keratitis, bilateral

    H16.329 Diffuse interstitial keratitis, unspecified eye

● **H16.33** **Sclerosing keratitis**

    H16.331 Sclerosing keratitis, right eye

    H16.332 Sclerosing keratitis, left eye

    H16.333 Sclerosing keratitis, bilateral

    H16.339 Sclerosing keratitis, unspecified eye

● **H16.39** **Other interstitial and deep keratitis**

    H16.391 Other interstitial and deep keratitis, right eye

    H16.392 Other interstitial and deep keratitis, left eye

    H16.393 Other interstitial and deep keratitis, bilateral

    H16.399 Other interstitial and deep keratitis, unspecified eye

● **H16.4** **Corneal neovascularization**

● **H16.40** **Unspecified corneal neovascularization**

    H16.401 Unspecified corneal neovascularization, right eye

    H16.402 Unspecified corneal neovascularization, left eye

    H16.403 Unspecified corneal neovascularization, bilateral

    H16.409 Unspecified corneal neovascularization, unspecified eye

● **H16.41** **Ghost vessels (corneal)**

    H16.411 Ghost vessels (corneal), right eye

    H16.412 Ghost vessels (corneal), left eye

    H16.413 Ghost vessels (corneal), bilateral

    H16.419 Ghost vessels (corneal), unspecified eye

● **H16.42** **Pannus (corneal)**

    H16.421 Pannus (corneal), right eye

    H16.422 Pannus (corneal), left eye

    H16.423 Pannus (corneal), bilateral

    H16.429 Pannus (corneal), unspecified eye

● **H16.43** **Localized vascularization of cornea**

    H16.431 Localized vascularization of cornea, right eye

    H16.432 Localized vascularization of cornea, left eye

    H16.433 Localized vascularization of cornea, bilateral

    H16.439 Localized vascularization of cornea, unspecified eye

● **H16.44** **Deep vascularization of cornea**

    H16.441 Deep vascularization of cornea, right eye

    H16.442 Deep vascularization of cornea, left eye

    H16.443 Deep vascularization of cornea, bilateral

    H16.449 Deep vascularization of cornea, unspecified eye

H16.8 **Other keratitis**

H16.9 **Unspecified keratitis**

● **H17** **Corneal scars and opacities**

● **H17.0** **Adherent leukoma**

    H17.00 Adherent leukoma, unspecified eye

    H17.01 Adherent leukoma, right eye

    H17.02 Adherent leukoma, left eye

    H17.03 Adherent leukoma, bilateral

● **H17.1** **Central corneal opacity**

    H17.10 Central corneal opacity, unspecified eye

    H17.11 Central corneal opacity, right eye

    H17.12 Central corneal opacity, left eye

    H17.13 Central corneal opacity, bilateral

● **H17.8** **Other corneal scars and opacities**

● **H17.81** **Minor opacity of cornea**

    Corneal nebula

    H17.811 Minor opacity of cornea, right eye

    H17.812 Minor opacity of cornea, left eye

    H17.813 Minor opacity of cornea, bilateral

    H17.819 Minor opacity of cornea, unspecified eye

● **H17.82** **Peripheral opacity of cornea**

    H17.821 Peripheral opacity of cornea, right eye

    H17.822 Peripheral opacity of cornea, left eye

    H17.823 Peripheral opacity of cornea, bilateral

    H17.829 Peripheral opacity of cornea, unspecified eye

    H17.89 Other corneal scars and opacities

H17.9 **Unspecified corneal scar and opacity**

● **H18** **Other disorders of cornea**

● **H18.0** **Corneal pigmentations and deposits**

● **H18.00** **Unspecified corneal deposit**

    H18.001 Unspecified corneal deposit, right eye

    H18.002 Unspecified corneal deposit, left eye

    H18.003 Unspecified corneal deposit, bilateral

    H18.009 Unspecified corneal deposit, unspecified eye

▶ New   ⇒ Revised   ~~deleted~~ Deleted   Excludes 1   Excludes 2   Includes   Use additional   Code first   Code also   Key words

OGCR Official Guidelines   X Assign placeholder X   ● Use Additional Character(s)   ▶ Manifestation Code   🅗 Hierarchical Condition Category   **Coding Clinic**

● **H18.01**   **Anterior corneal pigmentations**
Staehli's line

    H18.011   Anterior corneal pigmentations, right eye

    H18.012   Anterior corneal pigmentations, left eye

    H18.013   Anterior corneal pigmentations, bilateral

    H18.019   Anterior corneal pigmentations, unspecified eye

● **H18.02**   **Argentous corneal deposits**

    H18.021   Argentous corneal deposits, right eye

    H18.022   Argentous corneal deposits, left eye

    H18.023   Argentous corneal deposits, bilateral

    H18.029   Argentous corneal deposits, unspecified eye

● **H18.03**   **Corneal deposits in metabolic disorders**
Code also associated metabolic disorder

    H18.031   Corneal deposits in metabolic disorders, right eye

    H18.032   Corneal deposits in metabolic disorders, left eye

    H18.033   Corneal deposits in metabolic disorders, bilateral

    H18.039   Corneal deposits in metabolic disorders, unspecified eye

● **H18.04**   **Kayser-Fleischer ring**
Code also associated Wilson's disease (E83.01)

    H18.041   Kayser-Fleischer ring, right eye

    H18.042   Kayser-Fleischer ring, left eye

    H18.043   Kayser-Fleischer ring, bilateral

    H18.049   Kayser-Fleischer ring, unspecified eye

● **H18.05**   **Posterior corneal pigmentations**
Krukenberg's spindle

    H18.051   Posterior corneal pigmentations, right eye

    H18.052   Posterior corneal pigmentations, left eye

    H18.053   Posterior corneal pigmentations, bilateral

    H18.059   Posterior corneal pigmentations, unspecified eye

● **H18.06**   **Stromal corneal pigmentations**
Hematocornea

    H18.061   Stromal corneal pigmentations, right eye

    H18.062   Stromal corneal pigmentations, left eye

    H18.063   Stromal corneal pigmentations, bilateral

    H18.069   Stromal corneal pigmentations, unspecified eye

● **H18.1**   **Bullous keratopathy**

    H18.10   Bullous keratopathy, unspecified eye

    H18.11   Bullous keratopathy, right eye

    H18.12   Bullous keratopathy, left eye

    H18.13   Bullous keratopathy, bilateral

● **H18.2**   **Other and unspecified corneal edema**

    H18.20   Unspecified corneal edema

●   H18.21   Corneal edema secondary to contact lens

      Excludes2   other corneal disorders due to contact lens (H18.82-)

    H18.211   Corneal edema secondary to contact lens, right eye

    H18.212   Corneal edema secondary to contact lens, left eye

    H18.213   Corneal edema secondary to contact lens, bilateral

    H18.219   Corneal edema secondary to contact lens, unspecified eye

● **H18.22**   **Idiopathic corneal edema**

    H18.221   Idiopathic corneal edema, right eye

    H18.222   Idiopathic corneal edema, left eye

    H18.223   Idiopathic corneal edema, bilateral

    H18.229   Idiopathic corneal edema, unspecified eye

● **H18.23**   **Secondary corneal edema**

    H18.231   Secondary corneal edema, right eye

    H18.232   Secondary corneal edema, left eye

    H18.233   Secondary corneal edema, bilateral

    H18.239   Secondary corneal edema, unspecified eye

● **H18.3**   **Changes of corneal membranes**

    H18.30   Unspecified corneal membrane change

● **H18.31**   **Folds and rupture in Bowman's membrane**

    H18.311   Folds and rupture in Bowman's membrane, right eye

    H18.312   Folds and rupture in Bowman's membrane, left eye

    H18.313   Folds and rupture in Bowman's membrane, bilateral

    H18.319   Folds and rupture in Bowman's membrane, unspecified eye

● **H18.32**   **Folds in Descemet's membrane**

    H18.321   Folds in Descemet's membrane, right eye

    H18.322   Folds in Descemet's membrane, left eye

    H18.323   Folds in Descemet's membrane, bilateral

    H18.329   Folds in Descemet's membrane, unspecified eye

● **H18.33**   **Rupture in Descemet's membrane**

    H18.331   Rupture in Descemet's membrane, right eye

    H18.332   Rupture in Descemet's membrane, left eye

    H18.333   Rupture in Descemet's membrane, bilateral

    H18.339   Rupture in Descemet's membrane, unspecified eye

● **H18.4**   **Corneal degeneration**

      Excludes1   Mooren's ulcer (H16.0-)
        recurrent erosion of cornea (H18.83-)

    H18.40   Unspecified corneal degeneration

● **H18.41**   **Arcus senilis**
Senile corneal changes

    H18.411   Arcus senilis, right eye

    H18.412   Arcus senilis, left eye

    H18.413   Arcus senilis, bilateral

    H18.419   Arcus senilis, unspecified eye

● **H18.42**   **Band keratopathy**

    H18.421   Band keratopathy, right eye

    H18.422   Band keratopathy, left eye

    H18.423   Band keratopathy, bilateral

    H18.429   Band keratopathy, unspecified eye

    H18.43   Other calcerous corneal degeneration

● **H18.44**   **Keratomalacia**

      Excludes1   keratomalacia due to vitamin A deficiency (E50.4)

    H18.441   Keratomalacia, right eye

    H18.442   Keratomalacia, left eye

    H18.443   Keratomalacia, bilateral

    H18.449   Keratomalacia, unspecified eye

● **H18.45**   Nodular corneal degeneration

    H18.451   Nodular corneal degeneration, right eye

    H18.452   Nodular corneal degeneration, left eye

    H18.453   Nodular corneal degeneration, bilateral

    H18.459   Nodular corneal degeneration, unspecified eye

● **H18.46**   Peripheral corneal degeneration

    H18.461   Peripheral corneal degeneration, right eye

    H18.462   Peripheral corneal degeneration, left eye

    H18.463   Peripheral corneal degeneration, bilateral

    H18.469   Peripheral corneal degeneration, unspecified eye

  H18.49   Other corneal degeneration

● **H18.5**   Hereditary corneal dystrophies

● **H18.50**   Unspecified hereditary corneal dystrophies

    ▶ H18.501   Unspecified hereditary corneal dystrophies, right eye

    ▶ H18.502   Unspecified hereditary corneal dystrophies, left eye

    ▶ H18.503   Unspecified hereditary corneal dystrophies, bilateral

    ▶ H18.509   Unspecified hereditary corneal dystrophies, unspecified eye

● **H18.51**   Endothelial corneal dystrophy
       Fuchs' dystrophy

    ▶ H18.511   Endothelial corneal dystrophy, right eye

    ▶ H18.512   Endothelial corneal dystrophy, left eye

    ▶ H18.513   Endothelial corneal dystrophy, bilateral

    ▶ H18.519   Endothelial corneal dystrophy, unspecified eye

● **H18.52**   Epithelial (juvenile) corneal dystrophy

    ▶ H18.521   Epithelial (juvenile) corneal dystrophy, right eye

    ▶ H18.522   Epithelial (juvenile) corneal dystrophy, left eye

    ▶ H18.523   Epithelial (juvenile) corneal dystrophy, bilateral

    ▶ H18.529   Epithelial (juvenile) corneal dystrophy, unspecified eye

● **H18.53**   Granular corneal dystrophy

    ▶ H18.531   Granular corneal dystrophy, right eye

    ▶ H18.532   Granular corneal dystrophy, left eye

    ▶ H18.533   Granular corneal dystrophy, bilateral

    ▶ H18.539   Granular corneal dystrophy, unspecified eye

● **H18.54**   Lattice corneal dystrophy

    ▶ H18.541   Lattice corneal dystrophy, right eye

    ▶ H18.542   Lattice corneal dystrophy, left eye

    ▶ H18.543   Lattice corneal dystrophy, bilateral

    ▶ H18.549   Lattice corneal dystrophy, unspecified eye

● **H18.55**   Macular corneal dystrophy

    ▶ H18.551   Macular corneal dystrophy, right eye

    ▶ H18.552   Macular corneal dystrophy, left eye

    ▶ H18.553   Macular corneal dystrophy, bilateral

    ▶ H18.559   Macular corneal dystrophy, unspecified eye

● **H18.59**   Other hereditary corneal dystrophies

    ▶ H18.591   Other hereditary corneal dystrophies, right eye

    ▶ H18.592   Other hereditary corneal dystrophies, left eye

    ▶ H18.593   Other hereditary corneal dystrophies, bilateral

    ▶ H18.599   Other hereditary corneal dystrophies, unspecified eye

● **H18.6**   Keratoconus

● **H18.60**   Keratoconus, unspecified

    H18.601   Keratoconus, unspecified, right eye

    H18.602   Keratoconus, unspecified, left eye

    H18.603   Keratoconus, unspecified, bilateral

    H18.609   Keratoconus, unspecified, unspecified eye

● **H18.61**   Keratoconus, stable

    H18.611   Keratoconus, stable, right eye

    H18.612   Keratoconus, stable, left eye

    H18.613   Keratoconus, stable, bilateral

    H18.619   Keratoconus, stable, unspecified eye

● **H18.62**   Keratoconus, unstable
       Acute hydrops

    H18.621   Keratoconus, unstable, right eye

    H18.622   Keratoconus, unstable, left eye

    H18.623   Keratoconus, unstable, bilateral

    H18.629   Keratoconus, unstable, unspecified eye

● **H18.7**   Other and unspecified corneal deformities

    Excludes1   congenital malformations of cornea (Q13.3-Q13.4)

  H18.70   Unspecified corneal deformity

● **H18.71**   Corneal ectasia

    H18.711   Corneal ectasia, right eye

    H18.712   Corneal ectasia, left eye

    H18.713   Corneal ectasia, bilateral

    H18.719   Corneal ectasia, unspecified eye

● **H18.72**   Corneal staphyloma

    H18.721   Corneal staphyloma, right eye

    H18.722   Corneal staphyloma, left eye

    H18.723   Corneal staphyloma, bilateral

    H18.729   Corneal staphyloma, unspecified eye

● **H18.73**   Descemetocele

    H18.731   Descemetocele, right eye

    H18.732   Descemetocele, left eye

    H18.733   Descemetocele, bilateral

    H18.739   Descemetocele, unspecified eye

● **H18.79**   Other corneal deformities

    H18.791   Other corneal deformities, right eye

    H18.792   Other corneal deformities, left eye

    H18.793   Other corneal deformities, bilateral

    H18.799   Other corneal deformities, unspecified eye

Figure 7-8   Lateral view of the displacement of the cone apex in keratoconus. (From Yanoff: Ophthalmology, ed 3, Mosby, Inc., 2008)

Item 7-4 Keratoconus results in corneal degeneration that begins in childhood, gradually changes the cornea from a round to cone shape, decreasing visual acuity. Treatment includes contact lenses. In severe cases the need for corneal transplant may be the treatment of choice; however, newer technologies may use high-frequency radio energy to shrink the edges of the cornea, pulling the central area back to a more normal shape. It can help delay or avoid the need for a corneal transplantation.

● **H18.8   Other specified disorders of cornea**
   ● **H18.81   Anesthesia and hypoesthesia of cornea**
     H18.811   Anesthesia and hypoesthesia of cornea, right eye
     H18.812   Anesthesia and hypoesthesia of cornea, left eye
     H18.813   Anesthesia and hypoesthesia of cornea, bilateral
     H18.819   Anesthesia and hypoesthesia of cornea, unspecified eye
   ● **H18.82   Corneal disorder due to contact lens**
     Excludes2   corneal edema due to contact lens (H18.21-)
     H18.821   Corneal disorder due to contact lens, right eye
     H18.822   Corneal disorder due to contact lens, left eye
     H18.823   Corneal disorder due to contact lens, bilateral
     H18.829   Corneal disorder due to contact lens, unspecified eye
   ● **H18.83   Recurrent erosion of cornea**
     H18.831   Recurrent erosion of cornea, right eye
     H18.832   Recurrent erosion of cornea, left eye
     H18.833   Recurrent erosion of cornea, bilateral
     H18.839   Recurrent erosion of cornea, unspecified eye
   ● **H18.89   Other specified disorders of cornea**
     H18.891   Other specified disorders of cornea, right eye
     H18.892   Other specified disorders of cornea, left eye
     H18.893   Other specified disorders of cornea, bilateral
     H18.899   Other specified disorders of cornea, unspecified eye
   H18.9   Unspecified disorder of cornea

● **H20   Iridocyclitis**
   ● **H20.0   Acute and subacute iridocyclitis**
     Acute anterior uveitis
     Acute cyclitis
     Acute iritis
     Subacute anterior uveitis
     Subacute cyclitis
     Subacute iritis
     Excludes1   iridocyclitis, iritis, uveitis (due to) (in) diabetes mellitus (E08-E13 with .39)
           iridocyclitis, iritis, uveitis (due to) (in) diphtheria (A36.89)
           iridocyclitis, iritis, uveitis (due to) (in) gonococcal (A54.32)
           iridocyclitis, iritis, uveitis (due to) (in) herpes (simplex) (B00.51)
           iridocyclitis, iritis, uveitis (due to) (in) herpes zoster (B02.32)
           iridocyclitis, iritis, uveitis (due to) (in) late congenital syphilis (A50.39)
           iridocyclitis, iritis, uveitis (due to) (in) late syphilis (A52.71)
           iridocyclitis, iritis, uveitis (due to) (in) sarcoidosis (D86.83)
           iridocyclitis, iritis, uveitis (due to) (in) syphilis (A51.43)
           iridocyclitis, iritis, uveitis (due to) (in) toxoplasmosis (B58.09)
           iridocyclitis, iritis, uveitis (due to) (in) tuberculosis (A18.54)
     H20.00   Unspecified acute and subacute iridocyclitis
     ● **H20.01   Primary iridocyclitis**
       H20.011   Primary iridocyclitis, right eye
       H20.012   Primary iridocyclitis, left eye
       H20.013   Primary iridocyclitis, bilateral
       H20.019   Primary iridocyclitis, unspecified eye
     ● **H20.02   Recurrent acute iridocyclitis**
       H20.021   Recurrent acute iridocyclitis, right eye
       H20.022   Recurrent acute iridocyclitis, left eye
       H20.023   Recurrent acute iridocyclitis, bilateral
       H20.029   Recurrent acute iridocyclitis, unspecified eye
     ● **H20.03   Secondary infectious iridocyclitis**
       H20.031   Secondary infectious iridocyclitis, right eye
       H20.032   Secondary infectious iridocyclitis, left eye
       H20.033   Secondary infectious iridocyclitis, bilateral
       H20.039   Secondary infectious iridocyclitis, unspecified eye
     ● **H20.04   Secondary noninfectious iridocyclitis**
       H20.041   Secondary noninfectious iridocyclitis, right eye
       H20.042   Secondary noninfectious iridocyclitis, left eye
       H20.043   Secondary noninfectious iridocyclitis, bilateral
       H20.049   Secondary noninfectious iridocyclitis, unspecified eye
     ● **H20.05   Hypopyon**
       H20.051   Hypopyon, right eye
       H20.052   Hypopyon, left eye
       H20.053   Hypopyon, bilateral
       H20.059   Hypopyon, unspecified eye
   ● **H20.1   Chronic iridocyclitis**
     Use additional code for any associated cataract (H26.21-)
     Excludes2   posterior cyclitis (H30.2-)
     H20.10   Chronic iridocyclitis, unspecified eye
     H20.11   Chronic iridocyclitis, right eye
     H20.12   Chronic iridocyclitis, left eye
     H20.13   Chronic iridocyclitis, bilateral
   ● **H20.2   Lens-induced iridocyclitis**
     H20.20   Lens-induced iridocyclitis, unspecified eye
     H20.21   Lens-induced iridocyclitis, right eye
     H20.22   Lens-induced iridocyclitis, left eye
     H20.23   Lens-induced iridocyclitis, bilateral
   ● **H20.8   Other iridocyclitis**
     Excludes2   glaucomatocyclitis crises (H40.4-)
           posterior cyclitis (H30.2-)
           sympathetic uveitis (H44.13-)
     ● **H20.81   Fuchs' heterochromic cyclitis**
       H20.811   Fuchs' heterochromic cyclitis, right eye
       H20.812   Fuchs' heterochromic cyclitis, left eye
       H20.813   Fuchs' heterochromic cyclitis, bilateral
       H20.819   Fuchs' heterochromic cyclitis, unspecified eye
     ● **H20.82   Vogt-Koyanagi syndrome**
       H20.821   Vogt-Koyanagi syndrome, right eye
       H20.822   Vogt-Koyanagi syndrome, left eye
       H20.823   Vogt-Koyanagi syndrome, bilateral
       H20.829   Vogt-Koyanagi syndrome, unspecified eye
   H20.9   Unspecified iridocyclitis
     Uveitis NOS

● **H21   Other disorders of iris and ciliary body**
     Excludes2   sympathetic uveitis (H44.1-)
   ● **H21.0   Hyphema**
       Excludes1   traumatic hyphema (S05.1-)
     H21.00   Hyphema, unspecified eye
     H21.01   Hyphema, right eye
     H21.02   Hyphema, left eye
     H21.03   Hyphema, bilateral
   ● **H21.1   Other vascular disorders of iris and ciliary body**
       Neovascularization of iris or ciliary body
       Rubeosis iridis
       Rubeosis of iris
     ● **H21.1X   Other vascular disorders of iris and ciliary body**
         H21.1X1   Other vascular disorders of iris and ciliary body, right eye
         H21.1X2   Other vascular disorders of iris and ciliary body, left eye
         H21.1X3   Other vascular disorders of iris and ciliary body, bilateral
         H21.1X9   Other vascular disorders of iris and ciliary body, unspecified eye
   ● **H21.2   Degeneration of iris and ciliary body**
     ● **H21.21   Degeneration of chamber angle**
         H21.211   Degeneration of chamber angle, right eye
         H21.212   Degeneration of chamber angle, left eye
         H21.213   Degeneration of chamber angle, bilateral
         H21.219   Degeneration of chamber angle, unspecified eye
     ● **H21.22   Degeneration of ciliary body**
         H21.221   Degeneration of ciliary body, right eye
         H21.222   Degeneration of ciliary body, left eye
         H21.223   Degeneration of ciliary body, bilateral
         H21.229   Degeneration of ciliary body, unspecified eye
     ● **H21.23   Degeneration of iris (pigmentary)**
         Translucency of iris
         H21.231   Degeneration of iris (pigmentary), right eye
         H21.232   Degeneration of iris (pigmentary), left eye
         H21.233   Degeneration of iris (pigmentary), bilateral
         H21.239   Degeneration of iris (pigmentary), unspecified eye
     ● **H21.24   Degeneration of pupillary margin**
         H21.241   Degeneration of pupillary margin, right eye
         H21.242   Degeneration of pupillary margin, left eye
         H21.243   Degeneration of pupillary margin, bilateral
         H21.249   Degeneration of pupillary margin, unspecified eye
     ● **H21.25   Iridoschisis**
         H21.251   Iridoschisis, right eye
         H21.252   Iridoschisis, left eye
         H21.253   Iridoschisis, bilateral
         H21.259   Iridoschisis, unspecified eye
     ● **H21.26   Iris atrophy (essential) (progressive)**
         H21.261   Iris atrophy (essential) (progressive), right eye
         H21.262   Iris atrophy (essential) (progressive), left eye

         H21.263   Iris atrophy (essential) (progressive), bilateral
         H21.269   Iris atrophy (essential) (progressive), unspecified eye
     ● **H21.27   Miotic pupillary cyst**
         H21.271   Miotic pupillary cyst, right eye
         H21.272   Miotic pupillary cyst, left eye
         H21.273   Miotic pupillary cyst, bilateral
         H21.279   Miotic pupillary cyst, unspecified eye
     H21.29   Other iris atrophy
   ● **H21.3   Cyst of iris, ciliary body and anterior chamber**
       Excludes2   miotic pupillary cyst (H21.27-)
     ● **H21.30   Idiopathic cysts of iris, ciliary body or anterior chamber**
         Cyst of iris, ciliary body or anterior chamber NOS
         H21.301   Idiopathic cysts of iris, ciliary body or anterior chamber, right eye
         H21.302   Idiopathic cysts of iris, ciliary body or anterior chamber, left eye
         H21.303   Idiopathic cysts of iris, ciliary body or anterior chamber, bilateral
         H21.309   Idiopathic cysts of iris, ciliary body or anterior chamber, unspecified eye
     ● **H21.31   Exudative cysts of iris or anterior chamber**
         H21.311   Exudative cysts of iris or anterior chamber, right eye
         H21.312   Exudative cysts of iris or anterior chamber, left eye
         H21.313   Exudative cysts of iris or anterior chamber, bilateral
         H21.319   Exudative cysts of iris or anterior chamber, unspecified eye
     ● **H21.32   Implantation cysts of iris, ciliary body or anterior chamber**
         H21.321   Implantation cysts of iris, ciliary body or anterior chamber, right eye
         H21.322   Implantation cysts of iris, ciliary body or anterior chamber, left eye
         H21.323   Implantation cysts of iris, ciliary body or anterior chamber, bilateral
         H21.329   Implantation cysts of iris, ciliary body or anterior chamber, unspecified eye
     ● **H21.33   Parasitic cyst of iris, ciliary body or anterior chamber**
         H21.331   Parasitic cyst of iris, ciliary body or anterior chamber, right eye
         H21.332   Parasitic cyst of iris, ciliary body or anterior chamber, left eye
         H21.333   Parasitic cyst of iris, ciliary body or anterior chamber, bilateral
         H21.339   Parasitic cyst of iris, ciliary body or anterior chamber, unspecified eye
     ● **H21.34   Primary cyst of pars plana**
         H21.341   Primary cyst of pars plana, right eye
         H21.342   Primary cyst of pars plana, left eye
         H21.343   Primary cyst of pars plana, bilateral
         H21.349   Primary cyst of pars plana, unspecified eye
     ● **H21.35   Exudative cyst of pars plana**
         H21.351   Exudative cyst of pars plana, right eye
         H21.352   Exudative cyst of pars plana, left eye
         H21.353   Exudative cyst of pars plana, bilateral
         H21.359   Exudative cyst of pars plana, unspecified eye

▶ New   ⇒ Revised   ~~deleted~~ Deleted   Excludes 1   Excludes 2   Includes   Use additional   Code first   Code also   Key words
OGCR Official Guidelines   X Assign placeholder X   ● Use Additional Character(s)   ▶ Manifestation Code   🏥 Hierarchical Condition Category   **Coding Clinic**

● **H21.4** **Pupillary membranes**
Iris bombé
Pupillary occlusion
Pupillary seclusion
  Excludes1   congenital pupillary membranes (Q13.8)
  H21.40 Pupillary membranes, unspecified eye
  H21.41 Pupillary membranes, right eye
  H21.42 Pupillary membranes, left eye
  H21.43 Pupillary membranes, bilateral

● **H21.5** **Other and unspecified adhesions and disruptions of iris and ciliary body**
  Excludes1   corectopia (Q13.2)
 ● **H21.50** **Unspecified adhesions of iris**
    Synechia (iris) NOS
    H21.501 Unspecified adhesions of iris, right eye
    H21.502 Unspecified adhesions of iris, left eye
    H21.503 Unspecified adhesions of iris, bilateral
    H21.509 Unspecified adhesions of iris and ciliary body, unspecified eye
 ● **H21.51** Anterior synechiae (iris)
    H21.511 Anterior synechiae (iris), right eye
    H21.512 Anterior synechiae (iris), left eye
    H21.513 Anterior synechiae (iris), bilateral
    H21.519 Anterior synechiae (iris), unspecified eye
 ● **H21.52** Goniosynechiae
    H21.521 Goniosynechiae, right eye
    H21.522 Goniosynechiae, left eye
    H21.523 Goniosynechiae, bilateral
    H21.529 Goniosynechiae, unspecified eye
 ● **H21.53** Iridodialysis
    H21.531 Iridodialysis, right eye
    H21.532 Iridodialysis, left eye
    H21.533 Iridodialysis, bilateral
    H21.539 Iridodialysis, unspecified eye
 ● **H21.54** Posterior synechiae (iris)
    H21.541 Posterior synechiae (iris), right eye
    H21.542 Posterior synechiae (iris), left eye
    H21.543 Posterior synechiae (iris), bilateral
    H21.549 Posterior synechiae (iris), unspecified eye
 ● **H21.55** Recession of chamber angle
    H21.551 Recession of chamber angle, right eye
    H21.552 Recession of chamber angle, left eye
    H21.553 Recession of chamber angle, bilateral
    H21.559 Recession of chamber angle, unspecified eye
 ● **H21.56** Pupillary abnormalities
    Deformed pupil
    Ectopic pupil
    Rupture of sphincter, pupil
    Excludes1   congenital deformity of pupil (Q13.2-)
    H21.561 Pupillary abnormality, right eye
    H21.562 Pupillary abnormality, left eye
    H21.563 Pupillary abnormality, bilateral
    H21.569 Pupillary abnormality, unspecified eye

● **H21.8** **Other specified disorders of iris and ciliary body**
  H21.81 Floppy iris syndrome
    Intraoperative floppy iris syndrome (IFIS)
    Use additional code for adverse effect, if applicable, to identify drug (T36-T50 with fifth or sixth character 5)
  H21.82 Plateau iris syndrome (post-iridectomy) (postprocedural)
  H21.89 Other specified disorders of iris and ciliary body
 H21.9 Unspecified disorder of iris and ciliary body

▶ **H22** *Disorders of iris and ciliary body in diseases classified elsewhere*
  Code first underlying disease, such as:
    gout (M1A.-, M10.-)
    leprosy (A30.-)
    parasitic disease (B89)

DISORDERS OF LENS (H25-H28)

● **H25** **Age-related cataract**
Senile cataract
  Excludes2   capsular glaucoma with pseudoexfoliation of lens (H40.1-)
 ● **H25.0** Age-related incipient cataract
  ● **H25.01** Cortical age-related cataract
    H25.011 Cortical age-related cataract, right eye   **A**
    H25.012 Cortical age-related cataract, left eye   **A**
    H25.013 Cortical age-related cataract, bilateral   **A**
    H25.019 Cortical age-related cataract, unspecified eye   **A**
  ● **H25.03** Anterior subcapsular polar age-related cataract
    H25.031 Anterior subcapsular polar age-related cataract, right eye   **A**
    H25.032 Anterior subcapsular polar age-related cataract, left eye   **A**
    H25.033 Anterior subcapsular polar age-related cataract, bilateral   **A**
    H25.039 Anterior subcapsular polar age-related cataract, unspecified eye   **A**
  ● **H25.04** Posterior subcapsular polar age-related cataract
    H25.041 Posterior subcapsular polar age-related cataract, right eye   **A**
    H25.042 Posterior subcapsular polar age-related cataract, left eye   **A**
    H25.043 Posterior subcapsular polar age-related cataract, bilateral   **A**
    H25.049 Posterior subcapsular polar age-related cataract, unspecified eye   **A**

Figure 7-9 Age-related cataract. Nuclear sclerosis and cortical lens opacities are present. (From Ignatavicius DD, Workman ML: Medical-Surgical Nursing: Patient-Centered Collaborative Care, St. Louis, MO, Saunders/Elsevier, 2010)

Item 7-5 Senile cataracts are linked to the aging process. The most common area for the formation of a cataract is the cortical area of the lens. **Polar cataracts** can be either anterior or posterior. **Anterior polar cataracts** are more common and are small, white, capsular cataracts located on the anterior portion of the lens. **Total cataracts,** also called **complete** or **mature,** cause an opacity of all fibers of the lens. **Hypermature** describes a mature cataract with a swollen, milky cortex that covers the entire lens. **Immature,** also called **incipient,** cataracts have a clear cortex and are only slightly opaque. Treatment for all cataracts is the removal of the lens.

● H25.09   Other age-related incipient cataract
      Coronary age-related cataract
      Punctate age-related cataract
      Water clefts
    H25.091   Other age-related incipient cataract, right eye   **A**
    H25.092   Other age-related incipient cataract, left eye   **A**
    H25.093   Other age-related incipient cataract, bilateral   **A**
    H25.099   Other age-related incipient cataract, unspecified eye   **A**

● H25.1   Age-related nuclear cataract
      Cataracta brunescens
      Nuclear sclerosis cataract
    H25.10   Age-related nuclear cataract, unspecified eye   **A**
    H25.11   Age-related nuclear cataract, right eye   **A**
      Coding Clinic: 2019, Q2, P30
    H25.12   Age-related nuclear cataract, left eye   **A**
      Coding Clinic: 2016, Q1, P33
    H25.13   Age-related nuclear cataract, bilateral   **A**
      Coding Clinic: 2016, Q1, P32

● H25.2   Age-related cataract, morgagnian type
      Age-related hypermature cataract
    H25.20   Age-related cataract, morgagnian type, unspecified eye   **A**
    H25.21   Age-related cataract, morgagnian type, right eye   **A**
    H25.22   Age-related cataract, morgagnian type, left eye   **A**
    H25.23   Age-related cataract, morgagnian type, bilateral   **A**

● H25.8   Other age-related cataract
   ● H25.81   Combined forms of age-related cataract
    H25.811   Combined forms of age-related cataract, right eye   **A**
    H25.812   Combined forms of age-related cataract, left eye   **A**
    H25.813   Combined forms of age-related cataract, bilateral   **A**
      Coding Clinic: 2019, Q2, P30
    H25.819   Combined forms of age-related cataract, unspecified eye   **A**
    H25.89   Other age-related cataract   **A**
   H25.9   Unspecified age-related cataract   **A**

● H26   Other cataract
   Excludes1   congenital cataract (Q12.0)
   ● H26.0   Infantile and juvenile cataract
   ● H26.00   Unspecified infantile and juvenile cataract
    H26.001   Unspecified infantile and juvenile cataract, right eye   **P**
    H26.002   Unspecified infantile and juvenile cataract, left eye   **P**
    H26.003   Unspecified infantile and juvenile cataract, bilateral   **P**
    H26.009   Unspecified infantile and juvenile cataract, unspecified eye   **P**
   ● H26.01   Infantile and juvenile cortical, lamellar, or zonular cataract
    H26.011   Infantile and juvenile cortical, lamellar, or zonular cataract, right eye   **P**
    H26.012   Infantile and juvenile cortical, lamellar, or zonular cataract, left eye   **P**
    H26.013   Infantile and juvenile cortical, lamellar, or zonular cataract, bilateral   **P**
    H26.019   Infantile and juvenile cortical, lamellar, or zonular cataract, unspecified eye   **P**

● H26.03   Infantile and juvenile nuclear cataract
    H26.031   Infantile and juvenile nuclear cataract, right eye   **P**
    H26.032   Infantile and juvenile nuclear cataract, left eye   **P**
    H26.033   Infantile and juvenile nuclear cataract, bilateral   **P**
    H26.039   Infantile and juvenile nuclear cataract, unspecified eye   **P**
● H26.04   Anterior subcapsular polar infantile and juvenile cataract
    H26.041   Anterior subcapsular polar infantile and juvenile cataract, right eye   **P**
    H26.042   Anterior subcapsular polar infantile and juvenile cataract, left eye   **P**
    H26.043   Anterior subcapsular polar infantile and juvenile cataract, bilateral   **P**
    H26.049   Anterior subcapsular polar infantile and juvenile cataract, unspecified eye   **P**
● H26.05   Posterior subcapsular polar infantile and juvenile cataract
    H26.051   Posterior subcapsular polar infantile and juvenile cataract, right eye   **P**
    H26.052   Posterior subcapsular polar infantile and juvenile cataract, left eye   **P**
    H26.053   Posterior subcapsular polar infantile and juvenile cataract, bilateral   **P**
    H26.059   Posterior subcapsular polar infantile and juvenile cataract, unspecified eye   **P**
● H26.06   Combined forms of infantile and juvenile cataract
    H26.061   Combined forms of infantile and juvenile cataract, right eye   **P**
    H26.062   Combined forms of infantile and juvenile cataract, left eye   **P**
    H26.063   Combined forms of infantile and juvenile cataract bilateral   **P**
    H26.069   Combined forms of infantile and juvenile cataract, unspecified eye   **P**
   H26.09   Other infantile and juvenile cataract   **P**
● H26.1   Traumatic cataract
    Use additional code (Chapter 20) to identify external cause
   ● H26.10   Unspecified traumatic cataract
    H26.101   Unspecified traumatic cataract, right eye
    H26.102   Unspecified traumatic cataract, left eye
    H26.103   Unspecified traumatic cataract, bilateral
    H26.109   Unspecified traumatic cataract, unspecified eye
   ● H26.11   Localized traumatic opacities
    H26.111   Localized traumatic opacities, right eye
    H26.112   Localized traumatic opacities, left eye
    H26.113   Localized traumatic opacities, bilateral
    H26.119   Localized traumatic opacities, unspecified eye
   ● H26.12   Partially resolved traumatic cataract
    H26.121   Partially resolved traumatic cataract, right eye
    H26.122   Partially resolved traumatic cataract, left eye
    H26.123   Partially resolved traumatic cataract, bilateral
    H26.129   Partially resolved traumatic cataract, unspecified eye

▶ New   ⇒ Revised   ~~deleted~~ Deleted   Excludes 1   Excludes 2   Includes   Use additional   Code first   Code also   Key words
OGCR Official Guidelines   X Assign placeholder X   ● Use Additional Character(s)   ▶ Manifestation Code   🏷 Hierarchical Condition Category   **Coding Clinic**

● **H26.13**   Total traumatic cataract
    H26.131   Total traumatic cataract, **right eye**
    H26.132   Total traumatic cataract, **left eye**
    H26.133   Total traumatic cataract, **bilateral**
    H26.139   Total traumatic cataract, **unspecified eye**

● **H26.2**   Complicated cataract
    H26.20   **Unspecified** complicated cataract
        Cataracta complicata NOS
   ● H26.21   Cataract with **neovascularization**
        Code also associated condition, such as:
          chronic iridocyclitis (H20.1-)
    H26.211   Cataract with neovascularization, **right eye**
    H26.212   Cataract with neovascularization, **left eye**
    H26.213   Cataract with neovascularization, **bilateral**
    H26.219   Cataract with neovascularization, **unspecified eye**
   ● H26.22   Cataract **secondary to ocular disorders** (degenerative) (inflammatory)
        Code also associated ocular disorder
    H26.221   Cataract secondary to ocular disorders (degenerative) (inflammatory), **right eye**
    H26.222   Cataract secondary to ocular disorders (degenerative) (inflammatory), **left eye**
    H26.223   Cataract secondary to ocular disorders (degenerative) (inflammatory), **bilateral**
    H26.229   Cataract secondary to ocular disorders (degenerative) (inflammatory), **unspecified eye**
   ● H26.23   **Glaucomatous flecks** (subcapsular)
        Code first underlying glaucoma (H40-H42)
    H26.231   Glaucomatous flecks (subcapsular), **right eye**
    H26.232   Glaucomatous flecks (subcapsular), **left eye**
    H26.233   Glaucomatous flecks (subcapsular), **bilateral**
    H26.239   Glaucomatous flecks (subcapsular), **unspecified eye**

● **H26.3**   **Drug-induced cataract**
     Toxic cataract
     Use additional code for adverse effect, if applicable, to identify drug (T36-T50 with fifth or sixth character 5)
    H26.30   Drug-induced cataract, **unspecified eye**
    H26.31   Drug-induced cataract, **right eye**
    H26.32   Drug-induced cataract, **left eye**
    H26.33   Drug-induced cataract, **bilateral**

● **H26.4**   **Secondary cataract**
     Coding Clinic: 2018, Q2, P14
    H26.40   **Unspecified** secondary cataract
   ● H26.41   **Soemmering's ring**
    H26.411   Soemmering's ring, **right eye**
    H26.412   Soemmering's ring, **left eye**
    H26.413   Soemmering's ring, **bilateral**
    H26.419   Soemmering's ring, **unspecified eye**

   ● H26.49   **Other** secondary cataract
    H26.491   Other secondary cataract, **right eye**
    H26.492   Other secondary cataract, **left eye**
         Coding Clinic: 2018, Q2, P13
    H26.493   Other secondary cataract, **bilateral**
    H26.499   Other secondary cataract, **unspecified eye**
  H26.8   **Other** specified cataract
  H26.9   **Unspecified** cataract

● **H27**   **Other disorders of lens**
    Excludes1   congenital lens malformations (Q12.-)
          mechanical complications of intraocular lens implant (T85.2)
          pseudophakia (Z96.1)
  ● **H27.0**   **Aphakia**
     Acquired absence of lens
     Acquired aphakia
     Aphakia due to trauma
     Excludes1   cataract extraction status (Z98.4-)
           congenital absence of lens (Q12.3)
           congenital aphakia (Q12.3)
    H27.00   Aphakia, **unspecified eye**
    H27.01   Aphakia, **right eye**
    H27.02   Aphakia, **left eye**
    H27.03   Aphakia, **bilateral**
  ● **H27.1**   **Dislocation of lens**
    H27.10   **Unspecified** dislocation of lens
   ● H27.11   **Subluxation** of lens
    H27.111   Subluxation of lens, **right eye**
    H27.112   Subluxation of lens, **left eye**
    H27.113   Subluxation of lens, **bilateral**
    H27.119   Subluxation of lens, **unspecified eye**
   ● H27.12   **Anterior** dislocation of lens
    H27.121   Anterior dislocation of lens, **right eye**
    H27.122   Anterior dislocation of lens, **left eye**
    H27.123   Anterior dislocation of lens, **bilateral**
    H27.129   Anterior dislocation of lens, **unspecified eye**
   ● H27.13   **Posterior** dislocation of lens
    H27.131   Posterior dislocation of lens, **right eye**
    H27.132   Posterior dislocation of lens, **left eye**
    H27.133   Posterior dislocation of lens, **bilateral**
    H27.139   Posterior dislocation of lens, **unspecified eye**
  H27.8   **Other** specified disorders of lens
  H27.9   **Unspecified** disorder of lens

▌ *H28*   *Cataract in diseases classified elsewhere*
    Code first underlying disease, such as:
     hypoparathyroidism (E20.-)
     myotonia (G71.1-)
     myxedema (E03.-)
     protein-calorie malnutrition (E40-E46)
    Excludes1   cataract in diabetes mellitus (E08.36, E09.36, E10.36, E11.36, E13.36)

DISORDERS OF CHOROID AND RETINA (H30-H36)

★ **(See Plate 16 of the Anatomy Illustrations.)**

● H30   Chorioretinal inflammation

   ● H30.0   **Focal chorioretinal inflammation**
       Focal chorioretinitis
       Focal choroiditis
       Focal retinitis
       Focal retinochoroiditis

     ● H30.00   Unspecified focal chorioretinal inflammation
         Focal chorioretinitis NOS
         Focal choroiditis NOS
         Focal retinitis NOS
         Focal retinochoroiditis NOS

         H30.001   Unspecified focal chorioretinal inflammation, **right eye**
         H30.002   Unspecified focal chorioretinal inflammation, **left eye**
         H30.003   Unspecified focal chorioretinal inflammation, **bilateral**
         H30.009   Unspecified focal chorioretinal inflammation, **unspecified eye**

     ● H30.01   Focal chorioretinal inflammation, **juxtapapillary**
         H30.011   Focal chorioretinal inflammation, juxtapapillary, **right eye**
         H30.012   Focal chorioretinal inflammation, juxtapapillary, **left eye**
         H30.013   Focal chorioretinal inflammation, juxtapapillary, **bilateral**
         H30.019   Focal chorioretinal inflammation, juxtapapillary, **unspecified eye**

     ● H30.02   Focal chorioretinal inflammation of **posterior pole**
         H30.021   Focal chorioretinal inflammation of posterior pole, **right eye**
         H30.022   Focal chorioretinal inflammation of posterior pole, **left eye**
         H30.023   Focal chorioretinal inflammation of posterior pole, **bilateral**
         H30.029   Focal chorioretinal inflammation of posterior pole, **unspecified eye**

     ● H30.03   Focal chorioretinal inflammation, **peripheral**
         H30.031   Focal chorioretinal inflammation, peripheral, **right eye**
         H30.032   Focal chorioretinal inflammation, peripheral, **left eye**
         H30.033   Focal chorioretinal inflammation, peripheral, **bilateral**
         H30.039   Focal chorioretinal inflammation, peripheral, **unspecified eye**

     ● H30.04   Focal chorioretinal inflammation, **macular or paramacular**
         H30.041   Focal chorioretinal inflammation, macular or paramacular, **right eye**
         H30.042   Focal chorioretinal inflammation, macular or paramacular, **left eye**
         H30.043   Focal chorioretinal inflammation, macular or paramacular, **bilateral**
         H30.049   Focal chorioretinal inflammation, macular or paramacular, **unspecified eye**

● H30.1   Disseminated chorioretinal inflammation
       Disseminated chorioretinitis
       Disseminated choroiditis
       Disseminated retinitis
       Disseminated retinochoroiditis

     Excludes2   exudative retinopathy (H35.02-)

   ● H30.10   Unspecified disseminated chorioretinal inflammation
       Disseminated chorioretinitis NOS
       Disseminated choroiditis NOS
       Disseminated retinitis NOS
       Disseminated retinochoroiditis NOS

       H30.101   Unspecified disseminated chorioretinal inflammation, **right eye**
       H30.102   Unspecified disseminated chorioretinal inflammation, **left eye**
       H30.103   Unspecified disseminated chorioretinal inflammation, **bilateral**
       H30.109   Unspecified disseminated chorioretinal inflammation, **unspecified eye**

   ● H30.11   Disseminated chorioretinal inflammation of **posterior pole**
       H30.111   Disseminated chorioretinal inflammation of posterior pole, **right eye**
       H30.112   Disseminated chorioretinal inflammation of posterior pole, **left eye**
       H30.113   Disseminated chorioretinal inflammation of posterior pole, **bilateral**
       H30.119   Disseminated chorioretinal inflammation of posterior pole, **unspecified eye**

   ● H30.12   Disseminated chorioretinal inflammation, **peripheral**
       H30.121   Disseminated chorioretinal inflammation, peripheral **right eye**
       H30.122   Disseminated chorioretinal inflammation, peripheral, **left eye**
       H30.123   Disseminated chorioretinal inflammation, peripheral, **bilateral**
       H30.129   Disseminated chorioretinal inflammation, peripheral, **unspecified eye**

   ● H30.13   Disseminated chorioretinal inflammation, **generalized**
       H30.131   Disseminated chorioretinal inflammation, generalized, **right eye**
       H30.132   Disseminated chorioretinal inflammation, generalized, **left eye**
       H30.133   Disseminated chorioretinal inflammation, generalized, **bilateral**
       H30.139   Disseminated chorioretinal inflammation, generalized, **unspecified eye**

   ● H30.14   Acute posterior multifocal placoid pigment epitheliopathy
       H30.141   Acute posterior multifocal placoid pigment epitheliopathy, **right eye**
       H30.142   Acute posterior multifocal placoid pigment epitheliopathy, **left eye**
       H30.143   Acute posterior multifocal placoid pigment epitheliopathy, **bilateral**
       H30.149   Acute posterior multifocal placoid pigment epitheliopathy, **unspecified eye**

▶ New   ⯈ Revised   ~~deleted~~ Deleted   Excludes 1   Excludes 2   Includes   Use additional   Code first   Code also   Key words

OGCR Official Guidelines   X Assign placeholder X   ● Use Additional Character(s)   ▶ Manifestation Code   🏷 Hierarchical Condition Category   **Coding Clinic**

● **H30.2**   Posterior cyclitis
     Pars planitis
     H30.20   Posterior cyclitis, unspecified eye
     H30.21   Posterior cyclitis, right eye
     H30.22   Posterior cyclitis, left eye
     H30.23   Posterior cyclitis, bilateral

● **H30.8**   Other chorioretinal inflammations
   ● **H30.81**   Harada's disease
     H30.811   Harada's disease, right eye
     H30.812   Harada's disease, left eye
     H30.813   Harada's disease, bilateral
     H30.819   Harada's disease, unspecified eye

   ● **H30.89**   Other chorioretinal inflammations
     H30.891   Other chorioretinal inflammations, right eye
     H30.892   Other chorioretinal inflammations, left eye
     H30.893   Other chorioretinal inflammations, bilateral
     H30.899   Other chorioretinal inflammations, unspecified eye

● **H30.9**   Unspecified chorioretinal inflammation
     Chorioretinitis NOS
     Choroiditis NOS
     Neuroretinitis NOS
     Retinitis NOS
     Retinochoroiditis NOS
     H30.90   Unspecified chorioretinal inflammation, unspecified eye
     H30.91   Unspecified chorioretinal inflammation, right eye
     H30.92   Unspecified chorioretinal inflammation, left eye
     H30.93   Unspecified chorioretinal inflammation, bilateral

● **H31**   Other disorders of choroid
   ● **H31.0**   Chorioretinal scars
     Excludes2   postsurgical chorioretinal scars (H59.81-)
   ● **H31.00**   Unspecified chorioretinal scars
     H31.001   Unspecified chorioretinal scars, right eye
     H31.002   Unspecified chorioretinal scars, left eye
     H31.003   Unspecified chorioretinal scars, bilateral
     H31.009   Unspecified chorioretinal scars, unspecified eye

   ● **H31.01**   Macula scars of posterior pole (postinflammatory) (post-traumatic)
     Excludes1   postprocedural chorioretinal scar (H59.81-)
     H31.011   Macula scars of posterior pole (postinflammatory) (post-traumatic), right eye
     H31.012   Macula scars of posterior pole (postinflammatory) (post-traumatic), left eye
     H31.013   Macula scars of posterior pole (postinflammatory) (post-traumatic), bilateral
     H31.019   Macula scars of posterior pole (postinflammatory) (post-traumatic), unspecified eye

   ● **H31.02**   Solar retinopathy
     H31.021   Solar retinopathy, right eye
     H31.022   Solar retinopathy, left eye
     H31.023   Solar retinopathy, bilateral
     H31.029   Solar retinopathy, unspecified eye

● **H31.09**   Other chorioretinal scars
     H31.091   Other chorioretinal scars, right eye
     H31.092   Other chorioretinal scars, left eye
     H31.093   Other chorioretinal scars, bilateral
     H31.099   Other chorioretinal scars, unspecified eye

● **H31.1**   Choroidal degeneration
     Excludes2   angioid streaks of macula (H35.33)
   ● **H31.10**   Unspecified choroidal degeneration
     Choroidal sclerosis NOS
     H31.101   Choroidal degeneration, unspecified, right eye
     H31.102   Choroidal degeneration, unspecified, left eye
     H31.103   Choroidal degeneration, unspecified, bilateral
     H31.109   Choroidal degeneration, unspecified, unspecified eye

   ● **H31.11**   Age-related choroidal atrophy
     H31.111   Age-related choroidal atrophy, right eye   A
     H31.112   Age-related choroidal atrophy, left eye   A
     H31.113   Age-related choroidal atrophy, bilateral   A
     H31.119   Age-related choroidal atrophy, unspecified eye   A

   ● **H31.12**   Diffuse secondary atrophy of choroid
     H31.121   Diffuse secondary atrophy of choroid, right eye
     H31.122   Diffuse secondary atrophy of choroid, left eye
     H31.123   Diffuse secondary atrophy of choroid, bilateral
     H31.129   Diffuse secondary atrophy of choroid, unspecified eye

● **H31.2**   Hereditary choroidal dystrophy
     Excludes2   hyperornithinemia (E72.4)
              ornithinemia (E72.4)
     H31.20   Hereditary choroidal dystrophy, unspecified
     H31.21   Choroideremia
     H31.22   Choroidal dystrophy (central areolar) (generalized) (peripapillary)
     H31.23   Gyrate atrophy, choroid
     H31.29   Other hereditary choroidal dystrophy

● **H31.3**   Choroidal hemorrhage and rupture
   ● **H31.30**   Unspecified choroidal hemorrhage
     H31.301   Unspecified choroidal hemorrhage, right eye
     H31.302   Unspecified choroidal hemorrhage, left eye
     H31.303   Unspecified choroidal hemorrhage, bilateral
     H31.309   Unspecified choroidal hemorrhage, unspecified eye

   ● **H31.31**   Expulsive choroidal hemorrhage
     H31.311   Expulsive choroidal hemorrhage, right eye
     H31.312   Expulsive choroidal hemorrhage, left eye
     H31.313   Expulsive choroidal hemorrhage, bilateral
     H31.319   Expulsive choroidal hemorrhage, unspecified eye

   ● **H31.32**   Choroidal rupture
     H31.321   Choroidal rupture, right eye
     H31.322   Choroidal rupture, left eye
     H31.323   Choroidal rupture, bilateral
     H31.329   Choroidal rupture, unspecified eye

● **H31.4**   **Choroidal detachment**
    ● **H31.40**   **Unspecified** choroidal detachment
       H31.401   **Unspecified** choroidal detachment, **right eye**
       H31.402   **Unspecified** choroidal detachment, **left eye**
       H31.403   **Unspecified** choroidal detachment, **bilateral**
       H31.409   **Unspecified** choroidal detachment, **unspecified eye**
    ● **H31.41**   **Hemorrhagic** choroidal detachment
       H31.411   **Hemorrhagic** choroidal detachment, **right eye**
       H31.412   **Hemorrhagic** choroidal detachment, **left eye**
       H31.413   **Hemorrhagic** choroidal detachment, **bilateral**
       H31.419   **Hemorrhagic** choroidal detachment, **unspecified eye**
    ● **H31.42**   **Serous** choroidal detachment
       H31.421   **Serous** choroidal detachment, **right eye**
       H31.422   **Serous** choroidal detachment, **left eye**
       H31.423   **Serous** choroidal detachment, **bilateral**
       H31.429   **Serous** choroidal detachment, **unspecified eye**
    H31.8   **Other specified** disorders of choroid
    H31.9   **Unspecified** disorder of choroid

▶ *H32*   *Chorioretinal disorders in diseases classified elsewhere*
    Code first underlying disease, such as:
      congenital toxoplasmosis (P37.1)
      histoplasmosis (B39.-)
      leprosy (A30.-)
    Excludes1   chorioretinitis (in):
         toxoplasmosis (acquired) (B58.01)
         tuberculosis (A18.53)

● **H33**   **Retinal detachments and breaks**
    Excludes1   detachment of retinal pigment epithelium (H35.72-, H35.73-)
    ● **H33.0**   **Retinal detachment with retinal break**
       Rhegmatogenous retinal detachment
       Excludes1   serous retinal detachment (without retinal break) (H33.2-)
     ● **H33.00**   **Unspecified** retinal detachment with retinal break
         H33.001   **Unspecified** retinal detachment with retinal break, **right eye**
         H33.002   **Unspecified** retinal detachment with retinal break, **left eye**
         H33.003   **Unspecified** retinal detachment with retinal break, **bilateral**
         H33.009   **Unspecified** retinal detachment with retinal break, **unspecified eye**
     ● **H33.01**   Retinal detachment with **single break**
         H33.011   Retinal detachment with single break, **right eye**
         H33.012   Retinal detachment with single break, **left eye**
         H33.013   Retinal detachment with single break, **bilateral**
         H33.019   Retinal detachment with single break, **unspecified eye**

NON-RHEGMATOGENOUS
RETINAL DETACHMENT

— Vitreous
— Retina
— Protein-rich fluid in sub-retinal space
Retinal pigment epithelium

VITREOUS DETACHMENT

— Vitreous
— Posterior hyaloid
— Internal limiting membrane

RHEGMATOGENOUS
RETINAL
DETACHMENT

Blood
— Vitreous
— Posterior hyaloid
— Retina
— Retinal tear
— Liquified vitreous
— Retinal pigment epithelium

Figure 7-10   Retinal detachment. (From Kumar: Robbins and Cotran: Pathologic Basis of Disease, ed 7, Saunders, 2005)

Item 7–6   Retinal detachments and defects are conditions of the eye in which the retina separates from the underlying tissue. Initial detachment may be localized, requiring rapid treatment (medical emergency) to avoid the entire retina from detaching, which leads to vision loss and blindness.

    ● **H33.02**   Retinal detachment with **multiple breaks**
       H33.021   Retinal detachment with multiple breaks, **right eye**
       H33.022   Retinal detachment with multiple breaks, **left eye**
       H33.023   Retinal detachment with multiple breaks, **bilateral**
       H33.029   Retinal detachment with multiple breaks, **unspecified eye**
    ● **H33.03**   Retinal detachment with **giant retinal tear**
       H33.031   Retinal detachment with giant retinal tear, **right eye**
       H33.032   Retinal detachment with giant retinal tear, **left eye**
       H33.033   Retinal detachment with giant retinal tear, **bilateral**
       H33.039   Retinal detachment with giant retinal tear, **unspecified eye**
    ● **H33.04**   Retinal detachment with **retinal dialysis**
       H33.041   Retinal detachment with retinal dialysis, **right eye**
       H33.042   Retinal detachment with retinal dialysis, **left eye**
       H33.043   Retinal detachment with retinal dialysis, **bilateral**
       H33.049   Retinal detachment with retinal dialysis, **unspecified eye**

● **H33.05** **Total** retinal detachment
　　H33.051　Total retinal detachment, right eye
　　H33.052　Total retinal detachment, left eye
　　H33.053　Total retinal detachment, bilateral
　　H33.059　Total retinal detachment, unspecified eye

● **H33.1** **Retinoschisis and retinal cysts**
　　Excludes1　congenital retinoschisis (Q14.1)
　　　　　　microcystoid degeneration of retina (H35.42-)

● **H33.10** **Unspecified** retinoschisis
　　H33.101　Unspecified retinoschisis, right eye
　　H33.102　Unspecified retinoschisis, left eye
　　H33.103　Unspecified retinoschisis, bilateral
　　H33.109　Unspecified retinoschisis, unspecified eye

● **H33.11** **Cyst of ora serrata**
　　H33.111　Cyst of ora serrata, right eye
　　H33.112　Cyst of ora serrata, left eye
　　H33.113　Cyst of ora serrata, bilateral
　　H33.119　Cyst of ora serrata, unspecified eye

● **H33.12** **Parasitic cyst of retina**
　　H33.121　Parasitic cyst of retina, right eye
　　H33.122　Parasitic cyst of retina, left eye
　　H33.123　Parasitic cyst of retina, bilateral
　　H33.129　Parasitic cyst of retina, unspecified eye

● **H33.19** **Other** retinoschisis and retinal cysts
　　Pseudocyst of retina
　　H33.191　Other retinoschisis and retinal cysts, right eye
　　H33.192　Other retinoschisis and retinal cysts, left eye
　　H33.193　Other retinoschisis and retinal cysts, bilateral
　　H33.199　Other retinoschisis and retinal cysts, unspecified eye

● **H33.2** **Serous retinal detachment**
　　Retinal detachment NOS
　　Retinal detachment without retinal break
　　Excludes1　central serous chorioretinopathy (H35.71-)
　　H33.20　Serous retinal detachment, unspecified eye
　　H33.21　Serous retinal detachment, right eye
　　H33.22　Serous retinal detachment, left eye
　　H33.23　Serous retinal detachment, bilateral

● **H33.3** **Retinal breaks without detachment**
　　Excludes1　chorioretinal scars after surgery for detachment (H59.81-)
　　　　　　peripheral retinal degeneration without break (H35.4-)

● **H33.30** **Unspecified** retinal break
　　H33.301　Unspecified retinal break, right eye
　　H33.302　Unspecified retinal break, left eye
　　H33.303　Unspecified retinal break, bilateral
　　H33.309　Unspecified retinal break, unspecified eye

● **H33.31** **Horseshoe tear** of retina without detachment
　　Operculum of retina without detachment
　　H33.311　Horseshoe tear of retina without detachment, right eye
　　H33.312　Horseshoe tear of retina without detachment, left eye
　　H33.313　Horseshoe tear of retina without detachment, bilateral
　　H33.319　Horseshoe tear of retina without detachment, unspecified eye

● **H33.32** **Round hole of retina without detachment**
　　H33.321　Round hole, right eye
　　H33.322　Round hole, left eye
　　H33.323　Round hole, bilateral
　　H33.329　Round hole, unspecified eye

● **H33.33** **Multiple defects** of retina without detachment
　　H33.331　Multiple defects of retina without detachment, right eye
　　H33.332　Multiple defects of retina without detachment, left eye
　　H33.333　Multiple defects of retina without detachment, bilateral
　　H33.339　Multiple defects of retina without detachment, unspecified eye

● **H33.4** **Traction** detachment of retina
　　Proliferative vitreo-retinopathy with retinal detachment
　　H33.40　Traction detachment of retina, unspecified eye
　　H33.41　Traction detachment of retina, right eye
　　H33.42　Traction detachment of retina, left eye
　　H33.43　Traction detachment of retina, bilateral

　　H33.8　**Other retinal detachments**

● **H34** **Retinal vascular occlusions**
　　Blockage in vessel of the retina
　　Excludes1　amaurosis fugax (G45.3)

● **H34.0** **Transient retinal artery occlusion**
　　H34.00　Transient retinal artery occlusion, unspecified eye
　　H34.01　Transient retinal artery occlusion, right eye
　　H34.02　Transient retinal artery occlusion, left eye
　　H34.03　Transient retinal artery occlusion, bilateral

● **H34.1** **Central** retinal artery occlusion
　　H34.10　Central retinal artery occlusion, unspecified eye
　　H34.11　Central retinal artery occlusion, right eye
　　H34.12　Central retinal artery occlusion, left eye
　　H34.13　Central retinal artery occlusion, bilateral

● **H34.2** **Other retinal artery occlusions**

● **H34.21** **Partial retinal artery occlusion**
　　Hollenhorst's plaque
　　Retinal microembolism
　　H34.211　Partial retinal artery occlusion, right eye
　　H34.212　Partial retinal artery occlusion, left eye
　　H34.213　Partial retinal artery occlusion, bilateral
　　H34.219　Partial retinal artery occlusion, unspecified eye

● **H34.23** **Retinal artery branch occlusion**
　　H34.231　Retinal artery branch occlusion, right eye
　　H34.232　Retinal artery branch occlusion, left eye
　　H34.233　Retinal artery branch occlusion, bilateral
　　H34.239　Retinal artery branch occlusion, unspecified eye

- H34.8 **Other retinal vascular occlusions**
  Coding Clinic: 2016, Q4, P19
  - H34.81 **Central retinal vein occlusion**
    One of the following 7th characters is to be
    assigned to codes in subcategory H34.81
    to designate the severity of the occlusion:

    > Ø with macular edema
    > 1 with retinal neovascularization
    > 2 stable
    >   Old central retinal vein occlusion

    - H34.811 Central retinal vein occlusion, **right**
      eye
    - H34.812 Central retinal vein occlusion, **left eye**
    - H34.813 Central retinal vein occlusion,
      bilateral
    - H34.819 Central retinal vein occlusion,
      unspecified eye
  - H34.82 **Venous** engorgement
    Incipient retinal vein occlusion
    Partial retinal vein occlusion
    - H34.821 Venous engorgement, **right eye**
    - H34.822 Venous engorgement, **left eye**
    - H34.823 Venous engorgement, **bilateral**
    - H34.829 Venous engorgement, **unspecified** eye
  - H34.83 **Tributary (branch) retinal vein occlusion**
    One of the following 7th characters is to be
    assigned to codes in subcategory H34.83
    to designate the severity of the occlusion:

    > Ø with macular edema
    > 1 with retinal neovascularization
    > 2 stable
    >   Old tributary (branch) retinal vein
    >   occlusion

    - H34.831 Tributary (branch) retinal vein
      occlusion, **right eye**
    - H34.832 Tributary (branch) retinal vein
      occlusion, **left eye**
    - H34.833 Tributary (branch) retinal vein
      occlusion, **bilateral**
    - H34.839 Tributary (branch) retinal vein
      occlusion, **unspecified** eye
- H34.9 **Unspecified** retinal vascular occlusion

- H35 **Other retinal disorders**
  Excludes2 diabetic retinal disorders (E08.311-E08.359,
  E09.311-E09.359, E10.311-E10.359,
  E11.311-E11.359, E13.311-E13.359)
  - H35.0 **Background retinopathy and retinal vascular changes**
    Code also any associated hypertension (I10.-)
    OGCR Section I. C.9.a.5.

    > Hypertensive Retinopathy
    > Subcategory H35.0, Background retinopathy and
    > retinal vascular changes, should be used with a
    > code from category I10–I15, Hypertensive disease to
    > include the systemic hypertension. The sequencing is
    > based on the reason for the encounter.

    - H35.00 **Unspecified** background retinopathy
    - H35.01 **Changes in retinal vascular appearance**
      Retinal vascular sheathing
      - H35.011 Changes in retinal vascular
        appearance, **right eye**
      - H35.012 Changes in retinal vascular
        appearance, **left eye**
      - H35.013 Changes in retinal vascular
        appearance, **bilateral**
      - H35.019 Changes in retinal vascular
        appearance, **unspecified** eye

- H35.02 **Exudative retinopathy**
  Coats retinopathy
  - H35.021 Exudative retinopathy, **right eye**
  - H35.022 Exudative retinopathy, **left eye**
  - H35.023 Exudative retinopathy, **bilateral**
  - H35.029 Exudative retinopathy, **unspecified**
    eye
- H35.03 **Hypertensive** retinopathy
  - H35.031 Hypertensive retinopathy, **right eye**
  - H35.032 Hypertensive retinopathy, **left eye**
  - H35.033 Hypertensive retinopathy, **bilateral**
  - H35.039 Hypertensive retinopathy, **unspecified**
    eye
- H35.04 Retinal **micro-aneurysms, unspecified**
  - H35.041 Retinal micro-aneurysms,
    unspecified, **right eye**
  - H35.042 Retinal micro-aneurysms,
    unspecified, **left eye**
  - H35.043 Retinal micro-aneurysms,
    unspecified, **bilateral**
  - H35.049 Retinal micro-aneurysms,
    unspecified, **unspecified** eye
- H35.05 Retinal **neovascularization, unspecified**
  - H35.051 Retinal neovascularization,
    unspecified, **right eye**
  - H35.052 Retinal neovascularization,
    unspecified, **left eye**
  - H35.053 Retinal neovascularization,
    unspecified, **bilateral**
  - H35.059 Retinal neovascularization,
    unspecified, **unspecified** eye
- H35.06 Retinal **vasculitis**
  Eales disease
  Retinal perivasculitis
  - H35.061 Retinal vasculitis, **right eye**
  - H35.062 Retinal vasculitis, **left eye**
  - H35.063 Retinal vasculitis, **bilateral**
  - H35.069 Retinal vasculitis, **unspecified** eye
- H35.07 Retinal **telangiectasis**
  - H35.071 Retinal telangiectasis, **right eye**
  - H35.072 Retinal telangiectasis, **left eye**
  - H35.073 Retinal telangiectasis, **bilateral**
  - H35.079 Retinal telangiectasis, **unspecified** eye
- H35.09 **Other** intraretinal microvascular abnormalities
  Retinal varices
- H35.1 **Retinopathy of prematurity**
  - H35.10 Retinopathy of prematurity, **unspecified**
    Retinopathy of prematurity NOS
    - H35.101 Retinopathy of prematurity,
      unspecified, **right eye**
    - H35.102 Retinopathy of prematurity,
      unspecified, **left eye**
    - H35.103 Retinopathy of prematurity,
      unspecified, **bilateral**
    - H35.109 Retinopathy of prematurity,
      unspecified, **unspecified** eye
  - H35.11 Retinopathy of prematurity, **stage Ø**
    - H35.111 Retinopathy of prematurity, stage Ø,
      right eye
    - H35.112 Retinopathy of prematurity, stage Ø,
      left eye
    - H35.113 Retinopathy of prematurity, stage Ø,
      bilateral
    - H35.119 Retinopathy of prematurity, stage Ø,
      unspecified eye

▶ New   ⇒ Revised   ~~deleted~~ Deleted   Excludes 1   Excludes 2   Includes   Use additional   Code first   Code also   Key words

OGCR Official Guidelines   X Assign placeholder X   ● Use Additional Character(s)   ▶ Manifestation Code   🅰 Hierarchical Condition Category   **Coding Clinic**

● **H35.12**   **Retinopathy of prematurity, stage 1**
     H35.121   Retinopathy of prematurity, stage 1, right eye
     H35.122   Retinopathy of prematurity, stage 1, left eye
     H35.123   Retinopathy of prematurity, stage 1, bilateral
     H35.129   Retinopathy of prematurity, stage 1, unspecified eye

● **H35.13**   **Retinopathy of prematurity, stage 2**
     H35.131   Retinopathy of prematurity, stage 2, right eye
     H35.132   Retinopathy of prematurity, stage 2, left eye
     H35.133   Retinopathy of prematurity, stage 2, bilateral
     H35.139   Retinopathy of prematurity, stage 2, unspecified eye

● **H35.14**   **Retinopathy of prematurity, stage 3**
     H35.141   Retinopathy of prematurity, stage 3, right eye
     H35.142   Retinopathy of prematurity, stage 3, left eye
     H35.143   Retinopathy of prematurity, stage 3, bilateral
     H35.149   Retinopathy of prematurity, stage 3, unspecified eye

● **H35.15**   **Retinopathy of prematurity, stage 4**
     H35.151   Retinopathy of prematurity, stage 4, right eye
     H35.152   Retinopathy of prematurity, stage 4, left eye
     H35.153   Retinopathy of prematurity, stage 4, bilateral
     H35.159   Retinopathy of prematurity, stage 4, unspecified eye

● **H35.16**   **Retinopathy of prematurity, stage 5**
     H35.161   Retinopathy of prematurity, stage 5, right eye
     H35.162   Retinopathy of prematurity, stage 5, left eye
     H35.163   Retinopathy of prematurity, stage 5, bilateral
     H35.169   Retinopathy of prematurity, stage 5, unspecified eye

● **H35.17**   **Retrolental fibroplasia**
     H35.171   Retrolental fibroplasia, right eye
     H35.172   Retrolental fibroplasia, left eye
     H35.173   Retrolental fibroplasia, bilateral
     H35.179   Retrolental fibroplasia, unspecified eye

● **H35.2**   **Other non-diabetic proliferative retinopathy**
     Proliferative vitreo-retinopathy

     Excludes1   proliferative vitreo-retinopathy with retinal detachment (H33.4-)

     H35.20   Other non-diabetic proliferative retinopathy, unspecified eye
     H35.21   Other non-diabetic proliferative retinopathy, right eye
     H35.22   Other non-diabetic proliferative retinopathy, left eye
     H35.23   Other non-diabetic proliferative retinopathy, bilateral

● **H35.3**   **Degeneration of macula and posterior pole**
     H35.30   **Unspecified macular degeneration**   A
                Age-related macular degeneration

● **H35.31**   **Nonexudative age-related macular degeneration**
     Atrophic age-related macular degeneration
     Dry age-related macular degeneration
     One of the following 7th characters is to be assigned to codes in subcategory H35.31 to designate the stage of the disease:

Ø	stage unspecified
1	early dry stage
2	intermediate dry stage
3	advanced atrophic without subfoveal involvement
	advanced dry stage
4	advanced atrophic with subfoveal involvement

     ● H35.311   Nonexudative age-related macular degeneration, **right eye**   A
                Coding Clinic: 2016, Q4, P20-21
     ● H35.312   Nonexudative age-related macular degeneration, **left eye**   A
                Coding Clinic: 2016, Q4, P20-21
     ● H35.313   Nonexudative age-related macular degeneration, **bilateral**   A
                Coding Clinic: 2016, Q4, P20
     ● H35.319   Nonexudative age-related macular degeneration, **unspecified** eye   A
                Coding Clinic: 2016, Q4, P20

● **H35.32**   **Exudative age-related macular degeneration**
     Wet age-related macular degeneration
     One of the following 7th characters is to be assigned to codes in subcategory H35.32 to designate the stage of the disease:

Ø	stage unspecified
1	with active choroidal neovascularization
2	with inactive choroidal neovascularization
	with involuted or regressed neovascularization
3	with inactive scar

     Coding Clinic: 2016, Q4, P20
     ● H35.321   Exudative age-related macular degeneration, **right eye** 🔁   A
     ● H35.322   Exudative age-related macular degeneration, **left eye** 🔁   A
     ● H35.323   Exudative age-related macular degeneration, **bilateral** 🔁   A
     ● H35.329   Exudative age-related macular degeneration, **unspecified** eye 🔁   A

     H35.33   **Angioid streaks of macula**
● **H35.34**   **Macular cyst, hole, or pseudohole**
     H35.341   Macular cyst, hole, or pseudohole, **right** eye
     H35.342   Macular cyst, hole, or pseudohole, **left** eye
     H35.343   Macular cyst, hole, or pseudohole, **bilateral**
     H35.349   Macular cyst, hole, or pseudohole, **unspecified** eye

Item 7-7   Macular degeneration is typically age-related, chronic, and is evidenced by deterioration of the macula (the part of the retina that provides for central field vision), resulting in blurred vision or a blind spot in the center of visual field while not affecting peripheral vision.

● **H35.35**   Cystoid macular degeneration
    Excludes1   cystoid macular edema
                      following cataract surgery
                      (H59.Ø3-)
    H35.351   Cystoid macular degeneration, right eye
    H35.352   Cystoid macular degeneration, left eye
    H35.353   Cystoid macular degeneration, bilateral
    H35.359   Cystoid macular degeneration, unspecified eye

● **H35.36**   Drusen (degenerative) of macula
    H35.361   Drusen (degenerative) of macula, right eye
           Coding Clinic: 2Ø16, Q4, P21
    H35.362   Drusen (degenerative) of macula, left eye
           Coding Clinic: 2Ø16, Q4, P21
    H35.363   Drusen (degenerative) of macula, bilateral
           Coding Clinic: 2Ø17, Q1, P51
    H35.369   Drusen (degenerative) of macula, unspecified eye

● **H35.37**   Puckering of macula
    H35.371   Puckering of macula, right eye
    H35.372   Puckering of macula, left eye
    H35.373   Puckering of macula, bilateral
    H35.379   Puckering of macula, unspecified eye

● **H35.38**   Toxic maculopathy
    Code first poisoning due to drug or toxin, if
       applicable (T36-T65 with fifth or sixth
       character 1-4 or 6)
    Use additional code for adverse effect, if
       applicable, to identify drug (T36-T5Ø
       with fifth or sixth character 5)
    H35.381   Toxic maculopathy, right eye
    H35.382   Toxic maculopathy, left eye
    H35.383   Toxic maculopathy, bilateral
    H35.389   Toxic maculopathy, unspecified eye

● **H35.4**   Peripheral retinal degeneration
    Excludes1   hereditary retinal degeneration
                      (dystrophy) (H35.5-)
                      peripheral retinal degeneration with
                      retinal break (H33.3-)
   H35.4Ø   Unspecified peripheral retinal degeneration
●   H35.41   Lattice degeneration of retina
        Palisade degeneration of retina
    H35.411   Lattice degeneration of retina, right eye
    H35.412   Lattice degeneration of retina, left eye
    H35.413   Lattice degeneration of retina, bilateral
    H35.419   Lattice degeneration of retina, unspecified eye

● **H35.42**   Microcystoid degeneration of retina
    H35.421   Microcystoid degeneration of retina, right eye
    H35.422   Microcystoid degeneration of retina, left eye
    H35.423   Microcystoid degeneration of retina, bilateral
    H35.429   Microcystoid degeneration of retina, unspecified eye

● **H35.43**   Paving stone degeneration of retina
    H35.431   Paving stone degeneration of retina, right eye
    H35.432   Paving stone degeneration of retina, left eye

    H35.433   Paving stone degeneration of retina, bilateral
    H35.439   Paving stone degeneration of retina, unspecified eye

● **H35.44**   Age-related reticular degeneration of retina
    H35.441   Age-related reticular degeneration of retina, right eye   A
    H35.442   Age-related reticular degeneration of retina, left eye   A
    H35.443   Age-related reticular degeneration of retina, bilateral   A
    H35.449   Age-related reticular degeneration of retina, unspecified eye   A

● **H35.45**   Secondary pigmentary degeneration
    H35.451   Secondary pigmentary degeneration, right eye
    H35.452   Secondary pigmentary degeneration, left eye
    H35.453   Secondary pigmentary degeneration, bilateral
    H35.459   Secondary pigmentary degeneration, unspecified eye

● **H35.46**   Secondary vitreoretinal degeneration
    H35.461   Secondary vitreoretinal degeneration, right eye
    H35.462   Secondary vitreoretinal degeneration, left eye
    H35.463   Secondary vitreoretinal degeneration, bilateral
    H35.469   Secondary vitreoretinal degeneration, unspecified eye

● **H35.5**   Hereditary retinal dystrophy
    Excludes1   dystrophies primarily involving Bruch's
                      membrane (H31.1-)
   H35.5Ø   Unspecified hereditary retinal dystrophy
   H35.51   Vitreoretinal dystrophy
   H35.52   Pigmentary retinal dystrophy
        Albipunctate retinal dystrophy
        Retinitis pigmentosa
        Tapetoretinal dystrophy
   H35.53   Other dystrophies primarily involving the sensory retina
        Stargardt's disease
   H35.54   Dystrophies primarily involving the retinal pigment epithelium
        Vitelliform retinal dystrophy

● **H35.6**   Retinal hemorrhage
   H35.6Ø   Retinal hemorrhage, unspecified eye
   H35.61   Retinal hemorrhage, right eye
   H35.62   Retinal hemorrhage, left eye
   H35.63   Retinal hemorrhage, bilateral

● **H35.7**   Separation of retinal layers
    Excludes1   retinal detachment (serous) (H33.2-)
                      rhegmatogenous retinal detachment
                      (H33.Ø-)
   H35.7Ø   Unspecified separation of retinal layers
●   H35.71   Central serous chorioretinopathy
    H35.711   Central serous chorioretinopathy, right eye
    H35.712   Central serous chorioretinopathy, left eye
    H35.713   Central serous chorioretinopathy, bilateral
    H35.719   Central serous chorioretinopathy, unspecified eye

---

▶ New   ⟹ Revised   ~~deleted~~ Deleted   Excludes 1   Excludes 2   Includes   Use additional   Code first   Code also   Key words

OGCR Official Guidelines   X Assign placeholder X   ● Use Additional Character(s)   ▷ Manifestation Code   🅚 Hierarchical Condition Category   **Coding Clinic**

● **H35.72**   **Serous detachment of retinal pigment epithelium**

    H35.721   Serous detachment of retinal pigment epithelium, **right eye**

    H35.722   Serous detachment of retinal pigment epithelium, **left eye**

    H35.723   Serous detachment of retinal pigment epithelium, **bilateral**

    H35.729   Serous detachment of retinal pigment epithelium, **unspecified eye**

● **H35.73**   **Hemorrhagic detachment of retinal pigment epithelium**

    H35.731   Hemorrhagic detachment of retinal pigment epithelium, **right eye**

    H35.732   Hemorrhagic detachment of retinal pigment epithelium, **left eye**

    H35.733   Hemorrhagic detachment of retinal pigment epithelium, **bilateral**

    H35.739   Hemorrhagic detachment of retinal pigment epithelium, **unspecified eye**

● **H35.8**   **Other specified retinal disorders**

    Excludes2   retinal hemorrhage (H35.6-)

    H35.81   **Retinal edema**
       Retinal cotton wool spots

    H35.82   **Retinal ischemia**

    H35.89   **Other specified retinal disorders**

H35.9   **Unspecified retinal disorder**

▶ **H36**   *Retinal disorders in diseases classified elsewhere*

    Code first underlying disease, such as:
      lipid storage disorders (E75.-)
      sickle-cell disorders (D57.-)

    Excludes1   arteriosclerotic retinopathy (H35.0-)
              diabetic retinopathy (E08.3-, E09.3-, E10.3-, E11.3-, E13.3-)

GLAUCOMA (H40-H42)

● **H40**   **Glaucoma**

    Intraocular pressure (IOP) that is too high results from too much aqueous humor and because of excess production or inadequate drainage, optic nerve damage and vision loss may occur.

    Excludes1   absolute glaucoma (H44.51-)
              congenital glaucoma (Q15.0)
              traumatic glaucoma due to birth injury (P15.3)

● **H40.0**   **Glaucoma suspect**

   ● **H40.00**   **Preglaucoma, unspecified**

      H40.001   Preglaucoma, unspecified, **right eye**

      H40.002   Preglaucoma, unspecified, **left eye**

      H40.003   Preglaucoma, unspecified, **bilateral**

      H40.009   Preglaucoma, unspecified, **unspecified eye**

   ● **H40.01**   **Open angle with borderline findings, low risk**
       Open angle, low risk

      H40.011   Open angle with borderline findings, low risk, **right eye**

      H40.012   Open angle with borderline findings, low risk, **left eye**

      H40.013   Open angle with borderline findings, low risk, **bilateral**

      H40.019   Open angle with borderline findings, low risk, **unspecified eye**

   ● **H40.02**   **Open angle with borderline findings, high risk**
       Open angle, high risk

      H40.021   Open angle with borderline findings, high risk, **right eye**

      H40.022   Open angle with borderline findings, high risk, **left eye**

      H40.023   Open angle with borderline findings, high risk, **bilateral**

      H40.029   Open angle with borderline findings, high risk, **unspecified eye**

   ● **H40.03**   **Anatomical narrow angle**
       Primary angle closure suspect

      H40.031   Anatomical narrow angle, **right eye**

      H40.032   Anatomical narrow angle, **left eye**

      H40.033   Anatomical narrow angle, **bilateral**

      H40.039   Anatomical narrow angle, **unspecified eye**

   ● **H40.04**   **Steroid responder**

      H40.041   Steroid responder, **right eye**

      H40.042   Steroid responder, **left eye**

      H40.043   Steroid responder, **bilateral**

      H40.049   Steroid responder, **unspecified eye**

   ● **H40.05**   **Ocular hypertension**

      H40.051   Ocular hypertension, **right eye**

      H40.052   Ocular hypertension, **left eye**

      H40.053   Ocular hypertension, **bilateral**

      H40.059   Ocular hypertension, **unspecified eye**

   ● **H40.06**   **Primary angle closure without glaucoma damage**

      H40.061   Primary angle closure without glaucoma damage, **right eye**

      H40.062   Primary angle closure without glaucoma damage, **left eye**

      H40.063   Primary angle closure without glaucoma damage, **bilateral**

      H40.069   Primary angle closure without glaucoma damage, **unspecified eye**

● **H40.1**   **Open-angle glaucoma**

   X ● **H40.10**   **Unspecified open-angle glaucoma**

      One of the following 7th characters is to be assigned to code H40.10 to designate the stage of glaucoma

0	stage unspecified
1	mild stage
2	moderate stage
3	severe stage
4	indeterminate stage

   ● **H40.11**   **Primary open-angle glaucoma**
       Chronic simple glaucoma

      One of the following 7th characters is to be assigned to each code in subcategory H40.11 to designate the stage of glaucoma

0	stage unspecified
1	mild stage
2	moderate stage
3	severe stage
4	indeterminate stage

      Coding Clinic: 2016, Q4, P22

   ● **H40.111**   Primary open-angle glaucoma, **right eye**
          Coding Clinic: 2019, Q2, P31

   ● **H40.112**   Primary open-angle glaucoma, **left eye**

   ● **H40.113**   Primary open-angle glaucoma, **bilateral**

   ● **H40.119**   Primary open-angle glaucoma, **unspecified eye**

● **H40.12**   Low-tension glaucoma

One of the following 7th characters is to be assigned to each code in subcategory H40.12 to designate the stage of glaucoma

0	stage unspecified
1	mild stage
2	moderate stage
3	severe stage
4	indeterminate stage

  ● **H40.121**   Low-tension glaucoma, right eye

  ● **H40.122**   Low-tension glaucoma, left eye

  ● **H40.123**   Low-tension glaucoma, bilateral

  ● **H40.129**   Low-tension glaucoma, unspecified eye

● **H40.13**   Pigmentary glaucoma

One of the following 7th characters is to be assigned to each code in subcategory H40.13 to designate the stage of glaucoma

0	stage unspecified
1	mild stage
2	moderate stage
3	severe stage
4	indeterminate stage

  ● **H40.131**   Pigmentary glaucoma, right eye

  ● **H40.132**   Pigmentary glaucoma, left eye

  ● **H40.133**   Pigmentary glaucoma, bilateral

  ● **H40.139**   Pigmentary glaucoma, unspecified eye

● **H40.14**   Capsular glaucoma with pseudoexfoliation of lens

One of the following 7th characters is to be assigned to each code in subcategory H40.14 to designate the stage of glaucoma

0	stage unspecified
1	mild stage
2	moderate stage
3	severe stage
4	indeterminate stage

  ● **H40.141**   Capsular glaucoma with pseudoexfoliation of lens, right eye

  ● **H40.142**   Capsular glaucoma with pseudoexfoliation of lens, left eye

  ● **H40.143**   Capsular glaucoma with pseudoexfoliation of lens, bilateral

  ● **H40.149**   Capsular glaucoma with pseudoexfoliation of lens, unspecified eye

● **H40.15**   Residual stage of open-angle glaucoma

  H40.151   Residual stage of open-angle glaucoma, right eye

  H40.152   Residual stage of open-angle glaucoma, left eye

  H40.153   Residual stage of open-angle glaucoma, bilateral

  H40.159   Residual stage of open-angle glaucoma, unspecified eye

● **H40.2**   Primary angle-closure glaucoma

Excludes1   aqueous misdirection (H40.83-)
           malignant glaucoma (H40.83-)

X● **H40.20**   Unspecified primary angle-closure glaucoma

One of the following 7th characters is to be assigned to code H40.20 to designate the stage of glaucoma

0	stage unspecified
1	mild stage
2	moderate stage
3	severe stage
4	indeterminate stage

● **H40.21**   Acute angle-closure glaucoma

Acute angle-closure glaucoma attack
Acute angle-closure glaucoma crisis

  H40.211   Acute angle-closure glaucoma, right eye

  H40.212   Acute angle-closure glaucoma, left eye

  H40.213   Acute angle-closure glaucoma, bilateral

  H40.219   Acute angle-closure glaucoma, unspecified eye

● **H40.22**   Chronic angle-closure glaucoma

Chronic primary angle closure glaucoma

One of the following 7th characters is to be assigned to each code in subcategory H40.22 to designate the stage of glaucoma

0	stage unspecified
1	mild stage
2	moderate stage
3	severe stage
4	indeterminate stage

  ● **H40.221**   Chronic angle-closure glaucoma, right eye

  ● **H40.222**   Chronic angle-closure glaucoma, left eye

  ● **H40.223**   Chronic angle-closure glaucoma, bilateral

  ● **H40.229**   Chronic angle-closure glaucoma, unspecified eye

● **H40.23**   Intermittent angle-closure glaucoma

  H40.231   Intermittent angle-closure glaucoma, right eye

  H40.232   Intermittent angle-closure glaucoma, left eye

  H40.233   Intermittent angle-closure glaucoma, bilateral

  H40.239   Intermittent angle-closure glaucoma, unspecified eye

● **H40.24**   Residual stage of angle-closure glaucoma

  H40.241   Residual stage of angle-closure glaucoma, right eye

  H40.242   Residual stage of angle-closure glaucoma, left eye

  H40.243   Residual stage of angle-closure glaucoma, bilateral

  H40.249   Residual stage of angle-closure glaucoma, unspecified eye

▶ New   ⇒ Revised   ~~deleted~~ Deleted   Excludes 1   Excludes 2   Includes   Use additional   Code first   Code also   Key words

OGCR Official Guidelines   X Assign placeholder X   ● Use Additional Character(s)   ⫽ Manifestation Code   🔖 Hierarchical Condition Category   Coding Clinic

● **H40.3 Glaucoma secondary to eye trauma**

    Code also underlying condition

    One of the following 7th characters is to be assigned to each code in subcategory H40.3 to designate the stage of glaucoma

0	stage unspecified
1	mild stage
2	moderate stage
3	severe stage
4	indeterminate stage

X● **H40.30** Glaucoma secondary to eye trauma, **unspecified eye**

X● **H40.31** Glaucoma secondary to eye trauma, **right eye**

X● **H40.32** Glaucoma secondary to eye trauma, **left eye**

X● **H40.33** Glaucoma secondary to eye trauma, **bilateral**

● **H40.4 Glaucoma secondary to eye inflammation**

    Code also underlying condition

    One of the following 7th characters is to be assigned to each code in subcategory H40.4 to designate the stage of glaucoma

0	stage unspecified
1	mild stage
2	moderate stage
3	severe stage
4	indeterminate stage

X● **H40.40** Glaucoma secondary to eye inflammation, **unspecified eye**

X● **H40.41** Glaucoma secondary to eye inflammation, **right eye**

X● **H40.42** Glaucoma secondary to eye inflammation, **left eye**

X● **H40.43** Glaucoma secondary to eye inflammation, **bilateral**

● **H40.5 Glaucoma secondary to other eye disorders**

    Code also underlying eye disorder

    One of the following 7th characters is to be assigned to each code in subcategory H40.5 to designate the stage of glaucoma

0	stage unspecified
1	mild stage
2	moderate stage
3	severe stage
4	indeterminate stage

X● **H40.50** Glaucoma secondary to other eye disorders, **unspecified eye**

X● **H40.51** Glaucoma secondary to other eye disorders, **right eye**

X● **H40.52** Glaucoma secondary to other eye disorders, **left eye**

X● **H40.53** Glaucoma secondary to other eye disorders, **bilateral**

● **H40.6 Glaucoma secondary to drugs**

    Use additional code for adverse effect, if applicable, to identify drug (T36-T50 with fifth or sixth character 5)

    One of the following 7th characters is to be assigned to each code in subcategory H40.6 to designate the stage of glaucoma

0	stage unspecified
1	mild stage
2	moderate stage
3	severe stage
4	indeterminate stage

X● **H40.60** Glaucoma secondary to drugs, **unspecified** eye

X● **H40.61** Glaucoma secondary to drugs, **right eye**

X● **H40.62** Glaucoma secondary to drugs, **left eye**

X● **H40.63** Glaucoma secondary to drugs, **bilateral**

● **H40.8 Other glaucoma**

  ● **H40.81** Glaucoma with **increased episcleral venous pressure**

    H40.811 Glaucoma with increased episcleral venous pressure, **right eye**

    H40.812 Glaucoma with increased episcleral venous pressure, **left eye**

    H40.813 Glaucoma with increased episcleral venous pressure, **bilateral**

    H40.819 Glaucoma with increased episcleral venous pressure, **unspecified** eye

  ● **H40.82** **Hypersecretion** glaucoma

    H40.821 Hypersecretion glaucoma, **right eye**

    H40.822 Hypersecretion glaucoma, **left eye**

    H40.823 Hypersecretion glaucoma, **bilateral**

    H40.829 Hypersecretion glaucoma, **unspecified** eye

  ● **H40.83** **Aqueous misdirection**

    Malignant glaucoma

    H40.831 Aqueous misdirection, **right eye**

    H40.832 Aqueous misdirection, **left eye**

    H40.833 Aqueous misdirection, **bilateral**

    H40.839 Aqueous misdirection, **unspecified** eye

    H40.89 **Other** specified glaucoma

  H40.9 Unspecified glaucoma

▷ *H42 Glaucoma in diseases classified elsewhere*

    Code first underlying condition, such as:
    amyloidosis (E85.-)
    aniridia (Q13.1)
    glaucoma (in) diabetes mellitus (E08.39, E09.39, E10.39, E11.39, E13.39)
    Lowe's syndrome (E72.03)
    Reiger's anomaly (Q13.81)
    specified metabolic disorder (E70-E88)

    Excludes1   glaucoma (in) onchocerciasis (B73.02)
                glaucoma (in) syphilis (A52.71)
                glaucoma (in) tuberculous (A18.59)

DISORDERS OF VITREOUS BODY AND GLOBE (H43-H44)

● **H43 Disorders of vitreous body**

  ● **H43.0 Vitreous prolapse**

    Excludes1   vitreous syndrome following cataract surgery (H59.0-)
                traumatic vitreous prolapse (S05.2-)

    H43.00 Vitreous prolapse, **unspecified eye**

    H43.01 Vitreous prolapse, **right eye**

    H43.02 Vitreous prolapse, **left eye**

    H43.03 Vitreous prolapse, **bilateral**

● **H43.1**   Vitreous hemorrhage
    H43.10   Vitreous hemorrhage, unspecified eye 🝫
    H43.11   Vitreous hemorrhage, right eye
    H43.12   Vitreous hemorrhage, left eye 🝫
    H43.13   Vitreous hemorrhage, bilateral 🝫

● **H43.2**   Crystalline deposits in vitreous body
    H43.20   Crystalline deposits in vitreous body, unspecified eye
    H43.21   Crystalline deposits in vitreous body, right eye
    H43.22   Crystalline deposits in vitreous body, left eye
    H43.23   Crystalline deposits in vitreous body, bilateral

● **H43.3**   Other vitreous opacities
   ● H43.31   Vitreous membranes and strands
      H43.311   Vitreous membranes and strands, right eye
      H43.312   Vitreous membranes and strands, left eye
      H43.313   Vitreous membranes and strands, bilateral
      H43.319   Vitreous membranes and strands, unspecified eye
   ● H43.39   Other vitreous opacities
      Vitreous floaters
      Small clumps of cells that float in the vitreous of the eye, appearing as black specks or dots in the field of vision and common in the aging eye.
      H43.391   Other vitreous opacities, right eye
      H43.392   Other vitreous opacities, left eye
      H43.393   Other vitreous opacities, bilateral
      H43.399   Other vitreous opacities, unspecified eye

● **H43.8**   Other disorders of vitreous body
    Excludes1   proliferative vitreo-retinopathy with retinal detachment (H33.4)
    Excludes2   vitreous abscess (H44.02-)
   ● H43.81   Vitreous degeneration
      Vitreous detachment
      H43.811   Vitreous degeneration, right eye
      H43.812   Vitreous degeneration, left eye
      H43.813   Vitreous degeneration, bilateral
      H43.819   Vitreous degeneration, unspecified eye
   ● H43.82   Vitreomacular adhesion
      Vitreomacular traction
      H43.821   Vitreomacular adhesion, right eye   A
      H43.822   Vitreomacular adhesion, left eye   A
      H43.823   Vitreomacular adhesion, bilateral   A
      H43.829   Vitreomacular adhesion, unspecified eye   A
    H43.89   Other disorders of vitreous body
    H43.9   Unspecified disorder of vitreous body

● **H44**   Disorders of globe
    Includes   disorders affecting multiple structures of eye
   ● H44.0   Purulent endophthalmitis
      Use additional code to identify organism
      Excludes1   bleb associated endophthalmitis (H59.4-)
    ● H44.00   Unspecified purulent endophthalmitis
      H44.001   Unspecified purulent endophthalmitis, right eye
      H44.002   Unspecified purulent endophthalmitis, left eye
      H44.003   Unspecified purulent endophthalmitis, bilateral
      H44.009   Unspecified purulent endophthalmitis, unspecified eye

   ● H44.01   Panophthalmitis (acute)
      H44.011   Panophthalmitis (acute), right eye
      H44.012   Panophthalmitis (acute), left eye
      H44.013   Panophthalmitis (acute), bilateral
      H44.019   Panophthalmitis (acute), unspecified eye
   ● H44.02   Vitreous abscess (chronic)
      H44.021   Vitreous abscess (chronic), right eye
      H44.022   Vitreous abscess (chronic), left eye
      H44.023   Vitreous abscess (chronic), bilateral
      H44.029   Vitreous abscess (chronic), unspecified eye

● **H44.1**   Other endophthalmitis
    Excludes1   bleb associated endophthalmitis (H59.4-)
    Excludes2   ophthalmia nodosa (H16.2-)
   ● H44.11   Panuveitis
      H44.111   Panuveitis, right eye
      H44.112   Panuveitis, left eye
      H44.113   Panuveitis, bilateral
      H44.119   Panuveitis, unspecified eye
   ● H44.12   Parasitic endophthalmitis, unspecified
      H44.121   Parasitic endophthalmitis, unspecified, right eye
      H44.122   Parasitic endophthalmitis, unspecified, left eye
      H44.123   Parasitic endophthalmitis, unspecified, bilateral
      H44.129   Parasitic endophthalmitis, unspecified, unspecified eye
   ● H44.13   Sympathetic uveitis
      H44.131   Sympathetic uveitis, right eye
      H44.132   Sympathetic uveitis, left eye
      H44.133   Sympathetic uveitis, bilateral
      H44.139   Sympathetic uveitis, unspecified eye
    H44.19   Other endophthalmitis

● **H44.2**   Degenerative myopia
    Malignant myopia
    H44.20   Degenerative myopia, unspecified eye
    H44.21   Degenerative myopia, right eye
    H44.22   Degenerative myopia, left eye
    H44.23   Degenerative myopia, bilateral
   ● H44.2A   Degenerative myopia with choroidal neovascularization
      Use Additional code for any associated choroid disorders (H31.-)
      H44.2A1   Degenerative myopia with choroidal neovascularization, right eye
      H44.2A2   Degenerative myopia with choroidal neovascularization, left eye
      H44.2A3   Degenerative myopia with choroidal neovascularization, bilateral eye
      H44.2A9   Degenerative myopia with choroidal neovascularization, unspecified eye
   ● H44.2B   Degenerative myopia with macular hole
      H44.2B1   Degenerative myopia with macular hole, right eye
      H44.2B2   Degenerative myopia with macular hole, left eye
      H44.2B3   Degenerative myopia with macular hole, bilateral eye
      H44.2B9   Degenerative myopia with macular hole, unspecified eye

▶ New   ⇒ Revised   ~~deleted~~ Deleted   Excludes 1   Excludes 2   Includes   Use additional   Code first   Code also   Key words
OGCR Official Guidelines   X Assign placeholder X   ● Use Additional Character(s)   》 Manifestation Code   🝫 Hierarchical Condition Category   **Coding Clinic**

● H44.2C **Degenerative myopia with retinal detachment**
   Use Additional code to identify the retinal
   detachment (H33.-)
   H44.2C1 Degenerative myopia with retinal
            detachment, right eye
   H44.2C2 Degenerative myopia with retinal
            detachment, left eye
   H44.2C3 Degenerative myopia with retinal
            detachment, bilateral eye
   H44.2C9 Degenerative myopia with retinal
            detachment, unspecified eye
● H44.2D **Degenerative myopia with foveoschisis**
   H44.2D1 Degenerative myopia with
            foveoschisis, right eye
   H44.2D2 Degenerative myopia with
            foveoschisis, left eye
   H44.2D3 Degenerative myopia with
            foveoschisis, bilateral eye
   H44.2D9 Degenerative myopia with
            foveoschisis, unspecified eye
● H44.2E **Degenerative myopia with other maculopathy**
   H44.2E1 Degenerative myopia with other
            maculopathy, right eye
   H44.2E2 Degenerative myopia with other
            maculopathy, left eye
   H44.2E3 Degenerative myopia with other
            maculopathy, bilateral eye
   H44.2E9 Degenerative myopia with other
            maculopathy, unspecified eye
● H44.3 **Other and unspecified degenerative disorders of globe**
   H44.30   Unspecified degenerative disorder of globe
● H44.31 Chalcosis
   H44.311 Chalcosis, right eye
   H44.312 Chalcosis, left eye
   H44.313 Chalcosis, bilateral
   H44.319 Chalcosis, unspecified eye
● H44.32 Siderosis of eye
   H44.321 Siderosis of eye, right eye
   H44.322 Siderosis of eye, left eye
   H44.323 Siderosis of eye, bilateral
   H44.329 Siderosis of eye, unspecified eye
● H44.39 Other degenerative disorders of globe
   H44.391 Other degenerative disorders of
            globe, right eye
   H44.392 Other degenerative disorders of
            globe, left eye
   H44.393 Other degenerative disorders of
            globe, bilateral
   H44.399 Other degenerative disorders of
            globe, unspecified eye
● H44.4 **Hypotony of eye**
   H44.40   Unspecified hypotony of eye
● H44.41 Flat anterior chamber hypotony of eye
   H44.411 Flat anterior chamber hypotony of
            right eye
   H44.412 Flat anterior chamber hypotony of left
            eye
   H44.413 Flat anterior chamber hypotony of
            eye, bilateral
   H44.419 Flat anterior chamber hypotony of
            unspecified eye
● H44.42 Hypotony of eye due to ocular fistula
   H44.421 Hypotony of right eye due to ocular
            fistula
   H44.422 Hypotony of left eye due to ocular
            fistula

   H44.423 Hypotony of eye due to ocular fistula,
            bilateral
   H44.429 Hypotony of unspecified eye due to
            ocular fistula
● H44.43 Hypotony of eye due to other ocular disorders
   H44.431 Hypotony of eye due to other ocular
            disorders, right eye
   H44.432 Hypotony of eye due to other ocular
            disorders, left eye
   H44.433 Hypotony of eye due to other ocular
            disorders, bilateral
   H44.439 Hypotony of eye due to other ocular
            disorders, unspecified eye
● H44.44 Primary hypotony of eye
   H44.441 Primary hypotony of right eye
   H44.442 Primary hypotony of left eye
   H44.443 Primary hypotony of eye, bilateral
   H44.449 Primary hypotony of unspecified eye
● H44.5 **Degenerated conditions of globe**
   H44.50   Unspecified degenerated conditions of globe
● H44.51 Absolute glaucoma
   H44.511 Absolute glaucoma, right eye
   H44.512 Absolute glaucoma, left eye
   H44.513 Absolute glaucoma, bilateral
   H44.519 Absolute glaucoma, unspecified eye
● H44.52 Atrophy of globe
            Phthisis bulbi
   H44.521 Atrophy of globe, right eye
   H44.522 Atrophy of globe, left eye
   H44.523 Atrophy of globe, bilateral
   H44.529 Atrophy of globe, unspecified eye
● H44.53 Leucocoria
   H44.531 Leucocoria, right eye
   H44.532 Leucocoria, left eye
   H44.533 Leucocoria, bilateral
   H44.539 Leucocoria, unspecified eye
● H44.6 **Retained (old) intraocular foreign body, magnetic**
   Use additional code to identify magnetic foreign body
   (Z18.11)
   Excludes1 current intraocular foreign body (S05.-)
   Excludes2 retained foreign body in eyelid (H02.81-)
                retained (old) foreign body following
                    penetrating wound of orbit (H05.5-)
                retained (old) intraocular foreign body,
                    nonmagnetic (H44.7-)
● H44.60 Unspecified retained (old) intraocular foreign
          body, magnetic
   H44.601 Unspecified retained (old) intraocular
            foreign body, magnetic, right eye
   H44.602 Unspecified retained (old) intraocular
            foreign body, magnetic, left eye
   H44.603 Unspecified retained (old) intraocular
            foreign body, magnetic, bilateral
   H44.609 Unspecified retained (old) intraocular
            foreign body, magnetic, unspecified
            eye
● H44.61 Retained (old) magnetic foreign body in
          anterior chamber
   H44.611 Retained (old) magnetic foreign body
            in anterior chamber, right eye
   H44.612 Retained (old) magnetic foreign body
            in anterior chamber, left eye
   H44.613 Retained (old) magnetic foreign body
            in anterior chamber, bilateral
   H44.619 Retained (old) magnetic foreign body
            in anterior chamber, unspecified eye

● **H44.62** Retained (old) magnetic foreign body in iris or ciliary body

     H44.621 Retained (old) magnetic foreign body in iris or ciliary body, right eye

     H44.622 Retained (old) magnetic foreign body in iris or ciliary body, left eye

     H44.623 Retained (old) magnetic foreign body in iris or ciliary body, bilateral

     H44.629 Retained (old) magnetic foreign body in iris or ciliary body, unspecified eye

● **H44.63** Retained (old) magnetic foreign body in lens

     H44.631 Retained (old) magnetic foreign body in lens, right eye

     H44.632 Retained (old) magnetic foreign body in lens, left eye

     H44.633 Retained (old) magnetic foreign body in lens, bilateral

     H44.639 Retained (old) magnetic foreign body in lens, unspecified eye

● **H44.64** Retained (old) magnetic foreign body in posterior wall of globe

     H44.641 Retained (old) magnetic foreign body in posterior wall of globe, right eye

     H44.642 Retained (old) magnetic foreign body in posterior wall of globe, left eye

     H44.643 Retained (old) magnetic foreign body in posterior wall of globe, bilateral

     H44.649 Retained (old) magnetic foreign body in posterior wall of globe, unspecified eye

● **H44.65** Retained (old) magnetic foreign body in vitreous body

     H44.651 Retained (old) magnetic foreign body in vitreous body, right eye

     H44.652 Retained (old) magnetic foreign body in vitreous body, left eye

     H44.653 Retained (old) magnetic foreign body in vitreous body, bilateral

     H44.659 Retained (old) magnetic foreign body in vitreous body, unspecified eye

● **H44.69** Retained (old) intraocular foreign body, magnetic, in other or multiple sites

     H44.691 Retained (old) intraocular foreign body, magnetic, in other or multiple sites, right eye

     H44.692 Retained (old) intraocular foreign body, magnetic, in other or multiple sites, left eye

     H44.693 Retained (old) intraocular foreign body, magnetic, in other or multiple sites, bilateral

     H44.699 Retained (old) intraocular foreign body, magnetic, in other or multiple sites, unspecified eye

● **H44.7** Retained (old) intraocular foreign body, nonmagnetic

Use additional code to identify nonmagnetic foreign body (Z18.01-Z18.10, Z18.12, Z18.2-Z18.9)

Excludes1 current intraocular foreign body (S05.-)

Excludes2 retained foreign body in eyelid (H02.81-)
retained (old) foreign body following penetrating wound of orbit (H05.5-)
retained (old) intraocular foreign body, magnetic (H44.6-)

● **H44.70** Unspecified retained (old) intraocular foreign body, nonmagnetic

     H44.701 Unspecified retained (old) intraocular foreign body, nonmagnetic, right eye

     H44.702 Unspecified retained (old) intraocular foreign body, nonmagnetic, left eye

     H44.703 Unspecified retained (old) intraocular foreign body, nonmagnetic, bilateral

     H44.709 Unspecified retained (old) intraocular foreign body, nonmagnetic, unspecified eye

         Retained (old) intraocular foreign body NOS

● **H44.71** Retained (nonmagnetic) (old) foreign body in anterior chamber

     H44.711 Retained (nonmagnetic) (old) foreign body in anterior chamber, right eye

     H44.712 Retained (nonmagnetic) (old) foreign body in anterior chamber, left eye

     H44.713 Retained (nonmagnetic) (old) foreign body in anterior chamber, bilateral

     H44.719 Retained (nonmagnetic) (old) foreign body in anterior chamber, unspecified eye

● **H44.72** Retained (nonmagnetic) (old) foreign body in iris or ciliary body

     H44.721 Retained (nonmagnetic) (old) foreign body in iris or ciliary body, right eye

     H44.722 Retained (nonmagnetic) (old) foreign body in iris or ciliary body, left eye

     H44.723 Retained (nonmagnetic) (old) foreign body in iris or ciliary body, bilateral

     H44.729 Retained (nonmagnetic) (old) foreign body in iris or ciliary body, unspecified eye

● **H44.73** Retained (nonmagnetic) (old) foreign body in lens

     H44.731 Retained (nonmagnetic) (old) foreign body in lens, right eye

     H44.732 Retained (nonmagnetic) (old) foreign body in lens, left eye

     H44.733 Retained (nonmagnetic) (old) foreign body in lens, bilateral

     H44.739 Retained (nonmagnetic) (old) foreign body in lens, unspecified eye

● **H44.74** Retained (nonmagnetic) (old) foreign body in posterior wall of globe

     H44.741 Retained (nonmagnetic) (old) foreign body in posterior wall of globe, right eye

     H44.742 Retained (nonmagnetic) (old) foreign body in posterior wall of globe, left eye

     H44.743 Retained (nonmagnetic) (old) foreign body in posterior wall of globe, bilateral

     H44.749 Retained (nonmagnetic) (old) foreign body in posterior wall of globe, unspecified eye

● **H44.75** Retained (nonmagnetic) (old) foreign body in vitreous body

     H44.751 Retained (nonmagnetic) (old) foreign body in vitreous body, right eye

     H44.752 Retained (nonmagnetic) (old) foreign body in vitreous body, left eye

     H44.753 Retained (nonmagnetic) (old) foreign body in vitreous body, bilateral

     H44.759 Retained (nonmagnetic) (old) foreign body in vitreous body, unspecified eye

▶ New   ⇛ Revised   ~~deleted~~ Deleted   Excludes 1   Excludes 2   Includes   Use additional   Code first   Code also   Key words

OGCR Official Guidelines   X Assign placeholder X   ● Use Additional Character(s)   ▶ Manifestation Code   ℞ Hierarchical Condition Category   **Coding Clinic**

● **H44.79**   Retained (old) intraocular foreign body, nonmagnetic, in other or multiple sites

    H44.791   Retained (old) intraocular foreign body, nonmagnetic, in other or multiple sites, right eye

    H44.792   Retained (old) intraocular foreign body, nonmagnetic, in other or multiple sites, left eye

    H44.793   Retained (old) intraocular foreign body, nonmagnetic, in other or multiple sites, bilateral

    H44.799   Retained (old) intraocular foreign body, nonmagnetic, in other or multiple sites, unspecified eye

● **H44.8**   Other disorders of globe

  ● **H44.81**   Hemophthalmos

    H44.811   Hemophthalmos, right eye

    H44.812   Hemophthalmos, left eye

    H44.813   Hemophthalmos, bilateral

    H44.819   Hemophthalmos, unspecified eye

  ● **H44.82**   Luxation of globe

    H44.821   Luxation of globe, right eye

    H44.822   Luxation of globe, left eye

    H44.823   Luxation of globe, bilateral

    H44.829   Luxation of globe, unspecified eye

  H44.89   Other disorders of globe

H44.9   Unspecified disorder of globe

★**(See Plate 7 of the Anatomy Illustrations.)**

DISORDERS OF OPTIC NERVE AND VISUAL PATHWAYS (H46-H47)

● **H46**   Optic neuritis

    Excludes2   ischemic optic neuropathy (H47.01-)
             neuromyelitis optica [Devic] (G36.0)

  ● **H46.0**   Optic papillitis

    H46.00   Optic papillitis, unspecified eye

    H46.01   Optic papillitis, right eye

    H46.02   Optic papillitis, left eye

    H46.03   Optic papillitis, bilateral

  ● **H46.1**   Retrobulbar neuritis
    Retrobulbar neuritis NOS

    Excludes1   syphilitic retrobulbar neuritis (A52.15)

    H46.10   Retrobulbar neuritis, unspecified eye

    H46.11   Retrobulbar neuritis, right eye

    H46.12   Retrobulbar neuritis, left eye

    H46.13   Retrobulbar neuritis, bilateral

  H46.2   Nutritional optic neuropathy

  H46.3   Toxic optic neuropathy
    Code first (T51-T65) to identify cause

  H46.8   Other optic neuritis

  H46.9   Unspecified optic neuritis

● **H47**   Other disorders of optic [2nd] nerve and visual pathways

  ● **H47.0**   Disorders of optic nerve, not elsewhere classified

    ● **H47.01**   Ischemic optic neuropathy

      H47.011   Ischemic optic neuropathy, right eye

      H47.012   Ischemic optic neuropathy, left eye

      H47.013   Ischemic optic neuropathy, bilateral

      H47.019   Ischemic optic neuropathy, unspecified eye

    ● **H47.02**   Hemorrhage in optic nerve sheath

      H47.021   Hemorrhage in optic nerve sheath, right eye

      H47.022   Hemorrhage in optic nerve sheath, left eye

      H47.023   Hemorrhage in optic nerve sheath, bilateral

      H47.029   Hemorrhage in optic nerve sheath, unspecified eye

  ● **H47.03**   Optic nerve hypoplasia

    H47.031   Optic nerve hypoplasia, right eye

    H47.032   Optic nerve hypoplasia, left eye

    H47.033   Optic nerve hypoplasia, bilateral

    H47.039   Optic nerve hypoplasia, unspecified eye

  ● **H47.09**   Other disorders of optic nerve, not elsewhere classified
    Compression of optic nerve

    H47.091   Other disorders of optic nerve, not elsewhere classified, right eye

    H47.092   Other disorders of optic nerve, not elsewhere classified, left eye

    H47.093   Other disorders of optic nerve, not elsewhere classified, bilateral

    H47.099   Other disorders of optic nerve, not elsewhere classified, unspecified eye

● **H47.1**   Papilledema

  H47.10   Unspecified papilledema

  H47.11   Papilledema associated with increased intracranial pressure

  H47.12   Papilledema associated with decreased ocular pressure

  H47.13   Papilledema associated with retinal disorder

  ● **H47.14**   Foster-Kennedy syndrome

    H47.141   Foster-Kennedy syndrome, right eye

    H47.142   Foster-Kennedy syndrome, left eye

    H47.143   Foster-Kennedy syndrome, bilateral

    H47.149   Foster-Kennedy syndrome, unspecified eye

● **H47.2**   Optic atrophy

  H47.20   Unspecified optic atrophy

  ● **H47.21**   Primary optic atrophy

    H47.211   Primary optic atrophy, right eye

    H47.212   Primary optic atrophy, left eye

    H47.213   Primary optic atrophy, bilateral

    H47.219   Primary optic atrophy, unspecified eye

  H47.22   Hereditary optic atrophy
    Leber's optic atrophy

Figure 7-11   Stages of papilledema according to the Frisén grading scale. **A,** Very eary papilledema (Frisén stage 1). **B,** Early papilledema (Frisén stage 2). **C,** Moderate papilledema (Frisén stage 3). **D,** Marked papilledema (Frisén stage 4). **E,** Severe papilledema. (From Youmans JR, Winn HR: Youmans Neurological Surgery, Philadelphia, PA, Elsevier/Saunders, 2011)

Item 7-8   Papilledema is swelling of the optic disc caused by increased intracranial pressure. It is most often bilateral and occurs quickly (hours) or over weeks of time. It is a common symptom of a brain tumor. The term should not be used to describe optic disc swelling with underlying infectious, infiltrative, or inflammatory etiologies.

● H47.23   Glaucomatous optic atrophy
     H47.231   Glaucomatous optic atrophy, right eye
     H47.232   Glaucomatous optic atrophy, left eye
     H47.233   Glaucomatous optic atrophy, bilateral
     H47.239   Glaucomatous optic atrophy, unspecified eye
● H47.29   Other optic atrophy
     Temporal pallor of optic disc
     H47.291   Other optic atrophy, right eye
     H47.292   Other optic atrophy, left eye
     H47.293   Other optic atrophy, bilateral
     H47.299   Other optic atrophy, unspecified eye
● H47.3   Other disorders of optic disc
   ● H47.31   Coloboma of optic disc
     H47.311   Coloboma of optic disc, right eye
     H47.312   Coloboma of optic disc, left eye
     H47.313   Coloboma of optic disc, bilateral
     H47.319   Coloboma of optic disc, unspecified eye
   ● H47.32   Drusen of optic disc
     H47.321   Drusen of optic disc, right eye
     H47.322   Drusen of optic disc, left eye
     H47.323   Drusen of optic disc, bilateral
     H47.329   Drusen of optic disc, unspecified eye
   ● H47.33   Pseudopapilledema of optic disc
     H47.331   Pseudopapilledema of optic disc, right eye
     H47.332   Pseudopapilledema of optic disc, left eye
     H47.333   Pseudopapilledema of optic disc, bilateral
     H47.339   Pseudopapilledema of optic disc, unspecified eye
   ● H47.39   Other disorders of optic disc
     H47.391   Other disorders of optic disc, right eye
     H47.392   Other disorders of optic disc, left eye
     H47.393   Other disorders of optic disc, bilateral
     H47.399   Other disorders of optic disc, unspecified eye
● H47.4   Disorders of optic chiasm
     Code also underlying condition
   H47.41   Disorders of optic chiasm in (due to) inflammatory disorders
   H47.42   Disorders of optic chiasm in (due to) neoplasm
   H47.43   Disorders of optic chiasm in (due to) vascular disorders
   H47.49   Disorders of optic chiasm in (due to) other disorders
● H47.5   Disorders of other visual pathways
     Disorders of optic tracts, geniculate nuclei and optic radiations
     Code also underlying condition
   ● H47.51   Disorders of visual pathways in (due to) inflammatory disorders
     H47.511   Disorders of visual pathways in (due to) inflammatory disorders, right side
     H47.512   Disorders of visual pathways in (due to) inflammatory disorders, left side
     H47.519   Disorders of visual pathways in (due to) inflammatory disorders, unspecified side

   ● H47.52   Disorders of visual pathways in (due to) neoplasm
     H47.521   Disorders of visual pathways in (due to) neoplasm, right side
     H47.522   Disorders of visual pathways in (due to) neoplasm, left side
     H47.529   Disorders of visual pathways in (due to) neoplasm, unspecified side
   ● H47.53   Disorders of visual pathways in (due to) vascular disorders
     H47.531   Disorders of visual pathways in (due to) vascular disorders, right side
     H47.532   Disorders of visual pathways in (due to) vascular disorders, left side
     H47.539   Disorders of visual pathways in (due to) vascular disorders, unspecified side
● H47.6   Disorders of visual cortex
     Code also underlying condition
     Excludes1   injury to visual cortex S04.04-
   ● H47.61   Cortical blindness
     H47.611   Cortical blindness, right side of brain
     H47.612   Cortical blindness, left side of brain
     H47.619   Cortical blindness, unspecified side of brain
   ● H47.62   Disorders of visual cortex in (due to) inflammatory disorders
     H47.621   Disorders of visual cortex in (due to) inflammatory disorders, right side of brain
     H47.622   Disorders of visual cortex in (due to) inflammatory disorders, left side of brain
     H47.629   Disorders of visual cortex in (due to) inflammatory disorders, unspecified side of brain
   ● H47.63   Disorders of visual cortex in (due to) neoplasm
     H47.631   Disorders of visual cortex in (due to) neoplasm, right side of brain
     H47.632   Disorders of visual cortex in (due to) neoplasm, left side of brain
     H47.639   Disorders of visual cortex in (due to) neoplasm, unspecified side of brain
   ● H47.64   Disorders of visual cortex in (due to) vascular disorders
     H47.641   Disorders of visual cortex in (due to) vascular disorders, right side of brain
     H47.642   Disorders of visual cortex in (due to) vascular disorders, left side of brain
     H47.649   Disorders of visual cortex in (due to) vascular disorders, unspecified side of brain
   H47.9   Unspecified disorder of visual pathways

DISORDERS OF OCULAR MUSCLES, BINOCULAR MOVEMENT, ACCOMMODATION AND REFRACTION (H49-H52)

Excludes2   nystagmus and other irregular eye movements (H55)

● H49   Paralytic strabismus
   Excludes2   internal ophthalmoplegia (H52.51-)
               internuclear ophthalmoplegia (H51.2-)
               progressive supranuclear ophthalmoplegia (G23.1)
   ● H49.0   Third [oculomotor] nerve palsy
     H49.00   Third [oculomotor] nerve palsy, unspecified eye
     H49.01   Third [oculomotor] nerve palsy, right eye
     H49.02   Third [oculomotor] nerve palsy, left eye
     H49.03   Third [oculomotor] nerve palsy, bilateral

Item 7–9 Strabismus or esotropia (crossed eyes) is a condition of the extraocular eye muscles, resulting in an inability of the eyes to focus and also affects depth perception.

A

B

Figure 7-12 A. Image of strabismus. **B.** Exotropia. (**A** from Yanoff: Ophthalmology, ed 3, Mosby, Inc., 2008. **B** from Zitelli BJ, Davis HW, Pediatric Physical Diagnosis: Atlas of Pediatric Physical Diagnosis, Philadelphia, Elsevier Saunders, 2012)

- ● H49.1 Fourth [trochlear] nerve palsy
  - H49.10 Fourth [trochlear] nerve palsy, unspecified eye
  - H49.11 Fourth [trochlear] nerve palsy, right eye
  - H49.12 Fourth [trochlear] nerve palsy, left eye
  - H49.13 Fourth [trochlear] nerve palsy, bilateral
- ● H49.2 Sixth [abducent] nerve palsy
  - H49.20 Sixth [abducent] nerve palsy, unspecified eye
  - H49.21 Sixth [abducent] nerve palsy, right eye
  - H49.22 Sixth [abducent] nerve palsy, left eye
  - H49.23 Sixth [abducent] nerve palsy, bilateral
- ● H49.3 Total (external) ophthalmoplegia
  - H49.30 Total (external) ophthalmoplegia, unspecified eye
  - H49.31 Total (external) ophthalmoplegia, right eye
  - H49.32 Total (external) ophthalmoplegia, left eye
  - H49.33 Total (external) ophthalmoplegia, bilateral
- ● H49.4 Progressive external ophthalmoplegia
  - **Excludes1** Kearns-Sayre syndrome (H49.81-)
  - H49.40 Progressive external ophthalmoplegia, unspecified eye
  - H49.41 Progressive external ophthalmoplegia, right eye
  - H49.42 Progressive external ophthalmoplegia, left eye
  - H49.43 Progressive external ophthalmoplegia, bilateral
- ● H49.8 Other paralytic strabismus
  - ● H49.81 Kearns-Sayre syndrome
    - Progressive external ophthalmoplegia with pigmentary retinopathy
    - Use additional code for other manifestation, such as:
      - heart block (I45.9)
    - H49.811 Kearns-Sayre syndrome, right eye ⚭
    - H49.812 Kearns-Sayre syndrome, left eye ⚭
    - H49.813 Kearns-Sayre syndrome, bilateral ⚭
    - H49.819 Kearns-Sayre syndrome, unspecified eye ⚭
  - ● H49.88 Other paralytic strabismus
    - External ophthalmoplegia NOS
    - H49.881 Other paralytic strabismus, right eye
    - H49.882 Other paralytic strabismus, left eye
    - H49.883 Other paralytic strabismus, bilateral
    - H49.889 Other paralytic strabismus, unspecified eye
  - H49.9 Unspecified paralytic strabismus

- ● H50 Other strabismus
  - ● H50.0 Esotropia
    - Convergent concomitant strabismus
    - **Excludes1** intermittent esotropia (H50.31-, H50.32)
    - H50.00 Unspecified esotropia
    - ● H50.01 Monocular esotropia
      - H50.011 Monocular esotropia, right eye
      - H50.012 Monocular esotropia, left eye
    - ● H50.02 Monocular esotropia with A pattern
      - H50.021 Monocular esotropia with A pattern, right eye
      - H50.022 Monocular esotropia with A pattern, left eye
    - ● H50.03 Monocular esotropia with V pattern
      - H50.031 Monocular esotropia with V pattern, right eye
      - H50.032 Monocular esotropia with V pattern, left eye
    - ● H50.04 Monocular esotropia with other noncomitancies
      - H50.041 Monocular esotropia with other noncomitancies, right eye
      - H50.042 Monocular esotropia with other noncomitancies, left eye
    - H50.05 Alternating esotropia
    - H50.06 Alternating esotropia with A pattern
    - H50.07 Alternating esotropia with V pattern
    - H50.08 Alternating esotropia with other noncomitancies
  - ● H50.1 Exotropia
    - *Misalignment in which one eye deviates outward (away from nose) while the other fixates normally*
    - Divergent concomitant strabismus
    - **Excludes1** intermittent exotropia (H50.33-, H50.34)
    - H50.10 Unspecified exotropia
    - ● H50.11 Monocular exotropia
      - H50.111 Monocular exotropia, right eye
      - H50.112 Monocular exotropia, left eye
    - ● H50.12 Monocular exotropia with A pattern
      - H50.121 Monocular exotropia with A pattern, right eye
      - H50.122 Monocular exotropia with A pattern, left eye
    - ● H50.13 Monocular exotropia with V pattern
      - H50.131 Monocular exotropia with V pattern, right eye
      - H50.132 Monocular exotropia with V pattern, left eye
    - ● H50.14 Monocular exotropia with other noncomitancies
      - H50.141 Monocular exotropia with other noncomitancies, right eye
      - H50.142 Monocular exotropia with other noncomitancies, left eye
    - H50.15 Alternating exotropia
    - H50.16 Alternating exotropia with A pattern
    - H50.17 Alternating exotropia with V pattern
    - H50.18 Alternating exotropia with other noncomitancies
  - ● H50.2 Vertical strabismus
    - Hypertropia
    - H50.21 Vertical strabismus, right eye
    - H50.22 Vertical strabismus, left eye

- **H50.3**   Intermittent heterotropia
    - *Displacement of an organ or part of an organ from its normal position*
    - **H50.30**   Unspecified intermittent heterotropia
    - **H50.31**   Intermittent monocular esotropia
        - H50.311   Intermittent monocular esotropia, right eye
        - H50.312   Intermittent monocular esotropia, left eye
    - **H50.32**   Intermittent alternating esotropia
    - **H50.33**   Intermittent monocular exotropia
        - H50.331   Intermittent monocular exotropia, right eye
        - H50.332   Intermittent monocular exotropia, left eye
    - **H50.34**   Intermittent alternating exotropia
- **H50.4**   Other and unspecified heterotropia
    - **H50.40**   Unspecified heterotropia
    - **H50.41**   Cyclotropia
        - H50.411   Cyclotropia, right eye
        - H50.412   Cyclotropia, left eye
    - **H50.42**   Monofixation syndrome
    - **H50.43**   Accommodative component in esotropia
- **H50.5**   Heterophoria
    - *One or both eyes wander away from the position where both eyes are looking together in the same direction*
    - **H50.50**   Unspecified heterophoria
    - **H50.51**   Esophoria
        - *Eye deviates inward (toward the nose)*
    - **H50.52**   Exophoria
        - *Eye deviates outward (toward the ear)*
    - **H50.53**   Vertical heterophoria
    - **H50.54**   Cyclophoria
    - **H50.55**   Alternating heterophoria
- **H50.6**   Mechanical strabismus
    - **H50.60**   Mechanical strabismus, unspecified
    - **H50.61**   Brown's sheath syndrome
        - H50.611   Brown's sheath syndrome, right eye
        - H50.612   Brown's sheath syndrome, left eye
    - **H50.69**   Other mechanical strabismus
        - Strabismus due to adhesions
        - Traumatic limitation of duction of eye muscle
- **H50.8**   Other specified strabismus
    - **H50.81**   Duane's syndrome
        - H50.811   Duane's syndrome, right eye
        - H50.812   Duane's syndrome, left eye
    - **H50.89**   Other specified strabismus
    - **H50.9**   Unspecified strabismus
- **H51**   Other disorders of binocular movement
    - **H51.0**   Palsy (spasm) of conjugate gaze
    - **H51.1**   Convergence insufficiency and excess
        - **H51.11**   Convergence insufficiency
        - **H51.12**   Convergence excess
    - **H51.2**   Internuclear ophthalmoplegia
        - H51.20   Internuclear ophthalmoplegia, unspecified eye
        - H51.21   Internuclear ophthalmoplegia, right eye
        - H51.22   Internuclear ophthalmoplegia, left eye
        - H51.23   Internuclear ophthalmoplegia, bilateral
    - **H51.8**   Other specified disorders of binocular movement
    - **H51.9**   Unspecified disorder of binocular movement

Item 7–10   Disorders of refraction: **Hypermetropia,** or farsightedness, means focus at a distance is adequate but not on close objects. **Myopia** is near-sightedness or short-sightedness and means the focus on nearby objects is clear but distant objects appear blurred. **Astigmatism** is warping of the curvature of the cornea so light rays entering do not meet a single focal point, resulting in a distorted image. **Anisometropia** is unequal refractive power in which one eye may be myopic (near-sighted) and the other hyperopic (far-sighted). **Presbyopia** is the loss of focus on near objects, which occurs with age because the lens loses elasticity.

- **H52**   Disorders of refraction and accommodation
    - **H52.0**   Hypermetropia
        - H52.00   Hypermetropia, unspecified eye
        - H52.01   Hypermetropia, right eye
        - H52.02   Hypermetropia, left eye
        - H52.03   Hypermetropia, bilateral
    - **H52.1**   Myopia
        - **Excludes1**   degenerative myopia (H44.2-)
        - H52.10   Myopia, unspecified eye
        - H52.11   Myopia, right eye
        - H52.12   Myopia, left eye
        - H52.13   Myopia, bilateral
    - **H52.2**   Astigmatism
        - **H52.20**   Unspecified astigmatism
            - H52.201   Unspecified astigmatism, right eye
            - H52.202   Unspecified astigmatism, left eye
            - H52.203   Unspecified astigmatism, bilateral
            - H52.209   Unspecified astigmatism, unspecified eye
        - **H52.21**   Irregular astigmatism
            - H52.211   Irregular astigmatism, right eye
            - H52.212   Irregular astigmatism, left eye
            - H52.213   Irregular astigmatism, bilateral
            - H52.219   Irregular astigmatism, unspecified eye
        - **H52.22**   Regular astigmatism
            - H52.221   Regular astigmatism, right eye
            - H52.222   Regular astigmatism, left eye
            - H52.223   Regular astigmatism, bilateral
            - H52.229   Regular astigmatism, unspecified eye
    - **H52.3**   Anisometropia and aniseikonia
        - H52.31   Anisometropia
        - H52.32   Aniseikonia
    - **H52.4**   Presbyopia
    - **H52.5**   Disorders of accommodation
        - **H52.51**   Internal ophthalmoplegia (complete) (total)
            - H52.511   Internal ophthalmoplegia (complete) (total), right eye
            - H52.512   Internal ophthalmoplegia (complete) (total), left eye
            - H52.513   Internal ophthalmoplegia (complete) (total), bilateral
            - H52.519   Internal ophthalmoplegia (complete) (total), unspecified eye
        - **H52.52**   Paresis of accommodation
            - H52.521   Paresis of accommodation, right eye
            - H52.522   Paresis of accommodation, left eye
            - H52.523   Paresis of accommodation, bilateral
            - H52.529   Paresis of accommodation, unspecified eye
        - **H52.53**   Spasm of accommodation
            - H52.531   Spasm of accommodation, right eye
            - H52.532   Spasm of accommodation, left eye
            - H52.533   Spasm of accommodation, bilateral
            - H52.539   Spasm of accommodation, unspecified eye

▶ New   ⇒ Revised   ~~deleted~~ Deleted   Excludes 1   Excludes 2   Includes   Use additional   Code first   Code also   Key words

OGCR Official Guidelines   X Assign placeholder X   ● Use Additional Character(s)   ▮ Manifestation Code   ✎ Hierarchical Condition Category   **Coding Clinic**

H52.6   **Other disorders of refraction**

H52.7   **Unspecified disorder of refraction**

VISUAL DISTURBANCES AND BLINDNESS (H53-H54)

- ● H53   **Visual disturbances**
  - ● H53.0   **Amblyopia ex anopsia**
    - **Excludes1**   amblyopia due to vitamin A deficiency (E50.5)
    - ● H53.00   **Unspecified amblyopia**
      - H53.001   Unspecified amblyopia, right eye
      - H53.002   Unspecified amblyopia, left eye
      - H53.003   Unspecified amblyopia, bilateral
      - H53.009   Unspecified amblyopia, unspecified eye
    - ● H53.01   **Deprivation amblyopia**
      - H53.011   Deprivation amblyopia, right eye
      - H53.012   Deprivation amblyopia, left eye
      - H53.013   Deprivation amblyopia, bilateral
      - H53.019   Deprivation amblyopia, unspecified eye
    - ● H53.02   **Refractive amblyopia**
      - H53.021   Refractive amblyopia, right eye
      - H53.022   Refractive amblyopia, left eye
      - H53.023   Refractive amblyopia, bilateral
      - H53.029   Refractive amblyopia, unspecified eye
    - ● H53.03   **Strabismic amblyopia**
      - **Excludes1**   strabismus (H50.-)
      - H53.031   Strabismic amblyopia, right eye
      - H53.032   Strabismic amblyopia, left eye
      - H53.033   Strabismic amblyopia, bilateral
      - H53.039   Strabismic amblyopia, unspecified eye
    - ● H53.04   **Amblyopia suspect**
      - Coding Clinic: 2016, Q4, P22
      - H53.041   Amblyopia suspect, right eye
      - H53.042   Amblyopia suspect, left eye
      - H53.043   Amblyopia suspect, bilateral
      - H53.049   Amblyopia suspect, unspecified eye
  - ● H53.1   **Subjective visual disturbances**
    - **Excludes1**   subjective visual disturbances due to vitamin A deficiency (E50.5)
    - visual hallucinations (R44.1)
    - H53.10   Unspecified subjective visual disturbances
    - H53.11   **Day blindness**
      - Hemeralopia
    - ● H53.12   **Transient visual loss**
      - Scintillating scotoma
      - **Excludes1**   amaurosis fugax (G45.3-)
        - transient retinal artery occlusion (H34.0-)
      - H53.121   Transient visual loss, right eye
      - H53.122   Transient visual loss, left eye
      - H53.123   Transient visual loss, bilateral
      - H53.129   Transient visual loss, unspecified eye
    - ● H53.13   **Sudden visual loss**
      - H53.131   Sudden visual loss, right eye
      - H53.132   Sudden visual loss, left eye
      - H53.133   Sudden visual loss, bilateral
      - H53.139   Sudden visual loss, unspecified eye
    - ● H53.14   **Visual discomfort**
      - Asthenopia
      - Photophobia
      - H53.141   Visual discomfort, right eye
      - H53.142   Visual discomfort, left eye

H53.143   Visual discomfort, bilateral

H53.149   Visual discomfort, unspecified

- H53.15   **Visual distortions of shape and size**
  - Metamorphopsia
- H53.16   **Psychophysical visual disturbances**
- H53.19   **Other subjective visual disturbances**
  - Visual halos
- H53.2   **Diplopia**
  - Double vision
- ● H53.3   **Other and unspecified disorders of binocular vision**
  - H53.30   Unspecified disorder of binocular vision
  - H53.31   Abnormal retinal correspondence
  - H53.32   Fusion with defective stereopsis
  - H53.33   Simultaneous visual perception without fusion
  - H53.34   Suppression of binocular vision
- ● H53.4   **Visual field defects**
  - H53.40   Unspecified visual field defects
  - ● H53.41   Scotoma involving central area
    - Central scotoma
    - H53.411   Scotoma involving central area, right eye
    - H53.412   Scotoma involving central area, left eye
    - H53.413   Scotoma involving central area, bilateral
    - H53.419   Scotoma involving central area, unspecified eye
  - ● H53.42   Scotoma of blind spot area
    - Enlarged blind spot
    - H53.421   Scotoma of blind spot area, right eye
    - H53.422   Scotoma of blind spot area, left eye
    - H53.423   Scotoma of blind spot area, bilateral
    - H53.429   Scotoma of blind spot area, unspecified eye
  - ● H53.43   Sector or arcuate defects
    - Arcuate scotoma
    - Bjerrum scotoma
    - H53.431   Sector or arcuate defects, right eye
    - H53.432   Sector or arcuate defects, left eye
    - H53.433   Sector or arcuate defects, bilateral
    - H53.439   Sector or arcuate defects, unspecified eye
  - ● H53.45   Other localized visual field defect
    - Peripheral visual field defect
    - Ring scotoma NOS
    - Scotoma NOS
    - H53.451   Other localized visual field defect, right eye
    - H53.452   Other localized visual field defect, left eye
    - H53.453   Other localized visual field defect, bilateral
    - H53.459   Other localized visual field defect, unspecified eye
  - ● H53.46   Homonymous bilateral field defects
    - Homonymous hemianopia
    - Homonymous hemianopsia
    - Quadrant anopia
    - Quadrant anopsia
    - H53.461   Homonymous bilateral field defects, right side
    - H53.462   Homonymous bilateral field defects, left side
    - H53.469   Homonymous bilateral field defects, unspecified side
      - Homonymous bilateral field defects NOS
  - H53.47   Heteronymous bilateral field defects
    - Heteronymous hemianop(s)ia

● **H53.48   Generalized contraction of visual field**
  H53.481   Generalized contraction of visual field, **right** eye
  H53.482   Generalized contraction of visual field, **left** eye
  H53.483   Generalized contraction of visual field, **bilateral**
  H53.489   Generalized contraction of visual field, **unspecified** eye

● H53.5   Color vision deficiencies
  Color blindness
  Excludes2   day blindness (H53.11)
  H53.50   **Unspecified** color vision deficiencies
  Color blindness NOS
  H53.51   Achromatopsia
  H53.52   Acquired color vision deficiency
  H53.53   Deuteranomaly
  Deuteranopia
  H53.54   Protanomaly
  Protanopia
  H53.55   Tritanomaly
  Tritanopia
  H53.59   **Other** color vision deficiencies

● H53.6   Night blindness
  Excludes1   night blindness due to vitamin A deficiency (E50.5)
  H53.60   **Unspecified** night blindness
  H53.61   **Abnormal dark adaptation curve**
  H53.62   **Acquired** night blindness
  H53.63   **Congenital** night blindness
  H53.69   **Other** night blindness

● H53.7   Vision sensitivity deficiencies
  H53.71   **Glare** sensitivity
  H53.72   **Impaired contrast** sensitivity

  H53.8   **Other** visual disturbances
  H53.9   **Unspecified** visual disturbance

● H54   Blindness and low vision
  Note: For definition of visual impairment categories see table below.
  Code first any associated underlying cause of the blindness
  Excludes1   amaurosis fugax (G45.3)

● H54.0   **Blindness, both eyes**
  Visual impairment categories 3, 4, 5 in both eyes.
  ● H54.0X   Blindness, both eyes, **different category levels**
    H54.0X3   Blindness right eye, category 3
      H54.0X33   Blindness right eye category 3, blindness **left** eye category 3
      H54.0X34   Blindness right eye category 3, blindness **left** eye category 4
      H54.0X35   Blindness right eye category 3, blindness **left** eye category 5
    ● H54.0X4   Blindness right eye, category 4
      H54.0X43   Blindness right eye category 4, blindness **left** eye category 3
      H54.0X44   Blindness right eye category 4, blindness **left** eye category 4
      H54.0X45   Blindness right eye category 4, blindness **left** eye category 5

● H54.0X5   Blindness **right eye, category 5**
    H54.0X53   Blindness right eye category 5, blindness **left** eye category 3
    H54.0X54   Blindness right eye category 5, blindness **left** eye category 4
    H54.0X55   Blindness right eye category 5, blindness **left** eye category 5

● H54.1   **Blindness, one eye, low vision other eye**
  Visual impairment categories 3, 4, 5 in one eye, with categories 1 or 2 in the other eye.
  H54.10   Blindness, one eye, low vision other eye, **unspecified** eyes
  ● H54.11   Blindness, **right eye, low vision left eye**
    ● H54.113   Blindness **right eye category 3, low vision left eye**
      H54.1131   Blindness right eye category 3, low vision left eye category 1
      H54.1132   Blindness right eye category 3, low vision left eye category 2
    ● H54.114   Blindness **right eye category 4, low vision left eye**
      H54.1141   Blindness right eye category 4, low vision left eye category 1
      H54.1142   Blindness right eye category 4, low vision left eye category 2
    ● H54.115   Blindness **right eye category 5, low vision left eye**
      H54.1151   Blindness right eye category 5, low vision left eye category 1
      H54.1152   Blindness right eye category 5, low vision left eye category 2
  ● H54.12   Blindness, **left** eye, low vision right eye
    ● H54.121   **Low vision right eye category 1, blindness left eye**
      H54.1213   Low vision right eye category 1, blindness left eye category 3
      H54.1214   Low vision right eye category 1, blindness left eye category 4
      H54.1215   Low vision right eye category 1, blindness left eye category 5
    ● H54.122   **Low vision right eye category 2, blindness left eye**
      H54.1223   Low vision right eye category 2, blindness left eye category 3
      H54.1224   Low vision right eye category 2, blindness left eye category 4
      H54.1225   Low vision right eye category 2, blindness left eye category 5

● H54.2   **Low vision, both eyes**
  Visual impairment categories 1 or 2 in both eyes.
  ● H54.2X   Low vision, both eyes, **different category levels**
    ● H54.2X1   Low vision, **right eye, category 1**
      H54.2X11   Low vision right eye category 1, low vision left eye category 1
      H54.2X12   Low vision right eye category 1, low vision left eye category 2

▶ New   ⇒ Revised   ~~deleted~~ Deleted   Excludes 1   Excludes 2   Includes   Use additional   Code first   Code also   Key words

OGCR Official Guidelines   X Assign placeholder X   ● Use Additional Character(s)   ▶ Manifestation Code   🅚 Hierarchical Condition Category   **Coding Clinic**

OGCR Section I.C.7.b.

Blindness

If "blindness" or "low vision" of both eyes is documented but the visual impairment category is not documented, assign code H54.3, Unqualified visual loss, both eyes. If "blindness" or "low vision" in one eye is documented but the visual impairment category is not documented, assign a code from H54.6-, Unqualified visual loss, one eye. If "blindness" or "visual loss" is documented without any information about whether one or both eyes are affected, assign code H54.7, Unspecified visual loss.

● H54.2X2   Low vision, right eye, category 2
    H54.2X21   Low vision right eye category 2, low vision left eye category 1
    H54.2X22   Low vision right eye category 2, low vision left eye category 2
H54.3   Unqualified visual loss, both eyes
    Visual impairment category 9 in both eyes.
● H54.4   Blindness, one eye
    Visual impairment categories 3, 4, 5 in one eye [normal vision in other eye]
   H54.40   Blindness, one eye, unspecified eye
● H54.41   Blindness, right eye, normal vision left eye
   ● H54.413   Blindness, right eye, category 3
     H54.413A   Blindness right eye category 3, normal vision left eye
   ● H54.414   Blindness, right eye, category 4
     H54.414A   Blindness right eye category 4, normal vision left eye
   ● H54.415   Blindness, right eye, category 5
     H54.415A   Blindness right eye category 5, normal vision left eye
● H54.42   Blindness, left eye, normal vision right eye
   ● H54.42A   Blindness, left eye, category 3-5
     H54.42A3   Blindness left eye category 3, normal vision right eye
     H54.42A4   Blindness left eye category 4, normal vision right eye
     H54.42A5   Blindness left eye category 5, normal vision right eye
● H54.5   Low vision, one eye
    Visual impairment categories 1 or 2 in one eye [normal vision in other eye].
   H54.50   Low vision, one eye, unspecified eye
● H54.51   Low vision, right eye, normal vision left eye
   ● H54.511   Low vision, right eye, category 1-2
     H54.511A   Low vision right eye category 1, normal vision left eye
     H54.512A   Low vision right eye category 2, normal vision left eye
● H54.52   Low vision, left eye, normal vision right eye
   ● H54.52A   Low vision, left eye, category 1-2
     H54.52A1   Low vision left eye category 1, normal vision right eye
     H54.52A2   Low vision left eye category 2, normal vision right eye
● H54.6   Unqualified visual loss, one eye
    Visual impairment category 9 in one eye [normal vision in other eye].
   H54.60   Unqualified visual loss, one eye, unspecified
   H54.61   Unqualified visual loss, right eye, normal vision left eye
   H54.62   Unqualified visual loss, left eye, normal vision right eye

H54.7   **Unspecified visual loss**
    Visual impairment category 9 NOS
H54.8   **Legal blindness, as defined in USA**
    Blindness NOS according to USA definition
   Excludes1   legal blindness with specification of impairment level (H54.0-H54.7)
   Note: The table below gives a classification of severity of visual impairment recommended by a WHO Study Group on the Prevention of Blindness, Geneva, 6-10 November 1972.

   The term "low vision" in category H54 comprises categories 1 and 2 of the table, the term "blindness" categories 3, 4, and 5, and the term "unqualified visual loss" category 9.

   If the extent of the visual field is taken into account, patients with a field no greater than 10 but greater than 5 around central fixation should be placed in category 3 and patients with a field no greater than 5 around central fixation should be placed in category 4, even if the central acuity is not impaired.

(Document 508 compliance requires all cells in the following table to be filled.)

Category of visual impairment	Visual acuity with best possible correction	
	Maximum less than:	**Minimum equal to or better than:**
—	6/18	6/60
3/10 (0.3)	1/10 (0.1)	—
20/70	20/200	—
—	6/60	3/60
1/10 (0.1)	1/20 (0.05)	—
20/200	20/400	—
—	3/60	1/60 (finger counting at one meter)
1/20 (0.05)	1/50 (0.02)	—
20/400	5/300 (20/1200)	—
—	1/60 (finger counting at one meter)	Light perception
1/50 (0.02)	—	—
5/300	—	—
—	No light perception	—
—	Undetermined or unspecified	—

OTHER DISORDERS OF EYE AND ADNEXA (H55-H57)

● H55   Nystagmus and other irregular eye movements
   ● H55.0   Nystagmus
    Rapid, involuntary movements of the eyes in the horizontal or vertical direction
    H55.00   Unspecified nystagmus
    H55.01   Congenital nystagmus
    H55.02   Latent nystagmus
    H55.03   Visual deprivation nystagmus
    H55.04   Dissociated nystagmus
    H55.09   Other forms of nystagmus
   ● H55.8   Other irregular eye movements
    ⇒ H55.81   Deficient saccadic eye movements
    ▶ H55.82   Deficient smooth pursuit eye movements
    H55.89   Other irregular eye movements

● H57   Other disorders of eye and adnexa
    ● H57.0   Anomalies of pupillary function
         H57.00   Unspecified anomaly of pupillary function
         H57.01   Argyll Robertson pupil, atypical
             Excludes1   syphilitic Argyll Robertson pupil (A52.19)
         H57.02   Anisocoria
         H57.03   Miosis
         H57.04   Mydriasis
         ● H57.05   Tonic pupil
             H57.051   Tonic pupil, right eye
             H57.052   Tonic pupil, left eye
             H57.053   Tonic pupil, bilateral
             H57.059   Tonic pupil, unspecified eye
         H57.09   Other anomalies of pupillary function
    ● H57.1   Ocular pain
         H57.10   Ocular pain, unspecified eye
         H57.11   Ocular pain, right eye
         H57.12   Ocular pain, left eye
         H57.13   Ocular pain, bilateral
    ● H57.8   Other specified disorders of eye and adnexa
         ● H57.81   Brow ptosis
             H57.811   Brow ptosis, right
             H57.812   Brow ptosis, left
             H57.813   Brow ptosis, bilateral
             H57.819   Brow ptosis, unspecified
         H57.89   Other specified disorders of eye and adnexa
    H57.9   Unspecified disorder of eye and adnexa

INTRAOPERATIVE AND POSTPROCEDURAL COMPLICATIONS AND DISORDERS OF EYE AND ADNEXA, NOT ELSEWHERE CLASSIFIED (H59)

● H59   Intraoperative and postprocedural complications and disorders of eye and adnexa, not elsewhere classified
     Excludes1   mechanical complication of intraocular lens (T85.2)
             mechanical complication of other ocular prosthetic devices, implants and grafts (T85.3)
             pseudophakia (Z96.1)
             secondary cataracts (H26.4-)
    ● H59.0   Disorders of the eye following cataract surgery
         ● H59.01   Keratopathy (bullous aphakic) following cataract surgery
             Vitreal corneal syndrome
             Vitreous (touch) syndrome
             H59.011   Keratopathy (bullous aphakic) following cataract surgery, right eye
             H59.012   Keratopathy (bullous aphakic) following cataract surgery, left eye
             H59.013   Keratopathy (bullous aphakic) following cataract surgery, bilateral
             H59.019   Keratopathy (bullous aphakic) following cataract surgery, unspecified eye
         ● H59.02   Cataract (lens) fragments in eye following cataract surgery
             H59.021   Cataract (lens) fragments in eye following cataract surgery, right eye
             H59.022   Cataract (lens) fragments in eye following cataract surgery, left eye
             H59.023   Cataract (lens) fragments in eye following cataract surgery, bilateral
             H59.029   Cataract (lens) fragments in eye following cataract surgery, unspecified eye

● H59.03   Cystoid macular edema following cataract surgery
     H59.031   Cystoid macular edema following cataract surgery, right eye
     H59.032   Cystoid macular edema following cataract surgery, left eye
     H59.033   Cystoid macular edema following cataract surgery, bilateral
     H59.039   Cystoid macular edema following cataract surgery, unspecified eye
● H59.09   Other disorders of the eye following cataract surgery
     H59.091   Other disorders of the right eye following cataract surgery
     H59.092   Other disorders of the left eye following cataract surgery
     H59.093   Other disorders of the eye following cataract surgery, bilateral
     H59.099   Other disorders of unspecified eye following cataract surgery
● H59.1   Intraoperative hemorrhage and hematoma of eye and adnexa complicating a procedure
     Excludes1   intraoperative hemorrhage and hematoma of eye and adnexa due to accidental puncture or laceration during a procedure (H59.2-)
    ● H59.11   Intraoperative hemorrhage and hematoma of eye and adnexa complicating an ophthalmic procedure
         H59.111   Intraoperative hemorrhage and hematoma of right eye and adnexa complicating an ophthalmic procedure
         H59.112   Intraoperative hemorrhage and hematoma of left eye and adnexa complicating an ophthalmic procedure
         H59.113   Intraoperative hemorrhage and hematoma of eye and adnexa complicating an ophthalmic procedure, bilateral
         H59.119   Intraoperative hemorrhage and hematoma of unspecified eye and adnexa complicating an ophthalmic procedure
    ● H59.12   Intraoperative hemorrhage and hematoma of eye and adnexa complicating other procedure
         H59.121   Intraoperative hemorrhage and hematoma of right eye and adnexa complicating other procedure
         H59.122   Intraoperative hemorrhage and hematoma of left eye and adnexa complicating other procedure
         H59.123   Intraoperative hemorrhage and hematoma of eye and adnexa complicating other procedure, bilateral
         H59.129   Intraoperative hemorrhage and hematoma of unspecified eye and adnexa complicating other procedure

---

▶ New   ⇒ Revised   ~~deleted~~ Deleted   Excludes 1   Excludes 2   Includes   Use additional   Code first   Code also   Key words

OGCR Official Guidelines   X Assign placeholder X   ● Use Additional Character(s)   ▶ Manifestation Code   Hierarchical Condition Category   **Coding Clinic**

● **H59.2**   **Accidental puncture and laceration** of eye and adnexa during a procedure

  ● **H59.21**   Accidental puncture and laceration of eye and adnexa during an ophthalmic procedure

     H59.211   Accidental puncture and laceration of right eye and adnexa during an ophthalmic procedure

     H59.212   Accidental puncture and laceration of left eye and adnexa during an ophthalmic procedure

     H59.213   Accidental puncture and laceration of eye and adnexa during an ophthalmic procedure, bilateral

     H59.219   Accidental puncture and laceration of unspecified eye and adnexa during an ophthalmic procedure

  ● **H59.22**   Accidental puncture and laceration of eye and adnexa during other procedure

     H59.221   Accidental puncture and laceration of right eye and adnexa during other procedure

     H59.222   Accidental puncture and laceration of left eye and adnexa during other procedure

     H59.223   Accidental puncture and laceration of eye and adnexa during other procedure, bilateral

     H59.229   Accidental puncture and laceration of unspecified eye and adnexa during other procedure

● **H59.3**   **Postprocedural hemorrhage, hematoma, and seroma** of eye and adnexa following other procedure
     Coding Clinic: 2016, Q4, P10

  ● **H59.31**   Postprocedural hemorrhage of eye and adnexa following an ophthalmic procedure

     H59.311   Postprocedural hemorrhage of right eye and adnexa following an ophthalmic procedure

     H59.312   Postprocedural hemorrhage of left eye and adnexa following an ophthalmic procedure

     H59.313   Postprocedural hemorrhage of eye and adnexa following an ophthalmic procedure, bilateral

     H59.319   Postprocedural hemorrhage of unspecified eye and adnexa following an ophthalmic procedure

  ● **H59.32**   Postprocedural hemorrhage of eye and adnexa following other procedure

     H59.321   Postprocedural hemorrhage of right eye and adnexa following other procedure

     H59.322   Postprocedural hemorrhage of left eye and adnexa following other procedure

     H59.323   Postprocedural hemorrhage of eye and adnexa following other procedure, bilateral

     H59.329   Postprocedural hemorrhage of unspecified eye and adnexa following other procedure

  ● **H59.33**   Postprocedural hematoma of eye and adnexa following an ophthalmic procedure

     H59.331   Postprocedural hematoma of right eye and adnexa following an ophthalmic procedure

     H59.332   Postprocedural hematoma of left eye and adnexa following an ophthalmic procedure

     H59.333   Postprocedural hematoma of eye and adnexa following an ophthalmic procedure, bilateral

     H59.339   Postprocedural hematoma of unspecified eye and adnexa following an ophthalmic procedure

  ● **H59.34**   Postprocedural hematoma of eye and adnexa following other procedure

     H59.341   Postprocedural hematoma of right eye and adnexa following other procedure

     H59.342   Postprocedural hematoma of left eye and adnexa following other procedure

     H59.343   Postprocedural hematoma of eye and adnexa following other procedure, bilateral

     H59.349   Postprocedural hematoma of unspecified eye and adnexa following other procedure

  ● **H59.35**   Postprocedural seroma of eye and adnexa following an ophthalmic procedure

     H59.351   Postprocedural seroma of right eye and adnexa following an ophthalmic procedure

     H59.352   Postprocedural seroma of left eye and adnexa following an ophthalmic procedure

     H59.353   Postprocedural seroma of eye and adnexa following an ophthalmic procedure, bilateral

     H59.359   Postprocedural seroma of unspecified eye and adnexa following an ophthalmic procedure

  ● **H59.36**   Postprocedural seroma of eye and adnexa following other procedure

     H59.361   Postprocedural seroma of right eye and adnexa following other procedure

     H59.362   Postprocedural seroma of left eye and adnexa following other procedure

     H59.363   Postprocedural seroma of eye and adnexa following other procedure, bilateral

     H59.369   Postprocedural seroma of unspecified eye and adnexa following other procedure

● **H59.4**   **Inflammation (infection) of postprocedural bleb**
     Postprocedural blebitis

     Excludes1   filtering (vitreous) bleb after glaucoma surgery status (Z98.83)

     H59.40   Inflammation (infection) of postprocedural bleb, unspecified

     H59.41   Inflammation (infection) of postprocedural bleb, stage 1

     H59.42   Inflammation (infection) of postprocedural bleb, stage 2

     H59.43   Inflammation (infection) of postprocedural bleb, stage 3
       Bleb endophthalmitis

● **H59.8**   **Other intraoperative and postprocedural complications** and disorders of eye and adnexa, not elsewhere classified

  ● **H59.81**   Chorioretinal scars after surgery for detachment

     H59.811   Chorioretinal scars after surgery for detachment, right eye

     H59.812   Chorioretinal scars after surgery for detachment, left eye

     H59.813   Chorioretinal scars after surgery for detachment, bilateral

     H59.819   Chorioretinal scars after surgery for detachment, unspecified eye

     H59.88   Other intraoperative complications of eye and adnexa, not elsewhere classified

     H59.89   Other postprocedural complications and disorders of eye and adnexa, not elsewhere classified

CHAPTER 8

DISEASES OF THE EAR AND MASTOID PROCESS (H60-H95)

OGCR Chapter-Specific Coding Guidelines

8. Chapter 8: Diseases of the Ear and Mastoid Process (H60-H95)
   Reserved for future guideline expansion

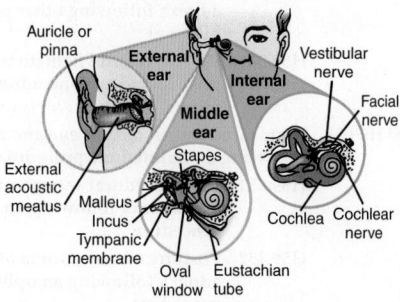

Figure 8-1 Auditory system. (From Buck CJ: Step-by-Step Medical Coding, ed 2016, St. Louis, Elsevier, 2016)

★ **(See Plate 20 of the Anatomy Illustrations.)**

CHAPTER 8

DISEASES OF THE EAR AND MASTOID PROCESS (H60-H95)

Note: Use an external cause code following the code for the ear condition, if applicable, to identify the cause of the ear condition

Excludes2   certain conditions originating in the perinatal period (P04-P96)
certain infectious and parasitic diseases (A00-B99)
complications of pregnancy, childbirth and the puerperium (O00-O9A)
congenital malformations, deformations and chromosomal abnormalities (Q00-Q99)
endocrine, nutritional and metabolic diseases (E00-E88)
injury, poisoning and certain other consequences of external causes (S00-T88)
neoplasms (C00-D49)
symptoms, signs and abnormal clinical and laboratory findings, not elsewhere classified (R00-R94)

This chapter contains the following blocks:

H60-H62	Diseases of external ear
H65-H75	Diseases of middle ear and mastoid
H80-H83	Diseases of inner ear
H90-H94	Other disorders of ear
H95	Intraoperative and postprocedural complications and disorders of ear and mastoid process, not elsewhere classified

DISEASES OF EXTERNAL EAR (H60-H62)

● **H60**   **Otitis externa**

  ● **H60.0**   **Abscess of external ear**
      Boil of external ear
      Carbuncle of auricle or external auditory canal
      Furuncle of external ear

     H60.00   Abscess of external ear, **unspecified ear**
     H60.01   Abscess of **right** external ear
     H60.02   Abscess of **left** external ear
     H60.03   Abscess of external ear, **bilateral**

● **H60.1**   **Cellulitis of external ear**
      Cellulitis of auricle
      Cellulitis of external auditory canal

     H60.10   Cellulitis of external ear, **unspecified ear**
     H60.11   Cellulitis of **right** external ear
     H60.12   Cellulitis of **left** external ear
     H60.13   Cellulitis of external ear, **bilateral**

● **H60.2**   **Malignant otitis externa**

     H60.20   Malignant otitis externa, **unspecified ear**
     H60.21   Malignant otitis externa, **right ear**
     H60.22   Malignant otitis externa, **left ear**
     H60.23   Malignant otitis externa, **bilateral**

● **H60.3**   **Other infective otitis externa**

  ● **H60.31**   **Diffuse otitis externa**
      H60.311   Diffuse otitis externa, **right ear**
      H60.312   Diffuse otitis externa, **left ear**
      H60.313   Diffuse otitis externa, **bilateral**
      H60.319   Diffuse otitis externa, **unspecified ear**

  ● **H60.32**   **Hemorrhagic otitis externa**
      H60.321   Hemorrhagic otitis externa, **right ear**
      H60.322   Hemorrhagic otitis externa, **left ear**
      H60.323   Hemorrhagic otitis externa, **bilateral**
      H60.329   Hemorrhagic otitis externa, **unspecified ear**

  ● **H60.33**   **Swimmer's ear**
      H60.331   Swimmer's ear, **right ear**
      H60.332   Swimmer's ear, **left ear**
      H60.333   Swimmer's ear, **bilateral**
      H60.339   Swimmer's ear, **unspecified ear**

  ● **H60.39**   **Other infective otitis externa**
      H60.391   Other infective otitis externa, **right ear**
      H60.392   Other infective otitis externa, **left ear**
      H60.393   Other infective otitis externa, **bilateral**
      H60.399   Other infective otitis externa, **unspecified ear**

● **H60.4**   **Cholesteatoma of external ear**
      Keratosis obturans of external ear (canal)

     Excludes2   cholesteatoma of middle ear (H71.-)
              recurrent cholesteatoma of postmastoidectomy cavity (H95.0-)

     H60.40   Cholesteatoma of external ear, **unspecified ear**
     H60.41   Cholesteatoma of **right** external ear
     H60.42   Cholesteatoma of **left** external ear
     H60.43   Cholesteatoma of external ear, **bilateral**

● **H60.5**   **Acute noninfective otitis externa**

  ● **H60.50**   **Unspecified acute noninfective otitis externa**
      Acute otitis externa NOS

      H60.501   Unspecified acute noninfective otitis externa, **right ear**
      H60.502   Unspecified acute noninfective otitis externa, **left ear**
      H60.503   Unspecified acute noninfective otitis externa, **bilateral**
      H60.509   Unspecified acute noninfective otitis externa, **unspecified ear**

  ● **H60.51**   **Acute actinic otitis externa**
      H60.511   Acute actinic otitis externa, **right ear**
      H60.512   Acute actinic otitis externa, **left ear**
      H60.513   Acute actinic otitis externa, **bilateral**
      H60.519   Acute actinic otitis externa, **unspecified ear**

● **H60.52   Acute chemical otitis externa**
    H60.521   Acute chemical otitis externa, **right ear**
    H60.522   Acute chemical otitis externa, **left ear**
    H60.523   Acute chemical otitis externa, **bilateral**
    H60.529   Acute chemical otitis externa, **unspecified** ear

● **H60.53   Acute contact otitis externa**
    H60.531   Acute contact otitis externa, **right ear**
    H60.532   Acute contact otitis externa, **left ear**
    H60.533   Acute contact otitis externa, **bilateral**
    H60.539   Acute contact otitis externa, **unspecified** ear

● **H60.54   Acute eczematoid otitis externa**
    H60.541   Acute eczematoid otitis externa, **right ear**
    H60.542   Acute eczematoid otitis externa, **left ear**
    H60.543   Acute eczematoid otitis externa, **bilateral**
    H60.549   Acute eczematoid otitis externa, **unspecified** ear

● **H60.55   Acute reactive otitis externa**
    H60.551   Acute reactive otitis externa, **right ear**
    H60.552   Acute reactive otitis externa, **left ear**
    H60.553   Acute reactive otitis externa, **bilateral**
    H60.559   Acute reactive otitis externa, **unspecified** ear

● **H60.59   Other noninfective acute otitis externa**
    H60.591   Other noninfective acute otitis externa, **right ear**
    H60.592   Other noninfective acute otitis externa, **left ear**
    H60.593   Other noninfective acute otitis externa, **bilateral**
    H60.599   Other noninfective acute otitis externa, **unspecified** ear

● **H60.6   Unspecified chronic otitis externa**
    H60.60   Unspecified chronic otitis externa, **unspecified** ear
    H60.61   Unspecified chronic otitis externa, **right ear**
    H60.62   Unspecified chronic otitis externa, **left ear**
    H60.63   Unspecified chronic otitis externa, **bilateral**

● **H60.8   Other otitis externa**
   ● **H60.8X   Other otitis externa**
    H60.8X1   Other otitis externa, **right ear**
    H60.8X2   Other otitis externa, **left ear**
    H60.8X3   Other otitis externa, **bilateral**
    H60.8X9   Other otitis externa, **unspecified** ear

● **H60.9   Unspecified otitis externa**
    H60.90   Unspecified otitis externa, **unspecified** ear
    H60.91   Unspecified otitis externa, **right ear**
    H60.92   Unspecified otitis externa, **left ear**
    H60.93   Unspecified otitis externa, **bilateral**

● **H61   Other disorders of external ear**
   ● **H61.0   Chondritis and perichondritis of external ear**
     Chondrodermatitis nodularis chronica helicis
     Perichondritis of auricle
     Perichondritis of pinna
    ● **H61.00   Unspecified perichondritis of external ear**
     H61.001   Unspecified perichondritis of **right** external ear
     H61.002   Unspecified perichondritis of **left** external ear
     H61.003   Unspecified perichondritis of external ear, **bilateral**
     H61.009   Unspecified perichondritis of external ear, **unspecified** ear

● **H61.01   Acute perichondritis of external ear**
    H61.011   Acute perichondritis of **right** external ear
    H61.012   Acute perichondritis of **left** external ear
    H61.013   Acute perichondritis of external ear, **bilateral**
    H61.019   Acute perichondritis of external ear, **unspecified** ear

● **H61.02   Chronic perichondritis of external ear**
    H61.021   Chronic perichondritis of **right** external ear
    H61.022   Chronic perichondritis of **left** external ear
    H61.023   Chronic perichondritis of external ear, **bilateral**
    H61.029   Chronic perichondritis of external ear, **unspecified** ear

● **H61.03   Chondritis of external ear**
     Chondritis of auricle
     Chondritis of pinna
    H61.031   Chondritis of **right** external ear
    H61.032   Chondritis of **left** external ear
     Coding Clinic: 2015, Q1, P18
    H61.033   Chondritis of external ear, **bilateral**
    H61.039   Chondritis of external ear, **unspecified** ear

● **H61.1   Noninfective disorders of pinna**
    Excludes2   cauliflower ear (M95.1-)
             gouty tophi of ear (M1A.-)
   ● **H61.10   Unspecified noninfective disorders of pinna**
     Disorder of pinna NOS
    H61.101   Unspecified noninfective disorders of pinna, **right ear**
    H61.102   Unspecified noninfective disorders of pinna, **left ear**
    H61.103   Unspecified noninfective disorders of pinna, **bilateral**
    H61.109   Unspecified noninfective disorders of pinna, **unspecified** ear

● **H61.11   Acquired deformity of pinna**
     Acquired deformity of auricle
    Excludes2   cauliflower ear (M95.1-)
    H61.111   Acquired deformity of pinna, **right ear**
    H61.112   Acquired deformity of pinna, **left ear**
    H61.113   Acquired deformity of pinna, **bilateral**
    H61.119   Acquired deformity of pinna, **unspecified** ear

● **H61.12   Hematoma of pinna**
     Hematoma of auricle
    H61.121   Hematoma of pinna, **right ear**
    H61.122   Hematoma of pinna, **left ear**
    H61.123   Hematoma of pinna, **bilateral**
    H61.129   Hematoma of pinna, **unspecified** ear

● **H61.19   Other noninfective disorders of pinna**
    H61.191   Noninfective disorders of pinna, **right ear**
    H61.192   Noninfective disorders of pinna, **left ear**
    H61.193   Noninfective disorders of pinna, **bilateral**
    H61.199   Noninfective disorders of pinna, **unspecified** ear

CHAPTER 8 (H60–H95)

● **H61.2**   **Impacted cerumen**
Wax in ear
    H61.20   Impacted cerumen, unspecified ear
    H61.21   Impacted cerumen, right ear
    H61.22   Impacted cerumen, left ear
    H61.23   Impacted cerumen, bilateral

● **H61.3**   **Acquired stenosis of external ear canal**
Collapse of external ear canal

    Excludes1   postprocedural stenosis of external ear canal (H95.81-)

  ● **H61.30**   **Acquired stenosis of external ear canal, unspecified**
      H61.301   Acquired stenosis of right external ear canal, unspecified
      H61.302   Acquired stenosis of left external ear canal, unspecified
      H61.303   Acquired stenosis of external ear canal, unspecified, bilateral
      H61.309   Acquired stenosis of external ear canal, unspecified, unspecified ear

  ● **H61.31**   **Acquired stenosis of external ear canal secondary to trauma**
      H61.311   Acquired stenosis of right external ear canal secondary to trauma
      H61.312   Acquired stenosis of left external ear canal secondary to trauma
      H61.313   Acquired stenosis of external ear canal secondary to trauma, bilateral
      H61.319   Acquired stenosis of external ear canal secondary to trauma, unspecified ear

  ● **H61.32**   **Acquired stenosis of external ear canal secondary to inflammation and infection**
      H61.321   Acquired stenosis of right external ear canal secondary to inflammation and infection
      H61.322   Acquired stenosis of left external ear canal secondary to inflammation and infection
      H61.323   Acquired stenosis of external ear canal secondary to inflammation and infection, bilateral
      H61.329   Acquired stenosis of external ear canal secondary to inflammation and infection, unspecified ear

  ● **H61.39**   **Other** acquired stenosis of external ear canal
      H61.391   Other acquired stenosis of right external ear canal
      H61.392   Other acquired stenosis of left external ear canal
      H61.393   Other acquired stenosis of external ear canal, bilateral
      H61.399   Other acquired stenosis of external ear canal, unspecified ear

● **H61.8**   **Other specified disorders of external ear**
  ● **H61.81**   **Exostosis of external canal**
      H61.811   Exostosis of right external canal
      H61.812   Exostosis of left external canal
      H61.813   Exostosis of external canal, bilateral
      H61.819   Exostosis of external canal, unspecified ear

  ● **H61.89**   **Other specified disorders of external ear**
      H61.891   Other specified disorders of right external ear
      H61.892   Other specified disorders of left external ear
      H61.893   Other specified disorders of external ear, bilateral
      H61.899   Other specified disorders of external ear, unspecified ear

● **H61.9**   **Disorder of external ear, unspecified**
    H61.90   Disorder of external ear, unspecified, unspecified ear
    H61.91   Disorder of right external ear, unspecified
    H61.92   Disorder of left external ear, unspecified
    H61.93   Disorder of external ear, unspecified, bilateral

● **H62**   **Disorders of external ear in diseases classified elsewhere**
  ● **H62.4**   **Otitis externa in other diseases classified elsewhere**
    Code first underlying disease, such as:
    erysipelas (A46)
    impetigo (L01.0)

    Excludes1   otitis externa (in):
        candidiasis (B37.84)
        herpes viral [herpes simplex] (B00.1)
        herpes zoster (B02.8)

    ▶ **H62.40**   *Otitis externa in other diseases classified elsewhere, unspecified ear*
    ▶ **H62.41**   *Otitis externa in other diseases classified elsewhere, right ear*
    ▶ **H62.42**   *Otitis externa in other diseases classified elsewhere, left ear*
    ▶ **H62.43**   *Otitis externa in other diseases classified elsewhere, bilateral*

  ● **H62.8**   **Other disorders of external ear in diseases classified elsewhere**
    Code first underlying disease, such as:
    gout (M1A.-, M10.-)

  ● **H62.8X**   **Other disorders of external ear in diseases classified elsewhere**
    ▶ **H62.8X1**   *Other disorders of right external ear in diseases classified elsewhere*
    ▶ **H62.8X2**   *Other disorders of left external ear in diseases classified elsewhere*
    ▶ **H62.8X3**   *Other disorders of external ear in diseases classified elsewhere, bilateral*
    ▶ **H62.8X9**   *Other disorders of external ear in diseases classified elsewhere, unspecified ear*

DISEASES OF MIDDLE EAR AND MASTOID (H65-H75)

★ **(See Plate 21 of the Anatomy Illustrations.)**

● **H65**   **Nonsuppurative otitis media**
Bacterial or viral infection or inflammation of the middle ear; may result in fluid accumulation with pain and temporary hearing loss.

    Includes   nonsuppurative otitis media with myringitis

  Use additional code for any associated perforated tympanic membrane (H72.-)

  Use additional code to identify:
    exposure to environmental tobacco smoke (Z77.22)
    exposure to tobacco smoke in the perinatal period (P96.81)
    history of tobacco dependence (Z87.891)
    infectious agent (B95-B97)
    occupational exposure to environmental tobacco smoke (Z57.31)
    tobacco dependence (F17.-)
    tobacco use (Z72.0)

  ● **H65.0**   **Acute serous otitis media**
    Acute and subacute secretory otitis
    H65.00   Acute serous otitis media, unspecified ear
    H65.01   Acute serous otitis media, right ear
    H65.02   Acute serous otitis media, left ear
    H65.03   Acute serous otitis media, bilateral
    H65.04   Acute serous otitis media, recurrent, right ear
    H65.05   Acute serous otitis media, recurrent, left ear
    H65.06   Acute serous otitis media, recurrent, bilateral
    H65.07   Acute serous otitis media, recurrent, unspecified ear

▶ New   ⇒ Revised   ~~deleted~~ Deleted   Excludes 1   Excludes 2   Includes   Use additional   Code first   Code also   Key words

OGCR Official Guidelines   X Assign placeholder X   ● Use Additional Character(s)   ▶ Manifestation Code   🔖 Hierarchical Condition Category   Coding Clinic

● **H65.1 Other acute nonsuppurative otitis media**
> **Excludes1** otitic barotrauma (T70.0)
> otitis media (acute) NOS (H66.9)

● **H65.11 Acute and subacute allergic otitis media (mucoid) (sanguinous) (serous)**

　　H65.111 Acute and subacute allergic otitis media (mucoid) (sanguinous) (serous), right ear

　　H65.112 Acute and subacute allergic otitis media (mucoid) (sanguinous) (serous), left ear

　　H65.113 Acute and subacute allergic otitis media (mucoid) (sanguinous) (serous), bilateral

　　H65.114 Acute and subacute allergic otitis media (mucoid) (sanguinous) (serous), recurrent, right ear

　　H65.115 Acute and subacute allergic otitis media (mucoid) (sanguinous) (serous), recurrent, left ear

　　H65.116 Acute and subacute allergic otitis media (mucoid) (sanguinous) (serous), recurrent, bilateral

　　H65.117 Acute and subacute allergic otitis media (mucoid) (sanguinous) (serous), recurrent, unspecified ear

　　H65.119 Acute and subacute allergic otitis media (mucoid) (sanguinous) (serous), unspecified ear

● **H65.19 Other acute nonsuppurative otitis media**
　Acute and subacute mucoid otitis media
　Acute and subacute nonsuppurative otitis media NOS
　Acute and subacute sanguinous otitis media
　Acute and subacute seromucinous otitis media

　　H65.191 Other acute nonsuppurative otitis media, right ear

　　H65.192 Other acute nonsuppurative otitis media, left ear

　　H65.193 Other acute nonsuppurative otitis media, bilateral

　　H65.194 Other acute nonsuppurative otitis media, recurrent, right ear

　　H65.195 Other acute nonsuppurative otitis media, recurrent, left ear

　　H65.196 Other acute nonsuppurative otitis media, recurrent, bilateral

　　H65.197 Other acute nonsuppurative otitis media recurrent, unspecified ear

　　H65.199 Other acute nonsuppurative otitis media, unspecified ear

● **H65.2 Chronic serous otitis media**
　Chronic tubotympanal catarrh

　H65.20 Chronic serous otitis media, unspecified ear

　H65.21 Chronic serous otitis media, right ear

　H65.22 Chronic serous otitis media, left ear

　H65.23 Chronic serous otitis media, bilateral

● **H65.3 Chronic mucoid otitis media**
　Chronic mucinous otitis media
　Chronic secretory otitis media
　Chronic transudative otitis media
　Glue ear
> **Excludes1** adhesive middle ear disease (H74.1)

　H65.30 Chronic mucoid otitis media, unspecified ear

　H65.31 Chronic mucoid otitis media, right ear

　H65.32 Chronic mucoid otitis media, left ear

　H65.33 Chronic mucoid otitis media, bilateral

● **H65.4 Other chronic nonsuppurative otitis media**

● **H65.41 Chronic allergic otitis media**

　　H65.411 Chronic allergic otitis media, right ear

　　H65.412 Chronic allergic otitis media, left ear

　　H65.413 Chronic allergic otitis media, bilateral

　　H65.419 Chronic allergic otitis media, unspecified ear

● **H65.49 Other chronic nonsuppurative otitis media**
　Chronic exudative otitis media
　Chronic nonsuppurative otitis media NOS
　Chronic otitis media with effusion (nonpurulent)
　Chronic seromucinous otitis media

　　H65.491 Other chronic nonsuppurative otitis media, right ear

　　H65.492 Other chronic nonsuppurative otitis media, left ear

　　H65.493 Other chronic nonsuppurative otitis media, bilateral

　　H65.499 Other chronic nonsuppurative otitis media, unspecified ear

● **H65.9 Unspecified nonsuppurative otitis media**
　Allergic otitis media NOS
　Catarrhal otitis media NOS
　Exudative otitis media NOS
　Mucoid otitis media NOS
　Otitis media with effusion (nonpurulent) NOS
　Secretory otitis media NOS
　Seromucinous otitis media NOS
　Serous otitis media NOS
　Transudative otitis media NOS

　H65.90 Unspecified nonsuppurative otitis media, unspecified ear

　H65.91 Unspecified nonsuppurative otitis media, right ear

　H65.92 Unspecified nonsuppurative otitis media, left ear

　H65.93 Unspecified nonsuppurative otitis media, bilateral

● **H66 Suppurative and unspecified otitis media**
> *Suppurative: Discharging pus*
> **Includes** suppurative and unspecified otitis media with myringitis

Use additional code to identify:
　exposure to environmental tobacco smoke (Z77.22)
　exposure to tobacco smoke in the perinatal period (P96.81)
　history of tobacco dependence (Z87.891)
　occupational exposure to environmental tobacco smoke (Z57.31)
　tobacco dependence (F17.-)
　tobacco use (Z72.0)

● **H66.0 Acute suppurative otitis media**

● **H66.00 Acute suppurative otitis media without spontaneous rupture of ear drum**

　　H66.001 Acute suppurative otitis media without spontaneous rupture of ear drum, right ear
　　　Coding Clinic: 2016, Q1, P34

　　H66.002 Acute suppurative otitis media without spontaneous rupture of ear drum, left ear

　　H66.003 Acute suppurative otitis media without spontaneous rupture of ear drum, bilateral

　　H66.004 Acute suppurative otitis media without spontaneous rupture of ear drum, recurrent, right ear

　　H66.005 Acute suppurative otitis media without spontaneous rupture of ear drum, recurrent, left ear

　　H66.006 Acute suppurative otitis media without spontaneous rupture of ear drum, recurrent, bilateral

　　H66.007 Acute suppurative otitis media without spontaneous rupture of ear drum, recurrent, unspecified ear

　　H66.009 Acute suppurative otitis media without spontaneous rupture of ear drum, unspecified ear

● **H66.01**   **Acute suppurative otitis media with spontaneous rupture of ear drum**

    H66.011   Acute suppurative otitis media with spontaneous rupture of ear drum, right ear

    H66.012   Acute suppurative otitis media with spontaneous rupture of ear drum, left ear

    H66.013   Acute suppurative otitis media with spontaneous rupture of ear drum, bilateral

    H66.014   Acute suppurative otitis media with spontaneous rupture of ear drum, recurrent, right ear

    H66.015   Acute suppurative otitis media with spontaneous rupture of ear drum, recurrent, left ear

    H66.016   Acute suppurative otitis media with spontaneous rupture of ear drum, recurrent, bilateral

    H66.017   Acute suppurative otitis media with spontaneous rupture of ear drum, recurrent, unspecified ear

    H66.019   Acute suppurative otitis media with spontaneous rupture of ear drum, unspecified ear

● **H66.1**   **Chronic tubotympanic suppurative otitis media**

    Benign chronic suppurative otitis media
    Chronic tubotympanic disease

    Use additional code for any associated perforated tympanic membrane (H72.-)

    H66.10   Chronic tubotympanic suppurative otitis media, unspecified

    H66.11   Chronic tubotympanic suppurative otitis media, right ear

    H66.12   Chronic tubotympanic suppurative otitis media, left ear

    H66.13   Chronic tubotympanic suppurative otitis media, bilateral

● **H66.2**   **Chronic atticoantral suppurative otitis media**

    Chronic atticoantral disease

    Use additional code for any associated perforated tympanic membrane (H72.-)

    H66.20   Chronic atticoantral suppurative otitis media, unspecified ear

    H66.21   Chronic atticoantral suppurative otitis media, right ear

    H66.22   Chronic atticoantral suppurative otitis media, left ear

    H66.23   Chronic atticoantral suppurative otitis media, bilateral

● **H66.3**   **Other chronic suppurative otitis media**

    Chronic suppurative otitis media NOS

    Use additional code for any associated perforated tympanic membrane (H72.-)

    Excludes1   tuberculous otitis media (A18.6)

● **H66.3X**   **Other chronic suppurative otitis media**

    H66.3X1   Other chronic suppurative otitis media, right ear

    H66.3X2   Other chronic suppurative otitis media, left ear

    H66.3X3   Other chronic suppurative otitis media, bilateral

    H66.3X9   Other chronic suppurative otitis media, unspecified ear

● **H66.4**   **Suppurative otitis media, unspecified**

    Purulent otitis media NOS

    Use additional code for any associated perforated tympanic membrane (H72.-)

    H66.40   Suppurative otitis media, unspecified, unspecified ear

    H66.41   Suppurative otitis media, unspecified, right ear

    H66.42   Suppurative otitis media, unspecified, left ear

    H66.43   Suppurative otitis media, unspecified, bilateral

● **H66.9**   **Otitis media, unspecified**

    Otitis media NOS
    Acute otitis media NOS
    Chronic otitis media NOS

    Use additional code for any associated perforated tympanic membrane (H72.-)

    H66.90   Otitis media, unspecified, unspecified ear

    H66.91   Otitis media, unspecified, right ear

    H66.92   Otitis media, unspecified, left ear

    H66.93   Otitis media, unspecified, bilateral

● **H67**   **Otitis media in diseases classified elsewhere**

    Code first underlying disease, such as:
    plasminogen deficiency (E88.02)
    viral disease NEC (B00-B34)

    Use additional code for any associated perforated tympanic membrane (H72.-)

    Excludes1   otitis media in:
       influenza (J09.X9, J10.83, J11.83)
       measles (B05.3)
       scarlet fever (A38.0)
       tuberculosis (A18.6)

▌ *H67.1*   *Otitis media in diseases classified elsewhere, right ear*

▌ *H67.2*   *Otitis media in diseases classified elsewhere, left ear*

▌ *H67.3*   *Otitis media in diseases classified elsewhere, bilateral*

▌ *H67.9*   *Otitis media in diseases classified elsewhere, unspecified ear*

● **H68**   **Eustachian salpingitis and obstruction**

    ● **H68.0**   **Eustachian salpingitis**

       ● **H68.00**   **Unspecified Eustachian salpingitis**

       H68.001   Unspecified Eustachian salpingitis, right ear

       H68.002   Unspecified Eustachian salpingitis, left ear

       H68.003   Unspecified Eustachian salpingitis, bilateral

       H68.009   Unspecified Eustachian salpingitis, unspecified ear

       ● **H68.01**   **Acute Eustachian salpingitis**

       H68.011   Acute Eustachian salpingitis, right ear

       H68.012   Acute Eustachian salpingitis, left ear

       H68.013   Acute Eustachian salpingitis, bilateral

       H68.019   Acute Eustachian salpingitis, unspecified ear

       ● **H68.02**   **Chronic Eustachian salpingitis**

       H68.021   Chronic Eustachian salpingitis, right ear

       H68.022   Chronic Eustachian salpingitis, left ear

       H68.023   Chronic Eustachian salpingitis, bilateral

       H68.029   Chronic Eustachian salpingitis, unspecified ear

▶ New   ⇒ Revised   ~~deleted~~ Deleted   Excludes 1   Excludes 2   Includes   Use additional   Code first   Code also   Key words

OGCR Official Guidelines   X Assign placeholder X   ● Use Additional Character(s)   ▌ Manifestation Code   ℂ Hierarchical Condition Category   Coding Clinic

● **H68.1   Obstruction of Eustachian tube**
    Stenosis of Eustachian tube
    Stricture of Eustachian tube

  ● **H68.10   Unspecified obstruction of Eustachian tube**

     H68.101   Unspecified obstruction of Eustachian tube, right ear

     H68.102   Unspecified obstruction of Eustachian tube, left ear

     H68.103   Unspecified obstruction of Eustachian tube, bilateral

     H68.109   Unspecified obstruction of Eustachian tube, unspecified ear

  ● **H68.11   Osseous obstruction of Eustachian tube**

     H68.111   Osseous obstruction of Eustachian tube, right ear

     H68.112   Osseous obstruction of Eustachian tube, left ear

     H68.113   Osseous obstruction of Eustachian tube, bilateral

     H68.119   Osseous obstruction of Eustachian tube, unspecified ear

  ● **H68.12   Intrinsic cartilagenous obstruction of Eustachian tube**

     H68.121   Intrinsic cartilagenous obstruction of Eustachian tube, right ear

     H68.122   Intrinsic cartilagenous obstruction of Eustachian tube, left ear

     H68.123   Intrinsic cartilagenous obstruction of Eustachian tube, bilateral

     H68.129   Intrinsic cartilagenous obstruction of Eustachian tube, unspecified ear

  ● **H68.13   Extrinsic cartilagenous obstruction of Eustachian tube**
     Compression of Eustachian tube

     H68.131   Extrinsic cartilagenous obstruction of Eustachian tube, right ear

     H68.132   Extrinsic cartilagenous obstruction of Eustachian tube, left ear

     H68.133   Extrinsic cartilagenous obstruction of Eustachian tube, bilateral

     H68.139   Extrinsic cartilagenous obstruction of Eustachian tube, unspecified ear

● **H69   Other and unspecified disorders of Eustachian tube**

  ● **H69.0   Patulous Eustachian tube**

     H69.00   Patulous Eustachian tube, unspecified ear

     H69.01   Patulous Eustachian tube, right ear

     H69.02   Patulous Eustachian tube, left ear

     H69.03   Patulous Eustachian tube, bilateral

  ● **H69.8   Other specified disorders of Eustachian tube**

     H69.80   Other specified disorders of Eustachian tube, unspecified ear

     H69.81   Other specified disorders of Eustachian tube, right ear

     H69.82   Other specified disorders of Eustachian tube, left ear

     H69.83   Other specified disorders of Eustachian tube, bilateral

  ● **H69.9   Unspecified Eustachian tube disorder**

     H69.90   Unspecified Eustachian tube disorder, unspecified ear

     H69.91   Unspecified Eustachian tube disorder, right ear

     H69.92   Unspecified Eustachian tube disorder, left ear

     H69.93   Unspecified Eustachian tube disorder, bilateral

● **H70   Mastoiditis and related conditions**

  ● **H70.0   Acute mastoiditis**
     Abscess of mastoid
     Empyema of mastoid

  ● **H70.00   Acute mastoiditis without complications**

     H70.001   Acute mastoiditis without complications, right ear

     H70.002   Acute mastoiditis without complications, left ear

     H70.003   Acute mastoiditis without complications, bilateral

     H70.009   Acute mastoiditis without complications, unspecified ear

  ● **H70.01   Subperiosteal abscess of mastoid**

     H70.011   Subperiosteal abscess of mastoid, right ear

     H70.012   Subperiosteal abscess of mastoid, left ear

     H70.013   Subperiosteal abscess of mastoid, bilateral

     H70.019   Subperiosteal abscess of mastoid, unspecified ear

  ● **H70.09   Acute mastoiditis with other complications**

     H70.091   Acute mastoiditis with other complications, right ear

     H70.092   Acute mastoiditis with other complications, left ear

     H70.093   Acute mastoiditis with other complications, bilateral

     H70.099   Acute mastoiditis with other complications, unspecified ear

  ● **H70.1   Chronic mastoiditis**
     Caries of mastoid
     Fistula of mastoid

     Excludes1   tuberculous mastoiditis (A18.03)

     H70.10   Chronic mastoiditis, unspecified ear

     H70.11   Chronic mastoiditis, right ear

     H70.12   Chronic mastoiditis, left ear

     H70.13   Chronic mastoiditis, bilateral

  ● **H70.2   Petrositis**
     Inflammation of petrous bone

  ● **H70.20   Unspecified petrositis**

     H70.201   Unspecified petrositis, right ear

     H70.202   Unspecified petrositis, left ear

     H70.203   Unspecified petrositis, bilateral

     H70.209   Unspecified petrositis, unspecified ear

  ● **H70.21   Acute petrositis**

     H70.211   Acute petrositis, right ear

     H70.212   Acute petrositis, left ear

     H70.213   Acute petrositis, bilateral

     H70.219   Acute petrositis, unspecified ear

  ● **H70.22   Chronic petrositis**

     H70.221   Chronic petrositis, right ear

     H70.222   Chronic petrositis, left ear

     H70.223   Chronic petrositis, bilateral

     H70.229   Chronic petrositis, unspecified ear

Item 8–1   Mastoiditis is an infection of the portion of the temporal bone of the skull that is behind the ear (mastoid process) caused by an untreated otitis media, leading to an infection of the surrounding structures which may include the brain.

CHAPTER 8 (H60-H95)

CHAPTER 8 (H60–H95)

- **H70.8 Other mastoiditis and related conditions**
  - **Excludes1** preauricular sinus and cyst (Q18.1)
    sinus, fistula, and cyst of branchial cleft
    (Q18.0)
  - **H70.81 Postauricular fistula**
    - H70.811 Postauricular fistula, **right ear**
    - H70.812 Postauricular fistula, **left ear**
    - H70.813 Postauricular fistula, **bilateral**
    - H70.819 Postauricular fistula, **unspecified ear**
  - **H70.89 Other mastoiditis and related conditions**
    - H70.891 Other mastoiditis and related
      conditions, **right ear**
    - H70.892 Other mastoiditis and related
      conditions, **left ear**
    - H70.893 Other mastoiditis and related
      conditions, **bilateral**
    - H70.899 Other mastoiditis and related
      conditions, **unspecified ear**
- **H70.9 Unspecified mastoiditis**
  - H70.90 Unspecified mastoiditis, **unspecified ear**
  - H70.91 Unspecified mastoiditis, **right ear**
  - H70.92 Unspecified mastoiditis, **left ear**
  - H70.93 Unspecified mastoiditis, **bilateral**

- **H71 Cholesteatoma of middle ear**
  - **Excludes2** cholesteatoma of external ear (H60.4-)
    recurrent cholesteatoma of postmastoidectomy
    cavity (H95.0-)
  - **H71.0 Cholesteatoma of attic**
    - H71.00 Cholesteatoma of attic, **unspecified** ear
    - H71.01 Cholesteatoma of attic, **right ear**
    - H71.02 Cholesteatoma of attic, **left ear**
    - H71.03 Cholesteatoma of attic, **bilateral**
  - **H71.1 Cholesteatoma of tympanum**
    - H71.10 Cholesteatoma of tympanum, **unspecified ear**
    - H71.11 Cholesteatoma of tympanum, **right ear**
    - H71.12 Cholesteatoma of tympanum, **left ear**
    - H71.13 Cholesteatoma of tympanum, **bilateral**
  - **H71.2 Cholesteatoma of mastoid**
    - H71.20 Cholesteatoma of mastoid, **unspecified ear**
    - H71.21 Cholesteatoma of mastoid, **right ear**
    - H71.22 Cholesteatoma of mastoid, **left ear**
    - H71.23 Cholesteatoma of mastoid, **bilateral**
  - **H71.3 Diffuse cholesteatosis**
    - H71.30 Diffuse cholesteatosis, **unspecified ear**
    - H71.31 Diffuse cholesteatosis, **right ear**
    - H71.32 Diffuse cholesteatosis, **left ear**
    - H71.33 Diffuse cholesteatosis, **bilateral**
  - **H71.9 Unspecified cholesteatoma**
    - H71.90 Unspecified cholesteatoma, **unspecified ear**
    - H71.91 Unspecified cholesteatoma, **right ear**
    - H71.92 Unspecified cholesteatoma, **left ear**
    - H71.93 Unspecified cholesteatoma, **bilateral**

★ **(See Plate 22 of the Anatomy Illustrations.)**

- **H72 Perforation of tympanic membrane**
  Hole or rupture in ear drum
  - **Includes** persistent post-traumatic perforation of ear drum
    postinflammatory perforation of ear drum
  - *Code first any associated otitis media (H65.-, H66.1-, H66.2-,
    H66.3-, H66.4-, H66.9-, H67.-)*
  - **Excludes1** acute suppurative otitis media with rupture of
    the tympanic membrane (H66.01-)
    traumatic rupture of ear drum (S09.2-)
  - **H72.0 Central perforation of tympanic membrane**
    - H72.00 Central perforation of tympanic membrane,
      unspecified ear
    - H72.01 Central perforation of tympanic membrane,
      right ear
    - H72.02 Central perforation of tympanic membrane, **left
      ear**
    - H72.03 Central perforation of tympanic membrane,
      bilateral
  - **H72.1 Attic perforation of tympanic membrane**
    Perforation of pars flaccida
    - H72.10 Attic perforation of tympanic membrane,
      unspecified ear
    - H72.11 Attic perforation of tympanic membrane, **right
      ear**
    - H72.12 Attic perforation of tympanic membrane, **left
      ear**
    - H72.13 Attic perforation of tympanic membrane,
      bilateral
  - **H72.2 Other marginal perforations of tympanic membrane**
    - **H72.2X Other marginal perforations of tympanic
      membrane**
      - H72.2X1 Other marginal perforations of
        tympanic membrane, **right ear**
      - H72.2X2 Other marginal perforations of
        tympanic membrane, **left ear**
      - H72.2X3 Other marginal perforations of
        tympanic membrane, **bilateral**
      - H72.2X9 Other marginal perforations of
        tympanic membrane, **unspecified ear**
  - **H72.8 Other perforations of tympanic membrane**
    - **H72.81 Multiple perforations of tympanic membrane**
      - H72.811 Multiple perforations of tympanic
        membrane, **right ear**
      - H72.812 Multiple perforations of tympanic
        membrane, **left ear**
      - H72.813 Multiple perforations of tympanic
        membrane, **bilateral**
      - H72.819 Multiple perforations of tympanic
        membrane, **unspecified ear**
    - **H72.82 Total perforations of tympanic membrane**
      - H72.821 Total perforations of tympanic
        membrane, **right ear**
      - H72.822 Total perforations of tympanic
        membrane, **left ear**
      - H72.823 Total perforations of tympanic
        membrane, **bilateral**
      - H72.829 Total perforations of tympanic
        membrane, **unspecified ear**
  - **H72.9 Unspecified perforation of tympanic membrane**
    - H72.90 Unspecified perforation of tympanic
      membrane, **unspecified ear**
    - H72.91 Unspecified perforation of tympanic
      membrane, **right ear**
    - H72.92 Unspecified perforation of tympanic
      membrane, **left ear**
    - H72.93 Unspecified perforation of tympanic
      membrane, **bilateral**

▶ New   ⇒ Revised   ~~deleted~~ Deleted   Excludes 1   Excludes 2   Includes   Use additional   Code first   Code also   Key words
OGCR Official Guidelines   X Assign placeholder X   ● Use Additional Character(s)   ▶ Manifestation Code   ⓗ Hierarchical Condition Category   Coding Clinic

● H73   **Other disorders of tympanic membrane**
  ● H73.0   **Acute myringitis**
      Excludes1   acute myringitis with otitis media (H65, H66)
    ● H73.00   **Unspecified acute myringitis**
         Acute tympanitis NOS
         H73.001   Acute myringitis, right ear
         H73.002   Acute myringitis, left ear
         H73.003   Acute myringitis, bilateral
         H73.009   Acute myringitis, unspecified ear
    ● H73.01   **Bullous myringitis**
         H73.011   Bullous myringitis, right ear
         H73.012   Bullous myringitis, left ear
         H73.013   Bullous myringitis, bilateral
         H73.019   Bullous myringitis, unspecified ear
    ● H73.09   **Other acute myringitis**
         H73.091   Other acute myringitis, right ear
         H73.092   Other acute myringitis, left ear
         H73.093   Other acute myringitis, bilateral
         H73.099   Other acute myringitis, unspecified ear
  ● H73.1   **Chronic myringitis**
       Chronic tympanitis
      Excludes1   chronic myringitis with otitis media (H65, H66)
     H73.10   Chronic myringitis, unspecified ear
     H73.11   Chronic myringitis, right ear
     H73.12   Chronic myringitis, left ear
     H73.13   Chronic myringitis, bilateral
  ● H73.2   **Unspecified myringitis**
     H73.20   Unspecified myringitis, unspecified ear
     H73.21   Unspecified myringitis, right ear
     H73.22   Unspecified myringitis, left ear
     H73.23   Unspecified myringitis, bilateral
  ● H73.8   **Other specified disorders of tympanic membrane**
    ● H73.81   **Atrophic flaccid tympanic membrane**
         H73.811   Atrophic flaccid tympanic membrane, right ear
         H73.812   Atrophic flaccid tympanic membrane, left ear
         H73.813   Atrophic flaccid tympanic membrane, bilateral
         H73.819   Atrophic flaccid tympanic membrane, unspecified ear
    ● H73.82   **Atrophic nonflaccid tympanic membrane**
         H73.821   Atrophic nonflaccid tympanic membrane, right ear
         H73.822   Atrophic nonflaccid tympanic membrane, left ear
         H73.823   Atrophic nonflaccid tympanic membrane, bilateral
         H73.829   Atrophic nonflaccid tympanic membrane, unspecified ear
    ● H73.89   **Other specified disorders of tympanic membrane**
         H73.891   Other specified disorders of tympanic membrane, right ear
         H73.892   Other specified disorders of tympanic membrane, left ear
         H73.893   Other specified disorders of tympanic membrane, bilateral
         H73.899   Other specified disorders of tympanic membrane, unspecified ear

● H73.9   **Unspecified disorder of tympanic membrane**
     H73.90   Unspecified disorder of tympanic membrane, unspecified ear
     H73.91   Unspecified disorder of tympanic membrane, right ear
     H73.92   Unspecified disorder of tympanic membrane, left ear
     H73.93   Unspecified disorder of tympanic membrane, bilateral

● H74   **Other disorders of middle ear mastoid**
      Excludes2   mastoiditis (H70.-)
  ● H74.0   **Tympanosclerosis**
     H74.01   Tympanosclerosis, right ear
     H74.02   Tympanosclerosis, left ear
     H74.03   Tympanosclerosis, bilateral
     H74.09   Tympanosclerosis, unspecified ear
  ● H74.1   **Adhesive middle ear disease**
       Adhesive otitis
      Excludes1   glue ear (H65.3-)
     H74.11   Adhesive right middle ear disease
     H74.12   Adhesive left middle ear disease
     H74.13   Adhesive middle ear disease, bilateral
     H74.19   Adhesive middle ear disease, unspecified ear
  ● H74.2   **Discontinuity and dislocation of ear ossicles**
     H74.20   Discontinuity and dislocation of ear ossicles, unspecified ear
     H74.21   Discontinuity and dislocation of right ear ossicles
     H74.22   Discontinuity and dislocation of left ear ossicles
     H74.23   Discontinuity and dislocation of ear ossicles, bilateral
  ● H74.3   **Other acquired abnormalities of ear ossicles**
    ● H74.31   **Ankylosis of ear ossicles**
         H74.311   Ankylosis of ear ossicles, right ear
         H74.312   Ankylosis of ear ossicles, left ear
         H74.313   Ankylosis of ear ossicles, bilateral
         H74.319   Ankylosis of ear ossicles, unspecified ear
    ● H74.32   **Partial loss of ear ossicles**
         H74.321   Partial loss of ear ossicles, right ear
         H74.322   Partial loss of ear ossicles, left ear
         H74.323   Partial loss of ear ossicles, bilateral
         H74.329   Partial loss of ear ossicles, unspecified ear
    ● H74.39   **Other acquired abnormalities of ear ossicles**
         H74.391   Other acquired abnormalities of right ear ossicles
         H74.392   Other acquired abnormalities of left ear ossicles
         H74.393   Other acquired abnormalities of ear ossicles, bilateral
         H74.399   Other acquired abnormalities of ear ossicles, unspecified ear
  ● H74.4   **Polyp of middle ear**
     H74.40   Polyp of middle ear, unspecified ear
     H74.41   Polyp of right middle ear
     H74.42   Polyp of left middle ear
     H74.43   Polyp of middle ear, bilateral

CHAPTER 8 (H60-H95)

N Newborn Age: 0   **P** Pediatric Age: 0–17   **M** Maternity DX: 12–55   **A** Adult Age: 15–124   ♀ Females Only   ♂ Males Only

867

● H74.8   Other specified disorders of middle ear and mastoid

    ● H74.8X   Other specified disorders of middle ear and mastoid

       H74.8X1   Other specified disorders of right middle ear and mastoid

       H74.8X2   Other specified disorders of left middle ear and mastoid

       H74.8X3   Other specified disorders of middle ear and mastoid, bilateral

       H74.8X9   Other specified disorders of middle ear and mastoid, unspecified ear

● H74.9   Unspecified disorder of middle ear and mastoid

    H74.90   Unspecified disorder of middle ear and mastoid, unspecified ear

    H74.91   Unspecified disorder of right middle ear and mastoid

    H74.92   Unspecified disorder of left middle ear and mastoid

    H74.93   Unspecified disorder of middle ear and mastoid, bilateral

● H75   Other disorders of middle ear and mastoid in diseases classified elsewhere

    Code first underlying disease

    ● H75.0   Mastoiditis in infectious and parasitic diseases classified elsewhere

       Excludes1   mastoiditis (in):
                         syphilis (A52.77)
                         tuberculosis (A18.03)

      ▷ *H75.00*   *Mastoiditis in infectious and parasitic diseases classified elsewhere, unspecified ear*

      ▷ *H75.01*   *Mastoiditis in infectious and parasitic diseases classified elsewhere, right ear*

      ▷ *H75.02*   *Mastoiditis in infectious and parasitic diseases classified elsewhere, left ear*

      ▷ *H75.03*   *Mastoiditis in infectious and parasitic diseases classified elsewhere, bilateral*

    ● H75.8   Other specified disorders of middle ear and mastoid in diseases classified elsewhere

      ▷ *H75.80*   *Other specified disorders of middle ear and mastoid in diseases classified elsewhere, unspecified ear*

      ▷ *H75.81*   *Other specified disorders of right middle ear and mastoid in diseases classified elsewhere*

      ▷ *H75.82*   *Other specified disorders of left middle ear and mastoid in diseases classified elsewhere*

      ▷ *H75.83*   *Other specified disorders of middle ear and mastoid in diseases classified elsewhere, bilateral*

DISEASES OF INNER EAR (H80-H83)

★ **(See Plate 23 of the Anatomy Illustrations.)**

● H80   Otosclerosis

    Inherited middle ear spongelike bone growth causing hearing loss

    Includes   Otospongiosis

    ● H80.0   Otosclerosis involving oval window, nonobliterative

      H80.00   Otosclerosis involving oval window, nonobliterative, unspecified ear

      H80.01   Otosclerosis involving oval window, nonobliterative, right ear

      H80.02   Otosclerosis involving oval window, nonobliterative, left ear

      H80.03   Otosclerosis involving oval window, nonobliterative, bilateral

● H80.1   Otosclerosis involving oval window, obliterative

    H80.10   Otosclerosis involving oval window, obliterative, unspecified ear

    H80.11   Otosclerosis involving oval window, obliterative, right ear

    H80.12   Otosclerosis involving oval window, obliterative, left ear

    H80.13   Otosclerosis involving oval window, obliterative, bilateral

● H80.2   Cochlear otosclerosis

    Otosclerosis involving otic capsule
    Otosclerosis involving round window

    H80.20   Cochlear otosclerosis, unspecified ear

    H80.21   Cochlear otosclerosis, right ear

    H80.22   Cochlear otosclerosis, left ear

    H80.23   Cochlear otosclerosis, bilateral

● H80.8   Other otosclerosis

    H80.80   Other otosclerosis, unspecified ear

    H80.81   Other otosclerosis, right ear

    H80.82   Other otosclerosis, left ear

    H80.83   Other otosclerosis, bilateral

● H80.9   Unspecified otosclerosis

    H80.90   Unspecified otosclerosis, unspecified ear

    H80.91   Unspecified otosclerosis, right ear

    H80.92   Unspecified otosclerosis, left ear

    H80.93   Unspecified otosclerosis, bilateral

● H81   Disorders of vestibular function

    Excludes1   epidemic vertigo (A88.1)
                  vertigo NOS (R42)

    ● H81.0   Ménière's disease

      Vestibular disorder that produces recurring symptoms including severe and intermittent hearing loss including the feeling of ear pressure or pain

      Labyrinthine hydrops
      Ménière's syndrome or vertigo

      H81.01   Ménière's disease, right ear

      H81.02   Ménière's disease, left ear

      H81.03   Ménière's disease, bilateral

      H81.09   Ménière's disease, unspecified ear

    ● H81.1   Benign paroxysmal vertigo

      H81.10   Benign paroxysmal vertigo, unspecified ear

      H81.11   Benign paroxysmal vertigo, right ear

      H81.12   Benign paroxysmal vertigo, left ear

      H81.13   Benign paroxysmal vertigo, bilateral

    ● H81.2   Vestibular neuronitis

      H81.20   Vestibular neuronitis, unspecified ear

      H81.21   Vestibular neuronitis, right ear

      H81.22   Vestibular neuronitis, left ear

      H81.23   Vestibular neuronitis, bilateral

    ● H81.3   Other peripheral vertigo

      ● H81.31   Aural vertigo

        H81.311   Aural vertigo, right ear

        H81.312   Aural vertigo, left ear

        H81.313   Aural vertigo, bilateral

        H81.319   Aural vertigo, unspecified ear

      ● H81.39   Other peripheral vertigo

        Lermoyez' syndrome
        Otogenic vertigo
        Peripheral vertigo NOS

        H81.391   Other peripheral vertigo, right ear

        H81.392   Other peripheral vertigo, left ear

        H81.393   Other peripheral vertigo, bilateral

        H81.399   Other peripheral vertigo, unspecified ear

    H81.4   Vertigo of central origin
      Central positional nystagmus

CHAPTER 8 (H60-H95)

▶ New   ⫸ Revised   ~~deleted~~ Deleted   Excludes 1   Excludes 2   Includes   Use additional   Code first   Code also   Key words

OGCR Official Guidelines   X Assign placeholder X   ● Use Additional Character(s)   ▷ Manifestation Code   🔗 Hierarchical Condition Category   **Coding Clinic**

● H81.8   Other disorders of vestibular function
    ● H81.8X   Other disorders of vestibular function
       H81.8X1   Other disorders of vestibular function, right ear
       H81.8X2   Other disorders of vestibular function, left ear
       H81.8X3   Other disorders of vestibular function, bilateral
       H81.8X9   Other disorders of vestibular function, unspecified ear

● H81.9   Unspecified disorder of vestibular function
       Vertiginous syndrome NOS
    H81.90   Unspecified disorder of vestibular function, unspecified ear
    H81.91   Unspecified disorder of vestibular function, right ear
    H81.92   Unspecified disorder of vestibular function, left ear
    H81.93   Unspecified disorder of vestibular function, bilateral

● H82   Vertiginous syndromes in diseases classified elsewhere
    Code first underlying disease
    Excludes1   epidemic vertigo (A88.1)
    ▶ *H82.1*   *Vertiginous syndromes in diseases classified elsewhere, right ear*
    ▶ *H82.2*   *Vertiginous syndromes in diseases classified elsewhere, left ear*
    ▶ *H82.3*   *Vertiginous syndromes in diseases classified elsewhere, bilateral*
    ▶ *H82.9*   *Vertiginous syndromes in diseases classified elsewhere, unspecified ear*

● H83   Other diseases of inner ear
    ● H83.0   Labyrinthitis
       Balance disorder that follows URI or head injury
       H83.01   Labyrinthitis, right ear
       H83.02   Labyrinthitis, left ear
       H83.03   Labyrinthitis, bilateral
       H83.09   Labyrinthitis, unspecified ear
    ● H83.1   Labyrinthine fistula
       H83.11   Labyrinthine fistula, right ear
       H83.12   Labyrinthine fistula, left ear
       H83.13   Labyrinthine fistula, bilateral
       H83.19   Labyrinthine fistula, unspecified ear
    ● H83.2   Labyrinthine dysfunction
       Labyrinthine hypersensitivity
       Labyrinthine hypofunction
       Labyrinthine loss of function
      ● H83.2X   Labyrinthine dysfunction
         H83.2X1   Labyrinthine dysfunction, right ear
         H83.2X2   Labyrinthine dysfunction, left ear
         H83.2X3   Labyrinthine dysfunction, bilateral
         H83.2X9   Labyrinthine dysfunction, unspecified ear
    ● H83.3   Noise effects on inner ear
       Acoustic trauma of inner ear
       Noise-induced hearing loss of inner ear
      ● H83.3X   Noise effects on inner ear
         H83.3X1   Noise effects on right inner ear
         H83.3X2   Noise effects on left inner ear
         H83.3X3   Noise effects on inner ear, bilateral
         H83.3X9   Noise effects on inner ear, unspecified ear

● H83.8   Other specified diseases of inner ear
    ● H83.8X   Other specified diseases of inner ear
       H83.8X1   Other specified diseases of right inner ear
       H83.8X2   Other specified diseases of left inner ear
       H83.8X3   Other specified diseases of inner ear, bilateral
       H83.8X9   Other specified diseases of inner ear, unspecified ear

● H83.9   Unspecified disease of inner ear
    H83.90   Unspecified disease of inner ear, unspecified ear
    H83.91   Unspecified disease of right inner ear
    H83.92   Unspecified disease of left inner ear
    H83.93   Unspecified disease of inner ear, bilateral

OTHER DISORDERS OF EAR (H90-H94)

● H90   Conductive and sensorineural hearing loss
    Excludes1   deaf nonspeaking NEC (H91.3)
       deafness NOS (H91.9-)
       hearing loss NOS (H91.9-)
       noise-induced hearing loss (H83.3-)
       ototoxic hearing loss (H91.0-)
       sudden (idiopathic) hearing loss (H91.2-)
    H90.0   Conductive hearing loss, bilateral
    ● H90.1   Conductive hearing loss, unilateral with unrestricted hearing on the contralateral side
       H90.11   Conductive hearing loss, unilateral, right ear, with unrestricted hearing on the contralateral side
       H90.12   Conductive hearing loss, unilateral, left ear, with unrestricted hearing on the contralateral side
    H90.2   Conductive hearing loss, unspecified
       Conductive deafness NOS
    H90.3   Sensorineural hearing loss, bilateral
    ● H90.4   Sensorineural hearing loss, unilateral with unrestricted hearing on the contralateral side
       H90.41   Sensorineural hearing loss, unilateral, right ear, with unrestricted hearing on the contralateral side
       H90.42   Sensorineural hearing loss, unilateral, left ear, with unrestricted hearing on the contralateral side
    H90.5   Unspecified sensorineural hearing loss
       Central hearing loss NOS
       Congenital deafness NOS
       Neural hearing loss NOS
       Perceptive hearing loss NOS
       Sensorineural deafness NOS
       Sensory hearing loss NOS
       Excludes1   abnormal auditory perception (H93.2-)
         psychogenic deafness (F44.6)
    H90.6   Mixed conductive and sensorineural hearing loss, bilateral
       Coding Clinic: 2015, Q2, P7
    ● H90.7   Mixed conductive and sensorineural hearing loss, unilateral with unrestricted hearing on the contralateral side
       H90.71   Mixed conductive and sensorineural hearing loss, unilateral, right ear, with unrestricted hearing on the contralateral side
       H90.72   Mixed conductive and sensorineural hearing loss, unilateral, left ear, with unrestricted hearing on the contralateral side
    H90.8   Mixed conductive and sensorineural hearing loss, unspecified

● **H90.A** **Conductive and sensorineural hearing loss with restricted hearing on the contralateral side**
Coding Clinic: 2016, Q4, P23-24

   ● **H90.A1** Conductive hearing loss, unilateral, with restricted hearing on the contralateral side

      H90.A11 Conductive hearing loss, unilateral, right ear with restricted hearing on the contralateral side

      H90.A12 Conductive hearing loss, unilateral, left ear with restricted hearing on the contralateral side
Coding Clinic: 2016, Q4, P25

   ● **H90.A2** Sensorineural hearing loss, unilateral, with restricted hearing on the contralateral side

      H90.A21 Sensorineural hearing loss, unilateral, right ear, with restricted hearing on the contralateral side

      H90.A22 Sensorineural hearing loss, unilateral, left ear, with restricted hearing on the contralateral side

   ● **H90.A3** Mixed conductive and sensorineural hearing loss, unilateral with restricted hearing on the contralateral side

      H90.A31 Mixed conductive and sensorineural hearing loss, unilateral, right ear with restricted hearing on the contralateral side

      H90.A32 Mixed conductive and sensorineural hearing loss, unilateral, left ear with restricted hearing on the contralateral side

● **H91** **Other and unspecified hearing loss**

   Excludes1 abnormal auditory perception (H93.2-)
hearing loss as classified in H90.-
impacted cerumen (H61.2-)
noise-induced hearing loss (H83.3-)
psychogenic deafness (F44.6)
transient ischemic deafness (H93.01-)

   ● **H91.0** Ototoxic hearing loss

      Code first poisoning due to drug or toxin, if applicable (T36-T65 with fifth or sixth character 1-4 or 6)

      Use additional code for adverse effect, if applicable, to identify drug (T36-T50 with fifth or sixth character 5)

      H91.01 Ototoxic hearing loss, right ear

      H91.02 Ototoxic hearing loss, left ear

      H91.03 Ototoxic hearing loss, bilateral

      H91.09 Ototoxic hearing loss, unspecified ear

   ● **H91.1** Presbycusis
Presbyacusia

      H91.10 Presbycusis, unspecified ear

      H91.11 Presbycusis, right ear

      H91.12 Presbycusis, left ear

      H91.13 Presbycusis, bilateral

   ● **H91.2** Sudden idiopathic hearing loss
Sudden hearing loss NOS

      H91.20 Sudden idiopathic hearing loss, unspecified ear

      H91.21 Sudden idiopathic hearing loss, right ear

      H91.22 Sudden idiopathic hearing loss, left ear

      H91.23 Sudden idiopathic hearing loss, bilateral

   H91.3 Deaf nonspeaking, not elsewhere classified

   ● **H91.8** Other specified hearing loss

      ● **H91.8X** Other specified hearing loss

         H91.8X1 Other specified hearing loss, right ear

         H91.8X2 Other specified hearing loss, left ear

         H91.8X3 Other specified hearing loss, bilateral

         H91.8X9 Other specified hearing loss, unspecified ear

● **H91.9** **Unspecified hearing loss**
Deafness NOS
High frequency deafness
Low frequency deafness

      H91.90 Unspecified hearing loss, unspecified ear

      H91.91 Unspecified hearing loss, right ear

      H91.92 Unspecified hearing loss, left ear

      H91.93 Unspecified hearing loss, bilateral

● **H92** **Otalgia and effusion of ear**

   ● **H92.0** Otalgia

      H92.01 Otalgia, right ear

      H92.02 Otalgia, left ear

      H92.03 Otalgia, bilateral

      H92.09 Otalgia, unspecified ear

   ● **H92.1** Otorrhea

      Excludes1 leakage of cerebrospinal fluid through ear (G96.0)

      H92.10 Otorrhea, unspecified ear

      H92.11 Otorrhea, right ear

      H92.12 Otorrhea, left ear

      H92.13 Otorrhea, bilateral

   ● **H92.2** Otorrhagia

      Excludes1 traumatic otorrhagia - code to injury

      H92.20 Otorrhagia, unspecified ear

      H92.21 Otorrhagia, right ear

      H92.22 Otorrhagia, left ear

      H92.23 Otorrhagia, bilateral

● **H93** **Other disorders of ear, not elsewhere classified**

   ● **H93.0** Degenerative and vascular disorders of ear

      Excludes1 presbycusis (H91.1)

     ● **H93.01** Transient ischemic deafness

         H93.011 Transient ischemic deafness, right ear

         H93.012 Transient ischemic deafness, left ear

         H93.013 Transient ischemic deafness, bilateral

         H93.019 Transient ischemic deafness, unspecified ear

     ● **H93.09** Unspecified degenerative and vascular disorders of ear

         H93.091 Unspecified degenerative and vascular disorders of right ear

         H93.092 Unspecified degenerative and vascular disorders of left ear

         H93.093 Unspecified degenerative and vascular disorders of ear, bilateral

         H93.099 Unspecified degenerative and vascular disorders of unspecified ear

   ● **H93.1** Tinnitus
Perception of sound (ringing, buzzing, humming, whistling tunes, or singing)

      H93.11 Tinnitus, right ear

      H93.12 Tinnitus, left ear

      H93.13 Tinnitus, bilateral

      H93.19 Tinnitus, unspecified ear

   ● **H93.A** Pulsatile tinnitus
Coding Clinic: 2016, Q4, P25

      H93.A1 Pulsatile tinnitus, right ear
Coding Clinic: 2016, Q4, P26

      H93.A2 Pulsatile tinnitus, left ear

      H93.A3 Pulsatile tinnitus, bilateral

      H93.A9 Pulsatile tinnitus, unspecified ear

▶ New   ⇒ Revised   ~~deleted~~ Deleted   Excludes 1   Excludes 2   Includes   Use additional   Code first   Code also   Key words

OGCR Official Guidelines   X Assign placeholder X   ● Use Additional Character(s)   ▶ Manifestation Code   🏥 Hierarchical Condition Category   **Coding Clinic**

● **H93.2**   **Other abnormal auditory perceptions**
     Excludes2   auditory hallucinations (R44.0)
  ● **H93.21**   Auditory recruitment
       H93.211   Auditory recruitment, right ear
       H93.212   Auditory recruitment, left ear
       H93.213   Auditory recruitment, bilateral
       H93.219   Auditory recruitment, unspecified ear
  ● **H93.22**   Diplacusis
       H93.221   Diplacusis, right ear
       H93.222   Diplacusis, left ear
       H93.223   Diplacusis, bilateral
       H93.229   Diplacusis, unspecified ear
  ● **H93.23**   Hyperacusis
       H93.231   Hyperacusis, right ear
       H93.232   Hyperacusis, left ear
       H93.233   Hyperacusis, bilateral
       H93.239   Hyperacusis, unspecified ear
  ● **H93.24**   Temporary auditory threshold shift
       H93.241   Temporary auditory threshold shift, right ear
       H93.242   Temporary auditory threshold shift, left ear
       H93.243   Temporary auditory threshold shift, bilateral
       H93.249   Temporary auditory threshold shift, unspecified ear
    H93.25   Central auditory processing disorder
         Congenital auditory imperception
         Word deafness
         Excludes1   mixed receptive-expressive language disorder (F80.2)
  ● **H93.29**   Other abnormal auditory perceptions
       H93.291   Other abnormal auditory perceptions, right ear
       H93.292   Other abnormal auditory perceptions, left ear
       H93.293   Other abnormal auditory perceptions, bilateral
       H93.299   Other abnormal auditory perceptions, unspecified ear
● **H93.3**   **Disorders of acoustic nerve**
     Disorder of 8th cranial nerve
     Excludes1   acoustic neuroma (D33.3)
             syphilitic acoustic neuritis (A52.15)
  ● **H93.3X**   Disorders of acoustic nerve
       H93.3X1   Disorders of right acoustic nerve
       H93.3X2   Disorders of left acoustic nerve
       H93.3X3   Disorders of bilateral acoustic nerves
       H93.3X9   Disorders of unspecified acoustic nerve
● **H93.8**   **Other specified disorders of ear**
  ● **H93.8X**   Other specified disorders of ear
       H93.8X1   Other specified disorders of right ear
       H93.8X2   Other specified disorders of left ear
       H93.8X3   Other specified disorders of ear, bilateral
       H93.8X9   Other specified disorders of ear, unspecified ear
● **H93.9**   **Unspecified disorder of ear**
     H93.90   Unspecified disorder of ear, unspecified ear
     H93.91   Unspecified disorder of right ear
     H93.92   Unspecified disorder of left ear
     H93.93   Unspecified disorder of ear, bilateral

● **H94**   **Other disorders of ear in diseases classified elsewhere**
  ● **H94.0**   Acoustic neuritis in infectious and parasitic diseases classified elsewhere
       Code first underlying disease, such as:
         parasitic disease (B65-B89)
       Excludes1   acoustic neuritis (in):
                 herpes zoster (B02.29)
                 syphilis (A52.15)
     ▷ *H94.00*   *Acoustic neuritis in infectious and parasitic diseases classified elsewhere, unspecified ear*
     ▷ *H94.01*   *Acoustic neuritis in infectious and parasitic diseases classified elsewhere, right ear*
     ▷ *H94.02*   *Acoustic neuritis in infectious and parasitic diseases classified elsewhere, left ear*
     ▷ *H94.03*   *Acoustic neuritis in infectious and parasitic diseases classified elsewhere, bilateral*
  ● **H94.8**   Other specified disorders of ear in diseases classified elsewhere
       Code first underlying disease, such as:
         congenital syphilis (A50.0)
       Excludes1   aural myiasis (B87.4)
                 syphilitic labyrinthitis (A52.79)
     ▷ *H94.80*   *Other specified disorders of ear in diseases classified elsewhere, unspecified ear*
     ▷ *H94.81*   *Other specified disorders of right ear in diseases classified elsewhere*
     ▷ *H94.82*   *Other specified disorders of left ear in diseases classified elsewhere*
     ▷ *H94.83*   *Other specified disorders of ear in diseases classified elsewhere, bilateral*

INTRAOPERATIVE AND POSTPROCEDURAL COMPLICATIONS AND DISORDERS OF EAR AND MASTOID PROCESS, NOT ELSEWHERE CLASSIFIED (H95)

● **H95**   Intraoperative and postprocedural complications and disorders of ear and mastoid process, not elsewhere classified
     Coding Clinic: 2016, Q4, P10
  ● **H95.0**   Recurrent cholesteatoma of postmastoidectomy cavity
       H95.00   Recurrent cholesteatoma of postmastoidectomy cavity, unspecified ear
       H95.01   Recurrent cholesteatoma of postmastoidectomy cavity, right ear
       H95.02   Recurrent cholesteatoma of postmastoidectomy cavity, left ear
       H95.03   Recurrent cholesteatoma of postmastoidectomy cavity, bilateral ears
  ● **H95.1**   Other disorders of ear and mastoid process following mastoidectomy
   ● **H95.11**   Chronic inflammation of postmastoidectomy cavity
       H95.111   Chronic inflammation of postmastoidectomy cavity, right ear
       H95.112   Chronic inflammation of postmastoidectomy cavity, left ear
       H95.113   Chronic inflammation of postmastoidectomy cavity, bilateral ears
       H95.119   Chronic inflammation of postmastoidectomy cavity, unspecified ear
   ● **H95.12**   Granulation of postmastoidectomy cavity
       H95.121   Granulation of postmastoidectomy cavity, right ear
       H95.122   Granulation of postmastoidectomy cavity, left ear
       H95.123   Granulation of postmastoidectomy cavity, bilateral ears
       H95.129   Granulation of postmastoidectomy cavity, unspecified ear

● **H95.13** Mucosal cyst of postmastoidectomy cavity
    H95.131 Mucosal cyst of postmastoidectomy cavity, **right ear**
    H95.132 Mucosal cyst of postmastoidectomy cavity, **left ear**
    H95.133 Mucosal cyst of postmastoidectomy cavity, **bilateral ears**
    H95.139 Mucosal cyst of postmastoidectomy cavity, **unspecified ear**
● **H95.19** Other disorders following mastoidectomy
    H95.191 Other disorders following mastoidectomy, **right ear**
    H95.192 Other disorders following mastoidectomy, **left ear**
    H95.193 Other disorders following mastoidectomy, **bilateral ears**
    H95.199 Other disorders following mastoidectomy, **unspecified ear**
● **H95.2** Intraoperative hemorrhage and hematoma of ear and mastoid process complicating a procedure

Excludes1 intraoperative hemorrhage and hematoma of ear and mastoid process due to accidental puncture or laceration during a procedure (H95.3-)

    H95.21 Intraoperative hemorrhage and hematoma of ear and mastoid process complicating a procedure on the ear and mastoid process
    H95.22 Intraoperative hemorrhage and hematoma of ear and mastoid process complicating other procedure
● **H95.3** Accidental puncture and laceration of ear and mastoid process during a procedure
    H95.31 Accidental puncture and laceration of the ear and mastoid process during a procedure on the ear and mastoid process
    H95.32 Accidental puncture and laceration of the ear and mastoid process during other procedure
● **H95.4** Postprocedural hemorrhage of ear and mastoid process following a procedure
    H95.41 Postprocedural hemorrhage of ear and mastoid process following a procedure on the ear and mastoid process
    H95.42 Postprocedural hemorrhage of ear and mastoid process following other procedure
● **H95.5** Postprocedural hematoma and seroma of ear and mastoid process following a procedure

H95.51 Postprocedural hematoma of ear and mastoid process following a procedure on the ear and mastoid process
H95.52 Postprocedural hematoma of ear and mastoid process following other procedure
H95.53 Postprocedural seroma of ear and mastoid process following a procedure on the ear and mastoid process
H95.54 Postprocedural seroma of ear and mastoid process following other procedure
● **H95.8** Other intraoperative and postprocedural complications and disorders of the ear and mastoid process, not elsewhere classified

Excludes2 postprocedural complications and disorders following mastoidectomy (H95.0-, H95.1-)

● **H95.81** Postprocedural stenosis of external ear canal
    H95.811 Postprocedural stenosis of right external ear canal
    H95.812 Postprocedural stenosis of left external ear canal
    H95.813 Postprocedural stenosis of external ear canal, bilateral
    H95.819 Postprocedural stenosis of unspecified external ear canal
    H95.88 Other intraoperative complications and disorders of the ear and mastoid process, not elsewhere classified

Use additional code, if applicable, to further specify disorder

    H95.89 Other postprocedural complications and disorders of the ear and mastoid process, not elsewhere classified

Use additional code, if applicable, to further specify disorder

CHAPTER 9

DISEASES OF THE CIRCULATORY SYSTEM
(I00-I99)

OGCR Chapter-Specific Coding Guidelines

9. Chapter 9: Diseases of the Circulatory System (I00-I99)

a. Hypertension

The classification presumes a causal relationship between hypertension and heart involvement and between hypertension and kidney involvement, as the two conditions are linked by the term "with" in the Alphabetic Index. These conditions should be coded as related even in the absence of provider documentation explicitly linking them, unless the documentation clearly states the conditions are unrelated.

For hypertension and conditions not specifically linked by relational terms such as "with," "associated with" or "due to" in the classification, provider documentation must link the conditions in order to code them as related.

1) Hypertension with Heart Disease

Hypertension with heart conditions classified to I50.- or I51.4-I51.7, I51.89, I51.9, are assigned to, a code from category I11, Hypertensive heart disease. Use additional code(s) from category I50, Heart failure, to identify the type(s) of heart failure in those patients with heart failure.

The same heart conditions (I50.-, I51.4-I51.7, I51.89, I51.9) with hypertension, are coded separately if the provider has documented they are unrelated to the hypertension. Sequence according to the circumstances of the admission/encounter.

2) Hypertensive Chronic Kidney Disease

Assign codes from category I12, Hypertensive chronic kidney disease, when both hypertension and a condition classifiable to category N18, Chronic kidney disease (CKD), are present. CKD should not be coded as hypertension if the provider indicates the CKD is not related to the hypertension.

The appropriate code from category N18 should be used as a secondary code with a code from category I12 to identify the stage of chronic kidney disease.

See Section I.C.14. Chronic kidney disease.

If a patient has hypertensive chronic kidney disease and acute renal failure, an additional code for the acute renal failure is required.

3) Hypertensive Heart and Chronic Kidney Disease

Assign codes from combination category I13, Hypertensive heart and chronic kidney disease, when there is hypertension with both heart and kidney involvement. If heart failure is present, assign an additional code from category I50 to identify the type of heart failure.

The appropriate code from category N18, Chronic kidney disease, should be used as a secondary code with a code from category I13 to identify the stage of chronic kidney disease.

See Section I.C.14. Chronic kidney disease.

The codes in category I13, Hypertensive heart and chronic kidney disease, are combination codes that include hypertension, heart disease and chronic kidney disease. The Includes note at I13 specifies that the conditions included at I11 and I12 are included together in I13. If a patient has hypertension, heart disease and chronic kidney disease then a code from I13 should be used, not individual codes for hypertension, heart disease and chronic kidney disease, or codes from I11 or I12.

For patients with both acute renal failure and chronic kidney disease an additional code for acute renal failure is required.

4) Hypertensive Cerebrovascular Disease

For hypertensive cerebrovascular disease, first assign the appropriate code from categories I60-I69, followed by the appropriate hypertension code.

5) Hypertensive Retinopathy

Subcategory H35.0, Background retinopathy and retinal vascular changes, should be used with a code from category I10 – I15, Hypertensive disease to include the systemic hypertension. The sequencing is based on the reason for the encounter.

6) Hypertension, Secondary

Secondary hypertension is due to an underlying condition. Two codes are required: one to identify the underlying etiology and one from category I15 to identify the hypertension. Sequencing of codes is determined by the reason for admission/encounter.

7) Hypertension, Transient

Assign code R03.0, Elevated blood pressure reading without diagnosis of hypertension, unless patient has an established diagnosis of hypertension. Assign code O13.-, Gestational [pregnancy-induced] hypertension without significant proteinuria, or O14.-, Pre-eclampsia, for transient hypertension of pregnancy.

8) Hypertension, Controlled

This diagnostic statement usually refers to an existing state of hypertension under control by therapy. Assign the appropriate code from categories I10-I15, Hypertensive diseases.

9) Hypertension, Uncontrolled

Uncontrolled hypertension may refer to untreated hypertension or hypertension not responding to current therapeutic regimen. In either case, assign the appropriate code from categories I10-I15, Hypertensive diseases.

10) Hypertensive Crisis

Assign a code from category I16, Hypertensive crisis, for documented hypertensive urgency, hypertensive emergency or unspecified hypertensive crisis. Code also any identified hypertensive disease (I10-I15). The sequencing is based on the reason for the encounter.

11) Pulmonary Hypertension

Pulmonary hypertension is classified to category I27, Other pulmonary heart diseases. For secondary pulmonary hypertension (I27.1, I27.2-), code also any associated conditions or adverse effects of drugs or toxins. The sequencing is based on the reason for the encounter, except for adverse effects of drugs.

See Section I.C.19.e Adverse Effects, Poisoning, Underdosing and Toxic Effects.

b. Atherosclerotic Coronary Artery Disease and Angina

ICD-10-CM has combination codes for atherosclerotic heart disease with angina pectoris. The subcategories for these codes are I25.11, Atherosclerotic heart disease of native coronary artery with angina pectoris and I25.7, Atherosclerosis of coronary artery bypass graft(s) and coronary artery of transplanted heart with angina pectoris.

When using one of these combination codes it is not necessary to use an additional code for angina pectoris. A causal relationship can be assumed in a patient with both atherosclerosis and angina pectoris, unless the documentation indicates the angina is due to something other than the atherosclerosis.

If a patient with coronary artery disease is admitted due to an acute myocardial infarction (AMI), the AMI should be sequenced before the coronary artery disease.

See Section I.C.9. Acute myocardial infarction (AMI).

c. Intraoperative and Postprocedural Cerebrovascular Accident

Medical record documentation should clearly specify the cause-and-effect relationship between the medical intervention and the cerebrovascular accident in order to assign a code for intraoperative or postprocedural cerebrovascular accident.

Proper code assignment depends on whether it was an infarction or hemorrhage and whether it occurred intraoperatively or postoperatively. If it was a cerebral hemorrhage, code assignment depends on the type of procedure performed.

d. Sequelae of Cerebrovascular Disease

1) Category I69, Sequelae of Cerebrovascular disease

Category I69 is used to indicate conditions classifiable to categories I60-I67 as the causes of sequela (neurologic deficits), themselves classified elsewhere. These "late effects" include neurologic deficits that persist after initial onset of conditions classifiable to categories I60-I67. The neurologic deficits caused by cerebrovascular disease may be present from the onset or may arise at any time after the onset of the condition classifiable to categories I60-I67.

Codes from category I69, Sequelae of cerebrovascular disease, that specify hemiplegia, hemiparesis and monoplegia identify whether the dominant or nondominant side is affected. Should the affected side be documented, but not specified as dominant or nondominant, and the classification system does not indicate a default, code selection is as follows:

- For ambidextrous patients, the default should be dominant.
- If the left side is affected, the default is nondominant.
- If the right side is affected, the default is dominant.

2) Codes from category I69 with codes from I60-I67

Codes from category I69 may be assigned on a health care record with codes from I60-I67, if the patient has a current cerebrovascular disease and deficits from an old cerebrovascular disease.

3) **Codes from category I69 and Personal history of transient ischemic attack (TIA) and cerebral infarction (Z86.73)**

Codes from category I69 should not be assigned if the patient does not have neurologic deficits.

See Section I.C.21. 4. History (of) for use of personal history codes.

e. **Acute myocardial infarction (AMI)**

1) **Type 1 ST elevation myocardial infarction (STEMI) and non-ST elevation myocardial infarction (NSTEMI)**

The ICD-10-CM codes for acute type 1 myocardial infarction (AMI) identify the site, such as anterolateral wall or true posterior wall. Subcategories I21.0-I21.2 and code I21.3 are used for type 1 ST elevation myocardial infarction (STEMI). Code I21.4, non-ST elevation (NSTEMI) myocardial infarction, is used for type 1 non-ST elevation myocardial infarction (NSTEMI) and nontransmural MIs.

If a type 1 NSTEMI evolves to STEMI, assign the STEMI code. If a type 1 STEMI converts to NSTEMI due to thrombolytic therapy, it is still coded as STEMI.

For encounters occurring while the myocardial infarction is equal to, or less than, four weeks old, including transfers to another acute setting or a postacute setting, and the myocardial infarction meets the definition for "other diagnoses" (see Section III, Reporting Additional Diagnoses), codes from category I21 may continue to be reported. For encounters after the 4-week time frame and the patient is still receiving care related to the myocardial infarction, the appropriate aftercare code should be assigned, rather than a code from category I21. For old or healed myocardial infarctions not requiring further care, code I25.2, Old myocardial infarction, may be assigned.

2) **Acute myocardial infarction, unspecified**

Code I21.9, Acute myocardial infarction, unspecified, is the default for unspecified acute myocardial infarction or unspecified type. If only type 1 STEMI or transmural MI without the site is documented, assign code I21.3, ST elevation (STEMI) myocardial infarction of unspecified site.

3) **AMI documented as nontransmural or subendocardial but site provided**

If an AMI is documented as nontransmural or subendocardial, but the site is provided, it is still coded as a subendocardial AMI.

See Section I.C.21.3 for information on coding status post administration of tPA in a different facility within the last 24 hours.

4) **Subsequent acute myocardial infarction**

A code from category I22, Subsequent ST elevation (STEMI) and non-ST elevation (NSTEMI) myocardial infarction, is to be used when a patient who has suffered a type 1 or unspecified AMI has a new AMI within the 4-week time frame of the initial AMI. A code from category I22 must be used in conjunction with a code from category I21. The sequencing of the I22 and I21 codes depends on the circumstances of the encounter.

Do not assign code I22 for subsequent myocardial infarctions other than type 1 or unspecified. For subsequent type 2 AMI assign only code I21.A1. For subsequent type 4 or type 5 AMI, assign only code I21.A9.

If a subsequent myocardial infarction of one type occurs within 4 weeks of a myocardial infarction of a different type, assign the appropriate codes from category I21 to identify each type. Do not assign a code from category I22. Codes from category I22 should only be assigned if both the initial and subsequent myocardial infarctions are type 1 or unspecified.

5) **Other Types of Myocardial Infarction**

The ICD-10-CM provides codes for different types of myocardial infarction. Type 1 myocardial infarctions are assigned to codes I21.0-I21.4 and I21.9.

Type 2 myocardial infarction, and myocardial infarction due to demand ischemia or secondary to ischemic balance, is assigned to code I21.A1, Myocardial infarction type 2 with a code for the underlying cause. Do not assign code I24.8, Other forms of acute ischemic heart disease for the demand ischemia. Sequencing of type 2 AMI or the underlying cause is dependent on the circumstances of admission. When a type 2 AMI code is described as NSTEMI or STEMI, only assign code I21.A1. Codes I21.01-I21.4 should only be assigned for type 1 AMIs.

Acute myocardial infarctions type 3, 4a, 4b, 4c, and 5 are assigned to code I21.A9, Other myocardial infarction type.

The "Code also" and "Code first" notes should be followed related to complications, and for coding of postprocedural myocardial infarctions during or following cardiac surgery.

Figure 9-1   Cardiovascular valves.

Item 9–1 Rheumatic fever is the inflammation of the valve(s) of the heart, usually the mitral or aortic, which leads to valve damage. Rheumatic heart inflammations are usually **pericarditis** (sac surrounding heart), **endocarditis** (heart cavity), or **myocarditis** (heart muscle).

CHAPTER 9

DISEASES OF THE CIRCULATORY SYSTEM (I00-I99)

Excludes2   certain conditions originating in the perinatal period (P04-P96)
certain infectious and parasitic diseases (A00-B99)
complications of pregnancy, childbirth and the puerperium (O00-O9A)
congenital malformations, deformations, and chromosomal abnormalities (Q00-Q99)
endocrine, nutritional and metabolic diseases (E00-E88)
injury, poisoning and certain other consequences of external causes (S00-T88)
neoplasms (C00-D49)
symptoms, signs and abnormal clinical and laboratory findings, not elsewhere classified (R00-R94)
systemic connective tissue disorders (M30-M36)
transient cerebral ischemic attacks and related syndromes (G45.-)

This chapter contains the following blocks:

I00-I02	Acute rheumatic fever
I05-I09	Chronic rheumatic heart diseases
I10-I16	Hypertensive diseases
I20-I25	Ischemic heart diseases
I26-I28	Pulmonary heart disease and diseases of pulmonary circulation
I30-I52	Other forms of heart disease
I60-I69	Cerebrovascular diseases
I70-I79	Diseases of arteries, arterioles and capillaries
I80-I89	Diseases of veins, lymphatic vessels and lymph nodes, not elsewhere classified
I95-I99	Other and unspecified disorders of the circulatory system

ACUTE RHEUMATIC FEVER (I00-I02)

I00   **Rheumatic fever without heart involvement**

    Includes   arthritis, rheumatic, acute or subacute

    Excludes1   rheumatic fever with heart involvement (I01.0-I01.9)

● **I01**   **Rheumatic fever with heart involvement**

    Excludes1   chronic diseases of rheumatic origin (I05-I09) unless rheumatic fever is also present or there is evidence of reactivation or activity of the rheumatic process.

    I01.0   **Acute rheumatic pericarditis**
      Any condition in I00 with pericarditis
      Rheumatic pericarditis (acute)

      Excludes1   acute pericarditis not specified as rheumatic (I30.-)

    I01.1   **Acute rheumatic endocarditis**
      Any condition in I00 with endocarditis or valvulitis
      Acute rheumatic valvulitis

▶ New   ⇒ Revised   ~~deleted~~ Deleted   Excludes 1   Excludes 2   Includes   Use additional   Code first   Code also   Key words

OGCR Official Guidelines   X Assign placeholder X   ● Use Additional Character(s)   ❱ Manifestation Code   ⬢ Hierarchical Condition Category   **Coding Clinic**

Item 9–2 Rheumatic chorea, also called Sydenham's, juvenile, minor, simple, or St. Vitus' dance, is a major symptom of rheumatic fever and is characterized by ceaseless, involuntary, jerky, purposeless movements.

I01.2   **Acute rheumatic myocarditis**
Any condition in I00 with myocarditis

I01.8   **Other acute rheumatic heart disease**
Any condition in I00 with other or multiple types of heart involvement
Acute rheumatic pancarditis

I01.9   **Acute rheumatic heart disease, unspecified**
Any condition in I00 with unspecified type of heart involvement
Rheumatic carditis, acute
Rheumatic heart disease, active or acute

● **I02**   **Rheumatic chorea**

    Includes   Sydenham's chorea

    Excludes1   chorea NOS (G25.5)
Huntington's chorea (G10)

I02.0   **Rheumatic chorea with heart involvement**
Chorea NOS with heart involvement
Rheumatic chorea with heart involvement of any type classifiable under I01.-

I02.9   **Rheumatic chorea without heart involvement**
Rheumatic chorea NOS

CHRONIC RHEUMATIC HEART DISEASES (I05-I09)

● **I05**   **Rheumatic mitral valve diseases**

    Includes   conditions classifiable to both I05.0 and I05.2-I05.9, whether specified as rheumatic or not

    Excludes1   mitral valve disease specified as nonrheumatic (I34.-)
mitral valve disease with aortic and/or tricuspid valve involvement (I08.-)

I05.0   **Rheumatic mitral stenosis**
Mitral (valve) obstruction (rheumatic)

I05.1   **Rheumatic mitral insufficiency**
Rheumatic mitral incompetence
Rheumatic mitral regurgitation

    Excludes1   mitral insufficiency not specified as rheumatic (I34.0)

I05.2   **Rheumatic mitral stenosis with insufficiency**
Rheumatic mitral stenosis with incompetence or regurgitation

I05.8   **Other rheumatic mitral valve diseases**
Rheumatic mitral (valve) failure

I05.9   **Rheumatic mitral valve disease, unspecified**
Rheumatic mitral (valve) disorder (chronic) NOS

● **I06**   **Rheumatic aortic valve diseases**

    Excludes1   aortic valve disease not specified as rheumatic (I35.-)
aortic valve disease with mitral and/or tricuspid valve involvement (I08.-)

I06.0   **Rheumatic aortic stenosis**
Rheumatic aortic (valve) obstruction

I06.1   **Rheumatic aortic insufficiency**
Rheumatic aortic incompetence
Rheumatic aortic regurgitation

I06.2   **Rheumatic aortic stenosis with insufficiency**
Rheumatic aortic stenosis with incompetence or regurgitation

I06.8   **Other rheumatic aortic valve diseases**

I06.9   **Rheumatic aortic valve disease, unspecified**
Rheumatic aortic (valve) disease NOS

★**(See Plate 33 of the Anatomy Illustrations.)**

Item 9–3 Mitral stenosis is the narrowing of the mitral valve separating the left atrium from the left ventricle. **Mitral insufficiency** is the improper closure of the mitral valve, which may lead to enlargement (hypertrophy) of the left atrium.

Item 9–4 Aortic stenosis is the narrowing of the aortic valve located between the left ventricle and the aorta. **Aortic insufficiency** is the improper closure of the aortic valve, which may lead to enlargement (hypertrophy) of the left ventricle.

● **I07**   **Rheumatic tricuspid valve diseases**

    Includes   rheumatic tricuspid valve diseases specified as rheumatic or unspecified

    Excludes1   tricuspid valve disease specified as nonrheumatic (I36.-)
tricuspid valve disease with aortic and/or mitral valve involvement (I08.-)

I07.0   **Rheumatic tricuspid stenosis**
Tricuspid (valve) stenosis (rheumatic)

I07.1   **Rheumatic tricuspid insufficiency**
Tricuspid (valve) insufficiency (rheumatic)

I07.2   **Rheumatic tricuspid stenosis and insufficiency**

I07.8   **Other rheumatic tricuspid valve diseases**

I07.9   **Rheumatic tricuspid valve disease, unspecified**
Rheumatic tricuspid valve disorder NOS

● **I08**   **Multiple valve diseases**

    Includes   multiple valve diseases specified as rheumatic or unspecified

    Excludes1   endocarditis, valve unspecified (I38)
multiple valve disease specified a nonrheumatic (I34.-, I35.-, I36.-, I37.-, I38.-, Q22.-, Q23.-, Q24.8-)
rheumatic valve disease NOS (I09.1)

    Coding Clinic: 2019, Q2, P5

I08.0   **Rheumatic disorders of both mitral and aortic valves**
Involvement of both mitral and aortic valves specified as rheumatic or unspecified
    Coding Clinic: 2019, Q2, P5

I08.1   **Rheumatic disorders of both mitral and tricuspid valves**

I08.2   **Rheumatic disorders of both aortic and tricuspid valves**

I08.3   **Combined rheumatic disorders of mitral, aortic and tricuspid valves**

I08.8   **Other rheumatic multiple valve diseases**

I08.9   **Rheumatic multiple valve disease, unspecified**

● **I09**   **Other rheumatic heart diseases**

I09.0   **Rheumatic myocarditis**

    Excludes1   myocarditis not specified as rheumatic (I51.4)

I09.1   **Rheumatic diseases of endocardium, valve unspecified**
Rheumatic endocarditis (chronic)
Rheumatic valvulitis (chronic)

    Excludes1   endocarditis, valve unspecified (I38)

I09.2   **Chronic rheumatic pericarditis**
Adherent pericardium, rheumatic
Chronic rheumatic mediastinopericarditis
Chronic rheumatic myopericarditis

    Excludes1   chronic pericarditis not specified as rheumatic (I31.-)

● **I09.8**   **Other specified rheumatic heart diseases**

I09.81   **Rheumatic heart failure** 🔗
Use additional code to identify type of heart failure (I50.-)

I09.89   **Other specified rheumatic heart diseases**
Rheumatic disease of pulmonary valve

I09.9   **Rheumatic heart disease, unspecified**
Rheumatic carditis

    Excludes1   rheumatoid carditis (M05.31)

Item 9–5 Hypertension is caused by high arterial blood pressure in the arteries. **Essential, primary,** or **idiopathic** hypertension occurs without identifiable organic cause. **Secondary** hypertension is that which has an organic cause. **Malignant** hypertension is severely elevated blood pressure. **Benign** hypertension is mildly elevated blood pressure.

HYPERTENSIVE DISEASES (I10-I16)

Use additional code to identify:
exposure to environmental tobacco smoke (Z77.22)
history of tobacco dependence (Z87.891)
occupational exposure to environmental tobacco smoke (Z57.31)
tobacco dependence (F17.-)
tobacco use (Z72.0)

Excludes1   neonatal hypertension (P29.2)
primary pulmonary hypertension (I27.0)

Excludes2   hypertensive disease complicating pregnancy, childbirth and the puerperium (O10-O11, O13-O16)

I10   **Essential (primary) hypertension**
Includes   high blood pressure
hypertension (arterial) (benign) (essential) (malignant) (primary) (systemic)

Excludes1   hypertensive disease complicating pregnancy, childbirth and the puerperium (O10-O11, O13-O16)

Excludes2   essential (primary) hypertension involving vessels of brain (I60-I69)
essential (primary) hypertension involving vessels of eye (H35.0-)

● **I11**   **Hypertensive heart disease**
➡ **Includes**   any condition in I50.- or I51.4-I51.7, I51.89, I51.9 due to hypertension

I11.0   **Hypertensive heart disease with heart failure** 🔵
Hypertensive heart failure
Use additional code to identify type of heart failure (I50.-)
Coding Clinic: 2017, Q1, P47

I11.9   **Hypertensive heart disease without heart failure**
Hypertensive heart disease NOS

OGCR Section I.C.9.a.2.

Hypertensive Chronic Kidney Disease

Assign codes from category I12, Hypertensive chronic kidney disease, when both hypertension and a condition classifiable to category N18, Chronic kidney disease (CKD), are present. **CKD should not be coded as hypertensive if the physician has specifically documented a different cause.**

The appropriate code from category N18 should be used as a secondary code with a code from category I12 to identify the stage of chronic kidney disease.

See Section I.C.14. Chronic kidney disease.

If a patient has hypertensive chronic kidney disease and acute renal failure, an additional code for the acute renal failure is required.

● **I12**   **Hypertensive chronic kidney disease**
Includes   any condition in N18 and N26 - due to hypertension
arteriosclerosis of kidney
arteriosclerotic nephritis (chronic) (interstitial)
hypertensive nephropathy
nephrosclerosis

Excludes1   hypertension due to kidney disease (I15.0, I15.1)
renovascular hypertension (I15.0)
secondary hypertension (I15.-)

Excludes2   acute kidney failure (N17.-)

Coding Clinic: 2018, Q4, P89; 2016, Q4, P123

I12.0   **Hypertensive chronic kidney disease with stage 5 chronic kidney disease or end stage renal disease** 🔵
Use additional code to identify the stage of chronic kidney disease (N18.5, N18.6)
Coding Clinic: 2016, Q3, P23

I12.9   **Hypertensive chronic kidney disease with stage 1 through stage 4 chronic kidney disease, or unspecified chronic kidney disease**
Hypertensive chronic kidney disease NOS
Hypertensive renal disease NOS
Use additional code to identify the stage of chronic kidney disease (N18.1-N18.4, N18.9)
Coding Clinic: 2018, Q4, P88

OGCR Section I.c.9.a.3.

Hypertensive Heart and Chronic Kidney Disease

Assign codes from combination category I13, Hypertensive heart and chronic kidney disease, when **there is hypertension with both heart and kidney involvement.** If heart failure is present, assign an additional code from category I50 to identify the type of heart failure.

The appropriate code from category N18, Chronic kidney disease, should be used as a secondary code with a code from category I13 to identify the stage of chronic kidney disease. See Section I.C.14. Chronic kidney disease.

The codes in category I13, Hypertensive heart and chronic kidney disease, are combination codes that include hypertension, heart disease and chronic kidney disease. The Includes note at I13 specifies that the conditions included at I11 and I12 are included together in I13. If a patient has hypertension, heart disease and chronic kidney disease then a code from I13 should be used, not individual codes for hypertension, heart disease and chronic kidney disease, or codes from I11 or I12.

For patients with both acute renal failure and chronic kidney disease an additional code for acute renal failure is required.

● **I13**   **Hypertensive heart and chronic kidney disease**
Includes   any condition in I11.- with any condition in I12.-
cardiorenal disease
cardiovascular renal disease
Coding Clinic: 2016, Q4, P123

I13.0   **Hypertensive heart and chronic kidney disease with heart failure and stage 1 through stage 4 chronic kidney disease, or unspecified chronic kidney disease** 🔵
Use additional code to identify type of heart failure (I50.-)
Use additional code to identify stage of chronic kidney disease (N18.1-N18.4, N18.9)

● **I13.1**   **Hypertensive heart and chronic kidney disease without heart failure**
I13.10   **Hypertensive heart and chronic kidney disease without heart failure, with stage 1 through stage 4 chronic kidney disease, or unspecified chronic kidney disease**
Hypertensive heart disease and hypertensive chronic kidney disease NOS
Use additional code to identify the stage of chronic kidney disease (N18.1-N18.4, N18.9)

I13.11   **Hypertensive heart and chronic kidney disease without heart failure, with stage 5 chronic kidney disease, or end stage renal disease** 🔵
Use additional code to identify the stage of chronic kidney disease (N18.5, N18.6)

I13.2   **Hypertensive heart and chronic kidney disease with heart failure and with stage 5 chronic kidney disease, or end stage renal disease** 🔵
Use additional code to identify type of heart failure (I50.-)
Use additional code to identify the stage of chronic kidney disease (N18.5, N18.6)

▶ New   ➡ Revised   ~~deleted~~ Deleted   Excludes 1   Excludes 2   Includes   Use additional   Code first   Code also   Key words

OGCR Official Guidelines   X Assign placeholder X   ● Use Additional Character(s)   ▌ Manifestation Code   🔵 Hierarchical Condition Category   **Coding Clinic**

OGCR Section I.9.a.6.

Hypertension, Secondary
Secondary hypertension is due to an underlying condition.
Two codes are required: one to identify the underlying
etiology and one from category I15 to identify the
hypertension. Sequencing of codes is determined by the
reason for admission/encounter.

● **I15** **Secondary hypertension**
Code also underlying condition
Excludes1 postprocedural hypertension (I97.3)
Excludes2 secondary hypertension involving vessels of
brain (I60-I69)
secondary hypertension involving vessels of eye
(H35.0-)

I15.0 **Renovascular hypertension**
I15.1 **Hypertension secondary to other renal disorders**
Coding Clinic: 2016, Q3, P23
I15.2 **Hypertension secondary to endocrine disorders**
I15.8 **Other secondary hypertension**
I15.9 **Secondary hypertension, unspecified**

● **I16** **Hypertensive crisis**
Code also any identified hypertensive disease (I10-I15)
Coding Clinic: 2016, Q4, P26-27, 123

I16.0 **Hypertensive urgency**
I16.1 **Hypertensive emergency**
I16.9 **Hypertensive crisis, unspecified**

ISCHEMIC HEART DISEASES (I20-I25)

Use additional code to identify presence of hypertension (I10-I16)

● **I20** **Angina pectoris**
Chest pain/discomfort due to lack of oxygen to the heart muscle.
Principal symptom of myocardial infarction.
Use additional code to identify:
exposure to environmental tobacco smoke (Z77.22)
history of tobacco dependence (Z87.891)
occupational exposure to environmental tobacco smoke
(Z57.31)
tobacco dependence (F17.-)
tobacco use (Z72.0)

Excludes1 angina pectoris with atherosclerotic heart disease
of native coronary arteries (I25.1-)
atherosclerosis of coronary artery bypass graft(s)
and coronary artery of transplanted heart
with angina pectoris (I25.7-)
postinfarction angina (I23.7)

I20.0 **Unstable angina** 🔊
Accelerated angina
Crescendo angina
De novo effort angina
Intermediate coronary syndrome
Preinfarction syndrome
Worsening effort angina

I20.1 **Angina pectoris with documented spasm** 🔊
Angiospastic angina
Prinzmetal angina
Spasm-induced angina
Variant angina

I20.8 **Other forms of angina pectoris** 🔊
Angina equivalent
Angina of effort
Coronary slow flow syndrome
Stable angina
Stenocardia
Use additional code(s) for symptoms associated with
angina equivalent

I20.9 **Angina pectoris, unspecified** 🔊
Angina NOS
Anginal syndrome
Cardiac angina
Ischemic chest pain

● **I21** **Acute myocardial infarction**
Includes cardiac infarction
coronary (artery) embolism
coronary (artery) occlusion
coronary (artery) rupture
coronary (artery) thrombosis
infarction of heart, myocardium, or ventricle
myocardial infarction specified as acute or with a
stated duration of 4 weeks (28 days) or less
from onset

Use additional code, if applicable, to identify:
exposure to environmental tobacco smoke (Z77.22)
history of tobacco dependence (Z87.891)
occupational exposure to environmental tobacco smoke
(Z57.31)
status post administration of tPA (rtPA) in a different facility
within the last 24 hours prior to admission to current
facility (Z92.82)
tobacco dependence (F17.-)
tobacco use (Z72.0)

Excludes2 old myocardial infarction (I25.2)
postmyocardial infarction syndrome (I24.1)
subsequent type 1 myocardial infarction (I22.-)
Coding Clinic: 2016, Q4, P140; 2013, Q1, P25-26; 2012, Q4, P103

● **I21.0** **ST elevation (STEMI) myocardial infarction of anterior
wall**
Type 1 ST elevation myocardial infarction of anterior
wall
Coding Clinic: 2013, Q1, P26

I21.01 **ST elevation (STEMI) myocardial infarction
involving left main coronary artery** 🔊
I21.02 **ST elevation (STEMI) myocardial infarction
involving left anterior descending coronary
artery** 🔊
ST elevation (STEMI) myocardial infarction
involving diagonal coronary artery
Coding Clinic: 2013, Q1, P26
I21.09 **ST elevation (STEMI) myocardial infarction
involving other coronary artery of anterior
wall** 🔊
Acute transmural myocardial infarction of
anterior wall
Anteroapical transmural (Q wave) infarction
(acute)
Anterolateral transmural (Q wave) infarction
(acute)
Anteroseptal transmural (Q wave) infarction
(acute)
Transmural (Q wave) infarction (acute) (of)
anterior (wall) NOS
Coding Clinic: 2012, Q4, P102, 104

● **I21.1** **ST elevation (STEMI) myocardial infarction of inferior
wall**
Type 1 ST elevation myocardial infarction of inferior
wall
Coding Clinic: 2013, Q1, P26

I21.11 **ST elevation (STEMI) myocardial infarction
involving right coronary artery** 🔊
Inferoposterior transmural (Q wave) infarction
(acute)
I21.19 **ST elevation (STEMI) myocardial infarction
involving other coronary artery of inferior
wall** 🔊
Acute transmural myocardial infarction of
inferior wall
Inferolateral transmural (Q wave) infarction
(acute)
Transmural (Q wave) infarction (acute) (of)
diaphragmatic wall
Transmural (Q wave) infarction (acute) (of)
inferior (wall) NOS
Excludes2 ST elevation (STEMI)
myocardial infarction involving
left circumflex coronary
artery (I21.21)
Coding Clinic: 2012, Q4, P97

CHAPTER 9 (I00-I99)

● **I21.2** **ST elevation (STEMI) myocardial infarction of other sites**

Type 1 ST elevation myocardial infarction of other sites
Coding Clinic: 2013, Q1, P26

I21.21 **ST elevation (STEMI) myocardial infarction involving left circumflex coronary artery** 🐾

ST elevation (STEMI) myocardial infarction involving oblique marginal coronary artery

I21.29 **ST elevation (STEMI) myocardial infarction involving other sites** 🐾

Acute transmural myocardial infarction of other sites

Apical-lateral transmural (Q wave) infarction (acute)

Basal-lateral transmural (Q wave) infarction (acute)

High lateral transmural (Q wave) infarction (acute)

Lateral (wall) NOS transmural (Q wave) infarction (acute)

Posterior (true) transmural (Q wave) infarction (acute)

Posterobasal transmural (Q wave) infarction (acute)

Posterolateral transmural (Q wave) infarction (acute)

Posteroseptal transmural (Q wave) infarction (acute)

Septal transmural (Q wave) infarction (acute) NOS

OGCR Section I.c.9.e.2.

Acute myocardial infarction, unspecified

Code I21.9, Acute myocardial infarction, unspecified, is the default for unspecified acute myocardial infarction or unspecified type. If only type 1 STEMI or transmural MI without the site is documented, assign I21.3, ST elevation (STEMI) myocardial infarction of unspecified site.

I21.3 **ST elevation (STEMI) myocardial infarction of unspecified site** 🐾

Acute transmural myocardial infarction of unspecified site

Transmural (Q wave) myocardial infarction NOS

Type 1 ST elevation myocardial infarction of unspecified site
Coding Clinic: 2013, Q1, P26

I21.4 **Non-ST elevation (NSTEMI) myocardial infarction** 🐾

Acute subendocardial myocardial infarction

Non-Q wave myocardial infarction NOS

Nontransmural myocardial infarction NOS

Type 1 non-ST elevation myocardial infarction
Coding Clinic: 2017, Q1, P44; 2015, Q2, P16; 2013, Q1, P26

I21.9 **Acute myocardial infarction, unspecified** 🐾

Myocardial infarction (acute) NOS

● **I21.A** **Other type of myocardial infarction**

I21.A1 **Myocardial infarction type 2** 🐾

Myocardial infarction due to demand ischemia

Myocardial infarction secondary to ischemic imbalance

Code first the underlying cause, such as:
anemia (D50.0-D64.9)
chronic obstructive pulmonary disease (J44.-)
paroxysmal tachycardia (I47.0-I47.9)
shock (R57.0-R57.9)
Coding Clinic: 2017, Q4, P13-14

I21.A9 **Other myocardial infarction type** 🐾

Myocardial infarction associated with revascularization procedure

Myocardial infarction type 3

Myocardial infarction type 4a

Myocardial infarction type 4b

Myocardial infarction type 4c

Myocardial infarction type 5

Code first, if applicable, postprocedural myocardial infarction following cardiac surgery (I97.190), or postprocedural myocardial infarction during cardiac surgery (I97.790)

Code also complication, if known and applicable, such as:
(acute) stent occlusion (T82.897-)
(acute) stent stenosis (T82.857-)
(acute) stent thrombosis (T82.865-)
cardiac arrest due to underlying cardiac condition (I46.2)
complication of percutaneous coronary intervention (PCI) (I97.89)
occlusion of coronary artery bypass graft (T82.218-)
Coding Clinic: 2019, Q2, P32-33

● **I22** **Subsequent ST elevation (STEMI) and non-ST elevation (NSTEMI) myocardial infarction**

Includes acute myocardial infarction occurring within four weeks (28 days) of a previous acute myocardial infarction, regardless of site
cardiac infarction
coronary (artery) embolism
coronary (artery) occlusion
coronary (artery) rupture
coronary (artery) thrombosis
infarction of heart, myocardium, or ventricle
recurrent myocardial infarction
reinfarction of myocardium
rupture of heart, myocardium, or ventricle
subsequent type 1 myocardial infarction

Excludes1 subsequent myocardial infarction, type 2 (I21.A1)
subsequent myocardial infarction of other type (type 3) (type 4) (type 5) (I21.A9)

Use additional code, if applicable, to identify:
exposure to environmental tobacco smoke (Z77.22)
history of tobacco dependence (Z87.891)
occupational exposure to environmental tobacco smoke (Z57.31)
status post administration of tPA (rtPA) in a different facility within the last 24 hours prior to admission to current facility (Z92.82)
tobacco dependence (F17.-)
tobacco use (Z72.0)
Coding Clinic: 2017, Q4, P14; 2013, Q1, P25; 2012, Q4, P103

I22.0 **Subsequent ST elevation (STEMI) myocardial infarction of anterior wall** 🐾

Subsequent acute transmural myocardial infarction of anterior wall

Subsequent transmural (Q wave) infarction (acute)(of) anterior (wall) NOS

Subsequent anteroapical transmural (Q wave) infarction (acute)

Subsequent anterolateral transmural (Q wave) infarction (acute)

Subsequent anteroseptal transmural (Q wave) infarction (acute)

I22.1 **Subsequent ST elevation (STEMI) myocardial infarction of inferior wall** 🐾

Subsequent acute transmural myocardial infarction of inferior wall

Subsequent transmural (Q wave) infarction (acute)(of) diaphragmatic wall

Subsequent transmural (Q wave) infarction (acute)(of) inferior (wall) NOS

Subsequent inferolateral transmural (Q wave) infarction (acute)

Subsequent inferoposterior transmural (Q wave) infarction (acute)
Coding Clinic: 2012, Q4, P97, 102, 104

▶ New   ⇒ Revised   ~~deleted~~ Deleted   Excludes 1   Excludes 2   Includes   Use additional   Code first   Code also   Key words
OGCR Official Guidelines   X Assign placeholder X   ● Use Additional Character(s)   ▶ Manifestation Code   🐾 Hierarchical Condition Category   Coding Clinic

I22.2 **Subsequent non-ST elevation (NSTEMI) myocardial infarction** 🦟
     Subsequent acute subendocardial myocardial infarction
     Subsequent non-Q wave myocardial infarction NOS
     Subsequent nontransmural myocardial infarction NOS

I22.8 **Subsequent ST elevation (STEMI) myocardial infarction of other sites** 🦟
     Subsequent acute transmural myocardial infarction of other sites
     Subsequent apical-lateral transmural (Q wave) myocardial infarction (acute)
     Subsequent basal-lateral transmural (Q wave) myocardial infarction (acute)
     Subsequent high lateral transmural (Q wave) myocardial infarction (acute)
     Subsequent transmural (Q wave) myocardial infarction (acute)(of) lateral (wall) NOS
     Subsequent posterior (true) transmural (Q wave) myocardial infarction (acute)
     Subsequent posterobasal transmural (Q wave) myocardial infarction (acute)
     Subsequent posterolateral transmural (Q wave) myocardial infarction (acute)
     Subsequent posteroseptal transmural (Q wave) myocardial infarction (acute)
     Subsequent septal NOS transmural (Q wave) myocardial infarction (acute)

I22.9 **Subsequent ST elevation (STEMI) myocardial infarction of unspecified site** 🦟
     Subsequent acute myocardial infarction of unspecified site
     Subsequent myocardial infarction (acute) NOS

● **I23** **Certain current complications following ST elevation (STEMI) and non-ST elevation (NSTEMI) myocardial infarction (within the 28 day period)**
     Coding Clinic: 2017, Q2, P11

I23.0 **Hemopericardium as current complication following acute myocardial infarction** 🦟   A
     Excludes1   hemopericardium not specified as current complication following acute myocardial infarction (I31.2)

I23.1 **Atrial septal defect as current complication following acute myocardial infarction** 🦟   A
     Excludes1   acquired atrial septal defect not specified as current complication following acute myocardial infarction (I51.0)

I23.2 **Ventricular septal defect as current complication following acute myocardial infarction** 🦟   A
     Excludes1   acquired ventricular septal defect not specified as current complication following acute myocardial infarction (I51.0)

I23.3 **Rupture of cardiac wall without hemopericardium as current complication following acute myocardial infarction** 🦟   A
     Coding Clinic: 2017, Q2, P11

I23.4 **Rupture of chordae tendineae as current complication following acute myocardial infarction** 🦟
     Excludes1   rupture of chordae tendineae not specified as current complication following acute myocardial infarction (I51.1)

I23.5 **Rupture of papillary muscle as current complication following acute myocardial infarction** 🦟
     Excludes1   rupture of papillary muscle not specified as current complication following acute myocardial infarction (I51.2)

I23.6 **Thrombosis of atrium, auricular appendage, and ventricle as current complications following acute myocardial infarction** 🦟   A
     Excludes1   thrombosis of atrium, auricular appendage, and ventricle not specified as current complication following acute myocardial infarction (I51.3)

I23.7 **Postinfarction angina** 🦟   A
     Coding Clinic: 2015, Q2, P16-17

I23.8 **Other current complications following acute myocardial infarction** 🦟   A

● **I24** **Other acute ischemic heart diseases**
     Excludes1   angina pectoris (I20.-)
               transient myocardial ischemia in newborn (P29.4)

I24.0 **Acute coronary thrombosis not resulting in myocardial infarction** 🦟
     Acute coronary (artery) (vein) embolism not resulting in myocardial infarction
     Acute coronary (artery) (vein) occlusion not resulting in myocardial infarction
     Acute coronary (artery) (vein) thromboembolism not resulting in myocardial infarction
     Excludes1   atherosclerotic heart disease (I25.1-)
     Coding Clinic: 2013, Q1, P24

I24.1 **Dressler's syndrome** 🦟
     Postmyocardial infarction syndrome
     Excludes1   postinfarction angina (I23.7)

I24.8 **Other forms of acute ischemic heart disease** 🦟
     Excludes1   myocardial infarction due to demand ischemia (I21.A1)
     Coding Clinic: 2017, Q4, P13

I24.9 **Acute ischemic heart disease, unspecified** 🦟
     Excludes1   ischemic heart disease (chronic) NOS (I25.9)

● **I25** **Chronic ischemic heart disease**
     Use additional code to identify:
     chronic total occlusion of coronary artery (I25.82)
     exposure to environmental tobacco smoke (Z77.22)
     history of tobacco dependence (Z87.891)
     occupational exposure to environmental tobacco smoke (Z57.31)
     tobacco dependence (F17.-)
     tobacco use (Z72.0)

★ **(See Plates 218 and 219 on pages 74 and 75.)**

● **I25.1** **Atherosclerotic heart disease of native coronary artery**
     Disease in which fatty deposits form on the walls of arteries
     Atherosclerotic cardiovascular disease
     Coronary (artery) atheroma
     Coronary (artery) atherosclerosis
     Coronary (artery) disease
     Coronary (artery) sclerosis
     Use additional code, if applicable, to identify:
     coronary atherosclerosis due to calcified coronary lesion (I25.84)
     coronary atherosclerosis due to lipid rich plaque (I25.83)
     Excludes2   atheroembolism (I75.-)
               atherosclerosis of coronary artery bypass graft(s) and transplanted heart (I25.7-)

I25.10 **Atherosclerotic heart disease of native coronary artery without angina pectoris**   A
     Atherosclerotic heart disease NOS
     Coding Clinic: 2015, Q2, P17; 2012, Q4, P92

Item 9–6 Classification is based on the location of the atherosclerosis. **"Of native coronary artery"** indicates the atherosclerosis is within an original heart artery. **"Of autologous vein bypass graft"** indicates that the atherosclerosis is within a vein graft that was taken from within the patient. **"Of nonautologous biological bypass graft"** indicates the atherosclerosis is within a vessel grafted from other than the patient. **"Of artery bypass graft"** indicates the atherosclerosis is within an artery that was grafted from within the patient.

CHAPTER 9 (I00–I99)

Figure 9-2 Atherosclerotic plaque.

Atherosclerotic
plaque
(atheromas)

OGCR See Section I.9.b.

Atherosclerotic Coronary Artery Disease and Angina

ICD-10-CM has combination codes for atherosclerotic heart disease with angina pectoris. The subcategories for these codes are I25.11, Atherosclerotic heart disease of native coronary artery with angina pectoris and I25.7, Atherosclerosis of coronary artery bypass graft(s) and coronary artery of transplanted heart with angina pectoris.

When using one of these combination codes it is not necessary to use an additional code for angina pectoris. A causal relationship can be assumed in a patient with both atherosclerosis and angina pectoris, unless the documentation indicates the angina is due to something other than the atherosclerosis.

If a patient with coronary artery disease is admitted due to an acute myocardial infarction (AMI), the AMI should be sequenced before the coronary artery disease.

See Section I.C.9. Acute myocardial infarction (AMI).

● **I25.11   Atherosclerotic heart disease of native coronary artery with angina pectoris**

    I25.110   Atherosclerotic heart disease of native coronary artery with unstable angina pectoris 🅫   A

        Excludes1 unstable angina without atherosclerotic heart disease (I20.0)

    I25.111   Atherosclerotic heart disease of native coronary artery with angina pectoris with documented spasm 🅫 A

        Excludes1 angina pectoris with documented spasm without atherosclerotic heart disease (I20.1)

    I25.118   Atherosclerotic heart disease of native coronary artery with other forms of angina pectoris 🅫   A

        Excludes1 other forms of angina pectoris without atherosclerotic heart disease (I20.8)

        Coding Clinic: 2015, Q2, P16-17

    I25.119   Atherosclerotic heart disease of native coronary artery with unspecified angina pectoris 🅫   A

        Atherosclerotic heart disease with angina NOS
        Atherosclerotic heart disease with ischemic chest pain

        Excludes1 unspecified angina pectoris without atherosclerotic heart disease (I20.9)

I25.2   Old myocardial infarction
    Healed myocardial infarction
    Past myocardial infarction diagnosed by ECG or other investigation, but currently presenting no symptoms

I25.3   Aneurysm of heart
    Mural aneurysm
    Ventricular aneurysm

● **I25.4   Coronary artery aneurysm and dissection**

    I25.41   Coronary artery aneurysm
        Coronary arteriovenous fistula, acquired

        Excludes1 congenital coronary (artery) aneurysm (Q24.5)

    I25.42   Coronary artery dissection

I25.5   Ischemic cardiomyopathy

    Excludes2 coronary atherosclerosis (I25.1-, I25.7-)

I25.6   Silent myocardial ischemia

● **I25.7   Atherosclerosis of coronary artery bypass graft(s) and coronary artery of transplanted heart with angina pectoris**

    Use additional code, if applicable, to identify:
        coronary atherosclerosis due to calcified coronary lesion (I25.84)
        coronary atherosclerosis due to lipid rich plaque (I25.83)

    Excludes1 atherosclerosis of bypass graft(s) of transplanted heart without angina pectoris (I25.812)
        atherosclerosis of coronary artery bypass graft(s) without angina pectoris (I25.810)
        atherosclerosis of native coronary artery of transplanted heart without angina pectoris (I25.811)

● **I25.70   Atherosclerosis of coronary artery bypass graft(s), unspecified, with angina pectoris**

    I25.700   Atherosclerosis of coronary artery bypass graft(s), unspecified, with unstable angina pectoris 🅫   A

        Excludes1 unstable angina pectoris without atherosclerosis of coronary artery bypass graft (I20.0)

    I25.701   Atherosclerosis of coronary artery bypass graft(s), unspecified, with angina pectoris with documented spasm 🅫   A

        Excludes1 angina pectoris with documented spasm without atherosclerosis of coronary artery bypass graft (I20.1)

    I25.708   Atherosclerosis of coronary artery bypass graft(s), unspecified, with other forms of angina pectoris 🅫 A

        Excludes1 other forms of angina pectoris without atherosclerosis of coronary artery bypass graft (I20.8)

    I25.709   Atherosclerosis of coronary artery bypass graft(s), unspecified, with unspecified angina pectoris 🅫 A

        Excludes1 unspecified angina pectoris without atherosclerosis of coronary artery bypass graft (I20.9)

▶ New   ➠ Revised   ~~deleted~~ Deleted   Excludes 1   Excludes 2   Includes   Use additional   Code first   Code also   Key words
OGCR Official Guidelines   X Assign placeholder X   ● Use Additional Character(s)   ▶ Manifestation Code   🅫 Hierarchical Condition Category   Coding Clinic

● **I25.71**   **Atherosclerosis of autologous vein coronary artery bypass graft(s) with angina pectoris**

   I25.710   **Atherosclerosis of autologous vein coronary artery bypass graft(s) with unstable angina pectoris** 🔲   A

    Excludes1   unstable angina without atherosclerosis of autologous vein coronary artery bypass graft(s) (I20.0)

    Excludes2   embolism or thrombus of coronary artery bypass graft(s) (T82.8-)

   I25.711   **Atherosclerosis of autologous vein coronary artery bypass graft(s) with angina pectoris with documented spasm** 🔲   A

    Excludes1   angina pectoris with documented spasm without atherosclerosis of autologous vein coronary artery bypass graft(s) (I20.1)

   I25.718   **Atherosclerosis of autologous vein coronary artery bypass graft(s) with other forms of angina pectoris** 🔲   A

    Excludes1   other forms of angina pectoris without atherosclerosis of autologous vein coronary artery bypass graft(s) (I20.8)

   I25.719   **Atherosclerosis of autologous vein coronary artery bypass graft(s) with unspecified angina pectoris** 🔲   A

    Excludes1   unspecified angina pectoris without atherosclerosis of autologous vein coronary artery bypass graft(s) (I20.9)

● **I25.72**   **Atherosclerosis of autologous artery coronary artery bypass graft(s) with angina pectoris**
   Atherosclerosis of internal mammary artery graft with angina pectoris

   I25.720   **Atherosclerosis of autologous artery coronary artery bypass graft(s) with unstable angina pectoris** 🔲   A

    Excludes1   unstable angina without atherosclerosis of autologous artery coronary artery bypass graft(s) (I20.0)

   I25.721   **Atherosclerosis of autologous artery coronary artery bypass graft(s) with angina pectoris with documented spasm** 🔲   A

    Excludes1   angina pectoris with documented spasm without atherosclerosis of autologous artery coronary artery bypass graft(s) (I20.1)

   I25.728   **Atherosclerosis of autologous artery coronary artery bypass graft(s) with other forms of angina pectoris** 🔲   A

    Excludes1   other forms of angina pectoris without atherosclerosis of autologous artery coronary artery bypass graft(s) (I20.8)

   I25.729   **Atherosclerosis of autologous artery coronary artery bypass graft(s) with unspecified angina pectoris** 🔲   A

    Excludes1   unspecified angina pectoris without atherosclerosis of autologous artery coronary artery bypass graft(s) (I20.9)

● **I25.73**   **Atherosclerosis of nonautologous biological coronary artery bypass graft(s) with angina pectoris**

   I25.730   **Atherosclerosis of nonautologous biological coronary artery bypass graft(s) with unstable angina pectoris** 🔲   A

    Excludes1   unstable angina without atherosclerosis of nonautologous biological coronary artery bypass graft(s) (I20.0)

   I25.731   **Atherosclerosis of nonautologous biological coronary artery bypass graft(s) with angina pectoris with documented spasm** 🔲   A

    Excludes1   angina pectoris with documented spasm without atherosclerosis of nonautologous biological coronary artery bypass graft(s) (I20.1)

   I25.738   **Atherosclerosis of nonautologous biological coronary artery bypass graft(s) with other forms of angina pectoris** 🔲   A

    Excludes1   other forms of angina pectoris without atherosclerosis of nonautologous biological coronary artery bypass graft(s) (I20.8)

   I25.739   **Atherosclerosis of nonautologous biological coronary artery bypass graft(s) with unspecified angina pectoris** 🔲   A

    Excludes1   unspecified angina pectoris without atherosclerosis of nonautologous biological coronary artery bypass graft(s) (I20.9)

CHAPTER 9 (I00-I99)

● **I25.75 Atherosclerosis of native coronary artery of transplanted heart with angina pectoris**

> **Excludes1** atherosclerosis of native coronary artery of transplanted heart without angina pectoris (I25.811)

I25.750 Atherosclerosis of native coronary artery of transplanted heart with unstable angina 🐾

I25.751 Atherosclerosis of native coronary artery of transplanted heart with angina pectoris with documented spasm 🐾

I25.758 Atherosclerosis of native coronary artery of transplanted heart with other forms of angina pectoris 🐾

I25.759 Atherosclerosis of native coronary artery of transplanted heart with unspecified angina pectoris 🐾

● **I25.76 Atherosclerosis of bypass graft of coronary artery of transplanted heart with angina pectoris**

> **Excludes1** atherosclerosis of bypass graft of coronary artery of transplanted heart without angina pectoris (I25.812)

I25.760 Atherosclerosis of bypass graft of coronary artery of transplanted heart with unstable angina 🐾   A

I25.761 Atherosclerosis of bypass graft of coronary artery of transplanted heart with angina pectoris with documented spasm 🐾   A

I25.768 Atherosclerosis of bypass graft of coronary artery of transplanted heart with other forms of angina pectoris 🐾   A

I25.769 Atherosclerosis of bypass graft of coronary artery of transplanted heart with unspecified angina pectoris 🐾   A

● **I25.79 Atherosclerosis of other coronary artery bypass graft(s) with angina pectoris**   A

I25.790 Atherosclerosis of other coronary artery bypass graft(s) with unstable angina pectoris 🐾

> **Excludes1** unstable angina without atherosclerosis of other coronary artery bypass graft(s) (I20.0)

I25.791 Atherosclerosis of other coronary artery bypass graft(s) with angina pectoris with documented spasm 🐾   A

> **Excludes1** angina pectoris with documented spasm without atherosclerosis of other coronary artery bypass graft(s) (I20.1)

I25.798 Atherosclerosis of other coronary artery bypass graft(s) with other forms of angina pectoris 🐾   A

> **Excludes1** other forms of angina pectoris without atherosclerosis of other coronary artery bypass graft(s) (I20.8)

I25.799 Atherosclerosis of other coronary artery bypass graft(s) with unspecified angina pectoris 🐾   A

> **Excludes1** unspecified angina pectoris without atherosclerosis of other coronary artery bypass graft(s) (I20.9)

● **I25.8 Other forms of chronic ischemic heart disease**

● **I25.81 Atherosclerosis of other coronary vessels without angina pectoris**

Use additional code, if applicable, to identify:
coronary atherosclerosis due to calcified coronary lesion (I25.84)
coronary atherosclerosis due to lipid rich plaque (I25.83)

> **Excludes2** atherosclerotic heart disease of native coronary artery without angina pectoris (I25.10)

I25.810 Atherosclerosis of coronary artery bypass graft(s) without angina pectoris   A

Atherosclerosis of coronary artery bypass graft NOS

> **Excludes1** atherosclerosis of coronary bypass graft(s) with angina pectoris (I25.70- -I25.73-, I25.79-)

Coding Clinic: 2016, Q4, P86

I25.811 Atherosclerosis of native coronary artery of transplanted heart without angina pectoris

Atherosclerosis of native coronary artery of transplanted heart NOS

> **Excludes1** atherosclerosis of native coronary artery of transplanted heart with angina pectoris (I25.75-)

I25.812 Atherosclerosis of bypass graft of coronary artery of transplanted heart without angina pectoris   A

Atherosclerosis of bypass graft of transplanted heart NOS

> **Excludes1** atherosclerosis of bypass graft of transplanted heart with angina pectoris (I25.76)

I25.82   Chronic total occlusion of coronary artery
Complete occlusion of coronary artery
Total occlusion of coronary artery
Code first coronary atherosclerosis (I25.1-, I25.7-, I25.81-)

> **Excludes1**   acute coronary occlusion with myocardial infarction (I21.0-I21.9, I22.-)
> acute coronary occlusion without myocardial infarction (I24.0)

I25.83   Coronary atherosclerosis due to lipid rich plaque   A
Code first coronary atherosclerosis (I25.1-, I25.7-, I25.81-)

I25.84   Coronary atherosclerosis due to calcified coronary lesion
Coronary atherosclerosis due to severely calcified coronary lesion
Code first coronary atherosclerosis (I25.1-, I25.7-, I25.81-)

I25.89   Other forms of chronic ischemic heart disease

I25.9   Chronic ischemic heart disease, unspecified
Ischemic heart disease (chronic) NOS

PULMONARY HEART DISEASE AND DISEASES OF PULMONARY CIRCULATION (I26-I28)

● **I26   Pulmonary embolism**

> **Includes**   pulmonary (acute)(artery)(vein) infarction
> pulmonary (acute)(artery)(vein) thromboembolism
> pulmonary (acute)(artery)(vein) thrombosis

> **Excludes2**   chronic pulmonary embolism (I27.82)
> personal history of pulmonary embolism (Z86.711)
> pulmonary embolism due to trauma (T79.0, T79.1)
> pulmonary embolism due to complications of surgical and medical care (T80.0, T81.7-, T82.8-)
> pulmonary embolism complicating abortion, ectopic or molar pregnancy (O00-O07, O08.2)
> pulmonary embolism complicating pregnancy, childbirth and the puerperium (O88.-)
> septic (non-pulmonary) arterial embolism (I76)

● **I26.0   Pulmonary embolism with acute cor pulmonale**

I26.01   Septic pulmonary embolism with acute cor pulmonale 🔍
Code first underlying infection

I26.02   Saddle embolus of pulmonary artery with acute cor pulmonale 🔍

I26.09   Other pulmonary embolism with acute cor pulmonale 🔍
Acute cor pulmonale NOS

● **I26.9   Pulmonary embolism without acute cor pulmonale**

I26.90   Septic pulmonary embolism without acute cor pulmonale 🔍
Code first underlying infection

I26.92   Saddle embolus of pulmonary artery without acute cor pulmonale 🔍

I26.93   Single subsegmental pulmonary embolism without acute cor pulmonale 🔍
Subsegmental pulmonary embolism NOS

I26.94   Multiple subsegmental pulmonary emboli without acute cor pulmonale 🔍

I26.99   Other pulmonary embolism without acute cor pulmonale 🔍
Acute pulmonary embolism NOS
Pulmonary embolism NOS
Coding Clinic: 2019, Q2, P22-23

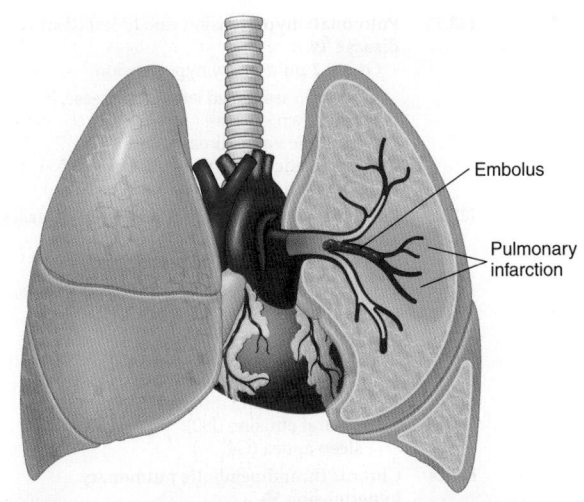

Figure 9-3   Pulmonary embolism. (From Chabner: The Language of Medicine, ed 8, St. Louis, Saunders, 2007)

Item 9-7   Pulmonary heart disease or **cor pulmonale** is right ventricle hypertrophy or RVH as a result of a respiratory disorder increasing back flow pressure to the right ventricle. Left untreated, cor pulmonale leads to right-heart failure and death.

● **I27   Other pulmonary heart diseases**

I27.0   Primary pulmonary hypertension 🔍
Heritable pulmonary arterial hypertension
Idiopathic pulmonary arterial hypertension
Primary group 1 pulmonary hypertension
Primary pulmonary arterial hypertension

> **Excludes1**   persistent pulmonary hypertension of newborn (P29.30)
> pulmonary hypertension NOS (I27.20)
> secondary pulmonary arterial hypertension (I27.21)
> secondary pulmonary hypertension (I27.29)

I27.1   Kyphoscoliotic heart disease 🔍

● **I27.2   Other secondary pulmonary hypertension**
Code also associated underlying condition
> **Excludes1**   Eisenmenger's syndrome (I27.83)
Coding Clinic: 2016, Q2, P8

I27.20   Pulmonary hypertension, unspecified 🔍
Pulmonary hypertension NOS

I27.21   Secondary pulmonary arterial hypertension 🔍
(Associated) (drug-induced) (toxin-induced) pulmonary arterial hypertension NOS
(Associated) (drug-induced) (toxin-induced) (secondary) group 1 pulmonary hypertension
Code also associated conditions if applicable, or adverse effects of drugs or toxins, such as:
adverse effect of appetite depressants (T50.5X5)
congenital heart disease (Q20-Q28)
human immunodeficiency virus [HIV] disease (B20)
polymyositis (M33.2-)
portal hypertension (K76.6)
rheumatoid arthritis (M05.-)
schistosomiasis (B65.-)
Sjögren syndrome (M35.0-)
systemic sclerosis (M34.-)

N   Newborn Age: 0   **P**   Pediatric Age: 0–17   **M**   Maternity DX: 12–55   **A**   Adult Age: 15–124   ♀   Females Only   ♂   Males Only   **883**

I27.22   **Pulmonary hypertension due to left heart disease** 🐾
    Group 2 pulmonary hypertension
    Code also associated left heart disease, if known, such as:
      multiple valve disease (I08.-)
      rheumatic mitral valve diseases (I05.-)
      rheumatic aortic valve diseases (I06.-)

I27.23   **Pulmonary hypertension due to lung diseases and hypoxia** 🐾
    Group 3 pulmonary hypertension
    Code also associated lung disease, if known, such as:
      bronchiectasis (J47.-)
      cystic fibrosis with pulmonary manifestations (E84.0)
      interstitial lung disease (J84.-)
      pleural effusion (J90)
      sleep apnea (G47.3-)

I27.24   **Chronic thromboembolic pulmonary hypertension** 🐾
    Group 4 pulmonary hypertension
    Code also associated pulmonary embolism, if applicable (I26.-, I27.82)

I27.29   **Other secondary pulmonary hypertension** 🐾
    Group 5 pulmonary hypertension
    Pulmonary hypertension with unclear multifactorial mechanisms
    Pulmonary hypertension due to hematologic disorders
    Pulmonary hypertension due to metabolic disorders
    Pulmonary hypertension due to other systemic disorders
    Code also other associated disorders, if known, such as:
      chronic myeloid leukemia (C92.10-C92.22)
      essential thrombocythemia (D47.3)
      Gaucher disease (E75.22)
      hypertensive chronic kidney disease with end stage renal disease (I12.0, I13.11, I13.2)
      hyperthyroidism (E05.-)
      hypothyroidism (E00-E03)
      polycythemia vera (D45)
      sarcoidosis (D86.-)

● **I27.8**   **Other specified pulmonary heart diseases**

I27.81   **Cor pulmonale (chronic)** 🐾
    Cor pulmonale NOS
    Excludes1   acute cor pulmonale (I26.0-)

I27.82   **Chronic pulmonary embolism** 🐾
    Use additional code, if applicable, for associated long-term (current) use of anticoagulants (Z79.01)
    Excludes1   personal history of pulmonary embolism (Z86.711)

I27.83   **Eisenmenger's syndrome** 🐾
    Eisenmenger's complex
    (Irreversible) Eisenmenger's disease
    Pulmonary hypertension with right to left shunt related to congenital heart disease
    Code also underlying heart defect, if known, such as:
      atrial septal defect (Q21.1)
      Eisenmenger's defect (Q21.8)
      patent ductus arteriosus (Q25.0)
      ventricular septal defect (Q21.0)

I27.89   **Other specified pulmonary heart diseases** 🐾

● **I27.9**   **Pulmonary heart disease, unspecified** 🐾
    Chronic cardiopulmonary disease

● **I28**   **Other diseases of pulmonary vessels**

I28.0   **Arteriovenous fistula of pulmonary vessels** 🐾
    Excludes1   congenital arteriovenous fistula (Q25.72)

I28.1   **Aneurysm of pulmonary artery** 🐾
    Excludes1   congenital aneurysm (Q25.79)
      congenital arteriovenous aneurysm (Q25.72)

I28.8   **Other diseases of pulmonary vessels** 🐾
    Pulmonary arteritis
    Pulmonary endarteritis
    Rupture of pulmonary vessels
    Stenosis of pulmonary vessels
    Stricture of pulmonary vessels

I28.9   **Disease of pulmonary vessels, unspecified** 🐾

OTHER FORMS OF HEART DISEASE (I30-I52)

● **I30**   **Acute pericarditis**
    Inflammation of pericardium (sac surrounding the heart) caused by an infection
    Includes   acute mediastinopericarditis
      acute myopericarditis
      acute pericardial effusion
      acute pleuropericarditis
      acute pneumopericarditis
    Excludes1   Dressler's syndrome (I24.1)
      rheumatic pericarditis (acute) (I01.0)
      viral pericarditis due to Coxsakie virus (B33.23)

I30.0   **Acute nonspecific idiopathic pericarditis**

I30.1   **Infective pericarditis**
    Pneumococcal pericarditis
    Pneumopyopericardium
    Purulent pericarditis
    Pyopericarditis
    Pyopericardium
    Pyopneumopericardium
    Staphylococcal pericarditis
    Streptococcal pericarditis
    Suppurative pericarditis
    Viral pericarditis
    Use additional code (B95-B97) to identify infectious agent

I30.8   **Other forms of acute pericarditis**

I30.9   **Acute pericarditis, unspecified**

● **I31**   **Other diseases of pericardium**
    Excludes1   diseases of pericardium specified as rheumatic (I09.2)
      postcardiotomy syndrome (I97.0)
      traumatic injury to pericardium (S26.-)

I31.0   **Chronic adhesive pericarditis**
    Accretio cordis
    Adherent pericardium
    Adhesive mediastinopericarditis

I31.1   **Chronic constrictive pericarditis**
    Concretio cordis
    Pericardial calcification

I31.2   **Hemopericardium, not elsewhere classified**
    Excludes1   hemopericardium as current complication following acute myocardial infarction (I23.0)

I31.3   **Pericardial effusion (noninflammatory)**
    Chylopericardium
    Excludes1   acute pericardial effusion (I30.9)
    Coding Clinic: 2019, Q1, P16

I31.4   **Cardiac tamponade**
    Code first underlying cause

I31.8   **Other specified diseases of pericardium**
    Epicardial plaques
    Focal pericardial adhesions

I31.9   **Disease of pericardium, unspecified**
    Pericarditis (chronic) NOS

▶ New   ⇒ Revised   ~~deleted~~ Deleted   Excludes 1   Excludes 2   Includes   Use additional   Code first   Code also   Key words

OGCR Official Guidelines   X Assign placeholder X   ● Use Additional Character(s)   ▶ Manifestation Code   🐾 Hierarchical Condition Category   Coding Clinic

▷ **I32**   *Pericarditis in diseases classified elsewhere*
        Code first underlying disease
        Excludes1   pericarditis (in):
                            coxsackie (virus) (B33.23)
                            gonococcal (A54.83)
                            meningococcal (A39.53)
                            rheumatoid (arthritis) (M05.31)
                            syphilitic (A52.06)
                            systemic lupus erythematosus (M32.12)
                            tuberculosis (A18.84)

● **I33**   **Acute and subacute endocarditis**
        *Inflammation/infection of lining of heart, affecting heart valves
        including replacement valves and is usually caused by a
        bacterial infection*
        Excludes1   acute rheumatic endocarditis (I01.1)
                            endocarditis NOS (I38)

    I33.0   **Acute and subacute infective endocarditis**
                Bacterial endocarditis (acute) (subacute)
                Infective endocarditis (acute) (subacute) NOS
                Endocarditis lenta (acute) (subacute)
                Malignant endocarditis (acute) (subacute)
                Purulent endocarditis (acute) (subacute)
                Septic endocarditis (acute) (subacute)
                Ulcerative endocarditis (acute) (subacute)
                Vegetative endocarditis (acute) (subacute)
                Use additional code (B95-B97) to identify infectious
                agent

    I33.9   **Acute and subacute endocarditis, unspecified**
                Acute endocarditis NOS
                Acute myoendocarditis NOS
                Acute periendocarditis NOS
                Subacute endocarditis NOS
                Subacute myoendocarditis NOS
                Subacute periendocarditis NOS

● **I34**   **Nonrheumatic mitral valve disorders**
        Excludes1   mitral valve disease (I05.9)
                            mitral valve failure (I05.8)
                            mitral valve stenosis (I05.0)
                            mitral valve disorder of unspecified cause with
                                diseases of aortic and/or tricuspid valve(s)
                                (I08.-)
                            mitral valve disorder of unspecified cause with
                                mitral stenosis or obstruction (I05.0)
                            mitral valve disorder specified as congenital
                                (Q23.2, Q23.9)
                            mitral valve disorder specified as rheumatic
                                (I05.-)

    I34.0   **Nonrheumatic mitral (valve) insufficiency**
                Nonrheumatic mitral (valve) incompetence NOS
                Nonrheumatic mitral (valve) regurgitation NOS

    I34.1   **Nonrheumatic mitral (valve) prolapse**
                Floppy nonrheumatic mitral valve syndrome
                Excludes1   Marfan's syndrome (Q87.4-)

    I34.2   **Nonrheumatic mitral (valve) stenosis**
    I34.8   **Other nonrheumatic mitral valve disorders**
    I34.9   **Nonrheumatic mitral valve disorder, unspecified**

● **I35**   **Nonrheumatic aortic valve disorders**
        Excludes1   aortic valve disorder of unspecified cause but
                                with diseases of mitral and/or tricuspid
                                valve(s) (I08.-)
                            aortic valve disorder specified as congenital
                                (Q23.0, Q23.1)
                            aortic valve disorder specified as rheumatic (I06.-)
                            hypertrophic subaortic stenosis (I42.1)

    I35.0   **Nonrheumatic aortic (valve) stenosis**
    I35.1   **Nonrheumatic aortic (valve) insufficiency**
                Nonrheumatic aortic (valve) incompetence NOS
                Nonrheumatic aortic (valve) regurgitation NOS

    I35.2   **Nonrheumatic aortic (valve) stenosis with insufficiency**
    I35.8   **Other nonrheumatic aortic valve disorders**
    I35.9   **Nonrheumatic aortic valve disorder, unspecified**

● **I36**   **Nonrheumatic tricuspid valve disorders**
        Excludes1   tricuspid valve disorders of unspecified cause
                                (I07.-)
                            tricuspid valve disorders specified as congenital
                                (Q22.4, Q22.8, Q22.9)
                            tricuspid valve disorders specified as rheumatic
                                (I07.-)
                            tricuspid valve disorders with aortic and/or
                                mitral valve involvement (I08.-)

    I36.0   **Nonrheumatic tricuspid (valve) stenosis**
    I36.1   **Nonrheumatic tricuspid (valve) insufficiency**
                Nonrheumatic tricuspid (valve) incompetence
                Nonrheumatic tricuspid (valve) regurgitation

    I36.2   **Nonrheumatic tricuspid (valve) stenosis with insufficiency**
    I36.8   **Other nonrheumatic tricuspid valve disorders**
    I36.9   **Nonrheumatic tricuspid valve disorder, unspecified**

● **I37**   **Nonrheumatic pulmonary valve disorders**
        Excludes1   pulmonary valve disorder specified as congenital
                                (Q22.1, Q22.2, Q22.3)
                            pulmonary valve disorder specified as rheumatic
                                (I09.89)

    I37.0   **Nonrheumatic pulmonary valve stenosis**
    I37.1   **Nonrheumatic pulmonary valve insufficiency**
                Nonrheumatic pulmonary valve incompetence
                Nonrheumatic pulmonary valve regurgitation

    I37.2   **Nonrheumatic pulmonary valve stenosis with insufficiency**
    I37.8   **Other nonrheumatic pulmonary valve disorders**
    I37.9   **Nonrheumatic pulmonary valve disorder, unspecified**

    I38   **Endocarditis, valve unspecified**
        Includes   endocarditis (chronic) NOS
                            valvular incompetence NOS
                            valvular insufficiency NOS
                            valvular regurgitation NOS
                            valvular stenosis NOS
                            valvulitis (chronic) NOS
        Excludes1   congenital insufficiency of cardiac valve NOS
                                (Q24.8)
                            congenital stenosis of cardiac valve NOS (Q24.8)
                            endocardial fibroelastosis (I42.4)
                            endocarditis specified as rheumatic (I09.1)

▷ **I39**   *Endocarditis and heart valve disorders in diseases classified
        elsewhere*
        Code first underlying disease, such as:
        Q fever (A78)
        Excludes1   endocardial involvement in:
                            candidiasis (B37.6)
                            gonococcal infection (A54.83)
                            Libman-Sacks disease (M32.11)
                            listerosis (A32.82)
                            meningococcal infection (A39.51)
                            rheumatoid arthritis (M05.31)
                            syphilis (A52.03)
                            tuberculosis (A18.84)
                            typhoid fever (A01.02)

● **I40**   **Acute myocarditis**
        Inflammation of heart muscle due to infection (viral/bacterial)
        Includes   subacute myocarditis
        Excludes1   acute rheumatic myocarditis (I01.2)

    I40.0   **Infective myocarditis**
                Septic myocarditis
                Use additional code (B95-B97) to identify infectious
                agent

    I40.1   **Isolated myocarditis**
                Fiedler's myocarditis
                Giant cell myocarditis
                Idiopathic myocarditis

    I40.8   **Other acute myocarditis**
    I40.9   **Acute myocarditis, unspecified**

CHAPTER 9 (I00-I99)

▶ **I41   *Myocarditis in diseases classified elsewhere***

Code first underlying disease, such as:
    typhus (A75.0-A75.9)

> **Excludes1**   myocarditis (in):
>   Chagas' disease (chronic) (B57.2)
>   acute (B57.0)
>   coxsackie (virus) infection (B33.22)
>   diphtheritic (A36.81)
>   gonococcal (A54.83)
>   influenzal (J09.X9, J10.82, J11.82)
>   meningococcal (A39.52)
>   mumps (B26.82)
>   rheumatoid arthritis (M05.31)
>   sarcoid (D86.85)
>   syphilis (A52.06)
>   toxoplasmosis (B58.81)
>   tuberculous (A18.84)

● **I42   Cardiomyopathy**

Disease of the heart muscle resulting in an abnormally enlarged, weakened, thickened, and/or stiffened muscles

> **Includes**   myocardiopathy

Code first pre-existing cardiomyopathy complicating pregnancy and puerperium (O99.4)

> **Excludes2**   ischemic cardiomyopathy (I25.5)
>   peripartum cardiomyopathy (O90.3)
>   ventricular hypertrophy (I51.7)

I42.0   Dilated cardiomyopathy 🅗
    Congestive cardiomyopathy

I42.1   Obstructive hypertrophic cardiomyopathy 🅗
    Hypertrophic subaortic stenosis (idiopathic)

I42.2   Other hypertrophic cardiomyopathy 🅗
    Nonobstructive hypertrophic cardiomyopathy

I42.3   Endomyocardial (eosinophilic) disease 🅗
    Endomyocardial (tropical) fibrosis
    Löffler's endocarditis

I42.4   Endocardial fibroelastosis 🅗
    Congenital cardiomyopathy
    Elastomyofibrosis

I42.5   Other restrictive cardiomyopathy 🅗
    Constrictive cardiomyopathy NOS

I42.6   Alcoholic cardiomyopathy 🅗
    Code also presence of alcoholism (F10.-)

I42.7   Cardiomyopathy due to drug and external agent 🅗
    Code first poisoning due to drug or toxin, if applicable (T36-T65 with fifth or sixth character 1-4 or 6)
    Use additional code for adverse effect, if applicable, to identify drug (T36-T50 with fifth or sixth character 5)

I42.8   Other cardiomyopathies 🅗

I42.9   Cardiomyopathy, unspecified 🅗
    Cardiomyopathy (primary) (secondary) NOS

▶ **I43   *Cardiomyopathy in diseases classified elsewhere*** 🅗

Code first underlying disease, such as:
    amyloidosis (E85.-)
    glycogen storage disease (E74.0)
    gout (M10.0-)
    thyrotoxicosis (E05.0-E05.9-)

> **Excludes1**   cardiomyopathy (in):
>   coxsackie (virus) (B33.24)
>   diphtheria (A36.81)
>   sarcoidosis (D86.85)
>   tuberculosis (A18.84)

● **I44   Atrioventricular and left bundle-branch block**

Conduction problem resulting in arrhythmias/dysrhythmias due to a lack of electrical impulses being transmitted normally through the heart

I44.0   Atrioventricular block, first degree

I44.1   Atrioventricular block, second degree
    Atrioventricular block, type I and II
    Möbitz block, type I and II
    Second degree block, type I and II
    Wenckebach's block

I44.2   Atrioventricular block, complete 🅗
    Complete heart block NOS
    Third degree block
    Coding Clinic: 2019, Q2, P4

● **I44.3   Other and unspecified atrioventricular block**
    Atrioventricular block NOS

    I44.30   Unspecified atrioventricular block

    I44.39   Other atrioventricular block

I44.4   Left anterior fascicular block

I44.5   Left posterior fascicular block

● **I44.6   Other and unspecified fascicular block**

    I44.60   Unspecified fascicular block
        Left bundle-branch hemiblock NOS

    I44.69   Other fascicular block

I44.7   Left bundle-branch block, unspecified

● **I45   Other conduction disorders**

I45.0   Right fascicular block

● **I45.1   Other and unspecified right bundle-branch block**

    I45.10   Unspecified right bundle-branch block
        Right bundle-branch block NOS

    I45.19   Other right bundle-branch block

I45.2   Bifascicular block

I45.3   Trifascicular block

I45.4   Nonspecific intraventricular block
    Bundle-branch block NOS

I45.5   Other specified heart block
    Sinoatrial block
    Sinoauricular block

> **Excludes1**   heart block NOS (I45.9)

I45.6   Pre-excitation syndrome
    Accelerated atrioventricular conduction
    Accessory atrioventricular conduction
    Anomalous atrioventricular excitation
    Lown-Ganong-Levine syndrome
    Pre-excitation atrioventricular conduction
    Wolff-Parkinson-White syndrome

● **I45.8   Other specified conduction disorders**

    I45.81   Long QT syndrome

    I45.89   Other specified conduction disorders
        Atrioventricular [AV] dissociation
        Interference dissociation
        Isorhythmic dissociation
        Nonparoxysmal AV nodal tachycardia
        Coding Clinic: 2013, Q2, P32

I45.9   Conduction disorder, unspecified
    Heart block NOS
    Stokes-Adams syndrome

● **I46   Cardiac arrest**

> ~~**Excludes1**   cardiogenic shock (R57.0)~~

> ▶ **Excludes2**   cardiogenic shock (R57.0)

I46.2   Cardiac arrest due to underlying cardiac condition 🅗
    Code first underlying cardiac condition

I46.8   Cardiac arrest due to other underlying condition 🅗
    Code first underlying condition

I46.9   Cardiac arrest, cause unspecified 🅗

▶ New   ⇒ Revised   ~~deleted~~ Deleted   Excludes 1   Excludes 2   Includes   Use additional   Code first   Code also   Key words

OGCR Official Guidelines   X Assign placeholder X   ● Use Additional Character(s)   ▶ Manifestation Code   🅗 Hierarchical Condition Category   Coding Clinic

● **I47 Paroxysmal tachycardia**
> *Code first tachycardia complicating:*
> abortion or ectopic or molar pregnancy (O00-O07, O08.8)
> obstetric surgery and procedures (O75.4)

> **Excludes1**   tachycardia NOS (R00.0)
>   sinoauricular tachycardia NOS (R00.0)
>   sinus [sinusal] tachycardia NOS (R00.0)

I47.0 Re-entry ventricular arrhythmia 🔖

I47.1 Supraventricular tachycardia 🔖
   Atrial (paroxysmal) tachycardia
   Atrioventricular [AV] (paroxysmal) tachycardia
   Atrioventricular re-entrant (nodal) tachycardia
     [AVNRT] [AVRT]
   Junctional (paroxysmal) tachycardia
   Nodal (paroxysmal) tachycardia

I47.2 Ventricular tachycardia 🔖
   Coding Clinic: 2013, Q3, P23

I47.9 Paroxysmal tachycardia, unspecified 🔖
   Bouveret (-Hoffman) syndrome

● **I48 Atrial fibrillation and flutter**
> *Most common abnormal heart rhythm (arrhythmia) presenting*
> *as irregular, rapid beating (tachycardia) of the heart's upper*
> *chamber.*

I48.0 Paroxysmal atrial fibrillation 🔖
● **I48.1 Persistent atrial fibrillation** 🔖
> *Rapid contractions of the upper heart chamber*

> **Excludes1**   Permanent atrial fibrillation (I48.21)
> **Coding Clinic: 2019, Q2, P3-4**

I48.11 Longstanding persistent atrial fibrillation

I48.19 Other persistent atrial fibrillation
   Chronic persistent atrial fibrillation
   Persistent atrial fibrillation, NOS

● **I48.2 Chronic atrial fibrillation** 🔖
   Coding Clinic: 2019, Q2, P3

I48.20 Chronic atrial fibrillation, unspecified
> **Excludes1**   Chronic persistent atrial
>   fibrillation (I48.19)

I48.21 Permanent atrial fibrillation

I48.3 Typical atrial flutter 🔖
   Type I atrial flutter

I48.4 Atypical atrial flutter 🔖
   Type II atrial flutter

● **I48.9 Unspecified atrial fibrillation and atrial flutter**
I48.91 Unspecified atrial fibrillation 🔖
I48.92 Unspecified atrial flutter 🔖

● **I49 Other cardiac arrhythmias**
> *Code first cardiac arrhythmia complicating:*
> abortion or ectopic or molar pregnancy (O00-O07, O08.8)
> obstetric surgery and procedures (O75.4)

> **Excludes1**   neonatal dysrhythmia (P29.1-)
>   sinoatrial bradycardia (R00.1)
>   sinus bradycardia (R00.1)
>   vagal bradycardia (R00.1)

> **Excludes2**   bradycardia NOS (R00.1)

● **I49.0 Ventricular fibrillation and flutter**
I49.01 Ventricular fibrillation 🔖
I49.02 Ventricular flutter 🔖

I49.1 Atrial premature depolarization
   Atrial premature beats

I49.2 Junctional premature depolarization 🔖

I49.3 Ventricular premature depolarization

● **I49.4 Other and unspecified premature depolarization**
I49.40 Unspecified premature depolarization
   Premature beats NOS

I49.49 Other premature depolarization
   Ectopic beats
   Extrasystoles
   Extrasystolic arrhythmias
   Premature contractions

I49.5 Sick sinus syndrome 🔖
   Tachycardia-bradycardia syndrome
   Coding Clinic: 2019, Q1, P33

I49.8 Other specified cardiac arrhythmias
   Brugada syndrome
   Coronary sinus rhythm disorder
   Ectopic rhythm disorder
   Nodal rhythm disorder

I49.9 Cardiac arrhythmia, unspecified
   Arrhythmia (cardiac) NOS

● **I50 Heart failure**
> *Code first heart failure complicating abortion or ectopic or molar*
> *pregnancy (O00-O07, O08.8)*
> heart failure due to hypertension (I11.0)
> heart failure due to hypertension with chronic kidney disease
>   (I13.-)
> heart failure following surgery (I97.13-)
> obstetric surgery and procedures (O75.4)
> rheumatic heart failure (I09.81)

> **Excludes1**   neonatal cardiac failure (P29.0)

> **Excludes2**   cardiac arrest (I46.-)

Coding Clinic: 2017, Q1, P47; 2016, Q4, P122-123, Q1, P38; 2015, Q2, P15

I50.1 Left ventricular failure, unspecified 🔖
   Cardiac asthma
   Edema of lung with heart disease NOS
   Edema of lung with heart failure
   Left heart failure
   Pulmonary edema with heart disease NOS
   Pulmonary edema with heart failure

> **Excludes1**   edema of lung without heart disease or
>   heart failure (J81.-)
>   pulmonary edema without heart disease
>   or failure (J81.-)

● **I50.2 Systolic (congestive) heart failure**
   Heart failure with reduced ejection fraction [HFrEF]
   Systolic left ventricular heart failure

   Code also end stage heart failure, if applicable (I50.84)

> **Excludes1**   combined systolic (congestive) and
>   diastolic (congestive) heart failure
>   (I50.4-)

I50.20 Unspecified systolic (congestive) heart failure 🔖

I50.21 Acute systolic (congestive) heart failure 🔖
> *Presenting a short and relatively severe episode*

I50.22 Chronic systolic (congestive) heart failure 🔖
> *Long-lasting, presenting over time*

I50.23 Acute on chronic systolic (congestive) heart failure 🔖
> *Combination code. What was a chronic condition*
> *now has an acute exacerbation (to make more*
> *severe).*
> **Coding Clinic: 2013, Q2, P33**

● **I50.3 Diastolic (congestive) heart failure**
   Diastolic left ventricular heart failure
   Heart failure with normal ejection fraction
   Heart failure with preserved ejection fraction [HFpEF]

   Code also end stage heart failure, if applicable (I50.84)

> **Excludes1**   combined systolic (congestive) and
>   diastolic (congestive) heart failure
>   (I50.4-)

I50.30 Unspecified diastolic (congestive) heart failure 🔖

I50.31 Acute diastolic (congestive) heart failure 🔖
   Coding Clinic: 2017, Q1, P46

I50.32 Chronic diastolic (congestive) heart failure 🔖

I50.33 Acute on chronic diastolic (congestive) heart failure 🔖

Item 9–8 Congestive heart failure (CHF) is a condition in which the left ventricle of the heart cannot pump enough blood to the body. The blood flow from the heart slows or returns to the heart from the venous system (back flow) resulting in congestion (fluid accumulation) particularly in the abdomen. Most commonly, fluid collects in the lungs and results in shortness of breath, especially when in a reclining position.

● I50.4　**Combined systolic (congestive) and diastolic (congestive) heart failure**
Combined systolic and diastolic left ventricular heart failure
Heart failure with reduced ejection fraction and diastolic dysfunction
Code also end stage heart failure, if applicable (I50.84)

I50.40　**Unspecified combined systolic (congestive) and diastolic (congestive) heart failure** 🐾

I50.41　**Acute combined systolic (congestive) and diastolic (congestive) heart failure** 🐾

I50.42　**Chronic combined systolic (congestive) and diastolic (congestive) heart failure** 🐾

I50.43　**Acute on chronic combined systolic (congestive) and diastolic (congestive) heart failure** 🐾

● I50.8　**Other heart failure**
● I50.81　**Right heart failure**
Right ventricular failure

I50.810　**Right heart failure, unspecified** 🐾
Right heart failure without mention of left heart failure
Right ventricular failure NOS

I50.811　**Acute right heart failure** 🐾
Acute isolated right heart failure
Acute (isolated) right ventricular failure

I50.812　**Chronic right heart failure** 🐾
Chronic isolated right heart failure
Chronic (isolated) right ventricular failure

I50.813　**Acute on chronic right heart failure** 🐾
Acute on chronic isolated right heart failure
Acute on chronic (isolated) right ventricular failure
Acute decompensation of chronic (isolated) right ventricular failure
Acute exacerbation of chronic (isolated) right ventricular failure

I50.814　**Right heart failure due to left heart failure** 🐾
Right ventricular failure secondary to left ventricular failure
Code also the type of left ventricular failure, if known (I50.2-I50.43)

Excludes1　Right heart failure with but not due to left heart failure (I50.82)

I50.82　**Biventricular heart failure** 🐾
Code also the type of left ventricular failure as systolic, diastolic, or combined, if known **(I50.2-I50.43)**

I50.83　**High output heart failure** 🐾
I50.84　**End stage heart failure** 🐾
Stage D heart failure
Code also the type of heart failure as systolic, diastolic, or combined, if known (I50.2-I50.43)

I50.89　**Other heart failure** 🐾

I50.9　**Heart failure, unspecified** 🐾
Cardiac, heart or myocardial failure NOS
Congestive heart disease
Congestive heart failure NOS

Excludes2　fluid overload unrelated to congestive heart failure (E87.70)

Coding Clinic: 2017, Q1, P45-46; 2015, Q2, P15; 2012, Q4, P92

● I51　**Complications and ill-defined descriptions of heart disease**

Excludes1　any condition in I51.4-I51.9 due to hypertension (I11.-)
any condition in I51.4-I51.9 due to hypertension and chronic kidney disease (I13.-)
heart disease specified as rheumatic (I00-I09)

I51.0　**Cardiac septal defect, acquired**　　　　　　A
Acquired septal atrial defect (old)
Acquired septal auricular defect (old)
Acquired septal ventricular defect (old)

Excludes1　cardiac septal defect as current complication following acute myocardial infarction (I23.1, I23.2)

I51.1　**Rupture of chordae tendineae, not elsewhere classified** 🐾

Excludes1　rupture of chordae tendineae as current complication following acute myocardial infarction (I23.4)

I51.2　**Rupture of papillary muscle, not elsewhere classified** 🐾

Excludes1　rupture of papillary muscle as current complication following acute myocardial infarction (I23.5)

I51.3　**Intracardiac thrombosis, not elsewhere classified**
Apical thrombosis (old)
Atrial thrombosis (old)
Auricular thrombosis (old)
Mural thrombosis (old)
Ventricular thrombosis (old)

Excludes1　intracardiac thrombosis as current complication following acute myocardial infarction (I23.6)

Coding Clinic: 2013, Q1, P24

I51.4　**Myocarditis, unspecified** 🐾
Chronic (interstitial) myocarditis
Myocardial fibrosis
Myocarditis NOS

Excludes1　acute or subacute myocarditis (I40.-)

Coding Clinic: 2016, Q4, P122

I51.5　**Myocardial degeneration** 🐾
Fatty degeneration of heart or myocardium
Myocardial disease
Senile degeneration of heart or myocardium
Coding Clinic: 2016, Q4, P122

I51.7　**Cardiomegaly**
Cardiac dilatation
Cardiac hypertrophy
Ventricular dilatation
Coding Clinic: 2016, Q4, P122

● I51.8　**Other ill-defined heart diseases**
Coding Clinic: 2016, Q4, P122

I51.81　**Takotsubo syndrome**
Reversible left ventricular dysfunction following sudden emotional stress
Stress induced cardiomyopathy
Takotsubo cardiomyopathy
Transient left ventricular apical ballooning syndrome

I51.89　**Other ill-defined heart diseases**
Carditis (acute)(chronic)
Pancarditis (acute)(chronic)
Coding Clinic: 2019, Q2, P6

I51.9　**Heart disease, unspecified**
Coding Clinic: 2016, Q4, P122

▶ New　　➠ Revised　　~~deleted~~ Deleted　　Excludes 1　　Excludes 2　　Includes　　Use additional　　Code first　　Code also　　Key words

OGCR Official Guidelines　　X Assign placeholder X　　● Use Additional Character(s)　　▌ Manifestation Code　　🐾 Hierarchical Condition Category　　**Coding Clinic**

▶ **I52** *Other heart disorders in diseases classified elsewhere*

Code first underlying disease, such as:
congenital syphilis (A50.5)
mucopolysaccharidosis (E76.3)
schistosomiasis (B65.0-B65.9)

Excludes1 heart disease (in):
gonococcal infection (A54.83)
meningococcal infection (A39.50)
rheumatoid arthritis (M05.31)
syphilis (A52.06)

CEREBROVASCULAR DISEASES (I60-I69)

Use additional code to identify presence of:
alcohol abuse and dependence (F10.-)
exposure to environmental tobacco smoke (Z77.22)
history of tobacco dependence (Z87.891)
hypertension (I10-I16)
occupational exposure to environmental tobacco smoke (Z57.31)
tobacco dependence (F17.-)
tobacco use (Z72.0)

Excludes1 traumatic intracranial hemorrhage (S06.-)

Coding Clinic: 2015, Q4, P40

● **I60** Nontraumatic subarachnoid hemorrhage

Excludes1 syphilitic ruptured cerebral aneurysm (A52.05)

Excludes2 sequelae of subarachnoid hemorrhage (I69.0-)

● **I60.0** Nontraumatic subarachnoid hemorrhage from carotid siphon and bifurcation

I60.00 Nontraumatic subarachnoid hemorrhage from unspecified carotid siphon and bifurcation

I60.01 Nontraumatic subarachnoid hemorrhage from right carotid siphon and bifurcation

I60.02 Nontraumatic subarachnoid hemorrhage from left carotid siphon and bifurcation

● **I60.1** Nontraumatic subarachnoid hemorrhage from middle cerebral artery

I60.10 Nontraumatic subarachnoid hemorrhage from unspecified middle cerebral artery

I60.11 Nontraumatic subarachnoid hemorrhage from right middle cerebral artery

I60.12 Nontraumatic subarachnoid hemorrhage from left middle cerebral artery

I60.2 Nontraumatic subarachnoid hemorrhage from anterior communicating artery

● **I60.3** Nontraumatic subarachnoid hemorrhage from posterior communicating artery

I60.30 Nontraumatic subarachnoid hemorrhage from unspecified posterior communicating artery

I60.31 Nontraumatic subarachnoid hemorrhage from right posterior communicating artery

I60.32 Nontraumatic subarachnoid hemorrhage from left posterior communicating artery

I60.4 Nontraumatic subarachnoid hemorrhage from basilar artery

● **I60.5** Nontraumatic subarachnoid hemorrhage from vertebral artery

I60.50 Nontraumatic subarachnoid hemorrhage from unspecified vertebral artery

I60.51 Nontraumatic subarachnoid hemorrhage from right vertebral artery

I60.52 Nontraumatic subarachnoid hemorrhage from left vertebral artery

I60.6 Nontraumatic subarachnoid hemorrhage from other intracranial arteries

I60.7 Nontraumatic subarachnoid hemorrhage from unspecified intracranial artery
Ruptured (congenital) berry aneurysm
Ruptured (congenital) cerebral aneurysm
Subarachnoid hemorrhage (nontraumatic) from cerebral artery NOS
Subarachnoid hemorrhage (nontraumatic) from communicating artery NOS

Excludes1 berry aneurysm, nonruptured (I67.1)

I60.8 Other nontraumatic subarachnoid hemorrhage
Meningeal hemorrhage
Rupture of cerebral arteriovenous malformation

I60.9 Nontraumatic subarachnoid hemorrhage, unspecified

● **I61** Nontraumatic intracerebral hemorrhage

Excludes2 sequelae of intracerebral hemorrhage (I69.1-)

Coding Clinic: 2017, Q2, P10

I61.0 Nontraumatic intracerebral hemorrhage in hemisphere, subcortical
Deep intracerebral hemorrhage (nontraumatic)
Coding Clinic: 2016, Q4, P27

I61.1 Nontraumatic intracerebral hemorrhage in hemisphere, cortical
Cerebral lobe hemorrhage (nontraumatic)
Superficial intracerebral hemorrhage (nontraumatic)
Coding Clinic: 2016, Q4, P28

I61.2 Nontraumatic intracerebral hemorrhage in hemisphere, unspecified

I61.3 Nontraumatic intracerebral hemorrhage in brain stem

I61.4 Nontraumatic intracerebral hemorrhage in cerebellum

I61.5 Nontraumatic intracerebral hemorrhage, intraventricular

I61.6 Nontraumatic intracerebral hemorrhage, multiple localized

I61.8 Other nontraumatic intracerebral hemorrhage

I61.9 Nontraumatic intracerebral hemorrhage, unspecified

● **I62** Other and unspecified nontraumatic intracranial hemorrhage

Excludes2 sequelae of intracranial hemorrhage (I69.2)

● **I62.0** Nontraumatic subdural hemorrhage

I62.00 Nontraumatic subdural hemorrhage, unspecified

I62.01 Nontraumatic acute subdural hemorrhage

I62.02 Nontraumatic subacute subdural hemorrhage

I62.03 Nontraumatic chronic subdural hemorrhage

I62.1 Nontraumatic extradural hemorrhage
Nontraumatic epidural hemorrhage

I62.9 Nontraumatic intracranial hemorrhage, unspecified

★ **(See Plate 31 of the Anatomy Illustrations.)**

● **I63** Cerebral infarction

▶ **Excludes1** neonatal cerebral infarction (P91.82-)

Includes occlusion and stenosis of cerebral and precerebral arteries, resulting in cerebral infarction

Use additional code, if applicable, to identify status post administration of tPA (rtPA) in a different facility within the last 24 hours prior to admission to current facility (Z92.82)

Use additional code, if known, to indicate National Institutes of Health Stroke Scale (NIHSS) score (R29.7-)

Excludes2 sequelae of cerebral infarction (I69.3-)

Coding Clinic: 2016, Q4, P28, 61, 127

● **I63.0** Cerebral infarction due to thrombosis of precerebral arteries

I63.00 Cerebral infarction due to thrombosis of unspecified precerebral artery

Cerebral embolus

Cerebral hemorrhage

Cerebral thrombosis

Figure 9-4 Events causing a stroke. (From Shiland: Mastering Healthcare Terminology, ed 1, St. Louis, Mosby, 2003)

● I63.01   Cerebral infarction due to thrombosis of vertebral artery
     I63.011   Cerebral infarction due to thrombosis of right vertebral artery 🐾
     I63.012   Cerebral infarction due to thrombosis of left vertebral artery 🐾
     I63.013   Cerebral infarction due to thrombosis of bilateral vertebral arteries 🐾
     I63.019   Cerebral infarction due to thrombosis of unspecified vertebral artery 🐾
   I63.02   Cerebral infarction due to thrombosis of basilar artery 🐾
● I63.03   Cerebral infarction due to thrombosis of carotid artery
     I63.031   Cerebral infarction due to thrombosis of right carotid artery 🐾
     I63.032   Cerebral infarction due to thrombosis of left carotid artery 🐾
     I63.033   Cerebral infarction due to thrombosis of bilateral carotid arteries 🐾
     I63.039   Cerebral infarction due to thrombosis of unspecified carotid artery 🐾
   I63.09   Cerebral infarction due to thrombosis of other precerebral artery 🐾
● I63.1   Cerebral infarction due to embolism of precerebral arteries
   I63.10   Cerebral infarction due to embolism of unspecified precerebral artery 🐾
● I63.11   Cerebral infarction due to embolism of vertebral artery
     I63.111   Cerebral infarction due to embolism of right vertebral artery 🐾
     I63.112   Cerebral infarction due to embolism of left vertebral artery 🐾
     I63.113   Cerebral infarction due to embolism of bilateral vertebral arteries 🐾
     I63.119   Cerebral infarction due to embolism of unspecified vertebral artery 🐾
   I63.12   Cerebral infarction due to embolism of basilar artery 🐾
● I63.13   Cerebral infarction due to embolism of carotid artery
     I63.131   Cerebral infarction due to embolism of right carotid artery 🐾
     I63.132   Cerebral infarction due to embolism of left carotid artery 🐾

     I63.133   Cerebral infarction due to embolism of bilateral carotid arteries 🐾
     I63.139   Cerebral infarction due to embolism of unspecified carotid artery 🐾
   I63.19   Cerebral infarction due to embolism of other precerebral artery 🐾
● I63.2   Cerebral infarction due to unspecified occlusion or stenosis of precerebral arteries
   I63.20   Cerebral infarction due to unspecified occlusion or stenosis of unspecified precerebral arteries 🐾
● I63.21   Cerebral infarction due to unspecified occlusion or stenosis of vertebral arteries
     I63.211   Cerebral infarction due to unspecified occlusion or stenosis of right vertebral artery 🐾
     I63.212   Cerebral infarction due to unspecified occlusion or stenosis of left vertebral artery 🐾
     I63.213   Cerebral infarction due to unspecified occlusion or stenosis of bilateral vertebral arteries 🐾
     I63.219   Cerebral infarction due to unspecified occlusion or stenosis of unspecified vertebral artery 🐾
   I63.22   Cerebral infarction due to unspecified occlusion or stenosis of basilar artery 🐾
● I63.23   Cerebral infarction due to unspecified occlusion or stenosis of carotid arteries
     I63.231   Cerebral infarction due to unspecified occlusion or stenosis of right carotid arteries 🐾
     I63.232   Cerebral infarction due to unspecified occlusion or stenosis of left carotid arteries 🐾
     I63.233   Cerebral infarction due to unspecified occlusion or stenosis of bilateral carotid arteries 🐾
     I63.239   Cerebral infarction due to unspecified occlusion or stenosis of unspecified carotid artery 🐾
   I63.29   Cerebral infarction due to unspecified occlusion or stenosis of other precerebral arteries 🐾
● I63.3   Cerebral infarction due to thrombosis of cerebral arteries
   I63.30   Cerebral infarction due to thrombosis of unspecified cerebral artery 🐾
● I63.31   Cerebral infarction due to thrombosis of middle cerebral artery
     I63.311   Cerebral infarction due to thrombosis of right middle cerebral artery 🐾
     I63.312   Cerebral infarction due to thrombosis of left middle cerebral artery 🐾
     I63.313   Cerebral infarction due to thrombosis of bilateral middle cerebral arteries 🐾
     I63.319   Cerebral infarction due to thrombosis of unspecified middle cerebral artery 🐾
● I63.32   Cerebral infarction due to thrombosis of anterior cerebral artery
     I63.321   Cerebral infarction due to thrombosis of right anterior cerebral artery 🐾
     I63.322   Cerebral infarction due to thrombosis of left anterior cerebral artery 🐾
     I63.323   Cerebral infarction due to thrombosis of bilateral anterior cerebral arteries 🐾
     I63.329   Cerebral infarction due to thrombosis of unspecified anterior cerebral artery 🐾

▶ New   ⇒ Revised   ~~deleted~~ Deleted   Excludes 1   Excludes 2   Includes   Use additional   Code first   Code also   Key words
OGCR Official Guidelines   X Assign placeholder X   ● Use Additional Character(s)   ▶ Manifestation Code   🐾 Hierarchical Condition Category   **Coding Clinic**

● **I63.33** Cerebral infarction due to thrombosis of posterior cerebral artery

　　I63.331 Cerebral infarction due to thrombosis of right posterior cerebral artery ℞

　　I63.332 Cerebral infarction due to thrombosis of left posterior cerebral artery ℞

　　I63.333 Cerebral infarction due to thrombosis of bilateral posterior cerebral arteries ℞

　　I63.339 Cerebral infarction due to thrombosis of unspecified posterior cerebral artery ℞

● **I63.34** Cerebral infarction due to thrombosis of cerebellar artery

　　I63.341 Cerebral infarction due to thrombosis of right cerebellar artery ℞

　　I63.342 Cerebral infarction due to thrombosis of left cerebellar artery ℞

　　I63.343 Cerebral infarction due to thrombosis of bilateral cerebellar arteries ℞

　　I63.349 Cerebral infarction due to thrombosis of unspecified cerebellar artery ℞

　I63.39 Cerebral infarction due to thrombosis of other cerebral artery ℞

● **I63.4** Cerebral infarction due to embolism of cerebral arteries

　I63.40 Cerebral infarction due to embolism of unspecified cerebral artery ℞

● **I63.41** Cerebral infarction due to embolism of middle cerebral artery

　　I63.411 Cerebral infarction due to embolism of right middle cerebral artery ℞

　　I63.412 Cerebral infarction due to embolism of left middle cerebral artery ℞

　　I63.413 Cerebral infarction due to embolism of bilateral middle cerebral arteries ℞

　　I63.419 Cerebral infarction due to embolism of unspecified middle cerebral artery ℞

● **I63.42** Cerebral infarction due to embolism of anterior cerebral artery

　　I63.421 Cerebral infarction due to embolism of right anterior cerebral artery ℞

　　I63.422 Cerebral infarction due to embolism of left anterior cerebral artery ℞

　　I63.423 Cerebral infarction due to embolism of bilateral anterior cerebral arteries ℞

　　I63.429 Cerebral infarction due to embolism of unspecified anterior cerebral artery ℞

● **I63.43** Cerebral infarction due to embolism of posterior cerebral artery

　　I63.431 Cerebral infarction due to embolism of right posterior cerebral artery ℞

　　I63.432 Cerebral infarction due to embolism of left posterior cerebral artery ℞

　　I63.433 Cerebral infarction due to embolism of bilateral posterior cerebral arteries ℞

　　I63.439 Cerebral infarction due to embolism of unspecified posterior cerebral artery ℞

● **I63.44** Cerebral infarction due to embolism of cerebellar artery

　　I63.441 Cerebral infarction due to embolism of right cerebellar artery ℞

　　I63.442 Cerebral infarction due to embolism of left cerebellar artery ℞

　　I63.443 Cerebral infarction due to embolism of bilateral cerebellar arteries ℞

　　I63.449 Cerebral infarction due to embolism of unspecified cerebellar artery ℞

　I63.49 Cerebral infarction due to embolism of other cerebral artery ℞

● **I63.5** Cerebral infarction due to unspecified occlusion or stenosis of cerebral arteries

　I63.50 Cerebral infarction due to unspecified occlusion or stenosis of unspecified cerebral artery ℞

● **I63.51** Cerebral infarction due to unspecified occlusion or stenosis of middle cerebral artery

　　I63.511 Cerebral infarction due to unspecified occlusion or stenosis of right middle cerebral artery ℞

　　I63.512 Cerebral infarction due to unspecified occlusion or stenosis of left middle cerebral artery ℞

　　I63.513 Cerebral infarction due to unspecified occlusion or stenosis of bilateral middle cerebral arteries ℞

　　I63.519 Cerebral infarction due to unspecified occlusion or stenosis of unspecified middle cerebral artery ℞

● **I63.52** Cerebral infarction due to unspecified occlusion or stenosis of anterior cerebral artery

　　I63.521 Cerebral infarction due to unspecified occlusion or stenosis of right anterior cerebral artery ℞

　　I63.522 Cerebral infarction due to unspecified occlusion or stenosis of left anterior cerebral artery ℞

　　I63.523 Cerebral infarction due to unspecified occlusion or stenosis of bilateral anterior cerebral arteries ℞

　　I63.529 Cerebral infarction due to unspecified occlusion or stenosis of unspecified anterior cerebral artery ℞

● **I63.53** Cerebral infarction due to unspecified occlusion or stenosis of posterior cerebral artery

　　I63.531 Cerebral infarction due to unspecified occlusion or stenosis of right posterior cerebral artery ℞

　　I63.532 Cerebral infarction due to unspecified occlusion or stenosis of left posterior cerebral artery ℞
　　　　　Coding Clinic: 2017, Q2, P10

　　I63.533 Cerebral infarction due to unspecified occlusion or stenosis of bilateral posterior cerebral arteries ℞

　　I63.539 Cerebral infarction due to unspecified occlusion or stenosis of unspecified posterior cerebral artery ℞

CHAPTER 9 (I00-I99)

● **I63.54** Cerebral infarction due to unspecified occlusion or stenosis of cerebellar artery
- **I63.541** Cerebral infarction due to unspecified occlusion or stenosis of right cerebellar artery ⦿
- **I63.542** Cerebral infarction due to unspecified occlusion or stenosis of left cerebellar artery ⦿
- **I63.543** Cerebral infarction due to unspecified occlusion or stenosis of bilateral cerebellar arteries ⦿
- **I63.549** Cerebral infarction due to unspecified occlusion or stenosis of unspecified cerebellar artery ⦿

I63.59 Cerebral infarction due to unspecified occlusion or stenosis of other cerebral artery ⦿

I63.6 Cerebral infarction due to cerebral venous thrombosis, nonpyogenic ⦿

● **I63.8** Other cerebral infarction ⦿
- **I63.81** Other cerebral infarction due to occlusion or stenosis of small artery ⦿
  Lacunar infarction
  Coding Clinic: 2018, Q4, P16
- **I63.89** Other cerebral infarction ⦿
  Coding Clinic: 2017, Q2, P9

I63.9 Cerebral infarction, unspecified ⦿
  Stroke NOS
  > **Excludes2** transient cerebral ischemic attacks and related syndromes (G45.-)
  Coding Clinic: 2016, Q4, P62; 2015, Q1, P26

● **I65** Occlusion and stenosis of precerebral arteries, not resulting in cerebral infarction
  > **Includes** embolism of precerebral artery
  > narrowing of precerebral artery
  > obstruction (complete) (partial) of precerebral artery
  > thrombosis of precerebral artery
  > **Excludes1** insufficiency, NOS, of precerebral artery (G45.-)
  > insufficiency of precerebral arteries causing cerebral infarction (I63.0-I63.2)

● **I65.0** Occlusion and stenosis of vertebral artery
- **I65.01** Occlusion and stenosis of right vertebral artery
- **I65.02** Occlusion and stenosis of left vertebral artery
- **I65.03** Occlusion and stenosis of bilateral vertebral arteries
- **I65.09** Occlusion and stenosis of unspecified vertebral artery

I65.1 Occlusion and stenosis of basilar artery

● **I65.2** Occlusion and stenosis of carotid artery
- **I65.21** Occlusion and stenosis of right carotid artery
- **I65.22** Occlusion and stenosis of left carotid artery
- **I65.23** Occlusion and stenosis of bilateral carotid arteries
- **I65.29** Occlusion and stenosis of unspecified carotid artery

I65.8 Occlusion and stenosis of other precerebral arteries

I65.9 Occlusion and stenosis of unspecified precerebral artery
  Occlusion and stenosis of precerebral artery NOS

● **I66** Occlusion and stenosis of cerebral arteries, not resulting in cerebral infarction
  > **Includes** embolism of cerebral artery
  > narrowing of cerebral artery
  > obstruction (complete) (partial) of cerebral artery
  > thrombosis of cerebral artery
  > **Excludes1** occlusion and stenosis of cerebral artery causing cerebral infarction (I63.3-I63.5)

● **I66.0** Occlusion and stenosis of middle cerebral artery
- **I66.01** Occlusion and stenosis of right middle cerebral artery
- **I66.02** Occlusion and stenosis of left middle cerebral artery
- **I66.03** Occlusion and stenosis of bilateral middle cerebral arteries
- **I66.09** Occlusion and stenosis of unspecified middle cerebral artery

● **I66.1** Occlusion and stenosis of anterior cerebral artery
- **I66.11** Occlusion and stenosis of right anterior cerebral artery
- **I66.12** Occlusion and stenosis of left anterior cerebral artery
- **I66.13** Occlusion and stenosis of bilateral anterior cerebral arteries
- **I66.19** Occlusion and stenosis of unspecified anterior cerebral artery

● **I66.2** Occlusion and stenosis of posterior cerebral artery
- **I66.21** Occlusion and stenosis of right posterior cerebral artery
- **I66.22** Occlusion and stenosis of left posterior cerebral artery
- **I66.23** Occlusion and stenosis of bilateral posterior cerebral arteries
- **I66.29** Occlusion and stenosis of unspecified posterior cerebral artery

I66.3 Occlusion and stenosis of cerebellar arteries

I66.8 Occlusion and stenosis of other cerebral arteries
  Occlusion and stenosis of perforating arteries

I66.9 Occlusion and stenosis of unspecified cerebral artery

● **I67** Other cerebrovascular diseases
  > **Excludes2** sequelae of the listed conditions (I69.8)

I67.0 Dissection of cerebral arteries, nonruptured ⦿
  > **Excludes1** ruptured cerebral arteries (I60.7)

I67.1 Cerebral aneurysm, nonruptured
  Cerebral aneurysm NOS
  Cerebral arteriovenous fistula, acquired
  Internal carotid artery aneurysm, intracranial portion
  Internal carotid artery aneurysm, NOS
  > **Excludes1** congenital cerebral aneurysm, nonruptured (Q28.-)
  > ruptured cerebral aneurysm (I60.7)

I67.2 Cerebral atherosclerosis   A
  Atheroma of cerebral and precerebral arteries

I67.3 Progressive vascular leukoencephalopathy
  Binswanger's disease

I67.4 Hypertensive encephalopathy
  > **Excludes2** insufficiency, NOS, of precerebral arteries (G45.2)

I67.5 Moyamoya disease

I67.6 Nonpyogenic thrombosis of intracranial venous system
  Nonpyogenic thrombosis of cerebral vein
  Nonpyogenic thrombosis of intracranial venous sinus
  > **Excludes1** nonpyogenic thrombosis of intracranial venous system causing infarction (I63.6)

I67.7 Cerebral arteritis, not elsewhere classified
  Granulomatous angiitis of the nervous system
  > **Excludes1** allergic granulomatous angiitis (M30.1)

▶ New ⫸ Revised ~~deleted~~ Deleted Excludes 1 Excludes 2 Includes Use additional Code first Code also Key words
OGCR Official Guidelines X Assign placeholder X ● Use Additional Character(s) ▶ Manifestation Code ⦿ Hierarchical Condition Category Coding Clinic

● **I67.8**   **Other specified cerebrovascular diseases**

    I67.81   **Acute cerebrovascular insufficiency**
        Acute cerebrovascular insufficiency unspecified as to location or reversibility

    I67.82   **Cerebral ischemia**
        Chronic cerebral ischemia

    I67.83   **Posterior reversible encephalopathy syndrome**
        PRES

    ● **I67.84**   **Cerebral vasospasm and vasoconstriction**

        I67.841   **Reversible cerebrovascular vasoconstriction syndrome**
            Call-Fleming syndrome

            Code first underlying condition, if applicable, such as eclampsia (O15.00-O15.9)

        I67.848   **Other cerebrovascular vasospasm and vasoconstriction**

    ● **I67.85**   **Hereditary cerebrovascular diseases**

        I67.850   **Cerebral autosomal dominant arteriopathy with subcortical infarcts and leukoencephalopathy**
            CADASIL

            Code also any associated diagnoses, such as:
                epilepsy (G40.-), stroke (I63.-) vascular dementia (F01.-)

        I67.858   **Other hereditary cerebrovascular disease**

    I67.89   **Other cerebrovascular disease**

  I67.9   **Cerebrovascular disease, unspecified**

● **I68**   **Cerebrovascular disorders in diseases classified elsewhere**

  ▷ **I68.0**   *Cerebral amyloid angiopathy*
      Code first underlying amyloidosis (E85.-)

  ▷ **I68.2**   *Cerebral arteritis in other diseases classified elsewhere*
      Code first underlying disease

      Excludes1   cerebral arteritis (in):
          listerosis (A32.89)
          systemic lupus erythematosus (M32.19)
          syphilis (A52.04)
          tuberculosis (A18.89)

  ▷ **I68.8**   *Other cerebrovascular disorders in diseases classified elsewhere*
      Code first underlying disease

      Excludes1   syphilitic cerebral aneurysm (A52.05)

OGCR Section I.c.9.d.

Sequelae of Cerebrovascular Disease

1) Category I69, Sequelae of Cerebrovascular disease

Category I69 is used to indicate conditions classifiable to categories I60-I67 as the causes of sequela (neurologic deficits), themselves classified elsewhere. These "late effects" include neurologic deficits that persist after initial onset of conditions classifiable to categories I60-I67. The neurologic deficits caused by cerebrovascular disease may be present from the onset of may arise at any time after the onset of the condition classifiable to categories I60-I67.

Codes from category I69, Sequelae of cerebrovascular disease, that specify hemiplegia, hemiparesis and monoplegia identify whether the dominant or nondominant side is affected. Should the affected side be documented, but not specified as dominant or nondominant, and the classification system does not indicate a default, code selection is as follows:

For ambidextrous patients, the default should be dominant.

If the left side is affected, the default is nondominant.

If the right side is affected, the default is dominant.

2) Codes from category I69 with codes from I60-I67

Codes from category I69 may be assigned on a health care record with codes from I60-I67, if the patient has a current cerebrovascular disease and deficits from an old cerebrovascular disease.

● **I69**   **Sequelae of cerebrovascular disease**
    Note: Category I69 is to be used to indicate conditions in I60-I67 as the cause of sequelae. The 'sequelae' include conditions specified as such or as residuals which may occur at any time after the onset of the causal condition.

    Excludes1   personal history of cerebral infarction without residual deficit (Z86.73)
         personal history of prolonged reversible ischemic neurologic deficit (PRIND) (Z86.73)
         personal history of reversible ischemic neurologcial deficit (RIND) (Z86.73)
         sequelae of traumatic intracranial injury (S06.-)

Coding Clinic: 2016, Q4, P28; 2015, Q4, P40; 2012, Q4, P107

● **I69.0**   **Sequelae of nontraumatic subarachnoid hemorrhage**

    I69.00   **Unspecified sequelae of nontraumatic subarachnoid hemorrhage**

    ● **I69.01**   **Cognitive deficits** following nontraumatic subarachnoid hemorrhage

        I69.010   **Attention and concentration** deficit following nontraumatic subarachnoid hemorrhage

        I69.011   **Memory deficit** following nontraumatic subarachnoid hemorrhage

        I69.012   **Visuospatial deficit** and spatial neglect following nontraumatic subarachnoid hemorrhage

        I69.013   **Psychomotor** deficit following nontraumatic subarachnoid hemorrhage

        I69.014   **Frontal lobe and executive function** deficit following nontraumatic subarachnoid hemorrhage

        I69.015   **Cognitive social or emotional** deficit following nontraumatic subarachnoid hemorrhage

        I69.018   **Other symptoms and signs** involving cognitive functions following nontraumatic subarachnoid hemorrhage

        I69.019   **Unspecified** symptoms and signs involving cognitive functions following nontraumatic subarachnoid hemorrhage

    ● **I69.02**   **Speech and language deficits** following nontraumatic subarachnoid hemorrhage

        I69.020   **Aphasia** following nontraumatic subarachnoid hemorrhage

        I69.021   **Dysphasia** following nontraumatic subarachnoid hemorrhage

        I69.022   **Dysarthria** following nontraumatic subarachnoid hemorrhage

        I69.023   **Fluency disorder** following nontraumatic subarachnoid hemorrhage
            Stuttering following nontraumatic subarachnoid hemorrhage

        I69.028   **Other speech and language deficits** following nontraumatic subarachnoid hemorrhage

CHAPTER 9 (I00-I99)

● **I69.03 Monoplegia of upper limb following nontraumatic subarachnoid hemorrhage**

    I69.031 **Monoplegia of upper limb following nontraumatic subarachnoid hemorrhage affecting right dominant side** 🐾

    I69.032 **Monoplegia of upper limb following nontraumatic subarachnoid hemorrhage affecting left dominant side** 🐾

    I69.033 **Monoplegia of upper limb following nontraumatic subarachnoid hemorrhage affecting right non-dominant side** 🐾

    I69.034 **Monoplegia of upper limb following nontraumatic subarachnoid hemorrhage affecting left non-dominant side** 🐾

    I69.039 **Monoplegia of upper limb following nontraumatic subarachnoid hemorrhage affecting unspecified side** 🐾

● **I69.04 Monoplegia of lower limb following nontraumatic subarachnoid hemorrhage**

    I69.041 **Monoplegia of lower limb following nontraumatic subarachnoid hemorrhage affecting right dominant side** 🐾

    I69.042 **Monoplegia of lower limb following nontraumatic subarachnoid hemorrhage affecting left dominant side** 🐾

    I69.043 **Monoplegia of lower limb following nontraumatic subarachnoid hemorrhage affecting right non-dominant side** 🐾

    I69.044 **Monoplegia of lower limb following nontraumatic subarachnoid hemorrhage affecting left non-dominant side** 🐾

    I69.049 **Monoplegia of lower limb following nontraumatic subarachnoid hemorrhage affecting unspecified side** 🐾

● **I69.05 Hemiplegia and hemiparesis following nontraumatic subarachnoid hemorrhage**

    I69.051 **Hemiplegia and hemiparesis following nontraumatic subarachnoid hemorrhage affecting right dominant side** 🐾

    I69.052 **Hemiplegia and hemiparesis following nontraumatic subarachnoid hemorrhage affecting left dominant side** 🐾

    I69.053 **Hemiplegia and hemiparesis following nontraumatic subarachnoid hemorrhage affecting right non-dominant side** 🐾

    I69.054 **Hemiplegia and hemiparesis following nontraumatic subarachnoid hemorrhage affecting left non-dominant side** 🐾

    I69.059 **Hemiplegia and hemiparesis following nontraumatic subarachnoid hemorrhage affecting unspecified side** 🐾

● **I69.06 Other paralytic syndrome following nontraumatic subarachnoid hemorrhage**

Use additional code to identify type of paralytic syndrome, such as:
locked-in state (G83.5)
quadriplegia (G82.5-)

Excludes1   hemiplegia/hemiparesis following nontraumatic subarachnoid hemorrhage (I69.05-)
monoplegia of lower limb following nontraumatic subarachnoid hemorrhage (I69.04-)
monoplegia of upper limb following nontraumatic subarachnoid hemorrhage (I69.03-)

    I69.061 **Other paralytic syndrome following nontraumatic subarachnoid hemorrhage affecting right dominant side** 🐾

    I69.062 **Other paralytic syndrome following nontraumatic subarachnoid hemorrhage affecting left dominant side** 🐾

    I69.063 **Other paralytic syndrome following nontraumatic subarachnoid hemorrhage affecting right non-dominant side** 🐾

    I69.064 **Other paralytic syndrome following nontraumatic subarachnoid hemorrhage affecting left non-dominant side** 🐾

    I69.065 **Other paralytic syndrome following nontraumatic subarachnoid hemorrhage, bilateral** 🐾

    I69.069 **Other paralytic syndrome following nontraumatic subarachnoid hemorrhage affecting unspecified side** 🐾

● **I69.09 Other sequelae of nontraumatic subarachnoid hemorrhage**

    I69.090 **Apraxia following nontraumatic subarachnoid hemorrhage**

    I69.091 **Dysphagia following nontraumatic subarachnoid hemorrhage**

        Use additional code to identify the type of dysphagia, if known (R13.1-)

    I69.092 **Facial weakness following nontraumatic subarachnoid hemorrhage**
        Facial droop following nontraumatic subarachnoid hemorrhage

    I69.093 **Ataxia following nontraumatic subarachnoid hemorrhage**

    I69.098 **Other sequelae following nontraumatic subarachnoid hemorrhage**
        Alterations of sensation following nontraumatic subarachnoid hemorrhage
        Disturbance of vision following nontraumatic subarachnoid hemorrhage
        Use additional code to identify the sequelae

▶ New   ⇒ Revised   ~~deleted~~ Deleted   Excludes 1   Excludes 2   Includes   Use additional   Code first   Code also   Key words
OGCR Official Guidelines   X Assign placeholder X   ● Use Additional Character(s)   ▷ Manifestation Code   🐾 Hierarchical Condition Category   **Coding Clinic**

● **I69.1**   Sequelae of nontraumatic intracerebral hemorrhage

  I69.10   Unspecified sequelae of nontraumatic intracerebral hemorrhage

● **I69.11**   Cognitive deficits following nontraumatic intracerebral hemorrhage

  I69.110   Attention and concentration deficit following nontraumatic intracerebral hemorrhage

  I69.111   Memory deficit following nontraumatic intracerebral hemorrhage

  I69.112   Visuospatial deficit and spatial neglect following nontraumatic intracerebral hemorrhage

  I69.113   Psychomotor deficit following nontraumatic intracerebral hemorrhage

  I69.114   Frontal lobe and executive function deficit following nontraumatic intracerebral hemorrhage

  I69.115   Cognitive social or emotional deficit following nontraumatic intracerebral hemorrhage

  I69.118   Other symptoms and signs involving cognitive functions following nontraumatic intracerebral hemorrhage

  I69.119   Unspecified symptoms and signs involving cognitive functions following nontraumatic intracerebral hemorrhage

● **I69.12**   Speech and language deficits following nontraumatic intracerebral hemorrhage

  I69.120   Aphasia following nontraumatic intracerebral hemorrhage

  I69.121   Dysphasia following nontraumatic intracerebral hemorrhage

  I69.122   Dysarthria following nontraumatic intracerebral hemorrhage

  I69.123   Fluency disorder following nontraumatic intracerebral hemorrhage
      Stuttering following nontraumatic intracerebral hemorrhage

  I69.128   Other speech and language deficits following nontraumatic intracerebral hemorrhage

● **I69.13**   Monoplegia of upper limb following nontraumatic intracerebral hemorrhage

  I69.131   Monoplegia of upper limb following nontraumatic intracerebral hemorrhage affecting right dominant side 🔄

  I69.132   Monoplegia of upper limb following nontraumatic intracerebral hemorrhage affecting left dominant side 🔄

  I69.133   Monoplegia of upper limb following nontraumatic intracerebral hemorrhage affecting right non-dominant side 🔄

  I69.134   Monoplegia of upper limb following nontraumatic intracerebral hemorrhage affecting left non-dominant side 🔄

  I69.139   Monoplegia of upper limb following nontraumatic intracerebral hemorrhage affecting unspecified side 🔄

● **I69.14**   Monoplegia of lower limb following nontraumatic intracerebral hemorrhage

  I69.141   Monoplegia of lower limb following nontraumatic intracerebral hemorrhage affecting right dominant side 🔄

  I69.142   Monoplegia of lower limb following nontraumatic intracerebral hemorrhage affecting left dominant side 🔄

  I69.143   Monoplegia of lower limb following nontraumatic intracerebral hemorrhage affecting right non-dominant side 🔄

  I69.144   Monoplegia of lower limb following nontraumatic intracerebral hemorrhage affecting left non-dominant side 🔄

  I69.149   Monoplegia of lower limb following nontraumatic intracerebral hemorrhage affecting unspecified side 🔄

● **I69.15**   Hemiplegia and hemiparesis following nontraumatic intracerebral hemorrhage

  I69.151   Hemiplegia and hemiparesis following nontraumatic intracerebral hemorrhage affecting right dominant side 🔄

  I69.152   Hemiplegia and hemiparesis following nontraumatic intracerebral hemorrhage affecting left dominant side 🔄

  I69.153   Hemiplegia and hemiparesis following nontraumatic intracerebral hemorrhage affecting right non-dominant side 🔄

  I69.154   Hemiplegia and hemiparesis following nontraumatic intracerebral hemorrhage affecting left non-dominant side 🔄

  I69.159   Hemiplegia and hemiparesis following nontraumatic intracerebral hemorrhage affecting unspecified side 🔄

● **I69.16**   Other paralytic syndrome following nontraumatic intracerebral hemorrhage
      Use additional code to identify type of paralytic syndrome, such as:
      locked-in state (G83.5)
      quadriplegia (G82.5-)
      Excludes1   hemiplegia/hemiparesis following nontraumatic intracerebral hemorrhage (I69.15-)
              monoplegia of lower limb following nontraumatic intracerebral hemorrhage (I69.14-)
              monoplegia of upper limb following nontraumatic intracerebral hemorrhage (I69.13-)

  I69.161   Other paralytic syndrome following nontraumatic intracerebral hemorrhage affecting right dominant side 🔄

  I69.162   Other paralytic syndrome following nontraumatic intracerebral hemorrhage affecting left dominant side 🔄

  I69.163   Other paralytic syndrome following nontraumatic intracerebral hemorrhage affecting right non-dominant side 🔄

I69.164　Other paralytic syndrome following nontraumatic intracerebral hemorrhage affecting left non-dominant side 🐾

I69.165　Other paralytic syndrome following nontraumatic intracerebral hemorrhage, bilateral 🐾

I69.169　Other paralytic syndrome following nontraumatic intracerebral hemorrhage affecting unspecified side 🐾

● I69.19　Other sequelae of nontraumatic intracerebral hemorrhage

I69.190　Apraxia following nontraumatic intracerebral hemorrhage

I69.191　Dysphagia following nontraumatic intracerebral hemorrhage

Use additional code to identify the type of dysphagia, if known (R13.1-)

I69.192　Facial weakness following nontraumatic intracerebral hemorrhage

Facial droop following nontraumatic intracerebral hemorrhage

I69.193　Ataxia following nontraumatic intracerebral hemorrhage

I69.198　Other sequelae of nontraumatic intracerebral hemorrhage

Alteration of sensations following nontraumatic intracerebral hemorrhage

Disturbance of vision following nontraumatic intracerebral hemorrhage

Use additional code to identify the sequelae

● I69.2　Sequelae of other nontraumatic intracranial hemorrhage

I69.20　Unspecified sequelae of other nontraumatic intracranial hemorrhage

● I69.21　Cognitive deficits following other nontraumatic intracranial hemorrhage

I69.210　Attention and concentration deficit following other nontraumatic intracranial hemorrhage

I69.211　Memory deficit following other nontraumatic intracranial hemorrhage

I69.212　Visuospatial deficit and spatial neglect following other nontraumatic intracranial hemorrhage

I69.213　Psychomotor deficit following other nontraumatic intracranial hemorrhage

I69.214　Frontal lobe and executive function deficit following other nontraumatic intracranial hemorrhage

I69.215　Cognitive social or emotional deficit following other nontraumatic intracranial hemorrhage

I69.218　Other symptoms and signs involving cognitive functions following other nontraumatic intracranial hemorrhage

I69.219　Unspecified symptoms and signs involving cognitive functions following other nontraumatic intracranial hemorrhage

● I69.22　Speech and language deficits following other nontraumatic intracranial hemorrhage

I69.220　Aphasia following other nontraumatic intracranial hemorrhage

I69.221　Dysphasia following other nontraumatic intracranial hemorrhage

I69.222　Dysarthria following other nontraumatic intracranial hemorrhage

I69.223　Fluency disorder following other nontraumatic intracranial hemorrhage

Stuttering following other nontraumatic intracranial hemorrhage

I69.228　Other speech and language deficits following other nontraumatic intracranial hemorrhage

● I69.23　Monoplegia of upper limb following other nontraumatic intracranial hemorrhage

I69.231　Monoplegia of upper limb following other nontraumatic intracranial hemorrhage affecting right dominant side 🐾

I69.232　Monoplegia of upper limb following other nontraumatic intracranial hemorrhage affecting left dominant side 🐾

I69.233　Monoplegia of upper limb following other nontraumatic intracranial hemorrhage affecting right non-dominant side 🐾

I69.234　Monoplegia of upper limb following other nontraumatic intracranial hemorrhage affecting left non-dominant side 🐾

I69.239　Monoplegia of upper limb following other nontraumatic intracranial hemorrhage affecting unspecified side 🐾

● I69.24　Monoplegia of lower limb following other nontraumatic intracranial hemorrhage

I69.241　Monoplegia of lower limb following other nontraumatic intracranial hemorrhage affecting right dominant side 🐾

I69.242　Monoplegia of lower limb following other nontraumatic intracranial hemorrhage affecting left dominant side 🐾

I69.243　Monoplegia of lower limb following other nontraumatic intracranial hemorrhage affecting right non-dominant side 🐾

I69.244　Monoplegia of lower limb following other nontraumatic intracranial hemorrhage affecting left non-dominant side 🐾

I69.249　Monoplegia of lower limb following other nontraumatic intracranial hemorrhage affecting unspecified side 🐾

● I69.25　Hemiplegia and hemiparesis following other nontraumatic intracranial hemorrhage

I69.251　Hemiplegia and hemiparesis following other nontraumatic intracranial hemorrhage affecting right dominant side 🐾

I69.252　Hemiplegia and hemiparesis following other nontraumatic intracranial hemorrhage affecting left dominant side 🐾

I69.253　Hemiplegia and hemiparesis following other nontraumatic intracranial hemorrhage affecting right non-dominant side 🐾

I69.254　Hemiplegia and hemiparesis following other nontraumatic intracranial hemorrhage affecting left non-dominant side 🐾

I69.259　Hemiplegia and hemiparesis following other nontraumatic intracranial hemorrhage affecting unspecified side 🐾

● **I69.26 Other paralytic syndrome following other nontraumatic intracranial hemorrhage**

Use additional code to identify type of paralytic syndrome, such as:
locked-in state (G83.5)
quadriplegia (G82.5-)

Excludes1 hemiplegia/hemiparesis following other nontraumatic intracranial hemorrhage (I69.25-)
monoplegia of lower limb following other nontraumatic intracranial hemorrhage (I69.24-)
monoplegia of upper limb following other nontraumatic intracranial hemorrhage (I69.23-)

I69.261 Other paralytic syndrome following other nontraumatic intracranial hemorrhage affecting **right dominant side** 🔁

I69.262 Other paralytic syndrome following other nontraumatic intracranial hemorrhage affecting **left dominant side** 🔁

I69.263 Other paralytic syndrome following other nontraumatic intracranial hemorrhage affecting **right non-dominant side** 🔁

I69.264 Other paralytic syndrome following other nontraumatic intracranial hemorrhage affecting **left non-dominant side** 🔁

I69.265 Other paralytic syndrome following other nontraumatic intracranial hemorrhage, **bilateral** 🔁

I69.269 Other paralytic syndrome following other nontraumatic intracranial hemorrhage affecting **unspecified side** 🔁

● **I69.29 Other sequelae of other nontraumatic intracranial hemorrhage**

I69.290 Apraxia following other nontraumatic intracranial hemorrhage

I69.291 Dysphagia following other nontraumatic intracranial hemorrhage

Use additional code to identify the type of dysphagia, if known (R13.1-)

I69.292 Facial weakness following other nontraumatic intracranial hemorrhage
Facial droop following other nontraumatic intracranial hemorrhage

I69.293 Ataxia following other nontraumatic intracranial hemorrhage

I69.298 Other sequelae of other nontraumatic intracranial hemorrhage
Alteration of sensation following other nontraumatic intracranial hemorrhage
Disturbance of vision following other nontraumatic intracranial hemorrhage

Use additional code to identify the sequelae

● **I69.3 Sequelae of cerebral infarction**
Sequelae of stroke NOS
Coding Clinic: 2012, Q4, P92, 95

I69.30 Unspecified sequelae of cerebral infarction

● **I69.31 Cognitive deficits following cerebral infarction**

I69.310 **Attention and concentration deficit** following cerebral infarction

I69.311 **Memory deficit** following cerebral infarction

I69.312 **Visuospatial deficit and spatial neglect** following cerebral infarction

I69.313 **Psychomotor deficit** following cerebral infarction

I69.314 **Frontal lobe and executive function deficit** following cerebral infarction

I69.315 **Cognitive social or emotional deficit** following cerebral infarction

I69.318 **Other symptoms and signs involving cognitive functions** following cerebral infarction

I69.319 **Unspecified symptoms and signs involving cognitive functions** following cerebral infarction

● **I69.32 Speech and language deficits following cerebral infarction**

I69.320 **Aphasia** following cerebral infarction

I69.321 **Dysphasia** following cerebral infarction
Coding Clinic: 2012, Q4, P91

I69.322 **Dysarthria** following cerebral infarction

Excludes2 transient ischemic attack (TIA) (G45.9)

I69.323 **Fluency disorder** following cerebral infarction
Stuttering following cerebral infarction

I69.328 **Other speech and language deficits** following cerebral infarction

● **I69.33 Monoplegia of upper limb following cerebral infarction**
Coding Clinic: 2017, Q1, P47

I69.331 Monoplegia of upper limb following cerebral infarction affecting **right dominant side** 🔁

I69.332 Monoplegia of upper limb following cerebral infarction affecting **left dominant side** 🔁

I69.333 Monoplegia of upper limb following cerebral infarction affecting **right non-dominant side** 🔁

I69.334 Monoplegia of upper limb following cerebral infarction affecting **left non-dominant side** 🔁

I69.339 Monoplegia of upper limb following cerebral infarction affecting **unspecified side** 🔁

● **I69.34 Monoplegia of lower limb following cerebral infarction**
Coding Clinic: 2017, Q1, P47

I69.341 Monoplegia of lower limb following cerebral infarction affecting **right dominant side** 🔁

I69.342 Monoplegia of lower limb following cerebral infarction affecting **left dominant side** 🔁

I69.343 Monoplegia of lower limb following cerebral infarction affecting **right non-dominant side** 🔁

CHAPTER 9 (I00-I99)

I69.344 **Monoplegia** of lower limb following cerebral infarction affecting **left non-dominant side** 🕮

I69.349 **Monoplegia** of lower limb following cerebral infarction affecting **unspecified side** 🕮

● I69.35 **Hemiplegia and hemiparesis** following cerebral infarction

I69.351 **Hemiplegia and hemiparesis** following cerebral infarction affecting **right dominant side** 🕮

Excludes2 transient ischemic attack (TIA) (G45.9)

Coding Clinic: 2015, Q1, P25

I69.352 **Hemiplegia and hemiparesis** following cerebral infarction affecting **left dominant side** 🕮

I69.353 **Hemiplegia and hemiparesis** following cerebral infarction affecting **right non-dominant side** 🕮

I69.354 **Hemiplegia and hemiparesis** following cerebral infarction affecting **left non-dominant side** 🕮

Coding Clinic: 2012, Q4, P91

I69.359 **Hemiplegia and hemiparesis** following cerebral infarction affecting **unspecified side** 🕮

● I69.36 **Other paralytic syndrome** following cerebral infarction

Use additional code to identify type of paralytic syndrome, such as:
locked-in state (G83.5)
quadriplegia (G82.5-)

Excludes1 hemiplegia/hemiparesis following cerebral infarction (I69.35-)
monoplegia of lower limb following cerebral infarction (I69.34-)
monoplegia of upper limb following cerebral infarction (I69.33-)

I69.361 **Other paralytic syndrome** following cerebral infarction affecting **right dominant side** 🕮

I69.362 **Other paralytic syndrome** following cerebral infarction affecting **left dominant side** 🕮

I69.363 **Other paralytic syndrome** following cerebral infarction affecting **right non-dominant side** 🕮

I69.364 **Other paralytic syndrome** following cerebral infarction affecting **left non-dominant side** 🕮

I69.365 **Other paralytic syndrome** following cerebral infarction, **bilateral** 🕮

I69.369 **Other paralytic syndrome** following cerebral infarction affecting **unspecified side** 🕮

● I69.39 **Other sequelae** of cerebral infarction

I69.390 **Apraxia** following cerebral infarction

I69.391 **Dysphagia** following cerebral infarction

Use additional code to identify the type of dysphagia, if known (R13.1-)

I69.392 **Facial weakness** following cerebral infarction

Facial droop following cerebral infarction

I69.393 **Ataxia** following cerebral infarction

I69.398 **Other sequelae** of cerebral infarction

Alteration of sensation following cerebral infarction
Disturbance of vision following cerebral infarction

Use additional code to identify the sequelae

● I69.8 **Sequelae of other cerebrovascular diseases**

Excludes1 sequelae of traumatic intracranial injury (S06.-)

I69.80 **Unspecified** sequelae of other cerebrovascular disease

● I69.81 **Cognitive deficits** following other cerebrovascular disease

I69.810 **Attention and concentration** deficit following other cerebrovascular disease

I69.811 **Memory** deficit following other cerebrovascular disease

I69.812 **Visuospatial** deficit and spatial neglect following other cerebrovascular disease

I69.813 **Psychomotor** deficit following other cerebrovascular disease

I69.814 **Frontal lobe and executive function** deficit following other cerebrovascular disease

I69.815 **Cognitive social or emotional** deficit following other cerebrovascular disease

I69.818 **Other symptoms and signs** involving cognitive functions following other cerebrovascular disease

I69.819 **Unspecified symptoms and signs** involving cognitive functions following other cerebrovascular disease

● I69.82 **Speech and language** deficits following other cerebrovascular disease

I69.820 **Aphasia** following other cerebrovascular disease

I69.821 **Dysphasia** following other cerebrovascular disease

I69.822 **Dysarthria** following other cerebrovascular disease

I69.823 **Fluency disorder** following other cerebrovascular disease

Stuttering following other cerebrovascular disease

I69.828 **Other speech and language deficits** following other cerebrovascular disease

Coding Clinic: 2019, Q3, P9

● I69.83 **Monoplegia of upper limb** following other cerebrovascular disease

I69.831 **Monoplegia** of upper limb following other cerebrovascular disease affecting **right dominant side** 🕮

I69.832 **Monoplegia** of upper limb following other cerebrovascular disease affecting **left dominant side** 🕮

I69.833 **Monoplegia** of upper limb following other cerebrovascular disease affecting **right non-dominant side** 🕮

I69.834 **Monoplegia** of upper limb following other cerebrovascular disease affecting **left non-dominant side** 🕮

I69.839 **Monoplegia** of upper limb following other cerebrovascular disease affecting **unspecified side** 🕮

▶ New   ⇒ Revised   ~~deleted~~ Deleted   Excludes 1   Excludes 2   Includes   Use additional   Code first   Code also   Key words

OGCR Official Guidelines   X Assign placeholder X   ● Use Additional Character(s)   ▶ Manifestation Code   🕮 Hierarchical Condition Category   Coding Clinic

CHAPTER 9 (I00-I99)

● **I69.84   Monoplegia of lower limb following other cerebrovascular disease**

I69.841   Monoplegia of lower limb following other cerebrovascular disease affecting right dominant side 🐾

I69.842   Monoplegia of lower limb following other cerebrovascular disease affecting left dominant side 🐾

I69.843   Monoplegia of lower limb following other cerebrovascular disease affecting right non-dominant side 🐾

I69.844   Monoplegia of lower limb following other cerebrovascular disease affecting left non-dominant side 🐾

I69.849   Monoplegia of lower limb following other cerebrovascular disease affecting unspecified side 🐾

● **I69.85   Hemiplegia and hemiparesis following other cerebrovascular disease**

I69.851   Hemiplegia and hemiparesis following other cerebrovascular disease affecting right dominant side 🐾

I69.852   Hemiplegia and hemiparesis following other cerebrovascular disease affecting left dominant side 🐾

I69.853   Hemiplegia and hemiparesis following other cerebrovascular disease affecting right non-dominant side 🐾

I69.854   Hemiplegia and hemiparesis following other cerebrovascular disease affecting left non-dominant side 🐾

I69.859   Hemiplegia and hemiparesis following other cerebrovascular disease affecting unspecified side 🐾

● **I69.86   Other paralytic syndrome following other cerebrovascular disease**

Use additional code to identify type of paralytic syndrome, such as:
locked-in state (G83.5)
quadriplegia (G82.5-)

Excludes1   hemiplegia/hemiparesis following other cerebrovascular disease (I69.85-)
monoplegia of lower limb following other cerebrovascular disease (I69.84-)
monoplegia of upper limb following other cerebrovascular disease (I69.83-)

I69.861   Other paralytic syndrome following other cerebrovascular disease affecting right dominant side 🐾

I69.862   Other paralytic syndrome following other cerebrovascular disease affecting left dominant side 🐾

I69.863   Other paralytic syndrome following other cerebrovascular disease affecting right non-dominant side 🐾

I69.864   Other paralytic syndrome following other cerebrovascular disease affecting left non-dominant side 🐾

I69.865   Other paralytic syndrome following other cerebrovascular disease, bilateral 🐾

I69.869   Other paralytic syndrome following other cerebrovascular disease affecting unspecified side 🐾

● **I69.89   Other sequelae of other cerebrovascular disease**

I69.890   Apraxia following other cerebrovascular disease

I69.891   Dysphagia following other cerebrovascular disease
Use additional code to identify the type of dysphagia, if known (R13.1-)

I69.892   Facial weakness following other cerebrovascular disease
Facial droop following other cerebrovascular disease

I69.893   Ataxia following other cerebrovascular disease

I69.898   Other sequelae of other cerebrovascular disease
Alteration of sensation following other cerebrovascular disease
Disturbance of vision following other cerebrovascular disease
Use additional code to identify the sequelae

● **I69.9   Sequelae of unspecified cerebrovascular diseases**

Excludes1   sequelae of stroke (I69.3)
sequelae of traumatic intracranial injury (S06.-)

I69.90   Unspecified sequelae of unspecified cerebrovascular disease

● **I69.91   Cognitive deficits following unspecified cerebrovascular disease**

I69.910   Attention and concentration deficit following unspecified cerebrovascular disease

I69.911   Memory deficit following unspecified cerebrovascular disease

I69.912   Visuospatial deficit and spatial neglect following unspecified cerebrovascular disease

I69.913   Psychomotor deficit following unspecified cerebrovascular disease

I69.914   Frontal lobe and executive function deficit following unspecified cerebrovascular disease

I69.915   Cognitive social or emotional deficit following unspecified cerebrovascular disease

I69.918   Other symptoms and signs involving cognitive functions following unspecified cerebrovascular disease

I69.919   Unspecified symptoms and signs involving cognitive functions following unspecified cerebrovascular disease

CHAPTER 9 (I00-I99)

● **I69.92**   **Speech and language deficits following unspecified cerebrovascular disease**

    I69.920   Aphasia following unspecified cerebrovascular disease

    I69.921   Dysphasia following unspecified cerebrovascular disease

    I69.922   Dysarthria following unspecified cerebrovascular disease

    I69.923   Fluency disorder following unspecified cerebrovascular disease
              Stuttering following unspecified cerebrovascular disease

    I69.928   Other speech and language deficits following unspecified cerebrovascular disease

● **I69.93**   **Monoplegia of upper limb following unspecified cerebrovascular disease**

    I69.931   Monoplegia of upper limb following unspecified cerebrovascular disease affecting right dominant side 🐾

    I69.932   Monoplegia of upper limb following unspecified cerebrovascular disease affecting left dominant side 🐾

    I69.933   Monoplegia of upper limb following unspecified cerebrovascular disease affecting right non-dominant side 🐾

    I69.934   Monoplegia of upper limb following unspecified cerebrovascular disease affecting left non-dominant side 🐾

    I69.939   Monoplegia of upper limb following unspecified cerebrovascular disease affecting unspecified side 🐾

● **I69.94**   **Monoplegia of lower limb following unspecified cerebrovascular disease**

    I69.941   Monoplegia of lower limb following unspecified cerebrovascular disease affecting right dominant side 🐾

    I69.942   Monoplegia of lower limb following unspecified cerebrovascular disease affecting left dominant side 🐾

    I69.943   Monoplegia of lower limb following unspecified cerebrovascular disease affecting right non-dominant side 🐾

    I69.944   Monoplegia of lower limb following unspecified cerebrovascular disease affecting left non-dominant side 🐾

    I69.949   Monoplegia of lower limb following unspecified cerebrovascular disease affecting unspecified side 🐾

● **I69.95**   **Hemiplegia and hemiparesis following unspecified cerebrovascular disease**

    I69.951   Hemiplegia and hemiparesis following unspecified cerebrovascular disease affecting right dominant side 🐾

    I69.952   Hemiplegia and hemiparesis following unspecified cerebrovascular disease affecting left dominant side 🐾

    I69.953   Hemiplegia and hemiparesis following unspecified cerebrovascular disease affecting right non-dominant side 🐾

    I69.954   Hemiplegia and hemiparesis following unspecified cerebrovascular disease affecting left non-dominant side 🐾

    I69.959   Hemiplegia and hemiparesis following unspecified cerebrovascular disease affecting unspecified side 🐾

● **I69.96**   **Other paralytic syndrome following unspecified cerebrovascular disease**
      Use additional code to identify type of paralytic syndrome, such as:
      locked-in state (G83.5)
      quadriplegia (G82.5-)

      Excludes1   hemiplegia/hemiparesis following unspecified cerebrovascular disease (I69.95-)
                monoplegia of lower limb following unspecified cerebrovascular disease (I69.94-)
                monoplegia of upper limb following unspecified cerebrovascular disease (I69.93-)

    I69.961   Other paralytic syndrome following unspecified cerebrovascular disease affecting right dominant side 🐾

    I69.962   Other paralytic syndrome following unspecified cerebrovascular disease affecting left dominant side 🐾

    I69.963   Other paralytic syndrome following unspecified cerebrovascular disease affecting right non-dominant side 🐾

    I69.964   Other paralytic syndrome following unspecified cerebrovascular disease affecting left non-dominant side 🐾

    I69.965   Other paralytic syndrome following unspecified cerebrovascular disease, bilateral 🐾

    I69.969   Other paralytic syndrome following unspecified cerebrovascular disease affecting unspecified side 🐾

● **I69.99**   **Other sequelae of unspecified cerebrovascular disease**

    I69.990   Apraxia following unspecified cerebrovascular disease

    I69.991   Dysphagia following unspecified cerebrovascular disease
           Use additional code to identify the type of dysphagia, if known (R13.1-)

    I69.992   Facial weakness following unspecified cerebrovascular disease
           Facial droop following unspecified cerebrovascular disease

    I69.993   Ataxia following unspecified cerebrovascular disease

    I69.998   Other sequelae following unspecified cerebrovascular disease
           Alteration in sensation following unspecified cerebrovascular disease
           Disturbance of vision following unspecified cerebrovascular disease
           Use additional code to identify the sequelae

▶ New   ⇒ Revised   ~~deleted~~ Deleted   Excludes 1   Excludes 2   Includes   Use additional   Code first   Code also   Key words

OGCR Official Guidelines   X Assign placeholder X   ● Use Additional Character(s)   ▶ Manifestation Code   🐾 Hierarchical Condition Category   Coding Clinic

DISEASES OF ARTERIES, ARTERIOLES AND CAPILLARIES (I70-I79)

● I70 **Atherosclerosis**

Includes arteriolosclerosis
arterial degeneration
arteriosclerosis
arteriosclerotic vascular disease
arteriovascular degeneration
atheroma
endarteritis deformans or obliterans
senile arteritis
senile endarteritis
vascular degeneration

Use additional code to identify:
exposure to environmental tobacco smoke (Z77.22)
history of tobacco dependence (Z87.891)
occupational exposure to environmental tobacco smoke
(Z57.31)
tobacco dependence (F17.-)
tobacco use (Z72.0)

Excludes2 arteriosclerotic cardiovascular disease (I25.1-)
arteriosclerotic heart disease (I25.1-)
atheroembolism (I75.-)
cerebral atherosclerosis (I67.2)
coronary atherosclerosis (I25.1-)
mesenteric atherosclerosis (K55.1)
precerebral atherosclerosis (I67.2)
primary pulmonary atherosclerosis (I27.0)

I70.0 **Atherosclerosis of aorta** 🔎   A

I70.1 **Atherosclerosis of renal artery** 🔎   A
Goldblatt's kidney

    Excludes2 atherosclerosis of renal arterioles (I12.-)

★ **(See Plates 500, 501, and 502 on pages 60 – 62.)**

● I70.2 **Atherosclerosis of native arteries of the extremities**
Mönckeberg's (medial) sclerosis

Use additional code, if applicable, to identify chronic
total occlusion of artery of extremity (I70.92)

    Excludes2 atherosclerosis of bypass graft of
extremities (I70.30-I70.79)

  ● I70.20 **Unspecified atherosclerosis of native arteries of
extremities**

    I70.201 **Unspecified atherosclerosis of native
arteries of extremities, right leg** 🔎   A

    I70.202 **Unspecified atherosclerosis of native
arteries of extremities, left leg** 🔎   A

    I70.203 **Unspecified atherosclerosis of native
arteries of extremities, bilateral
legs** 🔎   A

    I70.208 **Unspecified atherosclerosis of native
arteries of extremities, other
extremity** 🔎   A

    I70.209 **Unspecified atherosclerosis of native
arteries of extremities, unspecified
extremity** 🔎   A

  ● I70.21 **Atherosclerosis of native arteries of extremities
with intermittent claudication**

    I70.211 **Atherosclerosis of native arteries of
extremities with intermittent
claudication, right leg** 🔎   A

    I70.212 **Atherosclerosis of native arteries of
extremities with intermittent
claudication, left leg** 🔎   A

    I70.213 **Atherosclerosis of native arteries of
extremities with intermittent
claudication, bilateral legs** 🔎   A

    I70.218 **Atherosclerosis of native arteries of
extremities with intermittent
claudication, other extremity** 🔎   A

    I70.219 **Atherosclerosis of native arteries of
extremities with intermittent
claudication, unspecified
extremity** 🔎   A

● I70.22 **Atherosclerosis of native arteries of extremities
with rest pain**

    Includes any condition classifiable to
I70.21-
▶chronic limb-threatening
ischemia NOS of native
arteries of extremities
▶chronic limb-threatening
ischemia of native arteries
of extremities with rest pain
▶critical limb ischemia NOS of
native arteries of extremities
▶critical limb ischemia of native
arteries of extremities with
rest pain

    I70.221 **Atherosclerosis of native arteries of
extremities with rest pain, right leg** 🔎
A

    I70.222 **Atherosclerosis of native arteries of
extremities with rest pain, left leg** 🔎 A

    I70.223 **Atherosclerosis of native arteries of
extremities with rest pain, bilateral
legs** 🔎   A

    I70.228 **Atherosclerosis of native arteries of
extremities with rest pain, other
extremity** 🔎   A

    I70.229 **Atherosclerosis of native arteries of
extremities with rest pain, unspecified
extremity** 🔎   A

● I70.23 **Atherosclerosis of native arteries of right leg
with ulceration**

    Includes any condition classifiable to
I70.211 and I70.221
▶chronic limb-threatening
ischemia of native arteries
of right leg with ulceration
▶critical limb ischemia of native
arteries of right leg with
ulceration

Use additional code to identify severity of
ulcer (L97.-)

    I70.231 **Atherosclerosis of native arteries of
right leg with ulceration of thigh** 🔎 A

    I70.232 **Atherosclerosis of native arteries of
right leg with ulceration of calf** 🔎   A

    I70.233 **Atherosclerosis of native arteries of
right leg with ulceration of ankle** 🔎 A

    I70.234 **Atherosclerosis of native arteries of
right leg with ulceration of heel and
midfoot** 🔎   A
Atherosclerosis of native arteries
of right leg with ulceration of
plantar surface of midfoot

    I70.235 **Atherosclerosis of native arteries of
right leg with ulceration of other part
of foot** 🔎   A
Atherosclerosis of native arteries
of right leg extremities with
ulceration of toe

    I70.238 **Atherosclerosis of native arteries of
right leg with ulceration of other part
of lower leg** 🔎   A

    I70.239 **Atherosclerosis of native arteries of
right leg with ulceration of
unspecified site** 🔎   A

CHAPTER 9 (I00–I99)

● **I70.24** **Atherosclerosis of native arteries of left leg with ulceration**

> **Includes**   any condition classifiable to I70.212 and I70.222
>
> ▶chronic limb-threatening ischemia of native arteries of left leg with ulceration
>
> ▶critical limb ischemia of native arteries of left leg with ulceration

Use additional code to identify severity of ulcer (L97.-)

I70.241 **Atherosclerosis of native arteries of left leg with ulceration of thigh** 🕮   A

I70.242 **Atherosclerosis of native arteries of left leg with ulceration of calf** 🕮   A

I70.243 **Atherosclerosis of native arteries of left leg with ulceration of ankle** 🕮   A

I70.244 **Atherosclerosis of native arteries of left leg with ulceration of heel and midfoot** 🕮   A

> Atherosclerosis of native arteries of left leg with ulceration of plantar surface of midfoot

I70.245 **Atherosclerosis of native arteries of left leg with ulceration of other part of foot** 🕮   A

> Atherosclerosis of native arteries of left leg extremities with ulceration of toe

I70.248 **Atherosclerosis of native arteries of left leg with ulceration of other part of lower leg** 🕮   A

I70.249 **Atherosclerosis of native arteries of left leg with ulceration of unspecified site** 🕮   A

I70.25 **Atherosclerosis of native arteries of other extremities with ulceration** 🕮   A

> **Includes**   any condition classifiable to I70.218 and I70.228

Use additional code to identify the severity of the ulcer (L98.49-)

● **I70.26** **Atherosclerosis of native arteries of extremities with gangrene**

> **Includes**   any condition classifiable to I70.21-, I70.22-, I70.23-, I70.24-, and I70.25-
>
> ▶chronic limb-threatening ischemia of native arteries of extremities with gangrene
>
> ▶critical limb ischemia of native arteries of extremities with gangrene

Use additional code to identify the severity of any ulcer (L97.-, L98.49-), if applicable

I70.261 **Atherosclerosis of native arteries of extremities with gangrene, right leg**   A

I70.262 **Atherosclerosis of native arteries of extremities with gangrene, left leg** 🕮A

I70.263 **Atherosclerosis of native arteries of extremities with gangrene, bilateral legs** 🕮   A

I70.268 **Atherosclerosis of native arteries of extremities with gangrene, other extremity** 🕮   A

I70.269 **Atherosclerosis of native arteries of extremities with gangrene, unspecified extremity** 🕮   A

● **I70.29** **Other atherosclerosis of native arteries of extremities**

I70.291 **Other atherosclerosis of native arteries of extremities, right leg** 🕮   A

I70.292 **Other atherosclerosis of native arteries of extremities, left leg** 🕮   A

I70.293 **Other atherosclerosis of native arteries of extremities, bilateral legs** 🕮   A

I70.298 **Other atherosclerosis of native arteries of extremities, other extremity** 🕮   A

I70.299 **Other atherosclerosis of native arteries of extremities, unspecified extremity** 🕮   A

● **I70.3** **Atherosclerosis of unspecified type of bypass graft(s) of the extremities**

> Use additional code, if applicable, to identify chronic total occlusion of artery of extremity (I70.92)
>
> **Excludes1**   embolism or thrombus of bypass graft(s) of extremities (T82.8-)

● **I70.30** **Unspecified atherosclerosis of unspecified type of bypass graft(s) of the extremities**

I70.301 **Unspecified atherosclerosis of unspecified type of bypass graft(s) of the extremities, right leg** 🕮   A

I70.302 **Unspecified atherosclerosis of unspecified type of bypass graft(s) of the extremities, left leg** 🕮   A

I70.303 **Unspecified atherosclerosis of unspecified type of bypass graft(s) of the extremities, bilateral legs** 🕮   A

I70.308 **Unspecified atherosclerosis of unspecified type of bypass graft(s) of the extremities, other extremity** 🕮   A

I70.309 **Unspecified atherosclerosis of unspecified type of bypass graft(s) of the extremities, unspecified extremity** 🕮   A

● **I70.31** **Atherosclerosis of unspecified type of bypass graft(s) of the extremities with intermittent claudication**

I70.311 **Atherosclerosis of unspecified type of bypass graft(s) of the extremities with intermittent claudication, right leg** 🕮   A

I70.312 **Atherosclerosis of unspecified type of bypass graft(s) of the extremities with intermittent claudication, left leg** 🕮   A

I70.313 **Atherosclerosis of unspecified type of bypass graft(s) of the extremities with intermittent claudication, bilateral legs** 🕮   A

I70.318 **Atherosclerosis of unspecified type of bypass graft(s) of the extremities with intermittent claudication, other extremity** 🕮   A

I70.319 **Atherosclerosis of unspecified type of bypass graft(s) of the extremities with intermittent claudication, unspecified extremity** 🕮   A

● **I70.32**   **Atherosclerosis of unspecified type of bypass graft(s) of the extremities with rest pain**

> **Includes**   any condition classifiable to I70.31-
> ▶ chronic limb-threatening ischemia NOS of unspecified type of bypass graft(s) of the extremities
> ▶ chronic limb-threatening ischemia of unspecified type of bypass graft(s) of the extremities with rest pain, right leg
> ▶ critical limb ischemia NOS of unspecified type of bypass graft(s) of the extremities
> ▶ critical limb ischemia of unspecified type of bypass graft(s) of the extremities with rest pain

I70.321   Atherosclerosis of unspecified type of bypass graft(s) of the extremities with rest pain, right leg 🌸   A

I70.322   Atherosclerosis of unspecified type of bypass graft(s) of the extremities with rest pain, left leg 🌸   A

I70.323   Atherosclerosis of unspecified type of bypass graft(s) of the extremities with rest pain, bilateral legs 🌸   A

I70.328   Atherosclerosis of unspecified type of bypass graft(s) of the extremities with rest pain, other extremity 🌸   A

I70.329   Atherosclerosis of unspecified type of bypass graft(s) of the extremities with rest pain, unspecified extremity 🌸   A

● **I70.33**   **Atherosclerosis of unspecified type of bypass graft(s) of the right leg with ulceration**

> **Includes**   any condition classifiable to I70.311 and I70.321
> ▶ chronic limb-threatening ischemia of unspecified type of bypass graft(s) of the right leg with ulceration
> ▶ critical limb ischemia of unspecified type of bypass graft(s) of the right leg with ulceration

Use additional code to identify severity of ulcer (L97.-)

I70.331   Atherosclerosis of unspecified type of bypass graft(s) of the right leg with ulceration of thigh 🌸   A

I70.332   Atherosclerosis of unspecified type of bypass graft(s) of the right leg with ulceration of calf 🌸   A

I70.333   Atherosclerosis of unspecified type of bypass graft(s) of the right leg with ulceration of ankle 🌸   A

I70.334   Atherosclerosis of unspecified type of bypass graft(s) of the right leg with ulceration of heel and midfoot 🌸   A
> Atherosclerosis of unspecified type of bypass graft(s) of right leg with ulceration of plantar surface of midfoot

I70.335   Atherosclerosis of unspecified type of bypass graft(s) of the right leg with ulceration of other part of foot 🌸   A
> Atherosclerosis of unspecified type of bypass graft(s) of the right leg with ulceration of toe

I70.338   Atherosclerosis of unspecified type of bypass graft(s) of the right leg with ulceration of other part of lower leg 🌸   A

I70.339   Atherosclerosis of unspecified type of bypass graft(s) of the right leg with ulceration of unspecified site 🌸   A

● **I70.34**   **Atherosclerosis of unspecified type of bypass graft(s) of the left leg with ulceration**

> **Includes**   any condition classifiable to I70.312 and I70.322
> ▶ chronic limb-threatening ischemia of unspecified type of bypass graft(s) of the left leg with ulceration
> ▶ critical limb ischemia of unspecified type of bypass graft(s) of the left leg with ulceration

Use additional code to identify severity of ulcer (L97.-)

I70.341   Atherosclerosis of unspecified type of bypass graft(s) of the left leg with ulceration of thigh 🌸   A

I70.342   Atherosclerosis of unspecified type of bypass graft(s) of the left leg with ulceration of calf 🌸   A

I70.343   Atherosclerosis of unspecified type of bypass graft(s) of the left leg with ulceration of ankle 🌸   A

I70.344   Atherosclerosis of unspecified type of bypass graft(s) of the left leg with ulceration of heel and midfoot 🌸   A
> Atherosclerosis of unspecified type of bypass graft(s) of left leg with ulceration of plantar surface of midfoot

I70.345   Atherosclerosis of unspecified type of bypass graft(s) of the left leg with ulceration of other part of foot 🌸   A
> Atherosclerosis of unspecified type of bypass graft(s) of the left leg with ulceration of toe

I70.348   Atherosclerosis of unspecified type of bypass graft(s) of the left leg with ulceration of other part of lower leg 🌸   A

I70.349   Atherosclerosis of unspecified type of bypass graft(s) of the left leg with ulceration of unspecified site 🌸   A

I70.35   Atherosclerosis of unspecified type of bypass graft(s) of other extremity with ulceration 🌸   A

> **Includes**   any condition classifiable to I70.318 and I70.328

Use additional code to identify severity of ulcer (L98.49-)

CHAPTER 9 (I00-I99)

CHAPTER 9 (I00-I99)

● **I70.36** **Atherosclerosis of unspecified type of bypass graft(s) of the extremities with gangrene**

     Includes   any condition classifiable to I70.31-, I70.32-, I70.33-, I70.34-, I70.35

         ▶chronic limb-threatening ischemia of unspecified type of bypass graft(s) of the extremities with gangrene

         ▶critical limb ischemia of unspecified type of bypass graft(s) of the extremities with gangrene

     Use additional code to identify the severity of any ulcer (L97.-, L98.49-), if applicable

     I70.361   **Atherosclerosis of unspecified type of bypass graft(s) of the extremities with gangrene, right leg** 🗇   A

     I70.362   **Atherosclerosis of unspecified type of bypass graft(s) of the extremities with gangrene, left leg** 🗇   A

     I70.363   **Atherosclerosis of unspecified type of bypass graft(s) of the extremities with gangrene, bilateral legs** 🗇   A

     I70.368   **Atherosclerosis of unspecified type of bypass graft(s) of the extremities with gangrene, other extremity** 🗇   A

     I70.369   **Atherosclerosis of unspecified type of bypass graft(s) of the extremities with gangrene, unspecified extremity** 🗇 A

● **I70.39** **Other atherosclerosis of unspecified type of bypass graft(s) of the extremities**

     I70.391   **Other atherosclerosis of unspecified type of bypass graft(s) of the extremities, right leg** 🗇   A

     I70.392   **Other atherosclerosis of unspecified type of bypass graft(s) of the extremities, left leg** 🗇   A

     I70.393   **Other atherosclerosis of unspecified type of bypass graft(s) of the extremities, bilateral legs** 🗇   A

     I70.398   **Other atherosclerosis of unspecified type of bypass graft(s) of the extremities, other extremity** 🗇   A

     I70.399   **Other atherosclerosis of unspecified type of bypass graft(s) of the extremities, unspecified extremity** 🗇 A

● **I70.4** **Atherosclerosis of autologous vein bypass graft(s) of the extremities**

     Use additional code, if applicable, to identify chronic total occlusion of artery of extremity (I70.92)

● **I70.40** **Unspecified atherosclerosis of autologous vein bypass graft(s) of the extremities**

     I70.401   **Unspecified atherosclerosis of autologous vein bypass graft(s) of the extremities, right leg** 🗇   A

     I70.402   **Unspecified atherosclerosis of autologous vein bypass graft(s) of the extremities, left leg** 🗇   A

     I70.403   **Unspecified atherosclerosis of autologous vein bypass graft(s) of the extremities, bilateral legs** 🗇   A

     I70.408   **Unspecified atherosclerosis of autologous vein bypass graft(s) of the extremities, other extremity** 🗇   A

     I70.409   **Unspecified atherosclerosis of autologous vein bypass graft(s) of the extremities, unspecified extremity** 🗇 A

● **I70.41** **Atherosclerosis of autologous vein bypass graft(s) of the extremities with intermittent claudication**

     I70.411   **Atherosclerosis of autologous vein bypass graft(s) of the extremities with intermittent claudication, right leg** 🗇 A

     I70.412   **Atherosclerosis of autologous vein bypass graft(s) of the extremities with intermittent claudication, left leg** 🗇 A

     I70.413   **Atherosclerosis of autologous vein bypass graft(s) of the extremities with intermittent claudication, bilateral legs** 🗇   A

     I70.418   **Atherosclerosis of autologous vein bypass graft(s) of the extremities with intermittent claudication, other extremity** 🗇   A

     I70.419   **Atherosclerosis of autologous vein bypass graft(s) of the extremities with intermittent claudication, unspecified extremity** 🗇   A

● **I70.42** **Atherosclerosis of autologous vein bypass graft(s) of the extremities with rest pain**

     Includes   any condition classifiable to I70.41-

         ▶chronic limb-threatening ischemia NOS of autologous vein bypass graft(s) of the extremities

         ▶chronic limb-threatening ischemia of autologous vein bypass graft(s) of the extremities with rest pain

         ▶critical limb ischemia NOS of autologous vein bypass graft(s) of the extremities

         ▶critical limb ischemia of autologous vein bypass graft(s) of the extremities with rest pain

     I70.421   **Atherosclerosis of autologous vein bypass graft(s) of the extremities with rest pain, right leg** 🗇   A

     I70.422   **Atherosclerosis of autologous vein bypass graft(s) of the extremities with rest pain, left leg** 🗇   A

     I70.423   **Atherosclerosis of autologous vein bypass graft(s) of the extremities with rest pain, bilateral legs** 🗇   A

     I70.428   **Atherosclerosis of autologous vein bypass graft(s) of the extremities with rest pain, other extremity** 🗇   A

     I70.429   **Atherosclerosis of autologous vein bypass graft(s) of the extremities with rest pain, unspecified extremity** 🗇   A

● **I70.43** **Atherosclerosis of autologous vein bypass graft(s) of the right leg with ulceration**

     Includes   any condition classifiable to I70.411 and I70.421

         ▶chronic limb-threatening ischemia of autologous vein bypass graft(s) of the right leg with ulceration

         ▶critical limb ischemia of autologous vein bypass graft(s) of the right leg with ulceration

     Use additional code to identify severity of ulcer (L97.-)

     I70.431   **Atherosclerosis of autologous vein bypass graft(s) of the right leg with ulceration of thigh**   A

     I70.432   **Atherosclerosis of autologous vein bypass graft(s) of the right leg with ulceration of calf** 🗇   A

▶ New   ➠ Revised   ~~deleted~~ Deleted   Excludes 1   Excludes 2   Includes   Use additional   Code first   Code also   Key words

OGCR Official Guidelines   X Assign placeholder X   ● Use Additional Character(s)   ▶ Manifestation Code   🗇 Hierarchical Condition Category   Coding Clinic

I70.433 Atherosclerosis of autologous vein bypass graft(s) of the right leg with ulceration of ankle 🔖　　A

I70.434 Atherosclerosis of autologous vein bypass graft(s) of the right leg with ulceration of heel and midfoot 🔖　A
　　　Atherosclerosis of autologous vein bypass graft(s) of right leg with ulceration of plantar surface of midfoot

I70.435 Atherosclerosis of autologous vein bypass graft(s) of the right leg with ulceration of other part of foot 🔖　A
　　　Atherosclerosis of autologous vein bypass graft(s) of right leg with ulceration of toe

I70.438 Atherosclerosis of autologous vein bypass graft(s) of the right leg with ulceration of other part of lower leg 🔖　　A

I70.439 Atherosclerosis of autologous vein bypass graft(s) of the right leg with ulceration of unspecified site 🔖　A

● **I70.44** Atherosclerosis of autologous vein bypass graft(s) of the left leg with ulceration

　　Includes any condition classifiable to I70.412 and I70.422
　　　▶ chronic limb-threatening ischemia of autologous vein bypass graft(s) of the left leg with ulceration
　　　▶ critical limb ischemia of autologous vein bypass graft(s) of the left leg with ulceration

　　Use additional code to identify severity of ulcer (L97.-)

I70.441 Atherosclerosis of autologous vein bypass graft(s) of the left leg with ulceration of thigh 🔖　　A

I70.442 Atherosclerosis of autologous vein bypass graft(s) of the left leg with ulceration of calf 🔖　　A

I70.443 Atherosclerosis of autologous vein bypass graft(s) of the left leg with ulceration of ankle 🔖　　A

I70.444 Atherosclerosis of autologous vein bypass graft(s) of the left leg with ulceration of heel and midfoot 🔖　A
　　　Atherosclerosis of autologous vein bypass graft(s) of left leg with ulceration of plantar surface of midfoot

I70.445 Atherosclerosis of autologous vein bypass graft(s) of the left leg with ulceration of other part of foot 🔖　A
　　　Atherosclerosis of autologous vein bypass graft(s) of left leg with ulceration of toe

I70.448 Atherosclerosis of autologous vein bypass graft(s) of the left leg with ulceration of other part of lower leg 🔖　　A

I70.449 Atherosclerosis of autologous vein bypass graft(s) of the left leg with ulceration of unspecified site 🔖　A

I70.45 Atherosclerosis of autologous vein bypass graft(s) of other extremity with ulceration 🔖　A

　　Includes any condition classifiable to I70.418, I70.428, and I70.438

　　Use additional code to identify severity of ulcer (L98.49-)

● **I70.46** Atherosclerosis of autologous vein bypass graft(s) of the extremities with gangrene

　　Includes any condition classifiable to I70.41-, I70.42-, and I70.43-, I70.44-, I70.45
　　　▶ chronic limb-threatening ischemia of autologous vein bypass graft(s) of the extremities with gangrene
　　　▶ critical limb ischemia of autologous vein bypass graft(s) of the extremities with gangrene

　　Use additional code to identify the severity of any ulcer (L97.-, L98.49-), if applicable

I70.461 Atherosclerosis of autologous vein bypass graft(s) of the extremities with gangrene, right leg　　A

I70.462 Atherosclerosis of autologous vein bypass graft(s) of the extremities with gangrene, left leg 🔖　　A

I70.463 Atherosclerosis of autologous vein bypass graft(s) of the extremities with gangrene, bilateral legs 🔖　　A

I70.468 Atherosclerosis of autologous vein bypass graft(s) of the extremities with gangrene, other extremity 🔖　　A

I70.469 Atherosclerosis of autologous vein bypass graft(s) of the extremities with gangrene, unspecified extremity 🔖　A

● **I70.49** Other atherosclerosis of autologous vein bypass graft(s) of the extremities

I70.491 Other atherosclerosis of autologous vein bypass graft(s) of the extremities, right leg 🔖　　A

I70.492 Other atherosclerosis of autologous vein bypass graft(s) of the extremities, left leg 🔖　　A

I70.493 Other atherosclerosis of autologous vein bypass graft(s) of the extremities, bilateral legs 🔖　　A

I70.498 Other atherosclerosis of autologous vein bypass graft(s) of the extremities, other extremity 🔖　　A

I70.499 Other atherosclerosis of autologous vein bypass graft(s) of the extremities, unspecified extremity 🔖　　A

● **I70.5** Atherosclerosis of nonautologous biological bypass graft(s) of the extremities

　　Use additional code, if applicable, to identify chronic total occlusion of artery of extremity (I70.92)

● **I70.50** Unspecified atherosclerosis of nonautologous biological bypass graft(s) of the extremities

I70.501 Unspecified atherosclerosis of nonautologous biological bypass graft(s) of the extremities, right leg 🔖　　A

I70.502 Unspecified atherosclerosis of nonautologous biological bypass graft(s) of the extremities, left leg 🔖　A

I70.503 Unspecified atherosclerosis of nonautologous biological bypass graft(s) of the extremities, bilateral legs 🔖　　A

I70.508 Unspecified atherosclerosis of nonautologous biological bypass graft(s) of the extremities, other extremity 🔖　　A

I70.509 Unspecified atherosclerosis of nonautologous biological bypass graft(s) of the extremities, unspecified extremity 🔖　　A

CHAPTER 9 (I00-I99)

CHAPTER 9 (I00-I99)

● **I70.51** **Atherosclerosis of nonautologous biological bypass graft(s) of the extremities intermittent claudication**

     I70.511 Atherosclerosis of nonautologous biological bypass graft(s) of the extremities with intermittent claudication, right leg 🦠   A

     I70.512 Atherosclerosis of nonautologous biological bypass graft(s) of the extremities with intermittent claudication, left leg 🦠   A

     I70.513 Atherosclerosis of nonautologous biological bypass graft(s) of the extremities with intermittent claudication, bilateral legs 🦠   A

     I70.518 Atherosclerosis of nonautologous biological bypass graft(s) of the extremities with intermittent claudication, other extremity 🦠   A

     I70.519 Atherosclerosis of nonautologous biological bypass graft(s) of the extremities with intermittent claudication, unspecified extremity 🦠 A

● **I70.52** **Atherosclerosis of nonautologous biological bypass graft(s) of the extremities with rest pain**

     Includes   any condition classifiable to I70.51-

       ▶ chronic limb-threatening ischemia NOS of nonautologous biological bypass graft(s) of the extremities

       ▶ chronic limb-threatening ischemia of nonautologous biological bypass graft(s) of the extremities with rest pain

       ▶ critical limb ischemia NOS of nonautologous biological bypass graft(s) of the extremities

       ▶ critical limb ischemia of nonautologous biological bypass graft(s) of the extremities with rest pain

     I70.521 Atherosclerosis of nonautologous biological bypass graft(s) of the extremities with rest pain, right leg 🦠 A

     I70.522 Atherosclerosis of nonautologous biological bypass graft(s) of the extremities with rest pain, left leg 🦠 A

     I70.523 Atherosclerosis of nonautologous biological bypass graft(s) of the extremities with rest pain, bilateral legs 🦠   A

     I70.528 Atherosclerosis of nonautologous biological bypass graft(s) of the extremities with rest pain, other extremity 🦠   A

     I70.529 Atherosclerosis of nonautologous biological bypass graft(s) of the extremities with rest pain, unspecified extremity 🦠   A

● **I70.53** **Atherosclerosis of nonautologous biological bypass graft(s) of the right leg with ulceration**

     Includes   any condition classifiable to I70.511 and I70.521

       ▶ chronic limb-threatening ischemia of nonautologous biological bypass graft(s) of the right leg with ulceration

       ▶ critical limb ischemia of nonautologous biological bypass graft(s) of the right leg with ulceration

   Use additional code to identify severity of ulcer (L97.-)

     I70.531 Atherosclerosis of nonautologous biological bypass graft(s) of the right leg with ulceration of thigh 🦠   A

     I70.532 Atherosclerosis of nonautologous biological bypass graft(s) of the right leg with ulceration of calf 🦠   A

     I70.533 Atherosclerosis of nonautologous biological bypass graft(s) of the right leg with ulceration of ankle 🦠   A

     I70.534 Atherosclerosis of nonautologous biological bypass graft(s) of the right leg with ulceration of heel and midfoot 🦠   A

       Atherosclerosis of nonautologous biological bypass graft(s) of right leg with ulceration of plantar surface of midfoot

     I70.535 Atherosclerosis of nonautologous biological bypass graft(s) of the right leg with ulceration of other part of foot 🦠   A

       Atherosclerosis of nonautologous biological bypass graft(s) of the right leg with ulceration of toe

     I70.538 Atherosclerosis of nonautologous biological bypass graft(s) of the right leg with ulceration of other part of lower leg 🦠   A

     I70.539 Atherosclerosis of nonautologous biological bypass graft(s) of the right leg with ulceration of unspecified site 🦠   A

● **I70.54** **Atherosclerosis of nonautologous biological bypass graft(s) of the left leg with ulceration**

     Includes   any condition classifiable to I70.512 and I70.522

       ▶ chronic limb-threatening ischemia of nonautologous biological bypass graft(s) of the left leg with ulceration

       ▶ critical limb ischemia of nonautologous biological bypass graft(s) of the left leg with ulceration

   Use additional code to identify severity of ulcer (L97.-)

     I70.541 Atherosclerosis of nonautologous biological bypass graft(s) of the left leg with ulceration of thigh 🦠   A

     I70.542 Atherosclerosis of nonautologous biological bypass graft(s) of the left leg with ulceration of calf 🦠   A

     I70.543 Atherosclerosis of nonautologous biological bypass graft(s) of the left leg with ulceration of ankle 🦠   A

▶ New   ⇒ Revised   ~~deleted~~ Deleted   Excludes 1   Excludes 2   Includes   Use additional   Code first   Code also   Key words

OGCR Official Guidelines   X Assign placeholder X   ● Use Additional Character(s)   ▶ Manifestation Code   🦠 Hierarchical Condition Category   **Coding Clinic**

I70.544   Atherosclerosis of nonautologous biological bypass graft(s) of the left leg with ulceration of heel and midfoot ✎   A

    Atherosclerosis of nonautologous biological bypass graft(s) of left leg with ulceration of plantar surface of midfoot

I70.545   Atherosclerosis of nonautologous biological bypass graft(s) of the left leg with ulceration of other part of foot ✎   A

    Atherosclerosis of nonautologous biological bypass graft(s) of the left leg with ulceration of toe

I70.548   Atherosclerosis of nonautologous biological bypass graft(s) of the left leg with ulceration of other part of lower leg ✎   A

I70.549   Atherosclerosis of nonautologous biological bypass graft(s) of the left leg with ulceration of unspecified site ✎   A

I70.55   Atherosclerosis of nonautologous biological bypass graft(s) of other extremity with ulceration ✎   A

    Includes   any condition classifiable to I70.518, I70.528, and I70.538

Use additional code to identify severity of ulcer (L98.49)

● I70.56   Atherosclerosis of nonautologous biological bypass graft(s) of the extremities with gangrene

    Includes   any condition classifiable to I70.51-, I70.52-, and I70.53-, I70.54-, I70.55

    ▶ chronic limb-threatening ischemia of nonautologous biological bypass graft(s) of the extremities with gangrene

    ▶ critical limb ischemia of nonautologous biological bypass graft(s) of the extremities with gangrene

Use additional code to identify the severity of any ulcer (L97.-, L98.49-), if applicable

I70.561   Atherosclerosis of nonautologous biological bypass graft(s) of the extremities with gangrene, right leg ✎   A

I70.562   Atherosclerosis of nonautologous biological bypass graft(s) of the extremities with gangrene, left leg ✎ A

I70.563   Atherosclerosis of nonautologous biological bypass graft(s) of the extremities with gangrene, bilateral legs ✎   A

I70.568   Atherosclerosis of nonautologous biological bypass graft(s) of the extremities with gangrene, other extremity ✎   A

I70.569   Atherosclerosis of nonautologous biological bypass graft(s) of the extremities with gangrene, unspecified extremity ✎   A

● I70.59   Other atherosclerosis of nonautologous biological bypass graft(s) of the extremities

I70.591   Other atherosclerosis of nonautologous biological bypass graft(s) of the extremities, right leg ✎   A

I70.592   Other atherosclerosis of nonautologous biological bypass graft(s) of the extremities, left leg ✎   A

I70.593   Other atherosclerosis of nonautologous biological bypass graft(s) of the extremities, bilateral legs ✎   A

I70.598   Other atherosclerosis of nonautologous biological bypass graft(s) of the extremities, other extremity ✎   A

I70.599   Other atherosclerosis of nonautologous biological bypass graft(s) of the extremities, unspecified extremity ✎ A

● I70.6   Atherosclerosis of nonbiological bypass graft(s) of the extremities

    Use additional code, if applicable, to identify chronic total occlusion of artery of extremity (I70.92)

● I70.60   Unspecified atherosclerosis of nonbiological bypass graft(s) of the extremities

I70.601   Unspecified atherosclerosis of nonbiological bypass graft(s) of the extremities, right leg ✎   A

I70.602   Unspecified atherosclerosis of nonbiological bypass graft(s) of the extremities, left leg ✎   A

I70.603   Unspecified atherosclerosis of nonbiological bypass graft(s) of the extremities, bilateral legs ✎   A

I70.608   Unspecified atherosclerosis of nonbiological bypass graft(s) of the extremities, other extremity ✎   A

I70.609   Unspecified atherosclerosis of nonbiological bypass graft(s) of the extremities, unspecified extremity ✎ A

● I70.61   Atherosclerosis of nonbiological bypass graft(s) of the extremities with intermittent claudication

I70.611   Atherosclerosis of nonbiological bypass graft(s) of the extremities with intermittent claudication, right leg ✎   A

I70.612   Atherosclerosis of nonbiological bypass graft(s) of the extremities with intermittent claudication, left leg ✎ A

I70.613   Atherosclerosis of nonbiological bypass graft(s) of the extremities with intermittent claudication, bilateral legs ✎   A

I70.618   Atherosclerosis of nonbiological bypass graft(s) of the extremities with intermittent claudication, other extremity ✎   A

I70.619   Atherosclerosis of nonbiological bypass graft(s) of the extremities with intermittent claudication, unspecified extremity ✎   A

CHAPTER 9 (I00-I99)

● **I70.62** **Atherosclerosis of nonbiological bypass graft(s) of the extremities with rest pain**

> **Includes**   any condition classifiable to I70.61-
> - ▶chronic limb-threatening ischemia NOS of nonbiological bypass graft(s) of the extremities
> - ▶chronic limb-threatening ischemia of nonbiological bypass graft(s) of the extremities with rest pain
> - ▶critical limb ischemia NOS of nonbiological bypass graft(s) of the extremities
> - ▶critical limb ischemia of nonbiological bypass graft(s) of the extremities with rest pain

I70.621   **Atherosclerosis of nonbiological bypass graft(s) of the extremities with rest pain, right leg** 🐾   A

I70.622   **Atherosclerosis of nonbiological bypass graft(s) of the extremities with rest pain, left leg** 🐾   A

I70.623   **Atherosclerosis of nonbiological bypass graft(s) of the extremities with rest pain, bilateral legs** 🐾   A

I70.628   **Atherosclerosis of nonbiological bypass graft(s) of the extremities with rest pain, other extremity** 🐾   A

I70.629   **Atherosclerosis of nonbiological bypass graft(s) of the extremities with rest pain, unspecified extremity** 🐾   A

● **I70.63** **Atherosclerosis of nonbiological bypass graft(s) of the right leg with ulceration**

> **Includes**   any condition classifiable to I70.611 and I70.621
> - ▶chronic limb-threatening ischemia of nonbiological bypass graft(s) of the right leg with ulceration
> - ▶critical limb ischemia of nonbiological bypass graft(s) of the right leg with ulceration

> Use additional code to identify severity of ulcer (L97.-)

I70.631   **Atherosclerosis of nonbiological bypass graft(s) of the right leg with ulceration of thigh** 🐾   A

I70.632   **Atherosclerosis of nonbiological bypass graft(s) of the right leg with ulceration of calf** 🐾   A

I70.633   **Atherosclerosis of nonbiological bypass graft(s) of the right leg with ulceration of ankle** 🐾   A

I70.634   **Atherosclerosis of nonbiological bypass graft(s) of the right leg with ulceration of heel and midfoot** 🐾   A

> Atherosclerosis of nonbiological bypass graft(s) of right leg with ulceration of plantar surface of midfoot

I70.635   **Atherosclerosis of nonbiological bypass graft(s) of the right leg with ulceration of other part of foot** 🐾   A

> Atherosclerosis of nonbiological bypass graft(s) of the right leg with ulceration of toe

I70.638   **Atherosclerosis of nonbiological bypass graft(s) of the right leg with ulceration of other part of lower leg** 🐾   A

I70.639   **Atherosclerosis of nonbiological bypass graft(s) of the right leg with ulceration of unspecified site** 🐾   A

● **I70.64** **Atherosclerosis of nonbiological bypass graft(s) of the left leg with ulceration**

> **Includes**   any condition classifiable to I70.612 and I70.622
> - ▶chronic limb-threatening ischemia of nonbiological bypass graft(s) of the left leg with ulceration
> - ▶critical limb ischemia of nonbiological bypass graft(s) of the left leg with ulceration

> Use additional code to identify severity of ulcer (L97.-)

I70.641   **Atherosclerosis of nonbiological bypass graft(s) of the left leg with ulceration of thigh** 🐾   A

I70.642   **Atherosclerosis of nonbiological bypass graft(s) of the left leg with ulceration of calf** 🐾   A

I70.643   **Atherosclerosis of nonbiological bypass graft(s) of the left leg with ulceration of ankle** 🐾   A

I70.644   **Atherosclerosis of nonbiological bypass graft(s) of the left leg with ulceration of heel and midfoot** 🐾   A

> Atherosclerosis of nonbiological bypass graft(s) of left leg with ulceration of plantar surface of midfoot

I70.645   **Atherosclerosis of nonbiological bypass graft(s) of the left leg with ulceration of other part of foot** 🐾   A

> Atherosclerosis of nonbiological bypass graft(s) of the left leg with ulceration of toe

I70.648   **Atherosclerosis of nonbiological bypass graft(s) of the left leg with ulceration of other part of lower leg** 🐾   A

I70.649   **Atherosclerosis of nonbiological bypass graft(s) of the left leg with ulceration of unspecified site** 🐾   A

I70.65   **Atherosclerosis of nonbiological bypass graft(s) of other extremity with ulceration** 🐾   A

> **Includes**   any condition classifiable to I70.618 and I70.628

> Use additional code to identify severity of ulcer (L98.49-)

▶ New   ➡ Revised   ~~deleted~~ Deleted   Excludes 1   Excludes 2   Includes   Use additional   Code first   Code also   Key words

OGCR Official Guidelines   X Assign placeholder X   ● Use Additional Character(s)   ▌ Manifestation Code   🐾 Hierarchical Condition Category   **Coding Clinic**

● **I70.66** **Atherosclerosis of nonbiological bypass graft(s) of the extremities with gangrene**

> **Includes**   any condition classifiable to I70.61-, I70.62-, I70.63-, I70.64-, I70.65
> ▶ chronic limb-threatening ischemia of nonbiological bypass graft(s) of the extremities with gangrene
> ▶ critical limb ischemia of nonbiological bypass graft(s) of the extremities with gangrene

> Use additional code to identify the severity of any ulcer (L97.-, L98.49-), if applicable

   I70.661   Atherosclerosis of nonbiological bypass graft(s) of the extremities with gangrene, right leg 🔍   A

   I70.662   Atherosclerosis of nonbiological bypass graft(s) of the extremities with gangrene, left leg 🔍   A

   I70.663   Atherosclerosis of nonbiological bypass graft(s) of the extremities with gangrene, bilateral legs 🔍   A

   I70.668   Atherosclerosis of nonbiological bypass graft(s) of the extremities with gangrene, other extremity 🔍   A

   I70.669   Atherosclerosis of nonbiological bypass graft(s) of the extremities with gangrene, unspecified extremity 🔍   A

● **I70.69** **Other atherosclerosis of nonbiological bypass graft(s) of the extremities**

   I70.691   Other atherosclerosis of nonbiological bypass graft(s) of the extremities, right leg 🔍   A

   I70.692   Other atherosclerosis of nonbiological bypass graft(s) of the extremities, left leg 🔍   A

   I70.693   Other atherosclerosis of nonbiological bypass graft(s) of the extremities, bilateral legs 🔍   A

   I70.698   Other atherosclerosis of nonbiological bypass graft(s) of the extremities, other extremity 🔍   A

   I70.699   Other atherosclerosis of nonbiological bypass graft(s) of the extremities, unspecified extremity 🔍   A

● **I70.7** **Atherosclerosis of other type of bypass graft(s) of the extremities**

> Use additional code, if applicable, to identify chronic total occlusion of artery of extremity (I70.92)

● **I70.70** **Unspecified atherosclerosis of other type of bypass graft(s) of the extremities**

   I70.701   Unspecified atherosclerosis of other type of bypass graft(s) of the extremities, right leg 🔍   A

   I70.702   Unspecified atherosclerosis of other type of bypass graft(s) of the extremities, left leg 🔍   A

   I70.703   Unspecified atherosclerosis of other type of bypass graft(s) of the extremities, bilateral legs 🔍   A

   I70.708   Unspecified atherosclerosis of other type of bypass graft(s) of the extremities, other extremity 🔍   A

   I70.709   Unspecified atherosclerosis of other type of bypass graft(s) of the extremities, unspecified extremity 🔍 A

● **I70.71** **Atherosclerosis of other type of bypass graft(s) of the extremities with intermittent claudication**

   I70.711   Atherosclerosis of other type of bypass graft(s) of the extremities with intermittent claudication, right leg 🔍   A

   I70.712   Atherosclerosis of other type of bypass graft(s) of the extremities with intermittent claudication, left leg 🔍 A

   I70.713   Atherosclerosis of other type of bypass graft(s) of the extremities with intermittent claudication, bilateral legs 🔍   A

   I70.718   Atherosclerosis of other type of bypass graft(s) of the extremities with intermittent claudication, other extremity 🔍   A

   I70.719   Atherosclerosis of other type of bypass graft(s) of the extremities with intermittent claudication, unspecified extremity 🔍   A

● **I70.72** **Atherosclerosis of other type of bypass graft(s) of the extremities with rest pain**

> **Includes**   any condition classifiable to I70.71-
> ▶ chronic limb-threatening ischemia NOS of other type of bypass graft(s) of the extremities
> ▶ chronic limb-threatening ischemia of other type of bypass graft(s) of the extremities with rest pain
> ▶ critical limb ischemia NOS of other type of bypass graft(s) of the extremities
> ▶ critical limb ischemia of other type of bypass graft(s) of the extremities with rest pain

   I70.721   Atherosclerosis of other type of bypass graft(s) of the extremities with rest pain, right leg 🔍   A

   I70.722   Atherosclerosis of other type of bypass graft(s) of the extremities with rest pain, left leg 🔍   A

   I70.723   Atherosclerosis of other type of bypass graft(s) of the extremities with rest pain, bilateral legs 🔍   A

   I70.728   Atherosclerosis of other type of bypass graft(s) of the extremities with rest pain, other extremity 🔍   A

   I70.729   Atherosclerosis of other type of bypass graft(s) of the extremities with rest pain, unspecified extremity 🔍   A

● **I70.73** **Atherosclerosis of other type of bypass graft(s) of the right leg with ulceration**

> **Includes**   any condition classifiable to I70.711 and I70.721
> ▶ chronic limb-threatening ischemia of other type of bypass graft(s) of the right leg with ulceration
> ▶ critical limb ischemia of other type of bypass graft(s) of the right leg with ulceration

> Use additional code to identify severity of ulcer (L97.-)

   I70.731   Atherosclerosis of other type of bypass graft(s) of the right leg with ulceration of thigh 🔍   A

   I70.732   Atherosclerosis of other type of bypass graft(s) of the right leg with ulceration of calf 🔍   A

CHAPTER 9 (I00–I99)

I70.733   **Atherosclerosis of other type of bypass graft(s) of the right leg with ulceration of** ancle 🦠   A

I70.734   **Atherosclerosis of other type of bypass graft(s) of the right leg with ulceration of** heel and midfoot 🦠   A
     Atherosclerosis of other type of bypass graft(s) of right leg with ulceration of plantar surface of midfoot

I70.735   **Atherosclerosis of other type of bypass graft(s) of the right leg with ulceration of** other part of foot 🦠   A
     Atherosclerosis of other type of bypass graft(s) of right leg with ulceration of toe

I70.738   **Atherosclerosis of other type of bypass graft(s) of the right leg with ulceration of** other part of lower leg 🦠   A

I70.739   **Atherosclerosis of other type of bypass graft(s) of the right leg with ulceration of** unspecified site 🦠   A

● I70.74   **Atherosclerosis of other type of bypass graft(s) of the left leg with ulceration**
     Includes   any condition classifiable to I70.712 and I70.722
        ▶ chronic limb-threatening ischemia of other type of bypass graft(s) of the left leg with ulceration
        ▶ critical limb ischemia of other type of bypass graft(s) of the left leg with ulceration
     Use additional code to identify severity of ulcer (L97.-)

I70.741   **Atherosclerosis of other type of bypass graft(s) of the left leg with ulceration of** thigh 🦠   A

I70.742   **Atherosclerosis of other type of bypass graft(s) of the left leg with ulceration of** calf 🦠   A

I70.743   **Atherosclerosis of other type of bypass graft(s) of the left leg with ulceration of** ankle 🦠   A

I70.744   **Atherosclerosis of other type of bypass graft(s) of the left leg with ulceration of** heel and midfoot 🦠   A
     Atherosclerosis of other type of bypass graft(s) of left leg with ulceration of plantar surface of midfoot

I70.745   **Atherosclerosis of other type of bypass graft(s) of the left leg with ulceration of** other part of foot 🦠   A
     Atherosclerosis of other type of bypass graft(s) of left leg with ulceration of toe

I70.748   **Atherosclerosis of other type of bypass graft(s) of the left leg with ulceration of** other part of lower leg 🦠   A

I70.749   **Atherosclerosis of other type of bypass graft(s) of the left leg with ulceration of** unspecified site 🦠   A

I70.75   **Atherosclerosis of other type of bypass graft(s) of other extremity with ulceration** 🦠   A
     Includes   any condition classifiable to I70.718 and I70.728
     Use additional code to identify severity of ulcer (L98.49)

● I70.76   **Atherosclerosis of other type of bypass graft(s) of the extremities with gangrene**
     Includes   any condition classifiable to I70.71-, I70.72-, I70.73-, I70.74-, I70.75
        ▶ chronic limb-threatening ischemia of other type of bypass graft(s) of the extremities with gangrene
        ▶ critical limb ischemia of other type of bypass graft(s) of the extremities with gangrene
     Use additional code to identify the severity of any ulcer (L97.-, L98.49-), if applicable

I70.761   **Atherosclerosis of other type of bypass graft(s) of the extremities with gangrene, right leg** 🦠   A

I70.762   **Atherosclerosis of other type of bypass graft(s) of the extremities with gangrene, left leg** 🦠   A

I70.763   **Atherosclerosis of other type of bypass graft(s) of the extremities with gangrene, bilateral legs** 🦠   A

I70.768   **Atherosclerosis of other type of bypass graft(s) of the extremities with gangrene, other extremity** 🦠   A

I70.769   **Atherosclerosis of other type of bypass graft(s) of the extremities with gangrene, unspecified extremity** 🦠   A

● I70.79   **Other atherosclerosis of other type of bypass graft(s) of the extremities**

I70.791   **Other atherosclerosis of other type of bypass graft(s) of the extremities, right leg** 🦠   A

I70.792   **Other atherosclerosis of other type of bypass graft(s) of the extremities, left leg** 🦠   A

I70.793   **Other atherosclerosis of other type of bypass graft(s) of the extremities, bilateral legs** 🦠   A

I70.798   **Other atherosclerosis of other type of bypass graft(s) of the extremities, other extremity** 🦠   A

I70.799   **Other atherosclerosis of other type of bypass graft(s) of the extremities, unspecified extremity** 🦠   A

I70.8   **Atherosclerosis of other arteries**   A

● I70.9   **Other and unspecified atherosclerosis**

I70.90   **Unspecified atherosclerosis**   A

I70.91   **Generalized atherosclerosis**   A

I70.92   **Chronic total occlusion of artery of the extremities** 🦠   A
     Complete occlusion of artery of the extremities
     Total occlusion of artery of the extremities
     Code first atherosclerosis of arteries of the extremities (I70.2-, I70.3-, I70.4-, I70.5-, I70.6-, I70.7-)

● I71   **Aortic aneurysm and dissection**
     Excludes1   aortic ectasia (I77.81-)
           syphilitic aortic aneurysm (A52.01)
           traumatic aortic aneurysm (S25.09, S35.09)

● I71.0   **Dissection of aorta**

I71.00   **Dissection of unspecified site of aorta** 🦠

I71.01   **Dissection of thoracic aorta** 🦠

I71.02   **Dissection of abdominal aorta** 🦠

I71.03   **Dissection of thoracoabdominal aorta** 🦠

I71.1   **Thoracic aortic aneurysm, ruptured** 🦠

I71.2   **Thoracic aortic aneurysm, without rupture** 🦠

I71.3   **Abdominal aortic aneurysm, ruptured** 🦠

I71.4   **Abdominal aortic aneurysm, without rupture** 🦠

I71.5   **Thoracoabdominal aortic aneurysm, ruptured** 🦠

I71.6   **Thoracoabdominal aortic aneurysm, without rupture** 🦠

▶ New   ⇒ Revised   ~~deleted~~ Deleted   Excludes 1   Excludes 2   Includes   Use additional   Code first   Code also   Key words

910

OGCR Official Guidelines   X Assign placeholder X   ● Use Additional Character(s)   ▶ Manifestation Code   🦠 Hierarchical Condition Category   **Coding Clinic**

I71.8 Aortic aneurysm of unspecified site, ruptured 🔗
Rupture of aorta NOS

I71.9 Aortic aneurysm of unspecified site, without rupture 🔗
Aneurysm of aorta
Dilatation of aorta
Hyaline necrosis of aorta

● **I72 Other aneurysm**
   Includes   aneurysm (cirsoid) (false) (ruptured)
   Excludes2   acquired aneurysm (I77.0)
       aneurysm (of) aorta (I71.-)
       aneurysm (of) arteriovenous NOS (Q27.3-)
       carotid artery dissection (I77.71)
       cerebral (nonruptured) aneurysm (I67.1)
       coronary aneurysm (I25.4)
       coronary artery dissection (I25.42)
       dissection of artery NEC (I77.79)
       dissection of precerebral artery, congenital
         (nonruptured) (Q28.1)
       heart aneurysm (I25.3)
       iliac artery dissection (I77.72)
       precerebral artery, congential (nonruptured) (Q28.1)
       pulmonary artery aneurysm (I28.1)
       renal artery dissection (I77.73)
       retinal aneurysm (H35.0)
       ruptured cerebral aneurysm (I60.7)
       varicose aneurysm (I77.0)
       vertebral artery dissection (I77.74)

I72.0 Aneurysm of carotid artery 🔗
Aneurysm of common carotid artery
Aneurysm of external carotid artery
Aneurysm of internal carotid artery, extracranial
   portion
   Excludes1   aneurysm of internal carotid artery,
       intracranial portion (I67.1)
       aneurysm of internal carotid artery NOS
       (I67.1)

I72.1 Aneurysm of artery of upper extremity 🔗
I72.2 Aneurysm of renal artery 🔗
I72.3 Aneurysm of iliac artery 🔗
I72.4 Aneurysm of artery of lower extremity 🔗
   Coding Clinic: 2019, Q2, P22

I72.5 Aneurysm of other precerebral arteries 🔗
Aneurysm of basilar artery (trunk)
   Excludes2   aneurysm of carotid artery (I72.0)
       aneurysm of vertebral artery (I72.6)
       dissection of carotid artery (I77.71)
       dissection of other precerebral arteries
       (I77.75)
       dissection of vertebral artery (I77.74)
   Coding Clinic 2016, Q4, P28

I72.6 Aneurysm of vertebral artery 🔗
   Excludes2   dissection of vertebral artery (I77.74)
   Coding Clinic 2016, Q4, P28

I72.8 Aneurysm of other specified arteries 🔗
I72.9 Aneurysm of unspecified site 🔗

● **I73 Other peripheral vascular diseases**
   Excludes2   chilblains (T69.1)
       frostbite (T33-T34)
       immersion hand or foot (T69.0-)
       spasm of cerebral artery (G45.9)
   Coding Clinic: 2018, Q4, P87-88

● **I73.0 Raynaud's syndrome**
*Diminishing oxygen supply to fingers, toes, nose, and ears
     when exposed to temperature changes or stress*
Raynaud's disease
Raynaud's phenomenon (secondary)
   I73.00 Raynaud's syndrome without gangrene
   I73.01 Raynaud's syndrome with gangrene 🔗

I73.1 Thromboangiitis obliterans [Buerger's disease] 🔗
*Inflammatory occlusive disease resulting in poor circulation
    to the legs, feet, and sometimes the hands due to
    progressive inflammatory narrowing and eventually
    obliteration of the small arteries*

Figure 9-5 Raynaud's syndrome. (From Hallett: Comprehensive Vascular and Endovascular Surgery, ed 2, Philadelphia, Mosby Ltd., 2010)

● **I73.8 Other specified peripheral vascular diseases**
   Excludes1   diabetic (peripheral) angiopathy
       (E08-E13 with .51-.52)
   I73.81 Erythromelalgia 🔗
   I73.89 Other specified peripheral vascular diseases 🔗
     Acrocyanosis
     Erythrocyanosis
     Simple acroparesthesia [Schultze's type]
     Vasomotor acroparesthesia [Nothnagel's type]

I73.9 Peripheral vascular disease, unspecified 🔗
Intermittent claudication
Peripheral angiopathy NOS
Spasm of artery
   Excludes1   atherosclerosis of the extremities
       (I70.2—I70.7-)
   Coding Clinic: 2018, Q4, P87

● **I74 Arterial embolism and thrombosis**
   Includes   embolic infarction
       embolic occlusion
       thrombotic infarction
       thrombotic occlusion

Code first embolism and thrombosis complicating abortion or
   ectopic or molar pregnancy (O00-O07, O08.2)
   embolism and thrombosis complicating pregnancy, childbirth
   and the puerperium (O88.-)

   Excludes2   atheroembolism (I75.-)
       basilar embolism and thrombosis (I63.0-I63.2, I65.1)
       carotid embolism and thrombosis (I63.0-I63.2, I65.2)
       cerebral embolism and thrombosis (I63.3-I63.5,
         I66.-)
       coronary embolism and thrombosis (I21-I25)
       mesenteric embolism and thrombosis (K55.0-)
       ophthalmic embolism and thrombosis (H34.-)
       precerebral embolism and thrombosis NOS
         (I63.0-I63.2, I65.9)
       pulmonary embolism and thrombosis (I26.-)
       renal embolism and thrombosis (N28.0)
       retinal embolism and thrombosis (H34.-)
       septic embolism and thrombosis (I76)
       vertebral embolism and thrombosis (I63.0-I63.2,
         I65.0)

● **I74.0 Embolism and thrombosis of abdominal aorta**
   I74.01 Saddle embolus of abdominal aorta 🔗
   **I74.09 Other arterial embolism and thrombosis of
     abdominal aorta** 🔗
     Aortic bifurcation syndrome
     Aortoiliac obstruction
     Leriche's syndrome

CHAPTER 9 (I00-I99)

Item 9–9 An **embolus** is a mass of undissolved matter present in the blood that is transported by the blood current. A **thrombus** is a blood clot that occludes or shuts off a vessel. When a thrombus is dislodged, it becomes an embolus.

Embolus

Figure 9-6   An arterial embolus.

- **I74.1** **Embolism and thrombosis of other and unspecified parts of aorta**
  - **I74.10** Embolism and thrombosis of unspecified parts of aorta 🐾
  - **I74.11** Embolism and thrombosis of thoracic aorta 🐾
  - **I74.19** Embolism and thrombosis of other parts of aorta 🐾
  - **I74.2** Embolism and thrombosis of arteries of the upper extremities 🐾
  - **I74.3** Embolism and thrombosis of arteries of the lower extremities 🐾
  - **I74.4** Embolism and thrombosis of arteries of extremities, unspecified 🐾
    - Peripheral arterial embolism NOS
  - **I74.5** Embolism and thrombosis of iliac artery 🐾
  - **I74.8** Embolism and thrombosis of other arteries 🐾
  - **I74.9** Embolism and thrombosis of unspecified artery 🐾

- **I75** **Atheroembolism**
  - **Includes**   atherothrombotic microembolism
    - cholesterol embolism
  - **I75.0** **Atheroembolism of extremities**
    - **I75.01** **Atheroembolism of upper extremity**
      - **I75.011** Atheroembolism of right upper extremity 🐾
      - **I75.012** Atheroembolism of left upper extremity 🐾
      - **I75.013** Atheroembolism of bilateral upper extremities 🐾
      - **I75.019** Atheroembolism of unspecified upper extremity 🐾
    - **I75.02** **Atheroembolism of lower extremity**
      - **I75.021** Atheroembolism of right lower extremity 🐾
      - **I75.022** Atheroembolism of left lower extremity 🐾
      - **I75.023** Atheroembolism of bilateral lower extremities 🐾
      - **I75.029** Atheroembolism of unspecified lower extremity 🐾
  - **I75.8** **Atheroembolism of other sites**
    - **I75.81** Atheroembolism of kidney 🐾
      - Use additional code for any associated acute kidney failure and chronic kidney disease (N17.-, N18.-)
    - **I75.89** Atheroembolism of other site 🐾

- **I76** **Septic arterial embolism** 🐾
  - *Code first underlying infection, such as:*
    - infective endocarditis (I33.0)
    - lung abscess (J85.-)
  - Use additional code to identify the site of the embolism (I74.-)
  - **Excludes2**   septic pulmonary embolism (I26.01, I26.90)

- **I77** **Other disorders of arteries and arterioles**
  - **Excludes2**   collagen (vascular) diseases (M30-M36)
    - hypersensitivity angiitis (M31.0)
    - pulmonary artery (I28.-)
  - **I77.0** **Arteriovenous fistula, acquired** 🐾
    - Aneurysmal varix
    - Arteriovenous aneurysm, acquired
    - **Excludes1**   arteriovenous aneurysm NOS (Q27.3-)
      - presence of arteriovenous shunt (fistula) for dialysis (Z99.2)
      - traumatic - see injury of blood vessel by body region
    - **Excludes2**   cerebral (I67.1)
      - coronary (I25.4)
  - **I77.1** **Stricture of artery** 🐾
    - Narrowing of artery
  - **I77.2** **Rupture of artery** 🐾
    - Erosion of artery
    - Fistula of artery
    - Ulcer of artery
    - **Excludes1**   traumatic rupture of artery - see injury of blood vessel by body region
  - **I77.3** **Arterial fibromuscular dysplasia** 🐾
    - Fibromuscular hyperplasia (of) carotid artery
    - Fibromuscular hyperplasia (of) renal artery
  - **I77.4** **Celiac artery compression syndrome** 🐾
  - **I77.5** **Necrosis of artery** 🐾
  - **I77.6** **Arteritis, unspecified** 🐾
    - Aortitis NOS
    - Endarteritis NOS
    - **Excludes1**   arteritis or endarteritis:
      - aortic arch (M31.4)
      - cerebral NEC (I67.7)
      - coronary (I25.89)
      - deformans (I70.-)
      - giant cell (M31.5, M31.6)
      - obliterans (I70.-)
      - senile (I70.-)
  - **I77.7** **Other arterial dissection**
    - **Excludes2**   dissection of aorta (I71.0-)
      - dissection of coronary artery (I25.42)
    - **I77.70** Dissection of unspecified artery 🐾
      - Coding Clinic 2016, Q4, P28
    - **I77.71** Dissection of carotid artery 🐾
    - **I77.72** Dissection of iliac artery 🐾
    - **I77.73** Dissection of renal artery 🐾
    - **I77.74** Dissection of vertebral artery 🐾
      - **Excludes2**   aneurysm of vertebral artery (I72.6)
    - **I77.75** Dissection of other precerebral arteries 🐾
      - Dissection of basilar artery (trunk)
      - **Excludes2**   aneurysm of carotid artery (I72.0)
        - aneurysm of other precerebral arteries (I72.5)
        - aneurysm of vertebral artery (I72.6)
        - dissection of carotid artery (I77.71)
        - dissection of vertebral artery (I77.74)
      - Coding Clinic 2016, Q4, P28
    - **I77.76** Dissection of artery of upper extremity 🐾
      - Coding Clinic 2016, Q4, P28
    - **I77.77** Dissection of artery of lower extremity 🐾
      - Coding Clinic 2016, Q4, P28
    - **I77.79** Dissection of other specified artery 🐾
      - Coding Clinic 2016, Q4, P28

▶ New   ⇒ Revised   ~~deleted~~ Deleted   Excludes 1   Excludes 2   Includes   Use additional   Code first   Code also   Key words
OGCR Official Guidelines   X Assign placeholder X   ● Use Additional Character(s)   ▌ Manifestation Code   🐾 Hierarchical Condition Category   Coding Clinic

I77.8   **Other specified disorders of arteries and arterioles**
     I77.81   **Aortic ectasia**
         Ectasis aorta
         Excludes1   aortic aneurysm and dissection (I71.0-)
         I77.810   **Thoracic aortic ectasia** 🔾
         I77.811   **Abdominal aortic ectasia** 🔾
         I77.812   **Thoracoabdominal aortic ectasia** 🔾
         I77.819   **Aortic ectasia, unspecified site** 🔾
     I77.89   **Other specified disorders of arteries and arterioles** 🔾
   I77.9   **Disorder of arteries and arterioles, unspecified** 🔾

● **I78**   **Diseases of capillaries**
   I78.0   **Hereditary hemorrhagic telangiectasia** 🔾
     Rendu-Osler-Weber disease
   I78.1   **Nevus, non-neoplastic**
     Araneus nevus   Spider nevus
     Senile nevus   Stellar nevus
     Excludes1   nevus NOS (D22.-)
         vascular NOS (Q82.5)
     Excludes2   blue nevus (D22.-)
         flammeus nevus (Q82.5)
         hairy nevus (D22.-)
         melanocytic nevus (D22.-)
         pigmented nevus (D22.-)
         portwine nevus (Q82.5)
         sanguineous nevus (Q82.5)
         strawberry nevus (Q82.5)
         verrucous nevus (Q82.5)
     Coding Clinic: 2019, Q1, P21
   I78.8   **Other diseases of capillaries**
   I78.9   **Disease of capillaries, unspecified**

● **I79**   **Disorders of arteries, arterioles and capillaries in diseases classified elsewhere**
   ▷ *I79.0*   *Aneurysm of aorta in diseases classified elsewhere* 🔾
     Code first underlying disease
     Excludes1   syphilitic aneurysm (A52.01)
   ▷ *I79.1*   *Aortitis in diseases classified elsewhere* 🔾
     Code first underlying disease
     Excludes1   syphilitic aortitis (A52.02)
   ▷ *I79.8*   *Other disorders of arteries, arterioles and capillaries in diseases classified elsewhere* 🔾
     Code first underlying disease, such as:
         amyloidosis (E85.-)
     Excludes1   diabetic (peripheral) angiopathy (E08-E13 with .51-.52)
         syphilitic endarteritis (A52.09)
         tuberculous endarteritis (A18.89)

DISEASES OF VEINS, LYMPHATIC VESSELS AND LYMPH NODES, NOT ELSEWHERE CLASSIFIED (I80-I89)

● **I80**   **Phlebitis and thrombophlebitis**
   Inflammation of a vein with infiltration of walls (phlebitis)
   Includes   endophlebitis
         inflammation, vein
         periphlebitis
         suppurative phlebitis
   Code first phlebitis and thrombophlebitis complicating abortion, ectopic or molar pregnancy (O00-O07, O08.7)
     phlebitis and thrombophlebitis complicating pregnancy, childbirth and the puerperium (O22.-, O87.-)
   Excludes1   venous embolism and thrombosis of lower extremities (I82.4-, I82.5-, I82.81-)
   ● **I80.0**   **Phlebitis and thrombophlebitis of superficial vessels of lower extremities**
     Phlebitis and thrombophlebitis of femoropopliteal vein
     I80.00   **Phlebitis and thrombophlebitis of superficial vessels of unspecified lower extremity**

     I80.01   **Phlebitis and thrombophlebitis of superficial vessels of right lower extremity**
     I80.02   **Phlebitis and thrombophlebitis of superficial vessels of left lower extremity**
     I80.03   **Phlebitis and thrombophlebitis of superficial vessels of lower extremities, bilateral**
   ● **I80.1**   **Phlebitis and thrombophlebitis of femoral vein**
     Phlebitis and thrombophlebitis of common femoral vein
     Phlebitis and thrombophlebitis of deep femoral vein
     I80.10   **Phlebitis and thrombophlebitis of unspecified femoral vein** 🔾
     I80.11   **Phlebitis and thrombophlebitis of right femoral vein** 🔾
     I80.12   **Phlebitis and thrombophlebitis of left femoral vein** 🔾
     I80.13   **Phlebitis and thrombophlebitis of femoral vein, bilateral** 🔾
   ● **I80.2**   **Phlebitis and thrombophlebitis of other and unspecified deep vessels of lower extremities**
     ● **I80.20**   **Phlebitis and thrombophlebitis of unspecified deep vessels of lower extremities**
         I80.201   **Phlebitis and thrombophlebitis of unspecified deep vessels of right lower extremity** 🔾
         I80.202   **Phlebitis and thrombophlebitis of unspecified deep vessels of left lower extremity** 🔾
         I80.203   **Phlebitis and thrombophlebitis of unspecified deep vessels of lower extremities, bilateral** 🔾
         I80.209   **Phlebitis and thrombophlebitis of unspecified deep vessels of unspecified lower extremity** 🔾
     ● **I80.21**   **Phlebitis and thrombophlebitis of iliac vein**
         Phlebitis and thrombophlebitis of common iliac vein
         Phlebitis and thrombophlebitis of external iliac vein
         Phlebitis and thrombophlebitis of internal iliac vein
         I80.211   **Phlebitis and thrombophlebitis of right iliac vein** 🔾
         I80.212   **Phlebitis and thrombophlebitis of left iliac vein** 🔾
         I80.213   **Phlebitis and thrombophlebitis of iliac vein, bilateral** 🔾
         I80.219   **Phlebitis and thrombophlebitis of unspecified iliac vein** 🔾
     ● **I80.22**   **Phlebitis and thrombophlebitis of popliteal vein**
         I80.221   **Phlebitis and thrombophlebitis of right popliteal vein** 🔾
         I80.222   **Phlebitis and thrombophlebitis of left popliteal vein** 🔾
         I80.223   **Phlebitis and thrombophlebitis of popliteal vein, bilateral** 🔾
         I80.229   **Phlebitis and thrombophlebitis of unspecified popliteal vein** 🔾
     ● **I80.23**   **Phlebitis and thrombophlebitis of tibial vein**
         Phlebitis and thrombophlebitis of anterior tibial vein
         Phlebitis and thrombophlebitis of posterior tibial vein
         I80.231   **Phlebitis and thrombophlebitis of right tibial vein** 🔾
         I80.232   **Phlebitis and thrombophlebitis of left tibial vein** 🔾
         I80.233   **Phlebitis and thrombophlebitis of tibial vein, bilateral** 🔾
         I80.239   **Phlebitis and thrombophlebitis of unspecified tibial vein** 🔾

CHAPTER 9 (I00-I99)

● I80.24   **Phlebitis and thrombophlebitis of peroneal vein**

     I80.241   **Phlebitis and thrombophlebitis of right peroneal vein**

     I80.242   **Phlebitis and thrombophlebitis of left peroneal vein**

     I80.243   **Phlebitis and thrombophlebitis of peroneal vein, bilateral**

     I80.249   **Phlebitis and thrombophlebitis of unspecified peroneal vein**

● I80.25   **Phlebitis and thrombophlebitis of calf muscular vein**

     Phlebitis and thrombophlebitis of calf muscular vein, NOS
     Phlebitis and thrombophlebitis of gastrocnemial vein
     Phlebitis and thrombophlebitis of soleal vein

     I80.251   **Phlebitis and thrombophlebitis of right calf muscular vein**

     I80.252   **Phlebitis and thrombophlebitis of left calf muscular vein**

     I80.253   **Phlebitis and thrombophlebitis of calf muscular vein, bilateral**

     I80.259   **Phlebitis and thrombophlebitis of unspecified calf muscular vein**

● I80.29   **Phlebitis and thrombophlebitis of other deep vessels of lower extremities**

     I80.291   **Phlebitis and thrombophlebitis of other deep vessels of right lower extremity** 🔧

     I80.292   **Phlebitis and thrombophlebitis of other deep vessels of left lower extremity** 🔧

     I80.293   **Phlebitis and thrombophlebitis of other deep vessels of lower extremity, bilateral** 🔧

     I80.299   **Phlebitis and thrombophlebitis of other deep vessels of unspecified lower extremity** 🔧

I80.3   **Phlebitis and thrombophlebitis of lower extremities, unspecified**

I80.8   **Phlebitis and thrombophlebitis of other sites**

I80.9   **Phlebitis and thrombophlebitis of unspecified site**

I81   **Portal vein thrombosis**
     Portal (vein) obstruction

     Excludes2   hepatic vein thrombosis (I82.0)
                      phlebitis of portal vein (K75.1)
     Coding Clinic: 2019, Q4, P68

● I82   **Other venous embolism and thrombosis**

     Code first venous embolism and thrombosis complicating:
     abortion, ectopic or molar pregnancy (O00-O07, O08.7)
     pregnancy, childbirth and the puerperium (O22.-, O87.-)

     Excludes2   venous embolism and thrombosis (of):
                      cerebral (I63.6, I67.6)
                      coronary (I21-I25)
                      intracranial and intraspinal, septic or NOS (G08)
                      intracranial, nonpyogenic (I67.6)
                      intraspinal, nonpyogenic (G95.1)
                      mesenteric (K55.0-)
                      portal (I81)
                      pulmonary (I26.-)

I82.0   **Budd-Chiari syndrome** 🔧
     Hepatic vein thrombosis

I82.1   **Thrombophlebitis migrans**
     "White leg" is the other term to describe a migrating thrombus.

● I82.2   **Embolism and thrombosis of vena cava and other thoracic veins**

● I82.21   **Embolism and thrombosis of superior vena cava**

     I82.210   **Acute embolism and thrombosis of superior vena cava** 🔧
              Embolism and thrombosis of superior vena cava NOS

     I82.211   **Chronic embolism and thrombosis of superior vena cava** 🔧

● I82.22   **Embolism and thrombosis of inferior vena cava**

     I82.220   **Acute embolism and thrombosis of inferior vena cava** 🔧
              Embolism and thrombosis of inferior vena cava NOS

     I82.221   **Chronic embolism and thrombosis of inferior vena cava** 🔧

● I82.29   **Embolism and thrombosis of other thoracic veins**
     Embolism and thrombosis of brachiocephalic (innominate) vein

     I82.290   **Acute embolism and thrombosis of other thoracic veins** 🔧

     I82.291   **Chronic embolism and thrombosis of other thoracic veins** 🔧

I82.3   **Embolism and thrombosis of renal vein** 🔧

● I82.4   **Acute embolism and thrombosis of deep veins of lower extremity**

     I82.40   **Acute embolism and thrombosis of unspecified deep veins of lower extremity**
     Deep vein thrombosis NOS
     DVT NOS

         Excludes1   acute embolism and thrombosis of unspecified deep veins of distal lower extremity (I82.4Z-)
                      acute embolism and thrombosis of unspecified deep veins of proximal lower extremity (I82.4Y-)

     I82.401   **Acute embolism and thrombosis of unspecified deep veins of right lower extremity** 🔧

     I82.402   **Acute embolism and thrombosis of unspecified deep veins of left lower extremity** 🔧

     I82.403   **Acute embolism and thrombosis of unspecified deep veins of lower extremity, bilateral** 🔧

     I82.409   **Acute embolism and thrombosis of unspecified deep veins of unspecified lower extremity** 🔧

● I82.41   **Acute embolism and thrombosis of femoral vein**
     Acute embolism and thrombosis of common femoral vein
     Acute embolism and thrombosis of deep femoral vein

     I82.411   **Acute embolism and thrombosis of right femoral vein** 🔧

     I82.412   **Acute embolism and thrombosis of left femoral vein** 🔧

     I82.413   **Acute embolism and thrombosis of femoral vein, bilateral** 🔧

     I82.419   **Acute embolism and thrombosis of unspecified femoral vein** 🔧

▶ New   ⇒ Revised   ~~deleted~~ Deleted   Excludes 1   Excludes 2   Includes   Use additional   Code first   Code also   Key words

OGCR Official Guidelines   X Assign placeholder X   ● Use Additional Character(s)   ❙ Manifestation Code   🔧 Hierarchical Condition Category   **Coding Clinic**

● **I82.42** **Acute embolism and thrombosis of iliac vein**
　　Acute embolism and thrombosis of common
　　　　iliac vein
　　Acute embolism and thrombosis of external
　　　　iliac vein
　　Acute embolism and thrombosis of internal
　　　　iliac vein

　I82.421 Acute embolism and thrombosis of
　　　　right iliac vein 🦠

　I82.422 Acute embolism and thrombosis of
　　　　left iliac vein 🦠

　I82.423 Acute embolism and thrombosis of
　　　　iliac vein, bilateral 🦠

　I82.429 Acute embolism and thrombosis of
　　　　unspecified iliac vein 🦠

● **I82.43** **Acute embolism and thrombosis of popliteal
vein**

　I82.431 Acute embolism and thrombosis of
　　　　right popliteal vein 🦠

　I82.432 Acute embolism and thrombosis of
　　　　left popliteal vein 🦠

　I82.433 Acute embolism and thrombosis of
　　　　popliteal vein, bilateral 🦠

　I82.439 Acute embolism and thrombosis of
　　　　unspecified popliteal vein 🦠

● **I82.44** **Acute embolism and thrombosis of tibial vein**
　　Acute embolism and thrombosis of anterior
　　　　tibial vein
　　Acute embolism and thrombosis of posterior
　　　　tibial vein

　I82.441 Acute embolism and thrombosis of
　　　　right tibial vein 🦠

　I82.442 Acute embolism and thrombosis of
　　　　left tibial vein 🦠

　I82.443 Acute embolism and thrombosis of
　　　　tibial vein, bilateral 🦠

　I82.449 Acute embolism and thrombosis of
　　　　unspecified tibial vein 🦠

● **I82.45** **Acute embolism and thrombosis of peroneal
vein**

　I82.451 Acute embolism and thrombosis of
　　　　right peroneal vein

　I82.452 Acute embolism and thrombosis of
　　　　left peroneal vein

　I82.453 Acute embolism and thrombosis of
　　　　peroneal vein, bilateral

　I82.459 Acute embolism and thrombosis of
　　　　unspecified peroneal vein

● **I82.46** **Acute embolism and thrombosis of calf
muscular vein**
　　Acute embolism and thrombosis of calf
　　　　muscular vein, NOS
　　Acute embolism and thrombosis of
　　　　gastrocnemial vein
　　Acute embolism and thrombosis of soleal vein

　I82.461 Acute embolism and thrombosis of
　　　　right calf muscular vein

　I82.462 Acute embolism and thrombosis of
　　　　left calf muscular vein

　I82.463 Acute embolism and thrombosis of
　　　　calf muscular vein, bilateral

　I82.469 Acute embolism and thrombosis of
　　　　unspecified calf muscular vein

● **I82.49** **Acute embolism and thrombosis of other
specified deep vein of lower extremity**

　I82.491 Acute embolism and thrombosis of
　　　　other specified deep vein of right
　　　　lower extremity 🦠

　I82.492 Acute embolism and thrombosis of
　　　　other specified deep vein of left lower
　　　　extremity 🦠

　I82.493 Acute embolism and thrombosis of
　　　　other specified deep vein of lower
　　　　extremity, bilateral 🦠

　I82.499 Acute embolism and thrombosis of
　　　　other specified deep vein of
　　　　unspecified lower extremity 🦠

● **I82.4Y** **Acute embolism and thrombosis of unspecified
deep veins of proximal lower extremity**
　　Acute embolism and thrombosis of deep vein
　　　　of thigh NOS
　　Acute embolism and thrombosis of deep vein
　　　　of upper leg NOS

　I82.4Y1 Acute embolism and thrombosis of
　　　　unspecified deep veins of right
　　　　proximal lower extremity 🦠

　I82.4Y2 Acute embolism and thrombosis of
　　　　unspecified deep veins of left
　　　　proximal lower extremity 🦠

　I82.4Y3 Acute embolism and thrombosis of
　　　　unspecified deep veins of proximal
　　　　lower extremity, bilateral 🦠

　I82.4Y9 Acute embolism and thrombosis of
　　　　unspecified deep veins of unspecified
　　　　proximal lower extremity 🦠

● **I82.4Z** **Acute embolism and thrombosis of unspecified
deep veins of distal lower extremity**
　　Acute embolism and thrombosis of deep vein
　　　　of calf NOS
　　Acute embolism and thrombosis of deep vein
　　　　of lower leg NOS

　I82.4Z1 Acute embolism and thrombosis of
　　　　unspecified deep veins of right distal
　　　　lower extremity 🦠

　I82.4Z2 Acute embolism and thrombosis of
　　　　unspecified deep veins of left distal
　　　　lower extremity 🦠

　I82.4Z3 Acute embolism and thrombosis of
　　　　unspecified deep veins of distal lower
　　　　extremity, bilateral 🦠

　I82.4Z9 Acute embolism and thrombosis of
　　　　unspecified deep veins of unspecified
　　　　distal lower extremity 🦠

● **I82.5** **Chronic embolism and thrombosis of deep veins of
lower extremity**
　　Use additional code, if applicable, for associated long-
　　　　term (current) use of anticoagulants (Z79.01)

　Excludes1 personal history of venous embolism and
　　　　　　thrombosis (Z86.718)

● **I82.50** **Chronic embolism and thrombosis of
unspecified deep veins of lower extremity**

　　Excludes1 chronic embolism and
　　　　　　　thrombosis of unspecified
　　　　　　　deep veins of distal lower
　　　　　　　extremity (I82.5Z-)
　　　　　　chronic embolism and
　　　　　　　thrombosis of unspecified
　　　　　　　deep veins of proximal
　　　　　　　lower extremity (I82.5Y-)

　I82.501 Chronic embolism and thrombosis of
　　　　unspecified deep veins of right lower
　　　　extremity 🦠

　I82.502 Chronic embolism and thrombosis of
　　　　unspecified deep veins of left lower
　　　　extremity 🦠

　I82.503 Chronic embolism and thrombosis of
　　　　unspecified deep veins of lower
　　　　extremity, bilateral 🦠

　I82.509 Chronic embolism and thrombosis of
　　　　unspecified deep veins of unspecified
　　　　lower extremity 🦠

● I82.51   **Chronic embolism and thrombosis of femoral vein**
          Chronic embolism and thrombosis of common femoral vein
          Chronic embolism and thrombosis of deep femoral vein

   I82.511   **Chronic embolism and thrombosis of right femoral vein** 🐾

   I82.512   **Chronic embolism and thrombosis of left femoral vein** 🐾

   I82.513   **Chronic embolism and thrombosis of femoral vein, bilateral** 🐾

   I82.519   **Chronic embolism and thrombosis of unspecified femoral vein** 🐾

● I82.52   **Chronic embolism and thrombosis of iliac vein**
          Chronic embolism and thrombosis of common iliac vein
          Chronic embolism and thrombosis of external iliac vein
          Chronic embolism and thrombosis of internal iliac vein

   I82.521   **Chronic embolism and thrombosis of right iliac vein** 🐾

   I82.522   **Chronic embolism and thrombosis of left iliac vein** 🐾

   I82.523   **Chronic embolism and thrombosis of iliac vein, bilateral** 🐾

   I82.529   **Chronic embolism and thrombosis of unspecified iliac vein** 🐾

● I82.53   **Chronic embolism and thrombosis of popliteal vein**

   I82.531   **Chronic embolism and thrombosis of right popliteal vein** 🐾

   I82.532   **Chronic embolism and thrombosis of left popliteal vein** 🐾

   I82.533   **Chronic embolism and thrombosis of popliteal vein, bilateral** 🐾

   I82.539   **Chronic embolism and thrombosis of unspecified popliteal vein** 🐾

● I82.54   **Chronic embolism and thrombosis of tibial vein**
          Chronic embolism and thrombosis of anterior tibial vein
          Chronic embolism and thrombosis of posterior tibial vein

   I82.541   **Chronic embolism and thrombosis of right tibial vein** 🐾

   I82.542   **Chronic embolism and thrombosis of left tibial vein** 🐾

   I82.543   **Chronic embolism and thrombosis of tibial vein, bilateral** 🐾

   I82.549   **Chronic embolism and thrombosis of unspecified tibial vein** 🐾

● I82.55   **Chronic embolism and thrombosis of peroneal vein**

   I82.551   **Chronic embolism and thrombosis of right peroneal vein**

   I82.552   **Chronic embolism and thrombosis of left peroneal vein**

   I82.553   **Chronic embolism and thrombosis of peroneal vein, bilateral**

   I82.559   **Chronic embolism and thrombosis of unspecified peroneal vein**

Item 9–10 Varicose/Varicosities (varix = singular, varices = plural): Enlarged, engorged, tortuous, twisted vascular vessels (veins, arteries, lymphatics). As such, the condition can present in various parts of the body, although the most familiar locations are the lower extremities. A common complication of varices is thrombophlebitis. Varicosities of the anus and rectum are called hemorrhoids.

Figure 9-7 Varicose veins of the legs. (Getty Image)

● I82.56   **Chronic embolism and thrombosis of calf muscular vein**
          Chronic embolism and thrombosis of calf muscular vein NOS
          Chronic embolism and thrombosis of gastrocnemial vein
          Chronic embolism and thrombosis of soleal vein

   I82.561   **Chronic embolism and thrombosis of right calf muscular vein**

   I82.562   **Chronic embolism and thrombosis of left calf muscular vein**

   I82.563   **Chronic embolism and thrombosis of calf muscular vein, bilateral**

   I82.569   **Chronic embolism and thrombosis of unspecified calf muscular vein**

● I82.59   **Chronic embolism and thrombosis of other specified deep vein of lower extremity**

   I82.591   **Chronic embolism and thrombosis of other specified deep vein of right lower extremity** 🐾

   I82.592   **Chronic embolism and thrombosis of other specified deep vein of left lower extremity** 🐾

   I82.593   **Chronic embolism and thrombosis of other specified deep vein of lower extremity, bilateral** 🐾

   I82.599   **Chronic embolism and thrombosis of other specified deep vein of unspecified lower extremity** 🐾

● I82.5Y   **Chronic embolism and thrombosis of unspecified deep veins of proximal lower extremity**
          Chronic embolism and thrombosis of deep veins of thigh NOS
          Chronic embolism and thrombosis of deep veins of upper leg NOS

   I82.5Y1   **Chronic embolism and thrombosis of unspecified deep veins of right proximal lower extremity** 🐾

   I82.5Y2   **Chronic embolism and thrombosis of unspecified deep veins of left proximal lower extremity** 🐾

   I82.5Y3   **Chronic embolism and thrombosis of unspecified deep veins of proximal lower extremity, bilateral** 🐾

   I82.5Y9   **Chronic embolism and thrombosis of unspecified deep veins of unspecified proximal lower extremity** 🐾

▶ New   ⇒ Revised   ~~deleted~~ Deleted   Excludes 1   Excludes 2   Includes   Use additional   Code first   Code also   Key words

OGCR Official Guidelines   X Assign placeholder X   ● Use Additional Character(s)   ❱ Manifestation Code   🐾 Hierarchical Condition Category   Coding Clinic

● **I82.5Z** **Chronic embolism and thrombosis of unspecified deep veins of distal lower extremity**
Chronic embolism and thrombosis of deep veins of calf NOS
Chronic embolism and thrombosis of deep veins of lower leg NOS

I82.5Z1 Chronic embolism and thrombosis of unspecified deep veins of right distal lower extremity 🔖

I82.5Z2 Chronic embolism and thrombosis of unspecified deep veins of left distal lower extremity 🔖

I82.5Z3 Chronic embolism and thrombosis of unspecified deep veins of distal lower extremity, bilateral 🔖

I82.5Z9 Chronic embolism and thrombosis of unspecified deep veins of unspecified distal lower extremity 🔖

● **I82.6** **Acute embolism and thrombosis of veins of upper extremity**

● **I82.60** **Acute embolism and thrombosis of unspecified veins of upper extremity**

I82.601 Acute embolism and thrombosis of unspecified veins of right upper extremity

I82.602 Acute embolism and thrombosis of unspecified veins of left upper extremity

I82.603 Acute embolism and thrombosis of unspecified veins of upper extremity, bilateral

I82.609 Acute embolism and thrombosis of unspecified veins of unspecified upper extremity

● **I82.61** **Acute embolism and thrombosis of superficial veins of upper extremity**
Acute embolism and thrombosis of antecubital vein
Acute embolism and thrombosis of basilic vein
Acute embolism and thrombosis of cephalic vein

I82.611 Acute embolism and thrombosis of superficial veins of right upper extremity

I82.612 Acute embolism and thrombosis of superficial veins of left upper extremity

I82.613 Acute embolism and thrombosis of superficial veins of upper extremity, bilateral

I82.619 Acute embolism and thrombosis of superficial veins of unspecified upper extremity

● **I82.62** **Acute embolism and thrombosis of deep veins of upper extremity**
Acute embolism and thrombosis of brachial vein
Acute embolism and thrombosis of radial vein
Acute embolism and thrombosis of ulnar vein

I82.621 Acute embolism and thrombosis of deep veins of right upper extremity 🔖

I82.622 Acute embolism and thrombosis of deep veins of left upper extremity 🔖

I82.623 Acute embolism and thrombosis of deep veins of upper extremity, bilateral 🔖

I82.629 Acute embolism and thrombosis of deep veins of unspecified upper extremity 🔖

● **I82.7** **Chronic embolism and thrombosis of veins of upper extremity**
Use additional code, if applicable, for associated long-term (current) use of anticoagulants (Z79.01)

Excludes1 personal history of venous embolism and thrombosis (Z86.718)

● **I82.70** **Chronic embolism and thrombosis of unspecified veins of upper extremity**

I82.701 Chronic embolism and thrombosis of unspecified veins of right upper extremity

I82.702 Chronic embolism and thrombosis of unspecified veins of left upper extremity

I82.703 Chronic embolism and thrombosis of unspecified veins of upper extremity, bilateral

I82.709 Chronic embolism and thrombosis of unspecified veins of unspecified upper extremity

● **I82.71** **Chronic embolism and thrombosis of superficial veins of upper extremity**
Chronic embolism and thrombosis of antecubital vein
Chronic embolism and thrombosis of basilic vein
Chronic embolism and thrombosis of cephalic vein

I82.711 Chronic embolism and thrombosis of superficial veins of right upper extremity

I82.712 Chronic embolism and thrombosis of superficial veins of left upper extremity

I82.713 Chronic embolism and thrombosis of superficial veins of upper extremity, bilateral

I82.719 Chronic embolism and thrombosis of superficial veins of unspecified upper extremity

● **I82.72** **Chronic embolism and thrombosis of deep veins of upper extremity**
Chronic embolism and thrombosis of brachial vein
Chronic embolism and thrombosis of radial vein
Chronic embolism and thrombosis of ulnar vein

I82.721 Chronic embolism and thrombosis of deep veins of right upper extremity 🔖

I82.722 Chronic embolism and thrombosis of deep veins of left upper extremity 🔖

I82.723 Chronic embolism and thrombosis of deep veins of upper extremity, bilateral 🔖

I82.729 Chronic embolism and thrombosis of deep veins of unspecified upper extremity 🔖

● **I82.A** **Embolism and thrombosis of axillary vein**

● **I82.A1** **Acute embolism and thrombosis of axillary vein**

I82.A11 Acute embolism and thrombosis of right axillary vein 🔖

I82.A12 Acute embolism and thrombosis of left axillary vein 🔖

I82.A13 Acute embolism and thrombosis of axillary vein, bilateral 🔖

I82.A19 Acute embolism and thrombosis of unspecified axillary vein 🔖

● **I82.A2**   **Chronic** embolism and thrombosis of axillary vein

I82.A21   Chronic embolism and thrombosis of right axillary vein 🦚

I82.A22   Chronic embolism and thrombosis of left axillary vein 🦚

I82.A23   Chronic embolism and thrombosis of axillary vein, bilateral 🦚

I82.A29   Chronic embolism and thrombosis of unspecified axillary vein 🦚

● **I82.B**   Embolism and thrombosis of subclavian vein

● **I82.B1**   Acute embolism and thrombosis of subclavian vein

I82.B11   Acute embolism and thrombosis of right subclavian vein 🦚

I82.B12   Acute embolism and thrombosis of left subclavian vein 🦚

I82.B13   Acute embolism and thrombosis of subclavian vein, bilateral 🦚

I82.B19   Acute embolism and thrombosis of unspecified subclavian vein 🦚

● **I82.B2**   Chronic embolism and thrombosis of subclavian vein

I82.B21   Chronic embolism and thrombosis of right subclavian vein 🦚

I82.B22   Chronic embolism and thrombosis of left subclavian vein 🦚

I82.B23   Chronic embolism and thrombosis of subclavian vein, bilateral 🦚

I82.B29   Chronic embolism and thrombosis of unspecified subclavian vein 🦚

● **I82.C**   Embolism and thrombosis of internal jugular vein

● **I82.C1**   Acute embolism and thrombosis of internal jugular vein

I82.C11   Acute embolism and thrombosis of right internal jugular vein 🦚

I82.C12   Acute embolism and thrombosis of left internal jugular vein 🦚

I82.C13   Acute embolism and thrombosis of internal jugular vein, bilateral 🦚

I82.C19   Acute embolism and thrombosis of unspecified internal jugular vein 🦚

● **I82.C2**   Chronic embolism and thrombosis of internal jugular vein

I82.C21   Chronic embolism and thrombosis of right internal jugular vein 🦚

I82.C22   Chronic embolism and thrombosis of left internal jugular vein 🦚

I82.C23   Chronic embolism and thrombosis of internal jugular vein, bilateral 🦚

I82.C29   Chronic embolism and thrombosis of unspecified internal jugular vein 🦚

● **I82.8**   Embolism and thrombosis of other specified veins

Use additional code, if applicable, for associated long-term (current) use of anticoagulants (Z79.01)

● **I82.81**   Embolism and thrombosis of superficial veins of lower extremities

Embolism and thrombosis of saphenous vein (greater) (lesser)

I82.811   Embolism and thrombosis of superficial veins of right lower extremity

I82.812   Embolism and thrombosis of superficial veins of left lower extremity

I82.813   Embolism and thrombosis of superficial veins of lower extremities, bilateral

I82.819   Embolism and thrombosis of superficial veins of unspecified lower extremity

● **I82.89**   Embolism and thrombosis of other specified veins

I82.890   Acute embolism and thrombosis of other specified veins

I82.891   Chronic embolism and thrombosis of other specified veins

● **I82.9**   Embolism and thrombosis of unspecified vein

I82.90   Acute embolism and thrombosis of unspecified vein

Embolism of vein NOS
Thrombosis (vein) NOS

I82.91   Chronic embolism and thrombosis of unspecified vein

● **I83**   Varicose veins of lower extremities

Excludes1   varicose veins complicating pregnancy (O22.0-)
varicose veins complicating the puerperium (O87.4)

● **I83.0**   Varicose veins of lower extremities with ulcer

Use additional code to identify severity of ulcer (L97.-)

● **I83.00**   Varicose veins of unspecified lower extremity with ulcer

I83.001   Varicose veins of unspecified lower extremity with ulcer of thigh 🦚   A

I83.002   Varicose veins of unspecified lower extremity with ulcer of calf 🦚   A

I83.003   Varicose veins of unspecified lower extremity with ulcer of ankle 🦚   A

I83.004   Varicose veins of unspecified lower extremity with ulcer of heel and midfoot 🦚   A

Varicose veins of unspecified lower extremity with ulcer of plantar surface of midfoot

I83.005   Varicose veins of unspecified lower extremity with ulcer other part of foot 🦚   A

Varicose veins of unspecified lower extremity with ulcer of toe

I83.008   Varicose veins of unspecified lower extremity with ulcer other part of lower leg 🦚   A

I83.009   Varicose veins of unspecified lower extremity with ulcer of unspecified site 🦚   A

● **I83.01**   Varicose veins of right lower extremity with ulcer

I83.011   Varicose veins of right lower extremity with ulcer of thigh 🦚   A

I83.012   Varicose veins of right lower extremity with ulcer of calf 🦚   A

I83.013   Varicose veins of right lower extremity with ulcer of ankle 🦚   A

I83.014   Varicose veins of right lower extremity with ulcer of heel and midfoot 🦚   A

Varicose veins of right lower extremity with ulcer of plantar surface of midfoot

I83.015   Varicose veins of right lower extremity with ulcer other part of foot 🦚   A

Varicose veins of right lower extremity with ulcer of toe

I83.018   Varicose veins of right lower extremity with ulcer other part of lower leg 🦚   A

I83.019   Varicose veins of right lower extremity with ulcer of unspecified site 🦚   A

▶ New   ⇒ Revised   ~~deleted~~ Deleted   Excludes 1   Excludes 2   Includes   Use additional   Code first   Code also   Key words

OGCR Official Guidelines   X Assign placeholder X   ● Use Additional Character(s)   ▶ Manifestation Code   🦚 Hierarchical Condition Category   Coding Clinic

● I83.02   Varicose veins of left lower extremity with ulcer

    I83.021   Varicose veins of left lower extremity with ulcer of thigh ⚕   A

    I83.022   Varicose veins of left lower extremity with ulcer of calf ⚕   A

    I83.023   Varicose veins of left lower extremity with ulcer of ankle ⚕   A

    I83.024   Varicose veins of left lower extremity with ulcer of heel and midfoot ⚕   A
        Varicose veins of left lower extremity with ulcer of plantar surface of midfoot

    I83.025   Varicose veins of left lower extremity with ulcer other part of foot ⚕   A
        Varicose veins of left lower extremity with ulcer of toe

    I83.028   Varicose veins of left lower extremity with ulcer other part of lower leg ⚕   A

    I83.029   Varicose veins of left lower extremity with ulcer of unspecified site ⚕   A

● I83.1   Varicose veins of lower extremities with inflammation

    I83.10   Varicose veins of unspecified lower extremity with inflammation   A

    I83.11   Varicose veins of right lower extremity with inflammation   A

    I83.12   Varicose veins of left lower extremity with inflammation   A

● I83.2   Varicose veins of lower extremities with both ulcer and inflammation
    Use additional code to identify severity of ulcer (L97.-)

  ● I83.20   Varicose veins of unspecified lower extremity with both ulcer and inflammation

    I83.201   Varicose veins of unspecified lower extremity with both ulcer of thigh and inflammation ⚕   A

    I83.202   Varicose veins of unspecified lower extremity with both ulcer of calf and inflammation ⚕   A

    I83.203   Varicose veins of unspecified lower extremity with both ulcer of ankle and inflammation ⚕   A

    I83.204   Varicose veins of unspecified lower extremity with both ulcer of heel and midfoot and inflammation ⚕   A
        Varicose veins of unspecified lower extremity with both ulcer of plantar surface of midfoot and inflammation

    I83.205   Varicose veins of unspecified lower extremity with both ulcer other part of foot and inflammation ⚕   A
        Varicose veins of unspecified lower extremity with both ulcer of toe and inflammation

    I83.208   Varicose veins of unspecified lower extremity with both ulcer of other part of lower extremity and inflammation ⚕   A

    I83.209   Varicose veins of unspecified lower extremity with both ulcer of unspecified site and inflammation ⚕   A

  ● I83.21   Varicose veins of right lower extremity with both ulcer and inflammation

    I83.211   Varicose veins of right lower extremity with both ulcer of thigh and inflammation ⚕   A

    I83.212   Varicose veins of right lower extremity with both ulcer of calf and inflammation ⚕   A

    I83.213   Varicose veins of right lower extremity with both ulcer of ankle and inflammation ⚕   A

    I83.214   Varicose veins of right lower extremity with both ulcer of heel and midfoot and inflammation ⚕   A
        Varicose veins of right lower extremity with both ulcer of plantar surface of midfoot and inflammation

    I83.215   Varicose veins of right lower extremity with both ulcer other part of foot and inflammation ⚕   A
        Varicose veins of right lower extremity with both ulcer of toe and inflammation

    I83.218   Varicose veins of right lower extremity with both ulcer of other part of lower extremity and inflammation ⚕   A

    I83.219   Varicose veins of right lower extremity with both ulcer of unspecified site and inflammation ⚕   A

● I83.22   Varicose veins of left lower extremity with both ulcer and inflammation

    I83.221   Varicose veins of left lower extremity with both ulcer of thigh and inflammation ⚕   A

    I83.222   Varicose veins of left lower extremity with both ulcer of calf and inflammation ⚕   A

    I83.223   Varicose veins of left lower extremity with both ulcer of ankle and inflammation ⚕   A

    I83.224   Varicose veins of left lower extremity with both ulcer of heel and midfoot and inflammation ⚕   A
        Varicose veins of left lower extremity with both ulcer of plantar surface of midfoot and inflammation

    I83.225   Varicose veins of left lower extremity with both ulcer other part of foot and inflammation ⚕   A
        Varicose veins of left lower extremity with both ulcer of toe and inflammation

    I83.228   Varicose veins of left lower extremity with both ulcer of other part of lower extremity and inflammation ⚕   A

    I83.229   Varicose veins of left lower extremity with both ulcer of unspecified site and inflammation ⚕   A

● I83.8   Varicose veins of lower extremities with other complications

  ● I83.81   Varicose veins of lower extremities with pain

    I83.811   Varicose veins of right lower extremity with pain   A

    I83.812   Varicose veins of left lower extremity with pain   A

    I83.813   Varicose veins of bilateral lower extremities with pain   A

    I83.819   Varicose veins of unspecified lower extremity with pain   A

  ● I83.89   Varicose veins of lower extremities with other complications
    Varicose veins of lower extremities with edema
    Varicose veins of lower extremities with swelling

    I83.891   Varicose veins of right lower extremity with other complications   A

    I83.892   Varicose veins of left lower extremity with other complications   A

    I83.893   Varicose veins of bilateral lower extremities with other complications   A

    I83.899   Varicose veins of unspecified lower extremity with other complications   A

CHAPTER 9 (I00-I99)

● **I83.9**   **Asymptomatic varicose veins of lower extremities**
Phlebectasia of lower extremities
Varicose veins of lower extremities
Varix of lower extremities

    I83.90   **Asymptomatic varicose veins of unspecified lower extremity**   A
        Varicose veins NOS

    I83.91   **Asymptomatic varicose veins of right lower extremity**   A

    I83.92   **Asymptomatic varicose veins of left lower extremity**   A

    I83.93   **Asymptomatic varicose veins of bilateral lower extremities**   A

● **I85**   **Esophageal varices**
Use additional code to identify:
    alcohol abuse and dependence (F10.-)

● **I85.0**   **Esophageal varices**
Idiopathic esophageal varices
Primary esophageal varices

    I85.00   **Esophageal varices without bleeding** 🐾
        Esophageal varices NOS

    I85.01   **Esophageal varices with bleeding** 🐾

● **I85.1**   **Secondary esophageal varices**
Esophageal varices secondary to alcoholic liver disease
Esophageal varices secondary to cirrhosis of liver
Esophageal varices secondary to schistosomiasis
Esophageal varices secondary to toxic liver disease
Code first underlying disease

    I85.10   **Secondary esophageal varices without bleeding** 🐾

    I85.11   **Secondary esophageal varices with bleeding** 🐾

● **I86**   **Varicose veins of other sites**
    Excludes1   varicose veins of unspecified site (I83.9-)
    Excludes2   retinal varices (H35.0-)

I86.0   **Sublingual varices**

I86.1   **Scrotal varices** ♂
    Varicocele

I86.2   **Pelvic varices**

I86.3   **Vulval varices** ♀
    Excludes1   vulval varices complicating childbirth and the puerperium (O87.8)
            vulval varices complicating pregnancy (O22.1-)

I86.4   **Gastric varices**

I86.8   **Varicose veins of other specified sites**   A
    Varicose ulcer of nasal septum

● **I87**   **Other disorders of veins**

● **I87.0**   **Postthrombotic syndrome**
Chronic venous hypertension due to deep vein thrombosis
Postphlebitic syndrome
    Excludes1   chronic venous hypertension without deep vein thrombosis (I87.3-)

    ● **I87.00**   **Postthrombotic syndrome without complications**
        Asymptomatic Postthrombotic syndrome

      I87.001   **Postthrombotic syndrome without complications of right lower extremity**

      I87.002   **Postthrombotic syndrome without complications of left lower extremity**

      I87.003   **Postthrombotic syndrome without complications of bilateral lower extremity**

      I87.009   **Postthrombotic syndrome without complications of unspecified extremity**
         Postthrombotic syndrome NOS

● **I87.01**   **Postthrombotic syndrome with ulcer**
Use additional code to specify site and severity of ulcer (L97.-)

    I87.011   **Postthrombotic syndrome with ulcer of right lower extremity** 🐾

    I87.012   **Postthrombotic syndrome with ulcer of left lower extremity** 🐾

    I87.013   **Postthrombotic syndrome with ulcer of bilateral lower extremity** 🐾

    I87.019   **Postthrombotic syndrome with ulcer of unspecified lower extremity** 🐾

● **I87.02**   **Postthrombotic syndrome with inflammation**

    I87.021   **Postthrombotic syndrome with inflammation of right lower extremity**

    I87.022   **Postthrombotic syndrome with inflammation of left lower extremity**

    I87.023   **Postthrombotic syndrome with inflammation of bilateral lower extremity**

    I87.029   **Postthrombotic syndrome with inflammation of unspecified lower extremity**

● **I87.03**   **Postthrombotic syndrome with ulcer and inflammation**
Use additional code to specify site and severity of ulcer (L97.-)

    I87.031   **Postthrombotic syndrome with ulcer and inflammation of right lower extremity** 🐾

    I87.032   **Postthrombotic syndrome with ulcer and inflammation of left lower extremity** 🐾

    I87.033   **Postthrombotic syndrome with ulcer and inflammation of bilateral lower extremity** 🐾

    I87.039   **Postthrombotic syndrome with ulcer and inflammation of unspecified lower extremity** 🐾

● **I87.09**   **Postthrombotic syndrome with other complications**

    I87.091   **Postthrombotic syndrome with other complications of right lower extremity**

    I87.092   **Postthrombotic syndrome with other complications of left lower extremity**

    I87.093   **Postthrombotic syndrome with other complications of bilateral lower extremity**

    I87.099   **Postthrombotic syndrome with other complications of unspecified lower extremity**

I87.1   **Compression of vein**
Stricture of vein
Vena cava syndrome (inferior) (superior)
    Excludes2   compression of pulmonary vein (I28.8)

I87.2   **Venous insufficiency (chronic) (peripheral)**
Stasis dermatitis
    Excludes1   stasis dermatitis with varicose veins of lower extremities (I83.1-, I83.2-)

▶ New   ⇒ Revised   ~~deleted~~ Deleted   Excludes 1   Excludes 2   Includes   Use additional   Code first   Code also   Key words
OGCR Official Guidelines   X Assign placeholder X   ● Use Additional Character(s)   ▷ Manifestation Code   🐾 Hierarchical Condition Category   **Coding Clinic**

● **I87.3   Chronic venous hypertension (idiopathic)**
Stasis edema

Excludes1   chronic venous hypertension due to deep vein thrombosis (I87.0-)
varicose veins of lower extremities (I83.-)

● **I87.30   Chronic venous hypertension (idiopathic) without complications**
Asymptomatic chronic venous hypertension (idiopathic)

I87.301   Chronic venous hypertension (idiopathic) without complications of right lower extremity

I87.302   Chronic venous hypertension (idiopathic) without complications of left lower extremity

I87.303   Chronic venous hypertension (idiopathic) without complications of bilateral lower extremity

I87.309   Chronic venous hypertension (idiopathic) without complications of unspecified lower extremity
Chronic venous hypertension NOS

● **I87.31   Chronic venous hypertension (idiopathic) with ulcer**
Use additional code to specify site and severity of ulcer (L97.-)

I87.311   Chronic venous hypertension (idiopathic) with ulcer of right lower extremity ℞

I87.312   Chronic venous hypertension (idiopathic) with ulcer of left lower extremity ℞

I87.313   Chronic venous hypertension (idiopathic) with ulcer of bilateral lower extremity ℞

I87.319   Chronic venous hypertension (idiopathic) with ulcer of unspecified lower extremity ℞

● **I87.32   Chronic venous hypertension (idiopathic) with inflammation**

I87.321   Chronic venous hypertension (idiopathic) with inflammation of right lower extremity

I87.322   Chronic venous hypertension (idiopathic) with inflammation of left lower extremity

I87.323   Chronic venous hypertension (idiopathic) with inflammation of bilateral lower extremity

I87.329   Chronic venous hypertension (idiopathic) with inflammation of unspecified lower extremity

● **I87.33   Chronic venous hypertension (idiopathic) with ulcer and inflammation**
Use additional code to specify site and severity of ulcer (L97.-)

I87.331   Chronic venous hypertension (idiopathic) with ulcer and inflammation of right lower extremity ℞

I87.332   Chronic venous hypertension (idiopathic) with ulcer and inflammation of left lower extremity ℞

I87.333   Chronic venous hypertension (idiopathic) with ulcer and inflammation of bilateral lower extremity ℞

I87.339   Chronic venous hypertension (idiopathic) with ulcer and inflammation of unspecified lower extremity ℞

● **I87.39   Chronic venous hypertension (idiopathic) with other complications**

I87.391   Chronic venous hypertension (idiopathic) with other complications of right lower extremity

I87.392   Chronic venous hypertension (idiopathic) with other complications of left lower extremity

I87.393   Chronic venous hypertension (idiopathic) with other complications of bilateral lower extremity

I87.399   Chronic venous hypertension (idiopathic) with other complications of unspecified lower extremity

I87.8   Other specified disorders of veins
Phlebosclerosis
Venofibrosis

I87.9   Disorder of vein, unspecified

● **I88   Nonspecific lymphadenitis**

Excludes1   acute lymphadenitis, except mesenteric (L04.-)
enlarged lymph nodes NOS (R59.-)
human immunodeficiency virus [HIV] disease resulting in generalized lymphadenopathy (B20)

I88.0   Nonspecific mesenteric lymphadenitis
Mesenteric lymphadenitis (acute)(chronic)

I88.1   Chronic lymphadenitis, except mesenteric
Adenitis
Lymphadenitis

I88.8   Other nonspecific lymphadenitis

I88.9   Nonspecific lymphadenitis, unspecified
Lymphadenitis NOS

● **I89   Other noninfective disorders of lymphatic vessels and lymph nodes**

Excludes1   chylocele, tunica vaginalis (nonfilarial) NOS (N50.89)
enlarged lymph nodes NOS (R59.-)
filarial chylocele (B74.-)
hereditary lymphedema (Q82.0)

I89.0   Lymphedema, not elsewhere classified
Elephantiasis (nonfilarial) NOS
Lymphangiectasis
Obliteration, lymphatic vessel
Praecox lymphedema
Secondary lymphedema

Excludes1   postmastectomy lymphedema (I97.2)

I89.1   Lymphangitis
Chronic lymphangitis
Lymphangitis NOS
Subacute lymphangitis

Excludes1   acute lymphangitis (L03.-)

I89.8   Other specified noninfective disorders of lymphatic vessels and lymph nodes
Chylocele (nonfilarial)
Chylous ascites
Chylous cyst
Lipomelanotic reticulosis
Lymph node or vessel fistula
Lymph node or vessel infarction
Lymph node or vessel rupture

I89.9   Noninfective disorder of lymphatic vessels and lymph nodes, unspecified
Disease of lymphatic vessels NOS

OTHER AND UNSPECIFIED DISORDERS OF THE CIRCULATORY SYSTEM (I95-I99)

- **I95**   **Hypotension**
  Subnormal arterial blood pressure
  > **Excludes1**   cardiovascular collapse (R57.9)
  > maternal hypotension syndrome (O26.5-)
  > nonspecific low blood pressure reading NOS (R03.1)

  I95.0   **Idiopathic hypotension**

  I95.1   **Orthostatic hypotension**
  Hypotension, postural
  > *Moving from a sitting or reclining position to a standing position precipitates a sudden drop in blood pressure (hypotension).*
  >> **Excludes1**   neurogenic orthostatic hypotension [Shy-Drager] (G90.3)
  >> orthostatic hypotension due to drugs (I95.2)

  I95.2   **Hypotension due to drugs**
  Orthostatic hypotension due to drugs
  > Use additional code for adverse effect, if applicable, to identify drug (T36-T50 with fifth or sixth character 5)

  I95.3   **Hypotension of hemodialysis**
  Intra-dialytic hypotension

- **I95.8**   **Other hypotension**
  I95.81   **Postprocedural hypotension**
  I95.89   **Other hypotension**
  Chronic hypotension

  I95.9   **Hypotension, unspecified**

- **I96**   **Gangrene, not elsewhere classified**
  Gangrenous cellulitis
  > **Excludes1**   gangrene in atherosclerosis of native arteries of the extremities (I70.26)
  > gangrene of certain specified sites - *see* Alphabetical Index
  > gangrene in hernia (K40.1, K40.4, K41.1, K41.4, K42.1, K43.1-, K44.1, K45.1, K46.1)
  > gangrene in other peripheral vascular diseases (I73.-)
  > gas gangrene (A48.0)
  > pyoderma gangrenosum (L88)
  > **Excludes2**   gangrene in diabetes mellitus (E08-E13 with .52)
  > Coding Clinic: 2018, Q4, P87; 2017, Q3, P6; 2013, Q2, P35

- **I97**   **Intraoperative and postprocedural complications and disorders of circulatory system, not elsewhere classified**
  > **Excludes2**   postprocedural shock (T81.1-)
  > Coding Clinic: 2019, Q2, P22

  I97.0   **Postcardiotomy syndrome**

- **I97.1**   **Other postprocedural cardiac functional disturbances**
  > **Excludes2**   acute pulmonary insufficiency following thoracic surgery (J95.1)
  > intraoperative cardiac functional disturbances (I97.7-)

  - **I97.11**   **Postprocedural cardiac insufficiency**
    I97.110   **Postprocedural cardiac insufficiency following cardiac surgery**
    I97.111   **Postprocedural cardiac insufficiency following other surgery**

  - **I97.12**   **Postprocedural cardiac arrest**
    I97.120   **Postprocedural cardiac arrest following cardiac surgery**
    I97.121   **Postprocedural cardiac arrest following other surgery**

- **I97.13**   **Postprocedural heart failure**
  > Use additional code to identify the heart failure (I50.-)
  I97.130   **Postprocedural heart failure following cardiac surgery**
  I97.131   **Postprocedural heart failure following other surgery**

- **I97.19**   **Other postprocedural cardiac functional disturbances**
  > Use additional code, if applicable, to further specify disorder
  I97.190   **Other postprocedural cardiac functional disturbances following cardiac surgery**
  > Use Additional code, if applicable, for type 4 or type 5 myocardial infarction, to further specify disorder
  > Coding Clinic: 2019, Q2, P32-33
  I97.191   **Other postprocedural cardiac functional disturbances following other surgery**

  I97.2   **Postmastectomy lymphedema syndrome**   A
  Elephantiasis due to mastectomy
  Obliteration of lymphatic vessels

  I97.3   **Postprocedural hypertension**

- **I97.4**   **Intraoperative hemorrhage and hematoma of a circulatory system organ or structure complicating a procedure**
  > **Excludes1**   intraoperative hemorrhage and hematoma of a circulatory system organ or structure due to accidental puncture and laceration during a procedure (I97.5-)
  > **Excludes2**   intraoperative cerebrovascular hemorrhage complicating a procedure (G97.3-)

  - **I97.41**   **Intraoperative hemorrhage and hematoma of a circulatory system organ or structure complicating a circulatory system procedure**
    I97.410   **Intraoperative hemorrhage and hematoma of a circulatory system organ or structure complicating a cardiac catheterization**
    I97.411   **Intraoperative hemorrhage and hematoma of a circulatory system organ or structure complicating a cardiac bypass**
    I97.418   **Intraoperative hemorrhage and hematoma of a circulatory system organ or structure complicating other circulatory system procedure**

  - **I97.42**   **Intraoperative hemorrhage and hematoma of a circulatory system organ or structure complicating other procedure**
    Coding Clinic: 2020, Q1, P20; 2016, Q4, P100

- **I97.5**   **Accidental puncture and laceration of a circulatory system organ or structure during a procedure**
  > **Excludes2**   accidental puncture and laceration of brain during a procedure (G97.4-)

  I97.51   **Accidental puncture and laceration of a circulatory system organ or structure during a circulatory system procedure**
  Coding Clinic: 2019, Q2, P24

  I97.52   **Accidental puncture and laceration of a circulatory system organ or structure during other procedure**

● I97.6 **Postprocedural hemorrhage, hematoma and seroma of a circulatory system organ or structure following a procedure**

Excludes2   postprocedural cerebrovascular hemorrhage complicating a procedure (G97.5-)

Coding Clinic: 2016, Q4, P10

● I97.61 **Postprocedural hemorrhage of a circulatory system organ or structure following a circulatory system procedure**

I97.610 **Postprocedural hemorrhage of a circulatory system organ or structure following a cardiac catheterization**

I97.611 **Postprocedural hemorrhage of a circulatory system organ or structure following cardiac bypass**

I97.618 **Postprocedural hemorrhage of a circulatory system organ or structure following other circulatory system procedure**

● I97.62 **Postprocedural hemorrhage, hematoma and seroma of a circulatory system organ or structure following other procedure**

I97.620 **Postprocedural hemorrhage of a circulatory system organ or structure following other procedure**

I97.621 **Postprocedural hematoma of a circulatory system organ or structure following other procedure**

I97.622 **Postprocedural seroma of a circulatory system organ or structure following other procedure**

● I97.63 **Postprocedural hematoma of a circulatory system organ or structure following a circulatory system procedure**

I97.630 **Postprocedural hematoma of a circulatory system organ or structure following a cardiac catheterization**

I97.631 **Postprocedural hematoma of a circulatory system organ or structure following cardiac bypass**

I97.638 **Postprocedural hematoma of a circulatory system organ or structure following other circulatory system procedure**

● I97.64 **Postprocedural seroma of a circulatory system organ or structure following a circulatory system procedure**

I97.640 **Postprocedural seroma of a circulatory system organ or structure following a cardiac catheterization**

I97.641 **Postprocedural seroma of a circulatory system organ or structure following cardiac bypass**

I97.648 **Postprocedural seroma of a circulatory system organ or structure following other circulatory system procedure**

● I97.7 **Intraoperative cardiac functional disturbances**

Excludes2   acute pulmonary insufficiency following thoracic surgery (J95.1)
postprocedural cardiac functional disturbances (I97.1-)

● I97.71 **Intraoperative cardiac arrest**

I97.710 **Intraoperative cardiac arrest during cardiac surgery**

I97.711 **Intraoperative cardiac arrest during other surgery**

● I97.79 **Other intraoperative cardiac functional disturbances**

Use additional code, if applicable, to further specify disorder

I97.790 **Other intraoperative cardiac functional disturbances during cardiac surgery**

I97.791 **Other intraoperative cardiac functional disturbances during other surgery**

● I97.8 **Other intraoperative and postprocedural complications and disorders of the circulatory system, not elsewhere classified**

Use additional code, if applicable, to further specify disorder

● I97.81 **Intraoperative cerebrovascular infarction**

I97.810 **Intraoperative cerebrovascular infarction during cardiac surgery** 🔖

I97.811 **Intraoperative cerebrovascular infarction during other surgery** 🔖

● I97.82 **Postprocedural cerebrovascular infarction**

I97.820 **Postprocedural cerebrovascular infarction following cardiac surgery** 🔖

I97.821 **Postprocedural cerebrovascular infarction following other surgery** 🔖

I97.88 **Other intraoperative complications of the circulatory system, not elsewhere classified**

I97.89 **Other postprocedural complications and disorders of the circulatory system, not elsewhere classified**

Coding Clinic: 2019, Q2, P32-33

● I99 **Other and unspecified disorders of circulatory system**

I99.8 **Other disorder of circulatory system**

I99.9 **Unspecified disorder of circulatory system**

CHAPTER 9 (I00-I99)

CHAPTER 10

DISEASES OF THE RESPIRATORY SYSTEM (J00-J99)

OGCR Chapter-Specific Coding Guidelines

10. **Chapter 10: Diseases of the Respiratory System (J00-J99)**

a. **Chronic Obstructive Pulmonary Disease [COPD] and Asthma**

1) **Acute exacerbation of chronic obstructive bronchitis and asthma**

The codes in categories J44 and J45 distinguish between uncomplicated cases and those in acute exacerbation. An acute exacerbation is a worsening or a decompensation of a chronic condition. An acute exacerbation is not equivalent to an infection superimposed on a chronic condition, though an exacerbation may be triggered by an infection.

b. **Acute Respiratory Failure**

1) **Acute respiratory failure as principal diagnosis**

A code from subcategory J96.0, Acute respiratory failure, or subcategory J96.2, Acute and chronic respiratory failure, may be assigned as a principal diagnosis when it is the condition established after study to be chiefly responsible for occasioning the admission to the hospital, and the selection is supported by the Alphabetic Index and Tabular List. However, chapter-specific coding guidelines (such as obstetrics, poisoning, HIV, newborn) that provide sequencing direction take precedence.

2) **Acute respiratory failure as secondary diagnosis**

Respiratory failure may be listed as a secondary diagnosis if it occurs after admission, or if it is present on admission, but does not meet the definition of principal diagnosis.

3) **Sequencing of acute respiratory failure and another acute condition**

When a patient is admitted with respiratory failure and another acute condition (e.g., myocardial infarction, cerebrovascular accident, aspiration pneumonia), the principal diagnosis will not be the same in every situation. This applies whether the other acute condition is a respiratory or nonrespiratory condition. Selection of the principal diagnosis will be dependent on the circumstances of admission. If both the respiratory failure and the other acute condition are equally responsible for occasioning the admission to the hospital, and there are no chapter-specific sequencing rules, the guideline regarding two or more diagnoses that equally meet the definition for principal diagnosis (*Section II, C.*) may be applied in these situations.

If the documentation is not clear as to whether acute respiratory failure and another condition are equally responsible for occasioning the admission, query the provider for clarification.

c. **Influenza due to certain identified influenza viruses**

Code only confirmed cases of influenza due to certain identified influenza viruses (category J09), and due to other identified influenza virus (category J10). This is an exception to the hospital inpatient guideline Section II, H. (Uncertain Diagnosis).

In this context, "confirmation" does not require documentation of positive laboratory testing specific for avian or other novel influenza A or other identified influenza virus. However, coding should be based on the provider's diagnostic statement that the patient has avian influenza, or other novel influenza A, for category J09, or has another particular identified strain of influenza, such as H1N1 or H3N2, but not identified as novel or variant, for category J10.

If the provider records "suspected" or "possible" or "probable" avian influenza, or novel influenza, or other identified influenza, then the appropriate influenza code from category J11, Influenza due to unidentified influenza virus, should be assigned. A code from category J09, Influenza due to certain identified influenza viruses, should not be assigned nor should a code from category J10, Influenza due to other identified influenza virus.

d. **Ventilator associated Pneumonia**

1) **Documentation of Ventilator associated Pneumonia**

As with all procedural or postprocedural complications, code assignment is based on the provider's documentation of the relationship between the condition and the procedure.

Code J95.851, Ventilator associated pneumonia, should be assigned only when the provider has documented ventilator associated pneumonia (VAP). An additional code to identify the organism (e.g., Pseudomonas aeruginosa, code B96.5) should also be assigned. Do not assign an additional code from categories J12-J18 to identify the type of pneumonia.

Code J95.851 should not be assigned for cases where the patient has pneumonia and is on a mechanical ventilator and the provider has not specifically stated that the pneumonia is ventilator associated pneumonia. If the documentation is unclear as to whether the patient has a pneumonia that is a complication attributable to the mechanical ventilator, query the provider.

2) **Ventilator associated Pneumonia Develops after Admission**

A patient may be admitted with one type of pneumonia (e.g., code J13, Pneumonia due to Streptococcus pneumonia) and subsequently develop VAP. In this instance, the principal diagnosis would be the appropriate code from categories J12-J18 for the pneumonia diagnosed at the time of admission. Code J95.851, Ventilator associated pneumonia, would be assigned as an additional diagnosis when the provider has also documented the presence of ventilator associated pneumonia.

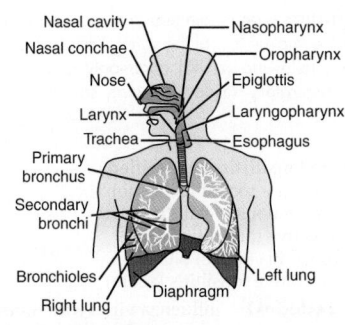

Figure 10-1 Respiratory system. (From Buck CJ: Step-by-Step Medical Coding, ed 2016, St. Louis, Elsevier, 2016)

Figure 10-2 Paranasal sinuses. (From Buck CJ: Step-by-Step Medical Coding, ed 2016, St. Louis, Elsevier, 2016)

Item 10–1 Pharyngitis is painful inflammation of the pharynx (sore throat). Ninety percent of the infections are caused by a virus with the remaining being bacterial and rarely a fungus (candidiasis). Other irritants such as pollutants, chemicals, or smoke may cause similar symptoms.

CHAPTER 10

DISEASES OF THE RESPIRATORY SYSTEM (J00-J99)

Note: When a respiratory condition is described as occurring in more than one site and is not specifically indexed, it should be classified to the lower anatomic site (e.g., tracheobronchitis to bronchitis in J40).

Use additional code, where applicable, to identify:
exposure to environmental tobacco smoke (Z77.22)
exposure to tobacco smoke in the perinatal period (P96.81)
history of tobacco dependence (Z87.891)
occupational exposure to environmental tobacco smoke (Z57.31)
tobacco dependence (F17.-)
tobacco use (Z72.0)

Excludes2   certain conditions originating in the perinatal period (P04-P96)
certain infectious and parasitic diseases (A00-B99)
complications of pregnancy, childbirth and the puerperium (O00-O99A)
congenital malformations, deformations and chromosomal abnormalities (Q00-Q99)
endocrine, nutritional and metabolic diseases (E00-E88)
injury, poisoning and certain other consequences of external causes (S00-T88)
neoplasms (C00-D49)
smoke inhalation (T59.81-)
symptoms, signs and abnormal clinical and laboratory findings, not elsewhere classified (R00-R94)

This chapter contains the following blocks:

J00-J06	Acute upper respiratory infections
J09-J18	Influenza and pneumonia
J20-J22	Other acute lower respiratory infections
J30-J39	Other diseases of upper respiratory tract
J40-J47	Chronic lower respiratory diseases
J60-J70	Lung diseases due to external agents
J80-J84	Other respiratory diseases principally affecting the interstitium
J85-J86	Suppurative and necrotic conditions of the lower respiratory tract
J90-J94	Other diseases of the pleura
J95	Intraoperative and postprocedural complications and disorders of respiratory system, not elsewhere classified
J96-J99	Other diseases of the respiratory system

ACUTE UPPER RESPIRATORY INFECTIONS (J00-J06)

Excludes1   chronic obstructive pulmonary disease with acute lower respiratory infection (J44.0)
~~influenza virus with other respiratory manifestations (J09.X2, J10.1, J11.1)~~

J00   **Acute nasopharyngitis [common cold]**
Acute rhinitis
Coryza (acute)
Infective nasopharyngitis NOS
Infective rhinitis
Nasal catarrh, acute
Nasopharyngitis NOS

Excludes1   acute pharyngitis (J02.-)
acute sore throat NOS (J02.9)
▶influenza virus with other respiratory manifestations (J09.X2, J10.1, J11.1)
pharyngitis NOS (J02.9)
rhinitis NOS (J31.0)
sore throat NOS (J02.9)

Excludes2   allergic rhinitis (J30.1-J30.9)
chronic pharyngitis (J31.2)
chronic rhinitis (J31.0)
chronic sore throat (J31.2)
nasopharyngitis, chronic (J31.1)
vasomotor rhinitis (J30.0)

★**(See Plate 27 of the Anatomy Illustrations.)**

●**J01**   **Acute sinusitis**
Includes   acute abscess of sinus
acute empyema of sinus
acute infection of sinus
acute inflammation of sinus
acute suppuration of sinus

Use additional code (B95-B97) to identify infectious agent.
Excludes1   sinusitis NOS (J32.9)
Excludes2   chronic sinusitis (J32.0-J32.8)

●**J01.0**   **Acute maxillary sinusitis**
Acute antritis
        J01.00   Acute maxillary sinusitis, **unspecified**
        J01.01   Acute **recurrent** maxillary sinusitis
●**J01.1**   **Acute frontal sinusitis**
        J01.10   Acute frontal sinusitis, **unspecified**
        J01.11   Acute **recurrent** frontal sinusitis
●**J01.2**   **Acute ethmoidal sinusitis**
        J01.20   Acute ethmoidal sinusitis, **unspecified**
        J01.21   Acute **recurrent** ethmoidal sinusitis
●**J01.3**   **Acute sphenoidal sinusitis**
        J01.30   Acute sphenoidal sinusitis, **unspecified**
        J01.31   Acute **recurrent** sphenoidal sinusitis
●**J01.4**   **Acute pansinusitis**
        J01.40   Acute pansinusitis, **unspecified**
        J01.41   Acute **recurrent** pansinusitis

CHAPTER 10 (J00-J99)

● **J01.8 Other acute sinusitis**

J01.80 Other acute sinusitis
Acute sinusitis involving more than one sinus but not pansinusitis

J01.81 Other acute recurrent sinusitis
Acute recurrent sinusitis involving more than one sinus but not pansinusitis

● **J01.9 Acute sinusitis, unspecified**

J01.90 Acute sinusitis, unspecified

J01.91 Acute recurrent sinusitis, unspecified

● **J02 Acute pharyngitis**

Includes acute sore throat

Excludes1 acute laryngopharyngitis (J06.0)
peritonsillar abscess (J36)
pharyngeal abscess (J39.1)
retropharyngeal abscess (J39.0)

Excludes2 chronic pharyngitis (J31.2)

J02.0 Streptococcal pharyngitis
Septic pharyngitis
Streptococcal sore throat

Excludes2 scarlet fever (A38.-)

J02.8 Acute pharyngitis due to other specified organisms
Use additional code (B95-B97) to identify infectious agent

Excludes1 pharyngitis due to coxsackie virus (B08.5)
pharyngitis due to gonococcus (A54.5)
acute pharyngitis due to herpes [simplex] virus (B00.2)
acute pharyngitis due to infectious mononucleosis (B27.-)
enteroviral vesicular pharyngitis (B08.5)

J02.9 Acute pharyngitis, unspecified
Gangrenous pharyngitis (acute)
Infective pharyngitis (acute) NOS
Pharyngitis (acute) NOS
Sore throat (acute) NOS
Suppurative pharyngitis (acute)
Ulcerative pharyngitis (acute)

Excludes1 influenza virus with other respiratory manifestations (J09.X2, J10.1, J11.1)

● **J03 Acute tonsillitis**
Inflammation of pharyngeal tonsils caused by virus or bacteria

Excludes1 acute sore throat (J02.-)
hypertrophy of tonsils (J35.1)
peritonsillar abscess (J36)
sore throat NOS (J02.9)
streptococcal sore throat (J02.0)

Excludes2 chronic tonsillitis (J35.0)

● **J03.0 Streptococcal tonsillitis**

J03.00 Acute streptococcal tonsillitis, unspecified

J03.01 Acute recurrent streptococcal tonsillitis

● **J03.8 Acute tonsillitis due to other specified organisms**
Use additional code (B95-B97) to identify infectious agent.

Excludes1 diphtheritic tonsillitis (A36.0)
herpesviral pharyngotonsillitis (B00.2)
streptococcal tonsillitis (J03.0)
tuberculous tonsillitis (A15.8)
Vincent's tonsillitis (A69.1)

J03.80 Acute tonsillitis due to other specified organisms

J03.81 Acute recurrent tonsillitis due to other specified organisms

Item 10–2 Laryngitis is an inflammation of the larynx (voice box) resulting in hoarse voice or the complete loss of the voice. **Tracheitis** is an inflammation of the trachea (often following a URI) commonly caused by *staphylococcus aureus* resulting in inspiratory stridor (crowing sound on inspiration) and a crouplike cough.

● **J03.9 Acute tonsillitis, unspecified**
Follicular tonsillitis (acute)
Gangrenous tonsillitis (acute)
Infective tonsillitis (acute)
Tonsillitis (acute) NOS
Ulcerative tonsillitis (acute)

Excludes1 influenza virus with other respiratory manifestations (J09.X2, J10.1, J11.1)

J03.90 Acute tonsillitis, unspecified

J03.91 Acute recurrent tonsillitis, unspecified

● **J04 Acute laryngitis and tracheitis**
Use additional code (B95-B97) to identify infectious agent.
Code also influenza, if present, such as:
influenza due to identified novel influenza A virus with other respiratory manifestations (J09.X2)
influenza due to other identified influenza virus with other respiratory manifestations (J10.1)
influenza due to unidentified influenza virus with other respiratory manifestations (J11.1)

Excludes1 acute obstructive laryngitis [croup] and epiglottitis (J05.-)

Excludes2 laryngismus (stridulus) (J38.5)

J04.0 Acute laryngitis
Edematous laryngitis (acute)
Laryngitis (acute) NOS
Subglottic laryngitis (acute)
Suppurative laryngitis (acute)
Ulcerative laryngitis (acute)

Excludes1 acute obstructive laryngitis (J05.0)

Excludes2 chronic laryngitis (J37.0)

● **J04.1 Acute tracheitis**
Acute viral tracheitis
Catarrhal tracheitis (acute)
Tracheitis (acute) NOS

Excludes2 chronic tracheitis (J42)

J04.10 Acute tracheitis without obstruction

J04.11 Acute tracheitis with obstruction

J04.2 Acute laryngotracheitis
Laryngotracheitis NOS
Tracheitis (acute) with laryngitis (acute)

Excludes1 acute obstructive laryngotracheitis (J05.0)

Excludes2 chronic laryngotracheitis (J37.1)

● **J04.3 Supraglottitis, unspecified**

J04.30 Supraglottitis, unspecified, without obstruction

J04.31 Supraglottitis, unspecified, with obstruction

● **J05 Acute obstructive laryngitis [croup] and epiglottitis**
Use additional code (B95-B97) to identify infectious agent.
Code also if present, such as:
influenza due to identified novel influenza A virus with other respiratory manifestations (J09.X2)
influenza due to other identified influenza virus with other respiratory manifestations (J10.1)
influenza due to unidentified influenza virus with other respiratory manifestations (J11.1)

J05.0 Acute obstructive laryngitis [croup]
Obstructive laryngitis (acute) NOS
Obstructive laryngotracheitis NOS

● **J05.1   Acute epiglottitis**

  Excludes2 epiglottitis, chronic (J37.0)

  J05.10   Acute epiglottitis without obstruction
      Epiglottitis NOS

  J05.11   Acute epiglottitis with obstruction

● **J06   Acute upper respiratory infections of multiple and unspecified sites**

  Excludes1 acute respiratory infection NOS (J22)
      ▶ influenza virus with other respiratory
         manifestations (J09.X2, J10.1, J11.1)
      streptococcal pharyngitis (J02.0)
  Coding Clinic: 2020, Q1, P22

  J06.0   Acute laryngopharyngitis

  J06.9   Acute upper respiratory infection, unspecified
      Upper respiratory disease, acute
      Upper respiratory infection NOS

      Use additional code (B95-B97) to identify infectious
         agent, if known, such as:
         respiratory syncytial virus (RSV) (B97.4)

INFLUENZA AND PNEUMONIA (J09-J18)

  Excludes2 allergic or eosinophilic pneumonia (J82)
      aspiration pneumonia NOS (J69.0)
      meconium pneumonia (P24.01)
      neonatal aspiration pneumonia (P24.-)
      pneumonia due to solids and liquids (J69.-)
      congenital pneumonia (P23.9)
      lipid pneumonia (J69.1)
      rheumatic pneumonia (I00)
      ventilator associated pneumonia (J95.851)
  Coding Clinic: 2020, Q1, P22

● **J09   Influenza due to certain identified influenza viruses**

  Excludes1 influenza A/H1N1 (J10.-)
      influenza due to other influenza viruses (J10.-)
      influenza due to unidentified influenza virus
         (J11.-)
      seasonal influenza due to other identified
         influenza virus (J10.-)
      seasonal influenza due to unidentified influenza
         virus (J11.-)

● **J09.X   Influenza due to identified novel influenza A virus**
      Avian influenza
      Bird influenza
      Influenza A/H5N1
      Influenza of other animal origin, not bird or swine
      Swine influenza virus (viruses that normally cause
         infections in pigs)
      Coding Clinic: 2016, Q3, P11

  J09.X1   Influenza due to identified novel influenza A virus with pneumonia
      Code also , if applicable, associated:
         lung abscess (J85.1)
         other specified type of pneumonia

  J09.X2   Influenza due to identified novel influenza A virus with other respiratory manifestations
      Influenza due to identified novel influenza A
         virus NOS
      Influenza due to identified novel influenza A
         virus with laryngitis
      Influenza due to identified novel influenza A
         virus with pharyngitis
      Influenza due to identified novel influenza A
         virus with upper respiratory symptoms

      Use additional code, if applicable, for
         associated:
         pleural effusion (J91.8)
         sinusitis (J01.-)

  J09.X3   Influenza due to identified novel influenza A virus with gastrointestinal manifestations
      Influenza due to identified novel influenza A
         virus gastroenteritis

      Excludes1 'intestinal flu' [viral
                 gastroenteritis] (A08.-)

  J09.X9   Influenza due to identified novel influenza A virus with other manifestations
      Influenza due to identified novel influenza A
         virus with encephalopathy
      Influenza due to identified novel influenza A
         virus with myocarditis
      Influenza due to identified novel influenza A
         virus with otitis media

      Use additional code to identify manifestation

● **J10   Influenza due to other identified influenza virus**

  ▶ **Includes**   influenza A (non-novel)
      ▶ influenza B
      ▶ influenza C

  Excludes1 influenza due to avian influenza virus (J09.X-)
      influenza due to swine flu (J09.X-)
      influenza due to unidentified influenza virus
         (J11.-)

● **J10.0   Influenza due to other identified influenza virus with pneumonia**
      Code also associated lung abscess, if applicable (J85.1)

  J10.00   Influenza due to other identified influenza virus with unspecified type of pneumonia

  J10.01   Influenza due to other identified influenza virus with the same other identified influenza virus pneumonia

  J10.08   Influenza due to other identified influenza virus with other specified pneumonia
      Code also other specified type of pneumonia
      Coding Clinic: 2017, Q4, P96

  J10.1   Influenza due to other identified influenza virus with other respiratory manifestations
      Influenza due to other identified influenza virus NOS
      Influenza due to other identified influenza virus with
         laryngitis
      Influenza due to other identified influenza virus with
         pharyngitis
      Influenza due to other identified influenza virus with
         upper respiratory symptoms

      Use additional code for associated pleural effusion, if
         applicable (J91.8)

      Use additional code for associated sinusitis, if
         applicable (J01.-)
      Coding Clinic: 2016, Q3, P11

  J10.2   Influenza due to other identified influenza virus with gastrointestinal manifestations
      Influenza due to other identified influenza virus
         gastroenteritis

      Excludes1 'intestinal flu' [viral gastroenteritis]
                 (A08.-)

● **J10.8   Influenza due to other identified influenza virus with other manifestations**

  J10.81   Influenza due to other identified influenza virus with encephalopathy

  J10.82   Influenza due to other identified influenza virus with myocarditis

  J10.83   Influenza due to other identified influenza virus with otitis media
      Use additional code for any associated
         perforated tympanic membrane (H72.-)

  J10.89   Influenza due to other identified influenza virus with other manifestations
      Use additional codes to identify the
         manifestations

CHAPTER 10 (J00-J99)

CHAPTER 10 (J00-J99)

● **J11 Influenza due to unidentified influenza virus**
  ● **J11.0 Influenza due to unidentified influenza virus with pneumonia**
      Code also associated lung abscess, if applicable (J85.1)
      J11.00 Influenza due to unidentified influenza virus with unspecified type of pneumonia
          Influenza with pneumonia NOS
          Coding Clinic: 2016, Q3, P12
      J11.08 Influenza due to unidentified influenza virus with specified pneumonia
          Code also other specified type of pneumonia
  J11.1 Influenza due to unidentified influenza virus with other respiratory manifestations
      Influenza NOS
      Influenzal laryngitis NOS
      Influenzal pharyngitis NOS
      Influenza with upper respiratory symptoms NOS
      Use additional code for associated pleural effusion, if applicable (J91.8)
      Use additional code for associated sinusitis, if applicable (J01.-)
  J11.2 Influenza due to unidentified influenza virus with gastrointestinal manifestations
      Influenza gastroenteritis NOS
      Excludes1 'intestinal flu' [viral gastroenteritis] (A08.-)
  ● **J11.8 Influenza due to unidentified influenza virus with other manifestations**
      J11.81 Influenza due to unidentified influenza virus with encephalopathy
          Influenzal encephalopathy NOS
      J11.82 Influenza due to unidentified influenza virus with myocarditis
          Influenzal myocarditis NOS
      J11.83 Influenza due to unidentified influenza virus with otitis media
          Influenzal otitis media NOS
          Use additional code for any associated perforated tympanic membrane (H72.-)
      J11.89 Influenza due to unidentified influenza virus with other manifestations
          Use additional codes to identify the manifestations

● **J12 Viral pneumonia, not elsewhere classified**
  Includes bronchopneumonia due to viruses other than influenza viruses
  Code first associated influenza, if applicable (J09.X1, J10.0-, J11.0-)
  Code also associated abscess, if applicable (J85.1)
  Excludes1 aspiration pneumonia due to anesthesia during labor and delivery (O74.0)
      aspiration pneumonia due to anesthesia during pregnancy (O29)
      aspiration pneumonia due to anesthesia during puerperium (O89.0)
      aspiration pneumonia due to solids and liquids (J69.-)
      aspiration pneumonia NOS (J69.0)
      congenital pneumonia (P23.0)
      congenital rubella pneumonitis (P35.0)
      interstitial pneumonia NOS (J84.9)
      lipid pneumonia (J69.1)
      neonatal aspiration pneumonia (P24.-)
  J12.0 Adenoviral pneumonia
  J12.1 Respiratory syncytial virus pneumonia
      RSV pneumonia
  J12.2 Parainfluenza virus pneumonia
  J12.3 Human metapneumovirus pneumonia
  ● **J12.8 Other viral pneumonia**
      J12.81 Pneumonia due to SARS-associated coronavirus
          Severe acute respiratory syndrome NOS
      J12.89 Other viral pneumonia
  J12.9 Viral pneumonia, unspecified

Item 10–3 Pneumonia is an infection of the lungs, caused by a variety of microorganisms, including viruses, most commonly the Streptococcus pneumoniae (pneumococcus) bacteria, fungi, and parasites. Pneumonia occurs when the immune system is weakened, often by a URI or influenza.

J13 Pneumonia due to Streptococcus pneumoniae 🦠
  Bronchopneumonia due to S. pneumoniae
  Code first associated influenza, if applicable (J09.X1, J10.0-, J11.0-)
  Code also associated abscess, if applicable (J85.1)
  Excludes1 congenital pneumonia due to S. pneumoniae (P23.6)
      lobar pneumonia, unspecified organism (J18.1)
      pneumonia due to other streptococci (J15.3-J15.4)

J14 Pneumonia due to Hemophilus influenzae 🦠
  Bronchopneumonia due to H. influenzae
  Code first associated influenza, if applicable (J09.X1, J10.0-, J11.0-)
  Code also associated abscess, if applicable (J85.1)
  Excludes1 congenital pneumonia due to H. influenzae (P23.6)

● **J15 Bacterial pneumonia, not elsewhere classified**
  Includes bronchopneumonia due to bacteria other than S. pneumoniae and H. influenzae
  Code first associated influenza, if applicable (J09.X1, J10.0-, J11.0-)
  Code also associated abscess, if applicable (J85.1)
  Excludes1 chlamydial pneumonia (J16.0)
      congenital pneumonia (P23.-)
      Legionnaires' disease (A48.1)
      spirochetal pneumonia (A69.8)
  J15.0 Pneumonia due to Klebsiella pneumoniae 🦠
  J15.1 Pneumonia due to Pseudomonas 🦠
  ● **J15.2 Pneumonia due to staphylococcus**
      J15.20 Pneumonia due to staphylococcus, unspecified 🦠
      ● **J15.21 Pneumonia due to staphylococcus aureus**
          J15.211 Pneumonia due to Methicillin susceptible Staphylococcus aureus 🦠
             MSSA pneumonia
             Pneumonia due to Staphylococcus aureus NOS
          J15.212 Pneumonia due to Methicillin resistant Staphylococcus aureus 🦠
      J15.29 Pneumonia due to other staphylococcus 🦠
  J15.3 Pneumonia due to streptococcus, group B
  J15.4 Pneumonia due to other streptococci 🦠
      Excludes1 pneumonia due to streptococcus, group B (J15.3)
          pneumonia due to Streptococcus pneumoniae (J13)
  J15.5 Pneumonia due to Escherichia coli 🦠
  J15.6 Pneumonia due to other Gram-negative bacteria 🦠
      Pneumonia due to other aerobic Gram-negative bacteria
      Pneumonia due to Serratia marcescens
  J15.7 Pneumonia due to Mycoplasma pneumoniae
  J15.8 Pneumonia due to other specified bacteria 🦠
  J15.9 Unspecified bacterial pneumonia
      Pneumonia due to gram-positive bacteria
      Coding Clinic: 2017, Q4, P96

● **J16 Pneumonia due to other infectious organisms, not elsewhere classified**
  Code first associated influenza, if applicable (J09.X1, J10.0-, J11.0-)
  Code also associated abscess, if applicable (J85.1)
  Excludes1 congenital pneumonia (P23.-)
      ornithosis (A70)
      pneumocystosis (B59)
      pneumonia NOS (J18.9)
  J16.0 Chlamydial pneumonia
  J16.8 Pneumonia due to other specified infectious organisms

---

▶ New   ⇒ Revised   ~~deleted~~ Deleted   Excludes 1   Excludes 2   Includes   Use additional   Code first   Code also   Key words

   OGCR Official Guidelines   X Assign placeholder X   ● Use Additional Character(s)   ▶ Manifestation Code   🦠 Hierarchical Condition Category   **Coding Clinic**

▶ **J17**   *Pneumonia in diseases classified elsewhere*
    Code first underlying disease, such as:
      Q fever (A78)
      rheumatic fever (I00)
      schistosomiasis (B65.0-B65.9)

    Excludes1   candidial pneumonia (B37.1)
        chlamydial pneumonia (J16.0)
        gonorrheal pneumonia (A54.84)
        histoplasmosis pneumonia (B39.0-B39.2)
        measles pneumonia (B05.2)
        nocardiosis pneumonia (A43.0)
        pneumocystosis (B59)
        pneumonia due to Pneumocystis carinii (B59)
        pneumonia due to Pneumocystis jiroveci (B59)
        pneumonia in actinomycosis (A42.0)
        pneumonia in anthrax (A22.1)
        pneumonia in ascariasis (B77.81)
        pneumonia in aspergillosis (B44.0-B44.1)
        pneumonia in coccidioidomycosis (B38.0-B38.2)
        pneumonia in cytomegalovirus disease (B25.0)
        pneumonia in toxoplasmosis (B58.3)
        rubella pneumonia (B06.81)
        salmonella pneumonia (A02.22)
        spirochetal infection NEC with pneumonia (A69.8)
        tularemia pneumonia (A21.2)
        typhoid fever with pneumonia (A01.03)
        varicella pneumonia (B01.2)
        whooping cough with pneumonia (A37 with
          fifth-character 1)

● **J18**   Pneumonia, **unspecified organism**
    Code first associated influenza, if applicable (J09.X1, J10.0-, J11.0-)

    Excludes1   abscess of lung with pneumonia (J85.1)
        aspiration pneumonia due to anesthesia during
          labor and delivery (O74.0)
        aspiration pneumonia due to anesthesia during
          pregnancy (O29)
        aspiration pneumonia due to anesthesia during
          puerperium (O89.0)
        aspiration pneumonia due to solids and liquids
          (J69.-)
        aspiration pneumonia NOS (J69.0)
        congenital pneumonia (P23.0)
        drug-induced interstitial lung disorder (J70.2-J70.4)
        interstitial pneumonia NOS (J84.9)
        lipid pneumonia (J69.1)
        neonatal aspiration pneumonia (P24.-)
        pneumonitis due to external agents (J67-J70)
        pneumonitis due to fumes and vapors (J68.0)
    ⇒ usual interstitial pneumonia (J84.178)

    J18.0   Bronchopneumonia, **unspecified organism**
        Excludes1   hypostatic bronchopneumonia (J18.2)
            lipid pneumonia (J69.1)
        Excludes2   acute bronchiolitis (J21.-)
            chronic bronchiolitis (J44.9)

    J18.1   Lobar pneumonia, **unspecified organism** ⓦ
        Coding Clinic: 2016, Q3, P15

    J18.2   Hypostatic pneumonia, **unspecified organism**
        Hypostatic bronchopneumonia
        Passive pneumonia

    J18.8   Other pneumonia, **unspecified organism**

    J18.9   Pneumonia, **unspecified organism**
        Coding Clinic: Q3, P15; 2019, Q2, P28; Q1, P36; 2016, Q3, P15;
        2012, Q4, P94

OTHER ACUTE LOWER RESPIRATORY INFECTIONS (J20-J22)

    Excludes2   chronic obstructive pulmonary disease with acute
        lower respiratory infection (J44.0)

● **J20**   Acute bronchitis
    *Inflammation/irritation of the bronchial tubes lasting 2-3 weeks, most
    commonly caused by a virus*

    Includes   acute and subacute bronchitis (with)
        bronchospasm
        acute and subacute bronchitis (with) tracheitis
        acute and subacute bronchitis (with)
        tracheobronchitis, acute
        acute and subacute fibrinous bronchitis
        acute and subacute membranous bronchitis
        acute and subacute purulent bronchitis
        acute and subacute septic bronchitis

    Excludes1   bronchitis NOS (J40)
        tracheobronchitis NOS (J40)

    Excludes2   acute bronchitis with bronchiectasis (J47.0)
        acute bronchitis with chronic obstructive asthma
        (J44.0)
        acute bronchitis with chronic obstructive
        pulmonary disease (J44.0)
        allergic bronchitis NOS (J45.909-)
        bronchitis due to chemicals, fumes and vapors
        (J68.0)
        chronic bronchitis NOS (J42)
        chronic mucopurulent bronchitis (J41.1)
        chronic obstructive bronchitis (J44.-)
        chronic obstructive tracheobronchitis (J44.-)
        chronic simple bronchitis (J41.0)
        chronic tracheobronchitis (J42)

    J20.0   Acute bronchitis due to Mycoplasma pneumoniae
    J20.1   Acute bronchitis due to Hemophilus influenzae
    J20.2   Acute bronchitis due to streptococcus
    J20.3   Acute bronchitis due to coxsackievirus
    J20.4   Acute bronchitis due to parainfluenza virus
    J20.5   Acute bronchitis due to respiratory syncytial virus
        Acute bronchitis due to RSV
    J20.6   Acute bronchitis due to rhinovirus
        Coding Clinic: 2016, Q3, P10
    J20.7   Acute bronchitis due to echovirus
    J20.8   Acute bronchitis due to other specified organisms
        Coding Clinic: 2016, Q3, P11
    J20.9   Acute bronchitis, **unspecified**
        Coding Clinic: 2019, Q1, P35; 2016, Q3, P16

● **J21**   Acute bronchiolitis
    *Bronchiolitis obliterans with organizing pneumonia (BOOP)
    inflammation of bronchioles and surrounding tissue in lung*

    Includes   acute bronchiolitis with bronchospasm
    Excludes2   respiratory bronchiolitis interstitial lung disease
        (J84.115)

    J21.0   Acute bronchiolitis due to respiratory syncytial virus
        Acute bronchitis due to RSV
    J21.1   Acute bronchiolitis due to human metapneumovirus
    J21.8   Acute bronchiolitis due to other specified organisms
    J21.9   Acute bronchiolitis, **unspecified**
        Bronchiolitis (acute)
        Excludes1   chronic bronchiolitis (J44.-)

    J22   Unspecified acute lower respiratory infection
        Acute (lower) respiratory (tract) infection NOS
        Excludes1   upper respiratory infection (acute) (J06.9)
        Coding Clinic: 2020, Q1, P22-23

CHAPTER 10 (J00-J99)

OTHER DISEASES OF UPPER RESPIRATORY TRACT (J30-J39)

● **J30 Vasomotor and allergic rhinitis**
  Includes spasmodic rhinorrhea
  Excludes1 allergic rhinitis with asthma (bronchial) (J45.909)
  rhinitis NOS (J31.0)

  J30.0 Vasomotor rhinitis
  J30.1 Allergic rhinitis due to pollen
    Allergy NOS due to pollen
    Hay fever
    Pollinosis
  J30.2 Other seasonal allergic rhinitis
  J30.5 Allergic rhinitis due to food
● **J30.8 Other allergic rhinitis**
    J30.81 Allergic rhinitis due to animal (cat) (dog) hair and dander
    J30.89 Other allergic rhinitis
      Perennial allergic rhinitis
  J30.9 Allergic rhinitis, unspecified

● **J31 Chronic rhinitis, nasopharyngitis and pharyngitis**
  Use additional code to identify:
    exposure to environmental tobacco smoke (Z77.22)
    exposure to tobacco smoke in the perinatal period (P96.81)
    history of tobacco dependence (Z87.891)
    occupational exposure to environmental tobacco smoke (Z57.31)
    tobacco dependence (F17.-)
    tobacco use (Z72.0)

  J31.0 Chronic rhinitis
    Atrophic rhinitis (chronic)
    Granulomatous rhinitis (chronic)
    Hypertrophic rhinitis (chronic)
    Obstructive rhinitis (chronic)
    Ozena
    Purulent rhinitis (chronic)
    Rhinitis (chronic) NOS
    Ulcerative rhinitis (chronic)
    Excludes1 allergic rhinitis (J30.1-J30.9)
      vasomotor rhinitis (J30.0)

  J31.1 Chronic nasopharyngitis
    Excludes2 acute nasopharyngitis (J00)

  J31.2 Chronic pharyngitis
    Chronic sore throat
    Atrophic pharyngitis (chronic)
    Granular pharyngitis (chronic)
    Hypertrophic pharyngitis (chronic)
    Excludes2 acute pharyngitis (J02.9)

● **J32 Chronic sinusitis**
  Includes sinus abscess
    sinus empyema
    sinus infection
    sinus suppuration
  Use additional code to identify:
    exposure to environmental tobacco smoke (Z77.22)
    exposure to tobacco smoke in the perinatal period (P96.81)
    history of tobacco dependence (Z87.891)
    infectious agent (B95-B97)
    occupational exposure to environmental tobacco smoke (Z57.31)
    tobacco dependence (F17.-)
    tobacco use (Z72.0)
  Excludes2 acute sinusitis (J01.-)

  J32.0 Chronic maxillary sinusitis
    Antritis (chronic)
    Maxillary sinusitis NOS
  J32.1 Chronic frontal sinusitis
    Frontal sinusitis NOS

Item 10-4 Nasal polyps are an abnormal growth of tissue (tumor) projecting from a mucous membrane and attached to the surface by a narrow elongated stalk (pedunculated). Nasal polyps usually originate in the ethmoid sinus but also may occur in the maxillary sinus. Symptoms are nasal block, sinusitis, anosmia, and secondary infections.

  J32.2 Chronic ethmoidal sinusitis
    Ethmoidal sinusitis NOS
    Excludes1 Woakes' ethmoiditis (J33.1)
  J32.3 Chronic sphenoidal sinusitis
    Sphenoidal sinusitis NOS
  J32.4 Chronic pansinusitis
    Pansinusitis NOS
  J32.8 Other chronic sinusitis
    Sinusitis (chronic) involving more than one sinus but not pansinusitis
  J32.9 Chronic sinusitis, unspecified
    Sinusitis (chronic) NOS

● **J33 Nasal polyp**
  Use additional code to identify:
    exposure to environmental tobacco smoke (Z77.22)
    exposure to tobacco smoke in the perinatal period (P96.81)
    history of tobacco dependence (Z87.891)
    occupational exposure to environmental tobacco smoke (Z57.31)
    tobacco dependence (F17.-)
    tobacco use (Z72.0)
  Excludes1 adenomatous polyps (D14.0)

  J33.0 Polyp of nasal cavity
    Choanal polyp
    Nasopharyngeal polyp
  J33.1 Polypoid sinus degeneration
    Woakes' syndrome or ethmoiditis
  J33.8 Other polyp of sinus
    Accessory polyp of sinus
    Ethmoidal polyp of sinus
    Maxillary polyp of sinus
    Sphenoidal polyp of sinus
  J33.9 Nasal polyp, unspecified

● **J34 Other and unspecified disorders of nose and nasal sinuses**
  Excludes2 varicose ulcer of nasal septum (I86.8)

  J34.0 Abscess, furuncle and carbuncle of nose
    Cellulitis of nose
    Necrosis of nose
    Ulceration of nose
  J34.1 Cyst and mucocele of nose and nasal sinus
  J34.2 Deviated nasal septum
    Deflection or deviation of septum (nasal) (acquired)
    Excludes1 congenital deviated nasal septum (Q67.4)
  J34.3 Hypertrophy of nasal turbinates

Deviated septal cartilage

Figure 10-3 Deviated nasal septum.

Item 10-5 A **deviated nasal septum** is the displacement of the septal cartilage that separates the nares. This displacement causes obstructed air flow through the nasal passages. A child can be born with this displacement (congenital), or the condition may be acquired through trauma, such as a sports injury. Symptoms include nasal block, sinusitis, and related secondary infections. Septoplasty is surgical repair of this condition.

▶ New ⇒ Revised ~~deleted~~ Deleted Excludes 1 Excludes 2 Includes Use additional Code first Code also Key words
OGCR Official Guidelines X Assign placeholder X ● Use Additional Character(s) ▶ Manifestation Code 🖤 Hierarchical Condition Category Coding Clinic
930

● **J34.8   Other specified disorders of nose and nasal sinuses**

　　J34.81   Nasal mucositis (ulcerative)

　　　　Code also type of associated therapy, such as:
　　　　　antineoplastic and immunosuppressive
　　　　　drugs (T45.1X-)
　　　　　radiological procedure and radiotherapy
　　　　　(Y84.2)

　　　　Excludes2 gastrointestinal mucositis
　　　　　　　　　(ulcerative) (K92.81)
　　　　　　　　mucositis (ulcerative) of vagina
　　　　　　　　　and vulva (N76.81)
　　　　　　　　oral mucositis (ulcerative)
　　　　　　　　　(K12.3-)

　　**J34.89   Other specified disorders of nose and nasal
　　　　　　sinuses**
　　　　　Perforation of nasal septum NOS
　　　　　Rhinolith

J34.9   Unspecified disorder of nose and nasal sinuses

● **J35   Chronic diseases of tonsils and adenoids**
　　Use additional code to identify:
　　　exposure to environmental tobacco smoke (Z77.22)
　　　exposure to tobacco smoke in the perinatal period (P96.81)
　　　history of tobacco dependence (Z87.891)
　　　occupational exposure to environmental tobacco smoke
　　　　(Z57.31)
　　　tobacco dependence (F17.-)
　　　tobacco use (Z72.0)

● **J35.0   Chronic tonsillitis and adenoiditis**
　　　　Excludes2 acute tonsillitis (J03.-)

　　J35.01   Chronic tonsillitis
　　J35.02   Chronic adenoiditis
　　J35.03   Chronic tonsillitis and adenoiditis

J35.1   Hypertrophy of tonsils
　　　Enlargement of tonsils
　　　Excludes1 hypertrophy of tonsils with tonsillitis
　　　　　　　　　(J35.0-)

J35.2   Hypertrophy of adenoids
　　　Enlargement of adenoids
　　　Excludes1 hypertrophy of adenoids with adenoiditis
　　　　　　　　　(J35.0-)

J35.3   Hypertrophy of tonsils with hypertrophy of adenoids
　　　Excludes1 hypertrophy of tonsils and adenoids with
　　　　　　　　　tonsillitis and adenoiditis (J35.03)

J35.8   Other chronic diseases of tonsils and adenoids
　　　Adenoid vegetations
　　　Amygdalolith
　　　Calculus, tonsil
　　　Cicatrix of tonsil (and adenoid)
　　　Tonsillar tag
　　　Ulcer of tonsil

J35.9   Chronic disease of tonsils and adenoids, unspecified
　　　Disease (chronic) of tonsils and adenoids NOS

J36   Peritonsillar abscess
　　Includes   abscess of tonsil
　　　　　　　peritonsillar cellulitis
　　　　　　　quinsy
　　Use additional code (B95-B97) to identify infectious agent.
　　Excludes1 acute tonsillitis (J03.-)
　　　　　　　chronic tonsillitis (J35.0)
　　　　　　　retropharyngeal abscess (J39.0)
　　　　　　　tonsillitis NOS (J03.9-)

● **J37   Chronic laryngitis and laryngotracheitis**
　　Use additional code to identify:
　　　exposure to environmental tobacco smoke (Z77.22)
　　　exposure to tobacco smoke in the perinatal period (P96.81)
　　　history of tobacco dependence (Z87.891)
　　　infectious agent (B95-B97)
　　　occupational exposure to environmental tobacco smoke
　　　　(Z57.31)
　　　tobacco dependence (F17.-)
　　　tobacco use (Z72.0)

　　J37.0   Chronic laryngitis
　　　　Catarrhal laryngitis
　　　　Hypertrophic laryngitis
　　　　Sicca laryngitis
　　　　Excludes2 acute laryngitis (J04.0)
　　　　　　　　　obstructive (acute) laryngitis (J05.0)

　　J37.1   Chronic laryngotracheitis
　　　　Laryngitis, chronic, with tracheitis (chronic)
　　　　Tracheitis, chronic, with laryngitis
　　　　Excludes1 chronic tracheitis (J42)
　　　　Excludes2 acute laryngotracheitis (J04.2)
　　　　　　　　　acute tracheitis (J04.1)

● **J38   Diseases of vocal cords and larynx, not elsewhere classified**
　　Use additional code to identify:
　　　exposure to environmental tobacco smoke (Z77.22)
　　　exposure to tobacco smoke in the perinatal period (P96.81)
　　　history of tobacco dependence (Z87.891)
　　　occupational exposure to environmental tobacco smoke
　　　　(Z57.31)
　　　tobacco dependence (F17.-)
　　　tobacco use (Z72.0)

　　Excludes1 congenital laryngeal stridor (P28.89)
　　　　　　　obstructive laryngitis (acute) (J05.0)
　　　　　　　postprocedural subglottic stenosis (J95.5)
　　　　　　　stridor (R06.1)
　　　　　　　ulcerative laryngitis (J04.0)

● **J38.0   Paralysis of vocal cords and larynx**
　　　　Laryngoplegia
　　　　Paralysis of glottis

　　J38.00   Paralysis of vocal cords and larynx, unspecified
　　J38.01   Paralysis of vocal cords and larynx, unilateral
　　J38.02   Paralysis of vocal cords and larynx, bilateral

J38.1   Polyp of vocal cord and larynx
　　　Excludes1 adenomatous polyps (D14.1)

J38.2   Nodules of vocal cords
　　　Chorditis (fibrinous)(nodosa)(tuberosa)
　　　Singer's nodes
　　　Teacher's nodes

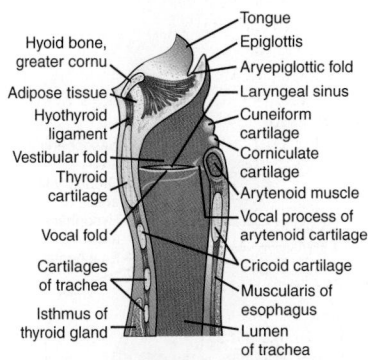

Hyoid bone,
greater cornu

Adipose tissue

Hyothyroid
ligament

Vestibular fold

Thyroid
cartilage

Vocal fold

Cartilages
of trachea

Isthmus of
thyroid gland

Tongue
Epiglottis
Aryepiglottic fold
Laryngeal sinus
Cuneiform
cartilage
Corniculate
cartilage
Arytenoid muscle
Vocal process of
arytenoid cartilage
Cricoid cartilage
Muscularis of
esophagus
Lumen
of trachea

Figure 10-4   Coronal section of the larynx.

Item 10–6   The **larynx** extends from the tongue to the trachea and is
divided into an upper and lower portion separated by folds. The framework
of the larynx is cartilage composed of the single cricoid, thyroid, and epiglottic
cartilages, and the paired arytenoid, cuneiform, and corniculate cartilages.

CHAPTER 10 (J00-J99)

J38.3   Other diseases of vocal cords
Abscess of vocal cords
Cellulitis of vocal cords
Granuloma of vocal cords
Leukokeratosis of vocal cords
Leukoplakia of vocal cords

J38.4   Edema of larynx
Edema (of) glottis
Subglottic edema
Supraglottic edema

> **Excludes1**   acute obstructive laryngitis [croup] (J05.0)
> edematous laryngitis (J04.0)

J38.5   Laryngeal spasm
Laryngismus (stridulus)

J38.6   Stenosis of larynx

J38.7   Other diseases of larynx
Abscess of larynx
Cellulitis of larynx
Disease of larynx NOS
Necrosis of larynx
Pachyderma of larynx
Perichondritis of larynx
Ulcer of larynx

● J39   Other diseases of upper respiratory tract

> **Excludes1**   acute respiratory infection NOS (J22)
> acute upper respiratory infection (J06.9)
> upper respiratory inflammation due to chemicals, gases, fumes or vapors (J68.2)

J39.0   Retropharyngeal and parapharyngeal abscess
Peripharyngeal abscess

> **Excludes1**   peritonsillar abscess (J36)

J39.1   Other abscess of pharynx
Cellulitis of pharynx
Nasopharyngeal abscess

J39.2   Other diseases of pharynx
Cyst of pharynx
Edema of pharynx

> **Excludes2**   chronic pharyngitis (J31.2)
> ulcerative pharyngitis (J02.9)

J39.3   Upper respiratory tract hypersensitivity reaction, site unspecified

> **Excludes1**   hypersensitivity reaction of upper respiratory tract, such as:
> extrinsic allergic alveolitis (J67.9)
> pneumoconiosis (J60-J67.9)

J39.8   Other specified diseases of upper respiratory tract

J39.9   Disease of upper respiratory tract, unspecified

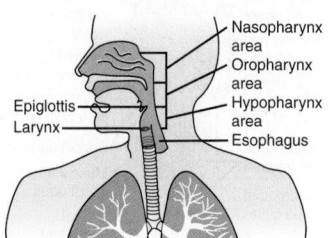

Figure 10-5 The pharynx.

Item 10-7   The **pharynx** is the passage for both food and air between the mouth and the esophagus and is divided into three areas: nasopharynx, oropharynx, and hypopharynx. The hypopharynx branches into the esophagus and the voice box.

Item 10-8   **Chronic bronchitis** is usually defined as being present in any patient who has persistent cough with sputum production for at least three months in at least two consecutive years. **Simple chronic bronchitis** is marked by a productive cough but no pathological airflow obstruction. **Chronic obstructive pulmonary disease (COPD)** is a group of conditions—bronchitis, emphysema, asthma, bronchiectasis, allergic alveolitis—marked by dyspnea. **Catarrhal** bronchitis is an acute form of bronchitis marked by profuse mucus and pus production (**mucopurulent** discharge). **Croupous** bronchitis, also known as pseudomembranous, fibrinous, plastic, exudative, or membranous, is marked by a violent cough and dyspnea.

CHRONIC LOWER RESPIRATORY DISEASES (J40-J47)

> **Excludes1**   bronchitis due to chemicals, gases, fumes and vapors (J68.0)
>
> **Excludes2**   cystic fibrosis (E84.-)

J40   Bronchitis, not specified as acute or chronic
Bronchitis NOS
Catarrhal bronchitis
Bronchitis with tracheitis NOS
Tracheobronchitis NOS

Use additional code to identify:
exposure to environmental tobacco smoke (Z77.22)
exposure to tobacco smoke in the perinatal period (P96.81)
history of tobacco dependence (Z87.891)
occupational exposure to environmental tobacco smoke (Z57.31)
tobacco dependence (F17.-)
tobacco use (Z72.0)

> **Excludes1**   acute bronchitis (J20.-)
> allergic bronchitis NOS (J45.909-)
> asthmatic bronchitis NOS (J45.9-)
> bronchitis due to chemicals, gases, fumes and vapors (J68.0)

● J41   Simple and mucopurulent chronic bronchitis
Use additional code to identify:
exposure to environmental tobacco smoke (Z77.22)
exposure to tobacco smoke in the perinatal period (P96.81)
history of tobacco dependence (Z87.891)
occupational exposure to environmental tobacco smoke (Z57.31)
tobacco dependence (F17.-)
tobacco use (Z72.0)

> **Excludes1**   chronic bronchitis NOS (J42)
> chronic obstructive bronchitis (J44.-)

J41.0   Simple chronic bronchitis 🏷

J41.1   Mucopurulent chronic bronchitis 🏷

J41.8   Mixed simple and mucopurulent chronic bronchitis 🏷

J42   Unspecified chronic bronchitis 🏷
Chronic bronchitis NOS
Chronic tracheitis
Chronic tracheobronchitis

Use additional code to identify:
exposure to environmental tobacco smoke (Z77.22)
exposure to tobacco smoke in the perinatal period (P96.81)
history of tobacco dependence (Z87.891)
occupational exposure to environmental tobacco smoke (Z57.31)
tobacco dependence (F17.-)
tobacco use (Z72.0)

> **Excludes1**   chronic asthmatic bronchitis (J44.-)
> chronic bronchitis with airways obstruction (J44.-)
> chronic emphysematous bronchitis (J44.-)
> chronic obstructive pulmonary disease NOS (J44.9)
> simple and mucopurulent chronic bronchitis (J41.-)

▶ New   ➡ Revised   ~~deleted~~ Deleted   Excludes 1   Excludes 2   Includes   Use additional   Code first   Code also   Key words

OGCR Official Guidelines   X Assign placeholder X   ● Use Additional Character(s)   ▶ Manifestation Code   🏷 Hierarchical Condition Category   **Coding Clinic**

● **J43 Emphysema**

    Use additional code to identify:
      exposure to environmental tobacco smoke (Z77.22)
      history of tobacco dependence (Z87.891)
      occupational exposure to environmental tobacco smoke
        (Z57.31)
      tobacco dependence (F17.-)
      tobacco use (Z72.0)

    Excludes1 compensatory emphysema (J98.3)
          emphysema due to inhalation of chemicals, gases,
            fumes or vapors (J68.4)
          emphysema with chronic (obstructive) bronchitis
            (J44.-)
          emphysematous (obstructive) bronchitis (J44.-)
          interstitial emphysema (J98.2)
          mediastinal emphysema (J98.2)
          neonatal interstitial emphysema (P25.0)
          surgical (subcutaneous) emphysema (T81.82)
          ~~traumatic subcutaneous emphysema (T79.7)~~

   ▶ **Excludes2** traumatic subcutaneous emphysema (T79.7)

**J43.0 Unilateral pulmonary emphysema [MacLeod's
      syndrome]** 🔲
      Swyer-James syndrome
      Unilateral emphysema
      Unilateral hyperlucent lung
      Unilateral pulmonary artery functional hypoplasia
      Unilateral transparency of lung

J43.1 Panlobular emphysema 🔲
      Panacinar emphysema

J43.2 Centrilobular emphysema 🔲

J43.8 Other emphysema 🔲

J43.9 Emphysema, unspecified 🔲
      Bullous emphysema (lung)(pulmonary)
      Emphysema (lung)(pulmonary) NOS
      Emphysematous bleb
      Vesicular emphysema (lung)(pulmonary)
      Coding Clinic: 2019, Q1, P35-37; 2017, Q4, P97-98

● **J44 Other chronic obstructive pulmonary disease**

    Includes   asthma with chronic obstructive pulmonary
            disease
         chronic asthmatic (obstructive) bronchitis
         chronic bronchitis with airways obstruction
         chronic bronchitis with emphysema
         chronic emphysematous bronchitis
         chronic obstructive asthma
         chronic obstructive bronchitis
         chronic obstructive tracheobronchitis

    Code also type of asthma, if applicable (J45.-)

    Use additional code to identify:
      exposure to environmental tobacco smoke (Z77.22)
      history of tobacco dependence (Z87.891)
      occupational exposure to environmental tobacco smoke
        (Z57.31)
      tobacco dependence (F17.-)
      tobacco use (Z72.0)

    Excludes1 bronchiectasis (J47.-)
          chronic bronchitis NOS (J42)
          chronic simple and mucopurulent bronchitis
           (J41.-)
          chronic tracheitis (J42)
          chronic tracheobronchitis (J42)
          emphysema without chronic bronchitis (J43.-)
    Coding Clinic: 2019, Q1, P34-36; 2017, Q4, P97; 2017, Q1, P25; 2016, Q3, P16

**J44.0 Chronic obstructive pulmonary disease with (acute)
      lower respiratory infection** 🔲
      Code also to identify the infection
      **Coding Clinic: 2019, Q1, P35-36; 2017, Q4, P96; 2017, Q2, P30, Q1,
      P24-25; 2016, Q3, P15-16**

                              — Walls of
                                alveoli enlarge
                                and fuse into
                                large air spaces
  Normal alveoli

                      Emphysema

Figure 10-6   Emphysema. (From Shiland, BJ: Medical Terminology &
Anatomy for ICD-10 Coding, ed 2, Mosby, 2015)

**J44.1 Chronic obstructive pulmonary disease with (acute)
      exacerbation** 🔲
      Decompensated COPD
      Decompensated COPD with (acute) exacerbation

      Excludes2 chronic obstructive pulmonary disease
             [COPD] with acute bronchitis (J44.0)
            lung diseases due to external agents
             (J60-J70)
    **Coding Clinic: 2019, Q1, P34-35; 2017, Q4, P96; 2017, Q1, P26; 2016,
    Q3, P15-16, Q1, P36**

J44.9 Chronic obstructive pulmonary disease, unspecified 🔲
      Chronic obstructive airway disease NOS
      Chronic obstructive lung disease NOS

      Excludes2 lung diseases due to external agents
            (J60-J70)
    **Coding Clinic: 2019, Q1, P36; 2017, Q4, P96-97; 2017, Q1, P24-25;
    2016, Q1, P37**

● **J45 Asthma**
    Allergic (predominantly) asthma
    Allergic bronchitis NOS
    Allergic rhinitis with asthma
    Atopic asthma
    Extrinsic allergic asthma
    Hay fever with asthma
    Idiosyncratic asthma
    Intrinsic nonallergic asthma
    Nonallergic asthma

    Use additional code to identify:
   ▶eosinophilic asthma (J82.83)
      exposure to environmental tobacco smoke (Z77.22)
      exposure to tobacco smoke in the perinatal period (P96.81)
      history of tobacco dependence (Z87.891)
      occupational exposure to environmental tobacco smoke (Z57.31)
      tobacco dependence (F17.-)
      tobacco use (Z72.0)

    Excludes1 detergent asthma (J69.8)
          eosinophilic asthma (J82)
          miner's asthma (J60)
          wheezing NOS (R06.2)
          wood asthma (J67.8)

    Excludes2 asthma with chronic obstructive pulmonary
            disease (J44.9)
          chronic asthmatic (obstructive) bronchitis (J44.9)
          chronic obstructive asthma (J44.9)
    Coding Clinic: 2019, Q1, P37; 2017, Q1, P25

● **J45.2 Mild intermittent asthma**

    J45.20 Mild intermittent asthma, uncomplicated
          Mild intermittent asthma NOS

    **J45.21 Mild intermittent asthma with (acute)
         exacerbation**

    **J45.22 Mild intermittent asthma with status
         asthmaticus**

Item 10–9 Asthma is a bronchial condition marked by airway obstruction, hyper-responsiveness, and inflammation. **Extrinsic** asthma, also known as allergic asthma, is characterized by the same symptoms that occur with exposure to allergens and is divided into the following types: **atopic, occupational,** and **allergic bronchopulmonary aspergillosis.** **Intrinsic** asthma occurs in patients who have no history of allergy or sensitivities to allergens and is divided into the following types: **nonreaginic** and **pharmacologic.** **Status asthmaticus** is the most severe form of asthma attack and can last for days or weeks.

Figure 10-7   Factors causing expiratory obstruction in asthma. **A.** Cross section of a bronchiole occluded by muscle spasm, swollen mucosa, and mucus. **B.** Longitudinal section of an obstructed bronchiole. **C.** Cross section of a clear bronchiole. (From Shiland: Mastering Healthcare Terminology, ed 1, St. Louis, Mosby, 2003)

● **J45.3**   **Mild persistent** asthma

     J45.30   **Mild persistent asthma, uncomplicated**
               Mild persistent asthma NOS

     J45.31   **Mild persistent asthma with (acute) exacerbation**
               Coding Clinic: 2016, Q1, P35

     J45.32   **Mild persistent asthma with status asthmaticus**

● **J45.4**   **Moderate persistent** asthma

     J45.40   **Moderate persistent asthma, uncomplicated**
               Moderate persistent asthma NOS

     J45.41   **Moderate persistent asthma with (acute) exacerbation**
               Coding Clinic: 2017, Q1, P26

     J45.42   **Moderate persistent asthma with status asthmaticus**

● **J45.5**   **Severe persistent** asthma

     J45.50   **Severe persistent asthma, uncomplicated**
               Severe persistent asthma NOS

     J45.51   **Severe persistent asthma with (acute) exacerbation**

     J45.52   **Severe persistent asthma with status asthmaticus**

● **J45.9**   **Other and unspecified** asthma

     ● **J45.90**   **Unspecified asthma**
               Asthmatic bronchitis NOS
               Childhood asthma NOS
               Late onset asthma

         J45.901   **Unspecified asthma with (acute) exacerbation**
                   Coding Clinic: 2017, Q4, P96

         J45.902   **Unspecified asthma with status asthmaticus**

         J45.909   **Unspecified asthma, uncomplicated**
                   Asthma NOS

                 Excludes2   lung diseases due to external agents (J60-J70)
                   Coding Clinic: 2017, Q4, P96; 2017, Q1, P25

     ● **J45.99**   **Other asthma**

         J45.990   **Exercise induced bronchospasm**

         J45.991   **Cough variant asthma**

         J45.998   **Other asthma**

● **J47**   **Bronchiectasis**

     Includes   bronchiolectasis

     Use additional code to identify:
         exposure to environmental tobacco smoke (Z77.22)
         exposure to tobacco smoke in the perinatal period (P96.81)
         history of tobacco dependence (Z87.891)
         occupational exposure to environmental tobacco smoke (Z57.31)
         tobacco dependence (F17.-)
         tobacco use (Z72.0)

     Excludes1   congenital bronchiectasis (Q33.4)
                  tuberculous bronchiectasis (current disease) (A15.0)

     J47.0   **Bronchiectasis with acute lower respiratory infection** 🐾
               Bronchiectasis with acute bronchitis
               Use additional code to identify the infection

     J47.1   **Bronchiectasis with (acute) exacerbation** 🐾

     J47.9   **Bronchiectasis, uncomplicated** 🐾
               Bronchiectasis NOS

LUNG DISEASES DUE TO EXTERNAL AGENTS (J60-J70)

     Excludes2   asthma (J45.-)
                  malignant neoplasm of bronchus and lung (C34.-)

J60   **Coalworker's pneumoconiosis** 🐾   A
     Anthracosilicosis
     Anthracosis
     Black lung disease
     Coalworker's lung

     Excludes1   coalworker pneumoconiosis with tuberculosis, any type in A15 (J65)

J61   **Pneumoconiosis due to asbestos and other mineral fibers** 🐾   A
     Asbestosis

     Excludes1   pleural plaque with asbestosis (J92.0)
                  pneumoconiosis with tuberculosis, any type in A15 (J65)

● **J62**   **Pneumoconiosis due to dust containing silica**

     Includes   silicotic fibrosis (massive) of lung

     Excludes1   pneumoconiosis with tuberculosis, any type in A15 (J65)

     J62.0   **Pneumoconiosis due to talc dust** 🐾

     J62.8   **Pneumoconiosis due to other dust containing silica** 🐾
               Silicosis NOS

● **J63**   **Pneumoconiosis due to other inorganic dusts**

     Excludes1   pneumoconiosis with tuberculosis, any type in A15 (J65)
     Coding Clinic: 2019, Q3, P8

     J63.0   **Aluminosis (of lung)** 🐾

     J63.1   **Bauxite fibrosis (of lung)** 🐾

     J63.2   **Berylliosis** 🐾

     J63.3   **Graphite fibrosis (of lung)** 🐾

     J63.4   **Siderosis** 🐾
               Coding Clinic: 2019, Q3, P8

     J63.5   **Stannosis** 🐾

     J63.6   **Pneumoconiosis due to other specified inorganic dusts** 🐾

Figure 10-8   Progressive massive fibrosis superimposed on coal workers' pneumoconiosis. The large, blackened scars are located principally in the upper lobe. (From Frazier MS, Drzymkowski JW: Essentials of Human Diseases and Conditions, St. Louis, MO, Saunders, 2004)

Item 10–10   Pneumoconiosis refers to a lung condition resulting from exposure to inorganic or organic airborne particles, such as coal dust or moldy hay, as well as chemical fumes and vapors, such as insecticides. In this condition, the lungs retain the airborne particles.

▶ New   ⇨ Revised   ~~deleted~~ Deleted   Excludes 1   Excludes 2   Includes   Use additional   Code first   Code also   Key words

OGCR   Official Guidelines   X   Assign placeholder X   ● Use Additional Character(s)   ▌ Manifestation Code   🐾 Hierarchical Condition Category   **Coding Clinic**

J64   **Unspecified pneumoconiosis** 🦠
> **Excludes1**   pneumonoconiosis with tuberculosis, any type in A15 (J65)

J65   **Pneumoconiosis associated with tuberculosis** 🦠
> Any condition in J60-J64 with tuberculosis, any type in A15
> Silicotuberculosis

● **J66**   **Airway disease due to specific organic dust**
> **Excludes2**   allergic alveolitis (J67.-)
>   asbestosis (J61)
>   bagassosis (J67.1)
>   farmer's lung (J67.0)
>   hypersensitivity pneumonitis due to organic dust (J67.-)
>   reactive airways dysfunction syndrome (J68.3)

J66.0   **Byssinosis** 🦠
> Airway disease due to cotton dust

J66.1   **Flax-dressers' disease** 🦠

J66.2   **Cannabinosis** 🦠

J66.8   **Airway disease due to other specific organic dusts** 🦠

● **J67**   **Hypersensitivity pneumonitis due to organic dust**
> **Includes**   allergic alveolitis and pneumonitis due to inhaled organic dust and particles of fungal, actinomycetic or other origin
> **Excludes1**   pneumonitis due to inhalation of chemicals, gases, fumes or vapors (J68.0)

J67.0   **Farmer's lung** 🦠
> Harvester's lung
> Haymaker's lung
> Moldy hay disease

J67.1   **Bagassosis** 🦠
> Bagasse disease
> Bagasse pneumonitis

J67.2   **Bird fancier's lung** 🦠
> Budgerigar fancier's disease or lung
> Pigeon fancier's disease or lung

J67.3   **Suberosis** 🦠
> Corkhandler's disease or lung
> Corkworker's disease or lung

J67.4   **Maltworker's lung** 🦠
> Alveolitis due to Aspergillus clavatus

J67.5   **Mushroom-worker's lung** 🦠

J67.6   **Maple-bark-stripper's lung** 🦠
> Alveolitis due to Cryptostroma corticale
> Cryptostromosis

J67.7   **Air conditioner and humidifier lung** 🦠
> Allergic alveolitis due to fungal, thermophilic actinomycetes and other organisms growing in ventilation [air conditioning] systems

J67.8   **Hypersensitivity pneumonitis due to other organic dusts** 🦠
> Cheese-washer's lung
> Coffee-worker's lung
> Fish-meal worker's lung
> Furrier's lung
> Sequoiosis

J67.9   **Hypersensitivity pneumonitis due to unspecified organic dust** 🦠
> Allergic alveolitis (extrinsic) NOS
> Hypersensitivity pneumonitis NOS

● **J68**   **Respiratory conditions due to inhalation of chemicals, gases, fumes and vapors**
> *Code first (T51-T65) to identify cause*
> Use additional code to identify associated respiratory conditions, such as:
> acute respiratory failure (J96.0-)

J68.0   **Bronchitis and pneumonitis due to chemicals, gases, fumes and vapors** 🦠
> Chemical bronchitis (acute)
> **Coding Clinic: 2019, Q2, P31-32**

J68.1   **Pulmonary edema due to chemicals, gases, fumes and vapors** 🦠
> Chemical pulmonary edema (acute) (chronic)
> **Excludes1**   pulmonary edema (acute) (chronic) NOS (J81.-)

J68.2   **Upper respiratory inflammation due to chemicals, gases, fumes and vapors, not elsewhere classified** 🦠

J68.3   **Other acute and subacute respiratory conditions due to chemicals, gases, fumes and vapors** 🦠
> Reactive airways dysfunction syndrome

J68.4   **Chronic respiratory conditions due to chemicals, gases, fumes and vapors** 🦠
> Emphysema (diffuse) (chronic) due to inhalation of chemicals, gases, fumes and vapors
> Obliterative bronchiolitis (chronic) (subacute) due to inhalation of chemicals, gases, fumes and vapors
> Pulmonary fibrosis (chronic) due to inhalation of chemicals, gases, fumes and vapors
> **Excludes1**   chronic pulmonary edema due to chemicals, gases, fumes and vapors (J68.1)

J68.8   **Other respiratory conditions due to chemicals, gases, fumes and vapors** 🦠

J68.9   **Unspecified respiratory condition due to chemicals, gases, fumes and vapors** 🦠

● **J69**   **Pneumonitis due to solids and liquids**
> **Excludes1**   neonatal aspiration syndromes (P24.-)
>   postprocedural pneumonitis (J95.4)

J69.0   **Pneumonitis due to inhalation of food and vomit** 🦠
> Aspiration pneumonia NOS
> Aspiration pneumonia (due to) food (regurgitated)
> Aspiration pneumonia (due to) gastric secretions
> Aspiration pneumonia (due to) milk
> Aspiration pneumonia (due to) vomit
> Code also any associated foreign body in respiratory tract (T17.-)
> **Excludes1**   chemical pneumonitis due to anesthesia (J95.4)
>   obstetric aspiration pneumonitis (O74.0)
> **Coding Clinic: 2019, Q2, P7, 31-32; 2017, Q1, P24**

J69.1   **Pneumonitis due to inhalation of oils and essences** 🦠
> Exogenous lipoid pneumonia
> Lipid pneumonia NOS
> *Code first (T51-T65) to identify substance*
> **Excludes1**   endogenous lipoid pneumonia (J84.89)

J69.8   **Pneumonitis due to inhalation of other solids and liquids** 🦠
> Pneumonitis due to aspiration of blood
> Pneumonitis due to aspiration of detergent
> *Code first (T51-T65) to identify substance*

N Newborn Age: 0   **P** Pediatric Age: 0–17   **M** Maternity DX: 12–55   **A** Adult Age: 15–124   ♀ Females Only   ♂ Males Only

935

● **J70**   **Respiratory conditions due to other external agents**

     J70.0   **Acute pulmonary manifestations due to radiation** 🐾
           Radiation pneumonitis
           Use additional code (W88-W90, X39.0-) to identify the external cause

     J70.1   **Chronic and other pulmonary manifestations due to radiation** 🐾
           Fibrosis of lung following radiation
           Use additional code (W88-W90, X39.0-) to identify the external cause

     J70.2   **Acute drug-induced interstitial lung disorders** 🐾
           Use additional code for adverse effect, if applicable, to identify drug (T36-T50 with fifth or sixth character 5)
           Excludes1   interstitial pneumonia NOS (J84.9)
                         lymphoid interstitial pneumonia (J84.2)
           Coding Clinic: 2019, Q2, P28

     J70.3   **Chronic drug-induced interstitial lung disorders** 🐾
           Use additional code for adverse effect, if applicable, to identify drug (T36-T50 with fifth or sixth character 5)
           Excludes1   interstitial pneumonia NOS (J84.9)
                         lymphoid interstitial pneumonia (J84.2)

     J70.4   **Drug-induced interstitial lung disorders, unspecified** 🐾
           Use additional code for adverse effect, if applicable, to identify drug (T36-T50 with fifth or sixth character 5)
           Excludes1   interstitial pneumonia NOS (J84.9)
                         lymphoid interstitial pneumonia (J84.2)
           Coding Clinic: 2019, Q2, P28

     J70.5   **Respiratory conditions due to smoke inhalation** 🐾
           ▶ *Code first* smoke inhalation (T59.81-)
           ▶ **Excludes2**   smoke inhalation due to chemicals, gases, fumes and vapors (J68.9)
           ~~Smoke inhalation NOS~~
           ~~Excludes1~~   ~~smoke inhalation due to chemicals, gases, fumes and vapors (J68.9)~~

     J70.8   **Respiratory conditions due to other specified external agents** 🐾
           Code first (T51-T65) *to identify the external agent*

     J70.9   **Respiratory conditions due to unspecified external agent** 🐾
           Code first (T51-T65) *to identify the external agent*

OTHER RESPIRATORY DISEASES PRINCIPALLY AFFECTING THE INTERSTITIUM (J80-J84)

J80   **Acute respiratory distress syndrome** 🐾
     Acute respiratory distress syndrome in adult or child
     Adult hyaline membrane disease
     Excludes1   respiratory distress syndrome in newborn (perinatal) (P22.0)
     Coding Clinic: 2017, Q1, P26-27

● **J81**   **Pulmonary edema**
     Use additional code to identify:
         exposure to environmental tobacco smoke (Z77.22)
         history of tobacco dependence (Z87.891)
         occupational exposure to environmental tobacco smoke (Z57.31)
         tobacco dependence (F17.-)
         tobacco use (Z72.0)
     Excludes1   chemical (acute) pulmonary edema (J68.1)
                   hypostatic pneumonia (J18.2)
                   passive pneumonia (J18.2)
                   pulmonary edema due to external agents (J60-J70)
                   pulmonary edema with heart disease NOS (I50.1)
                   pulmonary edema with heart failure (I50.1)

     J81.0   **Acute pulmonary edema** 🐾
           Acute edema of lung
           Coding Clinic: 2017, Q1, P26

     J81.1   **Chronic pulmonary edema**
           Pulmonary congestion (chronic) (passive)
           Pulmonary edema NOS

Figure 10-9   Bullous emphysema with large subpleural bullae *(upper left)*. (From Kumar: Robbins and Cotran: Pathologic Basis of Disease, ed 8, Saunders, An Imprint of Elsevier, 2009)

J82   **Pulmonary eosinophilia, not elsewhere classified** 🐾
     ▶ **Excludes2**   pulmonary eosinophilia due to aspergillosis (B44.-)
           ▶ pulmonary eosinophilia due to drugs (J70.2-J70.4)
           ▶ pulmonary eosinophilia due to specified parasitic infection (B50-B83)
           ▶ pulmonary eosinophilia due to systemic connective tissue disorders (M30-M36)
           ▶ pulmonary infiltrate NOS (R91.8)

▶ ● **J82.8**   **Pulmonary eosinophilia, not elsewhere classified**

     ▶ **J82.81**   **Chronic eosinophilic pneumonia**
           ▶ Eosinophilic pneumonia, NOS

     ▶ **J82.82**   **Acute eosinophilic pneumonia**

     ▶ **J82.83**   **Eosinophilic asthma**
           ▶ *Code first asthma, by type, such as:*
              ▶ mild intermittent asthma (J45.2-)
              ▶ mild persistent asthma (J45.3-)
              ▶ moderate persistent asthma (J45.4-)
              ▶ severe persistent asthma (J45.5-)

     ▶ **J82.89**   **Other pulmonary eosinophilia, not elsewhere classified**
           ▶ Allergic pneumonia
           ▶ Löffler's pneumonia
           ▶ Tropical (pulmonary) eosinophilia NOS

     ~~Allergic pneumonia~~
     ~~Eosinophilic asthma~~
     ~~Eosinophilic pneumonia~~
     ~~Löffler's pneumonia~~
     ~~Tropical (pulmonary) eosinophilia NOS~~
     ~~Excludes1~~   ~~pulmonary eosinophilia due to aspergillosis (B44.-)~~
                   ~~pulmonary eosinophilia due to drugs (J70.2-J70.4)~~
                   ~~pulmonary eosinophilia due to specified parasitic infection (B50-B83)~~
                   ~~pulmonary eosinophilia due to systemic connective tissue disorders (M30-M36)~~
                   ~~pulmonary infiltrate NOS (R91.8)~~

● **J84**   **Other interstitial pulmonary diseases**
     Excludes1   drug-induced interstitial lung disorders (J70.2-J70.4)
                   interstitial emphysema (J98.2)
     Excludes2   lung diseases due to external agents (J60-J70)
     Coding Clinic: 2019, Q2, P28

     ● **J84.0**   **Alveolar and parieto-alveolar conditions**

         J84.01   **Alveolar proteinosis** 🐾

         J84.02   **Pulmonary alveolar microlithiasis** 🐾

     ▷   **J84.03**   *Idiopathic pulmonary hemosiderosis* 🐾
           Essential brown induration of lung
           Code first underlying disease, such as:
           disorders of iron metabolism (E83.1-)
           Excludes1   acute idiopathic pulmonary hemorrhage in infants [AIPHI] (R04.81)

         J84.09   **Other alveolar and parieto-alveolar conditions** 🐾

▶ New   ⮕ Revised   ~~deleted~~ Deleted   Excludes 1   Excludes 2   Includes   Use additional   Code first   Code also   Key words

936   OGCR Official Guidelines   X Assign placeholder X   ● Use Additional Character(s)   ▷ Manifestation Code   🐾 Hierarchical Condition Category   Coding Clinic

● J84.1   **Other interstitial pulmonary diseases with fibrosis**
     Excludes1   pulmonary fibrosis (chronic) due to inhalation of chemicals, gases, fumes or vapors (J68.4)
             pulmonary fibrosis (chronic) following radiation (J70.1)

   J84.10   **Pulmonary fibrosis, unspecified** 🔍
     Capillary fibrosis of lung
     Cirrhosis of lung (chronic) NOS
     Fibrosis of lung (atrophic) (chronic) (confluent) (massive) (perialveolar) (peribronchial) NOS
     Induration of lung (chronic) NOS
     Postinflammatory pulmonary fibrosis

● J84.11   **Idiopathic interstitial pneumonia**
     Excludes1   lymphoid interstitial pneumonia (J84.2)
             pneumocystis pneumonia (B59)

   J84.111   **Idiopathic interstitial pneumonia, not otherwise specified** 🔍

   J84.112   **Idiopathic pulmonary fibrosis** 🔍
     Cryptogenic fibrosing alveolitis
     Idiopathic fibrosing alveolitis

   J84.113   **Idiopathic non-specific interstitial pneumonitis** 🔍
     Excludes1   non-specific interstitial pneumonia NOS, or due to known underlying cause (J84.89)

   J84.114   **Acute interstitial pneumonitis** 🔍
     Hamman-Rich syndrome
     Excludes1   pneumocystis pneumonia (B59)

   J84.115   **Respiratory bronchiolitis interstitial lung disease** 🔍

   J84.116   **Cryptogenic organizing pneumonia** 🔍
     Excludes1   organizing pneumonia NOS, or due to known underlying cause (J84.89)

   J84.117   **Desquamative interstitial pneumonia** 🔍

●◗ J84.17   *Other interstitial pulmonary diseases with fibrosis in diseases classified elsewhere* 🔍
   ▷ J84.170   **Interstitial lung disease with progressive fibrotic phenotype in diseases classified elsewhere**
     ▷ Progressive fibrotic interstitial lung disease
     ▷ *Code first underlying disease, such as:*
     ▷ lung diseases due to external agents (J60-J70)
     ▷ rheumatoid arthritis (M05.00-M06.9)
     ▷ sarcoidosis (D86)
     ▷ systemic connective tissue disorders (M30-M36)

▷ J84.178   **Other interstitial pulmonary diseases with fibrosis in diseases classified elsewhere**
     ▷ Interstitial pneumonia (nonspecific) (usual) due to collagen vascular disease
     ▷ Interstitial pneumonia (nonspecific) (usual) in diseases classified elsewhere
     ▷ Organizing pneumonia due to collagen vascular disease
     ▷ Organizing pneumonia in diseases classified elsewhere
     ▷ *Code first underlying disease, such as:*
     ▷ progressive systemic sclerosis (M34.0)
     ▷ rheumatoid arthritis (M05.00-M06.9)
     ▷ systemic lupus erythematosis (M32.0-M32.9)
     ~~Interstitial pneumonia (nonspecific) (usual) due to collagen vascular disease~~
     ~~Interstitial pneumonia (nonspecific) (usual) in diseases classified elsewhere~~
     ~~Organizing pneumonia due to collagen vascular disease~~
     ~~Organizing pneumonia in diseases classified elsewhere~~
     ~~Code first underlying disease, such as:~~
     ~~progressive systemic sclerosis (M34.0)~~
     ~~rheumatoid arthritis (M05.00-M06.9)~~
     ~~systemic lupus erythematosis (M32.0-M32.9)~~

J84.2   **Lymphoid interstitial pneumonia** 🔍
     Lymphoid interstitial pneumonitis

● J84.8   **Other specified interstitial pulmonary diseases**
     Excludes1   exogenous lipoid pneumonia (J69.1)
             unspecified lipoid pneumonia (J69.1)

   J84.81   **Lymphangioleiomyomatosis** 🔍
     Lymphangiomyomatosis

   J84.82   **Adult pulmonary Langerhans cell histiocytosis** 🔍   A
     Adult PLCH

   J84.83   **Surfactant mutations of the lung** 🔍

● J84.84   **Other interstitial lung diseases of childhood**
   J84.841   **Neuroendocrine cell hyperplasia of infancy** 🔍
   J84.842   **Pulmonary interstitial glycogenosis** 🔍
   J84.843   **Alveolar capillary dysplasia with vein misalignment** 🔍
   J84.848   **Other interstitial lung diseases of childhood** 🔍

   J84.89   **Other specified interstitial pulmonary diseases** 🔍
     Endogenous lipoid pneumonia
     Interstitial pneumonitis
     Non-specific interstitial pneumonitis NOS
     Organizing pneumonia NOS
     Code first, if applicable:
     poisoning due to drug or toxin (T51-T65 with fifth or sixth character to indicate intent), for toxic pneumonopathy underlying cause of pneumonopathy, if known
     Use additional code, for adverse effect, to identify drug (T36-T50 with fifth or sixth character 5), if drug-induced
     Excludes1   cryptogenic organizing pneumonia (J84.116)
             idiopathic non-specific interstitial pneumonitis (J84.113)
             lipoid pneumonia, exogenous or unspecified (J69.1)
             lymphoid interstitial pneumonia (J84.2)

     Coding Clinic: 2019, Q2, P28

J84.9   **Interstitial pulmonary disease, unspecified** 🔍
     Interstitial pneumonia NOS

CHAPTER 10 (J00-J99)

CHAPTER 10 (J00-J99)

Item 10–11 **Empyema** is a condition in which pus accumulates in a body cavity. Empyema **with fistula** occurs when the pus passes from one cavity to another organ or structure.

SUPPURATIVE AND NECROTIC CONDITIONS OF THE LOWER RESPIRATORY TRACT (J85-J86)

● **J85** **Abscess of lung and mediastinum**
Use additional code (B95-B97) to identify infectious agent.

    J85.0 **Gangrene and necrosis of lung** 🐾

    J85.1 **Abscess of lung with pneumonia** 🐾
        Code also the type of pneumonia

    J85.2 **Abscess of lung without pneumonia** 🐾
        Abscess of lung NOS

    J85.3 **Abscess of mediastinum** 🐾

● **J86** **Pyothorax**
Use additional code (B95-B97) to identify infectious agent.

    Excludes1 abscess of lung (J85.-)
            pyothorax due to tuberculosis (A15.6)

    J86.0 **Pyothorax with fistula** 🐾
        Bronchocutaneous fistula
        Bronchopleural fistula
        Hepatopleural fistula
        Mediastinal fistula
        Pleural fistula
        Thoracic fistula
        Any condition classifiable to J86.9 with fistula

    J86.9 **Pyothorax without fistula** 🐾
        Abscess of pleura
        Abscess of thorax
        Empyema (chest) (lung) (pleura)
        Fibrinopurulent pleurisy
        Purulent pleurisy
        Pyopneumothorax
        Septic pleurisy
        Seropurulent pleurisy
        Suppurative pleurisy

OTHER DISEASES OF THE PLEURA (J90-J94)

J90 **Pleural effusion, not elsewhere classified**
    Encysted pleurisy
    Pleural effusion NOS
    Pleurisy with effusion (exudative) (serous)

    Excludes1 chylous (pleural) effusion (J94.0)
            malignant pleural effusion (J91.0))
            pleurisy NOS (R09.1)
            tuberculous pleural effusion (A15.6)
    Coding Clinic: 2015, Q2, P16

● **J91** **Pleural effusion in conditions classified elsewhere**
    Excludes2 pleural effusion in heart failure (I50.-)
            pleural effusion in systemic lupus erythematosus
              (M32.13)

   ▸ **J91.0** *Malignant pleural effusion*
        Code first underlying neoplasm

   ▸ **J91.8** *Pleural effusion in other conditions classified elsewhere*
        Code first underlying disease, such as:
          filariasis (B74.0-B74.9)
          influenza (J09.X2, J10.1, J11.1)
        Coding Clinic: 2015, Q2, P16

● **J92** **Pleural plaque**
    Includes pleural thickening

    J92.0 **Pleural plaque with presence of asbestos**

    J92.9 **Pleural plaque without asbestos**
        Pleural plaque NOS

● **J93** **Pneumothorax and air leak**
    Collapsed lung

    Excludes1 congenital or perinatal pneumothorax (P25.1)
            postprocedural air leak (J95.812)
            postprocedural pneumothorax (J95.811)
            traumatic pneumothorax (S27.0)
            tuberculous (current disease) pneumothorax
              (A15.-)
            pyopneumothorax (J86.-)

    J93.0 **Spontaneous tension pneumothorax**
        Tension pneumothorax (most serious type) occurs when air
          (positive pressure) collects in the pleural space

●   **J93.1** **Other spontaneous pneumothorax**

      J93.11 **Primary spontaneous pneumothorax**

      J93.12 **Secondary spontaneous pneumothorax**
         Code first underlying condition, such as:
          catamenial pneumothorax due to
            endometriosis (N80.8)
          cystic fibrosis (E84.-)
          eosinophilic pneumonia (J82)
          lymphangioleiomyomatosis (J84.81)
          malignant neoplasm of bronchus and lung
            (C34.-)
          Marfan's syndrome (Q87.4)
          pneumonia due to Pneumocystis carinii
            (B59)
          secondary malignant neoplasm of lung
            (C78.0-)
          spontaneous rupture of the esophagus
            (K22.3)

●   **J93.8** **Other pneumothorax and air leak**

      J93.81 **Chronic pneumothorax**

      J93.82 **Other air leak**
         Persistent air leak

      J93.83 **Other pneumothorax**
         Acute pneumothorax
         Spontaneous pneumothorax NOS

    J93.9 **Pneumothorax, unspecified**
        Pneumothorax NOS

● **J94** **Other pleural conditions**
    Excludes1 pleurisy NOS (R09.1)
            traumatic hemopneumothorax (S27.2)
            traumatic hemothorax (S27.1)
            tuberculous pleural conditions (current disease)
             (A15.-)

    J94.0 **Chylous effusion**
        Chyliform effusion

    J94.1 **Fibrothorax**

    J94.2 **Hemothorax**
        Hemopneumothorax

    J94.8 **Other specified pleural conditions**
        Hydropneumothorax
        Hydrothorax

    J94.9 **Pleural condition, unspecified**

INTRAOPERATIVE AND POSTPROCEDURAL COMPLICATIONS AND DISORDERS OF RESPIRATORY SYSTEM, NOT ELSEWHERE CLASSIFIED (J95)

● **J95** **Intraoperative and postprocedural complications and disorders of respiratory system, not elsewhere classified**
    Excludes2 aspiration pneumonia (J69.-)
            emphysema (subcutaneous) resulting from a
              procedure (T81.82)
            hypostatic pneumonia (J18.2)
            pulmonary manifestations due to radiation
              (J70.0- J70.1)

● **J95.0** **Tracheostomy complications**

    J95.00 **Unspecified tracheostomy complication** 🐾

    J95.01 **Hemorrhage from tracheostomy stoma** 🐾

▶ New   ➡ Revised   ~~deleted~~ Deleted   Excludes 1   Excludes 2   Includes   Use additional   Code first   Code also   Key words

OGCR Official Guidelines   X Assign placeholder X   ● Use Additional Character(s)   ▸ Manifestation Code   🐾 Hierarchical Condition Category   **Coding Clinic**

J95.02 Infection of tracheostomy stoma 🦠
    Use additional code to identify type of
      infection, such as:
        cellulitis of neck (L03.221)
        sepsis (A40, A41.-)

J95.03 Malfunction of tracheostomy stoma 🦠
    Mechanical complication of tracheostomy
      stoma
    Obstruction of tracheostomy airway
    Tracheal stenosis due to tracheostomy

J95.04 Tracheo-esophageal fistula following
    tracheostomy 🦠

J95.09 Other tracheostomy complication 🦠

J95.1 Acute pulmonary insufficiency following thoracic
surgery 🦠
    Excludes2   functional disturbances following cardiac
             surgery (I97.0, I97.1-)

J95.2 Acute pulmonary insufficiency following nonthoracic
surgery 🦠
    Excludes2   functional disturbances following cardiac
             surgery (I97.0, I97.1-)

J95.3 Chronic pulmonary insufficiency following surgery 🦠
    Excludes2   functional disturbances following cardiac
             surgery (I97.0, I97.1-)

J95.4 Chemical pneumonitis due to anesthesia
    Mendelson's syndrome
    Postprocedural aspiration pneumonia
    Use additional code for adverse effect, if applicable, to
      identify drug (T41.- with fifth or sixth character 5)
    Excludes1   aspiration pneumonitis due to anesthesia
             complicating labor and delivery
             (O74.0)
             aspiration pneumonitis due to anesthesia
             complicating pregnancy (O29)
             aspiration pneumonitis due to anesthesia
             complicating the puerperium
             (O89.01)

J95.5 Postprocedural subglottic stenosis

J95.6 Intraoperative hemorrhage and hematoma of a
respiratory system organ or structure complicating a
procedure
    Excludes1   intraoperative hemorrhage and
             hematoma of a respiratory system
             organ or structure due to accidental
             puncture and laceration during
             procedure (J95.7-)

    J95.61 Intraoperative hemorrhage and hematoma
        of a respiratory system organ or structure
        complicating a respiratory system procedure

    J95.62 Intraoperative hemorrhage and hematoma
        of a respiratory system organ or structure
        complicating other procedure

J95.7 Accidental puncture and laceration of a respiratory
system organ or structure during a procedure
    Excludes2   postprocedural pneumothorax (J95.811)

    J95.71 Accidental puncture and laceration of a
        respiratory system organ or structure during a
        respiratory system procedure

    J95.72 Accidental puncture and laceration of a
        respiratory system organ or structure during
        other procedure

J95.8 Other intraoperative and postprocedural complications
and disorders of respiratory system, not elsewhere
classified
    Coding Clinic: 2016, Q4, P10

    J95.81 Postprocedural pneumothorax and air leak
        J95.811 Postprocedural pneumothorax
        J95.812 Postprocedural air leak

J95.82 Postprocedural respiratory failure
    Excludes1   Respiratory failure in other
             conditions (J96.-)

    J95.821 Acute postprocedural respiratory
        failure 🦠
        Postprocedural respiratory failure
          NOS

    J95.822 Acute and chronic postprocedural
        respiratory failure 🦠

J95.83 Postprocedural hemorrhage of a respiratory
system organ or structure following a procedure
    J95.830 Postprocedural hemorrhage of a
        respiratory system organ or structure
        following a respiratory system
        procedure

    J95.831 Postprocedural hemorrhage of a
        respiratory system organ or structure
        following other procedure

J95.84 Transfusion-related acute lung injury (TRALI)

J95.85 Complication of respirator [ventilator]
    J95.850 Mechanical complication of
        respirator 🦠
        Excludes1   encounter for
             respirator
             [ventilator]
             dependence
             during power
             failure (Z99.12)

    J95.851 Ventilator associated pneumonia 🦠
        Ventilator associated pneumonitis
        Use additional code to identify the
          organism, if known (B95.-,
          B96.-, B97.-)
        Excludes1   ventilator lung in
             newborn (P27.8)
        Coding Clinic: 2017, Q1, P25

    J95.859 Other complication of respirator
        [ventilator] 🦠

J95.86 Postprocedural hematoma and seroma of a
respiratory system organ or structure following
a procedure
    J95.860 Postprocedural hematoma of a
        respiratory system organ or structure
        following a respiratory system
        procedure

    J95.861 Postprocedural hematoma of a
        respiratory system organ or structure
        following other procedure

    J95.862 Postprocedural seroma of a
        respiratory system organ or structure
        following a respiratory system
        procedure

    J95.863 Postprocedural seroma of a
        respiratory system organ or structure
        following other procedure

J95.88 Other intraoperative complications of
respiratory system, not elsewhere classified

J95.89 Other postprocedural complications and
disorders of respiratory system, not elsewhere
classified
    Use additional code to identify disorder,
      such as:
      aspiration pneumonia (J69.-)
      bacterial or viral pneumonia (J12-J18)
    Excludes2   acute pulmonary insufficiency
             following thoracic surgery
             (J95.1)
             postprocedural subglottic
             stenosis (J95.5)

CHAPTER 10 (J00-J99)

CHAPTER 10 (J00-J99)

OTHER DISEASES OF THE RESPIRATORY SYSTEM (J96-J99)

● **J96**   **Respiratory failure, not elsewhere classified**

     Excludes1   acute respiratory distress syndrome (J80)
                  cardiorespiratory failure (R09.2)
                  newborn respiratory distress syndrome (P22.0)
                  postprocedural respiratory failure (J95.82-)
                  respiratory arrest (R09.2)
                  respiratory arrest of newborn (P28.81)
                  respiratory failure of newborn (P28.5)

● **J96.0**   **Acute respiratory failure**

     J96.00   **Acute respiratory failure, unspecified whether with hypoxia or hypercapnia** 🔖
              Coding Clinic: 2016, Q3, P14

     J96.01   **Acute respiratory failure with hypoxia** 🔖

     J96.02   **Acute respiratory failure with hypercapnia** 🔖

● **J96.1**   **Chronic respiratory failure**

     J96.10   **Chronic respiratory failure, unspecified whether with hypoxia or hypercapnia** 🔖
              Coding Clinic: 2016, Q1, P38; 2015, Q1, P21

     J96.11   **Chronic respiratory failure with hypoxia** 🔖

     J96.12   **Chronic respiratory failure with hypercapnia** 🔖

● **J96.2**   **Acute and chronic respiratory failure**
     Acute on chronic respiratory failure

     J96.20   **Acute and chronic respiratory failure, unspecified whether with hypoxia or hypercapnia** 🔖

     J96.21   **Acute and chronic respiratory failure with hypoxia** 🔖

     J96.22   **Acute and chronic respiratory failure with hypercapnia** 🔖

● **J96.9**   **Respiratory failure, unspecified**

     J96.90   **Respiratory failure, unspecified, unspecified whether with hypoxia or hypercapnia** 🔖

     J96.91   **Respiratory failure, unspecified with hypoxia** 🔖

     J96.92   **Respiratory failure, unspecified with hypercapnia** 🔖

● **J98**   **Other respiratory disorders**
     Use additional code to identify:
       exposure to environmental tobacco smoke (Z77.22)
       exposure to tobacco smoke in the perinatal period (P96.81)
       history of tobacco dependence (Z87.891)
       occupational exposure to environmental tobacco smoke (Z57.31)
       tobacco dependence (F17.-)
       tobacco use (Z72.0)

     Excludes1   newborn apnea (P28.4)
                  newborn sleep apnea (P28.3)

     Excludes2   apnea NOS (R06.81)
                  sleep apnea (G47.3-)

● **J98.0**   **Diseases of bronchus, not elsewhere classified**

     J98.01   **Acute bronchospasm**

         Excludes1   acute bronchiolitis with bronchospasm (J21.-)
                    acute bronchitis with bronchospasm (J20.-)
                    asthma (J45.-)
                    exercise induced bronchospasm (J45.990)

     J98.09   **Other diseases of bronchus, not elsewhere classified**
              Broncholithiasis
              Calcification of bronchus
              Stenosis of bronchus
              Tracheobronchial collapse
              Tracheobronchial dyskinesia
              Ulcer of bronchus

● **J98.1**   **Pulmonary collapse**

     Excludes1   therapeutic collapse of lung status (Z98.3)

     J98.11   **Atelectasis**

         Excludes1   newborn atelectasis
                    tuberculous atelectasis (current disease) (A15)

     J98.19   **Other pulmonary collapse**

   J98.2   **Interstitial emphysema** 🔖
     Mediastinal emphysema

     Excludes1   emphysema NOS (J43.9)
                  emphysema in newborn (P25.0)
                  surgical emphysema (subcutaneous) (T81.82)
                  traumatic subcutaneous emphysema (T79.7)

   J98.3   **Compensatory emphysema** 🔖

   J98.4   **Other disorders of lung**
     Calcification of lung
     Cystic lung disease (acquired)
     Lung disease NOS
     Pulmolithiasis

     Excludes1   acute interstitial pneumonitis (J84.114)
                  pulmonary insufficiency following surgery (J95.1-J95.2)

● **J98.5**   **Diseases of mediastinum, not elsewhere classified**

     Excludes2   abscess of mediastinum (J85.3)

     Coding Clinic: 2016, Q4, P29

     J98.51   **Mediastinitis**

         Code first underlying condition, if applicable, such as postoperative mediastinitis (T81.-)

     J98.59   **Other diseases of mediastinum, not elsewhere classified**
         Fibrosis of mediastinum
         Hernia of mediastinum
         Retraction of mediastinum

   J98.6   **Disorders of diaphragm**
     Diaphragmatitis
     Paralysis of diaphragm
     Relaxation of diaphragm

     Excludes1   congenital malformation of diaphragm NEC (Q79.1)
                  congenital diaphragmatic hernia (Q79.0)

     Excludes2   diaphragmatic hernia (K44.-)

   J98.8   **Other specified respiratory disorders**

   J98.9   **Respiratory disorder, unspecified**
     Respiratory disease (chronic) NOS

▶ *J99*   *Respiratory disorders in diseases classified elsewhere* 🔖

     Code first underlying disease, such as:
       amyloidosis (E85.-)
       ankylosing spondylitis (M45)
       congenital syphilis (A50.5)
       cryoglobulinemia (D89.1)
       early congenital syphilis (A50.0)
       plasminogen deficiency (E88.02)
       schistosomiasis (B65.0-B65.9)

     Excludes1   respiratory disorders in:
                  amebiasis (A06.5)
                  blastomycosis (B40.0-B40.2)
                  candidiasis (B37.1)
                  coccidioidomycosis (B38.0-B38.2)
                  cystic fibrosis with pulmonary manifestations (E84.0)
                  dermatomyositis (M33.01, M33.11)
                  histoplasmosis (B39.0-B39.2)
                  late syphilis (A52.72, A52.73)
                  polymyositis (M33.21)
                  sicca syndrome (M35.02)
                  systemic lupus erythematosus (M32.13)
                  systemic sclerosis (M34.81)
                  Wegener's granulomatosis (M31.30-M31.31)

▶ New   ⟹ Revised   ~~deleted~~ Deleted   Excludes 1   Excludes 2   Includes   Use additional   Code first   Code also   Key words
OGCR Official Guidelines   X Assign placeholder X   ● Use Additional Character(s)   ▶ Manifestation Code   🔖 Hierarchical Condition Category   Coding Clinic

CHAPTER 11

DISEASES OF THE DIGESTIVE SYSTEM
(K00-K95)

OGCR Chapter-Specific Coding Guidelines

11. Chapter 11: Diseases of the Digestive System (K00-K95)
Reserved for future guideline expansion

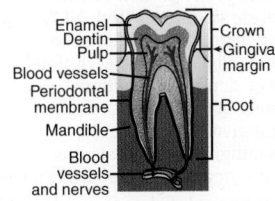

Figure 11-1 Anatomy of a tooth.

Item 11-1 Anodontia is the congenital absence of teeth. **Hypodontia** is partial anodontia. **Oligodontia** is the congenital absence of some teeth, whereas **supernumerary** is having more teeth than the normal number. **Mesiodens** are small extra teeth that often appear in pairs, although single small teeth are not uncommon.

CHAPTER 11

DISEASES OF THE DIGESTIVE SYSTEM
(K00-K95)

Excludes2 certain conditions originating in the perinatal period (P04-P96)
certain infectious and parasitic diseases (A00-B99)
complications of pregnancy, childbirth and the puerperium (O00-O9A)
congenital malformations, deformations and chromosomal abnormalities (Q00-Q99)
endocrine, nutritional and metabolic diseases (E00-E88)
injury, poisoning and certain other consequences of external causes (S00-T88)
neoplasms (C00-D49)
symptoms, signs and abnormal clinical and laboratory findings, not elsewhere classified (R00-R94)

This chapter contains the following blocks:

K00-K14	Diseases of oral cavity and salivary glands
K20-K31	Diseases of esophagus, stomach and duodenum
K35-K38	Diseases of appendix
K40-K46	Hernia
K50-K52	Noninfective enteritis and colitis
K55-K64	Other diseases of intestines
K65-K68	Diseases of peritoneum and retroperitoneum
K70-K77	Diseases of liver
K80-K87	Disorders of gallbladder, biliary tract and pancreas
K90-K95	Other diseases of the digestive system

DISEASES OF ORAL CAVITY AND SALIVARY GLANDS (K00-K14)

● **K00 Disorders of tooth development and eruption**
Excludes2 embedded and impacted teeth (K01.-)

K00.0 Anodontia
Hypodontia
Oligodontia
Excludes1 acquired absence of teeth (K08.1-)

K00.1 Supernumerary teeth
Distomolar
Fourth molar
Mesiodens
Paramolar
Supplementary teeth
Excludes2 supernumerary roots (K00.2)

K00.2 Abnormalities of size and form of teeth
Concrescence of teeth
Fusion of teeth
Gemination of teeth
Dens evaginatus
Dens in dente
Dens invaginatus
Enamel pearls
Macrodontia
Microdontia
Peg-shaped [conical] teeth
Supernumerary roots
Taurodontism
Tuberculum paramolare
Excludes1 abnormalities of teeth due to congenital syphilis (A50.5)
tuberculum Carabelli, which is regarded as a normal variation and should not be coded

K00.3 Mottled teeth
Dental fluorosis
Mottling of enamel
Nonfluoride enamel opacities
Excludes2 deposits [accretions] on teeth (K03.6)

K00.4 Disturbances in tooth formation
Aplasia and hypoplasia of cementum
Dilaceration of tooth
Enamel hypoplasia (neonatal) (postnatal) (prenatal)
Regional odontodysplasia
Turner's tooth
Excludes1 Hutchinson's teeth and mulberry molars in congenital syphilis (A50.5)
Excludes2 mottled teeth (K00.3)

K00.5 Hereditary disturbances in tooth structure, not elsewhere classified
Amelogenesis imperfecta
Dentinogenesis imperfecta
Odontogenesis imperfecta
Dentinal dysplasia
Shell teeth

K00.6 Disturbances in tooth eruption
Dentia praecox
Natal tooth
Neonatal tooth
Premature eruption of tooth
Premature shedding of primary [deciduous] tooth
Prenatal teeth
Retained [persistent] primary tooth
Excludes2 embedded and impacted teeth (K01.-)

K00.7 Teething syndrome

K00.8 Other disorders of tooth development
Color changes during tooth formation
Intrinsic staining of teeth NOS
Excludes2 posteruptive color changes (K03.7)

K00.9 Disorder of tooth development, unspecified
Disorder of odontogenesis NOS

● **K01 Embedded and impacted teeth**
Excludes1 abnormal position of fully erupted teeth (M26.3-)

K01.0 Embedded teeth

K01.1 Impacted teeth

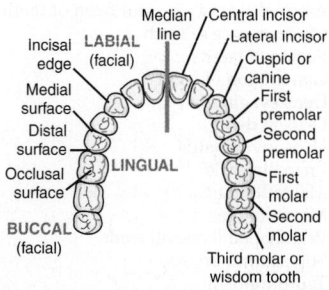

Figure 11-2 The permanent teeth within the dental arch.

Item 11-2 Each dental arch (jaw) normally contains 16 teeth. Tooth decay or **dental caries** is a disease of the enamel, dentin, and cementum of the tooth and can result in a cavity.

● **K02 Dental caries**

Includes caries of dentine
dental cavities
early childhood caries
pre-eruptive caries
recurrent caries (dentino enamel junction) (enamel) (to the pulp)
tooth decay

K02.3 Arrested dental caries
Arrested coronal and root caries

● **K02.5 Dental caries on pit and fissure surface**
Dental caries on chewing surface of tooth

K02.51 Dental caries on pit and fissure surface limited to enamel
White spot lesions [initial caries] on pit and fissure surface of tooth

K02.52 Dental caries on pit and fissure surface penetrating into dentin
Primary dental caries, cervical origin

K02.53 Dental caries on pit and fissure surface penetrating into pulp

● **K02.6 Dental caries on smooth surface**

K02.61 Dental caries on smooth surface limited to enamel
White spot lesions [initial caries] on smooth surface of tooth

K02.62 Dental caries on smooth surface penetrating into dentin

K02.63 Dental caries on smooth surface penetrating into pulp

K02.7 Dental root caries

K02.9 Dental caries, unspecified

● **K03 Other diseases of hard tissues of teeth**

Excludes2 bruxism (F45.8)
dental caries (K02.-)
teeth-grinding NOS (F45.8)

K03.0 Excessive attrition of teeth
Approximal wear of teeth
Occlusal wear of teeth

K03.1 Abrasion of teeth
Dentifrice abrasion of teeth
Habitual abrasion of teeth
Occupational abrasion of teeth
Ritual abrasion of teeth
Traditional abrasion of teeth
Wedge defect NOS

K03.2 Erosion of teeth
Erosion of teeth due to diet
Erosion of teeth due to drugs and medicaments
Erosion of teeth due to persistent vomiting
Erosion of teeth NOS
Idiopathic erosion of teeth
Occupational erosion of teeth

K03.3 Pathological resorption of teeth
Internal granuloma of pulp
Resorption of teeth (external)

K03.4 Hypercementosis
Cementation hyperplasia

K03.5 Ankylosis of teeth

K03.6 Deposits [accretions] on teeth
Betel deposits [accretions] on teeth
Black deposits [accretions] on teeth
Extrinsic staining of teeth NOS
Green deposits [accretions] on teeth
Materia alba deposits [accretions] on teeth
Orange deposits [accretions] on teeth
Staining of teeth NOS
Subgingival dental calculus
Supragingival dental calculus
Tobacco deposits [accretions] on teeth

K03.7 Posteruptive color changes of dental hard tissues

Excludes2 deposits [accretions] on teeth (K03.6)

● **K03.8 Other specified diseases of hard tissues of teeth**

K03.81 Cracked tooth

Excludes1 asymptomatic craze lines in enamel - omit code
broken or fractured tooth due to trauma (S02.5)

K03.89 Other specified diseases of hard tissues of teeth

K03.9 Disease of hard tissues of teeth, unspecified

● **K04 Diseases of pulp and periapical tissues**
Coding Clinic: 2016, Q4, P29

● **K04.0 Pulpitis**
Acute pulpitis
Chronic (hyperplastic) (ulcerative) pulpitis

K04.01 Reversible pulpitis

K04.02 Irreversible pulpitis

K04.1 Necrosis of pulp
Pulpal gangrene

K04.2 Pulp degeneration
Denticles
Pulpal calcifications
Pulpal stones

K04.3 Abnormal hard tissue formation in pulp
Secondary or irregular dentine

K04.4 Acute apical periodontitis of pulpal origin
Acute apical periodontitis NOS

Excludes1 acute periodontitis (K05.2-)

K04.5 Chronic apical periodontitis
Apical or periapical granuloma
Apical periodontitis NOS

Excludes1 chronic periodontitis (K05.3-)

K04.6 Periapical abscess with sinus
Dental abscess with sinus
Dentoalveolar abscess with sinus

K04.7 Periapical abscess without sinus
Dental abscess without sinus
Dentoalveolar abscess without sinus

K04.8 Radicular cyst
Apical (periodontal) cyst
Periapical cyst
Residual radicular cyst

Excludes2 lateral periodontal cyst (K09.0)

● **K04.9 Other and unspecified diseases of pulp and periapical tissues**

K04.90 Unspecified diseases of pulp and periapical tissues

K04.99 Other diseases of pulp and periapical tissues

▶ New ➡ Revised d̶e̶l̶e̶t̶e̶d̶ Deleted Excludes 1 Excludes 2 Includes Use additional Code first Code also Key words

OGCR Official Guidelines X Assign placeholder X ● Use Additional Character(s) ▶ Manifestation Code 🔖 Hierarchical Condition Category Coding Clinic

Item 11–3 Acute gingivitis, also known as orilitis or ulitis, is the short-term, severe inflammation of the gums (gingiva) caused by bacteria. **Chronic gingivitis** is persistent inflammation of the gums. When the gingivitis moves into the periodontium it is called periodontitis, also known as paradentitis.

● **K05   Gingivitis and periodontal diseases**
     Use additional code to identify:
       alcohol abuse and dependence (F10.-)
       exposure to environmental tobacco smoke (Z77.22)
       exposure to tobacco smoke in the perinatal period (P96.81)
       history of tobacco dependence (Z87.891)
       occupational exposure to environmental tobacco smoke (Z57.31)
       tobacco dependence (F17.-)
       tobacco use (Z72.0)
     Coding Clinic: 2016, Q4, P29

● **K05.0   Acute gingivitis**
     Excludes1   acute necrotizing ulcerative gingivitis (A69.1)
              herpesviral [herpes simplex] gingivostomatitis (B00.2)
     K05.00   Acute gingivitis, plaque induced
       Acute gingivitis NOS
       Plaque induced gingival disease
     K05.01   Acute gingivitis, non-plaque induced

● **K05.1   Chronic gingivitis**
     Desquamative gingivitis (chronic)
     Gingivitis (chronic) NOS
     Hyperplastic gingivitis (chronic)
     Pregnancy associated gingivitis
     Simple marginal gingivitis (chronic)
     Ulcerative gingivitis (chronic)
     Code first, if applicable, diseases of the digestive system complicating pregnancy (O99.61-)
     K05.10   Chronic gingivitis, plaque induced
       Chronic gingivitis NOS
       Gingivitis NOS
     K05.11   Chronic gingivitis, non-plaque induced

● **K05.2   Aggressive periodontitis**
     Acute pericoronitis
     Excludes1   acute apical periodontitis (K04.4)
              periapical abscess (K04.7)
              periapical abscess with sinus (K04.6)
     K05.20   Aggressive periodontitis, unspecified
     ● **K05.21   Aggressive periodontitis, localized**
       Periodontal abscess
       K05.211   Aggressive periodontitis, localized, slight
       K05.212   Aggressive periodontitis, localized, moderate
       K05.213   Aggressive periodontitis, localized, severe
       K05.219   Aggressive periodontitis, localized, unspecified severity
     ● **K05.22   Aggressive periodontitis, generalized**
       K05.221   Aggressive periodontitis, generalized, slight
       K05.222   Aggressive periodontitis, generalized, moderate
       K05.223   Aggressive periodontitis, generalized, severe
       K05.229   Aggressive periodontitis, generalized, unspecified severity

● **K05.3   Chronic periodontitis**
     Chronic pericoronitis
     Complex periodontitis
     Periodontitis NOS
     Simplex periodontitis
     Excludes1   chronic apical periodontitis (K04.5)
     K05.30   Chronic periodontitis, unspecified
     ● **K05.31   Chronic periodontitis, localized**
       K05.311   Chronic periodontitis, localized, slight
       K05.312   Chronic periodontitis, localized, moderate
       K05.313   Chronic periodontitis, localized, severe
       K05.319   Chronic periodontitis, localized, unspecified severity
     ● **K05.32   Chronic periodontitis, generalized**
       K05.321   Chronic periodontitis, generalized, slight
       K05.322   Chronic periodontitis, generalized, moderate
       K05.323   Chronic periodontitis, generalized, severe
       K05.329   Chronic periodontitis, generalized, unspecified severity

K05.4   Periodontosis
     Juvenile periodontosis

K05.5   Other periodontal diseases
     Combined periodontic-endodontic lesion
     Narrow gingival width (of periodontal soft tissue)
     Excludes2   leukoplakia of gingiva (K13.21)

K05.6   Periodontal disease, unspecified

● **K06   Other disorders of gingiva and edentulous alveolar ridge**
     Excludes2   acute gingivitis (K05.0)
              atrophy of edentulous alveolar ridge (K08.2)
              chronic gingivitis (K05.1)
              gingivitis NOS (K05.1)
     Coding Clinic: 2016, Q4, P29

● **K06.0   Gingival recession**
     Gingival recession (postinfective) (postprocedural)
     ● **K06.01   Gingival recession, localized**
       K06.010   Localized gingival recession, unspecified
         Localized gingival recession, NOS
       K06.011   Localized gingival recession, minimal
       K06.012   Localized gingival recession, moderate
       K06.013   Localized gingival recession, severe
     ● **K06.02   Gingival recession, generalized**
       K06.020   Generalized gingival recession, unspecified
         Generalized gingival recession, NOS
       K06.021   Generalized gingival recession, minimal
       K06.022   Generalized gingival recession, moderate
       K06.023   Generalized gingival recession, severe

K06.1   Gingival enlargement
     Gingival fibromatosis

K06.2   Gingival and edentulous alveolar ridge lesions associated with trauma
     Irritative hyperplasia of edentulous ridge [denture hyperplasia]
     Use additional code (Chapter 20) to identify external cause or denture status (Z97.2)

K06.3   Horizontal alveolar bone loss

K06.8   **Other specified disorders of gingiva and edentulous alveolar ridge**
  Fibrous epulis
  Flabby alveolar ridge
  Giant cell epulis
  Peripheral giant cell granuloma of gingiva
  Pyogenic granuloma of gingiva
  Vertical ridge deficiency
  Excludes2   gingival cyst (K09.0)

K06.9   **Disorder of gingiva and edentulous alveolar ridge, unspecified**

● **K08**   **Other disorders of teeth and supporting structures**
  Excludes2   dentofacial anomalies [including malocclusion] (M26.-)
               disorders of jaw (M27.-)
  Coding Clinic: 2016, Q4, P29

K08.0   **Exfoliation of teeth due to systemic causes**
  Code also underlying systemic condition

● **K08.1**   **Complete loss of teeth**
  Acquired loss of teeth, complete
  Excludes1   congenital absence of teeth (K00.0)
               exfoliation of teeth due to systemic causes (K08.0)
               partial loss of teeth (K08.4-)

  ● **K08.10**   **Complete loss of teeth, unspecified cause**
       K08.101   Complete loss of teeth, unspecified cause, class I
       K08.102   Complete loss of teeth, unspecified cause, class II
       K08.103   Complete loss of teeth, unspecified cause, class III
       K08.104   Complete loss of teeth, unspecified cause, class IV
       K08.109   Complete loss of teeth, unspecified cause, unspecified class
            Edentulism NOS

  ● **K08.11**   **Complete loss of teeth due to trauma**
       K08.111   Complete loss of teeth due to trauma, class I
       K08.112   Complete loss of teeth due to trauma, class II
       K08.113   Complete loss of teeth due to trauma, class III
       K08.114   Complete loss of teeth due to trauma, class IV
       K08.119   Complete loss of teeth due to trauma, unspecified class

  ● **K08.12**   **Complete loss of teeth due to periodontal diseases**
       K08.121   Complete loss of teeth due to periodontal diseases, class I
       K08.122   Complete loss of teeth due to periodontal diseases, class II
       K08.123   Complete loss of teeth due to periodontal diseases, class III
       K08.124   Complete loss of teeth due to periodontal diseases, class IV
       K08.129   Complete loss of teeth due to periodontal diseases, unspecified class

  ● **K08.13**   **Complete loss of teeth due to caries**
       K08.131   Complete loss of teeth due to caries, class I
       K08.132   Complete loss of teeth due to caries, class II
       K08.133   Complete loss of teeth due to caries, class III
       K08.134   Complete loss of teeth due to caries, class IV
       K08.139   Complete loss of teeth due to caries, unspecified class

  ● **K08.19**   **Complete loss of teeth due to other specified cause**
       K08.191   Complete loss of teeth due to other specified cause, class I
       K08.192   Complete loss of teeth due to other specified cause, class II
       K08.193   Complete loss of teeth due to other specified cause, class III
       K08.194   Complete loss of teeth due to other specified cause, class IV
       K08.199   Complete loss of teeth due to other specified cause, unspecified class

● **K08.2**   **Atrophy of edentulous alveolar ridge**
   K08.20   **Unspecified atrophy of edentulous alveolar ridge**
         Atrophy of the mandible NOS
         Atrophy of the maxilla NOS
   K08.21   **Minimal atrophy of the mandible**
         Minimal atrophy of the edentulous mandible
   K08.22   **Moderate atrophy of the mandible**
         Moderate atrophy of the edentulous mandible
   K08.23   **Severe atrophy of the mandible**
         Severe atrophy of the edentulous mandible
   K08.24   **Minimal atrophy of maxilla**
         Minimal atrophy of the edentulous maxilla
   K08.25   **Moderate atrophy of the maxilla**
         Moderate atrophy of the edentulous maxilla
   K08.26   **Severe atrophy of the maxilla**
         Severe atrophy of the edentulous maxilla

K08.3   **Retained dental root**

● **K08.4**   **Partial loss of teeth**
  Acquired loss of teeth, partial
  Excludes1   complete loss of teeth (K08.1-)
               congenital absence of teeth (K00.0)
  Excludes2   exfoliation of teeth due to systemic causes (K08.0)

  ● **K08.40**   **Partial loss of teeth, unspecified cause**
       K08.401   Partial loss of teeth, unspecified cause, class I
       K08.402   Partial loss of teeth, unspecified cause, class II
       K08.403   Partial loss of teeth, unspecified cause, class III
       K08.404   Partial loss of teeth, unspecified cause, class IV
       K08.409   Partial loss of teeth, unspecified cause, unspecified class
            Tooth extraction status NOS

  ● **K08.41**   **Partial loss of teeth due to trauma**
       K08.411   Partial loss of teeth due to trauma, class I
       K08.412   Partial loss of teeth due to trauma, class II
       K08.413   Partial loss of teeth due to trauma, class III
       K08.414   Partial loss of teeth due to trauma, class IV
       K08.419   Partial loss of teeth due to trauma, unspecified class

  ● **K08.42**   **Partial loss of teeth due to periodontal diseases**
       K08.421   Partial loss of teeth due to periodontal diseases, class I
       K08.422   Partial loss of teeth due to periodontal diseases, class II
       K08.423   Partial loss of teeth due to periodontal diseases, class III
       K08.424   Partial loss of teeth due to periodontal diseases, class IV
       K08.429   Partial loss of teeth due to periodontal diseases, unspecified class

---

▶ New   ⇒ Revised   ~~deleted~~ Deleted   Excludes 1   Excludes 2   Includes   Use additional   Code first   Code also   Key words
OGCR Official Guidelines   X Assign placeholder X   ● Use Additional Character(s)   ▷ Manifestation Code   🔒 Hierarchical Condition Category   **Coding Clinic**

● **K08.43** Partial loss of teeth due to caries
  K08.431 Partial loss of teeth due to caries, class I
  K08.432 Partial loss of teeth due to caries, class II
  K08.433 Partial loss of teeth due to caries, class III
  K08.434 Partial loss of teeth due to caries, class IV
  K08.439 Partial loss of teeth due to caries, unspecified class

● **K08.49** Partial loss of teeth due to other specified cause
  K08.491 Partial loss of teeth due to other specified cause, class I
  K08.492 Partial loss of teeth due to other specified cause, class II
  K08.493 Partial loss of teeth due to other specified cause, class III
  K08.494 Partial loss of teeth due to other specified cause, class IV
  K08.499 Partial loss of teeth due to other specified cause, unspecified class

● **K08.5** Unsatisfactory restoration of tooth
 Defective bridge, crown, filling
 Defective dental restoration
 Excludes1 dental restoration status (Z98.811)
 Excludes2 endosseous dental implant failure (M27.6-)
    unsatisfactory endodontic treatment (M27.5-)

 K08.50 Unsatisfactory restoration of tooth, unspecified
  Defective dental restoration NOS

 K08.51 Open restoration margins of tooth
  Dental restoration failure of marginal integrity
  Open margin on tooth restoration
  Poor gingival margin to tooth restoration

 K08.52 Unrepairable overhanging of dental restorative materials
  Overhanging of tooth restoration

● **K08.53** Fractured dental restorative material
  Excludes1 cracked tooth (K03.81)
    traumatic fracture of tooth (S02.5)

  K08.530 Fractured dental restorative material without loss of material
  K08.531 Fractured dental restorative material with loss of material
  K08.539 Fractured dental restorative material, unspecified

 K08.54 Contour of existing restoration of tooth biologically incompatible with oral health
  Dental restoration failure of periodontal anatomical integrity
  Unacceptable contours of existing restoration of tooth
  Unacceptable morphology of existing restoration of tooth

 K08.55 Allergy to existing dental restorative material
  Use additional code to identify the specific type of allergy

 K08.56 Poor aesthetic of existing restoration of tooth
  Dental restoration aesthetically inadequate or displeasing

 K08.59 Other unsatisfactory restoration of tooth
  Other defective dental restoration

● **K08.8** Other specified disorders of teeth and supporting structures
 K08.81 Primary occlusal trauma
 K08.82 Secondary occlusal trauma
 K08.89 Other specified disorders of teeth and supporting structures
  Enlargement of alveolar ridge NOS
  Insufficient anatomic crown height
  Insufficient clinical crown length
  Irregular alveolar process
  Toothache NOS

 K08.9 Disorder of teeth and supporting structures, unspecified

● **K09** Cysts of oral region, not elsewhere classified
 Includes lesions showing histological features both of aneurysmal cyst and of another fibro-osseous lesion
 Excludes2 cysts of jaw (M27.0-, M27.4-)
    radicular cyst (K04.8)

 K09.0 Developmental odontogenic cysts
  Dentigerous cyst
  Eruption cyst
  Follicular cyst
  Gingival cyst
  Lateral periodontal cyst
  Primordial cyst
  Excludes2 keratocysts (D16.4, D16.5)
    odontogenic keratocystic tumors (D16.4, D16.5)

 K09.1 Developmental (nonodontogenic) cysts of oral region
  Cyst (of) incisive canal
  Cyst (of) palatine of papilla
  Globulomaxillary cyst
  Median palatal cyst
  Nasoalveolar cyst
  Nasolabial cyst
  Nasopalatine duct cyst

 K09.8 Other cysts of oral region, not elsewhere classified
  Dermoid cyst
  Epidermoid cyst
  Lymphoepithelial cyst
  Epstein's pearl

 K09.9 Cyst of oral region, unspecified

★**(See Plate 28 of the Anatomy Illustrations.)**

● **K11** Diseases of salivary glands
 Use additional code to identify:
  alcohol abuse and dependence (F10.-)
  exposure to environmental tobacco smoke (Z77.22)
  exposure to tobacco smoke in the perinatal period (P96.81)
  history of tobacco dependence (Z87.891)
  occupational exposure to environmental tobacco smoke (Z57.31)
  tobacco dependence (F17.-)
  tobacco use (Z72.0)

 K11.0 Atrophy of salivary gland
 K11.1 Hypertrophy of salivary gland

Item 11-4 **Atrophy** is wasting away of a tissue or organ, whereas **hypertrophy** is overdevelopment or enlargement of a tissue or organ. **Sialoadenitis** is salivary gland inflammation. **Parotitis** is the inflammation of the parotid gland. In the epidemic form, parotitis is also known as mumps. **Sialolithiasis** is the formation of calculus within a salivary gland. **Mucocele** is a polyp composed of mucus.

Figure 11-3 Major salivary glands.

Parotid gland
Sublingual gland
Submandibular gland

CHAPTER 11 (K00-K95)

● **K11.2   Sialoadenitis**
     Parotitis

     Excludes1   epidemic parotitis (B26.-)
                      mumps (B26.-)
                      uveoparotid fever [Heerfordt] (D86.89)

     K11.20   Sialoadenitis, unspecified

     K11.21   Acute sialoadenitis

         Excludes1   acute recurrent sialoadenitis
                          (K11.22)

     K11.22   Acute recurrent sialoadenitis

     K11.23   Chronic sialoadenitis

K11.3   Abscess of salivary gland

K11.4   Fistula of salivary gland

     Excludes1   congenital fistula of salivary gland
                      (Q38.4)

K11.5   Sialolithiasis
     Calculus of salivary gland or duct
     Stone of salivary gland or duct

K11.6   Mucocele of salivary gland
     Mucous extravasation cyst of salivary gland
     Mucous retention cyst of salivary gland
     Ranula

K11.7   Disturbances of salivary secretion
     Hypoptyalism
     Ptyalism
     Xerostomia

     Excludes2   dry mouth NOS (R68.2)

K11.8   Other diseases of salivary glands
     Benign lymphoepithelial lesion of salivary gland
     Mikulicz' disease
     Necrotizing sialometaplasia
     Sialectasia
     Stenosis of salivary duct
     Stricture of salivary duct

     Excludes1   sicca syndrome [Sjögren] (M35.0-)

K11.9   Disease of salivary gland, unspecified
     Sialoadenopathy NOS

● **K12   Stomatitis and related lesions**
     Use additional code to identify:
         alcohol abuse and dependence (F10.-)
         exposure to environmental tobacco smoke (Z77.22)
         exposure to tobacco smoke in the perinatal period (P96.81)
         history of tobacco dependence (Z87.891)
         occupational exposure to environmental tobacco smoke (Z57.31)
         tobacco dependence (F17.-)
         tobacco use (Z72.0)

     Excludes1   cancrum oris (A69.0)
                      cheilitis (K13.0)
                      gangrenous stomatitis (A69.0)
                      herpesviral [herpes simplex] gingivostomatitis
                          (B00.2)
                      noma (A69.0)

K12.0   Recurrent oral aphthae
     Aphthous stomatitis (major) (minor)
     Bednar's aphthae
     Periadenitis mucosa necrotica recurrens
     Recurrent aphthous ulcer
     Stomatitis herpetiformis

K12.1   Other forms of stomatitis
     Stomatitis NOS
     Denture stomatitis
     Ulcerative stomatitis
     Vesicular stomatitis

     Excludes1   acute necrotizing ulcerative stomatitis
                      (A69.1)
                      Vincent's stomatitis (A69.1)

K12.2   Cellulitis and abscess of mouth
     Cellulitis of mouth (floor)
     Submandibular abscess

     Excludes2   abscess of salivary gland (K11.3)
                       abscess of tongue (K14.0)
                       periapical abscess (K04.6-K04.7)
                       periodontal abscess (K05.21)
                       peritonsillar abscess (J36)

● **K12.3   Oral mucositis (ulcerative)**
     Mucositis (oral) (oropharyneal)

     Excludes2   gastrointestinal mucositis (ulcerative)
                       (K92.81)
                       mucositis (ulcerative) of vagina and vulva
                       (N76.81)
                       nasal mucositis (ulcerative) (J34.81)

     K12.30   Oral mucositis (ulcerative), unspecified

     K12.31   Oral mucositis (ulcerative) due to antineoplastic therapy
         Use additional code for adverse effect, if
             applicable, to identify antineoplastic and
             immunosuppressive drugs (T45.1X5)
         Use additional code for other antineoplastic
             therapy, such as:
             radiological procedure and radiotherapy
             (Y84.2)

     K12.32   Oral mucositis (ulcerative) due to other drugs
         Use additional code for adverse effect, if
             applicable, to identify drug (T36-T50 with
             fifth or sixth character 5)

     K12.33   Oral mucositis (ulcerative) due to radiation
         Use additional external cause code (W88-W90,
             X39.0-) to identify cause

     K12.39   Other oral mucositis (ulcerative)
         Viral oral mucositis (ulcerative)

● **K13   Other diseases of lip and oral mucosa**

     Includes   epithelial disturbances of tongue
     Use additional code to identify:
         alcohol abuse and dependence (F10.-)
         exposure to environmental tobacco smoke (Z77.22)
         exposure to tobacco smoke in the perinatal period (P96.81)
         history of tobacco dependence (Z87.891)
         occupational exposure to environmental tobacco smoke
             (Z57.31)
         tobacco dependence (F17.-)
         tobacco use (Z72.0)

     Excludes2   certain disorders of gingiva and edentulous
                       alveolar ridge (K05-K06)
                       cysts of oral region (K09.-)
                       diseases of tongue (K14.-)
                       stomatitis and related lesions (K12.-)

K13.0   Diseases of lips

Abscess of lips	Exfoliative cheilitis
Angular cheilitis	Fistula of lips
Cellulitis of lips	Glandular cheilitis
Cheilitis NOS	Hypertrophy of lips
Cheilodynia	Perlèche NEC
Cheilosis	

     Excludes1   ariboflavinosis (E53.0)
                       cheilitis due to radiation-related disorders
                         (L55-L59)
                       congenital fistula of lips (Q38.0)
                       congenital hypertrophy of lips (Q18.6)
                       Perlèche due to candidiasis (B37.83)
                       Perlèche due to riboflavin deficiency
                         (E53.0)

K13.1   Cheek and lip biting

Item 11-5   Stomatitis is the inflammation of the oral mucosa. **Mucositis** is the inflammation of the mucous membranes lining the digestive tract from the mouth to the anus. It is a common side effect of chemotherapy and of radiotherapy that involves any part of the digestive tract.

▶ New   ⇒ Revised   ~~deleted~~ Deleted   Excludes 1   Excludes 2   Includes   Use additional   Code first   Code also   Key words
OGCR Official Guidelines   X Assign placeholder X   ● Use Additional Character(s)   ▶ Manifestation Code   Hierarchical Condition Category   **Coding Clinic**

Figure 11-4   Oral leukoplakia and associated. (From Swartz MH: Textbook of Physical Diagnosis: History and Examination, Philadelphia, PA, Saunders/Elsevier, 2010)

● **K13.2 Leukoplakia and other disturbances of oral epithelium, including tongue**

> **Excludes1**   carcinoma in situ of oral epithelium (D00.0-)
> hairy leukoplakia (K13.3)

K13.21 Leukoplakia of oral mucosa, including tongue
Considered precancerous and evidenced by thickened white patches of epithelium on mucous membranes
Leukokeratosis of oral mucosa
Leukoplakia of gingiva, lips, tongue

> **Excludes1**   hairy leukoplakia (K13.3)
> leukokeratosis nicotina palati (K13.24)

K13.22 Minimal keratinized residual ridge mucosa
Minimal keratinization of alveolar ridge mucosa

K13.23 Excessive keratinized residual ridge mucosa
Excessive keratinization of alveolar ridge mucosa

K13.24 Leukokeratosis nicotina palati
Smoker's palate

K13.29 Other disturbances of oral epithelium, including tongue
Erythroplakia of mouth or tongue
Focal epithelial hyperplasia of mouth or tongue
Leukoedema of mouth or tongue
Other oral epithelium disturbances

K13.3 Hairy leukoplakia

K13.4 Granuloma and granuloma-like lesions of oral mucosa
Eosinophilic granuloma
Granuloma pyogenicum
Verrucous xanthoma

K13.5 Oral submucous fibrosis
Submucous fibrosis of tongue

K13.6 Irritative hyperplasia of oral mucosa

> **Excludes2**   irritative hyperplasia of edentulous ridge [denture hyperplasia] (K06.2)

● **K13.7 Other and unspecified lesions of oral mucosa**

K13.70 Unspecified lesions of oral mucosa

K13.79 Other lesions of oral mucosa
Focal oral mucinosis

★ **(See Plate 26 of the Anatomy Illustrations.)**

● **K14 Diseases of tongue**
Use additional code to identify:
alcohol abuse and dependence (F10.-)
exposure to environmental tobacco smoke (Z77.22)
history of tobacco dependence (Z87.891)
occupational exposure to environmental tobacco smoke (Z57.31)
tobacco dependence (F17.-)
tobacco use (Z72.0)

> **Excludes2**   erythroplakia (K13.29)
> focal epithelial hyperplasia (K13.29)
> leukedema of tongue (K13.29)
> leukoplakia of tongue (K13.21)
> hairy leukoplakia (K13.3)
> macroglossia (congenital) (Q38.2)
> submucous fibrosis of tongue (K13.5)

K14.0 Glossitis
Abscess of tongue
Ulceration (traumatic) of tongue

> **Excludes1**   atrophic glossitis (K14.4)

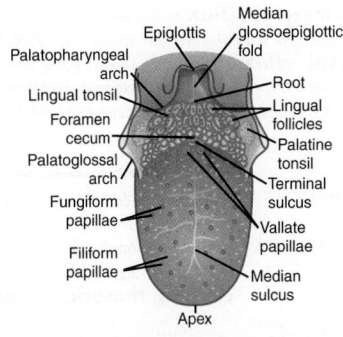

Figure 11-5   Structure of the tongue.

K14.1 Geographic tongue
Benign migratory glossitis
Glossitis areata exfoliativa

K14.2 Median rhomboid glossitis

K14.3 Hypertrophy of tongue papillae
Black hairy tongue
Coated tongue
Hypertrophy of foliate papillae
Lingua villosa nigra

K14.4 Atrophy of tongue papillae
Atrophic glossitis

K14.5 Plicated tongue
Fissured tongue   Scrotal tongue
Furrowed tongue

> **Excludes1**   fissured tongue, congenital (Q38.3)

K14.6 Glossodynia
Glossopyrosis   Painful tongue

K14.8 Other diseases of tongue
Atrophy of tongue   Glossocele
Crenated tongue   Glossoptosis
Enlargement of tongue   Hypertrophy of tongue

K14.9 Disease of tongue, unspecified
Glossopathy NOS

DISEASES OF ESOPHAGUS, STOMACH AND DUODENUM (K20-K31)

> **Excludes2**   hiatus hernia (K44.-)

● **K20 Esophagitis**
Use additional code to identify:
alcohol abuse and dependence (F10.-)

> **Excludes1**   erosion of esophagus (K22.1-)
> esophagitis with gastro-esophageal reflux disease (K21.0-)
> reflux esophagitis (K21.0-)
> ulcerative esophagitis (K22.1-)

> **Excludes2**   eosinophilic gastritis or gastroenteritis (K52.81)

K20.0 Eosinophilic esophagitis

● **K20.8 Other esophagitis**

▶ **K20.80 Other esophagitis without bleeding**
▶ Abscess of esophagus
▶ Other esophagitis NOS

▶ **K20.81 Other esophagitis with bleeding**
~~Abscess of esophagus~~

● **K20.9 Esophagitis, unspecified**

▶ **K20.90 Esophagitis, unspecified without bleeding**
▶ Esophagitis NOS

▶ **K20.91 Esophagitis, unspecified with bleeding**
~~Esophagitis NOS~~

Item 11–6 Esophageal reflux is the return flow of the contents of the stomach to the esophagus and is referred to as GERD and/or "heartburn." **Gastroesophageal reflux** is the return flow of the contents of the stomach and duodenum to the esophagus. **Esophageal leukoplakia** are white areas on the mucous membrane of the esophagus for which no specific cause can be identified.

CERVICAL
ESOPHAGUS
Left
subclavian
artery
First rib
Arch of
aorta
Diaphragm
THORACIC
ESOPHAGUS
ABDOMINAL
ESOPHAGUS
Stomach

Figure 11-6 The esophagus is the muscular tube that connects the pharynx and the stomach. The 10-inch (25 cm) long esophagus is divided into three parts: **cervical, thoracic,** and **abdominal.**

● **K21   Gastro-esophageal reflux disease**
　　Excludes1   newborn esophageal reflux (P78.83)
● **K21.0   Gastro-esophageal reflux disease with esophagitis**
▶ **K21.00   Gastro-esophageal reflux disease with esophagitis, without bleeding**
▶ Reflux esophagitis
▶ **K21.01   Gastro-esophageal reflux disease with esophagitis, with bleeding**
~~Reflux esophagitis~~

K21.9   Gastro-esophageal reflux disease without esophagitis
　　Esophageal reflux NOS
　　Coding Clinic: 2016, Q1, P18

● **K22   Other diseases of esophagus**
　　Excludes2   esophageal varices (I85.-)

K22.0   Achalasia of cardia
　　Achalasia NOS
　　Cardiospasm
　　Excludes1   congenital cardiospasm (Q39.5)

● **K22.1   Ulcer of esophagus**
　　Barrett's ulcer
　　Erosion of esophagus
　　Fungal ulcer of esophagus
　　Peptic ulcer of esophagus
　　Ulcer of esophagus due to ingestion of chemicals
　　Ulcer of esophagus due to ingestion of drugs and
　　　medicaments
　　Ulcerative esophagitis
　　*Code first poisoning due to drug or toxin, if applicable
　　(T36-T65 with fifth or sixth character 1-4 or 6)*
　　Use additional code for adverse effect, if applicable,
　　　to identify drug (T36-T50 with fifth or sixth
　　　character 5)
　　Excludes1   Barrett's esophagus (K22.87-)

K22.10   Ulcer of esophagus without bleeding
　　Ulcer of esophagus NOS

K22.11   Ulcer of esophagus with bleeding
　　Excludes2   bleeding esophageal varices
　　　　　　　　(I85.01, I85.11)

K22.2   Esophageal obstruction
　　Compression of esophagus
　　Constriction of esophagus
　　Stenosis of esophagus
　　Stricture of esophagus
　　Excludes1   congenital stenosis or stricture of
　　　　　　　　esophagus (Q39.3)

K22.3   Perforation of esophagus
　　Rupture of esophagus
　　Excludes1   traumatic perforation of (thoracic)
　　　　　　　　esophagus (S27.8-)

K22.4   Dyskinesia of esophagus
　　Difficulty in moving
　　Corkscrew esophagus
　　Diffuse esophageal spasm
　　Spasm of esophagus
　　Excludes1   cardiospasm (K22.0)

K22.5   Diverticulum of esophagus, acquired
　　Esophageal pouch, acquired
　　Excludes1   diverticulum of esophagus (congenital)
　　　　　　　　(Q39.6)

K22.6   Gastro-esophageal laceration-hemorrhage syndrome
　　Mallory-Weiss syndrome

● **K22.7   Barrett's esophagus**
　　Barrett's disease
　　Barrett's syndrome
　　Excludes1   Barrett's ulcer (K22.1)
　　　　　　　　malignant neoplasm of esophagus (C15.-)

K22.70   Barrett's esophagus without dysplasia
　　Barrett's esophagus NOS

● **K22.71   Barrett's esophagus with dysplasia**
　　**K22.710   Barrett's esophagus with low grade
　　　　　　　dysplasia**
　　**K22.711   Barrett's esophagus with high grade
　　　　　　　dysplasia**
　　**K22.719   Barrett's esophagus with dysplasia,
　　　　　　　unspecified**

K22.8   Other specified diseases of esophagus
　　Hemorrhage of esophagus NOS
　　Excludes2   esophageal varices (I85.-)
　　　　　　　　Paterson-Kelly syndrome (D50.1)
　　Coding Clinic: 2020, Q1, P16

K22.9   Disease of esophagus, unspecified

▶ **K23   Disorders of esophagus in diseases classified elsewhere**
　　Code first underlying disease, such as:
　　congenital syphilis (A50.5)
　　Excludes1   late syphilis (A52.79)
　　　　　　　　megaesophagus due to Chagas' disease (B57.31)
　　　　　　　　tuberculosis (A18.83)

● **K25   Gastric ulcer**
　　Includes   erosion (acute) of stomach
　　　　　　　pylorus ulcer (peptic)
　　　　　　　stomach ulcer (peptic)
　　Use additional code to identify:
　　　alcohol abuse and dependence (F10.-)
　　Excludes1   acute gastritis (K29.0-)
　　　　　　　　peptic ulcer NOS (K27.-)

K25.0   Acute gastric ulcer with hemorrhage

K25.1   Acute gastric ulcer with perforation 🔲

Item 11–7 Achalasia is a condition in which the smooth muscle fibers of the esophagus do not relax. Most frequently, this condition occurs at the esophagogastric sphincter. **Cardiospasm,** also known as **megaesophagus,** is achalasia of the thoracic esophagus.

A   B   C

Figure 11-7   A. Ulcer. **B.** Perforated ulcer. **C.** Laparoscopic view of a perforated duodenal ulcer *(arrow)* with fibrinous exudate on the adjacent peritoneum. (**C** from Feldman: Sleisenger & Fordtran's Gastrointestinal and Liver Disease, ed 8, Saunders, An Imprint of Elsevier, 2006)

▶ New   ⇒ Revised   ~~deleted~~ Deleted   Excludes 1   Excludes 2   Includes   Use additional   Code first   Code also   Key words

OGCR Official Guidelines   X Assign placeholder X   ● Use Additional Character(s)   ▶ Manifestation Code   🔲 Hierarchical Condition Category   Coding Clinic

Item 11–8   Gastric ulcers are lesions of the stomach that result in the death of the tissue and a defect of the surface. **Perforated ulcers** are those in which the lesion penetrates the gastric wall, leaving a hole. **Peptic ulcers** are lesions of the stomach or the duodenum. **Peptic** refers to the gastric juice, pepsin.

K25.2   Acute gastric ulcer with both hemorrhage and perforation 📎

K25.3   Acute gastric ulcer without hemorrhage or perforation

K25.4   Chronic or unspecified gastric ulcer with hemorrhage
     Coding Clinic: 2017, Q3, P27

K25.5   Chronic or unspecified gastric ulcer with perforation 📎

K25.6   Chronic or unspecified gastric ulcer with both hemorrhage and perforation 📎

K25.7   Chronic gastric ulcer without hemorrhage or perforation

K25.9   Gastric ulcer, unspecified as acute or chronic, without hemorrhage or perforation

● **K26**   Duodenal ulcer

     Includes   erosion (acute) of duodenum
               duodenum ulcer (peptic)
               postpyloric ulcer (peptic)

     Use additional code to identify:
         alcohol abuse and dependence (F10.-)

     Excludes1   peptic ulcer NOS (K27.-)

K26.0   Acute duodenal ulcer with hemorrhage

K26.1   Acute duodenal ulcer with perforation 📎

K26.2   Acute duodenal ulcer with both hemorrhage and perforation 📎

K26.3   Acute duodenal ulcer without hemorrhage or perforation

K26.4   Chronic or unspecified duodenal ulcer with hemorrhage
     Coding Clinic: 2016, Q1, P14

K26.5   Chronic or unspecified duodenal ulcer with perforation 📎

K26.6   Chronic or unspecified duodenal ulcer with both hemorrhage and perforation 📎

K26.7   Chronic duodenal ulcer without hemorrhage or perforation

K26.9   Duodenal ulcer, unspecified as acute or chronic, without hemorrhage or perforation

● **K27**   Peptic ulcer, site unspecified

     Includes   gastroduodenal ulcer NOS
               peptic ulcer NOS

     Use additional code to identify:
         alcohol abuse and dependence (F10.-)

     Excludes1   peptic ulcer of newborn (P78.82)

K27.0   Acute peptic ulcer, site unspecified, with hemorrhage

K27.1   Acute peptic ulcer, site unspecified, with perforation 📎

K27.2   Acute peptic ulcer, site unspecified, with both hemorrhage and perforation 📎

K27.3   Acute peptic ulcer, site unspecified, without hemorrhage or perforation

K27.4   Chronic or unspecified peptic ulcer, site unspecified, with hemorrhage

K27.5   Chronic or unspecified peptic ulcer, site unspecified, with perforation 📎

K27.6   Chronic or unspecified peptic ulcer, site unspecified, with both hemorrhage and perforation 📎

K27.7   Chronic peptic ulcer, site unspecified, without hemorrhage or perforation

K27.9   Peptic ulcer, site unspecified, unspecified as acute or chronic, without hemorrhage or perforation

● **K28**   Gastrojejunal ulcer

     Includes   anastomotic ulcer (peptic) or erosion
               gastrocolic ulcer (peptic) or erosion
               gastrointestinal ulcer (peptic) or erosion
               gastrojejunal ulcer (peptic) or erosion
               jejunal ulcer (peptic) or erosion
               marginal ulcer (peptic) or erosion
               stomal ulcer (peptic) or erosion

     Use additional code to identify:
         alcohol abuse and dependence (F10.-)

     Excludes1   primary ulcer of small intestine (K63.3)

K28.0   Acute gastrojejunal ulcer with hemorrhage

K28.1   Acute gastrojejunal ulcer with perforation 📎

K28.2   Acute gastrojejunal ulcer with both hemorrhage and perforation 📎

K28.3   Acute gastrojejunal ulcer without hemorrhage or perforation

K28.4   Chronic or unspecified gastrojejunal ulcer with hemorrhage

K28.5   Chronic or unspecified gastrojejunal ulcer with perforation 📎

K28.6   Chronic or unspecified gastrojejunal ulcer with both hemorrhage and perforation 📎

K28.7   Chronic gastrojejunal ulcer without hemorrhage or perforation

K28.9   Gastrojejunal ulcer, unspecified as acute or chronic, without hemorrhage or perforation

● **K29**   Gastritis and duodenitis

     Excludes1   eosinophilic gastritis or gastroenteritis (K52.81)
                    Zollinger-Ellison syndrome (E16.4)

● **K29.0**   Acute gastritis

     Use additional code to identify:
         alcohol abuse and dependence (F10.-)

     Excludes1   erosion (acute) of stomach (K25.-)

     K29.00   Acute gastritis without bleeding

     K29.01   Acute gastritis with bleeding

● **K29.2**   Alcoholic gastritis

     Use additional code to identify:
         alcohol abuse and dependence (F10.-)

     K29.20   Alcoholic gastritis without bleeding

     K29.21   Alcoholic gastritis with bleeding

● **K29.3**   Chronic superficial gastritis

     K29.30   Chronic superficial gastritis without bleeding

     K29.31   Chronic superficial gastritis with bleeding

● **K29.4**   Chronic atrophic gastritis
     Gastric atrophy

     K29.40   Chronic atrophic gastritis without bleeding

     K29.41   Chronic atrophic gastritis with bleeding

● **K29.5**   Unspecified chronic gastritis
     Chronic antral gastritis
     Chronic fundal gastritis

     K29.50   Unspecified chronic gastritis without bleeding

     K29.51   Unspecified chronic gastritis with bleeding

● **K29.6**   Other gastritis
     Giant hypertrophic gastritis
     Granulomatous gastritis
     Ménétrier's disease

     K29.60   Other gastritis without bleeding

     K29.61   Other gastritis with bleeding

● **K29.7**   Gastritis, unspecified

     K29.70   Gastritis, unspecified, without bleeding

     K29.71   Gastritis, unspecified, with bleeding

Item 11–9   Gastritis is a severe inflammation of the stomach. **Atrophic gastritis** is a chronic inflammation of the stomach that results in destruction of the cells of the mucosa of the stomach. Duodenitis is an inflammation of the duodenum, the first section of the small intestine.

● **K29.8   Duodenitis**

    K29.80   Duodenitis without bleeding

    K29.81   Duodenitis with bleeding

● **K29.9   Gastroduodenitis, unspecified**

    K29.90   Gastroduodenitis, unspecified, without bleeding

    K29.91   Gastroduodenitis, unspecified, with bleeding

K30   Functional dyspepsia
    Indigestion

    Excludes1   dyspepsia NOS (R10.13)
               heartburn (R12)
               nervous dyspepsia (F45.8)
               neurotic dyspepsia (F45.8)
               psychogenic dyspepsia (F45.8)

● **K31   Other diseases of stomach and duodenum**
    Includes   functional disorders of stomach

    Excludes2   diabetic gastroparesis (E08.43, E09.43, E10.43, E11.43, E13.43)
               diverticulum of duodenum (K57.00-K57.13)

    K31.0   Acute dilatation of stomach
        Acute distention of stomach

    K31.1   Adult hypertrophic pyloric stenosis   A
        Pyloric stenosis NOS

        Excludes1   congenital or infantile pyloric stenosis (Q40.0)

    K31.2   Hourglass stricture and stenosis of stomach

        Excludes1   congenital hourglass stomach (Q40.2)
               hourglass contraction of stomach (K31.89)

    K31.3   Pylorospasm, not elsewhere classified

        Excludes1   congenital or infantile pylorospasm (Q40.0)
               neurotic pylorospasm (F45.8)
               psychogenic pylorospasm (F45.8)

    K31.4   Gastric diverticulum

        Excludes1   congenital diverticulum of stomach (Q40.2)

    K31.5   Obstruction of duodenum
        Constriction of duodenum
        Duodenal ileus (chronic)
        Stenosis of duodenum
            Narrowing
        Stricture of duodenum
            Narrowing
        Volvulus of duodenum
            Twisting/knotting

        Excludes1   congenital stenosis of duodenum (Q41.0)

    K31.6   Fistula of stomach and duodenum
        Gastrocolic fistula
        Gastrojejunocolic fistula

    K31.7   Polyp of stomach and duodenum

        Excludes1   adenomatous polyp of stomach (D13.1)
        Coding Clinic: 2020, Q1, P16

●   **K31.8   Other specified diseases of stomach and duodenum**

    ● **K31.81   Angiodysplasia of stomach and duodenum**

        K31.811   Angiodysplasia of stomach and duodenum with bleeding

        K31.819   Angiodysplasia of stomach and duodenum without bleeding
               Angiodysplasia of stomach and duodenum NOS

    K31.82   Dieulafoy lesion (hemorrhagic) of stomach and duodenum

        Excludes2   Dieulafoy lesion of intestine (K63.81)

    K31.83   Achlorhydria

    K31.84   Gastroparesis
        Gastroparalysis

        Code first underlying disease, if known, such as:
          anorexia nervosa (F50.0-)
          diabetes mellitus (E08.43, E09.43, E10.43, E11.43, E13.43)
          scleroderma (M34.-)

    K31.89   Other diseases of stomach and duodenum
        Coding Clinic: 2020, Q1, P16; 2017, Q1, P28

    K31.9   Disease of stomach and duodenum, unspecified

DISEASES OF APPENDIX (K35-K38)

● **K35   Acute appendicitis**

  ● **K35.2   Acute appendicitis with generalized peritonitis**
      Appendicitis (acute) with generalized (diffuse) peritonitis following rupture or perforation of appendix

    K35.20   Acute appendicitis with generalized peritonitis, without abscess (Acute) appendicitis with generalized peritonitis NOS
        Coding Clinic: 2018, Q4, P18

    K35.21   Acute appendicitis with generalized peritonitis, with abscess

  ● **K35.3   Acute appendicitis with localized peritonitis**

    K35.30   Acute appendicitis with localized peritonitis, without perforation or gangrene
        Acute appendicitis with localized peritonitis NOS

    K35.31   Acute appendicitis with localized peritonitis and gangrene, without perforation

    K35.32   Acute appendicitis with perforation and localized peritonitis, without abscess
        (Acute) appendicitis with perforation NOS
        Perforated appendix NOS
        Ruptured appendix (with localized peritonitis) NOS
        Coding Clinic: 2020, Q1, P16; 2018, Q4, P18

    K35.33   Acute appendicitis with perforation and localized peritonitis, with abscess
        (Acute) appendicitis with (peritoneal) abscess NOS
        Ruptured appendix with localized peritonitis and abscess

  ● **K35.8   Other and unspecified acute appendicitis**

    K35.80   Unspecified acute appendicitis
        Acute appendicitis NOS
        Acute appendicitis without (localized) (generalized) peritonitis

    ● **K35.89   Other acute appendicitis**

        K35.890   Other acute appendicitis without perforation or gangrene

        K35.891   Other acute appendicitis without perforation, with gangrene
            (Acute) appendicitis with gangrene NOS

K36   Other appendicitis
    Chronic appendicitis
    Recurrent appendicitis

K37   Unspecified appendicitis

    Excludes1   -unspecified appendicitis with peritonitis (K35.2-, K35.3)

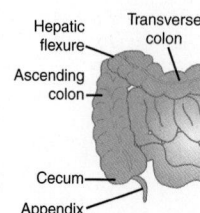

Figure 11-8   Acute appendicitis is the inflammation of the appendix, usually associated with obstruction. Most often this is a disease of adolescents and young adults.

Hepatic flexure — Transverse colon — Ascending colon — Cecum — Appendix

---

Item 11–10   Achlorhydria, also known as gastric anacidity, is the absence of gastric acid.

▶ New   ➠ Revised   ~~deleted~~ Deleted   Excludes 1   Excludes 2   Includes   Use additional   Code first   Code also   Key words

OGCR Official Guidelines   X Assign placeholder X   ● Use Additional Character(s)   ▶ Manifestation Code   🔒 Hierarchical Condition Category   Coding Clinic

● **K38**   **Other diseases of appendix**

     K38.0   **Hyperplasia of appendix**

     K38.1   **Appendicular concretions**
         Fecalith of appendix
         Stercolith of appendix

     K38.2   **Diverticulum of appendix**

     K38.3   **Fistula of appendix**

     K38.8   **Other specified diseases of appendix**
         Intussusception of appendix

     K38.9   **Disease of appendix, unspecified**

HERNIA (K40-K46)

Note: Hernia with both gangrene and obstruction is classified to hernia with gangrene.

> **Includes**   acquired hernia
>   congenital [except diaphragmatic or hiatus] hernia
>   recurrent hernia

● **K40**   **Inguinal hernia**

> **Includes**   bubonocele
>   direct inguinal hernia
>   double inguinal hernia
>   indirect inguinal hernia
>   inguinal hernia NOS
>   oblique inguinal hernia
>   scrotal hernia

● **K40.0**   **Bilateral inguinal hernia, with obstruction, without gangrene**
     Inguinal hernia (bilateral) causing obstruction without gangrene
     Incarcerated inguinal hernia (bilateral) without gangrene
     Irreducible inguinal hernia (bilateral) without gangrene
     Strangulated inguinal hernia (bilateral) without gangrene

     K40.00   **Bilateral inguinal hernia, with obstruction, without gangrene, not specified as recurrent**
         Bilateral inguinal hernia, with obstruction, without gangrene NOS

     K40.01   **Bilateral inguinal hernia, with obstruction, without gangrene, recurrent**

● **K40.1**   **Bilateral inguinal hernia, with gangrene**

     K40.10   **Bilateral inguinal hernia, with gangrene, not specified as recurrent**
         Bilateral inguinal hernia, with gangrene NOS

     K40.11   **Bilateral inguinal hernia, with gangrene, recurrent**

● **K40.2**   **Bilateral inguinal hernia, without obstruction or gangrene**

     K40.20   **Bilateral inguinal hernia, without obstruction or gangrene, not specified as recurrent**
         Bilateral inguinal hernia NOS

     K40.21   **Bilateral inguinal hernia, without obstruction or gangrene, recurrent**

● **K40.3**   **Unilateral inguinal hernia, with obstruction, without gangrene**
     Inguinal hernia (unilateral) causing obstruction without gangrene
     Incarcerated inguinal hernia (unilateral) without gangrene
     Irreducible inguinal hernia (unilateral) without gangrene
     Strangulated inguinal hernia (unilateral) without gangrene

     K40.30   **Unilateral inguinal hernia, with obstruction, without gangrene, not specified as recurrent**
         Inguinal hernia, with obstruction NOS
         Unilateral inguinal hernia, with obstruction, without gangrene NOS

     K40.31   **Unilateral inguinal hernia, with obstruction, without gangrene, recurrent**

Item 11-11   **Hernias** of the groin are the most common type, accounting for 80 percent of all hernias. There are two major types of inguinal hernias: indirect (oblique) affecting men only and direct. **Indirect inguinal hernias** result when the intestines emerge through the abdominal wall in an indirect fashion through the inguinal canal. **Direct inguinal hernias** penetrate through the abdominal wall in a direct fashion. **Femoral hernias** occur at the femoral ring where the femoral vessels enter the thigh and is most common in women. An abdominal wall hernia is also called a ventral or epigastric hernia and occurs in both sexes. Classification is based on location of the hernia and whether there is obstruction or gangrene.

     Ventral, epigastric, or incisional hernia occurs on the abdominal surface caused by musculature weakness or a tear at a previous surgical site and is evidenced by a bulge that changes in size, becoming larger with exertion. An **incarcerated** hernia is one in which the intestines become trapped in the hernia. A **strangulated** hernia is one in which the blood supply to the intestines is lost. **Hiatal hernia** occurs when a loop of the stomach protrudes upward through the small opening in the diaphragm through which the esophagus passes, leaving the abdominal cavity and entering the chest. It occurs in both sexes.

Figure 11-9   Inguinal hernias are those that are located in the inguinal , or iliac areas of the abdomen.

● **K40.4**   **Unilateral inguinal hernia, with gangrene**

     K40.40   **Unilateral inguinal hernia, with gangrene, not specified as recurrent**
         Inguinal hernia with gangrene NOS
         Unilateral inguinal hernia with gangrene NOS

     K40.41   **Unilateral inguinal hernia, with gangrene, recurrent**

● **K40.9**   **Unilateral inguinal hernia, without obstruction or gangrene**

     K40.90   **Unilateral inguinal hernia, without obstruction or gangrene, not specified as recurrent**
         Inguinal hernia NOS
         Unilateral inguinal hernia NOS

     K40.91   **Unilateral inguinal hernia, without obstruction or gangrene, recurrent**

● **K41**   **Femoral hernia**

● **K41.0**   **Bilateral femoral hernia, with obstruction, without gangrene**
     Femoral hernia (bilateral) causing obstruction, without gangrene
     Incarcerated femoral hernia (bilateral), without gangrene
     Irreducible femoral hernia (bilateral), without gangrene
     Strangulated femoral hernia (bilateral), without gangrene

     K41.00   **Bilateral femoral hernia, with obstruction, without gangrene, not specified as recurrent**
         Bilateral femoral hernia, with obstruction, without gangrene NOS

     K41.01   **Bilateral femoral hernia, with obstruction, without gangrene, recurrent**

● **K41.1**   **Bilateral femoral hernia, with gangrene**
    K41.10   Bilateral femoral hernia, with gangrene, not specified as recurrent
         Bilateral femoral hernia, with gangrene NOS
    K41.11   Bilateral femoral hernia, with gangrene, recurrent

● **K41.2**   **Bilateral femoral hernia, without obstruction or gangrene**
    K41.20   Bilateral femoral hernia, without obstruction or gangrene, not specified as recurrent
         Bilateral femoral hernia NOS
    K41.21   Bilateral femoral hernia, without obstruction or gangrene, recurrent

● **K41.3**   **Unilateral femoral hernia, with obstruction, without gangrene**
       Femoral hernia (unilateral) causing obstruction, without gangrene
       Incarcerated femoral hernia (unilateral), without gangrene
       Irreducible femoral hernia (unilateral), without gangrene
       Strangulated femoral hernia (unilateral), without gangrene
    K41.30   Unilateral femoral hernia, with obstruction, without gangrene, not specified as recurrent
         Femoral hernia, with obstruction NOS
         Unilateral femoral hernia, with obstruction NOS
    K41.31   Unilateral femoral hernia, with obstruction, without gangrene, recurrent

● **K41.4**   **Unilateral femoral hernia, with gangrene**
    K41.40   Unilateral femoral hernia, with gangrene, not specified as recurrent
         Femoral hernia, with gangrene NOS
         Unilateral femoral hernia, with gangrene NOS
    K41.41   Unilateral femoral hernia, with gangrene, recurrent

● **K41.9**   **Unilateral femoral hernia, without obstruction or gangrene**
    K41.90   Unilateral femoral hernia, without obstruction or gangrene, not specified as recurrent
         Femoral hernia NOS
         Unilateral femoral hernia NOS
    K41.91   Unilateral femoral hernia, without obstruction or gangrene, recurrent

● **K42**   **Umbilical hernia**
    Includes   paraumbilical hernia
    Excludes1   omphalocele (Q79.2)
    K42.0   **Umbilical hernia with obstruction, without gangrene**
       Umbilical hernia causing obstruction, without gangrene
       Incarcerated umbilical hernia, without gangrene
       Irreducible umbilical hernia, without gangrene
       Strangulated umbilical hernia, without gangrene
    K42.1   **Umbilical hernia with gangrene**
       Gangrenous umbilical hernia
    K42.9   **Umbilical hernia without obstruction or gangrene**
       Umbilical hernia NOS

● **K43**   **Ventral hernia**
    K43.0   **Incisional hernia with obstruction, without gangrene**
       Incisional hernia causing obstruction, without gangrene
       Incarcerated incisional hernia, without gangrene
       Irreducible incisional hernia, without gangrene
       Strangulated incisional hernia, without gangrene
    K43.1   **Incisional hernia with gangrene**
       Gangrenous incisional hernia
    K43.2   **Incisional hernia without obstruction or gangrene**
       Incisional hernia NOS

    K43.3   **Parastomal hernia with obstruction, without gangrene**
       Incarcerated parastomal hernia, without gangrene
       Irreducible parastomal hernia, without gangrene
       Parastomal hernia causing obstruction, without gangrene
       Strangulated parastomal hernia, without gangrene
    K43.4   **Parastomal hernia with gangrene**
       Gangrenous parastomal hernia
    K43.5   **Parastomal hernia without obstruction or gangrene**
       Parastomal hernia NOS
    K43.6   **Other and unspecified ventral hernia with obstruction, without gangrene**
       Epigastric hernia causing obstruction, without gangrene
       Hypogastric hernia causing obstruction, without gangrene
       Incarcerated epigastric hernia without gangrene
       Incarcerated hypogastric hernia without gangrene
       Incarcerated midline hernia without gangrene
       Incarcerated spigelian hernia without gangrene
       Incarcerated subxiphoid hernia without gangrene
       Irreducible epigastric hernia without gangrene
       Irreducible hypogastric hernia without gangrene
       Irreducible midline hernia without gangrene
       Irreducible spigelian hernia without gangrene
       Irreducible subxiphoid hernia without gangrene
       Midline hernia causing obstruction, without gangrene
       Spigelian hernia causing obstruction, without gangrene
       Strangulated epigastric hernia without gangrene
       Strangulated hypogastric hernia without gangrene
       Strangulated midline hernia without gangrene
       Strangulated spigelian hernia without gangrene
       Strangulated subxiphoid hernia without gangrene
       Subxiphoid hernia causing obstruction, without gangrene
    K43.7   **Other and unspecified ventral hernia with gangrene**
       Any condition listed under K43.6 specified as gangrenous
    K43.9   **Ventral hernia without obstruction or gangrene**
       Epigastric hernia
       Ventral hernia NOS

● **K44**   **Diaphragmatic hernia**
    Includes   hiatus hernia (esophageal) (sliding)
          paraesophageal hernia
    Excludes1   congenital diaphragmatic hernia (Q79.0)
          congenital hiatus hernia (Q40.1)
    K44.0   **Diaphragmatic hernia with obstruction, without gangrene**
       Diaphragmatic hernia causing obstruction
       Incarcerated diaphragmatic hernia
       Irreducible diaphragmatic hernia
       Strangulated diaphragmatic hernia
    K44.1   **Diaphragmatic hernia with gangrene**
       Gangrenous diaphragmatic hernia
    K44.9   **Diaphragmatic hernia without obstruction or gangrene**
       Diaphragmatic hernia NOS
       Coding Clinic: 2017, Q1, P7

● **K45**   **Other abdominal hernia**
    Includes   abdominal hernia, specified site NEC
          lumbar hernia
          obturator hernia
          pudendal hernia
          retroperitoneal hernia
          sciatic hernia
    K45.0   **Other specified abdominal hernia with obstruction, without gangrene**
       Other specified abdominal hernia causing obstruction
       Other specified incarcerated abdominal hernia
       Other specified irreducible abdominal hernia
       Other specified strangulated abdominal hernia
    K45.1   **Other specified abdominal hernia with gangrene**
       Any condition listed under K45 specified as gangrenous
    K45.8   **Other specified abdominal hernia without obstruction or gangrene**

▶ New   ⇒ Revised   ~~deleted~~ Deleted   Excludes 1   Excludes 2   Includes   Use additional   Code first   Code also   Key words
OGCR Official Guidelines   **X** Assign placeholder X   ● Use Additional Character(s)   ▷ Manifestation Code   ⦿ Hierarchical Condition Category   **Coding Clinic**

● **K46   Unspecified abdominal hernia**

      Includes   enterocele
                    epiplocele
                    hernia NOS
                    interstitial hernia
                    intestinal hernia
                    intra-abdominal hernia

      Excludes1   vaginal enterocele (N81.5)

    K46.0   Unspecified abdominal hernia with obstruction, without gangrene
             Unspecified abdominal hernia causing obstruction
             Unspecified incarcerated abdominal hernia
             Unspecified irreducible abdominal hernia
             Unspecified strangulated abdominal hernia

    K46.1   Unspecified abdominal hernia with gangrene
             Any condition listed under K46 specified as gangrenous

    K46.9   Unspecified abdominal hernia without obstruction or gangrene
             Abdominal hernia NOS

★ **(See Plate 32 of the Anatomy Illustrations.)**

NONINFECTIVE ENTERITIS AND COLITIS (K50-K52)

      Includes   noninfective inflammatory bowel disease
      Excludes1   irritable bowel syndrome (K58.-)
                   megacolon (K59.3-)

● **K50   Crohn's disease [regional enteritis]**
      Includes   granulomatous enteritis
      Use additional code to identify manifestations, such as:
          pyoderma gangrenosum (L88)
      Excludes1   ulcerative colitis (K51.-)

 ● **K50.0   Crohn's disease of small intestine**
             Crohn's disease [regional enteritis] of duodenum
             Crohn's disease [regional enteritis] of ileum
             Crohn's disease [regional enteritis] of jejunum
             Regional ileitis
             Terminal ileitis
        Excludes1   Crohn's disease of both small and large intestine (K50.8-)

      K50.00   Crohn's disease of small intestine without complications 🔲

   ● **K50.01   Crohn's disease of small intestine with complications**

        K50.011   Crohn's disease of small intestine with rectal bleeding 🔲

        K50.012   Crohn's disease of small intestine with intestinal obstruction 🔲

        K50.013   Crohn's disease of small intestine with fistula 🔲

        K50.014   Crohn's disease of small intestine with abscess 🔲
                 Coding Clinic: 2012, Q4, P104

        K50.018   Crohn's disease of small intestine with other complication 🔲

        K50.019   Crohn's disease of small intestine with unspecified complications 🔲

Item 11-12   Crohn's disease, also known as **regional enteritis,** is a chronic inflammatory disease of the intestines. Classification is based on location in the small (duodenum, ileum, jejunum) or large (cecum, colon, rectum, anal canal) intestine.

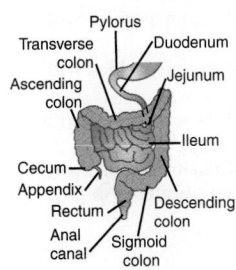

Figure 11-10   Small and large intestines.

● **K50.1   Crohn's disease of large intestine**
          Crohn's disease [regional enteritis] of colon
         Crohn's disease [regional enteritis] of large bowel
         Crohn's disease [regional enteritis] of rectum
         Granulomatous colitis
         Regional colitis
      Excludes1   Crohn's disease of both small and large intestine (K50.8)

    K50.10   Crohn's disease of large intestine without complications 🔲

 ● **K50.11   Crohn's disease of large intestine with complications**

      K50.111   Crohn's disease of large intestine with rectal bleeding 🔲

      K50.112   Crohn's disease of large intestine with intestinal obstruction 🔲

      K50.113   Crohn's disease of large intestine with fistula 🔲

      K50.114   Crohn's disease of large intestine with abscess 🔲
               Coding Clinic: 2012, Q4, P104

      K50.118   Crohn's disease of large intestine with other complication 🔲

      K50.119   Crohn's disease of large intestine with unspecified complications 🔲

● **K50.8   Crohn's disease of both small and large intestine**

    K50.80   Crohn's disease of both small and large intestine without complications 🔲

 ● **K50.81   Crohn's disease of both small and large intestine with complications**

      K50.811   Crohn's disease of both small and large intestine with rectal bleeding 🔲

      K50.812   Crohn's disease of both small and large intestine with intestinal obstruction 🔲

      K50.813   Crohn's disease of both small and large intestine with fistula 🔲

      K50.814   Crohn's disease of both small and large intestine with abscess 🔲
               Coding Clinic: 2012, Q4, P104

      K50.818   Crohn's disease of both small and large intestine with other complication 🔲

      K50.819   Crohn's disease of both small and large intestine with unspecified complications 🔲

● **K50.9   Crohn's disease, unspecified**

    K50.90   Crohn's disease, unspecified, without complications 🔲
             Crohn's disease NOS
             Regional enteritis NOS

 ● **K50.91   Crohn's disease, unspecified, with complications**

      K50.911   Crohn's disease, unspecified, with rectal bleeding 🔲

      K50.912   Crohn's disease, unspecified, with intestinal obstruction 🔲

      K50.913   Crohn's disease, unspecified, with fistula 🔲

      K50.914   Crohn's disease, unspecified, with abscess 🔲
               Coding Clinic: 2012, Q4, P104

      K50.918   Crohn's disease, unspecified, with other complication 🔲

      K50.919   Crohn's disease, unspecified, with unspecified complications 🔲

Item 11–13 Ulcerative colitis attacks the colonic mucosa and forms abscesses. The disease involves the intestines. Classification is based on the location:
- Enterocolitis: large and small intestine
- Ileocolitis: ileum and colon
- Proctitis: rectum
- Proctosigmoiditis: sigmoid colon and rectum

● **K51   Ulcerative colitis**

Use additional code to identify manifestations, such as: pyoderma gangrenosum (L88)

Excludes1   Crohn's disease [regional enteritis] (K50.-)

● **K51.0   Ulcerative (chronic) pancolitis**
Backwash ileitis

     K51.00   Ulcerative (chronic) pancolitis without complications 🦠
         Ulcerative (chronic) pancolitis NOS

    ● **K51.01   Ulcerative (chronic) pancolitis with complications**

         K51.011   Ulcerative (chronic) pancolitis with rectal bleeding 🦠

         K51.012   Ulcerative (chronic) pancolitis with intestinal obstruction 🦠

         K51.013   Ulcerative (chronic) pancolitis with fistula 🦠

         K51.014   Ulcerative (chronic) pancolitis with abscess 🦠

         K51.018   Ulcerative (chronic) pancolitis with other complication 🦠

         K51.019   Ulcerative (chronic) pancolitis with unspecified complications 🦠

● **K51.2   Ulcerative (chronic) proctitis**

     K51.20   Ulcerative (chronic) proctitis without complications 🦠
         Ulcerative (chronic) proctitis NOS

    ● **K51.21   Ulcerative (chronic) proctitis with complications**

         K51.211   Ulcerative (chronic) proctitis with rectal bleeding 🦠

         K51.212   Ulcerative (chronic) proctitis with intestinal obstruction 🦠

         K51.213   Ulcerative (chronic) proctitis with fistula 🦠

         K51.214   Ulcerative (chronic) proctitis with abscess 🦠

         K51.218   Ulcerative (chronic) proctitis with other complication 🦠

         K51.219   Ulcerative (chronic) proctitis with unspecified complications 🦠

● **K51.3   Ulcerative (chronic) rectosigmoiditis**

     K51.30   Ulcerative (chronic) rectosigmoiditis without complications 🦠
         Ulcerative (chronic) rectosigmoiditis NOS

    ● **K51.31   Ulcerative (chronic) rectosigmoiditis with complications**

         K51.311   Ulcerative (chronic) rectosigmoiditis with rectal bleeding 🦠

         K51.312   Ulcerative (chronic) rectosigmoiditis with intestinal obstruction 🦠

         K51.313   Ulcerative (chronic) rectosigmoiditis with fistula 🦠

         K51.314   Ulcerative (chronic) rectosigmoiditis with abscess 🦠

         K51.318   Ulcerative (chronic) rectosigmoiditis with other complication 🦠

         K51.319   Ulcerative (chronic) rectosigmoiditis with unspecified complications 🦠

● **K51.4   Inflammatory polyps of colon**

     Excludes1   adenomatous polyp of colon (D12.6)
         polyposis of colon (D12.6)
         polyps of colon NOS (K63.5)

     K51.40   Inflammatory polyps of colon without complications 🦠
         Inflammatory polyps of colon NOS

    ● **K51.41   Inflammatory polyps of colon with complications**

         K51.411   Inflammatory polyps of colon with rectal bleeding 🦠

         K51.412   Inflammatory polyps of colon with intestinal obstruction 🦠

         K51.413   Inflammatory polyps of colon with fistula 🦠

         K51.414   Inflammatory polyps of colon with abscess 🦠

         K51.418   Inflammatory polyps of colon with other complication 🦠

         K51.419   Inflammatory polyps of colon with unspecified complications 🦠

● **K51.5   Left sided colitis**
Left hemicolitis

     K51.50   Left sided colitis without complications 🦠
         Left sided colitis NOS

    ● **K51.51   Left sided colitis with complications**

         K51.511   Left sided colitis with rectal bleeding 🦠

         K51.512   Left sided colitis with intestinal obstruction 🦠

         K51.513   Left sided colitis with fistula 🦠

         K51.514   Left sided colitis with abscess 🦠

         K51.518   Left sided colitis with other complication 🦠

         K51.519   Left sided colitis with unspecified complications 🦠

● **K51.8   Other ulcerative colitis**

     K51.80   Other ulcerative colitis without complications 🦠

    ● **K51.81   Other ulcerative colitis with complications**

         K51.811   Other ulcerative colitis with rectal bleeding 🦠

         K51.812   Other ulcerative colitis with intestinal obstruction 🦠

         K51.813   Other ulcerative colitis with fistula 🦠

         K51.814   Other ulcerative colitis with abscess 🦠

         K51.818   Other ulcerative colitis with other complication 🦠

         K51.819   Other ulcerative colitis with unspecified complications 🦠

● **K51.9   Ulcerative colitis, unspecified**

     K51.90   Ulcerative colitis, unspecified, without complications 🦠

    ● **K51.91   Ulcerative colitis, unspecified, with complications**

         K51.911   Ulcerative colitis, unspecified with rectal bleeding 🦠

         K51.912   Ulcerative colitis, unspecified with intestinal obstruction 🦠

         K51.913   Ulcerative colitis, unspecified with fistula 🦠

         K51.914   Ulcerative colitis, unspecified with abscess 🦠

         K51.918   Ulcerative colitis, unspecified with other complication 🦠

         K51.919   Ulcerative colitis, unspecified with unspecified complications 🦠

▶ New   ⇒ Revised   ~~deleted~~ Deleted   Excludes 1   Excludes 2   Includes   Use additional   Code first   Code also   Key words

OGCR Official Guidelines   X Assign placeholder X   ● Use Additional Character(s)   ▸ Manifestation Code   🦠 Hierarchical Condition Category   **Coding Clinic**

● **K52**   **Other and unspecified noninfective gastroenteritis and colitis**

   K52.0   **Gastroenteritis and colitis due to radiation**

   K52.1   **Toxic gastroenteritis and colitis**
      Drug-induced gastroenteritis and colitis
      Code first (T51-T65) to identify toxic agent
      Use additional code for adverse effect, if applicable, to identify drug (T36-T50 with fifth or sixth character 5)
      Coding Clinic: 2019, Q1, P17

● **K52.2**   **Allergic and dietetic gastroenteritis and colitis**
      Food hypersensitivity gastroenteritis or colitis
      Use additional code to identify type of food allergy (Z91.01-, Z91.02-)
      Excludes2   allergic eosinophilic colitis (K52.82)
                        allergic eosinophilic esophagitis (K20.0)
                        allergic eosinophilic gastritis (K52.81)
                        allergic eosinophilic gastroenteritis (K52.81)
                        food protein-induced proctocolitis (K52.82)
      Coding Clinic: 2016, Q4, P30-31

     K52.21   **Food protein-induced enterocolitis syndrome**
         FPIES
         Use additional code for hypovolemic shock, if present (R57.1)

     K52.22   **Food protein-induced enteropathy**

     K52.29   **Other allergic and dietetic gastroenteritis and colitis**
         Food hypersensitivity gastroenteritis or colitis
         Immediate gastrointestinal hypersensitivity

   K52.3   **Indeterminate colitis**
      Colonic inflammatory bowel disease unclassified (IBDU)
      Excludes1   unspecified colitis (K52.9)

● **K52.8**   **Other specified noninfective gastroenteritis and colitis**

     K52.81   **Eosinophilic gastritis or gastroenteritis**
         Eosinophilic enteritis
         Excludes2   eosinophilic esophagitis (K20.0)

     K52.82   **Eosinophilic colitis**
         Allergic proctocolitis
         Food-induced eosinophilic proctocolitis
         Food protein-induced proctocolitis
         Milk protein-induced proctocolitis

   ● **K52.83**   **Microscopic colitis**
         Coding Clinic: 2016, Q4, P30-31

       K52.831   **Collagenous colitis**

       K52.832   **Lymphocytic colitis**

       K52.838   **Other microscopic colitis**

       K52.839   **Microscopic colitis, unspecified**

     K52.89   **Other specified noninfective gastroenteritis and colitis**
         Coding Clinic: 2019, Q1, P21

   K52.9   **Noninfective gastroenteritis and colitis, unspecified**
      Colitis NOS   Ileitis NOS
      Enteritis NOS   Jejunitis NOS
      Gastroenteritis NOS   Sigmoiditis NOS
      Excludes1   diarrhea NOS (R19.7)
                        functional diarrhea (K59.1)
                        infectious gastroenteritis and colitis NOS (A09)
                        neonatal diarrhea (noninfective) (P78.3)
                        psychogenic diarrhea (F45.8)

OTHER DISEASES OF INTESTINES (K55-K64)

● **K55**   **Vascular disorders of intestine**
      Excludes1   necrotizing enterocolitis of newborn (P77.-)

● **K55.0**   **Acute vascular disorders of intestine**
      Infarction of appendices epiploicae
      Mesenteric (artery) (vein) embolism
      Mesenteric (artery) (vein) infarction
      Mesenteric (artery) (vein) thrombosis
      Coding Clinic: 2019, Q4, P68

  ● **K55.01**   **Acute (reversible) ischemia of small intestine**
         Coding Clinic: 2016, Q4, P32

       K55.011   **Focal (segmental) acute (reversible) ischemia of small intestine** 🐾

       K55.012   **Diffuse acute (reversible) ischemia of small intestine** 🐾

       K55.019   **Acute (reversible) ischemia of small intestine, extent unspecified** 🐾

  ● **K55.02**   **Acute infarction of small intestine**
         Gangrene of small intestine
         Necrosis of small intestine
         Coding Clinic: 2016, Q4, P32

       K55.021   **Focal (segmental) acute infarction of small intestine** 🐾

       K55.022   **Diffuse acute infarction of small intestine** 🐾

       K55.029   **Acute infarction of small intestine, extent unspecified** 🐾

  ● **K55.03**   **Acute (reversible) ischemia of large intestine**
         Acute fulminant ischemic colitis
         Subacute ischemic colitis
         Coding Clinic: 2016, Q4, P32

       K55.031   **Focal (segmental) acute (reversible) ischemia of large intestine** 🐾

       K55.032   **Diffuse acute (reversible) ischemia of large intestine** 🐾

       K55.039   **Acute (reversible) ischemia of large intestine, extent unspecified** 🐾
          Coding Clinic: 2019, Q4, P68

  ● **K55.04**   **Acute infarction of large intestine**
         Gangrene of large intestine
         Necrosis of large intestine
         Coding Clinic: 2016, Q4, P32

       K55.041   **Focal (segmental) acute infarction of large intestine** 🐾

       K55.042   **Diffuse acute infarction of large intestine** 🐾

       K55.049   **Acute infarction of large intestine, extent unspecified** 🐾

  ● **K55.05**   **Acute (reversible) ischemia of intestine, part unspecified**

       K55.051   **Focal (segmental) acute (reversible) ischemia of intestine, part unspecified** 🐾

       K55.052   **Diffuse acute (reversible) ischemia of intestine, part unspecified** 🐾

       K55.059   **Acute (reversible) ischemia of intestine, part and extent unspecified** 🐾

N Newborn Age: 0   **P** Pediatric Age: 0–17   **M** Maternity DX: 12–55   **A** Adult Age: 15–124   ♀ Females Only   ♂ Males Only

●**K55.06**   **Acute infarction of intestine, part unspecified**
             Acute intestinal infarction
             Gangrene of intestine
             Necrosis of intestine

   K55.061   **Focal (segmental) acute infarction of intestine, part unspecified** 🦠

   K55.062   **Diffuse acute infarction of intestine, part unspecified** 🦠

   K55.069   **Acute infarction of intestine, part and extent unspecified** 🦠

K55.1   **Chronic vascular disorders of intestine** 🦠
             Chronic ischemic colitis
             Chronic ischemic enteritis
             Chronic ischemic enterocolitis
             Ischemic stricture of intestine
             Mesenteric atherosclerosis
             Mesenteric vascular insufficiency

●**K55.2**   **Angiodysplasia of colon**

   K55.20   **Angiodysplasia of colon without hemorrhage**

   K55.21   **Angiodysplasia of colon with hemorrhage**

●**K55.3**   **Necrotizing enterocolitis**

   Excludes1   necrotizing enterocolitis of newborn (P77.-)

   Excludes2   necrotizing enterocolitis due to Clostridium difficile (A04.7-)

   K55.30   **Necrotizing enterocolitis, unspecified** 🦠
             Necrotizing enterocolitis, NOS

   K55.31   **Stage 1 necrotizing enterocolitis** 🦠
             Necrotizing enterocolitis without pneumatosis, without perforation
             Coding Clinic: 2016, Q4, P32

   K55.32   **Stage 2 necrotizing enterocolitis** 🦠
             Necrotizing enterocolitis with pneumatosis, without perforation
             Coding Clinic: 2016, Q4, P32

   K55.33   **Stage 3 necrotizing enterocolitis** 🦠
             Necrotizing enterocolitis with perforation
             Necrotizing enterocolitis with pneumatosis and perforation
             Coding Clinic: 2016, Q4, P32

K55.8   **Other vascular disorders of intestine** 🦠

K55.9   **Vascular disorder of intestine, unspecified** 🦠
             Ischemic colitis
             Ischemic enteritis
             Ischemic enterocolitis

●**K56**   **Paralytic ileus and intestinal obstruction without hernia**

   Excludes1   congenital stricture or stenosis of intestine (Q41-Q42)
                   cystic fibrosis with meconium ileus (E84.11)
                   ischemic stricture of intestine (K55.1)
                   meconium ileus NOS (P76.0)
                   neonatal intestinal obstructions classifiable to P76.-
                   obstruction of duodenum (K31.5)
                   postprocedural intestinal obstruction (K91.3-)
                   ~~stenosis of anus or rectum (K62.4)~~

   ▶ **Excludes2**   stenosis of anus or rectum (K62.4)

K56.0   **Paralytic ileus** 🦠
             Paralysis of bowel
             Paralysis of colon
             Paralysis of intestine
   Excludes1   gallstone ileus (K56.3)
                   ileus NOS (K56.7)
                   obstructive ileus NOS (K56.69-)

K56.1   **Intussusception** 🦠
             Intussusception or invagination of bowel
             Intussusception or invagination of colon
             Intussusception or invagination of intestine
             Intussusception or invagination of rectum
   Excludes2   intussusception of appendix (K38.8)

Figure 11-11   Types of intussusception.

Item 11–14   Intussusception is the prolapse (telescoping) of a part of the intestine into another adjacent part of the intestine. Intussusception may be enteric (ileoileal, jejunoileal, jejunojejunal), colic (colocolic), or intracolic (ileocecal, ileocolic).

Item 11–15   Volvulus is the twisting of a segment of the intestine, resulting in obstruction. Paralytic ileus is paralysis of the intestine. It need not be a complete paralysis, but it must prohibit the passage of food through the intestine and lead to intestinal blockage. It is a common aftermath of some types of surgery.

K56.2   **Volvulus** 🦠
             Strangulation of colon or intestine
             Torsion of colon or intestine
             Twist of colon or intestine
   Excludes2   volvulus of duodenum (K31.5)

K56.3   **Gallstone ileus** 🦠
             Obstruction of intestine by gallstone

●**K56.4**   **Other impaction of intestine**

   K56.41   **Fecal impaction** 🦠
      Excludes1   constipation (K59.0-)
                      incomplete defecation (R15.0)

   K56.49   **Other impaction of intestine** 🦠

●**K56.5**   **Intestinal adhesions [bands] with obstruction (postinfection)**
             Abdominal hernia due to adhesions with obstruction
             Peritoneal adhesions [bands] with intestinal obstruction (postinfection)

   K56.50   **Intestinal adhesions [bands], unspecified as to partial versus complete obstruction** 🦠
             Intestinal adhesions with obstruction NOS

   K56.51   **Intestinal adhesions [bands], with partial obstruction** 🦠
             Intestinal adhesions with incomplete obstruction

   K56.52   **Intestinal adhesions [bands] with complete obstruction** 🦠

●**K56.6**   **Other and unspecified intestinal obstruction**

   ●**K56.60**   **Unspecified intestinal obstruction**
      ~~**Excludes1**   intestinal obstruction due to specified condition-code to condition~~

      Coding Clinic: 2017, Q2, P12

      K56.600   **Partial intestinal obstruction, unspecified as to cause** 🦠
                Incomplete intestinal obstruction, NOS

      K56.601   **Complete intestinal obstruction, unspecified as to cause** 🦠

      K56.609   **Unspecified intestinal obstruction, unspecified as to partial versus complete obstruction** 🦠
                Intestinal obstruction NOS

▶ New   ⇒ Revised   ~~deleted~~ Deleted   Excludes 1   Excludes 2   Includes   Use additional   Code first   Code also   Key words
OGCR Official Guidelines   X Assign placeholder X   ● Use Additional Character(s)   ▶ Manifestation Code   🦠 Hierarchical Condition Category   **Coding Clinic**

● **K56.69** **Other intestinal obstruction**
Enterostenosis NOS
Obstructive ileus NOS
Occlusion of colon or intestine NOS
Stenosis of colon or intestine NOS
Stricture of colon or intestine NOS

> **Excludes1** intestinal obstruction due to
specified condition-code to
condition
>
> **Coding Clinic: 2017, Q2, P12**

 K56.690 **Other partial intestinal obstruction** 🔗
Other incomplete intestinal
obstruction

 K56.691 **Other complete intestinal
obstruction** 🔗

 K56.699 **Other intestinal obstruction
unspecified as to partial versus
complete obstruction** 🔗
Other intestinal obstruction, NEC

K56.7 **Ileus, unspecified** 🔗

> **Excludes1** obstructive ileus (K56.69-)
>
> **Excludes2** intestinal obstruction with hernia
(K40-K46)
>
> **Coding Clinic: 2017, Q1, P41**

● **K57** **Diverticular disease of intestine**
Code also if applicable peritonitis K65.-

> **Excludes1** congenital diverticulum of intestine (Q43.8)
Meckel's diverticulum (Q43.0)
>
> **Excludes2** diverticulum of appendix (K38.2)

● **K57.0** **Diverticulitis of small intestine with perforation and
abscess**
~~Diverticulitis of small intestine with peritonitis~~

> **Excludes1** diverticulitis of both small and large
intestine with perforation and
abscess (K57.4-)

 K57.00 **Diverticulitis of small intestine with
perforation and abscess without bleeding**

 K57.01 **Diverticulitis of small intestine with
perforation and abscess with bleeding**

● **K57.1** **Diverticular disease of small intestine without
perforation or abscess**

> **Excludes1** diverticular disease of both small and
large intestine without perforation or
abscess (K57.5-)

 K57.10 **Diverticulosis of small intestine without
perforation or abscess without bleeding**
Diverticular disease of small intestine NOS

 K57.11 **Diverticulosis of small intestine without
perforation or abscess with bleeding**

 K57.12 **Diverticulitis of small intestine without
perforation or abscess without bleeding**

 K57.13 **Diverticulitis of small intestine without
perforation or abscess with bleeding**

● **K57.2** **Diverticulitis of large intestine with perforation and
abscess**
~~Diverticulitis of colon with peritonitis~~

> **Excludes1** diverticulitis of both small and large
intestine with perforation and
abscess (K57.4-)

 K57.20 **Diverticulitis of large intestine with perforation
and abscess without bleeding**

 K57.21 **Diverticulitis of large intestine with perforation
and abscess with bleeding**

Figure 11-12 Diverticulosis. (From Shiland: Mastering Healthcare
Terminology, ed 4, St. Louis, Mosby, 2012)

Item 11-16 **Diverticula** of the intestines are acquired herniations of the
mucosa. Diverticulum (singular): Pocket or pouch that bulges outward through
a weak spot (herniation) in the colon. Diverticula (plural). **Diverticulosis** is
the condition of having diverticula. **Diverticulitis** is inflammation of these
pouches or herniations. Classification is based on location (small intestine or
colon) and whether it occurs with or without hemorrhage.

● **K57.3** **Diverticular disease of large intestine without
perforation or abscess**

> **Excludes1** diverticular disease of both small and
large intestine without perforation or
abscess (K57.5-)

 K57.30 **Diverticulosis of large intestine without
perforation or abscess without bleeding**
Diverticular disease of colon NOS

 K57.31 **Diverticulosis of large intestine without
perforation or abscess with bleeding**

 K57.32 **Diverticulitis of large intestine without
perforation or abscess without bleeding**

 K57.33 **Diverticulitis of large intestine without
perforation or abscess with bleeding**

● **K57.4** **Diverticulitis of both small and large intestine with
perforation and abscess**
~~Diverticulitis of both small and large intestine with
peritonitis~~

 K57.40 **Diverticulitis of both small and large intestine
with perforation and abscess without bleeding**

 K57.41 **Diverticulitis of both small and large intestine
with perforation and abscess with bleeding**

● **K57.5** **Diverticular disease of both small and large intestine
without perforation or abscess**

 K57.50 **Diverticulosis of both small and large intestine
without perforation or abscess without
bleeding**
Diverticular disease of both small and large
intestine NOS

 K57.51 **Diverticulosis of both small and large intestine
without perforation or abscess with bleeding**

 K57.52 **Diverticulitis of both small and large intestine
without perforation or abscess without
bleeding**

 K57.53 **Diverticulitis of both small and large intestine
without perforation or abscess with bleeding**

● **K57.8** **Diverticulitis of intestine, part unspecified, with
perforation and abscess**
~~Diverticulitis of intestine NOS with peritonitis~~

 K57.80 **Diverticulitis of intestine, part unspecified,
with perforation and abscess without bleeding**

 K57.81 **Diverticulitis of intestine, part unspecified,
with perforation and abscess with bleeding**

● **K57.9**   **Diverticular disease of intestine, part unspecified, without perforation or abscess**

     K57.90   **Diverticulosis of intestine, part unspecified, without perforation or abscess without bleeding**
         Diverticular disease of intestine NOS

     K57.91   **Diverticulosis of intestine, part unspecified, without perforation or abscess with bleeding**

     K57.92   **Diverticulitis of intestine, part unspecified, without perforation or abscess without bleeding**

     K57.93   **Diverticulitis of intestine, part unspecified, without perforation or abscess with bleeding**

● **K58**   **Irritable bowel syndrome**

     Includes   irritable colon
                   spastic colon

     K58.0   **Irritable bowel syndrome with diarrhea**

     K58.1   **Irritable bowel syndrome with constipation**
         Coding Clinic: 2016, Q4, P32

     K58.2   **Mixed irritable bowel syndrome**
         Coding Clinic: 2016, Q4, P32

     K58.8   **Other irritable bowel syndrome**
         Coding Clinic: 2016, Q4, P32

     K58.9   **Irritable bowel syndrome without diarrhea**
         Irritable bowel syndrome NOS

● **K59**   **Other functional intestinal disorders**

     Excludes1   change in bowel habit NOS (R19.4)
                 intestinal malabsorption (K90.-)
                 psychogenic intestinal disorders (F45.8)

     Excludes2   functional disorders of stomach (K31.-)

●   **K59.0**   **Constipation**

         Excludes1   fecal impaction (K56.41)
                     incomplete defecation (R15.0)

         K59.00   **Constipation, unspecified**

         K59.01   **Slow transit constipation**

         K59.02   **Outlet dysfunction constipation**

         K59.03   **Drug induced constipation**
               Use additional code for adverse effect, if applicable, to identify drug (T36-T50 with fifth or sixth character 5)
               Coding Clinic: 2016, Q4, P33

         K59.04   **Chronic idiopathic constipation**
               Functional constipation
               Coding Clinic: 2016, Q4, P33

         K59.09   **Other constipation**
               Chronic constipation

     K59.1   **Functional diarrhea**

         Excludes1   diarrhea NOS (R19.7)
                    irritable bowel syndrome with diarrhea (K58.0)

     K59.2   **Neurogenic bowel, not elsewhere classified**

●   **K59.3**   **Megacolon, not elsewhere classified**
         Dilatation of colon

         Code first, if applicable (T51-T65) to identify toxic agent

         Excludes1   congenital megacolon (aganglionic) (Q43.1)
                  megacolon (due to) (in) Chagas' disease (B57.32)
                  megacolon (due to) (in) Clostridium difficile (A04.7-)
                  megacolon (due to) (in) Hirschsprung's disease (Q43.1)

         Coding Clinic: 2016, Q4, P33

         K59.31   **Toxic megacolon** 🅗🅒

         K59.39   **Other megacolon**
               Megacolon NOS

     K59.4   **Anal spasm**
         Proctalgia fugax

Item 11-17   A **fissure** is a groove in the surface, whereas a **fistula** is an abnormal passage. An **abscess** is an accumulation of pus in a tissue cavity resulting from a bacterial or parasitic infection.

● **K59.8**   **Other specified functional intestinal disorders**
     ~~Atony of colon~~
     ~~Pseudo-obstruction (acute) (chronic) of intestine~~

     ▶ **K59.81 Ogilvie syndrome**
         ▶ Acute colonic pseudo-obstruction (ACPO)

     ▶ **K59.89 Other specified functional intestinal disorders**
         ▶ Atony of colon
         ▶ Pseudo-obstruction (acute) (chronic) of intestine

     K59.9   **Functional intestinal disorder, unspecified**

● **K60**   **Fissure and fistula of anal and rectal regions**

     Excludes1   fissure and fistula of anal and rectal regions with abscess or cellulitis (K61.-)

     Excludes2   anal sphincter tear (healed) (nontraumatic) (old) (K62.81)

     K60.0   **Acute anal fissure**

     K60.1   **Chronic anal fissure**

     K60.2   **Anal fissure, unspecified**

     K60.3   **Anal fistula**

     K60.4   **Rectal fistula**
         Fistula of rectum to skin

         Excludes1   rectovaginal fistula (N82.3)
                  vesicorectal fistula (N32.1)

     K60.5   **Anorectal fistula**

● **K61**   **Abscess of anal and rectal regions**

     Includes   abscess of anal and rectal regions
                cellulitis of anal and rectal regions

     K61.0   **Anal abscess**
         Perianal abscess

         Excludes2   intrasphincteric abscess (K61.4)

     K61.1   **Rectal abscess**
         Perirectal abscess

         Excludes1   ischiorectal abscess (K61.39)

         Coding Clinic: 2012, Q4, P104

     K61.2   **Anorectal abscess**

     K61.3   **Ischiorectal abscess**

         K61.31   **Horseshoe abscess**

         K61.39   **Other ischiorectal abscess**
               Abscess of ischiorectal fossa
               Ischiorectal abscess, NOS

     K61.4   **Intrasphincteric abscess**
         Intersphincteric abscess

     K61.5   **Supralevator abscess**

● **K62**   **Other diseases of anus and rectum**

     Includes   anal canal

     Excludes2   colostomy and enterostomy malfunction (K94.0-, K91.4-)
                  fecal incontinence (R15.-)
                  hemorrhoids (K64.-)

     K62.0   **Anal polyp**
         Coding Clinic: 2018, Q1, P7

     K62.1   **Rectal polyp**

         Excludes1   adenomatous polyp (D12.8)

         Coding Clinic: 2018, Q1, P7

     K62.2   **Anal prolapse**
         Prolapse of anal canal

     K62.3   **Rectal prolapse**
         Prolapse of rectal mucosa

     K62.4   **Stenosis of anus and rectum**
         Stricture of anus (sphincter)
         Coding Clinic: 2019, Q2, P13

▶ New   ⟹ Revised   ~~deleted~~ Deleted   Excludes 1   Excludes 2   Includes   Use additional   Code first   Code also   Key words

OGCR Official Guidelines   X Assign placeholder X   ● Use Additional Character(s)   ▶ Manifestation Code   🅗🅒 Hierarchical Condition Category   Coding Clinic

K62.5   **Hemorrhage of anus and rectum**
> **Excludes1**   gastrointestinal bleeding NOS (K92.2)
>   melena (K92.1)
>   neonatal rectal hemorrhage (P54.2)

K62.6   **Ulcer of anus and rectum**
> Solitary ulcer of anus and rectum
> Stercoral ulcer of anus and rectum
> > **Excludes1**   fissure and fistula of anus and rectum
> >   (K60.-)
> >   ulcerative colitis (K51.-)

K62.7   **Radiation proctitis**
> ➠Use additional code to identify the type of radiation
>   (W88.-) or radiation therapy (Y84.2)
> **Coding Clinic: 2019, Q1, P21**

● **K62.8**   **Other specified diseases of anus and rectum**
> **Excludes2**   ulcerative proctitis (K51.2)

> **K62.81**   **Anal sphincter tear (healed) (nontraumatic) (old)**
> > Tear of anus, nontraumatic
> > Use additional code for any associated fecal
> >   incontinence (R15.-)
> > > **Excludes2**   anal fissure (K60.-)
> > >   anal sphincter tear (healed)
> > >   (old) complicating delivery
> > >   (O34.7-)
> > >   traumatic tear of anal sphincter
> > >   (S31.831)

> **K62.82**   **Dysplasia of anus**
> > Anal intraepithelial neoplasia I and II (AIN I
> >   and II) (histologically confirmed)
> > Dysplasia of anus NOS
> > Mild and moderate dysplasia of anus
> >   (histologically confirmed)
> > > **Excludes1**   abnormal results from anal
> > >   cytologic examination
> > >   without histologic
> > >   confirmation (R85.61-)
> > >   anal intraepithelial neoplasia III
> > >   (D01.3)
> > >   carcinoma in situ of anus (D01.3)
> > >   HGSIL of anus (R85.613)
> > >   severe dysplasia of anus (D01.3)

> **K62.89**   **Other specified diseases of anus and rectum**
> > Proctitis NOS
> > Use additional code for any associated fecal
> >   incontinence (R15.-)

K62.9   **Disease of anus and rectum, unspecified**

● **K63**   **Other diseases of intestine**

K63.0   **Abscess of intestine**
> > **Excludes1**   abscess of intestine with Crohn's disease
> >   (K50.014, K50.114, K50.814, K50.914)
> >   abscess of intestine with diverticular
> >   disease (K57.0, K57.2, K57.4, K57.8)
> >   abscess of intestine with ulcerative colitis
> >   (K51.014, K51.214, K51.314, K51.414,
> >   K51.514, K51.814, K51.914)
> > **Excludes2**   abscess of anal and rectal regions (K61.-)
> >   abscess of appendix (K35.3-)

K63.1   **Perforation of intestine (nontraumatic)** 🔃
> Perforation (nontraumatic) of rectum
> > **Excludes1**   perforation (nontraumatic) of duodenum
> >   (K26.-)
> >   perforation (nontraumatic) of intestine
> >   with diverticular disease (K57.0,
> >   K57.2, K57.4, K57.8)
> > **Excludes2**   perforation (nontraumatic) of appendix
> >   (K35.2-, K35.3)

K63.2   **Fistula of intestine**
> > **Excludes1**   fistula of duodenum (K31.6)
> >   fistula of intestine with Crohn's disease
> >   (K50.013, K50.113, K50.813, K50.913)
> >   fistula of intestine with ulcerative colitis
> >   (K51.013, K51.213, K51.313, K51.413,
> >   K51.513, K51.813, K51.913)
> > **Excludes2**   fistula of anal and rectal regions (K60.-)
> >   fistula of appendix (K38.3)
> >   intestinal-genital fistula, female
> >   (N82.2-N82.4)
> >   vesicointestinal fistula (N32.1)
> **Coding Clinic: 2017, Q3, P4**

K63.3   **Ulcer of intestine**
> Primary ulcer of small intestine
> > **Excludes1**   duodenal ulcer (K26.-)
> >   gastrointestinal ulcer (K28.-)
> >   gastrojejunal ulcer (K28.-)
> >   jejunal ulcer (K28.-)
> >   peptic ulcer, site unspecified (K27.-)
> >   ulcer of intestine with perforation (K63.1)
> >   ulcer of anus or rectum (K62.6)
> >   ulcerative colitis (K51.-)

K63.4   **Enteroptosis**

K63.5   **Polyp of colon**
> > **Excludes1**   adenomatous polyp of colon (D12.-)
> >   inflammatory polyp of colon (K51.4-)
> >   polyposis of colon (D12.6)
> **Coding Clinic: 2019, Q1, P33; 2017, Q1, P15-16; 2015, Q2, P14**

● **K63.8**   **Other specified diseases of intestine**
> **K63.81**   **Dieulafoy lesion of intestine**
> > **Excludes2**   Dieulafoy lesion of stomach and
> >   duodenum (K31.82)

> **K63.89**   **Other specified diseases of intestine**
> > **Coding Clinic: 2013, Q2, P31**

K63.9   **Disease of intestine, unspecified**

● **K64**   **Hemorrhoids and perianal venous thrombosis**
> **Includes**   piles
> **Excludes1**   hemorrhoids complicating childbirth and the
>   puerperium (O87.2)
>   hemorrhoids complicating pregnancy (O22.4)

K64.0   **First degree hemorrhoids**
> Grade/stage I hemorrhoids
> Hemorrhoids (bleeding) without prolapse outside of
>   anal canal

K64.1   **Second degree hemorrhoids**
> Grade/stage II hemorrhoids
> Hemorrhoids (bleeding) that prolapse with straining,
>   but retract spontaneously

K64.2   **Third degree hemorrhoids**
> Grade/stage III hemorrhoids
> Hemorrhoids (bleeding) that prolapse with straining
>   and require manual replacement back inside anal
>   canal

K64.3   **Fourth degree hemorrhoids**
> Grade/stage IV hemorrhoids
> Hemorrhoids (bleeding) with prolapsed tissue that
>   cannot be manually replaced

K64.4   **Residual hemorrhoidal skin tags**
> External hemorrhoids, NOS
> Skin tags of anus

K64.5   **Perianal venous thrombosis**
> External hemorrhoids with thrombosis
> Perianal hematoma
> Thrombosed hemorrhoids NOS

K64.8   **Other hemorrhoids**
> Internal hemorrhoids, without mention of degree
> Prolapsed hemorrhoids, degree not specified

K64.9   **Unspecified hemorrhoids**
> Hemorrhoids (bleeding) NOS
> Hemorrhoids (bleeding) without mention of degree

N   Newborn Age: 0   **P**   Pediatric Age: 0–17   **M**   Maternity DX: 12–55   **A**   Adult Age: 15–124   ♀   Females Only   ♂   Males Only

CHAPTER 11 (K00-K95)

Item 11–18 Peritonitis is an inflammation of the lining (peritoneum) of the abdominal cavity and surface of the intestines.

DISEASES OF PERITONEUM AND RETROPERITONEUM (K65-K68)

● **K65** **Peritonitis**

Use additional code (B95-B97), to identify infectious agent, if known

Code also if applicable diverticular disease of intestine (K57.-)

Excludes1   acute appendicitis with generalized peritonitis (K35.2-)
aseptic peritonitis (T81.6)
benign paroxysmal peritonitis (E85.0)
chemical peritonitis (T81.6)
gonococcal peritonitis (A54.85)
neonatal peritonitis (P78.0-P78.1)
pelvic peritonitis, female (N73.3-N73.5)
periodic familial peritonitis (E85.0)
peritonitis due to talc or other foreign substance (T81.6)
peritonitis in chlamydia (A74.81)
peritonitis in diphtheria (A36.89)
peritonitis in syphilis (late) (A52.74)
peritonitis in tuberculosis (A18.31)
peritonitis with or following abortion or ectopic or molar pregnancy (O00-O07, O08.0)
peritonitis with or following appendicitis (K35.-)
puerperal peritonitis (O85)
retroperitoneal infections (K68.-)

K65.0 **Generalized (acute) peritonitis** 🅥
Pelvic peritonitis (acute), male
Subphrenic peritonitis (acute)
Suppurative peritonitis (acute)

K65.1 **Peritoneal abscess** 🅥
Abdominopelvic abscess
Abscess (of) omentum
Abscess (of) peritoneum
Mesenteric abscess
Retrocecal abscess
Subdiaphragmatic abscess
Subhepatic abscess
Subphrenic abscess
Coding Clinic: 2019, Q1, P15

K65.2 **Spontaneous bacterial peritonitis** 🅥
Excludes1   bacterial peritonitis NOS (K65.9)

K65.3 **Choleperitonitis** 🅥
Peritonitis due to bile

K65.4 **Sclerosing mesenteritis** 🅥
Fat necrosis of peritoneum
(Idiopathic) sclerosing mesenteric fibrosis
Mesenteric lipodystrophy
Mesenteric panniculitis
Retractile mesenteritis

K65.8 **Other peritonitis** 🅥
Chronic proliferative peritonitis
Peritonitis due to urine

K65.9 **Peritonitis, unspecified** 🅥
Bacterial peritonitis NOS
Coding Clinic: 2013, Q2, P31

● **K66** **Other disorders of peritoneum**

Excludes2   ascites (R18.-)
peritoneal effusion (chronic) (R18.8)

K66.0 **Peritoneal adhesions (postprocedural) (postinfection)**
Adhesions (of) abdominal (wall)
Adhesions (of) diaphragm
Adhesions (of) intestine
Adhesions (of) male pelvis
Adhesions (of) omentum
Adhesions (of) stomach
Adhesive bands
Mesenteric adhesions
Excludes1   female pelvic adhesions [bands] (N73.6)
peritoneal adhesions with intestinal obstruction (K56.5-)

K66.1 **Hemoperitoneum**
Excludes1   traumatic hemoperitoneum (S36.8-)

K66.8 **Other specified disorders of peritoneum**

K66.9 **Disorder of peritoneum, unspecified**

▷ **K67** *Disorders of peritoneum in infectious diseases classified elsewhere* 🅥
Code first underlying disease, such as:
congenital syphilis (A50.0)
helminthiasis (B65.0-B83.9)
Excludes1   peritonitis in chlamydia (A74.81)
peritonitis in diphtheria (A36.89)
peritonitis in gonococcal (A54.85)
peritonitis in syphilis (late) (A52.74)
peritonitis in tuberculosis (A18.31)

● **K68** **Disorders of retroperitoneum**

● **K68.1** **Retroperitoneal abscess**

K68.11 **Postprocedural retroperitoneal abscess**
Excludes2   infection following procedure (T81.44)

K68.12 **Psoas muscle abscess** 🅥

K68.19 **Other retroperitoneal abscess** 🅥
Coding Clinic: 2019, Q1, P15

K68.9 **Other disorders of retroperitoneum**

DISEASES OF LIVER (K70-K77)

Excludes1   jaundice NOS (R17)

Excludes2   hemochromatosis (E83.11-)
Reye's syndrome (G93.7)
viral hepatitis (B15-B19)
Wilson's disease (E83.0)

● **K70** **Alcoholic liver disease**
Use additional code to identify:
alcohol abuse and dependence (F10.-)

K70.0 **Alcoholic fatty liver**   A

● **K70.1** **Alcoholic hepatitis**
K70.10 **Alcoholic hepatitis without ascites**   A
K70.11 **Alcoholic hepatitis with ascites**   A

K70.2 **Alcoholic fibrosis and sclerosis of liver**   A

● **K70.3** **Alcoholic cirrhosis of liver**
Alcoholic cirrhosis NOS
K70.30 **Alcoholic cirrhosis of liver without ascites** 🅥   A
K70.31 **Alcoholic cirrhosis of liver with ascites** 🅥   A
Coding Clinic: 2018, Q1, P5

● **K70.4** **Alcoholic hepatic failure**
Acute alcoholic hepatic failure
Alcoholic hepatic failure NOS
Chronic alcoholic hepatic failure
Subacute alcoholic hepatic failure
K70.40 **Alcoholic hepatic failure without coma** 🅥   A
K70.41 **Alcoholic hepatic failure with coma** 🅥   A

K70.9 **Alcoholic liver disease, unspecified** 🅥   A

Item 11-19 Retroperitoneal infections occur between the posterior parietal peritoneum and posterior abdominal wall where the kidneys, adrenal glands, ureters, duodenum, ascending colon, descending colon, pancreas, and the large vessels and nerves are located.

▶ New   ⇒ Revised   ~~deleted~~ Deleted   Excludes 1   Excludes 2   Includes   Use additional   Code first   Code also   Key words
OGCR Official Guidelines   X Assign placeholder X   ● Use Additional Character(s)   ▷ Manifestation Code   🅥 Hierarchical Condition Category   Coding Clinic

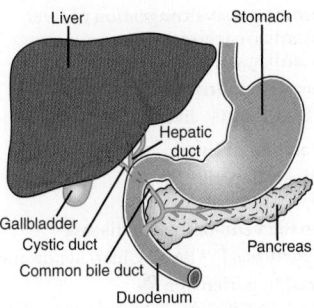

Figure 11-13   Liver and bile ducts.

Item 11-20 Cirrhosis is the progressive fibrosis of the liver resulting in loss of liver function. The main causes of cirrhosis of the liver are alcohol abuse, chronic hepatitis (inflammation of the liver), biliary disease, and excessive amounts of iron. **Alcoholic cirrhosis of the liver** is also called portal, Laënnec's, or fatty nutritional cirrhosis.

● **K71   Toxic liver disease**

     Includes   drug-induced idiosyncratic (unpredictable) liver disease
                   drug-induced toxic (predictable) liver disease

     Code first poisoning due to drug or toxin, if applicable (T36-T65 with fifth or sixth character 1-4 or 6)

     Use additional code for adverse effect, if applicable, to identify drug (T36-T50 with fifth or sixth character 5)

     Excludes2   alcoholic liver disease (K70.-)
                    Budd-Chiari syndrome (I82.0)

   K71.0   Toxic liver disease with cholestasis
        Cholestasis with hepatocyte injury
        'Pure' cholestasis

● **K71.1   Toxic liver disease with hepatic necrosis**
        Hepatic failure (acute) (chronic) due to drugs

     K71.10   Toxic liver disease with hepatic necrosis, without coma

     K71.11   Toxic liver disease with hepatic necrosis, with coma 🝔

   K71.2   Toxic liver disease with acute hepatitis

   K71.3   Toxic liver disease with chronic persistent hepatitis

   K71.4   Toxic liver disease with chronic lobular hepatitis

● **K71.5   Toxic liver disease with chronic active hepatitis**
        Toxic liver disease with lupoid hepatitis

     K71.50   Toxic liver disease with chronic active hepatitis without ascites

     K71.51   Toxic liver disease with chronic active hepatitis with ascites
            Coding Clinic: 2018, Q1, P4

   K71.6   Toxic liver disease with hepatitis, not elsewhere classified

   K71.7   Toxic liver disease with fibrosis and cirrhosis of liver

   K71.8   Toxic liver disease with other disorders of liver
        Toxic liver disease with focal nodular hyperplasia
        Toxic liver disease with hepatic granulomas
        Toxic liver disease with peliosis hepatis
        Toxic liver disease with veno-occlusive disease of liver

   K71.9   Toxic liver disease, unspecified

● **K72   Hepatic failure, not elsewhere classified**

     Includes   fulminant hepatitis NEC, with hepatic failure
                   hepatic encephalopathy NOS
                   liver (cell) necrosis with hepatic failure
                   malignant hepatitis NEC, with hepatic failure
                   yellow liver atrophy or dystrophy

     Excludes1   alcoholic hepatic failure (K70.4)
                    hepatic failure with toxic liver disease (K71.1-)
                    icterus of newborn (P55-P59)
                    postprocedural hepatic failure (K91.82)

     Excludes2   hepatic failure complicating abortion or ectopic or molar pregnancy (O00-O07, O08.8)
                    hepatic failure complicating pregnancy, childbirth and the puerperium (O26.6-)
                    viral hepatitis with hepatic coma (B15-B19)

● **K72.0   Acute and subacute hepatic failure**
        Acute non-viral hepatitis NOS
        Coding Clinic: 2015, Q2, P17

     K72.00   Acute and subacute hepatic failure without coma
            Coding Clinic: 2015, Q2, P17

     K72.01   Acute and subacute hepatic failure with coma 🝔

● **K72.1   Chronic hepatic failure**

     K72.10   Chronic hepatic failure without coma 🝔
            Coding Clinic: 2017, Q1, P41

     K72.11   Chronic hepatic failure with coma 🝔
            Coding Clinic: 2020, Q1, P15

● **K72.9   Hepatic failure, unspecified**

     K72.90   Hepatic failure, unspecified without coma 🝔
            Coding Clinic: 2018, Q4, P21

     K72.91   Hepatic failure, unspecified with coma 🝔
            Hepatic coma NOS
            Coding Clinic: 2016, Q2, P35

● **K73   Chronic hepatitis, not elsewhere classified**

     Excludes1   alcoholic hepatitis (chronic) (K70.1-)
                    drug-induced hepatitis (chronic) (K71.-)
                    granulomatous hepatitis (chronic) NEC (K75.3)
                    reactive, nonspecific hepatitis (chronic) (K75.2)
                    viral hepatitis (chronic) (B15-B19)

   K73.0   Chronic persistent hepatitis, not elsewhere classified 🝔
   K73.1   Chronic lobular hepatitis, not elsewhere classified 🝔
   K73.2   Chronic active hepatitis, not elsewhere classified 🝔
   K73.8   Other chronic hepatitis, not elsewhere classified 🝔
   K73.9   Chronic hepatitis, unspecified 🝔

● **K74   Fibrosis and cirrhosis of liver**

     Code also, if applicable, viral hepatitis (acute) (chronic) (B15-B19)

     Excludes1   alcoholic cirrhosis (of liver) (K70.3)
                    alcoholic fibrosis of liver (K70.2)
                    cardiac sclerosis of liver (K76.1)
                    cirrhosis (of liver) with toxic liver disease (K71.7)
                    congenital cirrhosis (of liver) (P78.81)
                    pigmentary cirrhosis (of liver) (E83.110)

● **K74.0   Hepatic fibrosis**

     ▶ *Code first underlying liver disease, such as:*
       ▶ nonalcoholic steatohepatitis (NASH) (K75.81)

     ▶ **K74.00   Hepatic fibrosis, unspecified**

     ▶ **K74.01   Hepatic fibrosis, early fibrosis**
           ▶ Hepatic fibrosis, stage F1 or stage F2

     ▶ **K74.02   Hepatic fibrosis, advanced fibrosis**
           ▶ Hepatic fibrosis, stage F3

         ▶ **Excludes1**   cirrhosis of liver (K74.6-)
                      ▶ hepatic fibrosis, stage F4 (K74.6-)

   K74.1   Hepatic sclerosis

   K74.2   Hepatic fibrosis with hepatic sclerosis

K74.3 Primary biliary cirrhosis 🅗
Chronic nonsuppurative destructive cholangitis
Primary biliary cholangitis
> **Excludes2**   primary sclerosing cholangitis (K83.01)

K74.4 Secondary biliary cirrhosis 🅗

K74.5 Biliary cirrhosis, unspecified 🅗

● **K74.6 Other and unspecified cirrhosis of liver**

     K74.60 Unspecified cirrhosis of liver 🅗
         Cirrhosis (of liver) NOS
         Coding Clinic: 2018, Q1, P4

     K74.69 Other cirrhosis of liver 🅗
         Cryptogenic cirrhosis (of liver)
         Macronodular cirrhosis (of liver)
         Micronodular cirrhosis (of liver)
         Mixed type cirrhosis (of liver)
         Portal cirrhosis (of liver)
         Postnecrotic cirrhosis (of liver)

● **K75 Other inflammatory liver diseases**
> **Excludes2**   toxic liver disease (K71.-)

K75.0 Abscess of liver
Cholangitic hepatic abscess
Hematogenic hepatic abscess
Hepatic abscess NOS
Lymphogenic hepatic abscess
Pylephlebitic hepatic abscess
> **Excludes1**   amebic liver abscess (A06.4)
>   cholangitis without liver abscess (K83.09)
>   pylephlebitis without liver abscess (K75.1)

> **Excludes2**   acute or subacute hepatitis NOS (B17.9)
>   acute or subacute non-viral hepatitis
>   (K72.0)
>   chronic hepatitis NEC (K73.8)

K75.1 Phlebitis of portal vein
Pylephlebitis
> **Excludes1**   pylephlebitic liver abscess (K75.0)

K75.2 Nonspecific reactive hepatitis
> **Excludes1**   acute or subacute hepatitis (K72.0-)
>   chronic hepatitis NEC (K73.-)
>   viral hepatitis (B15-B19)

K75.3 Granulomatous hepatitis, not elsewhere classified
> **Excludes1**   acute or subacute hepatitis (K72.0-)
>   chronic hepatitis NEC (K73.-)
>   viral hepatitis (B15-B19)

K75.4 Autoimmune hepatitis 🅗
Lupoid hepatitis NEC

● **K75.8 Other specified inflammatory liver diseases**

     K75.81 Nonalcoholic steatohepatitis (NASH)
         ▶Use additional code, if applicable, hepatic
         fibrosis (K74.0-)

     K75.89 Other specified inflammatory liver diseases

K75.9 Inflammatory liver disease, unspecified
Hepatitis NOS
> **Excludes1**   acute or subacute hepatitis (K72.0-)
>   chronic hepatitis NEC (K73.-)
>   viral hepatitis (B15-B19)
> **Coding Clinic: 2015, Q2, P17**

● **K76 Other diseases of liver**
> **Excludes2**   alcoholic liver disease (K70.-)
>   amyloid degeneration of liver (E85.-)
>   cystic disease of liver (congenital) (Q44.6)
>   hepatic vein thrombosis (I82.0)
>   hepatomegaly NOS (R16.0)
>   pigmentary cirrhosis (of liver) (E83.110)
>   portal vein thrombosis (I81)
>   toxic liver disease (K71.-)

K76.0 Fatty (change of) liver, not elsewhere classified
Nonalcoholic fatty liver disease (NAFLD)
> **Excludes1**   nonalcoholic steatohepatitis (NASH)
>   (K75.81)

K76.1 Chronic passive congestion of liver
Cardiac cirrhosis
Cardiac sclerosis

K76.2 Central hemorrhagic necrosis of liver
> **Excludes1**   liver necrosis with hepatic failure (K72.-)

K76.3 Infarction of liver

K76.4 Peliosis hepatis
Hepatic angiomatosis

K76.5 Hepatic veno-occlusive disease
> **Excludes1**   Budd-Chiari syndrome (I82.0)

K76.6 Portal hypertension 🅗
Use additional code for any associated complications,
such as:
     portal hypertensive gastropathy (K31.89)
Coding Clinic: 2020, Q1, P15

K76.7 Hepatorenal syndrome 🅗
> **Excludes1**   hepatorenal syndrome following labor
>   and delivery (O90.4)
>   postprocedural hepatorenal syndrome
>   (K91.83)

● **K76.8 Other specified diseases of liver**

     K76.81 Hepatopulmonary syndrome 🅗
         Code first underlying liver disease, such as:
         alcoholic cirrhosis of liver (K70.3-)
         cirrhosis of liver without mention of alcohol
         (K74.6-)

     K76.89 Other specified diseases of liver
         Cyst (simple) of liver
         Focal nodular hyperplasia of liver
         Hepatoptosis

K76.9 Liver disease, unspecified

▶ **K77 Liver disorders in diseases classified elsewhere**
Code first underlying disease, such as:
     amyloidosis (E85.-)
     congenital syphilis (A50.0, A50.5)
     congenital toxoplasmosis (P37.1)
     schistosomiasis (B65.0-B65.9)
> **Excludes1**   alcoholic hepatitis (K70.1-)
>   alcoholic liver disease (K70.-)
>   cytomegaloviral hepatitis (B25.1)
>   herpesviral [herpes simplex] hepatitis (B00.81)
>   infectious mononucleosis with liver disease
>   (B27.0-B27.9 with .9)
>   mumps hepatitis (B26.81)
>   sarcoidosis with liver disease (D86.89)
>   secondary syphilis with liver disease (A51.45)
>   syphilis (late) with liver disease (A52.74)
>   toxoplasmosis (acquired) hepatitis (B58.1)
>   tuberculosis with liver disease (A18.83)

DISORDERS OF GALLBLADDER, BILIARY TRACT AND PANCREAS (K80–K87)

● **K80 Cholelithiasis**
Presence or formation of gallstones
> **Excludes1**   retained cholelithiasis following cholecystectomy
>   (K91.86)

● **K80.0 Calculus of gallbladder with acute cholecystitis**
Any condition listed in K80.2 with acute cholecystitis
Use additional code if applicable for associated
gangrene of gallbladder (K82.A1), or perforation of
gallbladder (K82.A2)
*Check documentation for acute/chronic gallbladder/common
bile duct either with or without obstruction.*

     **K80.00 Calculus of gallbladder with acute cholecystitis
without obstruction**
         Coding Clinic: 2018, Q4, P20

     **K80.01 Calculus of gallbladder with acute cholecystitis
with obstruction**

▶ New   ⟹ Revised   ~~deleted~~ Deleted   Excludes 1   Excludes 2   Includes   Use additional   Code first   Code also   Key words
OGCR Official Guidelines   X Assign placeholder X   ● Use Additional Character(s)   ▶ Manifestation Code   🅗 Hierarchical Condition Category   Coding Clinic

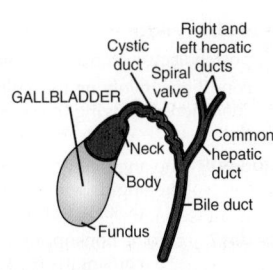

Figure 11-14 Gallbladder and bile ducts.

● **K80.1   Calculus of gallbladder with other cholecystitis**
    Use additional code if applicable for associated
    gangrene of gallbladder (K82.A1), or perforation of
    gallbladder (K82.A2)

    **K80.10   Calculus of gallbladder with chronic
           cholecystitis without obstruction**
              Cholelithiasis with cholecystitis NOS

    **K80.11   Calculus of gallbladder with chronic
           cholecystitis with obstruction**

    **K80.12   Calculus of gallbladder with acute and chronic
           cholecystitis without obstruction**

    **K80.13   Calculus of gallbladder with acute and chronic
           cholecystitis with obstruction**

    **K80.18   Calculus of gallbladder with other cholecystitis
           without obstruction**

    **K80.19   Calculus of gallbladder with other cholecystitis
           with obstruction**

● **K80.2   Calculus of gallbladder without cholecystitis**
    Cholecystolithiasis without cholecystitis
    Cholelithiasis (without cholecystitis)
    Colic (recurrent) of gallbladder (without cholecystitis)
    Gallstone (impacted) of cystic duct (without
        cholecystitis)
    Gallstone (impacted) of gallbladder (without
        cholecystitis)

    **K80.20   Calculus of gallbladder without cholecystitis
           without obstruction**

    **K80.21   Calculus of gallbladder without cholecystitis
           with obstruction**

● **K80.3   Calculus of bile duct with cholangitis**
    Any condition listed in K80.5 with cholangitis

    **K80.30   Calculus of bile duct with cholangitis,
           unspecified, without obstruction**

    **K80.31   Calculus of bile duct with cholangitis,
           unspecified, with obstruction**

    **K80.32   Calculus of bile duct with acute cholangitis
           without obstruction**

    **K80.33   Calculus of bile duct with acute cholangitis
           with obstruction**

    **K80.34   Calculus of bile duct with chronic cholangitis
           without obstruction**

    **K80.35   Calculus of bile duct with chronic cholangitis
           with obstruction**

    **K80.36   Calculus of bile duct with acute and chronic
           cholangitis without obstruction**

    **K80.37   Calculus of bile duct with acute and chronic
           cholangitis with obstruction**

● **K80.4   Calculus of bile duct with cholecystitis**
    Any condition listed in K80.5 with cholecystitis (with
    cholangitis)

    ▶Code also fistula of bile duct (K83.3)

    Use additional code if applicable for associated
    gangrene of gallbladder (K82.A1), or perforation of
    gallbladder (K82.A2)

    **K80.40   Calculus of bile duct with cholecystitis,
           unspecified, without obstruction**

    **K80.41   Calculus of bile duct with cholecystitis,
           unspecified, with obstruction**
           Coding Clinic: 2019, Q1, P18

    **K80.42   Calculus of bile duct with acute cholecystitis
           without obstruction**

    **K80.43   Calculus of bile duct with acute cholecystitis
           with obstruction**

    **K80.44   Calculus of bile duct with chronic cholecystitis
           without obstruction**

    **K80.45   Calculus of bile duct with chronic cholecystitis
           with obstruction**

    **K80.46   Calculus of bile duct with acute and chronic
           cholecystitis without obstruction**

    **K80.47   Calculus of bile duct with acute and chronic
           cholecystitis with obstruction**

● **K80.5   Calculus of bile duct without cholangitis or cholecystitis**
    Choledocholithiasis (without cholangitis or cholecystitis)
    Gallstone (impacted) of bile duct NOS (without
        cholangitis or cholecystitis)
    Gallstone (impacted) of common duct (without
        cholangitis or cholecystitis)
    Gallstone (impacted) of hepatic duct (without cholangitis
        or cholecystitis)
    Hepatic cholelithiasis (without cholangitis or cholecystitis)
    Hepatic colic (recurrent) (without cholangitis or
        cholecystitis)

    **K80.50   Calculus of bile duct without cholangitis or
           cholecystitis without obstruction**

    **K80.51   Calculus of bile duct without cholangitis or
           cholecystitis with obstruction**

● **K80.6   Calculus of gallbladder and bile duct with cholecystitis**
    Use additional code if applicable for associated
    gangrene of gallbladder (K82.A1), or perforation of
    gallbladder (K82.A2)

    **K80.60   Calculus of gallbladder and bile duct with
           cholecystitis, unspecified, without obstruction**

    **K80.61   Calculus of gallbladder and bile duct with
           cholecystitis, unspecified, with obstruction**

    **K80.62   Calculus of gallbladder and bile duct with
           acute cholecystitis without obstruction**

    **K80.63   Calculus of gallbladder and bile duct with
           acute cholecystitis with obstruction**

    **K80.64   Calculus of gallbladder and bile duct with
           chronic cholecystitis without obstruction**

    **K80.65   Calculus of gallbladder and bile duct with
           chronic cholecystitis with obstruction**

    **K80.66   Calculus of gallbladder and bile duct with
           acute and chronic cholecystitis without
           obstruction**

    **K80.67   Calculus of gallbladder and bile duct with
           acute and chronic cholecystitis with obstruction**

● **K80.7   Calculus of gallbladder and bile duct without
cholecystitis**

    **K80.70   Calculus of gallbladder and bile duct without
           cholecystitis without obstruction**

    **K80.71   Calculus of gallbladder and bile duct without
           cholecystitis with obstruction**

● **K80.8   Other cholelithiasis**

    K80.80   Other cholelithiasis without obstruction

    K80.81   Other cholelithiasis with obstruction

CHAPTER 11 (K00-K95)

● **K81 Cholecystitis**
Chronic or acute inflammation of the gallbladder

Use additional code if applicable for associated gangrene of gallbladder (K82.A1), or perforation of gallbladder (K82.A2)

Excludes1   cholecystitis with cholelithiasis (K80.-)

K81.0   Acute cholecystitis
Abscess of gallbladder
Angiocholecystitis
Emphysematous (acute) cholecystitis
Empyema of gallbladder
Gangrene of gallbladder
Gangrenous cholecystitis
Suppurative cholecystitis

K81.1   Chronic cholecystitis

K81.2   Acute cholecystitis with chronic cholecystitis

K81.9   Cholecystitis, unspecified

● **K82 Other diseases of gallbladder**

Excludes1   nonvisualization of gallbladder (R93.2)
postcholecystectomy syndrome (K91.5)

K82.0   Obstruction of gallbladder
Occlusion of cystic duct or gallbladder without cholelithiasis
Stenosis of cystic duct or gallbladder without cholelithiasis
Stricture of cystic duct or gallbladder without cholelithiasis

     Excludes1   obstruction of gallbladder with cholelithiasis (K80.-)

K82.1   Hydrops of gallbladder
Mucocele of gallbladder

K82.2   Perforation of gallbladder
Rupture of cystic duct or gallbladder

     Excludes1   Perforation of gallbladder in cholecystitis (K82.A2)

K82.3   Fistula of gallbladder
Cholecystocolic fistula
Cholecystoduodenal fistula
Coding Clinic: 2019, Q1, P18

K82.4   Cholesterolosis of gallbladder
Strawberry gallbladder

     Excludes1   cholesterolosis of gallbladder with cholecystitis (K81.-)
cholesterolosis of gallbladder with cholelithiasis (K80.-)

K82.8   Other specified diseases of gallbladder
Adhesions of cystic duct or gallbladder
Atrophy of cystic duct or gallbladder
Cyst of cystic duct or gallbladder
Dyskinesia of cystic duct or gallbladder
Hypertrophy of cystic duct or gallbladder
Nonfunctioning of cystic duct or gallbladder
Ulcer of cystic duct or gallbladder

K82.9   Disease of gallbladder, unspecified

● **K82.A Disorders of gallbladder in diseases classified elsewhere**
Code first the type of cholecystitis (K81.-), or cholelithiasis with cholecystitis (K80.00-K80.19, K80.40-K80.47, K80.60-K80.67)

▶ **K82.A1   Gangrene of gallbladder in cholecystitis**
Coding Clinic: 2018, Q4, P20

● **K82.A2   Perforation of gallbladder in cholecystitis**
Coding Clinic: 2018, Q4, P20

● **K83 Other diseases of biliary tract**

Excludes1   postcholecystectomy syndrome (K91.5)

Excludes2   conditions involving the gallbladder (K81-K82)
conditions involving the cystic duct (K81-K82)

● **K83.0   Cholangitis**

     Excludes1   cholangitic liver abscess (K75.0)
cholangitis with choledocholithiasis (K80.3-, K80.4-)

     Excludes2   chronic nonsuppurative destructive cholangitis (K74.3)
primary biliary cholangitis (K74.3)
primary biliary cirrhosis (K74.3)

K83.01   Primary sclerosing cholangitis
Coding Clinic: 2018, Q4, P21

K83.09   Other cholangitis
Ascending cholangitis
Cholangitis NOS
Primary cholangitis
Recurrent cholangitis
Sclerosing cholangitis
Secondary cholangitis
Stenosing cholangitis
Suppurative cholangitis

K83.1   Obstruction of bile duct
Occlusion of bile duct without cholelithiasis
Stenosis of bile duct without cholelithiasis
Stricture of bile duct without cholelithiasis

     Excludes1   congenital obstruction of bile duct (Q44.3)
obstruction of bile duct with cholelithiasis (K80.-)

     Coding Clinic: 2016, Q1, P18

K83.2   Perforation of bile duct
Rupture of bile duct

K83.3   Fistula of bile duct
Choledochoduodenal fistula

K83.4   Spasm of sphincter of Oddi

K83.5   Biliary cyst

K83.8   Other specified diseases of biliary tract
Adhesions of biliary tract
Atrophy of biliary tract
Hypertrophy of biliary tract
Ulcer of biliary tract

K83.9   Disease of biliary tract, unspecified

● **K85 Acute pancreatitis**
Inflammatory process in which pancreatic enzymes autodigest the gland

Includes   acute (recurrent) pancreatitis
subacute pancreatitis
Coding Clinic: 2016, Q4, P34

● **K85.0   Idiopathic acute pancreatitis**

K85.00   Idiopathic acute pancreatitis without necrosis or infection

K85.01   Idiopathic acute pancreatitis with uninfected necrosis

K85.02   Idiopathic acute pancreatitis with infected necrosis

● **K85.1   Biliary acute pancreatitis**
Gallstone pancreatitis

K85.10   Biliary acute pancreatitis without necrosis or infection

K85.11   Biliary acute pancreatitis with uninfected necrosis

K85.12   Biliary acute pancreatitis with infected necrosis

▶ New   ⇒ Revised   ~~deleted~~ Deleted   Excludes 1   Excludes 2   Includes   Use additional   Code first   Code also   Key words
OGCR Official Guidelines   X Assign placeholder X   ● Use Additional Character(s)   ▶ Manifestation Code   🔖 Hierarchical Condition Category   Coding Clinic

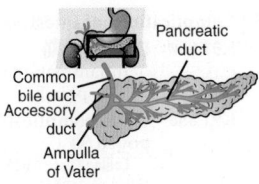

Figure 11-15 Pancreatic ductal system.

● **K85.2   Alcohol induced acute pancreatitis**
   Excludes2   alcohol induced chronic pancreatitis (K86.0)

   K85.20   Alcohol induced acute pancreatitis without necrosis or infection
      Coding Clinic: 2020, Q1, P9

   K85.21   Alcohol induced acute pancreatitis with uninfected necrosis

   K85.22   Alcohol induced acute pancreatitis with infected necrosis

● **K85.3   Drug induced acute pancreatitis**
   Use additional code for adverse effect, if applicable, to identify drug (T36-T50 with fifth or sixth character 5)
   Use additional code to identify drug abuse and dependence (F11.-F17.-)

   K85.30   Drug induced acute pancreatitis without necrosis or infection

   K85.31   Drug induced acute pancreatitis with uninfected necrosis

   K85.32   Drug induced acute pancreatitis with infected necrosis

● **K85.8   Other acute pancreatitis**

   K85.80   Other acute pancreatitis without necrosis or infection

   K85.81   Other acute pancreatitis with uninfected necrosis

   K85.82   Other acute pancreatitis with infected necrosis

● **K85.9   Acute pancreatitis, unspecified**
      Pancreatitis NOS

   K85.90   Acute pancreatitis without necrosis or infection, unspecified

   K85.91   Acute pancreatitis with uninfected necrosis, unspecified

   K85.92   Acute pancreatitis with infected necrosis, unspecified

● **K86   Other diseases of pancreas**
   Excludes2   fibrocystic disease of pancreas (E84.-)
                   islet cell tumor (of pancreas) (D13.7)
                   pancreatic steatorrhea (K90.3)

   K86.0   Alcohol-induced chronic pancreatitis 🔁
      Use additional code to identify:
         alcohol abuse and dependence (F10.-)
      Code also exocrine pancreatic insufficiency (K86.81)
      Excludes2   alcohol induced acute pancreatitis (K85.2-)

   K86.1   Other chronic pancreatitis 🔁
      Chronic pancreatitis NOS
      Infectious chronic pancreatitis
      Recurrent chronic pancreatitis
      Relapsing chronic pancreatitis
      Code also exocrine pancreatic insufficiency (K86.81)

   K86.2   Cyst of pancreas

   K86.3   Pseudocyst of pancreas

● **K86.8   Other specified diseases of pancreas**
      Coding Clinic: 2016, Q4, P34

   K86.81   Exocrine pancreatic insufficiency

   K86.89   Other specified diseases of pancreas
      Aseptic pancreatic necrosis, unrelated to acute pancreatitis
      Atrophy of pancreas
      Calculus of pancreas
      Cirrhosis of pancreas
      Fibrosis of pancreas
      Pancreatic fat necrosis, unrelated to acute pancreatitis
      Pancreatic infantilism
      Pancreatic necrosis NOS, unrelated to acute pancreatitis

   K86.9   Disease of pancreas, unspecified

▷ **K87   Disorders of gallbladder, biliary tract and pancreas in diseases classified elsewhere**
      Code first underlying disease
      Excludes1   cytomegaloviral pancreatitis (B25.2)
                      mumps pancreatitis (B26.3)
                      syphilitic gallbladder (A52.74)
                      syphilitic pancreas (A52.74)
                      tuberculosis of gallbladder (A18.83)
                      tuberculosis of pancreas (A18.83)

OTHER DISEASES OF THE DIGESTIVE SYSTEM (K90-K95)

● **K90   Intestinal malabsorption**
   Excludes1   intestinal malabsorption following gastrointestinal surgery (K91.2)

   K90.0   Celiac disease
      Celiac disease with steatorrhea
      Celiac gluten-sensitive enteropathy
      Nontropical sprue
      Use additional code for associated disorders including:
         dermatitis herpetiformis (L13.0)
         gluten ataxia (G32.81)
      Code also exocrine pancreatic insufficiency (K86.81)

   K90.1   Tropical sprue
      Sprue NOS
      Tropical steatorrhea

   K90.2   Blind loop syndrome, not elsewhere classified
      Blind loop syndrome NOS
      Excludes1   congenital blind loop syndrome (Q43.8)
                      postsurgical blind loop syndrome (K91.2)

   K90.3   Pancreatic steatorrhea

● **K90.4   Other malabsorption due to intolerance**
      Excludes2   celiac gluten-sensitive enteropathy (K90.0)
                      lactose intolerance (E73.-)
      Coding Clinic: 2016, Q4, P35-36

   K90.41   Non-celiac gluten sensitivity
      Gluten sensitivity NOS
      Non-celiac gluten sensitive enteropathy

   K90.49   Malabsorption due to intolerance, not elsewhere classified
      Malabsorption due to intolerance to carbohydrate
      Malabsorption due to intolerance to fat
      Malabsorption due to intolerance to protein
      Malabsorption due to intolerance to starch

● **K90.8   Other intestinal malabsorption**

   K90.81   Whipple's disease

   K90.89   Other intestinal malabsorption

   K90.9   Intestinal malabsorption, unspecified
      Coding Clinic: 2017, Q4, P108-109

● **K91   Intraoperative and postprocedural complications and disorders of digestive system, not elsewhere classified**

    Excludes2   complications of artificial opening of digestive system (K94.-)
                    complications of bariatric procedures (K95.-)
                    gastrojejunal ulcer (K28.-)
                    postprocedural (radiation) retroperitoneal abscess (K68.11)
                    radiation colitis (K52.0)
                    radiation gastroenteritis (K52.0)
                    radiation proctitis (K62.7)

    Coding Clinic: 2016, Q4, P10

  K91.0   Vomiting following gastrointestinal surgery

  K91.1   Postgastric surgery syndromes
      Dumping syndrome
      Postgastrectomy syndrome
      Postvagotomy syndrome

  K91.2   Postsurgical malabsorption, not elsewhere classified
      Postsurgical blind loop syndrome

      Excludes1   malabsorption osteomalacia in adults (M83.2)
                    malabsorption osteoporosis, postsurgical (M80.8-, M81.8)

● **K91.3   Postprocedural intestinal obstruction**
    Coding Clinic: 2017, Q1, P40-41

    K91.30   Postprocedural intestinal obstruction, unspecified as to partial versus complete
        Postprocedural intestinal obstruction NOS

    K91.31   Postprocedural partial intestinal obstruction
        Postprocedural incomplete intestinal obstruction

    K91.32   Postprocedural complete intestinal obstruction

  K91.5   Postcholecystectomy syndrome

● **K91.6   Intraoperative hemorrhage and hematoma of a digestive system organ or structure complicating a procedure**

      Excludes1   intraoperative hemorrhage and hematoma of a digestive system organ or structure due to accidental puncture and laceration during a procedure (K91.7-)

    K91.61   Intraoperative hemorrhage and hematoma of a digestive system organ or structure complicating a digestive system procedure
        Coding Clinic: 2020, Q1, P20

    K91.62   Intraoperative hemorrhage and hematoma of a digestive system organ or structure complicating other procedure

● **K91.7   Accidental puncture and laceration of a digestive system organ or structure during a procedure**

    K91.71   Accidental puncture and laceration of a digestive system organ or structure during a digestive system procedure

    K91.72   Accidental puncture and laceration of a digestive system organ or structure during other procedure
        Coding Clinic: 2019, Q2, P24

● **K91.8   Other intraoperative and postprocedural complications and disorders of digestive system**

    K91.81   Other intraoperative complications of digestive system

    K91.82   Postprocedural hepatic failure

    K91.83   Postprocedural hepatorenal syndrome

  ● **K91.84   Postprocedural hemorrhage of a digestive system organ or structure following a procedure**

      K91.840   Postprocedural hemorrhage of a digestive system organ or structure following a digestive system procedure
          Coding Clinic: 2016, Q1, P15

      K91.841   Postprocedural hemorrhage of a digestive system organ or structure following other procedure

● **K91.85   Complications of intestinal pouch**

    K91.850   Pouchitis 🔒
        Inflammation of internal ileoanal pouch

    K91.858   Other complications of intestinal pouch 🔒
        Coding Clinic: 2019, Q2, P13

  K91.86   Retained cholelithiasis following cholecystectomy

● **K91.87   Postprocedural hematoma and seroma of a digestive system organ or structure following a procedure**

    K91.870   Postprocedural hematoma of a digestive system organ or structure following a digestive system procedure

    K91.871   Postprocedural hematoma of a digestive system organ or structure following other procedure

    K91.872   Postprocedural seroma of a digestive system organ or structure following a digestive system procedure

    K91.873   Postprocedural seroma of a digestive system organ or structure following other procedure

  K91.89   Other postprocedural complications and disorders of digestive system

      Use additional code, if applicable, to further specify disorder

      Excludes2   postprocedural retroperitoneal abscess (K68.11)
      Coding Clinic: 2017, Q1, P41

● **K92   Other diseases of digestive system**

    Excludes1   neonatal gastrointestinal hemorrhage (P54.0-P54.3)

  K92.0   Hematemesis

  K92.1   Melena

      Excludes1   occult blood in feces (R19.5)

  K92.2   Gastrointestinal hemorrhage, unspecified
      Gastric hemorrhage NOS
      Intestinal hemorrhage NOS

      Excludes1   acute hemorrhagic gastritis (K29.01)
                  hemorrhage of anus and rectum (K62.5)
                  angiodysplasia of stomach with hemorrhage (K31.811)
                  diverticular disease with hemorrhage (K57.-)
                  gastritis and duodenitis with hemorrhage (K29.-)
                  peptic ulcer with hemorrhage (K25-K28)

● **K92.8   Other specified diseases of the digestive system**

    K92.81   Gastrointestinal mucositis (ulcerative)

      Code also type of associated therapy, such as:
        antineoplastic and immunosuppressive drugs (T45.1X-)
        radiological procedure and radiotherapy (Y84.2)

      Excludes2   mucositis (ulcerative) of vagina and vulva (N76.81)
                nasal mucositis (ulcerative) (J34.81)
                oral mucositis (ulcerative) (K12.3-)

    K92.89   Other specified diseases of the digestive system

  K92.9   Disease of digestive system, unspecified

▶ New   ⧯ Revised   ~~deleted~~ Deleted   Excludes 1   Excludes 2   Includes   Use additional   Code first   Code also   Key words

OGCR Official Guidelines   X Assign placeholder X   ● Use Additional Character(s)   ▶ Manifestation Code   🔒 Hierarchical Condition Category   Coding Clinic

● **K94**   **Complications of artificial openings of the digestive system**
  ● **K94.0**   Colostomy complications
     K94.00   Colostomy complication, unspecified 🗑
     K94.01   Colostomy hemorrhage 🗑
     K94.02   Colostomy infection 🗑
         Use additional code to specify type of
           infection, such as:
           cellulitis of abdominal wall (L03.311)
           sepsis (A40.-, A41.-)
     K94.03   Colostomy malfunction 🗑
         Mechanical complication of colostomy
     K94.09   Other complications of colostomy 🗑
  ● **K94.1**   Enterostomy complications
     K94.10   Enterostomy complication, unspecified 🗑
     K94.11   Enterostomy hemorrhage 🗑
     K94.12   Enterostomy infection 🗑
         Use additional code to specify type of
           infection, such as:
           cellulitis of abdominal wall (L03.311)
           sepsis (A40.-, A41.-)
     K94.13   Enterostomy malfunction 🗑
         Mechanical complication of enterostomy
     K94.19   Other complications of enterostomy 🗑
  ● **K94.2**   Gastrostomy complications
     K94.20   Gastrostomy complication, unspecified 🗑
     K94.21   Gastrostomy hemorrhage 🗑
     K94.22   Gastrostomy infection 🗑
         Use additional code to specify type of
           infection, such as:
           cellulitis of abdominal wall (L03.311)
           sepsis (A40.-, A41.-)
     K94.23   Gastrostomy malfunction 🗑
         Mechanical complication of gastrostomy
     K94.29   Other complications of gastrostomy 🗑
  ● **K94.3**   Esophagostomy complications
     K94.30   Esophagostomy complications, unspecified 🗑
     K94.31   Esophagostomy hemorrhage 🗑
     K94.32   Esophagostomy infection 🗑
         Use additional code to identify the infection
     K94.33   Esophagostomy malfunction 🗑
         Mechanical complication of esophagostomy
     K94.39   Other complications of esophagostomy 🗑

● **K95**   **Complications of bariatric procedures**
  ● **K95.0**   Complications of gastric band procedure
     K95.01   Infection due to gastric band procedure
         Use additional code to specify type of infection
           or organism, such as:
           bacterial and viral infectious agents (B95.-,
           B96.-)
           cellulitis of abdominal wall (L03.311)
           sepsis (A40.-, A41.-)
     K95.09   Other complications of gastric band procedure
         Use additional code, if applicable, to further
           specify complication
  ● **K95.8**   Complications of other bariatric procedure
     Excludes1   complications of gastric band surgery
             (K95.0-)
     K95.81   Infection due to other bariatric procedure
         Use additional code to specify type of infection
           or organism, such as:
           bacterial and viral infectious agents (B95.-,
           B96.-)
           cellulitis of abdominal wall (L03.311)
           sepsis (A40.-, A41.-)
     K95.89   Other complications of other bariatric
         procedure
         Use additional code, if applicable, to further
           specify complication

CHAPTER 11 (K00-K95)

CHAPTER 12

DISEASES OF THE SKIN AND SUBCUTANEOUS TISSUE (L00-L99)

OGCR Chapter-Specific Coding Guidelines

12. Chapter 12: Diseases of the Skin and Subcutaneous Tissue (L00-L99)

a. **Pressure ulcer stage codes**

1) **Pressure ulcer stages**
Codes from category L89, Pressure ulcer, identify the site of the pressure ulcer as well as the stage of the ulcer.

The ICD-10-CM classifies pressure ulcer stages based on severity, which is designated by stages 1-4, unspecified stage and unstageable.

Assign as many codes from category L89 as needed to identify all the pressure ulcers the patient has, if applicable.

See Section I.B.14 for pressure ulcer stage documentation by clinicians other than patient's provider.

2) **Unstageable pressure ulcers**
Assignment of the code for unstageable pressure ulcer (L89.–0) should be based on the clinical documentation. These codes are used for pressure ulcers whose stage cannot be clinically determined (e.g., the ulcer is covered by eschar or has been treated with a skin or muscle graft) and pressure ulcers that are documented as deep tissue injury but not documented as due to trauma. This code should not be confused with the codes for unspecified stage (L89.–9). When there is no documentation regarding the stage of the pressure ulcer, assign the appropriate code for unspecified stage (L89.–9).

3) **Documented pressure ulcer stage**
Assignment of the pressure ulcer stage code should be guided by clinical documentation of the stage or documentation of the terms found in the Alphabetic Index. For clinical terms describing the stage that are not found in the Alphabetic Index, and there is no documentation of the stage, the provider should be queried.

4) **Patients admitted with pressure ulcers documented as healed**
No code is assigned if the documentation states that the pressure ulcer is completely healed.

5) **Patients admitted with pressure ulcers documented as healing**
Pressure ulcers described as healing should be assigned the appropriate pressure ulcer stage code based on the documentation in the medical record. If the documentation does not provide information about the stage of the healing pressure ulcer, assign the appropriate code for unspecified stage.

If the documentation is unclear as to whether the patient has a current (new) pressure ulcer or if the patient is being treated for a healing pressure ulcer, query the provider.

For ulcers that were present on admission but healed at the time of discharge, assign the code for the site and stage of the pressure ulcer at the time of admission.

6) **Patient admitted with pressure ulcer evolving into another stage during the admission**
If a patient is admitted to an inpatient hospital with a pressure ulcer at one stage and it progresses to a higher stage, two separate codes should be assigned: one code for the site and stage of the ulcer on admission and a second code for the same ulcer site and the highest stage reported during the stay.

b. **Non-Pressure Chronic Ulcers**

1) **Patients admitted with non-pressure ulcers documented as healed**
No code is assigned if the documentation states that the non-pressure ulcer is completely healed.

2) **Patients admitted with non-pressure ulcers documented as healing**
Non-pressure ulcers described as healing should be assigned the appropriate non-pressure ulcer code based on the documentation in the medical record. If the documentation does not provide information about the severity of the healing non-pressure ulcer, assign the appropriate code for unspecified severity.

If the documentation is unclear as to whether the patient has a current (new) non-pressure ulcer or if the patient is being treated for a healing non-pressure ulcer, query the provider.

For ulcers that were present on admission but healed at the time of discharge, assign the code for the site and severity of the non-pressure ulcer at the time of admission.

3) **Patient admitted with non-pressure ulcer that progresses to another severity level during the admission**
If a patient is admitted to an inpatient hospital with a non-pressure ulcer at one severity level and it progresses to a higher severity level, two separate codes should be assigned: one code for the site and severity level of the ulcer on admission and a second code for the same ulcer site and the highest severity level reported during the stay.

See Section I.B.14 for pressure ulcer stage documentation by clinicians other than patient's provider.

Figure 12-1 Furuncle, also known as a boil, is a staphylococcal infection. The organism enters the body through a hair follicle and so furuncles usually appear in hairy areas of the body. A cluster of furuncles is known as a carbuncle and involves infection into the deep subcutaneous fascia. These usually appear on the back and neck. (**B** from Habif TP, Binnick AN, Meyerson LB: Clinical Dermatology: A Color Guide to Diagnosis and Therapy, S.I., Mosby Elsevier, 2010)

CHAPTER 12

DISEASES OF THE SKIN AND SUBCUTANEOUS TISSUE (L00-L99)

Excludes2 certain conditions originating in the perinatal period (P04-P96)
certain infectious and parasitic diseases (A00-B99)
complications of pregnancy, childbirth and the puerperium (O00-O9A)
congenital malformations, deformations, and chromosomal abnormalities (Q00-Q99)
endocrine, nutritional and metabolic diseases (E00-E88)
lipomelanotic reticulosis (I89.8)
neoplasms (C00-D49)
symptoms, signs and abnormal clinical and laboratory findings, not elsewhere classified (R00-R94)
systemic connective tissue disorders (M30-M36)
viral warts (B07.-)

This chapter contains the following blocks:

L00-L08	Infections of the skin and subcutaneous tissue
L10-L14	Bullous disorders
L20-L30	Dermatitis and eczema
L40-L45	Papulosquamous disorders
L49-L54	Urticaria and erythema
L55-L59	Radiation-related disorders of the skin and subcutaneous tissue
L60-L75	Disorders of skin appendages
L76	Intraoperative and postprocedural complications of skin and subcutaneous tissue
L80-L99	Other disorders of the skin and subcutaneous tissue

▶ New ⇒ Revised ~~deleted~~ Deleted Excludes 1 Excludes 2 Includes Use additional Code first Code also Key words
OGCR Official Guidelines X Assign placeholder X ● Use Additional Character(s) ▷ Manifestation Code ℚ Hierarchical Condition Category Coding Clinic

INFECTIONS OF THE SKIN AND SUBCUTANEOUS TISSUE (L00-L08)

Use additional code (B95-B97) to identify infectious agent.

Excludes2 hordeolum (H00.0)
infective dermatitis (L30.3)
local infections of skin classified in Chapter 1
lupus panniculitis (L93.2)
panniculitis NOS (M79.3)
panniculitis of neck and back (M54.0-)
Perlèche NOS (K13.0)
Perlèche due to candidiasis (B37.0)
Perlèche due to riboflavin deficiency (E53.0)
pyogenic granuloma (L98.0)
relapsing panniculitis [Weber-Christian] (M35.6)
viral warts (B07.-)
zoster (B02.-)

L00 **Staphylococcal scalded skin syndrome**
Ritter's disease

Use additional code to identify percentage of skin exfoliation
(L49.-)

Excludes1 bullous impetigo (L01.03)
pemphigus neonatorum (L01.03)
toxic epidermal necrolysis [Lyell] (L51.2)

● **L01** **Impetigo**
*Contagious skin infection caused by a streptococcus or staphylococcus
aureus, common skin infections among children*

Excludes1 impetigo herpetiformis (L40.1)

● **L01.0** **Impetigo**
Impetigo contagiosa
Impetigo vulgaris

L01.00 **Impetigo, unspecified**
Impetigo NOS

L01.01 **Non-bullous impetigo**

L01.02 **Bockhart's impetigo**
Impetigo follicularis
Perifolliculitis NOS
Superficial pustular perifolliculitis

L01.03 **Bullous impetigo**
Impetigo neonatorum
Pemphigus neonatorum
Neonate = newborn

L01.09 **Other impetigo**
Ulcerative impetigo

L01.1 **Impetiginization of other dermatoses**

● **L02** **Cutaneous abscess, furuncle and carbuncle**
Use additional code to identify organism (B95-B96)

Excludes2 abscess of anus and rectal regions (K61.-)
abscess of female genital organs (external) (N76.4)
abscess of male genital organs (external) (N48.2,
N49.-)

● **L02.0** **Cutaneous abscess, furuncle and carbuncle of face**
Excludes2 abscess of ear, external (H60.0)
abscess of eyelid (H00.0)
abscess of head [any part, except face]
(L02.8)
abscess of lacrimal gland (H04.0)
abscess of lacrimal passages (H04.3)
abscess of mouth (K12.2)
abscess of nose (J34.0)
abscess of orbit (H05.0)
submandibular abscess (K12.2)

L02.01 **Cutaneous abscess of face**

L02.02 **Furuncle of face**
Boil of face
Folliculitis of face

L02.03 **Carbuncle of face**

● **L02.1** **Cutaneous abscess, furuncle and carbuncle of neck**

L02.11 **Cutaneous abscess of neck**

L02.12 **Furuncle of neck**
Boil of neck
Folliculitis of neck

L02.13 **Carbuncle of neck**

● **L02.2** **Cutaneous abscess, furuncle and carbuncle of trunk**
Excludes1 non-newborn omphalitis (L08.82)
omphalitis of newborn (P38.-)

Excludes2 abscess of breast (N61.1)
abscess of buttocks (L02.3)
abscess of female external genital organs
(N76.4)
abscess of male external genital organs
(N48.2, N49.-)
abscess of hip (L02.4)

● **L02.21** **Cutaneous abscess of trunk**

L02.211 **Cutaneous abscess of abdominal wall**

L02.212 **Cutaneous abscess of back [any part, except buttock]**

L02.213 **Cutaneous abscess of chest wall**

L02.214 **Cutaneous abscess of groin**

L02.215 **Cutaneous abscess of perineum**

L02.216 **Cutaneous abscess of umbilicus**

L02.219 **Cutaneous abscess of trunk, unspecified**

● **L02.22** **Furuncle of trunk**
Boil of trunk
Folliculitis of trunk

L02.221 **Furuncle of abdominal wall**

L02.222 **Furuncle of back [any part, except buttock]**

L02.223 **Furuncle of chest wall**

L02.224 **Furuncle of groin**

L02.225 **Furuncle of perineum**

L02.226 **Furuncle of umbilicus**

L02.229 **Furuncle of trunk, unspecified**

● **L02.23** **Carbuncle of trunk**

L02.231 **Carbuncle of abdominal wall**

L02.232 **Carbuncle of back [any part, except buttock]**

L02.233 **Carbuncle of chest wall**

L02.234 **Carbuncle of groin**

L02.235 **Carbuncle of perineum**

L02.236 **Carbuncle of umbilicus**

L02.239 **Carbuncle of trunk, unspecified**

● **L02.3** **Cutaneous abscess, furuncle and carbuncle of buttock**
Excludes1 pilonidal cyst with abscess (L05.01)

L02.31 **Cutaneous abscess of buttock**
Cutaneous abscess of gluteal region

L02.32 **Furuncle of buttock**
Boil of buttock
Folliculitis of buttock
Furuncle of gluteal region

L02.33 **Carbuncle of buttock**
Carbuncle of gluteal region

Figure 12-2 Impetigo. A thick,
honey-yellow adherent crust covers the entire
eroded surface. (From James WD, Elston DM,
Berger TG, Andrews GC: Andrews' Diseases
of the Skin: Clinical Dermatology, London,
Saunders/Elsevier, 2011)

CHAPTER 12 (L00-L99)

● **L02.4**   **Cutaneous abscess, furuncle and carbuncle of limb**
     Excludes2   Cutaneous abscess, furuncle and carbuncle of groin (L02.214, L02.224, L02.234)
                Cutaneous abscess, furuncle and carbuncle of hand (L02.5-)
                Cutaneous abscess, furuncle and carbuncle of foot (L02.6-)

    ● **L02.41**   **Cutaneous abscess of limb**
       L02.411   Cutaneous abscess of right axilla
       L02.412   Cutaneous abscess of left axilla
       L02.413   Cutaneous abscess of right upper limb
       L02.414   Cutaneous abscess of left upper limb
       L02.415   Cutaneous abscess of right lower limb
       L02.416   Cutaneous abscess of left lower limb
       L02.419   Cutaneous abscess of limb, unspecified

    ● **L02.42**   **Furuncle of limb**
       Boil of limb
       Folliculitis of limb
       L02.421   Furuncle of right axilla
       L02.422   Furuncle of left axilla
       L02.423   Furuncle of right upper limb
       L02.424   Furuncle of left upper limb
       L02.425   Furuncle of right lower limb
       L02.426   Furuncle of left lower limb
       L02.429   Furuncle of limb, unspecified

    ● **L02.43**   **Carbuncle of limb**
       L02.431   Carbuncle of right axilla
       L02.432   Carbuncle of left axilla
       L02.433   Carbuncle of right upper limb
       L02.434   Carbuncle of left upper limb
       L02.435   Carbuncle of right lower limb
       L02.436   Carbuncle of left lower limb
       L02.439   Carbuncle of limb, unspecified

● **L02.5**   **Cutaneous abscess, furuncle and carbuncle of hand**
    ● **L02.51**   **Cutaneous abscess of hand**
       L02.511   Cutaneous abscess of right hand
       L02.512   Cutaneous abscess of left hand
       L02.519   Cutaneous abscess of unspecified hand

    ● **L02.52**   **Furuncle hand**
       Boil of hand
       Folliculitis of hand
       L02.521   Furuncle right hand
       L02.522   Furuncle left hand
       L02.529   Furuncle unspecified hand

    ● **L02.53**   **Carbuncle of hand**
       L02.531   Carbuncle of right hand
       L02.532   Carbuncle of left hand
       L02.539   Carbuncle of unspecified hand

● **L02.6**   **Cutaneous abscess, furuncle and carbuncle of foot**
    ● **L02.61**   **Cutaneous abscess of foot**
       L02.611   Cutaneous abscess of right foot
       L02.612   Cutaneous abscess of left foot
       L02.619   Cutaneous abscess of unspecified foot

    ● **L02.62**   **Furuncle of foot**
       Boil of foot
       Folliculitis of foot
       L02.621   Furuncle of right foot
       L02.622   Furuncle of left foot
       L02.629   Furuncle of unspecified foot

    ● **L02.63**   **Carbuncle of foot**
       L02.631   Carbuncle of right foot
       L02.632   Carbuncle of left foot
       L02.639   Carbuncle of unspecified foot

● **L02.8**   **Cutaneous abscess, furuncle and carbuncle of other sites**
    ● **L02.81**   **Cutaneous abscess of other sites**
       L02.811   Cutaneous abscess of head [any part, except face]
       L02.818   Cutaneous abscess of other sites

    ● **L02.82**   **Furuncle of other sites**
       Boil of other sites
       Folliculitis of other sites
       L02.821   Furuncle of head [any part, except face]
       L02.828   Furuncle of other sites

    ● **L02.83**   **Carbuncle of other sites**
       L02.831   Carbuncle of head [any part, except face]
       L02.838   Carbuncle of other sites

● **L02.9**   **Cutaneous abscess, furuncle and carbuncle, unspecified**
       L02.91   **Cutaneous abscess, unspecified**
       L02.92   **Furuncle, unspecified**
          Boil NOS
          Furunculosis NOS
       L02.93   **Carbuncle, unspecified**

● **L03**   **Cellulitis and acute lymphangitis**
     Excludes2   cellulitis of anal and rectal region (K61.-)
               cellulitis of external auditory canal (H60.1)
               cellulitis of eyelid (H00.0)
               cellulitis of female external genital organs (N76.4)
               cellulitis of lacrimal apparatus (H04.3)
               cellulitis of male external genital organs (N48.2, N49.-)
               cellulitis of mouth (K12.2)
               cellulitis of nose (J34.0)
               eosinophilic cellulitis [Wells] (L98.3)
               febrile neutrophilic dermatosis [Sweet] (L98.2)
               lymphangitis (chronic) (subacute) (I89.1)

● **L03.0**   **Cellulitis and acute lymphangitis of finger and toe**
       Infection of nail
       Onychia
       Paronychia
       Perionychia
    ● **L03.01**   **Cellulitis of finger**
       Felon
       Whitlow
       Excludes1   herpetic whitlow (B00.89)
       L03.011   Cellulitis of right finger
       L03.012   Cellulitis of left finger
       L03.019   Cellulitis of unspecified finger

    ● **L03.02**   **Acute lymphangitis of finger**
       Hangnail with lymphangitis of finger
       L03.021   Acute lymphangitis of right finger
       L03.022   Acute lymphangitis of left finger
       L03.029   Acute lymphangitis of unspecified finger

    ● **L03.03**   **Cellulitis of toe**
       L03.031   Cellulitis of right toe
       L03.032   Cellulitis of left toe
       L03.039   Cellulitis of unspecified toe

    ● **L03.04**   **Acute lymphangitis of toe**
       Hangnail with lymphangitis of toe
       L03.041   Acute lymphangitis of right toe
       L03.042   Acute lymphangitis of left toe
       L03.049   Acute lymphangitis of unspecified toe

Item 12-1   **Onychia** is an inflammation of the tissue surrounding the nail with pus accumulation and loss of the nail, resulting from microscopic pathogens entering through small wounds. **Paronychia** is a nail disease also known as felon or whitlow and is a bacterial or fungal infection.

▶ New   ⇒ Revised   ~~deleted~~ Deleted   Excludes 1   Excludes 2   Includes   Use additional   Code first   Code also   Key words

OGCR Official Guidelines   X Assign placeholder X   ● Use Additional Character(s)   ▶ Manifestation Code   ⮾ Hierarchical Condition Category   **Coding Clinic**

Item 12–2 Cellulitis is an acute spreading bacterial infection below the surface of the skin characterized by redness (erythema), warmth, swelling, pain, fever, chills, and enlarged lymph nodes ("swollen glands").

● **L03.1   Cellulitis and acute lymphangitis of other parts of limb**
  ● **L03.11   Cellulitis of other parts of limb**
    Excludes2 cellulitis of fingers (L03.01-)
          cellulitis of toes (L03.03-)
          groin (L03.314)

    L03.111   Cellulitis of right axilla
    L03.112   Cellulitis of left axilla
    L03.113   Cellulitis of right upper limb
    L03.114   Cellulitis of left upper limb
        Coding Clinic: 2019, Q1, P13
    L03.115   Cellulitis of right lower limb
    L03.116   Cellulitis of left lower limb
    L03.119   Cellulitis of unspecified part of limb
  ● **L03.12   Acute lymphangitis of other parts of limb**
    Excludes2 acute lymphangitis of fingers (L03.2-)
          acute lymphangitis of toes (L03.04-)
          acute lymphangitis of groin (L03.324)

    L03.121   Acute lymphangitis of right axilla
    L03.122   Acute lymphangitis of left axilla
    L03.123   Acute lymphangitis of right upper limb
    L03.124   Acute lymphangitis of left upper limb
    L03.125   Acute lymphangitis of right lower limb
    L03.126   Acute lymphangitis of left lower limb
    L03.129   Acute lymphangitis of unspecified part of limb
● **L03.2   Cellulitis and acute lymphangitis of face and neck**
  ● **L03.21   Cellulitis and acute lymphangitis of face**
    L03.211   Cellulitis of face
        Excludes2 abscess of orbit (H05.01-)
          cellulitis of ear (H60.1-)
          cellulitis of eyelid (H00.0-)
          cellulitis of head (L03.81)
          cellulitis of lacrimal apparatus (H04.3)
          cellulitis of lip (K13.0)
          cellulitis of mouth (K12.2)
          cellulitis of nose (internal) (J34.0)
          cellulitis of orbit (H05.01-)
          cellulitis of scalp (L03.81)

    L03.212   Acute lymphangitis of face
    L03.213   Periorbital cellulitis
        Preseptal cellulitis
        Coding Clinic: 2016, Q4, P36
  ● **L03.22   Cellulitis and acute lymphangitis of neck**
    L03.221   Cellulitis of neck
    L03.222   Acute lymphangitis of neck

● **L03.3   Cellulitis and acute lymphangitis of trunk**
  ● **L03.31   Cellulitis of trunk**
    Excludes2 cellulitis of anal and rectal regions (K61.-)
          cellulitis of breast NOS (N61.0)
          cellulitis of female external genital organs (N76.4)
          cellulitis of male external genital organs (N48.2, N49.-)
          omphalitis of newborn (P38.-)
          puerperal cellulitis of breast (O91.2)

    L03.311   Cellulitis of abdominal wall
        Excludes2 cellulitis of umbilicus (L03.316)
          cellulitis of groin (L03.314)
    L03.312   Cellulitis of back [any part except buttock]
    L03.313   Cellulitis of chest wall
    L03.314   Cellulitis of groin
    L03.315   Cellulitis of perineum
    L03.316   Cellulitis of umbilicus
    L03.317   Cellulitis of buttock
    L03.319   Cellulitis of trunk, unspecified
  ● **L03.32   Acute lymphangitis of trunk**
    L03.321   Acute lymphangitis of abdominal wall
    L03.322   Acute lymphangitis of back [any part except buttock]
    L03.323   Acute lymphangitis of chest wall
    L03.324   Acute lymphangitis of groin
    L03.325   Acute lymphangitis of perineum
    L03.326   Acute lymphangitis of umbilicus
    L03.327   Acute lymphangitis of buttock
    L03.329   Acute lymphangitis of trunk, unspecified
● **L03.8   Cellulitis and acute lymphangitis of other sites**
  ● **L03.81   Cellulitis of other sites**
    L03.811   Cellulitis of head [any part, except face]
        Cellulitis of scalp
        Excludes2 cellulitis of face (L03.211)
    L03.818   Cellulitis of other sites
  ● **L03.89   Acute lymphangitis of other sites**
    L03.891   Acute lymphangitis of head [any part, except face]
    L03.898   Acute lymphangitis of other sites
● **L03.9   Cellulitis and acute lymphangitis, unspecified**
  L03.90   Cellulitis, unspecified
  L03.91   Acute lymphangitis, unspecified
    Excludes1 lymphangitis NOS (I89.1)

CHAPTER 12 (L00-L99)

Item 12–3   Abscess is a localized collection of pus in tissues or organs and is a sign of infection, resulting in swelling and inflammation.

Item 12–4   Pilonidal cyst, also called a coccygeal cyst, is the result of a disorder called pilonidal disease. The cyst usually contains hair and pus.

● **L04   Acute lymphadenitis**
    Short-term inflammation of lymph nodes which can be regionalized to involve a given area of the lymph system or systemic involving much of the body

    Includes   abscess (acute) of lymph nodes, except mesenteric
                   acute lymphadenitis, except mesenteric

    Excludes1   chronic or subacute lymphadenitis, except mesenteric (I88.1)
                   enlarged lymph nodes (R59.-)
                   human immunodeficiency virus [HIV] disease resulting in generalized lymphadenopathy (B20)
                   lymphadenitis NOS (I88.9)
                   nonspecific mesenteric lymphadenitis (I88.0)

    L04.0   Acute lymphadenitis of face, head and neck
    L04.1   Acute lymphadenitis of trunk
    L04.2   Acute lymphadenitis of upper limb
        Acute lymphadenitis of axilla
        Acute lymphadenitis of shoulder
    L04.3   Acute lymphadenitis of lower limb
        Acute lymphadenitis of hip
        Excludes2   acute lymphadenitis of groin (L04.1)
    L04.8   Acute lymphadenitis of other sites
    L04.9   Acute lymphadenitis, unspecified

● **L05   Pilonidal cyst and sinus**
  ● **L05.0   Pilonidal cyst and sinus with abscess**
    L05.01   Pilonidal cyst with abscess
        Pilonidal abscess
        Pilonidal dimple with abscess
        Postanal dimple with abscess
        Excludes2   congenital sacral dimple (Q82.6)
                        parasacral dimple (Q82.6)
    L05.02   Pilonidal sinus with abscess
        Coccygeal fistula with abscess
        Coccygeal sinus with abscess
        Pilonidal fistula with abscess
  ● **L05.9   Pilonidal cyst and sinus without abscess**
    L05.91   Pilonidal cyst without abscess
        Pilonidal dimple
        Postanal dimple
        Pilonidal cyst NOS
        Excludes2   congenital sacral dimple (Q82.6)
                        parasacral dimple (Q82.6)
    L05.92   Pilonidal sinus without abscess
        Coccygeal fistula
        Coccygeal sinus without abscess
        Pilonidal fistula

● **L08   Other local infections of skin and subcutaneous tissue**
    L08.0   Pyoderma
        Dermatitis gangrenosa
        Purulent dermatitis
        Septic dermatitis
        Suppurative dermatitis
        Excludes1   pyoderma gangrenosum (L88)
                      pyoderma vegetans (L08.81)
    L08.1   Erythrasma

    L08.8   Other specified local infections of the skin and subcutaneous tissue
      L08.81   Pyoderma vegetans
         Excludes1   pyoderma gangrenosum (L88)
                      pyoderma NOS (L08.0)
      L08.82   Omphalitis not of newborn
         Excludes1   omphalitis of newborn (P38.-)
      L08.89   Other specified local infections of the skin and subcutaneous tissue
    L08.9   Local infection of the skin and subcutaneous tissue, unspecified

---

BULLOUS DISORDERS (L10-L14)

    Excludes1   benign familial pemphigus [Hailey-Hailey] (Q82.8)
                  staphylococcal scalded skin syndrome (L00)
                  toxic epidermal necrolysis [Lyell] (L51.2)

● **L10   Pemphigus**
    Excludes1   pemphigus neonatorum (L01.03)

    L10.0   Pemphigus vulgaris
    L10.1   Pemphigus vegetans
    L10.2   Pemphigus foliaceous
    L10.3   Brazilian pemphigus [fogo selvagem]
    L10.4   Pemphigus erythematosus
        Senear-Usher syndrome
    L10.5   Drug-induced pemphigus
        Use additional code for adverse effect, if applicable, to identify drug (T36-T50 with fifth or sixth character 5)
  ● **L10.8   Other pemphigus**
      L10.81   Paraneoplastic pemphigus
      L10.89   Other pemphigus
    L10.9   Pemphigus, unspecified

● **L11   Other acantholytic disorders**
    L11.0   Acquired keratosis follicularis
        Excludes1   keratosis follicularis (congenital) [Darier-White] (Q82.8)
    L11.1   Transient acantholytic dermatosis [Grover]
    L11.8   Other specified acantholytic disorders
    L11.9   Acantholytic disorder, unspecified

● **L12   Pemphigoid**
    Excludes1   herpes gestationis (O26.4-)
                  impetigo herpetiformis (L40.1)
    L12.0   Bullous pemphigoid
    L12.1   Cicatricial pemphigoid
        Benign mucous membrane pemphigoid
    L12.2   Chronic bullous disease of childhood   P
        Juvenile dermatitis herpetiformis
  ● **L12.3   Acquired epidermolysis bullosa**
      Excludes1   epidermolysis bullosa (congenital) (Q81.-)
      L12.30   Acquired epidermolysis bullosa, unspecified ⬡
      L12.31   Epidermolysis bullosa due to drug ⬡
        Use additional code for adverse effect, if applicable, to identify drug (T36-T50 with fifth or sixth character 5)
      L12.35   Other acquired epidermolysis bullosa ⬡
    L12.8   Other pemphigoid
    L12.9   Pemphigoid, unspecified

▶ New   ⯈ Revised   ~~deleted~~ Deleted   Excludes 1   Excludes 2   Includes   Use additional   Code first   Code also   Key words

OGCR Official Guidelines   X Assign placeholder X   ● Use Additional Character(s)   ▶ Manifestation Code   ⬡ Hierarchical Condition Category   **Coding Clinic**

Item 12–5 Dermatitis herpetiformis, also known as Duhring's disease, is a systemic disease characterized by small blisters (3 to 5 mm) and occasionally large bullae (> 5 mm).

Figure 12-3 Dermatitis herpetiformis. (From Terhorst D: BASICS Dermatologie, München, Elsevier, Urban & Fischer, 2011)

● **L13   Other bullous disorders**

    L13.0   Dermatitis herpetiformis
       Duhring's disease
       Hydroa herpetiformis
       Excludes1   juvenile dermatitis herpetiformis (L12.2)
                  senile dermatitis herpetiformis (L12.0)

    L13.1   Subcorneal pustular dermatitis
       Sneddon-Wilkinson disease

    L13.8   Other specified bullous disorders

    L13.9   Bullous disorder, unspecified

▷ *L14   **Bullous disorders in diseases classified elsewhere***
      Code first underlying disease

DERMATITIS AND ECZEMA (L20-L30)

Note: In this block the terms dermatitis and eczema are used synonymously and interchangeably.

    Excludes2   chronic (childhood) granulomatous disease (D71)
              dermatitis gangrenosa (L08.0)
              dermatitis herpetiformis (L13.0)
              dry skin dermatitis (L85.3)
              factitial dermatitis (L98.1)
              perioral dermatitis (L71.0)
              radiation-related disorders of the skin and
                 subcutaneous tissue (L55-L59)
              stasis dermatitis (I87.2)

● **L20   Atopic dermatitis**

    L20.0   Besnier's prurigo

●   **L20.8   Other atopic dermatitis**
       Excludes2   circumscribed neurodermatitis (L28.0)

      L20.81   Atopic neurodermatitis
           Diffuse neurodermatitis

      L20.82   Flexural eczema

      L20.83   Infantile (acute) (chronic) eczema   P

      L20.84   Intrinsic (allergic) eczema

      L20.89   Other atopic dermatitis

    L20.9   Atopic dermatitis, unspecified

● **L21   Seborrheic dermatitis**

    Excludes2   infective dermatitis (L30.3)
              seborrheic keratosis (L82.-)

    L21.0   Seborrhea capitis
       Cradle cap
       Coding Clinic: 2018, Q1, P6

    L21.1   Seborrheic infantile dermatitis   P

    L21.8   Other seborrheic dermatitis

    L21.9   Seborrheic dermatitis, unspecified
       Seborrhea NOS

Item 12–6 Seborrheic dermatitis is characterized by greasy, scaly, red patches and is associated with oily skin and scalp.

Figure 12-4 Seborrheic dermatitis. (Getty Image)

Item 12–7 Atopic dermatitis, also known as atopic eczema, infantile eczema, disseminated neuro dermatitis, flexural eczema, and *prurigo diathesique* (Besnier), is characterized by intense itching and is often hereditary.

Figure 12-5 Atopic dermatitis. (From Chabner D-E: The Language of Medicine, St. Louis, MO, Saunders/Elsevier, 2007)

   L22   Diaper dermatitis
       Diaper erythema
       Diaper rash
       Psoriasiform diaper rash

● **L23   Allergic contact dermatitis**

    Excludes1   allergy NOS (T78.40)
              contact dermatitis NOS (L25.9)
              dermatitis NOS (L30.9)

    Excludes2   dermatitis due to substances taken internally
                 (L27.-)
              dermatitis of eyelid (H01.1-)
              diaper dermatitis (L22)
              eczema of external ear (H60.5-)
              irritant contact dermatitis (L24.-)
              perioral dermatitis (L71.0)
              radiation-related disorders of the skin and
                 subcutaneous tissue (L55-L59)

    L23.0   Allergic contact dermatitis due to metals
       Allergic contact dermatitis due to chromium
       Allergic contact dermatitis due to nickel

    L23.1   Allergic contact dermatitis due to adhesives

    L23.2   Allergic contact dermatitis due to cosmetics

    L23.3   Allergic contact dermatitis due to drugs in contact with skin

       Use additional code for adverse effect, if applicable,
       to identify drug (T36-T50 with fifth or sixth
       character 5)

       Excludes2   dermatitis due to ingested drugs and
                 medicaments (L27.0-L27.1)

    L23.4   Allergic contact dermatitis due to dyes

    L23.5   Allergic contact dermatitis due to other chemical products
       Allergic contact dermatitis due to cement
       Allergic contact dermatitis due to insecticide
       Allergic contact dermatitis due to plastic
       Allergic contact dermatitis due to rubber

    L23.6   Allergic contact dermatitis due to food in contact with the skin
       Excludes2   dermatitis due to ingested food (L27.2)

    L23.7   Allergic contact dermatitis due to plants, except food
       Excludes2   allergy NOS due to pollen (J30.1)

●   **L23.8   Allergic contact dermatitis due to other agents**

      L23.81   Allergic contact dermatitis due to animal (cat) (dog) dander
           Allergic contact dermatitis due to animal (cat) (dog) hair

      L23.89   Allergic contact dermatitis due to other agents

    L23.9   Allergic contact dermatitis, unspecified cause
       Allergic contact eczema NOS

CHAPTER 12 (L00-L99)

CHAPTER 12 (L00-L99)

● **L24** **Irritant contact dermatitis**

    Excludes1   allergy NOS (T78.40)
                     contact dermatitis NOS (L25.9)
                     dermatitis NOS (L30.9)

    Excludes2   allergic contact dermatitis (L23.-)
                     dermatitis due to substances taken internally
                         (L27.-)
                     dermatitis of eyelid (H01.1-)
                     diaper dermatitis (L22)
                     eczema of external ear (H60.5-)
                     perioral dermatitis (L71.0)
                     radiation-related disorders of the skin and
                         subcutaneous tissue (L55-L59)

    L24.0   **Irritant contact dermatitis due to detergents**

    L24.1   **Irritant contact dermatitis due to oils and greases**

    L24.2   **Irritant contact dermatitis due to solvents**
           Irritant contact dermatitis due to chlorocompound
           Irritant contact dermatitis due to cyclohexane
           Irritant contact dermatitis due to ester
           Irritant contact dermatitis due to glycol
           Irritant contact dermatitis due to hydrocarbon
           Irritant contact dermatitis due to ketone

    L24.3   **Irritant contact dermatitis due to cosmetics**

    L24.4   **Irritant contact dermatitis due to drugs in contact with skin**
           Use additional code for adverse effect, if applicable,
              to identify drug (T36-T50 with fifth or sixth
              character 5)

    L24.5   **Irritant contact dermatitis due to other chemical products**
           Irritant contact dermatitis due to cement
           Irritant contact dermatitis due to insecticide
           Irritant contact dermatitis due to plastic
           Irritant contact dermatitis due to rubber

    L24.6   **Irritant contact dermatitis due to food in contact with skin**
        Excludes2   dermatitis due to ingested food (L27.2)

    L24.7   **Irritant contact dermatitis due to plants, except food**
        Excludes2   allergy NOS to pollen (J30.1)

  ● **L24.8**   **Irritant contact dermatitis due to other agents**

        L24.81   **Irritant contact dermatitis due to metals**
              Irritant contact dermatitis due to chromium
              Irritant contact dermatitis due to nickel

        L24.89   **Irritant contact dermatitis due to other agents**
              Irritant contact dermatitis due to dyes

    L24.9   **Irritant contact dermatitis, unspecified cause**
           Irritant contact eczema NOS

● **L25** **Unspecified contact dermatitis**

    Excludes1   allergic contact dermatitis (L23.-)
                     allergy NOS (T78.40)
                     dermatitis NOS (L30.9)
                     irritant contact dermatitis (L24.-)

    Excludes2   dermatitis due to ingested substances (L27.-)
                     dermatitis of eyelid (H01.1-)
                     eczema of external ear (H60.5-)
                     perioral dermatitis (L71.0)
                     radiation-related disorders of the skin and
                       subcutaneous tissue (L55-L59)

    L25.0   **Unspecified contact dermatitis due to cosmetics**

    L25.1   **Unspecified contact dermatitis due to drugs in contact with skin**
           Use additional code for adverse effect, if applicable,
              to identify drug (T36-T50 with fifth or sixth
              character 5)
        Excludes2   dermatitis due to ingested drugs and
                     medicaments (L27.0-L27.1)

    L25.2   **Unspecified contact dermatitis due to dyes**

    L25.3   **Unspecified contact dermatitis due to other chemical products**
           Unspecified contact dermatitis due to cement
           Unspecified contact dermatitis due to insecticide

    Ł25.4   **Unspecified contact dermatitis due to food in contact with skin**
        Excludes2   dermatitis due to ingested food (L27.2)

    L25.5   **Unspecified contact dermatitis due to plants, except food**
        Excludes1   nettle rash (L50.9)
        Excludes2   allergy NOS due to pollen (J30.1)

    L25.8   **Unspecified contact dermatitis due to other agents**

    L25.9   **Unspecified contact dermatitis, unspecified cause**
           Contact dermatitis (occupational) NOS
           Contact eczema (occupational) NOS

  L26 **Exfoliative dermatitis**
           Hebra's pityriasis
    Excludes1   Ritter's disease (L00)

● **L27** **Dermatitis due to substances taken internally**

    Excludes1   allergy NOS (T78.40)

    Excludes2   adverse food reaction, except dermatitis
                       (T78.0-T78.1)
                     contact dermatitis (L23-L25)
                     drug photoallergic response (L56.1)
                     drug phototoxic response (L56.0)
                     urticaria (L50.-)

    L27.0   **Generalized skin eruption due to drugs and medicaments taken internally**
           Use additional code for adverse effect, if applicable,
              to identify drug (T36-T50 with fifth or sixth
              character 5)

    L27.1   **Localized skin eruption due to drugs and medicaments taken internally**
           Use additional code for adverse effect, if applicable,
              to identify drug (T36-T50 with fifth or sixth
              character 5)

    L27.2   **Dermatitis due to ingested food**
        Excludes2   dermatitis due to food in contact with
                         skin (L23.6, L24.6, L25.4)

    L27.8   **Dermatitis due to other substances taken internally**

    L27.9   **Dermatitis due to unspecified substance taken internally**

● **L28** **Lichen simplex chronicus and prurigo**

    L28.0   **Lichen simplex chronicus**
           Circumscribed neurodermatitis
           Lichen NOS

    L28.1   **Prurigo nodularis**

    L28.2   **Other prurigo**
           Prurigo NOS   Prurigo mitis
           Prurigo Hebra   Urticaria papulosa

● **L29** **Pruritus**

    Excludes1   neurotic excoriation (L98.1)
                     psychogenic pruritus (F45.8)

    L29.0   **Pruritus ani**

    L29.1   **Pruritus scroti** ♂

    L29.2   **Pruritus vulvae** ♀

    L29.3   **Anogenital pruritus, unspecified**

    L29.8   **Other pruritus**

    L29.9   **Pruritus, unspecified**
           Itch NOS

▶ New   ⇒ Revised   ~~deleted~~ Deleted   Excludes 1   Excludes 2   Includes   Use additional   Code first   Code also   Key words

OGCR Official Guidelines   X Assign placeholder X   ● Use Additional Character(s)   ❩ Manifestation Code   🔖 Hierarchical Condition Category   **Coding Clinic**

● **L30**   **Other and unspecified dermatitis**

> **Excludes2**   contact dermatitis (L23-L25)
> dry skin dermatitis (L85.3)
> small plaque parapsoriasis (L41.3)
> stasis dermatitis (I87.2)

L30.0   **Nummular dermatitis**

L30.1   **Dyshidrosis [pompholyx]**

L30.2   **Cutaneous autosensitization**
    Candidid [levurid]   Eczematid
    Dermatophytid

L30.3   **Infective dermatitis**
    Infectious eczematoid dermatitis

L30.4   **Erythema intertrigo**

L30.5   **Pityriasis alba**
    Coding Clinic: 2018, Q1, P6

L30.8   **Other specified dermatitis**

L30.9   **Dermatitis, unspecified**
    Eczema NOS

PAPULOSQUAMOUS DISORDERS (L40-L45)

● **L40**   **Psoriasis**

L40.0   **Psoriasis vulgaris**
    Nummular psoriasis   Plaque psoriasis

L40.1   **Generalized pustular psoriasis**
    Impetigo herpetiformis   Von Zumbusch's disease

L40.2   **Acrodermatitis continua**

L40.3   **Pustulosis palmaris et plantaris**

L40.4   **Guttate psoriasis**

● **L40.5**   **Arthropathic psoriasis**

    L40.50   Arthropathic psoriasis, unspecified 🔖

    L40.51   Distal interphalangeal psoriatic arthropathy 🔖

    L40.52   Psoriatic arthritis mutilans 🔖

    L40.53   Psoriatic spondylitis 🔖

    L40.54   Psoriatic juvenile arthropathy 🔖

    L40.59   Other psoriatic arthropathy 🔖

L40.8   **Other psoriasis**
    Flexural psoriasis

L40.9   **Psoriasis, unspecified**

● **L41**   **Parapsoriasis**

> **Excludes1**   poikiloderma vasculare atrophicans (L94.5)

L41.0   **Pityriasis lichenoides et varioliformis acuta**
    Mucha-Habermann disease

L41.1   **Pityriasis lichenoides chronica**

L41.3   **Small plaque parapsoriasis**

L41.4   **Large plaque parapsoriasis**

L41.5   **Retiform parapsoriasis**

L41.8   **Other parapsoriasis**

L41.9   **Parapsoriasis, unspecified**

L42   **Pityriasis rosea**

● **L43**   **Lichen planus**

> **Excludes1**   lichen planopilaris (L66.1)

L43.0   **Hypertrophic lichen planus**

L43.1   **Bullous lichen planus**

L43.2   **Lichenoid drug reaction**
    Use additional code for adverse effect, if applicable, to identify drug (T36-T50 with fifth or sixth character 5)

L43.3   **Subacute (active) lichen planus**
    Lichen planus tropicus

L43.8   **Other lichen planus**

L43.9   **Lichen planus, unspecified**

Item 12–8 Psoriasis is a chronic, recurrent inflammatory skin disease characterized by small patches covered with thick, silvery scales. **Parapsoriasis** is a treatment-resistant erythroderma. **Pityriasis rosea** is characterized by a herald patch that is a single large lesion and that usually appears on the trunk and is followed by scattered, smaller lesions.

● **L44**   **Other papulosquamous disorders**

L44.0   **Pityriasis rubra pilaris**

L44.1   **Lichen nitidus**

L44.2   **Lichen striatus**

L44.3   **Lichen ruber moniliformis**

L44.4   **Infantile papular acrodermatitis [Gianotti-Crosti]**   P

L44.8   **Other specified papulosquamous disorders**

L44.9   **Papulosquamous disorder, unspecified**

▷ **L45**   *Papulosquamous disorders in diseases classified elsewhere*
> *Code first* underlying disease

URTICARIA AND ERYTHEMA (L49-L54)

> **Excludes1**   Lyme disease (A69.2-)
> rosacea (L71.-)

● **L49**   **Exfoliation due to erythematous conditions according to extent of body surface involved**

> *Code first erythematous condition causing exfoliation, such as:*
> Ritter's disease (L00)
> (Staphylococcal) scalded skin syndrome (L00)
> Stevens-Johnson syndrome (L51.1)
> Stevens-Johnson syndrome-toxic epidermal necrolysis overlap syndrome (L51.3)
> Toxic epidermal necrolysis (L51.2)

L49.0   **Exfoliation due to erythematous condition involving less than 10 percent of body surface**
    Exfoliation due to erythematous condition NOS

L49.1   **Exfoliation due to erythematous condition involving 10-19 percent of body surface**

L49.2   **Exfoliation due to erythematous condition involving 20-29 percent of body surface**

L49.3   **Exfoliation due to erythematous condition involving 30-39 percent of body surface**

L49.4   **Exfoliation due to erythematous condition involving 40-49 percent of body surface**

L49.5   **Exfoliation due to erythematous condition involving 50-59 percent of body surface**

L49.6   **Exfoliation due to erythematous condition involving 60-69 percent of body surface**

L49.7   **Exfoliation due to erythematous condition involving 70-79 percent of body surface**

L49.8   **Exfoliation due to erythematous condition involving 80-89 percent of body surface**

L49.9   **Exfoliation due to erythematous condition involving 90 or more percent of body surface**

Figure 12-6 Erythematous plaques with silvery scales in a patient with psoriasis. (Getty Image)

CHAPTER 12 (L00-L99)

Figure 12-7 Urticaria (hives). *(Courtesy of David Effron, MD.)* (Getty Image)

Item 12–9 Urticaria is a vascular reaction in which wheals surrounded by a red halo appear and cause severe itching. The causes of urticaria or hives are extensive and varied (e.g., food, heat, cold, drugs, stress, infections).

● **L50   Urticaria**
> **Excludes1**   allergic contact dermatitis (L23.-)
>   angioneurotic edema (T78.3)
>   giant urticaria (T78.3)
>   hereditary angio-edema (D84.1)
>   Quincke's edema (T78.3)
>   serum urticaria (T80.6-)
>   solar urticaria (L56.3)
>   urticaria neonatorum (P83.8)
>   urticaria papulosa (L28.2)
>   urticaria pigmentosa (D47.01)

   L50.0   Allergic urticaria
   L50.1   Idiopathic urticaria
   L50.2   Urticaria due to cold and heat
> **Excludes2**   familial cold urticaria (M04.2)

   L50.3   Dermatographic urticaria
   L50.4   Vibratory urticaria
   L50.5   Cholinergic urticaria
   L50.6   Contact urticaria
   L50.8   Other urticaria
         Chronic urticaria
         Recurrent periodic urticaria
   L50.9   Urticaria, unspecified

● **L51   Erythema multiforme**
> Use additional code for adverse effect, if applicable, to identify drug (T36-T50 with fifth or sixth character 5)
> Use additional code to identify associated manifestations, such as:
>   arthropathy associated with dermatological disorders (M14.8-)
>   conjunctival edema (H11.42)
>   conjunctivitis (H10.22-)
>   corneal scars and opacities (H17.-)
>   corneal ulcer (H16.0-)
>   edema of eyelid (H02.84-)
>   inflammation of eyelid (H01.8)
>   keratoconjunctivitis sicca (H16.22-)
>   mechanical lagophthalmos (H02.22-)
>   stomatitis (K12.-)
>   symblepharon (H11.23-)
> Use additional code to identify percentage of skin exfoliation (L49.-)
> **Excludes1**   staphylococcal scalded skin syndrome (L00)
>   Ritter's disease (L00)

   L51.0   Nonbullous erythema multiforme
   L51.1   Stevens-Johnson syndrome 🅒🅒
   L51.2   Toxic epidermal necrolysis [Lyell] 🅒🅒
   L51.3   Stevens-Johnson syndrome-toxic epidermal necrolysis overlap syndrome 🅒🅒
         SJS-TEN overlap syndrome
   L51.8   Other erythema multiforme
   L51.9   Erythema multiforme, unspecified
         Erythema iris
         Erythema multiforme major NOS
         Erythema multiforme minor NOS
         Herpes iris

   L52   Erythema nodosum
> **Excludes1**   tuberculous erythema nodosum (A18.4)

● **L53   Other erythematous conditions**
> **Excludes1**   erythema ab igne (L59.0)
>   erythema due to external agents in contact with skin (L23-L25)
>   erythema intertrigo (L30.4)

   L53.0   Toxic erythema
> *Code first poisoning due to drug or toxin, if applicable (T36-T65 with fifth or sixth character 1-4 or 6)*
> Use additional code for adverse effect, if applicable, to identify drug (T36-T50 with fifth or sixth character 5)
> **Excludes1**   neonatal erythema toxicum (P83.1)

   L53.1   Erythema annulare centrifugum
   L53.2   Erythema marginatum
   L53.3   Other chronic figurate erythema
   L53.8   Other specified erythematous conditions
   L53.9   Erythematous condition, unspecified
         Erythema NOS
         Erythroderma NOS

▷ *L54   Erythema in diseases classified elsewhere*
> *Code first underlying disease*

RADIATION-RELATED DISORDERS OF THE SKIN AND SUBCUTANEOUS TISSUE (L55-L59)

● **L55   Sunburn**
   L55.0   Sunburn of first degree
   L55.1   Sunburn of second degree
   L55.2   Sunburn of third degree
   L55.9   Sunburn, unspecified

● **L56   Other acute skin changes due to ultraviolet radiation**
> Use additional code to identify the source of the ultraviolet radiation (W89, X32)

   L56.0   Drug phototoxic response
> Use additional code for adverse effect, if applicable, to identify drug (T36-T50 with fifth or sixth character 5)

   L56.1   Drug photoallergic response
> Use additional code for adverse effect, if applicable, to identify drug (T36-T50 with fifth or sixth character 5)

   L56.2   Photocontact dermatitis [berloque dermatitis]
   L56.3   Solar urticaria
   L56.4   Polymorphous light eruption
   L56.5   Disseminated superficial actinic porokeratosis (DSAP)
   L56.8   Other specified acute skin changes due to ultraviolet radiation
   L56.9   Acute skin change due to ultraviolet radiation, unspecified

● **L57   Skin changes due to chronic exposure to nonionizing radiation**
> ⇒ Use additional code to identify the source of the ultraviolet radiation (W89), or other nonionizing radiation (W90)

   L57.0   Actinic keratosis
         Keratosis NOS   Solar keratosis
         Senile keratosis
   L57.1   Actinic reticuloid
   L57.2   Cutis rhomboidalis nuchae
   L57.3   Poikiloderma of Civatte
   L57.4   Cutis laxa senilis
         Elastosis senilis
   L57.5   Actinic granuloma
   L57.8   Other skin changes due to chronic exposure to nonionizing radiation
         Farmer's skin   Solar dermatitis
         Sailor's skin
   L57.9   Skin changes due to chronic exposure to nonionizing radiation, unspecified

▶ New   ⇒ Revised   ~~deleted~~ Deleted   Excludes 1   Excludes 2   Includes   Use additional   Code first   Code also   Key words
OGCR Official Guidelines   X Assign placeholder X   ● Use Additional Character(s)   ▷ Manifestation Code   🅒🅒 Hierarchical Condition Category   **Coding Clinic**

● **L58 Radiodermatitis**

> Use additional code to identify the source of the radiation (W88, W9Ø)

     L58.0 Acute radiodermatitis

     L58.1 Chronic radiodermatitis

     L58.9 Radiodermatitis, unspecified

● **L59 Other disorders of skin and subcutaneous tissue related to radiation**

     L59.0 Erythema ab igne [dermatitis ab igne]

     L59.8 Other specified disorders of the skin and subcutaneous tissue related to radiation
         Coding Clinic: 2017, Q1, P34

     L59.9 Disorder of the skin and subcutaneous tissue related to radiation, unspecified

DISORDERS OF SKIN APPENDAGES (L6Ø-L75)

> **Excludes1**   congenital malformations of integument (Q84.-)

● **L60 Nail disorders**

> **Excludes2**   clubbing of nails (R68.3)
>   onychia and paronychia (LØ3.Ø-)

     L60.0 Ingrowing nail

     L60.1 Onycholysis

     L60.2 Onychogryphosis

     L60.3 Nail dystrophy

     L60.4 Beau's lines

     L60.5 Yellow nail syndrome

     L60.8 Other nail disorders

     L60.9 Nail disorder, unspecified

◗ *L62 Nail disorders in diseases classified elsewhere*

> *Code first underlying disease, such as:*
>   pachydermoperiostosis (M89.4-)

● **L63 Alopecia areata**

     L63.0 Alopecia (capitis) totalis

     L63.1 Alopecia universalis

     L63.2 Ophiasis

     L63.8 Other alopecia areata

     L63.9 Alopecia areata, unspecified

● **L64 Androgenic alopecia**

> **Includes**   male-pattern baldness

     L64.0 Drug-induced androgenic alopecia

> Use additional code for adverse effect, if applicable, to identify drug (T36-T5Ø with fifth or sixth character 5)

     L64.8 Other androgenic alopecia

     L64.9 Androgenic alopecia, unspecified

● **L65 Other nonscarring hair loss**

> Use additional code for adverse effect, if applicable, to identify drug (T36-T5Ø with fifth or sixth character 5)

> **Excludes1**   trichotillomania (F63.3)

     L65.0 Telogen effluvium

     L65.1 Anagen effluvium

     L65.2 Alopecia mucinosa

     L65.8 Other specified nonscarring hair loss

     L65.9 Nonscarring hair loss, unspecified
         Alopecia NOS

● **L66 Cicatricial alopecia [scarring hair loss]**

     L66.0 Pseudopelade

     L66.1 Lichen planopilaris
         Follicular lichen planus

     L66.2 Folliculitis decalvans

     L66.3 Perifolliculitis capitis abscedens

     L66.4 Folliculitis ulerythematosa reticulata

     L66.8 Other cicatricial alopecia
         Coding Clinic: 2015, Q1, P19

     L66.9 Cicatricial alopecia, unspecified

● **L67 Hair color and hair shaft abnormalities**

> **Excludes1**   monilethrix (Q84.1)
>   pili annulati (Q84.1)
>   telogen effluvium (L65.Ø)

     L67.0 Trichorrhexis nodosa

     L67.1 Variations in hair color
         Canities
         Greyness, hair (premature)
         Heterochromia of hair
         Poliosis circumscripta, acquired
         Poliosis NOS

     L67.8 Other hair color and hair shaft abnormalities
         Fragilitas crinium

     L67.9 Hair color and hair shaft abnormality, unspecified

● **L68 Hypertrichosis**

> **Includes**   excess hair

> **Excludes1**   congenital hypertrichosis (Q84.2)
>   persistent lanugo (Q84.2)

     L68.0 Hirsutism
         Excessive growth of hair

     L68.1 Acquired hypertrichosis lanuginosa

     L68.2 Localized hypertrichosis

     L68.3 Polytrichia

     L68.8 Other hypertrichosis

     L68.9 Hypertrichosis, unspecified

Item 12–10 Alopecia is lack of hair and takes many forms. The most common is male pattern alopecia, also known as **androgenetic alopecia. Telogen effluvium** is early and excessive loss of hair resulting from a trauma to the hair follicle (fever, drugs, surgery, etc.).

Figure 12-8 Male pattern alopecia.

CHAPTER 12 (LØØ-L99)

CHAPTER 12 (L00–L99)

● **L70**   **Acne**
> **Excludes2**   acne keloid (L73.0)

L70.0   **Acne vulgaris**

L70.1   **Acne conglobata**

L70.2   **Acne varioliformis**
> Acne necrotica miliaris

L70.3   **Acne tropica**

L70.4   **Infantile acne**   **P**

L70.5   **Acné excoriée**
> Acné excoriée des jeunes filles
> Picker's acne

L70.8   **Other acne**

L70.9   **Acne, unspecified**

● **L71**   **Rosacea**
> Use additional code for adverse effect, if applicable, to identify drug (T36-T50 with fifth or sixth character 5)

L71.0   **Perioral dermatitis**

L71.1   **Rhinophyma**

L71.8   **Other rosacea**
> Coding Clinic: 2018, Q4, P15

L71.9   **Rosacea, unspecified**

● **L72**   **Follicular cysts of skin and subcutaneous tissue**

L72.0   **Epidermal cyst**

● L72.1   **Pilar and trichodermal cyst**

     L72.11   **Pilar cyst**

     L72.12   **Trichodermal cyst**
> Trichilemmal (proliferating) cyst

L72.3   **Sebaceous cyst**
> **Excludes2**   pilar cyst (L72.11)
> trichilemmal (proliferating) cyst (L72.12)

L72.2   **Steatocystoma multiplex**

L72.8   **Other follicular cysts of the skin and subcutaneous tissue**

L72.9   **Follicular cyst of the skin and subcutaneous tissue, unspecified**

● **L73**   **Other follicular disorders**

L73.0   **Acne keloid**

L73.1   **Pseudofolliculitis barbae**

L73.2   **Hidradenitis suppurativa**

L73.8   **Other specified follicular disorders**
> Sycosis barbae

L73.9   **Follicular disorder, unspecified**

● **L74**   **Eccrine sweat disorders**
> **Excludes2**   generalized hyperhidrosis (R61)

L74.0   **Miliaria rubra**

L74.1   **Miliaria crystallina**

L74.2   **Miliaria profunda**
> Miliaria tropicalis

L74.3   **Miliaria, unspecified**

L74.4   **Anhidrosis**
> Hypohidrosis

● L74.5   **Focal hyperhidrosis**

     ● L74.51   **Primary focal hyperhidrosis**

         L74.510   **Primary focal hyperhidrosis, axilla**

         L74.511   **Primary focal hyperhidrosis, face**

         L74.512   **Primary focal hyperhidrosis, palms**

         L74.513   **Primary focal hyperhidrosis, soles**

         L74.519   **Primary focal hyperhidrosis, unspecified**

     L74.52   **Secondary focal hyperhidrosis**
> Frey's syndrome

L74.8   **Other eccrine sweat disorders**

L74.9   **Eccrine sweat disorder, unspecified**
> Sweat gland disorder NOS

● **L75**   **Apocrine sweat disorders**
> **Excludes1**   dyshidrosis (L30.1)
> hidradenitis suppurativa (L73.2)

L75.0   **Bromhidrosis**

L75.1   **Chromhidrosis**

L75.2   **Apocrine miliaria**
> Fox-Fordyce disease

L75.8   **Other apocrine sweat disorders**

L75.9   **Apocrine sweat disorder, unspecified**
> Intraoperative and postprocedural complications of skin and subcutaneous tissue (L76)

INTRAOPERATIVE AND POSTPROCEDURAL COMPLICATIONS OF SKIN AND SUBCUTANEOUS TISSUE (L76)

● **L76**   **Intraoperative and postprocedural complications of skin and subcutaneous tissue**
> Coding Clinic: 2016, Q4, P10

● L76.0   **Intraoperative hemorrhage and hematoma of skin and subcutaneous tissue complicating a procedure**
> **Excludes1**   intraoperative hemorrhage and hematoma of skin and subcutaneous tissue due to accidental puncture and laceration during a procedure (L76.1-)

     L76.01   **Intraoperative hemorrhage and hematoma of skin and subcutaneous tissue complicating a dermatologic procedure**

     L76.02   **Intraoperative hemorrhage and hematoma of skin and subcutaneous tissue complicating other procedure**

● L76.1   **Accidental puncture and laceration of skin and subcutaneous tissue during a procedure**

     L76.11   **Accidental puncture and laceration of skin and subcutaneous tissue during a dermatologic procedure**

     L76.12   **Accidental puncture and laceration of skin and subcutaneous tissue during other procedure**

● L76.2   **Postprocedural hemorrhage of skin and subcutaneous tissue following a procedure**

     L76.21   **Postprocedural hemorrhage of skin and subcutaneous tissue following a dermatologic procedure**

     L76.22   **Postprocedural hemorrhage of skin and subcutaneous tissue following other procedure**

● L76.3   **Postprocedural hematoma and seroma of skin and subcutaneous tissue following a procedure**

     L76.31   **Postprocedural hematoma of skin and subcutaneous tissue following a dermatologic procedure**

     L76.32   **Postprocedural hematoma of skin and subcutaneous tissue following other procedure**

     L76.33   **Postprocedural seroma of skin and subcutaneous tissue following a dermatologic procedure**

     L76.34   **Postprocedural seroma of skin and subcutaneous tissue following other procedure**

● L76.8   **Other intraoperative and postprocedural complications of skin and subcutaneous tissue**
> Use additional code, if applicable, to further specify disorder

     L76.81   **Other intraoperative complications of skin and subcutaneous tissue**

     L76.82   **Other postprocedural complications of skin and subcutaneous tissue**
> Coding Clinic: 2017, Q3, P6

▶ New   ⇒ Revised   ~~deleted~~ Deleted   Excludes 1   Excludes 2   Includes   Use additional   Code first   Code also   Key words

OGCR Official Guidelines   X Assign placeholder X   ● Use Additional Character(s)   ▶ Manifestation Code   🍂 Hierarchical Condition Category   **Coding Clinic**

OTHER DISORDERS OF THE SKIN AND SUBCUTANEOUS TISSUE (L80-L99)

L80   **Vitiligo**
> **Excludes2**   vitiligo of eyelids (H02.73-)
> vitiligo of vulva (N90.89)

● **L81**   **Other disorders of pigmentation**
> **Excludes1**   birthmark NOS (Q82.5)
> Peutz-Jeghers syndrome (Q85.8)
>
> **Excludes2**   nevus - see Alphabetical Index

L81.0   **Postinflammatory hyperpigmentation**

L81.1   **Chloasma**

L81.2   **Freckles**

L81.3   **Café au lait spots**

L81.4   **Other melanin hyperpigmentation**
> Lentigo

L81.5   **Leukoderma, not elsewhere classified**

L81.6   **Other disorders of diminished melanin formation**

L81.7   **Pigmented purpuric dermatosis**
> Angioma serpiginosum

L81.8   **Other specified disorders of pigmentation**
> Iron pigmentation
> Tattoo pigmentation

L81.9   **Disorder of pigmentation, unspecified**

● **L82**   **Seborrheic keratosis**
> **Includes**   basal cell papilloma
> dermatosis papulosa nigra
> Leser-Trélat disease
>
> **Excludes2**   seborrheic dermatitis (L21.-)

L82.0   **Inflamed seborrheic keratosis**

L82.1   **Other seborrheic keratosis**
> Seborrheic keratosis NOS

L83   **Acanthosis nigricans**
> Confluent and reticulated papillomatosis

L84   **Corns and callosities**
> Callus
> Clavus

● **L85**   **Other epidermal thickening**
> **Excludes2**   hypertrophic disorders of the skin (L91.-)

L85.0   **Acquired ichthyosis**
> **Excludes1**   congenital ichthyosis (Q80.-)

L85.1   **Acquired keratosis [keratoderma] palmaris et plantaris**
> **Excludes1**   inherited keratosis palmaris et plantaris (Q82.8)

L85.2   **Keratosis punctata (palmaris et plantaris)**

L85.3   **Xerosis cutis**
> Dry skin dermatitis

L85.8   **Other specified epidermal thickening**
> Cutaneous horn

L85.9   **Epidermal thickening, unspecified**

▷ **L86**   *Keratoderma in diseases classified elsewhere*
> *Firm horny papules that have a cobblestone appearance*
> *Code first underlying disease, such as:*
> Reiter's disease (M02.3-)
>
> **Excludes1**   gonococcal keratoderma (A54.89)
> gonococcal keratosis (A54.89)
> keratoderma due to vitamin A deficiency (E50.8)
> keratosis due to vitamin A deficiency (E50.8)
> xeroderma due to vitamin A deficiency (E50.8)

● **L87**   **Transepidermal elimination disorders**
> **Excludes1**   granuloma annulare (perforating) (L92.0)

L87.0   **Keratosis follicularis et parafollicularis in cutem penetrans**
> Kyrle disease
> Hyperkeratosis follicularis penetrans

L87.1   **Reactive perforating collagenosis**

L87.2   **Elastosis perforans serpiginosa**

L87.8   **Other transepidermal elimination disorders**

L87.9   **Transepidermal elimination disorder, unspecified**

L88   **Pyoderma gangrenosum**
> Phagedenic pyoderma
>
> **Excludes1**   dermatitis gangrenosa (L08.0)

OGCR   Section I.B.14.

> General Coding Guidelines
>
> Documentation for BMI, *Depth of* Non-pressure ulcers, Pressure Ulcer Stages, Coma Scale, and *NIH Stroke Scale*
>
> For the Body Mass Index (BMI), depth of non-pressure chronic ulcers, pressure ulcer stage, coma scale, and NIH stroke scale (NIHSS) codes, code assignment may be based on medical record documentation from clinicians who are not the patient's provider (i.e., physician or other qualified healthcare practitioner legally accountable for establishing the patient's diagnosis), since this information is typically documented by other clinicians involved in the care of the patient (e.g., a dietitian often documents the BMI, a nurse often documents the pressure ulcer stages, and an emergency medical technician often documents the coma scale). However, the associated diagnosis (such as overweight, obesity, acute stroke, or pressure ulcer) must be documented by the patient's provider. If there is conflicting medical record documentation, either from the same clinician or different clinicians, the patient's attending provider should be queried for clarification. The BMI, coma scale, and NHSS codes should only be reported as secondary diagnoses.

● **L89**   **Pressure ulcer**
> **Includes**   bed sore   pressure area
> decubitus ulcer   pressure sore
> plaster ulcer
>
> *Code first any associated gangrene (I96)*
>
> **Excludes2**   decubitus (trophic) ulcer of cervix (uteri) (N86)
> diabetic ulcers (E08.621, E08.622, E09.621,
>   E09.622, E10.621, E10.622, E11.621, E11.622,
>   E13.621, E13.622)
> non-pressure chronic ulcer of skin (L97.-)
> skin infections (L00-L08)
> varicose ulcer (I83.0, I83.2)
>
> Coding Clinic: 2019, Q4, P11; 2018, Q2, P22; 2016, Q4, P124

● **L89.0**   **Pressure ulcer of elbow**

     ● **L89.00**   **Pressure ulcer of unspecified elbow**

         L89.000   **Pressure ulcer of unspecified elbow, unstageable** 🔁

         L89.001   **Pressure ulcer of unspecified elbow, stage 1**
> Healing pressure ulcer of unspecified elbow, stage 1
> Pressure pre-ulcer skin changes limited to persistent focal edema, unspecified elbow

         L89.002   **Pressure ulcer of unspecified elbow, stage 2**
> Healing pressure ulcer of unspecified elbow, stage 2
> Pressure ulcer with abrasion, blister, partial thickness skin loss involving epidermis and/or dermis, unspecified elbow

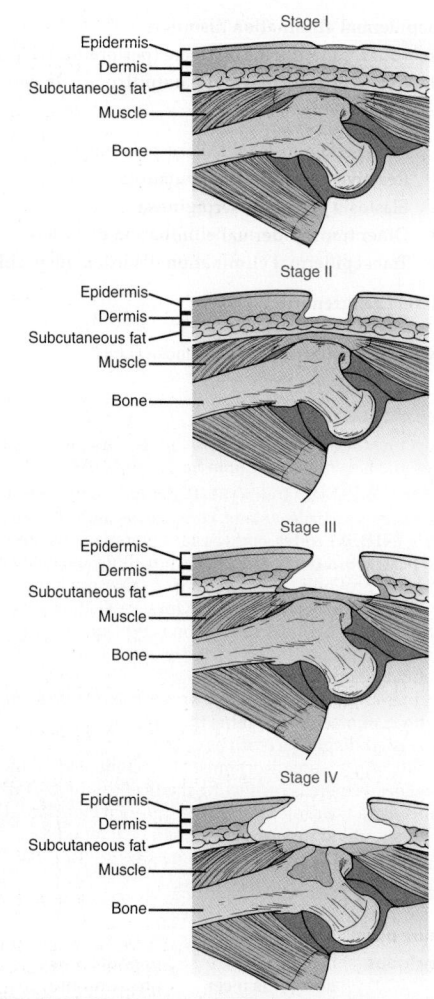

Figure 12-9 Stage I, II, III, and IV of pressure ulcers.

L89.003   **Pressure ulcer of unspecified elbow, stage 3** 🏵
           Healing pressure ulcer of
              unspecified elbow, stage 3
           Pressure ulcer with full thickness
              skin loss involving damage or
              necrosis of subcutaneous tissue,
              unspecified elbow

L89.004   **Pressure ulcer of unspecified elbow, stage 4** 🏵
           Healing pressure ulcer of
              unspecified elbow, stage 4
           Pressure ulcer with necrosis of soft
              tissues through to underlying
              muscle, tendon, or bone,
              unspecified elbow

L89.006   **Pressure-induced deep tissue damage of unspecified elbow**

L89.009   **Pressure ulcer of unspecified elbow, unspecified stage**
           Healing pressure ulcer of elbow
              NOS
           Healing pressure ulcer of
              unspecified elbow, unspecified
              stage

● L89.01   **Pressure ulcer of right elbow**

L89.010   **Pressure ulcer of right elbow, unstageable** 🏵

L89.011   **Pressure ulcer of right elbow, stage 1**
           Healing pressure ulcer of right
              elbow, stage 1
           Pressure pre-ulcer skin changes
              limited to persistent focal
              edema, right elbow

L89.012   **Pressure ulcer of right elbow, stage 2**
           Healing pressure ulcer of right
              elbow, stage 2
           Pressure ulcer with abrasion, blister,
              partial thickness skin loss
              involving epidermis and/or
              dermis, right elbow

L89.013   **Pressure ulcer of right elbow, stage 3** 🏵
           Healing pressure ulcer of right
              elbow, stage 3
           Pressure ulcer with full thickness
              skin loss involving damage or
              necrosis of subcutaneous tissue,
              right elbow

L89.014   **Pressure ulcer of right elbow, stage 4** 🏵
           Healing pressure ulcer of right
              elbow, stage 4
           Pressure ulcer with necrosis of soft
              tissues through to underlying
              muscle, tendon, or bone, right
              elbow

L89.016   **Pressure-induced deep tissue damage of right elbow**

L89.019   **Pressure ulcer of right elbow, unspecified stage**
           Healing pressure right of elbow
              NOS
           Healing pressure ulcer of right
              elbow, unspecified stage

● L89.02   **Pressure ulcer of left elbow**

L89.020   **Pressure ulcer of left elbow, unstageable** 🏵

L89.021   **Pressure ulcer of left elbow, stage 1**
           Healing pressure ulcer of left elbow,
              stage 1
           Pressure pre-ulcer skin changes
              limited to persistent focal
              edema, left elbow

L89.022   **Pressure ulcer of left elbow, stage 2**
           Healing pressure ulcer of left elbow,
              stage 2
           Pressure ulcer with abrasion, blister,
              partial thickness skin loss
              involving epidermis and/or
              dermis, left elbow

L89.023   **Pressure ulcer of left elbow, stage 3** 🏵
           Healing pressure ulcer of left elbow,
              stage 3
           Pressure ulcer with full thickness
              skin loss involving damage or
              necrosis of subcutaneous tissue,
              left elbow

L89.024   **Pressure ulcer of left elbow, stage 4** 🏵
           Healing pressure ulcer of left elbow,
              stage 4
           Pressure ulcer with necrosis of soft
              tissues through to underlying
              muscle, tendon, or bone, left
              elbow

▶ New   ⇒ Revised   ~~deleted~~ Deleted   Excludes 1   Excludes 2   Includes   Use additional   Code first   Code also   Key words
OGCR Official Guidelines   X Assign placeholder X   ● Use Additional Character(s)   ▶ Manifestation Code   🏵 Hierarchical Condition Category   **Coding Clinic**

L89.026   **Pressure-induced deep tissue damage of left elbow**

L89.029   **Pressure ulcer of left elbow, unspecified stage**
> Healing pressure ulcer of left of elbow NOS
> Healing pressure ulcer of left elbow, unspecified stage

● **L89.1   Pressure ulcer of back**

  ● **L89.10   Pressure ulcer of unspecified part of back**

L89.100   **Pressure ulcer of unspecified part of back, unstageable** 🔒

L89.101   **Pressure ulcer of unspecified part of back, stage 1**
> Healing pressure ulcer of unspecified part of back, stage 1
> Pressure pre-ulcer skin changes limited to persistent focal edema, unspecified part of back

L89.102   **Pressure ulcer of unspecified part of back, stage 2**
> Healing pressure ulcer of unspecified part of back, stage 2
> Pressure ulcer with abrasion, blister, partial thickness skin loss involving epidermis and/or dermis, unspecified part of back

L89.103   **Pressure ulcer of unspecified part of back, stage 3** 🔒
> Healing pressure ulcer of unspecified part of back, stage 3
> Pressure ulcer with full thickness skin loss involving damage or necrosis of subcutaneous tissue, unspecified part of back

L89.104   **Pressure ulcer of unspecified part of back, stage 4** 🔒
> Healing pressure ulcer of unspecified part of back, stage 4
> Pressure ulcer with necrosis of soft tissues through to underlying muscle, tendon, or bone, unspecified part of back

L89.106   **Pressure-induced deep tissue damage of unspecified part of back**

L89.109   **Pressure ulcer of unspecified part of back, unspecified stage**
> Healing pressure ulcer of unspecified part of back NOS
> Healing pressure ulcer of unspecified part of back, unspecified stage

  ● **L89.11   Pressure ulcer of right upper back**
> Pressure ulcer of right shoulder blade

L89.110   **Pressure ulcer of right upper back, unstageable** 🔒

L89.111   **Pressure ulcer of right upper back, stage 1**
> Healing pressure ulcer of right upper back, stage 1
> Pressure pre-ulcer skin changes limited to persistent focal edema, right upper back

L89.112   **Pressure ulcer of right upper back, stage 2**
> Healing pressure ulcer of right upper back, stage 2
> Pressure ulcer with abrasion, blister, partial thickness skin loss involving epidermis and/or dermis, right upper back

L89.113   **Pressure ulcer of right upper back, stage 3** 🔒
> Healing pressure ulcer of right upper back, stage 3
> Pressure ulcer with full thickness skin loss involving damage or necrosis of subcutaneous tissue, right upper back

L89.114   **Pressure ulcer of right upper back, stage 4** 🔒
> Healing pressure ulcer of right upper back, stage 4
> Pressure ulcer with necrosis of soft tissues through to underlying muscle, tendon, or bone, right upper back

L89.116   **Pressure-induced deep tissue damage of right upper back**

L89.119   **Pressure ulcer of right upper back, unspecified stage**
> Healing pressure ulcer of right upper back NOS
> Healing pressure ulcer of right upper back, unspecified stage

  ● **L89.12   Pressure ulcer of left upper back**
> Pressure ulcer of left shoulder blade

L89.120   **Pressure ulcer of left upper back, unstageable** 🔒

L89.121   **Pressure ulcer of left upper back, stage 1**
> Healing pressure ulcer of left upper back, stage 1
> Pressure pre-ulcer skin changes limited to persistent focal edema, left upper back

L89.122   **Pressure ulcer of left upper back, stage 2**
> Healing pressure ulcer of left upper back, stage 2
> Pressure ulcer with abrasion, blister, partial thickness skin loss involving epidermis and/or dermis, left upper back

L89.123   **Pressure ulcer of left upper back, stage 3** 🔒
> Healing pressure ulcer of left upper back, stage 3
> Pressure ulcer with full thickness skin loss involving damage or necrosis of subcutaneous tissue, left upper back

L89.124   **Pressure ulcer of left upper back, stage 4** 🔒
> Healing pressure ulcer of left upper back, stage 4
> Pressure ulcer with necrosis of soft tissues through to underlying muscle, tendon, or bone, left upper back

L89.126   **Pressure-induced deep tissue damage of left upper back**

L89.129   **Pressure ulcer of left upper back, unspecified stage**
> Healing pressure ulcer of left upper back NOS
> Healing pressure ulcer of left upper back, unspecified stage

N Newborn Age: 0   **P** Pediatric Age: 0–17   **M** Maternity DX: 12–55   **A** Adult Age: 15–124   ♀ Females Only   ♂ Males Only

981

CHAPTER 12 (L00–L99)

● **L89.13 Pressure ulcer of right lower back**

    L89.130 Pressure ulcer of right lower back, unstageable 🐾

    L89.131 Pressure ulcer of right lower back, stage 1
        Healing pressure ulcer of right lower back, stage 1
        Pressure pre-ulcer skin changes limited to persistent focal edema, right lower back

    L89.132 Pressure ulcer of right lower back, stage 2
        Healing pressure ulcer of right lower back, stage 2
        Pressure ulcer with abrasion, blister, partial thickness skin loss involving epidermis and/or dermis, right lower back

    L89.133 Pressure ulcer of right lower back, stage 3 🐾
        Healing pressure ulcer of right lower back, stage 3
        Pressure ulcer with full thickness skin loss involving damage or necrosis of subcutaneous tissue, right lower back

    L89.134 Pressure ulcer of right lower back, stage 4 🐾
        Healing pressure ulcer of right lower back, stage 4
        Pressure ulcer with necrosis of soft tissues through to underlying muscle, tendon, or bone, right lower back

    L89.136 Pressure-induced deep tissue damage of right lower back

    L89.139 Pressure ulcer of right lower back, unspecified stage
        Healing pressure ulcer of right lower back NOS
        Healing pressure ulcer of right lower back, unspecified stage

● **L89.14 Pressure ulcer of left lower back**

    L89.140 Pressure ulcer of left lower back, unstageable 🐾

    L89.141 Pressure ulcer of left lower back, stage 1
        Healing pressure ulcer of left lower back, stage 1
        Pressure pre-ulcer skin changes limited to persistent focal edema, left lower back

    L89.142 Pressure ulcer of left lower back, stage 2
        Healing pressure ulcer of left lower back, stage 2
        Pressure ulcer with abrasion, blister, partial thickness skin loss involving epidermis and/or dermis, left lower back

    L89.143 Pressure ulcer of left lower back, stage 3 🐾
        Healing pressure ulcer of left lower back, stage 3
        Pressure ulcer with full thickness skin loss involving damage or necrosis of subcutaneous tissue, left lower back

    L89.144 Pressure ulcer of left lower back, stage 4 🐾
        Healing pressure ulcer of left lower back, stage 4
        Pressure ulcer with necrosis of soft tissues through to underlying muscle, tendon, or bone, left lower back

    L89.146 Pressure-induced deep tissue damage of left lower back

    L89.149 Pressure ulcer of left lower back, unspecified stage
        Healing pressure ulcer of left lower back NOS
        Healing pressure ulcer of left lower back, unspecified stage

● **L89.15 Pressure ulcer of sacral region**
    Pressure ulcer of coccyx
    Pressure ulcer of tailbone

    L89.150 Pressure ulcer of sacral region, unstageable 🐾

    L89.151 Pressure ulcer of sacral region, stage 1
        Healing pressure ulcer of sacral region, stage 1
        Pressure pre-ulcer skin changes limited to persistent focal edema, sacral region

    L89.152 Pressure ulcer of sacral region, stage 2
        Healing pressure ulcer of sacral region, stage 2
        Pressure ulcer with abrasion, blister, partial thickness skin loss involving epidermis and/or dermis, sacral region

    L89.153 Pressure ulcer of sacral region, stage 3 🐾
        Healing pressure ulcer of sacral region, stage 3
        Pressure ulcer with full thickness skin loss involving damage or necrosis of subcutaneous tissue, sacral region

    L89.154 Pressure ulcer of sacral region, stage 4 🐾
        Healing pressure ulcer of sacral region, stage 4
        Pressure ulcer with necrosis of soft tissues through to underlying muscle, tendon, or bone, sacral region

    L89.156 Pressure-induced deep tissue damage of sacral region

    L89.159 Pressure ulcer of sacral region, unspecified stage
        Healing pressure ulcer of sacral region NOS
        Healing pressure ulcer of sacral region, unspecified stage

● **L89.2 Pressure ulcer of hip**

● **L89.20 Pressure ulcer of unspecified hip**

    L89.200 Pressure ulcer of unspecified hip, unstageable 🐾

    L89.201 Pressure ulcer of unspecified hip, stage 1
        Healing pressure ulcer of unspecified hip back, stage 1
        Pressure pre-ulcer skin changes limited to persistent focal edema, unspecified hip

▶ New   ⇒ Revised   ~~deleted~~ Deleted   Excludes 1   Excludes 2   Includes   Use additional   Code first   Code also   Key words

OGCR Official Guidelines   X Assign placeholder X   ● Use Additional Character(s)   ▷ Manifestation Code   🐾 Hierarchical Condition Category   **Coding Clinic**

L89.202   **Pressure ulcer of unspecified hip, stage 2**
Healing pressure ulcer of unspecified hip, stage 2
Pressure ulcer with abrasion, blister, partial thickness skin loss involving epidermis and/or dermis, unspecified hip

L89.203   **Pressure ulcer of unspecified hip, stage 3 🔍**
Healing pressure ulcer of unspecified hip, stage 3
Pressure ulcer with full thickness skin loss involving damage or necrosis of subcutaneous tissue, unspecified hip

L89.204   **Pressure ulcer of unspecified hip, stage 4 🔍**
Healing pressure ulcer of unspecified hip, stage 4
Pressure ulcer with necrosis of soft tissues through to underlying muscle, tendon, or bone, unspecified hip

L89.206   **Pressure-induced deep tissue damage of unspecified hip**

L89.209   **Pressure ulcer of unspecified hip, unspecified stage**
Healing pressure ulcer of unspecified hip NOS
Healing pressure ulcer of unspecified hip, unspecified stage

● **L89.21**   Pressure ulcer of **right hip**

L89.210   **Pressure ulcer of right hip, unstageable 🔍**

L89.211   **Pressure ulcer of right hip, stage 1**
Healing pressure ulcer of right hip back, stage 1
Pressure pre-ulcer skin changes limited to persistent focal edema, right hip

L89.212   **Pressure ulcer of right hip, stage 2**
Healing pressure ulcer of right hip, stage 2
Pressure ulcer with abrasion, blister, partial thickness skin loss involving epidermis and/or dermis, right hip

L89.213   **Pressure ulcer of right hip, stage 3 🔍**
Healing pressure ulcer of right hip, stage 3
Pressure ulcer with full thickness skin loss involving damage or necrosis of subcutaneous tissue, right hip

L89.214   **Pressure ulcer of right hip, stage 4 🔍**
Healing pressure ulcer of right hip, stage 4
Pressure ulcer with necrosis of soft tissues through to underlying muscle, tendon, or bone, right hip

L89.216   **Pressure-induced deep tissue damage of right hip**

L89.219   **Pressure ulcer of right hip, unspecified stage**
Healing pressure ulcer of right hip NOS
Healing pressure ulcer of right hip, unspecified stage

● **L89.22**   Pressure ulcer of **left hip**

L89.220   **Pressure ulcer of left hip, unstageable 🔍**

L89.221   **Pressure ulcer of left hip, stage 1**
Healing pressure ulcer of left hip back, stage 1
Pressure pre-ulcer skin changes limited to persistent focal edema, left hip

L89.222   **Pressure ulcer of left hip, stage 2**
Healing pressure ulcer of left hip, stage 2
Pressure ulcer with abrasion, blister, partial thickness skin loss involving epidermis and/or dermis, left hip

L89.223   **Pressure ulcer of left hip, stage 3 🔍**
Healing pressure ulcer of left hip, stage 3
Pressure ulcer with full thickness skin loss involving damage or necrosis of subcutaneous tissue, left hip

L89.224   **Pressure ulcer of left hip, stage 4 🔍**
Healing pressure ulcer of left hip, stage 4
Pressure ulcer with necrosis of soft tissues through to underlying muscle, tendon, or bone, left hip

L89.226   **Pressure-induced deep tissue damage of left hip**

L89.229   **Pressure ulcer of left hip, unspecified stage**
Healing pressure ulcer of left hip NOS
Healing pressure ulcer of left hip, unspecified stage

● **L89.3**   Pressure ulcer of **buttock**

● **L89.30**   Pressure ulcer of **unspecified** buttock

L89.300   **Pressure ulcer of unspecified buttock, unstageable 🔍**

L89.301   **Pressure ulcer of unspecified buttock, stage 1**
Healing pressure ulcer of unspecified buttock, stage 1
Pressure pre-ulcer skin changes limited to persistent focal edema, unspecified buttock

L89.302   **Pressure ulcer of unspecified buttock, stage 2**
Healing pressure ulcer of unspecified buttock, stage 2
Pressure ulcer with abrasion, blister, partial thickness skin loss involving epidermis and/or dermis, unspecified buttock

L89.303   **Pressure ulcer of unspecified buttock, stage 3 🔍**
Healing pressure ulcer of unspecified buttock, stage 3
Pressure ulcer with full thickness skin loss involving damage or necrosis of subcutaneous tissue, unspecified buttock

L89.304   **Pressure ulcer of unspecified buttock, stage 4 🔍**
Healing pressure ulcer of unspecified buttock, stage 4
Pressure ulcer with necrosis of soft tissues through to underlying muscle, tendon, or bone, unspecified buttock

L89.306   Pressure-induced deep tissue damage of unspecified buttock

L89.309   Pressure ulcer of unspecified buttock, unspecified stage

      Healing pressure ulcer of unspecified buttock NOS

      Healing pressure ulcer of unspecified buttock, unspecified stage

● **L89.31**   Pressure ulcer of right buttock

L89.310   Pressure ulcer of right buttock, unstageable 🦠

L89.311   Pressure ulcer of right buttock, stage 1

      Healing pressure ulcer of right buttock, stage 1

      Pressure pre-ulcer skin changes limited to persistent focal edema, right buttock

L89.312   Pressure ulcer of right buttock, stage 2

      Healing pressure ulcer of right buttock, stage 2

      Pressure ulcer with abrasion, blister, partial thickness skin loss involving epidermis and/or dermis, right buttock

L89.313   Pressure ulcer of right buttock, stage 3 🦠

      Healing pressure ulcer of right buttock, stage 3

      Pressure ulcer with full thickness skin loss involving damage or necrosis of subcutaneous tissue, right buttock

L89.314   Pressure ulcer of right buttock, stage 4 🦠

      Healing pressure ulcer of right buttock, stage 4

      Pressure ulcer with necrosis of soft tissues through to underlying muscle, tendon, or bone, right buttock

L89.316 Pressure-induced deep tissue damage of right buttock

L89.319   Pressure ulcer of right buttock, unspecified stage

      Healing pressure ulcer of right buttock NOS

      Healing pressure ulcer of right buttock, unspecified stage

● **L89.32**   Pressure ulcer of left buttock

L89.320   Pressure ulcer of left buttock, unstageable 🦠

L89.321   Pressure ulcer of left buttock, stage 1

      Healing pressure ulcer of left buttock, stage 1

      Pressure pre-ulcer skin changes limited to persistent focal edema, left buttock

L89.322   Pressure ulcer of left buttock, stage 2

      Healing pressure ulcer of left buttock, stage 2

      Pressure ulcer with abrasion, blister, partial thickness skin loss involving epidermis and/or dermis, left buttock

L89.323   Pressure ulcer of left buttock, stage 3 🦠

      Healing pressure ulcer of left buttock, stage 3

      Pressure ulcer with full thickness skin loss involving damage or necrosis of subcutaneous tissue, left buttock

L89.324   Pressure ulcer of left buttock, stage 4 🦠

      Healing pressure ulcer of left buttock, stage 4

      Pressure ulcer with necrosis of soft tissues through to underlying muscle, tendon, or bone, left buttock

L89.326   Pressure-induced deep tissue damage of left buttock

L89.329   Pressure ulcer of left buttock, unspecified stage

      Healing pressure ulcer of left buttock NOS

      Healing pressure ulcer of left buttock, unspecified stage

● **L89.4**   Pressure ulcer of contiguous site of back, buttock and hip

L89.40   Pressure ulcer of contiguous site of back, buttock and hip, unspecified stage

      Healing pressure ulcer of contiguous site of back, buttock and hip NOS

      Healing pressure ulcer of contiguous site of back, buttock and hip, unspecified stage

L89.41   Pressure ulcer of contiguous site of back, buttock and hip, stage 1

      Healing pressure ulcer of contiguous site of back, buttock and hip, stage 1

      Pressure pre-ulcer skin changes limited to persistent focal edema, contiguous site of back, buttock and hip

L89.42   Pressure ulcer of contiguous site of back, buttock and hip, stage 2

      Healing pressure ulcer of contiguous site of back, buttock and hip, stage 2

      Pressure ulcer with abrasion, blister, partial thickness skin loss involving epidermis and/or dermis, contiguous site of back, buttock and hip

L89.43   Pressure ulcer of contiguous site of back, buttock and hip, stage 3 🦠

      Healing pressure ulcer of contiguous site of back, buttock and hip, stage 3

      Pressure ulcer with full thickness skin loss involving damage or necrosis of subcutaneous tissue, contiguous site of back, buttock and hip

L89.44   Pressure ulcer of contiguous site of back, buttock and hip, stage 4 🦠

      Healing pressure ulcer of contiguous site of back, buttock and hip, stage 4

      Pressure ulcer with necrosis of soft tissues through to underlying muscle, tendon, or bone, contiguous site of back, buttock and hip

L89.45   Pressure ulcer of contiguous site of back, buttock and hip, unstageable 🦠

L89.46   Pressure-induced deep tissue damage of contiguous site of back, buttock and hip

CHAPTER 12 (L00-L99)

▶ New   ⇒ Revised   ~~deleted~~ Deleted   Excludes 1   Excludes 2   Includes   Use additional   Code first   Code also   Key words

OGCR Official Guidelines   X Assign placeholder X   ● Use Additional Character(s)   ▶ Manifestation Code   🦠 Hierarchical Condition Category   **Coding Clinic**

● **L89.5**   **Pressure ulcer of ankle**

   ● **L89.50**   **Pressure ulcer of unspecified ankle**

     L89.500   **Pressure ulcer of unspecified ankle, unstageable** 🔲

     L89.501   **Pressure ulcer of unspecified ankle, stage 1**
         Healing pressure ulcer of unspecified ankle, stage 1
         Pressure pre-ulcer skin changes limited to persistent focal edema, unspecified ankle

     L89.502   **Pressure ulcer of unspecified ankle, stage 2**
         Healing pressure ulcer of unspecified ankle, stage 2
         Pressure ulcer with abrasion, blister, partial thickness skin loss involving epidermis and/or dermis, unspecified ankle

     L89.503   **Pressure ulcer of unspecified ankle, stage 3** 🔲
         Healing pressure ulcer of unspecified ankle, stage 3
         Pressure ulcer with full thickness skin loss involving damage or necrosis of subcutaneous tissue, unspecified ankle

     L89.504   **Pressure ulcer of unspecified ankle, stage 4** 🔲
         Healing pressure ulcer of unspecified ankle, stage 4
         Pressure ulcer with necrosis of soft tissues through to underlying muscle, tendon, or bone, unspecified ankle

     L89.506   **Pressure-induced deep tissue damage of unspecified ankle**

     L89.509   **Pressure ulcer of unspecified ankle, unspecified stage**
         Healing pressure ulcer of unspecified ankle NOS
         Healing pressure ulcer of unspecified ankle, unspecified stage

   ● **L89.51**   **Pressure ulcer of right ankle**

     L89.510   **Pressure ulcer of right ankle, unstageable** 🔲

     L89.511   **Pressure ulcer of right ankle, stage 1**
         Healing pressure ulcer of right ankle, stage 1
         Pressure pre-ulcer skin changes limited to persistent focal edema, right ankle

     L89.512   **Pressure ulcer of right ankle, stage 2**
         Healing pressure ulcer of right ankle, stage 2
         Pressure ulcer with abrasion, blister, partial thickness skin loss involving epidermis and/or dermis, right ankle

     L89.513   **Pressure ulcer of right ankle, stage 3** 🔲
         Healing pressure ulcer of right ankle, stage 3
         Pressure ulcer with full thickness skin loss involving damage or necrosis of subcutaneous tissue, right ankle

     L89.514   **Pressure ulcer of right ankle, stage 4** 🔲
         Healing pressure ulcer of right ankle, stage 4
         Pressure ulcer with necrosis of soft tissues through to underlying muscle, tendon, or bone, right ankle

     L89.516   **Pressure-induced deep tissue damage of right ankle**

     L89.519   **Pressure ulcer of right ankle, unspecified stage**
         Healing pressure ulcer of right ankle NOS
         Healing pressure ulcer of right ankle, unspecified stage

   ● **L89.52**   **Pressure ulcer of left ankle**

     L89.520   **Pressure ulcer of left ankle, unstageable**

     L89.521   **Pressure ulcer of left ankle, stage 1**
         Healing pressure ulcer of left ankle, stage 1
         Pressure pre-ulcer skin changes limited to persistent focal edema, left ankle

     L89.522   **Pressure ulcer of left ankle, stage 2**
         Healing pressure ulcer of left ankle, stage 2
         Pressure ulcer with abrasion, blister, partial thickness skin loss involving epidermis and/or dermis, left ankle

     L89.523   **Pressure ulcer of left ankle, stage 3** 🔲
         Healing pressure ulcer of left ankle, stage 3
         Pressure ulcer with full thickness skin loss involving damage or necrosis of subcutaneous tissue, left ankle

     L89.524   **Pressure ulcer of left ankle, stage 4** 🔲
         Healing pressure ulcer of left ankle, stage 4
         Pressure ulcer with necrosis of soft tissues through to underlying muscle, tendon, or bone, left ankle

     L89.526   **Pressure-induced deep tissue damage of left ankle**

     L89.529   **Pressure ulcer of left ankle, unspecified stage**
         Healing pressure ulcer of left ankle NOS
         Healing pressure ulcer of left ankle, unspecified stage

● **L89.6**   **Pressure ulcer of heel**

   ● **L89.60**   **Pressure ulcer of unspecified heel**

     L89.600   **Pressure ulcer of unspecified heel, unstageable** 🔲

     L89.601   **Pressure ulcer of unspecified heel, stage 1**
         Healing pressure ulcer of unspecified heel, stage 1
         Pressure pre-ulcer skin changes limited to persistent focal edema, unspecified heel

     L89.602   **Pressure ulcer of unspecified heel, stage 2**
         Healing pressure ulcer of unspecified heel, stage 2
         Pressure ulcer with abrasion, blister, partial thickness skin loss involving epidermis and/or dermis, unspecified heel

     L89.603   **Pressure ulcer of unspecified heel, stage 3** 🔲
         Healing pressure ulcer of unspecified heel, stage 3
         Pressure ulcer with full thickness skin loss involving damage or necrosis of subcutaneous tissue, unspecified heel

CHAPTER 12 (L00-L99)

CHAPTER 12 (L00-L99)

L89.604 **Pressure ulcer of unspecified heel, stage 4** 🝙
    Healing pressure ulcer of unspecified heel, stage 4
    Pressure ulcer with necrosis of soft tissues through to underlying muscle, tendon, or bone, unspecified heel

L89.606 **Pressure-induced deep tissue damage of unspecified heel**

L89.609 **Pressure ulcer of unspecified heel, unspecified stage**
    Healing pressure ulcer of unspecified heel NOS
    Healing pressure ulcer of unspecified heel, unspecified stage

● L89.61 **Pressure ulcer of right heel**

L89.610 **Pressure ulcer of right heel, unstageable** 🝙

L89.611 **Pressure ulcer of right heel, stage 1**
    Healing pressure ulcer of right heel, stage 1
    Pressure pre-ulcer skin changes limited to persistent focal edema, right heel

L89.612 **Pressure ulcer of right heel, stage 2**
    Healing pressure ulcer of right heel, stage 2
    Pressure ulcer with abrasion, blister, partial thickness skin loss involving epidermis and/or dermis, right heel

L89.613 **Pressure ulcer of right heel, stage 3** 🝙
    Healing pressure ulcer of right heel, stage 3
    Pressure ulcer with full thickness skin loss involving damage or necrosis of subcutaneous tissue, right heel

L89.614 **Pressure ulcer of right heel, stage 4** 🝙
    Healing pressure ulcer of right heel, stage 4
    Pressure ulcer with necrosis of soft tissues through to underlying muscle, tendon, or bone, right heel

L89.616 **Pressure-induced deep tissue damage of right heel**

L89.619 **Pressure ulcer of right heel, unspecified stage**
    Healing pressure ulcer of right heel NOS
    Healing pressure ulcer of right heel, unspecified stage

● L89.62 **Pressure ulcer of left heel**

L89.620 **Pressure ulcer of left heel, unstageable** 🝙

L89.621 **Pressure ulcer of left heel, stage 1**
    Healing pressure ulcer of left heel, stage 1
    Pressure pre-ulcer skin changes limited to persistent focal edema, left heel

L89.622 **Pressure ulcer of left heel, stage 2**
    Healing pressure ulcer of left heel, stage 2
    Pressure ulcer with abrasion, blister, partial thickness skin loss involving epidermis and/or dermis, left heel
    Coding Clinic: 2016, Q4, P142

L89.623 **Pressure ulcer of left heel, stage 3** 🝙
    Healing pressure ulcer of left heel, stage 3
    Pressure ulcer with full thickness skin loss involving damage or necrosis of subcutaneous tissue, left heel
    Coding Clinic: 2016, Q4, P142

L89.624 **Pressure ulcer of left heel, stage 4** 🝙
    Healing pressure ulcer of left heel, stage 4
    Pressure ulcer with necrosis of soft tissues through to underlying muscle, tendon, or bone, left heel

L89.626 **Pressure-induced deep tissue damage of left heel**

L89.629 **Pressure ulcer of left heel, unspecified stage**
    Healing pressure ulcer of left heel NOS
    Healing pressure ulcer of left heel, unspecified stage

● L89.8 **Pressure ulcer of other site**

● L89.81 **Pressure ulcer of head**
    Pressure ulcer of face

L89.810 **Pressure ulcer of head, unstageable** 🝙

L89.811 **Pressure ulcer of head, stage 1**
    Healing pressure ulcer of head, stage 1
    Pressure pre-ulcer skin changes limited to persistent focal edema, head

L89.812 **Pressure ulcer of head, stage 2**
    Healing pressure ulcer of head, stage 2
    Pressure ulcer with abrasion, blister, partial thickness skin loss involving epidermis and/or dermis, head

L89.813 **Pressure ulcer of head, stage 3** 🝙
    Healing pressure ulcer of head, stage 3
    Pressure ulcer with full thickness skin loss involving damage or necrosis of subcutaneous tissue, head

L89.814 **Pressure ulcer of head, stage 4** 🝙
    Healing pressure ulcer of head, stage 4
    Pressure ulcer with necrosis of soft tissues through to underlying muscle, tendon, or bone, head

L89.816 **Pressure-induced deep tissue damage of head**

L89.819 **Pressure ulcer of head, unspecified stage**
    Healing pressure ulcer of head NOS
    Healing pressure ulcer of head, unspecified stage

● L89.89 **Pressure ulcer of other site**

L89.890 **Pressure ulcer of other site, unstageable** 🝙

L89.891 **Pressure ulcer of other site, stage 1**
    Healing pressure ulcer of other site, stage 1
    Pressure pre-ulcer skin changes limited to persistent focal edema, other site

L89.892 **Pressure ulcer of other site, stage 2**
    Healing pressure ulcer of other site, stage 2
    Pressure ulcer with abrasion, blister, partial thickness skin loss involving epidermis and/or dermis, other site

▶ New   ⇒ Revised   ~~deleted~~ Deleted   Excludes 1   Excludes 2   Includes   Use additional   Code first   Code also   Key words

OGCR Official Guidelines   X Assign placeholder X   ● Use Additional Character(s)   ▷ Manifestation Code   🝙 Hierarchical Condition Category   Coding Clinic

L89.893   **Pressure ulcer of other site, stage 3** 🔁
          Healing pressure ulcer of other site,
          stage 3
          Pressure ulcer with full thickness
          skin loss involving damage or
          necrosis of subcutaneous tissue,
          other site

L89.894   **Pressure ulcer of other site, stage 4** 🔁
          Healing pressure ulcer of other site,
          stage 4
          Pressure ulcer with necrosis of soft
          tissues through to underlying
          muscle, tendon, or bone, other
          site

L89.899   **Pressure ulcer of other site,
          unspecified stage**
          Healing pressure ulcer of other site
          NOS
          Healing pressure ulcer of other site,
          unspecified stage

● **L89.9   Pressure ulcer of unspecified site**

L89.90   **Pressure ulcer of unspecified site, unspecified
          stage**
          Healing pressure ulcer of unspecified site NOS
          Healing pressure ulcer of unspecified site,
          unspecified stage

L89.91   **Pressure ulcer of unspecified site, stage 1**
          Healing pressure ulcer of unspecified site,
          stage 1
          Pressure pre-ulcer skin changes limited to
          persistent focal edema, unspecified site

L89.92   **Pressure ulcer of unspecified site, stage 2**
          Healing pressure ulcer of unspecified site,
          stage 2
          Pressure ulcer with abrasion, blister, partial
          thickness skin loss involving epidermis
          and/or dermis, unspecified site

L89.93   **Pressure ulcer of unspecified site, stage 3** 🔁
          Healing pressure ulcer of unspecified site,
          stage 3
          Pressure ulcer with full thickness skin
          loss involving damage or necrosis of
          subcutaneous tissue, unspecified site

L89.94   **Pressure ulcer of unspecified site, stage 4** 🔁
          Healing pressure ulcer of unspecified site,
          stage 4
          Pressure ulcer with necrosis of soft tissues
          through to underlying muscle, tendon, or
          bone, unspecified site

L89.95   **Pressure ulcer of unspecified site,
          unstageable** 🔁

L89.96   **Pressure-induced deep tissue damage of
          unspecified site**

● **L90   Atrophic disorders of skin**

L90.0   **Lichen sclerosus et atrophicus**
        Excludes2   lichen sclerosus of external female genital
                        organs (N90.4)
                        lichen sclerosus of external male genital
                        organs (N48.0)

L90.1   **Anetoderma of Schweninger-Buzzi**

L90.2   **Anetoderma of Jadassohn-Pellizzari**

L90.3   **Atrophoderma of Pasini and Pierini**

L90.4   **Acrodermatitis chronica atrophicans**

L90.5   **Scar conditions and fibrosis of skin**
        Adherent scar (skin)
        Cicatrix
        Disfigurement of skin due to scar
        Fibrosis of skin NOS
        Scar NOS
        Excludes2   hypertrophic scar (L91.0)
                        keloid scar (L91.0)
        Coding Clinic: 2016, Q2, P5; 2015, Q1, P19

Item 12–11   Scleroderma means hard skin. It is a group of diseases that causes abnormal growth of connective tissues that support the skin and organs. There are two types: localized scleroderma affecting the skin and systemic scleroderma affecting blood vessels and internal organs and the skin.

L90.6   **Striae atrophicae**

L90.8   **Other atrophic disorders of skin**

L90.9   **Atrophic disorder of skin, unspecified**

● **L91   Hypertrophic disorders of skin**

L91.0   **Keloid scar**
        Hypertrophic scar
        Keloid
        Excludes2   acne keloid (L73.0)
                        scar NOS (L90.5)

L91.8   **Other hypertrophic disorders of the skin**

L91.9   **Hypertrophic disorder of the skin, unspecified**

● **L92   Granulomatous disorders of skin and subcutaneous tissue**
        Excludes2   actinic granuloma (L57.5)

L92.0   **Granuloma annulare**
        Perforating granuloma annulare

L92.1   **Necrobiosis lipoidica, not elsewhere classified**
        Excludes1   necrobiosis lipoidica associated with
                        diabetes mellitus (E08-E13 with .620)

L92.2   **Granuloma faciale [eosinophilic granuloma of skin]**

L92.3   **Foreign body granuloma of the skin and subcutaneous
        tissue**
        Use additional code to identify the type of retained
        foreign body (Z18.-)

L92.8   **Other granulomatous disorders of the skin and
        subcutaneous tissue**

L92.9   **Granulomatous disorder of the skin and subcutaneous
        tissue, unspecified**
        Excludes2   umbilical granuloma (P83.81)

● **L93   Lupus erythematosus**
        Use additional code for adverse effect, if applicable, to identify
        drug (T36-T50 with fifth or sixth character 5)
        Excludes1   lupus exedens (A18.4)
                        lupus vulgaris (A18.4)
                        scleroderma (M34.-)
                        systemic lupus erythematosus (M32.-)

L93.0   **Discoid lupus erythematosus**
        Lupus erythematosus NOS

L93.1   **Subacute cutaneous lupus erythematosus**

L93.2   **Other local lupus erythematosus**
        Lupus erythematosus profundus
        Lupus panniculitis

● **L94   Other localized connective tissue disorders**
        Excludes1   systemic connective tissue disorders (M30-M36)

L94.0   **Localized scleroderma [morphea]**
        Circumscribed scleroderma

L94.1   **Linear scleroderma**
        En coup de sabre lesion

L94.2   **Calcinosis cutis**

L94.3   **Sclerodactyly**

L94.4   **Gottron's papules**

L94.5   **Poikiloderma vasculare atrophicans**

L94.6   **Ainhum**

L94.8   **Other specified localized connective tissue disorders**

L94.9   **Localized connective tissue disorder, unspecified**

CHAPTER 12 (L00–L99)

● **L95   Vasculitis limited to skin, not elsewhere classified**

    Excludes 1   angioma serpiginosum (L81.7)
                Henoch(-Schönlein) purpura (D69.0)
                hypersensitivity angiitis (M31.0)
                lupus panniculitis (L93.2)
                panniculitis NOS (M79.3)
                panniculitis of neck and back (M54.0-)
                polyarteritis nodosa (M30.0)
                relapsing panniculitis (M35.6)
                rheumatoid vasculitis (M05.2)
                serum sickness (T80.6-)
                urticaria (L50.-)
                Wegener's granulomatosis (M31.3-)

    L95.0   Livedoid vasculitis
            Atrophie blanche (en plaque)

    L95.1   Erythema elevatum diutinum

    L95.8   Other vasculitis limited to the skin

    L95.9   Vasculitis limited to the skin, unspecified

● **L97   Non-pressure chronic ulcer of lower limb, not elsewhere classified**

    Includes   chronic ulcer of skin of lower limb NOS
              non-healing ulcer of skin
              non-infected sinus of skin
              trophic ulcer NOS
              tropical ulcer NOS
              ulcer of skin of lower limb NOS

    Code first any associated underlying condition, such as:
      any associated gangrene (I96)
      atherosclerosis of the lower extremities (I70.23-, I70.24-,
        I70.33-, I70.34-, I70.43-, I70.44-, I70.53-, I70.54-, I70.63-,
        I70.64-, I70.73-, I70.74-)
      chronic venous hypertension (I87.31-, I87.33-)
      diabetic ulcers (E08.621, E08.622, E09.621, E09.622, E10.621,
        E10.622, E11.621, E11.622, E13.621, E13.622)
      postphlebitic syndrome (I87.01-, I87.03-)
      postthrombotic syndrome (I87.01-, I87.03-)
      varicose ulcer (I83.0-, I83.2-)

    Excludes 2   pressure ulcer (pressure area) (L89.-)
                skin infections (L00-L08)
                specific infections classified to A00-B99

● **L97.1   Non-pressure chronic ulcer of thigh**

  ● **L97.10   Non-pressure chronic ulcer of unspecified thigh**

      L97.101   Non-pressure chronic ulcer of unspecified thigh limited to breakdown of skin 🦠

      L97.102   Non-pressure chronic ulcer of unspecified thigh with fat layer exposed 🦠

      L97.103   Non-pressure chronic ulcer of unspecified thigh with necrosis of muscle 🦠

      L97.104   Non-pressure chronic ulcer of unspecified thigh with necrosis of bone 🦠

      L97.105   Non-pressure chronic ulcer of unspecified thigh with muscle involvement without evidence of necrosis 🦠

      L97.106   Non-pressure chronic ulcer of unspecified thigh with bone involvement without evidence of necrosis 🦠

      L97.108   Non-pressure chronic ulcer of unspecified thigh with other specified severity 🦠

      L97.109   Non-pressure chronic ulcer of unspecified thigh with unspecified severity 🦠

● **L97.11   Non-pressure chronic ulcer of right thigh**

      L97.111   Non-pressure chronic ulcer of right thigh limited to breakdown of skin 🦠

      L97.112   Non-pressure chronic ulcer of right thigh with fat layer exposed 🦠

      L97.113   Non-pressure chronic ulcer of right thigh with necrosis of muscle 🦠

      L97.114   Non-pressure chronic ulcer of right thigh with necrosis of bone 🦠

      L97.115   Non-pressure chronic ulcer of right thigh with muscle involvement without evidence of necrosis 🦠

      L97.116   Non-pressure chronic ulcer of right thigh with bone involvement without evidence of necrosis 🦠

      L97.118   Non-pressure chronic ulcer of right thigh with other specified severity 🦠

      L97.119   Non-pressure chronic ulcer of right thigh with unspecified severity 🦠

● **L97.12   Non-pressure chronic ulcer of left thigh**

      L97.121   Non-pressure chronic ulcer of left thigh limited to breakdown of skin 🦠

      L97.122   Non-pressure chronic ulcer of left thigh with fat layer exposed 🦠

      L97.123   Non-pressure chronic ulcer of left thigh with necrosis of muscle 🦠

      L97.124   Non-pressure chronic ulcer of left thigh with necrosis of bone 🦠

      L97.125   Non-pressure chronic ulcer of left thigh with muscle involvement without evidence of necrosis 🦠

      L97.126   Non-pressure chronic ulcer of left thigh with bone involvement without evidence of necrosis 🦠

      L97.128   Non-pressure chronic ulcer of left thigh with other specified severity 🦠

      L97.129   Non-pressure chronic ulcer of left thigh with unspecified severity 🦠

● **L97.2   Non-pressure chronic ulcer of calf**

  ● **L97.20   Non-pressure chronic ulcer of unspecified calf**

      L97.201   Non-pressure chronic ulcer of unspecified calf limited to breakdown of skin 🦠

      L97.202   Non-pressure chronic ulcer of unspecified calf with fat layer exposed 🦠

      L97.203   Non-pressure chronic ulcer of unspecified calf with necrosis of muscle 🦠

      L97.204   Non-pressure chronic ulcer of unspecified calf with necrosis of bone 🦠

      L97.205   Non-pressure chronic ulcer of unspecified calf with muscle involvement without evidence of necrosis 🦠

      L97.206   Non-pressure chronic ulcer of unspecified calf with bone involvement without evidence of necrosis 🦠

      L97.208   Non-pressure chronic ulcer of unspecified calf with other specified severity 🦠

      L97.209   Non-pressure chronic ulcer of unspecified calf with unspecified severity 🦠

▶ New   ⇒ Revised   ~~deleted~~ Deleted   Excludes 1   Excludes 2   Includes   Use additional   Code first   Code also   Key words

OGCR Official Guidelines   X Assign placeholder X   ● Use Additional Character(s)   ▶ Manifestation Code   🦠 Hierarchical Condition Category   Coding Clinic

● **L97.21**   Non-pressure chronic ulcer of right calf
     L97.211   Non-pressure chronic ulcer of right calf limited to breakdown of skin 🐾
     L97.212   Non-pressure chronic ulcer of right calf with fat layer exposed 🐾
     L97.213   Non-pressure chronic ulcer of right calf with necrosis of muscle 🐾
     L97.214   Non-pressure chronic ulcer of right calf with necrosis of bone 🐾
     L97.215   Non-pressure chronic ulcer of right calf with muscle involvement without evidence of necrosis 🐾
     L97.216   Non-pressure chronic ulcer of right calf with bone involvement without evidence of necrosis 🐾
     L97.218   Non-pressure chronic ulcer of right calf with other specified severity 🐾
     L97.219   Non-pressure chronic ulcer of right calf with unspecified severity 🐾

● **L97.22**   Non-pressure chronic ulcer of left calf
     L97.221   Non-pressure chronic ulcer of left calf limited to breakdown of skin 🐾
     L97.222   Non-pressure chronic ulcer of left calf with fat layer exposed 🐾
     L97.223   Non-pressure chronic ulcer of left calf with necrosis of muscle 🐾
     L97.224   Non-pressure chronic ulcer of left calf with necrosis of bone 🐾
     L97.225   Non-pressure chronic ulcer of left calf with muscle involvement without evidence of necrosis 🐾
     L97.226   Non-pressure chronic ulcer of left calf with bone involvement without evidence of necrosis 🐾
     L97.228   Non-pressure chronic ulcer of left calf with other specified severity 🐾
     L97.229   Non-pressure chronic ulcer of left calf with unspecified severity 🐾

● **L97.3**   Non-pressure chronic ulcer of ankle
   ● **L97.30**   Non-pressure chronic ulcer of unspecified ankle
     L97.301   Non-pressure chronic ulcer of unspecified ankle limited to breakdown of skin 🐾
     L97.302   Non-pressure chronic ulcer of unspecified ankle with fat layer exposed 🐾
     L97.303   Non-pressure chronic ulcer of unspecified ankle with necrosis of muscle 🐾
     L97.304   Non-pressure chronic ulcer of unspecified ankle with necrosis of bone 🐾
     L97.305   Non-pressure chronic ulcer of unspecified ankle with muscle involvement without evidence of necrosis 🐾
     L97.306   Non-pressure chronic ulcer of unspecified ankle with bone involvement without evidence of necrosis 🐾
     L97.308   Non-pressure chronic ulcer of unspecified ankle with other specified severity 🐾
     L97.309   Non-pressure chronic ulcer of unspecified ankle with unspecified severity 🐾

● **L97.31**   Non-pressure chronic ulcer of right ankle
     L97.311   Non-pressure chronic ulcer of right ankle limited to breakdown of skin 🐾
     L97.312   Non-pressure chronic ulcer of right ankle with fat layer exposed 🐾
     L97.313   Non-pressure chronic ulcer of right ankle with necrosis of muscle 🐾
     L97.314   Non-pressure chronic ulcer of right ankle with necrosis of bone 🐾
     L97.315   Non-pressure chronic ulcer of right ankle with muscle involvement without evidence of necrosis 🐾
         Coding Clinic: 2017, Q4, P17
     L97.316   Non-pressure chronic ulcer of right ankle with bone involvement without evidence of necrosis 🐾
     L97.318   Non-pressure chronic ulcer of right ankle with other specified severity 🐾
     L97.319   Non-pressure chronic ulcer of right ankle with unspecified severity 🐾

● **L97.32**   Non-pressure chronic ulcer of left ankle
     L97.321   Non-pressure chronic ulcer of left ankle limited to breakdown of skin 🐾
     L97.322   Non-pressure chronic ulcer of left ankle with fat layer exposed 🐾
     L97.323   Non-pressure chronic ulcer of left ankle with necrosis of muscle 🐾
     L97.324   Non-pressure chronic ulcer of left ankle with necrosis of bone 🐾
     L97.325   Non-pressure chronic ulcer of left ankle with muscle involvement without evidence of necrosis 🐾
     L97.326   Non-pressure chronic ulcer of left ankle with bone involvement without evidence of necrosis 🐾
     L97.328   Non-pressure chronic ulcer of left ankle with other specified severity 🐾
     L97.329   Non-pressure chronic ulcer of left ankle with unspecified severity 🐾

● **L97.4**   Non-pressure chronic ulcer of heel and midfoot
     Non-pressure chronic ulcer of plantar surface of midfoot
   ● **L97.40**   Non-pressure chronic ulcer of unspecified heel and midfoot
     L97.401   Non-pressure chronic ulcer of unspecified heel and midfoot limited to breakdown of skin 🐾
     L97.402   Non-pressure chronic ulcer of unspecified heel and midfoot with fat layer exposed 🐾
     L97.403   Non-pressure chronic ulcer of unspecified heel and midfoot with necrosis of muscle 🐾
     L97.404   Non-pressure chronic ulcer of unspecified heel and midfoot with necrosis of bone 🐾
     L97.405   Non-pressure chronic ulcer of unspecified heel and midfoot with muscle involvement without evidence of necrosis 🐾
     L97.406   Non-pressure chronic ulcer of unspecified heel and midfoot with bone involvement without evidence of necrosis 🐾
     L97.408   Non-pressure chronic ulcer of unspecified heel and midfoot with other specified severity 🐾
     L97.409   Non-pressure chronic ulcer of unspecified heel and midfoot with unspecified severity 🐾

CHAPTER 12 (L00-L99)

● **L97.41**   Non-pressure chronic ulcer of right heel and midfoot

    L97.411   Non-pressure chronic ulcer of right heel and midfoot limited to breakdown of skin 🝙

    L97.412   Non-pressure chronic ulcer of right heel and midfoot with fat layer exposed 🝙

    L97.413   Non-pressure chronic ulcer of right heel and midfoot with necrosis of muscle 🝙

    L97.414   Non-pressure chronic ulcer of right heel and midfoot with necrosis of bone 🝙

    L97.415   Non-pressure chronic ulcer of right heel and midfoot with muscle involvement without evidence of necrosis 🝙

    L97.416   Non-pressure chronic ulcer of right heel and midfoot with bone involvement without evidence of necrosis 🝙

    L97.418   Non-pressure chronic ulcer of right heel and midfoot with other specified severity 🝙

    L97.419   Non-pressure chronic ulcer of right heel and midfoot with unspecified severity 🝙

● **L97.42**   Non-pressure chronic ulcer of left heel and midfoot

    L97.421   Non-pressure chronic ulcer of left heel and midfoot limited to breakdown of skin 🝙
       Coding Clinic: 2016, Q1, P13

    L97.422   Non-pressure chronic ulcer of left heel and midfoot with fat layer exposed 🝙

    L97.423   Non-pressure chronic ulcer of left heel and midfoot with necrosis of muscle 🝙

    L97.424   Non-pressure chronic ulcer of left heel and midfoot with necrosis of bone 🝙

    L97.425   Non-pressure chronic ulcer of left heel and midfoot with muscle involvement without evidence of necrosis 🝙

    L97.426   Non-pressure chronic ulcer of left heel and midfoot with bone involvement without evidence of necrosis 🝙

    L97.428   Non-pressure chronic ulcer of left heel and midfoot with other specified severity 🝙

    L97.429   Non-pressure chronic ulcer of left heel and midfoot with unspecified severity 🝙

● **L97.5**   Non-pressure chronic ulcer of other part of foot
    Non-pressure chronic ulcer of toe

● **L97.50**   Non-pressure chronic ulcer of other part of unspecified foot

    L97.501   Non-pressure chronic ulcer of other part of unspecified foot limited to breakdown of skin 🝙

    L97.502   Non-pressure chronic ulcer of other part of unspecified foot with fat layer exposed 🝙

    L97.503   Non-pressure chronic ulcer of other part of unspecified foot with necrosis of muscle 🝙

    L97.504   Non-pressure chronic ulcer of other part of unspecified foot with necrosis of bone 🝙

    L97.505   Non-pressure chronic ulcer of other part of unspecified foot with muscle involvement without evidence of necrosis 🝙

    L97.506   Non-pressure chronic ulcer of other part of unspecified foot with bone involvement without evidence of necrosis 🝙

    L97.508   Non-pressure chronic ulcer of other part of unspecified foot with other specified severity 🝙

    L97.509   Non-pressure chronic ulcer of other part of unspecified foot with unspecified severity 🝙

● **L97.51**   Non-pressure chronic ulcer of other part of right foot

    L97.511   Non-pressure chronic ulcer of other part of right foot limited to breakdown of skin 🝙
       Coding Clinic: 2020, Q1, P12

    L97.512   Non-pressure chronic ulcer of other part of right foot with fat layer exposed 🝙

    L97.513   Non-pressure chronic ulcer of other part of right foot with necrosis of muscle 🝙

    L97.514   Non-pressure chronic ulcer of other part of right foot with necrosis of bone 🝙

    L97.515   Non-pressure chronic ulcer of other part of right foot with muscle involvement without evidence of necrosis 🝙

    L97.516   Non-pressure chronic ulcer of other part of right foot with bone involvement without evidence of necrosis 🝙

    L97.518   Non-pressure chronic ulcer of other part of right foot with other specified severity 🝙

    L97.519   Non-pressure chronic ulcer of other part of right foot with unspecified severity 🝙

● **L97.52**   Non-pressure chronic ulcer of other part of left foot

    L97.521   Non-pressure chronic ulcer of other part of left foot limited to breakdown of skin 🝙

    L97.522   Non-pressure chronic ulcer of other part of left foot with fat layer exposed 🝙

    L97.523   Non-pressure chronic ulcer of other part of left foot with necrosis of muscle 🝙

    L97.524   Non-pressure chronic ulcer of other part of left foot with necrosis of bone 🝙

    L97.525   Non-pressure chronic ulcer of other part of left foot with muscle involvement without evidence of necrosis 🝙

    L97.526   Non-pressure chronic ulcer of other part of left foot with bone involvement without evidence of necrosis 🝙

    L97.528   Non-pressure chronic ulcer of other part of left foot with other specified severity 🝙

    L97.529   Non-pressure chronic ulcer of other part of left foot with unspecified severity 🝙

▶ New   ⇛ Revised   ~~deleted~~ Deleted   Excludes 1   Excludes 2   Includes   Use additional   Code first   Code also   Key words

OGCR Official Guidelines   X Assign placeholder X   ● Use Additional Character(s)   ⫸ Manifestation Code   🝙 Hierarchical Condition Category   **Coding Clinic**

● **L97.8**   Non-pressure chronic ulcer of other part of lower leg

  ● **L97.80**   Non-pressure chronic ulcer of other part of unspecified lower leg

    L97.801   Non-pressure chronic ulcer of other part of unspecified lower leg limited to breakdown of skin 🔍

    L97.802   Non-pressure chronic ulcer of other part of unspecified lower leg with fat layer exposed 🔍

    L97.803   Non-pressure chronic ulcer of other part of unspecified lower leg with necrosis of muscle 🔍

    L97.804   Non-pressure chronic ulcer of other part of unspecified lower leg with necrosis of bone 🔍

    L97.805   Non-pressure chronic ulcer of other part of unspecified lower leg with muscle involvement without evidence of necrosis 🔍

    L97.806   Non-pressure chronic ulcer of other part of unspecified lower leg with bone involvement without evidence of necrosis 🔍

    L97.808   Non-pressure chronic ulcer of other part of unspecified lower leg with other specified severity 🔍

    L97.809   Non-pressure chronic ulcer of other part of unspecified lower leg with unspecified severity 🔍

  ● **L97.81**   Non-pressure chronic ulcer of other part of right lower leg

    L97.811   Non-pressure chronic ulcer of other part of right lower leg limited to breakdown of skin 🔍

    L97.812   Non-pressure chronic ulcer of other part of right lower leg with fat layer exposed 🔍

    L97.813   Non-pressure chronic ulcer of other part of right lower leg with necrosis of muscle 🔍

    L97.814   Non-pressure chronic ulcer of other part of right lower leg with necrosis of bone 🔍

    L97.815   Non-pressure chronic ulcer of other part of right lower leg with muscle involvement without evidence of necrosis 🔍

    L97.816   Non-pressure chronic ulcer of other part of right lower leg with bone involvement without evidence of necrosis 🔍

    L97.818   Non-pressure chronic ulcer of other part of right lower leg with other specified severity 🔍

    L97.819   Non-pressure chronic ulcer of other part of right lower leg with unspecified severity 🔍

  ● **L97.82**   Non-pressure chronic ulcer of other part of left lower leg

    L97.821   Non-pressure chronic ulcer of other part of left lower leg limited to breakdown of skin 🔍

    L97.822   Non-pressure chronic ulcer of other part of left lower leg with fat layer exposed 🔍

    L97.823   Non-pressure chronic ulcer of other part of left lower leg with necrosis of muscle 🔍

    L97.824   Non-pressure chronic ulcer of other part of left lower leg with necrosis of bone 🔍

    L97.825   Non-pressure chronic ulcer of other part of left lower leg with muscle involvement without evidence of necrosis 🔍

    L97.826   Non-pressure chronic ulcer of other part of left lower leg with bone involvement without evidence of necrosis 🔍

    L97.828   Non-pressure chronic ulcer of other part of left lower leg with other specified severity 🔍

    L97.829   Non-pressure chronic ulcer of other part of left lower leg with unspecified severity 🔍

● **L97.9**   Non-pressure chronic ulcer of unspecified part of lower leg

  ● **L97.90**   Non-pressure chronic ulcer of unspecified part of unspecified lower leg

    L97.901   Non-pressure chronic ulcer of unspecified part of unspecified lower leg limited to breakdown of skin 🔍

    L97.902   Non-pressure chronic ulcer of unspecified part of unspecified lower leg with fat layer exposed 🔍

    L97.903   Non-pressure chronic ulcer of unspecified part of unspecified lower leg with necrosis of muscle 🔍

    L97.904   Non-pressure chronic ulcer of unspecified part of unspecified lower leg with necrosis of bone 🔍

    L97.905   Non-pressure chronic ulcer of unspecified part of unspecified lower leg with muscle involvement without evidence of necrosis 🔍

    L97.906   Non-pressure chronic ulcer of unspecified part of unspecified lower leg with bone involvement without evidence of necrosis 🔍

    L97.908   Non-pressure chronic ulcer of unspecified part of unspecified lower leg with other specified severity 🔍

    L97.909   Non-pressure chronic ulcer of unspecified part of unspecified lower leg with unspecified severity 🔍

  ● **L97.91**   Non-pressure chronic ulcer of unspecified part of right lower leg

    L97.911   Non-pressure chronic ulcer of unspecified part of right lower leg limited to breakdown of skin 🔍

    L97.912   Non-pressure chronic ulcer of unspecified part of right lower leg with fat layer exposed 🔍

    L97.913   Non-pressure chronic ulcer of unspecified part of right lower leg with necrosis of muscle 🔍

    L97.914   Non-pressure chronic ulcer of unspecified part of right lower leg with necrosis of bone 🔍

    L97.915   Non-pressure chronic ulcer of unspecified part of right lower leg with muscle involvement without evidence of necrosis 🔍

    L97.916   Non-pressure chronic ulcer of unspecified part of right lower leg with bone involvement without evidence of necrosis 🔍

    L97.918   Non-pressure chronic ulcer of unspecified part of right lower leg with other specified severity 🔍

    L97.919   Non-pressure chronic ulcer of unspecified part of right lower leg with unspecified severity 🔍

CHAPTER 12 (L00-L99)

● **L97.92** Non-pressure chronic ulcer of unspecified part of left lower leg

    L97.921 Non-pressure chronic ulcer of unspecified part of left lower leg limited to breakdown of skin 🐾

    L97.922 Non-pressure chronic ulcer of unspecified part of left lower leg with fat layer exposed 🐾

    L97.923 Non-pressure chronic ulcer of unspecified part of left lower leg with necrosis of muscle 🐾

    L97.924 Non-pressure chronic ulcer of unspecified part of left lower leg with necrosis of bone 🐾

    L97.925 Non-pressure chronic ulcer of unspecified part of left lower leg with muscle involvement without evidence of necrosis 🐾

    L97.926 Non-pressure chronic ulcer of unspecified part of left lower leg with bone involvement without evidence of necrosis 🐾

    L97.928 Non-pressure chronic ulcer of unspecified part of left lower leg with other specified severity 🐾

    L97.929 Non-pressure chronic ulcer of unspecified part of left lower leg with unspecified severity 🐾

● **L98** Other disorders of skin and subcutaneous tissue, not elsewhere classified

  L98.0 Pyogenic granuloma

    Excludes2 pyogenic granuloma of gingiva (K06.8)
                 pyogenic granuloma of maxillary alveolar ridge (K04.5)
                  pyogenic granuloma of oral mucosa (K13.4)

  L98.1 Factitial dermatitis
    Neurotic excoriation

    Excludes1 Excoriation (skin-picking) disorder (F42.4)

    Coding Clinic: 2016, Q4, P15

  L98.2 Febrile neutrophilic dermatosis [Sweet]

  L98.3 Eosinophilic cellulitis [Wells]

● **L98.4** Non-pressure chronic ulcer of skin, not elsewhere classified
    Chronic ulcer of skin NOS
    Tropical ulcer NOS
    Ulcer of skin NOS

    Excludes2 pressure ulcer (pressure area) (L89.-)
                  gangrene (I96) 🐾
                  skin infections (L00-L08)
                  specific infections classified to A00-B99
                  ulcer of lower limb NEC (L97.-)
             ⇒ varicose ulcer (I83.0-I83.93)

● **L98.41** Non-pressure chronic ulcer of buttock

    L98.411 Non-pressure chronic ulcer of buttock limited to breakdown of skin 🐾

    L98.412 Non-pressure chronic ulcer of buttock with fat layer exposed 🐾

    L98.413 Non-pressure chronic ulcer of buttock with necrosis of muscle 🐾

    L98.414 Non-pressure chronic ulcer of buttock with necrosis of bone 🐾

    L98.415 Non-pressure chronic ulcer of buttock with muscle involvement without evidence of necrosis 🐾

    L98.416 Non-pressure chronic ulcer of buttock with bone involvement without evidence of necrosis 🐾

    L98.418 Non-pressure chronic ulcer of buttock with other specified severity 🐾

    L98.419 Non-pressure chronic ulcer of buttock with unspecified severity 🐾

● **L98.42** Non-pressure chronic ulcer of back

    L98.421 Non-pressure chronic ulcer of back limited to breakdown of skin 🐾

    L98.422 Non-pressure chronic ulcer of back with fat layer exposed 🐾

    L98.423 Non-pressure chronic ulcer of back with necrosis of muscle 🐾

    L98.424 Non-pressure chronic ulcer of back with necrosis of bone 🐾

    L98.425 Non-pressure chronic ulcer of back with muscle involvement without evidence of necrosis 🐾

    L98.426 Non-pressure chronic ulcer of back with bone involvement without evidence of necrosis 🐾

    L98.428 Non-pressure chronic ulcer of back with other specified severity 🐾

    L98.429 Non-pressure chronic ulcer of back with unspecified severity 🐾

● **L98.49** Non-pressure chronic ulcer of skin of other sites
    Non-pressure chronic ulcer of skin NOS

    L98.491 Non-pressure chronic ulcer of skin of other sites limited to breakdown of skin 🐾

    L98.492 Non-pressure chronic ulcer of skin of other sites with fat layer exposed 🐾

    L98.493 Non-pressure chronic ulcer of skin of other sites with necrosis of muscle 🐾

    L98.494 Non-pressure chronic ulcer of skin of other sites with necrosis of bone 🐾

    L98.495 Non-pressure chronic ulcer of skin of other sites with muscle involvement without evidence of necrosis 🐾

    L98.496 Non-pressure chronic ulcer of skin of other sites with bone involvement without evidence of necrosis 🐾

    L98.498 Non-pressure chronic ulcer of skin of other sites with other specified severity 🐾

    L98.499 Non-pressure chronic ulcer of skin of other sites with unspecified severity 🐾

  L98.5 Mucinosis of the skin
    Focal mucinosis
    Lichen myxedematosus
    Reticular erythematous mucinosis

    Excludes1 focal oral mucinosis (K13.79)
                  myxedema (E03.9)

  L98.6 Other infiltrative disorders of the skin and subcutaneous tissue

    Excludes1 hyalinosis cutis et mucosae (E78.89)

▶ New   ⇒ Revised   ~~deleted~~ Deleted   Excludes 1   Excludes 2   Includes   Use additional   Code first   Code also   Key words

992   OGCR Official Guidelines   X Assign placeholder X   ● Use Additional Character(s)   ⫸ Manifestation Code   🐾 Hierarchical Condition Category   **Coding Clinic**

L98.7   **Excessive and redundant skin and subcutaneous tissue**
     Loose or sagging skin following bariatric surgery
       weight loss
     Loose or sagging skin following dietary weight loss
     Loose or sagging skin, NOS

     Excludes2   acquired excess or redundant skin of
                   eyelid (H02.3-)
                   congenital excess or redundant skin of
                   eyelid (Q10.3)
                   skin changes due to chronic exposure to
                   nonionizing radiation (L57.-)
     Coding Clinic: 2016, Q4, P36

L98.8   **Other specified disorders of the skin and subcutaneous tissue**
     Coding Clinic: 2013, Q2, P32

L98.9   **Disorder of the skin and subcutaneous tissue, unspecified**

L99   *Other disorders of skin and subcutaneous tissue in diseases classified elsewhere*
     Code first underlying disease, such as:
       amyloidosis (E85.-)

     Excludes1   skin disorders in diabetes (E08-E13 with .62)
                   skin disorders in gonorrhea (A54.89)
                   skin disorders in syphilis (A51.31, A52.79)

CHAPTER 12 (L00-L99)

CHAPTER 13

DISEASES OF THE MUSCULOSKELETAL SYSTEM AND CONNECTIVE TISSUE (M00-M99)

OGCR Chapter-Specific Coding Guidelines

13. **Chapter 13: Diseases of the Musculoskeletal System and Connective Tissue (M00-M99)**

  a. Site and laterality
  Most of the codes within Chapter 13 have site and laterality designations. The site represents the bone, joint or the muscle involved. For some conditions where more than one bone, joint or muscle is usually involved, such as osteoarthritis, there is a "multiple sites" code available. For categories where no multiple site code is provided and more than one bone, joint or muscle is involved, multiple codes should be used to indicate the different sites involved.

  1) Bone versus joint
  For certain conditions, the bone may be affected at the upper or lower end (e.g., avascular necrosis of bone, M87, Osteoporosis, M80, M81). Though the portion of the bone affected may be at the joint, the site designation will be the bone, not the joint.

  b. Acute traumatic versus chronic or recurrent musculoskeletal conditions
  Many musculoskeletal conditions are a result of previous injury or trauma to a site, or are recurrent conditions. Bone, joint or muscle conditions that are the result of a healed injury are usually found in Chapter 13. Recurrent bone, joint or muscle conditions are also usually found in Chapter 13. Any current, acute injury should be coded to the appropriate injury code from Chapter 19. Chronic or recurrent conditions should generally be coded with a code from Chapter 13. If it is difficult to determine from the documentation in the record which code is best to describe a condition, query the provider.

  c. Coding of Pathologic Fractures
  7th character A is for use as long as the patient is receiving active treatment for the fracture. While the patient may be seen by a new or different provider over the course of treatment for a pathological fracture, assignment of the 7th character is based on whether the patient is undergoing active treatment and not whether the provider is seeing the patient for the first time.

  7th character, D is to be used for encounters after the patient has completed active treatment for the fracture and is receiving routine care for the fracture during the healing or recovery phase. The other 7th characters, listed under each subcategory in the Tabular List, are to be used for subsequent encounters for treatment of problems associated with the healing, such as malunions, nonunions, and sequelae.

  Care for complications of surgical treatment for fracture repairs during the healing or recovery phase should be coded with the appropriate complication codes.

  See Section I.C.19. Coding of traumatic fractures.

  d. Osteoporosis
  Osteoporosis is a systemic condition, meaning that all bones of the musculoskeletal system are affected. Therefore, site is not a component of the codes under category M81, Osteoporosis without current pathological fracture. The site codes under category M80, Osteoporosis with current pathological fracture, identify the site of the fracture, not the osteoporosis.

  1) Osteoporosis without pathological fracture
  Category M81, Osteoporosis without current pathological fracture, is for use for patients with osteoporosis who do not currently have a pathologic fracture due to the osteoporosis, even if they have had a fracture in the past. For patients with a history of osteoporosis fractures, status code Z87.310, Personal history of (healed) osteoporosis fracture, should follow the code from M81.

  2) Osteoporosis with current pathological fracture
  Category M80, Osteoporosis with current pathological fracture, is for patients who have a current pathologic fracture at the time of an encounter. The codes under M80 identify the site of the fracture. A code from category M80, not a traumatic fracture code, should be used for any patient with known osteoporosis who suffers a fracture, even if the patient had a minor fall or trauma, if that fall or trauma would not usually break a normal, healthy bone.

CHAPTER 13

DISEASES OF THE MUSCULOSKELETAL SYSTEM AND CONNECTIVE TISSUE (M00-M99)

Note: Use an external cause code following the code for the musculoskeletal condition, if applicable, to identify the cause of the musculoskeletal condition

Excludes2 arthropathic psoriasis (L40.5-)
certain conditions originating in the perinatal period (P04-P96)
certain infectious and parasitic diseases (A00-B99)
compartment syndrome (traumatic) (T79.A-)
complications of pregnancy, childbirth and the puerperium (O00-O9A)
congenital malformations, deformations, and chromosomal abnormalities (Q00-Q99)
endocrine, nutritional and metabolic diseases (E00-E88)
injury, poisoning and certain other consequences of external causes (S00-T88)
neoplasms (C00-D49)
symptoms, signs and abnormal clinical and laboratory findings, not elsewhere classified (R00-R94)

This chapter contains the following blocks:

M00-M02	Infectious arthropathies
M04	Autoinflammatory syndromes
M05-M14	Inflammatory polyarthropathies
M15-M19	Osteoarthritis
M20-M25	Other joint disorders
M26-M27	Dentofacial anomalies [including malocclusion] and other disorders of jaw
M30-M36	Systemic connective tissue disorders
M40-M43	Deforming dorsopathies
M45-M49	Spondylopathies
M50-M54	Other dorsopathies
M60-M63	Disorders of muscles
M65-M67	Disorders of synovium and tendon
M70-M79	Other soft tissue disorders
M80-M85	Disorders of bone density and structure
M86-M90	Other osteopathies
M91-M94	Chondropathies
M95	Other disorders of the musculoskeletal system and connective tissue
M96	Intraoperative and postprocedural complications and disorders of musculoskeletal system, not elsewhere classified
M97	Periprosthetic fracture around internal prosthetic joint
M99	Biomechanical lesions, not elsewhere classified

Coding Clinic: 2016, Q4, P124

ARTHROPATHIES (M00-M25)

Includes Disorders affecting predominantly peripheral (limb) joints

INFECTIOUS ARTHROPATHIES (M00-M02)

Note: This block comprises arthropathies due to microbiological agents.

Distinction is made between the following types of etiological relationship:

a) direct infection of joint, where organisms invade synovial tissue and microbial antigen is present in the joint;

b) indirect infection, which may be of two types: a reactive arthropathy, where microbial infection of the body is established but neither organisms nor antigens can be identified in the joint, and a postinfective arthropathy, where microbial antigen is present but recovery of an organism is inconstant and evidence of local multiplication is lacking.

▶ New ⇒ Revised deleted Deleted | Excludes 1 | Excludes 2 | Includes | Use additional | Code first | Code also | Key words
OGCR Official Guidelines   X Assign placeholder X   ● Use Additional Character(s)   ▶ Manifestation Code   Ⓗ Hierarchical Condition Category   **Coding Clinic**

● **M00 Pyogenic arthritis**
> ▶ **Excludes2** infection and inflammatory reaction due to internal joint prosthesis (T84.5-)

● **M00.0 Staphylococcal arthritis and polyarthritis**
     Use additional code (B95.61-B95.8) to identify bacterial agent
     ~~Excludes2 infection and inflammatory reaction due to internal joint prosthesis (T84.5-)~~

     M00.00 Staphylococcal arthritis, unspecified joint ℞

     ● M00.01 Staphylococcal arthritis, shoulder
         M00.011 Staphylococcal arthritis, right shoulder ℞
         M00.012 Staphylococcal arthritis, left shoulder ℞
         M00.019 Staphylococcal arthritis, unspecified shoulder ℞

     ● M00.02 Staphylococcal arthritis, elbow
         M00.021 Staphylococcal arthritis, right elbow ℞
         M00.022 Staphylococcal arthritis, left elbow ℞
         M00.029 Staphylococcal arthritis, unspecified elbow ℞

     ● M00.03 Staphylococcal arthritis, wrist
         Staphylococcal arthritis of carpal bones
         M00.031 Staphylococcal arthritis, right wrist ℞
         M00.032 Staphylococcal arthritis, left wrist ℞
         M00.039 Staphylococcal arthritis, unspecified wrist ℞

     ● M00.04 Staphylococcal arthritis, hand
         Staphylococcal arthritis of metacarpus and phalanges
         M00.041 Staphylococcal arthritis, right hand ℞
         M00.042 Staphylococcal arthritis, left hand ℞
         M00.049 Staphylococcal arthritis, unspecified hand ℞

     ● M00.05 Staphylococcal arthritis, hip
         M00.051 Staphylococcal arthritis, right hip ℞
         M00.052 Staphylococcal arthritis, left hip ℞
         M00.059 Staphylococcal arthritis, unspecified hip ℞

     ● M00.06 Staphylococcal arthritis, knee
         M00.061 Staphylococcal arthritis, right knee ℞
         M00.062 Staphylococcal arthritis, left knee ℞
         M00.069 Staphylococcal arthritis, unspecified knee ℞

     ● M00.07 Staphylococcal arthritis, ankle and foot
         Staphylococcal arthritis, tarsus, metatarsus and phalanges
         M00.071 Staphylococcal arthritis, right ankle and foot ℞
         M00.072 Staphylococcal arthritis, left ankle and foot ℞
         M00.079 Staphylococcal arthritis, unspecified ankle and foot ℞

     M00.08 Staphylococcal arthritis, vertebrae ℞
     M00.09 Staphylococcal polyarthritis ℞

● **M00.1 Pneumococcal arthritis and polyarthritis**
     M00.10 Pneumococcal arthritis, unspecified joint ℞

     ● M00.11 Pneumococcal arthritis, shoulder
         M00.111 Pneumococcal arthritis, right shoulder ℞
         M00.112 Pneumococcal arthritis, left shoulder ℞
         M00.119 Pneumococcal arthritis, unspecified shoulder ℞

     ● M00.12 Pneumococcal arthritis, elbow
         M00.121 Pneumococcal arthritis, right elbow ℞
         M00.122 Pneumococcal arthritis, left elbow ℞
         M00.129 Pneumococcal arthritis, unspecified elbow ℞

     ● M00.13 Pneumococcal arthritis, wrist
         Pneumococcal arthritis of carpal bones
         M00.131 Pneumococcal arthritis, right wrist ℞
         M00.132 Pneumococcal arthritis, left wrist ℞
         M00.139 Pneumococcal arthritis, unspecified wrist ℞

     ● M00.14 Pneumococcal arthritis, hand
         Pneumococcal arthritis of metacarpus and phalanges
         M00.141 Pneumococcal arthritis, right hand ℞
         M00.142 Pneumococcal arthritis, left hand ℞
         M00.149 Pneumococcal arthritis, unspecified hand ℞

     ● M00.15 Pneumococcal arthritis, hip
         M00.151 Pneumococcal arthritis, right hip ℞
         M00.152 Pneumococcal arthritis, left hip ℞
         M00.159 Pneumococcal arthritis, unspecified hip ℞

     ● M00.16 Pneumococcal arthritis, knee
         M00.161 Pneumococcal arthritis, right knee ℞
         M00.162 Pneumococcal arthritis, left knee ℞
         M00.169 Pneumococcal arthritis, unspecified knee ℞

     ● M00.17 Pneumococcal arthritis, ankle and foot
         Pneumococcal arthritis, tarsus, metatarsus and phalanges
         M00.171 Pneumococcal arthritis, right ankle and foot ℞
         M00.172 Pneumococcal arthritis, left ankle and foot ℞
         M00.179 Pneumococcal arthritis, unspecified ankle and foot ℞

     M00.18 Pneumococcal arthritis, vertebrae ℞
     M00.19 Pneumococcal polyarthritis ℞

● **M00.2 Other streptococcal arthritis and polyarthritis**
     Use additional code (B95.0-B95.2, B95.4-B95.5) to identify bacterial agent

     M00.20 Other streptococcal arthritis, unspecified joint ℞

     ● M00.21 Other streptococcal arthritis, shoulder
         M00.211 Other streptococcal arthritis, right shoulder ℞
         M00.212 Other streptococcal arthritis, left shoulder ℞
         M00.219 Other streptococcal arthritis, unspecified shoulder ℞

     ● M00.22 Other streptococcal arthritis, elbow
         M00.221 Other streptococcal arthritis, right elbow ℞
         M00.222 Other streptococcal arthritis, left elbow ℞
         M00.229 Other streptococcal arthritis, unspecified elbow ℞

     ● M00.23 Other streptococcal arthritis, wrist
         Other streptococcal arthritis of carpal bones
         M00.231 Other streptococcal arthritis, right wrist ℞
         M00.232 Other streptococcal arthritis, left wrist ℞
         M00.239 Other streptococcal arthritis, unspecified wrist ℞

● **M00.24** Other streptococcal arthritis, hand
  Other streptococcal arthritis metacarpus and phalanges
  M00.241 Other streptococcal arthritis, right hand 🦠
  M00.242 Other streptococcal arthritis, left hand 🦠
  M00.249 Other streptococcal arthritis, unspecified hand 🦠

● **M00.25** Other streptococcal arthritis, hip
  M00.251 Other streptococcal arthritis, right hip 🦠
  M00.252 Other streptococcal arthritis, left hip 🦠
  M00.259 Other streptococcal arthritis, unspecified hip 🦠

● **M00.26** Other streptococcal arthritis, knee
  M00.261 Other streptococcal arthritis, right knee 🦠
  M00.262 Other streptococcal arthritis, left knee 🦠
  M00.269 Other streptococcal arthritis, unspecified knee 🦠

● **M00.27** Other streptococcal arthritis, ankle and foot
  Other streptococcal arthritis, tarsus, metatarsus and phalanges
  M00.271 Other streptococcal arthritis, right ankle and foot 🦠
  M00.272 Other streptococcal arthritis, left ankle and foot 🦠
  M00.279 Other streptococcal arthritis, unspecified ankle and foot 🦠
  M00.28 Other streptococcal arthritis, vertebrae 🦠
  M00.29 Other streptococcal polyarthritis 🦠

● **M00.8** Arthritis and polyarthritis due to other bacteria
  Use additional code (B96) to identify bacteria
  M00.80 Arthritis due to other bacteria, unspecified joint 🦠

● **M00.81** Arthritis due to other bacteria, shoulder
  M00.811 Arthritis due to other bacteria, right shoulder 🦠
  M00.812 Arthritis due to other bacteria, left shoulder 🦠
  M00.819 Arthritis due to other bacteria, unspecified shoulder 🦠

● **M00.82** Arthritis due to other bacteria, elbow
  M00.821 Arthritis due to other bacteria, right elbow 🦠
  M00.822 Arthritis due to other bacteria, left elbow 🦠
  M00.829 Arthritis due to other bacteria, unspecified elbow 🦠

● **M00.83** Arthritis due to other bacteria, wrist
  Arthritis due to other bacteria, carpal bones
  M00.831 Arthritis due to other bacteria, right wrist 🦠
  M00.832 Arthritis due to other bacteria, left wrist 🦠
  M00.839 Arthritis due to other bacteria, unspecified wrist 🦠

● **M00.84** Arthritis due to other bacteria, hand
  Arthritis due to other bacteria, metacarpus and phalanges
  M00.841 Arthritis due to other bacteria, right hand 🦠
  M00.842 Arthritis due to other bacteria, left hand 🦠
  M00.849 Arthritis due to other bacteria, unspecified hand 🦠

● **M00.85** Arthritis due to other bacteria, hip
  M00.851 Arthritis due to other bacteria, right hip 🦠
  M00.852 Arthritis due to other bacteria, left hip 🦠
  M00.859 Arthritis due to other bacteria, unspecified hip 🦠

● **M00.86** Arthritis due to other bacteria, knee
  M00.861 Arthritis due to other bacteria, right knee 🦠
  M00.862 Arthritis due to other bacteria, left knee 🦠
    Coding Clinic: 2019, Q3, P16
  M00.869 Arthritis due to other bacteria, unspecified knee 🦠

● **M00.87** Arthritis due to other bacteria, ankle and foot
  Arthritis due to other bacteria, tarsus, metatarsus, and phalanges
  M00.871 Arthritis due to other bacteria, right ankle and foot 🦠
  M00.872 Arthritis due to other bacteria, left ankle and foot 🦠
  M00.879 Arthritis due to other bacteria, unspecified ankle and foot 🦠
  M00.88 Arthritis due to other bacteria, vertebrae 🦠
  M00.89 Polyarthritis due to other bacteria 🦠

M00.9 Pyogenic arthritis, unspecified 🦠
  Infective arthritis NOS

● **M01** Direct infections of joint in infectious and parasitic diseases classified elsewhere
  Code first underlying disease, such as:
    leprosy [Hansen's disease] (A30.-)
    mycoses (B35-B49)
    O'nyong-nyong fever (A92.1)
    paratyphoid fever (A01.1-A01.4)

  Excludes1 arthropathy in Lyme disease (A69.23)
    gonococcal arthritis (A54.42)
    meningococcal arthritis (A39.83)
    mumps arthritis (B26.85)
    postinfective arthropathy (M02.-)
    postmeningococcal arthritis (A39.84)
    reactive arthritis (M02.3)
    rubella arthritis (B06.82)
    sarcoidosis arthritis (D86.86)
    typhoid fever arthritis (A01.04)
    tuberculosis arthritis (A18.01-A18.02)

● **M01.X** Direct infection of joint in infectious and parasitic diseases classified elsewhere
  ▸ *M01.X0* Direct infection of unspecified joint in infectious and parasitic diseases classified elsewhere 🦠

  ● *M01.X1* Direct infection of shoulder joint in infectious and parasitic diseases classified elsewhere
    ▸ *M01.X11* Direct infection of right shoulder in infectious and parasitic diseases classified elsewhere 🦠
    ▸ *M01.X12* Direct infection of left shoulder in infectious and parasitic diseases classified elsewhere 🦠
    ▸ *M01.X19* Direct infection of unspecified shoulder in infectious and parasitic diseases classified elsewhere 🦠

  ● *M01.X2* Direct infection of elbow in infectious and parasitic diseases classified elsewhere
    ▸ *M01.X21* Direct infection of right elbow in infectious and parasitic diseases classified elsewhere 🦠
    ▸ *M01.X22* Direct infection of left elbow in infectious and parasitic diseases classified elsewhere 🦠
    ▸ *M01.X29* Direct infection of unspecified elbow in infectious and parasitic diseases classified elsewhere 🦠

▶ New   ⟹ Revised   ~~deleted~~ Deleted   Excludes 1   Excludes 2   Includes   Use additional   Code first   Code also   Key words
OGCR Official Guidelines   X Assign placeholder X   ● Use Additional Character(s)   ▸ Manifestation Code   🦠 Hierarchical Condition Category   **Coding Clinic**

● **M01.X3**   **Direct infection of wrist in infectious and parasitic diseases classified elsewhere**
Direct infection of carpal bones in infectious and parasitic diseases classified elsewhere

▷ *M01.X31*   *Direct infection of right wrist in infectious and parasitic diseases classified elsewhere* 🔖

▷ *M01.X32*   *Direct infection of left wrist in infectious and parasitic diseases classified elsewhere* 🔖

▷ *M01.X39*   *Direct infection of unspecified wrist in infectious and parasitic diseases classified elsewhere* 🔖

● **M01.X4**   **Direct infection of hand in infectious and parasitic diseases classified elsewhere**
Direct infection of metacarpus and phalanges in infectious and parasitic diseases classified elsewhere

▷ *M01.X41*   *Direct infection of right hand in infectious and parasitic diseases classified elsewhere* 🔖

▷ *M01.X42*   *Direct infection of left hand in infectious and parasitic diseases classified elsewhere* 🔖

▷ *M01.X49*   *Direct infection of unspecified hand in infectious and parasitic diseases classified elsewhere* 🔖

● **M01.X5**   **Direct infection of hip in infectious and parasitic diseases classified elsewhere**

▷ *M01.X51*   *Direct infection of right hip in infectious and parasitic diseases classified elsewhere* 🔖

▷ *M01.X52*   *Direct infection of left hip in infectious and parasitic diseases classified elsewhere* 🔖

▷ *M01.X59*   *Direct infection of unspecified hip in infectious and parasitic diseases classified elsewhere* 🔖

● **M01.X6**   **Direct infection of knee in infectious and parasitic diseases classified elsewhere**

▷ *M01.X61*   *Direct infection of right knee in infectious and parasitic diseases classified elsewhere* 🔖

▷ *M01.X62*   *Direct infection of left knee in infectious and parasitic diseases classified elsewhere* 🔖

▷ *M01.X69*   *Direct infection of unspecified knee in infectious and parasitic diseases classified elsewhere* 🔖

● **M01.X7**   **Direct infection of ankle and foot in infectious and parasitic diseases classified elsewhere**
Direct infection of tarsus, metatarsus and phalanges in infectious and parasitic diseases classified elsewhere

▷ *M01.X71*   *Direct infection of right ankle and foot in infectious and parasitic diseases classified elsewhere* 🔖

▷ *M01.X72*   *Direct infection of left ankle and foot in infectious and parasitic diseases classified elsewhere* 🔖

▷ *M01.X79*   *Direct infection of unspecified ankle and foot in infectious and parasitic diseases classified elsewhere* 🔖

▷ *M01.X8*   *Direct infection of vertebrae in infectious and parasitic diseases classified elsewhere* 🔖

▷ *M01.X9*   *Direct infection of multiple joints in infectious and parasitic diseases classified elsewhere* 🔖

● **M02**   **Postinfective and reactive arthropathies**
Code first underlying disease, such as:
congenital syphilis [Clutton's joints] (A50.5)
enteritis due to Yersinia enterocolitica (A04.6)
infective endocarditis (I33.0)
viral hepatitis (B15-B19)

Excludes 1   Behçet's disease (M35.2)
direct infections of joint in infectious and parasitic diseases classified elsewhere (M01.-)
postmeningococcal arthritis (A39.84)
mumps arthritis (B26.85)
rubella arthritis (B06.82)
syphilis arthritis (late) (A52.77)
rheumatic fever (I00)
tabetic arthropathy [Charcôt's] (A52.16)

● **M02.0**   **Arthropathy following intestinal bypass**

   M02.00   **Arthropathy following intestinal bypass, unspecified site**

● **M02.01**   **Arthropathy following intestinal bypass, shoulder**

   M02.011   **Arthropathy following intestinal bypass, right shoulder**

   M02.012   **Arthropathy following intestinal bypass, left shoulder**

   M02.019   **Arthropathy following intestinal bypass, unspecified shoulder**

● **M02.02**   **Arthropathy following intestinal bypass, elbow**

   M02.021   **Arthropathy following intestinal bypass, right elbow**

   M02.022   **Arthropathy following intestinal bypass, left elbow**

   M02.029   **Arthropathy following intestinal bypass, unspecified elbow**

● **M02.03**   **Arthropathy following intestinal bypass, wrist**
Arthropathy following intestinal bypass, carpal bones

   M02.031   **Arthropathy following intestinal bypass, right wrist**

   M02.032   **Arthropathy following intestinal bypass, left wrist**

   M02.039   **Arthropathy following intestinal bypass, unspecified wrist**

● **M02.04**   **Arthropathy following intestinal bypass, hand**
Arthropathy following intestinal bypass, metacarpals and phalanges

   M02.041   **Arthropathy following intestinal bypass, right hand**

   M02.042   **Arthropathy following intestinal bypass, left hand**

   M02.049   **Arthropathy following intestinal bypass, unspecified hand**

● **M02.05**   **Arthropathy following intestinal bypass, hip**

   M02.051   **Arthropathy following intestinal bypass, right hip**

   M02.052   **Arthropathy following intestinal bypass, left hip**

   M02.059   **Arthropathy following intestinal bypass, unspecified hip**

● **M02.06**   **Arthropathy following intestinal bypass, knee**

   M02.061   **Arthropathy following intestinal bypass, right knee**

   M02.062   **Arthropathy following intestinal bypass, left knee**

   M02.069   **Arthropathy following intestinal bypass, unspecified knee**

● **M02.07** **Arthropathy following intestinal bypass, ankle and foot**
    Arthropathy following intestinal bypass, tarsus, metatarsus and phalanges
    M02.071 **Arthropathy following intestinal bypass, right ankle and foot**
    M02.072 **Arthropathy following intestinal bypass, left ankle and foot**
    M02.079 **Arthropathy following intestinal bypass, unspecified ankle and foot**
   M02.08 **Arthropathy following intestinal bypass, vertebrae**
   M02.09 **Arthropathy following intestinal bypass, multiple sites**

● **M02.1** **Postdysenteric arthropathy**
   M02.10 **Postdysenteric arthropathy, unspecified site**
● **M02.11** **Postdysenteric arthropathy, shoulder**
    M02.111 **Postdysenteric arthropathy, right shoulder**
    M02.112 **Postdysenteric arthropathy, left shoulder**
    M02.119 **Postdysenteric arthropathy, unspecified shoulder**
● **M02.12** **Postdysenteric arthropathy, elbow**
    M02.121 **Postdysenteric arthropathy, right elbow**
    M02.122 **Postdysenteric arthropathy, left elbow**
    M02.129 **Postdysenteric arthropathy, unspecified elbow**
● **M02.13** **Postdysenteric arthropathy, wrist**
    Postdysenteric arthropathy, carpal bones
    M02.131 **Postdysenteric arthropathy, right wrist**
    M02.132 **Postdysenteric arthropathy, left wrist**
    M02.139 **Postdysenteric arthropathy, unspecified wrist**
● **M02.14** **Postdysenteric arthropathy, hand**
    Postdysenteric arthropathy, metacarpus and phalanges
    M02.141 **Postdysenteric arthropathy, right hand**
    M02.142 **Postdysenteric arthropathy, left hand**
    M02.149 **Postdysenteric arthropathy, unspecified hand**
● **M02.15** **Postdysenteric arthropathy, hip**
    M02.151 **Postdysenteric arthropathy, right hip**
    M02.152 **Postdysenteric arthropathy, left hip**
    M02.159 **Postdysenteric arthropathy, unspecified hip**
● **M02.16** **Postdysenteric arthropathy, knee**
    M02.161 **Postdysenteric arthropathy, right knee**
    M02.162 **Postdysenteric arthropathy, left knee**
    M02.169 **Postdysenteric arthropathy, unspecified knee**
● **M02.17** **Postdysenteric arthropathy, ankle and foot**
    Postdysenteric arthropathy, tarsus, metatarsus and phalanges
    M02.171 **Postdysenteric arthropathy, right ankle and foot**
    M02.172 **Postdysenteric arthropathy, left ankle and foot**
    M02.179 **Postdysenteric arthropathy, unspecified ankle and foot**
   M02.18 **Postdysenteric arthropathy, vertebrae**
   M02.19 **Postdysenteric arthropathy, multiple sites**

● **M02.2** **Postimmunization arthropathy**
   M02.20 **Postimmunization arthropathy, unspecified site**
● **M02.21** **Postimmunization arthropathy, shoulder**
    M02.211 **Postimmunization arthropathy, right shoulder**
    M02.212 **Postimmunization arthropathy, left shoulder**
    M02.219 **Postimmunization arthropathy, unspecified shoulder**
● **M02.22** **Postimmunization arthropathy, elbow**
    M02.221 **Postimmunization arthropathy, right elbow**
    M02.222 **Postimmunization arthropathy, left elbow**
    M02.229 **Postimmunization arthropathy, unspecified elbow**
● **M02.23** **Postimmunization arthropathy, wrist**
    Postimmunization arthropathy, carpal bones
    M02.231 **Postimmunization arthropathy, right wrist**
    M02.232 **Postimmunization arthropathy, left wrist**
    M02.239 **Postimmunization arthropathy, unspecified wrist**
● **M02.24** **Postimmunization arthropathy, hand**
    Postimmunization arthropathy, metacarpus and phalanges
    M02.241 **Postimmunization arthropathy, right hand**
    M02.242 **Postimmunization arthropathy, left hand**
    M02.249 **Postimmunization arthropathy, unspecified hand**
● **M02.25** **Postimmunization arthropathy, hip**
    M02.251 **Postimmunization arthropathy, right hip**
    M02.252 **Postimmunization arthropathy, left hip**
    M02.259 **Postimmunization arthropathy, unspecified hip**
● **M02.26** **Postimmunization arthropathy, knee**
    M02.261 **Postimmunization arthropathy, right knee**
    M02.262 **Postimmunization arthropathy, left knee**
    M02.269 **Postimmunization arthropathy, unspecified knee**
● **M02.27** **Postimmunization arthropathy, ankle and foot**
    Postimmunization arthropathy, tarsus, metatarsus and phalanges
    M02.271 **Postimmunization arthropathy, right ankle and foot**
    M02.272 **Postimmunization arthropathy, left ankle and foot**
    M02.279 **Postimmunization arthropathy, unspecified ankle and foot**
   M02.28 **Postimmunization arthropathy, vertebrae**
   M02.29 **Postimmunization arthropathy, multiple sites**

● **M02.3** **Reiter's disease**
   Reactive arthritis
   M02.30 **Reiter's disease, unspecified site**
● **M02.31** **Reiter's disease, shoulder**
    M02.311 **Reiter's disease, right shoulder**
    M02.312 **Reiter's disease, left shoulder**
    M02.319 **Reiter's disease, unspecified shoulder**

▶ New   ⇒ Revised   ~~deleted~~ Deleted   Excludes 1   Excludes 2   Includes   Use additional   Code first   Code also   Key words
OGCR Official Guidelines   X Assign placeholder X   ● Use Additional Character(s)   ▷ Manifestation Code   Hierarchical Condition Category   **Coding Clinic**

● **M02.32   Reiter's disease, elbow**
    M02.321   Reiter's disease, right elbow
    M02.322   Reiter's disease, left elbow
    M02.329   Reiter's disease, unspecified elbow

● **M02.33   Reiter's disease, wrist**
    Reiter's disease, carpal bones
    M02.331   Reiter's disease, right wrist
    M02.332   Reiter's disease, left wrist
    M02.339   Reiter's disease, unspecified wrist

● **M02.34   Reiter's disease, hand**
    Reiter's disease, metacarpus and phalanges
    M02.341   Reiter's disease, right hand
    M02.342   Reiter's disease, left hand
    M02.349   Reiter's disease, unspecified hand

● **M02.35   Reiter's disease, hip**
    M02.351   Reiter's disease, right hip
    M02.352   Reiter's disease, left hip
    M02.359   Reiter's disease, unspecified hip

● **M02.36   Reiter's disease, knee**
    M02.361   Reiter's disease, right knee
    M02.362   Reiter's disease, left knee
    M02.369   Reiter's disease, unspecified knee

● **M02.37   Reiter's disease, ankle and foot**
    Reiter's disease, tarsus, metatarsus and phalanges
    M02.371   Reiter's disease, right ankle and foot
    M02.372   Reiter's disease, left ankle and foot
    M02.379   Reiter's disease, unspecified ankle and foot

    M02.38   Reiter's disease, vertebrae
    M02.39   Reiter's disease, multiple sites

● **M02.8   Other reactive arthropathies**
    M02.80   Other reactive arthropathies, unspecified site

● **M02.81   Other reactive arthropathies, shoulder**
    M02.811   Other reactive arthropathies, right shoulder
    M02.812   Other reactive arthropathies, left shoulder
    M02.819   Other reactive arthropathies, unspecified shoulder

● **M02.82   Other reactive arthropathies, elbow**
    M02.821   Other reactive arthropathies, right elbow
    M02.822   Other reactive arthropathies, left elbow
    M02.829   Other reactive arthropathies, unspecified elbow

● **M02.83   Other reactive arthropathies, wrist**
    Other reactive arthropathies, carpal bones
    M02.831   Other reactive arthropathies, right wrist
    M02.832   Other reactive arthropathies, left wrist
    M02.839   Other reactive arthropathies, unspecified wrist

● **M02.84   Other reactive arthropathies, hand**
    Other reactive arthropathies, metacarpus and phalanges
    M02.841   Other reactive arthropathies, right hand
    M02.842   Other reactive arthropathies, left hand
    M02.849   Other reactive arthropathies, unspecified hand

● **M02.85   Other reactive arthropathies, hip**
    M02.851   Other reactive arthropathies, right hip
    M02.852   Other reactive arthropathies, left hip
    M02.859   Other reactive arthropathies, unspecified hip

● **M02.86   Other reactive arthropathies, knee**
    M02.861   Other reactive arthropathies, right knee
    M02.862   Other reactive arthropathies, left knee
    M02.869   Other reactive arthropathies, unspecified knee

● **M02.87   Other reactive arthropathies, ankle and foot**
    Other reactive arthropathies, tarsus, metatarsus and phalanges
    M02.871   Other reactive arthropathies, right ankle and foot
    M02.872   Other reactive arthropathies, left ankle and foot
    M02.879   Other reactive arthropathies, unspecified ankle and foot

    M02.88   Other reactive arthropathies, vertebrae
    M02.89   Other reactive arthropathies, multiple sites
    M02.9   Reactive arthropathy, unspecified

AUTOINFLAMMATORY SYNDROMES (M04)

● **M04   Autoinflammatory syndromes**
    Excludes2   Crohn's disease (K50.-)
    Coding Clinic: 2016, Q4, P37

    M04.1   Periodic fever syndromes
      Familial Mediterranean fever
      Hyperimmunoglobin D syndrome
      Mevalonate kinase deficiency
      Tumor necrosis factor receptor associated periodic syndrome [TRAPS]

    M04.2   Cryopyrin-associated periodic syndromes
      Chronic infantile neurological, cutaneous and articular syndrome [CINCA]
      Familial cold autoinflammatory syndrome
      Familial cold urticaria
      Muckle-Wells syndrome
      Neonatal onset multisystemic inflammatory disorder [NOMID]

    M04.8   Other autoinflammatory syndromes
      Blau syndrome
      Deficiency of interleukin 1 receptor antagonist [DIRA]
      Majeed syndrome
      Periodic fever, aphthous stomatitis, pharyngitis, and adenopathy syndrome [PFAPA]
      Pyogenic arthritis, pyoderma gangrenosum, and acne syndrome [PAPA]

    M04.9   Autoinflammatory syndrome, unspecified

INFLAMMATORY POLYARTHROPATHIES (M05-M14)

● **M05   Rheumatoid arthritis with rheumatoid factor**
    Excludes1   rheumatic fever (I00)
      juvenile rheumatoid arthritis (M08.-)
      rheumatoid arthritis of spine (M45.-)

   ● **M05.0   Felty's syndrome**
    Rheumatoid arthritis with splenoadenomegaly and leukopenia
    M05.00   Felty's syndrome, unspecified site
   ● **M05.01   Felty's syndrome, shoulder**
      M05.011   Felty's syndrome, right shoulder
      M05.012   Felty's syndrome, left shoulder
      M05.019   Felty's syndrome, unspecified shoulder

● M05.02　Felty's syndrome, elbow
　　　M05.021　Felty's syndrome, right elbow 🐾
　　　M05.022　Felty's syndrome, left elbow 🐾
　　　M05.029　Felty's syndrome, unspecified elbow 🐾
● M05.03　Felty's syndrome, wrist
　　　　Felty's syndrome, carpal bones
　　　M05.031　Felty's syndrome, right wrist 🐾
　　　M05.032　Felty's syndrome, left wrist 🐾
　　　M05.039　Felty's syndrome, unspecified wrist 🐾
● M05.04　Felty's syndrome, hand
　　　　Felty's syndrome, metacarpus and phalanges
　　　M05.041　Felty's syndrome, right hand 🐾
　　　M05.042　Felty's syndrome, left hand 🐾
　　　M05.049　Felty's syndrome, unspecified hand 🐾
● M05.05　Felty's syndrome, hip
　　　M05.051　Felty's syndrome, right hip 🐾
　　　M05.052　Felty's syndrome, left hip 🐾
　　　M05.059　Felty's syndrome, unspecified hip 🐾
● M05.06　Felty's syndrome, knee
　　　M05.061　Felty's syndrome, right knee 🐾
　　　M05.062　Felty's syndrome, left knee 🐾
　　　M05.069　Felty's syndrome, unspecified knee 🐾
● M05.07　Felty's syndrome, ankle and foot
　　　　Felty's syndrome, tarsus, metatarsus and phalanges
　　　M05.071　Felty's syndrome, right ankle and foot 🐾
　　　M05.072　Felty's syndrome, left ankle and foot 🐾
　　　M05.079　Felty's syndrome, unspecified ankle and foot 🐾
　　M05.09　Felty's syndrome, multiple sites 🐾
● M05.1　Rheumatoid lung disease with rheumatoid arthritis
　　M05.10　Rheumatoid lung disease with rheumatoid arthritis of unspecified site 🐾
● M05.11　Rheumatoid lung disease with rheumatoid arthritis of shoulder
　　　M05.111　Rheumatoid lung disease with rheumatoid arthritis of right shoulder 🐾
　　　M05.112　Rheumatoid lung disease with rheumatoid arthritis of left shoulder 🐾
　　　M05.119　Rheumatoid lung disease with rheumatoid arthritis of unspecified shoulder 🐾
● M05.12　Rheumatoid lung disease with rheumatoid arthritis of elbow
　　　M05.121　Rheumatoid lung disease with rheumatoid arthritis of right elbow 🐾
　　　M05.122　Rheumatoid lung disease with rheumatoid arthritis of left elbow 🐾
　　　M05.129　Rheumatoid lung disease with rheumatoid arthritis of unspecified elbow 🐾

● M05.13　Rheumatoid lung disease with rheumatoid arthritis of wrist
　　　　Rheumatoid lung disease with rheumatoid arthritis, carpal bones
　　　M05.131　Rheumatoid lung disease with rheumatoid arthritis of right wrist 🐾
　　　M05.132　Rheumatoid lung disease with rheumatoid arthritis of left wrist 🐾
　　　M05.139　Rheumatoid lung disease with rheumatoid arthritis of unspecified wrist 🐾
● M05.14　Rheumatoid lung disease with rheumatoid arthritis of hand
　　　　Rheumatoid lung disease with rheumatoid arthritis, metacarpus and phalanges
　　　M05.141　Rheumatoid lung disease with rheumatoid arthritis of right hand 🐾
　　　M05.142　Rheumatoid lung disease with rheumatoid arthritis of left hand 🐾
　　　M05.149　Rheumatoid lung disease with rheumatoid arthritis of unspecified hand 🐾
● M05.15　Rheumatoid lung disease with rheumatoid arthritis of hip
　　　M05.151　Rheumatoid lung disease with rheumatoid arthritis of right hip 🐾
　　　M05.152　Rheumatoid lung disease with rheumatoid arthritis of left hip 🐾
　　　M05.159　Rheumatoid lung disease with rheumatoid arthritis of unspecified hip 🐾
● M05.16　Rheumatoid lung disease with rheumatoid arthritis of knee
　　　M05.161　Rheumatoid lung disease with rheumatoid arthritis of right knee 🐾
　　　M05.162　Rheumatoid lung disease with rheumatoid arthritis of left knee 🐾
　　　M05.169　Rheumatoid lung disease with rheumatoid arthritis of unspecified knee 🐾
● M05.17　Rheumatoid lung disease with rheumatoid arthritis of ankle and foot
　　　　Rheumatoid lung disease with rheumatoid arthritis, tarsus, metatarsus and phalanges
　　　M05.171　Rheumatoid lung disease with rheumatoid arthritis of right ankle and foot 🐾
　　　M05.172　Rheumatoid lung disease with rheumatoid arthritis of left ankle and foot 🐾
　　　M05.179　Rheumatoid lung disease with rheumatoid arthritis of unspecified ankle and foot 🐾
　　M05.19　Rheumatoid lung disease with rheumatoid arthritis of multiple sites 🐾
● M05.2　Rheumatoid vasculitis with rheumatoid arthritis
　　M05.20　Rheumatoid vasculitis with rheumatoid arthritis of unspecified site 🐾
● M05.21　Rheumatoid vasculitis with rheumatoid arthritis of shoulder
　　　M05.211　Rheumatoid vasculitis with rheumatoid arthritis of right shoulder 🐾
　　　M05.212　Rheumatoid vasculitis with rheumatoid arthritis of left shoulder 🐾
　　　M05.219　Rheumatoid vasculitis with rheumatoid arthritis of unspecified shoulder 🐾

Item 13–1　Rheumatoid arthritis (RA) is a chronic systemic inflammatory autoimmune disease of undetermined etiology involving primarily the synovial membranes and articular structures of multiple joints. It can also affect other organs, including the eyes, blood vessels, heart, and lungs. The disease is often progressive. In late stages, deformity, ankylosis, and other **inflammatory polyarthropathies** develop.

▶ New　⟹ Revised　~~deleted~~ Deleted　Excludes 1　Excludes 2　Includes　Use additional　Code first　Code also　Key words
OGCR Official Guidelines　X Assign placeholder X　● Use Additional Character(s)　⟩ Manifestation Code　🐾 Hierarchical Condition Category　Coding Clinic

● **M05.22** Rheumatoid vasculitis with rheumatoid arthritis of elbow

     M05.221 Rheumatoid vasculitis with rheumatoid arthritis of right elbow 🔖

     M05.222 Rheumatoid vasculitis with rheumatoid arthritis of left elbow 🔖

     M05.229 Rheumatoid vasculitis with rheumatoid arthritis of unspecified elbow 🔖

● **M05.23** Rheumatoid vasculitis with rheumatoid arthritis of wrist
Rheumatoid vasculitis with rheumatoid arthritis, carpal bones

     M05.231 Rheumatoid vasculitis with rheumatoid arthritis of right wrist 🔖

     M05.232 Rheumatoid vasculitis with rheumatoid arthritis of left wrist 🔖

     M05.239 Rheumatoid vasculitis with rheumatoid arthritis of unspecified wrist 🔖

● **M05.24** Rheumatoid vasculitis with rheumatoid arthritis of hand
Rheumatoid vasculitis with rheumatoid arthritis, metacarpus and phalanges

     M05.241 Rheumatoid vasculitis with rheumatoid arthritis of right hand 🔖

     M05.242 Rheumatoid vasculitis with rheumatoid arthritis of left hand 🔖

     M05.249 Rheumatoid vasculitis with rheumatoid arthritis of unspecified hand 🔖

● **M05.25** Rheumatoid vasculitis with rheumatoid arthritis of hip

     M05.251 Rheumatoid vasculitis with rheumatoid arthritis of right hip 🔖

     M05.252 Rheumatoid vasculitis with rheumatoid arthritis of left hip 🔖

     M05.259 Rheumatoid vasculitis with rheumatoid arthritis of unspecified hip 🔖

● **M05.26** Rheumatoid vasculitis with rheumatoid arthritis of knee

     M05.261 Rheumatoid vasculitis with rheumatoid arthritis of right knee 🔖

     M05.262 Rheumatoid vasculitis with rheumatoid arthritis of left knee 🔖

     M05.269 Rheumatoid vasculitis with rheumatoid arthritis of unspecified knee 🔖

● **M05.27** Rheumatoid vasculitis with rheumatoid arthritis of ankle and foot
Rheumatoid vasculitis with rheumatoid arthritis, tarsus, metatarsus and phalanges

     M05.271 Rheumatoid vasculitis with rheumatoid arthritis of right ankle and foot 🔖

     M05.272 Rheumatoid vasculitis with rheumatoid arthritis of left ankle and foot 🔖

     M05.279 Rheumatoid vasculitis with rheumatoid arthritis of unspecified ankle and foot 🔖

M05.29 Rheumatoid vasculitis with rheumatoid arthritis of multiple sites 🔖

● **M05.3** Rheumatoid heart disease with rheumatoid arthritis
Rheumatoid carditis
Rheumatoid endocarditis
Rheumatoid myocarditis
Rheumatoid pericarditis

     M05.30 Rheumatoid heart disease with rheumatoid arthritis of unspecified site 🔖

● **M05.31** Rheumatoid heart disease with rheumatoid arthritis of shoulder

     M05.311 Rheumatoid heart disease with rheumatoid arthritis of right shoulder 🔖

     M05.312 Rheumatoid heart disease with rheumatoid arthritis of left shoulder 🔖

     M05.319 Rheumatoid heart disease with rheumatoid arthritis of unspecified shoulder 🔖

● **M05.32** Rheumatoid heart disease with rheumatoid arthritis of elbow

     M05.321 Rheumatoid heart disease with rheumatoid arthritis of right elbow 🔖

     M05.322 Rheumatoid heart disease with rheumatoid arthritis of left elbow 🔖

     M05.329 Rheumatoid heart disease with rheumatoid arthritis of unspecified elbow 🔖

● **M05.33** Rheumatoid heart disease with rheumatoid arthritis of wrist
Rheumatoid heart disease with rheumatoid arthritis, carpal bones

     M05.331 Rheumatoid heart disease with rheumatoid arthritis of right wrist 🔖

     M05.332 Rheumatoid heart disease with rheumatoid arthritis of left wrist 🔖

     M05.339 Rheumatoid heart disease with rheumatoid arthritis of unspecified wrist 🔖

● **M05.34** Rheumatoid heart disease with rheumatoid arthritis of hand
Rheumatoid heart disease with rheumatoid arthritis, metacarpus and phalanges

     M05.341 Rheumatoid heart disease with rheumatoid arthritis of right hand 🔖

     M05.342 Rheumatoid heart disease with rheumatoid arthritis of left hand 🔖

     M05.349 Rheumatoid heart disease with rheumatoid arthritis of unspecified hand 🔖

● **M05.35** Rheumatoid heart disease with rheumatoid arthritis of hip

     M05.351 Rheumatoid heart disease with rheumatoid arthritis of right hip 🔖

     M05.352 Rheumatoid heart disease with rheumatoid arthritis of left hip 🔖

     M05.359 Rheumatoid heart disease with rheumatoid arthritis of unspecified hip 🔖

● **M05.36** Rheumatoid heart disease with rheumatoid arthritis of knee

     M05.361 Rheumatoid heart disease with rheumatoid arthritis of right knee 🔖

     M05.362 Rheumatoid heart disease with rheumatoid arthritis of left knee 🔖

     M05.369 Rheumatoid heart disease with rheumatoid arthritis of unspecified knee 🔖

● **M05.37**   Rheumatoid heart disease with rheumatoid arthritis of ankle and foot
Rheumatoid heart disease with rheumatoid arthritis, tarsus, metatarsus and phalanges

     M05.371   Rheumatoid heart disease with rheumatoid arthritis of right ankle and foot 🐾

     M05.372   Rheumatoid heart disease with rheumatoid arthritis of left ankle and foot 🐾

     M05.379   Rheumatoid heart disease with rheumatoid arthritis of unspecified ankle and foot 🐾

   M05.39   Rheumatoid heart disease with rheumatoid arthritis of multiple sites 🐾

● **M05.4**   Rheumatoid myopathy with rheumatoid arthritis

   M05.40   Rheumatoid myopathy with rheumatoid arthritis of unspecified site 🐾

● **M05.41**   Rheumatoid myopathy with rheumatoid arthritis of shoulder

     M05.411   Rheumatoid myopathy with rheumatoid arthritis of right shoulder 🐾

     M05.412   Rheumatoid myopathy with rheumatoid arthritis of left shoulder 🐾

     M05.419   Rheumatoid myopathy with rheumatoid arthritis of unspecified shoulder 🐾

● **M05.42**   Rheumatoid myopathy with rheumatoid arthritis of elbow

     M05.421   Rheumatoid myopathy with rheumatoid arthritis of right elbow 🐾

     M05.422   Rheumatoid myopathy with rheumatoid arthritis of left elbow 🐾

     M05.429   Rheumatoid myopathy with rheumatoid arthritis of unspecified elbow 🐾

● **M05.43**   Rheumatoid myopathy with rheumatoid arthritis of wrist
Rheumatoid myopathy with rheumatoid arthritis, carpal bones

     M05.431   Rheumatoid myopathy with rheumatoid arthritis of right wrist 🐾

     M05.432   Rheumatoid myopathy with rheumatoid arthritis of left wrist 🐾

     M05.439   Rheumatoid myopathy with rheumatoid arthritis of unspecified wrist 🐾

● **M05.44**   Rheumatoid myopathy with rheumatoid arthritis of hand
Rheumatoid myopathy with rheumatoid arthritis, metacarpus and phalanges

     M05.441   Rheumatoid myopathy with rheumatoid arthritis of right hand 🐾

     M05.442   Rheumatoid myopathy with rheumatoid arthritis of left hand 🐾

     M05.449   Rheumatoid myopathy with rheumatoid arthritis of unspecified hand 🐾

● **M05.45**   Rheumatoid myopathy with rheumatoid arthritis of hip

     M05.451   Rheumatoid myopathy with rheumatoid arthritis of right hip 🐾

     M05.452   Rheumatoid myopathy with rheumatoid arthritis of left hip 🐾

     M05.459   Rheumatoid myopathy with rheumatoid arthritis of unspecified hip 🐾

● **M05.46**   Rheumatoid myopathy with rheumatoid arthritis of knee

     M05.461   Rheumatoid myopathy with rheumatoid arthritis of right knee 🐾

     M05.462   Rheumatoid myopathy with rheumatoid arthritis of left knee 🐾

     M05.469   Rheumatoid myopathy with rheumatoid arthritis of unspecified knee 🐾

● **M05.47**   Rheumatoid myopathy with rheumatoid arthritis of ankle and foot
Rheumatoid myopathy with rheumatoid arthritis, tarsus, metatarsus and phalanges

     M05.471   Rheumatoid myopathy with rheumatoid arthritis of right ankle and foot 🐾

     M05.472   Rheumatoid myopathy with rheumatoid arthritis of left ankle and foot 🐾

     M05.479   Rheumatoid myopathy with rheumatoid arthritis of unspecified ankle and foot 🐾

   M05.49   Rheumatoid myopathy with rheumatoid arthritis of multiple sites 🐾

● **M05.5**   Rheumatoid polyneuropathy with rheumatoid arthritis

   M05.50   Rheumatoid polyneuropathy with rheumatoid arthritis of unspecified site 🐾

● **M05.51**   Rheumatoid polyneuropathy with rheumatoid arthritis of shoulder

     M05.511   Rheumatoid polyneuropathy with rheumatoid arthritis of right shoulder 🐾

     M05.512   Rheumatoid polyneuropathy with rheumatoid arthritis of left shoulder 🐾

     M05.519   Rheumatoid polyneuropathy with rheumatoid arthritis of unspecified shoulder 🐾

● **M05.52**   Rheumatoid polyneuropathy with rheumatoid arthritis of elbow

     M05.521   Rheumatoid polyneuropathy with rheumatoid arthritis of right elbow 🐾

     M05.522   Rheumatoid polyneuropathy with rheumatoid arthritis of left elbow 🐾

     M05.529   Rheumatoid polyneuropathy with rheumatoid arthritis of unspecified elbow 🐾

● **M05.53**   Rheumatoid polyneuropathy with rheumatoid arthritis of wrist
Rheumatoid polyneuropathy with rheumatoid arthritis, carpal bones

     M05.531   Rheumatoid polyneuropathy with rheumatoid arthritis of right wrist 🐾

     M05.532   Rheumatoid polyneuropathy with rheumatoid arthritis of left wrist 🐾

     M05.539   Rheumatoid polyneuropathy with rheumatoid arthritis of unspecified wrist 🐾

● **M05.54**   Rheumatoid polyneuropathy with rheumatoid arthritis of hand
Rheumatoid polyneuropathy with rheumatoid arthritis, metacarpus and phalanges

     M05.541   Rheumatoid polyneuropathy with rheumatoid arthritis of right hand 🐾

     M05.542   Rheumatoid polyneuropathy with rheumatoid arthritis of left hand 🐾

     M05.549   Rheumatoid polyneuropathy with rheumatoid arthritis of unspecified hand 🐾

▶ New   ⇒ Revised   ~~deleted~~ Deleted   Excludes 1   Excludes 2   Includes   Use additional   Code first   Code also   Key words

OGCR Official Guidelines   X Assign placeholder X   ● Use Additional Character(s)   ▷ Manifestation Code   🐾 Hierarchical Condition Category   **Coding Clinic**

● **M05.55** Rheumatoid polyneuropathy with rheumatoid arthritis of hip

   M05.551 Rheumatoid polyneuropathy with rheumatoid arthritis of right hip ℞

   M05.552 Rheumatoid polyneuropathy with rheumatoid arthritis of left hip ℞

   M05.559 Rheumatoid polyneuropathy with rheumatoid arthritis of unspecified hip ℞

● **M05.56** Rheumatoid polyneuropathy with rheumatoid arthritis of knee

   M05.561 Rheumatoid polyneuropathy with rheumatoid arthritis of right knee ℞

   M05.562 Rheumatoid polyneuropathy with rheumatoid arthritis of left knee ℞

   M05.569 Rheumatoid polyneuropathy with rheumatoid arthritis of unspecified knee ℞

● **M05.57** Rheumatoid polyneuropathy with rheumatoid arthritis of ankle and foot

   Rheumatoid polyneuropathy with rheumatoid arthritis, tarsus, metatarsus and phalanges

   M05.571 Rheumatoid polyneuropathy with rheumatoid arthritis of right ankle and foot ℞

   M05.572 Rheumatoid polyneuropathy with rheumatoid arthritis of left ankle and foot ℞

   M05.579 Rheumatoid polyneuropathy with rheumatoid arthritis of unspecified ankle and foot ℞

   M05.59 Rheumatoid polyneuropathy with rheumatoid arthritis of multiple sites ℞

● **M05.6** Rheumatoid arthritis with involvement of other organs and systems

   M05.60 Rheumatoid arthritis of unspecified site with involvement of other organs and systems ℞

● **M05.61** Rheumatoid arthritis of shoulder with involvement of other organs and systems

   M05.611 Rheumatoid arthritis of right shoulder with involvement of other organs and systems ℞

   M05.612 Rheumatoid arthritis of left shoulder with involvement of other organs and systems ℞

   M05.619 Rheumatoid arthritis of unspecified shoulder with involvement of other organs and systems ℞

● **M05.62** Rheumatoid arthritis of elbow with involvement of other organs and systems

   M05.621 Rheumatoid arthritis of right elbow with involvement of other organs and systems ℞

   M05.622 Rheumatoid arthritis of left elbow with involvement of other organs and systems ℞

   M05.629 Rheumatoid arthritis of unspecified elbow with involvement of other organs and systems ℞

● **M05.63** Rheumatoid arthritis of wrist with involvement of other organs and systems

   Rheumatoid arthritis of carpal bones with involvement of other organs and systems

   M05.631 Rheumatoid arthritis of right wrist with involvement of other organs and systems ℞

   M05.632 Rheumatoid arthritis of left wrist with involvement of other organs and systems ℞

   M05.639 Rheumatoid arthritis of unspecified wrist with involvement of other organs and systems ℞

● **M05.64** Rheumatoid arthritis of hand with involvement of other organs and systems

   Rheumatoid arthritis of metacarpus and phalanges with involvement of other organs and systems

   M05.641 Rheumatoid arthritis of right hand with involvement of other organs and systems ℞

   M05.642 Rheumatoid arthritis of left hand with involvement of other organs and systems ℞

   M05.649 Rheumatoid arthritis of unspecified hand with involvement of other organs and systems ℞

● **M05.65** Rheumatoid arthritis of hip with involvement of other organs and systems

   M05.651 Rheumatoid arthritis of right hip with involvement of other organs and systems ℞

   M05.652 Rheumatoid arthritis of left hip with involvement of other organs and systems ℞

   M05.659 Rheumatoid arthritis of unspecified hip with involvement of other organs and systems ℞

● **M05.66** Rheumatoid arthritis of knee with involvement of other organs and systems

   M05.661 Rheumatoid arthritis of right knee with involvement of other organs and systems ℞

   M05.662 Rheumatoid arthritis of left knee with involvement of other organs and systems ℞

   M05.669 Rheumatoid arthritis of unspecified knee with involvement of other organs and systems ℞

● **M05.67** Rheumatoid arthritis of ankle and foot with involvement of other organs and systems

   Rheumatoid arthritis of tarsus, metatarsus and phalanges with involvement of other organs and systems

   M05.671 Rheumatoid arthritis of right ankle and foot with involvement of other organs and systems ℞

   M05.672 Rheumatoid arthritis of left ankle and foot with involvement of other organs and systems ℞

   M05.679 Rheumatoid arthritis of unspecified ankle and foot with involvement of other organs and systems ℞

   M05.69 Rheumatoid arthritis of multiple sites with involvement of other organs and systems ℞

● **M05.7** Rheumatoid arthritis with rheumatoid factor without organ or systems involvement

   M05.70 Rheumatoid arthritis with rheumatoid factor of unspecified site without organ or systems involvement ℞

● **M05.71** Rheumatoid arthritis with rheumatoid factor of shoulder without organ or systems involvement

   M05.711 Rheumatoid arthritis with rheumatoid factor of right shoulder without organ or systems involvement ℞

   M05.712 Rheumatoid arthritis with rheumatoid factor of left shoulder without organ or systems involvement ℞

   M05.719 Rheumatoid arthritis with rheumatoid factor of unspecified shoulder without organ or systems involvement ℞

● M05.72 Rheumatoid arthritis with rheumatoid factor of elbow without organ or systems involvement

    M05.721 Rheumatoid arthritis with rheumatoid factor of right elbow without organ or systems involvement ✎

    M05.722 Rheumatoid arthritis with rheumatoid factor of left elbow without organ or systems involvement ✎

    M05.729 Rheumatoid arthritis with rheumatoid factor of unspecified elbow without organ or systems involvement ✎

● M05.73 Rheumatoid arthritis with rheumatoid factor of wrist without organ or systems involvement

    M05.731 Rheumatoid arthritis with rheumatoid factor of right wrist without organ or systems involvement ✎

    M05.732 Rheumatoid arthritis with rheumatoid factor of left wrist without organ or systems involvement ✎

    M05.739 Rheumatoid arthritis with rheumatoid factor of unspecified wrist without organ or systems involvement ✎

● M05.74 Rheumatoid arthritis with rheumatoid factor of hand without organ or systems involvement

    M05.741 Rheumatoid arthritis with rheumatoid factor of right hand without organ or systems involvement ✎

    M05.742 Rheumatoid arthritis with rheumatoid factor of left hand without organ or systems involvement ✎

    M05.749 Rheumatoid arthritis with rheumatoid factor of unspecified hand without organ or systems involvement ✎

● M05.75 Rheumatoid arthritis with rheumatoid factor of hip without organ or systems involvement

    M05.751 Rheumatoid arthritis with rheumatoid factor of right hip without organ or systems involvement ✎

    M05.752 Rheumatoid arthritis with rheumatoid factor of left hip without organ or systems involvement ✎

    M05.759 Rheumatoid arthritis with rheumatoid factor of unspecified hip without organ or systems involvement ✎

● M05.76 Rheumatoid arthritis with rheumatoid factor of knee without organ or systems involvement

    M05.761 Rheumatoid arthritis with rheumatoid factor of right knee without organ or systems involvement ✎

    M05.762 Rheumatoid arthritis with rheumatoid factor of left knee without organ or systems involvement ✎

    M05.769 Rheumatoid arthritis with rheumatoid factor of unspecified knee without organ or systems involvement ✎

● M05.77 Rheumatoid arthritis with rheumatoid factor of ankle and foot without organ or systems involvement

    M05.771 Rheumatoid arthritis with rheumatoid factor of right ankle and foot without organ or systems involvement ✎

    M05.772 Rheumatoid arthritis with rheumatoid factor of left ankle and foot without organ or systems involvement ✎

    M05.779 Rheumatoid arthritis with rheumatoid factor of unspecified ankle and foot without organ or systems involvement ✎

  M05.79 Rheumatoid arthritis with rheumatoid factor of multiple sites without organ or systems involvement ✎

▶ M05.7A Rheumatoid arthritis with rheumatoid factor of other specified site without organ or systems involvement

● M05.8 Other rheumatoid arthritis with rheumatoid factor

  M05.80 Other rheumatoid arthritis with rheumatoid factor of unspecified site ✎

● M05.81 Other rheumatoid arthritis with rheumatoid factor of shoulder

    M05.811 Other rheumatoid arthritis with rheumatoid factor of right shoulder ✎

    M05.812 Other rheumatoid arthritis with rheumatoid factor of left shoulder ✎

    M05.819 Other rheumatoid arthritis with rheumatoid factor of unspecified shoulder ✎

● M05.82 Other rheumatoid arthritis with rheumatoid factor of elbow

    M05.821 Other rheumatoid arthritis with rheumatoid factor of right elbow ✎

    M05.822 Other rheumatoid arthritis with rheumatoid factor of left elbow ✎

    M05.829 Other rheumatoid arthritis with rheumatoid factor of unspecified elbow ✎

● M05.83 Other rheumatoid arthritis with rheumatoid factor of wrist

    M05.831 Other rheumatoid arthritis with rheumatoid factor of right wrist ✎

    M05.832 Other rheumatoid arthritis with rheumatoid factor of left wrist ✎

    M05.839 Other rheumatoid arthritis with rheumatoid factor of unspecified wrist ✎

● M05.84 Other rheumatoid arthritis with rheumatoid factor of hand

    M05.841 Other rheumatoid arthritis with rheumatoid factor of right hand ✎

    M05.842 Other rheumatoid arthritis with rheumatoid factor of left hand ✎

    M05.849 Other rheumatoid arthritis with rheumatoid factor of unspecified hand ✎

● M05.85 Other rheumatoid arthritis with rheumatoid factor of hip

    M05.851 Other rheumatoid arthritis with rheumatoid factor of right hip ✎

    M05.852 Other rheumatoid arthritis with rheumatoid factor of left hip ✎

    M05.859 Other rheumatoid arthritis with rheumatoid factor of unspecified hip ✎

▶ New   ⇒ Revised   ~~deleted~~ Deleted   Excludes 1   Excludes 2   Includes   Use additional   Code first   Code also   Key words

OGCR Official Guidelines   X Assign placeholder X   ● Use Additional Character(s)   ▶ Manifestation Code   ✎ Hierarchical Condition Category   **Coding Clinic**

● **M05.86** Other rheumatoid arthritis with rheumatoid factor of knee

    M05.861 Other rheumatoid arthritis with rheumatoid factor of right knee ℞

    M05.862 Other rheumatoid arthritis with rheumatoid factor of left knee ℞

    M05.869 Other rheumatoid arthritis with rheumatoid factor of unspecified knee ℞

● **M05.87** Other rheumatoid arthritis with rheumatoid factor of ankle and foot

    M05.871 Other rheumatoid arthritis with rheumatoid factor of right ankle and foot ℞

    M05.872 Other rheumatoid arthritis with rheumatoid factor of left ankle and foot ℞

    M05.879 Other rheumatoid arthritis with rheumatoid factor of unspecified ankle and foot ℞

  M05.89 Other rheumatoid arthritis with rheumatoid factor of multiple sites ℞

▶ **M05.8A** Other rheumatoid arthritis with rheumatoid factor of other specified site

  M05.9 Rheumatoid arthritis with rheumatoid factor, unspecified ℞

● **M06** Other rheumatoid arthritis

  ● **M06.0** Rheumatoid arthritis without rheumatoid factor

    M06.00 Rheumatoid arthritis without rheumatoid factor, unspecified site ℞

    ● **M06.01** Rheumatoid arthritis without rheumatoid factor, shoulder

      M06.011 Rheumatoid arthritis without rheumatoid factor, right shoulder ℞

      M06.012 Rheumatoid arthritis without rheumatoid factor, left shoulder ℞

      M06.019 Rheumatoid arthritis without rheumatoid factor, unspecified shoulder ℞

    ● **M06.02** Rheumatoid arthritis without rheumatoid factor, elbow

      M06.021 Rheumatoid arthritis without rheumatoid factor, right elbow ℞

      M06.022 Rheumatoid arthritis without rheumatoid factor, left elbow ℞

      M06.029 Rheumatoid arthritis without rheumatoid factor, unspecified elbow ℞

    ● **M06.03** Rheumatoid arthritis without rheumatoid factor, wrist

      M06.031 Rheumatoid arthritis without rheumatoid factor, right wrist ℞

      M06.032 Rheumatoid arthritis without rheumatoid factor, left wrist ℞

      M06.039 Rheumatoid arthritis without rheumatoid factor, unspecified wrist ℞

    ● **M06.04** Rheumatoid arthritis without rheumatoid factor, hand

      M06.041 Rheumatoid arthritis without rheumatoid factor, right hand ℞

      M06.042 Rheumatoid arthritis without rheumatoid factor, left hand ℞

      M06.049 Rheumatoid arthritis without rheumatoid factor, unspecified hand ℞

● **M06.05** Rheumatoid arthritis without rheumatoid factor, hip

    M06.051 Rheumatoid arthritis without rheumatoid factor, right hip ℞

    M06.052 Rheumatoid arthritis without rheumatoid factor, left hip ℞

    M06.059 Rheumatoid arthritis without rheumatoid factor, unspecified hip ℞

● **M06.06** Rheumatoid arthritis without rheumatoid factor, knee

    M06.061 Rheumatoid arthritis without rheumatoid factor, right knee ℞

    M06.062 Rheumatoid arthritis without rheumatoid factor, left knee ℞

    M06.069 Rheumatoid arthritis without rheumatoid factor, unspecified knee ℞

● **M06.07** Rheumatoid arthritis without rheumatoid factor, ankle and foot

    M06.071 Rheumatoid arthritis without rheumatoid factor, right ankle and foot ℞

    M06.072 Rheumatoid arthritis without rheumatoid factor, left ankle and foot ℞

    M06.079 Rheumatoid arthritis without rheumatoid factor, unspecified ankle and foot ℞

  M06.08 Rheumatoid arthritis without rheumatoid factor, vertebrae ℞

  M06.09 Rheumatoid arthritis without rheumatoid factor, multiple sites ℞

▶ **M06.0A** Rheumatoid arthritis without rheumatoid factor, other specified site

M06.1 Adult-onset Still's disease ℞   **A**

    Excludes1 Still's disease NOS (M08.2-)

● **M06.2** Rheumatoid bursitis

  M06.20 Rheumatoid bursitis, unspecified site ℞

  ● **M06.21** Rheumatoid bursitis, shoulder

    M06.211 Rheumatoid bursitis, right shoulder ℞

    M06.212 Rheumatoid bursitis, left shoulder ℞

    M06.219 Rheumatoid bursitis, unspecified shoulder ℞

  ● **M06.22** Rheumatoid bursitis, elbow

    M06.221 Rheumatoid bursitis, right elbow ℞

    M06.222 Rheumatoid bursitis, left elbow ℞

    M06.229 Rheumatoid bursitis, unspecified elbow ℞

  ● **M06.23** Rheumatoid bursitis, wrist

    M06.231 Rheumatoid bursitis, right wrist ℞

    M06.232 Rheumatoid bursitis, left wrist ℞

    M06.239 Rheumatoid bursitis, unspecified wrist ℞

  ● **M06.24** Rheumatoid bursitis, hand

    M06.241 Rheumatoid bursitis, right hand ℞

    M06.242 Rheumatoid bursitis, left hand ℞

    M06.249 Rheumatoid bursitis, unspecified hand ℞

  ● **M06.25** Rheumatoid bursitis, hip

    M06.251 Rheumatoid bursitis, right hip ℞

    M06.252 Rheumatoid bursitis, left hip ℞

    M06.259 Rheumatoid bursitis, unspecified hip ℞

  ● **M06.26** Rheumatoid bursitis, knee

    M06.261 Rheumatoid bursitis, right knee ℞

    M06.262 Rheumatoid bursitis, left knee ℞

    M06.269 Rheumatoid bursitis, unspecified knee ℞

● **M06.27** Rheumatoid bursitis, ankle and foot
  - M06.271 Rheumatoid bursitis, right ankle and foot 🦪
  - M06.272 Rheumatoid bursitis, left ankle and foot 🦪
  - M06.279 Rheumatoid bursitis, unspecified ankle and foot 🦪
- M06.28 Rheumatoid bursitis, vertebrae 🦪
- M06.29 Rheumatoid bursitis, multiple sites 🦪

● **M06.3** **Rheumatoid nodule**
- M06.30 Rheumatoid nodule, unspecified site 🦪
● **M06.31** Rheumatoid nodule, shoulder
  - M06.311 Rheumatoid nodule, right shoulder 🦪
  - M06.312 Rheumatoid nodule, left shoulder 🦪
  - M06.319 Rheumatoid nodule, unspecified shoulder 🦪
● **M06.32** Rheumatoid nodule, elbow
  - M06.321 Rheumatoid nodule, right elbow 🦪
  - M06.322 Rheumatoid nodule, left elbow 🦪
  - M06.329 Rheumatoid nodule, unspecified elbow 🦪
● **M06.33** Rheumatoid nodule, wrist
  - M06.331 Rheumatoid nodule, right wrist 🦪
  - M06.332 Rheumatoid nodule, left wrist 🦪
  - M06.339 Rheumatoid nodule, unspecified wrist 🦪
● **M06.34** Rheumatoid nodule, hand
  - M06.341 Rheumatoid nodule, right hand 🦪
  - M06.342 Rheumatoid nodule, left hand 🦪
  - M06.349 Rheumatoid nodule, unspecified hand 🦪
● **M06.35** Rheumatoid nodule, hip
  - M06.351 Rheumatoid nodule, right hip 🦪
  - M06.352 Rheumatoid nodule, left hip 🦪
  - M06.359 Rheumatoid nodule, unspecified hip 🦪
● **M06.36** Rheumatoid nodule, knee
  - M06.361 Rheumatoid nodule, right knee 🦪
  - M06.362 Rheumatoid nodule, left knee 🦪
  - M06.369 Rheumatoid nodule, unspecified knee 🦪
● **M06.37** Rheumatoid nodule, ankle and foot
  - M06.371 Rheumatoid nodule, right ankle and foot 🦪
  - M06.372 Rheumatoid nodule, left ankle and foot 🦪
  - M06.379 Rheumatoid nodule, unspecified ankle and foot 🦪
- M06.38 Rheumatoid nodule, vertebrae 🦪
- M06.39 Rheumatoid nodule, multiple sites 🦪

M06.4 **Inflammatory polyarthropathy** 🦪
  > **Excludes1**   polyarthritis NOS (M13.0)

● **M06.8** **Other specified rheumatoid arthritis**
- M06.80 Other specified rheumatoid arthritis, unspecified site 🦪
● **M06.81** Other specified rheumatoid arthritis, shoulder
  - M06.811 Other specified rheumatoid arthritis, right shoulder 🦪
  - M06.812 Other specified rheumatoid arthritis, left shoulder 🦪
  - M06.819 Other specified rheumatoid arthritis, unspecified shoulder 🦪

● **M06.82** Other specified rheumatoid arthritis, elbow
  - M06.821 Other specified rheumatoid arthritis, right elbow 🦪
  - M06.822 Other specified rheumatoid arthritis, left elbow 🦪
  - M06.829 Other specified rheumatoid arthritis, unspecified elbow 🦪
● **M06.83** Other specified rheumatoid arthritis, wrist
  - M06.831 Other specified rheumatoid arthritis, right wrist 🦪
  - M06.832 Other specified rheumatoid arthritis, left wrist 🦪
  - M06.839 Other specified rheumatoid arthritis, unspecified wrist 🦪
● **M06.84** Other specified rheumatoid arthritis, hand
  - M06.841 Other specified rheumatoid arthritis, right hand 🦪
  - M06.842 Other specified rheumatoid arthritis, left hand 🦪
  - M06.849 Other specified rheumatoid arthritis, unspecified hand 🦪
● **M06.85** Other specified rheumatoid arthritis, hip
  - M06.851 Other specified rheumatoid arthritis, right hip 🦪
  - M06.852 Other specified rheumatoid arthritis, left hip 🦪
  - M06.859 Other specified rheumatoid arthritis, unspecified hip 🦪
● **M06.86** Other specified rheumatoid arthritis, knee
  - M06.861 Other specified rheumatoid arthritis, right knee 🦪
  - M06.862 Other specified rheumatoid arthritis, left knee 🦪
  - M06.869 Other specified rheumatoid arthritis, unspecified knee 🦪
● **M06.87** Other specified rheumatoid arthritis, ankle and foot
  - M06.871 Other specified rheumatoid arthritis, right ankle and foot 🦪
  - M06.872 Other specified rheumatoid arthritis, left ankle and foot 🦪
  - M06.879 Other specified rheumatoid arthritis, unspecified ankle and foot 🦪
- M06.88 Other specified rheumatoid arthritis, vertebrae 🦪
- M06.89 Other specified rheumatoid arthritis, multiple sites 🦪
- ▶ M06.8A Other specified rheumatoid arthritis, other specified site

M06.9 **Rheumatoid arthritis, unspecified** 🦪

● **M07** **Enteropathic arthropathies**
  Code also associated enteropathy, such as:
    regional enteritis [Crohn's disease] (K50.-)
    ulcerative colitis (K51.-)
  > **Excludes1**   psoriatic arthropathies (L40.5-)

● **M07.6** **Enteropathic arthropathies**
- M07.60 Enteropathic arthropathies, unspecified site
● **M07.61** Enteropathic arthropathies, shoulder
  - M07.611 Enteropathic arthropathies, right shoulder
  - M07.612 Enteropathic arthropathies, left shoulder
  - M07.619 Enteropathic arthropathies, unspecified shoulder
● **M07.62** Enteropathic arthropathies, elbow
  - M07.621 Enteropathic arthropathies, right elbow
  - M07.622 Enteropathic arthropathies, left elbow
  - M07.629 Enteropathic arthropathies, unspecified elbow

▶ New   ⇒ Revised   ~~deleted~~ Deleted   Excludes 1   Excludes 2   Includes   Use additional   Code first   Code also   Key words
OGCR Official Guidelines   X Assign placeholder X   ● Use Additional Character(s)   ▷ Manifestation Code   🦪 Hierarchical Condition Category   **Coding Clinic**

● **M07.63** Enteropathic arthropathies, wrist

    M07.631 Enteropathic arthropathies, right wrist

    M07.632 Enteropathic arthropathies, left wrist

    M07.639 Enteropathic arthropathies, unspecified wrist

● **M07.64** Enteropathic arthropathies, hand

    M07.641 Enteropathic arthropathies, right hand

    M07.642 Enteropathic arthropathies, left hand

    M07.649 Enteropathic arthropathies, unspecified hand

● **M07.65** Enteropathic arthropathies, hip

    M07.651 Enteropathic arthropathies, right hip

    M07.652 Enteropathic arthropathies, left hip

    M07.659 Enteropathic arthropathies, unspecified hip

● **M07.66** Enteropathic arthropathies, knee

    M07.661 Enteropathic arthropathies, right knee

    M07.662 Enteropathic arthropathies, left knee

    M07.669 Enteropathic arthropathies, unspecified knee

● **M07.67** Enteropathic arthropathies, ankle and foot

    M07.671 Enteropathic arthropathies, right ankle and foot

    M07.672 Enteropathic arthropathies, left ankle and foot

    M07.679 Enteropathic arthropathies, unspecified ankle and foot

  M07.68 Enteropathic arthropathies, vertebrae

  M07.69 Enteropathic arthropathies, multiple sites

● **M08** Juvenile arthritis

Code also any associated underlying condition, such as:
regional enteritis [Crohn's disease] (K50.-)
ulcerative colitis (K51.-)

  Excludes1   arthropathy in Whipple's disease (M14.8)
Felty's syndrome (M05.0)
juvenile dermatomyositis (M33.0-)
psoriatic juvenile arthropathy (L40.54)

● **M08.0** Unspecified juvenile rheumatoid arthritis

Juvenile rheumatoid arthritis with or without rheumatoid factor

  M08.00 Unspecified juvenile rheumatoid arthritis of unspecified site 🦟

● **M08.01** Unspecified juvenile rheumatoid arthritis, shoulder

    M08.011 Unspecified juvenile rheumatoid arthritis, right shoulder 🦟

    M08.012 Unspecified juvenile rheumatoid arthritis, left shoulder 🦟

    M08.019 Unspecified juvenile rheumatoid arthritis, unspecified shoulder 🦟

● **M08.02** Unspecified juvenile rheumatoid arthritis of elbow

    M08.021 Unspecified juvenile rheumatoid arthritis, right elbow 🦟

    M08.022 Unspecified juvenile rheumatoid arthritis, left elbow 🦟

    M08.029 Unspecified juvenile rheumatoid arthritis, unspecified elbow 🦟

● **M08.03** Unspecified juvenile rheumatoid arthritis, wrist

    M08.031 Unspecified juvenile rheumatoid arthritis, right wrist 🦟

    M08.032 Unspecified juvenile rheumatoid arthritis, left wrist 🦟

    M08.039 Unspecified juvenile rheumatoid arthritis, unspecified wrist 🦟

● **M08.04** Unspecified juvenile rheumatoid arthritis, hand

    M08.041 Unspecified juvenile rheumatoid arthritis, right hand 🦟

    M08.042 Unspecified juvenile rheumatoid arthritis, left hand 🦟

    M08.049 Unspecified juvenile rheumatoid arthritis, unspecified hand 🦟

● **M08.05** Unspecified juvenile rheumatoid arthritis, hip

    M08.051 Unspecified juvenile rheumatoid arthritis, right hip 🦟

    M08.052 Unspecified juvenile rheumatoid arthritis, left hip 🦟

    M08.059 Unspecified juvenile rheumatoid arthritis, unspecified hip 🦟

● **M08.06** Unspecified juvenile rheumatoid arthritis, knee

    M08.061 Unspecified juvenile rheumatoid arthritis, right knee 🦟

    M08.062 Unspecified juvenile rheumatoid arthritis, left knee 🦟

    M08.069 Unspecified juvenile rheumatoid arthritis, unspecified knee 🦟

● **M08.07** Unspecified juvenile rheumatoid arthritis, ankle and foot

    M08.071 Unspecified juvenile rheumatoid arthritis, right ankle and foot 🦟

    M08.072 Unspecified juvenile rheumatoid arthritis, left ankle and foot 🦟

    M08.079 Unspecified juvenile rheumatoid arthritis, unspecified ankle and foot 🦟

  M08.08 Unspecified juvenile rheumatoid arthritis, vertebrae 🦟

  M08.09 Unspecified juvenile rheumatoid arthritis, multiple sites 🦟

▶ **M08.0A** Unspecified juvenile rheumatoid arthritis, other specified site

M08.1 Juvenile ankylosing spondylitis 🦟

  Excludes1   ankylosing spondylitis in adults (M45.0-)

● **M08.2** Juvenile rheumatoid arthritis with systemic onset

Still's disease NOS

  Excludes1   adult-onset Still's disease (M06.1-)

  M08.20 Juvenile rheumatoid arthritis with systemic onset, unspecified site 🦟

● **M08.21** Juvenile rheumatoid arthritis with systemic onset, shoulder

    M08.211 Juvenile rheumatoid arthritis with systemic onset, right shoulder 🦟

    M08.212 Juvenile rheumatoid arthritis with systemic onset, left shoulder 🦟

    M08.219 Juvenile rheumatoid arthritis with systemic onset, unspecified shoulder 🦟

● **M08.22** Juvenile rheumatoid arthritis with systemic onset, elbow

    M08.221 Juvenile rheumatoid arthritis with systemic onset, right elbow 🦟

    M08.222 Juvenile rheumatoid arthritis with systemic onset, left elbow 🦟

    M08.229 Juvenile rheumatoid arthritis with systemic onset, unspecified elbow 🦟

● **M08.23** Juvenile rheumatoid arthritis with systemic onset, wrist

    M08.231 Juvenile rheumatoid arthritis with systemic onset, right wrist 🦟

    M08.232 Juvenile rheumatoid arthritis with systemic onset, left wrist 🦟

    M08.239 Juvenile rheumatoid arthritis with systemic onset, unspecified wrist 🦟

● M08.24 Juvenile rheumatoid arthritis with systemic onset, hand

   M08.241 Juvenile rheumatoid arthritis with systemic onset, right hand 🐾

   M08.242 Juvenile rheumatoid arthritis with systemic onset, left hand 🐾

   M08.249 Juvenile rheumatoid arthritis with systemic onset, unspecified hand 🐾

● M08.25 Juvenile rheumatoid arthritis with systemic onset, hip

   M08.251 Juvenile rheumatoid arthritis with systemic onset, right hip 🐾

   M08.252 Juvenile rheumatoid arthritis with systemic onset, left hip 🐾

   M08.259 Juvenile rheumatoid arthritis with systemic onset, unspecified hip 🐾

● M08.26 Juvenile rheumatoid arthritis with systemic onset, knee

   M08.261 Juvenile rheumatoid arthritis with systemic onset, right knee 🐾

   M08.262 Juvenile rheumatoid arthritis with systemic onset, left knee 🐾

   M08.269 Juvenile rheumatoid arthritis with systemic onset, unspecified knee 🐾

● M08.27 Juvenile rheumatoid arthritis with systemic onset, ankle and foot

   M08.271 Juvenile rheumatoid arthritis with systemic onset, right ankle and foot 🐾

   M08.272 Juvenile rheumatoid arthritis with systemic onset, left ankle and foot 🐾

   M08.279 Juvenile rheumatoid arthritis with systemic onset, unspecified ankle and foot 🐾

  M08.28 Juvenile rheumatoid arthritis with systemic onset, vertebrae 🐾

  M08.29 Juvenile rheumatoid arthritis with systemic onset, multiple sites 🐾

▶ M08.2A Juvenile rheumatoid arthritis with systemic onset, other specified site

M08.3 Juvenile rheumatoid polyarthritis (seronegative)

● M08.4 Pauciarticular juvenile rheumatoid arthritis

  M08.40 Pauciarticular juvenile rheumatoid arthritis, unspecified site 🐾

● M08.41 Pauciarticular juvenile rheumatoid arthritis, shoulder

   M08.411 Pauciarticular juvenile rheumatoid arthritis, right shoulder 🐾

   M08.412 Pauciarticular juvenile rheumatoid arthritis, left shoulder 🐾

   M08.419 Pauciarticular juvenile rheumatoid arthritis, unspecified shoulder 🐾

● M08.42 Pauciarticular juvenile rheumatoid arthritis, elbow

   M08.421 Pauciarticular juvenile rheumatoid arthritis, right elbow 🐾

   M08.422 Pauciarticular juvenile rheumatoid arthritis, left elbow 🐾

   M08.429 Pauciarticular juvenile rheumatoid arthritis, unspecified elbow 🐾

● M08.43 Pauciarticular juvenile rheumatoid arthritis, wrist

   M08.431 Pauciarticular juvenile rheumatoid arthritis, right wrist 🐾

   M08.432 Pauciarticular juvenile rheumatoid arthritis, left wrist 🐾

   M08.439 Pauciarticular juvenile rheumatoid arthritis, unspecified wrist 🐾

● M08.44 Pauciarticular juvenile rheumatoid arthritis, hand

   M08.441 Pauciarticular juvenile rheumatoid arthritis, right hand 🐾

   M08.442 Pauciarticular juvenile rheumatoid arthritis, left hand 🐾

   M08.449 Pauciarticular juvenile rheumatoid arthritis, unspecified hand 🐾

● M08.45 Pauciarticular juvenile rheumatoid arthritis, hip

   M08.451 Pauciarticular juvenile rheumatoid arthritis, right hip 🐾

   M08.452 Pauciarticular juvenile rheumatoid arthritis, left hip 🐾

   M08.459 Pauciarticular juvenile rheumatoid arthritis, unspecified hip 🐾

● M08.46 Pauciarticular juvenile rheumatoid arthritis, knee

   M08.461 Pauciarticular juvenile rheumatoid arthritis, right knee 🐾

   M08.462 Pauciarticular juvenile rheumatoid arthritis, left knee 🐾

   M08.469 Pauciarticular juvenile rheumatoid arthritis, unspecified knee 🐾

● M08.47 Pauciarticular juvenile rheumatoid arthritis, ankle and foot

   M08.471 Pauciarticular juvenile rheumatoid arthritis, right ankle and foot 🐾

   M08.472 Pauciarticular juvenile rheumatoid arthritis, left ankle and foot 🐾

   M08.479 Pauciarticular juvenile rheumatoid arthritis, unspecified ankle and foot 🐾

  M08.48 Pauciarticular juvenile rheumatoid arthritis, vertebrae 🐾

▶ M08.4A Pauciarticular juvenile rheumatoid arthritis, other specified site

● M08.8 Other juvenile arthritis

  M08.80 Other juvenile arthritis, unspecified site 🐾

● M08.81 Other juvenile arthritis, shoulder

   M08.811 Other juvenile arthritis, right shoulder 🐾

   M08.812 Other juvenile arthritis, left shoulder 🐾

   M08.819 Other juvenile arthritis, unspecified shoulder 🐾

● M08.82 Other juvenile arthritis, elbow

   M08.821 Other juvenile arthritis, right elbow 🐾

   M08.822 Other juvenile arthritis, left elbow 🐾

   M08.829 Other juvenile arthritis, unspecified elbow 🐾

● M08.83 Other juvenile arthritis, wrist

   M08.831 Other juvenile arthritis, right wrist 🐾

   M08.832 Other juvenile arthritis, left wrist 🐾

   M08.839 Other juvenile arthritis, unspecified wrist 🐾

● M08.84 Other juvenile arthritis, hand

   M08.841 Other juvenile arthritis, right hand 🐾

   M08.842 Other juvenile arthritis, left hand 🐾

   M08.849 Other juvenile arthritis, unspecified hand 🐾

● M08.85 Other juvenile arthritis, hip

   M08.851 Other juvenile arthritis, right hip 🐾

   M08.852 Other juvenile arthritis, left hip 🐾

   M08.859 Other juvenile arthritis, unspecified hip 🐾

● **M08.86** Other juvenile arthritis, knee
　　M08.861 Other juvenile arthritis, right knee 🔧
　　M08.862 Other juvenile arthritis, left knee 🔧
　　M08.869 Other juvenile arthritis, unspecified knee 🔧
● **M08.87** Other juvenile arthritis, ankle and foot
　　M08.871 Other juvenile arthritis, right ankle and foot 🔧
　　M08.872 Other juvenile arthritis, left ankle and foot 🔧
　　M08.879 Other juvenile arthritis, unspecified ankle and foot 🔧
　M08.88 Other juvenile arthritis, other specified site 🔧
　　Other juvenile arthritis, vertebrae
　M08.89 Other juvenile arthritis, multiple sites 🔧
● **M08.9** Juvenile arthritis, unspecified

> **Excludes1**　juvenile rheumatoid arthritis, unspecified (M08.0-)

　M08.90 Juvenile arthritis, unspecified, unspecified site 🔧
● **M08.91** Juvenile arthritis, unspecified, shoulder
　　M08.911 Juvenile arthritis, unspecified, right shoulder 🔧
　　M08.912 Juvenile arthritis, unspecified, left shoulder 🔧
　　M08.919 Juvenile arthritis, unspecified, unspecified shoulder 🔧
● **M08.92** Juvenile arthritis, unspecified, elbow
　　M08.921 Juvenile arthritis, unspecified, right elbow 🔧
　　M08.922 Juvenile arthritis, unspecified, left elbow 🔧
　　M08.929 Juvenile arthritis, unspecified, unspecified elbow 🔧
● **M08.93** Juvenile arthritis, unspecified, wrist
　　M08.931 Juvenile arthritis, unspecified, right wrist 🔧
　　M08.932 Juvenile arthritis, unspecified, left wrist 🔧
　　M08.939 Juvenile arthritis, unspecified, unspecified wrist 🔧
● **M08.94** Juvenile arthritis, unspecified, hand
　　M08.941 Juvenile arthritis, unspecified, right hand 🔧
　　M08.942 Juvenile arthritis, unspecified, left hand 🔧
　　M08.949 Juvenile arthritis, unspecified, unspecified hand 🔧
● **M08.95** Juvenile arthritis, unspecified, hip
　　M08.951 Juvenile arthritis, unspecified, right hip 🔧
　　M08.952 Juvenile arthritis, unspecified, left hip 🔧
　　M08.959 Juvenile arthritis, unspecified, unspecified hip 🔧
● **M08.96** Juvenile arthritis, unspecified, knee
　　M08.961 Juvenile arthritis, unspecified, right knee 🔧
　　M08.962 Juvenile arthritis, unspecified, left knee 🔧
　　M08.969 Juvenile arthritis, unspecified, unspecified knee 🔧
● **M08.97** Juvenile arthritis, unspecified, ankle and foot
　　M08.971 Juvenile arthritis, unspecified, right ankle and foot 🔧
　　M08.972 Juvenile arthritis, unspecified, left ankle and foot 🔧
　　M08.979 Juvenile arthritis, unspecified, unspecified ankle and foot 🔧

　　M08.98 Juvenile arthritis, unspecified, vertebrae 🔧
　　M08.99 Juvenile arthritis, unspecified, multiple sites 🔧
　▶ **M08.9A** Juvenile arthritis, unspecified, other specified site

● **M1A** Chronic gout

Use additional code to identify:
Autonomic neuropathy in diseases classified elsewhere (G99.0)
Calculus of urinary tract in diseases classified elsewhere (N22)
Cardiomyopathy in diseases classified elsewhere (I43)
Disorders of external ear in diseases classified elsewhere (H61.1-, H62.8-)
Disorders of iris and ciliary body in diseases classified elsewhere (H22)
Glomerular disorders in diseases classified elsewhere (N08)

> **Excludes1**　gout NOS (M10.-)

> **Excludes2**　acute gout (M10.-)

The appropriate 7th character is to be added to each code from category M1A

0	without tophus (tophi)
1	with tophus (tophi)

● **M1A.0** Idiopathic chronic gout
　Chronic gouty bursitis
　Primary chronic gout
　X ● **M1A.00** Idiopathic chronic gout, unspecified site
　● **M1A.01** Idiopathic chronic gout, shoulder
　　　● **M1A.011** Idiopathic chronic gout, right shoulder
　　　● **M1A.012** Idiopathic chronic gout, left shoulder
　　　● **M1A.019** Idiopathic chronic gout, unspecified shoulder
　● **M1A.02** Idiopathic chronic gout, elbow
　　　● **M1A.021** Idiopathic chronic gout, right elbow
　　　● **M1A.022** Idiopathic chronic gout, left elbow
　　　● **M1A.029** Idiopathic chronic gout, unspecified elbow
　● **M1A.03** Idiopathic chronic gout, wrist
　　　● **M1A.031** Idiopathic chronic gout, right wrist
　　　● **M1A.032** Idiopathic chronic gout, left wrist
　　　● **M1A.039** Idiopathic chronic gout, unspecified wrist
　● **M1A.04** Idiopathic chronic gout, hand
　　　● **M1A.041** Idiopathic chronic gout, right hand
　　　● **M1A.042** Idiopathic chronic gout, left hand
　　　● **M1A.049** Idiopathic chronic gout, unspecified hand
　● **M1A.05** Idiopathic chronic gout, hip
　　　● **M1A.051** Idiopathic chronic gout, right hip
　　　● **M1A.052** Idiopathic chronic gout, left hip
　　　● **M1A.059** Idiopathic chronic gout, unspecified hip
　● **M1A.06** Idiopathic chronic gout, knee
　　　● **M1A.061** Idiopathic chronic gout, right knee
　　　● **M1A.062** Idiopathic chronic gout, left knee
　　　● **M1A.069** Idiopathic chronic gout, unspecified knee
　● **M1A.07** Idiopathic chronic gout, ankle and foot
　　　● **M1A.071** Idiopathic chronic gout, right ankle and foot
　　　● **M1A.072** Idiopathic chronic gout, left ankle and foot
　　　● **M1A.079** Idiopathic chronic gout, unspecified ankle and foot
　X ● **M1A.08** Idiopathic chronic gout, vertebrae
　X ● **M1A.09** Idiopathic chronic gout, multiple sites

● M1A.1 Lead-induced chronic gout
> *Code first toxic effects of lead and its compounds (T56.0-)*

X● M1A.10 Lead-induced chronic gout, unspecified site
● M1A.11 Lead-induced chronic gout, shoulder
   ● M1A.111 Lead-induced chronic gout, right shoulder
   ● M1A.112 Lead-induced chronic gout, left shoulder
   ● M1A.119 Lead-induced chronic gout, unspecified shoulder
● M1A.12 Lead-induced chronic gout, elbow
   ● M1A.121 Lead-induced chronic gout, right elbow
   ● M1A.122 Lead-induced chronic gout, left elbow
   ● M1A.129 Lead-induced chronic gout, unspecified elbow
● M1A.13 Lead-induced chronic gout, wrist
   ● M1A.131 Lead-induced chronic gout, right wrist
   ● M1A.132 Lead-induced chronic gout, left wrist
   ● M1A.139 Lead-induced chronic gout, unspecified wrist
● M1A.14 Lead-induced chronic gout, hand
   ● M1A.141 Lead-induced chronic gout, right hand
   ● M1A.142 Lead-induced chronic gout, left hand
   ● M1A.149 Lead-induced chronic gout, unspecified hand
● M1A.15 Lead-induced chronic gout, hip
   ● M1A.151 Lead-induced chronic gout, right hip
   ● M1A.152 Lead-induced chronic gout, left hip
   ● M1A.159 Lead-induced chronic gout, unspecified hip
● M1A.16 Lead-induced chronic gout, knee
   ● M1A.161 Lead-induced chronic gout, right knee
   ● M1A.162 Lead-induced chronic gout, left knee
   ● M1A.169 Lead-induced chronic gout, unspecified knee
● M1A.17 Lead-induced chronic gout, ankle and foot
   ● M1A.171 Lead-induced chronic gout, right ankle and foot
   ● M1A.172 Lead-induced chronic gout, left ankle and foot
   ● M1A.179 Lead-induced chronic gout, unspecified ankle and foot
X● M1A.18 Lead-induced chronic gout, vertebrae
X● M1A.19 Lead-induced chronic gout, multiple sites

● M1A.2 Drug-induced chronic gout
> Use additional code for adverse effect, if applicable, to identify drug (T36-T50 with fifth or sixth character 5)

X● M1A.20 Drug-induced chronic gout, unspecified site
● M1A.21 Drug-induced chronic gout, shoulder
   ● M1A.211 Drug-induced chronic gout, right shoulder
   ● M1A.212 Drug-induced chronic gout, left shoulder
   ● M1A.219 Drug-induced chronic gout, unspecified shoulder
● M1A.22 Drug-induced chronic gout, elbow
   ● M1A.221 Drug-induced chronic gout, right elbow
   ● M1A.222 Drug-induced chronic gout, left elbow
   ● M1A.229 Drug-induced chronic gout, unspecified elbow

● M1A.23 Drug-induced chronic gout, wrist
   ● M1A.231 Drug-induced chronic gout, right wrist
   ● M1A.232 Drug-induced chronic gout, left wrist
   ● M1A.239 Drug-induced chronic gout, unspecified wrist
● M1A.24 Drug-induced chronic gout, hand
   ● M1A.241 Drug-induced chronic gout, right hand
   ● M1A.242 Drug-induced chronic gout, left hand
   ● M1A.249 Drug-induced chronic gout, unspecified hand
● M1A.25 Drug-induced chronic gout, hip
   ● M1A.251 Drug-induced chronic gout, right hip
   ● M1A.252 Drug-induced chronic gout, left hip
   ● M1A.259 Drug-induced chronic gout, unspecified hip
● M1A.26 Drug-induced chronic gout, knee
   ● M1A.261 Drug-induced chronic gout, right knee
   ● M1A.262 Drug-induced chronic gout, left knee
   ● M1A.269 Drug-induced chronic gout, unspecified knee
● M1A.27 Drug-induced chronic gout, ankle and foot
   ● M1A.271 Drug-induced chronic gout, right ankle and foot
   ● M1A.272 Drug-induced chronic gout, left ankle and foot
   ● M1A.279 Drug-induced chronic gout, unspecified ankle and foot
X● M1A.28 Drug-induced chronic gout, vertebrae
X● M1A.29 Drug-induced chronic gout, multiple sites

● M1A.3 Chronic gout due to renal impairment
> *Code first associated renal disease*

X● M1A.30 Chronic gout due to renal impairment, unspecified site
● M1A.31 Chronic gout due to renal impairment, shoulder
   ● M1A.311 Chronic gout due to renal impairment, right shoulder
   ● M1A.312 Chronic gout due to renal impairment, left shoulder
   ● M1A.319 Chronic gout due to renal impairment, unspecified shoulder
● M1A.32 Chronic gout due to renal impairment, elbow
   ● M1A.321 Chronic gout due to renal impairment, right elbow
   ● M1A.322 Chronic gout due to renal impairment, left elbow
   ● M1A.329 Chronic gout due to renal impairment, unspecified elbow
● M1A.33 Chronic gout due to renal impairment, wrist
   ● M1A.331 Chronic gout due to renal impairment, right wrist
   ● M1A.332 Chronic gout due to renal impairment, left wrist
   ● M1A.339 Chronic gout due to renal impairment, unspecified wrist
● M1A.34 Chronic gout due to renal impairment, hand
   ● M1A.341 Chronic gout due to renal impairment, right hand
   ● M1A.342 Chronic gout due to renal impairment, left hand
   ● M1A.349 Chronic gout due to renal impairment, unspecified hand

▶ New   ⇒ Revised   ~~deleted~~ Deleted   Excludes 1   Excludes 2   Includes   Use additional   Code first   Code also   Key words
OGCR Official Guidelines   X Assign placeholder X   ● Use Additional Character(s)   ▶ Manifestation Code   🦠 Hierarchical Condition Category   **Coding Clinic**

● M1A.35 Chronic gout due to renal impairment, hip
  ● M1A.351 Chronic gout due to renal impairment, right hip
  ● M1A.352 Chronic gout due to renal impairment, left hip
  ● M1A.359 Chronic gout due to renal impairment, unspecified hip
● M1A.36 Chronic gout due to renal impairment, knee
  ● M1A.361 Chronic gout due to renal impairment, right knee
  ● M1A.362 Chronic gout due to renal impairment, left knee
  ● M1A.369 Chronic gout due to renal impairment, unspecified knee
● M1A.37 Chronic gout due to renal impairment, ankle and foot
  ● M1A.371 Chronic gout due to renal impairment, right ankle and foot
  ● M1A.372 Chronic gout due to renal impairment, left ankle and foot
  ● M1A.379 Chronic gout due to renal impairment, unspecified ankle and foot
X ● M1A.38 Chronic gout due to renal impairment, vertebrae
X ● M1A.39 Chronic gout due to renal impairment, multiple sites
● M1A.4 Other secondary chronic gout
  Code first associated condition
X ● M1A.40 Other secondary chronic gout, unspecified site
● M1A.41 Other secondary chronic gout, shoulder
  ● M1A.411 Other secondary chronic gout, right shoulder
  ● M1A.412 Other secondary chronic gout, left shoulder
  ● M1A.419 Other secondary chronic gout, unspecified shoulder
● M1A.42 Other secondary chronic gout, elbow
  ● M1A.421 Other secondary chronic gout, right elbow
  ● M1A.422 Other secondary chronic gout, left elbow
  ● M1A.429 Other secondary chronic gout, unspecified elbow
● M1A.43 Other secondary chronic gout, wrist
  ● M1A.431 Other secondary chronic gout, right wrist
  ● M1A.432 Other secondary chronic gout, left wrist
  ● M1A.439 Other secondary chronic gout, unspecified wrist
● M1A.44 Other secondary chronic gout, hand
  ● M1A.441 Other secondary chronic gout, right hand
  ● M1A.442 Other secondary chronic gout, left hand
  ● M1A.449 Other secondary chronic gout, unspecified hand
● M1A.45 Other secondary chronic gout, hip
  ● M1A.451 Other secondary chronic gout, right hip
  ● M1A.452 Other secondary chronic gout, left hip
  ● M1A.459 Other secondary chronic gout, unspecified hip

● M1A.46 Other secondary chronic gout, knee
  ● M1A.461 Other secondary chronic gout, right knee
  ● M1A.462 Other secondary chronic gout, left knee
  ● M1A.469 Other secondary chronic gout, unspecified knee
● M1A.47 Other secondary chronic gout, ankle and foot
  ● M1A.471 Other secondary chronic gout, right ankle and foot
  ● M1A.472 Other secondary chronic gout, left ankle and foot
  ● M1A.479 Other secondary chronic gout, unspecified ankle and foot
X ● M1A.48 Other secondary chronic gout, vertebrae
X ● M1A.49 Other secondary chronic gout, multiple sites
X ● M1A.9 Chronic gout, unspecified

● **M10**   **Gout**
  Accumulation of uric acid that results in swollen, red, hot, painful, stiff joints
  Acute gout
  Gout attack
  Gout flare
  Podagra
  Use additional code to identify:
    Autonomic neuropathy in diseases classified elsewhere (G99.0)
    Calculus of urinary tract in diseases classified elsewhere (N22)
    Cardiomyopathy in diseases classified elsewhere (I43)
    Disorders of external ear in diseases classified elsewhere (H61.1-, H62.8-)
    Disorders of iris and ciliary body in diseases classified elsewhere (H22)
    Glomerular disorders in diseases classified elsewhere (N08)
  Excludes2   chronic gout (M1A.-)
● **M10.0**   **Idiopathic gout**
  Gouty bursitis
  Primary gout
  M10.00 Idiopathic gout, unspecified site
  ● M10.01 Idiopathic gout, shoulder
    M10.011 Idiopathic gout, right shoulder
    M10.012 Idiopathic gout, left shoulder
    M10.019 Idiopathic gout, unspecified shoulder
  ● M10.02 Idiopathic gout, elbow
    M10.021 Idiopathic gout, right elbow
    M10.022 Idiopathic gout, left elbow
    M10.029 Idiopathic gout, unspecified elbow
  ● M10.03 Idiopathic gout, wrist
    M10.031 Idiopathic gout, right wrist
    M10.032 Idiopathic gout, left wrist
    M10.039 Idiopathic gout, unspecified wrist
  ● M10.04 Idiopathic gout, hand
    M10.041 Idiopathic gout, right hand
    M10.042 Idiopathic gout, left hand
    M10.049 Idiopathic gout, unspecified hand
  ● M10.05 Idiopathic gout, hip
    M10.051 Idiopathic gout, right hip
    M10.052 Idiopathic gout, left hip
    M10.059 Idiopathic gout, unspecified hip
  ● M10.06 Idiopathic gout, knee
    M10.061 Idiopathic gout, right knee
    M10.062 Idiopathic gout, left knee
    M10.069 Idiopathic gout, unspecified knee

● **M10.07** Idiopathic gout, ankle and foot
    M10.071 Idiopathic gout, right ankle and foot
    M10.072 Idiopathic gout, left ankle and foot
    M10.079 Idiopathic gout, unspecified ankle and foot
  M10.08 Idiopathic gout, vertebrae
  M10.09 Idiopathic gout, multiple sites
● **M10.1** Lead-induced gout
    Code first toxic effects of lead and its compounds (T56.0-)
  M10.10 Lead-induced gout, unspecified site
● **M10.11** Lead-induced gout, shoulder
    M10.111 Lead-induced gout, right shoulder
    M10.112 Lead-induced gout, left shoulder
    M10.119 Lead-induced gout, unspecified shoulder
● **M10.12** Lead-induced gout, elbow
    M10.121 Lead-induced gout, right elbow
    M10.122 Lead-induced gout, left elbow
    M10.129 Lead-induced gout, unspecified elbow
● **M10.13** Lead-induced gout, wrist
    M10.131 Lead-induced gout, right wrist
    M10.132 Lead-induced gout, left wrist
    M10.139 Lead-induced gout, unspecified wrist
● **M10.14** Lead-induced gout, hand
    M10.141 Lead-induced gout, right hand
    M10.142 Lead-induced gout, left hand
    M10.149 Lead-induced gout, unspecified hand
● **M10.15** Lead-induced gout, hip
    M10.151 Lead-induced gout, right hip
    M10.152 Lead-induced gout, left hip
    M10.159 Lead-induced gout, unspecified hip
● **M10.16** Lead-induced gout, knee
    M10.161 Lead-induced gout, right knee
    M10.162 Lead-induced gout, left knee
    M10.169 Lead-induced gout, unspecified knee
● **M10.17** Lead-induced gout, ankle and foot
    M10.171 Lead-induced gout, right ankle and foot
    M10.172 Lead-induced gout, left ankle and foot
    M10.179 Lead-induced gout, unspecified ankle and foot
  M10.18 Lead-induced gout, vertebrae
  M10.19 Lead-induced gout, multiple sites
● **M10.2** Drug-induced gout
    Use additional code for adverse effect, if applicable, to identify drug (T36-T50 with fifth or sixth character 5)
  M10.20 Drug-induced gout, unspecified site
● **M10.21** Drug-induced gout, shoulder
    M10.211 Drug-induced gout, right shoulder
    M10.212 Drug-induced gout, left shoulder
    M10.219 Drug-induced gout, unspecified shoulder
● **M10.22** Drug-induced gout, elbow
    M10.221 Drug-induced gout, right elbow
    M10.222 Drug-induced gout, left elbow
    M10.229 Drug-induced gout, unspecified elbow
● **M10.23** Drug-induced gout, wrist
    M10.231 Drug-induced gout, right wrist
    M10.232 Drug-induced gout, left wrist
    M10.239 Drug-induced gout, unspecified wrist

● **M10.24** Drug-induced gout, hand
    M10.241 Drug-induced gout, right hand
    M10.242 Drug-induced gout, left hand
    M10.249 Drug-induced gout, unspecified hand
● **M10.25** Drug-induced gout, hip
    M10.251 Drug-induced gout, right hip
    M10.252 Drug-induced gout, left hip
    M10.259 Drug-induced gout, unspecified hip
● **M10.26** Drug-induced gout, knee
    M10.261 Drug-induced gout, right knee
    M10.262 Drug-induced gout, left knee
    M10.269 Drug-induced gout, unspecified knee
● **M10.27** Drug-induced gout, ankle and foot
    M10.271 Drug-induced gout, right ankle and foot
    M10.272 Drug-induced gout, left ankle and foot
    M10.279 Drug-induced gout, unspecified ankle and foot
  M10.28 Drug-induced gout, vertebrae
  M10.29 Drug-induced gout, multiple sites
● **M10.3** Gout due to renal impairment
    Code also associated renal disease
  M10.30 Gout due to renal impairment, unspecified site
● **M10.31** Gout due to renal impairment, shoulder
    M10.311 Gout due to renal impairment, right shoulder
    M10.312 Gout due to renal impairment, left shoulder
    M10.319 Gout due to renal impairment, unspecified shoulder
● **M10.32** Gout due to renal impairment, elbow
    M10.321 Gout due to renal impairment, right elbow
    M10.322 Gout due to renal impairment, left elbow
    M10.329 Gout due to renal impairment, unspecified elbow
● **M10.33** Gout due to renal impairment, wrist
    M10.331 Gout due to renal impairment, right wrist
    M10.332 Gout due to renal impairment, left wrist
    M10.339 Gout due to renal impairment, unspecified wrist
● **M10.34** Gout due to renal impairment, hand
    M10.341 Gout due to renal impairment, right hand
    M10.342 Gout due to renal impairment, left hand
    M10.349 Gout due to renal impairment, unspecified hand
● **M10.35** Gout due to renal impairment, hip
    M10.351 Gout due to renal impairment, right hip
    M10.352 Gout due to renal impairment, left hip
    M10.359 Gout due to renal impairment, unspecified hip
● **M10.36** Gout due to renal impairment, knee
    M10.361 Gout due to renal impairment, right knee
    M10.362 Gout due to renal impairment, left knee
    M10.369 Gout due to renal impairment, unspecified knee

▶ New   ⇒ Revised   ~~deleted~~ Deleted   Excludes 1   Excludes 2   Includes   Use additional   Code first   Code also   Key words
OGCR Official Guidelines   X Assign placeholder X   ● Use Additional Character(s)   ▷ Manifestation Code   🏷 Hierarchical Condition Category   **Coding Clinic**

● M10.37 Gout due to renal impairment, ankle and foot
     M10.371 Gout due to renal impairment, right ankle and foot
     M10.372 Gout due to renal impairment, left ankle and foot
     M10.379 Gout due to renal impairment, unspecified ankle and foot
   M10.38 Gout due to renal impairment, vertebrae
   M10.39 Gout due to renal impairment, multiple sites
● M10.4 Other secondary gout
     Code first associated condition
   M10.40 Other secondary gout, unspecified site
● M10.41 Other secondary gout, shoulder
     M10.411 Other secondary gout, right shoulder
     M10.412 Other secondary gout, left shoulder
     M10.419 Other secondary gout, unspecified shoulder
● M10.42 Other secondary gout, elbow
     M10.421 Other secondary gout, right elbow
     M10.422 Other secondary gout, left elbow
     M10.429 Other secondary gout, unspecified elbow
● M10.43 Other secondary gout, wrist
     M10.431 Other secondary gout, right wrist
     M10.432 Other secondary gout, left wrist
     M10.439 Other secondary gout, unspecified wrist
● M10.44 Other secondary gout, hand
     M10.441 Other secondary gout, right hand
     M10.442 Other secondary gout, left hand
     M10.449 Other secondary gout, unspecified hand
● M10.45 Other secondary gout, hip
     M10.451 Other secondary gout, right hip
     M10.452 Other secondary gout, left hip
     M10.459 Other secondary gout, unspecified hip
● M10.46 Other secondary gout, knee
     M10.461 Other secondary gout, right knee
     M10.462 Other secondary gout, left knee
     M10.469 Other secondary gout, unspecified knee
● M10.47 Other secondary gout, ankle and foot
     M10.471 Other secondary gout, right ankle and foot
     M10.472 Other secondary gout, left ankle and foot
     M10.479 Other secondary gout, unspecified ankle and foot
   M10.48 Other secondary gout, vertebrae
   M10.49 Other secondary gout, multiple sites
M10.9 Gout, unspecified
     Gout NOS

● M11 Other crystal arthropathies
● M11.0 Hydroxyapatite deposition disease
   M11.00 Hydroxyapatite deposition disease, unspecified site
● M11.01 Hydroxyapatite deposition disease, shoulder
     M11.011 Hydroxyapatite deposition disease, right shoulder
     M11.012 Hydroxyapatite deposition disease, left shoulder
     M11.019 Hydroxyapatite deposition disease, unspecified shoulder

● M11.02 Hydroxyapatite deposition disease, elbow
     M11.021 Hydroxyapatite deposition disease, right elbow
     M11.022 Hydroxyapatite deposition disease, left elbow
     M11.029 Hydroxyapatite deposition disease, unspecified elbow
● M11.03 Hydroxyapatite deposition disease, wrist
     M11.031 Hydroxyapatite deposition disease, right wrist
     M11.032 Hydroxyapatite deposition disease, left wrist
     M11.039 Hydroxyapatite deposition disease, unspecified wrist
● M11.04 Hydroxyapatite deposition disease, hand
     M11.041 Hydroxyapatite deposition disease, right hand
     M11.042 Hydroxyapatite deposition disease, left hand
     M11.049 Hydroxyapatite deposition disease, unspecified hand
● M11.05 Hydroxyapatite deposition disease, hip
     M11.051 Hydroxyapatite deposition disease, right hip
     M11.052 Hydroxyapatite deposition disease, left hip
     M11.059 Hydroxyapatite deposition disease, unspecified hip
● M11.06 Hydroxyapatite deposition disease, knee
     M11.061 Hydroxyapatite deposition disease, right knee
     M11.062 Hydroxyapatite deposition disease, left knee
     M11.069 Hydroxyapatite deposition disease, unspecified knee
● M11.07 Hydroxyapatite deposition disease, ankle and foot
     M11.071 Hydroxyapatite deposition disease, right ankle and foot
     M11.072 Hydroxyapatite deposition disease, left ankle and foot
     M11.079 Hydroxyapatite deposition disease, unspecified ankle and foot
   M11.08 Hydroxyapatite deposition disease, vertebrae
   M11.09 Hydroxyapatite deposition disease, multiple sites
● M11.1 Familial chondrocalcinosis
   M11.10 Familial chondrocalcinosis, unspecified site
● M11.11 Familial chondrocalcinosis, shoulder
     M11.111 Familial chondrocalcinosis, right shoulder
     M11.112 Familial chondrocalcinosis, left shoulder
     M11.119 Familial chondrocalcinosis, unspecified shoulder
● M11.12 Familial chondrocalcinosis, elbow
     M11.121 Familial chondrocalcinosis, right elbow
     M11.122 Familial chondrocalcinosis, left elbow
     M11.129 Familial chondrocalcinosis, unspecified elbow
● M11.13 Familial chondrocalcinosis, wrist
     M11.131 Familial chondrocalcinosis, right wrist
     M11.132 Familial chondrocalcinosis, left wrist
     M11.139 Familial chondrocalcinosis, unspecified wrist

● M11.14   Familial chondrocalcinosis, hand
      M11.141   Familial chondrocalcinosis, right hand
      M11.142   Familial chondrocalcinosis, left hand
      M11.149   Familial chondrocalcinosis, unspecified hand
● M11.15   Familial chondrocalcinosis, hip
      M11.151   Familial chondrocalcinosis, right hip
      M11.152   Familial chondrocalcinosis, left hip
      M11.159   Familial chondrocalcinosis, unspecified hip
● M11.16   Familial chondrocalcinosis, knee
      M11.161   Familial chondrocalcinosis, right knee
      M11.162   Familial chondrocalcinosis, left knee
      M11.169   Familial chondrocalcinosis, unspecified knee
● M11.17   Familial chondrocalcinosis, ankle and foot
      M11.171   Familial chondrocalcinosis, right ankle and foot
      M11.172   Familial chondrocalcinosis, left ankle and foot
      M11.179   Familial chondrocalcinosis, unspecified ankle and foot
   M11.18   Familial chondrocalcinosis, vertebrae
   M11.19   Familial chondrocalcinosis, multiple sites
● M11.2   Other chondrocalcinosis
      Chondrocalcinosis NOS
   M11.20   Other chondrocalcinosis, unspecified site
● M11.21   Other chondrocalcinosis, shoulder
      M11.211   Other chondrocalcinosis, right shoulder
      M11.212   Other chondrocalcinosis, left shoulder
      M11.219   Other chondrocalcinosis, unspecified shoulder
● M11.22   Other chondrocalcinosis, elbow
      M11.221   Other chondrocalcinosis, right elbow
      M11.222   Other chondrocalcinosis, left elbow
      M11.229   Other chondrocalcinosis, unspecified elbow
● M11.23   Other chondrocalcinosis, wrist
      M11.231   Other chondrocalcinosis, right wrist
      M11.232   Other chondrocalcinosis, left wrist
      M11.239   Other chondrocalcinosis, unspecified wrist
● M11.24   Other chondrocalcinosis, hand
      M11.241   Other chondrocalcinosis, right hand
      M11.242   Other chondrocalcinosis, left hand
      M11.249   Other chondrocalcinosis, unspecified hand
● M11.25   Other chondrocalcinosis, hip
      M11.251   Other chondrocalcinosis, right hip
      M11.252   Other chondrocalcinosis, left hip
      M11.259   Other chondrocalcinosis, unspecified hip
● M11.26   Other chondrocalcinosis, knee
      M11.261   Other chondrocalcinosis, right knee
      M11.262   Other chondrocalcinosis, left knee
      M11.269   Other chondrocalcinosis, unspecified knee

● M11.27   Other chondrocalcinosis, ankle and foot
      M11.271   Other chondrocalcinosis, right ankle and foot
      M11.272   Other chondrocalcinosis, left ankle and foot
      M11.279   Other chondrocalcinosis, unspecified ankle and foot
   M11.28   Other chondrocalcinosis, vertebrae
   M11.29   Other chondrocalcinosis, multiple sites
● M11.8   Other specified crystal arthropathies
   M11.80   Other specified crystal arthropathies, unspecified site
● M11.81   Other specified crystal arthropathies, shoulder
      M11.811   Other specified crystal arthropathies, right shoulder
      M11.812   Other specified crystal arthropathies, left shoulder
      M11.819   Other specified crystal arthropathies, unspecified shoulder
● M11.82   Other specified crystal arthropathies, elbow
      M11.821   Other specified crystal arthropathies, right elbow
      M11.822   Other specified crystal arthropathies, left elbow
      M11.829   Other specified crystal arthropathies, unspecified elbow
● M11.83   Other specified crystal arthropathies, wrist
      M11.831   Other specified crystal arthropathies, right wrist
      M11.832   Other specified crystal arthropathies, left wrist
      M11.839   Other specified crystal arthropathies, unspecified wrist
● M11.84   Other specified crystal arthropathies, hand
      M11.841   Other specified crystal arthropathies, right hand
      M11.842   Other specified crystal arthropathies, left hand
      M11.849   Other specified crystal arthropathies, unspecified hand
● M11.85   Other specified crystal arthropathies, hip
      M11.851   Other specified crystal arthropathies, right hip
      M11.852   Other specified crystal arthropathies, left hip
      M11.859   Other specified crystal arthropathies, unspecified hip
● M11.86   Other specified crystal arthropathies, knee
      M11.861   Other specified crystal arthropathies, right knee
      M11.862   Other specified crystal arthropathies, left knee
      M11.869   Other specified crystal arthropathies, unspecified knee
● M11.87   Other specified crystal arthropathies, ankle and foot
      M11.871   Other specified crystal arthropathies, right ankle and foot
      M11.872   Other specified crystal arthropathies, left ankle and foot
      M11.879   Other specified crystal arthropathies, unspecified ankle and foot
   M11.88   Other specified crystal arthropathies, vertebrae
   M11.89   Other specified crystal arthropathies, multiple sites
   M11.9   Crystal arthropathy, unspecified

▶ New   ⇒ Revised   ~~deleted~~ Deleted   Excludes 1   Excludes 2   Includes   Use additional   Code first   Code also   Key words
OGCR Official Guidelines   X Assign placeholder X   ● Use Additional Character(s)   ▶ Manifestation Code   🏷 Hierarchical Condition Category   **Coding Clinic**

● M12 Other and unspecified arthropathy
  Excludes1 arthrosis (M15-M19)
           cricoarytenoid arthropathy (J38.7)
  ● M12.0 Chronic postrheumatic arthropathy [Jaccoud]
    M12.00 Chronic postrheumatic arthropathy [Jaccoud], unspecified site %
    ● M12.01 Chronic postrheumatic arthropathy [Jaccoud], shoulder
      M12.011 Chronic postrheumatic arthropathy [Jaccoud], right shoulder %
      M12.012 Chronic postrheumatic arthropathy [Jaccoud], left shoulder %
      M12.019 Chronic postrheumatic arthropathy [Jaccoud], unspecified shoulder %
    ● M12.02 Chronic postrheumatic arthropathy [Jaccoud], elbow
      M12.021 Chronic postrheumatic arthropathy [Jaccoud], right elbow %
      M12.022 Chronic postrheumatic arthropathy [Jaccoud], left elbow %
      M12.029 Chronic postrheumatic arthropathy [Jaccoud], unspecified elbow %
    ● M12.03 Chronic postrheumatic arthropathy [Jaccoud], wrist
      M12.031 Chronic postrheumatic arthropathy [Jaccoud], right wrist %
      M12.032 Chronic postrheumatic arthropathy [Jaccoud], left wrist %
      M12.039 Chronic postrheumatic arthropathy [Jaccoud], unspecified wrist %
    ● M12.04 Chronic postrheumatic arthropathy [Jaccoud], hand
      M12.041 Chronic postrheumatic arthropathy [Jaccoud], right hand %
      M12.042 Chronic postrheumatic arthropathy [Jaccoud], left hand %
      M12.049 Chronic postrheumatic arthropathy [Jaccoud], unspecified hand %
    ● M12.05 Chronic postrheumatic arthropathy [Jaccoud], hip
      M12.051 Chronic postrheumatic arthropathy [Jaccoud], right hip %
      M12.052 Chronic postrheumatic arthropathy [Jaccoud], left hip %
      M12.059 Chronic postrheumatic arthropathy [Jaccoud], unspecified hip %
    ● M12.06 Chronic postrheumatic arthropathy [Jaccoud], knee
      M12.061 Chronic postrheumatic arthropathy [Jaccoud], right knee %
      M12.062 Chronic postrheumatic arthropathy [Jaccoud], left knee %
      M12.069 Chronic postrheumatic arthropathy [Jaccoud], unspecified knee %
    ● M12.07 Chronic postrheumatic arthropathy [Jaccoud], ankle and foot
      M12.071 Chronic postrheumatic arthropathy [Jaccoud], right ankle and foot %
      M12.072 Chronic postrheumatic arthropathy [Jaccoud], left ankle and foot %
      M12.079 Chronic postrheumatic arthropathy [Jaccoud], unspecified ankle and foot %
    M12.08 Chronic postrheumatic arthropathy [Jaccoud], other specified site %
           Chronic postrheumatic arthropathy [Jaccoud], vertebrae
    M12.09 Chronic postrheumatic arthropathy [Jaccoud], multiple sites %

● M12.1 Kaschin-Beck disease
       Osteochondroarthrosis deformans endemica
  M12.10 Kaschin-Beck disease, unspecified site
  ● M12.11 Kaschin-Beck disease, shoulder
    M12.111 Kaschin-Beck disease, right shoulder
    M12.112 Kaschin-Beck disease, left shoulder
    M12.119 Kaschin-Beck disease, unspecified shoulder
  ● M12.12 Kaschin-Beck disease, elbow
    M12.121 Kaschin-Beck disease, right elbow
    M12.122 Kaschin-Beck disease, left elbow
    M12.129 Kaschin-Beck disease, unspecified elbow
  ● M12.13 Kaschin-Beck disease, wrist
    M12.131 Kaschin-Beck disease, right wrist
    M12.132 Kaschin-Beck disease, left wrist
    M12.139 Kaschin-Beck disease, unspecified wrist
  ● M12.14 Kaschin-Beck disease, hand
    M12.141 Kaschin-Beck disease, right hand
    M12.142 Kaschin-Beck disease, left hand
    M12.149 Kaschin-Beck disease, unspecified hand
  ● M12.15 Kaschin-Beck disease, hip
    M12.151 Kaschin-Beck disease, right hip
    M12.152 Kaschin-Beck disease, left hip
    M12.159 Kaschin-Beck disease, unspecified hip
  ● M12.16 Kaschin-Beck disease, knee
    M12.161 Kaschin-Beck disease, right knee
    M12.162 Kaschin-Beck disease, left knee
    M12.169 Kaschin-Beck disease, unspecified knee
  ● M12.17 Kaschin-Beck disease, ankle and foot
    M12.171 Kaschin-Beck disease, right ankle and foot
    M12.172 Kaschin-Beck disease, left ankle and foot
    M12.179 Kaschin-Beck disease, unspecified ankle and foot
  M12.18 Kaschin-Beck disease, vertebrae
  M12.19 Kaschin-Beck disease, multiple sites
● M12.2 Villonodular synovitis (pigmented)
  M12.20 Villonodular synovitis (pigmented), unspecified site
  ● M12.21 Villonodular synovitis (pigmented), shoulder
    M12.211 Villonodular synovitis (pigmented), right shoulder
    M12.212 Villonodular synovitis (pigmented), left shoulder
    M12.219 Villonodular synovitis (pigmented), unspecified shoulder
  ● M12.22 Villonodular synovitis (pigmented), elbow
    M12.221 Villonodular synovitis (pigmented), right elbow
    M12.222 Villonodular synovitis (pigmented), left elbow
    M12.229 Villonodular synovitis (pigmented), unspecified elbow
  ● M12.23 Villonodular synovitis (pigmented), wrist
    M12.231 Villonodular synovitis (pigmented), right wrist
    M12.232 Villonodular synovitis (pigmented), left wrist
    M12.239 Villonodular synovitis (pigmented), unspecified wrist

● M12.24   Villonodular synovitis (pigmented), hand
     M12.241   Villonodular synovitis (pigmented), right hand
     M12.242   Villonodular synovitis (pigmented), left hand
     M12.249   Villonodular synovitis (pigmented), unspecified hand

● M12.25   Villonodular synovitis (pigmented), hip
     M12.251   Villonodular synovitis (pigmented), right hip
     M12.252   Villonodular synovitis (pigmented), left hip
     M12.259   Villonodular synovitis (pigmented), unspecified hip

● M12.26   Villonodular synovitis (pigmented), knee
     M12.261   Villonodular synovitis (pigmented), right knee
     M12.262   Villonodular synovitis (pigmented), left knee
     M12.269   Villonodular synovitis (pigmented), unspecified knee

● M12.27   Villonodular synovitis (pigmented), ankle and foot
     M12.271   Villonodular synovitis (pigmented), right ankle and foot
     M12.272   Villonodular synovitis (pigmented), left ankle and foot
     M12.279   Villonodular synovitis (pigmented), unspecified ankle and foot

     M12.28   Villonodular synovitis (pigmented), other specified site
        Villonodular synovitis (pigmented), vertebrae

     M12.29   Villonodular synovitis (pigmented), multiple sites

● M12.3   Palindromic rheumatism
     M12.30   Palindromic rheumatism, unspecified site

● M12.31   Palindromic rheumatism, shoulder
     M12.311   Palindromic rheumatism, right shoulder
     M12.312   Palindromic rheumatism, left shoulder
     M12.319   Palindromic rheumatism, unspecified shoulder

● M12.32   Palindromic rheumatism, elbow
     M12.321   Palindromic rheumatism, right elbow
     M12.322   Palindromic rheumatism, left elbow
     M12.329   Palindromic rheumatism, unspecified elbow

● M12.33   Palindromic rheumatism, wrist
     M12.331   Palindromic rheumatism, right wrist
     M12.332   Palindromic rheumatism, left wrist
     M12.339   Palindromic rheumatism, unspecified wrist

● M12.34   Palindromic rheumatism, hand
     M12.341   Palindromic rheumatism, right hand
     M12.342   Palindromic rheumatism, left hand
     M12.349   Palindromic rheumatism, unspecified hand

● M12.35   Palindromic rheumatism, hip
     M12.351   Palindromic rheumatism, right hip
     M12.352   Palindromic rheumatism, left hip
     M12.359   Palindromic rheumatism, unspecified hip

● M12.36   Palindromic rheumatism, knee
     M12.361   Palindromic rheumatism, right knee
     M12.362   Palindromic rheumatism, left knee
     M12.369   Palindromic rheumatism, unspecified knee

● M12.37   Palindromic rheumatism, ankle and foot
     M12.371   Palindromic rheumatism, right ankle and foot
     M12.372   Palindromic rheumatism, left ankle and foot
     M12.379   Palindromic rheumatism, unspecified ankle and foot

     M12.38   Palindromic rheumatism, other specified site
        Palindromic rheumatism, vertebrae

     M12.39   Palindromic rheumatism, multiple sites

● M12.4   Intermittent hydrarthrosis
     M12.40   Intermittent hydrarthrosis, unspecified site

● M12.41   Intermittent hydrarthrosis, shoulder
     M12.411   Intermittent hydrarthrosis, right shoulder
     M12.412   Intermittent hydrarthrosis, left shoulder
     M12.419   Intermittent hydrarthrosis, unspecified shoulder

● M12.42   Intermittent hydrarthrosis, elbow
     M12.421   Intermittent hydrarthrosis, right elbow
     M12.422   Intermittent hydrarthrosis, left elbow
     M12.429   Intermittent hydrarthrosis, unspecified elbow

● M12.43   Intermittent hydrarthrosis, wrist
     M12.431   Intermittent hydrarthrosis, right wrist
     M12.432   Intermittent hydrarthrosis, left wrist
     M12.439   Intermittent hydrarthrosis, unspecified wrist

● M12.44   Intermittent hydrarthrosis, hand
     M12.441   Intermittent hydrarthrosis, right hand
     M12.442   Intermittent hydrarthrosis, left hand
     M12.449   Intermittent hydrarthrosis, unspecified hand

● M12.45   Intermittent hydrarthrosis, hip
     M12.451   Intermittent hydrarthrosis, right hip
     M12.452   Intermittent hydrarthrosis, left hip
     M12.459   Intermittent hydrarthrosis, unspecified hip

● M12.46   Intermittent hydrarthrosis, knee
     M12.461   Intermittent hydrarthrosis, right knee
     M12.462   Intermittent hydrarthrosis, left knee
     M12.469   Intermittent hydrarthrosis, unspecified knee

● M12.47   Intermittent hydrarthrosis, ankle and foot
     M12.471   Intermittent hydrarthrosis, right ankle and foot
     M12.472   Intermittent hydrarthrosis, left ankle and foot
     M12.479   Intermittent hydrarthrosis, unspecified ankle and foot

     M12.48   Intermittent hydrarthrosis, other site
     M12.49   Intermittent hydrarthrosis, multiple sites

▶ New   ⇒ Revised   deleted Deleted   Excludes 1   Excludes 2   Includes   Use additional   Code first   Code also   Key words
OGCR Official Guidelines   X Assign placeholder X   ● Use Additional Character(s)   ▷ Manifestation Code   🦜 Hierarchical Condition Category   Coding Clinic

● M12.5   Traumatic arthropathy
    Excludes1   current injury-see Alphabetic Index
                post-traumatic osteoarthritis of first
                    carpometacarpal joint (M18.2-M18.3)
                post-traumatic osteoarthritis of hip
                    (M16.4-M16.5)
                post-traumatic osteoarthritis of knee
                    (M17.2-M17.3)
                post-traumatic osteoarthritis NOS
                    (M19.1-)
                post-traumatic osteoarthritis of other
                    single joints (M19.1-)
    M12.50   Traumatic arthropathy, unspecified site
● M12.51   Traumatic arthropathy, shoulder
        M12.511   Traumatic arthropathy, right shoulder
        M12.512   Traumatic arthropathy, left shoulder
        M12.519   Traumatic arthropathy, unspecified
                    shoulder
● M12.52   Traumatic arthropathy, elbow
        M12.521   Traumatic arthropathy, right elbow
        M12.522   Traumatic arthropathy, left elbow
        M12.529   Traumatic arthropathy, unspecified
                    elbow
● M12.53   Traumatic arthropathy, wrist
        M12.531   Traumatic arthropathy, right wrist
        M12.532   Traumatic arthropathy, left wrist
        M12.539   Traumatic arthropathy, unspecified
                    wrist
● M12.54   Traumatic arthropathy, hand
        M12.541   Traumatic arthropathy, right hand
        M12.542   Traumatic arthropathy, left hand
        M12.549   Traumatic arthropathy, unspecified
                    hand
● M12.55   Traumatic arthropathy, hip
        M12.551   Traumatic arthropathy, right hip
        M12.552   Traumatic arthropathy, left hip
                    Coding Clinic: 2015, Q1, P17
        M12.559   Traumatic arthropathy, unspecified
                    hip
● M12.56   Traumatic arthropathy, knee
        M12.561   Traumatic arthropathy, right knee
        M12.562   Traumatic arthropathy, left knee
        M12.569   Traumatic arthropathy, unspecified
                    knee
● M12.57   Traumatic arthropathy, ankle and foot
        M12.571   Traumatic arthropathy, right ankle
                    and foot
        M12.572   Traumatic arthropathy, left ankle and
                    foot
        M12.579   Traumatic arthropathy, unspecified
                    ankle and foot
    M12.58   Traumatic arthropathy, other specified site
                Traumatic arthropathy, vertebrae
    M12.59   Traumatic arthropathy, multiple sites
● M12.8   Other specific arthropathies, not elsewhere classified
            Transient arthropathy
    M12.80   Other specific arthropathies, not elsewhere
                classified, unspecified site
● M12.81   Other specific arthropathies, not elsewhere
                classified, shoulder
        M12.811   Other specific arthropathies, not
                    elsewhere classified, right shoulder
        M12.812   Other specific arthropathies, not
                    elsewhere classified, left shoulder
        M12.819   Other specific arthropathies, not
                    elsewhere classified, unspecified
                    shoulder

● M12.82   Other specific arthropathies, not elsewhere
                classified, elbow
        M12.821   Other specific arthropathies, not
                    elsewhere classified, right elbow
        M12.822   Other specific arthropathies, not
                    elsewhere classified, left elbow
        M12.829   Other specific arthropathies, not
                    elsewhere classified, unspecified
                    elbow
● M12.83   Other specific arthropathies, not elsewhere
                classified, wrist
        M12.831   Other specific arthropathies, not
                    elsewhere classified, right wrist
        M12.832   Other specific arthropathies, not
                    elsewhere classified, left wrist
        M12.839   Other specific arthropathies, not
                    elsewhere classified, unspecified wrist
● M12.84   Other specific arthropathies, not elsewhere
                classified, hand
        M12.841   Other specific arthropathies, not
                    elsewhere classified, right hand
        M12.842   Other specific arthropathies, not
                    elsewhere classified, left hand
        M12.849   Other specific arthropathies, not
                    elsewhere classified, unspecified hand
● M12.85   Other specific arthropathies, not elsewhere
                classified, hip
        M12.851   Other specific arthropathies, not
                    elsewhere classified, right hip
        M12.852   Other specific arthropathies, not
                    elsewhere classified, left hip
        M12.859   Other specific arthropathies, not
                    elsewhere classified, unspecified hip
● M12.86   Other specific arthropathies, not elsewhere
                classified, knee
        M12.861   Other specific arthropathies, not
                    elsewhere classified, right knee
        M12.862   Other specific arthropathies, not
                    elsewhere classified, left knee
        M12.869   Other specific arthropathies, not
                    elsewhere classified, unspecified knee
● M12.87   Other specific arthropathies, not elsewhere
                classified, ankle and foot
        M12.871   Other specific arthropathies, not
                    elsewhere classified, right ankle and
                    foot
        M12.872   Other specific arthropathies, not
                    elsewhere classified, left ankle and
                    foot
        M12.879   Other specific arthropathies, not
                    elsewhere classified, unspecified
                    ankle and foot
    M12.88   Other specific arthropathies, not elsewhere
                classified, other specified site
                    Other specific arthropathies, not elsewhere
                    classified, vertebrae
    M12.89   Other specific arthropathies, not elsewhere
                classified, multiple sites
    M12.9   Arthropathy, unspecified

M13   Other arthritis

> **Excludes1**   arthrosis (M15-M19)
> osteoarthritis (M15-M19)

M13.0   Polyarthritis, unspecified

M13.1   Monoarthritis, not elsewhere classified

    M13.10   Monoarthritis, not elsewhere classified, unspecified site

    M13.11   Monoarthritis, not elsewhere classified, shoulder

       M13.111   Monoarthritis, not elsewhere classified, right shoulder

       M13.112   Monoarthritis, not elsewhere classified, left shoulder

       M13.119   Monoarthritis, not elsewhere classified, unspecified shoulder

    M13.12   Monoarthritis, not elsewhere classified, elbow

       M13.121   Monoarthritis, not elsewhere classified, right elbow

       M13.122   Monoarthritis, not elsewhere classified, left elbow

       M13.129   Monoarthritis, not elsewhere classified, unspecified elbow

    M13.13   Monoarthritis, not elsewhere classified, wrist

       M13.131   Monoarthritis, not elsewhere classified, right wrist

       M13.132   Monoarthritis, not elsewhere classified, left wrist

       M13.139   Monoarthritis, not elsewhere classified, unspecified wrist

    M13.14   Monoarthritis, not elsewhere classified, hand

       M13.141   Monoarthritis, not elsewhere classified, right hand

       M13.142   Monoarthritis, not elsewhere classified, left hand

       M13.149   Monoarthritis, not elsewhere classified, unspecified hand

    M13.15   Monoarthritis, not elsewhere classified, hip

       M13.151   Monoarthritis, not elsewhere classified, right hip

       M13.152   Monoarthritis, not elsewhere classified, left hip

       M13.159   Monoarthritis, not elsewhere classified, unspecified hip

    M13.16   Monoarthritis, not elsewhere classified, knee

       M13.161   Monoarthritis, not elsewhere classified, right knee

       M13.162   Monoarthritis, not elsewhere classified, left knee

       M13.169   Monoarthritis, not elsewhere classified, unspecified knee

    M13.17   Monoarthritis, not elsewhere classified, ankle and foot

       M13.171   Monoarthritis, not elsewhere classified, right ankle and foot

       M13.172   Monoarthritis, not elsewhere classified, left ankle and foot

       M13.179   Monoarthritis, not elsewhere classified, unspecified ankle and foot

M13.8   Other specified arthritis

    Allergic arthritis

> **Excludes1**   osteoarthritis (M15-M19)

    M13.80   Other specified arthritis, unspecified site

    M13.81   Other specified arthritis, shoulder

       M13.811   Other specified arthritis, right shoulder

       M13.812   Other specified arthritis, left shoulder

       M13.819   Other specified arthritis, unspecified shoulder

    M13.82   Other specified arthritis, elbow

       M13.821   Other specified arthritis, right elbow

       M13.822   Other specified arthritis, left elbow

       M13.829   Other specified arthritis, unspecified elbow

    M13.83   Other specified arthritis, wrist

       M13.831   Other specified arthritis, right wrist

       M13.832   Other specified arthritis, left wrist

       M13.839   Other specified arthritis, unspecified wrist

    M13.84   Other specified arthritis, hand

       M13.841   Other specified arthritis, right hand

       M13.842   Other specified arthritis, left hand

       M13.849   Other specified arthritis, unspecified hand

    M13.85   Other specified arthritis, hip

       M13.851   Other specified arthritis, right hip

       M13.852   Other specified arthritis, left hip

       M13.859   Other specified arthritis, unspecified hip

    M13.86   Other specified arthritis, knee

       M13.861   Other specified arthritis, right knee

       M13.862   Other specified arthritis, left knee

       M13.869   Other specified arthritis, unspecified knee

    M13.87   Other specified arthritis, ankle and foot

       M13.871   Other specified arthritis, right ankle and foot

       M13.872   Other specified arthritis, left ankle and foot

       M13.879   Other specified arthritis, unspecified ankle and foot

    M13.88   Other specified arthritis, other site

    M13.89   Other specified arthritis, multiple sites

M14   Arthropathies in other diseases classified elsewhere

> **Excludes1**   arthropathy in:
> diabetes mellitus (E08-E13 with .61-)
> hematological disorders (M36.2-M36.3)
> hypersensitivity reactions (M36.4)
> neoplastic disease (M36.1)
> neurosyphillis (A52.16)
> sarcoidosis (D86.86)
> enteropathic arthropathies (M07.0-)
> juvenile psoriatic arthropathy (L40.54)
> lipoid dermatoarthritis (E78.81)

M14.6   Charcôt's joint

    Neuropathic arthropathy

> **Excludes1**   Charcôt's joint in diabetes mellitus (E08-E13 with .610)
> Charcôt's joint in tabes dorsalis (A52.16)

    M14.60   Charcôt's joint, unspecified site

    M14.61   Charcôt's joint, shoulder

       M14.611   Charcôt's joint, right shoulder

       M14.612   Charcôt's joint, left shoulder

       M14.619   Charcôt's joint, unspecified shoulder

    M14.62   Charcôt's joint, elbow

       M14.621   Charcôt's joint, right elbow

       M14.622   Charcôt's joint, left elbow

       M14.629   Charcôt's joint, unspecified elbow

    M14.63   Charcôt's joint, wrist

       M14.631   Charcôt's joint, right wrist

       M14.632   Charcôt's joint, left wrist

       M14.639   Charcôt's joint, unspecified wrist

▶ New   ⟹ Revised   ~~deleted~~ Deleted   Excludes 1   Excludes 2   Includes   Use additional   Code first   Code also   Key words

OGCR Official Guidelines   X Assign placeholder X   ● Use Additional Character(s)   ⟩ Manifestation Code   🗨 Hierarchical Condition Category   **Coding Clinic**

● M14.64 Charcôt's joint, hand
     M14.641 Charcôt's joint, right hand
     M14.642 Charcôt's joint, left hand
     M14.649 Charcôt's joint, unspecified hand
● M14.65 Charcôt's joint, hip
     M14.651 Charcôt's joint, right hip
     M14.652 Charcôt's joint, left hip
     M14.659 Charcôt's joint, unspecified hip
● M14.66 Charcôt's joint, knee
     M14.661 Charcôt's joint, right knee
     M14.662 Charcôt's joint, left knee
     M14.669 Charcôt's joint, unspecified knee
● M14.67 Charcôt's joint, ankle and foot
     M14.671 Charcôt's joint, right ankle and foot
     M14.672 Charcôt's joint, left ankle and foot
     M14.679 Charcôt's joint, unspecified ankle and foot
   M14.68 Charcôt's joint, vertebrae
   M14.69 Charcôt's joint, multiple sites
● M14.8 Arthropathies in other specified diseases classified elsewhere

> *Code first underlying disease, such as:*
> amyloidosis (E85.-)
> erythema multiforme (L51.-)
> erythema nodosum (L52)
> hemochromatosis (E83.11-)
> hyperparathyroidism (E21.-)
> hypothyroidism (E00-E03)
> sickle-cell disorders (D57.-)
> thyrotoxicosis [hyperthyroidism] (E05.-)
> Whipple's disease (K90.81)

   ▶ *M14.80*   *Arthropathies in other specified diseases classified elsewhere, unspecified site*
● M14.81 Arthropathies in other specified diseases classified elsewhere, shoulder
   ▶ *M14.811*   *Arthropathies in other specified diseases classified elsewhere, right shoulder*
   ▶ *M14.812*   *Arthropathies in other specified diseases classified elsewhere, left shoulder*
   ▶ *M14.819*   *Arthropathies in other specified diseases classified elsewhere, unspecified shoulder*
● M14.82 Arthropathies in other specified diseases classified elsewhere, elbow
   ▶ *M14.821*   *Arthropathies in other specified diseases classified elsewhere, right elbow*
   ▶ *M14.822*   *Arthropathies in other specified diseases classified elsewhere, left elbow*
   ▶ *M14.829*   *Arthropathies in other specified diseases classified elsewhere, unspecified elbow*
● M14.83 Arthropathies in other specified diseases classified elsewhere, wrist
   ▶ *M14.831*   *Arthropathies in other specified diseases classified elsewhere, right wrist*
   ▶ *M14.832*   *Arthropathies in other specified diseases classified elsewhere, left wrist*
   ▶ *M14.839*   *Arthropathies in other specified diseases classified elsewhere, unspecified wrist*

● M14.84 Arthropathies in other specified diseases classified elsewhere, hand
   ▶ *M14.841*   *Arthropathies in other specified diseases classified elsewhere, right hand*
   ▶ *M14.842*   *Arthropathies in other specified diseases classified elsewhere, left hand*
   ▶ *M14.849*   *Arthropathies in other specified diseases classified elsewhere, unspecified hand*
● M14.85 Arthropathies in other specified diseases classified elsewhere, hip
   ▶ *M14.851*   *Arthropathies in other specified diseases classified elsewhere, right hip*
   ▶ *M14.852*   *Arthropathies in other specified diseases classified elsewhere, left hip*
   ▶ *M14.859*   *Arthropathies in other specified diseases classified elsewhere, unspecified hip*
● M14.86 Arthropathies in other specified diseases classified elsewhere, knee
   ▶ *M14.861*   *Arthropathies in other specified diseases classified elsewhere, right knee*
   ▶ *M14.862*   *Arthropathies in other specified diseases classified elsewhere, left knee*
   ▶ *M14.869*   *Arthropathies in other specified diseases classified elsewhere, unspecified knee*
● M14.87 Arthropathies in other specified diseases classified elsewhere, ankle and foot
   ▶ *M14.871*   *Arthropathies in other specified diseases classified elsewhere, right ankle and foot*
   ▶ *M14.872*   *Arthropathies in other specified diseases classified elsewhere, left ankle and foot*
   ▶ *M14.879*   *Arthropathies in other specified diseases classified elsewhere, unspecified ankle and foot*
   ▶ *M14.88*   *Arthropathies in other specified diseases classified elsewhere, vertebrae*
   ▶ *M14.89*   *Arthropathies in other specified diseases classified elsewhere, multiple sites*

OSTEOARTHRITIS (M15-M19)

Osteoarthritis is the most common degenerative joint disease and form of arthritis that breaks down the cartilage causing pain, swelling, and reduced motion in the joints.

   Excludes2   osteoarthritis of spine (M47.-)

● M15 Polyosteoarthritis
   Includes   arthritis of multiple sites
   Excludes1   bilateral involvement of single joint (M16-M19)
   M15.0 Primary generalized (osteo)arthritis
   M15.1 Heberden's nodes (with arthropathy)
      Interphalangeal distal osteoarthritis
   M15.2 Bouchard's nodes (with arthropathy)
      Juxtaphalangeal distal osteoarthritis
   M15.3 Secondary multiple arthritis
      Post-traumatic polyosteoarthritis
   M15.4 Erosive (osteo)arthritis
   M15.8 Other polyosteoarthritis
   M15.9 Polyosteoarthritis, unspecified
      Generalized osteoarthritis NOS

CHAPTER 13 (M00-M99)

CHAPTER 13 (M00-M99)

● M16 **Osteoarthritis of hip**

   M16.0 **Bilateral primary osteoarthritis of hip**
      Coding Clinic: 2018, Q2, P15; 2016, Q4, P146

  ● M16.1 **Unilateral primary osteoarthritis of hip**
      Primary osteoarthritis of hip NOS

     M16.10 **Unilateral primary osteoarthritis, unspecified hip**

     M16.11 **Unilateral primary osteoarthritis, right hip**

     M16.12 **Unilateral primary osteoarthritis, left hip**

   M16.2 **Bilateral osteoarthritis resulting from hip dysplasia**

  ● M16.3 **Unilateral osteoarthritis resulting from hip dysplasia**
      Dysplastic osteoarthritis of hip NOS

     M16.30 **Unilateral osteoarthritis resulting from hip dysplasia, unspecified hip**

     M16.31 **Unilateral osteoarthritis resulting from hip dysplasia, right hip**

     M16.32 **Unilateral osteoarthritis resulting from hip dysplasia, left hip**

   M16.4 **Bilateral post-traumatic osteoarthritis of hip**

  ● M16.5 **Unilateral post-traumatic osteoarthritis of hip**
      Post-traumatic osteoarthritis of hip NOS

     M16.50 **Unilateral post-traumatic osteoarthritis, unspecified hip**

     M16.51 **Unilateral post-traumatic osteoarthritis, right hip**

     M16.52 **Unilateral post-traumatic osteoarthritis, left hip**

   M16.6 **Other bilateral secondary osteoarthritis of hip**

   M16.7 **Other unilateral secondary osteoarthritis of hip**
      Secondary osteoarthritis of hip NOS

   M16.9 **Osteoarthritis of hip, unspecified**

● M17 **Osteoarthritis of knee**

   M17.0 **Bilateral primary osteoarthritis of knee**

  ● M17.1 **Unilateral primary osteoarthritis of knee**
      Primary osteoarthritis of knee NOS

     M17.10 **Unilateral primary osteoarthritis, unspecified knee**
        Coding Clinic: 2016, Q4, P147

     M17.11 **Unilateral primary osteoarthritis, right knee**

     M17.12 **Unilateral primary osteoarthritis, left knee**
        Coding Clinic: 2016, Q4, P146

   M17.2 **Bilateral post-traumatic osteoarthritis of knee**

  ● M17.3 **Unilateral post-traumatic osteoarthritis of knee**
      Post-traumatic osteoarthritis of knee NOS

     M17.30 **Unilateral post-traumatic osteoarthritis, unspecified knee**

     M17.31 **Unilateral post-traumatic osteoarthritis, right knee**

     M17.32 **Unilateral post-traumatic osteoarthritis, left knee**

   M17.4 **Other bilateral secondary osteoarthritis of knee**

   M17.5 **Other unilateral secondary osteoarthritis of knee**
      Secondary osteoarthritis of knee NOS

   M17.9 **Osteoarthritis of knee, unspecified**
      Coding Clinic: 2016, Q4, P146

● M18 **Osteoarthritis of first carpometacarpal joint**

   M18.0 **Bilateral primary osteoarthritis of first carpometacarpal joints**

  ● M18.1 **Unilateral primary osteoarthritis of first carpometacarpal joint**
      Primary osteoarthritis of first carpometacarpal joint NOS

     M18.10 **Unilateral primary osteoarthritis of first carpometacarpal joint, unspecified hand**

     M18.11 **Unilateral primary osteoarthritis of first carpometacarpal joint, right hand**

     M18.12 **Unilateral primary osteoarthritis of first carpometacarpal joint, left hand**

   M18.2 **Bilateral post-traumatic osteoarthritis of first carpometacarpal joints**

  ● M18.3 **Unilateral post-traumatic osteoarthritis of first carpometacarpal joint**
      Post-traumatic osteoarthritis of first carpometacarpal joint NOS

     M18.30 **Unilateral post-traumatic osteoarthritis of first carpometacarpal joint, unspecified hand**

     M18.31 **Unilateral post-traumatic osteoarthritis of first carpometacarpal joint, right hand**

     M18.32 **Unilateral post-traumatic osteoarthritis of first carpometacarpal joint, left hand**

   M18.4 **Other bilateral secondary osteoarthritis of first carpometacarpal joints**

  ● M18.5 **Other unilateral secondary osteoarthritis of first carpometacarpal joint**
      Secondary osteoarthritis of first carpometacarpal joint NOS

     M18.50 **Other unilateral secondary osteoarthritis of first carpometacarpal joint, unspecified hand**

     M18.51 **Other unilateral secondary osteoarthritis of first carpometacarpal joint, right hand**

     M18.52 **Other unilateral secondary osteoarthritis of first carpometacarpal joint, left hand**

   M18.9 **Osteoarthritis of first carpometacarpal joint, unspecified**

● M19 **Other and unspecified osteoarthritis**

   Excludes1 polyarthritis (M15.-)

   Excludes2 arthrosis of spine (M47.-)
        hallux rigidus (M20.2)
        osteoarthritis of spine (M47.-)

  ● M19.0 **Primary osteoarthritis of other joints**

    ● M19.01 **Primary osteoarthritis, shoulder**

      M19.011 **Primary osteoarthritis, right shoulder**
         Coding Clinic: 2016, Q4, P145

      M19.012 **Primary osteoarthritis, left shoulder**

      M19.019 **Primary osteoarthritis, unspecified shoulder**

    ● M19.02 **Primary osteoarthritis, elbow**

      M19.021 **Primary osteoarthritis, right elbow**

      M19.022 **Primary osteoarthritis, left elbow**

      M19.029 **Primary osteoarthritis, unspecified elbow**

    ● M19.03 **Primary osteoarthritis, wrist**

      M19.031 **Primary osteoarthritis, right wrist**

      M19.032 **Primary osteoarthritis, left wrist**

      M19.039 **Primary osteoarthritis, unspecified wrist**

    ● M19.04 **Primary osteoarthritis, hand**

      Excludes2 primary osteoarthritis of first carpometacarpal joint (M18.0-, M18.1-)

      M19.041 **Primary osteoarthritis, right hand**

      M19.042 **Primary osteoarthritis, left hand**

      M19.049 **Primary osteoarthritis, unspecified hand**

    ● M19.07 **Primary osteoarthritis ankle and foot**

      M19.071 **Primary osteoarthritis, right ankle and foot**

      M19.072 **Primary osteoarthritis, left ankle and foot**

      M19.079 **Primary osteoarthritis, unspecified ankle and foot**

    ▶ M19.09 **Primary osteoarthritis, other specified site**

▶ New   ⇒ Revised   ~~deleted~~ Deleted   Excludes 1   Excludes 2   Includes   Use additional   Code first   Code also   Key words

OGCR Official Guidelines   X Assign placeholder X   ● Use Additional Character(s)   ▌ Manifestation Code   Hierarchical Condition Category   **Coding Clinic**

● **M19.1** Post-traumatic osteoarthritis of other joints
  ● **M19.11**   Post-traumatic osteoarthritis, shoulder
      M19.111   Post-traumatic osteoarthritis, right shoulder
      M19.112   Post-traumatic osteoarthritis, left shoulder
      M19.119   Post-traumatic osteoarthritis, unspecified shoulder
  ● **M19.12**   Post-traumatic osteoarthritis, elbow
      M19.121   Post-traumatic osteoarthritis, right elbow
      M19.122   Post-traumatic osteoarthritis, left elbow
      M19.129   Post-traumatic osteoarthritis, unspecified elbow
  ● **M19.13**   Post-traumatic osteoarthritis, wrist
      M19.131   Post-traumatic osteoarthritis, right wrist
      M19.132   Post-traumatic osteoarthritis, left wrist
      M19.139   Post-traumatic osteoarthritis, unspecified wrist
  ● **M19.14**   Post-traumatic osteoarthritis, hand

> **Excludes2**   post-traumatic osteoarthritis of first carpometacarpal joint (M18.2-, M18.3-)

      M19.141   Post-traumatic osteoarthritis, right hand
      M19.142   Post-traumatic osteoarthritis, left hand
      M19.149   Post-traumatic osteoarthritis, unspecified hand
  ● **M19.17**   Post-traumatic osteoarthritis, ankle and foot
      M19.171   Post-traumatic osteoarthritis, right ankle and foot
      M19.172   Post-traumatic osteoarthritis, left ankle and foot
      M19.179   Post-traumatic osteoarthritis, unspecified ankle and foot
  ▶ **M19.19**   Post-traumatic osteoarthritis, other specified site
● **M19.2** Secondary osteoarthritis of other joints
  ● **M19.21**   Secondary osteoarthritis, shoulder
      M19.211   Secondary osteoarthritis, right shoulder
      M19.212   Secondary osteoarthritis, left shoulder
      M19.219   Secondary osteoarthritis, unspecified shoulder
  ● **M19.22**   Secondary osteoarthritis, elbow
      M19.221   Secondary osteoarthritis, right elbow
      M19.222   Secondary osteoarthritis, left elbow
      M19.229   Secondary osteoarthritis, unspecified elbow
  ● **M19.23**   Secondary osteoarthritis, wrist
      M19.231   Secondary osteoarthritis, right wrist
      M19.232   Secondary osteoarthritis, left wrist
      M19.239   Secondary osteoarthritis, unspecified wrist
  ● **M19.24**   Secondary osteoarthritis, hand
      M19.241   Secondary osteoarthritis, right hand
      M19.242   Secondary osteoarthritis, left hand
      M19.249   Secondary osteoarthritis, unspecified hand
  ● **M19.27**   Secondary osteoarthritis, ankle and foot
      M19.271   Secondary osteoarthritis, right ankle and foot
      M19.272   Secondary osteoarthritis, left ankle and foot
      M19.279   Secondary osteoarthritis, unspecified ankle and foot
  ▶ **M19.29**   Secondary osteoarthritis, other specified site

● **M19.9** Osteoarthritis, unspecified site
     M19.90   Unspecified osteoarthritis, unspecified site
        Arthrosis NOS
        Arthritis NOS
        Osteoarthritis NOS
        Coding Clinic: 2016, Q4, P147
     M19.91   Primary osteoarthritis, unspecified site
        Primary osteoarthritis NOS
     M19.92   Post-traumatic osteoarthritis, unspecified site
        Post-traumatic osteoarthritis NOS
     M19.93   Secondary osteoarthritis, unspecified site
        Secondary osteoarthritis NOS

OTHER JOINT DISORDERS (M20-M25)

> **Excludes2**   joints of the spine (M40-M54)

● **M20** Acquired deformities of fingers and toes

> **Excludes1**   acquired absence of fingers and toes (Z89.-)
> congenital absence of fingers and toes (Q71.3-, Q72.3-)
> congenital deformities and malformations of fingers and toes (Q66.-, Q68-Q70, Q74.-)

● **M20.0** Deformity of finger(s)

> **Excludes1**   clubbing of fingers (R68.3)
> palmar fascial fibromatosis [Dupuytren] (M72.0)
> trigger finger (M65.3)

  ● **M20.00**   Unspecified deformity of finger(s)
      M20.001   Unspecified deformity of right finger(s)
      M20.002   Unspecified deformity of left finger(s)
      M20.009   Unspecified deformity of unspecified finger(s)
  ● **M20.01**   Mallet finger
      M20.011   Mallet finger of right finger(s)
      M20.012   Mallet finger of left finger(s)
      M20.019   Mallet finger of unspecified finger(s)
  ● **M20.02**   Boutonnière deformity
      M20.021   Boutonnière deformity of right finger(s)
      M20.022   Boutonnière deformity of left finger(s)
      M20.029   Boutonnière deformity of unspecified finger(s)
  ● **M20.03**   Swan-neck deformity
      M20.031   Swan-neck deformity of right finger(s)
      M20.032   Swan-neck deformity of left finger(s)
      M20.039   Swan-neck deformity of unspecified finger(s)
  ● **M20.09**   Other deformity of finger(s)
      M20.091   Other deformity of right finger(s)
      M20.092   Other deformity of left finger(s)
      M20.099   Other deformity of finger(s), unspecified finger(s)
● **M20.1** Hallux valgus (acquired)

> **Excludes2**   bunion (M21.6-)
> Coding Clinic: 2016, Q4, P38

     M20.10   Hallux valgus (acquired), unspecified foot
     M20.11   Hallux valgus (acquired), right foot
     M20.12   Hallux valgus (acquired), left foot
● **M20.2** Hallux rigidus
     M20.20   Hallux rigidus, unspecified foot
     M20.21   Hallux rigidus, right foot
     M20.22   Hallux rigidus, left foot

Figure 13-1   Hallux valgus.

Item 13–2 Hallux valgus is a sometimes painful structural deformity caused by an inflammation of the bursal sac at the base of the metatarsophalangeal joint (big toe). **Hallus varus** is a deviation of the great toe to the inner side of the foot or away from the next toe.

- ● **M20.3 Hallux varus (acquired)**
  - M20.30   Hallux varus (acquired), unspecified foot
  - M20.31   Hallux varus (acquired), right foot
  - M20.32   Hallux varus (acquired), left foot
- ● **M20.4 Other hammer toe(s) (acquired)**
  - M20.40   Other hammer toe(s) (acquired), unspecified foot
  - M20.41   Other hammer toe(s) (acquired), right foot
  - M20.42   Other hammer toe(s) (acquired), left foot
- ● **M20.5 Other deformities of toe(s) (acquired)**
  - ● **M20.5X Other deformities of toe(s) (acquired)**
    - M20.5X1   Other deformities of toe(s) (acquired), right foot
    - M20.5X2   Other deformities of toe(s) (acquired), left foot
    - M20.5X9   Other deformities of toe(s) (acquired), unspecified foot
- ● **M20.6 Acquired deformities of toe(s), unspecified**
  - M20.60   Acquired deformities of toe(s), unspecified, unspecified foot
  - M20.61   Acquired deformities of toe(s), unspecified, right foot
  - M20.62   Acquired deformities of toe(s), unspecified, left foot
- ● **M21 Other acquired deformities of limbs**
  - **Excludes1**   acquired absence of limb (Z89.-)
    congenital absence of limbs (Q71-Q73)
    congenital deformities and malformations of limbs (Q65-Q66, Q68-Q74)
  - **Excludes2**   acquired deformities of fingers or toes (M20.-)
    coxa plana (M91.2)
  - ● **M21.0 Valgus deformity, not elsewhere classified**
    - **Excludes1**   metatarsus valgus (Q66.6)
      talipes calcaneovalgus (Q66.4-)
    - M21.00   Valgus deformity, not elsewhere classified, unspecified site
    - ● **M21.02 Valgus deformity, not elsewhere classified, elbow**
      Cubitus valgus
      - M21.021   Valgus deformity, not elsewhere classified, right elbow
      - M21.022   Valgus deformity, not elsewhere classified, left elbow
      - M21.029   Valgus deformity, not elsewhere classified, unspecified elbow

Item 13–3 Cubitus valgus is a deformity of the elbow resulting in an increased carrying angle in which the arm extends at the side and the palm faces forward, which results in the forearm and hand extended at greater than 15 degrees.

Item 13–4 Cubitus varus is a deformity of the elbow resulting in the arm extended at the side and the palm facing forward so that the forearm and hand are held at less than 5 degrees, decreasing the carrying angle.

- ● **M21.05 Valgus deformity, not elsewhere classified, hip**
  - M21.051   Valgus deformity, not elsewhere classified, right hip
  - M21.052   Valgus deformity, not elsewhere classified, left hip
  - M21.059   Valgus deformity, not elsewhere classified, unspecified hip
- ● **M21.06 Valgus deformity, not elsewhere classified, knee**
  Genu valgum
  Knock knee
  - M21.061   Valgus deformity, not elsewhere classified, right knee
  - M21.062   Valgus deformity, not elsewhere classified, left knee
  - M21.069   Valgus deformity, not elsewhere classified, unspecified knee
- ● **M21.07 Valgus deformity, not elsewhere classified, ankle**
  - M21.071   Valgus deformity, not elsewhere classified, right ankle
  - M21.072   Valgus deformity, not elsewhere classified, left ankle
  - M21.079   Valgus deformity, not elsewhere classified, unspecified ankle
- ● **M21.1 Varus deformity, not elsewhere classified**
  - **Excludes1**   metatarsus varus (Q66.22-)
    ⮕ tibia vara (M92.51-)
  - M21.10   Varus deformity, not elsewhere classified, unspecified site
  - ● **M21.12 Varus deformity, not elsewhere classified, elbow**
    Cubitus varus, elbow
    - M21.121   Varus deformity, not elsewhere classified, right elbow
    - M21.122   Varus deformity, not elsewhere classified, left elbow
    - M21.129   Varus deformity, not elsewhere classified, unspecified elbow
  - ● **M21.15 Varus deformity, not elsewhere classified, hip**
    - M21.151   Varus deformity, not elsewhere classified, right hip
    - M21.152   Varus deformity, not elsewhere classified, left hip
    - M21.159   Varus deformity, not elsewhere classified, unspecified
  - ● **M21.16 Varus deformity, not elsewhere classified, knee**
    Bow leg
    Genu varum
    - M21.161   Varus deformity, not elsewhere classified, right knee
    - M21.162   Varus deformity, not elsewhere classified, left knee
    - M21.169   Varus deformity, not elsewhere classified, unspecified knee
  - ● **M21.17 Varus deformity, not elsewhere classified, ankle**
    - M21.171   Varus deformity, not elsewhere classified, right ankle
    - M21.172   Varus deformity, not elsewhere classified, left ankle
    - M21.179   Varus deformity, not elsewhere classified, unspecified ankle

▶ New   ⮕ Revised   ~~deleted~~ Deleted   Excludes 1   Excludes 2   Includes   Use additional   Code first   Code also   Key words

OGCR Official Guidelines   X Assign placeholder X   ● Use Additional Character(s)   ▶ Manifestation Code   ⓠ Hierarchical Condition Category   **Coding Clinic**

● **M21.2 Flexion deformity**
     M21.20 Flexion deformity, unspecified site
     ● M21.21 Flexion deformity, shoulder
         M21.211 Flexion deformity, right shoulder
         M21.212 Flexion deformity, left shoulder
         M21.219 Flexion deformity, unspecified shoulder
     ● M21.22 Flexion deformity, elbow
         M21.221 Flexion deformity, right elbow
         M21.222 Flexion deformity, left elbow
         M21.229 Flexion deformity, unspecified elbow
     ● M21.23 Flexion deformity, wrist
         M21.231 Flexion deformity, right wrist
         M21.232 Flexion deformity, left wrist
         M21.239 Flexion deformity, unspecified wrist
     ● M21.24 Flexion deformity, finger joints
         M21.241 Flexion deformity, right finger joints
         M21.242 Flexion deformity, left finger joints
         M21.249 Flexion deformity, unspecified finger joints
     ● M21.25 Flexion deformity, hip
         M21.251 Flexion deformity, right hip
         M21.252 Flexion deformity, left hip
         M21.259 Flexion deformity, unspecified hip
     ● M21.26 Flexion deformity, knee
         M21.261 Flexion deformity, right knee
         M21.262 Flexion deformity, left knee
         M21.269 Flexion deformity, unspecified knee
     ● M21.27 Flexion deformity, ankle and toes
         M21.271 Flexion deformity, right ankle and toes
         M21.272 Flexion deformity, left ankle and toes
         M21.279 Flexion deformity, unspecified ankle and toes
● **M21.3 Wrist or foot drop (acquired)**
     ● M21.33 Wrist drop (acquired)
         M21.331 Wrist drop, right wrist
         M21.332 Wrist drop, left wrist
         M21.339 Wrist drop, unspecified wrist
     ● M21.37 Foot drop (acquired)
         M21.371 Foot drop, right foot
         M21.372 Foot drop, left foot
         M21.379 Foot drop, unspecified foot
● **M21.4 Flat foot [pes planus] (acquired)**
     Excludes1   congenital pes planus (Q66.5-)
     M21.40 Flat foot [pes planus] (acquired), unspecified foot
     M21.41 Flat foot [pes planus] (acquired), right foot
     M21.42 Flat foot [pes planus] (acquired), left foot
● **M21.5 Acquired clawhand, clubhand, clawfoot and clubfoot**
     Excludes1   clubfoot, not specified as acquired (Q66.89)
     ● M21.51 Acquired clawhand
         M21.511 Acquired clawhand, right hand
         M21.512 Acquired clawhand, left hand
         M21.519 Acquired clawhand, unspecified hand
     ● M21.52 Acquired clubhand
         M21.521 Acquired clubhand, right hand
         M21.522 Acquired clubhand, left hand
         M21.529 Acquired clubhand, unspecified hand
     ● M21.53 Acquired clawfoot
         M21.531 Acquired clawfoot, right foot
         M21.532 Acquired clawfoot, left foot
         M21.539 Acquired clawfoot, unspecified foot

     ● M21.54 Acquired clubfoot
         M21.541 Acquired clubfoot, right foot
         M21.542 Acquired clubfoot, left foot
         M21.549 Acquired clubfoot, unspecified foot
● **M21.6 Other acquired deformities of foot**
     Excludes2   deformities of toe (acquired) (M20.1-M20.6-)
     ● M21.61 Bunion
         Coding Clinic: 2016, Q4, P38
         M21.611 Bunion of right foot
         M21.612 Bunion of left foot
         M21.619 Bunion of unspecified foot
     ● M21.62 Bunionette
         Coding Clinic: 2016, Q4, P38
         M21.621 Bunionette of right foot
         M21.622 Bunionette of left foot
         M21.629 Bunionette of unspecified foot
     ● M21.6X Other acquired deformities of foot
         M21.6X1 Other acquired deformities of right foot
         M21.6X2 Other acquired deformities of left foot
         M21.6X9 Other acquired deformities of unspecified foot
● **M21.7 Unequal limb length (acquired)**
     Note: The site used should correspond to the shorter limb.
     M21.70 Unequal limb length (acquired), unspecified site
     ● M21.72 Unequal limb length (acquired), humerus
         M21.721 Unequal limb length (acquired), right humerus
         M21.722 Unequal limb length (acquired), left humerus
         M21.729 Unequal limb length (acquired), unspecified humerus
     ● M21.73 Unequal limb length (acquired), ulna and radius
         M21.731 Unequal limb length (acquired), right ulna
         M21.732 Unequal limb length (acquired), left ulna
         M21.733 Unequal limb length (acquired), right radius
         M21.734 Unequal limb length (acquired), left radius
         M21.739 Unequal limb length (acquired), unspecified ulna and radius
     ● M21.75 Unequal limb length (acquired), femur
         M21.751 Unequal limb length (acquired), right femur
         M21.752 Unequal limb length (acquired), left femur
         M21.759 Unequal limb length (acquired), unspecified femur
     ● M21.76 Unequal limb length (acquired), tibia and fibula
         M21.761 Unequal limb length (acquired), right tibia
         M21.762 Unequal limb length (acquired), left tibia
         M21.763 Unequal limb length (acquired), right fibula
         M21.764 Unequal limb length (acquired), left fibula
         M21.769 Unequal limb length (acquired), unspecified tibia and fibula

● **M21.8　Other specified acquired deformities of limbs**
　　Excludes2　coxa plana (M91.2)
　　M21.80　Other specified acquired deformities of unspecified limb
● 　M21.82　Other specified acquired deformities of upper arm
　　　　M21.821　Other specified acquired deformities of right upper arm
　　　　M21.822　Other specified acquired deformities of left upper arm
　　　　M21.829　Other specified acquired deformities of unspecified upper arm
● 　M21.83　Other specified acquired deformities of forearm
　　　　M21.831　Other specified acquired deformities of right forearm
　　　　M21.832　Other specified acquired deformities of left forearm
　　　　M21.839　Other specified acquired deformities of unspecified forearm
● 　M21.85　Other specified acquired deformities of thigh
　　　　M21.851　Other specified acquired deformities of right thigh
　　　　M21.852　Other specified acquired deformities of left thigh
　　　　M21.859　Other specified acquired deformities of unspecified thigh
● 　M21.86　Other specified acquired deformities of lower leg
　　　　M21.861　Other specified acquired deformities of right lower leg
　　　　M21.862　Other specified acquired deformities of left lower leg
　　　　M21.869　Other specified acquired deformities of unspecified lower leg

● **M21.9　Unspecified acquired deformity of limb and hand**
　　M21.90　Unspecified acquired deformity of unspecified limb
● 　M21.92　Unspecified acquired deformity of upper arm
　　　　M21.921　Unspecified acquired deformity of right upper arm
　　　　M21.922　Unspecified acquired deformity of left upper arm
　　　　M21.929　Unspecified acquired deformity of unspecified upper arm
● 　M21.93　Unspecified acquired deformity of forearm
　　　　M21.931　Unspecified acquired deformity of right forearm
　　　　M21.932　Unspecified acquired deformity of left forearm
　　　　M21.939　Unspecified acquired deformity of unspecified forearm
● 　M21.94　Unspecified acquired deformity of hand
　　　　M21.941　Unspecified acquired deformity of hand, right hand
　　　　M21.942　Unspecified acquired deformity of hand, left hand
　　　　M21.949　Unspecified acquired deformity of hand, unspecified hand

● 　M21.95　Unspecified acquired deformity of thigh
　　　　M21.951　Unspecified acquired deformity of right thigh
　　　　M21.952　Unspecified acquired deformity of left thigh
　　　　M21.959　Unspecified acquired deformity of unspecified thigh
● 　M21.96　Unspecified acquired deformity of lower leg
　　　　M21.961　Unspecified acquired deformity of right lower leg
　　　　M21.962　Unspecified acquired deformity of left lower leg
　　　　M21.969　Unspecified acquired deformity of unspecified lower leg

● **M22　Disorder of patella**
　　Excludes1　traumatic dislocation of patella (S83.0-)
　▶ **Excludes2**　traumatic dislocation of patella (S83.0-)
● **M22.0　Recurrent dislocation of patella**
　　M22.00　Recurrent dislocation of patella, unspecified knee
　　M22.01　Recurrent dislocation of patella, right knee
　　M22.02　Recurrent dislocation of patella, left knee
● **M22.1　Recurrent subluxation of patella**
　　Incomplete dislocation of patella
　　M22.10　Recurrent subluxation of patella, unspecified knee
　　M22.11　Recurrent subluxation of patella, right knee
　　M22.12　Recurrent subluxation of patella, left knee
● **M22.2　Patellofemoral disorders**
● 　M22.2X　Patellofemoral disorders
　　　　M22.2X1　Patellofemoral disorders, right knee
　　　　M22.2X2　Patellofemoral disorders, left knee
　　　　M22.2X9　Patellofemoral disorders, unspecified knee
● **M22.3　Other derangements of patella**
● 　M22.3X　Other derangements of patella
　　　　M22.3X1　Other derangements of patella, right knee
　　　　M22.3X2　Other derangements of patella, left knee
　　　　M22.3X9　Other derangements of patella, unspecified knee
● **M22.4　Chondromalacia patellae**
　　M22.40　Chondromalacia patellae, unspecified knee
　　M22.41　Chondromalacia patellae, right knee
　　M22.42　Chondromalacia patellae, left knee
● **M22.8　Other disorders of patella**
● 　M22.8X　Other disorders of patella
　　　　M22.8X1　Other disorders of patella, right knee
　　　　M22.8X2　Other disorders of patella, left knee
　　　　M22.8X9　Other disorders of patella, unspecified knee
● **M22.9　Unspecified disorder of patella**
　　M22.90　Unspecified disorder of patella, unspecified knee
　　M22.91　Unspecified disorder of patella, right knee
　　M22.92　Unspecified disorder of patella, left knee

▶ New　▥ Revised　deleted Deleted　Excludes 1　Excludes 2　Includes　Use additional　Code first　Code also　Key words
OGCR Official Guidelines　X Assign placeholder X　● Use Additional Character(s)　▌Manifestation Code　🅗 Hierarchical Condition Category　**Coding Clinic**

● **M23**   **Internal derangement of knee**
    Excludes1   ankylosis (M24.66)
            deformity of knee (M21.-)
            osteochondritis dissecans (M93.2)
            ~~current injury - see injury of knee and lower leg~~
              ~~(S80-S89)~~
            ~~recurrent dislocation or subluxation of joints~~
              ~~(M24.4)~~
            ~~recurrent dislocation or subluxation of patella~~
              ~~(M22.0-M22.1)~~

   ▶ **Excludes2**   current injury - see injury of knee and lower leg
              (S80-S89)
         ▶ recurrent dislocation or subluxation of joints
              (M24.4)
         ▶ recurrent dislocation or subluxation of patella
              (M22.0-M22.1)

     Coding Clinic: 2019, Q2, P26

● **M23.0**   **Cystic meniscus**
   ● **M23.00**   Cystic meniscus, unspecified meniscus
          Cystic meniscus, unspecified lateral meniscus
          Cystic meniscus, unspecified medial meniscus
      M23.000   Cystic meniscus, unspecified lateral meniscus, right knee
      M23.001   Cystic meniscus, unspecified lateral meniscus, left knee
      M23.002   Cystic meniscus, unspecified lateral meniscus, unspecified knee
      M23.003   Cystic meniscus, unspecified medial meniscus, right knee
      M23.004   Cystic meniscus, unspecified medial meniscus, left knee
      M23.005   Cystic meniscus, unspecified medial meniscus, unspecified knee
      M23.006   Cystic meniscus, unspecified meniscus, right knee
      M23.007   Cystic meniscus, unspecified meniscus, left knee
      M23.009   Cystic meniscus, unspecified meniscus, unspecified knee

   ● **M23.01**   Cystic meniscus, anterior horn of medial meniscus
      M23.011   Cystic meniscus, anterior horn of medial meniscus, right knee
      M23.012   Cystic meniscus, anterior horn of medial meniscus, left knee
      M23.019   Cystic meniscus, anterior horn of medial meniscus, unspecified knee

   ● **M23.02**   Cystic meniscus, posterior horn of medial meniscus
      M23.021   Cystic meniscus, posterior horn of medial meniscus, right knee
      M23.022   Cystic meniscus, posterior horn of medial meniscus, left knee
      M23.029   Cystic meniscus, posterior horn of medial meniscus, unspecified knee

   ● **M23.03**   Cystic meniscus, other medial meniscus
      M23.031   Cystic meniscus, other medial meniscus, right knee
      M23.032   Cystic meniscus, other medial meniscus, left knee
      M23.039   Cystic meniscus, other medial meniscus, unspecified knee

   ● **M23.04**   Cystic meniscus, anterior horn of lateral meniscus
      M23.041   Cystic meniscus, anterior horn of lateral meniscus, right knee
      M23.042   Cystic meniscus, anterior horn of lateral meniscus, left knee
      M23.049   Cystic meniscus, anterior horn of lateral meniscus, unspecified knee

● **M23.05**   Cystic meniscus, posterior horn of lateral meniscus
      M23.051   Cystic meniscus, posterior horn of lateral meniscus, right knee
      M23.052   Cystic meniscus, posterior horn of lateral meniscus, left knee
      M23.059   Cystic meniscus, posterior horn of lateral meniscus, unspecified knee

● **M23.06**   Cystic meniscus, other lateral meniscus
      M23.061   Cystic meniscus, other lateral meniscus, right knee
      M23.062   Cystic meniscus, other lateral meniscus, left knee
      M23.069   Cystic meniscus, other lateral meniscus, unspecified knee

★ **(See Plate 34 of the Anatomy Illustrations.)**

   ● **M23.2**   Derangement of meniscus due to old tear or injury
        Old bucket-handle tear
   ● **M23.20**   Derangement of unspecified meniscus due to old tear or injury
        Derangement of unspecified lateral meniscus due to old tear or injury
        Derangement of unspecified medial meniscus due to old tear or injury
      M23.200   Derangement of unspecified lateral meniscus due to old tear or injury, right knee
      M23.201   Derangement of unspecified lateral meniscus due to old tear or injury, left knee
      M23.202   Derangement of unspecified lateral meniscus due to old tear or injury, unspecified knee
      M23.203   Derangement of unspecified medial meniscus due to old tear or injury, right knee
      M23.204   Derangement of unspecified medial meniscus due to old tear or injury, left knee
      M23.205   Derangement of unspecified medial meniscus due to old tear or injury, unspecified knee
      M23.206   Derangement of unspecified meniscus due to old tear or injury, right knee
      M23.207   Derangement of unspecified meniscus due to old tear or injury, left knee
      M23.209   Derangement of unspecified meniscus due to old tear or injury, unspecified knee

   ● **M23.21**   Derangement of anterior horn of medial meniscus due to old tear or injury
      M23.211   Derangement of anterior horn of medial meniscus due to old tear or injury, right knee
      M23.212   Derangement of anterior horn of medial meniscus due to old tear or injury, left knee
      M23.219   Derangement of anterior horn of medial meniscus due to old tear or injury, unspecified knee

   ● **M23.22**   Derangement of posterior horn of medial meniscus due to old tear or injury
      M23.221   Derangement of posterior horn of medial meniscus due to old tear or injury, right knee
      M23.222   Derangement of posterior horn of medial meniscus due to old tear or injury, left knee
      M23.229   Derangement of posterior horn of medial meniscus due to old tear or injury, unspecified knee

● M23.23 Derangement of other medial meniscus due to old tear or injury

    M23.231 Derangement of other medial meniscus due to old tear or injury, right knee

    M23.232 Derangement of other medial meniscus due to old tear or injury, left knee

    M23.239 Derangement of other medial meniscus due to old tear or injury, unspecified knee

● M23.24 Derangement of anterior horn of lateral meniscus due to old tear or injury

    M23.241 Derangement of anterior horn of lateral meniscus due to old tear or injury, right knee

    M23.242 Derangement of anterior horn of lateral meniscus due to old tear or injury, left knee

    M23.249 Derangement of anterior horn of lateral meniscus due to old tear or injury, unspecified knee

● M23.25 Derangement of posterior horn of lateral meniscus due to old tear or injury

    M23.251 Derangement of posterior horn of lateral meniscus due to old tear or injury, right knee

    M23.252 Derangement of posterior horn of lateral meniscus due to old tear or injury, left knee

    M23.259 Derangement of posterior horn of lateral meniscus due to old tear or injury, unspecified knee

● M23.26 Derangement of other lateral meniscus due to old tear or injury

    M23.261 Derangement of other lateral meniscus due to old tear or injury, right knee

    M23.262 Derangement of other lateral meniscus due to old tear or injury, left knee

    M23.269 Derangement of other lateral meniscus due to old tear or injury, unspecified knee

● M23.3 Other meniscus derangements

    Degenerate meniscus
    Detached meniscus
    Retained meniscus

● M23.30 Other meniscus derangements, unspecified meniscus

    Other meniscus derangements, unspecified lateral meniscus
    Other meniscus derangements, unspecified medial meniscus

    M23.300 Other meniscus derangements, unspecified lateral meniscus, right knee

    M23.301 Other meniscus derangements, unspecified lateral meniscus, left knee

    M23.302 Other meniscus derangements, unspecified lateral meniscus, unspecified knee

    M23.303 Other meniscus derangements, unspecified medial meniscus, right knee

    M23.304 Other meniscus derangements, unspecified medial meniscus, left knee

    M23.305 Other meniscus derangements, unspecified medial meniscus, unspecified knee

    M23.306 Other meniscus derangements, unspecified meniscus, right knee

    M23.307 Other meniscus derangements, unspecified meniscus, left knee

    M23.309 Other meniscus derangements, unspecified meniscus, unspecified knee

● M23.31 Other meniscus derangements, anterior horn of medial meniscus

    M23.311 Other meniscus derangements, anterior horn of medial meniscus, right knee

    M23.312 Other meniscus derangements, anterior horn of medial meniscus, left knee

    M23.319 Other meniscus derangements, anterior horn of medial meniscus, unspecified knee

● M23.32 Other meniscus derangements, posterior horn of medial meniscus

    M23.321 Other meniscus derangements, posterior horn of medial meniscus, right knee

    M23.322 Other meniscus derangements, posterior horn of medial meniscus, left knee

    M23.329 Other meniscus derangements, posterior horn of medial meniscus, unspecified knee

● M23.33 Other meniscus derangements, other medial meniscus

    M23.331 Other meniscus derangements, other medial meniscus, right knee

    M23.332 Other meniscus derangements, other medial meniscus, left knee

    M23.339 Other meniscus derangements, other medial meniscus, unspecified knee

● M23.34 Other meniscus derangements, anterior horn of lateral meniscus

    M23.341 Other meniscus derangements, anterior horn of lateral meniscus, right knee

    M23.342 Other meniscus derangements, anterior horn of lateral meniscus, left knee

    M23.349 Other meniscus derangements, anterior horn of lateral meniscus, unspecified knee

● M23.35 Other meniscus derangements, posterior horn of lateral meniscus

    M23.351 Other meniscus derangements, posterior horn of lateral meniscus, right knee

    M23.352 Other meniscus derangements, posterior horn of lateral meniscus, left knee

    M23.359 Other meniscus derangements, posterior horn of lateral meniscus, unspecified knee

● M23.36 Other meniscus derangements, other lateral meniscus

    M23.361 Other meniscus derangements, other lateral meniscus, right knee

    M23.362 Other meniscus derangements, other lateral meniscus, left knee

    M23.369 Other meniscus derangements, other lateral meniscus, unspecified knee

▶ New   ⇛ Revised   ~~deleted~~ Deleted   Excludes 1   Excludes 2   Includes   Use additional   Code first   Code also   Key words

OGCR Official Guidelines   X Assign placeholder X   ● Use Additional Character(s)   ▶ Manifestation Code   🅠 Hierarchical Condition Category   **Coding Clinic**

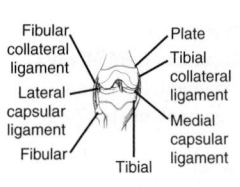

Fibular collateral ligament
Lateral capsular ligament
Fibular
Plate
Tibial collateral ligament
Medial capsular ligament
Tibial

Figure 13-2 Collateral and cruciate ligament of knee. (From DeLee: DeLee and Drez's Orthopaedic Sports Medicine, ed 3, Saunders, 2009)

● M23.4 Loose body in knee
    M23.40 Loose body in knee, unspecified knee
    M23.41 Loose body in knee, right knee
    M23.42 Loose body in knee, left knee
● M23.5 Chronic instability of knee
    M23.50 Chronic instability of knee, unspecified knee
    M23.51 Chronic instability of knee, right knee
    M23.52 Chronic instability of knee, left knee
● M23.6 Other spontaneous disruption of ligament(s) of knee
    ● M23.60 Other spontaneous disruption of unspecified ligament of knee
      M23.601 Other spontaneous disruption of unspecified ligament of right knee
      M23.602 Other spontaneous disruption of unspecified ligament of left knee
      M23.609 Other spontaneous disruption of unspecified ligament of unspecified knee
    ● M23.61 Other spontaneous disruption of anterior cruciate ligament of knee
      M23.611 Other spontaneous disruption of anterior cruciate ligament of right knee
      M23.612 Other spontaneous disruption of anterior cruciate ligament of left knee
      M23.619 Other spontaneous disruption of anterior cruciate ligament of unspecified knee
    ● M23.62 Other spontaneous disruption of posterior cruciate ligament of knee
      M23.621 Other spontaneous disruption of posterior cruciate ligament of right knee
      M23.622 Other spontaneous disruption of posterior cruciate ligament of left knee
      M23.629 Other spontaneous disruption of posterior cruciate ligament of unspecified knee
    ● M23.63 Other spontaneous disruption of medial collateral ligament of knee
      M23.631 Other spontaneous disruption of medial collateral ligament of right knee
      M23.632 Other spontaneous disruption of medial collateral ligament of left knee
      M23.639 Other spontaneous disruption of medial collateral ligament of unspecified knee
    ● M23.64 Other spontaneous disruption of lateral collateral ligament of knee
      M23.641 Other spontaneous disruption of lateral collateral ligament of right knee
      M23.642 Other spontaneous disruption of lateral collateral ligament of left knee
      M23.649 Other spontaneous disruption of lateral collateral ligament of unspecified knee

    ● M23.67 Other spontaneous disruption of capsular ligament of knee
      M23.671 Other spontaneous disruption of capsular ligament of right knee
      M23.672 Other spontaneous disruption of capsular ligament of left knee
      M23.679 Other spontaneous disruption of capsular ligament of unspecified knee
● M23.8 Other internal derangements of knee
    Laxity of ligament of knee
    Snapping knee
    ● M23.8X Other internal derangements of knee
      M23.8X1 Other internal derangements of right knee
      M23.8X2 Other internal derangements of left knee
      M23.8X9 Other internal derangements of unspecified knee
● M23.9 Unspecified internal derangement of knee
    M23.90 Unspecified internal derangement of unspecified knee
    M23.91 Unspecified internal derangement of right knee
    M23.92 Unspecified internal derangement of left knee
● M24 Other specific joint derangements
    Excludes1 current injury - see injury of joint by body region
    Excludes2 ganglion (M67.4)
      snapping knee (M23.8-)
      temporomandibular joint disorders (M26.6-)
    ● M24.0 Loose body in joint
      Excludes2 loose body in knee (M23.4)
      M24.00 Loose body in unspecified joint
      ● M24.01 Loose body in shoulder
        M24.011 Loose body in right shoulder
        M24.012 Loose body in left shoulder
        M24.019 Loose body in unspecified shoulder
      ● M24.02 Loose body in elbow
        M24.021 Loose body in right elbow
        M24.022 Loose body in left elbow
        M24.029 Loose body in unspecified elbow
      ● M24.03 Loose body in wrist
        M24.031 Loose body in right wrist
        M24.032 Loose body in left wrist
        M24.039 Loose body in unspecified wrist
      ● M24.04 Loose body in finger joints
        M24.041 Loose body in right finger joint(s)
        M24.042 Loose body in left finger joint(s)
        M24.049 Loose body in unspecified finger joint(s)
      ● M24.05 Loose body in hip
        M24.051 Loose body in right hip
        M24.052 Loose body in left hip
        M24.059 Loose body in unspecified hip
      ● M24.07 Loose body in ankle and toe joints
        M24.071 Loose body in right ankle
        M24.072 Loose body in left ankle
        M24.073 Loose body in unspecified ankle
        M24.074 Loose body in right toe joint(s)
        M24.075 Loose body in left toe joint(s)
        M24.076 Loose body in unspecified toe joints
      M24.08 Loose body, other site

CHAPTER 13 (M00-M99)

CHAPTER 13 (M00-M99)

● **M24.1 Other articular cartilage disorders**
    Excludes2   chondrocalcinosis (M11.1, M11.2-)
                   internal derangement of knee (M23.-)
                   metastatic calcification (E83.5)
                   ochronosis (E70.2)

  M24.10 Other articular cartilage disorders, unspecified site

● **M24.11 Other articular cartilage disorders, shoulder**
    M24.111 Other articular cartilage disorders, right shoulder
    M24.112 Other articular cartilage disorders, left shoulder
    M24.119 Other articular cartilage disorders, unspecified shoulder

● **M24.12 Other articular cartilage disorders, elbow**
    M24.121 Other articular cartilage disorders, right elbow
    M24.122 Other articular cartilage disorders, left elbow
    M24.129 Other articular cartilage disorders, unspecified elbow

● **M24.13 Other articular cartilage disorders, wrist**
    M24.131 Other articular cartilage disorders, right wrist
    M24.132 Other articular cartilage disorders, left wrist
    M24.139 Other articular cartilage disorders, unspecified wrist

● **M24.14 Other articular cartilage disorders, hand**
    M24.141 Other articular cartilage disorders, right hand
    M24.142 Other articular cartilage disorders, left hand
    M24.149 Other articular cartilage disorders, unspecified hand

● **M24.15 Other articular cartilage disorders, hip**
    M24.151 Other articular cartilage disorders, right hip
    M24.152 Other articular cartilage disorders, left hip
    M24.159 Other articular cartilage disorders, unspecified hip

● **M24.17 Other articular cartilage disorders, ankle and foot**
    M24.171 Other articular cartilage disorders, right ankle
    M24.172 Other articular cartilage disorders, left ankle
    M24.173 Other articular cartilage disorders, unspecified ankle
    M24.174 Other articular cartilage disorders, right foot
    M24.175 Other articular cartilage disorders, left foot
    M24.176 Other articular cartilage disorders, unspecified foot

▶ **M24.19 Other articular cartilage disorders, other specified site**

● **M24.2 Disorder of ligament**
  Instability secondary to old ligament injury
  Ligamentous laxity NOS
    Excludes1   familial ligamentous laxity (M35.7)
    Excludes2   internal derangement of knee (M23.5-M23.8X9)

  M24.20 Disorder of ligament, unspecified site

● **M24.21 Disorder of ligament, shoulder**
    M24.211 Disorder of ligament, right shoulder
    M24.212 Disorder of ligament, left shoulder
    M24.219 Disorder of ligament, unspecified shoulder

● **M24.22 Disorder of ligament, elbow**
    M24.221 Disorder of ligament, right elbow
    M24.222 Disorder of ligament, left elbow
    M24.229 Disorder of ligament, unspecified elbow

● **M24.23 Disorder of ligament, wrist**
    M24.231 Disorder of ligament, right wrist
    M24.232 Disorder of ligament, left wrist
    M24.239 Disorder of ligament, unspecified wrist

● **M24.24 Disorder of ligament, hand**
    M24.241 Disorder of ligament, right hand
    M24.242 Disorder of ligament, left hand
    M24.249 Disorder of ligament, unspecified hand

● **M24.25 Disorder of ligament, hip**
    M24.251 Disorder of ligament, right hip
    M24.252 Disorder of ligament, left hip
    M24.259 Disorder of ligament, unspecified hip

● **M24.27 Disorder of ligament, ankle and foot**
    M24.271 Disorder of ligament, right ankle
    M24.272 Disorder of ligament, left ankle
    M24.273 Disorder of ligament, unspecified ankle
    M24.274 Disorder of ligament, right foot
    M24.275 Disorder of ligament, left foot
    M24.276 Disorder of ligament, unspecified foot

  M24.28 Disorder of ligament, vertebrae

▶ **M24.29 Disorder of ligament, other specified site**

● **M24.3 Pathological dislocation of joint, not elsewhere classified**
    Excludes1   congenital dislocation or displacement of joint - see congenital malformations and deformations of the musculoskeletal system (Q65-Q79)
                   current injury - see injury of joints and ligaments by body region
                   recurrent dislocation of joint (M24.4-)

  M24.30 Pathological dislocation of unspecified joint, not elsewhere classified

● **M24.31 Pathological dislocation of shoulder, not elsewhere classified**
    M24.311 Pathological dislocation of right shoulder, not elsewhere classified
    M24.312 Pathological dislocation of left shoulder, not elsewhere classified
    M24.319 Pathological dislocation of unspecified shoulder, not elsewhere classified

● **M24.32 Pathological dislocation of elbow, not elsewhere classified**
    M24.321 Pathological dislocation of right elbow, not elsewhere classified
    M24.322 Pathological dislocation of left elbow, not elsewhere classified
    M24.329 Pathological dislocation of unspecified elbow, not elsewhere classified

● **M24.33 Pathological dislocation of wrist, not elsewhere classified**
    M24.331 Pathological dislocation of right wrist, not elsewhere classified
    M24.332 Pathological dislocation of left wrist, not elsewhere classified
    M24.339 Pathological dislocation of unspecified wrist, not elsewhere classified

● **M24.34** Pathological dislocation of hand, not elsewhere classified

     M24.341 Pathological dislocation of right hand, not elsewhere classified

     M24.342 Pathological dislocation of left hand, not elsewhere classified

     M24.349 Pathological dislocation of unspecified hand, not elsewhere classified

● **M24.35** Pathological dislocation of hip, not elsewhere classified

     M24.351 Pathological dislocation of right hip, not elsewhere classified

     M24.352 Pathological dislocation of left hip, not elsewhere classified

     M24.359 Pathological dislocation of unspecified hip, not elsewhere classified

● **M24.36** Pathological dislocation of knee, not elsewhere classified

     M24.361 Pathological dislocation of right knee, not elsewhere classified

     M24.362 Pathological dislocation of left knee, not elsewhere classified

     M24.369 Pathological dislocation of unspecified knee, not elsewhere classified

● **M24.37** Pathological dislocation of ankle and foot, not elsewhere classified

     M24.371 Pathological dislocation of right ankle, not elsewhere classified

     M24.372 Pathological dislocation of left ankle, not elsewhere classified

     M24.373 Pathological dislocation of unspecified ankle, not elsewhere classified

     M24.374 Pathological dislocation of right foot, not elsewhere classified

     M24.375 Pathological dislocation of left foot, not elsewhere classified

     M24.376 Pathological dislocation of unspecified foot, not elsewhere classified

▶ **M24.39** Pathological dislocation of other specified joint, not elsewhere classified

● **M24.4** **Recurrent dislocation of joint**

     Recurrent subluxation of joint

     Excludes2   recurrent dislocation of patella (M22.0-M22.1)

                 recurrent vertebral dislocation (M43.3-, M43.4, M43.5-)

     M24.40 Recurrent dislocation, unspecified joint

● **M24.41** Recurrent dislocation, shoulder

     M24.411 Recurrent dislocation, right shoulder

     M24.412 Recurrent dislocation, left shoulder

     M24.419 Recurrent dislocation, unspecified shoulder

● **M24.42** Recurrent dislocation, elbow

     M24.421 Recurrent dislocation, right elbow

     M24.422 Recurrent dislocation, left elbow

     M24.429 Recurrent dislocation, unspecified elbow

● **M24.43** Recurrent dislocation, wrist

     M24.431 Recurrent dislocation, right wrist

     M24.432 Recurrent dislocation, left wrist

     M24.439 Recurrent dislocation, unspecified wrist

● **M24.44** Recurrent dislocation, hand and finger(s)

     M24.441 Recurrent dislocation, right hand

     M24.442 Recurrent dislocation, left hand

     M24.443 Recurrent dislocation, unspecified hand

     M24.444 Recurrent dislocation, right finger

     M24.445 Recurrent dislocation, left finger

     M24.446 Recurrent dislocation, unspecified finger

● **M24.45** Recurrent dislocation, hip

     M24.451 Recurrent dislocation, right hip

     M24.452 Recurrent dislocation, left hip

     M24.459 Recurrent dislocation, unspecified hip

● **M24.46** Recurrent dislocation, knee

     M24.461 Recurrent dislocation, right knee

     M24.462 Recurrent dislocation, left knee

     M24.469 Recurrent dislocation, unspecified knee

● **M24.47** Recurrent dislocation, ankle, foot and toes

     M24.471 Recurrent dislocation, right ankle

     M24.472 Recurrent dislocation, left ankle

     M24.473 Recurrent dislocation, unspecified ankle

     M24.474 Recurrent dislocation, right foot

     M24.475 Recurrent dislocation, left foot

     M24.476 Recurrent dislocation, unspecified foot

     M24.477 Recurrent dislocation, right toe(s)

     M24.478 Recurrent dislocation, left toe(s)

     M24.479 Recurrent dislocation, unspecified toe(s)

▶ **M24.49** Recurrent dislocation, other specified joint

● **M24.5** **Contracture of joint**

     Excludes1   contracture of muscle without contracture of joint (M62.4-)

                 contracture of tendon (sheath) without contracture of joint (M62.4-)

                 Dupuytren's contracture (M72.0)

     Excludes2   acquired deformities of limbs (M20-M21)

     M24.50 Contracture, unspecified joint

● **M24.51** Contracture, shoulder

     M24.511 Contracture, right shoulder

     M24.512 Contracture, left shoulder

     M24.519 Contracture, unspecified shoulder

● **M24.52** Contracture, elbow

     M24.521 Contracture, right elbow

     M24.522 Contracture, left elbow

     M24.529 Contracture, unspecified elbow

● **M24.53** Contracture, wrist

     M24.531 Contracture, right wrist

     M24.532 Contracture, left wrist

     M24.539 Contracture, unspecified wrist

● **M24.54** Contracture, hand

     M24.541 Contracture, right hand

     M24.542 Contracture, left hand

     M24.549 Contracture, unspecified hand

● **M24.55** Contracture, hip

     M24.551 Contracture, right hip

         Coding Clinic: 2016, Q2, P6

     M24.552 Contracture, left hip

         Coding Clinic: 2016, Q2, P6

     M24.559 Contracture, unspecified hip

Item 13-5   **Ankylosis** or arthrokleisis is a consolidation of a joint due to disease, injury, or surgical procedure. Spondylosis is the degeneration of the vertebral processes and formation of osteophytes and commonly occurs with age. **Spondylitis** or ankylosing spondylitis is a type of arthritis that affects the spine or backbone, causing back pain and stiffness.

● **M24.56**   Contracture, knee

     M24.561   Contracture, right knee
          Coding Clinic: 2016, Q2, P6

     M24.562   Contracture, left knee
          Coding Clinic: 2016, Q2, P6

     M24.569   Contracture, unspecified knee

● **M24.57**   Contracture, ankle and foot

     M24.571   Contracture, right ankle

     M24.572   Contracture, left ankle

     M24.573   Contracture, unspecified ankle

     M24.574   Contracture, right foot

     M24.575   Contracture, left foot

     M24.576   Contracture, unspecified foot

▶ M24.59   Contracture, other specified joint

● **M24.6**   Ankylosis of joint

     Excludes1   stiffness of joint without ankylosis (M25.6-)

     Excludes2   spine (M43.2-)

     M24.60   Ankylosis, unspecified joint

● **M24.61**   Ankylosis, shoulder

     M24.611   Ankylosis, right shoulder

     M24.612   Ankylosis, left shoulder

     M24.619   Ankylosis, unspecified shoulder

● **M24.62**   Ankylosis, elbow

     M24.621   Ankylosis, right elbow

     M24.622   Ankylosis, left elbow

     M24.629   Ankylosis, unspecified elbow

● **M24.63**   Ankylosis, wrist

     M24.631   Ankylosis, right wrist

     M24.632   Ankylosis, left wrist

     M24.639   Ankylosis, unspecified wrist

● **M24.64**   Ankylosis, hand

     M24.641   Ankylosis, right hand

     M24.642   Ankylosis, left hand

     M24.649   Ankylosis, unspecified hand

● **M24.65**   Ankylosis, hip

     M24.651   Ankylosis, right hip

     M24.652   Ankylosis, left hip

     M24.659   Ankylosis, unspecified hip

● **M24.66**   Ankylosis, knee

     M24.661   Ankylosis, right knee

     M24.662   Ankylosis, left knee

     M24.669   Ankylosis, unspecified knee

● **M24.67**   Ankylosis, ankle and foot

     M24.671   Ankylosis, right ankle

     M24.672   Ankylosis, left ankle

     M24.673   Ankylosis, unspecified ankle

     M24.674   Ankylosis, right foot

     M24.675   Ankylosis, left foot

     M24.676   Ankylosis, unspecified foot

▶ M24.69   Ankylosis, other specified joint

M24.7   Protrusio acetabuli

● **M24.8**   Other specific joint derangements, not elsewhere classified

     Excludes2   iliotibial band syndrome (M76.3)

     M24.80   Other specific joint derangements of unspecified joint, not elsewhere classified

● **M24.81**   Other specific joint derangements of shoulder, not elsewhere classified

     M24.811   Other specific joint derangements of right shoulder, not elsewhere classified

     M24.812   Other specific joint derangements of left shoulder, not elsewhere classified

     M24.819   Other specific joint derangements of unspecified shoulder, not elsewhere classified

● **M24.82**   Other specific joint derangements of elbow, not elsewhere classified

     M24.821   Other specific joint derangements of right elbow, not elsewhere classified

     M24.822   Other specific joint derangements of left elbow, not elsewhere classified

     M24.829   Other specific joint derangements of unspecified elbow, not elsewhere classified

● **M24.83**   Other specific joint derangements of wrist, not elsewhere classified

     M24.831   Other specific joint derangements of right wrist, not elsewhere classified

     M24.832   Other specific joint derangements of left wrist, not elsewhere classified

     M24.839   Other specific joint derangements of unspecified wrist, not elsewhere classified

● **M24.84**   Other specific joint derangements of hand, not elsewhere classified

     M24.841   Other specific joint derangements of right hand, not elsewhere classified

     M24.842   Other specific joint derangements of left hand, not elsewhere classified

     M24.849   Other specific joint derangements of unspecified hand, not elsewhere classified

● **M24.85**   Other specific joint derangements of hip, not elsewhere classified

     Irritable hip

     M24.851   Other specific joint derangements of right hip, not elsewhere classified

     M24.852   Other specific joint derangements of left hip, not elsewhere classified

     M24.859   Other specific joint derangements of unspecified hip, not elsewhere classified

● **M24.87**   Other specific joint derangements of ankle and foot, not elsewhere classified

     M24.871   Other specific joint derangements of right ankle, not elsewhere classified

     M24.872   Other specific joint derangements of left ankle, not elsewhere classified

     M24.873   Other specific joint derangements of unspecified ankle, not elsewhere classified

     M24.874   Other specific joint derangements of right foot, not elsewhere classified

     M24.875   Other specific joint derangements left foot, not elsewhere classified

     M24.876   Other specific joint derangements of unspecified foot, not elsewhere classified

▶ M24.89   Other specific joint derangement of other specified joint, not elsewhere classified

M24.9   Joint derangement, unspecified

▶ New   ⟹ Revised   ~~deleted~~ Deleted   Excludes 1   Excludes 2   Includes   Use additional   Code first   Code also   Key words

OGCR Official Guidelines   X Assign placeholder X   ● Use Additional Character(s)   ▷ Manifestation Code   🇶 Hierarchical Condition Category   **Coding Clinic**

● **M25   Other joint disorder, not elsewhere classified**

     Excludes2   abnormality of gait and mobility (R26.-)
                  acquired deformities of limb (M20-M21)
                  calcification of bursa (M71.4-)
                  calcification of shoulder (joint) (M75.3)
                  calcification of tendon (M65.2-)
                  difficulty in walking (R26.2)
                  temporomandibular joint disorder (M26.6-)

● **M25.0   Hemarthrosis**

     Excludes1   current injury - see injury of joint by body
                  region
                  hemophilic arthropathy (M36.2)

    M25.00   Hemarthrosis, unspecified joint

    ● M25.01   Hemarthrosis, shoulder
       M25.011   Hemarthrosis, right shoulder
       M25.012   Hemarthrosis, left shoulder
       M25.019   Hemarthrosis, unspecified shoulder

    ● M25.02   Hemarthrosis, elbow
       M25.021   Hemarthrosis, right elbow
       M25.022   Hemarthrosis, left elbow
       M25.029   Hemarthrosis, unspecified elbow

    ● M25.03   Hemarthrosis, wrist
       M25.031   Hemarthrosis, right wrist
       M25.032   Hemarthrosis, left wrist
       M25.039   Hemarthrosis, unspecified wrist

    ● M25.04   Hemarthrosis, hand
       M25.041   Hemarthrosis, right hand
       M25.042   Hemarthrosis, left hand
       M25.049   Hemarthrosis, unspecified hand

    ● M25.05   Hemarthrosis, hip
       M25.051   Hemarthrosis, right hip
       M25.052   Hemarthrosis, left hip
       M25.059   Hemarthrosis, unspecified hip

    ● M25.06   Hemarthrosis, knee
       M25.061   Hemarthrosis, right knee
       M25.062   Hemarthrosis, left knee
       M25.069   Hemarthrosis, unspecified knee

    ● M25.07   Hemarthrosis, ankle and foot
       M25.071   Hemarthrosis, right ankle
       M25.072   Hemarthrosis, left ankle
       M25.073   Hemarthrosis, unspecified ankle
       M25.074   Hemarthrosis, right foot
       M25.075   Hemarthrosis, left foot
       M25.076   Hemarthrosis, unspecified foot

    M25.08   Hemarthrosis, other specified site
          Hemarthrosis, vertebrae

● **M25.1   Fistula of joint**

    M25.10   Fistula, unspecified joint

    ● M25.11   Fistula, shoulder
       M25.111   Fistula, right shoulder
       M25.112   Fistula, left shoulder
       M25.119   Fistula, unspecified shoulder

    ● M25.12   Fistula, elbow
       M25.121   Fistula, right elbow
       M25.122   Fistula, left elbow
       M25.129   Fistula, unspecified elbow

    ● M25.13   Fistula, wrist
       M25.131   Fistula, right wrist
       M25.132   Fistula, left wrist
       M25.139   Fistula, unspecified wrist

    ● M25.14   Fistula, hand
       M25.141   Fistula, right hand
       M25.142   Fistula, left hand
       M25.149   Fistula, unspecified hand

    ● M25.15   Fistula, hip
       M25.151   Fistula, right hip
       M25.152   Fistula, left hip
       M25.159   Fistula, unspecified hip

    ● M25.16   Fistula, knee
       M25.161   Fistula, right knee
       M25.162   Fistula, left knee
       M25.169   Fistula, unspecified knee

    ● M25.17   Fistula, ankle and foot
       M25.171   Fistula, right ankle
       M25.172   Fistula, left ankle
       M25.173   Fistula, unspecified ankle
       M25.174   Fistula, right foot
       M25.175   Fistula, left foot
       M25.176   Fistula, unspecified foot

    M25.18   Fistula, other specified site
          Fistula, vertebrae

● **M25.2   Flail joint**

    M25.20   Flail joint, unspecified joint

    ● M25.21   Flail joint, shoulder
       M25.211   Flail joint, right shoulder
       M25.212   Flail joint, left shoulder
       M25.219   Flail joint, unspecified shoulder

    ● M25.22   Flail joint, elbow
       M25.221   Flail joint, right elbow
       M25.222   Flail joint, left elbow
       M25.229   Flail joint, unspecified elbow

    ● M25.23   Flail joint, wrist
       M25.231   Flail joint, right wrist
       M25.232   Flail joint, left wrist
       M25.239   Flail joint, unspecified wrist

    ● M25.24   Flail joint, hand
       M25.241   Flail joint, right hand
       M25.242   Flail joint, left hand
       M25.249   Flail joint, unspecified hand

    ● M25.25   Flail joint, hip
       M25.251   Flail joint, right hip
       M25.252   Flail joint, left hip
       M25.259   Flail joint, unspecified hip

    ● M25.26   Flail joint, knee
       M25.261   Flail joint, right knee
       M25.262   Flail joint, left knee
       M25.269   Flail joint, unspecified knee

    ● M25.27   Flail joint, ankle and foot
       M25.271   Flail joint, right ankle and foot
       M25.272   Flail joint, left ankle and foot
       M25.279   Flail joint, unspecified ankle and foot

    M25.28   Flail joint, other site

● **M25.3   Other instability of joint**

     Excludes1   instability of joint secondary to old
                  ligament injury (M24.2-)
                  instability of joint secondary to removal
                  of joint prosthesis (M96.8-)

     Excludes2   spinal instabilities (M53.2-)

    M25.30   Other instability, unspecified joint

    ● M25.31   Other instability, shoulder
       M25.311   Other instability, right shoulder
       M25.312   Other instability, left shoulder
       M25.319   Other instability, unspecified
                shoulder

    ● M25.32   Other instability, elbow
       M25.321   Other instability, right elbow
       M25.322   Other instability, left elbow
       M25.329   Other instability, unspecified elbow

M25.33 Other instability, wrist
    M25.331 Other instability, right wrist
    M25.332 Other instability, left wrist
    M25.339 Other instability, unspecified wrist
M25.34 Other instability, hand
    M25.341 Other instability, right hand
    M25.342 Other instability, left hand
    M25.349 Other instability, unspecified hand
M25.35 Other instability, hip
    M25.351 Other instability, right hip
    M25.352 Other instability, left hip
    M25.359 Other instability, unspecified hip
M25.36 Other instability, knee
    M25.361 Other instability, right knee
    M25.362 Other instability, left knee
    M25.369 Other instability, unspecified knee
M25.37 Other instability, ankle and foot
    M25.371 Other instability, right ankle
    M25.372 Other instability, left ankle
    M25.373 Other instability, unspecified ankle
    M25.374 Other instability, right foot
    M25.375 Other instability, left foot
    M25.376 Other instability, unspecified foot
▶ M25.39 Other instability of joint
M25.4 Effusion of joint
    Excludes1 hydrarthrosis in yaws (A66.6)
               intermittent hydrarthrosis (M12.4-)
               other infective (teno)synovitis (M65.1-)
  M25.40 Effusion, unspecified joint
M25.41 Effusion, shoulder
    M25.411 Effusion, right shoulder
    M25.412 Effusion, left shoulder
    M25.419 Effusion, unspecified shoulder
M25.42 Effusion, elbow
    M25.421 Effusion, right elbow
    M25.422 Effusion, left elbow
    M25.429 Effusion, unspecified elbow
M25.43 Effusion, wrist
    M25.431 Effusion, right wrist
    M25.432 Effusion, left wrist
    M25.439 Effusion, unspecified wrist
M25.44 Effusion, hand
    M25.441 Effusion, right hand
    M25.442 Effusion, left hand
    M25.449 Effusion, unspecified hand
M25.45 Effusion, hip
    M25.451 Effusion, right hip
    M25.452 Effusion, left hip
    M25.459 Effusion, unspecified hip
M25.46 Effusion, knee
    M25.461 Effusion, right knee
    M25.462 Effusion, left knee
    M25.469 Effusion, unspecified knee
M25.47 Effusion, ankle and foot
    M25.471 Effusion, right ankle
    M25.472 Effusion, left ankle
    M25.473 Effusion, unspecified ankle
    M25.474 Effusion, right foot
    M25.475 Effusion, left foot
    M25.476 Effusion, unspecified foot
  M25.48 Effusion, other site

M25.5 Pain in joint
    Excludes2 pain in hand (M79.64-)
               pain in fingers (M79.64-)
               pain in foot (M79.67-)
               pain in limb (M79.6-)
               pain in toes (M79.67-)
  M25.50 Pain in unspecified joint
M25.51 Pain in shoulder
    M25.511 Pain in right shoulder
    M25.512 Pain in left shoulder
    M25.519 Pain in unspecified shoulder
M25.52 Pain in elbow
    M25.521 Pain in right elbow
    M25.522 Pain in left elbow
    M25.529 Pain in unspecified elbow
M25.53 Pain in wrist
    M25.531 Pain in right wrist
    M25.532 Pain in left wrist
    M25.539 Pain in unspecified wrist
M25.54 Pain in joints of hand
    Coding Clinic: 2016, Q4, P38
    M25.541 Pain in joints of right hand
    M25.542 Pain in joints of left hand
    M25.549 Pain in joints of unspecified hand
             Pain in joints of hand NOS
M25.55 Pain in hip
    M25.551 Pain in right hip
    M25.552 Pain in left hip
    M25.559 Pain in unspecified hip
M25.56 Pain in knee
    M25.561 Pain in right knee
    M25.562 Pain in left knee
    M25.569 Pain in unspecified knee
M25.57 Pain in ankle and joints of foot
    M25.571 Pain in right ankle and joints of right foot
    M25.572 Pain in left ankle and joints of left foot
    M25.579 Pain in unspecified ankle and joints of unspecified foot
▶ M25.59 Pain in other specified joint
M25.6 Stiffness of joint, not elsewhere classified
    Excludes1 ankylosis of joint (M24.6-)
               contracture of joint (M24.5-)
  M25.60 Stiffness of unspecified joint, not elsewhere classified
M25.61 Stiffness of shoulder, not elsewhere classified
    M25.611 Stiffness of right shoulder, not elsewhere classified
    M25.612 Stiffness of left shoulder, not elsewhere classified
    M25.619 Stiffness of unspecified shoulder, not elsewhere classified
M25.62 Stiffness of elbow, not elsewhere classified
    M25.621 Stiffness of right elbow, not elsewhere classified
    M25.622 Stiffness of left elbow, not elsewhere classified
    M25.629 Stiffness of unspecified elbow, not elsewhere classified
M25.63 Stiffness of wrist, not elsewhere classified
    M25.631 Stiffness of right wrist, not elsewhere classified
    M25.632 Stiffness of left wrist, not elsewhere classified
    M25.639 Stiffness of unspecified wrist, not elsewhere classified

▶ New ⇒ Revised ~~deleted~~ Deleted Excludes 1 Excludes 2 Includes Use additional Code first Code also Key words
OGCR Official Guidelines X Assign placeholder X ● Use Additional Character(s) ▌ Manifestation Code 🔖 Hierarchical Condition Category Coding Clinic

● M25.64　Stiffness of hand, not elsewhere classified
　　　M25.641　Stiffness of right hand, not elsewhere classified
　　　M25.642　Stiffness of left hand, not elsewhere classified
　　　M25.649　Stiffness of unspecified hand, not elsewhere classified
● M25.65　Stiffness of hip, not elsewhere classified
　　　M25.651　Stiffness of right hip, not elsewhere classified
　　　M25.652　Stiffness of left hip, not elsewhere classified
　　　M25.659　Stiffness of unspecified hip, not elsewhere classified
● M25.66　Stiffness of knee, not elsewhere classified
　　　M25.661　Stiffness of right knee, not elsewhere classified
　　　M25.662　Stiffness of left knee, not elsewhere classified
　　　M25.669　Stiffness of unspecified knee, not elsewhere classified
● M25.67　Stiffness of ankle and foot, not elsewhere classified
　　　M25.671　Stiffness of right ankle, not elsewhere classified
　　　M25.672　Stiffness of left ankle, not elsewhere classified
　　　M25.673　Stiffness of unspecified ankle, not elsewhere classified
　　　M25.674　Stiffness of right foot, not elsewhere classified
　　　M25.675　Stiffness of left foot, not elsewhere classified
　　　M25.676　Stiffness of unspecified foot, not elsewhere classified
▶ M25.69　Stiffness of other specified joint, not elsewhere classified
● M25.7　Osteophyte
　　　M25.70　Osteophyte, unspecified joint
● M25.71　Osteophyte, shoulder
　　　M25.711　Osteophyte, right shoulder
　　　M25.712　Osteophyte, left shoulder
　　　M25.719　Osteophyte, unspecified shoulder
● M25.72　Osteophyte, elbow
　　　M25.721　Osteophyte, right elbow
　　　M25.722　Osteophyte, left elbow
　　　M25.729　Osteophyte, unspecified elbow
● M25.73　Osteophyte, wrist
　　　M25.731　Osteophyte, right wrist
　　　M25.732　Osteophyte, left wrist
　　　M25.739　Osteophyte, unspecified wrist
● M25.74　Osteophyte, hand
　　　M25.741　Osteophyte, right hand
　　　M25.742　Osteophyte, left hand
　　　M25.749　Osteophyte, unspecified hand
● M25.75　Osteophyte, hip
　　　M25.751　Osteophyte, right hip
　　　M25.752　Osteophyte, left hip
　　　M25.759　Osteophyte, unspecified hip
● M25.76　Osteophyte, knee
　　　M25.761　Osteophyte, right knee
　　　M25.762　Osteophyte, left knee
　　　M25.769　Osteophyte, unspecified knee

● M25.77　Osteophyte, ankle and foot
　　　M25.771　Osteophyte, right ankle
　　　M25.772　Osteophyte, left ankle
　　　M25.773　Osteophyte, unspecified ankle
　　　M25.774　Osteophyte, right foot
　　　M25.775　Osteophyte, left foot
　　　M25.776　Osteophyte, unspecified foot
　　　M25.78　Osteophyte, vertebrae
● M25.8　Other specified joint disorders
　　　M25.80　Other specified joint disorders, unspecified joint
● M25.81　Other specified joint disorders, shoulder
　　　M25.811　Other specified joint disorders, right shoulder
　　　M25.812　Other specified joint disorders, left shoulder
　　　M25.819　Other specified joint disorders, unspecified shoulder
● M25.82　Other specified joint disorders, elbow
　　　M25.821　Other specified joint disorders, right elbow
　　　M25.822　Other specified joint disorders, left elbow
　　　M25.829　Other specified joint disorders, unspecified elbow
● M25.83　Other specified joint disorders, wrist
　　　M25.831　Other specified joint disorders, right wrist
　　　M25.832　Other specified joint disorders, left wrist
　　　M25.839　Other specified joint disorders, unspecified wrist
● M25.84　Other specified joint disorders, hand
　　　M25.841　Other specified joint disorders, right hand
　　　M25.842　Other specified joint disorders, left hand
　　　M25.849　Other specified joint disorders, unspecified hand
● M25.85　Other specified joint disorders, hip
　　　M25.851　Other specified joint disorders, right hip
　　　M25.852　Other specified joint disorders, left hip
　　　M25.859　Other specified joint disorders, unspecified hip
● M25.86　Other specified joint disorders, knee
　　　M25.861　Other specified joint disorders, right knee
　　　M25.862　Other specified joint disorders, left knee
　　　M25.869　Other specified joint disorders, unspecified knee
● M25.87　Other specified joint disorders, ankle and foot
　　　M25.871　Other specified joint disorders, right ankle and foot
　　　M25.872　Other specified joint disorders, left ankle and foot
　　　M25.879　Other specified joint disorders, unspecified ankle and foot
　　M25.9　Joint disorder, unspecified

Figure 13-3   Dentofacial malocclusion.

Item 13–6 **Hyperplasia** is a condition of overdevelopment, whereas **hypoplasia** is a condition of underdevelopment. **Macrogenia** is overdevelopment of the chin, whereas **microgenia** is underdevelopment of the chin.

DENTOFACIAL ANOMALIES [INCLUDING MALOCCLUSION] AND OTHER DISORDERS OF JAW (M26-M27)

> **Excludes1**   hemifacial atrophy or hypertrophy (Q67.4)
> unilateral condylar hyperplasia or hypoplasia (M27.8)

● **M26 Dentofacial anomalies [including malocclusion]**

● **M26.0 Major anomalies of jaw size**

> **Excludes1**   acromegaly (E22.0)
> Robin's syndrome (Q87.0)

M26.00 Unspecified anomaly of jaw size

M26.01 Maxillary hyperplasia

M26.02 Maxillary hypoplasia

M26.03 Mandibular hyperplasia

M26.04 Mandibular hypoplasia

M26.05 Macrogenia

M26.06 Microgenia

M26.07 Excessive tuberosity of jaw
Entire maxillary tuberosity

M26.09 Other specified anomalies of jaw size

● **M26.1 Anomalies of jaw-cranial base relationship**

M26.10 Unspecified anomaly of jaw-cranial base relationship

M26.11 Maxillary asymmetry

M26.12 Other jaw asymmetry

M26.19 Other specified anomalies of jaw-cranial base relationship
Coding Clinic: 2020, Q1, P21

● **M26.2 Anomalies of dental arch relationship**

M26.20 Unspecified anomaly of dental arch relationship

● **M26.21 Malocclusion, Angle's class**

M26.211 Malocclusion, Angle's class I
Neutro-occlusion

M26.212 Malocclusion, Angle's class II
Disto-occlusion Division I
Disto-occlusion Division II

M26.213 Malocclusion, Angle's class III
Mesio-occlusion

M26.219 Malocclusion, Angle's class, unspecified

● **M26.22 Open occlusal relationship**

M26.220 Open anterior occlusal relationship
Anterior open bite

M26.221 Open posterior occlusal relationship
Posterior open bite

M26.23 Excessive horizontal overlap
Excessive horizontal overjet

M26.24 Reverse articulation
Crossbite (anterior) (posterior)

M26.25 Anomalies of interarch distance

M26.29 Other anomalies of dental arch relationship
Midline deviation of dental arch
Overbite (excessive) deep
Overbite (excessive) horizontal
Overbite (excessive) vertical
Posterior lingual occlusion of mandibular teeth

● **M26.3 Anomalies of tooth position of fully erupted tooth or teeth**

> **Excludes2**   embedded and impacted teeth (K01.-)

M26.30 Unspecified anomaly of tooth position of fully erupted tooth or teeth
Abnormal spacing of fully erupted tooth or teeth NOS
Displacement of fully erupted tooth or teeth NOS
Transposition of fully erupted tooth or teeth NOS

M26.31 Crowding of fully erupted teeth

M26.32 Excessive spacing of fully erupted teeth
Diastema of fully erupted tooth or teeth NOS

M26.33 Horizontal displacement of fully erupted tooth or teeth
Tipped tooth or teeth
Tipping of fully erupted tooth

M26.34 Vertical displacement of fully erupted tooth or teeth
Extruded tooth
Infraeruption of tooth or teeth
Supraeruption of tooth or teeth

M26.35 Rotation of fully erupted tooth or teeth

M26.36 Insufficient interocclusal distance of fully erupted teeth (ridge)
Lack of adequate intermaxillary vertical dimension of fully erupted teeth

M26.37 Excessive interocclusal distance of fully erupted teeth
Excessive intermaxillary vertical dimension of fully erupted teeth
Loss of occlusal vertical dimension of fully erupted teeth

M26.39 Other anomalies of tooth position of fully erupted tooth or teeth

M26.4 Malocclusion, unspecified

● **M26.5 Dentofacial functional abnormalities**

> **Excludes1**   bruxism (F45.8)
> teeth-grinding NOS (F45.8)

M26.50 Dentofacial functional abnormalities, unspecified

M26.51 Abnormal jaw closure

M26.52 Limited mandibular range of motion

M26.53 Deviation in opening and closing of the mandible

M26.54 Insufficient anterior guidance
Insufficient anterior occlusal guidance

M26.55 Centric occlusion maximum intercuspation discrepancy

> **Excludes1**   centric occlusion NOS (M26.59)

M26.56 Non-working side interference
Balancing side interference

M26.57 Lack of posterior occlusal support

M26.59 Other dentofacial functional abnormalities
Centric occlusion (of teeth) NOS
Malocclusion due to abnormal swallowing
Malocclusion due to mouth breathing
Malocclusion due to tongue, lip or finger habits

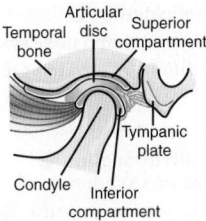

Figure 13-4   Temporomandibular joint.

Item 13–7 Dysfunction of the temporomandibular joint is termed **temporomandibular joint (TMJ) syndrome** and is characterized by pain and tenderness/spasm of the muscles of mastication, joint noise, and in the later stages, limited mandibular movement.

● **M26.6   Temporomandibular joint disorders**

     Excludes2   current temporomandibular joint
                      dislocation (S03.0)
                    current temporomandibular joint sprain
                      (S03.4)

     Coding Clinic: 2016, Q4, P38-39

     ● **M26.60   Temporomandibular joint disorder, unspecified**

         M26.601   **Right** temporomandibular joint disorder, unspecified

         M26.602   **Left** temporomandibular joint disorder, unspecified

         M26.603   **Bilateral** temporomandibular joint disorder, unspecified

         M26.609   **Unspecified** temporomandibular joint disorder, unspecified side
                   Temporomandibular joint disorder NOS

     ● **M26.61   Adhesions and ankylosis of temporomandibular joint**

         M26.611   **Adhesions and ankylosis of right** temporomandibular joint

         M26.612   **Adhesions and ankylosis of left** temporomandibular joint

         M26.613   **Adhesions and ankylosis of bilateral** temporomandibular joint

         M26.619   **Adhesions and ankylosis of** temporomandibular joint, **unspecified side**

     ● **M26.62   Arthralgia of temporomandibular joint**

         M26.621   **Arthralgia of right** temporomandibular joint

         M26.622   **Arthralgia of left** temporomandibular joint

         M26.623   **Arthralgia of bilateral** temporomandibular joint

         M26.629   **Arthralgia of** temporomandibular joint, **unspecified side**

     ● **M26.63   Articular disc disorder of temporomandibular joint**

         M26.631   **Articular disc disorder of right** temporomandibular joint

         M26.632   **Articular disc disorder of left** temporomandibular joint

         M26.633   **Articular disc disorder of bilateral** temporomandibular joint

         M26.639   **Articular disc disorder of** temporomandibular joint, **unspecified side**

▶● **M26.64   Arthritis of temporomandibular joint**

     ▶ M26.641   **Arthritis of right temporomandibular joint**

     ▶ M26.642   **Arthritis of left temporomandibular joint**

     ▶ M26.643   **Arthritis of bilateral temporomandibular joint**

     ▶ M26.649   **Arthritis of unspecified temporomandibular joint**

▶● **M26.65   Arthropathy of temporomandibular joint**

     ▶ M26.651   **Arthropathy of right temporomandibular joint**

     ▶ M26.652   **Arthropathy of left temporomandibular joint**

     ▶ M26.653   **Arthropathy of bilateral temporomandibular joint**

     ▶ M26.659   **Arthropathy of unspecified temporomandibular joint**

     M26.69   **Other specified disorders of temporomandibular joint**

● **M26.7   Dental alveolar anomalies**

     M26.70   Unspecified alveolar anomaly

     M26.71   Alveolar maxillary hyperplasia

     M26.72   Alveolar mandibular hyperplasia

     M26.73   Alveolar maxillary hypoplasia

     M26.74   Alveolar mandibular hypoplasia

     M26.79   Other specified alveolar anomalies

● **M26.8   Other dentofacial anomalies**

     M26.81   **Anterior soft tissue impingement**
                 Anterior soft tissue impingement on teeth

     M26.82   **Posterior soft tissue impingement**
                 Posterior soft tissue impingement on teeth

     M26.89   **Other dentofacial anomalies**

     M26.9   Dentofacial anomaly, unspecified

● **M27   Other diseases of jaws**

     M27.0   **Developmental disorders of jaws**
              Latent bone cyst of jaw
              Stafne's cyst
              Torus mandibularis
              Torus palatinus

     M27.1   **Giant cell granuloma, central**
              Giant cell granuloma NOS

         Excludes1   peripheral giant cell granuloma (K06.8)

     M27.2   **Inflammatory conditions of jaws**
              Osteitis of jaw(s)
              Osteomyelitis (neonatal) jaw(s)
              Osteoradionecrosis jaw(s)
              Periostitis jaw(s)
              Sequestrum of jaw bone

         Use additional code (W88-W90, X39.0) to identify radiation, if radiation-induced

         Excludes2   osteonecrosis of jaw due to drug (M87.180)

     M27.3   **Alveolitis of jaws**
              Alveolar osteitis
              Dry socket

●   M27.4   **Other and unspecified cysts of jaw**

         Excludes1   cysts of oral region (K09.-)
                    latent bone cyst of jaw (M27.0)
                    Stafne's cyst (M27.0)

     M27.40   **Unspecified cyst of jaw**
                Cyst of jaw NOS

     M27.49   **Other cysts of jaw**
                Aneurysmal cyst of jaw
                Hemorrhagic cyst of jaw
                Traumatic cyst of jaw

- M27.5 **Periradicular pathology associated with previous endodontic treatment**
    - M27.51 Perforation of root canal space due to endodontic treatment
    - M27.52 Endodontic overfill
    - M27.53 Endodontic underfill
    - M27.59 Other periradicular pathology associated with previous endodontic treatment
- M27.6 **Endosseous dental implant failure**
    - M27.61 **Osseointegration failure of dental implant**
        - Hemorrhagic complications of dental implant placement
        - Iatrogenic osseointegration failure of dental implant
        - Osseointegration failure of dental implant due to complications of systemic disease
        - Osseointegration failure of dental implant due to poor bone quality
        - Pre-integration failure of dental implant NOS
        - Pre-osseointegration failure of dental implant
    - M27.62 **Post-osseointegration biological failure of dental implant**
        - Failure of dental implant due to lack of attached gingiva
        - Failure of dental implant due to occlusal trauma (caused by poor prosthetic design)
        - Failure of dental implant due to parafunctional habits
        - Failure of dental implant due to periodontal infection (peri mplantitis)
        - Failure of dental implant due to poor oral hygiene
        - Iatrogenic post-osseointegration failure of dental implant
        - Post-osseointegration failure of dental implant due to complications of systemic disease
    - M27.63 **Post-osseointegration mechanical failure of dental implant**
        - Failure of dental prosthesis causing loss of dental implant
        - Fracture of dental implant
        - **Excludes2** cracked tooth (K03.81)
            - fractured dental restorative material with loss of material (K08.531)
            - fractured dental restorative material without loss of material (K08.530)
            - fractured tooth (S02.5)
    - M27.69 **Other endosseous dental implant failure**
        - Dental implant failure NOS
- M27.8 **Other specified diseases of jaws**
    - Cherubism
    - Exostosis
    - Fibrous dysplasia
    - Unilateral condylar hyperplasia
    - Unilateral condylar hypoplasia
    - **Excludes1** jaw pain (R68.84)
- M27.9 **Disease of jaws, unspecified**

SYSTEMIC CONNECTIVE TISSUE DISORDERS (M30-M36)

Includes autoimmune disease NOS
collagen (vascular) disease NOS
systemic autoimmune disease
systemic collagen (vascular) disease

Excludes1 autoimmune disease, single organ or single cell-type - code to relevant condition category

- M30 **Polyarteritis nodosa and related conditions**
    - **Excludes1** microscopic polyarteritis (M31.7)
    - M30.0 **Polyarteritis nodosa** 🦠
    - M30.1 **Polyarteritis with lung involvement [Churg-Strauss]** 🦠
        - Allergic granulomatous angiitis
        - ▶Eosinophilic granulomatosis with polyangiitis [EGPA]

- M30.2 **Juvenile polyarteritis** 🦠
- M30.3 **Mucocutaneous lymph node syndrome [Kawasaki]** 🦠
- M30.8 **Other conditions related to polyarteritis nodosa** 🦠
    - Polyangiitis overlap syndrome
- M31 **Other necrotizing vasculopathies**
    - M31.0 **Hypersensitivity angiitis** 🦠
        - Goodpasture's syndrome
    - M31.1 **Thrombotic microangiopathy** 🦠
        - Thrombotic thrombocytopenic purpura
    - M31.2 **Lethal midline granuloma** 🦠
    - M31.3 **Wegener's granulomatosis**
        - ▶Granulomatosis with polyangiitis
        - Necrotizing respiratory granulomatosis
        - M31.30 **Wegener's granulomatosis without renal involvement** 🦠
            - Wegener's granulomatosis NOS
        - M31.31 **Wegener's granulomatosis with renal involvement** 🦠
    - M31.4 **Aortic arch syndrome [Takayasu]** 🦠
    - M31.5 **Giant cell arteritis with polymyalgia rheumatica** 🦠
    - M31.6 **Other giant cell arteritis** 🦠
    - M31.7 **Microscopic polyangiitis** 🦠
        - Microscopic polyarteritis
        - **Excludes1** polyarteritis nodosa (M30.0)
    - M31.8 **Other specified necrotizing vasculopathies** 🦠
        - Hypocomplementemic vasculitis
        - Septic vasculitis
    - M31.9 **Necrotizing vasculopathy, unspecified** 🦠
- M32 **Systemic lupus erythematosus (SLE)**
    - *Autoimmune inflammatory connective tissue disease of unknown cause that occurs most often in women*
    - **Excludes1** lupus erythematosus (discoid) (NOS) (L93.0)
    - M32.0 **Drug-induced systemic lupus erythematosus** 🦠
        - Use additional code for adverse effect, if applicable, to identify drug (T36-T50 with fifth or sixth character 5)
    - M32.1 **Systemic lupus erythematosus with organ or system involvement**
        - M32.10 **Systemic lupus erythematosus, organ or system involvement unspecified** 🦠
        - M32.11 **Endocarditis in systemic lupus erythematosus** 🦠
            - Libman-Sacks disease
        - M32.12 **Pericarditis in systemic lupus erythematosus** 🦠
            - Lupus pericarditis
        - M32.13 **Lung involvement in systemic lupus erythematosus** 🦠
            - Pleural effusion due to systemic lupus erythematosus
        - M32.14 **Glomerular disease in systemic lupus erythematosus** 🦠
            - Lupus renal disease NOS
        - M32.15 **Tubulo-interstitial nephropathy in systemic lupus erythematosus** 🦠
        - M32.19 **Other organ or system involvement in systemic lupus erythematosus** 🦠
    - M32.8 **Other forms of systemic lupus erythematosus** 🦠
    - M32.9 **Systemic lupus erythematosus, unspecified** 🦠
        - SLE NOS
        - Systemic lupus erythematosus NOS
        - Systemic lupus erythematosus without organ involvement

---

▶ New ⟱ Revised ~~deleted~~ Deleted Excludes 1 Excludes 2 Includes Use additional Code first Code also Key words

OGCR Official Guidelines X Assign placeholder X ● Use Additional Character(s) ▶ Manifestation Code 🦠 Hierarchical Condition Category **Coding Clinic**

● **M33　Dermatopolymyositis**
　● **M33.0　Juvenile dermatomyositis**
　　　M33.00　Juvenile dermatomyositis, organ involvement unspecified ⊘
　　　M33.01　Juvenile dermatomyositis with respiratory involvement ⊘
　　　M33.02　Juvenile dermatomyositis with myopathy ⊘
　　　M33.03　Juvenile dermatomyositis without myopathy ⊘
　　　M33.09　Juvenile dermatomyositis with other organ involvement ⊘
　● **M33.1　Other dermatomyositis**
　　　Adult dermatomyositis
　　　M33.10　Other dermatomyositis, organ involvement unspecified ⊘
　　　M33.11　Other dermatomyositis with respiratory involvement ⊘
　　　M33.12　Other dermatomyositis with myopathy ⊘
　　　M33.13　Other dermatomyositis without myopathy ⊘
　　　　　　Dermatomyositis NOS
　　　M33.19　Other dermatomyositis with other organ involvement ⊘
　● **M33.2　Polymyositis**
　　　M33.20　Polymyositis, organ involvement unspecified ⊘
　　　M33.21　Polymyositis with respiratory involvement ⊘
　　　M33.22　Polymyositis with myopathy ⊘
　　　M33.29　Polymyositis with other organ involvement ⊘
　● **M33.9　Dermatopolymyositis, unspecified**
　　　M33.90　Dermatopolymyositis, unspecified, organ involvement unspecified ⊘
　　　M33.91　Dermatopolymyositis, unspecified with respiratory involvement ⊘
　　　M33.92　Dermatopolymyositis, unspecified with myopathy ⊘
　　　M33.93　Dermatopolymyositis, unspecified without myopathy ⊘
　　　M33.99　Dermatopolymyositis, unspecified with other organ involvement ⊘

Item 13–8　Polymyalgia rheumatica is a syndrome characterized by aching and morning stiffness and is related to aging and hereditary predisposition.

● **M34　Systemic sclerosis [scleroderma]**
　　Excludes1　circumscribed scleroderma (L94.0)
　　　　　　　　　neonatal scleroderma (P83.88)
　　M34.0　Progressive systemic sclerosis ⊘
　　M34.1　CR(E)ST syndrome ⊘
　　　　　Combination of calcinosis, Raynaud's phenomenon, esophageal dysfunction, sclerodactyly, telangiectasia
　　M34.2　Systemic sclerosis induced by drug and chemical ⊘
　　　　　Code first poisoning due to drug or toxin, if applicable (T36-T65 with fifth or sixth character 1-4 or 6)
　　　　　Use additional code for adverse effect, if applicable, to identify drug (T36-T50 with fifth or sixth character 5)
　● **M34.8　Other forms of systemic sclerosis**
　　　M34.81　Systemic sclerosis with lung involvement ⊘
　　　M34.82　Systemic sclerosis with myopathy ⊘
　　　M34.83　Systemic sclerosis with polyneuropathy ⊘
　　　M34.89　Other systemic sclerosis ⊘
　　M34.9　Systemic sclerosis, unspecified ⊘

● **M35　Other systemic involvement of connective tissue**
　　Excludes1　reactive perforating collagenosis (L87.1)
　● **M35.0　Sicca syndrome [Sjögren]**
　　　M35.00　Sicca syndrome, unspecified ⊘
　　　M35.01　Sicca syndrome with keratoconjunctivitis ⊘
　　　M35.02　Sicca syndrome with lung involvement ⊘
　　　M35.03　Sicca syndrome with myopathy ⊘
　　　M35.04　Sicca syndrome with tubulo-interstitial nephropathy ⊘
　　　　　　Renal tubular acidosis in sicca syndrome
　　　M35.09　Sicca syndrome with other organ involvement ⊘
　　M35.1　Other overlap syndromes ⊘
　　　　　Mixed connective tissue disease
　　　　Excludes1　polyangiitis overlap syndrome (M30.8)
　　M35.2　Behçet's disease ⊘
　　M35.3　Polymyalgia rheumatica ⊘
　　　　Excludes1　polymyalgia rheumatica with giant cell arteritis (M31.5)
　　M35.4　Diffuse (eosinophilic) fasciitis
　　M35.5　Multifocal fibrosclerosis ⊘
　　M35.6　Relapsing panniculitis [Weber-Christian]
　　　　Excludes1　lupus panniculitis (L93.2)
　　　　　　　　　panniculitis NOS (M79.3-)
　　M35.7　Hypermobility syndrome
　　　　　Familial ligamentous laxity
　　　➠ **Excludes1**　Ehlers-Danlos syndromes (Q79.6-)
　　　　　　　　　ligamentous laxity, NOS (M24.2-)
　　M35.8　Other specified systemic involvement of connective tissue ⊘
　　M35.9　Systemic involvement of connective tissue, unspecified ⊘
　　　　　Autoimmune disease (systemic) NOS
　　　　　Collagen (vascular) disease NOS

● **M36　Systemic disorders of connective tissue in diseases classified elsewhere**
　　Excludes2　arthropathies in diseases classified elsewhere (M14.-)
　▶ **M36.0　*Dermato(poly)myositis in neoplastic disease* ⊘**
　　　　Code first underlying neoplasm (C00-D49)
　▶ **M36.1　*Arthropathy in neoplastic disease***
　　　　Code first underlying neoplasm, such as:
　　　　　leukemia (C91-C95)
　　　　　malignant histiocytosis (C96.A)
　　　　　multiple myeloma (C90.0)
　▶ **M36.2　*Hemophilic arthropathy***
　　　　Hemarthrosis in hemophilic arthropathy
　　　　Code first underlying disease, such as:
　　　　　factor VIII deficiency (D66)
　　　　　with vascular defect (D68.0)
　　　　　factor IX deficiency (D67)
　　　　　hemophilia (classical) (D66)
　　　　　hemophilia B (D67)
　　　　　hemophilia C (D68.1)
　▶ **M36.3　*Arthropathy in other blood disorders***
　▶ **M36.4　*Arthropathy in hypersensitivity reactions classified elsewhere***
　　　　Code first underlying disease, such as:
　　　　　Henoch (-Schönlein) purpura (D69.0)
　　　　　serum sickness (T80.6-)
　▶ **M36.8　*Systemic disorders of connective tissue in other diseases classified elsewhere* ⊘**
　　　　Code first underlying disease, such as:
　　　　　alkaptonuria (E70.2)
　　　　　hypogammaglobulinemia (D80.-)
　　　　　ochronosis (E70.2)

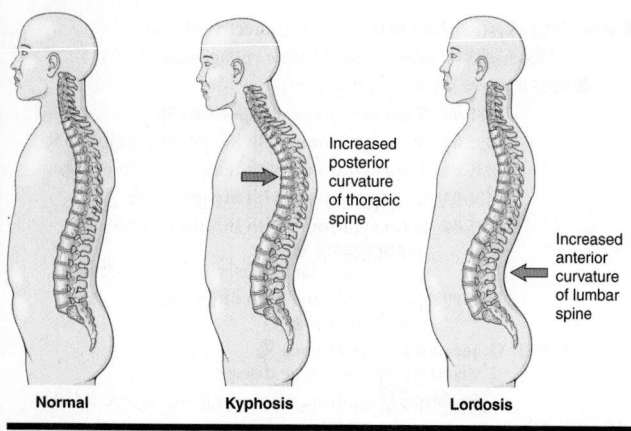

Figure 13-5   Kyphosis, Lordosis, Scoliosis. (From Chabner: The Language of Medicine, ed 8, St. Louis, Saunders, 2007)

Item 13–9 Kyphosis is an abnormal curvature of the spine. **Senile kyphosis** is a result of disc degeneration causing ossification (turning to bone). **Adolescent** or **juvenile** kyphosis is also known as **Scheuermann's disease,** a condition in which the discs of the lower thoracic spine herniate, causing the disc space to narrow and the spine to tilt forward. This condition is attributed to poor posture. **Lordosis or swayback** is an abnormal curvature of the spine resulting in an inward curve of the lumbar spine just above the buttocks. **Scoliosis** causes a sideways curve to the spine. The curves are S- or C-shaped, and it is most commonly acquired in late childhood and early teen years, when growth is fast.

DORSOPATHIES (M40-M54)

DEFORMING DORSOPATHIES (M40-M43)

● **M40 Kyphosis and lordosis**

    Excludes1   congenital kyphosis and lordosis (Q76.4)
                 kyphoscoliosis (M41.-)
                 postprocedural kyphosis and lordosis (M96.-)

 ● **M40.0 Postural kyphosis**

      Excludes1   osteochondrosis of spine (M42.-)

    M40.00 Postural kyphosis, site unspecified
    M40.03 Postural kyphosis, cervicothoracic region
    M40.04 Postural kyphosis, thoracic region
    M40.05 Postural kyphosis, thoracolumbar region

 ● **M40.1 Other secondary kyphosis**

    M40.10 Other secondary kyphosis, site unspecified
    M40.12 Other secondary kyphosis, cervical region
    M40.13 Other secondary kyphosis, cervicothoracic region
    M40.14 Other secondary kyphosis, thoracic region
    M40.15 Other secondary kyphosis, thoracolumbar region

 ● **M40.2 Other and unspecified kyphosis**

  ● **M40.20 Unspecified kyphosis**

     M40.202 Unspecified kyphosis, cervical region
     M40.203 Unspecified kyphosis, cervicothoracic region
     M40.204 Unspecified kyphosis, thoracic region
     M40.205 Unspecified kyphosis, thoracolumbar region
     M40.209 Unspecified kyphosis, site unspecified

  ● **M40.29 Other kyphosis**

     M40.292 Other kyphosis, cervical region
     M40.293 Other kyphosis, cervicothoracic region
     M40.294 Other kyphosis, thoracic region
     M40.295 Other kyphosis, thoracolumbar region
     M40.299 Other kyphosis, site unspecified

 ● **M40.3 Flatback syndrome**

    M40.30 Flatback syndrome, site unspecified
    M40.35 Flatback syndrome, thoracolumbar region
    M40.36 Flatback syndrome, lumbar region
    M40.37 Flatback syndrome, lumbosacral region

 ● **M40.4 Postural lordosis**

    Abnormal increase in the normal curvature of the lumbar spine (sway back)
    Acquired lordosis

    M40.40 Postural lordosis, site unspecified
    M40.45 Postural lordosis, thoracolumbar region
    M40.46 Postural lordosis, lumbar region
    M40.47 Postural lordosis, lumbosacral region

 ● **M40.5 Lordosis, unspecified**

    M40.50 Lordosis, unspecified, site unspecified
    M40.55 Lordosis, unspecified, thoracolumbar region
    M40.56 Lordosis, unspecified, lumbar region
    M40.57 Lordosis, unspecified, lumbosacral region

● **M41 Scoliosis**

   Includes   kyphoscoliosis

   Excludes1   congenital scoliosis NOS (Q67.5)
               congenital scoliosis due to bony malformation (Q76.3)
               postural congenital scoliosis (Q67.5)
               kyphoscoliotic heart disease (I27.1)
               postprocedural scoliosis (M96.-)

 ● **M41.0 Infantile idiopathic scoliosis**

    M41.00 Infantile idiopathic scoliosis, site unspecified
    M41.02 Infantile idiopathic scoliosis, cervical region
    M41.03 Infantile idiopathic scoliosis, cervicothoracic region
    M41.04 Infantile idiopathic scoliosis, thoracic region
    M41.05 Infantile idiopathic scoliosis, thoracolumbar region
    M41.06 Infantile idiopathic scoliosis, lumbar region
    M41.07 Infantile idiopathic scoliosis, lumbosacral region
    M41.08 Infantile idiopathic scoliosis, sacral and sacrococcygeal region

 ● **M41.1 Juvenile and adolescent idiopathic scoliosis**

  ● **M41.11 Juvenile idiopathic scoliosis**

     M41.112 Juvenile idiopathic scoliosis, cervical region
     M41.113 Juvenile idiopathic scoliosis, cervicothoracic region
     M41.114 Juvenile idiopathic scoliosis, thoracic region
     M41.115 Juvenile idiopathic scoliosis, thoracolumbar region
     M41.116 Juvenile idiopathic scoliosis, lumbar region
     M41.117 Juvenile idiopathic scoliosis, lumbosacral region
     M41.119 Juvenile idiopathic scoliosis, site unspecified

▶ New   ⇒ Revised   ~~deleted~~ Deleted   Excludes 1   Excludes 2   Includes   Use additional   Code first   Code also   Key words

OGCR Official Guidelines   X Assign placeholder X   ● Use Additional Character(s)   ▷ Manifestation Code   🅗🅒 Hierarchical Condition Category   **Coding Clinic**

●M41.12 **Adolescent scoliosis**
  M41.122 Adolescent idiopathic scoliosis, cervical region
  M41.123 Adolescent idiopathic scoliosis, cervicothoracic region
  M41.124 Adolescent idiopathic scoliosis, thoracic region
  M41.125 Adolescent idiopathic scoliosis, thoracolumbar region
  M41.126 Adolescent idiopathic scoliosis, lumbar region
  M41.127 Adolescent idiopathic scoliosis, lumbosacral region
  M41.129 Adolescent idiopathic scoliosis, site unspecified

●M41.2 **Other idiopathic scoliosis**
  M41.20 Other idiopathic scoliosis, site unspecified
  M41.22 Other idiopathic scoliosis, cervical region
  M41.23 Other idiopathic scoliosis, cervicothoracic region
  M41.24 Other idiopathic scoliosis, thoracic region
  M41.25 Other idiopathic scoliosis, thoracolumbar region
  M41.26 Other idiopathic scoliosis, lumbar region
  M41.27 Other idiopathic scoliosis, lumbosacral region

●M41.3 **Thoracogenic scoliosis**
  M41.30 Thoracogenic scoliosis, site unspecified
  M41.34 Thoracogenic scoliosis, thoracic region
  M41.35 Thoracogenic scoliosis, thoracolumbar region

●M41.4 **Neuromuscular scoliosis**
  Scoliosis secondary to cerebral palsy, Friedreich's ataxia, poliomyelitis and other neuromuscular disorders
  Code also underlying condition
  M41.40 Neuromuscular scoliosis, site unspecified
  M41.41 Neuromuscular scoliosis, occipito-atlanto-axial region
  M41.42 Neuromuscular scoliosis, cervical region
  M41.43 Neuromuscular scoliosis, cervicothoracic region
  M41.44 Neuromuscular scoliosis, thoracic region
  M41.45 Neuromuscular scoliosis, thoracolumbar region
  M41.46 Neuromuscular scoliosis, lumbar region
  M41.47 Neuromuscular scoliosis, lumbosacral region

●M41.5 **Other secondary scoliosis**
  Coding Clinic: 2019, Q1, P19
  M41.50 Other secondary scoliosis, site unspecified
  M41.52 Other secondary scoliosis, cervical region
  M41.53 Other secondary scoliosis, cervicothoracic region
  M41.54 Other secondary scoliosis, thoracic region
  M41.55 Other secondary scoliosis, thoracolumbar region
  M41.56 Other secondary scoliosis, lumbar region
  M41.57 Other secondary scoliosis, lumbosacral region

●M41.8 **Other forms of scoliosis**
  M41.80 Other forms of scoliosis, site unspecified
  M41.82 Other forms of scoliosis, cervical region
  M41.83 Other forms of scoliosis, cervicothoracic region
  M41.84 Other forms of scoliosis, thoracic region
  M41.85 Other forms of scoliosis, thoracolumbar region
  M41.86 Other forms of scoliosis, lumbar region
  M41.87 Other forms of scoliosis, lumbosacral region

 M41.9 Scoliosis, unspecified

●M42 **Spinal osteochondrosis**
●M42.0 **Juvenile osteochondrosis of spine**
  Calvé's disease
  Scheuermann's disease
  Excludes1 postural kyphosis (M40.0)
  M42.00 Juvenile osteochondrosis of spine, site unspecified
  M42.01 Juvenile osteochondrosis of spine, occipito-atlanto-axial region
  M42.02 Juvenile osteochondrosis of spine, cervical region
  M42.03 Juvenile osteochondrosis of spine, cervicothoracic region
  M42.04 Juvenile osteochondrosis of spine, thoracic region
  M42.05 Juvenile osteochondrosis of spine, thoracolumbar region
  M42.06 Juvenile osteochondrosis of spine, lumbar region
  M42.07 Juvenile osteochondrosis of spine, lumbosacral region
  M42.08 Juvenile osteochondrosis of spine, sacral and sacrococcygeal region
  M42.09 Juvenile osteochondrosis of spine, multiple sites in spine

●M42.1 **Adult osteochondrosis of spine**
  M42.10 Adult osteochondrosis of spine, site unspecified   A
  M42.11 Adult osteochondrosis of spine, occipitoatlanto-axial region   A
  M42.12 Adult osteochondrosis of spine, cervical region   A
  M42.13 Adult osteochondrosis of spine, cervicothoracic region   A
  M42.14 Adult osteochondrosis of spine, thoracic region   A
  M42.15 Adult osteochondrosis of spine, thoracolumbar region   A
  M42.16 Adult osteochondrosis of spine, lumbar region   A
  M42.17 Adult osteochondrosis of spine, lumbosacral region   A
  M42.18 Adult osteochondrosis of spine, sacral and sacrococcygeal region   A
  M42.19 Adult osteochondrosis of spine, multiple sites in spine   A

 M42.9 Spinal osteochondrosis, unspecified

●M43 **Other deforming dorsopathies**
  Excludes1 congenital spondylolysis and spondylolisthesis (Q76.2)
    hemivertebra (Q76.3-Q76.4)
    Klippel-Feil syndrome (Q76.1)
    lumbarization and sacralization (Q76.4)
    platyspondylisis (Q76.4)
    spina bifida occulta (Q76.0)
    spinal curvature in osteoporosis (M80.-)
    spinal curvature in Paget's disease of bone [osteitis deformans] (M88.-)

●M43.0 **Spondylolysis**
  Excludes1 congenital spondylolysis (Q76.2)
    spondylolisthesis (M43.1)
  M43.00 Spondylolysis, site unspecified
  M43.01 Spondylolysis, occipito-atlanto-axial region
  M43.02 Spondylolysis, cervical region
  M43.03 Spondylolysis, cervicothoracic region
  M43.04 Spondylolysis, thoracic region
  M43.05 Spondylolysis, thoracolumbar region

M43.06   Spondylolysis, lumbar region
M43.07   Spondylolysis, lumbosacral region
M43.08   Spondylolysis, sacral and sacrococcygeal region
M43.09   Spondylolysis, multiple sites in spine
● M43.1   Spondylolisthesis
     Excludes1   acute traumatic of lumbosacral region
                          (S33.1)
                     acute traumatic of sites other than
                          lumbosacral - code to Fracture,
                          vertebra, by region
                     congenital spondylolisthesis (Q76.2)

M43.10   Spondylolisthesis, site unspecified
M43.11   Spondylolisthesis, occipito-atlanto-axial region
M43.12   Spondylolisthesis, cervical region
M43.13   Spondylolisthesis, cervicothoracic region
M43.14   Spondylolisthesis, thoracic region
M43.15   Spondylolisthesis, thoracolumbar region
M43.16   Spondylolisthesis, lumbar region
M43.17   Spondylolisthesis, lumbosacral region
M43.18   Spondylolisthesis, sacral and sacrococcygeal
         region
M43.19   Spondylolisthesis, multiple sites in spine

Item 13-10 **Spondylolisthesis** is a condition caused by the slipping forward of one disc over another.

● M43.2   Fusion of spine
          Ankylosis of spinal joint
     Excludes1   ankylosing spondylitis (M45.0-)
                     congenital fusion of spine (Q76.4)
     Excludes2   arthrodesis status (Z98.1)
                     pseudoarthrosis after fusion or
                          arthrodesis (M96.0)
M43.20   Fusion of spine, site unspecified
M43.21   Fusion of spine, occipito-atlanto-axial region
M43.22   Fusion of spine, cervical region
M43.23   Fusion of spine, cervicothoracic region
M43.24   Fusion of spine, thoracic region
M43.25   Fusion of spine, thoracolumbar region
M43.26   Fusion of spine, lumbar region
M43.27   Fusion of spine, lumbosacral region
M43.28   Fusion of spine, sacral and sacrococcygeal region
M43.3   Recurrent atlantoaxial dislocation with myelopathy
M43.4   Other recurrent atlantoaxial dislocation
● M43.5   Other recurrent vertebral dislocation
     Excludes1   biomechanical lesions NEC (M99.-)
     ● M43.5X   Other recurrent vertebral dislocation
          M43.5X2   Other recurrent vertebral dislocation,
                    cervical region
          M43.5X3   Other recurrent vertebral dislocation,
                    cervicothoracic region
          M43.5X4   Other recurrent vertebral dislocation,
                    thoracic region
          M43.5X5   Other recurrent vertebral dislocation,
                    thoracolumbar region
          M43.5X6   Other recurrent vertebral dislocation,
                    lumbar region
          M43.5X7   Other recurrent vertebral dislocation,
                    lumbosacral region
          M43.5X8   Other recurrent vertebral dislocation,
                    sacral and sacrococcygeal region
          M43.5X9   Other recurrent vertebral dislocation,
                    site unspecified

M43.6   Torticollis
     Excludes1   congenital (sternomastoid) torticollis
                          (Q68.0)
                     current injury - see Injury, of spine, by body
                          region ocular torticollis (R29.891)
                     psychogenic torticollis (F45.8)
                     spasmodic torticollis (G24.3)
                     torticollis due to birth injury (P15.2)
● M43.8   Other specified deforming dorsopathies
     Excludes2   kyphosis and lordosis (M40.-)
                     scoliosis (M41.-)
     ● M43.8X   Other specified deforming dorsopathies
          M43.8X1   Other specified deforming
                    dorsopathies, occipito-atlanto-axial
                    region
          M43.8X2   Other specified deforming
                    dorsopathies, cervical region
          M43.8X3   Other specified deforming
                    dorsopathies, cervicothoracic region
          M43.8X4   Other specified deforming
                    dorsopathies, thoracic region
          M43.8X5   Other specified deforming
                    dorsopathies, thoracolumbar region
          M43.8X6   Other specified deforming
                    dorsopathies, lumbar region
          M43.8X7   Other specified deforming
                    dorsopathies, lumbosacral region
          M43.8X8   Other specified deforming
                    dorsopathies, sacral and
                    sacrococcygeal region
          M43.8X9   Other specified deforming
                    dorsopathies, site unspecified
M43.9   Deforming dorsopathy, unspecified
        Curvature of spine NOS

SPONDYLOPATHIES (M45-M49)

● M45   Ankylosing spondylitis
        Rheumatoid arthritis of spine
     Excludes1   arthropathy in Reiter's disease (M02.3-)
                     juvenile (ankylosing) spondylitis (M08.1)
     Excludes2   Behçet's disease (M35.2)
M45.0   Ankylosing spondylitis of multiple sites in spine ℞
M45.1   Ankylosing spondylitis of occipito-atlanto-axial
        region ℞
M45.2   Ankylosing spondylitis of cervical region ℞
M45.3   Ankylosing spondylitis of cervicothoracic region ℞
M45.4   Ankylosing spondylitis of thoracic region ℞
M45.5   Ankylosing spondylitis of thoracolumbar region ℞
M45.6   Ankylosing spondylitis lumbar region ℞
M45.7   Ankylosing spondylitis of lumbosacral region ℞
M45.8   Ankylosing spondylitis sacral and sacrococcygeal
        region ℞
M45.9   Ankylosing spondylitis of unspecified sites in spine ℞

● M46   Other inflammatory spondylopathies
● M46.0   Spinal enthesopathy
          Disorder of ligamentous or muscular attachments of
          spine
          M46.00   Spinal enthesopathy, site unspecified ℞
          M46.01   Spinal enthesopathy, occipito-atlanto-axial
                   region ℞
          M46.02   Spinal enthesopathy, cervical region ℞
          M46.03   Spinal enthesopathy, cervicothoracic region ℞
          M46.04   Spinal enthesopathy, thoracic region ℞
          M46.05   Spinal enthesopathy, thoracolumbar region ℞
          M46.06   Spinal enthesopathy, lumbar region ℞
          M46.07   Spinal enthesopathy, lumbosacral region ℞
          M46.08   Spinal enthesopathy, sacral and sacrococcygeal
                   region ℞
          M46.09   Spinal enthesopathy, multiple sites in spine ℞

▶ New   ⇛ Revised   ~~deleted~~ Deleted   Excludes 1   Excludes 2   Includes   Use additional   Code first   Code also   Key words
OGCR Official Guidelines   X Assign placeholder X   ● Use Additional Character(s)   ▮ Manifestation Code   ℞ Hierarchical Condition Category   **Coding Clinic**

M46.1   Sacroiliitis, not elsewhere classified 🔍

● M46.2   Osteomyelitis of vertebra
    M46.20   Osteomyelitis of vertebra, site unspecified 🔍
    M46.21   Osteomyelitis of vertebra, occipito-atlanto-axial region 🔍
    M46.22   Osteomyelitis of vertebra, cervical region 🔍
    M46.23   Osteomyelitis of vertebra, cervicothoracic region 🔍
    M46.24   Osteomyelitis of vertebra, thoracic region 🔍
    M46.25   Osteomyelitis of vertebra, thoracolumbar region 🔍
    M46.26   Osteomyelitis of vertebra, lumbar region 🔍
    M46.27   Osteomyelitis of vertebra, lumbosacral region 🔍
    M46.28   Osteomyelitis of vertebra, sacral and sacrococcygeal region 🔍

● M46.3   Infection of intervertebral disc (pyogenic)
    Use additional code (B95-B97) to identify infectious agent
    M46.30   Infection of intervertebral disc (pyogenic), site unspecified 🔍
    M46.31   Infection of intervertebral disc (pyogenic), occipito-atlanto-axial region 🔍
    M46.32   Infection of intervertebral disc (pyogenic), cervical region 🔍
    M46.33   Infection of intervertebral disc (pyogenic), cervicothoracic region 🔍
    M46.34   Infection of intervertebral disc (pyogenic), thoracic region 🔍
    M46.35   Infection of intervertebral disc (pyogenic), thoracolumbar region 🔍
    M46.36   Infection of intervertebral disc (pyogenic), lumbar region 🔍
    M46.37   Infection of intervertebral disc (pyogenic), lumbosacral region 🔍
    M46.38   Infection of intervertebral disc (pyogenic), sacral and sacrococcygeal region 🔍
    M46.39   Infection of intervertebral disc (pyogenic), multiple sites in spine 🔍

● M46.4   Discitis, unspecified
    M46.40   Discitis, unspecified, site unspecified
    M46.41   Discitis, unspecified, occipito-atlanto-axial region
    M46.42   Discitis, unspecified, cervical region
    M46.43   Discitis, unspecified, cervicothoracic region
    M46.44   Discitis, unspecified, thoracic region
    M46.45   Discitis, unspecified, thoracolumbar region
    M46.46   Discitis, unspecified, lumbar region
    M46.47   Discitis, unspecified, lumbosacral region
    M46.48   Discitis, unspecified, sacral and sacrococcygeal region
    M46.49   Discitis, unspecified, multiple sites in spine

● M46.5   Other infective spondylopathies
    M46.50   Other infective spondylopathies, site unspecified 🔍
    M46.51   Other infective spondylopathies, occipitoatlanto-axial region 🔍
    M46.52   Other infective spondylopathies, cervical region 🔍
    M46.53   Other infective spondylopathies, cervicothoracic region 🔍
    M46.54   Other infective spondylopathies, thoracic region 🔍
    M46.55   Other infective spondylopathies, thoracolumbar region 🔍
    M46.56   Other infective spondylopathies, lumbar region 🔍
    M46.57   Other infective spondylopathies, lumbosacral region 🔍

    M46.58   Other infective spondylopathies, sacral and sacrococcygeal region 🔍
    M46.59   Other infective spondylopathies, multiple sites in spine 🔍

● M46.8   Other specified inflammatory spondylopathies
    M46.80   Other specified inflammatory spondylopathies, site unspecified 🔍
    M46.81   Other specified inflammatory spondylopathies, occipito-atlanto-axial region 🔍
    M46.82   Other specified inflammatory spondylopathies, cervical region 🔍
    M46.83   Other specified inflammatory spondylopathies, cervicothoracic region 🔍
    M46.84   Other specified inflammatory spondylopathies, thoracic region 🔍
    M46.85   Other specified inflammatory spondylopathies, thoracolumbar region 🔍
    M46.86   Other specified inflammatory spondylopathies, lumbar region 🔍
    M46.87   Other specified inflammatory spondylopathies, lumbosacral region 🔍
    M46.88   Other specified inflammatory spondylopathies, sacral and sacrococcygeal region 🔍
    M46.89   Other specified inflammatory spondylopathies, multiple sites in spine 🔍

● M46.9   Unspecified inflammatory spondylopathy
    M46.90   Unspecified inflammatory spondylopathy, site unspecified 🔍
    M46.91   Unspecified inflammatory spondylopathy, occipito-atlanto-axial region 🔍
    M46.92   Unspecified inflammatory spondylopathy, cervical region 🔍
       Coding Clinic: 2019, Q3, P10
    M46.93   Unspecified inflammatory spondylopathy, cervicothoracic region 🔍
    M46.94   Unspecified inflammatory spondylopathy, thoracic region 🔍
    M46.95   Unspecified inflammatory spondylopathy, thoracolumbar region 🔍
    M46.96   Unspecified inflammatory spondylopathy, lumbar region 🔍
    M46.97   Unspecified inflammatory spondylopathy, lumbosacral region 🔍
    M46.98   Unspecified inflammatory spondylopathy, sacral and sacrococcygeal region 🔍
    M46.99   Unspecified inflammatory spondylopathy, multiple sites in spine 🔍

● M47   Spondylosis
    Includes   arthrosis or osteoarthritis of spine degeneration of facet joints

● M47.0   Anterior spinal and vertebral artery compression syndromes
       Coding Clinic: 2019, Q3, P10
    ● M47.01   Anterior spinal artery compression syndromes
       M47.011   Anterior spinal artery compression syndromes, occipito-atlanto-axial region
       M47.012   Anterior spinal artery compression syndromes, cervical region
       M47.013   Anterior spinal artery compression syndromes, cervicothoracic region
       M47.014   Anterior spinal artery compression syndromes, thoracic region
       M47.015   Anterior spinal artery compression syndromes, thoracolumbar region
       M47.016   Anterior spinal artery compression syndromes, lumbar region
       M47.019   Anterior spinal artery compression syndromes, site unspecified

CHAPTER 13 (M00-M99)

CHAPTER 13 (M00-M99)

● **M47.02** Vertebral artery compression syndromes

     M47.021 Vertebral artery compression syndromes, occipito-atlanto-axial region

     M47.022 Vertebral artery compression syndromes, cervical region

     M47.029 Vertebral artery compression syndromes, site unspecified

● **M47.1** Other spondylosis with myelopathy

     Spondylogenic compression of spinal cord

     Excludes1   vertebral subluxation (M43.3-M43.5X9)

     M47.10 Other spondylosis with myelopathy, site unspecified

     M47.11 Other spondylosis with myelopathy, occipito-atlanto-axial region

     M47.12 Other spondylosis with myelopathy, cervical region

       Coding Clinic: 2020, Q1, P17

     M47.13 Other spondylosis with myelopathy, cervicothoracic region

     M47.14 Other spondylosis with myelopathy, thoracic region

     M47.15 Other spondylosis with myelopathy, thoracolumbar region

     M47.16 Other spondylosis with myelopathy, lumbar region

● **M47.2** Other spondylosis with radiculopathy

     M47.20 Other spondylosis with radiculopathy, site unspecified

     M47.21 Other spondylosis with radiculopathy, occipito-atlanto-axial region

     M47.22 Other spondylosis with radiculopathy, cervical region

       Coding Clinic: 2020, Q1, P17

     M47.23 Other spondylosis with radiculopathy, cervicothoracic region

     M47.24 Other spondylosis with radiculopathy, thoracic region

     M47.25 Other spondylosis with radiculopathy, thoracolumbar region

     M47.26 Other spondylosis with radiculopathy, lumbar region

     M47.27 Other spondylosis with radiculopathy, lumbosacral region

     M47.28 Other spondylosis with radiculopathy, sacral and sacrococcygeal region

● **M47.8** Other spondylosis

  ● **M47.81** Spondylosis without myelopathy or radiculopathy

     M47.811 Spondylosis without myelopathy or radiculopathy, occipito-atlanto-axial region

     M47.812 Spondylosis without myelopathy or radiculopathy, cervical region

       Coding Clinic: 2019, Q3, P10-11; 2018, Q2, P15

     M47.813 Spondylosis without myelopathy or radiculopathy, cervicothoracic region

     M47.814 Spondylosis without myelopathy or radiculopathy, thoracic region

     M47.815 Spondylosis without myelopathy or radiculopathy, thoracolumbar region

     M47.816 Spondylosis without myelopathy or radiculopathy, lumbar region

     M47.817 Spondylosis without myelopathy or radiculopathy, lumbosacral region

     M47.818 Spondylosis without myelopathy or radiculopathy, sacral and sacrococcygeal region

     M47.819 Spondylosis without myelopathy or radiculopathy, site unspecified

  ● **M47.89** Other spondylosis

     M47.891 Other spondylosis, occipito-atlanto-axial region

     M47.892 Other spondylosis, cervical region

     M47.893 Other spondylosis, cervicothoracic region

     M47.894 Other spondylosis, thoracic region

     M47.895 Other spondylosis, thoracolumbar region

     M47.896 Other spondylosis, lumbar region

     M47.897 Other spondylosis, lumbosacral region

     M47.898 Other spondylosis, sacral and sacrococcygeal region

     M47.899 Other spondylosis, site unspecified

  M47.9 Spondylosis, unspecified

● **M48** Other spondylopathies

  ● **M48.0** Spinal stenosis

     Caudal stenosis

     M48.00 Spinal stenosis, site unspecified

     M48.01 Spinal stenosis, occipito-atlanto-axial region

     M48.02 Spinal stenosis, cervical region

       Coding Clinic: 2020, Q1, P17

     M48.03 Spinal stenosis, cervicothoracic region

     M48.04 Spinal stenosis, thoracic region

     M48.05 Spinal stenosis, thoracolumbar region

  ● M48.06 Spinal stenosis, lumbar region

       Coding Clinic: 2017, Q3, P24

     M48.061 Spinal stenosis, lumbar region without neurogenic claudication

       Spinal stenosis, lumbar region NOS

     M48.062 Spinal stenosis, lumbar region with neurogenic claudication

       Coding Clinic: 2017, Q4, P19

     M48.07 Spinal stenosis, lumbosacral region

     M48.08 Spinal stenosis, sacral and sacrococcygeal region

  ● **M48.1** Ankylosing hyperostosis [Forestier]

     Diffuse idiopathic skeletal hyperostosis [DISH]

     M48.10 Ankylosing hyperostosis [Forestier], site unspecified

     M48.11 Ankylosing hyperostosis [Forestier], occipito-atlanto-axial region

     M48.12 Ankylosing hyperostosis [Forestier], cervical region

     M48.13 Ankylosing hyperostosis [Forestier], cervicothoracic region

     M48.14 Ankylosing hyperostosis [Forestier], thoracic region

     M48.15 Ankylosing hyperostosis [Forestier], thoracolumbar region

     M48.16 Ankylosing hyperostosis [Forestier], lumbar region

     M48.17 Ankylosing hyperostosis [Forestier], lumbosacral region

     M48.18 Ankylosing hyperostosis [Forestier], sacral and sacrococcygeal region

     M48.19 Ankylosing hyperostosis [Forestier], multiple sites in spine

▶ New   ⇒ Revised   ~~deleted~~ Deleted   Excludes 1   Excludes 2   Includes   Use additional   Code first   Code also   Key words

OGCR Official Guidelines   X Assign placeholder X   ● Use Additional Character(s)   ▶ Manifestation Code   🔖 Hierarchical Condition Category   Coding Clinic

● **M48.2 Kissing spine**
> **M48.20 Kissing spine, site unspecified**
> **M48.21 Kissing spine, occipito-atlanto-axial region**
> **M48.22 Kissing spine, cervical region**
> **M48.23 Kissing spine, cervicothoracic region**
> **M48.24 Kissing spine, thoracic region**
> **M48.25 Kissing spine, thoracolumbar region**
> **M48.26 Kissing spine, lumbar region**
> **M48.27 Kissing spine, lumbosacral region**

● **M48.3 Traumatic spondylopathy**
> **M48.30 Traumatic spondylopathy, site unspecified**
> **M48.31 Traumatic spondylopathy, occipito-atlanto-axial region**
> **M48.32 Traumatic spondylopathy, cervical region**
> **M48.33 Traumatic spondylopathy, cervicothoracic region**
> **M48.34 Traumatic spondylopathy, thoracic region**
> **M48.35 Traumatic spondylopathy, thoracolumbar region**
> **M48.36 Traumatic spondylopathy, lumbar region**
> **M48.37 Traumatic spondylopathy, lumbosacral region**
> **M48.38 Traumatic spondylopathy, sacral and sacrococcygeal region**

● **M48.4 Fatigue fracture of vertebra**
Stress fracture of vertebra

Excludes1 pathological fracture NOS (M84.4-)
pathological fracture of vertebra due to neoplasm (M84.58)
pathological fracture of vertebra due to other diagnosis (M84.68)
pathological fracture of vertebra due to osteoporosis (M80.-)
traumatic fracture of vertebrae (S12.0-S12.3-, S22.0-, S32.0-)

The appropriate 7th character is to be added to each code from subcategory M48.4:

A	initial encounter for fracture
D	subsequent encounter for fracture with routine healing
G	subsequent encounter for fracture with delayed healing
S	sequela of fracture

X● **M48.40 Fatigue fracture of vertebra, site unspecified**
X● **M48.41 Fatigue fracture of vertebra, occipitoatlanto-axial region**
X● **M48.42 Fatigue fracture of vertebra, cervical region**
X● **M48.43 Fatigue fracture of vertebra, cervicothoracic region**
X● **M48.44 Fatigue fracture of vertebra, thoracic region**
X● **M48.45 Fatigue fracture of vertebra, thoracolumbar region**
X● **M48.46 Fatigue fracture of vertebra, lumbar region**
X● **M48.47 Fatigue fracture of vertebra, lumbosacral region**
X● **M48.48 Fatigue fracture of vertebra, sacral and sacrococcygeal region**

● **M48.5 Collapsed vertebra, not elsewhere classified**
Collapsed vertebra NOS
Compression fracture of vertebra NOS
Wedging of vertebra NOS

Excludes1 current injury - see Injury of spine, by body region
fatigue fracture of vertebra (M48.4)
pathological fracture of vertebra due to neoplasm (M84.58)
pathological fracture of vertebra due to other diagnosis (M84.68)
pathological fracture of vertebra due to osteoporosis (M80.-)
pathological fracture NOS (M84.4-)
stress fracture of vertebra (M48.4-)
traumatic fracture of vertebra (S12.-, S22.-, S32.-)

The appropriate 7th character is to be added to each code from subcategory M48.5:

A	initial encounter for fracture
D	subsequent encounter for fracture with routine healing
G	subsequent encounter for fracture with delayed healing
S	sequela of fracture

X● **M48.50 Collapsed vertebra, not elsewhere classified, site unspecified A** 🔁
X● **M48.51 Collapsed vertebra, not elsewhere classified, occipito-atlanto-axial region A** 🔁
X● **M48.52 Collapsed vertebra, not elsewhere classified, cervical region A** 🔁
X● **M48.53 Collapsed vertebra, not elsewhere classified, cervicothoracic region A** 🔁
X● **M48.54 Collapsed vertebra, not elsewhere classified, thoracic region A** 🔁
X● **M48.55 Collapsed vertebra, not elsewhere classified, thoracolumbar region A** 🔁
X● **M48.56 Collapsed vertebra, not elsewhere classified, lumbar region A** 🔁
X● **M48.57 Collapsed vertebra, not elsewhere classified, lumbosacral region A** 🔁
X● **M48.58 Collapsed vertebra, not elsewhere classified, sacral and sacrococcygeal region A** 🔁

● **M48.8 Other specified spondylopathies**
Ossification of posterior longitudinal ligament
> ● **M48.8X Other specified spondylopathies**
> > **M48.8X1 Other specified spondylopathies, occipito-atlanto-axial region** 🔁
> > **M48.8X2 Other specified spondylopathies, cervical region** 🔁
> > **M48.8X3 Other specified spondylopathies, cervicothoracic region** 🔁
> > **M48.8X4 Other specified spondylopathies, thoracic region** 🔁
> > **M48.8X5 Other specified spondylopathies, thoracolumbar region** 🔁
> > **M48.8X6 Other specified spondylopathies, lumbar region** 🔁
> > **M48.8X7 Other specified spondylopathies, lumbosacral region** 🔁
> > **M48.8X8 Other specified spondylopathies, sacral and sacrococcygeal region** 🔁
> > **M48.8X9 Other specified spondylopathies, site unspecified** 🔁

M48.9 Spondylopathy, unspecified

● **M49 Spondylopathies in diseases classified elsewhere**

     Includes   curvature of spine in diseases classified elsewhere
                         deformity of spine in diseases classified
                             elsewhere
                         kyphosis in diseases classified elsewhere
                         scoliosis in diseases classified elsewhere
                         spondylopathy in diseases classified elsewhere

     Code first underlying disease, such as:
         brucellosis (A23.-)
         Charcot-Marie-Tooth disease (G60.0)
         enterobacterial infections (A01-A04)
         osteitis fibrosa cystica (E21.0)

     Excludes1   curvature of spine in tuberculosis [Pott's]
                         (A18.01)
                         enteropathic arthropathies (M07.-)
                         gonococcal spondylitis (A54.41)
                         neuropathic [tabes dorsalis] spondylitis (A52.11)
                         neuropathic spondylopathy in syringomyelia
                         (G95.0)
                         neuropathic spondylopathy in tabes dorsalis
                         (A52.11)
                         nonsyphilitic neuropathic spondylopathy NEC
                         (G98.0)
                         spondylitis in syphilis (acquired) (A52.77)
                         tuberculous spondylitis (A18.01)
                         typhoid fever spondylitis (A01.05)

● **M49.8 Spondylopathy in diseases classified elsewhere**

    ▌ *M49.80 Spondylopathy in diseases classified elsewhere, site unspecified* ℞

    ▌ *M49.81 Spondylopathy in diseases classified elsewhere, occipito-atlanto-axial region* ℞

    ▌ *M49.82 Spondylopathy in diseases classified elsewhere, cervical region* ℞

    ▌ *M49.83 Spondylopathy in diseases classified elsewhere, cervicothoracic region* ℞

    ▌ *M49.84 Spondylopathy in diseases classified elsewhere, thoracic region* ℞

    ▌ *M49.85 Spondylopathy in diseases classified elsewhere, thoracolumbar region* ℞

    ▌ *M49.86 Spondylopathy in diseases classified elsewhere, lumbar region* ℞

    ▌ *M49.87 Spondylopathy in diseases classified elsewhere, lumbosacral region* ℞

    ▌ *M49.88 Spondylopathy in diseases classified elsewhere, sacral and sacrococcygeal region* ℞

    ▌ *M49.89 Spondylopathy in diseases classified elsewhere, multiple sites in spine* ℞

OTHER DORSOPATHIES (M50-M54)

     Excludes1   current injury - see injury of spine by body region
                         discitis NOS (M46.4-)

● **M50 Cervical disc disorders**

     Note: Code to the most superior level of disorder.

     Includes   cervicothoracic disc disorders with cervicalgia
                         cervicothoracic disc disorders
     Coding Clinic: 2016, Q1, P17

● **M50.0 Cervical disc disorder with myelopathy**

     M50.00 Cervical disc disorder with myelopathy, unspecified cervical region

     M50.01 Cervical disc disorder with myelopathy, high cervical region
            C2-C3 disc disorder with myelopathy
            C3-C4 disc disorder with myelopathy
            Coding Clinic: 2016, Q1, P17

● **M50.02 Cervical disc disorder with myelopathy, mid-cervical region**
         Coding Clinic: 2016, Q4, P39-40

     M50.020 Cervical disc disorder with myelopathy, mid-cervical region, unspecified level

     M50.021 Cervical disc disorder at C4-C5 level with myelopathy
            C4-C5 disc disorder with myelopathy

     M50.022 Cervical disc disorder at C5-C6 level with myelopathy
            C5-C6 disc disorder with myelopathy

     M50.023 Cervical disc disorder at C6-C7 level with myelopathy
            C6-C7 disc disorder with myelopathy

     M50.03 Cervical disc disorder with myelopathy, cervicothoracic region
            C7-T1 disc disorder with myelopathy

● **M50.1 Cervical disc disorder with radiculopathy**

     Excludes2   brachial radiculitis NOS (M54.13)

     M50.10 Cervical disc disorder with radiculopathy, unspecified cervical region

     M50.11 Cervical disc disorder with radiculopathy, high cervical region
            C2-C3 disc disorder with radiculopathy
            C3 radiculopathy due to disc disorder
            C3-C4 disc disorder with radiculopathy
            C4 radiculopathy due to disc disorder

● **M50.12 Cervical disc disorder with radiculopathy, mid-cervical region**
         Coding Clinic: 2016, Q4, P39-40

     M50.120 Mid-cervical disc disorder, unspecified level

     M50.121 Cervical disc disorder at C4-C5 level with radiculopathy
            C4-C5 disc disorder with radiculopathy
            C5 radiculopathy due to disc disorder

     M50.122 Cervical disc disorder at C5-C6 level with radiculopathy
            C5-C6 disc disorder with radiculopathy
            C6 radiculopathy due to disc disorder

     M50.123 Cervical disc disorder at C6-C7 level with radiculopathy
            C6-C7 disc disorder with radiculopathy
            C7 radiculopathy due to disc disorder

     M50.13 Cervical disc disorder with radiculopathy, cervicothoracic region
            C7-T1 disc disorder with radiculopathy
            C8 radiculopathy due to disc disorder

● **M50.2 Other cervical disc displacement**
         Coding Clinic: 2016, Q4, P40

     M50.20 Other cervical disc displacement, unspecified cervical region

     M50.21 Other cervical disc displacement, high cervical region
            Other C2-C3 cervical disc displacement
            Other C3-C4 cervical disc displacement

▶ New   ⇒ Revised   ~~deleted~~ Deleted   Excludes 1   Excludes 2   Includes   Use additional   Code first   Code also   Key words
OGCR Official Guidelines   X Assign placeholder X   ● Use Additional Character(s)   ▌ Manifestation Code   ℞ Hierarchical Condition Category   Coding Clinic

● **M50.22 Other cervical disc displacement, mid-cervical region**

     M50.220 Other cervical disc displacement, mid-cervical region, unspecified level

     M50.221 Other cervical disc displacement at C4-C5 level
         Other C4-C5 cervical disc displacement

     M50.222 Other cervical disc displacement at C5-C6 level
         Other C5-C6 cervical disc displacement

     M50.223 Other cervical disc displacement at C6-C7 level
         Other C6-C7 cervical disc displacement

   M50.23 Other cervical disc displacement, cervicothoracic region
     Other C7-T1 cervical disc displacement

● **M50.3 Other cervical disc degeneration**
   Coding Clinic: 2016, Q4, P40

   M50.30 Other cervical disc degeneration, unspecified cervical region

   M50.31 Other cervical disc degeneration, high cervical region
     Other C2-C3 cervical disc degeneration
     Other C3-C4 cervical disc degeneration

● **M50.32 Other cervical disc degeneration, mid-cervical region**

     M50.320 Other cervical disc degeneration, mid-cervical region, unspecified level

     M50.321 Other cervical disc degeneration at C4-C5 level
         Other C4-C5 cervical disc degeneration

     M50.322 Other cervical disc degeneration at C5-C6 level
         Other C5-C6 cervical disc degeneration

     M50.323 Other cervical disc degeneration at C6-C7 level
         Other C6-C7 cervical disc degeneration

   M50.33 Other cervical disc degeneration, cervicothoracic region
     Other C7-T1 cervical disc degeneration

● **M50.8 Other cervical disc disorders**
   Coding Clinic: 2016, Q4, P40

   M50.80 Other cervical disc disorders, unspecified cervical region

   M50.81 Other cervical disc disorders, high cervical region
     Other C2-C3 cervical disc disorders
     Other C3-C4 cervical disc disorders

● **M50.82 Other cervical disc disorders, mid-cervical region**

     M50.820 Other cervical disc disorders, mid-cervical region, unspecified level

     M50.821 Other cervical disc disorders at C4-C5 level
         Other C4-C5 cervical disc disorders

     M50.822 Other cervical disc disorders at C5-C6 level
         Other C5-C6 cervical disc disorders

     M50.823 Other cervical disc disorders at C6-C7 level
         Other C6-C7 cervical disc disorders

   M50.83 Other cervical disc disorders, cervicothoracic region
     Other C7-T1 cervical disc disorders

● **M50.9 Cervical disc disorder, unspecified**
   Coding Clinic: 2016, Q4, P40

   M50.90 Cervical disc disorder, unspecified, unspecified cervical region

   M50.91 Cervical disc disorder, unspecified, high cervical region
     C2-C3 cervical disc disorder, unspecified
     C3-C4 cervical disc disorder, unspecified

● **M50.92 Cervical disc disorder, unspecified, mid-cervical region**

     M50.920 Unspecified cervical disc disorder, mid-cervical region, unspecified level

     M50.921 Unspecified cervical disc disorder at C4-C5 level
         Unspecified C4-C5 cervical disc disorder

     M50.922 Unspecified cervical disc disorder at C5-C6 level
         Unspecified C5-C6 cervical disc disorder

     M50.923 Unspecified cervical disc disorder at C6-C7 level
         Unspecified C6-C7 cervical disc disorder

   M50.93 Cervical disc disorder, unspecified, cervicothoracic region
     C7-T1 cervical disc disorder, unspecified

● **M51 Thoracic, thoracolumbar, and lumbosacral intervertebral disc disorders**

   Excludes2   cervical and cervicothoracic disc disorders (M50.-)
         sacral and sacrococcygeal disorders (M53.3)

● **M51.0 Thoracic, thoracolumbar and lumbosacral intervertebral disc disorders with myelopathy**

   M51.04 Intervertebral disc disorders with myelopathy, thoracic region

   M51.05 Intervertebral disc disorders with myelopathy, thoracolumbar region

   M51.06 Intervertebral disc disorders with myelopathy, lumbar region

● **M51.1 Thoracic, thoracolumbar and lumbosacral intervertebral disc disorders with radiculopathy**
   Sciatica due to intervertebral disc disorder

   Excludes1   lumbar radiculitis NOS (M54.16)
         sciatica NOS (M54.3)

   M51.14 Intervertebral disc disorders with radiculopathy, thoracic region

   M51.15 Intervertebral disc disorders with radiculopathy, thoracolumbar region

   M51.16 Intervertebral disc disorders with radiculopathy, lumbar region

   M51.17 Intervertebral disc disorders with radiculopathy, lumbosacral region

● **M51.2** **Other thoracic, thoracolumbar and lumbosacral intervertebral disc displacement**
Lumbago due to displacement of intervertebral disc

M51.24 Other intervertebral disc displacement, thoracic region

M51.25 Other intervertebral disc displacement, thoracolumbar region

M51.26 Other intervertebral disc displacement, lumbar region

M51.27 Other intervertebral disc displacement, lumbosacral region

● **M51.3** **Other thoracic, thoracolumbar and lumbosacral intervertebral disc degeneration**
Coding Clinic: 2013, Q3, P22

M51.34 Other intervertebral disc degeneration, thoracic region

M51.35 Other intervertebral disc degeneration, thoracolumbar region

M51.36 Other intervertebral disc degeneration, lumbar region
Coding Clinic: 2018, Q2, P15

M51.37 Other intervertebral disc degeneration, lumbosacral region

● **M51.4** **Schmorl's nodes**

M51.44 Schmorl's nodes, thoracic region

M51.45 Schmorl's nodes, thoracolumbar region

M51.46 Schmorl's nodes, lumbar region

M51.47 Schmorl's nodes, lumbosacral region

● **M51.8** **Other thoracic, thoracolumbar and lumbosacral intervertebral disc disorders**

M51.84 Other intervertebral disc disorders, thoracic region

M51.85 Other intervertebral disc disorders, thoracolumbar region

M51.86 Other intervertebral disc disorders, lumbar region

M51.87 Other intervertebral disc disorders, lumbosacral region

M51.9 Unspecified thoracic, thoracolumbar and lumbosacral intervertebral disc disorder

● **M53** **Other and unspecified dorsopathies, not elsewhere classified**

M53.0 Cervicocranial syndrome
Posterior cervical sympathetic syndrome

M53.1 Cervicobrachial syndrome

Excludes2   cervical disc disorder (M50.-)
thoracic outlet syndrome (G54.0)

● **M53.2** **Spinal instabilities**

● **M53.2X** **Spinal instabilities**

M53.2X1 Spinal instabilities, occipito-atlanto-axial region

M53.2X2 Spinal instabilities, cervical region

M53.2X3 Spinal instabilities, cervicothoracic region

M53.2X4 Spinal instabilities, thoracic region

M53.2X5 Spinal instabilities, thoracolumbar region

M53.2X6 Spinal instabilities, lumbar region

M53.2X7 Spinal instabilities, lumbosacral region

M53.2X8 Spinal instabilities, sacral and sacrococcygeal region

M53.2X9 Spinal instabilities, site unspecified

M53.3 Sacrococcygeal disorders, not elsewhere classified
Coccygodynia

● **M53.8** **Other specified dorsopathies**

M53.80 Other specified dorsopathies, site unspecified

M53.81 Other specified dorsopathies, occipito-atlanto-axial region

M53.82 Other specified dorsopathies, cervical region

M53.83 Other specified dorsopathies, cervicothoracic region

M53.84 Other specified dorsopathies, thoracic region

M53.85 Other specified dorsopathies, thoracolumbar region

M53.86 Other specified dorsopathies, lumbar region

M53.87 Other specified dorsopathies, lumbosacral region

M53.88 Other specified dorsopathies, sacral and sacrococcygeal region

M53.9 Dorsopathy, unspecified

● **M54** **Dorsalgia**

Excludes1   psychogenic dorsalgia (F45.41)

● **M54.0** **Panniculitis affecting regions of neck and back**

Excludes1   lupus panniculitis (L93.2)
panniculitis NOS (M79.3)
relapsing [Weber-Christian] panniculitis (M35.6)

M54.00 Panniculitis affecting regions of neck and back, site unspecified

M54.01 Panniculitis affecting regions of neck and back, occipito-atlanto-axial region

M54.02 Panniculitis affecting regions of neck and back, cervical region

M54.03 Panniculitis affecting regions of neck and back, cervicothoracic region

M54.04 Panniculitis affecting regions of neck and back, thoracic region

M54.05 Panniculitis affecting regions of neck and back, thoracolumbar region

M54.06 Panniculitis affecting regions of neck and back, lumbar region

M54.07 Panniculitis affecting regions of neck and back, lumbosacral region

M54.08 Panniculitis affecting regions of neck and back, sacral and sacrococcygeal region

M54.09 Panniculitis affecting regions, neck and back, multiple sites in spine

● **M54.1** **Radiculopathy**
Brachial neuritis or radiculitis NOS
Lumbar neuritis or radiculitis NOS
Lumbosacral neuritis or radiculitis NOS
Thoracic neuritis or radiculitis NOS
Radiculitis NOS

Excludes1   neuralgia and neuritis NOS (M79.2)
radiculopathy with cervical disc disorder (M50.1)
radiculopathy with lumbar and other intervertebral disc disorder (M51.1-)
radiculopathy with spondylosis (M47.2-)

M54.10 Radiculopathy, site unspecified

M54.11 Radiculopathy, occipito-atlanto-axial region

M54.12 Radiculopathy, cervical region

M54.13 Radiculopathy, cervicothoracic region

M54.14 Radiculopathy, thoracic region

M54.15 Radiculopathy, thoracolumbar region

M54.16 Radiculopathy, lumbar region

M54.17 Radiculopathy, lumbosacral region

M54.18 Radiculopathy, sacral and sacrococcygeal region

▶ New   ⇒ Revised   ~~deleted~~ Deleted   Excludes 1   Excludes 2   Includes   Use additional   Code first   Code also   Key words
OGCR Official Guidelines   X Assign placeholder X   ● Use Additional Character(s)   ▶ Manifestation Code   🏷 Hierarchical Condition Category   Coding Clinic

M54.2 Cervicalgia

> **Excludes1**   cervicalgia due to intervertebral cervical disc disorder (M50.-)

M54.3 Sciatica

> **Excludes1**   lesion of sciatic nerve (G57.0)
> sciatica due to intervertebral disc disorder (M51.1-)
> sciatica with lumbago (M54.4-)

     M54.30   Sciatica, unspecified side
     M54.31   Sciatica, right side
     M54.32   Sciatica, left side

M54.4 Lumbago with sciatica

> **Excludes1**   lumbago with sciatica due to intervertebral disc disorder (M51.1-)

     M54.40   Lumbago with sciatica, unspecified side
     M54.41   Lumbago with sciatica, right side
     M54.42   Lumbago with sciatica, left side
         Coding Clinic: 2016, Q2, P7

M54.5 Low back pain
     Loin pain
     Lumbago NOS

> **Excludes1**   low back strain (S39.012)
> lumbago due to intervertebral disc displacement (M51.2-)
> lumbago with sciatica (M54.4-)

M54.6 Pain in thoracic spine

> **Excludes1**   pain in thoracic spine due to intervertebral disc disorder (M51.)

M54.8 Other dorsalgia

> **Excludes1**   dorsalgia in thoracic region (M54.6)
> low back pain (M54.5)

     M54.81   Occipital neuralgia
     M54.89   Other dorsalgia

M54.9 Dorsalgia, unspecified
     Backache NOS
     Back pain NOS

SOFT TISSUE DISORDERS (M60-M79)

DISORDERS OF MUSCLES (M60-M63)

> **Excludes1**   dermatopolymyositis (M33.-)
> muscular dystrophies and myopathies (G71-G72)
> myopathy in amyloidosis (E85.-)
> myopathy in polyarteritis nodosa (M30.0)
> myopathy in rheumatoid arthritis (M05.32)
> myopathy in scleroderma (M34.-)
> myopathy in Sjögren's syndrome (M35.03)
> myopathy in systemic lupus erythematosus (M32.-)

M60 Myositis

> **Excludes2**   inclusion body myositis [IBM] (G72.41)

M60.0 Infective myositis
     Tropical pyomyositis
     Use additional code (B95-B97) to identify infectious agent

     M60.00   Infective myositis, unspecified site
         M60.000   Infective myositis, unspecified right arm
             Infective myositis, right upper limb NOS
         M60.001   Infective myositis, unspecified left arm
             Infective myositis, left upper limb NOS
         M60.002   Infective myositis, unspecified arm
             Infective myositis, upper limb NOS
         M60.003   Infective myositis, unspecified right leg
             Infective myositis, right lower limb NOS

         M60.004   Infective myositis, unspecified left leg
             Infective myositis, left lower limb NOS
         M60.005   Infective myositis, unspecified leg
             Infective myositis, lower limb NOS
         M60.009   Infective myositis, unspecified site

     M60.01   Infective myositis, shoulder
         M60.011   Infective myositis, right shoulder
         M60.012   Infective myositis, left shoulder
         M60.019   Infective myositis, unspecified shoulder

     M60.02   Infective myositis, upper arm
         M60.021   Infective myositis, right upper arm
         M60.022   Infective myositis, left upper arm
         M60.029   Infective myositis, unspecified upper arm

     M60.03   Infective myositis, forearm
         M60.031   Infective myositis, right forearm
         M60.032   Infective myositis, left forearm
         M60.039   Infective myositis, unspecified forearm

     M60.04   Infective myositis, hand and fingers
         M60.041   Infective myositis, right hand
         M60.042   Infective myositis, left hand
         M60.043   Infective myositis, unspecified hand
         M60.044   Infective myositis, right finger(s)
         M60.045   Infective myositis, left finger(s)
         M60.046   Infective myositis, unspecified finger(s)

     M60.05   Infective myositis, thigh
         M60.051   Infective myositis, right thigh
         M60.052   Infective myositis, left thigh
         M60.059   Infective myositis, unspecified thigh

     M60.06   Infective myositis, lower leg
         M60.061   Infective myositis, right lower leg
         M60.062   Infective myositis, left lower leg
         M60.069   Infective myositis, unspecified lower leg

     M60.07   Infective myositis, ankle, foot and toes
         M60.070   Infective myositis, right ankle
         M60.071   Infective myositis, left ankle
         M60.072   Infective myositis, unspecified ankle
         M60.073   Infective myositis, right foot
         M60.074   Infective myositis, left foot
         M60.075   Infective myositis, unspecified foot
         M60.076   Infective myositis, right toe(s)
         M60.077   Infective myositis, left toe(s)
         M60.078   Infective myositis, unspecified toe(s)

     M60.08   Infective myositis, other site
     M60.09   Infective myositis, multiple sites

M60.1 Interstitial myositis
     M60.10   Interstitial myositis of unspecified site

     M60.11   Interstitial myositis, shoulder
         M60.111   Interstitial myositis, right shoulder
         M60.112   Interstitial myositis, left shoulder
         M60.119   Interstitial myositis, unspecified shoulder

     M60.12   Interstitial myositis, upper arm
         M60.121   Interstitial myositis, right upper arm
         M60.122   Interstitial myositis, left upper arm
         M60.129   Interstitial myositis, unspecified upper arm

● M60.13   Interstitial myositis, forearm
     M60.131   Interstitial myositis, right forearm
     M60.132   Interstitial myositis, left forearm
     M60.139   Interstitial myositis, unspecified forearm

● M60.14   Interstitial myositis, hand
     M60.141   Interstitial myositis, right hand
     M60.142   Interstitial myositis, left hand
     M60.149   Interstitial myositis, unspecified hand

● M60.15   Interstitial myositis, thigh
     M60.151   Interstitial myositis, right thigh
     M60.152   Interstitial myositis, left thigh
     M60.159   Interstitial myositis, unspecified thigh

● M60.16   Interstitial myositis, lower leg
     M60.161   Interstitial myositis, right lower leg
     M60.162   Interstitial myositis, left lower leg
     M60.169   Interstitial myositis, unspecified lower leg

● M60.17   Interstitial myositis, ankle and foot
     M60.171   Interstitial myositis, right ankle and foot
     M60.172   Interstitial myositis, left ankle and foot
     M60.179   Interstitial myositis, unspecified ankle and foot

   M60.18   Interstitial myositis, other site

   M60.19   Interstitial myositis, multiple sites

● M60.2   **Foreign body granuloma of soft tissue, not elsewhere classified**

     Use additional code to identify the type of retained foreign body (Z18.-)

     Excludes1   foreign body granuloma of skin and subcutaneous tissue (L92.3)

   M60.20   Foreign body granuloma of soft tissue, not elsewhere classified, unspecified site

● M60.21   Foreign body granuloma of soft tissue, not elsewhere classified, shoulder
     M60.211   Foreign body granuloma of soft tissue, not elsewhere classified, right shoulder
     M60.212   Foreign body granuloma of soft tissue, not elsewhere classified, left shoulder
     M60.219   Foreign body granuloma of soft tissue, not elsewhere classified, unspecified shoulder

● M60.22   Foreign body granuloma of soft tissue, not elsewhere classified, upper arm
     M60.221   Foreign body granuloma of soft tissue, not elsewhere classified, right upper arm
     M60.222   Foreign body granuloma of soft tissue, not elsewhere classified, left upper arm
     M60.229   Foreign body granuloma of soft tissue, not elsewhere classified, unspecified upper arm

● M60.23   Foreign body granuloma of soft tissue, not elsewhere classified, forearm
     M60.231   Foreign body granuloma of soft tissue, not elsewhere classified, right forearm
     M60.232   Foreign body granuloma of soft tissue, not elsewhere classified, left forearm
     M60.239   Foreign body granuloma of soft tissue, not elsewhere classified, unspecified forearm

● M60.24   Foreign body granuloma of soft tissue, not elsewhere classified, hand
     M60.241   Foreign body granuloma of soft tissue, not elsewhere classified, right hand
     M60.242   Foreign body granuloma of soft tissue, not elsewhere classified, left hand
     M60.249   Foreign body granuloma of soft tissue, not elsewhere classified, unspecified hand

● M60.25   Foreign body granuloma of soft tissue, not elsewhere classified, thigh
     M60.251   Foreign body granuloma of soft tissue, not elsewhere classified, right thigh
     M60.252   Foreign body granuloma of soft tissue, not elsewhere classified, left thigh
     M60.259   Foreign body granuloma of soft tissue, not elsewhere classified, unspecified thigh

● M60.26   Foreign body granuloma of soft tissue, not elsewhere classified, lower leg
     M60.261   Foreign body granuloma of soft tissue, not elsewhere classified, right lower leg
     M60.262   Foreign body granuloma of soft tissue, not elsewhere classified, left lower leg
     M60.269   Foreign body granuloma of soft tissue, not elsewhere classified, unspecified lower leg

● M60.27   Foreign body granuloma of soft tissue, not elsewhere classified, ankle and foot
     M60.271   Foreign body granuloma of soft tissue, not elsewhere classified, right ankle and foot
     M60.272   Foreign body granuloma of soft tissue, not elsewhere classified, left ankle and foot
     M60.279   Foreign body granuloma of soft tissue, not elsewhere classified, unspecified ankle and foot

   M60.28   Foreign body granuloma of soft tissue, not elsewhere classified, other site

● M60.8   **Other myositis**

   M60.80   Other myositis, unspecified site

● M60.81   Other myositis shoulder
     M60.811   Other myositis, right shoulder
     M60.812   Other myositis, left shoulder
     M60.819   Other myositis, unspecified shoulder

● M60.82   Other myositis, upper arm
     M60.821   Other myositis, right upper arm
     M60.822   Other myositis, left upper arm
     M60.829   Other myositis, unspecified upper arm

● M60.83   Other myositis, forearm
     M60.831   Other myositis, right forearm
     M60.832   Other myositis, left forearm
     M60.839   Other myositis, unspecified forearm

● M60.84   Other myositis, hand
     M60.841   Other myositis, right hand
     M60.842   Other myositis, left hand
     M60.849   Other myositis, unspecified hand

● M60.85   Other myositis, thigh
     M60.851   Other myositis, right thigh
     M60.852   Other myositis, left thigh
     M60.859   Other myositis, unspecified thigh

- M60.86   Other myositis, lower leg
  - M60.861   Other myositis, right lower leg
  - M60.862   Other myositis, left lower leg
  - M60.869   Other myositis, unspecified lower leg
- M60.87   Other myositis, ankle and foot
  - M60.871   Other myositis, right ankle and foot
  - M60.872   Other myositis, left ankle and foot
  - M60.879   Other myositis, unspecified ankle and foot
  - M60.88   Other myositis, other site
  - M60.89   Other myositis, multiple sites
- M60.9   Myositis, unspecified

- M61   Calcification and ossification of muscle
  - M61.0   Myositis ossificans traumatica
    - M61.00   Myositis ossificans traumatica, unspecified site
    - M61.01   Myositis ossificans traumatica, shoulder
      - M61.011   Myositis ossificans traumatica, right shoulder
      - M61.012   Myositis ossificans traumatica, left shoulder
      - M61.019   Myositis ossificans traumatica, unspecified shoulder
    - M61.02   Myositis ossificans traumatica, upper arm
      - M61.021   Myositis ossificans traumatica, right upper arm
      - M61.022   Myositis ossificans traumatica, left upper arm
      - M61.029   Myositis ossificans traumatica, unspecified upper arm
    - M61.03   Myositis ossificans traumatica, forearm
      - M61.031   Myositis ossificans traumatica, right forearm
      - M61.032   Myositis ossificans traumatica, left forearm
      - M61.039   Myositis ossificans traumatica, unspecified forearm
    - M61.04   Myositis ossificans traumatica, hand
      - M61.041   Myositis ossificans traumatica, right hand
      - M61.042   Myositis ossificans traumatica, left hand
      - M61.049   Myositis ossificans traumatica, unspecified hand
    - M61.05   Myositis ossificans traumatica, thigh
      - M61.051   Myositis ossificans traumatica, right thigh
      - M61.052   Myositis ossificans traumatica, left thigh
      - M61.059   Myositis ossificans traumatica, unspecified thigh
    - M61.06   Myositis ossificans traumatica, lower leg
      - M61.061   Myositis ossificans traumatica, right lower leg
      - M61.062   Myositis ossificans traumatica, left lower leg
      - M61.069   Myositis ossificans traumatica, unspecified lower leg
    - M61.07   Myositis ossificans traumatica, ankle and foot
      - M61.071   Myositis ossificans traumatica, right ankle and foot
      - M61.072   Myositis ossificans traumatica, left ankle and foot
      - M61.079   Myositis ossificans traumatica, unspecified ankle and foot
    - M61.08   Myositis ossificans traumatica, other site
    - M61.09   Myositis ossificans traumatica, multiple sites

- M61.1   Myositis ossificans progressiva
  Fibrodysplasia ossificans progressiva
  - M61.10   Myositis ossificans progressiva, unspecified site
  - M61.11   Myositis ossificans progressiva, shoulder
    - M61.111   Myositis ossificans progressiva, right shoulder
    - M61.112   Myositis ossificans progressiva, left shoulder
    - M61.119   Myositis ossificans progressiva, unspecified shoulder
  - M61.12   Myositis ossificans progressiva, upper arm
    - M61.121   Myositis ossificans progressiva, right upper arm
    - M61.122   Myositis ossificans progressiva, left upper arm
    - M61.129   Myositis ossificans progressiva, unspecified arm
  - M61.13   Myositis ossificans progressiva, forearm
    - M61.131   Myositis ossificans progressiva, right forearm
    - M61.132   Myositis ossificans progressiva, left forearm
    - M61.139   Myositis ossificans progressiva, unspecified forearm
  - M61.14   Myositis ossificans progressiva, hand and finger(s)
    - M61.141   Myositis ossificans progressiva, right hand
    - M61.142   Myositis ossificans progressiva, left hand
    - M61.143   Myositis ossificans progressiva, unspecified hand
    - M61.144   Myositis ossificans progressiva, right finger(s)
    - M61.145   Myositis ossificans progressiva, left finger(s)
    - M61.146   Myositis ossificans progressiva, unspecified finger(s)
  - M61.15   Myositis ossificans progressiva, thigh
    - M61.151   Myositis ossificans progressiva, right thigh
    - M61.152   Myositis ossificans progressiva, left thigh
    - M61.159   Myositis ossificans progressiva, unspecified thigh
  - M61.16   Myositis ossificans progressiva, lower leg
    - M61.161   Myositis ossificans progressiva, right lower leg
    - M61.162   Myositis ossificans progressiva, left lower leg
    - M61.169   Myositis ossificans progressiva, unspecified lower leg
  - M61.17   Myositis ossificans progressiva, ankle, foot and toe(s)
    - M61.171   Myositis ossificans progressiva, right ankle
    - M61.172   Myositis ossificans progressiva, left ankle
    - M61.173   Myositis ossificans progressiva, unspecified ankle
    - M61.174   Myositis ossificans progressiva, right foot
    - M61.175   Myositis ossificans progressiva, left foot
    - M61.176   Myositis ossificans progressiva, unspecified foot
    - M61.177   Myositis ossificans progressiva, right toe(s)
    - M61.178   Myositis ossificans progressiva, left toe(s)
    - M61.179   Myositis ossificans progressiva, unspecified toe(s)

CHAPTER 13 (MØØ-M99)

M61.18 Myositis ossificans progressiva, other site

M61.19 Myositis ossificans progressiva, multiple sites

● M61.2 **Paralytic calcification and ossification of muscle**
Myositis ossificans associated with quadriplegia or paraplegia

M61.20 Paralytic calcification and ossification of muscle, unspecified site

● M61.21 Paralytic calcification and ossification of muscle, shoulder

M61.211 Paralytic calcification and ossification of muscle, right shoulder

M61.212 Paralytic calcification and ossification of muscle, left shoulder

M61.219 Paralytic calcification and ossification of muscle, unspecified shoulder

● M61.22 Paralytic calcification and ossification of muscle, upper arm

M61.221 Paralytic calcification and ossification of muscle, right upper arm

M61.222 Paralytic calcification and ossification of muscle, left upper arm

M61.229 Paralytic calcification and ossification of muscle, unspecified upper arm

● M61.23 Paralytic calcification and ossification of muscle, forearm

M61.231 Paralytic calcification and ossification of muscle, right forearm

M61.232 Paralytic calcification and ossification of muscle, left forearm

M61.239 Paralytic calcification and ossification of muscle, unspecified forearm

● M61.24 Paralytic calcification and ossification of muscle, hand

M61.241 Paralytic calcification and ossification of muscle, right hand

M61.242 Paralytic calcification and ossification of muscle, left hand

M61.249 Paralytic calcification and ossification of muscle, unspecified hand

● M61.25 Paralytic calcification and ossification of muscle, thigh

M61.251 Paralytic calcification and ossification of muscle, right thigh

M61.252 Paralytic calcification and ossification of muscle, left thigh

M61.259 Paralytic calcification and ossification of muscle, unspecified thigh

● M61.26 Paralytic calcification and ossification of muscle, lower leg

M61.261 Paralytic calcification and ossification of muscle, right lower leg

M61.262 Paralytic calcification and ossification of muscle, left lower leg

M61.269 Paralytic calcification and ossification of muscle, unspecified lower leg

● M61.27 Paralytic calcification and ossification of muscle, ankle and foot

M61.271 Paralytic calcification and ossification of muscle, right ankle and foot

M61.272 Paralytic calcification and ossification of muscle, left ankle and foot

M61.279 Paralytic calcification and ossification of muscle, unspecified ankle and foot

M61.28 Paralytic calcification and ossification of muscle, other site

M61.29 Paralytic calcification and ossification of muscle, multiple sites

● M61.3 Calcification and ossification of muscles associated with burns
Myositis ossificans associated with burns

M61.30 Calcification and ossification of muscles associated with burns, unspecified site

● M61.31 Calcification and ossification of muscles associated with burns, shoulder

M61.311 Calcification and ossification of muscles associated with burns, right shoulder

M61.312 Calcification and ossification of muscles associated with burns, left shoulder

M61.319 Calcification and ossification of muscles associated with burns, unspecified shoulder

● M61.32 Calcification and ossification of muscles associated with burns, upper arm

M61.321 Calcification and ossification of muscles associated with burns, right upper arm

M61.322 Calcification and ossification of muscles associated with burns, left upper arm

M61.329 Calcification and ossification of muscles associated with burns, unspecified upper arm

● M61.33 Calcification and ossification of muscles associated with burns, forearm

M61.331 Calcification and ossification of muscles associated with burns, right forearm

M61.332 Calcification and ossification of muscles associated with burns, left forearm

M61.339 Calcification and ossification of muscles associated with burns, unspecified forearm

● M61.34 Calcification and ossification of muscles associated with burns, hand

M61.341 Calcification and ossification of muscles associated with burns, right hand

M61.342 Calcification and ossification of muscles associated with burns, left hand

M61.349 Calcification and ossification of muscles associated with burns, unspecified hand

● M61.35 Calcification and ossification of muscles associated with burns, thigh

M61.351 Calcification and ossification of muscles associated with burns, right thigh

M61.352 Calcification and ossification of muscles associated with burns, left thigh

M61.359 Calcification and ossification of muscles associated with burns, unspecified thigh

● M61.36 Calcification and ossification of muscles associated with burns, lower leg

M61.361 Calcification and ossification of muscles associated with burns, right lower leg

M61.362 Calcification and ossification of muscles associated with burns, left lower leg

M61.369 Calcification and ossification of muscles associated with burns, unspecified lower leg

▶ New   ⇒ Revised   ~~deleted~~ Deleted   Excludes 1   Excludes 2   Includes   Use additional   Code first   Code also   Key words

OGCR Official Guidelines   X Assign placeholder X   ● Use Additional Character(s)   ▌ Manifestation Code   ⚕ Hierarchical Condition Category   Coding Clinic

● **M61.37 Calcification and ossification of muscles associated with burns, ankle and foot**
    M61.371 Calcification and ossification of muscles associated with burns, right ankle and foot
    M61.372 Calcification and ossification of muscles associated with burns, left ankle and foot
    M61.379 Calcification and ossification of muscles associated with burns, unspecified ankle and foot
  M61.38 Calcification and ossification of muscles associated with burns, other site
  M61.39 Calcification and ossification of muscles associated with burns, multiple sites
● **M61.4 Other calcification of muscle**
    Excludes1   calcific tendinitis NOS (M65.2-)
                 calcific tendinitis of shoulder (M75.3)
  M61.40 Other calcification of muscle, unspecified site
● **M61.41 Other calcification of muscle, shoulder**
    M61.411 Other calcification of muscle, right shoulder
    M61.412 Other calcification of muscle, left shoulder
    M61.419 Other calcification of muscle, unspecified shoulder
● **M61.42 Other calcification of muscle, upper arm**
    M61.421 Other calcification of muscle, right upper arm
    M61.422 Other calcification of muscle, left upper arm
    M61.429 Other calcification of muscle, unspecified upper arm
● **M61.43 Other calcification of muscle, forearm**
    M61.431 Other calcification of muscle, right forearm
    M61.432 Other calcification of muscle, left forearm
    M61.439 Other calcification of muscle, unspecified forearm
● **M61.44 Other calcification of muscle, hand**
    M61.441 Other calcification of muscle, right hand
    M61.442 Other calcification of muscle, left hand
    M61.449 Other calcification of muscle, unspecified hand
● **M61.45 Other calcification of muscle, thigh**
    M61.451 Other calcification of muscle, right thigh
    M61.452 Other calcification of muscle, left thigh
    M61.459 Other calcification of muscle, unspecified thigh
● **M61.46 Other calcification of muscle, lower leg**
    M61.461 Other calcification of muscle, right lower leg
    M61.462 Other calcification of muscle, left lower leg
    M61.469 Other calcification of muscle, unspecified lower leg

● **M61.47 Other calcification of muscle, ankle and foot**
    M61.471 Other calcification of muscle, right ankle and foot
    M61.472 Other calcification of muscle, left ankle and foot
    M61.479 Other calcification of muscle, unspecified ankle and foot
  M61.48 Other calcification of muscle, other site
  M61.49 Other calcification of muscle, multiple sites
● **M61.5 Other ossification of muscle**
  M61.50 Other ossification of muscle, unspecified site
● **M61.51 Other ossification of muscle, shoulder**
    M61.511 Other ossification of muscle, right shoulder
    M61.512 Other ossification of muscle, left shoulder
    M61.519 Other ossification of muscle, unspecified shoulder
● **M61.52 Other ossification of muscle, upper arm**
    M61.521 Other ossification of muscle, right upper arm
    M61.522 Other ossification of muscle, left upper arm
    M61.529 Other ossification of muscle, unspecified upper arm
● **M61.53 Other ossification of muscle, forearm**
    M61.531 Other ossification of muscle, right forearm
    M61.532 Other ossification of muscle, left forearm
    M61.539 Other ossification of muscle, unspecified forearm
● **M61.54 Other ossification of muscle, hand**
    M61.541 Other ossification of muscle, right hand
    M61.542 Other ossification of muscle, left hand
    M61.549 Other ossification of muscle, unspecified hand
● **M61.55 Other ossification of muscle, thigh**
    M61.551 Other ossification of muscle, right thigh
    M61.552 Other ossification of muscle, left thigh
    M61.559 Other ossification of muscle, unspecified thigh
● **M61.56 Other ossification of muscle, lower leg**
    M61.561 Other ossification of muscle, right lower leg
    M61.562 Other ossification of muscle, left lower leg
    M61.569 Other ossification of muscle, unspecified lower leg
● **M61.57 Other ossification of muscle, ankle and foot**
    M61.571 Other ossification of muscle, right ankle and foot
    M61.572 Other ossification of muscle, left ankle and foot
    M61.579 Other ossification of muscle, unspecified ankle and foot
  M61.58 Other ossification of muscle, other site
  M61.59 Other ossification of muscle, multiple sites
  M61.9 Calcification and ossification of muscle, unspecified

● **M62 Other disorders of muscle**

    Excludes1   alcoholic myopathy (G72.1)
                    cramp and spasm (R25.2)
                    drug-induced myopathy (G72.0)
                    myalgia (M79.1-)
                    stiff-man syndrome (G25.82)

    Excludes2   nontraumatic hematoma of muscle (M79.81)

  ● **M62.0 Separation of muscle (nontraumatic)**
        Diastasis of muscle

        Excludes1   diastasis recti complicating pregnancy, labor and delivery (O71.8)
                              traumatic separation of muscle - see strain of muscle by body region

      M62.00 Separation of muscle (nontraumatic), unspecified site

    ● **M62.01** Separation of muscle (nontraumatic), shoulder

        M62.011 Separation of muscle (nontraumatic), right shoulder

        M62.012 Separation of muscle (nontraumatic), left shoulder

        M62.019 Separation of muscle (nontraumatic), unspecified shoulder

    ● **M62.02** Separation of muscle (nontraumatic), upper arm

        M62.021 Separation of muscle (nontraumatic), right upper arm

        M62.022 Separation of muscle (nontraumatic), left upper arm

        M62.029 Separation of muscle (nontraumatic), unspecified upper arm

    ● **M62.03** Separation of muscle (nontraumatic), forearm

        M62.031 Separation of muscle (nontraumatic), right forearm

        M62.032 Separation of muscle (nontraumatic), left forearm

        M62.039 Separation of muscle (nontraumatic), unspecified forearm

    ● **M62.04** Separation of muscle (nontraumatic), hand

        M62.041 Separation of muscle (nontraumatic), right hand

        M62.042 Separation of muscle (nontraumatic), left hand

        M62.049 Separation of muscle (nontraumatic), unspecified hand

    ● **M62.05** Separation of muscle (nontraumatic), thigh

        M62.051 Separation of muscle (nontraumatic), right thigh

        M62.052 Separation of muscle (nontraumatic), left thigh

        M62.059 Separation of muscle (nontraumatic), unspecified thigh

    ● **M62.06** Separation of muscle (nontraumatic), lower leg

        M62.061 Separation of muscle (nontraumatic), right lower leg

        M62.062 Separation of muscle (nontraumatic), left lower leg

        M62.069 Separation of muscle (nontraumatic), unspecified lower leg

    ● **M62.07** Separation of muscle (nontraumatic), ankle and foot

        M62.071 Separation of muscle (nontraumatic), right ankle and foot

        M62.072 Separation of muscle (nontraumatic), left ankle and foot

        M62.079 Separation of muscle (nontraumatic), unspecified ankle and foot

      M62.08 Separation of muscle (nontraumatic), other site

● **M62.1 Other rupture of muscle (nontraumatic)**

    Excludes1   traumatic rupture of muscle - see strain of muscle by body region

    Excludes2   rupture of tendon (M66.-)

    M62.10 Other rupture of muscle (nontraumatic), unspecified site

  ● **M62.11** Other rupture of muscle (nontraumatic), shoulder

      M62.111 Other rupture of muscle (nontraumatic), right shoulder

      M62.112 Other rupture of muscle (nontraumatic), left shoulder

      M62.119 Other rupture of muscle (nontraumatic), unspecified shoulder

  ● **M62.12** Other rupture of muscle (nontraumatic), upper arm

      M62.121 Other rupture of muscle (nontraumatic), right upper arm

      M62.122 Other rupture of muscle (nontraumatic), left upper arm

      M62.129 Other rupture of muscle (nontraumatic), unspecified upper arm

  ● **M62.13** Other rupture of muscle (nontraumatic), forearm

      M62.131 Other rupture of muscle (nontraumatic), right forearm

      M62.132 Other rupture of muscle (nontraumatic), left forearm

      M62.139 Other rupture of muscle (nontraumatic), unspecified forearm

  ● **M62.14** Other rupture of muscle (nontraumatic), hand

      M62.141 Other rupture of muscle (nontraumatic), right hand

      M62.142 Other rupture of muscle (nontraumatic), left hand

      M62.149 Other rupture of muscle (nontraumatic), unspecified hand

  ● **M62.15** Other rupture of muscle (nontraumatic), thigh

      M62.151 Other rupture of muscle (nontraumatic), right thigh

      M62.152 Other rupture of muscle (nontraumatic), left thigh

      M62.159 Other rupture of muscle (nontraumatic), unspecified thigh

  ● **M62.16** Other rupture of muscle (nontraumatic), lower leg

      M62.161 Other rupture of muscle (nontraumatic), right lower leg

      M62.162 Other rupture of muscle (nontraumatic), left lower leg

      M62.169 Other rupture of muscle (nontraumatic), unspecified lower leg

  ● **M62.17** Other rupture of muscle (nontraumatic), ankle and foot

      M62.171 Other rupture of muscle (nontraumatic), right ankle and foot

      M62.172 Other rupture of muscle (nontraumatic), left ankle and foot

      M62.179 Other rupture of muscle (nontraumatic), unspecified ankle and foot

    M62.18 Other rupture of muscle (nontraumatic), other site

▶ New   ⇒ Revised   ~~deleted~~ Deleted   Excludes 1   Excludes 2   Includes   Use additional   Code first   Code also   Key words

OGCR Official Guidelines   X Assign placeholder X   ● Use Additional Character(s)   ▶ Manifestation Code   🐾 Hierarchical Condition Category   **Coding Clinic**

● **M62.2 Nontraumatic ischemic infarction of muscle**

    Excludes1   compartment syndrome (traumatic) (T79.A-)

         nontraumatic compartment syndrome (M79.A-)

         traumatic ischemia of muscle (T79.6)

         rhabdomyolysis (M62.82)

         Volkmann's ischemic contracture (T79.6)

     M62.20   Nontraumatic ischemic infarction of muscle, unspecified site

●   **M62.21**   Nontraumatic ischemic infarction of muscle, shoulder

       M62.211   Nontraumatic ischemic infarction of muscle, right shoulder

       M62.212   Nontraumatic ischemic infarction of muscle, left shoulder

       M62.219   Nontraumatic ischemic infarction of muscle, unspecified shoulder

●   **M62.22**   Nontraumatic ischemic infarction of muscle, upper arm

       M62.221   Nontraumatic ischemic infarction of muscle, right upper arm

       M62.222   Nontraumatic ischemic infarction of muscle, left upper arm

       M62.229   Nontraumatic ischemic infarction of muscle, unspecified upper arm

●   **M62.23**   Nontraumatic ischemic infarction of muscle, forearm

       M62.231   Nontraumatic ischemic infarction of muscle, right forearm

       M62.232   Nontraumatic ischemic infarction of muscle, left forearm

       M62.239   Nontraumatic ischemic infarction of muscle, unspecified forearm

●   **M62.24**   Nontraumatic ischemic infarction of muscle, hand

       M62.241   Nontraumatic ischemic infarction of muscle, right hand

       M62.242   Nontraumatic ischemic infarction of muscle, left hand

       M62.249   Nontraumatic ischemic infarction of muscle, unspecified hand

●   **M62.25**   Nontraumatic ischemic infarction of muscle, thigh

       M62.251   Nontraumatic ischemic infarction of muscle, right thigh

       M62.252   Nontraumatic ischemic infarction of muscle, left thigh

       M62.259   Nontraumatic ischemic infarction of muscle, unspecified thigh

●   **M62.26**   Nontraumatic ischemic infarction of muscle, lower leg

       M62.261   Nontraumatic ischemic infarction of muscle, right lower leg

       M62.262   Nontraumatic ischemic infarction of muscle, left lower leg

       M62.269   Nontraumatic ischemic infarction of muscle, unspecified lower leg

●   **M62.27**   Nontraumatic ischemic infarction of muscle, ankle and foot

       M62.271   Nontraumatic ischemic infarction of muscle, right ankle and foot

       M62.272   Nontraumatic ischemic infarction of muscle, left ankle and foot

       M62.279   Nontraumatic ischemic infarction of muscle, unspecified ankle and foot

     M62.28   Nontraumatic ischemic infarction of muscle, other site

M62.3   Immobility syndrome (paraplegic)

M62.4   Contracture of muscle

     Contracture of tendon (sheath)

    Excludes1   contracture of joint (M24.5-)

     M62.40   Contracture of muscle, unspecified site

●   **M62.41**   Contracture of muscle, shoulder

       M62.411   Contracture of muscle, right shoulder

       M62.412   Contracture of muscle, left shoulder

       M62.419   Contracture of muscle, unspecified shoulder

●   **M62.42**   Contracture of muscle, upper arm

       M62.421   Contracture of muscle, right upper arm

       M62.422   Contracture of muscle, left upper arm

       M62.429   Contracture of muscle, unspecified upper arm

●   **M62.43**   Contracture of muscle, forearm

       M62.431   Contracture of muscle, right forearm

       M62.432   Contracture of muscle, left forearm

       M62.439   Contracture of muscle, unspecified forearm

●   **M62.44**   Contracture of muscle, hand

       M62.441   Contracture of muscle, right hand

       M62.442   Contracture of muscle, left hand

       M62.449   Contracture of muscle, unspecified hand

●   **M62.45**   Contracture of muscle, thigh

       M62.451   Contracture of muscle, right thigh

       M62.452   Contracture of muscle, left thigh

       M62.459   Contracture of muscle, unspecified thigh

●   **M62.46**   Contracture of muscle, lower leg

       M62.461   Contracture of muscle, right lower leg

       M62.462   Contracture of muscle, left lower leg

       M62.469   Contracture of muscle, unspecified lower leg

●   **M62.47**   Contracture of muscle, ankle and foot

       M62.471   Contracture of muscle, right ankle and foot

       M62.472   Contracture of muscle, left ankle and foot

       M62.479   Contracture of muscle, unspecified ankle and foot

     M62.48   Contracture of muscle, other site

     M62.49   Contracture of muscle, multiple sites

● **M62.5   Muscle wasting and atrophy, not elsewhere classified**

     Disuse atrophy NEC

    Excludes1   neuralgic amyotrophy (G54.5)

         progressive muscular atrophy (G12.21)

         sarcopenia (M62.84)

    Excludes2   pelvic muscle wasting (N81.84)

     M62.50   Muscle wasting and atrophy, not elsewhere classified, unspecified site

●   **M62.51**   Muscle wasting and atrophy, not elsewhere classified, shoulder

       M62.511   Muscle wasting and atrophy, not elsewhere classified, right shoulder

       M62.512   Muscle wasting and atrophy, not elsewhere classified, left shoulder

       M62.519   Muscle wasting and atrophy, not elsewhere classified, unspecified shoulder

● **M62.52**   Muscle wasting and atrophy, not elsewhere classified, upper arm

    M62.521   Muscle wasting and atrophy, not elsewhere classified, right upper arm

    M62.522   Muscle wasting and atrophy, not elsewhere classified, left upper arm

    M62.529   Muscle wasting and atrophy, not elsewhere classified, unspecified upper arm

● **M62.53**   Muscle wasting and atrophy, not elsewhere classified, forearm

    M62.531   Muscle wasting and atrophy, not elsewhere classified, right forearm

    M62.532   Muscle wasting and atrophy, not elsewhere classified, left forearm

    M62.539   Muscle wasting and atrophy, not elsewhere classified, unspecified forearm

● **M62.54**   Muscle wasting and atrophy, not elsewhere classified, hand

    M62.541   Muscle wasting and atrophy, not elsewhere classified, right hand

    M62.542   Muscle wasting and atrophy, not elsewhere classified, left hand

    M62.549   Muscle wasting and atrophy, not elsewhere classified, unspecified hand

● **M62.55**   Muscle wasting and atrophy, not elsewhere classified, thigh

    M62.551   Muscle wasting and atrophy, not elsewhere classified, right thigh

    M62.552   Muscle wasting and atrophy, not elsewhere classified, left thigh

    M62.559   Muscle wasting and atrophy, not elsewhere classified, unspecified thigh

● **M62.56**   Muscle wasting and atrophy, not elsewhere classified, lower leg

    M62.561   Muscle wasting and atrophy, not elsewhere classified, right lower leg

    M62.562   Muscle wasting and atrophy, not elsewhere classified, left lower leg

    M62.569   Muscle wasting and atrophy, not elsewhere classified, unspecified lower leg

● **M62.57**   Muscle wasting and atrophy, not elsewhere classified, ankle and foot

    M62.571   Muscle wasting and atrophy, not elsewhere classified, right ankle and foot

    M62.572   Muscle wasting and atrophy, not elsewhere classified, left ankle and foot

    M62.579   Muscle wasting and atrophy, not elsewhere classified, unspecified ankle and foot

    M62.58   Muscle wasting and atrophy, not elsewhere classified, other site

    M62.59   Muscle wasting and atrophy, not elsewhere classified, multiple sites

● **M62.8**   Other specified disorders of muscle

    Excludes2   nontraumatic hematoma of muscle (M79.81)

    M62.81   Muscle weakness (generalized)

      Excludes1   muscle weakness in sarcopenia (M62.84)

    M62.82   Rhabdomyolysis

      Excludes1   traumatic rhabdomyolysis (T79.6)

      Coding Clinic: 2019, Q2, P12

● **M62.83**   Muscle spasm

    M62.830   Muscle spasm of back

    M62.831   Muscle spasm of calf
       Charley-horse

    M62.838   Other muscle spasm

    M62.84   Sarcopenia
      Age-related sarcopenia
      Code first underlying disease, if applicable, such as:
       disorders of myoneural junction and muscle disease in diseases classified elsewhere (G73.-)
       other and unspecified myopathies (G72.-)
       primary disorders of muscles (G71.-)
      Coding Clinic: 2016, Q4, P41

    M62.89   Other specified disorders of muscle
      Muscle (sheath) hernia

   M62.9   Disorder of muscle, unspecified

● **M63**   Disorders of muscle in diseases classified elsewhere

   Code first underlying disease, such as:
    leprosy (A30.-)
    neoplasm (C49.-, C79.89, D21.-, D48.1)
    schistosomiasis (B65.-)
    trichinellosis (B75)

   Excludes1   myopathy in cysticercosis (B69.81)
      myopathy in endocrine diseases (G73.7)
      myopathy in metabolic diseases (G73.7)
      myopathy in sarcoidosis (D86.87)
      myopathy in secondary syphilis (A51.49)
      myopathy in syphilis (late) (A52.78)
      myopathy in toxoplasmosis (B58.82)
      myopathy in tuberculosis (A18.09)

● **M63.8**   Disorders of muscle in diseases classified elsewhere

 ▷ *M63.80*   *Disorders of muscle in diseases classified elsewhere, unspecified site*

● *M63.81*   Disorders of muscle in diseases classified elsewhere, shoulder

 ▷ *M63.811*   *Disorders of muscle in diseases classified elsewhere, right shoulder*

 ▷ *M63.812*   *Disorders of muscle in diseases classified elsewhere, left shoulder*

 ▷ *M63.819*   *Disorders of muscle in diseases classified elsewhere, unspecified shoulder*

● *M63.82*   Disorders of muscle in diseases classified elsewhere, upper arm

 ▷ *M63.821*   *Disorders of muscle in diseases classified elsewhere, right upper arm*

 ▷ *M63.822*   *Disorders of muscle in diseases classified elsewhere, left upper arm*

 ▷ *M63.829*   *Disorders of muscle in diseases classified elsewhere, unspecified upper arm*

● *M63.83*   Disorders of muscle in diseases classified elsewhere, forearm

 ▷ *M63.831*   *Disorders of muscle in diseases classified elsewhere, right forearm*

 ▷ *M63.832*   *Disorders of muscle in diseases classified elsewhere, left forearm*

 ▷ *M63.839*   *Disorders of muscle in diseases classified elsewhere, unspecified forearm*

● *M63.84*   Disorders of muscle in diseases classified elsewhere, hand

 ▷ *M63.841*   *Disorders of muscle in diseases classified elsewhere, right hand*

 ▷ *M63.842*   *Disorders of muscle in diseases classified elsewhere, left hand*

 ▷ *M63.849*   *Disorders of muscle in diseases classified elsewhere, unspecified hand*

▶ New   ⇒ Revised   ~~deleted~~ Deleted   Excludes 1   Excludes 2   Includes   Use additional   Code first   Code also   Key words

OGCR Official Guidelines   X Assign placeholder X   ● Use Additional Character(s)   ▷ Manifestation Code   🅗🅒 Hierarchical Condition Category   **Coding Clinic**

● **M63.85** Disorders of muscle in diseases classified elsewhere, **thigh**
  ▶ *M63.851 Disorders of muscle in diseases classified elsewhere, right thigh*
  ▶ *M63.852 Disorders of muscle in diseases classified elsewhere, left thigh*
  ▶ *M63.859 Disorders of muscle in diseases classified elsewhere, unspecified thigh*
● **M63.86** Disorders of muscle in diseases classified elsewhere, **lower leg**
  ▶ *M63.861 Disorders of muscle in diseases classified elsewhere, right lower leg*
  ▶ *M63.862 Disorders of muscle in diseases classified elsewhere, left lower leg*
  ▶ *M63.869 Disorders of muscle in diseases classified elsewhere, unspecified lower leg*
● **M63.87** Disorders of muscle in diseases classified elsewhere, **ankle and foot**
  ▶ *M63.871 Disorders of muscle in diseases classified elsewhere, right ankle and foot*
  ▶ *M63.872 Disorders of muscle in diseases classified elsewhere, left ankle and foot*
  ▶ *M63.879 Disorders of muscle in diseases classified elsewhere, unspecified ankle and foot*
  ▶ *M63.88 Disorders of muscle in diseases classified elsewhere, other site*
  ▶ *M63.89 Disorders of muscle in diseases classified elsewhere, multiple sites*

DISORDERS OF SYNOVIUM AND TENDON (M65-M67)

● **M65** Synovitis and tenosynovitis
  | Excludes1 | chronic crepitant synovitis of hand and wrist (M70.0-) |
  current injury - see injury of ligament or tendon by body region
  soft tissue disorders related to use, overuse and pressure (M70.-)
● **M65.0** Abscess of tendon sheath
  Use additional code (B95-B96) to identify bacterial agent
  M65.00 Abscess of tendon sheath, unspecified site
  ● **M65.01** Abscess of tendon sheath, shoulder
  M65.011 Abscess of tendon sheath, right shoulder
  M65.012 Abscess of tendon sheath, left shoulder
  M65.019 Abscess of tendon sheath, unspecified shoulder
  ● **M65.02** Abscess of tendon sheath, upper arm
  M65.021 Abscess of tendon sheath, right upper arm
  M65.022 Abscess of tendon sheath, left upper arm
  M65.029 Abscess of tendon sheath, unspecified upper arm

● **M65.03** Abscess of tendon sheath, forearm
  M65.031 Abscess of tendon sheath, right forearm
  M65.032 Abscess of tendon sheath, left forearm
  M65.039 Abscess of tendon sheath, unspecified forearm
● **M65.04** Abscess of tendon sheath, hand
  M65.041 Abscess of tendon sheath, right hand
  M65.042 Abscess of tendon sheath, left hand
  M65.049 Abscess of tendon sheath, unspecified hand
● **M65.05** Abscess of tendon sheath, thigh
  M65.051 Abscess of tendon sheath, right thigh
  M65.052 Abscess of tendon sheath, left thigh
  M65.059 Abscess of tendon sheath, unspecified thigh
● **M65.06** Abscess of tendon sheath, lower leg
  M65.061 Abscess of tendon sheath, right lower leg
  M65.062 Abscess of tendon sheath, left lower leg
  M65.069 Abscess of tendon sheath, unspecified lower leg
● **M65.07** Abscess of tendon sheath, ankle and foot
  M65.071 Abscess of tendon sheath, right ankle and foot
  M65.072 Abscess of tendon sheath, left ankle and foot
  M65.079 Abscess of tendon sheath, unspecified ankle and foot
  M65.08 Abscess of tendon sheath, other site
● **M65.1** Other infective (teno)synovitis
  M65.10 Other infective (teno)synovitis, unspecified site
  ● **M65.11** Other infective (teno)synovitis, shoulder
  M65.111 Other infective (teno)synovitis, right shoulder
  M65.112 Other infective (teno)synovitis, left shoulder
  M65.119 Other infective (teno)synovitis, unspecified shoulder
  ● **M65.12** Other infective (teno)synovitis, elbow
  M65.121 Other infective (teno)synovitis, right elbow
  M65.122 Other infective (teno)synovitis, left elbow
  M65.129 Other infective (teno)synovitis, unspecified elbow
  ● **M65.13** Other infective (teno)synovitis, wrist
  M65.131 Other infective (teno)synovitis, right wrist
  M65.132 Other infective (teno)synovitis, left wrist
  M65.139 Other infective (teno)synovitis, unspecified wrist
  ● **M65.14** Other infective (teno)synovitis, hand
  M65.141 Other infective (teno)synovitis, right hand
  M65.142 Other infective (teno)synovitis, left hand
  M65.149 Other infective (teno)synovitis, unspecified hand
  ● **M65.15** Other infective (teno)synovitis, hip
  M65.151 Other infective (teno)synovitis, right hip
  M65.152 Other infective (teno)synovitis, left hip
  M65.159 Other infective (teno)synovitis, unspecified hip

Item 13-11 Synovitis is an inflammation of a synovial membrane resulting in pain on motion and is characterized by fluctuating swelling due to effusion in a synovial sac. **Tenosynovitis** is an inflammation of a tendon sheath and occurs most commonly in the wrists, hands, and feet. Bursitis is inflammation of a bursa (fluid-filled sac) caused by repetitive use, trauma, infection, or systemic inflammatory disease. Bursae act as protectors and facilitate movement between bones and overlapping muscles (deep bursae) or between bones and tendons/skin (superficial bursae).

● M65.16 Other infective (teno)synovitis, knee
    M65.161 Other infective (teno)synovitis, right knee
    M65.162 Other infective (teno)synovitis, left knee
    M65.169 Other infective (teno)synovitis, unspecified knee
● M65.17 Other infective (teno)synovitis, ankle and foot
    M65.171 Other infective (teno)synovitis, right ankle and foot
    M65.172 Other infective (teno)synovitis, left ankle and foot
    M65.179 Other infective (teno)synovitis, unspecified ankle and foot
  M65.18 Other infective (teno)synovitis, other site
  M65.19 Other infective (teno)synovitis, multiple sites
● M65.2 Calcific tendinitis
    Excludes1   tendinitis as classified in M75-M77
                 calcified tendinitis of shoulder (M75.3)
  M65.20 Calcific tendinitis, unspecified site
● M65.22 Calcific tendinitis, upper arm
    M65.221 Calcific tendinitis, right upper arm
    M65.222 Calcific tendinitis, left upper arm
    M65.229 Calcific tendinitis, unspecified upper arm
● M65.23 Calcific tendinitis, forearm
    M65.231 Calcific tendinitis, right forearm
    M65.232 Calcific tendinitis, left forearm
    M65.239 Calcific tendinitis, unspecified forearm
● M65.24 Calcific tendinitis, hand
    M65.241 Calcific tendinitis, right hand
    M65.242 Calcific tendinitis, left hand
    M65.249 Calcific tendinitis, unspecified hand
● M65.25 Calcific tendinitis, thigh
    M65.251 Calcific tendinitis, right thigh
    M65.252 Calcific tendinitis, left thigh
    M65.259 Calcific tendinitis, unspecified thigh
● M65.26 Calcific tendinitis, lower leg
    M65.261 Calcific tendinitis, right lower leg
    M65.262 Calcific tendinitis, left lower leg
    M65.269 Calcific tendinitis, unspecified lower leg
● M65.27 Calcific tendinitis, ankle and foot
    M65.271 Calcific tendinitis, right ankle and foot
    M65.272 Calcific tendinitis, left ankle and foot
    M65.279 Calcific tendinitis, unspecified ankle and foot
  M65.28 Calcific tendinitis, other site
  M65.29 Calcific tendinitis, multiple sites
● M65.3 Trigger finger
    Nodular tendinous disease
  M65.30 Trigger finger, unspecified finger
● M65.31 Trigger thumb
    M65.311 Trigger thumb, right thumb
    M65.312 Trigger thumb, left thumb
    M65.319 Trigger thumb, unspecified thumb
● M65.32 Trigger finger, index finger
    M65.321 Trigger finger, right index finger
    M65.322 Trigger finger, left index finger
    M65.329 Trigger finger, unspecified index finger
● M65.33 Trigger finger, middle finger
    M65.331 Trigger finger, right middle finger
    M65.332 Trigger finger, left middle finger
    M65.339 Trigger finger, unspecified middle finger

● M65.34 Trigger finger, ring finger
    M65.341 Trigger finger, right ring finger
    M65.342 Trigger finger, left ring finger
    M65.349 Trigger finger, unspecified ring finger
● M65.35 Trigger finger, little finger
    M65.351 Trigger finger, right little finger
    M65.352 Trigger finger, left little finger
    M65.359 Trigger finger, unspecified little finger
  M65.4 Radial styloid tenosynovitis [de Quervain]
● M65.8 Other synovitis and tenosynovitis
  M65.80 Other synovitis and tenosynovitis, unspecified site
● M65.81 Other synovitis and tenosynovitis, shoulder
    M65.811 Other synovitis and tenosynovitis, right shoulder
    M65.812 Other synovitis and tenosynovitis, left shoulder
    M65.819 Other synovitis and tenosynovitis, unspecified shoulder
● M65.82 Other synovitis and tenosynovitis, upper arm
    M65.821 Other synovitis and tenosynovitis, right upper arm
    M65.822 Other synovitis and tenosynovitis, left upper arm
    M65.829 Other synovitis and tenosynovitis, unspecified upper arm
● M65.83 Other synovitis and tenosynovitis, forearm
    M65.831 Other synovitis and tenosynovitis, right forearm
    M65.832 Other synovitis and tenosynovitis, left forearm
    M65.839 Other synovitis and tenosynovitis, unspecified forearm
● M65.84 Other synovitis and tenosynovitis, hand
    M65.841 Other synovitis and tenosynovitis, right hand
    M65.842 Other synovitis and tenosynovitis, left hand
    M65.849 Other synovitis and tenosynovitis, unspecified hand
● M65.85 Other synovitis and tenosynovitis, thigh
    M65.851 Other synovitis and tenosynovitis, right thigh
    M65.852 Other synovitis and tenosynovitis, left thigh
    M65.859 Other synovitis and tenosynovitis, unspecified thigh
● M65.86 Other synovitis and tenosynovitis, lower leg
    M65.861 Other synovitis and tenosynovitis, right lower leg
    M65.862 Other synovitis and tenosynovitis, left lower leg
    M65.869 Other synovitis and tenosynovitis, unspecified lower leg
● M65.87 Other synovitis and tenosynovitis, ankle and foot
    M65.871 Other synovitis and tenosynovitis, right ankle and foot
    M65.872 Other synovitis and tenosynovitis, left ankle and foot
    M65.879 Other synovitis and tenosynovitis, unspecified ankle and foot
  M65.88 Other synovitis and tenosynovitis, other site
  M65.89 Other synovitis and tenosynovitis, multiple sites
  M65.9 Synovitis and tenosynovitis, unspecified

▶ New   ⇛ Revised   ~~deleted~~ Deleted   Excludes 1   Excludes 2   Includes   Use additional   Code first   Code also   Key words

OGCR Official Guidelines   X Assign placeholder X   ● Use Additional Character(s)   ▶ Manifestation Code   🅗 Hierarchical Condition Category   **Coding Clinic**

● **M66 Spontaneous rupture of synovium and tendon**

    Includes   rupture that occurs when a normal force is applied to tissues that are inferred to have less than normal strength

    Excludes2   rotator cuff syndrome (M75.1-)

             rupture where an abnormal force is applied to normal tissue - see injury of tendon by body region

    M66.0 Rupture of popliteal cyst

● **M66.1 Rupture of synovium**

       Rupture of synovial cyst

        Excludes2   rupture of popliteal cyst (M66.0)

       M66.10   Rupture of synovium, unspecified joint

    ● M66.11   Rupture of synovium, shoulder

         M66.111   Rupture of synovium, right shoulder

         M66.112   Rupture of synovium, left shoulder

         M66.119   Rupture of synovium, unspecified shoulder

    ● M66.12   Rupture of synovium, elbow

         M66.121   Rupture of synovium, right elbow

         M66.122   Rupture of synovium, left elbow

         M66.129   Rupture of synovium, unspecified elbow

    ● M66.13   Rupture of synovium, wrist

         M66.131   Rupture of synovium, right wrist

         M66.132   Rupture of synovium, left wrist

         M66.139   Rupture of synovium, unspecified wrist

    ● M66.14   Rupture of synovium, hand and fingers

         M66.141   Rupture of synovium, right hand

         M66.142   Rupture of synovium, left hand

         M66.143   Rupture of synovium, unspecified hand

         M66.144   Rupture of synovium, right finger(s)

         M66.145   Rupture of synovium, left finger(s)

         M66.146   Rupture of synovium, unspecified finger(s)

    ● M66.15   Rupture of synovium, hip

         M66.151   Rupture of synovium, right hip

         M66.152   Rupture of synovium, left hip

         M66.159   Rupture of synovium, unspecified hip

    ● M66.17   Rupture of synovium, ankle, foot and toes

         M66.171   Rupture of synovium, right ankle

         M66.172   Rupture of synovium, left ankle

         M66.173   Rupture of synovium, unspecified ankle

         M66.174   Rupture of synovium, right foot

         M66.175   Rupture of synovium, left foot

         M66.176   Rupture of synovium, unspecified foot

         M66.177   Rupture of synovium, right toe(s)

         M66.178   Rupture of synovium, left toe(s)

         M66.179   Rupture of synovium, unspecified toe(s)

       M66.18   Rupture of synovium, other site

● **M66.2 Spontaneous rupture of extensor tendons**

       M66.20   Spontaneous rupture of extensor tendons, unspecified site

    ● M66.21   Spontaneous rupture of extensor tendons, shoulder

         M66.211   Spontaneous rupture of extensor tendons, right shoulder

         M66.212   Spontaneous rupture of extensor tendons, left shoulder

         M66.219   Spontaneous rupture of extensor tendons, unspecified shoulder

● M66.22   Spontaneous rupture of extensor tendons, upper arm

         M66.221   Spontaneous rupture of extensor tendons, right upper arm

         M66.222   Spontaneous rupture of extensor tendons, left upper arm

         M66.229   Spontaneous rupture of extensor tendons, unspecified upper arm

● M66.23   Spontaneous rupture of extensor tendons, forearm

         M66.231   Spontaneous rupture of extensor tendons, right forearm

         M66.232   Spontaneous rupture of extensor tendons, left forearm

         M66.239   Spontaneous rupture of extensor tendons, unspecified forearm

● M66.24   Spontaneous rupture of extensor tendons, hand

         M66.241   Spontaneous rupture of extensor tendons, right hand

         M66.242   Spontaneous rupture of extensor tendons, left hand

         M66.249   Spontaneous rupture of extensor tendons, unspecified hand

● M66.25   Spontaneous rupture of extensor tendons, thigh

         M66.251   Spontaneous rupture of extensor tendons, right thigh

         M66.252   Spontaneous rupture of extensor tendons, left thigh

         M66.259   Spontaneous rupture of extensor tendons, unspecified thigh

● M66.26   Spontaneous rupture of extensor tendons, lower leg

         M66.261   Spontaneous rupture of extensor tendons, right lower leg

         M66.262   Spontaneous rupture of extensor tendons, left lower leg

         M66.269   Spontaneous rupture of extensor tendons, unspecified lower leg

● M66.27   Spontaneous rupture of extensor tendons, ankle and foot

         M66.271   Spontaneous rupture of extensor tendons, right ankle and foot

         M66.272   Spontaneous rupture of extensor tendons, left ankle and foot

         M66.279   Spontaneous rupture of extensor tendons, unspecified ankle and foot

       M66.28   Spontaneous rupture of extensor tendons, other site

       M66.29   Spontaneous rupture of extensor tendons, multiple sites

● **M66.3 Spontaneous rupture of flexor tendons**

       M66.30   Spontaneous rupture of flexor tendons, unspecified site

    ● M66.31   Spontaneous rupture of flexor tendons, shoulder

         M66.311   Spontaneous rupture of flexor tendons, right shoulder

         M66.312   Spontaneous rupture of flexor tendons, left shoulder

         M66.319   Spontaneous rupture of flexor tendons, unspecified shoulder

    ● M66.32   Spontaneous rupture of flexor tendons, upper arm

         M66.321   Spontaneous rupture of flexor tendons, right upper arm

         M66.322   Spontaneous rupture of flexor tendons, left upper arm

         M66.329   Spontaneous rupture of flexor tendons, unspecified upper arm

● **M66.33** Spontaneous rupture of flexor tendons, forearm

     M66.331   Spontaneous rupture of flexor tendons, right forearm

     M66.332   Spontaneous rupture of flexor tendons, left forearm

     M66.339   Spontaneous rupture of flexor tendons, unspecified forearm

● **M66.34** Spontaneous rupture of flexor tendons, hand

     M66.341   Spontaneous rupture of flexor tendons, right hand

     M66.342   Spontaneous rupture of flexor tendons, left hand

     M66.349   Spontaneous rupture of flexor tendons, unspecified hand

● **M66.35** Spontaneous rupture of flexor tendons, thigh

     M66.351   Spontaneous rupture of flexor tendons, right thigh

     M66.352   Spontaneous rupture of flexor tendons, left thigh

     M66.359   Spontaneous rupture of flexor tendons, unspecified thigh

● **M66.36** Spontaneous rupture of flexor tendons, lower leg

     M66.361   Spontaneous rupture of flexor tendons, right lower leg

     M66.362   Spontaneous rupture of flexor tendons, left lower leg

     M66.369   Spontaneous rupture of flexor tendons, unspecified lower leg

● **M66.37** Spontaneous rupture of flexor tendons, ankle and foot

     M66.371   Spontaneous rupture of flexor tendons, right ankle and foot

     M66.372   Spontaneous rupture of flexor tendons, left ankle and foot

     M66.379   Spontaneous rupture of flexor tendons, unspecified ankle and foot

     M66.38   Spontaneous rupture of flexor tendons, other site

     M66.39   Spontaneous rupture of flexor tendons, multiple sites

● **M66.8** Spontaneous rupture of other tendons

     M66.80   Spontaneous rupture of other tendons, unspecified site

● **M66.81** Spontaneous rupture of other tendons, shoulder

     M66.811   Spontaneous rupture of other tendons, right shoulder

     M66.812   Spontaneous rupture of other tendons, left shoulder

     M66.819   Spontaneous rupture of other tendons, unspecified shoulder

● **M66.82** Spontaneous rupture of other tendons, upper arm

     M66.821   Spontaneous rupture of other tendons, right upper arm

     M66.822   Spontaneous rupture of other tendons, left upper arm

     M66.829   Spontaneous rupture of other tendons, unspecified upper arm

● **M66.83** Spontaneous rupture of other tendons, forearm

     M66.831   Spontaneous rupture of other tendons, right forearm

     M66.832   Spontaneous rupture of other tendons, left forearm

     M66.839   Spontaneous rupture of other tendons, unspecified forearm

● **M66.84** Spontaneous rupture of other tendons, hand

     M66.841   Spontaneous rupture of other tendons, right hand

     M66.842   Spontaneous rupture of other tendons, left hand

     M66.849   Spontaneous rupture of other tendons, unspecified hand

● **M66.85** Spontaneous rupture of other tendons, thigh

     M66.851   Spontaneous rupture of other tendons, right thigh

     M66.852   Spontaneous rupture of other tendons, left thigh

     M66.859   Spontaneous rupture of other tendons, unspecified thigh

● **M66.86** Spontaneous rupture of other tendons, lower leg

     M66.861   Spontaneous rupture of other tendons, right lower leg

     M66.862   Spontaneous rupture of other tendons, left lower leg

     M66.869   Spontaneous rupture of other tendons, unspecified lower leg

● **M66.87** Spontaneous rupture of other tendons, ankle and foot

     M66.871   Spontaneous rupture of other tendons, right ankle and foot

     M66.872   Spontaneous rupture of other tendons, left ankle and foot

     M66.879   Spontaneous rupture of other tendons, unspecified ankle and foot

     M66.88   Spontaneous rupture of other tendons, other sites

     M66.89   Spontaneous rupture of other tendons, multiple sites

   M66.9 Spontaneous rupture of unspecified tendon

     Rupture at musculotendinous junction, nontraumatic

● **M67** Other disorders of synovium and tendon

     Excludes1   palmar fascial fibromatosis [Dupuytren] (M72.0)

                 tendinitis NOS (M77.9-)

                  xanthomatosis localized to tendons (E78.2)

● **M67.0** Short Achilles tendon (acquired)

     M67.00   Short Achilles tendon (acquired), unspecified ankle

     M67.01   Short Achilles tendon (acquired), right ankle

     M67.02   Short Achilles tendon (acquired), left ankle

● **M67.2** Synovial hypertrophy, not elsewhere classified

     Excludes1   villonodular synovitis (pigmented) (M12.2-)

     M67.20   Synovial hypertrophy, not elsewhere classified, unspecified site

● **M67.21** Synovial hypertrophy, not elsewhere classified, shoulder

     M67.211   Synovial hypertrophy, not elsewhere classified, right shoulder

     M67.212   Synovial hypertrophy, not elsewhere classified, left shoulder

     M67.219   Synovial hypertrophy, not elsewhere classified, unspecified shoulder

● **M67.22** Synovial hypertrophy, not elsewhere classified, upper arm

     M67.221   Synovial hypertrophy, not elsewhere classified, right upper arm

     M67.222   Synovial hypertrophy, not elsewhere classified, left upper arm

     M67.229   Synovial hypertrophy, not elsewhere classified, unspecified upper arm

▶ New   ⇒ Revised   ~~deleted~~ Deleted   Excludes 1   Excludes 2   Includes   Use additional   Code first   Code also   Key words

OGCR Official Guidelines   X Assign placeholder X   ● Use Additional Character(s)   ▶ Manifestation Code   ●ᴴᶜᶜ Hierarchical Condition Category   **Coding Clinic**

● **M67.23** Synovial hypertrophy, not elsewhere classified, forearm
     M67.231 Synovial hypertrophy, not elsewhere classified, right forearm
     M67.232 Synovial hypertrophy, not elsewhere classified, left forearm
     M67.239 Synovial hypertrophy, not elsewhere classified, unspecified forearm

● **M67.24** Synovial hypertrophy, not elsewhere classified, hand
     M67.241 Synovial hypertrophy, not elsewhere classified, right hand
     M67.242 Synovial hypertrophy, not elsewhere classified, left hand
     M67.249 Synovial hypertrophy, not elsewhere classified, unspecified hand

● **M67.25** Synovial hypertrophy, not elsewhere classified, thigh
     M67.251 Synovial hypertrophy, not elsewhere classified, right thigh
     M67.252 Synovial hypertrophy, not elsewhere classified, left thigh
     M67.259 Synovial hypertrophy, not elsewhere classified, unspecified thigh

● **M67.26** Synovial hypertrophy, not elsewhere classified, lower leg
     M67.261 Synovial hypertrophy, not elsewhere classified, right lower leg
     M67.262 Synovial hypertrophy, not elsewhere classified, left lower leg
     M67.269 Synovial hypertrophy, not elsewhere classified, unspecified lower leg

● **M67.27** Synovial hypertrophy, not elsewhere classified, ankle and foot
     M67.271 Synovial hypertrophy, not elsewhere classified, right ankle and foot
     M67.272 Synovial hypertrophy, not elsewhere classified, left ankle and foot
     M67.279 Synovial hypertrophy, not elsewhere classified, unspecified ankle and foot

     M67.28 Synovial hypertrophy, not elsewhere classified, other site

     M67.29 Synovial hypertrophy, not elsewhere classified, multiple sites

● **M67.3** Transient synovitis
     Toxic synovitis
     Excludes1   palindromic rheumatism (M12.3-)

     M67.30 Transient synovitis, unspecified site

● **M67.31** Transient synovitis, shoulder
     M67.311 Transient synovitis, right shoulder
     M67.312 Transient synovitis, left shoulder
     M67.319 Transient synovitis, unspecified shoulder

● **M67.32** Transient synovitis, elbow
     M67.321 Transient synovitis, right elbow
     M67.322 Transient synovitis, left elbow
     M67.329 Transient synovitis, unspecified elbow

● **M67.33** Transient synovitis, wrist
     M67.331 Transient synovitis, right wrist
     M67.332 Transient synovitis, left wrist
     M67.339 Transient synovitis, unspecified wrist

● **M67.34** Transient synovitis, hand
     M67.341 Transient synovitis, right hand
     M67.342 Transient synovitis, left hand
     M67.349 Transient synovitis, unspecified hand

● **M67.35** Transient synovitis, hip
     M67.351 Transient synovitis, right hip
     M67.352 Transient synovitis, left hip
     M67.359 Transient synovitis, unspecified hip

● **M67.36** Transient synovitis, knee
     M67.361 Transient synovitis, right knee
     M67.362 Transient synovitis, left knee
     M67.369 Transient synovitis, unspecified knee

● **M67.37** Transient synovitis, ankle and foot
     M67.371 Transient synovitis, right ankle and foot
     M67.372 Transient synovitis, left ankle and foot
     M67.379 Transient synovitis, unspecified ankle and foot

     M67.38 Transient synovitis, other site

     M67.39 Transient synovitis, multiple sites

● **M67.4** Ganglion
     Ganglion of joint or tendon (sheath)
     Excludes1   ganglion in yaws (A66.6)
     Excludes2   cyst of bursa (M71.2-M71.3)
                       cyst of synovium (M71.2-M71.3)

     M67.40 Ganglion, unspecified site

● **M67.41** Ganglion, shoulder
     M67.411 Ganglion, right shoulder
     M67.412 Ganglion, left shoulder
     M67.419 Ganglion, unspecified shoulder

● **M67.42** Ganglion, elbow
     M67.421 Ganglion, right elbow
     M67.422 Ganglion, left elbow
     M67.429 Ganglion, unspecified elbow

● **M67.43** Ganglion, wrist
     M67.431 Ganglion, right wrist
     M67.432 Ganglion, left wrist
     M67.439 Ganglion, unspecified wrist

● **M67.44** Ganglion, hand
     M67.441 Ganglion, right hand
     M67.442 Ganglion, left hand
     M67.449 Ganglion, unspecified hand

● **M67.45** Ganglion, hip
     M67.451 Ganglion, right hip
     M67.452 Ganglion, left hip
     M67.459 Ganglion, unspecified hip

● **M67.46** Ganglion, knee
     M67.461 Ganglion, right knee
     M67.462 Ganglion, left knee
     M67.469 Ganglion, unspecified knee

● **M67.47** Ganglion, ankle and foot
     M67.471 Ganglion, right ankle and foot
     M67.472 Ganglion, left ankle and foot
     M67.479 Ganglion, unspecified ankle and foot

     M67.48 Ganglion, other site

     M67.49 Ganglion, multiple sites

● **M67.5** Plica syndrome
     Plica knee
     M67.50 Plica syndrome, unspecified knee
     M67.51 Plica syndrome, right knee
     M67.52 Plica syndrome, left knee

● M67.8 **Other specified disorders of synovium and tendon**

M67.80 Other specified disorders of synovium and tendon, unspecified site

● M67.81 Other specified disorders of synovium and tendon, shoulder

M67.811 Other specified disorders of synovium, right shoulder

M67.812 Other specified disorders of synovium, left shoulder

M67.813 Other specified disorders of tendon, right shoulder

M67.814 Other specified disorders of tendon, left shoulder

M67.819 Other specified disorders of synovium and tendon, unspecified shoulder

● M67.82 Other specified disorders of synovium and tendon, elbow

M67.821 Other specified disorders of synovium, right elbow

M67.822 Other specified disorders of synovium, left elbow

M67.823 Other specified disorders of tendon, right elbow

M67.824 Other specified disorders of tendon, left elbow

M67.829 Other specified disorders of synovium and tendon, unspecified elbow

● M67.83 Other specified disorders of synovium and tendon, wrist

M67.831 Other specified disorders of synovium, right wrist

M67.832 Other specified disorders of synovium, left wrist

M67.833 Other specified disorders of tendon, right wrist

M67.834 Other specified disorders of tendon, left wrist

M67.839 Other specified disorders of synovium and tendon, unspecified wrist

● M67.84 Other specified disorders of synovium and tendon, hand

M67.841 Other specified disorders of synovium, right hand

M67.842 Other specified disorders of synovium, left hand

M67.843 Other specified disorders of tendon, right hand

M67.844 Other specified disorders of tendon, left hand

M67.849 Other specified disorders of synovium and tendon, unspecified hand

● M67.85 Other specified disorders of synovium and tendon, hip

M67.851 Other specified disorders of synovium, right hip

M67.852 Other specified disorders of synovium, left hip

M67.853 Other specified disorders of tendon, right hip

M67.854 Other specified disorders of tendon, left hip

M67.859 Other specified disorders of synovium and tendon, unspecified hip

● M67.86 Other specified disorders of synovium and tendon, knee

M67.861 Other specified disorders of synovium, right knee

M67.862 Other specified disorders of synovium, left knee

M67.863 Other specified disorders of tendon, right knee

M67.864 Other specified disorders of tendon, left knee

M67.869 Other specified disorders of synovium and tendon, unspecified knee

● M67.87 Other specified disorders of synovium and tendon, ankle and foot

M67.871 Other specified disorders of synovium, right ankle and foot

M67.872 Other specified disorders of synovium, left ankle and foot

M67.873 Other specified disorders of tendon, right ankle and foot

M67.874 Other specified disorders of tendon, left ankle and foot

M67.879 Other specified disorders of synovium and tendon, unspecified ankle and foot

M67.88 Other specified disorders of synovium and tendon, other site

M67.89 Other specified disorders of synovium and tendon, multiple sites

● M67.9 **Unspecified disorder of synovium and tendon**

M67.90 Unspecified disorder of synovium and tendon, unspecified site

● M67.91 Unspecified disorder of synovium and tendon, shoulder

M67.911 Unspecified disorder of synovium and tendon, right shoulder

M67.912 Unspecified disorder of synovium and tendon, left shoulder

M67.919 Unspecified disorder of synovium and tendon, unspecified shoulder

● M67.92 Unspecified disorder of synovium and tendon, upper arm

M67.921 Unspecified disorder of synovium and tendon, right upper arm

M67.922 Unspecified disorder of synovium and tendon, left upper arm

M67.929 Unspecified disorder of synovium and tendon, unspecified upper arm

● M67.93 Unspecified disorder of synovium and tendon, forearm

M67.931 Unspecified disorder of synovium and tendon, right forearm

M67.932 Unspecified disorder of synovium and tendon, left forearm

M67.939 Unspecified disorder of synovium and tendon, unspecified forearm

● M67.94 Unspecified disorder of synovium and tendon, hand

M67.941 Unspecified disorder of synovium and tendon, right hand

M67.942 Unspecified disorder of synovium and tendon, left hand

M67.949 Unspecified disorder of synovium and tendon, unspecified hand

▶ New ⇨ Revised ~~deleted~~ Deleted | Excludes 1 | Excludes 2 | Includes | Use additional | Code first | Code also | Key words

OGCR Official Guidelines X Assign placeholder X ● Use Additional Character(s) ▷ Manifestation Code 🔖 Hierarchical Condition Category **Coding Clinic**

● M67.95   Unspecified disorder of synovium and tendon, thigh

    M67.951   Unspecified disorder of synovium and tendon, right thigh

    M67.952   Unspecified disorder of synovium and tendon, left thigh

    M67.959   Unspecified disorder of synovium and tendon, unspecified thigh

● M67.96   Unspecified disorder of synovium and tendon, lower leg

    M67.961   Unspecified disorder of synovium and tendon, right lower leg

    M67.962   Unspecified disorder of synovium and tendon, left lower leg

    M67.969   Unspecified disorder of synovium and tendon, unspecified lower leg

● M67.97   Unspecified disorder of synovium and tendon, ankle and foot

    M67.971   Unspecified disorder of synovium and tendon, right ankle and foot

    M67.972   Unspecified disorder of synovium and tendon, left ankle and foot

    M67.979   Unspecified disorder of synovium and tendon, unspecified ankle and foot

   M67.98   Unspecified disorder of synovium and tendon, other site

   M67.99   Unspecified disorder of synovium and tendon, multiple sites

---

OTHER SOFT TISSUE DISORDERS (M70-M79)

● M70   Soft tissue disorders related to use, overuse and pressure

    Includes   soft tissue disorders of occupational origin

    Use additional external cause code to identify activity causing disorder (Y93.-)

    Excludes1   bursitis NOS (M71.9-)

    Excludes2   bursitis of shoulder (M75.5)
                enthesopathies (M76-M77)
                pressure ulcer (pressure area) (L89.-)

● M70.0   Crepitant synovitis (acute) (chronic) of hand and wrist

   ● M70.03   Crepitant synovitis (acute) (chronic), wrist

     M70.031   Crepitant synovitis (acute) (chronic), right wrist

     M70.032   Crepitant synovitis (acute) (chronic), left wrist

     M70.039   Crepitant synovitis (acute) (chronic), unspecified wrist

   ● M70.04   Crepitant synovitis (acute) (chronic), hand

     M70.041   Crepitant synovitis (acute) (chronic), right hand

     M70.042   Crepitant synovitis (acute) (chronic), left hand

     M70.049   Crepitant synovitis (acute) (chronic), unspecified hand

● M70.1   Bursitis of hand

   M70.10   Bursitis, unspecified hand

   M70.11   Bursitis, right hand

   M70.12   Bursitis, left hand

● M70.2   Olecranon bursitis

   M70.20   Olecranon bursitis, unspecified elbow

   M70.21   Olecranon bursitis, right elbow

   M70.22   Olecranon bursitis, left elbow

● M70.3   Other bursitis of elbow

   M70.30   Other bursitis of elbow, unspecified elbow

   M70.31   Other bursitis of elbow, right elbow

   M70.32   Other bursitis of elbow, left elbow

● M70.4   Prepatellar bursitis

   M70.40   Prepatellar bursitis, unspecified knee

   M70.41   Prepatellar bursitis, right knee

   M70.42   Prepatellar bursitis, left knee

● M70.5   Other bursitis of knee

   M70.50   Other bursitis of knee, unspecified knee

   M70.51   Other bursitis of knee, right knee

   M70.52   Other bursitis of knee, left knee

● M70.6   Trochanteric bursitis

    Trochanteric tendinitis

   M70.60   Trochanteric bursitis, unspecified hip

   M70.61   Trochanteric bursitis, right hip

   M70.62   Trochanteric bursitis, left hip

● M70.7   Other bursitis of hip

    Ischial bursitis

   M70.70   Other bursitis of hip, unspecified hip

   M70.71   Other bursitis of hip, right hip

   M70.72   Other bursitis of hip, left hip

● M70.8   Other soft tissue disorders related to use, overuse and pressure

   M70.80   Other soft tissue disorders related to use, overuse and pressure of unspecified site

   ● M70.81   Other soft tissue disorders related to use, overuse and pressure of shoulder

     M70.811   Other soft tissue disorders related to use, overuse and pressure, right shoulder

     M70.812   Other soft tissue disorders related to use, overuse and pressure, left shoulder

     M70.819   Other soft tissue disorders related to use, overuse and pressure, unspecified shoulder

   ● M70.82   Other soft tissue disorders related to use, overuse and pressure of upper arm

     M70.821   Other soft tissue disorders related to use, overuse and pressure, right upper arm

     M70.822   Other soft tissue disorders related to use, overuse and pressure, left upper arm

     M70.829   Other soft tissue disorders related to use, overuse and pressure, unspecified upper arms

   ● M70.83   Other soft tissue disorders related to use, overuse and pressure of forearm

     M70.831   Other soft tissue disorders related to use, overuse and pressure, right forearm

     M70.832   Other soft tissue disorders related to use, overuse and pressure, left forearm

     M70.839   Other soft tissue disorders related to use, overuse and pressure, unspecified forearm

   ● M70.84   Other soft tissue disorders related to use, overuse and pressure of hand

     M70.841   Other soft tissue disorders related to use, overuse and pressure, right hand

     M70.842   Other soft tissue disorders related to use, overuse and pressure, left hand

     M70.849   Other soft tissue disorders related to use, overuse and pressure, unspecified hand

● **M70.85** Other soft tissue disorders related to use, overuse and pressure of thigh

    M70.851 Other soft tissue disorders related to use, overuse and pressure, right thigh

    M70.852 Other soft tissue disorders related to use, overuse and pressure, left thigh

    M70.859 Other soft tissue disorders related to use, overuse and pressure, unspecified thigh

● **M70.86** Other soft tissue disorders related to use, overuse and pressure lower leg

    M70.861 Other soft tissue disorders related to use, overuse and pressure, right lower leg

    M70.862 Other soft tissue disorders related to use, overuse and pressure, left lower leg

    M70.869 Other soft tissue disorders related to use, overuse and pressure, unspecified leg

● **M70.87** Other soft tissue disorders related to use, overuse and pressure of ankle and foot

    M70.871 Other soft tissue disorders related to use, overuse and pressure, right ankle and foot

    M70.872 Other soft tissue disorders related to use, overuse and pressure, left ankle and foot

    M70.879 Other soft tissue disorders related to use, overuse and pressure, unspecified ankle and foot

    M70.88 Other soft tissue disorders related to use, overuse and pressure other site

    M70.89 Other soft tissue disorders related to use, overuse and pressure multiple sites

● **M70.9** Unspecified soft tissue disorder related to use, overuse and pressure

    M70.90 Unspecified soft tissue disorder related to use, overuse and pressure of unspecified site

● **M70.91** Unspecified soft tissue disorder related to use, overuse and pressure of shoulder

    M70.911 Unspecified soft tissue disorder related to use, overuse and pressure, right shoulder

    M70.912 Unspecified soft tissue disorder related to use, overuse and pressure, left shoulder

    M70.919 Unspecified soft tissue disorder related to use, overuse and pressure, unspecified shoulder

● **M70.92** Unspecified soft tissue disorder related to use, overuse and pressure of upper arm

    M70.921 Unspecified soft tissue disorder related to use, overuse and pressure, right upper arm

    M70.922 Unspecified soft tissue disorder related to use, overuse and pressure, left upper arm

    M70.929 Unspecified soft tissue disorder related to use, overuse and pressure, unspecified upper arm

● **M70.93** Unspecified soft tissue disorder related to use, overuse and pressure of forearm

    M70.931 Unspecified soft tissue disorder related to use, overuse and pressure, right forearm

    M70.932 Unspecified soft tissue disorder related to use, overuse and pressure, left forearm

    M70.939 Unspecified soft tissue disorder related to use, overuse and pressure, unspecified forearm

● **M70.94** Unspecified soft tissue disorder related to use, overuse and pressure of hand

    M70.941 Unspecified soft tissue disorder related to use, overuse and pressure, right hand

    M70.942 Unspecified soft tissue disorder related to use, overuse and pressure, left hand

    M70.949 Unspecified soft tissue disorder related to use, overuse and pressure, unspecified hand

● **M70.95** Unspecified soft tissue disorder related to use, overuse and pressure of thigh

    M70.951 Unspecified soft tissue disorder related to use, overuse and pressure, right thigh

    M70.952 Unspecified soft tissue disorder related to use, overuse and pressure, left thigh

    M70.959 Unspecified soft tissue disorder related to use, overuse and pressure, unspecified thigh

● **M70.96** Unspecified soft tissue disorder related to use, overuse and pressure lower leg

    M70.961 Unspecified soft tissue disorder related to use, overuse and pressure, right lower leg

    M70.962 Unspecified soft tissue disorder related to use, overuse and pressure, left lower leg

    M70.969 Unspecified soft tissue disorder related to use, overuse and pressure, unspecified lower leg

● **M70.97** Unspecified soft tissue disorder related to use, overuse and pressure of ankle and foot

    M70.971 Unspecified soft tissue disorder related to use, overuse and pressure, right ankle and foot

    M70.972 Unspecified soft tissue disorder related to use, overuse and pressure, left ankle and foot

    M70.979 Unspecified soft tissue disorder related to use, overuse and pressure, unspecified ankle and foot

    M70.98 Unspecified soft tissue disorder related to use, overuse and pressure other

    M70.99 Unspecified soft tissue disorder related to use, overuse and pressure multiple sites

● **M71**   Other bursopathies

    Excludes1   bunion (M20.1)
            bursitis related to use, overuse or pressure (M70.-)
            enthesopathies (M76-M77)

● **M71.0** Abscess of bursa

    Use additional code (B95.-, B96.-) to identify causative organism

    M71.00 Abscess of bursa, unspecified site

● **M71.01** Abscess of bursa, shoulder

    M71.011 Abscess of bursa, right shoulder

    M71.012 Abscess of bursa, left shoulder

    M71.019 Abscess of bursa, unspecified shoulder

● **M71.02** Abscess of bursa, elbow

    M71.021 Abscess of bursa, right elbow

    M71.022 Abscess of bursa, left elbow

    M71.029 Abscess of bursa, unspecified elbow

● **M71.03** Abscess of bursa, wrist

    M71.031 Abscess of bursa, right wrist

    M71.032 Abscess of bursa, left wrist

    M71.039 Abscess of bursa, unspecified wrist

▶ New   ⇒ Revised   ~~deleted~~ Deleted   Excludes 1   Excludes 2   Includes   Use additional   Code first   Code also   Key words

OGCR Official Guidelines   X Assign placeholder X   ● Use Additional Character(s)   ▶ Manifestation Code   ✎ Hierarchical Condition Category   Coding Clinic

● **M71.04**   **Abscess of bursa, hand**
    M71.041   Abscess of bursa, right hand
    M71.042   Abscess of bursa, left hand
    M71.049   Abscess of bursa, unspecified hand

● **M71.05**   **Abscess of bursa, hip**
    M71.051   Abscess of bursa, right hip
    M71.052   Abscess of bursa, left hip
    M71.059   Abscess of bursa, unspecified hip

● **M71.06**   **Abscess of bursa, knee**
    M71.061   Abscess of bursa, right knee
    M71.062   Abscess of bursa, left knee
    M71.069   Abscess of bursa, unspecified knee

● **M71.07**   **Abscess of bursa, ankle and foot**
    M71.071   Abscess of bursa, right ankle and foot
    M71.072   Abscess of bursa, left ankle and foot
    M71.079   Abscess of bursa, unspecified ankle and foot

   M71.08   **Abscess of bursa, other site**

   M71.09   **Abscess of bursa, multiple sites**

● **M71.1**   **Other infective bursitis**

    Use additional code (B95.-, B96.-) to identify causative organism

   M71.10   **Other infective bursitis, unspecified site**

● **M71.11**   **Other infective bursitis, shoulder**
    M71.111   Other infective bursitis, right shoulder
    M71.112   Other infective bursitis, left shoulder
    M71.119   Other infective bursitis, unspecified shoulder

● **M71.12**   **Other infective bursitis, elbow**
    M71.121   Other infective bursitis, right elbow
    M71.122   Other infective bursitis, left elbow
    M71.129   Other infective bursitis, unspecified elbow

● **M71.13**   **Other infective bursitis, wrist**
    M71.131   Other infective bursitis, right wrist
    M71.132   Other infective bursitis, left wrist
    M71.139   Other infective bursitis, unspecified wrist

● **M71.14**   **Other infective bursitis, hand**
    M71.141   Other infective bursitis, right hand
    M71.142   Other infective bursitis, left hand
    M71.149   Other infective bursitis, unspecified hand

● **M71.15**   **Other infective bursitis, hip**
    M71.151   Other infective bursitis, right hip
    M71.152   Other infective bursitis, left hip
    M71.159   Other infective bursitis, unspecified hip

● **M71.16**   **Other infective bursitis, knee**
    M71.161   Other infective bursitis, right knee
    M71.162   Other infective bursitis, left knee
    M71.169   Other infective bursitis, unspecified knee

● **M71.17**   **Other infective bursitis, ankle and foot**
    M71.171   Other infective bursitis, right ankle and foot
    M71.172   Other infective bursitis, left ankle and foot
    M71.179   Other infective bursitis, unspecified ankle and foot

   M71.18   **Other infective bursitis, other site**

   M71.19   **Other infective bursitis, multiple sites**

● **M71.2**   **Synovial cyst of popliteal space [Baker]**
    Popliteal space = popliteal cavity, popliteal fossa. Depression in the posterior aspect of the knee (behind the knee).

    Excludes1   synovial cyst of popliteal space with rupture (M66.0)

   M71.20   **Synovial cyst of popliteal space [Baker], unspecified knee**

   M71.21   **Synovial cyst of popliteal space [Baker], right knee**

   M71.22   **Synovial cyst of popliteal space [Baker], left knee**

● **M71.3**   **Other bursal cyst**
    Synovial cyst NOS

    Excludes1   synovial cyst with rupture (M66.1-)

   M71.30   **Other bursal cyst, unspecified site**

● **M71.31**   **Other bursal cyst, shoulder**
    M71.311   Other bursal cyst, right shoulder
    M71.312   Other bursal cyst, left shoulder
    M71.319   Other bursal cyst, unspecified shoulder

● **M71.32**   **Other bursal cyst, elbow**
    M71.321   Other bursal cyst, right elbow
    M71.322   Other bursal cyst, left elbow
    M71.329   Other bursal cyst, unspecified elbow

● **M71.33**   **Other bursal cyst, wrist**
    M71.331   Other bursal cyst, right wrist
    M71.332   Other bursal cyst, left wrist
    M71.339   Other bursal cyst, unspecified wrist

● **M71.34**   **Other bursal cyst, hand**
    M71.341   Other bursal cyst, right hand
    M71.342   Other bursal cyst, left hand
    M71.349   Other bursal cyst, unspecified hand

● **M71.35**   **Other bursal cyst, hip**
    M71.351   Other bursal cyst, right hip
    M71.352   Other bursal cyst, left hip
    M71.359   Other bursal cyst, unspecified hip

● **M71.37**   **Other bursal cyst, ankle and foot**
    M71.371   Other bursal cyst, right ankle and foot
    M71.372   Other bursal cyst, left ankle and foot
    M71.379   Other bursal cyst, unspecified ankle and foot

   M71.38   **Other bursal cyst, other site**

   M71.39   **Other bursal cyst, multiple sites**

● **M71.4**   **Calcium deposit in bursa**

    Excludes2   calcium deposit in bursa of shoulder (M75.3)

   M71.40   **Calcium deposit in bursa, unspecified site**

● **M71.42**   **Calcium deposit in bursa, elbow**
    M71.421   Calcium deposit in bursa, right elbow
    M71.422   Calcium deposit in bursa, left elbow
    M71.429   Calcium deposit in bursa, unspecified elbow

● **M71.43**   **Calcium deposit in bursa, wrist**
    M71.431   Calcium deposit in bursa, right wrist
    M71.432   Calcium deposit in bursa, left wrist
    M71.439   Calcium deposit in bursa, unspecified wrist

● **M71.44**   **Calcium deposit in bursa, hand**
    M71.441   Calcium deposit in bursa, right hand
    M71.442   Calcium deposit in bursa, left hand
    M71.449   Calcium deposit in bursa, unspecified hand

● M71.45 Calcium deposit in bursa, hip
    M71.451 Calcium deposit in bursa, right hip
    M71.452 Calcium deposit in bursa, left hip
    M71.459 Calcium deposit in bursa, unspecified hip
● M71.46 Calcium deposit in bursa, knee
    M71.461 Calcium deposit in bursa, right knee
    M71.462 Calcium deposit in bursa, left knee
    M71.469 Calcium deposit in bursa, unspecified knee
● M71.47 Calcium deposit in bursa, ankle and foot
    M71.471 Calcium deposit in bursa, right ankle and foot
    M71.472 Calcium deposit in bursa, left ankle and foot
    M71.479 Calcium deposit in bursa, unspecified ankle and foot
  M71.48 Calcium deposit in bursa, other site
  M71.49 Calcium deposit in bursa, multiple sites
● M71.5 Other bursitis, not elsewhere classified

Excludes1 bursitis NOS (M71.9-)
Excludes2 bursitis of shoulder (M75.5)
              bursitis of tibial collateral [Pellegrini-Stieda] (M76.4-)

  M71.50 Other bursitis, not elsewhere classified, unspecified site
● M71.52 Other bursitis, not elsewhere classified, elbow
    M71.521 Other bursitis, not elsewhere classified, right elbow
    M71.522 Other bursitis, not elsewhere classified, left elbow
    M71.529 Other bursitis, not elsewhere classified, unspecified elbow
● M71.53 Other bursitis, not elsewhere classified, wrist
    M71.531 Other bursitis, not elsewhere classified, right wrist
    M71.532 Other bursitis, not elsewhere classified, left wrist
    M71.539 Other bursitis, not elsewhere classified, unspecified wrist
● M71.54 Other bursitis, not elsewhere classified, hand
    M71.541 Other bursitis, not elsewhere classified, right hand
    M71.542 Other bursitis, not elsewhere classified, left hand
    M71.549 Other bursitis, not elsewhere classified, unspecified hand
● M71.55 Other bursitis, not elsewhere classified, hip
    M71.551 Other bursitis, not elsewhere classified, right hip
    M71.552 Other bursitis, not elsewhere classified, left hip
    M71.559 Other bursitis, not elsewhere classified, unspecified hip
● M71.56 Other bursitis, not elsewhere classified, knee
    M71.561 Other bursitis, not elsewhere classified, right knee
    M71.562 Other bursitis, not elsewhere classified, left knee
    M71.569 Other bursitis, not elsewhere classified, unspecified knee

● M71.57 Other bursitis, not elsewhere classified, ankle and foot
    M71.571 Other bursitis, not elsewhere classified, right ankle and foot
    M71.572 Other bursitis, not elsewhere classified, left ankle and foot
    M71.579 Other bursitis, not elsewhere classified, unspecified ankle and foot
  M71.58 Other bursitis, not elsewhere classified, other site
● M71.8 Other specified bursopathies
  M71.80 Other specified bursopathies, unspecified site
● M71.81 Other specified bursopathies, shoulder
    M71.811 Other specified bursopathies, right shoulder
    M71.812 Other specified bursopathies, left shoulder
    M71.819 Other specified bursopathies, unspecified shoulder
● M71.82 Other specified bursopathies, elbow
    M71.821 Other specified bursopathies, right elbow
    M71.822 Other specified bursopathies, left elbow
    M71.829 Other specified bursopathies, unspecified elbow
● M71.83 Other specified bursopathies, wrist
    M71.831 Other specified bursopathies, right wrist
    M71.832 Other specified bursopathies, left wrist
    M71.839 Other specified bursopathies, unspecified wrist
● M71.84 Other specified bursopathies, hand
    M71.841 Other specified bursopathies, right hand
    M71.842 Other specified bursopathies, left hand
    M71.849 Other specified bursopathies, unspecified hand
● M71.85 Other specified bursopathies, hip
    M71.851 Other specified bursopathies, right hip
    M71.852 Other specified bursopathies, left hip
    M71.859 Other specified bursopathies, unspecified hip
● M71.86 Other specified bursopathies, knee
    M71.861 Other specified bursopathies, right knee
    M71.862 Other specified bursopathies, left knee
    M71.869 Other specified bursopathies, unspecified knee
● M71.87 Other specified bursopathies, ankle and foot
    M71.871 Other specified bursopathies, right ankle and foot
    M71.872 Other specified bursopathies, left ankle and foot
    M71.879 Other specified bursopathies, unspecified ankle and foot
  M71.88 Other specified bursopathies, other site
  M71.89 Other specified bursopathies, multiple sites
  M71.9 Bursopathy, unspecified
    Bursitis NOS

▶ New   ⟹ Revised   ~~deleted~~ Deleted   Excludes 1   Excludes 2   Includes   Use additional   Code first   Code also   Key words

OGCR Official Guidelines   X Assign placeholder X   ● Use Additional Character(s)   ⟫ Manifestation Code   🅠 Hierarchical Condition Category   Coding Clinic

1064

● **M72 Fibroblastic disorders**
> **Excludes2**   retroperitoneal fibromatosis (D48.3)

    M72.0 Palmar fascial fibromatosis [Dupuytren]   **A**

    M72.1 Knuckle pads

    M72.2 Plantar fascial fibromatosis
       Plantar fasciitis

    M72.4 Pseudosarcomatous fibromatosis
       Nodular fasciitis

    M72.6 Necrotizing fasciitis 🔗
       Use additional code (B95.-, B96.-) to identify causative organism

    M72.8 Other fibroblastic disorders
       Abscess of fascia
       Fasciitis NEC
       Other infective fasciitis
       Use additional code to (B95.-, B96.-) identify causative organism
>   **Excludes1**   diffuse (eosinophilic) fasciitis (M35.4)
>   necrotizing fasciitis (M72.6)
>   nodular fasciitis (M72.4)
>   perirenal fasciitis NOS (N13.5)
>   perirenal fasciitis with infection (N13.6)
>   plantar fasciitis (M72.2)

    M72.9 Fibroblastic disorder, unspecified
       Fasciitis NOS
       Fibromatosis NOS

● **M75 Shoulder lesions**
> **Excludes2**   shoulder-hand syndrome (M89.0-)

   ● **M75.0 Adhesive capsulitis of shoulder**
       Frozen shoulder
       Periarthritis of shoulder

      M75.00 Adhesive capsulitis of unspecified shoulder

      M75.01 Adhesive capsulitis of right shoulder

      M75.02 Adhesive capsulitis of left shoulder
          Coding Clinic: 2015, Q2, P23

   ● **M75.1 Rotator cuff tear or rupture, not specified as traumatic**
       Rotator cuff syndrome
       Supraspinatus syndrome
       Supraspinatus tear or rupture, not specified as traumatic
>   **Excludes1**   tear of rotator cuff, traumatic (S46.01-)
>   *Gradual onset due to repetitive stress to rotator cuff*

    ● **M75.10 Unspecified rotator cuff tear or rupture, not specified as traumatic**

       M75.100 Unspecified rotator cuff tear or rupture of unspecified shoulder, not specified as traumatic

       M75.101 Unspecified rotator cuff tear or rupture of right shoulder, not specified as traumatic

       M75.102 Unspecified rotator cuff tear or rupture of left shoulder, not specified as traumatic

    ● **M75.11 Incomplete rotator cuff tear or rupture not specified as traumatic**

       M75.110 Incomplete rotator cuff tear or rupture of unspecified shoulder, not specified as traumatic

       M75.111 Incomplete rotator cuff tear or rupture of right shoulder, not specified as traumatic

       M75.112 Incomplete rotator cuff tear or rupture of left shoulder, not specified as traumatic

   ● **M75.12 Complete rotator cuff tear or rupture not specified as traumatic**

       M75.120 Complete rotator cuff tear or rupture of unspecified shoulder, not specified as traumatic

       M75.121 Complete rotator cuff tear or rupture of right shoulder, not specified as traumatic

       M75.122 Complete rotator cuff tear or rupture of left shoulder, not specified as traumatic

   ● **M75.2 Bicipital tendinitis**

      M75.20 Bicipital tendinitis, unspecified shoulder

      M75.21 Bicipital tendinitis, right shoulder

      M75.22 Bicipital tendinitis, left shoulder

   ● **M75.3 Calcific tendinitis of shoulder**
       Calcified bursa of shoulder

      M75.30 Calcific tendinitis of unspecified shoulder

      M75.31 Calcific tendinitis of right shoulder

      M75.32 Calcific tendinitis of left shoulder

   ● **M75.4 Impingement syndrome of shoulder**

      M75.40 Impingement syndrome of unspecified shoulder

      M75.41 Impingement syndrome of right shoulder

      M75.42 Impingement syndrome of left shoulder

   ● **M75.5 Bursitis of shoulder**

      M75.50 Bursitis of unspecified shoulder

      M75.51 Bursitis of right shoulder

      M75.52 Bursitis of left shoulder

   ● **M75.8 Other shoulder lesions**

      M75.80 Other shoulder lesions, unspecified shoulder

      M75.81 Other shoulder lesions, right shoulder

      M75.82 Other shoulder lesions, left shoulder

   ● **M75.9 Shoulder lesion, unspecified**

      M75.90 Shoulder lesion, unspecified, unspecified shoulder

      M75.91 Shoulder lesion, unspecified, right shoulder

      M75.92 Shoulder lesion, unspecified, left shoulder

● **M76 Enthesopathies, lower limb, excluding foot**
> **Excludes2**   bursitis due to use, overuse and pressure (M70.-)
>   enthesopathies of ankle and foot (M77.5-)

   ● **M76.0 Gluteal tendinitis**

      M76.00 Gluteal tendinitis, unspecified hip

      M76.01 Gluteal tendinitis, right hip

      M76.02 Gluteal tendinitis, left hip

   ● **M76.1 Psoas tendinitis**

      M76.10 Psoas tendinitis, unspecified hip

      M76.11 Psoas tendinitis, right hip

      M76.12 Psoas tendinitis, left hip

   ● **M76.2 Iliac crest spur**

      M76.20 Iliac crest spur, unspecified hip

      M76.21 Iliac crest spur, right hip

      M76.22 Iliac crest spur, left hip

   ● **M76.3 Iliotibial band syndrome**

      M76.30 Iliotibial band syndrome, unspecified leg

      M76.31 Iliotibial band syndrome, right leg

      M76.32 Iliotibial band syndrome, left leg

   ● **M76.4 Tibial collateral bursitis [Pellegrini-Stieda]**

      M76.40 Tibial collateral bursitis [Pellegrini-Stieda], unspecified leg

      M76.41 Tibial collateral bursitis [Pellegrini-Stieda], right leg

      M76.42 Tibial collateral bursitis [Pellegrini-Stieda], left leg

---

● **M76.5 Patellar tendinitis**
  M76.50 Patellar tendinitis, unspecified knee
  M76.51 Patellar tendinitis, right knee
  M76.52 Patellar tendinitis, left knee
● **M76.6 Achilles tendinitis**
    Achilles bursitis
  M76.60 Achilles tendinitis, unspecified leg
  M76.61 Achilles tendinitis, right leg
  M76.62 Achilles tendinitis, left leg
● **M76.7 Peroneal tendinitis**
  M76.70 Peroneal tendinitis, unspecified leg
  M76.71 Peroneal tendinitis, right leg
  M76.72 Peroneal tendinitis, left leg
● **M76.8 Other specified enthesopathies of lower limb, excluding foot**
  ● **M76.81 Anterior tibial syndrome**
    M76.811 Anterior tibial syndrome, right leg
    M76.812 Anterior tibial syndrome, left leg
    M76.819 Anterior tibial syndrome, unspecified leg
  ● **M76.82 Posterior tibial tendinitis**
    M76.821 Posterior tibial tendinitis, right leg
    M76.822 Posterior tibial tendinitis, left leg
    M76.829 Posterior tibial tendinitis, unspecified leg
  ● **M76.89 Other specified enthesopathies of lower limb, excluding foot**
    M76.891 Other specified enthesopathies of right lower limb, excluding foot
    M76.892 Other specified enthesopathies of left lower limb, excluding foot
    M76.899 Other specified enthesopathies of unspecified lower limb, excluding foot
  M76.9 Unspecified enthesopathy, lower limb, excluding foot

● **M77 Other enthesopathies**
  Excludes1 bursitis NOS (M71.9-)
  Excludes2 bursitis due to use, overuse and pressure (M70.-)
            osteophyte (M25.7)
            spinal enthesopathy (M46.0-)
  ● **M77.0 Medial epicondylitis**
    M77.00 Medial epicondylitis, unspecified elbow
    M77.01 Medial epicondylitis, right elbow
    M77.02 Medial epicondylitis, left elbow
  ● **M77.1 Lateral epicondylitis**
      Tennis elbow
    M77.10 Lateral epicondylitis, unspecified elbow
    M77.11 Lateral epicondylitis, right elbow
    M77.12 Lateral epicondylitis, left elbow
  ● **M77.2 Periarthritis of wrist**
    M77.20 Periarthritis, unspecified wrist
    M77.21 Periarthritis, right wrist
    M77.22 Periarthritis, left wrist
  ● **M77.3 Calcaneal spur**
    M77.30 Calcaneal spur, unspecified foot
    M77.31 Calcaneal spur, right foot
    M77.32 Calcaneal spur, left foot
  ● **M77.4 Metatarsalgia**
    Excludes1 Morton's metatarsalgia (G57.6)
    M77.40 Metatarsalgia, unspecified foot
    M77.41 Metatarsalgia, right foot
    M77.42 Metatarsalgia, left foot

● **M77.5 Other enthesopathy of foot and ankle**
  M77.50 Other enthesopathy of unspecified foot and ankle
  M77.51 Other enthesopathy of right foot and ankle
  M77.52 Other enthesopathy of left foot and ankle
M77.8 Other enthesopathies, not elsewhere classified
M77.9 Enthesopathy, unspecified
    Bone spur NOS
    Capsulitis NOS
    Periarthritis NOS
    Tendinitis NOS

● **M79 Other and unspecified soft tissue disorders, not elsewhere classified**
    Excludes1 psychogenic rheumatism (F45.8)
              soft tissue pain, psychogenic (F45.41)
  M79.0 Rheumatism, unspecified
      Excludes1 fibromyalgia (M79.7)
                palindromic rheumatism (M12.3-)
  ● **M79.1 Myalgia**
      Myofascial pain syndrome
    M79.10 Myalgia, unspecified site
    M79.11 Myalgia of mastication muscle
    M79.12 Myalgia of auxiliary muscles, head and neck
    M79.18 Myalgia, other site
        Excludes1 fibromyalgia (M79.7)
                  myositis (M60.-)
  M79.2 Neuralgia and neuritis, unspecified
      Excludes1 brachial radiculitis NOS (M54.1)
                lumbosacral radiculitis NOS (M54.1)
                mononeuropathies (G56-G58)
                radiculitis NOS (M54.1)
                sciatica (M54.3-M54.4)
  M79.3 Panniculitis, unspecified
      Excludes1 lupus panniculitis (L93.2)
                neck and back panniculitis (M54.0-)
                relapsing [Weber-Christian] panniculitis (M35.6)
  M79.4 Hypertrophy of (infrapatellar) fat pad
  M79.5 Residual foreign body in soft tissue
      Excludes1 foreign body granuloma of skin and subcutaneous tissue (L92.3)
                foreign body granuloma of soft tissue (M60.2-)
  ● **M79.6 Pain in limb, hand, foot, fingers and toes**
      Excludes2 pain in joint (M25.5-)
    ● **M79.60 Pain in limb, unspecified**
        M79.601 Pain in right arm
            Pain in right upper limb NOS
        M79.602 Pain in left arm
            Pain in left upper limb NOS
        M79.603 Pain in arm, unspecified
            Pain in upper limb NOS
        M79.604 Pain in right leg
            Pain in right lower limb NOS
        M79.605 Pain in left leg
            Pain in left lower limb NOS
        M79.606 Pain in leg, unspecified
            Pain in lower limb NOS
        M79.609 Pain in unspecified limb
            Pain in limb NOS
    ● **M79.62 Pain in upper arm**
        Pain in axillary region
        M79.621 Pain in right upper arm
        M79.622 Pain in left upper arm
        M79.629 Pain in unspecified upper arm
    ● **M79.63 Pain in forearm**
        M79.631 Pain in right forearm
        M79.632 Pain in left forearm
        M79.639 Pain in unspecified forearm

▶ New   ➡ Revised   ~~deleted~~ Deleted   Excludes 1   Excludes 2   Includes   Use additional   Code first   Code also   Key words
OGCR Official Guidelines   X Assign placeholder X   ● Use Additional Character(s)   ❚ Manifestation Code   🅗 Hierarchical Condition Category   **Coding Clinic**

● **M79.64** Pain in hand and fingers
    M79.641 Pain in right hand
    M79.642 Pain in left hand
    M79.643 Pain in unspecified hand
    M79.644 Pain in right finger(s)
    M79.645 Pain in left finger(s)
    M79.646 Pain in unspecified finger(s)
● **M79.65** Pain in thigh
    M79.651 Pain in right thigh
    M79.652 Pain in left thigh
    M79.659 Pain in unspecified thigh
● **M79.66** Pain in lower leg
    M79.661 Pain in right lower leg
    M79.662 Pain in left lower leg
    M79.669 Pain in unspecified lower leg
● **M79.67** Pain in foot and toes
    M79.671 Pain in right foot
    M79.672 Pain in left foot
    M79.673 Pain in unspecified foot
    M79.674 Pain in right toe(s)
    M79.675 Pain in left toe(s)
    M79.676 Pain in unspecified toe(s)
M79.7 Fibromyalgia
    Fibromyositis
    Fibrositis
    Myofibrositis
● **M79.A** Nontraumatic compartment syndrome
    Code first, if applicable, associated postprocedural
      complication
    Excludes1   compartment syndrome NOS (T79.A-)
           fibromyalgia (M79.7) nontraumatic
             ischemic infarction of muscle (M62.2-)
           traumatic compartment syndrome (T79.A-)
   ● **M79.A1** Nontraumatic compartment syndrome of upper extremity
       Nontraumatic compartment syndrome of shoulder, arm, forearm, wrist, hand, and fingers
     M79.A11 Nontraumatic compartment syndrome of right upper extremity
     M79.A12 Nontraumatic compartment syndrome of left upper extremity
     M79.A19 Nontraumatic compartment syndrome of unspecified upper extremity
   ● **M79.A2** Nontraumatic compartment syndrome of lower extremity
       Nontraumatic compartment syndrome of hip, buttock, thigh, leg, foot, and toes
     M79.A21 Nontraumatic compartment syndrome of right lower extremity
     M79.A22 Nontraumatic compartment syndrome of left lower extremity
     M79.A29 Nontraumatic compartment syndrome of unspecified lower extremity
     M79.A3 Nontraumatic compartment syndrome of abdomen
     M79.A9 Nontraumatic compartment syndrome of other sites
● **M79.8** Other specified soft tissue disorders
     M79.81 Nontraumatic hematoma of soft tissue
       Nontraumatic hematoma of muscle
       Nontraumatic seroma of muscle and soft tissue
     M79.89 Other specified soft tissue disorders
       Polyalgia
M79.9 Soft tissue disorder, unspecified

OGCR See Section I.C., Chapter 13.d.

Osteoporosis

Osteoporosis is a systemic condition, meaning that all bones of the musculoskeletal system are affected. Therefore, site is not a component of the codes under category M81, Osteoporosis without current pathological fracture. The site codes under category M80, Osteoporosis with current pathological fracture, identify the site of the fracture, not the osteoporosis.

1) Osteoporosis without pathological fracture

Category M81, Osteoporosis without current pathological fracture, is for use for patients with osteoporosis who do not currently have a pathologic fracture due to the osteoporosis, even if they have had a fracture in the past. For patients with a history of osteoporosis fractures, status code Z87.310, Personal history of (healed) osteoporosis fracture, should follow the code from M81.

2) Osteoporosis with current pathological fracture

Category M80, Osteoporosis with current pathological fracture, is for patients who have a current pathologic fracture at the time of an encounter. The codes under M80 identify the site of the fracture. A code from category M80, not a traumatic fracture code, should be used for any patient with known osteoporosis who suffers a fracture, even if the patient had a minor fall or trauma, if that fall or trauma would not usually break a normal, healthy bone.

OSTEOPATHIES AND CHONDROPATHIES (M80-M94)

DISORDERS OF BONE DENSITY AND STRUCTURE (M80-M85)

M80 Osteoporosis with current pathological fracture
Excessive skeletal fragility (porous bone) resulting in bone fractures
   Includes   osteoporosis with current fragility fracture
   Use additional code to identify major osseous defect, if applicable (M89.7-)
   Excludes1   collapsed vertebra NOS (M48.5)
           pathological fracture NOS (M84.4)
           wedging of vertebra NOS (M48.5)
   Excludes2   personal history of (healed) osteoporosis fracture (Z87.310)
   Coding Clinic: 2018, Q2, P12

The appropriate 7th character is to be added to each code from category M80:

Char	Meaning
A	initial encounter for fracture *All encounters involving diagnosis and treatment*
D	subsequent encounter for fracture with routine healing
G	subsequent encounter for fracture with delayed healing *Encounters for attention to casting or fixation devices, medication, and follow-up visits during the healing phase*
K	subsequent encounter for fracture with nonunion *Total failure of fracture healing*
P	subsequent encounter for fracture with malunion *Fracture ends do not heal together correctly.*
S	sequela

● **M80.0** Age-related osteoporosis with current pathological fracture
     Involutional osteoporosis with current pathological fracture
     Osteoporosis NOS with current pathological fracture
     Postmenopausal osteoporosis with current pathological fracture
     Senile osteoporosis with current pathological fracture
   X ● **M80.00** Age-related osteoporosis with current pathological fracture, unspecified site   A
   ● **M80.01** Age-related osteoporosis with current pathological fracture, shoulder
     ● M80.011 Age-related osteoporosis with current pathological fracture, right shoulder   A
     ● M80.012 Age-related osteoporosis with current pathological fracture, left shoulder   A
     ● M80.019 Age-related osteoporosis with current pathological fracture, unspecified shoulder   A

● **M80.02 Age-related osteoporosis with current pathological fracture, humerus**
  ● **M80.021 Age-related osteoporosis with current pathological fracture, right humerus** A
  ● **M80.022 Age-related osteoporosis with current pathological fracture, left humerus** A
  ● **M80.029 Age-related osteoporosis with current pathological fracture, unspecified humerus** A

● **M80.03 Age-related osteoporosis with current pathological fracture, forearm**
  Age-related osteoporosis with current pathological fracture of wrist
  ● **M80.031 Age-related osteoporosis with current pathological fracture, right forearm** A
  ● **M80.032 Age-related osteoporosis with current pathological fracture, left forearm** A
  ● **M80.039 Age-related osteoporosis with current pathological fracture, unspecified forearm** A

● **M80.04 Age-related osteoporosis with current pathological fracture, hand**
  ● **M80.041 Age-related osteoporosis with current pathological fracture, right hand** A
  ● **M80.042 Age-related osteoporosis with current pathological fracture, left hand** A
  ● **M80.049 Age-related osteoporosis with current pathological fracture, unspecified hand** A

● **M80.05 Age-related osteoporosis with current pathological fracture, femur**
  Age-related osteoporosis with current pathological fracture of hip
  ● **M80.051 Age-related osteoporosis with current pathological fracture, right femur** A 🗞
  ● **M80.052 Age-related osteoporosis with current pathological fracture, left femur** A 🗞 A
    Coding Clinic: 2018, Q2, P12
  ● **M80.059 Age-related osteoporosis with current pathological fracture, unspecified femur** A 🗞 A

● **M80.06 Age-related osteoporosis with current pathological fracture, lower leg**
  ● **M80.061 Age-related osteoporosis with current pathological fracture, right lower leg** A
  ● **M80.062 Age-related osteoporosis with current pathological fracture, left lower leg** A
  ● **M80.069 Age-related osteoporosis with current pathological fracture, unspecified lower leg** A

● **M80.07 Age-related osteoporosis with current pathological fracture, ankle and foot**
  ● **M80.071 Age-related osteoporosis with current pathological fracture, right ankle and foot** A
  ● **M80.072 Age-related osteoporosis with current pathological fracture, left ankle and foot** A
  ● **M80.079 Age-related osteoporosis with current pathological fracture, unspecified ankle and foot** A

X ● **M80.08 Age-related osteoporosis with current pathological fracture, vertebra(e)** A 🗞 A
▶ **M80.0A Age-related osteoporosis with current pathological fracture, other site**

● **M80.8 Other osteoporosis with current pathological fracture**
  Drug-induced osteoporosis with current pathological fracture
  Idiopathic osteoporosis with current pathological fracture
  Osteoporosis of disuse with current pathological fracture
  Postoophorectomy osteoporosis with current pathological fracture
  Postsurgical malabsorption osteoporosis with current pathological fracture
  Post-traumatic osteoporosis with current pathological fracture
  Use additional code for adverse effect, if applicable, to identify drug (T36-T50 with fifth or sixth character 5)

X ● **M80.80 Other osteoporosis with current pathological fracture, unspecified site** A
● **M80.81 Other osteoporosis with pathological fracture, shoulder**
  ● **M80.811 Other osteoporosis with current pathological fracture, right shoulder**
  ● **M80.812 Other osteoporosis with current pathological fracture, left shoulder**
  ● **M80.819 Other osteoporosis with current pathological fracture, unspecified shoulder**

● **M80.82 Other osteoporosis with current pathological fracture, humerus**
  ● **M80.821 Other osteoporosis with current pathological fracture, right humerus**
  ● **M80.822 Other osteoporosis with current pathological fracture, left humerus**
  ● **M80.829 Other osteoporosis with current pathological fracture, unspecified humerus**

● **M80.83 Other osteoporosis with current pathological fracture, forearm**
  Other osteoporosis with current pathological fracture of wrist
  ● **M80.831 Other osteoporosis with current pathological fracture, right forearm**
  ● **M80.832 Other osteoporosis with current pathological fracture, left forearm**
  ● **M80.839 Other osteoporosis with current pathological fracture, unspecified forearm**

▶ **M80.8A Other osteoporosis with current pathological fracture, other site**
● **M80.84 Other osteoporosis with current pathological fracture, hand**
  ● **M80.841 Other osteoporosis with current pathological fracture, right hand**
  ● **M80.842 Other osteoporosis with current pathological fracture, left hand**
  ● **M80.849 Other osteoporosis with current pathological fracture, unspecified hand**

● **M80.85 Other osteoporosis with current pathological fracture, femur**
  Other osteoporosis with current pathological fracture of hip
  ● **M80.851 Other osteoporosis with current pathological fracture, right femur** A 🗞
  ● **M80.852 Other osteoporosis with current pathological fracture, left femur** A 🗞
  ● **M80.859 Other osteoporosis with current pathological fracture, unspecified femur** A 🗞

▶ New ⇒ Revised ~~deleted~~ Deleted Excludes 1 Excludes 2 Includes Use additional Code first Code also Key words
OGCR Official Guidelines X Assign placeholder X ● Use Additional Character(s) ▶ Manifestation Code 🗞 Hierarchical Condition Category **Coding Clinic**

● **M80.86   Other osteoporosis with current pathological fracture, lower leg**
    ● **M80.861   Other osteoporosis with current pathological fracture, right lower leg**
    ● **M80.862   Other osteoporosis with current pathological fracture, left lower leg**
    ● **M80.869   Other osteoporosis with current pathological fracture, unspecified lower leg**

● **M80.87   Other osteoporosis with current pathological fracture, ankle and foot**
    ● **M80.871   Other osteoporosis with current pathological fracture, right ankle and foot**
    ● **M80.872   Other osteoporosis with current pathological fracture, left ankle and foot**
    ● **M80.879   Other osteoporosis with current pathological fracture, unspecified ankle and foot**

X ● **M80.88   Other osteoporosis with current pathological fracture, vertebra(e) A** 🔳

● **M81   Osteoporosis without current pathological fracture**
    Use additional code to identify:
    major osseous defect, if applicable (M89.7-)
    personal history of (healed) osteoporosis fracture, if applicable (Z87.310)

    Excludes1   osteoporosis with current pathological fracture (M80.-)
              Sudeck's atrophy (M89.0)

M81.0   Age-related osteoporosis without current pathological fracture   A
    Involutional osteoporosis without current pathological fracture
    Osteoporosis NOS
    Postmenopausal osteoporosis without current pathological fracture
    Senile osteoporosis without current pathological fracture

M81.6   Localized osteoporosis [Lequesne]
    Excludes1   Sudeck's atrophy (M89.0)

M81.8   Other osteoporosis without current pathological fracture
    Drug-induced osteoporosis without current pathological fracture
    Idiopathic osteoporosis without current pathological fracture
    Osteoporosis of disuse without current pathological fracture
    Postoophorectomy osteoporosis without current pathological fracture
    Postsurgical malabsorption osteoporosis without current pathological fracture
    Post-traumatic osteoporosis without current pathological fracture
    Use additional code for adverse effect, if applicable, to identify drug (T36-T50 with fifth or sixth character 5)

● **M83   Adult osteomalacia**
    Excludes1   infantile and juvenile osteomalacia (E55.0)
              renal osteodystrophy (N25.0)
              rickets (active) (E55.0)
              rickets (active) sequelae (E64.3)
              vitamin D-resistant osteomalacia (E83.3)
              vitamin D-resistant rickets (active) (E83.3)

M83.0   Puerperal osteomalacia ♀   M

M83.1   Senile osteomalacia   A

M83.2   Adult osteomalacia due to malabsorption   A
    Postsurgical malabsorption osteomalacia in adults

M83.3   Adult osteomalacia due to malnutrition   A

M83.4   Aluminum bone disease

M83.5   Other drug-induced osteomalacia in adults   A
    Use additional code for adverse effect, if applicable, to identify drug (T36-T50 with fifth or sixth character 5)

M83.8   Other adult osteomalacia   A

M83.9   Adult osteomalacia, unspecified   A

● **M84   Disorder of continuity of bone**
    Excludes2   traumatic fracture of bone–see fracture, by site

● **M84.3   Stress fracture**
    Fatigue fracture
    March fracture
    Stress fracture NOS
    Stress reaction
    Use additional external cause code(s) to identify the cause of the stress fracture

    Excludes1   pathological fracture NOS (M84.4.-)
              pathological fracture due to osteoporosis (M80.-)
              traumatic fracture (S12.-, S22.-, S32.-, S42.-, S52.-, S62.-, S72.-, S82.-, S92.-)

    Excludes2   personal history of (healed) stress (fatigue) fracture (Z87.312)
              stress fracture of vertebra (M48.4-)

    The appropriate 7th character is to be added to each code from subcategory M84.3:

A	initial encounter for fracture
D	subsequent encounter for fracture with routine healing
G	subsequent encounter for fracture with delayed healing
K	subsequent encounter for fracture with nonunion
P	subsequent encounter for fracture with malunion
S	sequela

X ● **M84.30   Stress fracture, unspecified site**

● **M84.31   Stress fracture, shoulder**
    ● **M84.311   Stress fracture, right shoulder**
    ● **M84.312   Stress fracture, left shoulder**
    ● **M84.319   Stress fracture, unspecified shoulder**

● **M84.32   Stress fracture, humerus**
    ● **M84.321   Stress fracture, right humerus**
    ● **M84.322   Stress fracture, left humerus**
    ● **M84.329   Stress fracture, unspecified humerus**

● **M84.33   Stress fracture, ulna and radius**
    ● **M84.331   Stress fracture, right ulna**
    ● **M84.332   Stress fracture, left ulna**
    ● **M84.333   Stress fracture, right radius**
    ● **M84.334   Stress fracture, left radius**
    ● **M84.339   Stress fracture, unspecified ulna and radius**

● **M84.34   Stress fracture, hand and fingers**
    ● **M84.341   Stress fracture, right hand**
    ● **M84.342   Stress fracture, left hand**
    ● **M84.343   Stress fracture, unspecified hand**
    ● **M84.344   Stress fracture, right finger(s)**
    ● **M84.345   Stress fracture, left finger(s)**
    ● **M84.346   Stress fracture, unspecified finger(s)**

● **M84.35   Stress fracture, pelvis and femur**
    Stress fracture, hip
    ● **M84.350   Stress fracture, pelvis**
    ● **M84.351   Stress fracture, right femur**
    ● **M84.352   Stress fracture, left femur**
    ● **M84.353   Stress fracture, unspecified femur**
    ● **M84.359   Stress fracture, hip, unspecified**

● **M84.36   Stress fracture, tibia and fibula**
    ● **M84.361   Stress fracture, right tibia**
    ● **M84.362   Stress fracture, left tibia**
    ● **M84.363   Stress fracture, right fibula**
    ● **M84.364   Stress fracture, left fibula**
    ● **M84.369   Stress fracture, unspecified tibia and fibula**

● **M84.37**   Stress fracture, ankle, foot and toes
- ● **M84.371**   Stress fracture, right ankle
- ● **M84.372**   Stress fracture, left ankle
- ● **M84.373**   Stress fracture, unspecified ankle
- ● **M84.374**   Stress fracture, right foot
- ● **M84.375**   Stress fracture, left foot
- ● **M84.376**   Stress fracture, unspecified foot
- ● **M84.377**   Stress fracture, right toe(s)
- ● **M84.378**   Stress fracture, left toe(s)
- ● **M84.379**   Stress fracture, unspecified toe(s)

X ● **M84.38**   Stress fracture, other site

> **Excludes2**   stress fracture of vertebra (M48.4-)

● **M84.4**   Pathological fracture, not elsewhere classified
Chronic fracture
Pathological fracture NOS

> **Excludes1**   collapsed vertebra NEC (M48.5)
> pathological fracture in neoplastic disease (M84.5-)
> pathological fracture in osteoporosis (M80.-)
> pathological fracture in other disease (M84.6-)
> stress fracture (M84.3-)
> traumatic fracture (S12.-, S22.-, S32.-, S42.-, S52.-, S62.-, S72.-, S82.-, S92.-)

> **Excludes2**   personal history of (healed) pathological fracture (Z87.311)

The appropriate 7th character is to be added to each code from subcategory M84.4:

A	initial encounter for fracture
D	subsequent encounter for fracture with routine healing
G	subsequent encounter for fracture with delayed healing
K	subsequent encounter for fracture with nonunion
P	subsequent encounter for fracture with malunion
S	sequela

X ● **M84.40**   Pathological fracture, unspecified site

● **M84.41**   Pathological fracture, shoulder
- ● **M84.411**   Pathological fracture, right shoulder
- ● **M84.412**   Pathological fracture, left shoulder
- ● **M84.419**   Pathological fracture, unspecified shoulder

● **M84.42**   Pathological fracture, humerus
- ● **M84.421**   Pathological fracture, right humerus
- ● **M84.422**   Pathological fracture, left humerus
- ● **M84.429**   Pathological fracture, unspecified humerus

● **M84.43**   Pathological fracture, ulna and radius
- ● **M84.431**   Pathological fracture, right ulna
- ● **M84.432**   Pathological fracture, left ulna
- ● **M84.433**   Pathological fracture, right radius
- ● **M84.434**   Pathological fracture, left radius
- ● **M84.439**   Pathological fracture, unspecified ulna and radius

● **M84.44**   Pathological fracture, hand and fingers
- ● **M84.441**   Pathological fracture, right hand
- ● **M84.442**   Pathological fracture, left hand
- ● **M84.443**   Pathological fracture, unspecified hand
- ● **M84.444**   Pathological fracture, right finger(s)
- ● **M84.445**   Pathological fracture, left finger(s)
- ● **M84.446**   Pathological fracture, unspecified finger(s)

● **M84.45**   Pathological fracture, femur and pelvis
- ● **M84.451**   Pathological fracture, right femur A 🏵
- ● **M84.452**   Pathological fracture, left femur A 🏵
- ● **M84.453**   Pathological fracture, unspecified femur A 🏵
- ● **M84.454**   Pathological fracture, pelvis A 🏵
  Coding Clinic: 2016, Q4, P43
- ● **M84.459**   Pathological fracture, hip, unspecified A 🏵

● **M84.46**   Pathological fracture, tibia and fibula
- ● **M84.461**   Pathological fracture, right tibia
- ● **M84.462**   Pathological fracture, left tibia
- ● **M84.463**   Pathological fracture, right fibula
- ● **M84.464**   Pathological fracture, left fibula
- ● **M84.469**   Pathological fracture, unspecified tibia and fibula

● **M84.47**   Pathological fracture, ankle, foot and toes
- ● **M84.471**   Pathological fracture, right ankle
- ● **M84.472**   Pathological fracture, left ankle
- ● **M84.473**   Pathological fracture, unspecified ankle
- ● **M84.474**   Pathological fracture, right foot
- ● **M84.475**   Pathological fracture, left foot
- ● **M84.476**   Pathological fracture, unspecified foot
- ● **M84.477**   Pathological fracture, right toe(s)
- ● **M84.478**   Pathological fracture, left toe(s)
- ● **M84.479**   Pathological fracture, unspecified toe(s)

X ● **M84.48**   Pathological fracture, other site

OGCR   Section I.C. 13.C.

Coding of Pathologic Fractures

7th character A is for use as long as the patient is receiving active treatment for the fracture. While the patient may be seen by a new or different provider over the course of treatment for a pathological fracture, assignment of the 7th character is based on whether the patient is undergoing active treatment and not whether the provider is seeing the patient for the first time.

7th character, D is to be used for encounters after the patient has completed active treatment for the fracture and is receiving routine care for the fracture during the healing or recovery phase. The other 7th characters, listed under each subcategory in the Tabular List, are to be used for subsequent encounters for treatment of problems associated with the healing, such as malunions, nonunions, and sequelae.

Care for complications of surgical treatment for fracture repairs during the healing or recovery phase should be coded with the appropriate complication codes.

See Section I.C.19. Coding of traumatic fractures.

● **M84.5**   Pathological fracture in neoplastic disease
Code also underlying neoplasm
The appropriate 7th character is to be added to each code from subcategory M84.5:

A	initial encounter for fracture
D	subsequent encounter for fracture with routine healing
G	subsequent encounter for fracture with delayed healing
K	subsequent encounter for fracture with nonunion
P	subsequent encounter for fracture with malunion
S	sequela

X ● **M84.50**   Pathological fracture in neoplastic disease, unspecified site

● **M84.51**   Pathological fracture in neoplastic disease, shoulder
- ● **M84.511**   Pathological fracture in neoplastic disease, right shoulder
- ● **M84.512**   Pathological fracture in neoplastic disease, left shoulder
- ● **M84.519**   Pathological fracture in neoplastic disease, unspecified shoulder

▶ New   ⇒ Revised   ~~deleted~~ Deleted   Excludes 1   Excludes 2   Includes   Use additional   Code first   Code also   Key words

OGCR Official Guidelines   X Assign placeholder X   ● Use Additional Character(s)   ▶ Manifestation Code   🏵 Hierarchical Condition Category   **Coding Clinic**

● **M84.52 Pathological fracture in neoplastic disease, humerus**
    ● M84.521 Pathological fracture in neoplastic disease, **right humerus**
    ● M84.522 Pathological fracture in neoplastic disease, **left humerus**
    ● M84.529 Pathological fracture in neoplastic disease, **unspecified** humerus

● **M84.53 Pathological fracture in neoplastic disease, ulna and radius**
    ● M84.531 Pathological fracture in neoplastic disease, **right ulna**
    ● M84.532 Pathological fracture in neoplastic disease, **left ulna**
    ● M84.533 Pathological fracture in neoplastic disease, **right radius**
    ● M84.534 Pathological fracture in neoplastic disease, **left radius**
    ● M84.539 Pathological fracture in neoplastic disease, **unspecified ulna and radius**

● **M84.54 Pathological fracture in neoplastic disease, hand**
    ● M84.541 Pathological fracture in neoplastic disease, **right hand**
    ● M84.542 Pathological fracture in neoplastic disease, **left hand**
    ● M84.549 Pathological fracture in neoplastic disease, **unspecified** hand

● **M84.55 Pathological fracture in neoplastic disease, pelvis and femur**
    ● M84.550 Pathological fracture in neoplastic disease, **pelvis**
    ● M84.551 Pathological fracture in neoplastic disease, **right femur** A 🜛
    ● M84.552 Pathological fracture in neoplastic disease, **left femur** A 🜛
    ● M84.553 Pathological fracture in neoplastic disease, **unspecified femur** A 🜛
    ● M84.559 Pathological fracture in neoplastic disease, **hip, unspecified** A 🜛

● **M84.56 Pathological fracture in neoplastic disease, tibia and fibula**
    ● M84.561 Pathological fracture in neoplastic disease, **right tibia**
    ● M84.562 Pathological fracture in neoplastic disease, **left tibia**
    ● M84.563 Pathological fracture in neoplastic disease, **right fibula**
    ● M84.564 Pathological fracture in neoplastic disease, **left fibula**
    ● M84.569 Pathological fracture in neoplastic disease, **unspecified tibia and fibula**

● **M84.57 Pathological fracture in neoplastic disease, ankle and foot**
    ● M84.571 Pathological fracture in neoplastic disease, **right ankle**
    ● M84.572 Pathological fracture in neoplastic disease, **left ankle**
    ● M84.573 Pathological fracture in neoplastic disease, **unspecified ankle**
    ● M84.574 Pathological fracture in neoplastic disease, **right foot**
    ● M84.575 Pathological fracture in neoplastic disease, **left foot**
    ● M84.576 Pathological fracture in neoplastic disease, **unspecified foot**

X● **M84.58 Pathological fracture in neoplastic disease, other specified site**
    Pathological fracture in neoplastic disease, vertebrae

● **M84.6 Pathological fracture in other disease**
Code also underlying condition
Excludes1 pathological fracture in osteoporosis (M80.-)

The appropriate 7th character is to be added to each code from subcategory M84.6:

A	initial encounter for fracture
D	subsequent encounter for fracture with routine healing
G	subsequent encounter for fracture with delayed healing
K	subsequent encounter for fracture with nonunion
P	subsequent encounter for fracture with malunion
S	sequela

X● **M84.60 Pathological fracture in other disease, unspecified site**

● **M84.61 Pathological fracture in other disease, shoulder**
    ● M84.611 Pathological fracture in other disease, **right shoulder**
    ● M84.612 Pathological fracture in other disease, **left shoulder**
    ● M84.619 Pathological fracture in other disease, **unspecified shoulder**

● **M84.62 Pathological fracture in other disease, humerus**
    ● M84.621 Pathological fracture in other disease, **right humerus**
    ● M84.622 Pathological fracture in other disease, **left humerus**
    ● M84.629 Pathological fracture in other disease, **unspecified humerus**

● **M84.63 Pathological fracture in other disease, ulna and radius**
    ● M84.631 Pathological fracture in other disease, **right ulna**
    ● M84.632 Pathological fracture in other disease, **left ulna**
    ● M84.633 Pathological fracture in other disease, **right radius**
    ● M84.634 Pathological fracture in other disease, **left radius**
    ● M84.639 Pathological fracture in other disease, **unspecified ulna and radius**

● **M84.64 Pathological fracture in other disease, hand**
    ● M84.641 Pathological fracture in other disease, **right hand**
    ● M84.642 Pathological fracture in other disease, **left hand**
    ● M84.649 Pathological fracture in other disease, **unspecified hand**

● **M84.65 Pathological fracture in other disease, pelvis and femur**
    ● M84.650 Pathological fracture in other disease, **pelvis**
    ● M84.651 Pathological fracture in other disease, **right femur** A 🜛
    ● M84.652 Pathological fracture in other disease, **left femur** A 🜛
    ● M84.653 Pathological fracture in other disease, **unspecified femur** A 🜛
    ● M84.659 Pathological fracture in other disease, **hip, unspecified** A 🜛

● **M84.66** Pathological fracture in other disease, tibia and fibula

  ● **M84.661** Pathological fracture in other disease, right tibia

  ● **M84.662** Pathological fracture in other disease, left tibia

  ● **M84.663** Pathological fracture in other disease, right fibula

  ● **M84.664** Pathological fracture in other disease, left fibula

  ● **M84.669** Pathological fracture in other disease, unspecified tibia and fibula

● **M84.67** Pathological fracture in other disease, ankle and foot

  ● **M84.671** Pathological fracture in other disease, right ankle

  ● **M84.672** Pathological fracture in other disease, left ankle

  ● **M84.673** Pathological fracture in other disease, unspecified ankle

  ● **M84.674** Pathological fracture in other disease, right foot

  ● **M84.675** Pathological fracture in other disease, left foot

  ● **M84.676** Pathological fracture in other disease, unspecified foot

X ● **M84.68** Pathological fracture in other disease, other site

● **M84.7** Nontraumatic fracture, not elsewhere classified

  ● **M84.75** **Atypical femoral fracture**

    The appropriate 7th character is to be added to each code from M84.75:

> A   initial encounter for fracture
> D   subsequent encounter for fracture with routine healing
> G   subsequent encounter for fracture with delayed healing
> K   subsequent encounter for fracture with nonunion
> P   subsequent encounter for fracture with malunion
> S   sequela

Coding Clinic: 2016, Q4, P41

  ● **M84.750** Atypical femoral fracture, unspecified

  ● **M84.751** Incomplete atypical femoral fracture, right leg

  ● **M84.752** Incomplete atypical femoral fracture, left leg

  ● **M84.753** Incomplete atypical femoral fracture, unspecified leg

  ● **M84.754** Complete transverse atypical femoral fracture, right leg A 🅗

  ● **M84.755** Complete transverse atypical femoral fracture, left leg A 🅗

  ● **M84.756** Complete transverse atypical femoral fracture, unspecified leg A 🅗

  ● **M84.757** Complete oblique atypical femoral fracture, right leg A 🅗

  ● **M84.758** Complete oblique atypical femoral fracture, left leg A 🅗

  ● **M84.759** Complete oblique atypical femoral fracture, unspecified leg , A 🅗

● **M84.8** Other disorders of continuity of bone

  M84.80 Other disorders of continuity of bone, unspecified site

  ● **M84.81** Other disorders of continuity of bone, shoulder

    M84.811 Other disorders of continuity of bone, right shoulder

    M84.812 Other disorders of continuity of bone, left shoulder

    M84.819 Other disorders of continuity of bone, unspecified shoulder

  ● **M84.82** Other disorders of continuity of bone, humerus

    M84.821 Other disorders of continuity of bone, right humerus

    M84.822 Other disorders of continuity of bone, left humerus

    M84.829 Other disorders of continuity of bone, unspecified humerus

  ● **M84.83** Other disorders of continuity of bone, ulna and radius

    M84.831 Other disorders of continuity of bone, right ulna

    M84.832 Other disorders of continuity of bone, left ulna

    M84.833 Other disorders of continuity of bone, right radius

    M84.834 Other disorders of continuity of bone, left radius

    M84.839 Other disorders of continuity of bone, unspecified ulna and radius

  ● **M84.84** Other disorders of continuity of bone, hand

    M84.841 Other disorders of continuity of bone, right hand

    M84.842 Other disorders of continuity of bone, left hand

    M84.849 Other disorders of continuity of bone, unspecified hand

  ● **M84.85** Other disorders of continuity of bone, pelvic region and thigh

    M84.851 Other disorders of continuity of bone, right pelvic region and thigh

    M84.852 Other disorders of continuity of bone, left pelvic region and thigh

    M84.859 Other disorders of continuity of bone, unspecified pelvic region and thigh

  ● **M84.86** Other disorders of continuity of bone, tibia and fibula

    M84.861 Other disorders of continuity of bone, right tibia

    M84.862 Other disorders of continuity of bone, left tibia

    M84.863 Other disorders of continuity of bone, right fibula

    M84.864 Other disorders of continuity of bone, left fibula

    M84.869 Other disorders of continuity of bone, unspecified tibia and fibula

  ● **M84.87** Other disorders of continuity of bone, ankle and foot

    M84.871 Other disorders of continuity of bone, right ankle and foot

    M84.872 Other disorders of continuity of bone, left ankle and foot

    M84.879 Other disorders of continuity of bone, unspecified ankle and foot

  M84.88 Other disorders of continuity of bone, other site

M84.9 Disorder of continuity of bone, unspecified

▶ New   ⇰ Revised   ~~deleted~~ Deleted   Excludes 1   Excludes 2   Includes   Use additional   Code first   Code also   Key words

OGCR Official Guidelines   X Assign placeholder X   ● Use Additional Character(s)   ❯ Manifestation Code   🅗 Hierarchical Condition Category   **Coding Clinic**

● **M85   Other disorders of bone density and structure**

     Excludes1   osteogenesis imperfecta (Q78.0)
                osteopetrosis (Q78.2)
                osteopoikilosis (Q78.8)
                polyostotic fibrous dysplasia (Q78.1)

   ● **M85.0   Fibrous dysplasia (monostotic)**

       Excludes2   fibrous dysplasia of jaw (M27.8)

     M85.00   Fibrous dysplasia (monostotic), unspecified site

    ● M85.01   Fibrous dysplasia (monostotic), shoulder

       M85.011   Fibrous dysplasia (monostotic), right shoulder

       M85.012   Fibrous dysplasia (monostotic), left shoulder

       M85.019   Fibrous dysplasia (monostotic), unspecified shoulder

    ● M85.02   Fibrous dysplasia (monostotic), upper arm

       M85.021   Fibrous dysplasia (monostotic), right upper arm

       M85.022   Fibrous dysplasia (monostotic), left upper arm

       M85.029   Fibrous dysplasia (monostotic), unspecified upper arm

    ● M85.03   Fibrous dysplasia (monostotic), forearm

       M85.031   Fibrous dysplasia (monostotic), right forearm

       M85.032   Fibrous dysplasia (monostotic), left forearm

       M85.039   Fibrous dysplasia (monostotic), unspecified forearm

    ● M85.04   Fibrous dysplasia (monostotic), hand

       M85.041   Fibrous dysplasia (monostotic), right hand

       M85.042   Fibrous dysplasia (monostotic), left hand

       M85.049   Fibrous dysplasia (monostotic), unspecified hand

    ● M85.05   Fibrous dysplasia (monostotic), thigh

       M85.051   Fibrous dysplasia (monostotic), right thigh

       M85.052   Fibrous dysplasia (monostotic), left thigh

       M85.059   Fibrous dysplasia (monostotic), unspecified thigh

    ● M85.06   Fibrous dysplasia (monostotic), lower leg

       M85.061   Fibrous dysplasia (monostotic), right lower leg

       M85.062   Fibrous dysplasia (monostotic), left lower leg

       M85.069   Fibrous dysplasia (monostotic), unspecified lower leg

    ● M85.07   Fibrous dysplasia (monostotic), ankle and foot

       M85.071   Fibrous dysplasia (monostotic), right ankle and foot

       M85.072   Fibrous dysplasia (monostotic), left ankle and foot

       M85.079   Fibrous dysplasia (monostotic), unspecified ankle and foot

     M85.08   Fibrous dysplasia (monostotic), other site

     M85.09   Fibrous dysplasia (monostotic), multiple sites

   ● **M85.1   Skeletal fluorosis**

     M85.10   Skeletal fluorosis, unspecified site

    ● M85.11   Skeletal fluorosis, shoulder

       M85.111   Skeletal fluorosis, right shoulder

       M85.112   Skeletal fluorosis, left shoulder

       M85.119   Skeletal fluorosis, unspecified shoulder

    ● M85.12   Skeletal fluorosis, upper arm

       M85.121   Skeletal fluorosis, right upper arm

       M85.122   Skeletal fluorosis, left upper arm

       M85.129   Skeletal fluorosis, unspecified upper arm

    ● M85.13   Skeletal fluorosis, forearm

       M85.131   Skeletal fluorosis, right forearm

       M85.132   Skeletal fluorosis, left forearm

       M85.139   Skeletal fluorosis, unspecified forearm

    ● M85.14   Skeletal fluorosis, hand

       M85.141   Skeletal fluorosis, right hand

       M85.142   Skeletal fluorosis, left hand

       M85.149   Skeletal fluorosis, unspecified hand

    ● M85.15   Skeletal fluorosis, thigh

       M85.151   Skeletal fluorosis, right thigh

       M85.152   Skeletal fluorosis, left thigh

       M85.159   Skeletal fluorosis, unspecified thigh

    ● M85.16   Skeletal fluorosis, lower leg

       M85.161   Skeletal fluorosis, right lower leg

       M85.162   Skeletal fluorosis, left lower leg

       M85.169   Skeletal fluorosis, unspecified lower leg

    ● M85.17   Skeletal fluorosis, ankle and foot

       M85.171   Skeletal fluorosis, right ankle and foot

       M85.172   Skeletal fluorosis, left ankle and foot

       M85.179   Skeletal fluorosis, unspecified ankle and foot

     M85.18   Skeletal fluorosis, other site

     M85.19   Skeletal fluorosis, multiple sites

     M85.2   Hyperostosis of skull

   ● **M85.3   Osteitis condensans**

     M85.30   Osteitis condensans, unspecified site

    ● M85.31   Osteitis condensans, shoulder

       M85.311   Osteitis condensans, right shoulder

       M85.312   Osteitis condensans, left shoulder

       M85.319   Osteitis condensans, unspecified shoulder

    ● M85.32   Osteitis condensans, upper arm

       M85.321   Osteitis condensans, right upper arm

       M85.322   Osteitis condensans, left upper arm

       M85.329   Osteitis condensans, unspecified upper arm

    ● M85.33   Osteitis condensans, forearm

       M85.331   Osteitis condensans, right forearm

       M85.332   Osteitis condensans, left forearm

       M85.339   Osteitis condensans, unspecified forearm

    ● M85.34   Osteitis condensans, hand

       M85.341   Osteitis condensans, right hand

       M85.342   Osteitis condensans, left hand

       M85.349   Osteitis condensans, unspecified hand

    ● M85.35   Osteitis condensans, thigh

       M85.351   Osteitis condensans, right thigh

       M85.352   Osteitis condensans, left thigh

       M85.359   Osteitis condensans, unspecified thigh

    ● M85.36   Osteitis condensans, lower leg

       M85.361   Osteitis condensans, right lower leg

       M85.362   Osteitis condensans, left lower leg

       M85.369   Osteitis condensans, unspecified lower leg

● M85.37   Osteitis condensans, ankle and foot
     M85.371   Osteitis condensans, right ankle and foot
     M85.372   Osteitis condensans, left ankle and foot
     M85.379   Osteitis condensans, unspecified ankle and foot
   M85.38   Osteitis condensans, other site
   M85.39   Osteitis condensans, multiple sites
● M85.4   Solitary bone cyst
     Excludes2   solitary cyst of jaw (M27.4)
   M85.40   Solitary bone cyst, unspecified site
● M85.41   Solitary bone cyst, shoulder
     M85.411   Solitary bone cyst, right shoulder
     M85.412   Solitary bone cyst, left shoulder
     M85.419   Solitary bone cyst, unspecified shoulder
● M85.42   Solitary bone cyst, humerus
     M85.421   Solitary bone cyst, right humerus
     M85.422   Solitary bone cyst, left humerus
     M85.429   Solitary bone cyst, unspecified humerus
● M85.43   Solitary bone cyst, ulna and radius
     M85.431   Solitary bone cyst, right ulna and radius
     M85.432   Solitary bone cyst, left ulna and radius
     M85.439   Solitary bone cyst, unspecified ulna and radius
● M85.44   Solitary bone cyst, hand
     M85.441   Solitary bone cyst, right hand
     M85.442   Solitary bone cyst, left hand
     M85.449   Solitary bone cyst, unspecified hand
● M85.45   Solitary bone cyst, pelvis
     M85.451   Solitary bone cyst, right pelvis
     M85.452   Solitary bone cyst, left pelvis
     M85.459   Solitary bone cyst, unspecified pelvis
● M85.46   Solitary bone cyst, tibia and fibula
     M85.461   Solitary bone cyst, right tibia and fibula
     M85.462   Solitary bone cyst, left tibia and fibula
     M85.469   Solitary bone cyst, unspecified tibia and fibula
● M85.47   Solitary bone cyst, ankle and foot
     M85.471   Solitary bone cyst, right ankle and foot
     M85.472   Solitary bone cyst, left ankle and foot
     M85.479   Solitary bone cyst, unspecified ankle and foot
   M85.48   Solitary bone cyst, other site
● M85.5   Aneurysmal bone cyst
     Excludes2   aneurysmal cyst of jaw (M27.4)
   M85.50   Aneurysmal bone cyst, unspecified site
● M85.51   Aneurysmal bone cyst, shoulder
     M85.511   Aneurysmal bone cyst, right shoulder
     M85.512   Aneurysmal bone cyst, left shoulder
     M85.519   Aneurysmal bone cyst, unspecified shoulder
● M85.52   Aneurysmal bone cyst, upper arm
     M85.521   Aneurysmal bone cyst, right upper arm
     M85.522   Aneurysmal bone cyst, left upper arm
     M85.529   Aneurysmal bone cyst, unspecified upper arm

● M85.53   Aneurysmal bone cyst, forearm
     M85.531   Aneurysmal bone cyst, right forearm
     M85.532   Aneurysmal bone cyst, left forearm
     M85.539   Aneurysmal bone cyst, unspecified forearm
● M85.54   Aneurysmal bone cyst, hand
     M85.541   Aneurysmal bone cyst, right hand
     M85.542   Aneurysmal bone cyst, left hand
     M85.549   Aneurysmal bone cyst, unspecified hand
● M85.55   Aneurysmal bone cyst, thigh
     M85.551   Aneurysmal bone cyst, right thigh
     M85.552   Aneurysmal bone cyst, left thigh
     M85.559   Aneurysmal bone cyst, unspecified thigh
● M85.56   Aneurysmal bone cyst, lower leg
     M85.561   Aneurysmal bone cyst, right lower leg
     M85.562   Aneurysmal bone cyst, left lower leg
     M85.569   Aneurysmal bone cyst, unspecified lower leg
● M85.57   Aneurysmal bone cyst, ankle and foot
     M85.571   Aneurysmal bone cyst, right ankle and foot
     M85.572   Aneurysmal bone cyst, left ankle and foot
     M85.579   Aneurysmal bone cyst, unspecified ankle and foot
   M85.58   Aneurysmal bone cyst, other site
   M85.59   Aneurysmal bone cyst, multiple sites
● M85.6   Other cyst of bone
     Excludes1   cyst of jaw NEC (M27.4)
                  osteitis fibrosa cystica generalisata [von Recklinghausen's disease of bone] (E21.0)
   M85.60   Other cyst of bone, unspecified site
● M85.61   Other cyst of bone, shoulder
     M85.611   Other cyst of bone, right shoulder
     M85.612   Other cyst of bone, left shoulder
     M85.619   Other cyst of bone, unspecified shoulder
● M85.62   Other cyst of bone, upper arm
     M85.621   Other cyst of bone, right upper arm
     M85.622   Other cyst of bone, left upper arm
     M85.629   Other cyst of bone, unspecified upper arm
● M85.63   Other cyst of bone, forearm
     M85.631   Other cyst of bone, right forearm
     M85.632   Other cyst of bone, left forearm
     M85.639   Other cyst of bone, unspecified forearm
● M85.64   Other cyst of bone, hand
     M85.641   Other cyst of bone, right hand
     M85.642   Other cyst of bone, left hand
     M85.649   Other cyst of bone, unspecified hand
● M85.65   Other cyst of bone, thigh
     M85.651   Other cyst of bone, right thigh
     M85.652   Other cyst of bone, left thigh
     M85.659   Other cyst of bone, unspecified thigh
● M85.66   Other cyst of bone, lower leg
     M85.661   Other cyst of bone, right lower leg
     M85.662   Other cyst of bone, left lower leg
     M85.669   Other cyst of bone, unspecified lower leg

▶ New   ⇒ Revised   ~~deleted~~ Deleted   Excludes 1   Excludes 2   Includes   Use additional   Code first   Code also   Key words

OGCR Official Guidelines   X Assign placeholder X   ● Use Additional Character(s)   ▷ Manifestation Code   Ⓗⓒ Hierarchical Condition Category   Coding Clinic

● M85.67 Other cyst of bone, ankle and foot

    M85.671 Other cyst of bone, right ankle and foot

    M85.672 Other cyst of bone, left ankle and foot

    M85.679 Other cyst of bone, unspecified ankle and foot

M85.68 Other cyst of bone, other site

M85.69 Other cyst of bone, multiple sites

● M85.8 Other specified disorders of bone density and structure

    Hyperostosis of bones, except skull

    Osteosclerosis, acquired

    Excludes1 diffuse idiopathic skeletal hyperostosis [DISH] (M48.1)

               osteosclerosis congenita (Q77.4)

               osteosclerosis fragilitas (generalista) (Q78.2)

               osteosclerosis myelofibrosis (D75.81)

M85.80 Other specified disorders of bone density and structure, unspecified site

● M85.81 Other specified disorders of bone density and structure, shoulder

    M85.811 Other specified disorders of bone density and structure, right shoulder

    M85.812 Other specified disorders of bone density and structure, left shoulder

    M85.819 Other specified disorders of bone density and structure, unspecified shoulder

● M85.82 Other specified disorders of bone density and structure, upper arm

    M85.821 Other specified disorders of bone density and structure, right upper arm

    M85.822 Other specified disorders of bone density and structure, left upper arm

    M85.829 Other specified disorders of bone density and structure, unspecified upper arm

● M85.83 Other specified disorders of bone density and structure, forearm

    M85.831 Other specified disorders of bone density and structure, right forearm

    M85.832 Other specified disorders of bone density and structure, left forearm

    M85.839 Other specified disorders of bone density and structure, unspecified forearm

● M85.84 Other specified disorders of bone density and structure, hand

    M85.841 Other specified disorders of bone density and structure, right hand

    M85.842 Other specified disorders of bone density and structure, left hand

    M85.849 Other specified disorders of bone density and structure, unspecified hand

● M85.85 Other specified disorders of bone density and structure, thigh

    M85.851 Other specified disorders of bone density and structure, right thigh

    M85.852 Other specified disorders of bone density and structure, left thigh

    M85.859 Other specified disorders of bone density and structure, unspecified thigh

● M85.86 Other specified disorders of bone density and structure, lower leg

    M85.861 Other specified disorders of bone density and structure, right lower leg

    M85.862 Other specified disorders of bone density and structure, left lower leg

    M85.869 Other specified disorders of bone density and structure, unspecified lower leg

● M85.87 Other specified disorders of bone density and structure, ankle and foot

    M85.871 Other specified disorders of bone density and structure, right ankle and foot

    M85.872 Other specified disorders of bone density and structure, left ankle and foot

    M85.879 Other specified disorders of bone density and structure, unspecified ankle and foot

M85.88 Other specified disorders of bone density and structure, other site

M85.89 Other specified disorders of bone density and structure, multiple sites

M85.9 Disorder of bone density and structure, unspecified

OTHER OSTEOPATHIES (M86-M90)

Excludes1 postprocedural osteopathies (M96.-)

● M86 Osteomyelitis

  Use additional code (B95-B97) to identify infectious agent

  Use additional code to identify major osseous defect, if applicable (M89.7-)

  Excludes1 osteomyelitis due to:

          echinococcus (B67.2)

          gonococcus (A54.43)

          salmonella (A02.24)

  Excludes2 ostemyelitis of:

          orbit (H05.0-)

          petrous bone (H70.2-)

          vertebra (M46.2-)

● M86.0 Acute hematogenous osteomyelitis

    M86.00 Acute hematogenous osteomyelitis, unspecified site

  ● M86.01 Acute hematogenous osteomyelitis, shoulder

      M86.011 Acute hematogenous osteomyelitis, right shoulder

      M86.012 Acute hematogenous osteomyelitis, left shoulder

      M86.019 Acute hematogenous osteomyelitis, unspecified shoulder

Figure 13-6 Osteomyelitis of the spine. A lateral view of the lower thoracic spine demonstrates destruction of the disk space *(arrow)* as well as destruction of the adjoining vertebral bodies. (From Mettler: Essentials of Radiology, ed 2, Saunders, An Imprint of Elsevier, 2005)

Item 13-12 Osteomyelitis is an inflammation of the bone. **Acute osteomyelitis** is a rapidly destructive, pus-producing infection capable of causing severe bone destruction. **Chronic osteomyelitis** can remain long after the initial acute episode has passed and may lead to a recurrence of the acute phase. **Brodie's abscess** is an encapsulated focal abscess that must be surgically drained. **Periostitis** is an inflammation of the periosteum, a dense membrane composed of fibrous connective tissue that closely wraps all bone, except those with articulating surfaces in joints, which are covered by synovial membranes.

● **M86.02** Acute hematogenous osteomyelitis, humerus
- **M86.021** Acute hematogenous osteomyelitis, right humerus 🐾
- **M86.022** Acute hematogenous osteomyelitis, left humerus 🐾
- **M86.029** Acute hematogenous osteomyelitis, unspecified humerus 🐾

● **M86.03** Acute hematogenous osteomyelitis, radius and ulna
- **M86.031** Acute hematogenous osteomyelitis, right radius and ulna 🐾
- **M86.032** Acute hematogenous osteomyelitis, left radius and ulna 🐾
- **M86.039** Acute hematogenous osteomyelitis, unspecified radius and ulna 🐾

● **M86.04** Acute hematogenous osteomyelitis, hand
- **M86.041** Acute hematogenous osteomyelitis, right hand 🐾
- **M86.042** Acute hematogenous osteomyelitis, left hand 🐾
- **M86.049** Acute hematogenous osteomyelitis, unspecified hand 🐾

● **M86.05** Acute hematogenous osteomyelitis, femur
- **M86.051** Acute hematogenous osteomyelitis, right femur 🐾
- **M86.052** Acute hematogenous osteomyelitis, left femur 🐾
- **M86.059** Acute hematogenous osteomyelitis, unspecified femur 🐾

● **M86.06** Acute hematogenous osteomyelitis, tibia and fibula
- **M86.061** Acute hematogenous osteomyelitis, right tibia and fibula 🐾
- **M86.062** Acute hematogenous osteomyelitis, left tibia and fibula 🐾
- **M86.069** Acute hematogenous osteomyelitis, unspecified tibia and fibula 🐾

● **M86.07** Acute hematogenous osteomyelitis, ankle and foot
- **M86.071** Acute hematogenous osteomyelitis, right ankle and foot 🐾
- **M86.072** Acute hematogenous osteomyelitis, left ankle and foot 🐾
- **M86.079** Acute hematogenous osteomyelitis, unspecified ankle and foot 🐾

M86.08 Acute hematogenous osteomyelitis, other sites 🐾

M86.09 Acute hematogenous osteomyelitis, multiple sites 🐾

● **M86.1** Other acute osteomyelitis

M86.10 Other acute osteomyelitis, unspecified site 🐾

● **M86.11** Other acute osteomyelitis, shoulder
- **M86.111** Other acute osteomyelitis, right shoulder 🐾
- **M86.112** Other acute osteomyelitis, left shoulder 🐾
- **M86.119** Other acute osteomyelitis, unspecified shoulder 🐾

● **M86.12** Other acute osteomyelitis, humerus
- **M86.121** Other acute osteomyelitis, right humerus 🐾
- **M86.122** Other acute osteomyelitis, left humerus 🐾
- **M86.129** Other acute osteomyelitis, unspecified humerus 🐾

● **M86.13** Other acute osteomyelitis, radius and ulna
- **M86.131** Other acute osteomyelitis, right radius and ulna 🐾
- **M86.132** Other acute osteomyelitis, left radius and ulna 🐾
- **M86.139** Other acute osteomyelitis, unspecified radius and ulna 🐾

● **M86.14** Other acute osteomyelitis, hand
- **M86.141** Other acute osteomyelitis, right hand 🐾
- **M86.142** Other acute osteomyelitis, left hand 🐾
- **M86.149** Other acute osteomyelitis, unspecified hand 🐾

● **M86.15** Other acute osteomyelitis, femur
- **M86.151** Other acute osteomyelitis, right femur 🐾
- **M86.152** Other acute osteomyelitis, left femur 🐾
- **M86.159** Other acute osteomyelitis, unspecified femur 🐾

● **M86.16** Other acute osteomyelitis, tibia and fibula
- **M86.161** Other acute osteomyelitis, right tibia and fibula 🐾
- **M86.162** Other acute osteomyelitis, left tibia and fibula 🐾
- **M86.169** Other acute osteomyelitis, unspecified tibia and fibula 🐾

● **M86.17** Other acute osteomyelitis, ankle and foot
- **M86.171** Other acute osteomyelitis, right ankle and foot 🐾
  - Coding Clinic: 2020, Q1, P12
- **M86.172** Other acute osteomyelitis, left ankle and foot 🐾
- **M86.179** Other acute osteomyelitis, unspecified ankle and foot 🐾

M86.18 Other acute osteomyelitis, other site 🐾

M86.19 Other acute osteomyelitis, multiple sites 🐾

● **M86.2** Subacute osteomyelitis

M86.20 Subacute osteomyelitis, unspecified site 🐾

● **M86.21** Subacute osteomyelitis, shoulder
- **M86.211** Subacute osteomyelitis, right shoulder 🐾
- **M86.212** Subacute osteomyelitis, left shoulder 🐾
- **M86.219** Subacute osteomyelitis, unspecified shoulder 🐾

● **M86.22** Subacute osteomyelitis, humerus
- **M86.221** Subacute osteomyelitis, right humerus 🐾
- **M86.222** Subacute osteomyelitis, left humerus 🐾
- **M86.229** Subacute osteomyelitis, unspecified humerus 🐾

● **M86.23** Subacute osteomyelitis, radius and ulna
- **M86.231** Subacute osteomyelitis, right radius and ulna 🐾
- **M86.232** Subacute osteomyelitis, left radius and ulna 🐾
- **M86.239** Subacute osteomyelitis, unspecified radius and ulna 🐾

● **M86.24** Subacute osteomyelitis, hand
- **M86.241** Subacute osteomyelitis, right hand 🐾
- **M86.242** Subacute osteomyelitis, left hand 🐾
- **M86.249** Subacute osteomyelitis, unspecified hand 🐾

● M86.25   Subacute osteomyelitis, femur

    M86.251   Subacute osteomyelitis, right femur 🔖

    M86.252   Subacute osteomyelitis, left femur 🔖

    M86.259   Subacute osteomyelitis, unspecified femur 🔖

● M86.26   Subacute osteomyelitis, tibia and fibula

    M86.261   Subacute osteomyelitis, right tibia and fibula 🔖

    M86.262   Subacute osteomyelitis, left tibia and fibula 🔖

    M86.269   Subacute osteomyelitis, unspecified tibia and fibula 🔖

● M86.27   Subacute osteomyelitis, ankle and foot

    M86.271   Subacute osteomyelitis, right ankle and foot 🔖

    M86.272   Subacute osteomyelitis, left ankle and foot 🔖

    M86.279   Subacute osteomyelitis, unspecified ankle and foot 🔖

    M86.28   Subacute osteomyelitis, other site 🔖

    M86.29   Subacute osteomyelitis, multiple sites 🔖

● M86.3   Chronic multifocal osteomyelitis

    M86.30   Chronic multifocal osteomyelitis, unspecified site 🔖

● M86.31   Chronic multifocal osteomyelitis, shoulder

    M86.311   Chronic multifocal osteomyelitis, right shoulder 🔖

    M86.312   Chronic multifocal osteomyelitis, left shoulder 🔖

    M86.319   Chronic multifocal osteomyelitis, unspecified shoulder 🔖

● M86.32   Chronic multifocal osteomyelitis, humerus

    M86.321   Chronic multifocal osteomyelitis, right humerus 🔖

    M86.322   Chronic multifocal osteomyelitis, left humerus 🔖

    M86.329   Chronic multifocal osteomyelitis, unspecified humerus 🔖

● M86.33   Chronic multifocal osteomyelitis, radius and ulna

    M86.331   Chronic multifocal osteomyelitis, right radius and ulna 🔖

    M86.332   Chronic multifocal osteomyelitis, left radius and ulna 🔖

    M86.339   Chronic multifocal osteomyelitis, unspecified radius and ulna 🔖

● M86.34   Chronic multifocal osteomyelitis, hand

    M86.341   Chronic multifocal osteomyelitis, right hand 🔖

    M86.342   Chronic multifocal osteomyelitis, left hand 🔖

    M86.349   Chronic multifocal osteomyelitis, unspecified hand 🔖

● M86.35   Chronic multifocal osteomyelitis, femur

    M86.351   Chronic multifocal osteomyelitis, right femur 🔖

    M86.352   Chronic multifocal osteomyelitis, left femur 🔖

    M86.359   Chronic multifocal osteomyelitis, unspecified femur 🔖

● M86.36   Chronic multifocal osteomyelitis, tibia and fibula

    M86.361   Chronic multifocal osteomyelitis, right tibia and fibula 🔖

    M86.362   Chronic multifocal osteomyelitis, left tibia and fibula 🔖

    M86.369   Chronic multifocal osteomyelitis, unspecified tibia and fibula 🔖

● M86.37   Chronic multifocal osteomyelitis, ankle and foot

    M86.371   Chronic multifocal osteomyelitis, right ankle and foot 🔖

    M86.372   Chronic multifocal osteomyelitis, left ankle and foot 🔖

    M86.379   Chronic multifocal osteomyelitis, unspecified ankle and foot 🔖

    M86.38   Chronic multifocal osteomyelitis, other site 🔖

    M86.39   Chronic multifocal osteomyelitis, multiple sites 🔖

● M86.4   Chronic osteomyelitis with draining sinus

    M86.40   Chronic osteomyelitis with draining sinus, unspecified site 🔖

● M86.41   Chronic osteomyelitis with draining sinus, shoulder

    M86.411   Chronic osteomyelitis with draining sinus, right shoulder 🔖

    M86.412   Chronic osteomyelitis with draining sinus, left shoulder 🔖

    M86.419   Chronic osteomyelitis with draining sinus, unspecified shoulder 🔖

● M86.42   Chronic osteomyelitis with draining sinus, humerus

    M86.421   Chronic osteomyelitis with draining sinus, right humerus 🔖

    M86.422   Chronic osteomyelitis with draining sinus, left humerus 🔖

    M86.429   Chronic osteomyelitis with draining sinus, unspecified humerus 🔖

● M86.43   Chronic osteomyelitis with draining sinus, radius and ulna

    M86.431   Chronic osteomyelitis with draining sinus, right radius and ulna 🔖

    M86.432   Chronic osteomyelitis with draining sinus, left radius and ulna 🔖

    M86.439   Chronic osteomyelitis with draining sinus, unspecified radius and ulna 🔖

● M86.44   Chronic osteomyelitis with draining sinus, hand

    M86.441   Chronic osteomyelitis with draining sinus, right hand 🔖

    M86.442   Chronic osteomyelitis with draining sinus, left hand 🔖

    M86.449   Chronic osteomyelitis with draining sinus, unspecified hand 🔖

● M86.45   Chronic osteomyelitis with draining sinus, femur

    M86.451   Chronic osteomyelitis with draining sinus, right femur 🔖

    M86.452   Chronic osteomyelitis with draining sinus, left femur 🔖

    M86.459   Chronic osteomyelitis with draining sinus, unspecified femur 🔖

● M86.46   Chronic osteomyelitis with draining sinus, tibia and fibula

    M86.461   Chronic osteomyelitis with draining sinus, right tibia and fibula 🔖

    M86.462   Chronic osteomyelitis with draining sinus, left tibia and fibula 🔖

    M86.469   Chronic osteomyelitis with draining sinus, unspecified tibia and fibula 🔖

● M86.47 Chronic osteomyelitis with draining sinus, ankle and foot
    M86.471 Chronic osteomyelitis with draining sinus, right ankle and foot ⚕
    M86.472 Chronic osteomyelitis with draining sinus, left ankle and foot ⚕
    M86.479 Chronic osteomyelitis with draining sinus, unspecified ankle and foot ⚕
  M86.48 Chronic osteomyelitis with draining sinus, other site ⚕
  M86.49 Chronic osteomyelitis with draining sinus, multiple sites ⚕

● M86.5 Other chronic hematogenous osteomyelitis
  M86.50 Other chronic hematogenous osteomyelitis, unspecified site ⚕
  ● M86.51 Other chronic hematogenous osteomyelitis, shoulder
    M86.511 Other chronic hematogenous osteomyelitis, right shoulder ⚕
    M86.512 Other chronic hematogenous osteomyelitis, left shoulder ⚕
    M86.519 Other chronic hematogenous osteomyelitis, unspecified shoulder ⚕
  ● M86.52 Other chronic hematogenous osteomyelitis, humerus
    M86.521 Other chronic hematogenous osteomyelitis, right humerus ⚕
    M86.522 Other chronic hematogenous osteomyelitis, left humerus ⚕
    M86.529 Other chronic hematogenous osteomyelitis, unspecified humerus ⚕
  ● M86.53 Other chronic hematogenous osteomyelitis, radius and ulna
    M86.531 Other chronic hematogenous osteomyelitis, right radius and ulna ⚕
    M86.532 Other chronic hematogenous osteomyelitis, left radius and ulna ⚕
    M86.539 Other chronic hematogenous osteomyelitis, unspecified radius and ulna ⚕
  ● M86.54 Other chronic hematogenous osteomyelitis, hand
    M86.541 Other chronic hematogenous osteomyelitis, right hand ⚕
    M86.542 Other chronic hematogenous osteomyelitis, left hand ⚕
    M86.549 Other chronic hematogenous osteomyelitis, unspecified hand ⚕
  ● M86.55 Other chronic hematogenous osteomyelitis, femur
    M86.551 Other chronic hematogenous osteomyelitis, right femur ⚕
    M86.552 Other chronic hematogenous osteomyelitis, left femur ⚕
    M86.559 Other chronic hematogenous osteomyelitis, unspecified femur ⚕
  ● M86.56 Other chronic hematogenous osteomyelitis, tibia and fibula
    M86.561 Other chronic hematogenous osteomyelitis, right tibia and fibula ⚕
    M86.562 Other chronic hematogenous osteomyelitis, left tibia and fibula ⚕
    M86.569 Other chronic hematogenous osteomyelitis, unspecified tibia and fibula ⚕

● M86.57 Other chronic hematogenous osteomyelitis, ankle and foot
    M86.571 Other chronic hematogenous osteomyelitis, right ankle and foot ⚕
    M86.572 Other chronic hematogenous osteomyelitis, left ankle and foot ⚕
    M86.579 Other chronic hematogenous osteomyelitis, unspecified ankle and foot ⚕
  M86.58 Other chronic hematogenous osteomyelitis, other site ⚕
  M86.59 Other chronic hematogenous osteomyelitis, multiple sites ⚕

● M86.6 Other chronic osteomyelitis
  M86.60 Other chronic osteomyelitis, unspecified site ⚕
  ● M86.61 Other chronic osteomyelitis, shoulder
    M86.611 Other chronic osteomyelitis, right shoulder ⚕
    M86.612 Other chronic osteomyelitis, left shoulder ⚕
    M86.619 Other chronic osteomyelitis, unspecified shoulder ⚕
  ● M86.62 Other chronic osteomyelitis, humerus
    M86.621 Other chronic osteomyelitis, right humerus ⚕
    M86.622 Other chronic osteomyelitis, left humerus ⚕
    M86.629 Other chronic osteomyelitis, unspecified humerus ⚕
  ● M86.63 Other chronic osteomyelitis, radius and ulna
    M86.631 Other chronic osteomyelitis, right radius and ulna ⚕
    M86.632 Other chronic osteomyelitis, left radius and ulna ⚕
    M86.639 Other chronic osteomyelitis, unspecified radius and ulna ⚕
  ● M86.64 Other chronic osteomyelitis, hand
    M86.641 Other chronic osteomyelitis, right hand ⚕
    M86.642 Other chronic osteomyelitis, left hand ⚕
    M86.649 Other chronic osteomyelitis, unspecified hand ⚕
  ● M86.65 Other chronic osteomyelitis, thigh
    M86.651 Other chronic osteomyelitis, right thigh ⚕
    M86.652 Other chronic osteomyelitis, left thigh ⚕
    M86.659 Other chronic osteomyelitis, unspecified thigh ⚕
  ● M86.66 Other chronic osteomyelitis, tibia and fibula
    M86.661 Other chronic osteomyelitis, right tibia and fibula ⚕
    M86.662 Other chronic osteomyelitis, left tibia and fibula ⚕
    M86.669 Other chronic osteomyelitis, unspecified tibia and fibula ⚕
  ● M86.67 Other chronic osteomyelitis, ankle and foot
    M86.671 Other chronic osteomyelitis, right ankle and foot ⚕
      Coding Clinic: 2016, Q1, P13
    M86.672 Other chronic osteomyelitis, left ankle and foot ⚕
    M86.679 Other chronic osteomyelitis, unspecified ankle and foot ⚕
  M86.68 Other chronic osteomyelitis, other site ⚕
  M86.69 Other chronic osteomyelitis, multiple sites ⚕

▶ New   ⇒ Revised   ~~deleted~~ Deleted   Excludes 1   Excludes 2   Includes   Use additional   Code first   Code also   Key words
OGCR Official Guidelines   X Assign placeholder X   ● Use Additional Character(s)   ▶ Manifestation Code   ⚕ Hierarchical Condition Category   Coding Clinic

● **M86.8**   Other osteomyelitis
     Brodie's abscess
  ● **M86.8X**   Other osteomyelitis
       M86.8X0   Other osteomyelitis, multiple sites ⚕
       M86.8X1   Other osteomyelitis, shoulder ⚕
       M86.8X2   Other osteomyelitis, upper arm ⚕
       M86.8X3   Other osteomyelitis, forearm ⚕
       M86.8X4   Other osteomyelitis, hand ⚕
       M86.8X5   Other osteomyelitis, thigh ⚕
       M86.8X6   Other osteomyelitis, lower leg ⚕
       M86.8X7   Other osteomyelitis, ankle and foot ⚕
       M86.8X8   Other osteomyelitis, other site ⚕
       M86.8X9   Other osteomyelitis, unspecified sites ⚕
   M86.9   Osteomyelitis, unspecified ⚕
     Infection of bone NOS
     Periostitis without osteomyelitis

● **M87**   Osteonecrosis
     Includes   avascular necrosis of bone
     Use additional code to identify major osseous defect, if applicable (M89.7-)
     Excludes1   juvenile osteonecrosis (M91-M92)
                osteochondropathies (M90-M93)
  ● **M87.0**   Idiopathic aseptic necrosis of bone
     M87.00   Idiopathic aseptic necrosis of unspecified bone ⚕
    ● **M87.01**   Idiopathic aseptic necrosis of shoulder
       Idiopathic aseptic necrosis of clavicle and scapula
       M87.011   Idiopathic aseptic necrosis of right shoulder ⚕
       M87.012   Idiopathic aseptic necrosis of left shoulder ⚕
       M87.019   Idiopathic aseptic necrosis of unspecified shoulder ⚕
    ● **M87.02**   Idiopathic aseptic necrosis of humerus
       M87.021   Idiopathic aseptic necrosis of right humerus ⚕
       M87.022   Idiopathic aseptic necrosis of left humerus ⚕
       M87.029   Idiopathic aseptic necrosis of unspecified humerus ⚕
    ● **M87.03**   Idiopathic aseptic necrosis of radius, ulna and carpus
       M87.031   Idiopathic aseptic necrosis of right radius ⚕
       M87.032   Idiopathic aseptic necrosis of left radius ⚕
       M87.033   Idiopathic aseptic necrosis of unspecified radius ⚕
       M87.034   Idiopathic aseptic necrosis of right ulna ⚕
       M87.035   Idiopathic aseptic necrosis of left ulna ⚕
       M87.036   Idiopathic aseptic necrosis of unspecified ulna ⚕
       M87.037   Idiopathic aseptic necrosis of right carpus ⚕
       M87.038   Idiopathic aseptic necrosis of left carpus ⚕
       M87.039   Idiopathic aseptic necrosis of unspecified carpus ⚕

● **M87.04**   Idiopathic aseptic necrosis of hand and fingers
     Idiopathic aseptic necrosis of metacarpals and phalanges of hands
     M87.041   Idiopathic aseptic necrosis of right hand ⚕
     M87.042   Idiopathic aseptic necrosis of left hand ⚕
     M87.043   Idiopathic aseptic necrosis of unspecified hand ⚕
     M87.044   Idiopathic aseptic necrosis of right finger(s) ⚕
     M87.045   Idiopathic aseptic necrosis of left finger(s) ⚕
     M87.046   Idiopathic aseptic necrosis of unspecified finger(s) ⚕
● **M87.05**   Idiopathic aseptic necrosis of pelvis and femur
     M87.050   Idiopathic aseptic necrosis of pelvis ⚕
     M87.051   Idiopathic aseptic necrosis of right femur ⚕
     M87.052   Idiopathic aseptic necrosis of left femur ⚕
     M87.059   Idiopathic aseptic necrosis of unspecified femur ⚕
       Idiopathic aseptic necrosis of hip NOS
● **M87.06**   Idiopathic aseptic necrosis of tibia and fibula
     M87.061   Idiopathic aseptic necrosis of right tibia ⚕
     M87.062   Idiopathic aseptic necrosis of left tibia ⚕
     M87.063   Idiopathic aseptic necrosis of unspecified tibia ⚕
     M87.064   Idiopathic aseptic necrosis of right fibula ⚕
     M87.065   Idiopathic aseptic necrosis of left fibula ⚕
     M87.066   Idiopathic aseptic necrosis of unspecified fibula ⚕
● **M87.07**   Idiopathic aseptic necrosis of ankle, foot and toes
     Idiopathic aseptic necrosis of metatarsus, tarsus, and phalanges of toes
     M87.071   Idiopathic aseptic necrosis of right ankle ⚕
     M87.072   Idiopathic aseptic necrosis of left ankle ⚕
     M87.073   Idiopathic aseptic necrosis of unspecified ankle ⚕
     M87.074   Idiopathic aseptic necrosis of right foot ⚕
     M87.075   Idiopathic aseptic necrosis of left foot ⚕
     M87.076   Idiopathic aseptic necrosis of unspecified foot ⚕
     M87.077   Idiopathic aseptic necrosis of right toe(s) ⚕
     M87.078   Idiopathic aseptic necrosis of left toe(s) ⚕
     M87.079   Idiopathic aseptic necrosis of unspecified toe(s) ⚕
   M87.08   Idiopathic aseptic necrosis of bone, other site ⚕
   M87.09   Idiopathic aseptic necrosis of bone, multiple sites ⚕

● **M87.1   Osteonecrosis due to drugs**

> Use additional code for adverse effect, if applicable, to identify drug (T36-T50 with fifth or sixth character 5)

     M87.10   Osteonecrosis due to drugs, unspecified bone 🐾

● **M87.11   Osteonecrosis due to drugs, shoulder**

       M87.111   Osteonecrosis due to drugs, right shoulder 🐾

       M87.112   Osteonecrosis due to drugs, left shoulder 🐾

       M87.119   Osteonecrosis due to drugs, unspecified shoulder 🐾

● **M87.12   Osteonecrosis due to drugs, humerus**

       M87.121   Osteonecrosis due to drugs, right humerus 🐾

       M87.122   Osteonecrosis due to drugs, left humerus 🐾

       M87.129   Osteonecrosis due to drugs, unspecified humerus 🐾

● **M87.13   Osteonecrosis due to drugs of radius, ulna and carpus**

       M87.131   Osteonecrosis due to drugs of right radius 🐾

       M87.132   Osteonecrosis due to drugs of left radius 🐾

       M87.133   Osteonecrosis due to drugs of unspecified radius 🐾

       M87.134   Osteonecrosis due to drugs of right ulna 🐾

       M87.135   Osteonecrosis due to drugs of left ulna 🐾

       M87.136   Osteonecrosis due to drugs of unspecified ulna 🐾

       M87.137   Osteonecrosis due to drugs of right carpus 🐾

       M87.138   Osteonecrosis due to drugs of left carpus 🐾

       M87.139   Osteonecrosis due to drugs of unspecified carpus 🐾

● **M87.14   Osteonecrosis due to drugs, hand and fingers**

       M87.141   Osteonecrosis due to drugs, right hand 🐾

       M87.142   Osteonecrosis due to drugs, left hand 🐾

       M87.143   Osteonecrosis due to drugs, unspecified hand 🐾

       M87.144   Osteonecrosis due to drugs, right finger(s) 🐾

       M87.145   Osteonecrosis due to drugs, left finger(s) 🐾

       M87.146   Osteonecrosis due to drugs, unspecified finger(s) 🐾

● **M87.15   Osteonecrosis due to drugs, pelvis and femur**

       M87.150   Osteonecrosis due to drugs, pelvis 🐾

       M87.151   Osteonecrosis due to drugs, right femur 🐾

       M87.152   Osteonecrosis due to drugs, left femur 🐾

       M87.159   Osteonecrosis due to drugs, unspecified femur 🐾

● **M87.16   Osteonecrosis due to drugs, tibia and fibula**

       M87.161   Osteonecrosis due to drugs, right tibia 🐾

       M87.162   Osteonecrosis due to drugs, left tibia 🐾

       M87.163   Osteonecrosis due to drugs, unspecified tibia 🐾

       M87.164   Osteonecrosis due to drugs, right fibula 🐾

       M87.165   Osteonecrosis due to drugs, left fibula 🐾

       M87.166   Osteonecrosis due to drugs, unspecified fibula 🐾

● **M87.17   Osteonecrosis due to drugs, ankle, foot and toes**

       M87.171   Osteonecrosis due to drugs, right ankle 🐾

       M87.172   Osteonecrosis due to drugs, left ankle 🐾

       M87.173   Osteonecrosis due to drugs, unspecified ankle 🐾

       M87.174   Osteonecrosis due to drugs, right foot 🐾

       M87.175   Osteonecrosis due to drugs, left foot 🐾

       M87.176   Osteonecrosis due to drugs, unspecified foot 🐾

       M87.177   Osteonecrosis due to drugs, right toe(s) 🐾

       M87.178   Osteonecrosis due to drugs, left toe(s) 🐾

       M87.179   Osteonecrosis due to drugs, unspecified toe(s) 🐾

● **M87.18   Osteonecrosis due to drugs, other site**

       M87.180   Osteonecrosis due to drugs, jaw 🐾

       M87.188   Osteonecrosis due to drugs, other site 🐾

     M87.19   Osteonecrosis due to drugs, multiple sites 🐾

● **M87.2   Osteonecrosis due to previous trauma**

     M87.20   Osteonecrosis due to previous trauma, unspecified bone 🐾

● **M87.21   Osteonecrosis due to previous trauma, shoulder**

       M87.211   Osteonecrosis due to previous trauma, right shoulder 🐾

       M87.212   Osteonecrosis due to previous trauma, left shoulder 🐾

       M87.219   Osteonecrosis due to previous trauma, unspecified shoulder 🐾

● **M87.22   Osteonecrosis due to previous trauma, humerus**

       M87.221   Osteonecrosis due to previous trauma, right humerus 🐾

       M87.222   Osteonecrosis due to previous trauma, left humerus 🐾

       M87.229   Osteonecrosis due to previous trauma, unspecified humerus 🐾

● **M87.23   Osteonecrosis due to previous trauma of radius, ulna and carpus**

       M87.231   Osteonecrosis due to previous trauma of right radius 🐾

       M87.232   Osteonecrosis due to previous trauma of left radius 🐾

       M87.233   Osteonecrosis due to previous trauma of unspecified radius 🐾

       M87.234   Osteonecrosis due to previous trauma of right ulna 🐾

       M87.235   Osteonecrosis due to previous trauma of left ulna 🐾

       M87.236   Osteonecrosis due to previous trauma of unspecified ulna 🐾

       M87.237   Osteonecrosis due to previous trauma of right carpus 🐾

       M87.238   Osteonecrosis due to previous trauma of left carpus 🐾

       M87.239   Osteonecrosis due to previous trauma of unspecified carpus 🐾

● M87.24 Osteonecrosis due to previous trauma, hand and fingers

    M87.241 Osteonecrosis due to previous trauma, right hand 🦴

    M87.242 Osteonecrosis due to previous trauma, left hand 🦴

    M87.243 Osteonecrosis due to previous trauma, unspecified hand 🦴

    M87.244 Osteonecrosis due to previous trauma, right finger(s) 🦴

    M87.245 Osteonecrosis due to previous trauma, left finger(s) 🦴

    M87.246 Osteonecrosis due to previous trauma, unspecified finger(s) 🦴

● M87.25 Osteonecrosis due to previous trauma, pelvis and femur

    M87.250 Osteonecrosis due to previous trauma, pelvis 🦴

    M87.251 Osteonecrosis due to previous trauma, right femur 🦴

    M87.252 Osteonecrosis due to previous trauma, left femur 🦴

    M87.256 Osteonecrosis due to previous trauma, unspecified femur 🦴

● M87.26 Osteonecrosis due to previous trauma, tibia and fibula

    M87.261 Osteonecrosis due to previous trauma, right tibia 🦴

    M87.262 Osteonecrosis due to previous trauma, left tibia 🦴

    M87.263 Osteonecrosis due to previous trauma, unspecified tibia 🦴

    M87.264 Osteonecrosis due to previous trauma, right fibula 🦴

    M87.265 Osteonecrosis due to previous trauma, left fibula 🦴

    M87.266 Osteonecrosis due to previous trauma, unspecified fibula 🦴

● M87.27 Osteonecrosis due to previous trauma, ankle, foot and toes

    M87.271 Osteonecrosis due to previous trauma, right ankle 🦴

    M87.272 Osteonecrosis due to previous trauma, left ankle 🦴

    M87.273 Osteonecrosis due to previous trauma, unspecified ankle 🦴

    M87.274 Osteonecrosis due to previous trauma, right foot 🦴

    M87.275 Osteonecrosis due to previous trauma, left foot 🦴

    M87.276 Osteonecrosis due to previous trauma, unspecified foot 🦴

    M87.277 Osteonecrosis due to previous trauma, right toe(s) 🦴

    M87.278 Osteonecrosis due to previous trauma, left toe(s) 🦴

    M87.279 Osteonecrosis due to previous trauma, unspecified toe(s) 🦴

M87.28 Osteonecrosis due to previous trauma, other site 🦴

M87.29 Osteonecrosis due to previous trauma, multiple sites 🦴

● M87.3 Other secondary osteonecrosis

    M87.30 Other secondary osteonecrosis, unspecified bone 🦴

● M87.31 Other secondary osteonecrosis, shoulder

    M87.311 Other secondary osteonecrosis, right shoulder 🦴

    M87.312 Other secondary osteonecrosis, left shoulder 🦴

    M87.319 Other secondary osteonecrosis, unspecified shoulder 🦴

● M87.32 Other secondary osteonecrosis, humerus

    M87.321 Other secondary osteonecrosis, right humerus 🦴

    M87.322 Other secondary osteonecrosis, left humerus 🦴

    M87.329 Other secondary osteonecrosis, unspecified humerus 🦴

● M87.33 Other secondary osteonecrosis of radius, ulna and carpus

    M87.331 Other secondary osteonecrosis of right radius 🦴

    M87.332 Other secondary osteonecrosis of left radius 🦴

    M87.333 Other secondary osteonecrosis of unspecified radius 🦴

    M87.334 Other secondary osteonecrosis of right ulna 🦴

    M87.335 Other secondary osteonecrosis of left ulna 🦴

    M87.336 Other secondary osteonecrosis of unspecified ulna 🦴

    M87.337 Other secondary osteonecrosis of right carpus 🦴

    M87.338 Other secondary osteonecrosis of left carpus 🦴

    M87.339 Other secondary osteonecrosis of unspecified carpus 🦴

● M87.34 Other secondary osteonecrosis, hand and fingers

    M87.341 Other secondary osteonecrosis, right hand 🦴

    M87.342 Other secondary osteonecrosis, left hand 🦴

    M87.343 Other secondary osteonecrosis, unspecified hand 🦴

    M87.344 Other secondary osteonecrosis, right finger(s) 🦴

    M87.345 Other secondary osteonecrosis, left finger(s) 🦴

    M87.346 Other secondary osteonecrosis, unspecified finger(s) 🦴

● M87.35 Other secondary osteonecrosis, pelvis and femur

    M87.350 Other secondary osteonecrosis, pelvis 🦴

    M87.351 Other secondary osteonecrosis, right femur 🦴

    M87.352 Other secondary osteonecrosis, left femur 🦴

    M87.353 Other secondary osteonecrosis, unspecified femur 🦴

● M87.36   Other secondary osteonecrosis, tibia and fibula
     M87.361   Other secondary osteonecrosis, right tibia 🐾
     M87.362   Other secondary osteonecrosis, left tibia 🐾
     M87.363   Other secondary osteonecrosis, unspecified tibia 🐾
     M87.364   Other secondary osteonecrosis, right fibula 🐾
     M87.365   Other secondary osteonecrosis, left fibula 🐾
     M87.366   Other secondary osteonecrosis, unspecified fibula 🐾

● M87.37   Other secondary osteonecrosis, ankle and foot
     M87.371   Other secondary osteonecrosis, right ankle 🐾
     M87.372   Other secondary osteonecrosis, left ankle 🐾
     M87.373   Other secondary osteonecrosis, unspecified ankle 🐾
     M87.374   Other secondary osteonecrosis, right foot 🐾
     M87.375   Other secondary osteonecrosis, left foot 🐾
     M87.376   Other secondary osteonecrosis, unspecified foot 🐾
     M87.377   Other secondary osteonecrosis, right toe(s) 🐾
     M87.378   Other secondary osteonecrosis, left toe(s) 🐾
     M87.379   Other secondary osteonecrosis, unspecified toe(s) 🐾

   M87.38   Other secondary osteonecrosis, other site 🐾
   M87.39   Other secondary osteonecrosis, multiple sites 🐾

● M87.8   Other osteonecrosis
   M87.80   Other osteonecrosis, unspecified bone 🐾

● M87.81   Other osteonecrosis, shoulder
     M87.811   Other osteonecrosis, right shoulder 🐾
     M87.812   Other osteonecrosis, left shoulder 🐾
     M87.819   Other osteonecrosis, unspecified shoulder 🐾

● M87.82   Other osteonecrosis, humerus
     M87.821   Other osteonecrosis, right humerus 🐾
     M87.822   Other osteonecrosis, left humerus 🐾
     M87.829   Other osteonecrosis, unspecified humerus 🐾

● M87.83   Other osteonecrosis of radius, ulna and carpus
     M87.831   Other osteonecrosis of right radius 🐾
     M87.832   Other osteonecrosis of left radius 🐾
     M87.833   Other osteonecrosis of unspecified radius 🐾
     M87.834   Other osteonecrosis of right ulna 🐾
     M87.835   Other osteonecrosis of left ulna 🐾
     M87.836   Other osteonecrosis of unspecified ulna 🐾
     M87.837   Other osteonecrosis of right carpus 🐾
     M87.838   Other osteonecrosis of left carpus 🐾
     M87.839   Other osteonecrosis of unspecified carpus 🐾

● M87.84   Other osteonecrosis, hand and fingers
     M87.841   Other osteonecrosis, right hand 🐾
     M87.842   Other osteonecrosis, left hand 🐾
     M87.843   Other osteonecrosis, unspecified hand 🐾
     M87.844   Other osteonecrosis, right finger(s) 🐾
     M87.845   Other osteonecrosis, left finger(s) 🐾
     M87.849   Other osteonecrosis, unspecified finger(s) 🐾

● M87.85   Other osteonecrosis, pelvis and femur
     M87.850   Other osteonecrosis, pelvis 🐾
     M87.851   Other osteonecrosis, right femur 🐾
     M87.852   Other osteonecrosis, left femur 🐾
     M87.859   Other osteonecrosis, unspecified femur 🐾

● M87.86   Other osteonecrosis, tibia and fibula
     M87.861   Other osteonecrosis, right tibia 🐾
     M87.862   Other osteonecrosis, left tibia 🐾
     M87.863   Other osteonecrosis, unspecified tibia 🐾
     M87.864   Other osteonecrosis, right fibula 🐾
     M87.865   Other osteonecrosis, left fibula 🐾
     M87.869   Other osteonecrosis, unspecified fibula 🐾

● M87.87   Other osteonecrosis, ankle, foot and toes
     M87.871   Other osteonecrosis, right ankle 🐾
     M87.872   Other osteonecrosis, left ankle 🐾
     M87.873   Other osteonecrosis, unspecified ankle 🐾
     M87.874   Other osteonecrosis, right foot 🐾
     M87.875   Other osteonecrosis, left foot 🐾
     M87.876   Other osteonecrosis, unspecified foot 🐾
     M87.877   Other osteonecrosis, right toe(s) 🐾
     M87.878   Other osteonecrosis, left toe(s) 🐾
     M87.879   Other osteonecrosis, unspecified toe(s) 🐾

   M87.88   Other osteonecrosis, other site 🐾
   M87.89   Other osteonecrosis, multiple sites 🐾

   M87.9   Osteonecrosis, unspecified 🐾
     Necrosis of bone NOS

● M88   **Osteitis deformans [Paget's disease of bone]**
Chronic disorder that results in enlarged and deformed bones. The excessive breakdown and formation of bone tissue causes bones to weaken and results in bone pain, arthritis, deformities, and fractures.

   Excludes 1   osteitis deformans in neoplastic disease (M90.6)

   M88.0   Osteitis deformans of skull
   M88.1   Osteitis deformans of vertebrae

● M88.8   Osteitis deformans of other bones

● M88.81   Osteitis deformans of shoulder
     M88.811   Osteitis deformans of right shoulder
     M88.812   Osteitis deformans of left shoulder
     M88.819   Osteitis deformans of unspecified shoulder

● M88.82   Osteitis deformans of upper arm
     M88.821   Osteitis deformans of right upper arm
     M88.822   Osteitis deformans of left upper arm
     M88.829   Osteitis deformans of unspecified upper arm

● M88.83   Osteitis deformans of forearm
     M88.831   Osteitis deformans of right forearm
     M88.832   Osteitis deformans of left forearm
     M88.839   Osteitis deformans of unspecified forearm

● M88.84   Osteitis deformans of hand
     M88.841   Osteitis deformans of right hand
     M88.842   Osteitis deformans of left hand
     M88.849   Osteitis deformans of unspecified hand

● M88.85   Osteitis deformans of thigh
     M88.851   Osteitis deformans of right thigh
     M88.852   Osteitis deformans of left thigh
     M88.859   Osteitis deformans of unspecified thigh

▶ New   ⇒ Revised   ~~deleted~~ Deleted   Excludes 1   Excludes 2   Includes   Use additional   Code first   Code also   Key words
OGCR Official Guidelines   X Assign placeholder X   ● Use Additional Character(s)   ▷ Manifestation Code   🐾 Hierarchical Condition Category   **Coding Clinic**

● M88.86   Osteitis deformans of lower leg
    M88.861   Osteitis deformans of right lower leg
    M88.862   Osteitis deformans of left lower leg
    M88.869   Osteitis deformans of unspecified lower leg

● M88.87   Osteitis deformans of ankle and foot
    M88.871   Osteitis deformans of right ankle and foot
    M88.872   Osteitis deformans of left ankle and foot
    M88.879   Osteitis deformans of unspecified ankle and foot

  M88.88   Osteitis deformans of other bones
    Excludes2   osteitis deformans of skull (M88.0)
              osteitis deformans of vertebrae (M88.1)

  M88.89   Osteitis deformans of multiple sites

M88.9   Osteitis deformans of unspecified bone

● M89   Other disorders of bone

● M89.0   Algoneurodystrophy
    Shoulder-hand syndrome
    Sudeck's atrophy
    Excludes1   causalgia, lower limb (G57.7-)
              causalgia, upper limb (G56.4-)
              complex regional pain syndrome II, lower limb (G57.7-)
              complex regional pain syndrome II, upper limb (G56.4-)
              reflex sympathetic dystrophy (G90.5-)

  M89.00   Algoneurodystrophy, unspecified site

● M89.01   Algoneurodystrophy, shoulder
    M89.011   Algoneurodystrophy, right shoulder
    M89.012   Algoneurodystrophy, left shoulder
    M89.019   Algoneurodystrophy, unspecified shoulder

● M89.02   Algoneurodystrophy, upper arm
    M89.021   Algoneurodystrophy, right upper arm
    M89.022   Algoneurodystrophy, left upper arm
    M89.029   Algoneurodystrophy, unspecified upper arm

● M89.03   Algoneurodystrophy, forearm
    M89.031   Algoneurodystrophy, right forearm
    M89.032   Algoneurodystrophy, left forearm
    M89.039   Algoneurodystrophy, unspecified forearm

● M89.04   Algoneurodystrophy, hand
    M89.041   Algoneurodystrophy, right hand
    M89.042   Algoneurodystrophy, left hand
    M89.049   Algoneurodystrophy, unspecified hand

● M89.05   Algoneurodystrophy, thigh
    M89.051   Algoneurodystrophy, right thigh
    M89.052   Algoneurodystrophy, left thigh
    M89.059   Algoneurodystrophy, unspecified thigh

● M89.06   Algoneurodystrophy, lower leg
    M89.061   Algoneurodystrophy, right lower leg
    M89.062   Algoneurodystrophy, left lower leg
    M89.069   Algoneurodystrophy, unspecified lower leg

● M89.07   Algoneurodystrophy, ankle and foot
    M89.071   Algoneurodystrophy, right ankle and foot
    M89.072   Algoneurodystrophy, left ankle and foot
    M89.079   Algoneurodystrophy, unspecified ankle and foot

  M89.08   Algoneurodystrophy, other site

  M89.09   Algoneurodystrophy, multiple sites

● M89.1   Physeal arrest
    Arrest of growth plate
    Epiphyseal arrest
    Growth plate arrest

● M89.12   Physeal arrest, humerus
    M89.121   Complete physeal arrest, right proximal humerus
    M89.122   Complete physeal arrest, left proximal humerus
    M89.123   Partial physeal arrest, right proximal humerus
    M89.124   Partial physeal arrest, left proximal humerus
    M89.125   Complete physeal arrest, right distal humerus
    M89.126   Complete physeal arrest, left distal humerus
    M89.127   Partial physeal arrest, right distal humerus
    M89.128   Partial physeal arrest, left distal humerus
    M89.129   Physeal arrest, humerus, unspecified

● M89.13   Physeal arrest, forearm
    M89.131   Complete physeal arrest, right distal radius
    M89.132   Complete physeal arrest, left distal radius
    M89.133   Partial physeal arrest, right distal radius
    M89.134   Partial physeal arrest, left distal radius
    M89.138   Other physeal arrest of forearm
    M89.139   Physeal arrest, forearm, unspecified

● M89.15   Physeal arrest, femur
    M89.151   Complete physeal arrest, right proximal femur
    M89.152   Complete physeal arrest, left proximal femur
    M89.153   Partial physeal arrest, right proximal femur
    M89.154   Partial physeal arrest, left proximal femur
    M89.155   Complete physeal arrest, right distal femur
    M89.156   Complete physeal arrest, left distal femur
    M89.157   Partial physeal arrest, right distal femur
    M89.158   Partial physeal arrest, left distal femur
    M89.159   Physeal arrest, femur, unspecified

● M89.16   Physeal arrest, lower leg

     M89.160   Complete physeal arrest, right proximal tibia

     M89.161   Complete physeal arrest, left proximal tibia

     M89.162   Partial physeal arrest, right proximal tibia

     M89.163   Partial physeal arrest, left proximal tibia

     M89.164   Complete physeal arrest, right distal tibia

     M89.165   Complete physeal arrest, left distal tibia

     M89.166   Partial physeal arrest, right distal tibia

     M89.167   Partial physeal arrest, left distal tibia

     M89.168   Other physeal arrest of lower leg

     M89.169   Physeal arrest, lower leg, unspecified

     M89.18   Physeal arrest, other site

● M89.2   Other disorders of bone development and growth

     M89.20   Other disorders of bone development and growth, unspecified site

● M89.21   Other disorders of bone development and growth, shoulder

     M89.211   Other disorders of bone development and growth, right shoulder

     M89.212   Other disorders of bone development and growth, left shoulder

     M89.219   Other disorders of bone development and growth, unspecified shoulder

● M89.22   Other disorders of bone development and growth, humerus

     M89.221   Other disorders of bone development and growth, right humerus

     M89.222   Other disorders of bone development and growth, left humerus

     M89.229   Other disorders of bone development and growth, unspecified humerus

● M89.23   Other disorders of bone development and growth, ulna and radius

     M89.231   Other disorders of bone development and growth, right ulna

     M89.232   Other disorders of bone development and growth, left ulna

     M89.233   Other disorders of bone development and growth, right radius

     M89.234   Other disorders of bone development and growth, left radius

     M89.239   Other disorders of bone development and growth, unspecified ulna and radius

● M89.24   Other disorders of bone development and growth, hand

     M89.241   Other disorders of bone development and growth, right hand

     M89.242   Other disorders of bone development and growth, left hand

     M89.249   Other disorders of bone development and growth, unspecified hand

● M89.25   Other disorders of bone development and growth, femur

     M89.251   Other disorders of bone development and growth, right femur

     M89.252   Other disorders of bone development and growth, left femur

     M89.259   Other disorders of bone development and growth, unspecified femur

● M89.26   Other disorders of bone development and growth, tibia and fibula

     M89.261   Other disorders of bone development and growth, right tibia

     M89.262   Other disorders of bone development and growth, left tibia

     M89.263   Other disorders of bone development and growth, right fibula

     M89.264   Other disorders of bone development and growth, left fibula

     M89.269   Other disorders of bone development and growth, unspecified lower leg

● M89.27   Other disorders of bone development and growth, ankle and foot

     M89.271   Other disorders of bone development and growth, right ankle and foot

     M89.272   Other disorders of bone development and growth, left ankle and foot

     M89.279   Other disorders of bone development and growth, unspecified ankle and foot

     M89.28   Other disorders of bone development and growth, other site

     M89.29   Other disorders of bone development and growth, multiple sites

● M89.3   Hypertrophy of bone

     M89.30   Hypertrophy of bone, unspecified site

● M89.31   Hypertrophy of bone, shoulder

     M89.311   Hypertrophy of bone, right shoulder

     M89.312   Hypertrophy of bone, left shoulder

     M89.319   Hypertrophy of bone, unspecified shoulder

● M89.32   Hypertrophy of bone, humerus

     M89.321   Hypertrophy of bone, right humerus

     M89.322   Hypertrophy of bone, left humerus

     M89.329   Hypertrophy of bone, unspecified humerus

● M89.33   Hypertrophy of bone, ulna and radius

     M89.331   Hypertrophy of bone, right ulna

     M89.332   Hypertrophy of bone, left ulna

     M89.333   Hypertrophy of bone, right radius

     M89.334   Hypertrophy of bone, left radius

     M89.339   Hypertrophy of bone, unspecified ulna and radius

● M89.34   Hypertrophy of bone, hand

     M89.341   Hypertrophy of bone, right hand

     M89.342   Hypertrophy of bone, left hand

     M89.349   Hypertrophy of bone, unspecified hand

● M89.35   Hypertrophy of bone, femur

     M89.351   Hypertrophy of bone, right femur

     M89.352   Hypertrophy of bone, left femur

     M89.359   Hypertrophy of bone, unspecified femur

● M89.36   Hypertrophy of bone, tibia and fibula

     M89.361   Hypertrophy of bone, right tibia

     M89.362   Hypertrophy of bone, left tibia

     M89.363   Hypertrophy of bone, right fibula

     M89.364   Hypertrophy of bone, left fibula

     M89.369   Hypertrophy of bone, unspecified tibia and fibula

▶ New   ⇒ Revised   ~~deleted~~ Deleted   Excludes 1   Excludes 2   Includes   Use additional   Code first   Code also   Key words

OGCR Official Guidelines   X Assign placeholder X   ● Use Additional Character(s)   ▶ Manifestation Code   ℆ Hierarchical Condition Category   **Coding Clinic**

● M89.37   Hypertrophy of bone, ankle and foot
     M89.371   Hypertrophy of bone, right ankle and foot
     M89.372   Hypertrophy of bone, left ankle and foot
     M89.379   Hypertrophy of bone, unspecified ankle and foot
   M89.38   Hypertrophy of bone, other site
   M89.39   Hypertrophy of bone, multiple sites

● M89.4   Other hypertrophic osteoarthropathy
     Marie-Bamberger disease
     Pachydermoperiostosis
   M89.40   Other hypertrophic osteoarthropathy, unspecified site
● M89.41   Other hypertrophic osteoarthropathy, shoulder
     M89.411   Other hypertrophic osteoarthropathy, right shoulder
     M89.412   Other hypertrophic osteoarthropathy, left shoulder
     M89.419   Other hypertrophic osteoarthropathy, unspecified shoulder
● M89.42   Other hypertrophic osteoarthropathy, upper arm
     M89.421   Other hypertrophic osteoarthropathy, right upper arm
     M89.422   Other hypertrophic osteoarthropathy, left upper arm
     M89.429   Other hypertrophic osteoarthropathy, unspecified upper arm
● M89.43   Other hypertrophic osteoarthropathy, forearm
     M89.431   Other hypertrophic osteoarthropathy, right forearm
     M89.432   Other hypertrophic osteoarthropathy, left forearm
     M89.439   Other hypertrophic osteoarthropathy, unspecified forearm
● M89.44   Other hypertrophic osteoarthropathy, hand
     M89.441   Other hypertrophic osteoarthropathy, right hand
     M89.442   Other hypertrophic osteoarthropathy, left hand
     M89.449   Other hypertrophic osteoarthropathy, unspecified hand
● M89.45   Other hypertrophic osteoarthropathy, thigh
     M89.451   Other hypertrophic osteoarthropathy, right thigh
     M89.452   Other hypertrophic osteoarthropathy, left thigh
     M89.459   Other hypertrophic osteoarthropathy, unspecified thigh
● M89.46   Other hypertrophic osteoarthropathy, lower leg
     M89.461   Other hypertrophic osteoarthropathy, right lower leg
     M89.462   Other hypertrophic osteoarthropathy, left lower leg
     M89.469   Other hypertrophic osteoarthropathy, unspecified lower leg
● M89.47   Other hypertrophic osteoarthropathy, ankle and foot
     M89.471   Other hypertrophic osteoarthropathy, right ankle and foot
     M89.472   Other hypertrophic osteoarthropathy, left ankle and foot
     M89.479   Other hypertrophic osteoarthropathy, unspecified ankle and foot
   M89.48   Other hypertrophic osteoarthropathy, other site
   M89.49   Other hypertrophic osteoarthropathy, multiple sites

● M89.5   Osteolysis
     Use additional code to identify major osseous defect, if applicable (M89.7-)
     Excludes2   periprosthetic osteolysis of internal prosthetic joint (T84.05-)
   M89.50   Osteolysis, unspecified site
● M89.51   Osteolysis, shoulder
     M89.511   Osteolysis, right shoulder
     M89.512   Osteolysis, left shoulder
     M89.519   Osteolysis, unspecified shoulder
● M89.52   Osteolysis, upper arm
     M89.521   Osteolysis, right upper arm
     M89.522   Osteolysis, left upper arm
     M89.529   Osteolysis, unspecified upper arm
● M89.53   Osteolysis, forearm
     M89.531   Osteolysis, right forearm
     M89.532   Osteolysis, left forearm
     M89.539   Osteolysis, unspecified forearm
● M89.54   Osteolysis, hand
     M89.541   Osteolysis, right hand
     M89.542   Osteolysis, left hand
     M89.549   Osteolysis, unspecified hand
● M89.55   Osteolysis, thigh
     M89.551   Osteolysis, right thigh
     M89.552   Osteolysis, left thigh
     M89.559   Osteolysis, unspecified thigh
● M89.56   Osteolysis, lower leg
     M89.561   Osteolysis, right lower leg
     M89.562   Osteolysis, left lower leg
     M89.569   Osteolysis, unspecified lower leg
● M89.57   Osteolysis, ankle and foot
     M89.571   Osteolysis, right ankle and foot
     M89.572   Osteolysis, left ankle and foot
     M89.579   Osteolysis, unspecified ankle and foot
   M89.58   Osteolysis, other site
   M89.59   Osteolysis, multiple sites

● M89.6   Osteopathy after poliomyelitis
     Use additional code (B91) to identify previous poliomyelitis
     Excludes1   postpolio syndrome (G14)
   M89.60   Osteopathy after poliomyelitis, unspecified site 🦠
● M89.61   Osteopathy after poliomyelitis, shoulder
     M89.611   Osteopathy after poliomyelitis, right shoulder 🦠
     M89.612   Osteopathy after poliomyelitis, left shoulder 🦠
     M89.619   Osteopathy after poliomyelitis, unspecified shoulder 🦠
● M89.62   Osteopathy after poliomyelitis, upper arm
     M89.621   Osteopathy after poliomyelitis, right upper arm 🦠
     M89.622   Osteopathy after poliomyelitis, left upper arm 🦠
     M89.629   Osteopathy after poliomyelitis, unspecified upper arm 🦠
● M89.63   Osteopathy after poliomyelitis, forearm
     M89.631   Osteopathy after poliomyelitis, right forearm 🦠
     M89.632   Osteopathy after poliomyelitis, left forearm 🦠
     M89.639   Osteopathy after poliomyelitis, unspecified forearm 🦠

● **M89.64** Osteopathy after poliomyelitis, hand
  M89.641 Osteopathy after poliomyelitis, right hand 🦠
  M89.642 Osteopathy after poliomyelitis, left hand 🦠
  M89.649 Osteopathy after poliomyelitis, unspecified hand 🦠

● **M89.65** Osteopathy after poliomyelitis, thigh
  M89.651 Osteopathy after poliomyelitis, right thigh 🦠
  M89.652 Osteopathy after poliomyelitis, left thigh 🦠
  M89.659 Osteopathy after poliomyelitis, unspecified thigh 🦠

● **M89.66** Osteopathy after poliomyelitis, lower leg
  M89.661 Osteopathy after poliomyelitis, right lower leg 🦠
  M89.662 Osteopathy after poliomyelitis, left lower leg 🦠
  M89.669 Osteopathy after poliomyelitis, unspecified lower leg 🦠

● **M89.67** Osteopathy after poliomyelitis, ankle and foot
  M89.671 Osteopathy after poliomyelitis, right ankle and foot 🦠
  M89.672 Osteopathy after poliomyelitis, left ankle and foot 🦠
  M89.679 Osteopathy after poliomyelitis, unspecified ankle and foot 🦠

M89.68 Osteopathy after poliomyelitis, other site 🦠

M89.69 Osteopathy after poliomyelitis, multiple sites 🦠

● **M89.7** Major osseous defect

  Code first underlying disease, if known, such as:
    aseptic necrosis of bone (M87.-)
    malignant neoplasm of bone (C40.-)
    osteolysis (M89.5)
    osteomyelitis (M86.-)
    osteonecrosis (M87.-)
    osteoporosis (M80.-, M81.-)
    periprosthetic osteolysis (T84.05-)

  M89.70 Major osseous defect, unspecified site

● **M89.71** Major osseous defect, shoulder region
    Major osseous defect clavicle or scapula
  M89.711 Major osseous defect, right shoulder region
  M89.712 Major osseous defect, left shoulder region
  M89.719 Major osseous defect, unspecified shoulder region

● **M89.72** Major osseous defect, humerus
  M89.721 Major osseous defect, right humerus
  M89.722 Major osseous defect, left humerus
  M89.729 Major osseous defect, unspecified humerus

● **M89.73** Major osseous defect, forearm
    Major osseous defect of radius and ulna
  M89.731 Major osseous defect, right forearm
  M89.732 Major osseous defect, left forearm
  M89.739 Major osseous defect, unspecified forearm

● **M89.74** Major osseous defect, hand
    Major osseous defect of carpus, fingers, metacarpus
  M89.741 Major osseous defect, right hand
  M89.742 Major osseous defect, left hand
  M89.749 Major osseous defect, unspecified hand

● **M89.75** Major osseous defect, pelvic region and thigh
    Major osseous defect of femur and pelvis
  M89.751 Major osseous defect, right pelvic region and thigh
  M89.752 Major osseous defect, left pelvic region and thigh
  M89.759 Major osseous defect, unspecified pelvic region and thigh

● **M89.76** Major osseous defect, lower leg
    Major osseous defect of fibula and tibia
  M89.761 Major osseous defect, right lower leg
  M89.762 Major osseous defect, left lower leg
  M89.769 Major osseous defect, unspecified lower leg

● **M89.77** Major osseous defect, ankle and foot
    Major osseous defect of metatarsus, tarsus, toes
  M89.771 Major osseous defect, right ankle and foot
  M89.772 Major osseous defect, left ankle and foot
  M89.779 Major osseous defect, unspecified ankle and foot

M89.78 Major osseous defect, other site

M89.79 Major osseous defect, multiple sites

● **M89.8** Other specified disorders of bone
    Infantile cortical hyperostoses
    Post-traumatic subperiosteal ossification

● **M89.8X** Other specified disorders of bone
  M89.8X0 Other specified disorders of bone, multiple sites
  M89.8X1 Other specified disorders of bone, shoulder
  M89.8X2 Other specified disorders of bone, upper arm
  M89.8X3 Other specified disorders of bone, forearm
        Coding Clinic: 2019, Q3, P10
  M89.8X4 Other specified disorders of bone, hand
  M89.8X5 Other specified disorders of bone, thigh
  M89.8X6 Other specified disorders of bone, lower leg
  M89.8X7 Other specified disorders of bone, ankle and foot
  M89.8X8 Other specified disorders of bone, other site
  M89.8X9 Other specified disorders of bone, unspecified site

M89.9 Disorder of bone, unspecified

▶ New   ⇒ Revised   ~~deleted~~ Deleted   Excludes 1   Excludes 2   Includes   Use additional   Code first   Code also   Key words
OGCR Official Guidelines   X Assign placeholder X   ● Use Additional Character(s)   ⟩ Manifestation Code   🦠 Hierarchical Condition Category   Coding Clinic

● **M90   Osteopathies in diseases classified elsewhere**

     Excludes1   osteochondritis, osteomyelitis, and osteopathy (in):
         cryptococcosis (B45.3)
         diabetes mellitus (E08-E13 with .69-)
         gonococcal (A54.43)
         neurogenic syphilis (A52.11)
         renal osteodystrophy (N25.0)
         salmonellosis (A02.24)
         secondary syphilis (A51.46)
         syphilis (late) (A52.77)

● **M90.5   Osteonecrosis in diseases classified elsewhere**

     Code first underlying disease, such as:
         caisson disease (T70.3)
         hemoglobinopathy (D50-D64)

   ▷ *M90.50   Osteonecrosis in diseases classified elsewhere, unspecified site* 🔎

   ● **M90.51   Osteonecrosis in diseases classified elsewhere, shoulder**

     ▷ *M90.511   Osteonecrosis in diseases classified elsewhere, right shoulder* 🔎

     ▷ *M90.512   Osteonecrosis in diseases classified elsewhere, left shoulder* 🔎

     ▷ *M90.519   Osteonecrosis in diseases classified elsewhere, unspecified shoulder* 🔎

   ● **M90.52   Osteonecrosis in diseases classified elsewhere, upper arm**

     ▷ *M90.521   Osteonecrosis in diseases classified elsewhere, right upper arm* 🔎

     ▷ *M90.522   Osteonecrosis in diseases classified elsewhere, left upper arm* 🔎

     ▷ *M90.529   Osteonecrosis in diseases classified elsewhere, unspecified upper arm* 🔎

   ● **M90.53   Osteonecrosis in diseases classified elsewhere, forearm**

     ▷ *M90.531   Osteonecrosis in diseases classified elsewhere, right forearm* 🔎

     ▷ *M90.532   Osteonecrosis in diseases classified elsewhere, left forearm* 🔎

     ▷ *M90.539   Osteonecrosis in diseases classified elsewhere, unspecified forearm* 🔎

   ● **M90.54   Osteonecrosis in diseases classified elsewhere, hand**

     ▷ *M90.541   Osteonecrosis in diseases classified elsewhere, right hand* 🔎

     ▷ *M90.542   Osteonecrosis in diseases classified elsewhere, left hand* 🔎

     ▷ *M90.549   Osteonecrosis in diseases classified elsewhere, unspecified hand* 🔎

   ● **M90.55   Osteonecrosis in diseases classified elsewhere, thigh**

     ▷ *M90.551   Osteonecrosis in diseases classified elsewhere, right thigh* 🔎

     ▷ *M90.552   Osteonecrosis in diseases classified elsewhere, left thigh* 🔎

     ▷ *M90.559   Osteonecrosis in diseases classified elsewhere, unspecified thigh* 🔎

   ● **M90.56   Osteonecrosis in diseases classified elsewhere, lower leg**

     ▷ *M90.561   Osteonecrosis in diseases classified elsewhere, right lower leg* 🔎

     ▷ *M90.562   Osteonecrosis in diseases classified elsewhere, left lower leg* 🔎

     ▷ *M90.569   Osteonecrosis in diseases classified elsewhere, unspecified lower leg* 🔎

   ● **M90.57   Osteonecrosis in diseases classified elsewhere, ankle and foot**

     ▷ *M90.571   Osteonecrosis in diseases classified elsewhere, right ankle and foot* 🔎

     ▷ *M90.572   Osteonecrosis in diseases classified elsewhere, left ankle and foot* 🔎

     ▷ *M90.579   Osteonecrosis in diseases classified elsewhere, unspecified ankle and foot* 🔎

   ▷ *M90.58   Osteonecrosis in diseases classified elsewhere, other site* 🔎

   ▷ *M90.59   Osteonecrosis in diseases classified elsewhere, multiple sites* 🔎

● **M90.6   Osteitis deformans in neoplastic diseases**

     Osteitis deformans in malignant neoplasm of bone

     Code first the neoplasm (C40.-, C41.-)

     Excludes1   osteitis deformans [Paget's disease of bone] (M88.-)

   ▷ *M90.60   Osteitis deformans in neoplastic diseases, unspecified site*

   ● **M90.61   Osteitis deformans in neoplastic diseases, shoulder**

     ▷ *M90.611   Osteitis deformans in neoplastic diseases, right shoulder*

     ▷ *M90.612   Osteitis deformans in neoplastic diseases, left shoulder*

     ▷ *M90.619   Osteitis deformans in neoplastic diseases, unspecified shoulder*

   ● **M90.62   Osteitis deformans in neoplastic diseases, upper arm**

     ▷ *M90.621   Osteitis deformans in neoplastic diseases, right upper arm*

     ▷ *M90.622   Osteitis deformans in neoplastic diseases, left upper arm*

     ▷ *M90.629   Osteitis deformans in neoplastic diseases, unspecified upper arm*

   ● **M90.63   Osteitis deformans in neoplastic diseases, forearm**

     ▷ *M90.631   Osteitis deformans in neoplastic diseases, right forearm*

     ▷ *M90.632   Osteitis deformans in neoplastic diseases, left forearm*

     ▷ *M90.639   Osteitis deformans in neoplastic diseases, unspecified forearm*

   ● **M90.64   Osteitis deformans in neoplastic diseases, hand**

     ▷ *M90.641   Osteitis deformans in neoplastic diseases, right hand*

     ▷ *M90.642   Osteitis deformans in neoplastic diseases, left hand*

     ▷ *M90.649   Osteitis deformans in neoplastic diseases, unspecified hand*

   ● **M90.65   Osteitis deformans in neoplastic diseases, thigh**

     ▷ *M90.651   Osteitis deformans in neoplastic diseases, right thigh*

     ▷ *M90.652   Osteitis deformans in neoplastic diseases, left thigh*

     ▷ *M90.659   Osteitis deformans in neoplastic diseases, unspecified thigh*

   ● **M90.66   Osteitis deformans in neoplastic diseases, lower leg**

     ▷ *M90.661   Osteitis deformans in neoplastic diseases, right lower leg*

     ▷ *M90.662   Osteitis deformans in neoplastic diseases, left lower leg*

     ▷ *M90.669   Osteitis deformans in neoplastic diseases, unspecified lower leg*

● **M90.67** **Osteitis deformans in neoplastic diseases, ankle and foot**

▷ *M90.671* *Osteitis deformans in neoplastic diseases, right ankle and foot*

▷ *M90.672* *Osteitis deformans in neoplastic diseases, left ankle and foot*

▷ *M90.679* *Osteitis deformans in neoplastic diseases, unspecified ankle and foot*

▷ *M90.68* *Osteitis deformans in neoplastic diseases, other site*

▷ *M90.69* *Osteitis deformans in neoplastic diseases, multiple sites*

● **M90.8** **Osteopathy in diseases classified elsewhere**

Code first underlying disease, such as:
rickets (E55.0)
vitamin-D-resistant rickets (E83.3)

▷ *M90.80* *Osteopathy in diseases classified elsewhere, unspecified site*

● **M90.81** **Osteopathy in diseases classified elsewhere, shoulder**

▷ *M90.811* *Osteopathy in diseases classified elsewhere, right shoulder*

▷ *M90.812* *Osteopathy in diseases classified elsewhere, left shoulder*

▷ *M90.819* *Osteopathy in diseases classified elsewhere, unspecified shoulder*

● **M90.82** **Osteopathy in diseases classified elsewhere, upper arm**

▷ *M90.821* *Osteopathy in diseases classified elsewhere, right upper arm*

▷ *M90.822* *Osteopathy in diseases classified elsewhere, left upper arm*

▷ *M90.829* *Osteopathy in diseases classified elsewhere, unspecified upper arm*

● **M90.83** **Osteopathy in diseases classified elsewhere, forearm**

▷ *M90.831* *Osteopathy in diseases classified elsewhere, right forearm*

▷ *M90.832* *Osteopathy in diseases classified elsewhere, left forearm*

▷ *M90.839* *Osteopathy in diseases classified elsewhere, unspecified forearm*

● **M90.84** **Osteopathy in diseases classified elsewhere, hand**

▷ *M90.841* *Osteopathy in diseases classified elsewhere, right hand*

▷ *M90.842* *Osteopathy in diseases classified elsewhere, left hand*

▷ *M90.849* *Osteopathy in diseases classified elsewhere, unspecified hand*

● **M90.85** **Osteopathy in diseases classified elsewhere, thigh**

▷ *M90.851* *Osteopathy in diseases classified elsewhere, right thigh*

▷ *M90.852* *Osteopathy in diseases classified elsewhere, left thigh*

▷ *M90.859* *Osteopathy in diseases classified elsewhere, unspecified thigh*

● **M90.86** **Osteopathy in diseases classified elsewhere, lower leg**

▷ *M90.861* *Osteopathy in diseases classified elsewhere, right lower leg*

▷ *M90.862* *Osteopathy in diseases classified elsewhere, left lower leg*

▷ *M90.869* *Osteopathy in diseases classified elsewhere, unspecified lower leg*

● **M90.87** **Osteopathy in diseases classified elsewhere, ankle and foot**

▷ *M90.871* *Osteopathy in diseases classified elsewhere, right ankle and foot*

▷ *M90.872* *Osteopathy in diseases classified elsewhere, left ankle and foot*

▷ *M90.879* *Osteopathy in diseases classified elsewhere, unspecified ankle and foot*

▷ *M90.88* *Osteopathy in diseases classified elsewhere, other site*

▷ *M90.89* *Osteopathy in diseases classified elsewhere, multiple sites*

CHONDROPATHIES (M91-M94)

Excludes1   postprocedural chondropathies (M96.-)

● **M91** **Juvenile osteochondrosis of hip and pelvis**

Excludes1   slipped upper femoral epiphysis (nontraumatic) (M93.0)

M91.0 **Juvenile osteochondrosis of pelvis**
Osteochondrosis (juvenile) of acetabulum
Osteochondrosis (juvenile) of iliac crest [Buchanan]
Osteochondrosis (juvenile) of ischiopubic synchondrosis [van Neck]
Osteochondrosis (juvenile) of symphysis pubis [Pierson]

● **M91.1** **Juvenile osteochondrosis of head of femur [Legg-Calvé-Perthes]**

M91.10 Juvenile osteochondrosis of head of femur [Legg-Calvé-Perthes], unspecified leg

M91.11 Juvenile osteochondrosis of head of femur [Legg-Calvé-Perthes], right leg

M91.12 Juvenile osteochondrosis of head of femur [Legg-Calvé-Perthes], left leg

● **M91.2** **Coxa plana**
Hip deformity due to previous juvenile osteochondrosis

M91.20 Coxa plana, unspecified hip

M91.21 Coxa plana, right hip

M91.22 Coxa plana, left hip

● **M91.3** **Pseudocoxalgia**

M91.30 Pseudocoxalgia, unspecified hip

M91.31 Pseudocoxalgia, right hip

M91.32 Pseudocoxalgia, left hip

● **M91.4** **Coxa magna**

M91.40 Coxa magna, unspecified hip

M91.41 Coxa magna, right hip

M91.42 Coxa magna, left hip

● **M91.8** **Other juvenile osteochondrosis of hip and pelvis**
Juvenile osteochondrosis after reduction of congenital dislocation of hip

M91.80 Other juvenile osteochondrosis of hip and pelvis, unspecified leg

M91.81 Other juvenile osteochondrosis of hip and pelvis, right leg

M91.82 Other juvenile osteochondrosis of hip and pelvis, left leg

● **M91.9** **Juvenile osteochondrosis of hip and pelvis, unspecified**

M91.90 Juvenile osteochondrosis of hip and pelvis, unspecified, unspecified leg

M91.91 Juvenile osteochondrosis of hip and pelvis, unspecified, right leg

M91.92 Juvenile osteochondrosis of hip and pelvis, unspecified, left leg

▶ New   ⇒ Revised   ~~deleted~~ Deleted   Excludes 1   Excludes 2   Includes   Use additional   Code first   Code also   Key words

OGCR Official Guidelines   X Assign placeholder X   ● Use Additional Character(s)   ▷ Manifestation Code   🖢 Hierarchical Condition Category   Coding Clinic

● **M92 Other juvenile osteochondrosis**

● **M92.0 Juvenile osteochondrosis of humerus**
Osteochondrosis (juvenile) of capitulum of humerus [Panner]
Osteochondrosis (juvenile) of head of humerus [Haas]

     M92.00 Juvenile osteochondrosis of humerus, unspecified arm

     M92.01 Juvenile osteochondrosis of humerus, right arm

     M92.02 Juvenile osteochondrosis of humerus, left arm

● **M92.1 Juvenile osteochondrosis of radius and ulna**
Osteochondrosis (juvenile) of lower ulna [Burns]
Osteochondrosis (juvenile) of radial head [Brailsford]

     M92.10 Juvenile osteochondrosis of radius and ulna, unspecified arm

     M92.11 Juvenile osteochondrosis of radius and ulna, right arm

     M92.12 Juvenile osteochondrosis of radius and ulna, left arm

● **M92.2 Juvenile osteochondrosis, hand**

     ● **M92.20 Unspecified juvenile osteochondrosis, hand**

         M92.201 Unspecified juvenile osteochondrosis, right hand

         M92.202 Unspecified juvenile osteochondrosis, left hand

         M92.209 Unspecified juvenile osteochondrosis, unspecified hand

     ● **M92.21 Osteochondrosis (juvenile) of carpal lunate [Kienböck]**

         M92.211 Osteochondrosis (juvenile) of carpal lunate [Kienböck], right hand

         M92.212 Osteochondrosis (juvenile) of carpal lunate [Kienböck], left hand

         M92.219 Osteochondrosis (juvenile) of carpal lunate [Kienböck], unspecified hand

     ● **M92.22 Osteochondrosis (juvenile) of metacarpal heads [Mauclaire]**

         M92.221 Osteochondrosis (juvenile) of metacarpal heads [Mauclaire], right hand

         M92.222 Osteochondrosis (juvenile) of metacarpal heads [Mauclaire], left hand

         M92.229 Osteochondrosis (juvenile) of metacarpal heads [Mauclaire], unspecified hand

     ● **M92.29 Other juvenile osteochondrosis, hand**

         M92.291 Other juvenile osteochondrosis, right hand

         M92.292 Other juvenile osteochondrosis, left hand

         M92.299 Other juvenile osteochondrosis, unspecified hand

● **M92.3 Other juvenile osteochondrosis, upper limb**

     M92.30 Other juvenile osteochondrosis, unspecified upper limb

     M92.31 Other juvenile osteochondrosis, right upper limb

     M92.32 Other juvenile osteochondrosis, left upper limb

● **M92.4 Juvenile osteochondrosis of patella**
Osteochondrosis (juvenile) of primary patellar center [Köhler]
Osteochondrosis (juvenile) of secondary patellar center [Sinding Larsen]

     M92.40 Juvenile osteochondrosis of patella, unspecified knee

     M92.41 Juvenile osteochondrosis of patella, right knee

     M92.42 Juvenile osteochondrosis of patella, left knee

● **M92.5 Juvenile osteochondrosis of tibia and fibula**
~~Osteochondrosis (juvenile) of proximal tibia [Blount]~~
~~Osteochondrosis (juvenile) of tibial tubercle [Osgood-Schlatter]~~
~~Tibia vara~~

     ➡ ● **M92.50 Unspecified juvenile osteochondrosis of tibia and fibula**

         ▶ **M92.501 Unspecified juvenile osteochondrosis, right leg**

         ▶ **M92.502 Unspecified juvenile osteochondrosis, left leg**

         ▶ **M92.503 Unspecified juvenile osteochondrosis, bilateral leg**

         ▶ **M92.509 Unspecified juvenile osteochondrosis, unspecified leg**

     ➡ ● **M92.51 Juvenile osteochondrosis of proximal tibia**
         ▶ Blount disease
         ▶ Tibia vara

         ▶ **M92.511 Juvenile osteochondrosis of proximal tibia, right leg**

         ▶ **M92.512 Juvenile osteochondrosis of proximal tibia, left leg**

         ▶ **M92.513 Juvenile osteochondrosis of proximal tibia, bilateral**

         ▶ **M92.519 Juvenile osteochondrosis of proximal tibia, unspecified leg**

     ➡ ● **M92.52 Juvenile osteochondrosis of tibia tubercle**
         ▶ Osgood-Schlatter disease

         ▶ **M92.521 Juvenile osteochondrosis of tibia tubercle, right leg**

         ▶ **M92.522 Juvenile osteochondrosis of tibia tubercle, left leg**

         ▶ **M92.523 Juvenile osteochondrosis of tibia tubercle, bilateral**

         ▶ **M92.529 Juvenile osteochondrosis of tibia tubercle, unspecified leg**

     ▶ **M92.59 Other juvenile osteochondrosis of tibia and fibula**

         ▶ **M92.591 Other juvenile osteochondrosis of tibia and fibula, right leg**

         ▶ **M92.592 Other juvenile osteochondrosis of tibia and fibula, left leg**

         ▶ **M92.593 Other juvenile osteochondrosis of tibia and fibula, bilateral**

         ▶ **M92.599 Other juvenile osteochondrosis of tibia and fibula, unspecified leg**

● **M92.6 Juvenile osteochondrosis of tarsus**
Osteochondrosis (juvenile) of calcaneum [Sever]
Osteochondrosis (juvenile) of os tibiale externum [Haglund]
Osteochondrosis (juvenile) of talus [Diaz]
Osteochondrosis (juvenile) of tarsal navicular [Köhler]

     M92.60 Juvenile osteochondrosis of tarsus, unspecified ankle

     M92.61 Juvenile osteochondrosis of tarsus, right ankle

     M92.62 Juvenile osteochondrosis of tarsus, left ankle

● **M92.7 Juvenile osteochondrosis of metatarsus**
Osteochondrosis (juvenile) of fifth metatarsus [Iselin]
Osteochondrosis (juvenile) of second metatarsus [Freiberg]

     M92.70 Juvenile osteochondrosis of metatarsus, unspecified foot

     M92.71 Juvenile osteochondrosis of metatarsus, right foot

     M92.72 Juvenile osteochondrosis of metatarsus, left foot

● **M92.8 Other specified juvenile osteochondrosis**
Calcaneal apophysitis

● **M92.9 Juvenile osteochondrosis, unspecified**
Juvenile apophysitis NOS
Juvenile epiphysitis NOS
Juvenile osteochondritis NOS
Juvenile osteochondrosis NOS

● **M93**   **Other osteochondropathies**
    Excludes2   osteochondrosis of spine (M42.-)
  ● **M93.0**   **Slipped upper femoral epiphysis (nontraumatic)**
      Use additional code for associated chondrolysis (M94.3)
   ● **M93.00**   **Unspecified** slipped upper femoral epiphysis (nontraumatic)
      M93.001   Unspecified slipped upper femoral epiphysis (nontraumatic), **right hip**
      M93.002   Unspecified slipped upper femoral epiphysis (nontraumatic), **left hip**
      M93.003   Unspecified slipped upper femoral epiphysis (nontraumatic), **unspecified hip**
   ● **M93.01**   **Acute** slipped upper femoral epiphysis (nontraumatic)
      M93.011   Acute slipped upper femoral epiphysis (nontraumatic), **right hip**
      M93.012   Acute slipped upper femoral epiphysis (nontraumatic), **left hip**
      M93.013   Acute slipped upper femoral epiphysis (nontraumatic), **unspecified** hip
   ● **M93.02**   **Chronic** slipped upper femoral epiphysis (nontraumatic)
      M93.021   Chronic slipped upper femoral epiphysis (nontraumatic), **right hip**
      M93.022   Chronic slipped upper femoral epiphysis (nontraumatic), **left hip**
      M93.023   Chronic slipped upper femoral epiphysis (nontraumatic), **unspecified** hip
   ● **M93.03**   **Acute on chronic** slipped upper femoral epiphysis (nontraumatic)
      M93.031   Acute on chronic slipped upper femoral epiphysis (nontraumatic), **right hip**
      M93.032   Acute on chronic slipped upper femoral epiphysis (nontraumatic), **left hip**
      M93.033   Acute on chronic slipped upper femoral epiphysis (nontraumatic), **unspecified hip**
  M93.1   **Kienböck's disease of adults**   A
      Adult osteochondrosis of carpal lunates
  ● **M93.2**   **Osteochondritis dissecans**
     M93.20   Osteochondritis dissecans of **unspecified** site
   ● **M93.21**   Osteochondritis dissecans of **shoulder**
      M93.211   Osteochondritis dissecans, **right shoulder**
      M93.212   Osteochondritis dissecans, **left shoulder**
      M93.219   Osteochondritis dissecans, **unspecified shoulder**
   ● **M93.22**   Osteochondritis dissecans of **elbow**
      M93.221   Osteochondritis dissecans, **right elbow**
      M93.222   Osteochondritis dissecans, **left elbow**
      M93.229   Osteochondritis dissecans, **unspecified elbow**
   ● **M93.23**   Osteochondritis dissecans of **wrist**
      M93.231   Osteochondritis dissecans, **right wrist**
      M93.232   Osteochondritis dissecans, **left wrist**
      M93.239   Osteochondritis dissecans, **unspecified** wrist
   ● **M93.24**   Osteochondritis dissecans of joints of **hand**
      M93.241   Osteochondritis dissecans, joints of **right hand**
      M93.242   Osteochondritis dissecans, joints of **left hand**
      M93.249   Osteochondritis dissecans, joints of **unspecified hand**

● **M93.25**   Osteochondritis dissecans of **hip**
    M93.251   Osteochondritis dissecans, **right hip**
    M93.252   Osteochondritis dissecans, **left hip**
    M93.259   Osteochondritis dissecans, **unspecified hip**
● **M93.26**   Osteochondritis dissecans **knee**
    M93.261   Osteochondritis dissecans, **right knee**
    M93.262   Osteochondritis dissecans, **left knee**
    M93.269   Osteochondritis dissecans, **unspecified knee**
● **M93.27**   Osteochondritis dissecans of **ankle and joints of foot**
    M93.271   Osteochondritis dissecans, **right ankle** and joints of right foot
    M93.272   Osteochondritis dissecans, **left ankle** and joints of left foot
    M93.279   Osteochondritis dissecans, **unspecified ankle and joints of foot**
  M93.28   Osteochondritis dissecans **other site**
  M93.29   Osteochondritis dissecans **multiple sites**
● **M93.8**   **Other specified osteochondropathies**
  M93.80   Other specified osteochondropathies of **unspecified site**
● **M93.81**   Other specified osteochondropathies of **shoulder**
    M93.811   Other specified osteochondropathies, **right shoulder**
    M93.812   Other specified osteochondropathies, **left shoulder**
    M93.819   Other specified osteochondropathies, **unspecified shoulder**
● **M93.82**   Other specified osteochondropathies of **upper arm**
    M93.821   Other specified osteochondropathies, **right upper arm**
    M93.822   Other specified osteochondropathies, **left upper arm**
    M93.829   Other specified osteochondropathies, **unspecified upper arm**
● **M93.83**   Other specified osteochondropathies of **forearm**
    M93.831   Other specified osteochondropathies, **right forearm**
    M93.832   Other specified osteochondropathies, **left forearm**
    M93.839   Other specified osteochondropathies, **unspecified forearm**
● **M93.84**   Other specified osteochondropathies of **hand**
    M93.841   Other specified osteochondropathies, **right hand**
    M93.842   Other specified osteochondropathies, **left hand**
    M93.849   Other specified osteochondropathies, **unspecified hand**
● **M93.85**   Other specified osteochondropathies of **thigh**
    M93.851   Other specified osteochondropathies, **right thigh**
    M93.852   Other specified osteochondropathies, **left thigh**
    M93.859   Other specified osteochondropathies, **unspecified thigh**
● **M93.86**   Other specified osteochondropathies **lower leg**
    M93.861   Other specified osteochondropathies, **right lower leg**
    M93.862   Other specified osteochondropathies, **left lower leg**
    M93.869   Other specified osteochondropathies, **unspecified lower leg**

▶ New   ⇒ Revised   ~~deleted~~ Deleted   Excludes 1   Excludes 2   Includes   Use additional   Code first   Code also   Key words
OGCR Official Guidelines   X Assign placeholder X   ● Use Additional Character(s)   ▷ Manifestation Code   🔗 Hierarchical Condition Category   **Coding Clinic**

● M93.87 Other specified osteochondropathies of ankle and foot
- M93.871 Other specified osteochondropathies, right ankle and foot
- M93.872 Other specified osteochondropathies, left ankle and foot
- M93.879 Other specified osteochondropathies, unspecified ankle and foot

M93.88 Other specified osteochondropathies other

M93.89 Other specified osteochondropathies multiple sites

M93.9 Osteochondropathy, unspecified
Apophysitis NOS
Epiphysitis NOS
Osteochondritis NOS
Osteochondrosis NOS

M93.90 Osteochondropathy, unspecified of unspecified site

● M93.91 Osteochondropathy, unspecified of shoulder
- M93.911 Osteochondropathy, unspecified, right shoulder
- M93.912 Osteochondropathy, unspecified, left shoulder
- M93.919 Osteochondropathy, unspecified, unspecified shoulder

● M93.92 Osteochondropathy, unspecified of upper arm
- M93.921 Osteochondropathy, unspecified, right upper arm
- M93.922 Osteochondropathy, unspecified, left upper arm
- M93.929 Osteochondropathy, unspecified, unspecified upper arm

● M93.93 Osteochondropathy, unspecified of forearm
- M93.931 Osteochondropathy, unspecified, right forearm
- M93.932 Osteochondropathy, unspecified, left forearm
- M93.939 Osteochondropathy, unspecified, unspecified forearm

● M93.94 Osteochondropathy, unspecified of hand
- M93.941 Osteochondropathy, unspecified, right hand
- M93.942 Osteochondropathy, unspecified, left hand
- M93.949 Osteochondropathy, unspecified, unspecified hand

● M93.95 Osteochondropathy, unspecified of thigh
- M93.951 Osteochondropathy, unspecified, right thigh
- M93.952 Osteochondropathy, unspecified, left thigh
- M93.959 Osteochondropathy, unspecified, unspecified thigh

● M93.96 Osteochondropathy, unspecified lower leg
- M93.961 Osteochondropathy, unspecified, right lower leg
- M93.962 Osteochondropathy, unspecified, left lower leg
- M93.969 Osteochondropathy, unspecified, unspecified lower leg

● M93.97 Osteochondropathy, unspecified of ankle and foot
- M93.971 Osteochondropathy, unspecified, right ankle and foot
- M93.972 Osteochondropathy, unspecified, left ankle and foot
- M93.979 Osteochondropathy, unspecified, unspecified ankle and foot

M93.98 Osteochondropathy, unspecified other

M93.99 Osteochondropathy, unspecified multiple sites

● M94 Other disorders of cartilage

M94.0 Chondrocostal junction syndrome [Tietze]
Costochondritis

M94.1 Relapsing polychondritis

● M94.2 Chondromalacia
Excludes1 chondromalacia patellae (M22.4)

M94.20 Chondromalacia, unspecified site

● M94.21 Chondromalacia, shoulder
- M94.211 Chondromalacia, right shoulder
- M94.212 Chondromalacia, left shoulder
- M94.219 Chondromalacia, unspecified shoulder

● M94.22 Chondromalacia, elbow
- M94.221 Chondromalacia, right elbow
- M94.222 Chondromalacia, left elbow
- M94.229 Chondromalacia, unspecified elbow

● M94.23 Chondromalacia, wrist
- M94.231 Chondromalacia, right wrist
- M94.232 Chondromalacia, left wrist
- M94.239 Chondromalacia, unspecified wrist

● M94.24 Chondromalacia, joints of hand
- M94.241 Chondromalacia, joints of right hand
- M94.242 Chondromalacia, joints of left hand
- M94.249 Chondromalacia, joints of unspecified hand

● M94.25 Chondromalacia, hip
- M94.251 Chondromalacia, right hip
- M94.252 Chondromalacia, left hip
- M94.259 Chondromalacia, unspecified hip

● M94.26 Chondromalacia, knee
- M94.261 Chondromalacia, right knee
- M94.262 Chondromalacia, left knee
- M94.269 Chondromalacia, unspecified knee

● M94.27 Chondromalacia, ankle and joints of foot
- M94.271 Chondromalacia, right ankle and joints of right foot
- M94.272 Chondromalacia, left ankle and joints of left foot
- M94.279 Chondromalacia, unspecified ankle and joints of foot

M94.28 Chondromalacia, other site

M94.29 Chondromalacia, multiple sites

● M94.3 Chondrolysis
Code first any associated slipped upper femoral epiphysis (nontraumatic) (M93.0-)

● M94.35 Chondrolysis, hip
- M94.351 Chondrolysis, right hip
- M94.352 Chondrolysis, left hip
- M94.359 Chondrolysis, unspecified hip

● M94.8 Other specified disorders of cartilage
    ● M94.8X Other specified disorders of cartilage
        M94.8X0 Other specified disorders of cartilage, multiple sites
        M94.8X1 Other specified disorders of cartilage, shoulder
        M94.8X2 Other specified disorders of cartilage, upper arm
        M94.8X3 Other specified disorders of cartilage, forearm
        M94.8X4 Other specified disorders of cartilage, hand
        M94.8X5 Other specified disorders of cartilage, thigh
        M94.8X6 Other specified disorders of cartilage, lower leg
        M94.8X7 Other specified disorders of cartilage, ankle and foot
        M94.8X8 Other specified disorders of cartilage, other site
        M94.8X9 Other specified disorders of cartilage, unspecified sites
    M94.9 Disorder of cartilage, unspecified

OTHER DISORDERS OF THE MUSCULOSKELETAL SYSTEM AND CONNECTIVE TISSUE (M95)

● M95 Other acquired deformities of musculoskeletal system and connective tissue
    Excludes2 acquired absence of limbs and organs (Z89-Z90)
        acquired deformities of limbs (M20-M21)
        congenital malformations and deformations of the musculoskeletal system (Q65-Q79)
        deforming dorsopathies (M40-M43)
        dentofacial anomalies [including malocclusion] (M26.-)
        postprocedural musculoskeletal disorders (M96.-)
    M95.0 Acquired deformity of nose
        Excludes2 deviated nasal septum (J34.2)
    ● M95.1 Cauliflower ear
        Excludes2 other acquired deformities of ear (H61.1)
        M95.10 Cauliflower ear, unspecified ear
        M95.11 Cauliflower ear, right ear
        M95.12 Cauliflower ear, left ear
    M95.2 Other acquired deformity of head
    M95.3 Acquired deformity of neck
    M95.4 Acquired deformity of chest and rib
    M95.5 Acquired deformity of pelvis
        Excludes1 maternal care for known or suspected disproportion (O33.-)
    M95.8 Other specified acquired deformities of musculoskeletal system
    M95.9 Acquired deformity of musculoskeletal system, unspecified

INTRAOPERATIVE AND POSTPROCEDURAL COMPLICATIONS AND DISORDERS OF MUSCULOSKELETAL SYSTEM, NOT ELSEWHERE CLASSIFIED (M96)

● M96 Intraoperative and postprocedural complications and disorders of musculoskeletal system, not elsewhere classified
    Excludes2 arthropathy following intestinal bypass (M02.0-)
        complications of internal orthopedic prosthetic devices, implants and grafts (T84.-)
        disorders associated with osteoporosis (M80)
        periprosthetic fracture around internal prosthetic joint (M97.-)
        presence of functional implants and other devices (Z96-Z97)
    M96.0 Pseudarthrosis after fusion or arthrodesis
    M96.1 Postlaminectomy syndrome, not elsewhere classified

M96.2 Postradiation kyphosis
M96.3 Postlaminectomy kyphosis
M96.4 Postsurgical lordosis
M96.5 Postradiation scoliosis
● M96.6 Fracture of bone following insertion of orthopedic implant, joint prosthesis, or bone plate
    Intraoperative fracture of bone during insertion of orthopedic implant, joint prosthesis, or bone plate
    Excludes2 complication of internal orthopedic devices, implants or grafts (T84.-)
    ● M96.62 Fracture of humerus following insertion of orthopedic implant, joint prosthesis, or bone plate
        M96.621 Fracture of humerus following insertion of orthopedic implant, joint prosthesis, or bone plate, right arm 🦠
        M96.622 Fracture of humerus following insertion of orthopedic implant, joint prosthesis, or bone plate, left arm 🦠
        M96.629 Fracture of humerus following insertion of orthopedic implant, joint prosthesis, or bone plate, unspecified arm 🦠
    ● M96.63 Fracture of radius or ulna following insertion of orthopedic implant, joint prosthesis, or bone plate
        M96.631 Fracture of radius or ulna following insertion of orthopedic implant, joint prosthesis, or bone plate, right arm 🦠
        M96.632 Fracture of radius or ulna following insertion of orthopedic implant, joint prosthesis, or bone plate, left arm 🦠
        M96.639 Fracture of radius or ulna following insertion of orthopedic implant, joint prosthesis, or bone plate, unspecified arm 🦠
    M96.65 Fracture of pelvis following insertion of orthopedic implant, joint prosthesis, or bone plate 🦠
    ● M96.66 Fracture of femur following insertion of orthopedic implant, joint prosthesis, or bone plate
        M96.661 Fracture of femur following insertion of orthopedic implant, joint prosthesis, or bone plate, right leg 🦠
        M96.662 Fracture of femur following insertion of orthopedic implant, joint prosthesis, or bone plate, left leg 🦠
        M96.669 Fracture of femur following insertion of orthopedic implant, joint prosthesis, or bone plate, unspecified leg 🦠
    ● M96.67 Fracture of tibia or fibula following insertion of orthopedic implant, joint prosthesis, or bone plate
        M96.671 Fracture of tibia or fibula following insertion of orthopedic implant, joint prosthesis, or bone plate, right leg 🦠
        M96.672 Fracture of tibia or fibula following insertion of orthopedic implant, joint prosthesis, or bone plate, left leg 🦠
        M96.679 Fracture of tibia or fibula following insertion of orthopedic implant, joint prosthesis, or bone plate, unspecified leg 🦠
    M96.69 Fracture of other bone following insertion of orthopedic implant, joint prosthesis, or bone plate 🦠

▶ New   ⇒ Revised   ~~deleted~~ Deleted   Excludes 1   Excludes 2   Includes   Use additional   Code first   Code also   Key words
OGCR Official Guidelines   X Assign placeholder X   ● Use Additional Character(s)   ▶ Manifestation Code   🦠 Hierarchical Condition Category   **Coding Clinic**

● M96.8 Other intraoperative and postprocedural complications and disorders of musculoskeletal system, not elsewhere classified
Coding Clinic: 2016, Q4, P10

● M96.81 Intraoperative hemorrhage and hematoma of a musculoskeletal structure complicating a procedure

Excludes1 intraoperative hemorrhage and hematoma of a musculoskeletal structure due to accidental puncture and laceration during a procedure (M96.82-)

M96.810 Intraoperative hemorrhage and hematoma of a musculoskeletal structure complicating a musculoskeletal system procedure

M96.811 Intraoperative hemorrhage and hematoma of a musculoskeletal structure complicating other procedure

● M96.82 Accidental puncture and laceration of a musculoskeletal structure during a procedure

M96.820 Accidental puncture and laceration of a musculoskeletal structure during a musculoskeletal system procedure

M96.821 Accidental puncture and laceration of a musculoskeletal structure during other procedure

● M96.83 Postprocedural hemorrhage of a musculoskeletal structure following a procedure

M96.830 Postprocedural hemorrhage of a musculoskeletal structure following a musculoskeletal system procedure

M96.831 Postprocedural hemorrhage of a musculoskeletal structure following other procedure

● M96.84 Postprocedural hematoma and seroma of a musculoskeletal structure following a procedure

M96.840 Postprocedural hematoma of a musculoskeletal structure following a musculoskeletal system procedure

M96.841 Postprocedural hematoma of a musculoskeletal structure following other procedure
Coding Clinic: 2016, Q4, P10

M96.842 Postprocedural seroma of a musculoskeletal structure following a musculoskeletal system procedure

M96.843 Postprocedural seroma of a musculoskeletal structure following other procedure

M96.89 Other intraoperative and postprocedural complications and disorders of the musculoskeletal system
Instability of joint secondary to removal of joint prosthesis
Use additional code, if applicable, to further specify disorder

PERIPROSTHETIC FRACTURE AROUND INTERNAL PROSTHETIC JOINT (M97)

● M97 Periprosthetic fracture around internal prosthetic joint

Excludes2 fracture of bone following insertion of orthopedic implant, joint prosthesis or bone plate (M96.6-)
breakage (fracture) of prosthetic joint (T84.01-)
Coding Clinic: 2016, Q4, P42

The appropriate 7th character is to be added to each code from category M97:

A	initial encounter
D	subsequent encounter
S	sequela

● M97.0 Periprosthetic fracture around internal prosthetic hip joint

X● M97.01 Periprosthetic fracture around internal prosthetic right hip joint 🔗
Coding Clinic: 2016, Q4, P43

X● M97.02 Periprosthetic fracture around internal prosthetic left hip joint 🔗

● M97.1 Periprosthetic fracture around internal prosthetic knee joint

X● M97.11 Periprosthetic fracture around internal prosthetic right knee joint

X● M97.12 Periprosthetic fracture around internal prosthetic left knee joint

● M97.2 Periprosthetic fracture around internal prosthetic ankle joint

X● M97.21 Periprosthetic fracture around internal prosthetic right ankle joint

X● M97.22 Periprosthetic fracture around internal prosthetic left ankle joint

● M97.3 Periprosthetic fracture around internal prosthetic shoulder joint

X● M97.31 Periprosthetic fracture around internal prosthetic right shoulder joint

X● M97.32 Periprosthetic fracture around internal prosthetic left shoulder joint

● M97.4 Periprosthetic fracture around internal prosthetic elbow joint

X● M97.41 Periprosthetic fracture around internal prosthetic right elbow joint

X● M97.42 Periprosthetic fracture around internal prosthetic left elbow joint

X● M97.8 Periprosthetic fracture around other internal prosthetic joint
Periprosthetic fracture around internal prosthetic finger joint
Periprosthetic fracture around internal prosthetic spinal joint
Periprosthetic fracture around internal prosthetic toe joint
Periprosthetic fracture around internal prosthetic wrist joint
Use additional code to identify the joint (Z96.6-)

X● M97.9 Periprosthetic fracture around unspecified internal prosthetic joint

BIOMECHANICAL LESIONS, NOT ELSEWHERE CLASSIFIED (M99)

● **M99 Biomechanical lesions, not elsewhere classified**

Note: This category should not be used if the condition can be classified elsewhere.

● **M99.0 Segmental and somatic dysfunction**

M99.00   Segmental and somatic dysfunction of head region

M99.01   Segmental and somatic dysfunction of cervical region

M99.02   Segmental and somatic dysfunction of thoracic region

M99.03   Segmental and somatic dysfunction of lumbar region

M99.04   Segmental and somatic dysfunction of sacral region

M99.05   Segmental and somatic dysfunction of pelvic region

M99.06   Segmental and somatic dysfunction of lower extremity

M99.07   Segmental and somatic dysfunction of upper extremity

M99.08   Segmental and somatic dysfunction of rib cage

M99.09   Segmental and somatic dysfunction of abdomen and other regions

● **M99.1 Subluxation complex (vertebral)**

M99.10   Subluxation complex (vertebral) of head region

M99.11   Subluxation complex (vertebral) of cervical region

M99.12   Subluxation complex (vertebral) of thoracic region

M99.13   Subluxation complex (vertebral) of lumbar region

M99.14   Subluxation complex (vertebral) of sacral region

M99.15   Subluxation complex (vertebral) of pelvic region

M99.16   Subluxation complex (vertebral) of lower extremity

M99.17   Subluxation complex (vertebral) of upper extremity

M99.18   Subluxation complex (vertebral) of rib cage

M99.19   Subluxation complex (vertebral) of abdomen and other regions

● **M99.2 Subluxation stenosis of neural canal**

M99.20   Subluxation stenosis of neural canal of head region

M99.21   Subluxation stenosis of neural canal of cervical region

M99.22   Subluxation stenosis of neural canal of thoracic region

M99.23   Subluxation stenosis of neural canal of lumbar region

M99.24   Subluxation stenosis of neural canal of sacral region

M99.25   Subluxation stenosis of neural canal of pelvic region

M99.26   Subluxation stenosis of neural canal of lower extremity

M99.27   Subluxation stenosis of neural canal of upper extremity

M99.28   Subluxation stenosis of neural canal of rib cage

M99.29   Subluxation stenosis of neural canal of abdomen and other regions

● **M99.3 Osseous stenosis of neural canal**

M99.30   Osseous stenosis of neural canal of head region

M99.31   Osseous stenosis of neural canal of cervical region

M99.32   Osseous stenosis of neural canal of thoracic region

M99.33   Osseous stenosis of neural canal of lumbar region

M99.34   Osseous stenosis of neural canal of sacral region

M99.35   Osseous stenosis of neural canal of pelvic region

M99.36   Osseous stenosis of neural canal of lower extremity

M99.37   Osseous stenosis of neural canal of upper extremity

M99.38   Osseous stenosis of neural canal of rib cage

M99.39   Osseous stenosis of neural canal of abdomen and other regions

● **M99.4 Connective tissue stenosis of neural canal**

M99.40   Connective tissue stenosis of neural canal of head region

M99.41   Connective tissue stenosis of neural canal of cervical region

M99.42   Connective tissue stenosis of neural canal of thoracic region

M99.43   Connective tissue stenosis of neural canal of lumbar region

M99.44   Connective tissue stenosis of neural canal of sacral region

M99.45   Connective tissue stenosis of neural canal of pelvic region

M99.46   Connective tissue stenosis of neural canal of lower extremity

M99.47   Connective tissue stenosis of neural canal of upper extremity

M99.48   Connective tissue stenosis of neural canal of rib cage

M99.49   Connective tissue stenosis of neural canal of abdomen and other regions

● **M99.5 Intervertebral disc stenosis of neural canal**

M99.50   Intervertebral disc stenosis of neural canal of head region

M99.51   Intervertebral disc stenosis of neural canal of cervical region

M99.52   Intervertebral disc stenosis of neural canal of thoracic region

M99.53   Intervertebral disc stenosis of neural canal of lumbar region

M99.54   Intervertebral disc stenosis of neural canal of sacral region

M99.55   Intervertebral disc stenosis of neural canal of pelvic region

M99.56   Intervertebral disc stenosis of neural canal of lower extremity

M99.57   Intervertebral disc stenosis of neural canal of upper extremity

M99.58   Intervertebral disc stenosis of neural canal of rib cage

M99.59   Intervertebral disc stenosis of neural canal of abdomen and other regions

▶ New   ⇒ Revised   ~~deleted~~ Deleted   Excludes 1   Excludes 2   Includes   Use additional   Code first   Code also   Key words

OGCR Official Guidelines   X Assign placeholder X   ● Use Additional Character(s)   ▶ Manifestation Code   🏷 Hierarchical Condition Category   **Coding Clinic**

● **M99.6 Osseous and subluxation stenosis of intervertebral foramina**

  M99.60 Osseous and subluxation stenosis of intervertebral foramina of head region

  M99.61 Osseous and subluxation stenosis of intervertebral foramina of cervical region

  M99.62 Osseous and subluxation stenosis of intervertebral foramina of thoracic region

  M99.63 Osseous and subluxation stenosis of intervertebral foramina of lumbar region

  M99.64 Osseous and subluxation stenosis of intervertebral foramina of sacral region

  M99.65 Osseous and subluxation stenosis of intervertebral foramina of pelvic region

  M99.66 Osseous and subluxation stenosis of intervertebral foramina of lower extremity

  M99.67 Osseous and subluxation stenosis of intervertebral foramina of upper extremity

  M99.68 Osseous and subluxation stenosis of intervertebral foramina of rib cage

  M99.69 Osseous and subluxation stenosis of intervertebral foramina of abdomen and other regions

● **M99.7 Connective tissue and disc stenosis of intervertebral foramina**

  M99.70 Connective tissue and disc stenosis of intervertebral foramina of head region

  M99.71 Connective tissue and disc stenosis of intervertebral foramina of cervical region

  M99.72 Connective tissue and disc stenosis of intervertebral foramina of thoracic region

  M99.73 Connective tissue and disc stenosis of intervertebral foramina of lumbar region

  M99.74 Connective tissue and disc stenosis of intervertebral foramina of sacral region

  M99.75 Connective tissue and disc stenosis of intervertebral foramina of pelvic region

  M99.76 Connective tissue and disc stenosis of intervertebral foramina of lower extremity

  M99.77 Connective tissue and disc stenosis of intervertebral foramina of upper extremity

  M99.78 Connective tissue and disc stenosis of intervertebral foramina of rib cage

  M99.79 Connective tissue and disc stenosis of intervertebral foramina of abdomen and other regions

● **M99.8 Other biomechanical lesions**

  M99.80 Other biomechanical lesions of head region

  M99.81 Other biomechanical lesions of cervical region

  M99.82 Other biomechanical lesions of thoracic region

  M99.83 Other biomechanical lesions of lumbar region

  M99.84 Other biomechanical lesions of sacral region

  M99.85 Other biomechanical lesions of pelvic region

  M99.86 Other biomechanical lesions of lower extremity

  M99.87 Other biomechanical lesions of upper extremity

  M99.88 Other biomechanical lesions of rib cage

  M99.89 Other biomechanical lesions of abdomen and other regions

M99.9 Biomechanical lesion, unspecified

CHAPTER 14

DISEASES OF THE GENITOURINARY SYSTEM (N00-N99)

OGCR   Chapter-Specific Coding Guidelines

14. Chapter 14: Diseases of Genitourinary System (N00-N99)

a. Chronic kidney disease

1) Stages of chronic kidney disease (CKD)

The ICD-10-CM classifies CKD based on severity. The severity of CKD is designated by stages 1-5. Stage 2, code N18.2, equates to mild CKD; stage 3, code N18.3, equates to moderate CKD; and stage 4, code N18.4, equates to severe CKD. Code N18.6, End stage renal disease (ESRD), is assigned when the provider has documented end-stage-renal disease (ESRD).

If both a stage of CKD and ESRD are documented, assign code N18.6 only.

2) Chronic kidney disease and kidney transplant status

Patients who have undergone kidney transplant may still have some form of chronic kidney disease CKD because the kidney transplant may not fully restore kidney function. Therefore, the presence of CKD alone does not constitute a transplant complication. Assign the appropriate N18 code for the patient's stage of CKD and code Z94.0, Kidney transplant status. If a transplant complication such as failure or rejection or other transplant complication is documented, see Section I.C.19.g for information on coding complications of a kidney transplant. If the documentation is unclear as to whether the patient has a complication of the transplant, query the provider.

3) Chronic kidney disease with other conditions

Patients with CKD may also suffer from other serious conditions, most commonly diabetes mellitus and hypertension. The sequencing of the CKD code in relationship to codes for other contributing conditions is based on the conventions in the Tabular List.

See I.C.9. Hypertensive chronic kidney disease.
See I.C.19. Chronic kidney disease and kidney transplant complications.

Item 14-1 Nephritis (inflammation) or **nephropathy** (disease) **with lesion of proliferative glomerulonephritis** results from a streptococcal infection.

Nephritis (inflammation) or **nephropathy** (disease) **with lesion of membranous glomerulonephritis** is characterized by deposits along the epithelial side of the basement membrane.

Nephritis (inflammation) or **nephropathy** (disease) **with lesion of membranoproliferative glomerulonephritis** is characterized by alterations in the basement membranes of the kidney and the glomerular cells.

Nephritis (inflammation) or **nephropathy** (disease) **with lesion of rapidly progressive glomerulonephritis** is characterized by rapid and progressive decline in renal function.

Nephritis (inflammation) or **nephropathy** (disease) **with lesion of renal cortical necrosis** is characterized by death of the cortical tissues.

Nephritis (inflammation) or **nephropathy** (disease) **with lesion of renal medullary necrosis** is characterized by death of the tissues that collect urine.

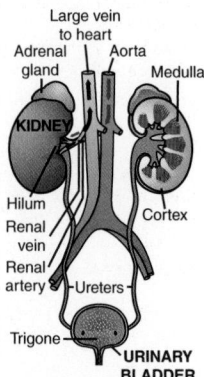

Figure 14-1   Kidneys within the urinary system.

Item 14-2 Glomerulonephritis is nephritis accompanied by inflammation of the glomeruli of the kidney, resulting in the degeneration of the glomeruli and the nephrons.

Acute glomerulonephritis primarily affects children and young adults and is usually a result of a streptococcal infection.

Proliferative glomerulonephritis is the acute form of the disease resulting from a streptococcal infection.

Rapidly progressive glomerulonephritis, also known as **crescentic** or **malignant glomerulonephritis**, is the acute form of the disease, which leads quickly to rapid and progressive decline in renal function.

CHAPTER 14

DISEASES OF THE GENITOURINARY SYSTEM (N00-N99)

Excludes2	certain conditions originating in the perinatal period (P04-P96)
	certain infectious and parasitic diseases (A00-B99)
	complications of pregnancy, childbirth and the puerperium (O00-O9A)
	congenital malformations, deformations and chromosomal abnormalities (Q00-Q99)
	endocrine, nutritional and metabolic diseases (E00-E88)
	injury, poisoning and certain other consequences of external causes (S00-T88)
	neoplasms (C00-D49)
	symptoms, signs and abnormal clinical and laboratory findings, not elsewhere classified (R00-R94)

This chapter contains the following blocks:

N00-N08	Glomerular diseases
N10-N16	Renal tubulo-interstitial diseases
N17-N19	Acute kidney failure and chronic kidney disease
N20-N23	Urolithiasis
N25-N29	Other disorders of kidney and ureter
N30-N39	Other diseases of the urinary system
N40-N53	Diseases of male genital organs
N60-N65	Disorders of breast
N70-N77	Inflammatory diseases of female pelvic organs
N80-N98	Noninflammatory disorders of female genital tract
N99	Intraoperative and postprocedural complications and disorders of genitourinary system, not elsewhere classified

GLOMERULAR DISEASES (N00-N08)

Code also any associated kidney failure (N17-N19)

| **Excludes1** | hypertensive chronic kidney disease (I12.-) |

● **N00 Acute nephritic syndrome**

Includes	acute glomerular disease
	acute glomerulonephritis
	acute nephritis
Excludes1	acute tubulo-interstitial nephritis (N10)
	nephritic syndrome NOS (N05.-)

N00.0 Acute nephritic syndrome with minor glomerular abnormality
     Acute nephritic syndrome with minimal change lesion

N00.1 Acute nephritic syndrome with focal and segmental glomerular lesions
     Acute nephritic syndrome with focal and segmental hyalinosis
     Acute nephritic syndrome with focal and segmental sclerosis
     Acute nephritic syndrome with focal glomerulonephritis

N00.2 Acute nephritic syndrome with diffuse membranous glomerulonephritis

N00.3 Acute nephritic syndrome with diffuse mesangial proliferative glomerulonephritis

N00.4 Acute nephritic syndrome with diffuse endocapillary proliferative glomerulonephritis

N00.5　**Acute nephritic syndrome with diffuse mesangiocapillary glomerulonephritis**
　　　Acute nephritic syndrome with membranoproliferative glomerulonephritis, types 1 and 3, or NOS
　　　▶ **Excludes1**　Acute nephritic syndrome with C3 glomerulonephritis (N00.A)
　　　　　　▶ Acute nephritic syndrome with C3 glomerulopathy (N00.A)

N00.6　**Acute nephritic syndrome with dense deposit disease**
　　　▶ Acute nephritic syndrome with C3 glomerulopathy with dense deposit disease
　　　Acute nephritic syndrome with membranoproliferative glomerulonephritis, type 2

N00.7　**Acute nephritic syndrome with diffuse crescentic glomerulonephritis**
　　　Acute nephritic syndrome with extracapillary glomerulonephritis

N00.8　**Acute nephritic syndrome with other morphologic changes**
　　　Acute nephritic syndrome with proliferative glomerulonephritis NOS

N00.9　**Acute nephritic syndrome with unspecified morphologic changes**

▶ **N00.A**　**Acute nephritic syndrome with C3 glomerulonephritis**
　　　▶ Acute nephritic syndrome with C3 glomerulopathy, NOS
　　　▶ **Excludes1**　Acute nephritic syndrome (with C3 glomerulopathy) with dense deposit disease(N00.6)

● **N01**　**Rapidly progressive nephritic syndrome**
　　　Includes　rapidly progressive glomerular disease
　　　　　　rapidly progressive glomerulonephritis
　　　　　　rapidly progressive nephritis
　　　Excludes1　nephritic syndrome NOS (N05.-)

N01.0　**Rapidly progressive nephritic syndrome with minor glomerular abnormality**
　　　Rapidly progressive nephritic syndrome with minimal change lesion

N01.1　**Rapidly progressive nephritic syndrome with focal and segmental glomerular lesions**
　　　Rapidly progressive nephritic syndrome with focal and segmental hyalinosis
　　　Rapidly progressive nephritic syndrome with focal and segmental sclerosis
　　　Rapidly progressive nephritic syndrome with focal glomerulonephritis

N01.2　**Rapidly progressive nephritic syndrome with diffuse membranous glomerulonephritis**

N01.3　**Rapidly progressive nephritic syndrome with diffuse mesangial proliferative glomerulonephritis**

N01.4　**Rapidly progressive nephritic syndrome with diffuse endocapillary proliferative glomerulonephritis**

N01.5　**Rapidly progressive nephritic syndrome with diffuse mesangiocapillary glomerulonephritis**
　　　Rapidly progressive nephritic syndrome with membranoproliferative glomerulonephritis, types 1 and 3, or NOS
　　　▶ **Excludes1**　Rapidly progressive nephritic syndrome with C3 glomerulonephritis (N01.A)
　　　　　　▶ Rapidly progressive nephritic syndrome with C3 glomerulopathy (N01.A)

N01.6　**Rapidly progressive nephritic syndrome with dense deposit disease**
　　　▶ Rapidly progressive nephritic syndrome with C3 glomerulopathy with dense deposit disease
　　　Rapidly progressive nephritic syndrome with membranoproliferative glomerulonephritis, type 2

N01.7　**Rapidly progressive nephritic syndrome with diffuse crescentic glomerulonephritis**
　　　Rapidly progressive nephritic syndrome with extracapillary glomerulonephritis

N01.8　**Rapidly progressive nephritic syndrome with other morphologic changes**
　　　Rapidly progressive nephritic syndrome with proliferative glomerulonephritis NOS

N01.9　**Rapidly progressive nephritic syndrome with unspecified morphologic changes**

▶ **N01.A**　**Rapidly progressive nephritic syndrome with C3 glomerulonephritis**
　　　▶ Rapidly progressive nephritic syndrome with C3 glomerulopathy, NOS
　　　▶ **Excludes1**　Rapidly progressive nephritic syndrome (with C3 glomerulopathy) with dense deposit disease (N01.6)

● **N02**　**Recurrent and persistent hematuria**
　　　Excludes1　acute cystitis with hematuria (N30.01)
　　　　　　hematuria NOS (R31.9)
　　　　　　hematuria not associated with specified morphologic lesions (R31.-)

N02.0　**Recurrent and persistent hematuria with minor glomerular abnormality**
　　　Recurrent and persistent hematuria with minimal change lesion

N02.1　**Recurrent and persistent hematuria with focal and segmental glomerular lesions**
　　　Recurrent and persistent hematuria with focal and segmental hyalinosis
　　　Recurrent and persistent hematuria with focal and segmental sclerosis
　　　Recurrent and persistent hematuria with focal glomerulonephritis

N02.2　**Recurrent and persistent hematuria with diffuse membranous glomerulonephritis**

N02.3　**Recurrent and persistent hematuria with diffuse mesangial proliferative glomerulonephritis**

N02.4　**Recurrent and persistent hematuria with diffuse endocapillary proliferative glomerulonephritis**

N02.5　**Recurrent and persistent hematuria with diffuse mesangiocapillary glomerulonephritis**
　　　Recurrent and persistent hematuria with membranoproliferative glomerulonephritis, types 1 and 3, or NOS
　　　▶ **Excludes1**　Recurrent and persistent hematuria with C3 glomerulonephritis (N02.A)
　　　　　　▶ Recurrent and persistent hematuria with C3 glomerulopathy (N02.A)

N02.6　**Recurrent and persistent hematuria with dense deposit disease**
　　　▶ Recurrent and persistent hematuria with C3 glomerulopathy with dense deposit disease
　　　Recurrent and persistent hematuria with membranoproliferative glomerulonephritis, type 2

N02.7　**Recurrent and persistent hematuria with diffuse crescentic glomerulonephritis**
　　　Recurrent and persistent hematuria with extracapillary glomerulonephritis

N02.8　**Recurrent and persistent hematuria with other morphologic changes**
　　　Recurrent and persistent hematuria with proliferative glomerulonephritis NOS

N02.9　**Recurrent and persistent hematuria with unspecified morphologic changes**
　　　Coding Clinic: 2017, Q2, P5

▶ **N02.A**　**Recurrent and persistent hematuria with C3 glomerulonephritis**
　　　▶ Recurrent and persistent hematuria with C3 glomerulopathy
　　　▶ **Excludes1**　Recurrent and persistent hematuria (with C3 glomerulopathy) with dense deposit disease (N02.6)

CHAPTER 14 (N00-N99)

Item 14–3 Chronic glomerulonephritis (GN) persists over a period of years, with remissions and exacerbation.

Chronic GN with lesion of proliferative glomerulonephritis results from a streptococcal infection.

Chronic GN with lesion of membranous glomerulonephritis, also known as membranous nephropathy, is characterized by deposits along the epithelial side of the basement membrane.

Chronic GN with lesion of membrano-proliferative glomerulonephritis (MPGN) is a group of disorders characterized by alterations in the basement membranes of the kidney and the glomerular cells.

Chronic GN with lesion of rapidly progressive glomerulonephritis is characterized by necrosis, endothelial proliferation, and mesangial proliferation. The condition is marked by rapid and progressive decline in renal function.

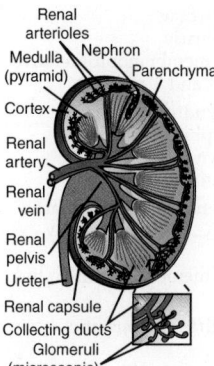

Figure 14-2 Kidney cross section.

● **N03   Chronic nephritic syndrome**

> **Includes**   chronic glomerular disease
> chronic glomerulonephritis
> chronic nephritis

> **Excludes1**   chronic tubulo-interstitial nephritis (N11.-)
> diffuse sclerosing glomerulonephritis (N05.8-)
> nephritic syndrome NOS (N05.-)

N03.0   Chronic nephritic syndrome with minor glomerular abnormality
> Chronic nephritic syndrome with minimal change lesion

N03.1   Chronic nephritic syndrome with focal and segmental glomerular lesions
> Chronic nephritic syndrome with focal and segmental hyalinosis
> Chronic nephritic syndrome with focal and segmental sclerosis
> Chronic nephritic syndrome with focal glomerulonephritis

N03.2   Chronic nephritic syndrome with diffuse membranous glomerulonephritis

N03.3   Chronic nephritic syndrome with diffuse mesangial proliferative glomerulonephritis

N03.4   Chronic nephritic syndrome with diffuse endocapillary proliferative glomerulonephritis

N03.5   Chronic nephritic syndrome with diffuse mesangiocapillary glomerulonephritis
> Chronic nephritic syndrome with membranoproliferative glomerulonephritis, types 1 and 3, or NOS

> ▶ **Excludes1**   Chronic nephritic syndrome with C3 glomerulonephritis (N03.A)
> ▶Chronic nephritic syndrome with C3 glomerulopathy (N03.A)

N03.6   Chronic nephritic syndrome with dense deposit disease
> ▶Chronic nephritic syndrome with C3 glomerulopathy with dense deposit disease
> Chronic nephritic syndrome with membranoproliferative glomerulonephritis, type 2

N03.7   Chronic nephritic syndrome with diffuse crescentic glomerulonephritis
> Chronic nephritic syndrome with extracapillary glomerulonephritis

N03.8   Chronic nephritic syndrome with other morphologic changes
> Chronic nephritic syndrome with proliferative glomerulonephritis NOS

N03.9   Chronic nephritic syndrome with unspecified morphologic changes

▶ **N03.A   Chronic nephritic syndrome with C3 glomerulonephritis**
> ▶ Chronic nephritic syndrome with C3 glomerulopathy

> ▶ **Excludes1**   Chronic nephritic syndrome (with C3 glomerulopathy) with dense deposit disease(N03.6)

Item 14–4 Nephrotic syndrome (NS) is marked by massive proteinuria (protein in the urine) and water retention. Patients with NS are particularly vulnerable to staphylococcal and pneumococcal infections. NS with lesion of proliferative glomerulonephritis results from a streptococcal infection. NS with lesion of membranous glomerulonephritis results in thickening of the capillary walls. NS with lesion of minimal change glomerulonephritis is usually a benign disorder that occurs mostly in children and requires electron microscopy (biopsy) to verify changes in the glomeruli.

● **N04   Nephrotic syndrome**

> **Includes**   congenital nephrotic syndrome
> lipoid nephrosis

N04.0   Nephrotic syndrome with minor glomerular abnormality
> Nephrotic syndrome with minimal change lesion

N04.1   Nephrotic syndrome with focal and segmental glomerular lesions
> Nephrotic syndrome with focal and segmental hyalinosis
> Nephrotic syndrome with focal and segmental sclerosis
> Nephrotic syndrome with focal glomerulonephritis

N04.2   Nephrotic syndrome with diffuse membranous glomerulonephritis

N04.3   Nephrotic syndrome with diffuse mesangial proliferative glomerulonephritis

N04.4   Nephrotic syndrome with diffuse endocapillary proliferative glomerulonephritis

N04.5   Nephrotic syndrome with diffuse mesangiocapillary glomerulonephritis
> Nephrotic syndrome with membranoproliferative glomerulonephritis, types 1 and 3, or NOS

> ▶ **Excludes1**   Nephrotic syndrome with C3 glomerulonephritis (N04.A)
> ▶Nephrotic syndrome with C3 glomerulopathy (N04.A)

N04.6   Nephrotic syndrome with dense deposit disease
> ▶Nephrotic syndrome with C3 glomerulopathy with dense deposit disease
> Nephrotic syndrome with membranoproliferative glomerulonephritis, type 2

N04.7   Nephrotic syndrome with diffuse crescentic glomerulonephritis
> Nephrotic syndrome with extracapillary glomerulonephritis

N04.8   Nephrotic syndrome with other morphologic changes
> Nephrotic syndrome with proliferative glomerulonephritis NOS

N04.9   Nephrotic syndrome with unspecified morphologic changes

▶ **N04.A   Nephrotic syndrome with C3 glomerulonephritis**
> ▶ Nephrotic syndrome with C3 glomerulopathy

> ▶ **Excludes1**   Nephrotic syndrome (with C3 glomerulopathy) with dense deposit disease (N04.6)

▶ New   ⇒ Revised   ~~deleted~~ Deleted   Excludes 1   Excludes 2   Includes   Use additional   Code first   Code also   Key words

OGCR Official Guidelines   X Assign placeholder X   ● Use Additional Character(s)   ▶ Manifestation Code   Hierarchical Condition Category   **Coding Clinic**

● **N05　Unspecified nephritic syndrome**

　　Includes　　glomerular disease NOS
　　　　　　　　　glomerulonephritis NOS
　　　　　　　　　nephritis NOS
　　　　　　　　　nephropathy NOS and renal disease NOS with
　　　　　　　　　　　morphological lesion specified in .0–.8

　　Excludes1　　nephropathy NOS with no stated morphological
　　　　　　　　　　lesion (N28.9)
　　　　　　　　　renal disease NOS with no stated morphological
　　　　　　　　　　lesion (N28.9)
　　　　　　　　　tubulo-interstitial nephritis NOS (N12)

N05.0　Unspecified nephritic syndrome with minor glomerular abnormality
　　　Unspecified nephritic syndrome with minimal change lesion

N05.1　Unspecified nephritic syndrome with focal and segmental glomerular lesions
　　　Unspecified nephritic syndrome with focal and segmental hyalinosis
　　　Unspecified nephritic syndrome with focal and segmental sclerosis
　　　Unspecified nephritic syndrome with focal glomerulonephritis

N05.2　Unspecified nephritic syndrome with diffuse membranous glomerulonephritis

N05.3　Unspecified nephritic syndrome with diffuse mesangial proliferative glomerulonephritis

N05.4　Unspecified nephritic syndrome with diffuse endocapillary proliferative glomerulonephritis

N05.5　Unspecified nephritic syndrome with diffuse mesangiocapillary glomerulonephritis
　　　Unspecified nephritic syndrome with membranoproliferative glomerulonephritis, types 1 and 3, or NOS

　　▶ **Excludes1**　　Unspecified nephritic syndrome with C3 glomerulonephritis (N05.A)
　　　　　　　　　▶Unspecified nephritic syndrome with C3 glomerulopathy (N05.A)

N05.6　Unspecified nephritic syndrome with dense deposit disease
　　　▶Unspecified nephritic syndrome with C3 glomerulopathy with dense deposit disease
　　　Unspecified nephritic syndrome with membranoproliferative glomerulonephritis, type 2

N05.7　Unspecified nephritic syndrome with diffuse crescentic glomerulonephritis
　　　Unspecified nephritic syndrome with extracapillary glomerulonephritis

N05.8　Unspecified nephritic syndrome with other morphologic changes
　　　Unspecified nephritic syndrome with proliferative glomerulonephritis NOS

N05.9　Unspecified nephritic syndrome with unspecified morphologic changes

▶ **N05.A　Unspecified nephritic syndrome with C3 glomerulonephritis**
　　　▶Unspecified nephritic syndrome with C3 glomerulopathy

　　▶ **Excludes1**　　Unspecified nephritic syndrome (with C3 glomerulopathy) with dense deposit disease(N05.6)

● **N06　Isolated proteinuria with specified morphological lesion**

　　Excludes1　　proteinuria not associated with specific morphologic lesions (R80.0)

N06.0　Isolated proteinuria with minor glomerular abnormality
　　　Isolated proteinuria with minimal change lesion

N06.1　Isolated proteinuria with focal and segmental glomerular lesions
　　　Isolated proteinuria with focal and segmental hyalinosis
　　　Isolated proteinuria with focal and segmental sclerosis
　　　Isolated proteinuria with focal glomerulonephritis

N06.2　Isolated proteinuria with diffuse membranous glomerulonephritis

N06.3　Isolated proteinuria with diffuse mesangial proliferative glomerulonephritis

N06.4　Isolated proteinuria with diffuse endocapillary proliferative glomerulonephritis

N06.5　Isolated proteinuria with diffuse mesangiocapillary glomerulonephritis
　　　Isolated proteinuria with membranoproliferative glomerulonephritis, types 1 and 3, or NOS

　　▶ **Excludes1**　　Isolated proteinuria with C3 glomerulonephritis (N06.A)
　　　　　　　　　▶Isolated proteinuria with C3 glomerulopathy (N06.A)

N06.6　Isolated proteinuria with dense deposit disease
　　　▶Isolated proteinuria with C3 glomerulopathy with dense deposit disease
　　　Isolated proteinuria with membranoproliferative glomerulonephritis, type 2

N06.7　Isolated proteinuria with diffuse crescentic glomerulonephritis
　　　Isolated proteinuria with extracapillary glomerulonephritis

N06.8　Isolated proteinuria with other morphologic lesion
　　　Isolated proteinuria with proliferative glomerulonephritis NOS

N06.9　Isolated proteinuria with unspecified morphologic lesion

▶ **N06.A　Isolated proteinuria with C3 glomerulonephritis**
　　　▶Isolated proteinuria with C3 glomerulopathy

　　▶ **Excludes1**　　Isolated proteinuria (with C3 glomerulopathy) with dense deposit disease (N06.6)

● **N07　Hereditary nephropathy, not elsewhere classified**

　　Excludes2　　Alport's syndrome (Q87.81-)
　　　　　　　　　hereditary amyloid nephropathy (E85.-)
　　　　　　　　　nail patella syndrome (Q87.2)
　　　　　　　　　non-neuropathic heredofamilial amyloidosis (E85.-)

N07.0　Hereditary nephropathy, not elsewhere classified with minor glomerular abnormality
　　　Hereditary nephropathy, not elsewhere classified with minimal change lesion

N07.1　Hereditary nephropathy, not elsewhere classified with focal and segmental glomerular lesions
　　　Hereditary nephropathy, not elsewhere classified with focal and segmental hyalinosis
　　　Hereditary nephropathy, not elsewhere classified with focal and segmental sclerosis
　　　Hereditary nephropathy, not elsewhere classified with focal glomerulonephritis

CHAPTER 14 (N00-N99)

N07.2   **Hereditary nephropathy, not elsewhere classified with diffuse membranous glomerulonephritis**

N07.3   **Hereditary nephropathy, not elsewhere classified with diffuse mesangial proliferative glomerulonephritis**

N07.4   **Hereditary nephropathy, not elsewhere classified with diffuse endocapillary proliferative glomerulonephritis**

N07.5   **Hereditary nephropathy, not elsewhere classified with diffuse mesangiocapillary glomerulonephritis**
Hereditary nephropathy, not elsewhere classified with membranoproliferative glomerulonephritis, types 1 and 3, or NOS

> **Excludes1**   Hereditary nephropathy, not elsewhere classified with C3 glomerulonephritis (N07.A)
> ▶Hereditary nephropathy, not elsewhere classified with C3 glomerulopathy (N07.A)

N07.6   **Hereditary nephropathy, not elsewhere classified with dense deposit disease**
> ▶Hereditary nephropathy, not elsewhere classified with C3 glomerulopathy with dense deposit disease
Hereditary nephropathy, not elsewhere classified with membranoproliferative glomerulonephritis, type 2

N07.7   **Hereditary nephropathy, not elsewhere classified with diffuse crescentic glomerulonephritis**
Hereditary nephropathy, not elsewhere classified with extracapillary glomerulonephritis

N07.8   **Hereditary nephropathy, not elsewhere classified with other morphologic lesions**
Hereditary nephropathy, not elsewhere classified with proliferative glomerulonephritis NOS

N07.9   **Hereditary nephropathy, not elsewhere classified with unspecified morphologic lesions**

▶ **N07.A**   **Hereditary nephropathy, not elsewhere classified with C3 glomerulonephritis**
> ▶Hereditary nephropathy, not elsewhere classified with C3 glomerulopathy

> **Excludes1**   Hereditary nephropathy, not elsewhere classified (with C3 glomerulopathy) with dense deposit disease (N07.6)

▷ **N08**   *Glomerular disorders in diseases classified elsewhere*
Glomerulonephritis
Nephritis
Nephropathy

Code first underlying disease, such as:
amyloidosis (E85.-)
congenital syphilis (A50.5)
cryoglobulinemia (D89.1)
disseminated intravascular coagulation (D65)
gout (M1A.-, M10.-)
microscopic polyangiitis (M31.7)
multiple myeloma (C90.0-)
sepsis (A40.0-A41.9)
sickle-cell disease (D57.0-D57.8)

> **Excludes1**   glomerulonephritis, nephritis and nephropathy (in):
> antiglomerular basement membrane disease (M31.0)
> diabetes (E08-E13 with .21)
> gonococcal (A54.21)
> Goodpasture's syndrome (M31.0)
> hemolytic-uremic syndrome (D59.3)
> lupus (M32.14)
> mumps (B26.83)
> syphilis (A52.75)
> systemic lupus erythematosus (M32.14)
> Wegener's granulomatosis (M31.31)
> pyelonephritis in diseases classified elsewhere (N16)
> renal tubulo-interstitial disorders classified elsewhere (N16)

Figure 14-3   Acute pyelonephritis. Cortical surface exhibits grayish white areas of inflammation and abscess formation. (From Frazier MS, Drzymkowski JW: Essentials of Human Diseases and Conditions, St. Louis, Saunders/Elsevier, 2009)

Item 14-5 Pyelonephritis is an infection of the kidneys and ureters and may be chronic or acute in one or both kidneys.

RENAL TUBULO-INTERSTITIAL DISEASES (N10-N16)

Includes   pyelonephritis

Excludes1   pyeloureteritis cystica (N28.85)

N10   **Acute pyelonephritis**
Acute infectious interstitial nephritis
Acute pyelitis
Acute tubulo-interstitial nephritis
Hemoglobin nephrosis
Myoglobin nephrosis
Use additional code (B95-B97), to identify infectious agent
Coding Clinic: 2019, Q3, P13-14

● **N11**   **Chronic tubulo-interstitial nephritis**

Includes   chronic infectious interstitial nephritis
chronic pyelitis
chronic pyelonephritis

Use additional code (B95-B97), to identify infectious agent

N11.0   **Nonobstructive reflux-associated chronic pyelonephritis**
Pyelonephritis (chronic) associated with (vesicoureteral) reflux

> **Excludes1**   vesicoureteral reflux NOS (N13.70)

N11.1   **Chronic obstructive pyelonephritis**
Pyelonephritis (chronic) associated with anomaly of pelviureteric junction
Pyelonephritis (chronic) associated with anomaly of pyeloureteric junction
Pyelonephritis (chronic) associated with crossing of vessel
Pyelonephritis (chronic) associated with kinking of ureter
Pyelonephritis (chronic) associated with obstruction of ureter
Pyelonephritis (chronic) associated with stricture of pelviureteric junction
Pyelonephritis (chronic) associated with stricture of ureter

> **Excludes1**   calculous pyelonephritis (N20.9)
> obstructive uropathy (N13.-)

N11.8   **Other chronic tubulo-interstitial nephritis**
Nonobstructive chronic pyelonephritis NOS

N11.9   **Chronic tubulo-interstitial nephritis, unspecified**
Chronic interstitial nephritis NOS
Chronic pyelitis NOS
Chronic pyelonephritis NOS

N12   **Tubulo-interstitial nephritis, not specified as acute or chronic**
Interstitial nephritis NOS
Pyelitis NOS
Pyelonephritis NOS

> **Excludes1**   calculous pyelonephritis (N20.9)

> New   ▰ Revised   ~~deleted~~ Deleted   Excludes 1   Excludes 2   Includes   Use additional   Code first   Code also   Key words
OGCR Official Guidelines   X Assign placeholder X   ● Use Additional Character(s)   ▷ Manifestation Code   ❧ Hierarchical Condition Category   Coding Clinic

Figure 14-4 Hydronephrosis of the kidney, with marked dilatation of pelvis and calyces and thinning of renal parenchyma. (From Kumar: Robbins and Cotran: Pathologic Basis of Disease, ed 8, Saunders, An Imprint of Elsevier, 2009)

● **N13   Obstructive and reflux uropathy**
   Excludes2   calculus of kidney and ureter without hydronephrosis (N20.-)
         congenital obstructive defects of renal pelvis and ureter (Q62.0-Q62.3)
         hydronephrosis with ureteropelvic junction obstruction (Q62.11)
         obstructive pyelonephritis (N11.1)

   N13.0   Hydronephrosis with ureteropelvic junction obstruction
      Hydronephrosis due to acquired occlusion of ureteropelvic junction
      Excludes2   Hydronephrosis with ureteropelvic junction obstruction due to calculus (N13.2)
      Coding Clinic: 2016, Q4, P43

   N13.1   Hydronephrosis with ureteral stricture, not elsewhere classified
      Excludes1   hydronephrosis with ureteral stricture with infection (N13.6)

   N13.2   Hydronephrosis with renal and ureteral calculous obstruction
      Excludes1   hydronephrosis with renal and ureteral calculous obstruction with infection (N13.6)

● **N13.3   Other and unspecified hydronephrosis**
      Excludes1   hydronephrosis with infection (N13.6)
      N13.30   Unspecified hydronephrosis
      N13.39   Other hydronephrosis

   N13.4   Hydroureter
      Excludes1   congenital hydroureter (Q62.3-)
         hydroureter with infection (N13.6)
         vesicoureteral-reflux with hydroureter (N13.73-)

   N13.5   Crossing vessel and stricture of ureter without hydronephrosis
      Kinking and stricture of ureter without hydronephrosis
      Excludes1   crossing vessel and stricture of ureter without hydronephrosis with infection (N13.6)
      Coding Clinic: 2016, Q4, P43

   N13.6   Pyonephrosis
      Conditions in N13.0-N13.5 with infection
      Obstructive uropathy with infection
      Use additional code (B95-B97), to identify infectious agent
      Coding Clinic: 2018, Q2, P21

● **N13.7   Vesicoureteral-reflux**
      Excludes1   reflux-associated pyelonephritis (N11.0)
      N13.70   Vesicoureteral-reflux, unspecified
         Occurs when urine flows from bladder back into ureters
         Vesicoureteral-reflux NOS
      N13.71   Vesicoureteral-reflux without reflux nephropathy
   ● **N13.72   Vesicoureteral-reflux with reflux nephropathy without hydroureter**
         N13.721   Vesicoureteral-reflux with reflux nephropathy without hydroureter, unilateral
         N13.722   Vesicoureteral-reflux with reflux nephropathy without hydroureter, bilateral
         N13.729   Vesicoureteral-reflux with reflux nephropathy without hydroureter, unspecified
   ● **N13.73   Vesicoureteral-reflux with reflux nephropathy with hydroureter**
         N13.731   Vesicoureteral-reflux with reflux nephropathy with hydroureter, unilateral
         N13.732   Vesicoureteral-reflux with reflux nephropathy with hydroureter, bilateral
         N13.739   Vesicoureteral-reflux with reflux nephropathy with hydroureter, unspecified

   N13.8   Other obstructive and reflux uropathy
      Urinary tract obstruction due to specified cause
      Code first, if applicable, any causal condition first, such as: enlarged prostate (N40.1)

   N13.9   Obstructive and reflux uropathy, unspecified
      Urinary tract obstruction NOS

● **N14   Drug- and heavy-metal-induced tubulo-interstitial and tubular conditions**
      Code first poisoning due to drug or toxin, if applicable (T36-T65 with fifth or sixth character 1-4 or 6)
      Use additional code for adverse effect, if applicable, to identify drug (T36-T50 with fifth or sixth character 5)

   N14.0   Analgesic nephropathy
   N14.1   Nephropathy induced by other drugs, medicaments and biological substances
   N14.2   Nephropathy induced by unspecified drug, medicament or biological substance
   N14.3   Nephropathy induced by heavy metals
   N14.4   Toxic nephropathy, not elsewhere classified

● **N15   Other renal tubulo-interstitial diseases**
   N15.0   Balkan nephropathy
      Balkan endemic nephropathy
   N15.1   Renal and perinephric abscess
   N15.8   Other specified renal tubulo-interstitial diseases
   N15.9   Renal tubulo-interstitial disease, unspecified
      Infection of kidney NOS
      Excludes1   urinary tract infection NOS (N39.0)

CHAPTER 14 (N00-N99)

▶**N16**   *Renal tubulo-interstitial disorders in diseases classified elsewhere*
    Pyelonephritis
    Tubulo-interstitial nephritis

    Code first underlying disease, such as:
      brucellosis (A23.0-A23.9)
      cryoglobulinemia (D89.1)
      glycogen storage disease (E74.0)
      leukemia (C91-C95)
      lymphoma (C81.0-C85.9, C96.0-C96.9)
      multiple myeloma (C90.0-)
      sepsis (A40.0-A41.9)
      Wilson's disease (E83.0)

    Excludes1   diphtheritic pyelonephritis and tubulo-interstitial nephritis (A36.84)
       pyelonephritis and tubulo-interstitial nephritis in candidiasis (B37.49)
       pyelonephritis and tubulo-interstitial nephritis in cystinosis (E72.04)
       pyelonephritis and tubulo-interstitial nephritis in salmonella infection (A02.25)
       pyelonephritis and tubulo-interstitial nephritis in sarcoidosis (D86.84)
       pyelonephritis and tubulo-interstitial nephritis in sicca syndrome [Sjogren's] (M35.04)
       pyelonephritis and tubulo-interstitial nephritis in systemic lupus erythematosus (M32.15)
       pyelonephritis and tubulo-interstitial nephritis in toxoplasmosis (B58.83)
       renal tubular degeneration in diabetes (E08-E13 with .29)
       syphilitic pyelonephritis and tubulo-interstitial nephritis (A52.75)

ACUTE KIDNEY FAILURE AND CHRONIC KIDNEY DISEASE (N17-N19)

    Excludes2   congenital renal failure (P96.0)
       drug- and heavy-metal-induced tubulo-interstitial and tubular conditions (N14.-)
       extrarenal uremia (R39.2)
       hemolytic-uremic syndrome (D59.3)
       hepatorenal syndrome (K76.7)
       postpartum hepatorenal syndrome (O90.4)
       posttraumatic renal failure (T79.5)
       prerenal uremia (R39.2)
       renal failure complicating abortion or ectopic or molar pregnancy (O00-O07, O08.4)
       renal failure following labor and delivery (O90.4)
       renal failure postprocedural (N99.0)

●**N17**   **Acute kidney failure**
    Code also associated underlying condition
    Excludes1   posttraumatic renal failure (T79.5)

    N17.0   **Acute kidney failure with tubular necrosis** 🝗
      Acute tubular necrosis
      Renal tubular necrosis
      Tubular necrosis NOS

    N17.1   **Acute kidney failure with acute cortical necrosis** 🝗
      Acute cortical necrosis
      Cortical necrosis NOS
      Renal cortical necrosis

    N17.2   **Acute kidney failure with medullary necrosis** 🝗
      Medullary [papillary] necrosis NOS
      Acute medullary [papillary] necrosis
      Renal medullary [papillary] necrosis

    N17.8   **Other acute kidney failure** 🝗

    N17.9   **Acute kidney failure, unspecified** 🝗
      Acute kidney injury (nontraumatic)
      Excludes2   traumatic kidney injury (S37.0-)
      Coding Clinic: 2019, Q2, P7,25

●**N18**   **Chronic kidney disease (CKD)**
    Code first any associated:
      diabetic chronic kidney disease (E08.22, E09.22, E10.22, E11.22, E13.22)
      hypertensive chronic kidney disease (I12.-, I13.-)
    Use additional code to identify kidney transplant status, if applicable, (Z94.0)
    Coding Clinic: 2018, Q4, P89; 2016, Q4, P123

    N18.1   **Chronic kidney disease, stage 1**
    N18.2   **Chronic kidney disease, stage 2 (mild)**
    ●**N18.3**   **Chronic kidney disease, stage 3 (moderate)**
      ▶**N18.30**   **Chronic kidney disease, stage 3 unspecified**
      ▶**N18.31**   **Chronic kidney disease, stage 3a**
      ▶**N18.32**   **Chronic kidney disease, stage 3b**

    N18.4   **Chronic kidney disease, stage 4 (severe)** 🝗
      Coding Clinic: 2013, Q1, P24

    N18.5   **Chronic kidney disease, stage 5** 🝗
      Excludes1   chronic kidney disease, stage 5 requiring chronic dialysis (N18.6)

    N18.6   **End stage renal disease** 🝗
      Chronic kidney disease requiring chronic dialysis
      Use additional code to identify dialysis status (Z99.2)
      Coding Clinic: 2016, Q3, P23, Q1, P13

    N18.9   **Chronic kidney disease, unspecified**
      Chronic renal disease
      Chronic renal failure NOS
      Chronic renal insufficiency
      Chronic uremia NOS
      Diffuse sclerosing glomerulonephritis NOS
      Coding Clinic: 2018, Q4, P88

N19   **Unspecified kidney failure**
    Uremia NOS
    Excludes1   acute kidney failure (N17.-)
       chronic kidney disease (N18.-)
       chronic uremia (N18.9)
       extrarenal uremia (R39.2)
       prerenal uremia (R39.2)
       renal insufficiency (acute) (N28.9)
       uremia of newborn (P96.0)

UROLITHIASIS (N20-N23)

●**N20**   **Calculus of kidney and ureter**
    Calculous pyelonephritis
    Excludes1   nephrocalcinosis (E83.5)
       that with hydronephrosis (N13.2)
    Coding Clinic: 2019, Q3, P14

    N20.0   **Calculus of kidney**
      Nephrolithiasis NOS   Staghorn calculus
      Renal calculus   Stone in kidney
      Renal stone
      Coding Clinic: 2019, Q3, P13; 2017, Q1, P5

    N20.1   **Calculus of ureter**
      ▶Calculus of the ureteropelvic junction
      Ureteric stone
      Coding Clinic: 2016, Q3, P24

    N20.2   **Calculus of kidney with calculus of ureter**
    N20.9   **Urinary calculus, unspecified**

Multiple calculi

Figure 14-5   Multiple urinary calculi.

Item 14–6 Decreased blood flow is the usual cause of **acute renal failure** that offers a good prognosis for recovery.
    Chronic renal failure is usually the result of long-standing kidney disease and is a very serious condition that generally results in death.

▶ New   ➧ Revised   ~~deleted~~ Deleted   Excludes 1   Excludes 2   Includes   Use additional   Code first   Code also   Key words

   OGCR Official Guidelines   X Assign placeholder X   ● Use Additional Character(s)   ▶ Manifestation Code   🝗 Hierarchical Condition Category   Coding Clinic

● **N21 Calculus of lower urinary tract**
> **Includes**   calculus of lower urinary tract with cystitis and urethritis

N21.0 Calculus in bladder
> Calculus in diverticulum of bladder
> Urinary bladder stone
> **Excludes2**   staghorn calculus (N20.0)
> Coding Clinic: 2015, Q2, P9

N21.1 Calculus in urethra
> **Excludes2**   calculus of prostate (N42.0)

N21.8 Other lower urinary tract calculus

N21.9 Calculus of lower urinary tract, unspecified
> **Excludes1**   calculus of urinary tract NOS (N20.9)

▌**N22 *Calculus of urinary tract in diseases classified elsewhere***
> *Code first underlying disease, such as:*
> gout (M1A.-, M10.-)
> schistosomiasis (B65.0-B65.9)

N23 Unspecified renal colic

OTHER DISORDERS OF KIDNEY AND URETER (N25-N29)

> **Excludes2**   disorders of kidney and ureter with urolithiasis (N20-N23)

● **N25 Disorders resulting from impaired renal tubular function**

N25.0 Renal osteodystrophy
> Azotemic osteodystrophy
> Phosphate-losing tubular disorders
> Renal rickets
> Renal short stature
> **Excludes2**   metabolic disorders classifiable to E70-E88

N25.1 Nephrogenic diabetes insipidus 🔲
> **Excludes1**   diabetes insipidus NOS (E23.2)

● **N25.8 Other disorders resulting from impaired renal tubular function**

N25.81 Secondary hyperparathyroidism of renal origin 🔲
> **Excludes1**   secondary hyperparathyroidism, non-renal (E21.1)
> **Excludes2**   metabolic disorders classifiable to E70-E88

N25.89 Other disorders resulting from impaired renal tubular function
> Hypokalemic nephropathy
> Lightwood-Albright syndrome
> Renal tubular acidosis NOS

N25.9 Disorder resulting from impaired renal tubular function, unspecified

● **N26 Unspecified contracted kidney**
> **Excludes1**   contracted kidney due to hypertension (I12.-)
> diffuse sclerosing glomerulonephritis (N05.8.-)
> hypertensive nephrosclerosis (arteriolar) (arteriosclerotic) (I12.-)
> small kidney of unknown cause (N27.-)

N26.1 Atrophy of kidney (terminal)

N26.2 Page kidney

N26.9 Renal sclerosis, unspecified

● **N27 Small kidney of unknown cause**
> **Includes**   oligonephronia

N27.0 Small kidney, unilateral

N27.1 Small kidney, bilateral

N27.9 Small kidney, unspecified

● **N28 Other disorders of kidney and ureter, not elsewhere classified**

N28.0 Ischemia and infarction of kidney 🔲
> Renal artery embolism
> Renal artery obstruction
> Renal artery occlusion
> Renal artery thrombosis
> Renal infarct
> **Excludes1**   atherosclerosis of renal artery (extrarenal part) (I70.1)
> congenital stenosis of renal artery (Q27.1)
> Goldblatt's kidney (I70.1)

N28.1 Cyst of kidney, acquired
> Cyst (multiple) (solitary) of kidney, (acquired)
> **Excludes1**   cystic kidney disease (congenital) (Q61.-)

● **N28.8 Other specified disorders of kidney and ureter**
> **Excludes1**   hydroureter (N13.4)
> ureteric stricture with hydronephrosis (N13.1)
> ureteric stricture without hydronephrosis (N13.5)

N28.81 Hypertrophy of kidney

N28.82 Megaloureter

N28.83 Nephroptosis

N28.84 Pyelitis cystica

N28.85 Pyeloureteritis cystica

N28.86 Ureteritis cystica

N28.89 Other specified disorders of kidney and ureter

N28.9 Disorder of kidney and ureter, unspecified
> Nephropathy NOS
> Renal disease (acute) NOS
> Renal insufficiency (acute)
> **Excludes1**   chronic renal insufficiency (N18.9)
> unspecified nephritic syndrome (N05.-)
> Coding Clinic: 2016, Q1, P13

▌**N29 *Other disorders of kidney and ureter in diseases classified elsewhere***
> *Code first underlying disease, such as:*
> amyloidosis (E85.-)
> nephrocalcinosis (E83.5)
> schistosomiasis (B65.0-B65.9)
> **Excludes1**   disorders of kidney and ureter in:
> cystinosis (E72.0)
> gonorrhea (A54.21)
> syphilis (A52.75)
> tuberculosis (A18.11)

OTHER DISEASES OF THE URINARY SYSTEM (N30-N39)

> **Excludes1**   urinary infection (complicating):
> abortion or ectopic or molar pregnancy (O00-O07, O08.8)
> pregnancy, childbirth and the puerperium (O23.-, O75.3, O86.2-)

● **N30 Cystitis**
> *Infection of bladder and irritation in lower urinary tract*
> Use additional code to identify infectious agent (B95-B97)
> **Excludes1**   prostatocystitis (N41.3)

● **N30.0 Acute cystitis**
> **Excludes1**   irradiation cystitis (N30.4-)
> trigonitis (N30.3-)

N30.00 Acute cystitis without hematuria

N30.01 Acute cystitis with hematuria

● **N30.1 Interstitial cystitis (chronic)**
> *Ongoing infection of kidney glomeruli and tubules*

N30.10 Interstitial cystitis (chronic) without hematuria

N30.11 Interstitial cystitis (chronic) with hematuria

CHAPTER 14 (N00-N99)

● **N30.2**   **Other chronic cystitis**
     N30.20   **Other chronic cystitis without hematuria**
     N30.21   **Other chronic cystitis with hematuria**

● **N30.3**   **Trigonitis**
     Inflammation of triangular area of bladder (where the ureters
        and urethra come together)
     Urethrotrigonitis
     N30.30   **Trigonitis without hematuria**
     N30.31   **Trigonitis with hematuria**

● **N30.4**   **Irradiation cystitis**
     N30.40   **Irradiation cystitis without hematuria**
     N30.41   **Irradiation cystitis with hematuria**

● **N30.8**   **Other cystitis**
     Abscess of bladder
     N30.80   **Other cystitis without hematuria**
     N30.81   **Other cystitis with hematuria**

● **N30.9**   **Cystitis, unspecified**
     N30.90   **Cystitis, unspecified without hematuria**
     N30.91   **Cystitis, unspecified with hematuria**

● **N31**   **Neuromuscular dysfunction of bladder, not elsewhere classified**
     Use additional code to identify any associated urinary
     incontinence (N39.3-N39.4-)
     Excludes1   cord bladder NOS (G95.89)
                neurogenic bladder due to cauda equina
                   syndrome (G83.4)
                neuromuscular dysfunction due to spinal cord
                   lesion (G95.89)
     N31.0   **Uninhibited neuropathic bladder, not elsewhere classified**
     N31.1   **Reflex neuropathic bladder, not elsewhere classified**
     N31.2   **Flaccid neuropathic bladder, not elsewhere classified**
         Atonic (motor) (sensory) neuropathic bladder
         Diminished tone of bladder muscle
         Autonomous neuropathic bladder
         Nonreflex neuropathic bladder
     N31.8   **Other neuromuscular dysfunction of bladder**
     N31.9   **Neuromuscular dysfunction of bladder, unspecified**
         Neurogenic bladder dysfunction NOS

● **N32**   **Other disorders of bladder**
     Excludes2   calculus of bladder (N21.0)
                cystocele (N81.1-)
                hernia or prolapse of bladder, female (N81.1-)
     N32.0   **Bladder-neck obstruction**
         Bladder-neck stenosis (acquired)
         Excludes1   congenital bladder-neck obstruction
                    (Q64.3-)
     N32.1   **Vesicointestinal fistula**
         Vesicorectal fistula
     N32.2   **Vesical fistula, not elsewhere classified**
         Excludes1   fistula between bladder and female
                    genital tract (N82.0-N82.1)
     N32.3   **Diverticulum of bladder**
         Formation of sac from a herniation of wall of bladder
         Excludes1   congenital diverticulum of bladder (Q64.6)
                    diverticulitis of bladder (N30.8-)
● **N32.8**   **Other specified disorders of bladder**
     N32.81   **Overactive bladder**
         Detrusor muscle hyperactivity
         Excludes1   frequent urination due to
                    specified bladder condition-
                    code to condition
     N32.89   **Other specified disorders of bladder**
         Bladder hemorrhage
         Bladder hypertrophy
         Calcified bladder
         Contracted bladder
     N32.9   **Bladder disorder, unspecified**

▷ **N33**   *Bladder disorders in diseases classified elsewhere*
     Code first underlying disease, such as:
         schistosomiasis (B65.0-B65.9)
     Excludes1   bladder disorder in syphilis (A52.76)
                bladder disorder in tuberculosis (A18.12)
                candidal cystitis (B37.41)
                chlamydial cystitis(A56.01)
                cystitis in gonorrhea (A54.01)
                cystitis in neurogenic bladder (N31.-)
                diphtheritic cystitis (A36.85)
                syphilitic cystitis (A52.76)
                trichomonal cystitis (A59.03)

● **N34**   **Urethritis and urethral syndrome**
     Use additional code (B95-B97), to identify infectious agent
     Excludes2   Reiter's disease (M02.3-)
                urethritis in diseases with a predominantly sexual
                   mode of transmission (A50-A64)
                urethrotrigonitis (N30.3-)
     N34.0   **Urethral abscess**
         Abscess (of) Cowper's gland
         Abscess (of) Littré's gland
         Abscess (of) urethral (gland)
         Periurethral abscess
         Excludes1   urethral caruncle (N36.2)
     N34.1   **Nonspecific urethritis**
         Nongonococcal urethritis
         Nonvenereal urethritis
     N34.2   **Other urethritis**
         Inflammation of urethra
         Meatitis, urethral
         Postmenopausal urethritis
         Ulcer of urethra (meatus)
         Urethritis NOS
     N34.3   **Urethral syndrome, unspecified**

● **N35**   **Urethral stricture**
     Narrowing of lumen of urethra caused by scarring due to infection or
     injury
     Excludes1   congenital urethral stricture (Q64.3-)
                postprocedural urethral stricture (N99.1-)
● **N35.0**   **Post-traumatic urethral stricture**
     Urethral stricture due to injury
     Excludes1   postprocedural urethral stricture (N99.1-)
     ● **N35.01**   **Post-traumatic urethral stricture, male**
         N35.010   **Post-traumatic urethral stricture,**
                  male, meatal ♂
         N35.011   **Post-traumatic bulbous urethral**
                  stricture ♂
         N35.012   **Post-traumatic membranous urethral**
                  stricture ♂
         N35.013   **Post-traumatic anterior urethral**
                  stricture ♂
         N35.014   **Post-traumatic urethral stricture,**
                  male, unspecified ♂
         N35.016   **Post-traumatic urethral stricture,**
                  male, overlapping sites ♂
     ● **N35.02**   **Post-traumatic urethral stricture, female**
         N35.021   **Urethral stricture due to childbirth** ♀
         N35.028   **Other post-traumatic urethral**
                  stricture, female ♀
● **N35.1**   **Postinfective urethral stricture, not elsewhere classified**
     Excludes1   urethral stricture associated with
                   schistosomiasis (B65.-, N29)
                gonococcal urethral stricture (A54.01)
                syphilitic urethral stricture (A52.76)
     ● **N35.11**   **Postinfective urethral stricture, not elsewhere classified, male**
         N35.111   **Postinfective urethral stricture, not**
                  elsewhere classified, male, meatal ♂
         N35.112   **Postinfective bulbous urethral stricture,**
                  not elsewhere classified, male ♂

▶ New   ⟹ Revised   ̶d̶e̶l̶e̶t̶e̶d̶ Deleted   Excludes 1   Excludes 2   Includes   Use additional   Code first   Code also   Key words

OGCR Official Guidelines   X Assign placeholder X   ● Use Additional Character(s)   ▷ Manifestation Code   🄗 Hierarchical Condition Category   **Coding Clinic**

N35.113   **Postinfective membranous urethral stricture, not elsewhere classified, male** ♂

N35.114   **Postinfective anterior urethral stricture, not elsewhere classified, male** ♂

N35.116   **Postinfective urethral stricture, not elsewhere classified, male, overlapping sites** ♂

N35.119   **Postinfective urethral stricture, not elsewhere classified, male, unspecified** ♂

N35.12   **Postinfective urethral stricture, not elsewhere classified, female** ♀

● N35.8   **Other urethral stricture**

    Excludes1   postprocedural urethral stricture (N99.1-)

   ● N35.81   **Other urethral stricture, male**

     N35.811   **Other urethral stricture, male, meatal** ♂

     N35.812   **Other urethral bulbous stricture, male** ♂

     N35.813   **Other membranous urethral stricture, male** ♂

     N35.814   **Other anterior urethral stricture, male** ♂

     N35.816   **Other urethral stricture, male, overlapping sites** ♂

     N35.819   **Other urethral stricture, male, unspecified site** ♂

   N35.82   **Other urethral stricture, female** ♀

● N35.9   **Urethral stricture, unspecified**

   ● N35.91   **Urethral stricture, unspecified, male**

     N35.911   **Unspecified urethral stricture, male, meatal** ♂

     N35.912   **Unspecified bulbous urethral stricture, male** ♂

     N35.913   **Unspecified membranous urethral stricture, male** ♂

     N35.914   **Unspecified anterior urethral stricture, male** ♂

     N35.916   **Unspecified urethral stricture, male, overlapping sites** ♂

     N35.919   **Unspecified urethral stricture, male, unspecified site** ♂
        Pinhole meatus NOS
        Urethral stricture NOS

   N35.92   **Unspecified urethral stricture, female** ♀

● N36   **Other disorders of urethra**

   N36.0   **Urethral fistula**
     Urethroperineal fistula
     Urethrorectal fistula
     Urinary fistula NOS

     Excludes1   urethroscrotal fistula (N50.89)
        urethrovaginal fistula (N82.1)
        urethrovesicovaginal fistula (N82.1)

   N36.1   **Urethral diverticulum**

   N36.2   **Urethral caruncle**

   ● N36.4   **Urethral functional and muscular disorders**
     Use additional code to identify associated urinary stress incontinence (N39.3)

     N36.41   **Hypermobility of urethra**

     N36.42   **Intrinsic sphincter deficiency (ISD)**

     N36.43   **Combined hypermobility of urethra and intrinsic sphincter deficiency**

     N36.44   **Muscular disorders of urethra**
        Bladder sphincter dyssynergy

N36.5   **Urethral false passage**

N36.8   **Other specified disorders of urethra**

    Excludes1   congenital urethrocele (Q64.7)
        female urethrocele (N81.0)

N36.9   **Urethral disorder, unspecified**

▷ N37   *Urethral disorders in diseases classified elsewhere*
    Code first underlying disease

    Excludes1   urethritis (in):
        candidal infection (B37.41)
        chlamydial (A56.01)
        gonorrhea (A54.01)
        syphilis (A52.76)
        trichomonal infection (A59.03)
        tuberculosis (A18.13)

● N39   **Other disorders of urinary system**

    Excludes2   hematuria NOS (R31.-)
        recurrent or persistent hematuria (N02.-)
        recurrent or persistent hematuria with specified morphological lesion (N02.-)
        proteinuria NOS (R80.-)

   N39.0   **Urinary tract infection, site not specified**
     Use additional code (B95-B97), to identify infectious agent

     Excludes1   candidiasis of urinary tract (B37.4-)
        neonatal urinary tract infection (P39.3)
        pyuria (R82.81)
        urinary tract infection of specified site, such as:
          cystitis (N30.-)
          urethritis (N34.-)
     Coding Clinic: 2018, Q2, P22; Q1, P16; 2012, Q4, P94

   N39.3   **Stress incontinence (female) (male)**
     Code also any associated overactive bladder (N32.81)

     Excludes1   mixed incontinence (N39.46)

   ● N39.4   **Other specified urinary incontinence**
     Code also any associated overactive bladder (N32.81)

     Excludes1   enuresis NOS (R32)
        functional urinary incontinence (R39.81)
        urinary incontinence associated with cognitive impairment (R39.81)
        urinary incontinence NOS (R32)
        urinary incontinence of nonorganic origin (F98.0)

     N39.41   **Urge incontinence**

       Excludes1   mixed incontinence (N39.46)

     N39.42   **Incontinence without sensory awareness**
        Insensible (urinary) incontinence

     N39.43   **Post-void dribbling**

     N39.44   **Nocturnal enuresis**

     N39.45   **Continuous leakage**

     N39.46   **Mixed incontinence**
        Urge and stress incontinence

     ● N39.49   **Other specified urinary incontinence**

       N39.490   **Overflow incontinence**

       N39.491   **Coital incontinence**
         Coding Clinic: 2016, Q4, P44

       N39.492   **Postural (urinary) incontinence**
         Coding Clinic: 2016, Q4, P44

       N39.498   **Other specified urinary incontinence**
         Reflex incontinence
         Total incontinence

   N39.8   **Other specified disorders of urinary system**

   N39.9   **Disorder of urinary system, unspecified**

CHAPTER 14 (N00-N99)

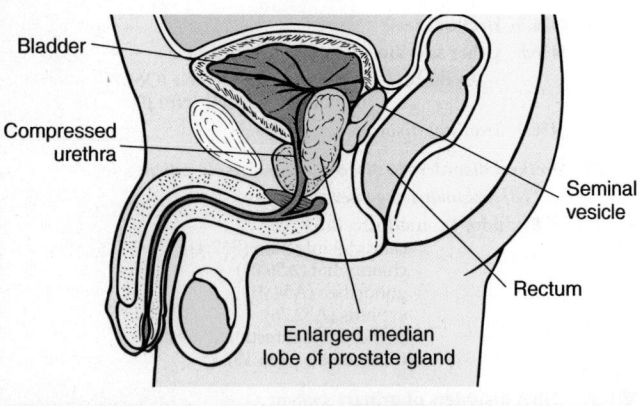

Figure 14-6 Benign prostatic hyperplasia. (From Shiland: Mastering Healthcare Terminology, ed 3, St. Louis, Mosby, 2010)

DISEASES OF MALE GENITAL ORGANS (N40-N53)

★ **(See Plate 5 of the Anatomy Illustrations.)**

● **N40 Benign prostatic hyperplasia**

    Includes   adenofibromatous hypertrophy of prostate
                   benign hypertrophy of the prostate
                   Enlargement of prostate gland usually occurring with age and causing obstructed urine flow
                   benign prostatic hypertrophy
                   BPH
                   enlarged prostate
                   nodular prostate
                   polyp of prostate

    Excludes1   benign neoplasms of prostate (adenoma, benign) (fibroadenoma) (fibroma) (myoma) (D29.1)
                  malignant neoplasm of prostate (C61)

  N40.0 Benign prostatic hyperplasia without lower urinary tract symptoms ♂   A
       Enlarged prostate without LUTS
       Enlarged prostate NOS

  N40.1 Benign prostatic hyperplasia with lower urinary tract symptoms ♂   A
       Enlarged prostate with LUTS
       Use additional code for associated symptoms, when specified:
          incomplete bladder emptying (R39.14)
          nocturia (R35.1)
          straining on urination (R39.16)
          urinary frequency (R35.0)
          urinary hesitancy (R39.11)
          urinary incontinence (N39.4-)
          urinary obstruction (N13.8)
          urinary retention (R33.8)
          urinary urgency (R39.15)
          weak urinary stream (R39.12)
       Coding Clinic: 2018, Q4, P55

  N40.2 Nodular prostate without lower urinary tract symptoms ♂   A
       Nodular prostate without LUTS

  N40.3 Nodular prostate with lower urinary tract symptoms ♂ A
       Use additional code for associated symptoms, when specified:
          incomplete bladder emptying (R39.14)
          nocturia (R35.1)
          straining on urination (R39.16)
          urinary frequency (R35.0)
          urinary hesitancy (R39.11)
          urinary incontinence (N39.4-)
          urinary obstruction (N13.8)
          urinary retention (R33.8)
          urinary urgency (R39.15)
          weak urinary stream (R39.12)

● **N41 Inflammatory diseases of prostate**
       Use additional code (B95-B97), to identify infectious agent
  N41.0 Acute prostatitis ♂   A
  N41.1 Chronic prostatitis ♂   A
  N41.2 Abscess of prostate ♂   A
  N41.3 Prostatocystitis ♂   A
  N41.4 Granulomatous prostatitis ♂   A
  N41.8 Other inflammatory diseases of prostate ♂   A
  N41.9 Inflammatory disease of prostate, unspecified ♂   A
       Prostatitis NOS

● **N42 Other and unspecified disorders of prostate**
  N42.0 Calculus of prostate ♂   A
       Prostatic stone

  N42.1 Congestion and hemorrhage of prostate ♂   A
       Excludes1   enlarged prostate (N40.-)
                 hematuria (R31.-)
                 hyperplasia of prostate (N40.-)
                 inflammatory diseases of prostate (N41.-)

● **N42.3 Dysplasia of prostate**
      Coding Clinic: 2016, Q4, P44
  N42.30 Unspecified dysplasia of prostate ♂
  N42.31 Prostatic intraepithelial neoplasia ♂
       PIN
       Prostatic intraepithelial neoplasia I (PIN I)
       Prostatic intraepithelial neoplasia II (PIN II)
       Excludes1   prostatic intraepithelial neoplasia III (PIN III) (D07.5)
  N42.32 Atypical small acinar proliferation of prostate ♂
  N42.39 Other dysplasia of prostate ♂

● **N42.8 Other specified disorders of prostate**
  N42.81 Prostatodynia syndrome ♂   A
       Painful prostate syndrome
  N42.82 Prostatosis syndrome ♂   A
  N42.83 Cyst of prostate ♂   A
  N42.89 Other specified disorders of prostate ♂   A

  N42.9 Disorder of prostate, unspecified ♂   A

● **N43 Hydrocele and spermatocele**
    Includes   hydrocele of spermatic cord, testis or tunica vaginalis
    Excludes1   congenital hydrocele (P83.5)
  N43.0 Encysted hydrocele ♂
  N43.1 Infected hydrocele ♂
       Use additional code (B95-B97), to identify infectious agent
  N43.2 Other hydrocele ♂
  N43.3 Hydrocele, unspecified ♂
● **N43.4 Spermatocele of epididymis ♂**
       Spermatic cyst
  N43.40 Spermatocele of epididymis, unspecified ♂
  N43.41 Spermatocele of epididymis, single ♂
  N43.42 Spermatocele of epididymis, multiple ♂

Item 14-7 Hydrocele is a sac of fluid accumulating in the testes membrane.

Figure 14-7 A. Hydrocele. **B.** Newborn with large right hydrocele. (**B** from Nelson WE, Kliegman R: Nelson Textbook of Pediatrics, Philadelphia, Saunders Elsevier, 2011)

▶ New   ⟹ Revised   ~~deleted~~ Deleted   Excludes 1   Excludes 2   Includes   Use additional   Code first   Code also   Key words

OGCR Official Guidelines   X Assign placeholder X   ● Use Additional Character(s)   ▷ Manifestation Code   🄗 Hierarchical Condition Category   Coding Clinic

CHAPTER 14 (N00-N99)

● N44 Noninflammatory disorders of testis
    ● N44.0 Torsion of testis
        N44.00 Torsion of testis, unspecified ♂
        N44.01 Extravaginal torsion of spermatic cord ♂
        N44.02 Intravaginal torsion of spermatic cord ♂
            Torsion of spermatic cord NOS
        N44.03 Torsion of appendix testis ♂
        N44.04 Torsion of appendix epididymis ♂
    N44.1 Cyst of tunica albuginea testis ♂
    N44.2 Benign cyst of testis ♂
    N44.8 Other noninflammatory disorders of the testis ♂

● N45 Orchitis and epididymitis
    *Orchitis is inflammation of one or both of the testes as a result of mumps or other infection, trauma, or metastasis. **Epididymitis** is inflammation of the tubular structure that connects the testicle with the vas deferens.*
    Use additional code (B95-B97), to identify infectious agent
    N45.1 Epididymitis ♂
    N45.2 Orchitis ♂
    N45.3 Epididymo-orchitis ♂
    N45.4 Abscess of epididymis or testis ♂

● N46 Male infertility
    Excludes1 vasectomy status (Z98.52)
    ● N46.0 Azoospermia
        Absolute male infertility
        Male infertility due to germinal (cell) aplasia
        Male infertility due to spermatogenic arrest (complete)
        N46.01 Organic azoospermia ♂   A
            Azoospermia NOS
      ● N46.02 Azoospermia due to extratesticular causes
            Code also associated cause
        N46.021 Azoospermia due to drug therapy ♂ A
        N46.022 Azoospermia due to infection ♂ A
        N46.023 Azoospermia due to obstruction of efferent ducts ♂ A
        N46.024 Azoospermia due to radiation ♂ A
        N46.025 Azoospermia due to systemic disease ♂ A
        N46.029 Azoospermia due to other extratesticular causes ♂ A
    ● N46.1 Oligospermia
        Male infertility due to germinal cell desquamation
        Male infertility due to hypospermatogenesis
        Male infertility due to incomplete spermatogenic arrest
        N46.11 Organic oligospermia ♂   A
            Oligospermia NOS
      ● N46.12 Oligospermia due to extratesticular causes
            Code also associated cause
        N46.121 Oligospermia due to drug therapy ♂ A
        N46.122 Oligospermia due to infection ♂ A
        N46.123 Oligospermia due to obstruction of efferent ducts ♂ A
        N46.124 Oligospermia due to radiation ♂ A
        N46.125 Oligospermia due to systemic disease ♂ A
        N46.129 Oligospermia due to other extratesticular causes ♂ A
    N46.8 Other male infertility ♂ A
    N46.9 Male infertility, unspecified ♂ A

● N47 Disorders of prepuce
    N47.0 Adherent prepuce, newborn ♂   N
    N47.1 Phimosis ♂
    N47.2 Paraphimosis ♂
    N47.3 Deficient foreskin ♂
    N47.4 Benign cyst of prepuce ♂
    N47.5 Adhesions of prepuce and glans penis ♂
    N47.6 Balanoposthitis ♂
        Use additional code (B95-B97), to identify infectious agent
        Excludes1 balanitis (N48.1)
    N47.7 Other inflammatory diseases of prepuce ♂
        Use additional code (B95-B97), to identify infectious agent
    N47.8 Other disorders of prepuce ♂

● N48 Other disorders of penis
    N48.0 Leukoplakia of penis ♂
        Balanitis xerotica obliterans
        Kraurosis of penis
        Lichen sclerosus of external male genital organs
        Excludes1 carcinoma in situ of penis (D07.4)
    N48.1 Balanitis ♂
        Use additional code (B95-B97), to identify infectious agent
        Excludes1 amebic balanitis (A06.8)
            balanitis xerotica obliterans (N48.0)
            candidal balanitis (B37.42)
            gonococcal balanitis (A54.23)
            herpesviral [herpes simplex] balanitis (A60.01)
    ● N48.2 Other inflammatory disorders of penis
        Use additional code (B95-B97), to identify infectious agent
        Excludes1 balanitis (N48.1)
            balanitis xerotica obliterans (N48.0)
            balanoposthitis (N47.6)
        N48.21 Abscess of corpus cavernosum and penis ♂
        N48.22 Cellulitis of corpus cavernosum and penis ♂
        N48.29 Other inflammatory disorders of penis ♂
    ● N48.3 Priapism
        Painful erection
        Code first underlying cause
        N48.30 Priapism, unspecified ♂
        N48.31 Priapism due to trauma ♂
        N48.32 Priapism due to disease classified elsewhere ♂
        N48.33 Priapism, drug-induced ♂
        N48.39 Other priapism ♂
    N48.5 Ulcer of penis ♂
    N48.6 Induration penis plastica ♂
        Peyronie's disease
        Plastic induration of penis
    ● N48.8 Other specified disorders of penis
        N48.81 Thrombosis of superficial vein of penis ♂
        N48.82 Acquired torsion of penis ♂
            Acquired torsion of penis NOS
            Excludes1 congenital torsion of penis (Q55.63)
        N48.83 Acquired buried penis ♂
            Excludes1 congenital hidden penis (Q55.64)
        N48.89 Other specified disorders of penis ♂
    N48.9 Disorder of penis, unspecified ♂

Item 14–8 Male infertility is the inability of the female sex partner to conceive after one year of unprotected intercourse.
    Azoospermia is no sperm ejaculated and **oligospermia** is few sperm ejaculated—both resulting in infertility. Extratesticular causes such as injury, infections, radiation, and chemotherapy may also cause male infertility.

CHAPTER 14 (N00-N99)

● **N49　Inflammatory disorders of male genital organs, not elsewhere classified**

Use additional code (B95-B97), to identify infectious agent

Excludes1　inflammation of penis (N48.1, N48.2-)
orchitis and epididymitis (N45.-)

N49.0　Inflammatory disorders of seminal vesicle ♂
Vesiculitis NOS

N49.1　Inflammatory disorders of spermatic cord, tunica vaginalis and vas deferens ♂
Vasitis

N49.2　Inflammatory disorders of scrotum ♂

N49.3　Fournier gangrene ♂

N49.8　Inflammatory disorders of other specified male genital organs ♂
Inflammation of multiple sites in male genital organs

N49.9　Inflammatory disorder of unspecified male genital organ ♂
Abscess of unspecified male genital organ
Boil of unspecified male genital organ
Carbuncle of unspecified male genital organ
Cellulitis of unspecified male genital organ

● **N50　Other and unspecified disorders of male genital organs**

Excludes2　torsion of testis (N44.0-)

N50.0　Atrophy of testis ♂

N50.1　Vascular disorders of male genital organs ♂
Hematocele, NOS, of male genital organs
Hemorrhage of male genital organs
Thrombosis of male genital organs

N50.3　Cyst of epididymis ♂

● **N50.8　Other specified disorders of male genital organs**
Coding Clinic: 2016, Q4, P45

● **N50.81　Testicular pain**

　　　N50.811　Right testicular pain ♂
　　　N50.812　Left testicular pain ♂
　　　N50.819　Testicular pain, unspecified ♂

N50.82　Scrotal pain ♂

N50.89　Other specified disorders of the male genital organs ♂
Atrophy of scrotum, seminal vesicle, spermatic cord, tunica vaginalis and vas deferens
Chylocele, tunica vaginalis (nonfilarial) NOS
Edema of scrotum, seminal vesicle, spermatic cord, tunica vaginalis and vas deferens
Hypertrophy of scrotum, seminal vesicle, spermatic cord, tunica vaginalis and vas deferens
Stricture of spermatic cord, tunica vaginalis, and vas deferens
Ulcer of scrotum, seminal vesicle, spermatic cord, testis, tunica vaginalis and vas deferens
Urethroscrotal fistula

N50.9　Disorder of male genital organs, unspecified ♂

▶ **N51　Disorders of male genital organs in diseases classified elsewhere** ♂

Code first underlying disease, such as:
filariasis (B74.0-B74.9)

Excludes1　amebic balanitis (A06.8)
candidal balanitis (B37.42)
gonococcal balanitis (A54.23)
gonococcal prostatitis (A54.22)
herpesviral [herpes simplex] balanitis (A60.01)
trichomonal prostatitis (A59.02)
tuberculous prostatitis (A18.14)

Item 14–9 Seminal vesiculitis is an inflammation of the seminal vesicle. **Spermatocele** is a benign cystic accumulation of sperm arising from the head of the epididymis. **Torsion of the testis** is a medical emergency occurring most commonly in boys 7 to 12 years of age and results from a congenital abnormality of the covering of the testis allowing the testis to twist within its sac and cutting off the blood supply to the testis.

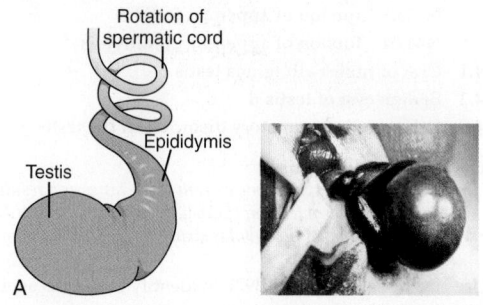

Figure 14-8　A. Torsion of testis. **B.** Torsion of the testis. (**B** from Kliegman R, Nelson WE: Nelson Textbook of Pediatrics, Philadelphia, Saunders, 2007)

● **N52　Male erectile dysfunction**

Excludes1　psychogenic impotence (F52.21)

● **N52.0　Vasculogenic erectile dysfunction**

N52.01　Erectile dysfunction due to arterial insufficiency ♂　　　　　A
N52.02　Corporo-venous occlusive erectile dysfunction ♂　　　　　A
N52.03　Combined arterial insufficiency and corporo-venous occlusive erectile dysfunction ♂　　　　　A

▶ **N52.1　Erectile dysfunction due to diseases classified elsewhere** ♂　　　　　A
Code first underlying disease

N52.2　Drug-induced erectile dysfunction ♂　　　　　A

● **N52.3　Postprocedural erectile dysfunction**

N52.31　Erectile dysfunction following radical prostatectomy ♂　　　　　A
N52.32　Erectile dysfunction following radical cystectomy ♂　　　　　A
N52.33　Erectile dysfunction following urethral surgery ♂　　　　　A
N52.34　Erectile dysfunction following simple prostatectomy ♂　　　　　A
N52.35　Erectile dysfunction following radiation therapy ♂　　　　　A
Coding Clinic: 2016, Q4, P45
N52.36　Erectile dysfunction following interstitial seed therapy ♂　　　　　A
Coding Clinic: 2016, Q4, P45
N52.37　Erectile dysfunction following prostate ablative therapy ♂　　　　　A
Erectile dysfunction following cryotherapy
Erectile dysfunction following other prostate ablative therapies
Erectile dysfunction following ultrasound ablative therapies
Coding Clinic: 2016, Q4, P45
N52.39　Other and unspecified postprocedural erectile dysfunction ♂　　　　　A

N52.8　Other male erectile dysfunction ♂　　　　　A

N52.9　Male erectile dysfunction, unspecified ♂　　　　　A
Impotence NOS

▶ New　⇒ Revised　deleted Deleted　Excludes 1　Excludes 2　Includes　Use additional　Code first　Code also　Key words
OGCR Official Guidelines　X Assign placeholder X　● Use Additional Character(s)　▶ Manifestation Code　🄗 Hierarchical Condition Category　Coding Clinic

● **N53　Other male sexual dysfunction**

　　Excludes1　psychogenic sexual dysfunction (F52.-)

　● **N53.1　Ejaculatory dysfunction**

　　　Excludes1　premature ejaculation (F52.4)

　　　N53.11　**Retarded ejaculation** ♂

　　　N53.12　**Painful ejaculation** ♂

　　　N53.13　**Anejaculatory orgasm** ♂

　　　N53.14　**Retrograde ejaculation** ♂

　　　N53.19　**Other ejaculatory dysfunction** ♂
　　　　　　　Ejaculatory dysfunction NOS

　　N53.8　**Other male sexual dysfunction** ♂

　　N53.9　**Unspecified male sexual dysfunction** ♂

DISORDERS OF BREAST (N60-N65)

　　Excludes1　disorders of breast associated with childbirth
　　　　　　　(O91-O92)

● **N60　Benign mammary dysplasia**
　　　Benign lumpiness of breast

　　Includes　fibrocystic mastopathy

　● **N60.0　Solitary cyst of breast**
　　　　Cyst of breast

　　　N60.01　**Solitary cyst of right breast**

　　　N60.02　**Solitary cyst of left breast**

　　　N60.09　**Solitary cyst of unspecified breast**

　● **N60.1　Diffuse cystic mastopathy**
　　　　Cystic breast
　　　　Fibrocystic disease of breast

　　　Excludes1　diffuse cystic mastopathy with epithelial
　　　　　　　proliferation (N60.3-)

　　　N60.11　**Diffuse cystic mastopathy of right breast**　　A

　　　N60.12　**Diffuse cystic mastopathy of left breast**　　A

　　　N60.19　**Diffuse cystic mastopathy of unspecified
　　　　　　　breast**　　A

　● **N60.2　Fibroadenosis of breast**
　　　　Adenofibrosis of breast

　　　Excludes2　fibroadenoma of breast (D24.-)

　　　N60.21　**Fibroadenosis of right breast**

　　　N60.22　**Fibroadenosis of left breast**

　　　N60.29　**Fibroadenosis of unspecified breast**

　● **N60.3　Fibrosclerosis of breast**
　　　　Cystic mastopathy with epithelial proliferation

　　　N60.31　**Fibrosclerosis of right breast**

　　　N60.32　**Fibrosclerosis of left breast**

　　　N60.39　**Fibrosclerosis of unspecified breast**

　● **N60.4　Mammary duct ectasia**

　　　N60.41　**Mammary duct ectasia of right breast**

　　　N60.42　**Mammary duct ectasia of left breast**

　　　N60.49　**Mammary duct ectasia of unspecified breast**

　● **N60.8　Other benign mammary dysplasias**

　　　N60.81　**Other benign mammary dysplasias of right
　　　　　　　breast**

　　　N60.82　**Other benign mammary dysplasias of left breast**

　　　N60.89　**Other benign mammary dysplasias of
　　　　　　　unspecified breast**

　● **N60.9　Unspecified benign mammary dysplasia**

　　　N60.91　**Unspecified benign mammary dysplasia of
　　　　　　　right breast**

　　　N60.92　**Unspecified benign mammary dysplasia of left
　　　　　　　breast**

　　　N60.99　**Unspecified benign mammary dysplasia of
　　　　　　　unspecified breast**

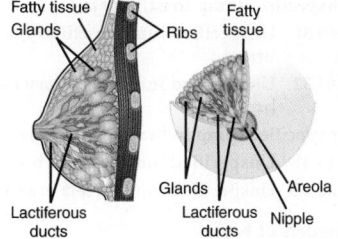

Figure 14-9　Breast.

● **N61　Inflammatory disorders of breast**

　　Excludes1　inflammatory carcinoma of breast (C50.9)
　　　　　　　inflammatory disorder of breast associated with
　　　　　　　　childbirth (O91.-)
　　　　　　　neonatal infective mastitis (P39.0)
　　　　　　　thrombophlebitis of breast [Mondor's disease]
　　　　　　　　(I80.8)

　　N61.0　**Mastitis without abscess**
　　　　Infective mastitis (acute) (nonpuerperal) (subacute)
　　　　Mastitis (acute) (nonpuerperal) (subacute) NOS
　　　　Cellulitis (acute) (nonpuerperal) (subacute) of breast NOS
　　　　Cellulitis (acute) (nonpuerperal) (subacute) of nipple NOS

　　N61.1　**Abscess of the breast and nipple**
　　　　Abscess (acute) (chronic) (nonpuerperal) of areola
　　　　Abscess (acute) (chronic) (nonpuerperal) of breast
　　　　Carbuncle of breast
　　　　Mastitis with abscess

　▶● **N61.2　Granulomatous mastitis**

　　　▶ N61.20　**Granulomatous mastitis, unspecified breast**

　　　▶ N61.21　**Granulomatous mastitis, right breast**

　　　▶ N61.22　**Granulomatous mastitis, left breast**

　　　▶ N61.23　**Granulomatous mastitis, bilateral breast**

　N62　**Hypertrophy of breast**
　　　　Gynecomastia
　　　　Hypertrophy of breast NOS
　　　　Massive pubertal hypertrophy of breast

　　　Excludes1　breast engorgement of newborn (P83.4)
　　　　　　　disproportion of reconstructed breast (N65.1)

● **N63　Unspecified lump in breast**
　　　Nodule(s) NOS in breast

　　N63.0　**Unspecified lump in unspecified breast**

　● **N63.1　Unspecified lump in the right breast**

　　　N63.10　**Unspecified lump in the right breast,
　　　　　　　unspecified quadrant**

　　　N63.11　**Unspecified lump in the right breast, upper
　　　　　　　outer quadrant**
　　　　　　　Coding Clinic: 2017, Q4, P19

　　　N63.12　**Unspecified lump in the right breast, upper
　　　　　　　inner quadrant**

　　　N63.13　**Unspecified lump in the right breast, lower
　　　　　　　outer quadrant**

　　　N63.14　**Unspecified lump in the right breast, lower
　　　　　　　inner quadrant**

　　　N63.15　**Unspecified lump in the right breast,
　　　　　　　overlapping quadrants**

　● **N63.2　Unspecified lump in the left breast**

　　　N63.20　**Unspecified lump in the left breast, unspecified
　　　　　　　quadrant**

　　　N63.21　**Unspecified lump in the left breast, upper outer
　　　　　　　quadrant**

　　　N63.22　**Unspecified lump in the left breast, upper inner
　　　　　　　quadrant**

　　　N63.23　**Unspecified lump in the left breast, lower outer
　　　　　　　quadrant**

　　　N63.24　**Unspecified lump in the left breast, lower inner
　　　　　　　quadrant**

　　　N63.25　**Unspecified lump in the left breast, overlapping
　　　　　　　quadrants**

CHAPTER 14 (N00-N99)

● **N63.3**   Unspecified lump in axillary tail
    N63.31   Unspecified lump in axillary tail of the right breast
    N63.32   Unspecified lump in axillary tail of the left breast

● **N63.4**   Unspecified lump in breast, subareolar
    N63.41   Unspecified lump in right breast, subareolar
    N63.42   Unspecified lump in left breast, subareolar

● **N64**   **Other disorders of breast**
    Excludes2   mechanical complication of breast prosthesis and implant (T85.4-)

N64.0   **Fissure and fistula of nipple**

N64.1   **Fat necrosis of breast**
    Fat necrosis (segmental) of breast
    Code first breast necrosis due to breast graft (T85.898)

N64.2   **Atrophy of breast**

N64.3   **Galactorrhea not associated with childbirth**
    Excessive or spontaneous flow of milk

N64.4   **Mastodynia**

● **N64.5**   **Other signs and symptoms in breast**
    Excludes2   abnormal findings on diagnostic imaging of breast (R92.-)
    N64.51   **Induration of breast**
    N64.52   **Nipple discharge**
       Excludes1   abnormal findings in nipple discharge (R89.-)
    N64.53   **Retraction of nipple**
    N64.59   **Other signs and symptoms in breast**

● **N64.8**   **Other specified disorders of breast**
    N64.81   **Ptosis of breast**   A
       Excludes1   ptosis of native breast in relation to reconstructed breast (N65.1)
    N64.82   **Hypoplasia of breast**   A
       Micromastia
       Excludes1   congenital absence of breast (Q83.0)
           hypoplasia of native breast in relation to reconstructed breast (N65.1)
    N64.89   **Other specified disorders of breast**
       Galactocele
       Subinvolution of breast (postlactational)
       Coding Clinic: 2019, Q1, P32; 2018, Q1, P4

N64.9   **Disorder of breast, unspecified**
    Coding Clinic: 2018, Q1, P4

● **N65**   **Deformity and disproportion of reconstructed breast**
    N65.0   **Deformity of reconstructed breast**   A
       Contour irregularity in reconstructed breast
       Excess tissue in reconstructed breast
       Misshapen reconstructed breast
    N65.1   **Disproportion of reconstructed breast**   A
       Breast asymmetry between native breast and reconstructed breast
       Disproportion between native breast and reconstructed breast

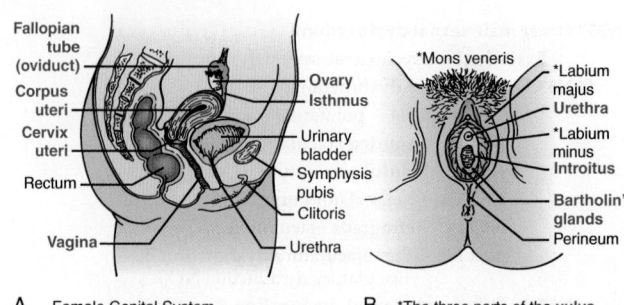

Figure 14-10   **A.** Female genital system. **B.** External female genital system. (From Buck CJ: Step-by-Step Medical Coding, ed 2016, St. Louis, Elsevier, 2016)

Item 14-10   **Salpingitis** is an infection of one or both fallopian tubes. **Oophoritis** is an infection of one or both ovaries.

INFLAMMATORY DISEASES OF FEMALE PELVIC ORGANS (N70-N77)

    Excludes1   inflammatory diseases of female pelvic organs complicating:
       abortion or ectopic or molar pregnancy (O00-O07, O08.0)
       pregnancy, childbirth and the puerperium (O23.-, O75.3, O85, O86.-)

★**(See Plate 35 of the Anatomy Illustrations.)**

● **N70**   **Salpingitis and oophoritis**
    Oophoritis = inflammation of ovary
    Salpingitis = inflammation of falloplan tube
    Includes   abscess (of) fallopian tube
       abscess (of) ovary
       pyosalpinx
       salpingo-oophoritis
       tubo-ovarian abscess
       tubo-ovarian inflammatory disease
    Use additional code (B95-B97), to identify infectious agent
    Excludes1   gonococcal infection (A54.24)
       tuberculous infection (A18.17)

● **N70.0**   **Acute salpingitis and oophoritis**
    N70.01   Acute salpingitis ♀
    N70.02   Acute oophoritis ♀
    N70.03   Acute salpingitis and oophoritis ♀

● **N70.1**   **Chronic salpingitis and oophoritis**
    Hydrosalpinx
    N70.11   Chronic salpingitis ♀
    N70.12   Chronic oophoritis ♀
    N70.13   Chronic salpingitis and oophoritis ♀

● **N70.9**   **Salpingitis and oophoritis, unspecified**
    N70.91   Salpingitis, unspecified ♀
    N70.92   Oophoritis, unspecified ♀
    N70.93   Salpingitis and oophoritis, unspecified ♀

● **N71 Inflammatory disease of uterus, except cervix**
  Includes   endo (myo) metritis
                  metritis
                  myometritis
                  pyometra
                  uterine abscess
  Use additional code (B95-B97), to identify infectious agent
  Excludes1   hyperplastic endometritis (N85.0-)
                  infection of uterus following delivery (O85, O86.-)
  N71.0 Acute inflammatory disease of uterus ♀
  N71.1 Chronic inflammatory disease of uterus ♀
  N71.9 Inflammatory disease of uterus, unspecified ♀

N72 Inflammatory disease of cervix uteri ♀
  Includes   cervicitis (with or without erosion or ectropion)
                  endocervicitis (with or without erosion or
                      ectropion)
                  exocervicitis (with or without erosion or ectropion)
  Use additional code (B95-B97), to identify infectious agent
  Excludes1   erosion and ectropion of cervix without cervicitis
                  (N86)

● **N73 Other female pelvic inflammatory diseases**
  Use additional code (B95-B97), to identify infectious agent
  N73.0 Acute parametritis and pelvic cellulitis ♀
          Abscess of broad ligament
          Abscess of parametrium
          Pelvic cellulitis, female
  N73.1 Chronic parametritis and pelvic cellulitis ♀
          Any condition in N73.0 specified as chronic
          Excludes1   tuberculous parametritis and pelvic
                          cellultis (A18.17)
  N73.2 Unspecified parametritis and pelvic cellulitis ♀
          Any condition in N73.0 unspecified whether acute or
          chronic
  N73.3 Female acute pelvic peritonitis ♀
  N73.4 Female chronic pelvic peritonitis ♀
          Excludes1   tuberculous pelvic (female) peritonitis
                          (A18.17)
  N73.5 Female pelvic peritonitis, unspecified ♀
  N73.6 Female pelvic peritoneal adhesions (postinfective) ♀
          Excludes2   postprocedural pelvic peritoneal
                          adhesions (N99.4)
  N73.8 Other specified female pelvic inflammatory diseases ♀
  N73.9 Female pelvic inflammatory disease, unspecified ♀
          Female pelvic infection or inflammation NOS

▸ **N74 Female pelvic inflammatory disorders in diseases classified
      elsewhere** ♀
      Code first underlying disease
      Excludes1   chlamydial cervicitis (A56.02)
                      chlamydial pelvic inflammatory disease (A56.11)
                      gonococcal cervicitis (A54.03)
                      gonococcal pelvic inflammatory disease (A54.24)
                      herpesviral [herpes simplex] cervicitis (A60.03)
                      herpesviral [herpes simplex] pelvic inflammatory
                          disease (A60.09)
                      syphilitic cervicitis (A52.76)
                      syphilitic pelvic inflammatory disease (A52.76)
                      trichomonal cervicitis (A59.09)
                      tuberculous cervicitis (A18.16)
                      tuberculous pelvic inflammatory disease (A18.17)

● **N75 Diseases of Bartholin's gland**
  N75.0 Cyst of Bartholin's gland ♀
          Cysts filled with liquid or semisolid material
  N75.1 Abscess of Bartholin's gland ♀
          Localized collection of pus
  N75.8 Other diseases of Bartholin's gland ♀
          Bartholinitis
  N75.9 Disease of Bartholin's gland, unspecified ♀

● **N76 Other inflammation of vagina and vulva**
      Use additional code (B95-B97), to identify infectious agent
      Excludes2   senile (atrophic) vaginitis (N95.2)
                      vulvar vestibulitis (N94.810)
  N76.0 Acute vaginitis ♀
          Acute vulvovaginitis
          Vaginitis NOS
          Vulvovaginitis NOS
  N76.1 Subacute and chronic vaginitis ♀
          Chronic vulvovaginitis
          Subacute vulvovaginitis
  N76.2 Acute vulvitis ♀
          Vulvitis NOS
  N76.3 Subacute and chronic vulvitis ♀
  N76.4 Abscess of vulva ♀
          Furuncle of vulva
  N76.5 Ulceration of vagina ♀
  N76.6 Ulceration of vulva ♀
  ● **N76.8 Other specified inflammation of vagina and vulva**
      N76.81 Mucositis (ulcerative) of vagina and vulva ♀
              Code also type of associated therapy, such as:
                  antineoplastic and immunosuppressive
                      drugs (T45.1X-)
                  radiological procedure and radiotherapy
                      (Y84.2)
              Excludes2   gastrointestinal mucositis
                              (ulcerative) (K92.81)
                              nasal mucositis (ulcerative)
                              (J34.81)
                              oral mucositis (ulcerative) (K12.3-)
      **N76.89 Other specified inflammation of vagina and
              vulva** ♀

● **N77 Vulvovaginal ulceration and inflammation in diseases classified
      elsewhere**
  ▸ **N77.0 Ulceration of vulva in diseases classified elsewhere** ♀
          Code first underlying disease, such as:
              Behçet's disease (M35.2)
          Excludes1   ulceration of vulva in gonococcal
                              infection (A54.02)
                          ulceration of vulva in herpesviral [herpes
                              simplex] infection (A60.04)
                          ulceration of vulva in syphilis (A51.0)
                          ulceration of vulva in tuberculosis (A18.18)
  ▸ **N77.1 Vaginitis, vulvitis and vulvovaginitis in diseases
          classified elsewhere** ♀
          Code first underlying disease, such as:
              pinworm (B80)
          Excludes1   candidial vulvovaginitis (B37.3)
                          chlamydial vulvovaginitis (A56.02)
                          gonococcal vulvovaginitis (A54.02)
                          herpesviral [herpes simplex]
                              vulvovaginitis (A60.04)
                          trichomonal vulvovaginitis (A59.01)
                          tuberculous vulvovaginitis (A18.18)
                          vulvovaginitis in early syphilis (A51.0)
                          vulvovaginitis in late syphilis (A52.76)

CHAPTER 14 (N00-N99)

Item 14–11 Endometriosis is a condition for which no clear cause has been identified. Endometrial tissue is expelled from the uterus into the abdominal cavity and can implant onto a variety of organs. Classification is based on the site of implant of the endometrial tissue.

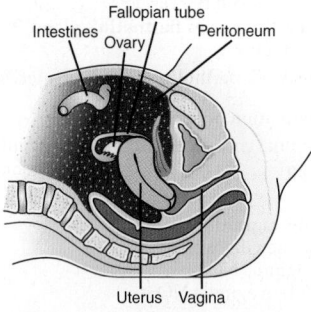

Fallopian tube
Intestines   Ovary   Peritoneum

Uterus   Vagina

Figure 14-11   Sites of potential endometrial implants.

NONINFLAMMATORY DISORDERS OF FEMALE GENITAL TRACT (N80-N98)

● **N80**   **Endometriosis**
    N80.0   **Endometriosis of uterus** ♀
       Adenomyosis
       Excludes1   stromal endometriosis (D39.0)
    N80.1   **Endometriosis of ovary** ♀
    N80.2   **Endometriosis of fallopian tube** ♀
    N80.3   **Endometriosis of pelvic peritoneum** ♀
    N80.4   **Endometriosis of rectovaginal septum and vagina** ♀
    N80.5   **Endometriosis of intestine** ♀
    N80.6   **Endometriosis in cutaneous scar** ♀
    N80.8   **Other endometriosis** ♀
       Endometriosis of thorax
    N80.9   **Endometriosis, unspecified** ♀

● **N81**   **Female genital prolapse**
    Excludes1   genital prolapse complicating pregnancy, labor or delivery (O34.5-)
          prolapse and hernia of ovary and fallopian tube (N83.4-)
          prolapse of vaginal vault after hysterectomy (N99.3)
    N81.0   **Urethrocele** ♀
       Excludes1   urethrocele with cystocele (N81.1-)
          urethrocele with prolapse of uterus (N81.2-N81.4)
   ● **N81.1**   **Cystocele**
       Cystocele with urethrocele
       Cystourethrocele
       Excludes1   cystocele with prolapse of uterus (N81.2-N81.4)
      N81.10   **Cystocele, unspecified** ♀
         Prolapse of (anterior) vaginal wall NOS
      N81.11   **Cystocele, midline** ♀
      N81.12   **Cystocele, lateral** ♀
         Paravaginal cystocele

A   B   C

Figure 14-12   Three stages of uterine prolapse. **A.** Uterus is prolapsed. **B.** Vagina and uterus are prolapsed (incomplete uterovaginal prolapse). **C.** Vagina and uterus are completely prolapsed and are exposed through the external genitalia (complete uterovaginal prolapse).

    N81.2   **Incomplete uterovaginal prolapse** ♀
       First degree uterine prolapse
       Prolapse of cervix NOS
       Second degree uterine prolapse
       Excludes1   cervical stump prolapse (N81.85)
    N81.3   **Complete uterovaginal prolapse** ♀
       Procidentia (uteri) NOS
       Third degree uterine prolapse
    N81.4   **Uterovaginal prolapse, unspecified** ♀
       Prolapse of uterus NOS
    N81.5   **Vaginal enterocele** ♀
       Excludes1   enterocele with prolapse of uterus (N81.2-N81.4)
    N81.6   **Rectocele** ♀
       Prolapse of posterior vaginal wall
       Use additional code for any associated fecal incontinence, if applicable (R15.-)
       Excludes2   perineocele (N81.81)
          rectal prolapse (K62.3)
          rectocele with prolapse of uterus (N81.2-N81.4)
   ● **N81.8**   **Other female genital prolapse**
      N81.81   **Perineocele** ♀
      N81.82   **Incompetence or weakening of pubocervical tissue** ♀
      N81.83   **Incompetence or weakening of rectovaginal tissue** ♀
      N81.84   **Pelvic muscle wasting** ♀
         Disuse atrophy of pelvic muscles and anal sphincter
      N81.85   **Cervical stump prolapse** ♀
      N81.89   **Other female genital prolapse** ♀
         Deficient perineum
         Old laceration of muscles of pelvic floor
    N81.9   **Female genital prolapse, unspecified** ♀

● **N82**   **Fistulae involving female genital tract**
    Excludes1   vesicointestinal fistulae (N32.1)
    N82.0   **Vesicovaginal fistula** ♀
    N82.1   **Other female urinary-genital tract fistulae** ♀
       Cervicovesical fistula
       Ureterovaginal fistula
       Urethrovaginal fistula
       Uteroureteric fistula
       Uterovesical fistula
       Coding Clinic: 2017, Q3, P4
    N82.2   **Fistula of vagina to small intestine** ♀
    N82.3   **Fistula of vagina to large intestine** ♀
       Rectovaginal fistula
    N82.4   **Other female intestinal-genital tract fistulae** ♀
       Intestinouterine fistula
    N82.5   **Female genital tract-skin fistulae** ♀
       Uterus to abdominal wall fistula
       Vaginoperineal fistula
    N82.8   **Other female genital tract fistulae** ♀
    N82.9   **Female genital tract fistula, unspecified** ♀

● **N83**   **Noninflammatory disorders of ovary, fallopian tube and broad ligament**
    Excludes2   hydrosalpinx (N70.1-)
   ● **N83.0**   **Follicular cyst of ovary**
       Cyst of graafian follicle
       Hemorrhagic follicular cyst (of ovary)
       Coding Clinic: 2016, Q4, P46
      N83.00   **Follicular cyst of ovary, unspecified side** ♀
      N83.01   **Follicular cyst of right ovary** ♀
      N83.02   **Follicular cyst of left ovary** ♀

▶ New   ⟩ Revised   ~~deleted~~ Deleted   Excludes 1   Excludes 2   Includes   Use additional   Code first   Code also   Key words

OGCR Official Guidelines   X Assign placeholder X   ● Use Additional Character(s)   ⟩ Manifestation Code   🄷🄲 Hierarchical Condition Category   **Coding Clinic**

● **N83.1**   **Corpus luteum cyst**
     Hemorrhagic corpus luteum cyst
     Coding Clinic: 2016, Q4, P46

     N83.10   **Corpus luteum cyst of ovary, unspecified side** ♀
     N83.11   **Corpus luteum cyst of right ovary** ♀
     N83.12   **Corpus luteum cyst of left ovary** ♀

● **N83.2**   **Other and unspecified ovarian cysts**
     Excludes1   developmental ovarian cyst (Q50.1)
               neoplastic ovarian cyst (D27.-)
               polycystic ovarian syndrome (E28.2)
               Stein-Leventhal syndrome (E28.2)
     Coding Clinic: 2016, Q4, P46

    ● **N83.20**   **Unspecified ovarian cysts**
        N83.201   **Unspecified ovarian cyst, right side** ♀
        N83.202   **Unspecified ovarian cyst, left side** ♀
        N83.209   **Unspecified ovarian cyst, unspecified side** ♀
            Ovarian cyst, NOS

    ● **N83.29**   **Other ovarian cysts**
            Retention cyst of ovary
            Simple cyst of ovary
        N83.291   **Other ovarian cyst, right side** ♀
        N83.292   **Other ovarian cyst, left side** ♀
        N83.299   **Other ovarian cyst, unspecified side** ♀

● **N83.3**   **Acquired atrophy of ovary and fallopian tube**
     Coding Clinic: 2016, Q4, P46

    ● **N83.31**   **Acquired atrophy of ovary**
        N83.311   **Acquired atrophy of right ovary** ♀
        N83.312   **Acquired atrophy of left ovary** ♀
        N83.319   **Acquired atrophy of ovary, unspecified side** ♀
            Acquired atrophy of ovary, NOS

    ● **N83.32**   **Acquired atrophy of fallopian tube**
        N83.321   **Acquired atrophy of right fallopian tube** ♀
        N83.322   **Acquired atrophy of left fallopian tube** ♀
        N83.329   **Acquired atrophy of fallopian tube, unspecified side** ♀
            Acquired atrophy of fallopian tube, NOS

    ● **N83.33**   **Acquired atrophy of ovary and fallopian tube**
        N83.331   **Acquired atrophy of right ovary and fallopian tube** ♀
        N83.332   **Acquired atrophy of left ovary and fallopian tube** ♀
        N83.339   **Acquired atrophy of ovary and fallopian tube, unspecified side** ♀
            Acquired atrophy of ovary and fallopian tube, NOS

● **N83.4**   **Prolapse and hernia of ovary and fallopian tube**
     Coding Clinic: 2016, Q4, P46

     N83.40   **Prolapse and hernia of ovary and fallopian tube, unspecified side** ♀
            Prolapse and hernia of ovary and fallopian tube, NOS
     N83.41   **Prolapse and hernia of right ovary and fallopian tube** ♀
     N83.42   **Prolapse and hernia of left ovary and fallopian tube** ♀

● **N83.5**   **Torsion of ovary, ovarian pedicle and fallopian tube**
     Torsion of accessory tube
     Coding Clinic: 2016, Q4, P46

    ● **N83.51**   **Torsion of ovary and ovarian pedicle**
        N83.511   **Torsion of right ovary and ovarian pedicle** ♀
        N83.512   **Torsion of left ovary and ovarian pedicle** ♀
        N83.519   **Torsion of ovary and ovarian pedicle, unspecified side** ♀
            Torsion of ovary and ovarian pedicle, NOS

● **N83.52**   **Torsion of fallopian tube**
     Torsion of hydatid of Morgagni
     N83.521   **Torsion of right fallopian tube** ♀
     N83.522   **Torsion of left fallopian tube** ♀
     N83.529   **Torsion of fallopian tube, unspecified side** ♀
            Torsion of fallopian tube, NOS

     N83.53   **Torsion of ovary, ovarian pedicle and fallopian tube** ♀

● **N83.6**   **Hematosalpinx** ♀
     Excludes1   hematosalpinx (with) (in):
               hematocolpos (N89.7)
               hematometra (N85.7)
               tubal pregnancy (O00.1-)

● **N83.7**   **Hematoma of broad ligament** ♀

● **N83.8**   **Other noninflammatory disorders of ovary, fallopian tube and broad ligament** ♀
     Broad ligament laceration syndrome [Allen-Masters]

● **N83.9**   **Noninflammatory disorder of ovary, fallopian tube and broad ligament, unspecified** ♀

● **N84**   **Polyp of female genital tract**
     Excludes1   adenomatous polyp (D28.-)
               placental polyp (O90.89)

     N84.0   **Polyp of corpus uteri** ♀
            Polyp of endometrium
            Polyp of uterus NOS
        Excludes1   polypoid endometrial hyperplasia (N85.0-)

     N84.1   **Polyp of cervix uteri** ♀
            Mucous polyp of cervix
     N84.2   **Polyp of vagina** ♀
     N84.3   **Polyp of vulva** ♀
            Polyp of labia
     N84.8   **Polyp of other parts of female genital tract** ♀
     N84.9   **Polyp of female genital tract, unspecified** ♀

● **N85**   **Other noninflammatory disorders of uterus, except cervix**
     Excludes1   endometriosis (N80.-)
               inflammatory diseases of uterus (N71.-)
               noninflammatory disorders of cervix, except malposition (N86-N88)
               polyp of corpus uteri (N84.0)
               uterine prolapse (N81.-)

    ● **N85.0**   **Endometrial hyperplasia**
        N85.00   **Endometrial hyperplasia, unspecified** ♀
            Hyperplasia (adenomatous) (cystic) (glandular) of endometrium
            Hyperplastic endometritis
        N85.01   **Benign endometrial hyperplasia** ♀
            Endometrial hyperplasia (complex) (simple) without atypia
        N85.02   **Endometrial intraepithelial neoplasia [EIN]** ♀
            Endometrial hyperplasia with atypia
            Excludes1   malignant neoplasm of endometrium (with endometrial intraepithelial neoplasia [EIN]) (C54.1)

     N85.2   **Hypertrophy of uterus** ♀
            Bulky or enlarged uterus
        Excludes1   puerperal hypertrophy of uterus (O90.89)
     N85.3   **Subinvolution of uterus** ♀
        Excludes1   puerperal subinvolution of uterus (O90.89)
     N85.4   **Malposition of uterus** ♀
            Anteversion of uterus
            Retroflexion of uterus
            Retroversion of uterus
        Excludes1   malposition of uterus complicating pregnancy, labor or delivery (O34.5-, O65.5)

CHAPTER 14 (N00-N99)

CHAPTER 14 (N00–N99)

N85.5　Inversion of uterus ♀
　　Excludes1　current obstetric trauma (O71.2)
　　　　　　　　postpartum inversion of uterus (O71.2)

N85.6　Intrauterine synechiae ♀

N85.7　Hematometra ♀
　　Hematosalpinx with hematometra
　　Excludes1　hematometra with hematocolpos (N89.7)

N85.8　Other specified noninflammatory disorders of uterus ♀
　　Atrophy of uterus, acquired
　　Fibrosis of uterus NOS

N85.9　Noninflammatory disorder of uterus, unspecified ♀
　　Disorder of uterus NOS

N86　Erosion and ectropion of cervix uteri ♀
　　Decubitus (trophic) ulcer of cervix
　　Eversion of cervix
　　Excludes1　erosion and ectropion of cervix with cervicitis
　　　　　　　　(N72)

● **N87　Dysplasia of cervix uteri**
　　Excludes1　abnormal results from cervical cytologic
　　　　　　　　examination without histologic confirmation
　　　　　　　　(R87.61-)
　　　　　　　　carcinoma in situ of cervix uteri (D06.-)
　　　　　　　　cervical intraepithelial neoplasia III [CIN III]
　　　　　　　　(D06.-)
　　　　　　　　HGSIL of cervix (R87.613)
　　　　　　　　severe dysplasia of cervix uteri (D06.-)

N87.0　Mild cervical dysplasia ♀
　　Cervical intraepithelial neoplasia I [CIN I]

N87.1　Moderate cervical dysplasia ♀
　　Cervical intraepithelial neoplasia II [CIN II]

N87.9　Dysplasia of cervix uteri, unspecified ♀
　　Anaplasia of cervix
　　Cervical atypism
　　Cervical dysplasia NOS

● **N88　Other noninflammatory disorders of cervix uteri**
　　Excludes2　inflammatory disease of cervix (N72)
　　　　　　　　polyp of cervix (N84.1)

N88.0　Leukoplakia of cervix uteri ♀

N88.1　Old laceration of cervix uteri ♀
　　Adhesions of cervix
　　Excludes1　current obstetric trauma (O71.3)

N88.2　Stricture and stenosis of cervix uteri ♀
　　Excludes1　stricture and stenosis of cervix uteri
　　　　　　　　complicating labor (O65.5)

N88.3　Incompetence of cervix uteri ♀
　　Investigation and management of (suspected) cervical
　　　　incompetence in a nonpregnant woman
　　Excludes1　cervical incompetence complicating
　　　　　　　　pregnancy (O34.3-)

N88.4　Hypertrophic elongation of cervix uteri ♀

**N88.8　Other specified noninflammatory disorders of cervix
　　uteri ♀**
　　Excludes1　current obstetric trauma (O71.3)

N88.9　Noninflammatory disorder of cervix uteri, unspecified ♀

● **N89　Other noninflammatory disorders of vagina**
　　Excludes1　abnormal results from vaginal cytologic
　　　　　　　　examination without histologic confirmation
　　　　　　　　(R87.62-)
　　　　　　　　carcinoma in situ of vagina (D07.2)
　　　　　　　　HGSIL of vagina (R87.623)
　　　　　　　　inflammation of vagina (N76.-)
　　　　　　　　senile (atrophic) vaginitis (N95.2)
　　　　　　　　severe dysplasia of vagina (D07.2)
　　　　　　　　trichomonal leukorrhea (A59.00)
　　　　　　　　vaginal intraepithelial neoplasia [VAIN], grade
　　　　　　　　III (D07.2)

N89.0　Mild vaginal dysplasia ♀
　　Vaginal intraepithelial neoplasia [VAIN], grade I

N89.1　Moderate vaginal dysplasia ♀
　　Vaginal intraepithelial neoplasia [VAIN], grade II

N89.3　Dysplasia of vagina, unspecified ♀

N89.4　Leukoplakia of vagina ♀

N89.5　Stricture and atresia of vagina ♀
　　Vaginal adhesions　　　Vaginal stenosis
　　Excludes1　congenital atresia or stricture (Q52.4)
　　　　　　　　postprocedural adhesions of vagina
　　　　　　　　(N99.2)

N89.6　Tight hymenal ring ♀
　　Rigid hymen　　　　　　Tight introitus
　　Excludes1　imperforate hymen (Q52.3)

N89.7　Hematocolpos ♀
　　Hematocolpos with hematometra or hematosalpinx
　　Coding Clinic: 2016, Q4, P59

N89.8　Other specified noninflammatory disorders of vagina ♀
　　Leukorrhea NOS
　　Old vaginal laceration
　　Pessary ulcer of vagina
　　Excludes1　current obstetric trauma (O70.-, O71.4,
　　　　　　　　O71.7-O71.8)
　　　　　　　　old laceration involving muscles of pelvic
　　　　　　　　floor (N81.8)

N89.9　Noninflammatory disorder of vagina, unspecified ♀

● **N90　Other noninflammatory disorders of vulva and perineum**
　　Excludes1　anogenital (venereal) warts (A63.0)
　　　　　　　　carcinoma in situ of vulva (D07.1)
　　　　　　　　condyloma acuminatum (A63.0)
　　　　　　　　current obstetric trauma (O70.-, O71.7-O71.8)
　　　　　　　　inflammation of vulva (N76.-)
　　　　　　　　severe dysplasia of vulva (D07.1)
　　　　　　　　vulvar intraepithelial neoplasm III [VIN III]
　　　　　　　　(D07.1)

N90.0　Mild vulvar dysplasia ♀
　　Vulvar intraepithelial neoplasia [VIN], grade I

N90.1　Moderate vulvar dysplasia ♀
　　Vulvar intraepithelial neoplasia [VIN], grade II

N90.3　Dysplasia of vulva, unspecified ♀

N90.4　Leukoplakia of vulva ♀
　　Dystrophy of vulva
　　Kraurosis of vulva
　　Lichen sclerosus of external female genital organs

N90.5　Atrophy of vulva ♀
　　Stenosis of vulva

● **N90.6　Hypertrophy of vulva**
　　Coding Clinic: 2016, Q4, P46

　　N90.60　Unspecified hypertrophy of vulva ♀
　　　　Unspecified hypertrophy of labia

　　**N90.61　Childhood asymmetric labium majus
　　　　enlargement ♀**
　　　　CALME

　　N90.69　Other specified hypertrophy of vulva ♀
　　　　Other specified hypertrophy of labia

N90.7　Vulvar cyst ♀

● **N90.8　Other specified noninflammatory disorders of vulva and
　　perineum**
　　● **N90.81　Female genital mutilation status**
　　　　Female genital cutting status

　　　　**N90.810　Female genital mutilation status,
　　　　　　unspecified ♀**
　　　　　　Female genital cutting status,
　　　　　　unspecified
　　　　　　Female genital mutilation status NOS

　　　　**N90.811　Female genital mutilation Type I
　　　　　　status ♀**
　　　　　　Clitorectomy status
　　　　　　Female genital cutting Type I status

　　　　**N90.812　Female genital mutilation Type II
　　　　　　status ♀**
　　　　　　Clitorectomy with excision of labia
　　　　　　minora status
　　　　　　Female genital cutting Type II status

▶ New　⇒ Revised　~~deleted~~ Deleted　Excludes 1　Excludes 2　Includes　Use additional　Code first　Code also　Key words
OGCR Official Guidelines　X Assign placeholder X　● Use Additional Character(s)　▶ Manifestation Code　🅗 Hierarchical Condition Category　**Coding Clinic**

N90.813   **Female genital mutilation Type III status** ♀
Female genital cutting Type III status
Infibulation status

N90.818   **Other female genital mutilation status** ♀
Female genital cutting Type IV status
Female genital mutilation Type IV status
Other female genital cutting status

N90.89   **Other specified noninflammatory disorders of vulva and perineum** ♀
Adhesions of vulva
Hypertrophy of clitoris

N90.9   **Noninflammatory disorder of vulva and perineum, unspecified** ♀

● N91   **Absent, scanty and rare menstruation**
Excludes1   ovarian dysfunction (E28.-)

N91.0   **Primary amenorrhea** ♀

N91.1   **Secondary amenorrhea** ♀

N91.2   **Amenorrhea, unspecified** ♀

N91.3   **Primary oligomenorrhea** ♀

N91.4   **Secondary oligomenorrhea** ♀

N91.5   **Oligomenorrhea, unspecified** ♀
Hypomenorrhea NOS

● N92   **Excessive, frequent and irregular menstruation**
Excludes1   postmenopausal bleeding (N95.0)
precocious puberty (menstruation) (E30.1)

N92.0   **Excessive and frequent menstruation with regular cycle** ♀
Heavy periods NOS   Polymenorrhea
Menorrhagia NOS

N92.1   **Excessive and frequent menstruation with irregular cycle** ♀
Irregular intermenstrual bleeding
Irregular, shortened intervals between menstrual bleeding
Menometrorrhagia
Metrorrhagia

N92.2   **Excessive menstruation at puberty** ♀   P
Excessive bleeding associated with onset of menstrual periods
Pubertal menorrhagia
Puberty bleeding

N92.3   **Ovulation bleeding** ♀
Regular intermenstrual bleeding

N92.4   **Excessive bleeding in the premenopausal period** ♀
Climacteric menorrhagia or metrorrhagia
Menopausal menorrhagia or metrorrhagia
Perimenopausal bleeding
Perimenopausal menorrhagia or metrorrhagia
Preclimacteric menorrhagia or metrorrhagia
Premenopausal menorrhagia or metrorrhagia

N92.5   **Other specified irregular menstruation** ♀

N92.6   **Irregular menstruation, unspecified** ♀
Irregular bleeding NOS
Irregular periods NOS
Excludes1   irregular menstruation with:
lengthened intervals or scanty bleeding (N91.3-N91.5)
shortened intervals or excessive bleeding (N92.1)

● N93   **Other abnormal uterine and vaginal bleeding**
Excludes1   neonatal vaginal hemorrhage (P54.6)
precocious puberty (menstruation) (E30.1)
pseudomenses (P54.6)

N93.0   **Postcoital and contact bleeding** ♀

N93.1   **Pre-pubertal vaginal bleeding** ♀
Coding Clinic: 2016, Q4, P47

N93.8   **Other specified abnormal uterine and vaginal bleeding** ♀
Dysfunctional or functional uterine or vaginal bleeding NOS

N93.9   **Abnormal uterine and vaginal bleeding, unspecified** ♀

● N94   **Pain and other conditions associated with female genital organs and menstrual cycle**

N94.0   **Mittelschmerz** ♀
Ovulation pain

● N94.1   **Dyspareunia**
Painful intercourse/coitus
Excludes1   psychogenic dyspareunia (F52.6)
Coding Clinic: 2016, Q4, P47

N94.10   **Unspecified dyspareunia** ♀

N94.11   **Superficial (introital) dyspareunia** ♀

N94.12   **Deep dyspareunia** ♀

N94.19   **Other specified dyspareunia** ♀

N94.2   **Vaginismus** ♀
Vagina tightness
Excludes1   psychogenic vaginismus (F52.5)

N94.3   **Premenstrual tension syndrome** ♀
AKA: PMS
Code also associated menstrual migraine (G43.82-, G43.83-)
Excludes1   Premenstrual dysphoric disorder (F32.81)
Coding Clinic: 2016, Q4, P14

N94.4   **Primary dysmenorrhea** ♀
Lifelong painful menstruation

N94.5   **Secondary dysmenorrhea** ♀
Later onset of painful menstruation

N94.6   **Dysmenorrhea, unspecified** ♀
Excludes1   psychogenic dysmenorrhea (F45.8)

● N94.8   **Other specified conditions associated with female genital organs and menstrual cycle**

● N94.81   **Vulvodynia**

N94.810   **Vulvar vestibulitis** ♀

N94.818   **Other vulvodynia** ♀

N94.819   **Vulvodynia, unspecified** ♀
Vulvodynia NOS

N94.89   **Other specified conditions associated with female genital organs and menstrual cycle** ♀

N94.9   **Unspecified condition associated with female genital organs and menstrual cycle** ♀

● N95   **Menopausal and other perimenopausal disorders**
Menopausal and other perimenopausal disorders due to naturally occurring (age-related) menopause and perimenopause
Excludes1   excessive bleeding in the premenopausal period (N92.4)
menopausal and perimenopausal disorders due to artificial or premature menopause (E89.4-, E28.31-)
premature menopause (E28.31-)
Excludes2   postmenopausal osteoporosis (M81.0-)
postmenopausal osteoporosis with current pathological fracture (M80.0-)
postmenopausal urethritis (N34.2)

N95.0   **Postmenopausal bleeding** ♀

N95.1   **Menopausal and female climacteric states** ♀
Symptoms such as flushing, sleeplessness, headache, lack of concentration, associated with natural (age-related) menopause
Use additional code for associated symptoms
Excludes1   asymptomatic menopausal state (Z78.0)
symptoms associated with artificial menopause (E89.41)
symptoms associated with premature menopause (E28.310)

N95.2   **Postmenopausal atrophic vaginitis** ♀
Senile (atrophic) vaginitis

N95.8   **Other specified menopausal and perimenopausal disorders** ♀

N95.9   **Unspecified menopausal and perimenopausal disorder** ♀

CHAPTER 14 (N00-N99)

N96 **Recurrent pregnancy loss** ♀

Investigation or care in a nonpregnant woman with history of recurrent pregnancy loss

> **Excludes1**   recurrent pregnancy loss with current pregnancy (O26.2-)

● **N97** **Female infertility**

> **Includes**   inability to achieve a pregnancy
> sterility, female NOS

> **Excludes1**   female infertility associated with:
>   hypopituitarism (E23.0)
>   Stein-Leventhal syndrome (E28.2)

> **Excludes2**   incompetence of cervix uteri (N88.3)

N97.0 **Female infertility associated with anovulation** ♀

N97.1 **Female infertility of tubal origin** ♀

Female infertility associated with congenital anomaly of tube
Female infertility due to tubal block
Female infertility due to tubal occlusion
Female infertility due to tubal stenosis

N97.2 **Female infertility of uterine origin** ♀

Female infertility associated with congenital anomaly of uterus
Female infertility due to nonimplantation of ovum

N97.8 **Female infertility of other origin** ♀

N97.9 **Female infertility, unspecified** ♀

● **N98** **Complications associated with artificial fertilization**

N98.0 **Infection associated with artificial insemination** ♀

N98.1 **Hyperstimulation of ovaries** ♀

Hyperstimulation of ovaries NOS
Hyperstimulation of ovaries associated with induced ovulation

N98.2 **Complications of attempted introduction of fertilized ovum following in vitro fertilization** ♀

N98.3 **Complications of attempted introduction of embryo in embryo transfer** ♀

N98.8 **Other complications associated with artificial fertilization** ♀

N98.9 **Complication associated with artificial fertilization, unspecified** ♀

INTRAOPERATIVE AND POSTPROCEDURAL COMPLICATIONS AND DISORDERS OF GENITOURINARY SYSTEM, NOT ELSEWHERE CLASSIFIED (N99)

● **N99** **Intraoperative and postprocedural complications and disorders of genitourinary system, not elsewhere classified**

> **Excludes2**   irradiation cystitis (N30.4-)
> postoophorectomy osteoporosis with current pathological fracture (M80.8-)
> postoophorectomy osteoporosis without current pathological fracture (M81.8)

N99.0 **Postprocedural (acute) (chronic) kidney failure**

Use additional code to type of kidney disease

● **N99.1** **Postprocedural urethral stricture**

Postcatheterization urethral stricture

● **N99.11** **Postprocedural urethral stricture, male**

N99.110 **Postprocedural urethral stricture, male, meatal** ♂

N99.111 **Postprocedural bulbous urethral stricture, male** ♂

N99.112 **Postprocedural membranous urethral stricture, male** ♂

N99.113 **Postprocedural anterior bulbous urethral stricture, male** ♂
Coding Clinic: 2016, Q4, P48

N99.114 **Postprocedural urethral stricture, male, unspecified** ♂

N99.115 **Postprocedural fossa navicularis urethral stricture** ♂
Coding Clinic: 2016, Q4, P47

N99.116 **Postprocedural urethral stricture, male, overlapping sites** ♂

N99.12 **Postprocedural urethral stricture, female** ♀

N99.2 **Postprocedural adhesions of vagina** ♀

N99.3 **Prolapse of vaginal vault after hysterectomy** ♀

N99.4 **Postprocedural pelvic peritoneal adhesions**

> **Excludes2**   pelvic peritoneal adhesions NOS (N73.6)
> postinfective pelvic peritoneal adhesions (N73.6)

● **N99.5** **Complications of stoma of urinary tract**

> **Excludes2**   mechanical complication of urinary catheter (T83.0-)

● **N99.51** **Complication of cystostomy**

N99.510 **Cystostomy hemorrhage** 🄗

N99.511 **Cystostomy infection** 🄗

N99.512 **Cystostomy malfunction** 🄗

N99.518 **Other cystostomy complication** 🄗

● **N99.52** **Complication of incontinent external stoma of urinary tract** 🄗

N99.520 **Hemorrhage of incontinent external stoma of urinary tract** 🄗

N99.521 **Infection of incontinent external stoma of urinary tract** 🄗
Coding Clinic: 2016, Q4, P48

N99.522 **Malfunction of incontinent external stoma of urinary tract** 🄗

N99.523 **Herniation of incontinent stoma of urinary tract** 🄗
Coding Clinic: 2016, Q4, P48

N99.524 **Stenosis of incontinent stoma of urinary tract** 🄗
Coding Clinic: 2016, Q4, P48

N99.528 **Other complication of incontinent external stoma of urinary tract** 🄗

● **N99.53** **Complication of continent stoma of urinary tract**

N99.530 **Hemorrhage of continent stoma of urinary tract** 🄗

N99.531 **Infection of continent stoma of urinary tract** 🄗

N99.532 **Malfunction of continent stoma of urinary tract** 🄗

N99.533 **Herniation of continent stoma of urinary tract** 🄗
Coding Clinic: 2016, Q4, P48

N99.534 **Stenosis of continent stoma of urinary tract** 🄗
Coding Clinic: 2016, Q4, P48

N99.538 **Other complication of continent stoma of urinary tract** 🄗

● **N99.6** **Intraoperative hemorrhage and hematoma of a genitourinary system organ or structure complicating a procedure**

> **Excludes1**   intraoperative hemorrhage and hematoma of a genitourinary system organ or structure due to accidental puncture or laceration during a procedure (N99.7-)

N99.61 **Intraoperative hemorrhage and hematoma of a genitourinary system organ or structure complicating a genitourinary system procedure**

N99.62 **Intraoperative hemorrhage and hematoma of a genitourinary system organ or structure complicating other procedure**

● **N99.7** **Accidental puncture and laceration of a genitourinary system organ or structure during a procedure**

N99.71 **Accidental puncture and laceration of a genitourinary system organ or structure during a genitourinary system procedure**

N99.72 **Accidental puncture and laceration of a genitourinary system organ or structure during other procedure**

▶ New   ⇒ Revised   ~~deleted~~ Deleted   Excludes 1   Excludes 2   Includes   Use additional   Code first   Code also   Key words

OGCR Official Guidelines   X Assign placeholder X   ● Use Additional Character(s)   ❱ Manifestation Code   🄗 Hierarchical Condition Category   Coding Clinic

- N99.8   Other intraoperative and postprocedural complications and disorders of genitourinary system
  Coding Clinic: 2016, Q4, P10

  N99.81   Other intraoperative complications of genitourinary system

- N99.82   Postprocedural hemorrhage of a genitourinary system organ or structure following a procedure

  N99.820   Postprocedural hemorrhage of a genitourinary system organ or structure following a genitourinary system procedure

  N99.821   Postprocedural hemorrhage of a genitourinary system organ or structure following other procedure

  N99.83   Residual ovary syndrome ♀

- N99.84   Postprocedural hematoma and seroma of a genitourinary system organ or structure following a procedure

  N99.840   Postprocedural hematoma of a genitourinary system organ or structure following a genitourinary system procedure

  N99.841   Postprocedural hematoma of a genitourinary system organ or structure following other procedure

  N99.842   Postprocedural seroma of a genitourinary system organ or structure following a genitourinary system procedure

  N99.843   Postprocedural seroma of a genitourinary system organ or structure following other procedure

  N99.85   Post endometrial ablation syndrome
  Coding Clinic: 2019, Q4, P12

  N99.89   Other postprocedural complications and disorders of genitourinary system

CHAPTER 15

PREGNANCY, CHILDBIRTH, AND THE PUERPERIUM (O00-O9A)

OGCR Chapter-Specific Coding Guidelines

15. **Chapter 15: Pregnancy, Childbirth, and the Puerperium (O00-O9A)**

a. General Rules for Obstetric Cases

1) Codes from Chapter 15 and sequencing priority
Obstetric cases require codes from Chapter 15, codes in the range O00-O9A, Pregnancy, Childbirth, and the Puerperium. Chapter 15 codes have sequencing priority over codes from other chapters. Additional codes from other chapters may be used in conjunction with Chapter 15 codes to further specify conditions. Should the provider document that the pregnancy is incidental to the encounter, then code Z33.1, Pregnant state, incidental, should be used in place of any Chapter 15 codes. It is the provider's responsibility to state that the condition being treated is not affecting the pregnancy.

2) Chapter 15 codes used only on the maternal record
Chapter 15 codes are to be used only on the maternal record, never on the record of the newborn.

3) Final character for trimester
The majority of codes in Chapter 15 have a final character indicating the trimester of pregnancy. The timeframes for the trimesters are indicated at the beginning of the chapter. If trimester is not a component of a code it is because the condition always occurs in a specific trimester, or the concept of trimester of pregnancy is not applicable. Certain codes have characters for only certain trimesters because the condition does not occur in all trimesters, but it may occur in more than just one.

Assignment of the final character for trimester should be based on the provider's documentation of the trimester (or number of weeks) for the current admission/encounter. This applies to the assignment of trimester for pre-existing conditions as well as those that develop during or are due to the pregnancy. The provider's documentation of the number of weeks may be used to assign the appropriate code identifying the trimester.

Whenever delivery occurs during the current admission, and there is an "in childbirth" option for the obstetric complication being coded, the "in childbirth" code should be assigned.

4) Selection of trimester for inpatient admissions that encompass more than one trimester
In instances when a patient is admitted to a hospital for complications of pregnancy during one trimester and remains in the hospital into a subsequent trimester, the trimester character for the antepartum complication code should be assigned on the basis of the trimester when the complication developed, not the trimester of the discharge. If the condition developed prior to the current admission/encounter or represents a pre-existing condition, the trimester character for the trimester at the time of the admission/encounter should be assigned.

5) Unspecified trimester
Each category that includes codes for trimester has a code for "unspecified trimester." The "unspecified trimester" code should rarely be used, such as when the documentation in the record is insufficient to determine the trimester and it is not possible to obtain clarification.

6) 7th character for Fetus Identification
Where applicable, a 7th character is to be assigned for certain categories (O31, O32, O33.3 - O33.6, O35, O36, O40, O41, O60.1, O60.2, O64, and O69) to identify the fetus for which the complication code applies.
Assign 7th character "0":
- For single gestations
- When the documentation in the record is insufficient to determine the fetus affected and it is not possible to obtain clarification.
- When it is not possible to clinically determine which fetus is affected.

b. Selection of OB Principal or First-listed Diagnosis

1) Routine outpatient prenatal visits
For routine outpatient prenatal visits when no complications are present, a code from category Z34, Encounter for supervision of normal pregnancy, should be used as the first-listed diagnosis. These codes should not be used in conjunction with Chapter 15 codes.

2) Supervision of High-Risk Pregnancy
Codes from category O09, Supervision of high-risk pregnancy, are intended for use only during the prenatal period. For complications during the labor or delivery episode as a result of a high-risk pregnancy, assign the applicable complication codes from Chapter 15. If there are no complications during the labor or delivery episode, assign code O80, Encounter for full-term uncomplicated delivery.

For routine prenatal outpatient visits for patients with high-risk pregnancies, a code from category O09, Supervision of high-risk pregnancy, should be used as the first-listed diagnosis. Secondary Chapter 15 codes may be used in conjunction with these codes if appropriate.

3) Episodes when no delivery occurs
In episodes when no delivery occurs, the principal diagnosis should correspond to the principal complication of the pregnancy which necessitated the encounter. Should more than one complication exist, all of which are treated or monitored, any of the complications codes may be sequenced first.

4) When a delivery occurs
When an obstetric patient is admitted and delivers during that admission, the condition that prompted the admission should be sequenced as the principal diagnosis. If multiple conditions prompted the admission, sequence the one most related to the delivery as the principal diagnosis. A code for any complication of the delivery should be assigned as an additional diagnosis. In cases of cesarean delivery, if the patient was admitted with a condition that resulted in the performance of a cesarean procedure, that condition should be selected as the principal diagnosis. If the reason for the admission was unrelated to the condition resulting in the cesarean delivery, the condition related to the reason for the admission should be selected as the principal diagnosis.

5) Outcome of delivery
A code from category Z37, Outcome of delivery, should be included on every maternal record when a delivery has occurred. These codes are not to be used on subsequent records or on the newborn record.

c. Pre-existing conditions versus conditions due to the pregnancy
Certain categories in Chapter 15 distinguish between conditions of the mother that existed prior to pregnancy (pre-existing) and those that are a direct result of pregnancy. When assigning codes from Chapter 15, it is important to assess if a condition was pre-existing prior to pregnancy or developed during or due to the pregnancy in order to assign the correct code.

Categories that do not distinguish between pre-existing and pregnancy-related conditions may be used for either. It is acceptable to use codes specifically for the puerperium with codes complicating pregnancy and childbirth if a condition arises postpartum during the delivery encounter.

d. Pre-existing hypertension in pregnancy
Category O10, Pre-existing hypertension complicating pregnancy, childbirth and the puerperium, includes codes for hypertensive heart and hypertensive chronic kidney disease. When assigning one of the O10 codes that includes hypertensive heart disease or hypertensive chronic kidney disease, it is necessary to add a secondary code from the appropriate hypertension category to specify the type of heart failure or chronic kidney disease.
See Section I.C.9. Hypertension.

e. Fetal Conditions Affecting the Management of the Mother

1) Codes from categories O35 and O36
Codes from categories O35, Maternal care for known or suspected fetal abnormality and damage, and O36, Maternal care for other fetal problems, are assigned only when the fetal condition is actually responsible for modifying the management of the mother, i.e., by requiring diagnostic studies, additional observation, special care, or termination of pregnancy. The fact that the fetal condition exists does not justify assigning a code from this series to the mother's record.

2) In utero surgery
In cases when surgery is performed on the fetus, a diagnosis code from category O35, Maternal care for known or suspected fetal abnormality and damage, should be assigned identifying the fetal condition. Assign the appropriate procedure code for the procedure performed.

No code from Chapter 16, the perinatal codes, should be used on the mother's record to identify fetal conditions. Surgery performed in utero on a fetus is still to be coded as an obstetric encounter.

f. HIV Infection in Pregnancy, Childbirth, and the Puerperium
During pregnancy, childbirth or the puerperium, a patient admitted because of an HIV-related illness should receive a principal diagnosis from subcategory O98.7-, Human immunodeficiency [HIV] disease complicating pregnancy, childbirth and the puerperium, followed by the code(s) for the HIV-related illness(es).

Patients with asymptomatic HIV infection status admitted during pregnancy, childbirth, or the puerperium should receive codes of O98.7- and Z21, Asymptomatic human immunodeficiency virus [HIV] infection status.

g. Diabetes mellitus in pregnancy
Diabetes mellitus is a significant complicating factor in pregnancy. Pregnant women who are diabetic should be assigned a code from category O24, Diabetes mellitus in pregnancy, childbirth, and the puerperium, first, followed by the appropriate diabetes code(s) (E08-E13) from Chapter 4.

h. Long-term use of insulin and oral hypoglycemics
See Section I.C.4.a.3 for information on the long-term use of insulin and oral hypoglycemic.

i. Gestational (pregnancy induced) diabetes
Gestational (pregnancy induced) diabetes can occur during the second and third trimester of pregnancy in women who were not diabetic prior to pregnancy. Gestational diabetes can cause complications in the pregnancy similar to those of pre-existing diabetes mellitus. It also puts the woman at greater risk of developing diabetes after the pregnancy. Codes for gestational diabetes are in subcategory O24.4, Gestational diabetes mellitus. No other code from category O24, Diabetes mellitus in pregnancy, childbirth, and the puerperium, should be used with a code from O24.4.

The codes under subcategory O24.4 include diet controlled, insulin controlled, and controlled by oral hypoglycemic drugs. If a patient with gestational diabetes is treated with both diet and insulin, only the code for insulin-controlled is required. If a patient with gestational diabetes is treated with both diet and oral hypoglycemic medications, only the code for "controlled by oral hypoglycemic drugs" is required. Code Z79.4, Long-term (current) use of insulin or code Z79.84, Long-term (current) use of oral hypoglycemic drugs, should not be assigned with codes from subcategory O24.4.

An abnormal glucose tolerance in pregnancy is assigned a code from subcategory O99.81, Abnormal glucose complicating pregnancy, childbirth, and the puerperium.

j. Sepsis and septic shock complicating abortion, pregnancy, childbirth and the puerperium
When assigning a Chapter 15 code for sepsis complicating abortion, pregnancy, childbirth, and the puerperium, a code for the specific type of infection should be assigned as an additional diagnosis. If severe sepsis is present, a code from subcategory R65.2, Severe sepsis, and code(s) for associated organ dysfunction(s) should also be assigned as additional diagnoses.

k. Puerperal sepsis
Code O85, Puerperal sepsis, should be assigned with a secondary code to identify the causal organism (e.g., for a bacterial infection, assign a code from category B95-B96, Bacterial infections in conditions classified elsewhere). A code from category A40, Streptococcal sepsis, or A41, Other sepsis, should not be used for puerperal sepsis. If applicable, use additional codes to identify severe sepsis (R65.2-) and any associated acute organ dysfunction.

l. Alcohol, tobacco and drug use during pregnancy, childbirth and the puerperium
1) Alcohol use during pregnancy, childbirth and the puerperium
Codes under subcategory O99.31, Alcohol use complicating pregnancy, childbirth, and the puerperium, should be assigned for any pregnancy case when a mother uses alcohol during the pregnancy or postpartum. A secondary code from category F10, Alcohol-related disorders, should also be assigned to identify manifestations of the alcohol use.

2) Tobacco use during pregnancy, childbirth, and the puerperium
Codes under subcategory O99.33, Smoking (tobacco) complicating pregnancy, childbirth, and the puerperium, should be assigned for any pregnancy case when a mother uses any type of tobacco product during the pregnancy or postpartum. A secondary code from category F17, Nicotine dependence, should also be assigned to identify the type of nicotine dependence.

3) Drug use during pregnancy, childbirth and the puerperium
Codes under subcategory O99.32, Drug use complicating pregnancy, childbirth, and the puerperium, should be assigned for any pregnancy case when a mother uses drugs during the pregnancy or postpartum. This can involve illegal drugs, or inappropriate use or abuse of prescription drugs. Secondary code(s) from categories F11-F16 and F18F19 should also be assigned to identify manifestations of the drug use.

m. Poisoning, toxic effects, adverse effects and underdosing in a pregnant patient
A code from subcategory O9A.2, Injury, poisoning and certain other consequences of external causes complicating pregnancy, childbirth, and the puerperium, should be sequenced first, followed by the appropriate injury, poisoning, toxic effect, adverse effect or underdosing code, and then the additional code(s) that specifies the condition caused by the poisoning, toxic effect, adverse effect or underdosing.
See Section I.C.19. Adverse effects, poisoning, underdosing and toxic effects.

n. Normal Delivery, Code O80
1) Encounter for full-term uncomplicated delivery
Code O80 should be assigned when a woman is admitted for a full-term normal delivery and delivers a single, healthy infant without any complications antepartum, during the delivery, or postpartum during the delivery episode. Code O80 is always a principal diagnosis. It is not to be used if any other code from Chapter 15 is needed to describe a current complication of the antenatal, delivery, or perinatal period. Additional codes from other chapters may be used with code O80 if they are not related to or are in any way complicating the pregnancy.

2) Uncomplicated delivery with resolved antepartum complication
Code O80 may be used if the patient had a complication at some point during the pregnancy, but the complication is not present at the time of the admission for delivery.

3) Outcome of delivery for O80
Z37.0, Single live birth, is the only outcome of delivery code appropriate for use with O80.

o. The Peripartum and Postpartum Periods
1) Peripartum and Postpartum periods
The postpartum period begins immediately after delivery and continues for six weeks following delivery. The peripartum period is defined as the last month of pregnancy to five months postpartum.

2) Peripartum and postpartum complication
A postpartum complication is any complication occurring within the six-week period.

3) Pregnancy-related complications after 6 week period
Chapter 15 codes may also be used to describe pregnancy-related complications after the peripartum or postpartum period if the provider documents that a condition is pregnancy related.

4) Admission for routine postpartum care following delivery outside hospital
When the mother delivers outside the hospital prior to admission and is admitted for routine postpartum care and no complications are noted, code Z39.0, Encounter for care and examination of mother immediately after delivery, should be assigned as the principal diagnosis.

5) Pregnancy associated cardiomyopathy
Pregnancy associated cardiomyopathy, code O90.3, is unique in that it may be diagnosed in the third trimester of pregnancy but may continue to progress months after delivery. For this reason, it is referred to as peripartum cardiomyopathy. Code O90.3 is only for use when the cardiomyopathy develops as a result of pregnancy in a woman who did not have pre-existing heart disease.

p. Code O94, Sequelae of complication of pregnancy, childbirth, and the puerperium
1) Code O94
Code O94, Sequelae of complication of pregnancy, childbirth, and the puerperium, is for use in those cases when an initial complication of a pregnancy develops a sequelae requiring care or treatment at a future date.

2) After the initial postpartum period
This code may be used at any time after the initial postpartum period.

3) Sequencing of Code O94
This code, like all sequela codes, is to be sequenced following the code describing the sequelae of the complication.

q. Termination of Pregnancy and Spontaneous abortions
1) Abortion with Liveborn Fetus
When an attempted termination of pregnancy results in a liveborn fetus assign code Z33.2, Encounter for elective termination of pregnancy and a code from category Z37, Outcome of Delivery.

2) Retained Products of Conception following an abortion
Subsequent encounters for retained products of conception following a spontaneous abortion or elective termination of pregnancy, without complications are assigned O03.4, Incomplete spontaneous, abortion without complication, or codes O07.4, Failed attempted termination of pregnancy without complication. This advice is appropriate even when the patient was discharged previously with a discharge diagnosis of complete abortion. If the patient has a specific complication associated with the spontaneous abortion or elective termination of pregnancy in addition to retained products of conception, assign the appropriate complication in category O03 or O07 instead of code O03.4 or O07.4

3) Complications leading to abortion
Codes from Chapter 15 may be used as additional codes to identify any documented complications of the pregnancy in conjunction with codes in categories O04, O07 and O08.

r. Abuse in a pregnant patient
For suspected or confirmed cases of abuse of a pregnant patient, a code(s) from subcategories O9A.3, Physical abuse complicating pregnancy, childbirth, and the puerperium, O9A.4, Sexual abuse complicating pregnancy, childbirth, and the puerperium, and O9A.5, Psychological abuse complicating pregnancy, childbirth, and the puerperium, should be sequenced first, followed by the appropriate codes (if applicable) to identify any associated current injury due to physical abuse, sexual abuse, and the perpetrator of abuse.
See Section I.C.19. Adult and child abuse, neglect and other maltreatment.

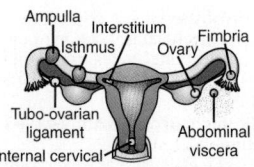

Figure 15-1   Implantation sites of ectopic pregnancy.

Item 15–1   Ectopic pregnancy most often occurs in the fallopian tube. Pregnancy outside the uterus may end in a lifethreatening rupture.

⭐**(See Plate 4 of the Anatomy Illustrations.)**

CHAPTER 15

PREGNANCY, CHILDBIRTH, AND THE PUERPERIUM (O00-O9A)

Note: CODES FROM THIS CHAPTER ARE FOR USE ONLY ON MATERNAL RECORDS, NEVER ON NEWBORN RECORDS

Codes from this chapter are for use for conditions related to or aggravated by the pregnancy, childbirth, or by the puerperium (maternal causes or obstetric causes)

Trimesters are counted from the first day of the last menstrual period. They are defined as follows:

1st trimester - less than 14 weeks 0 days

2nd trimester - 14 weeks 0 days to less than 28 weeks 0 days

3rd trimester - 28 weeks 0 days until delivery

Use additional code from category Z3A, Weeks of gestation, to identify the specific week of the pregnancy, if known.

Excludes1   supervision of normal pregnancy (Z34.-)

Excludes2   mental and behavioral disorders associated with the puerperium (F53.-)
obstetrical tetanus (A34)
postpartum necrosis of pituitary gland (E23.0)
puerperal osteomalacia (M83.0)

This chapter contains the following blocks:

O00-O08	Pregnancy with abortive outcome
O09	Supervision of high risk pregnancy
O10-O16	Edema, proteinuria and hypertensive disorders in pregnancy, childbirth and the puerperium
O20-O29	Other maternal disorders predominantly related to pregnancy
O30-O48	Maternal care related to the fetus and amniotic cavity and possible delivery problems
O60-O77	Complications of labor and delivery
O80, O82	Encounter for delivery
O85-O92	Complications predominantly related to the puerperium
O94-O9A	Other obstetric conditions, not elsewhere classified

PREGNANCY WITH ABORTIVE OUTCOME (O00-O08)

Excludes1   continuing pregnancy in multiple gestation after abortion of one fetus or more (O31.1-, O31.3-)
Coding Clinic: 2016, Q4, P130

● **O00   Ectopic pregnancy**
   Includes   ruptured ectopic pregnancy
   Use additional code from category O08 to identify any associated complication

   ● **O00.0   Abdominal pregnancy**
      Excludes1   maternal care for viable fetus in abdominal pregnancy (O36.7-)
      Coding Clinic: 2016, Q4, P49

      O00.00   Abdominal pregnancy without intrauterine pregnancy ♀   M
         Abdominal pregnancy NOS

      O00.01   Abdominal pregnancy with intrauterine pregnancy ♀   M

   ● **O00.1   Tubal pregnancy**
      Fallopian pregnancy
      Rupture of (fallopian) tube due to pregnancy
      Tubal abortion
      Coding Clinic: 2016, Q4, P49

      ● **O00.10   Tubal pregnancy without intrauterine pregnancy**
         Tubal pregnancy NOS

         O00.101   Right tubal pregnancy without intrauterine pregnancy ♀   M

         O00.102   Left tubal pregnancy without intrauterine pregnancy ♀   M

         O00.109   Unspecified tubal pregnancy without intrauterine pregnancy ♀   M

      ● **O00.11   Tubal pregnancy with intrauterine pregnancy**

         O00.111   Right tubal pregnancy with intrauterine pregnancy ♀   M

         O00.112   Left tubal pregnancy with intrauterine pregnancy ♀   M

         O00.119   Unspecified tubal pregnancy with intrauterine pregnancy ♀   M

   ● **O00.2   Ovarian pregnancy**
      Coding Clinic: 2016, Q4, P49

      ● **O00.20   Ovarian pregnancy without intrauterine pregnancy**
         Ovarian pregnancy NOS

         O00.201   Right ovarian pregnancy without intrauterine pregnancy ♀   M

         O00.202   Left ovarian pregnancy without intrauterine pregnancy ♀   M

         O00.209   Unspecified ovarian pregnancy without intrauterine pregnancy ♀   M

      ● **O00.21   Ovarian pregnancy with intrauterine pregnancy**

         O00.211   Right ovarian pregnancy with intrauterine pregnancy ♀   M

         O00.212   Left ovarian pregnancy with intrauterine pregnancy ♀   M

         O00.219   Unspecified ovarian pregnancy with intrauterine pregnancy ♀   M

   ● **O00.8   Other ectopic pregnancy**
      Cervical pregnancy
      Cornual pregnancy
      Intraligamentous pregnancy
      Mural pregnancy
      Coding Clinic: 2016, Q4, P49

      O00.80   Other ectopic pregnancy without intrauterine pregnancy ♀   M
         Other ectopic pregnancy NOS

      O00.81   Other ectopic pregnancy with intrauterine pregnancy ♀   M

▶ New   ⇒ Revised   ~~deleted~~ Deleted   Excludes 1   Excludes 2   Includes   Use additional   Code first   Code also   Key words

OGCR Official Guidelines   X Assign placeholder X   ● Use Additional Character(s)   ▶ Manifestation Code   � Hierarchical Condition Category   **Coding Clinic**

● **O00.9** **Ectopic pregnancy, unspecified**
    Coding Clinic: 2016, Q4, P49

    O00.90 **Unspecified ectopic pregnancy without intrauterine pregnancy** ♀   M
        Ectopic pregnancy NOS

    O00.91 **Unspecified ectopic pregnancy with intrauterine pregnancy** ♀   M

● **O01** **Hydatidiform mole**
    Use additional code from category O08 to identify any associated complication

    Excludes1   chorioadenoma (destruens) (D39.2)
                malignant hydatidiform mole (D39.2)

  O01.0 **Classical hydatidiform mole** ♀   M
    Complete hydatidiform mole

  O01.1 **Incomplete and partial hydatidiform mole** ♀   M

  O01.9 **Hydatidiform mole, unspecified** ♀   M
    Trophoblastic disease NOS
    Vesicular mole NOS

● **O02** **Other abnormal products of conception**
    Use additional code from category O08 to identify any associated complication

    Excludes1   papyraceous fetus (O31.0-)

  O02.0 **Blighted ovum and nonhydatidiform mole** ♀   M
    Carneous mole   Molar pregnancy NEC
    Fleshy mole   Pathological ovum
    Intrauterine mole NOS

  O02.1 **Missed abortion** ♀   M
    Early fetal death, before completion of 20 weeks of gestation, with retention of dead fetus

    Excludes1   failed induced abortion (O07.-)
                fetal death (intrauterine) (late) (O36.4)
                missed abortion with blighted ovum (O02.0)
                missed abortion with hydatidiform mole (O01.-)
                missed abortion with nonhydatidiform (O02.0)
                missed abortion with other abnormal products of conception (O02.8-)
                missed delivery (O36.4)
                stillbirth (P95)

    Coding Clinic: 2019, Q3, P12

● **O02.8** **Other specified abnormal products of conception**
    Excludes1   abnormal products of conception with blighted ovum (O02.0)
                abnormal products of conception with hydatidiform mole (O01.-)
                abnormal products of conception with nonhydatidiform mole (O02.0)

    O02.81 **Inappropriate change in quantitative human chorionic gonadotropin (hCG) in early pregnancy** ♀   M
        Biochemical pregnancy
        Chemical pregnancy
        Inappropriate level of quantitative human chorionic gonadotropin (hCG) for gestational age in early pregnancy

    O02.89 **Other abnormal products of conception** ♀   M

  O02.9 **Abnormal product of conception, unspecified** ♀   M

● **O03** **Spontaneous abortion**
    Note: Incomplete abortion includes retained products of conception following spontaneous abortion.

    Includes   miscarriage

  O03.0 **Genital tract and pelvic infection following incomplete spontaneous abortion** ♀   M
    Endometritis following incomplete spontaneous abortion
    Oophoritis following incomplete spontaneous abortion
    Parametritis following incomplete spontaneous abortion
    Pelvic peritonitis following incomplete spontaneous abortion
    Salpingitis following incomplete spontaneous abortion
    Salpingo-oophoritis following incomplete spontaneous abortion

    Excludes1   sepsis following incomplete spontaneous abortion (O03.37)
                urinary tract infection following incomplete spontaneous abortion (O03.38)

  O03.1 **Delayed or excessive hemorrhage following incomplete spontaneous abortion** ♀   M
    Afibrinogenemia following incomplete spontaneous abortion
    Defibrination syndrome following incomplete spontaneous abortion
    Hemolysis following incomplete spontaneous abortion
    Intravascular coagulation following incomplete spontaneous abortion

  O03.2 **Embolism following incomplete spontaneous abortion** ♀   M
    Air embolism following incomplete spontaneous abortion
    Amniotic fluid embolism following incomplete spontaneous abortion
    Blood-clot embolism following incomplete spontaneous abortion
    Embolism NOS following incomplete spontaneous abortion
    Fat embolism following incomplete spontaneous abortion
    Pulmonary embolism following incomplete spontaneous abortion
    Pyemic embolism following incomplete spontaneous abortion
    Septic or septicopyemic embolism following incomplete spontaneous abortion
    Soap embolism following incomplete spontaneous abortion

● **O03.3** **Other and unspecified complications following incomplete spontaneous abortion**
    O03.30 **Unspecified complication following incomplete spontaneous abortion** ♀   M

    O03.31 **Shock following incomplete spontaneous abortion** ♀   M
        Circulatory collapse following incomplete spontaneous abortion
        Shock (postprocedural) following incomplete spontaneous abortion

        Excludes1   shock due to infection following incomplete spontaneous abortion (O03.37)

    O03.32 **Renal failure following incomplete spontaneous abortion** ♀   M
        Kidney failure (acute) following incomplete spontaneous abortion
        Oliguria following incomplete spontaneous abortion
        Renal shutdown following incomplete spontaneous abortion
        Renal tubular necrosis following incomplete spontaneous abortion
        Uremia following incomplete spontaneous abortion

Item 15–2 A **hydatidiform** mole is an overproduction of placental tissue. The tumor secretes a hormone, chorionic gonadotropic hormone (CGH), that indicates a positive pregnancy test. There is no viable fetus. More than 80% of hydatidiform moles are noncancerous.

CHAPTER 15 (O00-O9A)

O03.33 Metabolic disorder following incomplete spontaneous abortion ♀ **M**

O03.34 Damage to pelvic organs following incomplete spontaneous abortion ♀ **M**

Laceration, perforation, tear or chemical damage of bladder following incomplete spontaneous abortion

Laceration, perforation, tear or chemical damage of bowel following incomplete spontaneous abortion

Laceration, perforation, tear or chemical damage of broad ligament following incomplete spontaneous abortion

Laceration, perforation, tear or chemical damage of cervix following incomplete spontaneous abortion

Laceration, perforation, tear or chemical damage of periurethral tissue following incomplete spontaneous abortion

Laceration, perforation, tear or chemical damage of uterus following incomplete spontaneous abortion

Laceration, perforation, tear or chemical damage of vagina following incomplete spontaneous abortion

O03.35 Other venous complications following incomplete spontaneous abortion ♀ **M**

O03.36 Cardiac arrest following incomplete spontaneous abortion ♀ **M**

O03.37 Sepsis following incomplete spontaneous abortion ♀ **M**

Use additional code to identify infectious agent (B95-B97)

Use additional code to identify severe sepsis, if applicable (R65.2-)

Excludes1 septic or septicopyemic embolism following incomplete spontaneous abortion (O03.2)

O03.38 Urinary tract infection following incomplete spontaneous abortion ♀ **M**

Cystitis following incomplete spontaneous abortion

O03.39 Incomplete spontaneous abortion with other complications ♀ **M**

O03.4 Incomplete spontaneous abortion without complication ♀ **M**

O03.5 Genital tract and pelvic infection following complete or unspecified spontaneous abortion ♀ **M**

Endometritis following complete or unspecified spontaneous abortion

Oophoritis following complete or unspecified spontaneous abortion

Parametritis following complete or unspecified spontaneous abortion

Pelvic peritonitis following complete or unspecified spontaneous abortion

Salpingitis following complete or unspecified spontaneous abortion

Salpingo-oophoritis following complete or unspecified spontaneous abortion

Excludes1 sepsis following complete or unspecified spontaneous abortion (O03.87)

urinary tract infection following complete or unspecified spontaneous abortion (O03.88)

O03.6 Delayed or excessive hemorrhage following complete or unspecified spontaneous abortion ♀ **M**

Afibrinogenemia following complete or unspecified spontaneous abortion

Defibrination syndrome following complete or unspecified spontaneous abortion

Hemolysis following complete or unspecified spontaneous abortion

Intravascular coagulation following complete or unspecified spontaneous abortion

O03.7 Embolism following complete or unspecified spontaneous abortion ♀ **M**

Air embolism following complete or unspecified spontaneous abortion

Amniotic fluid embolism following complete or unspecified spontaneous abortion

Blood-clot embolism following complete or unspecified spontaneous abortion

Embolism NOS following complete or unspecified spontaneous abortion

Fat embolism following complete or unspecified spontaneous abortion

Pulmonary embolism following complete or unspecified spontaneous abortion

Pyemic embolism following complete or unspecified spontaneous abortion

Septic or septicopyemic embolism following complete or unspecified spontaneous abortion

Soap embolism following complete or unspecified spontaneous abortion

● **O03.8 Other and unspecified complications following complete or unspecified spontaneous abortion**

O03.80 Unspecified complication following complete or unspecified spontaneous abortion ♀ **M**

O03.81 Shock following complete or unspecified spontaneous abortion ♀ **M**

Circulatory collapse following complete or unspecified spontaneous abortion

Shock (postprocedural) following complete or unspecified spontaneous abortion

Excludes1 shock due to infection following complete or unspecified spontaneous abortion (O03.87)

O03.82 Renal failure following complete or unspecified spontaneous abortion ♀ **M**

Kidney failure (acute) following complete or unspecified spontaneous abortion

Oliguria following complete or unspecified spontaneous abortion

Renal shutdown following complete or unspecified spontaneous abortion

Renal tubular necrosis following complete or unspecified spontaneous abortion

Uremia following complete or unspecified spontaneous abortion

O03.83 Metabolic disorder following complete or unspecified spontaneous abortion ♀ **M**

O03.84 Damage to pelvic organs following complete or unspecified spontaneous abortion ♀ **M**

Laceration, perforation, tear or chemical damage of bladder following complete or unspecified spontaneous abortion

Laceration, perforation, tear or chemical damage of bowel following complete or unspecified spontaneous abortion

Laceration, perforation, tear or chemical damage of broad ligament following complete or unspecified spontaneous abortion

Laceration, perforation, tear or chemical damage of cervix following complete or unspecified spontaneous abortion

Laceration, perforation, tear or chemical damage of periurethral tissue following complete or unspecified spontaneous abortion

Laceration, perforation, tear or chemical damage of uterus following complete or unspecified spontaneous abortion

Laceration, perforation, tear or chemical damage of vagina following complete or unspecified spontaneous abortion

▶ New ⇒ Revised ~~deleted~~ Deleted Excludes 1 Excludes 2 Includes Use additional Code first Code also Key words
OGCR Official Guidelines X Assign placeholder X ● Use Additional Character(s) ▷ Manifestation Code 🏥 Hierarchical Condition Category Coding Clinic

O03.85 **Other venous complications following complete or unspecified spontaneous abortion** ♀ **M**

O03.86 **Cardiac arrest following complete or unspecified spontaneous abortion** ♀ **M**

O03.87 **Sepsis following complete or unspecified spontaneous abortion** ♀ **M**

Use additional code to identify infectious agent (B95-B97)

Use additional code to identify severe sepsis, if applicable (R65.2-)

Excludes1 septic or septicopyemic embolism following complete or unspecified spontaneous abortion (O03.7)

O03.88 **Urinary tract infection following complete or unspecified spontaneous abortion** ♀ **M**

Cystitis following complete or unspecified spontaneous abortion

O03.89 **Complete or unspecified spontaneous abortion with other complications** ♀ **M**

O03.9 **Complete or unspecified spontaneous abortion without complication** ♀ **M**

Miscarriage NOS

Spontaneous abortion NOS

● **O04** **Complications following (induced) termination of pregnancy**

Includes complications following (induced) termination of pregnancy

Excludes1 encounter for elective termination of pregnancy, uncomplicated (Z33.2)

failed attempted termination of pregnancy (O07.-)

O04.5 **Genital tract and pelvic infection following (induced) termination of pregnancy** ♀ **M**

Endometritis following (induced) termination of pregnancy

Oophoritis following (induced) termination of pregnancy

Parametritis following (induced) termination of pregnancy

Pelvic peritonitis following (induced) termination of pregnancy

Salpingitis following (induced) termination of pregnancy

Salpingo-oophoritis following (induced) termination of pregnancy

Excludes1 sepsis following (induced) termination of pregnancy (O04.87)

urinary tract infection following (induced) termination of pregnancy (O04.88)

O04.6 **Delayed or excessive hemorrhage following (induced) termination of pregnancy** ♀ **M**

Afibrinogenemia following (induced) termination of pregnancy

Defibrination syndrome following (induced) termination of pregnancy

Hemolysis following (induced) termination of pregnancy

Intravascular coagulation following (induced) termination of pregnancy

Coding Clinic: 2019, Q3, P12

O04.7 **Embolism following (induced) termination of pregnancy** ♀ **M**

Air embolism following (induced) termination of pregnancy

Amniotic fluid embolism following (induced) termination of pregnancy

Blood-clot embolism following (induced) termination of pregnancy

Embolism NOS following (induced) termination of pregnancy

Fat embolism following (induced) termination of pregnancy

Pulmonary embolism following (induced) termination of pregnancy

Pyemic embolism following (induced) termination of pregnancy

Septic or septicopyemic embolism following (induced) termination of pregnancy

Soap embolism following (induced) termination of pregnancy

● **O04.8** **(Induced) termination of pregnancy with other and unspecified complications**

O04.80 **(Induced) termination of pregnancy with unspecified complications** ♀ **M**

O04.81 **Shock following (induced) termination of pregnancy** ♀ **M**

Circulatory collapse following (induced) termination of pregnancy

Shock (postprocedural) following (induced) termination of pregnancy

Excludes1 shock due to infection following (induced) termination of pregnancy (O04.87)

O04.82 **Renal failure following (induced) termination of pregnancy** ♀ **M**

Kidney failure (acute) following (induced) termination of pregnancy

Oliguria following (induced) termination of pregnancy

Renal shutdown following (induced) termination of pregnancy

Renal tubular necrosis following (induced) termination of pregnancy

Uremia following (induced) termination of pregnancy

O04.83 **Metabolic disorder following (induced) termination of pregnancy** ♀ **M**

O04.84 **Damage to pelvic organs following (induced) termination of pregnancy** ♀ **M**

Laceration, perforation, tear or chemical damage of bladder following (induced) termination of pregnancy

Laceration, perforation, tear or chemical damage of bowel following (induced) termination of pregnancy

Laceration, perforation, tear or chemical damage of broad ligament following (induced) termination of pregnancy

Laceration, perforation, tear or chemical damage of cervix following (induced) termination of pregnancy

Laceration, perforation, tear or chemical damage of periurethral tissue following (induced) termination of pregnancy

Laceration, perforation, tear or chemical damage of uterus following (induced) termination of pregnancy

Laceration, perforation, tear or chemical damage of vagina following (induced) termination of pregnancy

O04.85   **Other venous complications following (induced) termination of pregnancy** ♀   M

O04.86   **Cardiac arrest following (induced) termination of pregnancy** ♀   M

O04.87   **Sepsis following (induced) termination of pregnancy** ♀   M

     Use additional code to identify infectious agent (B95-B97)

     Use additional code to identify severe sepsis, if applicable (R65.2-)

     Excludes1   septic or septicopyemic embolism following (induced) termination of pregnancy (O04.7)

O04.88   **Urinary tract infection following (induced) termination of pregnancy** ♀   M

     Cystitis following (induced) termination of pregnancy

O04.89   **(Induced) termination of pregnancy with other complications** ♀   M

● **O07**   **Failed attempted termination of pregnancy**

     Includes   failure of attempted induction of termination of pregnancy
              incomplete elective abortion

     Excludes1   incomplete spontaneous abortion (O03.0-)

O07.0   **Genital tract and pelvic infection following failed attempted termination of pregnancy** ♀   M

     Endometritis following failed attempted termination of pregnancy

     Oophoritis following failed attempted termination of pregnancy

     Parametritis following failed attempted termination of pregnancy

     Pelvic peritonitis following failed attempted termination of pregnancy

     Salpingitis following failed attempted termination of pregnancy

     Salpingo-oophoritis following failed attempted termination of pregnancy

     Excludes1   sepsis following failed attempted termination of pregnancy (O07.37)
            urinary tract infection following failed attempted termination of pregnancy (O07.38)

O07.1   **Delayed or excessive hemorrhage following failed attempted termination of pregnancy** ♀   M

     Afibrinogenemia following failed attempted termination of pregnancy

     Defibrination syndrome following failed attempted termination of pregnancy

     Hemolysis following failed attempted termination of pregnancy

     Intravascular coagulation following failed attempted termination of pregnancy

O07.2   **Embolism following failed attempted termination of pregnancy** ♀   M

     Air embolism following failed attempted termination of pregnancy

     Amniotic fluid embolism following failed attempted termination of pregnancy

     Blood-clot embolism following failed attempted termination of pregnancy

     Embolism NOS following failed attempted termination of pregnancy

     Fat embolism following failed attempted termination of pregnancy

     Pulmonary embolism following failed attempted termination of pregnancy

     Pyemic embolism following failed attempted termination of pregnancy

     Septic or septicopyemic embolism following failed attempted termination of pregnancy

     Soap embolism following failed attempted termination of pregnancy

● **O07.3**   **Failed attempted termination of pregnancy with other and unspecified complications**

O07.30   **Failed attempted termination of pregnancy with unspecified complications** ♀   M

O07.31   **Shock following failed attempted termination of pregnancy** ♀   M

     Circulatory collapse following failed attempted termination of pregnancy

     Shock (postprocedural) following failed attempted termination of pregnancy

     Excludes1   shock due to infection following failed attempted termination of pregnancy (O07.37)

O07.32   **Renal failure following failed attempted termination of pregnancy** ♀   M

     Kidney failure (acute) following failed attempted termination of pregnancy

     Oliguria following failed attempted termination of pregnancy

     Renal shutdown following failed attempted termination of pregnancy

     Renal tubular necrosis following failed attempted termination of pregnancy

     Uremia following failed attempted termination of pregnancy

O07.33   **Metabolic disorder following failed attempted termination of pregnancy** ♀   M

O07.34   **Damage to pelvic organs following failed attempted termination of pregnancy** ♀   M

     Laceration, perforation, tear or chemical damage of bladder following failed attempted termination of pregnancy

     Laceration, perforation, tear or chemical damage of bowel following failed attempted termination of pregnancy

     Laceration, perforation, tear or chemical damage of broad ligament following failed attempted termination of pregnancy

     Laceration, perforation, tear or chemical damage of cervix following failed attempted termination of pregnancy

     Laceration, perforation, tear or chemical damage of periurethral tissue following failed attempted termination of pregnancy

     Laceration, perforation, tear or chemical damage of uterus following failed attempted termination of pregnancy

     Laceration, perforation, tear or chemical damage of vagina following failed attempted termination of pregnancy

O07.35   **Other venous complications following failed attempted termination of pregnancy** ♀   M

O07.36   **Cardiac arrest following failed attempted termination of pregnancy** ♀   M

O07.37   **Sepsis following failed attempted termination of pregnancy** ♀   M

     Use additional code (B95-B97), to identify infectious agent

     Use additional code (R65.2-) to identify severe sepsis, if applicable

     Excludes1   septic or septicopyemic embolism following failed attempted termination of pregnancy (O07.2)

O07.38   **Urinary tract infection following failed attempted termination of pregnancy** ♀   M

     Cystitis following failed attempted termination of pregnancy

O07.39   **Failed attempted termination of pregnancy with other complications** ♀   M

O07.4   **Failed attempted termination of pregnancy without complication** ♀   M

▶ New   ⇒ Revised   ~~deleted~~ Deleted   Excludes 1   Excludes 2   Includes   Use additional   Code first   Code also   Key words
OGCR Official Guidelines   X Assign placeholder X   ● Use Additional Character(s)   ▷ Manifestation Code   ℚ Hierarchical Condition Category   Coding Clinic

● **O08**   **Complications following ectopic and molar pregnancy**
This category is for use with categories O00-O02 to identify any associated complications.

O08.0   **Genital tract and pelvic infection following ectopic and molar pregnancy** ♀   M
Endometritis following ectopic and molar pregnancy
Oophoritis following ectopic and molar pregnancy
Parametritis following ectopic and molar pregnancy
Pelvic peritonitis following ectopic and molar pregnancy
Salpingitis following ectopic and molar pregnancy
Salpingo-oophoritis following ectopic and molar pregnancy
> **Excludes1**   sepsis following ectopic and molar pregnancy (O08.82)
> urinary tract infection (O08.83)

O08.1   **Delayed or excessive hemorrhage following ectopic and molar pregnancy** ♀   M
Afibrinogenemia following ectopic and molar pregnancy
Defibrination syndrome following ectopic and molar pregnancy
Hemolysis following ectopic and molar pregnancy
Intravascular coagulation following ectopic and molar pregnancy
> **Excludes1**   delayed or excessive hemorrhage due to incomplete abortion (O03.1)

O08.2   **Embolism following ectopic and molar pregnancy** ♀   M
Air embolism following ectopic and molar pregnancy
Amniotic fluid embolism following ectopic and molar pregnancy
Blood-clot embolism following ectopic and molar pregnancy
Embolism NOS following ectopic and molar pregnancy
Fat embolism following ectopic and molar pregnancy
Pulmonary embolism following ectopic and molar pregnancy
Pyemic embolism following ectopic and molar pregnancy
Septic or septicopyemic embolism following ectopic and molar pregnancy
Soap embolism following ectopic and molar pregnancy

O08.3   **Shock following ectopic and molar pregnancy** ♀   M
Circulatory collapse following ectopic and molar pregnancy
Shock (postprocedural) following ectopic and molar pregnancy
> **Excludes1**   shock due to infection following ectopic and molar pregnancy (O08.82)

O08.4   **Renal failure following ectopic and molar pregnancy** ♀   M
Kidney failure (acute) following ectopic and molar pregnancy
Oliguria following ectopic and molar pregnancy
Renal shutdown following ectopic and molar pregnancy
Renal tubular necrosis following ectopic and molar pregnancy
Uremia following ectopic and molar pregnancy

O08.5   **Metabolic disorders following an ectopic and molar pregnancy** ♀   M

O08.6   **Damage to pelvic organs and tissues following an ectopic and molar pregnancy** ♀   M
Laceration, perforation, tear or chemical damage of bladder following an ectopic and molar pregnancy
Laceration, perforation, tear or chemical damage of bowel following an ectopic and molar pregnancy
Laceration, perforation, tear or chemical damage of broad ligament following an ectopic and molar pregnancy
Laceration, perforation, tear or chemical damage of cervix following an ectopic and molar pregnancy
Laceration, perforation, tear or chemical damage of periurethral tissue following an ectopic and molar pregnancy
Laceration, perforation, tear or chemical damage of uterus following an ectopic and molar pregnancy
Laceration, perforation, tear or chemical damage of vagina following an ectopic and molar pregnancy

O08.7   **Other venous complications following an ectopic and molar pregnancy** ♀   M

● **O08.8**   **Other complications following an ectopic and molar pregnancy**

O08.81   **Cardiac arrest following an ectopic and molar pregnancy** ♀   M

O08.82   **Sepsis following ectopic and molar pregnancy** ♀   M
> Use additional code (B95-B97), to identify infectious agent
> Use additional code (R65.2-) to identify severe sepsis, if applicable
> **Excludes1**   septic or septicopyemic embolism following ectopic and molar pregnancy (O08.2)

O08.83   **Urinary tract infection following an ectopic and molar pregnancy** ♀   M
Cystitis following an ectopic and molar pregnancy

O08.89   **Other complications following an ectopic and molar pregnancy** ♀   M

O08.9   **Unspecified complication following an ectopic and molar pregnancy** ♀   M

SUPERVISION OF HIGH RISK PREGNANCY (O09)

● **O09**   **Supervision of high risk pregnancy**
Coding Clinic: 2016, Q4, P125, 150

● **O09.0**   **Supervision of pregnancy with history of infertility**

O09.00   **Supervision of pregnancy with history of infertility, unspecified trimester** ♀   M

O09.01   **Supervision of pregnancy with history of infertility, first trimester** ♀   M

O09.02   **Supervision of pregnancy with history of infertility, second trimester** ♀   M

O09.03   **Supervision of pregnancy with history of infertility, third trimester** ♀   M

● **O09.1**   **Supervision of pregnancy with history of ectopic pregnancy**
Coding Clinic: 2016, Q4, P49-50

O09.10   **Supervision of pregnancy with history of ectopic pregnancy, unspecified trimester** ♀   M

O09.11   **Supervision of pregnancy with history of ectopic pregnancy, first trimester** ♀   M

O09.12   **Supervision of pregnancy with history of ectopic pregnancy, second trimester** ♀   M

O09.13   **Supervision of pregnancy with history of ectopic pregnancy, third trimester** ♀   M

● **O09.A**   **Supervision of pregnancy with history of molar pregnancy**
Coding Clinic: 2016, Q4, P50

O09.A0   **Supervision of pregnancy with history of molar pregnancy, unspecified trimester** ♀   M

O09.A1   **Supervision of pregnancy with history of molar pregnancy, first trimester** ♀   M

O09.A2   **Supervision of pregnancy with history of molar pregnancy, second trimester** ♀   M

O09.A3   **Supervision of pregnancy with history of molar pregnancy, third trimester** ♀   M

CHAPTER 15 (O00-O9A)

● **O09.2 Supervision of pregnancy with other poor reproductive or obstetric history**
> **Excludes2** pregnancy care for patient with history of recurrent pregnancy loss (O26.2-)

● **O09.21 Supervision of pregnancy with history of pre-term labor**

O09.211 Supervision of pregnancy with history of pre-term labor, first trimester ♀   M

O09.212 Supervision of pregnancy with history of pre-term labor, second trimester ♀   M

O09.213 Supervision of pregnancy with history of pre-term labor, third trimester ♀   M

O09.219 Supervision of pregnancy with history of pre-term labor, unspecified trimester ♀   M

● **O09.29 Supervision of pregnancy with other poor reproductive or obstetric history**
> Supervision of pregnancy with history of neonatal death
> Supervision of pregnancy with history of stillbirth

O09.291 Supervision of pregnancy with other poor reproductive or obstetric history, first trimester ♀   M

O09.292 Supervision of pregnancy with other poor reproductive or obstetric history, second trimester ♀   M

O09.293 Supervision of pregnancy with other poor reproductive or obstetric history, third trimester ♀   M

O09.299 Supervision of pregnancy with other poor reproductive or obstetric history, unspecified trimester ♀   M

● **O09.3 Supervision of pregnancy with insufficient antenatal care**
> Supervision of concealed pregnancy
> Supervision of hidden pregnancy

O09.30 Supervision of pregnancy with insufficient antenatal care, unspecified trimester ♀   M

O09.31 Supervision of pregnancy with insufficient antenatal care, first trimester ♀   M

O09.32 Supervision of pregnancy with insufficient antenatal care, second trimester ♀   M

O09.33 Supervision of pregnancy with insufficient antenatal care, third trimester ♀   M

● **O09.4 Supervision of pregnancy with grand multiparity**

O09.40 Supervision of pregnancy with grand multiparity, unspecified trimester ♀   M

O09.41 Supervision of pregnancy with grand multiparity, first trimester ♀   M

O09.42 Supervision of pregnancy with grand multiparity, second trimester ♀   M

O09.43 Supervision of pregnancy with grand multiparity, third trimester ♀   M

● **O09.5 Supervision of elderly primigravida and multigravida**
> Pregnancy for a female 35 years and older at expected date of delivery

● **O09.51 Supervision of elderly primigravida**

O09.511 Supervision of elderly primigravida, first trimester ♀   M

O09.512 Supervision of elderly primigravida, second trimester ♀   M

O09.513 Supervision of elderly primigravida, third trimester ♀   M

O09.519 Supervision of elderly primigravida, unspecified trimester ♀   M

● **O09.52 Supervision of elderly multigravida**

O09.521 Supervision of elderly multigravida, first trimester ♀   M

O09.522 Supervision of elderly multigravida, second trimester ♀   M

O09.523 Supervision of elderly multigravida, third trimester ♀   M
> **Coding Clinic: 2016, Q4, P150**

O09.529 Supervision of elderly multigravida, unspecified trimester ♀   M

● **O09.6 Supervision of young primigravida and multigravida**
> Supervision of pregnancy for a female less than 16 years old at expected date of delivery

● **O09.61 Supervision of young primigravida**

O09.611 Supervision of young primigravida, first trimester ♀   M

O09.612 Supervision of young primigravida, second trimester ♀   M

O09.613 Supervision of young primigravida, third trimester ♀   M

O09.619 Supervision of young primigravida, unspecified trimester ♀   M

● **O09.62 Supervision of young multigravida**

O09.621 Supervision of young multigravida, first trimester ♀   M

O09.622 Supervision of young multigravida, second trimester ♀   M

O09.623 Supervision of young multigravida, third trimester ♀   M

O09.629 Supervision of young multigravida, unspecified trimester ♀   M

● **O09.7 Supervision of high risk pregnancy due to social problems**

O09.70 Supervision of high risk pregnancy due to social problems, unspecified trimester ♀   M

O09.71 Supervision of high risk pregnancy due to social problems, first trimester ♀   M

O09.72 Supervision of high risk pregnancy due to social problems, second trimester ♀   M

O09.73 Supervision of high risk pregnancy due to social problems, third trimester ♀   M

● **O09.8 Supervision of other high risk pregnancies**

● **O09.81 Supervision of pregnancy resulting from assisted reproductive technology**
> Supervision of pregnancy resulting from in-vitro fertilization

> **Excludes2** gestational carrier status (Z33.3)

O09.811 Supervision of pregnancy resulting from assisted reproductive technology, first trimester ♀   M

O09.812 Supervision of pregnancy resulting from assisted reproductive technology, second trimester ♀   M

O09.813 Supervision of pregnancy resulting from assisted reproductive technology, third trimester ♀   M

O09.819 Supervision of pregnancy resulting from assisted reproductive technology, unspecified trimester ♀   M

● **O09.82** **Supervision of pregnancy with history of in utero procedure during previous pregnancy**

O09.821 Supervision of pregnancy with history of in utero procedure during previous pregnancy, first trimester ♀   M

O09.822 Supervision of pregnancy with history of in utero procedure during previous pregnancy, second trimester ♀   M

O09.823 Supervision of pregnancy with history of in utero procedure during previous pregnancy, third trimester ♀   M

O09.829 Supervision of pregnancy with history of in utero procedure during previous pregnancy, unspecified trimester ♀   M

     Excludes1 supervision of pregnancy affected by in utero procedure during current pregnancy (O35.7)

● **O09.89** **Supervision of other high risk pregnancies**

O09.891 Supervision of other high risk pregnancies, first trimester ♀   M

O09.892 Supervision of other high risk pregnancies, second trimester ♀   M

O09.893 Supervision of other high risk pregnancies, third trimester ♀   M

O09.899 Supervision of other high risk pregnancies, unspecified trimester ♀   M

● **O09.9** **Supervision of high risk pregnancy, unspecified**

O09.90 Supervision of high risk pregnancy, unspecified, unspecified trimester ♀   M

O09.91 Supervision of high risk pregnancy, unspecified, first trimester ♀   M

O09.92 Supervision of high risk pregnancy, unspecified, second trimester ♀   M

O09.93 Supervision of high risk pregnancy, unspecified, third trimester ♀   M

EDEMA, PROTEINURIA AND HYPERTENSIVE DISORDERS IN PREGNANCY, CHILDBIRTH AND THE PUERPERIUM (O10-O16)

● **O10** **Pre-existing hypertension complicating pregnancy, childbirth and the puerperium**

     Includes pre-existing hypertension with pre-existing proteinuria complicating pregnancy, childbirth and the puerperium

     Excludes2 pre-existing hypertension with superimposed pre-eclampsia complicating pregnancy, childbirth and the puerperium (O11.-)

     Coding Clinic: 2016, Q4, P50

● **O10.0** **Pre-existing essential hypertension complicating pregnancy, childbirth and the puerperium**

     Any condition in I10 specified as a reason for obstetric care during pregnancy, childbirth or the puerperium

● **O10.01** **Pre-existing essential hypertension complicating pregnancy**

O10.011 Pre-existing essential hypertension complicating pregnancy, first trimester ♀   M

O10.012 Pre-existing essential hypertension complicating pregnancy, second trimester ♀   M

O10.013 Pre-existing essential hypertension complicating pregnancy, third trimester ♀   M

O10.019 Pre-existing essential hypertension complicating pregnancy, unspecified trimester ♀   M

O10.02 Pre-existing essential hypertension complicating childbirth ♀   M

O10.03 Pre-existing essential hypertension complicating the puerperium ♀   M

● **O10.1** **Pre-existing hypertensive heart disease complicating pregnancy, childbirth and the puerperium**

     Any condition in I11 specified as a reason for obstetric care during pregnancy, childbirth or the puerperium

     Use additional code from I11 to identify the type of hypertensive heart disease

● **O10.11** **Pre-existing hypertensive heart disease complicating pregnancy**

O10.111 Pre-existing hypertensive heart disease complicating pregnancy, first trimester ♀   M

O10.112 Pre-existing hypertensive heart disease complicating pregnancy, second trimester ♀   M

O10.113 Pre-existing hypertensive heart disease complicating pregnancy, third trimester ♀   M

O10.119 Pre-existing hypertensive heart disease complicating pregnancy, unspecified trimester ♀   M

O10.12 Pre-existing hypertensive heart disease complicating childbirth ♀   M

O10.13 Pre-existing hypertensive heart disease complicating the puerperium ♀   M

● **O10.2** **Pre-existing hypertensive chronic kidney disease complicating pregnancy, childbirth and the puerperium**

     Any condition in I12 specified as a reason for obstetric care during pregnancy, childbirth or the puerperium

     Use additional code from I12 to identify the type of hypertensive chronic kidney disease

● **O10.21** **Pre-existing hypertensive chronic kidney disease complicating pregnancy**

O10.211 Pre-existing hypertensive chronic kidney disease complicating pregnancy, first trimester ♀   M

O10.212 Pre-existing hypertensive chronic kidney disease complicating pregnancy, second trimester ♀   M

O10.213 Pre-existing hypertensive chronic kidney disease complicating pregnancy, third trimester ♀   M

O10.219 Pre-existing hypertensive chronic kidney disease complicating pregnancy, unspecified trimester ♀   M

O10.22 Pre-existing hypertensive chronic kidney disease complicating childbirth ♀   M

O10.23 Pre-existing hypertensive chronic kidney disease complicating the puerperium ♀   M

CHAPTER 15 (O00-O9A)

● **O10.3** **Pre-existing hypertensive heart and chronic kidney disease complicating pregnancy, childbirth and the puerperium**
  Any condition in I13 specified as a reason for obstetric care during pregnancy, childbirth or the puerperium
  Use additional code from I13 to identify the type of hypertensive heart and chronic kidney disease

  ● **O10.31** **Pre-existing hypertensive heart and chronic kidney disease complicating pregnancy**
    O10.311 Pre-existing hypertensive heart and chronic kidney disease complicating pregnancy, first trimester ♀   M
    O10.312 Pre-existing hypertensive heart and chronic kidney disease complicating pregnancy, second trimester ♀   M
    O10.313 Pre-existing hypertensive heart and chronic kidney disease complicating pregnancy, third trimester ♀   M
    O10.319 Pre-existing hypertensive heart and chronic kidney disease complicating pregnancy, unspecified trimester ♀   M

  O10.32 Pre-existing hypertensive heart and chronic kidney disease complicating childbirth ♀   M
  O10.33 Pre-existing hypertensive heart and chronic kidney disease complicating the puerperium ♀   M

● **O10.4** **Pre-existing secondary hypertension complicating pregnancy, childbirth and the puerperium**
  Any condition in I15 specified as a reason for obstetric care during pregnancy, childbirth or the puerperium
  Use additional code from I15 to identify the type of secondary hypertension

  ● **O10.41** **Pre-existing secondary hypertension complicating pregnancy**
    O10.411 Pre-existing secondary hypertension complicating pregnancy, first trimester ♀   M
    O10.412 Pre-existing secondary hypertension complicating pregnancy, second trimester ♀   M
    O10.413 Pre-existing secondary hypertension complicating pregnancy, third trimester ♀   M
    O10.419 Pre-existing secondary hypertension complicating pregnancy, unspecified trimester ♀   M

  O10.42 Pre-existing secondary hypertension complicating childbirth ♀   M
  O10.43 Pre-existing secondary hypertension complicating the puerperium ♀   M

● **O10.9** **Unspecified pre-existing hypertension complicating pregnancy, childbirth and the puerperium**

  ● **O10.91** **Unspecified pre-existing hypertension complicating pregnancy**
    O10.911 Unspecified pre-existing hypertension complicating pregnancy, first trimester ♀   M
    O10.912 Unspecified pre-existing hypertension complicating pregnancy, second trimester ♀   M
    O10.913 Unspecified pre-existing hypertension complicating pregnancy, third trimester ♀   M
    O10.919 Unspecified pre-existing hypertension complicating pregnancy, unspecified trimester ♀   M

  O10.92 Unspecified pre-existing hypertension complicating childbirth ♀   M
  O10.93 Unspecified pre-existing hypertension complicating the puerperium ♀   M

● **O11** **Pre-existing hypertension with pre-eclampsia**
  Includes   conditions in O10 complicated by pre-eclampsia
  pre-eclampsia superimposed pre-existing hypertension
  Use additional code from O10 to identify the type of hypertension
  Coding Clinic: 2016, Q4, P50

  O11.1 Pre-existing hypertension with pre-eclampsia, first trimester ♀   M
  O11.2 Pre-existing hypertension with pre-eclampsia, second trimester ♀   M
  O11.3 Pre-existing hypertension with pre-eclampsia, third trimester ♀   M
  O11.4 Pre-existing hypertension with pre-eclampsia, complicating childbirth ♀   M
  O11.5 Pre-existing hypertension with pre-eclampsia, complicating the puerperium ♀   M
  O11.9 Pre-existing hypertension with pre-eclampsia, unspecified trimester ♀   M

● **O12** **Gestational [pregnancy-induced] edema and proteinuria without hypertension**
  Coding Clinic: 2016, Q4, P50

  ● **O12.0** **Gestational edema**
    O12.00 Gestational edema, unspecified trimester ♀   M
    O12.01 Gestational edema, first trimester ♀   M
    O12.02 Gestational edema, second trimester ♀   M
    O12.03 Gestational edema, third trimester ♀   M
    O12.04 Gestational edema, complicating childbirth ♀ M
    O12.05 Gestational edema, complicating the puerperium ♀   M

  ● **O12.1** **Gestational proteinuria**
    O12.10 Gestational proteinuria, unspecified trimester ♀   M
    O12.11 Gestational proteinuria, first trimester ♀   M
    O12.12 Gestational proteinuria, second trimester ♀   M
    O12.13 Gestational proteinuria, third trimester ♀   M
    O12.14 Gestational proteinuria, complicating childbirth ♀   M
    O12.15 Gestational proteinuria, complicating the puerperium ♀   M

  ● **O12.2** **Gestational edema with proteinuria**
    O12.20 Gestational edema with proteinuria, unspecified trimester ♀   M
    O12.21 Gestational edema with proteinuria, first trimester ♀   M
    O12.22 Gestational edema with proteinuria, second trimester ♀   M
    O12.23 Gestational edema with proteinuria, third trimester ♀   M
    O12.24 Gestational edema with proteinuria, complicating childbirth ♀   M
    O12.25 Gestational edema with proteinuria, complicating the puerperium ♀   M

▶ New   ⇒ Revised   ~~deleted~~ Deleted   Excludes 1   Excludes 2   Includes   Use additional   Code first   Code also   Key words
OGCR Official Guidelines   X Assign placeholder X   ● Use Additional Character(s)   ▶ Manifestation Code   🅗 Hierarchical Condition Category   Coding Clinic

● **O13 Gestational [pregnancy-induced] hypertension without significant proteinuria**
    Includes   gestational hypertension NOS
        transient hypertension of pregnancy ♀
    Coding Clinic: 2016, Q4, P50

    O13.1 Gestational [pregnancy-induced] hypertension without significant proteinuria, first trimester ♀   **M**

    O13.2 Gestational [pregnancy-induced] hypertension without significant proteinuria, second trimester ♀   **M**

    O13.3 Gestational [pregnancy-induced] hypertension without significant proteinuria, third trimester ♀   **M**

    O13.4 Gestational [pregnancy-induced] hypertension without significant proteinuria, complicating childbirth ♀   **M**

    O13.5 Gestational [pregnancy-induced] hypertension without significant proteinuria, complicating the puerperium ♀   **M**

    O13.9 Gestational [pregnancy-induced] hypertension without significant proteinuria, unspecified trimester ♀   **M**

● **O14 Pre-eclampsia**
    Excludes1   pre-existing hypertension with pre-eclampsia (O11)
    Coding Clinic: 2016, Q4, P50

  ● **O14.0 Mild to moderate pre-eclampsia**
    O14.00 Mild to moderate pre-eclampsia, unspecified trimester ♀   **M**

    O14.02 Mild to moderate pre-eclampsia, second trimester ♀   **M**

    O14.03 Mild to moderate pre-eclampsia, third trimester ♀   **M**

    O14.04 Mild to moderate pre-eclampsia, complicating childbirth ♀
        Coding Clinic: 2019, Q2, P8   **M**

    O14.05 Mild to moderate pre-eclampsia, complicating the puerperium ♀   **M**

  ● **O14.1 Severe pre-eclampsia**
    Excludes1   HELLP syndrome (O14.2-)
    H=hemolysis, EL=elevated liver enzymes, LP=low platelet count
    Coding Clinic: 2019, Q3, P12

    O14.10 Severe pre-eclampsia, unspecified trimester ♀ **M**
    O14.12 Severe pre-eclampsia, second trimester ♀ **M**
    O14.13 Severe pre-eclampsia, third trimester ♀ **M**
    O14.14 Severe pre-eclampsia complicating childbirth ♀ **M**
    O14.15 Severe pre-eclampsia, complicating the puerperium ♀ **M**

  ● **O14.2 HELLP syndrome**
    Severe pre-eclampsia with hemolysis, elevated liver enzymes and low platelet count (HELLP)

    O14.20 HELLP syndrome (HELLP), unspecified trimester ♀   **M**

    O14.22 HELLP syndrome (HELLP), second trimester ♀   **M**

    O14.23 HELLP syndrome (HELLP), third trimester ♀ **M**
    O14.24 HELLP syndrome, complicating childbirth ♀ **M**
    O14.25 HELLP syndrome, complicating the puerperium ♀   **M**

  ● **O14.9 Unspecified pre-eclampsia**
    O14.90 Unspecified pre-eclampsia, unspecified trimester ♀   **M**

    O14.92 Unspecified pre-eclampsia, second trimester ♀   **M**

    O14.93 Unspecified pre-eclampsia, third trimester ♀ **M**
    O14.94 Unspecified pre-eclampsia, complicating childbirth ♀   **M**

    O14.95 Unspecified pre-eclampsia, complicating the puerperium ♀   **M**

● **O15 Eclampsia**
    Includes   convulsions following conditions in O10-O14 and O16

  ● **O15.0 Eclampsia complicating pregnancy**
    Coding Clinic: 2016, Q4, P50

    O15.00 Eclampsia complicating pregnancy, unspecified trimester ♀   **M**

    O15.02 Eclampsia complicating pregnancy, second trimester ♀   **M**

    O15.03 Eclampsia complicating pregnancy, third trimester ♀   **M**

    O15.1 Eclampsia complicating labor ♀   **M**
    O15.2 Eclampsia complicating the puerperium ♀   **M**
    O15.9 Eclampsia, unspecified as to time period ♀   **M**
        Eclampsia NOS

● **O16 Unspecified maternal hypertension**
    Coding Clinic: 2016, Q4, P50

    O16.1 Unspecified maternal hypertension, first trimester ♀   **M**
    O16.2 Unspecified maternal hypertension, second trimester ♀   **M**
    O16.3 Unspecified maternal hypertension, third trimester ♀   **M**
    O16.4 Unspecified maternal hypertension, complicating childbirth ♀   **M**
    O16.5 Unspecified maternal hypertension, complicating the puerperium ♀   **M**
    O16.9 Unspecified maternal hypertension, unspecified trimester ♀   **M**

OTHER MATERNAL DISORDERS PREDOMINANTLY RELATED TO PREGNANCY (O20-O29)

    Excludes2   maternal care related to the fetus and amniotic cavity and possible delivery problems (O30-O48)
        maternal diseases classifiable elsewhere but complicating pregnancy, labor and delivery, and the puerperium (O98-O99)

● **O20 Hemorrhage in early pregnancy**
    Includes   hemorrhage before completion of 20 weeks gestation
    Excludes1   pregnancy with abortive outcome (O00-O08)

    O20.0 Threatened abortion ♀   **M**
        Hemorrhage specified as due to threatened abortion

    O20.8 Other hemorrhage in early pregnancy ♀   **M**
    O20.9 Hemorrhage in early pregnancy, unspecified ♀   **M**

● **O21 Excessive vomiting in pregnancy**
    O21.0 Mild hyperemesis gravidarum ♀   **M**
        Hyperemesis gravidarum, mild or unspecified, starting before the end of the 20th week of gestation

    O21.1 Hyperemesis gravidarum with metabolic disturbance ♀   **M**
        Hyperemesis gravidarum, starting before the end of the 20th week of gestation, with metabolic disturbance such as carbohydrate depletion
        Hyperemesis gravidarum, starting before the end of the 20th week of gestation, with metabolic disturbance such as dehydration
        Hyperemesis gravidarum, starting before the end of the 20th week of gestation, with metabolic disturbance such as electrolyte imbalance

    O21.2 Late vomiting of pregnancy ♀   **M**
        Excessive vomiting starting after 20 completed weeks of gestation

    O21.8 Other vomiting complicating pregnancy ♀   **M**
        Vomiting due to diseases classified elsewhere, complicating pregnancy
        Use additional code, to identify cause

    O21.9 Vomiting of pregnancy, unspecified ♀   **M**

CHAPTER 15 (O00-O9A)

● **O22   Venous complications and hemorrhoids in pregnancy**

    Excludes1   venous complications of:
        abortion NOS (O03.9)
        ectopic or molar pregnancy (O08.7)
        failed attempted abortion (O07.35)
        induced abortion (O04.85)
        spontaneous abortion (O03.89)

    Excludes2   obstetric pulmonary embolism (O88.-)
        venous complications and hemorrhoids of
        childbirth and the puerperium (O87.-)

● **O22.0   Varicose veins of lower extremity in pregnancy**
    Varicose veins NOS in pregnancy

    O22.00   Varicose veins of lower extremity in pregnancy, unspecified trimester ♀   M

    O22.01   Varicose veins of lower extremity in pregnancy, first trimester ♀   M

    O22.02   Varicose veins of lower extremity in pregnancy, second trimester ♀   M

    O22.03   Varicose veins of lower extremity in pregnancy, third trimester ♀   M

● **O22.1   Genital varices in pregnancy**
    Perineal varices in pregnancy
    Vaginal varices in pregnancy
    Vulval varices in pregnancy

    O22.10   Genital varices in pregnancy, unspecified trimester ♀   M

    O22.11   Genital varices in pregnancy, first trimester ♀ M

    O22.12   Genital varices in pregnancy, second trimester ♀   M

    O22.13   Genital varices in pregnancy, third trimester ♀ M

● **O22.2   Superficial thrombophlebitis in pregnancy**
    Phlebitis in pregnancy NOS
    Thrombophlebitis of legs in pregnancy
    Thrombosis in pregnancy NOS

    Use additional code to identify the superficial thrombophlebitis (I80.0-)

    O22.20   Superficial thrombophlebitis in pregnancy, unspecified trimester ♀   M

    O22.21   Superficial thrombophlebitis in pregnancy, first trimester ♀   M

    O22.22   Superficial thrombophlebitis in pregnancy, second trimester ♀   M

    O22.23   Superficial thrombophlebitis in pregnancy, third trimester ♀   M

● **O22.3   Deep phlebothrombosis in pregnancy**
    Deep vein thrombosis, antepartum

    Use additional code to identify the deep vein thrombosis (I82.4-, I82.5-, I82.62-. I82.72-)

    Use additional code, if applicable, for associated long-term (current) use of anticoagulants (Z79.01)

    O22.30   Deep phlebothrombosis in pregnancy, unspecified trimester ♀   M

    O22.31   Deep phlebothrombosis in pregnancy, first trimester ♀   M

    O22.32   Deep phlebothrombosis in pregnancy, second trimester ♀   M

    O22.33   Deep phlebothrombosis in pregnancy, third trimester ♀   M

● **O22.4   Hemorrhoids in pregnancy**

    O22.40   Hemorrhoids in pregnancy, unspecified trimester ♀   M

    O22.41   Hemorrhoids in pregnancy, first trimester ♀   M

    O22.42   Hemorrhoids in pregnancy, second trimester ♀   M

    O22.43   Hemorrhoids in pregnancy, third trimester ♀   M

● **O22.5   Cerebral venous thrombosis in pregnancy**
    Cerebrovenous sinus thrombosis in pregnancy

    O22.50   Cerebral venous thrombosis in pregnancy, unspecified trimester ♀   M

    O22.51   Cerebral venous thrombosis in pregnancy, first trimester ♀   M

    O22.52   Cerebral venous thrombosis in pregnancy, second trimester ♀   M

    O22.53   Cerebral venous thrombosis in pregnancy, third trimester ♀   M

● **O22.8   Other venous complications in pregnancy**

    ● **O22.8X   Other venous complications in pregnancy**

        O22.8X1   Other venous complications in pregnancy, first trimester ♀   M

        O22.8X2   Other venous complications in pregnancy, second trimester ♀   M

        O22.8X3   Other venous complications in pregnancy, third trimester ♀   M

        O22.8X9   Other venous complications in pregnancy, unspecified trimester ♀   M

● **O22.9   Venous complication in pregnancy, unspecified**
    Gestational phlebitis NOS
    Gestational phlebopathy NOS
    Gestational thrombosis NOS

    O22.90   Venous complication in pregnancy, unspecified, unspecified trimester ♀   M

    O22.91   Venous complication in pregnancy, unspecified, first trimester ♀   M

    O22.92   Venous complication in pregnancy, unspecified, second trimester ♀   M

    O22.93   Venous complication in pregnancy, unspecified, third trimester ♀   M

● **O23   Infections of genitourinary tract in pregnancy**

    Use additional code to identify organism (B95.-, B96.-)

    Excludes2   gonococcal infections complicating pregnancy, childbirth and the puerperium (O98.2)
        infections with a predominantly sexual mode of transmission NOS complicating pregnancy, childbirth and the puerperium (O98.3)
        syphilis complicating pregnancy, childbirth and the puerperium (O98.1)
        tuberculosis of genitourinary system complicating pregnancy, childbirth and the puerperium (O98.0)
        venereal disease NOS complicating pregnancy, childbirth and the puerperium (O98.3)

● **O23.0   Infections of kidney in pregnancy**
    Pyelonephritis in pregnancy

    O23.00   Infections of kidney in pregnancy, unspecified trimester ♀   M

    O23.01   Infections of kidney in pregnancy, first trimester ♀   M

    O23.02   Infections of kidney in pregnancy, second trimester ♀   M

    O23.03   Infections of kidney in pregnancy, third trimester ♀   M

● **O23.1   Infections of bladder in pregnancy**

    O23.10   Infections of bladder in pregnancy, unspecified trimester ♀   M

    O23.11   Infections of bladder in pregnancy, first trimester ♀   M

    O23.12   Infections of bladder in pregnancy, second trimester ♀   M

    O23.13   Infections of bladder in pregnancy, third trimester ♀   M

● O23.2   Infections of urethra in pregnancy
     O23.20   Infections of urethra in pregnancy, unspecified trimester ♀   M
     O23.21   Infections of urethra in pregnancy, first trimester ♀   M
     O23.22   Infections of urethra in pregnancy, second trimester ♀   M
     O23.23   Infections of urethra in pregnancy, third trimester ♀   M

● O23.3   Infections of other parts of urinary tract in pregnancy
     O23.30   Infections of other parts of urinary tract in pregnancy, unspecified trimester ♀   M
     O23.31   Infections of other parts of urinary tract in pregnancy, first trimester ♀   M
     O23.32   Infections of other parts of urinary tract in pregnancy, second trimester ♀   M
     O23.33   Infections of other parts of urinary tract in pregnancy, third trimester ♀   M

● O23.4   Unspecified infection of urinary tract in pregnancy
     O23.40   Unspecified infection of urinary tract in pregnancy, unspecified trimester ♀   M
     O23.41   Unspecified infection of urinary tract in pregnancy, first trimester ♀   M
     O23.42   Unspecified infection of urinary tract in pregnancy, second trimester ♀   M
     O23.43   Unspecified infection of urinary tract in pregnancy, third trimester ♀   M

● O23.5   Infections of the genital tract in pregnancy
     ● O23.51   Infection of cervix in pregnancy
         O23.511   Infections of cervix in pregnancy, first trimester ♀   M
         O23.512   Infections of cervix in pregnancy, second trimester ♀   M
         O23.513   Infections of cervix in pregnancy, third trimester ♀   M
         O23.519   Infections of cervix in pregnancy, unspecified trimester ♀   M
     ● O23.52   Salpingo-oophoritis in pregnancy
         Oophoritis = inflammation of ovary
         Salpingitis = inflammation of fallopian tube
         Oophoritis in pregnancy
         Salpingitis in pregnancy
         O23.521   Salpingo-oophoritis in pregnancy, first trimester ♀   M
         O23.522   Salpingo-oophoritis in pregnancy, second trimester ♀   M
         O23.523   Salpingo-oophoritis in pregnancy, third trimester ♀   M
         O23.529   Salpingo-oophoritis in pregnancy, unspecified trimester ♀   M
     ● O23.59   Infection of other part of genital tract in pregnancy
         O23.591   Infection of other part of genital tract in pregnancy, first trimester ♀   M
         O23.592   Infection of other part of genital tract in pregnancy, second trimester ♀   M
         O23.593   Infection of other part of genital tract in pregnancy, third trimester ♀   M
         O23.599   Infection of other part of genital tract in pregnancy, unspecified trimester ♀   M

● O23.9   Unspecified genitourinary tract infection in pregnancy
     Genitourinary tract infection in pregnancy NOS
     O23.90   Unspecified genitourinary tract infection in pregnancy, unspecified trimester ♀   M
     O23.91   Unspecified genitourinary tract infection in pregnancy, first trimester ♀   M
     O23.92   Unspecified genitourinary tract infection in pregnancy, second trimester ♀   M
     O23.93   Unspecified genitourinary tract infection in pregnancy, third trimester ♀   M

OGCR Section I.C.15.g.

Diabetes mellitus in pregnancy
Diabetes mellitus is a significant complicating factor in pregnancy. Pregnant women who are diabetic should be assigned a code from category O24, Diabetes mellitus in pregnancy, childbirth, and the puerperium, first, followed by the appropriate diabetes code(s) (E08-E13) from Chapter 4.

● O24   Diabetes mellitus in pregnancy, childbirth, and the puerperium
     ● O24.0   Pre-existing type 1 diabetes mellitus, in pregnancy, childbirth and the puerperium
         Juvenile onset diabetes mellitus, in pregnancy, childbirth and the puerperium
         Ketosis-prone diabetes mellitus in pregnancy, childbirth and the puerperium
         Use additional code from category E10 to further identify any manifestations
         ● O24.01   Pre-existing type 1 diabetes mellitus, in pregnancy
             O24.011   Pre-existing type 1 diabetes mellitus, in pregnancy, first trimester ♀   M
             O24.012   Pre-existing type 1 diabetes mellitus, in pregnancy, second trimester ♀   M
             O24.013   Pre-existing type 1 diabetes mellitus, in pregnancy, third trimester ♀   M
             O24.019   Pre-existing type 1 diabetes mellitus, in pregnancy, unspecified trimester ♀   M
         O24.02   Pre-existing type 1 diabetes mellitus, in childbirth ♀   M
         O24.03   Pre-existing type 1 diabetes mellitus, in the puerperium ♀   M
     ● O24.1   Pre-existing type 2 diabetes mellitus, in pregnancy, childbirth and the puerperium
         Insulin-resistant diabetes mellitus in pregnancy, childbirth and the puerperium
         Use additional code (for):
         from category E11 to further identify any manifestations
         long-term (current) use of insulin (Z79.4)
         ● O24.11   Pre-existing type 2 diabetes mellitus, in pregnancy
             O24.111   Pre-existing type 2 diabetes mellitus, in pregnancy, first trimester ♀   M
             O24.112   Pre-existing type 2 diabetes mellitus, in pregnancy, second trimester ♀   M
             O24.113   Pre-existing type 2 diabetes mellitus, in pregnancy, third trimester ♀   M
             O24.119   Pre-existing type 2 diabetes mellitus, in pregnancy, unspecified trimester ♀   M
         O24.12   Pre-existing type 2 diabetes mellitus, in childbirth ♀   M
         O24.13   Pre-existing type 2 diabetes mellitus, in the puerperium ♀   M

● **O24.3 Unspecified pre-existing diabetes mellitus in pregnancy, childbirth and the puerperium**
Use additional code (for):
    from category E11 to further identify any manifestation
    long-term (current) use of insulin (Z79.4)

  ● **O24.31 Unspecified pre-existing diabetes mellitus in pregnancy**

    O24.311 Unspecified pre-existing diabetes mellitus in pregnancy, first trimester ♀   **M**

    O24.312 Unspecified pre-existing diabetes mellitus in pregnancy, second trimester ♀   **M**

    O24.313 Unspecified pre-existing diabetes mellitus in pregnancy, third trimester ♀   **M**

    O24.319 Unspecified pre-existing diabetes mellitus in pregnancy, unspecified trimester ♀   **M**

  O24.32 Unspecified pre-existing diabetes mellitus in childbirth ♀   **M**

  O24.33 Unspecified pre-existing diabetes mellitus in the puerperium ♀   **M**

● **O24.4 Gestational diabetes mellitus**
Diabetes mellitus arising in pregnancy
Gestational diabetes mellitus NOS
Coding Clinic: 2016, Q4, P50, 126

  ● **O24.41 Gestational diabetes mellitus in pregnancy**

    O24.410 Gestational diabetes mellitus in pregnancy, diet controlled ♀   **M**

    O24.414 Gestational diabetes mellitus in pregnancy, insulin controlled ♀   **M**

    O24.415 Gestational diabetes mellitus in pregnancy, controlled by oral hypoglycemic drugs ♀   **M**
        Gestational diabetes mellitus in pregnancy, controlled by oral antidiabetic drugs
        Coding Clinic: 2016, Q4, P50

    O24.419 Gestational diabetes mellitus in pregnancy, unspecified control ♀   **M**
        Coding Clinic: 2015, Q4, P34

  ● **O24.42 Gestational diabetes mellitus in childbirth**

    O24.420 Gestational diabetes mellitus in childbirth, diet controlled ♀   **M**

    O24.424 Gestational diabetes mellitus in childbirth, insulin controlled ♀   **M**

    O24.425 Gestational diabetes mellitus in childbirth, controlled by oral hypoglycemic drugs ♀   **M**
        Gestational diabetes mellitus in childbirth, controlled by oral antidiabetic drugs
        Coding Clinic: 2016, Q4, P50

    O24.429 Gestational diabetes mellitus in childbirth, unspecified control ♀   **M**

  ● **O24.43 Gestational diabetes mellitus in the puerperium**

    O24.430 Gestational diabetes mellitus in the puerperium, diet controlled ♀   **M**

    O24.434 Gestational diabetes mellitus in the puerperium, insulin controlled ♀   **M**

    O24.435 Gestational diabetes mellitus in puerperium, controlled by oral hypoglycemic drugs ♀   **M**
        Gestational diabetes mellitus in puerperium, controlled by oral antidiabetic drugs
        Coding Clinic: 2016, Q4, P50

    O24.439 Gestational diabetes mellitus in the puerperium, unspecified control ♀   **M**

● **O24.8 Other pre-existing diabetes mellitus in pregnancy, childbirth, and the puerperium**
Use additional code (for):
    from categories E08, E09 and E13 to further identify any manifestation
    long-term (current) use of insulin (Z79.4)

  ● **O24.81 Other pre-existing diabetes mellitus in pregnancy**

    O24.811 Other pre-existing diabetes mellitus in pregnancy, first trimester ♀   **M**

    O24.812 Other pre-existing diabetes mellitus in pregnancy, second trimester ♀   **M**

    O24.813 Other pre-existing diabetes mellitus in pregnancy, third trimester ♀   **M**

    O24.819 Other pre-existing diabetes mellitus in pregnancy, unspecified trimester ♀   **M**

  O24.82 Other pre-existing diabetes mellitus in childbirth ♀   **M**

  O24.83 Other pre-existing diabetes mellitus in the puerperium ♀   **M**

● **O24.9 Unspecified diabetes mellitus in pregnancy, childbirth and the puerperium**
Use additional code for long-term (current) use of insulin (Z79.4)
Unknown whether patient was diabetic before pregnancy occurred

  ● **O24.91 Unspecified diabetes mellitus in pregnancy**

    O24.911 Unspecified diabetes mellitus in pregnancy, first trimester ♀   **M**

    O24.912 Unspecified diabetes mellitus in pregnancy, second trimester ♀   **M**

    O24.913 Unspecified diabetes mellitus in pregnancy, third trimester ♀   **M**

    O24.919 Unspecified diabetes mellitus in pregnancy, unspecified trimester ♀   **M**

  O24.92 Unspecified diabetes mellitus in childbirth ♀   **M**

  O24.93 Unspecified diabetes mellitus in the puerperium ♀   **M**

▶ New   ⇒ Revised   ~~deleted~~ Deleted   Excludes 1   Excludes 2   Includes   Use additional   Code first   Code also   Key words
OGCR Official Guidelines   X Assign placeholder X   ● Use Additional Character(s)   ▶ Manifestation Code   🅠 Hierarchical Condition Category   **Coding Clinic**

● **O25   Malnutrition in pregnancy, childbirth and the puerperium**
  ● **O25.1   Malnutrition in pregnancy**
     O25.10   Malnutrition in pregnancy, unspecified trimester ♀   M
     O25.11   Malnutrition in pregnancy, first trimester ♀   M
     O25.12   Malnutrition in pregnancy, second trimester ♀ M
     O25.13   Malnutrition in pregnancy, third trimester ♀   M
    O25.2   Malnutrition in childbirth ♀   M
    O25.3   Malnutrition in the puerperium ♀   M

● **O26   Maternal care for other conditions predominantly related to pregnancy**
  ● **O26.0   Excessive weight gain in pregnancy**
      Excludes2   gestational edema (O12.0, O12.2)
     O26.00   Excessive weight gain in pregnancy, unspecified trimester ♀   M
     O26.01   Excessive weight gain in pregnancy, first trimester ♀   M
     O26.02   Excessive weight gain in pregnancy, second trimester ♀   M
     O26.03   Excessive weight gain in pregnancy, third trimester ♀   M
  ● **O26.1   Low weight gain in pregnancy**
     O26.10   Low weight gain in pregnancy, unspecified trimester ♀   M
     O26.11   Low weight gain in pregnancy, first trimester ♀   M
     O26.12   Low weight gain in pregnancy, second trimester ♀   M
     O26.13   Low weight gain in pregnancy, third trimester ♀   M
  ● **O26.2   Pregnancy care for patient with recurrent pregnancy loss**
     O26.20   Pregnancy care for patient with recurrent pregnancy loss, unspecified trimester ♀   M
     O26.21   Pregnancy care for patient with recurrent pregnancy loss, first trimester ♀   M
     O26.22   Pregnancy care for patient with recurrent pregnancy loss, second trimester ♀   M
     O26.23   Pregnancy care for patient with recurrent pregnancy loss, third trimester ♀   M
  ● **O26.3   Retained intrauterine contraceptive device in pregnancy**
     O26.30   Retained intrauterine contraceptive device in pregnancy, unspecified trimester ♀   M
     O26.31   Retained intrauterine contraceptive device in pregnancy, first trimester ♀   M
     O26.32   Retained intrauterine contraceptive device in pregnancy, second trimester ♀   M
     O26.33   Retained intrauterine contraceptive device in pregnancy, third trimester ♀   M
  ● **O26.4   Herpes gestationis**
     O26.40   Herpes gestationis, unspecified trimester ♀   M
     O26.41   Herpes gestationis, first trimester ♀   M
     O26.42   Herpes gestationis, second trimester ♀   M
     O26.43   Herpes gestationis, third trimester ♀   M
  ● **O26.5   Maternal hypotension syndrome**
     Supine hypotensive syndrome
     O26.50   Maternal hypotension syndrome, unspecified trimester ♀   M
     O26.51   Maternal hypotension syndrome, first trimester ♀   M
     O26.52   Maternal hypotension syndrome, second trimester ♀   M
     O26.53   Maternal hypotension syndrome, third trimester ♀   M

  ● **O26.6   Liver and biliary tract disorders in pregnancy, childbirth and the puerperium**
     Use additional code to identify the specific disorder
     Excludes2   hepatorenal syndrome following labor and delivery (O90.4)
   ● **O26.61   Liver and biliary tract disorders in pregnancy**
     O26.611   Liver and biliary tract disorders in pregnancy, first trimester ♀   M
     O26.612   Liver and biliary tract disorders in pregnancy, second trimester ♀   M
     O26.613   Liver and biliary tract disorders in pregnancy, third trimester ♀   M
     O26.619   Liver and biliary tract disorders in pregnancy, unspecified trimester ♀   M
    O26.62   Liver and biliary tract disorders in childbirth ♀   M
    O26.63   Liver and biliary tract disorders in the puerperium ♀   M
  ● **O26.7   Subluxation of symphysis (pubis) in pregnancy, childbirth and the puerperium**
     Excludes1   traumatic separation of symphysis (pubis) during childbirth (O71.6)
   ● **O26.71   Subluxation of symphysis (pubis) in pregnancy**
     O26.711   Subluxation of symphysis (pubis) in pregnancy, first trimester ♀   M
     O26.712   Subluxation of symphysis (pubis) in pregnancy, second trimester ♀   M
     O26.713   Subluxation of symphysis (pubis) in pregnancy, third trimester ♀   M
     O26.719   Subluxation of symphysis (pubis) in pregnancy, unspecified trimester ♀   M
    O26.72   Subluxation of symphysis (pubis) in childbirth ♀   M
    O26.73   Subluxation of symphysis (pubis) in the puerperium ♀   M
  ● **O26.8   Other specified pregnancy related conditions**
   ● **O26.81   Pregnancy related exhaustion and fatigue**
     O26.811   Pregnancy related exhaustion and fatigue, first trimester ♀   M
     O26.812   Pregnancy related exhaustion and fatigue, second trimester ♀   M
     O26.813   Pregnancy related exhaustion and fatigue, third trimester ♀   M
     O26.819   Pregnancy related exhaustion and fatigue, unspecified trimester ♀   M
   ● **O26.82   Pregnancy related peripheral neuritis**
     O26.821   Pregnancy related peripheral neuritis, first trimester ♀   M
     O26.822   Pregnancy related peripheral neuritis, second trimester ♀   M
     O26.823   Pregnancy related peripheral neuritis, third trimester ♀   M
     O26.829   Pregnancy related peripheral neuritis, unspecified trimester ♀   M
   ● **O26.83   Pregnancy related renal disease**
     Use additional code to identify the specific disorder
     O26.831   Pregnancy related renal disease, first trimester ♀   M
     O26.832   Pregnancy related renal disease, second trimester ♀   M
     O26.833   Pregnancy related renal disease, third trimester ♀   M
     O26.839   Pregnancy related renal disease, unspecified trimester ♀   M

● **O26.84** **Uterine size-date discrepancy complicating pregnancy**

     Excludes1   encounter for suspected problem with fetal growth ruled out (Z03.74)

     O26.841   Uterine size-date discrepancy, **first** trimester ♀   M

     O26.842   Uterine size-date discrepancy, **second** trimester ♀   M

     O26.843   Uterine size-date discrepancy, **third** trimester ♀   M

     O26.849   Uterine size-date discrepancy, **unspecified trimester** ♀   M

● **O26.85** **Spotting complicating pregnancy**

     O26.851   Spotting complicating pregnancy, **first** trimester ♀   M

     O26.852   Spotting complicating pregnancy, **second trimester** ♀   M

     O26.853   Spotting complicating pregnancy, **third trimester** ♀   M

     O26.859   Spotting complicating pregnancy, **unspecified trimester** ♀   M

O26.86   Pruritic urticarial papules and plaques of pregnancy (PUPPP) ♀   M
     Polymorphic eruption of pregnancy

● **O26.87** **Cervical shortening**

     Excludes1   encounter for suspected cervical shortening ruled out (Z03.75)

     O26.872   Cervical shortening, **second** trimester ♀   M

     O26.873   Cervical shortening, **third** trimester ♀   M

     O26.879   Cervical shortening, **unspecified** trimester ♀   M

● **O26.89** **Other specified pregnancy related conditions**

     O26.891   Other specified pregnancy related conditions, **first trimester** ♀   M

     O26.892   Other specified pregnancy related conditions, **second trimester** ♀   M

     O26.893   Other specified pregnancy related conditions, **third trimester** ♀   M
       Coding Clinic: 2015, Q3, P40

     O26.899   Other specified pregnancy related conditions, **unspecified trimester** ♀   M

● **O26.9**   **Pregnancy related conditions, unspecified**

     O26.90   Pregnancy related conditions, unspecified, **unspecified trimester** ♀   M

     O26.91   Pregnancy related conditions, unspecified, **first** trimester ♀   M

     O26.92   Pregnancy related conditions, unspecified, **second trimester** ♀   M

     O26.93   Pregnancy related conditions, unspecified, **third** trimester ♀   M

● **O28**   **Abnormal findings on antenatal screening of mother**

     Excludes1   diagnostic findings classified elsewhere - see Alphabetical Index

O28.0   Abnormal **hematological** finding on antenatal screening of mother ♀   M

O28.1   Abnormal **biochemical** finding on antenatal screening of mother ♀   M

O28.2   Abnormal **cytological** finding on antenatal screening of mother ♀   M

O28.3   Abnormal **ultrasonic** finding on antenatal screening of mother ♀   M
     Coding Clinic: 2016, Q4, P5

O28.4   Abnormal **radiological** finding on antenatal screening of mother ♀   M

O28.5   Abnormal **chromosomal and genetic** finding on antenatal screening of mother ♀   M

O28.8   Other abnormal findings on antenatal screening of mother ♀   M

O28.9   Unspecified abnormal findings on antenatal screening of mother ♀   M

● **O29**   **Complications of anesthesia during pregnancy**

     Includes   maternal complications arising from the administration of a general, regional or local anesthetic, analgesic or other sedation during pregnancy

     Use additional code, if necessary, to identify the complication

     Excludes2   complications of anesthesia during labor and delivery (O74.-)
       complications of anesthesia during the puerperium (O89.-)

● **O29.0**   **Pulmonary complications of anesthesia during pregnancy**

   ● **O29.01**   **Aspiration pneumonitis due to anesthesia during pregnancy**
       Inhalation of stomach contents or secretions NOS due to anesthesia during pregnancy
       Mendelson's syndrome due to anesthesia during pregnancy

     O29.011   Aspiration pneumonitis due to anesthesia during pregnancy, **first** trimester ♀   M

     O29.012   Aspiration pneumonitis due to anesthesia during pregnancy, **second** trimester ♀   M

     O29.013   Aspiration pneumonitis due to anesthesia during pregnancy, **third** trimester ♀   M

     O29.019   Aspiration pneumonitis due to anesthesia during pregnancy, **unspecified trimester** ♀   M

   ● **O29.02**   **Pressure collapse of lung due to anesthesia during pregnancy**

     O29.021   Pressure collapse of lung due to anesthesia during pregnancy, **first** trimester ♀   M

     O29.022   Pressure collapse of lung due to anesthesia during pregnancy, **second** trimester ♀   M

     O29.023   Pressure collapse of lung due to anesthesia during pregnancy, **third** trimester ♀   M

     O29.029   Pressure collapse of lung due to anesthesia during pregnancy, **unspecified trimester** ♀   M

   ● **O29.09**   **Other pulmonary complications of anesthesia during pregnancy**

     O29.091   Other pulmonary complications of anesthesia during pregnancy, **first** trimester ♀   M

     O29.092   Other pulmonary complications of anesthesia during pregnancy, **second** trimester ♀   M

     O29.093   Other pulmonary complications of anesthesia during pregnancy, **third** trimester ♀   M

     O29.099   Other pulmonary complications of anesthesia during pregnancy, **unspecified trimester** ♀   M

▶ New   ⇒ Revised   ~~deleted~~ Deleted   Excludes 1   Excludes 2   Includes   Use additional   Code first   Code also   Key words

OGCR Official Guidelines   X Assign placeholder X   ● Use Additional Character(s)   ▷ Manifestation Code   🖢 Hierarchical Condition Category   **Coding Clinic**

● **O29.1   Cardiac complications of anesthesia during pregnancy**
   ● **O29.11   Cardiac arrest due to anesthesia during pregnancy**
     O29.111   Cardiac arrest due to anesthesia during pregnancy, first trimester ♀ M
     O29.112   Cardiac arrest due to anesthesia during pregnancy, second trimester ♀   M
     O29.113   Cardiac arrest due to anesthesia during pregnancy, third trimester ♀ M
     O29.119   Cardiac arrest due to anesthesia during pregnancy, unspecified trimester ♀   M
   ● **O29.12   Cardiac failure due to anesthesia during pregnancy**
     O29.121   Cardiac failure due to anesthesia during pregnancy, first trimester ♀ M
     O29.122   Cardiac failure due to anesthesia during pregnancy, second trimester ♀   M
     O29.123   Cardiac failure due to anesthesia during pregnancy, third trimester ♀ M
     O29.129   Cardiac failure due to anesthesia during pregnancy, unspecified trimester ♀   M
   ● **O29.19   Other cardiac complications of anesthesia during pregnancy**
     O29.191   Other cardiac complications of anesthesia during pregnancy, first trimester ♀   M
     O29.192   Other cardiac complications of anesthesia during pregnancy, second trimester ♀   M
     O29.193   Other cardiac complications of anesthesia during pregnancy, third trimester ♀   M
     O29.199   Other cardiac complications of anesthesia during pregnancy, unspecified trimester ♀   M

● **O29.2   Central nervous system complications of anesthesia during pregnancy**
   ● **O29.21   Cerebral anoxia due to anesthesia during pregnancy**
     O29.211   Cerebral anoxia due to anesthesia during pregnancy, first trimester ♀ M
     O29.212   Cerebral anoxia due to anesthesia during pregnancy, second trimester ♀   M
     O29.213   Cerebral anoxia due to anesthesia during pregnancy, third trimester ♀ M
     O29.219   Cerebral anoxia due to anesthesia during pregnancy, unspecified trimester ♀   M
   ● **O29.29   Other central nervous system complications of anesthesia during pregnancy**
     O29.291   Other central nervous system complications of anesthesia during pregnancy, first trimester ♀   M
     O29.292   Other central nervous system complications of anesthesia during pregnancy, second trimester ♀   M
     O29.293   Other central nervous system complications of anesthesia during pregnancy, third trimester ♀   M
     O29.299   Other central nervous system complications of anesthesia during pregnancy, unspecified trimester ♀ M

● **O29.3   Toxic reaction to local anesthesia during pregnancy**
   ● **O29.3X   Toxic reaction to local anesthesia during pregnancy**
     O29.3X1   Toxic reaction to local anesthesia during pregnancy, first trimester ♀ M
     O29.3X2   Toxic reaction to local anesthesia during pregnancy, second trimester ♀   M
     O29.3X3   Toxic reaction to local anesthesia during pregnancy, third trimester ♀ M
     O29.3X9   Toxic reaction to local anesthesia during pregnancy, unspecified trimester ♀   M

● **O29.4   Spinal and epidural anesthesia induced headache during pregnancy**
     O29.40   Spinal and epidural anesthesia induced headache during pregnancy, unspecified trimester ♀   M
     O29.41   Spinal and epidural anesthesia induced headache during pregnancy, first trimester ♀ M
     O29.42   Spinal and epidural anesthesia induced headache during pregnancy, second trimester ♀   M
     O29.43   Spinal and epidural anesthesia induced headache during pregnancy, third trimester ♀ M

● **O29.5   Other complications of spinal and epidural anesthesia during pregnancy**
   ● **O29.5X   Other complications of spinal and epidural anesthesia during pregnancy**
     O29.5X1   Other complications of spinal and epidural anesthesia during pregnancy, first trimester ♀   M
     O29.5X2   Other complications of spinal and epidural anesthesia during pregnancy, second trimester ♀   M
     O29.5X3   Other complications of spinal and epidural anesthesia during pregnancy, third trimester ♀   M
     O29.5X9   Other complications of spinal and epidural anesthesia during pregnancy, unspecified trimester ♀   M

● **O29.6   Failed or difficult intubation for anesthesia during pregnancy**
     O29.60   Failed or difficult intubation for anesthesia during pregnancy, unspecified trimester ♀   M
     O29.61   Failed or difficult intubation for anesthesia during pregnancy, first trimester ♀   M
     O29.62   Failed or difficult intubation for anesthesia during pregnancy, second trimester ♀   M
     O29.63   Failed or difficult intubation for anesthesia during pregnancy, third trimester ♀   M

● **O29.8   Other complications of anesthesia during pregnancy**
   ● **O29.8X   Other complications of anesthesia during pregnancy**
     O29.8X1   Other complications of anesthesia during pregnancy, first trimester ♀ M
     O29.8X2   Other complications of anesthesia during pregnancy, second trimester ♀   M
     O29.8X3   Other complications of anesthesia during pregnancy, third trimester ♀ M
     O29.8X9   Other complications of anesthesia during pregnancy, unspecified trimester ♀   M

N   Newborn Age: 0   **P**   Pediatric Age: 0–17   **M**   Maternity DX: 12–55   **A**   Adult Age: 15–124   ♀   Females Only   ♂   Males Only   1135

CHAPTER 15 (O00–O9A)

● O29.9 Unspecified complication of anesthesia during pregnancy

O29.90 Unspecified complication of anesthesia during pregnancy, unspecified trimester ♀   M

O29.91 Unspecified complication of anesthesia during pregnancy, first trimester ♀   M

O29.92 Unspecified complication of anesthesia during pregnancy, second trimester ♀   M

O29.93 Unspecified complication of anesthesia during pregnancy, third trimester ♀   M

MATERNAL CARE RELATED TO THE FETUS AND AMNIOTIC CAVITY AND POSSIBLE DELIVERY PROBLEMS (O30-O48)

● O30 Multiple gestation

Code also any complications specific to multiple gestation
Coding Clinic: 2016, Q4, P51

● O30.0 Twin pregnancy

● O30.00 Twin pregnancy, unspecified number of placenta and unspecified number of amniotic sacs

O30.001 Twin pregnancy, unspecified number of placenta and unspecified number of amniotic sacs, first trimester ♀   M

O30.002 Twin pregnancy, unspecified number of placenta and unspecified number of amniotic sacs, second trimester ♀ M

O30.003 Twin pregnancy, unspecified number of placenta and unspecified number of amniotic sacs, third trimester ♀ M

O30.009 Twin pregnancy, unspecified number of placenta and unspecified number of amniotic sacs, unspecified trimester ♀   M

● O30.01 Twin pregnancy, monochorionic/monoamniotic
Twin pregnancy, one placenta, one amniotic sac

Excludes1   conjoined twins (O30.02-)

O30.011 Twin pregnancy, monochorionic/monoamniotic, first trimester ♀   M

O30.012 Twin pregnancy, monochorionic/monoamniotic, second trimester ♀   M

O30.013 Twin pregnancy, monochorionic/monoamniotic, third trimester ♀   M

O30.019 Twin pregnancy, monochorionic/monoamniotic, unspecified trimester ♀   M

● O30.02 Conjoined twin pregnancy

O30.021 Conjoined twin pregnancy, first trimester ♀   M

O30.022 Conjoined twin pregnancy, second trimester ♀   M

O30.023 Conjoined twin pregnancy, third trimester ♀   M

O30.029 Conjoined twin pregnancy, unspecified trimester ♀   M

● O30.03 Twin pregnancy, monochorionic/diamniotic
Twin pregnancy, one placenta, two amniotic sacs

O30.031 Twin pregnancy, monochorionic/diamniotic, first trimester ♀   M

O30.032 Twin pregnancy, monochorionic/diamniotic, second trimester ♀   M

O30.033 Twin pregnancy, monochorionic/diamniotic, third trimester ♀   M

O30.039 Twin pregnancy, monochorionic/diamniotic, unspecified trimester ♀ M

● O30.04 Twin pregnancy, dichorionic/diamniotic
Twin pregnancy, two placentae, two amniotic sacs

O30.041 Twin pregnancy, dichorionic/diamniotic, first trimester ♀   M

O30.042 Twin pregnancy, dichorionic/diamniotic, second trimester ♀   M

O30.043 Twin pregnancy, dichorionic/diamniotic, third trimester ♀   M

O30.049 Twin pregnancy, dichorionic/diamniotic, unspecified trimester ♀ M

● O30.09 Twin pregnancy, unable to determine number of placenta and number of amniotic sacs

O30.091 Twin pregnancy, unable to determine number of placenta and number of amniotic sacs, first trimester ♀   M

O30.092 Twin pregnancy, unable to determine number of placenta and number of amniotic sacs, second trimester ♀   M

O30.093 Twin pregnancy, unable to determine number of placenta and number of amniotic sacs, third trimester ♀   M

O30.099 Twin pregnancy, unable to determine number of placenta and number of amniotic sacs, unspecified trimester ♀   M

● O30.1 Triplet pregnancy

● O30.10 Triplet pregnancy, unspecified number of placenta and unspecified number of amniotic sacs

O30.101 Triplet pregnancy, unspecified number of placenta and unspecified number of amniotic sacs, first trimester ♀   M

O30.102 Triplet pregnancy, unspecified number of placenta and unspecified number of amniotic sacs, second trimester ♀   M

O30.103 Triplet pregnancy, unspecified number of placenta and unspecified number of amniotic sacs, third trimester ♀   M
Coding Clinic: 2016, Q2, P8

O30.109 Triplet pregnancy, unspecified number of placenta and unspecified number of amniotic sacs, unspecified trimester ♀   M

● O30.11 Triplet pregnancy with two or more monochorionic fetuses

O30.111 Triplet pregnancy with two or more monochorionic fetuses, first trimester ♀   M

O30.112 Triplet pregnancy with two or more monochorionic fetuses, second trimester ♀   M

O30.113 Triplet pregnancy with two or more monochorionic fetuses, third trimester ♀   M

O30.119 Triplet pregnancy with two or more monochorionic fetuses, unspecified trimester ♀   M

● O30.12 Triplet pregnancy with two or more monoamniotic fetuses

O30.121 Triplet pregnancy with two or more monoamniotic fetuses, first trimester ♀   M

O30.122 Triplet pregnancy with two or more monoamniotic fetuses, second trimester ♀   M

O30.123 Triplet pregnancy with two or more monoamniotic fetuses, third trimester ♀   M

O30.129 Triplet pregnancy with two or more monoamniotic fetuses, unspecified trimester ♀   M

▶ New   ➠ Revised   ~~deleted~~ Deleted   Excludes 1   Excludes 2   Includes   Use additional   Code first   Code also   Key words
OGCR Official Guidelines   X Assign placeholder X   ● Use Additional Character(s)   ▶ Manifestation Code   🅗 Hierarchical Condition Category   **Coding Clinic**

● **O30.13**   Triplet pregnancy, trichorionic/triamniotic
    O30.131   Triplet pregnancy, trichorionic/ triamniotic, first trimester ♀   M
    O30.132   Triplet pregnancy, trichorionic/ triamniotic, second trimester ♀   M
    O30.133   Triplet pregnancy, trichorionic/ triamniotic, third trimester ♀   M
    O30.139   Triplet pregnancy, trichorionic/ triamniotic, unspecified trimester ♀ M

● **O30.19**   Triplet pregnancy, unable to determine number of placenta and number of amniotic sacs
    O30.191   Triplet pregnancy, unable to determine number of placenta and number of amniotic sacs, first trimester ♀   M
    O30.192   Triplet pregnancy, unable to determine number of placenta and number of amniotic sacs, second trimester ♀   M
    O30.193   Triplet pregnancy, unable to determine number of placenta and number of amniotic sacs, third trimester ♀   M
    O30.199   Triplet pregnancy, unable to determine number of placenta and number of amniotic sacs, unspecified trimester ♀   M

● **O30.2**   Quadruplet pregnancy
   ● **O30.20**   Quadruplet pregnancy, unspecified number of placenta and unspecified number of amniotic sacs
    O30.201   Quadruplet pregnancy, unspecified number of placenta and unspecified number of amniotic sacs, first trimester ♀   M
    O30.202   Quadruplet pregnancy, unspecified number of placenta and unspecified number of amniotic sacs, second trimester ♀   M
    O30.203   Quadruplet pregnancy, unspecified number of placenta and unspecified number of amniotic sacs, third trimester ♀   M
    O30.209   Quadruplet pregnancy, unspecified number of placenta and unspecified number of amniotic sacs, unspecified trimester ♀   M

   ● **O30.21**   Quadruplet pregnancy with two or more monochorionic fetuses
    O30.211   Quadruplet pregnancy with two or more monochorionic fetuses, first trimester ♀   M
    O30.212   Quadruplet pregnancy with two or more monochorionic fetuses, second trimester ♀   M
    O30.213   Quadruplet pregnancy with two or more monochorionic fetuses, third trimester ♀   M
    O30.219   Quadruplet pregnancy with two or more monochorionic fetuses, unspecified trimester ♀   M

   ● **O30.22**   Quadruplet pregnancy with two or more monoamniotic fetuses
    O30.221   Quadruplet pregnancy with two or more monoamniotic fetuses, first trimester ♀   M
    O30.222   Quadruplet pregnancy with two or more monoamniotic fetuses, second trimester ♀   M
    O30.223   Quadruplet pregnancy with two or more monoamniotic fetuses, third trimester ♀   M
    O30.229   Quadruplet pregnancy with two or more monoamniotic fetuses, unspecified trimester ♀   M

● **O30.23**   Quadruplet pregnancy, quadrachorionic/ quadra-amniotic
    O30.231   Quadruplet pregnancy, quadrachorionic/quadra-amniotic, first trimester ♀   M
    O30.232   Quadruplet pregnancy, quadrachorionic/quadra-amniotic, second trimester ♀   M
    O30.233   Quadruplet pregnancy, quadrachorionic/quadra-amniotic, third trimester ♀   M
    O30.239   Quadruplet pregnancy, quadrachorionic/quadra-amniotic, unspecifiedtrimester ♀   M

● **O30.29**   Quadruplet pregnancy, unable to determine number of placenta and number of amniotic sacs
    O30.291   Quadruplet pregnancy, unable to determine number of placenta and number of amniotic sacs, first trimester ♀   M
    O30.292   Quadruplet pregnancy, unable to determine number of placenta and number of amniotic sacs, second trimester ♀   M
    O30.293   Quadruplet pregnancy, unable to determine number of placenta and number of amniotic sacs, third trimester ♀   M
    O30.299   Quadruplet pregnancy, unable to determine number of placenta and number of amniotic sacs, unspecified trimester ♀   M

● **O30.8**   Other specified multiple gestation
     Multiple gestation pregnancy greater then quadruplets
   ● **O30.80**   Other specified multiple gestation, unspecified number of placenta and unspecified number of amniotic sacs
    O30.801   Other specified multiple gestation, unspecified number of placenta and unspecified number of amniotic sacs, first trimester ♀   M
    O30.802   Other specified multiple gestation, unspecified number of placenta and unspecified number of amniotic sacs, second trimester ♀   M
    O30.803   Other specified multiple gestation, unspecified number of placenta and unspecified number of amniotic sacs, third trimester ♀   M
    O30.809   Other specified multiple gestation, unspecified number of placenta and unspecified number of amniotic sacs, unspecified trimester ♀   M

   ● **O30.81**   Other specified multiple gestation with two or more monochorionic fetuses
    O30.811   Other specified multiple gestation with two or more monochorionic fetuses, first trimester ♀   M
    O30.812   Other specified multiple gestation with two or more monochorionic fetuses, second trimester ♀   M
    O30.813   Other specified multiple gestation with two or more monochorionic fetuses, third trimester ♀   M
    O30.819   Other specified multiple gestation with two or more monochorionic fetuses, unspecified trimester ♀   M

CHAPTER 15 (O00-O9A)

O30.82 Other specified multiple gestation with two or more monoamniotic fetuses

O30.821 Other specified multiple gestation with two or more monoamniotic fetuses, first trimester ♀ M

O30.822 Other specified multiple gestation with two or more monoamniotic fetuses, second trimester ♀ M

O30.823 Other specified multiple gestation with two or more monoamniotic fetuses, third trimester ♀ M

O30.829 Other specified multiple gestation with two or more monoamniotic fetuses, unspecified trimester ♀ M

O30.83 Other specified multiple gestation, number of chorions and amnions are both equal to the number of fetuses
Pentachorionic, penta-amniotic pregnancy (quintuplets)
Hexachorionic, hexa-amniotic pregnancy (sextuplets)
Heptachorionic, hepta-amniotic pregnancy (septuplets)

O30.831 Other specified multiple gestation, number of chorions and amnions are both equal to the number of fetuses, first trimester ♀ M

O30.832 Other specified multiple gestation, number of chorions and amnions are both equal to the number of fetuses, second trimester ♀ M

O30.833 Other specified multiple gestation, number of chorions and amnions are both equal to the number of fetuses, third trimester ♀ M

O30.839 Other specified multiple gestation, number of chorions and amnions are both equal to the number of fetuses, unspecified trimester ♀ M

O30.89 Other specified multiple gestation, unable to determine number of placenta and number of amniotic sacs

O30.891 Other specified multiple gestation, unable to determine number of placenta and number of amniotic sacs, first trimester ♀ M

O30.892 Other specified multiple gestation, unable to determine number of placenta and number of amniotic sacs, second trimester ♀ M

O30.893 Other specified multiple gestation, unable to determine number of placenta and number of amniotic sacs, third trimester ♀ M

O30.899 Other specified multiple gestation, unable to determine number of placenta and number of amniotic sacs, unspecified trimester ♀ M

O30.9 Multiple gestation, unspecified
Multiple pregnancy NOS

O30.90 Multiple gestation, unspecified, unspecified trimester ♀ M

O30.91 Multiple gestation, unspecified, first trimester ♀ M

O30.92 Multiple gestation, unspecified, second trimester ♀ M

O30.93 Multiple gestation, unspecified, third trimester ♀ M

O31 Complications specific to multiple gestation

Excludes2 delayed delivery of second twin, triplet, etc. (O63.2)
malpresentation of one fetus or more (O32.9)
placental transfusion syndromes (O43.0-)

Coding Clinic: 2012, Q4, P107

One of the following 7th characters is to be assigned to each code under category O31. 7th character 0 is for single gestations and multiple gestations where the fetus is unspecified. 7th characters 1 through 9 are for cases of multiple gestations to identify the fetus for which the code applies. The appropriate code from category O30, Multiple gestation, must also be assigned when assigning a code from category O31 that has a 7th character of 1 through 9.

0	not applicable or unspecified
1	fetus 1
2	fetus 2
3	fetus 3
4	fetus 4
5	fetus 5
9	other fetus

O31.0 Papyraceous fetus
Fetus compressus

X● O31.00 Papyraceous fetus, unspecified trimester ♀ M

X● O31.01 Papyraceous fetus, first trimester ♀ M

X● O31.02 Papyraceous fetus, second trimester ♀ M

X● O31.03 Papyraceous fetus, third trimester ♀ M

O31.1 Continuing pregnancy after spontaneous abortion of one fetus or more

X● O31.10 Continuing pregnancy after spontaneous abortion of one fetus or more, unspecified trimester ♀ M

X● O31.11 Continuing pregnancy after spontaneous abortion of one fetus or more, first trimester ♀ M

X● O31.12 Continuing pregnancy after spontaneous abortion of one fetus or more, second trimester ♀ M

X● O31.13 Continuing pregnancy after spontaneous abortion of one fetus or more, third trimester ♀ M

O31.2 Continuing pregnancy after intrauterine death of one fetus or more

X● O31.20 Continuing pregnancy after intrauterine death of one fetus or more, unspecified trimester ♀ M

X● O31.21 Continuing pregnancy after intrauterine death of one fetus or more, first trimester ♀ M

X● O31.22 Continuing pregnancy after intrauterine death of one fetus or more, second trimester ♀ M

X● O31.23 Continuing pregnancy after intrauterine death of one fetus or more, third trimester ♀ M

O31.3 Continuing pregnancy after elective fetal reduction of one fetus or more
Continuing pregnancy after selective termination of one fetus or more

X● O31.30 Continuing pregnancy after elective fetal reduction of one fetus or more, unspecified trimester ♀ M

X● O31.31 Continuing pregnancy after elective fetal reduction of one fetus or more, first trimester ♀ M

X● O31.32 Continuing pregnancy after elective fetal reduction of one fetus or more, second trimester ♀ M

X● O31.33 Continuing pregnancy after elective fetal reduction of one fetus or more, third trimester ♀ M

CHAPTER 15 (O00-O9A)

▶ New   ⇛ Revised   ~~deleted~~ Deleted   Excludes 1   Excludes 2   Includes   Use additional   Code first   Code also   Key words

OGCR Official Guidelines   X Assign placeholder X   ● Use Additional Character(s)   ▶ Manifestation Code   🅠 Hierarchical Condition Category   Coding Clinic

● **O31.8 Other complications specific to multiple gestation**
  ● **O31.8X Other complications specific to multiple gestation**
    ● **O31.8X1 Other complications specific to multiple gestation, first trimester** ♀ M
    ● **O31.8X2 Other complications specific to multiple gestation, second trimester** ♀   M
    ● **O31.8X3 Other complications specific to multiple gestation, third trimester** ♀ M
    ● **O31.8X9 Other complications specific to multiple gestation, unspecified trimester** ♀   M

● **O32 Maternal care for malpresentation of fetus**

> **Includes** the listed conditions as a reason for observation, hospitalization or other obstetric care of the mother, or for cesarean delivery before onset of labor

> **Excludes1** malpresentation of fetus with obstructed labor (O64.-)

Coding Clinic: 2012, Q4, P107

One of the following 7th characters is to be assigned to each code under category O32. 7th character 0 is for single gestations and multiple gestations where the fetus is unspecified. 7th characters 1 through 9 are for cases of multiple gestations to identify the fetus for which the code applies. The appropriate code from category O30, Multiple gestation, must also be assigned when assigning a code from category O32 that has a 7th character of 1 through 9.

0	not applicable or unspecified
1	fetus 1
2	fetus 2
3	fetus 3
4	fetus 4
5	fetus 5
9	other fetus

X● **O32.0 Maternal care for unstable lie** ♀   M
X● **O32.1 Maternal care for breech presentation** ♀   M
  Maternal care for buttocks presentation
  Maternal care for complete breech
  Maternal care for frank breech
  > **Excludes1** footling presentation (O32.8)
  >   incomplete breech (O32.8)
X● **O32.2 Maternal care for transverse and oblique lie** ♀   M
  Maternal care for oblique presentation
  Maternal care for transverse presentation
X● **O32.3 Maternal care for face, brow and chin presentation** ♀   M
X● **O32.4 Maternal care for high head at term** ♀   M
  Maternal care for failure of head to enter pelvic brim
X● **O32.6 Maternal care for compound presentation** ♀   M
X● **O32.8 Maternal care for other malpresentation of fetus** ♀   M
  Maternal care for footling presentation
  Maternal care for incomplete breech
X● **O32.9 Maternal care for malpresentation of fetus, unspecified** ♀   M

● **O33 Maternal care for disproportion**

> **Includes** the listed conditions as a reason for observation, hospitalization or other obstetric care of the mother, or for cesarean delivery before onset of labor

> **Excludes1** disproportion with obstructed labor (O65-O66)

O33.0 Maternal care for disproportion due to deformity of maternal pelvic bones ♀   M
  Maternal care for disproportion due to pelvic deformity causing disproportion NOS

O33.1 Maternal care for disproportion due to generally contracted pelvis ♀   M
  Maternal care for disproportion due to contracted pelvis NOS causing disproportion

O33.2 Maternal care for disproportion due to inlet contraction of pelvis ♀   M
  Maternal care for disproportion due to inlet contraction (pelvis) causing disproportion

X● **O33.3 Maternal care for disproportion due to outlet contraction of pelvis** ♀   M
  Maternal care for disproportion due to mid-cavity contraction (pelvis)
  Maternal care for disproportion due to outlet contraction (pelvis)

One of the following 7th characters is to be assigned to code O33.3. 7th character 0 is for single gestations and multiple gestations where the fetus is unspecified. 7th characters 1 through 9 are for cases of multiple gestations to identify the fetus for which the code applies. The appropriate code from category O30, Multiple gestation, must also be assigned when assigning code O33.3 with a 7th character of 1 through 9.

0	not applicable or unspecified
1	fetus 1
2	fetus 2
3	fetus 3
4	fetus 4
5	fetus 5
9	other fetus

X● **O33.4 Maternal care for disproportion of mixed maternal and fetal origin** ♀   M

One of the following 7th characters is to be assigned to code O33.4. 7th character 0 is for single gestations and multiple gestations where the fetus is unspecified. 7th characters 1 through 9 are for cases of multiple gestations to identify the fetus for which the code applies. The appropriate code from category O30, Multiple gestation, must also be assigned when assigning code O33.4 with a 7th character of 1 through 9.

0	not applicable or unspecified
1	fetus 1
2	fetus 2
3	fetus 3
4	fetus 4
5	fetus 5
9	other fetus

X● **O33.5 Maternal care for disproportion due to unusually large fetus** ♀   M
  Maternal care for disproportion due to disproportion of fetal origin with normally formed fetus
  Maternal care for disproportion due to fetal disproportion NOS

One of the following 7th characters is to be assigned to code O33.5. 7th character 0 is for single gestations and multiple gestations where the fetus is unspecified. 7th characters 1 through 9 are for cases of multiple gestations to identify the fetus for which the code applies. The appropriate code from category O30, Multiple gestation, must also be assigned when assigning code O33.5 with a 7th character of 1 through 9.

0	not applicable or unspecified
1	fetus 1
2	fetus 2
3	fetus 3
4	fetus 4
5	fetus 5
9	other fetus

CHAPTER 15 (O00-O9A)

CHAPTER 15 (O00–O9A)

X ● **O33.6** **Maternal care for disproportion due to hydrocephalic fetus** ♀   M

One of the following 7th characters is to be assigned to code O33.6. 7th character Ø is for single gestations and multiple gestations where the fetus is unspecified. 7th characters 1 through 9 are for cases of multiple gestations to identify the fetus for which the code applies. The appropriate code from category O3Ø, Multiple gestation, must also be assigned when assigning code O33.6 with a 7th character of 1 through 9.

Ø	not applicable or unspecified
1	fetus 1
2	fetus 2
3	fetus 3
4	fetus 4
5	fetus 5
9	other fetus

X ● **O33.7** **Maternal care for disproportion due to other fetal deformities** ♀   M

Maternal care for disproportion due to fetal ascites
Maternal care for disproportion due to fetal hydrops
Maternal care for disproportion due to fetal meningomyelocele
Maternal care for disproportion due to fetal sacral teratoma
Maternal care for disproportion due to fetal tumor

Excludes1   obstructed labor due to other fetal deformities (O66.3)

Coding Clinic: 2016, Q4, P51

One of the following 7th characters is to be assigned to code O33.7. 7th character Ø is for single gestations and multiple gestations where the fetus is unspecified. 7th characters 1 through 9 are for cases of multiple gestations to identify the fetus for which the code applies. The appropriate code from category O3Ø, Multiple gestation, must also be assigned when assigning code O33.7 with a 7th character of 1 through 9.

Ø	not applicable or unspecified
1	fetus 1
2	fetus 2
3	fetus 3
4	fetus 4
5	fetus 5
9	other fetus

O33.8   **Maternal care for disproportion of other origin** ♀   M

O33.9   **Maternal care for disproportion, unspecified** ♀   M
Maternal care for disproportion due to cephalopelvic disproportion NOS
Maternal care for disproportion due to fetopelvic disproportion NOS

● **O34**   **Maternal care for abnormality of pelvic organs**

Includes   the listed conditions as a reason for hospitalization or other obstetric care of the mother, or for cesarean delivery before onset of labor

Code first any associated obstructed labor (O65.5)

Use additional code for specific condition

● **O34.0**   **Maternal care for congenital malformation of uterus**
Maternal care for double uterus
Maternal care for uterus bicornis

O34.00   Maternal care for unspecified congenital malformation of uterus, unspecified trimester ♀   M

O34.01   Maternal care for unspecified congenital malformation of uterus, first trimester ♀   M

O34.02   Maternal care for unspecified congenital malformation of uterus, second trimester ♀   M

O34.03   Maternal care for unspecified congenital malformation of uterus, third trimester ♀   M

● **O34.1**   **Maternal care for benign tumor of corpus uteri**

Excludes2   maternal care for benign tumor of cervix (O34.4-)
maternal care for malignant neoplasm of uterus (O9A.1-)

O34.10   Maternal care for benign tumor of corpus uteri, unspecified trimester ♀   M

O34.11   Maternal care for benign tumor of corpus uteri, first trimester ♀   M

O34.12   Maternal care for benign tumor of corpus uteri, second trimester ♀   M

O34.13   Maternal care for benign tumor of corpus uteri, third trimester ♀   M

● **O34.2**   **Maternal care due to uterine scar from previous surgery**
Coding Clinic: 2016, Q4, P76

● **O34.21**   **Maternal care for scar from previous cesarean delivery**
Coding Clinic: 2016, Q4, P51

O34.211   Maternal care for low transverse scar from previous cesarean delivery ♀   M

O34.212   Maternal care for vertical scar from previous cesarean delivery ♀   M
Maternal care for classical scar from previous cesarean delivery

▶ **O34.218**   Maternal care for other type scar from previous cesarean delivery
▶ Mid-transverse T incision

O34.219   Maternal care for unspecified type scar from previous cesarean delivery ♀   M

▶ **O34.22**   **Maternal care for cesarean scar defect (isthmocele)**

O34.29   **Maternal care due to uterine scar from other previous surgery** ♀   M
Maternal care due to uterine scar from other transmural uterine incision

● **O34.3**   **Maternal care for cervical incompetence**
Maternal care for cerclage with or without cervical incompetence
Maternal care for Shirodkar suture with or without cervical incompetence

O34.30   Maternal care for cervical incompetence, unspecified trimester ♀   M

O34.31   Maternal care for cervical incompetence, first trimester ♀   M

O34.32   Maternal care for cervical incompetence, second trimester ♀   M

O34.33   Maternal care for cervical incompetence, third trimester ♀   M

● **O34.4**   **Maternal care for other abnormalities of cervix**

O34.40   Maternal care for other abnormalities of cervix, unspecified trimester ♀   M

O34.41   Maternal care for other abnormalities of cervix, first trimester ♀   M

O34.42   Maternal care for other abnormalities of cervix, second trimester ♀   M

O34.43   Maternal care for other abnormalities of cervix, third trimester ♀   M

● **O34.5**   **Maternal care for other abnormalities of gravid uterus**

● **O34.51**   **Maternal care for incarceration of gravid uterus**

O34.511   Maternal care for incarceration of gravid uterus, first trimester ♀   M

O34.512   Maternal care for incarceration of gravid uterus, second trimester ♀   M

O34.513   Maternal care for incarceration of gravid uterus, third trimester ♀   M

O34.519   Maternal care for incarceration of gravid uterus, unspecified trimester ♀   M

▶ New   ⇒ Revised   ~~deleted~~ Deleted   Excludes 1   Excludes 2   Includes   Use additional   Code first   Code also   Key words

   OGCR Official Guidelines   X Assign placeholder X   ● Use Additional Character(s)   ▷ Manifestation Code   🅗 Hierarchical Condition Category   Coding Clinic

● **O34.52　Maternal care for prolapse of gravid uterus**
　　　O34.521　Maternal care for prolapse of gravid
　　　　　　　uterus, first trimester ♀　　　　M
　　　O34.522　Maternal care for prolapse of gravid
　　　　　　　uterus, second trimester ♀　　　M
　　　O34.523　Maternal care for prolapse of gravid
　　　　　　　uterus, third trimester ♀　　　　M
　　　O34.529　Maternal care for prolapse of gravid
　　　　　　　uterus, unspecified trimester ♀　M

● **O34.53　Maternal care for retroversion of gravid uterus**
　　　O34.531　Maternal care for retroversion of
　　　　　　　gravid uterus, first trimester ♀　M
　　　O34.532　Maternal care for retroversion of
　　　　　　　gravid uterus, second trimester ♀　M
　　　O34.533　Maternal care for retroversion of
　　　　　　　gravid uterus, third trimester ♀　M
　　　O34.539　Maternal care for retroversion
　　　　　　　of gravid uterus, unspecified
　　　　　　　trimester ♀　　　　　　　　M

● **O34.59　Maternal care for other abnormalities of gravid
　　　uterus**
　　　O34.591　Maternal care for other abnormalities
　　　　　　　of gravid uterus, first trimester ♀　M
　　　O34.592　Maternal care for other abnormalities
　　　　　　　of gravid uterus, second trimester ♀ M
　　　O34.593　Maternal care for other abnormalities
　　　　　　　of gravid uterus, third trimester ♀　M
　　　O34.599　Maternal care for other abnormalities
　　　　　　　of gravid uterus, unspecified
　　　　　　　trimester ♀　　　　　　　　M

● **O34.6　Maternal care for abnormality of vagina**
　　Excludes2　maternal care for vaginal varices in
　　　　　　　pregnancy (O22.1-)
　　　O34.60　Maternal care for abnormality of vagina,
　　　　　　　unspecified trimester ♀　　　　M
　　　O34.61　Maternal care for abnormality of vagina, first
　　　　　　　trimester ♀　　　　　　　　M
　　　O34.62　Maternal care for abnormality of vagina, second
　　　　　　　trimester ♀　　　　　　　　M
　　　O34.63　Maternal care for abnormality of vagina, third
　　　　　　　trimester ♀　　　　　　　　M

● **O34.7　Maternal care for abnormality of vulva and perineum**
　　Excludes2　maternal care for perineal and vulval
　　　　　　　varices in pregnancy (O22.1-)
　　　O34.70　Maternal care for abnormality of vulva and
　　　　　　　perineum, unspecified trimester ♀　M
　　　O34.71　Maternal care for abnormality of vulva and
　　　　　　　perineum, first trimester ♀　　　M
　　　O34.72　Maternal care for abnormality of vulva and
　　　　　　　perineum, second trimester ♀　　M
　　　O34.73　Maternal care for abnormality of vulva and
　　　　　　　perineum, third trimester ♀　　M

● **O34.8　Maternal care for other abnormalities of pelvic organs**
　　　O34.80　Maternal care for other abnormalities of pelvic
　　　　　　　organs, unspecified trimester ♀　M
　　　O34.81　Maternal care for other abnormalities of pelvic
　　　　　　　organs, first trimester ♀　　　　M
　　　O34.82　Maternal care for other abnormalities of pelvic
　　　　　　　organs, second trimester ♀　　　M
　　　O34.83　Maternal care for other abnormalities of pelvic
　　　　　　　organs, third trimester ♀　　　M

● **O34.9　Maternal care for abnormality of pelvic organ, unspecified**
　　　O34.90　Maternal care for abnormality of pelvic organ,
　　　　　　　unspecified, unspecified trimester ♀　M
　　　O34.91　Maternal care for abnormality of pelvic organ,
　　　　　　　unspecified, first trimester ♀　　M
　　　O34.92　Maternal care for abnormality of pelvic organ,
　　　　　　　unspecified, second trimester ♀　M
　　　O34.93　Maternal care for abnormality of pelvic organ,
　　　　　　　unspecified, third trimester ♀　　M

● **O35　Maternal care for known or suspected fetal abnormality and
　　damage**
　　Includes　the listed conditions in the fetus as a reason for
　　　　　　　hospitalization or other obstetric care to the
　　　　　　　mother, or for termination of pregnancy
　　Code also any associated maternal condition
　　Excludes1　encounter for suspected maternal and fetal
　　　　　　　conditions ruled out (Z03.7-)
　　One of the following 7th characters is to be assigned to each
　　　code under category O35. 7th character Ø is for single
　　　gestations and multiple gestations where the fetus is
　　　unspecified. 7th characters 1 through 9 are for cases of
　　　multiple gestations to identify the fetus for which the code
　　　applies. The appropriate code from category O30, Multiple
　　　gestation, must also be assigned when assigning a code
　　　from category O35 that has a 7th character of 1 through 9.

　　Ø　not applicable or unspecified
　　1　fetus 1
　　2　fetus 2
　　3　fetus 3
　　4　fetus 4
　　5　fetus 5
　　9　other fetus

X ● **O35.0　Maternal care for (suspected) central nervous system
　　malformation in fetus ♀　　　　　　　M**
　　　Maternal care for fetal anencephaly
　　　Maternal care for fetal hydrocephalus
　　　Maternal care for fetal spina bifida
　　Excludes2　chromosomal abnormality in fetus (O35.1)

X ● **O35.1　Maternal care for (suspected) chromosomal abnormality
　　in fetus ♀　　　　　　　　　　　　M**

X ● **O35.2　Maternal care for (suspected) hereditary disease in
　　fetus ♀　　　　　　　　　　　　　M**
　　Excludes2　chromosomal abnormality in fetus (O35.1)

X ● **O35.3　Maternal care for (suspected) damage to fetus from viral
　　disease in mother ♀　　　　　　　　M**
　　　Maternal care for damage to fetus from maternal
　　　　cytomegalovirus infection
　　　Maternal care for damage to fetus from maternal rubella
　　　Coding Clinic: 2016, Q4, P6

X ● **O35.4　Maternal care for (suspected) damage to fetus from
　　alcohol ♀　　　　　　　　　　　　M**

X ● **O35.5　Maternal care for (suspected) damage to fetus by
　　drugs ♀　　　　　　　　　　　　　M**
　　　Maternal care for damage to fetus from drug addiction

X ● **O35.6　Maternal care for (suspected) damage to fetus by
　　radiation ♀　　　　　　　　　　　M**

X ● **O35.7　Maternal care for (suspected) damage to fetus by other
　　medical procedures ♀　　　　　　　M**
　　　Maternal care for damage to fetus by amniocentesis
　　　Maternal care for damage to fetus by biopsy procedures
　　　Maternal care for damage to fetus by hematological
　　　　investigation
　　　Maternal care for damage to fetus by intrauterine
　　　　contraceptive device
　　　Maternal care for damage to fetus by intrauterine
　　　　surgery

X ● **O35.8　Maternal care for other (suspected) fetal abnormality
　　and damage ♀　　　　　　　　　　M**
　　　Maternal care for damage to fetus from maternal
　　　　listeriosis
　　　Maternal care for damage to fetus from maternal
　　　　toxoplasmosis

X ● **O35.9　Maternal care for (suspected) fetal abnormality and
　　damage, unspecified ♀　　　　　　　M**

N Newborn Age: Ø　**P** Pediatric Age: Ø–17　**M** Maternity DX: 12–55　**A** Adult Age: 15–124　♀ Females Only　♂ Males Only

OGCR Section I.C.15.e.l.

Fetal Conditions Affecting the Management of the Mother

1) Code from categories O35 and O36

Codes from categories O35, Maternal care for known or suspected fetal abnormality and damage, and O36, Maternal care for other fetal problems, are assigned only when the fetal condition is actually responsible for modifying the management of the mother, i.e., by requiring diagnostic studies, additional observation, special care, or termination of pregnancy. The fact that the fetal condition exists does not justify assigning a code from this series to the mother's record.

2) In utero surgery

In cases when surgery is performed on the fetus, a diagnosis code from category O35, Maternal care for known or suspected fetal abnormality and damage, should be assigned identifying the fetal condition. Assign the appropriate procedure code for the procedure performed.

No code from Chapter 16, the perinatal codes, should be used on the mother's record to identify fetal conditions. Surgery performed in utero on a fetus is still to be coded as an obstetric encounter.

● O36   **Maternal care for other fetal problems**

     Includes   the listed conditions in the fetus as a reason for hospitalization or other obstetric care of the mother, or for termination of pregnancy

     Excludes1   encounter for suspected maternal and fetal conditions ruled out (Z03.7-)
            placental transfusion syndromes (O43.0-)

     Excludes2   labor and delivery complicated by fetal stress (O77.-)

One of the following 7th characters is to be assigned to each code under category O36. 7th character 0 is for single gestations and multiple gestations where the fetus is unspecified. 7th characters 1 through 9 are for cases of multiple gestations to identify the fetus for which the code applies. The appropriate code from category O30, Multiple gestation, must also be assigned when assigning a code from category O36 that has a 7th character of 1 through 9.

0	not applicable or unspecified
1	fetus 1
2	fetus 2
3	fetus 3
4	fetus 4
5	fetus 5
9	other fetus

Coding Clinic: 2015, Q3, P40

● O36.0   **Maternal care for rhesus isoimmunization**
     Maternal care for Rh incompatibility (with hydrops fetalis)

     ● O36.01   **Maternal care for anti-D [Rh] antibodies**

         ● O36.011   Maternal care for anti-D [Rh] antibodies, **first trimester** ♀   M

         ● O36.012   Maternal care for anti-D [Rh] antibodies, **second trimester** ♀   M

         ● O36.013   Maternal care for anti-D [Rh] antibodies, **third trimester** ♀   M

         ● O36.019   Maternal care for anti-D [Rh] antibodies, **unspecified trimester** ♀   M

     ● O36.09   **Maternal care for other rhesus isoimmunization**

         ● O36.091   Maternal care for other rhesus isoimmunization, **first trimester** ♀   M

         ● O36.092   Maternal care for other rhesus isoimmunization, **second trimester** ♀   M

         ● O36.093   Maternal care for other rhesus isoimmunization, **third trimester** ♀   M
             Coding Clinic: 2015, Q3, P40

         ● O36.099   Maternal care for other rhesus isoimmunization, **unspecified trimester** ♀   M

● O36.1   **Maternal care for other isoimmunization**
     Maternal care for ABO isoimmunization

     ● O36.11   **Maternal care for Anti-A sensitization**
         Maternal care for isoimmunization NOS (with hydrops fetalis)

         ● O36.111   Maternal care for Anti-A sensitization, **first trimester** ♀   M

         ● O36.112   Maternal care for Anti-A sensitization, **second trimester** ♀   M

         ● O36.113   Maternal care for Anti-A sensitization, **third trimester** ♀   M

         ● O36.119   Maternal care for Anti-A sensitization, **unspecified trimester** ♀   M

     ● O36.19   **Maternal care for other isoimmunization**
         Maternal care for Anti-B sensitization

         ● O36.191   Maternal care for other isoimmunization, **first trimester** ♀   M

         ● O36.192   Maternal care for other isoimmunization, **second trimester** ♀   M

         ● O36.193   Maternal care for other isoimmunization, **third trimester** ♀   M

         ● O36.199   Maternal care for other isoimmunization, **unspecified trimester** ♀   M

● O36.2   **Maternal care for hydrops fetalis**
     Maternal care for hydrops fetalis NOS
     Maternal care for hydrops fetalis not associated with isoimmunization

     Excludes1   hydrops fetalis associated with ABO isoimmunization (O36.1-)
             hydrops fetalis associated with rhesus isoimmunization (O36.0-)

     ● O36.20   Maternal care for hydrops fetalis, **unspecified trimester** ♀   M

     ● O36.21   Maternal care for hydrops fetalis, **first trimester** ♀   M

     ● O36.22   Maternal care for hydrops fetalis, **second trimester** ♀   M

     ● O36.23   Maternal care for hydrops fetalis, **third trimester** ♀   M

● O36.4   **Maternal care for intrauterine death** ♀   M
     Maternal care for intrauterine fetal death NOS
     Maternal care for intrauterine fetal death after completion of 20 weeks of gestation
     Maternal care for late fetal death
     Maternal care for missed delivery

     Excludes1   missed abortion (O02.1)
             stillbirth (P95)

● O36.5   **Maternal care for known or suspected poor fetal growth**

     ● O36.51   **Maternal care for known or suspected placental insufficiency**

         ● O36.511   Maternal care for known or suspected placental insufficiency, **first trimester** ♀   M

         ● O36.512   Maternal care for known or suspected placental insufficiency, **second trimester** ♀   M

         ● O36.513   Maternal care for known or suspected placental insufficiency, **third trimester** ♀   M

         ● O36.519   Maternal care for known or suspected placental insufficiency, **unspecified trimester** ♀   M

▶ New   ⇒ Revised   ~~deleted~~ Deleted   Excludes 1   Excludes 2   Includes   Use additional   Code first   Code also   Key words

OGCR Official Guidelines   X Assign placeholder X   ● Use Additional Character(s)   ▶ Manifestation Code   🔖 Hierarchical Condition Category   **Coding Clinic**

● **O36.59   Maternal care for other known or suspected poor fetal growth**
    Maternal care for known or suspected light-for-dates NOS
    Maternal care for known or suspected small-for-dates NOS

  ● **O36.591   Maternal care for other known or suspected poor fetal growth, first trimester ♀**   **M**

  ● **O36.592   Maternal care for other known or suspected poor fetal growth, second trimester ♀**   **M**

  ● **O36.593   Maternal care for other known or suspected poor fetal growth, third trimester ♀**   **M**

  ● **O36.599   Maternal care for other known or suspected poor fetal growth, unspecified trimester ♀**   **M**

● **O36.6   Maternal care for excessive fetal growth**
    Maternal care for known or suspected large-for-dates

X ● **O36.60   Maternal care for excessive fetal growth, unspecified trimester ♀**   **M**

X ● **O36.61   Maternal care for excessive fetal growth, first trimester ♀**   **M**

X ● **O36.62   Maternal care for excessive fetal growth, second trimester ♀**   **M**

X ● **O36.63   Maternal care for excessive fetal growth, third trimester ♀**   **M**

● **O36.7   Maternal care for viable fetus in abdominal pregnancy**

X ● **O36.70   Maternal care for viable fetus in abdominal pregnancy, unspecified trimester ♀**   **M**

X ● **O36.71   Maternal care for viable fetus in abdominal pregnancy, first trimester ♀**   **M**

X ● **O36.72   Maternal care for viable fetus in abdominal pregnancy, second trimester ♀**   **M**

X ● **O36.73   Maternal care for viable fetus in abdominal pregnancy, third trimester ♀**   **M**

● **O36.8   Maternal care for other specified fetal problems**

X ● **O36.80   Pregnancy with inconclusive fetal viability ♀   M**
    Encounter to determine fetal viability of pregnancy
    Coding Clinic: 2019, Q2, P29

● **O36.81   Decreased fetal movements**

  ● **O36.812   Decreased fetal movements, second trimester ♀**   **M**

  ● **O36.813   Decreased fetal movements, third trimester ♀**   **M**

  ● **O36.819   Decreased fetal movements, unspecified trimester ♀**   **M**

● **O36.82   Fetal anemia and thrombocytopenia**

  ● **O36.821   Fetal anemia and thrombocytopenia, first trimester ♀**   **M**

  ● **O36.822   Fetal anemia and thrombocytopenia, second trimester ♀**   **M**

  ● **O36.823   Fetal anemia and thrombocytopenia, third trimester ♀**   **M**

  ● **O36.829   Fetal anemia and thrombocytopenia, unspecified trimester ♀**   **M**

● **O36.83   Maternal care for abnormalities of the fetal heart rate or rhythm**
    Maternal care for depressed fetal heart rate tones
    Maternal care for fetal bradycardia
    Maternal care for fetal heart rate abnormal variability
    Maternal care for fetal heart rate decelerations
    Maternal care for fetal heart rate irregularity
    Maternal care for fetal tachycardia
    Maternal care for non-reassuring fetal heart rate or rhythm

  ● **O36.831   Maternal care for abnormalities of the fetal heart rate or rhythm, first trimester ♀**   **M**

  ● **O36.832   Maternal care for abnormalities of the fetal heart rate or rhythm, second trimester ♀**   **M**

  ● **O36.833   Maternal care for abnormalities of the fetal heart rate or rhythm, third trimester ♀**   **M**

  ● **O36.839   Maternal care for abnormalities of the fetal heart rate or rhythm, unspecified trimester ♀**   **M**

● **O36.89   Maternal care for other specified fetal problems**

  ● **O36.891   Maternal care for other specified fetal problems, first trimester ♀**   **M**

  ● **O36.892   Maternal care for other specified fetal problems, second trimester ♀**   **M**

  ● **O36.893   Maternal care for other specified fetal problems, third trimester ♀**   **M**

  ● **O36.899   Maternal care for other specified fetal problems, unspecified trimester ♀   M**

● **O36.9   Maternal care for fetal problem, unspecified**

X ● **O36.90   Maternal care for fetal problem, unspecified, unspecified trimester ♀**   **M**

X ● **O36.91   Maternal care for fetal problem, unspecified, first trimester ♀**   **M**

X ● **O36.92   Maternal care for fetal problem, unspecified, second trimester ♀**   **M**

X ● **O36.93   Maternal care for fetal problem, unspecified, third trimester ♀**   **M**

● **O40   Polyhydramnios**
    Overabundance of amniotic fluid

    Includes   hydramnios

    Excludes1 encounter for suspected maternal and fetal conditions ruled out (Z03.7-)

One of the following 7th characters is to be assigned to each code under category O40. 7th character 0 is for single gestations and multiple gestations where the fetus is unspecified. 7th characters 1 through 9 are for cases of multiple gestations to identify the fetus for which the code applies. The appropriate code from category O30, Multiple gestation, must also be assigned when assigning a code from category O40 that has a 7th character of 1 through 9.

0	not applicable or unspecified
1	fetus 1
2	fetus 2
3	fetus 3
4	fetus 4
5	fetus 5
9	other fetus

X ● **O40.1   Polyhydramnios, first trimester ♀**   **M**

X ● **O40.2   Polyhydramnios, second trimester ♀**   **M**

X ● **O40.3   Polyhydramnios, third trimester ♀**   **M**

X ● **O40.9   Polyhydramnios, unspecified trimester ♀**   **M**

CHAPTER 15 (O00–O9A)

● **O41 Other disorders of amniotic fluid and membranes**

> **Excludes1**   encounter for suspected maternal and fetal conditions ruled out (Z03.7-)

> One of the following 7th characters is to be assigned to each code under category O41. 7th character Ø is for single gestations and multiple gestations where the fetus is unspecified. 7th characters 1 through 9 are for cases of multiple gestations to identify the fetus for which the code applies. The appropriate code from category O30, Multiple gestation, must also be assigned when assigning a code from category O41 that has a 7th character of 1 through 9.

> | | |
> |---|---|
> | Ø | not applicable or unspecified |
> | 1 | fetus 1 |
> | 2 | fetus 2 |
> | 3 | fetus 3 |
> | 4 | fetus 4 |
> | 5 | fetus 5 |
> | 9 | other fetus |

● **O41.0 Oligohydramnios**
> *Scant volume of amniotic fluid*
> Oligohydramnios without rupture of membranes

   X● **O41.00** Oligohydramnios, unspecified trimester ♀   M
   X● **O41.01** Oligohydramnios, first trimester ♀   M
   X● **O41.02** Oligohydramnios, second trimester ♀   M
   X● **O41.03** Oligohydramnios, third trimester ♀   M

● **O41.1 Infection of amniotic sac and membranes**
   ● **O41.10** Infection of amniotic sac and membranes, unspecified
     ● **O41.101** Infection of amniotic sac and membranes, unspecified, first trimester ♀   M
     ● **O41.102** Infection of amniotic sac and membranes, unspecified, second trimester ♀   M
     ● **O41.103** Infection of amniotic sac and membranes, unspecified, third trimester ♀   M
     ● **O41.109** Infection of amniotic sac and membranes, unspecified, unspecified trimester ♀   M
   ● **O41.12** Chorioamnionitis
     Coding Clinic: 2019, Q2, P34-35
     ● **O41.121** Chorioamnionitis, first trimester ♀   M
     ● **O41.122** Chorioamnionitis, second trimester ♀   M
     ● **O41.123** Chorioamnionitis, third trimester ♀   M
     ● **O41.129** Chorioamnionitis, unspecified trimester ♀   M
   ● **O41.14** Placentitis
     ● **O41.141** Placentitis, first trimester ♀   M
     ● **O41.142** Placentitis, second trimester ♀   M
     ● **O41.143** Placentitis, third trimester ♀   M
     ● **O41.149** Placentitis, unspecified trimester ♀   M

● **O41.8 Other specified disorders of amniotic fluid and membranes**
   ● **O41.8X** Other specified disorders of amniotic fluid and membranes
     ● **O41.8X1** Other specified disorders of amniotic fluid and membranes, first trimester ♀   M
     ● **O41.8X2** Other specified disorders of amniotic fluid and membranes, second trimester ♀   M
     ● **O41.8X3** Other specified disorders of amniotic fluid and membranes, third trimester ♀   M
     ● **O41.8X9** Other specified disorders of amniotic fluid and membranes, unspecified trimester ♀   M

● **O41.9 Disorder of amniotic fluid and membranes, unspecified**
   X● **O41.90** Disorder of amniotic fluid and membranes, unspecified, unspecified trimester ♀   M
   X● **O41.91** Disorder of amniotic fluid and membranes, unspecified, first trimester ♀   M
   X● **O41.92** Disorder of amniotic fluid and membranes, unspecified, second trimester ♀   M
   X● **O41.93** Disorder of amniotic fluid and membranes, unspecified, third trimester ♀   M

● **O42 Premature rupture of membranes**
   ● **O42.0 Premature rupture of membranes, onset of labor within 24 hours of rupture**
     O42.00 Premature rupture of membranes, onset of labor within 24 hours of rupture, unspecified weeks of gestation ♀   M
     ● **O42.01** Preterm premature rupture of membranes, onset of labor within 24 hours of rupture
      Premature rupture of membranes before 37 completed weeks of gestation
      O42.011 Preterm premature rupture of membranes, onset of labor within 24 hours of rupture, first trimester ♀   M
      O42.012 Preterm premature rupture of membranes, onset of labor within 24 hours of rupture, second trimester ♀ M
      O42.013 Preterm premature rupture of membranes, onset of labor within 24 hours of rupture, third trimester ♀   M
      O42.019 Preterm premature rupture of membranes, onset of labor within 24 hours of rupture, unspecified trimester ♀   M
     O42.02 Full-term premature rupture of membranes, onset of labor within 24 hours of rupture ♀   M
      Premature rupture of membranes at or after 37 completed weeks of gestation, onset of labor within 24 hours of rupture

   ● **O42.1 Premature rupture of membranes, onset of labor more than 24 hours following rupture**
     O42.10 Premature rupture of membranes, onset of labor more than 24 hours following rupture, unspecified weeks of gestation ♀   M
     ● **O42.11** Preterm premature rupture of membranes, onset of labor more than 24 hours following rupture
      Premature rupture of membranes before 37 completed weeks of gestation
      O42.111 Preterm premature rupture of membranes, onset of labor more than 24 hours following rupture, first trimester ♀   M
      O42.112 Preterm premature rupture of membranes, onset of labor more than 24 hours following rupture, second trimester ♀   M
      O42.113 Preterm premature rupture of membranes, onset of labor more than 24 hours following rupture, third trimester ♀   M
      O42.119 Preterm premature rupture of membranes, onset of labor more than 24 hours following rupture, unspecified trimester ♀   M
     O42.12 Full-term premature rupture of membranes, onset of labor more than 24 hours following rupture ♀   M
      Premature rupture of membranes at or after 37 completed weeks of gestation, onset of labor more than 24 hours following rupture

● **O42.9 Premature rupture of membranes, unspecified as to length of time between rupture and onset of labor**

  O42.90 Premature rupture of membranes, unspecified as to length of time between rupture and onset of labor, unspecified weeks of gestation ♀   M

  ● O42.91 Preterm premature rupture of membranes, unspecified as to length of time between rupture and onset of labor
    Premature rupture of membranes before 37 completed weeks of gestation

    O42.911 Preterm premature rupture of membranes, unspecified as to length of time between rupture and onset of labor, first trimester ♀   M

    O42.912 Preterm premature rupture of membranes, unspecified as to length of time between rupture and onset of labor, second trimester ♀   M

    O42.913 Preterm premature rupture of membranes, unspecified as to length of time between rupture and onset of labor, third trimester ♀   M

    O42.919 Preterm premature rupture of membranes, unspecified as to length of time between rupture and onset of labor, unspecified trimester ♀   M

  O42.92 Full-term premature rupture of membranes, unspecified as to length of time between rupture and onset of labor ♀   M
    Premature rupture of membranes at or after 37 completed weeks of gestation, unspecified as to length of time between rupture and onset of labor

● **O43 Placental disorders**

  Excludes2 maternal care for poor fetal growth due to placental insufficiency (O36.5-)
    placenta previa (O44.-)
    placental polyp (O90.89)
    placentitis (O41.14-)
    premature separation of placenta [abruptio placentae] (O45.-)

  ● **O43.0 Placental transfusion syndromes**

    ● O43.01 Fetomaternal placental transfusion syndrome
      Maternofetal placental transfusion syndrome

      O43.011 Fetomaternal placental transfusion syndrome, first trimester ♀   M

      O43.012 Fetomaternal placental transfusion syndrome, second trimester ♀   M

      O43.013 Fetomaternal placental transfusion syndrome, third trimester ♀   M

      O43.019 Fetomaternal placental transfusion syndrome, unspecified trimester ♀   M

    ● O43.02 Fetus-to-fetus placental transfusion syndrome

      O43.021 Fetus-to-fetus placental transfusion syndrome, first trimester ♀   M

      O43.022 Fetus-to-fetus placental transfusion syndrome, second trimester ♀   M

      O43.023 Fetus-to-fetus placental transfusion syndrome, third trimester ♀   M

      O43.029 Fetus-to-fetus placental transfusion syndrome, unspecified trimester ♀   M

  ● **O43.1 Malformation of placenta**

    ● O43.10 Malformation of placenta, unspecified
      Abnormal placenta NOS

      O43.101 Malformation of placenta, unspecified, first trimester ♀   M

      O43.102 Malformation of placenta, unspecified, second trimester ♀   M

      O43.103 Malformation of placenta, unspecified, third trimester ♀   M

      O43.109 Malformation of placenta, unspecified, unspecified trimester ♀ M

    ● O43.11 Circumvallate placenta

      O43.111 Circumvallate placenta, first trimester ♀   M

      O43.112 Circumvallate placenta, second trimester ♀   M

      O43.113 Circumvallate placenta, third trimester ♀   M

      O43.119 Circumvallate placenta, unspecified trimester ♀   M

    ● O43.12 Velamentous insertion of umbilical cord

      O43.121 Velamentous insertion of umbilical cord, first trimester ♀   M

      O43.122 Velamentous insertion of umbilical cord, second trimester ♀   M

      O43.123 Velamentous insertion of umbilical cord, third trimester ♀   M

      O43.129 Velamentous insertion of umbilical cord, unspecified trimester ♀   M

    ● O43.19 Other malformation of placenta

      O43.191 Other malformation of placenta, first trimester ♀   M

      O43.192 Other malformation of placenta, second trimester ♀   M

      O43.193 Other malformation of placenta, third trimester ♀   M

      O43.199 Other malformation of placenta, unspecified trimester ♀   M

● **O43.2 Morbidly adherent placenta**

  Code also associated third stage postpartum hemorrhage, if applicable (O72.0)

  Excludes1 retained placenta (O73.-)

  ● O43.21 Placenta accreta

    O43.211 Placenta accreta, first trimester ♀   M
    O43.212 Placenta accreta, second trimester ♀   M
    O43.213 Placenta accreta, third trimester ♀   M
    O43.219 Placenta accreta, unspecified trimester ♀   M

  ● O43.22 Placenta increta

    O43.221 Placenta increta, first trimester ♀   M
    O43.222 Placenta increta, second trimester ♀ M
    O43.223 Placenta increta, third trimester ♀   M
    O43.229 Placenta increta, unspecified trimester ♀   M

  ● O43.23 Placenta percreta

    O43.231 Placenta percreta, first trimester ♀   M
    O43.232 Placenta percreta, second trimester ♀ M
    O43.233 Placenta percreta, third trimester ♀   M
    O43.239 Placenta percreta, unspecified trimester ♀   M

● **O43.8 Other placental disorders**

  ● O43.81 Placental infarction

    O43.811 Placental infarction, first trimester ♀ M
    O43.812 Placental infarction, second trimester ♀   M
    O43.813 Placental infarction, third trimester ♀   M
    O43.819 Placental infarction, unspecified trimester ♀   M

  ● O43.89 Other placental disorders
    Placental dysfunction

    O43.891 Other placental disorders, first trimester ♀   M
    O43.892 Other placental disorders, second trimester ♀   M
    O43.893 Other placental disorders, third trimester ♀   M
    O43.899 Other placental disorders, unspecified trimester ♀   M

CHAPTER 15 (O00-O9A)

CHAPTER 15 (O00-O9A)

● **O43.9   Unspecified placental disorder**

     O43.90   Unspecified placental disorder, unspecified trimester ♀   M

     O43.91   Unspecified placental disorder, first trimester ♀   M

     O43.92   Unspecified placental disorder, second trimester ♀   M

     O43.93   Unspecified placental disorder, third trimester ♀   M

● **O44   Placenta previa**
    Coding Clinic: 2016, Q4, P52

   ● **O44.0   Complete placenta previa NOS or without hemorrhage**
       Placenta previa NOS

     O44.00   Complete placenta previa NOS or without hemorrhage, unspecified trimester ♀   M

     O44.01   Complete placenta previa NOS or without hemorrhage, first trimester ♀   M

     O44.02   Complete placenta previa NOS or without hemorrhage, second trimester ♀   M

     O44.03   Complete placenta previa NOS or without hemorrhage, third trimester ♀   M

   ● **O44.1   Complete placenta previa with hemorrhage**

     Excludes1   labor and delivery complicated by hemorrhage from vasa previa (O69.4)

     O44.10   Complete placenta previa with hemorrhage, unspecified trimester ♀   M

     O44.11   Complete placenta previa with hemorrhage, first trimester ♀   M

     O44.12   Complete placenta previa with hemorrhage, second trimester ♀   M

     O44.13   Complete placenta previa with hemorrhage, third trimester ♀   M

   ● **O44.2   Partial placenta previa without hemorrhage**
       Marginal placenta previa, NOS or without hemorrhage

     O44.20   Partial placenta previa NOS or without hemorrhage, unspecified trimester ♀   M

     O44.21   Partial placenta previa NOS or without hemorrhage, first trimester ♀   M

     O44.22   Partial placenta previa NOS or without hemorrhage, second trimester ♀   M

     O44.23   Partial placenta previa NOS or without hemorrhage, third trimester ♀   M

   ● **O44.3   Partial placenta previa with hemorrhage**
       Marginal placenta previa with hemorrhage

     O44.30   Partial placenta previa with hemorrhage, unspecified trimester ♀   M

     O44.31   Partial placenta previa with hemorrhage, first trimester ♀   M

     O44.32   Partial placenta previa with hemorrhage, second trimester ♀   M

     O44.33   Partial placenta previa with hemorrhage, third trimester ♀   M

● **O44.4   Low lying placenta NOS or without hemorrhage**
      Low implantation of placenta NOS or without hemorrhage

     O44.40   Low lying placenta NOS or without hemorrhage, unspecified trimester ♀   M

     O44.41   Low lying placenta NOS or without hemorrhage, first trimester ♀   M

     O44.42   Low lying placenta NOS or without hemorrhage, second trimester ♀   M

     O44.43   Low lying placenta NOS or without hemorrhage, third trimester ♀   M

● **O44.5   Low lying placenta with hemorrhage**
      Low implantation of placenta with hemorrhage

     O44.50   Low lying placenta with hemorrhage, unspecified trimester ♀   M

     O44.51   Low lying placenta with hemorrhage, first trimester ♀   M

     O44.52   Low lying placenta with hemorrhage, second trimester ♀   M

     O44.53   Low lying placenta with hemorrhage, third trimester ♀   M

● **O45   Premature separation of placenta [abruptio placentae]**

   ● **O45.0   Premature separation of placenta with coagulation defect**

    ● **O45.00   Premature separation of placenta with coagulation defect, unspecified**

      O45.001   Premature separation of placenta with coagulation defect, unspecified, first trimester ♀   M

      O45.002   Premature separation of placenta with coagulation defect, unspecified, second trimester ♀   M

      O45.003   Premature separation of placenta with coagulation defect, unspecified, third trimester ♀   M

      O45.009   Premature separation of placenta with coagulation defect, unspecified, unspecified trimester ♀   M

    ● **O45.01   Premature separation of placenta with afibrinogenemia**
       Premature separation of placenta with hypofibrinogenemia

      O45.011   Premature separation of placenta with afibrinogenemia, first trimester ♀   M

      O45.012   Premature separation of placenta with afibrinogenemia, second trimester ♀ M

      O45.013   Premature separation of placenta with afibrinogenemia, third trimester ♀   M

      O45.019   Premature separation of placenta with afibrinogenemia, unspecified trimester ♀   M

Figure 15-2   A. Marginal placenta previa. **B.** Partial placenta previa. **C.** Total placenta previa.

Item 15-3   Placenta previa is a condition in which the opening of the cervix is obstructed by the displaced placenta. The three types, marginal, partial, and total, are varying degrees of placenta displacement. Placenta abruption is the premature breaking away of the placenta from the site of the uterine implant before the delivery of the fetus.

Figure 15-3   Abruptio placentae is classified according to the grade of separation of the placenta from the uterine wall. **A.** Mild separation in which hemorrhage is internal. **B.** Moderate separation in which there is external hemorrhage. **C.** Severe separation in which there is external hemorrhage and extreme separation.

▶ New   ⇒ Revised   ~~deleted~~ Deleted   Excludes 1   Excludes 2   Includes   Use additional   Code first   Code also   Key words

   OGCR Official Guidelines   X Assign placeholder X   ● Use Additional Character(s)   ▷ Manifestation Code   🅗 Hierarchical Condition Category   **Coding Clinic**

● **O45.02   Premature separation of placenta with disseminated intravascular coagulation**

O45.021   Premature separation of placenta with disseminated intravascular coagulation, first trimester ♀   M

O45.022   Premature separation of placenta with disseminated intravascular coagulation, second trimester ♀   M

O45.023   Premature separation of placenta with disseminated intravascular coagulation, third trimester ♀   M

O45.029   Premature separation of placenta with disseminated intravascular coagulation, unspecified trimester ♀ M

● **O45.09   Premature separation of placenta with other coagulation defect**

O45.091   Premature separation of placenta with other coagulation defect, first trimester ♀   M

O45.092   Premature separation of placenta with other coagulation defect, second trimester ♀   M

O45.093   Premature separation of placenta with other coagulation defect, third trimester ♀   M

O45.099   Premature separation of placenta with other coagulation defect, unspecified trimester ♀   M

● **O45.8   Other premature separation of placenta**

● **O45.8X   Other premature separation of placenta**

O45.8X1   Other premature separation of placenta, first trimester ♀   M

O45.8X2   Other premature separation of placenta, second trimester ♀   M

O45.8X3   Other premature separation of placenta, third trimester ♀   M

O45.8X9   Other premature separation of placenta, unspecified trimester ♀   M

● **O45.9   Premature separation of placenta, unspecified**
Abruptio placentae NOS

O45.90   Premature separation of placenta, unspecified, unspecified trimester ♀   M

O45.91   Premature separation of placenta, unspecified, first trimester ♀   M

O45.92   Premature separation of placenta, unspecified, second trimester ♀   M

O45.93   Premature separation of placenta, unspecified, third trimester ♀   M

● **O46   Antepartum hemorrhage, not elsewhere classified**

Excludes1   hemorrhage in early pregnancy (O20.-)
intrapartum hemorrhage NEC (O67.-)
placenta previa (O44.-)
premature separation of placenta [abruptio placentae] (O45.-)

● **O46.0   Antepartum hemorrhage with coagulation defect**

● **O46.00   Antepartum hemorrhage with coagulation defect, unspecified**

O46.001   Antepartum hemorrhage with coagulation defect, unspecified, first trimester ♀   M

O46.002   Antepartum hemorrhage with coagulation defect, unspecified, second trimester ♀   M

O46.003   Antepartum hemorrhage with coagulation defect, unspecified, third trimester ♀   M

O46.009   Antepartum hemorrhage with coagulation defect, unspecified, unspecified trimester ♀   M

● **O46.01   Antepartum hemorrhage with afibrinogenemia**
Antepartum hemorrhage with hypofibrinogenemia

O46.011   Antepartum hemorrhage with afibrinogenemia, first trimester ♀   M

O46.012   Antepartum hemorrhage with afibrinogenemia, second trimester ♀ M

O46.013   Antepartum hemorrhage with afibrinogenemia, third trimester ♀   M

O46.019   Antepartum hemorrhage with afibrinogenemia, unspecified trimester ♀   M

● **O46.02   Antepartum hemorrhage with disseminated intravascular coagulation**

O46.021   Antepartum hemorrhage with disseminated intravascular coagulation, first trimester ♀   M

O46.022   Antepartum hemorrhage with disseminated intravascular coagulation, second trimester ♀   M

O46.023   Antepartum hemorrhage with disseminated intravascular coagulation, third trimester ♀   M

O46.029   Antepartum hemorrhage with disseminated intravascular coagulation, unspecified trimester ♀ M

● **O46.09   Antepartum hemorrhage with other coagulation defect**

O46.091   Antepartum hemorrhage with other coagulation defect, first trimester ♀ M

O46.092   Antepartum hemorrhage with other coagulation defect, second trimester ♀   M

O46.093   Antepartum hemorrhage with other coagulation defect, third trimester ♀ M

O46.099   Antepartum hemorrhage with other coagulation defect, unspecified trimester ♀   M

● **O46.8   Other antepartum hemorrhage**

● **O46.8x   Other antepartum hemorrhage**

O46.8x1   Other antepartum hemorrhage, first trimester ♀   M

O46.8x2   Other antepartum hemorrhage, second trimester ♀   M

O46.8x3   Other antepartum hemorrhage, third trimester ♀   M

O46.8x9   Other antepartum hemorrhage, unspecified trimester ♀   M

● **O46.9   Antepartum hemorrhage, unspecified**

O46.90   Antepartum hemorrhage, unspecified, unspecified trimester ♀   M

O46.91   Antepartum hemorrhage, unspecified, first trimester ♀   M

O46.92   Antepartum hemorrhage, unspecified, second trimester ♀   M

O46.93   Antepartum hemorrhage, unspecified, third trimester ♀   M

CHAPTER 15 (O00–O9A)

● **O47**   **False labor**

    Includes   Braxton Hicks contractions
                  threatened labor

    Excludes1   preterm labor (O60.-)

   ● **O47.0**   **False labor before 37 completed weeks of gestation**

      O47.00   False labor before 37 completed weeks of gestation, unspecified trimester ♀   M

      O47.02   False labor before 37 completed weeks of gestation, second trimester ♀   M

      O47.03   False labor before 37 completed weeks of gestation, third trimester ♀   M

   O47.1   **False labor at or after 37 completed weeks of gestation** ♀   M

   O47.9   **False labor, unspecified** ♀   M

● **O48**   **Late pregnancy**

   O48.0   **Post-term pregnancy** ♀   M
           Pregnancy over 40 completed weeks to 42 completed weeks gestation

   O48.1   **Prolonged pregnancy** ♀   M
           Pregnancy which has advanced beyond 42 completed weeks gestation

COMPLICATIONS OF LABOR AND DELIVERY (O60-O77)

● **O60**   **Preterm labor**

    Includes   onset (spontaneous) of labor before 37 completed weeks of gestation

    Excludes1   false labor (O47.0-)
                  threatened labor NOS (O47.0-)

   ● **O60.0**   **Preterm labor without delivery**

      O60.00   Preterm labor without delivery, unspecified trimester ♀   M

      O60.02   Preterm labor without delivery, second trimester ♀   M

      O60.03   Preterm labor without delivery, third trimester ♀   M

   ● **O60.1**   **Preterm labor with preterm delivery**

      One of the following 7th characters is to be assigned to each code under subcategory O60.1. 7th character 0 is for single gestations and multiple gestations where the fetus is unspecified. 7th characters 1 through 9 are for cases of multiple gestations to identify the fetus for which the code applies. The appropriate code from category O30, Multiple gestation, must also be assigned when assigning a code from subcategory O60.1 that has a 7th character of 1 through 9.

0	not applicable or unspecified
1	fetus 1
2	fetus 2
3	fetus 3
4	fetus 4
5	fetus 5
9	other fetus

      Coding Clinic: 2016, Q2, P11

   X● **O60.10**   Preterm labor with preterm delivery, unspecified trimester ♀   M
             Preterm labor with delivery NOS

   X● **O60.12**   Preterm labor second trimester with preterm delivery second trimester ♀   M

   X● **O60.13**   Preterm labor second trimester with preterm delivery third trimester ♀   M

   X● **O60.14**   Preterm labor third trimester with preterm delivery third trimester ♀   M
             Coding Clinic: 2016, Q2, P10

● **O60.2**   **Term delivery with preterm labor**

      One of the following 7th characters is to be assigned to each code under subcategory O60.2. 7th character 0 is for single gestations and multiple gestations where the fetus is unspecified. 7th characters 1 through 9 are for cases of multiple gestations to identify the fetus for which the code applies. The appropriate code from category O30, Multiple gestation, must also be assigned when assigning a code from subcategory O60.2 that has a 7th character of 1 through 9.

0	not applicable or unspecified
1	fetus 1
2	fetus 2
3	fetus 3
4	fetus 4
5	fetus 5
9	other fetus

   X● **O60.20**   Term delivery with preterm labor, unspecified trimester ♀   M

   X● **O60.22**   Term delivery with preterm labor, second trimester ♀   M

   X● **O60.23**   Term delivery with preterm labor, third trimester ♀   M

● **O61**   **Failed induction of labor**

   O61.0   **Failed medical induction of labor** ♀   M
           Failed induction (of labor) by oxytocin
           Failed induction (of labor) by prostaglandins

   O61.1   **Failed instrumental induction of labor** ♀   M
           Failed mechanical induction (of labor)
           Failed surgical induction (of labor)

   O61.8   **Other failed induction of labor** ♀   M

   O61.9   **Failed induction of labor, unspecified** ♀   M

● **O62**   **Abnormalities of forces of labor**

   O62.0   **Primary inadequate contractions** ♀   M
           Failure of cervical dilatation
           Primary hypotonic uterine dysfunction
           Uterine inertia during latent phase of labor

   O62.1   **Secondary uterine inertia** ♀   M
           Arrested active phase of labor
           Secondary hypotonic uterine dysfunction

   O62.2   **Other uterine inertia** ♀   M
           Atony of uterus without hemorrhage
           Atony of uterus NOS
           Desultory labor
           Hypotonic uterine dysfunction NOS
           Irregular labor
           Poor contractions
           Slow slope active phase of labor
           Uterine inertia NOS

      Excludes1   atony of uterus with hemorrhage (postpartum) (O72.1)
                  postpartum atony of uterus without hemorrhage (O75.89)

   O62.3   **Precipitate labor** ♀   M

   O62.4   **Hypertonic, incoordinate, and prolonged uterine contractions** ♀   M
           Cervical spasm
           Contraction ring dystocia
           Dyscoordinate labor
           Hour-glass contraction of uterus
           Hypertonic uterine dysfunction
           Incoordinate uterine action
           Tetanic contractions
           Uterine dystocia NOS
           Uterine spasm

      Excludes1   dystocia (fetal) (maternal) NOS (O66.9)

   O62.8   **Other abnormalities of forces of labor** ♀   M

   O62.9   **Abnormality of forces of labor, unspecified** ♀   M

▶ New   ➡ Revised   ~~deleted~~ Deleted   Excludes 1   Excludes 2   Includes   Use additional   Code first   Code also   Key words

OGCR Official Guidelines   X Assign placeholder X   ● Use Additional Character(s)   ▶ Manifestation Code   🅒🅒 Hierarchical Condition Category   Coding Clinic

Figure 15-4   Five types of malposition and malpresentation of the fetus: **A.** Breech. **B.** Vertex. **C.** Face. **D.** Brow. **E.** Shoulder.

● **O63**   **Long labor**
   O63.0   **Prolonged first stage (of labor)** ♀   M
   O63.1   **Prolonged second stage (of labor)** ♀   M
   O63.2   **Delayed delivery of second twin, triplet, etc.** ♀   M
   O63.9   **Long labor, unspecified** ♀   M
     Prolonged labor NOS

● **O64**   **Obstructed labor due to malposition and malpresentation of fetus**

   One of the following 7th characters is to be assigned to each code under category O64. 7th character Ø is for single gestations and multiple gestations where the fetus is unspecified. 7th characters 1 through 9 are for cases of multiple gestations to identify the fetus for which the code applies. The appropriate code from category O30, Multiple gestation, must also be assigned when assigning a code from category O64 that has a 7th character of 1 through 9.

   Ø   not applicable or unspecified
   1   fetus 1
   2   fetus 2
   3   fetus 3
   4   fetus 4
   5   fetus 5
   9   other fetus

X ● O64.0   **Obstructed labor due to incomplete rotation of fetal head** ♀   M
   Deep transverse arrest
   Obstructed labor due to persistent occipitoiliac (position)
   Obstructed labor due to persistent occipitoposterior (position)
   Obstructed labor due to persistent occipitosacral (position)
   Obstructed labor due to persistent occipitotransverse (position)
X ● O64.1   **Obstructed labor due to breech presentation** ♀   M
   Obstructed labor due to buttocks presentation
   Obstructed labor due to complete breech presentation
   Obstructed labor due to frank breech presentation
X ● O64.2   **Obstructed labor due to face presentation** ♀   M
   Obstructed labor due to chin presentation
X ● O64.3   **Obstructed labor due to brow presentation** ♀   M

X ● O64.4   **Obstructed labor due to shoulder presentation** ♀   M
   Prolapsed arm
   Excludes1   impacted shoulders (O66.0)
     shoulder dystocia (O66.0)
X ● O64.5   **Obstructed labor due to compound presentation** ♀   M
X ● O64.8   **Obstructed labor due to other malposition and malpresentation** ♀   M
   Obstructed labor due to footling presentation
   Obstructed labor due to incomplete breech presentation
X ● O64.9   **Obstructed labor due to malposition and malpresentation, unspecified** ♀   M

● **O65**   **Obstructed labor due to maternal pelvic abnormality**
   O65.0   **Obstructed labor due to deformed pelvis** ♀   M
   O65.1   **Obstructed labor due to generally contracted pelvis** ♀   M
   O65.2   **Obstructed labor due to pelvic inlet contraction** ♀   M
   O65.3   **Obstructed labor due to pelvic outlet and mid-cavity contraction** ♀   M
   O65.4   **Obstructed labor due to fetopelvic disproportion, unspecified** ♀   M
     Excludes1   dystocia due to abnormality of fetus (O66.2-O66.3)
   O65.5   **Obstructed labor due to abnormality of maternal pelvic organs** ♀   M
     Obstructed labor due to conditions listed in O34.-
     Use additional code to identify abnormality of pelvic organs O34.-
   O65.8   **Obstructed labor due to other maternal pelvic abnormalities** ♀   M
   O65.9   **Obstructed labor due to maternal pelvic abnormality, unspecified** ♀   M

● **O66**   **Other obstructed labor**
   O66.0   **Obstructed labor due to shoulder dystocia** ♀   M
     Impacted shoulders
   O66.1   **Obstructed labor due to locked twins** ♀   M
   O66.2   **Obstructed labor due to unusually large fetus** ♀   M
   O66.3   **Obstructed labor due to other abnormalities of fetus** ♀ M
     Dystocia due to fetal ascites
     Dystocia due to fetal hydrops
     Dystocia due to fetal meningomyelocele
     Dystocia due to fetal sacral teratoma
     Dystocia due to fetal tumor
     Dystocia due to hydrocephalic fetus
     Use additional code to identify cause of obstruction
   ● O66.4   **Failed trial of labor**
     O66.40   **Failed trial of labor, unspecified** ♀   M
     O66.41   **Failed attempted vaginal birth after previous cesarean delivery** ♀   M
       Code first rupture of uterus, if applicable (O71.0-, O71.1)
   O66.5   **Attempted application of vacuum extractor and forceps** ♀   M
     Attempted application of vacuum or forceps, with subsequent delivery by forceps or cesarean delivery
   O66.6   **Obstructed labor due to other multiple fetuses** ♀   M
   O66.8   **Other specified obstructed labor** ♀   M
     Use additional code to identify cause of obstruction
   O66.9   **Obstructed labor, unspecified** ♀   M
     Dystocia NOS
     Fetal dystocia NOS
     Maternal dystocia NOS

Figure 15-5   Hydrocephalic fetus causing disproportion.

CHAPTER 15 (OØØ-O9A)

● **O67** **Labor and delivery complicated by intrapartum hemorrhage, not elsewhere classified**

    Excludes1   antepartum hemorrhage NEC (O46.-)
               placenta previa (O44.-)
               premature separation of placenta [abruptio placentae] (O45.-)

    Excludes2   postpartum hemorrhage (O72.-)

   O67.0 **Intrapartum hemorrhage with coagulation defect** ♀   M
     Intrapartum hemorrhage (excessive) associated with afibrinogenemia
     Intrapartum hemorrhage (excessive) associated with disseminated intravascular coagulation
     Intrapartum hemorrhage (excessive) associated with hyperfibrinolysis
     Intrapartum hemorrhage (excessive) associated with hypofibrinogenemia

   O67.8 **Other intrapartum hemorrhage** ♀   M
     Excessive intrapartum hemorrhage

   O67.9 **Intrapartum hemorrhage, unspecified** ♀   M

O68 **Labor and delivery complicated by abnormality of fetal acid-base balance** ♀   M
     Fetal acidemia complicating labor and delivery
     Fetal acidosis complicating labor and delivery
     Fetal alkalosis complicating labor and delivery
     Fetal metabolic acidemia complicating labor and delivery

    Excludes1   fetal stress NOS (O77.9)
               labor and delivery complicated by electrocardiographic evidence of fetal stress (O77.8)
               labor and delivery complicated by ultrasonic evidence of fetal stress (O77.8)

    Excludes2   abnormality in fetal heart rate or rhythm (O76)
               labor and delivery complicated by meconium in amniotic fluid (O77.0)

● **O69** **Labor and delivery complicated by umbilical cord complications**

    One of the following 7th characters is to be assigned to each code under category O69. 7th character 0 is for single gestations and multiple gestations where the fetus is unspecified. 7th characters 1 through 9 are for cases of multiple gestations to identify the fetus for which the code applies. The appropriate code from category O30, Multiple gestation, must also be assigned when assigning a code from category O69 that has a 7th character of 1 through 9.

0	not applicable or unspecified
1	fetus 1
2	fetus 2
3	fetus 3
4	fetus 4
5	fetus 5
9	other fetus

X● **O69.0** **Labor and delivery complicated by prolapse of cord** ♀   M

X● **O69.1** **Labor and delivery complicated by cord around neck, with compression** ♀   M
    Excludes1   labor and delivery complicated by cord around neck, without compression (O69.81)

X● **O69.2** **Labor and delivery complicated by other cord entanglement, with compression** ♀   M
     Labor and delivery complicated by compression of cord NOS
     Labor and delivery complicated by entanglement of cords of twins in monoamniotic sac
     Labor and delivery complicated by knot in cord
    Excludes1   labor and delivery complicated by other cord entanglement, without compression (O69.82)

X● **O69.3** **Labor and delivery complicated by short cord** ♀   M

X● **O69.4** **Labor and delivery complicated by vasa previa** ♀   M
     Labor and delivery complicated by hemorrhage from vasa previa

X● **O69.5** **Labor and delivery complicated by vascular lesion of cord** ♀   M
     Labor and delivery complicated by cord bruising
     Labor and delivery complicated by cord hematoma
     Labor and delivery complicated by thrombosis of umbilical vessels

● **O69.8** **Labor and delivery complicated by other cord complications**

X● **O69.81** **Labor and delivery complicated by cord around neck, without compression** ♀   M

X● **O69.82** **Labor and delivery complicated by other cord entanglement, without compression** ♀   M

X● **O69.89** **Labor and delivery complicated by other cord complications** ♀   M

X● **O69.9** **Labor and delivery complicated by cord complication, unspecified** ♀   M

● **O70** **Perineal laceration during delivery**

    Includes   episiotomy extended by laceration
    Excludes1   obstetric high vaginal laceration alone (O71.4)

   O70.0 **First degree perineal laceration during delivery** ♀   M
     Perineal laceration, rupture or tear involving fourchette during delivery
     Perineal laceration, rupture or tear involving labia during delivery
     Perineal laceration, rupture or tear involving skin during delivery
     Perineal laceration, rupture or tear involving vagina during delivery
     Perineal laceration, rupture or tear involving vulva during delivery
     Slight perineal laceration, rupture or tear during delivery

   O70.1 **Second degree perineal laceration during delivery** ♀   M
     Perineal laceration, rupture or tear during delivery as in O70.0, also involving pelvic floor
     Perineal laceration, rupture or tear during delivery as in O70.0, also involving perineal muscles
     Perineal laceration, rupture or tear during delivery as in O70.0, also involving vaginal muscles
    Excludes1   perineal laceration involving anal sphincter (O70.2)
    Coding Clinic: 2016, CODING CIQ4, P53, Q2, P34

● **O70.2** **Third degree perineal laceration during delivery**
     Perineal laceration, rupture or tear during delivery as in O70.1, also involving anal sphincter
     Perineal laceration, rupture or tear during delivery as in O70.1, also involving rectovaginal septum
     Perineal laceration, rupture or tear during delivery as in O70.1, also involving sphincter NOS
    Excludes1   anal sphincter tear during delivery without third degree perineal laceration (O70.4)
               perineal laceration involving anal or rectal mucosa (O70.3)

   O70.20 **Third degree perineal laceration during delivery, unspecified** ♀   M

   O70.21 **Third degree perineal laceration during delivery, IIIa** ♀   M
     Third degree perineal laceration during delivery with less than 50% of external anal sphincter (EAS) thickness torn

   O70.22 **Third degree perineal laceration during delivery, IIIb** ♀   M
     Third degree perineal laceration during delivery with more than 50% external anal sphincter (EAS) thickness torn

   O70.23 **Third degree perineal laceration during delivery, IIIc** ♀   M
     Third degree perineal laceration during delivery with both external anal sphincter (EAS) and internal anal sphincter (IAS) torn

Vaginal opening   Urethral opening

A
B
C
D

Anus

Figure 15-6   Perineal lacerations: **A.** First-degree is laceration of superficial tissues. **B.** Second-degree is limited to the pelvic floor and may involve the perineal or vaginal muscles. **C.** Third-degree involves the anal sphincter. **D.** Fourth-degree involves anal or rectal mucosa.

O70.3   **Fourth degree perineal laceration during delivery** ♀   **M**
     Perineal laceration, rupture or tear during delivery as in O70.2, also involving anal mucosa
     Perineal laceration, rupture or tear during delivery as in O70.2, also involving rectal mucosa

O70.4   **Anal sphincter tear complicating delivery, not associated with third degree laceration** ♀   **M**
     Excludes1   anal sphincter tear with third degree perineal laceration (O70.2)

O70.9   **Perineal laceration during delivery, unspecified** ♀   **M**

● **O71**   **Other obstetric trauma**
     Includes   obstetric damage from instruments

● **O71.0**   **Rupture of uterus (spontaneous) before onset of labor**
     Excludes1   disruption of (current) cesarean delivery wound (O90.0)
              laceration of uterus, NEC (O71.81)

     O71.00   **Rupture of uterus before onset of labor, unspecified trimester** ♀   **M**

     O71.02   **Rupture of uterus before onset of labor, second trimester** ♀   **M**

     O71.03   **Rupture of uterus before onset of labor, third trimester** ♀   **M**

O71.1   **Rupture of uterus during labor** ♀   **M**
     Rupture of uterus not stated as occurring before onset of labor
     Excludes1   disruption of cesarean delivery wound (O90.0)
              laceration of uterus, NEC (O71.81)

O71.2   **Postpartum inversion of uterus** ♀   **M**

O71.3   **Obstetric laceration of cervix** ♀   **M**
     Annular detachment of cervix

O71.4   **Obstetric high vaginal laceration alone** ♀   **M**
     Laceration of vaginal wall without perineal laceration
     Excludes1   obstetric high vaginal laceration with perineal laceration (O70.-)

O71.5   **Other obstetric injury to pelvic organs** ♀   **M**
     Obstetric injury to bladder
     Obstetric injury to urethra
     Excludes2   obstetric periurethral trauma (O71.82)

O71.6   **Obstetric damage to pelvic joints and ligaments** ♀   **M**
     Obstetric avulsion of inner symphyseal cartilage
     Obstetric damage to coccyx
     Obstetric traumatic separation of symphysis (pubis)

O71.7   **Obstetric hematoma of pelvis** ♀   **M**
     Obstetric hematoma of perineum
     Obstetric hematoma of vagina
     Obstetric hematoma of vulva

● **O71.8**   **Other specified obstetric trauma**

     O71.81   **Laceration of uterus, not elsewhere classified** ♀   **M**

     O71.82   **Other specified trauma to perineum and vulva** ♀   **M**
         Obstetric periurethral trauma

     O71.89   **Other specified obstetric trauma** ♀   **M**

O71.9   **Obstetric trauma, unspecified** ♀   **M**

● **O72**   **Postpartum hemorrhage**
     Includes   hemorrhage after delivery of fetus or infant

O72.0   **Third-stage hemorrhage** ♀   **M**
     Hemorrhage associated with retained, trapped or adherent placenta
     Retained placenta NOS
     Code also type of adherent placenta (O43.2-)

O72.1   **Other immediate postpartum hemorrhage** ♀   **M**
     Hemorrhage following delivery of placenta
     Postpartum hemorrhage (atonic) NOS
     Uterine atony with hemorrhage
     Excludes1   uterine atony NOS (O62.2)
              uterine atony without hemorrhage (O62.2)
              postpartum atony of uterus without hemorrhage (O75.89)

O72.2   **Delayed and secondary postpartum hemorrhage** ♀   **M**
     Hemorrhage associated with retained portions of placenta or membranes after the first 24 hours following delivery of placenta
     Retained products of conception NOS, following delivery

O72.3   **Postpartum coagulation defects** ♀   **M**
     Postpartum afibrinogenemia
     Postpartum fibrinolysis

● **O73**   **Retained placenta and membranes, without hemorrhage**
     Excludes1   placenta accreta (O43.21-)
              placenta increta (O43.22-)
              placenta percreta (O43.23-)

O73.0   **Retained placenta without hemorrhage** ♀   **M**
     Adherent placenta, without hemorrhage
     Trapped placenta without hemorrhage

O73.1   **Retained portions of placenta and membranes, without hemorrhage** ♀   **M**
     Retained products of conception following delivery, without hemorrhage

● **O74**   **Complications of anesthesia during labor and delivery**
     Includes   maternal complications arising from the administration of a general, regional or local anesthetic, analgesic or other sedation during labor and delivery
     Use additional code, if applicable, to identify specific complication

O74.0   **Aspiration pneumonitis due to anesthesia during labor and delivery** ♀   **M**
     Inhalation of stomach contents or secretions NOS due to anesthesia during labor and delivery
     Mendelson's syndrome due to anesthesia during labor and delivery

O74.1   **Other pulmonary complications of anesthesia during labor and delivery** ♀   **M**

O74.2   **Cardiac complications of anesthesia during labor and delivery** ♀   **M**

O74.3   **Central nervous system complications of anesthesia during labor and delivery** ♀   **M**

O74.4   **Toxic reaction to local anesthesia during labor and delivery** ♀   **M**

O74.5   **Spinal and epidural anesthesia-induced headache during labor and delivery** ♀   **M**

O74.6   **Other complications of spinal and epidural anesthesia during labor and delivery** ♀   **M**

O74.7   **Failed or difficult intubation for anesthesia during labor and delivery** ♀   **M**

O74.8   **Other complications of anesthesia during labor and delivery** ♀   **M**

O74.9   **Complication of anesthesia during labor and delivery, unspecified** ♀   **M**

CHAPTER 15 (O00–O9A)

● **O75   Other complications of labor and delivery, not elsewhere classified**

  Excludes2   puerperal (postpartum) infection (O86.-)
                  puerperal (postpartum) sepsis (O85)

  O75.0   Maternal distress during labor and delivery ♀   M

  O75.1   Shock during or following labor and delivery ♀   M
            Obstetric shock following labor and delivery

  O75.2   Pyrexia during labor, not elsewhere classified ♀   M

  O75.3   Other infection during labor ♀   M
            Sepsis during labor

            Use additional code (B95-B97), to identify infectious
            agent

  **O75.4   Other complications of obstetric surgery and
            procedures ♀**   M
            Cardiac arrest following obstetric surgery or procedures
            Cardiac failure following obstetric surgery or
            procedures
            Cerebral anoxia following obstetric surgery or procedures
            Pulmonary edema following obstetric surgery or
            procedures

            Use additional code to identify specific complication

            Excludes2   complications of anesthesia during labor
                            and delivery (O74.-)
                            disruption of obstetrical (surgical) wound
                            (O90.0-O90.1)
                            hematoma of obstetrical (surgical) wound
                            (O90.2)
                            infection of obstetrical (surgical) wound
                            (O86.0-)

  **O75.5   Delayed delivery after artificial rupture of
            membranes ♀**   M

● **O75.8   Other specified complications of labor and delivery**

  **O75.81   Maternal exhaustion complicating labor and
             delivery ♀**   M

  **O75.82   Onset (spontaneous) of labor after 37 completed
             weeks of gestation but before 39 completed
             weeks gestation, with delivery by (planned)
             cesarean section ♀**   M
             Delivery by (planned) cesarean section occurring
             after 37 completed weeks of gestation but
             before 39 completed weeks gestation due to
             (spontaneous) onset of labor

             *Code first to specify reason for planned cesarean
             section such as:*
             cephalopelvic disproportion (normally
             formed fetus) (O33.9)
             previous cesarean delivery (O34.21)

  **O75.89   Other specified complications of labor and
             delivery ♀**   M

  O75.9   Complication of labor and delivery, unspecified ♀   M

**O76   Abnormality in fetal heart rate and rhythm complicating labor
        and delivery ♀**   M
        Depressed fetal heart rate tones complicating labor and
        delivery
        Fetal bradycardia complicating labor and delivery
        Fetal heart rate decelerations complicating labor and delivery
        Fetal heart rate irregularity complicating labor and delivery
        Fetal heart rate abnormal variability complicating labor and
        delivery
        Fetal tachycardia complicating labor and delivery
        Non-reassuring fetal heart rate or rhythm complicating labor
        and delivery

        Excludes1   fetal stress NOS (O77.9)
                        labor and delivery complicated by
                        electrocardiographic evidence of fetal stress
                        (O77.8)
                        labor and delivery complicated by ultrasonic
                        evidence of fetal stress (O77.8)

        Excludes2   fetal metabolic acidemia (O68)
                        other fetal stress (O77.0-O77.1)

● **O77   Other fetal stress complicating labor and delivery**

  **O77.0   Labor and delivery complicated by meconium in
            amniotic fluid ♀**   M

  **O77.1   Fetal stress in labor or delivery due to drug
            administration ♀**   M

  **O77.8   Labor and delivery complicated by other evidence of
            fetal stress ♀**   M
            Labor and delivery complicated by electrocardiographic
            evidence of fetal stress
            Labor and delivery complicated by ultrasonic evidence
            of fetal stress

            Excludes1   abnormality of fetal acid-base balance (O68)
                            abnormality in fetal heart rate or rhythm
                            (O76)
                            fetal metabolic acidemia (O68)

  **O77.9   Labor and delivery complicated by fetal stress,
            unspecified ♀**   M
            Excludes1   abnormality of fetal acid-base balance (O68)
                            abnormality in fetal heart rate or rhythm
                            (O76)
                            fetal metabolic acidemia (O68)

OGCR   Section I.C., Chapter 15.n.

Normal Delivery, Code O80

1) Encounter for full-term uncomplicated delivery

Code O80 should be assigned when a woman is admitted for a full-
term normal delivery and delivers a single, healthy infant without any
complications antepartum, during the delivery, or postpartum during
the delivery episode. Code O80 is always a principal diagnosis. It is
not to be used if any other code from Chapter 15 is needed to describe
a current complication of the antenatal, delivery, or perinatal period.
Additional codes from other chapters may be used with code O80 if
they are not related to or are in any way complicating the pregnancy.

2) Uncomplicated delivery with resolved antepartum complication

Code O80 may be used if the patient had a complication at some point
during the pregnancy, but the complication is not present at the time of
the admission for delivery.

3) Outcome of delivery for O80

Z37.0, Single live birth, is the only outcome of delivery code
appropriate for use with O80.

ENCOUNTER FOR DELIVERY (O80-O82)

O80   Encounter for full-term uncomplicated delivery ♀   M
        Delivery requiring minimal or no assistance, with or without
        episiotomy, without fetal manipulation [e.g., rotation
        version] or instrumentation [forceps] of a spontaneous,
        cephalic, vaginal, full-term, single, live-born infant. This
        code is for use as a single diagnosis code and is not to be
        used with any other code from Chapter 15.

        Use additional code to indicate outcome of delivery (Z37.0)
        Coding Clinic: 2016, Q4, P124, 150

O82   Encounter for cesarean delivery without indication ♀   M
        Use additional code to indicate outcome of delivery (Z37.0)

Figure 15-7   The four stages of normal delivery: **I.** Lightening, which
occurs 2 to 4 weeks before birth, at which time the fetus turns with head
toward the vagina. **II.** Regular contractions begin, the amniotic sac
ruptures, and dilation is complete. **III.** Delivery of the head and rotation.
IV. Expulsion of placenta.

▶ New   ⇒ Revised   ~~deleted~~ Deleted   Excludes 1   Excludes 2   Includes   Use additional   Code first   Code also   Key words

OGCR Official Guidelines   X Assign placeholder X   ● Use Additional Character(s)   ▶ Manifestation Code   🅗 Hierarchical Condition Category   **Coding Clinic**

COMPLICATIONS PREDOMINANTLY RELATED TO THE PUERPERIUM (O85-O92)

Excludes2   mental and behavioral disorders associated with the puerperium (F53.-)
obstetrical tetanus (A34)
puerperal osteomalacia (M83.0)

O85   Puerperal sepsis ♀   M
Postpartum sepsis
Puerperal peritonitis
Puerperal pyemia
Use additional code (B95-B97), to identify infectious agent
Use additional code (R65.2-) to identify severe sepsis, if applicable

Excludes1   fever of unknown origin following delivery (O86.4)
genital tract infection following delivery (O86.1-)
obstetric pyemic and septic embolism (O88.3-)
puerperal septic thrombophlebitis (O86.81)
urinary tract infection following delivery (O86.2-)

Excludes2   sepsis during labor (O75.3)

Coding Clinic: 2018, Q4, P23

● **O86   Other puerperal infections**
Use additional code (B95-B97), to identify infectious agent

Excludes2   infection during labor (O75.3)
obstetrical tetanus (A34)

● **O86.0   Infection of obstetric surgical wound**
Infected cesarean delivery wound following delivery
Infected perineal repair following delivery

Excludes1   complications of procedures, not elsewhere classified (T81.44)
postprocedural fever NOS (R50.82)
postprocedural retroperitoneal abscess (K68.11)

O86.00   **Infection of obstetric surgical wound, unspecified ♀**   M

O86.01   **Infection of obstetric surgical wound, superficial incisional site ♀**   M
Subcutaneous abscess following an obstetrical procedure
Stitch abscess following an obstetrical procedure

O86.02   **Infection of obstetric surgical wound, deep incisional site ♀**   M
Intramuscular abscess following an obstetrical procedure
Sub-fascial abscess following an obstetrical procedure
Coding Clinic: 2018, Q4, P23

O86.03   **Infection of obstetric surgical wound, organ and space site ♀**   M
Intraabdominal abscess following an obstetrical procedure
Subphrenic abscess following an obstetrical procedure

O86.04   **Sepsis following an obstetrical procedure ♀**   M
Use additional code to identify the sepsis

O86.09   **Infection of obstetric surgical wound, other surgical site ♀**   M

● **O86.1   Other infection of genital tract following delivery**
O86.11   **Cervicitis following delivery ♀**   M
O86.12   **Endometritis following delivery ♀**   M
O86.13   **Vaginitis following delivery ♀**   M
O86.19   **Other infection of genital tract following delivery ♀**   M

● **O86.2   Urinary tract infection following delivery**
O86.20   **Urinary tract infection following delivery, unspecified ♀**   M
Puerperal urinary tract infection NOS
O86.21   **Infection of kidney following delivery ♀**   M
O86.22   **Infection of bladder following delivery ♀**   M
Infection of urethra following delivery
O86.29   **Other urinary tract infection following delivery ♀**   M

● **O86.4   Pyrexia of unknown origin following delivery ♀**   M
Puerperal infection NOS following delivery
Puerperal pyrexia NOS following delivery

Excludes2   pyrexia during labor (O75.2)

● **O86.8   Other specified puerperal infections**
O86.81   **Puerperal septic thrombophlebitis ♀**   M
O86.89   **Other specified puerperal infections ♀**   M

● **O87   Venous complications and hemorrhoids in the puerperium**

Includes   venous complications in labor, delivery and the puerperium

Excludes2   obstetric embolism (O88.-)
puerperal septic thrombophlebitis (O86.81)
venous complications in pregnancy (O22.-)

O87.0   **Superficial thrombophlebitis in the puerperium ♀**   M
Puerperal phlebitis NOS
Puerperal thrombosis NOS

O87.1   **Deep phlebothrombosis in the puerperium ♀**   M
Deep vein thrombosis, postpartum
Pelvic thrombophlebitis, postpartum
Use additional code to identify the deep vein thrombosis (I82.4-, I82.5-, I82.62-. I82.72-)
Use additional code, if applicable, for associated long-term (current) use of anticoagulants (Z79.01)

O87.2   **Hemorrhoids in the puerperium ♀**   M
O87.3   **Cerebral venous thrombosis in the puerperium ♀**   M
Cerebrovenous sinus thrombosis in the puerperium
O87.4   **Varicose veins of lower extremity in the puerperium ♀** M
O87.8   **Other venous complications in the puerperium ♀**   M
Genital varices in the puerperium
O87.9   **Venous complication in the puerperium, unspecified ♀** M
Puerperal phlebopathy NOS

O88   **Obstetric embolism**

Excludes1   embolism complicating abortion NOS (O03.2)
embolism complicating ectopic or molar pregnancy (O08.2)
embolism complicating failed attempted abortion (O07.2)
embolism complicating induced abortion (O04.7)
embolism complicating spontaneous abortion (O03.2, O03.7)

● **O88.0   Obstetric air embolism**
● **O88.01   Obstetric air embolism in pregnancy**
O88.011   **Air embolism in pregnancy, first trimester ♀**   M
O88.012   **Air embolism in pregnancy, second trimester ♀**   M
O88.013   **Air embolism in pregnancy, third trimester ♀**   M
O88.019   **Air embolism in pregnancy, unspecified trimester ♀**   M
O88.02   **Air embolism in childbirth ♀**   M
O88.03   **Air embolism in the puerperium ♀**   M

CHAPTER 15 (O00-O9A)

● **O88.1**   **Amniotic fluid embolism**
      Anaphylactoid syndrome in pregnancy
   ● **O88.11**   **Amniotic fluid embolism in pregnancy**
       O88.111   **Amniotic fluid embolism in pregnancy, first trimester** ♀   M
       O88.112   **Amniotic fluid embolism in pregnancy, second trimester** ♀   M
       O88.113   **Amniotic fluid embolism in pregnancy, third trimester** ♀   M
       O88.119   **Amniotic fluid embolism in pregnancy, unspecified trimester** ♀   M
   O88.12   **Amniotic fluid embolism in childbirth** ♀   M
   O88.13   **Amniotic fluid embolism in the puerperium** ♀   M
● **O88.2**   **Obstetric thromboembolism**
   ● **O88.21**   **Thromboembolism in pregnancy**
       Obstetric (pulmonary) embolism NOS
       O88.211   **Thromboembolism in pregnancy, first trimester** ♀   M
       O88.212   **Thromboembolism in pregnancy, second trimester** ♀   M
       O88.213   **Thromboembolism in pregnancy, third trimester** ♀   M
       O88.219   **Thromboembolism in pregnancy, unspecified trimester** ♀   M
   O88.22   **Thromboembolism in childbirth** ♀   M
   O88.23   **Thromboembolism in the puerperium** ♀   M
      Puerperal (pulmonary) embolism NOS
● **O88.3**   **Obstetric pyemic and septic embolism**
   ● **O88.31**   **Pyemic and septic embolism in pregnancy**
       O88.311   **Pyemic and septic embolism in pregnancy, first trimester** ♀   M
       O88.312   **Pyemic and septic embolism in pregnancy, second trimester** ♀   M
       O88.313   **Pyemic and septic embolism in pregnancy, third trimester** ♀   M
       O88.319   **Pyemic and septic embolism in pregnancy, unspecified trimester** ♀   M
   O88.32   **Pyemic and septic embolism in childbirth** ♀   M
   O88.33   **Pyemic and septic embolism in the puerperium** ♀   M
● **O88.8**   **Other obstetric embolism**
      Obstetric fat embolism
   ● **O88.81**   **Other embolism in pregnancy**
       O88.811   **Other embolism in pregnancy, first trimester** ♀   M
       O88.812   **Other embolism in pregnancy, second trimester** ♀   M
       O88.813   **Other embolism in pregnancy, third trimester** ♀   M
       O88.819   **Other embolism in pregnancy, unspecified trimester** ♀   M
   O88.82   **Other embolism in childbirth** ♀   M
   O88.83   **Other embolism in the puerperium** ♀   M

● **O89**   **Complications of anesthesia during the puerperium**
   Includes   maternal complications arising from the administration of a general, regional or local anesthetic, analgesic or other sedation during the puerperium
   Use additional code, if applicable, to identify specific complication
   ● **O89.0**   **Pulmonary complications of anesthesia during the puerperium**
       O89.01   **Aspiration pneumonitis due to anesthesia during the puerperium** ♀   M
         Inhalation of stomach contents or secretions NOS due to anesthesia during the puerperium
         Mendelson's syndrome due to anesthesia during the puerperium
       O89.09   **Other pulmonary complications of anesthesia during the puerperium** ♀   M
   O89.1   **Cardiac complications of anesthesia during the puerperium** ♀   M
   O89.2   **Central nervous system complications of anesthesia during the puerperium** ♀   M
   O89.3   **Toxic reaction to local anesthesia during the puerperium** ♀   M
   O89.4   **Spinal and epidural anesthesia-induced headache during the puerperium** ♀   M
   O89.5   **Other complications of spinal and epidural anesthesia during the puerperium** ♀   M
   O89.6   **Failed or difficult intubation for anesthesia during the puerperium** ♀   M
   O89.8   **Other complications of anesthesia during the puerperium** ♀   M
   O89.9   **Complication of anesthesia during the puerperium, unspecified** ♀   M

● **O90**   **Complications of the puerperium, not elsewhere classified**
   O90.0   **Disruption of cesarean delivery wound** ♀   M
      Dehiscence of cesarean delivery wound
      Excludes1   rupture of uterus (spontaneous) before onset of labor (O71.0-)
          rupture of uterus during labor (O71.1)
   O90.1   **Disruption of perineal obstetric wound** ♀   M
      Disruption of wound of episiotomy
      Disruption of wound of perineal laceration
      Secondary perineal tear
   O90.2   **Hematoma of obstetric wound** ♀   M
   O90.3   **Peripartum cardiomyopathy** ♀   M
      Conditions in I42.- arising during pregnancy and the puerperium
      Excludes1   pre-existing heart disease complicating pregnancy and the puerperium (O99.4-)
   O90.4   **Postpartum acute kidney failure** ♀   M
      Hepatorenal syndrome following labor and delivery
   O90.5   **Postpartum thyroiditis** ♀   M
   O90.6   **Postpartum mood disturbance** ♀   M
      Postpartum blues   Postpartum sadness
      Postpartum dysphoria
      Excludes1   postpartum depression (F53.0)
          puerperal psychosis (F53.1)
   O90.8   **Other complications of the puerperium, not elsewhere classified**
       O90.81   **Anemia of the puerperium** ♀   M
         Postpartum anemia NOS
         Excludes1   pre-existing anemia complicating the puerperium (O99.03)
       O90.89   **Other complications of the puerperium, not elsewhere classified** ♀   M
         Placental polyp
   O90.9   **Complication of the puerperium, unspecified** ♀   M

▶ New   ⇒ Revised   ~~deleted~~ Deleted   Excludes 1   Excludes 2   Includes   Use additional   Code first   Code also   Key words
OGCR Official Guidelines   X Assign placeholder X   ● Use Additional Character(s)   ▷ Manifestation Code   🔲 Hierarchical Condition Category   **Coding Clinic**

● **O91**   **Infections of breast associated with pregnancy, the puerperium and lactation**
     Use additional code to identify infection

  ● **O91.0**   **Infection of nipple associated with pregnancy, the puerperium and lactation**

    ● **O91.01**   **Infection of nipple associated with pregnancy**
         Gestational abscess of nipple

       O91.011   **Infection of nipple associated with pregnancy, first trimester** ♀   M

       O91.012   **Infection of nipple associated with pregnancy, second trimester** ♀   M

       O91.013   **Infection of nipple associated with pregnancy, third trimester** ♀   M

       O91.019   **Infection of nipple associated with pregnancy, unspecified trimester** ♀   M

     O91.02   **Infection of nipple associated with the puerperium** ♀   M
         Puerperal abscess of nipple

     O91.03   **Infection of nipple associated with lactation** ♀ M
         Abscess of nipple associated with lactation

  ● **O91.1**   **Abscess of breast associated with pregnancy, the puerperium and lactation**

    ● **O91.11**   **Abscess of breast associated with pregnancy**
         Gestational mammary abscess
         Gestational purulent mastitis
         Gestational subareolar abscess

       O91.111   **Abscess of breast associated with pregnancy, first trimester** ♀   M

       O91.112   **Abscess of breast associated with pregnancy, second trimester** ♀   M

       O91.113   **Abscess of breast associated with pregnancy, third trimester** ♀   M

       O91.119   **Abscess of breast associated with pregnancy, unspecified trimester** ♀   M

     O91.12   **Abscess of breast associated with the puerperium** ♀   M
         Puerperal mammary abscess
         Puerperal purulent mastitis
         Puerperal subareolar abscess

     O91.13   **Abscess of breast associated with lactation** ♀   M
         Mammary abscess associated with lactation
         Purulent mastitis associated with lactation
         Subareolar abscess associated with lactation

  ● **O91.2**   **Nonpurulent mastitis associated with pregnancy, the puerperium and lactation**

    ● **O91.21**   **Nonpurulent mastitis associated with pregnancy**
         Gestational interstitial mastitis
         Gestational lymphangitis of breast
         Gestational mastitis NOS
         Gestational parenchymatous mastitis

       O91.211   **Nonpurulent mastitis associated with pregnancy, first trimester** ♀   M

       O91.212   **Nonpurulent mastitis associated with pregnancy, second trimester** ♀   M

       O91.213   **Nonpurulent mastitis associated with pregnancy, third trimester** ♀   M

       O91.219   **Nonpurulent mastitis associated with pregnancy, unspecified trimester** ♀   M

     O91.22   **Nonpurulent mastitis associated with the puerperium** ♀   M
         Puerperal interstitial mastitis
         Puerperal lymphangitis of breast
         Puerperal mastitis NOS
         Puerperal parenchymatous mastitis

     O91.23   **Nonpurulent mastitis associated with lactation** ♀   M
         Interstitial mastitis associated with lactation
         Lymphangitis of breast associated with lactation
         Mastitis NOS associated with lactation
         Parenchymatous mastitis associated with lactation

● **O92**   **Other disorders of breast and disorders of lactation associated with pregnancy and the puerperium**

  ● **O92.0**   **Retracted nipple associated with pregnancy, the puerperium, and lactation**

    ● **O92.01**   **Retracted nipple associated with pregnancy**

       O92.011   **Retracted nipple associated with pregnancy, first trimester** ♀   M

       O92.012   **Retracted nipple associated with pregnancy, second trimester** ♀   M

       O92.013   **Retracted nipple associated with pregnancy, third trimester** ♀   M

       O92.019   **Retracted nipple associated with pregnancy, unspecified trimester** ♀   M

     O92.02   **Retracted nipple associated with the puerperium** ♀   M

     O92.03   **Retracted nipple associated with lactation** ♀   M

  ● **O92.1**   **Cracked nipple associated with pregnancy, the puerperium, and lactation**
         Fissure of nipple, gestational or puerperal

    ● **O92.11**   **Cracked nipple associated with pregnancy**

       O92.111   **Cracked nipple associated with pregnancy, first trimester** ♀   M

       O92.112   **Cracked nipple associated with pregnancy, second trimester** ♀   M

       O92.113   **Cracked nipple associated with pregnancy, third trimester** ♀   M

       O92.119   **Cracked nipple associated with pregnancy, unspecified trimester** ♀   M

     O92.12   **Cracked nipple associated with the puerperium** ♀   M

     O92.13   **Cracked nipple associated with lactation** ♀   M

  ● **O92.2**   **Other and unspecified disorders of breast associated with pregnancy and the puerperium**

     O92.20   **Unspecified disorder of breast associated with pregnancy and the puerperium** ♀   M

     O92.29   **Other disorders of breast associated with pregnancy and the puerperium** ♀   M

   O92.3   **Agalactia** ♀   M
     Primary agalactia

     Excludes1   elective agalactia (O92.5)
                secondary agalactia (O92.5)
                therapeutic agalactia (O92.5)

   O92.4   **Hypogalactia** ♀   M

   O92.5   **Suppressed lactation** ♀   M
     Elective agalactia   Therapeutic agalactia
     Secondary agalactia

     Excludes1   primary agalactia (O92.3)

   O92.6   **Galactorrhea** ♀   M

  ● **O92.7**   **Other and unspecified disorders of lactation**

     O92.70   **Unspecified disorders of lactation** ♀   M

     O92.79   **Other disorders of lactation** ♀   M
         Puerperal galactocele

OTHER OBSTETRIC CONDITIONS, NOT ELSEWHERE CLASSIFIED (O94-O9A)

O94 Sequelae of complication of pregnancy, childbirth, and the puerperium ♀   M

    Note: This category is to be used to indicate conditions in O00-O77.-, O85-O94 and O98-O9A.- as the cause of late effects. The "sequelae" include conditions specified as such, or as late effects, which may occur at any time after the puerperium.

    Code first condition resulting from (sequela) of complication of pregnancy, childbirth, and the puerperium

O98 Maternal infectious and parasitic diseases classifiable elsewhere but complicating pregnancy, childbirth and the puerperium

    Includes   the listed conditions when complicating the pregnant state, when aggravated by the pregnancy, or as a reason for obstetric care

    Use additional code (Chapter 1), to identify specific infectious or parasitic disease

    Excludes2   herpes gestationis (O26.4-)
                       infectious carrier state (O99.82-, O99.83-)
                       obstetrical tetanus (A34)
                       puerperal infection (O86.-)
                       puerperal sepsis (O85)
                       when the reason for maternal care is that the disease is known or suspected to have affected the fetus (O35-O36)

● **O98.0** Tuberculosis complicating pregnancy, childbirth and the puerperium
    Conditions in A15-A19

  ● **O98.01** Tuberculosis complicating pregnancy

      O98.011 Tuberculosis complicating pregnancy, first trimester ♀   M

      O98.012 Tuberculosis complicating pregnancy, second trimester ♀   M

      O98.013 Tuberculosis complicating pregnancy, third trimester ♀   M

      O98.019 Tuberculosis complicating pregnancy, unspecified trimester ♀   M

    O98.02 Tuberculosis complicating childbirth ♀   M

    O98.03 Tuberculosis complicating the puerperium ♀   M

● **O98.1** Syphilis complicating pregnancy, childbirth and the puerperium
    Conditions in A50-A53

  ● **O98.11** Syphilis complicating pregnancy

      O98.111 Syphilis complicating pregnancy, first trimester ♀   M

      O98.112 Syphilis complicating pregnancy, second trimester ♀   M

      O98.113 Syphilis complicating pregnancy, third trimester ♀   M

      O98.119 Syphilis complicating pregnancy, unspecified trimester ♀   M

    O98.12 Syphilis complicating childbirth ♀   M

    O98.13 Syphilis complicating the puerperium ♀   M

● **O98.2** Gonorrhea complicating pregnancy, childbirth and the puerperium
    Conditions in A54.-

  ● **O98.21** Gonorrhea complicating pregnancy

      O98.211 Gonorrhea complicating pregnancy, first trimester ♀   M

      O98.212 Gonorrhea complicating pregnancy, second trimester ♀   M

      O98.213 Gonorrhea complicating pregnancy, third trimester ♀   M

      O98.219 Gonorrhea complicating pregnancy, unspecified trimester ♀   M

    O98.22 Gonorrhea complicating childbirth ♀   M

    O98.23 Gonorrhea complicating the puerperium ♀   M

● **O98.3** Other infections with a predominantly sexual mode of transmission complicating pregnancy, childbirth and the puerperium
    Conditions in A55-A64

  ● **O98.31** Other infections with a predominantly sexual mode of transmission complicating pregnancy

      O98.311 Other infections with a predominantly sexual mode of transmission complicating pregnancy, first trimester ♀   M

      O98.312 Other infections with a predominantly sexual mode of transmission complicating pregnancy, second trimester ♀   M

      O98.313 Other infections with a predominantly sexual mode of transmission complicating pregnancy, third trimester ♀   M

      O98.319 Other infections with a predominantly sexual mode of transmission complicating pregnancy, unspecified trimester ♀   M

    O98.32 Other infections with a predominantly sexual mode of transmission complicating childbirth ♀   M
        Coding Clinic: 2020, Q1, P20

    O98.33 Other infections with a predominantly sexual mode of transmission complicating the puerperium ♀   M

● **O98.4** Viral hepatitis complicating pregnancy, childbirth and the puerperium
    Conditions in B15-B19

  ● **O98.41** Viral hepatitis complicating pregnancy

      O98.411 Viral hepatitis complicating pregnancy, first trimester ♀   M

      O98.412 Viral hepatitis complicating pregnancy, second trimester ♀   M

      O98.413 Viral hepatitis complicating pregnancy, third trimester ♀   M

      O98.419 Viral hepatitis complicating pregnancy, unspecified trimester ♀   M

    O98.42 Viral hepatitis complicating childbirth ♀   M

    O98.43 Viral hepatitis complicating the puerperium ♀   M

● **O98.5** Other viral diseases complicating pregnancy, childbirth and the puerperium
    Conditions in A80-B09, B25-B34, R87.81-, R87.82-

    Excludes:1   human immunodeficiency virus [HIV] disease complicating pregnancy, childbirth and the puerperium (O98.7-)

  ● **O98.51** Other viral diseases complicating pregnancy

      O98.511 Other viral diseases complicating pregnancy, first trimester ♀   M

      O98.512 Other viral diseases complicating pregnancy, second trimester ♀   M
        Coding Clinic: 2016, Q4, P5-6

      O98.513 Other viral diseases complicating pregnancy, third trimester ♀   M
        Coding Clinic: 2016, Q4, P6

      O98.519 Other viral diseases complicating pregnancy, unspecified trimester ♀   M

    O98.52 Other viral diseases complicating childbirth ♀   M

    O98.53 Other viral diseases complicating the puerperium ♀   M

▶ New   ⇒ Revised   ~~deleted~~ Deleted   Excludes 1   Excludes 2   Includes   Use additional   Code first   Code also   Key words
OGCR Official Guidelines   X Assign placeholder X   ● Use Additional Character(s)   ▷ Manifestation Code   🝢 Hierarchical Condition Category   Coding Clinic

● **O98.6** **Protozoal diseases** complicating pregnancy, childbirth and the puerperium
Conditions in B50-B64

  ● **O98.61** Protozoal diseases complicating **pregnancy**

    O98.611   Protozoal diseases complicating pregnancy, **first trimester** ♀   M

    O98.612   Protozoal diseases complicating pregnancy, **second trimester** ♀   M

    O98.613   Protozoal diseases complicating pregnancy, **third trimester** ♀   M

    O98.619   Protozoal diseases complicating pregnancy, **unspecified trimester** ♀   M

    O98.62   Protozoal diseases complicating **childbirth** ♀   M

    O98.63   Protozoal diseases complicating the **puerperium** ♀   M

● **O98.7** **Human immunodeficiency virus [HIV]** disease complicating pregnancy, childbirth and the puerperium

  Use additional code to identify the type of HIV disease:
    Acquired immune deficiency syndrome (AIDS) (B20)
    Asymptomatic HIV status (Z21)
    HIV positive NOS (Z21)
    Symptomatic HIV disease (B20)

  OGCR Section I.C.15.f.

  HIV Infection in Pregnancy, Childbirth and the Puerperium

  During pregnancy, childbirth or the puerperium, a patient admitted because of an HIV-related illness should receive a principal diagnosis from subcategory O98.7-. Human immunodeficiency [HIV] disease complicating pregnancy, childbirth and the puerperium, followed by the code(s) for the HIV-related illness(es).

  Patients with asymptomatic HIV infection status admitted during pregnancy, childbirth, or the puerperium should receive codes of O98.7- and Z21, Asymptomatic human immunodeficiency virus [HIV] infection status.

  ● **O98.71** **Human immunodeficiency virus [HIV]** disease complicating **pregnancy**

    O98.711   Human immunodeficiency virus [HIV] disease complicating pregnancy, **first trimester** ♀   M

    O98.712   Human immunodeficiency virus [HIV] disease complicating pregnancy, **second trimester** ♀   M

    O98.713   Human immunodeficiency virus [HIV] disease complicating pregnancy, **third trimester** ♀   M

    O98.719   Human immunodeficiency virus [HIV] disease complicating pregnancy, **unspecified trimester** ♀   M

    O98.72   Human immunodeficiency virus [HIV] disease complicating **childbirth** ♀   M

    O98.73   Human immunodeficiency virus [HIV] disease complicating the **puerperium** ♀   M

● **O98.8** **Other maternal infectious** and parasitic diseases complicating pregnancy, childbirth and the puerperium

  ● **O98.81** Other maternal infectious and parasitic diseases complicating **pregnancy**

    O98.811   Other maternal infectious and parasitic diseases complicating pregnancy, **first trimester** ♀   M

    O98.812   Other maternal infectious and parasitic diseases complicating pregnancy, **second trimester** ♀   M

    O98.813   Other maternal infectious and parasitic diseases complicating pregnancy, **third trimester** ♀   M

    O98.819   Other maternal infectious and parasitic diseases complicating pregnancy, **unspecified trimester** ♀   M

    O98.82   Other maternal infectious and parasitic diseases complicating **childbirth** ♀   M
        Coding Clinic: 2020, Q1, P10

    O98.83   Other maternal infectious and parasitic diseases complicating the **puerperium** ♀   M

● **O98.9** **Unspecified** maternal infectious and parasitic disease complicating pregnancy, childbirth and the puerperium

  ● **O98.91** **Unspecified** maternal infectious and parasitic disease complicating **pregnancy**

    O98.911   Unspecified maternal infectious and parasitic disease complicating pregnancy, **first trimester** ♀   M

    O98.912   Unspecified maternal infectious and parasitic disease complicating pregnancy, **second trimester** ♀   M

    O98.913   Unspecified maternal infectious and parasitic disease complicating pregnancy, **third trimester** ♀   M

    O98.919   Unspecified maternal infectious and parasitic disease complicating pregnancy, **unspecified trimester** ♀   M

    O98.92   **Unspecified** maternal infectious and parasitic disease complicating **childbirth** ♀   M

    O98.93   **Unspecified** maternal infectious and parasitic disease complicating the **puerperium** ♀   M

● **O99** **Other maternal diseases** classifiable elsewhere but complicating pregnancy, childbirth and the puerperium

  Includes: conditions which complicate the pregnant state, are aggravated by the pregnancy or are a main reason for obstetric care

  Use additional code to identify specific condition

  Excludes2   when the reason for maternal care is that the condition is known or suspected to have affected the fetus (O35-O36)

  Coding Clinic: 2018, Q4, P8-9

● **O99.0** **Anemia** complicating pregnancy, childbirth and the puerperium
Conditions in D50-D64

  Excludes1   anemia arising in the puerperium (O90.81) postpartum anemia NOS (O90.81)

  ● **O99.01** Anemia complicating **pregnancy**

    O99.011   Anemia complicating pregnancy, **first trimester** ♀   M

    O99.012   Anemia complicating pregnancy, **second trimester** ♀   M

    O99.013   Anemia complicating pregnancy, **third trimester** ♀   M

    O99.019   Anemia complicating pregnancy, **unspecified trimester** ♀   M

    O99.02   Anemia complicating **childbirth** ♀   M

    O99.03   Anemia complicating the **puerperium** ♀   M

        Excludes1   postpartum anemia not pre-existing prior to delivery (O90.81)

● O99.1 Other diseases of the blood and blood-forming organs and certain disorders involving the immune mechanism complicating pregnancy, childbirth and the puerperium
    Conditions in D65-D89

    Excludes1   hemorrhage with coagulation defects (O45.-, O46.0-, O67.0, O72.3)

● O99.11 Other diseases of the blood and blood-forming organs and certain disorders involving the immune mechanism complicating pregnancy

    O99.111 Other diseases of the blood and blood-forming organs and certain disorders involving the immune mechanism complicating pregnancy, first trimester ♀   M

    O99.112 Other diseases of the blood and blood-forming organs and certain disorders involving the immune mechanism complicating pregnancy, second trimester ♀   M

    O99.113 Other diseases of the blood and blood-forming organs and certain disorders involving the immune mechanism complicating pregnancy, third trimester ♀   M

    O99.119 Other diseases of the blood and blood-forming organs and certain disorders involving the immune mechanism complicating pregnancy, unspecified trimester ♀   M

O99.12 Other diseases of the blood and blood-forming organs and certain disorders involving the immune mechanism complicating childbirth ♀   M

O99.13 Other diseases of the blood and blood-forming organs and certain disorders involving the immune mechanism complicating the puerperium ♀   M

● O99.2 Endocrine, nutritional and metabolic diseases complicating pregnancy, childbirth and the puerperium
    ⇒ Conditions in E00-E89

    Excludes2   diabetes mellitus (O24.-)
                  malnutrition (O25.-)
                  postpartum thyroiditis (O90.5)

● O99.21 Obesity complicating pregnancy, childbirth, and the puerperium
    Use additional code to identify the type of obesity (E66.-)

    O99.210 Obesity complicating pregnancy, unspecified trimester ♀   M

    O99.211 Obesity complicating pregnancy, first trimester ♀   M

    O99.212 Obesity complicating pregnancy, second trimester ♀   M

    O99.213 Obesity complicating pregnancy, third trimester ♀   M

    O99.214 Obesity complicating childbirth ♀   M
            Coding Clinic: 2018, Q4, P80

    O99.215 Obesity complicating the puerperium ♀   M

● O99.28 Other endocrine, nutritional and metabolic diseases complicating pregnancy, childbirth and the puerperium

    O99.280 Endocrine, nutritional and metabolic diseases complicating pregnancy, unspecified trimester ♀   M

    O99.281 Endocrine, nutritional and metabolic diseases complicating pregnancy, first trimester ♀   M

    O99.282 Endocrine, nutritional and metabolic diseases complicating pregnancy, second trimester ♀   M

    O99.283 Endocrine, nutritional and metabolic diseases complicating pregnancy, third trimester ♀   M

    O99.284 Endocrine, nutritional and metabolic diseases complicating childbirth ♀ M

    O99.285 Endocrine, nutritional and metabolic diseases complicating the puerperium ♀   M

● O99.3 Mental disorders and diseases of the nervous system complicating pregnancy, childbirth and the puerperium

● O99.31 Alcohol use complicating pregnancy, childbirth, and the puerperium
    Use additional code(s) from F10 to identify manifestations of the alcohol use

    O99.310 Alcohol use complicating pregnancy, unspecified trimester ♀   M

    O99.311 Alcohol use complicating pregnancy, first trimester ♀   M

    O99.312 Alcohol use complicating pregnancy, second trimester ♀   M

    O99.313 Alcohol use complicating pregnancy, third trimester ♀   M

    O99.314 Alcohol use complicating childbirth ♀   M

    O99.315 Alcohol use complicating the puerperium ♀   M

● O99.32 Drug use complicating pregnancy, childbirth, and the puerperium
    Use additional code(s) from F11-F16 and F18-F19 to identify manifestations of the drug use

    O99.320 Drug use complicating pregnancy, unspecified trimester ♀   M

    O99.321 Drug use complicating pregnancy, first trimester ♀   M

    O99.322 Drug use complicating pregnancy, second trimester ♀   M

    O99.323 Drug use complicating pregnancy, third trimester ♀   M

    O99.324 Drug use complicating childbirth ♀ M

    O99.325 Drug use complicating the puerperium ♀   M

● O99.33 Tobacco use disorder complicating pregnancy, childbirth, and the puerperium
    Smoking complicating pregnancy, childbirth, and the puerperium
    Use additional code from category F17 to identify type of tobacco nicotine dependence

    O99.330 Smoking (tobacco) complicating pregnancy, unspecified trimester ♀   M

    O99.331 Smoking (tobacco) complicating pregnancy, first trimester ♀   M

    O99.332 Smoking (tobacco) complicating pregnancy, second trimester ♀   M

    O99.333 Smoking (tobacco) complicating pregnancy, third trimester ♀   M

    O99.334 Smoking (tobacco) complicating childbirth ♀   M

    O99.335 Smoking (tobacco) complicating the puerperium ♀   M

CHAPTER 15 (O00-O9A)

▶ New   ⇒ Revised   ~~deleted~~ Deleted   Excludes 1   Excludes 2   Includes   Use additional   Code first   Code also   Key words

OGCR Official Guidelines   X Assign placeholder X   ● Use Additional Character(s)   ▶ Manifestation Code   🅦 Hierarchical Condition Category   **Coding Clinic**

● **O99.34**   **Other mental disorders complicating pregnancy, childbirth, and the puerperium**
➡ Conditions in F01-F09, F20-F52 and F54-F99

> **Excludes2**   postpartum mood disturbance (O90.6)
> postnatal psychosis (F53.1)
> puerperal psychosis (F53.1)

Coding Clinic: 2018, Q4, P9

    O99.340   Other mental disorders complicating pregnancy, unspecified trimester ♀   M

    O99.341   Other mental disorders complicating pregnancy, first trimester ♀   M

    O99.342   Other mental disorders complicating pregnancy, second trimester ♀   M

    O99.343   Other mental disorders complicating pregnancy, third trimester ♀   M

    O99.344   Other mental disorders complicating childbirth ♀   M

    O99.345   Other mental disorders complicating the puerperium ♀   M

Coding Clinic: 2018, Q4, P8-9

● **O99.35**   **Diseases of the nervous system complicating pregnancy, childbirth, and the puerperium**
Conditions in G00-G99

> **Excludes2**   pregnancy related peripheral neuritis (O26.8-)

    O99.350   Diseases of the nervous system complicating pregnancy, unspecified trimester ♀   M

    O99.351   Diseases of the nervous system complicating pregnancy, first trimester ♀   M

    O99.352   Diseases of the nervous system complicating pregnancy, second trimester ♀   M

    O99.353   Diseases of the nervous system complicating pregnancy, third trimester ♀   M

    O99.354   Diseases of the nervous system complicating childbirth ♀   M

    O99.355   Diseases of the nervous system complicating the puerperium ♀   M

● **O99.4**   **Diseases of the circulatory system complicating pregnancy, childbirth and the puerperium**
Conditions in I00-I99

> **Excludes1**   peripartum cardiomyopathy (O90.3)
> **Excludes2**   hypertensive disorders (O10-O16)
> obstetric embolism (O88.-)
> venous complications and cerebrovenous sinus thrombosis in labor, childbirth and the puerperium (O87.-)
> venous complications and cerebrovenous sinus thrombosis in pregnancy (O22.-)

● **O99.41**   **Diseases of the circulatory system complicating pregnancy**
Coding Clinic: 2016, Q2, P8

    O99.411   Diseases of the circulatory system complicating pregnancy, first trimester ♀   M

    O99.412   Diseases of the circulatory system complicating pregnancy, second trimester ♀   M

    O99.413   Diseases of the circulatory system complicating pregnancy, third trimester ♀   M

    O99.419   Diseases of the circulatory system complicating pregnancy, unspecified trimester ♀   M

    O99.42   Diseases of the circulatory system complicating childbirth ♀   M

    O99.43   Diseases of the circulatory system complicating the puerperium ♀   M

● **O99.5**   **Diseases of the respiratory system complicating pregnancy, childbirth and the puerperium**
Conditions in J00-J99

● **O99.51**   **Diseases of the respiratory system complicating pregnancy**

    O99.511   Diseases of the respiratory system complicating pregnancy, first trimester ♀   M

    O99.512   Diseases of the respiratory system complicating pregnancy, second trimester ♀   M

    O99.513   Diseases of the respiratory system complicating pregnancy, third trimester ♀   M

    O99.519   Diseases of the respiratory system complicating pregnancy, unspecified trimester ♀   M

    O99.52   Diseases of the respiratory system complicating childbirth ♀   M

    O99.53   Diseases of the respiratory system complicating the puerperium ♀   M

● **O99.6**   **Diseases of the digestive system complicating pregnancy, childbirth and the puerperium**
Conditions in K00-K93

> **Excludes2**   hemorrhoids in pregnancy (O22.4-)
> liver and biliary tract disorders in pregnancy, childbirth and the puerperium (O26.6-)

● **O99.61**   **Diseases of the digestive system complicating pregnancy**

    O99.611   Diseases of the digestive system complicating pregnancy, first trimester ♀   M

    O99.612   Diseases of the digestive system complicating pregnancy, second trimester ♀   M

    O99.613   Diseases of the digestive system complicating pregnancy, third trimester ♀   M

    O99.619   Diseases of the digestive system complicating pregnancy, unspecified trimester ♀   M

    O99.62   Diseases of the digestive system complicating childbirth ♀   M

    O99.63   Diseases of the digestive system complicating the puerperium ♀   M

● **O99.7**   **Diseases of the skin and subcutaneous tissue complicating pregnancy, childbirth and the puerperium**
Conditions in L00-L99

> **Excludes2**   herpes gestationis (O26.4)
> pruritic urticarial papules and plaques of pregnancy (PUPPP) (O26.86)

● **O99.71**   **Diseases of the skin and subcutaneous tissue complicating pregnancy**

    O99.711   Diseases of the skin and subcutaneous tissue complicating pregnancy, first trimester ♀   M

    O99.712   Diseases of the skin and subcutaneous tissue complicating pregnancy, second trimester ♀   M

    O99.713   Diseases of the skin and subcutaneous tissue complicating pregnancy, third trimester ♀   M

    O99.719   Diseases of the skin and subcutaneous tissue complicating pregnancy, unspecified trimester ♀   M

    O99.72   Diseases of the skin and subcutaneous tissue complicating childbirth ♀   M

    O99.73   Diseases of the skin and subcutaneous tissue complicating the puerperium ♀   M

● **O99.8   Other specified diseases and conditions complicating pregnancy, childbirth and the puerperium**
     Conditions in D00-D48, H00-H95, M00-N99, and Q00-Q99
     Use additional code to identify condition
     Excludes2   genitourinary infections in pregnancy (O23.-)
                 infection of genitourinary tract following delivery (O86.1-O86.4)
                 malignant neoplasm complicating pregnancy, childbirth and the puerperium (O9A.1-)
                 maternal care for known or suspected abnormality of maternal pelvic organs (O34.-)
                 postpartum acute kidney failure (O90.4)
                 traumatic injuries in pregnancy (O9A.2-)

● **O99.81   Abnormal glucose complicating pregnancy, childbirth and the puerperium**
     Excludes1   gestational diabetes (O24.4-)
     O99.810   Abnormal glucose complicating pregnancy ♀   M
     O99.814   Abnormal glucose complicating childbirth ♀   M
     O99.815   Abnormal glucose complicating the puerperium ♀   M

● **O99.82   Streptococcus B carrier state complicating pregnancy, childbirth and the puerperium**
     Excludes1   Carrier of streptococcus group B (GBS) in a nonpregnant woman (Z22.330)
     O99.820   Streptococcus B carrier state complicating pregnancy ♀   M
     O99.824   Streptococcus B carrier state complicating childbirth ♀   M
          Coding Clinic: 2019, Q2, P9
     O99.825   Streptococcus B carrier state complicating the puerperium ♀   M

● **O99.83   Other infection carrier state complicating pregnancy, childbirth and the puerperium**
     Use additional code to identify the carrier state (Z22.-)
     O99.830   Other infection carrier state complicating pregnancy ♀   M
     O99.834   Other infection carrier state complicating childbirth ♀   M
     O99.835   Other infection carrier state complicating the puerperium ♀   M

● **O99.84   Bariatric surgery status complicating pregnancy, childbirth and the puerperium**
     Gastric banding status complicating pregnancy, childbirth and the puerperium
     Gastric bypass status for obesity complicating pregnancy, childbirth and the puerperium
     Obesity surgery status complicating pregnancy, childbirth and the puerperium
     O99.840   Bariatric surgery status complicating pregnancy, unspecified trimester ♀   M
     O99.841   Bariatric surgery status complicating pregnancy, first trimester ♀   M
     O99.842   Bariatric surgery status complicating pregnancy, second trimester ♀   M
     O99.843   Bariatric surgery status complicating pregnancy, third trimester ♀   M
     O99.844   Bariatric surgery status complicating childbirth ♀   M
     O99.845   Bariatric surgery status complicating the puerperium ♀   M

● **O99.89   Other specified diseases and conditions complicating pregnancy, childbirth and the puerperium** ♀   M
     ▷ **O99.891   Other specified diseases and conditions complicating pregnancy**
     ▷ **O99.892   Other specified diseases and conditions complicating childbirth**
     ▷ **O99.893   Other specified diseases and conditions complicating puerperium**

OGCR   Section I.C.2.l.3.

> Malignant neoplasm in a pregnant patient
> When a pregnant woman has a malignant neoplasm, a code from subcategory O9A.1-, Malignant neoplasm complicating pregnancy, childbirth, and the puerperium, should be sequenced first, followed by the appropriate code from Chapter 2 to indicate the type of neoplasm.

● **O9A   Maternal malignant neoplasms, traumatic injuries and abuse classifiable elsewhere but complicating pregnancy, childbirth and the puerperium**

● **O9A.1   Malignant neoplasm complicating pregnancy, childbirth and the puerperium**
     Conditions in C00-C96
     Use additional code to identify neoplasm
     Excludes2   maternal care for benign tumor of corpus uteri (O34.1-)
                maternal care for benign tumor of cervix (O34.4-)

● **O9A.11   Malignant neoplasm complicating pregnancy**
     O9A.111   Malignant neoplasm complicating pregnancy, first trimester ♀   M
     O9A.112   Malignant neoplasm complicating pregnancy, second trimester ♀   M
     O9A.113   Malignant neoplasm complicating pregnancy, third trimester ♀   M
     O9A.119   Malignant neoplasm complicating pregnancy, unspecified trimester ♀   M

   O9A.12   Malignant neoplasm complicating childbirth ♀   M

   O9A.13   Malignant neoplasm complicating the puerperium ♀   M
       Coding Clinic: 2015, Q3, P19

● **O9A.2   Injury, poisoning and certain other consequences of external causes complicating pregnancy, childbirth and the puerperium**
     Conditions in S00-T88, except T74 and T76
     Use additional code(s) to identify the injury or poisoning
     Excludes2   physical, sexual and psychological abuse complicating pregnancy, childbirth and the puerperium (O9A.3-, O9A.4-, O9A.5-)

● **O9A.21   Injury, poisoning and certain other consequences of external causes complicating pregnancy**
     O9A.211   Injury, poisoning and certain other consequences of external causes complicating pregnancy, first trimester ♀   M
     O9A.212   Injury, poisoning and certain other consequences of external causes complicating pregnancy, second trimester ♀   M
     O9A.213   Injury, poisoning and certain other consequences of external causes complicating pregnancy, third trimester ♀   M
     O9A.219   Injury, poisoning and certain other consequences of external causes complicating pregnancy, unspecified trimester ♀   M

O9A.22 **Injury, poisoning and certain other consequences of external causes complicating childbirth** ♀   M

O9A.23 **Injury, poisoning and certain other consequences of external causes complicating the puerperium** ♀   M

● O9A.3 **Physical abuse complicating pregnancy, childbirth and the puerperium**
Conditions in T74.11 or T76.11

Use additional code (if applicable):
   to identify any associated current injury due to physical abuse
   to identify the perpetrator of abuse (Y07.-)

    Excludes2   sexual abuse complicating pregnancy, childbirth and the puerperium (O9A.4)

● O9A.31 **Physical abuse complicating pregnancy**

O9A.311 **Physical abuse complicating pregnancy, first trimester** ♀   M

O9A.312 **Physical abuse complicating pregnancy, second trimester** ♀   M

O9A.313 **Physical abuse complicating pregnancy, third trimester** ♀   M

O9A.319 **Physical abuse complicating pregnancy, unspecified trimester** ♀   M

O9A.32 **Physical abuse complicating childbirth** ♀   M

O9A.33 **Physical abuse complicating the puerperium** ♀   M

● O9A.4 **Sexual abuse complicating pregnancy, childbirth and the puerperium**
Conditions in T74.21 or T76.21

Use additional code (if applicable):
   to identify any associated current injury due to sexual abuse
   to identify the perpetrator of abuse (Y07.-)

● O9A.41 **Sexual abuse complicating pregnancy**

O9A.411 **Sexual abuse complicating pregnancy, first trimester** ♀   M

O9A.412 **Sexual abuse complicating pregnancy, second trimester** ♀   M

O9A.413 **Sexual abuse complicating pregnancy, third trimester** ♀   M

O9A.419 **Sexual abuse complicating pregnancy, unspecified trimester** ♀   M

O9A.42 **Sexual abuse complicating childbirth** ♀   M

O9A.43 **Sexual abuse complicating the puerperium** ♀   M

● O9A.5 **Psychological abuse complicating pregnancy, childbirth and the puerperium**
Conditions in T74.31 or T76.31

Use additional code to identify the perpetrator of abuse (Y07.-)

● O9A.51 **Psychological abuse complicating pregnancy**

O9A.511 **Psychological abuse complicating pregnancy, first trimester** ♀   M

O9A.512 **Psychological abuse complicating pregnancy, second trimester** ♀   M

O9A.513 **Psychological abuse complicating pregnancy, third trimester** ♀   M

O9A.519 **Psychological abuse complicating pregnancy, unspecified trimester** ♀   M

O9A.52 **Psychological abuse complicating childbirth** ♀ M

O9A.53 **Psychological abuse complicating the puerperium** ♀   M

N Newborn Age: 0   **P** Pediatric Age: 0–17   **M** Maternity DX: 12–55   **A** Adult Age: 15–124   ♀ Females Only   ♂ Males Only

CHAPTER 16

CERTAIN CONDITIONS ORIGINATING IN THE PERINATAL PERIOD (P00-P96)

OGCR Chapter-Specific Coding Guidelines

16. **Chapter 16: Certain Conditions Originating in the Perinatal Period (P00-P96)**
For coding and reporting purposes the perinatal period is defined as before birth through the 28th day following birth. The following guidelines are provided for reporting purposes

a. **General Perinatal Rules**

1) **Use of Chapter 16 Codes**
Codes in this chapter are <u>never</u> for use on the maternal record. Codes from Chapter 15, the obstetric chapter, are never permitted on the newborn record. Chapter 16 codes may be used throughout the life of the patient if the condition is still present.

2) **Principal Diagnosis for Birth Record**
When coding the birth episode in a newborn record, assign a code from category Z38, Liveborn infants according to place of birth and type of delivery, as the principal diagnosis. A code from category Z38 is assigned only once, to a newborn at the time of birth. If a newborn is transferred to another institution, a code from category Z38 should not be used at the receiving hospital.

A code from category Z38 is used only on the newborn record, not on the mother's record.

3) **Use of Codes from other Chapters with Codes from Chapter 16**
Codes from other chapters may be used with codes from chapter 16 if the codes from the other chapters provide more specific detail. Codes for signs and symptoms may be assigned when a definitive diagnosis has not been established. If the reason for the encounter is a perinatal condition, the code from Chapter 16 should be sequenced first.

4) **Use of Chapter 16 Codes after the Perinatal Period**
Should a condition originate in the perinatal period, and continue throughout the life of the patient, the perinatal code should continue to be used regardless of the patient's age.

5) **Birth process or community acquired conditions**
If a newborn has a condition that may be either due to the birth process or community acquired and the documentation does not indicate which it is, the default is due to the birth process and the code from Chapter 16 should be used. If the condition is community-acquired, a code from Chapter 16 should not be assigned.

6) **Code all clinically significant conditions**
All clinically significant conditions noted on routine newborn examination should be coded. A condition is clinically significant if it requires:
- clinical evaluation; or
- therapeutic treatment; or
- diagnostic procedures; or
- extended length of hospital stay; or
- increased nursing care and/or monitoring; or
- has implications for future health care needs

Note: The perinatal guidelines listed above are the same as the general coding guidelines for "additional diagnoses", except for the final point regarding implications for future health care needs. Codes should be assigned for conditions that have been specified by the provider as having implications for future health care needs.

b. **Observation and Evaluation of Newborns for Suspected Conditions Not Found**

1) **Use of Z05 codes**
Assign a code from category Z05, Observation and evaluation of newborns and infants for suspected conditions ruled out, to identify those instances when a healthy newborn is evaluated for a suspected condition that is determined after study not to be present. Do not use a code from category Z05 when the patient has identified signs or symptoms of a suspected problem; in such cases code the sign or symptom.

2) **Z05 on Other than the Birth Record**
A code from category Z05 may also be assigned as a principal or first-listed code for readmissions or encounters when the code from category Z38 code no longer applies. Codes from category Z05 are for use only for healthy newborns and infants for which no condition after study is found to be present.

3) **Z05 on a birth record**
A code from category Z05 is to be used as a secondary code after the code from category Z38, Liveborn infants according to place of birth and type of delivery.

c. **Coding Additional Perinatal Diagnoses**

1) **Assigning codes for conditions that require treatment**
Assign codes for conditions that require treatment or further investigation, prolong the length of stay, or require resource utilization.

2) **Codes for conditions specified as having implications for future health care needs**
Assign codes for conditions that have been specified by the provider as having implications for future health care needs.
Note: This guideline should not be used for adult patients.

d. **Prematurity and Fetal Growth Retardation**
Providers utilize different criteria in determining prematurity. A code for prematurity should not be assigned unless it is documented. Assignment of codes in categories P05, Disorders of newborn related to slow fetal growth and fetal malnutrition, and P07, Disorders of newborn related to short gestation and low birth weight, not elsewhere classified, should be based on the recorded birth weight and estimated gestational age.

When both birth weight and gestational age are available, two codes from category P07 should be assigned, with the code for birth weight sequenced before the code for gestational age.

e. **Low birth weight and immaturity status**
Codes from category P07, Disorders of newborn related to short gestation and low birth weight, not elsewhere classified, are for use for a child or adult who was premature or had a low birth weight as a newborn and this is affecting the patient's current health status.

See Section I.C.21. Factors influencing health status and contact with health services, Status.

f. **Bacterial Sepsis of Newborn**
Category P36, Bacterial sepsis of newborn, includes congenital sepsis. If a perinate is documented as having sepsis without documentation of congenital or community acquired, the default is congenital and a code from category P36 should be assigned. If the P36 code includes the causal organism, an additional code from category B95, Streptococcus, Staphylococcus, and Enterococcus as the cause of diseases classified elsewhere, or B96, Other bacterial agents as the cause of diseases classified elsewhere, should not be assigned. If the P36 code does not include the causal organism, assign an additional code from category B96. If applicable, use additional codes to identify severe sepsis (R65.2-) and any associated acute organ dysfunction.

g. **Stillbirth**
Code P95, Stillbirth, is only for use in institutions that maintain separate records for stillbirths. No other code should be used with P95. Code P95 should not be used on the mother's record.

CHAPTER 16

CERTAIN CONDITIONS ORIGINATING IN THE PERINATAL PERIOD (P00-P96)

Note: Codes from this chapter are for use on newborn records only, never on maternal records.

Includes conditions that have their origin in the fetal or perinatal period (before birth through the first 28 days after birth) even if morbidity occurs later

Excludes2 congenital malformations, deformations and chromosomal abnormalities (Q00-Q99)
endocrine, nutritional and metabolic diseases (E00-E88)
injury, poisoning and certain other consequences of external causes (S00-T88)
neoplasms (C00-D49)
tetanus neonatorum (A33)

This chapter contains the following blocks:

P00-P04	Newborn affected by maternal factors and by complications of pregnancy, labor, and delivery
P05-P08	Disorders of newborns related to length of gestation and fetal growth
P09	Abnormal findings on neonatal screening
P10-P15	Birth trauma
P19-P29	Respiratory and cardiovascular disorders specific to the perinatal period
P35-P39	Infections specific to the perinatal period
P50-P61	Hemorrhagic and hematological disorders of newborn
P70-P74	Transitory endocrine and metabolic disorders specific to newborn
P76-P78	Digestive system disorders of newborn
P80-P83	Conditions involving the integument and temperature regulation of newborn
P84	Other problems with newborn
P90-P96	Other disorders originating in the perinatal period

NEWBORN AFFECTED BY MATERNAL FACTORS AND BY COMPLICATIONS OF PREGNANCY, LABOR, AND DELIVERY (P00–P04)

Note: These codes are for use when the listed maternal conditions are specified as the cause of confirmed morbidity or potential morbidity which have their origin in the perinatal period (before birth through the first 28 days after birth).

● **P00** **Newborn affected by maternal conditions that may be unrelated to present pregnancy**

Code first any current condition in newborn

Excludes2 encounter for observation of newborn for suspected diseases and conditions ruled out (Z05.-)
newborn affected by maternal complications of pregnancy (P01.-)
newborn affected by maternal endocrine and metabolic disorders (P70–P74)
newborn affected by noxious substances transmitted via placenta or breast milk (P04.-)

Coding Clinic: 2016, Q4, P54

P00.0 **Newborn affected by maternal hypertensive disorders**
Newborn affected by maternal conditions classifiable to O10-O11, O13-O16

P00.1 **Newborn affected by maternal renal and urinary tract diseases**
Newborn affected by maternal conditions classifiable to N00-N39

P00.2 **Newborn affected by maternal infectious and parasitic diseases**
Newborn affected by maternal infectious disease classifiable to A00-B99, J09 and J10

Excludes1 maternal genital tract or other localized infections (P00.8)

Excludes2 infections specific to the perinatal period (P35-P39)

Coding Clinic: 2019, Q2, P10; 2015, Q3, P21

P00.3 **Newborn affected by other maternal circulatory and respiratory diseases**
Newborn affected by maternal conditions classifiable to I00-I99, J00-J99, Q20-Q34 and not included in P00.0, P00.2

P00.4 **Newborn affected by maternal nutritional disorders**
Newborn affected by maternal disorders classifiable to E40-E64
Maternal malnutrition NOS

P00.5 **Newborn affected by maternal injury**
Newborn affected by maternal conditions classifiable to O9A.2-

P00.6 **Newborn affected by surgical procedure on mother**
Newborn affected by amniocentesis

Excludes1 Cesarean delivery for present delivery (P03.4)
damage to placenta from amniocentesis, cesarean delivery or surgical induction (P02.1)
previous surgery to uterus or pelvic organs (P03.89)

Excludes2 newborn affected by complication of (fetal) intrauterine procedure (P96.5)

P00.7 **Newborn affected by other medical procedures on mother, not elsewhere classified**
Newborn affected by radiation to mother

Excludes1 damage to placenta from amniocentesis, cesarean delivery or surgical induction (P02.1)
newborn affected by other complications of labor and delivery (P03.-)

● **P00.8** **Newborn affected by other maternal conditions**

P00.81 **Newborn affected by periodontal disease in mother**

P00.89 **Newborn affected by other maternal conditions**
Newborn affected by conditions classifiable to T80-T88
Newborn affected by maternal genital tract or other localized infections
Newborn affected by maternal systemic lupus erythematosus

▶Use additional code to identify infectious agent, if known
Coding Clinic: 2019, Q2, P9

P00.9 **Newborn affected by unspecified maternal condition**

● **P01** **Newborn affected by maternal complications of pregnancy**

Code first any current condition in newborn

Excludes2 encounter for observation of newborn for suspected diseases and conditions ruled out (Z05.-)

Coding Clinic: 2016, Q4, P54

P01.0 **Newborn affected by incompetent cervix**

P01.1 **Newborn affected by premature rupture of membranes**

P01.2 **Newborn affected by oligohydramnios**

Excludes1 oligohydramnios due to premature rupture of membranes (P01.1)

P01.3 **Newborn affected by polyhydramnios**
Excess of amniotic fluid, usually > 2000 mL
Newborn affected by hydramnios

P01.4 **Newborn affected by ectopic pregnancy**
Newborn affected by abdominal pregnancy

P01.5 **Newborn affected by multiple pregnancy**
Newborn affected by triplet (pregnancy)
Newborn affected by twin (pregnancy)

P01.6 **Newborn affected by maternal death**

P01.7 **Newborn affected by malpresentation before labor**
Newborn affected by breech presentation before labor
Newborn affected by external version before labor
Newborn affected by face presentation before labor
Newborn affected by transverse lie before labor
Newborn affected by unstable lie before labor

P01.8   Newborn affected by other maternal complications of pregnancy

P01.9   Newborn affected by maternal complication of pregnancy, unspecified

● **P02**   Newborn affected by complications of placenta, cord and membranes

Code first any current condition in newborn

Excludes2   encounter for observation of newborn for suspected diseases and conditions ruled out (Z05.-)

Coding Clinic: 2016, Q4, P54

P02.0   Newborn affected by placenta previa

P02.1   Newborn affected by other forms of placental separation and hemorrhage

Newborn affected by abruptio placenta
Newborn affected by accidental hemorrhage
Newborn affected by antepartum hemorrhage
Newborn affected by damage to placenta from amniocentesis, cesarean delivery or surgical induction
Newborn affected by maternal blood loss
Newborn affected by premature separation of placenta

● **P02.2**   Newborn affected by other and unspecified morphological and functional abnormalities of placenta

P02.20   Newborn affected by unspecified morphological and functional abnormalities of placenta

P02.29   Newborn affected by other morphological and functional abnormalities of placenta
Newborn affected by placental dysfunction
Newborn affected by placental infarction
Newborn affected by placental insufficiency

P02.3   Newborn affected by placental transfusion syndromes
Newborn affected by placental and cord abnormalities resulting in twin-to-twin or other transplacental transfusion

P02.4   Newborn affected by prolapsed cord

P02.5   Newborn affected by other compression of umbilical cord
Newborn affected by umbilical cord (tightly) around neck
Newborn affected by entanglement of umbilical cord
Newborn affected by knot in umbilical cord

● **P02.6**   Newborn affected by other and unspecified conditions of umbilical cord

P02.60   Newborn affected by unspecified conditions of umbilical cord

P02.69   Newborn affected by other conditions of umbilical cord
Newborn affected by short umbilical cord
Newborn affected by vasa previa

Excludes1   newborn affected by single umbilical artery (Q27.0)

● **P02.7**   Newborn affected by chorioamnionitis
Inflammation of chorion and amnion

P02.70   Newborn affected by fetal inflammatory response syndrome 🅗
Newborn affected by FIRS

P02.78   Newborn affected by other conditions from chorioamnionitis
Newborn affected by amnionitis
Newborn affected by membranitis
Newborn affected by placentitis

P02.8   Newborn affected by other abnormalities of membranes

P02.9   Newborn affected by abnormality of membranes, unspecified

● **P03**   Newborn affected by other complications of labor and delivery

Code first any current condition in newborn

Excludes2   encounter for observation of newborn for suspected diseases and conditions ruled out (Z05.-)

Coding Clinic: 2016, Q4, P54

P03.0   Newborn affected by breech delivery and extraction

P03.1   Newborn affected by other malpresentation, malposition and disproportion during labor and delivery
Newborn affected by contracted pelvis
Newborn affected by conditions classifiable to O64-O66
Newborn affected by persistent occipitoposterior
Newborn affected by transverse lie

P03.2   Newborn affected by forceps delivery

P03.3   Newborn affected by delivery by vacuum extractor [ventouse]

P03.4   Newborn affected by Cesarean delivery

P03.5   Newborn affected by precipitate delivery
Newborn affected by rapid second stage

P03.6   Newborn affected by abnormal uterine contractions
Newborn affected by conditions classifiable to O62.-, except O62.3
Newborn affected by hypertonic labor
Newborn affected by uterine inertia

● **P03.8**   Newborn affected by other specified complications of labor and delivery

● **P03.81**   Newborn affected by abnormality in fetal (intrauterine) heart rate or rhythm

Excludes1   neonatal cardiac dysrhythmia (P29.1-)

P03.810   Newborn affected by abnormality in fetal (intrauterine) heart rate or rhythm before the onset of labor

P03.811   Newborn affected by abnormality in fetal (intrauterine) heart rate or rhythm during labor

P03.819   Newborn affected by abnormality in fetal (intrauterine) heart rate or rhythm, unspecified as to time of onset

P03.82   Meconium passage during delivery

Excludes1   meconium aspiration (P24.00, P24.01)
meconium staining (P96.83)

P03.89   Newborn affected by other specified complications of labor and delivery
Newborn affected by abnormality of maternal soft tissues
Newborn affected by conditions classifiable to O60-O75 and by procedures used in labor and delivery not included in P02.- and P03.0-P03.6
Newborn affected by induction of labor

P03.9   Newborn affected by complication of labor and delivery, unspecified

▶ New   ➡ Revised   ~~deleted~~ Deleted   Excludes 1   Excludes 2   Includes   Use additional   Code first   Code also   Key words

OGCR Official Guidelines   X Assign placeholder X   ● Use Additional Character(s)   ▶ Manifestation Code   🅗 Hierarchical Condition Category   Coding Clinic

● **P04 Newborn affected by noxious substances transmitted via placenta or breast milk**

> **Includes**   nonteratogenic effects of substances transmitted via placenta
>
> **Excludes2**   congenital malformations (Q00-Q99)
>   encounter for observation of newborn for suspected diseases and conditions ruled out (Z05.-)
>   neonatal jaundice from excessive hemolysis due to drugs or toxins transmitted from mother (P58.4)
>   newborn in contact with and (suspected) exposures hazardous to health not transmitted via placenta or breast milk (Z77.-)
>
> Coding Clinic: 2016, Q4, P54

P04.0 Newborn affected by maternal anesthesia and analgesia in pregnancy, labor and delivery

> Newborn affected by reactions and intoxications from maternal opiates and tranquilizers administered for procedures during pregnancy or labor and delivery
>
> **Excludes2**   newborn affected by other maternal medication (P04.1-)

● **P04.1 Newborn affected by other maternal medication**

> *Code first withdrawal symptoms from maternal use of drugs of addiction, if applicable (P96.1)*
>
> **Excludes1**   dysmorphism due to warfarin (Q86.2)
>   fetal hydantoin syndrome (Q86.1)
>
> **Excludes2**   maternal anesthesia and analgesia in pregnancy, labor and delivery (P04.0)
>   maternal use of drugs of addiction (P04.4-)

P04.11 Newborn affected by maternal antineoplastic chemotherapy

P04.12 Newborn affected by maternal cytotoxic drugs

P04.13 Newborn affected by maternal use of anticonvulsants

P04.14 Newborn affected by maternal use of opiates

P04.15 Newborn affected by maternal use of antidepressants

P04.16 Newborn affected by maternal use of amphetamines

P04.17 Newborn affected by maternal use of sedative-hypnotics

P04.1A Newborn affected by maternal use of anxiolytics

P04.18 Newborn affected by other maternal medication

P04.19 Newborn affected by maternal use of unspecified medication
> Coding Clinic: 2016, Q4, P55

P04.2 Newborn affected by maternal use of tobacco

> Newborn affected by exposure in utero to tobacco smoke
>
> **Excludes2**   newborn exposure to environmental tobacco smoke (P96.81)

P04.3 Newborn affected by maternal use of alcohol

> **Excludes1**   fetal alcohol syndrome (Q86.0)

● **P04.4 Newborn affected by maternal use of drugs of addiction**

P04.40 Newborn affected by maternal use of unspecified drugs of addiction

P04.41 Newborn affected by maternal use of cocaine

P04.42 Newborn affected by maternal use of hallucinogens

> **Excludes2**   newborn affected by other maternal medication (P04.1-)

P04.49 Newborn affected by maternal use of other drugs of addiction

> **Excludes2**   newborn affected by maternal anesthesia and analgesia (P04.0)
>   withdrawal symptoms from maternal use of drugs of addiction (P96.1)

P04.5 Newborn affected by maternal use of nutritional chemical substances

P04.6 Newborn affected by maternal exposure to environmental chemical substances

● **P04.8 Newborn affected by other maternal noxious substances**

P04.81 Newborn affected by maternal use of cannabis

P04.89 Newborn affected by other maternal noxious substances

P04.9 Newborn affected by maternal noxious substance, unspecified

OGCR Section I.C.16.d.

Prematurity and Fetal Growth Retardation

Providers utilize different criteria in determining prematurity. A code for prematurity should not be assigned unless it is documented. Assignment of codes in categories P05, Disorders of newborn related to slow fetal growth and fetal malnutrition, and P07, Disorders of newborn related to short gestation and low birth weight, not elsewhere classified, should be based on the recorded birth weight and estimated gestational age.

When both birth weight and gestational age are available, two codes from category P07 should be assigned, with the code for birth weight sequenced before the code for gestational age.

DISORDERS OF NEWBORN RELATED TO LENGTH OF GESTATION AND FETAL GROWTH (P05-P08)

● **P05 Disorders of newborn related to slow fetal growth and fetal malnutrition**
> Coding Clinic: 2016, Q4, P56

● **P05.0 Newborn light for gestational age**
> Newborn light-for-dates
> Weight below but length above 10th percentile for gestational age

P05.00 Newborn light for gestational age, unspecified weight

P05.01 Newborn light for gestational age, less than 500 grams

P05.02 Newborn light for gestational age, 500-749 grams

P05.03 Newborn light for gestational age, 750-999 grams

P05.04 Newborn light for gestational age, 1000-1249 grams

P05.05 Newborn light for gestational age, 1250-1499 grams

P05.06 Newborn light for gestational age, 1500-1749 grams

P05.07 Newborn light for gestational age, 1750-1999 grams

P05.08 Newborn light for gestational age, 2000-2499 grams

P05.09 Newborn light for gestational age, 2500 grams and over
> Newborn light for gestational age, other
> Coding Clinic: 2016, Q4, P55

CHAPTER 16 (P00–P96)

● **P05.1   Newborn small for gestational age**
Newborn small-and-light-for-dates
Newborn small-for-dates
Weight and length below 10th percentile for gestational age

    P05.10   Newborn small for gestational age, unspecified weight

    P05.11   Newborn small for gestational age, less than 500 grams

    P05.12   Newborn small for gestational age, 500-749 grams

    P05.13   Newborn small for gestational age, 750-999 grams

    P05.14   Newborn small for gestational age, 1000-1249 grams

    P05.15   Newborn small for gestational age, 1250-1499 grams

    P05.16   Newborn small for gestational age, 1500-1749 grams

    P05.17   Newborn small for gestational age, 1750-1999 grams

    P05.18   Newborn small for gestational age, 2000-2499 grams

    P05.19   Newborn small for gestational age, other
    Newborn small for gestational age, 2500 grams and over
    Coding Clinic: 2016, Q4, P55

P05.2   Newborn affected by fetal (intrauterine) malnutrition not light or small for gestational age
Infant, not light or small for gestational age, showing signs of fetal malnutrition, such as dry, peeling skin and loss of subcutaneous tissue

    Excludes1   newborn affected by fetal malnutrition with light for gestational age (P05.0-)
    newborn affected by fetal malnutrition with small for gestational age (P05.1-)

P05.9   Newborn affected by slow intrauterine growth, unspecified
Newborn affected by fetal growth retardation NOS

● **P07   Disorders of newborn related to short gestation and low birth weight, not elsewhere classified**

    Note: When both birth weight and gestational age of the newborn are available, both should be coded with birth weight sequenced before gestational age.

    Includes   the listed conditions, without further specification, as the cause of morbidity or additional care, in newborn

● **P07.0   Extremely low birth weight newborn**
Newborn birth weight 999 g. or less

    Excludes1   low birth weight due to slow fetal growth and fetal malnutrition (P05.-)

    P07.00   Extremely low birth weight newborn, unspecified weight

    P07.01   Extremely low birth weight newborn, less than 500 grams

    P07.02   Extremely low birth weight newborn, 500-749 grams

    P07.03   Extremely low birth weight newborn, 750-999 grams

● **P07.1   Other low birth weight newborn**
Newborn birth weight 1000-2499 g.

    Excludes1   low birth weight due to slow fetal growth and fetal malnutrition (P05.-)

    P07.10   Other low birth weight newborn, unspecified weight

    P07.14   Other low birth weight newborn, 1000-1249 grams

    P07.15   Other low birth weight newborn, 1250-1499 grams

    P07.16   Other low birth weight newborn, 1500-1749 grams

    P07.17   Other low birth weight newborn, 1750-1999 grams

    P07.18   Other low birth weight newborn, 2000-2499 grams

● **P07.2   Extreme immaturity of newborn**
Less than 28 completed weeks (less than 196 completed days) of gestation

    P07.20   Extreme immaturity of newborn, unspecified weeks of gestation
    Gestational age less than 28 completed weeks NOS

    P07.21   Extreme immaturity of newborn, gestational age less than 23 completed weeks
    Extreme immaturity of newborn, gestational age less than 23 weeks, 0 days

    P07.22   Extreme immaturity of newborn, gestational age 23 completed weeks
    Extreme immaturity of newborn, gestational age 23 weeks, 0 days through 23 weeks, 6 days

    P07.23   Extreme immaturity of newborn, gestational age 24 completed weeks
    Extreme immaturity of newborn, gestational age 24 weeks, 0 days through 24 weeks, 6 days

    P07.24   Extreme immaturity of newborn, gestational age 25 completed weeks
    Extreme immaturity of newborn, gestational age 25 weeks, 0 days through 25 weeks, 6 days

    P07.25   Extreme immaturity of newborn, gestational age 26 completed weeks
    Extreme immaturity of newborn, gestational age 26 weeks, 0 days through 26 weeks, 6 days

    P07.26   Extreme immaturity of newborn, gestational age 27 completed weeks
    Extreme immaturity of newborn, gestational age 27 weeks, 0 days through 27 weeks, 6 days

● **P07.3   Preterm [premature] newborn [other]**
28 completed weeks or more but less than 37 completed weeks (196 completed days but less than 259 completed days) of gestation
Prematurity NOS

    P07.30   Preterm newborn, unspecified weeks of gestation

    P07.31   Preterm newborn, gestational age 28 completed weeks
    Preterm newborn, gestational age 28 weeks, 0 days through 28 weeks, 6 days

▶ New   ⇛ Revised   ~~deleted~~ Deleted   Excludes 1   Excludes 2   Includes   Use additional   Code first   Code also   Key words
OGCR Official Guidelines   X Assign placeholder X   ● Use Additional Character(s)   ▶ Manifestation Code   🅚 Hierarchical Condition Category   Coding Clinic

P07.32 **Preterm newborn, gestational age 29 completed weeks**
Preterm newborn, gestational age 29 weeks, 0 days through 29 weeks, 6 days

P07.33 **Preterm newborn, gestational age 30 completed weeks**
Preterm newborn, gestational age 30 weeks, 0 days through 30 weeks, 6 days

P07.34 **Preterm newborn, gestational age 31 completed weeks**
Preterm newborn, gestational age 31 weeks, 0 days through 31 weeks, 6 days

P07.35 **Preterm newborn, gestational age 32 completed weeks**
Preterm newborn, gestational age 32 weeks, 0 days through 32 weeks, 6 days

P07.36 **Preterm newborn, gestational age 33 completed weeks**
Preterm newborn, gestational age 33 weeks, 0 days through 33 weeks, 6 days

P07.37 **Preterm newborn, gestational age 34 completed weeks**
Preterm newborn, gestational age 34 weeks, 0 days through 34 weeks, 6 days
Coding Clinic: 2017, Q2, P7

P07.38 **Preterm newborn, gestational age 35 completed weeks**
Preterm newborn, gestational age 35 weeks, 0 days through 35 weeks, 6 days

P07.39 **Preterm newborn, gestational age 36 completed weeks**
Preterm newborn, gestational age 36 weeks, 0 days through 36 weeks, 6 days
Coding Clinic: 2017, Q3, P26

● **P08** **Disorders of newborn related to long gestation and high birth weight**
Note: When both birth weight and gestational age of the newborn are available, priority of assignment should be given to birth weight.
Includes the listed conditions, without further specification, as causes of morbidity or additional care, in newborn

P08.0 **Exceptionally large newborn baby**
Usually implies a birth weight of 4500 g. or more
Excludes1 syndrome of infant of diabetic mother (P70.1)
syndrome of infant of mother with gestational diabetes (P70.0)

P08.1 **Other heavy for gestational age newborn**
Other newborn heavy- or large-for-dates regardless of period of gestation
Usually implies a birth weight of 4000 g. to 4499 g.
Excludes1 newborn with a birth weight of 4500 or more (P08.0)
syndrome of infant of diabetic mother (P70.1)
syndrome of infant of mother with gestational diabetes (P70.0)

● **P08.2** **Late newborn, not heavy for gestational age**

P08.21 **Post-term newborn**
Newborn with gestation period over 40 completed weeks to 42 completed weeks

P08.22 **Prolonged gestation of newborn**
Newborn with gestation period over 42 completed weeks (294 days or more), not heavy- or large-for-dates
Postmaturity NOS

P09 **Abnormal findings on neonatal screening**
Use additional code to identify signs, symptoms and conditions associated with the screening
Excludes2 nonspecific serologic evidence of human immunodeficiency virus [HIV] (R75)

BIRTH TRAUMA (P10-P15)

● **P10** **Intracranial laceration and hemorrhage due to birth injury**
Excludes1 intracranial hemorrhage of newborn NOS (P52.9)
intracranial hemorrhage of newborn due to anoxia or hypoxia (P52.-)
nontraumatic intracranial hemorrhage of newborn (P52.-)

P10.0 **Subdural hemorrhage due to birth injury**
Subdural hematoma (localized) due to birth injury
Excludes1 subdural hemorrhage accompanying tentorial tear (P10.4)

P10.1 **Cerebral hemorrhage due to birth injury**

P10.2 **Intraventricular hemorrhage due to birth injury**

P10.3 **Subarachnoid hemorrhage due to birth injury**

P10.4 **Tentorial tear due to birth injury**
Pertaining to tentorium of cerebellum (extension of dura mater that separates cerebellum from inferior portion of occipital lobes)

P10.8 **Other intracranial lacerations and hemorrhages due to birth injury**

P10.9 **Unspecified intracranial laceration and hemorrhage due to birth injury**

● **P11** **Other birth injuries to central nervous system**

P11.0 **Cerebral edema due to birth injury**

P11.1 **Other specified brain damage due to birth injury**

P11.2 **Unspecified brain damage due to birth injury**

P11.3 **Birth injury to facial nerve**
Facial palsy due to birth injury

P11.4 **Birth injury to other cranial nerves**

P11.5 **Birth injury to spine and spinal cord**
Fracture of spine due to birth injury

P11.9 **Birth injury to central nervous system, unspecified**

● **P12** **Birth injury to scalp**

P12.0 **Cephalhematoma due to birth injury**

P12.1 **Chignon (from vacuum extraction) due to birth injury**

P12.2 **Epicranial subaponeurotic hemorrhage due to birth injury**
Subgaleal hemorrhage

P12.3 **Bruising of scalp due to birth injury**

P12.4 **Injury of scalp of newborn due to monitoring equipment**
Sampling incision of scalp of newborn
Scalp clip (electrode) injury of newborn

● **P12.8** **Other birth injuries to scalp**

P12.81 **Caput succedaneum**

P12.89 **Other birth injuries to scalp**

P12.9 **Birth injury to scalp, unspecified**

● **P13** **Birth injury to skeleton**
Excludes2 birth injury to spine (P11.5)

P13.0 **Fracture of skull due to birth injury**

P13.1 **Other birth injuries to skull**
Excludes1 cephalhematoma (P12.0)

P13.2 **Birth injury to femur**

P13.3 **Birth injury to other long bones**

P13.4 **Fracture of clavicle due to birth injury**

P13.8 **Birth injuries to other parts of skeleton**

P13.9 **Birth injury to skeleton, unspecified**

CHAPTER 16 (P00-P96)

Item 16–1 The **peripheral nervous system** consists of 31 pairs of spinal nerves, 12 pairs of cranial nerves, and the autonomic nerves, which are divided into the parasympathetic and sympathetic nerves. The cranial nerves are: olfactory (I), optic (II), oculomotor (III), trochlear (IV), trigeminal (V), abducens (VI), facial (VII), vestibulocochlear (VIII), glossopharyngeal (IX), vagus (X), accessory (XI), and hypoglossal (XII).

Central
Nervous System

• Brain
• Spinal cord

Peripheral
Nervous System

• Cranial nerves (12)
• Spinal nerves
  cervical (8)
  thoracic (12)
  lumbar (5)
  sacral (5)
  coccyx (1)

Figure 16-1 The central nervous system consists of the brain and spinal cord. The peripheral nervous system consists of nerves that lie outside the skull and spinal cord. (From Stoy: Mosby's EMT-Basic Textbook, ed 2, St. Louis, Mosby, 2007)

● **P14**   **Birth injury to peripheral nervous system**
     P14.0   **Erb's paralysis due to birth injury**
     P14.1   **Klumpke's paralysis due to birth injury**
     P14.2   **Phrenic nerve paralysis due to birth injury**
     P14.3   **Other brachial plexus birth injuries**
     P14.8   **Birth injuries to other parts of peripheral nervous system**
     P14.9   **Birth injury to peripheral nervous system, unspecified**

● **P15**   **Other birth injuries**
     P15.0   **Birth injury to liver**
          Rupture of liver due to birth injury
     P15.1   **Birth injury to spleen**
          Rupture of spleen due to birth injury
     P15.2   **Sternomastoid injury due to birth injury**
     P15.3   **Birth injury to eye**
          Subconjunctival hemorrhage due to birth injury
          Traumatic glaucoma due to birth injury

     P15.4   **Birth injury to face**
          Facial congestion due to birth injury
     P15.5   **Birth injury to external genitalia**
     P15.6   **Subcutaneous fat necrosis due to birth injury**
     P15.8   **Other specified birth injuries**
     P15.9   **Birth injury, unspecified**

RESPIRATORY AND CARDIOVASCULAR DISORDERS SPECIFIC TO THE PERINATAL PERIOD (P19-P29)

● **P19**   **Metabolic acidemia in newborn**
     Includes   metabolic acidemia in newborn
     P19.0   **Metabolic acidemia in newborn first noted before onset of labor**
     P19.1   **Metabolic acidemia in newborn first noted during labor**
     P19.2   **Metabolic acidemia noted at birth**
     P19.9   **Metabolic acidemia, unspecified**

● **P22**   **Respiratory distress of newborn**
     Coding Clinic: 2019, Q2, P29
     P22.0   **Respiratory distress syndrome of newborn**
          Cardiorespiratory distress syndrome of newborn
          Hyaline membrane disease
          Idiopathic respiratory distress syndrome [IRDS or RDS] of newborn
          Pulmonary hypoperfusion syndrome
          Respiratory distress syndrome, type I
          Excludes2   respiratory arrest of newborn (P28.81)
                   respiratory failure of newborn NOS (P28.5)
          Coding Clinic: 2019, Q2, P29

     P22.1   **Transient tachypnea of newborn**
          Idiopathic tachypnea of newborn
          Respiratory distress syndrome, type II
          Wet lung syndrome

     P22.8   **Other respiratory distress of newborn**
          Excludes1   respiratory arrest of newborn (P28.81)
                   respiratory failure of newborn NOS (P28.5)

     P22.9   **Respiratory distress of newborn, unspecified**
          Excludes1   respiratory arrest of newborn (P28.81)
                   respiratory failure of newborn NOS (P28.5)

● **P23**   **Congenital pneumonia**
     Includes   infective pneumonia acquired in utero or during birth
     Excludes1   neonatal pneumonia resulting from aspiration (P24.-)
     P23.0   **Congenital pneumonia due to viral agent**
          Use additional code (B97) to identify organism
          Excludes1   congenital rubella pneumonitis (P35.0)
     P23.1   **Congenital pneumonia due to Chlamydia**
     P23.2   **Congenital pneumonia due to staphylococcus**
     P23.3   **Congenital pneumonia due to streptococcus, group B**
     P23.4   **Congenital pneumonia due to Escherichia coli**
     P23.5   **Congenital pneumonia due to Pseudomonas**
     P23.6   **Congenital pneumonia due to other bacterial agents**
          Congenital pneumonia due to Hemophilus influenzae
          Congenital pneumonia due to Klebsiella pneumoniae
          Congenital pneumonia due to Mycoplasma
          Congenital pneumonia due to Streptococcus, except group B
          Use additional code (B95-B96) to identify organism
     P23.8   **Congenital pneumonia due to other organisms**
     P23.9   **Congenital pneumonia, unspecified**

▶ New   ⇒ Revised   ~~deleted~~ Deleted   Excludes 1   Excludes 2   Includes   Use additional   Code first   Code also   Key words
OGCR Official Guidelines   X Assign placeholder X   ● Use Additional Character(s)   ▷ Manifestation Code   🔖 Hierarchical Condition Category   Coding Clinic

● **P24   Neonatal aspiration**
     Includes   aspiration in utero and during delivery
   ● **P24.0   Meconium aspiration**
         Excludes1   meconium passage (without aspiration)
                                 during delivery (P03.82)
                            meconium staining (P96.83)
      **P24.00   Meconium aspiration without respiratory
                    symptoms**
                    Meconium aspiration NOS
      **P24.01   Meconium aspiration with respiratory
                    symptoms**
                    Meconium aspiration pneumonia
                    Meconium aspiration pneumonitis
                    Meconium aspiration syndrome NOS
                    Use additional code to identify any secondary
                        pulmonary hypertension, if applicable
                        (I27.2-)
   ● **P24.1   Neonatal aspiration of (clear) amniotic fluid and mucus**
                Neonatal aspiration of liquor (amnii)
      **P24.10   Neonatal aspiration of (clear) amniotic fluid
                    and mucus without respiratory symptoms**
                    Neonatal aspiration of amniotic fluid and
                        mucus NOS
      **P24.11   Neonatal aspiration of (clear) amniotic fluid
                    and mucus with respiratory symptoms**
                    Neonatal aspiration of amniotic fluid and
                        mucus with pneumonia
                    Neonatal aspiration of amniotic fluid and
                        mucus with pneumonitis
                    Use additional code to identify any secondary
                        pulmonary hypertension, if applicable
                        (I27.2-)
   ● **P24.2   Neonatal aspiration of blood**
      **P24.20   Neonatal aspiration of blood without
                    respiratory symptoms**
                    Neonatal aspiration of blood NOS
      **P24.21   Neonatal aspiration of blood with respiratory
                    symptoms**
                    Neonatal aspiration of blood with pneumonia
                    Neonatal aspiration of blood with pneumonitis
                    Use additional code to identify any secondary
                        pulmonary hypertension, if applicable
                        (I27.2-)
   ● **P24.3   Neonatal aspiration of milk and regurgitated food**
                Neonatal aspiration of stomach contents
      **P24.30   Neonatal aspiration of milk and regurgitated
                    food without respiratory symptoms**
                    Neonatal aspiration of milk and regurgitated
                        food NOS
      **P24.31   Neonatal aspiration of milk and regurgitated
                    food with respiratory symptoms**
                    Neonatal aspiration of milk and regurgitated
                        food with pneumonia
                    Neonatal aspiration of milk and regurgitated
                        food with pneumonitis
                    Use additional code to identify any secondary
                        pulmonary hypertension, if applicable
                        (I27.2-)
   ● **P24.8   Other neonatal aspiration**
      **P24.80   Other neonatal aspiration without respiratory
                    symptoms**
                    Neonatal aspiration NEC
      **P24.81   Other neonatal aspiration with respiratory
                    symptoms**
                    Neonatal aspiration pneumonia NEC
                    Neonatal aspiration with pneumonitis NEC
                    Neonatal aspiration with pneumonia NOS
                    Neonatal aspiration with pneumonitis NOS
                    Use additional code to identify any secondary
                        pulmonary hypertension, if applicable
                        (I27.2-)
      P24.9   Neonatal aspiration, unspecified

● **P25   Interstitial emphysema and related conditions originating in the
            perinatal period**
      **P25.0   Interstitial emphysema originating in the perinatal
                    period**
      P25.1   Pneumothorax originating in the perinatal period
      P25.2   Pneumomediastinum originating in the perinatal period
      P25.3   Pneumopericardium originating in the perinatal period
      **P25.8   Other conditions related to interstitial emphysema
                    originating in the perinatal period**

● **P26   Pulmonary hemorrhage originating in the perinatal period**
         Excludes1   acute idiopathic hemorrhage in infants over 28
                                 days old (R04.81)
      **P26.0   Tracheobronchial hemorrhage originating in the
                    perinatal period**
      **P26.1   Massive pulmonary hemorrhage originating in the
                    perinatal period**
      **P26.8   Other pulmonary hemorrhages originating in the
                    perinatal period**
      **P26.9   Unspecified pulmonary hemorrhage originating in the
                    perinatal period**

● **P27   Chronic respiratory disease originating in the perinatal period**
         Excludes2   respiratory distress of newborn (P22.0-P22.9)
      P27.0   Wilson-Mikity syndrome
                    Pulmonary dysmaturity
      **P27.1   Bronchopulmonary dysplasia originating in the
                    perinatal period**
      **P27.8   Other chronic respiratory diseases originating in the
                    perinatal period**
                    Congenital pulmonary fibrosis
                    Ventilator lung in newborn
      **P27.9   Unspecified chronic respiratory disease originating in
                    the perinatal period**

● **P28   Other respiratory conditions originating in the perinatal period**
         Excludes1   congenital malformations of the respiratory
                                 system (Q30-Q34)
      P28.0   Primary atelectasis of newborn
                    Failure of lungs to expand properly at birth
                    Primary failure to expand terminal respiratory units
                    Pulmonary hypoplasia associated with short gestation
                    Pulmonary immaturity NOS
   ● **P28.1   Other and unspecified atelectasis of newborn**
      P28.10   Unspecified atelectasis of newborn
                    Atelectasis of newborn NOS
      **P28.11   Resorption atelectasis without respiratory
                    distress syndrome**
                    Excludes1   resorption atelectasis with
                                            respiratory distress
                                            syndrome (P22.0)
      P28.19   Other atelectasis of newborn
                    Partial atelectasis of newborn
                    Secondary atelectasis of newborn
      P28.2   Cyanotic attacks of newborn
                    Excludes1   apnea of newborn (P28.3-P28.4)
      P28.3   Primary sleep apnea of newborn
                    Central sleep apnea of newborn
                    Obstructive sleep apnea of newborn
                    Sleep apnea of newborn NOS
      P28.4   Other apnea of newborn
                    Apnea of prematurity
                    Obstructive apnea of newborn
                    Excludes1   obstructive sleep apnea of newborn
                                            (P28.3)
      P28.5   Respiratory failure of newborn
                    Excludes1   respiratory arrest of newborn (P28.81)
                                            respiratory distress of newborn (P22.0-)
                    Coding Clinic: 2019, Q2, P29

● P28.8 **Other specified respiratory conditions of newborn**

    P28.81 **Respiratory arrest of newborn**
       Coding Clinic: 2017, Q2, P6

    P28.89 **Other specified respiratory conditions of newborn**
       Congenital laryngeal stridor
       Sniffles in newborn
       Snuffles in newborn

        Excludes1 early congenital syphilitic rhinitis (A50.05)

P28.9 **Respiratory condition of newborn, unspecified**
    Respiratory depression in newborn

● **P29 Cardiovascular disorders originating in the perinatal period**

    Excludes1 congenital malformations of the circulatory system (Q20-Q28)

P29.0 **Neonatal cardiac failure**

● P29.1 **Neonatal cardiac dysrhythmia**

    P29.11 **Neonatal tachycardia**
    P29.12 **Neonatal bradycardia**

P29.2 **Neonatal hypertension**

● P29.3 **Persistent fetal circulation**

    P29.30 **Pulmonary hypertension of newborn**
       Persistent pulmonary hypertension of newborn

    P29.38 **Other persistent fetal circulation**
       Delayed closure of ductus arteriosus

P29.4 **Transient myocardial ischemia in newborn**

● P29.8 **Other cardiovascular disorders originating in the perinatal period**

    P29.81 **Cardiac arrest of newborn**

    P29.89 **Other cardiovascular disorders originating in the perinatal period**

P29.9 **Cardiovascular disorder originating in the perinatal period, unspecified**

INFECTIONS SPECIFIC TO THE PERINATAL PERIOD (P35-P39)

Infections acquired in utero, during birth via the umbilicus, or during the first 28 days after birth

    Excludes2 asymptomatic human immunodeficiency virus [HIV] infection status (Z21)
       congenital gonococcal infection (A54.-)
       congenital pneumonia (P23.-)
       congenital syphilis (A50.-)
       human immunodeficiency virus [HIV] disease (B20)
       infant botulism (A48.51)
       infectious diseases not specific to the perinatal period (A00-B99, J09, J10.-)
       intestinal infectious disease (A00-A09)
       laboratory evidence of human immunodeficiency virus [HIV] (R75)
       tetanus neonatorum (A33)

● **P35 Congenital viral diseases**

    Includes infections acquired in utero or during birth

P35.0 **Congenital rubella syndrome**
    Congenital rubella pneumonitis

P35.1 **Congenital cytomegalovirus infection**
    Viruses transmitted by multiple routes that cause mild/subclinical infection

P35.2 **Congenital herpesviral [herpes simplex] infection**

P35.3 **Congenital viral hepatitis**

P35.4 **Congenital Zika virus disease**
    Use additional code to identify manifestations of congenital Zika virus disease
    Coding Clinic: 2018, Q4, P26

P35.8 **Other congenital viral diseases**
    Congenital varicella [chickenpox]
    Coding Clinic: 2016, Q4, P7

P35.9 **Congenital viral disease, unspecified**

● P36 **Bacterial sepsis of newborn**

    Includes congenital sepsis
    Use additional code(s), if applicable, to identify severe sepsis (R65.2-) and associated acute organ dysfunction(s)

P36.0 **Sepsis of newborn due to streptococcus, group B** 🦠

● P36.1 **Sepsis of newborn due to other and unspecified streptococci**

    P36.10 **Sepsis of newborn due to unspecified streptococci** 🦠

    P36.19 **Sepsis of newborn due to other streptococci** 🦠

P36.2 **Sepsis of newborn due to Staphylococcus aureus** 🦠

● P36.3 **Sepsis of newborn due to other and unspecified staphylococci**

    P36.30 **Sepsis of newborn due to unspecified staphylococci** 🦠

    P36.39 **Sepsis of newborn due to other staphylococci** 🦠

P36.4 **Sepsis of newborn due to Escherichia coli** 🦠

P36.5 **Sepsis of newborn due to anaerobes** 🦠

P36.8 **Other bacterial sepsis of newborn** 🦠
    Use additional code from category B96 to identify organism

P36.9 **Bacterial sepsis of newborn, unspecified** 🦠

● P37 **Other congenital infectious and parasitic diseases**

    Excludes2 congenital syphilis (A50.-)
       infectious neonatal diarrhea (A00-A09)
       necrotizing enterocolitis in newborn (P77.-)
       noninfectious neonatal diarrhea (P78.3)
       ophthalmia neonatorum due to gonococcus (A54.31)
       tetanus neonatorum (A33)

P37.0 **Congenital tuberculosis**

P37.1 **Congenital toxoplasmosis**
    Parasitic infection, often causing mild flu-like illness
    Hydrocephalus due to congenital toxoplasmosis

P37.2 **Neonatal (disseminated) listeriosis**
    Acquired transplacentally or during/after parturition in which symptoms are those of sepsis

P37.3 **Congenital falciparum malaria**

P37.4 **Other congenital malaria**

P37.5 **Neonatal candidiasis**

P37.8 **Other specified congenital infectious and parasitic diseases**

P37.9 **Congenital infectious or parasitic disease, unspecified**

● P38 **Omphalitis of newborn**
    Inflammation of umbilicus

    Excludes1 omphalitis not of newborn (L08.82)
       tetanus omphalitis (A33)
       umbilical hemorrhage of newborn (P51.-)

P38.1 **Omphalitis with mild hemorrhage**

P38.9 **Omphalitis without hemorrhage**
    Omphalitis of newborn NOS

● P39 **Other infections specific to the perinatal period**
    Use additional code to identify organism or specific infection

P39.0 **Neonatal infective mastitis**

    Excludes1 breast engorgement of newborn (P83.4)
       noninfective mastitis of newborn (P83.4)

P39.1 **Neonatal conjunctivitis and dacryocystitis**
    Neonatal chlamydial conjunctivitis
    Ophthalmia neonatorum NOS
    Neonate = newborn

    Excludes1 gonococcal conjunctivitis (A54.31)

P39.2 **Intra-amniotic infection affecting newborn, not elsewhere classified**

P39.3 **Neonatal urinary tract infection**

P39.4 **Neonatal skin infection**
Neonatal pyoderma
> **Excludes1**   pemphigus neonatorum (L00)
> staphylococcal scalded skin syndrome (L00)

P39.8 **Other specified infections specific to the perinatal period**

P39.9 **Infection specific to the perinatal period, unspecified**

HEMORRHAGIC AND HEMATOLOGICAL DISORDERS OF NEWBORN (P50-P61)

> **Excludes1**   congenital stenosis and stricture of bile ducts (Q44.3)
> Crigler-Najjar syndrome (E80.5)
> Dubin-Johnson syndrome (E80.6)
> Gilbert syndrome (E80.4)
> hereditary hemolytic anemias (D55-D58)

● **P50**   **Newborn affected by intrauterine (fetal) blood loss**
> **Excludes1**   congenital anemia from intrauterine (fetal) blood loss (P61.3)

P50.0 **Newborn affected by intrauterine (fetal) blood loss from vasa previa**

P50.1 **Newborn affected by intrauterine (fetal) blood loss from ruptured cord**

P50.2 **Newborn affected by intrauterine (fetal) blood loss from placenta**

P50.3 **Newborn affected by hemorrhage into co-twin**

P50.4 **Newborn affected by hemorrhage into maternal circulation**

P50.5 **Newborn affected by intrauterine (fetal) blood loss from cut end of co-twin's cord**

P50.8 **Newborn affected by other intrauterine (fetal) blood loss**

P50.9 **Newborn affected by intrauterine (fetal) blood loss, unspecified**
Newborn affected by fetal hemorrhage NOS

● **P51**   **Umbilical hemorrhage of newborn**
> **Excludes1**   omphalitis with mild hemorrhage (P38.1)
> umbilical hemorrhage from cut end of co-twins cord (P50.5)

P51.0 **Massive umbilical hemorrhage of newborn**

P51.8 **Other umbilical hemorrhages of newborn**
Slipped umbilical ligature NOS

P51.9 **Umbilical hemorrhage of newborn, unspecified**

● **P52**   **Intracranial nontraumatic hemorrhage of newborn**
> **Includes**   intracranial hemorrhage due to anoxia or hypoxia
> **Excludes1**   intracranial hemorrhage due to birth injury (P10.-)
> intracranial hemorrhage due to other injury (S06.-)

P52.0 **Intraventricular (nontraumatic) hemorrhage, grade 1, of newborn**
Subependymal hemorrhage (without intraventricular extension)
Bleeding into germinal matrix

P52.1 **Intraventricular (nontraumatic) hemorrhage, grade 2, of newborn**
Subependymal hemorrhage with intraventricular extension
Bleeding into ventricle

● P52.2 **Intraventricular (nontraumatic) hemorrhage, grade 3 and grade 4, of newborn**

P52.21 **Intraventricular (nontraumatic) hemorrhage, grade 3, of newborn**
Subependymal hemorrhage with intraventricular extension with enlargement of ventricle

P52.22 **Intraventricular (nontraumatic) hemorrhage, grade 4, of newborn**
Bleeding into cerebral cortex
Subependymal hemorrhage with intracerebral extension

P52.3 **Unspecified intraventricular (nontraumatic) hemorrhage of newborn**

P52.4 **Intracerebral (nontraumatic) hemorrhage of newborn**

P52.5 **Subarachnoid (nontraumatic) hemorrhage of newborn**

P52.6 **Cerebellar (nontraumatic) and posterior fossa hemorrhage of newborn**

P52.8 **Other intracranial (nontraumatic) hemorrhages of newborn**

P52.9 **Intracranial (nontraumatic) hemorrhage of newborn, unspecified**

P53 **Hemorrhagic disease of newborn**
Vitamin K deficiency of newborn

● **P54**   **Other neonatal hemorrhages**
> **Excludes1**   newborn affected by (intrauterine) blood loss (P50.-)
> pulmonary hemorrhage originating in the perinatal period (P26.-)

P54.0 **Neonatal hematemesis**
Vomiting of blood
> **Excludes1**   neonatal hematemesis due to swallowed maternal blood (P78.2)

P54.1 **Neonatal melena**
Dark-colored feces stained with blood pigments
> **Excludes1**   neonatal melena due to swallowed maternal blood (P78.2)

P54.2 **Neonatal rectal hemorrhage**

P54.3 **Other neonatal gastrointestinal hemorrhage**

P54.4 **Neonatal adrenal hemorrhage**

P54.5 **Neonatal cutaneous hemorrhage**
Neonatal bruising
Neonatal ecchymoses
Neonatal petechiae
Neonatal superficial hematomata
> **Excludes2**   bruising of scalp due to birth injury (P12.3)
> cephalhematoma due to birth injury (P12.0)

P54.6 **Neonatal vaginal hemorrhage ♀**
Neonatal pseudomenses

P54.8 **Other specified neonatal hemorrhages**

P54.9 **Neonatal hemorrhage, unspecified**

● **P55**   **Hemolytic disease of newborn**
AKA erythroblastosis fetalis and is due to Rh isoimmunization, result of Rh blood factor incompatibilities between mother (Rh negative) and fetus (Rh positive)

P55.0 **Rh isoimmunization of newborn**

P55.1 **ABO isoimmunization of newborn**
Coding Clinic: 2015, Q3, P20

P55.8 **Other hemolytic diseases of newborn**

P55.9 **Hemolytic disease of newborn, unspecified**

● **P56**   **Hydrops fetalis due to hemolytic disease**
Caused by maternal sensitization to fetal blood group antigen
> **Excludes1**   hydrops fetalis NOS (P83.2)

P56.0 **Hydrops fetalis due to isoimmunization**

● P56.9 **Hydrops fetalis due to other and unspecified hemolytic disease**

P56.90 **Hydrops fetalis due to unspecified hemolytic disease**

P56.99 **Hydrops fetalis due to other hemolytic disease**

● **P57**   **Kernicterus**
High levels of bilirubin in blood, with severe neural symptoms

P57.0 **Kernicterus due to isoimmunization**

P57.8 **Other specified kernicterus**
> **Excludes1**   Crigler-Najjar syndrome (E80.5)

P57.9 **Kernicterus, unspecified**

● **P58** **Neonatal jaundice due to other excessive hemolysis**

Excludes1 jaundice due to isoimmunization (P55-P57)

P58.0 **Neonatal jaundice due to bruising**

P58.1 **Neonatal jaundice due to bleeding**

P58.2 **Neonatal jaundice due to infection**

P58.3 **Neonatal jaundice due to polycythemia**

● **P58.4** **Neonatal jaundice due to drugs or toxins transmitted from mother or given to newborn**

Code first poisoning due to drug or toxin, if applicable (T36-T65 with fifth or sixth character 1-4 or 6)

Use additional code for adverse effect, if applicable, to identify drug (T36-T50 with fifth or sixth character 5)

P58.41 **Neonatal jaundice due to drugs or toxins transmitted from mother**

P58.42 **Neonatal jaundice due to drugs or toxins given to newborn**

P58.5 **Neonatal jaundice due to swallowed maternal blood**

P58.8 **Neonatal jaundice due to other specified excessive hemolysis**

P58.9 **Neonatal jaundice due to excessive hemolysis, unspecified**

● **P59** **Neonatal jaundice from other and unspecified causes**

Excludes1 jaundice due to inborn errors of metabolism (E70-E88)
kernicterus (P57.-)

P59.0 **Neonatal jaundice associated with preterm delivery**
Hyperbilirubinemia of prematurity
Jaundice due to delayed conjugation associated with preterm delivery

P59.1 **Inspissated bile syndrome**

● **P59.2** **Neonatal jaundice from other and unspecified hepatocellular damage**

Excludes1 congenital viral hepatitis (P35.3)

P59.20 **Neonatal jaundice from unspecified hepatocellular damage**

P59.29 **Neonatal jaundice from other hepatocellular damage**
Neonatal giant cell hepatitis
Neonatal (idiopathic) hepatitis

P59.3 **Neonatal jaundice from breast milk inhibitor**

P59.8 **Neonatal jaundice from other specified causes**

P59.9 **Neonatal jaundice, unspecified**
Neonatal physiological jaundice (intense)(prolonged) NOS
Coding Clinic: 2015, Q3, P20

P60 **Disseminated intravascular coagulation of newborn**
Defibrination syndrome of newborn

● **P61** **Other perinatal hematological disorders**

Excludes1 transient hypogammaglobulinemia of infancy (D80.7)

P61.0 **Transient neonatal thrombocytopenia**
Lack of sufficient numbers of circulating thrombocytes (platelets)
Neonatal thrombocytopenia due to exchange transfusion
Neonatal thrombocytopenia due to idiopathic maternal thrombocytopenia
Neonatal thrombocytopenia due to isoimmunization

P61.1 **Polycythemia neonatorum**
Neonate = newborn

P61.2 **Anemia of prematurity**

P61.3 **Congenital anemia from fetal blood loss**

P61.4 **Other congenital anemias, not elsewhere classified**
Congenital anemia NOS

P61.5 **Transient neonatal neutropenia**
Low levels of granulocytic neutrophilic white blood cells

Excludes1 congenital neutropenia (nontransient) (D70.0)

P61.6 **Other transient neonatal disorders of coagulation**

P61.8 **Other specified perinatal hematological disorders**

P61.9 **Perinatal hematological disorder, unspecified**

TRANSITORY ENDOCRINE AND METABOLIC DISORDERS SPECIFIC TO NEWBORN (P70-P74)

Includes transitory endocrine and metabolic disturbances caused by the infant's response to maternal endocrine and metabolic factors, or its adjustment to extrauterine environment

● **P70** **Transitory disorders of carbohydrate metabolism specific to newborn**

P70.0 **Syndrome of infant of mother with gestational diabetes**
Newborn (with hypoglycemia) affected by maternal gestational diabetes

Excludes1 newborn (with hypoglycemia) affected by maternal (pre-existing) diabetes mellitus (P70.1)
syndrome of infant of a diabetic mother (P70.1)

P70.1 **Syndrome of infant of a diabetic mother**
Newborn (with hypoglycemia) affected by maternal (pre-existing) diabetes mellitus

Excludes1 newborn (with hypoglycemia) affected by maternal gestational diabetes (P70.0)
syndrome of infant of mother with gestational diabetes (P70.0)

P70.2 **Neonatal diabetes mellitus**

P70.3 **Iatrogenic neonatal hypoglycemia**

P70.4 **Other neonatal hypoglycemia**
Transitory neonatal hypoglycemia

P70.8 **Other transitory disorders of carbohydrate metabolism of newborn**

P70.9 **Transitory disorder of carbohydrate metabolism of newborn, unspecified**

● **P71** **Transitory neonatal disorders of calcium and magnesium metabolism**

P71.0 **Cow's milk hypocalcemia in newborn**

P71.1 **Other neonatal hypocalcemia**

Excludes1 neonatal hypoparathyroidism (P71.4)

P71.2 **Neonatal hypomagnesemia**

P71.3 **Neonatal tetany without calcium or magnesium deficiency**
Neonatal tetany NOS

P71.4 **Transitory neonatal hypoparathyroidism**

P71.8 **Other transitory neonatal disorders of calcium and magnesium metabolism**
Coding Clinic: 2016, Q4, P55

P71.9 **Transitory neonatal disorder of calcium and magnesium metabolism, unspecified**

● **P72** **Other transitory neonatal endocrine disorders**

Excludes1 congenital hypothyroidism with or without goiter (E03.0-E03.1)
dyshormogenetic goiter (E07.1)
Pendred's syndrome (E07.1)

P72.0 **Neonatal goiter, not elsewhere classified**
Transitory congenital goiter with normal functioning

P72.1 **Transitory neonatal hyperthyroidism**
Neonatal thyrotoxicosis

P72.2 **Other transitory neonatal disorders of thyroid function, not elsewhere classified**
Transitory neonatal hypothyroidism

P72.8 **Other specified transitory neonatal endocrine disorders**

P72.9 **Transitory neonatal endocrine disorder, unspecified**

● **P74** **Other transitory neonatal electrolyte and metabolic disturbances**

P74.0 **Late metabolic acidosis of newborn**

Excludes1 (fetal) metabolic acidosis of newborn (P19)

P74.1 **Dehydration of newborn**

▶ New ⟹ Revised ~~deleted~~ Deleted Excludes 1 Excludes 2 Includes Use additional Code first Code also Key words

OGCR Official Guidelines X Assign placeholder X ● Use Additional Character(s) ▶ Manifestation Code 🝆 Hierarchical Condition Category Coding Clinic

P74.2   Disturbances of sodium balance of newborn
Coding Clinic: 2018, Q2, P6

   P74.21   Hypernatremia of newborn

   P74.22   Hyponatremia of newborn

P74.3   Disturbances of potassium balance of newborn

   P74.31   Hyperkalemia of newborn

   P74.32   Hypokalemia of newborn

P74.4   Other transitory electrolyte disturbances of newborn

   P74.41   Alkalosis of newborn
            Hyperbicarbonatemia

   P74.42   Disturbances of chlorine balance of newborn

      P74.421   Hyperchloremia of newborn
                Hyperchloremic metabolic acidosis

         Excludes2   late metabolic acidosis
                         of the newborn
                         (P74.0)

      P74.422   Hypochloremia of newborn

   P74.49   Other transitory electrolyte disturbance of
            newborn

P74.5   Transitory tyrosinemia of newborn

P74.6   Transitory hyperammonemia of newborn

P74.8   Other transitory metabolic disturbances of newborn
            Amino-acid metabolic disorders described as transitory

**P74.9   Transitory metabolic disturbance of newborn,
            unspecified**

DIGESTIVE SYSTEM DISORDERS OF NEWBORN (P76-P78)

P76   Other intestinal obstruction of newborn

   P76.0   Meconium plug syndrome
            *Fetal stool obstruction in large intestine, present at birth;
            may be symptom of organic disease.*
            Meconium ileus NOS

         Excludes1   meconium ileus in cystic fibrosis (E84.11)

   P76.1   Transitory ileus of newborn
            Temporary obstruction of ileus (small intestine)

         Excludes1   Hirschsprung's disease (Q43.1)

   P76.2   Intestinal obstruction due to inspissated milk
            Being thickened, dried, or made less fluid

   P76.8   Other specified intestinal obstruction of newborn

         Excludes1   intestinal obstruction classifiable to K56.-

   P76.9   Intestinal obstruction of newborn, unspecified

P77   Necrotizing enterocolitis of newborn

   P77.1   Stage 1 necrotizing enterocolitis in newborn
            Necrotizing enterocolitis without pneumatosis, without
            perforation

   P77.2   Stage 2 necrotizing enterocolitis in newborn
            Necrotizing enterocolitis with pneumatosis, without
            perforation

   P77.3   Stage 3 necrotizing enterocolitis in newborn
            Necrotizing enterocolitis with perforation
            Necrotizing enterocolitis with pneumatosis and
            perforation

   P77.9   Necrotizing enterocolitis in newborn, unspecified
            Necrotizing enterocolitis in newborn, NOS

P78   Other perinatal digestive system disorders

      Excludes1   cystic fibrosis (E84.0-E84.9)
                       neonatal gastrointestinal hemorrhages
                       (P54.0-P54.3)

   P78.0   Perinatal intestinal perforation
            Meconium peritonitis

   P78.1   Other neonatal peritonitis
            Neonatal peritonitis NOS

   **P78.2   Neonatal hematemesis and melena due to swallowed
            maternal blood**

   P78.3   Noninfective neonatal diarrhea
            Neonatal diarrhea NOS

P78.8   Other specified perinatal digestive system disorders

   P78.81   Congenital cirrhosis (of liver)

   P78.82   Peptic ulcer of newborn

   P78.83   Newborn esophageal reflux
            Neonatal esophageal reflux

   P78.84   Gestational alloimmune liver disease
            GALD
            Neonatal hemochromatosis

         Excludes1   hemochromatosis (E83.11-)

   P78.89   Other specified perinatal digestive system
            disorders

P78.9   Perinatal digestive system disorder, unspecified

CONDITIONS INVOLVING THE INTEGUMENT AND TEMPERATURE REGULATION OF NEWBORN (P80-P83)

P80   Hypothermia of newborn

   P80.0   Cold injury syndrome
            *Severe and usually chronic hypothermia associated
            with a pink flushed appearance, edema and
            neurological and biochemical abnormalities.*

         Excludes1   mild hypothermia of newborn (P80.8)

   P80.8   Other hypothermia of newborn
            Mild hypothermia of newborn

   P80.9   Hypothermia of newborn, unspecified

P81   Other disturbances of temperature regulation of newborn

   P81.0   Environmental hyperthermia of newborn

   **P81.8   Other specified disturbances of temperature regulation
            of newborn**

   **P81.9   Disturbance of temperature regulation of newborn,
            unspecified**
            Fever of newborn NOS

P83   Other conditions of integument specific to newborn

      Excludes1   congenital malformations of skin and integument
                       (Q80-Q84)
                       hydrops fetalis due to hemolytic disease (P56.-)
                       neonatal skin infection (P39.4)
                       staphylococcal scalded skin syndrome (L00)

      Excludes2   cradle cap (L21.0)
                       diaper [napkin] dermatitis (L22)

   P83.0   Sclerema neonatorum
            Neonate = newborn

   P83.1   Neonatal erythema toxicum
            *Benign, generalized, transient pustules that become firm
            vesicles*

   P83.2   Hydrops fetalis not due to hemolytic disease
            *Severe, life-threatening problem of severe edema (swelling)
            as a result of too much fluid leaving blood and entering
            tissue*
            Hydrops fetalis NOS

   P83.3   Other and unspecified edema specific to newborn

      P83.30   Unspecified edema specific to newborn

      P83.39   Other edema specific to newborn

   P83.4   Breast engorgement of newborn
            Noninfective mastitis of newborn

   P83.5   Congenital hydrocele ♂

   P83.6   Umbilical polyp of newborn

   **P83.8   Other specified conditions of integument specific to
            newborn**

      P83.81   Umbilical granuloma

         Excludes2   Granulomatous disorder of the
                         skin and subcutaneous
                         tissue, unspecified (L92.9)

      P83.88   Other specified conditions of integument
               specific to newborn
               Bronze baby syndrome
               Neonatal scleroderma
               Urticaria neonatorum

   **P83.9   Condition of the integument specific to newborn,
            unspecified**

CHAPTER 16 (P00-P96)

OTHER PROBLEMS WITH NEWBORN (P84)

P84   **Other problems with newborn**
Acidemia of newborn
Acidosis of newborn
Anoxia of newborn NOS
Asphyxia of newborn NOS
Hypercapnia of newborn
Hypoxemia of newborn
Hypoxia of newborn NOS
Mixed metabolic and respiratory acidosis of newborn

    Excludes1   intracranial hemorrhage due to anoxia or hypoxia (P52.-)
                hypoxic ischemic encephalopathy [HIE] (P91.6-)
                late metabolic acidosis of newborn (P74.0)

OTHER DISORDERS ORIGINATING IN THE PERINATAL PERIOD (P90-P96)

P90   **Convulsions of newborn**

    Excludes1   benign myoclonic epilepsy in infancy (G40.3-)
                benign neonatal convulsions (familial) (G40.3-)

●P91   **Other disturbances of cerebral status of newborn**

    P91.0   **Neonatal cerebral ischemia**

      ▶ **Excludes1**   Neonatal cerebral infarction (P91.82-)

    P91.1   **Acquired periventricular cysts of newborn**

    P91.2   **Neonatal cerebral leukomalacia**
         Degeneration of white matter adjacent to cerebral ventricles following cerebral hypoxia or brain ischemia in neonates
         Periventricular leukomalacia

    P91.3   **Neonatal cerebral irritability**

    P91.4   **Neonatal cerebral depression**

    P91.5   **Neonatal coma**

  ●P91.6   **Hypoxic ischemic encephalopathy [HIE]**

      Excludes1   Neonatal cerebral depression (P91.4)
                   Neonatal cerebral irritability (P91.3)
                   Neonatal coma (P91.5)

      P91.60   **Hypoxic ischemic encephalopathy [HIE], unspecified**

      P91.61   **Mild hypoxic ischemic encephalopathy [HIE]**

      P91.62   **Moderate hypoxic ischemic encephalopathy [HIE]**

      P91.63   **Severe hypoxic ischemic encephalopathy [HIE]**

  ●P91.8   **Other specified disturbances of cerebral status of newborn**

    ●P91.81   **Neonatal encephalopathy**

      ▷**P91.811**   *Neonatal encephalopathy in diseases classified elsewhere*
            Code first underlying condition, if known, such as:
                congenital cirrhosis (of liver) (P78.81)
                intracranial nontraumatic hemorrhage of newborn (P52.-)
                kernicterus (P57.-)

      P91.819   **Neonatal encephalopathy, unspecified**

  ▶**●P91.82**   **Neonatal cerebral infarction**
      ▶ Neonatal stroke
      ▶ Perinatal arterial ischemic stroke
      ▶ Perinatal cerebral infarction

      ▶**Excludes1**   cerebral infarction (I63.-)

      ▶**Excludes2**   intracranial hemorrhage of newborn (P52.-)

      ▶**P91.821**   **Neonatal cerebral infarction, right side of brain**

      ▶**P91.822**   **Neonatal cerebral infarction, left side of brain**

      ▶**P91.823**   **Neonatal cerebral infarction, bilateral**

      ▶**P91.829**   **Neonatal cerebral infarction, unspecified side**

    P91.88   **Other specified disturbances of cerebral status of newborn**

    P91.9   **Disturbance of cerebral status of newborn, unspecified**

●P92   **Feeding problems of newborn**

    Excludes1   eating disorders (F50.-)
                feeding problems in child over 28 days old (R63.3)
    Coding Clinic: 2017, Q1, P28; 2016, Q3, P19

  ●P92.0   **Vomiting of newborn**

      Excludes1   vomiting of child over 28 days old (R11.-)

    P92.01   **Bilious vomiting of newborn**

      Excludes1   bilious vomiting in child over 28 days old (R11.14)

    P92.09   **Other vomiting of newborn**

      Excludes1   regurgitation of food in newborn (P92.1)

    P92.1   **Regurgitation and rumination of newborn**

    P92.2   **Slow feeding of newborn**

    P92.3   **Underfeeding of newborn**

    P92.4   **Overfeeding of newborn**

    P92.5   **Neonatal difficulty in feeding at breast**
      Coding Clinic: 2017, Q1, P28; 2016, Q3, P19

    P92.6   **Failure to thrive in newborn**

      Excludes1   failure to thrive in child over 28 days old (R62.51)

    P92.8   **Other feeding problems of newborn**

    P92.9   **Feeding problem of newborn, unspecified**

●P93   **Reactions and intoxications due to drugs administered to newborn**

    Includes   reactions and intoxications due to drugs administered to fetus affecting newborn

    Excludes1   jaundice due to drugs or toxins transmitted from mother or given to newborn (P58.4-)
                reactions and intoxications from maternal opiates, tranquilizers and other medication (P04.0-P04.1, P04.4-)
                withdrawal symptoms from maternal use of drugs of addiction (P96.1)
                withdrawal symptoms from therapeutic use of drugs in newborn (P96.2)

    P93.0   **Grey baby syndrome**
      Grey syndrome from chloramphenicol administration in newborn

    P93.8   **Other reactions and intoxications due to drugs administered to newborn**
      Use additional code for adverse effect, if applicable, to identify drug (T36-T50 with fifth or sixth character 5)

▶ New   ⇛ Revised   ~~deleted~~ Deleted   Excludes 1   Excludes 2   Includes   Use additional   Code first   Code also   Key words
OGCR Official Guidelines   X Assign placeholder X   ● Use Additional Character(s)   ▷ Manifestation Code   🅗 Hierarchical Condition Category   Coding Clinic

● **P94　Disorders of muscle tone of newborn**

　　P94.0　Transient neonatal myasthenia gravis

　　　　　Excludes1　myasthenia gravis (G70.0)

　　P94.1　Congenital hypertonia

　　P94.2　Congenital hypotonia

　　　　　Floppy baby syndrome, unspecified

　　P94.8　Other disorders of muscle tone of newborn

　　P94.9　Disorder of muscle tone of newborn, unspecified

OGCR Section I.C.16.g.

Stillbirth

Code P95, Stillbirth, is only for use for institutions that maintain separate records for stillbirths. No other code should be used with P95. Code P95 should not be used on the mother's record.

P95　Stillbirth

　　　Deadborn fetus NOS

　　　Fetal death of unspecified cause

　　　Stillbirth NOS

　　　Excludes1　maternal care for intrauterine death (O36.4)

　　　　　　　　　missed abortion (O02.1)

　　　　　　　　　outcome of delivery, stillbirth (Z37.1, Z37.3,

　　　　　　　　　　　Z37.4, Z37.7)

● **P96　Other conditions originating in the perinatal period**

　　P96.0　Congenital renal failure

　　　　　Uremia of newborn

　　P96.1　Neonatal withdrawal symptoms from maternal use of drugs of addiction

　　　　　Drug withdrawal syndrome in infant of dependent
　　　　　　mother

　　　　　Neonatal abstinence syndrome

　　　　　Excludes1　reactions and intoxications from
　　　　　　　　　　　maternal opiates and tranquilizers
　　　　　　　　　　　administered during labor and
　　　　　　　　　　　delivery (P04.0)

　　P96.2　Withdrawal symptoms from therapeutic use of drugs in newborn

　　P96.3　Wide cranial sutures of newborn

　　　　　Neonatal craniotabes

　　P96.5　Complication to newborn due to (fetal) intrauterine procedure

　　　　　Excludes2　newborn affected by amniocentesis
　　　　　　　　　　　(P00.6)

● **P96.8　Other specified conditions originating in the perinatal period**

　　P96.81　Exposure to (parental) (environmental) tobacco smoke in the perinatal period

　　　　　Excludes2　newborn affected by in utero
　　　　　　　　　　　exposure to tobacco (P04.2)
　　　　　　　　　　　exposure to environmental
　　　　　　　　　　　tobacco smoke after the
　　　　　　　　　　　perinatal period (Z77.22)

　　P96.82　Delayed separation of umbilical cord

　　P96.83　Meconium staining

　　　　　Excludes1　meconium aspiration (P24.00,
　　　　　　　　　　　P24.01)
　　　　　　　　　　　meconium passage during
　　　　　　　　　　　delivery (P03.82)

　　P96.89　Other specified conditions originating in the perinatal period

　　　　　Use additional code to specify condition

　　P96.9　Condition originating in the perinatal period, unspecified

　　　　　Congenital debility NOS

CHAPTER 16 (P00-P96)

CHAPTER 17 (Q00-Q99)

CHAPTER 17

CONGENITAL MALFORMATIONS, DEFORMATIONS, AND CHROMOSOMAL ABNORMALITIES (Q00-Q99)

OGCR   Chapter-Specific Coding Guidelines

17. **Chapter 17: Congenital malformations, deformations, and chromosomal abnormalities (Q00-Q99)**

Assign an appropriate code(s) from categories Q00-Q99, Congenital malformations, deformations, and chromosomal abnormalities when a malformation/deformation or chromosomal abnormality is documented. A malformation/deformation/ or chromosomal abnormality may be the principal/first-listed diagnosis on a record or a secondary diagnosis.

When a malformation/deformation/or chromosomal abnormality does not have a unique code assignment, assign additional code(s) for any manifestations that may be present.

When the code assignment specifically identifies the malformation/deformation/or chromosomal abnormality, manifestations that are an inherent component of the anomaly should not be coded separately. Additional codes should be assigned for manifestations that are not an inherent component.

Codes from Chapter 17 may be used throughout the life of the patient. If a congenital malformation or deformity has been corrected, a personal history code should be used to identify the history of the malformation or deformity. Although present at birth, malformation/deformation/or chromosomal abnormality may not be identified until later in life. Whenever the condition is diagnosed by the physician, it is appropriate to assign a code from codes Q00-Q99.

For the birth admission, the appropriate code from category Z38, Liveborn infants, according to place of birth and type of delivery, should be sequenced as the principal diagnosis, followed by any congenital anomaly codes, Q00-Q99.

CHAPTER 17

CONGENITAL MALFORMATIONS, DEFORMATIONS, AND CHROMOSOMAL ABNORMALITIES (Q00-Q99)

Note: Codes from this chapter are not for use on maternal records

> **Excludes2**   inborn errors of metabolism (E70-E88)

This chapter contains the following blocks:

Q00-Q07	Congenital malformations of the nervous system
Q10-Q18	Congenital malformations of eye, ear, face and neck
Q20-Q28	Congenital malformations of the circulatory system
Q30-Q34	Congenital malformations of the respiratory system
Q35-Q37	Cleft lip and cleft palate
Q38-Q45	Other congenital malformations of the digestive system
Q50-Q56	Congenital malformations of genital organs
Q60-Q64	Congenital malformations of the urinary system
Q65-Q79	Congenital malformations and deformations of the musculoskeletal system
Q80-Q89	Other congenital malformations
Q90-Q99	Chromosomal abnormalities, not elsewhere classified

Figure 17-1   An infant with a large occipital encephalocele. The large skin-covered encephalocele is visible. (From Swaiman KF, Ashwal S, Ferriero DM: Pediatric Neurology: Principles and Practice, Philadelphia, Saunders, 2012)

CONGENITAL MALFORMATIONS OF THE NERVOUS SYSTEM (Q00-Q07)

● **Q00**   **Anencephaly and similar malformations**

Q00.0   **Anencephaly** 🐾
> *Absence of skull with cerebral hemispheres missing or reduced to small masses attached to base of cranium*
> Acephaly
> Acrania
> Amyelencephaly
> Hemianencephaly
> Hemicephaly

Q00.1   **Craniorachischisis** 🐾
> *Developmental anomaly consisting of fissure of cranium and vertebral column*

Q00.2   **Iniencephaly** 🐾
> *Developmental anomaly characterized by enlargement of foramen magnum and absence of laminae and spinous processes of cervical, dorsal*

● **Q01**   **Encephalocele**
> *Sac-like protrusions of brain and membranes visible through an opening in skull*

> **Includes**   Arnold-Chiari syndrome, type III
> encephalocystocele
> encephalomyelocele
> hydroencephalocele
> hydromeningocele, cranial
> meningocele, cerebral
> meningoencephalocele

> **Excludes1**   Meckel-Gruber syndrome (Q61.9)

Q01.0   **Frontal encephalocele** 🐾
Q01.1   **Nasofrontal encephalocele** 🐾
Q01.2   **Occipital encephalocele** 🐾
Q01.8   **Encephalocele of other sites** 🐾
Q01.9   **Encephalocele, unspecified** 🐾

Q02   **Microcephaly** 🐾
> *Head size measures significantly below normal based on standardized charts*

> **Includes**   hydromicrocephaly
> micrencephalon

> *Code first, if applicable, congenital Zika virus disease*

> **Excludes1**   Meckel-Gruber syndrome (Q61.9)

> **Coding Clinic: 2018, Q4, P26; 2016, Q4, P7**

● **Q03**   **Congenital hydrocephalus**
> *Accumulation of cerebrospinal fluid in ventricles resulting in swelling and enlargement*

> **Includes**   hydrocephalus in newborn
> **Excludes1**   Arnold-Chiari syndrome, type II (Q07.0-)
> acquired hydrocephalus (G91.-)
> hydrocephalus due to congenital toxoplasmosis (P37.1)
> hydrocephalus with spina bifida (Q05.0-Q05.4)

Q03.0   **Malformations of aqueduct of Sylvius** 🐾
> Anomaly of aqueduct of Sylvius
> Obstruction of aqueduct of Sylvius, congenital
> Stenosis of aqueduct of Sylvius

Q03.1   **Atresia of foramina of Magendie and Luschka** 🐾
> Dandy-Walker syndrome

Q03.8   **Other congenital hydrocephalus** 🐾
Q03.9   **Congenital hydrocephalus, unspecified** 🐾

▶ New   ⇒ Revised   ~~deleted~~ Deleted   Excludes 1   Excludes 2   Includes   Use additional   Code first   Code also   Key words

OGCR Official Guidelines   X Assign placeholder X   ● Use Additional Character(s)   ⟩ Manifestation Code   🐾 Hierarchical Condition Category   **Coding Clinic**

● **Q04 Other congenital malformations of brain**

    Excludes1 cyclopia (Q87.0)

              macrocephaly (Q75.3)

  Q04.0 Congenital malformations of corpus callosum 🐾

    Agenesis of corpus callosum

  Q04.1 Arhinencephaly 🐾

    Congenital absence of olfactory bulbs, tract, or nerves

  Q04.2 Holoprosencephaly 🐾

    Failure of cleavage of forebrain (prosencephalon) resulting in incomplete or absent cortical separation and deficits in midline facial development

  Q04.3 Other reduction deformities of brain 🐾

    Absence of part of brain

    Agenesis of part of brain

      Cerebral cortex are not fully formed, brain surface is smooth

    Agyria

    Aplasia of part of brain

    Hydranencephaly

    Hypoplasia of part of brain

    Lissencephaly

      Congenital malformation or absence of convolutions of cerebral cortex

    Microgyria

      Malformation of brain characterized by excessive number of small convolutions (gyri) on surface

    Pachygyria

      Reduction in number of sulci of cerebrum

    Excludes1 congenital malformations of corpus callosum (Q04.0)

  Q04.4 Septo-optic dysplasia of brain 🐾

  Q04.5 Megalencephaly 🐾

    Abnormally large brain

  Q04.6 Congenital cerebral cysts 🐾

    Porencephaly   Schizencephaly

    Excludes1 acquired porencephalic cyst (G93.0)

  Q04.8 Other specified congenital malformations of brain 🐾

    Arnold-Chiari syndrome, type IV

    Macrogyria

  Q04.9 Congenital malformation of brain, unspecified 🐾

    Congenital anomaly NOS of brain

    Congenital deformity NOS of brain

    Congenital disease or lesion NOS of brain

    Multiple anomalies NOS of brain, congenital

● **Q05 Spina bifida**

    Developmental anomaly characterized by defective closure of vertebral arch, through which spinal cord and meninges may protrude

    Includes hydromeningocele (spinal)

                meningocele (spinal)

                meningomyelocele

                myelocele

                myelomeningocele

                rachischisis

                spina bifida (aperta)(cystica)

                syringomyelocele

    Use additional code for any associated paraplegia (paraparesis) (G82.2-)

    Excludes1 Arnold-Chiari syndrome, type II (Q07.0-)

              spina bifida occulta (Q76.0)

  Q05.0 Cervical spina bifida with hydrocephalus 🐾

  Q05.1 Thoracic spina bifida with hydrocephalus 🐾

    Dorsal spina bifida with hydrocephalus

    Thoracolumbar spina bifida with hydrocephalus

  Q05.2 Lumbar spina bifida with hydrocephalus 🐾

    Lumbosacral spina bifida with hydrocephalus

  Q05.3 Sacral spina bifida with hydrocephalus 🐾

  Q05.4 Unspecified spina bifida with hydrocephalus 🐾

  Q05.5 Cervical spina bifida without hydrocephalus 🐾

  Q05.6 Thoracic spina bifida without hydrocephalus 🐾

    Dorsal spina bifida NOS

    Thoracolumbar spina bifida NOS

  Q05.7 Lumbar spina bifida without hydrocephalus 🐾

    Lumbosacral spina bifida NOS

  Q05.8 Sacral spina bifida without hydrocephalus 🐾

  Q05.9 Spina bifida, unspecified 🐾

● **Q06 Other congenital malformations of spinal cord**

  Q06.0 Amyelia 🐾

    Congenital absence of spinal cord

  Q06.1 Hypoplasia and dysplasia of spinal cord 🐾

    Underdevelopment of spinal cord

    Atelomyelia

      Congenitally incomplete development of spinal cord

    Myelatelia

    Myelodysplasia of spinal cord

      Defective development of spinal cord, especially lower segments

  Q06.2 Diastematomyelia 🐾

    Congenital anomaly, associated with spina bifida, in which spinal cord is split into halves and surrounded by dural sac

  Q06.3 Other congenital cauda equina malformations 🐾

  Q06.4 Hydromyelia 🐾

    Dilation of central canal of spinal cord with increased fluid accumulation

    Hydrorachis

  Q06.8 Other specified congenital malformations of spinal cord 🐾

  Q06.9 Congenital malformation of spinal cord, unspecified 🐾

    Congenital anomaly NOS of spinal cord

    Congenital deformity NOS of spinal cord

    Congenital disease or lesion NOS of spinal cord

● **Q07 Other congenital malformations of nervous system**

    Excludes2 congenital central alveolar hypoventilation syndrome (G47.35)

              familial dysautonomia [Riley-Day] (G90.1)

              neurofibromatosis (nonmalignant) (Q85.0-)

● **Q07.0 Arnold-Chiari syndrome**

    Herniation of cerebellar tonsils and vermis through foramen magnum into spinal canal

    Arnold-Chiari syndrome, type II

    Excludes1 Arnold-Chiari syndrome, type III (Q01.-)

              Arnold-Chiari syndrome, type IV (Q04.8)

  Q07.00 Arnold-Chiari syndrome without spina bifida or hydrocephalus 🐾

  Q07.01 Arnold-Chiari syndrome with spina bifida 🐾

  Q07.02 Arnold-Chiari syndrome with hydrocephalus 🐾

  Q07.03 Arnold-Chiari syndrome with spina bifida and hydrocephalus 🐾

  Q07.8 Other specified congenital malformations of nervous system 🐾

    Agenesis of nerve

    Displacement of brachial plexus

    Jaw-winking syndrome

    Marcus Gunn's syndrome

  Q07.9 Congenital malformation of nervous system, unspecified 🐾

    Congenital anomaly NOS of nervous system

    Congenital deformity NOS of nervous system

    Congenital disease or lesion NOS of nervous system

CHAPTER 17 (Q00-Q99)

CHAPTER 17 (Q00-Q99)

CONGENITAL MALFORMATIONS OF EYE, EAR, FACE AND NECK (Q10-Q18)

> **Excludes2**   cleft lip and cleft palate (Q35-Q37)
> congenital malformation of cervical spine (Q05.0, Q05.5, Q67.5, Q76.0-Q76.4)
> congenital malformation of larynx (Q31.-)
> congenital malformation of lip NEC (Q38.0)
> congenital malformation of nose (Q30.-)
> congenital malformation of parathyroid gland (Q89.2)
> congenital malformation of thyroid gland (Q89.2)

● **Q10 Congenital malformations of eyelid, lacrimal apparatus and orbit**

> **Excludes1**   cryptophthalmos NOS (Q11.2)
> cryptophthalmos syndrome (Q87.0)

Q10.0 Congenital ptosis
Prolapse or drooping of upper eyelid from paralysis of third nerve or from sympathetic innervations

Q10.1 Congenital ectropion
Outward turning of eyelid

Q10.2 Congenital entropion
Inward turning of eyelid

Q10.3 Other congenital malformations of eyelid
Ablepharon
Blepharophimosis, congenital
Coloboma of eyelid
Congenital absence or agenesis of cilia
Congenital absence or agenesis of eyelid
Congenital accessory eyelid
Congenital accessory eye muscle
Congenital malformation of eyelid NOS

Q10.4 Absence and agenesis of lacrimal apparatus
Congenital absence of punctum lacrimale

Q10.5 Congenital stenosis and stricture of lacrimal duct

Q10.6 Other congenital malformations of lacrimal apparatus
Congenital malformation of lacrimal apparatus NOS

Q10.7 Congenital malformation of orbit

● **Q11 Anophthalmos, microphthalmos and macrophthalmos**
Absence of eye and optic pit

Q11.0 Cystic eyeball

Q11.1 Other anophthalmos
Anophthalmos NOS
Agenesis of eye
    Absence of eye
Aplasia of eye

Q11.2 Microphthalmos
Partial absence of eye and optic pit
Cryptophthalmos NOS
Dysplasia of eye
Hypoplasia of eye
Rudimentary eye

> **Excludes1**   cryptophthalmos syndrome (Q87.0)

Q11.3 Macrophthalmos
Congenital enlargement of eyes

> **Excludes1**   macrophthalmos in congenital glaucoma (Q15.0)

● **Q12 Congenital lens malformations**

Q12.0 Congenital cataract

Q12.1 Congenital displaced lens

Q12.2 Coloboma of lens

Q12.3 Congenital aphakia

Q12.4 Spherophakia
Smaller, more spherical optic lens than normal

Q12.8 Other congenital lens malformations
Microphakia

Q12.9 Congenital lens malformation, unspecified

Figure 17-2   Bilateral congenital **hydrophthalmia,** in which the eyes are very large in comparison to the other facial features due to glaucoma.

● **Q13 Congenital malformations of anterior segment of eye**

Q13.0 Coloboma of iris
Coloboma NOS

Q13.1 Absence of iris
Aniridia
Use additional code for associated glaucoma (H42)

Q13.2 Other congenital malformations of iris
Anisocoria, congenital
Atresia of pupil
Congenital malformation of iris NOS
Corectopia

Q13.3 Congenital corneal opacity

Q13.4 Other congenital corneal malformations
Congenital malformation of cornea NOS
Microcornea
Peter's anomaly

Q13.5 Blue sclera
Condition of unusual blueness of sclera; not harmful

● **Q13.8 Other congenital malformations of anterior segment of eye**

    Q13.81 Rieger's anomaly
       Use additional code for associated glaucoma (H42)

    Q13.89 Other congenital malformations of anterior segment of eye

Q13.9 Congenital malformation of anterior segment of eye, unspecified

● **Q14 Congenital malformations of posterior segment of eye**

> **Excludes2**   optic nerve hypoplasia (H47.03-)

Q14.0 Congenital malformation of vitreous humor
Congenital vitreous opacity

Q14.1 Congenital malformation of retina
Congenital retinal aneurysm

Q14.2 Congenital malformation of optic disc
Coloboma of optic disc

Q14.3 Congenital malformation of choroid

Q14.8 Other congenital malformations of posterior segment of eye
Coloboma of the fundus

Q14.9 Congenital malformation of posterior segment of eye, unspecified

● **Q15 Other congenital malformations of eye**

> **Excludes1**   congenital nystagmus (H55.01)
> ocular albinism (E70.31-)
> optic nerve hypoplasia (H47.03-)
> retinitis pigmentosa (H35.52)

Q15.0 Congenital glaucoma
Axenfeld's anomaly
Buphthalmos
    Congenital syndrome characterized by enlargement of the eye with symptoms of glaucoma.
Glaucoma of childhood
Glaucoma of newborn
Hydrophthalmos
Keratoglobus, congenital, with glaucoma
Macrocornea with glaucoma
Macrophthalmos in congenital glaucoma
Megalocornea with glaucoma

▶ New   ⇒ Revised   ~~deleted~~ Deleted   Excludes 1   Excludes 2   Includes   Use additional   Code first   Code also   Key words

OGCR Official Guidelines   X Assign placeholder X   ● Use Additional Character(s)   ▌ Manifestation Code   ℞ Hierarchical Condition Category   Coding Clinic

Q15.8 Other specified congenital malformations of eye

Q15.9 Congenital malformation of eye, unspecified
Congenital anomaly of eye
Congenital deformity of eye

● **Q16** Congenital malformations of ear causing impairment of hearing
Excludes1 congenital deafness (H90.-)

Q16.0 Congenital absence of (ear) auricle

Q16.1 Congenital absence, atresia and stricture of auditory canal (external)
Congenital atresia or stricture of osseous meatus

Q16.2 Absence of eustachian tube

Q16.3 Congenital malformation of ear ossicles
Congenital fusion of ear ossicles

Q16.4 Other congenital malformations of middle ear
Congenital malformation of middle ear NOS

Q16.5 Congenital malformation of inner ear
Congenital anomaly of membranous labyrinth
Congenital anomaly of organ of Corti

Q16.9 Congenital malformation of ear causing impairment of hearing, unspecified
Congenital absence of ear NOS

● **Q17** Other congenital malformations of ear
Excludes1 congenital malformations of ear with impairment of hearing (Q16.0-Q16.9)
preauricular sinus (Q18.1)

Q17.0 Accessory auricle
Accessory tragus
Polyotia
Preauricular appendage or tag
Supernumerary ear
Supernumerary lobule

Q17.1 Macrotia
Enlarged ears

Q17.2 Microtia
An abnormally small or underdeveloped external ear

Q17.3 Other misshapen ear
Pointed ear

Q17.4 Misplaced ear
Low-set ears
Excludes1 cervical auricle (Q18.2)

Q17.5 Prominent ear
Bat ear

Q17.8 Other specified congenital malformations of ear
Congenital absence of lobe of ear

Q17.9 Congenital malformation of ear, unspecified
Congenital anomaly of ear NOS

● **Q18** Other congenital malformations of face and neck
Excludes1 cleft lip and cleft palate (Q35-Q37)
conditions classified to Q67.0-Q67.4
congenital malformations of skull and face bones (Q75.-)
cyclopia (Q87.0)
dentofacial anomalies [including malocclusion] (M26.-)
malformation syndromes affecting facial appearance (Q87.0)
persistent thyroglossal duct (Q89.2)

Q18.0 Sinus, fistula and cyst of branchial cleft
Branchial vestige
Brachial remnants (cysts, fistula, skin tags) that are developmental anomalies

Q18.1 Preauricular sinus and cyst
Fistula of auricle, congenital
Cervicoaural fistula
Abnormal passage in neck originating from first branchial cleft

Q18.2 Other branchial cleft malformations
Branchial cleft malformation NOS
Cervical auricle
Otocephaly

Q18.3 Webbing of neck
Pterygium colli
Thick fold of skin on side of neck

Q18.4 Macrostomia
Results from failure of union of maxillary and mandibular processes, results in abnormally large mouth

Q18.5 Microstomia

Q18.6 Macrocheilia
Excessive size of lips
Hypertrophy of lip, congenital

Q18.7 Microcheilia
Abnormal smallness of lips

Q18.8 Other specified congenital malformations of face and neck
Medial cyst of face and neck
Medial fistula of face and neck
Medial sinus of face and neck

Q18.9 Congenital malformation of face and neck, unspecified
Congenital anomaly NOS of face and neck

CONGENITAL MALFORMATIONS OF THE CIRCULATORY SYSTEM (Q20-Q28)

● **Q20** Congenital malformations of cardiac chambers and connections
Excludes1 dextrocardia with situs inversus (Q89.3)
mirror-image atrial arrangement with situs inversus (Q89.3)

Q20.0 Common arterial trunk
Persistent truncus arteriosus
Excludes1 aortic septal defect (Q21.4)

Q20.1 Double outlet right ventricle
Taussig-Bing syndrome

Q20.2 Double outlet left ventricle

Q20.3 Discordant ventriculoarterial connection
Dextrotransposition of aorta
Transposition of great vessels (complete)

Q20.4 Double inlet ventricle
Common ventricle
Cor triloculare biatriatum
Single ventricle

Q20.5 Discordant atrioventricular connection
Corrected transposition
Levotransposition
Ventricular inversion

Q20.6 Isomerism of atrial appendages
Isomerism of atrial appendages with asplenia or polysplenia

Q20.8 Other congenital malformations of cardiac chambers and connections
Cor binoculare

Q20.9 Congenital malformation of cardiac chambers and connections, unspecified

● **Q21   Congenital malformations of cardiac septa**

Excludes1   acquired cardiac septal defect (I51.0)

Q21.0   Ventricular septal defect
Roger's disease

Q21.1   Atrial septal defect
Coronary sinus defect
Patent or persistent foramen ovale
Patent or persistent ostium secundum defect (type II)
Patent or persistent sinus venosus defect

Q21.2   Atrioventricular septal defect
Common atrioventricular canal
Endocardial cushion defect
Ostium primum atrial septal defect (type I)

Q21.3   Tetralogy of Fallot
Ventricular septal defect with pulmonary stenosis or
atresia, dextroposition of aorta and hypertrophy of
right ventricle.

Q21.4   Aortopulmonary septal defect
Aortic septal defect
Aortopulmonary window

Q21.8   Other congenital malformations of cardiac septa
Eisenmenger's defect
Pentalogy of Fallot
Code also if applicable:
Eisenmenger's complex (I27.83)
Eisenmenger's syndrome (I27.83)

Q21.9   Congenital malformation of cardiac septum, unspecified
Septal (heart) defect NOS

● **Q22   Congenital malformations of pulmonary and tricuspid valves**

Q22.0   Pulmonary valve atresia

Q22.1   Congenital pulmonary valve stenosis

Q22.2   Congenital pulmonary valve insufficiency
Congenital pulmonary valve regurgitation

Q22.3   Other congenital malformations of pulmonary valve
Congenital malformation of pulmonary valve NOS
Supernumerary cusps of pulmonary valve

Q22.4   Congenital tricuspid stenosis
Congenital tricuspid atresia

Q22.5   Ebstein's anomaly
Malformation of tricuspid valve

Q22.6   Hypoplastic right heart syndrome

Q22.8   Other congenital malformations of tricuspid valve

Q22.9   Congenital malformation of tricuspid valve, unspecified

● **Q23   Congenital malformations of aortic and mitral valves**

Q23.0   Congenital stenosis of aortic valve
Congenital aortic atresia
Congenital aortic stenosis NOS

Excludes1   congenital stenosis of aortic valve in
hypoplastic left heart syndrome
(Q23.4)
congenital subaortic stenosis (Q24.4)
supravalvular aortic stenosis (congenital)
(Q25.3)

Q23.1   Congenital insufficiency of aortic valve
Bicuspid aortic valve
Congenital aortic insufficiency

Q23.2   Congenital mitral stenosis
Congenital mitral atresia

Q23.3   Congenital mitral insufficiency

Q23.4   Hypoplastic left heart syndrome

Q23.8   Other congenital malformations of aortic and mitral valves

Q23.9   Congenital malformation of aortic and mitral valves, unspecified

● **Q24   Other congenital malformations of heart**

Excludes1   endocardial fibroelastosis (I42.4)

Q24.0   Dextrocardia
Heart is located in right hemithorax

Excludes1   dextrocardia with situs inversus (Q89.3)
isomerism of atrial appendages (with
asplenia or polysplenia) (Q20.6)
mirror-image atrial arrangement with
situs inversus (Q89.3)

Q24.1   Levocardia
Normal position of heart but related structures on wrong side

Q24.2   Cor triatriatum
Congenital heart defect; left atrium is subdivided

Q24.3   Pulmonary infundibular stenosis
Subvalvular pulmonic stenosis

Q24.4   Congenital subaortic stenosis

Q24.5   Malformation of coronary vessels
Congenital coronary (artery) aneurysm

Q24.6   Congenital heart block

Q24.8   Other specified congenital malformations of heart
Congenital diverticulum of left ventricle
Congenital malformation of myocardium
Congenital malformation of pericardium
Malposition of heart
Uhl's disease

Q24.9   Congenital malformation of heart, unspecified
Congenital anomaly of heart
Congenital disease of heart

● **Q25   Congenital malformations of great arteries**

Q25.0   Patent ductus arteriosus
*Fetal blood vessel connecting left pulmonary artery directly
to descending aorta*
Patent ductus Botallo
Persistent ductus arteriosus

Q25.1   Coarctation of aorta
Coarctation of aorta (preductal) (postductal)
Stenosis of aorta
Coding Clinic: 2016, Q4, P56-57

● **Q25.2   Atresia of aorta**
Coding Clinic: 2016, Q4, P56

Q25.21   Interruption of aortic arch
Atresia of aortic arch

Q25.29   Other atresia of aorta
Atresia of aorta

Q25.3   Supravalvular aortic stenosis

Excludes1   congenital aortic stenosis NOS (Q23.0)
congenital stenosis of aortic valve (Q23.0)

● **Q25.4   Other congenital malformations of aorta**

Excludes1   hypoplasia of aorta in hypoplastic left
heart syndrome (Q23.4)
Coding Clinic: 2016, Q4, P57

Q25.40   Congenital malformation of aorta unspecified

Q25.41   Absence and aplasia of aorta

Q25.42   Hypoplasia of aorta

Q25.43   Congenital aneurysm of aorta
Congenital aneurysm of aortic root
Congenital aneurysm of aortic sinus

Q25.44   Congenital dilation of aorta

Q25.45   Double aortic arch
Vascular ring of aorta

Q25.46   Tortuous aortic arch
Persistent convolutions of aortic arch

Q25.47   Right aortic arch
Persistent right aortic arch

Q25.48   Anomalous origin of subclavian artery

Q25.49   Other congenital malformations of aorta
Aortic arch
Bovine arch

▶ New   ⇒ Revised   ~~deleted~~ Deleted   Excludes 1   Excludes 2   Includes   Use additional   Code first   Code also   Key words

OGCR Official Guidelines   X Assign placeholder X   ● Use Additional Character(s)   ▷ Manifestation Code   🅗 Hierarchical Condition Category   Coding Clinic

Q25.5   **Atresia of pulmonary artery**

Q25.6   **Stenosis of pulmonary artery**
Supravalvular pulmonary stenosis

● **Q25.7**   **Other congenital malformations of pulmonary artery**

    Q25.71   **Coarctation of pulmonary artery**

    Q25.72   **Congenital pulmonary arteriovenous malformation**
Congenital pulmonary arteriovenous aneurysm

    Q25.79   **Other congenital malformations of pulmonary artery**
Aberrant pulmonary artery
Agenesis of pulmonary artery
Congenital aneurysm of pulmonary artery
Congenital anomaly of pulmonary artery
Hypoplasia of pulmonary artery

Q25.8   **Other congenital malformations of other great arteries**

Q25.9   **Congenital malformation of great arteries, unspecified**

● **Q26**   **Congenital malformations of great veins**

Q26.0   **Congenital stenosis of vena cava**
Congenital stenosis of vena cava (inferior)(superior)

Q26.1   **Persistent left superior vena cava**

Q26.2   **Total anomalous pulmonary venous connection**
Total anomalous pulmonary venous return [TAPVR], subdiaphragmatic
Total anomalous pulmonary venous return [TAPVR], supradiaphragmatic

Q26.3   **Partial anomalous pulmonary venous connection**
Partial anomalous pulmonary venous return

Q26.4   **Anomalous pulmonary venous connection, unspecified**

Q26.5   **Anomalous portal venous connection**

Q26.6   **Portal vein-hepatic artery fistula**

Q26.8   **Other congenital malformations of great veins**
Absence of vena cava (inferior) (superior)
Azygos continuation of inferior vena cava
Persistent left posterior cardinal vein
Scimitar syndrome

Q26.9   **Congenital malformation of great vein, unspecified**
Congenital anomaly of vena cava (inferior) (superior) NOS

● **Q27**   **Other congenital malformations of peripheral vascular system**

    Excludes2   anomalies of cerebral and precerebral vessels (Q28.0-Q28.3)
anomalies of coronary vessels (Q24.5)
anomalies of pulmonary artery (Q25.5-Q25.7)
congenital retinal aneurysm (Q14.1)
hemangioma and lymphangioma (D18.-)

Q27.0   **Congenital absence and hypoplasia of umbilical artery**
Single umbilical artery

Q27.1   **Congenital renal artery stenosis**

Q27.2   **Other congenital malformations of renal artery**
Congenital malformation of renal artery NOS
Multiple renal arteries

● **Q27.3**   **Arteriovenous malformation (peripheral)**
Arteriovenous aneurysm

    Excludes1   acquired arteriovenous aneurysm (I77.0)

    Excludes2   arteriovenous malformation of cerebral vessels (Q28.2)
arteriovenous malformation of precerebral vessels (Q28.0)

    Q27.30   **Arteriovenous malformation, site unspecified**

    Q27.31   **Arteriovenous malformation of vessel of upper limb**

    Q27.32   **Arteriovenous malformation of vessel of lower limb**

    Q27.33   **Arteriovenous malformation of digestive system vessel**

    Q27.34   **Arteriovenous malformation of renal vessel**

    Q27.39   **Arteriovenous malformation, other site**

Q27.4   **Congenital phlebectasia**

Q27.8   **Other specified congenital malformations of peripheral vascular system**
Absence of peripheral vascular system
Atresia of peripheral vascular system
Congenital aneurysm (peripheral)
Congenital stricture, artery
Congenital varix

    Excludes1   arteriovenous malformation (Q27.3-)

Q27.9   **Congenital malformation of peripheral vascular system, unspecified**
Anomaly of artery or vein NOS

● **Q28**   **Other congenital malformations of circulatory system**

    Excludes1   congenital aneurysm NOS (Q27.8)
congenital coronary aneurysm (Q24.5)
ruptured cerebral arteriovenous malformation (I60.8)
ruptured malformation of precerebral vessels (I72.0)

    Excludes2   congenital peripheral aneurysm (Q27.8)
congenital pulmonary aneurysm (Q25.79)
congenital retinal aneurysm (Q14.1)

Q28.0   **Arteriovenous malformation of precerebral vessels**
Congenital arteriovenous precerebral aneurysm (nonruptured)

Q28.1   **Other malformations of precerebral vessels**
Congenital malformation of precerebral vessels NOS
Congenital precerebral aneurysm (nonruptured)

Q28.2   **Arteriovenous malformation of cerebral vessels**
Arteriovenous malformation of brain NOS
Congenital arteriovenous cerebral aneurysm (nonruptured)

Q28.3   **Other malformations of cerebral vessels**
Congenital cerebral aneurysm (nonruptured)
Congenital malformation of cerebral vessels NOS
Developmental venous anomaly

Q28.8   **Other specified congenital malformations of circulatory system**
Congenital aneurysm, specified site NEC
Spinal vessel anomaly

Q28.9   **Congenital malformation of circulatory system, unspecified**

CONGENITAL MALFORMATIONS OF THE RESPIRATORY SYSTEM (Q30-Q34)

● **Q30**   **Congenital malformations of nose**

    Excludes1   congenital deviation of nasal septum (Q67.4)

Q30.0   **Choanal atresia**
Atresia of nares (anterior) (posterior)
Congenital stenosis of nares (anterior) (posterior)

Q30.1   **Agenesis and underdevelopment of nose**
Congenital absent of nose

Q30.2   **Fissured, notched and cleft nose**

Q30.3   **Congenital perforated nasal septum**

Q30.8   **Other congenital malformations of nose**
Accessory nose
Congenital anomaly of nasal sinus wall

Q30.9   **Congenital malformation of nose, unspecified**

- **Q31 Congenital malformations of larynx**
  - **Excludes1** congenital laryngeal stridor NOS (P28.89)

  - **Q31.0 Web of larynx**
    Glottic web of larynx
    Subglottic web of larynx
    Web of larynx NOS
  - **Q31.1 Congenital subglottic stenosis**
  - **Q31.2 Laryngeal hypoplasia**
  - **Q31.3 Laryngocele**
  - **Q31.5 Congenital laryngomalacia**
  - **Q31.8 Other congenital malformations of larynx**
    Absence of larynx
    Agenesis of larynx
    Atresia of larynx
    Congenital cleft thyroid cartilage
    Congenital fissure of epiglottis
    Congenital stenosis of larynx NEC
    Posterior cleft of cricoid cartilage
  - **Q31.9 Congenital malformation of larynx, unspecified**

- **Q32 Congenital malformations of trachea and bronchus**
  - **Excludes1** congenital bronchiectasis (Q33.4)

  - **Q32.0 Congenital tracheomalacia**
  - **Q32.1 Other congenital malformations of trachea**
    Atresia of trachea
    Congenital anomaly of tracheal cartilage
    Congenital dilatation of trachea
    Congenital malformation of trachea
    Congenital stenosis of trachea
    Congenital tracheocele
  - **Q32.2 Congenital bronchomalacia**
  - **Q32.3 Congenital stenosis of bronchus**
  - **Q32.4 Other congenital malformations of bronchus**
    Absence of bronchus
    Agenesis of bronchus
    Atresia of bronchus
    Congenital diverticulum of bronchus
    Congenital malformation of bronchus NOS

- **Q33 Congenital malformations of lung**
  - **Q33.0 Congenital cystic lung**
    Congenital cystic lung disease
    Congenital honeycomb lung
    Congenital polycystic lung disease
    - **Excludes1** cystic fibrosis (E84.0)
      cystic lung disease, acquired or
      unspecified (J98.4)
  - **Q33.1 Accessory lobe of lung**
    Azygos lobe (fissured), lung
  - **Q33.2 Sequestration of lung**
  - **Q33.3 Agenesis of lung**
    Congenital absence of lung (lobe)
  - **Q33.4 Congenital bronchiectasis**
  - **Q33.5 Ectopic tissue in lung**
  - **Q33.6 Congenital hypoplasia and dysplasia of lung**
    - **Excludes1** pulmonary hypoplasia associated with
      short gestation (P28.0)
  - **Q33.8 Other congenital malformations of lung**
  - **Q33.9 Congenital malformation of lung, unspecified**

- **Q34 Other congenital malformations of respiratory system**
  - **Excludes2** congenital central alveolar hypoventilation
    syndrome (G47.35)
  - **Q34.0 Anomaly of pleura**
  - **Q34.1 Congenital cyst of mediastinum**
  - **Q34.8 Other specified congenital malformations of respiratory system**
    Atresia of nasopharynx
  - **Q34.9 Congenital malformation of respiratory system, unspecified**
    Congenital absence of respiratory system
    Congenital anomaly of respiratory system NOS

Figure 17-3 Cleft palate.

CLEFT LIP AND CLEFT PALATE (Q35-Q37)

Use additional code to identify associated malformation of the
nose (Q30.2)

~~**Excludes1** Robin's syndrome (Q87.0)~~

▶ **Excludes2** Robin's syndrome (Q87.0)

- **Q35 Cleft palate**
  - **Includes** fissure of palate
    palatoschisis
  - **Excludes1** cleft palate with cleft lip (Q37.-)
  - **Q35.1 Cleft hard palate**
  - **Q35.3 Cleft soft palate**
  - **Q35.5 Cleft hard palate with cleft soft palate**
  - **Q35.7 Cleft uvula**
  - **Q35.9 Cleft palate, unspecified**
    Cleft palate NOS

- **Q36 Cleft lip**
  - **Includes** cheiloschisis
    congenital fissure of lip
    harelip
    labium leporinum
  - **Excludes1** cleft lip with cleft palate (Q37.-)
  - **Q36.0 Cleft lip, bilateral**
  - **Q36.1 Cleft lip, median**
  - **Q36.9 Cleft lip, unilateral**
    Cleft lip NOS

- **Q37 Cleft palate with cleft lip**
  - **Includes** cheilopalatoschisis
  - **Q37.0 Cleft hard palate with bilateral cleft lip**
  - **Q37.1 Cleft hard palate with unilateral cleft lip**
    Cleft hard palate with cleft lip NOS
  - **Q37.2 Cleft soft palate with bilateral cleft lip**
  - **Q37.3 Cleft soft palate with unilateral cleft lip**
    Cleft soft palate with cleft lip NOS
  - **Q37.4 Cleft hard and soft palate with bilateral cleft lip**
  - **Q37.5 Cleft hard and soft palate with unilateral cleft lip**
    Cleft hard and soft palate with cleft lip NOS
  - **Q37.8 Unspecified cleft palate with bilateral cleft lip**
  - **Q37.9 Unspecified cleft palate with unilateral cleft lip**
    Cleft palate with cleft lip NOS

OTHER CONGENITAL MALFORMATIONS OF THE DIGESTIVE SYSTEM (Q38-Q45)

- **Q38 Other congenital malformations of tongue, mouth and pharynx**
  - **Excludes1** dentofacial anomalies (M26.-)
    macrostomia (Q18.4)
    microstomia (Q18.5)
  - **Q38.0 Congenital malformations of lips, not elsewhere classified**
    Congenital fistula of lip
    Congenital malformation of lip NOS
    Van der Woude's syndrome
    - **Excludes1** cleft lip (Q36.-)
      cleft lip with cleft palate (Q37.-)
      macrocheilia (Q18.6)
      microcheilia (Q18.7)

▶ New   ⇒ Revised   ~~deleted~~ Deleted | Excludes 1 | Excludes 2 | Includes | Use additional | Code first | Code also | Key words |

OGCR Official Guidelines   X Assign placeholder X   ● Use Additional Character(s)   ▌ Manifestation Code   ℞ Hierarchical Condition Category   **Coding Clinic**

Q38.1   **Ankyloglossia**
Restricted movement of tongue resulting in speech difficulty
Tongue tie

Q38.2   **Macroglossia**
Excessive size of tongue
Congenital hypertrophy of tongue

Q38.3   **Other congenital malformations of tongue**
Aglossia
Bifid tongue
Congenital adhesion of tongue
Congenital fissure of tongue
Congenital malformation of tongue NOS
Double tongue
Hypoglossia
Hypoplasia of tongue
Microglossia

Q38.4   **Congenital malformations of salivary glands and ducts**
Atresia of salivary glands and ducts
Congenital absence of salivary glands and ducts
Congenital accessory salivary glands and ducts
Congenital fistula of salivary gland

Q38.5   **Congenital malformations of palate, not elsewhere classified**
Congenital absence of uvula
Congenital malformation of palate NOS
Congenital high arched palate
>   **Excludes1**   cleft palate (Q35.-)
>   cleft palate with cleft lip (Q37.-)

Q38.6   **Other congenital malformations of mouth**
Congenital malformation of mouth NOS

Q38.7   **Congenital pharyngeal pouch**
Congenital diverticulum of pharynx
>   **Excludes1**   pharyngeal pouch syndrome (D82.1)

Q38.8   **Other congenital malformations of pharynx**
Congenital malformation of pharynx NOS
Imperforate pharynx

● Q39   **Congenital malformations of esophagus**

Q39.0   **Atresia of esophagus without fistula**
Atresia of esophagus NOS

Q39.1   **Atresia of esophagus with tracheo-esophageal fistula**
Atresia of esophagus with broncho-esophageal fistula

Q39.2   **Congenital tracheo-esophageal fistula without atresia**
Congenital tracheo-esophageal fistula NOS

Q39.3   **Congenital stenosis and stricture of esophagus**

Q39.4   **Esophageal web**

Q39.5   **Congenital dilatation of esophagus**
Congenital cardiospasm

Q39.6   **Congenital diverticulum of esophagus**
Congenital esophageal pouch

Q39.8   **Other congenital malformations of esophagus**
Congenital absence of esophagus
Congenital displacement of esophagus
Congenital duplication of esophagus

Q39.9   **Congenital malformation of esophagus, unspecified**

● Q40   **Other congenital malformations of upper alimentary tract**

Q40.0   **Congenital hypertrophic pyloric stenosis**
Congenital or infantile constriction
Congenital or infantile hypertrophy
Congenital or infantile spasm
Congenital or infantile stenosis
Congenital or infantile stricture

Q40.1   **Congenital hiatus hernia**
Congenital displacement of cardia through esophageal hiatus
>   **Excludes1**   congenital diaphragmatic hernia (Q79.0)

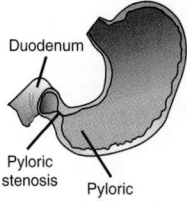

Duodenum

Pyloric stenosis

Pyloric part of stomach

Figure 17-4   Pyloric stenosis.

Q40.2   **Other specified congenital malformations of stomach**
Congenital displacement of stomach
Congenital diverticulum of stomach
Congenital hourglass stomach
Congenital duplication of stomach
Megalogastria
Microgastria

Q40.3   **Congenital malformation of stomach, unspecified**

Q40.8   **Other specified congenital malformations of upper alimentary tract**

Q40.9   **Congenital malformation of upper alimentary tract, unspecified**
Congenital anomaly of upper alimentary tract
Congenital deformity of upper alimentary tract

● Q41   **Congenital absence, atresia and stenosis of small intestine**
>   **Includes**   congenital obstruction, occlusion or stricture of small intestine or intestine NOS
>   **Excludes1**   cystic fibrosis with intestinal manifestation (E84.11)
>   meconium ileus NOS (without cystic fibrosis) (P76.0)

Q41.0   **Congenital absence, atresia and stenosis of duodenum**

Q41.1   **Congenital absence, atresia and stenosis of jejunum**
Apple peel syndrome
Imperforate jejunum

Q41.2   **Congenital absence, atresia and stenosis of ileum**

Q41.8   **Congenital absence, atresia and stenosis of other specified parts of small intestine**

Q41.9   **Congenital absence, atresia and stenosis of small intestine, part unspecified**
Congenital absence, atresia and stenosis of intestine NOS

● Q42   **Congenital absence, atresia and stenosis of large intestine**
>   **Includes**   congenital obstruction, occlusion and stricture of large intestine

Q42.0   **Congenital absence, atresia and stenosis of rectum with fistula**

Q42.1   **Congenital absence, atresia and stenosis of rectum without fistula**
Imperforate rectum

Q42.2   **Congenital absence, atresia and stenosis of anus with fistula**

Q42.3   **Congenital absence, atresia and stenosis of anus without fistula**
Imperforate anus

Q42.8   **Congenital absence, atresia and stenosis of other parts of large intestine**

Q42.9   **Congenital absence, atresia and stenosis of large intestine, part unspecified**

Q43   Other congenital malformations of intestine

Q43.0   Meckel's diverticulum (displaced) (hypertrophic)
Congenital abnormality in which a pouch remains on the lower end of the small intestine
Persistent omphalomesenteric duct
Persistent vitelline duct

Q43.1   Hirschsprung's disease
Developmental disorder of enteric nervous system characterized by absence of ganglion cells in distal colon resulting in functional obstruction
Aganglionosis
Congenital (aganglionic) megacolon

Q43.2   Other congenital functional disorders of colon
Congenital dilatation of colon

Q43.3   Congenital malformations of intestinal fixation
Congenital omental, anomalous adhesions [bands]
Congenital peritoneal adhesions [bands]
Incomplete rotation of cecum and colon
Insufficient rotation of cecum and colon
Jackson's membrane
Malrotation of colon
Rotation failure of cecum and colon
Universal mesentery

Q43.4   Duplication of intestine

Q43.5   Ectopic anus
Anal opening in abnormal location

Q43.6   Congenital fistula of rectum and anus
Excludes1   congenital fistula of anus with absence, atresia and stenosis (Q42.2)
congenital fistula of rectum with absence, atresia and stenosis (Q42.0)
congenital rectovaginal fistula (Q52.2)
congenital urethrorectal fistula (Q64.73)
pilonidal fistula or sinus (L05.-)

Q43.7   Persistent cloaca
Malformation in which rectum, vagina, and urinary tract form one channel; AKA congenital cloaca
Cloaca NOS

Q43.8   Other specified congenital malformations of intestine
Congenital blind loop syndrome
Congenital diverticulitis, colon
Congenital diverticulum, intestine
Dolichocolon
Megaloappendix
Megaloduodenum
Microcolon
Transposition of appendix
Transposition of colon
Transposition of intestine

Q43.9   Congenital malformation of intestine, unspecified

Q44   Congenital malformations of gallbladder, bile ducts and liver

Q44.0   Agenesis, aplasia and hypoplasia of gallbladder
Congenital absence of gallbladder

Q44.1   Other congenital malformations of gallbladder
Congenital malformation of gallbladder NOS
Intrahepatic gallbladder

Q44.2   Atresia of bile ducts

Q44.3   Congenital stenosis and stricture of bile ducts

Q44.4   Choledochal cyst

Q44.5   Other congenital malformations of bile ducts
Accessory hepatic duct
Biliary duct duplication
Congenital malformation of bile duct NOS
Cystic duct duplication

Q44.6   Cystic disease of liver
Fibrocystic disease of liver

Q44.7   Other congenital malformations of liver
Accessory liver
Alagille's syndrome
Congenital absence of liver
Congenital hepatomegaly
Congenital malformation of liver NOS

Q45   Other congenital malformations of digestive system
Excludes2   congenital diaphragmatic hernia (Q79.0)
congenital hiatus hernia (Q40.1)

Q45.0   Agenesis, aplasia and hypoplasia of pancreas
Congenital absence of pancreas

Q45.1   Annular pancreas

Q45.2   Congenital pancreatic cyst

Q45.3   Other congenital malformations of pancreas and pancreatic duct
Accessory pancreas
Congenital malformation of pancreas or pancreatic duct NOS
Excludes1   congenital diabetes mellitus (E10.-)
cystic fibrosis (E84.0-E84.9)
fibrocystic disease of pancreas (E84.-)
neonatal diabetes mellitus (P70.2)

Q45.8   Other specified congenital malformations of digestive system
Absence (complete) (partial) of alimentary tract NOS
Duplication of digestive system
Malposition, congenital of digestive system

Q45.9   Congenital malformation of digestive system, unspecified
Congenital anomaly of digestive system
Congenital deformity of digestive system

CONGENITAL MALFORMATIONS OF GENITAL ORGANS (Q50-Q56)

Excludes1   androgen insensitivity syndrome (E34.5-)
syndromes associated with anomalies in the number and form of chromosomes (Q90-Q99)

Q50   Congenital malformations of ovaries, fallopian tubes and broad ligaments

Q50.0   Congenital absence of ovary
Excludes1   Turner's syndrome (Q96.-)
Q50.01   Congenital absence of ovary, unilateral ♀
Q50.02   Congenital absence of ovary, bilateral ♀

Q50.1   Developmental ovarian cyst ♀

Q50.2   Congenital torsion of ovary ♀

Q50.3   Other congenital malformations of ovary
Q50.31   Accessory ovary ♀
Q50.32   Ovarian streak ♀
Inadequate ovaries with absent follicular and hormonal function
46, XX with streak gonads
Q50.39   Other congenital malformation of ovary ♀
Congenital malformation of ovary NOS

Q50.4   Embryonic cyst of fallopian tube ♀
Fimbrial cyst

Q50.5   Embryonic cyst of broad ligament ♀
Epoophoron cyst
Parovarian cyst

Q50.6   Other congenital malformations of fallopian tube and broad ligament ♀
Absence of fallopian tube and broad ligament
Accessory fallopian tube and broad ligament
Atresia of fallopian tube and broad ligament
Congenital malformation of fallopian tube or broad ligament NOS

Q51   Congenital malformations of uterus and cervix

Q51.0   Agenesis and aplasia of uterus ♀
Congenital absence of uterus

Q51.1   Doubling of uterus with doubling of cervix and vagina
Q51.10   Doubling of uterus with doubling of cervix and vagina without obstruction ♀
Doubling of uterus with doubling of cervix and vagina NOS
Q51.11   Doubling of uterus with doubling of cervix and vagina with obstruction ♀

▶ New   ⇒ Revised   ~~deleted~~ Deleted   Excludes 1   Excludes 2   Includes   Use additional   Code first   Code also   Key words
OGCR Official Guidelines   **X** Assign placeholder X   ● Use Additional Character(s)   ▶ Manifestation Code   🔖 Hierarchical Condition Category   **Coding Clinic**

Q51.2 Other doubling of uterus
Doubling of uterus NOS
Septate uterus
~~Q51.20 Other doubling of uterus, unspecified~~
~~Septate uterus, unspecified~~

➡ **Q51.21 Complete doubling of uterus** ♀
Complete septate uterus

➡ **Q51.22 Partial doubling of uterus** ♀
Partial septate uterus

➡ **Q51.28 Other and unspecified doubling of uterus** ♀
➡Septate uterus NOS

Q51.3 Bicornate uterus ♀
Bicornate uterus, complete or partial
Birth defect in which uterus has two separate "horns" that
form top of uterus

Q51.4 Unicornate uterus ♀
Unicornate uterus with or without a separate uterine
horn
Uterus with only one functioning horn
Uterus with half being undeveloped

Q51.5 Agenesis and aplasia of cervix ♀
Congenital absence of cervix

Q51.6 Embryonic cyst of cervix ♀

**Q51.7 Congenital fistulae between uterus and digestive and
urinary tracts** ♀

● **Q51.8 Other congenital malformations of uterus and cervix**

● **Q51.81 Other congenital malformations of uterus**

Q51.810 Arcuate uterus ♀
Arcuatus uterus

Q51.811 Hypoplasia of uterus ♀

**Q51.818 Other congenital malformations of
uterus** ♀
Müllerian anomaly of uterus NEC

● **Q51.82 Other congenital malformations of cervix**

Q51.820 Cervical duplication ♀

Q51.821 Hypoplasia of cervix ♀

**Q51.828 Other congenital malformations of
cervix** ♀

**Q51.9 Congenital malformation of uterus and cervix,
unspecified** ♀

● **Q52 Other congenital malformations of female genitalia**

Q52.0 Congenital absence of vagina ♀
Vaginal agenesis, total or partial

● **Q52.1 Doubling of vagina**

Excludes1 doubling of vagina with doubling of
uterus and cervix (Q51.1-)

Q52.10 Doubling of vagina, unspecified ♀
Septate vagina NOS

Q52.11 Transverse vaginal septum ♀

● **Q52.12 Longitudinal vaginal septum**
Coding Clinic: 2016, Q4, P58

**Q52.120 Longitudinal vaginal septum,
nonobstructing** ♀

**Q52.121 Longitudinal vaginal septum,
obstructing, right side** ♀

**Q52.122 Longitudinal vaginal septum,
obstructing, left side** ♀

**Q52.123 Longitudinal vaginal septum,
microperforate, right side** ♀

**Q52.124 Longitudinal vaginal septum,
microperforate, left side** ♀
Coding Clinic: 2016, Q4, P59

**Q52.129 Other and unspecified longitudinal
vaginal septum** ♀

Q52.2 Congenital rectovaginal fistula ♀
Excludes1 cloaca (Q43.7)

Q52.3 Imperforate hymen ♀
Membrane (hymen) completely closes vaginal orifice

Q52.4 Other congenital malformations of vagina ♀
Canal of Nuck cyst, congenital
Congenital malformation of vagina NOS
Embryonic vaginal cyst
Gartner's duct cyst

Q52.5 Fusion of labia ♀

Q52.6 Congenital malformation of clitoris ♀

● **Q52.7 Other and unspecified congenital malformations of
vulva**

**Q52.70 Unspecified congenital malformations of
vulva** ♀
Congenital malformation of vulva NOS

Q52.71 Congenital absence of vulva ♀

Q52.79 Other congenital malformations of vulva ♀
Congenital cyst of vulva

**Q52.8 Other specified congenital malformations of female
genitalia** ♀

**Q52.9 Congenital malformation of female genitalia,
unspecified** ♀

● **Q53 Undescended and ectopic testicle**

● **Q53.0 Ectopic testis**

Q53.00 Ectopic testis, unspecified ♂

Q53.01 Ectopic testis, unilateral ♂

Q53.02 Ectopic testes, bilateral ♂

● **Q53.1 Undescended testicle, unilateral**

Q53.10 Unspecified undescended testicle, unilateral ♂

● **Q53.11 Abdominal testis, unilateral**

Q53.111 Unilateral intraabdominal testis ♂

Q53.112 Unilateral inguinal testis ♂

Q53.12 Ectopic perineal testis, unilateral ♂

Q53.13 Unilateral high scrotal testis ♂

● **Q53.2 Undescended testicle, bilateral**

Q53.20 Undescended testicle, unspecified, bilateral ♂

● **Q53.21 Abdominal testis, bilateral**

Q53.211 Bilateral intraabdominal testes ♂

Q53.212 Bilateral inguinal testes ♂

Q53.22 Ectopic perineal testis, bilateral ♂

Q53.23 Bilateral high scrotal testes ♂

Q53.9 Undescended testicle, unspecified ♂
Cryptorchism NOS

Item 17-1 Testes form in the abdomen of the male and only descend into the scrotum during normal embryonic development. "Ectopic" testes are out of their normal place or "retained" (left behind) in the abdomen. Crypto (hidden) orchism (testicle) is a major risk factor for testicular cancer.

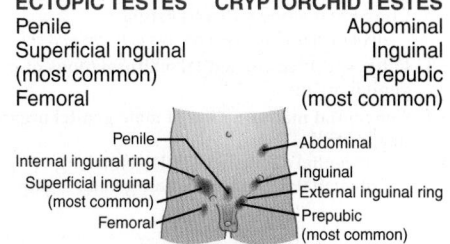

ECTOPIC TESTES	CRYPTORCHID TESTES
Penile	Abdominal
Superficial inguinal	Inguinal
(most common)	Prepubic
Femoral	(most common)

Figure 17-5 Undescended testes and the positions of the testes in various types of cryptorchidism or abnormal paths of descent.

Q54 Hypospadias
Birth defect of male; urethra opens in abnormal location on shaft
> **Excludes1** epispadias (Q64.0)

Q54.0 **Hypospadias, balanic** ♂
Hypospadias, coronal
Hypospadias, glandular

Q54.1 **Hypospadias, penile** ♂

Q54.2 **Hypospadias, penoscrotal** ♂

Q54.3 **Hypospadias, perineal** ♂

Q54.4 **Congenital chordee** ♂
Chordee without hypospadias

Q54.8 **Other hypospadias** ♂
Hypospadias with intersex state

Q54.9 **Hypospadias, unspecified** ♂

Q55 Other congenital malformations of male genital organs
> **Excludes1** congenital hydrocele (P83.5)
> hypospadias (Q54.-)

Q55.0 **Absence and aplasia of testis** ♂
Monorchism

Q55.1 **Hypoplasia of testis and scrotum** ♂
Fusion of testes

Q55.2 **Other and unspecified congenital malformations of testis and scrotum**

  Q55.20 **Unspecified congenital malformations of testis and scrotum** ♂
Congenital malformation of testis or scrotum NOS

  Q55.21 **Polyorchism** ♂
Developmental anomaly characterized by presence of more than two testes

  Q55.22 **Retractile testis** ♂

  Q55.23 **Scrotal transposition** ♂

  Q55.29 **Other congenital malformations of testis and scrotum** ♂

Q55.3 **Atresia of vas deferens** ♂
Code first any associated cystic fibrosis (E84.-)

Q55.4 **Other congenital malformations of vas deferens, epididymis, seminal vesicles and prostate** ♂
Absence or aplasia of prostate
Absence or aplasia of spermatic cord
Congenital malformation of vas deferens, epididymis, seminal vesicles or prostate NOS

Q55.5 **Congenital absence and aplasia of penis** ♂

Q55.6 **Other congenital malformations of penis**

  Q55.61 **Curvature of penis (lateral)** ♂

  Q55.62 **Hypoplasia of penis** ♂
Underdevelopment penis
Micropenis

  Q55.63 **Congenital torsion of penis** ♂
> **Excludes1** acquired torsion of penis (N48.82)

  Q55.64 **Hidden penis** ♂
Buried penis
Concealed penis
> **Excludes1** acquired buried penis (N48.83)

  Q55.69 **Other congenital malformation of penis** ♂
Congenital malformation of penis NOS

Q55.7 **Congenital vasocutaneous fistula** ♂
Abnormal opening between vas deferens and skin

Q55.8 **Other specified congenital malformations of male genital organs** ♂

Q55.9 **Congenital malformation of male genital organ, unspecified** ♂
Congenital anomaly of male genital organ
Congenital deformity of male genital organ

Q56 Indeterminate sex and pseudohermaphroditism
Internal reproductive organs are opposite external physical characteristics.
> **Excludes1** 46,XX true hermaphrodite (Q99.1)
> androgen insensitivity syndrome (E34.5-)
> chimera 46,XX/46,XY true hermaphrodite (Q99.0)
> female pseudohermaphroditism with adrenocortical disorder (E25.-)
> pseudohermaphroditism with specified chromosomal anomaly (Q96-Q99)
> pure gonadal dysgenesis (Q99.1)

Q56.0 **Hermaphroditism, not elsewhere classified**
Ovotestis

Q56.1 **Male pseudohermaphroditism, not elsewhere classified** ♂
46, XY with streak gonads
Male pseudohermaphroditism NOS

Q56.2 **Female pseudohermaphroditism, not elsewhere classified** ♀
Female pseudohermaphroditism NOS

Q56.3 **Pseudohermaphroditism, unspecified**

Q56.4 **Indeterminate sex, unspecified**
Ambiguous genitalia

CONGENITAL MALFORMATIONS OF THE URINARY SYSTEM (Q60-Q64)

Q60 Renal agenesis and other reduction defects of kidney
> **Includes** congenital absence of kidney
> congenital atrophy of kidney
> infantile atrophy of kidney

Q60.0 **Renal agenesis, unilateral**

Q60.1 **Renal agenesis, bilateral**

Q60.2 **Renal agenesis, unspecified**

Q60.3 **Renal hypoplasia, unilateral**

Q60.4 **Renal hypoplasia, bilateral**

Q60.5 **Renal hypoplasia, unspecified**

Q60.6 **Potter's syndrome**

Q61 Cystic kidney disease
Cysts that develop in failing kidney due to end-stage renal disease
> **Excludes1** acquired cyst of kidney (N28.1)
> Potter's syndrome (Q60.6)

Q61.0 **Congenital renal cyst**

  Q61.00 **Congenital renal cyst, unspecified**
Cyst of kidney NOS (congenital)

  Q61.01 **Congenital single renal cyst**

  Q61.02 **Congenital multiple renal cysts**

Q61.1 **Polycystic kidney, infantile type**
Polycystic kidney, autosomal recessive

  Q61.11 **Cystic dilatation of collecting ducts**

  Q61.19 **Other polycystic kidney, infantile type**

Q61.2 **Polycystic kidney, adult type**
Polycystic kidney, autosomal dominant

Q61.3 **Polycystic kidney, unspecified**
Coding Clinic: 2016, Q3, P23

Q61.4 **Renal dysplasia**
Multicystic dysplastic kidney
Multicystic kidney (development)
Multicystic kidney disease
Multicystic renal dysplasia
> **Excludes1** polycystic kidney disease (Q61.11-Q61.3)

Q61.5 **Medullary cystic kidney**
Nephronopthisis
Sponge kidney NOS

Q61.8 **Other cystic kidney diseases**
Fibrocystic kidney
Fibrocystic renal degeneration or disease

Q61.9 **Cystic kidney disease, unspecified**
Meckel-Gruber syndrome

▶ New   ⟼ Revised   ~~deleted~~ Deleted   Excludes 1   Excludes 2   Includes   Use additional   Code first   Code also   Key words
OGCR Official Guidelines   X Assign placeholder X   ● Use Additional Character(s)   ▶ Manifestation Code   🅗🅒 Hierarchical Condition Category   **Coding Clinic**

- **Q62** **Congenital obstructive defects of renal pelvis and congenital malformations of ureter**
  - **Q62.0** **Congenital hydronephrosis**
  - **Q62.1** **Congenital occlusion of ureter**
    Atresia and stenosis of ureter
    - **Q62.10** **Congenital occlusion of ureter, unspecified**
    - **Q62.11** **Congenital occlusion of ureteropelvic junction**
    - **Q62.12** **Congenital occlusion of ureterovesical orifice**
  - **Q62.2** **Congenital megaureter**
    Congenital dilatation of ureter
  - **Q62.3** **Other obstructive defects of renal pelvis and ureter**
    - **Q62.31** **Congenital ureterocele, orthotopic**
    - **Q62.32** **Cecoureterocele**
      Ectopic ureterocele
    - **Q62.39** **Other obstructive defects of renal pelvis and ureter**
      Ureteropelvic junction obstruction NOS
  - **Q62.4** **Agenesis of ureter**
    Congenital absence ureter
  - **Q62.5** **Duplication of ureter**
    Accessory ureter
    Double ureter
  - **Q62.6** **Malposition of ureter**
    - **Q62.60** **Malposition of ureter, unspecified**
    - **Q62.61** **Deviation of ureter**
    - **Q62.62** **Displacement of ureter**
    - **Q62.63** **Anomalous implantation of ureter**
      Ectopia of ureter
      Ectopic ureter
    - **Q62.69** **Other malposition of ureter**
  - **Q62.7** **Congenital vesico-uretero-renal reflux**
  - **Q62.8** **Other congenital malformations of ureter**
    Anomaly of ureter NOS

- **Q63** **Other congenital malformations of kidney**
  - **Excludes1** congenital nephrotic syndrome (N04.-)
  - **Q63.0** **Accessory kidney**
  - **Q63.1** **Lobulated, fused and horseshoe kidney**
  - **Q63.2** **Ectopic kidney**
    Congenital displaced kidney
    Malrotation of kidney
  - **Q63.3** **Hyperplastic and giant kidney**
    Compensatory hypertrophy of kidney
  - **Q63.8** **Other specified congenital malformations of kidney**
    Congenital renal calculi
  - **Q63.9** **Congenital malformation of kidney, unspecified**

- **Q64** **Other congenital malformations of urinary system**
  - **Q64.0** **Epispadias**
    Urethral opening somewhere on dorsum of penis
    - **Excludes1** hypospadias (Q54.-)
  - **Q64.1** **Exstrophy of urinary bladder**
    Bladder is exposed, inside out, and protrudes through abdominal wall
    - **Q64.10** **Exstrophy of urinary bladder, unspecified**
      Ectopia vesicae
    - **Q64.11** **Supravesical fissure of urinary bladder**
    - **Q64.12** **Cloacal exstrophy of urinary bladder**
    - **Q64.19** **Other exstrophy of urinary bladder**
      Extroversion of bladder
  - **Q64.2** **Congenital posterior urethral valves**

- **Q64.3** **Other atresia and stenosis of urethra and bladder neck**
  - **Q64.31** **Congenital bladder neck obstruction**
    Congenital obstruction of vesicourethral orifice
  - **Q64.32** **Congenital stricture of urethra**
  - **Q64.33** **Congenital stricture of urinary meatus**
  - **Q64.39** **Other atresia and stenosis of urethra and bladder neck**
    Atresia and stenosis of urethra and bladder neck NOS
  - **Q64.4** **Malformation of urachus**
    Cyst of urachus
    Patent urachus
    Prolapse of urachus
  - **Q64.5** **Congenital absence of bladder and urethra**
  - **Q64.6** **Congenital diverticulum of bladder**
  - **Q64.7** **Other and unspecified congenital malformations of bladder and urethra**
    - **Excludes1** congenital prolapse of bladder (mucosa) (Q79.4)
    - **Q64.70** **Unspecified congenital malformation of bladder and urethra**
      Malformation of bladder or urethra NOS
    - **Q64.71** **Congenital prolapse of urethra**
    - **Q64.72** **Congenital prolapse of urinary meatus**
    - **Q64.73** **Congenital urethrorectal fistula**
    - **Q64.74** **Double urethra**
    - **Q64.75** **Double urinary meatus**
    - **Q64.79** **Other congenital malformations of bladder and urethra**
  - **Q64.8** **Other specified congenital malformations of urinary system**
  - **Q64.9** **Congenital malformation of urinary system, unspecified**
    Congenital anomaly NOS of urinary system
    Congenital deformity NOS of urinary system

CONGENITAL MALFORMATIONS AND DEFORMATIONS OF THE MUSCULOSKELETAL SYSTEM (Q65-Q79)

- **Q65** **Congenital deformities of hip**
  - **Excludes1** clicking hip (R29.4)
  - **Q65.0** **Congenital dislocation of hip, unilateral**
    - **Q65.00** **Congenital dislocation of unspecified hip, unilateral**
    - **Q65.01** **Congenital dislocation of right hip, unilateral**
    - **Q65.02** **Congenital dislocation of left hip, unilateral**
  - **Q65.1** **Congenital dislocation of hip, bilateral**
  - **Q65.2** **Congenital dislocation of hip, unspecified**
  - **Q65.3** **Congenital partial dislocation of hip, unilateral**
    - **Q65.30** **Congenital partial dislocation of unspecified hip, unilateral**
    - **Q65.31** **Congenital partial dislocation of right hip, unilateral**
    - **Q65.32** **Congenital partial dislocation of left hip, unilateral**
  - **Q65.4** **Congenital partial dislocation of hip, bilateral**
  - **Q65.5** **Congenital partial dislocation of hip, unspecified**
  - **Q65.6** **Congenital unstable hip**
    Congenital dislocatable hip
  - **Q65.8** **Other congenital deformities of hip**
    - **Q65.81** **Congenital coxa valga**
    - **Q65.82** **Congenital coxa vara**
    - **Q65.89** **Other specified congenital deformities of hip**
      Anteversion of femoral neck
      Congenital acetabular dysplasia
  - **Q65.9** **Congenital deformity of hip, unspecified**

Item 17-2 **Equinus foot** is a term referring to the hoof of a horse. The deformity is usually congenital or spastic. **Talipes equinovarus** is referred to as clubfoot. The foot tends to be smaller than normal, with the heel pointing downward and the forefoot turning inward. The heel cord (Achilles tendon) is tight, causing the heel to be drawn up toward the leg.

Figure 17-6 Supination and cavus deformity of forefoot. (From Kliegman R, Nelson WE: Nelson Textbook of Pediatrics, Philadelphia, Saunders, 2007)

Figure 17-7 Talipes. (From Dorland: Dorland's Illustrated Medical Dictionary, ed 31, Saunders, 2007, p 1893)

● **Q66   Congenital deformities of feet**

   Excludes1   reduction defects of feet (Q72.-)
   valgus deformities (acquired) (M21.0-)
   varus deformities (acquired) (M21.1-)

● **Q66.0   Congenital talipes equinovarus**
   Heel is turned inward from midline and foot is plantar flexed; AKA clubfoot

   Q66.00   Congenital talipes equinovarus, unspecified foot

   Q66.01   Congenital talipes equinovarus, right foot

   Q66.02   Congenital talipes equinovarus, left foot

● **Q66.1   Congenital talipes calcaneovarus**
   Deformity of foot in which heel is turned toward midline of body and anterior of foot is elevated

   Q66.10   Congenital talipes calcaneovarus, unspecified foot

   Q66.11   Congenital talipes calcaneovarus, right foot

   Q66.12   Congenital talipes calcaneovarus, left foot

● **Q66.2   Congenital metatarsus (primus) varus**
   Angulation of first metatarsal bone toward midline of body
   Coding Clinic: 2016, Q4, P59

   ● **Q66.21   Congenital metatarsus primus varus**

      Q66.211   Congenital metatarsus primus varus, right foot

      Q66.212   Congenital metatarsus primus varus, left foot

      Q66.219   Congenital metatarsus primus varus, unspecified foot

   ● **Q66.22   Congenital metatarsus adductus**
      Congenital metatarsus varus

      Q66.221   Congenital metatarsus adductus, right foot

      Q66.222   Congenital metatarsus adductus, left foot

      Q66.229   Congenital metatarsus adductus, unspecified foot

● **Q66.3   Other congenital varus deformities of feet**
   Hallux varus, congenital

   Q66.30   Other congenital varus deformities of feet, unspecified foot

   Q66.31   Other congenital varus deformities of feet, right foot

   Q66.32   Other congenital varus deformities of feet, left foot

● **Q66.4   Congenital talipes calcaneovalgus**

   Q66.40   Congenital talipes calcaneovalgus, unspecified foot

   Q66.41   Congenital talipes calcaneovalgus, right foot

   Q66.42   Congenital talipes calcaneovalgus, left foot

● **Q66.5   Congenital pes planus**
   Congenital flat foot
   Congenital rigid flat foot
   Congenital spastic (everted) flat foot

   Excludes1   pes planus, acquired (M21.4)

   Q66.50   Congenital pes planus, unspecified foot

   Q66.51   Congenital pes planus, right foot

   Q66.52   Congenital pes planus, left foot

   Q66.6   Other congenital valgus deformities of feet
   Inward angulation
   Congenital metatarsus valgus

● **Q66.7   Congenital pes cavus**

   Q66.70   Congenital pes cavus, unspecified foot

   Q66.71   Congenital pes cavus, right foot

   Q66.72   Congenital pes cavus, left foot

● **Q66.8   Other congenital deformities of feet**

   Q66.80   Congenital vertical talus deformity, unspecified foot

   Q66.81   Congenital vertical talus deformity, right foot

   Q66.82   Congenital vertical talus deformity, left foot

   Q66.89   Other specified congenital deformities of feet
      Congenital asymmetric talipes
      Congenital clubfoot NOS
      Congenital talipes NOS
      Congenital tarsal coalition
      Hammer toe, congenital

● **Q66.9   Congenital deformity of feet, unspecified**

   Q66.90   Congenital deformity of feet, unspecified, unspecified foot

   Q66.91   Congenital deformity of feet, unspecified, right foot

   Q66.92   Congenital deformity of feet, unspecified, left foot

▶ New   ⟹ Revised   ~~deleted~~ Deleted   Excludes 1   Excludes 2   Includes   Use additional   Code first   Code also   Key words
OGCR Official Guidelines   X Assign placeholder X   ● Use Additional Character(s)   ▶ Manifestation Code   🅗🅒 Hierarchical Condition Category   Coding Clinic

Figure 17-8 Mild to moderate inbowing of the lower leg. (From Lissauer T, Clayden G: Illustrated Textbook of Paediatrics, Edinburgh, Mosby, 2011)

● **Q67   Congenital musculoskeletal deformities of head, face, spine and chest**

> **Excludes1** congenital malformation syndromes classified to Q87.-
> Potter's syndrome (Q60.6)

Q67.0   Congenital facial asymmetry

Q67.1   Congenital compression facies

Q67.2   Dolichocephaly
Long head dimension

Q67.3   Plagiocephaly
Asymmetric shape of head resulting from irregular closure of cranial sutures

Q67.4   Other congenital deformities of skull, face and jaw
Congenital depressions in skull
Congenital hemifacial atrophy or hypertrophy
Deviation of nasal septum, congenital
Squashed or bent nose, congenital

> **Excludes1** dentofacial anomalies [including malocclusion] (M26.-)
> syphilitic saddle nose (A50.5)

Q67.5   Congenital deformity of spine
Congenital postural scoliosis
Congenital scoliosis NOS

> **Excludes1** infantile idiopathic scoliosis (M41.0)
> scoliosis due to congenital bony malformation (Q76.3)

Q67.6   Pectus excavatum
Congenital funnel chest
Funnel-shaped chest depression

Q67.7   Pectus carinatum
Congenital pigeon chest

Q67.8   Other congenital deformities of chest
Congenital deformity of chest wall NOS

● **Q68   Other congenital musculoskeletal deformities**

> **Excludes1** reduction defects of limb(s) (Q71-Q73)
> **Excludes2** congenital myotonic chondrodystrophy (G71.13)

Q68.0   Congenital deformity of sternocleidomastoid muscle
Congenital contracture of sternocleidomastoid (muscle)
Congenital (sternomastoid) torticollis
Sternomastoid tumor (congenital)

Q68.1   Congenital deformity of finger(s) and hand
Congenital clubfinger
Spade-like hand (congenital)

Q68.2   Congenital deformity of knee
Congenital dislocation of knee
Congenital genu recurvatum
Hyperextension of knee resulting from hypermobility

Q68.3   Congenital bowing of femur

> **Excludes1** anteversion of femur (neck) (Q65.89)

Q68.4   Congenital bowing of tibia and fibula

Q68.5   Congenital bowing of long bones of leg, unspecified

Q68.6   Discoid meniscus

Q68.8   Other specified congenital musculoskeletal deformities
Congenital deformity of clavicle
Congenital deformity of elbow
Congenital deformity of forearm
Congenital deformity of scapula
Congenital deformity of wrist
Congenital dislocation of elbow
Congenital dislocation of shoulder
Congenital dislocation of wrist

● **Q69   Polydactyly**
AKA hyperdactyly, consists of supernumerary fingers or toes

Q69.0   Accessory finger(s)

Q69.1   Accessory thumb(s)

Q69.2   Accessory toe(s)
Accessory hallux

Q69.9   Polydactyly, unspecified
Supernumerary digit(s) NOS

● **Q70   Syndactyly**
Webbing between distal phalanges of adjacent digits

● **Q70.0   Fused fingers**
Complex syndactyly of fingers with synostosis

Q70.00   Fused fingers, unspecified hand

Q70.01   Fused fingers, right hand

Q70.02   Fused fingers, left hand

Q70.03   Fused fingers, bilateral

● **Q70.1   Webbed fingers**
Simple syndactyly of fingers without synostosis

Q70.10   Webbed fingers, unspecified hand

Q70.11   Webbed fingers, right hand

Q70.12   Webbed fingers, left hand

Q70.13   Webbed fingers, bilateral

● **Q70.2   Fused toes**
Complex syndactyly of toes with synostosis

Q70.20   Fused toes, unspecified foot

Q70.21   Fused toes, right foot

Q70.22   Fused toes, left foot

Q70.23   Fused toes, bilateral

● **Q70.3   Webbed toes**
Simple syndactyly of toes without synostosis

Q70.30   Webbed toes, unspecified foot

Q70.31   Webbed toes, right foot

Q70.32   Webbed toes, left foot

Q70.33   Webbed toes, bilateral

Q70.4   Polysyndactyly, unspecified

> **Excludes1** specified syndactyly of hand and feet - code to specified conditions (Q70.0- -Q70.3-)

Extra and webbed digits

Q70.9   Syndactyly, unspecified
Symphalangy NOS

Figure 17-9 Thumb and index finger. (From Chung K: Hand and Upper Extremity Reconstruction, 1e, Saunders, 2008)

● **Q71** **Reduction defects of upper limb**

  ● **Q71.0** Congenital complete absence of upper limb

    Q71.00   Congenital complete absence of unspecified upper limb

    Q71.01   Congenital complete absence of right upper limb

    Q71.02   Congenital complete absence of left upper limb

    Q71.03   Congenital complete absence of upper limb, bilateral

  ● **Q71.1** Congenital absence of upper arm and forearm with hand present

    Q71.10   Congenital absence of unspecified upper arm and forearm with hand present

    Q71.11   Congenital absence of right upper arm and forearm with hand present

    Q71.12   Congenital absence of left upper arm and forearm with hand present

    Q71.13   Congenital absence of upper arm and forearm with hand present, bilateral

  ● **Q71.2** Congenital absence of both forearm and hand

    Q71.20   Congenital absence of both forearm and hand, unspecified upper limb

    Q71.21   Congenital absence of both forearm and hand, right upper limb

    Q71.22   Congenital absence of both forearm and hand, left upper limb

    Q71.23   Congenital absence of both forearm and hand, bilateral

  ● **Q71.3** Congenital absence of hand and finger

    Q71.30   Congenital absence of unspecified hand and finger

    Q71.31   Congenital absence of right hand and finger

    Q71.32   Congenital absence of left hand and finger

    Q71.33   Congenital absence of hand and finger, bilateral

  ● **Q71.4** Longitudinal reduction defect of radius
      Clubhand (congenital)
      Radial clubhand

    Q71.40   Longitudinal reduction defect of unspecified radius

    Q71.41   Longitudinal reduction defect of right radius

    Q71.42   Longitudinal reduction defect of left radius

    Q71.43   Longitudinal reduction defect of radius, bilateral

  ● **Q71.5** Longitudinal reduction defect of ulna

    Q71.50   Longitudinal reduction defect of unspecified ulna

    Q71.51   Longitudinal reduction defect of right ulna

    Q71.52   Longitudinal reduction defect of left ulna

    Q71.53   Longitudinal reduction defect of ulna, bilateral

  ● **Q71.6** Lobster-claw hand

    Q71.60   Lobster-claw hand, unspecified hand

    Q71.61   Lobster-claw right hand

    Q71.62   Lobster-claw left hand

    Q71.63   Lobster-claw hand, bilateral

  ● **Q71.8** Other reduction defects of upper limb

    ● **Q71.81** Congenital shortening of upper limb

      Q71.811   Congenital shortening of right upper limb

      Q71.812   Congenital shortening of left upper limb

      Q71.813   Congenital shortening of upper limb, bilateral

      Q71.819   Congenital shortening of unspecified upper limb

    Q71.89   Other reduction defects of upper limb

      Q71.891   Other reduction defects of right upper limb

      Q71.892   Other reduction defects of left upper limb

      Q71.893   Other reduction defects of upper limb, bilateral

      Q71.899   Other reduction defects of unspecified upper limb

  ● **Q71.9** Unspecified reduction defect of upper limb

    Q71.90   Unspecified reduction defect of unspecified upper limb

    Q71.91   Unspecified reduction defect of right upper limb

    Q71.92   Unspecified reduction defect of left upper limb

    Q71.93   Unspecified reduction defect of upper limb, bilateral

● **Q72** **Reduction defects of lower limb**

  ● **Q72.0** Congenital complete absence of lower limb

    Q72.00   Congenital complete absence of unspecified lower limb

    Q72.01   Congenital complete absence of right lower limb

    Q72.02   Congenital complete absence of left lower limb

    Q72.03   Congenital complete absence of lower limb, bilateral

  ● **Q72.1** Congenital absence of thigh and lower leg with foot present

    Q72.10   Congenital absence of unspecified thigh and lower leg with foot present

    Q72.11   Congenital absence of right thigh and lower leg with foot present

    Q72.12   Congenital absence of left thigh and lower leg with foot present

    Q72.13   Congenital absence of thigh and lower leg with foot present, bilateral

  ● **Q72.2** Congenital absence of both lower leg and foot

    Q72.20   Congenital absence of both lower leg and foot, unspecified lower limb

    Q72.21   Congenital absence of both lower leg and foot, right lower limb

    Q72.22   Congenital absence of both left lower leg and foot, left lower limb

    Q72.23   Congenital absence of both lower leg and foot, bilateral

  ● **Q72.3** Congenital absence of foot and toe(s)

    Q72.30   Congenital absence of unspecified foot and toe(s)

    Q72.31   Congenital absence of right foot and toe(s)

    Q72.32   Congenital absence of left foot and toe(s)

    Q72.33   Congenital absence of foot and toe(s), bilateral

  ● **Q72.4** Longitudinal reduction defect of femur
      Proximal femoral focal deficiency

    Q72.40   Longitudinal reduction defect of unspecified femur

    Q72.41   Longitudinal reduction defect of right femur

    Q72.42   Longitudinal reduction defect of left femur

    Q72.43   Longitudinal reduction defect of femur, bilateral

  ● **Q72.5** Longitudinal reduction defect of tibia

    Q72.50   Longitudinal reduction defect of unspecified tibia

    Q72.51   Longitudinal reduction defect of right tibia

    Q72.52   Longitudinal reduction defect of left tibia

    Q72.53   Longitudinal reduction defect of tibia, bilateral

▶ New   ⇒ Revised   ~~deleted~~ Deleted   Excludes 1   Excludes 2   Includes   Use additional   Code first   Code also   Key words

OGCR Official Guidelines   X Assign placeholder X   ● Use Additional Character(s)   ▶ Manifestation Code   🅀 Hierarchical Condition Category   **Coding Clinic**

- **Q72.6**   Longitudinal reduction defect of fibula
  - **Q72.60**   Longitudinal reduction defect of unspecified fibula
  - **Q72.61**   Longitudinal reduction defect of right fibula
  - **Q72.62**   Longitudinal reduction defect of left fibula
  - **Q72.63**   Longitudinal reduction defect of fibula, bilateral
- **Q72.7**   Split foot
  - **Q72.70**   Split foot, unspecified lower limb
  - **Q72.71**   Split foot, right lower limb
  - **Q72.72**   Split foot, left lower limb
  - **Q72.73**   Split foot, bilateral
- **Q72.8**   Other reduction defects of lower limb
  - **Q72.81**   Congenital shortening of lower limb
    - **Q72.811**   Congenital shortening of right lower limb
    - **Q72.812**   Congenital shortening of left lower limb
    - **Q72.813**   Congenital shortening of lower limb, bilateral
    - **Q72.819**   Congenital shortening of unspecified lower limb
  - **Q72.89**   Other reduction defects of lower limb
    - **Q72.891**   Other reduction defects of right lower limb
    - **Q72.892**   Other reduction defects of left lower limb
    - **Q72.893**   Other reduction defects of lower limb, bilateral
    - **Q72.899**   Other reduction defects of unspecified lower limb
- **Q72.9**   Unspecified reduction defect of lower limb
  - **Q72.90**   Unspecified reduction defect of unspecified lower limb
  - **Q72.91**   Unspecified reduction defect of right lower limb
  - **Q72.92**   Unspecified reduction defect of left lower limb
  - **Q72.93**   Unspecified reduction defect of lower limb, bilateral

- **Q73**   Reduction defects of unspecified limb
  - **Q73.0**   Congenital absence of unspecified limb(s)
    - Amelia NOS
  - **Q73.1**   Phocomelia, unspecified limb(s)
    - Phocomelia NOS
    - *Absence/shortening of long bones primarily as a result of thalidomide*
  - **Q73.8**   Other reduction defects of unspecified limb(s)
    - Longitudinal reduction deformity of unspecified limb(s)
    - Ectromelia of limb NOS
    - *Gross hypoplasia or aplasia of one or more long bones of limb(s)*
    - Hemimelia of limb NOS
    - *Absence of one-half of long bone*
    - Reduction defect of limb NOS

- **Q74**   Other congenital malformations of limb(s)
  - **Excludes1**   polydactyly (Q69.-)
    - reduction defect of limb (Q71-Q73)
    - syndactyly (Q70.-)
  - **Q74.0**   Other congenital malformations of upper limb(s), including shoulder girdle
    - Accessory carpal bones
    - Cleidocranial dysostosis
    - Congenital pseudarthrosis of clavicle
    - Macrodactylia (fingers)
    - Madelung's deformity
    - Radioulnar synostosis
    - Sprengel's deformity
    - Triphalangeal thumb

- **Q74.1**   Congenital malformation of knee
  - Congenital absence of patella
  - Congenital dislocation of patella
  - Congenital genu valgum
  - Congenital genu varum
  - Rudimentary patella
  - **Excludes1**   congenital dislocation of knee (Q68.2)
    - congenital genu recurvatum (Q68.2)
    - nail patella syndrome (Q87.2)
- **Q74.2**   Other congenital malformations of lower limb(s), including pelvic girdle
  - Congenital fusion of sacroiliac joint
  - Congenital malformation of ankle joint
  - Congenital malformation of sacroiliac joint
  - **Excludes1**   anteversion of femur (neck) (Q65.89)
- **Q74.3**   Arthrogryposis multiplex congenita
- **Q74.8**   Other specified congenital malformations of limb(s)
- **Q74.9**   Unspecified congenital malformation of limb(s)
  - Congenital anomaly of limb(s) NOS

- **Q75**   Other congenital malformations of skull and face bones
  - **Excludes1**   congenital malformation of face NOS (Q18.-)
    - congenital malformation syndromes classified to Q87.-
    - dentofacial anomalies [including malocclusion] (M26.-)
    - musculoskeletal deformities of head and face (Q67.0-Q67.4)
    - skull defects associated with congenital anomalies of brain such as:
      - anencephaly (Q00.0)
      - encephalocele (Q01.-)
      - hydrocephalus (Q03.-)
      - microcephaly (Q02)
  - **Q75.0**   Craniosynostosis
    - *Premature closure of sutures of skull*
    - Acrocephaly
    - Imperfect fusion of skull
    - Oxycephaly
    - Trigonocephaly
  - **Q75.1**   Craniofacial dysostosis
    - *Congenital deformity of head*
    - Crouzon's disease
  - **Q75.2**   Hypertelorism
  - **Q75.3**   Macrocephaly
    - *Unusually large size of head; AKA megalocephaly*
  - **Q75.4**   Mandibulofacial dysostosis
    - Franceschetti syndrome
    - Treacher Collins syndrome
  - **Q75.5**   Oculomandibular dysostosis
    - *Ossification of occular and mandibular bones*

Item 17–3   **Anencephalus** is a congenital deformity of the cranial vault. **Craniosynostosis,** also known as craniostenosis and stenocephaly, signifies any form of congenital deformity of the skull that results from the premature closing of the sutures of the skull. **Iniencephaly** is a deformity in which the head and neck are flexed backward to a great extent and the head is very large in comparison to the shortened body.

Figure 17-10   Generalized craniosynostosis without symptoms or signs of increased intracranial pressure. (From Goetz C: Textbook of Clinical Neurology, St. Louis, MO, Elsevier, 2007)

Q75.8   Other specified congenital malformations of skull and face bones
Absence of skull bone, congenital
Congenital deformity of forehead
Platybasia

Q75.9   Congenital malformation of skull and face bones, unspecified
Congenital anomaly of face bones NOS
Congenital anomaly of skull NOS

● **Q76   Congenital malformations of spine and bony thorax**
Excludes1   congenital musculoskeletal deformities of spine and chest (Q67.5-Q67.8)

Q76.0   Spina bifida occulta
Excludes1   meningocele (spinal) (Q05.-)
spina bifida (aperta) (cystica) (Q05.-)

Q76.1   Klippel-Feil syndrome
Cervical fusion syndrome

Q76.2   Congenital spondylolisthesis
Congenital spondylolysis
Excludes1   spondylolisthesis (acquired) (M43.1-)
spondylolysis (acquired) (M43.0-)

Q76.3   Congenital scoliosis due to congenital bony malformation
Hemivertebra fusion or failure of segmentation with scoliosis

● **Q76.4   Other congenital malformations of spine, not associated with scoliosis**

● **Q76.41   Congenital kyphosis**
Abnormal increase in convexity curvature of thoracic spinal column; AKA humpback

Q76.411   Congenital kyphosis, occipito-atlanto-axial region

Q76.412   Congenital kyphosis, cervical region

Q76.413   Congenital kyphosis, cervicothoracic region

Q76.414   Congenital kyphosis, thoracic region

Q76.415   Congenital kyphosis, thoracolumbar region

Q76.419   Congenital kyphosis, unspecified region

● **Q76.42   Congenital lordosis**
An abnormal increase in curvature of lumbar spine (sway back)

Q76.425   Congenital lordosis, thoracolumbar region

Q76.426   Congenital lordosis, lumbar region

Q76.427   Congenital lordosis, lumbosacral region

Q76.428   Congenital lordosis, sacral and sacrococcygeal region

Q76.429   Congenital lordosis, unspecified region

Q76.49   Other congenital malformations of spine, not associated with scoliosis
Congenital absence of vertebra NOS
Congenital fusion of spine NOS
Congenital malformation of lumbosacral (joint) (region) NOS
Congenital malformation of spine NOS
Hemivertebra NOS
Malformation of spine NOS
Platyspondylisis NOS
Supernumerary vertebra NOS

Q76.5   Cervical rib
Supernumerary rib in cervical region

Q76.6   Other congenital malformations of ribs
Accessory rib
Congenital absence of rib
Congenital fusion of ribs
Congenital malformation of ribs NOS
Excludes1   short rib syndrome (Q77.2)

Q76.7   Congenital malformation of sternum
Congenital absence of sternum
Sternum bifidum

Q76.8   Other congenital malformations of bony thorax

Q76.9   Congenital malformation of bony thorax, unspecified

● **Q77   Osteochondrodysplasia with defects of growth of tubular bones and spine**
Excludes1   mucopolysaccharidosis (E76.0-E76.3)
Excludes2   congenital myotonic chondrodystrophy (G71.13)

Q77.0   Achondrogenesis
Hypochondrogenesis

Q77.1   Thanatophoric short stature

Q77.2   Short rib syndrome
Asphyxiating thoracic dysplasia [Jeune]

Q77.3   Chondrodysplasia punctata
Benign cartilaginous neoplasms
Excludes1   rhizomelic chondrodysplasia punctata (E71.43)

Q77.4   Achondroplasia
Disturbance of epiphyseal chondroblastic growth and maturation, results in dwarfism
Hypochondroplasia
Osteosclerosis congenita

Q77.5   Diastrophic dysplasia

Q77.6   Chondroectodermal dysplasia
Defective development of skin, hair, teeth, with polydactyly and defect of cardiac septum
Ellis-van Creveld syndrome

Q77.7   Spondyloepiphyseal dysplasia

Q77.8   Other osteochondrodysplasia with defects of growth of tubular bones and spine

Q77.9   Osteochondrodysplasia with defects of growth of tubular bones and spine, unspecified

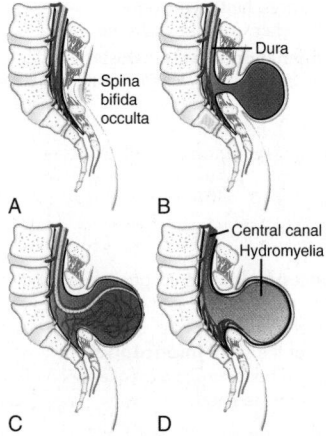

Figure 17-11   A. Spina bifida occulta. **B.** Meningocele.
C. Myelomeningocele. **D.** Myelocystocele (syringomyelocele) or hydromyelia.

Item 17-4   Spina bifida is a midline spinal defect in which one or more vertebrae fail to fuse, leaving an opening in the vertebral canal. When the defect is not visible, it is called spina bifida occulta, and when it is visible, it is called spina bifida cystica.

▶ New   ⇒ Revised   ~~deleted~~ Deleted   Excludes 1   Excludes 2   Includes   Use additional   Code first   Code also   Key words
OGCR Official Guidelines   X Assign placeholder X   ● Use Additional Character(s)   ) Manifestation Code   🔖 Hierarchical Condition Category   **Coding Clinic**

● **Q78 Other osteochondrodysplasias**
Disorder of development of bone and cartilage; common cause of dwarfism

>   **Excludes2**   congenital myotonic chondrodystrophy (G71.13)

Q78.0 Osteogenesis imperfecta
Fragilitas ossium
Osteopsathyrosis

Q78.1 Polyostotic fibrous dysplasia
Albright(-McCune)(-Sternberg) syndrome

Q78.2 Osteopetrosis
Abnormally dense bone; AKA marble bones disease, ivory bones
Albers-Schönberg syndrome
Osteosclerosis NOS

Q78.3 Progressive diaphyseal dysplasia
Camurati-Engelmann syndrome

Q78.4 Enchondromatosis
Thinning of overlying cortex of bone and distorted length
Maffucci's syndrome
Ollier's disease

Q78.5 Metaphyseal dysplasia
Disturbance in enchondral bone growth, causing ends of shafts to remain larger than normal in circumference
Pyle's syndrome

Q78.6 Multiple congenital exostoses
Diaphyseal aclasis

Q78.8 Other specified osteochondrodysplasias
Osteopoikilosis

Q78.9 Osteochondrodysplasia, unspecified
Chondrodystrophy NOS
AKA skeletal dysplasia (dwarfism) caused by genetic mutations affecting hyaline cartilage capping long bones and vertebrae
Osteodystrophy NOS

● **Q79 Congenital malformations of musculoskeletal system, not elsewhere classified**

>   **Excludes2**   congenital (sternomastoid) torticollis (Q68.0)

Q79.0 Congenital diaphragmatic hernia

>   **Excludes1**   congenital hiatus hernia (Q40.1)

Q79.1 Other congenital malformations of diaphragm
Absence of diaphragm
Congenital malformation of diaphragm NOS
Eventration of diaphragm

Q79.2 Exomphalos
Abdominal hernia in which part of intestine protrudes at umbilicus; AKA exomphalos and exumbilication
Omphalocele

>   **Excludes1**   umbilical hernia (K42.-)

Q79.3 Gastroschisis
Congenital fissure of anterior abdominal wall often with protrusion of small/large intestine

Q79.4 Prune belly syndrome
Congenital prolapse of bladder mucosa
Eagle-Barrett syndrome

● **Q79.5 Other congenital malformations of abdominal wall**

>   **Excludes1**   umbilical hernia (K42.-)

Q79.51 Congenital hernia of bladder

Q79.59 Other congenital malformations of abdominal wall

● **Q79.6 Ehlers-Danlos syndromes**
Group of inherited disorders of connective tissue; AKA cutis hyperelastica

Q79.60 Ehlers-Danlos syndrome, unspecified

Q79.61 Classical Ehlers-Danlos syndrome
Classical EDS (cEDS)

Q79.62 Hypermobile Ehlers-Danlos syndrome
Hypermobile EDS (hEDS)

Q79.63 Vascular Ehlers-Danlos syndrome
Vascular EDS (vEDS)

Q79.69 Other Ehlers-Danlos syndromes

Q79.8 Other congenital malformations of musculoskeletal system
Absence of muscle
Absence of tendon
Accessory muscle
Amyotrophia congenita
Congenital constricting bands
Congenital shortening of tendon
Poland syndrome

Q79.9 Congenital malformation of musculoskeletal system, unspecified
Congenital anomaly of musculoskeletal system NOS
Congenital deformity of musculoskeletal system NOS

OTHER CONGENITAL MALFORMATIONS (Q80-Q89)

● **Q80 Congenital ichthyosis**
Characterized by increased keratinization, resulting in noninflammatory scaling of skin

>   **Excludes1**   Refsum's disease (G60.1)

Q80.0 Ichthyosis vulgaris

Q80.1 X-linked ichthyosis

Q80.2 Lamellar ichthyosis
Collodion baby

Q80.3 Congenital bullous ichthyosiform erythroderma

Q80.4 Harlequin fetus

Q80.8 Other congenital ichthyosis

Q80.9 Congenital ichthyosis, unspecified

● **Q81 Epidermolysis bullosa**
Loosening of epidermis

Q81.0 Epidermolysis bullosa simplex

>   **Excludes1**   Cockayne's syndrome (Q87.19)

Q81.1 Epidermolysis bullosa letalis
Herlitz' syndrome

Q81.2 Epidermolysis bullosa dystrophica

Q81.8 Other epidermolysis bullosa

Q81.9 Epidermolysis bullosa, unspecified

● **Q82 Other congenital malformations of skin**

>   **Excludes1**   acrodermatitis enteropathica (E83.2)
>   congenital erythropoietic porphyria (E80.0)
>   pilonidal cyst or sinus (L05.-)
>   Sturge-Weber (-Dimitri) syndrome (Q85.8)

Q82.0 Hereditary lymphedema
Characterized by swelling of subcutaneous tissue caused by obstruction of lymphatic vessels and resulting edema of lymph fluid

Q82.1 Xeroderma pigmentosum
Extreme sensitivity to ultraviolet rays that most commonly affects the eyes and skin, but may also involve the nervous system

Q82.2 Congenital cutaneous mastocytosis
Characterized by infiltrates of mast cells in tissues/organs
Congenital diffuse cutaneous mastocytosis
Congenital maculopapular cutaneous mastocytosis
Congenital urticaria pigmentosa

>   **Excludes1**   cutaneous mastocytosis NOS (D47.01)
>   diffuse cutaneous mastocytosis (with onset after newborn period) (D47.01)
>   malignant mastocytosis (C96.2-)
>   systemic mastocytosis (D47.02)
>   urticaria pigmentosa (non-congenital) (with onset after newborn period) (D47.01)

Q82.3 Incontinentia pigmenti
Characterized by hypopigmented cutaneous in adults and early childhood

Q82.4 Ectodermal dysplasia (anhidrotic)
Absence/deficiency of tissues/structures, including teeth, hair, nails, and certain glands

>   **Excludes1**   Ellis-van Creveld syndrome (Q77.6)

Q82.5   **Congenital non-neoplastic nevus**
    Birthmark NOS
    Flammeus Nevus
    Portwine Nevus
    Sanguineous Nevus
    Strawberry Nevus
    Vascular Nevus NOS
    Verrucous Nevus
    Excludes2   Café au lait spots (L81.3)
              lentigo (L81.4)
              nevus NOS (D22.-)
              araneus nevus (I78.1)
              melanocytic nevus (D22.-)
              pigmented nevus (D22.-)
              spider nevus (I78.1)
              stellar nevus (I78.1)

Q82.6   **Congenital sacral dimple**
    Parasacral dimple
    Excludes2   pilonidal cyst with abscess (L05.01)
              pilonidal cyst without abscess (L05.91)
    Coding Clinic: 2016, Q4, P60

Q82.8   **Other specified congenital malformations of skin**
    Abnormal palmar creases
    Accessory skin tags
    Benign familial pemphigus [Hailey-Hailey]
    Congenital poikiloderma
    Cutis laxa (hyperelastica)
    Dermatoglyphic anomalies
    Inherited keratosis palmaris et plantaris
    Keratosis follicularis [Darier-White]
    Excludes1   Ehlers-Danlos syndromes (Q79.6-)
    Coding Clinic: 2016, Q1, P17

Q82.9   **Congenital malformation of skin, unspecified**

● Q83 Congenital malformations of breast
    Excludes2   absence of pectoral muscle (Q79.8)
              hypoplasia of breast (N64.82)
              micromastia (N64.82)

Q83.0   **Congenital absence of breast with absent nipple**

Q83.1   **Accessory breast**
    Supernumerary breast

Q83.2   **Absent nipple**

Q83.3   **Accessory nipple**
    Supernumerary nipple

Q83.8   **Other congenital malformations of breast**

Q83.9   **Congenital malformation of breast, unspecified**

● Q84 Other congenital malformations of integument

Q84.0   **Congenital alopecia**
    Congenital atrichosis

Q84.1   **Congenital morphological disturbances of hair, not elsewhere classified**
    Beaded hair
    Monilethrix
    Pili annulati
    Excludes1   Menkes' kinky hair syndrome (E83.0)

Q84.2   **Other congenital malformations of hair**
    Congenital hypertrichosis
    Congenital malformation of hair NOS
    Persistent lanugo

Q84.3   **Anonychia**
    Absence of nail
    Excludes1   nail patella syndrome (Q87.2)

Q84.4   **Congenital leukonychia**
    Opaque, whitish discoloration of nails; AKA leukopathia unguium

Q84.5   **Enlarged and hypertrophic nails**
    Congenital onychauxis
    Pachyonychia

Q84.6   **Other congenital malformations of nails**
    Congenital clubnail
    Congenital koilonychia
    Congenital malformation of nail NOS

Q84.8   **Other specified congenital malformations of integument**
    Aplasia cutis congenita

Q84.9   **Congenital malformation of integument, unspecified**
    Congenital anomaly of integument NOS
    Congenital deformity of integument NOS

● Q85 Phakomatoses, not elsewhere classified
    Excludes1   ataxia telangiectasia [Louis-Bar] (G11.3)
              familial dysautonomia [Riley-Day] (G90.1)

● Q85.0 Neurofibromatosis (nonmalignant)
    Developmental changes in nervous system and other structures, with formation of neurofibromas

Q85.00   **Neurofibromatosis, unspecified** 🐾

Q85.01   **Neurofibromatosis, type 1** 🐾
    Von Recklinghausen disease

Q85.02   **Neurofibromatosis, type 2** 🐾
    Acoustic neurofibromatosis

Q85.03   **Schwannomatosis** 🐾

Q85.09   **Other neurofibromatosis** 🐾

Q85.1   **Tuberous sclerosis** 🐾
    Bourneville's disease
    Epiloia

Q85.8   **Other phakomatoses, not elsewhere classified** 🐾
    Peutz-Jeghers Syndrome
    Sturge-Weber(-Dimitri) syndrome
    von Hippel-Lindau syndrome
    Excludes1   Meckel-Gruber syndrome (Q61.9)

Q85.9   **Phakomatosis, unspecified** 🐾
    Hamartosis NOS

● Q86 Congenital malformation syndromes due to known exogenous causes, not elsewhere classified
    Excludes2   iodine-deficiency-related hypothyroidism (E00-E02)
              nonteratogenic effects of substances transmitted via placenta or breast milk (P04.-)

Q86.0   **Fetal alcohol syndrome (dysmorphic)**

Q86.1   **Fetal hydantoin syndrome**
    Meadow's syndrome

Q86.2   **Dysmorphism due to warfarin**

Q86.8   **Other congenital malformation syndromes due to known exogenous causes**

● Q87 Other specified congenital malformation syndromes affecting multiple systems
    Use additional code(s) to identify all associated manifestations

Q87.0   **Congenital malformation syndromes predominantly affecting facial appearance**
    Acrocephalopolysyndactyly
    Acrocephalosyndactyly [Apert]
    Cryptophthalmos syndrome
    Cyclopia
    Goldenhar syndrome
    Moebius syndrome
    Oro-facial-digital syndrome
    Robin syndrome
    Whistling face

● Q87.1 Congenital malformation syndromes predominantly associated with short stature

Q87.11   **Prader-Willi syndrome**

Q87.19   **Other congenital malformation syndromes predominantly associated with short stature**
    Aarskog syndrome
    Cockayne syndrome
    De Lange syndrome
    Dubowitz syndrome
    Noonan syndrome
    Robinow-Silverman-Smith syndrome
    Russell-Silver syndrome
    Seckel syndrome
    Excludes1   Ellis-van Creveld syndrome (Q77.6)
              Smith-Lemli-Opitz syndrome (E78.72)

▶ New   ⇒ Revised   ~~deleted~~ Deleted   Excludes 1   Excludes 2   Includes   Use additional   Code first   Code also   Key words
OGCR Official Guidelines   **X** Assign placeholder X   ● Use Additional Character(s)   》 Manifestation Code   🐾 Hierarchical Condition Category   **Coding Clinic**

Q87.2   Congenital malformation syndromes predominantly involving limbs
    Holt-Oram syndrome
    Klippel-Trenaunay-Weber syndrome
    Nail patella syndrome
    Rubinstein-Taybi syndrome
    Sirenomelia syndrome
    Thrombocytopenia with absent radius [TAR] syndrome
    VATER syndrome

Q87.3   Congenital malformation syndromes involving early overgrowth
    Beckwith-Wiedemann syndrome
    Sotos' syndrome
    Weaver syndrome

● **Q87.4   Marfan's syndrome**

    Q87.40   Marfan's syndrome, unspecified

  ● **Q87.41   Marfan's syndrome with cardiovascular manifestations**

        Q87.410   Marfan's syndrome with aortic dilation

        Q87.418   Marfan's syndrome with other cardiovascular manifestations

    Q87.42   Marfan's syndrome with ocular manifestations

    Q87.43   Marfan's syndrome with skeletal manifestation

Q87.5   Other congenital malformation syndromes with other skeletal changes

● **Q87.8   Other specified congenital malformation syndromes, not elsewhere classified**

    Excludes1   Zellweger syndrome (E71.510)

    Q87.81   Alport syndrome
        Progressive sensorineural hearing loss, progressive pyelonephritis or glomerulonephritis, and ocular defects

        Use additional code to identify stage of chronic kidney disease (N18.1-N18.6)

    Q87.82   Arterial tortuosity syndrome
        Coding Clinic: 2016, Q4, P60-61

    Q87.89   Other specified congenital malformation syndromes, not elsewhere classified
        Laurence-Moon (-Bardet)-Biedl syndrome

● **Q89   Other congenital malformations, not elsewhere classified**

  ● **Q89.0   Congenital absence and malformations of spleen**

    Excludes1   isomerism of atrial appendages (with asplenia or polysplenia) (Q20.6)

    Q89.01   Asplenia (congenital)

    Q89.09   Congenital malformations of spleen
        Congenital splenomegaly

Q89.1   Congenital malformations of adrenal gland

    Excludes1   adrenogenital disorders (E25.-)
                 congenital adrenal hyperplasia (E25.0)

Q89.2   Congenital malformations of other endocrine glands
    Congenital malformation of parathyroid or thyroid gland
    Persistent thyroglossal duct
    Thyroglossal cyst

    Excludes1   congenital goiter (E03.0)
                 congenital hypothyroidism (E03.1)

Q89.3   Situs inversus
    Lateral transposition of viscera of thorax and abdomen
    Dextrocardia with situs inversus
    Mirror-image atrial arrangement with situs inversus
    Situs inversus or transversus abdominalis
    Situs inversus or transversus thoracis
    Transposition of abdominal viscera
    Transposition of thoracic viscera

    Excludes1   dextrocardia NOS (Q24.0)

Q89.4   Conjoined twins
    Craniopagus
    Dicephaly
    Pygopagus
    Thoracopagus

Q89.7   Multiple congenital malformations, not elsewhere classified
    Multiple congenital anomalies NOS
    Multiple congenital deformities NOS

    Excludes1   congenital malformation syndromes affecting multiple systems (Q87.-)

Q89.8   Other specified congenital malformations
    Use additional code(s) to identify all associated manifestations

Q89.9   Congenital malformation, unspecified
    Congenital anomaly NOS
    Congenital deformity NOS

CHROMOSOMAL ABNORMALITIES, NOT ELSEWHERE CLASSIFIED (Q90-Q99)

    Excludes2   mitochondrial metabolic disorders (E88.4-)

● **Q90   Down syndrome**
    Use additional code(s) to identify any associated physical conditions and degree of intellectual disabilities (F70-F79)

    Q90.0   Trisomy 21, nonmosaicism (meiotic nondisjunction)
        Trisomy 21, nondisjunction, accounts for 95% of Downs syndrome cases

    Q90.1   Trisomy 21, mosaicism (mitotic nondisjunction)

    Q90.2   Trisomy 21, translocation

    Q90.9   Down syndrome, unspecified
        Trisomy 21 NOS

● **Q91   Trisomy 18 and Trisomy 13**

    Q91.0   Trisomy 18, nonmosaicism (meiotic nondisjunction)

    Q91.1   Trisomy 18, mosaicism (mitotic nondisjunction)

    Q91.2   Trisomy 18, translocation

    Q91.3   Trisomy 18, unspecified

    Q91.4   Trisomy 13, nonmosaicism (meiotic nondisjunction)

    Q91.5   Trisomy 13, mosaicism (mitotic nondisjunction)

    Q91.6   Trisomy 13, translocation

    Q91.7   Trisomy 13, unspecified

● **Q92   Other trisomies and partial trisomies of the autosomes, not elsewhere classified**

    Includes   unbalanced translocations and insertions

    Excludes1   trisomies of chromosomes 13, 18, 21 (Q90-Q91)

    Q92.0   Whole chromosome trisomy, nonmosaicism (meiotic nondisjunction)

    Q92.1   Whole chromosome trisomy, mosaicism (mitotic nondisjunction)

    Q92.2   Partial trisomy
        Less than whole arm duplicated
        Whole arm or more duplicated

        Excludes1   partial trisomy due to unbalanced translocation (Q92.5)

    Q92.5   Duplications with other complex rearrangements
        Partial trisomy due to unbalanced translocations

        Code also any associated deletions due to unbalanced translocations, inversions and insertions (Q93.7)

● **Q92.6   Marker chromosomes**
        Trisomies due to dicentrics
        Trisomies due to extra rings
        Trisomies due to isochromosomes
        Individual with marker heterochromatin

        Q92.61   Marker chromosomes in normal individual

        Q92.62   Marker chromosomes in abnormal individual

    Q92.7   Triploidy and polyploidy

    Q92.8   Other specified trisomies and partial trisomies of autosomes
        Duplications identified by fluorescence in situ hybridization (FISH)
        Duplications identified by in situ hybridization (ISH)
        Duplications seen only at prometaphase

    Q92.9   Trisomy and partial trisomy of autosomes, unspecified

● Q93   **Monosomies and deletions from the autosomes, not elsewhere classified**

     Q93.0   **Whole chromosome monosomy, nonmosaicism (meiotic nondisjunction)**

     Q93.1   **Whole chromosome monosomy, mosaicism (mitotic nondisjunction)**

     Q93.2   **Chromosome replaced with ring, dicentric or isochromosome**

     Q93.3   **Deletion of short arm of chromosome 4**
             Wolff-Hirschorn syndrome

     Q93.4   **Deletion of short arm of chromosome 5**
             Cri-du-chat syndrome

●   Q93.5   **Other deletions of part of a chromosome**

         Q93.51   **Angelman syndrome**

         Q93.59   **Other deletions of part of a chromosome**

     Q93.7   **Deletions with other complex rearrangements**
             Deletions due to unbalanced translocations, inversions and insertions
             Code also any associated duplications due to unbalanced translocations, inversions and insertions (Q92.5)

●   Q93.8   **Other deletions from the autosomes**

         Q93.81   **Velo-cardio-facial syndrome**
                Deletion 22q11.2
                Coding Clinic: 2019, Q3, P14

         Q93.82   **Williams syndrome**

         Q93.88   **Other microdeletions Miller-Dieker syndrome**
                Smith-Magenis syndrome

         Q93.89   **Other deletions from the autosomes**
                Deletions identified by fluorescence in situ hybridization (FISH)
                Deletions identified by in situ hybridization (ISH)
                Deletions seen only at prometaphase

     Q93.9   **Deletion from autosomes, unspecified**

● Q95   **Balanced rearrangements and structural markers, not elsewhere classified**

     Includes   Robertsonian and balanced reciprocal translocations and insertions

     Q95.0   **Balanced translocation and insertion in normal individual**

     Q95.1   **Chromosome inversion in normal individual**

     Q95.2   **Balanced autosomal rearrangement in abnormal individual**

     Q95.3   **Balanced sex/autosomal rearrangement in abnormal individual**

     Q95.5   **Individual with autosomal fragile site**

     Q95.8   **Other balanced rearrangements and structural markers**

     Q95.9   **Balanced rearrangement and structural marker, unspecified**

● Q96   **Turner's syndrome**
     Caused by missing or incomplete X chromosome affecting growth and sexual development

     Excludes1   Noonan syndrome (Q87.19)

     Q96.0   **Karyotype 45, X ♀**

     Q96.1   **Karyotype 46, X iso (Xq) ♀**
             Karyotype 46, isochromosome Xq

     Q96.2   **Karyotype 46, X with abnormal sex chromosome, except iso (Xq) ♀**
             Karyotype 46, X with abnormal sex chromosome, except isochromosome Xq

     Q96.3   **Mosaicism, 45, X/46, XX or XY ♀**

     Q96.4   **Mosaicism, 45, X/other cell line(s) with abnormal sex chromosome ♀**

     Q96.8   **Other variants of Turner's syndrome ♀**

     Q96.9   **Turner's syndrome, unspecified ♀**

● Q97   **Other sex chromosome abnormalities, female phenotype, not elsewhere classified**

     Excludes1   Turner's syndrome (Q96.-)

     Q97.0   **Karyotype 47, XXX ♀**

     Q97.1   **Female with more than three X chromosomes ♀**

     Q97.2   **Mosaicism, lines with various numbers of X chromosomes ♀**

     Q97.3   **Female with 46, XY karyotype ♀**

     Q97.8   **Other specified sex chromosome abnormalities, female phenotype ♀**

     Q97.9   **Sex chromosome abnormality, female phenotype, unspecified ♀**

● Q98   **Other sex chromosome abnormalities, male phenotype, not elsewhere classified**

     Q98.0   **Klinefelter syndrome karyotype 47, XXY ♂**

     Q98.1   **Klinefelter syndrome, male with more than two X chromosomes ♂**

     Q98.3   **Other male with 46, XX karyotype ♂**

     Q98.4   **Klinefelter syndrome, unspecified ♂**

     Q98.5   **Karyotype 47, XYY**

     Q98.6   **Male with structurally abnormal sex chromosome ♂**

     Q98.7   **Male with sex chromosome mosaicism ♂**

     Q98.8   **Other specified sex chromosome abnormalities, male phenotype ♂**

     Q98.9   **Sex chromosome abnormality, male phenotype, unspecified ♂**

● Q99   **Other chromosome abnormalities, not elsewhere classified**

     Q99.0   **Chimera 46, XX/46, XY**
             Chimera 46, XX/46, XY true hermaphrodite

     Q99.1   **46, XX true hermaphrodite**
             46, XX with streak gonads
             46, XY with streak gonads
             Pure gonadal dysgenesis

     Q99.2   **Fragile X chromosome**
             Fragile X syndrome

     Q99.8   **Other specified chromosome abnormalities**

     Q99.9   **Chromosomal abnormality, unspecified**

▶ New   ⇒ Revised   ~~deleted~~ Deleted   Excludes 1   Excludes 2   Includes   Use additional   Code first   Code also   Key words

OGCR Official Guidelines   **X** Assign placeholder X   ● Use Additional Character(s)   ▶ Manifestation Code   🝞 Hierarchical Condition Category   **Coding Clinic**

CHAPTER 18

SYMPTOMS, SIGNS, AND ABNORMAL CLINICAL AND LABORATORY FINDINGS, NOT ELSEWHERE CLASSIFIED (R00-R99)

OGCR Chapter-Specific Coding Guidelines

18. **Chapter 18: Symptoms, signs, and abnormal clinical and laboratory findings, not elsewhere classified (R00-R99)**
Chapter 18 includes symptoms, signs, abnormal results of clinical or other investigative procedures, and ill-defined conditions regarding which no diagnosis classifiable elsewhere is recorded. Signs and symptoms that point to a specific diagnosis have been assigned to a category in other chapters of the classification.

    a. Use of symptom codes
    Codes that describe symptoms and signs are acceptable for reporting purposes when a related definitive diagnosis has not been established (confirmed) by the provider.

    b. Use of a symptom code with a definitive diagnosis code
    Codes for signs and symptoms may be reported in addition to a related definitive diagnosis when the sign or symptom is not routinely associated with that diagnosis, such as the various signs and symptoms associated with complex syndromes. The definitive diagnosis code should be sequenced before the symptom code.

    Signs or symptoms that are associated routinely with a disease process should not be assigned as additional codes, unless otherwise instructed by the classification.

    c. Combination codes that include symptoms
    ICD-10-CM contains a number of combination codes that identify both the definitive diagnosis and common symptoms of that diagnosis. When using one of these combination codes, an additional code should not be assigned for the symptom.

    d. Repeated falls
    Code R29.6, Repeated falls, is for use for encounters when a patient has recently fallen and the reason for the fall is being investigated.

    Code Z91.81, History of falling, is for use when a patient has fallen in the past and is at risk for future falls. When appropriate, both codes R29.6 and Z91.81 may be assigned together.

    e. Coma scale
    The coma scale codes (R40.2-) can be used in conjunction with traumatic brain injury codes, acute cerebrovascular disease or sequelae of cerebrovascular disease codes. These codes are primarily for use by trauma registries, but they may be used in any setting where this information is collected. The coma scale may also be used to assess the status of the central nervous system for other non-trauma conditions, such as monitoring patients in the intensive care unit regardless of medical condition. The coma scale codes should be sequenced after the diagnosis code(s).

    These codes, one from each subcategory, are needed to complete the scale. The 7th character indicates when the scale was recorded. The 7th character should match for all three codes.

    At a minimum, report the initial score documented on presentation at your facility. This may be a score from the emergency medicine technician (EMT) or in the emergency department. If desired, a facility may choose to capture multiple coma scale scores.

    Assign code R40.24, Glasgow coma scale, total score, when only the total score is documented in the medical record and not the individual score(s).

    Do not report codes for individual or total Glasgow coma scale scores for a patient with a medically induced coma or a sedated patient.

    See Section I.B.14 for coma scale documentation by clinicians other than patient's provider.

    f. Functional quadriplegia
    GUIDELINE HAS BEEN DELETED EFFECTIVE OCTOBER 1, 2017

    g. SIRS due to Non-Infectious Process
    The systemic inflammatory response syndrome (SIRS) can develop as a result of certain non-infectious disease processes, such as trauma, malignant neoplasm, or pancreatitis. When SIRS is documented with a noninfectious condition, and no subsequent infection is documented, the code for the underlying condition, such as an injury, should be assigned, followed by code R65.10, Systemic inflammatory response syndrome (SIRS) of non-infectious origin without acute organ dysfunction, or code R65.11, Systemic inflammatory response syndrome (SIRS) of non-infectious origin with acute organ dysfunction. If an associated acute organ dysfunction is documented, the appropriate code(s) for the specific type of organ dysfunction(s) should be assigned in addition to code R65.11. If acute organ dysfunction is documented, but it cannot be determined if the acute organ dysfunction is associated with SIRS or due to another condition (e.g., directly due to the trauma), the provider should be queried.

    h. Death NOS
    Code R99, Ill-defined and unknown cause of mortality, is only for use in the very limited circumstance when a patient who has already died is brought into an emergency department or other healthcare facility and is pronounced dead upon arrival. It does not represent the discharge disposition of death.

    i. NIHSS Stroke Scale
    The NIH stroke scale (NIHSS) codes (R29.7- -) can be used in conjunction with acute stroke codes (I63) to identify the patient's neurological status and the severity of the stroke. The stroke scale codes should be sequenced after the acute stroke diagnosis code(s).

    At a minimum, report the initial score documented. If desired, a facility may choose to capture multiple stroke scale scores.

    See Section I.B.14 for NIHSS stroke scale documentation by clinicians other than patient's provider.

OGCR Section I.B.4.

Signs and symptoms

Codes that describe symptoms and signs, as opposed to diagnoses, are acceptable for reporting purposes when a related definitive diagnosis has not been established (confirmed) by the provider. Chapter 18 of ICD-10-CM, Symptoms, Signs, and Abnormal Clinical and Laboratory Findings, Not Elsewhere Classified (codes R00.0-R99) contains many, but not all codes for symptoms.

CHAPTER 18

SYMPTOMS, SIGNS, AND ABNORMAL CLINICAL AND LABORATORY FINDINGS, NOT ELSEWHERE CLASSIFIED (R00-R99)

Note: This chapter includes symptoms, signs, abnormal results of clinical or other investigative procedures, and ill-defined conditions regarding which no diagnosis classifiable elsewhere is recorded.

Signs and symptoms that point rather definitely to a given diagnosis have been assigned to a category in other chapters of the classification. In general, categories in this chapter include the less well-defined conditions and symptoms that, without the necessary study of the case to establish a final diagnosis, point perhaps equally to two or more diseases or to two or more systems of the body. Practically all categories in the chapter could be designated "not otherwise specified", "unknown etiology" or "transient". The Alphabetical Index should be consulted to determine which symptoms and signs are to be allocated here and which to other chapters. The residual subcategories, numbered .8, are generally provided for other relevant symptoms that cannot be allocated elsewhere in the classification.

The conditions and signs or symptoms included in categories R00-R94 consist of:
(a) cases for which no more specific diagnosis can be made even after all the facts bearing on the case have been investigated;
(b) signs or symptoms existing at the time of initial encounter that proved to be transient and whose causes could not be determined;
(c) provisional diagnosis in a patient who failed to return for further investigation or care;
(d) cases referred elsewhere for investigation or treatment before the diagnosis was made;
(e) cases in which a more precise diagnosis was not available for any other reason;
(f) certain symptoms, for which supplementary information is provided, that represent important problems in medical care in their own right.

Excludes2 abnormal findings on antenatal screening of mother (O28.-)
certain conditions originating in the perinatal period (P04-P96)
signs and symptoms classified in the body system chapters
signs and symptoms of breast (N63, N64.5)

This chapter contains the following blocks:

R00-R09	Symptoms and signs involving the circulatory and respiratory systems
R10-R19	Symptoms and signs involving the digestive system and abdomen
R20-R23	Symptoms and signs involving the skin and subcutaneous tissue
R25-R29	Symptoms and signs involving the nervous and musculoskeletal systems
R30-R39	Symptoms and signs involving the genitourinary system
R40-R46	Symptoms and signs involving cognition, perception, emotional state and behavior
R47-R49	Symptoms and signs involving speech and voice
R50-R69	General symptoms and signs
R70-R79	Abnormal findings on examination of blood, without diagnosis
R80-R82	Abnormal findings on examination of urine, without diagnosis
R83-R89	Abnormal findings on examination of other body fluids, substances and tissues, without diagnosis
R90-R94	Abnormal findings on diagnostic imaging and in function studies, without diagnosis
R97	Abnormal tumor markers
R99	Ill-defined and unknown cause of mortality

SYMPTOMS AND SIGNS INVOLVING THE CIRCULATORY AND RESPIRATORY SYSTEMS (R00-R09)

● **R00   Abnormalities of heart beat**

    Excludes1   abnormalities originating in the perinatal period (P29.1-)

    Excludes2   specified arrhythmias (I47-I49)

  R00.0   Tachycardia, unspecified
    Rapid heart rate >100 beats
    Rapid heart beat
    Sinoauricular tachycardia NOS
    Sinus [sinusal] tachycardia NOS

      Excludes1   neonatal tachycardia (P29.11)
                  paroxysmal tachycardia (I47.-)

  R00.1   Bradycardia, unspecified
    Slow heart rate, <60
    Sinoatrial bradycardia
    Sinus bradycardia
    Slow heart beat
    Vagal bradycardia

    Use additional code for adverse effect, if applicable, to identify drug (T36-T50 with fifth or sixth character 5)

      Excludes1   neonatal bradycardia (P29.12)

  R00.2   Palpitations
    Awareness of heart beat

  R00.8   Other abnormalities of heart beat

  R00.9   Unspecified abnormalities of heart beat

● **R01   Cardiac murmurs and other cardiac sounds**

    Excludes1   cardiac murmurs and sounds originating in the perinatal period (P29.8)

  R01.0   Benign and innocent cardiac murmurs
    Functional cardiac murmur

  R01.1   Cardiac murmur, unspecified
    Cardiac bruit NOS
    Heart murmur NOS
    Systolic murmur NOS

  R01.2   Other cardiac sounds
    Cardiac dullness, increased or decreased
    Precordial friction

▶ New   ⇒ Revised   ~~deleted~~ Deleted   Excludes 1   Excludes 2   Includes   Use additional   Code first   Code also   Key words
OGCR Official Guidelines   X Assign placeholder X   ● Use Additional Character(s)   ▶ Manifestation Code   🔖 Hierarchical Condition Category   **Coding Clinic**

> **OGCR** Section I.C.9.a.7.
>
> Hypertension, Transient
> Assign code R03.0, Elevated blood pressure reading without
> diagnosis of hypertension, unless patient has an established
> diagnosis of hypertension. Assign code O13.-, Gestational
> [pregnancy-induced] hypertension with significant
> proteinuria, or O14.-, Pre-eclampsia, for transient hypertension
> of pregnancy.

● **R03** **Abnormal blood-pressure reading, without diagnosis**

    R03.0 **Elevated blood-pressure reading, without diagnosis of hypertension**

        Note: This category is to be used to record an episode of elevated blood pressure in a patient in whom no formal diagnosis of hypertension has been made, or as an isolated incidental finding.

    R03.1 **Nonspecific low blood-pressure reading**

        Excludes1   hypotension (I95.-)
                  maternal hypotension syndrome (O26.5-)
                  neurogenic orthostatic hypotension (G90.3)

● **R04** **Hemorrhage from respiratory passages**

    R04.0 **Epistaxis**
        Hemorrhage from nose
        Nosebleed
        Coding Clinic: 2018, Q4, P38

    R04.1 **Hemorrhage from throat**
        Excludes2   hemoptysis (R04.2)

    R04.2 **Hemoptysis**
        Blood-stained sputum
        Cough with hemorrhage

  ● **R04.8** **Hemorrhage from other sites in respiratory passages**

      R04.81 **Acute idiopathic pulmonary hemorrhage in infants**   **P**
          AIPHI
          Acute idiopathic hemorrhage in infants over 28 days old
          Excludes1   perinatal pulmonary hemorrhage (P26.-)
                     von Willebrand's disease (D68.0)

      R04.89 **Hemorrhage from other sites in respiratory passages**
          Pulmonary hemorrhage NOS

    R04.9 **Hemorrhage from respiratory passages, unspecified**

  R05 **Cough**
    Excludes1   cough with hemorrhage (R04.2)
                smoker's cough (J41.0)

● **R06** **Abnormalities of breathing**
    Excludes1   acute respiratory distress syndrome (J80)
                respiratory arrest (R09.2)
                respiratory arrest of newborn (P28.81)
                respiratory distress syndrome of newborn (P22.-)
                respiratory failure (J96.-)
                respiratory failure of newborn (P28.5)

  ● **R06.0** **Dyspnea**
      Excludes1   tachypnea NOS (R06.82)
                 transient tachypnea of newborn (P22.1)

      R06.00 **Dyspnea, unspecified**
          Coding Clinic: 2017, Q1, P26-27

      R06.01 **Orthopnea**
      R06.02 **Shortness of breath**
      R06.03 **Acute respiratory distress**
      R06.09 **Other forms of dyspnea**

    R06.1 **Stridor**
        Harsh, high-pitched breath sound
        Excludes1   congenital laryngeal stridor (P28.89)
                 laryngismus (stridulus) (J38.5)

    R06.2 **Wheezing**
        Excludes1   Asthma (J45.-)
        Coding Clinic: 2016, Q2, P34

    R06.3 **Periodic breathing**
        Cheyne-Stokes breathing
        An abnormal pattern of breathing with gradually increasing and decreasing tidal volume with some periods of apnea

    R06.4 **Hyperventilation**
        Excludes1   psychogenic hyperventilation (F45.8)

    R06.5 **Mouth breathing**
        Excludes2   dry mouth NOS (R68.2)

    R06.6 **Hiccough**
        Excludes1   psychogenic hiccough (F45.8)

    R06.7 **Sneezing**

  ● **R06.8** **Other abnormalities of breathing**

      R06.81 **Apnea, not elsewhere classified**
          Apnea NOS
          Excludes1   apnea (of) newborn (P28.4)
                     sleep apnea (G47.3-)
                     sleep apnea of newborn (primary) (P28.3)

      R06.82 **Tachypnea, not elsewhere classified**
          Tachypnea NOS
          Excludes1   transitory tachypnea of newborn (P22.1)

      R06.83 **Snoring**

      R06.89 **Other abnormalities of breathing**
          Breath-holding (spells)
          Sighing

    R06.9 **Unspecified abnormalities of breathing**

● **R07** **Pain in throat and chest**
    Excludes1   epidemic myalgia (B33.0)
    Excludes2   jaw pain R68.84
                pain in breast (N64.4)

    R07.0 **Pain in throat**
        Excludes1   chronic sore throat (J31.2)
                 sore throat (acute) NOS (J02.9)
        Excludes2   dysphagia (R13.1-)
                 pain in neck (M54.2)

    R07.1 **Chest pain on breathing**
        Painful respiration

    R07.2 **Precordial pain**

  ● **R07.8** **Other chest pain**

      R07.81 **Pleurodynia**
          Pleurodynia NOS
          Excludes1   epidemic pleurodynia (B33.0)

      R07.82 **Intercostal pain**

      R07.89 **Other chest pain**
          Anterior chest-wall pain NOS

    R07.9 **Chest pain, unspecified**

● **R09** **Other symptoms and signs involving the circulatory and respiratory system**
    Excludes1   acute respiratory distress syndrome (J80)
                respiratory arrest of newborn (P28.81)
                respiratory distress syndrome of newborn (P22.0)
                respiratory failure (J96.-)
                respiratory failure of newborn (P28.5)

  ● **R09.0** **Asphyxia and hypoxemia**
      Excludes1   asphyxia due to carbon monoxide (T58.-)
                 asphyxia due to foreign body in respiratory tract (T17.-)
                 birth (intrauterine) asphyxia (P84)
                 hyperventilation (R06.4)
                 traumatic asphyxia (T71.-)
      Excludes2   hypercapnia (R06.89)

      R09.01 **Asphyxia**

      R09.02 **Hypoxemia**
          Coding Clinic: 2019, Q3, P15

R09.1 **Pleurisy**
  Occurs when double membrane (pleura) lining chest cavity and lung surface becomes inflamed, causing sharp pain on inspiration/expiration
  Excludes1 pleurisy with effusion (J90)

R09.2 **Respiratory arrest** 🏷
  Cardiorespiratory failure
  Excludes1 cardiac arrest (I46.-)
            respiratory arrest of newborn (P28.81)
            respiratory distress of newborn (P22.0)
            respiratory failure (J96.-)
            respiratory failure of newborn (P28.5)
            respiratory insufficiency (R06.89)
            respiratory insufficiency of newborn (P28.5)

R09.3 **Abnormal sputum**
  Abnormal amount of sputum
  Abnormal color of sputum
  Abnormal odor of sputum
  Excessive sputum
  Excludes1 blood-stained sputum (R04.2)

● R09.8 **Other specified symptoms and signs involving the circulatory and respiratory systems**
  R09.81 **Nasal congestion**
  R09.82 **Postnasal drip**
  R09.89 **Other specified symptoms and signs involving the circulatory and respiratory systems**
            Bruit (arterial)
            Abnormal chest percussion
            Feeling of foreign body in throat
            Friction sounds in chest
            Chest tympany
            Choking sensation
            Rales
              Wet rattling, clicking, crackling sounds on auscultation
            Weak pulse
            Excludes2 foreign body in throat (T17.2-)
                      wheezing (R06.2)

SYMPTOMS AND SIGNS INVOLVING THE DIGESTIVE SYSTEM AND ABDOMEN (R10-R19)

  Excludes2 congenital or infantile pylorospasm (Q40.0)
            gastrointestinal hemorrhage (K92.0-K92.2)
            intestinal obstruction (K56.-)
            newborn gastrointestinal hemorrhage (P54.0-P54.3)
            newborn intestinal obstruction (P76.-)
            pylorospasm (K31.3)
            signs and symptoms involving the urinary system (R30-R39)
            symptoms referable to female genital organs (N94.-)
            symptoms referable to male genital organs (N48-N50)

● R10 **Abdominal and pelvic pain**
  Excludes1 renal colic (N23)
  Excludes2 dorsalgia (M54.-)
            flatulence and related conditions (R14.-)
  R10.0 **Acute abdomen**
    Severe abdominal pain (generalized) (with abdominal rigidity)
    Excludes1 abdominal rigidity NOS (R19.3)
              generalized abdominal pain NOS (R10.84)
              localized abdominal pain (R10.1-R10.3-)
● R10.1 **Pain localized to upper abdomen**
  R10.10 **Upper abdominal pain, unspecified**
  R10.11 **Right upper quadrant pain**
  R10.12 **Left upper quadrant pain**
  R10.13 **Epigastric pain**
            Dyspepsia
            Excludes1 functional dyspepsia (K30)

R10.2 **Pelvic and perineal pain**
  Excludes1 vulvodynia (N94.81)
● R10.3 **Pain localized to other parts of lower abdomen**
  R10.30 **Lower abdominal pain, unspecified**
  R10.31 **Right lower quadrant pain**
  R10.32 **Left lower quadrant pain**
  R10.33 **Periumbilical pain**
● R10.8 **Other abdominal pain**
  ● R10.81 **Abdominal tenderness**
            Abdominal tenderness NOS
    R10.811 **Right upper quadrant abdominal tenderness**
    R10.812 **Left upper quadrant abdominal tenderness**
    R10.813 **Right lower quadrant abdominal tenderness**
    R10.814 **Left lower quadrant abdominal tenderness**
    R10.815 **Periumbilic abdominal tenderness**
    R10.816 **Epigastric abdominal tenderness**
    R10.817 **Generalized abdominal tenderness**
    R10.819 **Abdominal tenderness, unspecified site**
  ● R10.82 **Rebound abdominal tenderness**
    R10.821 **Right upper quadrant rebound abdominal tenderness**
    R10.822 **Left upper quadrant rebound abdominal tenderness**
    R10.823 **Right lower quadrant rebound abdominal tenderness**
    R10.824 **Left lower quadrant rebound abdominal tenderness**
    R10.825 **Periumbilic rebound abdominal tenderness**
    R10.826 **Epigastric rebound abdominal tenderness**
    R10.827 **Generalized rebound abdominal tenderness**
    R10.829 **Rebound abdominal tenderness, unspecified site**
  R10.83 **Colic**   P
            Colic NOS
            Infantile colic
            Excludes1 colic in adult and child over 12 months old (R10.84)
  R10.84 **Generalized abdominal pain**
            Excludes1 generalized abdominal pain associated with acute abdomen (R10.0)
  R10.9 **Unspecified abdominal pain**

● R11 **Nausea and vomiting**
  Excludes1 cyclical vomiting associated with migraine (G43.A-)
            excessive vomiting in pregnancy (O21.-)
            hematemesis (K92.0)
            neonatal hematemesis (P54.0)
            newborn vomiting (P92.0-)
            psychogenic vomiting (F50.89)
            vomiting associated with bulimia nervosa (F50.2)
            vomiting following gastrointestinal surgery (K91.0)
  Coding Clinic: 2017, Q1, P27
● R11.0 **Nausea**
            Nausea NOS
            Nausea without vomiting

CHAPTER 18 (R00-R99)

▶ New   ⇒ Revised   ~~deleted~~ Deleted   Excludes 1   Excludes 2   Includes   Use additional   Code first   Code also   Key words
OGCR Official Guidelines   X Assign placeholder X   ● Use Additional Character(s)   ▶ Manifestation Code   🏷 Hierarchical Condition Category   **Coding Clinic**

● **R11.1   Vomiting**
    R11.10   Vomiting, unspecified
        Vomiting NOS
    R11.11   Vomiting without nausea
    R11.12   Projectile vomiting
    R11.13   Vomiting of fecal matter
    R11.14   Bilious vomiting
        Bilious emesis
    R11.15   Cyclical vomiting syndrome unrelated to migraine
        Cyclic vomiting syndrome NOS
        Persistent vomiting
        Excludes1   cyclical vomiting in migraine (G43.A-)
        Excludes2   bulimia nervosa (F50.2)
               diabetes mellitus due to underlying condition (E08.-)

R11.2   Nausea with vomiting, unspecified
    Persistent nausea with vomiting NOS
    Coding Clinic: 2020, Q1, P8

R12   Heartburn
    Excludes1   dyspepsia NOS (R10.13)
             functional dyspepsia (K30)

● **R13   Aphagia and dysphagia**
    R13.0   Aphagia
        Inability to swallow
        Excludes1   psychogenic aphagia (F50.9)
●   **R13.1   Dysphagia**
        Difficulty swallowing
        Code first, if applicable, dysphagia following cerebrovascular disease (I69. with final characters -91)
        Excludes1   psychogenic dysphagia (F45.8)
        R13.10   Dysphagia, unspecified
            Difficulty in swallowing NOS
        R13.11   Dysphagia, oral phase
        R13.12   Dysphagia, oropharyngeal phase
        R13.13   Dysphagia, pharyngeal phase
        R13.14   Dysphagia, pharyngoesophageal phase
        R13.19   Other dysphagia
            Cervical dysphagia
            Neurogenic dysphagia

● **R14   Flatulence and related conditions**
    Excludes1   psychogenic aerophagy (F45.8)
    R14.0   Abdominal distension (gaseous)
        Bloating
        Tympanites (abdominal) (intestinal)
    R14.1   Gas pain
    R14.2   Eructation
        Belching air from stomach through mouth
    R14.3   Flatulence

● **R15   Fecal incontinence**
    Includes   encopresis NOS
    Excludes1   fecal incontinence of nonorganic origin (F98.1)
    R15.0   Incomplete defecation
        Excludes1   constipation (K59.0-)
               fecal impaction (K56.41)
    R15.1   Fecal smearing
        Fecal soiling
    R15.2   Fecal urgency
    R15.9   Full incontinence of feces
        Fecal incontinence NOS

● **R16   Hepatomegaly and splenomegaly, not elsewhere classified**
    Enlargement of liver or spleen
    R16.0   Hepatomegaly, not elsewhere classified
        Hepatomegaly NOS
    R16.1   Splenomegaly, not elsewhere classified
        Splenomegaly NOS
    R16.2   Hepatomegaly with splenomegaly, not elsewhere classified
        Hepatosplenomegaly NOS

R17   Unspecified jaundice
    Excludes1   neonatal jaundice (P55, P57-P59)

● **R18   Ascites**
    Includes   fluid in peritoneal cavity
    Excludes1   ascites in alcoholic cirrhosis (K70.31)
             ascites in alcoholic hepatitis (K70.11)
             ascites in toxic liver disease with chronic active hepatitis (K71.51)
    R18.0   Malignant ascites
        Code first malignancy, such as:
            malignant neoplasm of ovary (C56.-)
            secondary malignant neoplasm of retroperitoneum and peritoneum (C78.6)
    R18.8   Other ascites
        Ascites NOS
        Peritoneal effusion (chronic)
        Coding Clinic: 2018, Q1, P4

● **R19   Other symptoms and signs involving the digestive system and abdomen**
    Excludes1   acute abdomen (R10.0)
●   **R19.0   Intra-abdominal and pelvic swelling, mass and lump**
        Excludes1   abdominal distension (gaseous) (R14.-)
               ascites (R18.-)
        R19.00   Intra-abdominal and pelvic swelling, mass and lump, unspecified site
        R19.01   Right upper quadrant abdominal swelling, mass and lump
        R19.02   Left upper quadrant abdominal swelling, mass and lump
        R19.03   Right lower quadrant abdominal swelling, mass and lump
        R19.04   Left lower quadrant abdominal swelling, mass and lump
        R19.05   Periumbilic swelling, mass or lump
            Diffuse or generalized umbilical swelling or mass
        R19.06   Epigastric swelling, mass or lump
        R19.07   Generalized intra-abdominal and pelvic swelling, mass and lump
            Diffuse or generalized intra-abdominal swelling or mass NOS
            Diffuse or generalized pelvic swelling or mass NOS
        R19.09   Other intra-abdominal and pelvic swelling, mass and lump
●   **R19.1   Abnormal bowel sounds**
        R19.11   Absent bowel sounds
        R19.12   Hyperactive bowel sounds
        R19.15   Other abnormal bowel sounds
            Abnormal bowel sounds NOS
    R19.2   Visible peristalsis
        Hyperperistalsis

CHAPTER 18 (R00-R99)

● **R19.3**   **Abdominal rigidity**

     Excludes1   abdominal rigidity with severe abdominal pain (R10.0)

     R19.30   Abdominal rigidity, **unspecified site**

     R19.31   **Right** upper quadrant abdominal rigidity

     R19.32   **Left** upper quadrant abdominal rigidity

     R19.33   **Right** lower quadrant abdominal rigidity

     R19.34   **Left** lower quadrant abdominal rigidity

     R19.35   **Periumbilic** abdominal rigidity

     R19.36   **Epigastric** abdominal rigidity

     R19.37   **Generalized** abdominal rigidity

R19.4   **Change in bowel habit**

     Excludes1   constipation (K59.0-)
                   functional diarrhea (K59.1)

R19.5   **Other fecal abnormalities**

     Abnormal stool color
     Bulky stools
     Mucus in stools
     Occult blood in feces
     Occult blood in stools

     Excludes1   melena (K92.1)
                   neonatal melena (P54.1)

     Coding Clinic: 2019, Q1, P32

R19.6   **Halitosis**

R19.7   **Diarrhea, unspecified**

     Diarrhea NOS

     Excludes1   functional diarrhea (K59.1)
                   neonatal diarrhea (P78.3)
                   psychogenic diarrhea (F45.8)

R19.8   **Other specified symptoms and signs involving the digestive system and abdomen**

SYMPTOMS AND SIGNS INVOLVING THE SKIN AND SUBCUTANEOUS TISSUE (R20-R23)

     Excludes2   symptoms relating to breast (N64.4-N64.5)

● **R20**   **Disturbances of skin sensation**

     Excludes1   dissociative anesthesia and sensory loss (F44.6)
                   psychogenic disturbances (F45.8)

     R20.0   **Anesthesia of skin**
           Loss of sensation

     R20.1   **Hypoesthesia of skin**
           Unpleasant abnormal sensation

     R20.2   **Paresthesia of skin**
           Abnormal touch sensation, including burning, prickling, often in absence of external stimulus
           Formication   Tingling skin
           Pins and needles

           Excludes1   acroparesthesia (I73.8)

     R20.3   **Hyperesthesia**

     R20.8   **Other disturbances of skin sensation**

     R20.9   **Unspecified disturbances of skin sensation**

R21   **Rash and other nonspecific skin eruption**

     Includes   rash NOS

     Excludes1   specified type of rash- code to condition
                   vesicular eruption (R23.8)

● **R22**   **Localized swelling, mass and lump of skin and subcutaneous tissue**

     Includes   subcutaneous nodules (localized) (superficial)

     Excludes1   abnormal findings on diagnostic imaging (R90-R93)
                   edema (R60.-)
                   enlarged lymph nodes (R59.-)
                   localized adiposity (E65)
                   swelling of joint (M25.4-)

     R22.0   Localized swelling, mass and lump, **head**

     R22.1   Localized swelling, mass and lump, **neck**

R22.2   Localized swelling, mass and lump, **trunk**

     Excludes1   intra-abdominal or pelvic mass and lump (R19.0-)
                   intra-abdominal or pelvic swelling (R19.0-)

     Excludes2   breast mass and lump (N63)

● **R22.3**   Localized swelling, mass and lump, **upper limb**

     R22.30   Localized swelling, mass and lump, **unspecified** upper limb

     R22.31   Localized swelling, mass and lump, **right** upper limb

     R22.32   Localized swelling, mass and lump, **left** upper limb

     R22.33   Localized swelling, mass and lump, upper limb, **bilateral**

● **R22.4**   Localized swelling, mass and lump, **lower limb**

     R22.40   Localized swelling, mass and lump, **unspecified** lower limb

     R22.41   Localized swelling, mass and lump, **right** lower limb

     R22.42   Localized swelling, mass and lump, **left** lower limb

     R22.43   Localized swelling, mass and lump, lower limb, **bilateral**

     R22.9   Localized swelling, mass and lump, **unspecified**

● **R23**   **Other skin changes**

     R23.0   **Cyanosis**

           Excludes1   acrocyanosis (I73.8)
                       cyanotic attacks of newborn (P28.2)

     R23.1   **Pallor**
           Clammy skin

     R23.2   **Flushing**
           Excessive blushing

           Code first, if applicable, menopausal and female climacteric states (N95.1)

     R23.3   **Spontaneous ecchymoses**
           Small hemorrhagic spot of skin; AKA black and blue spot
           Petechiae

           Excludes1   ecchymoses of newborn (P54.5)
                       purpura (D69.-)

     R23.4   **Changes in skin texture**
           Desquamation of skin   Scaling of skin
           Induration of skin

           Excludes1   epidermal thickening NOS (L85.9)

     R23.8   **Other skin changes**

     R23.9   **Unspecified skin changes**

SYMPTOMS AND SIGNS INVOLVING THE NERVOUS AND MUSCULOSKELETAL SYSTEMS (R25-R29)

● **R25**   **Abnormal involuntary movements**

     Excludes1   specific movement disorders (G20-G26)
                   stereotyped movement disorders (F98.4)
                   tic disorders (F95.-)

     R25.0   **Abnormal head movements**

     R25.1   **Tremor, unspecified**

           Excludes1   chorea NOS (G25.5)
                       essential tremor (G25.0)
                       hysterical tremor (F44.4)
                       intention tremor (G25.2)

     R25.2   **Cramp and spasm**

           Excludes2   carpopedal spasm (R29.0)
                       charley-horse (M62.831)
                       infantile spasms (G40.4-)
                       muscle spasm of back (M62.830)
                       muscle spasm of calf (M62.831)

     R25.3   **Fasciculation**
           Twitching NOS

     R25.8   **Other abnormal involuntary movements**

     R25.9   **Unspecified abnormal involuntary movements**

▶ New   ⟹ Revised   ~~deleted~~ Deleted   Excludes 1   Excludes 2   Includes   Use additional   Code first   Code also   Key words

1202   OGCR Official Guidelines   X Assign placeholder X   ● Use Additional Character(s)   ⟩ Manifestation Code   HCC Hierarchical Condition Category   Coding Clinic

● **R26 Abnormalities of gait and mobility**

    Excludes1 ataxia NOS (R27.0)
                hereditary ataxia (G11.-)
                locomotor (syphilitic) ataxia (A52.11)
                immobility syndrome (paraplegic) (M62.3)

  R26.0 Ataxic gait
      Staggering gait

  R26.1 Paralytic gait
      Spastic gait

  R26.2 Difficulty in walking, not elsewhere classified
      Excludes1 falling (R29.6)
                unsteadiness on feet (R26.81)
      Coding Clinic: 2016, Q2, P7

● **R26.8 Other abnormalities of gait and mobility**
    R26.81 Unsteadiness on feet
    R26.89 Other abnormalities of gait and mobility

  R26.9 Unspecified abnormalities of gait and mobility

● **R27 Other lack of coordination**

    Excludes1 ataxic gait (R26.0)
                hereditary ataxia (G11.-)
                vertigo NOS (R42)

  R27.0 Ataxia, unspecified
      Excludes1 ataxia following cerebrovascular disease
                    (I69. with final characters -93)

  R27.8 Other lack of coordination

  R27.9 Unspecified lack of coordination

● **R29 Other symptoms and signs involving the nervous and musculoskeletal systems**

  R29.0 Tetany
      Hyperexcitability of nerves and muscles characterized by spasm, twitching, and cramps
      Carpopedal spasm
      Excludes1 hysterical tetany (F44.5)
                neonatal tetany (P71.3)
                parathyroid tetany (E20.9)
                post-thyroidectomy tetany (E89.2)

  R29.1 Meningismus

  R29.2 Abnormal reflex
      Excludes2 abnormal pupillary reflex (H57.0)
                hyperactive gag reflex (J39.2)
                vasovagal reaction or syncope (R55)

  R29.3 Abnormal posture

  R29.4 Clicking hip
      Excludes1 congenital deformities of hip (Q65.-)

  R29.5 Transient paralysis
      Code first any associated spinal cord injury (S14.0, S14.1-, S24.0, S24.1-, S34.0-, S34.1-)
      Excludes1 transient ischemic attack (G45.9)

  R29.6 Repeated falls
      Falling
      Tendency to fall
      Excludes2 at risk for falling (Z91.81)
                history of falling (Z91.81)

OGCR Section I.C.18.d.

Repeated falls

Code R29.6, Repeated falls, is for use for encounters when a patient has recently fallen and the reason for the fall is being investigated.

Code Z91.81, History of falling, is for use when a patient has fallen in the past and is at risk for future falls. When appropriate, both codes R29.6 and Z91.81 may be assigned together.

Coding Clinic: 2016, Q2, P7

OGCR Section I.C.18.i.

NIHSS Stroke Scale

The NIH stroke scale (NIHSS) codes (R29.7- -) can be used in conjunction with acute stroke codes (I63) to identify the patient's neurological status and the severity of the stroke. The stroke scale codes should be sequenced after the acute stroke diagnosis code(s).

At a minimum, report the initial score documented. If desired, a facility may choose to capture multiple stroke scale scores.

● **R29.7 National Institutes of Health Stroke Scale (NIHSS) score**
    ➤ *Code first the type of cerebral infarction (I63.-)*
    Coding Clinic: 2016, Q4, P61, 127

● **R29.70 NIHSS score 0-9**
    R29.700 NIHSS score 0
    R29.701 NIHSS score 1
    R29.702 NIHSS score 2
    R29.703 NIHSS score 3
    R29.704 NIHSS score 4
    R29.705 NIHSS score 5
    R29.706 NIHSS score 6
    R29.707 NIHSS score 7
    R29.708 NIHSS score 8
    R29.709 NIHSS score 9

● **R29.71 NIHSS score 10-19**
    R29.710 NIHSS score 10
    R29.711 NIHSS score 11
    R29.712 NIHSS score 12
    R29.713 NIHSS score 13
    R29.714 NIHSS score 14
    R29.715 NIHSS score 15
    R29.716 NIHSS score 16
    R29.717 NIHSS score 17
    R29.718 NIHSS score 18
    R29.719 NIHSS score 19

● **R29.72 NIHSS score 20-29**
    R29.720 NIHSS score 20
    R29.721 NIHSS score 21
    R29.722 NIHSS score 22
    R29.723 NIHSS score 23
    R29.724 NIHSS score 24
    R29.725 NIHSS score 25
    R29.726 NIHSS score 26
    R29.727 NIHSS score 27
    R29.728 NIHSS score 28
    R29.729 NIHSS score 29

● **R29.73 NIHSS score 30-39**
    R29.730 NIHSS score 30
        Coding Clinic: 2016, Q4, P62
    R29.731 NIHSS score 31
    R29.732 NIHSS score 32
    R29.733 NIHSS score 33
    R29.734 NIHSS score 34
    R29.735 NIHSS score 35
    R29.736 NIHSS score 36
    R29.737 NIHSS score 37
    R29.738 NIHSS score 38
    R29.739 NIHSS score 39

● **R29.74 NIHSS score 40-42**
    R29.740 NIHSS score 40
    R29.741 NIHSS score 41
    R29.742 NIHSS score 42

CHAPTER 18 (R00-R99)

● **R29.8**   **Other symptoms and signs involving the nervous and musculoskeletal systems**

    ● **R29.81**   **Other symptoms and signs involving the nervous system**

       R29.810   **Facial weakness**
            Facial droop
            Excludes1   Bell's palsy (G51.0)
                         facial weakness following cerebrovascular disease (I69. with final characters -92)

       R29.818   **Other symptoms and signs involving the nervous system**

    ● **R29.89**   **Other symptoms and signs involving the musculoskeletal system**

       Excludes2   pain in limb (M79.6-)

       R29.890   **Loss of height**
            Excludes1   osteoporosis (M80-M81)

       R29.891   **Ocular torticollis**
            Excludes1   congenital (sterno-mastoid) torticollis Q68.0
                         psychogenic torticollis (F45.8)
                         spasmodic torticollis (G24.3)
                         torticollis due to birth injury (P15.8)
                         torticollis NOS M43.6

       R29.898   **Other symptoms and signs involving the musculoskeletal system**

    ● **R29.9**   **Unspecified symptoms and signs involving the nervous and musculoskeletal systems**

       R29.90   **Unspecified symptoms and signs involving the nervous system**

       R29.91   **Unspecified symptoms and signs involving the musculoskeletal system**

SYMPTOMS AND SIGNS INVOLVING THE GENITOURINARY SYSTEM (R30-R39)

● **R30**   **Pain associated with micturition**

    Excludes1   psychogenic pain associated with micturition (F45.8)

    R30.0   **Dysuria**
       Painful urination
       Strangury

    R30.1   **Vesical tenesmus**
       Straining to urinate, with sensation of a full bladder even when empty

    R30.9   **Painful micturition, unspecified**
       Painful urination NOS

● **R31**   **Hematuria**

    Excludes1   hematuria included with underlying conditions, such as:
                acute cystitis with hematuria (N30.01)
                recurrent and persistent hematuria in glomerular diseases (N02.-)

    R31.0   **Gross hematuria**
       Coding Clinic: 2017, Q1, P17

    R31.1   **Benign essential microscopic hematuria**

    ● **R31.2**   **Other microscopic hematuria**
       Coding Clinic: 2016, Q4, P62

       R31.21   **Asymptomatic microscopic hematuria**
            AMH

       R31.29   **Other microscopic hematuria**

    R31.9   **Hematuria, unspecified**
       Coding Clinic: 2017, Q1, P6

R32   **Unspecified urinary incontinence**
    Enuresis NOS

    Excludes1   functional urinary incontinence (R39.81)
                nonorganic enuresis (F98.0)
                stress incontinence and other specified urinary incontinence (N39.3-N39.4-)
                urinary incontinence associated with cognitive impairment (R39.81)

● **R33**   **Retention of urine**

    Excludes1   psychogenic retention of urine (F45.8)

    R33.0   **Drug induced retention of urine**
       Use additional code for adverse effect, if applicable, to identify drug (T36-T50 with fifth or sixth character 5)

    R33.8   **Other retention of urine**
       Code first, if applicable, any causal condition, such as:
           enlarged prostate (N40.1)
       Coding Clinic: 2018, Q4, P55

    R33.9   **Retention of urine, unspecified**

R34   **Anuria and oliguria**

    Excludes1   anuria and oliguria complicating abortion or ectopic or molar pregnancy (O00-O07, O08.4)
                anuria and oliguria complicating pregnancy (O26.83-)
                anuria and oliguria complicating the puerperium (O90.4)

● **R35**   **Polyuria**
    Passage of excessive volume of urine
    Code first, if applicable, any causal condition, such as:
       enlarged prostate (N40.1)

    Excludes1   psychogenic polyuria (F45.8)

    R35.0   **Frequency of micturition**
       Discharge or passage of urine; AKA uresis

    R35.1   **Nocturia**
       Urinary frequency at night

    R35.8   **Other polyuria**
       Polyuria NOS

● **R36**   **Urethral discharge**

    R36.0   **Urethral discharge without blood**

    R36.1   **Hematospermia** ♂
       Presence of blood in semen

    R36.9   **Urethral discharge, unspecified**
       Penile discharge NOS
       Urethrorrhea

R37   **Sexual dysfunction, unspecified**

▶ New   ⫸ Revised   ~~deleted~~ Deleted   Excludes 1   Excludes 2   Includes   Use additional   Code first   Code also   Key words

OGCR Official Guidelines   X Assign placeholder X   ● Use Additional Character(s)   ▶ Manifestation Code   🖸 Hierarchical Condition Category   Coding Clinic

● **R39**   **Other and unspecified symptoms and signs involving the genitourinary system**

     R39.0   **Extravasation of urine**
          Leakage, discharge

  ● **R39.1**   **Other difficulties with micturition**
         Code first, if applicable, any causal condition, such as:
           enlarged prostate (N40.1)

       R39.11   **Hesitancy of micturition**

       R39.12   **Poor urinary stream**
           Weak urinary steam

       R39.13   **Splitting of urinary stream**

       R39.14   **Feeling of incomplete bladder emptying**

       R39.15   **Urgency of urination**
           Excludes1   urge incontinence (N39.41, N39.46)

       R39.16   **Straining to void**

    ● **R39.19**   **Other difficulties with micturition**
           Coding Clinic: 2016, Q4, P63

         R39.191   **Need to immediately re-void**

         R39.192   **Position dependent micturition**

         R39.198   **Other difficulties with micturition**

     R39.2   **Extrarenal uremia**
          Prerenal uremia
          Excludes1   uremia NOS (N19)

  ● **R39.8**   **Other symptoms and signs involving the genitourinary system**

       R39.81   **Functional urinary incontinence**
           Urinary incontinence due to cognitive impairment, or severe physical disability or immobility
           Excludes1   stress incontinence and other specified urinary incontinence (N39.3-N39.4-)
                  urinary incontinence NOS (R32)

       R39.82   **Chronic bladder pain**
           Coding Clinic: 2016, Q4, P64

       R39.83   **Unilateral non-palpable testicle** ♂

       R39.84   **Bilateral non-palpable testicles** ♂

       R39.89   **Other symptoms and signs involving the genitourinary system**
           Coding Clinic: 2016, Q4, P64

     R39.9   **Unspecified symptoms and signs involving the genitourinary system**

SYMPTOMS AND SIGNS INVOLVING COGNITION, PERCEPTION, EMOTIONAL STATE AND BEHAVIOR (R40-R46)

     Excludes2   symptoms and signs constituting part of a pattern of mental disorder (F01-F99)
     Coding Clinic: 2015, Q4, P40

● **R40**   **Somnolence, stupor and coma**
     Excludes1   neonatal coma (P91.5)
               somnolence, stupor and coma in diabetes (E08-E13)
               somnolence, stupor and coma in hepatic failure (K72.-)
               somnolence, stupor and coma in hypoglycemia (nondiabetic) (E15)

     R40.0   **Somnolence**
          Drowsiness
          Excludes1   coma (R40.2-)

     R40.1   **Stupor**
          Lowered level of consciousness
          Catatonic stupor
          Semicoma
          Excludes1   catatonic schizophrenia (F20.2)
                  coma (R40.2-)
                  depressive stupor (F31-F33)
                  dissociative stupor (F44.2)
                  manic stupor (F30.2)

OGCR Section I.C.18.e.

Coma scale

The coma scale codes (R40.2-) can be used in conjunction with traumatic brain injury codes, acute cerebrovascular disease or sequelae of cerebrovascular disease codes. These codes are primarily for use by trauma registries, but they may be used in any setting where this information is collected. The coma scale may also be used to assess the status of the central nervous system for other non-trauma conditions, such as monitoring patients in the intensive care unit regardless of medical condition. The coma scale codes should be sequenced after the diagnosis code(s).

These codes, one from each subcategory, are needed to complete the scale. The 7th character indicates when the scale was recorded. The 7th character should match for all three codes.

At a minimum, report the initial score documented on presentation at your facility. This may be a score from the emergency medicine technician (EMT) or in the emergency department. If desired, a facility may choose to capture multiple coma scale scores.

Assign code R40.24, Glasgow coma scale, total score, when only the total score is documented in the medical record and not the individual score(s).

● **R40.2**   **Coma**
     Code first any associated:
       fracture of skull (S02.-)
       intracranial injury (S06.-)
     Note: One code from each subcategory R40.21-R40-23 is required to complete the coma scale
     Coding Clinic: 2016, Q4, P127

     R40.20   **Unspecified coma**
           Coma NOS
           Unconsciousness NOS

  ● **R40.21**   **Coma scale, eyes open**
          The following appropriate 7th character is to be added to subcategory R40.21-:

0	unspecified time
1	in the field [EMT or ambulance]
2	at arrival to emergency department
3	at hospital admission
4	24 hours or more after hospital admission

          Coding Clinic: 2017, Q4, P25; 2015, Q2, P18

    ● **R40.211**   **Coma scale, eyes open, never**
           Coma scale eye opening score of 1

    ● **R40.212**   **Coma scale, eyes open, to pain**
           Coma scale eye opening score of 2

    ● **R40.213**   **Coma scale, eyes open, to sound**
           Coma scale eye opening score of 3

    ● **R40.214**   **Coma scale, eyes open, spontaneous**
           Coma scale eye opening score of 4

  ● **R40.22**   **Coma scale, best verbal response**
          The following appropriate 7th character is to be added to subcategory R40.22-:

0	unspecified time
1	in the field [EMT or ambulance]
2	at arrival to emergency department
3	at hospital admission
4	24 hours or more after hospital admission

          Coding Clinic: 2017, Q4, P25; 2015, Q2, P18

    ● **R40.221**   **Coma scale, best verbal response, none**
           Coma scale verbal score of 1

    ● **R40.222**   **Coma scale, best verbal response, incomprehensible words**
           Coma scale verbal score of 2
           Incomprehensible sounds (2-5 years of age)
           Moans/grunts to pain; restless (<2 years old)

● **R40.223　Coma scale, best verbal response, inappropriate words**
　　Coma scale verbal score of 3
　　Inappropriate crying or screaming (< 2 years of age)
　　Screaming (2-5 years of age)

● **R40.224　Coma scale, best verbal response, confused conversation**
　　Coma scale verbal score of 4
　　Inappropriate words (2-5 years of age)
　　Irritable cries (< 2 years of age)

● **R40.225　Coma scale, best verbal response, oriented**
　　Coma scale verbal score of 5
　　Cooing or babbling or crying appropriately (< 2 years of age)
　　Uses appropriate words (2- 5 years of age)

● **R40.23　Coma scale, best motor response**
　　The following appropriate 7th character is to be added to subcategory R40.23-:

0	unspecified time
1	in the field [EMT or ambulance]
2	at arrival to emergency department
3	at hospital admission
4	24 hours or more after hospital admission

　　Coding Clinic: 2017, Q4, P25; 2015, Q2, P18

● **R40.231　Coma scale, best motor response, none** 🝙
　　Coma scale motor score of 1

● **R40.232　Coma scale, best motor response, extension** 🝙
　　Abnormal extensor posturing to pain or noxious stimuli (< 2 years of age)
　　Coma scale motor score of 2
　　Extensor posturing to pain or noxious stimuli (2-5 years of age)

● **R40.233　Coma scale, best motor response, abnormal flexion**
　　Coma scale motor score of 3
　　Abnormal flexure posturing to pain or noxious stimuli (2-5 years of age)
　　Flexion/decorticate posturing (< 2 years of age)

● **R40.234　Coma scale, best motor response, flexion withdrawal** 🝙
　　Coma scale motor score of 4
　　Withdraws from pain or noxious stimuli (2-5 years of age)

● **R40.235　Coma scale, best motor response, localizes pain**
　　Coma scale motor score of 5
　　Localizes pain (2-5 years of age)
　　Withdraws to touch (< 2 years of age)

● **R40.236　Coma scale, best motor response, obeys commands**
　　Coma scale motor score of 6
　　Normal or spontaneous movement (< 2 years of age)
　　Obeys commands (2-5 years of age)

Glasgow Coma Scale

Eye Opening Response	
• Spontaneous--open with blinking at baseline	4 points
• To verbal stimuli, command, speech	3 points
• To pain only (not applied to face)	2 points
• No response	1 point
Verbal Response	
• Oriented	5 points
• Confused conversation, but able to answer questions	4 points
• Inappropriate words	3 points
• Incomprehensible speech	2 points
• No response	1 point
Motor Response	
• Obeys commands for movement	6 points
• Purposeful movement to painful stimulus	5 points
• Withdraws in response to pain	4 points
• Flexion in response to pain (decorticate posturing)	3 points
• Extension response in response to pain (decerebrate posturing)	2 points
• No response	1 point
Categorization:	
Coma: No eye opening, no ability to follow commands, no word verbalizations (3-8)	
Head Injury Classification:	
Severe Head Injury--GCS score of 8 or less	
Moderate Head Injury--GCS score of 9 to 12	
Mild head injury--GCS score of 13 to 15	
(Adapted from: Advanced Trauma Life Support: Course for Physicians, American College of Surgeons, 1993). http://www.bt.cdc.gov/masscasulatires/gscale.asp	

Figure 18-1

● **R40.24　Glasgow coma scale, total score**
　　Note: Assign a code from subcategory R40.24, when only the total coma score is documented
　　The following appropriate 7th character is to be added to subcategory R40.24-:

0	unspecified time
1	in the field [EMT or ambulance]
2	at arrival to emergency department
3	at hospital admission
4	24 hours or more after hospital admission

　　Coding Clinic: 2016, Q4, P64; 2015, Q2, P18

● **R40.241　Glasgow coma scale score 13-15**
● **R40.242　Glasgow coma scale score 9-12**
● **R40.243　Glasgow coma scale score 3-8** 🝙
● **R40.244　Other coma, without documented Glasgow coma scale score, or with partial score reported** 🝙

R40.3　Persistent vegetative state 🝙

R40.4　Transient alteration of awareness

● **R41　Other symptoms and signs involving cognitive functions and awareness**

　　Excludes1　dissociative [conversion] disorders (F44.-)
　　　　　　　　mild cognitive impairment, so stated (G31.84)

　　R41.0　Disorientation, unspecified
　　　　Confusion NOS　　　　Delirium NOS
　　　　Coding Clinic: 2019, Q2, P34; 2016, Q4, P71

　　R41.1　Anterograde amnesia

　　R41.2　Retrograde amnesia

R41.3   Other amnesia
Amnesia NOS
Memory loss NOS

> **Excludes1**   amnestic disorder due to known physiologic condition (F04)
> amnestic syndrome due to psychoactive substance use (F10-F19 with 5th character .6)
> mild memory disturbance due to known physiological condition (F06.8)
> transient global amnesia (G45.4)

R41.4   Neurologic neglect syndrome

Asomatognosia	Left-sided neglect
Hemi-akinesia	Sensory neglect
Hemi-inattention	Visuospatial neglect
Hemispatial neglect	

> **Excludes1**   visuospatial deficit (R41.842)

● **R41.8   Other symptoms and signs involving cognitive functions and awareness**

R41.81   Age-related cognitive decline   **A**
Senility NOS

R41.82   Altered mental status, unspecified
Change in mental status NOS

> **Excludes1**   altered level of consciousness (R40.-)
> altered mental status due to known condition - code to condition
> delirium NOS (R41.0)

Coding Clinic: 2012, Q4, P98

R41.83   Borderline intellectual functioning
IQ level 71 to 84

> **Excludes1**   intellectual disabilities (F70-F79)

● **R41.84   Other specified cognitive deficit**

> **Excludes1**   cognitive deficits as sequelae of cerebrovascular disease (I69.01-, I69.11-, I69.21-, I69.31-, I69.81-, I69.91-)

R41.840   Attention and concentration deficit

> **Excludes1**   attention-deficit hyperactivity disorders (F90.-)

R41.841   Cognitive communication deficit

R41.842   Visuospatial deficit

R41.843   Psychomotor deficit

R41.844   Frontal lobe and executive function deficit

R41.89   Other symptoms and signs involving cognitive functions and awareness
Anosognosia

R41.9   Unspecified symptoms and signs involving cognitive functions and awareness
Unspecified neurocognitive disorder

R42   Dizziness and giddiness
Light-headedness
Vertigo NOS

> **Excludes1**   vertiginous syndromes (H81.-)
> vertigo from infrasound (T75.23)

Coding Clinic: 2015, Q4, P40

● **R43   Disturbances of smell and taste**

R43.0   Anosmia
Absence of sense of smell; AKA anosphresia and olfactory anesthesia

R43.1   Parosmia

R43.2   Parageusia
Perversion of sense of taste or bad taste in mouth; AKA dysgeusia

R43.8   Other disturbances of smell and taste
Mixed disturbance of smell and taste

R43.9   Unspecified disturbances of smell and taste

● **R44   Other symptoms and signs involving general sensations and perceptions**

> **Excludes1**   alcoholic hallucinations (F10.151, F10.251, F10.951)
> hallucinations in drug psychosis (F11-F19 with fifth to sixth characters 51)
> hallucinations in mood disorders with psychotic symptoms (F30.2, F31.5, F32.3, F33.3)
> hallucinations in schizophrenia, schizotypal and delusional disorders (F20-F29)

> **Excludes2**   disturbances of skin sensation (R20.-)

R44.0   Auditory hallucinations

R44.1   Visual hallucinations

R44.2   Other hallucinations

R44.3   Hallucinations, unspecified

R44.8   Other symptoms and signs involving general sensations and perceptions

R44.9   Unspecified symptoms and signs involving general sensations and perceptions

● **R45   Symptoms and signs involving emotional state**

R45.0   Nervousness
Nervous tension

R45.1   Restlessness and agitation

R45.2   Unhappiness

R45.3   Demoralization and apathy

> **Excludes1**   anhedonia (R45.84)

R45.4   Irritability and anger

R45.5   Hostility

R45.6   Violent behavior

R45.7   State of emotional shock and stress, unspecified

● **R45.8   Other symptoms and signs involving emotional state**

R45.81   Low self-esteem

R45.82   Worries

R45.83   Excessive crying of child, adolescent or adult

> **Excludes1**   excessive crying of infant (baby) R68.11

R45.84   Anhedonia
Total loss of feeling of pleasure in pleasurable acts

● **R45.85   Homicidal and suicidal ideations**

> **Excludes1**   suicide attempt (T14.91)

R45.850   Homicidal ideations

R45.851   Suicidal ideations

R45.86   Emotional lability

R45.87   Impulsiveness

R45.89   Other symptoms and signs involving emotional state

● **R46   Symptoms and signs involving appearance and behavior**

> **Excludes1**   appearance and behavior in schizophrenia, schizotypal and delusional disorders (F20-F29)
> mental and behavioral disorders (F01-F99)

R46.0   Very low level of personal hygiene

R46.1   Bizarre personal appearance

R46.2   Strange and inexplicable behavior

R46.3   Overactivity

R46.4   Slowness and poor responsiveness

> **Excludes1**   stupor (R40.1)

R46.5   Suspiciousness and marked evasiveness

R46.6   Undue concern and preoccupation with stressful events

R46.7   Verbosity and circumstantial detail obscuring reason for contact

● **R46.8   Other symptoms and signs involving appearance and behavior**

R46.81   Obsessive-compulsive behavior

> **Excludes1**   obsessive-compulsive disorder (F42.-)

R46.89   Other symptoms and signs involving appearance and behavior

CHAPTER 18 (R00-R99)

SYMPTOMS AND SIGNS INVOLVING SPEECH AND VOICE (R47-R49)

● **R47   Speech disturbances, not elsewhere classified**
     Excludes1   autism (F84.0)
              cluttering (F80.81)
              specific developmental disorders of speech and language (F80.-)
              stuttering (F80.81)

● **R47.0   Dysphasia and aphasia**
     R47.01   Aphasia
         Excludes1   aphasia following cerebrovascular disease (I69. with final characters -20)
              progressive isolated aphasia (G31.01)

     R47.02   Dysphasia
         Impairment in comprehension of speech, caused by left-sided brain damage
         Excludes1   dysphasia following cerebrovascular disease (I69. with final characters -21)

R47.1   Dysarthria and anarthria
     Motor speech disorder
     Excludes1   dysarthria following cerebrovascular disease (I69. with final characters -22)

● **R47.8   Other speech disturbances**
     Excludes1   dysarthria following cerebrovascular disease (I69. with final characters -28)
     R47.81   Slurred speech
▷   **R47.82   *Fluency disorder in conditions classified elsewhere***
         Stuttering in conditions classified elsewhere
         Code first underlying disease or condition, such as:
         Parkinson's disease (G20)
         Excludes1   adult onset fluency disorder (F98.5)
              childhood onset fluency disorder (F80.81)
              fluency disorder (stuttering) following cerebrovascular disease (I69. with final characters -23)
     R47.89   Other speech disturbances

R47.9   Unspecified speech disturbances

● **R48   Dyslexia and other symbolic dysfunctions, not elsewhere classified**
     Excludes1   specific developmental disorders of scholastic skills (F81.-)

R48.0   Dyslexia and alexia

R48.1   Agnosia
     Loss of ability to recognize objects, persons, sounds, shapes, or smells
     Astereognosia (astereognosis)
     Autotopagnosia
     Excludes1   visual object agnosia (R48.3)

R48.2   Apraxia
     Loss of ability to execute or carry out learned purposeful movements
     Excludes1   apraxia following cerebrovascular disease (I69. with final characters -90)

R48.3   Visual agnosia
     Prosopagnosia
     Simultanagnosia (asimultagnosia)

R48.8   Other symbolic dysfunctions
     Acalculia
     Difficulty performing simple mathematical tasks resulting from neurological injury
     Agraphia
     Coding Clinic: 2017, Q1, P27

R48.9   Unspecified symbolic dysfunctions

● **R49   Voice and resonance disorders**
     Excludes1   psychogenic voice and resonance disorders (F44.4)

R49.0   Dysphonia
     Hoarseness

R49.1   Aphonia
     Loss of voice

● **R49.2   Hypernasality and hyponasality**
     R49.21   Hypernasality
     R49.22   Hyponasality

R49.8   Other voice and resonance disorders

R49.9   Unspecified voice and resonance disorder
     Change in voice NOS
     Resonance disorder NOS

GENERAL SYMPTOMS AND SIGNS (R50-R69)

● **R50   Fever of other and unknown origin**
     Excludes1   chills without fever (R68.83)
              febrile convulsions (R56.0-)
              fever of unknown origin during labor (O75.2)
              fever of unknown origin in newborn (P81.9)
              hypothermia due to illness (R68.0)
              malignant hyperthermia due to anesthesia (T88.3)
              puerperal pyrexia NOS (O86.4)

R50.2   Drug induced fever
     Use additional code for adverse effect, if applicable, to identify drug (T36-T50 with fifth or sixth character 5)
     Excludes1   postvaccination (postimmunization) fever (R50.83)

● **R50.8   Other specified fever**
▷   **R50.81   *Fever presenting with conditions classified elsewhere***
         Code first underlying condition when associated fever is present, such as with:
         leukemia (C91-C95)
         neutropenia (D70.-)
         sickle-cell disease (D57.-)
         Coding Clinic: 2019, Q2, P25

     R50.82   Postprocedural fever
         Excludes1   postprocedural infection (T81.44)
              posttransfusion fever (R50.84)
              postvaccination (postimmunization) fever (R50.83)

     R50.83   Postvaccination fever
         Postimmunization fever

     R50.84   Febrile nonhemolytic transfusion reaction
         FNHTR
         Posttransfusion fever

R50.9   Fever, unspecified
     Fever NOS
     Fever of unknown origin [FUO]
     Fever with chills
     Fever with rigors
     Hyperpyrexia NOS
     Persistent fever
     Pyrexia NOS

● **R51   Headache**
  ▶ **Excludes2**   atypical face pain (G50.1)
                          ▶ migraine and other headache syndromes
                             (G43-G44)
                          ▶ trigeminal neuralgia (G50.0)
                 ~~Facial pain NOS~~
                 ~~**Excludes1**   atypical face pain (G50.1)~~
                             ~~migraine and other headache syndromes~~
                                ~~(G43-G44)~~
                             ~~trigeminal neuralgia (G50.0)~~

  ▶ **R51.0   Headache with orthostatic component, not elsewhere
             classified**
                 ▶ Headache with positional component, not elsewhere
                    classified
  ▶ **R51.9 Headache, unspecified**
                 ▶ Facial pain NOS

R52   Pain, unspecified
         Acute pain NOS
         Generalized pain NOS
         Excludes1   acute and chronic pain, not elsewhere classified
                          (G89.-)
                       localized pain, unspecified type - code to pain by
                          site, such as:
                          abdomen pain (R10.-)
                          back pain (M54.9)
                          breast pain (N64.4)
                          chest pain (R07.1-R07.9)
                          ear pain (H92.0-)
                          eye pain (H57.1)
                       ⇒ headache (R51.9)
                          joint pain (M25.5-)
                          limb pain (M79.6-)
                          lumbar region pain (M54.5)
                          pelvic and perineal pain (R10.2)
                          shoulder pain (M25.51-)
                          spine pain (M54.-)
                          throat pain (R07.0)
                          tongue pain (K14.6)
                          tooth pain (K08.8)
                          renal colic (N23)
                       pain disorders exclusively related to
                          psychological factors (F45.41)

● **R53   Malaise and fatigue**
  R53.0   Neoplastic (malignant) related fatigue
         Code first associated neoplasm
  R53.1   Weakness
         Asthenia NOS
         Excludes1   age-related weakness (R54)
                       ⇒ muscle weakness (generalized) (M62.81)
                          sarcopenia (M62.84)
                          senile asthenia (R54)
         Coding Clinic: 2017, Q1, P7
  R53.2   Functional quadriplegia 🐛
         Complete immobility due to severe physical disability
            or frailty
         Excludes1   frailty NOS (R54)
                          hysterical paralysis (F44.4)
                          immobility syndrome (M62.3)
                          neurologic quadriplegia (G82.5-)
                          quadriplegia (G82.50)
         Coding Clinic: 2016, Q2, P6

● **R53.8   Other malaise and fatigue**
         Excludes1   combat exhaustion and fatigue (F43.0)
                          congenital debility (P96.9)
                          exhaustion and fatigue due to excessive
                             exertion (T73.3)
                          exhaustion and fatigue due to exposure
                             (T73.2)
                          exhaustion and fatigue due to heat (T67.-)
                          exhaustion and fatigue due to pregnancy
                             (O26.8-)
                          exhaustion and fatigue due to recurrent
                             depressive episode (F33)
                          exhaustion and fatigue due to senile
                             debility (R54)
  R53.81   Other malaise
         Chronic debility
         Debility NOS
         General physical deterioration
         Malaise NOS
         Nervous debility
         Excludes1   age-related physical debility
                          (R54)
  R53.82   Chronic fatigue, unspecified
         Chronic fatigue syndrome NOS
         Excludes1   postviral fatigue syndrome
                          (G93.3)
  R53.83   Other fatigue
         Fatigue NOS   Lethargy
         Lack of energy   Tiredness
         Excludes2   exhaustion and fatigue due to
                          depressive episode (F32.-)
         Coding Clinic: 2017, Q1, P7

R54   Age-related physical debility   A
         Frailty   Senile asthenia
         Old age   Senile debility
         Senescence
         Excludes1   age-related cognitive decline (R41.81)
                          sarcopenia (M62.84)
                          senile psychosis (F03)
                          senility NOS (R41.81)

R55   Syncope and collapse
         Blackout
         Fainting
         Vasovagal attack
         Excludes1   cardiogenic shock (R57.0)
                          carotid sinus syncope (G90.01)
                          heat syncope (T67.1)
                          neurocirculatory asthenia (F45.8)
                          neurogenic orthostatic hypotension (G90.3)
                          orthostatic hypotension (I95.1)
                          postprocedural shock (T81.1-)
                          psychogenic syncope (F48.8)
                          shock NOS (R57.9)
                          shock complicating or following abortion or
                             ectopic or molar pregnancy (O00-O07, O08.3)
                          shock complicating or following labor and
                             delivery (O75.1)
                          Stokes-Adams attack (I45.9)
                          unconsciousness NOS (R40.2-)

● **R56   Convulsions, not elsewhere classified**
         Excludes1   dissociative convulsions and seizures (F44.5)
                          epileptic convulsions and seizures (G40.-)
                          newborn convulsions and seizures (P90)
  ● **R56.0   Febrile convulsions**
    R56.00   Simple febrile convulsions 🐛
             Febrile convulsion NOS
             Febrile seizure NOS
    R56.01   Complex febrile convulsions 🐛
             Atypical febrile seizure
             Complex febrile seizure
             Complicated febrile seizure
             Excludes1   status epilepticus (G40.901)

CHAPTER 18 (R00-R99)

N Newborn Age: 0   **P** Pediatric Age: 0–17   **M** Maternity DX: 12–55   **A** Adult Age: 15–124   ♀ Females Only   ♂ Males Only   **1209**

CHAPTER 18 (R00-R99)

R56.1   **Post traumatic seizures** 🦣
    Excludes1   post traumatic epilepsy (G40.-)

R56.9   **Unspecified convulsions**🦣
    Convulsion disorder   Recurrent convulsions
    Fit NOS   Seizure(s) (convulsive) NOS
    Coding Clinic: 2019, Q4, P18

● **R57   Shock, not elsewhere classified**
    Excludes1   anaphylactic shock NOS (T78.2)
        anaphylactic reaction or shock due to adverse
           food reaction (T78.0-)
        anaphylactic shock due to adverse effect of
           correct drug or medicament properly
           administered (T88.6)
        anaphylactic shock due to serum (T80.5-)
        anesthetic shock (T88.3)
        electric shock (T75.4)
        obstetric shock (O75.1)
        postprocedural shock (T81.1-)
        psychic shock (F43.0)
        shock complicating or following ectopic or molar
           pregnancy (O00-O07, O08.3)
        shock due to lightning (T75.01)
        traumatic shock (T79.4)
        toxic shock syndrome (A48.3)

R57.0   **Cardiogenic shock** 🦣
    Excludes2   septic shock (R65.21)

R57.1   **Hypovolemic shock** 🦣
    Decreased blood volume (loss)
    Coding Clinic: 2019, Q2, P7-8

R57.8   **Other shock** 🦣

R57.9   **Shock, unspecified** 🦣
    Failure of peripheral circulation NOS
    Resulting in significant blood pressure drop

R58   **Hemorrhage, not elsewhere classified**
    Hemorrhage NOS
    Excludes1   hemorrhage included with underlying
           conditions, such as:
        acute duodenal ulcer with hemorrhage (K26.0)
        acute gastritis with bleeding (K29.01)
        ulcerative enterocolitis with rectal bleeding
           (K51.01)

● **R59   Enlarged lymph nodes**
    Includes   swollen glands
    Excludes1   lymphadenitis NOS (I88.9)
        acute lymphadenitis (L04.-)
        chronic lymphadenitis (I88.1)
        mesenteric (acute) (chronic) lymphadenitis (I88.0)

R59.0   **Localized enlarged lymph nodes**

R59.1   **Generalized enlarged lymph nodes**
    Lymphadenopathy NOS

R59.9   **Enlarged lymph nodes, unspecified**

● **R60   Edema, not elsewhere classified**
    Excludes1   angioneurotic edema (T78.3)
        ascites (R18.-)
        cerebral edema (G93.6)
        cerebral edema due to birth injury (P11.0)
        edema of larynx (J38.4)
        edema of nasopharynx (J39.2)
        edema of pharynx (J39.2)
        gestational edema (O12.0-)
        hereditary edema (Q82.0)
        hydrops fetalis NOS (P83.2)
        hydrothorax (J94.8)
        hydrops fetalis NOS (P83.2)
        newborn edema (P83.3)
        pulmonary edema (J81.-)

R60.0   **Localized edema**

R60.1   **Generalized edema**
    Excludes2   nutritional edema (E40-E46)

R60.9   **Edema, unspecified**
    Fluid retention NOS

● R61   **Generalized hyperhidrosis**
    Excessive sweating
    Night sweats
    Secondary hyperhidrosis
    *Code first, if applicable, menopausal and female climacteric states
       (N95.1)*
    Excludes1   focal (primary) (secondary) hyperhidrosis
           (L74.5-)
        Frey's syndrome (L74.52)
        localized (primary) (secondary) hyperhidrosis
           (L74.5-)

● R62   **Lack of expected normal physiological development in
    childhood and adults**
    Excludes1   delayed puberty (E30.0)
        gonadal dysgenesis (Q99.1)
        hypopituitarism (E23.0)

R62.0   **Delayed milestone in childhood**   P
    Delayed attainment of expected physiological
        developmental stage
    Late talker
    Late walker

● R62.5   **Other and unspecified lack of expected normal
    physiological development in childhood**
    Excludes1   HIV disease resulting in failure to thrive
           (B20)
        physical retardation due to malnutrition
           (E45)

R62.50   **Unspecified lack of expected normal
    physiological development in childhood**
    Infantilism NOS

R62.51   **Failure to thrive (child)**   P
    Failure to gain weight
    Excludes1   failure to thrive in child under 28
           days old (P92.6)
    Coding Clinic: 2018, Q4, P82

R62.52   **Short stature (child)**
    Lack of growth   Short stature NOS
    Physical retardation
    Excludes1   short stature due to endocrine
           disorder (E34.3)

R62.59   **Other lack of expected normal physiological
    development in childhood**

R62.7   **Adult failure to thrive**   A

● R63   **Symptoms and signs concerning food and fluid intake**
    Excludes1   bulimia NOS (F50.2)

R63.0   **Anorexia**
    Loss of appetite
    Excludes1   anorexia nervosa (F50.0-)
        loss of appetite of nonorganic origin
           (F50.89)

R63.1   **Polydipsia**
    Excessive thirst

R63.2   **Polyphagia**
    Excessive eating   Hyperalimentation NOS

R63.3   **Feeding difficulties**
    Feeding problem (elderly) (infant) NOS
    Picky eater
    Excludes1   eating disorders (F50.-)
        feeding problems of newborn (P92.-)
        infant feeding disorder of nonorganic
           origin (F98.2-)
    Coding Clinic: 2017, Q1, P27; 2016, Q3, P19

R63.4   **Abnormal weight loss**

R63.5   **Abnormal weight gain**
    Excludes1   excessive weight gain in pregnancy
           (O26.0-)
        obesity (E66.-)

▶ New   ⇒ Revised   ~~deleted~~ Deleted   Excludes 1   Excludes 2   Includes   Use additional   Code first   Code also   Key words
OGCR Official Guidelines   X Assign placeholder X   ● Use Additional Character(s)   ▶ Manifestation Code   🦣 Hierarchical Condition Category   Coding Clinic

R63.6　Underweight

Use additional code to identify body mass index (BMI), if known (Z68.-)

> **Excludes1**　abnormal weight loss (R63.4)
> anorexia nervosa (F50.0-)
> malnutrition (E40-E46)

R63.8　Other symptoms and signs concerning food and fluid intake

R64　Cachexia 🏥

Wasting syndrome

Code first underlying condition, if known

> **Excludes1**　abnormal weight loss (R63.4)
> nutritional marasmus (E41)

Coding Clinic: 2017, Q3, P25

● **R65　Symptoms and signs specifically associated with systemic inflammation and infection**

● **R65.1　Systemic inflammatory response syndrome (SIRS) of non-infectious origin**

Code first underlying condition, such as:
heatstroke (T67.0-)
injury and trauma (S00-T88)

> **Excludes1**　sepsis - code to infection
> severe sepsis (R65.2)

Coding Clinic: 2019, Q2, P38

R65.10　Systemic inflammatory response syndrome (SIRS) of non-infectious origin without acute organ dysfunction 🏥

Systemic inflammatory response syndrome (SIRS) NOS

Coding Clinic: 2019, Q2, P25, 38

R65.11　Systemic inflammatory response syndrome (SIRS) of non-infectious origin with acute organ dysfunction 🏥

Use additional code to identify specific acute organ dysfunction, such as:
acute kidney failure (N17.-)
acute respiratory failure (J96.0-)
critical illness myopathy (G72.81)
critical illness polyneuropathy (G62.81)
disseminated intravascular coagulopathy [DIC] (D65)
encephalopathy (metabolic) (septic) (G93.41)
hepatic failure (K72.0-)

OGCR Section I.C.18.g.

SIRS due to Non-Infectious Process

The systemic inflammatory response syndrome (SIRS) can develop as a result of certain non-infectious disease processes, such as trauma, malignant neoplasm, or pancreatitis. When SIRS is documented with a noninfectious condition, and no subsequent infection is documented, the code for the underlying condition, such as an injury, should be assigned, followed by code R65.10, Systemic inflammatory response syndrome (SIRS) of non-infectious origin without acute organ dysfunction, or code R65.11, Systemic inflammatory response syndrome (SIRS) of non-infectious origin with acute organ dysfunction. If an associated acute organ dysfunction is documented, the appropriate code(s) for the specific type of organ dysfunction(s) should be assigned in addition to code R65.11. If acute organ dysfunction is documented, but it cannot be determined if the acute organ dysfunction is associated with SIRS or due to another condition (e.g., directly due to the trauma), the provider should be queried.

● **R65.2　Severe sepsis**

Infection with associated acute organ dysfunction
Sepsis with acute organ dysfunction
Sepsis with multiple organ dysfunction
Systemic inflammatory response syndrome due to infectious process with acute organ dysfunction

Code first underlying infection, such as:
infection following a procedure (T81.44)
infections following infusion, transfusion and therapeutic injection (T80.2-)
puerperal sepsis (O85)
sepsis following complete or unspecified spontaneous abortion (O03.87)
sepsis following ectopic and molar pregnancy (O08.82)
sepsis following incomplete spontaneous abortion (O03.37)
sepsis following (induced) termination of pregnancy (O04.87)
sepsis NOS (A41.9)

Use additional code to identify specific acute organ dysfunction, such as:
acute kidney failure (N17.-)
acute respiratory failure (J96.0-)
critical illness myopathy (G72.81)
critical illness polyneuropathy (G62.81)
disseminated intravascular coagulopathy [DIC] (D65)
encephalopathy (metabolic) (septic) (G93.41)
hepatic failure (K72.0-)

Coding Clinic: 2017, Q4, P99; 2016, Q3, P8

R65.20　Severe sepsis without septic shock 🏥

Severe sepsis NOS

Coding Clinic: 2019, Q1, P14; 2018, Q4, P90; 2016, Q3, P14

R65.21　Severe sepsis with septic shock 🏥

● **R68　Other general symptoms and signs**

R68.0　Hypothermia, not associated with low environmental temperature

> **Excludes1**　hypothermia NOS (accidental) (T68)
> hypothermia due to anesthesia (T88.51)
> hypothermia due to low environmental temperature (T68)
> newborn hypothermia (P80.-)

● **R68.1　Nonspecific symptoms peculiar to infancy**

> **Excludes1**　colic, infantile (R10.83)
> neonatal cerebral irritability (P91.3)
> teething syndrome (K00.7)

R68.11　Excessive crying of infant (baby)　　　　P

> **Excludes1**　excessive crying of child, adolescent, or adult (R45.83)

R68.12　Fussy infant (baby)　　　　P

Irritable infant

R68.13　Apparent life threatening event in infant (ALTE)　　　　P

Apparent life threatening event in newborn
Brief resolved unexplained event (BRUE)

Code first confirmed diagnosis, if known

Use additional code(s) for associated signs and symptoms if no confirmed diagnosis established, or if signs and symptoms are not associated routinely with confirmed diagnosis, or provide additional information for cause of ALTE

R68.19　Other nonspecific symptoms peculiar to infancy　　　　P

CHAPTER 18 (R00-R99)

CHAPTER 18 (R00-R99)

R68.2 **Dry mouth, unspecified**
> **Excludes1** dry mouth due to dehydration (E86.0)
> dry mouth due to sicca syndrome
> [Sjögren] (M35.0-)
> salivary gland hyposecretion (K11.7)

R68.3 **Clubbing of fingers**
Clubbing of nails
> **Excludes1** congenital clubfinger (Q68.1)

● **R68.8** **Other general symptoms and signs**

R68.81 **Early satiety**

R68.82 **Decreased libido**   A
Decreased sexual desire

R68.83 **Chills (without fever)**
Chills NOS
> **Excludes1** chills with fever (R50.9)

R68.84 **Jaw pain**
Mandibular pain
Maxilla pain
> **Excludes1** temporomandibular joint
> arthralgia (M26.62-)

R68.89 **Other general symptoms and signs**

R69 **Illness, unspecified**
Unknown and unspecified cases of morbidity

ABNORMAL FINDINGS ON EXAMINATION OF BLOOD, WITHOUT DIAGNOSIS (R70-R79)

> **Excludes2** abnormal findings on antenatal screening of
> mother (O28.-)
> abnormalities of lipids (E78.-)
> abnormalities of platelets and thrombocytes
> (D69.-)
> abnormalities of white blood cells classified
> elsewhere (D70-D72)
> coagulation hemorrhagic disorders (D65-D68)
> diagnostic abnormal findings classified
> elsewhere —*see* Alphabetical Index
> hemorrhagic and hematological disorders of
> newborn (P50-P61)

● **R70** **Elevated erythrocyte sedimentation rate and abnormality of plasma viscosity**

R70.0 **Elevated erythrocyte sedimentation rate**

R70.1 **Abnormal plasma viscosity**

● **R71** **Abnormality of red blood cells**
> **Excludes1** anemias (D50-D64)
> anemia of premature infant (P61.2)
> benign (familial) polycythemia (D75.0)
> congenital anemias (P61.2-P61.4)
> newborn anemia due to isoimmunization (P55.-)
> polycythemia neonatorum (P61.1)
> polycythemia NOS (D75.1)
> polycythemia vera (D45)
> secondary polycythemia (D75.1)

R71.0 **Precipitous drop in hematocrit**
Drop (precipitous) in hemoglobin
Drop in hematocrit
Blood volume that has decreased red blood cells

R71.8 **Other abnormality of red blood cells**
Abnormal red-cell morphology NOS
Abnormal red-cell volume NOS
Anisocytosis
Red blood cells of unequal size
Poikilocytosis
Red blood cells of abnormal shape

● **R73** **Elevated blood glucose level**
> **Excludes1** diabetes mellitus (E08-E13)
> diabetes mellitus in pregnancy, childbirth and the
> puerperium (O24.-)
> neonatal disorders (P70.0-P70.2)
> postsurgical hypoinsulinemia (E89.1)

● **R73.0** **Abnormal glucose**
> **Excludes1** abnormal glucose in pregnancy (O99.81-)
> diabetes mellitus (E08-E13)
> dysmetabolic syndrome X (E88.81)
> gestational diabetes (O24.4-)
> glycosuria (R81)
> hypoglycemia (E16.2)

R73.01 **Impaired fasting glucose**
Elevated fasting glucose

R73.02 **Impaired glucose tolerance (oral)**
Elevated glucose tolerance

R73.03 **Prediabetes**
Latent diabetes
Coding Clinic: 2016, Q4, P65

R73.09 **Other abnormal glucose**
Abnormal glucose NOS
Abnormal non-fasting glucose tolerance
Coding Clinic: 2016, Q4, P65

R73.9 **Hyperglycemia, unspecified**

● **R74** **Abnormal serum enzyme levels**

● **R74.0** **Nonspecific elevation of levels of transaminase and lactic acid dehydrogenase [LDH]**

▶ **R74.01** **Elevation of levels of liver transaminase levels**
▶Elevation of levels of alanine transaminase
(ALT)
▶Elevation of levels of aspartate transaminase
(AST)

▶ **R74.02** **Elevation of levels of lactic acid dehydrogenase [LDH]**

R74.8 **Abnormal levels of other serum enzymes**
Abnormal level of acid phosphatase
Abnormal level of alkaline phosphatase
Abnormal level of amylase
Abnormal level of lipase [triacylglycerol lipase]
Coding Clinic: 2019, Q2, P6

R74.9 **Abnormal serum enzyme level, unspecified**

R75 **Inconclusive laboratory evidence of human immunodeficiency virus [HIV]**
Nonconclusive HIV-test finding in infants
> **Excludes1** asymptomatic human immunodeficiency virus
> [HIV] infection status (Z21)
> human immunodeficiency virus [HIV] disease
> (B20)

OGCR Section I.C.1.e and f.

Patients with inconclusive HIV serology

e. Patients with inconclusive HIV serology, but no definitive
diagnosis or manifestations of the illness, may be assigned code R75,
Inconclusive laboratory evidence of human immunodeficiency virus
[HIV].

f. Previously diagnosed HIV-related illness

Patients with any known prior diagnosis of an HIV-related illness
should be coded to B20. Once a patient has developed an HIV-related
illness, the patient should always be assigned code B20 on every
subsequent admission/encounter. Patients previously diagnosed
with any HIV illness (B20) should never be assigned to R75 or Z21,
Asymptomatic human immunodeficiency virus [HIV] infection status.

▶ New   ⇒ Revised   ~~deleted~~ Deleted   Excludes 1   Excludes 2   Includes   Use additional   Code first   Code also   Key words
OGCR Official Guidelines   X Assign placeholder X   ● Use Additional Character(s)   ▌ Manifestation Code   **❊** Hierarchical Condition Category   **Coding Clinic**

● R76   Other abnormal immunological findings in serum

R76.0   Raised antibody titer

Excludes1   isoimmunization in pregnancy
(O36.0-O36.1)
isoimmunization affecting newborn
(P55.-)

● R76.1   Nonspecific reaction to test for tuberculosis

R76.11   Nonspecific reaction to tuberculin skin test
without active tuberculosis
Abnormal result of Mantoux test
PPD positive
Tuberculin (skin test) positive
Tuberculin (skin test) reactor

Excludes1   nonspecific reaction to cell
mediated immunity
measurement of gamma
interferon antigen response
without active tuberculosis
(R76.12)

R76.12   Nonspecific reaction to cell mediated immunity
measurement of gamma interferon antigen
response without active tuberculosis
Nonspecific reaction to QuantiFERON-TB test
(QFT) without active tuberculosis

Excludes1   nonspecific reaction to tuberculin
skin test without active
tuberculosis (R76.11)
positive tuberculin skin test
(R76.11)

R76.8   Other specified abnormal immunological findings in
serum
Raised level of immunoglobulins NOS

R76.9   Abnormal immunological finding in serum, unspecified

● R77   Other abnormalities of plasma proteins

Excludes1   disorders of plasma-protein metabolism (E88.0-)

R77.0   Abnormality of albumin

R77.1   Abnormality of globulin
Hyperglobulinemia NOS

R77.2   Abnormality of alphafetoprotein

R77.8   Other specified abnormalities of plasma proteins
Coding Clinic: 2019, Q2, P6

R77.9   Abnormality of plasma protein, unspecified
Coding Clinic: 2019, Q2, P6

● R78   Findings of drugs and other substances, not normally found in
blood
Use additional code to identify any retained foreign body, if
applicable (Z18.-)

Excludes1   mental or behavioral disorders due to
psychoactive substance use (F10-F19)

R78.0   Finding of alcohol in blood
Use additional external cause code (Y90.-), for detail
regarding alcohol level.

R78.1   Finding of opiate drug in blood

R78.2   Finding of cocaine in blood

R78.3   Finding of hallucinogen in blood

R78.4   Finding of other drugs of addictive potential in blood

R78.5   Finding of other psychotropic drug in blood

R78.6   Finding of steroid agent in blood

● R78.7   Finding of abnormal level of heavy metals in blood

R78.71   Abnormal lead level in blood

Excludes1   lead poisoning (T56.0-)

R78.79   Finding of abnormal level of heavy metals in
blood

● R78.8   Finding of other specified substances, not normally
found in blood

R78.81   Bacteremia
Blood poisoning/bacteremia

Excludes1   sepsis-code to specified
infection

R78.89   Finding of other specified substances, not
normally found in blood
Finding of abnormal level of lithium in blood

R78.9   Finding of unspecified substance, not normally found in
blood

● R79   Other abnormal findings of blood chemistry
Use additional code to identify any retained foreign body, if
applicable (Z18.-)

Excludes1   asymptomatic hyperuricemia (E79.0)
hyperglycemia NOS (R73.9)
hypoglycemia NOS (E16.2)
neonatal hypoglycemia (P70.3-P70.4)
specific findings indicating disorder of amino-
acid metabolism (E70-E72)
specific findings indicating disorder of
carbohydrate metabolism (E73-E74)
specific findings indicating disorder of lipid
metabolism (E75.-)

R79.0   Abnormal level of blood mineral
Abnormal blood level of cobalt
Abnormal blood level of copper
Abnormal blood level of iron
Abnormal blood level of magnesium
Abnormal blood level of mineral NEC
Abnormal blood level of zinc

Excludes1   abnormal level of lithium (R78.89)
disorders of mineral metabolism (E83.-)
neonatal hypomagnesemia (P71.2)
nutritional mineral deficiency (E58-E61)

R79.1   Abnormal coagulation profile
Abnormal or prolonged bleeding time
Abnormal or prolonged coagulation time
Abnormal or prolonged partial thromboplastin time
[PTT]
Abnormal or prolonged prothrombin time [PT]

Excludes1   coagulation defects (D68.-)

Excludes2   abnormality of fluid, electrolyte or acid-
base balance (E86-E87)

● R79.8   Other specified abnormal findings of blood chemistry

R79.81   Abnormal blood-gas level

R79.82   Elevated C-reactive protein (CRP)

R79.89   Other specified abnormal findings of blood
chemistry
Coding Clinic: 2019, Q2, P6

R79.9   Abnormal finding of blood chemistry, unspecified

CHAPTER 18 (R00-R99)

ABNORMAL FINDINGS ON EXAMINATION OF URINE, WITHOUT DIAGNOSIS (R80-R82)

Excludes1   abnormal findings on antenatal screening of mother (O28.-)
diagnostic abnormal findings classified elsewhere - see Alphabetical Index
specific findings indicating disorder of amino-acid metabolism (E70-E72)
specific findings indicating disorder of carbohydrate metabolism (E73-E74)

● **R80**   **Proteinuria**

     Excludes1   gestational proteinuria (O12.1-)

     R80.0   **Isolated proteinuria**
         Idiopathic proteinuria

         Excludes1   isolated proteinuria with specific morphological lesion (N06.-)

     R80.1   **Persistent proteinuria, unspecified**

     R80.2   **Orthostatic proteinuria, unspecified**
         Postural proteinuria

     R80.3   **Bence Jones proteinuria**

     R80.8   **Other proteinuria**

     R80.9   **Proteinuria, unspecified**
         Albuminuria NOS

 R81   **Glycosuria**

     ⇒ **Excludes1**   renal glycosuria (E74.818)

● **R82**   **Other and unspecified abnormal findings in urine**

     Includes   chromoabnormalities in urine

     Use additional code to identify any retained foreign body, if applicable (Z18.-)

     Excludes2   hematuria (R31.-)

     R82.0   **Chyluria**
         White milky urine

         Excludes1   filarial chyluria (B74.-)

     R82.1   **Myoglobinuria**
         Presence of myoglobin (iron containing protein) in urine

     R82.2   **Biliuria**
         Presence of bile pigments/salts in urine

     R82.3   **Hemoglobinuria**
         Presence of hemoglobin in urine

         Excludes1   hemoglobinuria due to hemolysis from external causes NEC (D59.6)
hemoglobinuria due to paroxysmal nocturnal [Marchiafava-Micheli] (D59.5)

     R82.4   **Acetonuria**
         Ketonuria

     R82.5   **Elevated urine levels of drugs, medicaments and biological substances**
         Elevated urine levels of catecholamines
         Elevated urine levels of indoleacetic acid
         Elevated urine levels of 17-ketosteroids
         Elevated urine levels of steroids

     R82.6   **Abnormal urine levels of substances chiefly nonmedicinal as to source**
         Abnormal urine level of heavy metals

     ● **R82.7**   **Abnormal findings on microbiological examination of urine**

         Excludes1   colonization status (Z22.-)

         Coding Clinic: 2016, Q4, P65

         R82.71   **Bacteriuria**

         R82.79   **Other abnormal findings on microbiological examination of urine**
             Positive culture findings of urine

     ● **R82.8**   **Abnormal findings on cytological and histological examination of urine**

         R82.81   **Pyuria**
             Sterile pyuria
             Coding Clinic: 2019, Q4, P16

         R82.89   **Other abnormal findings on cytological and histological examination of urine**

     ● **R82.9**   **Other and unspecified abnormal findings in urine**

         R82.90   **Unspecified abnormal findings in urine**

         R82.91   **Other chromoabnormalities of urine**
             Chromoconversion (dipstick)
             Idiopathic dipstick converts positive for blood with no cellular forms in sediment

             Excludes1   hemoglobinuria (R82.3)
                         myoglobinuria (R82.1)

     ● **R82.99**   **Other abnormal findings in urine**

         R82.991   **Hypocitraturia**

         R82.992   **Hyperoxaluria**

             Excludes1   Primary hyperoxaluria (E72.53)

         R82.993   **Hyperuricosuria**

         R82.994   **Hypercalciuria**
             Idiopathic hypercalciuria

         R82.998   **Other abnormal findings in urine**
             Cells and casts in urine
             Crystalluria
             Melanuria

ABNORMAL FINDINGS ON EXAMINATION OF OTHER BODY FLUIDS, SUBSTANCES AND TISSUES, WITHOUT DIAGNOSIS (R83-R89)

Excludes1   abnormal findings on antenatal screening of mother (O28.-)
diagnostic abnormal findings classified elsewhere - see Alphabetical Index

Excludes2   abnormal findings on examination of blood, without diagnosis (R70-R79)
abnormal findings on examination of urine, without diagnosis (R80-R82)
abnormal tumor markers (R97.-)

● **R83**   **Abnormal findings in cerebrospinal fluid**

     R83.0   **Abnormal level of enzymes in cerebrospinal fluid**

     R83.1   **Abnormal level of hormones in cerebrospinal fluid**

     R83.2   **Abnormal level of other drugs, medicaments and biological substances in cerebrospinal fluid**

     R83.3   **Abnormal level of substances chiefly nonmedicinal as to source in cerebrospinal fluid**

     R83.4   **Abnormal immunological findings in cerebrospinal fluid**

     R83.5   **Abnormal microbiological findings in cerebrospinal fluid**
         Positive culture findings in cerebrospinal fluid

         Excludes1   colonization status (Z22.-)

     R83.6   **Abnormal cytological findings in cerebrospinal fluid**

     R83.8   **Other abnormal findings in cerebrospinal fluid**
         Abnormal chromosomal findings in cerebrospinal fluid

     R83.9   **Unspecified abnormal finding in cerebrospinal fluid**

● **R84**   **Abnormal findings in specimens from respiratory organs and thorax**

     Includes   abnormal findings in bronchial washings
         abnormal findings in nasal secretions
         abnormal findings in pleural fluid
         abnormal findings in sputum
         abnormal findings in throat scrapings

     Excludes1   blood-stained sputum (R04.2)

     R84.0   **Abnormal level of enzymes in specimens from respiratory organs and thorax**

     R84.1   **Abnormal level of hormones in specimens from respiratory organs and thorax**

     R84.2   **Abnormal level of other drugs, medicaments and biological substances in specimens from respiratory organs and thorax**

     R84.3   **Abnormal level of substances chiefly nonmedicinal as to source in specimens from respiratory organs and thorax**

     R84.4   **Abnormal immunological findings in specimens from respiratory organs and thorax**

▶ New   ⇒ Revised   ~~deleted~~ Deleted   Excludes 1   Excludes 2   Includes   Use additional   Code first   Code also   Key words

OGCR Official Guidelines   X Assign placeholder X   ● Use Additional Character(s)   � Manifestation Code   ℞ Hierarchical Condition Category   Coding Clinic

R84.5   **Abnormal microbiological findings in specimens from respiratory organs and thorax**
    Positive culture findings in specimens from respiratory organs and thorax
    Excludes1   colonization status (Z22.-)

R84.6   **Abnormal cytological findings in specimens from respiratory organs and thorax**

R84.7   **Abnormal histological findings in specimens from respiratory organs and thorax**

R84.8   **Other abnormal findings in specimens from respiratory organs and thorax**
    Abnormal chromosomal findings in specimens from respiratory organs and thorax

R84.9   **Unspecified abnormal finding in specimens from respiratory organs and thorax**

● R85   **Abnormal findings in specimens from digestive organs and abdominal cavity**
    Includes   abnormal findings in peritoneal fluid
              abnormal findings in saliva
    Excludes1   cloudy peritoneal dialysis effluent (R88.0)
              fecal abnormalities (R19.5)

R85.0   **Abnormal level of enzymes in specimens from digestive organs and abdominal cavity**

R85.1   **Abnormal level of hormones in specimens from digestive organs and abdominal cavity**

R85.2   **Abnormal level of other drugs, medicaments and biological substances in specimens from digestive organs and abdominal cavity**

R85.3   **Abnormal level of substances chiefly nonmedicinal as to source in specimens from digestive organs and abdominal cavity**

R85.4   **Abnormal immunological findings in specimens from digestive organs and abdominal cavity**

R85.5   **Abnormal microbiological findings in specimens from digestive organs and abdominal cavity**
    Positive culture findings in specimens from digestive organs and abdominal cavity
    Excludes1   colonization status (Z22.-)

● R85.6   **Abnormal cytological findings in specimens from digestive organs and abdominal cavity**

● R85.61   **Abnormal cytologic smear of anus**
    Excludes1   abnormal cytological findings in specimens from other digestive organs and abdominal cavity (R85.69)
              carcinoma in situ of anus (histologically confirmed) (D01.3)
              anal intraepithelial neoplasia I [AIN I] (K62.82)
              anal intraepithelial neoplasia II [AIN II] (K62.82)
              anal intraepithelial neoplasia III [AIN III] (D01.3)
              dysplasia (mild) (moderate) of anus (histologically confirmed) (K62.82)
              severe dysplasia of anus (histologically confirmed) (D01.3)
    Excludes2   anal high risk human papillomavirus (HPV) DNA test positive (R85.81)
              anal low risk human papillomavirus (HPV) DNA test positive (R85.82)

R85.610   **Atypical squamous cells of undetermined significance on cytologic smear of anus (ASC-US)**

R85.611   **Atypical squamous cells cannot exclude high grade squamous intraepithelial lesion on cytologic smear of anus (ASC-H)**

R85.612   **Low grade squamous intraepithelial lesion on cytologic smear of anus (LGSIL)**

R85.613   **High grade squamous intraepithelial lesion on cytologic smear of anus (HGSIL)**

R85.614   **Cytologic evidence of malignancy on smear of anus**

R85.615   **Unsatisfactory cytologic smear of anus**
    Inadequate sample of cytologic smear of anus

R85.616   **Satisfactory anal smear but lacking transformation zone**

R85.618   **Other abnormal cytological findings on specimens from anus**

R85.619   **Unspecified abnormal cytological findings in specimens from anus**
    Abnormal anal cytology NOS
    Atypical glandular cells of anus NOS

R85.69   **Abnormal cytological findings in specimens from other digestive organs and abdominal cavity**

R85.7   **Abnormal histological findings in specimens from digestive organs and abdominal cavity**

● R85.8   **Other abnormal findings in specimens from digestive organs and abdominal cavity**

R85.81   **Anal high risk human papillomavirus (HPV) DNA test positive**
    Excludes1   anogenital warts due to human papillomavirus (HPV) (A63.0)
              condyloma acuminatum (A63.0)

R85.82   **Anal low risk human papillomavirus (HPV) DNA test positive**
    Use additional code for associated human papillomavirus (B97.7)

R85.89   **Other abnormal findings in specimens from digestive organs and abdominal cavity**
    Abnormal chromosomal findings in specimens from digestive organs and abdominal cavity

R85.9   **Unspecified abnormal finding in specimens from digestive organs and abdominal cavity**

● R86   **Abnormal findings in specimens from male genital organs**
    Includes   abnormal findings in prostatic secretions
              abnormal findings in semen, seminal fluid
              abnormal spermatozoa
    Excludes1   azoospermia (N46.0-)
              oligospermia (N46.1-)

R86.0   **Abnormal level of enzymes in specimens from male genital organs** ♂

R86.1   **Abnormal level of hormones in specimens from male genital organs** ♂

R86.2   **Abnormal level of other drugs, medicaments and biological substances in specimens from male genital organs** ♂

R86.3   **Abnormal level of substances chiefly nonmedicinal as to source in specimens from male genital organs** ♂

R86.4   **Abnormal immunological findings in specimens from male genital organs** ♂

R86.5   **Abnormal microbiological findings in specimens from male genital organs** ♂
    Positive culture findings in specimens from male genital organs
    Excludes1   colonization status (Z22.-)

R86.6   **Abnormal cytological findings in specimens from male genital organs** ♂

R86.7   **Abnormal histological findings in specimens from male genital organs** ♂

CHAPTER 18 (R00-R99)

R86.8 **Other abnormal findings in specimens from male genital organs** ♂

Abnormal chromosomal findings in specimens from male genital organs

R86.9 **Unspecified abnormal finding in specimens from male genital organs** ♂

● **R87** **Abnormal findings in specimens from female genital organs**

Includes abnormal findings in secretion and smears from cervix uteri

abnormal findings in secretion and smears from vagina

abnormal findings in secretion and smears from vulva

R87.0 **Abnormal level of enzymes in specimens from female genital organs** ♀

R87.1 **Abnormal level of hormones in specimens from female genital organs** ♀

R87.2 **Abnormal level of other drugs, medicaments and biological substances in specimens from female genital organs** ♀

R87.3 **Abnormal level of substances chiefly nonmedicinal as to source in specimens from female genital organs** ♀

R87.4 **Abnormal immunological findings in specimens from female genital organs** ♀

R87.5 **Abnormal microbiological findings in specimens from female genital organs** ♀

Positive culture findings in specimens from female genital organs

Excludes1 colonization status (Z22.-)

● **R87.6** **Abnormal cytological findings in specimens from female genital organs**

● **R87.61** **Abnormal cytological findings in specimens from cervix uteri**

Excludes1 abnormal cytological findings in specimens from other female genital organs (R87.69)

abnormal cytological findings in specimens from vagina (R87.62-)

carcinoma in situ of cervix uteri (histologically confirmed) (D06.-)

cervical intraepithelial neoplasia I [CIN I] (N87.0)

cervical intraepithelial neoplasia II [CIN II] (N87.1)

cervical intraepithelial neoplasia III [CIN III] (D06.-)

dysplasia (mild) (moderate) of cervix uteri (histologically confirmed) (N87.-)

severe dysplasia of cervix uteri (histologically confirmed) (D06.-)

Excludes2 cervical high risk human papillomavirus (HPV) DNA test positive (R87.810)

cervical low risk human papillomavirus (HPV) DNA test positive (R87.820)

R87.610 **Atypical squamous cells of undetermined significance on cytologic smear of cervix (ASC-US)** ♀

R87.611 **Atypical squamous cells cannot exclude high grade squamous intraepithelial lesion on cytologic smear of cervix (ASC-H)** ♀

R87.612 **Low grade squamous intraepithelial lesion on cytologic smear of cervix (LGSIL)** ♀

R87.613 **High grade squamous intraepithelial lesion on cytologic smear of cervix (HGSIL)** ♀

R87.614 **Cytologic evidence of malignancy on smear of cervix** ♀

R87.615 **Unsatisfactory cytologic smear of cervix** ♀

Inadequate sample of cytologic smear of cervix

R87.616 **Satisfactory cervical smear but lacking transformation zone** ♀

R87.618 **Other abnormal cytological findings on specimens from cervix uteri** ♀

R87.619 **Unspecified abnormal cytological findings in specimens from cervix uteri** ♀

Abnormal cervical cytology NOS

Abnormal Papanicolaou smear of cervix NOS

Abnormal thin preparation smear of cervix NOS

Atypical endocervial cells of cervix NOS

Atypical endometrial cells of cervix NOS

Atypical glandular cells of cervix NOS

● **R87.62** **Abnormal cytological findings in specimens from vagina**

Use additional code to identify acquired absence of uterus and cervix, if applicable (Z90.71-)

Excludes1 abnormal cytological findings in specimens from cervix uteri (R87.61-)

abnormal cytological findings in specimens from other female genital organs (R87.69)

carcinoma in situ of vagina (histologically confirmed) (D07.2)

vaginal intraepithelial neoplasia I [VAIN I] (N89.0)

vaginal intraepithelial neoplasia II [VAIN II] (N89.1)

vaginal intraepithelial neoplasia III [VAIN III] (D07.2)

dysplasia (mild) (moderate) of vagina (histologically confirmed) (N89.-)

severe dysplasia of vagina (histologically confirmed) (D07.2)

Excludes2 vaginal high risk human papillomavirus (HPV) DNA test positive (R87.811)

vaginal low risk human papillomavirus (HPV) DNA test positive (R87.821)

R87.620 **Atypical squamous cells of undetermined significance on cytologic smear of vagina (ASC-US)** ♀

R87.621 **Atypical squamous cells cannot exclude high grade squamous intraepithelial lesion on cytologic smear of vagina (ASC-H)** ♀

R87.622 **Low grade squamous intraepithelial lesion on cytologic smear of vagina (LGSIL)** ♀

R87.623 **High grade squamous intraepithelial lesion on cytologic smear of vagina (HGSIL)** ♀

R87.624 **Cytologic evidence of malignancy on smear of vagina** ♀

R87.625 **Unsatisfactory cytologic smear of vagina** ♀

Inadequate sample of cytologic smear of vagina

▶ New   ⟹ Revised   ~~deleted~~ Deleted   Excludes 1   Excludes 2   Includes   Use additional   Code first   Code also   Key words

OGCR Official Guidelines   X Assign placeholder X   ● Use Additional Character(s)   ▶ Manifestation Code   🝔 Hierarchical Condition Category   **Coding Clinic**

R87.628   Other abnormal cytological findings on specimens from vagina ♀

R87.629   Unspecified abnormal cytological findings in specimens from vagina ♀

Abnormal Papanicolaou smear of vagina NOS

Abnormal thin preparation smear of vagina NOS

Abnormal vaginal cytology NOS

Atypical endocervical cells of vagina NOS

Atypical endometrial cells of vagina NOS

Atypical glandular cells of vagina NOS

R87.69   Abnormal cytological findings in specimens from other female genital organs ♀

Abnormal cytological findings in specimens from female genital organs NOS

Excludes1   dysplasia of vulva (histologically confirmed) (N90.0-N90.3)

R87.7   Abnormal histological findings in specimens from female genital organs ♀

Excludes1   carcinoma in situ (histologically confirmed) of female genital organs (D06-D07.3)

cervical intraepithelial neoplasia I [CIN I] (N87.0)

cervical intraepithelial neoplasia II [CIN II] (N87.1)

cervical intraepithelial neoplasia III [CIN III] (D06.-)

dysplasia (mild) (moderate) of cervix uteri (histologically confirmed) (N87.-)

dysplasia (mild) (moderate) of vagina (histologically confirmed) (N89.-)

vaginal intraepithelial neoplasia I [VAIN I] (N89.0)

vaginal intraepithelial neoplasia II [VAIN II] (N89.1)

vaginal intraepithelial neoplasia III [VAIN III] (D07.2)

severe dysplasia of cervix uteri (histologically confirmed) (D06.-)

severe dysplasia of vagina (histologically confirmed) (D07.2)

● R87.8   Other abnormal findings in specimens from female genital organs

● R87.81   High risk human papillomavirus (HPV) DNA test positive from female genital organs

Excludes1   anogenital warts due to human papillomavirus (HPV) (A63.0)

condyloma acuminatum (A63.0)

R87.810   Cervical high risk human papillomavirus (HPV) DNA test positive ♀

R87.811   Vaginal high risk human papillomavirus (HPV) DNA test positive ♀

● R87.82   Low risk human papillomavirus (HPV) DNA test positive from female genital organs

Use additional code for associated human papillomavirus (B97.7)

R87.820   Cervical low risk human papillomavirus (HPV) DNA test positive ♀

R87.821   Vaginal low risk human papillomavirus (HPV) DNA test positive ♀

R87.89   Other abnormal findings in specimens from female genital organs ♀

Abnormal chromosomal findings in specimens from female genital organs

R87.9   Unspecified abnormal finding in specimens from female genital organs ♀

● R88   Abnormal findings in other body fluids and substances

R88.0   Cloudy (hemodialysis) (peritoneal) dialysis effluent

R88.8   Abnormal findings in other body fluids and substances

● R89   Abnormal findings in specimens from other organs, systems and tissues

Includes   abnormal findings in nipple discharge

abnormal findings in synovial fluid

abnormal findings in wound secretions

R89.0   Abnormal level of enzymes in specimens from other organs, systems and tissues

R89.1   Abnormal level of hormones in specimens from other organs, systems and tissues

R89.2   Abnormal level of other drugs, medicaments and biological substances in specimens from other organs, systems and tissues

R89.3   Abnormal level of substances chiefly nonmedicinal as to source in specimens from other organs, systems and tissues

R89.4   Abnormal immunological findings in specimens from other organs, systems and tissues

R89.5   Abnormal microbiological findings in specimens from other organs, systems and tissues

Positive culture findings in specimens from other organs, systems and tissues

Excludes1   colonization status (Z22.-)

R89.6   Abnormal cytological findings in specimens from other organs, systems and tissues

R89.7   Abnormal histological findings in specimens from other organs, systems and tissues

R89.8   Other abnormal findings in specimens from other organs, systems and tissues

Abnormal chromosomal findings in specimens from other organs, systems and tissues

R89.9   Unspecified abnormal finding in specimens from other organs, systems and tissues

---

ABNORMAL FINDINGS ON DIAGNOSTIC IMAGING AND IN FUNCTION STUDIES, WITHOUT DIAGNOSIS (R90-R94)

Includes   nonspecific abnormal findings on diagnostic imaging by computerized axial tomography [CAT scan]

nonspecific abnormal findings on diagnostic imaging by magnetic resonance imaging [MRI][NMR]

nonspecific abnormal findings on diagnostic imaging by positron emission tomography [PET scan]

nonspecific abnormal findings on diagnostic imaging by thermography

nonspecific abnormal findings on diagnostic imaging by ultrasound [echogram]

nonspecific abnormal findings on diagnostic imaging by X-ray examination

Excludes1   abnormal findings on antenatal screening of mother (O28.-)

diagnostic abnormal findings classified elsewhere - see Alphabetical Index

● R90   Abnormal findings on diagnostic imaging of central nervous system

R90.0   Intracranial space-occupying lesion found on diagnostic imaging of central nervous system

● R90.8   Other abnormal findings on diagnostic imaging of central nervous system

R90.81   Abnormal echoencephalogram

R90.82   White matter disease, unspecified

R90.89   Other abnormal findings on diagnostic imaging of central nervous system

Other cerebrovascular abnormality found on diagnostic imaging of central nervous system

CHAPTER 18 (R00-R99)

CHAPTER 18 (R00-R99)

● **R91**   **Abnormal findings on diagnostic imaging of lung**

    R91.1   **Solitary pulmonary nodule**
        Coin lesion lung
        Solitary pulmonary nodule, subsegmental branch of the bronchial tree

    R91.8   **Other nonspecific abnormal finding of lung field**
        Lung mass NOS found on diagnostic imaging of lung
        Pulmonary infiltrate NOS
        Shadow, lung

● **R92**   **Abnormal and inconclusive findings on diagnostic imaging of breast**

    R92.0   **Mammographic microcalcification found on diagnostic imaging of breast**
        Excludes2   mammographic calcification (calculus) found on diagnostic imaging of breast (R92.1)

    R92.1   **Mammographic calcification found on diagnostic imaging of breast**
        Mammographic calculus found on diagnostic imaging of breast

    R92.2   **Inconclusive mammogram**
        Dense breasts NOS
        Inconclusive mammogram NEC
        Inconclusive mammography due to dense breasts
        Inconclusive mammography NEC
        Coding Clinic: 2015, Q1, P24

    R92.8   **Other abnormal and inconclusive findings on diagnostic imaging of breast**

● **R93**   **Abnormal findings on diagnostic imaging of other body structures**

    R93.0   **Abnormal findings on diagnostic imaging of skull and head, not elsewhere classified**
        Excludes1   intracranial space-occupying lesion found on diagnostic imaging (R90.0)

    R93.1   **Abnormal findings on diagnostic imaging of heart and coronary circulation**
        Abnormal echocardiogram NOS
        Abnormal heart shadow

    R93.2   **Abnormal findings on diagnostic imaging of liver and biliary tract**
        Nonvisualization of gallbladder

    R93.3   **Abnormal findings on diagnostic imaging of other parts of digestive tract**

    ● **R93.4**   **Abnormal findings on diagnostic imaging of urinary organs**
        Excludes2   hypertrophy of kidney (N28.81)
        Coding Clinic: 2016, Q4, P66

        R93.41   **Abnormal radiologic findings on diagnostic imaging of renal pelvis, ureter, or bladder**
            Filling defect of bladder found on diagnostic imaging
            Filling defect of renal pelvis found on diagnostic imaging
            Filling defect of ureter found on diagnostic imaging

        ● **R93.42**   **Abnormal radiologic findings on diagnostic imaging of kidney**
            R93.421   **Abnormal radiologic findings on diagnostic imaging of right kidney**
            R93.422   **Abnormal radiologic findings on diagnostic imaging of left kidney**
            R93.429   **Abnormal radiologic findings on diagnostic imaging of unspecified kidney**

        R93.49   **Abnormal radiologic findings on diagnostic imaging of other urinary organs**

R93.5   **Abnormal findings on diagnostic imaging of other abdominal regions, including retroperitoneum**

R93.6   **Abnormal findings on diagnostic imaging of limbs**
    Excludes2   abnormal finding in skin and subcutaneous tissue (R93.8-)
    Coding Clinic: 2020, Q1, P14

R93.7   **Abnormal findings on diagnostic imaging of other parts of musculoskeletal system**
    Excludes2   abnormal findings on diagnostic imaging of skull (R93.0)

● **R93.8**   **Abnormal findings on diagnostic imaging of other specified body structures**

    ● **R93.81**   **Abnormal radiologic findings on diagnostic imaging of testis**
        R93.811   **Abnormal radiologic findings on diagnostic imaging of right testicle** ♂
        R93.812   **Abnormal radiologic findings on diagnostic imaging of left testicle** ♂
        R93.813   **Abnormal radiologic findings on diagnostic imaging of testicles, bilateral** ♂
        R93.819   **Abnormal radiologic findings on diagnostic imaging of unspecified testicle** ♂

    R93.89   **Abnormal findings on diagnostic imaging of other specified body structures**
        Abnormal finding by radioisotope localization of placenta
        Abnormal radiological finding in skin and subcutaneous tissue
        Mediastinal shift

    R93.9   **Diagnostic imaging inconclusive due to excess body fat of patient**

● **R94**   **Abnormal results of function studies**
    Includes   abnormal results of radionuclide [radioisotope] uptake studies
        abnormal results of scintigraphy

    ● **R94.0**   **Abnormal results of function studies of central nervous system**
        R94.01   **Abnormal electroencephalogram [EEG]**
        R94.02   **Abnormal brain scan**
        R94.09   **Abnormal results of other function studies of central nervous system**

    ● **R94.1**   **Abnormal results of function studies of peripheral nervous system and special senses**
        ● **R94.11**   **Abnormal results of function studies of eye**
            R94.110   **Abnormal electro-oculogram [EOG]**
            R94.111   **Abnormal electroretinogram [ERG]**
               Abnormal retinal function study
            R94.112   **Abnormal visually evoked potential [VEP]**
            R94.113   **Abnormal oculomotor study**
            R94.118   **Abnormal results of other function studies of eye**

        ● **R94.12**   **Abnormal results of function studies of ear and other special senses**
            R94.120   **Abnormal auditory function study**
               Coding Clinic: 2016, Q3, P17
            R94.121   **Abnormal vestibular function study**
            R94.128   **Abnormal results of other function studies of ear and other special senses**

▶ New   ⇒ Revised   ~~deleted~~ Deleted   Excludes 1   Excludes 2   Includes   Use additional   Code first   Code also   Key words

OGCR Official Guidelines   X Assign placeholder X   ● Use Additional Character(s)   ▶ Manifestation Code   ⬮ Hierarchical Condition Category   **Coding Clinic**

Figure 18-2 Cranial nerves. (From Patton and Thibodeau: Anatomy and physiology, ed 7, St. Louis, Mosby, 2009)

Trochlear nerve (IV)

Optic nerve (II)

Olfactory nerve (I)

Abducens nerve (VI)

Oculomotor nerve (III)

Facial nerve (VII)

Trigeminal nerve (V)

Vestibulocochlear nerve (VIII)

Glossopharyngeal nerve (IX)

Vagus nerve (X)

Accessory nerve (XI)

Hypoglossal nerve (XII)

Item 18–1 The **peripheral nervous system** consists of 31 pairs of spinal nerves, 12 pairs of cranial nerves, and the autonomic nerves, which are divided into the parasympathetic and sympathetic nerves. The cranial nerves are: olfactory (I), optic (II), oculomotor (III), trochlear (IV), trigeminal (V), abducens (VI), facial (VII), vestibulocochlear (VIII), glossopharyngeal (IX), vagus (X), accessory (XI), and hypoglossal (XII).

● R94.13   **Abnormal results of function studies of peripheral nervous system**

    R94.130   **Abnormal response to nerve stimulation, unspecified**

    R94.131   **Abnormal electromyogram [EMG]**

       Excludes1   electromyogram of eye (R94.113)

    R94.138   **Abnormal results of other function studies of peripheral nervous system**

R94.2   **Abnormal results of pulmonary function studies**
    Reduced ventilatory capacity
    Reduced vital capacity

● R94.3   **Abnormal results of cardiovascular function studies**

    R94.30   **Abnormal result of cardiovascular function study, unspecified**

    R94.31   **Abnormal electrocardiogram [ECG] [EKG]**

       Excludes1   long QT syndrome (I45.81)

    R94.39   **Abnormal result of other cardiovascular function study**
       Abnormal electrophysiological intracardiac studies
       Abnormal phonocardiogram
       Abnormal vectorcardiogram

R94.4   **Abnormal results of kidney function studies**
    Abnormal renal function test

R94.5   **Abnormal results of liver function studies**

R94.6   **Abnormal results of thyroid function studies**

R94.7   **Abnormal results of other endocrine function studies**
       Excludes2   abnormal glucose (R73.0-)

R94.8   **Abnormal results of function studies of other organs and systems**
    Abnormal basal metabolic rate [BMR]
    Abnormal bladder function test
    Abnormal splenic function test

ABNORMAL TUMOR MARKERS (R97)

● R97   **Abnormal tumor markers**
    Elevated tumor associated antigens [TAA]
    Elevated tumor specific antigens [TSA]

    R97.0   **Elevated carcinoembryonic antigen [CEA]**

    R97.1   **Elevated cancer antigen 125 [CA 125]**

●   R97.2   **Elevated prostate specific antigen [PSA]**
       Coding Clinic: 2016, Q4, P66

       R97.20   **Elevated prostate specific antigen [PSA]** ♂   A

       R97.21   **Rising PSA following treatment for malignant neoplasm of prostate** ♂   A

    R97.8   **Other abnormal tumor markers**

ILL-DEFINED AND UNKNOWN CAUSE OF MORTALITY (R99)

R99   **Ill-defined and unknown cause of mortality**
    Death (unexplained) NOS
    Unspecified cause of mortality

    OGCR Section I.C.18.h.

    Death NOS

    Code R99, Ill-defined and unknown cause of mortality, is only for use in the very limited circumstance when a patient who has already died is brought into the emergency department or other healthcare facility and is pronounced dead upon arrival. It does not represent the discharge disposition of death.

CHAPTER 18 (R00-R99)

CHAPTER 19

INJURY, POISONING AND CERTAIN OTHER CONSEQUENCES OF EXTERNAL CAUSES (S00-T88)

OGCR Chapter-Specific Coding Guidelines

19. Chapter 19: Injury, poisoning, and certain other consequences of external causes (S00-T88)

a. Application of 7th Characters in Chapter 19

Most categories in Chapter 19 have a 7th character requirement for each applicable code. Most categories in this chapter have three 7th character values (with the exception of fractures): A, initial encounter, D, subsequent encounter and S, sequela. Categories for traumatic fractures have additional 7th character values. While the patient may be seen by a new or different provider over the course of treatment for an injury, assignment of the 7th character is based on whether the patient is undergoing active treatment and not whether the provider is seeing the patient for the first time.

For complication codes, active treatment refers to treatment for the condition described by the code, even though it may be related to an earlier precipitating problem. For example, code T84.50XA, Infection and inflammatory reaction due to unspecified internal joint prosthesis, initial encounter, is used when active treatment is provided for the infection, even though the condition relates to the prosthetic device, implant or graft that was placed at a previous encounter.

7th character "A", initial encounter is used for each encounter where the patient is receiving active treatment for the condition.

7th character "D" subsequent encounter is used for encounters after the patient has completed active treatment of the condition and is receiving routine care for the condition during the healing or recovery phase.

The aftercare Z codes should not be used for aftercare for conditions such as injuries or poisonings, where 7th characters are provided to identify subsequent care. For example, for aftercare of an injury, assign the acute injury code with the 7th character "D" (subsequent encounter).

7th character "S", sequela, is for use for complications or conditions that arise as a direct result of a condition, such as scar formation after a burn. The scars are sequelae of the burn. When using 7th character "S", it is necessary to use both the injury code that precipitated the sequela and the code for the sequela itself. The "S" is added only to the injury code, not the sequela code. The 7th character "S" identifies the injury responsible for the sequela. The specific type of sequela (e.g. scar) is sequenced first, followed by the injury code.

See Section I.B.10. Sequelae, (Late Effects).

b. Coding of Injuries

When coding injuries, assign separate codes for each injury unless a combination code is provided, in which case the combination code is assigned. Codes from category T07, Unspecified multiple injuries should not be assigned in the inpatient setting unless information for a more specific code is not available. Traumatic injury codes (S00-T14.9) are not to be used for normal, healing surgical wounds or to identify complications of surgical wounds.

The code for the most serious injury, as determined by the provider and the focus of treatment, is sequenced first.

1) Superficial injuries

Superficial injuries such as abrasions or contusions are not coded when associated with more severe injuries of the same site.

2) Primary injury with damage to nerves/blood vessels

When a primary injury results in minor damage to peripheral nerves or blood vessels, the primary injury is sequenced first with additional code(s) for injuries to nerves and spinal cord (such as category S04), and/or injury to blood vessels (such as category S15). When the primary injury is to the blood vessels or nerves, that injury should be sequenced first.

c. Coding of Traumatic Fractures

The principles of multiple coding of injuries should be followed in coding fractures. Fractures of specified sites are coded individually by site in accordance with both the provisions within categories S02, S12, S22, S32, S42, S49, S52, S59, S62, S72, S79, S82, S89, S92 and the level of detail furnished by medical record content.

A fracture not indicated as open or closed should be coded to closed. A fracture not indicated whether displaced or not displaced should be coded to displaced.

More specific guidelines are as follows:

1) Initial vs. Subsequent Encounter for Fractures

Traumatic fractures are coded using the appropriate 7th character for initial encounter (A, B, C) for each encounter where the patient is receiving active treatment for the fracture. The appropriate 7th character for initial encounter should also be assigned for a patient who delayed seeking treatment for the fracture or nonunion.

Fractures are coded using the appropriate 7th character for subsequent care for encounters after the patient has completed active treatment of the fracture and is receiving routine care for the fracture during the healing or recovery phase.

Care for complications of surgical treatment for fracture repairs during the healing or recovery phase should be coded with the appropriate complication codes.

Care of complications of fractures, such as malunion and nonunion, should be reported with the appropriate 7th character for subsequent care with nonunion (K, M, N,) or subsequent care with malunion (P, Q, R).

Malunion/nonunion: The appropriate 7th character for initial encounter should also be assigned for a patient who delayed seeking treatment for the fracture or nonunion.

The open fracture designations in the assignment of the 7th character for fractures of the forearm, femur and lower leg, including ankle are based on the Gustilo open fracture classification. When the Gustilo classification type is not specified for an open fracture, the 7th character for open fracture type I or II should be assigned (B, E, H, M, Q).

A code from category M80, not a traumatic fracture code, should be used for any patient with known osteoporosis who suffers a fracture, even if the patient had a minor fall or trauma, if that fall or trauma would not usually break a normal, healthy bone.

See Section I.C.13. Osteoporosis.

The aftercare Z codes should not be used for aftercare for traumatic fractures. For aftercare of a traumatic fracture, assign the acute fracture code with the appropriate 7th character.

2) Multiple fractures sequencing

Multiple fractures are sequenced in accordance with the severity of the fracture.

d. Coding of Burns and Corrosions

The ICD-10-CM makes a distinction between burns and corrosions. The burn codes are for thermal burns, except sunburns, that come from a heat source, such as a fire or hot appliance. The burn codes are also for burns resulting from electricity and radiation. Corrosions are burns due to chemicals. The guidelines are the same for burns and corrosions.

Current burns (T20-T25) are classified by depth, extent and by agent (X code). Burns are classified by depth as first degree (erythema), second degree (blistering), and third degree (full-thickness involvement). Burns of the eye and internal organs (T26-T28) are classified by site, but not by degree.

1) Sequencing of burn and related condition codes

Sequence first the code that reflects the highest degree of burn when more than one burn is present.

  a. When the reason for the admission or encounter is for treatment of external multiple burns, sequence first the code that reflects the burn of the highest degree.

  b. When a patient has both internal and external burns, the circumstances of admission govern the selection of the principal diagnosis or first-listed diagnosis.

  c. When a patient is admitted for burn injuries and other related conditions such as smoke inhalation and/or respiratory failure, the circumstances of admission govern the selection of the principal or first-listed diagnosis.

2) Burns of the same *anatomic* site

Classify burns of the same anatomic site and on the same side but of different degrees to the subcategory identifying the highest degree recorded in the diagnosis (e.g., for second- and third-degree burns of right thigh, assign only code T24.311-).

3) Non-healing burns

Non-healing burns are coded as acute burns.

Necrosis of burned skin should be coded as a non-healed burn.

4) Infected Burn

For any documented infected burn site, use an additional code for the infection.

5) Assign separate codes for each burn site

When coding burns, assign separate codes for each burn site. Category T30, Burn and corrosion, body region unspecified is extremely vague and should rarely be used.

Codes for burns of "multiple sites" should only be assigned when the medical record documentation does not specify the individual sites.

6) Burns and Corrosions Classified According to Extent of Body Surface Involved

Assign codes from category T31, Burns classified according to extent of body surface involved, or T32, Corrosions classified according to extent of body surface involved, when the site of the burn is not specified or when there is a need for additional data. It is advisable to use category T31 as additional coding when needed to provide data for evaluating burn mortality, such as that needed by burn units. It is also advisable to use category T31 as an additional code for reporting purposes when there is mention of a third-degree burn involving 20 percent or more of the body surface.

Categories T31 and T32 are based on the classic "rule of nines" in estimating body surface involved: head and neck are assigned nine percent, each arm nine percent, each leg 18 percent, the anterior trunk 18 percent, posterior trunk 18 percent, and genitalia one percent. Providers may change these percentage assignments where necessary to accommodate infants and children who have proportionately larger heads than adults, and patients who have large buttocks, thighs, or abdomen that involve burns.

7) Encounters for treatment of sequela of burns

Encounters for the treatment of the late effects of burns or corrosions (i.e., scars or joint contractures) should be coded with a burn or corrosion code with the 7th character "S" for sequela.

8) Sequelae with a late effect code and current burn

When appropriate, both a code for a current burn or corrosion with 7th character "A" or "D" and a burn or corrosion code with 7th character "S" may be assigned on the same record (when both a current burn and sequelae of an old burn exist). Burns and corrosions do not heal at the same rate and a current healing wound may still exist with sequela of a healed burn or corrosion.

See Section I.B.10. Sequela, (Late Effects).

9) Use of an external cause code with burns and corrosions

An external cause code should be used with burns and corrosions to identify the source and intent of the burn, as well as the place where it occurred.

e. Adverse Effects, Poisoning , Underdosing and Toxic Effects

Codes in categories T36-T65 are combination codes that include the substance that was taken as well as the intent. No additional external cause code is required for poisonings, toxic effects, adverse effects and underdosing codes.

1) Do not code directly from the Table of Drugs

Do not code directly from the Table of Drugs and Chemicals. Always refer back to the Tabular List.

2) Use as many codes as necessary to describe

Use as many codes as necessary to describe completely all drugs, medicinal or biological substances.

3) If the same code would describe the causative agent

If the same code would describe the causative agent for more than one adverse reaction, poisoning, toxic effect or underdosing, assign the code only once.

4) If two or more drugs, medicinal or biological substances

If two or more drugs, medicinal or biological substances are reported, code each individually unless a combination code is listed in the Table of Drugs and Chemicals.

5) The occurrence of drug toxicity is classified in ICD-10-CM as follows:

(a) Adverse Effect

When coding an adverse effect of a drug that has been correctly prescribed and properly administered, assign the appropriate code for the nature of the adverse effect followed by the appropriate code for the adverse effect of the drug (T36-T50). The code for the drug should have a 5th or 6th character "5" (for example T36.0X5-) Examples of the nature of an adverse effect are tachycardia, delirium, gastrointestinal hemorrhaging, vomiting, hypokalemia, hepatitis, renal failure, or respiratory failure.

(b) Poisoning

When coding a poisoning or reaction to the improper use of a medication (e.g., overdose, wrong substance given or taken in error, wrong route of administration), first assign the appropriate code from categories T36-T50. The poisoning codes have an associated intent as their 5th or 6th character (accidental, intentional self-harm, assault and undetermined). If the intent of the poisoning is unknown or unspecified, code the intent as accidental intent. The undetermined intent is only for use if the documentation in the record specifies that the intent cannot be determined. Use additional code(s) for all manifestations of poisonings.

If there is also a diagnosis of abuse or dependence of the substance, the abuse or dependence is assigned as an additional code.

Examples of poisoning include:

(i) Error was made in drug prescription
Errors made in drug prescription or in the administration of the drug by provider, nurse, patient, or other person.

(ii) Overdose of a drug intentionally taken If an overdose of a drug was intentionally taken or administered and resulted in drug toxicity, it would be coded as a poisoning.

(iii) Nonprescribed drug taken with correctly prescribed and properly administered drug. If a nonprescribed drug or medicinal agent was taken in combination with a correctly prescribed and properly administered drug, any drug toxicity or other reaction resulting from the interaction of the two drugs would be classified as a poisoning.

(iv) Interaction of drug(s) and alcohol. When a reaction results from the interaction of a drug(s) and alcohol, this would be classified as poisoning.

See Section I.C.4. if poisoning is the result of insulin pump malfunctions.

(c) Underdosing

Underdosing refers to taking less of a medication than is prescribed by a provider or a manufacturer's instruction. Discontinuing the use of a prescribed medication on the patient's own initiative (not directed by the patient's provider) is also classified as an underdosing. For underdosing, assign the code from categories T36-T50 (fifth or sixth character "6").

Codes for underdosing should never be assigned as principal or first-listed codes. If a patient has a relapse or exacerbation of the medical condition for which the drug is prescribed because of the reduction in dose, then the medical condition itself should be coded.

Noncompliance (Z91.12-, Z91.13- and Z91.14-) or complication of care (Y63.6-Y63.9) codes are to be used with an underdosing code to indicate intent, if known.

(d) Toxic Effects

When a harmful substance is ingested or comes in contact with a person, this is classified as a toxic effect. The toxic effect codes are in categories T51-T65.

Toxic effect codes have an associated intent: accidental, intentional self-harm, assault and undetermined.

f. Adult and child abuse, neglect and other maltreatment

Sequence first the appropriate code from categories T74 (Adult and child abuse, neglect and other maltreatment, confirmed) or T76 (Adult and child abuse, neglect and other maltreatment, suspected) for abuse, neglect and other maltreatment, followed by any accompanying mental health or injury code(s).

If the documentation in the medical record states abuse or neglect it is coded as confirmed (T74.-). It is coded as suspected if it is documented as suspected (T76.-).

For cases of confirmed abuse or neglect an external cause code from the assault section (X92-Y09) should be added to identify the cause of any physical injuries. A perpetrator code (Y07) should be added when the perpetrator of the abuse is known. For suspected cases of abuse or neglect, do not report external cause or perpetrator code.

If a suspected case of abuse, neglect or mistreatment is ruled out during an encounter code Z04.71, Encounter for examination and observation following alleged physical adult abuse, ruled out, or code Z04.72, Encounter for examination and observation following alleged child physical abuse, ruled out, should be used, not a code from T76.

If a suspected case of alleged rape or sexual abuse is ruled out during an encounter code Z04.41, Encounter for examination and observation following alleged adult rape or code Z04.42, Encounter for examination and observation following alleged child rape, should be used, not a code from T76.

If a suspected case of forced sexual exploitation or forced labor exploitation is ruled out during an encounter, code Z04.81, Encounter for examination and observation of victim following forced sexual exploitation, or code Z04.82, Encounter for examination and observation of victim following forced labor exploitation, should be used, not a code from T76.

See Section I.C.15. Abuse in a pregnant patient.

g. Complications of care

1) General guidelines for complications of care

(a) Documentation of complications of care

See Section I.B.16. for information on documentation of complications of care.

2) Pain due to medical devices

Pain associated with devices, implants or grafts left in a surgical site (for example painful hip prosthesis) is assigned to the appropriate code(s) found in Chapter 19, Injury, poisoning, and certain other consequences of external causes. Specific codes for pain due to medical devices are found in the T code section of the ICD-10-CM. Use additional code(s) from category G89 to identify acute or chronic pain due to presence of the device, implant or graft (G89.18 or G89.28).

3) Transplant complications

(a) Transplant complications other than kidney

Codes under category T86, Complications of transplanted organs and tissues, are for use for both complications and rejection of transplanted organs. A transplant complication code is only assigned if the complication affects the function of the transplanted organ. Two codes are required to fully describe a transplant complication: the appropriate code from category T86 and a secondary code that identifies the complication.

Pre-existing conditions or conditions that develop after the transplant are not coded as complications unless they affect the function of the transplanted organs.

See I.C.21. for transplant organ removal status.
See I.C.2. for malignant neoplasm associated with transplanted organ.

(b) Kidney transplant complications

Patients who have undergone kidney transplant may still have some form of chronic kidney disease (CKD) because the kidney transplant may not fully restore kidney function. Code T86.1- should be assigned for documented complications of a kidney transplant, such as transplant failure or rejection or other transplant complication. Code T86.1- should not be assigned for post kidney transplant patients who have chronic kidney (CKD) unless a transplant complication such as transplant failure or rejection is documented. If the documentation is unclear as to whether the patient has a complication of the transplant, query the provider.

Conditions that affect the function of the transplanted kidney, other than CKD, should be assigned a code from subcategory T86.1, Complications of transplanted organ, Kidney, and a secondary code that identifies the complication.

For patients with CKD following a kidney transplant, but who do not have a complication such as failure or rejection, *see Section I.C.14. Chronic kidney disease and kidney transplant status.*

4) Complication codes that include the external cause

As with certain other T codes, some of the complications of care codes have the external cause included in the code. The code includes the nature of the complication as well as the type of procedure that caused the complication. No external cause code indicating the type of procedure is necessary for these codes.

5) Complications of care codes within the body system chapters

Intraoperative and postprocedural complication codes are found within the body system chapters with codes specific to the organs and structures of that body system. These codes should be sequenced first, followed by a code(s) for the specific complication, if applicable.

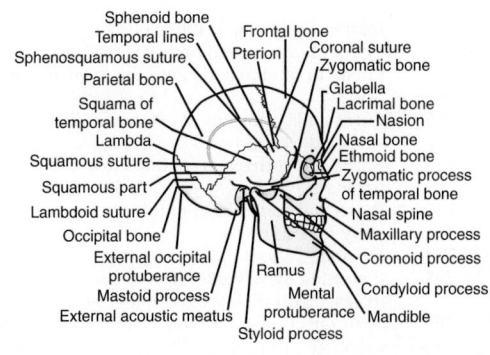

Figure 19-1 Lateral view of skull.

Figure 19-2 Frontal view of skull.

Figure 19-3 Anterior view of vertebral column.

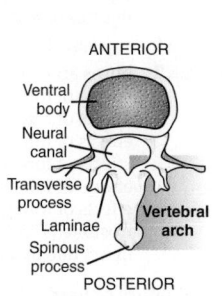

Figure 19-4 Vertebra viewed from above.

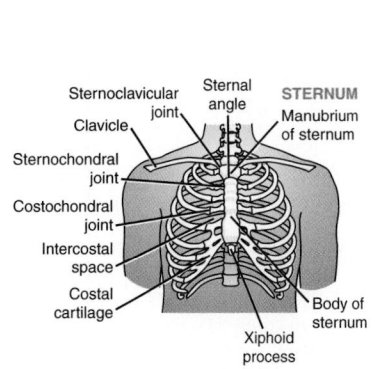

Figure 19-5 Anterior view of rib cage.

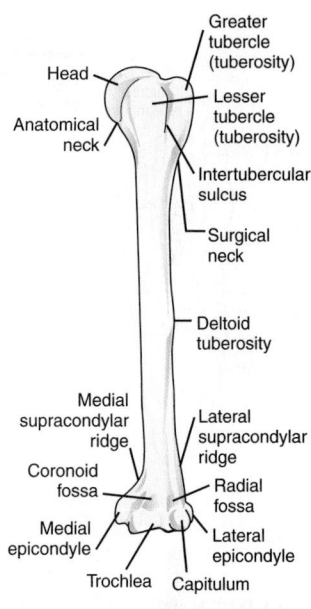

Figure 19-6 Anterior aspect of left humerus.

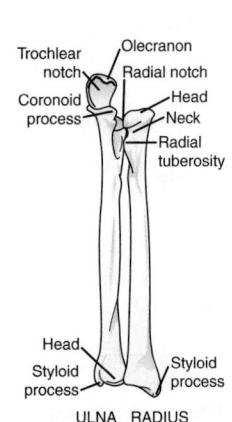

Figure 19-7 Anterior aspect of left radius and ulna.

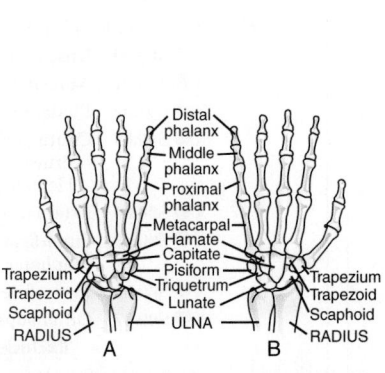

Figure 19-8 Right hand and wrist: **A.** Dorsal surface. **B.** Palmar surface.

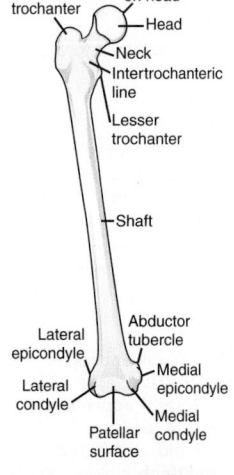

Figure 19-9 Anterior aspect of right femur.

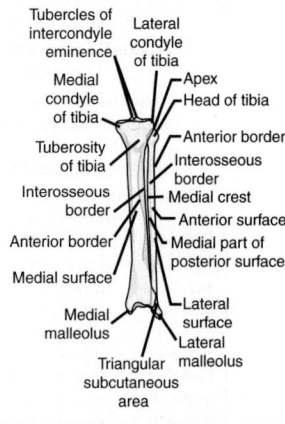

Figure 19-10 Anterior aspect of left tibia and fibula.

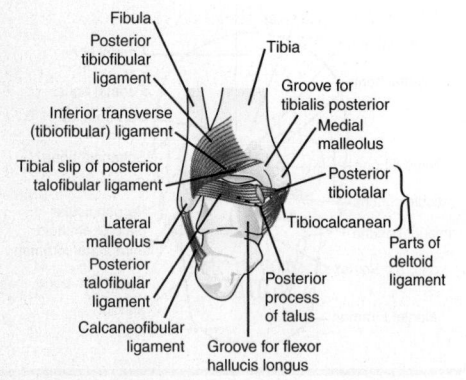

Figure 19-11 Posterior aspect of the left ankle joint.

Figure 19-12 Right foot viewed from above.

CHAPTER 19

INJURY, POISONING AND CERTAIN OTHER CONSEQUENCES OF EXTERNAL CAUSES (S00-T88)

Note: Use secondary code(s) from Chapter 20, External causes of morbidity, to indicate cause of injury. Codes within the T section that include the external cause do not require an additional external cause code.

Use additional code to identify any retained foreign body, if applicable (Z18.-)

Excludes1 birth trauma (P10-P15)
obstetric trauma (O70-O71)

Note: The chapter uses the S-section for coding different types of injuries related to single body regions and the T-section to cover injuries to unspecified body regions as well as poisoning and certain other consequences of external causes.

This chapter contains the following blocks:

S00-S09	Injuries to the head
S10-S19	Injuries to the neck
S20-S29	Injuries to the thorax
S30-S39	Injuries to the abdomen, lower back, lumbar spine, pelvis and external genitals
S40-S49	Injuries to the shoulder and upper arm
S50-S59	Injuries to the elbow and forearm
S60-S69	Injuries to the wrist, hand, and fingers
S70-S79	Injuries to the hip and thigh
S80-S89	Injuries to the knee and lower leg
S90-S99	Injuries to the ankle and foot

T07	Injuries involving multiple body regions
T14	Injury of unspecified body region
T15-T19	Effects of foreign body entering through natural orifice
T20-T25	Burns and corrosions of external body surface, specified by site
T26-T28	Burns and corrosions confined to eye and internal organs
T30-T32	Burns and corrosions of multiple and unspecified body regions
T33-T34	Frostbite
T36-T50	Poisoning by, adverse effect of and underdosing of drugs, medicaments and biological substances
T51-T65	Toxic effects of substances chiefly nonmedicinal as to source
T66-T78	Other and unspecified effects of external causes
T79	Certain early complications of trauma
T80-T88	Complications of surgical and medical care, not elsewhere classified

INJURIES TO THE HEAD (S00-S09)

Includes   injuries of ear
injuries of eye
injuries of face [any part]
injuries of gum
injuries of jaw
injuries of oral cavity
injuries of palate
injuries of periocular area
injuries of scalp
injuries of temporomandibular joint area
injuries of tongue
injuries of tooth

Code also for any associated infection

Excludes2   burns and corrosions (T20-T32)
effects of foreign body in ear (T16)
effects of foreign body in larynx (T17.3)
effects of foreign body in mouth NOS (T18.0)
effects of foreign body in nose (T17.0-T17.1)
effects of foreign body in pharynx (T17.2)
effects of foreign body on external eye (T15.-)
frostbite (T33-T34)
insect bite or sting, venomous (T63.4)

● **S00   Superficial injury of head**

Excludes1   diffuse cerebral contusion (S06.2-)
focal cerebral contusion (S06.3-)
injury of eye and orbit (S05.-)
open wound of head (S01.-)

The appropriate 7th character is to be added to each code from category S00

A	initial encounter
	All encounters involving diagnosis and treatment
D	subsequent encounter
	Encounters during the healing phase
S	sequela

● **S00.0   Superficial injury of scalp**

X● **S00.00   Unspecified superficial injury of scalp**

X● **S00.01   Abrasion of scalp**

X● **S00.02   Blister (nonthermal) of scalp**

X● **S00.03   Contusion of scalp**
Bruise of scalp
Hematoma of scalp

X● **S00.04   External constriction of part of scalp**

X● **S00.05   Superficial foreign body of scalp**
Splinter in the scalp

X● **S00.06   Insect bite (nonvenomous) of scalp**

X● **S00.07   Other superficial bite of scalp**
Excludes1   open bite of scalp (S01.05)

▶ New   ⇒ Revised   ~~deleted~~ Deleted   Excludes 1   Excludes 2   Includes   Use additional   Code first   Code also   Key words
OGCR Official Guidelines   X Assign placeholder X   ● Use Additional Character(s)   ▌ Manifestation Code   🔖 Hierarchical Condition Category   Coding Clinic

● **S00.1 Contusion of eyelid and periocular area**
Black eye

> **Excludes2** contusion of eyeball and orbital tissues (S05.1)

X● **S00.10 Contusion of unspecified eyelid and periocular area**

X● **S00.11 Contusion of right eyelid and periocular area**

X● **S00.12 Contusion of left eyelid and periocular area**

● **S00.2 Other and unspecified superficial injuries of eyelid and periocular area**

> **Excludes2** superficial injury of conjunctiva and cornea (S05.0-)

● **S00.20 Unspecified superficial injury of eyelid and periocular area**

  ● **S00.201 Unspecified superficial injury of right eyelid and periocular area**

  ● **S00.202 Unspecified superficial injury of left eyelid and periocular area**

  ● **S00.209 Unspecified superficial injury of unspecified eyelid and periocular area**

● **S00.21 Abrasion of eyelid and periocular area**

  ● **S00.211 Abrasion of right eyelid and periocular area**

  ● **S00.212 Abrasion of left eyelid and periocular area**

  ● **S00.219 Abrasion of unspecified eyelid and periocular area**

● **S00.22 Blister (nonthermal) of eyelid and periocular area**

  ● **S00.221 Blister (nonthermal) of right eyelid and periocular area**

  ● **S00.222 Blister (nonthermal) of left eyelid and periocular area**

  ● **S00.229 Blister (nonthermal) of unspecified eyelid and periocular area**

● **S00.24 External constriction of eyelid and periocular area**

  ● **S00.241 External constriction of right eyelid and periocular area**

  ● **S00.242 External constriction of left eyelid and periocular area**

  ● **S00.249 External constriction of unspecified eyelid and periocular area**

● **S00.25 Superficial foreign body of eyelid and periocular area**
Splinter of eyelid and periocular area

> **Excludes2** retained foreign body in eyelid (H02.81-)

  ● **S00.251 Superficial foreign body of right eyelid and periocular area**

  ● **S00.252 Superficial foreign body of left eyelid and periocular area**

  ● **S00.259 Superficial foreign body of unspecified eyelid and periocular area**

● **S00.26 Insect bite (nonvenomous) of eyelid and periocular area**

  ● **S00.261 Insect bite (nonvenomous) of right eyelid and periocular area**

  ● **S00.262 Insect bite (nonvenomous) of left eyelid and periocular area**

  ● **S00.269 Insect bite (nonvenomous) of unspecified eyelid and periocular area**

● **S00.27 Other superficial bite of eyelid and periocular area**

> **Excludes1** open bite of eyelid and periocular area (S01.15)

  ● **S00.271 Other superficial bite of right eyelid and periocular area**

  ● **S00.272 Other superficial bite of left eyelid and periocular area**

  ● **S00.279 Other superficial bite of unspecified eyelid and periocular area**

● **S00.3 Superficial injury of nose**

X● **S00.30 Unspecified superficial injury of nose**

X● **S00.31 Abrasion of nose**

X● **S00.32 Blister (nonthermal) of nose**

X● **S00.33 Contusion of nose**
Bruise of nose
Hematoma of nose

X● **S00.34 External constriction of nose**

X● **S00.35 Superficial foreign body of nose**
Splinter in the nose

X● **S00.36 Insect bite (nonvenomous) of nose**

X● **S00.37 Other superficial bite of nose**

> **Excludes1** open bite of nose (S01.25)

● **S00.4 Superficial injury of ear**

● **S00.40 Unspecified superficial injury of ear**

  ● **S00.401 Unspecified superficial injury of right ear**

  ● **S00.402 Unspecified superficial injury of left ear**

  ● **S00.409 Unspecified superficial injury of unspecified ear**

● **S00.41 Abrasion of ear**

  ● **S00.411 Abrasion of right ear**

  ● **S00.412 Abrasion of left ear**

  ● **S00.419 Abrasion of unspecified ear**

● **S00.42 Blister (nonthermal) of ear**

  ● **S00.421 Blister (nonthermal) of right ear**

  ● **S00.422 Blister (nonthermal) of left ear**

  ● **S00.429 Blister (nonthermal) of unspecified ear**

● **S00.43 Contusion of ear**
Bruise of ear
Hematoma of ear

  ● **S00.431 Contusion of right ear**

  ● **S00.432 Contusion of left ear**

  ● **S00.439 Contusion of unspecified ear**

● **S00.44 External constriction of ear**

  ● **S00.441 External constriction of right ear**

  ● **S00.442 External constriction of left ear**

  ● **S00.449 External constriction of unspecified ear**

● **S00.45 Superficial foreign body of ear**
Splinter in the ear

  ● **S00.451 Superficial foreign body of right ear**

  ● **S00.452 Superficial foreign body of left ear**

  ● **S00.459 Superficial foreign body of unspecified ear**

● **S00.46 Insect bite (nonvenomous) of ear**

  ● **S00.461 Insect bite (nonvenomous) of right ear**

  ● **S00.462 Insect bite (nonvenomous) of left ear**

  ● **S00.469 Insect bite (nonvenomous) of unspecified ear**

● **S00.47**   **Other superficial bite of ear**
> **Excludes1**   open bite of ear (S01.35)

  ● **S00.471**   Other superficial bite of **right ear**
  ● **S00.472**   Other superficial bite of **left ear**
  ● **S00.479**   Other superficial bite of **unspecified ear**

● **S00.5**   **Superficial injury of lip and oral cavity**

 ● **S00.50**   **Unspecified** superficial injury of lip and oral cavity

  ● **S00.501**   Unspecified superficial injury of **lip**
  ● **S00.502**   Unspecified superficial injury of **oral cavity**

 ● **S00.51**   **Abrasion** of lip and oral cavity

  ● **S00.511**   Abrasion of **lip**
  ● **S00.512**   Abrasion of **oral cavity**

 ● **S00.52**   **Blister (nonthermal)** of lip and oral cavity

  ● **S00.521**   Blister (nonthermal) of **lip**
  ● **S00.522**   Blister (nonthermal) of **oral cavity**

 ● **S00.53**   **Contusion** of lip and oral cavity

  ● **S00.531**   Contusion of **lip**
    Bruise of lip
    Hematoma of lip

  ● **S00.532**   Contusion of **oral cavity**
    Bruise of oral cavity
    Hematoma of oral cavity

 ● **S00.54**   **External constriction** of lip and oral cavity

  ● **S00.541**   External constriction of **lip**
  ● **S00.542**   External constriction of **oral cavity**

 ● **S00.55**   **Superficial foreign body** of lip and oral cavity

  ● **S00.551**   Superficial foreign body of **lip**
    Splinter of lip and oral cavity
  ● **S00.552**   Superficial foreign body of **oral cavity**
    Splinter of lip and oral cavity

 ● **S00.56**   **Insect bite (nonvenomous)** of lip and oral cavity

  ● **S00.561**   Insect bite (nonvenomous) of **lip**
  ● **S00.562**   Insect bite (nonvenomous) of **oral cavity**

 ● **S00.57**   **Other superficial bite** of lip and oral cavity

  ● **S00.571**   Other superficial bite of **lip**
> **Excludes1**   open bite of lip (S01.551)

  ● **S00.572**   Other superficial bite of **oral cavity**
> **Excludes1**   open bite of oral cavity (S01.552)

● **S00.8**   **Superficial injury of other parts of head**
   Superficial injuries of face [any part]

 X ● **S00.80**   **Unspecified** superficial injury of other part of head
 X ● **S00.81**   **Abrasion** of other part of head
 X ● **S00.82**   **Blister (nonthermal)** of other part of head
 X ● **S00.83**   **Contusion** of other part of head
    Bruise of other part of head
    Hematoma of other part of head
 X ● **S00.84**   **External constriction** of other part of head
 X ● **S00.85**   **Superficial foreign body** of other part of head
    Splinter in other part of head
 X ● **S00.86**   **Insect bite (nonvenomous)** of other part of head
 X ● **S00.87**   **Other superficial bite** of other part of head
> **Excludes1**   open bite of other part of head (S01.85)

● **S00.9**   **Superficial injury of unspecified part of head**

 X ● **S00.90**   **Unspecified** superficial injury of unspecified part of head
 X ● **S00.91**   **Abrasion** of unspecified part of head
 X ● **S00.92**   **Blister (nonthermal)** of unspecified part of head

 X ● **S00.93**   **Contusion** of unspecified part of head
    Bruise of head
    Hematoma of head
 X ● **S00.94**   **External constriction** of unspecified part of head
 X ● **S00.95**   **Superficial foreign body** of unspecified part of head
    Splinter of head
 X ● **S00.96**   **Insect bite (nonvenomous)** of unspecified part of head
 X ● **S00.97**   **Other superficial bite** of unspecified part of head
> **Excludes1**   open bite of head (S01.95)

● **S01**   **Open wound of head**
   Code also any associated:
    injury of cranial nerve (S04.-)
    injury of muscle and tendon of head (S09.1-)
    intracranial injury (S06.-)
    wound infection
> **Excludes1**   open skull fracture (S02.- with 7th character B)
> **Excludes2**   injury of eye and orbit (S05.-)
>   traumatic amputation of part of head (S08.-)

The appropriate 7th character is to be added to each code from category S01

> A   initial encounter
> D   subsequent encounter
> S   sequela

● **S01.0**   **Open wound of scalp**
> **Excludes1**   avulsion of scalp (S08.0)

 X ● **S01.00**   **Unspecified** open wound of scalp
 X ● **S01.01**   **Laceration without foreign body** of scalp
 X ● **S01.02**   **Laceration with foreign body** of scalp
    Coding Clinic: 2015, Q1, P5-7
 X ● **S01.03**   **Puncture wound without foreign body** of scalp
 X ● **S01.04**   **Puncture wound with foreign body** of scalp
 X ● **S01.05**   **Open bite** of scalp
    Bite of scalp NOS
> **Excludes1**   superficial bite of scalp (S00.06, S00.07-)

● **S01.1**   **Open wound of eyelid and periocular area**
   Open wound of eyelid and periocular area with or without involvement of lacrimal passages

 ● **S01.10**   **Unspecified** open wound of eyelid and periocular area

  ● **S01.101**   Unspecified open wound of **right** eyelid and periocular area
  ● **S01.102**   Unspecified open wound of **left** eyelid and periocular area
  ● **S01.109**   Unspecified open wound of **unspecified** eyelid and periocular area

 ● **S01.11**   **Laceration without foreign body** of eyelid and periocular area

  ● **S01.111**   Laceration without foreign body of **right** eyelid and periocular area
  ● **S01.112**   Laceration without foreign body of **left** eyelid and periocular area
  ● **S01.119**   Laceration without foreign body of **unspecified** eyelid and periocular area

 ● **S01.12**   **Laceration with foreign body** of eyelid and periocular area

  ● **S01.121**   Laceration with foreign body of **right** eyelid and periocular area
  ● **S01.122**   Laceration with foreign body of **left** eyelid and periocular area
  ● **S01.129**   Laceration with foreign body of **unspecified** eyelid and periocular area

▶ New   ⇒ Revised   ~~deleted~~ Deleted   Excludes 1   Excludes 2   Includes   Use additional   Code first   Code also   Key words
OGCR Official Guidelines   X Assign placeholder X   ● Use Additional Character(s)   ▶ Manifestation Code   🔖 Hierarchical Condition Category   **Coding Clinic**

● **S01.13**   **Puncture wound without foreign body** of eyelid and periocular area
   ● **S01.131**   Puncture wound without foreign body of **right** eyelid and periocular area
   ● **S01.132**   Puncture wound without foreign body of **left** eyelid and periocular area
   ● **S01.139**   Puncture wound without foreign body of **unspecified** eyelid and periocular area
● **S01.14**   **Puncture wound with foreign body** of eyelid and periocular area
   ● **S01.141**   Puncture wound with foreign body of **right** eyelid and periocular area
   ● **S01.142**   Puncture wound with foreign body of **left** eyelid and periocular area
   ● **S01.149**   Puncture wound with foreign body of **unspecified** eyelid and periocular area
● **S01.15**   **Open bite** of eyelid and periocular area
   Bite of eyelid and periocular area NOS
   Excludes1   superficial bite of eyelid and periocular area (S00.26, S00.27)
   ● **S01.151**   Open bite of **right** eyelid and periocular area
   ● **S01.152**   Open bite of **left** eyelid and periocular area
   ● **S01.159**   Open bite of **unspecified** eyelid and periocular area
● **S01.2**   **Open wound of nose**
  X ● **S01.20**   **Unspecified** open wound of nose
  X ● **S01.21**   **Laceration without foreign body** of nose
      Coding Clinic: 2015, Q1, P5-6
  X ● **S01.22**   **Laceration with foreign body** of nose
  X ● **S01.23**   **Puncture wound without foreign body** of nose
  X ● **S01.24**   **Puncture wound with foreign body** of nose
  X ● **S01.25**   **Open bite** of nose
      Bite of nose NOS
      Excludes1   superficial bite of nose (S00.36, S00.37)
● **S01.3**   **Open wound of ear**
  ● **S01.30**   **Unspecified** open wound of ear
   ● **S01.301**   Unspecified open wound of **right** ear
   ● **S01.302**   Unspecified open wound of **left** ear
   ● **S01.309**   Unspecified open wound of **unspecified** ear
  ● **S01.31**   **Laceration without foreign body** of ear
   ● **S01.311**   Laceration without foreign body of **right** ear
   ● **S01.312**   Laceration without foreign body of **left** ear
   ● **S01.319**   Laceration without foreign body of **unspecified** ear
  ● **S01.32**   **Laceration with foreign body** of ear
   ● **S01.321**   Laceration with foreign body of **right** ear
   ● **S01.322**   Laceration with foreign body of **left** ear
   ● **S01.329**   Laceration with foreign body of **unspecified** ear

● **S01.33**   **Puncture wound without foreign body** of ear
   ● **S01.331**   Puncture wound without foreign body of **right** ear
   ● **S01.332**   Puncture wound without foreign body of **left** ear
   ● **S01.339**   Puncture wound without foreign body of **unspecified** ear
● **S01.34**   **Puncture wound with foreign body** of ear
   ● **S01.341**   Puncture wound with foreign body of **right** ear
   ● **S01.342**   Puncture wound with foreign body of **left** ear
   ● **S01.349**   Puncture wound with foreign body of **unspecified** ear
● **S01.35**   **Open bite** of ear
   Bite of ear NOS
   Excludes1   superficial bite of ear (S00.46, S00.47)
   ● **S01.351**   Open bite of **right** ear
   ● **S01.352**   Open bite of **left** ear
   ● **S01.359**   Open bite of **unspecified** ear
● **S01.4**   **Open wound of cheek and temporomandibular area**
  ● **S01.40**   **Unspecified** open wound of cheek and temporomandibular area
   ● **S01.401**   Unspecified open wound of **right** cheek and temporomandibular area
   ● **S01.402**   Unspecified open wound of **left** cheek and temporomandibular area
   ● **S01.409**   Unspecified open wound of **unspecified** cheek and temporomandibular area
  ● **S01.41**   **Laceration without foreign body** of cheek and temporomandibular area
   ● **S01.411**   Laceration without foreign body of **right** cheek and temporomandibular area
      Coding Clinic: 2015, Q1, P5-7
   ● **S01.412**   Laceration without foreign body of **left** cheek and temporomandibular area
   ● **S01.419**   Laceration without foreign body of **unspecified** cheek and temporomandibular area
  ● **S01.42**   **Laceration with foreign body** of cheek and temporomandibular area
   ● **S01.421**   Laceration with foreign body of **right** cheek and temporomandibular area
   ● **S01.422**   Laceration with foreign body of **left** cheek and temporomandibular area
   ● **S01.429**   Laceration with foreign body of **unspecified** cheek and temporomandibular area
  ● **S01.43**   **Puncture wound without foreign body** of cheek and temporomandibular area
   ● **S01.431**   Puncture wound without foreign body of **right** cheek and temporomandibular area
   ● **S01.432**   Puncture wound without foreign body of **left** cheek and temporomandibular area
   ● **S01.439**   Puncture wound without foreign body of **unspecified** cheek and temporomandibular area

● **S01.44**   Puncture wound with foreign body of cheek and temporomandibular area
- ● **S01.441**   Puncture wound with foreign body of right cheek and temporomandibular area
- ● **S01.442**   Puncture wound with foreign body of left cheek and temporomandibular area
- ● **S01.449**   Puncture wound with foreign body of unspecified cheek and temporomandibular area

● **S01.45**   Open bite of cheek and temporomandibular area
> Bite of cheek and temporomandibular area NOS
>
> **Excludes2**   superficial bite of cheek and temporomandibular area (S00.86, S00.87)

- ● **S01.451**   Open bite of right cheek and temporomandibular area
- ● **S01.452**   Open bite of left cheek and temporomandibular area
- ● **S01.459**   Open bite of unspecified cheek and temporomandibular area

● **S01.5**   Open wound of lip and oral cavity
> **Excludes2**   tooth dislocation (S03.2)
> tooth fracture (S02.5)

- ● **S01.50**   Unspecified open wound of lip and oral cavity
  - ● **S01.501**   Unspecified open wound of lip
  - ● **S01.502**   Unspecified open wound of oral cavity
- ● **S01.51**   Laceration of lip and oral cavity without foreign body
  - ● **S01.511**   Laceration without foreign body of lip
  - ● **S01.512**   Laceration without foreign body of oral cavity
- ● **S01.52**   Laceration of lip and oral cavity with foreign body
  - ● **S01.521**   Laceration with foreign body of lip
  - ● **S01.522**   Laceration with foreign body of oral cavity
- ● **S01.53**   Puncture wound of lip and oral cavity without foreign body
  - ● **S01.531**   Puncture wound without foreign body of lip
  - ● **S01.532**   Puncture wound without foreign body of oral cavity
- ● **S01.54**   Puncture wound of lip and oral cavity with foreign body
  - ● **S01.541**   Puncture wound with foreign body of lip
  - ● **S01.542**   Puncture wound with foreign body of oral cavity
- ● **S01.55**   Open bite of lip and oral cavity
  - ● **S01.551**   Open bite of lip
    > Bite of lip NOS
    >
    > **Excludes1**   superficial bite of lip (S00.571)
  - ● **S01.552**   Open bite of oral cavity
    > Bite of oral cavity NOS
    >
    > **Excludes1**   superficial bite of oral cavity (S00.572)

● **S01.8**   Open wound of other parts of head
- X ● **S01.80**   Unspecified open wound of other part of head
- X ● **S01.81**   Laceration without foreign body of other part of head
- X ● **S01.82**   Laceration with foreign body of other part of head

- X ● **S01.83**   Puncture wound without foreign body of other part of head
- X ● **S01.84**   Puncture wound with foreign body of other part of head
- X ● **S01.85**   Open bite of other part of head
  > Bite of other part of head NOS
  >
  > **Excludes1**   superficial bite of other part of head (S00.87)

● **S01.9**   Open wound of unspecified part of head
- X ● **S01.90**   Unspecified open wound of unspecified part of head
- X ● **S01.91**   Laceration without foreign body of unspecified part of head
- X ● **S01.92**   Laceration with foreign body of unspecified part of head
- X ● **S01.93**   Puncture wound without foreign body of unspecified part of head
- X ● **S01.94**   Puncture wound with foreign body of unspecified part of head
- X ● **S01.95**   Open bite of unspecified part of head
  > Bite of head NOS
  >
  > **Excludes1**   superficial bite of head NOS (S00.97)

● **S02**   Fracture of skull and facial bones
> **Note:** A fracture not indicated as open or closed should be coded to closed
>
> The appropriate 7th character is to be added to each code from category S02

A	initial encounter for closed fracture
B	initial encounter for open fracture
D	subsequent encounter for fracture with routine healing
G	subsequent encounter for fracture with delayed healing
K	subsequent encounter for fracture with nonunion
S	sequela

> Code also any associated intracranial injury (S06.-)

- X ● **S02.0**   Fracture of vault of skull   A, B, S 🄗
  > Fracture of frontal bone
  > Fracture of parietal bone
- ● **S02.1**   Fracture of base of skull
  > **Excludes2**   lateral orbital wall (S02.84-)
  > medial orbital wall (S02.83-)
  > orbital floor (S02.3-)
  >
  > **Coding Clinic: 2016, Q4, P66**
  - ● **S02.10**   Unspecified fracture of base of skull
    - ● **S02.101**   Fracture of base of skull, right side A, B, S 🄗
    - ● **S02.102**   Fracture of base of skull, left side A, B, S 🄗
    - ● **S02.109**   Fracture of base of skull, unspecified side A, B, S 🄗
  - ● **S02.11**   Fracture of occiput
    - ● **S02.110**   Type I occipital condyle fracture, unspecified side A, B, S 🄗
    - ● **S02.111**   Type II occipital condyle fracture, unspecified side A, B, S 🄗
    - ● **S02.112**   Type III occipital condyle fracture, unspecified side A, B, S 🄗
    - ● **S02.113**   Unspecified occipital condyle fracture A, B, S 🄗
    - ● **S02.118**   Other fracture of occiput, unspecified side A, B, S 🄗
    - ● **S02.119**   Unspecified fracture of occiput A, B, S 🄗

▶ New   ⇒ Revised   ~~deleted~~ Deleted   Excludes 1   Excludes 2   Includes   Use additional   Code first   Code also   Key words

OGCR Official Guidelines   X Assign placeholder X   ● Use Additional Character(s)   ▶ Manifestation Code   🄗 Hierarchical Condition Category   **Coding Clinic**

● S02.11A Type I occipital condyle fracture, right side A, B, S 🔗

● S02.11B Type I occipital condyle fracture, left side A, B, S 🔗

● S02.11C Type II occipital condyle fracture, right side A, B, S 🔗

● S02.11D Type II occipital condyle fracture, left side A, B, S 🔗

● S02.11E Type III occipital condyle fracture, right side A, B, S 🔗

● S02.11F Type III occipital condyle fracture, left side A, B, S 🔗

● S02.11G Other fracture of occiput, right side A, B, S 🔗

● S02.11H Other fracture of occiput, left side A, B, S 🔗

S02.12 Fracture of orbital roof

S02.121 Fracture of orbital roof, right side

S02.122 Fracture of orbital roof, left side

S02.129 Fracture of orbital roof, unspecified side

X ● S02.19 Other fracture of base of skull A, B, S 🔗
Fracture of anterior fossa of base of skull
Fracture of ethmoid sinus
Fracture of frontal sinus
Fracture of middle fossa of base of skull
Fracture of posterior fossa of base of skull
Fracture of sphenoid
Fracture of temporal bone

X ● S02.2 Fracture of nasal bones

● S02.3 Fracture of orbital floor
Fracture of inferior orbital wall
Excludes1 orbit NOS (S02.85)
Excludes2 lateral orbital wall (S02.84-)
medial orbital wall (S02.83-)
orbital roof (S02.1-)
Coding Clinic: 2016, Q4, P66

X ● S02.30 Fracture of orbital floor, unspecified side A, B, S 🔗

X ● S02.31 Fracture of orbital floor, right side A, B, S 🔗

X ● S02.32 Fracture of orbital floor, left side A, B, S 🔗

● S02.4 Fracture of malar, maxillary and zygoma bones
Fracture of superior maxilla
Fracture of upper jaw (bone)
Fracture of zygomatic process of temporal bone
Coding Clinic: 2016, Q4, P66

● S02.40 Fracture of malar, maxillary and zygoma bones, unspecified

● S02.400 Malar fracture unspecified side A, B, S 🔗

● S02.401 Maxillary fracture, unspecified side A, B, S 🔗

● S02.402 Zygomatic fracture, unspecified side A, B, S 🔗

● S02.40A Malar fracture, right side A, B, S 🔗

● S02.40B Malar fracture, left side A, B, S 🔗

● S02.40C Maxillary fracture, right side A, B, S 🔗

● S02.40D Maxillary fracture, left side A, B, S 🔗

● S02.40E Zygomatic fracture, right side A, B, S 🔗

● S02.40F Zygomatic fracture, left side A, B, S 🔗

● S02.41 LeFort fracture

● S02.411 LeFort I fracture A, B, S 🔗

● S02.412 LeFort II fracture A, B, S 🔗

● S02.413 LeFort III fracture A, B, S 🔗

X ● S02.42 Fracture of alveolus of maxilla A, B, S 🔗

X ● S02.5 Fracture of tooth (traumatic) Broken tooth
Excludes1 cracked tooth (nontraumatic) (K03.81)

● S02.6 Fracture of mandible
Fracture of lower jaw (bone)
Coding Clinic: 2016, Q4, P66

● S02.60 Fracture of mandible of unspecified site

● S02.600 Fracture of unspecified part of body of mandible, unspecified side A, B, S 🔗

● S02.601 Fracture of unspecified part of body of right mandible A, B, S 🔗

● S02.602 Fracture of unspecified part of body of left mandible A, B, S 🔗

● S02.609 Fracture of mandible, unspecified A, B, S 🔗

● S02.61 Fracture of condylar process of mandible

● S02.610 Fracture of condylar process of mandible, unspecified side A, B, S 🔗

● S02.611 Fracture of condylar process of right mandible A, B, S 🔗

● S02.612 Fracture of condylar process of left mandible A, B, S 🔗

● S02.62 Fracture of subcondylar process of mandible

● S02.620 Fracture of subcondylar process of mandible, unspecified side A, B, S 🔗

● S02.621 Fracture of subcondylar process of right mandible A, B, S 🔗

● S02.622 Fracture of subcondylar process of left mandible A, B, S 🔗

● S02.63 Fracture of coronoid process of mandible

● S02.630 Fracture of coronoid process of mandible, unspecified side A, B, S 🔗

● S02.631 Fracture of coronoid process of right mandible A, B, S 🔗

● S02.632 Fracture of coronoid process of left mandible A, B, S 🔗

● S02.64 Fracture of ramus of mandible

● S02.640 Fracture of ramus of mandible, unspecified side A, B, S 🔗

● S02.641 Fracture of ramus of right mandible A, B, S 🔗

● S02.642 Fracture of ramus of left mandible A, B, S 🔗

● S02.65 Fracture of angle of mandible

● S02.650 Fracture of angle of mandible, unspecified side A, B, S 🔗

● S02.651 Fracture of angle of right mandible A, B, S 🔗

● S02.652 Fracture of angle of left mandible A, B, S 🔗

X ● S02.66 Fracture of symphysis of mandible A, B, S 🔗

● S02.67 Fracture of alveolus of mandible

● S02.670 Fracture of alveolus of mandible, unspecified side A, B, S 🔗

● S02.671 Fracture of alveolus of right mandible A, B, S 🔗

● S02.672 Fracture of alveolus of left mandible A, B, S 🔗

X ● S02.69 Fracture of mandible of other specified site A, B, S 🔗

CHAPTER 19 (S00–T88)

● **S02.8**   **Fractures of other specified skull and facial bones**
     Fracture of palate

     Excludes2   lateral orbital wall (S02.84-)
                      medial orbital wall (S02.83-)
     Coding Clinic: 2016, Q4, P66

    X● **S02.80**   Fracture of other specified skull and facial bones, unspecified side   A, B, S 🐾

    X● **S02.81**   Fracture of other specified skull and facial bones, right side   A, B, S 🐾

    X● **S02.82**   Fracture of other specified skull and facial bones, left side   A, B, S 🐾

    ● **S02.83** Fracture of medial orbital wall

        Excludes2   orbital floor (S02.3-)
                            orbital roof (S02.12-)

        S02.831   Fracture of medial orbital wall, right side

        S02.832   Fracture of medial orbital wall, left side

        S02.839   Fracture of medial orbital wall, unspecified side

    ● **S02.84** Fracture of lateral orbital wall

        Excludes2   orbital floor (S02.3-)
                            orbital roof (S02.12-)

        S02.841   Fracture of lateral orbital wall, right side

        S02.842   Fracture of lateral orbital wall, left side

        S02.849   Fracture of lateral orbital wall, unspecified side

    ● **S02.85** Fracture of orbit, unspecified
        Fracture of orbit NOS
        Fracture of orbit wall NOS

        Excludes1   lateral orbital wall (S02.84-)
                            medial orbital wall (S02.83-)
                            orbital floor (S02.3-)
                            orbital roof (S02.12-)

● **S02.9**   **Fracture of unspecified skull and facial bones**

    X● **S02.91**   Unspecified fracture of skull   A, B, S 🐾

    X● **S02.92**   Unspecified fracture of facial bones   A, B, S 🐾

● **S03**   **Dislocation and sprain of joints and ligaments of head**

    Includes   avulsion of joint (capsule) or ligament of head
                  laceration of cartilage, joint (capsule) or ligament of head
                  sprain of cartilage, joint (capsule) or ligament of head
                  traumatic hemarthrosis of joint or ligament of head
                  traumatic rupture of joint or ligament of head
                  traumatic subluxation of joint or ligament of head
                  traumatic tear of joint or ligament of head

    Code also any associated open wound

    Excludes2   Strain of muscle or tendon of head (S09.1)

    The appropriate 7th character is to be added to each code from category S03

       | A | initial encounter |
       | D | subsequent encounter |
       | S | sequela |

● **S03.0**   **Dislocation of jaw**
     Dislocation of jaw (cartilage) (meniscus)
     Dislocation of mandible
     Dislocation of temporomandibular (joint)
     Coding Clinic: 2016, Q4, P67

    X● **S03.00**   Dislocation of jaw, unspecified side

    X● **S03.01**   Dislocation of jaw, right side

    X● **S03.02**   Dislocation of jaw, left side

    X● **S03.03**   Dislocation of jaw, bilateral side

X● **S03.1**   **Dislocation of septal cartilage of nose**

X● **S03.2**   **Dislocation of tooth**

● **S03.4**   **Sprain of jaw**
     Sprain of temporomandibular (joint) (ligament)
     Coding Clinic: 2016, Q4, P67

    X● **S03.40**   Sprain of jaw, unspecified side

    X● **S03.41**   Sprain of jaw, right side

    X● **S03.42**   Sprain of jaw, left side

    X● **S03.43**   Sprain of jaw, bilateral side

X● **S03.8**   **Sprain of joints and ligaments of other parts of head**

X● **S03.9**   **Sprain of joints and ligaments of unspecified parts of head**

● **S04**   **Injury of cranial nerve**
     The selection of side should be based on the side of the body being affected

     Code first any associated intracranial injury (S06.-)

     Code also any associated:
       open wound of head (S01.-)
       skull fracture (S02.-)

     The appropriate 7th character is to be added to each code from category S04

       | A | initial encounter |
       | D | subsequent encounter |
       | S | sequela |

● **S04.0**   **Injury of optic nerve and pathways**
     Use additional code to identify any visual field defect or blindness (H53.4-, H54.-)

    ● **S04.01**   **Injury of optic nerve**
        Injury of 2nd cranial nerve

       ● **S04.011**   Injury of optic nerve, right eye

       ● **S04.012**   Injury of optic nerve, left eye

       ● **S04.019**   Injury of optic nerve, unspecified eye
               Injury of optic nerve NOS

    X● **S04.02**   **Injury of optic chiasm**

    ● **S04.03**   **Injury of optic tract and pathways**
        Injury of optic radiation

       ● **S04.031**   Injury of optic tract and pathways, right side

       ● **S04.032**   Injury of optic tract and pathways, left side

       ● **S04.039**   Injury of optic tract and pathways, unspecified side
              Injury of optic tract and pathways NOS

    ● **S04.04**   **Injury of visual cortex**

       ● **S04.041**   Injury of visual cortex, right side

       ● **S04.042**   Injury of visual cortex, left side

       ● **S04.049**   Injury of visual cortex, unspecified side
              Injury of visual cortex NOS

● **S04.1**   **Injury of oculomotor nerve**
     Injury of 3rd cranial nerve

    X● **S04.10**   Injury of oculomotor nerve, unspecified side

    X● **S04.11**   Injury of oculomotor nerve, right side

    X● **S04.12**   Injury of oculomotor nerve, left side

● **S04.2**   **Injury of trochlear nerve**
     Injury of 4th cranial nerve

    X● **S04.20**   Injury of trochlear nerve, unspecified side

    X● **S04.21**   Injury of trochlear nerve, right side

    X● **S04.22**   Injury of trochlear nerve, left side

● **S04.3**   **Injury of trigeminal nerve**
     Injury of 5th cranial nerve

    X● **S04.30**   Injury of trigeminal nerve, unspecified side

    X● **S04.31**   Injury of trigeminal nerve, right side

    X● **S04.32**   Injury of trigeminal nerve, left side

▶ New   ⇒ Revised   ~~deleted~~ Deleted   Excludes 1   Excludes 2   Includes   Use additional   Code first   Code also   Key words

OGCR Official Guidelines   X Assign placeholder X   ● Use Additional Character(s)   ▶ Manifestation Code   🐾 Hierarchical Condition Category   Coding Clinic

Trochlear nerve (IV)
Optic nerve (II)
Olfactory nerve (I)
Abducens nerve (VI)
Oculomotor nerve (III)
Trigeminal nerve (V)
Facial nerve (VII)
Vestibulocochlear nerve (VIII)
Glossopharyngeal nerve (IX)
Vagus nerve (X)
Accessory nerve (XI)
Hypoglossal nerve (XII)

Figure 19-13 Cranial nerves. (From Patton and Thibodeau: Anatomy and physiology, ed 7, St. Louis, Mosby, 2009)

● **S04.4   Injury of abducent nerve**
Injury of 6th cranial nerve
X ● **S04.40   Injury of abducent nerve, unspecified side**
X ● **S04.41   Injury of abducent nerve, right side**
X ● **S04.42   Injury of abducent nerve, left side**
● **S04.5   Injury of facial nerve**
Injury of 7th cranial nerve
X ● **S04.50   Injury of facial nerve, unspecified side**
X ● **S04.51   Injury of facial nerve, right side**
X ● **S04.52   Injury of facial nerve, left side**
● **S04.6   Injury of acoustic nerve**
Injury of auditory nerve
Injury of 8th cranial nerve
X ● **S04.60   Injury of acoustic nerve, unspecified side**
X ● **S04.61   Injury of acoustic nerve, right side**
X ● **S04.62   Injury of acoustic nerve, left side**
● **S04.7   Injury of accessory nerve**
Injury of 11th cranial nerve
X ● **S04.70   Injury of accessory nerve, unspecified side**
X ● **S04.71   Injury of accessory nerve, right side**
X ● **S04.72   Injury of accessory nerve, left side**
● **S04.8   Injury of other cranial nerves**
● **S04.81   Injury of olfactory [1st] nerve**
● **S04.811   Injury of olfactory [1st] nerve, right side**
● **S04.812   Injury of olfactory [1st] nerve, left side**
● **S04.819   Injury of olfactory [1st] nerve, unspecified side**
● **S04.89   Injury of other cranial nerves**
Injury of vagus [10th] nerve
● **S04.891   Injury of other cranial nerves, right side**
● **S04.892   Injury of other cranial nerves, left side**
● **S04.899   Injury of other cranial nerves, unspecified side**
X ● **S04.9   Injury of unspecified cranial nerve**

● **S05   Injury of eye and orbit**
Includes   open wound of eye and orbit
Excludes2   2nd cranial [optic] nerve injury (S04.0-)
3rd cranial [oculomotor] nerve injury (S04.1-)
open wound of eyelid and periocular area (S01.1-)
orbital bone fracture (S02.1-, S02.3-, S02.8-)
superficial injury of eyelid (S00.1-S00.2)

The appropriate 7th character is to be added to each code from category S05

A	initial encounter
D	subsequent encounter
S	sequela

● **S05.0   Injury of conjunctiva and corneal abrasion without foreign body**
Excludes1   foreign body in conjunctival sac (T15.1)
foreign body in cornea (T15.0)
X ● **S05.00   Injury of conjunctiva and corneal abrasion without foreign body, unspecified eye**
X ● **S05.01   Injury of conjunctiva and corneal abrasion without foreign body, right eye**
X ● **S05.02   Injury of conjunctiva and corneal abrasion without foreign body, left eye**
● **S05.1   Contusion of eyeball and orbital tissues**
Traumatic hyphema
Excludes2   black eye NOS (S00.1)
contusion of eyelid and periocular area (S00.1)
X ● **S05.10   Contusion of eyeball and orbital tissues, unspecified eye**
X ● **S05.11   Contusion of eyeball and orbital tissues, right eye**
X ● **S05.12   Contusion of eyeball and orbital tissues, left eye**
● **S05.2   Ocular laceration and rupture with prolapse or loss of intraocular tissue**

X ● **S05.20**   Ocular laceration and rupture with prolapse or loss of intraocular tissue, unspecified eye

X ● **S05.21**   Ocular laceration and rupture with prolapse or loss of intraocular tissue, right eye

X ● **S05.22**   Ocular laceration and rupture with prolapse or loss of intraocular tissue, left eye

● **S05.3**   Ocular laceration without prolapse or loss of intraocular tissue
      Laceration of eye NOS

X ● **S05.30**   Ocular laceration without prolapse or loss of intraocular tissue, unspecified eye

X ● **S05.31**   Ocular laceration without prolapse or loss of intraocular tissue, right eye

X ● **S05.32**   Ocular laceration without prolapse or loss of intraocular tissue, left eye

● **S05.4**   Penetrating wound of orbit with or without foreign body

    Excludes2   retained (old) foreign body following penetrating wound in orbit (H05.5-)

X ● **S05.40**   Penetrating wound of orbit with or without foreign body, unspecified eye

X ● **S05.41**   Penetrating wound of orbit with or without foreign body, right eye

X ● **S05.42**   Penetrating wound of orbit with or without foreign body, left eye

● **S05.5**   Penetrating wound with foreign body of eyeball

    Excludes2   retained (old) intraocular foreign body (H44.6-, H44.7)

X ● **S05.50**   Penetrating wound with foreign body of unspecified eyeball

X ● **S05.51**   Penetrating wound with foreign body of right eyeball

X ● **S05.52**   Penetrating wound with foreign body of left eyeball

● **S05.6**   Penetrating wound without foreign body of eyeball
      Ocular penetration NOS

X ● **S05.60**   Penetrating wound without foreign body of unspecified eyeball

X ● **S05.61**   Penetrating wound without foreign body of right eyeball

X ● **S05.62**   Penetrating wound without foreign body of left eyeball

● **S05.7**   Avulsion of eye
      Traumatic enucleation

X ● **S05.70**   Avulsion of unspecified eye

X ● **S05.71**   Avulsion of right eye

X ● **S05.72**   Avulsion of left eye

● **S05.8**   Other injuries of eye and orbit
      Lacrimal duct injury

   ● **S05.8X**   Other injuries of eye and orbit

     ● **S05.8X1**   Other injuries of right eye and orbit

     ● **S05.8X2**   Other injuries of left eye and orbit

     ● **S05.8X9**   Other injuries of unspecified eye and orbit

● **S05.9**   Unspecified injury of eye and orbit
      Injury of eye NOS

X ● **S05.90**   Unspecified injury of unspecified eye and orbit

X ● **S05.91**   Unspecified injury of right eye and orbit

X ● **S05.92**   Unspecified injury of left eye and orbit

● **S06**   Intracranial injury

   Includes   traumatic brain injury

Code also any associated:
   open wound of head (S01.-)
   skull fracture (S02.-)

   Excludes1   head injury NOS (S09.90)

The appropriate 7th character is to be added to each code from category S06

A	initial encounter
D	subsequent encounter
S	sequela

Note: 7th characters D and S do not apply to codes in category S06 with 6th character 7 - death due to brain injury prior to regaining consciousness, or 8 - death due to other cause prior to regaining consciousness.
Coding Clinic: 2015, Q4, P40

● **S06.0**   Concussion
      Commotio cerebri

   Excludes1   concussion with other intracranial injuries classified in subcategories S06.1- to S06.6- , S06.81- and S06.82- code to specified intracranial injury
      Coding Clinic: 2016, Q4, P67

   ● **S06.0X**   Concussion

     ● **S06.0X0**   Concussion without loss of consciousness S 🦠

     ● **S06.0X1**   Concussion with loss of consciousness of 30 minutes or less S 🦠

     ● **S06.0X9**   Concussion with loss of consciousness of unspecified duration S 🦠
         Concussion NOS
         Coding Clinic: 2016, Q4, P68

● **S06.1**   Traumatic cerebral edema
      Diffuse traumatic cerebral edema
      Focal traumatic cerebral edema
      Coding Clinic: 2016, Q4, P67

   ● **S06.1X**   Traumatic cerebral edema

     ● **S06.1X0**   Traumatic cerebral edema without loss of consciousness A, S 🦠
         Coding Clinic: 2015, Q1, P12

     ● **S06.1X1**   Traumatic cerebral edema with loss of consciousness of 30 minutes or less A, S 🦠

     ● **S06.1X2**   Traumatic cerebral edema with loss of consciousness of 31 minutes to 59 minutes A, S 🦠

     ● **S06.1X3**   Traumatic cerebral edema with loss of consciousness of 1 hour to 5 hours 59 minutes A, S 🦠

     ● **S06.1X4**   Traumatic cerebral edema with loss of consciousness of 6 hours to 24 hours A, S 🦠

     ● **S06.1X5**   Traumatic cerebral edema with loss of consciousness greater than 24 hours with return to pre-existing conscious level A, S 🦠

     ● **S06.1X6**   Traumatic cerebral edema with loss of consciousness greater than 24 hours without return to pre-existing conscious level with patient surviving A, S 🦠

▶ New   ⇒ Revised   ~~deleted~~ Deleted   Excludes 1   Excludes 2   Includes   Use additional   Code first   Code also   Key words

OGCR Official Guidelines   X Assign placeholder X   ● Use Additional Character(s)   ▶ Manifestation Code   🦠 Hierarchical Condition Category   Coding Clinic

● **S06.1X7**   **Traumatic cerebral edema with loss of consciousness of any duration with death due to brain injury prior to regaining consciousness**

● **S06.1X8**   **Traumatic cerebral edema with loss of consciousness of any duration with death due to other cause prior to regaining consciousness**

● **S06.1X9**   **Traumatic cerebral edema with loss of consciousness of unspecified duration A, S** 🐾
     Traumatic cerebral edema NOS

● **S06.2**   **Diffuse traumatic brain injury**
     Diffuse axonal brain injury
     Excludes1   traumatic diffuse cerebral edema (S06.1X-)

● **S06.2X**   **Diffuse traumatic brain injury**

● **S06.2X0**   **Diffuse traumatic brain injury without loss of consciousness A, S** 🐾

● **S06.2X1**   **Diffuse traumatic brain injury with loss of consciousness of 30 minutes or less A, S** 🐾

● **S06.2X2**   **Diffuse traumatic brain injury with loss of consciousness of 31 minutes to 59 minutes A, S** 🐾

● **S06.2X3**   **Diffuse traumatic brain injury with loss of consciousness of 1 hour to 5 hours 59 minutes A, S** 🐾

● **S06.2X4**   **Diffuse traumatic brain injury with loss of consciousness of 6 hours to 24 hours A, S** 🐾

● **S06.2X5**   **Diffuse traumatic brain injury with loss of consciousness greater than 24 hours with return to pre-existing conscious levels A, S** 🐾

● **S06.2X6**   **Diffuse traumatic brain injury with loss of consciousness greater than 24 hours without return to pre-existing conscious level with patient surviving A, S** 🐾

● **S06.2X7**   **Diffuse traumatic brain injury with loss of consciousness of any duration with death due to brain injury prior to regaining consciousness**

● **S06.2X8**   **Diffuse traumatic brain injury with loss of consciousness of any duration with death due to other cause prior to regaining consciousness**

● **S06.2X9**   **Diffuse traumatic brain injury with loss of consciousness of unspecified duration A, S** 🐾
     Diffuse traumatic brain injury NOS

● **S06.3**   **Focal traumatic brain injury**
     Excludes1   any condition classifiable to S06.4-S06.6
     ~~focal cerebral edema (S06.1)~~
     ▶ **Excludes2**   focal cerebral edema (S06.1)

● **S06.30**   **Unspecified focal traumatic brain injury**

● **S06.300**   **Unspecified focal traumatic brain injury without loss of consciousness A, S** 🐾

● **S06.301**   **Unspecified focal traumatic brain injury with loss of consciousness of 30 minutes or less A, S** 🐾

● **S06.302**   **Unspecified focal traumatic brain injury with loss of consciousness of 31 minutes to 59 minutes A, S** 🐾

● **S06.303**   **Unspecified focal traumatic brain injury with loss of consciousness of 1 hour to 5 hours 59 minutes A, S** 🐾

● **S06.304**   **Unspecified focal traumatic brain injury with loss of consciousness of 6 hours to 24 hours A, S** 🐾

● **S06.305**   **Unspecified focal traumatic brain injury with loss of consciousness greater than 24 hours with return to pre-existing conscious level A, S** 🐾

● **S06.306**   **Unspecified focal traumatic brain injury with loss of consciousness greater than 24 hours without return to pre-existing conscious level with patient surviving A, S** 🐾

● **S06.307**   **Unspecified focal traumatic brain injury with loss of consciousness of any duration with death due to brain injury prior to regaining consciousness**

● **S06.308**   **Unspecified focal traumatic brain injury with loss of consciousness of any duration with death due to other cause prior to regaining consciousness**

● **S06.309**   **Unspecified focal traumatic brain injury with loss of consciousness of unspecified duration A, S** 🐾
     Unspecified focal traumatic brain injury NOS

● **S06.31**   **Contusion and laceration of right cerebrum**

● **S06.310**   **Contusion and laceration of right cerebrum without loss of consciousness A, S** 🐾

● **S06.311**   **Contusion and laceration of right cerebrum with loss of consciousness of 30 minutes or less A, S** 🐾

● **S06.312**   **Contusion and laceration of right cerebrum with loss of consciousness of 31 minutes to 59 minutes A, S** 🐾

● **S06.313**   **Contusion and laceration of right cerebrum with loss of consciousness of 1 hour to 5 hours 59 minutes A, S** 🐾

● **S06.314**   **Contusion and laceration of right cerebrum with loss of consciousness of 6 hours to 24 hours A, S** 🐾

● **S06.315**   **Contusion and laceration of right cerebrum with loss of consciousness greater than 24 hours with return to pre-existing conscious level A, S** 🐾

● **S06.316**   **Contusion and laceration of right cerebrum with loss of consciousness greater than 24 hours without return to pre-existing conscious level with patient surviving A, S** 🐾

● **S06.317**   **Contusion and laceration of right cerebrum with loss of consciousness of any duration with death due to brain injury prior to regaining consciousness**

● **S06.318**   **Contusion and laceration of right cerebrum with loss of consciousness of any duration with death due to other cause prior to regaining consciousness**

● **S06.319**   **Contusion and laceration of right cerebrum with loss of consciousness of unspecified duration A, S** 🐾
     Contusion and laceration of right cerebrum NOS

● **S06.32**   Contusion and laceration of left cerebrum

● **S06.320**   Contusion and laceration of left cerebrum without loss of consciousness   A, S 🐾

● **S06.321**   Contusion and laceration of left cerebrum with loss of consciousness of 30 minutes or less   A, S 🐾

● **S06.322**   Contusion and laceration of left cerebrum with loss of consciousness of 31 minutes to 59 minutes   A, S 🐾

● **S06.323**   Contusion and laceration of left cerebrum with loss of consciousness of 1 hour to 5 hours 59 minutes   A, S 🐾

● **S06.324**   Contusion and laceration of left cerebrum with loss of consciousness of 6 hours to 24 hours   A, S 🐾

● **S06.325**   Contusion and laceration of left cerebrum with loss of consciousness greater than 24 hours with return to pre-existing conscious level   A, S 🐾

● **S06.326**   Contusion and laceration of left cerebrum with loss of consciousness greater than 24 hours without return to pre-existing conscious level with patient surviving   A, S 🐾

● **S06.327**   Contusion and laceration of left cerebrum with loss of consciousness of any duration with death due to brain injury prior to regaining consciousness

● **S06.328**   Contusion and laceration of left cerebrum with loss of consciousness of any duration with death due to other cause prior to regaining consciousness

● **S06.329**   Contusion and laceration of left cerebrum with loss of consciousness of unspecified duration   A, S 🐾
     Contusion and laceration of left cerebrum NOS

● **S06.33**   Contusion and laceration of cerebrum, unspecified

● **S06.330**   Contusion and laceration of cerebrum, unspecified, without loss of consciousness   A, S 🐾

● **S06.331**   Contusion and laceration of cerebrum, unspecified, with loss of consciousness of 30 minutes or less   A, S 🐾

● **S06.332**   Contusion and laceration of cerebrum, unspecified, with loss of consciousness of 31 minutes to 59 minutes   A, S 🐾

● **S06.333**   Contusion and laceration of cerebrum, unspecified, with loss of consciousness of 1 hour to 5 hours 59 minutes   A, S 🐾

● **S06.334**   Contusion and laceration of cerebrum, unspecified, with loss of consciousness of 6 hours to 24 hours   A, S 🐾

● **S06.335**   Contusion and laceration of cerebrum, unspecified, with loss of consciousness greater than 24 hours with return to pre-existing conscious level   A, S 🐾

● **S06.336**   Contusion and laceration of cerebrum, unspecified, with loss of consciousness greater than 24 hours without return to pre-existing conscious level with patient surviving   A, S 🐾

● **S06.337**   Contusion and laceration of cerebrum, unspecified, with loss of consciousness of any duration with death due to brain injury prior to regaining consciousness

● **S06.338**   Contusion and laceration of cerebrum, unspecified, with loss of consciousness of any duration with death due to other cause prior to regaining consciousness

● **S06.339**   Contusion and laceration of cerebrum, unspecified, with loss of consciousness of unspecified duration   A, S 🐾
     Contusion and laceration of cerebrum NOS

● **S06.34**   Traumatic hemorrhage of right cerebrum
     Traumatic intracerebral hemorrhage and hematoma of right cerebrum

● **S06.340**   Traumatic hemorrhage of right cerebrum without loss of consciousness   A, S 🐾
     Coding Clinic: 2015, Q1, P12

● **S06.341**   Traumatic hemorrhage of right cerebrum with loss of consciousness of 30 minutes or less   A, S 🐾

● **S06.342**   Traumatic hemorrhage of right cerebrum with loss of consciousness of 31 minutes to 59 minutes   A, S 🐾

● **S06.343**   Traumatic hemorrhage of right cerebrum with loss of consciousness of 1 hours to 5 hours 59 minutes   A, S 🐾

● **S06.344**   Traumatic hemorrhage of right cerebrum with loss of consciousness of 6 hours to 24 hours   A, S 🐾

● **S06.345**   Traumatic hemorrhage of right cerebrum with loss of consciousness greater than 24 hours with return to pre-existing conscious level   A, S 🐾

● **S06.346**   Traumatic hemorrhage of right cerebrum with loss of consciousness greater than 24 hours without return to pre-existing conscious level with patient surviving   A, S 🐾

● **S06.347**   Traumatic hemorrhage of right cerebrum with loss of consciousness of any duration with death due to brain injury prior to regaining consciousness

● **S06.348**   Traumatic hemorrhage of right cerebrum with loss of consciousness of any duration with death due to other cause prior to regaining consciousness

● **S06.349**   Traumatic hemorrhage of right cerebrum with loss of consciousness of unspecified duration   A, S 🐾
     Traumatic hemorrhage of right cerebrum NOS

▶ New   ⇒ Revised   ~~deleted~~ Deleted   Excludes 1   Excludes 2   Includes   Use additional   Code first   Code also   Key words
OGCR Official Guidelines   X Assign placeholder X   ● Use Additional Character(s)   ▷ Manifestation Code   🐾 Hierarchical Condition Category   Coding Clinic

● **S06.35**   **Traumatic hemorrhage of left cerebrum**
Traumatic intracerebral hemorrhage and hematoma of left cerebrum

  ● **S06.350**   Traumatic hemorrhage of left cerebrum without loss of consciousness   A, S 🔛

  ● **S06.351**   Traumatic hemorrhage of left cerebrum with loss of consciousness of 30 minutes or less   A, S 🔛

  ● **S06.352**   Traumatic hemorrhage of left cerebrum with loss of consciousness of 31 minutes to 59 minutes   A, S 🔛

  ● **S06.353**   Traumatic hemorrhage of left cerebrum with loss of consciousness of 1 hours to 5 hours 59 minutes   A, S 🔛

  ● **S06.354**   Traumatic hemorrhage of left cerebrum with loss of consciousness of 6 hours to 24 hours   A, S 🔛

  ● **S06.355**   Traumatic hemorrhage of left cerebrum with loss of consciousness greater than 24 hours with return to pre-existing conscious level   A, S 🔛

  ● **S06.356**   Traumatic hemorrhage of left cerebrum with loss of consciousness greater than 24 hours without return to pre-existing conscious level with patient surviving   A, S 🔛

  ● **S06.357**   Traumatic hemorrhage of left cerebrum with loss of consciousness of any duration with death due to brain injury prior to regaining consciousness

  ● **S06.358**   Traumatic hemorrhage of left cerebrum with loss of consciousness of any duration with death due to other cause prior to regaining consciousness

  ● **S06.359**   Traumatic hemorrhage of left cerebrum with loss of consciousness of unspecified duration   A, S 🔛
Traumatic hemorrhage of left cerebrum NOS

● **S06.36**   **Traumatic hemorrhage of cerebrum, unspecified**
Traumatic intracerebral hemorrhage and hematoma, unspecified

  ● **S06.360**   Traumatic hemorrhage of cerebrum, unspecified, without loss of consciousness   A, S 🔛

  ● **S06.361**   Traumatic hemorrhage of cerebrum, unspecified, with loss of consciousness of 30 minutes or less   A, S 🔛

  ● **S06.362**   Traumatic hemorrhage of cerebrum, unspecified, with loss of consciousness of 31 minutes to 59 minutes   A, S 🔛

  ● **S06.363**   Traumatic hemorrhage of cerebrum, unspecified, with loss of consciousness of 1 hours to 5 hours 59 minutes   A, S 🔛

  ● **S06.364**   Traumatic hemorrhage of cerebrum, unspecified, with loss of consciousness of 6 hours to 24 hours   A, S 🔛

  ● **S06.365**   Traumatic hemorrhage of cerebrum, unspecified, with loss of consciousness greater than 24 hours with return to pre-existing conscious level   A, S 🔛

  ● **S06.366**   Traumatic hemorrhage of cerebrum, unspecified, with loss of consciousness greater than 24 hours without return to pre-existing conscious level with patient surviving   A, S 🔛

  ● **S06.367**   Traumatic hemorrhage of cerebrum, unspecified, with loss of consciousness of any duration with death due to brain injury prior to regaining consciousness

  ● **S06.368**   Traumatic hemorrhage of cerebrum, unspecified, with loss of consciousness of any duration with death due to other cause prior to regaining consciousness

  ● **S06.369**   Traumatic hemorrhage of cerebrum, unspecified, with loss of consciousness of unspecified duration   A, S 🔛
Traumatic hemorrhage of cerebrum NOS

● **S06.37**   **Contusion, laceration, and hemorrhage of cerebellum**

  ● **S06.370**   Contusion, laceration, and hemorrhage of cerebellum without loss of consciousness   A, S 🔛

  ● **S06.371**   Contusion, laceration, and hemorrhage of cerebellum with loss of consciousness of 30 minutes or less   A, S 🔛

  ● **S06.372**   Contusion, laceration, and hemorrhage of cerebellum with loss of consciousness of 31 minutes to 59 minutes   A, S 🔛

  ● **S06.373**   Contusion, laceration, and hemorrhage of cerebellum with loss of consciousness of 1 hour to 5 hours 59 minutes   A, S 🔛

  ● **S06.374**   Contusion, laceration, and hemorrhage of cerebellum with loss of consciousness of 6 hours to 24 hours   A, S 🔛

  ● **S06.375**   Contusion, laceration, and hemorrhage of cerebellum with loss of consciousness greater than 24 hours with return to pre-existing conscious level   A, S 🔛

  ● **S06.376**   Contusion, laceration, and hemorrhage of cerebellum with loss of consciousness greater than 24 hours without return to pre-existing conscious level with patient surviving   A, S 🔛

  ● **S06.377**   Contusion, laceration, and hemorrhage of cerebellum with loss of consciousness of any duration with death due to brain injury prior to regaining consciousness

  ● **S06.378**   Contusion, laceration, and hemorrhage of cerebellum with loss of consciousness of any duration with death due to other cause prior to regaining consciousness

  ● **S06.379**   Contusion, laceration, and hemorrhage of cerebellum with loss of consciousness of unspecified duration   A, S 🔛
Contusion, laceration, and hemorrhage of cerebellum NOS

● **S06.38**   Contusion, laceration, and hemorrhage of brainstem

  ● **S06.380**   Contusion, laceration, and hemorrhage of brainstem without loss of consciousness   A, S 🦠

  ● **S06.381**   Contusion, laceration, and hemorrhage of brainstem with loss of consciousness of 30 minutes or less   A, S 🦠

  ● **S06.382**   Contusion, laceration, and hemorrhage of brainstem with loss of consciousness of 31 minutes to 59 minutes   A, S 🦠

  ● **S06.383**   Contusion, laceration, and hemorrhage of brainstem with loss of consciousness of 1 hour to 5 hours 59 minutes   A, S 🦠

  ● **S06.384**   Contusion, laceration, and hemorrhage of brainstem with loss of consciousness of 6 hours to 24 hours   A, S 🦠

  ● **S06.385**   Contusion, laceration, and hemorrhage of brainstem with loss of consciousness greater than 24 hours with return to pre-existing conscious level   A, S 🦠

  ● **S06.386**   Contusion, laceration, and hemorrhage of brainstem with loss of consciousness greater than 24 hours without return to pre-existing conscious level with patient surviving   A, S 🦠

  ● **S06.387**   Contusion, laceration, and hemorrhage of brainstem with loss of consciousness of any duration with death due to brain injury prior to regaining consciousness

  ● **S06.388**   Contusion, laceration, and hemorrhage of brainstem with loss of consciousness of any duration with death due to other cause prior to regaining consciousness

  ● **S06.389**   Contusion, laceration, and hemorrhage of brainstem with loss of consciousness of unspecified duration   A, S 🦠
      Contusion, laceration, and hemorrhage of brainstem NOS

● **S06.4**   **Epidural hemorrhage**
   Situated outside dura mater
   Extradural hemorrhage NOS
   Intracranial hemorrhage due to trauma
   Extradural hemorrhage (traumatic)

  ● **S06.4X**   Epidural hemorrhage

    ● **S06.4X0**   Epidural hemorrhage without loss of consciousness   A, S 🦠

    ● **S06.4X1**   Epidural hemorrhage with loss of consciousness of 30 minutes or less   A, S 🦠

    ● **S06.4X2**   Epidural hemorrhage with loss of consciousness of 31 minutes to 59 minutes   A, S 🦠

    ● **S06.4X3**   Epidural hemorrhage with loss of consciousness of 1 hour to 5 hours 59 minutes   A, S 🦠

    ● **S06.4X4**   Epidural hemorrhage with loss of consciousness of 6 hours to 24 hours   A, S 🦠

    ● **S06.4X5**   Epidural hemorrhage with loss of consciousness greater than 24 hours with return to pre-existing conscious level   A, S 🦠

    ● **S06.4X6**   Epidural hemorrhage with loss of consciousness greater than 24 hours without return to pre-existing conscious level with patient surviving   A, S 🦠

    ● **S06.4X7**   Epidural hemorrhage with loss of consciousness of any duration with death due to brain injury prior to regaining consciousness

    ● **S06.4X8**   Epidural hemorrhage with loss of consciousness of any duration with death due to other causes prior to regaining consciousness

    ● **S06.4X9**   Epidural hemorrhage with loss of consciousness of unspecified duration   A, S 🦠
       Epidural hemorrhage NOS

● **S06.5**   **Traumatic subdural hemorrhage**

  ● **S06.5X**   Traumatic subdural hemorrhage

    ● **S06.5X0**   Traumatic subdural hemorrhage without loss of consciousness   A, S 🦠
       Coding Clinic: 2018, Q2, P13; 2015, Q3, P37

    ● **S06.5X1**   Traumatic subdural hemorrhage with loss of consciousness of 30 minutes or less   A, S 🦠

    ● **S06.5X2**   Traumatic subdural hemorrhage with loss of consciousness of 31 minutes to 59 minutes   A, S 🦠

    ● **S06.5X3**   Traumatic subdural hemorrhage with loss of consciousness of 1 hour to 5 hours 59 minutes   A, S 🦠

    ● **S06.5X4**   Traumatic subdural hemorrhage with loss of consciousness of 6 hours to 24 hours   A, S 🦠

    ● **S06.5X5**   Traumatic subdural hemorrhage with loss of consciousness greater than 24 hours with return to pre-existing conscious level   A, S 🦠

    ● **S06.5X6**   Traumatic subdural hemorrhage with loss of consciousness greater than 24 hours without return to pre-existing conscious level with patient surviving   A, S 🦠

    ● **S06.5X7**   Traumatic subdural hemorrhage with loss of consciousness of any duration with death due to brain injury before regaining consciousness

    ● **S06.5X8**   Traumatic subdural hemorrhage with loss of consciousness of any duration with death due to other cause before regaining consciousness

    ● **S06.5X9**   Traumatic subdural hemorrhage with loss of consciousness of unspecified duration   A, S 🦠
       Traumatic subdural hemorrhage NOS

● **S06.6**   **Traumatic subarachnoid hemorrhage**
   Between arachnoid and pia mater
   Coding Clinic: 2016, Q4, P67

  ● **S06.6X**   Traumatic subarachnoid hemorrhage

    ● **S06.6X0**   Traumatic subarachnoid hemorrhage without loss of consciousness   A, S 🦠
       Coding Clinic: 2015, Q3, P37

    ● **S06.6X1**   Traumatic subarachnoid hemorrhage with loss of consciousness of 30 minutes or less   A, S 🦠

    ● **S06.6X2**   Traumatic subarachnoid hemorrhage with loss of consciousness of 31 minutes to 59 minutes   A, S 🦠

    ● **S06.6X3**   Traumatic subarachnoid hemorrhage with loss of consciousness of 1 hour to 5 hours 59 minutes   A, S 🦠

▶ New   ⇒ Revised   ~~deleted~~ Deleted   Excludes 1   Excludes 2   Includes   Use additional   Code first   Code also   Key words
OGCR Official Guidelines   X Assign placeholder X   ● Use Additional Character(s)   ▷ Manifestation Code   🦠 Hierarchical Condition Category   **Coding Clinic**

● **S06.6X4**   Traumatic subarachnoid hemorrhage with loss of consciousness of 6 hours to 24 hours   A, S

● **S06.6X5**   Traumatic subarachnoid hemorrhage with loss of consciousness greater than 24 hours with return to pre-existing conscious level   A, S

● **S06.6X6**   Traumatic subarachnoid hemorrhage with loss of consciousness greater than 24 hours without return to pre-existing conscious level with patient surviving   A, S

● **S06.6X7**   Traumatic subarachnoid hemorrhage with loss of consciousness of any duration with death due to brain injury prior to regaining consciousness

● **S06.6X8**   Traumatic subarachnoid hemorrhage with loss of consciousness of any duration with death due to other cause prior to regaining consciousness

● **S06.6X9**   Traumatic subarachnoid hemorrhage with loss of consciousness of unspecified duration   A, S

        Traumatic subarachnoid hemorrhage NOS

● **S06.8**   Other specified intracranial injuries

  ● **S06.81**   Injury of right internal carotid artery, intracranial portion, not elsewhere classified
      Coding Clinic: 2016, Q4, P67

    ● **S06.810**   Injury of right internal carotid artery, intracranial portion, not elsewhere classified without loss of consciousness   A, S

    ● **S06.811**   Injury of right internal carotid artery, intracranial portion, not elsewhere classified with loss of consciousness of 30 minutes or less   A, S

    ● **S06.812**   Injury of right internal carotid artery, intracranial portion, not elsewhere classified with loss of consciousness of 31 minutes to 59 minutes   A, S

    ● **S06.813**   Injury of right internal carotid artery, intracranial portion, not elsewhere classified with loss of consciousness of 1 hour to 5 hours 59 minutes   A, S

    ● **S06.814**   Injury of right internal carotid artery, intracranial portion, not elsewhere classified with loss of consciousness of 6 hours to 24 hours   A, S

    ● **S06.815**   Injury of right internal carotid artery, intracranial portion, not elsewhere classified with loss of consciousness greater than 24 hours with return to pre-existing conscious level   A, S

    ● **S06.816**   Injury of right internal carotid artery, intracranial portion, not elsewhere classified with loss of consciousness greater than 24 hours without return to pre-existing conscious level with patient surviving   A, S

    ● **S06.817**   Injury of right internal carotid artery, intracranial portion, not elsewhere classified with loss of consciousness of any duration with death due to brain injury prior to regaining consciousness

● **S06.818**   Injury of right internal carotid artery, intracranial portion, not elsewhere classified with loss of consciousness of any duration with death due to other cause prior to regaining consciousness

● **S06.819**   Injury of right internal carotid artery, intracranial portion, not elsewhere classified with loss of consciousness of unspecified duration   A, S

        Injury of right internal carotid artery, intracranial portion, not elsewhere classified NOS

● **S06.82**   Injury of left internal carotid artery, intracranial portion, not elsewhere classified
      Coding Clinic: 2016, Q4, P67

  ● **S06.820**   Injury of left internal carotid artery, intracranial portion, not elsewhere classified without loss of consciousness   A, S

  ● **S06.821**   Injury of left internal carotid artery, intracranial portion, not elsewhere classified with loss of consciousness of 30 minutes or less   A, S

  ● **S06.822**   Injury of left internal carotid artery, intracranial portion, not elsewhere classified with loss of consciousness of 31 minutes to 59 minutes   A, S

  ● **S06.823**   Injury of left internal carotid artery, intracranial portion, not elsewhere classified with loss of consciousness of 1 hour to 5 hours 59 minutes   A, S

  ● **S06.824**   Injury of left internal carotid artery, intracranial portion, not elsewhere classified with loss of consciousness of 6 hours to 24 hours   A, S

  ● **S06.825**   Injury of left internal carotid artery, intracranial portion, not elsewhere classified with loss of consciousness greater than 24 hours with return to pre-existing conscious level

  ● **S06.826**   Injury of left internal carotid artery, intracranial portion, not elsewhere classified with loss of consciousness greater than 24 hours without return to pre-existing conscious level with patient surviving   A, S

  ● **S06.827**   Injury of left internal carotid artery, intracranial portion, not elsewhere classified with loss of consciousness of any duration with death due to brain injury prior to regaining consciousness

  ● **S06.828**   Injury of left internal carotid artery, intracranial portion, not elsewhere classified with loss of consciousness of any duration with death due to other cause prior to regaining consciousness

  ● **S06.829**   Injury of left internal carotid artery, intracranial portion, not elsewhere classified with loss of consciousness of unspecified duration   A, S

        Injury of left internal carotid artery, intracranial portion, not elsewhere classified NOS

● **S06.89** **Other specified intracranial injury**
　　　　Excludes1 concussion (S06.0X-)
● S06.890 Other specified intracranial injury without loss of consciousness A, S 🦠
● S06.891 Other specified intracranial injury with loss of consciousness of 30 minutes or less A, S 🦠
● S06.892 Other specified intracranial injury with loss of consciousness of 31 minutes to 59 minutes A, S 🦠
● S06.893 Other specified intracranial injury with loss of consciousness of 1 hour to 5 hours 59 minutes A, S 🦠
● S06.894 Other specified intracranial injury with loss of consciousness of 6 hours to 24 hours A, S 🦠
● S06.895 Other specified intracranial injury with loss of consciousness greater than 24 hours with return to pre-existing conscious level A, S 🦠
● S06.896 Other specified intracranial injury with loss of consciousness greater than 24 hours without return to pre-existing conscious level with patient surviving A, S 🦠
● S06.897 Other specified intracranial injury with loss of consciousness of any duration with death due to brain injury prior to regaining consciousness
● S06.898 Other specified intracranial injury with loss of consciousness of any duration with death due to other cause prior to regaining consciousness
● S06.899 Other specified intracranial injury with loss of consciousness of unspecified duration A, S 🦠

● **S06.9** **Unspecified intracranial injury**
　　Brain injury NOS
　　Head injury NOS with loss of consciousness
　　Traumatic brain injury NOS
　　Excludes1 conditions classifiable to S06.0- to S06.8- code to specified intracranial injury head injury NOS (S09.90)
● **S06.9X** **Unspecified intracranial injury**
● S06.9X0 Unspecified intracranial injury without loss of consciousness A, S 🦠
● S06.9X1 Unspecified intracranial injury with loss of consciousness of 30 minutes or less A, S 🦠
● S06.9X2 Unspecified intracranial injury with loss of consciousness of 31 minutes to 59 minutes A, S 🦠
● S06.9X3 Unspecified intracranial injury with loss of consciousness of 1 hour to 5 hours 59 minutes A, S 🦠
● S06.9X4 Unspecified intracranial injury with loss of consciousness of 6 hours to 24 hours A, S 🦠
● S06.9X5 Unspecified intracranial injury with loss of consciousness greater than 24 hours with return to pre-existing conscious level A, S 🦠

● S06.9X6 Unspecified intracranial injury with loss of consciousness greater than 24 hours without return to pre-existing conscious level with patient surviving A, S 🦠
● S06.9X7 Unspecified intracranial injury with loss of consciousness of any duration with death due to brain injury prior to regaining consciousness
● S06.9X8 Unspecified intracranial injury with loss of consciousness of any duration with death due to other cause prior to regaining consciousness
● S06.9X9 Unspecified intracranial injury with loss of consciousness of unspecified duration A, S 🦠

● **S07** **Crushing injury of head**
　　Use additional code for all associated injuries, such as:
　　　intracranial injuries (S06.-)
　　　skull fractures (S02.-)
　　The appropriate 7th character is to be added to each code from category S07

> A　initial encounter
> D　subsequent encounter
> S　sequela

X ● **S07.0** **Crushing injury of face**
X ● **S07.1** **Crushing injury of skull**
X ● **S07.8** **Crushing injury of other parts of head**
X ● **S07.9** **Crushing injury of head, part unspecified**

● **S08** **Avulsion and traumatic amputation of part of head**
　　An amputation not identified as partial or complete should be coded to complete
　　The appropriate 7th character is to be added to each code from category S08

> A　initial encounter
> D　subsequent encounter
> S　sequela

X ● **S08.0** **Avulsion of scalp**
● **S08.1** **Traumatic amputation of ear**
● **S08.11** **Complete traumatic amputation of ear**
● S08.111 Complete traumatic amputation of right ear
● S08.112 Complete traumatic amputation of left ear
● S08.119 Complete traumatic amputation of unspecified ear
● **S08.12** **Partial traumatic amputation of ear**
● S08.121 Partial traumatic amputation of right ear
● S08.122 Partial traumatic amputation of left ear
● S08.129 Partial traumatic amputation of unspecified ear
● **S08.8** **Traumatic amputation of other parts of head**
● **S08.81** **Traumatic amputation of nose**
● S08.811 Complete traumatic amputation of nose
● S08.812 Partial traumatic amputation of nose
X ● **S08.89** **Traumatic amputation of other parts of head**

▶ New　⮕ Revised　deleted Deleted　Excludes 1　Excludes 2　Includes　Use additional　Code first　Code also　Key words

1238　OGCR Official Guidelines　X Assign placeholder X　● Use Additional Character(s)　▷ Manifestation Code　🦠 Hierarchical Condition Category　**Coding Clinic**

● **S09**   **Other and unspecified injuries of head**

The appropriate 7th character is to be added to each code from category S09

> A   initial encounter
> D   subsequent encounter
> S   sequela

X● **S09.0**   **Injury of blood vessels of head, not elsewhere classified**
>> **Excludes1**   injury of cerebral blood vessels (S06.-)
>> injury of precerebral blood vessels (S15.-)

● **S09.1**   **Injury of muscle and tendon of head**
> Code also any associated open wound (S01.-)
>> **Excludes2**   sprain to joints and ligament of head (S03.9)

X● **S09.10**   **Unspecified injury of muscle and tendon of head**
> Injury of muscle and tendon of head NOS

X● **S09.11**   **Strain of muscle and tendon of head**

X● **S09.12**   **Laceration of muscle and tendon of head**

X● **S09.19**   **Other specified injury of muscle and tendon of head**

● **S09.2**   **Traumatic rupture of ear drum**
>> **Excludes1**   traumatic rupture of ear drum due to blast injury (S09.31-)

X● **S09.20**   **Traumatic rupture of unspecified ear drum**

X● **S09.21**   **Traumatic rupture of right ear drum**

X● **S09.22**   **Traumatic rupture of left ear drum**

● **S09.3**   **Other specified and unspecified injury of middle and inner ear**
>> **Excludes1**   injury to ear NOS (S09.91-)
>> **Excludes2**   injury to external ear (S00.4-, S01.3-, S08.1-)

● **S09.30**   **Unspecified injury of middle and inner ear**

● **S09.301**   Unspecified injury of right middle and inner ear

● **S09.302**   Unspecified injury of left middle and inner ear

● **S09.309**   Unspecified injury of unspecified middle and inner ear

● **S09.31**   **Primary blast injury of ear**
> Blast injury of ear NOS

● **S09.311**   Primary blast injury of right ear

● **S09.312**   Primary blast injury of left ear

● **S09.313**   Primary blast injury of ear, bilateral

● **S09.319**   Primary blast injury of unspecified ear

● **S09.39**   **Other specified injury of middle and inner ear**
> Secondary blast injury to ear

● **S09.391**   Other specified injury of right middle and inner ear

● **S09.392**   Other specified injury of left middle and inner ear

● **S09.399**   Other specified injury of unspecified middle and inner ear

X● **S09.8**   **Other specified injuries of head**

● **S09.9**   **Unspecified injury of face and head**

X● **S09.90**   **Unspecified injury of head**
> Head injury NOS
>> **Excludes1**   brain injury NOS (S06.9-)
>> head injury NOS with loss of consciousness (S06.9-)
>> intracranial injury NOS (S06.9-)

X● **S09.91**   **Unspecified injury of ear**
> Injury of ear NOS

X● **S09.92**   **Unspecified injury of nose**
> Injury of nose NOS

X● **S09.93**   **Unspecified injury of face**
> Injury of face NOS

INJURIES TO THE NECK (S10-S19)

Includes	injuries of nape
	injuries of supraclavicular region
	injuries of throat
Excludes2	burns and corrosions (T20-T32)
	effects of foreign body in esophagus (T18.1)
	effects of foreign body in larynx (T17.3)
	effects of foreign body in pharynx (T17.2)
	effects of foreign body in trachea (T17.4)
	frostbite (T33-T34)
	insect bite or sting, venomous (T63.4)

● **S10**   **Superficial injury of neck**

The appropriate 7th character is to be added to each code from category S10

> A   initial encounter
> D   subsequent encounter
> S   sequela

X● **S10.0**   **Contusion of throat**
> Contusion of cervical esophagus
> Contusion of larynx
> Contusion of pharynx
> Contusion of trachea

● **S10.1**   **Other and unspecified superficial injuries of throat**

X● **S10.10**   **Unspecified superficial injuries of throat**

X● **S10.11**   **Abrasion of throat**

X● **S10.12**   **Blister (nonthermal) of throat**

X● **S10.14**   **External constriction of part of throat**

X● **S10.15**   **Superficial foreign body of throat**
> Splinter in the throat

X● **S10.16**   **Insect bite (nonvenomous) of throat**

X● **S10.17**   **Other superficial bite of throat**
>> **Excludes1**   open bite of throat (S11.85)

● **S10.8**   **Superficial injury of other specified parts of neck**

X● **S10.80**   **Unspecified superficial injury of other specified part of neck**

X● **S10.81**   **Abrasion of other specified part of neck**

X● **S10.82**   **Blister (nonthermal) of other specified part of neck**

X● **S10.83**   **Contusion of other specified part of neck**

X● **S10.84**   **External constriction of other specified part of neck**

X● **S10.85**   **Superficial foreign body of other specified part of neck**
> Splinter in other part of neck

X● **S10.86**   **Insect bite of other specified part of neck**

X● **S10.87**   **Other superficial bite of other specified part of neck**
>> **Excludes1**   open bite of other specified parts of neck (S11.85)

● **S10.9**   **Superficial injury of unspecified part of neck**

X● **S10.90**   **Unspecified superficial injury of unspecified part of neck**

X● **S10.91**   **Abrasion of unspecified part of neck**

X● **S10.92**   **Blister (nonthermal) of unspecified part of neck**

X● **S10.93**   **Contusion of unspecified part of neck**

X● **S10.94**   **External constriction of unspecified part of neck**

X● **S10.95**   **Superficial foreign body of unspecified part of neck**

X● **S10.96**   **Insect bite of unspecified part of neck**

X● **S10.97**   **Other superficial bite of unspecified part of neck**

● **S11   Open wound of neck**
    Code also any associated:
      spinal cord injury (S14.0, S14.1-)
      wound infection
    Excludes2   open fracture of vertebra (S12.- with 7th character B)
    The appropriate 7th character is to be added to each code from
        category S11

> A   initial encounter
> D   subsequent encounter
> S   sequela

● **S11.0   Open wound of larynx and trachea**
    ● **S11.01   Open wound of larynx**
          Excludes2   open wound of vocal cord
                                    (S11.03)
        ● **S11.011   Laceration without foreign body of
                        larynx**
        ● **S11.012   Laceration with foreign body of
                        larynx**
        ● **S11.013   Puncture wound without foreign
                        body of larynx**
        ● **S11.014   Puncture wound with foreign body of
                        larynx**
        ● **S11.015   Open bite of larynx**
                        Bite of larynx NOS
        ● **S11.019   Unspecified open wound of larynx**
    ● **S11.02   Open wound of trachea**
              Open wound of cervical trachea
              Open wound of trachea NOS
          Excludes2   open wound of thoracic trachea
                                    (S27.5-)
        ● **S11.021   Laceration without foreign body of
                        trachea**
        ● **S11.022   Laceration with foreign body of
                        trachea**
        ● **S11.023   Puncture wound without foreign
                        body of trachea**
        ● **S11.024   Puncture wound with foreign body of
                        trachea**
        ● **S11.025   Open bite of trachea**
                        Bite of trachea NOS
        ● **S11.029   Unspecified open wound of trachea**
    ● **S11.03   Open wound of vocal cord**
        ● **S11.031   Laceration without foreign body of
                        vocal cord**
        ● **S11.032   Laceration with foreign body of vocal
                        cord**
        ● **S11.033   Puncture wound without foreign
                        body of vocal cord**
        ● **S11.034   Puncture wound with foreign body of
                        vocal cord**
        ● **S11.035   Open bite of vocal cord**
                        Bite of vocal cord NOS
        ● **S11.039   Unspecified open wound of vocal
                        cord**

● **S11.1   Open wound of thyroid gland**
    X● **S11.10   Unspecified open wound of thyroid gland**
    X● **S11.11   Laceration without foreign body of thyroid
                    gland**
    X● **S11.12   Laceration with foreign body of thyroid gland**
    X● **S11.13   Puncture wound without foreign body of
                    thyroid gland**
    X● **S11.14   Puncture wound with foreign body of thyroid
                    gland**
    X● **S11.15   Open bite of thyroid gland**
                    Bite of thyroid gland NOS
● **S11.2   Open wound of pharynx and cervical esophagus**
          Excludes1   open wound of esophagus NOS (S27.8-)
    X● **S11.20   Unspecified open wound of pharynx and
                    cervical esophagus**
    X● **S11.21   Laceration without foreign body of pharynx
                    and cervical esophagus**
    X● **S11.22   Laceration with foreign body of pharynx and
                    cervical esophagus**
    X● **S11.23   Puncture wound without foreign body of
                    pharynx and cervical esophagus**
    X● **S11.24   Puncture wound with foreign body of pharynx
                    and cervical esophagus**
    X● **S11.25   Open bite of pharynx and cervical esophagus**
                    Bite of pharynx and cervical esophagus NOS
● **S11.8   Open wound of other specified parts of neck**
    X● **S11.80   Unspecified open specified wound of other part
                    of neck**
    X● **S11.81   Laceration without foreign body of other
                    specified part of neck**
    X● **S11.82   Laceration with foreign body of other specified
                    part of neck**
    X● **S11.83   Puncture wound without foreign body of other
                    specified part of neck**
    X● **S11.84   Puncture wound with foreign body of other
                    specified part of neck**
    X● **S11.85   Open bite of other specified part of neck**
                    Bite of other part of neck NOS
              Excludes1   superficial bite of other specified
                                    part of neck (S10.87)
    X● **S11.89   Other open wound of other part of neck**
● **S11.9   Open wound of unspecified part of neck**
    X● **S11.90   Unspecified open wound of unspecified part of
                    neck**
    X● **S11.91   Laceration without foreign body of unspecified
                    part of neck**
    X● **S11.92   Laceration with foreign body of unspecified
                    part of neck**
    X● **S11.93   Puncture wound without foreign body of
                    unspecified part of neck**
    X● **S11.94   Puncture wound with foreign body of
                    unspecified part of neck**
    X● **S11.95   Open bite of unspecified part of neck**
                    Bite of neck NOS
              Excludes1   superficial bite of neck (S10.97)

▶ New   ⇒ Revised   ~~deleted~~ Deleted   Excludes 1   Excludes 2   Includes   Use additional   Code first   Code also   Key words
OGCR Official Guidelines   X Assign placeholder X   ● Use Additional Character(s)   ⟩ Manifestation Code   ⬢ Hierarchical Condition Category   **Coding Clinic**

● S12 **Fracture of cervical vertebra and other parts of neck**

Note: A fracture not indicated as displaced or nondisplaced should be coded to displaced

A fracture not indicated as open or closed should be coded to closed

Includes   fracture of cervical neural arch
fracture of cervical spine
fracture of cervical spinous process
fracture of cervical transverse process
fracture of cervical vertebral arch
fracture of neck

Code first any associated cervical spinal cord injury (S14.0, S14.1-)

The appropriate 7th character is to be added to all codes from subcategories S12.0-S12.6

A	initial encounter for closed fracture
B	initial encounter for open fracture
D	subsequent encounter for fracture with routine healing
G	subsequent encounter for fracture with delayed healing
K	subsequent encounter for fracture with nonunion
S	sequela

● **S12.0** **Fracture of first cervical vertebra**
Atlas

  ● **S12.00** Unspecified fracture of first cervical vertebra

    ● S12.000 Unspecified displaced fracture of first cervical vertebra   A, B 🐾

    ● S12.001 Unspecified nondisplaced fracture of first cervical vertebra   A, B 🐾

  X ● **S12.01** Stable burst fracture of first cervical vertebra   A, B 🐾

  X ● **S12.02** Unstable burst fracture of first cervical vertebra   A, B 🐾

  ● **S12.03** Posterior arch fracture of first cervical vertebra

    ● S12.030 Displaced posterior arch fracture of first cervical vertebra   A, B 🐾

    ● S12.031 Nondisplaced posterior arch fracture of first cervical vertebra   A, B 🐾

  ● **S12.04** Lateral mass fracture of first cervical vertebra

    ● S12.040 Displaced lateral mass fracture of first cervical vertebra   A, B 🐾

    ● S12.041 Nondisplaced lateral mass fracture of first cervical vertebra   A, B 🐾

  ● **S12.09** Other fracture of first cervical vertebra

    ● S12.090 Other displaced fracture of first cervical vertebra   A, B 🐾

    ● S12.091 Other nondisplaced fracture of first cervical vertebra   A, B 🐾

● **S12.1** **Fracture of second cervical vertebra**
Axis

  ● **S12.10** Unspecified fracture of second cervical vertebra

    ● S12.100 Unspecified displaced fracture of second cervical vertebra   A, B 🐾

    ● S12.101 Unspecified nondisplaced fracture of second cervical vertebra   A, B 🐾

  ● **S12.11** Type II dens fracture

    ● S12.110 Anterior displaced Type II dens fracture   A, B 🐾

    ● S12.111 Posterior displaced Type II dens fracture   A, B 🐾

    ● S12.112 Nondisplaced Type II dens fracture   A, B 🐾

  ● **S12.12** Other dens fracture

    ● S12.120 Other displaced dens fracture   A, B 🐾

    ● S12.121 Other nondisplaced dens fracture   A, B 🐾

● **S12.13** Unspecified traumatic spondylolisthesis of second cervical vertebra

  ● S12.130 Unspecified traumatic displaced spondylolisthesis of second cervical vertebra   A, B 🐾

  ● S12.131 Unspecified traumatic nondisplaced spondylolisthesis of second cervical vertebra   A, B 🐾

X ● **S12.14** Type III traumatic spondylolisthesis of second cervical vertebra   A, B 🐾

● **S12.15** Other traumatic spondylolisthesis of second cervical vertebra

  ● S12.150 Other traumatic displaced spondylolisthesis of second cervical vertebra   A, B 🐾

  ● S12.151 Other traumatic nondisplaced spondylolisthesis of second cervical vertebra   A, B 🐾

● **S12.19** Other fracture of second cervical vertebra

  ● S12.190 Other displaced fracture of second cervical vertebra   A, B 🐾

  ● S12.191 Other nondisplaced fracture of second cervical vertebra   A, B 🐾

● **S12.2** **Fracture of third cervical vertebra**

  ● **S12.20** Unspecified fracture of third cervical vertebra

    ● S12.200 Unspecified displaced fracture of third cervical vertebra   A, B 🐾

    ● S12.201 Unspecified nondisplaced fracture of third cervical vertebra   A, B 🐾

  ● **S12.23** Unspecified traumatic spondylolisthesis of third cervical vertebra

    ● S12.230 Unspecified traumatic displaced spondylolisthesis of third cervical vertebra   A, B 🐾

    ● S12.231 Unspecified traumatic nondisplaced spondylolisthesis of third cervical vertebra   A, B 🐾

  X ● **S12.24** Type III traumatic spondylolisthesis of third cervical vertebra   A, B 🐾

  ● **S12.25** Other traumatic spondylolisthesis of third cervical vertebra

    ● S12.250 Other traumatic displaced spondylolisthesis of third cervical vertebra   A, B 🐾

    ● S12.251 Other traumatic nondisplaced spondylolisthesis of third cervical vertebra   A, B 🐾

  ● **S12.29** Other fracture of third cervical vertebra

    ● S12.290 Other displaced fracture of third cervical vertebra   A, B 🐾

    ● S12.291 Other nondisplaced fracture of third cervical vertebra   A, B 🐾

● **S12.3** **Fracture of fourth cervical vertebra**

  ● **S12.30** Unspecified fracture of fourth cervical vertebra

    ● S12.300 Unspecified displaced fracture of fourth cervical vertebra   A, B 🐾

    ● S12.301 Unspecified nondisplaced fracture of fourth cervical vertebra   A, B 🐾

  ● **S12.33** Unspecified traumatic spondylolisthesis of fourth cervical vertebra

    ● S12.330 Unspecified traumatic displaced spondylolisthesis of fourth cervical vertebra   A, B 🐾

    ● S12.331 Unspecified traumatic nondisplaced spondylolisthesis of fourth cervical vertebra   A, B 🐾

  X ● **S12.34** Type III traumatic spondylolisthesis of fourth cervical vertebra   A, B 🐾

N Newborn Age: 0   **P** Pediatric Age: 0–17   **M** Maternity DX: 12–55   **A** Adult Age: 15–124   ♀ Females Only   ♂ Males Only

1241

● S12.35   Other traumatic spondylolisthesis of fourth cervical vertebra

    ● S12.350   Other traumatic displaced spondylolisthesis of fourth cervical vertebra   A, B ⬤

    ● S12.351   Other traumatic nondisplaced spondylolisthesis of fourth cervical vertebra   A, B ⬤

● S12.39   Other fracture of fourth cervical vertebra

    ● S12.390   Other displaced fracture of fourth cervical vertebra   A, B ⬤

    ● S12.391   Other nondisplaced fracture of fourth cervical vertebra   A, B ⬤

● S12.4   Fracture of fifth cervical vertebra

   ● S12.40   Unspecified fracture of fifth cervical vertebra

    ● S12.400   Unspecified displaced fracture of fifth cervical vertebra   A, B ⬤

    ● S12.401   Unspecified nondisplaced fracture of fifth cervical vertebra   A, B ⬤

   ● S12.43   Unspecified traumatic spondylolisthesis of fifth cervical vertebra

    ● S12.430   Unspecified traumatic displaced spondylolisthesis of fifth cervical vertebra   A, B ⬤

    ● S12.431   Unspecified traumatic nondisplaced spondylolisthesis of fifth cervical vertebra   A, B ⬤

  X ● S12.44   Type III traumatic spondylolisthesis of fifth cervical vertebra   A, B ⬤

   ● S12.45   Other traumatic spondylolisthesis of fifth cervical vertebra

    ● S12.450   Other traumatic displaced spondylolisthesis of fifth cervical vertebra   A, B ⬤

    ● S12.451   Other traumatic nondisplaced spondylolisthesis of fifth cervical vertebra   A, B ⬤

   ● S12.49   Other fracture of fifth cervical vertebra

    ● S12.490   Other displaced fracture of fifth cervical vertebra   A, B ⬤

    ● S12.491   Other nondisplaced fracture of fifth cervical vertebra   A, B ⬤

● S12.5   Fracture of sixth cervical vertebra

   ● S12.50   Unspecified fracture of sixth cervical vertebra

    ● S12.500   Unspecified displaced fracture of sixth cervical vertebra   A, B ⬤

    ● S12.501   Unspecified nondisplaced fracture of sixth cervical vertebra   A, B ⬤

   ● S12.53   Unspecified traumatic spondylolisthesis of sixth cervical vertebra

    ● S12.530   Unspecified traumatic displaced spondylolisthesis of sixth cervical vertebra   A, B ⬤

    ● S12.531   Unspecified traumatic nondisplaced spondylolisthesis of sixth cervical vertebra   A, B ⬤

  X ● S12.54   Type III traumatic spondylolisthesis of sixth cervical vertebra   A, B ⬤

● S12.55   Other traumatic spondylolisthesis of sixth cervical vertebra

    ● S12.550   Other traumatic displaced spondylolisthesis of sixth cervical vertebra   A, B ⬤

    ● S12.551   Other traumatic nondisplaced spondylolisthesis of sixth cervical vertebra   A, B ⬤

● S12.59   Other fracture of sixth cervical vertebra

    ● S12.590   Other displaced fracture of sixth cervical vertebra   A, B ⬤

    ● S12.591   Other nondisplaced fracture of sixth cervical vertebra   A, B ⬤

● S12.6   Fracture of seventh cervical vertebra

   S12.60   Unspecified fracture of seventh cervical vertebra

    ● S12.600   Unspecified displaced fracture of seventh cervical vertebra   A, B ⬤

    ● S12.601   Unspecified nondisplaced fracture of seventh cervical vertebra   A, B ⬤

   ● S12.63   Unspecified traumatic spondylolisthesis of seventh cervical vertebra

    ● S12.630   Unspecified traumatic displaced spondylolisthesis of seventh cervical vertebra   A, B ⬤

    ● S12.631   Unspecified traumatic nondisplaced spondylolisthesis of seventh cervical vertebra   A, B ⬤

  X ● S12.64   Type III traumatic spondylolisthesis of seventh cervical vertebra   A, B ⬤

   ● S12.65   Other traumatic spondylolisthesis of seventh cervical vertebra

    ● S12.650   Other traumatic displaced spondylolisthesis of seventh cervical vertebra   A, B ⬤

    ● S12.651   Other traumatic nondisplaced spondylolisthesis of seventh cervical vertebra   A, B ⬤

   ● S12.69   Other fracture of seventh cervical vertebra

    ● S12.690   Other displaced fracture of seventh cervical vertebra   A, B ⬤

    ● S12.691   Other nondisplaced fracture of seventh cervical vertebra   A, B ⬤

X ● S12.8   Fracture of other parts of neck   A ⬤

   Hyoid bone   Thyroid cartilage

   Larynx   Trachea

   The appropriate 7th character is to be added to code S12.8

A	initial encounter
D	subsequent encounter
S	sequela

X ● S12.9   Fracture of neck, unspecified   A ⬤

   Fracture of neck NOS

   Fracture of cervical spine NOS

   Fracture of cervical vertebra NOS

   The appropriate 7th character is to be added to code S12.9

A	initial encounter
D	subsequent encounter
S	sequela

▶ New   ⇒ Revised   ~~deleted~~ Deleted   Excludes 1   Excludes 2   Includes   Use additional   Code first   Code also   Key words

1242   OGCR Official Guidelines   X Assign placeholder X   ● Use Additional Character(s)   ▷ Manifestation Code   ⬤ Hierarchical Condition Category   **Coding Clinic**

● S13   **Dislocation and sprain of joints and ligaments at neck level**
Includes   avulsion of joint or ligament at neck level
laceration of cartilage, joint or ligament at neck level
sprain of cartilage, joint or ligament at neck level
traumatic hemarthrosis of joint or ligament at neck level
traumatic rupture of joint or ligament at neck level
traumatic subluxation of joint or ligament at neck level
traumatic tear of joint or ligament at neck level
Code also any associated open wound
Excludes2   strain of muscle or tendon at neck level (S16.1)
The appropriate 7th character is to be added to each code from category S13

> A   initial encounter
> D   subsequent encounter
> S   sequela

X ● S13.0   **Traumatic rupture of cervical intervertebral disc**

> **Excludes1**   rupture or displacement (nontraumatic) of cervical intervertebral disc NOS (M50.-)

● S13.1   **Subluxation and dislocation of cervical vertebrae**
Code also any associated:
open wound of neck (S11.-)
spinal cord injury (S14.1-)
Excludes2   fracture of cervical vertebrae (S12.0-S12.3-)

● S13.10   **Subluxation and dislocation of unspecified cervical vertebrae**
● S13.100   **Subluxation of unspecified cervical vertebrae**
● S13.101   **Dislocation of unspecified cervical vertebrae**

● S13.11   **Subluxation and dislocation of C0/C1 cervical vertebrae**
Subluxation and dislocation of atlantooccipital joint
Subluxation and dislocation of atloidooccipital joint
Subluxation and dislocation of occipitoatloid joint
● S13.110   **Subluxation of C0/C1 cervical vertebrae**
● S13.111   **Dislocation of C0/C1 cervical vertebrae**

● S13.12   **Subluxation and dislocation of C1/C2 cervical vertebrae**
Subluxation and dislocation of atlantoaxial joint
● S13.120   **Subluxation of C1/C2 cervical vertebrae**
● S13.121   **Dislocation of C1/C2 cervical vertebrae**

● S13.13   **Subluxation and dislocation of C2/C3 cervical vertebrae**
● S13.130   **Subluxation of C2/C3 cervical vertebrae**
● S13.131   **Dislocation of C2/C3 cervical vertebrae**

● S13.14   **Subluxation and dislocation of C3/C4 cervical vertebrae**
● S13.140   **Subluxation of C3/C4 cervical vertebrae**
● S13.141   **Dislocation of C3/C4 cervical vertebrae**

● S13.15   **Subluxation and dislocation of C4/C5 cervical vertebrae**
● S13.150   **Subluxation of C4/C5 cervical vertebrae**
● S13.151   **Dislocation of C4/C5 cervical vertebrae**

● S13.16   **Subluxation and dislocation of C5/C6 cervical vertebrae**
● S13.160   **Subluxation of C5/C6 cervical vertebrae**
● S13.161   **Dislocation of C5/C6 cervical vertebrae**

● S13.17   **Subluxation and dislocation of C6/C7 cervical vertebrae**
● S13.170   **Subluxation of C6/C7 cervical vertebrae**
● S13.171   **Dislocation of C6/C7 cervical vertebrae**

● S13.18   **Subluxation and dislocation of C7/T1 cervical vertebrae**
● S13.180   **Subluxation of C7/T1 cervical vertebrae**
● S13.181   **Dislocation of C7/T1 cervical vertebrae**

● S13.2   **Dislocation of other and unspecified parts of neck**
X ● S13.20   **Dislocation of unspecified parts of neck**
X ● S13.29   **Dislocation of other parts of neck**

X ● S13.4   **Sprain of ligaments of cervical spine**
Sprain of anterior longitudinal (ligament), cervical
Sprain of atlanto-axial (joints)
Sprain of atlanto-occipital (joints)
Whiplash injury of cervical spine

X ● S13.5   **Sprain of thyroid region**
Sprain of cricoarytenoid (joint) (ligament)
Sprain of cricothyroid (joint) (ligament)
Sprain of thyroid cartilage

X ● S13.8   **Sprain of joints and ligaments of other parts of neck**
X ● S13.9   **Sprain of joints and ligaments of unspecified parts of neck**

● S14   **Injury of nerves and spinal cord at neck level**
Note: Code to highest level of cervical cord injury
Code also any associated:
fracture of cervical vertebra (S12.0--S12.6.-)
open wound of neck (S11.-)
transient paralysis (R29.5)
The appropriate 7th character is to be added to each code from category S14

> A   initial encounter
> D   subsequent encounter
> S   sequela

X ● S14.0   **Concussion and edema of cervical spinal cord** A, D, S ✇
● S14.1   **Other and unspecified injuries of cervical spinal cord**
● S14.10   **Unspecified injury of cervical spinal cord**
● S14.101   **Unspecified injury at C1 level of cervical spinal cord** A, D, S ✇
● S14.102   **Unspecified injury at C2 level of cervical spinal cord** A, D, S ✇
● S14.103   **Unspecified injury at C3 level of cervical spinal cord** A, D, S ✇
● S14.104   **Unspecified injury at C4 level of cervical spinal cord** A, D, S ✇
● S14.105   **Unspecified injury at C5 level of cervical spinal cord** A, D, S ✇
● S14.106   **Unspecified injury at C6 level of cervical spinal cord** A, D, S ✇
● S14.107   **Unspecified injury at C7 level of cervical spinal cord** A, D, S ✇
● S14.108   **Unspecified injury at C8 level of cervical spinal cord** A, D, S ✇
● S14.109   **Unspecified injury at unspecified level of cervical spinal cord** A, D, S ✇
Injury of cervical spinal cord NOS

● **S14.11**   **Complete lesion** of cervical spinal cord
   ● S14.111   Complete lesion at C1 level of cervical spinal cord   A, D, S 🐾
   ● S14.112   Complete lesion at C2 level of cervical spinal cord   A, D, S 🐾
   ● S14.113   Complete lesion at C3 level of cervical spinal cord   A, D, S 🐾
   ● S14.114   Complete lesion at C4 level of cervical spinal cord   A, D, S 🐾
   ● S14.115   Complete lesion at C5 level of cervical spinal cord   A, D, S 🐾
   ● S14.116   Complete lesion at C6 level of cervical spinal cord   A, D, S 🐾
   ● S14.117   Complete lesion at C7 level of cervical spinal cord   A, D, S 🐾
   ● S14.118   Complete lesion at C8 level of cervical spinal cord   A, D, S 🐾
   ● S14.119   Complete lesion at unspecified level of cervical spinal cord A, D, S 🐾

● **S14.12**   **Central cord syndrome** of cervical spinal cord
   ● S14.121   Central cord syndrome at C1 level of cervical spinal cord   A, D, S 🐾
   ● S14.122   Central cord syndrome at C2 level of cervical spinal cord   A, D, S 🐾
   ● S14.123   Central cord syndrome at C3 level of cervical spinal cord   A, D, S 🐾
   ● S14.124   Central cord syndrome at C4 level of cervical spinal cord   A, D, S 🐾
   ● S14.125   Central cord syndrome at C5 level of cervical spinal cord   A, D, S 🐾
   ● S14.126   Central cord syndrome at C6 level of cervical spinal cord   A, D, S 🐾
   ● S14.127   Central cord syndrome at C7 level of cervical spinal cord   A, D, S 🐾
   ● S14.128   Central cord syndrome at C8 level of cervical spinal cord   A, D, S 🐾
   ● S14.129   Central cord syndrome at unspecified level of cervical spinal cord A, D, S 🐾

● **S14.13**   **Anterior cord syndrome** of cervical spinal cord
   ● S14.131   Anterior cord syndrome at C1 level of cervical spinal cord   A, D, S 🐾
   ● S14.132   Anterior cord syndrome at C2 level of cervical spinal cord   A, D, S 🐾
   ● S14.133   Anterior cord syndrome at C3 level of cervical spinal cord   A, D, S 🐾
   ● S14.134   Anterior cord syndrome at C4 level of cervical spinal cord   A, D, S 🐾
   ● S14.135   Anterior cord syndrome at C5 level of cervical spinal cord   A, D, S 🐾
   ● S14.136   Anterior cord syndrome at C6 level of cervical spinal cord   A, D, S 🐾
   ● S14.137   Anterior cord syndrome at C7 level of cervical spinal cord   A, D, S 🐾
   ● S14.138   Anterior cord syndrome at C8 level of cervical spinal cord   A, D, S 🐾
   ● S14.139   Anterior cord syndrome at unspecified level of cervical spinal cord A, D, S 🐾

● **S14.14**   **Brown-Séquard syndrome** of cervical spinal cord
   ● S14.141   Brown-Séquard syndrome at C1 level of cervical spinal cord   A, D, S 🐾
   ● S14.142   Brown-Séquard syndrome at C2 level of cervical spinal cord   A, D, S 🐾
   ● S14.143   Brown-Séquard syndrome at C3 level of cervical spinal cord   A, D, S 🐾
   ● S14.144   Brown-Séquard syndrome at C4 level of cervical spinal cord   A, D, S 🐾
   ● S14.145   Brown-Séquard syndrome at C5 level of cervical spinal cord   A, D, S 🐾
   ● S14.146   Brown-Séquard syndrome at C6 level of cervical spinal cord   A, D, S 🐾
   ● S14.147   Brown-Séquard syndrome at C7 level of cervical spinal cord   A, D, S 🐾
   ● S14.148   Brown-Séquard syndrome at C8 level of cervical spinal cord   A, D, S 🐾
   ● S14.149   Brown-Séquard syndrome at unspecified level of cervical spinal cord A, D, S 🐾

● **S14.15**   **Other incomplete lesions** of cervical spinal cord
   Incomplete lesion of cervical spinal cord NOS
   Posterior cord syndrome of cervical spinal cord
   ● S14.151   Other incomplete lesion at C1 level of cervical spinal cord   A, D, S 🐾
   ● S14.152   Other incomplete lesion at C2 level of cervical spinal cord   A, D, S 🐾
   ● S14.153   Other incomplete lesion at C3 level of cervical spinal cord   A, D, S 🐾
   ● S14.154   Other incomplete lesion at C4 level of cervical spinal cord   A, D, S 🐾
   ● S14.155   Other incomplete lesion at C5 level of cervical spinal cord   A, D, S 🐾
   ● S14.156   Other incomplete lesion at C6 level of cervical spinal cord   A, D, S 🐾
   ● S14.157   Other incomplete lesion at C7 level of cervical spinal cord   A, D, S 🐾
   ● S14.158   Other incomplete lesion at C8 level of cervical spinal cord   A, D, S 🐾
   ● S14.159   Other incomplete lesion at unspecified level of cervical spinal cord A, D, S 🐾

X● **S14.2**   Injury of nerve root of cervical spine
X● **S14.3**   Injury of brachial plexus
X● **S14.4**   Injury of peripheral nerves of neck
X● **S14.5**   Injury of cervical sympathetic nerves
X● **S14.8**   Injury of other specified nerves of neck
X● **S14.9**   Injury of unspecified nerves of neck

● **S15**   **Injury of blood vessels at neck level**
   Code also any associated open wound (S11.-)
   The appropriate 7th character is to be added to each code from category S15

A	initial encounter
D	subsequent encounter
S	sequela

   ● **S15.0**   **Injury of carotid artery** of neck
     Injury of carotid artery (common) (external) (internal, extracranial portion)
     Injury of carotid artery NOS
     Excludes1   injury of internal carotid artery, intracranial portion (S06.8)
     ● **S15.00**   **Unspecified injury** of carotid artery
       ● S15.001   Unspecified injury of right carotid artery
       ● S15.002   Unspecified injury of left carotid artery
       ● S15.009   Unspecified injury of unspecified carotid artery
     ● **S15.01**   **Minor laceration** of carotid artery
       Incomplete transection of carotid artery
       Laceration of carotid artery NOS
       Superficial laceration of carotid artery
       ● S15.011   Minor laceration of right carotid artery
       ● S15.012   Minor laceration of left carotid artery
       ● S15.019   Minor laceration of unspecified carotid artery

▶ New   ⇒ Revised   ~~deleted~~ Deleted   Excludes 1   Excludes 2   Includes   Use additional   Code first   Code also   Key words

1244   OGCR Official Guidelines   X Assign placeholder X   ● Use Additional Character(s)   ▶ Manifestation Code   🐾 Hierarchical Condition Category   **Coding Clinic**

● **S15.02** **Major laceration of carotid artery**
Complete transection of carotid artery
Traumatic rupture of carotid artery

  ● **S15.021** Major laceration of right carotid artery

  ● **S15.022** Major laceration of left carotid artery

  ● **S15.029** Major laceration of unspecified carotid artery

● **S15.09** **Other specified injury of carotid artery**

  ● **S15.091** Other specified injury of right carotid artery

  ● **S15.092** Other specified injury of left carotid artery

  ● **S15.099** Other specified injury of unspecified carotid artery

● **S15.1** **Injury of vertebral artery**

  ● **S15.10** **Unspecified injury of vertebral artery**

    ● **S15.101** Unspecified injury of right vertebral artery

    ● **S15.102** Unspecified injury of left vertebral artery

    ● **S15.109** Unspecified injury of unspecified vertebral artery

  ● **S15.11** **Minor laceration of vertebral artery**
Incomplete transection of vertebral artery
Laceration of vertebral artery NOS
Superficial laceration of vertebral artery

    ● **S15.111** Minor laceration of right vertebral artery

    ● **S15.112** Minor laceration of left vertebral artery

    ● **S15.119** Minor laceration of unspecified vertebral artery

  ● **S15.12** **Major laceration of vertebral artery**
Complete transection of vertebral artery
Traumatic rupture of vertebral artery

    ● **S15.121** Major laceration of right vertebral artery

    ● **S15.122** Major laceration of left vertebral artery

    ● **S15.129** Major laceration of unspecified vertebral artery

  ● **S15.19** **Other specified injury of vertebral artery**

    ● **S15.191** Other specified injury of right vertebral artery

    ● **S15.192** Other specified injury of left vertebral artery

    ● **S15.199** Other specified injury of unspecified vertebral artery

● **S15.2** **Injury of external jugular vein**

  ● **S15.20** **Unspecified injury of external jugular vein**

    ● **S15.201** Unspecified injury of right external jugular vein

    ● **S15.202** Unspecified injury of left external jugular vein

    ● **S15.209** Unspecified injury of unspecified external jugular vein

  ● **S15.21** **Minor laceration of external jugular vein**
Incomplete transection of external jugular vein
Laceration of external jugular vein NOS
Superficial laceration of external jugular vein

    ● **S15.211** Minor laceration of right external jugular vein

    ● **S15.212** Minor laceration of left external jugular vein

    ● **S15.219** Minor laceration of unspecified external jugular vein

● **S15.22** **Major laceration of external jugular vein**
Complete transection of external jugular vein
Traumatic rupture of external jugular vein

  ● **S15.221** Major laceration of right external jugular vein

  ● **S15.222** Major laceration of left external jugular vein

  ● **S15.229** Major laceration of unspecified external jugular vein

● **S15.29** **Other specified injury of external jugular vein**

  ● **S15.291** Other specified injury of right external jugular vein

  ● **S15.292** Other specified injury of left external jugular vein

  ● **S15.299** Other specified injury of unspecified external jugular vein

● **S15.3** **Injury of internal jugular vein**

  ● **S15.30** **Unspecified injury of internal jugular vein**

    ● **S15.301** Unspecified injury of right internal jugular vein

    ● **S15.302** Unspecified injury of left internal jugular vein

    ● **S15.309** Unspecified injury of unspecified internal jugular vein

  ● **S15.31** **Minor laceration of internal jugular vein**
Incomplete transection of internal jugular vein
Laceration of internal jugular vein NOS
Superficial laceration of internal jugular vein

    ● **S15.311** Minor laceration of right internal jugular vein

    ● **S15.312** Minor laceration of left internal jugular vein

    ● **S15.319** Minor laceration of unspecified internal jugular vein

  ● **S15.32** **Major laceration of internal jugular vein**
Complete transection of internal jugular vein
Traumatic rupture of internal jugular vein

    ● **S15.321** Major laceration of right internal jugular vein

    ● **S15.322** Major laceration of left internal jugular vein

    ● **S15.329** Major laceration of unspecified internal jugular vein

  ● **S15.39** **Other specified injury of internal jugular vein**

    ● **S15.391** Other specified injury of right internal jugular vein

    ● **S15.392** Other specified injury of left internal jugular vein

    ● **S15.399** Other specified injury of unspecified internal jugular vein

X● **S15.8** **Injury of other specified blood vessels at neck level**

X● **S15.9** **Injury of unspecified blood vessel at neck level**

● **S16** **Injury of muscle, fascia and tendon at neck level**
Code also any associated open wound (S11.-)

  Excludes2   sprain of joint or ligament at neck level (S13.9)

The appropriate 7th character is to be added to each code from category S16

A	initial encounter
D	subsequent encounter
S	sequela

X● **S16.1** **Strain of muscle, fascia and tendon at neck level**

X● **S16.2** **Laceration of muscle, fascia and tendon at neck level**

X● **S16.8** **Other specified injury of muscle, fascia and tendon at neck level**

X● **S16.9** **Unspecified injury of muscle, fascia and tendon at neck level**

● **S17 Crushing injury of neck**

Use additional code for all associated injuries, such as:
injury of blood vessels (S15.-)
open wound of neck (S11.-)
spinal cord injury (S14.0, S14.1-)
vertebral fracture (S12.0--S12.3-)

The appropriate 7th character is to be added to each code from category S17

A	initial encounter
D	subsequent encounter
S	sequela

X● **S17.0 Crushing injury of larynx and trachea**
X● **S17.8 Crushing injury of other specified parts of neck**
X● **S17.9 Crushing injury of neck, part unspecified**

● **S19 Other and unspecified injuries of neck**

The appropriate 7th character is to be added to each code from category S19

A	initial encounter
D	subsequent encounter
S	sequela

● **S19.8 Other specified injuries of neck**
X● **S19.80 Other specified injuries of unspecified part of neck**
X● **S19.81 Other specified injuries of larynx**
X● **S19.82 Other specified injuries of cervical trachea**
　　　Excludes2 other specified injury of thoracic trachea (S27.5-)
X● **S19.83 Other specified injuries of vocal cord**
X● **S19.84 Other specified injuries of thyroid gland**
X● **S19.85 Other specified injuries of pharynx and cervical esophagus**
X● **S19.89 Other specified injuries of other specified part of neck**
X● **S19.9 Unspecified injury of neck**

INJURIES TO THE THORAX (S20-S29)

Includes injuries of breast
injuries of chest (wall)
injuries of interscapular area

Excludes2 burns and corrosions (T20-T32)
effects of foreign body in bronchus (T17.5)
effects of foreign body in esophagus (T18.1)
effects of foreign body in lung (T17.8)
effects of foreign body in trachea (T17.4)
frostbite (T33-T34)
injuries of axilla
injuries of clavicle
injuries of scapular region
injuries of shoulder
insect bite or sting, venomous (T63.4)

● **S20 Superficial injury of thorax**

The appropriate 7th character is to be added to each code from category S20

A	initial encounter
D	subsequent encounter
S	sequela

● **S20.0 Contusion of breast**
X● **S20.00 Contusion of breast, unspecified breast**
X● **S20.01 Contusion of right breast**
X● **S20.02 Contusion of left breast**

● **S20.1 Other and unspecified superficial injuries of breast**
● **S20.10 Unspecified superficial injuries of breast**
● **S20.101 Unspecified superficial injuries of breast, right breast**
● **S20.102 Unspecified superficial injuries of breast, left breast**
● **S20.109 Unspecified superficial injuries of breast, unspecified breast**
● **S20.11 Abrasion of breast**
● **S20.111 Abrasion of breast, right breast**
● **S20.112 Abrasion of breast, left breast**
● **S20.119 Abrasion of breast, unspecified breast**
● **S20.12 Blister (nonthermal) of breast**
● **S20.121 Blister (nonthermal) of breast, right breast**
● **S20.122 Blister (nonthermal) of breast, left breast**
● **S20.129 Blister (nonthermal) of breast, unspecified breast**
● **S20.14 External constriction of part of breast**
● **S20.141 External constriction of part of breast, right breast**
● **S20.142 External constriction of part of breast, left breast**
● **S20.149 External constriction of part of breast, unspecified breast**
● **S20.15 Superficial foreign body of breast**
Splinter in the breast
● **S20.151 Superficial foreign body of breast, right breast**
● **S20.152 Superficial foreign body of breast, left breast**
● **S20.159 Superficial foreign body of breast, unspecified breast**
● **S20.16 Insect bite (nonvenomous) of breast**
● **S20.161 Insect bite (nonvenomous) of breast, right breast**
● **S20.162 Insect bite (nonvenomous) of breast, left breast**
● **S20.169 Insect bite (nonvenomous) of breast, unspecified breast**
● **S20.17 Other superficial bite of breast**
　　　Excludes1 open bite of breast (S21.05-)
● **S20.171 Other superficial bite of breast, right breast**
● **S20.172 Other superficial bite of breast, left breast**
● **S20.179 Other superficial bite of breast, unspecified breast**
● **S20.2 Contusion of thorax**
X● **S20.20 Contusion of thorax, unspecified**
● **S20.21 Contusion of front wall of thorax**
● **S20.211 Contusion of right front wall of thorax**
● **S20.212 Contusion of left front wall of thorax**
▶ **S20.213 Contusion of bilateral front wall of thorax**
▶ **S20.214 Contusion of middle front wall of thorax**
● **S20.219 Contusion of unspecified front wall of thorax**
● **S20.22 Contusion of back wall of thorax**
● **S20.221 Contusion of right back wall of thorax**
● **S20.222 Contusion of left back wall of thorax**
▶ **S20.223 Contusion of bilateral back wall of thorax**
▶ **S20.224 Contusion of middle back wall of thorax**
● **S20.229 Contusion of unspecified back wall of thorax**

▶ New　⇒ Revised　~~deleted~~ Deleted　Excludes 1　Excludes 2　Includes　Use additional　Code first　Code also　Key words

OGCR Official Guidelines　X Assign placeholder X　● Use Additional Character(s)　▶ Manifestation Code　Hierarchical Condition Category　**Coding Clinic**

● S20.3 Other and unspecified superficial injuries of front wall of thorax
  ● S20.30 Unspecified superficial injuries of front wall of thorax
    ● S20.301 Unspecified superficial injuries of right front wall of thorax
    ● S20.302 Unspecified superficial injuries of left front wall of thorax
    ▷ S20.303 Unspecified superficial injuries of bilateral front wall of thorax
    ▷ S20.304 Unspecified superficial injuries of middle front wall of thorax
    ● S20.309 Unspecified superficial injuries of unspecified front wall of thorax
  ● S20.31 Abrasion of front wall of thorax
    ● S20.311 Abrasion of right front wall of thorax
    ● S20.312 Abrasion of left front wall of thorax
    ▷ S20.313 Abrasion of bilateral front wall of thorax
    ▷ S20.314 Abrasion of middle front wall of thorax
    ● S20.319 Abrasion of unspecified front wall of thorax
  ● S20.32 Blister (nonthermal) of front wall of thorax
    ● S20.321 Blister (nonthermal) of right front wall of thorax
    ● S20.322 Blister (nonthermal) of left front wall of thorax
    ▷ S20.323 Blister (nonthermal) of bilateral front wall of thorax
    ▷ S20.324 Blister (nonthermal) of middle front wall of thorax
    ● S20.329 Blister (nonthermal) of unspecified front wall of thorax
  ● S20.34 External constriction of front wall of thorax
    ● S20.341 External constriction of right front wall of thorax
    ● S20.342 External constriction of left front wall of thorax
    ▷ S20.343 External constriction of bilateral front wall of thorax
    ▷ S20.344 External constriction of middle front wall of thorax
    ● S20.349 External constriction of unspecified front wall of thorax
  ● S20.35 Superficial foreign body of front wall of thorax
    Splinter in front wall of thorax
    ● S20.351 Superficial foreign body of right front wall of thorax
    ● S20.352 Superficial foreign body of left front wall of thorax
    ▷ S20.353 Superficial foreign body of bilateral front wall of thorax
    ▷ S20.354 Superficial foreign body of middle front wall of thorax
    ● S20.359 Superficial foreign body of unspecified front wall of thorax
  ● S20.36 Insect bite (nonvenomous) of front wall of thorax
    ● S20.361 Insect bite (nonvenomous) of right front wall of thorax
    ● S20.362 Insect bite (nonvenomous) of left front wall of thorax
    ▷ S20.363 Insect bite (nonvenomous) of bilateral front wall of thorax
    ▷ S20.364 Insect bite (nonvenomous) of middle front wall of thorax
    ● S20.369 Insect bite (nonvenomous) of unspecified front wall of thorax

  ● S20.37 Other superficial bite of front wall of thorax
    Excludes1 open bite of front wall of thorax (S21.14)
    ● S20.371 Other superficial bite of right front wall of thorax
    ● S20.372 Other superficial bite of left front wall of thorax
    ▷ S20.373 Other superficial bite of bilateral front wall of thorax
    ▷ S20.374 Other superficial bite of middle front wall of thorax
    ● S20.379 Other superficial bite of unspecified front wall of thorax
● S20.4 Other and unspecified superficial injuries of back wall of thorax
  ● S20.40 Unspecified superficial injuries of back wall of thorax
    ● S20.401 Unspecified superficial injuries of right back wall of thorax
    ● S20.402 Unspecified superficial injuries of left back wall of thorax
    ● S20.409 Unspecified superficial injuries of unspecified back wall of thorax
  ● S20.41 Abrasion of back wall of thorax
    ● S20.411 Abrasion of right back wall of thorax
    ● S20.412 Abrasion of left back wall of thorax
    ● S20.419 Abrasion of unspecified back wall of thorax
  ● S20.42 Blister (nonthermal) of back wall of thorax
    ● S20.421 Blister (nonthermal) of right back wall of thorax
    ● S20.422 Blister (nonthermal) of left back wall of thorax
    ● S20.429 Blister (nonthermal) of unspecified back wall of thorax
  ● S20.44 External constriction of back wall of thorax
    ● S20.441 External constriction of right back wall of thorax
    ● S20.442 External constriction of left back wall of thorax
    ● S20.449 External constriction of unspecified back wall of thorax
  ● S20.45 Superficial foreign body of back wall of thorax
    Splinter of back wall of thorax
    ● S20.451 Superficial foreign body of right back wall of thorax
    ● S20.452 Superficial foreign body of left back wall of thorax
    ● S20.459 Superficial foreign body of unspecified back wall of thorax
  ● S20.46 Insect bite (nonvenomous) of back wall of thorax
    ● S20.461 Insect bite (nonvenomous) of right back wall of thorax
    ● S20.462 Insect bite (nonvenomous) of left back wall of thorax
    ● S20.469 Insect bite (nonvenomous) of unspecified back wall of thorax
  ● S20.47 Other superficial bite of back wall of thorax
    Excludes1 open bite of back wall of thorax (S21.24)
    ● S20.471 Other superficial bite of right back wall of thorax
    ● S20.472 Other superficial bite of left back wall of thorax
    ● S20.479 Other superficial bite of unspecified back wall of thorax

● **S20.9**   **Superficial injury of unspecified parts of thorax**
     Excludes1   contusion of thorax NOS (S20.20)
X● **S20.90**   **Unspecified superficial injury of unspecified parts of thorax**
     Superficial injury of thoracic wall NOS
X● **S20.91**   **Abrasion of unspecified parts of thorax**
X● **S20.92**   **Blister (nonthermal) of unspecified parts of thorax**
X● **S20.94**   **External constriction of unspecified parts of thorax**
X● **S20.95**   **Superficial foreign body of unspecified parts of thorax**
     Splinter in thorax NOS
X● **S20.96**   **Insect bite (nonvenomous) of unspecified parts of thorax**
X● **S20.97**   **Other superficial bite of unspecified parts of thorax**
     Excludes1   open bite of thorax NOS (S21.95)

● **S21**   **Open wound of thorax**
     Code also any associated injury such as:
       injury of heart (S26.-)
       injury of intrathoracic organs (S27.-)
       rib fracture (S22.3-, S22.4-)
       spinal cord injury (S24.0-, S24.1-)
       traumatic hemothorax (S27.1)
       traumatic hemopneumothorax (S27.3)
       traumatic pneumothorax (S27.0)
       wound infection
     Excludes1   traumatic amputation (partial) of thorax (S28.1)
     The appropriate 7th character is to be added to each code from category S21

A	initial encounter
D	subsequent encounter
S	sequela

● **S21.0**   **Open wound of breast**
 ● **S21.00**   **Unspecified open wound of breast**
  ● **S21.001**   **Unspecified open wound of right breast**
  ● **S21.002**   **Unspecified open wound of left breast**
  ● **S21.009**   **Unspecified open wound of unspecified breast**
 ● **S21.01**   **Laceration without foreign body of breast**
  ● **S21.011**   **Laceration without foreign body of right breast**
  ● **S21.012**   **Laceration without foreign body of left breast**
  ● **S21.019**   **Laceration without foreign body of unspecified breast**
 ● **S21.02**   **Laceration with foreign body of breast**
  ● **S21.021**   **Laceration with foreign body of right breast**
  ● **S21.022**   **Laceration with foreign body of left breast**
  ● **S21.029**   **Laceration with foreign body of unspecified breast**

● **S21.03**   **Puncture wound without foreign body of breast**
 ● **S21.031**   **Puncture wound without foreign body of right breast**
 ● **S21.032**   **Puncture wound without foreign body of left breast**
 ● **S21.039**   **Puncture wound without foreign body of unspecified breast**
● **S21.04**   **Puncture wound with foreign body of breast**
 ● **S21.041**   **Puncture wound with foreign body of right breast**
 ● **S21.042**   **Puncture wound with foreign body of left breast**
 ● **S21.049**   **Puncture wound with foreign body of unspecified breast**
● **S21.05**   **Open bite of breast**
     Bite of breast NOS
     Excludes1   superficial bite of breast (S20.17)
 ● **S21.051**   **Open bite of right breast**
 ● **S21.052**   **Open bite of left breast**
 ● **S21.059**   **Open bite of unspecified breast**
● **S21.1**   **Open wound of front wall of thorax without penetration into thoracic cavity**
     Open wound of chest without penetration into thoracic cavity
 ● **S21.10**   **Unspecified open wound of front wall of thorax without penetration into thoracic cavity**
  ● **S21.101**   **Unspecified open wound of right front wall of thorax without penetration into thoracic cavity**
  ● **S21.102**   **Unspecified open wound of left front wall of thorax without penetration into thoracic cavity**
  ● **S21.109**   **Unspecified open wound of unspecified front wall of thorax without penetration into thoracic cavity**
 ● **S21.11**   **Laceration without foreign body of front wall of thorax without penetration into thoracic cavity**
  ● **S21.111**   **Laceration without foreign body of right front wall of thorax without penetration into thoracic cavity**
  ● **S21.112**   **Laceration without foreign body of left front wall of thorax without penetration into thoracic cavity**
  ● **S21.119**   **Laceration without foreign body of unspecified front wall of thorax without penetration into thoracic cavity**
 ● **S21.12**   **Laceration with foreign body of front wall of thorax without penetration into thoracic cavity**
  ● **S21.121**   **Laceration with foreign body of right front wall of thorax without penetration into thoracic cavity**
  ● **S21.122**   **Laceration with foreign body of left front wall of thorax without penetration into thoracic cavity**
  ● **S21.129**   **Laceration with foreign body of unspecified front wall of thorax without penetration into thoracic cavity**

Item 19-1 Pneumothorax is a collection of gas (positive air pressure) in the pleural space, resulting in the lung collapsing. A **tension pneumothorax** is life-threatening and is a result of air in the pleural space causing a displacement in the mediastinal structures and cardiopulmonary function compromise. A **traumatic pneumothorax** results from blunt or penetrating injury that disrupts the parietal/visceral pleura. **Hemothorax** is blood or bloody fluid in the pleural cavity as a result of traumatic blood vessel rupture or inflammation of the lungs from pneumonia.

▶ New   ⇒ Revised   ~~deleted~~ Deleted   Excludes 1   Excludes 2   Includes   Use additional   Code first   Code also   Key words
OGCR Official Guidelines   X Assign placeholder X   ● Use Additional Character(s)   ▶ Manifestation Code   🏷 Hierarchical Condition Category   **Coding Clinic**

● **S21.13 Puncture wound without foreign body** of front wall of thorax without penetration into thoracic cavity

  ● **S21.131** Puncture wound without foreign body of **right** front wall of thorax without penetration into thoracic cavity

  ● **S21.132** Puncture wound without foreign body of **left** front wall of thorax without penetration into thoracic cavity

  ● **S21.139** Puncture wound without foreign body of **unspecified** front wall of thorax without penetration into thoracic cavity

● **S21.14 Puncture wound with foreign body** of front wall of thorax without penetration into thoracic cavity

  ● **S21.141** Puncture wound with foreign body of **right** front wall of thorax without penetration into thoracic cavity

  ● **S21.142** Puncture wound with foreign body of **left** front wall of thorax without penetration into thoracic cavity

  ● **S21.149** Puncture wound with foreign body of **unspecified** front wall of thorax without penetration into thoracic cavity

● **S21.15 Open bite** of front wall of thorax without penetration into thoracic cavity
    Bite of front wall of thorax NOS

    Excludes1 superficial bite of front wall of thorax (S20.37)

  ● **S21.151** Open bite of **right** front wall of thorax without penetration into thoracic cavity

  ● **S21.152** Open bite of **left** front wall of thorax without penetration into thoracic cavity

  ● **S21.159** Open bite of **unspecified** front wall of thorax without penetration into thoracic cavity

● **S21.2 Open wound of back wall** of thorax without **penetration into thoracic cavity**

  ● **S21.20 Unspecified** open wound of back wall of thorax without penetration into thoracic cavity

  ● **S21.201** Unspecified open wound of **right** back wall of thorax without penetration into thoracic cavity

  ● **S21.202** Unspecified open wound of **left** back wall of thorax without penetration into thoracic cavity

  ● **S21.209** Unspecified open wound of **unspecified** back wall of thorax without penetration into thoracic cavity

  ● **S21.21 Laceration without foreign body** of back wall of thorax without penetration into thoracic cavity

  ● **S21.211** Laceration without foreign body of **right** back wall of thorax without penetration into thoracic cavity

  ● **S21.212** Laceration without foreign body of **left** back wall of thorax without penetration into thoracic cavity

  ● **S21.219** Laceration without foreign body of **unspecified** back wall of thorax without penetration into thoracic cavity

● **S21.22 Laceration with foreign body** of back wall of thorax without penetration into thoracic cavity

  ● **S21.221** Laceration with foreign body of **right** back wall of thorax without penetration into thoracic cavity

  ● **S21.222** Laceration with foreign body of **left** back wall of thorax without penetration into thoracic cavity

  ● **S21.229** Laceration with foreign body of **unspecified** back wall of thorax without penetration into thoracic cavity

● **S21.23 Puncture wound without foreign body** of back wall of thorax without penetration into thoracic cavity

  ● **S21.231** Puncture wound without foreign body of **right** back wall of thorax without penetration into thoracic cavity

  ● **S21.232** Puncture wound without foreign body of **left** back wall of thorax without penetration into thoracic cavity

  ● **S21.239** Puncture wound without foreign body of **unspecified** back wall of thorax without penetration into thoracic cavity

● **S21.24 Puncture wound with foreign body** of back wall of thorax without penetration into thoracic cavity

  ● **S21.241** Puncture wound with foreign body of **right** back wall of thorax without penetration into thoracic cavity

  ● **S21.242** Puncture wound with foreign body of **left** back wall of thorax without penetration into thoracic cavity

  ● **S21.249** Puncture wound with foreign body of **unspecified** back wall of thorax without penetration into thoracic cavity

● **S21.25 Open bite** of back wall of thorax without penetration into thoracic cavity
    Bite of back wall of thorax NOS

    Excludes1 superficial bite of back wall of thorax (S20.47)

  ● **S21.251** Open bite of **right** back wall of thorax without penetration into thoracic cavity

  ● **S21.252** Open bite of **left** back wall of thorax without penetration into thoracic cavity

  ● **S21.259** Open bite of **unspecified** back wall of thorax without penetration into thoracic cavity

● **S21.3 Open wound of front wall** of thorax **with penetration into thoracic cavity**
    Open wound of chest with penetration into thoracic cavity

  ● **S21.30 Unspecified** open wound of front wall of thorax with penetration into thoracic cavity

  ● **S21.301** Unspecified open wound of **right** front wall of thorax with penetration into thoracic cavity

  ● **S21.302** Unspecified open wound of **left** front wall of thorax with penetration into thoracic cavity

  ● **S21.309** Unspecified open wound of **unspecified** front wall of thorax with penetration into thoracic cavity

● **S21.31** **Laceration without foreign body** of front wall of thorax with penetration into thoracic cavity

   ● **S21.311** Laceration without foreign body of **right** front wall of thorax with penetration into thoracic cavity

   ● **S21.312** Laceration without foreign body of **left** front wall of thorax with penetration into thoracic cavity

   ● **S21.319** Laceration without foreign body of **unspecified** front wall of thorax with penetration into thoracic cavity

● **S21.32** **Laceration with foreign body** of front wall of thorax with penetration into thoracic cavity

   ● **S21.321** Laceration with foreign body of **right** front wall of thorax with penetration into thoracic cavity

   ● **S21.322** Laceration with foreign body of **left** front wall of thorax with penetration into thoracic cavity

   ● **S21.329** Laceration with foreign body of **unspecified** front wall of thorax with penetration into thoracic cavity

● **S21.33** **Puncture wound without foreign body** of front wall of thorax with penetration into thoracic cavity

   ● **S21.331** Puncture wound without foreign body of **right** front wall of thorax with penetration into thoracic cavity

   ● **S21.332** Puncture wound without foreign body of **left** front wall of thorax with penetration into thoracic cavity

   ● **S21.339** Puncture wound without foreign body of **unspecified** front wall of thorax with penetration into thoracic cavity

● **S21.34** **Puncture wound with foreign body** of front wall of thorax with penetration into thoracic cavity

   ● **S21.341** Puncture wound with foreign body of **right** front wall of thorax with penetration into thoracic cavity

   ● **S21.342** Puncture wound with foreign body of **left** front wall of thorax with penetration into thoracic cavity

   ● **S21.349** Puncture wound with foreign body of **unspecified** front wall of thorax with penetration into thoracic cavity

● **S21.35** **Open bite** of front wall of thorax with penetration into thoracic cavity

   Excludes1   superficial bite of front wall of thorax (S20.37)

   ● **S21.351** Open bite of **right** front wall of thorax with penetration into thoracic cavity

   ● **S21.352** Open bite of **left** front wall of thorax with penetration into thoracic cavity

   ● **S21.359** Open bite of **unspecified** front wall of thorax with penetration into thoracic cavity

● **S21.4** Open wound of **back wall** of thorax with **penetration** into thoracic cavity

  ● **S21.40** **Unspecified** open wound of back wall of thorax with penetration into thoracic cavity

   ● **S21.401** Unspecified open wound of **right** back wall of thorax with penetration into thoracic cavity

   ● **S21.402** Unspecified open wound of **left** back wall of thorax with penetration into thoracic cavity

   ● **S21.409** Unspecified open wound of **unspecified** back wall of thorax with penetration into thoracic cavity

● **S21.41** **Laceration without foreign body** of back wall of thorax with penetration into thoracic cavity

   ● **S21.411** Laceration without foreign body of **right** back wall of thorax with penetration into thoracic cavity

   ● **S21.412** Laceration without foreign body of **left** back wall of thorax with penetration into thoracic cavity

   ● **S21.419** Laceration without foreign body of **unspecified** back wall of thorax with penetration into thoracic cavity

● **S21.42** **Laceration with foreign body** of back wall of thorax with penetration into thoracic cavity

   ● **S21.421** Laceration with foreign body of **right** back wall of thorax with penetration into thoracic cavity

   ● **S21.422** Laceration with foreign body of **left** back wall of thorax with penetration into thoracic cavity

   ● **S21.429** Laceration with foreign body of **unspecified** back wall of thorax with penetration into thoracic cavity

● **S21.43** **Puncture wound without foreign body** of back wall of thorax with penetration into thoracic cavity

   ● **S21.431** Puncture wound without foreign body of **right** back wall of thorax with penetration into thoracic cavity

   ● **S21.432** Puncture wound without foreign body of **left** back wall of thorax with penetration into thoracic cavity

   ● **S21.439** Puncture wound without foreign body of **unspecified** back wall of thorax with penetration into thoracic cavity

● **S21.44** **Puncture wound with foreign body** of back wall of thorax with penetration into thoracic cavity

   ● **S21.441** Puncture wound with foreign body of **right** back wall of thorax with penetration into thoracic cavity

   ● **S21.442** Puncture wound with foreign body of **left** back wall of thorax with penetration into thoracic cavity

   ● **S21.449** Puncture wound with foreign body of **unspecified** back wall of thorax with penetration into thoracic cavity

● **S21.45** **Open bite** of back wall of thorax with penetration into thoracic cavity
   Bite of back wall of thorax NOS

   Excludes1   superficial bite of back wall of thorax (S20.47)

   ● **S21.451** Open bite of **right** back wall of thorax with penetration into thoracic cavity

   ● **S21.452** Open bite of **left** back wall of thorax with penetration into thoracic cavity

   ● **S21.459** Open bite of **unspecified** back wall of thorax with penetration into thoracic cavity

● **S21.9** Open wound of **unspecified** part of thorax
   Open wound of thoracic wall NOS

X ● **S21.90** **Unspecified** open wound of unspecified part of thorax

X ● **S21.91** **Laceration without foreign body** of unspecified part of thorax

X ● **S21.92** **Laceration with foreign body** of unspecified part of thorax

X ● **S21.93** **Puncture wound without foreign body** of unspecified part of thorax

X ● **S21.94** **Puncture wound with foreign body** of unspecified part of thorax

X ● **S21.95** **Open bite** of unspecified part of thorax

   Excludes1   superficial bite of thorax (S20.97)

▶ New   ⇒ Revised   ~~deleted~~ Deleted   Excludes 1   Excludes 2   Includes   Use additional   Code first   Code also   Key words

1250   **OGCR** Official Guidelines   X Assign placeholder X   ● Use Additional Character(s)   ▶ Manifestation Code   🅀 Hierarchical Condition Category   **Coding Clinic**

● **S22 Fracture of rib(s), sternum and thoracic spine**

> **Note:** A fracture not indicated as displaced or nondisplaced should be coded to displaced
>
> A fracture not indicated as open or closed should be coded to closed

Includes	fracture of thoracic neural arch
	fracture of thoracic spinous process
	fracture of thoracic transverse process
	fracture of thoracic vertebra
	fracture of thoracic vertebral arch

Code first any associated:
injury of intrathoracic organ (S27.-)
spinal cord injury (S24.0-, S24.1-)

Excludes1	transection of thorax (S28.1)
Excludes2	fracture of clavicle (S42.0-)
	fracture of scapula (S42.1-)

The appropriate 7th character is to be added to each code from category S22

> A   initial encounter for closed fracture
> B   initial encounter for open fracture
> D   subsequent encounter for fracture with routine healing
> G   subsequent encounter for fracture with delayed healing
> K   subsequent encounter for fracture with nonunion
> S   sequela

● **S22.0 Fracture of thoracic vertebra**

  ● **S22.00 Fracture of unspecified thoracic vertebra**
    ● S22.000 Wedge compression fracture of unspecified thoracic vertebra   A, B 🔄
    ● S22.001 Stable burst fracture of unspecified thoracic vertebra   A, B 🔄
    ● S22.002 Unstable burst fracture of unspecified thoracic vertebra   A, B 🔄
    ● S22.008 Other fracture of unspecified thoracic vertebra   A, B 🔄
    ● S22.009 Unspecified fracture of unspecified thoracic vertebra   A, B 🔄

  ● **S22.01 Fracture of first thoracic vertebra**
    ● S22.010 Wedge compression fracture of first thoracic vertebra   A, B 🔄
    ● S22.011 Stable burst fracture of first thoracic vertebra   A, B 🔄
    ● S22.012 Unstable burst fracture of first thoracic vertebra   A, B 🔄
    ● S22.018 Other fracture of first thoracic vertebra   A, B 🔄
    ● S22.019 Unspecified fracture of first thoracic vertebra   A, B 🔄

  ● **S22.02 Fracture of second thoracic vertebra**
    ● S22.020 Wedge compression fracture of second thoracic vertebra   A, B 🔄
    ● S22.021 Stable burst fracture of second thoracic vertebra   A, B 🔄
    ● S22.022 Unstable burst fracture of second thoracic vertebra   A, B 🔄
    ● S22.028 Other fracture of second thoracic vertebra   A, B 🔄
    ● S22.029 Unspecified fracture of second thoracic vertebra   A, B 🔄

  ● **S22.03 Fracture of third thoracic vertebra**
    ● S22.030 Wedge compression fracture of third thoracic vertebra   A, B 🔄
    ● S22.031 Stable burst fracture of third thoracic vertebra   A, B 🔄
    ● S22.032 Unstable burst fracture of third thoracic vertebra   A, B 🔄
    ● S22.038 Other fracture of third thoracic vertebra   A, B 🔄
    ● S22.039 Unspecified fracture of third thoracic vertebra   A, B 🔄

● **S22.04 Fracture of fourth thoracic vertebra**
  ● S22.040 Wedge compression fracture of fourth thoracic vertebra   A, B 🔄
  ● S22.041 Stable burst fracture of fourth thoracic vertebra   A, B 🔄
  ● S22.042 Unstable burst fracture of fourth thoracic vertebra   A, B 🔄
  ● S22.048 Other fracture of fourth thoracic vertebra   A, B 🔄
  ● S22.049 Unspecified fracture of fourth thoracic vertebra   A, B 🔄

● **S22.05 Fracture of T5-T6 vertebra**
  ● S22.050 Wedge compression fracture of T5-T6 vertebra   A, B 🔄
  ● S22.051 Stable burst fracture of T5-T6 vertebra   A, B 🔄
  ● S22.052 Unstable burst fracture of T5-T6 vertebra   A, B 🔄
  ● S22.058 Other fracture of T5-T6 vertebra   A, B 🔄
  ● S22.059 Unspecified fracture of T5-T6 vertebra   A, B 🔄

● **S22.06 Fracture of T7-T8 vertebra**
  ● S22.060 Wedge compression fracture of T7-T8 vertebra   A, B 🔄
  ● S22.061 Stable burst fracture of T7-T8 vertebra   A, B 🔄
  ● S22.062 Unstable burst fracture of T7-T8 vertebra   A, B 🔄
  ● S22.068 Other fracture of T7-T8 thoracic vertebra   A, B 🔄
  ● S22.069 Unspecified fracture of T7-T8 vertebra   A, B 🔄

● **S22.07 Fracture of T9-T10 vertebra**
  ● S22.070 Wedge compression fracture of T9-T10 vertebra   A, B 🔄
  ● S22.071 Stable burst fracture of T9-T10 vertebra   A, B 🔄
  ● S22.072 Unstable burst fracture of T9-T10 vertebra   A, B 🔄
  ● S22.078 Other fracture of T9-T10 vertebra   A, B 🔄
  ● S22.079 Unspecified fracture of T9-T10 vertebra   A, B 🔄

● **S22.08 Fracture of T11-T12 vertebra**
  ● S22.080 Wedge compression fracture of T11-T12 vertebra   A, B 🔄
  ● S22.081 Stable burst fracture of T11-T12 vertebra   A, B 🔄
  ● S22.082 Unstable burst fracture of T11-T12 vertebra   A, B 🔄
  ● S22.088 Other fracture of T11-T12 vertebra   A, B 🔄
  ● S22.089 Unspecified fracture of T11-T12 vertebra   A, B 🔄

● **S22.2 Fracture of sternum**
  X ● S22.20 Unspecified fracture of sternum
  X ● S22.21 Fracture of manubrium
  X ● S22.22 Fracture of body of sternum
  X ● S22.23 Sternal manubrial dissociation
  X ● S22.24 Fracture of xiphoid process

● **S22.3 Fracture of one rib**
- X● S22.31 Fracture of one rib, **right side**
- X● S22.32 Fracture of one rib, **left side**
- X● S22.39 Fracture of one rib, **unspecified side**
- ● **S22.4 Multiple fractures of ribs**
  Fractures of two or more ribs
  > **Excludes1** flail chest (S22.5-)
  - X● S22.41 Multiple fractures of ribs, **right side**
  - X● S22.42 Multiple fractures of ribs, **left side**
  - X● S22.43 Multiple fractures of ribs, **bilateral**
  - X● S22.49 Multiple fractures of ribs, **unspecified side**
- X● **S22.5 Flail chest**
  Unstable chest due to sternum and/or rib fracture
- X● **S22.9 Fracture of bony thorax, part unspecified**

● **S23 Dislocation and sprain of joints and ligaments of thorax**
> **Includes** avulsion of joint or ligament of thorax
> laceration of cartilage, joint or ligament of thorax
> sprain of cartilage, joint or ligament of thorax
> traumatic hemarthrosis of joint or ligament of thorax
> traumatic rupture of joint or ligament of thorax
> traumatic subluxation of joint or ligament of thorax
> traumatic tear of joint or ligament of thorax

Code also any associated open wound
> **Excludes2** dislocation, sprain of sternoclavicular joint (S43.2, S43.6)
> strain of muscle or tendon of thorax (S29.01-)

The appropriate 7th character is to be added to each code from category S23

A	initial encounter
D	subsequent encounter
S	sequela

- X● **S23.0 Traumatic rupture of thoracic intervertebral disc**
  > **Excludes1** rupture or displacement (nontraumatic) of thoracic intervertebral disc NOS (M51.- with fifth character 4)
- ● **S23.1 Subluxation and dislocation of thoracic vertebra**
  Code also any associated
  open wound of thorax (S21.-)
  spinal cord injury (S24.0-, S24.1-)
  > **Excludes2** fracture of thoracic vertebrae (S22.0-)
  - ● S23.10 Subluxation and dislocation of **unspecified** thoracic vertebra
    - ● S23.100 Subluxation of unspecified thoracic vertebra
    - ● S23.101 Dislocation of unspecified thoracic vertebra
  - ● S23.11 Subluxation and dislocation of **T1/T2** thoracic vertebra
    - ● S23.110 Subluxation of T1/T2 thoracic vertebra
    - ● S23.111 Dislocation of T1/T2 thoracic vertebra
  - ● S23.12 Subluxation and dislocation of **T2/T3-T3/T4** thoracic vertebra
    - ● S23.120 Subluxation of T2/T3 thoracic vertebra
    - ● S23.121 Dislocation of T2/T3 thoracic vertebra
    - ● S23.122 Subluxation of T3/T4 thoracic vertebra
    - ● S23.123 Dislocation of T3/T4 thoracic vertebra

- ● S23.13 Subluxation and dislocation of **T4/T5-T5/T6** thoracic vertebra
  - ● S23.130 Subluxation of T4/T5 thoracic vertebra
  - ● S23.131 Dislocation of T4/T5 thoracic vertebra
  - ● S23.132 Subluxation of T5/T6 thoracic vertebra
  - ● S23.133 Dislocation of T5/T6 thoracic vertebra
- ● S23.14 Subluxation and dislocation of **T6/T7-T7/T8** thoracic vertebra
  - ● S23.140 Subluxation of T6/T7 thoracic vertebra
  - ● S23.141 Dislocation of T6/T7 thoracic vertebra
  - ● S23.142 Subluxation of T7/T8 thoracic vertebra
  - ● S23.143 Dislocation of T7/T8 thoracic vertebra
- ● S23.15 Subluxation and dislocation of **T8/T9-T9/T10** thoracic vertebra
  - ● S23.150 Subluxation of T8/T9 thoracic vertebra
  - ● S23.151 Dislocation of T8/T9 thoracic vertebra
  - ● S23.152 Subluxation of T9/T10 thoracic vertebra
  - ● S23.153 Dislocation of T9/T10 thoracic vertebra
- ● S23.16 Subluxation and dislocation of **T10/T11-T11/T12** thoracic vertebra
  - ● S23.160 Subluxation of T10/T11 thoracic vertebra
  - ● S23.161 Dislocation of T10/T11 thoracic vertebra
  - ● S23.162 Subluxation of T11/T12 thoracic vertebra
  - ● S23.163 Dislocation of T11/T12 thoracic vertebra
- ● S23.17 Subluxation and dislocation of **T12/L1** thoracic vertebra
  - ● S23.170 Subluxation of T12/L1 thoracic vertebra
  - ● S23.171 Dislocation of T12/L1 thoracic vertebra
- ● **S23.2 Dislocation of other and unspecified parts of thorax**
  - X● S23.20 Dislocation of **unspecified** part of thorax
  - X● S23.29 Dislocation of other parts of thorax
- X● **S23.3 Sprain of ligaments of thoracic spine**
- ● **S23.4 Sprain of ribs and sternum**
  - X● S23.41 Sprain of ribs
  - ● S23.42 Sprain of sternum
    - ● S23.420 Sprain of sternoclavicular (joint) (ligament)
    - ● S23.421 Sprain of chondrosternal joint
    - ● S23.428 Other sprain of sternum
    - ● S23.429 Unspecified sprain of sternum
- X● **S23.8 Sprain of other specified parts of thorax**
- X● **S23.9 Sprain of unspecified parts of thorax**

▶ New ⇒ Revised ~~deleted~~ Deleted Excludes 1 Excludes 2 Includes Use additional Code first Code also Key words
OGCR Official Guidelines X Assign placeholder X ● Use Additional Character(s) ▶ Manifestation Code 🐾 Hierarchical Condition Category **Coding Clinic**

● **S24   Injury of nerves and spinal cord at thorax level**
     Note: Code to highest level of thoracic spinal cord injury.

        Injuries to the spinal cord (S24.0 and S24.1) refer to the cord level and not bone level injury, and can affect nerve roots at and below the level given.

     Code also any associated:
        fracture of thoracic vertebra (S22.0-)
        open wound of thorax (S21.-)
        transient paralysis (R29.5)

     Excludes2   injury of brachial plexus (S14.3)

     The appropriate 7th character is to be added to each code from category S24

A	initial encounter
D	subsequent encounter
S	sequela

X● **S24.0**   Concussion and edema of thoracic spinal cord   A, D, S 🔲

● **S24.1**   Other and unspecified injuries of thoracic spinal cord
   ● **S24.10**   Unspecified injury of thoracic spinal cord
     ● **S24.101**   Unspecified injury at T1 level of thoracic spinal cord   A, D, S 🔲
     ● **S24.102**   Unspecified injury at T2-T6 level of thoracic spinal cord   A, D, S 🔲
     ● **S24.103**   Unspecified injury at T7-T10 level of thoracic spinal cord   A, D, S 🔲
     ● **S24.104**   Unspecified injury at T11-T12 level of thoracic spinal cord   A, D, S 🔲
     ● **S24.109**   Unspecified injury at unspecified level of thoracic spinal cord A, D, S 🔲
         Injury of thoracic spinal cord NOS

   ● **S24.11**   Complete lesion of thoracic spinal cord
     ● **S24.111**   Complete lesion at T1 level of thoracic spinal cord   A, D, S 🔲
     ● **S24.112**   Complete lesion at T2-T6 level of thoracic spinal cord   A, D, S 🔲
     ● **S24.113**   Complete lesion at T7-T10 level of thoracic spinal cord   A, D, S 🔲
     ● **S24.114**   Complete lesion at T11-T12 level of thoracic spinal cord   A, D, S 🔲
     ● **S24.119**   Complete lesion at unspecified level of thoracic spinal cord A, D, S 🔲

   ● **S24.13**   Anterior cord syndrome of thoracic spinal cord
     ● **S24.131**   Anterior cord syndrome at T1 level of thoracic spinal cord   A, D, S 🔲
     ● **S24.132**   Anterior cord syndrome at T2-T6 level of thoracic spinal cord   A, D, S 🔲
     ● **S24.133**   Anterior cord syndrome at T7-T10 level of thoracic spinal cord A, D, S 🔲
     ● **S24.134**   Anterior cord syndrome at T11-T12 level of thoracic spinal cord A, D, S 🔲
     ● **S24.139**   Anterior cord syndrome at unspecified level of thoracic spinal cord A, D, S 🔲

   ● **S24.14**   Brown-Séquard syndrome of thoracic spinal cord
     ● **S24.141**   Brown-Séquard syndrome at T1 level of thoracic spinal cord A, D, S 🔲
     ● **S24.142**   Brown-Séquard syndrome at T2-T6 level of thoracic spinal cord A, D, S 🔲
     ● **S24.143**   Brown-Séquard syndrome at T7-T10 level of thoracic spinal cord A, D, S 🔲
     ● **S24.144**   Brown-Séquard syndrome at T11-T12 level of thoracic spinal cord A, D, S 🔲
     ● **S24.149**   Brown-Séquard syndrome at unspecified level of thoracic spinal cord A, D, S 🔲

● **S24.15**   Other incomplete lesions of thoracic spinal cord
     Incomplete lesion of thoracic spinal cord NOS
     Posterior cord syndrome of thoracic spinal cord
   ● **S24.151**   Other incomplete lesion at T1 level of thoracic spinal cord   A, D, S 🔲
   ● **S24.152**   Other incomplete lesion at T2-T6 level of thoracic spinal cord A, D, S 🔲
   ● **S24.153**   Other incomplete lesion at T7-T10 level of thoracic spinal cord A, D, S 🔲
   ● **S24.154**   Other incomplete lesion at T11-T12 level of thoracic spinal cord A, D, S 🔲
   ● **S24.159**   Other incomplete lesion at unspecified level of thoracic spinal cord A, D, S 🔲

X● **S24.2**   Injury of nerve root of thoracic spine
X● **S24.3**   Injury of peripheral nerves of thorax
X● **S24.4**   Injury of thoracic sympathetic nervous system
     Injury of cardiac plexus
     Injury of esophageal plexus
     Injury of pulmonary plexus
     Injury of stellate ganglion
     Injury of thoracic sympathetic ganglion
X● **S24.8**   Injury of other specified nerves of thorax
X● **S24.9**   Injury of unspecified nerve of thorax

● **S25   Injury of blood vessels of thorax**
     The appropriate 7th character is to be added to each code from category S25

A	initial encounter
D	subsequent encounter
S	sequela

     Code also any associated open wound (S21.-)

● **S25.0**   Injury of thoracic aorta
     Injury of aorta NOS
   X● **S25.00**   Unspecified injury of thoracic aorta
   X● **S25.01**   Minor laceration of thoracic aorta
     Incomplete transection of thoracic aorta
     Laceration of thoracic aorta NOS
     Superficial laceration of thoracic aorta
   X● **S25.02**   Major laceration of thoracic aorta
     Complete transection of thoracic aorta
     Traumatic rupture of thoracic aorta
   X● **S25.09**   Other specified injury of thoracic aorta

● **S25.1**   Injury of innominate or subclavian artery
   ● **S25.10**   Unspecified injury of innominate or subclavian artery
     ● **S25.101**   Unspecified injury of right innominate or subclavian artery
     ● **S25.102**   Unspecified injury of left innominate or subclavian artery
     ● **S25.109**   Unspecified injury of unspecified innominate or subclavian artery
   ● **S25.11**   Minor laceration of innominate or subclavian artery
     Incomplete transection of innominate or subclavian artery
     Laceration of innominate or subclavian artery NOS
     Superficial laceration of innominate or subclavian artery
     ● **S25.111**   Minor laceration of right innominate or subclavian artery
     ● **S25.112**   Minor laceration of left innominate or subclavian artery
     ● **S25.119**   Minor laceration of unspecified innominate or subclavian artery

● **S25.12** **Major laceration of innominate or subclavian artery**
     Complete transection of innominate or subclavian artery
     Traumatic rupture of innominate or subclavian artery
     ● **S25.121** Major laceration of right innominate or subclavian artery
     ● **S25.122** Major laceration of left innominate or subclavian artery
     ● **S25.129** Major laceration of unspecified innominate or subclavian artery
● **S25.19** **Other specified injury of innominate or subclavian artery**
     ● **S25.191** Other specified injury of right innominate or subclavian artery
     ● **S25.192** Other specified injury of left innominate or subclavian artery
     ● **S25.199** Other specified injury of unspecified innominate or subclavian artery

● **S25.2** **Injury of superior vena cava**
     Injury of vena cava NOS
   X ● **S25.20** **Unspecified injury of superior vena cava**
   X ● **S25.21** **Minor laceration of superior vena cava**
     Incomplete transection of superior vena cava
     Laceration of superior vena cava NOS
     Superficial laceration of superior vena cava
   X ● **S25.22** **Major laceration of superior vena cava**
     Complete transection of superior vena cava
     Traumatic rupture of superior vena cava
   X ● **S25.29** **Other specified injury of superior vena cava**

● **S25.3** **Injury of innominate or subclavian vein**
     ● **S25.30** **Unspecified injury of innominate or subclavian vein**
       ● **S25.301** Unspecified injury of right innominate or subclavian vein
       ● **S25.302** Unspecified injury of left innominate or subclavian vein
       ● **S25.309** Unspecified injury of unspecified innominate or subclavian vein
     ● **S25.31** **Minor laceration of innominate or subclavian vein**
       Incomplete transection of innominate or subclavian vein
       Laceration of innominate or subclavian vein NOS
       Superficial laceration of innominate or subclavian vein
       ● **S25.311** Minor laceration of right innominate or subclavian vein
       ● **S25.312** Minor laceration of left innominate or subclavian vein
       ● **S25.319** Minor laceration of unspecified innominate or subclavian vein
     ● **S25.32** **Major laceration of innominate or subclavian vein**
       Complete transection of innominate or subclavian vein
       Traumatic rupture of innominate or subclavian vein
       ● **S25.321** Major laceration of right innominate or subclavian vein
       ● **S25.322** Major laceration of left innominate or subclavian vein
       ● **S25.329** Major laceration of unspecified innominate or subclavian vein

● **S25.39** **Other specified injury of innominate or subclavian vein**
     ● **S25.391** Other specified injury of right innominate or subclavian vein
     ● **S25.392** Other specified injury of left innominate or subclavian vein
     ● **S25.399** Other specified injury of unspecified innominate or subclavian vein

● **S25.4** **Injury of pulmonary blood vessels**
     ● **S25.40** **Unspecified injury of pulmonary blood vessels**
       ● **S25.401** Unspecified injury of right pulmonary blood vessels
       ● **S25.402** Unspecified injury of left pulmonary blood vessels
       ● **S25.409** Unspecified injury of unspecified pulmonary blood vessels
     ● **S25.41** **Minor laceration of pulmonary blood vessels**
       Incomplete transection of pulmonary blood vessels
       Laceration of pulmonary blood vessels NOS
       Superficial laceration of pulmonary blood vessels
       ● **S25.411** Minor laceration of right pulmonary blood vessels
       ● **S25.412** Minor laceration of left pulmonary blood vessels
       ● **S25.419** Minor laceration of unspecified pulmonary blood vessels
     ● **S25.42** **Major laceration of pulmonary blood vessels**
       Complete transection of pulmonary blood vessels
       Traumatic rupture of pulmonary blood vessels
       ● **S25.421** Major laceration of right pulmonary blood vessels
       ● **S25.422** Major laceration of left pulmonary blood vessels
       ● **S25.429** Major laceration of unspecified pulmonary blood vessels
     ● **S25.49** **Other specified injury of pulmonary blood vessels**
       ● **S25.491** Other specified injury of right pulmonary blood vessels
       ● **S25.492** Other specified injury of left pulmonary blood vessels
       ● **S25.499** Other specified injury of unspecified pulmonary blood vessels

● **S25.5** **Injury of intercostal blood vessels**
     ● **S25.50** **Unspecified injury of intercostal blood vessels**
       ● **S25.501** Unspecified injury of intercostal blood vessels, right side
       ● **S25.502** Unspecified injury of intercostal blood vessels, left side
       ● **S25.509** Unspecified injury of intercostal blood vessels, unspecified side
     ● **S25.51** **Laceration of intercostal blood vessels**
       ● **S25.511** Laceration of intercostal blood vessels, right side
       ● **S25.512** Laceration of intercostal blood vessels, left side
       ● **S25.519** Laceration of intercostal blood vessels, unspecified side
     ● **S25.59** **Other specified injury of intercostal blood vessels**
       ● **S25.591** Other specified injury of intercostal blood vessels, right side
       ● **S25.592** Other specified injury of intercostal blood vessels, left side
       ● **S25.599** Other specified injury of intercostal blood vessels, unspecified side

---

▶ New   ⇒ Revised   ~~deleted~~ Deleted   Excludes 1   Excludes 2   Includes   Use additional   Code first   Code also   Key words

OGCR Official Guidelines   X Assign placeholder X   ● Use Additional Character(s)   ▷ Manifestation Code   ℞ Hierarchical Condition Category   **Coding Clinic**

S25.8 Injury of other blood vessels of thorax
Injury of azygos vein
Injury of mammary artery or vein

  S25.80 Unspecified injury of other blood vessels of thorax

    S25.801 Unspecified injury of other blood vessels of thorax, right side

    S25.802 Unspecified injury of other blood vessels of thorax, left side

    S25.809 Unspecified injury of other blood vessels of thorax, unspecified side

  S25.81 Laceration of other blood vessels of thorax

    S25.811 Laceration of other blood vessels of thorax, right side

    S25.812 Laceration of other blood vessels of thorax, left side

    S25.819 Laceration of other blood vessels of thorax, unspecified side

  S25.89 Other specified injury of other blood vessels of thorax

    S25.891 Other specified injury of other blood vessels of thorax, right side

    S25.892 Other specified injury of other blood vessels of thorax, left side

    S25.899 Other specified injury of other blood vessels of thorax, unspecified side

S25.9 Injury of unspecified blood vessel of thorax

  X **S25.90** Unspecified injury of unspecified blood vessel of thorax

  X **S25.91** Laceration of unspecified blood vessel of thorax

  X **S25.99** Other specified injury of unspecified blood vessel of thorax

S26 Injury of heart

The appropriate 7th character is to be added to each code from category S26

> A   initial encounter
> D subsequent encounter
> S   sequela

Code also any associated:
open wound of thorax (S21.-)
traumatic hemopneumothorax (S27.2)
traumatic hemothorax (S27.1)
traumatic pneumothorax (S27.0)

S26.0 Injury of heart with hemopericardium
Hemopericardium: effusion of blood within pericardium

  X **S26.00** Unspecified injury of heart with hemopericardium

  X **S26.01** Contusion of heart with hemopericardium

  S26.02 Laceration of heart with hemopericardium

    S26.020 Mild laceration of heart with hemopericardium
Laceration of heart without penetration of heart chamber

    S26.021 Moderate laceration of heart with hemopericardium
Laceration of heart with penetration of heart chamber

    S26.022 Major laceration of heart with hemopericardium
Laceration of heart with penetration of multiple heart chambers

  X **S26.09** Other injury of heart with hemopericardium

S26.1 Injury of heart without hemopericardium
Hemopericardium: effusion of blood within pericardium

  X **S26.10** Unspecified injury of heart without hemopericardium

  X **S26.11** Contusion of heart without hemopericardium

  X **S26.12** Laceration of heart without hemopericardium

  X **S26.19** Other injury of heart without hemopericardium

Item 19–2 Pneumothorax is a collection of gas (positive air pressure) in the pleural space resulting in the lung collapsing. A **tension pneumothorax** is life-threatening and is a result of air in the pleural space causing a displacement in the mediastinal structures and cardiopulmonary function compromise. A **traumatic pneumothorax** results from blunt or penetrating injury that disrupts the parietal/visceral pleura. **Hemothorax** is blood or bloody fluid in the pleural cavity as a result of traumatic blood vessel rupture or inflammation of the lungs from pneumonia.

S26.9 Injury of heart, unspecified with or without hemopericardium
Hemopericardium: effusion of blood within pericardium

  X **S26.90** Unspecified injury of heart, unspecified with or without hemopericardium

  X **S26.91** Contusion of heart, unspecified with or without hemopericardium

  X **S26.92** Laceration of heart, unspecified with or without hemopericardium
Laceration of heart NOS

  X **S26.99** Other injury of heart, unspecified with or without hemopericardium

S27 Injury of other and unspecified intrathoracic organs
Code also any associated open wound of thorax (S21.-)

Excludes2 injury of cervical esophagus (S10-S19)
injury of trachea (cervical) (S10-S19)

The appropriate 7th character is to be added to each code from category S27

> A   initial encounter
> D subsequent encounter
> S   sequela

  X **S27.0** Traumatic pneumothorax
Excludes1 spontaneous pneumothorax (J93.-)

  X **S27.1** Traumatic hemothorax

  X **S27.2** Traumatic hemopneumothorax

S27.3 Other and unspecified injuries of lung

  S27.30 Unspecified injury of lung

    S27.301 Unspecified injury of lung, unilateral

    S27.302 Unspecified injury of lung, bilateral

    S27.309 Unspecified injury of lung, unspecified

  S27.31 Primary blast injury of lung
Blast injury of lung NOS

    S27.311 Primary blast injury of lung, unilateral

    S27.312 Primary blast injury of lung, bilateral

    S27.319 Primary blast injury of lung, unspecified

  S27.32 Contusion of lung

    S27.321 Contusion of lung, unilateral

    S27.322 Contusion of lung, bilateral

    S27.329 Contusion of lung, unspecified

  S27.33 Laceration of lung

    S27.331 Laceration of lung, unilateral

    S27.332 Laceration of lung, bilateral

    S27.339 Laceration of lung, unspecified

  S27.39 Other injuries of lung
Secondary blast injury of lung

    S27.391 Other injuries of lung, unilateral

    S27.392 Other injuries of lung, bilateral

    S27.399 Other injuries of lung, unspecified

- **S27.4   Injury of bronchus**
  - **S27.40   Unspecified injury of bronchus**
    - **S27.401   Unspecified injury of bronchus, unilateral**
    - **S27.402   Unspecified injury of bronchus, bilateral**
    - **S27.409   Unspecified injury of bronchus, unspecified**
  - **S27.41   Primary blast injury of bronchus**
    Blast injury of bronchus NOS
    - **S27.411   Primary blast injury of bronchus, unilateral**
    - **S27.412   Primary blast injury of bronchus, bilateral**
    - **S27.419   Primary blast injury of bronchus, unspecified**
  - **S27.42   Contusion of bronchus**
    - **S27.421   Contusion of bronchus, unilateral**
    - **S27.422   Contusion of bronchus, bilateral**
    - **S27.429   Contusion of bronchus, unspecified**
  - **S27.43   Laceration of bronchus**
    - **S27.431   Laceration of bronchus, unilateral**
    - **S27.432   Laceration of bronchus, bilateral**
    - **S27.439   Laceration of bronchus, unspecified**
  - **S27.49   Other injury of bronchus**
    Secondary blast injury of bronchus
    - **S27.491   Other injury of bronchus, unilateral**
    - **S27.492   Other injury of bronchus, bilateral**
    - **S27.499   Other injury of bronchus, unspecified**
- **S27.5   Injury of thoracic trachea**
  - X **S27.50   Unspecified injury of thoracic trachea**
  - X **S27.51   Primary blast injury of thoracic trachea**

    Blast injury of thoracic trachea NOS
  - X **S27.52   Contusion of thoracic trachea**
  - X **S27.53   Laceration of thoracic trachea**
  - X **S27.59   Other injury of thoracic trachea**
    Secondary blast injury of thoracic trachea
- **S27.6   Injury of pleura**
  - X **S27.60   Unspecified injury of pleura**
  - X **S27.63   Laceration of pleura**
  - X **S27.69   Other injury of pleura**
- **S27.8   Injury of other specified intrathoracic organs**
  - **S27.80   Injury of diaphragm**
    - **S27.802   Contusion of diaphragm**
    - **S27.803   Laceration of diaphragm**
    - **S27.808   Other injury of diaphragm**
    - **S27.809   Unspecified injury of diaphragm**
  - **S27.81   Injury of esophagus (thoracic part)**
    - **S27.812   Contusion of esophagus (thoracic part)**
    - **S27.813   Laceration of esophagus (thoracic part)**
    - **S27.818   Other injury of esophagus (thoracic part)**
    - **S27.819   Unspecified injury of esophagus (thoracic part)**
  - **S27.89   Injury of other specified intrathoracic organs**
    Injury of lymphatic thoracic duct
    Injury of thymus gland
    - **S27.892   Contusion of other specified intrathoracic organs**
    - **S27.893   Laceration of other specified intrathoracic organs**
    - **S27.898   Other injury of other specified intrathoracic organs**
    - **S27.899   Unspecified injury of other specified intrathoracic organs**
  - X **S27.9   Injury of unspecified intrathoracic organ**
- **S28   Crushing injury of thorax, and traumatic amputation of part of thorax**
  The appropriate 7th character is to be added to each code from category S28

  > A   initial encounter
  > D   subsequent encounter
  > S   sequela

  - X **S28.0   Crushed chest**
    Use additional code for all associated injuries
    Excludes1   flail chest (S22.5)
  - X **S28.1   Traumatic amputation (partial) of part of thorax, except breast**
  - **S28.2   Traumatic amputation of breast**
    - **S28.21   Complete traumatic amputation of breast**
      Traumatic amputation of breast NOS
      - **S28.211   Complete traumatic amputation of right breast**
      - **S28.212   Complete traumatic amputation of left breast**
      - **S28.219   Complete traumatic amputation of unspecified breast**
    - **S28.22   Partial traumatic amputation of breast**
      - **S28.221   Partial traumatic amputation of right breast**
      - **S28.222   Partial traumatic amputation of left breast**
      - **S28.229   Partial traumatic amputation of unspecified breast**
- **S29   Other and unspecified injuries of thorax**
  Code also any associated open wound (S21.-)
  The appropriate 7th character is to be added to each code from category S29

  > A   initial encounter
  > D   subsequent encounter
  > S   sequela

  - **S29.0   Injury of muscle and tendon at thorax level**
    - **S29.00   Unspecified injury of muscle and tendon of thorax**
      - **S29.001   Unspecified injury of muscle and tendon of front wall of thorax**
      - **S29.002   Unspecified injury of muscle and tendon of back wall of thorax**
      - **S29.009   Unspecified injury of muscle and tendon of unspecified wall of thorax**
    - **S29.01   Strain of muscle and tendon of thorax**
      - **S29.011   Strain of muscle and tendon of front wall of thorax**
      - **S29.012   Strain of muscle and tendon of back wall of thorax**
      - **S29.019   Strain of muscle and tendon of unspecified wall of thorax**
    - **S29.02   Laceration of muscle and tendon of thorax**
      - **S29.021   Laceration of muscle and tendon of front wall of thorax**
      - **S29.022   Laceration of muscle and tendon of back wall of thorax**
      - **S29.029   Laceration of muscle and tendon of unspecified wall of thorax**

▶ New   ⇒ Revised   ~~deleted~~ Deleted   Excludes 1   Excludes 2   Includes   Use additional   Code first   Code also   Key words

OGCR Official Guidelines   X Assign placeholder X   ● Use Additional Character(s)   ▷ Manifestation Code   🆀 Hierarchical Condition Category   **Coding Clinic**

● S29.09   Other injury of muscle and tendon of thorax
   ● S29.091   Other injury of muscle and tendon of front wall of thorax
   ● S29.092   Other injury of muscle and tendon of back wall of thorax
   ● S29.099   Other injury of muscle and tendon of unspecified wall of thorax
X● S29.8   Other specified injuries of thorax
X● S29.9   Unspecified injury of thorax

INJURIES TO THE ABDOMEN, LOWER BACK, LUMBAR SPINE PELVIS AND EXTERNAL GENITALS (S30-S39)

Includes   injuries to the abdominal wall
      injuries to the anus
      injuries to the buttock
      injuries to the external genitalia
      injuries to the flank
      injuries to the groin

Excludes2   burns and corrosions (T20-T32)
      effects of foreign body in anus and rectum (T18.5)
      effects of foreign body in genitourinary tract (T19.-)
      effects of foreign body in stomach, small intestine and colon (T18.2-T18.4)
      frostbite (T33-T34)
      insect bite or sting, venomous (T63.4)

● S30   **Superficial injury of abdomen, lower back, pelvis and external genitals**
   Excludes2   superficial injury of hip (S70.-)

The appropriate 7th character is to be added to each code from category S30

A	initial encounter
D	subsequent encounter
S	sequela

X● S30.0   Contusion of lower back and pelvis
   Contusion of buttock
X● S30.1   Contusion of abdominal wall
   Contusion of flank
   Contusion of groin
● S30.2   Contusion of external genital organs
   ● S30.20   Contusion of unspecified external genital organ
      ● S30.201   Contusion of unspecified external genital organ, male ♂
      ● S30.202   Contusion of unspecified external genital organ, female ♀
   X● S30.21   Contusion of penis ♂
   X● S30.22   Contusion of scrotum and testes ♂
   X● S30.23   Contusion of vagina and vulva ♀
X● S30.3   Contusion of anus
● S30.8   Other superficial injuries of abdomen, lower back, pelvis and external genitals
   ● S30.81   Abrasion of abdomen, lower back, pelvis and external genitals
      ● S30.810   Abrasion of lower back and pelvis
      ● S30.811   Abrasion of abdominal wall
      ● S30.812   Abrasion of penis ♂
      ● S30.813   Abrasion of scrotum and testes ♂
      ● S30.814   Abrasion of vagina and vulva ♀
      ● S30.815   Abrasion of unspecified external genital organs, male ♂
      ● S30.816   Abrasion of unspecified external genital organs, female ♀
      ● S30.817   Abrasion of anus
   ● S30.82   Blister (nonthermal) of abdomen, lower back, pelvis and external genitals
      ● S30.820   Blister (nonthermal) of lower back and pelvis
      ● S30.821   Blister (nonthermal) of abdominal wall

● S30.822   Blister (nonthermal) of penis ♂
● S30.823   Blister (nonthermal) of scrotum and testes ♂
● S30.824   Blister (nonthermal) of vagina and vulva ♀
● S30.825   Blister (nonthermal) of unspecified external genital organs, male ♂
● S30.826   Blister (nonthermal) of unspecified external genital organs, female ♀
● S30.827   Blister (nonthermal) of anus
● S30.84   External constriction of abdomen, lower back, pelvis and external genitals
   ● S30.840   External constriction of lower back and pelvis
   ● S30.841   External constriction of abdominal wall
   ● S30.842   External constriction of penis ♂
      Hair tourniquet syndrome of penis
      Use additional cause code to identify the constricting item (W49.0-)
   ● S30.843   External constriction of scrotum and testes ♂
   ● S30.844   External constriction of vagina and vulva ♀
   ● S30.845   External constriction of unspecified external genital organs, male ♂
   ● S30.846   External constriction of unspecified external genital organs, female ♀
● S30.85   Superficial foreign body of abdomen, lower back, pelvis and external genitals
   Splinter in the abdomen, lower back, pelvis and external genitals
   ● S30.850   Superficial foreign body of lower back and pelvis
   ● S30.851   Superficial foreign body of abdominal wall
   ● S30.852   Superficial foreign body of penis ♂
   ● S30.853   Superficial foreign body of scrotum and testes ♂
   ● S30.854   Superficial foreign body of vagina and vulva ♀
   ● S30.855   Superficial foreign body of unspecified external genital organs, male ♂
   ● S30.856   Superficial foreign body of unspecified external genital organs, female ♀
   ● S30.857   Superficial foreign body of anus
● S30.86   Insect bite (nonvenomous) of abdomen, lower back, pelvis and external genitals
   ● S30.860   Insect bite (nonvenomous) of lower back and pelvis
   ● S30.861   Insect bite (nonvenomous) of abdominal wall
   ● S30.862   Insect bite (nonvenomous) of penis ♂
   ● S30.863   Insect bite (nonvenomous) of scrotum and testes ♂
   ● S30.864   Insect bite (nonvenomous) of vagina and vulva ♀
   ● S30.865   Insect bite (nonvenomous) of unspecified external genital organs, male ♂
   ● S30.866   Insect bite (nonvenomous) of unspecified external genital organs, female ♀
   ● S30.867   Insect bite (nonvenomous) of anus

● **S30.87**   **Other superficial bite of abdomen, lower back, pelvis and external genitals**

     Excludes1   open bite of abdomen, lower back, pelvis and external genitals (S31.05, S31.15, S31.25, S31.35, S31.45, S31.55)

  ● **S30.870**   Other superficial bite of lower back and pelvis

  ● **S30.871**   Other superficial bite of abdominal wall

  ● **S30.872**   Other superficial bite of penis♂

  ● **S30.873**   Other superficial bite of scrotum and testes♂

  ● **S30.874**   Other superficial bite of vagina and vulva♀

  ● **S30.875**   Other superficial bite of unspecified external genital organs, male♂

  ● **S30.876**   Other superficial bite of unspecified external genital organs, female♀

  ● **S30.877**   Other superficial bite of anus

● **S30.9**   **Unspecified superficial injury of abdomen, lower back, pelvis and external genitals**

  X● **S30.91**   Unspecified superficial injury of lower back and pelvis

  X● **S30.92**   Unspecified superficial injury of abdominal wall

  X● **S30.93**   Unspecified superficial injury of penis♂

  X● **S30.94**   Unspecified superficial injury of scrotum and testes♂

  X● **S30.95**   Unspecified superficial injury of vagina and vulva♀

  X● **S30.96**   Unspecified superficial injury of unspecified external genital organs, male ♂

  X● **S30.97**   Unspecified superficial injury of unspecified external genital organs, female ♀

  X● **S30.98**   Unspecified superficial injury of anus

● **S31**   **Open wound of abdomen, lower back, pelvis and external genitals**

     Code also any associated:
       spinal cord injury (S24.0, S24.1-, S34.0-, S34.1-)
       wound infection

     Excludes1   traumatic amputation of part of abdomen, lower back and pelvis (S38.2-, S38.3)

     Excludes2   open wound of hip (S71.00-S71.02)
                 open fracture of pelvis (S32.1--S32.9 with 7th character B)

     The appropriate 7th character is to be added to each code from category S31

     | | |
     A   initial encounter
     D   subsequent encounter
     S   sequela

● **S31.0**   **Open wound of lower back and pelvis**

  ● **S31.00**   Unspecified open wound of lower back and pelvis

    ● **S31.000**   Unspecified open wound of lower back and pelvis without penetration into retroperitoneum
         Unspecified open wound of lower back and pelvis NOS

    ● **S31.001**   Unspecified open wound of lower back and pelvis with penetration into retroperitoneum

● **S31.01**   **Laceration without foreign body of lower back and pelvis**

  ● **S31.010**   Laceration without foreign body of lower back and pelvis without penetration into retroperitoneum
       Laceration without foreign body of lower back and pelvis NOS

  ● **S31.011**   Laceration without foreign body of lower back and pelvis with penetration into retroperitoneum

● **S31.02**   **Laceration with foreign body of lower back and pelvis**

  ● **S31.020**   Laceration with foreign body of lower back and pelvis without penetration into retroperitoneum
       Laceration with foreign body of lower back and pelvis NOS

  ● **S31.021**   Laceration with foreign body of lower back and pelvis with penetration into retroperitoneum

● **S31.03**   **Puncture wound without foreign body of lower back and pelvis**

  ● **S31.030**   Puncture wound without foreign body of lower back and pelvis without penetration into retroperitoneum
       Puncture wound without foreign body of lower back and pelvis NOS

  ● **S31.031**   Puncture wound without foreign body of lower back and pelvis with penetration into retroperitoneum

● **S31.04**   **Puncture wound with foreign body of lower back and pelvis**

  ● **S31.040**   Puncture wound with foreign body of lower back and pelvis without penetration into retroperitoneum
       Puncture wound with foreign body of lower back and pelvis NOS

  ● **S31.041**   Puncture wound with foreign body of lower back and pelvis with penetration into retroperitoneum

● **S31.05**   **Open bite of lower back and pelvis**
     Bite of lower back and pelvis NOS

     Excludes1   superficial bite of lower back and pelvis (S30.860, S30.870)

  ● **S31.050**   Open bite of lower back and pelvis without penetration into retroperitoneum
       Open bite of lower back and pelvis NOS

  ● **S31.051**   Open bite of lower back and pelvis with penetration into retroperitoneum

● **S31.1**   **Open wound of abdominal wall without penetration into peritoneal cavity**
     Open wound of abdominal wall NOS

     Excludes2   open wound of abdominal wall with penetration into peritoneal cavity (S31.6-)

  ● **S31.10**   Unspecified open wound of abdominal wall without penetration into peritoneal cavity

    ● **S31.100**   Unspecified open wound of abdominal wall, right upper quadrant without penetration into peritoneal cavity

    ● **S31.101**   Unspecified open wound of abdominal wall, left upper quadrant without penetration into peritoneal cavity

▶ New   ⟹ Revised   ~~deleted~~ Deleted   Excludes 1   Excludes 2   Includes   Use additional   Code first   Code also   Key words

OGCR Official Guidelines   X Assign placeholder X   ● Use Additional Character(s)   ▷ Manifestation Code   🐾 Hierarchical Condition Category   **Coding Clinic**

● S31.102 Unspecified open wound of abdominal wall, epigastric region without penetration into peritoneal cavity

● S31.103 Unspecified open wound of abdominal wall, right lower quadrant without penetration into peritoneal cavity

● S31.104 Unspecified open wound of abdominal wall, left lower quadrant without penetration into peritoneal cavity

● S31.105 Unspecified open wound of abdominal wall, periumbilic region without penetration into peritoneal cavity

● S31.109 Unspecified open wound of abdominal wall, unspecified quadrant without penetration into peritoneal cavity
Unspecified open wound of abdominal wall NOS

● S31.11 Laceration without foreign body of abdominal wall without penetration into peritoneal cavity

● S31.110 Laceration without foreign body of abdominal wall, right upper quadrant without penetration into peritoneal cavity

● S31.111 Laceration without foreign body of abdominal wall, left upper quadrant without penetration into peritoneal cavity

● S31.112 Laceration without foreign body of abdominal wall, epigastric region without penetration into peritoneal cavity

● S31.113 Laceration without foreign body of abdominal wall, right lower quadrant without penetration into peritoneal cavity

● S31.114 Laceration without foreign body of abdominal wall, left lower quadrant without penetration into peritoneal cavity

● S31.115 Laceration without foreign body of abdominal wall, periumbilic region without penetration into peritoneal cavity

● S31.119 Laceration without foreign body of abdominal wall, unspecified quadrant without penetration into peritoneal cavity

● S31.12 Laceration with foreign body of abdominal wall without penetration into peritoneal cavity

● S31.120 Laceration of abdominal wall with foreign body, right upper quadrant without penetration into peritoneal cavity

● S31.121 Laceration of abdominal wall with foreign body, left upper quadrant without penetration into peritoneal cavity

● S31.122 Laceration of abdominal wall with foreign body, epigastric region without penetration into peritoneal cavity

● S31.123 Laceration of abdominal wall with foreign body, right lower quadrant without penetration into peritoneal cavity

● S31.124 Laceration of abdominal wall with foreign body, left lower quadrant without penetration into peritoneal cavity

● S31.125 Laceration of abdominal wall with foreign body, periumbilic region without penetration into peritoneal cavity

● S31.129 Laceration of abdominal wall with foreign body, unspecified quadrant without penetration into peritoneal cavity

● S31.13 Puncture wound of abdominal wall without foreign body without penetration into peritoneal cavity

● S31.130 Puncture wound of abdominal wall without foreign body, right upper quadrant without penetration into peritoneal cavity

● S31.131 Puncture wound of abdominal wall without foreign body, left upper quadrant without penetration into peritoneal cavity

● S31.132 Puncture wound of abdominal wall without foreign body, epigastric region without penetration into peritoneal cavity

● S31.133 Puncture wound of abdominal wall without foreign body, right lower quadrant without penetration into peritoneal cavity

● S31.134 Puncture wound of abdominal wall without foreign body, left lower quadrant without penetration into peritoneal cavity

● S31.135 Puncture wound of abdominal wall without foreign body, periumbilic region without penetration into peritoneal cavity

● S31.139 Puncture wound of abdominal wall without foreign body, unspecified quadrant without penetration into peritoneal cavity

● S31.14 Puncture wound of abdominal wall with foreign body without penetration into peritoneal cavity

● S31.140 Puncture wound of abdominal wall with foreign body, right upper quadrant without penetration into peritoneal cavity

● S31.141 Puncture wound of abdominal wall with foreign body, left upper quadrant without penetration into peritoneal cavity

● S31.142 Puncture wound of abdominal wall with foreign body, epigastric region without penetration into peritoneal cavity

● S31.143 Puncture wound of abdominal wall with foreign body, right lower quadrant without penetration into peritoneal cavity

● S31.144 Puncture wound of abdominal wall with foreign body, left lower quadrant without penetration into peritoneal cavity

● S31.145 Puncture wound of abdominal wall with foreign body, periumbilic region without penetration into peritoneal cavity

● S31.149 Puncture wound of abdominal wall with foreign body, unspecified quadrant without penetration into peritoneal cavity

● **S31.15** **Open bite of abdominal wall without penetration into peritoneal cavity**
Bite of abdominal wall NOS

> **Excludes1** superficial bite of abdominal wall (S30.871)

● **S31.150** Open bite of abdominal wall, **right** upper quadrant without penetration into peritoneal cavity

● **S31.151** Open bite of abdominal wall, **left** upper quadrant without penetration into peritoneal cavity

● **S31.152** Open bite of abdominal wall, **epigastric region** without penetration into peritoneal cavity

● **S31.153** Open bite of abdominal wall, **right lower** quadrant without penetration into peritoneal cavity

● **S31.154** Open bite of abdominal wall, **left lower** quadrant without penetration into peritoneal cavity

● **S31.155** Open bite of abdominal wall, **periumbilic region** without penetration into peritoneal cavity

● **S31.159** Open bite of abdominal wall, **unspecified** quadrant without penetration into peritoneal cavity

● **S31.2** **Open wound of penis**
X ● **S31.20** Unspecified open wound of penis ♂
X ● **S31.21** Laceration without foreign body of penis ♂
X ● **S31.22** Laceration with foreign body of penis ♂
X ● **S31.23** Puncture wound without foreign body of penis ♂
X ● **S31.24** Puncture wound with foreign body of penis ♂
X ● **S31.25** Open bite of penis ♂
Bite of penis NOS

> **Excludes1** superficial bite of penis (S30.862, S30.872)

● **S31.3** **Open wound of scrotum and testes**
X ● **S31.30** Unspecified open wound of scrotum and testes ♂
X ● **S31.31** Laceration without foreign body of scrotum and testes ♂
X ● **S31.32** Laceration with foreign body of scrotum and testes ♂
X ● **S31.33** Puncture wound without foreign body of scrotum and testes ♂
X ● **S31.34** Puncture wound with foreign body of scrotum and testes ♂
X ● **S31.35** Open bite of scrotum and testes ♂
Bite of scrotum and testes NOS

> **Excludes1** superficial bite of scrotum and testes (S30.863, S30.873)

● **S31.4** **Open wound of vagina and vulva**

> **Excludes1** injury to vagina and vulva during delivery (O70.-, O71.4)

X ● **S31.40** Unspecified open wound of vagina and vulva ♀
X ● **S31.41** Laceration without foreign body of vagina and vulva ♀
X ● **S31.42** Laceration with foreign body of vagina and vulva ♀
X ● **S31.43** Puncture wound without foreign body of vagina and vulva ♀
X ● **S31.44** Puncture wound with foreign body of vagina and vulva ♀
X ● **S31.45** Open bite of vagina and vulva ♀
Bite of vagina and vulva NOS

> **Excludes1** superficial bite of vagina and vulva (S30.864, S30.874)

● **S31.5** **Open wound of unspecified external genital organs**

> **Excludes1** traumatic amputation of external genital organs (S38.21, S38.22)

● **S31.50** Unspecified open wound of unspecified external genital organs

● **S31.501** Unspecified open wound of unspecified external genital organs, **male** ♂

● **S31.502** Unspecified open wound of unspecified external genital organs, **female** ♀

● **S31.51** Laceration without foreign body of unspecified external genital organs

● **S31.511** Laceration without foreign body of unspecified external genital organs, **male** ♂

● **S31.512** Laceration without foreign body of unspecified external genital organs, **female** ♀

● **S31.52** Laceration with foreign body of unspecified external genital organs

● **S31.521** Laceration with foreign body of unspecified external genital organs, **male** ♂

● **S31.522** Laceration with foreign body of unspecified external genital organs, **female** ♀

● **S31.53** Puncture wound without foreign body of unspecified external genital organs

● **S31.531** Puncture wound without foreign body of unspecified external genital organs, **male** ♂

● **S31.532** Puncture wound without foreign body of unspecified external genital organs, **female** ♀

● **S31.54** Puncture wound with foreign body of unspecified external genital organs

● **S31.541** Puncture wound with foreign body of unspecified external genital organs, **male** ♂

● **S31.542** Puncture wound with foreign body of unspecified external genital organs, **female** ♀

● **S31.55** Open bite of unspecified external genital organs
Bite of unspecified external genital organs NOS

> **Excludes1** superficial bite of unspecified external genital organs (S30.865, S30.866, S30.875, S30.876)

● **S31.551** Open bite of unspecified external genital organs, **male** ♂

● **S31.552** Open bite of unspecified external genital organs, **female** ♀

● **S31.6** **Open wound of abdominal wall with penetration into peritoneal cavity**

● **S31.60** Unspecified open wound of abdominal wall with penetration into peritoneal cavity

● **S31.600** Unspecified open wound of abdominal wall, **right upper** quadrant with penetration into peritoneal cavity

● **S31.601** Unspecified open wound of abdominal wall, **left upper** quadrant with penetration into peritoneal cavity

● **S31.602** Unspecified open wound of abdominal wall, **epigastric region** with penetration into peritoneal cavity

▶ New   ⇒ Revised   ~~deleted~~ Deleted   Excludes 1   Excludes 2   Includes   Use additional   Code first   Code also   Key words
OGCR Official Guidelines   X Assign placeholder X   ● Use Additional Character(s)   ▷ Manifestation Code   🔖 Hierarchical Condition Category   **Coding Clinic**

● S31.603   Unspecified open wound of abdominal wall, **right lower** quadrant with penetration into peritoneal cavity

● S31.604   Unspecified open wound of abdominal wall, **left lower** quadrant with penetration into peritoneal cavity

● S31.605   Unspecified open wound of abdominal wall, **periumbilic region** with penetration into peritoneal cavity

● S31.609   Unspecified open wound of abdominal wall, **unspecified** quadrant with penetration into peritoneal cavity

● S31.61   Laceration without foreign body of abdominal wall with penetration into peritoneal cavity

● S31.610   Laceration without foreign body of abdominal wall, **right upper** quadrant with penetration into peritoneal cavity

● S31.611   Laceration without foreign body of abdominal wall, **left upper** quadrant with penetration into peritoneal cavity

● S31.612   Laceration without foreign body of abdominal wall, **epigastric region** with penetration into peritoneal cavity

● S31.613   Laceration without foreign body of abdominal wall, **right lower** quadrant with penetration into peritoneal cavity
     Coding Clinic: 2015, Q4, P37

● S31.614   Laceration without foreign body of abdominal wall, **left lower** quadrant with penetration into peritoneal cavity

● S31.615   Laceration without foreign body of abdominal wall, **periumbilic region** with penetration into peritoneal cavity

● S31.619   Laceration without foreign body of abdominal wall, **unspecified** quadrant with penetration into peritoneal cavity

● S31.62   Laceration with foreign body of abdominal wall with penetration into peritoneal cavity

● S31.620   Laceration with foreign body of abdominal wall, **right upper** quadrant with penetration into peritoneal cavity

● S31.621   Laceration with foreign body of abdominal wall, **left upper** quadrant with penetration into peritoneal cavity

● S31.622   Laceration with foreign body of abdominal wall, **epigastric region** with penetration into peritoneal cavity

● S31.623   Laceration with foreign body of abdominal wall, **right lower** quadrant with penetration into peritoneal cavity

● S31.624   Laceration with foreign body of abdominal wall, **left lower** quadrant with penetration into peritoneal cavity

● S31.625   Laceration with foreign body of abdominal wall, **periumbilic region** with penetration into peritoneal cavity

● S31.629   Laceration with foreign body of abdominal wall, **unspecified** quadrant with penetration into peritoneal cavity

● S31.63   Puncture wound without foreign body of abdominal wall with penetration into peritoneal cavity

● S31.630   Puncture wound without foreign body of abdominal wall, **right upper** quadrant with penetration into peritoneal cavity

● S31.631   Puncture wound without foreign body of abdominal wall, **left upper** quadrant with penetration into peritoneal cavity

● S31.632   Puncture wound without foreign body of abdominal wall, **epigastric region** with penetration into peritoneal cavity

● S31.633   Puncture wound without foreign body of abdominal wall, **right lower** quadrant with penetration into peritoneal cavity

● S31.634   Puncture wound without foreign body of abdominal wall, **left lower** quadrant with penetration into peritoneal cavity

● S31.635   Puncture wound without foreign body of abdominal wall, **periumbilic region** with penetration into peritoneal cavity

● S31.639   Puncture wound without foreign body of abdominal wall, **unspecified** quadrant with penetration into peritoneal cavity

● S31.64   Puncture wound with foreign body of abdominal wall with penetration into peritoneal cavity

● S31.640   Puncture wound with foreign body of abdominal wall, **right upper** quadrant with penetration into peritoneal cavity

● S31.641   Puncture wound with foreign body of abdominal wall, **left upper** quadrant with penetration into peritoneal cavity

● S31.642   Puncture wound with foreign body of abdominal wall, **epigastric region** with penetration into peritoneal cavity

● S31.643   Puncture wound with foreign body of abdominal wall, **right lower** quadrant with penetration into peritoneal cavity

● S31.644   Puncture wound with foreign body of abdominal wall, **left lower** quadrant with penetration into peritoneal cavity

● S31.645   Puncture wound with foreign body of abdominal wall, **periumbilic region** with penetration into peritoneal cavity

● S31.649   Puncture wound with foreign body of abdominal wall, **unspecified** quadrant with penetration into peritoneal cavity

● **S31.65**   **Open bite of abdominal wall with penetration into peritoneal cavity**

    Excludes1   superficial bite of abdominal wall (S30.861, S30.871)

   ● **S31.650**   **Open bite of abdominal wall, right upper quadrant with penetration into peritoneal cavity**

   ● **S31.651**   **Open bite of abdominal wall, left upper quadrant with penetration into peritoneal cavity**

   ● **S31.652**   **Open bite of abdominal wall, epigastric region with penetration into peritoneal cavity**

   ● **S31.653**   **Open bite of abdominal wall, right lower quadrant with penetration into peritoneal cavity**

   ● **S31.654**   **Open bite of abdominal wall, left lower quadrant with penetration into peritoneal cavity**

   ● **S31.655**   **Open bite of abdominal wall, periumbilic region with penetration into peritoneal cavity**

   ● **S31.659**   **Open bite of abdominal wall, unspecified quadrant with penetration into peritoneal cavity**

● **S31.8**   **Open wound of other parts of abdomen, lower back and pelvis**

  ● **S31.80**   **Open wound of unspecified buttock**

   ● **S31.801**   **Laceration without foreign body of unspecified buttock**

   ● **S31.802**   **Laceration with foreign body of unspecified buttock**

   ● **S31.803**   **Puncture wound without foreign body of unspecified buttock**

   ● **S31.804**   **Puncture wound with foreign body of unspecified buttock**

   ● **S31.805**   **Open bite of unspecified buttock**
      Bite of buttock NOS

      Excludes1   superficial bite of buttock (S30.870)

   ● **S31.809**   **Unspecified open wound of unspecified buttock**

  ● **S31.81**   **Open wound of right buttock**

   ● **S31.811**   **Laceration without foreign body of right buttock**

   ● **S31.812**   **Laceration with foreign body of right buttock**

   ● **S31.813**   **Puncture wound without foreign body of right buttock**

   ● **S31.814**   **Puncture wound with foreign body of right buttock**

   ● **S31.815**   **Open bite of right buttock**
      Bite of right buttock NOS

      Excludes1   superficial bite of buttock (S30.870)

   ● **S31.819**   **Unspecified open wound of right buttock**

  ● **S31.82**   **Open wound of left buttock**

   ● **S31.821**   **Laceration without foreign body of left buttock**

   ● **S31.822**   **Laceration with foreign body of left buttock**

   ● **S31.823**   **Puncture wound without foreign body of left buttock**

   ● **S31.824**   **Puncture wound with foreign body of left buttock**

   ● **S31.825**   **Open bite of left buttock**
      Bite of left buttock NOS

      Excludes1   superficial bite of buttock (S30.870)

   ● **S31.829**   **Unspecified open wound of left buttock**

● **S31.83**   **Open wound of anus**

   ● **S31.831**   **Laceration without foreign body of anus**

   ● **S31.832**   **Laceration with foreign body of anus**

   ● **S31.833**   **Puncture wound without foreign body of anus**

   ● **S31.834**   **Puncture wound with foreign body of anus**

   ● **S31.835**   **Open bite of anus**
      Bite of anus NOS

      Excludes1   superficial bite of anus (S30.877)

   ● **S31.839**   **Unspecified open wound of anus**

● **S32**   **Fracture of lumbar spine and pelvis**

   Note: A fracture not indicated as displaced or nondisplaced should be coded to displaced

     A fracture not indicated as opened or closed should be coded to closed

   Includes   fracture of lumbosacral neural arch
         fracture of lumbosacral spinous process
         fracture of lumbosacral transverse process
         fracture of lumbosacral vertebra
         fracture of lumbosacral vertebral arch

  Code first any associated spinal cord and spinal nerve injury (S34.-)

   Excludes1   transection of abdomen (S38.3)

   Excludes2   fracture of hip NOS (S72.0-)

  The appropriate 7th character is to be added to each code from category S32

A	initial encounter for closed fracture
B	initial encounter for open fracture
D	subsequent encounter for fracture with routine healing
G	subsequent encounter for fracture with delayed healing
K	subsequent encounter for fracture with nonunion
S	sequela

● **S32.0**   **Fracture of lumbar vertebra**
   Fracture of lumbar spine NOS

  ● **S32.00**   **Fracture of unspecified lumbar vertebra**

   ● **S32.000**   **Wedge compression fracture of unspecified lumbar vertebra** A, B 🐾

   ● **S32.001**   **Stable burst fracture of unspecified lumbar vertebra** A, B 🐾

   ● **S32.002**   **Unstable burst fracture of unspecified lumbar vertebra** A, B 🐾

   ● **S32.008**   **Other fracture of unspecified lumbar vertebra** A, B 🐾

   ● **S32.009**   **Unspecified fracture of unspecified lumbar vertebra** A, B 🐾

  ● **S32.01**   **Fracture of first lumbar vertebra**

   ● **S32.010**   **Wedge compression fracture of first lumbar vertebra** A, B 🐾

   ● **S32.011**   **Stable burst fracture of first lumbar vertebra** A, B 🐾

   ● **S32.012**   **Unstable burst fracture of first lumbar vertebra** A, B 🐾

   ● **S32.018**   **Other fracture of first lumbar vertebra** A, B 🐾

   ● **S32.019**   **Unspecified fracture of first lumbar vertebra** A, B 🐾

  ● **S32.02**   **Fracture of second lumbar vertebra**

   ● **S32.020**   **Wedge compression fracture of second lumbar vertebra** A, B 🐾

   ● **S32.021**   **Stable burst fracture of second lumbar vertebra** A, B 🐾

   ● **S32.022**   **Unstable burst fracture of second lumbar vertebra** A, B 🐾

   ● **S32.028**   **Other fracture of second lumbar vertebra** A, B 🐾

   ● **S32.029**   **Unspecified fracture of second lumbar vertebra** A, B 🐾

▶ New   ⟹ Revised   ~~deleted~~ Deleted   Excludes 1   Excludes 2   Includes   Use additional   Code first   Code also   Key words

1262   OGCR Official Guidelines   X Assign placeholder X   ● Use Additional Character(s)   ▷ Manifestation Code   🐾 Hierarchical Condition Category   **Coding Clinic**

● **S32.03**   Fracture of third lumbar vertebra
  ● **S32.030**   Wedge compression fracture of third lumbar vertebra   A, B 🗲
  ● **S32.031**   Stable burst fracture of third lumbar vertebra   A, B 🗲
  ● **S32.032**   Unstable burst fracture of third lumbar vertebra   A, B 🗲
  ● **S32.038**   Other fracture of third lumbar vertebra   A, B 🗲
  ● **S32.039**   Unspecified fracture of third lumbar vertebra   A, B 🗲

● **S32.04**   Fracture of fourth lumbar vertebra
  ● **S32.040**   Wedge compression fracture of fourth lumbar vertebra   A, B 🗲
  ● **S32.041**   Stable burst fracture of fourth lumbar vertebra   A, B 🗲
  ● **S32.042**   Unstable burst fracture of fourth lumbar vertebra   A, B 🗲
  ● **S32.048**   Other fracture of fourth lumbar vertebra   A, B 🗲
  ● **S32.049**   Unspecified fracture of fourth lumbar vertebra   A, B 🗲

● **S32.05**   Fracture of fifth lumbar vertebra
  ● **S32.050**   Wedge compression fracture of fifth lumbar vertebra   A, B 🗲
  ● **S32.051**   Stable burst fracture of fifth lumbar vertebra   A, B 🗲
  ● **S32.052**   Unstable burst fracture of fifth lumbar vertebra   A, B 🗲
  ● **S32.058**   Other fracture of fifth lumbar vertebra   A, B 🗲
  ● **S32.059**   Unspecified fracture of fifth lumbar vertebra   A, B 🗲

● **S32.1**   Fracture of sacrum
  For vertical fractures, code to most medial fracture extension
  Use two codes if both a vertical and transverse fracture are present
  Code also any associated fracture of pelvic ring (S32.8-)
  X ● **S32.10**   Unspecified fracture of sacrum   A, B 🗲
  ● **S32.11**   Zone I fracture of sacrum
    Vertical sacral ala fracture of sacrum
    ● **S32.110**   Nondisplaced Zone I fracture of sacrum   A, B 🗲
    ● **S32.111**   Minimally displaced Zone I fracture of sacrum   A, B 🗲
    ● **S32.112**   Severely displaced Zone I fracture of sacrum   A, B 🗲
    ● **S32.119**   Unspecified Zone I fracture of sacrum   A, B 🗲
  ● **S32.12**   Zone II fracture of sacrum
    Vertical foraminal region fracture of sacrum
    ● **S32.120**   Nondisplaced Zone II fracture of sacrum   A, B 🗲
    ● **S32.121**   Minimally displaced Zone II fracture of sacrum   A, B 🗲
    ● **S32.122**   Severely displaced Zone II fracture of sacrum   A, B 🗲
    ● **S32.129**   Unspecified Zone II fracture of sacrum   A, B 🗲
  ● **S32.13**   Zone III fracture of sacrum
    Vertical fracture into spinal canal region of sacrum
    ● **S32.130**   Nondisplaced Zone III fracture of sacrum   A, B 🗲
    ● **S32.131**   Minimally displaced Zone III fracture of sacrum   A, B 🗲
    ● **S32.132**   Severely displaced Zone III fracture of sacrum   A, B 🗲
    ● **S32.139**   Unspecified Zone III fracture of sacrum   A, B 🗲

X ● **S32.14**   Type 1 fracture of sacrum   A, B 🗲
  Transverse flexion fracture of sacrum without displacement
X ● **S32.15**   Type 2 fracture of sacrum   A, B 🗲
  Transverse flexion fracture of sacrum with posterior displacement
X ● **S32.16**   Type 3 fracture of sacrum   A, B 🗲
  Transverse extension fracture of sacrum with anterior displacement
X ● **S32.17**   Type 4 fracture of sacrum   A, B 🗲
  Transverse segmental comminution of upper sacrum
X ● **S32.19**   Other fracture of sacrum   A, B 🗲

X ● **S32.2**   Fracture of coccyx   A, B 🗲
● **S32.3**   Fracture of ilium
  Excludes1   fracture of ilium with associated disruption of pelvic ring (S32.8-)
  ● **S32.30**   Unspecified fracture of ilium
    ● **S32.301**   Unspecified fracture of right ilium   A, B 🗲
    ● **S32.302**   Unspecified fracture of left ilium   A, B 🗲
    ● **S32.309**   Unspecified fracture of unspecified ilium   A, B 🗲
  ● **S32.31**   Avulsion fracture of ilium
    ● **S32.311**   Displaced avulsion fracture of right ilium   A, B 🗲
    ● **S32.312**   Displaced avulsion fracture of left ilium   A, B 🗲
    ● **S32.313**   Displaced avulsion fracture of unspecified ilium   A, B 🗲
    ● **S32.314**   Nondisplaced avulsion fracture of right ilium   A, B 🗲
    ● **S32.315**   Nondisplaced avulsion fracture of left ilium   A, B 🗲
    ● **S32.316**   Nondisplaced avulsion fracture of unspecified ilium   A, B 🗲
  ● **S32.39**   Other fracture of ilium
    ● **S32.391**   Other fracture of right ilium   A, B 🗲
    ● **S32.392**   Other fracture of left ilium   A, B 🗲
    ● **S32.399**   Other fracture of unspecified ilium   A, B 🗲

● **S32.4**   Fracture of acetabulum
  Code also any associated fracture of pelvic ring (S32.8-)
  ● **S32.40**   Unspecified fracture of acetabulum
    ● **S32.401**   Unspecified fracture of right acetabulum   A, B 🗲
    ● **S32.402**   Unspecified fracture of left acetabulum   A, B 🗲
    ● **S32.409**   Unspecified fracture of unspecified acetabulum   A, B 🗲
  ● **S32.41**   Fracture of anterior wall of acetabulum
    ● **S32.411**   Displaced fracture of anterior wall of right acetabulum   A, B 🗲
    ● **S32.412**   Displaced fracture of anterior wall of left acetabulum   A, B 🗲
    ● **S32.413**   Displaced fracture of anterior wall of unspecified acetabulum   A, B 🗲
    ● **S32.414**   Nondisplaced fracture of anterior wall of right acetabulum   A, B 🗲
    ● **S32.415**   Nondisplaced fracture of anterior wall of left acetabulum   A, B 🗲
    ● **S32.416**   Nondisplaced fracture of anterior wall of unspecified acetabulum   A, B 🗲

●S32.42   Fracture of posterior wall of acetabulum
   ●S32.421   Displaced fracture of posterior wall of right acetabulum   A, B 🐾
   ●S32.422   Displaced fracture of posterior wall of left acetabulum   A, B 🐾
   ●S32.423   Displaced fracture of posterior wall of unspecified acetabulum   A, B 🐾
   ●S32.424   Nondisplaced fracture of posterior wall of right acetabulum   A, B 🐾
   ●S32.425   Nondisplaced fracture of posterior wall of left acetabulum   A, B 🐾
   ●S32.426   Nondisplaced fracture of posterior wall of unspecified acetabulum   A, B 🐾

●S32.43   Fracture of anterior column [iliopubic] of acetabulum
   ●S32.431   Displaced fracture of anterior column [iliopubic] of right acetabulum   A, B 🐾
   ●S32.432   Displaced fracture of anterior column [iliopubic] of left acetabulum   A, B 🐾
   ●S32.433   Displaced fracture of anterior column [iliopubic] of unspecified acetabulum   A, B 🐾
   ●S32.434   Nondisplaced fracture of anterior column [iliopubic] of right acetabulum   A, B 🐾
   ●S32.435   Nondisplaced fracture of anterior column [iliopubic] of left acetabulum   A, B 🐾
   ●S32.436   Nondisplaced fracture of anterior column [iliopubic] of unspecified acetabulum   A, B 🐾

●S32.44   Fracture of posterior column [ilioischial] of acetabulum
   ●S32.441   Displaced fracture of posterior column [ilioischial] of right acetabulum   A, B 🐾
   ●S32.442   Displaced fracture of posterior column [ilioischial] of left acetabulum   A, B 🐾
   ●S32.443   Displaced fracture of posterior column [ilioischial] of unspecified acetabulum   A, B 🐾
   ●S32.444   Nondisplaced fracture of posterior column [ilioischial] of right acetabulum   A, B 🐾
   ●S32.445   Nondisplaced fracture of posterior column [ilioischial] of left acetabulum   A, B 🐾
   ●S32.446   Nondisplaced fracture of posterior column [ilioischial] of unspecified acetabulum   A, B 🐾

●S32.45   Transverse fracture of acetabulum
   ●S32.451   Displaced transverse fracture of right acetabulum   A, B 🐾
   ●S32.452   Displaced transverse fracture of left acetabulum   A, B 🐾
   ●S32.453   Displaced transverse fracture of unspecified acetabulum   A, B 🐾
   ●S32.454   Nondisplaced transverse fracture of right acetabulum   A, B 🐾
   ●S32.455   Nondisplaced transverse fracture of left acetabulum   A, B 🐾
   ●S32.456   Nondisplaced transverse fracture of unspecified acetabulum   A, B 🐾

●S32.46   Associated transverse-posterior fracture of acetabulum
   ●S32.461   Displaced associated transverse-posterior fracture of right acetabulum   A, B 🐾
   ●S32.462   Displaced associated transverse-posterior fracture of left acetabulum   A, B 🐾
   ●S32.463   Displaced associated transverse-posterior fracture of unspecified acetabulum   A, B 🐾
   ●S32.464   Nondisplaced associated transverse-posterior fracture of right acetabulum   A, B 🐾
   ●S32.465   Nondisplaced associated transverse-posterior fracture of left acetabulum   A, B 🐾
   ●S32.466   Nondisplaced associated transverse-posterior fracture of unspecified acetabulum   A, B 🐾

●S32.47   Fracture of medial wall of acetabulum
   ●S32.471   Displaced fracture of medial wall of right acetabulum   A, B 🐾
   ●S32.472   Displaced fracture of medial wall of left acetabulum   A, B 🐾
   ●S32.473   Displaced fracture of medial wall of unspecified acetabulum   A, B 🐾
   ●S32.474   Nondisplaced fracture of medial wall of right acetabulum   A, B 🐾
   ●S32.475   Nondisplaced fracture of medial wall of left acetabulum   A, B 🐾
   ●S32.476   Nondisplaced fracture of medial wall of unspecified acetabulum   A, B 🐾

●S32.48   Dome fracture of acetabulum
   ●S32.481   Displaced dome fracture of right acetabulum   A, B 🐾
   ●S32.482   Displaced dome fracture of left acetabulum   A, B 🐾
   ●S32.483   Displaced dome fracture of unspecified acetabulum   A, B 🐾
   ●S32.484   Nondisplaced dome fracture of right acetabulum   A, B 🐾
   ●S32.485   Nondisplaced dome fracture of left acetabulum   A, B 🐾
   ●S32.486   Nondisplaced dome fracture of unspecified acetabulum   A, B 🐾

●S32.49   Other fracture of acetabulum
   ●S32.491   Other fracture of right acetabulum   A, B 🐾
   ●S32.492   Other fracture of left acetabulum   A, B 🐾
   ●S32.499   Other fracture of unspecified acetabulum   A, B 🐾

●S32.5   Fracture of pubis
   Excludes1   fracture of pubis with associated disruption of pelvic ring (S32.8-)
  ●S32.50   Unspecified fracture of pubis
   ●S32.501   Unspecified fracture of right pubis   A, B 🐾
   ●S32.502   Unspecified fracture of left pubis   A, B 🐾
   ●S32.509   Unspecified fracture of unspecified pubis   A, B 🐾
  ●S32.51   Fracture of superior rim of pubis
   ●S32.511   Fracture of superior rim of right pubis   A, B 🐾
   ●S32.512   Fracture of superior rim of left pubis   A, B 🐾
   ●S32.519   Fracture of superior rim of unspecified pubis   A, B 🐾

▶ New   ⇒ Revised   ~~deleted~~ Deleted   Excludes 1   Excludes 2   Includes   Use additional   Code first   Code also   Key words
OGCR Official Guidelines   X Assign placeholder X   ● Use Additional Character(s)   ▷ Manifestation Code   🐾 Hierarchical Condition Category   **Coding Clinic**

● **S32.59**   Other specified fracture of pubis
     ● **S32.591**   Other specified fracture of right pubis A, B 🔒
     ● **S32.592**   Other specified fracture of left pubis A, B 🔒
     ● **S32.599**   Other specified fracture of unspecified pubis   A, B 🔒

● **S32.6**   Fracture of ischium
    Excludes1   fracture of ischium with associated disruption of pelvic ring (S32.8-)

    ● **S32.60**   Unspecified fracture of ischium
     ● **S32.601**   Unspecified fracture of right ischium A, B 🔒
     ● **S32.602**   Unspecified fracture of left ischium A, B 🔒
     ● **S32.609**   Unspecified fracture of unspecified ischium   A, B 🔒

    ● **S32.61**   Avulsion fracture of ischium
     ● **S32.611**   Displaced avulsion fracture of right ischium   A, B 🔒
     ● **S32.612**   Displaced avulsion fracture of left ischium   A, B 🔒
     ● **S32.613**   Displaced avulsion fracture of unspecified ischium   A, B 🔒
     ● **S32.614**   Nondisplaced avulsion fracture of right ischium   A, B 🔒
     ● **S32.615**   Nondisplaced avulsion fracture of left ischium   A, B 🔒
     ● **S32.616**   Nondisplaced avulsion fracture of unspecified ischium   A, B 🔒

    ● **S32.69**   Other specified fracture of ischium
     ● **S32.691**   Other specified fracture of right ischium   A, B 🔒
     ● **S32.692**   Other specified fracture of left ischium   A, B 🔒
     ● **S32.699**   Other specified fracture of unspecified ischium   A, B 🔒

● **S32.8**   Fracture of other parts of pelvis
    Code also any associated:
     fracture of acetabulum (S32.4-)
     sacral fracture (S32.1-)

    ● **S32.81**   Multiple fractures of pelvis with disruption of pelvic ring
      Multiple pelvic fractures with disruption of pelvic circle
     ● **S32.810**   Multiple fractures of pelvis with stable disruption of pelvic ring A, B 🔒
     ● **S32.811**   Multiple fractures of pelvis with unstable disruption of pelvic ring A, B 🔒

    X ● **S32.82**   Multiple fractures of pelvis without disruption of pelvic ring   A, B 🔒
      Multiple pelvic fractures without disruption of pelvic circle

    X ● **S32.89**   Fracture of other parts of pelvis   A, B 🔒

X ● **S32.9**   Fracture of unspecified parts of lumbosacral spine and pelvis   A, B 🔒
    Fracture of lumbosacral spine NOS
    Fracture of pelvis NOS
    Coding Clinic: 2012, Q4, P93

● **S33**   Dislocation and sprain of joints and ligaments of lumbar spine and pelvis
    Includes   avulsion of joint or ligament of lumbar spine and pelvis
      laceration of cartilage, joint or ligament of lumbar spine and pelvis
      sprain of cartilage, joint or ligament of lumbar spine and pelvis
      traumatic hemarthrosis of joint or ligament of lumbar spine and pelvis
      traumatic rupture of joint or ligament of lumbar spine and pelvis
      traumatic subluxation of joint or ligament of lumbar spine and pelvis
      traumatic tear of joint or ligament of lumbar spine and pelvis

Code also any associated open wound
    Excludes1   nontraumatic rupture or displacement of lumbar intervertebral disc NOS (M51.-)
      obstetric damage to pelvic joints and ligaments (O71.6)

    Excludes2   dislocation and sprain of joints and ligaments of hip (S73.-)
      strain of muscle of lower back and pelvis (S39.01-)

The appropriate 7th character is to be added to each code from category S33

A	initial encounter
D	subsequent encounter
S	sequela

X ● **S33.0**   Traumatic rupture of lumbar intervertebral disc
    Excludes1   rupture or displacement (nontraumatic) of lumbar intervertebral disc NOS (M51.- with fifth character 6)

● **S33.1**   Subluxation and dislocation of lumbar vertebra
    Code also any associated:
     open wound of abdomen, lower back and pelvis (S31)
     spinal cord injury (S24.0, S24.1-, S34.0-, S34.1-)
    Excludes2   fracture of lumbar vertebrae (S32.0-)

    ● **S33.10**   Subluxation and dislocation of unspecified lumbar vertebra
     ● **S33.100**   Subluxation of unspecified lumbar vertebra
     ● **S33.101**   Dislocation of unspecified lumbar vertebra

    ● **S33.11**   Subluxation and dislocation of L1/L2 lumbar vertebra
     ● **S33.110**   Subluxation of L1/L2 lumbar vertebra
     ● **S33.111**   Dislocation of L1/L2 lumbar vertebra

    ● **S33.12**   Subluxation and dislocation of L2/L3 lumbar vertebra
     ● **S33.120**   Subluxation of L2/L3 lumbar vertebra
     ● **S33.121**   Dislocation of L2/L3 lumbar vertebra

    ● **S33.13**   Subluxation and dislocation of L3/L4 lumbar vertebra
     ● **S33.130**   Subluxation of L3/L4 lumbar vertebra
     ● **S33.131**   Dislocation of L3/L4 lumbar vertebra

    ● **S33.14**   Subluxation and dislocation of L4/L5 lumbar vertebra
     ● **S33.140**   Subluxation of L4/L5 lumbar vertebra
     ● **S33.141**   Dislocation of L4/L5 lumbar vertebra

X ● **S33.2**   Dislocation of sacroiliac and sacrococcygeal joint

● **S33.3** Dislocation of other and unspecified parts of lumbar spine and pelvis

  X● **S33.30** Dislocation of unspecified parts of lumbar spine and pelvis

  X● **S33.39** Dislocation of other parts of lumbar spine and pelvis

X● **S33.4** Traumatic rupture of symphysis pubis

X● **S33.5** Sprain of ligaments of lumbar spine

X● **S33.6** Sprain of sacroiliac joint

X● **S33.8** Sprain of other parts of lumbar spine and pelvis

X● **S33.9** Sprain of unspecified parts of lumbar spine and pelvis

● **S34** Injury of lumbar and sacral spinal cord and nerves at abdomen, lower back and pelvis level

  Note: Code to highest level of lumbar cord injury

    Injuries to the spinal cord (S34.0 and S34.1) refer to the cord level and not bone level injury, and can affect nerve roots at and below the level given.

    The appropriate 7th character is to be added to each code from category S34

A	initial encounter
D	subsequent encounter
S	sequela

  Code also any associated:
    fracture of vertebra (S22.0-, S32.0-)
    open wound of abdomen, lower back and pelvis (S31.-)
    transient paralysis (R29.5)

● **S34.0** Concussion and edema of lumbar and sacral spinal cord

  X● **S34.01** Concussion and edema of lumbar spinal cord A, D, S 🐾

  X● **S34.02** Concussion and edema of sacral spinal cord A, D, S 🐾
      Concussion and edema of conus medullaris

● **S34.1** Other and unspecified injury of lumbar and sacral spinal cord

  ● **S34.10** Unspecified injury to lumbar spinal cord

    ● **S34.101** Unspecified injury to L_1 level of lumbar spinal cord A, D, S 🐾
        Unspecified injury to lumbar spinal cord level 1

    ● **S34.102** Unspecified injury to L_2 level of lumbar spinal cord A, D, S 🐾
        Unspecified injury to lumbar spinal cord level 2

    ● **S34.103** Unspecified injury to L_3 level of lumbar spinal cord A, D, S 🐾
        Unspecified injury to lumbar spinal cord level 3

    ● **S34.104** Unspecified injury to L_4 level of lumbar spinal cord A, D, S 🐾
        Unspecified injury to lumbar spinal cord level 4

    ● **S34.105** Unspecified injury to L_5 level of lumbar spinal cord A, D, S 🐾
        Unspecified injury to lumbar spinal cord level 5

    ● **S34.109** Unspecified injury to unspecified level of lumbar spinal cord A, D, S 🐾

  ● **S34.11** Complete lesion of lumbar spinal cord

    ● **S34.111** Complete lesion of L_1 level of lumbar spinal cord A, D, S 🐾
        Complete lesion of lumbar spinal cord level 1

    ● **S34.112** Complete lesion of L_2 level of lumbar spinal cord A, D, S 🐾
        Complete lesion of lumbar spinal cord level 2

    ● **S34.113** Complete lesion of L_3 level of lumbar spinal cord A, D, S 🐾
        Complete lesion of lumbar spinal cord level 3

    ● **S34.114** Complete lesion of L_4 level of lumbar spinal cord A, D, S 🐾
        Complete lesion of lumbar spinal cord level 4

    ● **S34.115** Complete lesion of L_5 level of lumbar spinal cord A, D, S 🐾
        Complete lesion of lumbar spinal cord level 5

    ● **S34.119** Complete lesion of unspecified level of lumbar spinal cord A, D, S 🐾

  ● **S34.12** Incomplete lesion of lumbar spinal cord

    ● **S34.121** Incomplete lesion of L_1 level of lumbar spinal cord A, D, S 🐾
        Incomplete lesion of lumbar spinal cord level 1

    ● **S34.122** Incomplete lesion of L_2 level of lumbar spinal cord A, D, S 🐾
        Incomplete lesion of lumbar spinal cord level 2

    ● **S34.123** Incomplete lesion of L_3 level of lumbar spinal cord A, D, S 🐾
        Incomplete lesion of lumbar spinal cord level 3

    ● **S34.124** Incomplete lesion of L_4 level of lumbar spinal cord A, D, S 🐾
        Incomplete lesion of lumbar spinal cord level 4

    ● **S34.125** Incomplete lesion of L_5 level of lumbar spinal cord A, D, S 🐾
        Incomplete lesion of lumbar spinal cord level 5

    ● **S34.129** Incomplete lesion of unspecified level of lumbar spinal cord A, D, S 🐾

  ● **S34.13** Other and unspecified injury to sacral spinal cord
    Other injury to conus medullaris

    ● **S34.131** Complete lesion of sacral spinal cord A, D, S 🐾
        Complete lesion of conus medullaris

    ● **S34.132** Incomplete lesion of sacral spinal cord A, D, S 🐾
        Incomplete lesion of conus medullaris

    ● **S34.139** Unspecified injury to sacral spinal cord A, D, S 🐾
        Unspecified injury of conus medullaris

● **S34.2** Injury of nerve root of lumbar and sacral spine

  X● **S34.21** Injury of nerve root of lumbar spine

  X● **S34.22** Injury of nerve root of sacral spine

X● **S34.3** Injury of cauda equina A, D, S 🐾

X● **S34.4** Injury of lumbosacral plexus

X● **S34.5** Injury of lumbar, sacral and pelvic sympathetic nerves
    Injury of celiac ganglion or plexus
    Injury of hypogastric plexus
    Injury of mesenteric plexus (inferior) (superior)
    Injury of splanchnic nerve

X● **S34.6** Injury of peripheral nerve(s) at abdomen, lower back and pelvis level

X● **S34.8** Injury of other nerves at abdomen, lower back and pelvis level

X● **S34.9** Injury of unspecified nerves at abdomen, lower back and pelvis level

▶ New   ⇒ Revised   ~~deleted~~ Deleted   Excludes 1   Excludes 2   Includes   Use additional   Code first   Code also   Key words

OGCR Official Guidelines   X Assign placeholder X   ● Use Additional Character(s)   ▶ Manifestation Code   🐾 Hierarchical Condition Category   **Coding Clinic**

● **S35   Injury of blood vessels at abdomen, lower back and pelvis level**

The appropriate 7th character is to be added to each code from category S35

A	initial encounter
D	subsequent encounter
S	sequela

Code also any associated open wound (S31.-)

● **S35.0   Injury of abdominal aorta**

Excludes1   injury of aorta NOS (S25.0)

X ● **S35.00   Unspecified injury of abdominal aorta**

X ● **S35.01   Minor laceration of abdominal aorta**
Incomplete transection of abdominal aorta
Laceration of abdominal aorta NOS
Superficial laceration of abdominal aorta

X ● **S35.02   Major laceration of abdominal aorta**
Complete transection of abdominal aorta
Traumatic rupture of abdominal aorta

X ● **S35.09   Other injury of abdominal aorta**

● **S35.1   Injury of inferior vena cava**
Injury of hepatic vein

Excludes1   injury of vena cava NOS (S25.2)

X ● **S35.10   Unspecified injury of inferior vena cava**

X ● **S35.11   Minor laceration of inferior vena cava**
Incomplete transection of inferior vena cava
Laceration of inferior vena cava NOS
Superficial laceration of inferior vena cava

X ● **S35.12   Major laceration of inferior vena cava**
Complete transection of inferior vena cava
Traumatic rupture of inferior vena cava

X ● **S35.19   Other injury of inferior vena cava**

● **S35.2   Injury of celiac or mesenteric artery and branches**

● **S35.21   Injury of celiac artery**

● **S35.211   Minor laceration of celiac artery**
Incomplete transection of celiac artery
Laceration of celiac artery NOS
Superficial laceration of celiac artery

● **S35.212   Major laceration of celiac artery**
Complete transection of celiac artery
Traumatic rupture of celiac artery

● **S35.218   Other injury of celiac artery**

● **S35.219   Unspecified injury of celiac artery**

● **S35.22   Injury of superior mesenteric artery**

● **S35.221   Minor laceration of superior mesenteric artery**
Incomplete transection of superior mesenteric artery
Laceration of superior mesenteric artery NOS
Superficial laceration of superior mesenteric artery

● **S35.222   Major laceration of superior mesenteric artery**
Complete transection of superior mesenteric artery
Traumatic rupture of superior mesenteric artery

● **S35.228   Other injury of superior mesenteric artery**

● **S35.229   Unspecified injury of superior mesenteric artery**

● **S35.23   Injury of inferior mesenteric artery**

● **S35.231   Minor laceration of inferior mesenteric artery**
Incomplete transection of inferior mesenteric artery
Laceration of inferior mesenteric artery NOS
Superficial laceration of inferior mesenteric artery

● **S35.232   Major laceration of inferior mesenteric artery**
Complete transection of inferior mesenteric artery
Traumatic rupture of inferior mesenteric artery

● **S35.238   Other injury of inferior mesenteric artery**

● **S35.239   Unspecified injury of inferior mesenteric artery**

● **S35.29   Injury of branches of celiac and mesenteric artery**
Injury of gastric artery
Injury of gastroduodenal artery
Injury of hepatic artery
Injury of splenic artery

● **S35.291   Minor laceration of branches of celiac and mesenteric artery**
Incomplete transection of branches of celiac and mesenteric artery
Laceration of branches of celiac and mesenteric artery NOS
Superficial laceration of branches of celiac and mesenteric artery

● **S35.292   Major laceration of branches of celiac and mesenteric artery**
Complete transection of branches of celiac and mesenteric artery
Traumatic rupture of branches of celiac and mesenteric artery

● **S35.298   Other injury of branches of celiac and mesenteric artery**

● **S35.299   Unspecified injury of branches of celiac and mesenteric artery**

● **S35.3   Injury of portal or splenic vein and branches**

● **S35.31   Injury of portal vein**

● **S35.311   Laceration of portal vein**

● **S35.318   Other specified injury of portal vein**

● **S35.319   Unspecified injury of portal vein**

● **S35.32   Injury of splenic vein**

● **S35.321   Laceration of splenic vein**

● **S35.328   Other specified injury of splenic vein**

● **S35.329   Unspecified injury of splenic vein**

● **S35.33   Injury of superior mesenteric vein**

● **S35.331   Laceration of superior mesenteric vein**

● **S35.338   Other specified injury of superior mesenteric vein**

● **S35.339   Unspecified injury of superior mesenteric vein**

● **S35.34   Injury of inferior mesenteric vein**

● **S35.341   Laceration of inferior mesenteric vein**

● **S35.348   Other specified injury of inferior mesenteric vein**

● **S35.349   Unspecified injury of inferior mesenteric vein**

S35.4 **Injury of renal blood vessels**
  S35.40 **Unspecified injury of renal blood vessel**
    S35.401 Unspecified injury of **right renal artery**
    S35.402 Unspecified injury of left renal artery
    S35.403 Unspecified injury of **unspecified** renal **artery**
    S35.404 Unspecified injury of **right renal vein**
    S35.405 Unspecified injury of **left renal vein**
    S35.406 Unspecified injury of **unspecified** renal **vein**
  S35.41 **Laceration** of renal blood vessel
    S35.411 **Laceration** of **right renal artery**
    S35.412 **Laceration** of **left renal artery**
    S35.413 **Laceration** of **unspecified renal artery**
    S35.414 **Laceration** of **right renal vein**
    S35.415 **Laceration** of **left renal vein**
    S35.416 **Laceration** of **unspecified renal vein**
  S35.49 **Other specified injury of renal blood vessel**
    S35.491 **Other specified injury of right renal artery**
    S35.492 **Other specified injury of left renal artery**
    S35.493 **Other specified injury of unspecified** renal **artery**
    S35.494 **Other specified injury of right renal vein**
    S35.495 **Other specified injury of left renal vein**
    S35.496 **Other specified injury of unspecified** renal **vein**
S35.5 **Injury of iliac blood vessels**
  X S35.50 **Injury of unspecified iliac blood vessel(s)**
  S35.51 **Injury of iliac artery or vein**
        Injury of hypogastric artery or vein
    S35.511 Injury of **right iliac artery**
    S35.512 Injury of **left iliac artery**
    S35.513 Injury of **unspecified iliac artery**
    S35.514 Injury of **right iliac vein**
    S35.515 Injury of **left iliac vein**
    S35.516 Injury of **unspecified iliac vein**
  S35.53 **Injury of uterine artery or vein**
    S35.531 Injury of **right uterine artery** ♀
    S35.532 Injury of **left uterine artery** ♀
    S35.533 Injury of **unspecified uterine artery** ♀
    S35.534 Injury of **right uterine vein** ♀
    S35.535 Injury of **left uterine vein** ♀
    S35.536 Injury of **unspecified uterine vein** ♀
  X S35.59 **Injury of other iliac blood vessels**
S35.8 **Injury of other blood vessels at abdomen, lower back and pelvis level**
        Injury of ovarian artery or vein
  S35.8X **Injury of other blood vessels at abdomen, lower back and pelvis level**
    S35.8X1 **Laceration** of other blood vessels at abdomen, lower back and pelvis level
    S35.8X8 **Other specified injury of other blood vessels at abdomen, lower back and pelvis level**
    S35.8X9 **Unspecified injury of other blood vessels at abdomen, lower back and pelvis level**

S35.9 **Injury of unspecified blood vessel at abdomen, lower back and pelvis level**
  X S35.90 **Unspecified injury of unspecified blood vessel at abdomen, lower back and pelvis level**
  X S35.91 **Laceration of unspecified blood vessel at abdomen, lower back and pelvis level**
  X S35.99 **Other specified injury of unspecified blood vessel at abdomen, lower back and pelvis level**
S36 **Injury of intra-abdominal organs**
    The appropriate 7th character is to be added to each code from category S36

A	initial encounter
D	subsequent encounter
S	sequela

    Code also any associated open wound (S31.-)
S36.0 **Injury of spleen**
  X S36.00 **Unspecified injury of spleen**
  S36.02 **Contusion of spleen**
    S36.020 **Minor contusion of spleen**
        Contusion of spleen less than 2 cm
    S36.021 **Major contusion of spleen**
        Contusion of spleen greater than 2 cm
    S36.029 **Unspecified contusion of spleen**
        Coding Clinic: 2015, Q2, P36, Q1, P11
  S36.03 **Laceration of spleen**
    S36.030 **Superficial (capsular) laceration of spleen**
        Laceration of spleen less than 1 cm
        Minor laceration of spleen
    S36.031 **Moderate laceration of spleen**
        Laceration of spleen 1 to 3 cm
        Coding Clinic: 2015, Q2, P36, Q1, P11
    S36.032 **Major laceration of spleen**
        Avulsion of spleen
        Laceration of spleen greater than 3 cm
        Massive laceration of spleen
        Multiple moderate lacerations of spleen
        Stellate laceration of spleen
    S36.039 **Unspecified laceration of spleen**
  X S36.09 **Other injury of spleen**
S36.1 **Injury of liver and gallbladder and bile duct**
  S36.11 **Injury of liver**
    S36.112 **Contusion of liver**
    S36.113 **Laceration of liver, unspecified degree**
    S36.114 **Minor laceration of liver**
        Laceration involving capsule only, or, without significant involvement of hepatic parenchyma [i.e., less than 1 cm deep]
    S36.115 **Moderate laceration of liver**
        Laceration involving parenchyma but without major disruption of parenchyma [i.e., less than 10 cm long and less than 3 cm deep]
    S36.116 **Major laceration of liver**
        Laceration with significant disruption of hepatic parenchyma [i.e., greater than 10 cm long and 3 cm deep]
        Multiple moderate lacerations, with or without hematoma
        Stellate laceration of liver
    S36.118 **Other injury of liver**
    S36.119 **Unspecified injury of liver**
        Coding Clinic: 2015, Q2, P17

▶ New   ⇒ Revised   ~~deleted~~ Deleted   Excludes 1   Excludes 2   Includes   Use additional   Code first   Code also   Key words

OGCR Official Guidelines   X Assign placeholder X   ● Use Additional Character(s)   ▷ Manifestation Code   🐴 Hierarchical Condition Category   Coding Clinic

● S36.12　Injury of gallbladder
  ● S36.122　Contusion of gallbladder
  ● S36.123　Laceration of gallbladder
  ● S36.128　Other injury of gallbladder
  ● S36.129　Unspecified injury of gallbladder
X ● S36.13　Injury of bile duct
● S36.2　Injury of pancreas
  ● S36.20　Unspecified injury of pancreas
    ● S36.200　Unspecified injury of head of pancreas
    ● S36.201　Unspecified injury of body of pancreas
    ● S36.202　Unspecified injury of tail of pancreas
    ● S36.209　Unspecified injury of unspecified part of pancreas
  ● S36.22　Contusion of pancreas
    ● S36.220　Contusion of head of pancreas
    ● S36.221　Contusion of body of pancreas
    ● S36.222　Contusion of tail of pancreas
    ● S36.229　Contusion of unspecified part of pancreas
  ● S36.23　Laceration of pancreas, unspecified degree
    ● S36.230　Laceration of head of pancreas, unspecified degree
    ● S36.231　Laceration of body of pancreas, unspecified degree
    ● S36.232　Laceration of tail of pancreas, unspecified degree
    ● S36.239　Laceration of unspecified part of pancreas, unspecified degree
  ● S36.24　Minor laceration of pancreas
    ● S36.240　Minor laceration of head of pancreas
    ● S36.241　Minor laceration of body of pancreas
    ● S36.242　Minor laceration of tail of pancreas
    ● S36.249　Minor laceration of unspecified part of pancreas
  ● S36.25　Moderate laceration of pancreas
    ● S36.250　Moderate laceration of head of pancreas
    ● S36.251　Moderate laceration of body of pancreas
    ● S36.252　Moderate laceration of tail of pancreas
    ● S36.259　Moderate laceration of unspecified part of pancreas
  ● S36.26　Major laceration of pancreas
    ● S36.260　Major laceration of head of pancreas
    ● S36.261　Major laceration of body of pancreas
    ● S36.262　Major laceration of tail of pancreas
    ● S36.269　Major laceration of unspecified part of pancreas
  ● S36.29　Other injury of pancreas
    ● S36.290　Other injury of head of pancreas
    ● S36.291　Other injury of body of pancreas
    ● S36.292　Other injury of tail of pancreas
    ● S36.299　Other injury of unspecified part of pancreas
● S36.3　Injury of stomach
X ● S36.30　Unspecified injury of stomach
X ● S36.32　Contusion of stomach
X ● S36.33　Laceration of stomach
X ● S36.39　Other injury of stomach

● S36.4　Injury of small intestine
  ● S36.40　Unspecified injury of small intestine
    ● S36.400　Unspecified injury of duodenum
    ● S36.408　Unspecified injury of other part of small intestine
    ● S36.409　Unspecified injury of unspecified part of small intestine
  ● S36.41　Primary blast injury of small intestine
        Blast injury of small intestine NOS
    ● S36.410　Primary blast injury of duodenum
    ● S36.418　Primary blast injury of other part of small intestine
    ● S36.419　Primary blast injury of unspecified part of small intestine
  ● S36.42　Contusion of small intestine
    ● S36.420　Contusion of duodenum
    ● S36.428　Contusion of other part of small intestine
    ● S36.429　Contusion of unspecified part of small intestine
  ● S36.43　Laceration of small intestine
    ● S36.430　Laceration of duodenum
    ● S36.438　Laceration of other part of small intestine
    ● S36.439　Laceration of unspecified part of small intestine
  ● S36.49　Other injury of small intestine
    ● S36.490　Other injury of duodenum
    ● S36.498　Other injury of other part of small intestine
    ● S36.499　Other injury of unspecified part of small intestine
● S36.5　Injury of colon
      Excludes2　injury of rectum (S36.6-)
  ● S36.50　Unspecified injury of colon
    ● S36.500　Unspecified injury of ascending [right] colon
    ● S36.501　Unspecified injury of transverse colon
    ● S36.502　Unspecified injury of descending [left] colon
    ● S36.503　Unspecified injury of sigmoid colon
    ● S36.508　Unspecified injury of other part of colon
    ● S36.509　Unspecified injury of unspecified part of colon
  ● S36.51　Primary blast injury of colon
        Blast injury of colon NOS
    ● S36.510　Primary blast injury of ascending [right] colon
    ● S36.511　Primary blast injury of transverse colon
    ● S36.512　Primary blast injury of descending [left] colon
    ● S36.513　Primary blast injury of sigmoid colon
    ● S36.518　Primary blast injury of other part of colon
    ● S36.519　Primary blast injury of unspecified part of colon
  ● S36.52　Contusion of colon
    ● S36.520　Contusion of ascending [right] colon
    ● S36.521　Contusion of transverse colon
    ● S36.522　Contusion of descending [left] colon
    ● S36.523　Contusion of sigmoid colon
    ● S36.528　Contusion of other part of colon
    ● S36.529　Contusion of unspecified part of colon

● **S36.53**   Laceration of colon
- ● **S36.530**   Laceration of ascending [right] colon
- ● **S36.531**   Laceration of transverse colon
- ● **S36.532**   Laceration of descending [left] colon
- ● **S36.533**   Laceration of sigmoid colon
- ● **S36.538**   Laceration of other part of colon
- **S36.539**   Laceration of unspecified part of colon

● **S36.59**   Other injury of colon
Secondary blast injury of colon
- ● **S36.590**   Other injury of ascending [right] colon
- ● **S36.591**   Other injury of transverse colon
- ● **S36.592**   Other injury of descending [left] colon
- ● **S36.593**   Other injury of sigmoid colon
- ● **S36.598**   Other injury of other part of colon
- ● **S36.599**   Other injury of unspecified part of colon

● **S36.6**   Injury of rectum
- X ● **S36.60**   Unspecified injury of rectum
- X ● **S36.61**   Primary blast injury of rectum
  Blast injury of rectum NOS
- X ● **S36.62**   Contusion of rectum
- X ● **S36.63**   Laceration of rectum
- X ● **S36.69**   Other injury of rectum
  Secondary blast injury of rectum

● **S36.8**   Injury of other intra-abdominal organs
- X ● **S36.81**   Injury of peritoneum
- ● **S36.89**   Injury of other intra-abdominal organs
  Injury of retroperitoneum
  - ● **S36.892**   Contusion of other intra-abdominal organs
  - ● **S36.893**   Laceration of other intra-abdominal organs
  - ● **S36.898**   Other injury of other intra-abdominal organs
  - **S36.899**   Unspecified injury of other intra-abdominal organs

● **S36.9**   Injury of unspecified intra-abdominal organ
- X ● **S36.90**   Unspecified injury of unspecified intra-abdominal organ
- X ● **S36.92**   Contusion of unspecified intra-abdominal organ
- X ● **S36.93**   Laceration of unspecified intra-abdominal organ
- X ● **S36.99**   Other injury of unspecified intra-abdominal organ

● **S37**   **Injury of urinary and pelvic organs**
Code also any associated open wound (S31.-)
Excludes1   obstetric trauma to pelvic organs (O71.-)
Excludes2   injury of peritoneum (S36.81)
              injury of retroperitoneum (S36.89-)

The appropriate 7th character is to be added to each code from category S37

> A   initial encounter
> D   subsequent encounter
> S   sequela

● **S37.0**   Injury of kidney
Excludes2   acute kidney injury (nontraumatic) (N17.9)
- ● **S37.00**   Unspecified injury of kidney
  - ● **S37.001**   Unspecified injury of right kidney
  - ● **S37.002**   Unspecified injury of left kidney
  - ● **S37.009**   Unspecified injury of unspecified kidney

● **S37.01**   Minor contusion of kidney
Contusion of kidney less than 2 cm
Contusion of kidney NOS
- ● **S37.011**   Minor contusion of right kidney
- ● **S37.012**   Minor contusion of left kidney
- ● **S37.019**   Minor contusion of unspecified kidney

● **S37.02**   Major contusion of kidney
Contusion of kidney greater than 2 cm
- ● **S37.021**   Major contusion of right kidney
- ● **S37.022**   Major contusion of left kidney
- ● **S37.029**   Major contusion of unspecified kidney

● **S37.03**   Laceration of kidney, unspecified degree
- ● **S37.031**   Laceration of right kidney, unspecified degree
- ● **S37.032**   Laceration of left kidney, unspecified degree
- ● **S37.039**   Laceration of unspecified kidney, unspecified degree

● **S37.04**   Minor laceration of kidney
Laceration of kidney less than 1 cm
- ● **S37.041**   Minor laceration of right kidney
- ● **S37.042**   Minor laceration of left kidney
- ● **S37.049**   Minor laceration of unspecified kidney

● **S37.05**   Moderate laceration of kidney
Laceration of kidney 1 to 3 cm
- ● **S37.051**   Moderate laceration of right kidney
- ● **S37.052**   Moderate laceration of left kidney
- ● **S37.059**   Moderate laceration of unspecified kidney

● **S37.06**   Major laceration of kidney
Avulsion of kidney
Laceration of kidney greater than 3 cm
Massive laceration of kidney
Multiple moderate lacerations of kidney
Stellate laceration of kidney
- ● **S37.061**   Major laceration of right kidney
- ● **S37.062**   Major laceration of left kidney
- ● **S37.069**   Major laceration of unspecified kidney

● **S37.09**   Other injury of kidney
- ● **S37.091**   Other injury of right kidney
- ● **S37.092**   Other injury of left kidney
- ● **S37.099**   Other injury of unspecified kidney

● **S37.1**   Injury of ureter
- X ● **S37.10**   Unspecified injury of ureter
- X ● **S37.12**   Contusion of ureter
- X ● **S37.13**   Laceration of ureter
- X ● **S37.19**   Other injury of ureter

● **S37.2**   Injury of bladder
- X ● **S37.20**   Unspecified injury of bladder
- X ● **S37.22**   Contusion of bladder
- X ● **S37.23**   Laceration of bladder
- X ● **S37.29**   Other injury of bladder

● **S37.3**   Injury of urethra
- X ● **S37.30**   Unspecified injury of urethra
- X ● **S37.32**   Contusion of urethra
- X ● **S37.33**   Laceration of urethra
- X ● **S37.39**   Other injury of urethra

● **S37.4**   Injury of ovary
- ● **S37.40**   Unspecified injury of ovary
  - ● **S37.401**   Unspecified injury of ovary, unilateral ♀
  - ● **S37.402**   Unspecified injury of ovary, bilateral ♀
  - ● **S37.409**   Unspecified injury of ovary, unspecified ♀

▶ New   ⇒ Revised   ~~deleted~~ Deleted   Excludes 1   Excludes 2   Includes   Use additional   Code first   Code also   Key words
OGCR Official Guidelines   X Assign placeholder X   ● Use Additional Character(s)   ▷ Manifestation Code   🄗 Hierarchical Condition Category   **Coding Clinic**

● **S37.42**   Contusion of ovary
    ● S37.421   Contusion of ovary, unilateral ♀
    ● S37.422   Contusion of ovary, bilateral ♀
    ● S37.429   Contusion of ovary, unspecified ♀
● **S37.43**   Laceration of ovary
    ● S37.431   Laceration of ovary, unilateral ♀
    ● S37.432   Laceration of ovary, bilateral ♀
    ● S37.439   Laceration of ovary, unspecified ♀
● **S37.49**   Other injury of ovary
    ● S37.491   Other injury of ovary, unilateral ♀
    ● S37.492   Other injury of ovary, bilateral ♀
    ● S37.499   Other injury of ovary, unspecified ♀
● **S37.5**   Injury of fallopian tube
   ● **S37.50**   Unspecified injury of fallopian tube
    ● S37.501   Unspecified injury of fallopian tube, unilateral ♀
    ● S37.502   Unspecified injury of fallopian tube, bilateral ♀
    ● S37.509   Unspecified injury of fallopian tube, unspecified ♀
   ● **S37.51**   Primary blast injury of fallopian tube
     Blast injury of fallopian tube NOS
    ● S37.511   Primary blast injury of fallopian tube, unilateral ♀
    ● S37.512   Primary blast injury of fallopian tube, bilateral ♀
    ● S37.519   Primary blast injury of fallopian tube, unspecified ♀
   ● **S37.52**   Contusion of fallopian tube
    ● S37.521   Contusion of fallopian tube, unilateral ♀
    ● S37.522   Contusion of fallopian tube, bilateral ♀
    ● S37.529   Contusion of fallopian tube, unspecified ♀
   ● **S37.53**   Laceration of fallopian tube
    ● S37.531   Laceration of fallopian tube, unilateral ♀
    ● S37.532   Laceration of fallopian tube, bilateral ♀
    ● S37.539   Laceration of fallopian tube, unspecified ♀
   ● **S37.59**   Other injury of fallopian tube
     Secondary blast injury of fallopian tube
    ● S37.591   Other injury of fallopian tube, unilateral ♀
    ● S37.592   Other injury of fallopian tube, bilateral ♀
    ● S37.599   Other injury of fallopian tube, unspecified ♀
● **S37.6**   Injury of uterus
    Excludes1   injury to gravid uterus (O9A.2-)
             injury to uterus during delivery (O71.-)
X ● **S37.60**   Unspecified injury of uterus ♀
X ● **S37.62**   Contusion of uterus ♀
X ● **S37.63**   Laceration of uterus ♀
X ● **S37.69**   Other injury of uterus ♀
● **S37.8**   Injury of other urinary and pelvic organs
   ● **S37.81**   Injury of adrenal gland
    ● S37.812   Contusion of adrenal gland
    ● S37.813   Laceration of adrenal gland
    ● S37.818   Other injury of adrenal gland
    ● S37.819   Unspecified injury of adrenal gland
   ● **S37.82**   Injury of prostate
    ● S37.822   Contusion of prostate ♂
    ● S37.823   Laceration of prostate ♂
    ● S37.828   Other injury of prostate ♂
    ● S37.829   Unspecified injury of prostate ♂

● **S37.89**   Injury of other urinary and pelvic organ
    ● S37.892   Contusion of other urinary and pelvic organ
    ● S37.893   Laceration of other urinary and pelvic organ
    ● S37.898   Other injury of other urinary and pelvic organ
    ● S37.899   Unspecified injury of other urinary and pelvic organ
● **S37.9**   Injury of unspecified urinary and pelvic organ
X ● **S37.90**   Unspecified injury of unspecified urinary and pelvic organ
X ● **S37.92**   Contusion of unspecified urinary and pelvic organ
X ● **S37.93**   Laceration of unspecified urinary and pelvic organ
X ● **S37.99**   Other injury of unspecified urinary and pelvic organ
● **S38**   **Crushing injury and traumatic amputation of abdomen, lower back, pelvis and external genitals**
    An amputation not identified as partial or complete should be coded to complete
    The appropriate 7th character is to be added to each code from category S38

> A   initial encounter
> D   subsequent encounter
> S   sequela

● **S38.0**   Crushing injury of external genital organs
    Use additional code for any associated injuries
   ● **S38.00**   Crushing injury of unspecified external genital organs
    ● S38.001   Crushing injury of unspecified external genital organs, male ♂
    ● S38.002   Crushing injury of unspecified external genital organs, female ♀
X ● **S38.01**   Crushing injury of penis ♂
X ● **S38.02**   Crushing injury of scrotum and testis ♂
X ● **S38.03**   Crushing injury of vulva ♀
X ● **S38.1**   Crushing injury of abdomen, lower back, and pelvis
    Use additional code for all associated injuries, such as:
     fracture of thoracic or lumbar spine and pelvis (S22.0-, S32.-)
     injury to intra-abdominal organs (S36.-)
     injury to urinary and pelvic organs (S37.-)
     open wound of abdominal wall (S31.-)
     spinal cord injury (S34.0, S34.1-)
    Excludes2   crushing injury of external genital organs (S38.0-)
● **S38.2**   Traumatic amputation of external genital organs
   ● **S38.21**   Traumatic amputation of female external genital organs
     Traumatic amputation of clitoris
     Traumatic amputation of labium (majus) (minus)
     Traumatic amputation of vulva
    ● S38.211   Complete traumatic amputation of female external genital organs ♀
    ● S38.212   Partial traumatic amputation of female external genital organs ♀
   ● **S38.22**   Traumatic amputation of penis
    ● S38.221   Complete traumatic amputation of penis ♂
    ● S38.222   Partial traumatic amputation of penis ♂
   ● **S38.23**   Traumatic amputation of scrotum and testis
    ● S38.231   Complete traumatic amputation of scrotum and testis ♂
    ● S38.232   Partial traumatic amputation of scrotum and testis ♂
X ● **S38.3**   Transection (partial) of abdomen

● **S39 Other and unspecified injuries of abdomen, lower back, pelvis and external genitals**

Code also any associated open wound (S31.-)

Excludes2 sprain of joints and ligaments of lumbar spine and pelvis (S33.-)

The appropriate 7th character is to be added to each code from category S39

A	initial encounter
D	subsequent encounter
S	sequela

● **S39.0 Injury of muscle, fascia and tendon of abdomen, lower back and pelvis**

● **S39.00 Unspecified injury of muscle, fascia and tendon of abdomen, lower back and pelvis**

● S39.001 Unspecified injury of muscle, fascia and tendon of abdomen

● S39.002 Unspecified injury of muscle, fascia and tendon of lower back

● S39.003 Unspecified injury of muscle, fascia and tendon of pelvis

● **S39.01 Strain of muscle, fascia and tendon of abdomen, lower back and pelvis**

● S39.011 Strain of muscle, fascia and tendon of abdomen

● S39.012 Strain of muscle, fascia and tendon of lower back
Coding Clinic: 2016, Q4, P74

● S39.013 Strain of muscle, fascia and tendon of pelvis

● **S39.02 Laceration of muscle, fascia and tendon of abdomen, lower back and pelvis**

● S39.021 Laceration of muscle, fascia and tendon of abdomen

● S39.022 Laceration of muscle, fascia and tendon of lower back

● S39.023 Laceration of muscle, fascia and tendon of pelvis

● **S39.09 Other injury of muscle, fascia and tendon of abdomen, lower back and pelvis**

● S39.091 Other injury of muscle, fascia and tendon of abdomen

● S39.092 Other injury of muscle, fascia and tendon of lower back

● S39.093 Other injury of muscle, fascia and tendon of pelvis

● **S39.8 Other specified injuries of abdomen, lower back, pelvis and external genitals**

X● S39.81 Other specified injuries of abdomen

X● S39.82 Other specified injuries of lower back

X● S39.83 Other specified injuries of pelvis

● S39.84 Other specified injuries of external genitals

● S39.840 Fracture of corpus cavernosum penis ♂

● S39.848 Other specified injuries of external genitals

● **S39.9 Unspecified injury of abdomen, lower back, pelvis and external genitals**

X● S39.91 Unspecified injury of abdomen

X● S39.92 Unspecified injury of lower back

X● S39.93 Unspecified injury of pelvis

X● S39.94 Unspecified injury of external genitals

INJURIES TO THE SHOULDER AND UPPER ARM (S40-S49)

Includes injuries of axilla injuries of scapular region

Excludes2 burns and corrosions (T20-T32)
frostbite (T33-T34)
injuries of elbow (S50-S59)
insect bite or sting, venomous (T63.4)

● **S40 Superficial injury of shoulder and upper arm**

The appropriate 7th character is to be added to each code from category S40

A	initial encounter
D	subsequent encounter
S	sequela

● **S40.0 Contusion of shoulder and upper arm**

● **S40.01 Contusion of shoulder**

● S40.011 Contusion of right shoulder

● S40.012 Contusion of left shoulder

● S40.019 Contusion of unspecified shoulder

● **S40.02 Contusion of upper arm**

● S40.021 Contusion of right upper arm

● S40.022 Contusion of left upper arm

● S40.029 Contusion of unspecified upper arm

● **S40.2 Other superficial injuries of shoulder**

● **S40.21 Abrasion of shoulder**

● S40.211 Abrasion of right shoulder

● S40.212 Abrasion of left shoulder

● S40.219 Abrasion of unspecified shoulder

● **S40.22 Blister (nonthermal) of shoulder**

● S40.221 Blister (nonthermal) of right shoulder

● S40.222 Blister (nonthermal) of left shoulder

● S40.229 Blister (nonthermal) of unspecified shoulder

● **S40.24 External constriction of shoulder**

● S40.241 External constriction of right shoulder

● S40.242 External constriction of left shoulder

● S40.249 External constriction of unspecified shoulder

● **S40.25 Superficial foreign body of shoulder**
Splinter in the shoulder

● S40.251 Superficial foreign body of right shoulder

● S40.252 Superficial foreign body of left shoulder

● S40.259 Superficial foreign body of unspecified shoulder

● **S40.26 Insect bite (nonvenomous) of shoulder**

● S40.261 Insect bite (nonvenomous) of right shoulder

● S40.262 Insect bite (nonvenomous) of left shoulder

● S40.269 Insect bite (nonvenomous) of unspecified shoulder

● **S40.27 Other superficial bite of shoulder**

Excludes1 open bite of shoulder (S41.05)

● S40.271 Other superficial bite of right shoulder

● S40.272 Other superficial bite of left shoulder

● S40.279 Other superficial bite of unspecified shoulder

▶ New ⇒ Revised deleted Deleted Excludes 1 Excludes 2 Includes Use additional Code first Code also Key words
OGCR Official Guidelines X Assign placeholder X ● Use Additional Character(s) ▷ Manifestation Code 🔵 Hierarchical Condition Category Coding Clinic

● **S40.8**   Other superficial injuries of upper arm
   ● **S40.81**   Abrasion of upper arm
     ● S40.811   Abrasion of right upper arm
     ● S40.812   Abrasion of left upper arm
     ● S40.819   Abrasion of unspecified upper arm
   ● **S40.82**   Blister (nonthermal) of upper arm
     ● S40.821   Blister (nonthermal) of right upper arm
     ● S40.822   Blister (nonthermal) of left upper arm
     ● S40.829   Blister (nonthermal) of unspecified upper arm
   ● **S40.84**   External constriction of upper arm
     ● S40.841   External constriction of right upper arm
     ● S40.842   External constriction of left upper arm
     ● S40.849   External constriction of unspecified upper arm
   ● **S40.85**   Superficial foreign body of upper arm
       Splinter in the upper arm
     ● S40.851   Superficial foreign body of right upper arm
     ● S40.852   Superficial foreign body of left upper arm
     ● S40.859   Superficial foreign body of unspecified upper arm
   ● **S40.86**   Insect bite (nonvenomous) of upper arm
     ● S40.861   Insect bite (nonvenomous) of right upper arm
     ● S40.862   Insect bite (nonvenomous) of left upper arm
     ● S40.869   Insect bite (nonvenomous) of unspecified upper arm
   ● **S40.87**   Other superficial bite of upper arm
       Excludes1   open bite of upper arm (S41.14)
       Excludes2   other superficial bite of shoulder (S40.27-)
     ● S40.871   Other superficial bite of right upper arm
     ● S40.872   Other superficial bite of left upper arm
     ● S40.879   Other superficial bite of unspecified upper arm
● **S40.9**   Unspecified superficial injury of shoulder and upper arm
   ● **S40.91**   Unspecified superficial injury of shoulder
     ● S40.911   Unspecified superficial injury of right shoulder
     ● S40.912   Unspecified superficial injury of left shoulder
     ● S40.919   Unspecified superficial injury of unspecified shoulder
   ● **S40.92**   Unspecified superficial injury of upper arm
     ● S40.921   Unspecified superficial injury of right upper arm
     ● S40.922   Unspecified superficial injury of left upper arm
     ● S40.929   Unspecified superficial injury of unspecified upper arm

● **S41**   Open wound of shoulder and upper arm
     Code also any associated wound infection
     Excludes1   traumatic amputation of shoulder and upper arm (S48.-)
     Excludes2   open fracture of shoulder and upper arm (S42.- with 7th character B or C)
     The appropriate 7th character is to be added to each code from category S41

     | | |
     A   initial encounter
     D   subsequent encounter
     S   sequela

   ● **S41.0**   Open wound of shoulder
     ● **S41.00**   Unspecified open wound of shoulder
       ● S41.001   Unspecified open wound of right shoulder
       ● S41.002   Unspecified open wound of left shoulder
       ● S41.009   Unspecified open wound of unspecified shoulder
     ● **S41.01**   Laceration without foreign body of shoulder
       ● S41.011   Laceration without foreign body of right shoulder
       ● S41.012   Laceration without foreign body of left shoulder
       ● S41.019   Laceration without foreign body of unspecified shoulder
     ● **S41.02**   Laceration with foreign body of shoulder
       ● S41.021   Laceration with foreign body of right shoulder
       ● S41.022   Laceration with foreign body of left shoulder
       ● S41.029   Laceration with foreign body of unspecified shoulder
     ● **S41.03**   Puncture wound without foreign body of shoulder
       ● S41.031   Puncture wound without foreign body of right shoulder
       ● S41.032   Puncture wound without foreign body of left shoulder
       ● S41.039   Puncture wound without foreign body of unspecified shoulder
     ● **S41.04**   Puncture wound with foreign body of shoulder
       ● S41.041   Puncture wound with foreign body of right shoulder
       ● S41.042   Puncture wound with foreign body of left shoulder
       ● S41.049   Puncture wound with foreign body of unspecified shoulder
     ● **S41.05**   Open bite of shoulder
       Bite of shoulder NOS
       Excludes1   superficial bite of shoulder (S40.27)
       ● S41.051   Open bite of right shoulder
       ● S41.052   Open bite of left shoulder
       ● S41.059   Open bite of unspecified shoulder
   ● **S41.1**   Open wound of upper arm
     ● **S41.10**   Unspecified open wound of upper arm
       ● S41.101   Unspecified open wound of right upper arm
       ● S41.102   Unspecified open wound of left upper arm
       ● S41.109   Unspecified open wound of unspecified upper arm

- **S41.11**   **Laceration without foreign body of upper arm**
  - **S41.111**   Laceration without foreign body of right upper arm
  - **S41.112**   Laceration without foreign body of left upper arm
  - **S41.119**   Laceration without foreign body of unspecified upper arm
- **S41.12**   **Laceration with foreign body of upper arm**
  - **S41.121**   Laceration with foreign body of right upper arm
  - **S41.122**   Laceration with foreign body of left upper arm
  - **S41.129**   Laceration with foreign body of unspecified upper arm
- **S41.13**   **Puncture wound without foreign body of upper arm**
  - **S41.131**   Puncture wound without foreign body of right upper arm
  - **S41.132**   Puncture wound without foreign body of left upper arm
  - **S41.139**   Puncture wound without foreign body of unspecified upper arm
- **S41.14**   **Puncture wound with foreign body of upper arm**
  - **S41.141**   Puncture wound with foreign body of right upper arm
  - **S41.142**   Puncture wound with foreign body of left upper arm
  - **S41.149**   Puncture wound with foreign body of unspecified upper arm
- **S41.15**   **Open bite of upper arm**
  Bite of upper arm NOS
  - **Excludes1**   superficial bite of upper arm (S40.87)
  - **S41.151**   Open bite of right upper arm
  - **S41.152**   Open bite of left upper arm
  - **S41.159**   Open bite of unspecified upper arm

- **S42**   **Fracture of shoulder and upper arm**

  Note: A fracture not indicated as displaced or nondisplaced should be coded to displaced

  A fracture not indicated as open or closed should be coded to closed

  Excludes1   traumatic amputation of shoulder and upper arm (S48.-)

  The appropriate 7th character is to be added to all codes from category S42

A	initial encounter for closed fracture
B	initial encounter for open fracture
D	subsequent encounter for fracture with routine healing
G	subsequent encounter for fracture with delayed healing
K	subsequent encounter for fracture with nonunion
P	subsequent encounter for fracture with malunion
S	sequela

  - **S42.0**   **Fracture of clavicle**
    - **S42.00**   **Fracture of unspecified part of clavicle**
      - **S42.001**   Fracture of unspecified part of right clavicle
      - **S42.002**   Fracture of unspecified part of left clavicle
      - **S42.009**   Fracture of unspecified part of unspecified clavicle
        Coding Clinic: 2012, Q4, P3

  - **S42.01**   **Fracture of sternal end of clavicle**
    - **S42.011**   Anterior displaced fracture of sternal end of right clavicle
    - **S42.012**   Anterior displaced fracture of sternal end of left clavicle
    - **S42.013**   Anterior displaced fracture of sternal end of unspecified clavicle
      Displaced fracture of sternal end of clavicle NOS
    - **S42.014**   Posterior displaced fracture of sternal end of right clavicle
    - **S42.015**   Posterior displaced fracture of sternal end of left clavicle
    - **S42.016**   Posterior displaced fracture of sternal end of unspecified clavicle
    - **S42.017**   Nondisplaced fracture of sternal end of right clavicle
    - **S42.018**   Nondisplaced fracture of sternal end of left clavicle
    - **S42.019**   Nondisplaced fracture of sternal end of unspecified clavicle
  - **S42.02**   **Fracture of shaft of clavicle**
    - **S42.021**   Displaced fracture of shaft of right clavicle
    - **S42.022**   Displaced fracture of shaft of left clavicle
    - **S42.023**   Displaced fracture of shaft of unspecified clavicle
    - **S42.024**   Nondisplaced fracture of shaft of right clavicle
    - **S42.025**   Nondisplaced fracture of shaft of left clavicle
    - **S42.026**   Nondisplaced fracture of shaft of unspecified clavicle
  - **S42.03**   **Fracture of lateral end of clavicle**
    Fracture of acromial end of clavicle
    - **S42.031**   Displaced fracture of lateral end of right clavicle
    - **S42.032**   Displaced fracture of lateral end of left clavicle
    - **S42.033**   Displaced fracture of lateral end of unspecified clavicle
    - **S42.034**   Nondisplaced fracture of lateral end of right clavicle
    - **S42.035**   Nondisplaced fracture of lateral end of left clavicle
    - **S42.036**   Nondisplaced fracture of lateral end of unspecified clavicle
  - **S42.1**   **Fracture of scapula**
    - **S42.10**   **Fracture of unspecified part of scapula**
      - **S42.101**   Fracture of unspecified part of scapula, right shoulder
      - **S42.102**   Fracture of unspecified part of scapula, left shoulder
      - **S42.109**   Fracture of unspecified part of scapula, unspecified shoulder
    - **S42.11**   **Fracture of body of scapula**
      - **S42.111**   Displaced fracture of body of scapula, right shoulder
      - **S42.112**   Displaced fracture of body of scapula, left shoulder
      - **S42.113**   Displaced fracture of body of scapula, unspecified shoulder
      - **S42.114**   Nondisplaced fracture of body of scapula, right shoulder
      - **S42.115**   Nondisplaced fracture of body of scapula, left shoulder
      - **S42.116**   Nondisplaced fracture of body of scapula, unspecified shoulder

▶ New   ⇒ Revised   ~~deleted~~ Deleted   Excludes 1   Excludes 2   Includes   Use additional   Code first   Code also   Key words

OGCR Official Guidelines   X Assign placeholder X   ● Use Additional Character(s)   ▶ Manifestation Code   Hierarchical Condition Category   **Coding Clinic**

● **S42.12**   Fracture of acromial process
    ● S42.121   Displaced fracture of acromial process, right shoulder
    ● S42.122   Displaced fracture of acromial process, left shoulder
    ● S42.123   Displaced fracture of acromial process, unspecified shoulder
    ● S42.124   Nondisplaced fracture of acromial process, right shoulder
    ● S42.125   Nondisplaced fracture of acromial process, left shoulder
    ● S42.126   Nondisplaced fracture, of acromial process, unspecified shoulder

● **S42.13**   Fracture of coracoid process
    ● S42.131   Displaced fracture of coracoid process, right shoulder
    ● S42.132   Displaced fracture of coracoid process, left shoulder
    ● S42.133   Displaced fracture of coracoid process, unspecified shoulder
    ● S42.134   Nondisplaced fracture of coracoid process, right shoulder
    ● S42.135   Nondisplaced fracture of coracoid process, left shoulder
    ● S42.136   Nondisplaced fracture of coracoid process, unspecified shoulder

● **S42.14**   Fracture of glenoid cavity of scapula
    ● S42.141   Displaced fracture of glenoid cavity of scapula, right shoulder
    ● S42.142   Displaced fracture of glenoid cavity of scapula, left shoulder
    ● S42.143   Displaced fracture of glenoid cavity of scapula, unspecified shoulder
    ● S42.144   Nondisplaced fracture of glenoid cavity of scapula, right shoulder
    ● S42.145   Nondisplaced fracture of glenoid cavity of scapula, left shoulder
    ● S42.146   Nondisplaced fracture of glenoid cavity of scapula, unspecified shoulder

● **S42.15**   Fracture of neck of scapula
    ● S42.151   Displaced fracture of neck of scapula, right shoulder
    ● S42.152   Displaced fracture of neck of scapula, left shoulder
    ● S42.153   Displaced fracture of neck of scapula, unspecified shoulder
    ● S42.154   Nondisplaced fracture of neck of scapula, right shoulder
    ● S42.155   Nondisplaced fracture of neck of scapula, left shoulder
    ● S42.156   Nondisplaced fracture of neck of scapula, unspecified shoulder

● **S42.19**   Fracture of other part of scapula
    ● S42.191   Fracture of other part of scapula, right shoulder
    ● S42.192   Fracture of other part of scapula, left shoulder
    ● S42.199   Fracture of other part of scapula, unspecified shoulder

● **S42.2**   **Fracture of upper end of humerus**
    Fracture of proximal end of humerus
    Excludes2   fracture of shaft of humerus (S42.3-)
              physeal fracture of upper end of humerus (S49.0-)

● **S42.20**   Unspecified fracture of upper end of humerus
    ● S42.201   Unspecified fracture of upper end of right humerus
    ● S42.202   Unspecified fracture of upper end of left humerus
    ● S42.209   Unspecified fracture of upper end of unspecified humerus

● **S42.21**   Unspecified fracture of surgical neck of humerus
    Fracture of neck of humerus NOS
    ● S42.211   Unspecified displaced fracture of surgical neck of right humerus
    ● S42.212   Unspecified displaced fracture of surgical neck of left humerus
    ● S42.213   Unspecified displaced fracture of surgical neck of unspecified humerus
    ● S42.214   Unspecified nondisplaced fracture of surgical neck of right humerus
    ● S42.215   Unspecified nondisplaced fracture of surgical neck of left humerus
    ● S42.216   Unspecified nondisplaced fracture of surgical neck of unspecified humerus

●   S42.22   2-part fracture of surgical neck of humerus
    ● S42.221   2-part displaced fracture of surgical neck of right humerus
    ● S42.222   2-part displaced fracture of surgical neck of left humerus
    ● S42.223   2-part displaced fracture of surgical neck of unspecified humerus
    ● S42.224   2-part nondisplaced fracture of surgical neck of right humerus
    ● S42.225   2-part nondisplaced fracture of surgical neck of left humerus
    ● S42.226   2-part nondisplaced fracture of surgical neck of unspecified humerus

● **S42.23**   3-part fracture of surgical neck of humerus
    ● S42.231   3-part fracture of surgical neck of right humerus
    ● S42.232   3-part fracture of surgical neck of left humerus
    ● S42.239   3-part fracture of surgical neck of unspecified humerus

● **S42.24**   4-part fracture of surgical neck of humerus
    ● S42.241   4-part fracture of surgical neck of right humerus
    ● S42.242   4-part fracture of surgical neck of left humerus
    ● S42.249   4-part fracture of surgical neck of unspecified humerus

● **S42.25**   Fracture of greater tuberosity of humerus
    ● S42.251   Displaced fracture of greater tuberosity of right humerus
    ● S42.252   Displaced fracture of greater tuberosity of left humerus
    ● S42.253   Displaced fracture of greater tuberosity of unspecified humerus
    ● S42.254   Nondisplaced fracture of greater tuberosity of right humerus
    ● S42.255   Nondisplaced fracture of greater tuberosity of left humerus
    ● S42.256   Nondisplaced fracture of greater tuberosity of unspecified humerus

● **S42.26**   Fracture of lesser tuberosity of humerus
    ● S42.261   Displaced fracture of lesser tuberosity of right humerus
    ● S42.262   Displaced fracture of lesser tuberosity of left humerus
    ● S42.263   Displaced fracture of lesser tuberosity of unspecified humerus
    ● S42.264   Nondisplaced fracture of lesser tuberosity of right humerus
    ● S42.265   Nondisplaced fracture of lesser tuberosity of left humerus
    ● S42.266   Nondisplaced fracture of lesser tuberosity of unspecified humerus

CHAPTER 19 (S00–T88)

● **S42.27** **Torus fracture of upper end of humerus**
The appropriate 7th character is to be added to all codes in subcategory S42.27

A	initial encounter for closed fracture
D	subsequent encounter for fracture with routine healing
G	subsequent encounter for fracture with delayed healing
K	subsequent encounter for fracture with nonunion
P	subsequent encounter for fracture with malunion
S	sequela

  ● **S42.271** **Torus fracture of upper end of right humerus**
  ● **S42.272** **Torus fracture of upper end of left humerus**
  ● **S42.279** **Torus fracture of upper end of unspecified humerus**

● **S42.29** **Other fracture of upper end of humerus**
Fracture of anatomical neck of humerus
Fracture of articular head of humerus
  ● **S42.291** **Other displaced fracture of upper end of right humerus**
  ● **S42.292** **Other displaced fracture of upper end of left humerus**
  ● **S42.293** **Other displaced fracture of upper end of unspecified humerus**
  ● **S42.294** **Other nondisplaced fracture of upper end of right humerus**
  ● **S42.295** **Other nondisplaced fracture of upper end of left humerus**
      Coding Clinic: 2019, Q1, P19
  ● **S42.296** **Other nondisplaced fracture of upper end of unspecified humerus**

● **S42.3** **Fracture of shaft of humerus**
Fracture of humerus NOS
Fracture of upper arm NOS
  Excludes2 physeal fractures of upper end of humerus (S49.0-)
                physeal fractures of lower end of humerus (S49.1-)

● **S42.30** **Unspecified fracture of shaft of humerus**
  ● **S42.301** **Unspecified fracture of shaft of humerus, right arm**
  ● **S42.302** **Unspecified fracture of shaft of humerus, left arm**
  ● **S42.309** **Unspecified fracture of shaft of humerus, unspecified arm**

● **S42.31** **Greenstick fracture of shaft of humerus**
The appropriate 7th character is to be added to all codes in subcategory S42.31

A	initial encounter for closed fracture
D	subsequent encounter for fracture with routine healing
G	subsequent encounter for fracture with delayed healing
K	subsequent encounter for fracture with nonunion
P	subsequent encounter for fracture with malunion
S	sequela

  ● **S42.311** **Greenstick fracture of shaft of humerus, right arm**
  ● **S42.312** **Greenstick fracture of shaft of humerus, left arm**
  ● **S42.319** **Greenstick fracture of shaft of humerus, unspecified arm**

● **S42.32** **Transverse fracture of shaft of humerus**
  ● **S42.321** **Displaced transverse fracture of shaft of humerus, right arm**
  ● **S42.322** **Displaced transverse fracture of shaft of humerus, left arm**
  ● **S42.323** **Displaced transverse fracture of shaft of humerus, unspecified arm**
  ● **S42.324** **Nondisplaced transverse fracture of shaft of humerus, right arm**
  ● **S42.325** **Nondisplaced transverse fracture of shaft of humerus, left arm**
  ● **S42.326** **Nondisplaced transverse fracture of shaft of humerus, unspecified arm**

● **S42.33** **Oblique fracture of shaft of humerus**
  ● **S42.331** **Displaced oblique fracture of shaft of humerus, right arm**
  ● **S42.332** **Displaced oblique fracture of shaft of humerus, left arm**
  ● **S42.333** **Displaced oblique fracture of shaft of humerus, unspecified arm**
  ● **S42.334** **Nondisplaced oblique fracture of shaft of humerus, right arm**
  ● **S42.335** **Nondisplaced oblique fracture of shaft of humerus, left arm**
  ● **S42.336** **Nondisplaced oblique fracture of shaft of humerus, unspecified arm**

● **S42.34** **Spiral fracture of shaft of humerus**
  ● **S42.341** **Displaced spiral fracture of shaft of humerus, right arm**
  ● **S42.342** **Displaced spiral fracture of shaft of humerus, left arm**
  ● **S42.343** **Displaced spiral fracture of shaft of humerus, unspecified arm**
  ● **S42.344** **Nondisplaced spiral fracture of shaft of humerus, right arm**
  ● **S42.345** **Nondisplaced spiral fracture of shaft of humerus, left arm**
  ● **S42.346** **Nondisplaced spiral fracture of shaft of humerus, unspecified arm**

● **S42.35** **Comminuted fracture of shaft of humerus**
  ● **S42.351** **Displaced comminuted fracture of shaft of humerus, right arm**
  ● **S42.352** **Displaced comminuted fracture of shaft of humerus, left arm**
  ● **S42.353** **Displaced comminuted fracture of shaft of humerus, unspecified arm**
  ● **S42.354** **Nondisplaced comminuted fracture of shaft of humerus, right arm**
  ● **S42.355** **Nondisplaced comminuted fracture of shaft of humerus, left arm**
  ● **S42.356** **Nondisplaced comminuted fracture of shaft of humerus, unspecified arm**

● **S42.36** **Segmental fracture of shaft of humerus**
  ● **S42.361** **Displaced segmental fracture of shaft of humerus, right arm**
  ● **S42.362** **Displaced segmental fracture of shaft of humerus, left arm**
  ● **S42.363** **Displaced segmental fracture of shaft of humerus, unspecified arm**
  ● **S42.364** **Nondisplaced segmental fracture of shaft of humerus, right arm**
  ● **S42.365** **Nondisplaced segmental fracture of shaft of humerus, left arm**
  ● **S42.366** **Nondisplaced segmental fracture of shaft of humerus, unspecified arm**

▶ New   ⟹ Revised   ~~deleted~~ Deleted   Excludes 1   Excludes 2   Includes   Use additional   Code first   Code also   Key words
OGCR Official Guidelines   X Assign placeholder X   ● Use Additional Character(s)   ▷ Manifestation Code   ℞ᵉ Hierarchical Condition Category   **Coding Clinic**

● **S42.39**   Other fracture of shaft of humerus
   ● **S42.391**   Other fracture of shaft of right humerus
   ● **S42.392**   Other fracture of shaft of left humerus
   ● **S42.399**   Other fracture of shaft of unspecified humerus

● **S42.4**   Fracture of lower end of humerus
   Fracture of distal end of humerus
   Excludes2   fracture of shaft of humerus (S42.3-)
              physeal fracture of lower end of humerus (S49.1-)

   ● **S42.40**   Unspecified fracture of lower end of humerus
     Fracture of elbow NOS
     ● **S42.401**   Unspecified fracture of lower end of right humerus
     ● **S42.402**   Unspecified fracture of lower end of left humerus
     ● **S42.409**   Unspecified fracture of lower end of unspecified humerus

   ● **S42.41**   Simple supracondylar fracture without intercondylar fracture of humerus
     ● **S42.411**   Displaced simple supracondylar fracture without intercondylar fracture of right humerus
     ● **S42.412**   Displaced simple supracondylar fracture without intercondylar fracture of left humerus
     ● **S42.413**   Displaced simple supracondylar fracture without intercondylar fracture of unspecified humerus
     ● **S42.414**   Nondisplaced simple supracondylar fracture without intercondylar fracture of right humerus
     ● **S42.415**   Nondisplaced simple supracondylar fracture without intercondylar fracture of left humerus
     ● **S42.416**   Nondisplaced simple supracondylar fracture without intercondylar fracture of unspecified humerus

   ● **S42.42**   Comminuted supracondylar fracture without intercondylar fracture of humerus
     ● **S42.421**   Displaced comminuted supracondylar fracture without intercondylar fracture of right humerus
     ● **S42.422**   Displaced comminuted supracondylar fracture without intercondylar fracture of left humerus
     ● **S42.423**   Displaced comminuted supracondylar fracture without intercondylar fracture of unspecified humerus
     ● **S42.424**   Nondisplaced comminuted supracondylar fracture without intercondylar fracture of right humerus
     ● **S42.425**   Nondisplaced comminuted supracondylar fracture without intercondylar fracture of left humerus
     ● **S42.426**   Nondisplaced comminuted supracondylar fracture without intercondylar fracture of unspecified humerus

● **S42.43**   Fracture (avulsion) of lateral epicondyle of humerus
   ● **S42.431**   Displaced fracture (avulsion) of lateral epicondyle of right humerus
   ● **S42.432**   Displaced fracture (avulsion) of lateral epicondyle of left humerus
   ● **S42.433**   Displaced fracture (avulsion) of lateral epicondyle of unspecified humerus
   ● **S42.434**   Nondisplaced fracture (avulsion) of lateral epicondyle of right humerus
   ● **S42.435**   Nondisplaced fracture (avulsion) of lateral epicondyle of left humerus
   ● **S42.436**   Nondisplaced fracture (avulsion) of lateral epicondyle of unspecified humerus

● **S42.44**   Fracture (avulsion) of medial epicondyle of humerus
   ● **S42.441**   Displaced fracture (avulsion) of medial epicondyle of right humerus
   ● **S42.442**   Displaced fracture (avulsion) of medial epicondyle of left humerus
   ● **S42.443**   Displaced fracture (avulsion) of medial epicondyle of unspecified humerus
   ● **S42.444**   Nondisplaced fracture (avulsion) of medial epicondyle of right humerus
   ● **S42.445**   Nondisplaced fracture (avulsion) of medial epicondyle of left humerus
   ● **S42.446**   Nondisplaced fracture (avulsion) of medial epicondyle of unspecified humerus
   ● **S42.447**   Incarcerated fracture (avulsion) of medial epicondyle of right humerus
   ● **S42.448**   Incarcerated fracture (avulsion) of medial epicondyle of left humerus
   ● **S42.449**   Incarcerated fracture (avulsion) of medial epicondyle of unspecified humerus

● **S42.45**   Fracture of lateral condyle of humerus
   Fracture of capitellum of humerus
   ● **S42.451**   Displaced fracture of lateral condyle of right humerus
   ● **S42.452**   Displaced fracture of lateral condyle of left humerus
   ● **S42.453**   Displaced fracture of lateral condyle of unspecified humerus
   ● **S42.454**   Nondisplaced fracture of lateral condyle of right humerus
   ● **S42.455**   Nondisplaced fracture of lateral condyle of left humerus
   ● **S42.456**   Nondisplaced fracture of lateral condyle of unspecified humerus

● **S42.46**   Fracture of medial condyle of humerus
   Trochlea fracture of humerus
   ● **S42.461**   Displaced fracture of medial condyle of right humerus
   ● **S42.462**   Displaced fracture of medial condyle of left humerus
   ● **S42.463**   Displaced fracture of medial condyle of unspecified humerus
   ● **S42.464**   Nondisplaced fracture of medial condyle of right humerus
   ● **S42.465**   Nondisplaced fracture of medial condyle of left humerus
   ● **S42.466**   Nondisplaced fracture of medial condyle of unspecified humerus

● **S42.47**   Transcondylar fracture of humerus

    ● **S42.471**   Displaced transcondylar fracture of right humerus

    ● **S42.472**   Displaced transcondylar fracture of left humerus

    ● **S42.473**   Displaced transcondylar fracture of unspecified humerus

    ● **S42.474**   Nondisplaced transcondylar fracture of right humerus

    ● **S42.475**   Nondisplaced transcondylar fracture of left humerus

    ● **S42.476**   Nondisplaced transcondylar fracture of unspecified humerus

● **S42.48**   Torus fracture of lower end of humerus

    The appropriate 7th character is to be added to all codes in subcategory S42.48

A	initial encounter for closed fracture
D	subsequent encounter for fracture with routine healing
G	subsequent encounter for fracture with delayed healing
K	subsequent encounter for fracture with nonunion
P	subsequent encounter for fracture with malunion
S	sequela

    ● **S42.481**   Torus fracture of lower end of right humerus

    ● **S42.482**   Torus fracture of lower end of left humerus

    ● **S42.489**   Torus fracture of lower end of unspecified humerus

● **S42.49**   Other fracture of lower end of humerus

    ● **S42.491**   Other displaced fracture of lower end of right humerus

    ● **S42.492**   Other displaced fracture of lower end of left humerus

    ● **S42.493**   Other displaced fracture of lower end of unspecified humerus

    ● **S42.494**   Other nondisplaced fracture of lower end of right humerus

    ● **S42.495**   Other nondisplaced fracture of lower end of left humerus

    ● **S42.496**   Other nondisplaced fracture of lower end of unspecified humerus

● **S42.9**   Fracture of shoulder girdle, part unspecified

    Fracture of shoulder NOS

  X ● **S42.90**   Fracture of unspecified shoulder girdle, part unspecified

  X ● **S42.91**   Fracture of right shoulder girdle, part unspecified

  X ● **S42.92**   Fracture of left shoulder girdle, part unspecified

---

● **S43**   Dislocation and sprain of joints and ligaments of shoulder girdle

    Includes   avulsion of joint or ligament of shoulder girdle

        laceration of cartilage, joint or ligament of shoulder girdle

        sprain of cartilage, joint or ligament of shoulder girdle

        traumatic hemarthrosis of joint or ligament of shoulder girdle

        traumatic rupture of joint or ligament of shoulder girdle

        traumatic subluxation of joint or ligament of shoulder girdle

        traumatic tear of joint or ligament of shoulder girdle

    Code also any associated open wound

    Excludes2   strain of muscle, fascia and tendon of shoulder and upper arm (S46.-)

    The appropriate 7th character is to be added to each code from category S43

A	initial encounter
D	subsequent encounter
S	sequela

● **S43.0**   Subluxation and dislocation of shoulder joint

    Dislocation of glenohumeral joint

    Subluxation of glenohumeral joint

    ● **S43.00**   Unspecified subluxation and dislocation of shoulder joint

       Dislocation of humerus NOS

       Subluxation of humerus NOS

      ● **S43.001**   Unspecified subluxation of right shoulder joint

      ● **S43.002**   Unspecified subluxation of left shoulder joint

      ● **S43.003**   Unspecified subluxation of unspecified shoulder joint

      ● **S43.004**   Unspecified dislocation of right shoulder joint

      ● **S43.005**   Unspecified dislocation of left shoulder joint

      ● **S43.006**   Unspecified dislocation of unspecified shoulder joint

    ● **S43.01**   Anterior subluxation and dislocation of humerus

      ● **S43.011**   Anterior subluxation of right humerus

      ● **S43.012**   Anterior subluxation of left humerus

      ● **S43.013**   Anterior subluxation of unspecified humerus

      ● **S43.014**   Anterior dislocation of right humerus

      ● **S43.015**   Anterior dislocation of left humerus

      ● **S43.016**   Anterior dislocation of unspecified humerus

    ● **S43.02**   Posterior subluxation and dislocation of humerus

      ● **S43.021**   Posterior subluxation of right humerus

      ● **S43.022**   Posterior subluxation of left humerus

      ● **S43.023**   Posterior subluxation of unspecified humerus

      ● **S43.024**   Posterior dislocation of right humerus

      ● **S43.025**   Posterior dislocation of left humerus

      ● **S43.026**   Posterior dislocation of unspecified humerus

▶ New   ⟹ Revised   ~~deleted~~ Deleted   Excludes 1   Excludes 2   Includes   Use additional   Code first   Code also   Key words

OGCR Official Guidelines   X Assign placeholder X   ● Use Additional Character(s)   ⟩ Manifestation Code   ⓗ Hierarchical Condition Category   **Coding Clinic**

● S43.03   Inferior subluxation and dislocation of
            humerus
    ● S43.031   Inferior subluxation of right humerus
    ● S43.032   Inferior subluxation of left humerus
    ● S43.033   Inferior subluxation of unspecified
                 humerus
    ● S43.034   Inferior dislocation of right humerus
    ● S43.035   Inferior dislocation of left humerus
    ● S43.036   Inferior dislocation of unspecified
                 humerus
● S43.08   Other subluxation and dislocation of shoulder
            joint
    ● S43.081   Other subluxation of right shoulder
                 joint
    ● S43.082   Other subluxation of left shoulder
                 joint
    ● S43.083   Other subluxation of unspecified
                 shoulder joint
    ● S43.084   Other dislocation of right shoulder
                 joint
    ● S43.085   Other dislocation of left shoulder
                 joint
    ● S43.086   Other dislocation of unspecified
                 shoulder joint
● S43.1   Subluxation and dislocation of acromioclavicular joint
    ● S43.10   Unspecified dislocation of acromioclavicular
                joint
        ● S43.101   Unspecified dislocation of right
                     acromioclavicular joint
        ● S43.102   Unspecified dislocation of left
                     acromioclavicular joint
        ● S43.109   Unspecified dislocation of unspecified
                     acromioclavicular joint
    ● S43.11   Subluxation of acromioclavicular joint
        ● S43.111   Subluxation of right
                     acromioclavicular joint
        ● S43.112   Subluxation of left acromioclavicular
                     joint
        ● S43.119   Subluxation of unspecified
                     acromioclavicular joint
    ● S43.12   Dislocation of acromioclavicular joint,
                100%-200% displacement
        ● S43.121   Dislocation of right acromioclavicular
                     joint, 100%-200% displacement
        ● S43.122   Dislocation of left acromioclavicular
                     joint, 100%-200% displacement
        ● S43.129   Dislocation of unspecified
                     acromioclavicular joint, 100%-200%
                     displacement
    ● S43.13   Dislocation of acromioclavicular joint, greater
                than 200% displacement
        ● S43.131   Dislocation of right acromioclavicular
                     joint, greater than 200% displacement
        ● S43.132   Dislocation of left acromioclavicular
                     joint, greater than 200% displacement
        ● S43.139   Dislocation of unspecified
                     acromioclavicular joint, greater than
                     200% displacement
    ● S43.14   Inferior dislocation of acromioclavicular joint
        ● S43.141   Inferior dislocation of right
                     acromioclavicular joint
        ● S43.142   Inferior dislocation of left
                     acromioclavicular joint
        ● S43.149   Inferior dislocation of unspecified
                     acromioclavicular joint

● S43.15   Posterior dislocation of acromioclavicular joint
    ● S43.151   Posterior dislocation of right
                 acromioclavicular joint
    ● S43.152   Posterior dislocation of left
                 acromioclavicular joint
    ● S43.159   Posterior dislocation of unspecified
                 acromioclavicular joint
● S43.2   Subluxation and dislocation of sternoclavicular joint
    ● S43.20   Unspecified subluxation and dislocation of
                sternoclavicular joint
        ● S43.201   Unspecified subluxation of right
                     sternoclavicular joint
        ● S43.202   Unspecified subluxation of left
                     sternoclavicular joint
        ● S43.203   Unspecified subluxation of
                     unspecified sternoclavicular joint
        ● S43.204   Unspecified dislocation of right
                     sternoclavicular joint
        ● S43.205   Unspecified dislocation of left
                     sternoclavicular joint
        ● S43.206   Unspecified dislocation of unspecified
                     sternoclavicular joint
    ● S43.21   Anterior subluxation and dislocation of
                sternoclavicular joint
        ● S43.211   Anterior subluxation of right
                     sternoclavicular joint
        ● S43.212   Anterior subluxation of left
                     sternoclavicular joint
        ● S43.213   Anterior subluxation of unspecified
                     sternoclavicular joint
        ● S43.214   Anterior dislocation of right
                     sternoclavicular joint
        ● S43.215   Anterior dislocation of left
                     sternoclavicular joint
        ● S43.216   Anterior dislocation of unspecified
                     sternoclavicular joint
    ● S43.22   Posterior subluxation and dislocation of
                sternoclavicular joint
        ● S43.221   Posterior subluxation of right
                     sternoclavicular joint
        ● S43.222   Posterior subluxation of left
                     sternoclavicular joint
        ● S43.223   Posterior subluxation of unspecified
                     sternoclavicular joint
        ● S43.224   Posterior dislocation of right
                     sternoclavicular joint
        ● S43.225   Posterior dislocation of left
                     sternoclavicular joint
        ● S43.226   Posterior dislocation of unspecified
                     sternoclavicular joint
● S43.3   Subluxation and dislocation of other and unspecified
           parts of shoulder girdle
    ● S43.30   Subluxation and dislocation of unspecified
                parts of shoulder girdle
                Dislocation of shoulder girdle NOS
                Subluxation of shoulder girdle NOS
        ● S43.301   Subluxation of unspecified parts of
                     right shoulder girdle
        ● S43.302   Subluxation of unspecified parts of
                     left shoulder girdle
        ● S43.303   Subluxation of unspecified parts of
                     unspecified shoulder girdle
        ● S43.304   Dislocation of unspecified parts of
                     right shoulder girdle
        ● S43.305   Dislocation of unspecified parts of
                     left shoulder girdle
        ● S43.306   Dislocation of unspecified parts of
                     unspecified shoulder girdle

- **S43.31**   Subluxation and dislocation of scapula
  - **S43.311**   Subluxation of right scapula
  - **S43.312**   Subluxation of left scapula
  - **S43.313**   Subluxation of unspecified scapula
  - **S43.314**   Dislocation of right scapula
  - **S43.315**   Dislocation of left scapula
  - **S43.316**   Dislocation of unspecified scapula
- **S43.39**   Subluxation and dislocation of other parts of shoulder girdle
  - **S43.391**   Subluxation of other parts of right shoulder girdle
  - **S43.392**   Subluxation of other parts of left shoulder girdle
  - **S43.393**   Subluxation of other parts of unspecified shoulder girdle
  - **S43.394**   Dislocation of other parts of right shoulder girdle
  - **S43.395**   Dislocation of other parts of left shoulder girdle
  - **S43.396**   Dislocation of other parts of unspecified shoulder girdle
- **S43.4**   Sprain of shoulder joint
  - **S43.40**   Unspecified sprain of shoulder joint
    - **S43.401**   Unspecified sprain of right shoulder joint
    - **S43.402**   Unspecified sprain of left shoulder joint
    - **S43.409**   Unspecified sprain of unspecified shoulder joint
  - **S43.41**   Sprain of coracohumeral (ligament)
    - **S43.411**   Sprain of right coracohumeral (ligament)
    - **S43.412**   Sprain of left coracohumeral (ligament)
    - **S43.419**   Sprain of unspecified coracohumeral (ligament)
  - **S43.42**   Sprain of rotator cuff capsule
    Encounters during the healing phase
    > **Excludes1**   rotator cuff syndrome (complete) (incomplete), not specified as traumatic (M75.1-)
    > **Excludes2**   injury of tendon of rotator cuff (S46.0-)
    - **S43.421**   Sprain of right rotator cuff capsule
    - **S43.422**   Sprain of left rotator cuff capsule
    - **S43.429**   Sprain of unspecified rotator cuff capsule
  - **S43.43**   Superior glenoid labrum lesion
    SLAP lesion
    Coding Clinic: 2019, Q2, P27
    - **S43.431**   Superior glenoid labrum lesion of right shoulder
    - **S43.432**   Superior glenoid labrum lesion of left shoulder
    - **S43.439**   Superior glenoid labrum lesion of unspecified shoulder
  - **S43.49**   Other sprain of shoulder joint
    - **S43.491**   Other sprain of right shoulder joint
    - **S43.492**   Other sprain of left shoulder joint
    - **S43.499**   Other sprain of unspecified shoulder joint
- **S43.5**   Sprain of acromioclavicular joint
  Sprain of acromioclavicular ligament
  - X **S43.50**   Sprain of unspecified acromioclavicular joint
  - X **S43.51**   Sprain of right acromioclavicular joint
  - X **S43.52**   Sprain of left acromioclavicular joint
- **S43.6**   Sprain of sternoclavicular joint
  - X **S43.60**   Sprain of unspecified sternoclavicular joint
  - X **S43.61**   Sprain of right sternoclavicular joint
  - X **S43.62**   Sprain of left sternoclavicular joint
- **S43.8**   Sprain of other specified parts of shoulder girdle
  - X **S43.80**   Sprain of other specified parts of unspecified shoulder girdle
  - X **S43.81**   Sprain of other specified parts of right shoulder girdle
  - X **S43.82**   Sprain of other specified parts of left shoulder girdle
- **S43.9**   Sprain of unspecified parts of shoulder girdle
  - X **S43.90**   Sprain of unspecified parts of unspecified shoulder girdle
    Sprain of shoulder girdle NOS
  - X **S43.91**   Sprain of unspecified parts of right shoulder girdle
  - X **S43.92**   Sprain of unspecified parts of left shoulder girdle
- **S44**   **Injury of nerves at shoulder and upper arm level**
  Code also any associated open wound (S41.-)
  > **Excludes2**   injury of brachial plexus (S14.3-)

  The appropriate 7th character is to be added to each code from category S44

A	initial encounter
D	subsequent encounter
S	sequela

  - **S44.0**   Injury of ulnar nerve at upper arm level
    > **Excludes1**   ulnar nerve NOS (S54.0)
    - X **S44.00**   Injury of ulnar nerve at upper arm level, unspecified arm
    - X **S44.01**   Injury of ulnar nerve at upper arm level, right arm
    - X **S44.02**   Injury of ulnar nerve at upper arm level, left arm
  - **S44.1**   Injury of median nerve at upper arm level
    > **Excludes1**   median nerve NOS (S54.1)
    - X **S44.10**   Injury of median nerve at upper arm level, unspecified arm
    - X **S44.11**   Injury of median nerve at upper arm level, right arm
    - X **S44.12**   Injury of median nerve at upper arm level, left arm
  - **S44.2**   Injury of radial nerve at upper arm level
    > **Excludes1**   radial nerve NOS (S54.2)
    - X **S44.20**   Injury of radial nerve at upper arm level, unspecified arm
    - X **S44.21**   Injury of radial nerve at upper arm level, right arm
    - X **S44.22**   Injury of radial nerve at upper arm level, left arm
  - **S44.3**   Injury of axillary nerve
    - X **S44.30**   Injury of axillary nerve, unspecified arm
    - X **S44.31**   Injury of axillary nerve, right arm
    - X **S44.32**   Injury of axillary nerve, left arm
  - **S44.4**   Injury of musculocutaneous nerve
    - X **S44.40**   Injury of musculocutaneous nerve, unspecified arm
    - X **S44.41**   Injury of musculocutaneous nerve, right arm
    - X **S44.42**   Injury of musculocutaneous nerve, left arm

▶ New   ⇒ Revised   ~~deleted~~ Deleted   Excludes 1   Excludes 2   Includes   Use additional   Code first   Code also   Key words

OGCR Official Guidelines   X Assign placeholder X   ● Use Additional Character(s)   ▷ Manifestation Code   Hierarchical Condition Category   Coding Clinic

● **S44.5**   Injury of cutaneous sensory nerve at shoulder and upper arm level

   X● **S44.50**   Injury of cutaneous sensory nerve at shoulder and upper arm level, unspecified arm

   X● **S44.51**   Injury of cutaneous sensory nerve at shoulder and upper arm level, right arm

   X● **S44.52**   Injury of cutaneous sensory nerve at shoulder and upper arm level, left arm

● **S44.8**   Injury of other nerves at shoulder and upper arm level

   ● **S44.8X**   Injury of other nerves at shoulder and upper arm level

     ● **S44.8X1**   Injury of other nerves at shoulder and upper arm level, right arm

     ● **S44.8X2**   Injury of other nerves at shoulder and upper arm level, left arm

     ● **S44.8X9**   Injury of other nerves at shoulder and upper arm level, unspecified arm

● **S44.9**   Injury of unspecified nerve at shoulder and upper arm level

   X● **S44.90**   Injury of unspecified nerve at shoulder and upper arm level, unspecified arm

   X● **S44.91**   Injury of unspecified nerve at shoulder and upper arm level, right arm

   X● **S44.92**   Injury of unspecified nerve at shoulder and upper arm level, left arm

● **S45**   **Injury of blood vessels at shoulder and upper arm level**

   Code also any associated open wound (S41.-)

   Excludes2   injury of subclavian artery (S25.1)
           injury of subclavian vein (S25.3)

   The appropriate 7th character is to be added to each code from category S45

     | | |
     A   initial encounter
     D   subsequent encounter
     S   sequela

● **S45.0**   Injury of axillary artery

   ● **S45.00**   Unspecified injury of axillary artery

     ● **S45.001**   Unspecified injury of axillary artery, right side

     ● **S45.002**   Unspecified injury of axillary artery, left side

     ● **S45.009**   Unspecified injury of axillary artery, unspecified side

   ● **S45.01**   Laceration of axillary artery

     ● **S45.011**   Laceration of axillary artery, right side

     ● **S45.012**   Laceration of axillary artery, left side

     ● **S45.019**   Laceration of axillary artery, unspecified side

   ● **S45.09**   Other specified injury of axillary artery

     ● **S45.091**   Other specified injury of axillary artery, right side

     ● **S45.092**   Other specified injury of axillary artery, left side

     ● **S45.099**   Other specified injury of axillary artery, unspecified side

● **S45.1**   Injury of brachial artery

   ● **S45.10**   Unspecified injury of brachial artery

     ● **S45.101**   Unspecified injury of brachial artery, right side

     ● **S45.102**   Unspecified injury of brachial artery, left side

     ● **S45.109**   Unspecified injury of brachial artery, unspecified side

   ● **S45.11**   Laceration of brachial artery

     ● **S45.111**   Laceration of brachial artery, right side

     ● **S45.112**   Laceration of brachial artery, left side

     ● **S45.119**   Laceration of brachial artery, unspecified side

   ● **S45.19**   Other specified injury of brachial artery

     ● **S45.191**   Other specified injury of brachial artery, right side

     ● **S45.192**   Other specified injury of brachial artery, left side

     ● **S45.199**   Other specified injury of brachial artery, unspecified side

● **S45.2**   Injury of axillary or brachial vein

   ● **S45.20**   Unspecified injury of axillary or brachial vein

     ● **S45.201**   Unspecified injury of axillary or brachial vein, right side

     ● **S45.202**   Unspecified injury of axillary or brachial vein, left side

     ● **S45.209**   Unspecified injury of axillary or brachial vein, unspecified side

   ● **S45.21**   Laceration of axillary or brachial vein

     ● **S45.211**   Laceration of axillary or brachial vein, right side

     ● **S45.212**   Laceration of axillary or brachial vein, left side

     ● **S45.219**   Laceration of axillary or brachial vein, unspecified side

   ● **S45.29**   Other specified injury of axillary or brachial vein

     ● **S45.291**   Other specified injury of axillary or brachial vein, right side

     ● **S45.292**   Other specified injury of axillary or brachial vein, left side

     ● **S45.299**   Other specified injury of axillary or brachial vein, unspecified side

● **S45.3**   Injury of superficial vein at shoulder and upper arm level

   ● **S45.30**   Unspecified injury of superficial vein at shoulder and upper arm level

     ● **S45.301**   Unspecified injury of superficial vein at shoulder and upper arm level, right arm

     ● **S45.302**   Unspecified injury of superficial vein at shoulder and upper arm level, left arm

     ● **S45.309**   Unspecified injury of superficial vein at shoulder and upper arm level, unspecified arm

   ● **S45.31**   Laceration of superficial vein at shoulder and upper arm level

     ● **S45.311**   Laceration of superficial vein at shoulder and upper arm level, right arm

     ● **S45.312**   Laceration of superficial vein at shoulder and upper arm level, left arm

     ● **S45.319**   Laceration of superficial vein at shoulder and upper arm level, unspecified arm

   ● **S45.39**   Other specified injury of superficial vein at shoulder and upper arm level

     ● **S45.391**   Other specified injury of superficial vein at shoulder and upper arm level, right arm

     ● **S45.392**   Other specified injury of superficial vein at shoulder and upper arm level, left arm

     ● **S45.399**   Other specified injury of superficial vein at shoulder and upper arm level, unspecified arm

- **S45.8** **Injury of other specified blood vessels at shoulder and upper arm level**
  - **S45.80** **Unspecified injury of other specified blood vessels at shoulder and upper arm level**
    - **S45.801** Unspecified injury of other specified blood vessels at shoulder and upper arm level, right arm
    - **S45.802** Unspecified injury of other specified blood vessels at shoulder and upper arm level, left arm
    - **S45.809** Unspecified injury of other specified blood vessels at shoulder and upper arm level, unspecified arm
  - **S45.81** **Laceration of other specified blood vessels at shoulder and upper arm level**
    - **S45.811** Laceration of other specified blood vessels at shoulder and upper arm level, right arm
    - **S45.812** Laceration of other specified blood vessels at shoulder and upper arm level, left arm
    - **S45.819** Laceration of other specified blood vessels at shoulder and upper arm level, unspecified arm
  - **S45.89** **Other specified injury of other specified blood vessels at shoulder and upper arm level**
    - **S45.891** Other specified injury of other specified blood vessels at shoulder and upper arm level, right arm
    - **S45.892** Other specified injury of other specified blood vessels at shoulder and upper arm level, left arm
    - **S45.899** Other specified injury of other specified blood vessels at shoulder and upper arm level, unspecified arm
- **S45.9** **Injury of unspecified blood vessel at shoulder and upper arm level**
  - **S45.90** **Unspecified injury of unspecified blood vessel at shoulder and upper arm level**
    - **S45.901** Unspecified injury of unspecified blood vessel at shoulder and upper arm level, right arm
    - **S45.902** Unspecified injury of unspecified blood vessel at shoulder and upper arm level, left arm
    - **S45.909** Unspecified injury of unspecified blood vessel at shoulder and upper arm level, unspecified arm
  - **S45.91** **Laceration of unspecified blood vessel at shoulder and upper arm level**
    - **S45.911** Laceration of unspecified blood vessel at shoulder and upper arm level, right arm
    - **S45.912** Laceration of unspecified blood vessel at shoulder and upper arm level, left arm
    - **S45.919** Laceration of unspecified blood vessel at shoulder and upper arm level, unspecified arm
  - **S45.99** **Other specified injury of unspecified blood vessel at shoulder and upper arm level**
    - **S45.991** Other specified injury of unspecified blood vessel at shoulder and upper arm level, right arm
    - **S45.992** Other specified injury of unspecified blood vessel at shoulder and upper arm level, left arm
    - **S45.999** Other specified injury of unspecified blood vessel at shoulder and upper arm level, unspecified arm

- **S46** **Injury of muscle, fascia and tendon at shoulder and upper arm level**

  Code also any associated open wound (S41.-)

  Excludes2   injury of muscle, fascia and tendon at elbow (S56.-)

                  sprain of joints and ligaments of shoulder girdle (S43.9)

  The appropriate 7th character is to be added to each code from category S46

A	initial encounter
D	subsequent encounter
S	sequela

  - **S46.0** **Injury of muscle(s) and tendon(s) of the rotator cuff of shoulder**
    - **S46.00** **Unspecified injury of muscle(s) and tendon(s) of the rotator cuff of shoulder**
      - **S46.001** Unspecified injury of muscle(s) and tendon(s) of the rotator cuff of right shoulder
      - **S46.002** Unspecified injury of muscle(s) and tendon(s) of the rotator cuff of left shoulder
      - **S46.009** Unspecified injury of muscle(s) and tendon(s) of the rotator cuff of unspecified shoulder
    - **S46.01** **Strain of muscle(s) and tendon(s) of the rotator cuff of shoulder**
      Acute onset due to trauma to rotator cuff muscle/tendon
      - **S46.011** Strain of muscle(s) and tendon(s) of the rotator cuff of right shoulder
      - **S46.012** Strain of muscle(s) and tendon(s) of the rotator cuff of left shoulder
      - **S46.019** Strain of muscle(s) and tendon(s) of the rotator cuff of unspecified shoulder
    - **S46.02** **Laceration of muscle(s) and tendon(s) of the rotator cuff of shoulder**
      - **S46.021** Laceration of muscle(s) and tendon(s) of the rotator cuff of right shoulder
      - **S46.022** Laceration of muscle(s) and tendon(s) of the rotator cuff of left shoulder
      - **S46.029** Laceration of muscle(s) and tendon(s) of the rotator cuff of unspecified shoulder
    - **S46.09** **Other injury of muscle(s) and tendon(s) of the rotator cuff of shoulder**
      - **S46.091** Other injury of muscle(s) and tendon(s) of the rotator cuff of right shoulder
      - **S46.092** Other injury of muscle(s) and tendon(s) of the rotator cuff of left shoulder
      - **S46.099** Other injury of muscle(s) and tendon(s) of the rotator cuff of unspecified shoulder
  - **S46.1** **Injury of muscle, fascia and tendon of long head of biceps**
    - **S46.10** **Unspecified injury of muscle, fascia and tendon of long head of biceps**
      - **S46.101** Unspecified injury of muscle, fascia and tendon of long head of biceps, right arm
      - **S46.102** Unspecified injury of muscle, fascia and tendon of long head of biceps, left arm
      - **S46.109** Unspecified injury of muscle, fascia and tendon of long head of biceps, unspecified arm

▶ New   ⇒ Revised   ~~deleted~~ Deleted   Excludes 1   Excludes 2   Includes   Use additional   Code first   Code also   Key words

OGCR Official Guidelines   X Assign placeholder X   ● Use Additional Character(s)   ▷ Manifestation Code   🐄 Hierarchical Condition Category   **Coding Clinic**

● S46.11   Strain of muscle, fascia and tendon of long head of biceps
            Coding Clinic: 2019, Q2, P27
    ● S46.111   Strain of muscle, fascia and tendon of long head of biceps, right arm
    ● S46.112   Strain of muscle, fascia and tendon of long head of biceps, left arm
    ● S46.119   Strain of muscle, fascia and tendon of long head of biceps, unspecified arm
● S46.12   Laceration of muscle, fascia and tendon of long head of biceps
    ● S46.121   Laceration of muscle, fascia and tendon of long head of biceps, right arm
    ● S46.122   Laceration of muscle, fascia and tendon of long head of biceps, left arm
    ● S46.129   Laceration of muscle, fascia and tendon of long head of biceps, unspecified arm
● S46.19   Other injury of muscle, fascia and tendon of long head of biceps
    ● S46.191   Other injury of muscle, fascia and tendon of long head of biceps, right arm
    ● S46.192   Other injury of muscle, fascia and tendon of long head of biceps, left arm
    ● S46.199   Other injury of muscle, fascia and tendon of long head of biceps, unspecified arm
● S46.2   Injury of muscle, fascia and tendon of other parts of biceps
    ● S46.20   Unspecified injury of muscle, fascia and tendon of other parts of biceps
        ● S46.201   Unspecified injury of muscle, fascia and tendon of other parts of biceps, right arm
        ● S46.202   Unspecified injury of muscle, fascia and tendon of other parts of biceps, left arm
        ● S46.209   Unspecified injury of muscle, fascia and tendon of other parts of biceps, unspecified arm
    ● S46.21   Strain of muscle, fascia and tendon of other parts of biceps
        ● S46.211   Strain of muscle, fascia and tendon of other parts of biceps, right arm
        ● S46.212   Strain of muscle, fascia and tendon of other parts of biceps, left arm
        ● S46.219   Strain of muscle, fascia and tendon of other parts of biceps, unspecified arm
    ● S46.22   Laceration of muscle, fascia and tendon of other parts of biceps
        ● S46.221   Laceration of muscle, fascia and tendon of other parts of biceps, right arm
        ● S46.222   Laceration of muscle, fascia and tendon of other parts of biceps, left arm
        ● S46.229   Laceration of muscle, fascia and tendon of other parts of biceps, unspecified arm
    ● S46.29   Other injury of muscle, fascia and tendon of other parts of biceps
        ● S46.291   Other injury of muscle, fascia and tendon of other parts of biceps, right arm
        ● S46.292   Other injury of muscle, fascia and tendon of other parts of biceps, left arm
        ● S46.299   Other injury of muscle, fascia and tendon of other parts of biceps, unspecified arm

● S46.3   Injury of muscle, fascia and tendon of triceps
    ● S46.30   Unspecified injury of muscle, fascia and tendon of triceps
        ● S46.301   Unspecified injury of muscle, fascia and tendon of triceps, right arm
        ● S46.302   Unspecified injury of muscle, fascia and tendon of triceps, left arm
        ● S46.309   Unspecified injury of muscle, fascia and tendon of triceps, unspecified arm
    ● S46.31   Strain of muscle, fascia and tendon of triceps
        ● S46.311   Strain of muscle, fascia and tendon of triceps, right arm
        ● S46.312   Strain of muscle, fascia and tendon of triceps, left arm
        ● S46.319   Strain of muscle, fascia and tendon of triceps, unspecified arm
    ● S46.32   Laceration of muscle, fascia and tendon of triceps
        ● S46.321   Laceration of muscle, fascia and tendon of triceps, right arm
        ● S46.322   Laceration of muscle, fascia and tendon of triceps, left arm
        ● S46.329   Laceration of muscle, fascia and tendon of triceps, unspecified arm
    ● S46.39   Other injury of muscle, fascia and tendon of triceps
        ● S46.391   Other injury of muscle, fascia and tendon of triceps, right arm
        ● S46.392   Other injury of muscle, fascia and tendon of triceps, left arm
        ● S46.399   Other injury of muscle, fascia and tendon of triceps, unspecified arm
● S46.8   Injury of other muscles, fascia and tendons at shoulder and upper arm level
    ● S46.80   Unspecified injury of other muscles, fascia and tendons at shoulder and upper arm level
        ● S46.801   Unspecified injury of other muscles, fascia and tendons at shoulder and upper arm level, right arm
        ● S46.802   Unspecified injury of other muscles, fascia and tendons at shoulder and upper arm level, left arm
        ● S46.809   Unspecified injury of other muscles, fascia and tendons at shoulder and upper arm level, unspecified arm
    ● S46.81   Strain of other muscles, fascia and tendons at shoulder and upper arm level
        ● S46.811   Strain of other muscles, fascia and tendons at shoulder and upper arm level, right arm
        ● S46.812   Strain of other muscles, fascia and tendons at shoulder and upper arm level, left arm
        ● S46.819   Strain of other muscles, fascia and tendons at shoulder and upper arm level, unspecified arm
    ● S46.82   Laceration of other muscles, fascia and tendons at shoulder and upper arm level
        ● S46.821   Laceration of other muscles, fascia and tendons at shoulder and upper arm level, right arm
        ● S46.822   Laceration of other muscles, fascia and tendons at shoulder and upper arm level, left arm
        ● S46.829   Laceration of other muscles, fascia and tendons at shoulder and upper arm level, unspecified arm

● **S46.89**   Other injury of other muscles, fascia and tendons at shoulder and upper arm level

     ● **S46.891**   Other injury of other muscles, fascia and tendons at shoulder and upper arm level, **right arm**

     ● **S46.892**   Other injury of other muscles, fascia and tendons at shoulder and upper arm level, **left arm**

     ● **S46.899**   Other injury of other muscles, fascia and tendons at shoulder and upper arm level, **unspecified arm**

● **S46.9**   Injury of **unspecified** muscle, fascia and tendon at shoulder and upper arm level

   ● **S46.90**   **Unspecified** injury of unspecified muscle, fascia and tendon at shoulder and upper arm level

     ● **S46.901**   Unspecified injury of unspecified muscle, fascia and tendon at shoulder and upper arm level, **right arm**

     ● **S46.902**   Unspecified injury of unspecified muscle, fascia and tendon at shoulder and upper arm level, **left arm**

     ● **S46.909**   Unspecified injury of unspecified muscle, fascia and tendon at shoulder and upper arm level, **unspecified arm**

   ● **S46.91**   **Strain** of unspecified muscle, fascia and tendon at shoulder and upper arm level

     ● **S46.911**   Strain of unspecified muscle, fascia and tendon at shoulder and upper arm level, **right arm**

     ● **S46.912**   Strain of unspecified muscle, fascia and tendon at shoulder and upper arm level, **left arm**

     ● **S46.919**   Strain of unspecified muscle, fascia and tendon at shoulder and upper arm level, **unspecified arm**

   ● **S46.92**   **Laceration** of unspecified muscle, fascia and tendon at shoulder and upper arm level

     ● **S46.921**   Laceration of unspecified muscle, fascia and tendon at shoulder and upper arm level, **right arm**

     ● **S46.922**   Laceration of unspecified muscle, fascia and tendon at shoulder and upper arm level, **left arm**

     ● **S46.929**   Laceration of unspecified muscle, fascia and tendon at shoulder and upper arm level, **unspecified arm**

   ● **S46.99**   **Other** injury of unspecified muscle, fascia and tendon at shoulder and upper arm level

     ● **S46.991**   Other injury of unspecified muscle, fascia and tendon at shoulder and upper arm level, **right arm**

     ● **S46.992**   Other injury of unspecified muscle, fascia and tendon at shoulder and upper arm level, **left arm**

     ● **S46.999**   Other injury of unspecified muscle, fascia and tendon at shoulder and upper arm level, **unspecified arm**

● **S47**   **Crushing injury of shoulder and upper arm**

   Use additional code for all associated injuries

   Excludes2   crushing injury of elbow (S57.0-)

   The appropriate 7th character is to be added to each code from category S47

A	initial encounter
D	subsequent encounter
S	sequela

X ● **S47.1**   Crushing injury of **right** shoulder and upper arm

X ● **S47.2**   Crushing injury of **left** shoulder and upper arm

X ● **S47.9**   Crushing injury of shoulder and upper arm, **unspecified arm**

● **S48**   **Traumatic amputation of shoulder and upper arm**

   An amputation not identified as partial or complete should be coded to complete

   Excludes1   traumatic amputation at elbow level (S58.0)

   The appropriate 7th character is to be added to each code from category S48

A	initial encounter
D	subsequent encounter
S	sequela

● **S48.0**   Traumatic amputation at **shoulder joint**

   ● **S48.01**   **Complete** traumatic amputation at shoulder joint

     ● **S48.011**   Complete traumatic amputation at **right shoulder joint** A, S 🖙

     ● **S48.012**   Complete traumatic amputation at **left** shoulder joint A, S 🖙

     ● **S48.019**   Complete traumatic amputation at **unspecified shoulder joint** A, S 🖙

   ● **S48.02**   **Partial** traumatic amputation at shoulder joint

     ● **S48.021**   Partial traumatic amputation at **right** shoulder joint A, S 🖙

     ● **S48.022**   Partial traumatic amputation at **left** shoulder joint A, S 🖙

     ● **S48.029**   Partial traumatic amputation at **unspecified shoulder joint** A, S 🖙

● **S48.1**   Traumatic amputation at level **between shoulder and elbow**

   ● **S48.11**   **Complete** traumatic amputation at level between shoulder and elbow

     ● **S48.111**   Complete traumatic amputation at level between **right** shoulder and elbow A, S 🖙

     ● **S48.112**   Complete traumatic amputation at level between **left** shoulder and elbow A, S 🖙

     ● **S48.119**   Complete traumatic amputation at level between **unspecified** shoulder and elbow A, S 🖙

   ● **S48.12**   **Partial** traumatic amputation at level between shoulder and elbow

     ● **S48.121**   Partial traumatic amputation at level between **right** shoulder and elbow A, S 🖙

     ● **S48.122**   Partial traumatic amputation at level between **left** shoulder and elbow A, S 🖙

     ● **S48.129**   Partial traumatic amputation at level between **unspecified** shoulder and elbow A, S 🖙

● **S48.9**   Traumatic amputation of shoulder and upper arm, level **unspecified**

   ● **S48.91**   **Complete** traumatic amputation of shoulder and upper arm, level unspecified

     ● **S48.911**   Complete traumatic amputation of **right** shoulder and upper arm, level unspecified A, S 🖙

     ● **S48.912**   Complete traumatic amputation of **left** shoulder and upper arm, level unspecified A, S 🖙

     ● **S48.919**   Complete traumatic amputation of **unspecified** shoulder and upper arm, level unspecified A, S 🖙

   ● **S48.92**   **Partial** traumatic amputation of shoulder and upper arm, level unspecified

     ● **S48.921**   Partial traumatic amputation of **right** shoulder and upper arm, level unspecified A, S 🖙

     ● **S48.922**   Partial traumatic amputation of **left** shoulder and upper arm, level unspecified A, S 🖙

     ● **S48.929**   Partial traumatic amputation of **unspecified shoulder and upper arm**, level unspecified A, S 🖙

▶ New   ⠿ Revised   ~~deleted~~ Deleted   Excludes 1   Excludes 2   Includes   Use additional   Code first   Code also   Key words

OGCR Official Guidelines   X Assign placeholder X   ● Use Additional Character(s)   ▶ Manifestation Code   🖙 Hierarchical Condition Category   **Coding Clinic**

Item 19–3 SALTER-HARRIS TYPE 1: epiphysis is completely separated from end of bone, or metaphysic growth plate remains attached to epiphysis

SALTER-HARRIS TYPE 2: epiphysis and growth plate are partially separated from metaphysis, which is cracked—most common type

SALTER-HARRIS TYPE 3: fracture occurring through epiphysis and separates part of epiphysis and growth plate from metaphysis fracture, usually at distal end of tibia

SALTER-HARRIS TYPE 4: fracture runs through epiphysis, across growth plate, into metaphysic, surgery is required to restore joint surface to normal and align growth plate

● **S49 Other and unspecified injuries of shoulder and upper arm**

The appropriate 7th character is to be added to each code from subcategories S49.0 and S49.1

A	initial encounter for closed fracture
D	subsequent encounter for fracture with routine healing
G	subsequent encounter for fracture with delayed healing
K	subsequent encounter for fracture with nonunion
P	subsequent encounter for fracture with malunion
S	sequela

● **S49.0 Physeal fracture of upper end of humerus**

● **S49.00 Unspecified physeal fracture of upper end of humerus**

● S49.001 Unspecified physeal fracture of upper end of humerus, right arm

● S49.002 Unspecified physeal fracture of upper end of humerus, left arm

● S49.009 Unspecified physeal fracture of upper end of humerus, unspecified arm

● **S49.01 Salter-Harris Type I physeal fracture of upper end of humerus**

● S49.011 Salter-Harris Type I physeal fracture of upper end of humerus, right arm

● S49.012 Salter-Harris Type I physeal fracture of upper end of humerus, left arm

● S49.019 Salter-Harris Type I physeal fracture of upper end of humerus, unspecified arm

● **S49.02 Salter-Harris Type II physeal fracture of upper end of humerus**

● S49.021 Salter-Harris Type II physeal fracture of upper end of humerus, right arm

● S49.022 Salter-Harris Type II physeal fracture of upper end of humerus, left arm

● S49.029 Salter-Harris Type II physeal fracture of upper end of humerus, unspecified arm

● **S49.03 Salter-Harris Type III physeal fracture of upper end of humerus**

● S49.031 Salter-Harris Type III physeal fracture of upper end of humerus, right arm

● S49.032 Salter-Harris Type III physeal fracture of upper end of humerus, left arm

● S49.039 Salter-Harris Type III physeal fracture of upper end of humerus, unspecified arm

● **S49.04 Salter-Harris Type IV physeal fracture of upper end of humerus**

● S49.041 Salter-Harris Type IV physeal fracture of upper end of humerus, right arm

● S49.042 Salter-Harris Type IV physeal fracture of upper end of humerus, left arm

● S49.049 Salter-Harris Type IV physeal fracture of upper end of humerus, unspecified arm

● **S49.09 Other physeal fracture of upper end of humerus**

● S49.091 Other physeal fracture of upper end of humerus, right arm

● S49.092 Other physeal fracture of upper end of humerus, left arm

● S49.099 Other physeal fracture of upper end of humerus, unspecified arm

● **S49.1 Physeal fracture of lower end of humerus**

● **S49.10 Unspecified physeal fracture of lower end of humerus**

● S49.101 Unspecified physeal fracture of lower end of humerus, right arm

● S49.102 Unspecified physeal fracture of lower end of humerus, left arm

● S49.109 Unspecified physeal fracture of lower end of humerus, unspecified arm

● **S49.11 Salter-Harris Type I physeal fracture of lower end of humerus**

● S49.111 Salter-Harris Type I physeal fracture of lower end of humerus, right arm

● S49.112 Salter-Harris Type I physeal fracture of lower end of humerus, left arm

● S49.119 Salter-Harris Type I physeal fracture of lower end of humerus, unspecified arm

● **S49.12 Salter-Harris Type II physeal fracture of lower end of humerus**

● S49.121 Salter-Harris Type II physeal fracture of lower end of humerus, right arm

● S49.122 Salter-Harris Type II physeal fracture of lower end of humerus, left arm

● S49.129 Salter-Harris Type II physeal fracture of lower end of humerus, unspecified arm

● **S49.13 Salter-Harris Type III physeal fracture of lower end of humerus**

● S49.131 Salter-Harris Type III physeal fracture of lower end of humerus, right arm

● S49.132 Salter-Harris Type III physeal fracture of lower end of humerus, left arm

● S49.139 Salter-Harris Type III physeal fracture of lower end of humerus, unspecified arm

● **S49.14 Salter-Harris Type IV physeal fracture of lower end of humerus**

● S49.141 Salter-Harris Type IV physeal fracture of lower end of humerus, right arm

● S49.142 Salter-Harris Type IV physeal fracture of lower end of humerus, left arm

● S49.149 Salter-Harris Type IV physeal fracture of lower end of humerus, unspecified arm

● **S49.19 Other physeal fracture of lower end of humerus**

● S49.191 Other physeal fracture of lower end of humerus, right arm

● S49.192 Other physeal fracture of lower end of humerus, left arm

● S49.199 Other physeal fracture of lower end of humerus, unspecified arm

● **S49.8   Other specified injuries of shoulder and upper arm**
     The appropriate 7th character is to be added to each
         code in subcategory S49.8

A	initial encounter
D	subsequent encounter
S	sequela

X● **S49.80   Other specified injuries of shoulder and upper
                 arm, unspecified arm**
X● **S49.81   Other specified injuries of right shoulder and
                 upper arm**
X● **S49.82   Other specified injuries of left shoulder and
                 upper arm**

● **S49.9   Unspecified injury of shoulder and upper arm**
     The appropriate 7th character is to be added to each
         code in subcategory S49.9

A	initial encounter
D	subsequent encounter
S	sequela

X● **S49.90   Unspecified injury of shoulder and upper arm,
                 unspecified arm**
X● **S49.91   Unspecified injury of right shoulder and upper
                 arm**
X● **S49.92   Unspecified injury of left shoulder and upper
                 arm**

INJURIES TO THE ELBOW AND FOREARM (S50-S59)

Excludes2   burns and corrosions (T20-T32)
                 frostbite (T33-T34)
                 injuries of wrist and hand (S60-S69)
                 insect bite or sting, venomous (T63.4)

● **S50   Superficial injury of elbow and forearm**
     Excludes2   superficial injury of wrist and hand (S60.-)
     The appropriate 7th character is to be added to each code from
         category S50

A	initial encounter
D	subsequent encounter
S	sequela

● **S50.0   Contusion of elbow**
X● **S50.00   Contusion of unspecified elbow**
X● **S50.01   Contusion of right elbow**
X● **S50.02   Contusion of left elbow**
● **S50.1   Contusion of forearm**
X● **S50.10   Contusion of unspecified forearm**
X● **S50.11   Contusion of right forearm**
X● **S50.12   Contusion of left forearm**
● **S50.3   Other superficial injuries of elbow**
  ● **S50.31   Abrasion of elbow**
     ● **S50.311   Abrasion of right elbow**
     ● **S50.312   Abrasion of left elbow**
     ● **S50.319   Abrasion of unspecified elbow**
  ● **S50.32   Blister (nonthermal) of elbow**
     ● **S50.321   Blister (nonthermal) of right elbow**
     ● **S50.322   Blister (nonthermal) of left elbow**
     ● **S50.329   Blister (nonthermal) of unspecified
                    elbow**
  ● **S50.34   External constriction of elbow**
     ● **S50.341   External constriction of right elbow**
     ● **S50.342   External constriction of left elbow**
     ● **S50.349   External constriction of unspecified
                    elbow**

● **S50.35   Superficial foreign body of elbow**
         Splinter in the elbow
   ● **S50.351   Superficial foreign body of right
                  elbow**
   ● **S50.352   Superficial foreign body of left elbow**
   ● **S50.359   Superficial foreign body of
                  unspecified elbow**
● **S50.36   Insect bite (nonvenomous) of elbow**
   ● **S50.361   Insect bite (nonvenomous) of right
                  elbow**
   ● **S50.362   Insect bite (nonvenomous) of left
                  elbow**
   ● **S50.369   Insect bite (nonvenomous) of
                  unspecified elbow**
● **S50.37   Other superficial bite of elbow**
     Excludes1   open bite of elbow (S51.04)
   ● **S50.371   Other superficial bite of right elbow**
   ● **S50.372   Other superficial bite of left elbow**
   ● **S50.379   Other superficial bite of unspecified
                  elbow**
● **S50.8   Other superficial injuries of forearm**
  ● **S50.81   Abrasion of forearm**
     ● **S50.811   Abrasion of right forearm**
     ● **S50.812   Abrasion of left forearm**
     ● **S50.819   Abrasion of unspecified forearm**
  ● **S50.82   Blister (nonthermal) of forearm**
     ● **S50.821   Blister (nonthermal) of right forearm**
     ● **S50.822   Blister (nonthermal) of left forearm**
     ● **S50.829   Blister (nonthermal) of unspecified
                    forearm**
  ● **S50.84   External constriction of forearm**
     ● **S50.841   External constriction of right forearm**
     ● **S50.842   External constriction of left forearm**
     ● **S50.849   External constriction of unspecified
                    forearm**
  ● **S50.85   Superficial foreign body of forearm**
         Splinter in the forearm
     ● **S50.851   Superficial foreign body of right
                    forearm**
     ● **S50.852   Superficial foreign body of left
                    forearm**
     ● **S50.859   Superficial foreign body of
                    unspecified forearm**
  ● **S50.86   Insect bite (nonvenomous) of forearm**
     ● **S50.861   Insect bite (nonvenomous) of right
                    forearm**
     ● **S50.862   Insect bite (nonvenomous) of left
                    forearm**
     ● **S50.869   Insect bite (nonvenomous) of
                    unspecified forearm**
  ● **S50.87   Other superficial bite of forearm**
       Excludes1   open bite of forearm (S51.84)
     ● **S50.871   Other superficial bite of right forearm**
     ● **S50.872   Other superficial bite of left forearm**
     ● **S50.879   Other superficial bite of unspecified
                    forearm**
● **S50.9   Unspecified superficial injury of elbow and forearm**
  ● **S50.90   Unspecified superficial injury of elbow**
     ● **S50.901   Unspecified superficial injury of right
                    elbow**
     ● **S50.902   Unspecified superficial injury of left
                    elbow**
     ● **S50.909   Unspecified superficial injury of
                    unspecified elbow**

▶ New   ⇒ Revised   ~~deleted~~ Deleted   Excludes 1   Excludes 2   Includes   Use additional   Code first   Code also   Key words

OGCR Official Guidelines   X Assign placeholder X   ● Use Additional Character(s)   ▶ Manifestation Code   🄷🄲 Hierarchical Condition Category   **Coding Clinic**

● **S50.91　Unspecified superficial injury of forearm**
　　● **S50.911　Unspecified superficial injury of right forearm**
　　● **S50.912　Unspecified superficial injury of left forearm**
　　● **S50.919　Unspecified superficial injury of unspecified forearm**

● **S51　Open wound of elbow and forearm**
　　Code also any associated wound infection
　　Excludes1　open fracture of elbow and forearm (S52.- with open fracture 7th character)
　　　　　　traumatic amputation of elbow and forearm (S58.-)
　　Excludes2　open wound of wrist and hand (S61.-)
　　The appropriate 7th character is to be added to each code from category S51

A	initial encounter
D	subsequent encounter
S	sequela

● **S51.0　Open wound of elbow**
　　● **S51.00　Unspecified open wound of elbow**
　　　　● **S51.001　Unspecified open wound of right elbow**
　　　　　　Coding Clinic: 2012, Q4, P108
　　　　● **S51.002　Unspecified open wound of left elbow**
　　　　● **S51.009　Unspecified open wound of unspecified elbow**
　　　　　　Open wound of elbow NOS
　　● **S51.01　Laceration without foreign body of elbow**
　　　　● **S51.011　Laceration without foreign body of right elbow**
　　　　● **S51.012　Laceration without foreign body of left elbow**
　　　　● **S51.019　Laceration without foreign body of unspecified elbow**
　　● **S51.02　Laceration with foreign body of elbow**
　　　　● **S51.021　Laceration with foreign body of right elbow**
　　　　● **S51.022　Laceration with foreign body of left elbow**
　　　　● **S51.029　Laceration with foreign body of unspecified elbow**
　　● **S51.03　Puncture wound without foreign body of elbow**
　　　　● **S51.031　Puncture wound without foreign body of right elbow**
　　　　● **S51.032　Puncture wound without foreign body of left elbow**
　　　　● **S51.039　Puncture wound without foreign body of unspecified elbow**
　　● **S51.04　Puncture wound with foreign body of elbow**
　　　　● **S51.041　Puncture wound with foreign body of right elbow**
　　　　● **S51.042　Puncture wound with foreign body of left elbow**
　　　　● **S51.049　Puncture wound with foreign body of unspecified elbow**

● **S51.05　Open bite of elbow**
　　Bite of elbow NOS
　　Excludes1　superficial bite of elbow (S50.36, S50.37)
　　● **S51.051　Open bite, right elbow**
　　● **S51.052　Open bite, left elbow**
　　● **S51.059　Open bite, unspecified elbow**

● **S51.8　Open wound of forearm**
　　Excludes2　open wound of elbow (S51.0-)
　　● **S51.80　Unspecified open wound of forearm**
　　　　● **S51.801　Unspecified open wound of right forearm**
　　　　● **S51.802　Unspecified open wound of left forearm**
　　　　● **S51.809　Unspecified open wound of unspecified forearm**
　　　　　　Open wound of forearm NOS
　　● **S51.81　Laceration without foreign body of forearm**
　　　　● **S51.811　Laceration without foreign body of right forearm**
　　　　● **S51.812　Laceration without foreign body of left forearm**
　　　　● **S51.819　Laceration without foreign body of unspecified forearm**
　　● **S51.82　Laceration with foreign body of forearm**
　　　　● **S51.821　Laceration with foreign body of right forearm**
　　　　● **S51.822　Laceration with foreign body of left forearm**
　　　　● **S51.829　Laceration with foreign body of unspecified forearm**
　　● **S51.83　Puncture wound without foreign body of forearm**
　　　　● **S51.831　Puncture wound without foreign body of right forearm**
　　　　● **S51.832　Puncture wound without foreign body of left forearm**
　　　　● **S51.839　Puncture wound without foreign body of unspecified forearm**
　　● **S51.84　Puncture wound with foreign body of forearm**
　　　　● **S51.841　Puncture wound with foreign body of right forearm**
　　　　● **S51.842　Puncture wound with foreign body of left forearm**
　　　　● **S51.849　Puncture wound with foreign body of unspecified forearm**
　　● **S51.85　Open bite of forearm**
　　　　Bite of forearm NOS
　　　　Excludes1　superficial bite of forearm (S50.86, S50.87)
　　　　● **S51.851　Open bite of right forearm**
　　　　● **S51.852　Open bite of left forearm**
　　　　● **S51.859　Open bite of unspecified forearm**

● **S52 Fracture of forearm**

> **Note:** A fracture not identified as displaced or nondisplaced should be coded to displaced
>
> A fracture not designated as open or closed should be coded to closed
>
> The open fracture designations are based on the Gustilo open fracture classification

> **Excludes1**   traumatic amputation of forearm (S58.-)
>
> **Excludes2**   fracture at wrist and hand level (S62.-)

> The appropriate 7th character is to be added to all codes from category S52

A	initial encounter for closed fracture
B	initial encounter for open fracture type I or II
	initial encounter for open fracture NOS
C	initial encounter for open fracture type IIIA, IIIB, or IIIC
D	subsequent encounter for closed fracture with routine healing
E	subsequent encounter for open fracture type I or II with routine healing
F	subsequent encounter for open fracture type IIIA, IIIB, or IIIC with routine healing
G	subsequent encounter for closed fracture with delayed healing
H	subsequent encounter for open fracture type I or II with delayed healing
J	subsequent encounter for open fracture type IIIA, IIIB, or IIIC with delayed healing
K	subsequent encounter for closed fracture with nonunion
M	subsequent encounter for open fracture type I or II with nonunion
N	subsequent encounter for open fracture type IIIA, IIIB, or IIIC with nonunion
P	subsequent encounter for closed fracture with malunion
Q	subsequent encounter for open fracture type I or II with malunion
R	subsequent encounter for open fracture type IIIA, IIIB, or IIIC with malunion
S	sequela

> **Coding Clinic: 2016, Q1, P33**

● **S52.0 Fracture of upper end of ulna**

> Fracture of proximal end of ulna

> **Excludes2**   fracture of elbow NOS (S42.40-)
>
> fractures of shaft of ulna (S52.2-)

  ● **S52.00 Unspecified fracture of upper end of ulna**

    ● **S52.001 Unspecified fracture of upper end of right ulna**

    ● **S52.002 Unspecified fracture of upper end of left ulna**

    ● **S52.009 Unspecified fracture of upper end of unspecified ulna**

  ● **S52.01 Torus fracture of upper end of ulna**

> The appropriate 7th character is to be added to all codes in subcategory S52.01

A	initial encounter for closed fracture
D	subsequent encounter for fracture with routine healing
G	subsequent encounter for fracture with delayed healing
K	subsequent encounter for fracture with nonunion
P	subsequent encounter for fracture with malunion
S	sequela

    ● **S52.011 Torus fracture of upper end of right ulna**

    ● **S52.012 Torus fracture of upper end of left ulna**

    ● **S52.019 Torus fracture of upper end of unspecified ulna**

● **S52.02 Fracture of olecranon process without intraarticular extension of ulna**

  ● **S52.021 Displaced fracture of olecranon process without intraarticular extension of right ulna**

  ● **S52.022 Displaced fracture of olecranon process without intraarticular extension of left ulna**

  ● **S52.023 Displaced fracture of olecranon process without intraarticular extension of unspecified ulna**

  ● **S52.024 Nondisplaced fracture of olecranon process without intraarticular extension of right ulna**

  ● **S52.025 Nondisplaced fracture of olecranon process without intraarticular extension of left ulna**

  ● **S52.026 Nondisplaced fracture of olecranon process without intraarticular extension of unspecified ulna**

● **S52.03 Fracture of olecranon process with intraarticular extension of ulna**

  ● **S52.031 Displaced fracture of olecranon process with intraarticular extension of right ulna**

  ● **S52.032 Displaced fracture of olecranon process with intraarticular extension of left ulna**

  ● **S52.033 Displaced fracture of olecranon process with intraarticular extension of unspecified ulna**

  ● **S52.034 Nondisplaced fracture of olecranon process with intraarticular extension of right ulna**

  ● **S52.035 Nondisplaced fracture of olecranon process with intraarticular extension of left ulna**

  ● **S52.036 Nondisplaced fracture of olecranon process with intraarticular extension of unspecified ulna**

● **S52.04 Fracture of coronoid process of ulna**

  ● **S52.041 Displaced fracture of coronoid process of right ulna**

  ● **S52.042 Displaced fracture of coronoid process of left ulna**

  ● **S52.043 Displaced fracture of coronoid process of unspecified ulna**

  ● **S52.044 Nondisplaced fracture of coronoid process of right ulna**

  ● **S52.045 Nondisplaced fracture of coronoid process of left ulna**

  ● **S52.046 Nondisplaced fracture of coronoid process of unspecified ulna**

● **S52.09 Other fracture of upper end of ulna**

  ● **S52.091 Other fracture of upper end of right ulna**

  ● **S52.092 Other fracture of upper end of left ulna**

  ● **S52.099 Other fracture of upper end of unspecified ulna**

● **S52.1 Fracture of upper end of radius**

> Fracture of proximal end of radius

> **Excludes2**   physeal fractures of upper end of radius (S59.2-)
>
> fracture of shaft of radius (S52.3-)

  ● **S52.10 Unspecified fracture of upper end of radius**

    ● **S52.101 Unspecified fracture of upper end of right radius**

    ● **S52.102 Unspecified fracture of upper end of left radius**

    ● **S52.109 Unspecified fracture of upper end of unspecified radius**

▶ New   ⇒ Revised   ~~deleted~~ Deleted   Excludes 1   Excludes 2   Includes   Use additional   Code first   Code also   Key words

OGCR Official Guidelines   X Assign placeholder X   ● Use Additional Character(s)   ▶ Manifestation Code   ⍟ Hierarchical Condition Category   **Coding Clinic**

● **S52.11**   Torus fracture of upper end of radius

The appropriate 7th character is to be added to all codes in subcategory S52.11

A	initial encounter for closed fracture
D	subsequent encounter for fracture with routine healing
G	subsequent encounter for fracture with delayed healing
K	subsequent encounter for fracture with nonunion
P	subsequent encounter for fracture with malunion
S	sequela

● **S52.111**   Torus fracture of upper end of right radius

● **S52.112**   Torus fracture of upper end of left radius

● **S52.119**   Torus fracture of upper end of unspecified radius

● **S52.12**   Fracture of head of radius

● **S52.121**   Displaced fracture of head of right radius

● **S52.122**   Displaced fracture of head of left radius

● **S52.123**   Displaced fracture of head of unspecified radius

● **S52.124**   Nondisplaced fracture of head of right radius

● **S52.125**   Nondisplaced fracture of head of left radius

● **S52.126**   Nondisplaced fracture of head of unspecified radius

● **S52.13**   Fracture of neck of radius

● **S52.131**   Displaced fracture of neck of right radius

● **S52.132**   Displaced fracture of neck of left radius

● **S52.133**   Displaced fracture of neck of unspecified radius

● **S52.134**   Nondisplaced fracture of neck of right radius

● **S52.135**   Nondisplaced fracture of neck of left radius

● **S52.136**   Nondisplaced fracture of neck of unspecified radius

● **S52.18**   Other fracture of upper end of radius

● **S52.181**   Other fracture of upper end of right radius

● **S52.182**   Other fracture of upper end of left radius

● **S52.189**   Other fracture of upper end of unspecified radius

● **S52.2**   Fracture of shaft of ulna

● **S52.20**   Unspecified fracture of shaft of ulna
Fracture of ulna NOS

● **S52.201**   Unspecified fracture of shaft of right ulna

● **S52.202**   Unspecified fracture of shaft of left ulna

● **S52.209**   Unspecified fracture of shaft of unspecified ulna

● **S52.21**   Greenstick fracture of shaft of ulna

The appropriate 7th character is to be added to all codes in subcategory S52.21

A	initial encounter for closed fracture
D	subsequent encounter for fracture with routine healing
G	subsequent encounter for fracture with delayed healing
K	subsequent encounter for fracture with nonunion
P	subsequent encounter for fracture with malunion
S	sequela

● **S52.211**   Greenstick fracture of shaft of right ulna

● **S52.212**   Greenstick fracture of shaft of left ulna

● **S52.219**   Greenstick fracture of shaft of unspecified ulna

● **S52.22**   Transverse fracture of shaft of ulna

● **S52.221**   Displaced transverse fracture of shaft of right ulna

● **S52.222**   Displaced transverse fracture of shaft of left ulna

● **S52.223**   Displaced transverse fracture of shaft of unspecified ulna

● **S52.224**   Nondisplaced transverse fracture of shaft of right ulna

● **S52.225**   Nondisplaced transverse fracture of shaft of left ulna

● **S52.226**   Nondisplaced transverse fracture of shaft of unspecified ulna

● **S52.23**   Oblique fracture of shaft of ulna

● **S52.231**   Displaced oblique fracture of shaft of right ulna

● **S52.232**   Displaced oblique fracture of shaft of left ulna

● **S52.233**   Displaced oblique fracture of shaft of unspecified ulna

● **S52.234**   Nondisplaced oblique fracture of shaft of right ulna

● **S52.235**   Nondisplaced oblique fracture of shaft of left ulna

● **S52.236**   Nondisplaced oblique fracture of shaft of unspecified ulna

● **S52.24**   Spiral fracture of shaft of ulna

● **S52.241**   Displaced spiral fracture of shaft of ulna, right arm

● **S52.242**   Displaced spiral fracture of shaft of ulna, left arm

● **S52.243**   Displaced spiral fracture of shaft of ulna, unspecified arm

● **S52.244**   Nondisplaced spiral fracture of shaft of ulna, right arm

● **S52.245**   Nondisplaced spiral fracture of shaft of ulna, left arm

● **S52.246**   Nondisplaced spiral fracture of shaft of ulna, unspecified arm

● **S52.25**   Comminuted fracture of shaft of ulna

● **S52.251**   Displaced comminuted fracture of shaft of ulna, right arm

● **S52.252**   Displaced comminuted fracture of shaft of ulna, left arm

● **S52.253**   Displaced comminuted fracture of shaft of ulna, unspecified arm

● **S52.254**   Nondisplaced comminuted fracture of shaft of ulna, right arm

● **S52.255**   Nondisplaced comminuted fracture of shaft of ulna, left arm

● **S52.256**   Nondisplaced comminuted fracture of shaft of ulna, unspecified arm

● **S52.26**   Segmental fracture of shaft of ulna
- ● **S52.261**   Displaced segmental fracture of shaft of ulna, right arm
- ● **S52.262**   Displaced segmental fracture of shaft of ulna, left arm
- ● **S52.263**   Displaced segmental fracture of shaft of ulna, unspecified arm
- ● **S52.264**   Nondisplaced segmental fracture of shaft of ulna, right arm
- ● **S52.265**   Nondisplaced segmental fracture of shaft of ulna, left arm
- ● **S52.266**   Nondisplaced segmental fracture of shaft of ulna, unspecified arm

● **S52.27**   Monteggia's fracture of ulna
Fracture of upper shaft of ulna with dislocation of radial head
- ● **S52.271**   Monteggia's fracture of right ulna
- ● **S52.272**   Monteggia's fracture of left ulna
- ● **S52.279**   Monteggia's fracture of unspecified ulna

● **S52.28**   Bent bone of ulna
- ● **S52.281**   Bent bone of right ulna
- ● **S52.282**   Bent bone of left ulna
- ● **S52.283**   Bent bone of unspecified ulna

● **S52.29**   Other fracture of shaft of ulna
- ● **S52.291**   Other fracture of shaft of right ulna
- ● **S52.292**   Other fracture of shaft of left ulna
- ● **S52.299**   Other fracture of shaft of unspecified ulna

● **S52.3**   Fracture of shaft of radius

● **S52.30**   Unspecified fracture of shaft of radius
- ● **S52.301**   Unspecified fracture of shaft of right radius
- ● **S52.302**   Unspecified fracture of shaft of left radius
- ● **S52.309**   Unspecified fracture of shaft of unspecified radius

● **S52.31**   Greenstick fracture of shaft of radius
The appropriate 7th character is to be added to all codes in subcategory S52.31

A	initial encounter for closed fracture
D	subsequent encounter for fracture with routine healing
G	subsequent encounter for fracture with delayed healing
K	subsequent encounter for fracture with nonunion
P	subsequent encounter for fracture with malunion
S	sequela

- ● **S52.311**   Greenstick fracture of shaft of radius, right arm
- ● **S52.312**   Greenstick fracture of shaft of radius, left arm
- ● **S52.319**   Greenstick fracture of shaft of radius, unspecified arm

● **S52.32**   Transverse fracture of shaft of radius
- ● **S52.321**   Displaced transverse fracture of shaft of right radius
- ● **S52.322**   Displaced transverse fracture of shaft of left radius
- ● **S52.323**   Displaced transverse fracture of shaft of unspecified radius
- ● **S52.324**   Nondisplaced transverse fracture of shaft of right radius
- ● **S52.325**   Nondisplaced transverse fracture of shaft of left radius
- ● **S52.326**   Nondisplaced transverse fracture of shaft of unspecified radius

● **S52.33**   Oblique fracture of shaft of radius
- ● **S52.331**   Displaced oblique fracture of shaft of right radius
- ● **S52.332**   Displaced oblique fracture of shaft of left radius
- ● **S52.333**   Displaced oblique fracture of shaft of unspecified radius
- ● **S52.334**   Nondisplaced oblique fracture of shaft of right radius
- ● **S52.335**   Nondisplaced oblique fracture of shaft of left radius
- ● **S52.336**   Nondisplaced oblique fracture of shaft of unspecified radius

● **S52.34**   Spiral fracture of shaft of radius
- ● **S52.341**   Displaced spiral fracture of shaft of radius, right arm
- ● **S52.342**   Displaced spiral fracture of shaft of radius, left arm
- ● **S52.343**   Displaced spiral fracture of shaft of radius, unspecified arm
- ● **S52.344**   Nondisplaced spiral fracture of shaft of radius, right arm
- ● **S52.345**   Nondisplaced spiral fracture of shaft of radius, left arm
- ● **S52.346**   Nondisplaced spiral fracture of shaft of radius, unspecified arm

● **S52.35**   Comminuted fracture of shaft of radius
- ● **S52.351**   Displaced comminuted fracture of shaft of radius, right arm
- ● **S52.352**   Displaced comminuted fracture of shaft of radius, left arm
- ● **S52.353**   Displaced comminuted fracture of shaft of radius, unspecified arm
- ● **S52.354**   Nondisplaced comminuted fracture of shaft of radius, right arm
- ● **S52.355**   Nondisplaced comminuted fracture of shaft of radius, left arm
- ● **S52.356**   Nondisplaced comminuted fracture of shaft of radius, unspecified arm

● **S52.36**   Segmental fracture of shaft of radius
- ● **S52.361**   Displaced segmental fracture of shaft of radius, right arm
- ● **S52.362**   Displaced segmental fracture of shaft of radius, left arm
- ● **S52.363**   Displaced segmental fracture of shaft of radius, unspecified arm
- ● **S52.364**   Nondisplaced segmental fracture of shaft of radius, right arm
- ● **S52.365**   Nondisplaced segmental fracture of shaft of radius, left arm
- ● **S52.366**   Nondisplaced segmental fracture of shaft of radius, unspecified arm

● **S52.37**   Galeazzi's fracture
Fracture of lower shaft of radius with radioulnar joint dislocation
- ● **S52.371**   Galeazzi's fracture of right radius
- ● **S52.372**   Galeazzi's fracture of left radius
- ● **S52.379**   Galeazzi's fracture of unspecified radius

● **S52.38**   Bent bone of radius
- ● **S52.381**   Bent bone of right radius
- ● **S52.382**   Bent bone of left radius
- ● **S52.389**   Bent bone of unspecified radius

● **S52.39**   Other fracture of shaft of radius
- ● **S52.391**   Other fracture of shaft of radius, right arm
- ● **S52.392**   Other fracture of shaft of radius, left arm
- ● **S52.399**   Other fracture of shaft of radius, unspecified arm

▶ New   ⇒ Revised   ~~deleted~~ Deleted   Excludes 1   Excludes 2   Includes   Use additional   Code first   Code also   Key words

OGCR Official Guidelines   X Assign placeholder X   ● Use Additional Character(s)   ▷ Manifestation Code   🔖 Hierarchical Condition Category   **Coding Clinic**

- **S52.5**   Fracture of lower end of radius
  Fracture of distal end of radius
  > **Excludes2**   physeal fractures of lower end of radius
  > (S59.2-)
  - **S52.50**   Unspecified fracture of the lower end of radius
    - **S52.501**   Unspecified fracture of the lower end of right radius
    - **S52.502**   Unspecified fracture of the lower end of left radius
    - **S52.509**   Unspecified fracture of the lower end of unspecified radius
  - **S52.51**   Fracture of radial styloid process
    - **S52.511**   Displaced fracture of right radial styloid process
    - **S52.512**   Displaced fracture of left radial styloid process
    - **S52.513**   Displaced fracture of unspecified radial styloid process
    - **S52.514**   Nondisplaced fracture of right radial styloid process
    - **S52.515**   Nondisplaced fracture of left radial styloid process
    - **S52.516**   Nondisplaced fracture of unspecified radial styloid process
  - **S52.52**   Torus fracture of lower end of radius

    The appropriate 7th character is to be added to all codes in subcategory S52.52

A	initial encounter for closed fracture
D	subsequent encounter for fracture with routine healing
G	subsequent encounter for fracture with delayed healing
K	subsequent encounter for fracture with nonunion
P	subsequent encounter for fracture with malunion
S	sequela

    - **S52.521**   Torus fracture of lower end of right radius
    - **S52.522**   Torus fracture of lower end of left radius
    - **S52.529**   Torus fracture of lower end of unspecified radius
  - **S52.53**   Colles' fracture
    - **S52.531**   Colles' fracture of right radius
    - **S52.532**   Colles' fracture of left radius
      Coding Clinic: 2016, Q2, P5
    - **S52.539**   Colles' fracture of unspecified radius
  - **S52.54**   Smith's fracture
    - **S52.541**   Smith's fracture of right radius
    - **S52.542**   Smith's fracture of left radius
    - **S52.549**   Smith's fracture of unspecified radius
  - **S52.55**   Other extraarticular fracture of lower end of radius
    - **S52.551**   Other extraarticular fracture of lower end of right radius
    - **S52.552**   Other extraarticular fracture of lower end of left radius
    - **S52.559**   Other extraarticular fracture of lower end of unspecified radius
  - **S52.56**   Barton's fracture
    - **S52.561**   Barton's fracture of right radius
    - **S52.562**   Barton's fracture of left radius
    - **S52.569**   Barton's fracture of unspecified radius

- **S52.57**   Other intraarticular fracture of lower end of radius
  - **S52.571**   Other intraarticular fracture of lower end of right radius
  - **S52.572**   Other intraarticular fracture of lower end of left radius
  - **S52.579**   Other intraarticular fracture of lower end of unspecified radius
- **S52.59**   Other fractures of lower end of radius
  - **S52.591**   Other fractures of lower end of right radius
    Coding Clinic: 2019, Q3, P10
  - **S52.592**   Other fractures of lower end of left radius
  - **S52.599**   Other fractures of lower end of unspecified radius
- **S52.6**   Fracture of lower end of ulna
  - **S52.60**   Unspecified fracture of lower end of ulna
    - **S52.601**   Unspecified fracture of lower end of right ulna
    - **S52.602**   Unspecified fracture of lower end of left ulna
    - **S52.609**   Unspecified fracture of lower end of unspecified ulna
  - **S52.61**   Fracture of ulna styloid process
    - **S52.611**   Displaced fracture of right ulna styloid process
    - **S52.612**   Displaced fracture of left ulna styloid process
    - **S52.613**   Displaced fracture of unspecified ulna styloid process
    - **S52.614**   Nondisplaced fracture of right ulna styloid process
    - **S52.615**   Nondisplaced fracture of left ulna styloid process
    - **S52.616**   Nondisplaced fracture of unspecified ulna styloid process
  - **S52.62**   Torus fracture of lower end of ulna

    The appropriate 7th character is to be added to all codes in subcategory S52.62

A	initial encounter for closed fracture
D	subsequent encounter for fracture with routine healing
G	subsequent encounter for fracture with delayed healing
K	subsequent encounter for fracture with nonunion
P	subsequent encounter for fracture with malunion
S	sequela

    - **S52.621**   Torus fracture of lower end of right ulna
    - **S52.622**   Torus fracture of lower end of left ulna
    - **S52.629**   Torus fracture of lower end of unspecified ulna
  - **S52.69**   Other fracture of lower end of ulna
    - **S52.691**   Other fracture of lower end of right ulna
      Coding Clinic: 2019, Q3, P10
    - **S52.692**   Other fracture of lower end of left ulna
    - **S52.699**   Other fracture of lower end of unspecified ulna
- **S52.9**   Unspecified fracture of forearm
  - X **S52.90**   Unspecified fracture of unspecified forearm
  - X **S52.91**   Unspecified fracture of right forearm
  - X **S52.92**   Unspecified fracture of left forearm

● **S53**   **Dislocation and sprain of joints and ligaments of elbow**

     Includes   avulsion of joint or ligament of elbow
                       laceration of cartilage, joint or ligament of elbow
                       sprain of cartilage, joint or ligament of elbow
                       traumatic hemarthrosis of joint or ligament of
                           elbow
                       traumatic rupture of joint or ligament of elbow
                       traumatic subluxation of joint or ligament of
                           elbow
                       traumatic tear of joint or ligament of elbow

     Code also any associated open wound

     Excludes2   strain of muscle, fascia and tendon at forearm
                       level (S56.-)

     The appropriate 7th character is to be added to each code from
       category S53

> A   initial encounter
> D   subsequent encounter
> S   sequela

● **S53.0**   **Subluxation and dislocation of radial head**
             Dislocation of radiohumeral joint
             Subluxation of radiohumeral joint

            Excludes1   Monteggia's fracture-dislocation (S52.27-)

     ● **S53.00**   Unspecified subluxation and dislocation of
                radial head

       ● S53.001   Unspecified subluxation of right
                    radial head

       ● S53.002   Unspecified subluxation of left radial
                    head

       ● S53.003   Unspecified subluxation of
                    unspecified radial head

       ● S53.004   Unspecified dislocation of right radial
                    head

       ● S53.005   Unspecified dislocation of left radial
                    head

       ● S53.006   Unspecified dislocation of unspecified
                    radial head

     ● **S53.01**   Anterior subluxation and dislocation of radial
                head
                Anteriomedial subluxation and dislocation of
                    radial head

       ● S53.011   Anterior subluxation of right radial
                    head

       ● S53.012   Anterior subluxation of left radial
                    head

       ● S53.013   Anterior subluxation of unspecified
                    radial head

       ● S53.014   Anterior dislocation of right radial
                    head

       ● S53.015   Anterior dislocation of left radial
                    head

       ● S53.016   Anterior dislocation of unspecified
                    radial head

     ● **S53.02**   Posterior subluxation and dislocation of radial
                head
                Posteriolateral subluxation and dislocation of
                    radial head

       ● S53.021   Posterior subluxation of right radial
                    head

       ● S53.022   Posterior subluxation of left radial
                    head

       ● S53.023   Posterior subluxation of unspecified
                    radial head

       ● S53.024   Posterior dislocation of right radial
                    head

       ● S53.025   Posterior dislocation of left radial
                    head

       ● S53.026   Posterior dislocation of unspecified
                    radial head

● **S53.03**   Nursemaid's elbow

     ● S53.031   Nursemaid's elbow, right elbow
                  Coding Clinic: 2015, Q1, P7-8

     ● S53.032   Nursemaid's elbow, left elbow

     ● S53.033   Nursemaid's elbow, unspecified
                  elbow

● **S53.09**   Other subluxation and dislocation of radial
             head

     ● S53.091   Other subluxation of right radial head

     ● S53.092   Other subluxation of left radial head

     ● S53.093   Other subluxation of unspecified
                  radial head

     ● S53.094   Other dislocation of right radial head

     ● S53.095   Other dislocation of left radial head

     ● S53.096   Other dislocation of unspecified
                  radial head

● **S53.1**   **Subluxation and dislocation of ulnohumeral joint**
            Subluxation and dislocation of elbow NOS

            Excludes1   dislocation of radial head alone (S53.0-)

     ● **S53.10**   Unspecified subluxation and dislocation of
                ulnohumeral joint

       ● S53.101   Unspecified subluxation of right
                    ulnohumeral joint

       ● S53.102   Unspecified subluxation of left
                    ulnohumeral joint

       ● S53.103   Unspecified subluxation of
                    unspecified ulnohumeral joint

       ● S53.104   Unspecified dislocation of right
                    ulnohumeral joint

       ● S53.105   Unspecified dislocation of left
                    ulnohumeral joint

       ● S53.106   Unspecified dislocation of unspecified
                    ulnohumeral joint

     ● **S53.11**   Anterior subluxation and dislocation of
                ulnohumeral joint

       ● S53.111   Anterior subluxation of right
                    ulnohumeral joint

       ● S53.112   Anterior subluxation of left
                    ulnohumeral joint

       ● S53.113   Anterior subluxation of unspecified
                    ulnohumeral joint

       ● S53.114   Anterior dislocation of right
                    ulnohumeral joint
                    Coding Clinic: 2012, Q4, P108

       ● S53.115   Anterior dislocation of left
                    ulnohumeral joint

       ● S53.116   Anterior dislocation of unspecified
                    ulnohumeral joint

     ● **S53.12**   Posterior subluxation and dislocation of
                ulnohumeral joint

       ● S53.121   Posterior subluxation of right
                    ulnohumeral joint

       ● S53.122   Posterior subluxation of left
                    ulnohumeral joint

       ● S53.123   Posterior subluxation of unspecified
                    ulnohumeral joint

       ● S53.124   Posterior dislocation of right
                    ulnohumeral joint

       ● S53.125   Posterior dislocation of left
                    ulnohumeral joint

       ● S53.126   Posterior dislocation of unspecified
                    ulnohumeral joint

▶ New   ⟹ Revised   ~~deleted~~ Deleted   Excludes 1   Excludes 2   Includes   Use additional   Code first   Code also   Key words

OGCR Official Guidelines   X Assign placeholder X   ● Use Additional Character(s)   ▷ Manifestation Code   ⬤ Hierarchical Condition Category   **Coding Clinic**

● S53.13   **Medial** subluxation and dislocation of ulnohumeral joint
     ● S53.131   Medial subluxation of right ulnohumeral joint
     ● S53.132   Medial subluxation of left ulnohumeral joint
     ● S53.133   Medial subluxation of unspecified ulnohumeral joint
     ● S53.134   Medial dislocation of right ulnohumeral joint
     ● S53.135   Medial dislocation of left ulnohumeral joint
     ● S53.136   Medial dislocation of unspecified ulnohumeral joint

● S53.14   **Lateral** subluxation and dislocation of ulnohumeral joint
     ● S53.141   Lateral subluxation of right ulnohumeral joint
     ● S53.142   Lateral subluxation of left ulnohumeral joint
     ● S53.143   Lateral subluxation of unspecified ulnohumeral joint
     ● S53.144   Lateral dislocation of right ulnohumeral joint
     ● S53.145   Lateral dislocation of left ulnohumeral joint
     ● S53.146   Lateral dislocation of unspecified ulnohumeral joint

● S53.19   **Other** subluxation and dislocation of ulnohumeral joint
     ● S53.191   Other subluxation of right ulnohumeral joint
     ● S53.192   Other subluxation of left ulnohumeral joint
     ● S53.193   Other subluxation of unspecified ulnohumeral joint
     ● S53.194   Other dislocation of right ulnohumeral joint
     ● S53.195   Other dislocation of left ulnohumeral joint
     ● S53.196   Other dislocation of unspecified ulnohumeral joint

● S53.2   Traumatic rupture of **radial collateral ligament**
   Excludes1   sprain of radial collateral ligament NOS (S53.43-)
   X● S53.20   Traumatic rupture of unspecified radial collateral ligament
   X● S53.21   Traumatic rupture of right radial collateral ligament
   X● S53.22   Traumatic rupture of left radial collateral ligament

● S53.3   Traumatic rupture of **ulnar collateral ligament**
   Excludes1   sprain of ulnar collateral ligament (S53.44-)
   X● S53.30   Traumatic rupture of unspecified ulnar collateral ligament
   X● S53.31   Traumatic rupture of right ulnar collateral ligament
   X● S53.32   Traumatic rupture of left ulnar collateral ligament

● S53.4   Sprain of elbow
   Excludes2   traumatic rupture of radial collateral ligament (S53.2-)
             traumatic rupture of ulnar collateral ligament (S53.3-)
   ● S53.40   Unspecified sprain of elbow
     ● S53.401   Unspecified sprain of right elbow
     ● S53.402   Unspecified sprain of left elbow
     ● S53.409   Unspecified sprain of unspecified elbow
          Sprain of elbow NOS

● S53.41   **Radiohumeral** (joint) sprain
     ● S53.411   Radiohumeral (joint) sprain of right elbow
     ● S53.412   Radiohumeral (joint) sprain of left elbow
     ● S53.419   Radiohumeral (joint) sprain of unspecified elbow

● S53.42   **Ulnohumeral** (joint) sprain
     ● S53.421   Ulnohumeral (joint) sprain of right elbow
     ● S53.422   Ulnohumeral (joint) sprain of left elbow
     ● S53.429   Ulnohumeral (joint) sprain of unspecified elbow

● S53.43   **Radial collateral ligament** sprain
     ● S53.431   Radial collateral ligament sprain of right elbow
     ● S53.432   Radial collateral ligament sprain of left elbow
     ● S53.439   Radial collateral ligament sprain of unspecified elbow

● S53.44   **Ulnar collateral ligament** sprain
     ● S53.441   Ulnar collateral ligament sprain of right elbow
     ● S53.442   Ulnar collateral ligament sprain of left elbow
     ● S53.449   Ulnar collateral ligament sprain of unspecified elbow

● S53.49   **Other** sprain of elbow
     ● S53.491   Other sprain of right elbow
     ● S53.492   Other sprain of left elbow
     ● S53.499   Other sprain of unspecified elbow

● **S54**   **Injury of nerves at forearm level**
   Code also any associated open wound (S51.-)
   Excludes2   injury of nerves at wrist and hand level (S64.-)
   The appropriate 7th character is to be added to each code from category S54

A	initial encounter
D	subsequent encounter
S	sequela

● S54.0   **Injury of ulnar nerve at forearm level**
     Injury of ulnar nerve NOS
   X● S54.00   Injury of ulnar nerve at forearm level, unspecified arm
   X● S54.01   Injury of ulnar nerve at forearm level, right arm
   X● S54.02   Injury of ulnar nerve at forearm level, left arm

● S54.1   **Injury of median nerve at forearm level**
     Injury of median nerve NOS
   X● S54.10   Injury of median nerve at forearm level, unspecified arm
   X● S54.11   Injury of median nerve at forearm level, right arm
   X● S54.12   Injury of median nerve at forearm level, left arm

● S54.2   **Injury of radial nerve at forearm level**
     Injury of radial nerve NOS
   X● S54.20   Injury of radial nerve at forearm level, unspecified arm
   X● S54.21   Injury of radial nerve at forearm level, right arm
   X● S54.22   Injury of radial nerve at forearm level, left arm

● S54.3   **Injury of cutaneous sensory nerve at forearm level**
   X● S54.30   Injury of cutaneous sensory nerve at forearm level, unspecified arm
   X● S54.31   Injury of cutaneous sensory nerve at forearm level, right arm
   X● S54.32   Injury of cutaneous sensory nerve at forearm level, left arm

● S54.8   Injury of other nerves at forearm level
   ● S54.8X   Injury of other nerves at forearm level
     ● S54.8X1   Injury of other nerves at forearm level, **right arm**
     ● S54.8X2   Injury of other nerves at forearm level, **left arm**
     ● S54.8X9   Injury of other nerves at forearm level, **unspecified arm**
   ● S54.9   Injury of unspecified nerve at forearm level
    X ● S54.90   Injury of unspecified nerve at forearm level, **unspecified arm**
    X ● S54.91   Injury of unspecified nerve at forearm level, **right arm**
    X ● S54.92   Injury of unspecified nerve at forearm level, **left arm**

● S55   Injury of blood vessels at forearm level

     Code also any associated open wound (S51.-)

     Excludes2   injury of blood vessels at wrist and hand level (S65.-)
                injury of brachial vessels (S45.1-S45.2)

     The appropriate 7th character is to be added to each code from category S55

> A   initial encounter
> D   subsequent encounter
> S   sequela

   ● S55.0   Injury of ulnar artery at forearm level
    ● S55.00   Unspecified injury of ulnar artery at forearm level
     ● S55.001   Unspecified injury of ulnar artery at forearm level, **right arm**
     ● S55.002   Unspecified injury of ulnar artery at forearm level, **left arm**
     ● S55.009   Unspecified injury of ulnar artery at forearm level, **unspecified arm**
    ● S55.01   Laceration of ulnar artery at forearm level
     ● S55.011   Laceration of ulnar artery at forearm level, **right arm**
     ● S55.012   Laceration of ulnar artery at forearm level, **left arm**
     ● S55.019   Laceration of ulnar artery at forearm level, **unspecified arm**
    ● S55.09   Other specified injury of ulnar artery at forearm level
     ● S55.091   Other specified injury of ulnar artery at forearm level, **right arm**
     ● S55.092   Other specified injury of ulnar artery at forearm level, **left arm**
     ● S55.099   Other specified injury of ulnar artery at forearm level, **unspecified arm**
   ● S55.1   Injury of radial artery at forearm level
    ● S55.10   Unspecified injury of radial artery at forearm level
     ● S55.101   Unspecified injury of radial artery at forearm level, **right arm**
     ● S55.102   Unspecified injury of radial artery at forearm level, **left arm**
     ● S55.109   Unspecified injury of radial artery at forearm level, **unspecified arm**
    ● S55.11   Laceration of radial artery at forearm level
     ● S55.111   Laceration of radial artery at forearm level, **right arm**
     ● S55.112   Laceration of radial artery at forearm level, **left arm**
     ● S55.119   Laceration of radial artery at forearm level, **unspecified arm**

   ● S55.19   Other specified injury of radial artery at forearm level
     ● S55.191   Other specified injury of radial artery at forearm level, **right arm**
     ● S55.192   Other specified injury of radial artery at forearm level, **left arm**
     ● S55.199   Other specified injury of radial artery at forearm level, **unspecified arm**
   ● S55.2   Injury of vein at forearm level
    ● S55.20   Unspecified injury of vein at forearm level
     ● S55.201   Unspecified injury of vein at forearm level, **right arm**
     ● S55.202   Unspecified injury of vein at forearm level, **left arm**
     ● S55.209   Unspecified injury of vein at forearm level, **unspecified arm**
    ● S55.21   Laceration of vein at forearm level
     ● S55.211   Laceration of vein at forearm level, **right arm**
     ● S55.212   Laceration of vein at forearm level, **left arm**
     ● S55.219   Laceration of vein at forearm level, **unspecified arm**
    ● S55.29   Other specified injury of vein at forearm level
     ● S55.291   Other specified injury of vein at forearm level, **right arm**
     ● S55.292   Other specified injury of vein at forearm level, **left arm**
     ● S55.299   Other specified injury of vein at forearm level, **unspecified arm**
   ● S55.8   Injury of other blood vessels at forearm level
    ● S55.80   Unspecified injury of other blood vessels at forearm level
     ● S55.801   Unspecified injury of other blood vessels at forearm level, **right arm**
     ● S55.802   Unspecified injury of other blood vessels at forearm level, **left arm**
     ● S55.809   Unspecified injury of other blood vessels at forearm level, **unspecified arm**
    ● S55.81   Laceration of other blood vessels at forearm level
     ● S55.811   Laceration of other blood vessels at forearm level, **right arm**
     ● S55.812   Laceration of other blood vessels at forearm level, **left arm**
     ● S55.819   Laceration of other blood vessels at forearm level, **unspecified arm**
    ● S55.89   Other specified injury of other blood vessels at forearm level
     ● S55.891   Other specified injury of other blood vessels at forearm level, **right arm**
     ● S55.892   Other specified injury of other blood vessels at forearm level, **left arm**
     ● S55.899   Other specified injury of other blood vessels at forearm level, **unspecified arm**
   ● S55.9   Injury of unspecified blood vessel at forearm level
    ● S55.90   Unspecified injury of unspecified blood vessel at forearm level
     ● S55.901   Unspecified injury of unspecified blood vessel at forearm level, **right arm**
     ● S55.902   Unspecified injury of unspecified blood vessel at forearm level, **left arm**
     ● S55.909   Unspecified injury of unspecified blood vessel at forearm level, **unspecified arm**

▶ New   ⇒ Revised   ~~deleted~~ Deleted   Excludes 1   Excludes 2   Includes   Use additional   Code first   Code also   Key words
OGCR Official Guidelines   X Assign placeholder X   ● Use Additional Character(s)   ▶ Manifestation Code   🅀 Hierarchical Condition Category   **Coding Clinic**

● S55.91 Laceration of unspecified blood vessel at forearm level
  ● S55.911 Laceration of unspecified blood vessel at forearm level, right arm
  ● S55.912 Laceration of unspecified blood vessel at forearm level, left arm
  ● S55.919 Laceration of unspecified blood vessel at forearm level, unspecified arm
● S55.99 Other specified injury of unspecified blood vessel at forearm level
  ● S55.991 Other specified injury of unspecified blood vessel at forearm level, right arm
  ● S55.992 Other specified injury of unspecified blood vessel at forearm level, left arm
  ● S55.999 Other specified injury of unspecified blood vessel at forearm level, unspecified arm

● S56 Injury of muscle, fascia and tendon at forearm level
  Code also any associated open wound (S51.-)
  Excludes2 injury of muscle, fascia and tendon at or below wrist (S66.-)
  sprain of joints and ligaments of elbow (S53.4-)
  The appropriate 7th character is to be added to each code from category S56

A	initial encounter
D	subsequent encounter
S	sequela

  ● S56.0 Injury of flexor muscle, fascia and tendon of thumb at forearm level
    ● S56.00 Unspecified injury of flexor muscle, fascia and tendon of thumb at forearm level
      ● S56.001 Unspecified injury of flexor muscle, fascia and tendon of right thumb at forearm level
      ● S56.002 Unspecified injury of flexor muscle, fascia and tendon of left thumb at forearm level
      ● S56.009 Unspecified injury of flexor muscle, fascia and tendon of unspecified thumb at forearm level
    ● S56.01 Strain of flexor muscle, fascia and tendon of thumb at forearm level
      ● S56.011 Strain of flexor muscle, fascia and tendon of right thumb at forearm level
      ● S56.012 Strain of flexor muscle, fascia and tendon of left thumb at forearm level
      ● S56.019 Strain of flexor muscle, fascia and tendon of unspecified thumb at forearm level
    ● S56.02 Laceration of flexor muscle, fascia and tendon of thumb at forearm level
      ● S56.021 Laceration of flexor muscle, fascia and tendon of right thumb at forearm level
      ● S56.022 Laceration of flexor muscle, fascia and tendon of left thumb at forearm level
      ● S56.029 Laceration of flexor muscle, fascia and tendon of unspecified thumb at forearm level

  ● S56.09 Other injury of flexor muscle, fascia and tendon of thumb at forearm level
    ● S56.091 Other injury of flexor muscle, fascia and tendon of right thumb at forearm level
    ● S56.092 Other injury of flexor muscle, fascia and tendon of left thumb at forearm level
    ● S56.099 Other injury of flexor muscle, fascia and tendon of unspecified thumb at forearm level
● S56.1 Injury of flexor muscle, fascia and tendon of other and unspecified finger at forearm level
  ● S56.10 Unspecified injury of flexor muscle, fascia and tendon of other and unspecified finger at forearm level
    ● S56.101 Unspecified injury of flexor muscle, fascia and tendon of right index finger at forearm level
    ● S56.102 Unspecified injury of flexor muscle, fascia and tendon of left index finger at forearm level
    ● S56.103 Unspecified injury of flexor muscle, fascia and tendon of right middle finger at forearm level
    ● S56.104 Unspecified injury of flexor muscle, fascia and tendon of left middle finger at forearm level
    ● S56.105 Unspecified injury of flexor muscle, fascia and tendon of right ring finger at forearm level
    ● S56.106 Unspecified injury of flexor muscle, fascia and tendon of left ring finger at forearm level
    ● S56.107 Unspecified injury of flexor muscle, fascia and tendon of right little finger at forearm level
    ● S56.108 Unspecified injury of flexor muscle, fascia and tendon of left little finger at forearm level
    ● S56.109 Unspecified injury of flexor muscle, fascia and tendon of unspecified finger at forearm level
  ● S56.11 Strain of flexor muscle, fascia and tendon of other and unspecified finger at forearm level
    ● S56.111 Strain of flexor muscle, fascia and tendon of right index finger at forearm level
    ● S56.112 Strain of flexor muscle, fascia and tendon of left index finger at forearm level
    ● S56.113 Strain of flexor muscle, fascia and tendon of right middle finger at forearm level
    ● S56.114 Strain of flexor muscle, fascia and tendon of left middle finger at forearm level
    ● S56.115 Strain of flexor muscle, fascia and tendon of right ring finger at forearm level
    ● S56.116 Strain of flexor muscle, fascia and tendon of left ring finger at forearm level
    ● S56.117 Strain of flexor muscle, fascia and tendon of right little finger at forearm level
    ● S56.118 Strain of flexor muscle, fascia and tendon of left little finger at forearm level
    ● S56.119 Strain of flexor muscle, fascia and tendon of finger of unspecified finger at forearm level

● S56.12   Laceration of flexor muscle, fascia and tendon of other and unspecified finger at forearm level

    ● S56.121   Laceration of flexor muscle, fascia and tendon of right index finger at forearm level

    ● S56.122   Laceration of flexor muscle, fascia and tendon of left index finger at forearm level

    ● S56.123   Laceration of flexor muscle, fascia and tendon of right middle finger at forearm level

    ● S56.124   Laceration of flexor muscle, fascia and tendon of left middle finger at forearm level

    ● S56.125   Laceration of flexor muscle, fascia and tendon of right ring finger at forearm level

    ● S56.126   Laceration of flexor muscle, fascia and tendon of left ring finger at forearm level

    ● S56.127   Laceration of flexor muscle, fascia and tendon of right little finger at forearm level

    ● S56.128   Laceration of flexor muscle, fascia and tendon of left little finger at forearm level

    ● S56.129   Laceration of flexor muscle, fascia and tendon of unspecified finger at forearm level

● S56.19   Other injury of flexor muscle, fascia and tendon of other and unspecified finger at forearm level

    ● S56.191   Other injury of flexor muscle, fascia and tendon of right index finger at forearm level

    ● S56.192   Other injury of flexor muscle, fascia and tendon of left index finger at forearm level

    ● S56.193   Other injury of flexor muscle, fascia and tendon of right middle finger at forearm level

    ● S56.194   Other injury of flexor muscle, fascia and tendon of left middle finger at forearm level

    ● S56.195   Other injury of flexor muscle, fascia and tendon of right ring finger at forearm level

    ● S56.196   Other injury of flexor muscle, fascia and tendon of left ring finger at forearm level

    ● S56.197   Other injury of flexor muscle, fascia and tendon of right little finger at forearm level

    ● S56.198   Other injury of flexor muscle, fascia and tendon of left little finger at forearm level

    ● S56.199   Other injury of flexor muscle, fascia and tendon of unspecified finger at forearm level

● S56.2   Injury of other flexor muscle, fascia and tendon at forearm level

    ● S56.20   Unspecified injury of other flexor muscle, fascia and tendon at forearm level

    ● S56.201   Unspecified injury of other flexor muscle, fascia and tendon at forearm level, right arm

    ● S56.202   Unspecified injury of other flexor muscle, fascia and tendon at forearm level, left arm

    ● S56.209   Unspecified injury of other flexor muscle, fascia and tendon at forearm level, unspecified arm

● S56.21   Strain of other flexor muscle, fascia and tendon at forearm level

    ● S56.211   Strain of other flexor muscle, fascia and tendon at forearm level, right arm

    ● S56.212   Strain of other flexor muscle, fascia and tendon at forearm level, left arm

    ● S56.219   Strain of other flexor muscle, fascia and tendon at forearm level, unspecified arm

● S56.22   Laceration of other flexor muscle, fascia and tendon at forearm level

    ● S56.221   Laceration of other flexor muscle, fascia and tendon at forearm level, right arm

    ● S56.222   Laceration of other flexor muscle, fascia and tendon at forearm level, left arm

    ● S56.229   Laceration of other flexor muscle, fascia and tendon at forearm level, unspecified arm

● S56.29   Other injury of other flexor muscle, fascia and tendon at forearm level

    ● S56.291   Other injury of other flexor muscle, fascia and tendon at forearm level, right arm

    ● S56.292   Other injury of other flexor muscle, fascia and tendon at forearm level, left arm

    ● S56.299   Other injury of other flexor muscle, fascia and tendon at forearm level, unspecified arm

● S56.3   Injury of extensor or abductor muscles, fascia and tendons of thumb at forearm level

    ● S56.30   Unspecified injury of extensor or abductor muscles, fascia and tendons of thumb at forearm level

    ● S56.301   Unspecified injury of extensor or abductor muscles, fascia and tendons of right thumb at forearm level

    ● S56.302   Unspecified injury of extensor or abductor muscles, fascia and tendons of left thumb at forearm level

    ● S56.309   Unspecified injury of extensor or abductor muscles, fascia and tendons of unspecified thumb at forearm level

    ● S56.31   Strain of extensor or abductor muscles, fascia and tendons of thumb at forearm level

    ● S56.311   Strain of extensor or abductor muscles, fascia and tendons of right thumb at forearm level

    ● S56.312   Strain of extensor or abductor muscles, fascia and tendons of left thumb at forearm level

    ● S56.319   Strain of extensor or abductor muscles, fascia and tendons of unspecified thumb at forearm level

    ● S56.32   Laceration of extensor or abductor muscles, fascia and tendons of thumb at forearm level

    ● S56.321   Laceration of extensor or abductor muscles, fascia and tendons of right thumb at forearm level

    ● S56.322   Laceration of extensor or abductor muscles, fascia and tendons of left thumb at forearm level

    ● S56.329   Laceration of extensor or abductor muscles, fascia and tendons of unspecified thumb at forearm level

▶ New   ⇒ Revised   ~~deleted~~ Deleted   Excludes 1   Excludes 2   Includes   Use additional   Code first   Code also   Key words

OGCR Official Guidelines   X Assign placeholder X   ● Use Additional Character(s)   ▶ Manifestation Code   🅗 Hierarchical Condition Category   **Coding Clinic**

● S56.39   Other injury of extensor or abductor muscles, fascia and tendons of thumb at forearm level

     ● S56.391   Other injury of extensor or abductor muscles, fascia and tendons of right thumb at forearm level

     ● S56.392   Other injury of extensor or abductor muscles, fascia and tendons of left thumb at forearm level

     ● S56.399   Other injury of extensor or abductor muscles, fascia and tendons of unspecified thumb at forearm level

● S56.4   Injury of extensor muscle, fascia and tendon of other and unspecified finger at forearm level

     ● S56.40   Unspecified injury of extensor muscle, fascia and tendon of other and unspecified finger at forearm level

         ● S56.401   Unspecified injury of extensor muscle, fascia and tendon of right index finger at forearm level

         ● S56.402   Unspecified injury of extensor muscle, fascia and tendon of left index finger at forearm level

         ● S56.403   Unspecified injury of extensor muscle, fascia and tendon of right middle finger at forearm level

         ● S56.404   Unspecified injury of extensor muscle, fascia and tendon of left middle finger at forearm level

         ● S56.405   Unspecified injury of extensor muscle, fascia and tendon of right ring finger at forearm level

         ● S56.406   Unspecified injury of extensor muscle, fascia and tendon of left ring finger at forearm level

         ● S56.407   Unspecified injury of extensor muscle, fascia and tendon of right little finger at forearm level

         ● S56.408   Unspecified injury of extensor muscle, fascia and tendon of left little finger at forearm level

         ● S56.409   Unspecified injury of extensor muscle, fascia and tendon of unspecified finger at forearm level

     ● S56.41   Strain of extensor muscle, fascia and tendon of other and unspecified finger at forearm level

         ● S56.411   Strain of extensor muscle, fascia and tendon of right index finger at forearm level

         ● S56.412   Strain of extensor muscle, fascia and tendon of left index finger at forearm level

         ● S56.413   Strain of extensor muscle, fascia and tendon of right middle finger at forearm level

         ● S56.414   Strain of extensor muscle, fascia and tendon of left middle finger at forearm level

         ● S56.415   Strain of extensor muscle, fascia and tendon of right ring finger at forearm level

         ● S56.416   Strain of extensor muscle, fascia and tendon of left ring finger at forearm level

         ● S56.417   Strain of extensor muscle, fascia and tendon of right little finger at forearm level

         ● S56.418   Strain of extensor muscle, fascia and tendon of left little finger at forearm level

         ● S56.419   Strain of extensor muscle, fascia and tendon of finger, unspecified finger at forearm level

● S56.42   Laceration of extensor muscle, fascia and tendon of other and unspecified finger at forearm level

     ● S56.421   Laceration of extensor muscle, fascia and tendon of right index finger at forearm level

     ● S56.422   Laceration of extensor muscle, fascia and tendon of left index finger at forearm level

     ● S56.423   Laceration of extensor muscle, fascia and tendon of right middle finger at forearm level

     ● S56.424   Laceration of extensor muscle, fascia and tendon of left middle finger at forearm level

     ● S56.425   Laceration of extensor muscle, fascia and tendon of right ring finger at forearm level

     ● S56.426   Laceration of extensor muscle, fascia and tendon of left ring finger at forearm level

     ● S56.427   Laceration of extensor muscle, fascia and tendon of right little finger at forearm level

     ● S56.428   Laceration of extensor muscle, fascia and tendon of left little finger at forearm level

     ● S56.429   Laceration of extensor muscle, fascia and tendon of unspecified finger at forearm level

● S56.49   Other injury of extensor muscle, fascia and tendon of other and unspecified finger at forearm level

     ● S56.491   Other injury of extensor muscle, fascia and tendon of right index finger at forearm level

     ● S56.492   Other injury of extensor muscle, fascia and tendon of left index finger at forearm level

     ● S56.493   Other injury of extensor muscle, fascia and tendon of right middle finger at forearm level

     ● S56.494   Other injury of extensor muscle, fascia and tendon of left middle finger at forearm level

     ● S56.495   Other injury of extensor muscle, fascia and tendon of right ring finger at forearm level

     ● S56.496   Other injury of extensor muscle, fascia and tendon of left ring finger at forearm level

     ● S56.497   Other injury of extensor muscle, fascia and tendon of right little finger at forearm level

     ● S56.498   Other injury of extensor muscle, fascia and tendon of left little finger at forearm level

     ● S56.499   Other injury of extensor muscle, fascia and tendon of unspecified finger at forearm level

● S56.5   Injury of other extensor muscle, fascia and tendon at forearm level

     ● S56.50   Unspecified injury of other extensor muscle, fascia and tendon at forearm level

         ● S56.501   Unspecified injury of other extensor muscle, fascia and tendon at forearm level, right arm

         ● S56.502   Unspecified injury of other extensor muscle, fascia and tendon at forearm level, left arm

         ● S56.509   Unspecified injury of other extensor muscle, fascia and tendon at forearm level, unspecified arm

● S56.51   Strain of other extensor muscle, fascia and tendon at forearm level
- ● S56.511   Strain of other extensor muscle, fascia and tendon at forearm level, right arm
- ● S56.512   Strain of other extensor muscle, fascia and tendon at forearm level, left arm
- ● S56.519   Strain of other extensor muscle, fascia and tendon at forearm level, unspecified arm

● S56.52   Laceration of other extensor muscle, fascia and tendon at forearm level
- ● S56.521   Laceration of other extensor muscle, fascia and tendon at forearm level, right arm
- ● S56.522   Laceration of other extensor muscle, fascia and tendon at forearm level, left arm
- ● S56.529   Laceration of other extensor muscle, fascia and tendon at forearm level, unspecified arm

● S56.59   Other injury of other extensor muscle, fascia and tendon at forearm level
- ● S56.591   Other injury of other extensor muscle, fascia and tendon at forearm level, right arm
- ● S56.592   Other injury of other extensor muscle, fascia and tendon at forearm level, left arm
- ● S56.599   Other injury of other extensor muscle, fascia and tendon at forearm level, unspecified arm

● S56.8   Injury of other muscles, fascia and tendons at forearm level
- ● S56.80   Unspecified injury of other muscles, fascia and tendons at forearm level
  - ● S56.801   Unspecified injury of other muscles, fascia and tendons at forearm level, right arm
  - ● S56.802   Unspecified injury of other muscles, fascia and tendons at forearm level, left arm
  - ● S56.809   Unspecified injury of other muscles, fascia and tendons at forearm level, unspecified arm
- ● S56.81   Strain of other muscles, fascia and tendons at forearm level
  - ● S56.811   Strain of other muscles, fascia and tendons at forearm level, right arm
  - ● S56.812   Strain of other muscles, fascia and tendons at forearm level, left arm
  - ● S56.819   Strain of other muscles, fascia and tendons at forearm level, unspecified arm
- ● S56.82   Laceration of other muscles, fascia and tendons at forearm level
  - ● S56.821   Laceration of other muscles, fascia and tendons at forearm level, right arm
  - ● S56.822   Laceration of other muscles, fascia and tendons at forearm level, left arm
  - ● S56.829   Laceration of other muscles, fascia and tendons at forearm level, unspecified arm
- ● S56.89   Other injury of other muscles, fascia and tendons at forearm level
  - ● S56.891   Other injury of other muscles, fascia and tendons at forearm level, right arm
  - ● S56.892   Other injury of other muscles, fascia and tendons at forearm level, left arm
  - ● S56.899   Other injury of other muscles, fascia and tendons at forearm level, unspecified arm

● S56.9   Injury of unspecified muscles, fascia and tendons at forearm level
- ● S56.90   Unspecified injury of unspecified muscles, fascia and tendons at forearm level
  - ● S56.901   Unspecified injury of unspecified muscles, fascia and tendons at forearm level, right arm
  - ● S56.902   Unspecified injury of unspecified muscles, fascia and tendons at forearm level, left arm
  - ● S56.909   Unspecified injury of unspecified muscles, fascia and tendons at forearm level, unspecified arm
- ● S56.91   Strain of unspecified muscles, fascia and tendons at forearm level
  - ● S56.911   Strain of unspecified muscles, fascia and tendons at forearm level, right arm
  - ● S56.912   Strain of unspecified muscles, fascia and tendons at forearm level, left arm
  - ● S56.919   Strain of unspecified muscles, fascia and tendons at forearm level, unspecified arm
- ● S56.92   Laceration of unspecified muscles, fascia and tendons at forearm level
  - ● S56.921   Laceration of unspecified muscles, fascia and tendons at forearm level, right arm
  - ● S56.922   Laceration of unspecified muscles, fascia and tendons at forearm level, left arm
  - ● S56.929   Laceration of unspecified muscles, fascia and tendons at forearm level, unspecified arm
- ● S56.99   Other injury of unspecified muscles, fascia and tendons at forearm level
  - ● S56.991   Other injury of unspecified muscles, fascia and tendons at forearm level, right arm
  - ● S56.992   Other injury of unspecified muscles, fascia and tendons at forearm level, left arm
  - ● S56.999   Other injury of unspecified muscles, fascia and tendons at forearm level, unspecified arm

● S57   Crushing injury of elbow and forearm

Use additional code(s) for all associated injuries

Excludes2   crushing injury of wrist and hand (S67.-)

The appropriate 7th character is to be added to each code from category S57

A	initial encounter
D	subsequent encounter
S	sequela

● S57.0   Crushing injury of elbow
- X ● S57.00   Crushing injury of unspecified elbow
- X ● S57.01   Crushing injury of right elbow
- X ● S57.02   Crushing injury of left elbow

● S57.8   Crushing injury of forearm
- X ● S57.80   Crushing injury of unspecified forearm
- X ● S57.81   Crushing injury of right forearm
- X ● S57.82   Crushing injury of left forearm

▶ New   ⇒ Revised   ~~deleted~~ Deleted   Excludes 1   Excludes 2   Includes   Use additional   Code first   Code also   Key words

OGCR Official Guidelines   X Assign placeholder X   ● Use Additional Character(s)   ▶ Manifestation Code   🅗 Hierarchical Condition Category   **Coding Clinic**

● **S58   Traumatic amputation of elbow and forearm**

An amputation not identified as partial or complete should be coded to complete

Excludes1   traumatic amputation of wrist and hand (S68.-)

The appropriate 7th character is to be added to each code from category S58

> A   initial encounter
> D   subsequent encounter
> S   sequela

● **S58.0   Traumatic amputation at elbow level**

● **S58.01   Complete traumatic amputation at elbow level**

● **S58.011   Complete traumatic amputation at elbow level, right arm** A, S 🖧

● **S58.012   Complete traumatic amputation at elbow level, left arm** A, S 🖧

● **S58.019   Complete traumatic amputation at elbow level, unspecified arm** A, S 🖧

● **S58.02   Partial traumatic amputation at elbow level**

● **S58.021   Partial traumatic amputation at elbow level, right arm** A, S 🖧

● **S58.022   Partial traumatic amputation at elbow level, left arm** A, S 🖧

● **S58.029   Partial traumatic amputation at elbow level, unspecified arm** A, S 🖧

● **S58.1   Traumatic amputation at level between elbow and wrist**

● **S58.11   Complete traumatic amputation at level between elbow and wrist**

● **S58.111   Complete traumatic amputation at level between elbow and wrist, right arm** A, S 🖧

● **S58.112   Complete traumatic amputation at level between elbow and wrist, left arm** A, S 🖧

● **S58.119   Complete traumatic amputation at level between elbow and wrist, unspecified arm** A, S 🖧

● **S58.12   Partial traumatic amputation at level between elbow and wrist**

● **S58.121   Partial traumatic amputation at level between elbow and wrist, right arm** A, S 🖧

● **S58.122   Partial traumatic amputation at level between elbow and wrist, left arm** A, S 🖧

● **S58.129   Partial traumatic amputation at level between elbow and wrist, unspecified arm** A, S 🖧

● **S58.9   Traumatic amputation of forearm, level unspecified**

Excludes1   traumatic amputation of wrist (S68.-)

● **S58.91   Complete traumatic amputation of forearm, level unspecified**

● **S58.911   Complete traumatic amputation of right forearm, level unspecified** A, S 🖧

● **S58.912   Complete traumatic amputation of left forearm, level unspecified** A, S 🖧

● **S58.919   Complete traumatic amputation of unspecified forearm, level unspecified** A, S 🖧

● **S58.92   Partial traumatic amputation of forearm, level unspecified**

● **S58.921   Partial traumatic amputation of right forearm, level unspecified** A, S 🖧

● **S58.922   Partial traumatic amputation of left forearm, level unspecified** A, S 🖧

● **S58.929   Partial traumatic amputation of unspecified forearm, level unspecified** A, S 🖧

Item 19–4   SALTER-HARRIS TYPE 1: epiphysis is completely separated from end of bone, or metaphysic growth plate remains attached to epiphysis

SALTER-HARRIS TYPE 2: epiphysis and growth plate are partially separated from metaphysis, which is cracked—most common type

SALTER-HARRIS TYPE 3: fracture occurring through epiphysis and separates part of epiphysis and growth plate from metaphysis fracture, usually at distal end of tibia

SALTER-HARRIS TYPE 4: fracture runs through epiphysis, across growth plate, into metaphysic, surgery is required to restore joint surface to normal and align growth plate

● **S59   Other and unspecified injuries of elbow and forearm**

Excludes2   other and unspecified injuries of wrist and hand (S69.-)

The appropriate 7th character is to be added to each code from subcategories S59.0, S59.1, and S59.2

> A   initial encounter for closed fracture
> D   subsequent encounter for fracture with routine healing
> G   subsequent encounter for fracture with delayed healing
> K   subsequent encounter for fracture with nonunion
> P   subsequent encounter for fracture with malunion
> S   sequela

● **S59.0   Physeal fracture of lower end of ulna**

● **S59.00   Unspecified physeal fracture of lower end of ulna**

● **S59.001   Unspecified physeal fracture of lower end of ulna, right arm**

● **S59.002   Unspecified physeal fracture of lower end of ulna, left arm**

● **S59.009   Unspecified physeal fracture of lower end of ulna, unspecified arm**

● **S59.01   Salter-Harris Type I physeal fracture of lower end of ulna**

● **S59.011   Salter-Harris Type I physeal fracture of lower end of ulna, right arm**

● **S59.012   Salter-Harris Type I physeal fracture of lower end of ulna, left arm**

● **S59.019   Salter-Harris Type I physeal fracture of lower end of ulna, unspecified arm**

● **S59.02   Salter-Harris Type II physeal fracture of lower end of ulna**

● **S59.021   Salter-Harris Type II physeal fracture of lower end of ulna, right arm**

● **S59.022   Salter-Harris Type II physeal fracture of lower end of ulna, left arm**

● **S59.029   Salter-Harris Type II physeal fracture of lower end of ulna, unspecified arm**

● **S59.03   Salter-Harris Type III physeal fracture of lower end of ulna**

● **S59.031   Salter-Harris Type III physeal fracture of lower end of ulna, right arm**

● **S59.032   Salter-Harris Type III physeal fracture of lower end of ulna, left arm**

● **S59.039   Salter-Harris Type III physeal fracture of lower end of ulna, unspecified arm**

● **S59.04   Salter-Harris Type IV physeal fracture of lower end of ulna**

● **S59.041   Salter-Harris Type IV physeal fracture of lower end of ulna, right arm**

● **S59.042   Salter-Harris Type IV physeal fracture of lower end of ulna, left arm**

● **S59.049   Salter-Harris Type IV physeal fracture of lower end of ulna, unspecified arm**

● **S59.09   Other physeal fracture of lower end of ulna**

● **S59.091   Other physeal fracture of lower end of ulna, right arm**

● **S59.092   Other physeal fracture of lower end of ulna, left arm**

● **S59.099   Other physeal fracture of lower end of ulna, unspecified arm**

● **S59.1 Physeal fracture of upper end of radius**

  ● **S59.10 Unspecified physeal fracture of upper end of radius**

    ● S59.101 Unspecified physeal fracture of upper end of radius, right arm

    ● S59.102 Unspecified physeal fracture of upper end of radius, left arm

    ● S59.109 Unspecified physeal fracture of upper end of radius, unspecified arm

  ● **S59.11 Salter-Harris Type I physeal fracture of upper end of radius**

    ● S59.111 Salter-Harris Type I physeal fracture of upper end of radius, right arm

    ● S59.112 Salter-Harris Type I physeal fracture of upper end of radius, left arm

    ● S59.119 Salter-Harris Type I physeal fracture of upper end of radius, unspecified arm

  ● **S59.12 Salter-Harris Type II physeal fracture of upper end of radius**

    ● S59.121 Salter-Harris Type II physeal fracture of upper end of radius, right arm

    ● S59.122 Salter-Harris Type II physeal fracture of upper end of radius, left arm

    ● S59.129 Salter-Harris Type II physeal fracture of upper end of radius, unspecified arm

  ● **S59.13 Salter-Harris Type III physeal fracture of upper end of radius**

    ● S59.131 Salter-Harris Type III physeal fracture of upper end of radius, right arm

    ● S59.132 Salter-Harris Type III physeal fracture of upper end of radius, left arm

    ● S59.139 Salter-Harris Type III physeal fracture of upper end of radius, unspecified arm

  ● **S59.14 Salter-Harris Type IV physeal fracture of upper end of radius**

    ● S59.141 Salter-Harris Type IV physeal fracture of upper end of radius, right arm

    ● S59.142 Salter-Harris Type IV physeal fracture of upper end of radius, left arm

    ● S59.149 Salter-Harris Type IV physeal fracture of upper end of radius, unspecified arm

  ● **S59.19 Other physeal fracture of upper end of radius**

    ● S59.191 Other physeal fracture of upper end of radius, right arm

    ● S59.192 Other physeal fracture of upper end of radius, left arm

    ● S59.199 Other physeal fracture of upper end of radius, unspecified arm

● **S59.2 Physeal fracture of lower end of radius**

  ● **S59.20 Unspecified physeal fracture of lower end of radius**

    ● S59.201 Unspecified physeal fracture of lower end of radius, right arm

    ● S59.202 Unspecified physeal fracture of lower end of radius, left arm

    ● S59.209 Unspecified physeal fracture of lower end of radius, unspecified arm

  ● **S59.21 Salter-Harris Type I physeal fracture of lower end of radius**

    ● S59.211 Salter-Harris Type I physeal fracture of lower end of radius, right arm

    ● S59.212 Salter-Harris Type I physeal fracture of lower end of radius, left arm

    ● S59.219 Salter-Harris Type I physeal fracture of lower end of radius, unspecified arm

  ● **S59.22 Salter-Harris Type II physeal fracture of lower end of radius**

    ● S59.221 Salter-Harris Type II physeal fracture of lower end of radius, right arm

    ● S59.222 Salter-Harris Type II physeal fracture of lower end of radius, left arm

    ● S59.229 Salter-Harris Type II physeal fracture of lower end of radius, unspecified arm

  ● **S59.23 Salter-Harris Type III physeal fracture of lower end of radius**

    ● S59.231 Salter-Harris Type III physeal fracture of lower end of radius, right arm

    ● S59.232 Salter-Harris Type III physeal fracture of lower end of radius, left arm

    ● S59.239 Salter-Harris Type III physeal fracture of lower end of radius, unspecified arm

  ● **S59.24 Salter-Harris Type IV physeal fracture of lower end of radius**

    ● S59.241 Salter-Harris Type IV physeal fracture of lower end of radius, right arm

    ● S59.242 Salter-Harris Type IV physeal fracture of lower end of radius, left arm

    ● S59.249 Salter-Harris Type IV physeal fracture of lower end of radius, unspecified arm

  ● **S59.29 Other physeal fracture of lower end of radius**

    ● S59.291 Other physeal fracture of lower end of radius, right arm

    ● S59.292 Other physeal fracture of lower end of radius, left arm

    ● S59.299 Other physeal fracture of lower end of radius, unspecified arm

● **S59.8 Other specified injuries of elbow and forearm**

  The appropriate 7th character is to be added to each code in subcategory S59.8

A	initial encounter
D	subsequent encounter
S	sequela

  ● **S59.80 Other specified injuries of elbow**

    ● S59.801 Other specified injuries of right elbow

    ● S59.802 Other specified injuries of left elbow

    ● S59.809 Other specified injuries of unspecified elbow

  ● **S59.81 Other specified injuries of forearm**

    ● S59.811 Other specified injuries right forearm

    ● S59.812 Other specified injuries left forearm

    ● S59.819 Other specified injuries unspecified forearm

● **S59.9 Unspecified injury of elbow and forearm**

  The appropriate 7th character is to be added to each code in subcategory S59.9

A	initial encounter
D	subsequent encounter
S	sequela

  ● **S59.90 Unspecified injury of elbow**

    ● S59.901 Unspecified injury of right elbow

    ● S59.902 Unspecified injury of left elbow

    ● S59.909 Unspecified injury of unspecified elbow

  ● **S59.91 Unspecified injury of forearm**

    ● S59.911 Unspecified injury of right forearm

    ● S59.912 Unspecified injury of left forearm

    ● S59.919 Unspecified injury of unspecified forearm

▶ New   ⇒ Revised   ~~deleted~~ Deleted   Excludes 1   Excludes 2   Includes   Use additional   Code first   Code also   Key words

OGCR Official Guidelines   X Assign placeholder X   ● Use Additional Character(s)   ▶ Manifestation Code   🅗 Hierarchical Condition Category   Coding Clinic

INJURIES TO THE WRIST, HAND AND FINGERS (S60-S69)

Excludes2   burns and corrosions (T20-T32)
           frostbite (T33-T34)
           insect bite or sting, venomous (T63.4)

● **S60** **Superficial injury of wrist, hand and fingers**

The appropriate 7th character is to be added to each code from category S60

A	initial encounter
D	subsequent encounter
S	sequela

● **S60.0** Contusion of finger without damage to nail

       Excludes1 contusion involving nail (matrix) (S60.1)

X● **S60.00** Contusion of unspecified finger without damage to nail
        Contusion of finger(s) NOS

● **S60.01** Contusion of thumb without damage to nail

  ● **S60.011** Contusion of right thumb without damage to nail

  ● **S60.012** Contusion of left thumb without damage to nail

  ● **S60.019** Contusion of unspecified thumb without damage to nail

● **S60.02** Contusion of index finger without damage to nail

  ● **S60.021** Contusion of right index finger without damage to nail

  ● **S60.022** Contusion of left index finger without damage to nail

  ● **S60.029** Contusion of unspecified index finger without damage to nail

● **S60.03** Contusion of middle finger without damage to nail

  ● **S60.031** Contusion of right middle finger without damage to nail

  ● **S60.032** Contusion of left middle finger without damage to nail

  ● **S60.039** Contusion of unspecified middle finger without damage to nail

● **S60.04** Contusion of ring finger without damage to nail

  ● **S60.041** Contusion of right ring finger without damage to nail

  ● **S60.042** Contusion of left ring finger without damage to nail

  ● **S60.049** Contusion of unspecified ring finger without damage to nail

● **S60.05** Contusion of little finger without damage to nail

  ● **S60.051** Contusion of right little finger without damage to nail

  ● **S60.052** Contusion of left little finger without damage to nail

  ● **S60.059** Contusion of unspecified little finger without damage to nail

● **S60.1** Contusion of finger with damage to nail

X● **S60.10** Contusion of unspecified finger with damage to nail

● **S60.11** Contusion of thumb with damage to nail

  ● **S60.111** Contusion of right thumb with damage to nail

  ● **S60.112** Contusion of left thumb with damage to nail

  ● **S60.119** Contusion of unspecified thumb with damage to nail

● **S60.12** Contusion of index finger with damage to nail

  ● **S60.121** Contusion of right index finger with damage to nail

  ● **S60.122** Contusion of left index finger with damage to nail

  ● **S60.129** Contusion of unspecified index finger with damage to nail

● **S60.13** Contusion of middle finger with damage to nail

  ● **S60.131** Contusion of right middle finger with damage to nail

  ● **S60.132** Contusion of left middle finger with damage to nail

  ● **S60.139** Contusion of unspecified middle finger with damage to nail

● **S60.14** Contusion of ring finger with damage to nail

  ● **S60.141** Contusion of right ring finger with damage to nail

  ● **S60.142** Contusion of left ring finger with damage to nail

  ● **S60.149** Contusion of unspecified ring finger with damage to nail

● **S60.15** Contusion of little finger with damage to nail

  ● **S60.151** Contusion of right little finger with damage to nail

  ● **S60.152** Contusion of left little finger with damage to nail

  ● **S60.159** Contusion of unspecified little finger with damage to nail

● **S60.2** Contusion of wrist and hand

       Excludes2 contusion of fingers (S60.0-, S60.1-)

● **S60.21** Contusion of wrist

  ● **S60.211** Contusion of right wrist

  ● **S60.212** Contusion of left wrist

  ● **S60.219** Contusion of unspecified wrist

● **S60.22** Contusion of hand

  ● **S60.221** Contusion of right hand

  ● **S60.222** Contusion of left hand

  ● **S60.229** Contusion of unspecified hand

● **S60.3** Other superficial injuries of thumb

● **S60.31** Abrasion of thumb

  ● **S60.311** Abrasion of right thumb

  ● **S60.312** Abrasion of left thumb

  ● **S60.319** Abrasion of unspecified thumb

● **S60.32** Blister (nonthermal) of thumb

  ● **S60.321** Blister (nonthermal) of right thumb

  ● **S60.322** Blister (nonthermal) of left thumb

  ● **S60.329** Blister (nonthermal) of unspecified thumb

● **S60.34** External constriction of thumb
      Hair tourniquet syndrome of thumb
      Use additional cause code to identify the constricting item (W49.0-)

  ● **S60.341** External constriction of right thumb

  ● **S60.342** External constriction of left thumb

  ● **S60.349** External constriction of unspecified thumb

● **S60.35** Superficial foreign body of thumb
      Splinter in the thumb

  ● **S60.351** Superficial foreign body of right thumb

  ● **S60.352** Superficial foreign body of left thumb

  ● **S60.359** Superficial foreign body of unspecified thumb

● **S60.36**　**Insect bite (nonvenomous) of thumb**
　　● S60.361　Insect bite (nonvenomous) of **right thumb**
　　● S60.362　Insect bite (nonvenomous) of **left thumb**
　　● S60.369　Insect bite (nonvenomous) of **unspecified thumb**
● **S60.37**　**Other superficial bite of thumb**
　　　Excludes1　open bite of thumb (S61.05-, S61.15-)
　　● S60.371　Other superficial bite of **right thumb**
　　● S60.372　Other superficial bite of **left thumb**
　　● S60.379　Other superficial bite of **unspecified thumb**
● **S60.39**　**Other superficial injuries of thumb**
　　● S60.391　Other superficial injuries of **right thumb**
　　● S60.392　Other superficial injuries of **left thumb**
　　● S60.399　Other superficial injuries of **unspecified thumb**
● **S60.4**　**Other superficial injuries of other fingers**
　● **S60.41**　**Abrasion of fingers**
　　● S60.410　Abrasion of **right index** finger
　　● S60.411　Abrasion of **left index** finger
　　● S60.412　Abrasion of **right middle** finger
　　● S60.413　Abrasion of **left middle** finger
　　● S60.414　Abrasion of **right ring** finger
　　● S60.415　Abrasion of **left ring** finger
　　● S60.416　Abrasion of **right little** finger
　　● S60.417　Abrasion of **left little** finger
　　● S60.418　Abrasion of **other finger**
　　　　　Abrasion of specified finger with unspecified laterality
　　● S60.419　Abrasion of **unspecified finger**
　● **S60.42**　**Blister (nonthermal) of fingers**
　　● S60.420　Blister (nonthermal) of **right index** finger
　　● S60.421　Blister (nonthermal) of **left index** finger
　　● S60.422　Blister (nonthermal) of **right middle** finger
　　● S60.423　Blister (nonthermal) of **left middle** finger
　　● S60.424　Blister (nonthermal) of **right ring** finger
　　● S60.425　Blister (nonthermal) of **left ring** finger
　　● S60.426　Blister (nonthermal) of **right little** finger
　　● S60.427　Blister (nonthermal) of **left little** finger
　　● S60.428　Blister (nonthermal) of **other finger**
　　　　　Blister (nonthermal) of specified finger with unspecified laterality
　　● S60.429　Blister (nonthermal) of **unspecified finger**
　● **S60.44**　**External constriction of fingers**
　　　Hair tourniquet syndrome of finger
　　　Use additional cause code to identify the constricting item (W49.0-)
　　● S60.440　External constriction of **right index** finger
　　● S60.441　External constriction of **left index** finger

● S60.442　External constriction of **right middle** finger
● S60.443　External constriction of **left middle** finger
● S60.444　External constriction of **right ring** finger
● S60.445　External constriction of **left ring** finger
● S60.446　External constriction of **right little** finger
● S60.447　External constriction of **left little** finger
● S60.448　External constriction of **other finger**
　　　External constriction of specified finger with unspecified laterality
● S60.449　External constriction of **unspecified finger**
● **S60.45**　**Superficial foreign body of fingers**
　　Splinter in the finger(s)
　● S60.450　Superficial foreign body of **right index** finger
　● S60.451　Superficial foreign body of **left index** finger
　● S60.452　Superficial foreign body of **right middle** finger
　● S60.453　Superficial foreign body of **left middle** finger
　● S60.454　Superficial foreign body of **right ring** finger
　● S60.455　Superficial foreign body of **left ring** finger
　● S60.456　Superficial foreign body of **right little** finger
　● S60.457　Superficial foreign body of **left little** finger
　● S60.458　Superficial foreign body of **other finger**
　　　　Superficial foreign body of specified finger with unspecified laterality
　● S60.459　Superficial foreign body of **unspecified finger**
● **S60.46**　**Insect bite (nonvenomous) of fingers**
　● S60.460　Insect bite (nonvenomous) of **right index** finger
　● S60.461　Insect bite (nonvenomous) of **left index** finger
　● S60.462　Insect bite (nonvenomous) of **right middle** finger
　● S60.463　Insect bite (nonvenomous) of **left middle** finger
　● S60.464　Insect bite (nonvenomous) of **right ring** finger
　● S60.465　Insect bite (nonvenomous) of **left ring** finger
　● S60.466　Insect bite (nonvenomous) of **right little** finger
　● S60.467　Insect bite (nonvenomous) of **left little** finger
　● S60.468　Insect bite (nonvenomous) of **other finger**
　　　　Insect bite (nonvenomous) of specified finger with unspecified laterality
　● S60.469　Insect bite (nonvenomous) of **unspecified finger**

▶ New　⇛ Revised　~~deleted~~ Deleted　　Excludes 1　　Excludes 2　　Includes　　Use additional　　Code first　　Code also　　Key words
OGCR Official Guidelines　X Assign placeholder X　● Use Additional Character(s)　▶ Manifestation Code　Ⓗ Hierarchical Condition Category　**Coding Clinic**

● **S60.47**   **Other superficial bite of fingers**
     Excludes1   open bite of fingers (S61.25-, S61.35-)
   ● **S60.470**   Other superficial bite of right index finger
   ● **S60.471**   Other superficial bite of left index finger
   ● **S60.472**   Other superficial bite of right middle finger
   ● **S60.473**   Other superficial bite of left middle finger
   ● **S60.474**   Other superficial bite of right ring finger
   ● **S60.475**   Other superficial bite of left ring finger
   ● **S60.476**   Other superficial bite of right little finger
   ● **S60.477**   Other superficial bite of left little finger
   ● **S60.478**   Other superficial bite of other finger
       Other superficial bite of specified finger with unspecified laterality
   ● **S60.479**   Other superficial bite of unspecified finger

● **S60.5**   **Other superficial injuries of hand**
     Excludes2   superficial injuries of fingers (S60.3-, S60.4-)
  ● **S60.51**   **Abrasion of hand**
   ● **S60.511**   Abrasion of right hand
   ● **S60.512**   Abrasion of left hand
   ● **S60.519**   Abrasion of unspecified hand
  ● **S60.52**   **Blister (nonthermal) of hand**
   ● **S60.521**   Blister (nonthermal) of right hand
   ● **S60.522**   Blister (nonthermal) of left hand
   ● **S60.529**   Blister (nonthermal) of unspecified hand
  ● **S60.54**   **External constriction of hand**
   ● **S60.541**   External constriction of right hand
   ● **S60.542**   External constriction of left hand
   ● **S60.549**   External constriction of unspecified hand
  ● **S60.55**   **Superficial foreign body of hand**
     Splinter in the hand
   ● **S60.551**   Superficial foreign body of right hand
   ● **S60.552**   Superficial foreign body of left hand
   ● **S60.559**   Superficial foreign body of unspecified hand
  ● **S60.56**   **Insect bite (nonvenomous) of hand**
   ● **S60.561**   Insect bite (nonvenomous) of right hand
   ● **S60.562**   Insect bite (nonvenomous) of left hand
   ● **S60.569**   Insect bite (nonvenomous) of unspecified hand
  ● **S60.57**   **Other superficial bite of hand**
     Excludes1   open bite of hand (S61.45-)
   ● **S60.571**   Other superficial bite of hand of right hand
   ● **S60.572**   Other superficial bite of hand of left hand
   ● **S60.579**   Other superficial bite of hand of unspecified hand

● **S60.8**   **Other superficial injuries of wrist**
  ● **S60.81**   **Abrasion of wrist**
   ● **S60.811**   Abrasion of right wrist
   ● **S60.812**   Abrasion of left wrist
   ● **S60.819**   Abrasion of unspecified wrist
  ● **S60.82**   **Blister (nonthermal) of wrist**
   ● **S60.821**   Blister (nonthermal) of right wrist
   ● **S60.822**   Blister (nonthermal) of left wrist
   ● **S60.829**   Blister (nonthermal) of unspecified wrist
  ● **S60.84**   **External constriction of wrist**
   ● **S60.841**   External constriction of right wrist
   ● **S60.842**   External constriction of left wrist
   ● **S60.849**   External constriction of unspecified wrist
  ● **S60.85**   **Superficial foreign body of wrist**
     Splinter in the wrist
   ● **S60.851**   Superficial foreign body of right wrist
   ● **S60.852**   Superficial foreign body of left wrist
   ● **S60.859**   Superficial foreign body of unspecified wrist
  ● **S60.86**   **Insect bite (nonvenomous) of wrist**
   ● **S60.861**   Insect bite (nonvenomous) of right wrist
   ● **S60.862**   Insect bite (nonvenomous) of left wrist
   ● **S60.869**   Insect bite (nonvenomous) of unspecified wrist
  ● **S60.87**   **Other superficial bite of wrist**
     Excludes1   open bite of wrist (S61.55)
   ● **S60.871**   Other superficial bite of right wrist
   ● **S60.872**   Other superficial bite of left wrist
   ● **S60.879**   Other superficial bite of unspecified wrist

● **S60.9**   **Unspecified superficial injury of wrist, hand and fingers**
  ● **S60.91**   **Unspecified superficial injury of wrist**
   ● **S60.911**   Unspecified superficial injury of right wrist
   ● **S60.912**   Unspecified superficial injury of left wrist
   ● **S60.919**   Unspecified superficial injury of unspecified wrist
  ● **S60.92**   **Unspecified superficial injury of hand**
   ● **S60.921**   Unspecified superficial injury of right hand
   ● **S60.922**   Unspecified superficial injury of left hand
   ● **S60.929**   Unspecified superficial injury of unspecified hand
  ● **S60.93**   **Unspecified superficial injury of thumb**
   ● **S60.931**   Unspecified superficial injury of right thumb
   ● **S60.932**   Unspecified superficial injury of left thumb
   ● **S60.939**   Unspecified superficial injury of unspecified thumb

● **S60.94 Unspecified superficial injury of other fingers**
- ● **S60.940** Unspecified superficial injury of right index finger
- ● **S60.941** Unspecified superficial injury of left index finger
- ● **S60.942** Unspecified superficial injury of right middle finger
- ● **S60.943** Unspecified superficial injury of left middle finger
- ● **S60.944** Unspecified superficial injury of right ring finger
- ● **S60.945** Unspecified superficial injury of left ring finger
- ● **S60.946** Unspecified superficial injury of right little finger
- ● **S60.947** Unspecified superficial injury of left little finger
- ● **S60.948** Unspecified superficial injury of other finger
  Unspecified superficial injury of specified finger with unspecified laterality
- ● **S60.949** Unspecified superficial injury of unspecified finger

● **S61 Open wound of wrist, hand and fingers**
Code also any associated wound infection
Excludes1 open fracture of wrist, hand and finger (S62.- with 7th character B)
traumatic amputation of wrist and hand (S68.-)

The appropriate 7th character is to be added to each code from category S61

A	initial encounter
D	subsequent encounter
S	sequela

● **S61.0 Open wound of thumb without damage to nail**
Excludes1 open wound of thumb with damage to nail (S61.1-)
- ● **S61.00** Unspecified open wound of thumb without damage to nail
  - ● **S61.001** Unspecified open wound of right thumb without damage to nail
  - ● **S61.002** Unspecified open wound of left thumb without damage to nail
  - ● **S61.009** Unspecified open wound of unspecified thumb without damage to nail
- ● **S61.01** Laceration without foreign body of thumb without damage to nail
  - ● **S61.011** Laceration without foreign body of right thumb without damage to nail
  - ● **S61.012** Laceration without foreign body of left thumb without damage to nail
  - ● **S61.019** Laceration without foreign body of unspecified thumb without damage to nail
- ● **S61.02** Laceration with foreign body of thumb without damage to nail
  - ● **S61.021** Laceration with foreign body of right thumb without damage to nail
  - ● **S61.022** Laceration with foreign body of left thumb without damage to nail
  - ● **S61.029** Laceration with foreign body of unspecified thumb without damage to nail

● **S61.03 Puncture wound without foreign body of thumb without damage to nail**
- ● **S61.031** Puncture wound without foreign body of right thumb without damage to nail
- ● **S61.032** Puncture wound without foreign body of left thumb without damage to nail
- ● **S61.039** Puncture wound without foreign body of unspecified thumb without damage to nail
● **S61.04 Puncture wound with foreign body of thumb without damage to nail**
- ● **S61.041** Puncture wound with foreign body of right thumb without damage to nail
- ● **S61.042** Puncture wound with foreign body of left thumb without damage to nail
- ● **S61.049** Puncture wound with foreign body of unspecified thumb without damage to nail
● **S61.05 Open bite of thumb without damage to nail**
  Bite of thumb NOS
  Excludes1 superficial bite of thumb (S60.36-, S60.37-)
- ● **S61.051** Open bite of right thumb without damage to nail
- ● **S61.052** Open bite of left thumb without damage to nail
- ● **S61.059** Open bite of unspecified thumb without damage to nail
● **S61.1 Open wound of thumb with damage to nail**
- ● **S61.10** Unspecified open wound of thumb with damage to nail
  - ● **S61.101** Unspecified open wound of right thumb with damage to nail
  - ● **S61.102** Unspecified open wound of left thumb with damage to nail
  - ● **S61.109** Unspecified open wound of unspecified thumb with damage to nail
- ● **S61.11** Laceration without foreign body of thumb with damage to nail
  - ● **S61.111** Laceration without foreign body of right thumb with damage to nail
  - ● **S61.112** Laceration without foreign body of left thumb with damage to nail
  - ● **S61.119** Laceration without foreign body of unspecified thumb with damage to nail
- ● **S61.12** Laceration with foreign body of thumb with damage to nail
  - ● **S61.121** Laceration with foreign body of right thumb with damage to nail
  - ● **S61.122** Laceration with foreign body of left thumb with damage to nail
  - ● **S61.129** Laceration with foreign body of unspecified thumb with damage to nail
- ● **S61.13** Puncture wound without foreign body of thumb with damage to nail
  - ● **S61.131** Puncture wound without foreign body of right thumb with damage to nail
  - ● **S61.132** Puncture wound without foreign body of left thumb with damage to nail
  - ● **S61.139** Puncture wound without foreign body of unspecified thumb with damage to nail

▶ New ⇒ Revised ~~deleted~~ Deleted Excludes 1 Excludes 2 Includes Use additional Code first Code also Key words
OGCR Official Guidelines X Assign placeholder X ● Use Additional Character(s) ▷ Manifestation Code 🔖 Hierarchical Condition Category **Coding Clinic**

● **S61.14   Puncture wound with foreign body of thumb with damage to nail**
     ● **S61.141   Puncture wound with foreign body of right thumb with damage to nail**
     ● **S61.142   Puncture wound with foreign body of left thumb with damage to nail**
     ● **S61.149   Puncture wound with foreign body of unspecified thumb with damage to nail**

● **S61.15   Open bite of thumb with damage to nail**
     Bite of thumb with damage to nail NOS
       Excludes1   superficial bite of thumb (S60.36-, S60.37-)
     ● **S61.151   Open bite of right thumb with damage to nail**
     ● **S61.152   Open bite of left thumb with damage to nail**
     ● **S61.159   Open bite of unspecified thumb with damage to nail**

● **S61.2   Open wound of other finger without damage to nail**
       Excludes1   open wound of finger involving nail (matrix) (S61.3-)
       Excludes2   open wound of thumb without damage to nail (S61.0-)
     ● **S61.20   Unspecified open wound of other finger without damage to nail**
       ● **S61.200   Unspecified open wound of right index finger without damage to nail**
       ● **S61.201   Unspecified open wound of left index finger without damage to nail**
       ● **S61.202   Unspecified open wound of right middle finger without damage to nail**
       ● **S61.203   Unspecified open wound of left middle finger without damage to nail**
       ● **S61.204   Unspecified open wound of right ring finger without damage to nail**
       ● **S61.205   Unspecified open wound of left ring finger without damage to nail**
       ● **S61.206   Unspecified open wound of right little finger without damage to nail**
       ● **S61.207   Unspecified open wound of left little finger without damage to nail**
       ● **S61.208   Unspecified open wound of other finger without damage to nail**
         Unspecified open wound of specified finger with unspecified laterality without damage to nail
       ● **S61.209   Unspecified open wound of unspecified finger without damage to nail**

     ● **S61.21   Laceration without foreign body of finger without damage to nail**
       ● **S61.210   Laceration without foreign body of right index finger without damage to nail**
       ● **S61.211   Laceration without foreign body of left index finger without damage to nail**
       ● **S61.212   Laceration without foreign body of right middle finger without damage to nail**
       ● **S61.213   Laceration without foreign body of left middle finger without damage to nail**
       ● **S61.214   Laceration without foreign body of right ring finger without damage to nail**
       ● **S61.215   Laceration without foreign body of left ring finger without damage to nail**
       ● **S61.216   Laceration without foreign body of right little finger without damage to nail**

       ● **S61.217   Laceration without foreign body of left little finger without damage to nail**
       ● **S61.218   Laceration without foreign body of other finger without damage to nail**
         Laceration without foreign body of specified finger with unspecified laterality without damage to nail
       ● **S61.219   Laceration without foreign body of unspecified finger without damage to nail**

     ● **S61.22   Laceration with foreign body of finger without damage to nail**
       ● **S61.220   Laceration with foreign body of right index finger without damage to nail**
       ● **S61.221   Laceration with foreign body of left index finger without damage to nail**
       ● **S61.222   Laceration with foreign body of right middle finger without damage to nail**
       ● **S61.223   Laceration with foreign body of left middle finger without damage to nail**
       ● **S61.224   Laceration with foreign body of right ring finger without damage to nail**
       ● **S61.225   Laceration with foreign body of left ring finger without damage to nail**
       ● **S61.226   Laceration with foreign body of right little finger without damage to nail**
       ● **S61.227   Laceration with foreign body of left little finger without damage to nail**
       ● **S61.228   Laceration with foreign body of other finger without damage to nail**
         Laceration with foreign body of specified finger with unspecified laterality without damage to nail
       ● **S61.229   Laceration with foreign body of unspecified finger without damage to nail**

     ● **S61.23   Puncture wound without foreign body of finger without damage to nail**
       ● **S61.230   Puncture wound without foreign body of right index finger without damage to nail**
       ● **S61.231   Puncture wound without foreign body of left index finger without damage to nail**
       ● **S61.232   Puncture wound without foreign body of right middle finger without damage to nail**
       ● **S61.233   Puncture wound without foreign body of left middle finger without damage to nail**
       ● **S61.234   Puncture wound without foreign body of right ring finger without damage to nail**
       ● **S61.235   Puncture wound without foreign body of left ring finger without damage to nail**
       ● **S61.236   Puncture wound without foreign body of right little finger without damage to nail**
       ● **S61.237   Puncture wound without foreign body of left little finger without damage to nail**
       ● **S61.238   Puncture wound without foreign body of other finger without damage to nail**
         Puncture wound without foreign body of specified finger with unspecified laterality without damage to nail
       ● **S61.239   Puncture wound without foreign body of unspecified finger without damage to nail**

CHAPTER 19 (S00–T88)

● **S61.24**   **Puncture wound with foreign body of finger without damage to nail**

   ● **S61.240**   **Puncture wound with foreign body of right index finger without damage to nail**

   ● **S61.241**   **Puncture wound with foreign body of left index finger without damage to nail**

   ● **S61.242**   **Puncture wound with foreign body of right middle finger without damage to nail**

   ● **S61.243**   **Puncture wound with foreign body of left middle finger without damage to nail**

   ● **S61.244**   **Puncture wound with foreign body of right ring finger without damage to nail**

   ● **S61.245**   **Puncture wound with foreign body of left ring finger without damage to nail**

   ● **S61.246**   **Puncture wound with foreign body of right little finger without damage to nail**

   ● **S61.247**   **Puncture wound with foreign body of left little finger without damage to nail**

   ● **S61.248**   **Puncture wound with foreign body of other finger without damage to nail**
      Puncture wound with foreign body of specified finger with unspecified laterality without damage to nail

   ● **S61.249**   **Puncture wound with foreign body of unspecified finger without damage to nail**

● **S61.25**   **Open bite of finger without damage to nail**
      Bite of finger without damage to nail NOS

      Excludes1   superficial bite of finger (S60.46-, S60.47-)

   ● **S61.250**   **Open bite of right index finger without damage to nail**

   ● **S61.251**   **Open bite of left index finger without damage to nail**

   ● **S61.252**   **Open bite of right middle finger without damage to nail**

   ● **S61.253**   **Open bite of left middle finger without damage to nail**

   ● **S61.254**   **Open bite of right ring finger without damage to nail**

   ● **S61.255**   **Open bite of left ring finger without damage to nail**

   ● **S61.256**   **Open bite of right little finger without damage to nail**

   ● **S61.257**   **Open bite of left little finger without damage to nail**

   ● **S61.258**   **Open bite of other finger without damage to nail**
      Open bite of specified finger with unspecified laterality without damage to nail

   ● **S61.259**   **Open bite of unspecified finger without damage to nail**

● **S61.3**   **Open wound of other finger with damage to nail**

   ● **S61.30**   **Unspecified open wound of finger with damage to nail**

     ● **S61.300**   **Unspecified open wound of right index finger with damage to nail**

     ● **S61.301**   **Unspecified open wound of left index finger with damage to nail**

     ● **S61.302**   **Unspecified open wound of right middle finger with damage to nail**

     ● **S61.303**   **Unspecified open wound of left middle finger with damage to nail**

     ● **S61.304**   **Unspecified open wound of right ring finger with damage to nail**

     ● **S61.305**   **Unspecified open wound of left ring finger with damage to nail**

     ● **S61.306**   **Unspecified open wound of right little finger with damage to nail**

     ● **S61.307**   **Unspecified open wound of left little finger with damage to nail**

     ● **S61.308**   **Unspecified open wound of other finger with damage to nail**
      Unspecified open wound of specified finger with unspecified laterality with damage to nail

     ● **S61.309**   **Unspecified open wound of unspecified finger with damage to nail**

● **S61.31**   **Laceration without foreign body of finger with damage to nail**

   ● **S61.310**   **Laceration without foreign body of right index finger with damage to nail**

   ● **S61.311**   **Laceration without foreign body of left index finger with damage to nail**

   ● **S61.312**   **Laceration without foreign body of right middle finger with damage to nail**

   ● **S61.313**   **Laceration without foreign body of left middle finger with damage to nail**

   ● **S61.314**   **Laceration without foreign body of right ring finger with damage to nail**

   ● **S61.315**   **Laceration without foreign body of left ring finger with damage to nail**

   ● **S61.316**   **Laceration without foreign body of right little finger with damage to nail**

   ● **S61.317**   **Laceration without foreign body of left little finger with damage to nail**

   ● **S61.318**   **Laceration without foreign body of other finger with damage to nail**
      Laceration without foreign body of specified finger with unspecified laterality with damage to nail

   ● **S61.319**   **Laceration without foreign body of unspecified finger with damage to nail**

● **S61.32**   **Laceration with foreign body of finger with damage to nail**

   ● **S61.320**   **Laceration with foreign body of right index finger with damage to nail**

   ● **S61.321**   **Laceration with foreign body of left index finger with damage to nail**

   ● **S61.322**   **Laceration with foreign body of right middle finger with damage to nail**

   ● **S61.323**   **Laceration with foreign body of left middle finger with damage to nail**

   ● **S61.324**   **Laceration with foreign body of right ring finger with damage to nail**

   ● **S61.325**   **Laceration with foreign body of left ring finger with damage to nail**

   ● **S61.326**   **Laceration with foreign body of right little finger with damage to nail**

   ● **S61.327**   **Laceration with foreign body of left little finger with damage to nail**

   ● **S61.328**   **Laceration with foreign body of other finger with damage to nail**
      Laceration with foreign body of specified finger with unspecified laterality with damage to nail

   ● **S61.329**   **Laceration with foreign body of unspecified finger with damage to nail**

▶ New   ⇒ Revised   ~~deleted~~ Deleted   Excludes 1   Excludes 2   Includes   Use additional   Code first   Code also   Key words

OGCR Official Guidelines   X Assign placeholder X   ● Use Additional Character(s)   ▷ Manifestation Code   ⓗⓒ Hierarchical Condition Category   **Coding Clinic**

1306

● S61.33   **Puncture wound without foreign body** of finger with damage to nail

  ● S61.330   Puncture wound without foreign body of right index finger with damage to nail

  ● S61.331   Puncture wound without foreign body of left index finger with damage to nail

  ● S61.332   Puncture wound without foreign body of right middle finger with damage to nail

  ● S61.333   Puncture wound without foreign body of left middle finger with damage to nail

  ● S61.334   Puncture wound without foreign body of right ring finger with damage to nail

  ● S61.335   Puncture wound without foreign body of left ring finger with damage to nail

  ● S61.336   Puncture wound without foreign body of right little finger with damage to nail

  ● S61.337   Puncture wound without foreign body of left little finger with damage to nail

  ● S61.338   Puncture wound without foreign body of other finger with damage to nail

         Puncture wound without foreign body of specified finger with unspecified laterality with damage to nail

  ● S61.339   Puncture wound without foreign body of unspecified finger with damage to nail

● S61.34   **Puncture wound with foreign body of finger** with damage to nail

  ● S61.340   Puncture wound with foreign body of right index finger with damage to nail

  ● S61.341   Puncture wound with foreign body of left index finger with damage to nail

  ● S61.342   Puncture wound with foreign body of right middle finger with damage to nail

  ● S61.343   Puncture wound with foreign body of left middle finger with damage to nail

  ● S61.344   Puncture wound with foreign body of right ring finger with damage to nail

  ● S61.345   Puncture wound with foreign body of left ring finger with damage to nail

  ● S61.346   Puncture wound with foreign body of right little finger with damage to nail

  ● S61.347   Puncture wound with foreign body of left little finger with damage to nail

  ● S61.348   Puncture wound with foreign body of other finger with damage to nail

         Puncture wound with foreign body of specified finger with unspecified laterality with damage to nail

  ● S61.349   Puncture wound with foreign body of unspecified finger with damage to nail

● S61.35   **Open bite of finger** with damage to nail

       Bite of finger with damage to nail NOS

       Excludes1   superficial bite of finger (S60.46-, S60.47-)

  ● S61.350   Open bite of right index finger with damage to nail

  ● S61.351   Open bite of left index finger with damage to nail

  ● S61.352   Open bite of right middle finger with damage to nail

  ● S61.353   Open bite of left middle finger with damage to nail

  ● S61.354   Open bite of right ring finger with damage to nail

  ● S61.355   Open bite of left ring finger with damage to nail

  ● S61.356   Open bite of right little finger with damage to nail

  ● S61.357   Open bite of left little finger with damage to nail

  ● S61.358   Open bite of other finger with damage to nail

         Open bite of specified finger with unspecified laterality with damage to nail

  ● S61.359   Open bite of unspecified finger with damage to nail

● S61.4   **Open wound of hand**

 ● S61.40   **Unspecified open wound of hand**

  ● S61.401   Unspecified open wound of right hand

  ● S61.402   Unspecified open wound of left hand

  ● S61.409   Unspecified open wound of unspecified hand

 ● S61.41   **Laceration without foreign body** of hand

  ● S61.411   Laceration without foreign body of right hand

  ● S61.412   Laceration without foreign body of left hand

  ● S61.419   Laceration without foreign body of unspecified hand

 ● S61.42   **Laceration with foreign body** of hand

  ● S61.421   Laceration with foreign body of right hand

  ● S61.422   Laceration with foreign body of left hand

  ● S61.429   Laceration with foreign body of unspecified hand

 ● S61.43   **Puncture wound without foreign body** of hand

  ● S61.431   Puncture wound without foreign body of right hand

  ● S61.432   Puncture wound without foreign body of left hand

  ● S61.439   Puncture wound without foreign body of unspecified hand

 ● S61.44   **Puncture wound with foreign body** of hand

  ● S61.441   Puncture wound with foreign body of right hand

  ● S61.442   Puncture wound with foreign body of left hand

  ● S61.449   Puncture wound with foreign body of unspecified hand

 ● S61.45   **Open bite of hand**

      Bite of hand NOS

      Excludes1   superficial bite of hand (S60.56-, S60.57-)

  ● S61.451   Open bite of right hand

  ● S61.452   Open bite of left hand

  ● S61.459   Open bite of unspecified hand

● **S61.5　Open wound of wrist**
　　● **S61.50　Unspecified open wound of wrist**
　　　　● S61.501　Unspecified open wound of right wrist
　　　　● S61.502　Unspecified open wound of left wrist
　　　　● S61.509　Unspecified open wound of unspecified wrist
　　● **S61.51　Laceration without foreign body of wrist**
　　　　● S61.511　Laceration without foreign body of right wrist
　　　　● S61.512　Laceration without foreign body of left wrist
　　　　● S61.519　Laceration without foreign body of unspecified wrist
　　● **S61.52　Laceration with foreign body of wrist**
　　　　● S61.521　Laceration with foreign body of right wrist
　　　　● S61.522　Laceration with foreign body of left wrist
　　　　● S61.529　Laceration with foreign body of unspecified wrist
　　● **S61.53　Puncture wound without foreign body of wrist**
　　　　● S61.531　Puncture wound without foreign body of right wrist
　　　　● S61.532　Puncture wound without foreign body of left wrist
　　　　● S61.539　Puncture wound without foreign body of unspecified wrist
　　● **S61.54　Puncture wound with foreign body of wrist**
　　　　● S61.541　Puncture wound with foreign body of right wrist
　　　　● S61.542　Puncture wound with foreign body of left wrist
　　　　● S61.549　Puncture wound with foreign body of unspecified wrist
　　● **S61.55　Open bite of wrist**
　　　　Bite of wrist NOS
　　　　　Excludes1　superficial bite of wrist (S60.86-, S60.87-)
　　　　● S61.551　Open bite of right wrist
　　　　● S61.552　Open bite of left wrist
　　　　● S61.559　Open bite of unspecified wrist

● **S62　Fracture at wrist and hand level**
　　Note: A fracture not indicated as displaced or nondisplaced should be coded to displaced
　　　A fracture not indicated as open or closed should be coded to closed
　　Excludes1　traumatic amputation of wrist and hand (S68.-)
　　Excludes2　fracture of distal parts of ulna and radius (S52.-)
　　The appropriate 7th character is to be added to each code from category S62

A	initial encounter for closed fracture
B	initial encounter for open fracture
D	subsequent encounter for fracture with routine healing
G	subsequent encounter for fracture with delayed healing
K	subsequent encounter for fracture with nonunion
P	subsequent encounter for fracture with malunion
S	sequela

　　● **S62.0　Fracture of navicular [scaphoid] bone of wrist**
　　　　● **S62.00　Unspecified fracture of navicular [scaphoid] bone of wrist**
　　　　　　● S62.001　Unspecified fracture of navicular [scaphoid] bone of right wrist
　　　　　　● S62.002　Unspecified fracture of navicular [scaphoid] bone of left wrist
　　　　　　　　Coding Clinic: 2012, Q4, P106
　　　　　　● S62.009　Unspecified fracture of navicular [scaphoid] bone of unspecified wrist

　　● **S62.01　Fracture of distal pole of navicular [scaphoid] bone of wrist**
　　　　Fracture of volar tuberosity of navicular [scaphoid] bone of wrist
　　　　● S62.011　Displaced fracture of distal pole of navicular [scaphoid] bone of right wrist
　　　　● S62.012　Displaced fracture of distal pole of navicular [scaphoid] bone of left wrist
　　　　● S62.013　Displaced fracture of distal pole of navicular [scaphoid] bone of unspecified wrist
　　　　● S62.014　Nondisplaced fracture of distal pole of navicular [scaphoid] bone of right wrist
　　　　● S62.015　Nondisplaced fracture of distal pole of navicular [scaphoid] bone of left wrist
　　　　● S62.016　Nondisplaced fracture of distal pole of navicular [scaphoid] bone of unspecified wrist
　　● **S62.02　Fracture of middle third of navicular [scaphoid] bone of wrist**
　　　　● S62.021　Displaced fracture of middle third of navicular [scaphoid] bone of right wrist
　　　　● S62.022　Displaced fracture of middle third of navicular [scaphoid] bone of left wrist
　　　　● S62.023　Displaced fracture of middle third of navicular [scaphoid] bone of unspecified wrist
　　　　● S62.024　Nondisplaced fracture of middle third of navicular [scaphoid] bone of right wrist
　　　　● S62.025　Nondisplaced fracture of middle third of navicular [scaphoid] bone of left wrist
　　　　● S62.026　Nondisplaced fracture of middle third of navicular [scaphoid] bone of unspecified wrist
　　● **S62.03　Fracture of proximal third of navicular [scaphoid] bone of wrist**
　　　　● S62.031　Displaced fracture of proximal third of navicular [scaphoid] bone of right wrist
　　　　● S62.032　Displaced fracture of proximal third of navicular [scaphoid] bone of left wrist
　　　　● S62.033　Displaced fracture of proximal third of navicular [scaphoid] bone of unspecified wrist
　　　　● S62.034　Nondisplaced fracture of proximal third of navicular [scaphoid] bone of right wrist
　　　　● S62.035　Nondisplaced fracture of proximal third of navicular [scaphoid] bone of left wrist
　　　　● S62.036　Nondisplaced fracture of proximal third of navicular [scaphoid] bone of unspecified wrist
● **S62.1　Fracture of other and unspecified carpal bone(s)**
　　Excludes2　fracture of scaphoid of wrist (S62.0-)
　　● **S62.10　Fracture of unspecified carpal bone**
　　　　Fracture of wrist NOS
　　　　● S62.101　Fracture of unspecified carpal bone, right wrist
　　　　● S62.102　Fracture of unspecified carpal bone, left wrist
　　　　　　Coding Clinic: 2012, Q4, P95
　　　　● S62.109　Fracture of unspecified carpal bone, unspecified wrist

▶ New　▥ Revised　d̶e̶l̶e̶t̶e̶d̶ Deleted　Excludes 1　Excludes 2　Includes　Use additional　Code first　Code also　Key words
OGCR Official Guidelines　X Assign placeholder X　● Use Additional Character(s)　▶ Manifestation Code　🝖 Hierarchical Condition Category　Coding Clinic

● **S62.11** Fracture of triquetrum [cuneiform] bone of wrist
  ● **S62.111** Displaced fracture of triquetrum [cuneiform] bone, right wrist
  ● **S62.112** Displaced fracture of triquetrum [cuneiform] bone, left wrist
  ● **S62.113** Displaced fracture of triquetrum [cuneiform] bone, unspecified wrist
  ● **S62.114** Nondisplaced fracture of triquetrum [cuneiform] bone, right wrist
  ● **S62.115** Nondisplaced fracture of triquetrum [cuneiform] bone, left wrist
  ● **S62.116** Nondisplaced fracture of triquetrum [cuneiform] bone, unspecified wrist
● **S62.12** Fracture of lunate [semilunar]
  ● **S62.121** Displaced fracture of lunate [semilunar], right wrist
  ● **S62.122** Displaced fracture of lunate [semilunar], left wrist
  ● **S62.123** Displaced fracture of lunate [semilunar], unspecified wrist
  ● **S62.124** Nondisplaced fracture of lunate [semilunar], right wrist
  ● **S62.125** Nondisplaced fracture of lunate [semilunar], left wrist
  ● **S62.126** Nondisplaced fracture of lunate [semilunar], unspecified wrist
● **S62.13** Fracture of capitate [os magnum] bone
  ● **S62.131** Displaced fracture of capitate [os magnum] bone, right wrist
  ● **S62.132** Displaced fracture of capitate [os magnum] bone, left wrist
  ● **S62.133** Displaced fracture of capitate [os magnum] bone, unspecified wrist
  ● **S62.134** Nondisplaced fracture of capitate [os magnum] bone, right wrist
  ● **S62.135** Nondisplaced fracture of capitate [os magnum] bone, left wrist
  ● **S62.136** Nondisplaced fracture of capitate [os magnum] bone, unspecified wrist
● **S62.14** Fracture of body of hamate [unciform] bone
  Fracture of hamate [unciform] bone NOS
  ● **S62.141** Displaced fracture of body of hamate [unciform] bone, right wrist
  ● **S62.142** Displaced fracture of body of hamate [unciform] bone, left wrist
  ● **S62.143** Displaced fracture of body of hamate [unciform] bone, unspecified wrist
  ● **S62.144** Nondisplaced fracture of body of hamate [unciform] bone, right wrist
  ● **S62.145** Nondisplaced fracture of body of hamate [unciform] bone, left wrist
  ● **S62.146** Nondisplaced fracture of body of hamate [unciform] bone, unspecified wrist
● **S62.15** Fracture of hook process of hamate [unciform] bone
  Fracture of unciform process of hamate [unciform] bone
  ● **S62.151** Displaced fracture of hook process of hamate [unciform] bone, right wrist
  ● **S62.152** Displaced fracture of hook process of hamate [unciform] bone, left wrist
  ● **S62.153** Displaced fracture of hook process of hamate [unciform] bone, unspecified wrist
  ● **S62.154** Nondisplaced fracture of hook process of hamate [unciform] bone, right wrist
  ● **S62.155** Nondisplaced fracture of hook process of hamate [unciform] bone, left wrist
  ● **S62.156** Nondisplaced fracture of hook process of hamate [unciform] bone, unspecified wrist

● **S62.16** Fracture of pisiform
  ● **S62.161** Displaced fracture of pisiform, right wrist
  ● **S62.162** Displaced fracture of pisiform, left wrist
  ● **S62.163** Displaced fracture of pisiform, unspecified wrist
  ● **S62.164** Nondisplaced fracture of pisiform, right wrist
  ● **S62.165** Nondisplaced fracture of pisiform, left wrist
  ● **S62.166** Nondisplaced fracture of pisiform, unspecified wrist
● **S62.17** Fracture of trapezium [larger multangular]
  ● **S62.171** Displaced fracture of trapezium [larger multangular], right wrist
  ● **S62.172** Displaced fracture of trapezium [larger multangular], left wrist
  ● **S62.173** Displaced fracture of trapezium [larger multangular], unspecified wrist
  ● **S62.174** Nondisplaced fracture of trapezium [larger multangular], right wrist
  ● **S62.175** Nondisplaced fracture of trapezium [larger multangular], left wrist
  ● **S62.176** Nondisplaced fracture of trapezium [larger multangular], unspecified wrist
● **S62.18** Fracture of trapezoid [smaller multangular]
  ● **S62.181** Displaced fracture of trapezoid [smaller multangular], right wrist
  ● **S62.182** Displaced fracture of trapezoid [smaller multangular], left wrist
  ● **S62.183** Displaced fracture of trapezoid [smaller multangular], unspecified wrist
  ● **S62.184** Nondisplaced fracture of trapezoid [smaller multangular], right wrist
  ● **S62.185** Nondisplaced fracture of trapezoid [smaller multangular], left wrist
  ● **S62.186** Nondisplaced fracture of trapezoid [smaller multangular], unspecified wrist
● **S62.2** Fracture of first metacarpal bone
  ● **S62.20** Unspecified fracture of first metacarpal bone
    ● **S62.201** Unspecified fracture of first metacarpal bone, right hand
    ● **S62.202** Unspecified fracture of first metacarpal bone, left hand
    ● **S62.209** Unspecified fracture of first metacarpal bone, unspecified hand
  ● **S62.21** Bennett's fracture
    ● **S62.211** Bennett's fracture, right hand
    ● **S62.212** Bennett's fracture, left hand
    ● **S62.213** Bennett's fracture, unspecified hand
  ● **S62.22** Rolando's fracture
    ● **S62.221** Displaced Rolando's fracture, right hand
    ● **S62.222** Displaced Rolando's fracture, left hand
    ● **S62.223** Displaced Rolando's fracture, unspecified hand
    ● **S62.224** Nondisplaced Rolando's fracture, right hand
    ● **S62.225** Nondisplaced Rolando's fracture, left hand
    ● **S62.226** Nondisplaced Rolando's fracture, unspecified hand

● **S62.23**　Other fracture of base of first metacarpal bone
- ● **S62.231**　Other displaced fracture of base of first metacarpal bone, right hand
- ● **S62.232**　Other displaced fracture of base of first metacarpal bone, left hand
- ● **S62.233**　Other displaced fracture of base of first metacarpal bone, unspecified hand
- ● **S62.234**　Other nondisplaced fracture of base of first metacarpal bone, right hand
- ● **S62.235**　Other nondisplaced fracture of base of first metacarpal bone, left hand
- ● **S62.236**　Other nondisplaced fracture of base of first metacarpal bone, unspecified hand

● **S62.24**　Fracture of shaft of first metacarpal bone
- ● **S62.241**　Displaced fracture of shaft of first metacarpal bone, right hand
- ● **S62.242**　Displaced fracture of shaft of first metacarpal bone, left hand
- ● **S62.243**　Displaced fracture of shaft of first metacarpal bone, unspecified hand
- ● **S62.244**　Nondisplaced fracture of shaft of first metacarpal bone, right hand
- ● **S62.245**　Nondisplaced fracture of shaft of first metacarpal bone, left hand
- ● **S62.246**　Nondisplaced fracture of shaft of first metacarpal bone, unspecified hand

● **S62.25**　Fracture of neck of first metacarpal bone
- ● **S62.251**　Displaced fracture of neck of first metacarpal bone, right hand
- ● **S62.252**　Displaced fracture of neck of first metacarpal bone, left hand
- ● **S62.253**　Displaced fracture of neck of first metacarpal bone, unspecified hand
- ● **S62.254**　Nondisplaced fracture of neck of first metacarpal bone, right hand
- ● **S62.255**　Nondisplaced fracture of neck of first metacarpal bone, left hand
- ● **S62.256**　Nondisplaced fracture of neck of first metacarpal bone, unspecified hand

● **S62.29**　Other fracture of first metacarpal bone
- ● **S62.291**　Other fracture of first metacarpal bone, right hand
- ● **S62.292**　Other fracture of first metacarpal bone, left hand
- ● **S62.299**　Other fracture of first metacarpal bone, unspecified hand

● **S62.3**　Fracture of other and unspecified metacarpal bone
　　Excludes2　fracture of first metacarpal bone (S62.2-)

● **S62.30**　Unspecified fracture of other metacarpal bone
- ● **S62.300**　Unspecified fracture of second metacarpal bone, right hand
- ● **S62.301**　Unspecified fracture of second metacarpal bone, left hand
- ● **S62.302**　Unspecified fracture of third metacarpal bone, right hand
- ● **S62.303**　Unspecified fracture of third metacarpal bone, left hand
- ● **S62.304**　Unspecified fracture of fourth metacarpal bone, right hand
- ● **S62.305**　Unspecified fracture of fourth metacarpal bone, left hand
- ● **S62.306**　Unspecified fracture of fifth metacarpal bone, right hand
- ● **S62.307**　Unspecified fracture of fifth metacarpal bone, left hand
- ● **S62.308**　Unspecified fracture of other metacarpal bone
　　　Unspecified fracture of specified metacarpal bone with unspecified laterality
- ● **S62.309**　Unspecified fracture of unspecified metacarpal bone

● **S62.31**　Displaced fracture of base of other metacarpal bone
- ● **S62.310**　Displaced fracture of base of second metacarpal bone, right hand
- ● **S62.311**　Displaced fracture of base of second metacarpal bone, left hand
- ● **S62.312**　Displaced fracture of base of third metacarpal bone, right hand
- ● **S62.313**　Displaced fracture of base of third metacarpal bone, left hand
- ● **S62.314**　Displaced fracture of base of fourth metacarpal bone, right hand
- ● **S62.315**　Displaced fracture of base of fourth metacarpal bone, left hand
- ● **S62.316**　Displaced fracture of base of fifth metacarpal bone, right hand
- ● **S62.317**　Displaced fracture of base of fifth metacarpal bone, left hand
- ● **S62.318**　Displaced fracture of base of other metacarpal bone
　　　Displaced fracture of base of specified metacarpal bone with unspecified laterality
- ● **S62.319**　Displaced fracture of base of unspecified metacarpal bone

● **S62.32**　Displaced fracture of shaft of other metacarpal bone
- ● **S62.320**　Displaced fracture of shaft of second metacarpal bone, right hand
- ● **S62.321**　Displaced fracture of shaft of second metacarpal bone, left hand
- ● **S62.322**　Displaced fracture of shaft of third metacarpal bone, right hand
- ● **S62.323**　Displaced fracture of shaft of third metacarpal bone, left hand
- ● **S62.324**　Displaced fracture of shaft of fourth metacarpal bone, right hand
- ● **S62.325**　Displaced fracture of shaft of fourth metacarpal bone, left hand
- ● **S62.326**　Displaced fracture of shaft of fifth metacarpal bone, right hand
- ● **S62.327**　Displaced fracture of shaft of fifth metacarpal bone, left hand
- ● **S62.328**　Displaced fracture of shaft of other metacarpal bone
　　　Displaced fracture of shaft of specified metacarpal bone with unspecified laterality
- ● **S62.329**　Displaced fracture of shaft of unspecified metacarpal bone

▶ New　⇨ Revised　~~deleted~~ Deleted　Excludes 1　Excludes 2　Includes　Use additional　Code first　Code also　Key words
OGCR Official Guidelines　X Assign placeholder X　● Use Additional Character(s)　▌ Manifestation Code　🅗 Hierarchical Condition Category　**Coding Clinic**

● **S62.33** Displaced fracture of neck of other metacarpal bone
  ● **S62.330** Displaced fracture of neck of second metacarpal bone, right hand
  ● **S62.331** Displaced fracture of neck of second metacarpal bone, left hand
  ● **S62.332** Displaced fracture of neck of third metacarpal bone, right hand
  ● **S62.333** Displaced fracture of neck of third metacarpal bone, left hand
  ● **S62.334** Displaced fracture of neck of fourth metacarpal bone, right hand
  ● **S62.335** Displaced fracture of neck of fourth metacarpal bone, left hand
  ● **S62.336** Displaced fracture of neck of fifth metacarpal bone, right hand
  ● **S62.337** Displaced fracture of neck of fifth metacarpal bone, left hand
  ● **S62.338** Displaced fracture of neck of other metacarpal bone
    Displaced fracture of neck of specified metacarpal bone with unspecified laterality
  ● **S62.339** Displaced fracture of neck of unspecified metacarpal bone
● **S62.34** Nondisplaced fracture of base of other metacarpal bone
  ● **S62.340** Nondisplaced fracture of base of second metacarpal bone, right hand
  ● **S62.341** Nondisplaced fracture of base of second metacarpal bone, left hand
  ● **S62.342** Nondisplaced fracture of base of third metacarpal bone, right hand
  ● **S62.343** Nondisplaced fracture of base of third metacarpal bone, left hand
  ● **S62.344** Nondisplaced fracture of base of fourth metacarpal bone, right hand
  ● **S62.345** Nondisplaced fracture of base of fourth metacarpal bone, left hand
  ● **S62.346** Nondisplaced fracture of base of fifth metacarpal bone, right hand
  ● **S62.347** Nondisplaced fracture of base of fifth metacarpal bone, left hand
  ● **S62.348** Nondisplaced fracture of base of other metacarpal bone
    Nondisplaced fracture of base of specified metacarpal bone with unspecified laterality
  ● **S62.349** Nondisplaced fracture of base of unspecified metacarpal bone
● **S62.35** Nondisplaced fracture of shaft of other metacarpal bone
  ● **S62.350** Nondisplaced fracture of shaft of second metacarpal bone, right hand
  ● **S62.351** Nondisplaced fracture of shaft of second metacarpal bone, left hand
  ● **S62.352** Nondisplaced fracture of shaft of third metacarpal bone, right hand
  ● **S62.353** Nondisplaced fracture of shaft of third metacarpal bone, left hand
  ● **S62.354** Nondisplaced fracture of shaft of fourth metacarpal bone, right hand
  ● **S62.355** Nondisplaced fracture of shaft of fourth metacarpal bone, left hand
  ● **S62.356** Nondisplaced fracture of shaft of fifth metacarpal bone, right hand

● **S62.357** Nondisplaced fracture of shaft of fifth metacarpal bone, left hand
● **S62.358** Nondisplaced fracture of shaft of other metacarpal bone
  Nondisplaced fracture of shaft of specified metacarpal bone with unspecified laterality
● **S62.359** Nondisplaced fracture of shaft of unspecified metacarpal bone
● **S62.36** Nondisplaced fracture of neck of other metacarpal bone
  ● **S62.360** Nondisplaced fracture of neck of second metacarpal bone, right hand
  ● **S62.361** Nondisplaced fracture of neck of second metacarpal bone, left hand
  ● **S62.362** Nondisplaced fracture of neck of third metacarpal bone, right hand
  ● **S62.363** Nondisplaced fracture of neck of third metacarpal bone, left hand
  ● **S62.364** Nondisplaced fracture of neck of fourth metacarpal bone, right hand
  ● **S62.365** Nondisplaced fracture of neck of fourth metacarpal bone, left hand
  ● **S62.366** Nondisplaced fracture of neck of fifth metacarpal bone, right hand
  ● **S62.367** Nondisplaced fracture of neck of fifth metacarpal bone, left hand
  ● **S62.368** Nondisplaced fracture of neck of other metacarpal bone
    Nondisplaced fracture of neck of specified metacarpal bone with unspecified laterality
  ● **S62.369** Nondisplaced fracture of neck of unspecified metacarpal bone
● **S62.39** Other fracture of other metacarpal bone
  ● **S62.390** Other fracture of second metacarpal bone, right hand
  ● **S62.391** Other fracture of second metacarpal bone, left hand
  ● **S62.392** Other fracture of third metacarpal bone, right hand
  ● **S62.393** Other fracture of third metacarpal bone, left hand
  ● **S62.394** Other fracture of fourth metacarpal bone, right hand
  ● **S62.395** Other fracture of fourth metacarpal bone, left hand
  ● **S62.396** Other fracture of fifth metacarpal bone, right hand
  ● **S62.397** Other fracture of fifth metacarpal bone, left hand
  ● **S62.398** Other fracture of other metacarpal bone
    Other fracture of specified metacarpal bone with unspecified laterality
  ● **S62.399** Other fracture of unspecified metacarpal bone
● **S62.5** Fracture of thumb
  ● **S62.50** Fracture of unspecified phalanx of thumb
    ● **S62.501** Fracture of unspecified phalanx of right thumb
    ● **S62.502** Fracture of unspecified phalanx of left thumb
    ● **S62.509** Fracture of unspecified phalanx of unspecified thumb

- S62.51   Fracture of proximal phalanx of thumb
  - S62.511   Displaced fracture of proximal phalanx of right thumb
  - S62.512   Displaced fracture of proximal phalanx of left thumb
  - S62.513   Displaced fracture of proximal phalanx of unspecified thumb
  - S62.514   Nondisplaced fracture of proximal phalanx of right thumb
  - S62.515   Nondisplaced fracture of proximal phalanx of left thumb
  - S62.516   Nondisplaced fracture of proximal phalanx of unspecified thumb
- S62.52   Fracture of distal phalanx of thumb
  - S62.521   Displaced fracture of distal phalanx of right thumb
  - S62.522   Displaced fracture of distal phalanx of left thumb
  - S62.523   Displaced fracture of distal phalanx of unspecified thumb
  - S62.524   Nondisplaced fracture of distal phalanx of right thumb
  - S62.525   Nondisplaced fracture of distal phalanx of left thumb
  - S62.526   Nondisplaced fracture of distal phalanx of unspecified thumb
- S62.6   Fracture of other and unspecified finger(s)
  - Excludes2   fracture of thumb (S62.5-)
  - S62.60   Fracture of unspecified phalanx of finger
    - S62.600   Fracture of unspecified phalanx of right index finger
    - S62.601   Fracture of unspecified phalanx of left index finger
    - S62.602   Fracture of unspecified phalanx of right middle finger
    - S62.603   Fracture of unspecified phalanx of left middle finger
    - S62.604   Fracture of unspecified phalanx of right ring finger
    - S62.605   Fracture of unspecified phalanx of left ring finger
    - S62.606   Fracture of unspecified phalanx of right little finger
    - S62.607   Fracture of unspecified phalanx of left little finger
    - S62.608   Fracture of unspecified phalanx of other finger
      Fracture of unspecified phalanx of specified finger with unspecified laterality
    - S62.609   Fracture of unspecified phalanx of unspecified finger
  - S62.61   Displaced fracture of proximal phalanx of finger
    - S62.610   Displaced fracture of proximal phalanx of right index finger
    - S62.611   Displaced fracture of proximal phalanx of left index finger
    - S62.612   Displaced fracture of proximal phalanx of right middle finger
    - S62.613   Displaced fracture of proximal phalanx of left middle finger
    - S62.614   Displaced fracture of proximal phalanx of right ring finger
    - S62.615   Displaced fracture of proximal phalanx of left ring finger
    - S62.616   Displaced fracture of proximal phalanx of right little finger

Figure 19-14 Dorsal dislocation of the distal phalanx of the index finger. (From Hardy M, Snaith B: Musculoskeletal Trauma: A Guide to Assessment and Diagnosis, 1e, Elsevier, 2011)

  - S62.617   Displaced fracture of proximal phalanx of left little finger
  - S62.618   Displaced fracture of proximal phalanx of other finger
    Displaced fracture of proximal phalanx of specified finger with unspecified laterality
  - S62.619   Displaced fracture of proximal phalanx of unspecified finger
- S62.62   Displaced fracture of middle phalanx of finger
  - S62.620   Displaced fracture of middle phalanx of right index finger
  - S62.621   Displaced fracture of middle phalanx of left index finger
  - S62.622   Displaced fracture of middle phalanx of right middle finger
  - S62.623   Displaced fracture of middle phalanx of left middle finger
  - S62.624   Displaced fracture of middle phalanx of right ring finger
  - S62.625   Displaced fracture of middle phalanx of left ring finger
  - S62.626   Displaced fracture of middle phalanx of right little finger
  - S62.627   Displaced fracture of middle phalanx of left little finger
  - S62.628   Displaced fracture of middle phalanx of other finger
    Displaced fracture of middle phalanx of specified finger with unspecified laterality
  - S62.629   Displaced fracture of middle phalanx of unspecified finger
- S62.63   Displaced fracture of distal phalanx of finger
  - S62.630   Displaced fracture of distal phalanx of right index finger
  - S62.631   Displaced fracture of distal phalanx of left index finger
  - S62.632   Displaced fracture of distal phalanx of right middle finger
  - S62.633   Displaced fracture of distal phalanx of left middle finger

▶ New   ⟹ Revised   ~~deleted~~ Deleted   Excludes 1   Excludes 2   Includes   Use additional   Code first   Code also   Key words
OGCR Official Guidelines   X Assign placeholder X   ● Use Additional Character(s)   ▶ Manifestation Code   HCC Hierarchical Condition Category   Coding Clinic

● **S62.634**   Displaced fracture of distal phalanx of right ring finger

● **S62.635**   Displaced fracture of distal phalanx of left ring finger

● **S62.636**   Displaced fracture of distal phalanx of right little finger

● **S62.637**   Displaced fracture of distal phalanx of left little finger

● **S62.638**   Displaced fracture of distal phalanx of other finger
    Displaced fracture of distal phalanx of specified finger with unspecified laterality

● **S62.639**   Displaced fracture of distal phalanx of unspecified finger

● **S62.64**   Nondisplaced fracture of proximal phalanx of finger

● **S62.640**   Nondisplaced fracture of proximal phalanx of right index finger

● **S62.641**   Nondisplaced fracture of proximal phalanx of left index finger

● **S62.642**   Nondisplaced fracture of proximal phalanx of right middle finger

● **S62.643**   Nondisplaced fracture of proximal phalanx of left middle finger

● **S62.644**   Nondisplaced fracture of proximal phalanx of right ring finger

● **S62.645**   Nondisplaced fracture of proximal phalanx of left ring finger

● **S62.646**   Nondisplaced fracture of proximal phalanx of right little finger

● **S62.647**   Nondisplaced fracture of proximal phalanx of left little finger

● **S62.648**   Nondisplaced fracture of proximal phalanx of other finger
    Nondisplaced fracture of proximal phalanx of specified finger with unspecified laterality

● **S62.649**   Nondisplaced fracture of proximal phalanx of unspecified finger

● **S62.65**   Nondisplaced fracture of middle phalanx of finger

● **S62.650**   Nondisplaced fracture of middle phalanx of right index finger

● **S62.651**   Nondisplaced fracture of middle phalanx of left index finger

● **S62.652**   Nondisplaced fracture of middle phalanx of right middle finger

● **S62.653**   Nondisplaced fracture of middle phalanx of left middle finger

● **S62.654**   Nondisplaced fracture of middle phalanx of right ring finger

● **S62.655**   Nondisplaced fracture of middle phalanx of left ring finger

● **S62.656**   Nondisplaced fracture of middle phalanx of right little finger

● **S62.657**   Nondisplaced fracture of middle phalanx of left little finger

● **S62.658**   Nondisplaced fracture of middle phalanx of other finger
    Nondisplaced fracture of middle phalanx of specified finger with unspecified laterality

● **S62.659**   Nondisplaced fracture of middle phalanx of unspecified finger

● **S62.66**   Nondisplaced fracture of distal phalanx of finger

● **S62.660**   Nondisplaced fracture of distal phalanx of right index finger

● **S62.661**   Nondisplaced fracture of distal phalanx of left index finger

● **S62.662**   Nondisplaced fracture of distal phalanx of right middle finger

● **S62.663**   Nondisplaced fracture of distal phalanx of left middle finger

● **S62.664**   Nondisplaced fracture of distal phalanx of right ring finger

● **S62.665**   Nondisplaced fracture of distal phalanx of left ring finger

● **S62.666**   Nondisplaced fracture of distal phalanx of right little finger

● **S62.667**   Nondisplaced fracture of distal phalanx of left little finger

● **S62.668**   Nondisplaced fracture of distal phalanx of other finger
    Nondisplaced fracture of distal phalanx of specified finger with unspecified laterality

● **S62.669**   Nondisplaced fracture of distal phalanx of unspecified finger

● **S62.9**   Unspecified fracture of wrist and hand

X● **S62.90**   Unspecified fracture of unspecified wrist and hand

X● **S62.91**   Unspecified fracture of right wrist and hand

X● **S62.92**   Unspecified fracture of left wrist and hand

● **S63**   **Dislocation and sprain of joints and ligaments at wrist and hand level**

Includes   avulsion of joint or ligament at wrist and hand level
    laceration of cartilage, joint or ligament at wrist and hand level
    sprain of cartilage, joint or ligament at wrist and hand level
    traumatic hemarthrosis of joint or ligament at wrist and hand level
    traumatic rupture of joint or ligament at wrist and hand level
    traumatic subluxation of joint or ligament at wrist and hand level
    traumatic tear of joint or ligament at wrist and hand level

Code also any associated open wound

Excludes2   strain of muscle, fascia and tendon of wrist and hand (S66.-)

The appropriate 7th character is to be added to each code from category S63

> A   initial encounter
> D   subsequent encounter
> S   sequela

● **S63.0**   **Subluxation and dislocation of wrist and hand joints**

● **S63.00**   Unspecified subluxation and dislocation of wrist and hand
    Dislocation of carpal bone NOS
    Dislocation of distal end of radius NOS
    Subluxation of carpal bone NOS
    Subluxation of distal end of radius NOS

● **S63.001**   Unspecified subluxation of right wrist and hand

● **S63.002**   Unspecified subluxation of left wrist and hand

● **S63.003**   Unspecified subluxation of unspecified wrist and hand

● **S63.004**   Unspecified dislocation of right wrist and hand

● **S63.005**   Unspecified dislocation of left wrist and hand

● **S63.006**   Unspecified dislocation of unspecified wrist and hand

● **S63.01** Subluxation and dislocation of distal radioulnar joint

- ● **S63.011** Subluxation of distal radioulnar joint of right wrist
- ● **S63.012** Subluxation of distal radioulnar joint of left wrist
- ● **S63.013** Subluxation of distal radioulnar joint of unspecified wrist
- ● **S63.014** Dislocation of distal radioulnar joint of right wrist
- ● **S63.015** Dislocation of distal radioulnar joint of left wrist
- ● **S63.016** Dislocation of distal radioulnar joint of unspecified wrist

● **S63.02** Subluxation and dislocation of radiocarpal joint

- ● **S63.021** Subluxation of radiocarpal joint of right wrist
- ● **S63.022** Subluxation of radiocarpal joint of left wrist
- ● **S63.023** Subluxation of radiocarpal joint of unspecified wrist
- ● **S63.024** Dislocation of radiocarpal joint of right wrist
- ● **S63.025** Dislocation of radiocarpal joint of left wrist
- ● **S63.026** Dislocation of radiocarpal joint of unspecified wrist

● **S63.03** Subluxation and dislocation of midcarpal joint

- ● **S63.031** Subluxation of midcarpal joint of right wrist
- ● **S63.032** Subluxation of midcarpal joint of left wrist
- ● **S63.033** Subluxation of midcarpal joint of unspecified wrist
- ● **S63.034** Dislocation of midcarpal joint of right wrist
- ● **S63.035** Dislocation of midcarpal joint of left wrist
- ● **S63.036** Dislocation of midcarpal joint of unspecified wrist

● **S63.04** Subluxation and dislocation of carpometacarpal joint of thumb

Excludes2 interphalangeal subluxation and dislocation of thumb (S63.1-)

- ● **S63.041** Subluxation of carpometacarpal joint of right thumb
- ● **S63.042** Subluxation of carpometacarpal joint of left thumb
- ● **S63.043** Subluxation of carpometacarpal joint of unspecified thumb
- ● **S63.044** Dislocation of carpometacarpal joint of right thumb
- ● **S63.045** Dislocation of carpometacarpal joint of left thumb
- ● **S63.046** Dislocation of carpometacarpal joint of unspecified thumb

● **S63.05** Subluxation and dislocation of other carpometacarpal joint

Excludes2 subluxation and dislocation of carpometacarpal joint of thumb (S63.04-)

- ● **S63.051** Subluxation of other carpometacarpal joint of right hand
- ● **S63.052** Subluxation of other carpometacarpal joint of left hand
- ● **S63.053** Subluxation of other carpometacarpal joint of unspecified hand
- ● **S63.054** Dislocation of other carpometacarpal joint of right hand
- ● **S63.055** Dislocation of other carpometacarpal joint of left hand
- ● **S63.056** Dislocation of other carpometacarpal joint of unspecified hand

● **S63.06** Subluxation and dislocation of metacarpal (bone), proximal end

- ● **S63.061** Subluxation of metacarpal (bone), proximal end of right hand
- ● **S63.062** Subluxation of metacarpal (bone), proximal end of left hand
- ● **S63.063** Subluxation of metacarpal (bone), proximal end of unspecified hand
- ● **S63.064** Dislocation of metacarpal (bone), proximal end of right hand
- ● **S63.065** Dislocation of metacarpal (bone), proximal end of left hand
- ● **S63.066** Dislocation of metacarpal (bone), proximal end of unspecified hand

● **S63.07** Subluxation and dislocation of distal end of ulna

- ● **S63.071** Subluxation of distal end of right ulna
- ● **S63.072** Subluxation of distal end of left ulna
- ● **S63.073** Subluxation of distal end of unspecified ulna
- ● **S63.074** Dislocation of distal end of right ulna
- ● **S63.075** Dislocation of distal end of left ulna
- ● **S63.076** Dislocation of distal end of unspecified ulna

● **S63.09** Other subluxation and dislocation of wrist and hand

- ● **S63.091** Other subluxation of right wrist and hand
- ● **S63.092** Other subluxation of left wrist and hand
- ● **S63.093** Other subluxation of unspecified wrist and hand
- ● **S63.094** Other dislocation of right wrist and hand
- ● **S63.095** Other dislocation of left wrist and hand
- ● **S63.096** Other dislocation of unspecified wrist and hand

● **S63.1** Subluxation and dislocation of thumb

● **S63.10** Unspecified subluxation and dislocation of thumb

- ● **S63.101** Unspecified subluxation of right thumb
- ● **S63.102** Unspecified subluxation of left thumb
- ● **S63.103** Unspecified subluxation of unspecified thumb
- ● **S63.104** Unspecified dislocation of right thumb
- ● **S63.105** Unspecified dislocation of left thumb
- ● **S63.106** Unspecified dislocation of unspecified thumb

● **S63.11** Subluxation and dislocation of metacarpophalangeal joint of thumb

- ● **S63.111** Subluxation of metacarpophalangeal joint of right thumb
- ● **S63.112** Subluxation of metacarpophalangeal joint of left thumb
- ● **S63.113** Subluxation of metacarpophalangeal joint of unspecified thumb
- ● **S63.114** Dislocation of metacarpophalangeal joint of right thumb
- ● **S63.115** Dislocation of metacarpophalangeal joint of left thumb
- ● **S63.116** Dislocation of metacarpophalangeal joint of unspecified thumb

▶ New ⇒ Revised ~~deleted~~ Deleted Excludes 1 Excludes 2 Includes Use additional Code first Code also Key words

OGCR Official Guidelines X Assign placeholder X ● Use Additional Character(s) ▷ Manifestation Code 🔾 Hierarchical Condition Category **Coding Clinic**

● S63.12   Subluxation and dislocation of interphalangeal joint of thumb
     ● S63.121   Subluxation of interphalangeal joint of right thumb
     ● S63.122   Subluxation of interphalangeal joint of left thumb
     ● S63.123   Subluxation of interphalangeal joint of unspecified thumb
     ● S63.124   Dislocation of interphalangeal joint of right thumb
     ● S63.125   Dislocation of interphalangeal joint of left thumb
     ● S63.126   Dislocation of interphalangeal joint of unspecified thumb

● S63.2   Subluxation and dislocation of other finger(s)
     Excludes2   subluxation and dislocation of thumb (S63.1-)

   ● S63.20   Unspecified subluxation of other finger
     ● S63.200   Unspecified subluxation of right index finger
     ● S63.201   Unspecified subluxation of left index finger
     ● S63.202   Unspecified subluxation of right middle finger
     ● S63.203   Unspecified subluxation of left middle finger
     ● S63.204   Unspecified subluxation of right ring finger
     ● S63.205   Unspecified subluxation of left ring finger
     ● S63.206   Unspecified subluxation of right little finger
     ● S63.207   Unspecified subluxation of left little finger
     ● S63.208   Unspecified subluxation of other finger
           Unspecified subluxation of specified finger with unspecified laterality
     ● S63.209   Unspecified subluxation of unspecified finger

   ● S63.21   Subluxation of metacarpophalangeal joint of finger
     ● S63.210   Subluxation of metacarpophalangeal joint of right index finger
     ● S63.211   Subluxation of metacarpophalangeal joint of left index finger
     ● S63.212   Subluxation of metacarpophalangeal joint of right middle finger
     ● S63.213   Subluxation of metacarpophalangeal joint of left middle finger
     ● S63.214   Subluxation of metacarpophalangeal joint of right ring finger
     ● S63.215   Subluxation of metacarpophalangeal joint of left ring finger
     ● S63.216   Subluxation of metacarpophalangeal joint of right little finger
     ● S63.217   Subluxation of metacarpophalangeal joint of left little finger
     ● S63.218   Subluxation of metacarpophalangeal joint of other finger
           Subluxation of metacarpophalangeal joint of specified finger with unspecified laterality
     ● S63.219   Subluxation of metacarpophalangeal joint of unspecified finger

● S63.22   Subluxation of unspecified interphalangeal joint of finger
     ● S63.220   Subluxation of unspecified interphalangeal joint of right index finger
     ● S63.221   Subluxation of unspecified interphalangeal joint of left index finger
     ● S63.222   Subluxation of unspecified interphalangeal joint of right middle finger
     ● S63.223   Subluxation of unspecified interphalangeal joint of left middle finger
     ● S63.224   Subluxation of unspecified interphalangeal joint of right ring finger
     ● S63.225   Subluxation of unspecified interphalangeal joint of left ring finger
     ● S63.226   Subluxation of unspecified interphalangeal joint of right little finger
     ● S63.227   Subluxation of unspecified interphalangeal joint of left little finger
     ● S63.228   Subluxation of unspecified interphalangeal joint of other finger
           Subluxation of unspecified interphalangeal joint of specified finger with unspecified laterality
     ● S63.229   Subluxation of unspecified interphalangeal joint of unspecified finger

   ● S63.23   Subluxation of proximal interphalangeal joint of finger
     ● S63.230   Subluxation of proximal interphalangeal joint of right index finger
     ● S63.231   Subluxation of proximal interphalangeal joint of left index finger
     ● S63.232   Subluxation of proximal interphalangeal joint of right middle finger
     ● S63.233   Subluxation of proximal interphalangeal joint of left middle finger
     ● S63.234   Subluxation of proximal interphalangeal joint of right ring finger
     ● S63.235   Subluxation of proximal interphalangeal joint of left ring finger
     ● S63.236   Subluxation of proximal interphalangeal joint of right little finger
     ● S63.237   Subluxation of proximal interphalangeal joint of left little finger
     ● S63.238   Subluxation of proximal interphalangeal joint of other finger
           Subluxation of proximal interphalangeal joint of specified finger with unspecified laterality
     ● S63.239   Subluxation of proximal interphalangeal joint of unspecified finger

● **S63.24**   Subluxation of distal interphalangeal joint of finger

  ● **S63.240**   Subluxation of distal interphalangeal joint of right index finger

  ● **S63.241**   Subluxation of distal interphalangeal joint of left index finger

  ● **S63.242**   Subluxation of distal interphalangeal joint of right middle finger

  ● **S63.243**   Subluxation of distal interphalangeal joint of left middle finger

  ● **S63.244**   Subluxation of distal interphalangeal joint of right ring finger

  ● **S63.245**   Subluxation of distal interphalangeal joint of left ring finger

  ● **S63.246**   Subluxation of distal interphalangeal joint of right little finger

  ● **S63.247**   Subluxation of distal interphalangeal joint of left little finger

  ● **S63.248**   Subluxation of distal interphalangeal joint of other finger

       Subluxation of distal interphalangeal joint of specified finger with unspecified laterality

  ● **S63.249**   Subluxation of distal interphalangeal joint of unspecified finger

● **S63.25**   Unspecified dislocation of other finger

  ● **S63.250**   Unspecified dislocation of right index finger

  ● **S63.251**   Unspecified dislocation of left index finger

  ● **S63.252**   Unspecified dislocation of right middle finger

  ● **S63.253**   Unspecified dislocation of left middle finger

  ● **S63.254**   Unspecified dislocation of right ring finger

  ● **S63.255**   Unspecified dislocation of left ring finger

  ● **S63.256**   Unspecified dislocation of right little finger

  ● **S63.257**   Unspecified dislocation of left little finger

  ● **S63.258**   Unspecified dislocation of other finger

       Unspecified dislocation of specified finger with unspecified laterality

  ● **S63.259**   Unspecified dislocation of unspecified finger

       Unspecified dislocation of unspecified finger with unspecified laterality

● **S63.26**   Dislocation of metacarpophalangeal joint of finger

  ● **S63.260**   Dislocation of metacarpophalangeal joint of right index finger

  ● **S63.261**   Dislocation of metacarpophalangeal joint of left index finger

  ● **S63.262**   Dislocation of metacarpophalangeal joint of right middle finger

  ● **S63.263**   Dislocation of metacarpophalangeal joint of left middle finger

  ● **S63.264**   Dislocation of metacarpophalangeal joint of right ring finger

  ● **S63.265**   Dislocation of metacarpophalangeal joint of left ring finger

  ● **S63.266**   Dislocation of metacarpophalangeal joint of right little finger

  ● **S63.267**   Dislocation of metacarpophalangeal joint of left little finger

  ● **S63.268**   Dislocation of metacarpophalangeal joint of other finger

       Dislocation of metacarpophalangeal joint of specified finger with unspecified laterality

  ● **S63.269**   Dislocation of metacarpophalangeal joint of unspecified finger

● **S63.27**   Dislocation of unspecified interphalangeal joint of finger

  ● **S63.270**   Dislocation of unspecified interphalangeal joint of right index finger

  ● **S63.271**   Dislocation of unspecified interphalangeal joint of left index finger

  ● **S63.272**   Dislocation of unspecified interphalangeal joint of right middle finger

  ● **S63.273**   Dislocation of unspecified interphalangeal joint of left middle finger

  ● **S63.274**   Dislocation of unspecified interphalangeal joint of right ring finger

  ● **S63.275**   Dislocation of unspecified interphalangeal joint of left ring finger

  ● **S63.276**   Dislocation of unspecified interphalangeal joint of right little finger

  ● **S63.277**   Dislocation of unspecified interphalangeal joint of left little finger

  ● **S63.278**   Dislocation of unspecified interphalangeal joint of other finger

       Dislocation of unspecified interphalangeal joint of specified finger with unspecified laterality

  ● **S63.279**   Dislocation of unspecified interphalangeal joint of unspecified finger

       Dislocation of unspecified interphalangeal joint of unspecified finger without specified laterality

● **S63.28**   Dislocation of proximal interphalangeal joint of finger

  ● **S63.280**   Dislocation of proximal interphalangeal joint of right index finger

  ● **S63.281**   Dislocation of proximal interphalangeal joint of left index finger

  ● **S63.282**   Dislocation of proximal interphalangeal joint of right middle finger

  ● **S63.283**   Dislocation of proximal interphalangeal joint of left middle finger

  ● **S63.284**   Dislocation of proximal interphalangeal joint of right ring finger

  ● **S63.285**   Dislocation of proximal interphalangeal joint of left ring finger

▶ New   ⇒ Revised   ~~deleted~~ Deleted   Excludes 1   Excludes 2   Includes   Use additional   Code first   Code also   Key words
OGCR Official Guidelines   X Assign placeholder X   ● Use Additional Character(s)   ▷ Manifestation Code   ⚭ Hierarchical Condition Category   **Coding Clinic**

● S63.286 Dislocation of proximal interphalangeal joint of right little finger

● S63.287 Dislocation of proximal interphalangeal joint of left little finger

● S63.288 Dislocation of proximal interphalangeal joint of other finger
Dislocation of proximal interphalangeal joint of specified finger with unspecified laterality

● S63.289 Dislocation of proximal interphalangeal joint of unspecified finger

● S63.29 Dislocation of distal interphalangeal joint of finger

● S63.290 Dislocation of distal interphalangeal joint of right index finger

● S63.291 Dislocation of distal interphalangeal joint of left index finger

● S63.292 Dislocation of distal interphalangeal joint of right middle finger

● S63.293 Dislocation of distal interphalangeal joint of left middle finger

● S63.294 Dislocation of distal interphalangeal joint of right ring finger

● S63.295 Dislocation of distal interphalangeal joint of left ring finger

● S63.296 Dislocation of distal interphalangeal joint of right little finger

● S63.297 Dislocation of distal interphalangeal joint of left little finger

● S63.298 Dislocation of distal interphalangeal joint of other finger
Dislocation of distal interphalangeal joint of specified finger with unspecified laterality

● S63.299 Dislocation of distal interphalangeal joint of unspecified finger

● S63.3 Traumatic rupture of ligament of wrist

● S63.30 Traumatic rupture of unspecified ligament of wrist

● S63.301 Traumatic rupture of unspecified ligament of right wrist

● S63.302 Traumatic rupture of unspecified ligament of left wrist

● S63.309 Traumatic rupture of unspecified ligament of unspecified wrist

● S63.31 Traumatic rupture of collateral ligament of wrist

● S63.311 Traumatic rupture of collateral ligament of right wrist

● S63.312 Traumatic rupture of collateral ligament of left wrist

● S63.319 Traumatic rupture of collateral ligament of unspecified wrist

● S63.32 Traumatic rupture of radiocarpal ligament

● S63.321 Traumatic rupture of right radiocarpal ligament

● S63.322 Traumatic rupture of left radiocarpal ligament

● S63.329 Traumatic rupture of unspecified radiocarpal ligament

● S63.33 Traumatic rupture of ulnocarpal (palmar) ligament

● S63.331 Traumatic rupture of right ulnocarpal (palmar) ligament

● S63.332 Traumatic rupture of left ulnocarpal (palmar) ligament

● S63.339 Traumatic rupture of unspecified ulnocarpal (palmar) ligament

● S63.39 Traumatic rupture of other ligament of wrist

● S63.391 Traumatic rupture of other ligament of right wrist

● S63.392 Traumatic rupture of other ligament of left wrist

● S63.399 Traumatic rupture of other ligament of unspecified wrist

● S63.4 Traumatic rupture of ligament of finger at metacarpophalangeal and interphalangeal joint(s)

● S63.40 Traumatic rupture of unspecified ligament of finger at metacarpophalangeal and interphalangeal joint

● S63.400 Traumatic rupture of unspecified ligament of right index finger at metacarpophalangeal and interphalangeal joint

● S63.401 Traumatic rupture of unspecified ligament of left index finger at metacarpophalangeal and interphalangeal joint

● S63.402 Traumatic rupture of unspecified ligament of right middle finger at metacarpophalangeal and interphalangeal joint

● S63.403 Traumatic rupture of unspecified ligament of left middle finger at metacarpophalangeal and interphalangeal joint

● S63.404 Traumatic rupture of unspecified ligament of right ring finger at metacarpophalangeal and interphalangeal joint

● S63.405 Traumatic rupture of unspecified ligament of left ring finger at metacarpophalangeal and interphalangeal joint

● S63.406 Traumatic rupture of unspecified ligament of right little finger at metacarpophalangeal and interphalangeal joint

● S63.407 Traumatic rupture of unspecified ligament of left little finger at metacarpophalangeal and interphalangeal joint

● S63.408 Traumatic rupture of unspecified ligament of other finger at metacarpophalangeal and interphalangeal joint
Traumatic rupture of unspecified ligament of specified finger with unspecified laterality at metacarpophalangeal and interphalangeal joint

● S63.409 Traumatic rupture of unspecified ligament of unspecified finger at metacarpophalangeal and interphalangeal joint

● **S63.41**   Traumatic rupture of collateral ligament of finger at metacarpophalangeal and interphalangeal joint

  ● **S63.410**   Traumatic rupture of collateral ligament of right index finger at metacarpophalangeal and interphalangeal joint

  ● **S63.411**   Traumatic rupture of collateral ligament of left index finger at metacarpophalangeal and interphalangeal joint

  ● **S63.412**   Traumatic rupture of collateral ligament of right middle finger at metacarpophalangeal and interphalangeal joint

  ● **S63.413**   Traumatic rupture of collateral ligament of left middle finger at metacarpophalangeal and interphalangeal joint

  ● **S63.414**   Traumatic rupture of collateral ligament of right ring finger at metacarpophalangeal and interphalangeal joint

  ● **S63.415**   Traumatic rupture of collateral ligament of left ring finger at metacarpophalangeal and interphalangeal joint

  ● **S63.416**   Traumatic rupture of collateral ligament of right little finger at metacarpophalangeal and interphalangeal joint

  ● **S63.417**   Traumatic rupture of collateral ligament of left little finger at metacarpophalangeal and interphalangeal joint

  ● **S63.418**   Traumatic rupture of collateral ligament of other finger at metacarpophalangeal and interphalangeal joint
      Traumatic rupture of collateral ligament of specified finger with unspecified laterality at metacarpophalangeal and interphalangeal joint

  ● **S63.419**   Traumatic rupture of collateral ligament of unspecified finger at metacarpophalangeal and interphalangeal joint

● **S63.42**   Traumatic rupture of palmar ligament of finger at metacarpophalangeal and interphalangeal joint

  ● **S63.420**   Traumatic rupture of palmar ligament of right index finger at metacarpophalangeal and interphalangeal joint

  ● **S63.421**   Traumatic rupture of palmar ligament of left index finger at metacarpophalangeal and interphalangeal joint

  ● **S63.422**   Traumatic rupture of palmar ligament of right middle finger at metacarpophalangeal and interphalangeal joint

  ● **S63.423**   Traumatic rupture of palmar ligament of left middle finger at metacarpophalangeal and interphalangeal joint

  ● **S63.424**   Traumatic rupture of palmar ligament of right ring finger at metacarpophalangeal and interphalangeal joint

  ● **S63.425**   Traumatic rupture of palmar ligament of left ring finger at metacarpophalangeal and interphalangeal joint

  ● **S63.426**   Traumatic rupture of palmar ligament of right little finger at metacarpophalangeal and interphalangeal joint

  ● **S63.427**   Traumatic rupture of palmar ligament of left little finger at metacarpophalangeal and interphalangeal joint

  ● **S63.428**   Traumatic rupture of palmar ligament of other finger at metacarpophalangeal and interphalangeal joint
      Traumatic rupture of palmar ligament of specified finger with unspecified laterality at metacarpophalangeal and interphalangeal joint

  ● **S63.429**   Traumatic rupture of palmar ligament of unspecified finger at metacarpophalangeal and interphalangeal joint

● **S63.43**   Traumatic rupture of volar plate of finger at metacarpophalangeal and interphalangeal joint

  ● **S63.430**   Traumatic rupture of volar plate of right index finger at metacarpophalangeal and interphalangeal joint

  ● **S63.431**   Traumatic rupture of volar plate of left index finger at metacarpophalangeal and interphalangeal joint

  ● **S63.432**   Traumatic rupture of volar plate of right middle finger at metacarpophalangeal and interphalangeal joint

  ● **S63.433**   Traumatic rupture of volar plate of left middle finger at metacarpophalangeal and interphalangeal joint

  ● **S63.434**   Traumatic rupture of volar plate of right ring finger at metacarpophalangeal and interphalangeal joint

  ● **S63.435**   Traumatic rupture of volar plate of left ring finger at metacarpophalangeal and interphalangeal joint

  ● **S63.436**   Traumatic rupture of volar plate of right little finger at metacarpophalangeal and interphalangeal joint

  ● **S63.437**   Traumatic rupture of volar plate of left little finger at metacarpophalangeal and interphalangeal joint

  ● **S63.438**   Traumatic rupture of volar plate of other finger at metacarpophalangeal and interphalangeal joint
      Traumatic rupture of volar plate of specified finger with unspecified laterality at metacarpophalangeal and interphalangeal joint

  ● **S63.439**   Traumatic rupture of volar plate of unspecified finger at metacarpophalangeal and interphalangeal joint

▶ New   ⇒ Revised   ~~deleted~~ Deleted   Excludes 1   Excludes 2   Includes   Use additional   Code first   Code also   Key words

OGCR Official Guidelines   X Assign placeholder X   ● Use Additional Character(s)   ▶ Manifestation Code   Ⓗ Hierarchical Condition Category   **Coding Clinic**

● **S63.49**   Traumatic rupture of other ligament of finger at metacarpophalangeal and interphalangeal joint

   ● **S63.490**   Traumatic rupture of other ligament of right index finger at metacarpophalangeal and interphalangeal joint

   ● **S63.491**   Traumatic rupture of other ligament of left index finger at metacarpophalangeal and interphalangeal joint

   ● **S63.492**   Traumatic rupture of other ligament of right middle finger at metacarpophalangeal and interphalangeal joint

   ● **S63.493**   Traumatic rupture of other ligament of left middle finger at metacarpophalangeal and interphalangeal joint

   ● **S63.494**   Traumatic rupture of other ligament of right ring finger at metacarpophalangeal and interphalangeal joint

   ● **S63.495**   Traumatic rupture of other ligament of left ring finger at metacarpophalangeal and interphalangeal joint

   ● **S63.496**   Traumatic rupture of other ligament of right little finger at metacarpophalangeal and interphalangeal joint

   ● **S63.497**   Traumatic rupture of other ligament of left little finger at metacarpophalangeal and interphalangeal joint

   ● **S63.498**   Traumatic rupture of other ligament of other finger at metacarpophalangeal and interphalangeal joint

        Traumatic rupture of ligament of specified finger with unspecified laterality at metacarpophalangeal and interphalangeal joint

   ● **S63.499**   Traumatic rupture of other ligament of unspecified finger at metacarpophalangeal and interphalangeal joint

● **S63.5**   Other and unspecified sprain of wrist

  ● **S63.50**   Unspecified sprain of wrist

   ● **S63.501**   Unspecified sprain of right wrist

   ● **S63.502**   Unspecified sprain of left wrist

   ● **S63.509**   Unspecified sprain of unspecified wrist

  ● **S63.51**   Sprain of carpal (joint)

   ● **S63.511**   Sprain of carpal joint of right wrist

   ● **S63.512**   Sprain of carpal joint of left wrist

   ● **S63.519**   Sprain of carpal joint of unspecified wrist

  ● **S63.52**   Sprain of radiocarpal joint

     Excludes1   traumatic rupture of radiocarpal ligament (S63.32-)

   ● **S63.521**   Sprain of radiocarpal joint of right wrist

   ● **S63.522**   Sprain of radiocarpal joint of left wrist

   ● **S63.529**   Sprain of radiocarpal joint of unspecified wrist

● **S63.59**   Other specified sprain of wrist

   ● **S63.591**   Other specified sprain of right wrist

   ● **S63.592**   Other specified sprain of left wrist

   ● **S63.599**   Other specified sprain of unspecified wrist

● **S63.6**   Other and unspecified sprain of finger(s)

     Excludes1   traumatic rupture of ligament of finger at metacarpophalangeal and interphalangeal joint(s) (S63.4-)

  ● **S63.60**   Unspecified sprain of thumb

   ● **S63.601**   Unspecified sprain of right thumb

   ● **S63.602**   Unspecified sprain of left thumb

   ● **S63.609**   Unspecified sprain of unspecified thumb

  ● **S63.61**   Unspecified sprain of other and unspecified finger(s)

   ● **S63.610**   Unspecified sprain of right index finger

   ● **S63.611**   Unspecified sprain of left index finger

   ● **S63.612**   Unspecified sprain of right middle finger

   ● **S63.613**   Unspecified sprain of left middle finger

   ● **S63.614**   Unspecified sprain of right ring finger

   ● **S63.615**   Unspecified sprain of left ring finger

   ● **S63.616**   Unspecified sprain of right little finger

   ● **S63.617**   Unspecified sprain of left little finger

   ● **S63.618**   Unspecified sprain of other finger

        Unspecified sprain of specified finger with unspecified laterality

   ● **S63.619**   Unspecified sprain of unspecified finger

  ● **S63.62**   Sprain of interphalangeal joint of thumb

   ● **S63.621**   Sprain of interphalangeal joint of right thumb

   ● **S63.622**   Sprain of interphalangeal joint of left thumb

   ● **S63.629**   Sprain of interphalangeal joint of unspecified thumb

  ● **S63.63**   Sprain of interphalangeal joint of other and unspecified finger(s)

   ● **S63.630**   Sprain of interphalangeal joint of right index finger

   ● **S63.631**   Sprain of interphalangeal joint of left index finger

   ● **S63.632**   Sprain of interphalangeal joint of right middle finger

   ● **S63.633**   Sprain of interphalangeal joint of left middle finger

   ● **S63.634**   Sprain of interphalangeal joint of right ring finger

   ● **S63.635**   Sprain of interphalangeal joint of left ring finger

   ● **S63.636**   Sprain of interphalangeal joint of right little finger

   ● **S63.637**   Sprain of interphalangeal joint of left little finger

   ● **S63.638**   Sprain of interphalangeal joint of other finger

   ● **S63.639**   Sprain of interphalangeal joint of unspecified finger

● **S63.64　Sprain of metacarpophalangeal joint of thumb**
- ● S63.641　Sprain of metacarpophalangeal joint of right thumb
- ● S63.642　Sprain of metacarpophalangeal joint of left thumb
- ● S63.649　Sprain of metacarpophalangeal joint of unspecified thumb

● **S63.65　Sprain of metacarpophalangeal joint of other and unspecified finger(s)**
- ● S63.650　Sprain of metacarpophalangeal joint of right index finger
- ● S63.651　Sprain of metacarpophalangeal joint of left index finger
- ● S63.652　Sprain of metacarpophalangeal joint of right middle finger
- ● S63.653　Sprain of metacarpophalangeal joint of left middle finger
- ● S63.654　Sprain of metacarpophalangeal joint of right ring finger
- ● S63.655　Sprain of metacarpophalangeal joint of left ring finger
- ● S63.656　Sprain of metacarpophalangeal joint of right little finger
- ● S63.657　Sprain of metacarpophalangeal joint of left little finger
- ● S63.658　Sprain of metacarpophalangeal joint of other finger
  - Sprain of metacarpophalangeal joint of specified finger with unspecified laterality
- ● S63.659　Sprain of metacarpophalangeal joint of unspecified finger

● **S63.68　Other sprain of thumb**
- ● S63.681　Other sprain of right thumb
- ● S63.682　Other sprain of left thumb
- ● S63.689　Other sprain of unspecified thumb

● **S63.69　Other sprain of other and unspecified finger(s)**
- ● S63.690　Other sprain of right index finger
- ● S63.691　Other sprain of left index finger
- ● S63.692　Other sprain of right middle finger
- ● S63.693　Other sprain of left middle finger
- ● S63.694　Other sprain of right ring finger
- ● S63.695　Other sprain of left ring finger
- ● S63.696　Other sprain of right little finger
- ● S63.697　Other sprain of left little finger
- ● S63.698　Other sprain of other finger
  - Other sprain of specified finger with unspecified laterality
- ● S63.699　Other sprain of unspecified finger

● **S63.8　Sprain of other part of wrist and hand**
- ● S63.8X　Sprain of other part of wrist and hand
  - ● S63.8X1　Sprain of other part of right wrist and hand
  - ● S63.8X2　Sprain of other part of left wrist and hand
  - ● S63.8X9　Sprain of other part of unspecified wrist and hand

● **S63.9　Sprain of unspecified part of wrist and hand**
- X ● S63.90　Sprain of unspecified part of unspecified wrist and hand
- X ● S63.91　Sprain of unspecified part of right wrist and hand
- X ● S63.92　Sprain of unspecified part of left wrist and hand

● **S64　Injury of nerves at wrist and hand level**

The appropriate 7th character is to be added to each code from category S64

A	initial encounter
D	subsequent encounter
S	sequela

Code also any associated open wound (S61.-)

● **S64.0　Injury of ulnar nerve at wrist and hand level**
- X ● S64.00　Injury of ulnar nerve at wrist and hand level of unspecified arm
- X ● S64.01　Injury of ulnar nerve at wrist and hand level of right arm
- X ● S64.02　Injury of ulnar nerve at wrist and hand level of left arm

● **S64.1　Injury of median nerve at wrist and hand level**
- X ● S64.10　Injury of median nerve at wrist and hand level of unspecified arm
- X ● S64.11　Injury of median nerve at wrist and hand level of right arm
- X ● S64.12　Injury of median nerve at wrist and hand level of left arm

● **S64.2　Injury of radial nerve at wrist and hand level**
- X ● S64.20　Injury of radial nerve at wrist and hand level of unspecified arm
- X ● S64.21　Injury of radial nerve at wrist and hand level of right arm
- X ● S64.22　Injury of radial nerve at wrist and hand level of left arm

● **S64.3　Injury of digital nerve of thumb**
- X ● S64.30　Injury of digital nerve of unspecified thumb
- X ● S64.31　Injury of digital nerve of right thumb
- X ● S64.32　Injury of digital nerve of left thumb

● **S64.4　Injury of digital nerve of other and unspecified finger**
- X ● S64.40　Injury of digital nerve of unspecified finger
- ● S64.49　Injury of digital nerve of other finger
  - ● S64.490　Injury of digital nerve of right index finger
  - ● S64.491　Injury of digital nerve of left index finger
  - ● S64.492　Injury of digital nerve of right middle finger
  - ● S64.493　Injury of digital nerve of left middle finger
  - ● S64.494　Injury of digital nerve of right ring finger
  - ● S64.495　Injury of digital nerve of left ring finger
  - ● S64.496　Injury of digital nerve of right little finger
  - ● S64.497　Injury of digital nerve of left little finger
  - ● S64.498　Injury of digital nerve of other finger
    - Injury of digital nerve of specified finger with unspecified laterality

● **S64.8　Injury of other nerves at wrist and hand level**
- ● S64.8X　Injury of other nerves at wrist and hand level
  - ● S64.8X1　Injury of other nerves at wrist and hand level of right arm
  - ● S64.8X2　Injury of other nerves at wrist and hand level of left arm
  - ● S64.8X9　Injury of other nerves at wrist and hand level of unspecified arm

▶ New　⇨ Revised　~~deleted~~ Deleted　Excludes 1　Excludes 2　Includes　Use additional　Code first　Code also　Key words
OGCR Official Guidelines　X Assign placeholder X　● Use Additional Character(s)　▷ Manifestation Code　🅗 Hierarchical Condition Category　Coding Clinic

- **S64.9**   Injury of unspecified nerve at wrist and hand level
  - X⬤ **S64.90**   Injury of unspecified nerve at wrist and hand level of unspecified arm
  - X⬤ **S64.91**   Injury of unspecified nerve at wrist and hand level of right arm
  - X⬤ **S64.92**   Injury of unspecified nerve at wrist and hand level of left arm
- ⬤ **S65**   Injury of blood vessels at wrist and hand level

  The appropriate 7th character is to be added to each code from category S65

A	initial encounter
D	subsequent encounter
S	sequela

  Code also any associated open wound (S61.-)

  - ⬤ **S65.0**   Injury of ulnar artery at wrist and hand level
    - ⬤ **S65.00**   Unspecified injury of ulnar artery at wrist and hand level
      - ⬤ **S65.001**   Unspecified injury of ulnar artery at wrist and hand level of right arm
      - ⬤ **S65.002**   Unspecified injury of ulnar artery at wrist and hand level of left arm
      - ⬤ **S65.009**   Unspecified injury of ulnar artery at wrist and hand level of unspecified arm
    - ⬤ **S65.01**   Laceration of ulnar artery at wrist and hand level
      - ⬤ **S65.011**   Laceration of ulnar artery at wrist and hand level of right arm
      - ⬤ **S65.012**   Laceration of ulnar artery at wrist and hand level of left arm
      - ⬤ **S65.019**   Laceration of ulnar artery at wrist and hand level of unspecified arm
    - ⬤ **S65.09**   Other specified injury of ulnar artery at wrist and hand level
      - ⬤ **S65.091**   Other specified injury of ulnar artery at wrist and hand level of right arm
      - ⬤ **S65.092**   Other specified injury of ulnar artery at wrist and hand level of left arm
      - ⬤ **S65.099**   Other specified injury of ulnar artery at wrist and hand level of unspecified arm
  - ⬤ **S65.1**   Injury of radial artery at wrist and hand level
    - ⬤ **S65.10**   Unspecified injury of radial artery at wrist and hand level
      - ⬤ **S65.101**   Unspecified injury of radial artery at wrist and hand level of right arm
      - ⬤ **S65.102**   Unspecified injury of radial artery at wrist and hand level of left arm
      - ⬤ **S65.109**   Unspecified injury of radial artery at wrist and hand level of unspecified arm
    - ⬤ **S65.11**   Laceration of radial artery at wrist and hand level
      - ⬤ **S65.111**   Laceration of radial artery at wrist and hand level of right arm
      - ⬤ **S65.112**   Laceration of radial artery at wrist and hand level of left arm
      - ⬤ **S65.119**   Laceration of radial artery at wrist and hand level of unspecified arm
    - ⬤ **S65.19**   Other specified injury of radial artery at wrist and hand level
      - ⬤ **S65.191**   Other specified injury of radial artery at wrist and hand level of right arm
      - ⬤ **S65.192**   Other specified injury of radial artery at wrist and hand level of left arm
      - ⬤ **S65.199**   Other specified injury of radial artery at wrist and hand level of unspecified arm

- ⬤ **S65.2**   Injury of superficial palmar arch
  - ⬤ **S65.20**   Unspecified injury of superficial palmar arch
    - ⬤ **S65.201**   Unspecified injury of superficial palmar arch of right hand
    - ⬤ **S65.202**   Unspecified injury of superficial palmar arch of left hand
    - ⬤ **S65.209**   Unspecified injury of superficial palmar arch of unspecified hand
  - ⬤ **S65.21**   Laceration of superficial palmar arch
    - ⬤ **S65.211**   Laceration of superficial palmar arch of right hand
    - ⬤ **S65.212**   Laceration of superficial palmar arch of left hand
    - ⬤ **S65.219**   Laceration of superficial palmar arch of unspecified hand
  - ⬤ **S65.29**   Other specified injury of superficial palmar arch
    - ⬤ **S65.291**   Other specified injury of superficial palmar arch of right hand
    - ⬤ **S65.292**   Other specified injury of superficial palmar arch of left hand
    - ⬤ **S65.299**   Other specified injury of superficial palmar arch of unspecified hand
- ⬤ **S65.3**   Injury of deep palmar arch
  - ⬤ **S65.30**   Unspecified injury of deep palmar arch
    - ⬤ **S65.301**   Unspecified injury of deep palmar arch of right hand
    - ⬤ **S65.302**   Unspecified injury of deep palmar arch of left hand
    - ⬤ **S65.309**   Unspecified injury of deep palmar arch of unspecified hand
  - ⬤ **S65.31**   Laceration of deep palmar arch
    - ⬤ **S65.311**   Laceration of deep palmar arch of right hand
    - ⬤ **S65.312**   Laceration of deep palmar arch of left hand
    - ⬤ **S65.319**   Laceration of deep palmar arch of unspecified hand
  - ⬤ **S65.39**   Other specified injury of deep palmar arch
    - ⬤ **S65.391**   Other specified injury of deep palmar arch of right hand
    - ⬤ **S65.392**   Other specified injury of deep palmar arch of left hand
    - ⬤ **S65.399**   Other specified injury of deep palmar arch of unspecified hand
- ⬤ **S65.4**   Injury of blood vessel of thumb
  - ⬤ **S65.40**   Unspecified injury of blood vessel of thumb
    - ⬤ **S65.401**   Unspecified injury of blood vessel of right thumb
    - ⬤ **S65.402**   Unspecified injury of blood vessel of left thumb
    - ⬤ **S65.409**   Unspecified injury of blood vessel of unspecified thumb
  - ⬤ **S65.41**   Laceration of blood vessel of thumb
    - ⬤ **S65.411**   Laceration of blood vessel of right thumb
    - ⬤ **S65.412**   Laceration of blood vessel of left thumb
    - ⬤ **S65.419**   Laceration of blood vessel of unspecified thumb
  - ⬤ **S65.49**   Other specified injury of blood vessel of thumb
    - ⬤ **S65.491**   Other specified injury of blood vessel of right thumb
    - ⬤ **S65.492**   Other specified injury of blood vessel of left thumb
    - ⬤ **S65.499**   Other specified injury of blood vessel of unspecified thumb

● **S65.5**   **Injury of blood vessel of other and unspecified finger**

  ● **S65.50**   Unspecified injury of blood vessel of other and unspecified finger

    ● **S65.500**   Unspecified injury of blood vessel of right index finger

    ● **S65.501**   Unspecified injury of blood vessel of left index finger

    ● **S65.502**   Unspecified injury of blood vessel of right middle finger

    ● **S65.503**   Unspecified injury of blood vessel of left middle finger

    ● **S65.504**   Unspecified injury of blood vessel of right ring finger

    ● **S65.505**   Unspecified injury of blood vessel of left ring finger

    ● **S65.506**   Unspecified injury of blood vessel of right little finger

    ● **S65.507**   Unspecified injury of blood vessel of left little finger

    ● **S65.508**   Unspecified injury of blood vessel of other finger
         Unspecified injury of blood vessel of specified finger with unspecified laterality

    ● **S65.509**   Unspecified injury of blood vessel of unspecified finger

  ● **S65.51**   Laceration of blood vessel of other and unspecified finger

    ● **S65.510**   Laceration of blood vessel of right index finger

    ● **S65.511**   Laceration of blood vessel of left index finger

    ● **S65.512**   Laceration of blood vessel of right middle finger

    ● **S65.513**   Laceration of blood vessel of left middle finger

    ● **S65.514**   Laceration of blood vessel of right ring finger

    ● **S65.515**   Laceration of blood vessel of left ring finger

    ● **S65.516**   Laceration of blood vessel of right little finger

    ● **S65.517**   Laceration of blood vessel of left little finger

    ● **S65.518**   Laceration of blood vessel of other finger
         Laceration of blood vessel of specified finger with unspecified laterality

    ● **S65.519**   Laceration of blood vessel of unspecified finger

  ● **S65.59**   Other specified injury of blood vessel of other and unspecified finger

    ● **S65.590**   Other specified injury of blood vessel of right index finger

    ● **S65.591**   Other specified injury of blood vessel of left index finger

    ● **S65.592**   Other specified injury of blood vessel of right middle finger

    ● **S65.593**   Other specified injury of blood vessel of left middle finger

    ● **S65.594**   Other specified injury of blood vessel of right ring finger

    ● **S65.595**   Other specified injury of blood vessel of left ring finger

    ● **S65.596**   Other specified injury of blood vessel of right little finger

    ● **S65.597**   Other specified injury of blood vessel of left little finger

    ● **S65.598**   Other specified injury of blood vessel of other finger
         Other specified injury of blood vessel of specified finger with unspecified laterality

    ● **S65.599**   Other specified injury of blood vessel of unspecified finger

● **S65.8**   **Injury of other blood vessels at wrist and hand level**

  ● **S65.80**   Unspecified injury of other blood vessels at wrist and hand level

    ● **S65.801**   Unspecified injury of other blood vessels at wrist and hand level of right arm

    ● **S65.802**   Unspecified injury of other blood vessels at wrist and hand level of left arm

    ● **S65.809**   Unspecified injury of other blood vessels at wrist and hand level of unspecified arm

  ● **S65.81**   Laceration of other blood vessels at wrist and hand level

    ● **S65.811**   Laceration of other blood vessels at wrist and hand level of right arm

    ● **S65.812**   Laceration of other blood vessels at wrist and hand level of left arm

    ● **S65.819**   Laceration of other blood vessels at wrist and hand level of unspecified arm

  ● **S65.89**   Other specified injury of other blood vessels at wrist and hand level

    ● **S65.891**   Other specified injury of other blood vessels at wrist and hand level of right arm

    ● **S65.892**   Other specified injury of other blood vessels at wrist and hand level of left arm

    ● **S65.899**   Other specified injury of other blood vessels at wrist and hand level of unspecified arm

● **S65.9**   **Injury of unspecified blood vessel at wrist and hand level**

  ● **S65.90**   Unspecified injury of unspecified blood vessel at wrist and hand level

    ● **S65.901**   Unspecified injury of unspecified blood vessel at wrist and hand level of right arm

    ● **S65.902**   Unspecified injury of unspecified blood vessel at wrist and hand level of left arm

    ● **S65.909**   Unspecified injury of unspecified blood vessel at wrist and hand level of unspecified arm

  ● **S65.91**   Laceration of unspecified blood vessel at wrist and hand level

    ● **S65.911**   Laceration of unspecified blood vessel at wrist and hand level of right arm

    ● **S65.912**   Laceration of unspecified blood vessel at wrist and hand level of left arm

    ● **S65.919**   Laceration of unspecified blood vessel at wrist and hand level of unspecified arm

  ● **S65.99**   Other specified injury of unspecified blood vessel at wrist and hand level

    ● **S65.991**   Other specified injury of unspecified blood vessel at wrist and hand of right arm

    ● **S65.992**   Other specified injury of unspecified blood vessel at wrist and hand of left arm

    ● **S65.999**   Other specified injury of unspecified blood vessel at wrist and hand of unspecified arm

---

▶ New   ⇒ Revised   ~~deleted~~ Deleted   Excludes 1   Excludes 2   Includes   Use additional   Code first   Code also   Key words

OGCR Official Guidelines   X Assign placeholder X   ● Use Additional Character(s)   ▸ Manifestation Code   🔖 Hierarchical Condition Category   **Coding Clinic**

● **S66**   **Injury of muscle, fascia and tendon at wrist and hand level**

     Code also any associated open wound (S61.-)

     Excludes2   sprain of joints and ligaments of wrist and hand (S63.-)

     The appropriate 7th character is to be added to each code from category S66

> A   initial encounter
> D   subsequent encounter
> S   sequela

● **S66.0**   **Injury of long flexor muscle, fascia and tendon of thumb at wrist and hand level**

   ● **S66.00**   **Unspecified injury of long flexor muscle, fascia and tendon of thumb at wrist and hand level**

     ● **S66.001**   Unspecified injury of long flexor muscle, fascia and tendon of right thumb at wrist and hand level

     ● **S66.002**   Unspecified injury of long flexor muscle, fascia and tendon of left thumb at wrist and hand level

     ● **S66.009**   Unspecified injury of long flexor muscle, fascia and tendon of unspecified thumb at wrist and hand level

   ● **S66.01**   **Strain of long flexor muscle, fascia and tendon of thumb at wrist and hand level**

     ● **S66.011**   Strain of long flexor muscle, fascia and tendon of right thumb at wrist and hand level

     ● **S66.012**   Strain of long flexor muscle, fascia and tendon of left thumb at wrist and hand level

     ● **S66.019**   Strain of long flexor muscle, fascia and tendon of unspecified thumb at wrist and hand level

   ● **S66.02**   **Laceration of long flexor muscle, fascia and tendon of thumb at wrist and hand level**

     ● **S66.021**   Laceration of long flexor muscle, fascia and tendon of right thumb at wrist and hand level

     ● **S66.022**   Laceration of long flexor muscle, fascia and tendon of left thumb at wrist and hand level

     ● **S66.029**   Laceration of long flexor muscle, fascia and tendon of unspecified thumb at wrist and hand level

   ● **S66.09**   **Other specified injury of long flexor muscle, fascia and tendon of thumb at wrist and hand level**

     ● **S66.091**   Other specified injury of long flexor muscle, fascia and tendon of right thumb at wrist and hand level

     ● **S66.092**   Other specified injury of long flexor muscle, fascia and tendon of left thumb at wrist and hand level

     ● **S66.099**   Other specified injury of long flexor muscle, fascia and tendon of unspecified thumb at wrist and hand level

● **S66.1**   **Injury of flexor muscle, fascia and tendon of other and unspecified finger at wrist and hand level**

     Excludes2   injury of long flexor muscle, fascia and tendon of thumb at wrist and hand level (S66.0-)

   ● **S66.10**   **Unspecified injury of flexor muscle, fascia and tendon of other and unspecified finger at wrist and hand level**

     ● **S66.100**   Unspecified injury of flexor muscle, fascia and tendon of right index finger at wrist and hand level

     ● **S66.101**   Unspecified injury of flexor muscle, fascia and tendon of left index finger at wrist and hand level

     ● **S66.102**   Unspecified injury of flexor muscle, fascia and tendon of right middle finger at wrist and hand level

     ● **S66.103**   Unspecified injury of flexor muscle, fascia and tendon of left middle finger at wrist and hand level

     ● **S66.104**   Unspecified injury of flexor muscle, fascia and tendon of right ring finger at wrist and hand level

     ● **S66.105**   Unspecified injury of flexor muscle, fascia and tendon of left ring finger at wrist and hand level

     ● **S66.106**   Unspecified injury of flexor muscle, fascia and tendon of right little finger at wrist and hand level

     ● **S66.107**   Unspecified injury of flexor muscle, fascia and tendon of left little finger at wrist and hand level

     ● **S66.108**   Unspecified injury of flexor muscle, fascia and tendon of other finger at wrist and hand level

        Unspecified injury of flexor muscle, fascia and tendon of specified finger with unspecified laterality at wrist and hand level

     ● **S66.109**   Unspecified injury of flexor muscle, fascia and tendon of unspecified finger at wrist and hand level

   ● **S66.11**   **Strain of flexor muscle, fascia and tendon of other and unspecified finger at wrist and hand level**

     ● **S66.110**   Strain of flexor muscle, fascia and tendon of right index finger at wrist and hand level

     ● **S66.111**   Strain of flexor muscle, fascia and tendon of left index finger at wrist and hand level

     ● **S66.112**   Strain of flexor muscle, fascia and tendon of right middle finger at wrist and hand level

     ● **S66.113**   Strain of flexor muscle, fascia and tendon of left middle finger at wrist and hand level

     ● **S66.114**   Strain of flexor muscle, fascia and tendon of right ring finger at wrist and hand level

     ● **S66.115**   Strain of flexor muscle, fascia and tendon of left ring finger at wrist and hand level

     ● **S66.116**   Strain of flexor muscle, fascia and tendon of right little finger at wrist and hand level

     ● **S66.117**   Strain of flexor muscle, fascia and tendon of left little finger at wrist and hand level

     ● **S66.118**   Strain of flexor muscle, fascia and tendon of other finger at wrist and hand level

        Strain of flexor muscle, fascia and tendon of specified finger with unspecified laterality at wrist and hand level

     ● **S66.119**   Strain of flexor muscle, fascia and tendon of unspecified finger at wrist and hand level

● **S66.12** Laceration of flexor muscle, fascia and tendon of other and unspecified finger at wrist and hand level

   ● **S66.120** Laceration of flexor muscle, fascia and tendon of right index finger at wrist and hand level

   ● **S66.121** Laceration of flexor muscle, fascia and tendon of left index finger at wrist and hand level

   ● **S66.122** Laceration of flexor muscle, fascia and tendon of right middle finger at wrist and hand level

   ● **S66.123** Laceration of flexor muscle, fascia and tendon of left middle finger at wrist and hand level

   ● **S66.124** Laceration of flexor muscle, fascia and tendon of right ring finger at wrist and hand level

   ● **S66.125** Laceration of flexor muscle, fascia and tendon of left ring finger at wrist and hand level

   ● **S66.126** Laceration of flexor muscle, fascia and tendon of right little finger at wrist and hand level

   ● **S66.127** Laceration of flexor muscle, fascia and tendon of left little finger at wrist and hand level

   ● **S66.128** Laceration of flexor muscle, fascia and tendon of other finger at wrist and hand level
        Laceration of flexor muscle, fascia and tendon of specified finger with unspecified laterality at wrist and hand level

   ● **S66.129** Laceration of flexor muscle, fascia and tendon of unspecified finger at wrist and hand level

● **S66.19** Other injury of flexor muscle, fascia and tendon of other and unspecified finger at wrist and hand level

   ● **S66.190** Other injury of flexor muscle, fascia and tendon of right index finger at wrist and hand level

   ● **S66.191** Other injury of flexor muscle, fascia and tendon of left index finger at wrist and hand level

   ● **S66.192** Other injury of flexor muscle, fascia and tendon of right middle finger at wrist and hand level

   ● **S66.193** Other injury of flexor muscle, fascia and tendon of left middle finger at wrist and hand level

   ● **S66.194** Other injury of flexor muscle, fascia and tendon of right ring finger at wrist and hand level

   ● **S66.195** Other injury of flexor muscle, fascia and tendon of left ring finger at wrist and hand level

   ● **S66.196** Other injury of flexor muscle, fascia and tendon of right little finger at wrist and hand level

   ● **S66.197** Other injury of flexor muscle, fascia and tendon of left little finger at wrist and hand level

   ● **S66.198** Other injury of flexor muscle, fascia and tendon of other finger at wrist and hand level
        Other injury of flexor muscle, fascia and tendon of specified finger with unspecified laterality at wrist and hand level

   ● **S66.199** Other injury of flexor muscle, fascia and tendon of unspecified finger at wrist and hand level

● **S66.2** Injury of extensor muscle, fascia and tendon of thumb at wrist and hand level

   ● **S66.20** Unspecified injury of extensor muscle, fascia and tendon of thumb at wrist and hand level

      ● **S66.201** Unspecified injury of extensor muscle, fascia and tendon of right thumb at wrist and hand level

      ● **S66.202** Unspecified injury of extensor muscle, fascia and tendon of left thumb at wrist and hand level

      ● **S66.209** Unspecified injury of extensor muscle, fascia and tendon of unspecified thumb at wrist and hand level

   ● **S66.21** Strain of extensor muscle, fascia and tendon of thumb at wrist and hand level

      ● **S66.211** Strain of extensor muscle, fascia and tendon of right thumb at wrist and hand level

      ● **S66.212** Strain of extensor muscle, fascia and tendon of left thumb at wrist and hand level

      ● **S66.219** Strain of extensor muscle, fascia and tendon of unspecified thumb at wrist and hand level

   ● **S66.22** Laceration of extensor muscle, fascia and tendon of thumb at wrist and hand level

      ● **S66.221** Laceration of extensor muscle, fascia and tendon of right thumb at wrist and hand level

      ● **S66.222** Laceration of extensor muscle, fascia and tendon of left thumb at wrist and hand level

      ● **S66.229** Laceration of extensor muscle, fascia and tendon of unspecified thumb at wrist and hand level

   ● **S66.29** Other specified injury of extensor muscle, fascia and tendon of thumb at wrist and hand level

      ● **S66.291** Other specified injury of extensor muscle, fascia and tendon of right thumb at wrist and hand level

      ● **S66.292** Other specified injury of extensor muscle, fascia and tendon of left thumb at wrist and hand level

      ● **S66.299** Other specified injury of extensor muscle, fascia and tendon of unspecified thumb at wrist and hand level

● **S66.3** Injury of extensor muscle, fascia and tendon of other and unspecified finger at wrist and hand level

   Excludes2 injury of extensor muscle, fascia and tendon of thumb at wrist and hand level (S66.2-)

   ● **S66.30** Unspecified injury of extensor muscle, fascia and tendon of other and unspecified finger at wrist and hand level

      ● **S66.300** Unspecified injury of extensor muscle, fascia and tendon of right index finger at wrist and hand level

      ● **S66.301** Unspecified injury of extensor muscle, fascia and tendon of left index finger at wrist and hand level

      ● **S66.302** Unspecified injury of extensor muscle, fascia and tendon of right middle finger at wrist and hand level

      ● **S66.303** Unspecified injury of extensor muscle, fascia and tendon of left middle finger at wrist and hand level

      ● **S66.304** Unspecified injury of extensor muscle, fascia and tendon of right ring finger at wrist and hand level

---

▶ New ⇒ Revised ~~deleted~~ Deleted Excludes 1 Excludes 2 Includes Use additional Code first Code also Key words

1324 **OGCR** Official Guidelines X Assign placeholder X ● Use Additional Character(s) ▶ Manifestation Code ⚕ Hierarchical Condition Category **Coding Clinic**

● **S66.305**   **Unspecified injury of extensor muscle, fascia and tendon of left ring finger at wrist and hand level**

● **S66.306**   **Unspecified injury of extensor muscle, fascia and tendon of right little finger at wrist and hand level**

● **S66.307**   **Unspecified injury of extensor muscle, fascia and tendon of left little finger at wrist and hand level**

● **S66.308**   **Unspecified injury of extensor muscle, fascia and tendon of other finger at wrist and hand level**
> Unspecified injury of extensor muscle, fascia and tendon of specified finger with unspecified laterality at wrist and hand level

● **S66.309**   **Unspecified injury of extensor muscle, fascia and tendon of unspecified finger at wrist and hand level**

● **S66.31**   **Strain of extensor muscle, fascia and tendon of other and unspecified finger at wrist and hand level**

● **S66.310**   **Strain of extensor muscle, fascia and tendon of right index finger at wrist and hand level**

● **S66.311**   **Strain of extensor muscle, fascia and tendon of left index finger at wrist and hand level**

● **S66.312**   **Strain of extensor muscle, fascia and tendon of right middle finger at wrist and hand level**

● **S66.313**   **Strain of extensor muscle, fascia and tendon of left middle finger at wrist and hand level**

● **S66.314**   **Strain of extensor muscle, fascia and tendon of right ring finger at wrist and hand level**

● **S66.315**   **Strain of extensor muscle, fascia and tendon of left ring finger at wrist and hand level**

● **S66.316**   **Strain of extensor muscle, fascia and tendon of right little finger at wrist and hand level**

● **S66.317**   **Strain of extensor muscle, fascia and tendon of left little finger at wrist and hand level**

● **S66.318**   **Strain of extensor muscle, fascia and tendon of other finger at wrist and hand level**
> Strain of extensor muscle, fascia and tendon of specified finger with unspecified laterality at wrist and hand level

● **S66.319**   **Strain of extensor muscle, fascia and tendon of unspecified finger at wrist and hand level**

● **S66.32**   **Laceration of extensor muscle, fascia and tendon of other and unspecified finger at wrist and hand level**

● **S66.320**   **Laceration of extensor muscle, fascia and tendon of right index finger at wrist and hand level**

● **S66.321**   **Laceration of extensor muscle, fascia and tendon of left index finger at wrist and hand level**

● **S66.322**   **Laceration of extensor muscle, fascia and tendon of right middle finger at wrist and hand level**

● **S66.323**   **Laceration of extensor muscle, fascia and tendon of left middle finger at wrist and hand level**

● **S66.324**   **Laceration of extensor muscle, fascia and tendon of right ring finger at wrist and hand level**

● **S66.325**   **Laceration of extensor muscle, fascia and tendon of left ring finger at wrist and hand level**

● **S66.326**   **Laceration of extensor muscle, fascia and tendon of right little finger at wrist and hand level**

● **S66.327**   **Laceration of extensor muscle, fascia and tendon of left little finger at wrist and hand level**

● **S66.328**   **Laceration of extensor muscle, fascia and tendon of other finger at wrist and hand level**
> Laceration of extensor muscle, fascia and tendon of specified finger with unspecified laterality at wrist and hand level

● **S66.329**   **Laceration of extensor muscle, fascia and tendon of unspecified finger at wrist and hand level**

● **S66.39**   **Other injury of extensor muscle, fascia and tendon of other and unspecified finger at wrist and hand level**

● **S66.390**   **Other injury of extensor muscle, fascia and tendon of right index finger at wrist and hand level**

● **S66.391**   **Other injury of extensor muscle, fascia and tendon of left index finger at wrist and hand level**

● **S66.392**   **Other injury of extensor muscle, fascia and tendon of right middle finger at wrist and hand level**

● **S66.393**   **Other injury of extensor muscle, fascia and tendon of left middle finger at wrist and hand level**

● **S66.394**   **Other injury of extensor muscle, fascia and tendon of right ring finger at wrist and hand level**

● **S66.395**   **Other injury of extensor muscle, fascia and tendon of left ring finger at wrist and hand level**

● **S66.396**   **Other injury of extensor muscle, fascia and tendon of right little finger at wrist and hand level**

● **S66.397**   **Other injury of extensor muscle, fascia and tendon of left little finger at wrist and hand level**

● **S66.398**   **Other injury of extensor muscle, fascia and tendon of other finger at wrist and hand level**
> Other injury of extensor muscle, fascia and tendon of specified finger with unspecified laterality at wrist and hand level

● **S66.399**   **Other injury of extensor muscle, fascia and tendon of unspecified finger at wrist and hand level**

● **S66.4**   **Injury of intrinsic muscle, fascia and tendon of thumb at wrist and hand level**

● **S66.40**   **Unspecified injury of intrinsic muscle, fascia and tendon of thumb at wrist and hand level**

● **S66.401**   **Unspecified injury of intrinsic muscle, fascia and tendon of right thumb at wrist and hand level**

● **S66.402**   **Unspecified injury of intrinsic muscle, fascia and tendon of left thumb at wrist and hand level**

● **S66.409**   **Unspecified injury of intrinsic muscle, fascia and tendon of unspecified thumb at wrist and hand level**

● **S66.41** **Strain** of intrinsic muscle, fascia and tendon of thumb at wrist and hand level

   ● **S66.411** Strain of intrinsic muscle, fascia and tendon of **right** thumb at wrist and hand level

   ● **S66.412** Strain of intrinsic muscle, fascia and tendon of **left** thumb at wrist and hand level

   ● **S66.419** Strain of intrinsic muscle, fascia and tendon of **unspecified** thumb at wrist and hand level

● **S66.42** **Laceration** of intrinsic muscle, fascia and tendon of thumb at wrist and hand level

   ● **S66.421** Laceration of intrinsic muscle, fascia and tendon of **right** thumb at wrist and hand level

   ● **S66.422** Laceration of intrinsic muscle, fascia and tendon of **left** thumb at wrist and hand level

   ● **S66.429** Laceration of intrinsic muscle, fascia and tendon of **unspecified** thumb at wrist and hand level

● **S66.49** **Other** specified injury of intrinsic muscle, fascia and tendon of thumb at wrist and hand level

   ● **S66.491** Other specified injury of intrinsic muscle, fascia and tendon of **right** thumb at wrist and hand level

   ● **S66.492** Other specified injury of intrinsic muscle, fascia and tendon of **left** thumb at wrist and hand level

   ● **S66.499** Other specified injury of intrinsic muscle, fascia and tendon of **unspecified** thumb at wrist and hand level

● **S66.5** Injury of **intrinsic** muscle, fascia and tendon of other and unspecified **finger** at wrist and hand level

   Excludes2 injury of intrinsic muscle, fascia and tendon of thumb at wrist and hand level (S66.4-)

  ● **S66.50** **Unspecified** injury of intrinsic muscle and tendon of other and unspecified finger at wrist and hand level

   ● **S66.500** Unspecified injury of intrinsic muscle, fascia and tendon of **right index** finger at wrist and hand level

   ● **S66.501** Unspecified injury of intrinsic muscle, fascia and tendon of **left index** finger at wrist and hand level

   ● **S66.502** Unspecified injury of intrinsic muscle, fascia and tendon of **right middle** finger at wrist and hand level

   ● **S66.503** Unspecified injury of intrinsic muscle, fascia and tendon of **left middle** finger at wrist and hand level

   ● **S66.504** Unspecified injury of intrinsic muscle, fascia and tendon of **right ring** finger at wrist and hand level

   ● **S66.505** Unspecified injury of intrinsic muscle, fascia and tendon of **left ring** finger at wrist and hand level

   ● **S66.506** Unspecified injury of intrinsic muscle, fascia and tendon of **right little** finger at wrist and hand level

   ● **S66.507** Unspecified injury of intrinsic muscle, fascia and tendon of **left little** finger at wrist and hand level

   ● **S66.508** Unspecified injury of intrinsic muscle, fascia and tendon of **other** finger at wrist and hand level

Unspecified injury of intrinsic muscle, fascia and tendon of specified finger with unspecified laterality at wrist and hand level

   ● **S66.509** Unspecified injury of intrinsic muscle, fascia and tendon of **unspecified** finger at wrist and hand level

  ● **S66.51** **Strain** of intrinsic muscle, fascia and tendon of other and unspecified finger at wrist and hand level

   ● **S66.510** Strain of intrinsic muscle, fascia and tendon of **right index** finger at wrist and hand level

   ● **S66.511** Strain of intrinsic muscle, fascia and tendon of **left index** finger at wrist and hand level

   ● **S66.512** Strain of intrinsic muscle, fascia and tendon of **right middle** finger at wrist and hand level

   ● **S66.513** Strain of intrinsic muscle, fascia and tendon of **left middle** finger at wrist and hand level

   ● **S66.514** Strain of intrinsic muscle, fascia and tendon of **right ring** finger at wrist and hand level

   ● **S66.515** Strain of intrinsic muscle, fascia and tendon of **left ring** finger at wrist and hand level

   ● **S66.516** Strain of intrinsic muscle, fascia and tendon of **right little** finger at wrist and hand level

   ● **S66.517** Strain of intrinsic muscle, fascia and tendon of **left little** finger at wrist and hand level

   ● **S66.518** Strain of intrinsic muscle, fascia and tendon of **other** finger at wrist and hand level

Strain of intrinsic muscle, fascia and tendon of specified finger with unspecified laterality at wrist and hand level

   ● **S66.519** Strain of intrinsic muscle, fascia and tendon of **unspecified** finger at wrist and hand level

  ● **S66.52** **Laceration** of intrinsic muscle, fascia and tendon of other and unspecified finger at wrist and hand level

   ● **S66.520** Laceration of intrinsic muscle, fascia and tendon of **right index** finger at wrist and hand level

   ● **S66.521** Laceration of intrinsic muscle, fascia and tendon of **left index** finger at wrist and hand level

   ● **S66.522** Laceration of intrinsic muscle, fascia and tendon of **right middle** finger at wrist and hand level

   ● **S66.523** Laceration of intrinsic muscle, fascia and tendon of **left middle** finger at wrist and hand level

   ● **S66.524** Laceration of intrinsic muscle, fascia and tendon of **right ring** finger at wrist and hand level

   ● **S66.525** Laceration of intrinsic muscle, fascia and tendon of **left ring** finger at wrist and hand level

▶ New   ⇒ Revised   ~~deleted~~ Deleted   Excludes 1   Excludes 2   Includes   Use additional   Code first   Code also   Key words
OGCR Official Guidelines   X Assign placeholder X   ● Use Additional Character(s)   ▶ Manifestation Code   🅗🅒 Hierarchical Condition Category   **Coding Clinic**

● S66.526   Laceration of intrinsic muscle, fascia and tendon of right little finger at wrist and hand level

● S66.527   Laceration of intrinsic muscle, fascia and tendon of left little finger at wrist and hand level

● S66.528   Laceration of intrinsic muscle, fascia and tendon of other finger at wrist and hand level

Laceration of intrinsic muscle, fascia and tendon of specified finger with unspecified laterality at wrist and hand level

● S66.529   Laceration of intrinsic muscle, fascia and tendon of unspecified finger at wrist and hand level

● S66.59   Other injury of intrinsic muscle, fascia and tendon of other and unspecified finger at wrist and hand level

● S66.590   Other injury of intrinsic muscle, fascia and tendon of right index finger at wrist and hand level

● S66.591   Other injury of intrinsic muscle, fascia and tendon of left index finger at wrist and hand level

● S66.592   Other injury of intrinsic muscle, fascia and tendon of right middle finger at wrist and hand level

● S66.593   Other injury of intrinsic muscle, fascia and tendon of left middle finger at wrist and hand level

● S66.594   Other injury of intrinsic muscle, fascia and tendon of right ring finger at wrist and hand level

● S66.595   Other injury of intrinsic muscle, fascia and tendon of left ring finger at wrist and hand level

● S66.596   Other injury of intrinsic muscle, fascia and tendon of right little finger at wrist and hand level

● S66.597   Other injury of intrinsic muscle, fascia and tendon of left little finger at wrist and hand level

● S66.598   Other injury of intrinsic muscle, fascia and tendon of other finger at wrist and hand level

Other injury of intrinsic muscle, fascia and tendon of specified finger with unspecified laterality at wrist and hand level

● S66.599   Other injury of intrinsic muscle, fascia and tendon of unspecified finger at wrist and hand level

● S66.8   Injury of other specified muscles, fascia and tendons at wrist and hand level

● S66.80   Unspecified injury of other specified muscles, fascia and tendons at wrist and hand level

● S66.801   Unspecified injury of other specified muscles, fascia and tendons at wrist and hand level, right hand

● S66.802   Unspecified injury of other specified muscles, fascia and tendons at wrist and hand level, left hand

● S66.809   Unspecified injury of other specified muscles, fascia and tendons at wrist and hand level, unspecified hand

● S66.81   Strain of other specified muscles, fascia and tendons at wrist and hand level

● S66.811   Strain of other specified muscles, fascia and tendons at wrist and hand level, right hand

● S66.812   Strain of other specified muscles, fascia and tendons at wrist and hand level, left hand

● S66.819   Strain of other specified muscles, fascia and tendons at wrist and hand level, unspecified hand

● S66.82   Laceration of other specified muscles, fascia and tendons at wrist and hand level

● S66.821   Laceration of other specified muscles, fascia and tendons at wrist and hand level, right hand

● S66.822   Laceration of other specified muscles, fascia and tendons at wrist and hand level, left hand

● S66.829   Laceration of other specified muscles, fascia and tendons at wrist and hand level, unspecified hand

● S66.89   Other injury of other specified muscles, fascia and tendons at wrist and hand level

● S66.891   Other injury of other specified muscles, fascia and tendons at wrist and hand level, right hand

● S66.892   Other injury of other specified muscles, fascia and tendons at wrist and hand level, left hand

● S66.899   Other injury of other specified muscles, fascia and tendons at wrist and hand level, unspecified hand

● S66.9   Injury of unspecified muscle, fascia and tendon at wrist and hand level

● S66.90   Unspecified injury of unspecified muscle, fascia and tendon at wrist and hand level

● S66.901   Unspecified injury of unspecified muscle, fascia and tendon at wrist and hand level, right hand

● S66.902   Unspecified injury of unspecified muscle, fascia and tendon at wrist and hand level, left hand

● S66.909   Unspecified injury of unspecified muscle, fascia and tendon at wrist and hand level, unspecified hand

● S66.91   Strain of unspecified muscle, fascia and tendon at wrist and hand level

● S66.911   Strain of unspecified muscle, fascia and tendon at wrist and hand level, right hand

● S66.912   Strain of unspecified muscle, fascia and tendon at wrist and hand level, left hand

● S66.919   Strain of unspecified muscle, fascia and tendon at wrist and hand level, unspecified hand

● S66.92   Laceration of unspecified muscle, fascia and tendon at wrist and hand level

● S66.921   Laceration of unspecified muscle, fascia and tendon at wrist and hand level, right hand

● S66.922   Laceration of unspecified muscle, fascia and tendon at wrist and hand level, left hand

● S66.929   Laceration of unspecified muscle, fascia and tendon at wrist and hand level, unspecified hand

● **S66.99**   **Other** injury of unspecified muscle, fascia and tendon at wrist and hand level

    ● **S66.991**   Other injury of unspecified muscle, fascia and tendon at wrist and hand level, **right** hand

    ● **S66.992**   Other injury of unspecified muscle, fascia and tendon at wrist and hand level, **left** hand

    ● **S66.999**   Other injury of unspecified muscle, fascia and tendon at wrist and hand level, **unspecified** hand

● **S67**   **Crushing injury** of wrist, hand and fingers

    Use additional code for all associated injuries, such as:
       fracture of wrist and hand (S62.-)
       open wound of wrist and hand (S61.-)

    The appropriate 7th character is to be added to each code from category S67

A	initial encounter
D	subsequent encounter
S	sequela

● **S67.0**   Crushing injury of **thumb**

  X ● **S67.00**   Crushing injury of **unspecified** thumb

  X ● **S67.01**   Crushing injury of **right** thumb

  X ● **S67.02**   Crushing injury of **left** thumb

● **S67.1**   Crushing injury of other and unspecified **finger(s)**

    Excludes2   crushing injury of thumb (S67.0-)

  X ● **S67.10**   Crushing injury of **unspecified** finger(s)

  ● **S67.19**   Crushing injury of other finger(s)

    ● **S67.190**   Crushing injury of **right index** finger

    ● **S67.191**   Crushing injury of **left index** finger

    ● **S67.192**   Crushing injury of **right middle** finger

    ● **S67.193**   Crushing injury of **left middle** finger

    ● **S67.194**   Crushing injury of **right ring** finger

    ● **S67.195**   Crushing injury of **left ring** finger

    ● **S67.196**   Crushing injury of **right little** finger

    ● **S67.197**   Crushing injury of **left little** finger

    ● **S67.198**   Crushing injury of **other** finger
       Crushing injury of specified finger with unspecified laterality

● **S67.2**   Crushing injury of **hand**

    Excludes2   crushing injury of fingers (S67.1-)
                  crushing injury of thumb (S67.0-)

  X ● **S67.20**   Crushing injury of **unspecified** hand

  X ● **S67.21**   Crushing injury of **right** hand

  X ● **S67.22**   Crushing injury of **left** hand

● **S67.3**   Crushing injury of **wrist**

  X ● **S67.30**   Crushing injury of **unspecified** wrist

  X ● **S67.31**   Crushing injury of **right** wrist

  X ● **S67.32**   Crushing injury of **left** wrist

● **S67.4**   Crushing injury of **wrist and hand**

    Excludes1   crushing injury of hand alone (S67.2-)
                  crushing injury of wrist alone (S67.3-)

    Excludes2   crushing injury of fingers (S67.1-)
                  crushing injury of thumb (S67.0-)

  X ● **S67.40**   Crushing injury of **unspecified** wrist and hand

  X ● **S67.41**   Crushing injury of **right** wrist and hand

  X ● **S67.42**   Crushing injury of **left** wrist and hand

● **S67.9**   Crushing injury of **unspecified** part(s) of wrist, hand and fingers

  X ● **S67.90**   Crushing injury of unspecified part(s) of **unspecified** wrist, hand and fingers

  X ● **S67.91**   Crushing injury of unspecified part(s) of **right** wrist, hand and fingers

  X ● **S67.92**   Crushing injury of unspecified part(s) of **left** wrist, hand and fingers

● **S68**   **Traumatic amputation** of wrist, hand and fingers

    An amputation not identified as partial or complete should be coded to complete

    The appropriate 7th character is to be added to each code from category S68

A	initial encounter
D	subsequent encounter
S	sequela

● **S68.0**   Traumatic **metacarpophalangeal amputation of thumb**
    Traumatic amputation of thumb NOS

  ● **S68.01**   **Complete** traumatic metacarpophalangeal amputation of thumb

    ● **S68.011**   Complete traumatic metacarpophalangeal amputation of **right thumb** S 🐾

    ● **S68.012**   Complete traumatic metacarpophalangeal amputation of **left thumb** S 🐾

    ● **S68.019**   Complete traumatic metacarpophalangeal amputation of **unspecified thumb** S 🐾

  ● **S68.02**   **Partial** traumatic metacarpophalangeal amputation of thumb

    ● **S68.021**   Partial traumatic metacarpophalangeal amputation of **right thumb** S 🐾

    ● **S68.022**   Partial traumatic metacarpophalangeal amputation of **left thumb** S 🐾

    ● **S68.029**   Partial traumatic metacarpophalangeal amputation of **unspecified thumb** S 🐾

● **S68.1**   Traumatic **metacarpophalangeal amputation of other and unspecified finger**
    Traumatic amputation of finger NOS

    Excludes2   traumatic metacarpophalangeal amputation of thumb (S68.0-)

  ● **S68.11**   **Complete** traumatic metacarpophalangeal amputation of other and unspecified finger

    ● **S68.110**   Complete traumatic metacarpophalangeal amputation of **right index** finger S 🐾

    ● **S68.111**   Complete traumatic metacarpophalangeal amputation of **left index** finger S 🐾

    ● **S68.112**   Complete traumatic metacarpophalangeal amputation of **right middle** finger S 🐾

    ● **S68.113**   Complete traumatic metacarpophalangeal amputation of **left middle** finger S 🐾

    ● **S68.114**   Complete traumatic metacarpophalangeal amputation of **right ring** finger S 🐾

    ● **S68.115**   Complete traumatic metacarpophalangeal amputation of **left ring** finger S 🐾

    ● **S68.116**   Complete traumatic metacarpophalangeal amputation of **right little** finger S 🐾

    ● **S68.117**   Complete traumatic metacarpophalangeal amputation of **left little** finger S 🐾

    ● **S68.118**   Complete traumatic metacarpophalangeal amputation of **other finger** S 🐾
       Complete traumatic metacarpophalangeal amputation of specified finger with unspecified laterality

    ● **S68.119**   Complete traumatic metacarpophalangeal amputation of **unspecified finger** S 🐾

▶ New   ⇒ Revised   ~~deleted~~ Deleted   Excludes 1   Excludes 2   Includes   Use additional   Code first   Code also   Key words

OGCR Official Guidelines   X Assign placeholder X   ● Use Additional Character(s)   〗 Manifestation Code   🐾 Hierarchical Condition Category   **Coding Clinic**

● **S68.12** **Partial traumatic metacarpophalangeal amputation of other and unspecified finger**

  ● **S68.120** Partial traumatic metacarpophalangeal amputation of right index finger S ⚕

  ● **S68.121** Partial traumatic metacarpophalangeal amputation of left index finger S ⚕

  ● **S68.122** Partial traumatic metacarpophalangeal amputation of right middle finger S ⚕

  ● **S68.123** Partial traumatic metacarpophalangeal amputation of left middle finger S ⚕

  ● **S68.124** Partial traumatic metacarpophalangeal amputation of right ring finger S ⚕

  ● **S68.125** Partial traumatic metacarpophalangeal amputation of left ring finger S ⚕

  ● **S68.126** Partial traumatic metacarpophalangeal amputation of right little finger S ⚕

  ● **S68.127** Partial traumatic metacarpophalangeal amputation of left little finger S ⚕

  ● **S68.128** Partial traumatic metacarpophalangeal amputation of other finger S ⚕

     Partial traumatic metacarpophalangeal amputation of specified finger with unspecified laterality

  ● **S68.129** Partial traumatic metacarpophalangeal amputation of unspecified finger S ⚕

● **S68.4** **Traumatic amputation of hand at wrist level**
  Traumatic amputation of hand NOS
  Traumatic amputation of wrist

 ● **S68.41** Complete traumatic amputation of hand at wrist level

  ● **S68.411** Complete traumatic amputation of right hand at wrist level A, S ⚕

  ● **S68.412** Complete traumatic amputation of left hand at wrist level A, S ⚕

  ● **S68.419** Complete traumatic amputation of unspecified hand at wrist level A, S ⚕

 ● **S68.42** Partial traumatic amputation of hand at wrist level

  ● **S68.421** Partial traumatic amputation of right hand at wrist level A, S ⚕

  ● **S68.422** Partial traumatic amputation of left hand at wrist level A, S ⚕

  ● **S68.429** Partial traumatic amputation of unspecified hand at wrist level A, S ⚕

● **S68.5** **Traumatic transphalangeal amputation of thumb**
  Traumatic interphalangeal joint amputation of thumb

 ● **S68.51** Complete traumatic transphalangeal amputation of thumb

  ● **S68.511** Complete traumatic transphalangeal amputation of right thumb S ⚕

  ● **S68.512** Complete traumatic transphalangeal amputation of left thumb S ⚕

  ● **S68.519** Complete traumatic transphalangeal amputation of unspecified thumb S ⚕

 ● **S68.52** Partial traumatic transphalangeal amputation of thumb

  ● **S68.521** Partial traumatic transphalangeal amputation of right thumb S ⚕

  ● **S68.522** Partial traumatic transphalangeal amputation of left thumb S ⚕

  ● **S68.529** Partial traumatic transphalangeal amputation of unspecified thumb S ⚕

● **S68.6** **Traumatic transphalangeal amputation of other and unspecified finger**

 ● **S68.61** Complete traumatic transphalangeal amputation of other and unspecified finger(s)

  ● **S68.610** Complete traumatic transphalangeal amputation of right index finger S ⚕

  ● **S68.611** Complete traumatic transphalangeal amputation of left index finger S ⚕

  ● **S68.612** Complete traumatic transphalangeal amputation of right middle finger S ⚕

  ● **S68.613** Complete traumatic transphalangeal amputation of left middle finger S ⚕

  ● **S68.614** Complete traumatic transphalangeal amputation of right ring finger S ⚕

  ● **S68.615** Complete traumatic transphalangeal amputation of left ring finger S ⚕

  ● **S68.616** Complete traumatic transphalangeal amputation of right little finger S ⚕

  ● **S68.617** Complete traumatic transphalangeal amputation of left little finger S ⚕

  ● **S68.618** Complete traumatic transphalangeal amputation of other finger S ⚕

     Complete traumatic transphalangeal amputation of specified finger with unspecified laterality

  ● **S68.619** Complete traumatic transphalangeal amputation of unspecified finger S ⚕

 ● **S68.62** Partial traumatic transphalangeal amputation of other and unspecified finger

  ● **S68.620** Partial traumatic transphalangeal amputation of right index finger S ⚕

  ● **S68.621** Partial traumatic transphalangeal amputation of left index finger S ⚕

  ● **S68.622** Partial traumatic transphalangeal amputation of right middle finger S ⚕

  ● **S68.623** Partial traumatic transphalangeal amputation of left middle finger S ⚕

  ● **S68.624** Partial traumatic transphalangeal amputation of right ring finger S ⚕

  ● **S68.625** Partial traumatic transphalangeal amputation of left ring finger S ⚕

  ● **S68.626** Partial traumatic transphalangeal amputation of right little finger S ⚕

  ● **S68.627** Partial traumatic transphalangeal amputation of left little finger S ⚕

  ● **S68.628** Partial traumatic transphalangeal amputation of other finger S ⚕

     Partial traumatic transphalangeal amputation of specified finger with unspecified laterality

  ● **S68.629** Partial traumatic transphalangeal amputation of unspecified finger S ⚕

CHAPTER 19 (S00-T88)

● S68.7   Traumatic transmetacarpal amputation of hand
- ● S68.71   Complete traumatic transmetacarpal amputation of hand
  - ● S68.711   Complete traumatic transmetacarpal amputation of right hand A, S 🝢
  - ● S68.712   Complete traumatic transmetacarpal amputation of left hand A, S 🝢
  - ● S68.719   Complete traumatic transmetacarpal amputation of unspecified hand A, S 🝢
- ● S68.72   Partial traumatic transmetacarpal amputation of hand
  - ● S68.721   Partial traumatic transmetacarpal amputation of right hand A, S 🝢
  - ● S68.722   Partial traumatic transmetacarpal amputation of left hand A, S 🝢
  - ● S68.729   Partial traumatic transmetacarpal amputation of unspecified hand A, S 🝢

● S69   Other and unspecified injuries of wrist, hand and finger(s)

The appropriate 7th character is to be added to each code from category S69

A	initial encounter
D	subsequent encounter
S	sequela

- ● S69.8   Other specified injuries of wrist, hand and finger(s)
  - X ● S69.80   Other specified injuries of unspecified wrist, hand and finger(s)
  - X ● S69.81   Other specified injuries of right wrist, hand and finger(s)
  - X ● S69.82   Other specified injuries of left wrist, hand and finger(s)
- ● S69.9   Unspecified injury of wrist, hand and finger(s)
  - X ● S69.90   Unspecified injury of unspecified wrist, hand and finger(s)
  - X ● S69.91   Unspecified injury of right wrist, hand and finger(s)
  - X ● S69.92   Unspecified injury of left wrist, hand and finger(s)

INJURIES TO THE HIP AND THIGH (S70-S79)

Excludes2   burns and corrosions (T20-T32)
frostbite (T33-T34)
snake bite (T63.0-)
venomous insect bite or sting (T63.4-)

● S70   Superficial injury of hip and thigh

The appropriate 7th character is to be added to each code from category S70

A	initial encounter
D	subsequent encounter
S	sequela

- ● S70.0   Contusion of hip
  - X ● S70.00   Contusion of unspecified hip
  - X ● S70.01   Contusion of right hip
  - X ● S70.02   Contusion of left hip
- ● S70.1   Contusion of thigh
  - X ● S70.10   Contusion of unspecified thigh
  - X ● S70.11   Contusion of right thigh
  - X ● S70.12   Contusion of left thigh

● S70.2   Other superficial injuries of hip
- ● S70.21   Abrasion of hip
  - ● S70.211   Abrasion, right hip
  - ● S70.212   Abrasion, left hip
  - ● S70.219   Abrasion, unspecified hip
- ● S70.22   Blister (nonthermal) of hip
  - ● S70.221   Blister (nonthermal), right hip
  - ● S70.222   Blister (nonthermal), left hip
  - ● S70.229   Blister (nonthermal), unspecified hip
- ● S70.24   External constriction of hip
  - ● S70.241   External constriction, right hip
  - ● S70.242   External constriction, left hip
  - ● S70.249   External constriction, unspecified hip
- ● S70.25   Superficial foreign body of hip
  Splinter in the hip
  - ● S70.251   Superficial foreign body, right hip
  - ● S70.252   Superficial foreign body, left hip
  - ● S70.259   Superficial foreign body, unspecified hip
- ● S70.26   Insect bite (nonvenomous) of hip
  - ● S70.261   Insect bite (nonvenomous), right hip
  - ● S70.262   Insect bite (nonvenomous), left hip
  - ● S70.269   Insect bite (nonvenomous), unspecified hip
- ● S70.27   Other superficial bite of hip
  Excludes1   open bite of hip (S71.05-)
  - ● S70.271   Other superficial bite of hip, right hip
  - ● S70.272   Other superficial bite of hip, left hip
  - ● S70.279   Other superficial bite of hip, unspecified hip

● S70.3   Other superficial injuries of thigh
- ● S70.31   Abrasion of thigh
  - ● S70.311   Abrasion, right thigh
  - ● S70.312   Abrasion, left thigh
  - ● S70.319   Abrasion, unspecified thigh
- ● S70.32   Blister (nonthermal) of thigh
  - ● S70.321   Blister (nonthermal), right thigh
  - ● S70.322   Blister (nonthermal), left thigh
  - ● S70.329   Blister (nonthermal), unspecified thigh
- ● S70.34   External constriction of thigh
  - ● S70.341   External constriction, right thigh
  - ● S70.342   External constriction, left thigh
  - ● S70.349   External constriction, unspecified thigh
- ● S70.35   Superficial foreign body of thigh
  Splinter in the thigh
  - ● S70.351   Superficial foreign body, right thigh
  - ● S70.352   Superficial foreign body, left thigh
  - ● S70.359   Superficial foreign body, unspecified thigh
- ● S70.36   Insect bite (nonvenomous) of thigh
  - ● S70.361   Insect bite (nonvenomous), right thigh
  - ● S70.362   Insect bite (nonvenomous), left thigh
  - ● S70.369   Insect bite (nonvenomous), unspecified thigh

▶ New   ⇒ Revised   ~~deleted~~ Deleted   Excludes 1   Excludes 2   Includes   Use additional   Code first   Code also   Key words

OGCR Official Guidelines   X Assign placeholder X   ● Use Additional Character(s)   ▷ Manifestation Code   🝢 Hierarchical Condition Category   Coding Clinic

● S70.37   Other superficial bite of thigh
          Excludes1   open bite of thigh (S71.15)
    ● S70.371   Other superficial bite of right thigh
    ● S70.372   Other superficial bite of left thigh
    ● S70.379   Other superficial bite of unspecified thigh
● S70.9   Unspecified superficial injury of hip and thigh
    ● S70.91   Unspecified superficial injury of hip
        ● S70.911   Unspecified superficial injury of right hip
        ● S70.912   Unspecified superficial injury of left hip
        ● S70.919   Unspecified superficial injury of unspecified hip
    ● S70.92   Unspecified superficial injury of thigh
        ● S70.921   Unspecified superficial injury of right thigh
        ● S70.922   Unspecified superficial injury of left thigh
        ● S70.929   Unspecified superficial injury of unspecified thigh

● S71   Open wound of hip and thigh
       Code also any associated wound infection
       Excludes1   open fracture of hip and thigh (S72.-)
                traumatic amputation of hip and thigh (S78.-)
       Excludes2   bite of venomous animal (T63.-)
                open wound of ankle, foot and toes (S91.-)
                open wound of knee and lower leg (S81.-)
       The appropriate 7th character is to be added to each code from
          category S71

       A   initial encounter
       D   subsequent encounter
       S   sequela

    ● S71.0   Open wound of hip
        ● S71.00   Unspecified open wound of hip
            ● S71.001   Unspecified open wound, right hip
            ● S71.002   Unspecified open wound, left hip
            ● S71.009   Unspecified open wound, unspecified hip
        ● S71.01   Laceration without foreign body of hip
            ● S71.011   Laceration without foreign body, right hip
            ● S71.012   Laceration without foreign body, left hip
            ● S71.019   Laceration without foreign body, unspecified hip
        ● S71.02   Laceration with foreign body of hip
            ● S71.021   Laceration with foreign body, right hip
            ● S71.022   Laceration with foreign body, left hip
            ● S71.029   Laceration with foreign body, unspecified hip
        ● S71.03   Puncture wound without foreign body of hip
            ● S71.031   Puncture wound without foreign body, right hip
            ● S71.032   Puncture wound without foreign body, left hip
            ● S71.039   Puncture wound without foreign body, unspecified hip

● S71.04   Puncture wound with foreign body of hip
    ● S71.041   Puncture wound with foreign body, right hip
    ● S71.042   Puncture wound with foreign body, left hip
    ● S71.049   Puncture wound with foreign body, unspecified hip
● S71.05   Open bite of hip
          Bite of hip NOS
          Excludes1   superficial bite of hip (S70.26, S70.27)
    ● S71.051   Open bite, right hip
    ● S71.052   Open bite, left hip
    ● S71.059   Open bite, unspecified hip
● S71.1   Open wound of thigh
    ● S71.10   Unspecified open wound of thigh
        ● S71.101   Unspecified open wound, right thigh
        ● S71.102   Unspecified open wound, left thigh
        ● S71.109   Unspecified open wound, unspecified thigh
    ● S71.11   Laceration without foreign body of thigh
        ● S71.111   Laceration without foreign body, right thigh
        ● S71.112   Laceration without foreign body, left thigh
        ● S71.119   Laceration without foreign body, unspecified thigh
    ● S71.12   Laceration with foreign body of thigh
        ● S71.121   Laceration with foreign body, right thigh
        ● S71.122   Laceration with foreign body, left thigh
        ● S71.129   Laceration with foreign body, unspecified thigh
    ● S71.13   Puncture wound without foreign body of thigh
        ● S71.131   Puncture wound without foreign body, right thigh
        ● S71.132   Puncture wound without foreign body, left thigh
        ● S71.139   Puncture wound without foreign body, unspecified thigh
    ● S71.14   Puncture wound with foreign body of thigh
        ● S71.141   Puncture wound with foreign body, right thigh
        ● S71.142   Puncture wound with foreign body, left thigh
        ● S71.149   Puncture wound with foreign body, unspecified thigh
    ● S71.15   Open bite of thigh
              Bite of thigh NOS
              Excludes1   superficial bite of thigh (S70.37-)
        ● S71.151   Open bite, right thigh
        ● S71.152   Open bite, left thigh
        ● S71.159   Open bite, unspecified thigh

● S72   Fracture of femur
          Note: A fracture not indicated as displaced or nondisplaced
                  should be coded to displaced
                  A fracture not indicated as open or closed should be coded
                  to closed
                  The open fracture designations are based on the Gustilo
                  open fracture classification
          Excludes1   traumatic amputation of hip and thigh (S78.-)
          Excludes2   fracture of lower leg and ankle (S82.-)
                       fracture of foot (S92.-)
                       periprosthetic fracture of prosthetic implant of
                            hip (M97.0-)
          The appropriate 7th character is to be added to all codes from
              category S72

A	initial encounter for closed fracture
B	initial encounter for open fracture type I or II
	initial encounter for open fracture NOS
C	initial encounter for open fracture type IIIA, IIIB, or IIIC
D	subsequent encounter for closed fracture with routine healing
E	subsequent encounter for open fracture type I or II with routine healing
F	subsequent encounter for open fracture type IIIA, IIIB, or IIIC with routine healing
G	subsequent encounter for closed fracture with delayed healing
H	subsequent encounter for open fracture type I or II with delayed healing
J	subsequent encounter for open fracture type IIIA, IIIB, or IIIC with delayed healing
K	subsequent encounter for closed fracture with nonunion
M	subsequent encounter for open fracture type I or II with nonunion
N	subsequent encounter for open fracture type IIIA, IIIB, or IIIC with nonunion
P	subsequent encounter for closed fracture with malunion
Q	subsequent encounter for open fracture type I or II with malunion
R	subsequent encounter for open fracture type IIIA, IIIB, or IIIC with malunion
S	sequela

● S72.0   Fracture of head and neck of femur
            Excludes2   physeal fracture of upper end of femur
                         (S79.0-)
      ● S72.00   Fracture of **unspecified part** of neck of femur
                  Fracture of hip NOS
                  Fracture of neck of femur NOS
            ● S72.001   Fracture of unspecified part of neck of
                         right femur   A, B, C 🝆
            ● S72.002   Fracture of unspecified part of neck of
                         left femur   A, B, C 🝆
                         Coding Clinic: 2015, Q4, P37, Q1, P17
            ● S72.009   Fracture of unspecified part of neck of
                         unspecified femur   A, B, C 🝆
      ● S72.01   Unspecified intracapsular fracture of femur
                  Subcapital fracture of femur
            ● S72.011   Unspecified intracapsular fracture of
                         right femur   A, B, C 🝆
            ● S72.012   Unspecified intracapsular fracture of
                         left femur   A, B, C 🝆
            ● S72.019   Unspecified intracapsular fracture of
                         unspecified femur   A, B, C 🝆

● S72.02   Fracture of **epiphysis** (separation) (upper) of
            femur
            Transepiphyseal fracture of femur
            Fracture and separation across growth plate
            Excludes1   capital femoral epiphyseal fracture
                         (pediatric) of femur (S79.01-)
                         Salter-Harris Type I physeal
                              fracture of upper end of
                              femur (S79.01-)
      ● S72.021   Displaced fracture of epiphysis
                   (separation) (upper) of **right** femur
                   A, B, C 🝆
      ● S72.022   Displaced fracture of epiphysis
                   (separation) (upper) of **left** femur
                   A, B, C 🝆
      ● S72.023   Displaced fracture of epiphysis
                   (separation) (upper) of **unspecified**
                   femur   A, B, C 🝆
      ● S72.024   Nondisplaced fracture of epiphysis
                   (separation) (upper) of **right** femur
                   A, B, C 🝆
      ● S72.025   Nondisplaced fracture of epiphysis
                   (separation) (upper) of **left** femur
                   A, B, C 🝆
      ● S72.026   Nondisplaced fracture of epiphysis
                   (separation) (upper) of **unspecified**
                   femur   A, B, C 🝆
● S72.03   **Midcervical** fracture of femur
            Transcervical fracture of femur NOS
      ● S72.031   Displaced midcervical fracture of
                   right femur A, B, C 🝆
      ● S72.032   Displaced midcervical fracture of **left**
                   femur A, B, C 🝆
      ● S72.033   Displaced midcervical fracture of
                   unspecified femur A, B, C 🝆
      ● S72.034   Nondisplaced midcervical fracture of
                   right femur A, B, C 🝆
      ● S72.035   Nondisplaced midcervical fracture of
                   left femur A, B, C 🝆
      ● S72.036   Nondisplaced midcervical fracture of
                   unspecified femur A, B, C 🝆
● S72.04   Fracture of **base of neck** of femur
            Cervicotrochanteric fracture of femur
      ● S72.041   Displaced fracture of base of neck of
                   right femur A, B, C 🝆
      ● S72.042   Displaced fracture of base of neck of
                   left femur A, B, C 🝆
      ● S72.043   Displaced fracture of base of neck of
                   unspecified femur A, B, C 🝆
      ● S72.044   Nondisplaced fracture of base of neck
                   of **right** femur A, B, C 🝆
      ● S72.045   Nondisplaced fracture of base of neck
                   of **left** femur A, B, C 🝆
      ● S72.046   Nondisplaced fracture of base of neck
                   of **unspecified** femur A, B, C 🝆
● S72.05   **Unspecified** fracture of **head** of femur
            Fracture of head of femur NOS
      ● S72.051   Unspecified fracture of head of **right**
                   femur A, B, C 🝆
      ● S72.052   Unspecified fracture of head of **left**
                   femur A, B, C 🝆
      ● S72.059   Unspecified fracture of head of
                   unspecified femur A, B, C 🝆

▶ New   ⇨ Revised   ~~deleted~~ Deleted   Excludes 1   Excludes 2   Includes   Use additional   Code first   Code also   Key words
OGCR Official Guidelines   X Assign placeholder X   ● Use Additional Character(s)   ▷ Manifestation Code   🝆 Hierarchical Condition Category   Coding Clinic

- **S72.06**   Articular fracture of head of femur
  - **S72.061**   Displaced articular fracture of head of right femur A, B, C ℞
  - **S72.062**   Displaced articular fracture of head of left femur A, B, C ℞
  - **S72.063**   Displaced articular fracture of head of unspecified femur A, B, C ℞
  - **S72.064**   Nondisplaced articular fracture of head of right femur A, B, C ℞
  - **S72.065**   Nondisplaced articular fracture of head of left femur A, B, C ℞
  - **S72.066**   Nondisplaced articular fracture of head of unspecified femur A, B, C ℞
- **S72.09**   Other fracture of head and neck of femur
  - **S72.091**   Other fracture of head and neck of right femur A, B, C ℞
  - **S72.092**   Other fracture of head and neck of left femur A, B, C ℞
  - **S72.099**   Other fracture of head and neck of unspecified femur A, B, C ℞
- **S72.1**   **Pertrochanteric fracture**
  Fracture extending close to, but not into, joint
  - **S72.10**   Unspecified trochanteric fracture of femur
    Fracture of trochanter NOS
    - **S72.101**   Unspecified trochanteric fracture of right femur A, B, C ℞
    - **S72.102**   Unspecified trochanteric fracture of left femur A, B, C ℞
    - **S72.109**   Unspecified trochanteric fracture of unspecified femur A, B, C ℞
  - **S72.11**   Fracture of greater trochanter of femur
    - **S72.111**   Displaced fracture of greater trochanter of right femur A, B, C ℞
    - **S72.112**   Displaced fracture of greater trochanter of left femur A, B, C ℞
    - **S72.113**   Displaced fracture of greater trochanter of unspecified femur A, B, C ℞
    - **S72.114**   Nondisplaced fracture of greater trochanter of right femur A, B, C ℞
    - **S72.115**   Nondisplaced fracture of greater trochanter of left femur A, B, C ℞
    - **S72.116**   Nondisplaced fracture of greater trochanter of unspecified femur A, B, C ℞
  - **S72.12**   Fracture of lesser trochanter of femur
    - **S72.121**   Displaced fracture of lesser trochanter of right femur A, B, C ℞
    - **S72.122**   Displaced fracture of lesser trochanter of left femur A, B, C ℞
    - **S72.123**   Displaced fracture of lesser trochanter of unspecified femur A, B, C ℞
    - **S72.124**   Nondisplaced fracture of lesser trochanter of right femur A, B, C ℞
    - **S72.125**   Nondisplaced fracture of lesser trochanter of left femur A, B, C ℞
    - **S72.126**   Nondisplaced fracture of lesser trochanter of unspecified femur A, B, C ℞
  - **S72.13**   Apophyseal fracture of femur
    Pertaining to articulations between articular facets of adjacent vertebrae
    Excludes1   chronic (nontraumatic) slipped upper femoral epiphysis (M93.0-)
    - **S72.131**   Displaced apophyseal fracture of right femur A, B, C ℞
    - **S72.132**   Displaced apophyseal fracture of left femur A, B, C ℞
    - **S72.133**   Displaced apophyseal fracture of unspecified femur A, B, C ℞

- **S72.134**   Nondisplaced apophyseal fracture of right femur A, B, C ℞
- **S72.135**   Nondisplaced apophyseal fracture of left femur A, B, C ℞
- **S72.136**   Nondisplaced apophyseal fracture of unspecified femur A, B, C ℞
- **S72.14**   Intertrochanteric fracture of femur
  - **S72.141**   Displaced intertrochanteric fracture of right femur A, B, C ℞
    Coding Clinic: 2016, Q3, P17
  - **S72.142**   Displaced intertrochanteric fracture of left femur A, B, C ℞
  - **S72.143**   Displaced intertrochanteric fracture of unspecified femur A, B, C ℞
  - **S72.144**   Nondisplaced intertrochanteric fracture of right femur A, B, C ℞
  - **S72.145**   Nondisplaced intertrochanteric fracture of left femur A, B, C ℞
  - **S72.146**   Nondisplaced intertrochanteric fracture of unspecified femur A, B, C ℞
- **S72.2**   **Subtrochanteric fracture of femur**
  Subtrochanteric: inferior to trochanter
  - X● **S72.21**   Displaced subtrochanteric fracture of right femur A, B, C ℞
  - X● **S72.22**   Displaced subtrochanteric fracture of left femur A, B, C ℞
  - X● **S72.23**   Displaced subtrochanteric fracture of unspecified femur A, B, C ℞
  - X● **S72.24**   Nondisplaced subtrochanteric fracture of right femur A, B, C ℞
  - X● **S72.25**   Nondisplaced subtrochanteric fracture of left femur A, B, C ℞
  - X● **S72.26**   Nondisplaced subtrochanteric fracture of unspecified femur A, B, C ℞
- **S72.3**   Fracture of shaft of femur
  - **S72.30**   Unspecified fracture of shaft of femur
    - **S72.301**   Unspecified fracture of shaft of right femur A, B, C ℞
      Coding Clinic: 2018, Q2, P12
    - **S72.302**   Unspecified fracture of shaft of left femur A, B, C ℞
    - **S72.309**   Unspecified fracture of shaft of unspecified femur A, B, C ℞
  - **S72.32**   Transverse fracture of shaft of femur
    - **S72.321**   Displaced transverse fracture of shaft of right femur A, B, C ℞
    - **S72.322**   Displaced transverse fracture of shaft of left femur A, B, C ℞
    - **S72.323**   Displaced transverse fracture of shaft of unspecified femur A, B, C ℞
    - **S72.324**   Nondisplaced transverse fracture of shaft of right femur A, B, C ℞
    - **S72.325**   Nondisplaced transverse fracture of shaft of left femur A, B, C ℞
    - **S72.326**   Nondisplaced transverse fracture of shaft of unspecified femur A, B, C ℞
  - **S72.33**   Oblique fracture of shaft of femur
    - **S72.331**   Displaced oblique fracture of shaft of right femur A, B, C ℞
    - **S72.332**   Displaced oblique fracture of shaft of left femur A, B, C ℞
    - **S72.333**   Displaced oblique fracture of shaft of unspecified femur A, B, C ℞
    - **S72.334**   Nondisplaced oblique fracture of shaft of right femur A, B, C ℞
    - **S72.335**   Nondisplaced oblique fracture of shaft of left femur A, B, C ℞
    - **S72.336**   Nondisplaced oblique fracture of shaft of unspecified femur A, B, C ℞

● **S72.34**   Spiral fracture of shaft of femur
- ● S72.341   Displaced spiral fracture of shaft of right femur A, B, C 🐾
- ● S72.342   Displaced spiral fracture of shaft of left femur A, B, C 🐾
- ● S72.343   Displaced spiral fracture of shaft of unspecified femur A, B, C 🐾
- ● S72.344   Nondisplaced spiral fracture of shaft of right femur A, B, C 🐾
- ● S72.345   Nondisplaced spiral fracture of shaft of left femur A, B, C 🐾
- ● S72.346   Nondisplaced spiral fracture of shaft of unspecified femur A, B, C 🐾

● **S72.35**   Comminuted fracture of shaft of femur
- ● S72.351   Displaced comminuted fracture of shaft of right femur A, B, C 🐾
- ● S72.352   Displaced comminuted fracture of shaft of left femur A, B, C 🐾
- ● S72.353   Displaced comminuted fracture of shaft of unspecified femur A, B, C 🐾
- ● S72.354   Nondisplaced comminuted fracture of shaft of right femur A, B, C 🐾
- ● S72.355   Nondisplaced comminuted fracture of shaft of left femur A, B, C 🐾
- ● S72.356   Nondisplaced comminuted fracture of shaft of unspecified femur A, B, C 🐾

● **S72.36**   Segmental fracture of shaft of femur
- ● S72.361   Displaced segmental fracture of shaft of right femur A, B, C 🐾
- ● S72.362   Displaced segmental fracture of shaft of left femur A, B, C 🐾
- ● S72.363   Displaced segmental fracture of shaft of unspecified femur A, B, C 🐾
- ● S72.364   Nondisplaced segmental fracture of shaft of right femur A, B, C 🐾
- ● S72.365   Nondisplaced segmental fracture of shaft of left femur A, B, C 🐾
- ● S72.366   Nondisplaced segmental fracture of shaft of unspecified femur A, B, C 🐾

● **S72.39**   Other fracture of shaft of femur
- ● S72.391   Other fracture of shaft of right femur A, B, C 🐾
- ● S72.392   Other fracture of shaft of left femur A, B, C 🐾
- ● S72.399   Other fracture of shaft of unspecified femur A, B, C 🐾

● **S72.4**   Fracture of lower end of femur
Fracture of distal end of femur

> **Excludes2**   fracture of shaft of femur (S72.3-)
> physeal fracture of lower end of femur (S79.1-)

● **S72.40**   Unspecified fracture of lower end of femur
- ● S72.401   Unspecified fracture of lower end of right femur A, B, C 🐾
  Coding Clinic: 2016, Q4, P43
- ● S72.402   Unspecified fracture of lower end of left femur A, B, C 🐾
- ● S72.409   Unspecified fracture of lower end of unspecified femur A, B, C 🐾

● **S72.41**   Unspecified condyle fracture of lower end of femur
Condyle fracture of femur NOS
- ● S72.411   Displaced unspecified condyle fracture of lower end of right femur A, B, C 🐾
- ● S72.412   Displaced unspecified condyle fracture of lower end of left femur A, B, C 🐾

- ● S72.413   Displaced unspecified condyle fracture of lower end of unspecified femur A, B, C 🐾
- ● S72.414   Nondisplaced unspecified condyle fracture of lower end of right femur A, B, C 🐾
- ● S72.415   Nondisplaced unspecified condyle fracture of lower end of left femur A, B, C 🐾
- ● S72.416   Nondisplaced unspecified condyle fracture of lower end of unspecified femur A, B, C 🐾

● **S72.42**   Fracture of lateral condyle of femur
- ● S72.421   Displaced fracture of lateral condyle of right femur A, B, C 🐾
- ● S72.422   Displaced fracture of lateral condyle of left femur A, B, C 🐾
- ● S72.423   Displaced fracture of lateral condyle of unspecified femur A, B, C 🐾
- ● S72.424   Nondisplaced fracture of lateral condyle of right femur A, B, C 🐾
- ● S72.425   Nondisplaced fracture of lateral condyle of left femur A, B, C 🐾
- ● S72.426   Nondisplaced fracture of lateral condyle of unspecified femur A, B, C 🐾

● **S72.43**   Fracture of medial condyle of femur
- ● S72.431   Displaced fracture of medial condyle of right femur A, B, C 🐾
- ● S72.432   Displaced fracture of medial condyle of left femur A, B, C 🐾
- ● S72.433   Displaced fracture of medial condyle of unspecified femur A, B, C 🐾
- ● S72.434   Nondisplaced fracture of medial condyle of right femur A, B, C 🐾
- ● S72.435   Nondisplaced fracture of medial condyle of left femur A, B, C 🐾
- ● S72.436   Nondisplaced fracture of medial condyle of unspecified femur A, B, C 🐾

● **S72.44**   Fracture of lower epiphysis (separation) of femur

> **Excludes1**   Salter-Harris Type I physeal fracture of lower end of femur (S79.11-)

- ● S72.441   Displaced fracture of lower epiphysis (separation) of right femur A, B, C 🐾
- ● S72.442   Displaced fracture of lower epiphysis (separation) of left femur A, B, C 🐾
- ● S72.443   Displaced fracture of lower epiphysis (separation) of unspecified femur A, B, C 🐾
- ● S72.444   Nondisplaced fracture of lower epiphysis (separation) of right femur A, B, C 🐾
- ● S72.445   Nondisplaced fracture of lower epiphysis (separation) of left femur A, B, C 🐾
- ● S72.446   Nondisplaced fracture of lower epiphysis (separation) of unspecified femur A, B, C 🐾

▶ New   ⇒ Revised   ~~deleted~~ Deleted   Excludes 1   Excludes 2   Includes   Use additional   Code first   Code also   Key words
OGCR Official Guidelines   X Assign placeholder X   ● Use Additional Character(s)   ▷ Manifestation Code   🐾 Hierarchical Condition Category   **Coding Clinic**

● **S72.45**   **Supracondylar fracture without intracondylar extension of lower end of femur**
Supracondylar fracture of lower end of femur NOS

> **Excludes1**   supracondylar fracture with intracondylar extension of lower end of femur (S72.46-)

  ● **S72.451**   **Displaced supracondylar fracture without intracondylar extension of lower end of right femur** A, B, C 🦴

  ● **S72.452**   **Displaced supracondylar fracture without intracondylar extension of lower end of left femur** A, B, C 🦴

  ● **S72.453**   **Displaced supracondylar fracture without intracondylar extension of lower end of unspecified femur** A, B, C 🦴

  ● **S72.454**   **Nondisplaced supracondylar fracture without intracondylar extension of lower end of right femur** A, B, C 🦴

  ● **S72.455**   **Nondisplaced supracondylar fracture without intracondylar extension of lower end of left femur** A, B, C 🦴

  ● **S72.456**   **Nondisplaced supracondylar fracture without intracondylar extension of lower end of unspecified femur** A, B, C 🦴

● **S72.46**   **Supracondylar fracture with intracondylar extension of lower end of femur**

> **Excludes1**   supracondylar fracture without intracondylar extension of lower end of femur (S72.45-)

  ● **S72.461**   **Displaced supracondylar fracture with intracondylar extension of lower end of right femur** A, B, C 🦴

  ● **S72.462**   **Displaced supracondylar fracture with intracondylar extension of lower end of left femur** A, B, C 🦴

  ● **S72.463**   **Displaced supracondylar fracture with intracondylar extension of lower end of unspecified femur** A, B, C 🦴

  ● **S72.464**   **Nondisplaced supracondylar fracture with intracondylar extension of lower end of right femur** A, B, C 🦴

  ● **S72.465**   **Nondisplaced supracondylar fracture with intracondylar extension of lower end of left femur** A, B, C 🦴

  ● **S72.466**   **Nondisplaced supracondylar fracture with intracondylar extension of lower end of unspecified femur** A, B, C 🦴

● **S72.47**   **Torus fracture of lower end of femur**
The appropriate 7th character is to be added to all codes in subcategory S72.47

A	initial encounter for closed fracture
D	subsequent encounter for fracture with routine healing
G	subsequent encounter for fracture with delayed healing
K	subsequent encounter for fracture with nonunion
P	subsequent encounter for fracture with malunion
S	sequela

  ● **S72.471**   **Torus fracture of lower end of right femur** A 🦴

  ● **S72.472**   **Torus fracture of lower end of left femur** A 🦴

  ● **S72.479**   **Torus fracture of lower end of unspecified femur** A 🦴

● **S72.49**   **Other fracture of lower end of femur**

  ● **S72.491**   **Other fracture of lower end of right femur** A, B, C 🦴

  ● **S72.492**   **Other fracture of lower end of left femur** A, B, C 🦴

  ● **S72.499**   **Other fracture of lower end of unspecified femur** A, B, C 🦴

● **S72.8**   **Other fracture of femur**

  ● **S72.8X**   **Other fracture of femur**

    ● **S72.8X1**   **Other fracture of right femur** A, B, C 🦴

    ● **S72.8X2**   **Other fracture of left femur** A, B, C 🦴

    ● **S72.8X9**   **Other fracture of unspecified femur** A, B, C 🦴

● **S72.9**   **Unspecified fracture of femur**
Fracture of thigh NOS
Fracture of upper leg NOS

> **Excludes1**   fracture of hip NOS (S72.00-, S72.01-)

X ● **S72.90**   **Unspecified fracture of unspecified femur** A, B, C 🦴
     Coding Clinic: 2012, Q4, P94

X ● **S72.91**   **Unspecified fracture of right femur** A, B, C 🦴

X ● **S72.92**   **Unspecified fracture of left femur** A, B, C 🦴

● **S73**   **Dislocation and sprain of joint and ligaments of hip**

> **Includes**   avulsion of joint or ligament of hip
> laceration of cartilage, joint or ligament of hip
> sprain of cartilage, joint or ligament of hip
> traumatic hemarthrosis of joint or ligament of hip
> traumatic rupture of joint or ligament of hip
> traumatic subluxation of joint or ligament of hip
> traumatic tear of joint or ligament of hip

Code also any associated open wound

> **Excludes2**   strain of muscle, fascia and tendon of hip and thigh (S76.-)

The appropriate 7th character is to be added to each code from category S73

A	initial encounter
D	subsequent encounter
S	sequela

● **S73.0**   **Subluxation and dislocation of hip**
Out of position

> **Excludes2**   dislocation and subluxation of hip prosthesis (T84.020, T84.021)

  ● **S73.00**   **Unspecified subluxation and dislocation of hip**
Dislocation of hip NOS
Subluxation of hip NOS

    ● **S73.001**   **Unspecified subluxation of right hip** A 🦴

    ● **S73.002**   **Unspecified subluxation of left hip** A 🦴

    ● **S73.003**   **Unspecified subluxation of unspecified hip** A 🦴

    ● **S73.004**   **Unspecified dislocation of right hip** A 🦴

    ● **S73.005**   **Unspecified dislocation of left hip** A 🦴

    ● **S73.006**   **Unspecified dislocation of unspecified hip** A 🦴

  ● **S73.01**   **Posterior subluxation and dislocation of hip**

    ● **S73.011**   **Posterior subluxation of right hip** A 🦴

    ● **S73.012**   **Posterior subluxation of left hip** A 🦴

    ● **S73.013**   **Posterior subluxation of unspecified hip** A 🦴

    ● **S73.014**   **Posterior dislocation of right hip** A 🦴

    ● **S73.015**   **Posterior dislocation of left hip** A 🦴

    ● **S73.016**   **Posterior dislocation of unspecified hip** A 🦴

S73.02 **Obturator subluxation and dislocation of hip**
- **S73.021** Obturator subluxation of right hip A 🐾
- **S73.022** Obturator subluxation of left hip A 🐾
- **S73.023** Obturator subluxation of unspecified hip A 🐾
- **S73.024** Obturator dislocation of right hip A 🐾
- **S73.025** Obturator dislocation of left hip A 🐾
- **S73.026** Obturator dislocation of unspecified hip A 🐾

S73.03 **Other anterior subluxation and dislocation of hip**
- **S73.031** Other anterior subluxation of right hip A 🐾
- **S73.032** Other anterior subluxation of left hip A 🐾
- **S73.033** Other anterior subluxation of unspecified hip A 🐾
- **S73.034** Other anterior dislocation of right hip A 🐾
- **S73.035** Other anterior dislocation of left hip A 🐾
- **S73.036** Other anterior dislocation of unspecified hip A 🐾

S73.04 **Central subluxation and dislocation of hip**
- **S73.041** Central subluxation of right hip A 🐾
- **S73.042** Central subluxation of left hip A 🐾
- **S73.043** Central subluxation of unspecified hip A 🐾
- **S73.044** Central dislocation of right hip A 🐾
- **S73.045** Central dislocation of left hip A 🐾
- **S73.046** Central dislocation of unspecified hip A 🐾

S73.1 **Sprain of hip**
- **S73.10** **Unspecified sprain of hip**
  - **S73.101** Unspecified sprain of right hip
  - **S73.102** Unspecified sprain of left hip
  - **S73.109** Unspecified sprain of unspecified hip
- **S73.11** **Iliofemoral ligament sprain of hip**
  - **S73.111** Iliofemoral ligament sprain of right hip
  - **S73.112** Iliofemoral ligament sprain of left hip
  - **S73.119** Iliofemoral ligament sprain of unspecified hip
- **S73.12** **Ischiocapsular (ligament) sprain of hip**
  - **S73.121** Ischiocapsular ligament sprain of right hip
  - **S73.122** Ischiocapsular ligament sprain of left hip
  - **S73.129** Ischiocapsular ligament sprain of unspecified hip
- **S73.19** **Other sprain of hip**
  - **S73.191** Other sprain of right hip
  - **S73.192** Other sprain of left hip
  - **S73.199** Other sprain of unspecified hip

S74 **Injury of nerves at hip and thigh level**
Code also any associated open wound (S71.-)
Excludes2   injury of nerves at ankle and foot level (S94.-)
          injury of nerves at lower leg level (S84.-)

The appropriate 7th character is to be added to each code from category S74

A	initial encounter
D	subsequent encounter
S	sequela

S74.0 **Injury of sciatic nerve at hip and thigh level**
- X **S74.00** Injury of sciatic nerve at hip and thigh level, unspecified leg
- X **S74.01** Injury of sciatic nerve at hip and thigh level, right leg
- X **S74.02** Injury of sciatic nerve at hip and thigh level, left leg

S74.1 **Injury of femoral nerve at hip and thigh level**
- X **S74.10** Injury of femoral nerve at hip and thigh level, unspecified leg
- X **S74.11** Injury of femoral nerve at hip and thigh level, right leg
- X **S74.12** Injury of femoral nerve at hip and thigh level, left leg

S74.2 **Injury of cutaneous sensory nerve at hip and thigh level**
- X **S74.20** Injury of cutaneous sensory nerve at hip and thigh level, unspecified leg
- X **S74.21** Injury of cutaneous sensory nerve at hip and high level, right leg
- X **S74.22** Injury of cutaneous sensory nerve at hip and thigh level, left leg

S74.8 **Injury of other nerves at hip and thigh level**
- **S74.8X** Injury of other nerves at hip and thigh level
  - **S74.8X1** Injury of other nerves at hip and thigh level, right leg
  - **S74.8X2** Injury of other nerves at hip and thigh level, left leg
  - **S74.8X9** Injury of other nerves at hip and thigh level, unspecified leg

S74.9 **Injury of unspecified nerve at hip and thigh level**
- X **S74.90** Injury of unspecified nerve at hip and thigh level, unspecified leg
- X **S74.91** Injury of unspecified nerve at hip and thigh level, right leg
- X **S74.92** Injury of unspecified nerve at hip and thigh level, left leg

S75 **Injury of blood vessels at hip and thigh level**
Code also any associated open wound (S71.-)
Excludes2   injury of blood vessels at lower leg level (S85.-)
          injury of popliteal artery (S85.0)

The appropriate 7th character is to be added to each code from category S75

A	initial encounter
D	subsequent encounter
S	sequela

S75.0 **Injury of femoral artery**
- **S75.00** **Unspecified injury of femoral artery**
  - **S75.001** Unspecified injury of femoral artery, right leg
  - **S75.002** Unspecified injury of femoral artery, left leg
  - **S75.009** Unspecified injury of femoral artery, unspecified leg

▶ New   ⇒ Revised   ~~deleted~~ Deleted   Excludes 1   Excludes 2   Includes   Use additional   Code first   Code also   Key words

OGCR Official Guidelines   X Assign placeholder X   ● Use Additional Character(s)   ▶ Manifestation Code   🐾 Hierarchical Condition Category   **Coding Clinic**

- **S75.01   Minor laceration of femoral artery**
  Incomplete transection of femoral artery
  Laceration of femoral artery NOS
  Superficial laceration of femoral artery
  - **S75.011   Minor laceration of femoral artery, right leg**
  - **S75.012   Minor laceration of femoral artery, left leg**
  - **S75.019   Minor laceration of femoral artery, unspecified leg**
- **S75.02   Major laceration of femoral artery**
  Complete transection of femoral artery
  Traumatic rupture of femoral artery
  - **S75.021   Major laceration of femoral artery, right leg**
  - **S75.022   Major laceration of femoral artery, left leg**
  - **S75.029   Major laceration of femoral artery, unspecified leg**
- **S75.09   Other specified injury of femoral artery**
  - **S75.091   Other specified injury of femoral artery, right leg**
  - **S75.092   Other specified injury of femoral artery, left leg**
  - **S75.099   Other specified injury of femoral artery, unspecified leg**
- **S75.1   Injury of femoral vein at hip and thigh level**
  - **S75.10   Unspecified injury of femoral vein at hip and thigh level**
    - **S75.101   Unspecified injury of femoral vein at hip and thigh level, right leg**
    - **S75.102   Unspecified injury of femoral vein at hip and thigh level, left leg**
    - **S75.109   Unspecified injury of femoral vein at hip and thigh level, unspecified leg**
  - **S75.11   Minor laceration of femoral vein at hip and thigh level**
    Incomplete transection of femoral vein at hip and thigh level
    Laceration of femoral vein at hip and thigh level NOS
    Superficial laceration of femoral vein at hip and thigh level
    - **S75.111   Minor laceration of femoral vein at hip and thigh level, right leg**
    - **S75.112   Minor laceration of femoral vein at hip and thigh level, left leg**
    - **S75.119   Minor laceration of femoral vein at hip and thigh level, unspecified leg**
  - **S75.12   Major laceration of femoral vein at hip and thigh level**
    Complete transection of femoral vein at hip and thigh level
    Traumatic rupture of femoral vein at hip and thigh level
    - **S75.121   Major laceration of femoral vein at hip and thigh level, right leg**
    - **S75.122   Major laceration of femoral vein at hip and thigh level, left leg**
    - **S75.129   Major laceration of femoral vein at hip and thigh level, unspecified leg**
  - **S75.19   Other specified injury of femoral vein at hip and thigh level**
    - **S75.191   Other specified injury of femoral vein at hip and thigh level, right leg**
    - **S75.192   Other specified injury of femoral vein at hip and thigh level, left leg**
    - **S75.199   Other specified injury of femoral vein at hip and thigh level, unspecified leg**

- **S75.2   Injury of greater saphenous vein at hip and thigh level**
  Excludes1   greater saphenous vein NOS (S85.3)
  - **S75.20   Unspecified injury of greater saphenous vein at hip and thigh level**
    - **S75.201   Unspecified injury of greater saphenous vein at hip and thigh level, right leg**
    - **S75.202   Unspecified injury of greater saphenous vein at hip and thigh level, left leg**
    - **S75.209   Unspecified injury of greater saphenous vein at hip and thigh level, unspecified leg**
  - **S75.21   Minor laceration of greater saphenous vein at hip and thigh level**
    Incomplete transection of greater saphenous vein at hip and thigh level
    Laceration of greater saphenous vein at hip and thigh level NOS
    Superficial laceration of greater saphenous vein at hip and thigh level
    - **S75.211   Minor laceration of greater saphenous vein at hip and thigh level, right leg**
    - **S75.212   Minor laceration of greater saphenous vein at hip and thigh level, left leg**
    - **S75.219   Minor laceration of greater saphenous vein at hip and thigh level, unspecified leg**
  - **S75.22   Major laceration of greater saphenous vein at hip and thigh level**
    Complete transection of greater saphenous vein at hip and thigh level
    Traumatic rupture of greater saphenous vein at hip and thigh level
    - **S75.221   Major laceration of greater saphenous vein at hip and thigh level, right leg**
    - **S75.222   Major laceration of greater saphenous vein at hip and thigh level, left leg**
    - **S75.229   Major laceration of greater saphenous vein at hip and thigh level, unspecified leg**
  - **S75.29   Other specified injury of greater saphenous vein at hip and thigh level**
    - **S75.291   Other specified injury of greater saphenous vein at hip and thigh level, right leg**
    - **S75.292   Other specified injury of greater saphenous vein at hip and thigh level, left leg**
    - **S75.299   Other specified injury of greater saphenous vein at hip and thigh level, unspecified leg**
- **S75.8   Injury of other blood vessels at hip and thigh level**
  - **S75.80   Unspecified injury of other blood vessels at hip and thigh level**
    - **S75.801   Unspecified injury of other blood vessels at hip and thigh level, right leg**
    - **S75.802   Unspecified injury of other blood vessels at hip and thigh level, left leg**
    - **S75.809   Unspecified injury of other blood vessels at hip and thigh level, unspecified leg**
  - **S75.81   Laceration of other blood vessels at hip and thigh level**
    - **S75.811   Laceration of other blood vessels at hip and thigh level, right leg**
    - **S75.812   Laceration of other blood vessels at hip and thigh level, left leg**
    - **S75.819   Laceration of other blood vessels at hip and thigh level, unspecified leg**

● **S75.89**   Other specified injury of other blood vessels at hip and thigh level
    ● S75.891   Other specified injury of other blood vessels at hip and thigh level, right leg
    ● S75.892   Other specified injury of other blood vessels at hip and thigh level, left leg
    ● S75.899   Other specified injury of other blood vessels at hip and thigh level, unspecified leg

● S75.9   Injury of unspecified blood vessel at hip and thigh level
   ● **S75.90**   Unspecified injury of unspecified blood vessel at hip and thigh level
    ● S75.901   Unspecified injury of unspecified blood vessel at hip and thigh level, right leg
    ● S75.902   Unspecified injury of unspecified blood vessel at hip and thigh level, left leg
    ● S75.909   Unspecified injury of unspecified blood vessel at hip and thigh level, unspecified leg
   ● **S75.91**   Laceration of unspecified blood vessel at hip and thigh level
    ● S75.911   Laceration of unspecified blood vessel at hip and thigh level, right leg
    ● S75.912   Laceration of unspecified blood vessel at hip and thigh level, left leg
    ● S75.919   Laceration of unspecified blood vessel at hip and thigh level, unspecified leg
   ● **S75.99**   Other specified injury of unspecified blood vessel at hip and thigh level
    ● S75.991   Other specified injury of unspecified blood vessel at hip and thigh level, right leg
    ● S75.992   Other specified injury of unspecified blood vessel at hip and thigh level, left leg
    ● S75.999   Other specified injury of unspecified blood vessel at hip and thigh level, unspecified leg

● **S76**   **Injury of muscle, fascia and tendon at hip and thigh level**
    Code also any associated open wound (S71.-)
    Excludes2   injury of muscle, fascia and tendon at lower leg level (S86)
             sprain of joint and ligament of hip (S73.1)
    The appropriate 7th character is to be added to each code from category S76

     | | |
     A   initial encounter
     D   subsequent encounter
     S   sequela

   ● S76.0   Injury of muscle, fascia and tendon of hip
    ● **S76.00**   Unspecified injury of muscle, fascia and tendon of hip
     ● S76.001   Unspecified injury of muscle, fascia and tendon of right hip
     ● S76.002   Unspecified injury of muscle, fascia and tendon of left hip
     ● S76.009   Unspecified injury of muscle, fascia and tendon of unspecified hip
    ● **S76.01**   Strain of muscle, fascia and tendon of hip
     ● S76.011   Strain of muscle, fascia and tendon of right hip
     ● S76.012   Strain of muscle, fascia and tendon of left hip
     ● S76.019   Strain of muscle, fascia and tendon of unspecified hip

    ● **S76.02**   Laceration of muscle, fascia and tendon of hip
     ● S76.021   Laceration of muscle, fascia and tendon of right hip
     ● S76.022   Laceration of muscle, fascia and tendon of left hip
     ● S76.029   Laceration of muscle, fascia and tendon of unspecified hip
    ● **S76.09**   Other specified injury of muscle, fascia and tendon of hip
     ● S76.091   Other specified injury of muscle, fascia and tendon of right hip
     ● S76.092   Other specified injury of muscle, fascia and tendon of left hip
     ● S76.099   Other specified injury of muscle, fascia and tendon of unspecified hip

   ● S76.1   Injury of quadriceps muscle, fascia and tendon
       Injury of patellar ligament (tendon)
    ● **S76.10**   Unspecified injury of quadriceps muscle, fascia and tendon
     ● S76.101   Unspecified injury of right quadriceps muscle, fascia and tendon
     ● S76.102   Unspecified injury of left quadriceps muscle, fascia and tendon
     ● S76.109   Unspecified injury of unspecified quadriceps muscle, fascia and tendon
    ● **S76.11**   Strain of quadriceps muscle, fascia and tendon
     ● S76.111   Strain of right quadriceps muscle, fascia and tendon
     ● S76.112   Strain of left quadriceps muscle, fascia and tendon
     ● S76.119   Strain of unspecified quadriceps muscle, fascia and tendon
    ● **S76.12**   Laceration of quadriceps muscle, fascia and tendon
     ● S76.121   Laceration of right quadriceps muscle, fascia and tendon
     ● S76.122   Laceration of left quadriceps muscle, fascia and tendon
     ● S76.129   Laceration of unspecified quadriceps muscle, fascia and tendon
    ● **S76.19**   Other specified injury of quadriceps muscle, fascia and tendon
     ● S76.191   Other specified injury of right quadriceps muscle, fascia and tendon
     ● S76.192   Other specified injury of left quadriceps muscle, fascia and tendon
     ● S76.199   Other specified injury of unspecified quadriceps muscle, fascia and tendon

   ● S76.2   Injury of adductor muscle, fascia and tendon of thigh
    ● **S76.20**   Unspecified injury of adductor muscle, fascia and tendon of thigh
     ● S76.201   Unspecified injury of adductor muscle, fascia and tendon of right thigh
     ● S76.202   Unspecified injury of adductor muscle, fascia and tendon of left thigh
     ● S76.209   Unspecified injury of adductor muscle, fascia and tendon of unspecified thigh
    ● **S76.21**   Strain of adductor muscle, fascia and tendon of thigh
     ● S76.211   Strain of adductor muscle, fascia and tendon of right thigh
     ● S76.212   Strain of adductor muscle, fascia and tendon of left thigh
     ● S76.219   Strain of adductor muscle, fascia and tendon of unspecified thigh

▶ New   ⟹ Revised   ~~deleted~~ Deleted   Excludes 1   Excludes 2   Includes   Use additional   Code first   Code also   Key words
OGCR Official Guidelines   X Assign placeholder X   ● Use Additional Character(s)   ▷ Manifestation Code   🏷 Hierarchical Condition Category   **Coding Clinic**

S76.22　Laceration of adductor muscle, fascia and tendon of thigh

　S76.221　Laceration of adductor muscle, fascia and tendon of right thigh

　S76.222　Laceration of adductor muscle, fascia and tendon of left thigh

　S76.229　Laceration of adductor muscle, fascia and tendon of unspecified thigh

S76.29　Other injury of adductor muscle, fascia and tendon of thigh

　S76.291　Other injury of adductor muscle, fascia and tendon of right thigh

　S76.292　Other injury of adductor muscle, fascia and tendon of left thigh

　S76.299　Other injury of adductor muscle, fascia and tendon of unspecified thigh

S76.3　Injury of muscle, fascia and tendon of the posterior muscle group at thigh level

S76.30　Unspecified injury of muscle, fascia and tendon of the posterior muscle group at thigh level

　S76.301　Unspecified injury of muscle, fascia and tendon of the posterior muscle group at thigh level, right thigh

　S76.302　Unspecified injury of muscle, fascia and tendon of the posterior muscle group at thigh level, left thigh

　S76.309　Unspecified injury of muscle, fascia and tendon of the posterior muscle group at thigh level, unspecified thigh

S76.31　Strain of muscle, fascia and tendon of the posterior muscle group at thigh level

　S76.311　Strain of muscle, fascia and tendon of the posterior muscle group at thigh level, right thigh

　S76.312　Strain of muscle, fascia and tendon of the posterior muscle group at thigh level, left thigh

　S76.319　Strain of muscle, fascia and tendon of the posterior muscle group at thigh level, unspecified thigh

S76.32　Laceration of muscle, fascia and tendon of the posterior muscle group at thigh level

　S76.321　Laceration of muscle, fascia and tendon of the posterior muscle group at thigh level, right thigh

　S76.322　Laceration of muscle, fascia and tendon of the posterior muscle group at thigh level, left thigh

　S76.329　Laceration of muscle, fascia and tendon of the posterior muscle group at thigh level, unspecified thigh

S76.39　Other specified injury of muscle, fascia and tendon of the posterior muscle group at thigh level

　S76.391　Other specified injury of muscle, fascia and tendon of the posterior muscle group at thigh level, right thigh

　S76.392　Other specified injury of muscle, fascia and tendon of the posterior muscle group at thigh level, left thigh

　S76.399　Other specified injury of muscle, fascia and tendon of the posterior muscle group at thigh level, unspecified thigh

S76.8　Injury of other specified muscles, fascia and tendons at thigh level

S76.80　Unspecified injury of other specified muscles, fascia and tendons at thigh level

　S76.801　Unspecified injury of other specified muscles, fascia and tendons at thigh level, right thigh

　S76.802　Unspecified injury of other specified muscles, fascia and tendons at thigh level, left thigh

　S76.809　Unspecified injury of other specified muscles, fascia and tendons at thigh level, unspecified thigh

S76.81　Strain of other specified specified muscles, fascia and tendons at thigh level

　S76.811　Strain of other specified muscles, fascia and tendons at thigh level, right thigh

　S76.812　Strain of other specified muscles, fascia and tendons at thigh level, left thigh

　S76.819　Strain of other specified muscles, fascia and tendons at thigh level, unspecified thigh

S76.82　Laceration of other specified muscles, fascia and tendons at thigh level

　S76.821　Laceration of other specified muscles, fascia and tendons at thigh level, right thigh

　S76.822　Laceration of other specified muscles, fascia and tendons at thigh level, left thigh

　S76.829　Laceration of other specified muscles, fascia and tendons at thigh level, unspecified thigh

S76.89　Other injury of other specified muscles, fascia and tendons at thigh level

　S76.891　Other injury of other specified muscles, fascia and tendons at thigh level, right thigh

　S76.892　Other injury of other specified muscles, fascia and tendons at thigh level, left thigh

　S76.899　Other injury of other specified muscles, fascia and tendons at thigh level, unspecified thigh

S76.9　Injury of unspecified muscles, fascia and tendons at thigh level

S76.90　Unspecified injury of unspecified muscles, fascia and tendons at thigh level

　S76.901　Unspecified injury of unspecified muscles, fascia and tendons at thigh level, right thigh

　S76.902　Unspecified injury of unspecified muscles, fascia and tendons at thigh level, left thigh

　S76.909　Unspecified injury of unspecified muscles, fascia and tendons at thigh level, unspecified thigh

S76.91　Strain of unspecified muscles, fascia and tendons at thigh level

　S76.911　Strain of unspecified muscles, fascia and tendons at thigh level, right thigh

　S76.912　Strain of unspecified muscles, fascia and tendons at thigh level, left thigh

　S76.919　Strain of unspecified muscles fascia and tendons at thigh level, unspecified thigh

● **S76.92** **Laceration** of unspecified muscles, fascia and tendons at thigh level
  - ● **S76.921** Laceration of unspecified muscles, fascia and tendons at thigh level, **right** thigh
  - ● **S76.922** Laceration of unspecified muscles, fascia and tendons at thigh level, **left** thigh
  - ● **S76.929** Laceration of unspecified muscles, fascia and tendons at thigh level, **unspecified** thigh

● **S76.99** Other specified injury of unspecified muscles, fascia and tendons at thigh level
  - ● **S76.991** Other specified injury of unspecified muscles, fascia and tendons at thigh level, **right** thigh
  - ● **S76.992** Other specified injury of unspecified muscles, fascia and tendons at thigh level, **left** thigh
  - ● **S76.999** Other specified injury of unspecified muscles, fascia and tendons at thigh level, **unspecified** thigh

● **S77** **Crushing injury of hip and thigh**
     Use additional code(s) for all associated injuries

     Excludes2   crushing injury of ankle and foot (S97.-)
                        crushing injury of lower leg (S87.-)

     The appropriate 7th character is to be added to each code from category S77

     | | |
     | A | initial encounter |
     | D | subsequent encounter |
     | S | sequela |

   ● **S77.0** Crushing injury of **hip**
     X ● **S77.00** Crushing injury of **unspecified** hip
     X ● **S77.01** Crushing injury of **right** hip
     X ● **S77.02** Crushing injury of **left** hip

   ● **S77.1** Crushing injury of **thigh**
     X ● **S77.10** Crushing injury of **unspecified** thigh
     X ● **S77.11** Crushing injury of **right** thigh
     X ● **S77.12** Crushing injury of **left** thigh

   ● **S77.2** Crushing injury of **hip with thigh**
     X ● **S77.20** Crushing injury of **unspecified** hip with thigh
     X ● **S77.21** Crushing injury of **right** hip with thigh
     X ● **S77.22** Crushing injury of **left** hip with thigh

● **S78** **Traumatic amputation** of hip and thigh
     An amputation not identified as partial or complete should be coded to complete

     Excludes1   traumatic amputation of knee (S88.0-)

     The appropriate 7th character is to be added to each code from category S78

     | | |
     | A | initial encounter |
     | D | subsequent encounter |
     | S | sequela |

   ● **S78.0** Traumatic amputation at **hip** joint
     ● **S78.01** **Complete** traumatic amputation at hip joint
       ● **S78.011** Complete traumatic amputation at right hip joint A, D, S 🐾
       ● **S78.012** Complete traumatic amputation at **left** hip joint A, D, S 🐾
       ● **S78.019** Complete traumatic amputation at **unspecified** hip joint A, D, S 🐾

     ● **S78.02** **Partial** traumatic amputation at hip joint
       ● **S78.021** Partial traumatic amputation at **right** hip joint A, D, S 🐾
       ● **S78.022** Partial traumatic amputation at **left** hip joint A, D, S 🐾
       ● **S78.029** Partial traumatic amputation at **unspecified** hip joint A, D, S 🐾

● **S78.1** Traumatic amputation at level **between hip and knee**
     Excludes1   traumatic amputation of knee (S88.0-)
   ● **S78.11** **Complete** traumatic amputation at level between hip and knee
     ● **S78.111** Complete traumatic amputation at level between **right** hip and knee A, D, S 🐾
     ● **S78.112** Complete traumatic amputation at level between **left** hip and knee A, D, S 🐾
     ● **S78.119** Complete traumatic amputation at level between **unspecified** hip and knee A, D, S 🐾

   ● **S78.12** **Partial** traumatic amputation at level between hip and knee
     ● **S78.121** Partial traumatic amputation at level between **right** hip and knee A, D, S 🐾
     ● **S78.122** Partial traumatic amputation at level between **left** hip and knee A, D, S 🐾
     ● **S78.129** Partial traumatic amputation at level between **unspecified** hip and knee A, D, S 🐾

● **S78.9** Traumatic amputation of hip and thigh, **level unspecified**
   ● **S78.91** **Complete** traumatic amputation of hip and thigh, level unspecified
     ● **S78.911** Complete traumatic amputation of **right** hip and thigh, level unspecified A, D, S 🐾
     ● **S78.912** Complete traumatic amputation of **left** hip and thigh, level unspecified A, D, S 🐾
     ● **S78.919** Complete traumatic amputation of **unspecified** hip and thigh, level unspecified A, D, S 🐾

   ● **S78.92** **Partial** traumatic amputation of hip and thigh, level unspecified
     ● **S78.921** Partial traumatic amputation of **right** hip and thigh, level unspecified A, D, S 🐾
     ● **S78.922** Partial traumatic amputation of **left** hip and thigh, level unspecified A, D, S 🐾
     ● **S78.929** Partial traumatic amputation of **unspecified** hip and thigh, level unspecified A, D, S 🐾

● **S79** Other and unspecified injuries of hip and thigh
     Note: A fracture not indicated as open or closed should be coded to closed
     The appropriate 7th character is to be added to each code from subcategories S79.0 and S79.1

     | | |
     | A | initial encounter for closed fracture |
     | D | subsequent encounter for fracture with routine healing |
     | G | subsequent encounter for fracture with delayed healing |
     | K | subsequent encounter for fracture with nonunion |
     | P | subsequent encounter for fracture with malunion |
     | S | sequela |

   ● **S79.0** **Physeal** fracture of **upper end of** femur
     Excludes1   apophyseal fracture of upper end of femur (S72.13-)
                   nontraumatic slipped upper femoral epiphysis (M93.0-)
     ● **S79.00** **Unspecified** physeal fracture of upper end of femur
       ● **S79.001** Unspecified physeal fracture of upper end of **right** femur A 🐾
       ● **S79.002** Unspecified physeal fracture of upper end of **left** femur A 🐾
       ● **S79.009** Unspecified physeal fracture of upper end of **unspecified** femur A 🐾

▶ New   ⇒ Revised   ~~deleted~~ Deleted   Excludes 1   Excludes 2   Includes   Use additional   Code first   Code also   Key words

OGCR Official Guidelines   X Assign placeholder X   ● Use Additional Character(s)   ▷ Manifestation Code   🐾 Hierarchical Condition Category   **Coding Clinic**

Item 19–5   **SALTER-HARRIS TYPE 1:** epiphysis is completely separated from end of bone, or metaphysic growth plate remains attached to epiphysis

    SALTER-HARRIS TYPE 2: epiphysis and growth plate are partially separated from metaphysis, which is cracked—most common type

    SALTER-HARRIS TYPE 3: fracture occurring through epiphysis and separates part of epiphysis and growth plate from metaphysis fracture, usually at distal end of tibia

    SALTER-HARRIS TYPE 4: fracture runs through epiphysis, across growth plate, into metaphysic; surgery is required to restore joint surface to normal and align growth plate

● **S79.01** Salter-Harris Type I physeal fracture of upper end of femur
- Acute on chronic slipped capital femoral epiphysis (traumatic)
- Acute slipped capital femoral epiphysis (traumatic)
- Capital femoral epiphyseal fracture

    Excludes1   chronic slipped upper femoral epiphysis (nontraumatic) (M93.02-)

    ● **S79.011** Salter-Harris Type I physeal fracture of upper end of right femur A 🦴

    ● **S79.012** Salter-Harris Type I physeal fracture of upper end of left femur A 🦴

    ● **S79.019** Salter-Harris Type I physeal fracture of upper end of unspecified femur A 🦴

● **S79.09** Other physeal fracture of upper end of femur

    ● **S79.091** Other physeal fracture of upper end of right femur A 🦴

    ● **S79.092** Other physeal fracture of upper end of left femur A 🦴

    ● **S79.099** Other physeal fracture of upper end of unspecified femur A 🦴

● **S79.1** Physeal fracture of lower end of femur

    ● **S79.10** Unspecified physeal fracture of lower end of femur

     ● **S79.101** Unspecified physeal fracture of lower end of right femur A 🦴

     ● **S79.102** Unspecified physeal fracture of lower end of left femur A 🦴

     ● **S79.109** Unspecified physeal fracture of lower end of unspecified femur A 🦴

    ● **S79.11** Salter-Harris Type I physeal fracture of lower end of femur

     ● **S79.111** Salter-Harris Type I physeal fracture of lower end of right femur A 🦴

     ● **S79.112** Salter-Harris Type I physeal fracture of lower end of left femur A 🦴

     ● **S79.119** Salter-Harris Type I physeal fracture of lower end of unspecified femur A 🦴

    ● **S79.12** Salter-Harris Type II physeal fracture of lower end of femur

     ● **S79.121** Salter-Harris Type II physeal fracture of lower end of right femur A 🦴

     ● **S79.122** Salter-Harris Type II physeal fracture of lower end of left femur A 🦴

     ● **S79.129** Salter-Harris Type II physeal fracture of lower end of unspecified femur A 🦴

    ● **S79.13** Salter-Harris Type III physeal fracture of lower end of femur

     ● **S79.131** Salter-Harris Type III physeal fracture of lower end of right femur A 🦴

     ● **S79.132** Salter-Harris Type III physeal fracture of lower end of left femur A 🦴

     ● **S79.139** Salter-Harris Type III physeal fracture of lower end of unspecified femur A 🦴

● **S79.14** Salter-Harris Type IV physeal fracture of lower end of femur

    ● **S79.141** Salter-Harris Type IV physeal fracture of lower end of right femur A 🦴

    ● **S79.142** Salter-Harris Type IV physeal fracture of lower end of left femur A 🦴

    ● **S79.149** Salter-Harris Type IV physeal fracture of lower end of unspecified femur A 🦴

● **S79.19** Other physeal fracture of lower end of femur

    ● **S79.191** Other physeal fracture of lower end of right femur A 🦴

    ● **S79.192** Other physeal fracture of lower end of left femur A 🦴

    ● **S79.199** Other physeal fracture of lower end of unspecified femur A 🦴

● **S79.8 Other specified injuries of hip and thigh**

    The appropriate 7th character is to be added to each code in subcategory S79.8

A	initial encounter
D	subsequent encounter
S	sequela

    ● **S79.81** Other specified injuries of hip

     ● **S79.811** Other specified injuries of right hip

     ● **S79.812** Other specified injuries of left hip

     ● **S79.819** Other specified injuries of unspecified hip

    ● **S79.82** Other specified injuries of thigh

     ● **S79.821** Other specified injuries of right thigh

     ● **S79.822** Other specified injuries of left thigh

     ● **S79.829** Other specified injuries of unspecified thigh

● **S79.9** Unspecified injury of hip and thigh

    The appropriate 7th character is to be added to each code in subcategory S79.9

A	initial encounter
D	subsequent encounter
S	sequela

    ● **S79.91** Unspecified injury of hip

     ● **S79.911** Unspecified injury of right hip

     ● **S79.912** Unspecified injury of left hip

     ● **S79.919** Unspecified injury of unspecified hip

    ● **S79.92** Unspecified injury of thigh

     ● **S79.921** Unspecified injury of right thigh

     ● **S79.922** Unspecified injury of left thigh

     ● **S79.929** Unspecified injury of unspecified thigh

INJURIES TO THE KNEE AND LOWER LEG (S80-S89)

    Excludes2   burns and corrosions (T20-T32)
         frostbite (T33-T34)
         injuries of ankle and foot, except fracture of ankle and malleolus (S90-S99)
         insect bite or sting, venomous (T63.4)

● **S80** Superficial injury of knee and lower leg

    Excludes2   superficial injury of ankle and foot (S90.-)

    The appropriate 7th character is to be added to each code from category S80

A	initial encounter
D	subsequent encounter
S	sequela

    ● **S80.0** Contusion of knee

    X ● **S80.00** Contusion of unspecified knee

    X ● **S80.01** Contusion of right knee

    X ● **S80.02** Contusion of left knee

● **S80.1 Contusion of lower leg**
   X ● **S80.10** Contusion of unspecified lower leg
   X ● **S80.11** Contusion of right lower leg
   X ● **S80.12** Contusion of left lower leg
● **S80.2 Other superficial injuries of knee**
   ● **S80.21** Abrasion of knee
     ● **S80.211** Abrasion, right knee
     ● **S80.212** Abrasion, left knee
     ● **S80.219** Abrasion, unspecified knee
   ● **S80.22** Blister (nonthermal) of knee
     ● **S80.221** Blister (nonthermal), right knee
     ● **S80.222** Blister (nonthermal), left knee
     ● **S80.229** Blister (nonthermal), unspecified knee
   ● **S80.24** External constriction of knee
     ● **S80.241** External constriction, right knee
     ● **S80.242** External constriction, left knee
     ● **S80.249** External constriction, unspecified knee
   ● **S80.25** Superficial foreign body of knee
     Splinter in the knee
     ● **S80.251** Superficial foreign body, right knee
     ● **S80.252** Superficial foreign body, left knee
     ● **S80.259** Superficial foreign body, unspecified knee
   ● **S80.26** Insect bite (nonvenomous) of knee
     ● **S80.261** Insect bite (nonvenomous), right knee
     ● **S80.262** Insect bite (nonvenomous), left knee
     ● **S80.269** Insect bite (nonvenomous), unspecified knee
   ● **S80.27** Other superficial bite of knee
     Excludes1 open bite of knee (S81.05-)
     ● **S80.271** Other superficial bite of right knee
     ● **S80.272** Other superficial bite of left knee
     ● **S80.279** Other superficial bite of unspecified knee
● **S80.8 Other superficial injuries of lower leg**
   ● **S80.81** Abrasion of lower leg
     ● **S80.811** Abrasion, right lower leg
     ● **S80.812** Abrasion, left lower leg
     ● **S80.819** Abrasion, unspecified lower leg
   ● **S80.82** Blister (nonthermal) of lower leg
     ● **S80.821** Blister (nonthermal), right lower leg
     ● **S80.822** Blister (nonthermal), left lower leg
     ● **S80.829** Blister (nonthermal), unspecified lower leg
   ● **S80.84** External constriction of lower leg
     ● **S80.841** External constriction, right lower leg
     ● **S80.842** External constriction, left lower leg
     ● **S80.849** External constriction, unspecified lower leg
   ● **S80.85** Superficial foreign body of lower leg
     Splinter in the lower leg
     ● **S80.851** Superficial foreign body, right lower leg
     ● **S80.852** Superficial foreign body, left lower leg
     ● **S80.859** Superficial foreign body, unspecified lower leg

● **S80.86** Insect bite (nonvenomous) of lower leg
     ● **S80.861** Insect bite (nonvenomous), right lower leg
     ● **S80.862** Insect bite (nonvenomous), left lower leg
     ● **S80.869** Insect bite (nonvenomous), unspecified lower leg
   ● **S80.87** Other superficial bite of lower leg
     Excludes1 open bite of lower leg (S81.85-)
     ● **S80.871** Other superficial bite, right lower leg
     ● **S80.872** Other superficial bite, left lower leg
     ● **S80.879** Other superficial bite, unspecified lower leg
● **S80.9 Unspecified superficial injury of knee and lower leg**
   ● **S80.91** Unspecified superficial injury of knee
     ● **S80.911** Unspecified superficial injury of right knee
     ● **S80.912** Unspecified superficial injury of left knee
     ● **S80.919** Unspecified superficial injury of unspecified knee
   ● **S80.92** Unspecified superficial injury of lower leg
     ● **S80.921** Unspecified superficial injury of right lower leg
     ● **S80.922** Unspecified superficial injury of left lower leg
     ● **S80.929** Unspecified superficial injury of unspecified lower leg

● **S81 Open wound of knee and lower leg**
   Code also any associated wound infection
   Excludes1 open fracture of knee and lower leg (S82.-)
               traumatic amputation of lower leg (S88.-)
   Excludes2 open wound of ankle and foot (S91.-)
   The appropriate 7th character is to be added to each code from category S81

A	initial encounter
D	subsequent encounter
S	sequela

   ● **S81.0 Open wound of knee**
     ● **S81.00** Unspecified open wound of knee
       ● **S81.001** Unspecified open wound, right knee
       ● **S81.002** Unspecified open wound, left knee
       ● **S81.009** Unspecified open wound, unspecified knee
     ● **S81.01** Laceration without foreign body of knee
       ● **S81.011** Laceration without foreign body, right knee
       ● **S81.012** Laceration without foreign body, left knee
       ● **S81.019** Laceration without foreign body, unspecified knee
     ● **S81.02** Laceration with foreign body of knee
       ● **S81.021** Laceration with foreign body, right knee
       ● **S81.022** Laceration with foreign body, left knee
       ● **S81.029** Laceration with foreign body, unspecified knee

▶ New   ⇒ Revised   ~~deleted~~ Deleted   Excludes 1   Excludes 2   Includes   Use additional   Code first   Code also   Key words
OGCR Official Guidelines   X Assign placeholder X   ● Use Additional Character(s)   ▷ Manifestation Code   🏷 Hierarchical Condition Category   **Coding Clinic**

● **S81.03**   Puncture wound without foreign body of knee
- ● **S81.031**   Puncture wound without foreign body, **right** knee
- ● **S81.032**   Puncture wound without foreign body, **left** knee
- ● **S81.039**   Puncture wound without foreign body, **unspecified** knee

● **S81.04**   Puncture wound with foreign body of knee
- ● **S81.041**   Puncture wound with foreign body, **right** knee
- ● **S81.042**   Puncture wound with foreign body, **left** knee
- ● **S81.049**   Puncture wound with foreign body, **unspecified** knee

● **S81.05**   Open bite of knee
Bite of knee NOS
> **Excludes1**   superficial bite of knee (S80.27-)
- ● **S81.051**   Open bite, **right** knee
- ● **S81.052**   Open bite, **left** knee
- ● **S81.059**   Open bite, **unspecified** knee

● **S81.8**   Open wound of lower leg
● **S81.80**   Unspecified open wound of lower leg
- ● **S81.801**   Unspecified open wound, **right** lower leg
- ● **S81.802**   Unspecified open wound, **left** lower leg
- ● **S81.809**   Unspecified open wound, **unspecified** lower leg

● **S81.81**   Laceration without foreign body of lower leg
- ● **S81.811**   Laceration without foreign body, **right** lower leg
- ● **S81.812**   Laceration without foreign body, **left** lower leg
- ● **S81.819**   Laceration without foreign body, **unspecified** lower leg

● **S81.82**   Laceration with foreign body of lower leg
- ● **S81.821**   Laceration with foreign body, **right** lower leg
- ● **S81.822**   Laceration with foreign body, **left** lower leg
- ● **S81.829**   Laceration with foreign body, **unspecified** lower leg

● **S81.83**   Puncture wound without foreign body of lower leg
- ● **S81.831**   Puncture wound without foreign body, **right** lower leg
- ● **S81.832**   Puncture wound without foreign body, **left** lower leg
- ● **S81.839**   Puncture wound without foreign body, **unspecified** lower leg

● **S81.84**   Puncture wound with foreign body of lower leg
- ● **S81.841**   Puncture wound with foreign body, **right** lower leg
  Coding Clinic: 2016, Q3, P46
- ● **S81.842**   Puncture wound with foreign body, **left** lower leg
- ● **S81.849**   Puncture wound with foreign body, **unspecified** lower leg

● **S81.85**   Open bite of lower leg
Bite of lower leg NOS
> **Excludes1**   superficial bite of lower leg (S80.86-, S80.87-)
- ● **S81.851**   Open bite, **right** lower leg
- ● **S81.852**   Open bite, **left** lower leg
- ● **S81.859**   Open bite, **unspecified** lower leg

● **S82**   Fracture of lower leg, including ankle
Note: A fracture not indicated as displaced or nondisplaced should be coded to displaced

A fracture not indicated as open or closed should be coded to closed

The open fracture designations are based on the Gustilo open fracture classification

Includes	fracture of malleolus
Excludes1	traumatic amputation of lower leg (S88.-)
Excludes2	fracture of foot, except ankle (S92.-)
	periprosthetic fracture of prosthetic implant of knee (M97.0-)

The appropriate 7th character is to be added to all codes from category S82

A	initial encounter for closed fracture
B	initial encounter for open fracture type I or II initial encounter for open fracture NOS
C	initial encounter for open fracture type IIIA, IIIB, or IIIC
D	subsequent encounter for closed fracture with routine healing
E	subsequent encounter for open fracture type I or II with routine healing
F	subsequent encounter for open fracture type IIIA, IIIB, or IIIC with routine healing
G	subsequent encounter for closed fracture with delayed healing
H	subsequent encounter for open fracture type I or II with delayed healing
J	subsequent encounter for open fracture type IIIA, IIIB, or IIIC with delayed healing
K	subsequent encounter for closed fracture with nonunion
M	subsequent encounter for open fracture type I or II with nonunion
N	subsequent encounter for open fracture type IIIA, IIIB, or IIIC with nonunion
P	subsequent encounter for closed fracture with malunion
Q	subsequent encounter for open fracture type I or II with malunion
R	subsequent encounter for open fracture type IIIA, IIIB, or IIIC with malunion
S	sequela

● **S82.0**   Fracture of patella
Knee cap
● **S82.00**   Unspecified fracture of patella
- ● **S82.001**   Unspecified fracture of **right** patella
- ● **S82.002**   Unspecified fracture of **left** patella
- ● **S82.009**   Unspecified fracture of **unspecified** patella

● **S82.01**   Osteochondral fracture of patella
- ● **S82.011**   Displaced osteochondral fracture of **right** patella
- ● **S82.012**   Displaced osteochondral fracture of **left** patella
- ● **S82.013**   Displaced osteochondral fracture of **unspecified** patella
- ● **S82.014**   Nondisplaced osteochondral fracture of **right** patella
- ● **S82.015**   Nondisplaced osteochondral fracture of **left** patella
- ● **S82.016**   Nondisplaced osteochondral fracture of **unspecified** patella

CHAPTER 19 (S00-T88)

● S82.02   Longitudinal fracture of patella
- ● S82.021   Displaced longitudinal fracture of right patella
- ● S82.022   Displaced longitudinal fracture of left patella
- ● S82.023   Displaced longitudinal fracture of unspecified patella
- ● S82.024   Nondisplaced longitudinal fracture of right patella
- ● S82.025   Nondisplaced longitudinal fracture of left patella
- ● S82.026   Nondisplaced longitudinal fracture of unspecified patella

● S82.03   Transverse fracture of patella
- ● S82.031   Displaced transverse fracture of right patella
- ● S82.032   Displaced transverse fracture of left patella
- ● S82.033   Displaced transverse fracture of unspecified patella
- ● S82.034   Nondisplaced transverse fracture of right patella
- ● S82.035   Nondisplaced transverse fracture of left patella
- ● S82.036   Nondisplaced transverse fracture of unspecified patella

● S82.04   Comminuted fracture of patella
- ● S82.041   Displaced comminuted fracture of right patella
- ● S82.042   Displaced comminuted fracture of left patella
- ● S82.043   Displaced comminuted fracture of unspecified patella
- ● S82.044   Nondisplaced comminuted fracture of right patella
- ● S82.045   Nondisplaced comminuted fracture of left patella
- ● S82.046   Nondisplaced comminuted fracture of unspecified patella

● S82.09   Other fracture of patella
- ● S82.091   Other fracture of right patella
- ● S82.092   Other fracture of left patella
- ● S82.099   Other fracture of unspecified patella

▶ S82.1   Fracture of upper end of tibia
Fracture of proximal end of tibia

Excludes2   fracture of shaft of tibia (S82.2-)
physeal fracture of upper end of tibia (S89.0-)

● S82.10   Unspecified fracture of upper end of tibia
- ● S82.101   Unspecified fracture of upper end of right tibia
- ● S82.102   Unspecified fracture of upper end of left tibia
- ● S82.109   Unspecified fracture of upper end of unspecified tibia

● S82.11   Fracture of tibial spine
- ● S82.111   Displaced fracture of right tibial spine
- ● S82.112   Displaced fracture of left tibial spine
- ● S82.113   Displaced fracture of unspecified tibial spine
- ● S82.114   Nondisplaced fracture of right tibial spine
- ● S82.115   Nondisplaced fracture of left tibial spine
- ● S82.116   Nondisplaced fracture of unspecified tibial spine

● S82.12   Fracture of lateral condyle of tibia
- ● S82.121   Displaced fracture of lateral condyle of right tibia
- ● S82.122   Displaced fracture of lateral condyle of left tibia
- ● S82.123   Displaced fracture of lateral condyle of unspecified tibia
- ● S82.124   Nondisplaced fracture of lateral condyle of right tibia
- ● S82.125   Nondisplaced fracture of lateral condyle of left tibia
- ● S82.126   Nondisplaced fracture of lateral condyle of unspecified tibia

● S82.13   Fracture of medial condyle of tibia
- ● S82.131   Displaced fracture of medial condyle of right tibia
- ● S82.132   Displaced fracture of medial condyle of left tibia
- ● S82.133   Displaced fracture of medial condyle of unspecified tibia
- ● S82.134   Nondisplaced fracture of medial condyle of right tibia
- ● S82.135   Nondisplaced fracture of medial condyle of left tibia
- ● S82.136   Nondisplaced fracture of medial condyle of unspecified tibia

● S82.14   Bicondylar fracture of tibia
Fracture of tibial plateau NOS
- ● S82.141   Displaced bicondylar fracture of right tibia
- ● S82.142   Displaced bicondylar fracture of left tibia
- ● S82.143   Displaced bicondylar fracture of unspecified tibia
- ● S82.144   Nondisplaced bicondylar fracture of right tibia
- ● S82.145   Nondisplaced bicondylar fracture of left tibia
- ● S82.146   Nondisplaced bicondylar fracture of unspecified tibia

● S82.15   Fracture of tibial tuberosity
- ● S82.151   Displaced fracture of right tibial tuberosity
- ● S82.152   Displaced fracture of left tibial tuberosity
- ● S82.153   Displaced fracture of unspecified tibial tuberosity
- ● S82.154   Nondisplaced fracture of right tibial tuberosity
- ● S82.155   Nondisplaced fracture of left tibial tuberosity
- ● S82.156   Nondisplaced fracture of unspecified tibial tuberosity

● S82.16   Torus fracture of upper end of tibia
The appropriate 7th character is to be added to all codes in subcategory S82.16

A	initial encounter for closed fracture
D	subsequent encounter for fracture with routine healing
G	subsequent encounter for fracture with delayed healing
K	subsequent encounter for fracture with nonunion
P	subsequent encounter for fracture with malunion
S	sequela

- ● S82.161   Torus fracture of upper end of right tibia
- ● S82.162   Torus fracture of upper end of left tibia
- ● S82.169   Torus fracture of upper end of unspecified tibia

▶ New   ⇒ Revised   ~~deleted~~ Deleted   Excludes 1   Excludes 2   Includes   Use additional   Code first   Code also   Key words
OGCR Official Guidelines   X Assign placeholder X   ● Use Additional Character(s)   》 Manifestation Code   HCC Hierarchical Condition Category   **Coding Clinic**

● **S82.19** Other fracture of upper end of tibia
　● **S82.191** Other fracture of upper end of right tibia
　● **S82.192** Other fracture of upper end of left tibia
　● **S82.199** Other fracture of upper end of unspecified tibia

● **S82.2** Fracture of shaft of tibia
　● **S82.20** Unspecified fracture of shaft of tibia
　　Fracture of tibia NOS
　　● **S82.201** Unspecified fracture of shaft of right tibia
　　● **S82.202** Unspecified fracture of shaft of left tibia
　　● **S82.209** Unspecified fracture of shaft of unspecified tibia
　● **S82.22** Transverse fracture of shaft of tibia
　　● **S82.221** Displaced transverse fracture of shaft of right tibia
　　● **S82.222** Displaced transverse fracture of shaft of left tibia
　　● **S82.223** Displaced transverse fracture of shaft of unspecified tibia
　　● **S82.224** Nondisplaced transverse fracture of shaft of right tibia
　　● **S82.225** Nondisplaced transverse fracture of shaft of left tibia
　　● **S82.226** Nondisplaced transverse fracture of shaft of unspecified tibia
　● **S82.23** Oblique fracture of shaft of tibia
　　● **S82.231** Displaced oblique fracture of shaft of right tibia
　　● **S82.232** Displaced oblique fracture of shaft of left tibia
　　● **S82.233** Displaced oblique fracture of shaft of unspecified tibia
　　● **S82.234** Nondisplaced oblique fracture of shaft of right tibia
　　　Coding Clinic: 2015, Q1, P9-10
　　● **S82.235** Nondisplaced oblique fracture of shaft of left tibia
　　● **S82.236** Nondisplaced oblique fracture of shaft of unspecified tibia
　● **S82.24** Spiral fracture of shaft of tibia
　　Toddler fracture
　　● **S82.241** Displaced spiral fracture of shaft of right tibia
　　● **S82.242** Displaced spiral fracture of shaft of left tibia
　　● **S82.243** Displaced spiral fracture of shaft of unspecified tibia
　　● **S82.244** Nondisplaced spiral fracture of shaft of right tibia
　　● **S82.245** Nondisplaced spiral fracture of shaft of left tibia
　　● **S82.246** Nondisplaced spiral fracture of shaft of unspecified tibia
　● **S82.25** Comminuted fracture of shaft of tibia
　　● **S82.251** Displaced comminuted fracture of shaft of right tibia
　　　Coding Clinic: 2015, Q2, P6
　　● **S82.252** Displaced comminuted fracture of shaft of left tibia
　　● **S82.253** Displaced comminuted fracture of shaft of unspecified tibia
　　● **S82.254** Nondisplaced comminuted fracture of shaft of right tibia
　　● **S82.255** Nondisplaced comminuted fracture of shaft of left tibia
　　● **S82.256** Nondisplaced comminuted fracture of shaft of unspecified tibia

● **S82.26** Segmental fracture of shaft of tibia
　● **S82.261** Displaced segmental fracture of shaft of right tibia
　● **S82.262** Displaced segmental fracture of shaft of left tibia
　● **S82.263** Displaced segmental fracture of shaft of unspecified tibia
　● **S82.264** Nondisplaced segmental fracture of shaft of right tibia
　● **S82.265** Nondisplaced segmental fracture of shaft of left tibia
　● **S82.266** Nondisplaced segmental fracture of shaft of unspecified tibia
● **S82.29** Other fracture of shaft of tibia
　● **S82.291** Other fracture of shaft of right tibia
　● **S82.292** Other fracture of shaft of left tibia
　● **S82.299** Other fracture of shaft of unspecified tibia

● **S82.3** Fracture of lower end of tibia
　Excludes1 bimalleolar fracture of lower leg (S82.84-)
　　　fracture of medial malleolus alone (S82.5-)
　　　Maisonneuve's fracture (S82.86-)
　　　pilon fracture of distal tibia (S82.87-)
　　　trimalleolar fractures of lower leg (S82.85-)
　● **S82.30** Unspecified fracture of lower end of tibia
　　● **S82.301** Unspecified fracture of lower end of right tibia
　　● **S82.302** Unspecified fracture of lower end of left tibia
　　● **S82.309** Unspecified fracture of lower end of unspecified tibia
　● **S82.31** Torus fracture of lower end of tibia
　　The appropriate 7th character is to be added to all codes in subcategory S82.31

A	initial encounter for closed fracture
D	subsequent encounter for fracture with routine healing
G	subsequent encounter for fracture with delayed healing
K	subsequent encounter for fracture with nonunion
P	subsequent encounter for fracture with malunion
S	sequela

　　● **S82.311** Torus fracture of lower end of right tibia
　　● **S82.312** Torus fracture of lower end of left tibia
　　● **S82.319** Torus fracture of lower end of unspecified tibia
　● **S82.39** Other fracture of lower end of tibia
　　● **S82.391** Other fracture of lower end of right tibia
　　● **S82.392** Other fracture of lower end of left tibia
　　　Coding Clinic: 2015, Q1, P25
　　● **S82.399** Other fracture of lower end of unspecified tibia

● **S82.4** Fracture of shaft of fibula
　Excludes2 fracture of lateral malleolus alone (S82.6-)
　● **S82.40** Unspecified fracture of shaft of fibula
　　● **S82.401** Unspecified fracture of shaft of right fibula
　　● **S82.402** Unspecified fracture of shaft of left fibula
　　● **S82.409** Unspecified fracture of shaft of unspecified fibula

● S82.42 Transverse fracture of shaft of fibula
   ● S82.421 Displaced transverse fracture of shaft of right fibula
   ● S82.422 Displaced transverse fracture of shaft of left fibula
   ● S82.423 Displaced transverse fracture of shaft of unspecified fibula
   ● S82.424 Nondisplaced transverse fracture of shaft of right fibula
   ● S82.425 Nondisplaced transverse fracture of shaft of left fibula
   ● S82.426 Nondisplaced transverse fracture of shaft of unspecified fibula

● S82.43 Oblique fracture of shaft of fibula
   ● S82.431 Displaced oblique fracture of shaft of right fibula
   ● S82.432 Displaced oblique fracture of shaft of left fibula
   ● S82.433 Displaced oblique fracture of shaft of unspecified fibula
   ● S82.434 Nondisplaced oblique fracture of shaft of right fibula
   ● S82.435 Nondisplaced oblique fracture of shaft of left fibula
   ● S82.436 Nondisplaced oblique fracture of shaft of unspecified fibula

● S82.44 Spiral fracture of shaft of fibula
   ● S82.441 Displaced spiral fracture of shaft of right fibula
   ● S82.442 Displaced spiral fracture of shaft of left fibula
   ● S82.443 Displaced spiral fracture of shaft of unspecified fibula
   ● S82.444 Nondisplaced spiral fracture of shaft of right fibula
   ● S82.445 Nondisplaced spiral fracture of shaft of left fibula
   ● S82.446 Nondisplaced spiral fracture of shaft of unspecified fibula

● S82.45 Comminuted fracture of shaft of fibula
   ● S82.451 Displaced comminuted fracture of shaft of right fibula
   ● S82.452 Displaced comminuted fracture of shaft of left fibula
   ● S82.453 Displaced comminuted fracture of shaft of unspecified fibula
   ● S82.454 Nondisplaced comminuted fracture of shaft of right fibula
   ● S82.455 Nondisplaced comminuted fracture of shaft of left fibula
   ● S82.456 Nondisplaced comminuted fracture of shaft of unspecified fibula

● S82.46 Segmental fracture of shaft of fibula
   ● S82.461 Displaced segmental fracture of shaft of right fibula
   ● S82.462 Displaced segmental fracture of shaft of left fibula
   ● S82.463 Displaced segmental fracture of shaft of unspecified fibula
   ● S82.464 Nondisplaced segmental fracture of shaft of right fibula
   ● S82.465 Nondisplaced segmental fracture of shaft of left fibula
   ● S82.466 Nondisplaced segmental fracture of shaft of unspecified fibula

● S82.49 Other fracture of shaft of fibula
   ● S82.491 Other fracture of shaft of right fibula
   ● S82.492 Other fracture of shaft of left fibula
   ● S82.499 Other fracture of shaft of unspecified fibula

● S82.5 Fracture of medial malleolus
   Excludes1 pilon fracture of distal tibia (S82.87-)
        Salter-Harris type III of lower end of tibia (S89.13-)
        Salter-Harris type IV of lower end of tibia (S89.14-)
   X● S82.51 Displaced fracture of medial malleolus of right tibia
   X● S82.52 Displaced fracture of medial malleolus of left tibia
   X● S82.53 Displaced fracture of medial malleolus of unspecified tibia
   X● S82.54 Nondisplaced fracture of medial malleolus of right tibia
   X● S82.55 Nondisplaced fracture of medial malleolus of left tibia
   X● S82.56 Nondisplaced fracture of medial malleolus of unspecified tibia

● S82.6 Fracture of lateral malleolus
   Excludes1 pilon fracture of distal tibia (S82.87-)
   X● S82.61 Displaced fracture of lateral malleolus of right fibula
   X● S82.62 Displaced fracture of lateral malleolus of left fibula
   X● S82.63 Displaced fracture of lateral malleolus of unspecified fibula
   X● S82.64 Nondisplaced fracture of lateral malleolus of right fibula
   X● S82.65 Nondisplaced fracture of lateral malleolus of left fibula
   X● S82.66 Nondisplaced fracture of lateral malleolus of unspecified fibula

● S82.8 Other fractures of lower leg
   ● S82.81 Torus fracture of upper end of fibula

      The appropriate 7th character is to be added to all codes in subcategory S82.81

> A initial encounter for closed fracture
> D subsequent encounter for fracture with routine healing
> G subsequent encounter for fracture with delayed healing
> K subsequent encounter for fracture with nonunion
> P subsequent encounter for fracture with malunion
> S sequela

     ● S82.811 Torus fracture of upper end of right fibula
     ● S82.812 Torus fracture of upper end of left fibula
     ● S82.819 Torus fracture of upper end of unspecified fibula

   ● S82.82 Torus fracture of lower end of fibula

      The appropriate 7th character is to be added to all codes in subcategory S82.82

> A initial encounter for closed fracture
> D subsequent encounter for fracture with routine healing
> G subsequent encounter for fracture with delayed healing
> K subsequent encounter for fracture with nonunion
> P subsequent encounter for fracture with malunion
> S sequela

     ● S82.821 Torus fracture of lower end of right fibula
     ● S82.822 Torus fracture of lower end of left fibula
     ● S82.829 Torus fracture of lower end of unspecified fibula

▶ New   ⇒ Revised   ~~deleted~~ Deleted   Excludes 1   Excludes 2   Includes   Use additional   Code first   Code also   Key words
OGCR Official Guidelines   X Assign placeholder X   ● Use Additional Character(s)   ) Manifestation Code   🐾 Hierarchical Condition Category   **Coding Clinic**

● S82.83 Other fracture of upper and lower end of fibula

   ● S82.831 Other fracture of upper and lower end of right fibula

   ● S82.832 Other fracture of upper and lower end of left fibula
      Coding Clinic: 2015, Q1, P9-10

   ● S82.839 Other fracture of upper and lower end of unspecified fibula

● S82.84 Bimalleolar fracture of lower leg

   ● S82.841 Displaced bimalleolar fracture of right lower leg

   ● S82.842 Displaced bimalleolar fracture of left lower leg

   ● S82.843 Displaced bimalleolar fracture of unspecified lower leg

   ● S82.844 Nondisplaced bimalleolar fracture of right lower leg

   ● S82.845 Nondisplaced bimalleolar fracture of left lower leg

   ● S82.846 Nondisplaced bimalleolar fracture of unspecified lower leg

● S82.85 Trimalleolar fracture of lower leg

   ● S82.851 Displaced trimalleolar fracture of right lower leg

   ● S82.852 Displaced trimalleolar fracture of left lower leg

   ● S82.853 Displaced trimalleolar fracture of unspecified lower leg

   ● S82.854 Nondisplaced trimalleolar fracture of right lower leg

   ● S82.855 Nondisplaced trimalleolar fracture of left lower leg

   ● S82.856 Nondisplaced trimalleolar fracture of unspecified lower leg

● S82.86 Maisonneuve's fracture

   ● S82.861 Displaced Maisonneuve's fracture of right leg

   ● S82.862 Displaced Maisonneuve's fracture of left leg

   ● S82.863 Displaced Maisonneuve's fracture of unspecified leg

   ● S82.864 Nondisplaced Maisonneuve's fracture of right leg

   ● S82.865 Nondisplaced Maisonneuve's fracture of left leg

   ● S82.866 Nondisplaced Maisonneuve's fracture of unspecified leg

● S82.87 Pilon fracture of tibia

   ● S82.871 Displaced pilon fracture of right tibia

   ● S82.872 Displaced pilon fracture of left tibia

   ● S82.873 Displaced pilon fracture of unspecified tibia

   ● S82.874 Nondisplaced pilon fracture of right tibia

   ● S82.875 Nondisplaced pilon fracture of left tibia

   ● S82.876 Nondisplaced pilon fracture of unspecified tibia

● S82.89 Other fractures of lower leg
      Fracture of ankle NOS

   ● S82.891 Other fracture of right lower leg

   ● S82.892 Other fracture of left lower leg

   ● S82.899 Other fracture of unspecified lower leg

● S82.9 Unspecified fracture of lower leg

  X● S82.90 Unspecified fracture of unspecified lower leg

  X● S82.91 Unspecified fracture of right lower leg

  X● S82.92 Unspecified fracture of left lower leg

● S83 Dislocation and sprain of joints and ligaments of knee

   Includes avulsion of joint or ligament of knee
      laceration of cartilage, joint or ligament of knee
      sprain of cartilage, joint or ligament of knee
      traumatic hemarthrosis of joint or ligament of knee
      traumatic rupture of joint or ligament of knee
      traumatic subluxation of joint or ligament of knee
      traumatic tear of joint or ligament of knee

   Code also any associated open wound

   ~~Excludes1~~ ~~derangement of patella (M22.0-M22.3)~~
      ~~injury of patellar ligament (tendon) (S76.1-)~~
      ~~internal derangement of knee (M23.-)~~
      ~~old dislocation of knee (M24.36)~~
      ~~pathological dislocation of knee (M24.36)~~
      ~~recurrent dislocation of knee (M22.0)~~

   ▶ **Excludes2** derangement of patella (M22.0-M22.3)
      ▶injury of patellar ligament (tendon) (S76.1-)
      ▶internal derangement of knee (M23.-)
      ▶old dislocation of knee (M24.36)
      ▶pathological dislocation of knee (M24.36)
      ▶recurrent dislocation of knee (M22.0)
      strain of muscle, fascia and tendon of lower leg (S86.-)

   Coding Clinic: 2019, Q2, P26

   The appropriate 7th character is to be added to each code from category S83

A	initial encounter
D	subsequent encounter
S	sequela

● S83.0 Subluxation and dislocation of patella

   ● S83.00 Unspecified subluxation and dislocation of patella

      ● S83.001 Unspecified subluxation of right patella

      ● S83.002 Unspecified subluxation of left patella

      ● S83.003 Unspecified subluxation of unspecified patella

      ● S83.004 Unspecified dislocation of right patella

      ● S83.005 Unspecified dislocation of left patella

      ● S83.006 Unspecified dislocation of unspecified patella

   ● S83.01 Lateral subluxation and dislocation of patella

      ● S83.011 Lateral subluxation of right patella

      ● S83.012 Lateral subluxation of left patella

      ● S83.013 Lateral subluxation of unspecified patella

      ● S83.014 Lateral dislocation of right patella

      ● S83.015 Lateral dislocation of left patella

      ● S83.016 Lateral dislocation of unspecified patella

   ● S83.09 Other subluxation and dislocation of patella

      ● S83.091 Other subluxation of right patella

      ● S83.092 Other subluxation of left patella

      ● S83.093 Other subluxation of unspecified patella

      ● S83.094 Other dislocation of right patella

      ● S83.095 Other dislocation of left patella

      ● S83.096 Other dislocation of unspecified patella

● **S83.1**   **Subluxation and dislocation of knee**

      Excludes2   instability of knee prosthesis (T84.022, T84.023)

  ● **S83.10**   **Unspecified subluxation and dislocation of knee**

     ● **S83.101**   Unspecified subluxation of right knee

     ● **S83.102**   Unspecified subluxation of left knee

     ● **S83.103**   Unspecified subluxation of unspecified knee

     ● **S83.104**   Unspecified dislocation of right knee

     ● **S83.105**   Unspecified dislocation of left knee

     ● **S83.106**   Unspecified dislocation of unspecified knee

  ● **S83.11**   **Anterior subluxation and dislocation of proximal end of tibia**

      Posterior subluxation and dislocation of distal end of femur

     ● **S83.111**   Anterior subluxation of proximal end of tibia, right knee

     ● **S83.112**   Anterior subluxation of proximal end of tibia, left knee

     ● **S83.113**   Anterior subluxation of proximal end of tibia, unspecified knee

     ● **S83.114**   Anterior dislocation of proximal end of tibia, right knee

     ● **S83.115**   Anterior dislocation of proximal end of tibia, left knee

     ● **S83.116**   Anterior dislocation of proximal end of tibia, unspecified knee

  ● **S83.12**   **Posterior subluxation and dislocation of proximal end of tibia**

      Anterior dislocation of distal end of femur

     ● **S83.121**   Posterior subluxation of proximal end of tibia, right knee

     ● **S83.122**   Posterior subluxation of proximal end of tibia, left knee

     ● **S83.123**   Posterior subluxation of proximal end of tibia, unspecified knee

     ● **S83.124**   Posterior dislocation of proximal end of tibia, right knee

     ● **S83.125**   Posterior dislocation of proximal end of tibia, left knee

     ● **S83.126**   Posterior dislocation of proximal end of tibia, unspecified knee

  ● **S83.13**   **Medial subluxation and dislocation of proximal end of tibia**

     ● **S83.131**   Medial subluxation of proximal end of tibia, right knee

     ● **S83.132**   Medial subluxation of proximal end of tibia, left knee

     ● **S83.133**   Medial subluxation of proximal end of tibia, unspecified knee

     ● **S83.134**   Medial dislocation of proximal end of tibia, right knee

     ● **S83.135**   Medial dislocation of proximal end of tibia, left knee

     ● **S83.136**   Medial dislocation of proximal end of tibia, unspecified knee

  ● **S83.14**   **Lateral subluxation and dislocation of proximal end of tibia**

     ● **S83.141**   Lateral subluxation of proximal end of tibia, right knee

     ● **S83.142**   Lateral subluxation of proximal end of tibia, left knee

     ● **S83.143**   Lateral subluxation of proximal end of tibia, unspecified knee

     ● **S83.144**   Lateral dislocation of proximal end of tibia, right knee

     ● **S83.145**   Lateral dislocation of proximal end of tibia, left knee

     ● **S83.146**   Lateral dislocation of proximal end of tibia, unspecified knee

  ● **S83.19**   **Other subluxation and dislocation of knee**

     ● **S83.191**   Other subluxation of right knee

     ● **S83.192**   Other subluxation of left knee

     ● **S83.193**   Other subluxation of unspecified knee

     ● **S83.194**   Other dislocation of right knee

     ● **S83.195**   Other dislocation of left knee

     ● **S83.196**   Other dislocation of unspecified knee

● **S83.2**   **Tear of meniscus, current injury**

      Excludes1   old bucket-handle tear (M23.2)

  ● **S83.20**   **Tear of unspecified meniscus, current injury**

      Tear of meniscus of knee NOS

     ● **S83.200**   Bucket-handle tear of unspecified meniscus, current injury, right knee

     ● **S83.201**   Bucket-handle tear of unspecified meniscus, current injury, left knee

     ● **S83.202**   Bucket-handle tear of unspecified meniscus, current injury, unspecified knee

     ● **S83.203**   Other tear of unspecified meniscus, current injury, right knee

     ● **S83.204**   Other tear of unspecified meniscus, current injury, left knee

     ● **S83.205**   Other tear of unspecified meniscus, current injury, unspecified knee

     ● **S83.206**   Unspecified tear of unspecified meniscus, current injury, right knee

     ● **S83.207**   Unspecified tear of unspecified meniscus, current injury, left knee

     ● **S83.209**   Unspecified tear of unspecified meniscus, current injury, unspecified knee

  ● **S83.21**   **Bucket-handle tear of medial meniscus, current injury**

     ● **S83.211**   Bucket-handle tear of medial meniscus, current injury, right knee

     ● **S83.212**   Bucket-handle tear of medial meniscus, current injury, left knee

     ● **S83.219**   Bucket-handle tear of medial meniscus, current injury, unspecified knee

  ● **S83.22**   **Peripheral tear of medial meniscus, current injury**

     ● **S83.221**   Peripheral tear of medial meniscus, current injury, right knee

     ● **S83.222**   Peripheral tear of medial meniscus, current injury, left knee

     ● **S83.229**   Peripheral tear of medial meniscus, current injury, unspecified knee

  ● **S83.23**   **Complex tear of medial meniscus, current injury**

     ● **S83.231**   Complex tear of medial meniscus, current injury, right knee

     ● **S83.232**   Complex tear of medial meniscus, current injury, left knee

       Coding Clinic: 2019, Q2, P26

     ● **S83.239**   Complex tear of medial meniscus, current injury, unspecified knee

  ● **S83.24**   **Other tear of medial meniscus, current injury**

     ● **S83.241**   Other tear of medial meniscus, current injury, right knee

     ● **S83.242**   Other tear of medial meniscus, current injury, left knee

     ● **S83.249**   Other tear of medial meniscus, current injury, unspecified knee

▶ New   ⇒ Revised   ~~deleted~~ Deleted   Excludes 1   Excludes 2   Includes   Use additional   Code first   Code also   Key words

OGCR Official Guidelines   X Assign placeholder X   ● Use Additional Character(s)   ▷ Manifestation Code   🖂 Hierarchical Condition Category   **Coding Clinic**

● **S83.25**   **Bucket-handle tear of lateral meniscus, current injury**
    ● **S83.251**   Bucket-handle tear of lateral meniscus, current injury, **right** knee
    ● **S83.252**   Bucket-handle tear of lateral meniscus, current injury, **left** knee
    ● **S83.259**   Bucket-handle tear of lateral meniscus, current injury, **unspecified** knee

● **S83.26**   **Peripheral tear of lateral meniscus, current injury**
    ● **S83.261**   Peripheral tear of lateral meniscus, current injury, **right** knee
    ● **S83.262**   Peripheral tear of lateral meniscus, current injury, **left** knee
    ● **S83.269**   Peripheral tear of lateral meniscus, current injury, **unspecified** knee

● **S83.27**   **Complex tear of lateral meniscus, current injury**
    ● **S83.271**   Complex tear of lateral meniscus, current injury, **right** knee
    ● **S83.272**   Complex tear of lateral meniscus, current injury, **left** knee
    ● **S83.279**   Complex tear of lateral meniscus, current injury, **unspecified** knee

● **S83.28**   **Other tear of lateral meniscus, current injury**
    ● **S83.281**   Other tear of lateral meniscus, current injury, **right** knee
    ● **S83.282**   Other tear of lateral meniscus, current injury, **left** knee
    ● **S83.289**   Other tear of lateral meniscus, current injury, **unspecified** knee

● **S83.3**   **Tear of articular cartilage of knee, current**
    X ● **S83.30**   Tear of articular cartilage of **unspecified** knee, current
    X ● **S83.31**   Tear of articular cartilage of **right** knee, current
    X ● **S83.32**   Tear of articular cartilage of **left** knee, current

● **S83.4**   **Sprain of collateral ligament of knee**
    ● **S83.40**   Sprain of **unspecified** collateral ligament of knee
      ● **S83.401**   Sprain of unspecified collateral ligament of **right** knee
      ● **S83.402**   Sprain of unspecified collateral ligament of **left** knee
      ● **S83.409**   Sprain of unspecified collateral ligament of **unspecified** knee
    ● **S83.41**   Sprain of **medial** collateral ligament of knee
      Sprain of tibial collateral ligament
      ● **S83.411**   Sprain of medial collateral ligament of **right** knee
      ● **S83.412**   Sprain of medial collateral ligament of **left** knee
      ● **S83.419**   Sprain of medial collateral ligament of **unspecified** knee
    ● **S83.42**   Sprain of **lateral** collateral ligament of knee
      Sprain of fibular collateral ligament
      ● **S83.421**   Sprain of lateral collateral ligament of **right** knee
      ● **S83.422**   Sprain of lateral collateral ligament of **left** knee
      ● **S83.429**   Sprain of lateral collateral ligament of **unspecified** knee

● **S83.5**   **Sprain of cruciate ligament of knee**
    ● **S83.50**   Sprain of **unspecified** cruciate ligament of knee
      ● **S83.501**   Sprain of unspecified cruciate ligament of **right** knee
      ● **S83.502**   Sprain of unspecified cruciate ligament of **left** knee
      ● **S83.509**   Sprain of unspecified cruciate ligament of **unspecified** knee

● **S83.51**   Sprain of **anterior** cruciate ligament of knee
    ● **S83.511**   Sprain of anterior cruciate ligament of **right** knee
      Coding Clinic: 2016, Q2, P4
    ● **S83.512**   Sprain of anterior cruciate ligament of **left** knee
    ● **S83.519**   Sprain of anterior cruciate ligament of **unspecified** knee

● **S83.52**   Sprain of **posterior** cruciate ligament of knee
    ● **S83.521**   Sprain of posterior cruciate ligament of **right** knee
    ● **S83.522**   Sprain of posterior cruciate ligament of **left** knee
    ● **S83.529**   Sprain of posterior cruciate ligament of **unspecified** knee

● **S83.6**   Sprain of the **superior tibiofibular** joint and ligament
    X ● **S83.60**   Sprain of the superior tibiofibular joint and ligament, **unspecified** knee
    X ● **S83.61**   Sprain of the superior tibiofibular joint and ligament, **right** knee
    X ● **S83.62**   Sprain of the superior tibiofibular joint and ligament, **left** knee

● **S83.8**   Sprain of other specified parts of knee
    ● **S83.8X**   Sprain of **other specified** parts of knee
      ● **S83.8X1**   Sprain of other specified parts of **right** knee
      ● **S83.8X2**   Sprain of other specified parts of **left** knee
      ● **S83.8X9**   Sprain of other specified parts of **unspecified** knee

● **S83.9**   Sprain of **unspecified site** of knee
    X ● **S83.90**   Sprain of unspecified site of **unspecified** knee
    X ● **S83.91**   Sprain of unspecified site of **right** knee
    X ● **S83.92**   Sprain of unspecified site of **left** knee

● **S84**   **Injury of nerves at lower leg level**
    Code also any associated open wound (S81.-)
    Excludes2   injury of nerves at ankle and foot level (S94.-)
    The appropriate 7th character is to be added to each code from category S84

A	initial encounter
D	subsequent encounter
S	sequela

● **S84.0**   **Injury of tibial nerve at lower leg level**
    X ● **S84.00**   Injury of tibial nerve at lower leg level, **unspecified** leg
    X ● **S84.01**   Injury of tibial nerve at lower leg level, **right** leg
    X ● **S84.02**   Injury of tibial nerve at lower leg level, **left** leg

● **S84.1**   **Injury of peroneal nerve at lower leg level**
    X ● **S84.10**   Injury of peroneal nerve at lower leg level, **unspecified** leg
    X ● **S84.11**   Injury of peroneal nerve at lower leg level, **right** leg
    X ● **S84.12**   Injury of peroneal nerve at lower leg level, **left** leg

● **S84.2**   **Injury of cutaneous sensory nerve at lower leg level**
    X ● **S84.20**   Injury of cutaneous sensory nerve at lower leg level, **unspecified** leg
    X ● **S84.21**   Injury of cutaneous sensory nerve at lower leg level, **right** leg
    X ● **S84.22**   Injury of cutaneous sensory nerve at lower leg level, **left** leg

● S84.8   Injury of other nerves at lower leg level
    ● S84.80   Injury of other nerves at lower leg level
       ● S84.801   Injury of other nerves at lower leg level, right leg
       ● S84.802   Injury of other nerves at lower leg level, left leg
       ● S84.809   Injury of other nerves at lower leg level, unspecified leg
    ● S84.9   Injury of unspecified nerve at lower leg level
       X ● S84.90   Injury of unspecified nerve at lower leg level, unspecified leg
       X ● S84.91   Injury of unspecified nerve at lower leg level, right leg
       X ● S84.92   Injury of unspecified nerve at lower leg level, left leg

● S85   Injury of blood vessels at lower leg level
    Code also any associated open wound (S81.-)
    Excludes2   injury of blood vessels at ankle and foot level (S95.-)
    The appropriate 7th character is to be added to each code from category S85

> A   initial encounter
> D   subsequent encounter
> S   sequela

    ● S85.0   Injury of popliteal artery
       ● S85.00   Unspecified injury of popliteal artery
          ● S85.001   Unspecified injury of popliteal artery, right leg
          ● S85.002   Unspecified injury of popliteal artery, left leg
          ● S85.009   Unspecified injury of popliteal artery, unspecified leg
       ● S85.01   Laceration of popliteal artery
          ● S85.011   Laceration of popliteal artery, right leg
          ● S85.012   Laceration of popliteal artery, left leg
          ● S85.019   Laceration of popliteal artery, unspecified leg
       ● S85.09   Other specified injury of popliteal artery
          ● S85.091   Other specified injury of popliteal artery, right leg
          ● S85.092   Other specified injury of popliteal artery, left leg
          ● S85.099   Other specified injury of popliteal artery, unspecified leg
    ● S85.1   Injury of tibial artery
       ● S85.10   Unspecified injury of unspecified tibial artery
          Injury of tibial artery NOS
          ● S85.101   Unspecified injury of unspecified tibial artery, right leg
          ● S85.102   Unspecified injury of unspecified tibial artery, left leg
          ● S85.109   Unspecified injury of unspecified tibial artery, unspecified leg
       ● S85.11   Laceration of unspecified tibial artery
          ● S85.111   Laceration of unspecified tibial artery, right leg
          ● S85.112   Laceration of unspecified tibial artery, left leg
          ● S85.119   Laceration of unspecified tibial artery, unspecified leg

       ● S85.12   Other specified injury of unspecified tibial artery
          ● S85.121   Other specified injury of unspecified tibial artery, right leg
          ● S85.122   Other specified injury of unspecified tibial artery, left leg
          ● S85.129   Other specified injury of unspecified tibial artery, unspecified leg
       ● S85.13   Unspecified injury of anterior tibial artery
          ● S85.131   Unspecified injury of anterior tibial artery, right leg
          ● S85.132   Unspecified injury of anterior tibial artery, left leg
          ● S85.139   Unspecified injury of anterior tibial artery, unspecified leg
       ● S85.14   Laceration of anterior tibial artery
          ● S85.141   Laceration of anterior tibial artery, right leg
          ● S85.142   Laceration of anterior tibial artery, left leg
          ● S85.149   Laceration of anterior tibial artery, unspecified leg
       ● S85.15   Other specified injury of anterior tibial artery
          ● S85.151   Other specified injury of anterior tibial artery, right leg
          ● S85.152   Other specified injury of anterior tibial artery, left leg
          ● S85.159   Other specified injury of anterior tibial artery, unspecified leg
       ● S85.16   Unspecified injury of posterior tibial artery
          ● S85.161   Unspecified injury of posterior tibial artery, right leg
          ● S85.162   Unspecified injury of posterior tibial artery, left leg
          ● S85.169   Unspecified injury of posterior tibial artery, unspecified leg
       ● S85.17   Laceration of posterior tibial artery
          ● S85.171   Laceration of posterior tibial artery, right leg
          ● S85.172   Laceration of posterior tibial artery, left leg
          ● S85.179   Laceration of posterior tibial artery, unspecified leg
       ● S85.18   Other specified injury of posterior tibial artery
          ● S85.181   Other specified injury of posterior tibial artery, right leg
          ● S85.182   Other specified injury of posterior tibial artery, left leg
          ● S85.189   Other specified injury of posterior tibial artery, unspecified leg
    ● S85.2   Injury of peroneal artery
       ● S85.20   Unspecified injury of peroneal artery
          ● S85.201   Unspecified injury of peroneal artery, right leg
          ● S85.202   Unspecified injury of peroneal artery, left leg
          ● S85.209   Unspecified injury of peroneal artery, unspecified leg
       ● S85.21   Laceration of peroneal artery
          ● S85.211   Laceration of peroneal artery, right leg
          ● S85.212   Laceration of peroneal artery, left leg
          ● S85.219   Laceration of peroneal artery, unspecified leg

▶ New   ⇒ Revised   ~~deleted~~ Deleted   Excludes 1   Excludes 2   Includes   Use additional   Code first   Code also   Key words
OGCR Official Guidelines   X Assign placeholder X   ● Use Additional Character(s)   ▶ Manifestation Code   Ⓗ Hierarchical Condition Category   **Coding Clinic**

● **S85.29**   Other specified injury of peroneal artery
　　● **S85.291**   Other specified injury of peroneal artery, right leg
　　● **S85.292**   Other specified injury of peroneal artery, left leg
　　● **S85.299**   Other specified injury of peroneal artery, unspecified leg
● **S85.3**   Injury of greater saphenous vein at lower leg level
　　Injury of greater saphenous vein NOS
　　Injury of saphenous vein NOS
　● **S85.30**   Unspecified injury of greater saphenous vein at lower leg level
　　● **S85.301**   Unspecified injury of greater saphenous vein at lower leg level, right leg
　　● **S85.302**   Unspecified injury of greater saphenous vein at lower leg level, left leg
　　● **S85.309**   Unspecified injury of greater saphenous vein at lower leg level, unspecified leg
　● **S85.31**   Laceration of greater saphenous vein at lower leg level
　　● **S85.311**   Laceration of greater saphenous vein at lower leg level, right leg
　　● **S85.312**   Laceration of greater saphenous vein at lower leg level, left leg
　　● **S85.319**   Laceration of greater saphenous vein at lower leg level, unspecified leg
　● **S85.39**   Other specified injury of greater saphenous vein at lower leg level
　　● **S85.391**   Other specified injury of greater saphenous vein at lower leg level, right leg
　　● **S85.392**   Other specified injury of greater saphenous vein at lower leg level, left leg
　　● **S85.399**   Other specified injury of greater saphenous vein at lower leg level, unspecified leg
● **S85.4**   Injury of lesser saphenous vein at lower leg level
　● **S85.40**   Unspecified injury of lesser saphenous vein at lower leg level
　　● **S85.401**   Unspecified injury of lesser saphenous vein at lower leg level, right leg
　　● **S85.402**   Unspecified injury of lesser saphenous vein at lower leg level, left leg
　　● **S85.409**   Unspecified injury of lesser saphenous vein at lower leg level, unspecified leg
　● **S85.41**   Laceration of lesser saphenous vein at lower leg level
　　● **S85.411**   Laceration of lesser saphenous vein at lower leg level, right leg
　　● **S85.412**   Laceration of lesser saphenous vein at lower leg level, left leg
　　● **S85.419**   Laceration of lesser saphenous vein at lower leg level, unspecified leg
　● **S85.49**   Other specified injury of lesser saphenous vein at lower leg level
　　● **S85.491**   Other specified injury of lesser saphenous vein at lower leg level, right leg
　　● **S85.492**   Other specified injury of lesser saphenous vein at lower leg level, left leg
　　● **S85.499**   Other specified injury of lesser saphenous vein at lower leg level, unspecified leg

● **S85.5**   Injury of popliteal vein
　● **S85.50**   Unspecified injury of popliteal vein
　　● **S85.501**   Unspecified injury of popliteal vein, right leg
　　● **S85.502**   Unspecified injury of popliteal vein, left leg
　　● **S85.509**   Unspecified injury of popliteal vein, unspecified leg
　● **S85.51**   Laceration of popliteal vein
　　● **S85.511**   Laceration of popliteal vein, right leg
　　● **S85.512**   Laceration of popliteal vein, left leg
　　● **S85.519**   Laceration of popliteal vein, unspecified leg
　● **S85.59**   Other specified injury of popliteal vein
　　● **S85.591**   Other specified injury of popliteal vein, right leg
　　● **S85.592**   Other specified injury of popliteal vein, left leg
　　● **S85.599**   Other specified injury of popliteal vein, unspecified leg
● **S85.8**   Injury of other blood vessels at lower leg level
　● **S85.80**   Unspecified injury of other blood vessels at lower leg level
　　● **S85.801**   Unspecified injury of other blood vessels at lower leg level, right leg
　　● **S85.802**   Unspecified injury of other blood vessels at lower leg level, left leg
　　● **S85.809**   Unspecified injury of other blood vessels at lower leg level, unspecified leg
　● **S85.81**   Laceration of other blood vessels at lower leg level
　　● **S85.811**   Laceration of other blood vessels at lower leg level, right leg
　　● **S85.812**   Laceration of other blood vessels at lower leg level, left leg
　　● **S85.819**   Laceration of other blood vessels at lower leg level, unspecified leg
　● **S85.89**   Other specified injury of other blood vessels at lower leg level
　　● **S85.891**   Other specified injury of other blood vessels at lower leg level, right leg
　　● **S85.892**   Other specified injury of other blood vessels at lower leg level, left leg
　　● **S85.899**   Other specified injury of other blood vessels at lower leg level, unspecified leg
● **S85.9**   Injury of unspecified blood vessel at lower leg level
　● **S85.90**   Unspecified injury of unspecified blood vessel at lower leg level
　　● **S85.901**   Unspecified injury of unspecified blood vessel at lower leg level, right leg
　　● **S85.902**   Unspecified injury of unspecified blood vessel at lower leg level, left leg
　　● **S85.909**   Unspecified injury of unspecified blood vessel at lower leg level, unspecified leg
　● **S85.91**   Laceration of unspecified blood vessel at lower leg level
　　● **S85.911**   Laceration of unspecified blood vessel at lower leg level, right leg
　　● **S85.912**   Laceration of unspecified blood vessel at lower leg level, left leg
　　● **S85.919**   Laceration of unspecified blood vessel at lower leg level, unspecified leg

● **S85.99**   Other specified injury of unspecified blood vessel at lower leg level
     ● **S85.991**   Other specified injury of unspecified blood vessel at lower leg level, right leg
     ● **S85.992**   Other specified injury of unspecified blood vessel at lower leg level, left leg
     ● **S85.999**   Other specified injury of unspecified blood vessel at lower leg level, unspecified leg

● **S86**   Injury of muscle, fascia and tendon at lower leg level

Code also any associated open wound (S81.-)

Excludes2   injury of muscle, fascia and tendon at ankle (S96.-)
               injury of patellar ligament (tendon) (S76.1-)
               sprain of joints and ligaments of knee (S83.-)

The appropriate 7th character is to be added to each code from category S86

A	initial encounter
D	subsequent encounter
S	sequela

● **S86.0**   Injury of Achilles tendon
   ● **S86.00**   Unspecified injury of Achilles tendon
     ● **S86.001**   Unspecified injury of right Achilles tendon
     ● **S86.002**   Unspecified injury of left Achilles tendon
     ● **S86.009**   Unspecified injury of unspecified Achilles tendon
   ● **S86.01**   Strain of Achilles tendon
     ● **S86.011**   Strain of right Achilles tendon
     ● **S86.012**   Strain of left Achilles tendon
     ● **S86.019**   Strain of unspecified Achilles tendon
   ● **S86.02**   Laceration of Achilles tendon
     ● **S86.021**   Laceration of right Achilles tendon
     ● **S86.022**   Laceration of left Achilles tendon
     ● **S86.029**   Laceration of unspecified Achilles tendon
   ● **S86.09**   Other specified injury of Achilles tendon
     ● **S86.091**   Other specified injury of right Achilles tendon
     ● **S86.092**   Other specified injury of left Achilles tendon
     ● **S86.099**   Other specified injury of unspecified Achilles tendon

● **S86.1**   Injury of other muscle(s) and tendon(s) of posterior muscle group at lower leg level
   ● **S86.10**   Unspecified injury of other muscle(s) and tendon(s) of posterior muscle group at lower leg level
     ● **S86.101**   Unspecified injury of other muscle(s) and tendon(s) of posterior muscle group at lower leg level, right leg
     ● **S86.102**   Unspecified injury of other muscle(s) and tendon(s) of posterior muscle group at lower leg level, left leg
     ● **S86.109**   Unspecified injury of other muscle(s) and tendon(s) of posterior muscle group at lower leg level, unspecified leg

● **S86.11**   Strain of other muscle(s) and tendon(s) of posterior muscle group at lower leg level
     ● **S86.111**   Strain of other muscle(s) and tendon(s) of posterior muscle group at lower leg level, right leg
     ● **S86.112**   Strain of other muscle(s) and tendon(s) of posterior muscle group at lower leg level, left leg
     ● **S86.119**   Strain of other muscle(s) and tendon(s) of posterior muscle group at lower leg level, unspecified leg
● **S86.12**   Laceration of other muscle(s) and tendon(s) of posterior muscle group at lower leg level
     ● **S86.121**   Laceration of other muscle(s) and tendon(s) of posterior muscle group at lower leg level, right leg
     ● **S86.122**   Laceration of other muscle(s) and tendon(s) of posterior muscle group at lower leg level, left leg
     ● **S86.129**   Laceration of other muscle(s) and tendon(s) of posterior muscle group at lower leg level, unspecified leg
● **S86.19**   Other injury of other muscle(s) and tendon(s) of posterior muscle group at lower leg level
     ● **S86.191**   Other injury of other muscle(s) and tendon(s) of posterior muscle group at lower leg level, right leg
     ● **S86.192**   Other injury of other muscle(s) and tendon(s) of posterior muscle group at lower leg level, left leg
     ● **S86.199**   Other injury of other muscle(s) and tendon(s) of posterior muscle group at lower leg level, unspecified leg

● **S86.2**   Injury of muscle(s) and tendon(s) of anterior muscle group at lower leg level
   ● **S86.20**   Unspecified injury of muscle(s) and tendon(s) of anterior muscle group at lower leg level
     ● **S86.201**   Unspecified injury of muscle(s) and tendon(s) of anterior muscle group at lower leg level, right leg
     ● **S86.202**   Unspecified injury of muscle(s) and tendon(s) of anterior muscle group at lower leg level, left leg
     ● **S86.209**   Unspecified injury of muscle(s) and tendon(s) of anterior muscle group at lower leg level, unspecified leg
   ● **S86.21**   Strain of muscle(s) and tendon(s) of anterior muscle group at lower leg level
     ● **S86.211**   Strain of muscle(s) and tendon(s) of anterior muscle group at lower leg level, right leg
     ● **S86.212**   Strain of muscle(s) and tendon(s) of anterior muscle group at lower leg level, left leg
     ● **S86.219**   Strain of muscle(s) and tendon(s) of anterior muscle group at lower leg level, unspecified leg
   ● **S86.22**   Laceration of muscle(s) and tendon(s) of anterior muscle group at lower leg level
     ● **S86.221**   Laceration of muscle(s) and tendon(s) of anterior muscle group at lower leg level, right leg
     ● **S86.222**   Laceration of muscle(s) and tendon(s) of anterior muscle group at lower leg level, left leg
     ● **S86.229**   Laceration of muscle(s) and tendon(s) of anterior muscle group at lower leg level, unspecified leg

▶ New   ⇒ Revised   ~~deleted~~ Deleted   Excludes 1   Excludes 2   Includes   Use additional   Code first   Code also   Key words
OGCR Official Guidelines   X Assign placeholder X   ● Use Additional Character(s)   ▶ Manifestation Code   🅗 Hierarchical Condition Category   **Coding Clinic**

- S86.29　Other injury of muscle(s) and tendon(s) of anterior muscle group at lower leg level
  - S86.291　Other injury of muscle(s) and tendon(s) of anterior muscle group at lower leg level, right leg
  - S86.292　Other injury of muscle(s) and tendon(s) of anterior muscle group at lower leg level, left leg
  - S86.299　Other injury of muscle(s) and tendon(s) of anterior muscle group at lower leg level, unspecified leg
- S86.3　Injury of muscle(s) and tendon(s) of peroneal muscle group at lower leg level
  - S86.30　Unspecified injury of muscle(s) and tendon(s) of peroneal muscle group at lower leg level
    - S86.301　Unspecified injury of muscle(s) and tendon(s) of peroneal muscle group at lower leg level, right leg
    - S86.302　Unspecified injury of muscle(s) and tendon(s) of peroneal muscle group at lower leg level, left leg
    - S86.309　Unspecified injury of muscle(s) and tendon(s) of peroneal muscle group at lower leg level, unspecified leg
  - S86.31　Strain of muscle(s) and tendon(s) of peroneal muscle group at lower leg level
    - S86.311　Strain of muscle(s) and tendon(s) of peroneal muscle group at lower leg level, right leg
    - S86.312　Strain of muscle(s) and tendon(s) of peroneal muscle group at lower leg level, left leg
    - S86.319　Strain of muscle(s) and tendon(s) of peroneal muscle group at lower leg level, unspecified leg
  - S86.32　Laceration of muscle(s) and tendon(s) of peroneal muscle group at lower leg level
    - S86.321　Laceration of muscle(s) and tendon(s) of peroneal muscle group at lower leg level, right leg
    - S86.322　Laceration of muscle(s) and tendon(s) of peroneal muscle group at lower leg level, left leg
    - S86.329　Laceration of muscle(s) and tendon(s) of peroneal muscle group at lower leg level, unspecified leg
  - S86.39　Other injury of muscle(s) and tendon(s) of peroneal muscle group at lower leg level
    - S86.391　Other injury of muscle(s) and tendon(s) of peroneal muscle group at lower leg level, right leg
    - S86.392　Other injury of muscle(s) and tendon(s) of peroneal muscle group at lower leg level, left leg
    - S86.399　Other injury of muscle(s) and tendon(s) of peroneal muscle group at lower leg level, unspecified leg
- S86.8　Injury of other muscles and tendons at lower leg level
  - S86.80　Unspecified injury of other muscles and tendons at lower leg level
    - S86.801　Unspecified injury of other muscle(s) and tendon(s) at lower leg level, right leg
    - S86.802　Unspecified injury of other muscle(s) and tendon(s) at lower leg level, left leg
    - S86.809　Unspecified injury of other muscle(s) and tendon(s) at lower leg level, unspecified leg

- S86.81　Strain of other muscles and tendons at lower leg level
  - S86.811　Strain of other muscle(s) and tendon(s) at lower leg level, right leg
  - S86.812　Strain of other muscle(s) and tendon(s) at lower leg level, left leg
  - S86.819　Strain of other muscle(s) and tendon(s) at lower leg level, unspecified leg
- S86.82　Laceration of other muscles and tendons at lower leg level
  - S86.821　Laceration of other muscle(s) and tendon(s) at lower leg level, right leg
  - S86.822　Laceration of other muscle(s) and tendon(s) at lower leg level, left leg
  - S86.829　Laceration of other muscle(s) and tendon(s) at lower leg level, unspecified leg
- S86.89　Other injury of other muscles and tendons at lower leg level
  - S86.891　Other injury of other muscle(s) and tendon(s) at lower leg level, right leg
  - S86.892　Other injury of other muscle(s) and tendon(s) at lower leg level, left leg
  - S86.899　Other injury of other muscle(s) and tendon(s) at lower leg level, unspecified leg
- S86.9　Injury of unspecified muscle and tendon at lower leg level
  - S86.90　Unspecified injury of unspecified muscle and tendon at lower leg level
    - S86.901　Unspecified injury of unspecified muscle(s) and tendon(s) at lower leg level, right leg
    - S86.902　Unspecified injury of unspecified muscle(s) and tendon(s) at lower leg level, left leg
    - S86.909　Unspecified injury of unspecified muscle(s) and tendon(s) at lower leg level, unspecified leg
  - S86.91　Strain of unspecified muscle and tendon at lower leg level
    - S86.911　Strain of unspecified muscle(s) and tendon(s) at lower leg level, right leg
    - S86.912　Strain of unspecified muscle(s) and tendon(s) at lower leg level, left leg
    - S86.919　Strain of unspecified muscle(s) and tendon(s) at lower leg level, unspecified leg
  - S86.92　Laceration of unspecified muscle and tendon at lower leg level
    - S86.921　Laceration of unspecified muscle(s) and tendon(s) at lower leg level, right leg
    - S86.922　Laceration of unspecified muscle(s) and tendon(s) at lower leg level, left leg
    - S86.929　Laceration of unspecified muscle(s) and tendon(s) at lower leg level, unspecified leg
  - S86.99　Other injury of unspecified muscle and tendon at lower leg level
    - S86.991　Other injury of unspecified muscle(s) and tendon(s) at lower leg level, right leg
    - S86.992　Other injury of unspecified muscle(s) and tendon(s) at lower leg level, left leg
    - S86.999　Other injury of unspecified muscle(s) and tendon(s) at lower leg level, unspecified leg

● **S87**   **Crushing injury of lower leg**
     Use additional code(s) for all associated injuries
     Excludes2   crushing injury of ankle and foot (S97.-)
     The appropriate 7th character is to be added to each code from
       category S87

A	initial encounter
D	subsequent encounter
S	sequela

  ● **S87.0**   **Crushing injury of knee**
     X● **S87.00**   Crushing injury of unspecified knee
     X● **S87.01**   Crushing injury of right knee
     X● **S87.02**   Crushing injury of left knee
  ● **S87.8**   **Crushing injury of lower leg**
     X● **S87.80**   Crushing injury of unspecified lower leg
     X● **S87.81**   Crushing injury of right lower leg
     X● **S87.82**   Crushing injury of left lower leg

● **S88**   **Traumatic amputation of lower leg**
     An amputation not identified as partial or complete should be
       coded to complete
     Excludes1   traumatic amputation of ankle and foot (S98.-)
     The appropriate 7th character is to be added to each code from
       category S88

A	initial encounter
D	subsequent encounter
S	sequela

  ● **S88.0**   **Traumatic amputation at knee level**
     ● **S88.01**   Complete traumatic amputation at knee level
       ● **S88.011**   Complete traumatic amputation at
         knee level, right lower leg A, D, S 🐄
       ● **S88.012**   Complete traumatic amputation at
         knee level, left lower leg A, D, S 🐄
       ● **S88.019**   Complete traumatic amputation at
         knee level, unspecified lower leg
         A, D, S 🐄
     ● **S88.02**   Partial traumatic amputation at knee level
       ● **S88.021**   Partial traumatic amputation at knee
         level, right lower leg A, D, S 🐄
       ● **S88.022**   Partial traumatic amputation at knee
         level, left lower leg A, D, S 🐄
       ● **S88.029**   Partial traumatic amputation at knee
         level, unspecified lower leg A, D, S 🐄
  ● **S88.1**   **Traumatic amputation at level between knee and ankle**
     ● **S88.11**   Complete traumatic amputation at level
       between knee and ankle
       ● **S88.111**   Complete traumatic amputation at
         level between knee and ankle, right
         lower leg A, D, S 🐄
       ● **S88.112**   Complete traumatic amputation at
         level between knee and ankle, left
         lower leg A, D, S 🐄
       ● **S88.119**   Complete traumatic amputation at
         level between knee and ankle,
         unspecified lower leg A, D, S 🐄
     ● **S88.12**   Partial traumatic amputation at level between
       knee and ankle
       ● **S88.121**   Partial traumatic amputation at level
         between knee and ankle, right lower
         leg A, D, S 🐄
       ● **S88.122**   Partial traumatic amputation at level
         between knee and ankle, left lower
         leg A, D, S 🐄
       ● **S88.129**   Partial traumatic amputation at level
         between knee and ankle, unspecified
         lower leg A, D, S 🐄

  ● **S88.9**   **Traumatic amputation of lower leg, level unspecified**
     ● **S88.91**   Complete traumatic amputation of lower leg,
       level unspecified
       ● **S88.911**   Complete traumatic amputation of
         right lower leg, level unspecified
         A, D, S 🐄
       ● **S88.912**   Complete traumatic amputation of
         left lower leg, level unspecified
         A, D, S 🐄
       ● **S88.919**   Complete traumatic amputation of
         unspecified lower leg, level
         unspecified A, D, S 🐄
     ● **S88.92**   Partial traumatic amputation of lower leg, level
       unspecified
       ● **S88.921**   Partial traumatic amputation of right
         lower leg, level unspecified A, D, S 🐄
       ● **S88.922**   Partial traumatic amputation of left
         lower leg, level unspecified A, D, S 🐄
       ● **S88.929**   Partial traumatic amputation of
         unspecified lower leg, level
         unspecified A, D, S 🐄

● **S89**   **Other and unspecified injuries of lower leg**
     Note: A fracture not indicated as open or closed should be
       coded to closed
     Excludes2   other and unspecified injuries of ankle and foot
       (S99.-)
     The appropriate 7th character is to be added to each code from
       subcategories S89.0, S89.1, S89.2, and S89.3

A	initial encounter for closed fracture
D	subsequent encounter for fracture with routine healing
G	subsequent encounter for fracture with delayed healing
K	subsequent encounter for fracture with nonunion
P	subsequent encounter for fracture with malunion
S	sequela

  ● **S89.0**   **Physeal fracture of upper end of tibia**
     ● **S89.00**   Unspecified physeal fracture of upper end of
       tibia
       ● **S89.001**   Unspecified physeal fracture of upper
         end of right tibia
       ● **S89.002**   Unspecified physeal fracture of upper
         end of left tibia
       ● **S89.009**   Unspecified physeal fracture of upper
         end of unspecified tibia
     ● **S89.01**   Salter-Harris Type I physeal fracture of upper
       end of tibia
       ● **S89.011**   Salter-Harris Type I physeal fracture
         of upper end of right tibia
       ● **S89.012**   Salter-Harris Type I physeal fracture
         of upper end of left tibia
       ● **S89.019**   Salter-Harris Type I physeal fracture
         of upper end of unspecified tibia
     ● **S89.02**   Salter-Harris Type II physeal fracture of upper
       end of tibia
       ● **S89.021**   Salter-Harris Type II physeal fracture
         of upper end of right tibia
       ● **S89.022**   Salter-Harris Type II physeal fracture
         of upper end of left tibia
       ● **S89.029**   Salter-Harris Type II physeal fracture
         of upper end of unspecified tibia
     ● **S89.03**   Salter-Harris Type III physeal fracture of upper
       end of tibia
       ● **S89.031**   Salter-Harris Type III physeal fracture
         of upper end of right tibia
       ● **S89.032**   Salter-Harris Type III physeal fracture
         of upper end of left tibia
       ● **S89.039**   Salter-Harris Type III physeal fracture
         of upper end of unspecified tibia

▶ New   ⇒ Revised   ~~deleted~~ Deleted   Excludes 1   Excludes 2   Includes   Use additional   Code first   Code also   Key words
OGCR Official Guidelines   X Assign placeholder X   ● Use Additional Character(s)   ▶ Manifestation Code   🐄 Hierarchical Condition Category   **Coding Clinic**

● **S89.04** Salter-Harris Type IV physeal fracture of upper end of tibia
- ● **S89.041** Salter-Harris Type IV physeal fracture of upper end of right tibia
- ● **S89.042** Salter-Harris Type IV physeal fracture of upper end of left tibia
- ● **S89.049** Salter-Harris Type IV physeal fracture of upper end of unspecified tibia

● **S89.09** Other physeal fracture of upper end of tibia
- ● **S89.091** Other physeal fracture of upper end of right tibia
- ● **S89.092** Other physeal fracture of upper end of left tibia
- ● **S89.099** Other physeal fracture of upper end of unspecified tibia

● **S89.1** Physeal fracture of lower end of tibia
- ● **S89.10** Unspecified physeal fracture of lower end of tibia
  - ● **S89.101** Unspecified physeal fracture of lower end of right tibia
  - ● **S89.102** Unspecified physeal fracture of lower end of left tibia
  - ● **S89.109** Unspecified physeal fracture of lower end of unspecified tibia
- ● **S89.11** Salter-Harris Type I physeal fracture of lower end of tibia
  - ● **S89.111** Salter-Harris Type I physeal fracture of lower end of right tibia
  - ● **S89.112** Salter-Harris Type I physeal fracture of lower end of left tibia
  - ● **S89.119** Salter-Harris Type I physeal fracture of lower end of unspecified tibia
- ● **S89.12** Salter-Harris Type II physeal fracture of lower end of tibia
  - ● **S89.121** Salter-Harris Type II physeal fracture of lower end of right tibia
  - ● **S89.122** Salter-Harris Type II physeal fracture of lower end of left tibia
  - ● **S89.129** Salter-Harris Type II physeal fracture of lower end of unspecified tibia
- ● **S89.13** Salter-Harris Type III physeal fracture of lower end of tibia
    Excludes1 fracture of medial malleolus (adult) (S82.5-)
  - ● **S89.131** Salter-Harris Type III physeal fracture of lower end of right tibia
  - ● **S89.132** Salter-Harris Type III physeal fracture of lower end of left tibia
  - ● **S89.139** Salter-Harris Type III physeal fracture of lower end of unspecified tibia
- ● **S89.14** Salter-Harris Type IV physeal fracture of lower end of tibia
    Excludes1 fracture of medial malleolus (adult) (S82.5-)
  - ● **S89.141** Salter-Harris Type IV physeal fracture of lower end of right tibia
  - ● **S89.142** Salter-Harris Type IV physeal fracture of lower end of left tibia
  - ● **S89.149** Salter-Harris Type IV physeal fracture of lower end of unspecified tibia
- ● **S89.19** Other physeal fracture of lower end of tibia
  - ● **S89.191** Other physeal fracture of lower end of right tibia
  - ● **S89.192** Other physeal fracture of lower end of left tibia
  - ● **S89.199** Other physeal fracture of lower end of unspecified tibia

● **S89.2** Physeal fracture of upper end of fibula
- ● **S89.20** Unspecified physeal fracture of upper end of fibula
  - ● **S89.201** Unspecified physeal fracture of upper end of right fibula
  - ● **S89.202** Unspecified physeal fracture of upper end of left fibula
  - ● **S89.209** Unspecified physeal fracture of upper end of unspecified fibula
- ● **S89.21** Salter-Harris Type I physeal fracture of upper end of fibula
  - ● **S89.211** Salter-Harris Type I physeal fracture of upper end of right fibula
  - ● **S89.212** Salter-Harris Type I physeal fracture of upper end of left fibula
  - ● **S89.219** Salter-Harris Type I physeal fracture of upper end of unspecified fibula
- ● **S89.22** Salter-Harris Type II physeal fracture of upper end of fibula
  - ● **S89.221** Salter-Harris Type II physeal fracture of upper end of right fibula
  - ● **S89.222** Salter-Harris Type II physeal fracture of upper end of left fibula
  - ● **S89.229** Salter-Harris Type II physeal fracture of upper end of unspecified fibula
- ● **S89.29** Other physeal fracture of upper end of fibula
  - ● **S89.291** Other physeal fracture of upper end of right fibula
  - ● **S89.292** Other physeal fracture of upper end of left fibula
  - ● **S89.299** Other physeal fracture of upper end of unspecified fibula

● **S89.3** Physeal fracture of lower end of fibula
- ● **S89.30** Unspecified physeal fracture of lower end of fibula
  - ● **S89.301** Unspecified physeal fracture of lower end of right fibula
  - ● **S89.302** Unspecified physeal fracture of lower end of left fibula
  - ● **S89.309** Unspecified physeal fracture of lower end of unspecified fibula
- ● **S89.31** Salter-Harris Type I physeal fracture of lower end of fibula
  - ● **S89.311** Salter-Harris Type I physeal fracture of lower end of right fibula
  - ● **S89.312** Salter-Harris Type I physeal fracture of lower end of left fibula
  - ● **S89.319** Salter-Harris Type I physeal fracture of lower end of unspecified fibula
- ● **S89.32** Salter-Harris Type II physeal fracture of lower end of fibula
  - ● **S89.321** Salter-Harris Type II physeal fracture of lower end of right fibula
  - ● **S89.322** Salter-Harris Type II physeal fracture of lower end of left fibula
  - ● **S89.329** Salter-Harris Type II physeal fracture of lower end of unspecified fibula
- ● **S89.39** Other physeal fracture of lower end of fibula
  - ● **S89.391** Other physeal fracture of lower end of right fibula
  - ● **S89.392** Other physeal fracture of lower end of left fibula
  - ● **S89.399** Other physeal fracture of lower end of unspecified fibula

● **S89.8** **Other specified injuries of lower leg**
　　The appropriate 7th character is to be added to each
　　code in subcategory S89.8

A	initial encounter
D	subsequent encounter
S	sequela

　X● **S89.80** **Other specified injuries of unspecified lower
　　　　　leg**
　X● **S89.81** **Other specified injuries of right lower leg**
　X● **S89.82** **Other specified injuries of left lower leg**
● **S89.9** **Unspecified injury of lower leg**
　　The appropriate 7th character is to be added to each
　　code in subcategory S89.9

A	initial encounter
D	subsequent encounter
S	sequela

　X● **S89.90** **Unspecified injury of unspecified lower leg**
　X● **S89.91** **Unspecified injury of right lower leg**
　X● **S89.92** **Unspecified injury of left lower leg**

INJURIES TO THE ANKLE AND FOOT (S90-S99)

Excludes2　　burns and corrosions (T20-T32)
　　　　　　　fracture of ankle and malleolus (S82.-)
　　　　　　　frostbite (T33-T34)
　　　　　　　insect bite or sting, venomous (T63.4)

● **S90** **Superficial injury of ankle, foot and toes**
　　The appropriate 7th character is to be added to each code from
　　category S90

A	initial encounter
D	subsequent encounter
S	sequela

● **S90.0** **Contusion of ankle**
　X● **S90.00** **Contusion of unspecified ankle**
　X● **S90.01** **Contusion of right ankle**
　X● **S90.02** **Contusion of left ankle**
● **S90.1** **Contusion of toe without damage to nail**
　● **S90.11** **Contusion of great toe without damage to nail**
　　● **S90.111** **Contusion of right great toe without
　　　　　　damage to nail**
　　● **S90.112** **Contusion of left great toe without
　　　　　　damage to nail**
　　● **S90.119** **Contusion of unspecified great toe
　　　　　　without damage to nail**
　● **S90.12** **Contusion of lesser toe without damage to nail**
　　● **S90.121** **Contusion of right lesser toe(s)
　　　　　　without damage to nail**
　　● **S90.122** **Contusion of left lesser toe(s) without
　　　　　　damage to nail**
　　● **S90.129** **Contusion of unspecified lesser toe(s)
　　　　　　without damage to nail**
　　　　　　Contusion of toe NOS
● **S90.2** **Contusion of toe with damage to nail**
　● **S90.21** **Contusion of great toe with damage to nail**
　　● **S90.211** **Contusion of right great toe with
　　　　　　damage to nail**
　　● **S90.212** **Contusion of left great toe with
　　　　　　damage to nail**
　　● **S90.219** **Contusion of unspecified great toe
　　　　　　with damage to nail**

● **S90.22** **Contusion of lesser toe with damage to nail**
　● **S90.221** **Contusion of right lesser toe(s) with
　　　　　damage to nail**
　● **S90.222** **Contusion of left lesser toe(s) with
　　　　　damage to nail**
　● **S90.229** **Contusion of unspecified lesser toe(s)
　　　　　with damage to nail**
● **S90.3** **Contusion of foot**
　　Excludes2　contusion of toes (S90.1-, S90.2-)
　X● **S90.30** **Contusion of unspecified foot**
　　　　　Contusion of foot NOS
　X● **S90.31** **Contusion of right foot**
　X● **S90.32** **Contusion of left foot**
● **S90.4** **Other superficial injuries of toe**
　● **S90.41** **Abrasion of toe**
　　● **S90.411** **Abrasion, right great toe**
　　● **S90.412** **Abrasion, left great toe**
　　● **S90.413** **Abrasion, unspecified great toe**
　　● **S90.414** **Abrasion, right lesser toe(s)**
　　● **S90.415** **Abrasion, left lesser toe(s)**
　　● **S90.416** **Abrasion, unspecified lesser toe(s)**
　● **S90.42** **Blister (nonthermal) of toe**
　　● **S90.421** **Blister (nonthermal), right great toe**
　　● **S90.422** **Blister (nonthermal), left great toe**
　　● **S90.423** **Blister (nonthermal), unspecified
　　　　　　great toe**
　　● **S90.424** **Blister (nonthermal), right lesser
　　　　　　toe(s)**
　　● **S90.425** **Blister (nonthermal), left lesser toe(s)**
　　● **S90.426** **Blister (nonthermal), unspecified
　　　　　　lesser toe(s)**
　● **S90.44** **External constriction of toe**
　　　　　Hair tourniquet syndrome of toe
　　● **S90.441** **External constriction, right great toe**
　　● **S90.442** **External constriction, left great toe**
　　● **S90.443** **External constriction, unspecified
　　　　　　great toe**
　　● **S90.444** **External constriction, right lesser
　　　　　　toe(s)**
　　● **S90.445** **External constriction, left lesser toe(s)**
　　● **S90.446** **External constriction, unspecified
　　　　　　lesser toe(s)**
　● **S90.45** **Superficial foreign body of toe**
　　　　　Splinter in the toe
　　● **S90.451** **Superficial foreign body, right great
　　　　　　toe**
　　● **S90.452** **Superficial foreign body, left great toe**
　　● **S90.453** **Superficial foreign body, unspecified
　　　　　　great toe**
　　● **S90.454** **Superficial foreign body, right lesser
　　　　　　toe(s)**
　　● **S90.455** **Superficial foreign body, left lesser
　　　　　　toe(s)**
　　● **S90.456** **Superficial foreign body, unspecified
　　　　　　lesser toe(s)**
　● **S90.46** **Insect bite (nonvenomous) of toe**
　　● **S90.461** **Insect bite (nonvenomous), right great
　　　　　　toe**
　　● **S90.462** **Insect bite (nonvenomous), left great
　　　　　　toe**
　　● **S90.463** **Insect bite (nonvenomous),
　　　　　　unspecified great toe**
　　● **S90.464** **Insect bite (nonvenomous), right
　　　　　　lesser toe(s)**
　　● **S90.465** **Insect bite (nonvenomous), left lesser
　　　　　　toe(s)**
　　● **S90.466** **Insect bite (nonvenomous),
　　　　　　unspecified lesser toe(s)**

▶ New　⟹ Revised　d̶e̶l̶e̶t̶e̶d̶ Deleted　Excludes 1　Excludes 2　Includes　Use additional　Code first　Code also　Key words

1356　　OGCR Official Guidelines　X Assign placeholder X　● Use Additional Character(s)　▷ Manifestation Code　🅗 Hierarchical Condition Category　**Coding Clinic**

●**S90.47**   Other superficial bite of toe
> **Excludes1**   open bite of toe (S91.15-, S91.25-)

●**S90.471**   Other superficial bite of right great toe

●**S90.472**   Other superficial bite of left great toe

●**S90.473**   Other superficial bite of unspecified great toe

●**S90.474**   Other superficial bite of right lesser toe(s)

●**S90.475**   Other superficial bite of left lesser toe(s)

●**S90.476**   Other superficial bite of unspecified lesser toe(s)

●**S90.5**   Other superficial injuries of ankle

●**S90.51**   Abrasion of ankle

●**S90.511**   Abrasion, right ankle

●**S90.512**   Abrasion, left ankle

●**S90.519**   Abrasion, unspecified ankle

●**S90.52**   Blister (nonthermal) of ankle

●**S90.521**   Blister (nonthermal), right ankle

●**S90.522**   Blister (nonthermal), left ankle

●**S90.529**   Blister (nonthermal), unspecified ankle

●**S90.54**   External constriction of ankle

●**S90.541**   External constriction, right ankle

●**S90.542**   External constriction, left ankle

●**S90.549**   External constriction, unspecified ankle

●**S90.55**   Superficial foreign body of ankle
> Splinter in the ankle

●**S90.551**   Superficial foreign body, right ankle

●**S90.552**   Superficial foreign body, left ankle

●**S90.559**   Superficial foreign body, unspecified ankle

●**S90.56**   Insect bite (nonvenomous) of ankle

●**S90.561**   Insect bite (nonvenomous), right ankle

●**S90.562**   Insect bite (nonvenomous), left ankle

●**S90.569**   Insect bite (nonvenomous), unspecified ankle

●**S90.57**   Other superficial bite of ankle
> **Excludes1**   open bite of ankle (S91.05-)

●**S90.571**   Other superficial bite of ankle, right ankle

●**S90.572**   Other superficial bite of ankle, left ankle

●**S90.579**   Other superficial bite of ankle, unspecified ankle

●**S90.8**   Other superficial injuries of foot

●**S90.81**   Abrasion of foot

●**S90.811**   Abrasion, right foot

●**S90.812**   Abrasion, left foot

●**S90.819**   Abrasion, unspecified foot

●**S90.82**   Blister (nonthermal) of foot

●**S90.821**   Blister (nonthermal), right foot

●**S90.822**   Blister (nonthermal), left foot

●**S90.829**   Blister (nonthermal), unspecified foot

●**S90.84**   External constriction of foot

●**S90.841**   External constriction, right foot

●**S90.842**   External constriction, left foot

●**S90.849**   External constriction, unspecified foot

●**S90.85**   Superficial foreign body of foot
> Splinter in the foot

●**S90.851**   Superficial foreign body, right foot

●**S90.852**   Superficial foreign body, left foot

●**S90.859**   Superficial foreign body, unspecified foot

●**S90.86**   Insect bite (nonvenomous) of foot

●**S90.861**   Insect bite (nonvenomous), right foot

●**S90.862**   Insect bite (nonvenomous), left foot

●**S90.869**   Insect bite (nonvenomous), unspecified foot

●**S90.87**   Other superficial bite of foot
> **Excludes1**   open bite of foot (S91.35-)

●**S90.871**   Other superficial bite of right foot

●**S90.872**   Other superficial bite of left foot

●**S90.879**   Other superficial bite of unspecified foot

●**S90.9**   Unspecified superficial injury of ankle, foot and toe

●**S90.91**   Unspecified superficial injury of ankle

●**S90.911**   Unspecified superficial injury of right ankle

●**S90.912**   Unspecified superficial injury of left ankle

●**S90.919**   Unspecified superficial injury of unspecified ankle

●**S90.92**   Unspecified superficial injury of foot

●**S90.921**   Unspecified superficial injury of right foot

●**S90.922**   Unspecified superficial injury of left foot

●**S90.929**   Unspecified superficial injury of unspecified foot

S90.93   Unspecified superficial injury of toes

●**S90.931**   Unspecified superficial injury of right great toe

●**S90.932**   Unspecified superficial injury of left great toe

●**S90.933**   Unspecified superficial injury of unspecified great toe

●**S90.934**   Unspecified superficial injury of right lesser toe(s)

●**S90.935**   Unspecified superficial injury of left lesser toe(s)

●**S90.936**   Unspecified superficial injury of unspecified lesser toe(s)

●**S91**   Open wound of ankle, foot and toes
> Code also any associated wound infection
> **Excludes1**   open fracture of ankle, foot and toes (S92.-with 7th character B)
> traumatic amputation of ankle and foot (S98.-)
>
> The appropriate 7th character is to be added to each code from category S91

A	initial encounter
D	subsequent encounter
S	sequela

●**S91.0**   Open wound of ankle

●**S91.00**   Unspecified open wound of ankle

●**S91.001**   Unspecified open wound, right ankle

●**S91.002**   Unspecified open wound, left ankle

●**S91.009**   Unspecified open wound, unspecified ankle

●**S91.01**   Laceration without foreign body of ankle

●**S91.011**   Laceration without foreign body, right ankle

●**S91.012**   Laceration without foreign body, left ankle

●**S91.019**   Laceration without foreign body, unspecified ankle

- S91.02   **Laceration with foreign body** of ankle
  - S91.021   Laceration with foreign body, **right ankle**
  - S91.022   Laceration with foreign body, **left ankle**
  - S91.029   Laceration with foreign body, **unspecified ankle**
- S91.03   **Puncture wound without foreign body** of ankle
  - S91.031   Puncture wound without foreign body, **right ankle**
  - S91.032   Puncture wound without foreign body, **left ankle**
  - S91.039   Puncture wound without foreign body, **unspecified ankle**
- S91.04   **Puncture wound with foreign body** of ankle
  - S91.041   Puncture wound with foreign body, **right ankle**
  - S91.042   Puncture wound with foreign body, **left ankle**
  - S91.049   Puncture wound with foreign body, **unspecified ankle**
- S91.05   **Open bite** of ankle
  - **Excludes1**   superficial bite of ankle (S90.56-, S90.57-)
  - S91.051   Open bite, **right ankle**
  - S91.052   Open bite, **left ankle**
  - S91.059   Open bite, **unspecified ankle**
- S91.1   **Open wound of toe without damage to nail**
  - S91.10   **Unspecified** open wound of toe without damage to nail
    - S91.101   Unspecified open wound of **right great toe** without damage to nail
    - S91.102   Unspecified open wound of **left great** toe without damage to nail
    - S91.103   Unspecified open wound of **unspecified great** toe without damage to nail
    - S91.104   Unspecified open wound of **right lesser** toe(s) without damage to nail
    - S91.105   Unspecified open wound of **left lesser** toe(s) without damage to nail
    - S91.106   Unspecified open wound of **unspecified lesser** toe(s) without damage to nail
    - S91.109   Unspecified open wound of **unspecified** toe(s) without damage to nail
  - S91.11   **Laceration without foreign body** of toe without damage to nail
    - S91.111   Laceration without foreign body of **right great** toe without damage to nail
    - S91.112   Laceration without foreign body of **left great** toe without damage to nail
    - S91.113   Laceration without foreign body of **unspecified great** toe without damage to nail
    - S91.114   Laceration without foreign body of **right lesser** toe(s) without damage to nail
    - S91.115   Laceration without foreign body of **left lesser** toe(s) without damage to nail
    - S91.116   Laceration without foreign body of **unspecified lesser** toe(s) without damage to nail
    - S91.119   Laceration without foreign body of **unspecified toe** without damage to nail

- S91.12   **Laceration with foreign body** of toe without damage to nail
  - S91.121   Laceration with foreign body of **right great toe** without damage to nail
  - S91.122   Laceration with foreign body of **left great toe** without damage to nail
  - S91.123   Laceration with foreign body of **unspecified great** toe without damage to nail
  - S91.124   Laceration with foreign body of **right lesser** toe(s) without damage to nail
  - S91.125   Laceration with foreign body of **left lesser** toe(s) without damage to nail
  - S91.126   Laceration with foreign body of **unspecified lesser** toe(s) without damage to nail
  - S91.129   Laceration with foreign body of **unspecified toe(s)** without damage to nail
- S91.13   **Puncture wound without foreign body** of toe without damage to nail
  - S91.131   Puncture wound without foreign body of **right great toe** without damage to nail
  - S91.132   Puncture wound without foreign body of **left great** toe without damage to nail
  - S91.133   Puncture wound without foreign body of **unspecified great** toe without damage to nail
  - S91.134   Puncture wound without foreign body of **right lesser** toe(s) without damage to nail
  - S91.135   Puncture wound without foreign body of **left lesser** toe(s) without damage to nail
  - S91.136   Puncture wound without foreign body of **unspecified lesser** toe(s) without damage to nail
  - S91.139   Puncture wound without foreign body of **unspecified** toe(s) without damage to nail
- S91.14   **Puncture wound with foreign body** of toe without damage to nail
  - S91.141   Puncture wound with foreign body of **right great toe** without damage to nail
  - S91.142   Puncture wound with foreign body of **left great toe** without damage to nail
  - S91.143   Puncture wound with foreign body of **unspecified great** toe without damage to nail
  - S91.144   Puncture wound with foreign body of **right lesser** toe(s) without damage to nail
  - S91.145   Puncture wound with foreign body of **left lesser** toe(s) without damage to nail
  - S91.146   Puncture wound with foreign body of **unspecified lesser** toe(s) without damage to nail
  - S91.149   Puncture wound with foreign body of **unspecified** toe(s) without damage to nail

▶ New   ⇒ Revised   ~~deleted~~ Deleted   Excludes 1   Excludes 2   Includes   Use additional   Code first   Code also   Key words

OGCR Official Guidelines   X Assign placeholder X   ● Use Additional Character(s)   ▷ Manifestation Code   ⦾ Hierarchical Condition Category   **Coding Clinic**

● **S91.15**   **Open bite of toe without damage to nail**
Bite of toe NOS

> **Excludes1**   superficial bite of toe (S90.46-, S90.47-)

  ● **S91.151**   Open bite of right great toe without damage to nail

  ● **S91.152**   Open bite of left great toe without damage to nail

  ● **S91.153**   Open bite of unspecified great toe without damage to nail

  ● **S91.154**   Open bite of right lesser toe(s) without damage to nail

  ● **S91.155**   Open bite of left lesser toe(s) without damage to nail

  ● **S91.156**   Open bite of unspecified lesser toe(s) without damage to nail

  ● **S91.159**   Open bite of unspecified toe(s) without damage to nail

● **S91.2**   **Open wound of toe with damage to nail**

  ● **S91.20**   Unspecified open wound of toe with damage to nail

    ● **S91.201**   Unspecified open wound of right great toe with damage to nail

    ● **S91.202**   Unspecified open wound of left great toe with damage to nail

    ● **S91.203**   Unspecified open wound of unspecified great toe with damage to nail

    ● **S91.204**   Unspecified open wound of right lesser toe(s) with damage to nail

    ● **S91.205**   Unspecified open wound of left lesser toe(s) with damage to nail

    ● **S91.206**   Unspecified open wound of unspecified lesser toe(s) with damage to nail

    ● **S91.209**   Unspecified open wound of unspecified toe(s) with damage to nail

  ● **S91.21**   Laceration without foreign body of toe with damage to nail

    ● **S91.211**   Laceration without foreign body of right great toe with damage to nail

    ● **S91.212**   Laceration without foreign body of left great toe with damage to nail

    ● **S91.213**   Laceration without foreign body of unspecified great toe with damage to nail

    ● **S91.214**   Laceration without foreign body of right lesser toe(s) with damage to nail

    ● **S91.215**   Laceration without foreign body of left lesser toe(s) with damage to nail

    ● **S91.216**   Laceration without foreign body of unspecified lesser toe(s) with damage to nail

    ● **S91.219**   Laceration without foreign body of unspecified toe(s) with damage to nail

  ● **S91.22**   Laceration with foreign body of toe with damage to nail

    ● **S91.221**   Laceration with foreign body of right great toe with damage to nail

    ● **S91.222**   Laceration with foreign body of left great toe with damage to nail

    ● **S91.223**   Laceration with foreign body of unspecified great toe with damage to nail

    ● **S91.224**   Laceration with foreign body of right lesser toe(s) with damage to nail

    ● **S91.225**   Laceration with foreign body of left lesser toe(s) with damage to nail

    ● **S91.226**   Laceration with foreign body of unspecified lesser toe(s) with damage to nail

    ● **S91.229**   Laceration with foreign body of unspecified toe(s) with damage to nail

● **S91.23**   **Puncture wound without foreign body of toe with damage to nail**

  ● **S91.231**   Puncture wound without foreign body of right great toe with damage to nail

  ● **S91.232**   Puncture wound without foreign body of left great toe with damage to nail

  ● **S91.233**   Puncture wound without foreign body of unspecified great toe with damage to nail

  ● **S91.234**   Puncture wound without foreign body of right lesser toe(s) with damage to nail

  ● **S91.235**   Puncture wound without foreign body of left lesser toe(s) with damage to nail

  ● **S91.236**   Puncture wound without foreign body of unspecified lesser toe(s) with damage to nail

  ● **S91.239**   Puncture wound without foreign body of unspecified toe(s) with damage to nail

● **S91.24**   **Puncture wound with foreign body of toe with damage to nail**

  ● **S91.241**   Puncture wound with foreign body of right great toe with damage to nail

  ● **S91.242**   Puncture wound with foreign body of left great toe with damage to nail

  ● **S91.243**   Puncture wound with foreign body of unspecified great toe with damage to nail

  ● **S91.244**   Puncture wound with foreign body of right lesser toe(s) with damage to nail

  ● **S91.245**   Puncture wound with foreign body of left lesser toe(s) with damage to nail

  ● **S91.246**   Puncture wound with foreign body of unspecified lesser toe(s) with damage to nail

  ● **S91.249**   Puncture wound with foreign body of unspecified toe(s) with damage to nail

● **S91.25**   **Open bite of toe with damage to nail**
Bite of toe with damage to nail NOS

> **Excludes1**   superficial bite of toe (S90.46-, S90.47-)

  ● **S91.251**   Open bite of right great toe with damage to nail

  ● **S91.252**   Open bite of left great toe with damage to nail

  ● **S91.253**   Open bite of unspecified great toe with damage to nail

  ● **S91.254**   Open bite of right lesser toe(s) with damage to nail

  ● **S91.255**   Open bite of left lesser toe(s) with damage to nail

  ● **S91.256**   Open bite of unspecified lesser toe(s) with damage to nail

  ● **S91.259**   Open bite of unspecified toe(s) with damage to nail

● **S91.3   Open wound of foot**
　　● **S91.30   Unspecified open wound of foot**
　　　　● S91.301   Unspecified open wound, right foot
　　　　● S91.302   Unspecified open wound, left foot
　　　　● S91.309   Unspecified open wound, unspecified foot
　　● **S91.31   Laceration without foreign body of foot**
　　　　● S91.311   Laceration without foreign body, right foot
　　　　● S91.312   Laceration without foreign body, left foot
　　　　● S91.319   Laceration without foreign body, unspecified foot
　　● **S91.32   Laceration with foreign body of foot**
　　　　● S91.321   Laceration with foreign body, right foot
　　　　● S91.322   Laceration with foreign body, left foot
　　　　● S91.329   Laceration with foreign body, unspecified foot
　　● **S91.33   Puncture wound without foreign body of foot**
　　　　● S91.331   Puncture wound without foreign body, right foot
　　　　● S91.332   Puncture wound without foreign body, left foot
　　　　● S91.339   Puncture wound without foreign body, unspecified foot
　　● **S91.34   Puncture wound with foreign body of foot**
　　　　● S91.341   Puncture wound with foreign body, right foot
　　　　● S91.342   Puncture wound with foreign body, left foot
　　　　● S91.349   Puncture wound with foreign body, unspecified foot
　　● **S91.35   Open bite of foot**
　　　　Excludes1   superficial bite of foot (S90.86-, S90.87-)
　　　　● S91.351   Open bite, right foot
　　　　● S91.352   Open bite, left foot
　　　　● S91.359   Open bite, unspecified foot

● **S92   Fracture of foot and toe, except ankle**
　　Note: A fracture not indicated as displaced or nondisplaced should be coded to displaced

　　A fracture not indicated as open or closed should be coded to closed

　　Excludes1   traumatic amputation of ankle and foot (S98.-)
　　Excludes2   fracture of ankle (S82.-)
　　　　　　　　 fracture of malleolus (S82.-)

　　The appropriate 7th character is to be added to each code from category S92

A	initial encounter for closed fracture
B	initial encounter for open fracture
D	subsequent encounter for fracture with routine healing
G	subsequent encounter for fracture with delayed healing
K	subsequent encounter for fracture with nonunion
P	subsequent encounter for fracture with malunion
S	sequela

● **S92.0   Fracture of calcaneus**
　　Heel bone   Os calcis
　　Excludes2   Physeal fracture of calcaneus (S99.0-)
　　● **S92.00   Unspecified fracture of calcaneus**
　　　　● S92.001   Unspecified fracture of right calcaneus
　　　　● S92.002   Unspecified fracture of left calcaneus
　　　　● S92.009   Unspecified fracture of unspecified calcaneus

● **S92.01   Fracture of body of calcaneus**
　　● S92.011   Displaced fracture of body of right calcaneus
　　● S92.012   Displaced fracture of body of left calcaneus
　　● S92.013   Displaced fracture of body of unspecified calcaneus
　　● S92.014   Nondisplaced fracture of body of right calcaneus
　　● S92.015   Nondisplaced fracture of body of left calcaneus
　　● S92.016   Nondisplaced fracture of body of unspecified calcaneus
● **S92.02   Fracture of anterior process of calcaneus**
　　● S92.021   Displaced fracture of anterior process of right calcaneus
　　● S92.022   Displaced fracture of anterior process of left calcaneus
　　● S92.023   Displaced fracture of anterior process of unspecified calcaneus
　　● S92.024   Nondisplaced fracture of anterior process of right calcaneus
　　● S92.025   Nondisplaced fracture of anterior process of left calcaneus
　　● S92.026   Nondisplaced fracture of anterior process of unspecified calcaneus
● **S92.03   Avulsion fracture of tuberosity of calcaneus**
　　● S92.031   Displaced avulsion fracture of tuberosity of right calcaneus
　　● S92.032   Displaced avulsion fracture of tuberosity of left calcaneus
　　● S92.033   Displaced avulsion fracture of tuberosity of unspecified calcaneus
　　● S92.034   Nondisplaced avulsion fracture of tuberosity of right calcaneus
　　● S92.035   Nondisplaced avulsion fracture of tuberosity of left calcaneus
　　● S92.036   Nondisplaced avulsion fracture of tuberosity of unspecified calcaneus
● **S92.04   Other fracture of tuberosity of calcaneus**
　　● S92.041   Displaced other fracture of tuberosity of right calcaneus
　　● S92.042   Displaced other fracture of tuberosity of left calcaneus
　　● S92.043   Displaced other fracture of tuberosity of unspecified calcaneus
　　● S92.044   Nondisplaced other fracture of tuberosity of right calcaneus
　　● S92.045   Nondisplaced other fracture of tuberosity of left calcaneus
　　● S92.046   Nondisplaced other fracture of tuberosity of unspecified calcaneus
● **S92.05   Other extraarticular fracture of calcaneus**
　　● S92.051   Displaced other extraarticular fracture of right calcaneus
　　● S92.052   Displaced other extraarticular fracture of left calcaneus
　　● S92.053   Displaced other extraarticular fracture of unspecified calcaneus
　　● S92.054   Nondisplaced other extraarticular fracture of right calcaneus
　　● S92.055   Nondisplaced other extraarticular fracture of left calcaneus
　　● S92.056   Nondisplaced other extraarticular fracture of unspecified calcaneus

▶ New　　⇒ Revised　　~~deleted~~ Deleted　　Excludes 1　　Excludes 2　　Includes　　Use additional　　Code first　　Code also　　Key words

OGCR Official Guidelines　　X Assign placeholder X　　● Use Additional Character(s)　　▷ Manifestation Code　　🅠 Hierarchical Condition Category　　**Coding Clinic**

● **S92.06**   Intraarticular fracture of calcaneus
    ● **S92.061**   Displaced intraarticular fracture of right calcaneus
    ● **S92.062**   Displaced intraarticular fracture of left calcaneus
    ● **S92.063**   Displaced intraarticular fracture of unspecified calcaneus
    ● **S92.064**   Nondisplaced intraarticular fracture of right calcaneus
    ● **S92.065**   Nondisplaced intraarticular fracture of left calcaneus
    ● **S92.066**   Nondisplaced intraarticular fracture of unspecified calcaneus
● **S92.1**   Fracture of talus
    Astragalus
    ● **S92.10**   Unspecified fracture of talus
      ● **S92.101**   Unspecified fracture of right talus
      ● **S92.102**   Unspecified fracture of left talus
      ● **S92.109**   Unspecified fracture of unspecified talus
    ● **S92.11**   Fracture of neck of talus
      ● **S92.111**   Displaced fracture of neck of right talus
      ● **S92.112**   Displaced fracture of neck of left talus
      ● **S92.113**   Displaced fracture of neck of unspecified talus
      ● **S92.114**   Nondisplaced fracture of neck of right talus
      ● **S92.115**   Nondisplaced fracture of neck of left talus
      ● **S92.116**   Nondisplaced fracture of neck of unspecified talus
    ● **S92.12**   Fracture of body of talus
      ● **S92.121**   Displaced fracture of body of right talus
      ● **S92.122**   Displaced fracture of body of left talus
      ● **S92.123**   Displaced fracture of body of unspecified talus
      ● **S92.124**   Nondisplaced fracture of body of right talus
      ● **S92.125**   Nondisplaced fracture of body of left talus
      ● **S92.126**   Nondisplaced fracture of body of unspecified talus
    ● **S92.13**   Fracture of posterior process of talus
      ● **S92.131**   Displaced fracture of posterior process of right talus
      ● **S92.132**   Displaced fracture of posterior process of left talus
      ● **S92.133**   Displaced fracture of posterior process of unspecified talus
      ● **S92.134**   Nondisplaced fracture of posterior process of right talus
      ● **S92.135**   Nondisplaced fracture of posterior process of left talus
      ● **S92.136**   Nondisplaced fracture of posterior process of unspecified talus
    ● **S92.14**   Dome fracture of talus
      Excludes1   osteochondritis dissecans (M93.2)
      ● **S92.141**   Displaced dome fracture of right talus
      ● **S92.142**   Displaced dome fracture of left talus
      ● **S92.143**   Displaced dome fracture of unspecified talus
      ● **S92.144**   Nondisplaced dome fracture of right talus

      ● **S92.145**   Nondisplaced dome fracture of left talus
      ● **S92.146**   Nondisplaced dome fracture of unspecified talus
    ● **S92.15**   Avulsion fracture (chip fracture) of talus
      ● **S92.151**   Displaced avulsion fracture (chip fracture) of right talus
      ● **S92.152**   Displaced avulsion fracture (chip fracture) of left talus
      ● **S92.153**   Displaced avulsion fracture (chip fracture) of unspecified talus
      ● **S92.154**   Nondisplaced avulsion fracture (chip fracture) of right talus
      ● **S92.155**   Nondisplaced avulsion fracture (chip fracture) of left talus
      ● **S92.156**   Nondisplaced avulsion fracture (chip fracture) of unspecified talus
    ● **S92.19**   Other fracture of talus
      ● **S92.191**   Other fracture of right talus
      ● **S92.192**   Other fracture of left talus
      ● **S92.199**   Other fracture of unspecified talus
● **S92.2**   Fracture of other and unspecified tarsal bone(s)
    ● **S92.20**   Fracture of unspecified tarsal bone(s)
      ● **S92.201**   Fracture of unspecified tarsal bone(s) of right foot
      ● **S92.202**   Fracture of unspecified tarsal bone(s) of left foot
      ● **S92.209**   Fracture of unspecified tarsal bone(s) of unspecified foot
    ● **S92.21**   Fracture of cuboid bone
      ● **S92.211**   Displaced fracture of cuboid bone of right foot
      ● **S92.212**   Displaced fracture of cuboid bone of left foot
      ● **S92.213**   Displaced fracture of cuboid bone of unspecified foot
      ● **S92.214**   Nondisplaced fracture of cuboid bone of right foot
      ● **S92.215**   Nondisplaced fracture of cuboid bone of left foot
      ● **S92.216**   Nondisplaced fracture of cuboid bone of unspecified foot
    ● **S92.22**   Fracture of lateral cuneiform
      ● **S92.221**   Displaced fracture of lateral cuneiform of right foot
      ● **S92.222**   Displaced fracture of lateral cuneiform of left foot
      ● **S92.223**   Displaced fracture of lateral cuneiform of unspecified foot
      ● **S92.224**   Nondisplaced fracture of lateral cuneiform of right foot
      ● **S92.225**   Nondisplaced fracture of lateral cuneiform of left foot
      ● **S92.226**   Nondisplaced fracture of lateral cuneiform of unspecified foot
    ● **S92.23**   Fracture of intermediate cuneiform
      ● **S92.231**   Displaced fracture of intermediate cuneiform of right foot
      ● **S92.232**   Displaced fracture of intermediate cuneiform of left foot
      ● **S92.233**   Displaced fracture of intermediate cuneiform of unspecified foot
      ● **S92.234**   Nondisplaced fracture of intermediate cuneiform of right foot
      ● **S92.235**   Nondisplaced fracture of intermediate cuneiform of left foot
      ● **S92.236**   Nondisplaced fracture of intermediate cuneiform of unspecified foot

- S92.24   Fracture of medial cuneiform
  - S92.241   Displaced fracture of medial cuneiform of right foot
  - S92.242   Displaced fracture of medial cuneiform of left foot
  - S92.243   Displaced fracture of medial cuneiform of unspecified foot
  - S92.244   Nondisplaced fracture of medial cuneiform of right foot
  - S92.245   Nondisplaced fracture of medial cuneiform of left foot
  - S92.246   Nondisplaced fracture of medial cuneiform of unspecified foot
- S92.25   Fracture of navicular [scaphoid] of foot
  - S92.251   Displaced fracture of navicular [scaphoid] of right foot
  - S92.252   Displaced fracture of navicular [scaphoid] of left foot
  - S92.253   Displaced fracture of navicular [scaphoid] unspecified foot
  - S92.254   Nondisplaced fracture of navicular [scaphoid] of right foot
  - S92.255   Nondisplaced fracture of navicular [scaphoid] of left foot
  - S92.256   Nondisplaced fracture of navicular [scaphoid] of unspecified foot

- S92.3   Fracture of metatarsal bone(s)
  - **Excludes2**   Physeal fracture of metatarsal (S99.1-)
  - S92.30   Fracture of unspecified metatarsal bone(s)
    - S92.301   Fracture of unspecified metatarsal bone(s), right foot
    - S92.302   Fracture of unspecified metatarsal bone(s), left foot
    - S92.309   Fracture of unspecified metatarsal bone(s), unspecified foot
  - S92.31   Fracture of first metatarsal bone
    - S92.311   Displaced fracture of first metatarsal bone, right foot
    - S92.312   Displaced fracture of first metatarsal bone, left foot
    - S92.313   Displaced fracture of first metatarsal bone, unspecified foot
    - S92.314   Nondisplaced fracture of first metatarsal bone, right foot
    - S92.315   Nondisplaced fracture of first metatarsal bone, left foot
    - S92.316   Nondisplaced fracture of first metatarsal bone, unspecified foot
  - S92.32   Fracture of second metatarsal bone
    - S92.321   Displaced fracture of second metatarsal bone, right foot
    - S92.322   Displaced fracture of second metatarsal bone, left foot
    - S92.323   Displaced fracture of second metatarsal bone, unspecified foot
    - S92.324   Nondisplaced fracture of second metatarsal bone, right foot
    - S92.325   Nondisplaced fracture of second metatarsal bone, left foot
    - S92.326   Nondisplaced fracture of second metatarsal bone, unspecified foot

- S92.33   Fracture of third metatarsal bone
  Coding Clinic: 2018, Q1, P3
  - S92.331   Displaced fracture of third metatarsal bone, right foot
  - S92.332   Displaced fracture of third metatarsal bone, left foot
  - S92.333   Displaced fracture of third metatarsal bone, unspecified foot
  - S92.334   Nondisplaced fracture of third metatarsal bone, right foot
  - S92.335   Nondisplaced fracture of third metatarsal bone, left foot
  - S92.336   Nondisplaced fracture of third metatarsal bone, unspecified foot
- S92.34   Fracture of fourth metatarsal bone
  - S92.341   Displaced fracture of fourth metatarsal bone, right foot
  - S92.342   Displaced fracture of fourth metatarsal bone, left foot
  - S92.343   Displaced fracture of fourth metatarsal bone, unspecified foot
  - S92.344   Nondisplaced fracture of fourth metatarsal bone, right foot
  - S92.345   Nondisplaced fracture of fourth metatarsal bone, left foot
  - S92.346   Nondisplaced fracture of fourth metatarsal bone, unspecified foot
- S92.35   Fracture of fifth metatarsal bone
  - S92.351   Displaced fracture of fifth metatarsal bone, right foot
  - S92.352   Displaced fracture of fifth metatarsal bone, left foot
  - S92.353   Displaced fracture of fifth metatarsal bone, unspecified foot
  - S92.354   Nondisplaced fracture of fifth metatarsal bone, right foot
  - S92.355   Nondisplaced fracture of fifth metatarsal bone, left foot
  - S92.356   Nondisplaced fracture of fifth metatarsal bone, unspecified foot

- S92.4   Fracture of great toe
  - **Excludes2**   Physeal fracture of phalanx of toe (S99.2-)
  - S92.40   Unspecified fracture of great toe
    - S92.401   Displaced unspecified fracture of right great toe
    - S92.402   Displaced unspecified fracture of left great toe
    - S92.403   Displaced unspecified fracture of unspecified great toe
    - S92.404   Nondisplaced unspecified fracture of right great toe
    - S92.405   Nondisplaced unspecified fracture of left great toe
    - S92.406   Nondisplaced unspecified fracture of unspecified great toe
  - S92.41   Fracture of proximal phalanx of great toe
    - S92.411   Displaced fracture of proximal phalanx of right great toe
    - S92.412   Displaced fracture of proximal phalanx of left great toe
    - S92.413   Displaced fracture of proximal phalanx of unspecified great toe
    - S92.414   Nondisplaced fracture of proximal phalanx of right great toe
    - S92.415   Nondisplaced fracture of proximal phalanx of left great toe
    - S92.416   Nondisplaced fracture of proximal phalanx of unspecified great toe

▶ New   ⟹ Revised   ~~deleted~~ Deleted   Excludes 1   Excludes 2   Includes   Use additional   Code first   Code also   Key words
OGCR Official Guidelines   X Assign placeholder X   ● Use Additional Character(s)   ▶ Manifestation Code   🔖 Hierarchical Condition Category   Coding Clinic

● S92.42　Fracture of distal phalanx of great toe
　● S92.421　Displaced fracture of distal phalanx of right great toe
　● S92.422　Displaced fracture of distal phalanx of left great toe
　● S92.423　Displaced fracture of distal phalanx of unspecified great toe
　● S92.424　Nondisplaced fracture of distal phalanx of right great toe
　● S92.425　Nondisplaced fracture of distal phalanx of left great toe
　● S92.426　Nondisplaced fracture of distal phalanx of unspecified great toe
● S92.49　Other fracture of great toe
　● S92.491　Other fracture of right great toe
　● S92.492　Other fracture of left great toe
　● S92.499　Other fracture of unspecified great toe
● S92.5　Fracture of lesser toe(s)
　　Excludes2　Physeal fracture of phalanx of toe (S99.2-)
　● S92.50　Unspecified fracture of lesser toe(s)
　　● S92.501　Displaced unspecified fracture of right lesser toe(s)
　　● S92.502　Displaced unspecified fracture of left lesser toe(s)
　　● S92.503　Displaced unspecified fracture of unspecified lesser toe(s)
　　● S92.504　Nondisplaced unspecified fracture of right lesser toe(s)
　　● S92.505　Nondisplaced unspecified fracture of left lesser toe(s)
　　● S92.506　Nondisplaced unspecified fracture of unspecified lesser toe(s)
　● S92.51　Fracture of proximal phalanx of lesser toe(s)
　　● S92.511　Displaced fracture of proximal phalanx of right lesser toe(s)
　　● S92.512　Displaced fracture of proximal phalanx of left lesser toe(s)
　　● S92.513　Displaced fracture of proximal phalanx of unspecified lesser toe(s)
　　● S92.514　Nondisplaced fracture of proximal phalanx of right lesser toe(s)
　　● S92.515　Nondisplaced fracture of proximal phalanx of left lesser toe(s)
　　● S92.516　Nondisplaced fracture of proximal phalanx of unspecified lesser toe(s)
　● S92.52　Fracture of middle phalanx of lesser toe(s)
　　● S92.521　Displaced fracture of middle phalanx of right lesser toe(s)
　　● S92.522　Displaced fracture of middle phalanx of left lesser toe(s)
　　● S92.523　Displaced fracture of middle phalanx of unspecified lesser toe(s)
　　● S92.524　Nondisplaced fracture of middle phalanx of right lesser toe(s)
　　● S92.525　Nondisplaced fracture of middle phalanx of left lesser toe(s)
　　● S92.526　Nondisplaced fracture of middle phalanx of unspecified lesser toe(s)
　● S92.53　Fracture of distal phalanx of lesser toe(s)
　　● S92.531　Displaced fracture of distal phalanx of right lesser toe(s)
　　● S92.532　Displaced fracture of distal phalanx of left lesser toe(s)
　　● S92.533　Displaced fracture of distal phalanx of unspecified lesser toe(s)

　　● S92.534　Nondisplaced fracture of distal phalanx of right lesser toe(s)
　　● S92.535　Nondisplaced fracture of distal phalanx of left lesser toe(s)
　　● S92.536　Nondisplaced fracture of distal phalanx of unspecified lesser toe(s)
　● S92.59　Other fracture of lesser toe(s)
　　● S92.591　Other fracture of right lesser toe(s)
　　● S92.592　Other fracture of left lesser toe(s)
　　● S92.599　Other fracture of unspecified lesser toe(s)
● S92.8　Other fracture of foot, except ankle
　● S92.81　Other fracture of foot
　　　Sesamoid fracture of foot
　　　Coding Clinic: 2016, Q4, P68
　　● S92.811　Other fracture of right foot
　　● S92.812　Other fracture of left foot
　　● S92.819　Other fracture of unspecified foot
● S92.9　Unspecified fracture of foot and toe
　● S92.90　Unspecified fracture of foot
　　● S92.901　Unspecified fracture of right foot
　　● S92.902　Unspecified fracture of left foot
　　● S92.909　Unspecified fracture of unspecified foot
　● S92.91　Unspecified fracture of toe
　　● S92.911　Unspecified fracture of right toe(s)
　　● S92.912　Unspecified fracture of left toe(s)
　　● S92.919　Unspecified fracture of unspecified toe(s)

● S93　Dislocation and sprain of joints and ligaments at ankle, foot and toe level
　　Includes　avulsion of joint or ligament of ankle, foot and toe
　　　　　　　laceration of cartilage, joint or ligament of ankle, foot and toe
　　　　　　　sprain of cartilage, joint or ligament of ankle, foot and toe
　　　　　　　traumatic hemarthrosis of joint or ligament of ankle, foot and toe
　　　　　　　traumatic rupture of joint or ligament of ankle, foot and toe
　　　　　　　traumatic subluxation of joint or ligament of ankle, foot and toe
　　　　　　　traumatic tear of joint or ligament of ankle, foot and toe
　　Code also any associated open wound
　　Excludes2　strain of muscle and tendon of ankle and foot (S96.-)
　　The appropriate 7th character is to be added to each code from category S93

　　　┌─────────────────────────────┐
　　　│ A　initial encounter   │
　　　│ D　subsequent encounter   │
　　　│ S　sequela   │
　　　└─────────────────────────────┘

● S93.0　Subluxation and dislocation of ankle joint
　　　Subluxation and dislocation of astragalus
　　　Subluxation and dislocation of fibula, lower end
　　　Subluxation and dislocation of talus
　　　Subluxation and dislocation of tibia, lower end
　X● S93.01　Subluxation of right ankle joint
　X● S93.02　Subluxation of left ankle joint
　X● S93.03　Subluxation of unspecified ankle joint
　X● S93.04　Dislocation of right ankle joint
　X● S93.05　Dislocation of left ankle joint
　X● S93.06　Dislocation of unspecified ankle joint

● **S93.1**   **Subluxation and dislocation of toe**
   ● **S93.10**   **Unspecified subluxation and dislocation of toe**
          Dislocation of toe NOS
          Subluxation of toe NOS
      ● **S93.101**   Unspecified subluxation of right toe(s)
      ● **S93.102**   Unspecified subluxation of left toe(s)
      ● **S93.103**   Unspecified subluxation of unspecified toe(s)
      ● **S93.104**   Unspecified dislocation of right toe(s)
      ● **S93.105**   Unspecified dislocation of left toe(s)
      ● **S93.106**   Unspecified dislocation of unspecified toe(s)

   ● **S93.11**   **Dislocation of interphalangeal joint**
      ● **S93.111**   Dislocation of interphalangeal joint of right great toe
      ● **S93.112**   Dislocation of interphalangeal joint of left great toe
      ● **S93.113**   Dislocation of interphalangeal joint of unspecified great toe
      ● **S93.114**   Dislocation of interphalangeal joint of right lesser toe(s)
      ● **S93.115**   Dislocation of interphalangeal joint of left lesser toe(s)
      ● **S93.116**   Dislocation of interphalangeal joint of unspecified lesser toe(s)
      ● **S93.119**   Dislocation of interphalangeal joint of unspecified toe(s)

   ● **S93.12**   **Dislocation of metatarsophalangeal joint**
      ● **S93.121**   Dislocation of metatarsophalangeal joint of right great toe
      ● **S93.122**   Dislocation of metatarsophalangeal joint of left great toe
      ● **S93.123**   Dislocation of metatarsophalangeal joint of unspecified great toe
      ● **S93.124**   Dislocation of metatarsophalangeal joint of right lesser toe(s)
      ● **S93.125**   Dislocation of metatarsophalangeal joint of left lesser toe(s)
      ● **S93.126**   Dislocation of metatarsophalangeal joint of unspecified lesser toe(s)
      ● **S93.129**   Dislocation of metatarsophalangeal joint of unspecified toe(s)

   ● **S93.13**   **Subluxation of interphalangeal joint**
      ● **S93.131**   Subluxation of interphalangeal joint of right great toe
      ● **S93.132**   Subluxation of interphalangeal joint of left great toe
      ● **S93.133**   Subluxation of interphalangeal joint of unspecified great toe
      ● **S93.134**   Subluxation of interphalangeal joint of right lesser toe(s)
      ● **S93.135**   Subluxation of interphalangeal joint of left lesser toe(s)
      ● **S93.136**   Subluxation of interphalangeal joint of unspecified lesser toe(s)
      ● **S93.139**   Subluxation of interphalangeal joint of unspecified toe(s)

   ● **S93.14**   **Subluxation of metatarsophalangeal joint**
      ● **S93.141**   Subluxation of metatarsophalangeal joint of right great toe
      ● **S93.142**   Subluxation of metatarsophalangeal joint of left great toe
      ● **S93.143**   Subluxation of metatarsophalangeal joint of unspecified great toe
      ● **S93.144**   Subluxation of metatarsophalangeal joint of right lesser toe(s)
      ● **S93.145**   Subluxation of metatarsophalangeal joint of left lesser toe(s)
      ● **S93.146**   Subluxation of metatarsophalangeal joint of unspecified lesser toe(s)
      ● **S93.149**   Subluxation of metatarsophalangeal joint of unspecified toe(s)

● **S93.3**   **Subluxation and dislocation of foot**
    Excludes2   dislocation of toe (S93.1-)
   ● **S93.30**   **Unspecified subluxation and dislocation of foot**
          Dislocation of foot NOS
          Subluxation of foot NOS
      ● **S93.301**   Unspecified subluxation of right foot
      ● **S93.302**   Unspecified subluxation of left foot
      ● **S93.303**   Unspecified subluxation of unspecified foot
      ● **S93.304**   Unspecified dislocation of right foot
      ● **S93.305**   Unspecified dislocation of left foot
      ● **S93.306**   Unspecified dislocation of unspecified foot

   ● **S93.31**   **Subluxation and dislocation of tarsal joint**
      ● **S93.311**   Subluxation of tarsal joint of right foot
      ● **S93.312**   Subluxation of tarsal joint of left foot
      ● **S93.313**   Subluxation of tarsal joint of unspecified foot
      ● **S93.314**   Dislocation of tarsal joint of right foot
      ● **S93.315**   Dislocation of tarsal joint of left foot
      ● **S93.316**   Dislocation of tarsal joint of unspecified foot

   ● **S93.32**   **Subluxation and dislocation of tarsometatarsal joint**
      ● **S93.321**   Subluxation of tarsometatarsal joint of right foot
      ● **S93.322**   Subluxation of tarsometatarsal joint of left foot
      ● **S93.323**   Subluxation of tarsometatarsal joint of unspecified foot
      ● **S93.324**   Dislocation of tarsometatarsal joint of right foot
      ● **S93.325**   Dislocation of tarsometatarsal joint of left foot
      ● **S93.326**   Dislocation of tarsometatarsal joint of unspecified foot

   ● **S93.33**   **Other subluxation and dislocation of foot**
      ● **S93.331**   Other subluxation of right foot
      ● **S93.332**   Other subluxation of left foot
      ● **S93.333**   Other subluxation of unspecified foot
      ● **S93.334**   Other dislocation of right foot
      ● **S93.335**   Other dislocation of left foot
      ● **S93.336**   Other dislocation of unspecified foot

● **S93.4**   **Sprain of ankle**
    Injury to ligaments when one or more is stretched/torn
    Excludes2   injury of Achilles tendon (S86.0-)
   ● **S93.40**   **Sprain of unspecified ligament of ankle**
          Sprain of ankle NOS
          Sprained ankle NOS
      ● **S93.401**   Sprain of unspecified ligament of right ankle
      ● **S93.402**   Sprain of unspecified ligament of left ankle
      ● **S93.409**   Sprain of unspecified ligament of unspecified ankle

   ● **S93.41**   **Sprain of calcaneofibular ligament**
      ● **S93.411**   Sprain of calcaneofibular ligament of right ankle
      ● **S93.412**   Sprain of calcaneofibular ligament of left ankle
      ● **S93.419**   Sprain of calcaneofibular ligament of unspecified ankle

---

▶ New   ⇒ Revised   ~~deleted~~ Deleted   Excludes 1   Excludes 2   Includes   Use additional   Code first   Code also   Key words

   OGCR Official Guidelines   X Assign placeholder X   ● Use Additional Character(s)   ▷ Manifestation Code   ⊕ Hierarchical Condition Category   **Coding Clinic**

● S93.42   Sprain of deltoid ligament
   ● S93.421   Sprain of deltoid ligament of right ankle
   ● S93.422   Sprain of deltoid ligament of left ankle
   ● S93.429   Sprain of deltoid ligament of unspecified ankle
● S93.43   Sprain of tibiofibular ligament
   ● S93.431   Sprain of tibiofibular ligament of right ankle
   ● S93.432   Sprain of tibiofibular ligament of left ankle
   ● S93.439   Sprain of tibiofibular ligament of unspecified ankle
● S93.49   Sprain of other ligament of ankle
   Sprain of internal collateral ligament
   Sprain of talofibular ligament
   ● S93.491   Sprain of other ligament of right ankle
   ● S93.492   Sprain of other ligament of left ankle
   ● S93.499   Sprain of other ligament of unspecified ankle

● S93.5   Sprain of toe
  ● S93.50   Unspecified sprain of toe
   ● S93.501   Unspecified sprain of right great toe
   ● S93.502   Unspecified sprain of left great toe
   ● S93.503   Unspecified sprain of unspecified great toe
   ● S93.504   Unspecified sprain of right lesser toe(s)
   ● S93.505   Unspecified sprain of left lesser toe(s)
   ● S93.506   Unspecified sprain of unspecified lesser toe(s)
   ● S93.509   Unspecified sprain of unspecified toe(s)
  ● S93.51   Sprain of interphalangeal joint of toe
   ● S93.511   Sprain of interphalangeal joint of right great toe
   ● S93.512   Sprain of interphalangeal joint of left great toe
   ● S93.513   Sprain of interphalangeal joint of unspecified great toe
   ● S93.514   Sprain of interphalangeal joint of right lesser toe(s)
   ● S93.515   Sprain of interphalangeal joint of left lesser toe(s)
   ● S93.516   Sprain of interphalangeal joint of unspecified lesser toe(s)
   ● S93.519   Sprain of interphalangeal joint of unspecified toe(s)
  ● S93.52   Sprain of metatarsophalangeal joint of toe
   ● S93.521   Sprain of metatarsophalangeal joint of right great toe
   ● S93.522   Sprain of metatarsophalangeal joint of left great toe
   ● S93.523   Sprain of metatarsophalangeal joint of unspecified great toe
   ● S93.524   Sprain of metatarsophalangeal joint of right lesser toe(s)
   ● S93.525   Sprain of metatarsophalangeal joint of left lesser toe(s)
   ● S93.526   Sprain of metatarsophalangeal joint of unspecified lesser toe(s)
   ● S93.529   Sprain of metatarsophalangeal joint of unspecified toe(s)

● S93.6   Sprain of foot
   Excludes2   sprain of metatarsophalangeal joint of toe (S93.52-)
                sprain of toe (S93.5-)
  ● S93.60   Unspecified sprain of foot
   ● S93.601   Unspecified sprain of right foot
   ● S93.602   Unspecified sprain of left foot
   ● S93.609   Unspecified sprain of unspecified foot
  ● S93.61   Sprain of tarsal ligament of foot
   ● S93.611   Sprain of tarsal ligament of right foot
   ● S93.612   Sprain of tarsal ligament of left foot
   ● S93.619   Sprain of tarsal ligament of unspecified foot
  ● S93.62   Sprain of tarsometatarsal ligament of foot
   ● S93.621   Sprain of tarsometatarsal ligament of right foot
   ● S93.622   Sprain of tarsometatarsal ligament of left foot
   ● S93.629   Sprain of tarsometatarsal ligament of unspecified foot
  ● S93.69   Other sprain of foot
   ● S93.691   Other sprain of right foot
   ● S93.692   Other sprain of left foot
   ● S93.699   Other sprain of unspecified foot

● **S94**   Injury of nerves at ankle and foot level
   The appropriate 7th character is to be added to each code from category S94

> A   initial encounter
> D   subsequent encounter
> S   sequela

   Code also any associated open wound (S91.-)
● S94.0   Injury of lateral plantar nerve
  X ● S94.00   Injury of lateral plantar nerve, unspecified leg
  X ● S94.01   Injury of lateral plantar nerve, right leg
  X ● S94.02   Injury of lateral plantar nerve, left leg
● S94.1   Injury of medial plantar nerve
  X ● S94.10   Injury of medial plantar nerve, unspecified leg
  X ● S94.11   Injury of medial plantar nerve, right leg
  X ● S94.12   Injury of medial plantar nerve, left leg
● S94.2   Injury of deep peroneal nerve at ankle and foot level
   Injury of terminal, lateral branch of deep peroneal nerve
  X ● S94.20   Injury of deep peroneal nerve at ankle and foot level, unspecified leg
  X ● S94.21   Injury of deep peroneal nerve at ankle and foot level, right leg
  X ● S94.22   Injury of deep peroneal nerve at ankle and foot level, left leg
● S94.3   Injury of cutaneous sensory nerve at ankle and foot level
  X ● S94.30   Injury of cutaneous sensory nerve at ankle and foot level, unspecified leg
  X ● S94.31   Injury of cutaneous sensory nerve at ankle and foot level, right leg
  X ● S94.32   Injury of cutaneous sensory nerve at ankle and foot level, left leg
● S94.8   Injury of other nerves at ankle and foot level
  ● S94.8X   Injury of other nerves at ankle and foot level
   ● S94.8X1   Injury of other nerves at ankle and foot level, right leg
   ● S94.8X2   Injury of other nerves at ankle and foot level, left leg
   ● S94.8X9   Injury of other nerves at ankle and foot level, unspecified leg

CHAPTER 19 (S00–T88)

● **S94.9**   Injury of unspecified nerve at ankle and foot level

    X ● **S94.90**   Injury of unspecified nerve at ankle and foot level, unspecified leg

    X ● **S94.91**   Injury of unspecified nerve at ankle and foot level, right leg

    X ● **S94.92**   Injury of unspecified nerve at ankle and foot level, left leg

● **S95**   Injury of blood vessels at ankle and foot level

    Code also any associated open wound (S91.-)

    Excludes2   injury of posterior tibial artery and vein (S85.1-, S85.8-)

    The appropriate 7th character is to be added to each code from category S95

> A   initial encounter
> D   subsequent encounter
> S   sequela

● **S95.0**   Injury of dorsal artery of foot

    ● **S95.00**   Unspecified injury of dorsal artery of foot

      ● **S95.001**   Unspecified injury of dorsal artery of right foot

      ● **S95.002**   Unspecified injury of dorsal artery of left foot

      ● **S95.009**   Unspecified injury of dorsal artery of unspecified foot

    ● **S95.01**   Laceration of dorsal artery of foot

      ● **S95.011**   Laceration of dorsal artery of right foot

      ● **S95.012**   Laceration of dorsal artery of left foot

      ● **S95.019**   Laceration of dorsal artery of unspecified foot

    ● **S95.09**   Other specified injury of dorsal artery of foot

      ● **S95.091**   Other specified injury of dorsal artery of right foot

      ● **S95.092**   Other specified injury of dorsal artery of left foot

      ● **S95.099**   Other specified injury of dorsal artery of unspecified foot

● **S95.1**   Injury of plantar artery of foot

    ● **S95.10**   Unspecified injury of plantar artery of foot

      ● **S95.101**   Unspecified injury of plantar artery of right foot

      ● **S95.102**   Unspecified injury of plantar artery of left foot

      ● **S95.109**   Unspecified injury of plantar artery of unspecified foot

    ● **S95.11**   Laceration of plantar artery of foot

      ● **S95.111**   Laceration of plantar artery of right foot

      ● **S95.112**   Laceration of plantar artery of left foot

      ● **S95.119**   Laceration of plantar artery of unspecified foot

    ● **S95.19**   Other specified injury of plantar artery of foot

      ● **S95.191**   Other specified injury of plantar artery of right foot

      ● **S95.192**   Other specified injury of plantar artery of left foot

      ● **S95.199**   Other specified injury of plantar artery of unspecified foot

● **S95.2**   Injury of dorsal vein of foot

    ● **S95.20**   Unspecified injury of dorsal vein of foot

      ● **S95.201**   Unspecified injury of dorsal vein of right foot

      ● **S95.202**   Unspecified injury of dorsal vein of left foot

      ● **S95.209**   Unspecified injury of dorsal vein of unspecified foot

    ● **S95.21**   Laceration of dorsal vein of foot

      ● **S95.211**   Laceration of dorsal vein of right foot

      ● **S95.212**   Laceration of dorsal vein of left foot

      ● **S95.219**   Laceration of dorsal vein of unspecified foot

    ● **S95.29**   Other specified injury of dorsal vein of foot

      ● **S95.291**   Other specified injury of dorsal vein of right foot

      ● **S95.292**   Other specified injury of dorsal vein of left foot

      ● **S95.299**   Other specified injury of dorsal vein of unspecified foot

● **S95.8**   Injury of other blood vessels at ankle and foot level

    ● **S95.80**   Unspecified injury of other blood vessels at ankle and foot level

      ● **S95.801**   Unspecified injury of other blood vessels at ankle and foot level, right leg

      ● **S95.802**   Unspecified injury of other blood vessels at ankle and foot level, left leg

      ● **S95.809**   Unspecified injury of other blood vessels at ankle and foot level, unspecified leg

    ● **S95.81**   Laceration of other blood vessels at ankle and foot level

      ● **S95.811**   Laceration of other blood vessels at ankle and foot level, right leg

      ● **S95.812**   Laceration of other blood vessels at ankle and foot level, left leg

      ● **S95.819**   Laceration of other blood vessels at ankle and foot level, unspecified leg

    ● **S95.89**   Other specified injury of other blood vessels at ankle and foot level

      ● **S95.891**   Other specified injury of other blood vessels at ankle and foot level, right leg

      ● **S95.892**   Other specified injury of other blood vessels at ankle and foot level, left leg

      ● **S95.899**   Other specified injury of other blood vessels at ankle and foot level, unspecified leg

● **S95.9**   Injury of unspecified blood vessel at ankle and foot level

    ● **S95.90**   Unspecified injury of unspecified blood vessel at ankle and foot level

      ● **S95.901**   Unspecified injury of unspecified blood vessel at ankle and foot level, right leg

      ● **S95.902**   Unspecified injury of unspecified blood vessel at ankle and foot level, left leg

      ● **S95.909**   Unspecified injury of unspecified blood vessel at ankle and foot level, unspecified leg

▶ New   ⇒ Revised   ~~deleted~~ Deleted   Excludes 1   Excludes 2   Includes   Use additional   Code first   Code also   Key words

1366   OGCR Official Guidelines   X Assign placeholder X   ● Use Additional Character(s)   ▶ Manifestation Code   ⓠ Hierarchical Condition Category   **Coding Clinic**

● **S95.91**   Laceration of unspecified blood vessel at ankle and foot level

  ● **S95.911**   Laceration of unspecified blood vessel at ankle and foot level, right leg

  ● **S95.912**   Laceration of unspecified blood vessel at ankle and foot level, left leg

  ● **S95.919**   Laceration of unspecified blood vessel at ankle and foot level, unspecified leg

● **S95.99**   Other specified injury of unspecified blood vessel at ankle and foot level

  ● **S95.991**   Other specified injury of unspecified blood vessel at ankle and foot level, right leg

  ● **S95.992**   Other specified injury of unspecified blood vessel at ankle and foot level, left leg

  ● **S95.999**   Other specified injury of unspecified blood vessel at ankle and foot level, unspecified leg

● **S96**   **Injury of muscle and tendon at ankle and foot level**

  Code also any associated open wound (S91.-)

  Excludes2   injury of Achilles tendon (S86.0-)
                 sprain of joints and ligaments of ankle and foot (S93.-)

  The appropriate 7th character is to be added to each code from category S96

A	initial encounter
D	subsequent encounter
S	sequela

● **S96.0**   Injury of muscle and tendon of long flexor muscle of toe at ankle and foot level

  ● **S96.00**   Unspecified injury of muscle and tendon of long flexor muscle of toe at ankle and foot level

    ● **S96.001**   Unspecified injury of muscle and tendon of long flexor muscle of toe at ankle and foot level, right foot

    ● **S96.002**   Unspecified injury of muscle and tendon of long flexor muscle of toe at ankle and foot level, left foot

    ● **S96.009**   Unspecified injury of muscle and tendon of long flexor muscle of toe at ankle and foot level, unspecified foot

  ● **S96.01**   Strain of muscle and tendon of long flexor muscle of toe at ankle and foot level

    ● **S96.011**   Strain of muscle and tendon of long flexor muscle of toe at ankle and foot level, right foot

    ● **S96.012**   Strain of muscle and tendon of long flexor muscle of toe at ankle and foot level, left foot

    ● **S96.019**   Strain of muscle and tendon of long flexor muscle of toe at ankle and foot level, unspecified foot

  ● **S96.02**   Laceration of muscle and tendon of long flexor muscle of toe at ankle and foot level

    ● **S96.021**   Laceration of muscle and tendon of long flexor muscle of toe at ankle and foot level, right foot

    ● **S96.022**   Laceration of muscle and tendon of long flexor muscle of toe at ankle and foot level, left foot

    ● **S96.029**   Laceration of muscle and tendon of long flexor muscle of toe at ankle and foot level, unspecified foot

● **S96.09**   Other injury of muscle and tendon of long flexor muscle of toe at ankle and foot level

  ● **S96.091**   Other injury of muscle and tendon of long flexor muscle of toe at ankle and foot level, right foot

  ● **S96.092**   Other injury of muscle and tendon of long flexor muscle of toe at ankle and foot level, left foot

  ● **S96.099**   Other injury of muscle and tendon of long flexor muscle of toe at ankle and foot level, unspecified foot

● **S96.1**   Injury of muscle and tendon of long extensor muscle of toe at ankle and foot level

  ● **S96.10**   Unspecified injury of muscle and tendon of long extensor muscle of toe at ankle and foot level

    ● **S96.101**   Unspecified injury of muscle and tendon of long extensor muscle of toe at ankle and foot level, right foot

    ● **S96.102**   Unspecified injury of muscle and tendon of long extensor muscle of toe at ankle and foot level, left foot

    ● **S96.109**   Unspecified injury of muscle and tendon of long extensor muscle of toe at ankle and foot level, unspecified foot

  ● **S96.11**   Strain of muscle and tendon of long extensor muscle of toe at ankle and foot level

    ● **S96.111**   Strain of muscle and tendon of long extensor muscle of toe at ankle and foot level, right foot

    ● **S96.112**   Strain of muscle and tendon of long extensor muscle of toe at ankle and foot level, left foot

    ● **S96.119**   Strain of muscle and tendon of long extensor muscle of toe at ankle and foot level, unspecified foot

  ● **S96.12**   Laceration of muscle and tendon of long extensor muscle of toe at ankle and foot level

    ● **S96.121**   Laceration of muscle and tendon of long extensor muscle of toe at ankle and foot level, right foot

    ● **S96.122**   Laceration of muscle and tendon of long extensor muscle of toe at ankle and foot level, left foot

    ● **S96.129**   Laceration of muscle and tendon of long extensor muscle of toe at ankle and foot level, unspecified foot

  ● **S96.19**   Other specified injury of muscle and tendon of long extensor muscle of toe at ankle and foot level

    ● **S96.191**   Other specified injury of muscle and tendon of long extensor muscle of toe at ankle and foot level, right foot

    ● **S96.192**   Other specified injury of muscle and tendon of long extensor muscle of toe at ankle and foot level, left foot

    ● **S96.199**   Other specified injury of muscle and tendon of long extensor muscle of toe at ankle and foot level, unspecified foot

● **S96.2**   Injury of intrinsic muscle and tendon at ankle and foot level

  ● **S96.20**   Unspecified injury of intrinsic muscle and tendon at ankle and foot level

    ● **S96.201**   Unspecified injury of intrinsic muscle and tendon at ankle and foot level, right foot

    ● **S96.202**   Unspecified injury of intrinsic muscle and tendon at ankle and foot level, left foot

    ● **S96.209**   Unspecified injury of intrinsic muscle and tendon at ankle and foot level, unspecified foot

● **S96.21** **Strain** of intrinsic muscle and tendon at ankle and foot level
- ● **S96.211** Strain of intrinsic muscle and tendon at ankle and foot level, **right** foot
- ● **S96.212** Strain of intrinsic muscle and tendon at ankle and foot level, **left** foot
- ● **S96.219** Strain of intrinsic muscle and tendon at ankle and foot level, **unspecified** foot

● **S96.22** **Laceration** of intrinsic muscle and tendon at ankle and foot level
- ● **S96.221** Laceration of intrinsic muscle and tendon at ankle and foot level, **right** foot
- ● **S96.222** Laceration of intrinsic muscle and tendon at left ankle and foot level, **left** foot
- ● **S96.229** Laceration of intrinsic muscle and tendon at ankle and foot level, **unspecified** foot

● **S96.29** **Other** specified injury of intrinsic muscle and tendon at ankle and foot level
- ● **S96.291** Other specified injury of intrinsic muscle and tendon at ankle and foot level, **right** foot
- ● **S96.292** Other specified injury of intrinsic muscle and tendon at ankle and foot level, **left** foot
- ● **S96.299** Other specified injury of intrinsic muscle and tendon at ankle and foot level, **unspecified** foot

● **S96.8** Injury of **other** specified muscles and tendons at ankle and foot level
- ● **S96.80** **Unspecified** injury of other specified muscles and tendons at ankle and foot level
  - ● **S96.801** Unspecified injury of other specified muscles and tendons at ankle and foot level, **right** foot
  - ● **S96.802** Unspecified injury of other specified muscles and tendons at ankle and foot level, **left** foot
  - ● **S96.809** Unspecified injury of other specified muscles and tendons at ankle and foot level, **unspecified** foot
- ● **S96.81** **Strain** of other specified muscles and tendons at ankle and foot level
  - ● **S96.811** Strain of other specified muscles and tendons at ankle and foot level, **right** foot
  - ● **S96.812** Strain of other specified muscles and tendons at ankle and foot level, **left** foot
  - ● **S96.819** Strain of other specified muscles and tendons at ankle and foot level, **unspecified** foot
- ● **S96.82** **Laceration** of other specified muscles and tendons at ankle and foot level
  - ● **S96.821** Laceration of other specified muscles and tendons at ankle and foot level, **right** foot
  - ● **S96.822** Laceration of other specified muscles and tendons at ankle and foot level, **left** foot
  - ● **S96.829** Laceration of other specified muscles and tendons at ankle and foot level, **unspecified** foot

● **S96.89** **Other** specified injury of other specified muscles and tendons at ankle and foot level
- ● **S96.891** Other specified injury of other specified muscles and tendons at ankle and foot level, **right** foot
- ● **S96.892** Other specified injury of other specified muscles and tendons at ankle and foot level, **left** foot
- ● **S96.899** Other specified injury of other specified muscles and tendons at ankle and foot level, **unspecified** foot

● **S96.9** Injury of **unspecified** muscle and tendon at ankle and foot level
- ● **S96.90** **Unspecified** injury of unspecified muscle and tendon at ankle and foot level
  - ● **S96.901** Unspecified injury of unspecified muscle and tendon at ankle and foot level, **right** foot
  - ● **S96.902** Unspecified injury of unspecified muscle and tendon at ankle and foot level, **left** foot
  - ● **S96.909** Unspecified injury of unspecified muscle and tendon at ankle and foot level, **unspecified** foot
- ● **S96.91** **Strain** of unspecified muscle and tendon at ankle and foot level
  - ● **S96.911** Strain of unspecified muscle and tendon at ankle and foot level, **right** foot
  - ● **S96.912** Strain of unspecified muscle and tendon at ankle and foot level, **left** foot
  - ● **S96.919** Strain of unspecified muscle and tendon at ankle and foot level, **unspecified** foot
- ● **S96.92** **Laceration** of unspecified muscle and tendon at ankle and foot level
  - ● **S96.921** Laceration of unspecified muscle and tendon at ankle and foot level, **right** foot
  - ● **S96.922** Laceration of unspecified muscle and tendon at ankle and foot level, **left** foot
  - ● **S96.929** Laceration of unspecified muscle and tendon at ankle and foot level, **unspecified** foot
- ● **S96.99** **Other** specified injury of unspecified muscle and tendon at ankle and foot level
  - ● **S96.991** Other specified injury of unspecified muscle and tendon at ankle and foot level, **right** foot
  - ● **S96.992** Other specified injury of unspecified muscle and tendon at ankle and foot level, **left** foot
  - ● **S96.999** Other specified injury of unspecified muscle and tendon at ankle and foot level, **unspecified** foot

● **S97** **Crushing injury** of ankle and foot

Use additional code(s) for all associated injuries

The appropriate 7th character is to be added to each code from category S97

> | | |
> |---|---|
> | A | initial encounter |
> | D | subsequent encounter |
> | S | sequela |

● **S97.0** Crushing injury of **ankle**
- X ● **S97.00** Crushing injury of **unspecified** ankle
- X ● **S97.01** Crushing injury of **right** ankle
- X ● **S97.02** Crushing injury of **left** ankle

▶ New　⇒ Revised　~~deleted~~ Deleted　Excludes 1　Excludes 2　Includes　Use additional　Code first　Code also　Key words

OGCR Official Guidelines　X Assign placeholder X　● Use Additional Character(s)　▶ Manifestation Code　🅠 Hierarchical Condition Category　**Coding Clinic**

● **S97.1**   **Crushing injury of toe**
  ● **S97.10**   Crushing injury of unspecified toe(s)
    ● **S97.101**   Crushing injury of unspecified right toe(s)
    ● **S97.102**   Crushing injury of unspecified left toe(s)
    ● **S97.109**   Crushing injury of unspecified toe(s)
         Crushing injury of toe NOS
  ● **S97.11**   Crushing injury of great toe
    ● **S97.111**   Crushing injury of right great toe
    ● **S97.112**   Crushing injury of left great toe
    ● **S97.119**   Crushing injury of unspecified great toe
  ● **S97.12**   Crushing injury of lesser toe(s)
    ● **S97.121**   Crushing injury of right lesser toe(s)
    ● **S97.122**   Crushing injury of left lesser toe(s)
    ● **S97.129**   Crushing injury of lesser toe(s), unspecified toe(s)
● **S97.8**   **Crushing injury of foot**
  X ● **S97.80**   Crushing injury of foot, unspecified side
         Crushing injury of foot NOS
  X ● **S97.81**   Crushing injury of right foot
  X ● **S97.82**   Crushing injury of left foot

● **S98**   **Traumatic amputation of ankle and foot**
   An amputation not identified as partial or complete should be coded to complete
   The appropriate 7th character is to be added to each code from category S98

> A   initial encounter
> D   subsequent encounter
> S   sequela

● **S98.0**   **Traumatic amputation of foot at ankle level**
  ● **S98.01**   Complete traumatic amputation of foot at ankle level
    ● **S98.011**   Complete traumatic amputation of right foot at ankle level A, D, S 🔧
    ● **S98.012**   Complete traumatic amputation of left foot at ankle level A, D, S 🔧
    ● **S98.019**   Complete traumatic amputation of unspecified foot at ankle level A, D, S 🔧
  ● **S98.02**   Partial traumatic amputation of foot at ankle level
    ● **S98.021**   Partial traumatic amputation of right foot at ankle level A, D, S 🔧
    ● **S98.022**   Partial traumatic amputation of left foot at ankle level A, D, S 🔧
    ● **S98.029**   Partial traumatic amputation of unspecified foot at ankle level A, D, S 🔧
● **S98.1**   **Traumatic amputation of one toe**
  ● **S98.11**   Complete traumatic amputation of great toe
    ● **S98.111**   Complete traumatic amputation of right great toe A, D, S 🔧
    ● **S98.112**   Complete traumatic amputation of left great toe A, D, S 🔧
    ● **S98.119**   Complete traumatic amputation of unspecified great toe A, D, S 🔧
  ● **S98.12**   Partial traumatic amputation of great toe
    ● **S98.121**   Partial traumatic amputation of right great toe A, D, S 🔧
    ● **S98.122**   Partial traumatic amputation of left great toe A, D, S 🔧
    ● **S98.129**   Partial traumatic amputation of unspecified great toe A, D, S 🔧

● **S98.13**   Complete traumatic amputation of one lesser toe
     Traumatic amputation of toe NOS
    ● **S98.131**   Complete traumatic amputation of one right lesser toe A, D, S 🔧
    ● **S98.132**   Complete traumatic amputation of one left lesser toe A, D, S 🔧
    ● **S98.139**   Complete traumatic amputation of one unspecified lesser toe A, D, S 🔧
  ● **S98.14**   Partial traumatic amputation of one lesser toe
    ● **S98.141**   Partial traumatic amputation of one right lesser toe A, D, S 🔧
    ● **S98.142**   Partial traumatic amputation of one left lesser toe A, D, S 🔧
    ● **S98.149**   Partial traumatic amputation of one unspecified lesser toe A, D, S 🔧
● **S98.2**   **Traumatic amputation of two or more lesser toes**
  ● **S98.21**   Complete traumatic amputation of two or more lesser toes
    ● **S98.211**   Complete traumatic amputation of two or more right lesser toes A, D, S 🔧
    ● **S98.212**   Complete traumatic amputation of two or more left lesser toes A, D, S 🔧
    ● **S98.219**   Complete traumatic amputation of two or more unspecified lesser toes A, D, S 🔧
  ● **S98.22**   Partial traumatic amputation of two or more lesser toes
    ● **S98.221**   Partial traumatic amputation of two or more right lesser toes A, D, S 🔧
    ● **S98.222**   Partial traumatic amputation of two or more left lesser toes A, D, S 🔧
    ● **S98.229**   Partial traumatic amputation of two or more unspecified lesser toes A, D, S 🔧
● **S98.3**   **Traumatic amputation of midfoot**
  ● **S98.31**   Complete traumatic amputation of midfoot
    ● **S98.311**   Complete traumatic amputation of right midfoot A, D, S 🔧
    ● **S98.312**   Complete traumatic amputation of left midfoot A, D, S 🔧
    ● **S98.319**   Complete traumatic amputation of unspecified midfoot A, D, S 🔧
  ● **S98.32**   Partial traumatic amputation of midfoot
    ● **S98.321**   Partial traumatic amputation of right midfoot A, D, S 🔧
    ● **S98.322**   Partial traumatic amputation of left midfoot A, D, S 🔧
    ● **S98.329**   Partial traumatic amputation of unspecified midfoot A, D, S 🔧
● **S98.9**   **Traumatic amputation of foot, level unspecified**
  ● **S98.91**   Complete traumatic amputation of foot, level unspecified
    ● **S98.911**   Complete traumatic amputation of right foot, level unspecified A, D, S 🔧
    ● **S98.912**   Complete traumatic amputation of left foot, level unspecified A, D, S 🔧
    ● **S98.919**   Complete traumatic amputation of unspecified foot, level unspecified A, D, S 🔧
  ● **S98.92**   Partial traumatic amputation of foot, level unspecified
    ● **S98.921**   Partial traumatic amputation of right foot, level unspecified A, D, S 🔧
    ● **S98.922**   Partial traumatic amputation of left foot, level unspecified A, D, S 🔧
    ● **S98.929**   Partial traumatic amputation of unspecified foot, level unspecified A, D, S 🔧

CHAPTER 19 (S00-T88)

● **S99**   **Other and unspecified injuries of ankle and foot**
      Coding Clinic: 2016, Q4, P68

  ● **S99.0**   **Physeal fracture of calcaneus**

        The appropriate 7th character is to be added to each
        code from subcategories S99.0

A	initial encounter for closed fracture
B	initial encounter for open fracture
D	subsequent encounter for fracture with routine healing
G	subsequent encounter for fracture with delayed healing
K	subsequent encounter for fracture with nonunion
P	subsequent encounter for fracture with malunion
S	sequela

    ● **S99.00**   **Unspecified physeal fracture of calcaneus**

      ● **S99.001**   Unspecified physeal fracture of right calcaneus

      ● **S99.002**   Unspecified physeal fracture of left calcaneus

      ● **S99.009**   Unspecified physeal fracture of unspecified calcaneus

    ● **S99.01**   **Salter-Harris Type I physeal fracture of calcaneus**
        Coding Clinic: 2016, Q4, P69

      ● **S99.011**   Salter-Harris Type I physeal fracture of right calcaneus

      ● **S99.012**   Salter-Harris Type I physeal fracture of left calcaneus

      ● **S99.019**   Salter-Harris Type I physeal fracture of unspecified calcaneus

    ● **S99.02**   **Salter-Harris Type II physeal fracture of calcaneus**
        Coding Clinic: 2016, Q4, P69

      ● **S99.021**   Salter-Harris Type II physeal fracture of right calcaneus

      ● **S99.022**   Salter-Harris Type II physeal fracture of left calcaneus

      ● **S99.029**   Salter-Harris Type II physeal fracture of unspecified calcaneus

    ● **S99.03**   **Salter-Harris Type III physeal fracture of calcaneus**
        Coding Clinic: 2016, Q4, P69

      ● **S99.031**   Salter-Harris Type III physeal fracture of right calcaneus

      ● **S99.032**   Salter-Harris Type III physeal fracture of left calcaneus

      ● **S99.039**   Salter-Harris Type III physeal fracture of unspecified calcaneus

    ● **S99.04**   **Salter-Harris Type IV physeal fracture of calcaneus**
        Coding Clinic: 2016, Q4, P69

      ● **S99.041**   Salter-Harris Type IV physeal fracture of right calcaneus

      ● **S99.042**   Salter-Harris Type IV physeal fracture of left calcaneus

      ● **S99.049**   Salter-Harris Type IV physeal fracture of unspecified calcaneus

    ● **S99.09**   **Other physeal fracture of calcaneus**
        Coding Clinic: 2016, Q4, P69

      ● **S99.091**   Other physeal fracture of right calcaneus

      ● **S99.092**   Other physeal fracture of left calcaneus

      ● **S99.099**   Other physeal fracture of unspecified calcaneus

  ● **S99.1**   **Physeal fracture of metatarsal**

        The appropriate 7th character is to be added to each
        code from subcategories S99.1

A	initial encounter for closed fracture
B	initial encounter for open fracture
D	subsequent encounter for fracture with routine healing
G	subsequent encounter for fracture with delayed healing
K	subsequent encounter for fracture with nonunion
P	subsequent encounter for fracture with malunion
S	sequela

    ● **S99.10**   **Unspecified physeal fracture of metatarsal**

      ● **S99.101**   Unspecified physeal fracture of right metatarsal

      ● **S99.102**   Unspecified physeal fracture of left metatarsal

      ● **S99.109**   Unspecified physeal fracture of unspecified metatarsal

    ● **S99.11**   **Salter-Harris Type I physeal fracture of metatarsal**
        Coding Clinic: 2016, Q4, P69

      ● **S99.111**   Salter-Harris Type I physeal fracture of right metatarsal

      ● **S99.112**   Salter-Harris Type I physeal fracture of left metatarsal
          Coding Clinic: 2018, Q1, P3

      ● **S99.119**   Salter-Harris Type I physeal fracture of unspecified metatarsal

    ● **S99.12**   **Salter-Harris Type II physeal fracture of metatarsal**
        Coding Clinic: 2016, Q4, P69

      ● **S99.121**   Salter-Harris Type II physeal fracture of right metatarsal

      ● **S99.122**   Salter-Harris Type II physeal fracture of left metatarsal

      ● **S99.129**   Salter-Harris Type II physeal fracture of unspecified metatarsal

    ● **S99.13**   **Salter-Harris Type III physeal fracture of metatarsal**
        Coding Clinic: 2016, Q4, P69

      ● **S99.131**   Salter-Harris Type III physeal fracture of right metatarsal

      ● **S99.132**   Salter-Harris Type III physeal fracture of left metatarsal

      ● **S99.139**   Salter-Harris Type III physeal fracture of unspecified metatarsal

    ● **S99.14**   **Salter-Harris Type IV physeal fracture of metatarsal**
        Coding Clinic: 2016, Q4, P69

      ● **S99.141**   Salter-Harris Type IV physeal fracture of right metatarsal

      ● **S99.142**   Salter-Harris Type IV physeal fracture of left metatarsal

      ● **S99.149**   Salter-Harris Type IV physeal fracture of unspecified metatarsal

    ● **S99.19**   **Other physeal fracture of metatarsal**
        Coding Clinic: 2016, Q4, P69

      ● **S99.191**   Other physeal fracture of right metatarsal

      ● **S99.192**   Other physeal fracture of left metatarsal

      ● **S99.199**   Other physeal fracture of unspecified metatarsal

---

▶ New   ⇒ Revised   ~~deleted~~ Deleted   Excludes 1   Excludes 2   Includes   Use additional   Code first   Code also   Key words

OGCR Official Guidelines   X Assign placeholder X   ● Use Additional Character(s)   ) Manifestation Code   🗞 Hierarchical Condition Category   Coding Clinic

● **S99.2**   **Physeal fracture of phalanx of toe**

The appropriate 7th character is to be added to each code from subcategories S99.2

> A   initial encounter for closed fracture
> B   initial encounter for open fracture
> D   subsequent encounter for fracture with routine healing
> G   subsequent encounter for fracture with delayed healing
> K   subsequent encounter for fracture with nonunion
> P   subsequent encounter for fracture with malunion
> S   sequela

● **S99.20**   **Unspecified** physeal fracture of phalanx of toe

     ● **S99.201**   Unspecified physeal fracture of phalanx of **right toe**

     ● **S99.202**   Unspecified physeal fracture of phalanx of **right toe**

     ● **S99.209**   Unspecified physeal fracture of phalanx of **unspecified toe**

● **S99.21**   **Salter-Harris Type I** physeal fracture of phalanx of toe
     Coding Clinic: 2016, Q4, P69

     ● **S99.211**   Salter-Harris Type I physeal fracture of phalanx of **right toe**

     ● **S99.212**   Salter-Harris Type I physeal fracture of phalanx of **left toe**

     ● **S99.219**   Salter-Harris Type I physeal fracture of phalanx of **unspecified toe**

● **S99.22**   **Salter-Harris Type II** physeal fracture of phalanx of toe
     Coding Clinic: 2016, Q4, P69

     ● **S99.221**   Salter-Harris Type II physeal fracture of phalanx of **right toe**

     ● **S99.222**   Salter-Harris Type II physeal fracture of phalanx of **left toe**

     ● **S99.229**   Salter-Harris Type II physeal fracture of phalanx of **unspecified toe**

● **S99.23**   **Salter-Harris Type III** physeal fracture of phalanx of toe
     Coding Clinic: 2016, Q4, P69

     ● **S99.231**   Salter-Harris Type III physeal fracture of phalanx of **right toe**

     ● **S99.232**   Salter-Harris Type III physeal fracture of phalanx of **left toe**

     ● **S99.239**   Salter-Harris Type III physeal fracture of phalanx of **unspecified toe**

● **S99.24**   **Salter-Harris Type IV** physeal fracture of phalanx of toe
     Coding Clinic: 2016, Q4, P69

     ● **S99.241**   Salter-Harris Type IV physeal fracture of phalanx of **right toe**

     ● **S99.242**   Salter-Harris Type IV physeal fracture of phalanx of **left toe**

     ● **S99.249**   Salter-Harris Type IV physeal fracture of phalanx of **unspecified toe**

● **S99.29**   **Other** physeal fracture of phalanx of toe
     Coding Clinic: 2016, Q4, P69

     ● **S99.291**   Other physeal fracture of phalanx of **right toe**

     ● **S99.292**   Other physeal fracture of phalanx of **left toe**

     ● **S99.299**   Other physeal fracture of phalanx of **unspecified toe**

● **S99.8**   **Other** specified injuries of ankle and foot

The appropriate 7th character is to be added to each code from subcategory S99.8

> A   initial encounter
> D   subsequent encounter
> S   sequela

     ● **S99.81**   Other specified injuries of **ankle**

         ● **S99.811**   Other specified injuries of **right ankle**

         ● **S99.812**   Other specified injuries of **left ankle**

         ● **S99.819**   Other specified injuries of **unspecified ankle**

     ● **S99.82**   Other specified injuries of **foot**

         ● **S99.821**   Other specified injuries of **right foot**

         ● **S99.822**   Other specified injuries of **left foot**

         ● **S99.829**   Other specified injuries of **unspecified foot**

● **S99.9**   **Unspecified** injury of ankle and foot

The appropriate 7th character is to be added to each code from subcategory S99.9

> A   initial encounter
> D   subsequent encounter
> S   sequela

     ● **S99.91**   Unspecified injury of **ankle**

         ● **S99.911**   Unspecified injury of **right ankle**

         ● **S99.912**   Unspecified injury of **left ankle**

         ● **S99.919**   Unspecified injury of **unspecified ankle**

     ● **S99.92**   Unspecified injury of **foot**

         ● **S99.921**   Unspecified injury of **right foot**

         ● **S99.922**   Unspecified injury of **left foot**

         ● **S99.929**   Unspecified injury of **unspecified foot**

INJURY, POISONING AND CERTAIN OTHER CONSEQUENCES OF EXTERNAL CAUSES (T07-T88)

INJURIES INVOLVING MULTIPLE BODY REGIONS (T07)

Excludes1   burns and corrosions (T20-T32)
                frostbite (T33-T34)
                insect bite or sting, venomous (T63.4)
                sunburn (L55.-)

X ● **T07**   **Unspecified** multiple injuries

The appropriate 7th character is to be added to code T07

> A   initial encounter
> D   subsequent encounter
> S   sequela

Excludes1   injury NOS (T14.90)

INJURY OF UNSPECIFIED BODY REGION (T14)

● **T14**   **Injury of unspecified body region**

The appropriate 7th character is to be added to each code from category T14

> A   initial encounter
> D   subsequent encounter
> S   sequela

Excludes1   multiple unspecified injuries (T07)

X ● **T14.8**   Other injury of unspecified body region
     Abrasion NOS   Skin injury NOS
     Contusion NOS   Vascular injury NOS
     Crush injury NOS   Wound NOS
     Fracture NOS

● **T14.9**   **Unspecified injury**

     X ● **T14.90**   Injury, **unspecified**
         Injury NOS

     X ● **T14.91**   **Suicide attempt** A, D, S
         Attempted suicide NOS

CHAPTER 19 (S00-T88)

EFFECTS OF FOREIGN BODY ENTERING THROUGH NATURAL ORIFICE (T15-T19)

Excludes2   foreign body accidentally left in operation wound (T81.5-)

foreign body in penetrating wound - see open wound by body region

residual foreign body in soft tissue (M79.5)

splinter, without open wound - see superficial injury by body region

● **T15**   **Foreign body on external eye**

Excludes2   foreign body in penetrating wound of orbit and eye ball (S05.4-, S05.5-)

open wound of eyelid and periocular area (S01.1-)

retained foreign body in eyelid (H02.8-)

retained (old) foreign body in penetrating wound of orbit and eye ball (H05.5-, H44.6-, H44.7-)

superficial foreign body of eyelid and periocular area (S00.25-)

The appropriate 7th character is to be added to each code from category T15

A	initial encounter
D	subsequent encounter
S	sequela

● **T15.0**   **Foreign body in cornea**

X ● **T15.00**   Foreign body in cornea, **unspecified eye**

X ● **T15.01**   Foreign body in cornea, **right eye**

X ● **T15.02**   Foreign body in cornea, **left eye**

● **T15.1**   **Foreign body in conjunctival sac**

X ● **T15.10**   Foreign body in conjunctival sac, **unspecified eye**

X ● **T15.11**   Foreign body in conjunctival sac, **right eye**

X ● **T15.12**   Foreign body in conjunctival sac, **left eye**

● **T15.8**   **Foreign body in other and multiple parts** of external eye

Foreign body in lacrimal punctum

X ● **T15.80**   Foreign body in other and multiple parts of external eye, **unspecified eye**

X ● **T15.81**   Foreign body in other and multiple parts of external eye, **right eye**

X ● **T15.82**   Foreign body in other and multiple parts of external eye, **left eye**

● **T15.9**   **Foreign body on external eye, part unspecified**

X ● **T15.90**   Foreign body on external eye, part unspecified, **unspecified eye**

X ● **T15.91**   Foreign body on external eye, part unspecified, **right eye**

X ● **T15.92**   Foreign body on external eye, part unspecified, **left eye**

● **T16**   **Foreign body in ear**

Includes   foreign body in auditory canal

The appropriate 7th character is to be added to each code from category T16

A	initial encounter
D	subsequent encounter
S	sequela

X ● **T16.1**   Foreign body in **right ear**

X ● **T16.2**   Foreign body in **left ear**

X ● **T16.9**   Foreign body in ear, **unspecified ear**

● **T17**   **Foreign body in respiratory tract**

The appropriate 7th character is to be added to each code from category T17

A	initial encounter
D	subsequent encounter
S	sequela

X ● **T17.0**   **Foreign body in nasal sinus**

X ● **T17.1**   **Foreign body in nostril**

Foreign body in nose NOS

● **T17.2**   **Foreign body in pharynx**

Foreign body in nasopharynx

Foreign body in throat NOS

● **T17.20**   **Unspecified foreign body in pharynx**

● **T17.200**   **Unspecified foreign body in pharynx causing asphyxiation**

● **T17.208**   **Unspecified foreign body in pharynx causing other injury**

● **T17.21**   **Gastric contents in pharynx**

Aspiration of gastric contents into pharynx

Vomitus in pharynx

● **T17.210**   **Gastric contents in pharynx causing asphyxiation**

● **T17.218**   **Gastric contents in pharynx causing other injury**

● **T17.22**   **Food in pharynx**

Bones in pharynx

Seeds in pharynx

● **T17.220**   **Food in pharynx causing asphyxiation**

● **T17.228**   **Food in pharynx causing other injury**

● **T17.29**   **Other foreign object in pharynx**

● **T17.290**   **Other foreign object in pharynx causing asphyxiation**

● **T17.298**   **Other foreign object in pharynx causing other injury**

● **T17.3**   **Foreign body in larynx**

● **T17.30**   **Unspecified foreign body in larynx**

● **T17.300**   **Unspecified foreign body in larynx causing asphyxiation**

● **T17.308**   **Unspecified foreign body in larynx causing other injury**

● **T17.31**   **Gastric contents in larynx**

Aspiration of gastric contents into larynx

Vomitus in larynx

● **T17.310**   **Gastric contents in larynx causing asphyxiation**

● **T17.318**   **Gastric contents in larynx causing other injury**

● **T17.32**   **Food in larynx**

Bones in larynx

Seeds in larynx

● **T17.320**   **Food in larynx causing asphyxiation**

● **T17.328**   **Food in larynx causing other injury**

● **T17.39**   **Other foreign object in larynx**

● **T17.390**   **Other foreign object in larynx causing asphyxiation**

● **T17.398**   **Other foreign object in larynx causing other injury**

● **T17.4**   **Foreign body in trachea**

● **T17.40**   **Unspecified foreign body in trachea**

● **T17.400**   **Unspecified foreign body in trachea causing asphyxiation**

● **T17.408**   **Unspecified foreign body in trachea causing other injury**

▶ New   ⇒ Revised   ~~deleted~~ Deleted | Excludes 1 | | Excludes 2 | | Includes | | Use additional | | Code first | | Code also | | Key words |

OGCR Official Guidelines   X Assign placeholder X   ● Use Additional Character(s)   ▶ Manifestation Code   🗝 Hierarchical Condition Category   **Coding Clinic**

- **T17.41**   Gastric contents in trachea
  - Aspiration of gastric contents into trachea
  - Vomitus in trachea
  - **T17.410**   Gastric contents in trachea causing asphyxiation
  - **T17.418**   Gastric contents in trachea causing other injury
- **T17.42**   Food in trachea
  - Bones in trachea
  - Seeds in trachea
  - **T17.420**   Food in trachea causing asphyxiation
  - **T17.428**   Food in trachea causing other injury
- **T17.49**   Other foreign object in trachea
  - **T17.490**   Other foreign object in trachea causing asphyxiation
  - **T17.498**   Other foreign object in trachea causing other injury
- **T17.5**   Foreign body in bronchus
  - **T17.50**   Unspecified foreign body in bronchus
    - **T17.500**   Unspecified foreign body in bronchus causing asphyxiation
    - **T17.508**   Unspecified foreign body in bronchus causing other injury
  - **T17.51**   Gastric contents in bronchus
    - Aspiration of gastric contents into bronchus
    - Vomitus in bronchus
    - **T17.510**   Gastric contents in bronchus causing asphyxiation
    - **T17.518**   Gastric contents in bronchus causing other injury
  - **T17.52**   Food in bronchus
    - Bones in bronchus
    - Seeds in bronchus
    - **T17.520**   Food in bronchus causing asphyxiation
    - **T17.528**   Food in bronchus causing other injury
  - **T17.59**   Other foreign object in bronchus
    - **T17.590**   Other foreign object in bronchus causing asphyxiation
    - **T17.598**   Other foreign object in bronchus causing other injury
- **T17.8**   Foreign body in other parts of respiratory tract
  - Foreign body in bronchioles
  - Foreign body in lung
  - **T17.80**   Unspecified foreign body in other parts of respiratory tract
    - **T17.800**   Unspecified foreign body in other parts of respiratory tract causing asphyxiation
    - **T17.808**   Unspecified foreign body in other parts of respiratory tract causing other injury
  - **T17.81**   Gastric contents in other parts of respiratory tract
    - Aspiration of gastric contents into other parts of respiratory tract
    - Vomitus in other parts of respiratory tract
    - **T17.810**   Gastric contents in other parts of respiratory tract causing asphyxiation
    - **T17.818**   Gastric contents in other parts of respiratory tract causing other injury
  - **T17.82**   Food in other parts of respiratory tract
    - Bones in other parts of respiratory tract
    - Seeds in other parts of respiratory tract
    - **T17.820**   Food in other parts of respiratory tract causing asphyxiation
    - **T17.828**   Food in other parts of respiratory tract causing other injury

- **T17.89**   Other foreign object in other parts of respiratory tract
  - **T17.890**   Other foreign object in other parts of respiratory tract causing asphyxiation
  - **T17.898**   Other foreign object in other parts of respiratory tract causing other injury
- **T17.9**   Foreign body in respiratory tract, part unspecified
  - **T17.90**   Unspecified foreign body in respiratory tract, part unspecified
    - **T17.900**   Unspecified foreign body in respiratory tract, part unspecified causing asphyxiation
    - **T17.908**   Unspecified foreign body in respiratory tract, part unspecified causing other injury
  - **T17.91**   Gastric contents in respiratory tract, part unspecified
    - Aspiration of gastric contents into respiratory tract, part unspecified
    - Vomitus in trachea respiratory tract, part unspecified
    - **T17.910**   Gastric contents in respiratory tract, part unspecified causing asphyxiation
    - **T17.918**   Gastric contents in respiratory tract, part unspecified causing other injury
  - **T17.92**   Food in respiratory tract, part unspecified
    - Bones in respiratory tract, part unspecified
    - Seeds in respiratory tract, part unspecified
    - **T17.920**   Food in respiratory tract, part unspecified causing asphyxiation
    - **T17.928**   Food in respiratory tract, part unspecified causing other injury
  - **T17.99**   Other foreign object in respiratory tract, part unspecified
    - **T17.990**   Other foreign object in respiratory tract, part unspecified in causing asphyxiation
      - Coding Clinic: 2019, Q3, P15
    - **T17.998**   Other foreign object in respiratory tract, part unspecified causing other injury

- **T18**   Foreign body in alimentary tract
  - **Excludes2**   foreign body in pharynx (T17.2-)
  - The appropriate 7th character is to be added to each code from category T18

A	initial encounter
D	subsequent encounter
S	sequela

  - X **T18.0**   Foreign body in mouth
  - X **T18.1**   Foreign body in esophagus
    - **Excludes2**   foreign body in respiratory tract (T17.-)
    - **T18.10**   Unspecified foreign body in esophagus
      - **T18.100**   Unspecified foreign body in esophagus causing compression of trachea
        - Unspecified foreign body in esophagus causing obstruction of respiration
      - **T18.108**   Unspecified foreign body in esophagus causing other injury
    - **T18.11**   Gastric contents in esophagus
      - Vomitus in esophagus
      - **T18.110**   Gastric contents in esophagus causing compression of trachea
        - Gastric contents in esophagus causing obstruction of respiration
      - **T18.118**   Gastric contents in esophagus causing other injury

---

● **T18.12　Food in esophagus**
　　　　Bones in esophagus
　　　　Seeds in esophagus
　　● **T18.120　Food in esophagus causing compression of trachea**
　　　　　　Food in esophagus causing obstruction of respiration
　　● **T18.128　Food in esophagus causing other injury**
● **T18.19　Other foreign object in esophagus**
　　● **T18.190　Other foreign object in esophagus causing compression of trachea**
　　　　　　Other foreign body in esophagus causing obstruction of respiration
　　　　　　Coding Clinic: 2015, Q1, P24
　　● **T18.198　Other foreign object in esophagus causing other injury**
　　　　　　Coding Clinic: 2015, Q1, P24
X● **T18.2　Foreign body in stomach**
X● **T18.3　Foreign body in small intestine**
X● **T18.4　Foreign body in colon**
X● **T18.5　Foreign body in anus and rectum**
　　　　Foreign body in rectosigmoid (junction)
X● **T18.8　Foreign body in other parts of alimentary tract**
X● **T18.9　Foreign body of alimentary tract, part unspecified**
　　　　Foreign body in digestive system NOS
　　　　Swallowed foreign body NOS

● **T19　Foreign body in genitourinary tract**
　　Excludes2　complications due to implanted mesh (T83.7-)
　　　　　　mechanical complications of contraceptive device (intrauterine) (vaginal) (T83.3-)
　　　　　　presence of contraceptive device (intrauterine) (vaginal) (Z97.5)

　　The appropriate 7th character is to be added to each code from category T19

A	initial encounter
D	subsequent encounter
S	sequela

X● **T19.0　Foreign body in urethra**
X● **T19.1　Foreign body in bladder**
X● **T19.2　Foreign body in vulva and vagina ♀**
X● **T19.3　Foreign body in uterus ♀**
X● **T19.4　Foreign body in penis ♂**
X● **T19.8　Foreign body in other parts of genitourinary tract**
X● **T19.9　Foreign body in genitourinary tract, part unspecified**

BURNS AND CORROSIONS (T20-T32)

　　Includes　burns (thermal) from electrical heating appliances
　　　　　　burns (thermal) from electricity
　　　　　　burns (thermal) from flame
　　　　　　burns (thermal) from friction
　　　　　　burns (thermal) from hot air and hot gases
　　　　　　burns (thermal) from hot objects
　　　　　　burns (thermal) from lightning
　　　　　　burns (thermal) from radiation chemical
　　　　　　burn [corrosion] (external) (internal) scalds

　　Excludes2　erythema [dermatitis] ab igne (L59.0)
　　　　　　radiation-related disorders of the skin and subcutaneous tissue (L55-L59)
　　　　　　sunburn (L55.-)

OGCR Section I.C.19.d.

Burns and Corrosions

The ICD-10-CM makes a distinction between burn and corrosions. The burn codes are for thermal burns, except sunburns, that come from a heat source, such as a fire or hot appliance. The burn codes are also for burns resulting from electricity and radiation. Corrosions are burns due to chemicals. The guidelines for burns and corrosions are the same.

Current burns (T20-T25) are classified by depth, extent and by agent (X code). Burns are classified by depth as first degree (erythema), second degree (blistering), and third degree (full-thickness involvement). Burns of the eye and internal organs (T26-T28) are classified by site, but not by degree.

1) Sequencing of burn and related condition codes

Sequence first the code that reflects the highest degree of burn when more than one burn is present.

a. When the reason for the admission or encounter is for treatment of external multiple burns, sequence first the code that reflects the burn of the highest degree.

b. When a patient has both internal and external burns, the circumstances of admission govern the selection of the principal diagnosis or first-listed diagnosis.

c. When a patient is admitted for burn injuries and other related conditions such as smoke inhalation and/or respiratory failure, the circumstances of admission govern the selection of the principal or first-listed diagnosis.

2) Burns of the same local site

Classify burns of the same local site (three-character category level, T20-T28) but of different degrees to the subcategory identifying the highest degree recorded in the diagnosis.

BURNS AND CORROSIONS OF EXTERNAL BODY SURFACE, SPECIFIED BY SITE (T20-T25)

　　Includes　burns and corrosions of first degree [erythema]
　　　　　　burns and corrosions of second degree [blisters] [epidermal loss]
　　　　　　burns and corrosions of third degree [deep necrosis of underlying tissue] [full-thickness skin loss]
　　Use additional code from category T31 or T32 to identify extent of body surface involved

● **T20　Burn and corrosion of head, face, and neck**
　　Excludes2　burn and corrosion of ear drum (T28.41, T28.91)
　　　　　　burn and corrosion of eye and adnexa (T26.-)
　　　　　　burn and corrosion of mouth and pharynx (T28.0)

　　The appropriate 7th character is to be added to each code from category T20

A	initial encounter
D	subsequent encounter
S	sequela

● **T20.0　Burn of unspecified degree of head, face, and neck**
　　　　Use additional external cause code to identify the source, place and intent of the burn (X00-X19, X75-X77, X96-X98, Y92)
　　X● **T20.00　Burn of unspecified degree of head, face, and neck, unspecified site**
　　● **T20.01　Burn of unspecified degree of ear [any part, except ear drum]**
　　　　Excludes2　burn of ear drum (T28.41-)
　　　　● **T20.011　Burn of unspecified degree of right ear [any part, except ear drum]**
　　　　● **T20.012　Burn of unspecified degree of left ear [any part, except ear drum]**
　　　　● **T20.019　Burn of unspecified degree of unspecified ear [any part, except ear drum]**

Figure 19-15 A. Second-degree burn. **B.** Third-degree burn. (A. From Black J, Hawks J: Medical-Surgical Nursing: Clinical Management for Positive Outcomes, 8e, Saunders, 2008. B. From Marx J, Hockberger R, Walls R: Rosen's Emergency Medicine - Concepts and Clinical Practice, 7e, Mosby, 2009)

X● **T20.02**   Burn of unspecified degree of lip(s)

X● **T20.03**   Burn of unspecified degree of chin

X● **T20.04**   Burn of unspecified degree of nose (septum)

X● **T20.05**   Burn of unspecified degree of scalp [any part]

X● **T20.06**   Burn of unspecified degree of forehead and cheek

X● **T20.07**   Burn of unspecified degree of neck

X● **T20.09**   Burn of unspecified degree of multiple sites of head, face, and neck

● **T20.1**   Burn of first degree of head, face, and neck

Use additional external cause code to identify the source, place and intent of the burn (X00-X19, X75-X77, X96-X98, Y92)

X● **T20.10**   Burn of first degree of head, face, and neck, unspecified site

● **T20.11**   Burn of first degree of ear [any part, except ear drum]

Excludes2   burn of ear drum (T28.41-)

● **T20.111**   Burn of first degree of right ear [any part, except ear drum]

● **T20.112**   Burn of first degree of left ear [any part, except ear drum]

● **T20.119**   Burn of first degree of unspecified ear [any part, except ear drum]

X● **T20.12**   Burn of first degree of lip(s)

X● **T20.13**   Burn of first degree of chin

X● **T20.14**   Burn of first degree of nose (septum)

X● **T20.15**   Burn of first degree of scalp [any part]

X● **T20.16**   Burn of first degree of forehead and cheek

X● **T20.17**   Burn of first degree of neck

X● **T20.19**   Burn of first degree of multiple sites of head, face, and neck

● **T20.2**   Burn of second degree of head, face, and neck

Use additional external cause code to identify the source, place and intent of the burn (X00-X19, X75-X77, X96-X98, Y92)

X● **T20.20**   Burn of second degree of head, face, and neck, unspecified site

● **T20.21**   Burn of second degree of ear [any part, except ear drum]

Excludes2   burn of ear drum (T28.41-)

● **T20.211**   Burn of second degree of right ear [any part, except ear drum]

● **T20.212**   Burn of second degree of left ear [any part, except ear drum]

● **T20.219**   Burn of second degree of unspecified ear [any part, except ear drum]

X● **T20.22**   Burn of second degree of lip(s)

X● **T20.23**   Burn of second degree of chin

X● **T20.24**   Burn of second degree of nose (septum)

X● **T20.25**   Burn of second degree of scalp [any part]
Coding Clinic: 2015, Q1, P19

X● **T20.26**   Burn of second degree of forehead and cheek

X● **T20.27**   Burn of second degree of neck

X● **T20.29**   Burn of second degree of multiple sites of head, face, and neck

● **T20.3**   Burn of third degree of head, face, and neck

Use additional external cause code to identify the source, place and intent of the burn (X00-X19, X75-X77, X96-X98, Y92)

X● **T20.30**   Burn of third degree of head, face, and neck, unspecified site

● **T20.31**   Burn of third degree of ear [any part, except ear drum]

Excludes2   burn of ear drum (T28.41-)

● **T20.311**   Burn of third degree of right ear [any part, except ear drum]

● **T20.312**   Burn of third degree of left ear [any part, except ear drum]
Coding Clinic: 2015, Q1, P18

● **T20.319**   Burn of third degree of unspecified ear [any part, except ear drum]

X● **T20.32**   Burn of third degree of lip(s)

X● **T20.33**   Burn of third degree of chin

X● **T20.34**   Burn of third degree of nose (septum)

X● **T20.35**   Burn of third degree of scalp [any part]

X● **T20.36**   Burn of third degree of forehead and cheek

X● **T20.37**   Burn of third degree of neck

X● **T20.39**   Burn of third degree of multiple sites of head, face, and neck

● **T20.4**   Corrosion of unspecified degree of head, face, and neck

Code first (T51-T65) to identify chemical and intent

Use additional external cause code to identify place (Y92)

X● **T20.40**   Corrosion of unspecified degree of head, face, and neck, unspecified site

● **T20.41**   Corrosion of unspecified degree of ear [any part, except ear drum]

Excludes2   corrosion of ear drum (T28.91-)

● **T20.411**   Corrosion of unspecified degree of right ear [any part, except ear drum]

● **T20.412**   Corrosion of unspecified degree of left ear [any part, except ear drum]

● **T20.419**   Corrosion of unspecified degree of unspecified ear [any part, except ear drum]

X● **T20.42**   Corrosion of unspecified degree of lip(s)

X● **T20.43**   Corrosion of unspecified degree of chin

X● **T20.44**   Corrosion of unspecified degree of nose (septum)

X● **T20.45**   Corrosion of unspecified degree of scalp [any part]

X● **T20.46**   Corrosion of unspecified degree of forehead and cheek

X● **T20.47**   Corrosion of unspecified degree of neck

X● **T20.49**   Corrosion of unspecified degree of multiple sites of head, face, and neck

● **T20.5**   Corrosion of first degree of head, face, and neck

Code first (T51-T65) to identify chemical and intent

Use additional external cause code to identify place (Y92)

X● **T20.50**   Corrosion of first degree of head, face, and neck, unspecified site

● **T20.51**   Corrosion of first degree of ear [any part, except ear drum]

Excludes2   corrosion of ear drum (T28.91-)

● **T20.511**   Corrosion of first degree of right ear [any part, except ear drum]

● **T20.512**   Corrosion of first degree of left ear [any part, except ear drum]

● **T20.519**   Corrosion of first degree of unspecified ear [any part, except ear drum]

X● **T20.52** Corrosion of first degree of lip(s)
X● **T20.53** Corrosion of first degree of chin
X● **T20.54** Corrosion of first degree of nose (septum)
X● **T20.55** Corrosion of first degree of scalp [any part]
X● **T20.56** Corrosion of first degree of forehead and cheek
X● **T20.57** Corrosion of first degree of neck
X● **T20.59** Corrosion of first degree of multiple sites of head, face, and neck

● **T20.6** **Corrosion of second degree of head, face, and neck**
Code first (T51-T65) to identify chemical and intent
Use additional external cause code to identify place (Y92)

X● **T20.60** Corrosion of second degree of head, face, and neck, **unspecified site**
● **T20.61** Corrosion of second degree of ear [any part, except ear drum]
   Excludes2 corrosion of ear drum (T28.91-)
   ● **T20.611** Corrosion of second degree of **right ear** [any part, except ear drum]
   ● **T20.612** Corrosion of second degree of **left ear** [any part, except ear drum]
   ● **T20.619** Corrosion of second degree of **unspecified ear** [any part, except ear drum]

X● **T20.62** Corrosion of second degree of lip(s)
X● **T20.63** Corrosion of second degree of chin
X● **T20.64** Corrosion of second degree of nose (septum)
X● **T20.65** Corrosion of second degree of scalp [any part]
X● **T20.66** Corrosion of second degree of forehead and cheek
X● **T20.67** Corrosion of second degree of neck
X● **T20.69** Corrosion of second degree of multiple sites of head, face, and neck

● **T20.7** **Corrosion of third degree of head, face, and neck**
Code first (T51-T65) to identify chemical and intent
Use additional external cause code to identify place (Y92)

X● **T20.70** Corrosion of third degree of head, face, and neck, **unspecified site**
● **T20.71** Corrosion of third degree of ear [any part, except ear drum]
   Excludes2 corrosion of ear drum (T28.91-)
   ● **T20.711** Corrosion of third degree of **right ear** [any part, except ear drum]
   ● **T20.712** Corrosion of third degree of **left ear** [any part, except ear drum]
   ● **T20.719** Corrosion of third degree of **unspecified ear** [any part, except ear drum]

X● **T20.72** Corrosion of third degree of lip(s)
X● **T20.73** Corrosion of third degree of chin
X● **T20.74** Corrosion of third degree of nose (septum)
X● **T20.75** Corrosion of third degree of scalp [any part]
X● **T20.76** Corrosion of third degree of forehead and cheek
X● **T20.77** Corrosion of third degree of neck
X● **T20.79** Corrosion of third degree of multiple sites of head, face, and neck

● **T21** **Burn and corrosion of trunk**
  Includes burns and corrosion of hip region
  Excludes2 burns and corrosion of axilla (T22.- with fifth character 4)
      burns and corrosion of scapular region (T22.- with fifth character 6)
      burns and corrosion of shoulder (T22.- with fifth character 5)

The appropriate 7th character is to be added to each code from category T21

A	initial encounter
D	subsequent encounter
S	sequela

● **T21.0** **Burn of unspecified degree of trunk**
Use additional external cause code to identify the source, place and intent of the burn (X00-X19, X75-X77, X96-X98, Y92)

X● **T21.00** Burn of unspecified degree of trunk, **unspecified site**
X● **T21.01** Burn of unspecified degree of **chest wall**
   Burn of unspecified degree of breast
X● **T21.02** Burn of unspecified degree of **abdominal wall**
   Burn of unspecified degree of flank
   Burn of unspecified degree of groin
X● **T21.03** Burn of unspecified degree of **upper back**
   Burn of unspecified degree of interscapular region
X● **T21.04** Burn of unspecified degree of **lower back**
X● **T21.05** Burn of unspecified degree of **buttock**
   Burn of unspecified degree of anus
X● **T21.06** Burn of unspecified degree of **male genital region** ♂
   Burn of unspecified degree of penis
   Burn of unspecified degree of scrotum
   Burn of unspecified degree of testis
X● **T21.07** Burn of unspecified degree of **female genital region** ♀
   Burn of unspecified degree of labium (majus) (minus)
   Burn of unspecified degree of perineum
   Burn of unspecified degree of vulva
   Excludes2 burn of vagina (T28.3)
X● **T21.09** Burn of unspecified degree of **other site of trunk**

● **T21.1** **Burn of first degree of trunk**
Use additional external cause code to identify the source, place and intent of the burn (X00-X19, X75-X77, X96-X98, Y92)

X● **T21.10** Burn of first degree of trunk, **unspecified site**
X● **T21.11** Burn of first degree of **chest wall**
   Burn of first degree of breast
X● **T21.12** Burn of first degree of **abdominal wall**
   Burn of first degree of flank
   Burn of first degree of groin
X● **T21.13** Burn of first degree of **upper back**
   Burn of first degree of interscapular region
X● **T21.14** Burn of first degree of **lower back**
X● **T21.15** Burn of first degree of **buttock**
   Burn of first degree of anus
X● **T21.16** Burn of first degree of **male genital region** ♂
   Burn of first degree of penis
   Burn of first degree of scrotum
   Burn of first degree of testis
X● **T21.17** Burn of first degree of **female genital region** ♀
   Burn of first degree of labium (majus) (minus)
   Burn of first degree of perineum
   Burn of first degree of vulva
   Excludes2 burn of vagina (T28.3)
X● **T21.19** Burn of first degree of **other site of trunk**

▶ New   ⇒ Revised   ~~deleted~~ Deleted   Excludes 1   Excludes 2   Includes   Use additional   Code first   Code also   Key words
OGCR Official Guidelines   X Assign placeholder X   ● Use Additional Character(s)   ▶ Manifestation Code   🦠 Hierarchical Condition Category   **Coding Clinic**

● **T21.2**   Burn of second degree of trunk

> Use additional external cause code to identify the source, place and intent of the burn (X00-X19, X75-X77, X96-X98, Y92)

X● **T21.20**   Burn of second degree of trunk, unspecified site

X● **T21.21**   Burn of second degree of chest wall
> Burn of second degree of breast

X● **T21.22**   Burn of second degree of abdominal wall
> Burn of second degree of flank
> Burn of second degree of groin

X● **T21.23**   Burn of second degree of upper back
> Burn of second degree of interscapular region

X● **T21.24**   Burn of second degree of lower back

X● **T21.25**   Burn of second degree of buttock
> Burn of second degree of anus

X● **T21.26**   Burn of second degree of male genital region ♂
> Burn of second degree of penis
> Burn of second degree of scrotum
> Burn of second degree of testis

X● **T21.27**   Burn of second degree of female genital region ♀
> Burn of second degree of labium (majus) (minus)
> Burn of second degree of perineum
> Burn of second degree of vulva
>
> **Excludes2**   burn of vagina (T28.3)

X● **T21.29**   Burn of second degree of other site of trunk

● **T21.3**   Burn of third degree of trunk

> Use additional external cause code to identify the source, place and intent of the burn (X00-X19, X75-X77, X96-X98, Y92)

X● **T21.30**   Burn of third degree of trunk, unspecified site

X● **T21.31**   Burn of third degree of chest wall
> Burn of third degree of breast
> **Coding Clinic: 2016, Q2, P6**

X● **T21.32**   Burn of third degree of abdominal wall
> Burn of third degree of flank
> Burn of third degree of groin

X● **T21.33**   Burn of third degree of upper back
> Burn of third degree of interscapular region

X● **T21.34**   Burn of third degree of lower back

X● **T21.35**   Burn of third degree of buttock
> Burn of third degree of anus

X● **T21.36**   Burn of third degree of male genital region ♂
> Burn of third degree of penis
> Burn of third degree of scrotum
> Burn of third degree of testis

X● **T21.37**   Burn of third degree of female genital region ♀
> Burn of third degree of labium (majus) (minus)
> Burn of third degree of perineum
> Burn of third degree of vulva
>
> **Excludes2**   burn of vagina (T28.3)

X● **T21.39**   Burn of third degree of other site of trunk

● **T21.4**   Corrosion of unspecified degree of trunk

> *Code first* (T51-T65) *to identify chemical and intent*
> Use additional external cause code to identify place (Y92)

X● **T21.40**   Corrosion of unspecified degree of trunk, unspecified site

X● **T21.41**   Corrosion of unspecified degree of chest wall
> Corrosion of unspecified degree of breast

X● **T21.42**   Corrosion of unspecified degree of abdominal wall
> Corrosion of unspecified degree of flank
> Corrosion of unspecified degree of groin

X● **T21.43**   Corrosion of unspecified degree of upper back
> Corrosion of unspecified degree of interscapular region

X● **T21.44**   Corrosion of unspecified degree of lower back

X● **T21.45**   Corrosion of unspecified degree of buttock
> Corrosion of unspecified degree of anus

X● **T21.46**   Corrosion of unspecified degree of male genital region ♂
> Corrosion of unspecified degree of penis
> Corrosion of unspecified degree of scrotum
> Corrosion of unspecified degree of testis

X● **T21.47**   Corrosion of unspecified degree of female genital region ♀
> Corrosion of unspecified degree of labium (majus) (minus)
> Corrosion of unspecified degree of perineum
> Corrosion of unspecified degree of vulva
>
> **Excludes2**   corrosion of vagina (T28.8)

X● **T21.49**   Corrosion of unspecified degree of other site of trunk

● **T21.5**   Corrosion of first degree of trunk

> *Code first* (T51-T65) *to identify chemical and intent*
> Use additional external cause code to identify place (Y92)

X● **T21.50**   Corrosion of first degree of trunk, unspecified site

X● **T21.51**   Corrosion of first degree of chest wall
> Corrosion of first degree of breast

X● **T21.52**   Corrosion of first degree of abdominal wall
> Corrosion of first degree of flank
> Corrosion of first degree of groin

X● **T21.53**   Corrosion of first degree of upper back
> Corrosion of first degree of interscapular region

X● **T21.54**   Corrosion of first degree of lower back

X● **T21.55**   Corrosion of first degree of buttock
> Corrosion of first degree of anus

X● **T21.56**   Corrosion of first degree of male genital region ♂
> Corrosion of first degree of penis
> Corrosion of first degree of scrotum
> Corrosion of first degree of testis

X● **T21.57**   Corrosion of first degree of female genital region ♀
> Corrosion of first degree of labium (majus) (minus)
> Corrosion of first degree of perineum
> Corrosion of first degree of vulva
>
> **Excludes2**   corrosion of vagina (T28.8)

X● **T21.59**   Corrosion of first degree of other site of trunk

● **T21.6**   Corrosion of second degree of trunk

> *Code first* (T51-T65) *to identify chemical and intent*
> Use additional external cause code to identify place (Y92)

X● **T21.60**   Corrosion of second degree of trunk, unspecified site

X● **T21.61**   Corrosion of second degree of chest wall
> Corrosion of second degree of breast

X● **T21.62**   Corrosion of second degree of abdominal wall
> Corrosion of second degree of flank
> Corrosion of second degree of groin

X● **T21.63**   Corrosion of second degree of upper back
> Corrosion of second degree of interscapular region

X● **T21.64**   Corrosion of second degree of lower back

X● **T21.65**   Corrosion of second degree of buttock
> Corrosion of second degree of anus

X● **T21.66**   Corrosion of second degree of male genital region ♂
> Corrosion of second degree of penis
> Corrosion of second degree of scrotum
> Corrosion of second degree of testis

X● **T21.67** **Corrosion of second degree of female genital region ♀**
  Corrosion of second degree of labium (majus) (minus)
  Corrosion of second degree of perineum
  Corrosion of second degree of vulva
  Excludes2 corrosion of vagina (T28.8)

X● **T21.69** **Corrosion of second degree of other site of trunk**

● **T21.7** **Corrosion of third degree of trunk**
  Code first (T51-T65) to identify chemical and intent
  Use additional external cause code to identify place (Y92)

X● **T21.70** **Corrosion of third degree of trunk, unspecified site**

X● **T21.71** **Corrosion of third degree of chest wall**
  Corrosion of third degree of breast

X● **T21.72** **Corrosion of third degree of abdominal wall**
  Corrosion of third degree of flank
  Corrosion of third degree of groin

X● **T21.73** **Corrosion of third degree of upper back**
  Corrosion of third degree of interscapular region

X● **T21.74** **Corrosion of third degree of lower back**

X● **T21.75** **Corrosion of third degree of buttock**
  Corrosion of third degree of anus

X● **T21.76** **Corrosion of third degree of male genital region ♂**
  Corrosion of third degree of penis
  Corrosion of third degree of scrotum
  Corrosion of third degree of testis

X● **T21.77** **Corrosion of third degree of female genital region ♀**
  Corrosion of third degree of labium (majus) (minus)
  Corrosion of third degree of perineum
  Corrosion of third degree of vulva
  Excludes2 corrosion of vagina (T28.8)

X● **T21.79** **Corrosion of third degree of other site of trunk**

● **T22** **Burn and corrosion of shoulder and upper limb, except wrist and hand**
  Excludes2 burn and corrosion of interscapular region (T21.-)
      burn and corrosion of wrist and hand (T23.-)
  The appropriate 7th character is to be added to each code from category T22

A	initial encounter
D	subsequent encounter
S	sequela

● **T22.0** **Burn of unspecified degree of shoulder and upper limb, except wrist and hand**
  Use additional external cause code to identify the source, place and intent of the burn (X00-X19, X75-X77, X96-X98, Y92)

X● **T22.00** **Burn of unspecified degree of shoulder and upper limb, except wrist and hand, unspecified site**

● **T22.01** **Burn of unspecified degree of forearm**

  ● **T22.011** **Burn of unspecified degree of right forearm**

  ● **T22.012** **Burn of unspecified degree of left forearm**

  ● **T22.019** **Burn of unspecified degree of unspecified forearm**

● **T22.02** **Burn of unspecified degree of elbow**

  ● **T22.021** **Burn of unspecified degree of right elbow**

  ● **T22.022** **Burn of unspecified degree of left elbow**

  ● **T22.029** **Burn of unspecified degree of unspecified elbow**

● **T22.03** **Burn of unspecified degree of upper arm**

  ● **T22.031** **Burn of unspecified degree of right upper arm**

  ● **T22.032** **Burn of unspecified degree of left upper arm**

  ● **T22.039** **Burn of unspecified degree of unspecified upper arm**

● **T22.04** **Burn of unspecified degree of axilla**

  ● **T22.041** **Burn of unspecified degree of right axilla**

  ● **T22.042** **Burn of unspecified degree of left axilla**

  ● **T22.049** **Burn of unspecified degree of unspecified axilla**

● **T22.05** **Burn of unspecified degree of shoulder**

  ● **T22.051** **Burn of unspecified degree of right shoulder**

  ● **T22.052** **Burn of unspecified degree of left shoulder**

  ● **T22.059** **Burn of unspecified degree of unspecified shoulder**

● **T22.06** **Burn of unspecified degree of scapular region**

  ● **T22.061** **Burn of unspecified degree of right scapular region**

  ● **T22.062** **Burn of unspecified degree of left scapular region**

  ● **T22.069** **Burn of unspecified degree of unspecified scapular region**

● **T22.09** **Burn of unspecified degree of multiple sites of shoulder and upper limb, except wrist and hand**

  ● **T22.091** **Burn of unspecified degree of multiple sites of right shoulder and upper limb, except wrist and hand**

  ● **T22.092** **Burn of unspecified degree of multiple sites of left shoulder and upper limb, except wrist and hand**

  ● **T22.099** **Burn of unspecified degree of multiple sites of unspecified shoulder and upper limb, except wrist and hand**

● **T22.1** **Burn of first degree of shoulder and upper limb, except wrist and hand**
  Use additional external cause code to identify the source, place and intent of the burn (X00-X19, X75-X77, X96-X98, Y92)

X● **T22.10** **Burn of first degree of shoulder and upper limb, except wrist and hand, unspecified site**

● **T22.11** **Burn of first degree of forearm**

  ● **T22.111** **Burn of first degree of right forearm**

  ● **T22.112** **Burn of first degree of left forearm**

  ● **T22.119** **Burn of first degree of unspecified forearm**

● **T22.12** **Burn of first degree of elbow**

  ● **T22.121** **Burn of first degree of right elbow**

  ● **T22.122** **Burn of first degree of left elbow**

  ● **T22.129** **Burn of first degree of unspecified elbow**

▶ New   ⇒ Revised   ~~deleted~~ Deleted   Excludes 1   Excludes 2   Includes   Use additional   Code first   Code also   Key words

1378   OGCR Official Guidelines   X Assign placeholder X   ● Use Additional Character(s)   ⟩ Manifestation Code   🅠 Hierarchical Condition Category   **Coding Clinic**

● **T22.13**   Burn of first degree of upper arm
   ● **T22.131**   Burn of first degree of right upper arm
   ● **T22.132**   Burn of first degree of left upper arm
   ● **T22.139**   Burn of first degree of unspecified upper arm
● **T22.14**   Burn of first degree of axilla
   ● **T22.141**   Burn of first degree of right axilla
   ● **T22.142**   Burn of first degree of left axilla
   ● **T22.149**   Burn of first degree of unspecified axilla
● **T22.15**   Burn of first degree of shoulder
   ● **T22.151**   Burn of first degree of right shoulder
   ● **T22.152**   Burn of first degree of left shoulder
   ● **T22.159**   Burn of first degree of unspecified shoulder
● **T22.16**   Burn of first degree of scapular region
   ● **T22.161**   Burn of first degree of right scapular region
   ● **T22.162**   Burn of first degree of left scapular region
   ● **T22.169**   Burn of first degree of unspecified scapular region
● **T22.19**   Burn of first degree of multiple sites of shoulder and upper limb, except wrist and hand
   ● **T22.191**   Burn of first degree of multiple sites of right shoulder and upper limb, except wrist and hand
   ● **T22.192**   Burn of first degree of multiple sites of left shoulder and upper limb, except wrist and hand
   ● **T22.199**   Burn of first degree of multiple sites of unspecified shoulder and upper limb, except wrist and hand
● **T22.2**   Burn of second degree of shoulder and upper limb, except wrist and hand
   Use additional external cause code to identify the source, place and intent of the burn (X00-X19, X75-X77, X96-X98, Y92)
   X● **T22.20**   Burn of second degree of shoulder and upper limb, except wrist and hand, unspecified site
   ● **T22.21**   Burn of second degree of forearm
     ● **T22.211**   Burn of second degree of right forearm
     ● **T22.212**   Burn of second degree of left forearm
     ● **T22.219**   Burn of second degree of unspecified forearm
   ● **T22.22**   Burn of second degree of elbow
     ● **T22.221**   Burn of second degree of right elbow
     ● **T22.222**   Burn of second degree of left elbow
     ● **T22.229**   Burn of second degree of unspecified elbow
   ● **T22.23**   Burn of second degree of upper arm
     ● **T22.231**   Burn of second degree of right upper arm
     ● **T22.232**   Burn of second degree of left upper arm
     ● **T22.239**   Burn of second degree of unspecified upper arm
   ● **T22.24**   Burn of second degree of axilla
     ● **T22.241**   Burn of second degree of right axilla
     ● **T22.242**   Burn of second degree of left axilla
     ● **T22.249**   Burn of second degree of unspecified axilla

● **T22.25**   Burn of second degree of shoulder
   ● **T22.251**   Burn of second degree of right shoulder
   ● **T22.252**   Burn of second degree of left shoulder
   ● **T22.259**   Burn of second degree of unspecified shoulder
● **T22.26**   Burn of second degree of scapular region
   ● **T22.261**   Burn of second degree of right scapular region
   ● **T22.262**   Burn of second degree of left scapular region
   ● **T22.269**   Burn of second degree of unspecified scapular region
● **T22.29**   Burn of second degree of multiple sites of shoulder and upper limb, except wrist and hand
   ● **T22.291**   Burn of second degree of multiple sites of right shoulder and upper limb, except wrist and hand
   ● **T22.292**   Burn of second degree of multiple sites of left shoulder and upper limb, except wrist and hand
   ● **T22.299**   Burn of second degree of multiple sites of unspecified shoulder and upper limb, except wrist and hand
● **T22.3**   Burn of third degree of shoulder and upper limb, except wrist and hand
   Use additional external cause code to identify the source, place and intent of the burn (X00-X19, X75-X77, X96-X98, Y92)
   X● **T22.30**   Burn of third degree of shoulder and upper limb, except wrist and hand, unspecified site
   ● **T22.31**   Burn of third degree of forearm
     ● **T22.311**   Burn of third degree of right forearm
     ● **T22.312**   Burn of third degree of left forearm
     ● **T22.319**   Burn of third degree of unspecified forearm
   ● **T22.32**   Burn of third degree of elbow
     ● **T22.321**   Burn of third degree of right elbow
     ● **T22.322**   Burn of third degree of left elbow
     ● **T22.329**   Burn of third degree of unspecified elbow
   ● **T22.33**   Burn of third degree of upper arm
     ● **T22.331**   Burn of third degree of right upper arm
     ● **T22.332**   Burn of third degree of left upper arm
     ● **T22.339**   Burn of third degree of unspecified upper arm
   ● **T22.34**   Burn of third degree of axilla
     ● **T22.341**   Burn of third degree of right axilla
     ● **T22.342**   Burn of third degree of left axilla
     ● **T22.349**   Burn of third degree of unspecified axilla
   ● **T22.35**   Burn of third degree of shoulder
     ● **T22.351**   Burn of third degree of right shoulder
     ● **T22.352**   Burn of third degree of left shoulder
     ● **T22.359**   Burn of third degree of unspecified shoulder
   ● **T22.36**   Burn of third degree of scapular region
     ● **T22.361**   Burn of third degree of right scapular region
     ● **T22.362**   Burn of third degree of left scapular region
     ● **T22.369**   Burn of third degree of unspecified scapular region

CHAPTER 19 (S00-T88)

● **T22.39**   **Burn of third degree of** multiple sites **of shoulder and upper limb, except wrist and hand**

     ● **T22.391**   Burn of third degree of multiple sites of right shoulder and upper limb, except wrist and hand

     ● **T22.392**   Burn of third degree of multiple sites of left shoulder and upper limb, except wrist and hand

     ● **T22.399**   Burn of third degree of multiple sites of unspecified shoulder and upper limb, except wrist and hand

● **T22.4**   **Corrosion of** unspecified degree **of shoulder and upper limb, except wrist and hand**

     Code first (T51-T65) to identify chemical and intent

     Use additional external cause code to identify place (Y92)

X ● **T22.40**   Corrosion of unspecified degree of shoulder and upper limb, except wrist and hand, **unspecified site**

● **T22.41**   Corrosion of unspecified degree of forearm

     ● **T22.411**   Corrosion of unspecified degree of right forearm

     ● **T22.412**   Corrosion of unspecified degree of left forearm

     ● **T22.419**   Corrosion of unspecified degree of unspecified forearm

● **T22.42**   Corrosion of unspecified degree of elbow

     ● **T22.421**   Corrosion of unspecified degree of right elbow

     ● **T22.422**   Corrosion of unspecified degree of left elbow

     ● **T22.429**   Corrosion of unspecified degree of unspecified elbow

● **T22.43**   Corrosion of unspecified degree of upper arm

     ● **T22.431**   Corrosion of unspecified degree of right upper arm

     ● **T22.432**   Corrosion of unspecified degree of left upper arm

     ● **T22.439**   Corrosion of unspecified degree of unspecified upper arm

● **T22.44**   Corrosion of unspecified degree of axilla

     ● **T22.441**   Corrosion of unspecified degree of right axilla

     ● **T22.442**   Corrosion of unspecified degree of left axilla

     ● **T22.449**   Corrosion of unspecified degree of unspecified axilla

● **T22.45**   Corrosion of unspecified degree of shoulder

     ● **T22.451**   Corrosion of unspecified degree of right shoulder

     ● **T22.452**   Corrosion of unspecified degree of left shoulder

     ● **T22.459**   Corrosion of unspecified degree of unspecified shoulder

● **T22.46**   Corrosion of unspecified degree of scapular region

     ● **T22.461**   Corrosion of unspecified degree of right scapular region

     ● **T22.462**   Corrosion of unspecified degree of left scapular region

     ● **T22.469**   Corrosion of unspecified degree of unspecified scapular region

● **T22.49**   **Corrosion of unspecified degree of** multiple sites **of shoulder and upper limb, except wrist and hand**

     ● **T22.491**   Corrosion of unspecified degree of multiple sites of right shoulder and upper limb, except wrist and hand

     ● **T22.492**   Corrosion of unspecified degree of multiple sites of left shoulder and upper limb, except wrist and hand

     ● **T22.499**   Corrosion of unspecified degree of multiple sites of unspecified shoulder and upper limb, except wrist and hand

● **T22.5**   **Corrosion of** first degree **of shoulder and upper limb, except wrist and hand**

     Code first (T51-T65) to identify chemical and intent

     Use additional external cause code to identify place (Y92)

X ● **T22.50**   Corrosion of first degree of shoulder and upper limb, except wrist and hand unspecified site

● **T22.51**   Corrosion of first degree of forearm

     ● **T22.511**   Corrosion of first degree of right forearm

     ● **T22.512**   Corrosion of first degree of left forearm

     ● **T22.519**   Corrosion of first degree of unspecified forearm

● **T22.52**   Corrosion of first degree of elbow

     ● **T22.521**   Corrosion of first degree of right elbow

     ● **T22.522**   Corrosion of first degree of left elbow

     ● **T22.529**   Corrosion of first degree of unspecified elbow

● **T22.53**   Corrosion of first degree of upper arm

     ● **T22.531**   Corrosion of first degree of right upper arm

     ● **T22.532**   Corrosion of first degree of left upper arm

     ● **T22.539**   Corrosion of first degree of unspecified upper arm

● **T22.54**   Corrosion of first degree of axilla

     ● **T22.541**   Corrosion of first degree of right axilla

     ● **T22.542**   Corrosion of first degree of left axilla

     ● **T22.549**   Corrosion of first degree of unspecified axilla

● **T22.55**   Corrosion of first degree of shoulder

     ● **T22.551**   Corrosion of first degree of right shoulder

     ● **T22.552**   Corrosion of first degree of left shoulder

     ● **T22.559**   Corrosion of first degree of unspecified shoulder

● **T22.56**   Corrosion of first degree of scapular region

     ● **T22.561**   Corrosion of first degree of right scapular region

     ● **T22.562**   Corrosion of first degree of left scapular region

     ● **T22.569**   Corrosion of first degree of unspecified scapular region

▶ New   ⇒ Revised   ~~deleted~~ Deleted   Excludes 1   Excludes 2   Includes   Use additional   Code first   Code also   Key words

OGCR Official Guidelines   X Assign placeholder X   ● Use Additional Character(s)   ▷ Manifestation Code   🗞 Hierarchical Condition Category   **Coding Clinic**

● **T22.59**   Corrosion of first degree of multiple sites of shoulder and upper limb, except wrist and hand

     ● **T22.591**   Corrosion of first degree of multiple sites of right shoulder and upper limb, except wrist and hand

     ● **T22.592**   Corrosion of first degree of multiple sites of left shoulder and upper limb, except wrist and hand

     ● **T22.599**   Corrosion of first degree of multiple sites of unspecified shoulder and upper limb, except wrist and hand

● **T22.6**   Corrosion of second degree of shoulder and upper limb, except wrist and hand

     Code first (T51-T65) *to identify chemical and intent*

     Use additional external cause code to identify place (Y92)

X● **T22.60**   Corrosion of second degree of shoulder and upper limb, except wrist and hand, unspecified site

     ● **T22.61**   Corrosion of second degree of forearm

         ● **T22.611**   Corrosion of second degree of right forearm

         ● **T22.612**   Corrosion of second degree of left forearm

         ● **T22.619**   Corrosion of second degree of unspecified forearm

     ● **T22.62**   Corrosion of second degree of elbow

         ● **T22.621**   Corrosion of second degree of right elbow

         ● **T22.622**   Corrosion of second degree of left elbow

         ● **T22.629**   Corrosion of second degree of unspecified elbow

     ● **T22.63**   Corrosion of second degree of upper arm

         ● **T22.631**   Corrosion of second degree of right upper arm

         ● **T22.632**   Corrosion of second degree of left upper arm

         ● **T22.639**   Corrosion of second degree of unspecified upper arm

     ● **T22.64**   Corrosion of second degree of axilla

         ● **T22.641**   Corrosion of second degree of right axilla

         ● **T22.642**   Corrosion of second degree of left axilla

         ● **T22.649**   Corrosion of second degree of unspecified axilla

     ● **T22.65**   Corrosion of second degree of shoulder

         ● **T22.651**   Corrosion of second degree of right shoulder

         ● **T22.652**   Corrosion of second degree of left shoulder

         ● **T22.659**   Corrosion of second degree of unspecified shoulder

     ● **T22.66**   Corrosion of second degree of scapular region

         ● **T22.661**   Corrosion of second degree of right scapular region

         ● **T22.662**   Corrosion of second degree of left scapular region

         ● **T22.669**   Corrosion of second degree of unspecified scapular region

● **T22.69**   Corrosion of second degree of multiple sites of shoulder and upper limb, except wrist and hand

     ● **T22.691**   Corrosion of second degree of multiple sites of right shoulder and upper limb, except wrist and hand

     ● **T22.692**   Corrosion of second degree of multiple sites of left shoulder and upper limb, except wrist and hand

     ● **T22.699**   Corrosion of second degree of multiple sites of unspecified shoulder and upper limb, except wrist and hand

● **T22.7**   Corrosion of third degree of shoulder and upper limb, except wrist and hand

     Code first (T51-T65) *to identify chemical and intent*

     Use additional external cause code to identify place (Y92)

X● **T22.70**   Corrosion of third degree of shoulder and upper limb, except wrist and hand, unspecified site

     ● **T22.71**   Corrosion of third degree of forearm

         ● **T22.711**   Corrosion of third degree of right forearm

         ● **T22.712**   Corrosion of third degree of left forearm

         ● **T22.719**   Corrosion of third degree of unspecified forearm

     ● **T22.72**   Corrosion of third degree of elbow

         ● **T22.721**   Corrosion of third degree of right elbow

         ● **T22.722**   Corrosion of third degree of left elbow

         ● **T22.729**   Corrosion of third degree of unspecified elbow

     ● **T22.73**   Corrosion of third degree of upper arm

         ● **T22.731**   Corrosion of third degree of right upper arm

         ● **T22.732**   Corrosion of third degree of left upper arm

         ● **T22.739**   Corrosion of third degree of unspecified upper arm

     ● **T22.74**   Corrosion of third degree of axilla

         ● **T22.741**   Corrosion of third degree of right axilla

         ● **T22.742**   Corrosion of third degree of left axilla

         ● **T22.749**   Corrosion of third degree of unspecified axilla

     ● **T22.75**   Corrosion of third degree of shoulder

         ● **T22.751**   Corrosion of third degree of right shoulder

         ● **T22.752**   Corrosion of third degree of left shoulder

         ● **T22.759**   Corrosion of third degree of unspecified shoulder

     ● **T22.76**   Corrosion of third degree of scapular region

         ● **T22.761**   Corrosion of third degree of right scapular region

         ● **T22.762**   Corrosion of third degree of left scapular region

         ● **T22.769**   Corrosion of third degree of unspecified scapular region

● T22.79   Corrosion of third degree of multiple sites of shoulder and upper limb, except wrist and hand

     ● T22.791   Corrosion of third degree of multiple sites of right shoulder and upper limb, except wrist and hand

     ● T22.792   Corrosion of third degree of multiple sites of left shoulder and upper limb, except wrist and hand

     ● T22.799   Corrosion of third degree of multiple sites of unspecified shoulder and upper limb, except wrist and hand

● T23   Burn and corrosion of wrist and hand

The appropriate 7th character is to be added to each code from category T23

> | | |
> |---|---|
> | A | initial encounter |
> | D | subsequent encounter |
> | S | sequela |

● T23.0   Burn of unspecified degree of wrist and hand

Use additional external cause code to identify the source, place and intent of the burn (X00-X19, X75-X77, X96-X98, Y92)

   ● T23.00   Burn of unspecified degree of hand, unspecified site

     ● T23.001   Burn of unspecified degree of right hand, unspecified site

     ● T23.002   Burn of unspecified degree of left hand, unspecified site

     ● T23.009   Burn of unspecified degree of unspecified hand, unspecified site

   ● T23.01   Burn of unspecified degree of thumb (nail)

     ● T23.011   Burn of unspecified degree of right thumb (nail)

     ● T23.012   Burn of unspecified degree of left thumb (nail)

     ● T23.019   Burn of unspecified degree of unspecified thumb (nail)

   ● T23.02   Burn of unspecified degree of single finger (nail) except thumb

     ● T23.021   Burn of unspecified degree of single right finger (nail) except thumb

     ● T23.022   Burn of unspecified degree of single left finger (nail) except thumb

     ● T23.029   Burn of unspecified degree of unspecified single finger (nail) except thumb

   ● T23.03   Burn of unspecified degree of multiple fingers (nail), not including thumb

     ● T23.031   Burn of unspecified degree of multiple right fingers (nail), not including thumb

     ● T23.032   Burn of unspecified degree of multiple left fingers (nail), not including thumb

     ● T23.039   Burn of unspecified degree of unspecified multiple fingers (nail), not including thumb

   ● T23.04   Burn of unspecified degree of multiple fingers (nail), including thumb

     ● T23.041   Burn of unspecified degree of multiple right fingers (nail), including thumb

     ● T23.042   Burn of unspecified degree of multiple left fingers (nail), including thumb

     ● T23.049   Burn of unspecified degree of unspecified multiple fingers (nail), including thumb

● T23.05   Burn of unspecified degree of palm

     ● T23.051   Burn of unspecified degree of right palm

     ● T23.052   Burn of unspecified degree of left palm

     ● T23.059   Burn of unspecified degree of unspecified palm

   ● T23.06   Burn of unspecified degree of back of hand

     ● T23.061   Burn of unspecified degree of back of right hand

     ● T23.062   Burn of unspecified degree of back of left hand

     ● T23.069   Burn of unspecified degree of back of unspecified hand

   ● T23.07   Burn of unspecified degree of wrist

     ● T23.071   Burn of unspecified degree of right wrist

     ● T23.072   Burn of unspecified degree of left wrist

     ● T23.079   Burn of unspecified degree of unspecified wrist

   ● T23.09   Burn of unspecified degree of multiple sites of wrist and hand

     ● T23.091   Burn of unspecified degree of multiple sites of right wrist and hand

     ● T23.092   Burn of unspecified degree of multiple sites of left wrist and hand

     ● T23.099   Burn of unspecified degree of multiple sites of unspecified wrist and hand

● T23.1   Burn of first degree of wrist and hand

Use additional external cause code to identify the source, place and intent of the burn (X00-X19, X75-X77, X96-X98, Y92)

   ● T23.10   Burn of first degree of hand, unspecified site

     ● T23.101   Burn of first degree of right hand, unspecified site

     ● T23.102   Burn of first degree of left hand, unspecified site

     ● T23.109   Burn of first degree of unspecified hand, unspecified site

   ● T23.11   Burn of first degree of thumb (nail)

     ● T23.111   Burn of first degree of right thumb (nail)

     ● T23.112   Burn of first degree of left thumb (nail)

     ● T23.119   Burn of first degree of unspecified thumb (nail)

   ● T23.12   Burn of first degree of single finger (nail) except thumb

     ● T23.121   Burn of first degree of single right finger (nail) except thumb

     ● T23.122   Burn of first degree of single left finger (nail) except thumb

     ● T23.129   Burn of first degree of unspecified single finger (nail) except thumb

   ● T23.13   Burn of first degree of multiple fingers (nail), not including thumb

     ● T23.131   Burn of first degree of multiple right fingers (nail), not including thumb

     ● T23.132   Burn of first degree of multiple left fingers (nail), not including thumb

     ● T23.139   Burn of first degree of unspecified multiple fingers (nail), not including thumb

● **T23.14**　Burn of first degree of multiple fingers (nail), including thumb
　● **T23.141**　Burn of first degree of multiple right fingers (nail), including thumb
　● **T23.142**　Burn of first degree of multiple left fingers (nail), including thumb
　● **T23.149**　Burn of first degree of unspecified multiple fingers (nail), including thumb
● **T23.15**　Burn of first degree of palm
　● **T23.151**　Burn of first degree of right palm
　● **T23.152**　Burn of first degree of left palm
　● **T23.159**　Burn of first degree of unspecified palm
● **T23.16**　Burn of first degree of back of hand
　● **T23.161**　Burn of first degree of back of right hand
　● **T23.162**　Burn of first degree of back of left hand
　● **T23.169**　Burn of first degree of back of unspecified hand
● **T23.17**　Burn of first degree of wrist
　● **T23.171**　Burn of first degree of right wrist
　● **T23.172**　Burn of first degree of left wrist
　● **T23.179**　Burn of first degree of unspecified wrist
● **T23.19**　Burn of first degree of multiple sites of wrist and hand
　● **T23.191**　Burn of first degree of multiple sites of right wrist and hand
　● **T23.192**　Burn of first degree of multiple sites of left wrist and hand
　● **T23.199**　Burn of first degree of multiple sites of unspecified wrist and hand

● **T23.2**　Burn of second degree of wrist and hand
　Use additional external cause code to identify the source, place and intent of the burn (X00-X19, X75-X77, X96-X98, Y92)
● **T23.20**　Burn of second degree of hand, unspecified site
　● **T23.201**　Burn of second degree of right hand, unspecified site
　● **T23.202**　Burn of second degree of left hand, unspecified site
　● **T23.209**　Burn of second degree of unspecified hand, unspecified site
● **T23.21**　Burn of second degree of thumb (nail)
　● **T23.211**　Burn of second degree of right thumb (nail)
　● **T23.212**　Burn of second degree of left thumb (nail)
　● **T23.219**　Burn of second degree of unspecified thumb (nail)
● **T23.22**　Burn of second degree of single finger (nail) except thumb
　● **T23.221**　Burn of second degree of single right finger (nail) except thumb
　● **T23.222**　Burn of second degree of single left finger (nail) except thumb
　● **T23.229**　Burn of second degree of unspecified single finger (nail) except thumb
● **T23.23**　Burn of second degree of multiple fingers (nail), not including thumb
　● **T23.231**　Burn of second degree of multiple right fingers (nail), not including thumb
　● **T23.232**　Burn of second degree of multiple left fingers (nail), not including thumb
　● **T23.239**　Burn of second degree of unspecified multiple fingers (nail), not including thumb

● **T23.24**　Burn of second degree of multiple fingers (nail), including thumb
　● **T23.241**　Burn of second degree of multiple right fingers (nail), including thumb
　● **T23.242**　Burn of second degree of multiple left fingers (nail), including thumb
　● **T23.249**　Burn of second degree of unspecified multiple fingers (nail), including thumb
● **T23.25**　Burn of second degree of palm
　● **T23.251**　Burn of second degree of right palm
　● **T23.252**　Burn of second degree of left palm
　● **T23.259**　Burn of second degree of unspecified palm
● **T23.26**　Burn of second degree of back of hand
　● **T23.261**　Burn of second degree of back of right hand
　● **T23.262**　Burn of second degree of back of left hand
　● **T23.269**　Burn of second degree of back of unspecified hand
● **T23.27**　Burn of second degree of wrist
　● **T23.271**　Burn of second degree of right wrist
　● **T23.272**　Burn of second degree of left wrist
　● **T23.279**　Burn of second degree of unspecified wrist
● **T23.29**　Burn of second degree of multiple sites of wrist and hand
　● **T23.291**　Burn of second degree of multiple sites of right wrist and hand
　● **T23.292**　Burn of second degree of multiple sites of left wrist and hand
　● **T23.299**　Burn of second degree of multiple sites of unspecified wrist and hand

● **T23.3**　Burn of third degree of wrist and hand
　Use additional external cause code to identify the source, place and intent of the burn (X00-X19, X75-X77, X96-X98, Y92)
● **T23.30**　Burn of third degree of hand, unspecified site
　● **T23.301**　Burn of third degree of right hand, unspecified site
　　Coding Clinic: 2015, Q1, P19
　● **T23.302**　Burn of third degree of left hand, unspecified site
　　Coding Clinic: 2016, Q2, P5
　● **T23.309**　Burn of third degree of unspecified hand, unspecified site
● **T23.31**　Burn of third degree of thumb (nail)
　● **T23.311**　Burn of third degree of right thumb (nail)
　● **T23.312**　Burn of third degree of left thumb (nail)
　● **T23.319**　Burn of third degree of unspecified thumb (nail)
● **T23.32**　Burn of third degree of single finger (nail) except thumb
　● **T23.321**　Burn of third degree of single right finger (nail) except thumb
　● **T23.322**　Burn of third degree of single left finger (nail) except thumb
　● **T23.329**　Burn of third degree of unspecified single finger (nail) except thumb
● **T23.33**　Burn of third degree of multiple fingers (nail), not including thumb
　● **T23.331**　Burn of third degree of multiple right fingers (nail), not including thumb
　● **T23.332**　Burn of third degree of multiple left fingers (nail), not including thumb
　● **T23.339**　Burn of third degree of unspecified multiple fingers (nail), not including thumb

● **T23.34** Burn of third degree of multiple fingers (nail), including thumb

  ● **T23.341** Burn of third degree of multiple right fingers (nail), including thumb

  ● **T23.342** Burn of third degree of multiple left fingers (nail), including thumb

  ● **T23.349** Burn of third degree of unspecified multiple fingers (nail), including thumb

● **T23.35** Burn of third degree of palm

  ● **T23.351** Burn of third degree of right palm

  ● **T23.352** Burn of third degree of left palm

  ● **T23.359** Burn of third degree of unspecified palm

● **T23.36** Burn of third degree of back of hand

  ● **T23.361** Burn of third degree of back of right hand

  ● **T23.362** Burn of third degree of back of left hand

  ● **T23.369** Burn of third degree of back of unspecified hand

● **T23.37** Burn of third degree of wrist

  ● **T23.371** Burn of third degree of right wrist

  ● **T23.372** Burn of third degree of left wrist

  ● **T23.379** Burn of third degree of unspecified wrist

● **T23.39** Burn of third degree of multiple sites of wrist and hand

  ● **T23.391** Burn of third degree of multiple sites of right wrist and hand

  ● **T23.392** Burn of third degree of multiple sites of left wrist and hand

  ● **T23.399** Burn of third degree of multiple sites of unspecified wrist and hand

● **T23.4** Corrosion of unspecified degree of wrist and hand

  Code first (T51-T65) to identify chemical and intent

  Use additional external cause code to identify place (Y92)

  ● **T23.40** Corrosion of unspecified degree of hand, unspecified site

  ● **T23.401** Corrosion of unspecified degree of right hand, unspecified site

  ● **T23.402** Corrosion of unspecified degree of left hand, unspecified site

  ● **T23.409** Corrosion of unspecified degree of unspecified hand, unspecified site

  ● **T23.41** Corrosion of unspecified degree of thumb (nail)

  ● **T23.411** Corrosion of unspecified degree of right thumb (nail)

  ● **T23.412** Corrosion of unspecified degree of left thumb (nail)

  ● **T23.419** Corrosion of unspecified degree of unspecified thumb (nail)

  ● **T23.42** Corrosion of unspecified degree of single finger (nail) except thumb

  ● **T23.421** Corrosion of unspecified degree of single right finger (nail) except thumb

  ● **T23.422** Corrosion of unspecified degree of single left finger (nail) except thumb

  ● **T23.429** Corrosion of unspecified degree of unspecified single finger (nail) except thumb

● **T23.43** Corrosion of unspecified degree of multiple fingers (nail), not including thumb

  ● **T23.431** Corrosion of unspecified degree of multiple right fingers (nail), not including thumb

  ● **T23.432** Corrosion of unspecified degree of multiple left fingers (nail), not including thumb

  ● **T23.439** Corrosion of unspecified degree of unspecified multiple fingers (nail), not including thumb

● **T23.44** Corrosion of unspecified degree of multiple fingers (nail), including thumb

  ● **T23.441** Corrosion of unspecified degree of multiple right fingers (nail), including thumb

  ● **T23.442** Corrosion of unspecified degree of multiple left fingers (nail), including thumb

  ● **T23.449** Corrosion of unspecified degree of unspecified multiple fingers (nail), including thumb

● **T23.45** Corrosion of unspecified degree of palm

  ● **T23.451** Corrosion of unspecified degree of right palm

  ● **T23.452** Corrosion of unspecified degree of left palm

  ● **T23.459** Corrosion of unspecified degree of unspecified palm

● **T23.46** Corrosion of unspecified degree of back of hand

  ● **T23.461** Corrosion of unspecified degree of back of right hand

  ● **T23.462** Corrosion of unspecified degree of back of left hand

  ● **T23.469** Corrosion of unspecified degree of back of unspecified hand

● **T23.47** Corrosion of unspecified degree of wrist

  ● **T23.471** Corrosion of unspecified degree of right wrist

  ● **T23.472** Corrosion of unspecified degree of left wrist

  ● **T23.479** Corrosion of unspecified degree of unspecified wrist

● **T23.49** Corrosion of unspecified degree of multiple sites of wrist and hand

  ● **T23.491** Corrosion of unspecified degree of multiple sites of right wrist and hand

  ● **T23.492** Corrosion of unspecified degree of multiple sites of left wrist and hand

  ● **T23.499** Corrosion of unspecified degree of multiple sites of unspecified wrist and hand

● **T23.5** Corrosion of first degree of wrist and hand

  Code first (T51-T65) to identify chemical and intent

  Use additional external cause code to identify place (Y92)

  ● **T23.50** Corrosion of first degree of hand, unspecified site

  ● **T23.501** Corrosion of first degree of right hand, unspecified site

  ● **T23.502** Corrosion of first degree of left hand, unspecified site

  ● **T23.509** Corrosion of first degree of unspecified hand, unspecified site

---

▶ New ⇨ Revised ~~deleted~~ Deleted | Excludes 1 | Excludes 2 | Includes | Use additional | Code first | Code also | Key words

OGCR Official Guidelines   X Assign placeholder X   ● Use Additional Character(s)   ▷ Manifestation Code   ℞ Hierarchical Condition Category   **Coding Clinic**

● **T23.51** Corrosion of first degree of thumb (nail)
- ● **T23.511** Corrosion of first degree of right thumb (nail)
- ● **T23.512** Corrosion of first degree of left thumb (nail)
- ● **T23.519** Corrosion of first degree of unspecified thumb (nail)

● **T23.52** Corrosion of first degree of single finger (nail) except thumb
- ● **T23.521** Corrosion of first degree of single right finger (nail) except thumb
- ● **T23.522** Corrosion of first degree of single left finger (nail) except thumb
- ● **T23.529** Corrosion of first degree of unspecified single finger (nail) except thumb

● **T23.53** Corrosion of first degree of multiple fingers (nail), not including thumb
- ● **T23.531** Corrosion of first degree of multiple right fingers (nail), not including thumb
- ● **T23.532** Corrosion of first degree of multiple left fingers (nail), not including thumb
- ● **T23.539** Corrosion of first degree of unspecified multiple fingers (nail), not including thumb

● **T23.54** Corrosion of first degree of multiple fingers (nail), including thumb
- ● **T23.541** Corrosion of first degree of multiple right fingers (nail), including thumb
- ● **T23.542** Corrosion of first degree of multiple left fingers (nail), including thumb
- ● **T23.549** Corrosion of first degree of unspecified multiple fingers (nail), including thumb

● **T23.55** Corrosion of first degree of palm
- ● **T23.551** Corrosion of first degree of right palm
- ● **T23.552** Corrosion of first degree of left palm
- ● **T23.559** Corrosion of first degree of unspecified palm

● **T23.56** Corrosion of first degree of back of hand
- ● **T23.561** Corrosion of first degree of back of right hand
- ● **T23.562** Corrosion of first degree of back of left hand
- ● **T23.569** Corrosion of first degree of back of unspecified hand

● **T23.57** Corrosion of first degree of wrist
- ● **T23.571** Corrosion of first degree of right wrist
- ● **T23.572** Corrosion of first degree of left wrist
- ● **T23.579** Corrosion of first degree of unspecified wrist

● **T23.59** Corrosion of first degree of multiple sites of wrist and hand
- ● **T23.591** Corrosion of first degree of multiple sites of right wrist and hand
- ● **T23.592** Corrosion of first degree of multiple sites of left wrist and hand
- ● **T23.599** Corrosion of first degree of multiple sites of unspecified wrist and hand

● **T23.6** Corrosion of second degree of wrist and hand
    Code first (T51-T65) to identify chemical and intent
    Use additional external cause code to identify place (Y92)
- ● **T23.60** Corrosion of second degree of hand, unspecified site
  - ● **T23.601** Corrosion of second degree of right hand, unspecified site
  - ● **T23.602** Corrosion of second degree of left hand, unspecified site
  - ● **T23.609** Corrosion of second degree of unspecified hand, unspecified site
- ● **T23.61** Corrosion of second degree of thumb (nail)
  - ● **T23.611** Corrosion of second degree of right thumb (nail)
  - ● **T23.612** Corrosion of second degree of left thumb (nail)
  - ● **T23.619** Corrosion of second degree of unspecified thumb (nail)
- ● **T23.62** Corrosion of second degree of single finger (nail) except thumb
  - ● **T23.621** Corrosion of second degree of single right finger (nail) except thumb
  - ● **T23.622** Corrosion of second degree of single left finger (nail) except thumb
  - ● **T23.629** Corrosion of second degree of unspecified single finger (nail) except thumb
- ● **T23.63** Corrosion of second degree of multiple fingers (nail), not including thumb
  - ● **T23.631** Corrosion of second degree of multiple right fingers (nail), not including thumb
  - ● **T23.632** Corrosion of second degree of multiple left fingers (nail), not including thumb
  - ● **T23.639** Corrosion of second degree of unspecified multiple fingers (nail), not including thumb
- ● **T23.64** Corrosion of second degree of multiple fingers (nail), including thumb
  - ● **T23.641** Corrosion of second degree of multiple right fingers (nail), including thumb
  - ● **T23.642** Corrosion of second degree of multiple left fingers (nail), including thumb
  - ● **T23.649** Corrosion of second degree of unspecified multiple fingers (nail), including thumb
- ● **T23.65** Corrosion of second degree of palm
  - ● **T23.651** Corrosion of second degree of right palm
  - ● **T23.652** Corrosion of second degree of left palm
  - ● **T23.659** Corrosion of second degree of unspecified palm
- ● **T23.66** Corrosion of second degree of back of hand
  - ● **T23.661** Corrosion of second degree back of right hand
  - ● **T23.662** Corrosion of second degree back of left hand
  - ● **T23.669** Corrosion of second degree back of unspecified hand

● T23.67 Corrosion of second degree of wrist

   ● T23.671 Corrosion of second degree of right wrist

   ● T23.672 Corrosion of second degree of left wrist

   ● T23.679 Corrosion of second degree of unspecified wrist

● T23.69 Corrosion of second degree of multiple sites of wrist and hand

   ● T23.691 Corrosion of second degree of multiple sites of right wrist and hand

   ● T23.692 Corrosion of second degree of multiple sites of left wrist and hand

   ● T23.699 Corrosion of second degree of multiple sites of unspecified wrist and hand

● T23.7 Corrosion of third degree of wrist and hand

Code first (T51-T65) to identify chemical and intent

Use additional external cause code to identify place (Y92)

● T23.70 Corrosion of third degree of hand, unspecified site

   ● T23.701 Corrosion of third degree of right hand, unspecified site

   ● T23.702 Corrosion of third degree of left hand, unspecified site

   ● T23.709 Corrosion of third degree of unspecified hand, unspecified site

● T23.71 Corrosion of third degree of thumb (nail)

   ● T23.711 Corrosion of third degree of right thumb (nail)

   ● T23.712 Corrosion of third degree of left thumb (nail)

   ● T23.719 Corrosion of third degree of unspecified thumb (nail)

● T23.72 Corrosion of third degree of single finger (nail) except thumb

   ● T23.721 Corrosion of third degree of single right finger (nail) except thumb

   ● T23.722 Corrosion of third degree of single left finger (nail) except thumb

   ● T23.729 Corrosion of third degree of unspecified single finger (nail) except thumb

● T23.73 Corrosion of third degree of multiple fingers (nail), not including thumb

   ● T23.731 Corrosion of third degree of multiple right fingers (nail), not including thumb

   ● T23.732 Corrosion of third degree of multiple left fingers (nail), not including thumb

   ● T23.739 Corrosion of third degree of unspecified multiple fingers (nail), not including thumb

● T23.74 Corrosion of third degree of multiple fingers (nail), including thumb

   ● T23.741 Corrosion of third degree of multiple right fingers (nail), including thumb

   ● T23.742 Corrosion of third degree of multiple left fingers (nail), including thumb

   ● T23.749 Corrosion of third degree of unspecified multiple fingers (nail), including thumb

● T23.75 Corrosion of third degree of palm

   ● T23.751 Corrosion of third degree of right palm

   ● T23.752 Corrosion of third degree of left palm

   ● T23.759 Corrosion of third degree of unspecified palm

● T23.76 Corrosion of third degree of back of hand

   ● T23.761 Corrosion of third degree of back of right hand

   ● T23.762 Corrosion of third degree of back of left hand

   ● T23.769 Corrosion of third degree of back of unspecified hand

● T23.77 Corrosion of third degree of wrist

   ● T23.771 Corrosion of third degree of right wrist

   ● T23.772 Corrosion of third degree of left wrist

   ● T23.779 Corrosion of third degree of unspecified wrist

● T23.79 Corrosion of third degree of multiple sites of wrist and hand

   ● T23.791 Corrosion of third degree of multiple sites of right wrist and hand

   ● T23.792 Corrosion of third degree of multiple sites of left wrist and hand

   ● T23.799 Corrosion of third degree of multiple sites of unspecified wrist and hand

● T24 Burn and corrosion of lower limb, except ankle and foot

Excludes2 burn and corrosion of ankle and foot (T25.-)
burn and corrosion of hip region (T21.-)

The appropriate 7th character is to be added to each code from category T24

A	initial encounter
D	subsequent encounter
S	sequela

● T24.0 Burn of unspecified degree of lower limb, except ankle and foot

Use additional external cause code to identify the source, place and intent of the burn (X00-X19, X75-X77, X96-X98, Y92)

● T24.00 Burn of unspecified degree of unspecified site of lower limb, except ankle and foot

   ● T24.001 Burn of unspecified degree of unspecified site of right lower limb, except ankle and foot

   ● T24.002 Burn of unspecified degree of unspecified site of left lower limb, except ankle and foot

   ● T24.009 Burn of unspecified degree of unspecified site of unspecified lower limb, except ankle and foot

● T24.01 Burn of unspecified degree of thigh

   ● T24.011 Burn of unspecified degree of right thigh

   ● T24.012 Burn of unspecified degree of left thigh

   ● T24.019 Burn of unspecified degree of unspecified thigh

● T24.02 Burn of unspecified degree of knee

   ● T24.021 Burn of unspecified degree of right knee

   ● T24.022 Burn of unspecified degree of left knee

   ● T24.029 Burn of unspecified degree of unspecified knee

● T24.03 Burn of unspecified degree of lower leg

   ● T24.031 Burn of unspecified degree of right lower leg

   ● T24.032 Burn of unspecified degree of left lower leg

   ● T24.039 Burn of unspecified degree of unspecified lower leg

▶ New ⇒ Revised ~~deleted~~ Deleted Excludes 1 Excludes 2 Includes Use additional Code first Code also Key words

OGCR Official Guidelines X Assign placeholder X ● Use Additional Character(s) ⟩ Manifestation Code 🕭 Hierarchical Condition Category **Coding Clinic**

● T24.09   Burn of unspecified degree of multiple sites of lower limb, except ankle and foot
  ● T24.091   Burn of unspecified degree of multiple sites of right lower limb, except ankle and foot
  ● T24.092   Burn of unspecified degree of multiple sites of left lower limb, except ankle and foot
  ● T24.099   Burn of unspecified degree of multiple sites of unspecified lower limb, except ankle and foot

● T24.1   Burn of first degree of lower limb, except ankle and foot

Use additional external cause code to identify the source, place and intent of the burn (X00-X19, X75-X77, X96-X98, Y92)

  ● T24.10   Burn of first degree of unspecified site of lower limb, except ankle and foot
    ● T24.101   Burn of first degree of unspecified site of right lower limb, except ankle and foot
    ● T24.102   Burn of first degree of unspecified site of left lower limb, except ankle and foot
    ● T24.109   Burn of first degree of unspecified site of unspecified lower limb, except ankle and foot
  ● T24.11   Burn of first degree of thigh
    ● T24.111   Burn of first degree of right thigh
    ● T24.112   Burn of first degree of left thigh
    ● T24.119   Burn of first degree of unspecified thigh
  ● T24.12   Burn of first degree of knee
    ● T24.121   Burn of first degree of right knee
    ● T24.122   Burn of first degree of left knee
    ● T24.129   Burn of first degree of unspecified knee
  ● T24.13   Burn of first degree of lower leg
    ● T24.131   Burn of first degree of right lower leg
    ● T24.132   Burn of first degree of left lower leg
    ● T24.139   Burn of first degree of unspecified lower leg
  ● T24.19   Burn of first degree of multiple sites of lower limb, except ankle and foot
    ● T24.191   Burn of first degree of multiple sites of right lower limb, except ankle and foot
    ● T24.192   Burn of first degree of multiple sites of left lower limb, except ankle and foot
    ● T24.199   Burn of first degree of multiple sites of unspecified lower limb, except ankle and foot

● T24.2   Burn of second degree of lower limb, except ankle and foot

Use additional external cause code to identify the source, place and intent of the burn (X00-X19, X75-X77, X96-X98, Y92)

  ● T24.20   Burn of second degree of unspecified site of lower limb, except ankle and foot
    ● T24.201   Burn of second degree of unspecified site of right lower limb, except ankle and foot
    ● T24.202   Burn of second degree of unspecified site of left lower limb, except ankle and foot
    ● T24.209   Burn of second degree of unspecified site of unspecified lower limb, except ankle and foot

● T24.21   Burn of second degree of thigh
  ● T24.211   Burn of second degree of right thigh
  ● T24.212   Burn of second degree of left thigh
  ● T24.219   Burn of second degree of unspecified thigh
● T24.22   Burn of second degree of knee
  ● T24.221   Burn of second degree of right knee
  ● T24.222   Burn of second degree of left knee
  ● T24.229   Burn of second degree of unspecified knee
● T24.23   Burn of second degree of lower leg
  ● T24.231   Burn of second degree of right lower leg
  ● T24.232   Burn of second degree of left lower leg
  ● T24.239   Burn of second degree of unspecified lower leg
● T24.29   Burn of second degree of multiple sites of lower limb, except ankle and foot
  ● T24.291   Burn of second degree of multiple sites of right lower limb, except ankle and foot
  ● T24.292   Burn of second degree of multiple sites of left lower limb, except ankle and foot
  ● T24.299   Burn of second degree of multiple sites of unspecified lower limb, except ankle and foot

● T24.3   Burn of third degree of lower limb, except ankle and foot

Use additional external cause code to identify the source, place and intent of the burn (X00-X19, X75-X77, X96-X98, Y92)

  ● T24.30   Burn of third degree of unspecified site of lower limb, except ankle and foot
    ● T24.301   Burn of third degree of unspecified site of right lower limb, except ankle and foot
    ● T24.302   Burn of third degree of unspecified site of left lower limb, except ankle and foot
    ● T24.309   Burn of third degree of unspecified site of unspecified lower limb, except ankle and foot
  ● T24.31   Burn of third degree of thigh
    ● T24.311   Burn of third degree of right thigh
    ● T24.312   Burn of third degree of left thigh
    ● T24.319   Burn of third degree of unspecified thigh
  ● T24.32   Burn of third degree of knee
    ● T24.321   Burn of third degree of right knee
    ● T24.322   Burn of third degree of left knee
    ● T24.329   Burn of third degree of unspecified knee
  ● T24.33   Burn of third degree of lower leg
    ● T24.331   Burn of third degree of right lower leg
    ● T24.332   Burn of third degree of left lower leg
    ● T24.339   Burn of third degree of unspecified lower leg
  ● T24.39   Burn of third degree of multiple sites of lower limb, except ankle and foot
    ● T24.391   Burn of third degree of multiple sites of right lower limb, except ankle and foot
       Coding Clinic: 2016, Q2, P5
    ● T24.392   Burn of third degree of multiple sites of left lower limb, except ankle and foot
    ● T24.399   Burn of third degree of multiple sites of unspecified lower limb, except ankle and foot

● **T24.4** **Corrosion of unspecified degree of lower limb, except ankle and foot**

Code first (T51-T65) to identify chemical and intent

Use additional external cause code to identify place (Y92)

● **T24.40** Corrosion of unspecified degree of unspecified site of lower limb, except ankle and foot

● T24.401 Corrosion of unspecified degree of unspecified site of right lower limb, except ankle and foot

● T24.402 Corrosion of unspecified degree of unspecified site of left lower limb, except ankle and foot

● T24.409 Corrosion of unspecified degree of unspecified site of unspecified lower limb, except ankle and foot

● **T24.41** Corrosion of unspecified degree of thigh

● T24.411 Corrosion of unspecified degree of right thigh

● T24.412 Corrosion of unspecified degree of left thigh

● T24.419 Corrosion of unspecified degree of unspecified thigh

● **T24.42** Corrosion of unspecified degree of knee

● T24.421 Corrosion of unspecified degree of right knee

● T24.422 Corrosion of unspecified degree of left knee

● T24.429 Corrosion of unspecified degree of unspecified knee

● **T24.43** Corrosion of unspecified degree of lower leg

● T24.431 Corrosion of unspecified degree of right lower leg

● T24.432 Corrosion of unspecified degree of left lower leg

● T24.439 Corrosion of unspecified degree of unspecified lower leg

● **T24.49** Corrosion of unspecified degree of multiple sites of lower limb, except ankle and foot

● T24.491 Corrosion of unspecified degree of multiple sites of right lower limb, except ankle and foot

● T24.492 Corrosion of unspecified degree of multiple sites of left lower limb, except ankle and foot

● T24.499 Corrosion of unspecified degree of multiple sites of unspecified lower limb, except ankle and foot

● **T24.5** **Corrosion of first degree of lower limb, except ankle and foot**

Code first (T51-T65) to identify chemical and intent

Use additional external cause code to identify place (Y92)

● **T24.50** Corrosion of first degree of unspecified site of lower limb, except ankle and foot

● T24.501 Corrosion of first degree of unspecified site of right lower limb, except ankle and foot

● T24.502 Corrosion of first degree of unspecified site of left lower limb, except ankle and foot

● T24.509 Corrosion of first degree of unspecified site of unspecified lower limb, except ankle and foot

● **T24.51** Corrosion of first degree of thigh

● T24.511 Corrosion of first degree of right thigh

● T24.512 Corrosion of first degree of left thigh

● T24.519 Corrosion of first degree of unspecified thigh

● **T24.52** Corrosion of first degree of knee

● T24.521 Corrosion of first degree of right knee

● T24.522 Corrosion of first degree of left knee

● T24.529 Corrosion of first degree of unspecified knee

● **T24.53** Corrosion of first degree of lower leg

● T24.531 Corrosion of first degree of right lower leg

● T24.532 Corrosion of first degree of left lower leg

● T24.539 Corrosion of first degree of unspecified lower leg

● **T24.59** Corrosion of first degree of multiple sites of lower limb, except ankle and foot

● T24.591 Corrosion of first degree of multiple sites of right lower limb, except ankle and foot

● T24.592 Corrosion of first degree of multiple sites of left lower limb, except ankle and foot

● T24.599 Corrosion of first degree of multiple sites of unspecified lower limb, except ankle and foot

● **T24.6** **Corrosion of second degree of lower limb, except ankle and foot**

Code first (T51-T65) to identify chemical and intent

Use additional external cause code to identify place (Y92)

● **T24.60** Corrosion of second degree of unspecified site of lower limb, except ankle and foot

● T24.601 Corrosion of second degree of unspecified site of right lower limb, except ankle and foot

● T24.602 Corrosion of second degree of unspecified site of left lower limb, except ankle and foot

● T24.609 Corrosion of second degree of unspecified site of unspecified lower limb, except ankle and foot

● **T24.61** Corrosion of second degree of thigh

● T24.611 Corrosion of second degree of right thigh

● T24.612 Corrosion of second degree of left thigh

● T24.619 Corrosion of second degree of unspecified thigh

● **T24.62** Corrosion of second degree of knee

● T24.621 Corrosion of second degree of right knee

● T24.622 Corrosion of second degree of left knee

● T24.629 Corrosion of second degree of unspecified knee

● **T24.63** Corrosion of second degree of lower leg

● T24.631 Corrosion of second degree of right lower leg

● T24.632 Corrosion of second degree of left lower leg

● T24.639 Corrosion of second degree of unspecified lower leg

● **T24.69** Corrosion of second degree of multiple sites of lower limb, except ankle and foot

● T24.691 Corrosion of second degree of multiple sites of right lower limb, except ankle and foot

● T24.692 Corrosion of second degree of multiple sites of left lower limb, except ankle and foot

● T24.699 Corrosion of second degree of multiple sites of unspecified lower limb, except ankle and foot

▶ New   ⇒ Revised   ~~deleted~~ Deleted   Excludes 1   Excludes 2   Includes   Use additional   Code first   Code also   Key words

1388   OGCR Official Guidelines   X Assign placeholder X   ● Use Additional Character(s)   ▷ Manifestation Code   🔴 Hierarchical Condition Category   **Coding Clinic**

- **T24.7**   Corrosion of third degree of lower limb, except ankle and foot
  Code first (T51-T65) to identify chemical and intent
  Use additional external cause code to identify place (Y92)
  - **T24.70**   Corrosion of third degree of unspecified site of lower limb, except ankle and foot
    - **T24.701**   Corrosion of third degree of unspecified site of right lower limb, except ankle and foot
    - **T24.702**   Corrosion of third degree of unspecified site of left lower limb, except ankle and foot
    - **T24.709**   Corrosion of third degree of unspecified site of unspecified lower limb, except ankle and foot
  - **T24.71**   Corrosion of third degree of thigh
    - **T24.711**   Corrosion of third degree of right thigh
    - **T24.712**   Corrosion of third degree of left thigh
    - **T24.719**   Corrosion of third degree of unspecified thigh
  - **T24.72**   Corrosion of third degree of knee
    - **T24.721**   Corrosion of third degree of right knee
    - **T24.722**   Corrosion of third degree of left knee
    - **T24.729**   Corrosion of third degree of unspecified knee
  - **T24.73**   Corrosion of third degree of lower leg
    - **T24.731**   Corrosion of third degree of right lower leg
    - **T24.732**   Corrosion of third degree of left lower leg
    - **T24.739**   Corrosion of third degree of unspecified lower leg
  - **T24.79**   Corrosion of third degree of multiple sites of lower limb, except ankle and foot
    - **T24.791**   Corrosion of third degree of multiple sites of right lower limb, except ankle and foot
    - **T24.792**   Corrosion of third degree of multiple sites of left lower limb, except ankle and foot
    - **T24.799**   Corrosion of third degree of multiple sites of unspecified lower limb, except ankle and foot

- **T25**   Burn and corrosion of ankle and foot
  The appropriate 7th character is to be added to each code from category T25

A	initial encounter
D	subsequent encounter
S	sequela

  - **T25.0**   Burn of unspecifed degree of ankle and foot
    Use additional external cause code to identify the source, place and intent of the burn (X00-X19, X75-X77, X96-X98, Y92)
    - **T25.01**   Burn of unspecified degree of ankle
      - **T25.011**   Burn of unspecified degree of right ankle
      - **T25.012**   Burn of unspecified degree of left ankle
      - **T25.019**   Burn of unspecified degree of unspecified ankle

- **T25.02**   Burn of unspecified degree of foot
  - **Excludes2**   burn of unspecified degree of toe(s) (nail) (T25.03-)
  - **T25.021**   Burn of unspecified degree of right foot
  - **T25.022**   Burn of unspecified degree of left foot
  - **T25.029**   Burn of unspecified degree of unspecified foot
- **T25.03**   Burn of unspecified degree of toe(s) (nail)
  - **T25.031**   Burn of unspecified degree of right toe(s) (nail)
  - **T25.032**   Burn of unspecified degree of left toe(s) (nail)
  - **T25.039**   Burn of unspecified degree of unspecified toe(s) (nail)
- **T25.09**   Burn of unspecified degree of multiple sites of ankle and foot
  - **T25.091**   Burn of unspecified degree of multiple sites of right ankle and foot
  - **T25.092**   Burn of unspecified degree of multiple sites of left ankle and foot
  - **T25.099**   Burn of unspecified degree of multiple sites of unspecified ankle and foot

- **T25.1**   Burn of first degree of ankle and foot
  Use additional external cause code to identify the source, place and intent of the burn (X00-X19, X75-X77, X96-X98, Y92)
  - **T25.11**   Burn of first degree of ankle
    - **T25.111**   Burn of first degree of right ankle
    - **T25.112**   Burn of first degree of left ankle
    - **T25.119**   Burn of first degree of unspecified ankle
  - **T25.12**   Burn of first degree of foot
    - **Excludes2**   burn of first degree of toe(s) (nail) (T25.13-)
    - **T25.121**   Burn of first degree of right foot
    - **T25.122**   Burn of first degree of left foot
    - **T25.129**   Burn of first degree of unspecified foot
  - **T25.13**   Burn of first degree of toe(s) (nail)
    - **T25.131**   Burn of first degree of right toe(s) (nail)
    - **T25.132**   Burn of first degree of left toe(s) (nail)
    - **T25.139**   Burn of first degree of unspecified toe(s) (nail)
  - **T25.19**   Burn of first degree of multiple sites of ankle and foot
    - **T25.191**   Burn of first degree of multiple sites of right ankle and foot
    - **T25.192**   Burn of first degree of multiple sites of left ankle and foot
    - **T25.199**   Burn of first degree of multiple sites of unspecified ankle and foot

- **T25.2**   Burn of second degree of ankle and foot
  Use additional external cause code to identify the source, place and intent of the burn (X00-X19, X75-X77, X96-X98, Y92)
  - **T25.21**   Burn of second degree of ankle
    - **T25.211**   Burn of second degree of right ankle
    - **T25.212**   Burn of second degree of left ankle
    - **T25.219**   Burn of second degree of unspecified ankle
  - **T25.22**   Burn of second degree of foot
    - **Excludes2**   burn of second degree of toe(s) (nail) (T25.23-)
    - **T25.221**   Burn of second degree of right foot
    - **T25.222**   Burn of second degree of left foot
    - **T25.229**   Burn of second degree of unspecified foot

● T25.23   Burn of second degree of toe(s) (nail)
   ● T25.231   Burn of second degree of right toe(s) (nail)
   ● T25.232   Burn of second degree of left toe(s) (nail)
   ● T25.239   Burn of second degree of unspecified toe(s) (nail)
● T25.29   Burn of second degree of multiple sites of ankle and foot
   ● T25.291   Burn of second degree of multiple sites of right ankle and foot
   ● T25.292   Burn of second degree of multiple sites of left ankle and foot
   ● T25.299   Burn of second degree of multiple sites of unspecified ankle and foot

● T25.3   Burn of third degree of ankle and foot
Use additional external cause code to identify the source, place and intent of the burn (X00-X19, X75-X77, X96-X98, Y92)
  ● T25.31   Burn of third degree of ankle
   ● T25.311   Burn of third degree of right ankle
   ● T25.312   Burn of third degree of left ankle
   ● T25.319   Burn of third degree of unspecified ankle
  ● T25.32   Burn of third degree of foot
    Excludes2   burn of third degree of toe(s) (nail) (T25.33-)
   ● T25.321   Burn of third degree of right foot
   ● T25.322   Burn of third degree of left foot
   ● T25.329   Burn of third degree of unspecified foot
  ● T25.33   Burn of third degree of toe(s) (nail)
   ● T25.331   Burn of third degree of right toe(s) (nail)
   ● T25.332   Burn of third degree of left toe(s) (nail)
   ● T25.339   Burn of third degree of unspecified toe(s) (nail)
  ● T25.39   Burn of third degree of multiple sites of ankle and foot
   ● T25.391   Burn of third degree of multiple sites of right ankle and foot
   ● T25.392   Burn of third degree of multiple sites of left ankle and foot
   ● T25.399   Burn of third degree of multiple sites of unspecified ankle and foot

● T25.4   Corrosion of unspecified degree of ankle and foot
Code first (T51-T65) to identify chemical and intent
Use additional external cause code to identify place (Y92)
  ● T25.41   Corrosion of unspecified degree of ankle
   ● T25.411   Corrosion of unspecified degree of right ankle
   ● T25.412   Corrosion of unspecified degree of left ankle
   ● T25.419   Corrosion of unspecified degree of unspecified ankle
  ● T25.42   Corrosion of unspecified degree of foot
    Excludes2   corrosion of unspecified degree of toe(s) (nail) (T25.43-)
   ● T25.421   Corrosion of unspecified degree of right foot
   ● T25.422   Corrosion of unspecified degree of left foot
   ● T25.429   Corrosion of unspecified degree of unspecified foot

● T25.43   Corrosion of unspecified degree of toe(s) (nail)
   ● T25.431   Corrosion of unspecified degree of right toe(s) (nail)
   ● T25.432   Corrosion of unspecified degree of left toe(s) (nail)
   ● T25.439   Corrosion of unspecified degree of unspecified toe(s) (nail)
● T25.49   Corrosion of unspecified degree of multiple sites of ankle and foot
   ● T25.491   Corrosion of unspecified degree of multiple sites of right ankle and foot
   ● T25.492   Corrosion of unspecified degree of multiple sites of left ankle and foot
   ● T25.499   Corrosion of unspecified degree of multiple sites of unspecified ankle and foot

● T25.5   Corrosion of first degree of ankle and foot
Code first (T51-T65) to identify chemical and intent
Use additional external cause code to identify place (Y92)
  ● T25.51   Corrosion of first degree of ankle
   ● T25.511   Corrosion of first degree of right ankle
   ● T25.512   Corrosion of first degree of left ankle
   ● T25.519   Corrosion of first degree of unspecified ankle
  ● T25.52   Corrosion of first degree of foot
    Excludes2   corrosion of first degree of toe(s) (nail) (T25.53-)
   ● T25.521   Corrosion of first degree of right foot
   ● T25.522   Corrosion of first degree of left foot
   ● T25.529   Corrosion of first degree of unspecified foot
  ● T25.53   Corrosion of first degree of toe(s) (nail)
   ● T25.531   Corrosion of first degree of right toe(s) (nail)
   ● T25.532   Corrosion of first degree of left toe(s) (nail)
   ● T25.539   Corrosion of first degree of unspecified toe(s) (nail)
  ● T25.59   Corrosion of first degree of multiple sites of ankle and foot
   ● T25.591   Corrosion of first degree of multiple sites of right ankle and foot
   ● T25.592   Corrosion of first degree of multiple sites of left ankle and foot
   ● T25.599   Corrosion of first degree of multiple sites of unspecified ankle and foot

● T25.6   Corrosion of second degree of ankle and foot
Code first (T51-T65) to identify chemical and intent
Use additional external cause code to identify place (Y92)
  ● T25.61   Corrosion of second degree of ankle
   ● T25.611   Corrosion of second degree of right ankle
   ● T25.612   Corrosion of second degree of left ankle
   ● T25.619   Corrosion of second degree of unspecified ankle
  ● T25.62   Corrosion of second degree of foot
    Excludes2   corrosion of second degree of toe(s) (nail) (T25.63-)
   ● T25.621   Corrosion of second degree of right foot
   ● T25.622   Corrosion of second degree of left foot
   ● T25.629   Corrosion of second degree of unspecified foot

▶ New   ⇒ Revised   ~~deleted~~ Deleted   Excludes 1   Excludes 2   Includes   Use additional   Code first   Code also   Key words
OGCR Official Guidelines   X Assign placeholder X   ● Use Additional Character(s)   ▷ Manifestation Code   🅚 Hierarchical Condition Category   **Coding Clinic**

● T25.63　Corrosion of second degree of toe(s) (nail)
　　● T25.631　Corrosion of second degree of right toe(s) (nail)
　　● T25.632　Corrosion of second degree of left toe(s) (nail)
　　● T25.639　Corrosion of second degree of unspecified toe(s) (nail)
● T25.69　Corrosion of second degree of multiple sites of ankle and foot
　　● T25.691　Corrosion of second degree of right ankle and foot
　　● T25.692　Corrosion of second degree of left ankle and foot
　　● T25.699　Corrosion of second degree of unspecified ankle and foot

● T25.7　Corrosion of third degree of ankle and foot
　　Code first (T51-T65) to identify chemical and intent
　　Use additional external cause code to identify place (Y92)
　● T25.71　Corrosion of third degree of ankle
　　● T25.711　Corrosion of third degree of right ankle
　　● T25.712　Corrosion of third degree of left ankle
　　● T25.719　Corrosion of third degree of unspecified ankle
　● T25.72　Corrosion of third degree of foot
　　　Excludes2　corrosion of third degree of toe(s) (nail) (T25.73-)
　　● T25.721　Corrosion of third degree of right foot
　　● T25.722　Corrosion of third degree of left foot
　　● T25.729　Corrosion of third degree of unspecified foot
　● T25.73　Corrosion of third degree of toe(s) (nail)
　　● T25.731　Corrosion of third degree of right toe(s) (nail)
　　● T25.732　Corrosion of third degree of left toe(s) (nail)
　　● T25.739　Corrosion of third degree of unspecified toe(s) (nail)
　● T25.79　Corrosion of third degree of multiple sites of ankle and foot
　　● T25.791　Corrosion of third degree of multiple sites of right ankle and foot
　　● T25.792　Corrosion of third degree of multiple sites of left ankle and foot
　　● T25.799　Corrosion of third degree of multiple sites of unspecified ankle and foot

BURNS AND CORROSIONS CONFINED TO EYE AND INTERNAL ORGANS (T26-T28)

● T26　Burn and corrosion confined to eye and adnexa
　　The appropriate 7th character is to be added to each code from category T26

A	initial encounter
D	subsequent encounter
S	sequela

● T26.0　Burn of eyelid and periocular area
　　Use additional external cause code to identify the source, place and intent of the burn (X00-X19, X75-X77, X96-X98, Y92)
　X● T26.00　Burn of unspecified eyelid and periocular area
　X● T26.01　Burn of right eyelid and periocular area
　X● T26.02　Burn of left eyelid and periocular area

● T26.1　Burn of cornea and conjunctival sac
　　Use additional external cause code to identify the source, place and intent of the burn (X00-X19, X75-X77, X96-X98, Y92)
　X● T26.10　Burn of cornea and conjunctival sac, unspecified eye
　X● T26.11　Burn of cornea and conjunctival sac, right eye
　X● T26.12　Burn of cornea and conjunctival sac, left eye
● T26.2　Burn with resulting rupture and destruction of eyeball
　　Use additional external cause code to identify the source, place and intent of the burn (X00-X19, X75-X77, X96-X98, Y92)
　X● T26.20　Burn with resulting rupture and destruction of unspecified eyeball
　X● T26.21　Burn with resulting rupture and destruction of right eyeball
　X● T26.22　Burn with resulting rupture and destruction of left eyeball
● T26.3　Burns of other specified parts of eye and adnexa
　　Use additional external cause code to identify the source, place and intent of the burn (X00-X19, X75-X77, X96-X98, Y92)
　X● T26.30　Burns of other specified parts of unspecified eye and adnexa
　X● T26.31　Burns of other specified parts of right eye and adnexa
　X● T26.32　Burns of other specified parts of left eye and adnexa
● T26.4　Burn of eye and adnexa, part unspecified
　　Use additional external cause code to identify the source, place and intent of the burn (X00-X19, X75-X77, X96-X98, Y92)
　X● T26.40　Burn of unspecified eye and adnexa, part unspecified
　X● T26.41　Burn of right eye and adnexa, part unspecified
　X● T26.42　Burn of left eye and adnexa, part unspecified
● T26.5　Corrosion of eyelid and periocular area
　　Code first (T51-T65) to identify chemical and intent
　　Use additional external cause code to identify place (Y92)
　X● T26.50　Corrosion of unspecified eyelid and periocular area
　X● T26.51　Corrosion of right eyelid and periocular area
　X● T26.52　Corrosion of left eyelid and periocular area
● T26.6　Corrosion of cornea and conjunctival sac
　　Code first (T51-T65) to identify chemical and intent
　　Use additional external cause code to identify place (Y92)
　X● T26.60　Corrosion of cornea and conjunctival sac, unspecified eye
　X● T26.61　Corrosion of cornea and conjunctival sac, right eye
　X● T26.62　Corrosion of cornea and conjunctival sac, left eye
● T26.7　Corrosion with resulting rupture and destruction of eyeball
　　Code first (T51-T65) to identify chemical and intent
　　Use additional external cause code to identify place (Y92)
　X● T26.70　Corrosion with resulting rupture and destruction of unspecified eyeball
　X● T26.71　Corrosion with resulting rupture and destruction of right eyeball
　X● T26.72　Corrosion with resulting rupture and destruction of left eyeball

● **T26.8**   Corrosions of other specified parts of eye and adnexa
    Code first (T51-T65) to identify chemical and intent
    Use additional external cause code to identify place (Y92)

   X● **T26.80**   Corrosions of other specified parts of unspecified eye and adnexa

   X● **T26.81**   Corrosions of other specified parts of right eye and adnexa

   X● **T26.82**   Corrosions of other specified parts of left eye and adnexa

● **T26.9**   Corrosion of eye and adnexa, part unspecified
    Code first (T51-T65) to identify chemical and intent
    Use additional external cause code to identify place (Y92)

   X● **T26.90**   Corrosion of unspecified eye and adnexa, part unspecified

   X● **T26.91**   Corrosion of right eye and adnexa, part unspecified

   X● **T26.92**   Corrosion of left eye and adnexa, part unspecified

● **T27**   Burn and corrosion of respiratory tract
    Use additional external cause code to identify the source and intent of the burn (X00-X19, X75-X77, X96-X98)
    Use additional external cause code to identify place (Y92)
    The appropriate 7th character is to be added to each code from category T27

A	initial encounter
D	subsequent encounter
S	sequela

   X● **T27.0**   **Burn of larynx and trachea**

   X● **T27.1**   **Burn involving larynx and trachea with lung**

   X● **T27.2**   **Burn of other parts of respiratory tract**
      Burn of thoracic cavity

   X● **T27.3**   **Burn of respiratory tract, part unspecified**

   X● **T27.4**   **Corrosion of larynx and trachea**
      Code first (T51-T65) to identify chemical and intent

   X● **T27.5**   **Corrosion involving larynx and trachea with lung**
      Code first (T51-T65) to identify chemical and intent

   X● **T27.6**   **Corrosion of other parts of respiratory tract**
      Code first (T51-T65) to identify chemical and intent

   X● **T27.7**   **Corrosion of respiratory tract, part unspecified**
      Code first (T51-T65) to identify chemical and intent

● **T28**   Burn and corrosion of other internal organs
    Use additional external cause code to identify the source and intent of the burn (X00-X19, X75-X77, X96-X98)
    Use additional external cause code to identify place (Y92)
    The appropriate 7th character is to be added to each code from category T28

A	initial encounter
D	subsequent encounter
S	sequela

   X● **T28.0**   **Burn of mouth and pharynx**

   X● **T28.1**   **Burn of esophagus**

   X● **T28.2**   **Burn of other parts of alimentary tract**

   X● **T28.3**   **Burn of internal genitourinary organs**

   X● **T28.4**   **Burns of other and unspecified internal organs**

     X● **T28.40**   Burn of unspecified internal organ

     ● **T28.41**   Burn of ear drum

       ● **T28.411**   Burn of right ear drum

       ● **T28.412**   Burn of left ear drum

       ● **T28.419**   Burn of unspecified ear drum

     X● **T28.49**   Burn of other internal organ

   X● **T28.5**   **Corrosion of mouth and pharynx**
      Code first (T51-T65) to identify chemical and intent

X● **T28.6**   **Corrosion of esophagus**
      Code first (T51-T65) to identify chemical and intent

X● **T28.7**   **Corrosion of other parts of alimentary tract**
      Code first (T51-T65) to identify chemical and intent

X● **T28.8**   **Corrosion of internal genitourinary organs**
      Code first (T51-T65) to identify chemical and intent

● **T28.9**   **Corrosions of other and unspecified internal organs**
      Code first (T51-T65) to identify chemical and intent

   X● **T28.90**   Corrosions of unspecified internal organs

   ● **T28.91**   Corrosions of ear drum

     ● **T28.911**   Corrosions of right ear drum

     ● **T28.912**   Corrosions of left ear drum

     ● **T28.919**   Corrosions of unspecified ear drum

   X● **T28.99**   Corrosions of other internal organs

OGCR Section I.C.19.d.5.

Assign separate code for each burn site
When coding burns, assign separate codes for each burn site. Category T30, Burn and corrosion, body region unspecified is extremely vague and should rarely be used.

BURNS AND CORROSIONS OF MULTIPLE AND UNSPECIFIED BODY REGIONS (T30-T32)

● **T30**   Burn and corrosion, body region unspecified

   T30.0   **Burn of unspecified body region, unspecified degree**
      This code is not for inpatient use. Code to specified site and degree of burns
      Burn NOS
      Multiple burns NOS

   T30.4   **Corrosion of unspecified body region, unspecified degree**
      This code is not for inpatient use. Code to specified site and degree of corrosion
      Corrosion NOS
      Multiple corrosion NOS

● **T31**   Burns classified according to extent of body surface involved
   Note: This category is to be used as the primary code only when the site of the burn is unspecified. It should be used as a supplementary code with categories T20-T25 when the site is specified.

   T31.0   **Burns involving less than 10% of body surface**

● **T31.1**   **Burns involving 10-19% of body surface**

   T31.10   **Burns involving 10-19% of body surface with 0% to 9% third degree burns**
      Burns involving 10-19% of body surface NOS

   T31.11   **Burns involving 10-19% of body surface with 10-19% third degree burns** 🔳

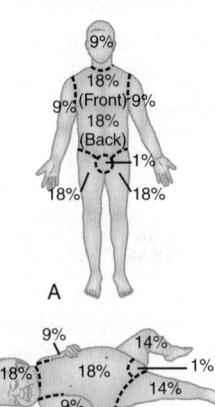

Figure 19-16   Rule of nines: percentages of total body area. (From Marx: Rosen's Emergency Medicine: Concepts and Clinical Practice, ed 6, Mosby, 2006)

▶ New   ⟲ Revised   ~~deleted~~ Deleted   Excludes 1   Excludes 2   Includes   Use additional   Code first   Code also   Key words

OGCR Official Guidelines   X Assign placeholder X   ● Use Additional Character(s)   ▷ Manifestation Code   🔳 Hierarchical Condition Category   **Coding Clinic**

● **T31.2 Burns involving 20-29% of body surface**

   T31.20 Burns involving 20-29% of body surface with 0% to 9% third degree burns
      Burns involving 20-29% of body surface NOS

   T31.21 Burns involving 20-29% of body surface with 10-19% third degree burns 🔏

   T31.22 Burns involving 20-29% of body surface with 20-29% third degree burns 🔏

● **T31.3 Burns involving 30-39% of body surface**

   T31.30 Burns involving 30-39% of body surface with 0% to 9% third degree burns
      Burns involving 30-39% of body surface NOS

   T31.31 Burns involving 30-39% of body surface with 10-19% third degree burns 🔏

   T31.32 Burns involving 30-39% of body surface with 20-29% third degree burns 🔏

   T31.33 Burns involving 30-39% of body surface with 30-39% third degree burns 🔏

● **T31.4 Burns involving 40-49% of body surface**

   T31.40 Burns involving 40-49% of body surface with 0% to 9% third degree burns
      Burns involving 40-49% of body surface NOS

   T31.41 Burns involving 40-49% of body surface with 10-19% third degree burns 🔏

   T31.42 Burns involving 40-49% of body surface with 20-29% third degree burns 🔏

   T31.43 Burns involving 40-49% of body surface with 30-39% third degree burns 🔏

   T31.44 Burns involving 40-49% of body surface with 40-49% third degree burns 🔏

● **T31.5 Burns involving 50-59% of body surface**

   T31.50 Burns involving 50-59% of body surface with 0% to 9% third degree burns
      Burns involving 50-59% of body surface NOS

   T31.51 Burns involving 50-59% of body surface with 10-19% third degree burns 🔏

   T31.52 Burns involving 50-59% of body surface with 20-29% third degree burns 🔏

   T31.53 Burns involving 50-59% of body surface with 30-39% third degree burns 🔏

   T31.54 Burns involving 50-59% of body surface with 40-49% third degree burns 🔏

   T31.55 Burns involving 50-59% of body surface with 50-59% third degree burns 🔏

● **T31.6 Burns involving 60-69% of body surface**

   T31.60 Burns involving 60-69% of body surface with 0% to 9% third degree burns
      Burns involving 60-69% of body surface NOS

   T31.61 Burns involving 60-69% of body surface with 10-19% third degree burns 🔏

   T31.62 Burns involving 60-69% of body surface with 20-29% third degree burns 🔏

   T31.63 Burns involving 60-69% of body surface with 30-39% third degree burns 🔏

   T31.64 Burns involving 60-69% of body surface with 40-49% third degree burns 🔏

   T31.65 Burns involving 60-69% of body surface with 50-59% third degree burns 🔏

   T31.66 Burns involving 60-69% of body surface with 60-69% third degree burns 🔏

● **T31.7 Burns involving 70-79% of body surface**

   T31.70 Burns involving 70-79% of body surface with 0% to 9% third degree burns
      Burns involving 70-79% of body surface NOS

   T31.71 Burns involving 70-79% of body surface with 10-19% third degree burns 🔏

   T31.72 Burns involving 70-79% of body surface with 20-29% third degree burns 🔏

   T31.73 Burns involving 70-79% of body surface with 30-39% third degree burns 🔏

   T31.74 Burns involving 70-79% of body surface with 40-49% third degree burns 🔏

   T31.75 Burns involving 70-79% of body surface with 50-59% third degree burns 🔏

   T31.76 Burns involving 70-79% of body surface with 60-69% third degree burns 🔏

   T31.77 Burns involving 70-79% of body surface with 70-79% third degree burns 🔏

● **T31.8 Burns involving 80-89% of body surface**

   T31.80 Burns involving 80-89% of body surface with 0% to 9% third degree burns
      Burns involving 80-89% of body surface NOS

   T31.81 Burns involving 80-89% of body surface with 10-19% third degree burns 🔏

   T31.82 Burns involving 80-89% of body surface with 20-29% third degree burns 🔏

   T31.83 Burns involving 80-89% of body surface with 30-39% third degree burns 🔏

   T31.84 Burns involving 80-89% of body surface with 40-49% third degree burns 🔏

   T31.85 Burns involving 80-89% of body surface with 50-59% third degree burns 🔏

   T31.86 Burns involving 80-89% of body surface with 60-69% third degree burns 🔏

   T31.87 Burns involving 80-89% of body surface with 70-79% third degree burns 🔏

   T31.88 Burns involving 80-89% of body surface with 80-89% third degree burns 🔏

● **T31.9 Burns involving 90% or more of body surface**

   T31.90 Burns involving 90% or more of body surface with 0% to 9% third degree burns
      Burns involving 90% or more of body surface NOS

   T31.91 Burns involving 90% or more of body surface with 10-19% third degree burns 🔏

   T31.92 Burns involving 90% or more of body surface with 20-29% third degree burns 🔏

   T31.93 Burns involving 90% or more of body surface with 30-39% third degree burns 🔏

   T31.94 Burns involving 90% or more of body surface with 40-49% third degree burns 🔏

   T31.95 Burns involving 90% or more of body surface with 50-59% third degree burns 🔏

   T31.96 Burns involving 90% or more of body surface with 60-69% third degree burns 🔏

   T31.97 Burns involving 90% or more of body surface with 70-79% third degree burns 🔏

   T31.98 Burns involving 90% or more of body surface with 80-89% third degree burns 🔏

   T31.99 Burns involving 90% or more of body surface with 90% or more third degree burns 🔏

CHAPTER 19 (S00-T88)

● **T32** **Corrosions** classified according to **extent of body surface involved**

> **Note:** This category is to be used as the primary code only when the site of the corrosion is unspecified. It may be used as a supplementary code with categories T20-T25 when the site is specified.

T32.0 Corrosions involving **less than 10%** of body surface

● **T32.1** Corrosions involving **10-19%** of body surface

T32.10 Corrosions involving **10-19%** of body surface with **0% to 9% third degree corrosion**
> Corrosions involving 10-19% of body surface NOS

T32.11 Corrosions involving **10-19%** of body surface with **10-19% third degree corrosion** 🔴

● **T32.2** Corrosions involving **20-29%** of body surface

T32.20 Corrosions involving **20-29%** of body surface with **0% to 9% third degree corrosion**

T32.21 Corrosions involving **20-29%** of body surface with **10-19% third degree corrosion** 🔴

T32.22 Corrosions involving **20-29%** of body surface with **20-29% third degree corrosion** 🔴

● **T32.3** Corrosions involving **30-39%** of body surface

T32.30 Corrosions involving **30-39%** of body surface with **0% to 9% third degree corrosion**

T32.31 Corrosions involving **30-39%** of body surface with **10-19% third degree corrosion** 🔴

T32.32 Corrosions involving **30-39%** of body surface with **20-29% third degree corrosion** 🔴

T32.33 Corrosions involving **30-39%** of body surface with **30-39% third degree corrosion** 🔴

● **T32.4** Corrosions involving **40-49%** of body surface

T32.40 Corrosions involving **40-49%** of body surface with **0% to 9% third degree corrosion**

T32.41 Corrosions involving **40-49%** of body surface with **10-19% third degree corrosion** 🔴

T32.42 Corrosions involving **40-49%** of body surface with **20-29% third degree corrosion** 🔴

T32.43 Corrosions involving **40-49%** of body surface with **30-39% third degree corrosion** 🔴

T32.44 Corrosions involving **40-49%** of body surface with **40-49% third degree corrosion** 🔴

● **T32.5** Corrosions involving **50-59%** of body surface

T32.50 Corrosions involving **50-59%** of body surface with **0% to 9% third degree corrosion**

T32.51 Corrosions involving **50-59%** of body surface with **10-19% third degree corrosion** 🔴

T32.52 Corrosions involving **50-59%** of body surface with **20-29% third degree corrosion** 🔴

T32.53 Corrosions involving **50-59%** of body surface with **30-39% third degree corrosion** 🔴

T32.54 Corrosions involving **50-59%** of body surface with **40-49% third degree corrosion** 🔴

T32.55 Corrosions involving **50-59%** of body surface with **50-59% third degree corrosion** 🔴

● **T32.6** Corrosions involving **60-69%** of body surface

T32.60 Corrosions involving **60-69%** of body surface with **0% to 9% third degree corrosion**

T32.61 Corrosions involving **60-69%** of body surface with **10-19% third degree corrosion** 🔴

T32.62 Corrosions involving **60-69%** of body surface with **20-29% third degree corrosion** 🔴

T32.63 Corrosions involving **60-69%** of body surface with **30-39% third degree corrosion** 🔴

T32.64 Corrosions involving **60-69%** of body surface with **40-49% third degree corrosion** 🔴

T32.65 Corrosions involving **60-69%** of body surface with **50-59% third degree corrosion** 🔴

T32.66 Corrosions involving **60-69%** of body surface with **60-69% third degree corrosion** 🔴

● **T32.7** Corrosions involving **70-79%** of body surface

T32.70 Corrosions involving **70-79%** of body surface with **0% to 9% third degree corrosion**

T32.71 Corrosions involving **70-79%** of body surface with **10-19% third degree corrosion** 🔴

T32.72 Corrosions involving **70-79%** of body surface with **20-29% third degree corrosion** 🔴

T32.73 Corrosions involving **70-79%** of body surface with **30-39% third degree corrosion** 🔴

T32.74 Corrosions involving **70-79%** of body surface with **40-49% third degree corrosion** 🔴

T32.75 Corrosions involving **70-79%** of body surface with **50-59% third degree corrosion** 🔴

T32.76 Corrosions involving **70-79%** of body surface with **60-69% third degree corrosion** 🔴

T32.77 Corrosions involving **70-79%** of body surface with **70-79% third degree corrosion** 🔴

● **T32.8** Corrosions involving **80-89%** of body surface

T32.80 Corrosions involving **80-89%** of body surface with **0% to 9% third degree corrosion**

T32.81 Corrosions involving **80-89%** of body surface with **10-19% third degree corrosion** 🔴

T32.82 Corrosions involving **80-89%** of body surface with **20-29% third degree corrosion** 🔴

T32.83 Corrosions involving **80-89%** of body surface with **30-39% third degree corrosion** 🔴

T32.84 Corrosions involving **80-89%** of body surface with **40-49% third degree corrosion** 🔴

T32.85 Corrosions involving **80-89%** of body surface with **50-59% third degree corrosion** 🔴

T32.86 Corrosions involving **80-89%** of body surface with **60-69% third degree corrosion** 🔴

T32.87 Corrosions involving **80-89%** of body surface with **70-79% third degree corrosion** 🔴

T32.88 Corrosions involving **80-89%** of body surface with **80-89% third degree corrosion** 🔴

● **T32.9** Corrosions involving **90% or more** of body surface

T32.90 Corrosions involving **90% or more** of body surface with **0% to 9% third degree corrosion**

T32.91 Corrosions involving **90% or more** of body surface with **10-19% third degree corrosion** 🔴

T32.92 Corrosions involving **90% or more** of body surface with **20-29% third degree corrosion** 🔴

T32.93 Corrosions involving **90% or more** of body surface with **30-39% third degree corrosion** 🔴

T32.94 Corrosions involving **90% or more** of body surface with **40-49% third degree corrosion** 🔴

T32.95 Corrosions involving **90% or more** of body surface with **50-59% third degree corrosion** 🔴

T32.96 Corrosions involving **90% or more** of body surface with **60-69% third degree corrosion** 🔴

T32.97 Corrosions involving **90% or more** of body surface with **70-79% third degree corrosion** 🔴

T32.98 Corrosions involving **90% or more** of body surface with **80-89% third degree corrosion** 🔴

T32.99 Corrosions involving **90% or more** of body surface with **90% or more third degree corrosion** 🔴

▶ New   ⇨ Revised   ~~deleted~~ Deleted   Excludes 1   Excludes 2   Includes   Use additional   Code first   Code also   Key words

OGCR Official Guidelines   X Assign placeholder X   ● Use Additional Character(s)   ▶ Manifestation Code   🔴 Hierarchical Condition Category   **Coding Clinic**

FROSTBITE (T33-T34)

Excludes2 hypothermia and other effects of reduced temperature (T68, T69.-)

● **T33 Superficial frostbite**

Includes frostbite with partial thickness skin loss

The appropriate 7th character is to be added to each code from category T33

A	initial encounter
D	subsequent encounter
S	sequela

- ● **T33.0 Superficial frostbite of head**
  - ● **T33.01 Superficial frostbite of ear**
    - ● T33.011 Superficial frostbite of right ear
    - ● T33.012 Superficial frostbite of left ear
    - ● T33.019 Superficial frostbite of unspecified ear
  - X● **T33.02 Superficial frostbite of nose**
  - X● **T33.09 Superficial frostbite of other part of head**
- X● **T33.1 Superficial frostbite of neck**
- X● **T33.2 Superficial frostbite of thorax**
- X● **T33.3 Superficial frostbite of abdominal wall, lower back and pelvis**
- ● **T33.4 Superficial frostbite of arm**

  Excludes2 superficial frostbite of wrist and hand (T33.5-)

  - X● **T33.40 Superficial frostbite of unspecified arm**
  - X● **T33.41 Superficial frostbite of right arm**
  - X● **T33.42 Superficial frostbite of left arm**
- ● **T33.5 Superficial frostbite of wrist, hand, and fingers**
  - ● **T33.51 Superficial frostbite of wrist**
    - ● T33.511 Superficial frostbite of right wrist
    - ● T33.512 Superficial frostbite of left wrist
    - ● T33.519 Superficial frostbite of unspecified wrist
  - ● **T33.52 Superficial frostbite of hand**

    Excludes2 superficial frostbite of fingers (T33.53-)

    - ● T33.521 Superficial frostbite of right hand
    - ● T33.522 Superficial frostbite of left hand
    - ● T33.529 Superficial frostbite of unspecified hand
  - ● **T33.53 Superficial frostbite of finger(s)**
    - ● T33.531 Superficial frostbite of right finger(s)
    - ● T33.532 Superficial frostbite of left finger(s)
    - ● T33.539 Superficial frostbite of unspecified finger(s)
- ● **T33.6 Superficial frostbite of hip and thigh**
  - X● **T33.60 Superficial frostbite of unspecified hip and thigh**
  - X● **T33.61 Superficial frostbite of right hip and thigh**
  - X● **T33.62 Superficial frostbite of left hip and thigh**
- ● **T33.7 Superficial frostbite of knee and lower leg**

  Excludes2 superficial frostbite of ankle and foot (T33.8-)

  - X● **T33.70 Superficial frostbite of unspecified knee and lower leg**
  - X● **T33.71 Superficial frostbite of right knee and lower leg**
  - X● **T33.72 Superficial frostbite of left knee and lower leg**
- ● **T33.8 Superficial frostbite of ankle, foot, and toe(s)**
  - ● **T33.81 Superficial frostbite of ankle**
    - ● T33.811 Superficial frostbite of right ankle
    - ● T33.812 Superficial frostbite of left ankle
    - ● T33.819 Superficial frostbite of unspecified ankle
  - ● **T33.82 Superficial frostbite of foot**
    - ● T33.821 Superficial frostbite of right foot
    - ● T33.822 Superficial frostbite of left foot
    - ● T33.829 Superficial frostbite of unspecified foot
  - ● **T33.83 Superficial frostbite of toe(s)**
    - ● T33.831 Superficial frostbite of right toe(s)
    - ● T33.832 Superficial frostbite of left toe(s)
    - ● T33.839 Superficial frostbite of unspecified toe(s)
- ● **T33.9 Superficial frostbite of other and unspecified sites**
  - X● **T33.90 Superficial frostbite of unspecified sites**

    Superficial frostbite NOS
  - X● **T33.99 Superficial frostbite of other sites**

    Superficial frostbite of leg NOS

    Superficial frostbite of trunk NOS

● **T34 Frostbite with tissue necrosis**

The appropriate 7th character is to be added to each code from category T34

A	initial encounter
D	subsequent encounter
S	sequela

- ● **T34.0 Frostbite with tissue necrosis of head**
  - ● **T34.01 Frostbite with tissue necrosis of ear**
    - ● T34.011 Frostbite with tissue necrosis of right ear
    - ● T34.012 Frostbite with tissue necrosis of left ear
    - ● T34.019 Frostbite with tissue necrosis of unspecified ear
  - X● **T34.02 Frostbite with tissue necrosis of nose**
  - X● **T34.09 Frostbite with tissue necrosis of other part of head**
- X● **T34.1 Frostbite with tissue necrosis of neck**
- X● **T34.2 Frostbite with tissue necrosis of thorax**
- X● **T34.3 Frostbite with tissue necrosis of abdominal wall, lower back and pelvis**
- ● **T34.4 Frostbite with tissue necrosis of arm**

  Excludes2 frostbite with tissue necrosis of wrist and hand (T34.5-)

  - X● **T34.40 Frostbite with tissue necrosis of unspecified arm**
  - X● **T34.41 Frostbite with tissue necrosis of right arm**
  - X● **T34.42 Frostbite with tissue necrosis of left arm**
- ● **T34.5 Frostbite with tissue necrosis of wrist, hand, and finger(s)**
  - ● **T34.51 Frostbite with tissue necrosis of wrist**
    - ● T34.511 Frostbite with tissue necrosis of right wrist
    - ● T34.512 Frostbite with tissue necrosis of left wrist
    - ● T34.519 Frostbite with tissue necrosis of unspecified wrist

● **T34.52** Frostbite with tissue necrosis of hand
  Excludes2 frostbite with tissue necrosis of finger(s) (T34.53-)

  ● **T34.521** Frostbite with tissue necrosis of right hand
  ● **T34.522** Frostbite with tissue necrosis of left hand
  ● **T34.529** Frostbite with tissue necrosis of unspecified hand

● **T34.53** Frostbite with tissue necrosis of finger(s)

  ● **T34.531** Frostbite with tissue necrosis of right finger(s)
  ● **T34.532** Frostbite with tissue necrosis of left finger(s)
  ● **T34.539** Frostbite with tissue necrosis of unspecified finger(s)

● **T34.6** Frostbite with tissue necrosis of hip and thigh

  X● **T34.60** Frostbite with tissue necrosis of unspecified hip and thigh
  X● **T34.61** Frostbite with tissue necrosis of right hip and thigh
  X● **T34.62** Frostbite with tissue necrosis of left hip and thigh

● **T34.7** Frostbite with tissue necrosis of knee and lower leg
  Excludes2 frostbite with tissue necrosis of ankle and foot (T34.8-)

  X● **T34.70** Frostbite with tissue necrosis of unspecified knee and lower leg
  X● **T34.71** Frostbite with tissue necrosis of right knee and lower leg
  X● **T34.72** Frostbite with tissue necrosis of left knee and lower leg

● **T34.8** Frostbite with tissue necrosis of ankle, foot, and toe(s)

  ● **T34.81** Frostbite with tissue necrosis of ankle

    ● **T34.811** Frostbite with tissue necrosis of right ankle
    ● **T34.812** Frostbite with tissue necrosis of left ankle
    ● **T34.819** Frostbite with tissue necrosis of unspecified ankle

  ● **T34.82** Frostbite with tissue necrosis of foot

    ● **T34.821** Frostbite with tissue necrosis of right foot
    ● **T34.822** Frostbite with tissue necrosis of left foot
    ● **T34.829** Frostbite with tissue necrosis of unspecified foot

  ● **T34.83** Frostbite with tissue necrosis of toe(s)

    ● **T34.831** Frostbite with tissue necrosis of right toe(s)
    ● **T34.832** Frostbite with tissue necrosis of left toe(s)
    ● **T34.839** Frostbite with tissue necrosis of unspecified toe(s)

● **T34.9** Frostbite with tissue necrosis of other and unspecified sites

  X● **T34.90** Frostbite with tissue necrosis of unspecified sites
    Frostbite with tissue necrosis NOS
  X● **T34.99** Frostbite with tissue necrosis of other sites
    Frostbite with tissue necrosis of leg NOS
    Frostbite with tissue necrosis of trunk NOS

OGCR See Section I.C.19.e.

Adverse Effects, Poisoning, Underdosing and Toxic Effects
Codes in categories T36-T65 are combination codes that include the substance that was taken as well as the intent. No additional external cause code is required for poisonings, toxic effects, adverse effects and underdosing codes.

POISONING BY, ADVERSE EFFECTS OF AND UNDERDOSING OF DRUGS MEDICAMENTS AND BIOLOGICAL SUBSTANCES (T36-T50)

Includes adverse effect of correct substance properly administered
poisoning by overdose of substance
poisoning by wrong substance given or taken in error
underdosing by (inadvertently) (deliberately) taking less substance than prescribed or instructed

Code first, for adverse effects, the nature of the adverse effect, such as:
adverse effect NOS (T88.7)
aspirin gastritis (K29.-)
blood disorders (D56-D76)
contact dermatitis (L23-L25)
dermatitis due to substances taken internally (L27.-)
nephropathy (N14.0-N14.2)

Note: The drug giving rise to the adverse effect should be identified by use of codes from categories T36-T50 with fifth or sixth character 5.

Use additional code(s) to specify:
manifestations of poisoning
underdosing or failure in dosage during medical and surgical care (Y63.6, Y63.8-Y63.9)
underdosing of medication regimen (Z91.12-, Z91.13-)

Excludes1 toxic reaction to local anesthesia in pregnancy (O29.3-)

Excludes2 abuse and dependence of psychoactive substances (F10-F19)
abuse of non-dependence-producing substances (F55.-)
drug reaction and poisoning affecting newborn (P00-P96)
▶immunodeficiency due to drugs (D84.821)
pathological drug intoxication (inebriation) (F10-F19)

● **T36** Poisoning by, adverse effect of and underdosing of systemic antibiotics
  Excludes1 antineoplastic antibiotics (T45.1-)
  locally applied antibiotic NEC (T49.0)
  topically used antibiotic for ear, nose and throat (T49.6)
  topically used antibiotic for eye (T49.5)

  The appropriate 7th character is to be added to each code from category T36

A	initial encounter
D	subsequent encounter
S	sequela

  ● **T36.0** Poisoning by, adverse effect of and underdosing of penicillins

    ● **T36.0X** Poisoning by, adverse effect of and underdosing of penicillins

      ● **T36.0X1** Poisoning by penicillins, **accidental (unintentional)**
        Poisoning by penicillins NOS
      ● **T36.0X2** Poisoning by penicillins, **intentional self-harm A, S** 🝅
      ● **T36.0X3** Poisoning by penicillins, **assault**
      ● **T36.0X4** Poisoning by penicillins, **undetermined**
      ● **T36.0X5** Adverse effect of penicillins
      ● **T36.0X6** Underdosing of penicillins

▶ New   ⇨ Revised   ~~deleted~~ Deleted   Excludes 1   Excludes 2   Includes   Use additional   Code first   Code also   Key words
OGCR Official Guidelines   X Assign placeholder X   ● Use Additional Character(s)   ▷ Manifestation Code   🝅 Hierarchical Condition Category   **Coding Clinic**

● **T36.1**   **Poisoning by, adverse effect of and underdosing of cephalosporins and other betalactam antibiotics**
  ● **T36.1X**   Poisoning by, adverse effect of and underdosing of cephalosporins and other beta-lactam antibiotics
    ● **T36.1X1**   Poisoning by cephalosporins and other beta-lactam antibiotics, accidental (unintentional)
         Poisoning by cephalosporins and other beta-lactam antibiotics NOS
    ● **T36.1X2**   Poisoning by cephalosporins and other beta-lactam antibiotics, intentional self-harm A, S 🔍
    ● **T36.1X3**   Poisoning by cephalosporins and other beta-lactam antibiotics, assault
    ● **T36.1X4**   Poisoning by cephalosporins and other beta-lactam antibiotics, undetermined
    ● **T36.1X5**   Adverse effect of cephalosporins and other beta-lactam antibiotics
    ● **T36.1X6**   Underdosing of cephalosporins and other beta-lactam antibiotics

● **T36.2**   **Poisoning by, adverse effect of and underdosing of chloramphenicol group**
  ● **T36.2X**   Poisoning by, adverse effect of and underdosing of chloramphenicol group
    ● **T36.2X1**   Poisoning by chloramphenicol group, accidental (unintentional)
         Poisoning by chloramphenicol group NOS
    ● **T36.2X2**   Poisoning by chloramphenicol group, intentional self-harm A, S 🔍
    ● **T36.2X3**   Poisoning by chloramphenicol group, assault
    ● **T36.2X4**   Poisoning by chloramphenicol group, undetermined
    ● **T36.2X5**   Adverse effect of chloramphenicol group
    ● **T36.2X6**   Underdosing of chloramphenicol group

● **T36.3**   **Poisoning by, adverse effect of and underdosing of macrolides**
  ● **T36.3X**   Poisoning by, adverse effect of and underdosing of macrolides
    ● **T36.3X1**   Poisoning by macrolides, accidental (unintentional)
         Poisoning by macrolides NOS
    ● **T36.3X2**   Poisoning by macrolides, intentional self-harm A, S 🔍
    ● **T36.3X3**   Poisoning by macrolides, assault
    ● **T36.3X4**   Poisoning by macrolides, undetermined
    ● **T36.3X5**   Adverse effect of macrolides
    ● **T36.3X6**   Underdosing of macrolides

● **T36.4**   **Poisoning by, adverse effect of and underdosing of tetracyclines**
  ● **T36.4X**   Poisoning by, adverse effect of and underdosing of tetracyclines
    ● **T36.4X1**   Poisoning by tetracyclines, accidental (unintentional)
         Poisoning by tetracyclines NOS
    ● **T36.4X2**   Poisoning by tetracyclines, intentional self-harm A, S 🔍
    ● **T36.4X3**   Poisoning by tetracyclines, assault
    ● **T36.4X4**   Poisoning by tetracyclines, undetermined
    ● **T36.4X5**   Adverse effect of tetracyclines
    ● **T36.4X6**   Underdosing of tetracyclines

● **T36.5**   **Poisoning by, adverse effect of and underdosing of aminoglycosides**
     Poisoning by, adverse effect of and underdosing of streptomycin
  ● **T36.5X**   Poisoning by, adverse effect of and underdosing of aminoglycosides
    ● **T36.5X1**   Poisoning by aminoglycosides, accidental (unintentional)
         Poisoning by aminoglycosides NOS
    ● **T36.5X2**   Poisoning by aminoglycosides, intentional self-harm A, S 🔍
    ● **T36.5X3**   Poisoning by aminoglycosides, assault
    ● **T36.5X4**   Poisoning by aminoglycosides, undetermined
    ● **T36.5X5**   Adverse effect of aminoglycosides
    ● **T36.5X6**   Underdosing of aminoglycosides

● **T36.6**   **Poisoning by, adverse effect of and underdosing of rifampicins**
  ● **T36.6X**   Poisoning by, adverse effect of and underdosing of rifampicins
    ● **T36.6X1**   Poisoning by rifampicins, accidental (unintentional)
         Poisoning by rifampicins NOS
    ● **T36.6X2**   Poisoning by rifampicins, intentional self-harm A, S 🔍
    ● **T36.6X3**   Poisoning by rifampicins, assault
    ● **T36.6X4**   Poisoning by rifampicins, undetermined
    ● **T36.6X5**   Adverse effect of rifampicins
    ● **T36.6X6**   Underdosing of rifampicins

● **T36.7**   **Poisoning by, adverse effect of and underdosing of antifungal antibiotics, systemically used**
  ● **T36.7X**   Poisoning by, adverse effect of and underdosing of antifungal antibiotics, systemically used
    ● **T36.7X1**   Poisoning by antifungal antibiotics, systemically used, accidental (unintentional)
         Poisoning by antifungal antibiotics, systemically used NOS
    ● **T36.7X2**   Poisoning by antifungal antibiotics, systemically used, intentional self-harm A, S 🔍
    ● **T36.7X3**   Poisoning by antifungal antibiotics, systemically used, assault
    ● **T36.7X4**   Poisoning by antifungal antibiotics, systemically used, undetermined
    ● **T36.7X5**   Adverse effect of antifungal antibiotics, systemically used
    ● **T36.7X6**   Underdosing of antifungal antibiotics, systemically used

● **T36.8**   **Poisoning by, adverse effect of and underdosing of other systemic antibiotics**
  ● **T36.8X**   Poisoning by, adverse effect of and underdosing of other systemic antibiotics
    ● **T36.8X1**   Poisoning by other systemic antibiotics, accidental (unintentional)
         Poisoning by other systemic antibiotics NOS
    ● **T36.8X2**   Poisoning by other systemic antibiotics, intentional self-harm A, S 🔍
    ● **T36.8X3**   Poisoning by other systemic antibiotics, assault
    ● **T36.8X4**   Poisoning by other systemic antibiotics, undetermined
    ● **T36.8X5**   Adverse effect of other systemic antibiotics
         Coding Clinic: 2017, Q1, P39
    ● **T36.8X6**   Underdosing of other systemic antibiotics

● T36.9 Poisoning by, adverse effect of and underdosing of unspecified systemic antibiotic

X ● **T36.91 Poisoning by unspecified systemic antibiotic, accidental (unintentional)**
Poisoning by systemic antibiotic NOS

X ● **T36.92 Poisoning by unspecified systemic antibiotic, intentional self-harm A, S** 🐾

X ● **T36.93 Poisoning by unspecified systemic antibiotic, assault**

X ● **T36.94 Poisoning by unspecified systemic antibiotic, undetermined**

X ● **T36.95 Adverse effect of unspecified systemic antibiotic**

X ● **T36.96 Underdosing of unspecified systemic antibiotic**

● T37 Poisoning by, adverse effect of and underdosing of other systemic anti-infectives and antiparasitics

> **Excludes1**   anti-infectives topically used for ear, nose and throat (T49.6-)
> anti-infectives topically used for eye (T49.5-)
> locally applied anti-infectives NEC (T49.0-)

The appropriate 7th character is to be added to each code from category T37

A	initial encounter
D	subsequent encounter
S	sequela

● T37.0 Poisoning by, adverse effect of and underdosing of sulfonamides

● T37.0X Poisoning by, adverse effect of and underdosing of sulfonamides

● **T37.0X1 Poisoning by sulfonamides, accidental (unintentional)**
Poisoning by sulfonamides NOS

● **T37.0X2 Poisoning by sulfonamides, intentional self-harm A, S** 🐾

● **T37.0X3 Poisoning by sulfonamides, assault**

● **T37.0X4 Poisoning by sulfonamides, undetermined**

● **T37.0X5 Adverse effect of sulfonamides**

● **T37.0X6 Underdosing of sulfonamides**

● T37.1 Poisoning by, adverse effect of and underdosing of antimycobacterial drugs

> **Excludes1**   rifampicins (T36.6-) streptomycin (T36.5-)

● T37.1X Poisoning by, adverse effect of and underdosing of antimycobacterial drugs

● **T37.1X1 Poisoning by antimycobacterial drugs, accidental (unintentional)**
Poisoning by antimycobacterial drugs NOS

● **T37.1X2 Poisoning by antimycobacterial drugs, intentional self-harm A, S** 🐾

● **T37.1X3 Poisoning by antimycobacterial drugs, assault**

● **T37.1X4 Poisoning by antimycobacterial drugs, undetermined**

● **T37.1X5 Adverse effect of antimycobacterial drugs**

● **T37.1X6 Underdosing of antimycobacterial drugs**

● T37.2 Poisoning by, adverse effect of and underdosing of antimalarials and drugs acting on other blood protozoa

> **Excludes1**   hydroxyquinoline derivatives (T37.8-)

● T37.2X Poisoning by, adverse effect of and underdosing of antimalarials and drugs acting on other blood protozoa

● **T37.2X1 Poisoning by antimalarials and drugs acting on other blood protozoa, accidental (unintentional)**
Poisoning by antimalarials and drugs acting on other blood protozoa NOS

● **T37.2X2 Poisoning by antimalarials and drugs acting on other blood protozoa, intentional self-harm A, S** 🐾

● **T37.2X3 Poisoning by antimalarials and drugs acting on other blood protozoa, assault**

● **T37.2X4 Poisoning by antimalarials and drugs acting on other blood protozoa, undetermined**

● **T37.2X5 Adverse effect of antimalarials and drugs acting on other blood protozoa**

● **T37.2X6 Underdosing of antimalarials and drugs acting on other blood protozoa**

● T37.3 Poisoning by, adverse effect of and underdosing of other antiprotozoal drugs

● T37.3X Poisoning by, adverse effect of and underdosing of other antiprotozoal drugs

● **T37.3X1 Poisoning by other antiprotozoal drugs, accidental (unintentional)**
Poisoning by other antiprotozoal drugs NOS

● **T37.3X2 Poisoning by other antiprotozoal drugs, intentional self-harm A, S** 🐾

● **T37.3X3 Poisoning by other antiprotozoal drugs, assault**

● **T37.3X4 Poisoning by other antiprotozoal drugs, undetermined**

● **T37.3X5 Adverse effect of other antiprotozoal drugs**

● **T37.3X6 Underdosing of other antiprotozoal drugs**

● T37.4 Poisoning by, adverse effect of and underdosing of anthelminthics

● T37.4X Poisoning by, adverse effect of and underdosing of anthelminthics

● **T37.4X1 Poisoning by anthelminthics, accidental (unintentional)**
Poisoning by anthelminthics NOS

● **T37.4X2 Poisoning by anthelminthics, intentional self-harm A, S** 🐾

● **T37.4X3 Poisoning by anthelminthics, assault**

● **T37.4X4 Poisoning by anthelminthics, undetermined**

● **T37.4X5 Adverse effect of anthelminthics**

● **T37.4X6 Underdosing of anthelminthics**

● T37.5 Poisoning by, adverse effect of and underdosing of antiviral drugs

> **Excludes1**   amantadine (T42.8-)
> cytarabine (T45.1-)

● T37.5X Poisoning by, adverse effect of and underdosing of antiviral drugs

● **T37.5X1 Poisoning by antiviral drugs, accidental (unintentional)**
Poisoning by antiviral drugs NOS

● **T37.5X2 Poisoning by antiviral drugs, intentional self-harm A, S** 🐾

● **T37.5X3 Poisoning by antiviral drugs, assault**

● **T37.5X4 Poisoning by antiviral drugs, undetermined**

● **T37.5X5 Adverse effect of antiviral drugs**

● **T37.5X6 Underdosing of antiviral drugs**

▶ New   ⇒ Revised   ~~deleted~~ Deleted   Excludes 1   Excludes 2   Includes   Use additional   Code first   Code also   Key words

OGCR Official Guidelines   X Assign placeholder X   ● Use Additional Character(s)   ▷ Manifestation Code   🐾 Hierarchical Condition Category   **Coding Clinic**

1398

● **T37.8** **Poisoning by, adverse effect of and underdosing of other specified systemic anti-infectives and antiparasitics**
Poisoning by, adverse effect of and underdosing of hydroxyquinoline derivatives
> **Excludes1** antimalarial drugs (T37.2-)

● **T37.8X** **Poisoning by, and adverse effect of and underdosing of other specified systemic anti-infectives and antiparasitics**

● **T37.8X1** Poisoning by other specified systemic anti-infectives and antiparasitics, accidental (unintentional)
Poisoning by other specified systemic anti-infectives and antiparasitics NOS

● **T37.8X2** Poisoning by other specified systemic anti-infectives and antiparasitics, intentional self-harm A, S 🖇

● **T37.8X3** Poisoning by other specified systemic anti-infectives and antiparasitics, assault

● **T37.8X4** Poisoning by other specified systemic anti-infectives and antiparasitics, undetermined

● **T37.8X5** Adverse effect of other specified systemic anti-infectives and antiparasitics

● **T37.8X6** Underdosing of other specified systemic anti-infectives and antiparasitics

● **T37.9** **Poisoning by, adverse effect of and underdosing of unspecified systemic anti-infective and antiparasitics**

X● **T37.91** Poisoning by unspecified systemic anti-infective and antiparasitics, accidental (unintentional)
Poisoning by, adverse effect of and underdosing of systemic anti-infective and antiparasitics NOS

X● **T37.92** Poisoning by unspecified systemic anti-infective and antiparasitics, intentional self-harm A, S 🖇

X● **T37.93** Poisoning by unspecified systemic anti-infective and antiparasitics, assault

X● **T37.94** Poisoning by unspecified systemic anti-infective and antiparasitics, undetermined

X● **T37.95** Adverse effect of unspecified systemic anti-infective and antiparasitic

X● **T37.96** Underdosing of unspecified systemic anti-infectives and antiparasitics

● **T38** **Poisoning by, adverse effect of and underdosing of hormones and their synthetic substitutes and antagonists, not elsewhere classified**
> **Excludes1** mineralocorticoids and their antagonists (T50.0-)
> oxytocic hormones (T48.0-)
> parathyroid hormones and derivatives (T50.9-)

The appropriate 7th character is to be added to each code from category T38

A	initial encounter
D	subsequent encounter
S	sequela

● **T38.0** **Poisoning by, adverse effect of and underdosing of glucocorticoids and synthetic analogues**
> **Excludes1** glucocorticoids, topically used (T49.-)

● **T38.0X** **Poisoning by, adverse effect of and underdosing of glucocorticoids and synthetic analogues**

● **T38.0X1** Poisoning by glucocorticoids and synthetic analogues, accidental (unintentional)
Poisoning by glucocorticoids and synthetic analogues NOS

● **T38.0X2** Poisoning by glucocorticoids and synthetic analogues, intentional self-harm A, S 🖇

● **T38.0X3** Poisoning by glucocorticoids and synthetic analogues, assault

● **T38.0X4** Poisoning by glucocorticoids and synthetic analogues, undetermined

● **T38.0X5** Adverse effect of glucocorticoids and synthetic analogues

● **T38.0X6** Underdosing of glucocorticoids and synthetic analogues

● **T38.1** **Poisoning by, adverse effect of and underdosing of thyroid hormones and substitutes**

● **T38.1X** **Poisoning by, adverse effect of and underdosing of thyroid hormones and substitutes**

● **T38.1X1** Poisoning by thyroid hormones and substitutes, accidental (unintentional)
Poisoning by thyroid hormones and substitutes NOS

● **T38.1X2** Poisoning by thyroid hormones and substitutes, intentional self-harm A, S 🖇

● **T38.1X3** Poisoning by thyroid hormones and substitutes, assault

● **T38.1X4** Poisoning by thyroid hormones and substitutes, undetermined

● **T38.1X5** Adverse effect of thyroid hormones and substitutes

● **T38.1X6** Underdosing of thyroid hormones and substitutes

● **T38.2** **Poisoning by, adverse effect of and underdosing of antithyroid drugs**

● **T38.2X** **Poisoning by, adverse effect of and underdosing of antithyroid drugs**

● **T38.2X1** Poisoning by antithyroid drugs, accidental (unintentional)
Poisoning by antithyroid drugs NOS

● **T38.2X2** Poisoning by antithyroid drugs, intentional self-harm A, S 🖇

● **T38.2X3** Poisoning by antithyroid drugs, assault

● **T38.2X4** Poisoning by antithyroid drugs, undetermined

● **T38.2X5** Adverse effect of antithyroid drugs

● **T38.2X6** Underdosing of antithyroid drugs

● **T38.3** **Poisoning by, adverse effect of and underdosing of insulin and oral hypoglycemic [antidiabetic] drugs**

● **T38.3X** **Poisoning by, adverse effect of and underdosing of insulin and oral hypoglycemic [antidiabetic] drugs**

● **T38.3X1** Poisoning by insulin and oral hypoglycemic [antidiabetic] drugs, accidental (unintentional)
Poisoning by insulin and oral hypoglycemic [antidiabetic] drugs NOS

● **T38.3X2** Poisoning by insulin and oral hypoglycemic [antidiabetic] drugs, intentional self-harm

● **T38.3X3** Poisoning by insulin and oral hypoglycemic [antidiabetic] drugs, assault A, S 🖇

● **T38.3X4** Poisoning by insulin and oral hypoglycemic [antidiabetic] drugs, undetermined

● **T38.3X5** Adverse effect of insulin and oral hypoglycemic [antidiabetic] drugs

● **T38.3X6** Underdosing of insulin and oral hypoglycemic [antidiabetic] drugs

● **T38.4** **Poisoning by, adverse effect of and underdosing of oral contraceptives**
     Poisoning by, adverse effect of and underdosing of multiple- and single-ingredient oral contraceptive preparations
   ● **T38.4X** **Poisoning by, adverse effect of and underdosing of oral contraceptives**
     ● **T38.4X1** **Poisoning by oral contraceptives, accidental (unintentional)**
        Poisoning by oral contraceptives NOS
     ● **T38.4X2** **Poisoning by oral contraceptives, intentional self-harm A, S** 🏥
     ● **T38.4X3** **Poisoning by oral contraceptives, assault**
     ● **T38.4X4** **Poisoning by oral contraceptives, undetermined**
     ● **T38.4X5** **Adverse effect of oral contraceptives**
     ● **T38.4X6** **Underdosing of oral contraceptives**

● **T38.5** **Poisoning by, adverse effect of and underdosing of other estrogens and progestogens**
     Poisoning by, adverse effect of and underdosing of estrogens and progestogens mixtures and substitutes
   ● **T38.5X** **Poisoning by, adverse effect of and underdosing of other estrogens and progestogens**
     ● **T38.5X1** **Poisoning by other estrogens and progestogens, accidental (unintentional)**
        Poisoning by other estrogens and progestogens NOS
     ● **T38.5X2** **Poisoning by other estrogens and progestogens, intentional self-harm A, S** 🏥
     ● **T38.5X3** **Poisoning by other estrogens and progestogens, assault**
     ● **T38.5X4** **Poisoning by other estrogens and progestogens, undetermined**
     ● **T38.5X5** **Adverse effect of other estrogens and progestogens**
     ● **T38.5X6** **Underdosing of other estrogens and progestogens**

● **T38.6** **Poisoning by, adverse effect of and underdosing of antigonadotrophins, antiestrogens, antiandrogens, not elsewhere classified**
     Poisoning by, adverse effect of and underdosing of tamoxifen
   ● **T38.6X** **Poisoning by, adverse effect of and underdosing of antigonadotrophins, antiestrogens, antiandrogens, not elsewhere classified**
     ● **T38.6X1** **Poisoning by antigonadotrophins, antiestrogens, antiandrogens, not elsewhere classified, accidental (unintentional)**
        Poisoning by antigonadotrophins, antiestrogens, antiandrogens, not elsewhere classified NOS
     ● **T38.6X2** **Poisoning by antigonadotrophins, antiestrogens, antiandrogens, not elsewhere classified, intentional self-harm A, S** 🏥
     ● **T38.6X3** **Poisoning by antigonadotrophins, antiestrogens, antiandrogens, not elsewhere classified, assault**
     ● **T38.6X4** **Poisoning by antigonadotrophins, antiestrogens, antiandrogens, not elsewhere classified, undetermined**

     ● **T38.6X5** **Adverse effect of antigonadotrophins, antiestrogens, antiandrogens, not elsewhere classified**
     ● **T38.6X6** **Underdosing of antigonadotrophins, antiestrogens, antiandrogens, not elsewhere classified**

● **T38.7** **Poisoning by, adverse effect of and underdosing of androgens and anabolic congeners**
   ● **T38.7X** **Poisoning by, adverse effect of and underdosing of androgens and anabolic congeners**
     ● **T38.7X1** **Poisoning by androgens and anabolic congeners, accidental (unintentional)**
        Poisoning by androgens and anabolic congeners NOS
     ● **T38.7X2** **Poisoning by androgens and anabolic congeners, intentional self-harm A, S** 🏥
     ● **T38.7X3** **Poisoning by androgens and anabolic congeners, assault**
     ● **T38.7X4** **Poisoning by androgens and anabolic congeners, undetermined**
     ● **T38.7X5** **Adverse effect of androgens and anabolic congeners**
     ● **T38.7X6** **Underdosing of androgens and anabolic congeners**

● **T38.8** **Poisoning by, adverse effect of and underdosing of other and unspecified hormones and synthetic substitutes**
   ● **T38.80** **Poisoning by, adverse effect of and underdosing of unspecified hormones and synthetic substitutes**
     ● **T38.801** **Poisoning by unspecified hormones and synthetic substitutes, accidental (unintentional)**
        Poisoning by unspecified hormones and synthetic substitutes NOS
     ● **T38.802** **Poisoning by unspecified hormones and synthetic substitutes, intentional self-harm A, S** 🏥
     ● **T38.803** **Poisoning by unspecified hormones and synthetic substitutes, assault**
     ● **T38.804** **Poisoning by unspecified hormones and synthetic substitutes, undetermined**
     ● **T38.805** **Adverse effect of unspecified hormones and synthetic substitutes**
     ● **T38.806** **Underdosing of unspecified hormones and synthetic substitutes**
   ● **T38.81** **Poisoning by, adverse effect of and underdosing of anterior pituitary [adenohypophyseal] hormones**
     ● **T38.811** **Poisoning by anterior pituitary [adenohypophyseal] hormones, accidental (unintentional)**
        Poisoning by anterior pituitary [adenohypophyseal] hormones NOS
     ● **T38.812** **Poisoning by anterior pituitary [adenohypophyseal] hormones, intentional self-harm A, S** 🏥
     ● **T38.813** **Poisoning by anterior pituitary [adenohypophyseal] hormones, assault**
     ● **T38.814** **Poisoning by anterior pituitary [adenohypophyseal] hormones, undetermined**
     ● **T38.815** **Adverse effect of anterior pituitary [adenohypophyseal] hormones**
     ● **T38.816** **Underdosing of anterior pituitary [adenohypophyseal] hormones**

▶ New   ⇒ Revised   ~~deleted~~ Deleted   Excludes 1   Excludes 2   Includes   Use additional   Code first   Code also   Key words
OGCR Official Guidelines   X Assign placeholder X   ● Use Additional Character(s)   ▶ Manifestation Code   🏥 Hierarchical Condition Category   **Coding Clinic**

- T38.89 Poisoning by, adverse effect of and underdosing of other hormones and synthetic substitutes
  - T38.891 Poisoning by other hormones and synthetic substitutes, accidental (unintentional)
    Poisoning by other hormones and synthetic substitutes NOS
  - T38.892 Poisoning by other hormones and synthetic substitutes, intentional self-harm A, S 🔒
  - T38.893 Poisoning by other hormones and synthetic substitutes, assault
  - T38.894 Poisoning by other hormones and synthetic substitutes, undetermined
  - T38.895 Adverse effect of other hormones and synthetic substitutes
  - T38.896 Underdosing of other hormones and synthetic substitutes
- T38.9 Poisoning by, adverse effect of and underdosing of other and unspecified hormone antagonists
  - T38.90 Poisoning by, adverse effect of and underdosing of unspecified hormone antagonists
    - T38.901 Poisoning by unspecified hormone antagonists, accidental (unintentional)
      Poisoning by unspecified hormone antagonists NOS
    - T38.902 Poisoning by unspecified hormone antagonists, intentional self-harm A, S 🔒
    - T38.903 Poisoning by unspecified hormone antagonists, assault
    - T38.904 Poisoning by unspecified hormone antagonists, undetermined
    - T38.905 Adverse effect of unspecified hormone antagonists
    - T38.906 Underdosing of unspecified hormone antagonists
  - T38.99 Poisoning by, adverse effect of and underdosing of other hormone antagonists
    - T38.991 Poisoning by other hormone antagonists, accidental (unintentional)
      Poisoning by other hormone antagonists NOS
    - T38.992 Poisoning by other hormone antagonists, intentional self-harm A, S 🔒
    - T38.993 Poisoning by other hormone antagonists, assault
    - T38.994 Poisoning by other hormone antagonists, undetermined
    - T38.995 Adverse effect of other hormone antagonists
    - T38.996 Underdosing of other hormone antagonists

- T39 Poisoning by, adverse effect of and underdosing of nonopioid analgesics, antipyretics and antirheumatics

  The appropriate 7th character is to be added to each code from category T39

A	initial encounter
D	subsequent encounter
S	sequela

  - T39.0 Poisoning by, adverse effect of and underdosing of salicylates
    - T39.01 Poisoning by, adverse effect of and underdosing of aspirin
      Poisoning by, adverse effect of and underdosing of acetylsalicylic acid
      - T39.011 Poisoning by aspirin, accidental (unintentional)
      - T39.012 Poisoning by aspirin, intentional self-harm A, S 🔒
      - T39.013 Poisoning by aspirin, assault
      - T39.014 Poisoning by aspirin, undetermined
      - T39.015 Adverse effect of aspirin
        Coding Clinic: 2016, Q1, P15
      - T39.016 Underdosing of aspirin
    - T39.09 Poisoning by, adverse effect of and underdosing of other salicylates
      - T39.091 Poisoning by salicylates, accidental (unintentional)
        Poisoning by salicylates NOS
      - T39.092 Poisoning by salicylates, intentional self-harm A, S 🔒
      - T39.093 Poisoning by salicylates, assault
      - T39.094 Poisoning by salicylates, undetermined
      - T39.095 Adverse effect of salicylates
      - T39.096 Underdosing of salicylates
  - T39.1 Poisoning by, adverse effect of and underdosing of 4-Aminophenol derivatives
    - T39.1X Poisoning by, adverse effect of and underdosing of 4-Aminophenol derivatives
      - T39.1X1 Poisoning by 4-Aminophenol derivatives, accidental (unintentional)
        Poisoning by 4-Aminophenol derivatives NOS
      - T39.1X2 Poisoning by 4-Aminophenol derivatives, intentional self-harm A, S 🔒
      - T39.1X3 Poisoning by 4-Aminophenol derivatives, assault
      - T39.1X4 Poisoning by 4-Aminophenol derivatives, undetermined
      - T39.1X5 Adverse effect of 4-Aminophenol derivatives
      - T39.1X6 Underdosing of 4-Aminophenol derivatives

● **T39.2 Poisoning by, adverse effect of and underdosing of pyrazolone derivatives**

● **T39.2X Poisoning by, adverse effect of and underdosing of pyrazolone derivatives**

● T39.2X1 Poisoning by pyrazolone derivatives, accidental (unintentional)
Poisoning by pyrazolone derivatives NOS

● T39.2X2 Poisoning by pyrazolone derivatives, intentional self-harm A, S 🦠

● T39.2X3 Poisoning by pyrazolone derivatives, assault

● T39.2X4 Poisoning by pyrazolone derivatives, undetermined

● T39.2X5 Adverse effect of pyrazolone derivatives

● T39.2X6 Underdosing of pyrazolone derivatives

● **T39.3 Poisoning by, adverse effect of and underdosing of other nonsteroidal anti-inflammatory drugs [NSAID]**

● **T39.31 Poisoning by, adverse effect of and underdosing of propionic acid derivatives**
Poisoning by, adverse effect of and underdosing of fenoprofen
Poisoning by, adverse effect of and underdosing of flurbiprofen
Poisoning by, adverse effect of and underdosing of ibuprofen
Poisoning by, adverse effect of and underdosing of ketoprofen
Poisoning by, adverse effect of and underdosing of naproxen
Poisoning by, adverse effect of and underdosing of oxaprozin

● T39.311 Poisoning by propionic acid derivatives, accidental (unintentional)

● T39.312 Poisoning by propionic acid derivatives, intentional self-harm A, S 🦠

● T39.313 Poisoning by propionic acid derivatives, assault

● T39.314 Poisoning by propionic acid derivatives, undetermined

● T39.315 Adverse effect of propionic acid derivatives

● T39.316 Underdosing of propionic acid derivatives

● **T39.39 Poisoning by, adverse effect of and underdosing of other nonsteroidal anti-inflammatory drugs [NSAID]**

● T39.391 Poisoning by other nonsteroidal anti-inflammatory drugs [NSAID], accidental (unintentional)
Poisoning by other nonsteroidal anti-inflammatory drugs NOS

● T39.392 Poisoning by other nonsteroidal anti-inflammatory drugs [NSAID], intentional self-harm A, S 🦠

● T39.393 Poisoning by other nonsteroidal anti-inflammatory drugs [NSAID], assault

● T39.394 Poisoning by other nonsteroidal anti-inflammatory drugs [NSAID], undetermined

● T39.395 Adverse effect of other nonsteroidal anti-inflammatory drugs [NSAID]

● T39.396 Underdosing of other nonsteroidal anti-inflammatory drugs [NSAID]

● **T39.4 Poisoning by, adverse effect of and underdosing of antirheumatics, not elsewhere classified**

Excludes1 poisoning by, adverse effect of and underdosing of glucocorticoids (T38.0-)
poisoning by, adverse effect of and underdosing of salicylates (T39.0-)

● **T39.4X Poisoning by, adverse effect of and underdosing of antirheumatics, not elsewhere classified**

● T39.4X1 Poisoning by antirheumatics, not elsewhere classified, accidental (unintentional)
Poisoning by antirheumatics, not elsewhere classified NOS

● T39.4X2 Poisoning by antirheumatics, not elsewhere classified, intentional self-harm A, S 🦠

● T39.4X3 Poisoning by antirheumatics, not elsewhere classified, assault

● T39.4X4 Poisoning by antirheumatics, not elsewhere classified, undetermined

● T39.4X5 Adverse effect of antirheumatics, not elsewhere classified

● T39.4X6 Underdosing of antirheumatics, not elsewhere classified

● **T39.8 Poisoning by, adverse effect of and underdosing of other nonopioid analgesics and antipyretics, not elsewhere classified**

● **T39.8X Poisoning by, adverse effect of and underdosing of other nonopioid analgesics and antipyretics, not elsewhere classified**

● T39.8X1 Poisoning by other nonopioid analgesics and antipyretics, not elsewhere classified, accidental (unintentional)
Poisoning by other nonopioid analgesics and antipyretics, not elsewhere classified NOS

● T39.8X2 Poisoning by other nonopioid analgesics and antipyretics, not elsewhere classified, intentional self-harm A, S 🦠

● T39.8X3 Poisoning by other nonopioid analgesics and antipyretics, not elsewhere classified, assault

● T39.8X4 Poisoning by other nonopioid analgesics and antipyretics, not elsewhere classified, undetermined

● T39.8X5 Adverse effect of other nonopioid analgesics and antipyretics, not elsewhere classified

● T39.8X6 Underdosing of other nonopioid analgesics and antipyretics, not elsewhere classified

● **T39.9 Poisoning by, adverse effect of and underdosing of unspecified nonopioid analgesic, antipyretic and antirheumatic**

X ● T39.91 Poisoning by unspecified nonopioid analgesic, antipyretic and antirheumatic, accidental (unintentional)
Poisoning by nonopioid analgesic, antipyretic and antirheumatic NOS

X ● T39.92 Poisoning by unspecified nonopioid analgesic, antipyretic and antirheumatic, intentional self-harm A, S 🦠

X ● T39.93 Poisoning by unspecified nonopioid analgesic, antipyretic and antirheumatic, assault

▶ New ⇒ Revised ~~deleted~~ Deleted Excludes 1 Excludes 2 Includes Use additional Code first Code also Key words
OGCR Official Guidelines X Assign placeholder X ● Use Additional Character(s)) Manifestation Code 🦠 Hierarchical Condition Category **Coding Clinic**

X ● **T39.94** Poisoning by unspecified nonopioid analgesic, antipyretic and antirheumatic, **undetermined**

X ● **T39.95** Adverse effect of unspecified nonopioid analgesic, antipyretic and antirheumatic

X ● **T39.96** Underdosing of unspecified nonopioid analgesic, antipyretic and antirheumatic

● **T40** Poisoning by, adverse effect of and underdosing of narcotics and psychodysleptics [hallucinogens]

Excludes2 drug dependence and related mental and behavioral disorders due to psychoactive substance use (F10.-F19.-)

The appropriate 7th character is to be added to each code from category T40

A	initial encounter
D	subsequent encounter
S	sequela

● **T40.0** Poisoning by, adverse effect of and underdosing of opium

● **T40.0X** Poisoning by, adverse effect of and underdosing of opium

● **T40.0X1** Poisoning by opium, **accidental (unintentional)**
Poisoning by opium NOS

● **T40.0X2** Poisoning by opium, **intentional self-harm A, S** 🔧

● **T40.0X3** Poisoning by opium, **assault**

● **T40.0X4** Poisoning by opium, **undetermined**

● **T40.0X5** Adverse effect of opium

● **T40.0X6** Underdosing of opium

● **T40.1** Poisoning by and adverse effect of heroin

● **T40.1X** Poisoning by and adverse effect of heroin

● **T40.1X1** Poisoning by heroin, **accidental (unintentional)**
Poisoning by heroin NOS

● **T40.1X2** Poisoning by heroin, **intentional self-harm A, S** 🔧

● **T40.1X3** Poisoning by heroin, **assault**

● **T40.1X4** Poisoning by heroin, **undetermined**

● **T40.2** Poisoning by, adverse effect of and underdosing of other opioids

● **T40.2X** Poisoning by, adverse effect of and underdosing of other opioids

● **T40.2X1** Poisoning by other opioids, **accidental (unintentional)**
Poisoning by other opioids NOS

● **T40.2X2** Poisoning by other opioids, **intentional self-harm A, S** 🔧

● **T40.2X3** Poisoning by other opioids, **assault**

● **T40.2X4** Poisoning by other opioids, **undetermined**

● **T40.2X5** Adverse effect of other opioids

● **T40.2X6** Underdosing of other opioids

● **T40.3** Poisoning by, adverse effect of and underdosing of methadone

● **T40.3X** Poisoning by, adverse effect of and underdosing of methadone

● **T40.3X1** Poisoning by methadone, **accidental (unintentional)**
Poisoning by methadone NOS

● **T40.3X2** Poisoning by methadone, **intentional self-harm A, S** 🔧

● **T40.3X3** Poisoning by methadone, **assault**

● **T40.3X4** Poisoning by methadone, **undetermined**

● **T40.3X5** Adverse effect of methadone

● **T40.3X6** Underdosing of methadone

● **T40.4** Poisoning by, adverse effect of and underdosing of other synthetic narcotics

▶ ● **T40.41** Poisoning by, adverse effect of and underdosing of fentanyl or fentanyl analogs

▶ **T40.411** Poisoning by fentanyl or fentanyl analogs, accidental (unintentional)

▶ **T40.412** Poisoning by fentanyl or fentanyl analogs, intentional self-harm

▶ **T40.413** Poisoning by fentanyl or fentanyl analogs, assault

▶ **T40.414** Poisoning by fentanyl or fentanyl analogs, undetermined

▶ **T40.415** Adverse effect of fentanyl or fentanyl analogs

▶ **T40.416** Underdosing of fentanyl or fentanyl analogs

▶ ● **T40.42** Poisoning by, adverse effect of and underdosing of tramadol

▶ **T40.421** Poisoning by tramadol, accidental (unintentional)

▶ **T40.422** Poisoning by tramadol, intentional self-harm

▶ **T40.423** Poisoning by tramadol, assault

▶ **T40.424** Poisoning by tramadol, undetermined

▶ **T40.425** Adverse effect of tramadol

▶ **T40.426** Underdosing of tramadol

▶ ● **T40.49** Poisoning by, adverse effect of and underdosing of other synthetic narcotics

▶ **T40.491** Poisoning by other synthetic narcotics, accidental (unintentional)

▶ **T40.492** Poisoning by other synthetic narcotics, intentional self-harm

▶ **T40.493** Poisoning by other synthetic narcotics, assault

▶ **T40.494** Poisoning by other synthetic narcotics, undetermined

▶ **T40.495** Adverse effect of other synthetic narcotics

▶ **T40.496** Underdosing of other synthetic narcotics

~~T40.4X~~ ~~Poisoning by, adverse effect of and underdosing of other synthetic narcotics~~

~~T40.4X1~~ ~~Poisoning by other synthetic narcotics, accidental (unintentional)~~
~~Poisoning by other synthetic narcotics NOS~~

~~T40.4X2~~ ~~Poisoning by other synthetic narcotics, intentional self-harm A, S~~

~~T40.4X3~~ ~~Poisoning by other synthetic narcotics, assault~~

~~T40.4X4~~ ~~Poisoning by other synthetic narcotics, undetermined~~

~~T40.4X5~~ ~~Adverse effect of other synthetic narcotics~~

~~T40.4X6~~ ~~Underdosing of other synthetic narcotics~~

● **T40.5** Poisoning by, adverse effect of and underdosing of cocaine

● **T40.5X** Poisoning by, adverse effect of and underdosing of cocaine

● **T40.5X1** Poisoning by cocaine, **accidental (unintentional)**
Poisoning by cocaine NOS
Coding Clinic: 2016, Q2, P9

● **T40.5X2** Poisoning by cocaine, **intentional self-harm A, S** 🔧

● **T40.5X3** Poisoning by cocaine, **assault**

● **T40.5X4** Poisoning by cocaine, **undetermined**

● **T40.5X5** Adverse effect of cocaine

● **T40.5X6** Underdosing of cocaine

CHAPTER 19 (S00-T88)

● **T40.6** **Poisoning by, adverse effect of and underdosing of other and unspecified narcotics**
  ● **T40.60** **Poisoning by, adverse effect of and underdosing of unspecified narcotics**
    ● **T40.601** **Poisoning by unspecified narcotics, accidental (unintentional)**
       Poisoning by narcotics NOS
    ● **T40.602** **Poisoning by unspecified narcotics, intentional self-harm A, S** 🦠
    ● **T40.603** **Poisoning by unspecified narcotics, assault**
    ● **T40.604** **Poisoning by unspecified narcotics, undetermined**
    ● **T40.605** **Adverse effect of unspecified narcotics**
    ● **T40.606** **Underdosing of unspecified narcotics**
  ● **T40.69** **Poisoning by, adverse effect of and underdosing of other narcotics**
    ● **T40.691** **Poisoning by other narcotics, accidental (unintentional)**
       Poisoning by other narcotics NOS
    ● **T40.692** **Poisoning by other narcotics, intentional self-harm A, S** 🦠
    ● **T40.693** **Poisoning by other narcotics, assault**
    ● **T40.694** **Poisoning by other narcotics, undetermined**
    ● **T40.695** **Adverse effect of other narcotics**
    ● **T40.696** **Underdosing of other narcotics**
● **T40.7** **Poisoning by, adverse effect of and underdosing of cannabis (derivatives)**
  ● **T40.7X** **Poisoning by, adverse effect of and underdosing of cannabis (derivatives)**
    ● **T40.7X1** **Poisoning by cannabis (derivatives), accidental (unintentional)**
       Poisoning by cannabis NOS
       Coding Clinic: 2020, Q1, P8
    ● **T40.7X2** **Poisoning by cannabis (derivatives), intentional self-harm A, S** 🦠
    ● **T40.7X3** **Poisoning by cannabis (derivatives), assault**
    ● **T40.7X4** **Poisoning by cannabis (derivatives), undetermined**
    ● **T40.7X5** **Adverse effect of cannabis (derivatives)**
    ● **T40.7X6** **Underdosing of cannabis (derivatives)**
● **T40.8** **Poisoning by and adverse effect of lysergide [LSD]**
  ● **T40.8X** **Poisoning by and adverse effect of lysergide [LSD]**
    ● **T40.8X1** **Poisoning by lysergide [LSD], accidental (unintentional)**
       Poisoning by lysergide [LSD] NOS
    ● **T40.8X2** **Poisoning by lysergide [LSD], intentional self-harm A, S** 🦠
    ● **T40.8X3** **Poisoning by lysergide [LSD], assault**
    ● **T40.8X4** **Poisoning by lysergide [LSD], undetermined**
● **T40.9** **Poisoning by, adverse effect of and underdosing of other and unspecified psychodysleptics [hallucinogens]**
  ● **T40.90** **Poisoning by, adverse effect of and underdosing of unspecified psychodysleptics [hallucinogens]**
    ● **T40.901** **Poisoning by unspecified psychodysleptics [hallucinogens], accidental (unintentional)**
    ● **T40.902** **Poisoning by unspecified psychodysleptics [hallucinogens], intentional self-harm A, S** 🦠

    ● **T40.903** **Poisoning by unspecified psychodysleptics [hallucinogens], assault**
    ● **T40.904** **Poisoning by unspecified psychodysleptics [hallucinogens], undetermined**
    ● **T40.905** **Adverse effect of unspecified psychodysleptics [hallucinogens]**
    ● **T40.906** **Underdosing of unspecified psychodysleptics [hallucinogens]**
  ● **T40.99** **Poisoning by, adverse effect of and underdosing of other psychodysleptics [hallucinogens]**
    ● **T40.991** **Poisoning by other psychodysleptics [hallucinogens], accidental (unintentional)**
       Poisoning by other psychodysleptics [hallucinogens] NOS
    ● **T40.992** **Poisoning by other psychodysleptics [hallucinogens], intentional self-harm A, S** 🦠
    ● **T40.993** **Poisoning by other psychodysleptics [hallucinogens], assault**
    ● **T40.994** **Poisoning by other psychodysleptics [hallucinogens], undetermined**
    ● **T40.995** **Adverse effect of other psychodysleptics [hallucinogens]**
    ● **T40.996** **Underdosing of other psychodysleptics [hallucinogens]**
● **T41** **Poisoning by, adverse effect of and underdosing of anesthetics and therapeutic gases**
   Excludes1   benzodiazepines (T42.4-)
       cocaine (T40.5-)
       complications of anesthesia during pregnancy (O29.-)
       complications of anesthesia during labor and delivery (O74.-)
       complications of anesthesia during the puerperium (O89.-) opioids (T40.0-T40.2-)
   The appropriate 7th character is to be added to each code from category T41

A	initial encounter
D	subsequent encounter
S	sequela

● **T41.0** **Poisoning by, adverse effect of and underdosing of inhaled anesthetics**
   Excludes1   oxygen (T41.5-)
  ● **T41.0X** **Poisoning by, adverse effect of and underdosing of inhaled anesthetics**
    ● **T41.0X1** **Poisoning by inhaled anesthetics, accidental (unintentional)**
       Poisoning by inhaled anesthetics NOS
    ● **T41.0X2** **Poisoning by inhaled anesthetics, intentional self-harm A, S** 🦠
    ● **T41.0X3** **Poisoning by inhaled anesthetics, assault**
    ● **T41.0X4** **Poisoning by inhaled anesthetics, undetermined**
    ● **T41.0X5** **Adverse effect of inhaled anesthetics**
    ● **T41.0X6** **Underdosing of inhaled anesthetics**

● **T41.1** **Poisoning by, adverse effect of and underdosing of intravenous anesthetics**
     Poisoning by, adverse effect of and underdosing of thiobarbiturates
  ● **T41.1X** **Poisoning by, adverse effect of and underdosing of intravenous anesthetics**
    ● **T41.1X1** **Poisoning by intravenous anesthetics, accidental (unintentional)**
       Poisoning by intravenous anesthetics NOS
    ● **T41.1X2** **Poisoning by intravenous anesthetics, intentional self-harm A, S** 📖
    ● **T41.1X3** **Poisoning by intravenous anesthetics, assault**
    ● **T41.1X4** **Poisoning by intravenous anesthetics, undetermined**
    ● **T41.1X5** **Adverse effect of intravenous anesthetics**
    ● **T41.1X6** **Underdosing of intravenous anesthetics**

● **T41.2** **Poisoning by, adverse effect of and underdosing of other and unspecified general anesthetics**
  ● **T41.20** **Poisoning by, adverse effect of and underdosing of unspecified general anesthetics**
    ● **T41.201** **Poisoning by unspecified general anesthetics, accidental (unintentional)**
       Poisoning by general anesthetics NOS
    ● **T41.202** **Poisoning by unspecified general anesthetics, intentional self-harm A, S** 📖
    ● **T41.203** **Poisoning by unspecified general anesthetics, assault**
    ● **T41.204** **Poisoning by unspecified general anesthetics, undetermined**
    ● **T41.205** **Adverse effect of unspecified general anesthetics**
       Coding Clinic: 2016, Q4, P73
    ● **T41.206** **Underdosing of unspecified general anesthetics**
  ● **T41.29** **Poisoning by, adverse effect of and underdosing of other general anesthetics**
    ● **T41.291** **Poisoning by other general anesthetics, accidental (unintentional)**
       Poisoning by other general anesthetics NOS
    ● **T41.292** **Poisoning by other general anesthetics, intentional self-harm A, S** 📖
    ● **T41.293** **Poisoning by other general anesthetics, assault**
    ● **T41.294** **Poisoning by other general anesthetics, undetermined**
    ● **T41.295** **Adverse effect of other general anesthetics**
    ● **T41.296** **Underdosing of other general anesthetics**

● **T41.3** **Poisoning by, adverse effect of and underdosing of local anesthetics**
     Cocaine (topical)
   Excludes2   poisoning by cocaine used as a central nervous system stimulant (T40.5X1-T40.5X4)
  ● **T41.3X** **Poisoning by, adverse effect of and underdosing of local anesthetics**
    ● **T41.3X1** **Poisoning by local anesthetics, accidental (unintentional)**
       Poisoning by local anesthetics NOS
    ● **T41.3X2** **Poisoning by local anesthetics, intentional self-harm A, S** 📖

● **T41.3X3** **Poisoning by local anesthetics, assault**
● **T41.3X4** **Poisoning by local anesthetics, undetermined**
● **T41.3X5** **Adverse effect of local anesthetics**
● **T41.3X6** **Underdosing of local anesthetics**

● **T41.4** **Poisoning by, adverse effect of and underdosing of unspecified anesthetic**
   X ● **T41.41** **Poisoning by unspecified anesthetic, accidental (unintentional)**
     Poisoning by anesthetic NOS
   X ● **T41.42** **Poisoning by unspecified anesthetic, intentional self-harm A, S** 📖
   X ● **T41.43** **Poisoning by unspecified anesthetic, assault**
   X ● **T41.44** **Poisoning by unspecified anesthetic, undetermined**
   X ● **T41.45** **Adverse effect of unspecified anesthetic**
   X ● **T41.46** **Underdosing of unspecified anesthetics**

● **T41.5** **Poisoning by, adverse effect of and underdosing of therapeutic gases**
  ● **T41.5X** **Poisoning by, adverse effect of and underdosing of therapeutic gases**
    ● **T41.5X1** **Poisoning by therapeutic gases, accidental (unintentional)**
       Poisoning by therapeutic gases NOS
    ● **T41.5X2** **Poisoning by therapeutic gases, intentional self-harm A, S** 📖
    ● **T41.5X3** **Poisoning by therapeutic gases, assault**
    ● **T41.5X4** **Poisoning by therapeutic gases, undetermined**
    ● **T41.5X5** **Adverse effect of therapeutic gases**
    ● **T41.5X6** **Underdosing of therapeutic gases**

● **T42** **Poisoning by, adverse effect of and underdosing of antiepileptic, sedative-hypnotic and antiparkinsonism drugs**
   Excludes2   drug dependence and related mental and behavioral disorders due to psychoactive substance use (F10.--F19.-)
   The appropriate 7th character is to be added to each code from category T42

A	initial encounter
D	subsequent encounter
S	sequela

● **T42.0** **Poisoning by, adverse effect of and underdosing of hydantoin derivatives**
  ● **T42.0X** **Poisoning by, adverse effect of and underdosing of hydantoin derivatives**
    ● **T42.0X1** **Poisoning by hydantoin derivatives, accidental (unintentional)**
       Poisoning by hydantoin derivatives NOS
    ● **T42.0X2** **Poisoning by hydantoin derivatives, intentional self-harm A, S** 📖
    ● **T42.0X3** **Poisoning by hydantoin derivatives, assault**
    ● **T42.0X4** **Poisoning by hydantoin derivatives, undetermined**
    ● **T42.0X5** **Adverse effect of hydantoin derivatives**
    ● **T42.0X6** **Underdosing of hydantoin derivatives**

● **T42.1** **Poisoning by, adverse effect of and underdosing of iminostilbenes**
Poisoning by, adverse effect of and underdosing of carbamazepine

  ● **T42.1X** **Poisoning by, adverse effect of and underdosing of iminostilbenes**

    ● **T42.1X1** **Poisoning by iminostilbenes, accidental (unintentional)**
Poisoning by iminostilbenes NOS

    ● **T42.1X2** **Poisoning by iminostilbenes, intentional self-harm A, S** 🦚

    ● **T42.1X3** **Poisoning by iminostilbenes, assault**

    ● **T42.1X4** **Poisoning by iminostilbenes, undetermined**

    ● **T42.1X5** **Adverse effect of iminostilbenes**

    ● **T42.1X6** **Underdosing of iminostilbenes**

● **T42.2** **Poisoning by, adverse effect of and underdosing of succinimides and oxazolidinediones**

  ● **T42.2X** **Poisoning by, adverse effect of and underdosing of succinimides and oxazolidinediones**

    ● **T42.2X1** **Poisoning by succinimides and oxazolidinediones, accidental (unintentional)**
Poisoning by succinimides and oxazolidinediones NOS

    ● **T42.2X2** **Poisoning by succinimides and oxazolidinediones, intentional self-harm A, S** 🦚

    ● **T42.2X3** **Poisoning by succinimides and oxazolidinediones, assault**

    ● **T42.2X4** **Poisoning by succinimides and oxazolidinediones, undetermined**

    ● **T42.2X5** **Adverse effect of succinimides and oxazolidinediones**

    ● **T42.2X6** **Underdosing of succinimides and oxazolidinediones**

● **T42.3** **Poisoning by, adverse effect of and underdosing of barbiturates**

  Excludes1 poisoning by, adverse effect of and underdosing of thiobarbiturates (T41.1-)

  ● **T42.3X** **Poisoning by, adverse effect of and underdosing of barbiturates**

    ● **T42.3X1** **Poisoning by barbiturates, accidental (unintentional)**
Poisoning by barbiturates NOS

    ● **T42.3X2** **Poisoning by barbiturates, intentional self-harm A, S** 🦚

    ● **T42.3X3** **Poisoning by barbiturates, assault**

    ● **T42.3X4** **Poisoning by barbiturates, undetermined**

    ● **T42.3X5** **Adverse effect of barbiturates**

    ● **T42.3X6** **Underdosing of barbiturates**

● **T42.4** **Poisoning by, adverse effect of and underdosing of benzodiazepines**

  ● **T42.4X** **Poisoning by, adverse effect of and underdosing of benzodiazepines**

    ● **T42.4X1** **Poisoning by benzodiazepines, accidental (unintentional)**
Poisoning by benzodiazepines NOS

    ● **T42.4X2** **Poisoning by benzodiazepines, intentional self-harm A, S** 🦚

    ● **T42.4X3** **Poisoning by benzodiazepines, assault**

    ● **T42.4X4** **Poisoning by benzodiazepines, undetermined**

    ● **T42.4X5** **Adverse effect of benzodiazepines**

    ● **T42.4X6** **Underdosing of benzodiazepines**

● **T42.5** **Poisoning by, adverse effect of and underdosing of mixed antiepileptics**

  ● **T42.5X** **Poisoning by, adverse effect of and underdosing of antiepileptics**

    ● **T42.5X1** **Poisoning by mixed antiepileptics, accidental (unintentional)**
Poisoning by mixed antiepileptics NOS

    ● **T42.5X2** **Poisoning by mixed antiepileptics, intentional self-harm A, S** 🦚

    ● **T42.5X3** **Poisoning by mixed antiepileptics, assault**

    ● **T42.5X4** **Poisoning by mixed antiepileptics, undetermined**

    ● **T42.5X5** **Adverse effect of mixed antiepileptics**

    ● **T42.5X6** **Underdosing of mixed antiepileptics**

● **T42.6** **Poisoning by, adverse effect of and underdosing of other antiepileptic and sedative-hypnotic drugs**
Poisoning by, adverse effect of and underdosing of methaqualone
Poisoning by, adverse effect of and underdosing of valproic acid

  Excludes1 poisoning by, adverse effect of and underdosing of carbamazepine (T42.1-)

  ● **T42.6X** **Poisoning by, adverse effect of and underdosing of other antiepileptic and sedative-hypnotic drugs**

    ● **T42.6X1** **Poisoning by other antiepileptic and sedative-hypnotic drugs, accidental (unintentional)**
Poisoning by other antiepileptic and sedative-hypnotic drugs NOS

    ● **T42.6X2** **Poisoning by other antiepileptic and sedative-hypnotic drugs, intentional self-harm A, S** 🦚

    ● **T42.6X3** **Poisoning by other antiepileptic and sedative-hypnotic drugs, assault**

    ● **T42.6X4** **Poisoning by other antiepileptic and sedative-hypnotic drugs, undetermined**

    ● **T42.6X5** **Adverse effect of other antiepileptic and sedative-hypnotic drugs**

    ● **T42.6X6** **Underdosing of other antiepileptic and sedative-hypnotic drugs**

● **T42.7** **Poisoning by, adverse effect of and underdosing of unspecified antiepileptic and sedative-hypnotic drugs**

  X ● **T42.71** **Poisoning by unspecified antiepileptic and sedative-hypnotic drugs, accidental (unintentional)**
Poisoning by antiepileptic and sedative-hypnotic drugs NOS

  X ● **T42.72** **Poisoning by unspecified antiepileptic and sedative-hypnotic drugs, intentional self-harm A, S** 🦚

  X ● **T42.73** **Poisoning by unspecified antiepileptic and sedative-hypnotic drugs, assault**

  X ● **T42.74** **Poisoning by unspecified antiepileptic and sedative-hypnotic drugs, undetermined**

  X ● **T42.75** **Adverse effect of unspecified antiepileptic and sedative-hypnotic drugs**

  X ● **T42.76** **Underdosing of unspecified antiepileptic and sedative-hypnotic drugs**

▶ New   ⇒ Revised   ~~deleted~~ Deleted   Excludes 1   Excludes 2   Includes   Use additional   Code first   Code also   Key words

OGCR Official Guidelines   X Assign placeholder X   ● Use Additional Character(s)   ▷ Manifestation Code   🦚 Hierarchical Condition Category   **Coding Clinic**

● **T42.8**   Poisoning by, adverse effect of and underdosing of antiparkinsonism drugs and other central muscle-tone depressants
> Poisoning by, adverse effect of and underdosing of amantadine

   ● **T42.8X**   Poisoning by, adverse effect of and underdosing of antiparkinsonism drugs and other central muscle-tone depressants

     ● **T42.8X1**   Poisoning by antiparkinsonism drugs and other central muscle-tone depressants, accidental (unintentional)
> Poisoning by antiparkinsonism drugs and other central muscle-tone depressants NOS

     ● **T42.8X2**   Poisoning by antiparkinsonism drugs and other central muscle-tone depressants, intentional self-harm A, S 🔒

     ● **T42.8X3**   Poisoning by antiparkinsonism drugs and other central muscle-tone depressants, assault

     ● **T42.8X4**   Poisoning by antiparkinsonism drugs and other central muscle-tone depressants, undetermined

     ● **T42.8X5**   Adverse effect of antiparkinsonism drugs and other central muscle-tone depressants

     ● **T42.8X6**   Underdosing of antiparkinsonism drugs and other central muscle-tone depressants

● **T43**   Poisoning by, adverse effect of and underdosing of psychotropic drugs, not elsewhere classified

     Excludes1   appetite depressants (T50.5-)
                 barbiturates (T42.3-)
                 benzodiazepines (T42.4-)
                 methaqualone (T42.6-)
                 psychodysleptics [hallucinogens] (T40.7-T40.9-)

     Excludes2   drug dependence and related mental and behavioral disorders due to psychoactive substance use (F10.--F19.-)

> The appropriate 7th character is to be added to each code from category T43

A	initial encounter
D	subsequent encounter
S	sequela

   ● **T43.0**   Poisoning by, adverse effect of and underdosing of tricyclic and tetracyclic antidepressants

     ● **T43.01**   Poisoning by, adverse effect of and underdosing of tricyclic antidepressants

       ● **T43.011**   Poisoning by tricyclic antidepressants, accidental (unintentional)
> Poisoning by tricyclic antidepressants NOS

       ● **T43.012**   Poisoning by tricyclic antidepressants, intentional self-harm A, S 🔒

       ● **T43.013**   Poisoning by tricyclic antidepressants, assault

       ● **T43.014**   Poisoning by tricyclic antidepressants, undetermined

       ● **T43.015**   Adverse effect of tricyclic antidepressants

       ● **T43.016**   Underdosing of tricyclic antidepressants

     ● **T43.02**   Poisoning by, adverse effect of and underdosing of tetracyclic antidepressants

       ● **T43.021**   Poisoning by tetracyclic antidepressants, accidental (unintentional)
> Poisoning by tetracyclic antidepressants NOS

       ● **T43.022**   Poisoning by tetracyclic antidepressants, intentional self-harm A, S 🔒

       ● **T43.023**   Poisoning by tetracyclic antidepressants, assault

       ● **T43.024**   Poisoning by tetracyclic antidepressants, undetermined

       ● **T43.025**   Adverse effect of tetracyclic antidepressants

       ● **T43.026**   Underdosing of tetracyclic antidepressants

   ● **T43.1**   Poisoning by, adverse effect of and underdosing of monoamine-oxidase-inhibitor antidepressants

     ● **T43.1X**   Poisoning by, adverse effect of and underdosing of monoamine-oxidase-inhibitor antidepressants

       ● **T43.1X1**   Poisoning by monoamine-oxidase-inhibitor antidepressants, accidental (unintentional)
> Poisoning by monoamine-oxidase-inhibitor antidepressants NOS

       ● **T43.1X2**   Poisoning by monoamine-oxidase-inhibitor antidepressants, intentional self-harm A, S 🔒

       ● **T43.1X3**   Poisoning by monoamine-oxidase-inhibitor antidepressants, assault

       ● **T43.1X4**   Poisoning by monoamine-oxidase-inhibitor antidepressants, undetermined

       ● **T43.1X5**   Adverse effect of monoamine-oxidase-inhibitor antidepressants

       ● **T43.1X6**   Underdosing of monoamine-oxidase-inhibitor antidepressants

   ● **T43.2**   Poisoning by, adverse effect of and underdosing of other and unspecified antidepressants

     ● **T43.20**   Poisoning by, adverse effect of and underdosing of unspecified antidepressants

       ● **T43.201**   Poisoning by unspecified antidepressants, accidental (unintentional)
> Poisoning by antidepressants NOS

       ● **T43.202**   Poisoning by unspecified antidepressants, intentional self-harm A, S 🔒

       ● **T43.203**   Poisoning by unspecified antidepressants, assault

       ● **T43.204**   Poisoning by unspecified antidepressants, undetermined

       ● **T43.205**   Adverse effect of unspecified antidepressants
> Antidepressant discontinuation syndrome

       ● **T43.206**   Underdosing of unspecified antidepressants

- **T43.21** Poisoning by, adverse effect of and underdosing of selective serotonin and norepinephrine reuptake inhibitors
  Poisoning by, adverse effect of and underdosing of SSNRI antidepressants
  - **T43.211** Poisoning by selective serotonin and norepinephrine reuptake inhibitors, accidental (unintentional)
  - **T43.212** Poisoning by selective serotonin and norepinephrine reuptake inhibitors, intentional self-harm A, S 🝅
  - **T43.213** Poisoning by selective serotonin and norepinephrine reuptake inhibitors, assault
  - **T43.214** Poisoning by selective serotonin and norepinephrine reuptake inhibitors, undetermined
  - **T43.215** Adverse effect of selective serotonin and norepinephrine reuptake inhibitors
  - **T43.216** Underdosing of selective serotonin and norepinephrine reuptake inhibitors
- **T43.22** Poisoning by, adverse effect of and underdosing of selective serotonin reuptake inhibitors
  Poisoning by, adverse effect of and underdosing of SSRI antidepressants
  - **T43.221** Poisoning by selective serotonin reuptake inhibitors, accidental (unintentional)
  - **T43.222** Poisoning by selective serotonin reuptake inhibitors, intentional self-harm A, S 🝅
  - **T43.223** Poisoning by selective serotonin reuptake inhibitors, assault
  - **T43.224** Poisoning by selective serotonin reuptake inhibitors, undetermined
  - **T43.225** Adverse effect of selective serotonin reuptake inhibitors
  - **T43.226** Underdosing of selective serotonin reuptake inhibitors
- **T43.29** Poisoning by, adverse effect of and underdosing of other antidepressants
  - **T43.291** Poisoning by other antidepressants, accidental (unintentional)
    Poisoning by other antidepressants NOS
  - **T43.292** Poisoning by other antidepressants, intentional self-harm A, S 🝅
  - **T43.293** Poisoning by other antidepressants, assault
  - **T43.294** Poisoning by other antidepressants, undetermined
  - **T43.295** Adverse effect of other antidepressants
  - **T43.296** Underdosing of other antidepressants
- **T43.3** Poisoning by, adverse effect of and underdosing of phenothiazine antipsychotics and neuroleptics
  - **T43.3X** Poisoning by, adverse effect of and underdosing of phenothiazine antipsychotics and neuroleptics
    - **T43.3X1** Poisoning by phenothiazine antipsychotics and neuroleptics, accidental (unintentional)
      Poisoning by phenothiazine antipsychotics and neuroleptics NOS
    - **T43.3X2** Poisoning by phenothiazine antipsychotics and neuroleptics, intentional self-harm A, S 🝅
    - **T43.3X3** Poisoning by phenothiazine antipsychotics and neuroleptics, assault
    - **T43.3X4** Poisoning by phenothiazine antipsychotics and neuroleptics, undetermined

- **T43.3X5** Adverse effect of phenothiazine antipsychotics and neuroleptics
- **T43.3X6** Underdosing of phenothiazine antipsychotics and neuroleptics
- **T43.4** Poisoning by, adverse effect of and underdosing of butyrophenone and thiothixene neuroleptics
  - **T43.4X** Poisoning by, adverse effect of and underdosing of butyrophenone and thiothixene neuroleptics
    - **T43.4X1** Poisoning by butyrophenone and thiothixene neuroleptics, accidental (unintentional)
      Poisoning by butyrophenone and thiothixene neuroleptics NOS
    - **T43.4X2** Poisoning by butyrophenone and thiothixene neuroleptics, intentional self-harm A, S 🝅
    - **T43.4X3** Poisoning by butyrophenone and thiothixene neuroleptics, assault
    - **T43.4X4** Poisoning by butyrophenone and thiothixene neuroleptics, undetermined
    - **T43.4X5** Adverse effect of butyrophenone and thiothixene neuroleptics
    - **T43.4X6** Underdosing of butyrophenone and thiothixene neuroleptics
- **T43.5** Poisoning by, adverse effect of and underdosing of other and unspecified antipsychotics and neuroleptics

  Excludes1   poisoning by, adverse effect of and underdosing of rauwolfia (T46.5-)

  - **T43.50** Poisoning by, adverse effect of and underdosing of unspecified antipsychotics and neuroleptics
    - **T43.501** Poisoning by unspecified antipsychotics and neuroleptics, accidental (unintentional)
      Poisoning by antipsychotics and neuroleptics NOS
    - **T43.502** Poisoning by unspecified antipsychotics and neuroleptics, intentional self-harm A, S 🝅
    - **T43.503** Poisoning by unspecified antipsychotics and neuroleptics, assault
    - **T43.504** Poisoning by unspecified antipsychotics and neuroleptics, undetermined
    - **T43.505** Adverse effect of unspecified antipsychotics and neuroleptics
    - **T43.506** Underdosing of unspecified antipsychotics and neuroleptics
  - **T43.59** Poisoning by, adverse effect of and underdosing of other antipsychotics and neuroleptics
    - **T43.591** Poisoning by other antipsychotics and neuroleptics, accidental (unintentional)
      Poisoning by other antipsychotics and neuroleptics NOS
    - **T43.592** Poisoning by other antipsychotics and neuroleptics, intentional self-harm A, S 🝅
      Coding Clinic: 2017, Q1, P40
    - **T43.593** Poisoning by other antipsychotics and neuroleptics, assault
    - **T43.594** Poisoning by other antipsychotics and neuroleptics, undetermined
    - **T43.595** Adverse effect of other antipsychotics and neuroleptics
    - **T43.596** Underdosing of other antipsychotics and neuroleptics

CHAPTER 19 (S00-T88)

▶ New   ⇉ Revised   ~~deleted~~ Deleted   Excludes 1   Excludes 2   Includes   Use additional   Code first   Code also   Key words

OGCR Official Guidelines   X Assign placeholder X   ● Use Additional Character(s)   ▶ Manifestation Code   🝅 Hierarchical Condition Category   **Coding Clinic**

● T43.6 Poisoning by, adverse effect of and underdosing of psychostimulants

> Excludes1 poisoning by, adverse effect of and underdosing of cocaine (T40.5-)

● T43.60 Poisoning by, adverse effect of and underdosing of unspecified psychostimulant

● T43.601 Poisoning by unspecified psychostimulants, accidental (unintentional)
> Poisoning by psychostimulants NOS

● T43.602 Poisoning by unspecified psychostimulants, intentional self-harm A, S 🔖

● T43.603 Poisoning by unspecified psychostimulants, assault

● T43.604 Poisoning by unspecified psychostimulants, undetermined

● T43.605 Adverse effect of unspecified psychostimulants

● T43.606 Underdosing of unspecified psychostimulants

● T43.61 Poisoning by, adverse effect of and underdosing of caffeine

● T43.611 Poisoning by caffeine, accidental (unintentional)
> Poisoning by caffeine NOS

● T43.612 Poisoning by caffeine, intentional self-harm A, S 🔖

● T43.613 Poisoning by caffeine, assault

● T43.614 Poisoning by caffeine, undetermined

● T43.615 Adverse effect of caffeine

● T43.616 Underdosing of caffeine

● T43.62 Poisoning by, adverse effect of and underdosing of amphetamines
> Poisoning by, adverse effect of and underdosing of methamphetamines

● T43.621 Poisoning by amphetamines, accidental (unintentional)
> Poisoning by amphetamines NOS

● T43.622 Poisoning by amphetamines, intentional self-harm A, S 🔖

● T43.623 Poisoning by amphetamines, assault

● T43.624 Poisoning by amphetamines, undetermined

● T43.625 Adverse effect of amphetamines

● T43.626 Underdosing of amphetamines

● T43.63 Poisoning by, adverse effect of and underdosing of methylphenidate

● T43.631 Poisoning by methylphenidate, accidental (unintentional)
> Poisoning by methylphenidate NOS

● T43.632 Poisoning by methylphenidate, intentional self-harm A, S 🔖

● T43.633 Poisoning by methylphenidate, assault

● T43.634 Poisoning by methylphenidate, undetermined

● T43.635 Adverse effect of methylphenidate

● T43.636 Underdosing of methylphenidate

● T43.64 Poisoning by ecstasy
> Poisoning by MDMA
> Poisoning by 3,4-methylenedioxymethamphetamine

● T43.641 Poisoning by ecstasy, accidental (unintentional)
> Poisoning by ecstasy NOS
> **Coding Clinic: 2018, Q4, P31**

● T43.642 Poisoning by ecstasy, intentional self-harm A, S 🔖

● T43.643 Poisoning by ecstasy, assault

● T43.644 Poisoning by ecstasy, undetermined

● T43.69 Poisoning by, adverse effect of and underdosing of other psychostimulants

● T43.691 Poisoning by other psychostimulants, accidental (unintentional)
> Poisoning by other psychostimulants NOS

● T43.692 Poisoning by other psychostimulants, intentional self-harm A, S 🔖

● T43.693 Poisoning by other psychostimulants, assault

● T43.694 Poisoning by other psychostimulants, undetermined

● T43.695 Adverse effect of other psychostimulants

● T43.696 Underdosing of other psychostimulants

● T43.8 Poisoning by, adverse effect of and underdosing of other psychotropic drugs

● T43.8X Poisoning by, adverse effect of and underdosing of other psychotropic drugs

● T43.8X1 Poisoning by other psychotropic drugs, accidental (unintentional)
> Poisoning by other psychotropic drugs NOS

● T43.8X2 Poisoning by other psychotropic drugs, intentional self-harm A, S 🔖

● T43.8X3 Poisoning by other psychotropic drugs, assault

● T43.8X4 Poisoning by other psychotropic drugs, undetermined

● T43.8X5 Adverse effect of other psychotropic drugs

● T43.8X6 Underdosing of other psychotropic drugs

● T43.9 Poisoning by, adverse effect of and underdosing of unspecified psychotropic drug

X ● T43.91 Poisoning by unspecified psychotropic drug, accidental (unintentional)
> Poisoning by psychotropic drug NOS

X ● T43.92 Poisoning by unspecified psychotropic drug, intentional self-harm A, S 🔖

X ● T43.93 Poisoning by unspecified psychotropic drug, assault

X ● T43.94 Poisoning by unspecified psychotropic drug, undetermined

X ● T43.95 Adverse effect of unspecified psychotropic drug

X ● T43.96 Underdosing of unspecified psychotropic drug

● T44 Poisoning by, adverse effect of and underdosing of drugs primarily affecting the autonomic nervous system

> The appropriate 7th character is to be added to each code from category T44

A	initial encounter
D	subsequent encounter
S	sequela

● T44.0 Poisoning by, adverse effect of and underdosing of anticholinesterase agents

● T44.0X Poisoning by, adverse effect of and underdosing of anticholinesterase agents

● T44.0X1 Poisoning by anticholinesterase agents, accidental (unintentional)
> Poisoning by anticholinesterase agents NOS

● T44.0X2 Poisoning by anticholinesterase agents, intentional self-harm A, S 🔖

● T44.0X3 Poisoning by anticholinesterase agents, assault

● T44.0X4 Poisoning by anticholinesterase agents, undetermined

● T44.0X5 Adverse effect of anticholinesterase agents

● T44.0X6 Underdosing of anticholinesterase agents

● **T44.1 Poisoning by, adverse effect of and underdosing of other parasympathomimetics [cholinergics]**
- ● **T44.1X Poisoning by, adverse effect of and underdosing of other parasympathomimetics [cholinergics]**
  - ● **T44.1X1 Poisoning by other parasympathomimetics [cholinergics], accidental (unintentional)**
    Poisoning by other parasympathomimetics [cholinergics] NOS
  - ● **T44.1X2 Poisoning by other parasympathomimetics [cholinergics], intentional self-harm A, S** 🏷
  - ● **T44.1X3 Poisoning by other parasympathomimetics [cholinergics], assault**
  - ● **T44.1X4 Poisoning by other parasympathomimetics [cholinergics], undetermined**
  - ● **T44.1X5 Adverse effect of other parasympathomimetics [cholinergics]**
  - ● **T44.1X6 Underdosing of other parasympathomimetics [cholinergics]**

● **T44.2 Poisoning by, adverse effect of and underdosing of ganglionic blocking drugs**
- ● **T44.2X Poisoning by, adverse effect of and underdosing of ganglionic blocking drugs**
  - ● **T44.2X1 Poisoning by ganglionic blocking drugs, accidental (unintentional)**
    Poisoning by ganglionic blocking drugs NOS
  - ● **T44.2X2 Poisoning by ganglionic blocking drugs, intentional self-harm A, S** 🏷
  - ● **T44.2X3 Poisoning by ganglionic blocking drugs, assault**
  - ● **T44.2X4 Poisoning by ganglionic blocking drugs, undetermined**
  - ● **T44.2X5 Adverse effect of ganglionic blocking drugs**
  - ● **T44.2X6 Underdosing of ganglionic blocking drugs**

● **T44.3 Poisoning by, adverse effect of and underdosing of other parasympatholytics [anticholinergics and antimuscarinics] and spasmolytics**
Poisoning by, adverse effect of and underdosing of papaverine
- ● **T44.3X Poisoning by, adverse effect of and underdosing of other parasympatholytics [anticholinergics and antimuscarinics] and spasmolytics**
  - ● **T44.3X1 Poisoning by other parasympatholytics [anticholinergics and antimuscarinics] and spasmolytics, accidental (unintentional)**
    Poisoning by other parasympatholytics [anticholinergics and antimuscarinics] and spasmolytics NOS
  - ● **T44.3X2 Poisoning by other parasympatholytics [anticholinergics and antimuscarinics] and spasmolytics, intentional self-harm A, S** 🏷

- ● **T44.3X3 Poisoning by other parasympatholytics [anticholinergics and antimuscarinics] and spasmolytics, assault**
- ● **T44.3X4 Poisoning by other parasympatholytics [anticholinergics and antimuscarinics] and spasmolytics, undetermined**
- ● **T44.3X5 Adverse effect of other parasympatholytics [anticholinergics and antimuscarinics] and spasmolytics**
- ● **T44.3X6 Underdosing of other parasympatholytics [anticholinergics and antimuscarinics] and spasmolytics**

● **T44.4 Poisoning by, adverse effect of and underdosing of predominantly alpha-adrenoreceptor agonists**
Poisoning by, adverse effect of and underdosing of metaraminol
- ● **T44.4X Poisoning by, adverse effect of and underdosing of predominantly alpha-adrenoreceptor agonists**
  - ● **T44.4X1 Poisoning by predominantly alpha-adrenoreceptor agonists, accidental (unintentional)**
    Poisoning by predominantly alpha-adrenoreceptor agonists NOS
  - ● **T44.4X2 Poisoning by predominantly alpha-adrenoreceptor agonists, intentional self-harm A, S** 🏷
  - ● **T44.4X3 Poisoning by predominantly alpha-adrenoreceptor agonists, assault**
  - ● **T44.4X4 Poisoning by predominantly alpha-adrenoreceptor agonists, undetermined**
  - ● **T44.4X5 Adverse effect of predominantly alpha-adrenoreceptor agonists**
  - ● **T44.4X6 Underdosing of predominantly alpha-adrenoreceptor agonists**

● **T44.5 Poisoning by, adverse effect of and underdosing of predominantly beta-adrenoreceptor agonists**
> **Excludes1**   poisoning by, adverse effect of and underdosing of beta-adrenoreceptor agonists used in asthma therapy (T48.6-)
- ● **T44.5X Poisoning by, adverse effect of and underdosing of predominantly beta-adrenoreceptor agonists**
  - ● **T44.5X1 Poisoning by predominantly beta-adrenoreceptor agonists, accidental (unintentional)**
    Poisoning by predominantly beta-adrenoreceptor agonists NOS
  - ● **T44.5X2 Poisoning by predominantly beta-adrenoreceptor agonists, intentional self-harm A, S** 🏷
  - ● **T44.5X3 Poisoning by predominantly beta-adrenoreceptor agonists, assault**
  - ● **T44.5X4 Poisoning by predominantly beta-adrenoreceptor agonists, undetermined**
  - ● **T44.5X5 Adverse effect of predominantly beta-adrenoreceptor agonists**
  - ● **T44.5X6 Underdosing of predominantly beta-adrenoreceptor agonists**

▶ New   ⇒ Revised   ~~deleted~~ Deleted   Excludes 1   Excludes 2   Includes   Use additional   Code first   Code also   Key words
OGCR Official Guidelines   X Assign placeholder X   ● Use Additional Character(s)   ▷ Manifestation Code   🏷 Hierarchical Condition Category   **Coding Clinic**

● T44.6   Poisoning by, adverse effect of and underdosing of alpha-adrenoreceptor antagonists
> **Excludes1**   poisoning by, adverse effect of and underdosing of ergot alkaloids (T48.0)

   ● T44.6X   Poisoning by, adverse effect of and underdosing of alpha-adrenoreceptor antagonists

     ● T44.6X1   Poisoning by alpha-adrenoreceptor antagonists, **accidental (unintentional)**
> Poisoning by alpha-adrenoreceptor antagonists NOS

     ● T44.6X2   Poisoning by alpha-adrenoreceptor antagonists, **intentional self-harm A, S** 🔓

     ● T44.6X3   Poisoning by alpha-adrenoreceptor antagonists, **assault**

     ● T44.6X4   Poisoning by alpha-adrenoreceptor antagonists, **undetermined**

     ● T44.6X5   **Adverse effect of alpha-adrenoreceptor antagonists**

     ● T44.6X6   **Underdosing of alpha-adrenoreceptor antagonists**

● T44.7   Poisoning by, adverse effect of and underdosing of beta-adrenoreceptor antagonists

   ● T44.7X   Poisoning by, adverse effect of and underdosing of **beta-adrenoreceptor antagonists**

     ● T44.7X1   Poisoning by beta-adrenoreceptor antagonists, **accidental (unintentional)**
> Poisoning by beta-adrenoreceptor antagonists NOS

     ● T44.7X2   Poisoning by beta-adrenoreceptor antagonists, **intentional self-harm A, S** 🔓

     ● T44.7X3   Poisoning by beta-adrenoreceptor antagonists, **assault**

     ● T44.7X4   Poisoning by beta-adrenoreceptor antagonists, **undetermined**

     ● T44.7X5   **Adverse effect of beta-adrenoreceptor antagonists**

     ● T44.7X6   **Underdosing of beta-adrenoreceptor antagonists**

● T44.8   Poisoning by, adverse effect of and underdosing of centrally-acting and adrenergic-neuron-blocking agents
> **Excludes1**   poisoning by, adverse effect of and underdosing of clonidine (T46.5)
> poisoning by, adverse effect of and underdosing of guanethidine (T46.5)

   ● T44.8X   Poisoning by, adverse effect of and underdosing of **centrally-acting and adrenergic-neuron-blocking agents**

     ● T44.8X1   Poisoning by centrally-acting and adrenergic-neuron-blocking agents, **accidental (unintentional)**
> Poisoning by centrally-acting and adrenergic-neuron-blocking agents NOS

     ● T44.8X2   Poisoning by centrally-acting and adrenergic-neuron-blocking agents, **intentional self-harm A, S** 🔓

     ● T44.8X3   Poisoning by centrally-acting and adrenergic-neuron-blocking agents, **assault**

     ● T44.8X4   Poisoning by centrally-acting and adrenergic-neuron-blocking agents, **undetermined**

     ● T44.8X5   **Adverse effect of centrally-acting and adrenergic-neuron-blocking agents**

     ● T44.8X6   **Underdosing of centrally-acting and adrenergic-neuron-blocking agents**

● T44.9   Poisoning by, adverse effect of and underdosing of other and unspecified drugs primarily affecting the autonomic nervous system
> Poisoning by, adverse effect of and underdosing of drug stimulating both alpha and beta-adrenoreceptors

   ● T44.90   Poisoning by, adverse effect of and underdosing of **unspecified drugs primarily affecting the autonomic nervous system**

     ● T44.901   Poisoning by unspecified drugs primarily affecting the autonomic nervous system, **accidental (unintentional)**
> Poisoning by unspecified drugs primarily affecting the autonomic nervous system NOS

     ● T44.902   Poisoning by unspecified drugs primarily affecting the autonomic nervous system, **intentional self-harm A, S** 🔓

     ● T44.903   Poisoning by unspecified drugs primarily affecting the autonomic nervous system, **assault**

     ● T44.904   Poisoning by unspecified drugs primarily affecting the autonomic nervous system, **undetermined**

     ● T44.905   **Adverse effect of unspecified drugs primarily affecting the autonomic nervous system**

     ● T44.906   **Underdosing of unspecified drugs primarily affecting the autonomic nervous system**

   ● T44.99   Poisoning by, adverse effect of and underdosing of **other drugs primarily affecting the autonomic nervous system**

     ● T44.991   Poisoning by other drug primarily affecting the autonomic nervous system, **accidental (unintentional)**
> Poisoning by other drugs primarily affecting the autonomic nervous system NOS

     ● T44.992   Poisoning by other drug primarily affecting the autonomic nervous system, **intentional self-harm A, S** 🔓

     ● T44.993   Poisoning by other drug primarily affecting the autonomic nervous system, **assault**

     ● T44.994   Poisoning by other drug primarily affecting the autonomic nervous system, **undetermined**

     ● T44.995   **Adverse effect of other drug primarily affecting the autonomic nervous system**

     ● T44.996   **Underdosing of other drug primarily affecting the autonomic nervous system**

CHAPTER 19 (S00-T88)

● **T45** **Poisoning by, adverse effect of and underdosing of primarily systemic and hematological agents, not elsewhere classified**

> The appropriate 7th character is to be added to each code from category T45
>
> | | |
> |---|---|
> | A | initial encounter |
> | D | subsequent encounter |
> | S | sequela |

● **T45.0** **Poisoning by, adverse effect of and underdosing of antiallergic and antiemetic drugs**

> **Excludes1**   poisoning by, adverse effect of and underdosing of phenothiazine-based neuroleptics (T43.3)

  ● **T45.0X** **Poisoning by, adverse effect of and underdosing of antiallergic and antiemetic drugs**

    ● **T45.0X1** **Poisoning by antiallergic and antiemetic drugs, accidental (unintentional)**
> Poisoning by antiallergic and antiemetic drugs NOS

    ● **T45.0X2** **Poisoning by antiallergic and antiemetic drugs, intentional self-harm A, S** 🐾

    ● **T45.0X3** **Poisoning by antiallergic and antiemetic drugs, assault**

    ● **T45.0X4** **Poisoning by antiallergic and antiemetic drugs, undetermined**

    ● **T45.0X5** **Adverse effect of antiallergic and antiemetic drugs**

    ● **T45.0X6** **Underdosing of antiallergic and antiemetic drugs**

● **T45.1** **Poisoning by, adverse effect of and underdosing of antineoplastic and immunosuppressive drugs**

> **Excludes1**   poisoning by, adverse effect of and underdosing of tamoxifen (T38.6)

  ● **T45.1X** **Poisoning by, adverse effect of and underdosing of antineoplastic and immunosuppressive drugs**

    ● **T45.1X1** **Poisoning by antineoplastic and immunosuppressive drugs, accidental (unintentional)**
> Poisoning by antineoplastic and immunosuppressive drugs NOS

    ● **T45.1X2** **Poisoning by antineoplastic and immunosuppressive drugs, intentional self-harm A, S** 🐾

    ● **T45.1X3** **Poisoning by antineoplastic and immunosuppressive drugs, assault**

    ● **T45.1X4** **Poisoning by antineoplastic and immunosuppressive drugs, undetermined**

    ● **T45.1X5** **Adverse effect of antineoplastic and immunosuppressive drugs**
> **Coding Clinic: 2019, Q2, P25, 28; Q1, P17, 21**

    ● **T45.1X6** **Underdosing of antineoplastic and immunosuppressive drugs**

● **T45.2** **Poisoning by, adverse effect of and underdosing of vitamins**

> **Excludes2**   poisoning by, adverse effect of and underdosing of nicotinic acid (derivatives) (T46.7)
> poisoning by, adverse effect of and underdosing of iron (T45.4)
> poisoning by, adverse effect of and underdosing of vitamin K (T45.7)

● **T45.2X** **Poisoning by, adverse effect of and underdosing of vitamins**

  ● **T45.2X1** **Poisoning by vitamins, accidental (unintentional)**
> Poisoning by vitamins NOS

  ● **T45.2X2** **Poisoning by vitamins, intentional self-harm A, S** 🐾

  ● **T45.2X3** **Poisoning by vitamins, assault**

  ● **T45.2X4** **Poisoning by vitamins, undetermined**

  ● **T45.2X5** **Adverse effect of vitamins**

  ● **T45.2X6** **Underdosing of vitamins**
> **Excludes1**   vitamin deficiencies (E50-E56)

● **T45.3** **Poisoning by, adverse effect of and underdosing of enzymes**

  ● **T45.3X** **Poisoning by, adverse effect of and underdosing of enzymes**

    ● **T45.3X1** **Poisoning by enzymes, accidental (unintentional)**
> Poisoning by enzymes NOS

    ● **T45.3X2** **Poisoning by enzymes, intentional self-harm A, S** 🐾

    ● **T45.3X3** **Poisoning by enzymes, assault**

    ● **T45.3X4** **Poisoning by enzymes, undetermined**

    ● **T45.3X5** **Adverse effect of enzymes**

    ● **T45.3X6** **Underdosing of enzymes**

● **T45.4** **Poisoning by, adverse effect of and underdosing of iron and its compounds**

  ● **T45.4X** **Poisoning by, adverse effect of and underdosing of iron and its compounds**

    ● **T45.4X1** **Poisoning by iron and its compounds, accidental (unintentional)**
> Poisoning by iron and its compounds NOS

    ● **T45.4X2** **Poisoning by iron and its compounds, intentional self-harm A, S** 🐾

    ● **T45.4X3** **Poisoning by iron and its compounds, assault**

    ● **T45.4X4** **Poisoning by iron and its compounds, undetermined**

    ● **T45.4X5** **Adverse effect of iron and its compounds**

    ● **T45.4X6** **Underdosing of iron and its compounds**
> **Excludes1**   iron deficiency (E61.1)

● **T45.5** **Poisoning by, adverse effect of and underdosing of anticoagulants and antithrombotic drugs**

  ● **T45.51** **Poisoning by, adverse effect of and underdosing of anticoagulants**

    ● **T45.511** **Poisoning by anticoagulants, accidental (unintentional)**
> Poisoning by anticoagulants NOS

    ● **T45.512** **Poisoning by anticoagulants, intentional self-harm A, S** 🐾

    ● **T45.513** **Poisoning by anticoagulants, assault**

    ● **T45.514** **Poisoning by anticoagulants, undetermined**

    ● **T45.515** **Adverse effect of anticoagulants**
> **Coding Clinic: 2016, Q1, P14; 2013, Q2, P35**

    ● **T45.516** **Underdosing of anticoagulants**

▶ New   ⟹ Revised   ~~deleted~~ Deleted   Excludes 1   Excludes 2   Includes   Use additional   Code first   Code also   Key words

OGCR Official Guidelines   X Assign placeholder X   ● Use Additional Character(s)   ▷ Manifestation Code   🐾 Hierarchical Condition Category   **Coding Clinic**

● **T45.52 Poisoning by, adverse effect of and underdosing of antithrombotic drugs**
Poisoning by, adverse effect of and underdosing of antiplatelet drugs

Excludes2 poisoning by, adverse effect of and underdosing of aspirin (T39.Ø1-)
poisoning by, adverse effect of and underdosing of acetylsalicylic acid (T39.Ø1-)

● **T45.521 Poisoning by antithrombotic drugs, accidental (unintentional)**
Poisoning by antithrombotic drug NOS

● **T45.522 Poisoning by antithrombotic drugs, intentional self-harm A, S** 🔒

● **T45.523 Poisoning by antithrombotic drugs, assault**

● **T45.524 Poisoning by antithrombotic drugs, undetermined**

● **T45.525 Adverse effect of antithrombotic drugs**
Coding Clinic: 2016, Q1, P15

● **T45.526 Underdosing of antithrombotic drugs**

● **T45.6 Poisoning by, adverse effect of and underdosing of fibrinolysis-affecting drugs**

● **T45.6Ø Poisoning by, adverse effect of and underdosing of unspecified fibrinolysis-affecting drugs**

● **T45.6Ø1 Poisoning by unspecified fibrinolysis-affecting drugs, accidental (unintentional)**
Poisoning by fibrinolysis-affecting drug NOS

● **T45.6Ø2 Poisoning by unspecified fibrinolysis-affecting drugs, intentional self-harm A, S** 🔒

● **T45.6Ø3 Poisoning by unspecified fibrinolysis-affecting drugs, assault**

● **T45.6Ø4 Poisoning by unspecified fibrinolysis-affecting drugs, undetermined**

● **T45.6Ø5 Adverse effect of unspecified fibrinolysis-affecting drugs**

● **T45.6Ø6 Underdosing of unspecified fibrinolysis-affecting drugs**

● **T45.61 Poisoning by, adverse effect of and underdosing of thrombolytic drugs**

● **T45.611 Poisoning by thrombolytic drug, accidental (unintentional)**
Poisoning by thrombolytic drug NOS

● **T45.612 Poisoning by thrombolytic drug, intentional self-harm A, S** 🔒

● **T45.613 Poisoning by thrombolytic drug, assault**

● **T45.614 Poisoning by thrombolytic drug, undetermined**

● **T45.615 Adverse effect of thrombolytic drugs**
Coding Clinic: 2017, Q2, P1Ø

● **T45.616 Underdosing of thrombolytic drugs**

● **T45.62 Poisoning by, adverse effect of and underdosing of hemostatic drugs**

● **T45.621 Poisoning by hemostatic drug, accidental (unintentional)**
Poisoning by hemostatic drug NOS

● **T45.622 Poisoning by hemostatic drug, intentional self-harm A, S** 🔒

● **T45.623 Poisoning by hemostatic drug, assault**

● **T45.624 Poisoning by hemostatic drug, undetermined**

● **T45.625 Adverse effect of hemostatic drug**

● **T45.626 Underdosing of hemostatic drugs**

● **T45.69 Poisoning by, adverse effect of and underdosing of other fibrinolysis-affecting drugs**

● **T45.691 Poisoning by other fibrinolysis-affecting drugs, accidental (unintentional)**
Poisoning by other fibrinolysis-affecting drug NOS

● **T45.692 Poisoning by other fibrinolysis-affecting drugs, intentional self-harm A, S** 🔒

● **T45.693 Poisoning by other fibrinolysis-affecting drugs, assault**

● **T45.694 Poisoning by other fibrinolysis-affecting drugs, undetermined**

● **T45.695 Adverse effect of other fibrinolysis-affecting drugs**

● **T45.696 Underdosing of other fibrinolysis-affecting drugs**

● **T45.7 Poisoning by, adverse effect of and underdosing of anticoagulant antagonists, vitamin K and other coagulants**

● **T45.7X Poisoning by, adverse effect of and underdosing of anticoagulant antagonists, vitamin K and other coagulants**

● **T45.7X1 Poisoning by anticoagulant antagonists, vitamin K and other coagulants, accidental (unintentional)**
Poisoning by anticoagulant antagonists, vitamin K and other coagulants NOS

● **T45.7X2 Poisoning by anticoagulant antagonists, vitamin K and other coagulants, intentional self-harm A, S** 🔒

● **T45.7X3 Poisoning by anticoagulant antagonists, vitamin K and other coagulants, assault**

● **T45.7X4 Poisoning by anticoagulant antagonists, vitamin K and other coagulants, undetermined**

● **T45.7X5 Adverse effect of anticoagulant antagonists, vitamin K and other coagulants**

● **T45.7X6 Underdosing of anticoagulant antagonist, vitamin K and other coagulants**
Excludes1 vitamin K deficiency (E56.1)

● **T45.8 Poisoning by, adverse effect of and underdosing of other primarily systemic and hematological agents**
Poisoning by, adverse effect of and underdosing of liver preparations and other antianemic agents
Poisoning by, adverse effect of and underdosing of natural blood and blood products
Poisoning by, adverse effect of and underdosing of plasma substitute

Excludes2 poisoning by, adverse effect of and underdosing of immunoglobulin (T5Ø.Z1)
poisoning by, adverse effect of and underdosing of iron (T45.4)
transfusion reactions (T8Ø.-)

● **T45.8X Poisoning by, adverse effect of and underdosing of other primarily systemic and hematological agents**

● **T45.8X1 Poisoning by other primarily systemic and hematological agents, accidental (unintentional)**
Poisoning by other primarily systemic and hematological agents NOS

● **T45.8X2 Poisoning by other primarily systemic and hematological agents, intentional self-harm A, S** 🔒

● **T45.8X3 Poisoning by other primarily systemic and hematological agents, assault**

● T45.8X4 Poisoning by other primarily systemic and hematological agents, undetermined

● T45.8X5 Adverse effect of other primarily systemic and hematological agents
Coding Clinic: 2016, Q4, P42

● T45.8X6 Underdosing of other primarily systemic and hematological agents

● T45.9 Poisoning by, adverse effect of and underdosing of unspecified primarily systemic and hematological agent

X ● T45.91 Poisoning by unspecified primarily systemic and hematological agent, accidental (unintentional)
Poisoning by primarily systemic and hematological agent NOS

X ● T45.92 Poisoning by unspecified primarily systemic and hematological agent, intentional self-harm A, S 🅒

X ● T45.93 Poisoning by unspecified primarily systemic and hematological agent, assault

X ● T45.94 Poisoning by unspecified primarily systemic and hematological agent, undetermined

X ● T45.95 Adverse effect of unspecified primarily systemic and hematological agent

X ● T45.96 Underdosing of unspecified primarily systemic and hematological agent

● T46 Poisoning by, adverse effect of and underdosing of agents primarily affecting the cardiovascular system
Excludes 1 poisoning by, adverse effect of and underdosing of metaraminol (T44.4)

The appropriate 7th character is to be added to each code from category T46

A	initial encounter
D	subsequent encounter
S	sequela

● T46.0 Poisoning by, adverse effect of and underdosing of cardiac-stimulant glycosides and drugs of similar action

● T46.0X Poisoning by, adverse effect of and underdosing of cardiac-stimulant glycosides and drugs of similar action

● T46.0X1 Poisoning by cardiac-stimulant glycosides and drugs of similar action, accidental (unintentional)
Poisoning by cardiac-stimulant glycosides and drugs of similar action NOS

● T46.0X2 Poisoning by cardiac-stimulant glycosides and drugs of similar action, intentional self-harm A, S 🅒

● T46.0X3 Poisoning by cardiac-stimulant glycosides and drugs of similar action, assault

● T46.0X4 Poisoning by cardiac-stimulant glycosides and drugs of similar action, undetermined

● T46.0X5 Adverse effect of cardiac-stimulant glycosides and drugs of similar action

● T46.0X6 Underdosing of cardiac-stimulant glycosides and drugs of similar action

● T46.1 Poisoning by, adverse effect of and underdosing of calcium-channel blockers

● T46.1X Poisoning by, adverse effect of and underdosing of calcium-channel blockers

● T46.1X1 Poisoning by calcium-channel blockers, accidental (unintentional)
Poisoning by calcium-channel blockers NOS

● T46.1X2 Poisoning by calcium-channel blockers, intentional self-harm A, S 🅒

● T46.1X3 Poisoning by calcium-channel blockers, assault

● T46.1X4 Poisoning by calcium-channel blockers, undetermined

● T46.1X5 Adverse effect of calcium-channel blockers

● T46.1X6 Underdosing of calcium-channel blockers

● T46.2 Poisoning by, adverse effect of and underdosing of other antidysrhythmic drugs, not elsewhere classified
Excludes 1 poisoning by, adverse effect of and underdosing of beta-adrenoreceptor antagonists (T44.7-)

● T46.2X Poisoning by, adverse effect of and underdosing of other antidysrhythmic drugs

● T46.2X1 Poisoning by other antidysrhythmic drugs, accidental (unintentional)
Poisoning by other antidysrhythmic drugs NOS

● T46.2X2 Poisoning by other antidysrhythmic drugs, intentional self-harm A, S 🅒

● T46.2X3 Poisoning by other antidysrhythmic drugs, assault

● T46.2X4 Poisoning by other antidysrhythmic drugs, undetermined

● T46.2X5 Adverse effect of other antidysrhythmic drugs

● T46.2X6 Underdosing of other antidysrhythmic drugs

● T46.3 Poisoning by, adverse effect of and underdosing of coronary vasodilators
Poisoning by, adverse effect of and underdosing of dipyridamole
Excludes 1 poisoning by, adverse effect of and underdosing of calcium-channel blockers (T46.1)

● T46.3X Poisoning by, adverse effect of and underdosing of coronary vasodilators

● T46.3X1 Poisoning by coronary vasodilators, accidental (unintentional)
Poisoning by coronary vasodilators NOS

● T46.3X2 Poisoning by coronary vasodilators, intentional self-harm A, S 🅒

● T46.3X3 Poisoning by coronary vasodilators, assault

● T46.3X4 Poisoning by coronary vasodilators, undetermined

● T46.3X5 Adverse effect of coronary vasodilators

● T46.3X6 Underdosing of coronary vasodilators

● T46.4 Poisoning by, adverse effect of and underdosing of angiotensin-converting-enzyme inhibitors

● T46.4X Poisoning by, adverse effect of and underdosing of angiotensin-converting-enzyme inhibitors

● T46.4X1 Poisoning by angiotensin-converting-enzyme inhibitors, accidental (unintentional)
Poisoning by angiotensin-converting-enzyme inhibitors NOS

● T46.4X2 Poisoning by angiotensin-converting-enzyme inhibitors, intentional self-harm A, S 🅒

● T46.4X3 Poisoning by angiotensin-converting-enzyme inhibitors, assault

● T46.4X4 Poisoning by angiotensin-converting-enzyme inhibitors, undetermined

● T46.4X5 Adverse effect of angiotensin-converting-enzyme inhibitors

● T46.4X6 Underdosing of angiotensin-converting-enzyme inhibitors

▶ New   ⇒ Revised   ~~deleted~~ Deleted   Excludes 1   Excludes 2   Includes   Use additional   Code first   Code also   Key words
OGCR Official Guidelines   X Assign placeholder X   ● Use Additional Character(s)   ▶ Manifestation Code   🅒 Hierarchical Condition Category   **Coding Clinic**

● T46.5 **Poisoning by, adverse effect of and underdosing of other antihypertensive drugs**

> **Excludes2** poisoning by, adverse effect of and underdosing of beta-adrenoreceptor antagonists (T44.7)
> poisoning by, adverse effect of and underdosing of calcium-channel blockers (T46.1)
> poisoning by, adverse effect of and underdosing of diuretics (T50.0-T50.2)

● T46.5X **Poisoning by, adverse effect of and underdosing of other antihypertensive drugs**

● T46.5X1 **Poisoning by other antihypertensive drugs, accidental (unintentional)**
> Poisoning by other antihypertensive drugs NOS

● T46.5X2 **Poisoning by other antihypertensive drugs, intentional self-harm A, S** 🔒

● T46.5X3 **Poisoning by other antihypertensive drugs, assault**

● T46.5X4 **Poisoning by other antihypertensive drugs, undetermined**

● T46.5X5 **Adverse effect of other antihypertensive drugs**

● T46.5X6 **Underdosing of other antihypertensive drugs**

● T46.6 **Poisoning by, adverse effect of and underdosing of antihyperlipidemic and antiarteriosclerotic drugs**

● T46.6X **Poisoning by, adverse effect of and underdosing of antihyperlipidemic and antiarteriosclerotic drugs**

● T46.6X1 **Poisoning by antihyperlipidemic and antiarteriosclerotic drugs, accidental (unintentional)**
> Poisoning by antihyperlipidemic and antiarteriosclerotic drugs NOS

● T46.6X2 **Poisoning by antihyperlipidemic and antiarteriosclerotic drugs, intentional self-harm A, S** 🔒

● T46.6X3 **Poisoning by antihyperlipidemic and antiarteriosclerotic drugs, assault**

● T46.6X4 **Poisoning by antihyperlipidemic and antiarteriosclerotic drugs, undetermined**

● T46.6X5 **Adverse effect of antihyperlipidemic and antiarteriosclerotic drugs**

● T46.6X6 **Underdosing of antihyperlipidemic and antiarteriosclerotic drugs**

● T46.7 **Poisoning by, adverse effect of and underdosing of peripheral vasodilators**
> Poisoning by, adverse effect of and underdosing of nicotinic acid (derivatives)

> **Excludes1** poisoning by, adverse effect of and underdosing of papaverine (T44.3)

● T46.7X **Poisoning by, adverse effect of and underdosing of peripheral vasodilators**

● T46.7X1 **Poisoning by peripheral vasodilators, accidental (unintentional)**
> Poisoning by peripheral vasodilators NOS

● T46.7X2 **Poisoning by peripheral vasodilators, intentional self-harm A, S** 🔒

● T46.7X3 **Poisoning by peripheral vasodilators, assault**

● T46.7X4 **Poisoning by peripheral vasodilators, undetermined**

● T46.7X5 **Adverse effect of peripheral vasodilators**

● T46.7X6 **Underdosing of peripheral vasodilators**

● T46.8 **Poisoning by, adverse effect of and underdosing of antivaricose drugs, including sclerosing agents**

● T46.8X **Poisoning by, adverse effect of and underdosing of antivaricose drugs, including sclerosing agents**

● T46.8X1 **Poisoning by antivaricose drugs, including sclerosing agents, accidental (unintentional)**
> Poisoning by antivaricose drugs, including sclerosing agents NOS

● T46.8X2 **Poisoning by antivaricose drugs, including sclerosing agents, intentional self-harm A, S** 🔒

● T46.8X3 **Poisoning by antivaricose drugs, including sclerosing agents, assault**

● T46.8X4 **Poisoning by antivaricose drugs, including sclerosing agents, undetermined**

● T46.8X5 **Adverse effect of antivaricose drugs, including sclerosing agents**

● T46.8X6 **Underdosing of antivaricose drugs, including sclerosing agents**

● T46.9 **Poisoning by, adverse effect of and underdosing of other and unspecified agents primarily affecting the cardiovascular system**

● T46.90 **Poisoning by, adverse effect of and underdosing of unspecified agents primarily affecting the cardiovascular system**

● T46.901 **Poisoning by unspecified agents primarily affecting the cardiovascular system, accidental (unintentional)**

● T46.902 **Poisoning by unspecified agents primarily affecting the cardiovascular system, intentional self-harm A, S** 🔒

● T46.903 **Poisoning by unspecified agents primarily affecting the cardiovascular system, assault**

● T46.904 **Poisoning by unspecified agents primarily affecting the cardiovascular system, undetermined**

● T46.905 **Adverse effect of unspecified agents primarily affecting the cardiovascular system**

● T46.906 **Underdosing of unspecified agents primarily affecting the cardiovascular system**

● T46.99 **Poisoning by, adverse effect of and underdosing of other agents primarily affecting the cardiovascular system**

● T46.991 **Poisoning by other agents primarily affecting the cardiovascular system, accidental (unintentional)**

● T46.992 **Poisoning by other agents primarily affecting the cardiovascular system, intentional self-harm A, S** 🔒

● T46.993 **Poisoning by other agents primarily affecting the cardiovascular system, assault**

● T46.994 **Poisoning by other agents primarily affecting the cardiovascular system, undetermined**

● T46.995 **Adverse effect of other agents primarily affecting the cardiovascular system**

● T46.996 **Underdosing of other agents primarily affecting the cardiovascular system**

● T47 **Poisoning by, adverse effect of and underdosing of agents primarily affecting the gastrointestinal system**

> The appropriate 7th character is to be added to each code from category T47

> | A | initial encounter |
> |---|---|
> | D | subsequent encounter |
> | S | sequela |

● T47.0 **Poisoning by, adverse effect of and underdosing of histamine H2-receptor blockers**

● T47.0X **Poisoning by, adverse effect of and underdosing of histamine H2-receptor blockers**

● T47.0X1 **Poisoning by histamine H2-receptor blockers, accidental (unintentional)**
Poisoning by histamine H2-receptor blockers NOS

● T47.0X2 **Poisoning by histamine H2-receptor blockers, intentional self-harm A, S** 🔵

● T47.0X3 **Poisoning by histamine H2-receptor blockers, assault**

● T47.0X4 **Poisoning by histamine H2-receptor blockers, undetermined**

● T47.0X5 **Adverse effect of histamine H2-receptor blockers**

● T47.0X6 **Underdosing of histamine H2-receptor blockers**

● T47.1 **Poisoning by, adverse effect of and underdosing of other antacids and anti-gastric-secretion drugs**

● T47.1X **Poisoning by, adverse effect of and underdosing of other antacids and anti-gastric-secretion drugs**

● T47.1X1 **Poisoning by other antacids and anti-gastric-secretion drugs, accidental (unintentional)**
Poisoning by other antacids and anti-gastric-secretion drugs NOS

● T47.1X2 **Poisoning by other antacids and anti-gastric-secretion drugs, intentional self-harm A, S** 🔵

● T47.1X3 **Poisoning by other antacids and anti-gastric-secretion drugs, assault**

● T47.1X4 **Poisoning by other antacids and anti-gastric-secretion drugs, undetermined**

● T47.1X5 **Adverse effect of other antacids and anti-gastric-secretion drugs**

● T47.1X6 **Underdosing of other antacids and anti-gastric-secretion drugs**

● T47.2 **Poisoning by, adverse effect of and underdosing of stimulant laxatives**

● T47.2X **Poisoning by, adverse effect of and underdosing of stimulant laxatives**

● T47.2X1 **Poisoning by stimulant laxatives, accidental (unintentional)**
Poisoning by stimulant laxatives NOS

● T47.2X2 **Poisoning by stimulant laxatives, intentional self-harm A, S** 🔵

● T47.2X3 **Poisoning by stimulant laxatives, assault**

● T47.2X4 **Poisoning by stimulant laxatives, undetermined**

● T47.2X5 **Adverse effect of stimulant laxatives**

● T47.2X6 **Underdosing of stimulant laxatives**

● T47.3 **Poisoning by, adverse effect of and underdosing of saline and osmotic laxatives**

● T47.3X **Poisoning by and adverse effect of saline and osmotic laxatives**

● T47.3X1 **Poisoning by saline and osmotic laxatives, accidental (unintentional)**
Poisoning by saline and osmotic laxatives NOS

● T47.3X2 **Poisoning by saline and osmotic laxatives, intentional self-harm**

● T47.3X3 **Poisoning by saline and osmotic laxatives, assault A, S** 🔵

● T47.3X4 **Poisoning by saline and osmotic laxatives, undetermined**

● T47.3X5 **Adverse effect of saline and osmotic laxatives**

● T47.3X6 **Underdosing of saline and osmotic laxatives**

● T47.4 **Poisoning by, adverse effect of and underdosing of other laxatives**

● T47.4X **Poisoning by, adverse effect of and underdosing of other laxatives**

● T47.4X1 **Poisoning by other laxatives, accidental (unintentional)**
Poisoning by other laxatives NOS

● T47.4X2 **Poisoning by other laxatives, intentional self-harm A, S** 🔵

● T47.4X3 **Poisoning by other laxatives, assault**

● T47.4X4 **Poisoning by other laxatives, undetermined**

● T47.4X5 **Adverse effect of other laxatives**

● T47.4X6 **Underdosing of other laxatives**

● T47.5 **Poisoning by, adverse effect of and underdosing of digestants**

● T47.5X **Poisoning by, adverse effect of and underdosing of digestants**

● T47.5X1 **Poisoning by digestants, accidental (unintentional)**
Poisoning by digestants NOS

● T47.5X2 **Poisoning by digestants, intentional self-harm A, S** 🔵

● T47.5X3 **Poisoning by digestants, assault**

● T47.5X4 **Poisoning by digestants, undetermined**

● T47.5X5 **Adverse effect of digestants**

● T47.5X6 **Underdosing of digestants**

● T47.6 **Poisoning by, adverse effect of and underdosing of antidiarrheal drugs**

> **Excludes2** poisoning by, adverse effect of and underdosing of systemic antibiotics and other anti-infectives (T36-T37)

● T47.6X **Poisoning by, adverse effect of and underdosing of antidiarrheal drugs**

● T47.6X1 **Poisoning by antidiarrheal drugs, accidental (unintentional)**
Poisoning by antidiarrheal drugs NOS

● T47.6X2 **Poisoning by antidiarrheal drugs, intentional self-harm A, S** 🔵

● T47.6X3 **Poisoning by antidiarrheal drugs, assault**

● T47.6X4 **Poisoning by antidiarrheal drugs, undetermined**

● T47.6X5 **Adverse effect of antidiarrheal drugs**

● T47.6X6 **Underdosing of antidiarrheal drugs**

▶ New ➡ Revised ~~deleted~~ Deleted Excludes 1 Excludes 2 Includes Use additional Code first Code also Key words
OGCR Official Guidelines X Assign placeholder X ● Use Additional Character(s) ▶ Manifestation Code 🔵 Hierarchical Condition Category Coding Clinic

● **T47.7**   Poisoning by, adverse effect of and underdosing of emetics
  ● **T47.7X**   Poisoning by, adverse effect of and underdosing of emetics
    ● **T47.7X1**   Poisoning by emetics, accidental (unintentional)
        Poisoning by emetics NOS
    ● **T47.7X2**   Poisoning by emetics, intentional self-harm A, S 🔖
    ● **T47.7X3**   Poisoning by emetics, assault
    ● **T47.7X4**   Poisoning by emetics, undetermined
    ● **T47.7X5**   Adverse effect of emetics
    ● **T47.7X6**   Underdosing of emetics

● **T47.8**   Poisoning by, adverse effect of and underdosing of other agents primarily affecting gastrointestinal system
  ● **T47.8X**   Poisoning by, adverse effect of and underdosing of other agents primarily affecting gastrointestinal system
    ● **T47.8X1**   Poisoning by other agents primarily affecting gastrointestinal system, accidental (unintentional)
        Poisoning by other agents primarily affecting gastrointestinal system NOS
    ● **T47.8X2**   Poisoning by other agents primarily affecting gastrointestinal system, intentional self-harm A, S 🔖
    ● **T47.8X3**   Poisoning by other agents primarily affecting gastrointestinal system, assault
    ● **T47.8X4**   Poisoning by other agents primarily affecting gastrointestinal system, undetermined
    ● **T47.8X5**   Adverse effect of other agents primarily affecting gastrointestinal system
    ● **T47.8X6**   Underdosing of other agents primarily affecting gastrointestinal system

● **T47.9**   Poisoning by, adverse effect of and underdosing of unspecified agents primarily affecting the gastrointestinal system
  X ● **T47.91**   Poisoning by unspecified agents primarily affecting the gastrointestinal system, accidental (unintentional)
        Poisoning by agents primarily affecting the gastrointestinal system NOS
  X ● **T47.92**   Poisoning by unspecified agents primarily affecting the gastrointestinal system, intentional self-harm A, S 🔖
  X ● **T47.93**   Poisoning by unspecified agents primarily affecting the gastrointestinal system, assault
  X ● **T47.94**   Poisoning by unspecified agents primarily affecting the gastrointestinal system, undetermined
  X ● **T47.95**   Adverse effect of unspecified agents primarily affecting the gastrointestinal system
  X ● **T47.96**   Underdosing of unspecified agents primarily affecting the gastrointestinal system

● **T48**   Poisoning by, adverse effect of and underdosing of agents primarily acting on smooth and skeletal muscles and the respiratory system
     The appropriate 7th character is to be added to each code from category T48

> A   initial encounter
> D   subsequent encounter
> S   sequela

● **T48.0**   Poisoning by, adverse effect of and underdosing of oxytocic drugs
     Excludes1   poisoning by, adverse effect of and underdosing of estrogens, progestogens and antagonists (T38.4-T38.6)
  ● **T48.0X**   Poisoning by, adverse effect of and underdosing of oxytocic drugs
    ● **T48.0X1**   Poisoning by oxytocic drugs, accidental (unintentional)
        Poisoning by oxytocic drugs NOS
    ● **T48.0X2**   Poisoning by oxytocic drugs, intentional self-harm A, S 🔖
    ● **T48.0X3**   Poisoning by oxytocic drugs, assault
    ● **T48.0X4**   Poisoning by oxytocic drugs, undetermined
    ● **T48.0X5**   Adverse effect of oxytocic drugs
    ● **T48.0X6**   Underdosing of oxytocic drugs

● **T48.1**   Poisoning by, adverse effect of and underdosing of skeletal muscle relaxants [neuromuscular blocking agents]
  ● **T48.1X**   Poisoning by, adverse effect of and underdosing of skeletal muscle relaxants [neuromuscular blocking agents]
    ● **T48.1X1**   Poisoning by skeletal muscle relaxants [neuromuscular blocking agents], accidental (unintentional)
        Poisoning by skeletal muscle relaxants [neuromuscular blocking agents] NOS
    ● **T48.1X2**   Poisoning by skeletal muscle relaxants [neuromuscular blocking agents], intentional self-harm A, S 🔖
    ● **T48.1X3**   Poisoning by skeletal muscle relaxants [neuromuscular blocking agents], assault
    ● **T48.1X4**   Poisoning by skeletal muscle relaxants [neuromuscular blocking agents], undetermined
    ● **T48.1X5**   Adverse effect of skeletal muscle relaxants [neuromuscular blocking agents]
    ● **T48.1X6**   Underdosing of skeletal muscle relaxants [neuromuscular blocking agents]

● **T48.2**   Poisoning by, adverse effect of and underdosing of other and unspecified drugs acting on muscles
  ● **T48.20**   Poisoning by, adverse effect of and underdosing of unspecified drugs acting on muscles
    ● **T48.201**   Poisoning by unspecified drugs acting on muscles, accidental (unintentional)
        Poisoning by unspecified drugs acting on muscles NOS
    ● **T48.202**   Poisoning by unspecified drugs acting on muscles, intentional self-harm A, S 🔖
    ● **T48.203**   Poisoning by unspecified drugs acting on muscles, assault
    ● **T48.204**   Poisoning by unspecified drugs acting on muscles, undetermined
    ● **T48.205**   Adverse effect of unspecified drugs acting on muscles
    ● **T48.206**   Underdosing of unspecified drugs acting on muscles

● **T48.29**   **Poisoning by, adverse effect of and underdosing of other drugs acting on muscles**

  ● **T48.291**   **Poisoning by other drugs acting on muscles, accidental (unintentional)**
       Poisoning by other drugs acting on muscles NOS

  ● **T48.292**   **Poisoning by other drugs acting on muscles, intentional self-harm A, S** 🏷

  ● **T48.293**   **Poisoning by other drugs acting on muscles, assault**

  ● **T48.294**   **Poisoning by other drugs acting on muscles, undetermined**

  ● **T48.295**   **Adverse effect of other drugs acting on muscles**

  ● **T48.296**   **Underdosing of other drugs acting on muscles**

● **T48.3**   **Poisoning by, adverse effect of and underdosing of antitussives**

 ● **T48.3X**   **Poisoning by, adverse effect of and underdosing of antitussives**

  ● **T48.3X1**   **Poisoning by antitussives, accidental (unintentional)**
       Poisoning by antitussives NOS

  ● **T48.3X2**   **Poisoning by antitussives, intentional self-harm A, S** 🏷

  ● **T48.3X3**   **Poisoning by antitussives, assault**

  ● **T48.3X4**   **Poisoning by antitussives, undetermined**

  ● **T48.3X5**   **Adverse effect of antitussives**

  ● **T48.3X6**   **Underdosing of antitussives**

● **T48.4**   **Poisoning by, adverse effect of and underdosing of expectorants**

 ● **T48.4X**   **Poisoning by, adverse effect of and underdosing of expectorants**

  ● **T48.4X1**   **Poisoning by expectorants, accidental (unintentional)**
       Poisoning by expectorants NOS

  ● **T48.4X2**   **Poisoning by expectorants, intentional self-harm A, S** 🏷

  ● **T48.4X3**   **Poisoning by expectorants, assault**

  ● **T48.4X4**   **Poisoning by expectorants, undetermined**

  ● **T48.4X5**   **Adverse effect of expectorants**

  ● **T48.4X6**   **Underdosing of expectorants**

● **T48.5**   **Poisoning by, adverse effect of and underdosing of other anti-common-cold drugs**
   Poisoning by, adverse effect of and underdosing of decongestants

   Excludes2   poisoning by, adverse effect of and underdosing of antipyretics, NEC (T39.9-)
       poisoning by, adverse effect of and underdosing of non-steroidal antiinflammatory drugs (T39.3-)
       poisoning by, adverse effect of and underdosing of salicylates (T39.0-)

 ● **T48.5X**   **Poisoning by, adverse effect of and underdosing of other anti-common-cold drugs**

  ● **T48.5X1**   **Poisoning by other anti-common-cold drugs, accidental (unintentional)**
       Poisoning by other anti-common-cold drugs NOS

  ● **T48.5X2**   **Poisoning by other anti-common-cold drugs, intentional self-harm A, S** 🏷

  ● **T48.5X3**   **Poisoning by other anti-common-cold drugs, assault**

  ● **T48.5X4**   **Poisoning by other anti-common-cold drugs, undetermined**

  ● **T48.5X5**   **Adverse effect of other anti-common-cold drugs**

  ● **T48.5X6**   **Underdosing of other anti-common-cold drugs**

● **T48.6**   **Poisoning by, adverse effect of and underdosing of antiasthmatics, not elsewhere classified**
   Poisoning by, adverse effect of and underdosing of beta-adrenoreceptor agonists used in asthma therapy

   Excludes1   poisoning by, adverse effect of and underdosing of beta-adrenoreceptor agonists not used in asthma therapy (T44.5)
       poisoning by, adverse effect of and underdosing of anterior pituitary [adenohypophyseal] hormones (T38.8)

 ● **T48.6X**   **Poisoning by, adverse effect of and underdosing of antiasthmatics**

  ● **T48.6X1**   **Poisoning by antiasthmatics, accidental (unintentional)**
       Poisoning by antiasthmatics NOS

  ● **T48.6X2**   **Poisoning by antiasthmatics, intentional self-harm A, S** 🏷

  ● **T48.6X3**   **Poisoning by antiasthmatics, assault**

  ● **T48.6X4**   **Poisoning by antiasthmatics, undetermined**

  ● **T48.6X5**   **Adverse effect of antiasthmatics**

  ● **T48.6X6**   **Underdosing of antiasthmatics**

● **T48.9**   **Poisoning by, adverse effect of and underdosing of other and unspecified agents primarily acting on the respiratory system**

 ● **T48.90**   **Poisoning by, adverse effect of and underdosing of unspecified agents primarily acting on the respiratory system**

  ● **T48.901**   **Poisoning by unspecified agents primarily acting on the respiratory system, accidental (unintentional)**

  ● **T48.902**   **Poisoning by unspecified agents primarily acting on the respiratory system, intentional self-harm A, S** 🏷

  ● **T48.903**   **Poisoning by unspecified agents primarily acting on the respiratory system, assault**

  ● **T48.904**   **Poisoning by unspecified agents primarily acting on the respiratory system, undetermined**

  ● **T48.905**   **Adverse effect of unspecified agents primarily acting on the respiratory system**

  ● **T48.906**   **Underdosing of unspecified agents primarily acting on the respiratory system**

 ● **T48.99**   **Poisoning by, adverse effect of and underdosing of other agents primarily acting on the respiratory system**

  ● **T48.991**   **Poisoning by other agents primarily acting on the respiratory system, accidental (unintentional)**

  ● **T48.992**   **Poisoning by other agents primarily acting on the respiratory system, intentional self-harm A, S** 🏷

  ● **T48.993**   **Poisoning by other agents primarily acting on the respiratory system, assault**

  ● **T48.994**   **Poisoning by other agents primarily acting on the respiratory system, undetermined**

  ● **T48.995**   **Adverse effect of other agents primarily acting on the respiratory system**

  ● **T48.996**   **Underdosing of other agents primarily acting on the respiratory system**

▶ New   ⇒ Revised   ~~deleted~~ Deleted   Excludes 1   Excludes 2   Includes   Use additional   Code first   Code also   Key words

OGCR Official Guidelines   X Assign placeholder X   ● Use Additional Character(s)   ▌ Manifestation Code   🏷 Hierarchical Condition Category   **Coding Clinic**

● **T49**   **Poisoning by, adverse effect of and underdosing of topical agents primarily affecting skin and mucous membrane and by ophthalmological, otorhinolaryngological and dental drugs**

     Includes   poisoning by, adverse effect of and underdosing of glucocorticoids, topically used

     The appropriate 7th character is to be added to each code from category T49

     A   initial encounter
     D   subsequent encounter
     S   sequela

● **T49.0**   **Poisoning by, adverse effect of and underdosing of local antifungal, anti-infective and anti-inflammatory drugs**

   ● **T49.0X**   Poisoning by, adverse effect of and underdosing of local antifungal, anti-infective and anti-inflammatory drugs

     ● **T49.0X1**   Poisoning by local antifungal, anti-infective and anti-inflammatory drugs, accidental (unintentional)
         Poisoning by local antifungal, anti-infective and anti-inflammatory drugs NOS

     ● **T49.0X2**   Poisoning by local antifungal, anti-infective and anti-inflammatory drugs, intentional self-harm A, S 🔂

     ● **T49.0X3**   Poisoning by local antifungal, anti-infective and anti-inflammatory drugs, assault

     ● **T49.0X4**   Poisoning by local antifungal, anti-infective and anti-inflammatory drugs, undetermined

     ● **T49.0X5**   Adverse effect of local antifungal, anti-infective and anti-inflammatory drugs

     ● **T49.0X6**   Underdosing of local antifungal, anti-infective and anti-inflammatory drugs

● **T49.1**   **Poisoning by, adverse effect of and underdosing of antipruritics**

   ● **T49.1X**   Poisoning by, adverse effect of and underdosing of antipruritics

     ● **T49.1X1**   Poisoning by antipruritics, accidental (unintentional)
         Poisoning by antipruritics NOS

     ● **T49.1X2**   Poisoning by antipruritics, intentional self-harm A, S 🔂

     ● **T49.1X3**   Poisoning by antipruritics, assault

     ● **T49.1X4**   Poisoning by antipruritics, undetermined

     ● **T49.1X5**   Adverse effect of antipruritics

     ● **T49.1X6**   Underdosing of antipruritics

● **T49.2**   **Poisoning by, adverse effect of and underdosing of local astringents and local detergents**

   ● **T49.2X**   Poisoning by, adverse effect of and underdosing of local astringents and local detergents

     ● **T49.2X1**   Poisoning by local astringents and local detergents, accidental (unintentional)
         Poisoning by local astringents and local detergents NOS

     ● **T49.2X2**   Poisoning by local astringents and local detergents, intentional self-harm A, S 🔂

     ● **T49.2X3**   Poisoning by local astringents and local detergents, assault

     ● **T49.2X4**   Poisoning by local astringents and local detergents, undetermined

     ● **T49.2X5**   Adverse effect of local astringents and local detergents

     ● **T49.2X6**   Underdosing of local astringents and local detergents

● **T49.3**   **Poisoning by, adverse effect of and underdosing of emollients, demulcents and protectants**

   ● **T49.3X**   Poisoning by, adverse effect of and underdosing of emollients, demulcents and protectants

     ● **T49.3X1**   Poisoning by emollients, demulcents and protectants, accidental (unintentional)
         Poisoning by emollients, demulcents and protectants NOS

     ● **T49.3X2**   Poisoning by emollients, demulcents and protectants, intentional self-harm A, S 🔂

     ● **T49.3X3**   Poisoning by emollients, demulcents and protectants, assault

     ● **T49.3X4**   Poisoning by emollients, demulcents and protectants, undetermined

     ● **T49.3X5**   Adverse effect of emollients, demulcents and protectants

     ● **T49.3X6**   Underdosing of emollients, demulcents and protectants

● **T49.4**   **Poisoning by, adverse effect of and underdosing of keratolytics, keratoplastics, and other hair treatment drugs and preparations**

   ● **T49.4X**   Poisoning by, adverse effect of and underdosing of keratolytics, keratoplastics, and other hair treatment drugs and preparations

     ● **T49.4X1**   Poisoning by keratolytics, keratoplastics, and other hair treatment drugs and preparations, accidental (unintentional)
         Poisoning by keratolytics, keratoplastics, and other hair treatment drugs and preparations NOS

     ● **T49.4X2**   Poisoning by keratolytics, keratoplastics, and other hair treatment drugs and preparations, intentional self-harm A, S 🔂

     ● **T49.4X3**   Poisoning by keratolytics, keratoplastics, and other hair treatment drugs and preparations, assault

     ● **T49.4X4**   Poisoning by keratolytics, keratoplastics, and other hair treatment drugs and preparations, undetermined

     ● **T49.4X5**   Adverse effect of keratolytics, keratoplastics, and other hair treatment drugs and preparations

     ● **T49.4X6**   Underdosing of keratolytics, keratoplastics, and other hair treatment drugs and preparations

● **T49.5**   **Poisoning by, adverse effect of and underdosing of ophthalmological drugs and preparations**

   ● **T49.5X**   Poisoning by, adverse effect of and underdosing of ophthalmological drugs and preparations

     ● **T49.5X1**   Poisoning by ophthalmological drugs and preparations, accidental (unintentional)
         Poisoning by ophthalmological drugs and preparations NOS

     ● **T49.5X2**   Poisoning by ophthalmological drugs and preparations, intentional self-harm A, S 🔂

     ● **T49.5X3**   Poisoning by ophthalmological drugs and preparations, assault

     ● **T49.5X4**   Poisoning by ophthalmological drugs and preparations, undetermined

     ● **T49.5X5**   Adverse effect of ophthalmological drugs and preparations

     ● **T49.5X6**   Underdosing of ophthalmological drugs and preparations

- **T49.6** Poisoning by, adverse effect of and underdosing of otorhinolaryngological drugs and preparations
  - **T49.6X** Poisoning by, adverse effect of and underdosing of otorhinolaryngological drugs and preparations
    - **T49.6X1** Poisoning by otorhinolaryngological drugs and preparations, accidental (unintentional)
      Poisoning by otorhinolaryngological drugs and preparations NOS
    - **T49.6X2** Poisoning by otorhinolaryngological drugs and preparations, intentional self-harm A, S ⊛
    - **T49.6X3** Poisoning by otorhinolaryngological drugs and preparations, assault
    - **T49.6X4** Poisoning by otorhinolaryngological drugs and preparations, undetermined
    - **T49.6X5** Adverse effect of otorhinolaryngological drugs and preparations
    - **T49.6X6** Underdosing of otorhinolaryngological drugs and preparations
- **T49.7** Poisoning by, adverse effect of and underdosing of dental drugs, topically applied
  - **T49.7X** Poisoning by, adverse effect of and underdosing of dental drugs, topically applied
    - **T49.7X1** Poisoning by dental drugs, topically applied, accidental (unintentional)
      Poisoning by dental drugs, topically applied NOS
    - **T49.7X2** Poisoning by dental drugs, topically applied, intentional self-harm A, S ⊛
    - **T49.7X3** Poisoning by dental drugs, topically applied, assault
    - **T49.7X4** Poisoning by dental drugs, topically applied, undetermined
    - **T49.7X5** Adverse effect of dental drugs, topically applied
    - **T49.7X6** Underdosing of dental drugs, topically applied
- **T49.8** Poisoning by, adverse effect of and underdosing of other topical agents
  Poisoning by, adverse effect of and underdosing of spermicides
  - **T49.8X** Poisoning by, adverse effect of and underdosing of other topical agents
    - **T49.8X1** Poisoning by other topical agents, accidental (unintentional)
      Poisoning by other topical agents NOS
    - **T49.8X2** Poisoning by other topical agents, intentional self-harm A, S ⊛
    - **T49.8X3** Poisoning by other topical agents, assault
    - **T49.8X4** Poisoning by other topical agents, undetermined
    - **T49.8X5** Adverse effect of other topical agents
    - **T49.8X6** Underdosing of other topical agents
- **T49.9** Poisoning by, adverse effect of and underdosing of unspecified topical agent
  - X● **T49.91** Poisoning by unspecified topical agent, accidental (unintentional)
  - X● **T49.92** Poisoning by unspecified topical agent, intentional self-harm A, S ⊛
  - X● **T49.93** Poisoning by unspecified topical agent, assault
  - X● **T49.94** Poisoning by unspecified topical agent, undetermined
  - X● **T49.95** Adverse effect of unspecified topical agent
  - X● **T49.96** Underdosing of unspecified topical agent

- **T50** Poisoning by, adverse effect of and underdosing of diuretics and other and unspecified drugs, medicaments and biological substances
  The appropriate 7th character is to be added to each code from category T50

A	initial encounter
D	subsequent encounter
S	sequela

  - **T50.0** Poisoning by, adverse effect of and underdosing of mineralocorticoids and their antagonists
    - **T50.0X** Poisoning by, adverse effect of and underdosing of mineralocorticoids and their antagonists
      - **T50.0X1** Poisoning by mineralocorticoids and their antagonists, accidental (unintentional)
        Poisoning by mineralocorticoids and their antagonists NOS
      - **T50.0X2** Poisoning by mineralocorticoids and their antagonists, intentional self-harm A, S ⊛
      - **T50.0X3** Poisoning by mineralocorticoids and their antagonists, assault
      - **T50.0X4** Poisoning by mineralocorticoids and their antagonists, undetermined
      - **T50.0X5** Adverse effect of mineralocorticoids and their antagonists
      - **T50.0X6** Underdosing of mineralocorticoids and their antagonists
  - **T50.1** Poisoning by, adverse effect of and underdosing of loop [high-ceiling] diuretics
    - **T50.1X** Poisoning by, adverse effect of and underdosing of loop [high-ceiling] diuretics
      - **T50.1X1** Poisoning by loop [high-ceiling] diuretics, accidental (unintentional)
        Poisoning by loop [high-ceiling] diuretics NOS
      - **T50.1X2** Poisoning by loop [high-ceiling] diuretics, intentional self-harm A, S ⊛
      - **T50.1X3** Poisoning by loop [high-ceiling] diuretics, assault
      - **T50.1X4** Poisoning by loop [high-ceiling] diuretics, undetermined
      - **T50.1X5** Adverse effect of loop [high-ceiling] diuretics
      - **T50.1X6** Underdosing of loop [high-ceiling] diuretics
  - **T50.2** Poisoning by, adverse effect of and underdosing of carbonic-anhydrase inhibitors, benzothiadiazides and other diuretics
    Poisoning by, adverse effect of and underdosing of acetazolamide
    - **T50.2X** Poisoning by, adverse effect of and underdosing of carbonic-anhydrase inhibitors, benzothiadiazides and other diuretics
      - **T50.2X1** Poisoning by carbonic-anhydrase inhibitors, benzothiadiazides and other diuretics, accidental (unintentional)
        Poisoning by carbonic-anhydrase inhibitors, benzothiadiazides and other diuretics NOS
      - **T50.2X2** Poisoning by carbonic-anhydrase inhibitors, benzothiadiazides and other diuretics, intentional self-harm A, S ⊛
      - **T50.2X3** Poisoning by carbonic-anhydrase inhibitors, benzothiadiazides and other diuretics, assault

▶ New   ⇒ Revised   ~~deleted~~ Deleted   Excludes 1   Excludes 2   Includes   Use additional   Code first   Code also   Key words

OGCR Official Guidelines   X Assign placeholder X   ● Use Additional Character(s)   ▷ Manifestation Code   ⊛ Hierarchical Condition Category   **Coding Clinic**

● **T50.2X4**   Poisoning by carbonic-anhydrase inhibitors, benzothiadiazides and other diuretics, undetermined

● **T50.2X5**   Adverse effect of carbonic-anhydrase inhibitors, benzothiadiazides and other diuretics

● **T50.2X6**   Underdosing of carbonic-anhydrase inhibitors, benzothiadiazides and other diuretics

● **T50.3**   Poisoning by, adverse effect of and underdosing of electrolytic, caloric and water-balance agents

Poisoning by, adverse effect of and underdosing of oral rehydration salts

● **T50.3X**   Poisoning by, adverse effect of and underdosing of electrolytic, caloric and water-balance agents

● **T50.3X1**   Poisoning by electrolytic, caloric and water-balance agents, accidental (unintentional)

Poisoning by electrolytic, caloric and water-balance agents NOS

● **T50.3X2**   Poisoning by electrolytic, caloric and water-balance agents, intentional self-harm A, S 🦠

● **T50.3X3**   Poisoning by electrolytic, caloric and water-balance agents, assault

● **T50.3X4**   Poisoning by electrolytic, caloric and water-balance agents, undetermined

● **T50.3X5**   Adverse effect of electrolytic, caloric and water-balance agents

● **T50.3X6**   Underdosing of electrolytic, caloric and water-balance agents

● **T50.4**   Poisoning by, adverse effect of and underdosing of drugs affecting uric acid metabolism

● **T50.4X**   Poisoning by, adverse effect of and underdosing of drugs affecting uric acid metabolism

● **T50.4X1**   Poisoning by drugs affecting uric acid metabolism, accidental (unintentional)

Poisoning by drugs affecting uric acid metabolism NOS

● **T50.4X2**   Poisoning by drugs affecting uric acid metabolism, intentional self-harm A, S 🦠

● **T50.4X3**   Poisoning by drugs affecting uric acid metabolism, assault

● **T50.4X4**   Poisoning by drugs affecting uric acid metabolism, undetermined

● **T50.4X5**   Adverse effect of drugs affecting uric acid metabolism

● **T50.4X6**   Underdosing of drugs affecting uric acid metabolism

● **T50.5**   Poisoning by, adverse effect of and underdosing of appetite depressants

● **T50.5X**   Poisoning by, adverse effect of and underdosing of appetite depressants

● **T50.5X1**   Poisoning by appetite depressants, accidental (unintentional)

Poisoning by appetite depressants NOS

● **T50.5X2**   Poisoning by appetite depressants, intentional self-harm A, S 🦠

● **T50.5X3**   Poisoning by appetite depressants, assault

● **T50.5X4**   Poisoning by appetite depressants, undetermined

● **T50.5X5**   Adverse effect of appetite depressants

● **T50.5X6**   Underdosing of appetite depressants

● **T50.6**   Poisoning by, adverse effect of and underdosing of antidotes and chelating agents

Poisoning by, adverse effect of and underdosing of alcohol deterrents

● **T50.6X**   Poisoning by, adverse effect of and underdosing of antidotes and chelating agents

● **T50.6X1**   Poisoning by antidotes and chelating agents, accidental (unintentional)

Poisoning by antidotes and chelating agents NOS

● **T50.6X2**   Poisoning by antidotes and chelating agents, intentional self-harm A, S 🦠

● **T50.6X3**   Poisoning by antidotes and chelating agents, assault

● **T50.6X4**   Poisoning by antidotes and chelating agents, undetermined

● **T50.6X5**   Adverse effect of antidotes and chelating agents

● **T50.6X6**   Underdosing of antidotes and chelating agents

● **T50.7**   Poisoning by, adverse effect of and underdosing of analeptics and opioid receptor antagonists

● **T50.7X**   Poisoning by, adverse effect of and underdosing of analeptics and opioid receptor antagonists

● **T50.7X1**   Poisoning by analeptics and opioid receptor antagonists, accidental (unintentional)

Poisoning by analeptics and opioid receptor antagonists NOS

● **T50.7X2**   Poisoning by analeptics and opioid receptor antagonists, intentional self-harm A, S 🦠

● **T50.7X3**   Poisoning by analeptics and opioid receptor antagonists, assault

● **T50.7X4**   Poisoning by analeptics and opioid receptor antagonists, undetermined

● **T50.7X5**   Adverse effect of analeptics and opioid receptor antagonists

● **T50.7X6**   Underdosing of analeptics and opioid receptor antagonists

● **T50.8**   Poisoning by, adverse effect of and underdosing of diagnostic agents

● **T50.8X**   Poisoning by, adverse effect of and underdosing of diagnostic agents

● **T50.8X1**   Poisoning by diagnostic agents, accidental (unintentional)

Poisoning by diagnostic agents NOS

● **T50.8X2**   Poisoning by diagnostic agents, intentional self-harm A, S 🦠

● **T50.8X3**   Poisoning by diagnostic agents, assault

● **T50.8X4**   Poisoning by diagnostic agents, undetermined

● **T50.8X5**   Adverse effect of diagnostic agents

● **T50.8X6**   Underdosing of diagnostic agents

● **T50.A**   Poisoning by, adverse effect of and underdosing of bacterial vaccines

● **T50.A1**   Poisoning by, adverse effect of and underdosing of pertussis vaccine, including combinations with a pertussis component

● **T50.A11**   Poisoning by pertussis vaccine, including combinations with a pertussis component, accidental (unintentional)

● **T50.A12**   Poisoning by pertussis vaccine, including combinations with a pertussis component, intentional self-harm A, S 🦠

● **T50.A13**   Poisoning by pertussis vaccine, including combinations with a pertussis component, assault

CHAPTER 19 (S00–T88)

● T50.A14   Poisoning by pertussis vaccine, including combinations with a pertussis component, **undetermined**

● T50.A15   Adverse effect of pertussis vaccine, including combinations with a pertussis component

● T50.A16   Underdosing of pertussis vaccine, including combinations with a pertussis component

● T50.A2   Poisoning by, adverse effect of and underdosing of mixed bacterial vaccines without a pertussis component

   ● T50.A21   Poisoning by mixed bacterial vaccines without a pertussis component, accidental (unintentional)

   ● T50.A22   Poisoning by mixed bacterial vaccines without a pertussis component, intentional self-harm A, S 🦠

   ● T50.A23   Poisoning by mixed bacterial vaccines without a pertussis component, assault

   ● T50.A24   Poisoning by mixed bacterial vaccines without a pertussis component, undetermined

   ● T50.A25   Adverse effect of mixed bacterial vaccines without a pertussis component

   ● T50.A26   Underdosing of mixed bacterial vaccines without a pertussis component

● T50.A9   Poisoning by, adverse effect of and underdosing of other bacterial vaccines

   ● T50.A91   Poisoning by other bacterial vaccines, accidental (unintentional)

   ● T50.A92   Poisoning by other bacterial vaccines, intentional self-harm A, S 🦠

   ● T50.A93   Poisoning by other bacterial vaccines, assault

   ● T50.A94   Poisoning by other bacterial vaccines, undetermined

   ● T50.A95   Adverse effect of other bacterial vaccines

   ● T50.A96   Underdosing of other bacterial vaccines

● T50.B   Poisoning by, adverse effect of and underdosing of viral vaccines

   ● T50.B1   Poisoning by, adverse effect of and underdosing of smallpox vaccines

      ● T50.B11   Poisoning by smallpox vaccines, accidental (unintentional)

      ● T50.B12   Poisoning by smallpox vaccines, intentional self-harm A, S 🦠

      ● T50.B13   Poisoning by smallpox vaccines, assault

      ● T50.B14   Poisoning by smallpox vaccines, undetermined

      ● T50.B15   Adverse effect of smallpox vaccines

      ● T50.B16   Underdosing of smallpox vaccines

   ● T50.B9   Poisoning by, adverse effect of and underdosing of other viral vaccines

      ● T50.B91   Poisoning by other viral vaccines, accidental (unintentional)

      ● T50.B92   Poisoning by other viral vaccines, intentional self-harm A, S 🦠

      ● T50.B93   Poisoning by other viral vaccines, assault

      ● T50.B94   Poisoning by other viral vaccines, undetermined

      ● T50.B95   Adverse effect of other viral vaccines

      ● T50.B96   Underdosing of other viral vaccines

● T50.Z   Poisoning by, adverse effect of and underdosing of other vaccines and biological substances

   ● T50.Z1   Poisoning by, adverse effect of and underdosing of immunoglobulin

      ● T50.Z11   Poisoning by immunoglobulin, accidental (unintentional)

      ● T50.Z12   Poisoning by immunoglobulin, intentional self-harm A, S 🦠

      ● T50.Z13   Poisoning by immunoglobulin, assault

      ● T50.Z14   Poisoning by immunoglobulin, undetermined

      ● T50.Z15   Adverse effect of immunoglobulin

      ● T50.Z16   Underdosing of immunoglobulin

   ● T50.Z9   Poisoning by, adverse effect of and underdosing of other vaccines and biological substances

      ● T50.Z91   Poisoning by other vaccines and biological substances, accidental (unintentional)

      ● T50.Z92   Poisoning by other vaccines and biological substances, intentional self-harm A, S 🦠

      ● T50.Z93   Poisoning by other vaccines and biological substances, assault

      ● T50.Z94   Poisoning by other vaccines and biological substances, undetermined

      ● T50.Z95   Adverse effect of other vaccines and biological substances
               Coding Clinic: 2020, Q1, P19

      ● T50.Z96   Underdosing of other vaccines and biological substances

● T50.9   Poisoning by, adverse effect of and underdosing of other and unspecified drugs, medicaments and biological substances

   ● T50.90   Poisoning by, adverse effect of and underdosing of unspecified drugs, medicaments and biological substances

      ● T50.901   Poisoning by unspecified drugs, medicaments and biological substances, accidental (unintentional)
               Coding Clinic: 2015, Q1, P21

      ● T50.902   Poisoning by unspecified drugs, medicaments and biological substances, intentional self-harm A, S 🦠

      ● T50.903   Poisoning by unspecified drugs, medicaments and biological substances, assault

      ● T50.904   Poisoning by unspecified drugs, medicaments and biological substances, undetermined

      ● T50.905   Adverse effect of unspecified drugs, medicaments and biological substances

      ● T50.906   Underdosing of unspecified drugs, medicaments and biological substances

   ● T50.91   Poisoning by, adverse effect of and underdosing of multiple unspecified drugs, medicaments and biological substances
            Multiple drug ingestion NOS
            Code also any specific drugs, medicaments and biological substances

      ● T50.911   Poisoning by multiple unspecified drugs, medicaments and biological substances, accidental (unintentional)

      ● T50.912   Poisoning by multiple unspecified drugs, medicaments and biological substances, intentional self-harm

      ● T50.913   Poisoning by multiple unspecified drugs, medicaments and biological substances, assault

▶ New   ⇒ Revised   ~~deleted~~ Deleted   Excludes 1   Excludes 2   Includes   Use additional   Code first   Code also   Key words
OGCR Official Guidelines   X Assign placeholder X   ● Use Additional Character(s)   ▶ Manifestation Code   🦠 Hierarchical Condition Category   Coding Clinic

● **T50.914** Poisoning by multiple unspecified drugs, medicaments and biological substances, undetermined

● **T50.915** Adverse effect of multiple unspecified drugs, medicaments and biological substances

● **T50.916** Underdosing of multiple unspecified drugs, medicaments and biological substances

● **T50.99** Poisoning by, adverse effect of and underdosing of other drugs, medicaments and biological substances

● **T50.991** Poisoning by other drugs, medicaments and biological substances, accidental (unintentional)

● **T50.992** Poisoning by other drugs, medicaments and biological substances, intentional self-harm A, S 🔖

● **T50.993** Poisoning by other drugs, medicaments and biological substances, assault

● **T50.994** Poisoning by other drugs, medicaments and biological substances, undetermined

● **T50.995** Adverse effect of other drugs, medicaments and biological substances

● **T50.996** Underdosing of other drugs, medicaments and biological substances

TOXIC EFFECTS OF SUBSTANCES CHIEFLY NONMEDICINAL AS TO SOURCE (T51–T65)

Note: When no intent is indicated code to accidental. Undetermined intent is only for use when there is specific documentation in the record that the intent of the toxic effect cannot be determined.

Use additional code(s): for all associated manifestations of toxic effect, such as:
respiratory conditions due to external agents (J60–J70)
personal history of foreign body fully removed (Z87.821)
to identify any retained foreign body, if applicable (Z18.-)

Excludes1 contact with and (suspected) exposure to toxic substances (Z77.-)

● **T51** **Toxic effect of alcohol**

The appropriate 7th character is to be added to each code from category T51

A	initial encounter
D	subsequent encounter
S	sequela

● **T51.0** **Toxic effect of ethanol**
Toxic effect of ethyl alcohol

Excludes2 acute alcohol intoxication or 'hangover' effects (F10.129, F10.229, F10.929)
drunkenness (F10.129, F10.229, F10.929)
pathological alcohol intoxication (F10.129, F10.229, F10.929)

● **T51.0X** **Toxic effect of ethanol**

● **T51.0X1** Toxic effect of ethanol, accidental (unintentional)
Toxic effect of ethanol NOS

● **T51.0X2** Toxic effect of ethanol, intentional self-harm A, S 🔖

● **T51.0X3** Toxic effect of ethanol, assault

● **T51.0X4** Toxic effect of ethanol, undetermined

● **T51.1** **Toxic effect of methanol**
Toxic effect of methyl alcohol

● **T51.1X** **Toxic effect of methanol**

● **T51.1X1** Toxic effect of methanol, accidental (unintentional)
Toxic effect of methanol NOS

● **T51.1X2** Toxic effect of methanol, intentional self-harm A, S 🔖

● **T51.1X3** Toxic effect of methanol, assault

● **T51.1X4** Toxic effect of methanol, undetermined

● **T51.2** **Toxic effect of 2-Propanol**
Toxic effect of isopropyl alcohol

● **T51.2X** **Toxic effect of 2-Propanol**

● **T51.2X1** Toxic effect of 2-Propanol, accidental (unintentional)
Toxic effect of 2-Propanol NOS

● **T51.2X2** Toxic effect of 2-Propanol, intentional self-harm A, S 🔖

● **T51.2X3** Toxic effect of 2-Propanol, assault

● **T51.2X4** Toxic effect of 2-Propanol, undetermined

● **T51.3** **Toxic effect of fusel oil**
Toxic effect of amyl alcohol
Toxic effect of butyl [1-butanol] alcohol
Toxic effect of propyl [1-propanol] alcohol

● **T51.3X** **Toxic effect of fusel oil**

● **T51.3X1** Toxic effect of fusel oil, accidental (unintentional)
Toxic effect of fusel oil NOS

● **T51.3X2** Toxic effect of fusel oil, intentional self-harm A, S 🔖

● **T51.3X3** Toxic effect of fusel oil, assault

● **T51.3X4** Toxic effect of fusel oil, undetermined

● **T51.8** **Toxic effect of other alcohols**

● **T51.8X** **Toxic effect of other alcohols**

● **T51.8X1** Toxic effect of other alcohols, accidental (unintentional)
Toxic effect of other alcohols NOS

● **T51.8X2** Toxic effect of other alcohols, intentional self-harm A, S 🔖

● **T51.8X3** Toxic effect of other alcohols, assault

● **T51.8X4** Toxic effect of other alcohols, undetermined

● **T51.9** **Toxic effect of unspecified alcohol**

X ● **T51.91** Toxic effect of unspecified alcohol, accidental (unintentional)

X ● **T51.92** Toxic effect of unspecified alcohol, intentional self-harm A, S 🔖

X ● **T51.93** Toxic effect of unspecified alcohol, assault

X ● **T51.94** Toxic effect of unspecified alcohol, undetermined

● **T52** **Toxic effect of organic solvents**

Excludes1 halogen derivatives of aliphatic and aromatic hydrocarbons (T53.-)

The appropriate 7th character is to be added to each code from category T52

A	initial encounter
D	subsequent encounter
S	sequela

● **T52.0** **Toxic effects of petroleum products**
Toxic effects of gasoline [petrol]
Toxic effects of kerosene [paraffin oil]
Toxic effects of paraffin wax
Toxic effects of ether petroleum
Toxic effects of naphtha petroleum
Toxic effects of spirit petroleum

● **T52.0X** **Toxic effects of petroleum products**

● **T52.0X1** Toxic effect of petroleum products, accidental (unintentional)
Toxic effects of petroleum products NOS

● **T52.0X2** Toxic effect of petroleum products, intentional self-harm A, S 🔖

● T52.0X3   Toxic effect of petroleum products, assault

● T52.0X4   Toxic effect of petroleum products, undetermined

● T52.1   **Toxic effects of benzene**

> **Excludes1**   homologues of benzene (T52.2)
> nitroderivatives and aminoderivatives of benzene and its homologues (T65.3)

● T52.1X   Toxic effects of benzene

  ● T52.1X1   Toxic effect of benzene, accidental (unintentional)
      Toxic effects of benzene NOS

  ● T52.1X2   Toxic effect of benzene, intentional self-harm A, S 🦠

  ● T52.1X3   Toxic effect of benzene, assault

  ● T52.1X4   Toxic effect of benzene, undetermined

● T52.2   **Toxic effects of homologues of benzene**
   Toxic effects of toluene [methylbenzene]
   Toxic effects of xylene [dimethylbenzene]

● T52.2X   Toxic effects of homologues of benzene

  ● T52.2X1   Toxic effect of homologues of benzene, accidental (unintentional)
      Toxic effects of homologues of benzene NOS

  ● T52.2X2   Toxic effect of homologues of benzene, intentional self-harm A, S 🦠

  ● T52.2X3   Toxic effect of homologues of benzene, assault

  ● T52.2X4   Toxic effect of homologues of benzene, undetermined

● T52.3   **Toxic effects of glycols**

● T52.3X   Toxic effects of glycols

  ● T52.3X1   Toxic effect of glycols, accidental (unintentional)
      Toxic effects of glycols NOS

  ● T52.3X2   Toxic effect of glycols, intentional self-harm A, S 🦠

  ● T52.3X3   Toxic effect of glycols, assault

  ● T52.3X4   Toxic effect of glycols, undetermined

● T52.4   **Toxic effects of ketones**

● T52.4X   Toxic effects of ketones

  ● T52.4X1   Toxic effect of ketones, accidental (unintentional)
      Toxic effects of ketones NOS

  ● T52.4X2   Toxic effect of ketones, intentional self-harm A, S 🦠

  ● T52.4X3   Toxic effect of ketones, assault

  ● T52.4X4   Toxic effect of ketones, undetermined

● T52.8   **Toxic effects of other organic solvents**

● T52.8X   Toxic effects of other organic solvents

  ● T52.8X1   Toxic effect of other organic solvents, accidental (unintentional)
      Toxic effects of other organic solvents NOS

  ● T52.8X2   Toxic effect of other organic solvents, intentional self-harm A, S 🦠

  ● T52.8X3   Toxic effect of other organic solvents, assault

  ● T52.8X4   Toxic effect of other organic solvents, undetermined

● T52.9   **Toxic effects of unspecified organic solvent**

X ● T52.91   Toxic effect of unspecified organic solvent, accidental (unintentional)

X ● T52.92   Toxic effect of unspecified organic solvent, intentional self-harm A, S 🦠

X ● T52.93   Toxic effect of unspecified organic solvent, assault

X ● T52.94   Toxic effect of unspecified organic solvent, undetermined

● T53   **Toxic effect of halogen derivatives of aliphatic and aromatic hydrocarbons**

> The appropriate 7th character is to be added to each code from category T53

> | A | initial encounter |
> |---|---|
> | D | subsequent encounter |
> | S | sequela |

● T53.0   **Toxic effects of carbon tetrachloride**
   Toxic effects of tetrachloromethane

● T53.0X   Toxic effects of carbon tetrachloride

  ● T53.0X1   Toxic effect of carbon tetrachloride, accidental (unintentional)
      Toxic effects of carbon tetrachloride NOS

  ● T53.0X2   Toxic effect of carbon tetrachloride, intentional self-harm A, S 🦠

  ● T53.0X3   Toxic effect of carbon tetrachloride, assault

  ● T53.0X4   Toxic effect of carbon tetrachloride, undetermined

● T53.1   **Toxic effects of chloroform**
   Toxic effects of trichloromethane

● T53.1X   Toxic effects of chloroform

  ● T53.1X1   Toxic effect of chloroform, accidental (unintentional)
      Toxic effects of chloroform NOS

  ● T53.1X2   Toxic effect of chloroform, intentional self-harm A, S 🦠

  ● T53.1X3   Toxic effect of chloroform, assault

  ● T53.1X4   Toxic effect of chloroform, undetermined

● T53.2   **Toxic effects of trichloroethylene**
   Toxic effects of trichloroethene

● T53.2X   Toxic effects of trichloroethylene

  ● T53.2X1   Toxic effect of trichloroethylene, accidental (unintentional)
      Toxic effects of trichloroethylene NOS

  ● T53.2X2   Toxic effect of trichloroethylene, intentional self-harm A, S 🦠

  ● T53.2X3   Toxic effect of trichloroethylene, assault

  ● T53.2X4   Toxic effect of trichloroethylene, undetermined

● T53.3   **Toxic effects of tetrachloroethylene**
   Toxic effects of perchloroethylene
   Toxic effect of tetrachloroethene

● T53.3X   Toxic effects of tetrachloroethylene

  ● T53.3X1   Toxic effect of tetrachloroethylene, accidental (unintentional)
      Toxic effects of tetrachloroethylene NOS

  ● T53.3X2   Toxic effect of tetrachloroethylene, intentional self-harm A, S 🦠

  ● T53.3X3   Toxic effect of tetrachloroethylene, assault

  ● T53.3X4   Toxic effect of tetrachloroethylene, undetermined

● T53.4   **Toxic effects of dichloromethane**
   Toxic effects of methylene chloride

● T53.4X   Toxic effects of dichloromethane

  ● T53.4X1   Toxic effect of dichloromethane, accidental (unintentional)
      Toxic effects of dichloromethane NOS

  ● T53.4X2   Toxic effect of dichloromethane, intentional self-harm A, S 🦠

  ● T53.4X3   Toxic effect of dichloromethane, assault

  ● T53.4X4   Toxic effect of dichloromethane, undetermined

▶ New   ⇛ Revised   ~~deleted~~ Deleted   Excludes 1   Excludes 2   Includes   Use additional   Code first   Code also   Key words

OGCR Official Guidelines   X Assign placeholder X   ● Use Additional Character(s)   ▷ Manifestation Code   🦠 Hierarchical Condition Category   **Coding Clinic**

● T53.5   Toxic effects of chlorofluorocarbons
   ● T53.5X   Toxic effects of chlorofluorocarbons
     ● T53.5X1   Toxic effect of chlorofluorocarbons, accidental (unintentional)
       Toxic effects of chlorofluorocarbons NOS
     ● T53.5X2   Toxic effect of chlorofluorocarbons, intentional self-harm A, S 🐾
     ● T53.5X3   Toxic effect of chlorofluorocarbons, assault
     ● T53.5X4   Toxic effect of chlorofluorocarbons, undetermined

● T53.6   Toxic effects of other halogen derivatives of aliphatic hydrocarbons
   ● T53.6X   Toxic effects of other halogen derivatives of aliphatic hydrocarbons
     ● T53.6X1   Toxic effect of other halogen derivatives of aliphatic hydrocarbons, accidental (unintentional)
       Toxic effects of other halogen derivatives of aliphatic hydrocarbons NOS
     ● T53.6X2   Toxic effect of other halogen derivatives of aliphatic hydrocarbons, intentional self-harm A, S 🐾
     ● T53.6X3   Toxic effect of other halogen derivatives of aliphatic hydrocarbons, assault
     ● T53.6X4   Toxic effect of other halogen derivatives of aliphatic hydrocarbons, undetermined

● T53.7   Toxic effects of other halogen derivatives of aromatic hydrocarbons
   ● T53.7X   Toxic effects of other halogen derivatives of aromatic hydrocarbons
     ● T53.7X1   Toxic effect of other halogen derivatives of aromatic hydrocarbons, accidental (unintentional)
       Toxic effects of other halogen derivatives of aromatic hydrocarbons NOS
     ● T53.7X2   Toxic effect of other halogen derivatives of aromatic hydrocarbons, intentional self-harm A, S 🐾
     ● T53.7X3   Toxic effect of other halogen derivatives of aromatic hydrocarbons, assault
     ● T53.7X4   Toxic effect of other halogen derivatives of aromatic hydrocarbons, undetermined

● T53.9   Toxic effects of unspecified halogen derivatives of aliphatic and aromatic hydrocarbons
   X ● T53.91   Toxic effect of unspecified halogen derivatives of aliphatic and aromatic hydrocarbons, accidental (unintentional)
   X ● T53.92   Toxic effect of unspecified halogen derivatives of aliphatic and aromatic hydrocarbons, intentional self-harm A, S 🐾
   X ● T53.93   Toxic effect of unspecified halogen derivatives of aliphatic and aromatic hydrocarbons, assault
   X ● T53.94   Toxic effect of unspecified halogen derivatives of aliphatic and aromatic hydrocarbons, undetermined

● T54   Toxic effect of corrosive substances
   The appropriate 7th character is to be added to each code from category T54

A	initial encounter
D	subsequent encounter
S	sequela

● T54.0   Toxic effects of phenol and phenol homologues
   ● T54.0X   Toxic effects of phenol and phenol homologues
     ● T54.0X1   Toxic effect of phenol and phenol homologues, accidental (unintentional)
       Toxic effects of phenol and phenol homologues NOS
     ● T54.0X2   Toxic effect of phenol and phenol homologues, intentional self-harm A, S 🐾
     ● T54.0X3   Toxic effect of phenol and phenol homologues, assault
     ● T54.0X4   Toxic effect of phenol and phenol homologues, undetermined

● T54.1   Toxic effects of other corrosive organic compounds
   ● T54.1X   Toxic effects of other corrosive organic compounds
     ● T54.1X1   Toxic effect of other corrosive organic compounds, accidental (unintentional)
       Toxic effects of other corrosive organic compounds NOS
     ● T54.1X2   Toxic effect of other corrosive organic compounds, intentional self-harm A, S 🐾
     ● T54.1X3   Toxic effect of other corrosive organic compounds, assault
     ● T54.1X4   Toxic effect of other corrosive organic compounds, undetermined

● T54.2   Toxic effects of corrosive acids and acid-like substances
   Toxic effects of hydrochloric acid
   Toxic effects of sulfuric acid
   ● T54.2X   Toxic effects of corrosive acids and acid-like substances
     ● T54.2X1   Toxic effect of corrosive acids and acid-like substances, accidental (unintentional)
       Toxic effects of corrosive acids and acid-like substances NOS
     ● T54.2X2   Toxic effect of corrosive acids and acid-like substances, intentional self-harm A, S 🐾
     ● T54.2X3   Toxic effect of corrosive acids and acid-like substances, assault
     ● T54.2X4   Toxic effect of corrosive acids and acid-like substances, undetermined

● T54.3   Toxic effects of corrosive alkalis and alkali-like substances
   Toxic effects of potassium hydroxide
   Toxic effects of sodium hydroxide
   ● T54.3X   Toxic effects of corrosive alkalis and alkali-like substances
     ● T54.3X1   Toxic effect of corrosive alkalis and alkali-like substances, accidental (unintentional)
       Toxic effects of corrosive alkalis and alkali-like substances NOS
     ● T54.3X2   Toxic effect of corrosive alkalis and alkali-like substances, intentional self-harm A, S 🐾
     ● T54.3X3   Toxic effect of corrosive alkalis and alkali-like substances, assault
     ● T54.3X4   Toxic effect of corrosive alkalis and alkali-like substances, undetermined

CHAPTER 19 (S00-T88)

● **T54.9** Toxic effects of unspecified corrosive substance

X● **T54.91** Toxic effect of unspecified corrosive substance, accidental (unintentional)

X● **T54.92** Toxic effect of unspecified corrosive substance, intentional self-harm A, S 🦠

X● **T54.93** Toxic effect of unspecified corrosive substance, assault

X● **T54.94** Toxic effect of unspecified corrosive substance, undetermined

● **T55** Toxic effect of soaps and detergents

The appropriate 7th character is to be added to each code from category T55

A	initial encounter
D	subsequent encounter
S	sequela

● **T55.0** Toxic effect of soaps

● **T55.0X** Toxic effect of soaps

● **T55.0X1** Toxic effect of soaps, accidental (unintentional)
Toxic effect of soaps NOS

● **T55.0X2** Toxic effect of soaps, intentional self-harm A, S 🦠

● **T55.0X3** Toxic effect of soaps, assault

● **T55.0X4** Toxic effect of soaps, undetermined

● **T55.1** Toxic effect of detergents

● **T55.1X** Toxic effect of detergents

● **T55.1X1** Toxic effect of detergents, accidental (unintentional)
Toxic effect of detergents NOS

● **T55.1X2** Toxic effect of detergents, intentional self-harm A, S 🦠

● **T55.1X3** Toxic effect of detergents, assault

● **T55.1X4** Toxic effect of detergents, undetermined

● **T56** Toxic effect of metals

Includes toxic effects of fumes and vapors of metals
toxic effects of metals from all sources, except medicinal substances

Use additional code to identify any retained metal foreign body, if applicable (Z18.0-, T18.1-)

Excludes1 arsenic and its compounds (T57.0)
manganese and its compounds (T57.2)

The appropriate 7th character is to be added to each code from category T56

A	initial encounter
D	subsequent encounter
S	sequela

● **T56.0** Toxic effects of lead and its compounds

● **T56.0X** Toxic effects of lead and its compounds

● **T56.0X1** Toxic effect of lead and its compounds, accidental (unintentional)
Toxic effects of lead and its compounds NOS

● **T56.0X2** Toxic effect of lead and its compounds, intentional self-harm A, S 🦠

● **T56.0X3** Toxic effect of lead and its compounds, assault

● **T56.0X4** Toxic effect of lead and its compounds, undetermined

● **T56.1** Toxic effects of mercury and its compounds

● **T56.1X** Toxic effects of mercury and its compounds

● **T56.1X1** Toxic effect of mercury and its compounds, accidental (unintentional)
Toxic effects of mercury and its compounds NOS

● **T56.1X2** Toxic effect of mercury and its compounds, intentional self-harm A, S 🦠

● **T56.1X3** Toxic effect of mercury and its compounds, assault

● **T56.1X4** Toxic effect of mercury and its compounds, undetermined

● **T56.2** Toxic effects of chromium and its compounds

● **T56.2X** Toxic effects of chromium and its compounds

● **T56.2X1** Toxic effect of chromium and its compounds, accidental (unintentional)
Toxic effects of chromium and its compounds NOS

● **T56.2X2** Toxic effect of chromium and its compounds, intentional self-harm A, S 🦠

● **T56.2X3** Toxic effect of chromium and its compounds, assault

● **T56.2X4** Toxic effect of chromium and its compounds, undetermined

● **T56.3** Toxic effects of cadmium and its compounds

● **T56.3X** Toxic effects of cadmium and its compounds

● **T56.3X1** Toxic effect of cadmium and its compounds, accidental (unintentional)
Toxic effects of cadmium and its compounds NOS

● **T56.3X2** Toxic effect of cadmium and its compounds, intentional self-harm A, S 🦠

● **T56.3X3** Toxic effect of cadmium and its compounds, assault

● **T56.3X4** Toxic effect of cadmium and its compounds, undetermined

● **T56.4** Toxic effects of copper and its compounds

● **T56.4X** Toxic effects of copper and its compounds

● **T56.4X1** Toxic effect of copper and its compounds, accidental (unintentional)
Toxic effects of copper and its compounds NOS

● **T56.4X2** Toxic effect of copper and its compounds, intentional self-harm A, S 🦠

● **T56.4X3** Toxic effect of copper and its compounds, assault

● **T56.4X4** Toxic effect of copper and its compounds, undetermined

● **T56.5** Toxic effects of zinc and its compounds

● **T56.5X** Toxic effects of zinc and its compounds

● **T56.5X1** Toxic effect of zinc and its compounds, accidental (unintentional)
Toxic effects of zinc and its compounds NOS

● **T56.5X2** Toxic effect of zinc and its compounds, intentional self-harm A, S 🦠

● **T56.5X3** Toxic effect of zinc and its compounds, assault

● **T56.5X4** Toxic effect of zinc and its compounds, undetermined

▶ New   ⇒ Revised   ~~deleted~~ Deleted   Excludes 1   Excludes 2   Includes   Use additional   Code first   Code also   Key words

OGCR Official Guidelines   X Assign placeholder X   ● Use Additional Character(s)   ▷ Manifestation Code   🦠 Hierarchical Condition Category   **Coding Clinic**

● **T56.6**   Toxic effects of tin and its compounds
   ● **T56.6X**   Toxic effects of tin and its compounds
     ● **T56.6X1**   Toxic effect of tin and its compounds, accidental (unintentional)
       Toxic effects of tin and its compounds NOS
     ● **T56.6X2**   Toxic effect of tin and its compounds, intentional self-harm A, S
     ● **T56.6X3**   Toxic effect of tin and its compounds, assault
     ● **T56.6X4**   Toxic effect of tin and its compounds, undetermined

● **T56.7**   Toxic effects of beryllium and its compounds
   ● **T56.7X**   Toxic effects of beryllium and its compounds
     ● **T56.7X1**   Toxic effect of beryllium and its compounds, accidental (unintentional)
       Toxic effects of beryllium and its compounds NOS
     ● **T56.7X2**   Toxic effect of beryllium and its compounds, intentional self-harm A, S
     ● **T56.7X3**   Toxic effect of beryllium and its compounds, assault
     ● **T56.7X4**   Toxic effect of beryllium and its compounds, undetermined

● **T56.8**   Toxic effects of other metals
   ● **T56.81**   Toxic effect of thallium
     ● **T56.811**   Toxic effect of thallium, accidental (unintentional)
       Toxic effect of thallium NOS
     ● **T56.812**   Toxic effect of thallium, intentional self-harm A, S
     ● **T56.813**   Toxic effect of thallium, assault
     ● **T56.814**   Toxic effect of thallium, undetermined
   ● **T56.89**   Toxic effects of other metals
     ● **T56.891**   Toxic effect of other metals, accidental (unintentional)
       Toxic effects of other metals NOS
     ● **T56.892**   Toxic effect of other metals, intentional self-harm A, S
     ● **T56.893**   Toxic effect of other metals, assault
     ● **T56.894**   Toxic effect of other metals, undetermined

● **T56.9**   Toxic effects of unspecified metal
   X ● **T56.91**   Toxic effect of unspecified metal, accidental (unintentional)
   X ● **T56.92**   Toxic effect of unspecified metal, intentional self-harm A, S
   X ● **T56.93**   Toxic effect of unspecified metal, assault
   X ● **T56.94**   Toxic effect of unspecified metal, undetermined

● **T57**   Toxic effect of other inorganic substances
   The appropriate 7th character is to be added to each code from category T57

A	initial encounter
D	subsequent encounter
S	sequela

● **T57.0**   Toxic effect of arsenic and its compounds
   ● **T57.0X**   Toxic effect of arsenic and its compounds
     ● **T57.0X1**   Toxic effect of arsenic and its compounds, accidental (unintentional)
       Toxic effect of arsenic and its compounds NOS
     ● **T57.0X2**   Toxic effect of arsenic and its compounds, intentional self-harm A, S

     ● **T57.0X3**   Toxic effect of arsenic and its compounds, assault
     ● **T57.0X4**   Toxic effect of arsenic and its compounds, undetermined

● **T57.1**   Toxic effect of phosphorus and its compounds
   Excludes1   organophosphate insecticides (T60.0)
   ● **T57.1X**   Toxic effect of phosphorus and its compounds
     ● **T57.1X1**   Toxic effect of phosphorus and its compounds, accidental (unintentional)
       Toxic effect of phosphorus and its compounds NOS
     ● **T57.1X2**   Toxic effect of phosphorus and its compounds, intentional self-harm A, S
     ● **T57.1X3**   Toxic effect of phosphorus and its compounds, assault
     ● **T57.1X4**   Toxic effect of phosphorus and its compounds, undetermined

● **T57.2**   Toxic effect of manganese and its compounds
   ● **T57.2X**   Toxic effect of manganese and its compounds
     ● **T57.2X1**   Toxic effect of manganese and its compounds, accidental (unintentional)
       Toxic effect of manganese and its compounds NOS
     ● **T57.2X2**   Toxic effect of manganese and its compounds, intentional self-harm A, S
     ● **T57.2X3**   Toxic effect of manganese and its compounds, assault
     ● **T57.2X4**   Toxic effect of manganese and its compounds, undetermined

● **T57.3**   Toxic effect of hydrogen cyanide
   ● **T57.3X**   Toxic effect of hydrogen cyanide
     ● **T57.3X1**   Toxic effect of hydrogen cyanide, accidental (unintentional)
       Toxic effect of hydrogen cyanide NOS
     ● **T57.3X2**   Toxic effect of hydrogen cyanide, intentional self-harm A, S
     ● **T57.3X3**   Toxic effect of hydrogen cyanide, assault
     ● **T57.3X4**   Toxic effect of hydrogen cyanide, undetermined

● **T57.8**   Toxic effect of other specified inorganic substances
   ● **T57.8X**   Toxic effect of other specified inorganic substances
     ● **T57.8X1**   Toxic effect of other specified inorganic substances, accidental (unintentional)
       Toxic effect of other specified inorganic substances NOS
     ● **T57.8X2**   Toxic effect of other specified inorganic substances, intentional self-harm A, S
     ● **T57.8X3**   Toxic effect of other specified inorganic substances, assault
     ● **T57.8X4**   Toxic effect of other specified inorganic substances, undetermined

● **T57.9**   Toxic effect of unspecified inorganic substance
   X ● **T57.91**   Toxic effect of unspecified inorganic substance, accidental (unintentional)
   X ● **T57.92**   Toxic effect of unspecified inorganic substance, intentional self-harm A, S
   X ● **T57.93**   Toxic effect of unspecified inorganic substance, assault
   X ● **T57.94**   Toxic effect of unspecified inorganic substance, undetermined

● **T58**   **Toxic effect of carbon monoxide**

> **Includes**   asphyxiation from carbon monoxide
> toxic effect of carbon monoxide from all sources
>
> The appropriate 7th character is to be added to each code from category T58
>
> | | |
> |---|---|
> | A | initial encounter |
> | D | subsequent encounter |
> | S | sequela |

> ● **T58.0**   **Toxic effect of carbon monoxide from motor vehicle exhaust**
> > Toxic effect of exhaust gas from gas engine
> > Toxic effect of exhaust gas from motor pump
>
> X ● **T58.01**   **Toxic effect of carbon monoxide from motor vehicle exhaust, accidental (unintentional)**
>
> X ● **T58.02**   **Toxic effect of carbon monoxide from motor vehicle exhaust, intentional self-harm A, S** 🐾
>
> X ● **T58.03**   **Toxic effect of carbon monoxide from motor vehicle exhaust, assault**
>
> X ● **T58.04**   **Toxic effect of carbon monoxide from motor vehicle exhaust, undetermined**
>
> ● **T58.1**   **Toxic effect of carbon monoxide from utility gas**
> > Toxic effect of acetylene
> > Toxic effect of gas NOS used for lighting, heating, cooking
> > Toxic effect of water gas
>
> X ● **T58.11**   **Toxic effect of carbon monoxide from utility gas, accidental (unintentional)**
>
> X ● **T58.12**   **Toxic effect of carbon monoxide from utility gas, intentional self-harm A, S** 🐾
>
> X ● **T58.13**   **Toxic effect of carbon monoxide from utility gas, assault**
>
> X ● **T58.14**   **Toxic effect of carbon monoxide from utility gas, undetermined**
>
> ● **T58.2**   **Toxic effect of carbon monoxide from incomplete combustion of other domestic fuels**
> > Toxic effect of carbon monoxide from incomplete combustion of coal, coke, kerosene, wood
>
> > ● **T58.2X**   **Toxic effect of carbon monoxide from incomplete combustion of other domestic fuels**
> >
> > ● **T58.2X1**   **Toxic effect of carbon monoxide from incomplete combustion of other domestic fuels, accidental (unintentional)**
> >
> > ● **T58.2X2**   **Toxic effect of carbon monoxide from incomplete combustion of other domestic fuels, intentional self-harm A, S** 🐾
> >
> > ● **T58.2X3**   **Toxic effect of carbon monoxide from incomplete combustion of other domestic fuels, assault**
> >
> > ● **T58.2X4**   **Toxic effect of carbon monoxide from incomplete combustion of other domestic fuels, undetermined**
>
> ● **T58.8**   **Toxic effect of carbon monoxide from other source**
> > Toxic effect of carbon monoxide from blast furnace gas
> > Toxic effect of carbon monoxide from fuels in industrial use
> > Toxic effect of carbon monoxide from kiln vapor
>
> > ● **T58.8X**   **Toxic effect of carbon monoxide from other source**
> >
> > ● **T58.8X1**   **Toxic effect of carbon monoxide from other source, accidental (unintentional)**
> >
> > ● **T58.8X2**   **Toxic effect of carbon monoxide from other source, intentional self-harm A, S** 🐾
> >
> > ● **T58.8X3**   **Toxic effect of carbon monoxide from other source, assault**
> >
> > ● **T58.8X4**   **Toxic effect of carbon monoxide from other source, undetermined**

● **T58.9**   **Toxic effect of carbon monoxide from unspecified source**

> X ● **T58.91**   **Toxic effect of carbon monoxide from unspecified source, accidental (unintentional)**
>
> X ● **T58.92**   **Toxic effect of carbon monoxide from unspecified source, intentional self-harm A, S** 🐾
>
> X ● **T58.93**   **Toxic effect of carbon monoxide from unspecified source, assault**
>
> X ● **T58.94**   **Toxic effect of carbon monoxide from unspecified source, undetermined**

● **T59**   **Toxic effect of other gases, fumes and vapors**

> **Includes**   aerosol propellants
>
> **Excludes1**   chlorofluorocarbons (T53.5)
>
> The appropriate 7th character is to be added to each code from category T59
>
> | | |
> |---|---|
> | A | initial encounter |
> | D | subsequent encounter |
> | S | sequela |

> ● **T59.0**   **Toxic effect of nitrogen oxides**
> > ● **T59.0X**   **Toxic effect of nitrogen oxides**
> >
> > ● **T59.0X1**   **Toxic effect of nitrogen oxides, accidental (unintentional)**
> > > Toxic effect of nitrogen oxides NOS
> >
> > ● **T59.0X2**   **Toxic effect of nitrogen oxides, intentional self-harm A, S** 🐾
> >
> > ● **T59.0X3**   **Toxic effect of nitrogen oxides, assault**
> >
> > ● **T59.0X4**   **Toxic effect of nitrogen oxides, undetermined**
>
> ● **T59.1**   **Toxic effect of sulfur dioxide**
> > ● **T59.1X**   **Toxic effect of sulfur dioxide**
> >
> > ● **T59.1X1**   **Toxic effect of sulfur dioxide, accidental (unintentional)**
> > > Toxic effect of sulfur dioxide NOS
> >
> > ● **T59.1X2**   **Toxic effect of sulfur dioxide, intentional self-harm A, S** 🐾
> >
> > ● **T59.1X3**   **Toxic effect of sulfur dioxide, assault**
> >
> > ● **T59.1X4**   **Toxic effect of sulfur dioxide, undetermined**
>
> ● **T59.2**   **Toxic effect of formaldehyde**
> > ● **T59.2X**   **Toxic effect of formaldehyde**
> >
> > ● **T59.2X1**   **Toxic effect of formaldehyde, accidental (unintentional)**
> > > Toxic effect of formaldehyde NOS
> >
> > ● **T59.2X2**   **Toxic effect of formaldehyde, intentional self-harm A, S** 🐾
> >
> > ● **T59.2X3**   **Toxic effect of formaldehyde, assault**
> >
> > ● **T59.2X4**   **Toxic effect of formaldehyde, undetermined**
>
> ● **T59.3**   **Toxic effect of lacrimogenic gas**
> > Toxic effect of tear gas
> >
> > ● **T59.3X**   **Toxic effect of lacrimogenic gas**
> >
> > ● **T59.3X1**   **Toxic effect of lacrimogenic gas, accidental (unintentional)**
> > > Toxic effect of lacrimogenic gas NOS
> >
> > ● **T59.3X2**   **Toxic effect of lacrimogenic gas, intentional self-harm A, S** 🐾
> >
> > ● **T59.3X3**   **Toxic effect of lacrimogenic gas, assault**
> >
> > ● **T59.3X4**   **Toxic effect of lacrimogenic gas, undetermined**
>
> ● **T59.4**   **Toxic effect of chlorine gas**
> > ● **T59.4X**   **Toxic effect of chlorine gas**
> >
> > ● **T59.4X1**   **Toxic effect of chlorine gas, accidental (unintentional)**
> > > Toxic effect of chlorine gas NOS
> >
> > ● **T59.4X2**   **Toxic effect of chlorine gas, intentional self-harm A, S** 🐾
> >
> > ● **T59.4X3**   **Toxic effect of chlorine gas, assault**
> >
> > ● **T59.4X4**   **Toxic effect of chlorine gas, undetermined**

▶ New   ⟹ Revised   ~~deleted~~ Deleted   Excludes 1   Excludes 2   Includes   Use additional   Code first   Code also   Key words

OGCR Official Guidelines   X Assign placeholder X   ● Use Additional Character(s)   ▶ Manifestation Code   🐾 Hierarchical Condition Category   **Coding Clinic**

T59.5   Toxic effect of fluorine gas and hydrogen fluoride

    T59.5X   Toxic effect of fluorine gas and hydrogen fluoride

       T59.5X1   Toxic effect of fluorine gas and hydrogen fluoride, accidental (unintentional)

          Toxic effect of fluorine gas and hydrogen fluoride NOS

       T59.5X2   Toxic effect of fluorine gas and hydrogen fluoride, intentional self-harm A, S 🔗

       T59.5X3   Toxic effect of fluorine gas and hydrogen fluoride, assault

       T59.5X4   Toxic effect of fluorine gas and hydrogen fluoride, undetermined

T59.6   Toxic effect of hydrogen sulfide

    T59.6X   Toxic effect of hydrogen sulfide

       T59.6X1   Toxic effect of hydrogen sulfide, accidental (unintentional)

          Toxic effect of hydrogen sulfide NOS

       T59.6X2   Toxic effect of hydrogen sulfide, intentional self-harm A, S 🔗

       T59.6X3   Toxic effect of hydrogen sulfide, assault

       T59.6X4   Toxic effect of hydrogen sulfide, undetermined

T59.7   Toxic effect of carbon dioxide

    T59.7X   Toxic effect of carbon dioxide

       T59.7X1   Toxic effect of carbon dioxide, accidental (unintentional)

          Toxic effect of carbon dioxide NOS

       T59.7X2   Toxic effect of carbon dioxide, intentional self-harm A, S 🔗

       T59.7X3   Toxic effect of carbon dioxide, assault

       T59.7X4   Toxic effect of carbon dioxide, undetermined

T59.8   Toxic effect of other specified gases, fumes and vapors

    T59.81   Toxic effect of smoke

       Smoke inhalation

       Excludes2   toxic effect of cigarette (tobacco) smoke (T65.22-)

       T59.811   Toxic effect of smoke, accidental (unintentional)

          Toxic effect of smoke NOS

       T59.812   Toxic effect of smoke, intentional self-harm A, S 🔗

       T59.813   Toxic effect of smoke, assault

       T59.814   Toxic effect of smoke, undetermined

    T59.89   Toxic effect of other specified gases, fumes and vapors

       T59.891   Toxic effect of other specified gases, fumes and vapors, accidental (unintentional)

       T59.892   Toxic effect of other specified gases, fumes and vapors, intentional self-harm A, S 🔗

       T59.893   Toxic effect of other specified gases, fumes and vapors, assault

       T59.894   Toxic effect of other specified gases, fumes and vapors, undetermined

T59.9   Toxic effect of unspecified gases, fumes and vapors

   X   **T59.91**   Toxic effect of unspecified gases, fumes and vapors, accidental (unintentional)

   X   **T59.92**   Toxic effect of unspecified gases, fumes and vapors, intentional self-harm A, S 🔗

   X   **T59.93**   Toxic effect of unspecified gases, fumes and vapors, assault

   X   **T59.94**   Toxic effect of unspecified gases, fumes and vapors, undetermined

T60   Toxic effect of pesticides

    Includes   toxic effect of wood preservatives

    The appropriate 7th character is to be added to each code from category T60

    | | |
    A   initial encounter
    D   subsequent encounter
    S   sequela

    T60.0   Toxic effect of organophosphate and carbamate insecticides

       T60.0X   Toxic effect of organophosphate and carbamate insecticides

          T60.0X1   Toxic effect of organophosphate and carbamate insecticides, accidental (unintentional)

             Toxic effect of organophosphate and carbamate insecticides NOS

          T60.0X2   Toxic effect of organophosphate and carbamate insecticides, intentional self-harm A, S 🔗

          T60.0X3   Toxic effect of organophosphate and carbamate insecticides, assault

          T60.0X4   Toxic effect of organophosphate and carbamate insecticides, undetermined

    T60.1   Toxic effect of halogenated insecticides

       Excludes1   chlorinated hydrocarbon (T53.-)

       T60.1X   Toxic effect of halogenated insecticides

          T60.1X1   Toxic effect of halogenated insecticides, accidental (unintentional)

             Toxic effect of halogenated insecticides NOS

          T60.1X2   Toxic effect of halogenated insecticides, intentional self-harm A, S 🔗

          T60.1X3   Toxic effect of halogenated insecticides, assault

          T60.1X4   Toxic effect of halogenated insecticides, undetermined

    T60.2   Toxic effect of other insecticides

       T60.2X   Toxic effect of other insecticides

          T60.2X1   Toxic effect of other insecticides, accidental (unintentional)

             Toxic effect of other insecticides NOS

          T60.2X2   Toxic effect of other insecticides, intentional self-harm A, S 🔗

          T60.2X3   Toxic effect of other insecticides, assault

          T60.2X4   Toxic effect of other insecticides, undetermined

    T60.3   Toxic effect of herbicides and fungicides

       T60.3X   Toxic effect of herbicides and fungicides

          T60.3X1   Toxic effect of herbicides and fungicides, accidental (unintentional)

             Toxic effect of herbicides and fungicides NOS

          T60.3X2   Toxic effect of herbicides and fungicides, intentional self-harm A, S 🔗

          T60.3X3   Toxic effect of herbicides and fungicides, assault

          T60.3X4   Toxic effect of herbicides and fungicides, undetermined

    T60.4   Toxic effect of rodenticides

       Excludes1   strychnine and its salts (T65.1)

          thallium (T56.81-)

       T60.4X   Toxic effect of rodenticides

          T60.4X1   Toxic effect of rodenticides, accidental (unintentional)

             Toxic effect of rodenticides NOS

          T60.4X2   Toxic effect of rodenticides, intentional self-harm A, S 🔗

CHAPTER 19 (S00-T88)

● **T60.4X3**   Toxic effect of rodenticides, assault

● **T60.4X4**   Toxic effect of rodenticides, undetermined

● **T60.8**   Toxic effect of other pesticides

  ● **T60.8X**   Toxic effect of other pesticides

    ● **T60.8X1**   Toxic effect of other pesticides, accidental (unintentional)
    Toxic effect of other pesticides NOS

    ● **T60.8X2**   Toxic effect of other pesticides, intentional self-harm A, S 🦠

    ● **T60.8X3**   Toxic effect of other pesticides, assault

    ● **T60.8X4**   Toxic effect of other pesticides, undetermined

● **T60.9**   Toxic effect of unspecified pesticide

  X● **T60.91**   Toxic effect of unspecified pesticide, accidental (unintentional)

  X● **T60.92**   Toxic effect of unspecified pesticide, intentional self-harm A, S 🦠

  X● **T60.93**   Toxic effect of unspecified pesticide, assault

  X● **T60.94**   Toxic effect of unspecified pesticide, undetermined

● **T61**   **Toxic effect of noxious substances eaten as seafood**

Excludes1	allergic reaction to food, such as:

    anaphylactic reaction or shock due to adverse food reaction (T78.0-)
    bacterial foodborne intoxications (A05.-)
    dermatitis (L23.6, L25.4, L27.2)
    food protein-induced enterocolitis syndrome (K52.21)
    food protein-induced enteropathy (K52.22)
    gastroenteritis (noninfective) (K52.29)
    toxic effect of aflatoxin and other mycotoxins (T64)
    toxic effect of cyanides (T65.0-)
    toxic effect of harmful algae bloom (T65.82-)
    toxic effect of hydrogen cyanide (T57.3-)
    toxic effect of mercury (T56.1-)
    toxic effect of red tide (T65.82-)

The appropriate 7th character is to be added to each code from category T61

A	initial encounter
D	subsequent encounter
S	sequela

● **T61.0**   **Ciguatera fish poisoning**

  X● **T61.01**   Ciguatera fish poisoning, accidental (unintentional)

  X● **T61.02**   Ciguatera fish poisoning, intentional self-harm A, S 🦠

  X● **T61.03**   Ciguatera fish poisoning, assault

  X● **T61.04**   Ciguatera fish poisoning, undetermined

● **T61.1**   **Scombroid fish poisoning**
Histamine-like syndrome

  X● **T61.11**   Scombroid fish poisoning, accidental (unintentional)

  X● **T61.12**   Scombroid fish poisoning, intentional self-harm A, S 🦠

  X● **T61.13**   Scombroid fish poisoning, assault

  X● **T61.14**   Scombroid fish poisoning, undetermined

● **T61.7**   Other fish and shellfish poisoning

  ● **T61.77**   Other fish poisoning

    ● **T61.771**   Other fish poisoning, accidental (unintentional)

    ● **T61.772**   Other fish poisoning, intentional self-harm A, S 🦠

    ● **T61.773**   Other fish poisoning, assault

    ● **T61.774**   Other fish poisoning, undetermined

● **T61.78**   Other shellfish poisoning

  ● **T61.781**   Other shellfish poisoning, accidental (unintentional)

  ● **T61.782**   Other shellfish poisoning, intentional self-harm A, S 🦠

  ● **T61.783**   Other shellfish poisoning, assault

  ● **T61.784**   Other shellfish poisoning, undetermined

● **T61.8**   Toxic effect of other seafood

  ● **T61.8X**   Toxic effect of other seafood

    ● **T61.8X1**   Toxic effect of other seafood, accidental (unintentional)

    ● **T61.8X2**   Toxic effect of other seafood, intentional self-harm A, S 🦠

    ● **T61.8X3**   Toxic effect of other seafood, assault

    ● **T61.8X4**   Toxic effect of other seafood, undetermined

● **T61.9**   Toxic effect of unspecified seafood

  X● **T61.91**   Toxic effect of unspecified seafood, accidental (unintentional)

  X● **T61.92**   Toxic effect of unspecified seafood, intentional self-harm A, S 🦠

  X● **T61.93**   Toxic effect of unspecified seafood, assault

  X● **T61.94**   Toxic effect of unspecified seafood, undetermined

● **T62**   **Toxic effect of other noxious substances eaten as food**

Excludes1	allergic reaction to food, such as:

    anaphylactic shock (reaction) due to adverse food reaction (T78.0-)
    dermatitis (L23.6, L25.4, L27.2)
    food protein-induced enterocolitis syndrome (K52.21)
    food protein-induced enteropathy (K52.22)
    gastroenteritis (noninfective) (K52.29)
    bacterial food borne intoxications (A05.-)
    toxic effect of aflatoxin and other mycotoxins (T64)
    toxic effect of cyanides (T65.0-)
    toxic effect of hydrogen cyanide (T57.3-)
    toxic effect of mercury (T56.1-)

The appropriate 7th character is to be added to each code from category T62

A	initial encounter
D	subsequent encounter
S	sequela

● **T62.0**   Toxic effect of ingested mushrooms

  ● **T62.0X**   Toxic effect of ingested mushrooms

    ● **T62.0X1**   Toxic effect of ingested mushrooms, accidental (unintentional)
    Toxic effect of ingested mushrooms NOS

    ● **T62.0X2**   Toxic effect of ingested mushrooms, intentional self-harm A, S 🦠

    ● **T62.0X3**   Toxic effect of ingested mushrooms, assault

    ● **T62.0X4**   Toxic effect of ingested mushrooms, undetermined

● **T62.1**   Toxic effect of ingested berries

  ● **T62.1X**   Toxic effect of ingested berries

    ● **T62.1X1**   Toxic effect of ingested berries, accidental (unintentional)
    Toxic effect of ingested berries NOS

    ● **T62.1X2**   Toxic effect of ingested berries, intentional self-harm A, S 🦠

    ● **T62.1X3**   Toxic effect of ingested berries, assault

    ● **T62.1X4**   Toxic effect of ingested berries, undetermined

▶ New   ⇒ Revised   ~~deleted~~ Deleted   Excludes 1   Excludes 2   Includes   Use additional   Code first   Code also   Key words

1430   OGCR Official Guidelines   X Assign placeholder X   ● Use Additional Character(s)   ▷ Manifestation Code   🦠 Hierarchical Condition Category   Coding Clinic

● **T62.2   Toxic effect of other ingested (parts of) plant(s)**
   ● **T62.2X   Toxic effect of other ingested (parts of) plant(s)**
     ● **T62.2X1   Toxic effect of other ingested (parts of) plant(s), accidental (unintentional)**
       Toxic effect of other ingested (parts of) plant(s) NOS
     ● **T62.2X2   Toxic effect of other ingested (parts of) plant(s), intentional self-harm A, S** 🔒
     ● **T62.2X3   Toxic effect of other ingested (parts of) plant(s), assault**
     ● **T62.2X4   Toxic effect of other ingested (parts of) plant(s), undetermined**
   ● **T62.8   Toxic effect of other specified noxious substances eaten as food**
     ● **T62.8X   Toxic effect of other specified noxious substances eaten as food**
       ● **T62.8X1   Toxic effect of other specified noxious substances eaten as food, accidental (unintentional)**
         Toxic effect of other specified noxious substances eaten as food NOS
       ● **T62.8X2   Toxic effect of other specified noxious substances eaten as food, intentional self-harm A, S** 🔒
       ● **T62.8X3   Toxic effect of other specified noxious substances eaten as food, assault**
       ● **T62.8X4   Toxic effect of other specified noxious substances eaten as food, undetermined**
   ● **T62.9   Toxic effect of unspecified noxious substance eaten as food**
     X ● **T62.91   Toxic effect of unspecified noxious substance eaten as food, accidental (unintentional)**
       Toxic effect of unspecified noxious substance eaten as food NOS
     X ● **T62.92   Toxic effect of unspecified noxious substance eaten as food, intentional self-harm A, S** 🔒
     X ● **T62.93   Toxic effect of unspecified noxious substance eaten as food, assault**
     X ● **T62.94   Toxic effect of unspecified noxious substance eaten as food, undetermined**
● **T63   Toxic effect of contact with venomous animals and plants**

> **Includes**   bite or touch of venomous animal
> pricked or stuck by thorn or leaf
>
> **Excludes2**   ingestion of toxic animal or plant (T61.-, T62.-)

The appropriate 7th character is to be added to each code from category T63

A	initial encounter
D	subsequent encounter
S	sequela

   ● **T63.0   Toxic effect of snake venom**
     ● **T63.00   Toxic effect of unspecified snake venom**
       ● **T63.001   Toxic effect of unspecified snake venom, accidental (unintentional)**
         Toxic effect of unspecified snake venom NOS
       ● **T63.002   Toxic effect of unspecified snake venom, intentional self-harm A, S** 🔒
       ● **T63.003   Toxic effect of unspecified snake venom, assault**
       ● **T63.004   Toxic effect of unspecified snake venom, undetermined**
     ● **T63.01   Toxic effect of rattlesnake venom**
       ● **T63.011   Toxic effect of rattlesnake venom, accidental (unintentional)**
         Toxic effect of rattlesnake venom NOS
       ● **T63.012   Toxic effect of rattlesnake venom, intentional self-harm A, S** 🔒

● **T63.013   Toxic effect of rattlesnake venom, assault**
● **T63.014   Toxic effect of rattlesnake venom, undetermined**
● **T63.02   Toxic effect of coral snake venom**
   ● **T63.021   Toxic effect of coral snake venom, accidental (unintentional)**
     Toxic effect of coral snake venom NOS
   ● **T63.022   Toxic effect of coral snake venom, intentional self-harm A, S** 🔒
   ● **T63.023   Toxic effect of coral snake venom, assault**
   ● **T63.024   Toxic effect of coral snake venom, undetermined**
● **T63.03   Toxic effect of taipan venom**
   ● **T63.031   Toxic effect of taipan venom, accidental (unintentional)**
     Toxic effect of taipan venom NOS
   ● **T63.032   Toxic effect of taipan venom, intentional self-harm A, S** 🔒
   ● **T63.033   Toxic effect of taipan venom, assault**
   ● **T63.034   Toxic effect of taipan venom, undetermined**
● **T63.04   Toxic effect of cobra venom**
   ● **T63.041   Toxic effect of cobra venom, accidental (unintentional)**
     Toxic effect of cobra venom NOS
   ● **T63.042   Toxic effect of cobra venom, intentional self-harm A, S** 🔒
   ● **T63.043   Toxic effect of cobra venom, assault**
   ● **T63.044   Toxic effect of cobra venom, undetermined**
● **T63.06   Toxic effect of venom of other North and South American snake**
   ● **T63.061   Toxic effect of venom of other North and South American snake, accidental (unintentional)**
     Toxic effect of venom of other North and South American snake NOS
   ● **T63.062   Toxic effect of venom of other North and South American snake, intentional self-harm A, S** 🔒
   ● **T63.063   Toxic effect of venom of other North and South American snake, assault**
   ● **T63.064   Toxic effect of venom of other North and South American snake, undetermined**
● **T63.07   Toxic effect of venom of other Australian snake**
   ● **T63.071   Toxic effect of venom of other Australian snake, accidental (unintentional)**
     Toxic effect of venom of other Australian snake NOS
   ● **T63.072   Toxic effect of venom of other Australian snake, intentional self-harm A, S** 🔒
   ● **T63.073   Toxic effect of venom of other Australian snake, assault**
   ● **T63.074   Toxic effect of venom of other Australian snake, undetermined**
● **T63.08   Toxic effect of venom of other African and Asian snake**
   ● **T63.081   Toxic effect of venom of other African and Asian snake, accidental (unintentional)**
     Toxic effect of venom of other African and Asian snake NOS
   ● **T63.082   Toxic effect of venom of other African and Asian snake, intentional self-harm A, S** 🔒

● T63.083   Toxic effect of venom of other African and Asian snake, assault

● T63.084   Toxic effect of venom of other African and Asian snake, undetermined

● T63.09   Toxic effect of venom of other snake

  ● T63.091   Toxic effect of venom of other snake, accidental (unintentional)
       Toxic effect of venom of other snake NOS

  ● T63.092   Toxic effect of venom of other snake, intentional self-harm A, S 🐾

  ● T63.093   Toxic effect of venom of other snake, assault

  ● T63.094   Toxic effect of venom of other snake, undetermined

● T63.1   Toxic effect of venom of other reptiles

  ● T63.11   Toxic effect of venom of gila monster

    ● T63.111   Toxic effect of venom of gila monster, accidental (unintentional)
         Toxic effect of venom of gila monster NOS

    ● T63.112   Toxic effect of venom of gila monster, intentional self-harm A, S 🐾

    ● T63.113   Toxic effect of venom of gila monster, assault

    ● T63.114   Toxic effect of venom of gila monster, undetermined

  ● T63.12   Toxic effect of venom of other venomous lizard

    ● T63.121   Toxic effect of venom of other venomous lizard, accidental (unintentional)
         Toxic effect of venom of other venomous lizard NOS

    ● T63.122   Toxic effect of venom of other venomous lizard, intentional self-harm A, S 🐾

    ● T63.123   Toxic effect of venom of other venomous lizard, assault

    ● T63.124   Toxic effect of venom of other venomous lizard, undetermined

  ● T63.19   Toxic effect of venom of other reptiles

    ● T63.191   Toxic effect of venom of other reptiles, accidental (unintentional)
         Toxic effect of venom of other reptiles NOS

    ● T63.192   Toxic effect of venom of other reptiles, intentional self-harm A, S 🐾

    ● T63.193   Toxic effect of venom of other reptiles, assault

    ● T63.194   Toxic effect of venom of other reptiles, undetermined

● T63.2   Toxic effect of venom of scorpion

  ● T63.2X   Toxic effect of venom of scorpion

    ● T63.2X1   Toxic effect of venom of scorpion, accidental (unintentional)
         Toxic effect of venom of scorpion NOS

    ● T63.2X2   Toxic effect of venom of scorpion, intentional self-harm A, S 🐾

    ● T63.2X3   Toxic effect of venom of scorpion, assault

    ● T63.2X4   Toxic effect of venom of scorpion, undetermined

● T63.3   Toxic effect of venom of spider

  ● T63.30   Toxic effect of unspecified spider venom

    ● T63.301   Toxic effect of unspecified spider venom, accidental (unintentional)

    ● T63.302   Toxic effect of unspecified spider venom, intentional self-harm A, S 🐾

    ● T63.303   Toxic effect of unspecified spider venom, assault

    ● T63.304   Toxic effect of unspecified spider venom, undetermined

● T63.31   Toxic effect of venom of black widow spider

  ● T63.311   Toxic effect of venom of black widow spider, accidental (unintentional)

  ● T63.312   Toxic effect of venom of black widow spider, intentional self-harm A, S 🐾

  ● T63.313   Toxic effect of venom of black widow spider, assault

  ● T63.314   Toxic effect of venom of black widow spider, undetermined

● T63.32   Toxic effect of venom of tarantula

  ● T63.321   Toxic effect of venom of tarantula, accidental (unintentional)

  ● T63.322   Toxic effect of venom of tarantula, intentional self-harm A, S 🐾

  ● T63.323   Toxic effect of venom of tarantula, assault

  ● T63.324   Toxic effect of venom of tarantula, undetermined

● T63.33   Toxic effect of venom of brown recluse spider

  ● T63.331   Toxic effect of venom of brown recluse spider, accidental (unintentional)

  ● T63.332   Toxic effect of venom of brown recluse spider, intentional self-harm A, S 🐾

  ● T63.333   Toxic effect of venom of brown recluse spider, assault

  ● T63.334   Toxic effect of venom of brown recluse spider, undetermined

● T63.39   Toxic effect of venom of other spider

  ● T63.391   Toxic effect of venom of other spider, accidental (unintentional)

  ● T63.392   Toxic effect of venom of other spider, intentional self-harm A, S 🐾

  ● T63.393   Toxic effect of venom of other spider, assault

  ● T63.394   Toxic effect of venom of other spider, undetermined

● T63.4   Toxic effect of venom of other arthropods

  ● T63.41   Toxic effect of venom of centipedes and venomous millipedes

    ● T63.411   Toxic effect of venom of centipedes and venomous millipedes, accidental (unintentional)

    ● T63.412   Toxic effect of venom of centipedes and venomous millipedes, intentional self-harm A, S 🐾

    ● T63.413   Toxic effect of venom of centipedes and venomous millipedes, assault

    ● T63.414   Toxic effect of venom of centipedes and venomous millipedes, undetermined

  ● T63.42   Toxic effect of venom of ants

    ● T63.421   Toxic effect of venom of ants, accidental (unintentional)

    ● T63.422   Toxic effect of venom of ants, intentional self-harm A, S 🐾

    ● T63.423   Toxic effect of venom of ants, assault

    ● T63.424   Toxic effect of venom of ants, undetermined

  ● T63.43   Toxic effect of venom of caterpillars

    ● T63.431   Toxic effect of venom of caterpillars, accidental (unintentional)

    ● T63.432   Toxic effect of venom of caterpillars, intentional self-harm A, S 🐾

    ● T63.433   Toxic effect of venom of caterpillars, assault

    ● T63.434   Toxic effect of venom of caterpillars, undetermined

▶ New   ⇒ Revised   ~~deleted~~ Deleted   Excludes 1   Excludes 2   Includes   Use additional   Code first   Code also   Key words

OGCR Official Guidelines   X Assign placeholder X   ● Use Additional Character(s)   ▷ Manifestation Code   🐾 Hierarchical Condition Category   **Coding Clinic**

● T63.44   Toxic effect of venom of bees
- ● T63.441   Toxic effect of venom of bees, accidental (unintentional)
- ● T63.442   Toxic effect of venom of bees, intentional self-harm A, S 🦠
- ● T63.443   Toxic effect of venom of bees, assault
- ● T63.444   Toxic effect of venom of bees, undetermined

● T63.45   Toxic effect of venom of hornets
- ● T63.451   Toxic effect of venom of hornets, accidental (unintentional)
- ● T63.452   Toxic effect of venom of hornets, intentional self-harm A, S 🦠
- ● T63.453   Toxic effect of venom of hornets, assault
- ● T63.454   Toxic effect of venom of hornets, undetermined

● T63.46   Toxic effect of venom of wasps
Toxic effect of yellow jacket
- ● T63.461   Toxic effect of venom of wasps, accidental (unintentional)
- ● T63.462   Toxic effect of venom of wasps, intentional self-harm A, S 🦠
- ● T63.463   Toxic effect of venom of wasps, assault
- ● T63.464   Toxic effect of venom of wasps, undetermined

● T63.48   Toxic effect of venom of other arthropod
- ● T63.481   Toxic effect of venom of other arthropod, accidental (unintentional)
- ● T63.482   Toxic effect of venom of other arthropod, intentional self-harm A, S 🦠
- ● T63.483   Toxic effect of venom of other arthropod, assault
- ● T63.484   Toxic effect of venom of other arthropod, undetermined

● T63.5   Toxic effect of contact with venomous fish
> **Excludes2**   poisoning by ingestion of fish (T61.-)

● T63.51   Toxic effect of contact with stingray
- ● T63.511   Toxic effect of contact with stingray, accidental (unintentional)
- ● T63.512   Toxic effect of contact with stingray, intentional self-harm A, S 🦠
- ● T63.513   Toxic effect of contact with stingray, assault
- ● T63.514   Toxic effect of contact with stingray, undetermined

● T63.59   Toxic effect of contact with other venomous fish
- ● T63.591   Toxic effect of contact with other venomous fish, accidental (unintentional)
- ● T63.592   Toxic effect of contact with other venomous fish, intentional self-harm A, S 🦠
- ● T63.593   Toxic effect of contact with other venomous fish, assault
- ● T63.594   Toxic effect of contact with other venomous fish, undetermined

● T63.6   Toxic effect of contact with other venomous marine animals
> **Excludes1**   sea-snake venom (T63.09)
> **Excludes2**   poisoning by ingestion of shellfish (T61.78-)

● T63.61   Toxic effect of contact with Portugese Man-o-war
Toxic effect of contact with bluebottle
- ● T63.611   Toxic effect of contact with Portugese Man-o-war, accidental (unintentional)
- ● T63.612   Toxic effect of contact with Portugese Man-o-war, intentional self-harm A, S 🦠

- ● T63.613   Toxic effect of contact with Portugese Man-o-war, assault
- ● T63.614   Toxic effect of contact with Portugese Man-o-war, undetermined

● T63.62   Toxic effect of contact with other jellyfish
- ● T63.621   Toxic effect of contact with other jellyfish, accidental (unintentional)
- ● T63.622   Toxic effect of contact with other jellyfish, intentional self-harm A, S 🦠
- ● T63.623   Toxic effect of contact with other jellyfish, assault
- ● T63.624   Toxic effect of contact with other jellyfish, undetermined

● T63.63   Toxic effect of contact with sea anemone
- ● T63.631   Toxic effect of contact with sea anemone, accidental (unintentional)
- ● T63.632   Toxic effect of contact with sea anemone, intentional self-harm A, S 🦠
- ● T63.633   Toxic effect of contact with sea anemone, assault
- ● T63.634   Toxic effect of contact with sea anemone, undetermined

● T63.69   Toxic effect of contact with other venomous marine animals
- ● T63.691   Toxic effect of contact with other venomous marine animals, accidental (unintentional)
- ● T63.692   Toxic effect of contact with other venomous marine animals, intentional self-harm A, S 🦠
- ● T63.693   Toxic effect of contact with other venomous marine animals, assault
- ● T63.694   Toxic effect of contact with other venomous marine animals, undetermined

● T63.7   Toxic effect of contact with venomous plant
● T63.71   Toxic effect of contact with venomous marine plant
- ● T63.711   Toxic effect of contact with venomous marine plant, accidental (unintentional)
- ● T63.712   Toxic effect of contact with venomous marine plant, intentional self-harm A, S 🦠
- ● T63.713   Toxic effect of contact with venomous marine plant, assault
- ● T63.714   Toxic effect of contact with venomous marine plant, undetermined

● T63.79   Toxic effect of contact with other venomous plant
- ● T63.791   Toxic effect of contact with other venomous plant, accidental (unintentional)
- ● T63.792   Toxic effect of contact with other venomous plant, intentional self-harm A, S 🦠
- ● T63.793   Toxic effect of contact with other venomous plant, assault
- ● T63.794   Toxic effect of contact with other venomous plant, undetermined

● T63.8   Toxic effect of contact with other venomous animals
● T63.81   Toxic effect of contact with venomous frog
> **Excludes1**   contact with nonvenomous frog (W62.0)
- ● T63.811   Toxic effect of contact with venomous frog, accidental (unintentional)
- ● T63.812   Toxic effect of contact with venomous frog, intentional self-harm A, S 🦠
- ● T63.813   Toxic effect of contact with venomous frog, assault
- ● T63.814   Toxic effect of contact with venomous frog, undetermined

CHAPTER 19 (S00-T88)

CHAPTER 19 (SØØ-T88)

- **T63.82** Toxic effect of contact with venomous toad
  - **Excludes1** contact with nonvenomous toad (W62.1)
  - **T63.821** Toxic effect of contact with venomous toad, accidental (unintentional)
  - **T63.822** Toxic effect of contact with venomous toad, intentional self-harm A, S 🔖
  - **T63.823** Toxic effect of contact with venomous toad, assault
  - **T63.824** Toxic effect of contact with venomous toad, undetermined
- **T63.83** Toxic effect of contact with other venomous amphibian
  - **Excludes1** contact with nonvenomous amphibian (W62.9)
  - **T63.831** Toxic effect of contact with other venomous amphibian, accidental (unintentional)
  - **T63.832** Toxic effect of contact with other venomous amphibian, intentional self-harm A, S 🔖
  - **T63.833** Toxic effect of contact with other venomous amphibian, assault
  - **T63.834** Toxic effect of contact with other venomous amphibian, undetermined
- **T63.89** Toxic effect of contact with other venomous animals
  - **T63.891** Toxic effect of contact with other venomous animals, accidental (unintentional)
  - **T63.892** Toxic effect of contact with other venomous animals, intentional self-harm A, S 🔖
  - **T63.893** Toxic effect of contact with other venomous animals, assault
  - **T63.894** Toxic effect of contact with other venomous animals, undetermined
- **T63.9** Toxic effect of contact with unspecified venomous animal
  - X● **T63.91** Toxic effect of contact with unspecified venomous animal, accidental (unintentional)
  - X● **T63.92** Toxic effect of contact with unspecified venomous animal, intentional self-harm A, S 🔖
  - X● **T63.93** Toxic effect of contact with unspecified venomous animal, assault
  - X● **T63.94** Toxic effect of contact with unspecified venomous animal, undetermined
- **T64** Toxic effect of aflatoxin and other mycotoxin food contaminants

  The appropriate 7th character is to be added to each code from category T64

A	initial encounter
D	subsequent encounter
S	sequela

  - **T64.0** Toxic effect of aflatoxin
    - X● **T64.01** Toxic effect of aflatoxin, accidental (unintentional)
    - X● **T64.02** Toxic effect of aflatoxin, intentional self-harm A, S 🔖
    - X● **T64.03** Toxic effect of aflatoxin, assault
    - X● **T64.04** Toxic effect of aflatoxin, undetermined
  - **T64.8** Toxic effect of other mycotoxin food contaminants
    - X● **T64.81** Toxic effect of other mycotoxin food contaminants, accidental (unintentional)
    - X● **T64.82** Toxic effect of other mycotoxin food contaminants, intentional self-harm A, S 🔖
    - X● **T64.83** Toxic effect of other mycotoxin food contaminants, assault
    - X● **T64.84** Toxic effect of other mycotoxin food contaminants, undetermined

- **T65** Toxic effect of other and unspecified substances

  The appropriate 7th character is to be added to each code from category T65

A	initial encounter
D	subsequent encounter
S	sequela

  - **T65.0** Toxic effect of cyanides
    - **Excludes1** hydrogen cyanide (T57.3-)
    - **T65.0X** Toxic effect of cyanides
      - **T65.0X1** Toxic effect of cyanides, accidental (unintentional)
        Toxic effect of cyanides NOS
      - **T65.0X2** Toxic effect of cyanides, intentional self-harm A, S 🔖
      - **T65.0X3** Toxic effect of cyanides, assault
      - **T65.0X4** Toxic effect of cyanides, undetermined
  - **T65.1** Toxic effect of strychnine and its salts
    - **T65.1X** Toxic effect of strychnine and its salts
      - **T65.1X1** Toxic effect of strychnine and its salts, accidental (unintentional)
        Toxic effect of strychnine and its salts NOS
      - **T65.1X2** Toxic effect of strychnine and its salts, intentional self-harm A, S 🔖
      - **T65.1X3** Toxic effect of strychnine and its salts, assault
      - **T65.1X4** Toxic effect of strychnine and its salts, undetermined
  - **T65.2** Toxic effect of tobacco and nicotine
    - **Excludes2** nicotine dependence (F17.-)
    - **T65.21** Toxic effect of chewing tobacco
      - **T65.211** Toxic effect of chewing tobacco, accidental (unintentional)
        Toxic effect of chewing tobacco NOS
      - **T65.212** Toxic effect of chewing tobacco, intentional self-harm A, S 🔖
      - **T65.213** Toxic effect of chewing tobacco, assault
      - **T65.214** Toxic effect of chewing tobacco, undetermined
    - **T65.22** Toxic effect of tobacco cigarettes
      Toxic effect of tobacco smoke
      Use additional code for exposure to second hand tobacco smoke (Z57.31, Z77.22)
      - **T65.221** Toxic effect of tobacco cigarettes, accidental (unintentional)
        Toxic effect of tobacco cigarettes NOS
      - **T65.222** Toxic effect of tobacco cigarettes, intentional self-harm A, S 🔖
      - **T65.223** Toxic effect of tobacco cigarettes, assault
      - **T65.224** Toxic effect of tobacco cigarettes, undetermined
    - **T65.29** Toxic effect of other tobacco and nicotine
      - **T65.291** Toxic effect of other tobacco and nicotine, accidental (unintentional)
        Toxic effect of other tobacco and nicotine NOS
      - **T65.292** Toxic effect of other tobacco and nicotine, intentional self-harm A, S 🔖
      - **T65.293** Toxic effect of other tobacco and nicotine, assault
      - **T65.294** Toxic effect of other tobacco and nicotine, undetermined

▶ New   ⇒ Revised   ~~deleted~~ Deleted   Excludes 1   Excludes 2   Includes   Use additional   Code first   Code also   Key words
OGCR Official Guidelines   X Assign placeholder X   ● Use Additional Character(s)   ❭ Manifestation Code   🔖 Hierarchical Condition Category   **Coding Clinic**

- **T65.3 Toxic effect of nitroderivatives and aminoderivatives of benzene and its homologues**
  Toxic effect of anilin [benzenamine]
  Toxic effect of nitrobenzene
  Toxic effect of trinitrotoluene
  - **T65.3X Toxic effect of nitroderivatives and aminoderivatives of benzene and its homologues**
    - **T65.3X1 Toxic effect of nitroderivatives and aminoderivatives of benzene and its homologues, accidental (unintentional)**
      Toxic effect of nitroderivatives and aminoderivatives of benzene and its homologues NOS
    - **T65.3X2 Toxic effect of nitroderivatives and aminoderivatives of benzene and its homologues, intentional self-harm A, S ▨**
    - **T65.3X3 Toxic effect of nitroderivatives and aminoderivatives of benzene and its homologues, assault**
    - **T65.3X4 Toxic effect of nitroderivatives and aminoderivatives of benzene and its homologues, undetermined**
- **T65.4 Toxic effect of carbon disulfide**
  - **T65.4X Toxic effect of carbon disulfide**
    - **T65.4X1 Toxic effect of carbon disulfide, accidental (unintentional)**
      Toxic effect of carbon disulfide NOS
    - **T65.4X2 Toxic effect of carbon disulfide, intentional self-harm A, S ▨**
    - **T65.4X3 Toxic effect of carbon disulfide, assault**
    - **T65.4X4 Toxic effect of carbon disulfide, undetermined**
- **T65.5 Toxic effect of nitroglycerin and other nitric acids and esters**
  Toxic effect of 1,2,3-Propanetriol trinitrate
  - **T65.5X Toxic effect of nitroglycerin and other nitric acids and esters**
    - **T65.5X1 Toxic effect of nitroglycerin and other nitric acids and esters, accidental (unintentional)**
      Toxic effect of nitroglycerin and other nitric acids and esters NOS
    - **T65.5X2 Toxic effect of nitroglycerin and other nitric acids and esters, intentional self-harm A, S ▨**
    - **T65.5X3 Toxic effect of nitroglycerin and other nitric acids and esters, assault**
    - **T65.5X4 Toxic effect of nitroglycerin and other nitric acids and esters, undetermined**
- **T65.6 Toxic effect of paints and dyes, not elsewhere classified**
  - **T65.6X Toxic effect of paints and dyes, not elsewhere classified**
    - **T65.6X1 Toxic effect of paints and dyes, not elsewhere classified, accidental (unintentional)**
      Toxic effect of paints and dyes NOS
    - **T65.6X2 Toxic effect of paints and dyes, not elsewhere classified, intentional self-harm A, S ▨**
    - **T65.6X3 Toxic effect of paints and dyes, not elsewhere classified, assault**
    - **T65.6X4 Toxic effect of paints and dyes, not elsewhere classified, undetermined**

- **T65.8 Toxic effect of other specified substances**
  - **T65.81 Toxic effect of latex**
    - **T65.811 Toxic effect of latex, accidental (unintentional)**
      Toxic effect of latex NOS
    - **T65.812 Toxic effect of latex, intentional self-harm A, S ▨**
    - **T65.813 Toxic effect of latex, assault**
    - **T65.814 Toxic effect of latex, undetermined**
  - **T65.82 Toxic effect of harmful algae and algae toxins**
    Toxic effect of (harmful) algae bloom NOS
    Toxic effect of blue-green algae bloom
    Toxic effect of brown tide
    Toxic effect of cyanobacteria bloom
    Toxic effect of Florida red tide
    Toxic effect of pfiesteria piscicida
    Toxic effect of red tide
    - **T65.821 Toxic effect of harmful algae and algae toxins, accidental (unintentional)**
      Toxic effect of harmful algae and algae toxins NOS
    - **T65.822 Toxic effect of harmful algae and algae toxins, intentional self-harm A, S ▨**
    - **T65.823 Toxic effect of harmful algae and algae toxins, assault**
    - **T65.824 Toxic effect of harmful algae and algae toxins, undetermined**
  - **T65.83 Toxic effect of fiberglass**
    - **T65.831 Toxic effect of fiberglass, accidental (unintentional)**
      Toxic effect of fiberglass NOS
    - **T65.832 Toxic effect of fiberglass, intentional self-harm A, S ▨**
    - **T65.833 Toxic effect of fiberglass, assault**
    - **T65.834 Toxic effect of fiberglass, undetermined**
  - **T65.89 Toxic effect of other specified substances**
    - **T65.891 Toxic effect of other specified substances, accidental (unintentional)**
      Toxic effect of other specified substances NOS
      Coding Clinic: 2018, Q1, P5
    - **T65.892 Toxic effect of other specified substances, intentional self-harm A, S ▨**
    - **T65.893 Toxic effect of other specified substances, assault**
    - **T65.894 Toxic effect of other specified substances, undetermined**
- **T65.9 Toxic effect of unspecified substance**
  - X **T65.91 Toxic effect of unspecified substance, accidental (unintentional)**
    Poisoning NOS
  - X **T65.92 Toxic effect of unspecified substance, intentional self-harm A, S ▨**
  - X **T65.93 Toxic effect of unspecified substance, assault**
  - X **T65.94 Toxic effect of unspecified substance, undetermined**

CHAPTER 19 (S00-T88)

CHAPTER 19 (S00-T88)

OTHER AND UNSPECIFIED EFFECTS OF EXTERNAL CAUSES (T66-T78)

● **T66   Radiation sickness, unspecified**

     Excludes1   specified adverse effects of radiation, such as:
              burns (T20-T31)
              leukemia (C91-C95)
              radiation gastroenteritis and colitis (K52.0)
              radiation pneumonitis (J70.0)
              radiation related disorders of the skin and
                subcutaneous tissue (L55-L59)
              sunburn (L55.-)

     The appropriate 7th character is to be added to code T66

A	initial encounter
D	subsequent encounter
S	sequela

● **T67   Effects of heat and light**

     Excludes1   erythema [dermatitis] ab igne (L59.0)
              malignant hyperpyrexia due to anesthesia (T88.3)
              radiation-related disorders of the skin and
                subcutaneous tissue (L55-L59)

     Excludes2   burns (T20-T31)
              sunburn (L55.-)
              sweat disorder due to heat (L74-L75)

     The appropriate 7th character is to be added to each code from
           category T67

A	initial encounter
D	subsequent encounter
S	sequela

   X ● **T67.0   Heatstroke and sunstroke**

         Use additional code(s) to identify any associated
            complications of heatstroke, such as:
         coma and stupor (R40.-)
         rhabdomyolysis (M62.82)
         systemic inflammatory response syndrome (R65.1-)
         Coding Clinic: 2019, Q4, P18

     X ● **T67.01   Heatstroke and sunstroke**
              Heat apoplexy
              Heat pyrexia
              Siriasis
              Thermoplegia

     X ● **T67.02   Exertional heatstroke**
              Coding Clinic: 2019, Q4, P18

     X ● **T67.09   Other heatstroke and sunstroke**

   X ● **T67.1   Heat syncope**
         Heat collapse

   X ● **T67.2   Heat cramp**

   X ● **T67.3   Heat exhaustion, anhydrotic**
         Heat prostration due to water depletion

       Excludes1   heat exhaustion due to salt depletion
                   (T67.4)

   X ● **T67.4   Heat exhaustion due to salt depletion**
         Heat prostration due to salt (and water) depletion

   X ● **T67.5   Heat exhaustion, unspecified**
         Heat prostration NOS

   X ● **T67.6   Heat fatigue, transient**

   X ● **T67.7   Heat edema**

   X ● **T67.8   Other effects of heat and light**

   X ● **T67.9   Effect of heat and light, unspecified**

X ● **T68   Hypothermia**
         Accidental hypothermia
         Hypothermia NOS
     Use additional code to identify source of exposure:
         Exposure to excessive cold of man-made origin (W93)
         Exposure to excessive cold of natural origin (X31)

     Excludes1   hypothermia following anesthesia (T88.51)
              hypothermia not associated with low
                environmental temperature (R68.0)
              hypothermia of newborn (P80.-)

     Excludes2   frostbite (T33-T34)

     The appropriate 7th character is to be added to code T68

A	initial encounter
D	subsequent encounter
S	sequela

● **T69   Other effects of reduced temperature**
     Use additional code to identify source of exposure:
         Exposure to excessive cold of man-made origin (W93)
         Exposure to excessive cold of natural origin (X31)

     Excludes2   frostbite (T33-T34)

     The appropriate 7th character is to be added to each code from
           category T69

A	initial encounter
D	subsequent encounter
S	sequela

   ● **T69.0   Immersion hand and foot**

     ● **T69.01   Immersion hand**

       ● **T69.011   Immersion hand, right hand**

       ● **T69.012   Immersion hand, left hand**

       ● **T69.019   Immersion hand, unspecified hand**

     ● **T69.02   Immersion foot**
              Trench foot

       ● **T69.021   Immersion foot, right foot**

       ● **T69.022   Immersion foot, left foot**

       ● **T69.029   Immersion foot, unspecified foot**

   X ● **T69.1   Chilblains**

   X ● **T69.8   Other specified effects of reduced temperature**

   X ● **T69.9   Effect of reduced temperature, unspecified**

● **T70   Effects of air pressure and water pressure**
     The appropriate 7th character is to be added to each code from
           category T70

A	initial encounter
D	subsequent encounter
S	sequela

   X ● **T70.0   Otitic barotrauma**
         Aero-otitis media
         Effects of change in ambient atmospheric pressure or
            water pressure on ears

   X ● **T70.1   Sinus barotrauma**
         Aerosinusitis
         Effects of change in ambient atmospheric pressure on
            sinuses

   ● **T70.2   Other and unspecified effects of high altitude**

       Excludes2   polycythemia due to high altitude (D75.1)

     X ● **T70.20   Unspecified effects of high altitude**

     X ● **T70.29   Other effects of high altitude**
              Alpine sickness
              Anoxia due to high altitude
              Barotrauma NOS
              Hypobaropathy
              Mountain sickness

▶ New   ⇒ Revised   ~~deleted~~ Deleted   Excludes 1   Excludes 2   Includes   Use additional   Code first   Code also   Key words

1436   OGCR Official Guidelines   X Assign placeholder X   ● Use Additional Character(s)   ) Manifestation Code   🔗 Hierarchical Condition Category   Coding

X ● **T70.3**   **Caisson disease [decompression sickness]**
     Compressed-air disease
     Diver's palsy or paralysis

X ● **T70.4**   **Effects of high-pressure fluids**
     Hydraulic jet injection (industrial)
     Pneumatic jet injection (industrial)
     Traumatic jet injection (industrial)

X ● **T70.8**   **Other effects of air pressure and water pressure**

X ● **T70.9**   **Effect of air pressure and water pressure, unspecified**

● **T71**   **Asphyxiation**
     Mechanical suffocation
     Traumatic suffocation

     Excludes1   acute respiratory distress (syndrome) (J80)
                anoxia due to high altitude (T70.2)
                asphyxia NOS (R09.01)
                asphyxia from carbon monoxide (T58.-)
                asphyxia from inhalation of food or foreign body
                  (T17.-)
                asphyxia from other gases, fumes and vapors
                  (T59.-)
                respiratory distress (syndrome) in newborn
                  (P22.-)

     The appropriate 7th character is to be added to each code from
     category T71

> A   initial encounter
> D   subsequent encounter
> S   sequela

● **T71.1**   **Asphyxiation due to mechanical threat to breathing**
     Suffocation due to mechanical threat to breathing

    ● **T71.11**   **Asphyxiation due to smothering under pillow**

       ● **T71.111**   **Asphyxiation due to smothering under pillow, accidental**
            Asphyxiation due to smothering under pillow NOS

       ● **T71.112**   **Asphyxiation due to smothering under pillow, intentional self-harm A, S** 🚫

       ● **T71.113**   **Asphyxiation due to smothering under pillow, assault**

       ● **T71.114**   **Asphyxiation due to smothering under pillow, undetermined**

    ● **T71.12**   **Asphyxiation due to plastic bag**

       ● **T71.121**   **Asphyxiation due to plastic bag, accidental**
            Asphyxiation due to plastic bag NOS

       ● **T71.122**   **Asphyxiation due to plastic bag, intentional self-harm A, S** 🚫

       ● **T71.123**   **Asphyxiation due to plastic bag, assault**

       ● **T71.124**   **Asphyxiation due to plastic bag, undetermined**

    ● **T71.13**   **Asphyxiation due to being trapped in bed linens**

       ● **T71.131**   **Asphyxiation due to being trapped in bed linens, accidental**
            Asphyxiation due to being trapped in bed linens NOS

       ● **T71.132**   **Asphyxiation due to being trapped in bed linens, intentional self-harm A, S** 🚫

       ● **T71.133**   **Asphyxiation due to being trapped in bed linens, assault**

       ● **T71.134**   **Asphyxiation due to being trapped in bed linens, undetermined**

    ● **T71.14**   **Asphyxiation due to smothering under another person's body (in bed)**

       ● **T71.141**   **Asphyxiation due to smothering under another person's body (in bed), accidental**
            Asphyxiation due to smothering under another person's body (in bed) NOS

       ● **T71.143**   **Asphyxiation due to smothering under another person's body (in bed), assault**

       ● **T71.144**   **Asphyxiation due to smothering under another person's body (in bed), undetermined**

    ● **T71.15**   **Asphyxiation due to smothering in furniture**

       ● **T71.151**   **Asphyxiation due to smothering in furniture, accidental**
            Asphyxiation due to smothering in furniture NOS

       ● **T71.152**   **Asphyxiation due to smothering in furniture, intentional self-harm A, S** 🚫

       ● **T71.153**   **Asphyxiation due to smothering in furniture, assault**

       ● **T71.154**   **Asphyxiation due to smothering in furniture, undetermined**

    ● **T71.16**   **Asphyxiation due to hanging**
       Hanging by window shade cord
       Use additional code for any associated injuries, such as:
         crushing injury of neck (S17.-)
         fracture of cervical vertebrae (S12.0-S12.2-)
         open wound of neck (S11.-)

       ● **T71.161**   **Asphyxiation due to hanging, accidental**
            Asphyxiation due to hanging NOS
            Hanging NOS

       ● **T71.162**   **Asphyxiation due to hanging, intentional self-harm A, S** 🚫

       ● **T71.163**   **Asphyxiation due to hanging, assault**

       ● **T71.164**   **Asphyxiation due to hanging, undetermined**

    ● **T71.19**   **Asphyxiation due to mechanical**
       Threat to breathing due to other causes

       ● **T71.191**   **Asphyxiation due to mechanical threat to breathing due to other causes, accidental**
            Asphyxiation due to other causes NOS
            Coding Clinic: 2016, Q4, P76

       ● **T71.192**   **Asphyxiation due to mechanical threat to breathing due to other causes, intentional self-harm A, S** 🚫

       ● **T71.193**   **Asphyxiation due to mechanical threat to breathing due to other causes, assault**

       ● **T71.194**   **Asphyxiation due to mechanical threat to breathing due to other causes, undetermined**

● **T71.2**   **Asphyxiation due to systemic oxygen deficiency due to low oxygen content in ambient air**
     Suffocation due to systemic oxygen deficiency due to low oxygen content in ambient air

X ● **T71.20**   **Asphyxiation due to systemic oxygen deficiency due to low oxygen content in ambient air due to unspecified cause**

X ● **T71.21**   **Asphyxiation due to cave-in or falling earth**
       Use additional code for any associated cataclysm (X34-X38)

● **T71.22** **Asphyxiation due to being** trapped in a car trunk

    ● **T71.221** Asphyxiation due to being trapped in a car trunk, accidental

    ● **T71.222** Asphyxiation due to being trapped in a car trunk, intentional self-harm A, S 🅗🅒

    ● **T71.223** Asphyxiation due to being trapped in a car trunk, assault

    ● **T71.224** Asphyxiation due to being trapped in a car trunk, undetermined

● **T71.23** **Asphyxiation due to being** trapped in a (discarded) refrigerator

    ● **T71.231** Asphyxiation due to being trapped in a (discarded) refrigerator, accidental

    ● **T71.232** Asphyxiation due to being trapped in a (discarded) refrigerator, intentional self-harm A, S 🅗🅒

    ● **T71.233** Asphyxiation due to being trapped in a (discarded) refrigerator, assault

    ● **T71.234** Asphyxiation due to being trapped in a (discarded) refrigerator, undetermined

X ● **T71.29** **Asphyxiation due to being** trapped in other low oxygen environment

X ● **T71.9** **Asphyxiation due to** unspecified cause

    Suffocation (by strangulation) due to unspecified cause

    Suffocation NOS

    Systemic oxygen deficiency due to low oxygen content in ambient air due to unspecified cause

    Systemic oxygen deficiency due to mechanical threat to breathing due to unspecified cause

    Traumatic asphyxia NOS

● **T73** **Effects of other deprivation**

The appropriate 7th character is to be added to each code from category T73

A	initial encounter
D	subsequent encounter
S	sequela

X ● **T73.0** **Starvation**
    Deprivation of food

X ● **T73.1** **Deprivation of water**

X ● **T73.2** **Exhaustion due to exposure**

X ● **T73.3** **Exhaustion due to excessive exertion**
    Exhaustion due to overexertion

X ● **T73.8** **Other effects of deprivation**

X ● **T73.9** **Effect of deprivation, unspecified**

● **T74** **Adult and child abuse, neglect and other maltreatment, confirmed**

Use additional code, if applicable, to identify any associated current injury

Use additional external cause code to identify perpetrator, if known (Y07.-)

Excludes1 abuse and maltreatment in pregnancy (O9A.3-, O9A.4-, O9A.5-)
    adult and child maltreatment, suspected (T76.-)

The appropriate 7th character is to be added to each code from category T74

A	initial encounter
D	subsequent encounter
S	sequela

● **T74.0** **Neglect or abandonment, confirmed**

X ● **T74.01** Adult neglect or abandonment, confirmed   A

X ● **T74.02** Child neglect or abandonment, confirmed   P

● **T74.1** **Physical abuse, confirmed**

    Excludes2 sexual abuse (T74.2-)

X ● **T74.11** Adult physical abuse, confirmed   A

X ● **T74.12** Child physical abuse, confirmed   P

    Excludes2 shaken infant syndrome (T74.4)

● **T74.2** **Sexual abuse, confirmed**
    Rape, confirmed
    Sexual assault, confirmed

X ● **T74.21** Adult sexual abuse, confirmed   A

X ● **T74.22** Child sexual abuse, confirmed   P

● **T74.3** **Psychological abuse, confirmed**
    Bullying and intimidation, confirmed
    Intimidation through social media, confirmed

X ● **T74.31** Adult psychological abuse, confirmed   A

X ● **T74.32** Child psychological abuse, confirmed   P

X ● **T74.4** **Shaken infant syndrome**   P

● **T74.5** **Forced sexual exploitation, confirmed**

X ● **T74.51** Adult forced sexual exploitation, confirmed   P

X ● **T74.52** Child sexual exploitation, confirmed   P

● **T74.6** **Forced labor exploitation, confirmed**

X ● **T74.61** Adult forced labor exploitation, confirmed   P

X ● **T74.62** Child forced labor exploitation, confirmed   P

● **T74.9** **Unspecified maltreatment, confirmed**

X ● **T74.91** Unspecified adult maltreatment, confirmed   A

X ● **T74.92** Unspecified child maltreatment, confirmed   P

● **T75** **Other and unspecified effects of other external causes**

    Excludes1 adverse effects NEC (T78.-)

    Excludes2 burns (electric) (T20-T31)

The appropriate 7th character is to be added to each code from category T75

A	initial encounter
D	subsequent encounter
S	sequela

● **T75.0** **Effects of lightning**
    Struck by lightning

X ● **T75.00** **Unspecified effects of lightning**
    Struck by lightning NOS

X ● **T75.01** **Shock due to being struck by lightning**

X ● **T75.09** **Other effects of lightning**
    Use additional code for other effects of lightning

X ● **T75.1** **Unspecified effects of drowning and nonfatal submersion**
    Immersion

    Excludes1 specified effects of drowning code to effects

● **T75.2** **Effects of vibration**

X ● **T75.20** **Unspecified effects of vibration**

X ● **T75.21** **Pneumatic hammer syndrome**

X ● **T75.22** **Traumatic vasospastic syndrome**

X ● **T75.23** **Vertigo from infrasound**

    Excludes1 vertigo NOS (R42)

X ● **T75.29** **Other effects of vibration**

▶ New   ⇒ Revised   ~~deleted~~ Deleted   Excludes 1   Excludes 2   Includes   Use additional   Code first   Code also   Key words

OGCR Official Guidelines   X Assign placeholder X   ● Use Additional Character(s)   ▌ Manifestation Code   🅗🅒 Hierarchical Condition Category   **Coding Clinic**

X● **T75.3** **Motion sickness**
Airsickness Travel sickness
Seasickness
Use additional external cause code to identify vehicle or
type of motion (Y92.81-, Y93.5-)

X● **T75.4** **Electrocution**
Shock from electric current
Shock from electroshock gun (taser)

●**T75.8** **Other specified effects of external causes**

X● **T75.81** **Effects of abnormal gravitation [G] forces**

X● **T75.82** **Effects of weightlessness**

X● **T75.89** **Other specified effects of external causes**

●**T76** **Adult and child abuse, neglect and other maltreatment, suspected**
Use additional code, if applicable, to identify any associated
current injury

Excludes1 adult and child maltreatment, confirmed (T74.-)
suspected abuse and maltreatment in pregnancy
(O9A.3-, O9A.4-, O9A.5-)
suspected adult physical abuse, ruled out (Z04.71)
suspected adult sexual abuse, ruled out (Z04.41)
suspected child physical abuse, ruled out (Z04.72)
suspected child sexual abuse, ruled out (Z04.42)

The appropriate 7th character is to be added to each code from
category T76

A	initial encounter
D	subsequent encounter
S	sequela

Coding Clinic: 2016, Q4, P129

●**T76.0** **Neglect or abandonment, suspected**

X● **T76.01** **Adult neglect or abandonment, suspected** A

X● **T76.02** **Child neglect or abandonment, suspected** P

●**T76.1** **Physical abuse, suspected**

X● **T76.11** **Adult physical abuse, suspected** A

X● **T76.12** **Child physical abuse, suspected** P
Coding Clinic: 2019, Q2, P12

●**T76.2** **Sexual abuse, suspected**
Rape, suspected
Excludes1 alleged abuse, ruled out (Z04.7)

X● **T76.21** **Adult sexual abuse, suspected** A

X● **T76.22** **Child sexual abuse, suspected** P

●**T76.3** **Psychological abuse, suspected**
Bullying and intimidation, suspected
Intimidation through social media, suspected

X● **T76.31** **Adult psychological abuse, suspected** A

X● **T76.32** **Child psychological abuse, suspected** P

●**T76.5** **Forced sexual exploitation, suspected**

X● **T76.51** **Adult forced sexual exploitation, suspected** P

X● **T76.52** **Child sexual exploitation, suspected** P

●**T76.6** **Forced labor exploitation, suspected**

X● **T76.61** **Adult forced labor exploitation, suspected** P

X● **T76.62** **Child forced labor exploitation, suspected** P

●**T76.9** **Unspecified maltreatment, suspected**

X● **T76.91** **Unspecified adult maltreatment, suspected** A

X● **T76.92** **Unspecified child maltreatment, suspected** P

●**T78** **Adverse effects, not elsewhere classified**
Excludes2 complications of surgical and medical care NEC
(T80-T88)

The appropriate 7th character is to be added to each code from
category T78

A	initial encounter
D	subsequent encounter
S	sequela

●**T78.0** **Anaphylactic reaction due to food**
Anaphylactic reaction due to adverse food reaction
Anaphylactic shock or reaction due to nonpoisonous
foods
Anaphylactoid reaction due to food

X● **T78.00** **Anaphylactic reaction due to unspecified food**

X● **T78.01** **Anaphylactic reaction due to peanuts**

X● **T78.02** **Anaphylactic reaction due to shellfish (crustaceans)**

X● **T78.03** **Anaphylactic reaction due to other fish**

X● **T78.04** **Anaphylactic reaction due to fruits and vegetables**

X● **T78.05** **Anaphylactic reaction due to tree nuts and seeds**
Excludes2 anaphylactic reaction due to
peanuts (T78.01)

X● **T78.06** **Anaphylactic reaction due to food additives**

X● **T78.07** **Anaphylactic reaction due to milk and dairy products**

X● **T78.08** **Anaphylactic reaction due to eggs**

X● **T78.09** **Anaphylactic reaction due to other food products**

X● **T78.1** **Other adverse food reactions, not elsewhere classified**
Use additional code to identify the type of reaction, if
applicable

Excludes1 anaphylactic reaction or shock due to
adverse food reaction (T78.0-)
anaphylactic reaction due to food (T78.0-)
bacterial food borne intoxications (A05.-)

Excludes2 allergic and dietetic gastroenteritis and
colitis (K52.29)
allergic rhinitis due to food (J30.5)
dermatitis due to food in contact with
skin (L23.6, L24.6, L25.4)
dermatitis due to ingested food (L27.2)
food protein-induced enterocolitis
syndrome (K52.21)
food protein-induced enteropathy
(K52.22)

X● **T78.2** **Anaphylactic shock, unspecified**
*Occurs when allergic response triggers large quantities of
histamines, prostaglandins, leukotrienes resulting in
systemic vasodilation*
Allergic shock
Anaphylactic reaction
Anaphylaxis

Excludes1 anaphylactic reaction or shock due to
adverse effect of correct medicinal
substance properly administered
(T88.6)
anaphylactic reaction or shock due to
adverse food reaction (T78.0-)
anaphylactic reaction or shock due to
serum (T80.5-)

X● **T78.3**   **Angioneurotic edema**
    Allergic angioedema
    Giant urticaria
    Vascular disorder resulting from abnormalities of autonomic
      nervous system fibers supplying blood vessels
    Quincke's edema
    Excludes1   serum urticaria (T80.6-)
             urticaria (L50.-)

● **T78.4**   **Other and unspecified allergy**
    Excludes1   specified types of allergic reaction
             such as:
             allergic diarrhea (K52.29)
             allergic gastroenteritis and colitis
               (K52.29)
             dermatitis (L23-L25, L27.-)
             food protein-induced enterocolitis
               syndrome (K52.21)
             food protein-induced enteropathy
               (K52.22)
             hay fever (J30.1)

   X● **T78.40**   **Allergy, unspecified**
         Allergic reaction NOS
         Hypersensitivity NOS

   X● **T78.41**   **Arthus phenomenon**
         Arthus reaction

   X● **T78.49**   **Other allergy**

X● **T78.8**   **Other adverse effects, not elsewhere classified**

CERTAIN EARLY COMPLICATIONS OF TRAUMA (T79)

● **T79**   **Certain early complications of trauma, not elsewhere classified**
    Excludes2   acute respiratory distress syndrome (J80)
             complications occurring during or following
               medical procedures (T80-T88)
             complications of surgical and medical care NEC
               (T80-T88)
             newborn respiratory distress syndrome (P22.0)

   The appropriate 7th character is to be added to each code from
   category T79

> | | |
> |---|---|
> | A | initial encounter |
> | D | subsequent encounter |
> | S | sequela |

X● **T79.0**   **Air embolism (traumatic) A** 🦠
    Excludes1   air embolism complicating abortion
             or ectopic or molar pregnancy
               (O00-O07, O08.2)
             air embolism complicating pregnancy,
               childbirth and the puerperium
               (O88.0)
             air embolism following infusion,
               transfusion, and therapeutic injection
               (T80.0)
             air embolism following procedure NEC
               (T81.7-)

X● **T79.1**   **Fat embolism (traumatic) A** 🦠
    Excludes1   fat embolism complicating:
             abortion or ectopic or molar pregnancy
               (O00-O07, O08.2)
             pregnancy, childbirth and the
               puerperium (O88.8)

X● **T79.2**   **Traumatic secondary and recurrent hemorrhage and**
    seroma A 🦠

X● **T79.4**   **Traumatic shock A** 🦠
    Shock (immediate) (delayed) following injury
    Excludes1   anaphylactic shock due to adverse food
               reaction (T78.0-)
             anaphylactic shock due to correct
               medicinal substance properly
               administered (T88.6)
             anaphylactic shock due to serum (T80.5-)
             anaphylactic shock NOS (T78.2)
             anesthetic shock (T88.2)
             electric shock (T75.4)
             nontraumatic shock NEC (R57.-)
             obstetric shock (O75.1)
             postprocedural shock (T81.1-)
             septic shock (R65.21)
             shock complicating abortion or ectopic or
               molar pregnancy (O00-O07, O08.3)
             shock due to lightning (T75.01)
             shock NOS (R57.9)

X● **T79.5**   **Traumatic anuria A** 🦠
    Crush syndrome
    Renal failure following crushing

X● **T79.6**   **Traumatic ischemia of muscle A** 🦠
    Traumatic rhabdomyolysis
    Volkmann's ischemic contracture
    Excludes2   anterior tibial syndrome (M76.8)
             compartment syndrome (traumatic)
               (T79.A-)
             nontraumatic ischemia of muscle (M62.2-)

X● **T79.7**   **Traumatic subcutaneous emphysema A** 🦠
    ~~**Excludes1**   emphysema NOS (J43)~~
             ~~emphysema (subcutaneous) resulting~~
               ~~from a procedure (T81.82)~~
    ▶ **Excludes2**   emphysema NOS (J43)
             emphysema (subcutaneous) resulting
               from a procedure (T81.82)

● **T79.A**   **Traumatic compartment syndrome**
    Excludes1   fibromyalgia (M79.7)
             nontraumatic compartment syndrome
               (M79.A-)
    Excludes2   traumatic ischemic infarction of muscle
             (T79.6)

   X● **T79.A0**   **Compartment syndrome, unspecified**
         Compartment syndrome NOS

   ● **T79.A1**   **Traumatic compartment syndrome of upper**
         extremity
         Traumatic compartment syndrome of shoulder,
           arm, forearm, wrist, hand, and fingers

     ● **T79.A11**   **Traumatic compartment syndrome of**
           right upper extremity A 🦠

     ● **T79.A12**   **Traumatic compartment syndrome of**
           left upper extremity A 🦠

     ● **T79.A19**   **Traumatic compartment syndrome of**
           unspecified upper extremity A 🦠

   ● **T79.A2**   **Traumatic compartment syndrome of lower**
         extremity
         Traumatic compartment syndrome of hip,
           buttock, thigh, leg, foot, and toes

     ● **T79.A21**   **Traumatic compartment syndrome of**
           right lower extremity A 🦠

     ● **T79.A22**   **Traumatic compartment syndrome of**
           left lower extremity A 🦠

     ● **T79.A29**   **Traumatic compartment syndrome of**
           unspecified lower extremity

   X● **T79.A3**   **Traumatic compartment syndrome of abdomen**
         A 🦠

   X● **T79.A9**   **Traumatic compartment syndrome of other sites**
         A 🦠

X● **T79.8**   **Other early complications of trauma A** 🦠

X● **T79.9**   **Unspecified early complication of trauma A** 🦠

▶ New   ⟹ Revised   ~~deleted~~ Deleted   Excludes 1   Excludes 2   Includes   Use additional   Code first   Code also   Key words

1440   OGCR Official Guidelines   X Assign placeholder X   ● Use Additional Character(s)   ▷ Manifestation Code   🦠 Hierarchical Condition Category   **Coding Clinic**

COMPLICATIONS OF SURGICAL AND MEDICAL CARE NOT ELSEWHERE CLASSIFIED (T80-T88)

Use additional code for adverse effect, if applicable, to identify drug (T36-T50 with fifth or sixth character 5)

Use additional code(s) to identify the specified condition resulting from the complication.

Use additional code to identify devices involved and details of circumstances (Y62-Y82)

Excludes2   any encounters with medical care for
postprocedural conditions in which no
complications are present, such as:
     artificial opening status (Z93.-)
     closure of external stoma (Z43.-)
     fitting and adjustment of external prosthetic
       device (Z44.-)
burns and corrosions from local applications and
     irradiation (T20-T32)
complications of surgical procedures during
     pregnancy, childbirth and the puerperium
     (O00-O9A)
mechanical complication of respirator [ventilator]
     (J95.850)
poisoning and toxic effects of drugs and
     chemicals (T36-T65 with fifth or sixth
     character 1-4 or 6)
postprocedural fever (R50.82)
specified complications classified elsewhere,
     such as:
     cerebrospinal fluid leak from spinal puncture
       (G97.0)
     colostomy malfunction (K94.0-)
     disorders of fluid and electrolyte imbalance
       (E86-E87)
     functional disturbances following cardiac
       surgery (I97.0-I97.1)
     intraoperative and postprocedural
       complications of specified body systems
       (D78.-, E36.-, E89.-, G97.3-, G97.4, H59.3-,
       H59.-, H95.2-, H95.3, I97.4-, I97.5, J95.6-,
       J95.7, K91.6-, L76.-, M96.-, N99.-)
     ostomy complications (J95.0-, K94.-, N99.5-)
     postgastric surgery syndromes (K91.1)
     postlaminectomy syndrome NEC (M96.1)
     postmastectomy lymphedema syndrome
       (I97.2)
     postsurgical blind-loop syndrome (K91.2)
     ventilator associated pneumonia (J95.851)

● **T80**   **Complications following infusion, transfusion and therapeutic injection**

     Includes   complications following perfusion

     Excludes2   bone marrow transplant rejection (T86.01)
       febrile nonhemolytic transfusion reaction (R50.84)
       fluid overload due to transfusion (E87.71)
       posttransfusion purpura (D69.51)
       transfusion associated circulatory overload
         (TACO) (E87.71)
       transfusion (red blood cell) associated
         hemochromatosis (E83.111)
       transfusion related acute lung injury (TRALI)
         (J95.84)

The appropriate 7th character is to be added to each code from category T80

A	initial encounter
D	subsequent encounter
S	sequela

X● **T80.0**   **Air embolism following infusion, transfusion and therapeutic injection**

X● **T80.1**   **Vascular complications** following infusion, transfusion and therapeutic injection

     Use additional code to identify the vascular
     complication

     Excludes2   extravasation of vesicant agent (T80.81-)
       infiltration of vesicant agent (T80.81-)
       vascular complications specified as due
         to prosthetic devices, implants and
         grafts (T82.8- T83.8-, T84.8-, T85.8-)
       postprocedural vascular complications
         (T81.7-)

● **T80.2**   **Infections** following infusion, transfusion and therapeutic injection

     Use additional code to identify the specific infection,
     such as:
       sepsis (A41.9)

     Use additional code (R65.2-) to identify severe sepsis, if
     applicable

     Excludes2   infections specified as due to
       prosthetic devices, implants and
       grafts (T82.6-T82.7, T83.5-T83.6,
       T84.5-T84.7, T85.7)
       postprocedural infections (T81.44)

     Coding Clinic: 2018, Q4, P89

● **T80.21**   **Infection due to central venous catheter**

     Infection due to pulmonary artery catheter
       (Swan-Ganz catheter)

     Coding Clinic: 2019, Q1, P13-14; 2018, Q4, P89

● **T80.211**   **Bloodstream infection due to central venous catheter**

     Catheter-related bloodstream
       infection (CRBSI) NOS
     Central line-associated bloodstream
       infection (CLABSI)
     Bloodstream infection due to
       Hickman catheter
     Bloodstream infection due to
       peripherally inserted central
       catheter (PICC)
     Bloodstream infection due to
       portacath (port-a-cath)
     Bloodstream infection due to
       pulmonary artery catheter
     Bloodstream infection due to triple
       lumen catheter
     Bloodstream infection due to
       umbilical venous catheter

     Coding Clinic: 2018, Q4, P89

● **T80.212**   **Local infection due to central venous catheter**

     Exit or insertion site infection
     Local infection due to Hickman
       catheter
     Local infection due to peripherally
       inserted central catheter (PICC)
     Local infection due to portacath
       (port-a-cath)
     Local infection due to pulmonary
       artery catheter
     Local infection due to triple lumen
       catheter
     Local infection due to umbilical
       venous catheter
     Port or reservoir infection
     Tunnel infection

● **T80.218 Other infection due to central venous catheter**
Other central line-associated infection
Other infection due to Hickman catheter
Other infection due to peripherally inserted central catheter (PICC)
Other infection due to portacath (port-a-cath)
Other infection due to pulmonary artery catheter
Other infection due to triple lumen catheter
Other infection due to umbilical venous catheter

● **T80.219 Unspecified infection due to central venous catheter**
Central line-associated infection NOS
Unspecified infection due to Hickman catheter
Unspecified infection due to peripherally inserted central catheter (PICC)
Unspecified infection due to portacath (port-a-cath)
Unspecified infection due to pulmonary artery catheter
Unspecified infection due to triple lumen catheter
Unspecified infection due to umbilical venous catheter

X● **T80.22 Acute infection following transfusion, infusion, or injection of blood and blood products**

X● **T80.29 Infection following other infusion, transfusion and therapeutic injection**

● **T80.3 ABO incompatibility reaction due to transfusion of blood or blood products**

Excludes1 minor blood group antigens reactions (Duffy) (E) (K) (Kell) (Kidd) (Lewis) (M) (N) (P) (S) (T80.A-)

X● **T80.30 ABO incompatibility reaction due to transfusion of blood or blood products, unspecified**
ABO incompatibility blood transfusion NOS
Reaction to ABO incompatibility from transfusion NOS

● **T80.31 ABO incompatibility with hemolytic transfusion reaction**

● **T80.310 ABO incompatibility with acute hemolytic transfusion reaction**
ABO incompatibility with hemolytic transfusion reaction less than 24 hours after transfusion
Acute hemolytic transfusion reaction (AHTR) due to ABO incompatibility

● **T80.311 ABO incompatibility with delayed hemolytic transfusion reaction**
ABO incompatibility with hemolytic transfusion reaction 24 hours or more after transfusion
Delayed hemolytic transfusion reaction (DHTR) due to ABO incompatibility

● **T80.319 ABO incompatibility with hemolytic transfusion reaction, unspecified**
ABO incompatibility with hemolytic transfusion reaction at unspecified time after transfusion
Hemolytic transfusion reaction (HTR) due to ABO incompatibility NOS

X● **T80.39 Other ABO incompatibility reaction due to transfusion of blood or blood products**
Delayed serologic transfusion reaction (DSTR) from ABO incompatibility
Other ABO incompatible blood transfusion
Other reaction to ABO incompatible blood transfusion

● **T80.4 Rh incompatibility reaction due to transfusion of blood or blood products**
Reaction due to incompatibility of Rh antigens (C) (c) (D) (E) (e)

X● **T80.40 Rh incompatibility reaction due to transfusion of blood or blood products, unspecified**
Reaction due to Rh factor in transfusion NOS
Rh incompatible blood transfusion NOS

● **T80.41 Rh incompatibility with hemolytic transfusion reaction**

● **T80.410 Rh incompatibility with acute hemolytic transfusion reaction**
Acute hemolytic transfusion reaction (AHTR) due to Rh incompatibility
Rh incompatibility with hemolytic transfusion reaction less than 24 hours after transfusion

● **T80.411 Rh incompatibility with delayed hemolytic transfusion reaction**
Delayed hemolytic transfusion reaction (DHTR) due to Rh incompatibility
Rh incompatibility with hemolytic transfusion reaction 24 hours or more after transfusion

● **T80.419 Rh incompatibility with hemolytic transfusion reaction, unspecified**
Rh incompatibility with hemolytic transfusion reaction at unspecified time after transfusion
Hemolytic transfusion reaction (HTR) due to Rh incompatibility NOS

X● **T80.49 Other Rh incompatibility reaction due to transfusion of blood or blood products**
Delayed serologic transfusion reaction (DSTR) from Rh incompatibility
Other reaction to Rh incompatible blood transfusion

● **T80.A Non-ABO incompatibility reaction due to transfusion of blood or blood products**
Reaction due to incompatibility of minor antigens (Duffy) (Kell) (Kidd) (Lewis) (M) (N) (P) (S)

X● **T80.A0 Non-ABO incompatibility reaction due to transfusion of blood or blood products, unspecified**
Non-ABO antigen incompatibility reaction from transfusion NOS

● **T80.A1 Non-ABO incompatibility with hemolytic transfusion reaction**

● **T80.A10 Non-ABO incompatibility with acute hemolytic transfusion reaction**
Acute hemolytic transfusion reaction (AHTR) due to non-ABO incompatibility
Non-ABO incompatibility with hemolytic transfusion reaction less than 24 hours after transfusion

▶ New ⇒ Revised ~~deleted~~ Deleted Excludes 1 Excludes 2 Includes Use additional Code first Code also Key words
OGCR Official Guidelines X Assign placeholder X ● Use Additional Character(s) ▶ Manifestation Code 🅚 Hierarchical Condition Category **Coding Clinic**

● **T80.A11 Non-ABO incompatibility with delayed hemolytic transfusion reaction**
> Delayed hemolytic transfusion reaction (DHTR) due to non-ABO incompatibility
> Non-ABO incompatibility with hemolytic transfusion reaction 24 or more hours after transfusion

● **T80.A19 Non-ABO incompatibility with hemolytic transfusion reaction, unspecified**
> Hemolytic transfusion reaction (HTR) due to non-ABO incompatibility NOS
> Non-ABO incompatibility with hemolytic transfusion reaction at unspecified time after transfusion

X ● **T80.A9 Other non-ABO incompatibility reaction due to transfusion of blood or blood products**
> Delayed serologic transfusion reaction (DSTR) from non-ABO incompatibility
> Other reaction to non-ABO incompatible blood transfusion

● **T80.5 Anaphylactic reaction due to serum**
> Allergic reaction due to serum
> Anaphylactic shock due to serum
> Anaphylactoid reaction due to serum
> Anaphylaxis due to serum

> **Excludes1**   ABO incompatibility reaction due to transfusion of blood or blood products (T80.3-)
> allergic reaction or shock NOS (T78.2)
> anaphylactic reaction or shock NOS (T78.2)
> anaphylactic reaction or shock due to adverse effect of correct medicinal substance properly administered (T88.6)
> other serum reaction (T80.6-)

X ● **T80.51 Anaphylactic reaction due to administration of blood and blood products**

X ● **T80.52 Anaphylactic reaction due to vaccination**

X ● **T80.59 Anaphylactic reaction due to other serum**

● **T80.6 Other serum reactions**
> Intoxication by serum   Serum sickness
> Protein sickness   Serum urticaria
> Serum rash

> **Excludes2**   serum hepatitis (B16-B19)

X ● **T80.61 Other serum reaction due to administration of blood and blood products**

X ● **T80.62 Other serum reaction due to vaccination**

X ● **T80.69 Other serum reaction due to other serum**
> Code also, if applicable, arthropathy in hypersensitivity reactions classified elsewhere (M36.4)

● **T80.8 Other complications following infusion, transfusion and therapeutic injection**

● **T80.81 Extravasation of vesicant agent**
> Infiltration of vesicant agent

● **T80.810 Extravasation of vesicant antineoplastic chemotherapy**
> Infiltration of vesicant antineoplastic chemotherapy

● **T80.818 Extravasation of other vesicant agent**
> Infiltration of other vesicant agent

X ● **T80.89 Other complications following infusion, transfusion and therapeutic injection**
> Delayed serologic transfusion reaction (DSTR), unspecified incompatibility
> Use additional code to identify graft-versus-host reaction, if applicable, (D89.81-)

● **T80.9 Unspecified complication following infusion, transfusion and therapeutic injection**

X ● **T80.90 Unspecified complication following infusion and therapeutic injection**

● **T80.91 Hemolytic transfusion reaction, unspecified incompatibility**

> **Excludes1**   ABO incompatibility with hemolytic transfusion reaction (T80.31-)
> Non-ABO incompatibility with hemolytic transfusion reaction (T80.A1-)
> Rh incompatibility with hemolytic transfusion reaction (T80.41-)

● **T80.910 Acute hemolytic transfusion reaction, unspecified incompatibility**

● **T80.911 Delayed hemolytic transfusion reaction, unspecified incompatibility**

● **T80.919 Hemolytic transfusion reaction, unspecified incompatibility, unspecified as acute or delayed**
> Hemolytic transfusion reaction NOS

X ● **T80.92 Unspecified transfusion reaction**
> Transfusion reaction NOS

● **T81 Complications of procedures, not elsewhere classified**
> Use additional code for adverse effect, if applicable, to identify drug (T36-T50 with fifth or sixth character 5)

> **Excludes2**   complications following immunization (T88.0-T88.1)
> complications following infusion, transfusion and therapeutic injection (T80.-)
> complications of transplanted organs and tissue (T86.-)
> poisoning and toxic effects of drugs and chemicals (T36-T65 with fifth or sixth character 1-4 or 6)
> specified complications classified elsewhere, such as:
>   complication of prosthetic devices, implants and grafts (T82-T85)
>   dermatitis due to drugs and medicaments (L23.3, L24.4, L25.1, L27.0-L27.1)
>   endosseous dental implant failure (M27.6-)
>   floppy iris syndrome (IFIS) (intraoperative) H21.81
>   intraoperative and postprocedural complications of specific body system (D78.-, E36.-, E89.-, G97.3-, G97.4, H59.3-, H59.-, H95.2-, H95.3, I97.4-, I97.5, J95, K91.-, L76.-, M96.-, N99.-)
>   ostomy complications (J95.0-, K94.-, N99.5-)
>   plateau iris syndrome (post-iridectomy) (postprocedural) H21.82

Coding Clinic: 2019, Q2, P21-22; 2016, Q4, P29

The appropriate 7th character is to be added to each code from category T81

> A   initial encounter
> D   subsequent encounter
> S   sequela

● **T81.1 Postprocedural shock**
> Shock during or resulting from a procedure, not elsewhere classified

> **Excludes1**   anaphylactic shock NOS (T78.2)
> anaphylactic shock due to correct substance properly administered (T88.6)
> anaphylactic shock due to serum (T80.5-)
> anesthetic shock (T88.2)
> electric shock (T75.4)
> obstetric shock (O75.1)
> septic shock (R65.21)
> shock following abortion or ectopic or molar pregnancy (O00-O07, O08.3)
> traumatic shock (T79.4)

X ● **T81.10**   **Postprocedural shock unspecified**
  Collapse NOS during or resulting from a
    procedure, not elsewhere classified
  Postprocedural failure of peripheral circulation
  Postprocedural shock NOS

X ● **T81.11**   **Postprocedural cardiogenic shock A** 🏷

X ● **T81.12**   **Postprocedural septic shock A** 🏷
  Postprocedural endotoxic shock resulting from
    a procedure, not elsewhere classified
  Postprocedural gram-negative shock resulting
    from a procedure, not elsewhere classified
  Code first underlying infection
  Use additional code, to identify any associated
    acute organ dysfunction, if applicable

X ● **T81.19**   **Other postprocedural shock**
  Postprocedural hypovolemic shock

● **T81.3**   **Disruption of wound, not elsewhere classified**
  Disruption of any suture materials or other closure
    methods

  Excludes1   breakdown (mechanical) of permanent
    sutures (T85.612)
  displacement of permanent sutures
    (T85.622)
  disruption of cesarean delivery wound
    (O90.0)
  disruption of perineal obstetric wound
    (O90.1)
  mechanical complication of permanent
    sutures NEC (T85.692)

X ● **T81.30**   **Disruption of wound, unspecified**
  Disruption of wound NOS

X ● **T81.31**   **Disruption of external operation (surgical)
    wound, not elsewhere classified**

  Excludes1   dehiscence of amputation stump
    (T87.81)
  Dehiscence of operation wound NOS
  Disruption of operation wound NOS
  Disruption or dehiscence of closure of cornea
  Disruption or dehiscence of closure of mucosa
  Disruption or dehiscence of closure of skin and
    subcutaneous tissue
  Full-thickness skin disruption or dehiscence
  Superficial disruption or dehiscence of
    operation wound
  Coding Clinic: 2015, Q1, P20

X ● **T81.32**   **Disruption of internal operation (surgical)
    wound, not elsewhere classified**
  Deep disruption or dehiscence of operation
    wound NOS
  Disruption or dehiscence of closure of internal
    organ or other internal tissue
  Disruption or dehiscence of closure of muscle
    or muscle flap
  Disruption or dehiscence of closure of ribs or
    rib cage
  Disruption or dehiscence of closure of skull or
    craniotomy
  Disruption or dehiscence of closure of sternum
    or sternotomy
  Disruption or dehiscence of closure of tendon
    or ligament
  Disruption or dehiscence of closure of
    superficial or muscular fascia
  Coding Clinic: 2017, Q3, P4

X ● **T81.33**   **Disruption of traumatic injury wound repair**
  Disruption or dehiscence of closure of
    traumatic laceration (external) (internal)

● **T81.4**   **Infection following a procedure**
  Use additional code to identify infection
  Use additional code (R65.2-) to identify severe sepsis, if
    applicable

  Excludes2   bleb associated endophthalmitis (H59.4-)
  infection due to infusion, transfusion and
    therapeutic injection (T80.2-)
  infection due to prosthetic devices,
    implants and grafts (T82.6-T82.7,
    T83.5-T83.6, T84.5-T84.7, T85.7)
  obstetric surgical wound infection
    (O86.0-)
  postprocedural fever NOS (R50.82)
  postprocedural retroperitoneal abscess
    (K68.11)

X ● **T81.40**   **Infection following a procedure, unspecified**

X ● **T81.41**   **Infection following a procedure, superficial
    incisional surgical site**
  Subcutaneous abscess following a procedure
  Stitch abscess following a procedure
  Coding Clinic: 2018, Q4, P34

X ● **T81.42**   **Infection following a procedure, deep
    incisional surgical site**
  Intra-muscular abscess following a procedure

X ● **T81.43**   **Infection following a procedure, organ and
    space surgical site**
  Intra-abdominal abscess following a procedure
  Subphrenic abscess following a procedure

X ● **T81.44**   **Sepsis following a procedure A** 🏷
  Use additional code to identify the sepsis

X ● **T81.49**   **Infection following a procedure, other surgical
    site**
  Coding Clinic: 2015, Q4, P37

● **T81.5**   **Complications of foreign body accidentally left in body
    following procedure**

● **T81.50**   **Unspecified complication of foreign body
    accidentally left in body following procedure**

  ● **T81.500**   Unspecified complication of foreign
    body accidentally left in body
    following surgical operation

  ● **T81.501**   Unspecified complication of foreign
    body accidentally left in body
    following infusion or transfusion

  ● **T81.502**   Unspecified complication of foreign
    body accidentally left in body
    following kidney dialysis A, D, S 🏷

  ● **T81.503**   Unspecified complication of foreign
    body accidentally left in body
    following injection or immunization

  ● **T81.504**   Unspecified complication of foreign
    body accidentally left in body
    following endoscopic examination

  ● **T81.505**   Unspecified complication of foreign
    body accidentally left in body
    following heart catheterization

  ● **T81.506**   Unspecified complication of foreign
    body accidentally left in body
    following aspiration, puncture or
    other catheterization

  ● **T81.507**   Unspecified complication of foreign
    body accidentally left in body
    following removal of catheter or
    packing

  ● **T81.508**   Unspecified complication of foreign
    body accidentally left in body
    following other procedure

  ● **T81.509**   Unspecified complication of foreign
    body accidentally left in body
    following unspecified procedure

▶ New   ⟹ Revised   ~~deleted~~ Deleted   Excludes 1   Excludes 2   Includes   Use additional   Code first   Code also   Key words
OGCR Official Guidelines   X Assign placeholder X   ● Use Additional Character(s)   ▷ Manifestation Code   🏷 Hierarchical Condition Category   **Coding Clinic**

● T81.51   **Adhesions** due to foreign body accidentally left in body following procedure

     ● T81.510   Adhesions due to foreign body accidentally left in body following **surgical operation**

     ● T81.511   Adhesions due to foreign body accidentally left in body following **infusion or transfusion**

     ● T81.512   Adhesions due to foreign body accidentally left in body following **kidney dialysis** A, D, S 🔟

     ● T81.513   Adhesions due to foreign body accidentally left in body following **injection or immunization**

     ● T81.514   Adhesions due to foreign body accidentally left in body following **endoscopic examination**

     ● T81.515   Adhesions due to foreign body accidentally left in body following **heart catheterization**

     ● T81.516   Adhesions due to foreign body accidentally left in body following **aspiration, puncture or other catheterization**

     ● T81.517   Adhesions due to foreign body accidentally left in body following **removal of catheter or packing**

     ● T81.518   Adhesions due to foreign body accidentally left in body following **other procedure**

     ● T81.519   Adhesions due to foreign body accidentally left in body following **unspecified** procedure

● T81.52   **Obstruction** due to foreign body accidentally left in body following procedure

     ● T81.520   Obstruction due to foreign body accidentally left in body following **surgical operation**

     ● T81.521   Obstruction due to foreign body accidentally left in body following **infusion or transfusion**

     ● T81.522   Obstruction due to foreign body accidentally left in body following **kidney dialysis** A, D, S 🔟

     ● T81.523   Obstruction due to foreign body accidentally left in body following **injection or immunization**

     ● T81.524   Obstruction due to foreign body accidentally left in body following **endoscopic examination**

     ● T81.525   Obstruction due to foreign body accidentally left in body following **heart catheterization**

     ● T81.526   Obstruction due to foreign body accidentally left in body following **aspiration, puncture or other catheterization**

     ● T81.527   Obstruction due to foreign body accidentally left in body following **removal of catheter or packing**

     ● T81.528   Obstruction due to foreign body accidentally left in body following **other procedure**

     ● T81.529   Obstruction due to foreign body accidentally left in body following **unspecified procedure**

● T81.53   **Perforation** due to foreign body accidentally left in body following procedure

     ● T81.530   Perforation due to foreign body accidentally left in body following **surgical operation**

     ● T81.531   Perforation due to foreign body accidentally left in body following **infusion or transfusion**

     ● T81.532   Perforation due to foreign body accidentally left in body following **kidney dialysis** A, D, S 🔟

     ● T81.533   Perforation due to foreign body accidentally left in body following **injection or immunization**

     ● T81.534   Perforation due to foreign body accidentally left in body following **endoscopic examination**

     ● T81.535   Perforation due to foreign body accidentally left in body following **heart catheterization**

     ● T81.536   Perforation due to foreign body accidentally left in body following **aspiration, puncture or other catheterization**

     ● T81.537   Perforation due to foreign body accidentally left in body following **removal of catheter or packing**

     ● T81.538   Perforation due to foreign body accidentally left in body following **other procedure**

     ● T81.539   Perforation due to foreign body accidentally left in body following **unspecified procedure**

● T81.59   **Other complications** of foreign body accidentally left in body following procedure

     Excludes2   obstruction or perforation due to prosthetic devices and implants intentionally left in body (T82.0-T82.5, T83.0-T83.4, T83.7, T84.0-T84.4, T85.0-T85.6)

     ● T81.590   Other complications of foreign body accidentally left in body following **surgical operation**

     ● T81.591   Other complications of foreign body accidentally left in body following **infusion or transfusion**

     ● T81.592   Other complications of foreign body accidentally left in body following **kidney dialysis** A, D, S 🔟

     ● T81.593   Other complications of foreign body accidentally left in body following **injection or immunization**

     ● T81.594   Other complications of foreign body accidentally left in body following **endoscopic examination**

     ● T81.595   Other complications of foreign body accidentally left in body following **heart catheterization**

     ● T81.596   Other complications of foreign body accidentally left in body following **aspiration, puncture or other catheterization**

     ● T81.597   Other complications of foreign body accidentally left in body following **removal of catheter or packing**

     ● T81.598   Other complications of foreign body accidentally left in body following **other procedure**

     ● T81.599   Other complications of foreign body accidentally left in body following **unspecified** procedure

● **T81.6**   **Acute reaction to foreign substance accidentally left during a procedure**

     Excludes2   complications of foreign body accidentally left in body cavity or operation wound following procedure (T81.5-)

X● **T81.60**   **Unspecified acute reaction to foreign substance accidentally left during a procedure**

X● **T81.61**   **Aseptic peritonitis due to foreign substance accidentally left during a procedure**

         Chemical peritonitis

X● **T81.69**   **Other acute reaction to foreign substance accidentally left during a procedure**

● **T81.7**   **Vascular complications following a procedure, not elsewhere classified**

     Air embolism following procedure NEC

     Phlebitis or thrombophlebitis resulting from a procedure

     Excludes1   embolism complicating abortion or ectopic or molar pregnancy (O00-O07, O08.2)

                   embolism complicating pregnancy, childbirth and the puerperium (O88.-)

                   traumatic embolism (T79.0)

     Excludes2   embolism due to prosthetic devices, implants and grafts (T82.8, T83.81, T84.8-, T85.1-)

                   embolism following infusion, transfusion and therapeutic injection (T80.0)

     Coding Clinic: 2019, Q2, P23

● **T81.71**   **Complication of artery following a procedure, not elsewhere classified**

     Coding Clinic: 2019, Q2, P22

     ● **T81.710**   **Complication of mesenteric artery following a procedure, not elsewhere classified**

     ● **T81.711**   **Complication of renal artery following a procedure, not elsewhere classified**

     ● **T81.718**   **Complication of other artery following a procedure, not elsewhere classified**

         Coding Clinic: 2019, Q2, P22-23

     ● **T81.719**   **Complication of unspecified artery following a procedure, not elsewhere classified**

X● **T81.72**   **Complication of vein following a procedure, not elsewhere classified**

     Coding Clinic: 2019, Q2, P22

● **T81.8**   **Other complications of procedures, not elsewhere classified**

     Excludes2   hypothermia following anesthesia (T88.51)

                   malignant hyperpyrexia due to anesthesia (T88.3)

X● **T81.81**   **Complication of inhalation therapy**

X● **T81.82**   **Emphysema (subcutaneous) resulting from a procedure**

X● **T81.83**   **Persistent postprocedural fistula**

     Coding Clinic: 2017, Q3, P3-5

X● **T81.89**   **Other complications of procedures, not elsewhere classified**

     Use additional code to specify complication, such as:

         postprocedural delirium (F05)

X● **T81.9**   **Unspecified complication of procedure**

● **T82**   **Complications of cardiac and vascular prosthetic devices, implants and grafts**

     Excludes2   failure and rejection of transplanted organs and tissue (T86.-)

     The appropriate 7th character is to be added to each code from category T82

A	initial encounter
D	subsequent encounter
S	sequela

● **T82.0**   **Mechanical complication of heart valve prosthesis**

     Mechanical complication of artificial heart valve

     Excludes1   mechanical complication of biological heart valve graft (T82.22-)

X● **T82.01**   **Breakdown (mechanical) of heart valve prosthesis**

X● **T82.02**   **Displacement of heart valve prosthesis**

     Malposition of heart valve prosthesis

X● **T82.03**   **Leakage of heart valve prosthesis**

X● **T82.09**   **Other mechanical complication of heart valve prosthesis**

     Obstruction (mechanical) of heart valve prosthesis

     Perforation of heart valve prosthesis

     Protrusion of heart valve prosthesis

● **T82.1**   **Mechanical complication of cardiac electronic device**

     ● **T82.11**   **Breakdown (mechanical) of cardiac electronic device**

         ● **T82.110**   **Breakdown (mechanical) of cardiac electrode**

         ● **T82.111**   **Breakdown (mechanical) of cardiac pulse generator (battery)**

         ● **T82.118**   **Breakdown (mechanical) of other cardiac electronic device**

         ● **T82.119**   **Breakdown (mechanical) of unspecified cardiac electronic device**

     ● **T82.12**   **Displacement of cardiac electronic device**

         Malposition of cardiac electronic device

         ● **T82.120**   **Displacement of cardiac electrode**

         ● **T82.121**   **Displacement of cardiac pulse generator (battery)**

         ● **T82.128**   **Displacement of other cardiac electronic device**

         ● **T82.129**   **Displacement of unspecified cardiac electronic device**

     ● **T82.19**   **Other mechanical complication of cardiac electronic device**

         Leakage of cardiac electronic device

         Obstruction of cardiac electronic device

         Perforation of cardiac electronic device

         Protrusion of cardiac electronic device

         ● **T82.190**   **Other mechanical complication of cardiac electrode**

         ● **T82.191**   **Other mechanical complication of cardiac pulse generator (battery)**

         ● **T82.198**   **Other mechanical complication of other cardiac electronic device**

         ● **T82.199**   **Other mechanical complication of unspecified cardiac device**

● **T82.2**   **Mechanical complication of coronary artery bypass graft and biological heart valve graft**

     Excludes1   mechanical complication of artificial heart valve prosthesis (T82.0-)

     ● **T82.21**   **Mechanical complication of coronary artery bypass graft**

         ● **T82.211**   **Breakdown (mechanical) of coronary artery bypass graft**

         ● **T82.212**   **Displacement of coronary artery bypass graft**

             Malposition of coronary artery bypass graft

▶ New   ⇒ Revised   ~~deleted~~ Deleted   Excludes 1   Excludes 2   Includes   Use additional   Code first   Code also   Key words

OGCR Official Guidelines   X Assign placeholder X   ● Use Additional Character(s)   ▶ Manifestation Code   Hierarchical Condition Category   **Coding Clinic**

● **T82.213**   Leakage of coronary artery bypass graft

● **T82.218**   Other mechanical complication of coronary artery bypass graft
     Obstruction, mechanical of coronary artery bypass graft
     Perforation of coronary artery bypass graft
     Protrusion of coronary artery bypass graft

● **T82.22**   Mechanical complication of biological heart valve graft

   ● **T82.221**   Breakdown (mechanical) of biological heart valve graft

   ● **T82.222**   Displacement of biological heart valve graft
      Malposition of biological heart valve graft

   ● **T82.223**   Leakage of biological heart valve graft

   ● **T82.228**   Other mechanical complication of biological heart valve graft
      Obstruction of biological heart valve graft
      Perforation of biological heart valve graft
      Protrusion of biological heart valve graft

● **T82.3**   Mechanical complication of other vascular grafts

 ● **T82.31**   Breakdown (mechanical) of other vascular grafts

   ● **T82.310**   Breakdown (mechanical) of aortic (bifurcation) graft (replacement) A 🐛

   ● **T82.311**   Breakdown (mechanical) of carotid arterial graft (bypass) A 🐛

   ● **T82.312**   Breakdown (mechanical) of femoral arterial graft (bypass) A 🐛

   ● **T82.318**   Breakdown (mechanical) of other vascular grafts A 🐛

   ● **T82.319**   Breakdown (mechanical) of unspecified vascular grafts A 🐛

 ● **T82.32**   Displacement of other vascular grafts
    Malposition of other vascular grafts

   ● **T82.320**   Displacement of aortic (bifurcation) graft (replacement) A 🐛

   ● **T82.321**   Displacement of carotid arterial graft (bypass) A 🐛

   ● **T82.322**   Displacement of femoral arterial graft (bypass) A 🐛

   ● **T82.328**   Displacement of other vascular grafts A 🐛

   ● **T82.329**   Displacement of unspecified vascular grafts A 🐛

 ● **T82.33**   Leakage of other vascular grafts

   ● **T82.330**   Leakage of aortic (bifurcation) graft (replacement) A 🐛

   ● **T82.331**   Leakage of carotid arterial graft (bypass) A 🐛

   ● **T82.332**   Leakage of femoral arterial graft (bypass) A 🐛

   ● **T82.338**   Leakage of other vascular grafts A 🐛

   ● **T82.339**   Leakage of unspecified vascular graft A 🐛

 ● **T82.39**   Other mechanical complication of other vascular grafts
    Obstruction (mechanical) of other vascular grafts
    Perforation of other vascular grafts
    Protrusion of other vascular grafts

   ● **T82.390**   Other mechanical complication of aortic (bifurcation) graft (replacement) A 🐛

   ● **T82.391**   Other mechanical complication of carotid arterial graft (bypass) A 🐛

   ● **T82.392**   Other mechanical complication of femoral arterial graft (bypass) A 🐛

   ● **T82.398**   Other mechanical complication of other vascular grafts A 🐛

   ● **T82.399**   Other mechanical complication of unspecified vascular grafts A 🐛

● **T82.4**   Mechanical complication of vascular dialysis catheter
   Mechanical complication of hemodialysis catheter

   Excludes1   mechanical complication of intraperitoneal dialysis catheter (T85.62)

X● **T82.41**   Breakdown (mechanical) of vascular dialysis catheter A, D, S 🐛

X● **T82.42**   Displacement of vascular dialysis catheter A, D, S 🐛
     Malposition of vascular dialysis catheter

X● **T82.43**   Leakage of vascular dialysis catheter A, D, S 🐛

X● **T82.49**   Other complication of vascular dialysis catheter A, D, S 🐛
     Obstruction (mechanical) of vascular dialysis catheter
     Perforation of vascular dialysis catheter
     Protrusion of vascular dialysis catheter

● **T82.5**   Mechanical complication of other cardiac and vascular devices and implants

   Excludes2   mechanical complication of epidural and subdural infusion catheter (T85.61)

 ● **T82.51**   Breakdown (mechanical) of other cardiac and vascular devices and implants

   ● **T82.510**   Breakdown (mechanical) of surgically created arteriovenous fistula A 🐛

   ● **T82.511**   Breakdown (mechanical) of surgically created arteriovenous shunt A 🐛

   ● **T82.512**   Breakdown (mechanical) of artificial heart

   ● **T82.513**   Breakdown (mechanical) of balloon (counterpulsation) device A 🐛

   ● **T82.514**   Breakdown (mechanical) of infusion catheter A 🐛

   ● **T82.515**   Breakdown (mechanical) of umbrella device A 🐛

   ● **T82.518**   Breakdown (mechanical) of other cardiac and vascular devices and implants A 🐛

   ● **T82.519**   Breakdown (mechanical) of unspecified cardiac and vascular devices and implants

 ● **T82.52**   Displacement of other cardiac and vascular devices and implants
    Malposition of other cardiac and vascular devices and implants

   ● **T82.520**   Displacement of surgically created arteriovenous fistula A 🐛

   ● **T82.521**   Displacement of surgically created arteriovenous shunt A 🐛

   ● **T82.522**   Displacement of artificial heart

   ● **T82.523**   Displacement of balloon (counterpulsation) device A 🐛

   ● **T82.524**   Displacement of infusion catheter A 🐛
      Coding Clinic: 2019, Q3, P15

   ● **T82.525**   Displacement of umbrella device A 🐛

   ● **T82.528**   Displacement of other cardiac and vascular devices and implants A 🐛

   ● **T82.529**   Displacement of unspecified cardiac and vascular devices and implants

● T82.53 **Leakage** of other cardiac and vascular devices and implants
- ● T82.530 Leakage of surgically created arteriovenous fistula A 🐾
- ● T82.531 Leakage of surgically created arteriovenous shunt A 🐾
- ● T82.532 Leakage of artificial heart
- ● T82.533 Leakage of balloon (counterpulsation) device A 🐾
- ● T82.534 Leakage of infusion catheter A 🐾
- ● T82.535 Leakage of umbrella device A 🐾
- ● T82.538 Leakage of other cardiac and vascular devices and implants A 🐾
- ● T82.539 Leakage of unspecified cardiac and vascular devices and implants

● T82.59 **Other mechanical complication** of other cardiac and vascular devices and implants
Obstruction (mechanical) of other cardiac and vascular devices and implants
Perforation of other cardiac and vascular devices and implants
Protrusion of other cardiac and vascular devices and implants
- ● T82.590 Other mechanical complication of surgically created arteriovenous fistula A 🐾
- ● T82.591 Other mechanical complication of surgically created arteriovenous shunt A 🐾
- ● T82.592 Other mechanical complication of artificial heart
- ● T82.593 Other mechanical complication of balloon (counterpulsation) device A 🐾
- ● T82.594 Other mechanical complication of infusion catheter A 🐾
- ● T82.595 Other mechanical complication of umbrella device A 🐾
- ● T82.598 Other mechanical complication of other cardiac and vascular devices and implants A 🐾
- ● T82.599 Other mechanical complication of unspecified cardiac and vascular devices and implants

X ● T82.6 **Infection** and inflammatory reaction due to cardiac valve prosthesis A 🐾
Use additional code to identify infection

X ● T82.7 **Infection** and inflammatory reaction due to other cardiac and vascular devices, implants and grafts A 🐾
Use additional code to identify infection
Coding Clinic: 2019, Q1, P13-14; 2018, Q4, P89

● T82.8 **Other specified complications** of cardiac and vascular prosthetic devices, implants and grafts
- ● T82.81 **Embolism** due to cardiac and vascular prosthetic devices, implants and grafts
  Coding Clinic: 2016, Q4, P70
  - ● T82.817 Embolism due to cardiac prosthetic devices, implants and grafts
    Coding Clinic: 2016, Q4, P70; 2015, Q1, P20
  - ● T82.818 Embolism due to vascular prosthetic devices, implants and grafts A 🐾
- ● T82.82 **Fibrosis** due to cardiac and vascular prosthetic devices, implants and grafts
  Coding Clinic: 2016, Q4, P70
  - ● T82.827 Fibrosis due to cardiac prosthetic devices, implants and grafts
  - ● T82.828 Fibrosis due to vascular prosthetic devices, implants and grafts A 🐾

● T82.83 **Hemorrhage** due to cardiac and vascular prosthetic devices, implants and grafts
Coding Clinic: 2016, Q4, P70
- ● T82.837 Hemorrhage due to cardiac prosthetic devices, implants and grafts
- ● T82.838 Hemorrhage due to vascular prosthetic devices, implants and grafts A 🐾

● T82.84 **Pain** due to cardiac and vascular prosthetic devices, implants and grafts
Coding Clinic: 2016, Q4, P70
- ● T82.847 Pain due to cardiac prosthetic devices, implants and grafts
- ● T82.848 Pain due to vascular prosthetic devices, implants and grafts A 🐾

● T82.85 **Stenosis** due to cardiac and vascular prosthetic devices, implants and grafts
- ● T82.855 Stenosis of coronary artery stent
  In-stent stenosis (restenosis) of coronary artery stent
  Restenosis of coronary artery stent
  Coding Clinic: 2016, Q4, P70
- ● T82.856 Stenosis of peripheral vascular stent A 🐾
  In-stent stenosis (restenosis) of peripheral vascular stent
  Restenosis of peripheral vascular stent
  Coding Clinic: 2016, Q4, P70
- ● T82.857 Stenosis of other cardiac prosthetic devices, implants and grafts
  Coding Clinic: 2016, Q4, P70
- ● T82.858 Stenosis of other vascular prosthetic devices, implants and grafts A 🐾
  Coding Clinic: 2016, Q4, P70

● T82.86 **Thrombosis** of cardiac and vascular prosthetic devices, implants and grafts
- ● T82.867 Thrombosis due to cardiac prosthetic devices, implants and grafts
- ● T82.868 Thrombosis due to vascular prosthetic devices, implants and grafts A 🐾

● T82.89 **Other specified complication** of cardiac and vascular prosthetic devices, implants and grafts
- ● T82.897 Other specified complication of cardiac prosthetic devices, implants and grafts
  Coding Clinic: 2019, Q2, P32-33
- ● T82.898 Other specified complication of vascular prosthetic devices, implants and grafts A 🐾

X ● T82.9 **Unspecified complication** of cardiac and vascular prosthetic device, implant and graft

● T83 **Complications of genitourinary prosthetic devices, implants and grafts**
Excludes2 failure and rejection of transplanted organs and tissue (T86.-)

The appropriate 7th character is to be added to each code from category T83

A	initial encounter
D	subsequent encounter
S	sequela

Coding Clinic: 2016, Q4, P70-71

● T83.0 **Mechanical complication** of urinary catheter
Excludes2 complications of stoma of urinary tract (N99.5-)
Coding Clinic: 2016, Q4, P70
- ● T83.01 **Breakdown (mechanical)** of urinary catheter
  - ● T83.010 Breakdown (mechanical) of cystostomy catheter A 🐾
  - ● T83.011 Breakdown (mechanical) of indwelling urethral catheter A 🐾

▶ New ⇒ Revised ~~deleted~~ Deleted | Excludes 1 | Excludes 2 | Includes | Use additional | Code first | Code also | Key words
OGCR Official Guidelines X Assign placeholder X ● Use Additional Character(s) ▸ Manifestation Code 🐾 Hierarchical Condition Category **Coding Clinic**

● **T83.012** Breakdown (mechanical) of nephrostomy catheter A 🐾

● **T83.018** Breakdown (mechanical) of other urinary catheter A 🐾
Breakdown (mechanical) of Hopkins catheter
Breakdown (mechanical) of ileostomy catheter
Breakdown (mechanical) urostomy catheter

● **T83.02** Displacement of urinary catheter
Malposition of urinary catheter

● **T83.020** Displacement of cystostomy catheter A 🐾

● **T83.021** Displacement of indwelling urethral catheter A 🐾

● **T83.022** Displacement of nephrostomy catheter A 🐾

● **T83.028** Displacement of other urinary catheter A 🐾
Displacement of Hopkins catheter
Displacement of ileostomy catheter
Displacement of urostomy catheter

● **T83.03** Leakage of urinary catheter

● **T83.030** Leakage of cystostomy catheter A 🐾

● **T83.031** Leakage of indwelling urethral catheter A 🐾

● **T83.032** Leakage of nephrostomy catheter A 🐾

● **T83.038** Leakage of other urinary catheter A 🐾
Leakage of Hopkins catheter
Leakage of ileostomy catheter
Leakage of urostomy catheter

● **T83.09** Other mechanical complication of urinary catheter
Obstruction (mechanical) of urinary catheter
Perforation of urinary catheter
Protrusion of urinary catheter

● **T83.090** Other mechanical complication of cystostomy catheter A 🐾

● **T83.091** Other mechanical complication of indwelling urethral catheter A 🐾

● **T83.092** Other mechanical complication of nephrostomy catheter A 🐾

● **T83.098** Other mechanical complication of other urinary catheter A 🐾
Other mechanical complication of Hopkins catheter
Other mechanical complication of ileostomy catheter
Other mechanical complication of urostomy catheter

● **T83.1** Mechanical complication of other urinary devices and implants
Coding Clinic: 2016, Q4, P70

● **T83.11** Breakdown (mechanical) of other urinary devices and implants

● **T83.110** Breakdown (mechanical) of urinary electronic stimulator device A 🐾
Excludes2 Breakdown (mechanical) of electrode (lead) for sacral nerve neurostimulator (T85.111)
Breakdown (mechanical) of implanted electronic sacral neurostimulator, pulse generator or receiver (T85.113)

● **T83.111** Breakdown (mechanical) of implanted urinary sphincter A 🐾

● **T83.112** Breakdown (mechanical) of indwelling ureteral stent A 🐾

● **T83.113** Breakdown (mechanical) of other urinary stents A 🐾
Breakdown (mechanical) of ileal conduit stent
Breakdown (mechanical) of nephroureteral stent

● **T83.118** Breakdown (mechanical) of other urinary devices and implants A 🐾

● **T83.12** Displacement of other urinary devices and implants
Malposition of other urinary devices and implants

● **T83.120** Displacement of urinary electronic stimulator device A 🐾
Excludes2 Displacement of electrode (lead) for sacral nerve neurostimulator (T85.121)
Displacement of implanted electronic sacral neurostimulator, pulse generator or receiver (T85.123)

● **T83.121** Displacement of implanted urinary sphincter A 🐾

● **T83.122** Displacement of indwelling ureteral stent A 🐾

● **T83.123** Displacement of other urinary stents A 🐾
Displacement of ileal conduit stent
Displacement of nephroureteral stent

● **T83.128** Displacement of other urinary devices and implants A 🐾

● **T83.19** Other mechanical complication of other urinary devices and implants
Leakage of other urinary devices and implants
Obstruction (mechanical) of other urinary devices and implants
Perforation of other urinary devices and implants
Protrusion of other urinary devices and implants

● **T83.190** Other mechanical complication of urinary electronic stimulator device A 🐾
Excludes2 Other mechanical complication of electrode (lead) for sacral nerve neurostimulator (T85.191)
Other mechanical complication of implanted electronic sacral neurostimulator, pulse generator or receiver (T85.193)

● **T83.191** Other mechanical complication of implanted urinary sphincter A 🐾

● **T83.192** Other mechanical complication of indwelling ureteral stent A 🐾

● T83.193 Other mechanical complication of
          other urinary stent A 🦠
          Other mechanical complication of
              ileal conduit stent
          Other mechanical complication of
              nephroureteral stent
      ● T83.198 Other mechanical complication of
                other urinary devices and implants
                A 🦠
● T83.2 Mechanical complication of graft of urinary organ
          Coding Clinic: 2016, Q4, P70
      X● T83.21 Breakdown (mechanical) of graft of urinary
                organ A 🦠
      X● T83.22 Displacement of graft of urinary organ A 🦠
                Malposition of graft of urinary organ
      X● T83.23 Leakage of graft of urinary organ A 🦠
      X● T83.24 Erosion of graft of urinary organ A 🦠
                Coding Clinic: 2016, Q4, P70
      X● T83.25 Exposure of graft of urinary organ A 🦠
                Coding Clinic: 2016, Q4, P70
      X● T83.29 Other mechanical complication of graft of
                urinary organ A 🦠
                Obstruction (mechanical) of graft of urinary
                    organ
                Perforation of graft of urinary organ
                Protrusion of graft of urinary organ
● T83.3 Mechanical complication of intrauterine contraceptive
        device
      X● T83.31 Breakdown (mechanical) of intrauterine
                contraceptive device ♀
      X● T83.32 Displacement of intrauterine contraceptive
                device ♀
                Malposition of intrauterine contraceptive
                    device
                Missing string of intrauterine contraceptive
                    device
      X● T83.39 Other mechanical complication of intrauterine
                contraceptive device ♀
                Leakage of intrauterine contraceptive device
                Obstruction (mechanical) of intrauterine
                    contraceptive device
                Perforation of intrauterine contraceptive
                    device
                Protrusion of intrauterine contraceptive device
● T83.4 Mechanical complication of other prosthetic devices,
        implants and grafts of genital tract
        Coding Clinic: 2016, Q4, P71
      ● T83.41 Breakdown (mechanical) of other prosthetic
                devices, implants and grafts of genital tract
              ● T83.410 Breakdown (mechanical) of
                        implanted penile prosthesis ♂ A 🦠
                        Breakdown (mechanical) of penile
                            prosthesis cylinder
                        Breakdown (mechanical) of penile
                            prosthesis pump
                        Breakdown (mechanical) of penile
                            prosthesis reservoir
              ● T83.411 Breakdown (mechanical) of
                        implanted testicular prosthesis A 🦠
              ● T83.418 Breakdown (mechanical) of other
                        prosthetic devices, implants and
                        grafts of genital tract A 🦠

● T83.42 Displacement of other prosthetic devices,
        implants and grafts of genital tract
        Malposition of other prosthetic devices,
            implants and grafts of genital tract
      ● T83.420 Displacement of implanted penile
                prosthesis ♂ A 🦠
                Displacement of penile prosthesis
                    cylinder
                Displacement of penile prosthesis
                    pump
                Displacement of penile prosthesis
                    reservoir
      ● T83.421 Displacement of implanted testicular
                prosthesis A 🦠
      ● T83.428 Displacement of other prosthetic
                devices, implants and grafts of genital
                tract A 🦠
                Coding Clinic: 2018, Q1, P6
● T83.49 Other mechanical complication of other
        prosthetic devices, implants and grafts of
        genital tract
        Leakage of other prosthetic devices, implants
            and grafts of genital tract
        Obstruction, mechanical of other prosthetic
            devices, implants and grafts of genital
            tract
        Perforation of other prosthetic devices,
            implants and grafts of genital tract
        Protrusion of other prosthetic devices,
            implants and grafts of genital tract
      ● T83.490 Other mechanical complication of
                implanted penile prosthesis ♂ A 🦠
                Other mechanical complication of
                    penile prosthesis cylinder
                Other mechanical complication of
                    penile prosthesis pump
                Other mechanical complication of
                    penile prosthesis reservoir
      ● T83.491 Other mechanical complication of
                implanted testicular prosthesis A 🦠
      ● T83.498 Other mechanical complication of
                other prosthetic devices, implants and
                grafts of genital tract A 🦠
● T83.5 Infection and inflammatory reaction due to prosthetic
        device, implant and graft in urinary system
        Use additional code to identify infection
        Coding Clinic: 2016, Q4, P71
      ● T83.51 Infection and inflammatory reaction due to
                urinary catheter
              Excludes2 complications of stoma of
                            urinary tract (N99.5-)
              ● T83.510 Infection and inflammatory reaction
                        due to cystostomy catheter A 🦠
              ● T83.511 Infection and inflammatory
                        reaction due to indwelling
                        urethral catheter A 🦠
              ● T83.512 Infection and inflammatory
                        reaction due to nephrostomy
                        catheter A 🦠
              ● T83.518 Infection and inflammatory
                        reaction due to other urinary
                        catheter A 🦠
                        Infection and inflammatory reaction
                            due to Hopkins catheter
                        Infection and inflammatory reaction
                            due to ileostomy catheter
                        Infection and inflammatory reaction
                            due to urostomy catheter

▶ New   ⇒ Revised   deleted Deleted   Excludes 1   Excludes 2   Includes   Use additional   Code first   Code also   Key words
OGCR Official Guidelines   X Assign placeholder X   ● Use Additional Character(s)   ▶ Manifestation Code   🦠 Hierarchical Condition Category   Coding Clinic

● **T83.59**   **Infection and inflammatory reaction due to prosthetic device, implant and graft in urinary system**

  ● **T83.590**   **Infection and inflammatory reaction due to implanted urinary neurostimulation device A** 🔖

     Excludes2   Infection and inflammatory reaction due to electrode lead of sacral nerve neurostimulator (T85.732)

                 Infection and inflammatory reaction due to pulse generator or receiver of sacral nerve neurostimulator (T85.734)

  ● **T83.591**   **Infection and inflammatory reaction due to implanted urinary sphincter A** 🔖

  ● **T83.592**   **Infection and inflammatory reaction due to indwelling ureteral stent A** 🔖

  ● **T83.593**   **Infection and inflammatory reaction due to other urinary stents A** 🔖

      Infection and inflammatory reaction due to ileal conduit stents

      Infection and inflammatory reaction due to nephroureteral stent

  ● **T83.598**   **Infection and inflammatory reaction due to other prosthetic device, implant and graft in urinary system A** 🔖

● **T83.6**   **Infection and inflammatory reaction due to prosthetic device, implant and graft in genital tract**

  Use additional code to identify infection

  Coding Clinic: 2016, Q4, P71

  ● **T83.61**   **Infection and inflammatory reaction due to implanted penile prosthesis A** 🔖

      Infection and inflammatory reaction due to penile prosthesis cylinder

      Infection and inflammatory reaction due to penile prosthesis pump

      Infection and inflammatory reaction due to penile prosthesis reservoir

  ● **T83.62**   **Infection and inflammatory reaction due to implanted testicular prosthesis A** 🔖

  ● **T83.69**   **Infection and inflammatory reaction due to other prosthetic device, implant and graft in genital tract A** 🔖

● **T83.7**   **Complications due to implanted mesh and other prosthetic materials**

  Coding Clinic: 2016, Q4, P71

  ● **T83.71**   **Erosion of implanted mesh and other prosthetic materials to surrounding organ or tissue**

    Coding Clinic: 2016, Q4, P71

    ● **T83.711**   **Erosion of implanted vaginal mesh to surrounding organ or tissue ♀ A** 🔖

       Erosion of implanted vaginal mesh into pelvic floor muscles

      Coding Clinic: 2016, Q4, P71

    ● **T83.712**   **Erosion of implanted urethral mesh to surrounding organ or tissue A** 🔖

       Erosion of implanted female urethral sling

       Erosion of implanted male urethral sling

       Erosion of implanted urethral mesh into pelvic floor muscles

    ● **T83.713**   **Erosion of implanted urethral bulking agent to surrounding organ or tissue A** 🔖

    ● **T83.714**   **Erosion of implanted ureteral bulking agent to surrounding organ or tissue A** 🔖

    ● **T83.718**   **Erosion of other implanted mesh to organ or tissue A** 🔖

      Coding Clinic: 2016, Q4, P71

    ● **T83.719**   **Erosion of other prosthetic materials to surrounding organ or tissue A** 🔖

      Coding Clinic: 2016, Q4, P71

  ● **T83.72**   **Exposure of implanted mesh and other prosthetic materials into surrounding organ or tissue**

    Extrusion of implanted mesh

    Coding Clinic: 2016, Q4, P71

    ● **T83.721**   **Exposure of implanted vaginal mesh into vagina ♀ A** 🔖

       Exposure of implanted vaginal mesh through vaginal wall

    ● **T83.722**   **Exposure of implanted urethral mesh into urethra A** 🔖

       Exposure of implanted female urethral sling

       Exposure of implanted male urethral sling

       Exposure of implanted urethral mesh through urethral wall

    ● **T83.723**   **Exposure of implanted urethral bulking agent into urethra A** 🔖

    ● **T83.724**   **Exposure of implanted ureteral bulking agent into ureter A** 🔖

    ● **T83.728**   **Exposure of other implanted mesh into organ or tissue A** 🔖

      Coding Clinic: 2016, Q4, P71

    ● **T83.729**   **Exposure of other prosthetic materials into organ or tissue A** 🔖

      Coding Clinic: 2016, Q4, P71

  X ● **T83.79**   **Other specified complications due to other genitourinary prosthetic materials A** 🔖

● **T83.8**   **Other specified complications of genitourinary prosthetic devices, implants and grafts**

  X ● **T83.81**   **Embolism due to genitourinary prosthetic devices, implants and grafts A** 🔖

  X ● **T83.82**   **Fibrosis due to genitourinary prosthetic devices, implants and grafts A** 🔖

  X ● **T83.83**   **Hemorrhage due to genitourinary prosthetic devices, implants and grafts A** 🔖

  X ● **T83.84**   **Pain due to genitourinary prosthetic devices, implants and grafts A** 🔖

  X ● **T83.85**   **Stenosis due to genitourinary prosthetic devices, implants and grafts A** 🔖

  X ● **T83.86**   **Thrombosis due to genitourinary prosthetic devices, implants and grafts A** 🔖

  X ● **T83.89**   **Other specified complication of genitourinary prosthetic devices, implants and grafts A** 🔖

X ● **T83.9**   **Unspecified complication of genitourinary prosthetic device, implant and graft A** 🔖

● **T84   Complications of internal orthopedic prosthetic devices, implants and grafts**

  Excludes2   failure and rejection of transplanted organs and tissues (T86.-)

               fracture of bone following insertion of orthopedic implant, joint prosthesis or bone plate (M96.6)

  The appropriate 7th character is to be added to each code from category T84

A	initial encounter
D	subsequent encounter
S	sequela

● **T84.0   Mechanical complication of internal joint prosthesis**

  ● **T84.01   Broken internal joint prosthesis**

      Breakage (fracture) of prosthetic joint

      Broken prosthetic joint implant

    ⇒ **Excludes1**   periprosthetic joint implant fracture (M97.-)

      Coding Clinic: 2016, Q4, P42

    ● T84.010   Broken internal **right hip** prosthesis A 🦟

    ● T84.011   Broken internal **left hip** prosthesis A 🦟

    ● T84.012   Broken internal **right knee** prosthesis A 🦟

    ● T84.013   Broken internal **left knee** prosthesis A 🦟

    ● T84.018   Broken internal joint prosthesis, **other** site A 🦟

        Use additional code to identify the joint (Z96.6-)

    ● T84.019   Broken internal joint prosthesis, **unspecified** site A 🦟

  ● **T84.02   Dislocation of internal joint prosthesis**

      Instability of internal joint prosthesis

      Subluxation of internal joint prosthesis

    ● T84.020   Dislocation of internal **right hip** prosthesis A 🦟

    ● T84.021   Dislocation of internal **left hip** prosthesis A 🦟

        Coding Clinic: 2019, Q2, P27

    ● T84.022   Instability of internal **right knee** prosthesis A 🦟

    ● T84.023   Instability of internal **left knee** prosthesis A 🦟

    ● T84.028   Dislocation of **other** internal joint prosthesis A 🦟

        Use additional code to identify the joint (Z96.6-)

    ● T84.029   Dislocation of **unspecified** internal joint prosthesis A 🦟

  ● **T84.03   Mechanical loosening of internal prosthetic joint**

      Aseptic loosening of prosthetic joint

    ● T84.030   Mechanical loosening of internal **right hip** prosthetic joint A 🦟

    ● T84.031   Mechanical loosening of internal **left hip** prosthetic joint A 🦟

    ● T84.032   Mechanical loosening of internal **right knee** prosthetic joint A 🦟

    ● T84.033   Mechanical loosening of internal **left knee** prosthetic joint A 🦟

    ● T84.038   Mechanical loosening of **other** internal prosthetic joint A 🦟

        Use additional code to identify the joint (Z96.6-)

    ● T84.039   Mechanical loosening of **unspecified** internal prosthetic joint A 🦟

● **T84.05   Periprosthetic osteolysis of internal prosthetic joint**

    Use additional code to identify major osseous defect, if applicable (M89.7-)

  ● T84.050   Periprosthetic osteolysis of internal prosthetic **right hip** joint A 🦟

  ● T84.051   Periprosthetic osteolysis of internal prosthetic **left hip** joint A 🦟

  ● T84.052   Periprosthetic osteolysis of internal prosthetic **right knee** joint A 🦟

  ● T84.053   Periprosthetic osteolysis of internal prosthetic **left knee** joint A 🦟

  ● T84.058   Periprosthetic osteolysis of **other** internal prosthetic joint A 🦟

      Use additional code to identify the joint (Z96.6-)

  ● T84.059   Periprosthetic osteolysis of **unspecified** internal prosthetic joint A 🦟

● **T84.06   Wear of articular bearing surface of internal prosthetic joint**

  ● T84.060   Wear of articular bearing surface of internal prosthetic **right hip** joint A 🦟

  ● T84.061   Wear of articular bearing surface of internal prosthetic **left hip** joint A 🦟

  ● T84.062   Wear of articular bearing surface of internal prosthetic **right knee** joint A 🦟

  ● T84.063   Wear of articular bearing surface of internal prosthetic **left knee** joint A 🦟

  ● T84.068   Wear of articular bearing surface of **other** internal prosthetic joint A 🦟

      Use additional code to identify the joint (Z96.6-)

  ● T84.069   Wear of articular bearing surface of **unspecified** internal prosthetic joint A 🦟

● **T84.09   Other mechanical complication of internal joint prosthesis**

    Prosthetic joint implant failure NOS

  ● T84.090   Other mechanical complication of internal **right hip** prosthesis A 🦟

      Coding Clinic: 2019, Q1, P20

  ● T84.091   Other mechanical complication of internal **left hip** prosthesis A 🦟

  ● T84.092   Other mechanical complication of internal **right knee** prosthesis A 🦟

  ● T84.093   Other mechanical complication of internal **left knee** prosthesis A 🦟

  ● T84.098   Other mechanical complication of **other** internal joint prosthesis A 🦟

      Use additional code to identify the joint (Z96.6-)

  ● T84.099   Other mechanical complication of **unspecified** internal joint prosthesis A 🦟

● **T84.1   Mechanical complication of internal fixation device of bones of limb**

  Excludes2   mechanical complication of internal fixation device of bones of feet (T84.2-)

            mechanical complication of internal fixation device of bones of fingers (T84.2-)

            mechanical complication of internal fixation device of bones of hands (T84.2-)

            mechanical complication of internal fixation device of bones of toes (T84.2-)

▶ New   ⇒ Revised   ~~deleted~~ Deleted   Excludes 1   Excludes 2   Includes   Use additional   Code first   Code also   Key words

OGCR Official Guidelines   X Assign placeholder X   ● Use Additional Character(s)   ▶ Manifestation Code   🦟 Hierarchical Condition Category   Coding Clinic

● **T84.11 Breakdown** (mechanical) of internal fixation device of bones of limb

  ● T84.110 Breakdown (mechanical) of internal fixation device of right humerus A 🔖

  ● T84.111 Breakdown (mechanical) of internal fixation device of left humerus A 🔖

  ● T84.112 Breakdown (mechanical) of internal fixation device of bone of right forearm A 🔖

  ● T84.113 Breakdown (mechanical) of internal fixation device of bone of left forearm A 🔖

  ● T84.114 Breakdown (mechanical) of internal fixation device of right femur A 🔖

  ● T84.115 Breakdown (mechanical) of internal fixation device of left femur A 🔖

  ● T84.116 Breakdown (mechanical) of internal fixation device of bone of right lower leg A 🔖

  ● T84.117 Breakdown (mechanical) of internal fixation device of bone of left lower leg A 🔖

  ● T84.119 Breakdown (mechanical) of internal fixation device of unspecified bone of limb A 🔖

● **T84.12 Displacement** of internal fixation device of bones of limb

  Malposition of internal fixation device of bones of limb

  ● T84.120 Displacement of internal fixation device of right humerus A 🔖

  ● T84.121 Displacement of internal fixation device of left humerus A 🔖

  ● T84.122 Displacement of internal fixation device of bone of right forearm A 🔖

  ● T84.123 Displacement of internal fixation device of bone of left forearm A 🔖

  ● T84.124 Displacement of internal fixation device of right femur A 🔖

  ● T84.125 Displacement of internal fixation device of left femur A 🔖

  ● T84.126 Displacement of internal fixation device of bone of right lower leg A 🔖

  ● T84.127 Displacement of internal fixation device of bone of left lower leg A 🔖

  ● T84.129 Displacement of internal fixation device of unspecified bone of limb A 🔖

● **T84.19 Other mechanical complication** of internal fixation device of bones of limb

  Obstruction (mechanical) of internal fixation device of bones of limb

  Perforation of internal fixation device of bones of limb

  Protrusion of internal fixation device of bones of limb

  ● T84.190 Other mechanical complication of internal fixation device of right humerus A 🔖

  ● T84.191 Other mechanical complication of internal fixation device of left humerus A 🔖

  ● T84.192 Other mechanical complication of internal fixation device of bone of right forearm A 🔖

  ● T84.193 Other mechanical complication of internal fixation device of bone of left forearm A 🔖

  ● T84.194 Other mechanical complication of internal fixation device of right femur A 🔖

  ● T84.195 Other mechanical complication of internal fixation device of left femur A 🔖

  ● T84.196 Other mechanical complication of internal fixation device of bone of right lower leg A 🔖

  ● T84.197 Other mechanical complication of internal fixation device of bone of left lower leg A 🔖

  ● T84.199 Other mechanical complication of internal fixation device of unspecified bone of limb A 🔖

● **T84.2 Mechanical complication** of internal fixation device of other bones

  ● **T84.21 Breakdown** (mechanical) of internal fixation device of other bones

    ● T84.210 Breakdown (mechanical) of internal fixation device of bones of hand and fingers A 🔖

    ● T84.213 Breakdown (mechanical) of internal fixation device of bones of foot and toes A 🔖

    ● T84.216 Breakdown (mechanical) of internal fixation device of vertebrae A 🔖

    ● T84.218 Breakdown (mechanical) of internal fixation device of other bones A 🔖

  ● **T84.22 Displacement** of internal fixation device of other bones

    Malposition of internal fixation device of other bones

    ● T84.220 Displacement of internal fixation device of bones of hand and fingers A 🔖

    ● T84.223 Displacement of internal fixation device of bones of foot and toes A 🔖

    ● T84.226 Displacement of internal fixation device of vertebrae A 🔖

    ● T84.228 Displacement of internal fixation device of other bones A 🔖

  ● **T84.29 Other mechanical complication** of internal fixation device of other bones

    Obstruction (mechanical) of internal fixation device of other bones

    Perforation of internal fixation device of other bones

    Protrusion of internal fixation device of other bones

    ● T84.290 Other mechanical complication of internal fixation device of bones of hand and fingers A 🔖

    ● T84.293 Other mechanical complication of internal fixation device of bones of foot and toes A 🔖

    ● T84.296 Other mechanical complication of internal fixation device of vertebrae A 🔖

    ● T84.298 Other mechanical complication of internal fixation device of other bones A 🔖

● **T84.3 Mechanical complication** of other bone devices, implants and grafts

  Excludes2 other complications of bone graft (T86.83-)

  ● **T84.31 Breakdown** (mechanical) of other bone devices, implants and grafts

    ● T84.310 Breakdown (mechanical) of electronic bone stimulator A 🔖

    ● T84.318 Breakdown (mechanical) of other bone devices, implants and grafts A 🔖

● **T84.32** **Displacement** of other bone devices, implants and grafts

    Malposition of other bone devices, implants and grafts

  ● **T84.320** Displacement of electronic bone stimulator A 🦠

  ● **T84.328** Displacement of other bone devices, implants and grafts A 🦠

● **T84.39** Other mechanical complication of other bone devices, implants and grafts

    Obstruction (mechanical) of other bone devices, implants and grafts

    Perforation of other bone devices, implants and grafts

    Protrusion of other bone devices, implants and grafts

  ● **T84.390** Other mechanical complication of electronic bone stimulator A 🦠

  ● **T84.398** Other mechanical complication of other bone devices, implants and grafts A 🦠

● **T84.4** Mechanical complication of other internal orthopedic devices, implants and grafts

  ● **T84.41** Breakdown (mechanical) of other internal orthopedic devices, implants and grafts

    ● **T84.410** Breakdown (mechanical) of muscle and tendon graft A 🦠

    ● **T84.418** Breakdown (mechanical) of other internal orthopedic devices, implants and grafts A 🦠

  ● **T84.42** Displacement of other internal orthopedic devices, implants and grafts

    Malposition of other internal orthopedic devices, implants and grafts

    ● **T84.420** Displacement of muscle and tendon graft A 🦠

    ● **T84.428** Displacement of other internal orthopedic devices, implants and grafts A 🦠

  ● **T84.49** Other mechanical complication of other internal orthopedic devices, implants and grafts

    Mechanical complication of other internal orthopedic devices, implants and grafts NOS

    Obstruction (mechanical) of other internal orthopedic devices, implants and grafts

    Perforation of other internal orthopedic devices, implants and grafts

    Protrusion of other internal orthopedic devices, implants and grafts

    ● **T84.490** Other mechanical complication of muscle and tendon graft A 🦠

    ● **T84.498** Other mechanical complication of other internal orthopedic devices, implants and grafts A 🦠

● **T84.5** Infection and inflammatory reaction due to internal joint prosthesis

    Use additional code to identify infection

    Coding Clinic: 2015, Q1, P16

  X ● **T84.50** Infection and inflammatory reaction due to unspecified internal joint prosthesis A 🦠

    Coding Clinic: 2015, Q1, P3

  X ● **T84.51** Infection and inflammatory reaction due to internal right hip prosthesis A 🦠

    Coding Clinic: 2015, Q4, P36

  X ● **T84.52** Infection and inflammatory reaction due to internal left hip prosthesis A 🦠

    Coding Clinic: 2015, Q1, P16-17

X ● **T84.53** Infection and inflammatory reaction due to internal right knee prosthesis A 🦠

X ● **T84.54** Infection and inflammatory reaction due to internal left knee prosthesis A 🦠

    Coding Clinic: 2019, Q3, P16

X ● **T84.59** Infection and inflammatory reaction due to other internal joint prosthesis A 🦠

● **T84.6** Infection and inflammatory reaction due to internal fixation device

    Use additional code to identify infection

  X ● **T84.60** Infection and inflammatory reaction due to internal fixation device of unspecified site A 🦠

  ● **T84.61** Infection and inflammatory reaction due to internal fixation device of arm

    ● **T84.610** Infection and inflammatory reaction due to internal fixation device of right humerus A 🦠

    ● **T84.611** Infection and inflammatory reaction due to internal fixation device of left humerus A 🦠

    ● **T84.612** Infection and inflammatory reaction due to internal fixation device of right radius A 🦠

    ● **T84.613** Infection and inflammatory reaction due to internal fixation device of left radius A 🦠

    ● **T84.614** Infection and inflammatory reaction due to internal fixation device of right ulna A 🦠

    ● **T84.615** Infection and inflammatory reaction due to internal fixation device of left ulna A 🦠

    ● **T84.619** Infection and inflammatory reaction due to internal fixation device of unspecified bone of arm A 🦠

  ● **T84.62** Infection and inflammatory reaction due to internal fixation device of leg

    ● **T84.620** Infection and inflammatory reaction due to internal fixation device of right femur A 🦠

    ● **T84.621** Infection and inflammatory reaction due to internal fixation device of left femur A 🦠

    ● **T84.622** Infection and inflammatory reaction due to internal fixation device of right tibia A 🦠

    ● **T84.623** Infection and inflammatory reaction due to internal fixation device of left tibia A 🦠

    ● **T84.624** Infection and inflammatory reaction due to internal fixation device of right fibula A 🦠

    ● **T84.625** Infection and inflammatory reaction due to internal fixation device of left fibula A 🦠

    ● **T84.629** Infection and inflammatory reaction due to internal fixation device of unspecified bone of leg A 🦠

  X ● **T84.63** Infection and inflammatory reaction due to internal fixation device of spine A 🦠

  X ● **T84.69** Infection and inflammatory reaction due to internal fixation device of other site A 🦠

● **T84.7** Infection and inflammatory reaction due to other internal orthopedic prosthetic devices, implants and grafts A 🦠

    Use additional code to identify infection

▶ New   ⇒ Revised   ~~deleted~~ Deleted   Excludes 1   Excludes 2   Includes   Use additional   Code first   Code also   Key words

OGCR Official Guidelines   X Assign placeholder X   ● Use Additional Character(s)   ▮ Manifestation Code   🦠 Hierarchical Condition Category   Coding Clinic

● **T84.8**   Other specified complications of internal orthopedic prosthetic devices, implants and grafts

   X ● **T84.81**   Embolism due to internal orthopedic prosthetic devices, implants and grafts A 🦠

   X ● **T84.82**   Fibrosis due to internal orthopedic prosthetic devices, implants and grafts A 🦠

   X ● **T84.83**   Hemorrhage due to internal orthopedic prosthetic devices, implants and grafts A 🦠

   X ● **T84.84**   Pain due to internal orthopedic prosthetic devices, implants and grafts A 🦠

   X ● **T84.85**   Stenosis due to internal orthopedic prosthetic devices, implants and grafts A 🦠

   X ● **T84.86**   Thrombosis due to internal orthopedic prosthetic devices, implants and grafts A 🦠

   X ● **T84.89**   Other specified complication of internal orthopedic prosthetic devices, implants and grafts A 🦠

  X ● **T84.9**   Unspecified complication of internal orthopedic prosthetic device, implant and graft A 🦠

● **T85**   Complications of other internal prosthetic devices, implants and grafts

   Excludes2   failure and rejection of transplanted organs and tissue (T86.-)

   The appropriate 7th character is to be added to each code from category T85

> | A | initial encounter |
> |---|---|
> | D | subsequent encounter |
> | S | sequela |

   Coding Clinic: 2016, Q4, P71

● **T85.0**   Mechanical complication of ventricular intracranial (communicating) shunt

   X ● **T85.01**   Breakdown (mechanical) of ventricular intracranial (communicating) shunt A 🦠

   X ● **T85.02**   Displacement of ventricular intracranial (communicating) shunt A 🦠
     Malposition of ventricular intracranial (communicating) shunt

   X ● **T85.03**   Leakage of ventricular intracranial (communicating) shunt A 🦠

   X ● **T85.09**   Other mechanical complication of ventricular intracranial (communicating) shunt A 🦠
     Obstruction (mechanical) of ventricular intracranial (communicating) shunt
     Perforation of ventricular intracranial (communicating) shunt
     Protrusion of ventricular intracranial (communicating) shunt

● **T85.1**   Mechanical complication of implanted electronic stimulator of nervous system
   Coding Clinic: 2016, Q4, P71

   ● **T85.11**   Breakdown (mechanical) of implanted electronic stimulator of nervous system

     ● **T85.110**   Breakdown (mechanical) of implanted electronic neurostimulator of brain electrode (lead) A 🦠

     ● **T85.111**   Breakdown (mechanical) of implanted electronic neurostimulator of peripheral nerve electrode (lead) A 🦠
       Breakdown of electrode (lead) for cranial nerve neurostimulators
       Breakdown of electrode (lead) for gastric neurostimulator
       Breakdown of electrode (lead) for sacral nerve neurostimulator
       Breakdown of electrode (lead) for vagal nerve neurostimulators

     ● **T85.112**   Breakdown (mechanical) of implanted electronic neurostimulator of spinal cord electrode (lead) A 🦠

     ● **T85.113**   Breakdown (mechanical) of implanted electronic neurostimulator, generator A 🦠
       Breakdown (mechanical) of implanted electronic neurostimulator generator, brain, peripheral, gastric, spinal
       Breakdown (mechanical) of implanted electronic sacral neurostimulator, pulse generator or receiver

     ● **T85.118**   Breakdown (mechanical) of other implanted electronic stimulator of nervous system A 🦠

   ● **T85.12**   Displacement of implanted electronic stimulator of nervous system
     Malposition of implanted electronic stimulator of nervous system

     ● **T85.120**   Displacement of implanted electronic neurostimulator of brain electrode (lead) A 🦠

     ● **T85.121**   Displacement of implanted electronic neurostimulator of peripheral nerve electrode (lead) A 🦠
       Displacement of electrode (lead) for cranial nerve neurostimulators
       Displacement of electrode (lead) for gastric neurostimulator
       Displacement of electrode (lead) for sacral nerve neurostimulator
       Displacement of electrode (lead) for vagal nerve neurostimulators

     ● **T85.122**   Displacement of implanted electronic neurostimulator of spinal cord electrode (lead) A 🦠

     ● **T85.123**   Displacement of implanted electronic neurostimulator, generator A 🦠
       Displacement of implanted electronic neurostimulator generator, brain, peripheral, gastric, spinal
       Displacement of implanted electronic sacral neurostimulator, pulse generator or receiver

     ● **T85.128**   Displacement of other implanted electronic stimulator of nervous system A 🦠

   ● **T85.19**   Other mechanical complication of implanted electronic stimulator of nervous system
     Leakage of implanted electronic stimulator of nervous system
     Obstruction (mechanical) of implanted electronic stimulator of nervous system
     Perforation of implanted electronic stimulator of nervous system
     Protrusion of implanted electronic stimulator of nervous system

     ● **T85.190**   Other mechanical complication of implanted electronic neurostimulator of brain electrode (lead) A 🦠

● T85.191   Other mechanical complication of
            implanted electronic neurostimulator
            of peripheral nerve electrode
            (lead) A 🐾
            Other mechanical complication
                of electrode (lead) for cranial
                nerve neurostimulators
            Other mechanical complication
                of electrode (lead) for gastric
                neurostimulator
            Other mechanical complication of
                electrode (lead) for sacral nerve
                neurostimulator
            Other mechanical complication of
                electrode (lead) for vagal nerve
                neurostimulators
● T85.192   Other mechanical complication of
            implanted electronic neurostimulator
            of spinal cord electrode (lead) A 🐾
● T85.193   Other mechanical complication of
            implanted electronic neurostimulator,
            generator A 🐾
            Other mechanical complication
                of implanted electronic
                neurostimulator generator,
                brain, peripheral, gastric, spinal
            Other mechanical complication
                of implanted electronic
                sacral neurostimulator, pulse
                generator or receiver
● T85.199   Other mechanical complication of
            other implanted electronic stimulator
            of nervous system A 🐾

● T85.2   Mechanical complication of intraocular lens
    X● T85.21   Breakdown (mechanical) of intraocular lens
    X● T85.22   Displacement of intraocular lens
               Malposition of intraocular lens
    X● T85.29   Other mechanical complication of intraocular
               lens
               Obstruction (mechanical) of intraocular lens
               Perforation of intraocular lens
               Protrusion of intraocular lens

● T85.3   Mechanical complication of other ocular prosthetic
          devices, implants and grafts
          Excludes2   other complications of corneal graft
                      (T86.84-)
    ● T85.31   Breakdown (mechanical) of other ocular
               prosthetic devices, implants and grafts
               ● T85.310   Breakdown (mechanical) of prosthetic
                           orbit of right eye
               ● T85.311   Breakdown (mechanical) of prosthetic
                           orbit of left eye
               ● T85.318   Breakdown (mechanical) of other
                           ocular prosthetic devices, implants
                           and grafts
    ● T85.32   Displacement of other ocular prosthetic
               devices, implants and grafts
               Malposition of other ocular prosthetic devices,
                   implants and grafts
               ● T85.320   Displacement of prosthetic orbit of
                           right eye
               ● T85.321   Displacement of prosthetic orbit of
                           left eye
               ● T85.328   Displacement of other ocular
                           prosthetic devices, implants and
                           grafts

● T85.39   Other mechanical complication of other ocular
           prosthetic devices, implants and grafts
           Obstruction (mechanical) of other ocular
               prosthetic devices, implants and grafts
           Perforation of other ocular prosthetic devices,
               implants and grafts
           Protrusion of other ocular prosthetic devices,
               implants and grafts
           ● T85.390   Other mechanical complication of
                       prosthetic orbit of right eye
           ● T85.391   Other mechanical complication of
                       prosthetic orbit of left eye
           ● T85.398   Other mechanical complication
                       of other ocular prosthetic devices,
                       implants and grafts

● T85.4   Mechanical complication of breast prosthesis and
          implant
    X● T85.41   Breakdown (mechanical) of breast prosthesis
               and implant
    X● T85.42   Displacement of breast prosthesis and implant
               Malposition of breast prosthesis and implant
    X● T85.43   Leakage of breast prosthesis and implant
    X● T85.44   Capsular contracture of breast implant
    X● T85.49   Other mechanical complication of breast
               prosthesis and implant
               Obstruction (mechanical) of breast prosthesis
                   and implant
               Perforation of breast prosthesis and implant
               Protrusion of breast prosthesis and implant

● T85.5   Mechanical complication of gastrointestinal prosthetic
          devices, implants and grafts
    ● T85.51   Breakdown (mechanical) of gastrointestinal
               prosthetic devices, implants and grafts
               ● T85.510   Breakdown (mechanical) of bile duct
                           prosthesis
               ● T85.511   Breakdown (mechanical) of
                           esophageal anti-reflux device
               ● T85.518   Breakdown (mechanical) of other
                           gastrointestinal prosthetic devices,
                           implants and grafts
    ● T85.52   Displacement of gastrointestinal prosthetic
               devices, implants and grafts
               Malposition of gastrointestinal prosthetic
                   devices, implants and grafts
               ● T85.520   Displacement of bile duct prosthesis
               ● T85.521   Displacement of esophageal anti-
                           reflux device
               ● T85.528   Displacement of other
                           gastrointestinal prosthetic devices,
                           implants and grafts
    ● T85.59   Other mechanical complication of
               gastrointestinal prosthetic devices, implants
               and
               Obstruction, mechanical of gastrointestinal
                   prosthetic devices, implants and grafts
               Perforation of gastrointestinal prosthetic
                   devices, implants and grafts
               Protrusion of gastrointestinal prosthetic
                   devices, implants and grafts
               ● T85.590   Other mechanical complication of
                           bile duct prosthesis
               ● T85.591   Other mechanical complication of
                           esophageal anti-reflux device
               ● T85.598   Other mechanical complication of
                           other gastrointestinal prosthetic
                           devices, implants and grafts

▶ New   ⇒ Revised   deleted Deleted   Excludes 1   Excludes 2   Includes   Use additional   Code first   Code also   Key words
OGCR Official Guidelines   X Assign placeholder X   ● Use Additional Character(s)   ▶ Manifestation Code   🐾 Hierarchical Condition Category   Coding Clinic

● **T85.6**   **Mechanical complication of other specified internal and external prosthetic devices, implants and grafts**
Coding Clinic: 2016, Q4, P71

  ● **T85.61**   **Breakdown (mechanical) of other specified internal prosthetic devices, implants and grafts**

    ● **T85.610**   **Breakdown (mechanical) of cranial or spinal infusion catheter**
Breakdown (mechanical) of epidural infusion catheter
Breakdown (mechanical) of intrathecal infusion catheter
Breakdown (mechanical) of subarachnoid infusion catheter
Breakdown (mechanical) of subdural infusion catheter

    ● **T85.611**   **Breakdown (mechanical) of intraperitoneal dialysis catheter A, D, S** 🔗
> **Excludes1**   mechanical complication of vascular dialysis catheter (T82.4-)

    ● **T85.612**   **Breakdown (mechanical) of permanent sutures**
> **Excludes1**   mechanical complication of permanent (wire) suture used in bone repair (T84.1-T84.2)

    ● **T85.613**   **Breakdown (mechanical) of artificial skin graft and decellularized allodermis**
Failure of artificial skin graft and decellularized allodermis
Non-adherence of artificial skin graft and decellularized allodermis
Poor incorporation of artificial skin graft and decellularized allodermis
Shearing of artificial skin graft and decellularized allodermis

    ● **T85.614**   **Breakdown (mechanical) of insulin pump**

    ● **T85.615**   **Breakdown (mechanical) of other nervous system device, implant or graft A** 🔗
Breakdown (mechanical) of intrathecal infusion pump

    ● **T85.618**   **Breakdown (mechanical) of other specified internal prosthetic devices, implants and grafts**

  ● **T85.62**   **Displacement of other specified internal prosthetic devices, implants and grafts**
Malposition of other specified internal prosthetic devices, implants and grafts

    ● **T85.620**   **Displacement of cranial or spinal infusion catheter**
Displacement of epidural infusion catheter
Displacement of intrathecal infusion catheter
Displacement of subarachnoid infusion catheter
Displacement of subdural infusion catheter

    ● **T85.621**   **Displacement of intraperitoneal dialysis catheter A, D, S** 🔗
> **Excludes1**   mechanical complication of vascular dialysis catheter (T82.4-)

    ● **T85.622**   **Displacement of permanent sutures**
> **Excludes1**   mechanical complication of permanent (wire) suture used in bone repair (T84.1-T84.2)

    ● **T85.623**   **Displacement of artificial skin graft and decellularized allodermis**
Dislodgement of artificial skin graft and decellularized allodermis

    ● **T85.624**   **Displacement of insulin pump**

    ● **T85.625**   **Displacement of other nervous system device, implant or graft A** 🔗
Displacement of intrathecal infusion pump

    ● **T85.628**   **Displacement of other specified internal prosthetic devices, implants and grafts**
Coding Clinic: 2015, Q1, P15

  ● **T85.63**   **Leakage of other specified internal prosthetic devices, implants and grafts**

    ● **T85.630**   **Leakage of cranial or spinal infusion catheter**
Leakage of epidural infusion catheter
Leakage of intrathecal infusion catheter
Leakage of subdural infusion catheter
Leakage of subarachnoid infusion catheter

    ● **T85.631**   **Leakage of intraperitoneal dialysis catheter A, D, S** 🔗
> **Excludes1**   mechanical complication of vascular dialysis catheter (T82.4)

    ● **T85.633**   **Leakage of insulin pump**

    ● **T85.635**   **Leakage of other nervous system device, implant or graft A** 🔗
Leakage of intrathecal infusion pump

    ● **T85.638**   **Leakage of other specified internal prosthetic devices, implants and grafts**

  ● **T85.69**   **Other mechanical complication of other specified internal prosthetic devices, implants and grafts**
Obstruction, mechanical of other specified internal prosthetic devices, implants and grafts
Perforation of other specified internal prosthetic devices, implants and grafts
Protrusion of other specified internal prosthetic devices, implants and grafts

    ● **T85.690**   **Other mechanical complication of cranial or spinal infusion catheter**
Other mechanical complication of epidural infusion catheter
Other mechanical complication of intrathecal infusion catheter
Other mechanical complication of subarachnoid infusion catheter
Other mechanical complication of subdural infusion catheter

● **T85.691** **Other mechanical complication of intraperitoneal dialysis catheter** A, D, S 🐾

> **Excludes1**   mechanical complication of vascular dialysis catheter (T82.4)

● **T85.692** **Other mechanical complication of permanent sutures**

> **Excludes1**   mechanical complication of permanent (wire) suture used in bone repair (T84.1-T84.2)

● **T85.693** **Other mechanical complication of artificial skin graft and decellularized allodermis**

● **T85.694** **Other mechanical complication of insulin pump**

● **T85.695** **Other mechanical complication of other nervous system device, implant or graft** A 🐾

> Other mechanical complication of intrathecal infusion pump

● **T85.698** **Other mechanical complication of other specified internal prosthetic devices, implants and grafts**

> Mechanical complication of nonabsorbable surgical material NOS

● **T85.7** **Infection and inflammatory reaction due to other internal prosthetic devices, implants and grafts**

> Use additional code to identify infection
>
> Coding Clinic: 2016, Q4, P72

X ● **T85.71** **Infection and inflammatory reaction due to peritoneal dialysis catheter** A, D, S 🐾

X ● **T85.72** **Infection and inflammatory reaction due to insulin pump** A 🐾

● **T85.73** **Infection and inflammatory reaction due to nervous system devices, implants and graft**

● **T85.730** **Infection and inflammatory reaction due to ventricular intracranial (communicating) shunt** A 🐾

● **T85.731** **Infection and inflammatory reaction due to implanted electronic neurostimulator of brain, electrode (lead)** A 🐾

● **T85.732** **Infection and inflammatory reaction due to implanted electronic neurostimulator of peripheral nerve, electrode (lead)** A 🐾

> Infection and inflammatory reaction due to electrode (lead) for cranial nerve neurostimulators
> Infection and inflammatory reaction due to electrode (lead) for gastric neurostimulator
> Infection and inflammatory reaction due to electrode (lead) for sacral nerve neurostimulator
> Infection and inflammatory reaction due to electrode (lead) for vagal nerve neurostimulators

● **T85.733** **Infection and inflammatory reaction due to implanted electronic neurostimulator of spinal cord, electrode (lead)** A 🐾

● **T85.734** **Infection and inflammatory reaction due to implanted electronic neurostimulator, generator** A 🐾

> Generator pocket infection

● **T85.735** **Infection and inflammatory reaction due to cranial or spinal infusion catheter** A 🐾

> Infection and inflammatory reaction due to epidural catheter
> Infection and inflammatory reaction due to intrathecal infusion catheter
> Infection and inflammatory reaction due to subarachnoid catheter
> Infection and inflammatory reaction due to subdural catheter

● **T85.738** **Infection and inflammatory reaction due to other nervous system device, implant or graft** A 🐾

> Infection and inflammatory reaction due to intrathecal infusion pump

X ● **T85.79** **Infection and inflammatory reaction due to other internal prosthetic devices, implants and grafts** A 🐾

> Coding Clinic: 2016, Q4, P72

● **T85.8** **Other specified complications of internal prosthetic devices, implants and grafts, not elsewhere classified**

> Coding Clinic: 2016, Q4, P72

● **T85.81** **Embolism due to internal prosthetic devices, implants and grafts, not elsewhere classified**

● **T85.810** **Embolism due to nervous system prosthetic devices, implants and grafts** A 🐾

● **T85.818** **Embolism due to other internal prosthetic devices, implants and grafts**

● **T85.82** **Fibrosis due to internal prosthetic devices, implants and grafts, not elsewhere classified**

● **T85.820** **Fibrosis due to nervous system prosthetic devices, implants and grafts** A 🐾

● **T85.828** **Fibrosis due to other internal prosthetic devices, implants and grafts**

● **T85.83** **Hemorrhage due to internal prosthetic devices, implants and grafts, not elsewhere classified**

● **T85.830** **Hemorrhage due to nervous system prosthetic devices, implants and grafts** A 🐾

● **T85.838** **Hemorrhage due to other internal prosthetic devices, implants and grafts**

● **T85.84** **Pain due to internal prosthetic devices, implants and grafts, not elsewhere classified**

● **T85.840** **Pain due to nervous system prosthetic devices, implants and grafts** A 🐾

● **T85.848** **Pain due to other internal prosthetic devices, implants and grafts**

● **T85.85** **Stenosis due to internal prosthetic devices, implants and grafts, not elsewhere classified**

● **T85.850** **Stenosis due to nervous system prosthetic devices, implants and grafts** A 🐾

● **T85.858** **Stenosis due to other internal prosthetic devices, implants and grafts**

● **T85.86** **Thrombosis due to internal prosthetic devices, implants and grafts, not elsewhere classified**

● **T85.860** **Thrombosis due to nervous system prosthetic devices, implants and grafts** A 🐾

● **T85.868** **Thrombosis due to other internal prosthetic devices, implants and grafts**

▶ New   ⟹ Revised   ~~deleted~~ Deleted   Excludes 1   Excludes 2   Includes   Use additional   Code first   Code also   Key words
OGCR Official Guidelines   X Assign placeholder X   ● Use Additional Character(s)   ▷ Manifestation Code   🐾 Hierarchical Condition Category   Coding Clinic

● T85.89 **Other specified** complication of internal prosthetic devices, implants and grafts, not elsewhere classified
Coding Clinic: 2016, Q4, P72

● T85.890 Other specified complication of **nervous system** prosthetic devices, implants and grafts A 🐾

● T85.898 Other specified complication of **other** internal prosthetic devices, implants and grafts

X● T85.9 **Unspecified** complication of internal prosthetic device, implant and graft
Complication of internal prosthetic device, implant and graft NOS

OGCR Section I.C.19.g.3.

Organ Transplant Complications

Transplant Complications

(a) Transplant complications other than kidney

Codes under category T86, Complications of transplanted organs and tissues, are for use for both complications and rejection of transplanted organs. A transplant complication code is only assigned if the complication affects the function of the transplanted organ. Two codes are required to fully describe a transplant complication: the appropriate code from category T86 and a secondary code that identifies the complication.

Pre-existing conditions or conditions that develop after the transplant are not coded as complications unless they affect the function of the transplanted organs.

See I.C.21 for transplant organ removal status.

See I.C.2 for malignant neoplasm associated with transplanted organ.

● T86 **Complications of transplanted organs and tissue**
Use additional code to identify other transplant complications, such as:
graft-versus-host disease (D89.81-)
malignancy associated with organ transplant (C80.2)
post-transplant lymphoproliferative disorders (PTLD) (D47.Z1)

● T86.0 Complications of **bone marrow** transplant

T86.00 **Unspecified** complication of bone marrow transplant 🐾

T86.01 Bone marrow transplant **rejection** 🐾

T86.02 Bone marrow transplant **failure** 🐾

T86.03 Bone marrow transplant **infection** 🐾

T86.09 **Other** complications of bone marrow transplant 🐾

● T86.1 Complications of **kidney** transplant

T86.10 **Unspecified** complication of kidney transplant

T86.11 Kidney transplant **rejection**

T86.12 Kidney transplant **failure**
Coding Clinic: 2013, Q1, P24

T86.13 Kidney transplant **infection**
Use additional code to specify infection

T86.19 **Other** complication of kidney transplant
Coding Clinic: 2019, Q2, P7

● T86.2 Complications of **heart** transplant

Excludes1 complication of:
artificial heart device (T82.5)
heart-lung transplant (T86.3)

T86.20 **Unspecified** complication of heart transplant 🐾

T86.21 Heart transplant **rejection** 🐾

T86.22 Heart transplant **failure** 🐾

T86.23 Heart transplant **infection** 🐾
Use additional code to specify infection

● T86.29 Other complications of heart transplant

T86.290 **Cardiac allograft vasculopathy** 🐾

Excludes1 atherosclerosis of coronary arteries (I25.75-, I25.76-, I25.81-)

T86.298 **Other** complications of heart transplant 🐾

● T86.3 Complications of **heart-lung** transplant

T86.30 **Unspecified** complication of heart-lung transplant 🐾

T86.31 Heart-lung transplant **rejection** 🐾

T86.32 Heart-lung transplant **failure** 🐾

T86.33 Heart-lung transplant **infection** 🐾
Use additional code to specify infection

T86.39 **Other** complications of heart-lung transplant 🐾

● T86.4 Complications of **liver** transplant

T86.40 **Unspecified** complication of liver transplant 🐾

T86.41 Liver transplant **rejection** 🐾

T86.42 Liver transplant **failure** 🐾

T86.43 Liver transplant **infection** 🐾
Use additional code to identify infection, such as:
Cytomegalovirus (CMV) infection (B25.-)

T86.49 **Other** complications of liver transplant 🐾

● T86.5 Complications of **stem cell transplant** 🐾
Complications from stem cells from peripheral blood
Complications from stem cells from umbilical cord

● T86.8 Complications of **other** transplanted organs and tissues

● T86.81 Complications of **lung** transplant

Excludes1 complication of heart-lung transplant (T86.3-)

T86.810 Lung transplant **rejection** 🐾

T86.811 Lung transplant **failure** 🐾

T86.812 Lung transplant **infection** 🐾
Use additional code to specify infection

T86.818 **Other** complications of lung transplant 🐾
Coding Clinic: 2019, Q2, P7

T86.819 **Unspecified** complication of lung transplant 🐾

● T86.82 Complications of **skin graft** (allograft) (autograft)

Excludes2 complication of artificial skin graft (T85.693)

T86.820 Skin graft (allograft) **rejection**

T86.821 Skin graft (allograft) (autograft) **failure**

T86.822 Skin graft (allograft) (autograft) **infection**
Use additional code to specify infection

T86.828 **Other** complications of skin graft (allograft) (autograft)

T86.829 **Unspecified** complication of skin graft (allograft) (autograft)

● T86.83 Complications of **bone graft**

Excludes2 mechanical complications of bone graft (T84.3-)

T86.830 Bone graft **rejection**

T86.831 Bone graft **failure**

T86.832 Bone graft **infection**
Use additional code to specify infection

T86.838 **Other** complications of bone graft

T86.839 **Unspecified** complication of bone graft

● T86.84   Complications of corneal transplant
            Excludes2   mechanical complications of
                             corneal graft (T85.3-)
    ● T86.840   Corneal transplant rejection
        ▶ T86.8401   Corneal transplant
                      rejection, right eye
        ▶ T86.8402   Corneal transplant
                      rejection, left eye
        ▶ T86.8403   Corneal transplant
                      rejection, bilateral
        ▶ T86.8409   Corneal transplant
                      rejection, unspecified eye
    ● T86.841   Corneal transplant failure
        ▶ T86.8411   Corneal transplant failure,
                      right eye
        ▶ T86.8412   Corneal transplant failure,
                      left eye
        ▶ T86.8413   Corneal transplant failure,
                      bilateral
        ▶ T86.8419   Corneal transplant failure,
                      unspecified eye
    ● T86.842   Corneal transplant infection 🐾
                 Use additional code to specify
                 infection
        ▶ T86.8421   Corneal transplant
                      infection, right eye
        ▶ T86.8422   Corneal transplant
                      infection, left eye
        ▶ T86.8423   Corneal transplant
                      infection, bilateral
        ▶ T86.8429   Corneal transplant
                      infection, unspecified eye
    ● T86.848   Other complications of corneal
                 transplant
        ▶ T86.8481   Other complications of
                      corneal transplant, right eye
        ▶ T86.8482   Other complications of
                      corneal transplant, left eye
        ▶ T86.8483   Other complications of
                      corneal transplant, bilateral
        ▶ T86.8489   Other complications of
                      corneal transplant,
                      unspecified eye
    ● T86.849   Unspecified complication of corneal
                 transplant
        ▶ T86.8491   Unspecified complication of
                      corneal transplant, right eye
        ▶ T86.8492   Unspecified complication of
                      corneal transplant, left eye
        ▶ T86.8493   Unspecified complication of
                      corneal transplant, bilateral
        ▶ T86.8499   Unspecified complication of
                      corneal transplant,
                      unspecified eye
● T86.85   Complication of intestine transplant
    T86.850   Intestine transplant rejection 🐾
    T86.851   Intestine transplant failure 🐾
    T86.852   Intestine transplant infection 🐾
               Use additional code to specify
               infection
    T86.858   Other complications of intestine
               transplant 🐾
    T86.859   Unspecified complication of intestine
               transplant 🐾

● T86.89   Complications of other transplanted tissue
            Transplant failure or rejection of pancreas
    T86.890   Other transplanted tissue rejection
    T86.891   Other transplanted tissue failure
    T86.892   Other transplanted tissue infection
               Use additional code to specify
               infection
    T86.898   Other complications of other
               transplanted tissue
    T86.899   Unspecified complication of other
               transplanted tissue
● T86.9   Complication of unspecified transplanted organ and
           tissue
    T86.90   Unspecified complication of unspecified
              transplanted organ and tissue
    T86.91   Unspecified transplanted organ and tissue
              rejection
    T86.92   Unspecified transplanted organ and tissue
              failure
    T86.93   Unspecified transplanted organ and tissue
              infection
              Use additional code to specify infection
    T86.99   Other complications of unspecified
              transplanted organ and tissue

● T87   Complications peculiar to reattachment and amputation
    ● T87.0   Complications of reattached (part of) upper extremity
        ● T87.0X   Complications of reattached (part of) upper
                    extremity
            T87.0X1   Complications of reattached (part of)
                       right upper extremity 🐾
            T87.0X2   Complications of reattached (part of)
                       left upper extremity 🐾
            T87.0X9   Complications of reattached (part of)
                       unspecified upper extremity 🐾
    ● T87.1   Complications of reattached (part of) lower extremity
        ● T87.1X   Complications of reattached (part of) lower
                    extremity
            T87.1X1   Complications of reattached (part of)
                       right lower extremity 🐾
            T87.1X2   Complications of reattached (part of)
                       left lower extremity 🐾
            T87.1X9   Complications of reattached (part of)
                       unspecified lower extremity 🐾
    T87.2   Complications of other reattached body part 🐾
    ● T87.3   Neuroma of amputation stump
        T87.30   Neuroma of amputation stump, unspecified
                  extremity 🐾
        T87.31   Neuroma of amputation stump, right upper
                  extremity 🐾
        T87.32   Neuroma of amputation stump, left upper
                  extremity 🐾
        T87.33   Neuroma of amputation stump, right lower
                  extremity 🐾
        T87.34   Neuroma of amputation stump, left lower
                  extremity 🐾
    ● T87.4   Infection of amputation stump
        T87.40   Infection of amputation stump, unspecified
                  extremity 🐾
        T87.41   Infection of amputation stump, right upper
                  extremity 🐾
        T87.42   Infection of amputation stump, left upper
                  extremity 🐾
        T87.43   Infection of amputation stump, right lower
                  extremity 🐾
        T87.44   Infection of amputation stump, left lower
                  extremity 🐾

▶ New   ⇒ Revised   ~~deleted~~ Deleted   Excludes 1   Excludes 2   Includes   Use additional   Code first   Code also   Key words
OGCR Official Guidelines   X Assign placeholder X   ● Use Additional Character(s)   ▶ Manifestation Code   🐾 Hierarchical Condition Category   Coding Clinic

● **T87.5**   **Necrosis of amputation stump**

     T87.50   Necrosis of amputation stump, **unspecified extremity** 🔁

     T87.51   Necrosis of amputation stump, **right upper extremity** 🔁

     T87.52   Necrosis of amputation stump, **left upper extremity** 🔁

     T87.53   Necrosis of amputation stump, **right lower extremity** 🔁

     T87.54   Necrosis of amputation stump, **left lower extremity** 🔁

● **T87.8**   **Other complications of amputation stump**

     T87.81   Dehiscence of amputation stump 🔁

     T87.89   Other complications of amputation stump 🔁
         Amputation stump contracture
         Amputation stump contracture of next proximal joint
         Amputation stump flexion
         Amputation stump edema
         Amputation stump hematoma
         Excludes2   phantom limb syndrome (G54.6-G54.7)

     T87.9   **Unspecified complications of amputation stump** 🔁

● **T88**   **Other complications of surgical and medical care, not elsewhere classified**

     Excludes2   complication following infusion, transfusion and therapeutic injection (T80.-)
         complication following procedure NEC (T81.-)
         complications of anesthesia in labor and delivery (O74.-)
         complications of anesthesia in pregnancy (O29.-)
         complications of anesthesia in puerperium (O89.-)
         complications of devices, implants and grafts (T82-T85)
         complications of obstetric surgery and procedure (O75.4)
         dermatitis due to drugs and medicaments (L23.3, L24.4, L25.1, L27.0-L27.1)
         poisoning and toxic effects of drugs and chemicals (T36-T65 with fifth or sixth character 1-4 or 6)
         specified complications classified elsewhere

     The appropriate 7th character is to be added to each code from category T88

> | | |
> |---|---|
> | A | initial encounter |
> | D | subsequent encounter |
> | S | sequela |

X● **T88.0**   **Infection following immunization**
     Sepsis following immunization
     Coding Clinic: 2019, Q1, P14;2018, Q4, P90

X● **T88.1**   **Other complications following immunization, not elsewhere classified**
     Generalized vaccinia
     Rash following immunization
     Excludes1   vaccinia not from vaccine (B08.011)
     Excludes2   anaphylactic shock due to serum (T80.5-)
         other serum reactions (T80.6-)
         postimmunization arthropathy (M02.2)
         postimmunization encephalitis (G04.02)
         postimmunization fever (R50.83)

X● **T88.2**   **Shock due to anesthesia**
     Use additional code for adverse effect, if applicable, to identify drug (T41.- with fifth or sixth character 5)
     Excludes1   complications of anesthesia (in):
         labor and delivery (O74.-)
         pregnancy (O29.-)
         puerperium (O89.-)
         postprocedural shock NOS (T81.1-)

X● **T88.3**   **Malignant hyperthermia due to anesthesia**
     Use additional code for adverse effect, if applicable, to identify drug (T41.- with fifth or sixth character 5)

X● **T88.4**   **Failed or difficult intubation**

● **T88.5**   **Other complications of anesthesia**
     Use additional code for adverse effect, if applicable, to identify drug (T41.- with fifth or sixth character 5)
     Coding Clinic: 2016, Q4, P72

     X● **T88.51**   Hypothermia following anesthesia

     X● **T88.52**   Failed moderate sedation during procedure
         Failed conscious sedation during procedure
         Excludes2   personal history of failed moderate sedation (Z92.83)

     X● **T88.53**   Unintended awareness under general anesthesia during procedure
         Excludes2   personal history of unintended awareness under general anesthesia (Z92.84)
         Coding Clinic: 2016, Q4, P72-73

     X● **T88.59**   Other complications of anesthesia

X● **T88.6**   **Anaphylactic reaction due to adverse effect of correct drug or medicament properly administered**
     Anaphylactic shock due to adverse effect of correct drug or medicament properly administered
     Anaphylactoid reaction NOS
     Use additional code for adverse effect, if applicable, to identify drug (T36-T50 with fifth or sixth character 5)
     Excludes1   anaphylactic reaction due to serum (T80.5-)
         anaphylactic shock or reaction due to adverse food reaction (T78.0-)
     Coding Clinic: 2020, Q1, P18

X● **T88.7**   **Unspecified adverse effect of drug or medicament**
     Drug hypersensitivity NOS
     Drug reaction NOS
     Use additional code for adverse effect, if applicable, to identify drug (T36-T50 with fifth or sixth character 5)
     Excludes1   specified adverse effects of drugs and medicaments (A00-R94 and T80-T88.6, T88.8)

X● **T88.8**   **Other specified complications of surgical and medical care, not elsewhere classified**
     Use additional code to identify the complication

X● **T88.9**   **Complication of surgical and medical care, unspecified**

CHAPTER 20

EXTERNAL CAUSES OF MORBIDITY (V00-Y99)

OGCR Chapter-Specific Coding Guidelines

20. **Chapter 20: External Causes of Morbidity (V00-Y99)**
The external causes of morbidity codes should never be sequenced as the first-listed or principal diagnosis.

External cause codes are intended to provide data for injury research and evaluation of injury prevention strategies. These codes capture how the injury or health condition happened (cause), the intent (unintentional or accidental; or intentional, such as suicide or assault), the place where the event occurred the activity of the patient at the time of the event, and the person's status (e.g., civilian, military).

There is no national requirement for mandatory ICD-10-CM external cause code reporting. Unless a provider is subject to a state-based external cause code reporting mandate or these codes are required by a particular payer, reporting of ICD-10-CM codes in Chapter 20, External Causes of Morbidity, is not required. In the absence of a mandatory reporting requirement, providers are encouraged to voluntarily report external cause codes, as they provide valuable data for injury research and evaluation of injury prevention strategies.

a. General External Cause Coding Guidelines

1) **Used with any code in the range of A00.0-T88.9, Z00-Z99**
An external cause code may be used with any code in the range of A00.0-T88.9, Z00-Z99, classification that represents a health condition due to an external cause. Though they are most applicable to injuries, they are also valid for use with such things as infections or diseases due to an external source, and other health conditions, such as a heart attack that occurs during strenuous physical activity.

2) **External cause code used for length of treatment**
Assign the external cause code, with the appropriate 7th character (initial encounter, subsequent encounter or sequela) for each encounter for which the injury or condition is being treated.

Most categories in Chapter 20 have a 7th character requirement for each applicable code. Most categories in this chapter have three 7th character values: A, initial encounter, D, subsequent encounter and S, sequela. While the patient may be seen by a new or different provider over the course of treatment for an injury or condition, assignment of the 7th character for external cause should match the 7th character of the code assigned for the associated injury or condition for the encounter.

3) **Use the full range of external cause codes**
Use the full range of external cause codes to completely describe the cause, the intent, the place of occurrence and if applicable, the activity of the patient at the time of the event, and the patient's status, for all injuries, and other health conditions due to an external cause.

4) **Assign as many external cause codes as necessary**
Assign as many external cause codes as necessary to fully explain each cause. If only one external code can be recorded, assign the code most related to the principal diagnosis.

5) **The selection of the appropriate external cause code**
The selection of the appropriate external cause code is guided by the Alphabetic Index of External Causes and by Inclusion and Exclusion notes in the Tabular List.

6) **External cause code can never be a principal diagnosis**
An external cause code can never be a principal (first-listed) diagnosis.

7) **Combination external cause codes**
Certain of the external cause codes are combination codes that identify sequential events that result in an injury, such as a fall which results in striking against an object. The injury may be due to either event or both. The combination external cause code used should correspond to the sequence of events regardless of which caused the most serious injury.

8) **No external cause code needed in certain circumstances**
No external cause code from Chapter 20 is needed if the external cause and intent are included in a code from another chapter (e.g., T36.0X1- Poisoning by penicillins, accidental (unintentional)).

b. Place of Occurrence Guideline
Codes from category Y92, Place of occurrence of the external cause, are secondary codes for use after other external cause codes to identify the location of the patient at the time of injury or other condition.

Generally, a place of occurrence code is assigned only once, at the initial encounter for treatment. However, in the rare instance that a new injury occurs during hospitalization, an additional place of occurrence code may be assigned. No 7th characters are used for Y92. Only one code from Y92 should be recorded on a medical record.

Do not use place of occurrence code Y92.9 if the place is not stated or is not applicable.

c. Activity Code
Assign a code from category Y93, Activity code, to describe the activity of the patient at the time the injury or other health condition occurred.

An activity code is used only once, at the initial encounter for treatment. Only one code from Y93 should be recorded on a medical record.

The activity codes are not applicable to poisonings, adverse effects, misadventures or sequela.

Do not assign Y93.9, Unspecified activity, if the activity is not stated.

A code from category Y93 is appropriate for use with external cause and intent codes if identifying the activity provides additional information about the event.

d. Place of Occurrence, Activity, and Status Codes Used with Other External Cause Code
When applicable, place of occurrence, activity, and external cause status codes are sequenced after the main external cause code(s). Regardless of the number of external cause codes assigned, there should be only one place of occurrence code, one activity code, and one external cause status code assigned to an encounter.

e. If the Reporting Format Limits the Number of External Cause Codes

If the reporting format limits the number of external cause codes that can be used in reporting clinical data, report the code for the cause/intent most related to the principal diagnosis. If the format permits capture of additional external cause codes, the cause/intent, including medical misadventures, of the additional events should be reported rather than the codes for place, activity, or external status.

f. Multiple External Cause Coding Guidelines

More than one external cause code is required to fully describe the external cause of an illness or injury. The assignment of external cause codes should be sequenced in the following priority:

If two or more events cause separate injuries, an external cause code should be assigned for each cause. The first-listed external cause code will be selected in the following order:

External codes for child and adult abuse take priority over all other external cause codes.

See Section I.C.19., Child and Adult abuse guidelines.

External codes for terrorism events take priority over all other external cause codes except child and adult abuse.

External cause codes for cataclysmic events take priority over all other external cause codes except child and adult abuse and terrorism.

External cause codes for transport accidents take priority over all other external cause codes except cataclysmic events, child and adult abuse and terrorism.

Activity and external cause status codes are assigned following all causal (intent) external cause codes.

The first-listed external cause code should correspond to the cause of the most serious diagnosis due to an assault, accident, or self-harm, following the order of hierarchy listed above.

g. Child and Adult Abuse Guideline

Adult and child abuse, neglect and maltreatment are classified as assault. Any of the assault codes may be used to indicate the external cause of any injury resulting from the confirmed abuse.

For confirmed cases of abuse, neglect and maltreatment, when the perpetrator is known, a code from Y07, Perpetrator of maltreatment and neglect, should accompany any other assault codes.

See Section I.C.19. Adult and child abuse, neglect and other maltreatment

h. Unknown or Undetermined Intent Guideline

If the intent (accident, self-harm, assault) of the cause of an injury or other condition is unknown or unspecified, code the intent as accidental intent. All transport accident categories assume accidental intent.

1) Use of undetermined intent

External cause codes for events of undetermined intent are only for use if the documentation in the record specifies that the intent cannot be determined.

i. Sequelae (Late Effects) of External Cause Guidelines

1) Sequelae external cause codes

Sequela are reported using the external cause code with the 7th character "S" for sequela. These codes should be used with any report of a late effect or sequela resulting from a previous injury.

See Section I.B.10. Sequela, (Late Effects).

2) Sequela external cause code with a related current injury

A sequela external cause code should never be used with a related current nature of injury code.

3) Use of sequela external cause codes for subsequent visits

Use a late effect external cause code for subsequent visits when a late effect of the initial injury is being treated. Do not use a late effect external cause code for subsequent visits for follow-up care (e.g., to assess healing, to receive rehabilitative therapy) of the injury when no late effect of the injury has been documented.

j. Terrorism Guidelines

1) Cause of injury identified by the Federal Government (FBI) as terrorism

When the cause of an injury is identified by the Federal Government (FBI) as terrorism, the first-listed external cause code should be a code from category Y38, Terrorism. The definition of terrorism employed by the FBI is found at the inclusion note at the beginning of category Y38. Use additional code for place of occurrence (Y92.-). More than one Y38 code may be assigned if the injury is the result of more than one mechanism of terrorism.

2) Cause of an injury is suspected to be the result of terrorism

When the cause of an injury is suspected to be the result of terrorism a code from category Y38 should not be assigned. Suspected cases should be classified as assault.

3) Code Y38.9, Terrorism, secondary effects

Assign code Y38.9, Terrorism, secondary effects, for conditions occurring subsequent to the terrorist event. This code should not be assigned for conditions that are due to the initial terrorist act.

It is acceptable to assign code Y38.9 with another code from Y38 if there is an injury due to the initial terrorist event and an injury that is a subsequent result of the terrorist event.

k. External cause status

A code from category Y99, External cause status, should be assigned whenever any other external cause code is assigned for an encounter, including an Activity code, except for the events noted below. Assign a code from category Y99, External cause status, to indicate the work status of the person at the time the event occurred. The status code indicates whether the event occurred during military activity, whether a non-military person was at work, whether an individual including a student or volunteer was involved in a non-work activity at the time of the causal event.

A code from Y99, External cause status, should be assigned, when applicable, with other external cause codes, such as transport accidents and falls. The external cause status codes are not applicable to poisonings, adverse effects, misadventures or late effects.

Do not assign a code from category Y99 if no other external cause codes (cause, activity) are applicable for the encounter.

An external cause status code is used only once, at the initial encounter for treatment. Only one code from Y99 should be recorded on a medical record.

Do not assign code Y99.9, Unspecified external cause status, if the status is not stated.

CHAPTER 20

EXTERNAL CAUSES OF MORBIDITY (V00-Y99)

Note: This chapter permits the classification of environmental events and circumstances as the cause of injury, and other adverse effects. Where a code from this section is applicable, it is intended that it shall be used secondary to a code from another chapter of the Classification indicating the nature of the condition. Most often, the condition will be classifiable to Chapter 19, Injury, poisoning and certain other consequences of external causes (S00-T88). Other conditions that may be stated to be due to external causes are classified in Chapters 1 to 18. For these conditions, codes from Chapter 20 should be used to provide additional information as to the cause of the condition.

This chapter contains the following blocks:

V00-X58	Accidents
V00-V99	Transport accidents
V00-V09	Pedestrian injured in transport accident
V10-V19	Pedal cycle rider injured in transport accident
V20-V29	Motorcycle rider injured in transport accident
V30-V39	Occupant of three-wheeled motor vehicle injured in transport accident
V40-V49	Car occupant injured in transport accident
V50-V59	Occupant of pick-up truck or van injured in transport accident
V60-V69	Occupant of heavy transport vehicle injured in transport accident
V70-V79	Bus occupant injured in transport accident
V80-V89	Other land transport accidents
V90-V94	Water transport accidents
V95-V97	Air and space transport accidents
V98-V99	Other and unspecified transport accidents
W00-X58	Other external causes of accidental injury
W00-W19	Slipping, tripping, stumbling and falls
W20-W49	Exposure to inanimate mechanical forces
W50-W64	Exposure to animate mechanical forces
W65-W74	Accidental non-transport drowning and submersion
W85-W99	Exposure to electric current, radiation and extreme ambient air temperature and pressure
X00-X08	Exposure to smoke, fire and flames
X10-X19	Contact with heat and hot substances
X30-X39	Exposure to forces of nature
X50	Overexertion and strenuous or repetitive movements
X52, X58	Accidental exposure to other specified factors
X71-X83	Intentional self-harm
X92-Y09	Assault
Y21-Y33	Event of undetermined intent
Y35-Y38	Legal intervention, operations of war, military operations, and terrorism
Y62-Y84	Complications of medical and surgical care
Y62-Y69	Misadventures to patients during surgical and medical care
Y70-Y82	Medical devices associated with adverse incidents in diagnostic and therapeutic use
Y83-Y84	Surgical and other medical procedures as the cause of abnormal reaction of the patient, or of later complication, without mention of misadventure at the time of the procedure
Y90-Y99	Supplementary factors related to causes of morbidity classified elsewhere

ACCIDENTS (V00-X58)

TRANSPORT ACCIDENTS (V00-V99)

Note: This section is structured in 12 groups. Those relating to land transport accidents (V00-V89) reflect the victim's mode of transport and are subdivided to identify the victim's 'counterpart' or the type of event. The vehicle of which the injured person is an occupant is identified in the first two characters since it is seen as the most important factor to identify for prevention purposes. A transport accident is one in which the vehicle involved must be moving or running or in use for transport purposes at the time of the accident.

Use additional code to identify:
Airbag injury (W22.1)
Type of street or road (Y92.4-)
Use of cellular telephone and other electronic equipment at the time of the transport accident (Y93.C-)

Excludes1   agricultural vehicles in stationary use or maintenance (W31.-)
assault by crashing of motor vehicle (Y03.-)
automobile or motor cycle in stationary use or maintenance - code to type of accident
crashing of motor vehicle, undetermined intent (Y32)
intentional self-harm by crashing of motor vehicle (X82)

Excludes2   transport accidents due to cataclysm (X34-X38)

Note: Definitions related to transport accidents:

(a) A transport accident (V00-V99) is any accident involving a device designed primarily for, or used at the time primarily for, conveying persons or good from one place to another.

(b) A public highway [trafficway] or street is the entire width between property lines (or other boundary lines) of land open to the public as a matter of right or custom for purposes of moving persons or property from one place to another. A roadway is that part of the public highway designed, improved and customarily used for vehicular traffic.

(c) A traffic accident is any vehicle accident occurring on the public highway [i.e., originating on, terminating on, or involving a vehicle partially on the highway]. A vehicle accident is assumed to have occurred on the public highway unless another place is specified, except in the case of accidents involving only off-road motor vehicles, which are classified as nontraffic accidents unless the contrary is stated.

(d) A nontraffic accident is any vehicle accident that occurs entirely in any place other than a public highway.

(e) A pedestrian is any person involved in an accident who was not at the time of the accident riding in or on a motor vehicle, railway train, streetcar or animal-drawn or other vehicle, or on a pedal cycle or animal. This includes, a person changing a tire, working on a parked car, or a person on foot. It also includes the user of a pedestrian conveyance such as a baby stroller, ice-skates, skis, sled, roller skates, a skateboard, nonmotorized or motorized wheelchair, motorized mobility scooter, or nonmotorized scooter.

(f) A driver is an occupant of a transport vehicle who is operating or intending to operate it.

(g) A passenger is any occupant of a transport vehicle other than the driver, except a person traveling on the outside of the vehicle.

(h) A person on the outside of a vehicle is any person being transported by a vehicle but not occupying the space normally reserved for the driver or passengers, or the space intended for the transport of property. This includes a person travelling on the bodywork, bumper, fender, roof, running board or step of a vehicle, as well as, hanging on the outside of the vehicle.

(i) A pedal cycle is any land transport vehicle operated solely by nonmotorized pedals including a bicycle or tricycle.

(j) A pedal cyclist is any person riding a pedal cycle or in a sidecar or trailer attached to a pedal cycle.

▶ New   ⇒ Revised   ~~deleted~~ Deleted   Excludes 1   Excludes 2   Includes   Use additional   Code first   Code also   Key words

1464   OGCR Official Guidelines   X Assign placeholder X   ● Use Additional Character(s)   ▶ Manifestation Code   🔖 Hierarchical Condition Category   Coding Clinic

(k) A motorcycle is a two-wheeled motor vehicle with one or two riding saddles and sometimes with a third wheel for the support of a sidecar. The sidecar is considered part of the motorcycle. This includes a moped, motor scooter, or motorized bicycle.

(l) A motorcycle rider is any person riding a motorcycle or in a sidecar or trailer attached to the motorcycle.

(m) A three-wheeled motor vehicle is a motorized tricycle designed primarily for on-road use. This includes a motor-driven tricycle, a motorized rickshaw, or a three-wheeled motor car.

(n) A car [automobile] is a four-wheeled motor vehicle designed primarily for carrying up to 7 persons. A trailer being towed by the car is considered part of the car. It does not include a van or minivan—see definition (o)

(o) A pick-up truck or van is a four or six-wheeled motor vehicle designed for carrying passengers as well as property or cargo weighing less than the local limit for classification as a heavy goods vehicle, and not requiring a special driver's license. This includes a minivan and a sport-utility vehicle (SUV).

(p) A heavy transport vehicle is a motor vehicle designed primarily for carrying property, meeting local criteria for classification as a heavy goods vehicle in terms of weight and requiring a special driver's license.

(q) A bus (coach) is a motor vehicle designed or adapted primarily for carrying more than 10 passengers, and requiring a special driver's license.

(r) A railway train or railway vehicle is any device, with or without freight or passenger cars coupled to it, designed for traffic on a railway track. This includes subterranean (subways) or elevated trains.

(s) A streetcar is a device designed and used primarily for transporting passengers within a municipality, running on rails, usually subject to normal traffic control signals, and operated principally on a right-of-way that forms part of the roadway. This includes a tram or trolley that runs on rails. A trailer being towed by a streetcar is considered part of the streetcar.

(t) A special vehicle mainly used on industrial premises is a motor vehicle designed primarily for use within the buildings and premises of industrial or commercial establishments. This includes battery-powered airport passenger vehicles or baggage/mail trucks, forklifts, coal-cars in a coal mine, logging cars and trucks used in mines or quarries.

(u) A special vehicle mainly used in agriculture is a motor vehicle designed specifically for use in farming and agriculture (horticulture), to work the land, tend and harvest crops and transport materials on the farm. This includes harvesters, farm machinery and tractor and trailers.

(v) A special construction vehicle is a motor vehicle designed specifically for use on construction and demolition sites. This includes bulldozers, diggers, earth levellers, dump trucks, backhoes, front-end loaders, pavers, and mechanical shovels.

(w) A special all-terrain vehicle is a motor vehicle of special design to enable it to negotiate over rough or soft terrain, snow or sand. Examples of special design are high construction, special wheels and tires, tracks, and support on a cushion of air. This includes snow mobiles, all-terrain vehicles (ATV), and dune buggies. It does not include passenger vehicle designated as sport utility vehicles (SUV).

(x) A watercraft is any device designed for transporting passengers or goods on water. This includes motor or sail boats, ships, and hovercraft.

(y) An aircraft is any device for transporting passengers or goods in the air. This includes hot-air balloons, gliders, helicopters and airplanes.

(z) A military vehicle is any motorized vehicle operating on a public roadway owned by the military and being operated by a member of the military.

PEDESTRIAN INJURED IN TRANSPORT ACCIDENT (V00-V09)

Includes person changing tire on transport vehicle
person examining engine of vehicle broken down in (on side of) road

Excludes1 fall due to non-transport collision with other person (W03)
pedestrian on foot falling (slipping) on ice and snow (W00.-)
struck or bumped by another person (W51)

● **V00 Pedestrian conveyance accident**

Use additional place of occurrence and activity external cause codes, if known (Y92.-, Y93.-)

Excludes1 collision with another person without fall (W51)
fall due to person on foot colliding with another person on foot (W03)
fall from non-moving wheelchair, nonmotorized scooter and motorized mobility scooter without collision (W05.-)
pedestrian (conveyance) collision with other land transport vehicle (V01-V09)
pedestrian on foot falling (slipping) on ice and snow (W00.-)

The appropriate 7th character is to be added to each code from category V00

A	initial encounter
D	subsequent encounter
S	sequela

● **V00.0 Pedestrian on foot injured in collision with pedestrian conveyance**

X ● **V00.01 Pedestrian on foot injured in collision with roller-skater**

X ● **V00.02 Pedestrian on foot injured in collision with skateboarder**

▶ ● **V00.03 Pedestrian on foot injured in collision with standing micro-mobility pedestrian conveyance**

  ▶ **V00.031 Pedestrian on foot injured in collision with rider of standing electric scooter**

  ▶ **V00.038 Pedestrian on foot injured in collision with rider of other standing micro-mobility pedestrian conveyance**
  ▶ Pedestrian on foot injured in collision with rider of hoverboard
  ▶ Pedestrian on foot injured in collision with rider of segway

X ● **V00.09 Pedestrian on foot injured in collision with other pedestrian conveyance**

● **V00.1 Rolling-type pedestrian conveyance accident**

Excludes1 accident with baby stroller (V00.82-)
accident with wheelchair (powered) (V00.81-)
accident with motorized mobility scooter (V00.83-)

● **V00.11 In-line roller-skate accident**

  ● **V00.111 Fall from in-line roller-skates**

  ● **V00.112 In-line roller-skater colliding with stationary object**

  ● **V00.118 Other in-line roller-skate accident**

  Excludes1 roller-skater collision with other land transport vehicle (V01-V09 with 5th character 1)

CHAPTER 20 (V00-Y99)

● **V00.12**   **Non-in-line roller-skate** accident
  ● **V00.121**   **Fall from non-in-line roller-skates**
  ● **V00.122**   **Non-in-line roller-skater colliding with stationary object**
  ● **V00.128**   **Other non-in-line roller-skating accident**
     Excludes1   roller-skater collision with other land transport vehicle (V01-V09 with 5th character 1)

● **V00.13**   **Skateboard accident**
  ● **V00.131**   **Fall from skateboard**
  ● **V00.132**   **Skateboarder colliding with stationary object**
  ● **V00.138**   **Other skateboard accident**
     Excludes1   skateboarder collision with other land transport vehicle (V01-V09 with 5th character 2)

● **V00.14**   **Scooter (nonmotorized) accident**
   Excludes1   motor scooter accident (V20-V29)
  ● **V00.141**   **Fall from scooter (nonmotorized)**
  ● **V00.142**   **Scooter (nonmotorized) colliding with stationary object**
  ● **V00.148**   **Other scooter (nonmotorized) accident**
     Excludes1   scooter (non-motorized) collision with other land transport vehicle (V01-V09 with fifth character 9)

● **V00.15**   **Heelies accident**
   Rolling shoe
   Wheeled shoe
   Wheelies accident
  ● **V00.151**   **Fall from heelies**
  ● **V00.152**   **Heelies colliding with stationary object**
  ● **V00.158**   **Other heelies accident**
● **V00.18**   **Accident on other rolling-type pedestrian conveyance**
  ● **V00.181**   **Fall from other rolling-type pedestrian conveyance**
  ● **V00.182**   **Pedestrian on other rolling-type pedestrian conveyance colliding with stationary object**
  ● **V00.188**   **Other accident on other rolling-type pedestrian conveyance**
● **V00.2**   **Gliding-type pedestrian conveyance accident**
  ● **V00.21**   **Ice-skates accident**
    ● **V00.211**   **Fall from ice-skates**
    ● **V00.212**   **Ice-skater colliding with stationary object**
    ● **V00.218**   **Other ice-skates accident**
       Excludes1   ice-skater collision with other land transport vehicle (V01-V09 with 5th character 9)

  ● **V00.22**   **Sled accident**
    ● **V00.221**   **Fall from sled**
    ● **V00.222**   **Sledder colliding with stationary object**
    ● **V00.228**   **Other sled accident**
       Excludes1   sled collision with other land transport vehicle (V01-V09 with 5th character 9)

● **V00.28**   **Other gliding-type pedestrian conveyance accident**
  ● **V00.281**   **Fall from other gliding-type pedestrian conveyance**
  ● **V00.282**   **Pedestrian on other gliding-type pedestrian conveyance colliding with stationary object**
  ● **V00.288**   **Other accident on other gliding-type pedestrian conveyance**
     Excludes1   gliding-type pedestrian conveyance collision with other land transport vehicle (V01-V09 with 5th character 9)

● **V00.3**   **Flat-bottomed pedestrian conveyance accident**
  ● **V00.31**   **Snowboard accident**
    ● **V00.311**   **Fall from snowboard**
    ● **V00.312**   **Snowboarder colliding with stationary object**
    ● **V00.318**   **Other snowboard accident**
       Excludes1   snowboarder collision with other land transport vehicle (V01-V09 with 5th character 9)

  ● **V00.32**   **Snow-ski accident**
    ● **V00.321**   **Fall from snow-skis**
       Coding Clinic: 2015, Q1, P12
    ● **V00.322**   **Snow-skier colliding with stationary object**
    ● **V00.328**   **Other snow-ski accident**
       Excludes1   snow-skier collision with other land transport vehicle (V01-V09 with 5th character 9)

  ● **V00.38**   **Other flat-bottomed pedestrian conveyance accident**
    ● **V00.381**   **Fall from other flat-bottomed pedestrian conveyance**
    ● **V00.382**   **Pedestrian on other flat-bottomed pedestrian conveyance colliding with stationary object**
    ● **V00.388**   **Other accident on other flat-bottomed pedestrian conveyance**
● **V00.8**   **Accident on other pedestrian conveyance**
  ● **V00.81**   **Accident with wheelchair (powered)**
    ● **V00.811**   **Fall from moving wheelchair (powered)**
       Excludes1   fall from non-moving wheelchair (W05.0)
    ● **V00.812**   **Wheelchair (powered) colliding with stationary object**
    ● **V00.818**   **Other accident with wheelchair (powered)**
  ● **V00.82**   **Accident with baby stroller**
    ● **V00.821**   **Fall from baby stroller**
    ● **V00.822**   **Baby stroller colliding with stationary object**
    ● **V00.828**   **Other accident with baby stroller**

▶ New   ⇒ Revised   ~~deleted~~ Deleted   Excludes 1   Excludes 2   Includes   Use additional   Code first   Code also   Key words
OGCR Official Guidelines   X Assign placeholder X   ● Use Additional Character(s)   ▸ Manifestation Code   🔖 Hierarchical Condition Category   **Coding Clinic**

● **V00.83**   Accident with motorized mobility scooter
     ● **V00.831**   **Fall from motorized mobility scooter**
         Excludes1   fall from non-moving motorized mobility scooter (W05.2)
     ● **V00.832**   **Motorized mobility scooter colliding with stationary object**
     ● **V00.838**   **Other accident with motorized mobility scooter**
▶ ● **V00.84**   **Accident with standing micro-mobility pedestrian conveyance**
     ▶ **V00.841**   **Fall from standing electric scooter**
     ▶ **V00.842**   **Pedestrian on standing electric scooter colliding with stationary object**
     ▶ **V00.848**   **Other accident with standing micro-mobility pedestrian conveyance**
         ▶ Accident with hoverboard
         ▶ Accident with segway
● **V00.89**   Accident on other pedestrian conveyance
     ● **V00.891**   **Fall from other pedestrian conveyance**
     ● **V00.892**   **Pedestrian on other pedestrian conveyance colliding with stationary object**
     ● **V00.898**   **Other accident on other pedestrian conveyance**
         Excludes1   other pedestrian (conveyance) collision with other land transport vehicle (V01-V09 with 5th character 9)

● **V01**   Pedestrian injured in collision with pedal cycle
     The appropriate 7th character is to be added to each code from category V01

     | | |
     A   initial encounter
     D   subsequent encounter
     S   sequela

   ● **V01.0**   **Pedestrian injured in collision with pedal cycle in nontraffic accident**
     X ● **V01.00**   **Pedestrian on foot injured in collision with pedal cycle in nontraffic accident**
         Pedestrian NOS injured in collision with pedal cycle in nontraffic accident
     X ● **V01.01**   **Pedestrian on roller-skates injured in collision with pedal cycle in nontraffic accident**
     X ● **V01.02**   **Pedestrian on skateboard injured in collision with pedal cycle in nontraffic accident**
     ▶ ● **V01.03**   **Pedestrian on standing micro-mobility pedestrian conveyance injured in collision with pedal cycle in nontraffic accident**
       ▶ **V01.031**   **Pedestrian on standing electric scooter injured in collision with pedal cycle in nontraffic accident**
       ▶ **V01.038**   **Pedestrian on other standing micro-mobility pedestrian conveyance injured in collision with pedal cycle in nontraffic accident**
         ▶ Pedestrian on hoverboard injured in collision with pedal cycle in nontraffic accident
         ▶ Pedestrian on segway injured in collision with pedal cycle in nontraffic accident

X ● **V01.09**   **Pedestrian with other conveyance injured in collision with pedal cycle in nontraffic accident**
     Pedestrian with baby stroller injured in collision with pedal cycle in nontraffic accident
     Pedestrian in wheelchair (powered) injured in collision with pedal cycle in nontraffic accident
     Pedestrian in motorized mobility scooter injured in collision with pedal cycle in nontraffic accident
     Pedestrian on ice-skates injured in collision with pedal cycle in nontraffic accident
     Pedestrian on nonmotorized scooter injured in collision with pedal cycle in nontraffic accident
     Pedestrian on sled injured in collision with pedal cycle in nontraffic accident
     Pedestrian on snowboard injured in collision with pedal cycle in nontraffic accident
     Pedestrian on snow-skis injured in collision with pedal cycle in nontraffic accident

● **V01.1**   Pedestrian injured in collision with pedal cycle in traffic accident
     X ● **V01.10**   **Pedestrian on foot injured in collision with pedal cycle in traffic accident**
         Pedestrian NOS injured in collision with pedal cycle in traffic accident
     X ● **V01.11**   **Pedestrian on roller-skates injured in collision with pedal cycle in traffic accident**
     X ● **V01.12**   **Pedestrian on skateboard injured in collision with pedal cycle in traffic accident**
     ▶ ● **V01.13**   **Pedestrian on standing micro-mobility pedestrian conveyance injured in collision with pedal cycle in traffic accident**
       ▶ **V01.131**   **Pedestrian on standing electric scooter injured in collision with pedal cycle in traffic accident**
       ▶ **V01.138**   **Pedestrian on other standing micro-mobility pedestrian conveyance injured in collision with pedal cycle in traffic accident**
         ▶ Pedestrian on hoverboard injured in collision with pedal cycle in traffic accident
         ▶ Pedestrian on segway injured in collision with pedal cycle in traffic accident

X ● **V01.19**   **Pedestrian with other conveyance injured in collision with pedal cycle in traffic accident**
     Pedestrian with baby stroller injured in collision with pedal cycle in traffic accident
     Pedestrian in wheelchair (powered) injured in collision with pedal cycle in traffic accident
     Pedestrian in motorized mobility scooter injured in collision with pedal cycle in traffic accident
     Pedestrian on ice-skates injured in collision with pedal cycle in traffic accident
     Pedestrian on nonmotorized scooter injured in collision with pedal cycle in traffic accident
     Pedestrian on sled injured in collision with pedal cycle in traffic accident
     Pedestrian on snowboard injured in collision with pedal cycle in traffic accident
     Pedestrian on snow-skis injured in collision with pedal cycle in traffic accident

CHAPTER 20 (V00-Y99)

● **V01.9**   **Pedestrian injured in collision with pedal cycle, unspecified whether traffic or nontraffic accident**

  X● **V01.90**   Pedestrian on foot injured in collision with pedal cycle, unspecified whether traffic or nontraffic accident
       Pedestrian NOS injured in collision with pedal cycle, unspecified whether traffic or nontraffic accident

  X● **V01.91**   Pedestrian on roller-skates injured in collision with pedal cycle, unspecified whether traffic or nontraffic accident

  X● **V01.92**   Pedestrian on skateboard injured in collision with pedal cycle, unspecified whether traffic or nontraffic accident

  ▶● **V01.93**   Pedestrian on standing micro-mobility pedestrian conveyance injured in collision with pedal cycle, unspecified whether traffic or nontraffic accident

    ▶ **V01.931**   Pedestrian on standing electric scooter injured in collision with pedal cycle, unspecified whether traffic or nontraffic accident

    ▶ **V01.938**   Pedestrian on other standing micro-mobility pedestrian conveyance injured in collision with pedal cycle, unspecified whether traffic or nontraffic accident
        ▶Pedestrian on hoverboard injured in collision with pedal cycle, unspecified whether traffic or nontraffic accident
        ▶Pedestrian on segway injured in collision with pedal cycle, unspecified whether traffic or nontraffic accident

  X● **V01.99**   Pedestrian with other conveyance injured in collision with pedal cycle, unspecified whether traffic or nontraffic accident
       Pedestrian with baby stroller injured in collision with pedal cycle, unspecified whether traffic or nontraffic accident
       Pedestrian in wheelchair (powered) injured in collision with pedal cycle, unspecified whether traffic or nontraffic accident
       Pedestrian in motorized mobility scooter injured in collision with pedal cycle, unspecified whether traffic or nontraffic accident
       Pedestrian on ice-skates injured in collision with pedal cycle unspecified, whether traffic or nontraffic accident
       Pedestrian on nonmotorized scooter injured in collision with pedal cycle, unspecified whether traffic or nontraffic accident
       Pedestrian on sled injured in collision with pedal cycle unspecified, whether traffic or nontraffic accident
       Pedestrian on snowboard injured in collision with pedal cycle, unspecified whether traffic or nontraffic accident
       Pedestrian on snow-skis injured in collision with pedal cycle, unspecified whether traffic or nontraffic accident

● **V02**   **Pedestrian injured in collision with two- or three-wheeled motor vehicle**
     The appropriate 7th character is to be added to each code from category V02

A	initial encounter
D	subsequent encounter
S	sequela

● **V02.0**   **Pedestrian injured in collision with two- or three-wheeled motor vehicle in nontraffic accident**

  X● **V02.00**   Pedestrian on foot injured in collision with two- or three-wheeled motor vehicle in nontraffic accident
       Pedestrian NOS injured in collision with two- or three-wheeled motor vehicle in nontraffic accident

  X● **V02.01**   Pedestrian on roller-skates injured in collision with two- or three-wheeled motor vehicle in nontraffic accident

  X● **V02.02**   Pedestrian on skateboard injured in collision with two- or three-wheeled motor vehicle in nontraffic accident

  ▶● **V02.03**   Pedestrian on standing micro-mobility pedestrian conveyance injured in collision with two- or three-wheeled motor vehicle in nontraffic accident

    ▶ **V02.031**   Pedestrian on standing electric scooter injured in collision with two- or three-wheeled motor vehicle in nontraffic accident

    ▶ **V02.038**   Pedestrian on other standing micro-mobility pedestrian conveyance injured in collision with two- or three-wheeled motor vehicle in nontraffic accident
        ▶Pedestrian on hoverboard injured in collision with two-or three wheeled motor vehicle in nontraffic accident
        ▶Pedestrian on segway injured in collision with two- or three-wheeled motor vehicle in nontraffic accident

  X● **V02.09**   Pedestrian with other conveyance injured in collision with two- or three-wheeled motor vehicle in nontraffic accident
       Pedestrian with baby stroller injured in collision with two- or three-wheeled motor vehicle in nontraffic accident
       Pedestrian on ice-skates injured in collision with two- or three-wheeled motor vehicle in nontraffic accident
       Pedestrian in wheelchair (powered) injured in collision with two- or three-wheeled motor vehicle in nontraffic accident
       Pedestrian in motorized mobility scooter injured in collision with two- or three-wheeled motor vehicle in nontraffic accident
       Pedestrian on nonmotorized scooter injured in collision with two- or three-wheeled motor vehicle in nontraffic accident
       Pedestrian on sled injured in collision with two- or three-wheeled motor vehicle in nontraffic accident
       Pedestrian on snowboard injured in collision with two- or three-wheeled motor vehicle in nontraffic accident
       Pedestrian on snow-skis injured in collision with two- or three-wheeled motor vehicle in nontraffic accident

▶ New   ⇒ Revised   ~~deleted~~ Deleted   Excludes 1   Excludes 2   Includes   Use additional   Code first   Code also   Key words

OGCR Official Guidelines   X Assign placeholder X   ● Use Additional Character(s)   ▶ Manifestation Code   🏷 Hierarchical Condition Category   **Coding Clinic**

● **V02.1** **Pedestrian injured in collision with two- or three-wheeled motor vehicle in traffic accident**

X ● **V02.10** Pedestrian on foot injured in collision with two- or three-wheeled motor vehicle in traffic accident

Pedestrian NOS injured in collision with two- or three-wheeled motor vehicle in traffic accident

X ● **V02.11** Pedestrian on roller-skates injured in collision with two- or three-wheeled motor vehicle in traffic accident

X ● **V02.12** Pedestrian on skateboard injured in collision with two- or three-wheeled motor vehicle in traffic accident

▶ ● **V02.13** Pedestrian on standing micro-mobility pedestrian conveyance injured in collision with two- or three-wheeled motor vehicle in traffic accident

　▶ **V02.131** Pedestrian on standing electric scooter injured in collision with two- or three-wheeled motor vehicle in traffic accident

　▶ **V02.138** Pedestrian on other standing micro-mobility pedestrian conveyance injured in collision with two- or three-wheeled motor vehicle in traffic accident

　　▶ Pedestrian on hoverboard injured in collision with two-or three wheeled motor vehicle in traffic accident

　　▶ Pedestrian on segway injured in collision with two- or three-wheeled motor vehicle in traffic accident

X ● **V02.19** Pedestrian with other conveyance injured in collision with two- or three-wheeled motor vehicle in traffic accident

Pedestrian with baby stroller injured in collision with two- or three-wheeled motor vehicle in traffic accident

Pedestrian in wheelchair (powered) injured in collision with two- or three-wheeled motor vehicle in traffic accident

Pedestrian in motorized mobility scooter injured in collision with two- or three-wheeled motor vehicle in traffic accident

Pedestrian on ice-skates injured in collision with two- or three-wheeled motor vehicle in traffic accident

Pedestrian on nonmotorized scooter injured in collision with two- or three-wheeled motor vehicle in traffic accident

Pedestrian on sled injured in collision with two- or three-wheeled motor vehicle in traffic accident

Pedestrian on snowboard injured in collision with two- or three-wheeled motor vehicle in traffic accident

Pedestrian on snow-skis injured in collision with two- or three-wheeled motor vehicle in traffic accident

● **V02.9** **Pedestrian injured in collision with two- or three-wheeled motor vehicle, unspecified whether traffic or nontraffic accident**

X ● **V02.90** Pedestrian on foot injured in collision with two- or three-wheeled motor vehicle, unspecified whether traffic or nontraffic accident

Pedestrian NOS injured in collision with two- or three-wheeled motor vehicle, unspecified whether traffic or nontraffic accident

X ● **V02.91** Pedestrian on roller-skates injured in collision with two- or three-wheeled motor vehicle, unspecified whether traffic or nontraffic accident

X ● **V02.92** Pedestrian on skateboard injured in collision with two- or three-wheeled motor vehicle, unspecified whether traffic or nontraffic accident

▶ ● **V02.93** Pedestrian on standing micro-mobility pedestrian conveyance injured in collision with two-or three-wheeled motor vehicle, unspecified whether traffic or nontraffic accident

　▶ **V02.931** Pedestrian on standing electric scooter injured in collision with two- or three wheeled motor vehicle, unspecified whether traffic or nontraffic accident

　▶ **V02.938** Pedestrian on other standing micro-mobility pedestrian conveyance injured in collision with two- or three wheeled motor vehicle, unspecified whether traffic or nontraffic accident

　　▶ Pedestrian on hoverboard injured in collision with two-three-wheeled motor vehicle, unspecified whether traffic or nontraffic accident

　　▶ Pedestrian on segway injured in collision with two- or three wheeled motor vehicle, unspecified whether traffic or nontraffic accident

X ● **V02.99** **Pedestrian with other conveyance injured in collision with two- or three-wheeled motor vehicle, unspecified whether traffic or nontraffic accident**

Pedestrian with baby stroller injured in collision with two- or three-wheeled motor vehicle, unspecified whether traffic or nontraffic accident

Pedestrian in wheelchair (powered) injured in collision with two- or three-wheeled motor vehicle, unspecified whether traffic or nontraffic accident

Pedestrian in motorized mobility scooter injured in collision with two- or three-wheeled motor vehicle, unspecified whether traffic or nontraffic accident

Pedestrian on ice-skates injured in collision with two- or three-wheeled motor vehicle, unspecified whether traffic or nontraffic accident

Pedestrian on nonmotorized scooter injured in collision with two- or three-wheeled motor vehicle, unspecified whether traffic or nontraffic accident

Pedestrian on sled injured in collision with two- or three-wheeled motor vehicle, unspecified whether traffic or nontraffic accident

Pedestrian on snowboard injured in collision with two- or three-wheeled motor vehicle, unspecified whether traffic or nontraffic accident

Pedestrian on snow-skis injured in collision with two- or three-wheeled motor vehicle, unspecified whether traffic or nontraffic accident

CHAPTER 20 (V00-Y99)

● **V03 Pedestrian injured in collision with car, pick-up truck or van**

The appropriate 7th character is to be added to each code from category V03

> A   initial encounter
> D   subsequent encounter
> S   sequela

● **V03.0 Pedestrian injured in collision with car, pick-up truck or van in nontraffic accident**

X ● **V03.00 Pedestrian on foot injured in collision with car, pick-up truck or van in nontraffic accident**
Pedestrian NOS injured in collision with car, pick-up truck or van in nontraffic accident

X ● **V03.01 Pedestrian on roller-skates injured in collision with car, pick-up truck or van in nontraffic accident**

X ● **V03.02 Pedestrian on skateboard injured in collision with car, pick-up truck or van in nontraffic accident**

▶ ● **V03.03 Pedestrian on standing micro-mobility pedestrian conveyance injured in collision with car, pick-up or van in nontraffic accident**

▶ **V03.031 Pedestrian on standing electric scooter injured in collision with car, pick-up or van in nontraffic accident**

▶ **V03.038 Pedestrian on other standing micro-mobility pedestrian conveyance injured in collision with car, pick-up or van in nontraffic accident**
▶Pedestrian on hoverboard injured in collision with car, pick-up or van in nontraffic accident
▶Pedestrian on segway injured in collision with car, pick-up or van in nontraffic accident

X ● **V03.09 Pedestrian with other conveyance injured in collision with car, pick-up truck or van in nontraffic accident**
Pedestrian with baby stroller injured in collision with car, pick-up truck or van in nontraffic accident
Pedestrian in wheelchair (powered) injured in collision with car, pick-up truck or van in nontraffic accident
Pedestrian in motorized mobility scooter injured in collision with car, pick-up truck or van in nontraffic accident
Pedestrian on ice-skates injured in collision with car, pick-up truck or van in nontraffic accident
Pedestrian on nonmotorized scooter injured in collision with car, pick-up truck or van in nontraffic accident
Pedestrian on sled injured in collision with car, pick-up truck or van in nontraffic accident
Pedestrian on snowboard injured in collision with car, pick-up truck or van in nontraffic accident
Pedestrian on snow-skis injured in collision with car, pick-up truck or van in nontraffic accident

● **V03.1 Pedestrian injured in collision with car, pick-up truck or van in traffic accident**

X ● **V03.10 Pedestrian on foot injured in collision with car, pick-up truck or van in traffic accident**
Pedestrian NOS injured in collision with car, pick-up truck or van in traffic accident

X ● **V03.11 Pedestrian on roller-skates injured in collision with car, pick-up truck or van in traffic accident**

X ● **V03.12 Pedestrian on skateboard injured in collision with car, pick-up truck or van in traffic accident**

▶ ● **V03.13 Pedestrian on standing micro-mobility pedestrian conveyance injured in collision with car, pick-up or van in traffic accident**

▶ **V03.131 Pedestrian on standing electric scooter injured in collision with car, pick-up or van in traffic accident**

▶ **V03.138 Pedestrian on other standing micro-mobility pedestrian conveyance injured in collision with car, pick-up or van in traffic accident**
▶Pedestrian on hoverboard injured in collision with car, pick-up or van in traffic accident
▶Pedestrian on segway injured in collision with car, pick-up or van in traffic accident

X ● **V03.19 Pedestrian with other conveyance injured in collision with car, pick-up truck or van in traffic accident**
Pedestrian with baby stroller injured in collision with car, pick-up truck or van in traffic accident
Pedestrian in wheelchair (powered) injured in collision with car, pick-up truck or van in traffic accident
Pedestrian in motorized mobility scooter injured in collision with car, pick-up truck or van in traffic accident
Pedestrian on ice-skates injured in collision with car, pick-up truck or van in traffic accident
Pedestrian on nonmotorized scooter injured in collision with car, pick-up truck or van in traffic accident
Pedestrian on sled injured in collision with car, pick-up truck or van in traffic accident
Pedestrian on snowboard injured in collision with car, pick-up truck or van in traffic accident
Pedestrian on snow-skis injured in collision with car, pick-up truck or van in traffic accident

● **V03.9 Pedestrian injured in collision with car, pick-up truck or van, unspecified whether traffic or nontraffic accident**

X ● **V03.90 Pedestrian on foot injured in collision with car, pick-up truck or van, unspecified whether traffic or nontraffic accident**
Pedestrian NOS injured in collision with car, pick-up truck or van, unspecified whether traffic or nontraffic accident

X ● **V03.91 Pedestrian on roller-skates injured in collision with car, pick-up truck or van, unspecified whether traffic or nontraffic accident**

X ● **V03.92 Pedestrian on skateboard injured in collision with car, pick-up truck or van, unspecified whether traffic or nontraffic accident**

▶ ● **V03.93 Pedestrian on standing micro-mobility pedestrian conveyance injured in collision with car, pick-up or van, unspecified whether traffic or nontraffic accident**

▶ **V03.931 Pedestrian on standing electric scooter injured in collision with car, pick-up or van, unspecified whether traffic or nontraffic accident**

▶ **V03.938 Pedestrian on other standing micro-mobility pedestrian conveyance injured in collision with car, pick-up or van, unspecified whether traffic or nontraffic accident**
▶Pedestrian on hoverboard injured in collision with car, pick-up or van, unspecified whether traffic or nontraffic accident
▶Pedestrian on segway injured in collision with car, pick-up or van, unspecified whether traffic or nontraffic accident

▶ New   ⇒ Revised   ~~deleted~~ Deleted   Excludes 1   Excludes 2   Includes   Use additional   Code first   Code also   Key words

OGCR Official Guidelines   X Assign placeholder X   ● Use Additional Character(s)   ▶ Manifestation Code   🅒 Hierarchical Condition Category   **Coding Clinic**

X● **V03.99** **Pedestrian with other conveyance injured in collision with car, pick-up truck or van, unspecified whether traffic or nontraffic accident**

Pedestrian with baby stroller injured in collision with car, pick-up truck or van, unspecified whether traffic or nontraffic accident

Pedestrian in wheelchair (powered) injured in collision with car, pick-up truck or van, unspecified whether traffic or nontraffic accident

Pedestrian in motorized mobility scooter injured in collision with car, pick-up truck or van, unspecified whether traffic or nontraffic accident

Pedestrian on ice-skates injured in collision with car, pick-up truck or van, unspecified whether traffic or nontraffic accident

Pedestrian on nonmotorized scooter injured in collision with car, pick-up truck or van, unspecified whether traffic or nontraffic accident

Pedestrian on sled injured in collision with car, pick-up truck or van in nontraffic accident

Pedestrian on snowboard injured in collision with car, pick-up truck or van, unspecified whether traffic or nontraffic accident

Pedestrian on snow-skis injured in collision with car, pick-up truck or van, unspecified whether traffic or nontraffic accident

● **V04** **Pedestrian injured in collision with heavy transport vehicle or bus**

> **Excludes1**   pedestrian injured in collision with military vehicle (V09.01, V09.21)

The appropriate 7th character is to be added to each code from category V04

A	initial encounter
D	subsequent encounter
S	sequela

● **V04.0** **Pedestrian injured in collision with heavy transport vehicle or bus in nontraffic accident**

X● **V04.00** **Pedestrian on foot injured in collision with heavy transport vehicle or bus in nontraffic accident**

Pedestrian NOS injured in collision with heavy transport vehicle or bus in nontraffic accident

X● **V04.01** **Pedestrian on roller-skates injured in collision with heavy transport vehicle or bus in nontraffic accident**

X● **V04.02** **Pedestrian on skateboard injured in collision with heavy transport vehicle or bus in nontraffic accident**

▶● **V04.03** **Pedestrian on standing micro-mobility pedestrian conveyance injured in collision with heavy transport vehicle or bus in nontraffic accident**

▶ **V04.031** **Pedestrian on standing electric scooter injured in collision with heavy transport vehicle or bus in nontraffic accident**

▶ **V04.038** **Pedestrian on other standing micro-mobility pedestrian conveyance injured in collision with heavy transport vehicle or bus in nontraffic accident**

▶Pedestrian on hoverboard injured in collision with heavy transport vehicle or bus in nontraffic accident

▶Pedestrian on segway injured in collision with heavy transport vehicle or bus in nontraffic accident

X● **V04.09** **Pedestrian with other conveyance injured in collision with heavy transport vehicle or bus in nontraffic accident**

Pedestrian with baby stroller injured in collision with heavy transport vehicle or bus in nontraffic accident

Pedestrian in wheelchair (powered) injured in collision with heavy transport vehicle or bus in nontraffic accident

Pedestrian in motorized mobility scooter injured in collision with heavy transport vehicle or bus in nontraffic accident

Pedestrian on ice-skates injured in collision with heavy transport vehicle or bus in nontraffic accident

Pedestrian on nonmotorized scooter injured in collision with heavy transport vehicle or bus in nontraffic accident

Pedestrian on sled injured in collision with heavy transport vehicle or bus in nontraffic accident

Pedestrian on snowboard injured in collision with heavy transport vehicle or bus in nontraffic accident

Pedestrian on snow-skis injured in collision with heavy transport vehicle or bus in nontraffic accident

● **V04.1** **Pedestrian injured in collision with heavy transport vehicle or bus in traffic accident**

X● **V04.10** **Pedestrian on foot injured in collision with heavy transport vehicle or bus in traffic accident**

Pedestrian NOS injured in collision with heavy transport vehicle or bus in traffic accident

X● **V04.11** **Pedestrian on roller-skates injured in collision with heavy transport vehicle or bus in traffic accident**

X● **V04.12** **Pedestrian on skateboard injured in collision with heavy transport vehicle or bus in traffic accident**

▶● **V04.13** **Pedestrian on standing micro-mobility pedestrian conveyance injured in collision with heavy transport vehicle or bus in traffic accident**

▶ **V04.131** **Pedestrian on standing electric scooter injured in collision with heavy transport vehicle or bus in traffic accident**

▶ **V04.138** **Pedestrian on other standing micro-mobility pedestrian conveyance injured in collision with heavy transport vehicle or bus in traffic accident**

▶Pedestrian on hoverboard injured in collision with heavy transport vehicle or bus in traffic accident

▶Pedestrian on segway injured in collision with heavy transport vehicle or bus in traffic accident

X● **V04.19** **Pedestrian with other conveyance injured in collision with heavy transport vehicle or bus in traffic accident**
  Pedestrian with baby stroller injured in collision with heavy transport vehicle or bus in traffic accident
  Pedestrian in wheelchair (powered) injured in collision with heavy transport vehicle or bus in traffic accident
  Pedestrian in motorized mobility scooter injured in collision with heavy transport vehicle or bus in traffic accident
  Pedestrian on ice-skates injured in collision with heavy transport vehicle or bus in traffic accident
  Pedestrian on nonmotorized scooter injured in collision with heavy transport vehicle or bus in traffic accident
  Pedestrian on sled injured in collision with heavy transport vehicle or bus in traffic accident
  Pedestrian on snowboard injured in collision with heavy transport vehicle or bus in traffic accident
  Pedestrian on snow-skis injured in collision with heavy transport vehicle or bus in traffic accident

● **V04.9** **Pedestrian injured in collision with heavy transport vehicle or bus, unspecified whether traffic or nontraffic accident**

X● **V04.90** **Pedestrian on foot injured in collision with heavy transport vehicle or bus, unspecified whether traffic or nontraffic accident**
  Pedestrian NOS injured in collision with heavy transport vehicle or bus, unspecified whether traffic or nontraffic accident

X● **V04.91** **Pedestrian on roller-skates injured in collision with heavy transport vehicle or bus, unspecified whether traffic or nontraffic accident**

X● **V04.92** **Pedestrian on skateboard injured in collision with heavy transport vehicle or bus, unspecified whether traffic or nontraffic accident**

▶● **V04.93** **Pedestrian on standing micro-mobility pedestrian conveyance injured in collision with heavy transport vehicle or bus, unspecified whether traffic or nontraffic accident**

  ▶ **V04.931** **Pedestrian on standing electric scooter injured in collision with heavy transport vehicle or bus, unspecified whether traffic or nontraffic accident**

  ▶ **V04.938** **Pedestrian on other standing micro-mobility pedestrian conveyance injured in collision with heavy transport vehicle or bus, unspecified whether traffic or nontraffic accident**
    ▶Pedestrian on hoverboard injured in collision with heavy transport vehicle or bus, unspecified whether traffic or nontraffic accident
    ▶Pedestrian on segway injured in collision with heavy transport vehicle or bus, unspecified whether traffic or nontraffic accident

X● **V04.99** **Pedestrian with other conveyance injured in collision with heavy transport vehicle or bus, unspecified whether traffic or nontraffic accident**
  Pedestrian with baby stroller injured in collision with heavy transport vehicle or bus, unspecified whether traffic or nontraffic accident
  Pedestrian in wheelchair (powered) injured in collision with heavy transport vehicle or bus, unspecified whether traffic or nontraffic accident
  Pedestrian in motorized mobility scooter injured in collision with heavy transport vehicle or bus, unspecified whether traffic or nontraffic accident
  Pedestrian on ice-skates injured in collision with heavy transport vehicle or bus, unspecified whether traffic or nontraffic accident
  Pedestrian on nonmotorized scooter injured in collision with heavy transport vehicle or bus, unspecified whether traffic or nontraffic accident
  Pedestrian on sled injured in collision with heavy transport vehicle or bus, unspecified whether traffic or nontraffic accident
  Pedestrian on snowboard injured in collision with heavy transport vehicle or bus, unspecified whether traffic or nontraffic accident
  Pedestrian on snow-skis injured in collision with heavy transport vehicle or bus, unspecified whether traffic or nontraffic accident

● **V05** **Pedestrian injured in collision with railway train or railway vehicle**
  The appropriate 7th character is to be added to each code from category V05

A	initial encounter
D	subsequent encounter
S	sequela

● **V05.0** **Pedestrian injured in collision with railway train or railway vehicle in nontraffic accident**

X● **V05.00** **Pedestrian on foot injured in collision with railway train or railway vehicle in nontraffic accident**
  Pedestrian NOS injured in collision with railway train or railway vehicle in nontraffic accident

X● **V05.01** **Pedestrian on roller-skates injured in collision with railway train or railway vehicle in nontraffic accident**

X● **V05.02** **Pedestrian on skateboard injured in collision with railway train or railway vehicle in nontraffic accident**

▶● **V05.03** **Pedestrian on standing micro-mobility pedestrian conveyance injured in collision with railway train or railway vehicle in nontraffic accident**

  ▶ **V05.031** **Pedestrian on standing electric scooter injured in collision with railway train or railway vehicle in nontraffic accident**

  ▶ **V05.038** **Pedestrian on other standing micro-mobility pedestrian conveyance injured in collision with railway train or railway vehicle in nontraffic accident**
    ▶Pedestrian on hoverboard injured in collision with railway train or railway vehicle in nontraffic accident
    ▶Pedestrian on segway injured in collision with railway train or railway vehicle in nontraffic accident

▶ New   ⇒ Revised   ~~deleted~~ Deleted   Excludes 1   Excludes 2   Includes   Use additional   Code first   Code also   Key words
OGCR Official Guidelines   X Assign placeholder X   ● Use Additional Character(s)   ▶ Manifestation Code   ℞ Hierarchical Condition Category   **Coding Clinic**

X● **V05.09** **Pedestrian with other conveyance injured in collision with railway train or railway vehicle in nontraffic accident**
Pedestrian with baby stroller injured in collision with railway train or railway vehicle in nontraffic accident
Pedestrian in wheelchair (powered) injured in collision with railway train or railway vehicle in nontraffic accident
Pedestrian in motorized mobility scooter injured in collision with railway train or railway vehicle in nontraffic accident
Pedestrian on ice-skates injured in collision with railway train or railway vehicle in nontraffic accident
Pedestrian on nonmotorized scooter injured in collision with railway train or railway vehicle in nontraffic accident
Pedestrian on sled injured in collision with railway train or railway vehicle in nontraffic accident
Pedestrian on snowboard injured in collision with railway train or railway vehicle in nontraffic accident
Pedestrian on snow-skis injured in collision with railway train or railway vehicle in nontraffic accident

● **V05.1** **Pedestrian injured in collision with railway train or railway vehicle in traffic accident**

X● **V05.10** **Pedestrian on foot injured in collision with railway train or railway vehicle in traffic accident**
Pedestrian NOS injured in collision with railway train or railway vehicle in traffic accident

X● **V05.11** **Pedestrian on roller-skates injured in collision with railway train or railway vehicle in traffic accident**

X● **V05.12** **Pedestrian on skateboard injured in collision with railway train or railway vehicle in traffic accident**

▶● **V05.13** **Pedestrian on standing micro-mobility pedestrian conveyance injured in collision with railway train or railway vehicle in traffic accident**

▶ **V05.131** **Pedestrian on standing electric scooter injured in collision with railway train or railway vehicle in traffic accident**

▶ **V05.138** **Pedestrian on other standing micro-mobility pedestrian conveyance injured in collision with railway train or railway vehicle in traffic accident**
▶Pedestrian on hoverboard injured in collision with railway train or railway vehicle in traffic accident
▶Pedestrian on segway injured in collision with railway train or railway vehicle in traffic accident

X● **V05.19** **Pedestrian with other conveyance injured in collision with railway train or railway vehicle in traffic accident**
Pedestrian with baby stroller injured in collision with railway train or railway vehicle in traffic accident
Pedestrian in wheelchair (powered) injured in collision with railway train or railway vehicle in traffic accident
Pedestrian in motorized mobility scooter injured in collision with railway train or railway vehicle in traffic accident
Pedestrian on ice-skates injured in collision with railway train or railway vehicle in traffic accident
Pedestrian on nonmotorized scooter injured in collision with railway train or railway vehicle in traffic accident
Pedestrian on sled injured in collision with railway train or railway vehicle in traffic accident
Pedestrian on snowboard injured in collision with railway train or railway vehicle in traffic accident
Pedestrian on snow-skis injured in collision with railway train or railway vehicle in traffic accident

● **V05.9** **Pedestrian injured in collision with railway train or railway vehicle, unspecified whether traffic or nontraffic accident**

X● **V05.90** **Pedestrian on foot injured in collision with railway train or railway vehicle, unspecified whether traffic or nontraffic accident**
Pedestrian NOS injured in collision with railway train or railway vehicle, unspecified whether traffic or nontraffic accident

X● **V05.91** **Pedestrian on roller-skates injured in collision with railway train or railway vehicle, unspecified whether traffic or nontraffic accident**

X● **V05.92** **Pedestrian on skateboard injured in collision with railway train or railway vehicle, unspecified whether traffic or nontraffic accident**

▶● **V05.93** **Pedestrian on standing micro-mobility pedestrian conveyance injured in collision with railway train or railway vehicle, unspecified whether traffic or nontraffic accident**

▶ **V05.931** **Pedestrian on standing electric scooter injured in collision with railway train or railway vehicle, unspecified whether traffic or nontraffic accident**

▶ **V05.938** **Pedestrian on other standing micro-mobility pedestrian conveyance injured in collision with railway train or railway vehicle, unspecified whether traffic or nontraffic accident**
▶Pedestrian on hoverboard injured in collision with railway train or railway vehicle, unspecified whether traffic or nontraffic accident
▶Pedestrian on segway injured in collision with railway train or railway vehicle, unspecified whether traffic or nontraffic accident

CHAPTER 20 (V00–Y99)

X● **V05.99** **Pedestrian with other conveyance injured in collision with railway train or railway vehicle, unspecified whether traffic or nontraffic accident**

Pedestrian with baby stroller injured in collision with railway train or railway vehicle, unspecified whether traffic or nontraffic

Pedestrian in wheelchair (powered) injured in collision with railway train or railway vehicle, unspecified whether traffic or nontraffic

Pedestrian in motorized mobility scooter injured in collision with railway train or railway vehicle, unspecified whether traffic or nontraffic

Pedestrian on ice-skates injured in collision with railway train or railway vehicle, unspecified whether traffic or nontraffic

Pedestrian on nonmotorized scooter injured in collision with railway train or railway vehicle, unspecified whether traffic or nontraffic

Pedestrian on sled injured in collision with railway train or railway vehicle, unspecified whether traffic or nontraffic

Pedestrian on snowboard injured in collision with railway train or railway vehicle, unspecified whether traffic or nontraffic

Pedestrian on snow-skis injured in collision with railway train or railway vehicle, unspecified whether traffic or nontraffic

● **V06** **Pedestrian injured in collision with other nonmotor vehicle**

    Includes   collision with animal-drawn vehicle, animal being ridden, nonpowered streetcar

    Excludes1   pedestrian injured in collision with pedestrian conveyance (V00.0-)

The appropriate 7th character is to be added to each code from category V06

A	initial encounter
D	subsequent encounter
S	sequela

● **V06.0** **Pedestrian injured in collision with other nonmotor vehicle in nontraffic accident**

X● **V06.00** **Pedestrian on foot injured in collision with other nonmotor vehicle in nontraffic accident**

Pedestrian NOS injured in collision with other nonmotor vehicle in nontraffic accident

X● **V06.01** **Pedestrian on roller-skates injured in collision with other nonmotor vehicle in nontraffic accident**

X● **V06.02** **Pedestrian on skateboard injured in collision with other nonmotor vehicle in nontraffic accident**

▶● **V06.03** **Pedestrian on standing micro-mobility pedestrian conveyance injured in collision with other nonmotor vehicle in nontraffic accident**

▶ **V06.031** **Pedestrian on standing electric scooter injured in collision with other nonmotor vehicle in nontraffic accident**

▶ **V06.038** **Pedestrian on other standing micro-mobility pedestrian conveyance injured in collision with other nonmotor vehicle in nontraffic accident**

▶ Pedestrian on hoverboard injured in collision with other nonmotor vehicle in nontraffic accident

▶ Pedestrian on segway injured in collision with other nonmotor vehicle in nontraffic accident

X● **V06.09** **Pedestrian with other conveyance injured in collision with other nonmotor vehicle in nontraffic accident**

Pedestrian with baby stroller injured in collision with other nonmotor vehicle in nontraffic accident

Pedestrian in wheelchair (powered) injured in collision with other nonmotor vehicle in nontraffic accident

Pedestrian in motorized mobility scooter injured in collision with other nonmotor vehicle in nontraffic accident

Pedestrian on ice-skates injured in collision with other nonmotor vehicle in nontraffic accident

Pedestrian on nonmotorized scooter injured in collision with other nonmotor vehicle in nontraffic accident

Pedestrian on sled injured in collision with other nonmotor vehicle in nontraffic accident

Pedestrian on snowboard injured in collision with other nonmotor vehicle in nontraffic accident

Pedestrian on snow-skis injured in collision with other nonmotor vehicle in nontraffic accident

● **V06.1** **Pedestrian injured in collision with other nonmotor vehicle in traffic accident**

X● **V06.10** **Pedestrian on foot injured in collision with other nonmotor vehicle in traffic accident**

Pedestrian NOS injured in collision with other nonmotor vehicle in traffic accident

X● **V06.11** **Pedestrian on roller-skates injured in collision with other nonmotor vehicle in traffic accident**

X● **V06.12** **Pedestrian on skateboard injured in collision with other nonmotor vehicle in traffic accident**

▶● **V06.13** **Pedestrian on standing micro-mobility pedestrian conveyance injured in collision with other nonmotor vehicle in traffic accident**

▶ **V06.131** **Pedestrian on standing electric scooter injured in collision with other nonmotor vehicle in traffic accident**

▶ **V06.138** **Pedestrian on other standing micro-mobility pedestrian conveyance injured in collision with other nonmotor vehicle in traffic accident**

▶ Pedestrian on hoverboard injured in collision with other nonmotor vehicle in traffic accident

▶ Pedestrian on segway injured in collision with other nonmotor vehicle in traffic accident

X● **V06.19** **Pedestrian with other conveyance injured in collision with other nonmotor vehicle in traffic accident**

Pedestrian with baby stroller injured in collision with other nonmotor vehicle in nontraffic accident

Pedestrian in wheelchair (powered) injured in collision with other nonmotor vehicle in traffic accident

Pedestrian in motorized mobility scooter injured in collision with other nonmotor vehicle in traffic accident

Pedestrian on ice-skates injured in collision with other nonmotor vehicle in traffic accident

Pedestrian on nonmotorized scooter injured in collision with other nonmotor vehicle in traffic accident

Pedestrian on sled injured in collision with other nonmotor vehicle in traffic accident

Pedestrian on snowboard injured in collision with other nonmotor vehicle in traffic accident

Pedestrian on snow-skis injured in collision with other nonmotor vehicle in traffic accident

▶ New   ⮕ Revised   ~~deleted~~ Deleted   Excludes 1   Excludes 2   Includes   Use additional   Code first   Code also   Key words

OGCR Official Guidelines   X Assign placeholder X   ● Use Additional Character(s)   ▶ Manifestation Code   🏥 Hierarchical Condition Category   **Coding Clinic**

● **V06.9**   **Pedestrian injured in collision with other nonmotor vehicle, unspecified whether traffic or nontraffic accident**

X● **V06.90**   **Pedestrian on foot injured in collision with other nonmotor vehicle, unspecified whether traffic or nontraffic accident**

Pedestrian NOS injured in collision with other nonmotor vehicle, unspecified whether traffic or nontraffic accident

X● **V06.91**   **Pedestrian on roller-skates injured in collision with other nonmotor vehicle, unspecified whether traffic or nontraffic accident**

X● **V06.92**   **Pedestrian on skateboard injured in collision with other nonmotor vehicle, unspecified whether traffic or nontraffic accident**

▶ ● **V06.93**   **Pedestrian on standing micro-mobility pedestrian conveyance injured in collision with other nonmotor vehicle, unspecified whether traffic or nontraffic accident**

    ▶ **V06.931**   **Pedestrian on standing electric scooter injured in collision with other nonmotor vehicle, unspecified whether traffic or nontraffic accident**

    ▶ **V06.938**   **Pedestrian on other standing micro-mobility pedestrian conveyance injured in collision with other nonmotor vehicle, unspecified whether traffic or nontraffic accident**

▶ Pedestrian on hoverboard injured in collision with other nonmotor, unspecified whether traffic or nontraffic accident

▶ Pedestrian on segway injured in collision with other nonmotor vehicle, unspecified whether traffic or nontraffic accident

X● **V06.99**   **Pedestrian with other conveyance injured in collision with other nonmotor vehicle, unspecified whether traffic or nontraffic accident**

Pedestrian with baby stroller injured in collision with other nonmotor vehicle, unspecified whether traffic or nontraffic accident

Pedestrian in wheelchair (powered) injured in collision with other nonmotor vehicle, unspecified whether traffic or nontraffic accident

Pedestrian in motorized mobility scooter injured in collision with other nonmotor vehicle, unspecified whether traffic or nontraffic accident

Pedestrian on ice-skates injured in collision with other nonmotor vehicle, unspecified whether traffic or nontraffic accident

Pedestrian on nonmotorized scooter injured in collision with other nonmotor vehicle, unspecified whether traffic or nontraffic accident

Pedestrian on sled injured in collision with other nonmotor vehicle, unspecified whether traffic or nontraffic accident

Pedestrian on snowboard injured in collision with other nonmotor vehicle, unspecified whether traffic or nontraffic accident

Pedestrian on snow-skis injured in collision with other nonmotor vehicle, unspecified whether traffic or nontraffic accident

● **V09**   **Pedestrian injured in other and unspecified transport accidents**

The appropriate 7th character is to be added to each code from category V09

A	initial encounter
D	subsequent encounter
S	sequela

● **V09.0**   **Pedestrian injured in nontraffic accident involving other and unspecified motor vehicles**

X● **V09.00**   **Pedestrian injured in nontraffic accident involving unspecified motor vehicles**

X● **V09.01**   **Pedestrian injured in nontraffic accident involving military vehicle**

X● **V09.09**   **Pedestrian injured in nontraffic accident involving other motor vehicles**

Pedestrian injured in nontraffic accident by special vehicle

X● **V09.1**   **Pedestrian injured in unspecified nontraffic accident**

● **V09.2**   **Pedestrian injured in traffic accident involving other and unspecified motor vehicles**

X● **V09.20**   **Pedestrian injured in traffic accident involving unspecified motor vehicles**

X● **V09.21**   **Pedestrian injured in traffic accident involving military vehicle**

X● **V09.29**   **Pedestrian injured in traffic accident involving other motor vehicles**

X● **V09.3**   **Pedestrian injured in unspecified traffic accident**

X● **V09.9**   **Pedestrian injured in unspecified transport accident**

PEDAL CYCLE RIDER INJURED IN TRANSPORT ACCIDENT (V10-V19)

Includes   any non-motorized vehicle, excluding an animal-drawn vehicle, or a sidecar or trailer attached to the pedal cycle

Excludes2   rupture of pedal cycle tire (W37.0)

● **V10**   **Pedal cycle rider injured in collision with pedestrian or animal**

Excludes1   pedal cycle rider collision with animal-drawn vehicle or animal being ridden (V16.-)

The appropriate 7th character is to be added to each code from category V10

A	initial encounter
D	subsequent encounter
S	sequela

X● **V10.0**   **Pedal cycle driver injured in collision with pedestrian or animal in nontraffic accident**

X● **V10.1**   **Pedal cycle passenger injured in collision with pedestrian or animal in nontraffic accident**

X● **V10.2**   **Unspecified pedal cyclist injured in collision with pedestrian or animal in nontraffic accident**

X● **V10.3**   **Person boarding or alighting a pedal cycle injured in collision with pedestrian or animal**

X● **V10.4**   **Pedal cycle driver injured in collision with pedestrian or animal in traffic accident**

X● **V10.5**   **Pedal cycle passenger injured in collision with pedestrian or animal in traffic accident**

X● **V10.9**   **Unspecified pedal cyclist injured in collision with pedestrian or animal in traffic accident**

CHAPTER 20 (V00-Y99)

● V11 Pedal cycle rider injured in collision with other pedal cycle

The appropriate 7th character is to be added to each code from category V11

> A   initial encounter
> D   subsequent encounter
> S   sequela

X● **V11.0** Pedal cycle driver injured in collision with other pedal cycle in nontraffic accident

X● **V11.1** Pedal cycle passenger injured in collision with other pedal cycle in nontraffic accident

X● **V11.2** Unspecified pedal cyclist injured in collision with other pedal cycle in nontraffic accident

X● **V11.3** Person boarding or alighting a pedal cycle injured in collision with other pedal cycle

X● **V11.4** Pedal cycle driver injured in collision with other pedal cycle in traffic accident

X● **V11.5** Pedal cycle passenger injured in collision with other pedal cycle in traffic accident

X● **V11.9** Unspecified pedal cyclist injured in collision with other pedal cycle in traffic accident

● V12 Pedal cycle rider injured in collision with two- or three-wheeled motor vehicle

The appropriate 7th character is to be added to each code from category V12

> A   initial encounter
> D   subsequent encounter
> S   sequela

X● **V12.0** Pedal cycle driver injured in collision with two- or three-wheeled motor vehicle in nontraffic accident

X● **V12.1** Pedal cycle passenger injured in collision with two- or three-wheeled motor vehicle in nontraffic accident

X● **V12.2** Unspecified pedal cyclist injured in collision with two- or three-wheeled motor vehicle in nontraffic accident

X● **V12.3** Person boarding or alighting a pedal cycle injured in collision with two- or three-wheeled motor vehicle

X● **V12.4** Pedal cycle driver injured in collision with two- or three-wheeled motor vehicle in traffic accident

X● **V12.5** Pedal cycle passenger injured in collision with two- or three-wheeled motor vehicle in traffic accident

X● **V12.9** Unspecified pedal cyclist injured in collision with two- or three-wheeled motor vehicle in traffic accident

● V13 Pedal cycle rider injured in collision with car, pick-up truck or van

The appropriate 7th character is to be added to each code from category V13

> A   initial encounter
> D   subsequent encounter
> S   sequela

X● **V13.0** Pedal cycle driver injured in collision with car, pick-up truck or van in nontraffic accident

X● **V13.1** Pedal cycle passenger injured in collision with car, pick-up truck or van in nontraffic accident

X● **V13.2** Unspecified pedal cyclist injured in collision with car, pick-up truck or van in nontraffic accident

X● **V13.3** Person boarding or alighting a pedal cycle injured in collision with car, pick-up truck or van

X● **V13.4** Pedal cycle driver injured in collision with car, pick-up truck or van in traffic accident

X● **V13.5** Pedal cycle passenger injured in collision with car, pick-up truck or van in traffic accident

X● **V13.9** Unspecified pedal cyclist injured in collision with car, pick-up truck or van in traffic accident

● V14 Pedal cycle rider injured in collision with heavy transport vehicle or bus

> **Excludes 1** pedal cycle rider injured in collision with military vehicle (V19.81)

The appropriate 7th character is to be added to each code from category V14

> A   initial encounter
> D   subsequent encounter
> S   sequela

X● **V14.0** Pedal cycle driver injured in collision with heavy transport vehicle or bus in nontraffic accident

X● **V14.1** Pedal cycle passenger injured in collision with heavy transport vehicle or bus in nontraffic accident

X● **V14.2** Unspecified pedal cyclist injured in collision with heavy transport vehicle or bus in nontraffic accident

X● **V14.3** Person boarding or alighting a pedal cycle injured in collision with heavy transport vehicle or bus

X● **V14.4** Pedal cycle driver injured in collision with heavy transport vehicle or bus in traffic accident

X● **V14.5** Pedal cycle passenger injured in collision with heavy transport vehicle or bus in traffic accident

X● **V14.9** Unspecified pedal cyclist injured in collision with heavy transport vehicle or bus in traffic accident

● V15 Pedal cycle rider injured in collision with railway train or railway vehicle

The appropriate 7th character is to be added to each code from category V15

> A   initial encounter
> D   subsequent encounter
> S   sequela

X● **V15.0** Pedal cycle driver injured in collision with railway train or railway vehicle in nontraffic accident

X● **V15.1** Pedal cycle passenger injured in collision with railway train or railway vehicle in nontraffic accident

X● **V15.2** Unspecified pedal cyclist injured in collision with railway train or railway vehicle in nontraffic accident

X● **V15.3** Person boarding or alighting a pedal cycle injured in collision with railway train or railway vehicle

X● **V15.4** Pedal cycle driver injured in collision with railway train or railway vehicle in traffic accident

X● **V15.5** Pedal cycle passenger injured in collision with railway train or railway vehicle in traffic accident

X● **V15.9** Unspecified pedal cyclist injured in collision with railway train or railway vehicle in traffic accident

● V16 Pedal cycle rider injured in collision with other nonmotor vehicle

> **Includes** collision with animal-drawn vehicle, animal being ridden, streetcar

The appropriate 7th character is to be added to each code from category V16

> A   initial encounter
> D   subsequent encounter
> S   sequela

X● **V16.0** Pedal cycle driver injured in collision with other nonmotor vehicle in nontraffic accident

X● **V16.1** Pedal cycle passenger injured in collision with other nonmotor vehicle in nontraffic accident

X● **V16.2** Unspecified pedal cyclist injured in collision with other nonmotor vehicle in nontraffic accident

X● **V16.3** Person boarding or alighting a pedal cycle injured in collision with other nonmotor vehicle in nontraffic accident

X● **V16.4** Pedal cycle driver injured in collision with other nonmotor vehicle in traffic accident

▶ New   ⇒ Revised   ~~deleted~~ Deleted   Excludes 1   Excludes 2   Includes   Use additional   Code first   Code also   Key words

OGCR Official Guidelines   X Assign placeholder X   ● Use Additional Character(s)   ▶ Manifestation Code   🔖 Hierarchical Condition Category   **Coding Clinic**

X● **V16.5** Pedal cycle passenger injured in collision with other nonmotor vehicle in traffic accident

X● **V16.9** Unspecified pedal cyclist injured in collision with other nonmotor vehicle in traffic accident

● **V17** Pedal cycle rider injured in collision with fixed or stationary object

The appropriate 7th character is to be added to each code from category V17

A	initial encounter
D	subsequent encounter
S	sequela

X● **V17.0** Pedal cycle driver injured in collision with fixed or stationary object in nontraffic accident

X● **V17.1** Pedal cycle passenger injured in collision with fixed or stationary object in nontraffic accident

X● **V17.2** Unspecified pedal cyclist injured in collision with fixed or stationary object in nontraffic accident

X● **V17.3** Person boarding or alighting a pedal cycle injured in collision with fixed or stationary object

X● **V17.4** Pedal cycle driver injured in collision with fixed or stationary object in traffic accident

X● **V17.5** Pedal cycle passenger injured in collision with fixed or stationary object in traffic accident

X● **V17.9** Unspecified pedal cyclist injured in collision with fixed or stationary object in traffic accident

● **V18** Pedal cycle rider injured in noncollision transport accident

Includes   fall or thrown from pedal cycle (without antecedent collision)
overturning pedal cycle NOS
overturning pedal cycle without collision

The appropriate 7th character is to be added to each code from category V18

A	initial encounter
D	subsequent encounter
S	sequela

X● **V18.0** Pedal cycle driver injured in noncollision transport accident in nontraffic accident

X● **V18.1** Pedal cycle passenger injured in noncollision transport accident in nontraffic accident

X● **V18.2** Unspecified pedal cyclist injured in noncollision transport accident in nontraffic accident

X● **V18.3** Person boarding or alighting a pedal cycle injured in noncollision transport accident

X● **V18.4** Pedal cycle driver injured in noncollision transport accident in traffic accident

X● **V18.5** Pedal cycle passenger injured in noncollision transport accident in traffic accident

X● **V18.9** Unspecified pedal cyclist injured in noncollision transport accident in traffic accident

● **V19** Pedal cycle rider injured in other and unspecified transport accidents

The appropriate 7th character is to be added to each code from category V19

A	initial encounter
D	subsequent encounter
S	sequela

● **V19.0** Pedal cycle driver injured in collision with other and unspecified motor vehicles in nontraffic accident

X● **V19.00** Pedal cycle driver injured in collision with unspecified motor vehicles in nontraffic accident

X● **V19.09** Pedal cycle driver injured in collision with other motor vehicles in nontraffic accident

● **V19.1** Pedal cycle passenger injured in collision with other and unspecified motor vehicles in nontraffic accident

X● **V19.10** Pedal cycle passenger injured in collision with unspecified motor vehicles in nontraffic accident

X● **V19.19** Pedal cycle passenger injured in collision with other motor vehicles in nontraffic accident

● **V19.2** Unspecified pedal cyclist injured in collision with other and unspecified motor vehicles in nontraffic accident

X● **V19.20** Unspecified pedal cyclist injured in collision with unspecified motor vehicles in nontraffic accident
Pedal cycle collision NOS, nontraffic

X● **V19.29** Unspecified pedal cyclist injured in collision with other motor vehicles in nontraffic accident

X● **V19.3** Pedal cyclist (driver) (passenger) injured in unspecified nontraffic accident
Pedal cycle accident NOS, nontraffic
Pedal cyclist injured in nontraffic accident NOS

● **V19.4** Pedal cycle driver injured in collision with other and unspecified motor vehicles in traffic accident

X● **V19.40** Pedal cycle driver injured in collision with unspecified motor vehicles in traffic accident

X● **V19.49** Pedal cycle driver injured in collision with other motor vehicles in traffic accident

● **V19.5** Pedal cycle passenger injured in collision with other and unspecified motor vehicles in traffic accident

X● **V19.50** Pedal cycle passenger injured in collision with unspecified motor vehicles in traffic accident

X● **V19.59** Pedal cycle passenger injured in collision with other motor vehicles in traffic accident

● **V19.6** Unspecified pedal cyclist injured in collision with other and unspecified motor vehicles in traffic accident

X● **V19.60** Unspecified pedal cyclist injured in collision with unspecified motor vehicles in traffic accident
Pedal cycle collision NOS (traffic)

X● **V19.69** Unspecified pedal cyclist injured in collision with other motor vehicles in traffic accident

● **V19.8** Pedal cyclist (driver) (passenger) injured in other specified transport accidents

X● **V19.81** Pedal cyclist (driver) (passenger) injured in transport accident with military vehicle

X● **V19.88** Pedal cyclist (driver) (passenger) injured in other specified transport accidents

X● **V19.9** Pedal cyclist (driver) (passenger) injured in unspecified traffic accident
Pedal cycle accident NOS

MOTORCYCLE RIDER INJURED IN TRANSPORT ACCIDENT (V20-V29)

Includes   moped motorcycle with sidecar motorized bicycle motor scooter

Excludes1   three-wheeled motor vehicle (V30-V39)

● **V20** Motorcycle rider injured in collision with pedestrian or animal

Excludes1   motorcycle rider collision with animal-drawn vehicle or animal being ridden (V26.-)

The appropriate 7th character is to be added to each code from category V20

A	initial encounter
D	subsequent encounter
S	sequela

X● **V20.0** Motorcycle driver injured in collision with pedestrian or animal in nontraffic accident

X● **V20.1** Motorcycle passenger injured in collision with pedestrian or animal in nontraffic accident

CHAPTER 20 (V00-Y99)

X ● **V20.2** Unspecified motorcycle rider injured in collision with pedestrian or animal in nontraffic accident

X ● **V20.3** Person boarding or alighting a motorcycle injured in collision with pedestrian or animal

X ● **V20.4** Motorcycle driver injured in collision with pedestrian or animal in traffic accident

X ● **V20.5** Motorcycle passenger injured in collision with pedestrian or animal in traffic accident

X ● **V20.9** Unspecified motorcycle rider injured in collision with pedestrian or animal in traffic accident

● **V21** Motorcycle rider injured in collision with pedal cycle

The appropriate 7th character is to be added to each code from category V21

A	initial encounter
D	subsequent encounter
S	sequela

X ● **V21.0** Motorcycle driver injured in collision with pedal cycle in nontraffic accident

X ● **V21.1** Motorcycle passenger injured in collision with pedal cycle in nontraffic accident

X ● **V21.2** Unspecified motorcycle rider injured in collision with pedal cycle in nontraffic accident

X ● **V21.3** Person boarding or alighting a motorcycle injured in collision with pedal cycle

X ● **V21.4** Motorcycle driver injured in collision with pedal cycle in traffic accident

X ● **V21.5** Motorcycle passenger injured in collision with pedal cycle in traffic accident

X ● **V21.9** Unspecified motorcycle rider injured in collision with pedal cycle in traffic accident

● **V22** Motorcycle rider injured in collision with two- or three-wheeled motor vehicle

The appropriate 7th character is to be added to each code from category V22

A	initial encounter
D	subsequent encounter
S	sequela

X ● **V22.0** Motorcycle driver injured in collision with two- or three-wheeled motor vehicle in nontraffic accident

X ● **V22.1** Motorcycle passenger injured in collision with two- or three-wheeled motor vehicle in nontraffic accident

X ● **V22.2** Unspecified motorcycle rider injured in collision with two- or three-wheeled motor vehicle in nontraffic accident

X ● **V22.3** Person boarding or alighting a motorcycle injured in collision with two- or three-wheeled motor vehicle

X ● **V22.4** Motorcycle driver injured in collision with two- or three-wheeled motor vehicle in traffic accident

X ● **V22.5** Motorcycle passenger injured in collision with two- or three-wheeled motor vehicle in traffic accident

X ● **V22.9** Unspecified motorcycle rider injured in collision with two- or three-wheeled motor vehicle in traffic accident

● **V23** Motorcycle rider injured in collision with car, pick-up truck or van

The appropriate 7th character is to be added to each code from category V23

A	initial encounter
D	subsequent encounter
S	sequela

X ● **V23.0** Motorcycle driver injured in collision with car, pick-up truck or van in nontraffic accident

X ● **V23.1** Motorcycle passenger injured in collision with car, pick-up truck or van in nontraffic accident

X ● **V23.2** Unspecified motorcycle rider injured in collision with car, pick-up truck or van in nontraffic accident

X ● **V23.3** Person boarding or alighting a motorcycle injured in collision with car, pick-up truck or van

X ● **V23.4** Motorcycle driver injured in collision with car, pick-up truck or van in traffic accident

X ● **V23.5** Motorcycle passenger injured in collision with car, pick-up truck or van in traffic accident

X ● **V23.9** Unspecified motorcycle rider injured in collision with car, pick-up truck or van in traffic accident

● **V24** Motorcycle rider injured in collision with heavy transport vehicle or bus

Excludes1 motorcycle rider injured in collision with military vehicle (V29.81)

The appropriate 7th character is to be added to each code from category V24

A	initial encounter
D	subsequent encounter
S	sequela

X ● **V24.0** Motorcycle driver injured in collision with heavy transport vehicle or bus in nontraffic accident

X ● **V24.1** Motorcycle passenger injured in collision with heavy transport vehicle or bus in nontraffic accident

X ● **V24.2** Unspecified motorcycle rider injured in collision with heavy transport vehicle or bus in nontraffic accident

X ● **V24.3** Person boarding or alighting a motorcycle injured in collision with heavy transport vehicle or bus

X ● **V24.4** Motorcycle driver injured in collision with heavy transport vehicle or bus in traffic accident

X ● **V24.5** Motorcycle passenger injured in collision with heavy transport vehicle or bus in traffic accident

X ● **V24.9** Unspecified motorcycle rider injured in collision with heavy transport vehicle or bus in traffic accident

● **V25** Motorcycle rider injured in collision with railway train or railway vehicle

The appropriate 7th character is to be added to each code from category V25

A	initial encounter
D	subsequent encounter
S	sequela

X ● **V25.0** Motorcycle driver injured in collision with railway train or railway vehicle in nontraffic accident

X ● **V25.1** Motorcycle passenger injured in collision with railway train or railway vehicle in nontraffic accident

X ● **V25.2** Unspecified motorcycle rider injured in collision with railway train or railway vehicle in nontraffic accident

X ● **V25.3** Person boarding or alighting a motorcycle injured in collision with railway train or railway vehicle

X ● **V25.4** Motorcycle driver injured in collision with railway train or railway vehicle in traffic accident

X ● **V25.5** Motorcycle passenger injured in collision with railway train or railway vehicle in traffic accident

X ● **V25.9** Unspecified motorcycle rider injured in collision with railway train or railway vehicle in traffic accident

▶ New　　⇒ Revised　　deleted Deleted　　Excludes 1　　Excludes 2　　Includes　　Use additional　　Code first　　Code also　　Key words

OGCR Official Guidelines　　X Assign placeholder X　　● Use Additional Character(s)　　▶ Manifestation Code　　🔒 Hierarchical Condition Category　　Coding Clinic

● **V26 Motorcycle rider injured in collision with other nonmotor vehicle**

> **Includes** collision with animal-drawn vehicle, animal being ridden, streetcar

> The appropriate 7th character is to be added to each code from category V26

> | A | initial encounter |
> |---|---|
> | D | subsequent encounter |
> | S | sequela |

X● **V26.0 Motorcycle driver injured in collision with other nonmotor vehicle in nontraffic accident**

X● **V26.1 Motorcycle passenger injured in collision with other nonmotor vehicle in nontraffic accident**

X● **V26.2 Unspecified motorcycle rider injured in collision with other nonmotor vehicle in nontraffic accident**

X● **V26.3 Person boarding or alighting a motorcycle injured in collision with other nonmotor vehicle**

X● **V26.4 Motorcycle driver injured in collision with other nonmotor vehicle in traffic accident**

X● **V26.5 Motorcycle passenger injured in collision with other nonmotor vehicle in traffic accident**

X● **V26.9 Unspecified motorcycle rider injured in collision with other nonmotor vehicle in traffic accident**

● **V27 Motorcycle rider injured in collision with fixed or stationary object**

> The appropriate 7th character is to be added to each code from category V27

> | A | initial encounter |
> |---|---|
> | D | subsequent encounter |
> | S | sequela |

X● **V27.0 Motorcycle driver injured in collision with fixed or stationary object in nontraffic accident**

X● **V27.1 Motorcycle passenger injured in collision with fixed or stationary object in nontraffic accident**

X● **V27.2 Unspecified motorcycle rider injured in collision with fixed or stationary object in nontraffic accident**

X● **V27.3 Person boarding or alighting a motorcycle injured in collision with fixed or stationary object**

X● **V27.4 Motorcycle driver injured in collision with fixed or stationary object in traffic accident**

X● **V27.5 Motorcycle passenger injured in collision with fixed or stationary object in traffic accident**

X● **V27.9 Unspecified motorcycle rider injured in collision with fixed or stationary object in traffic accident**

● **V28 Motorcycle rider injured in noncollision transport accident**

> **Includes** fall or thrown from motorcycle (without antecedent collision)
> overturning motorcycle NOS
> overturning motorcycle without collision

> The appropriate 7th character is to be added to each code from category V28

> | A | initial encounter |
> |---|---|
> | D | subsequent encounter |
> | S | sequela |

X● **V28.0 Motorcycle driver injured in noncollision transport accident in nontraffic accident**

X● **V28.1 Motorcycle passenger injured in noncollision transport accident in nontraffic accident**

X● **V28.2 Unspecified motorcycle rider injured in noncollision transport accident in nontraffic accident**

X● **V28.3 Person boarding or alighting a motorcycle injured in noncollision transport accident**

X● **V28.4 Motorcycle driver injured in noncollision transport accident in traffic accident**

X● **V28.5 Motorcycle passenger injured in noncollision transport accident in traffic accident**

X● **V28.9 Unspecified motorcycle rider injured in noncollision transport accident in traffic accident**

● **V29 Motorcycle rider injured in other and unspecified transport accidents**

> The appropriate 7th character is to be added to each code from category V29

> | A | initial encounter |
> |---|---|
> | D | subsequent encounter |
> | S | sequela |

> **Coding Clinic: 2015, Q3, P20**

● **V29.0 Motorcycle driver injured in collision with other and unspecified motor vehicles in nontraffic accident**

X● **V29.00 Motorcycle driver injured in collision with unspecified motor vehicles in nontraffic accident**

X● **V29.09 Motorcycle driver injured in collision with other motor vehicles in nontraffic accident**

● **V29.1 Motorcycle passenger injured in collision with other and unspecified motor vehicles in nontraffic accident**

X● **V29.10 Motorcycle passenger injured in collision with unspecified motor vehicles in nontraffic accident**

X● **V29.19 Motorcycle passenger injured in collision with other motor vehicles in nontraffic accident**

● **V29.2 Unspecified motorcycle rider injured in collision with other and unspecified motor vehicles in nontraffic accident**

X● **V29.20 Unspecified motorcycle rider injured in collision with unspecified motor vehicles in nontraffic accident**
> Motorcycle collision NOS, nontraffic

X● **V29.29 Unspecified motorcycle rider injured in collision with other motor vehicles in nontraffic accident**

X● **V29.3 Motorcycle rider (driver) (passenger) injured in unspecified nontraffic accident**
> Motorcycle accident NOS, nontraffic
> Motorcycle rider injured in nontraffic accident NOS

● **V29.4 Motorcycle driver injured in collision with other and unspecified motor vehicles in traffic accident**

X● **V29.40 Motorcycle driver injured in collision with unspecified motor vehicles in traffic accident**

X● **V29.49 Motorcycle driver injured in collision with other motor vehicles in traffic accident**

● **V29.5 Motorcycle passenger injured in collision with other and unspecified motor vehicles in traffic accident**

X● **V29.50 Motorcycle passenger injured in collision with unspecified motor vehicles in traffic accident**

X● **V29.59 Motorcycle passenger injured in collision with other motor vehicles in traffic accident**

● **V29.6 Unspecified motorcycle rider injured in collision with other and unspecified motor vehicles in traffic accident**

X● **V29.60 Unspecified motorcycle rider injured in collision with unspecified motor vehicles in traffic accident**
> Motorcycle collision NOS (traffic)

X● **V29.69 Unspecified motorcycle rider injured in collision with other motor vehicles in traffic accident**

● **V29.8 Motorcycle rider (driver) (passenger) injured in other specified transport accidents**

X● **V29.81 Motorcycle rider (driver) (passenger) injured in transport accident with military vehicle**

X● **V29.88 Motorcycle rider (driver) (passenger) injured in other specified transport accidents**

X● **V29.9 Motorcycle rider (driver) (passenger) injured in unspecified traffic accident**
> Motorcycle accident NOS

CHAPTER 20 (V00–Y99)

OCCUPANT OF THREE-WHEELED MOTOR VEHICLE INJURED IN TRANSPORT ACCIDENT (V30-V39)

Includes motorized tricycle
motorized rickshaw
three-wheeled motor car

Excludes1 all-terrain vehicles (V86.-)
motorcycle with sidecar (V20-V29)
vehicle designed primarily for off-road use
(V86.-)

● **V30** Occupant of three-wheeled motor vehicle injured in collision with pedestrian or animal

Excludes1 three-wheeled motor vehicle collision with animal-drawn vehicle or animal being ridden (V36.-)

The appropriate 7th character is to be added to each code from category V30

A	initial encounter
D	subsequent encounter
S	sequela

X● **V30.0** Driver of three-wheeled motor vehicle injured in collision with pedestrian or animal in nontraffic accident

X● **V30.1** Passenger in three-wheeled motor vehicle injured in collision with pedestrian or animal in nontraffic accident

X● **V30.2** Person on outside of three-wheeled motor vehicle injured in collision with pedestrian or animal in nontraffic accident

X● **V30.3** Unspecified occupant of three-wheeled motor vehicle injured in collision with pedestrian or animal in nontraffic accident

X● **V30.4** Person boarding or alighting a three-wheeled motor vehicle injured in collision with pedestrian or animal

X● **V30.5** Driver of three-wheeled motor vehicle injured in collision with pedestrian or animal in traffic accident

X● **V30.6** Passenger in three-wheeled motor vehicle injured in collision with pedestrian or animal in traffic accident

X● **V30.7** Person on outside of three-wheeled motor vehicle injured in collision with pedestrian or animal in traffic accident

X● **V30.9** Unspecified occupant of three-wheeled motor vehicle injured in collision with pedestrian or animal in traffic accident

● **V31** Occupant of three-wheeled motor vehicle injured in collision with pedal cycle

The appropriate 7th character is to be added to each code from category V31

A	initial encounter
D	subsequent encounter
S	sequela

X● **V31.0** Driver of three-wheeled motor vehicle injured in collision with pedal cycle in nontraffic accident

X● **V31.1** Passenger in three-wheeled motor vehicle injured in collision with pedal cycle in nontraffic accident

X● **V31.2** Person on outside of three-wheeled motor vehicle injured in collision with pedal cycle in nontraffic accident

X● **V31.3** Unspecified occupant of three-wheeled motor vehicle injured in collision with pedal cycle in nontraffic accident

X● **V31.4** Person boarding or alighting a three-wheeled motor vehicle injured in collision with pedal cycle

X● **V31.5** Driver of three-wheeled motor vehicle injured in collision with pedal cycle in traffic accident

X● **V31.6** Passenger in three-wheeled motor vehicle injured in collision with pedal cycle in traffic accident

X● **V31.7** Person on outside of three-wheeled motor vehicle injured in collision with pedal cycle in traffic accident

X● **V31.9** Unspecified occupant of three-wheeled motor vehicle injured in collision with pedal cycle in traffic accident

● **V32** Occupant of three-wheeled motor vehicle injured in collision with two- or three-wheeled motor vehicle

The appropriate 7th character is to be added to each code from category V32

A	initial encounter
D	subsequent encounter
S	sequela

X● **V32.0** Driver of three-wheeled motor vehicle injured in collision with two- or three-wheeled motor vehicle in nontraffic accident

X● **V32.1** Passenger in three-wheeled motor vehicle injured in collision with two- or three-wheeled motor vehicle in nontraffic accident

X● **V32.2** Person on outside of three-wheeled motor vehicle injured in collision with two- or three-wheeled motor vehicle in nontraffic accident

X● **V32.3** Unspecified occupant of three-wheeled motor vehicle injured in collision with two- or three-wheeled motor vehicle in nontraffic accident

X● **V32.4** Person boarding or alighting a three-wheeled motor vehicle injured in collision with two- or three-wheeled motor vehicle

X● **V32.5** Driver of three-wheeled motor vehicle injured in collision with two- or three-wheeled motor vehicle in traffic accident

X● **V32.6** Passenger in three-wheeled motor vehicle injured in collision with two- or three-wheeled motor vehicle in traffic accident

X● **V32.7** Person on outside of three-wheeled motor vehicle injured in collision with two- or three-wheeled motor vehicle in traffic accident

X● **V32.9** Unspecified occupant of three-wheeled motor vehicle injured in collision with two- or three-wheeled motor vehicle in traffic accident

● **V33** Occupant of three-wheeled motor vehicle injured in collision with car, pick-up truck or van

The appropriate 7th character is to be added to each code from category V33

A	initial encounter
D	subsequent encounter
S	sequela

X● **V33.0** Driver of three-wheeled motor vehicle injured in collision with car, pick-up truck or van in nontraffic accident

X● **V33.1** Passenger in three-wheeled motor vehicle injured in collision with car, pick-up truck or van in nontraffic accident

X● **V33.2** Person on outside of three-wheeled motor vehicle injured in collision with car, pick-up truck or van in nontraffic accident

X● **V33.3** Unspecified occupant of three-wheeled motor vehicle injured in collision with car, pick-up truck or van in nontraffic accident

X● **V33.4** Person boarding or alighting a three-wheeled motor vehicle injured in collision with car, pick-up truck or van

X● **V33.5** Driver of three-wheeled motor vehicle injured in collision with car, pick-up truck or van in traffic accident

X● **V33.6** Passenger in three-wheeled motor vehicle injured in collision with car, pick-up truck or van in traffic accident

X● **V33.7** Person on outside of three-wheeled motor vehicle injured in collision with car, pick-up truck or van in traffic accident

X● **V33.9** Unspecified occupant of three-wheeled motor vehicle injured in collision with car, pick-up truck or van in traffic accident

▶ New   ⇛ Revised   ~~deleted~~ Deleted   Excludes 1   Excludes 2   Includes   Use additional   Code first   Code also   Key words

1480   OGCR Official Guidelines   X Assign placeholder X   ● Use Additional Character(s)   》 Manifestation Code   🏥 Hierarchical Condition Category   Coding Clinic

● V34 Occupant of three-wheeled motor vehicle injured in collision with heavy transport vehicle or bus

Excludes1   occupant of three-wheeled motor vehicle injured in collision with military vehicle (V39.81)

The appropriate 7th character is to be added to each code from category V34

A	initial encounter
D	subsequent encounter
S	sequela

X ● **V34.0** Driver of three-wheeled motor vehicle injured in collision with heavy transport vehicle or bus in nontraffic accident

X ● **V34.1** Passenger in three-wheeled motor vehicle injured in collision with heavy transport vehicle or bus in nontraffic accident

X ● **V34.2** Person on outside of three-wheeled motor vehicle injured in collision with heavy transport vehicle or bus in nontraffic accident

X ● **V34.3** Unspecified occupant of three-wheeled motor vehicle injured in collision with heavy transport vehicle or bus in nontraffic accident

X ● **V34.4** Person boarding or alighting a three-wheeled motor vehicle injured in collision with heavy transport vehicle or bus

X ● **V34.5** Driver of three-wheeled motor vehicle injured in collision with heavy transport vehicle or bus in traffic accident

X ● **V34.6** Passenger in three-wheeled motor vehicle injured in collision with heavy transport vehicle or bus in traffic accident

X ● **V34.7** Person on outside of three-wheeled motor vehicle injured in collision with heavy transport vehicle or bus in traffic accident

X ● **V34.9** Unspecified occupant of three-wheeled motor vehicle injured in collision with heavy transport vehicle or bus in traffic accident

● V35 Occupant of three-wheeled motor vehicle injured in collision with railway train or railway vehicle

The appropriate 7th character is to be added to each code from category V35

A	initial encounter
D	subsequent encounter
S	sequela

X ● **V35.0** Driver of three-wheeled motor vehicle injured in collision with railway train or railway vehicle in nontraffic accident

X ● **V35.1** Passenger in three-wheeled motor vehicle injured in collision with railway train or railway vehicle in nontraffic accident

X ● **V35.2** Person on outside of three-wheeled motor vehicle injured in collision with railway train or railway vehicle in nontraffic accident

X ● **V35.3** Unspecified occupant of three-wheeled motor vehicle injured in collision with railway train or railway vehicle in nontraffic accident

X ● **V35.4** Person boarding or alighting a three-wheeled motor vehicle injured in collision with railway train or railway vehicle

X ● **V35.5** Driver of three-wheeled motor vehicle injured in collision with railway train or railway vehicle in traffic accident

X ● **V35.6** Passenger in three-wheeled motor vehicle injured in collision with railway train or railway vehicle in traffic accident

X ● **V35.7** Person on outside of three-wheeled motor vehicle injured in collision with railway train or railway vehicle in traffic accident

X ● **V35.9** Unspecified occupant of three-wheeled motor vehicle injured in collision with railway train or railway vehicle in traffic accident

● V36 Occupant of three-wheeled motor vehicle injured in collision with other nonmotor vehicle

Includes   collision with animal-drawn vehicle, animal being ridden, streetcar

The appropriate 7th character is to be added to each code from category V36

A	initial encounter
D	subsequent encounter
S	sequela

X ● **V36.0** Driver of three-wheeled motor vehicle injured in collision with other nonmotor vehicle in nontraffic accident

X ● **V36.1** Passenger in three-wheeled motor vehicle injured in collision with other nonmotor vehicle in nontraffic accident

X ● **V36.2** Person on outside of three-wheeled motor vehicle injured in collision with other nonmotor vehicle in nontraffic accident

X ● **V36.3** Unspecified occupant of three-wheeled motor vehicle injured in collision with other nonmotor vehicle in nontraffic accident

X ● **V36.4** Person boarding or alighting a three-wheeled motor vehicle injured in collision with other nonmotor vehicle

X ● **V36.5** Driver of three-wheeled motor vehicle injured in collision with other nonmotor vehicle in traffic accident

X ● **V36.6** Passenger in three-wheeled motor vehicle injured in collision with other nonmotor vehicle in traffic accident

X ● **V36.7** Person on outside of three-wheeled motor vehicle injured in collision with other nonmotor vehicle in traffic accident

X ● **V36.9** Unspecified occupant of three-wheeled motor vehicle injured in collision with other nonmotor vehicle in traffic accident

● V37 Occupant of three-wheeled motor vehicle injured in collision with fixed or stationary object

The appropriate 7th character is to be added to each code from category V37

A	initial encounter
D	subsequent encounter
S	sequela

X ● **V37.0** Driver of three-wheeled motor vehicle injured in collision with fixed or stationary object in nontraffic accident

X ● **V37.1** Passenger in three-wheeled motor vehicle injured in collision with fixed or stationary object in nontraffic accident

X ● **V37.2** Person on outside of three-wheeled motor vehicle injured in collision with fixed or stationary object in nontraffic accident

X ● **V37.3** Unspecified occupant of three-wheeled motor vehicle injured in collision with fixed or stationary object in nontraffic accident

X ● **V37.4** Person boarding or alighting a three-wheeled motor vehicle injured in collision with fixed or stationary object

X ● **V37.5** Driver of three-wheeled motor vehicle injured in collision with fixed or stationary object in traffic accident

X ● **V37.6** Passenger in three-wheeled motor vehicle injured in collision with fixed or stationary object in traffic accident

X ● **V37.7** Person on outside of three-wheeled motor vehicle injured in collision with fixed or stationary object in traffic accident

X ● **V37.9** Unspecified occupant of three-wheeled motor vehicle injured in collision with fixed or stationary object in traffic accident

CHAPTER 20 (V00–Y99)

CHAPTER 20 (V00-Y99)

● **V38** Occupant of three-wheeled motor vehicle injured in noncollision transport accident

> **Includes** fall or thrown from three-wheeled motor vehicle
> overturning of three-wheeled motor vehicle NOS
> overturning of three-wheeled motor vehicle without collision

The appropriate 7th character is to be added to each code from category V38

> A initial encounter
> D subsequent encounter
> S sequela

X● **V38.0** Driver of three-wheeled motor vehicle injured in noncollision transport accident in nontraffic accident

X● **V38.1** Passenger in three-wheeled motor vehicle injured in noncollision transport accident in nontraffic accident

X● **V38.2** Person on outside of three-wheeled motor vehicle injured in noncollision transport accident in nontraffic accident

X● **V38.3** Unspecified occupant of three-wheeled motor vehicle injured in noncollision transport accident in nontraffic accident

X● **V38.4** Person boarding or alighting a three-wheeled motor vehicle injured in noncollision transport accident

X● **V38.5** Driver of three-wheeled motor vehicle injured in noncollision transport accident in traffic accident

X● **V38.6** Passenger in three-wheeled motor vehicle injured in noncollision transport accident in traffic accident

X● **V38.7** Person on outside of three-wheeled motor vehicle injured in noncollision transport accident in traffic accident

X● **V38.9** Unspecified occupant of three-wheeled motor vehicle injured in noncollision transport accident in traffic accident

● **V39** Occupant of three-wheeled motor vehicle injured in other and unspecified transport accidents

The appropriate 7th character is to be added to each code from category V39

> A initial encounter
> D subsequent encounter
> S sequela

● **V39.0** Driver of three-wheeled motor vehicle injured in collision with other and unspecified motor vehicles in nontraffic accident

X● **V39.00** Driver of three-wheeled motor vehicle injured in collision with unspecified motor vehicles in nontraffic accident

X● **V39.09** Driver of three-wheeled motor vehicle injured in collision with other motor vehicles in nontraffic accident

● **V39.1** Passenger in three-wheeled motor vehicle injured in collision with other and unspecified motor vehicles in nontraffic accident

X● **V39.10** Passenger in three-wheeled motor vehicle injured in collision with unspecified motor vehicles in nontraffic accident

X● **V39.19** Passenger in three-wheeled motor vehicle injured in collision with other motor vehicles in nontraffic accident

● **V39.2** Unspecified occupant of three-wheeled motor vehicle injured in collision with other and unspecified motor vehicles in nontraffic accident

X● **V39.20** Unspecified occupant of three-wheeled motor vehicle injured in collision with unspecified motor vehicles in nontraffic accident
> Collision NOS involving three-wheeled motor vehicle, nontraffic

X● **V39.29** Unspecified occupant of three-wheeled motor vehicle injured in collision with other motor vehicles in nontraffic accident

X● **V39.3** Occupant (driver) (passenger) of three-wheeled motor vehicle injured in unspecified nontraffic accident
> Accident NOS involving three-wheeled motor vehicle, nontraffic
> Occupant of three-wheeled motor vehicle injured in nontraffic accident NOS

● **V39.4** Driver of three-wheeled motor vehicle injured in collision with other and unspecified motor vehicles in traffic accident

X● **V39.40** Driver of three-wheeled motor vehicle injured in collision with unspecified motor vehicles in traffic accident

X● **V39.49** Driver of three-wheeled motor vehicle injured in collision with other motor vehicles in traffic accident

● **V39.5** Passenger in three-wheeled motor vehicle injured in collision with other and unspecified motor vehicles in traffic accident

X● **V39.50** Passenger in three-wheeled motor vehicle injured in collision with unspecified motor vehicles in traffic accident

X● **V39.59** Passenger in three-wheeled motor vehicle injured in collision with other motor vehicles in traffic accident

● **V39.6** Unspecified occupant of three-wheeled motor vehicle injured in collision with other and unspecified motor vehicles in traffic accident

X● **V39.60** Unspecified occupant of three-wheeled motor vehicle injured in collision with unspecified motor vehicles in traffic accident
> Collision NOS involving three-wheeled motor vehicle (traffic)

X● **V39.69** Unspecified occupant of three-wheeled motor vehicle injured in collision with other motor vehicles in traffic accident

● **V39.8** Occupant (driver) (passenger) of three-wheeled motor vehicle injured in other specified transport accidents

X● **V39.81** Occupant (driver) (passenger) of three-wheeled motor vehicle injured in transport accident with military vehicle

X● **V39.89** Occupant (driver) (passenger) of three-wheeled motor vehicle injured in other specified transport accidents

X● **V39.9** Occupant (driver) (passenger) of three-wheeled motor vehicle injured in unspecified traffic accident
> Accident NOS involving three-wheeled motor vehicle

CAR OCCUPANT INJURED IN TRANSPORT ACCIDENT (V40-V49)

> **Includes** a four-wheeled motor vehicle designed primarily for carrying passengers
> automobile (pulling a trailer or camper)

> **Excludes1** bus (V50-V59)
> minibus (V50-V59)
> minivan (V50-V59)
> motorcoach (V70-V79)
> pick-up truck (V50-V59)
> sport utility vehicle (SUV) (V50-V59)

● **V40** Car occupant injured in collision with pedestrian or animal

> **Excludes1** car collision with animal-drawn vehicle or animal being ridden (V46.-)

The appropriate 7th character is to be added to each code from category V40

> A initial encounter
> D subsequent encounter
> S sequela

X● **V40.0** Car driver injured in collision with pedestrian or animal in nontraffic accident

X● **V40.1** Car passenger injured in collision with pedestrian or animal in nontraffic accident

---

▶ New ⇨ Revised ~~deleted~~ Deleted | Excludes 1 | Excludes 2 | Includes | Use additional | Code first | Code also | Key words

OGCR Official Guidelines X Assign placeholder X ● Use Additional Character(s) ⫯ Manifestation Code 🔖 Hierarchical Condition Category **Coding Clinic**

X● **V40.2**   **Person on outside** of car injured in collision with pedestrian or animal in nontraffic accident

X● **V40.3**   **Unspecified** car occupant injured in collision with pedestrian or animal in nontraffic accident

X● **V40.4**   Person **boarding or alighting** a car injured in collision with pedestrian or animal

X● **V40.5**   Car **driver** injured in collision with pedestrian or animal in traffic accident

X● **V40.6**   Car **passenger** injured in collision with pedestrian or animal in traffic accident

X● **V40.7**   **Person on outside** of car injured in collision with pedestrian or animal in traffic accident

X● **V40.9**   **Unspecified** car occupant injured in collision with pedestrian or animal in traffic accident

● **V41**   **Car occupant injured in collision with pedal cycle**

The appropriate 7th character is to be added to each code from category V41

> A   initial encounter
> D   subsequent encounter
> S   sequela

X● **V41.0**   Car **driver** injured in collision with pedal cycle in nontraffic accident

X● **V41.1**   Car **passenger** injured in collision with pedal cycle in nontraffic accident

X● **V41.2**   **Person on outside** of car injured in collision with pedal cycle in nontraffic accident

X● **V41.3**   **Unspecified** car occupant injured in collision with pedal cycle in nontraffic accident

X● **V41.4**   Person **boarding or alighting** a car injured in collision with pedal cycle

X● **V41.5**   Car **driver** injured in collision with pedal cycle in traffic accident

X● **V41.6**   Car **passenger** injured in collision with pedal cycle in traffic accident

X● **V41.7**   **Person on outside** of car injured in collision with pedal cycle in traffic accident

X● **V41.9**   **Unspecified** car occupant injured in collision with pedal cycle in traffic accident

● **V42**   **Car occupant injured in collision with two- or three-wheeled motor vehicle**

The appropriate 7th character is to be added to each code from category V42

> A   initial encounter
> D   subsequent encounter
> S   sequela

X● **V42.0**   Car **driver** injured in collision with two- or three-wheeled motor vehicle in nontraffic accident

X● **V42.1**   Car **passenger** injured in collision with two- or three-wheeled motor vehicle in nontraffic accident

X● **V42.2**   **Person on outside** of car injured in collision with two- or three-wheeled motor vehicle in nontraffic accident

X● **V42.3**   **Unspecified** car occupant injured in collision with two- or three-wheeled motor vehicle in nontraffic accident

X● **V42.4**   Person **boarding or alighting** a car injured in collision with two- or three-wheeled motor vehicle

X● **V42.5**   Car **driver** injured in collision with two- or three-wheeled motor vehicle in traffic accident

X● **V42.6**   Car **passenger** injured in collision with two- or three-wheeled motor vehicle in traffic accident

X● **V42.7**   **Person on outside** of car injured in collision with two- or three-wheeled motor vehicle in traffic accident

X● **V42.9**   **Unspecified** car occupant injured in collision with two- or three-wheeled motor vehicle in traffic accident

● **V43**   **Car occupant injured in collision with car, pick-up truck or van**

The appropriate 7th character is to be added to each code from category V43

> A   initial encounter
> D   subsequent encounter
> S   sequela

● **V43.0**   Car **driver** injured in collision with car, pick-up truck or van in nontraffic accident

    X● **V43.01**   Car driver injured in collision with sport utility vehicle in nontraffic accident

    X● **V43.02**   Car driver injured in collision with other type car in nontraffic accident

    X● **V43.03**   Car driver injured in collision with pick-up truck in nontraffic accident

    X● **V43.04**   Car driver injured in collision with van in nontraffic accident

● **V43.1**   Car **passenger** injured in collision with car, pick-up truck or van in nontraffic accident

    X● **V43.11**   Car passenger injured in collision with sport utility vehicle in nontraffic accident

    X● **V43.12**   Car passenger injured in collision with other type car in nontraffic accident

    X● **V43.13**   Car passenger injured in collision with pick-up truck in nontraffic accident

    X● **V43.14**   Car passenger injured in collision with van in nontraffic accident

● **V43.2**   **Person on outside** of car injured in collision with car, pick-up truck or van in nontraffic accident

    X● **V43.21**   Person on outside of car injured in collision with sport utility vehicle in nontraffic accident

    X● **V43.22**   Person on outside of car injured in collision with other type car in nontraffic accident

    X● **V43.23**   Person on outside of car injured in collision with pick-up truck in nontraffic accident

    X● **V43.24**   Person on outside of car injured in collision with van in nontraffic accident

● **V43.3**   **Unspecified** car occupant injured in collision with car, pick-up truck or van in nontraffic accident

    X● **V43.31**   Unspecified car occupant injured in collision with sport utility vehicle in nontraffic accident

    X● **V43.32**   Unspecified car occupant injured in collision with other type car in nontraffic accident

    X● **V43.33**   Unspecified car occupant injured in collision with pick-up truck in nontraffic accident

    X● **V43.34**   Unspecified car occupant injured in collision with van in nontraffic accident

● **V43.4**   Person **boarding or alighting** a car injured in collision with car, pick-up truck or van

    X● **V43.41**   Person boarding or alighting a car injured in collision with sport utility vehicle

    X● **V43.42**   Person boarding or alighting a car injured in collision with other type car

    X● **V43.43**   Person boarding or alighting a car injured in collision with pick-up truck

    X● **V43.44**   Person boarding or alighting a car injured in collision with van

● **V43.5**   Car **driver** injured in collision with car, pick-up truck or van in traffic accident

    X● **V43.51**   Car driver injured in collision with sport utility vehicle in traffic accident

    X● **V43.52**   Car driver injured in collision with other type car in traffic accident

    X● **V43.53**   Car driver injured in collision with pick-up truck in traffic accident

    X● **V43.54**   Car driver injured in collision with van in traffic accident

CHAPTER 20 (V00–Y99)

● **V43.6** Car passenger injured in collision with car, pick-up truck or van in traffic accident

X● **V43.61** Car passenger injured in collision with sport utility vehicle in traffic accident
Coding Clinic: 2015, Q1, P5-7

X● **V43.62** Car passenger injured in collision with other type car in traffic accident

X● **V43.63** Car passenger injured in collision with pick-up truck in traffic accident

X● **V43.64** Car passenger injured in collision with van in traffic accident

● **V43.7** Person on outside of car injured in collision with car, pick-up truck or van in traffic accident

X● **V43.71** Person on outside of car injured in collision with sport utility vehicle in traffic accident

X● **V43.72** Person on outside of car injured in collision with other type car in traffic accident

X● **V43.73** Person on outside of car injured in collision with pick-up truck in traffic accident

X● **V43.74** Person on outside of car injured in collision with van in traffic accident

● **V43.9** Unspecified car occupant injured in collision with car, pick-up truck or van in traffic accident

X● **V43.91** Unspecified car occupant injured in collision with sport utility vehicle in traffic accident

X● **V43.92** Unspecified car occupant injured in collision with other type car in traffic accident

X● **V43.93** Unspecified car occupant injured in collision with pick-up truck in traffic accident

X● **V43.94** Unspecified car occupant injured in collision with van in traffic accident

● **V44** Car occupant injured in collision with heavy transport vehicle or bus

Excludes1 car occupant injured in collision with military vehicle (V49.81)

The appropriate 7th character is to be added to each code from category V44

A	initial encounter
D	subsequent encounter
S	sequela

X● **V44.0** Car driver injured in collision with heavy transport vehicle or bus in nontraffic accident

X● **V44.1** Car passenger injured in collision with heavy transport vehicle or bus in nontraffic accident

X● **V44.2** Person on outside of car injured in collision with heavy transport vehicle or bus in nontraffic accident

X● **V44.3** Unspecified car occupant injured in collision with heavy transport vehicle or bus in nontraffic accident

X● **V44.4** Person boarding or alighting a car injured in collision with heavy transport vehicle or bus

X● **V44.5** Car driver injured in collision with heavy transport vehicle or bus in traffic accident

X● **V44.6** Car passenger injured in collision with heavy transport vehicle or bus in traffic accident

X● **V44.7** Person on outside of car injured in collision with heavy transport vehicle or bus in traffic accident

X● **V44.9** Unspecified car occupant injured in collision with heavy transport vehicle or bus in traffic accident

● **V45** Car occupant injured in collision with railway train or railway vehicle

The appropriate 7th character is to be added to each code from category V45

A	initial encounter
D	subsequent encounter
S	sequela

X● **V45.0** Car driver injured in collision with railway train or railway vehicle in nontraffic accident

X● **V45.1** Car passenger injured in collision with railway train or railway vehicle in nontraffic accident

X● **V45.2** Person on outside of car injured in collision with railway train or railway vehicle in nontraffic accident

X● **V45.3** Unspecified car occupant injured in collision with railway train or railway vehicle in nontraffic accident

X● **V45.4** Person boarding or alighting a car injured in collision with railway train or railway vehicle

X● **V45.5** Car driver injured in collision with railway train or railway vehicle in traffic accident

X● **V45.6** Car passenger injured in collision with railway train or railway vehicle in traffic accident

X● **V45.7** Person on outside of car injured in collision with railway train or railway vehicle in traffic accident

X● **V45.9** Unspecified car occupant injured in collision with railway train or railway vehicle in traffic accident

● **V46** Car occupant injured in collision with other nonmotor vehicle

Includes collision with animal-drawn vehicle, animal being ridden, streetcar

The appropriate 7th character is to be added to each code from category V46

A	initial encounter
D	subsequent encounter
S	sequela

X● **V46.0** Car driver injured in collision with other nonmotor vehicle in nontraffic accident

X● **V46.1** Car passenger injured in collision with other nonmotor vehicle in nontraffic accident

X● **V46.2** Person on outside of car injured in collision with other nonmotor vehicle in nontraffic accident

X● **V46.3** Unspecified car occupant injured in collision with other nonmotor vehicle in nontraffic accident

X● **V46.4** Person boarding or alighting a car injured in collision with other nonmotor vehicle

X● **V46.5** Car driver injured in collision with other nonmotor vehicle in traffic accident

X● **V46.6** Car passenger injured in collision with other nonmotor vehicle in traffic accident

X● **V46.7** Person on outside of car injured in collision with other nonmotor vehicle in traffic accident

X● **V46.9** Unspecified car occupant injured in collision with other nonmotor vehicle in traffic accident

● **V47** Car occupant injured in collision with fixed or stationary object

The appropriate 7th character is to be added to each code from category V47

A	initial encounter
D	subsequent encounter
S	sequela

Coding Clinic: 2016, Q4, P73

X● **V47.0** Car driver injured in collision with fixed or stationary object in nontraffic accident

X● **V47.1** Car passenger injured in collision with fixed or stationary object in nontraffic accident

X● **V47.2** Person on outside of car injured in collision with fixed or stationary object in nontraffic accident

X● **V47.3** Unspecified car occupant injured in collision with fixed or stationary object in nontraffic accident

X● **V47.4** Person boarding or alighting a car injured in collision with fixed or stationary object

X● **V47.5** Car driver injured in collision with fixed or stationary object in traffic accident

X● **V47.6** Car passenger injured in collision with fixed or stationary object in traffic accident

X● **V47.7** Person on outside of car injured in collision with fixed or stationary object in traffic accident

X● **V47.9** Unspecified car occupant injured in collision with fixed or stationary object in traffic accident

▶ New   ⇒ Revised   ~~deleted~~ Deleted   Excludes 1   Excludes 2   Includes   Use additional   Code first   Code also   Key words

OGCR Official Guidelines   X Assign placeholder X   ● Use Additional Character(s)   ▷ Manifestation Code   🔹 Hierarchical Condition Category   **Coding Clinic**

● **V48   Car occupant injured in noncollision transport accident**

   Includes   overturning car NOS
                   overturning car without collision

   The appropriate 7th character is to be added to each code from
   category V48

   > A   initial encounter
   > D   subsequent encounter
   > S   sequela

   X● **V48.0   Car driver injured in noncollision transport accident in
                nontraffic accident**

   X● **V48.1   Car passenger injured in noncollision transport accident
                in nontraffic accident**

   X● **V48.2   Person on outside of car injured in noncollision
                transport accident in nontraffic accident**

   X● **V48.3   Unspecified car occupant injured in noncollision
                transport accident in nontraffic accident**

   X● **V48.4   Person boarding or alighting a car injured in
                noncollision transport accident**

   X● **V48.5   Car driver injured in noncollision transport accident in
                traffic accident**

   X● **V48.6   Car passenger injured in noncollision transport accident
                in traffic accident**

   X● **V48.7   Person on outside of car injured in noncollision
                transport accident in traffic accident**

   X● **V48.9   Unspecified car occupant injured in noncollision
                transport accident in traffic accident**

● **V49   Car occupant injured in other and unspecified transport
           accidents**

   The appropriate 7th character is to be added to each code from
   category V49

   > A   initial encounter
   > D   subsequent encounter
   > S   sequela

   ● **V49.0   Driver injured in collision with other and unspecified
                motor vehicles in nontraffic accident**

      X● **V49.00   Driver injured in collision with unspecified
                    motor vehicles in nontraffic accident**

      X● **V49.09   Driver injured in collision with other motor
                    vehicles in nontraffic accident**

   ● **V49.1   Passenger injured in collision with other and
                unspecified motor vehicles in nontraffic accident**

      X● **V49.10   Passenger injured in collision with unspecified
                    motor vehicles in nontraffic accident**

      X● **V49.19   Passenger injured in collision with other motor
                    vehicles in nontraffic accident**

   ● **V49.2   Unspecified car occupant injured in collision with other
                and unspecified motor vehicles in nontraffic accident**

      X● **V49.20   Unspecified car occupant injured in collision
                    with unspecified motor vehicles in nontraffic
                    accident**
                    Car collision NOS, nontraffic

      X● **V49.29   Unspecified car occupant injured in collision
                    with other motor vehicles in nontraffic accident**

   X● **V49.3   Car occupant (driver) (passenger) injured in unspecified
                nontraffic accident**
                Car accident NOS, nontraffic
                Car occupant injured in nontraffic accident NOS

   ● **V49.4   Driver injured in collision with other and unspecified
                motor vehicles in traffic accident**

      X● **V49.40   Driver injured in collision with unspecified
                    motor vehicles in traffic accident**

      X● **V49.49   Driver injured in collision with other motor
                    vehicles in traffic accident**

● **V49.5   Passenger injured in collision with other and
             unspecified motor vehicles in traffic accident**

   X● **V49.50   Passenger injured in collision with unspecified
                 motor vehicles in traffic accident**

   X● **V49.59   Passenger injured in collision with other motor
                 vehicles in traffic accident**

● **V49.6   Unspecified car occupant injured in collision with other
             and unspecified motor vehicles in traffic accident**

   X● **V49.60   Unspecified car occupant injured in collision
                 with unspecified motor vehicles in traffic
                 accident**
                 Car collision NOS (traffic)

   X● **V49.69   Unspecified car occupant injured in collision
                 with other motor vehicles in traffic accident**

● **V49.8   Car occupant (driver) (passenger) injured in other
             specified transport accidents**

   X● **V49.81   Car occupant (driver) (passenger) injured in
                 transport accident with military vehicle**

   X● **V49.88   Car occupant (driver) (passenger) injured in
                 other specified transport accidents**

X● **V49.9   Car occupant (driver) (passenger) injured in unspecified
             traffic accident**
             Car accident NOS
             Coding Clinic: 2015, Q1, P11

OCCUPANT OF PICK-UP TRUCK OR VAN INJURED IN TRANSPORT ACCIDENT (V50-V59)

   Includes   a four- or six-wheel motor vehicle designed
                   primarily for carrying passengers and
                   property but weighing less than the local
                   limit for classification as a heavy goods
                   vehicle
                   minibus
                   minivan
                   sport utility vehicle (SUV)
                   truck
                   van

   Excludes1   heavy transport vehicle (V60-V69)

● **V50   Occupant of pick-up truck or van injured in collision with
           pedestrian or animal**

   Excludes1   pick-up truck or van collision with animal-drawn
                    vehicle or animal being ridden (V56.-)

   The appropriate 7th character is to be added to each code from
   category V50

   > A   initial encounter
   > D   subsequent encounter
   > S   sequela

   X● **V50.0   Driver of pick-up truck or van injured in collision with
                pedestrian or animal in nontraffic accident**

   X● **V50.1   Passenger in pick-up truck or van injured in collision
                with pedestrian or animal in nontraffic accident**

   X● **V50.2   Person on outside of pick-up truck or van injured in
                collision with pedestrian or animal in nontraffic accident**

   X● **V50.3   Unspecified occupant of pick-up truck or van injured in
                collision with pedestrian or animal in nontraffic accident**

   X● **V50.4   Person boarding or alighting a pick-up truck or van
                injured in collision with pedestrian or animal**

   X● **V50.5   Driver of pick-up truck or van injured in collision with
                pedestrian or animal in traffic accident**

   X● **V50.6   Passenger in pick-up truck or van injured in collision
                with pedestrian or animal in traffic accident**

   X● **V50.7   Person on outside of pick-up truck or van injured in
                collision with pedestrian or animal in traffic accident**

   X● **V50.9   Unspecified occupant of pick-up truck or van injured in
                collision with pedestrian or animal in traffic accident**

● **V51** **Occupant of pick-up truck or van injured in collision with pedal cycle**

The appropriate 7th character is to be added to each code from category V51

A	initial encounter
D	subsequent encounter
S	sequela

X● **V51.0** Driver of pick-up truck or van injured in collision with pedal cycle in nontraffic accident

X● **V51.1** Passenger in pick-up truck or van injured in collision with pedal cycle in nontraffic accident

X● **V51.2** Person on outside of pick-up truck or van injured in collision with pedal cycle in nontraffic accident

X● **V51.3** Unspecified occupant of pick-up truck or van injured in collision with pedal cycle in nontraffic accident

X● **V51.4** Person boarding or alighting a pick-up truck or van injured in collision with pedal cycle

X● **V51.5** Driver of pick-up truck or van injured in collision with pedal cycle in traffic accident

X● **V51.6** Passenger in pick-up truck or van injured in collision with pedal cycle in traffic accident

X● **V51.7** Person on outside of pick-up truck or van injured in collision with pedal cycle in traffic accident

X● **V51.9** Unspecified occupant of pick-up truck or van injured in collision with pedal cycle in traffic accident

● **V52** **Occupant of pick-up truck or van injured in collision with two- or three-wheeled motor vehicle**

The appropriate 7th character is to be added to each code from category V52

A	initial encounter
D	subsequent encounter
S	sequela

X● **V52.0** Driver of pick-up truck or van injured in collision with two- or three-wheeled motor vehicle in nontraffic accident

X● **V52.1** Passenger in pick-up truck or van injured in collision with two- or three-wheeled motor vehicle in nontraffic accident

X● **V52.2** Person on outside of pick-up truck or van injured in collision with two- or three-wheeled motor vehicle in nontraffic accident

X● **V52.3** Unspecified occupant of pick-up truck or van injured in collision with two- or three-wheeled motor vehicle in nontraffic accident

X● **V52.4** Person boarding or alighting a pick-up truck or van injured in collision with two- or three-wheeled motor vehicle

X● **V52.5** Driver of pick-up truck or van injured in collision with two- or three-wheeled motor vehicle in traffic accident

X● **V52.6** Passenger in pick-up truck or van injured in collision with two- or three-wheeled motor vehicle in traffic accident

X● **V52.7** Person on outside of pick-up truck or van injured in collision with two- or three-wheeled motor vehicle in traffic accident

X● **V52.9** Unspecified occupant of pick-up truck or van injured in collision with two- or three-wheeled motor vehicle in traffic accident

● **V53** **Occupant of pick-up truck or van injured in collision with car, pick-up truck or van**

The appropriate 7th character is to be added to each code from category V53

A	initial encounter
D	subsequent encounter
S	sequela

X● **V53.0** Driver of pick-up truck or van injured in collision with car, pick-up truck or van in nontraffic accident

X● **V53.1** Passenger in pick-up truck or van injured in collision with car, pick-up truck or van in nontraffic accident

X● **V53.2** Person on outside of pick-up truck or van injured in collision with car, pick-up truck or van in nontraffic accident

X● **V53.3** Unspecified occupant of pick-up truck or van injured in collision with car, pick-up truck or van in nontraffic accident

X● **V53.4** Person boarding or alighting a pick-up truck or van injured in collision with car, pick-up truck or van

X● **V53.5** Driver of pick-up truck or van injured in collision with car, pick-up truck or van in traffic accident

X● **V53.6** Passenger in pick-up truck or van injured in collision with car, pick-up truck or van in traffic accident

X● **V53.7** Person on outside of pick-up truck or van injured in collision with car, pick-up truck or van in traffic accident

X● **V53.9** Unspecified occupant of pick-up truck or van injured in collision with car, pick-up truck or van in traffic accident

● **V54** **Occupant of pick-up truck or van injured in collision with heavy transport vehicle or bus**

Excludes1 occupant of pick-up truck or van injured in collision with military vehicle (V59.81)

The appropriate 7th character is to be added to each code from category V54

A	initial encounter
D	subsequent encounter
S	sequela

X● **V54.0** Driver of pick-up truck or van injured in collision with heavy transport vehicle or bus in nontraffic accident

X● **V54.1** Passenger in pick-up truck or van injured in collision with heavy transport vehicle or bus in nontraffic accident

X● **V54.2** Person on outside of pick-up truck or van injured in collision with heavy transport vehicle or bus in nontraffic accident

X● **V54.3** Unspecified occupant of pick-up truck or van injured in collision with heavy transport vehicle or bus in nontraffic accident

X● **V54.4** Person boarding or alighting a pick-up truck or van injured in collision with heavy transport vehicle or bus

X● **V54.5** Driver of pick-up truck or van injured in collision with heavy transport vehicle or bus in traffic accident

X● **V54.6** Passenger in pick-up truck or van injured in collision with heavy transport vehicle or bus in traffic accident

X● **V54.7** Person on outside of pick-up truck or van injured in collision with heavy transport vehicle or bus in traffic accident

X● **V54.9** Unspecified occupant of pick-up truck or van injured in collision with heavy transport vehicle or bus in traffic accident

▶ New　⇒ Revised　~~deleted~~ Deleted　Excludes 1　Excludes 2　Includes　Use additional　Code first　Code also　Key words
OGCR Official Guidelines　X Assign placeholder X　● Use Additional Character(s)　▷ Manifestation Code　🅠 Hierarchical Condition Category　Coding Clinic

● **V55**   **Occupant of pick-up truck or van injured in collision with railway train or railway vehicle**

    The appropriate 7th character is to be added to each code from category V55

> A   initial encounter
> D   subsequent encounter
> S   sequela

X ● **V55.0**   Driver of pick-up truck or van injured in collision with railway train or railway vehicle in nontraffic accident

X ● **V55.1**   Passenger in pick-up truck or van injured in collision with railway train or railway vehicle in nontraffic accident

X ● **V55.2**   Person on outside of pick-up truck or van injured in collision with railway train or railway vehicle in nontraffic accident

X ● **V55.3**   Unspecified occupant of pick-up truck or van injured in collision with railway train or railway vehicle in nontraffic accident

X ● **V55.4**   Person boarding or alighting a pick-up truck or van injured in collision with railway train or railway vehicle

X ● **V55.5**   Driver of pick-up truck or van injured in collision with railway train or railway vehicle in traffic accident

X ● **V55.6**   Passenger in pick-up truck or van injured in collision with railway train or railway vehicle in traffic accident

X ● **V55.7**   Person on outside of pick-up truck or van injured in collision with railway train or railway vehicle in traffic accident

X ● **V55.9**   Unspecified occupant of pick-up truck or van injured in collision with railway train or railway vehicle in traffic accident

● **V56**   **Occupant of pick-up truck or van injured in collision with other nonmotor vehicle**

    Includes   collision with animal-drawn vehicle, animal being ridden, streetcar

    The appropriate 7th character is to be added to each code from category V56

> A   initial encounter
> D   subsequent encounter
> S   sequela

X ● **V56.0**   Driver of pick-up truck or van injured in collision with other nonmotor vehicle in nontraffic accident

X ● **V56.1**   Passenger in pick-up truck or van injured in collision with other nonmotor vehicle in nontraffic accident

X ● **V56.2**   Person on outside of pick-up truck or van injured in collision with other nonmotor vehicle in nontraffic accident

X ● **V56.3**   Unspecified occupant of pick-up truck or van injured in collision with other nonmotor vehicle in nontraffic accident

X ● **V56.4**   Person boarding or alighting a pick-up truck or van injured in collision with other nonmotor vehicle

X ● **V56.5**   Driver of pick-up truck or van injured in collision with other nonmotor vehicle in traffic accident

X ● **V56.6**   Passenger in pick-up truck or van injured in collision with other nonmotor vehicle in traffic accident

X ● **V56.7**   Person on outside of pick-up truck or van injured in collision with other nonmotor vehicle in traffic accident

X ● **V56.9**   Unspecified occupant of pick-up truck or van injured in collision with other nonmotor vehicle in traffic accident

● **V57**   **Occupant of pick-up truck or van injured in collision with fixed or stationary object**

    The appropriate 7th character is to be added to each code from category V57

> A   initial encounter
> D   subsequent encounter
> S   sequela

X ● **V57.0**   Driver of pick-up truck or van injured in collision with fixed or stationary object in nontraffic accident

X ● **V57.1**   Passenger in pick-up truck or van injured in collision with fixed or stationary object in nontraffic accident

X ● **V57.2**   Person on outside of pick-up truck or van injured in collision with fixed or stationary object in nontraffic accident

X ● **V57.3**   Unspecified occupant of pick-up truck or van injured in collision with fixed or stationary object in nontraffic accident

X ● **V57.4**   Person boarding or alighting a pick-up truck or van injured in collision with fixed or stationary object

X ● **V57.5**   Driver of pick-up truck or van injured in collision with fixed or stationary object in traffic accident

X ● **V57.6**   Passenger in pick-up truck or van injured in collision with fixed or stationary object in traffic accident

X ● **V57.7**   Person on outside of pick-up truck or van injured in collision with fixed or stationary object in traffic accident

X ● **V57.9**   Unspecified occupant of pick-up truck or van injured in collision with fixed or stationary object in traffic accident

● **V58**   **Occupant of pick-up truck or van injured in noncollision transport accident**

    Includes   overturning pick-up truck or van NOS
                 overturning pick-up truck or van without collision

    The appropriate 7th character is to be added to each code from category V58

> A   initial encounter
> D   subsequent encounter
> S   sequela

X ● **V58.0**   Driver of pick-up truck or van injured in noncollision transport accident in nontraffic accident

X ● **V58.1**   Passenger in pick-up truck or van injured in noncollision transport accident in nontraffic accident

X ● **V58.2**   Person on outside of pick-up truck or van injured in noncollision transport accident in nontraffic accident

X ● **V58.3**   Unspecified occupant of pick-up truck or van injured in noncollision transport accident in nontraffic accident

X ● **V58.4**   Person boarding or alighting a pick-up truck or van injured in noncollision transport accident

X ● **V58.5**   Driver of pick-up truck or van injured in noncollision transport accident in traffic accident

X ● **V58.6**   Passenger in pick-up truck or van injured in noncollision transport accident in traffic accident

X ● **V58.7**   Person on outside of pick-up truck or van injured in noncollision transport accident in traffic accident

X ● **V58.9**   Unspecified occupant of pick-up truck or van injured in noncollision transport accident in traffic accident

CHAPTER 20 (V00-Y99)

● **V59** **Occupant of pick-up truck or van injured in other and unspecified transport accidents**

> The appropriate 7th character is to be added to each code from category V59

> | A | initial encounter |
> |---|---|
> | D | subsequent encounter |
> | S | sequela |

  ● **V59.0** **Driver of pick-up truck or van injured in collision with other and unspecified motor vehicles in** nontraffic accident

    X● **V59.00** Driver of pick-up truck or van injured in collision with unspecified motor vehicles in nontraffic accident

    X● **V59.09** Driver of pick-up truck or van injured in collision with other motor vehicles in nontraffic accident

  ● **V59.1** **Passenger in pick-up truck or van injured in collision with other and unspecified motor vehicles in** nontraffic accident

    X● **V59.10** Passenger in pick-up truck or van injured in collision with unspecified motor vehicles in nontraffic accident

    X● **V59.19** Passenger in pick-up truck or van injured in collision with other motor vehicles in nontraffic accident

  ● **V59.2** **Unspecified occupant of pick-up truck or van injured in collision with other and unspecified motor vehicles in** nontraffic accident

    X● **V59.20** Unspecified occupant of pick-up truck or van injured in collision with unspecified motor vehicles in nontraffic accident
> Collision NOS involving pick-up truck or van, nontraffic

    X● **V59.29** Unspecified occupant of pick-up truck or van injured in collision with other motor vehicles in nontraffic accident

  X● **V59.3** Occupant (driver) (passenger) of pick-up truck or van injured in unspecified nontraffic accident
> Accident NOS involving pick-up truck or van, nontraffic
> Occupant of pick-up truck or van injured in nontraffic accident NOS

  ● **V59.4** **Driver of pick-up truck or van injured in collision with other and unspecified motor vehicles in** traffic accident

    X● **V59.40** Driver of pick-up truck or van injured in collision with unspecified motor vehicles in traffic accident

    X● **V59.49** Driver of pick-up truck or van injured in collision with other motor vehicles in traffic accident

  ● **V59.5** **Passenger in pick-up truck or van injured in collision with other and unspecified motor vehicles in** traffic accident

    X● **V59.50** Passenger in pick-up truck or van injured in collision with unspecified motor vehicles in traffic accident

    X● **V59.59** Passenger in pick-up truck or van injured in collision with other motor vehicles in traffic accident

  ● **V59.6** **Unspecified occupant of pick-up truck or van injured in collision with other and unspecified motor vehicles in** traffic accident

    X● **V59.60** Unspecified occupant of pick-up truck or van injured in collision with unspecified motor vehicles in traffic accident
> Collision NOS involving pick-up truck or van (traffic)

    X● **V59.69** Unspecified occupant of pick-up truck or van injured in collision with other motor vehicles in traffic accident

● **V59.8** **Occupant (driver) (passenger) of pick-up truck or van injured in other specified transport accidents**

  X● **V59.81** Occupant (driver) (passenger) of pick-up truck or van injured in transport accident with military vehicle

  X● **V59.88** Occupant (driver) (passenger) of pick-up truck or van injured in other specified transport accidents

X● **V59.9** Occupant (driver) (passenger) of pick-up truck or van injured in unspecified traffic accident
> Accident NOS involving pick-up truck or van

OCCUPANT OF HEAVY TRANSPORT VEHICLE INJURED IN TRANSPORT ACCIDENT (V60-V69)

> | **Includes** | 18 wheeler |
> |---|---|
> | | armored car |
> | | panel truck |
> | **Excludes1** | bus |
> | | motorcoach |

● **V60** **Occupant of heavy transport vehicle injured in collision with pedestrian or animal**

> **Excludes1** heavy transport vehicle collision with animal-drawn vehicle or animal being ridden (V66.-)

> The appropriate 7th character is to be added to each code from category V60

> | A | initial encounter |
> |---|---|
> | D | subsequent encounter |
> | S | sequela |

  X● **V60.0** **Driver of heavy transport vehicle injured in collision with pedestrian or animal in** nontraffic accident

  X● **V60.1** **Passenger in heavy transport vehicle injured in collision with pedestrian or animal in** nontraffic accident

  X● **V60.2** **Person on outside of heavy transport vehicle injured in collision with pedestrian or animal in** nontraffic accident

  X● **V60.3** **Unspecified occupant of heavy transport vehicle injured in collision with pedestrian or animal in** nontraffic accident

  X● **V60.4** **Person boarding or alighting a heavy transport vehicle injured in collision with pedestrian or animal**

  X● **V60.5** **Driver of heavy transport vehicle injured in collision with pedestrian or animal in** traffic accident

  X● **V60.6** **Passenger in heavy transport vehicle injured in collision with pedestrian or animal in** traffic accident

  X● **V60.7** **Person on outside of heavy transport vehicle injured in collision with pedestrian or animal in** traffic accident

  X● **V60.9** **Unspecified occupant of heavy transport vehicle injured in collision with pedestrian or animal in** traffic accident

● **V61** **Occupant of heavy transport vehicle injured in collision with pedal cycle**

> The appropriate 7th character is to be added to each code from category V61

> | A | initial encounter |
> |---|---|
> | D | subsequent encounter |
> | S | sequela |

  X● **V61.0** **Driver of heavy transport vehicle injured in collision with pedal cycle in** nontraffic accident

  X● **V61.1** **Passenger in heavy transport vehicle injured in collision with pedal cycle in** nontraffic accident

  X● **V61.2** **Person on outside of heavy transport vehicle injured in collision with pedal cycle in** nontraffic accident

  X● **V61.3** **Unspecified occupant of heavy transport vehicle injured in collision with pedal cycle in** nontraffic accident

  X● **V61.4** **Person boarding or alighting a heavy transport vehicle injured in collision with pedal cycle while boarding or alighting**

  X● **V61.5** **Driver of heavy transport vehicle injured in collision with pedal cycle in** traffic accident

▶ New   ⇒ Revised   ~~deleted~~ Deleted   Excludes 1   Excludes 2   Includes   Use additional   Code first   Code also   Key words

OGCR Official Guidelines   X Assign placeholder X   ● Use Additional Character(s)   ▶ Manifestation Code   🅗 Hierarchical Condition Category   **Coding Clinic**

X● **V61.6**   Passenger in heavy transport vehicle injured in collision with pedal cycle in traffic accident

X● **V61.7**   Person on outside of heavy transport vehicle injured in collision with pedal cycle in traffic accident

X● **V61.9**   Unspecified occupant of heavy transport vehicle injured in collision with pedal cycle in traffic accident

● **V62**   Occupant of heavy transport vehicle injured in collision with two- or three-wheeled motor vehicle

The appropriate 7th character is to be added to each code from category V62

> A   initial encounter
> D   subsequent encounter
> S   sequela

X● **V62.0**   Driver of heavy transport vehicle injured in collision with two- or three-wheeled motor vehicle in nontraffic accident

X● **V62.1**   Passenger in heavy transport vehicle injured in collision with two- or three-wheeled motor vehicle in nontraffic accident

X● **V62.2**   Person on outside of heavy transport vehicle injured in collision with two- or three-wheeled motor vehicle in nontraffic accident

X● **V62.3**   Unspecified occupant of heavy transport vehicle injured in collision with two- or three-wheeled motor vehicle in nontraffic accident

X● **V62.4**   Person boarding or alighting a heavy transport vehicle injured in collision with two- or three-wheeled motor vehicle

X● **V62.5**   Driver of heavy transport vehicle injured in collision with two- or three-wheeled motor vehicle in traffic accident

X● **V62.6**   Passenger in heavy transport vehicle injured in collision with two- or three-wheeled motor vehicle in traffic accident

X● **V62.7**   Person on outside of heavy transport vehicle injured in collision with two- or three-wheeled motor vehicle in traffic accident

X● **V62.9**   Unspecified occupant of heavy transport vehicle injured in collision with two- or three-wheeled motor vehicle in traffic accident

● **V63**   Occupant of heavy transport vehicle injured in collision with car, pick-up truck or van

The appropriate 7th character is to be added to each code from category V63

> A   initial encounter
> D   subsequent encounter
> S   sequela

X● **V63.0**   Driver of heavy transport vehicle injured in collision with car, pick-up truck or van in nontraffic accident

X● **V63.1**   Passenger in heavy transport vehicle injured in collision with car, pick-up truck or van in nontraffic accident

X● **V63.2**   Person on outside of heavy transport vehicle injured in collision with car, pick-up truck or van in nontraffic accident

X● **V63.3**   Unspecified occupant of heavy transport vehicle injured in collision with car, pick-up truck or van in nontraffic accident

X● **V63.4**   Person boarding or alighting a heavy transport vehicle injured in collision with car, pick-up truck or van

X● **V63.5**   Driver of heavy transport vehicle injured in collision with car, pick-up truck or van in traffic accident

X● **V63.6**   Passenger in heavy transport vehicle injured in collision with car, pick-up truck or van in traffic accident

X● **V63.7**   Person on outside of heavy transport vehicle injured in collision with car, pick-up truck or van in traffic accident

X● **V63.9**   Unspecified occupant of heavy transport vehicle injured in collision with car, pick-up truck or van in traffic accident

● **V64**   Occupant of heavy transport vehicle injured in collision with heavy transport vehicle or bus

> **Excludes1**   occupant of heavy transport vehicle injured in collision with military vehicle (V69.81)

The appropriate 7th character is to be added to each code from category V64

> A   initial encounter
> D   subsequent encounter
> S   sequela

X● **V64.0**   Driver of heavy transport vehicle injured in collision with heavy transport vehicle or bus in nontraffic accident

X● **V64.1**   Passenger in heavy transport vehicle injured in collision with heavy transport vehicle or bus in nontraffic accident

X● **V64.2**   Person on outside of heavy transport vehicle injured in collision with heavy transport vehicle or bus in nontraffic accident

X● **V64.3**   Unspecified occupant of heavy transport vehicle injured in collision with heavy transport vehicle or bus in nontraffic accident

X● **V64.4**   Person boarding or alighting a heavy transport vehicle injured in collision with heavy transport vehicle or bus while boarding or alighting

X● **V64.5**   Driver of heavy transport vehicle injured in collision with heavy transport vehicle or bus in traffic accident

X● **V64.6**   Passenger in heavy transport vehicle injured in collision with heavy transport vehicle or bus in traffic accident

X● **V64.7**   Person on outside of heavy transport vehicle injured in collision with heavy transport vehicle or bus in traffic accident

X● **V64.9**   Unspecified occupant of heavy transport vehicle injured in collision with heavy transport vehicle or bus in traffic accident

● **V65**   Occupant of heavy transport vehicle injured in collision with railway train or railway vehicle

The appropriate 7th character is to be added to each code from category V65

> A   initial encounter
> D   subsequent encounter
> S   sequela

X● **V65.0**   Driver of heavy transport vehicle injured in collision with railway train or railway vehicle in nontraffic accident

X● **V65.1**   Passenger in heavy transport vehicle injured in collision with railway train or railway vehicle in nontraffic accident

X● **V65.2**   Person on outside of heavy transport vehicle injured in collision with railway train or railway vehicle in nontraffic accident

X● **V65.3**   Unspecified occupant of heavy transport vehicle injured in collision with railway train or railway vehicle in nontraffic accident

X● **V65.4**   Person boarding or alighting a heavy transport vehicle injured in collision with railway train or railway vehicle

X● **V65.5**   Driver of heavy transport vehicle injured in collision with railway train or railway vehicle in traffic accident

X● **V65.6**   Passenger in heavy transport vehicle injured in collision with railway train or railway vehicle in traffic accident

X● **V65.7**   Person on outside of heavy transport vehicle injured in collision with railway train or railway vehicle in traffic accident

X● **V65.9**   Unspecified occupant of heavy transport vehicle injured in collision with railway train or railway vehicle in traffic accident

CHAPTER 20 (V00-Y99)

● **V66**   **Occupant of heavy transport vehicle injured in collision with other nonmotor vehicle**

> **Includes**   collision with animal-drawn vehicle, animal being ridden, streetcar

> The appropriate 7th character is to be added to each code from category V66

> | A | initial encounter |
> |---|---|
> | D | subsequent encounter |
> | S | sequela |

X● **V66.0**   Driver of heavy transport vehicle injured in collision with other nonmotor vehicle in nontraffic accident

X● **V66.1**   Passenger in heavy transport vehicle injured in collision with other nonmotor vehicle in nontraffic accident

X● **V66.2**   Person on outside of heavy transport vehicle injured in collision with other nonmotor vehicle in nontraffic accident

X● **V66.3**   Unspecified occupant of heavy transport vehicle injured in collision with other nonmotor vehicle in nontraffic accident

X● **V66.4**   Person boarding or alighting a heavy transport vehicle injured in collision with other nonmotor vehicle

X● **V66.5**   Driver of heavy transport vehicle injured in collision with other nonmotor vehicle in traffic accident

X● **V66.6**   Passenger in heavy transport vehicle injured in collision with other nonmotor vehicle in traffic accident

X● **V66.7**   Person on outside of heavy transport vehicle injured in collision with other nonmotor vehicle in traffic accident

X● **V66.9**   Unspecified occupant of heavy transport vehicle injured in collision with other nonmotor vehicle in traffic accident

● **V67**   **Occupant of heavy transport vehicle injured in collision with fixed or stationary object**

> The appropriate 7th character is to be added to each code from category V67

> | A | initial encounter |
> |---|---|
> | D | subsequent encounter |
> | S | sequela |

X● **V67.0**   Driver of heavy transport vehicle injured in collision with fixed or stationary object in nontraffic accident

X● **V67.1**   Passenger in heavy transport vehicle injured in collision with fixed or stationary object in nontraffic accident

X● **V67.2**   Person on outside of heavy transport vehicle injured in collision with fixed or stationary object in nontraffic accident

X● **V67.3**   Unspecified occupant of heavy transport vehicle injured in collision with fixed or stationary object in nontraffic accident

X● **V67.4**   Person boarding or alighting a heavy transport vehicle injured in collision with fixed or stationary object

X● **V67.5**   Driver of heavy transport vehicle injured in collision with fixed or stationary object in traffic accident

X● **V67.6**   Passenger in heavy transport vehicle injured in collision with fixed or stationary object in traffic accident

X● **V67.7**   Person on outside of heavy transport vehicle injured in collision with fixed or stationary object in traffic accident

X● **V67.9**   Unspecified occupant of heavy transport vehicle injured in collision with fixed or stationary object in traffic accident

● **V68**   **Occupant of heavy transport vehicle injured in noncollision transport accident**

> **Includes**   overturning heavy transport vehicle NOS overturning heavy transport vehicle without collision

> The appropriate 7th character is to be added to each code from category V68

> | A | initial encounter |
> |---|---|
> | D | subsequent encounter |
> | S | sequela |

X● **V68.0**   Driver of heavy transport vehicle injured in noncollision transport accident in nontraffic accident

X● **V68.1**   Passenger in heavy transport vehicle injured in noncollision transport accident in nontraffic accident

X● **V68.2**   Person on outside of heavy transport vehicle injured in noncollision transport accident in nontraffic accident

X● **V68.3**   Unspecified occupant of heavy transport vehicle injured in noncollision transport accident in nontraffic accident

X● **V68.4**   Person boarding or alighting a heavy transport vehicle injured in noncollision transport accident

X● **V68.5**   Driver of heavy transport vehicle injured in noncollision transport accident in traffic accident

X● **V68.6**   Passenger in heavy transport vehicle injured in noncollision transport accident in traffic accident

X● **V68.7**   Person on outside of heavy transport vehicle injured in noncollision transport accident in traffic accident

X● **V68.9**   Unspecified occupant of heavy transport vehicle injured in noncollision transport accident in traffic accident

● **V69**   **Occupant of heavy transport vehicle injured in other and unspecified transport accidents**

> The appropriate 7th character is to be added to each code from category V69

> | A | initial encounter |
> |---|---|
> | D | subsequent encounter |
> | S | sequela |

● **V69.0**   Driver of heavy transport vehicle injured in collision with other and unspecified motor vehicles in nontraffic accident

     X● **V69.00**   Driver of heavy transport vehicle injured in collision with unspecified motor vehicles in nontraffic accident

     X● **V69.09**   Driver of heavy transport vehicle injured in collision with other motor vehicles in nontraffic accident

● **V69.1**   Passenger in heavy transport vehicle injured in collision with other and unspecified motor vehicles in nontraffic accident

     X● **V69.10**   Passenger in heavy transport vehicle injured in collision with unspecified motor vehicles in nontraffic accident

     X● **V69.19**   Passenger in heavy transport vehicle injured in collision with other motor vehicles in nontraffic accident

● **V69.2**   Unspecified occupant of heavy transport vehicle injured in collision with other and unspecified motor vehicles in nontraffic accident

     X● **V69.20**   Unspecified occupant of heavy transport vehicle injured in collision with unspecified motor vehicles in nontraffic accident

         Collision NOS involving heavy transport vehicle, nontraffic

     X● **V69.29**   Unspecified occupant of heavy transport vehicle injured in collision with other motor vehicles in nontraffic accident

▶ New   ⇒ Revised   ~~deleted~~ Deleted   Excludes 1   Excludes 2   Includes   Use additional   Code first   Code also   Key words

OGCR Official Guidelines   X Assign placeholder X   ● Use Additional Character(s)   ▷ Manifestation Code   🔖 Hierarchical Condition Category   **Coding Clinic**

X● **V69.3** Occupant (driver) (passenger) of heavy transport vehicle injured in unspecified nontraffic accident

     Accident NOS involving heavy transport vehicle, nontraffic

     Occupant of heavy transport vehicle injured in nontraffic accident NOS

● **V69.4** Driver of heavy transport vehicle injured in collision with other and unspecified motor vehicles in traffic accident

   X● **V69.40** Driver of heavy transport vehicle injured in collision with unspecified motor vehicles in traffic accident

   X● **V69.49** Driver of heavy transport vehicle injured in collision with other motor vehicles in traffic accident

● **V69.5** Passenger in heavy transport vehicle injured in collision with other and unspecified motor vehicles in traffic accident

   X● **V69.50** Passenger in heavy transport vehicle injured in collision with unspecified motor vehicles in traffic accident

   X● **V69.59** Passenger in heavy transport vehicle injured in collision with other motor vehicles in traffic accident

● **V69.6** Unspecified occupant of heavy transport vehicle injured in collision with other and unspecified motor vehicles in traffic accident

   X● **V69.60** Unspecified occupant of heavy transport vehicle injured in collision with unspecified motor vehicles in traffic accident

     Collision NOS involving heavy transport vehicle (traffic)

   X● **V69.69** Unspecified occupant of heavy transport vehicle injured in collision with other motor vehicles in traffic accident

● **V69.8** Occupant (driver) (passenger) of heavy transport vehicle injured in other specified transport accidents

   X● **V69.81** Occupant (driver) (passenger) of heavy transport vehicle injured in transport accidents with military vehicle

   X● **V69.88** Occupant (driver) (passenger) of heavy transport vehicle injured in other specified transport accidents

X● **V69.9** Occupant (driver) (passenger) of heavy transport vehicle injured in unspecified traffic accident

     Accident NOS involving heavy transport vehicle

BUS OCCUPANT INJURED IN TRANSPORT ACCIDENT (V70-V79)

Includes	motorcoach
Excludes1	minibus (V50-V59)

● **V70** Bus occupant injured in collision with pedestrian or animal

   Excludes1   bus collision with animal-drawn vehicle or animal being ridden (V76.-)

   The appropriate 7th character is to be added to each code from category V70

A	initial encounter
D	subsequent encounter
S	sequela

X● **V70.0** Driver of bus injured in collision with pedestrian or animal in nontraffic accident

X● **V70.1** Passenger on bus injured in collision with pedestrian or animal in nontraffic accident

X● **V70.2** Person on outside of bus injured in collision with pedestrian or animal in nontraffic accident

X● **V70.3** Unspecified occupant of bus injured in collision with pedestrian or animal in nontraffic accident

X● **V70.4** Person boarding or alighting from bus injured in collision with pedestrian or animal

X● **V70.5** Driver of bus injured in collision with pedestrian or animal in traffic accident

X● **V70.6** Passenger on bus injured in collision with pedestrian or animal in traffic accident

X● **V70.7** Person on outside of bus injured in collision with pedestrian or animal in traffic accident

X● **V70.9** Unspecified occupant of bus injured in collision with pedestrian or animal in traffic accident

● **V71** Bus occupant injured in collision with pedal cycle

   The appropriate 7th character is to be added to each code from category V71

A	initial encounter
D	subsequent encounter
S	sequela

X● **V71.0** Driver of bus injured in collision with pedal cycle in nontraffic accident

X● **V71.1** Passenger on bus injured in collision with pedal cycle in nontraffic accident

X● **V71.2** Person on outside of bus injured in collision with pedal cycle in nontraffic accident

X● **V71.3** Unspecified occupant of bus injured in collision with pedal cycle in nontraffic accident

X● **V71.4** Person boarding or alighting from bus injured in collision with pedal cycle

X● **V71.5** Driver of bus injured in collision with pedal cycle in traffic accident

X● **V71.6** Passenger on bus injured in collision with pedal cycle in traffic accident

X● **V71.7** Person on outside of bus injured in collision with pedal cycle in traffic accident

X● **V71.9** Unspecified occupant of bus injured in collision with pedal cycle in traffic accident

● **V72** Bus occupant injured in collision with two- or three-wheeled motor vehicle

   The appropriate 7th character is to be added to each code from category V72

A	initial encounter
D	subsequent encounter
S	sequela

X● **V72.0** Driver of bus injured in collision with two- or three-wheeled motor vehicle in nontraffic accident

X● **V72.1** Passenger on bus injured in collision with two- or three-wheeled motor vehicle in nontraffic accident

X● **V72.2** Person on outside of bus injured in collision with two- or three-wheeled motor vehicle in nontraffic accident

X● **V72.3** Unspecified occupant of bus injured in collision with two- or three-wheeled motor vehicle in nontraffic accident

X● **V72.4** Person boarding or alighting from bus injured in collision with two- or three-wheeled motor vehicle

X● **V72.5** Driver of bus injured in collision with two- or three-wheeled motor vehicle in traffic accident

X● **V72.6** Passenger on bus injured in collision with two- or three-wheeled motor vehicle in traffic accident

X● **V72.7** Person on outside of bus injured in collision with two- or three-wheeled motor vehicle in traffic accident

X● **V72.9** Unspecified occupant of bus injured in collision with two- or three-wheeled motor vehicle in traffic accident

CHAPTER 20 (V00-Y99)

● **V73**   **Bus occupant injured in collision with car, pick-up truck or van**

The appropriate 7th character is to be added to each code from category V73

> A   initial encounter
> D   subsequent encounter
> S   sequela

X● **V73.0**   Driver of bus injured in collision with car, pick-up truck or van in nontraffic accident

X● **V73.1**   Passenger on bus injured in collision with car, pick-up truck or van in nontraffic accident

X● **V73.2**   Person on outside of bus injured in collision with car, pick-up truck or van in nontraffic accident

X● **V73.3**   Unspecified occupant of bus injured in collision with car, pick-up truck or van in nontraffic accident

X● **V73.4**   Person boarding or alighting from bus injured in collision with car, pick-up truck or van

X● **V73.5**   Driver of bus injured in collision with car, pick-up truck or van in traffic accident

X● **V73.6**   Passenger on bus injured in collision with car, pick-up truck or van in traffic accident

X● **V73.7**   Person on outside of bus injured in collision with car, pick-up truck or van in traffic accident

X● **V73.9**   Unspecified occupant of bus injured in collision with car, pick-up truck or van in traffic accident

● **V74**   **Bus occupant injured in collision with heavy transport vehicle or bus**

> **Excludes1**   bus occupant injured in collision with military vehicle (V79.81)

The appropriate 7th character is to be added to each code from category V74

> A   initial encounter
> D   subsequent encounter
> S   sequela

X● **V74.0**   Driver of bus injured in collision with heavy transport vehicle or bus in nontraffic accident

X● **V74.1**   Passenger on bus injured in collision with heavy transport vehicle or bus in nontraffic accident

X● **V74.2**   Person on outside of bus injured in collision with heavy transport vehicle or bus in nontraffic accident

X● **V74.3**   Unspecified occupant of bus injured in collision with heavy transport vehicle or bus in nontraffic accident

X● **V74.4**   Person boarding or alighting from bus injured in collision with heavy transport vehicle or bus

X● **V74.5**   Driver of bus injured in collision with heavy transport vehicle or bus in traffic accident

X● **V74.6**   Passenger on bus injured in collision with heavy transport vehicle or bus in traffic accident

X● **V74.7**   Person on outside of bus injured in collision with heavy transport vehicle or bus in traffic accident

X● **V74.9**   Unspecified occupant of bus injured in collision with heavy transport vehicle or bus in traffic accident

● **V75**   **Bus occupant injured in collision with railway train or railway vehicle**

The appropriate 7th character is to be added to each code from category V75

> A   initial encounter
> D   subsequent encounter
> S   sequela

X● **V75.0**   Driver of bus injured in collision with railway train or railway vehicle in nontraffic accident

X● **V75.1**   Passenger on bus injured in collision with railway train or railway vehicle in nontraffic accident

X● **V75.2**   Person on outside of bus injured in collision with railway train or railway vehicle in nontraffic accident

X● **V75.3**   Unspecified occupant of bus injured in collision with railway train or railway vehicle in nontraffic accident

X● **V75.4**   Person boarding or alighting from bus injured in collision with railway train or railway vehicle

X● **V75.5**   Driver of bus injured in collision with railway train or railway vehicle in traffic accident

X● **V75.6**   Passenger on bus injured in collision with railway train or railway vehicle in traffic accident

X● **V75.7**   Person on outside of bus injured in collision with railway train or railway vehicle in traffic accident

X● **V75.9**   Unspecified occupant of bus injured in collision with railway train or railway vehicle in traffic accident

● **V76**   **Bus occupant injured in collision with other nonmotor vehicle**

> **Includes**   collision with animal-drawn vehicle, animal being ridden, streetcar

The appropriate 7th character is to be added to each code from category V76

> A   initial encounter
> D   subsequent encounter
> S   sequela

X● **V76.0**   Driver of bus injured in collision with other nonmotor vehicle in nontraffic accident

X● **V76.1**   Passenger on bus injured in collision with other nonmotor vehicle in nontraffic accident

X● **V76.2**   Person on outside of bus injured in collision with other nonmotor vehicle in nontraffic accident

X● **V76.3**   Unspecified occupant of bus injured in collision with other nonmotor vehicle in nontraffic accident

X● **V76.4**   Person boarding or alighting from bus injured in collision with other nonmotor vehicle

X● **V76.5**   Driver of bus injured in collision with other nonmotor vehicle in traffic accident

X● **V76.6**   Passenger on bus injured in collision with other nonmotor vehicle in traffic accident

X● **V76.7**   Person on outside of bus injured in collision with other nonmotor vehicle in traffic accident

X● **V76.9**   Unspecified occupant of bus injured in collision with other nonmotor vehicle in traffic accident

● **V77**   **Bus occupant injured in collision with fixed or stationary object**

The appropriate 7th character is to be added to each code from category V77

> A   initial encounter
> D   subsequent encounter
> S   sequela

X● **V77.0**   Driver of bus injured in collision with fixed or stationary object in nontraffic accident

X● **V77.1**   Passenger on bus injured in collision with fixed or stationary object in nontraffic accident

X● **V77.2**   Person on outside of bus injured in collision with fixed or stationary object in nontraffic accident

X● **V77.3**   Unspecified occupant of bus injured in collision with fixed or stationary object in nontraffic accident

X● **V77.4**   Person boarding or alighting from bus injured in collision with fixed or stationary object

X● **V77.5**   Driver of bus injured in collision with fixed or stationary object in traffic accident

X● **V77.6**   Passenger on bus injured in collision with fixed or stationary object in traffic accident

X● **V77.7**   Person on outside of bus injured in collision with fixed or stationary object in traffic accident

X● **V77.9**   Unspecified occupant of bus injured in collision with fixed or stationary object in traffic accident

▶ New   ⇒ Revised   ~~deleted~~ Deleted   Excludes 1   Excludes 2   Includes   Use additional   Code first   Code also   Key words

OGCR Official Guidelines   X Assign placeholder X   ● Use Additional Character(s)   ▸ Manifestation Code   ⊗ Hierarchical Condition Category   **Coding Clinic**

● V78 **Bus occupant injured in noncollision transport accident**

Includes   overturning bus NOS
overturning bus without collision

The appropriate 7th character is to be added to each code from category V78

> A   initial encounter
> D   subsequent encounter
> S   sequela

X ● **V78.0**   Driver of bus injured in noncollision transport accident in nontraffic accident

X ● **V78.1**   Passenger on bus injured in noncollision transport accident in nontraffic accident

X ● **V78.2**   Person on outside of bus injured in noncollision transport accident in nontraffic accident

X ● **V78.3**   Unspecified occupant of bus injured in noncollision transport accident in nontraffic accident

X ● **V78.4**   Person boarding or alighting from bus injured in noncollision transport accident

X ● **V78.5**   Driver of bus injured in noncollision transport accident in traffic accident

X ● **V78.6**   Passenger on bus injured in noncollision transport accident in traffic accident

X ● **V78.7**   Person on outside of bus injured in noncollision transport accident in traffic accident

X ● **V78.9**   Unspecified occupant of bus injured in noncollision transport accident in traffic accident

● V79 **Bus occupant injured in other and unspecified transport accidents**

The appropriate 7th character is to be added to each code from category V79

> A   initial encounter
> D   subsequent encounter
> S   sequela

● **V79.0**   Driver of bus injured in collision with other and unspecified motor vehicles in nontraffic accident

X ● **V79.00**   Driver of bus injured in collision with unspecified motor vehicles in nontraffic accident

X ● **V79.09**   Driver of bus injured in collision with other motor vehicles in nontraffic accident

● **V79.1**   Passenger on bus injured in collision with other and unspecified motor vehicles in nontraffic accident

X ● **V79.10**   Passenger on bus injured in collision with unspecified motor vehicles in nontraffic accident

X ● **V79.19**   Passenger on bus injured in collision with other motor vehicles in nontraffic accident

● **V79.2**   Unspecified bus occupant injured in collision with other and unspecified motor vehicles in nontraffic accident

X ● **V79.20**   Unspecified bus occupant injured in collision with unspecified motor vehicles in nontraffic accident
Bus collision NOS, nontraffic

X ● **V79.29**   Unspecified bus occupant injured in collision with other motor vehicles in nontraffic accident

X ● **V79.3**   Bus occupant (driver) (passenger) injured in unspecified nontraffic accident
Bus accident NOS, nontraffic
Bus occupant injured in nontraffic accident NOS

● **V79.4**   Driver of bus injured in collision with other and unspecified motor vehicles in traffic accident

X ● **V79.40**   Driver of bus injured in collision with unspecified motor vehicles in traffic accident

X ● **V79.49**   Driver of bus injured in collision with other motor vehicles in traffic accident

● **V79.5**   Passenger on bus injured in collision with other and unspecified motor vehicles in traffic accident

X ● **V79.50**   Passenger on bus injured in collision with unspecified motor vehicles in traffic accident

X ● **V79.59**   Passenger on bus injured in collision with other motor vehicles in traffic accident

● **V79.6**   Unspecified bus occupant injured in collision with other and unspecified motor vehicles in traffic accident

X ● **V79.60**   Unspecified bus occupant injured in collision with unspecified motor vehicles in traffic accident
Bus collision NOS (traffic)

X ● **V79.69**   Unspecified bus occupant injured in collision with other motor vehicles in traffic accident

● **V79.8**   Bus occupant (driver) (passenger) injured in other specified transport accidents

X ● **V79.81**   Bus occupant (driver) (passenger) injured in transport accidents with military vehicle

X ● **V79.88**   Bus occupant (driver) (passenger) injured in other specified transport accidents

X ● **V79.9**   Bus occupant (driver) (passenger) injured in unspecified traffic accident
Bus accident NOS

OTHER LAND TRANSPORT ACCIDENTS (V80-V89)

● V80 **Animal-rider or occupant of animal-drawn vehicle injured in transport accident**

The appropriate 7th character is to be added to each code from category V80

> A   initial encounter
> D   subsequent encounter
> S   sequela

● **V80.0**   Animal-rider or occupant of animal drawn vehicle injured by fall from or being thrown from animal or animal-drawn vehicle in noncollision accident

● **V80.01**   Animal-rider injured by fall from or being thrown from animal in noncollision accident

● **V80.010**   Animal-rider injured by fall from or being thrown from horse in noncollision accident

● **V80.018**   Animal-rider injured by fall from or being thrown from other animal in noncollision accident

X ● **V80.02**   Occupant of animal-drawn vehicle injured by fall from or being thrown from animal-drawn vehicle in noncollision accident
Overturning animal-drawn vehicle NOS
Overturning animal-drawn vehicle without collision

● **V80.1**   Animal-rider or occupant of animal-drawn vehicle injured in collision with pedestrian or animal

Excludes 1   animal-rider or animal-drawn vehicle collision with animal-drawn vehicle or animal being ridden (V80.7)

X ● **V80.11**   Animal-rider injured in collision with pedestrian or animal

X ● **V80.12**   Occupant of animal-drawn vehicle injured in collision with pedestrian or animal

● **V80.2**   Animal-rider or occupant of animal-drawn vehicle injured in collision with pedal cycle

X ● **V80.21**   Animal-rider injured in collision with pedal cycle

X ● **V80.22**   Occupant of animal-drawn vehicle injured in collision with pedal cycle

● **V80.3** **Animal-rider or occupant of animal-drawn vehicle injured in collision with two- or three-wheeled motor vehicle**

  X● **V80.31** Animal-rider injured in collision with two- or three-wheeled motor vehicle

  X● **V80.32** Occupant of animal-drawn vehicle injured in collision with two- or three-wheeled motor vehicle

● **V80.4** **Animal-rider or occupant of animal-drawn vehicle injured in collision with car, pick-up truck, van, heavy transport vehicle or bus**

    Excludes1 animal-rider injured in collision with military vehicle (V80.910)
              occupant of animal-drawn vehicle injured in collision with military vehicle (V80.920)

  X● **V80.41** Animal-rider injured in collision with car, pick-up truck, van, heavy transport vehicle or bus

  X● **V80.42** Occupant of animal-drawn vehicle injured in collision with car, pick-up truck, van, heavy transport vehicle or bus

● **V80.5** **Animal-rider or occupant of animal-drawn vehicle injured in collision with other specified motor vehicle**

  X● **V80.51** Animal-rider injured in collision with other specified motor vehicle

  X● **V80.52** Occupant of animal-drawn vehicle injured in collision with other specified motor vehicle

● **V80.6** **Animal-rider or occupant of animal-drawn vehicle injured in collision with railway train or railway vehicle**

  X● **V80.61** Animal-rider injured in collision with railway train or railway vehicle

  X● **V80.62** Occupant of animal-drawn vehicle injured in collision with railway train or railway vehicle

● **V80.7** **Animal-rider or occupant of animal-drawn vehicle injured in collision with other nonmotor vehicles**

  ● **V80.71** Animal-rider or occupant of animal-drawn vehicle injured in collision with animal being ridden

    ● **V80.710** Animal-rider injured in collision with other animal being ridden

    ● **V80.711** Occupant of animal-drawn vehicle injured in collision with animal being ridden

  ● **V80.72** Animal-rider or occupant of animal-drawn vehicle injured in collision with other animal-drawn vehicle

    ● **V80.720** Animal-rider injured in collision with animal-drawn vehicle

    ● **V80.721** Occupant of animal-drawn vehicle injured in collision with other animal-drawn vehicle

  ● **V80.73** Animal-rider or occupant of animal-drawn vehicle injured in collision with streetcar

    ● **V80.730** Animal-rider injured in collision with streetcar

    ● **V80.731** Occupant of animal-drawn vehicle injured in collision with streetcar

  ● **V80.79** Animal-rider or occupant of animal-drawn vehicle injured in collision with other nonmotor vehicles

    ● **V80.790** Animal-rider injured in collision with other nonmotor vehicles

    ● **V80.791** Occupant of animal-drawn vehicle injured in collision with other nonmotor vehicles

● **V80.8** **Animal-rider or occupant of animal-drawn vehicle injured in collision with fixed or stationary object**

  X● **V80.81** Animal-rider injured in collision with fixed or stationary object

  X● **V80.82** Occupant of animal-drawn vehicle injured in collision with fixed or stationary object

● **V80.9** **Animal-rider or occupant of animal-drawn vehicle injured in other and unspecified transport accidents**

  ● **V80.91** Animal-rider injured in other and unspecified transport accidents

    ● **V80.910** Animal-rider injured in transport accident with military vehicle

    ● **V80.918** Animal-rider injured in other transport accident

    ● **V80.919** Animal-rider injured in unspecified transport accident
            Animal rider accident NOS

  ● **V80.92** Occupant of animal-drawn vehicle injured in other and unspecified transport accidents

    ● **V80.920** Occupant of animal-drawn vehicle injured in transport accident with military vehicle

    ● **V80.928** Occupant of animal-drawn vehicle injured in other transport accident

    ● **V80.929** Occupant of animal-drawn vehicle injured in unspecified transport accident
            Animal-drawn vehicle accident NOS

● **V81** **Occupant of railway train or railway vehicle injured in transport accident**

    Includes derailment of railway train or railway vehicle
             person on outside of train

    Excludes1 streetcar (V82.-)

  The appropriate 7th character is to be added to each code from category V81

A	initial encounter
D	subsequent encounter
S	sequela

  X● **V81.0** Occupant of railway train or railway vehicle injured in collision with motor vehicle in nontraffic accident

    Excludes1 occupant of railway train or railway vehicle injured due to collision with military vehicle (V81.83)

  X● **V81.1** Occupant of railway train or railway vehicle injured in collision with motor vehicle in traffic accident

    Excludes1 occupant of railway train or railway vehicle injured due to collision with military vehicle (V81.83)

  X● **V81.2** Occupant of railway train or railway vehicle injured in collision with or hit by rolling stock

  X● **V81.3** Occupant of railway train or railway vehicle injured in collision with other object
      Railway collision NOS

  X● **V81.4** Person injured while boarding or alighting from railway train or railway vehicle

  X● **V81.5** Occupant of railway train or railway vehicle injured by fall in railway train or railway vehicle

  X● **V81.6** Occupant of railway train or railway vehicle injured by fall from railway train or railway vehicle

  X● **V81.7** Occupant of railway train or railway vehicle injured in derailment without antecedent collision

● **V81.8** **Occupant of railway train or railway vehicle injured in other specified railway accidents**
- X● **V81.81** **Occupant of railway train or railway vehicle injured due to explosion or fire on train**
- X● **V81.82** **Occupant of railway train or railway vehicle injured due to object falling onto train**
  - Occupant of railway train or railway vehicle injured due to falling earth onto train
  - Occupant of railway train or railway vehicle injured due to falling rocks onto train
  - Occupant of railway train or railway vehicle injured due to falling snow onto train
  - Occupant of railway train or railway vehicle injured due to falling trees onto train
- X● **V81.83** **Occupant of railway train or railway vehicle injured due to collision with military vehicle**
- X● **V81.89** **Occupant of railway train or railway vehicle injured due to other specified railway accident**

X● **V81.9** **Occupant of railway train or railway vehicle injured in unspecified railway accident**
- Railway accident NOS

● **V82** **Occupant of powered streetcar injured in transport accident**
- **Includes**   interurban electric car
  - person on outside of streetcar
  - tram (car)
  - trolley (car)
- **Excludes1**   bus (V70-V79)
  - motorcoach (V70-V79)
  - nonpowered streetcar (V76.-)
  - train (V81.-)

The appropriate 7th character is to be added to each code from category V82

A	initial encounter
D	subsequent encounter
S	sequela

X● **V82.0** **Occupant of streetcar injured in collision with motor vehicle in nontraffic accident**

X● **V82.1** **Occupant of streetcar injured in collision with motor vehicle in traffic accident**

X● **V82.2** **Occupant of streetcar injured in collision with or hit by rolling stock**

X● **V82.3** **Occupant of streetcar injured in collision with other object**
- **Excludes1**   collision with animal-drawn vehicle or animal being ridden (V82.8)

X● **V82.4** **Person injured while boarding or alighting from streetcar**

X● **V82.5** **Occupant of streetcar injured by fall in streetcar**
- **Excludes1**   fall in streetcar:
  - while boarding or alighting (V82.4)
  - with antecedent collision (V82.0-V82.3)

X● **V82.6** **Occupant of streetcar injured by fall from streetcar**
- **Excludes1**   fall from streetcar:
  - while boarding or alighting (V82.4)
  - with antecedent collision (V82.0-V82.3)

X● **V82.7** **Occupant of streetcar injured in derailment without antecedent collision**
- **Excludes1**   occupant of streetcar injured in derailment with antecedent collision (V82.0-V82.3)

X● **V82.8** **Occupant of streetcar injured in other specified transport accidents**
- Streetcar collision with military vehicle
- Streetcar collision with train or nonmotor vehicles

X● **V82.9** **Occupant of streetcar injured in unspecified traffic accident**
- Streetcar accident NOS

● **V83** **Occupant of special vehicle mainly used on industrial premises injured in transport accident**
- **Includes**   battery-powered airport passenger vehicle
  - battery-powered truck (baggage) (mail)
  - coal-car in mine
  - forklift (truck)
  - logging car
  - self-propelled industrial truck
  - station baggage truck (powered)
  - tram, truck, or tub (powered) in mine or quarry
- **Excludes1**   special construction vehicles (V85.-)
  - special industrial vehicle in stationary use or maintenance (W31.-)

The appropriate 7th character is to be added to each code from category V83

A	initial encounter
D	subsequent encounter
S	sequela

X● **V83.0** **Driver of special industrial vehicle injured in traffic accident**

X● **V83.1** **Passenger of special industrial vehicle injured in traffic accident**

X● **V83.2** **Person on outside of special industrial vehicle injured in traffic accident**

X● **V83.3** **Unspecified occupant of special industrial vehicle injured in traffic accident**

X● **V83.4** **Person injured while boarding or alighting from special industrial vehicle**

X● **V83.5** **Driver of special industrial vehicle injured in nontraffic accident**

X● **V83.6** **Passenger of special industrial vehicle injured in nontraffic accident**

X● **V83.7** **Person on outside of special industrial vehicle injured in nontraffic accident**

X● **V83.9** **Unspecified occupant of special industrial vehicle injured in nontraffic accident**
- Special-industrial-vehicle accident NOS

● **V84** **Occupant of special vehicle mainly used in agriculture injured in transport accident**
- **Includes**   self-propelled farm machinery
  - tractor (and trailer)
- **Excludes1**   animal-powered farm machinery accident (W30.8-)
  - contact with combine harvester (W30.0)
  - special agricultural vehicle in stationary use or maintenance (W30.-)

The appropriate 7th character is to be added to each code from category V84

A	initial encounter
D	subsequent encounter
S	sequela

X● **V84.0** **Driver of special agricultural vehicle injured in traffic accident**

X● **V84.1** **Passenger of special agricultural vehicle injured in traffic accident**

X● **V84.2** **Person on outside of special agricultural vehicle injured in traffic accident**

X● **V84.3** **Unspecified occupant of special agricultural vehicle injured in traffic accident**

X● **V84.4** **Person injured while boarding or alighting from special agricultural vehicle**

X● **V84.5** **Driver of special agricultural vehicle injured in nontraffic accident**

X● **V84.6** **Passenger of special agricultural vehicle injured in nontraffic accident**

X● **V84.7** **Person on outside of special agricultural vehicle injured in nontraffic accident**

X● **V84.9** **Unspecified occupant of special agricultural vehicle injured in nontraffic accident**
- Special-agricultural vehicle accident NOS

CHAPTER 20 (V00-Y99)

● **V85** **Occupant of special construction vehicle injured in transport accident**

Includes	bulldozer
	digger
	dump truck
	earth-leveller
	mechanical shovel
	road-roller

Excludes1	special industrial vehicle (V83.-)
	special construction vehicle in stationary use or maintenance (W31.-)

The appropriate 7th character is to be added to each code from category V85

A	initial encounter
D	subsequent encounter
S	sequela

X ● **V85.0** **Driver of special construction vehicle injured in traffic accident**

X ● **V85.1** **Passenger of special construction vehicle injured in traffic accident**

X ● **V85.2** **Person on outside of special construction vehicle injured in traffic accident**

X ● **V85.3** **Unspecified occupant of special construction vehicle injured in traffic accident**

X ● **V85.4** **Person injured while boarding or alighting from special construction vehicle**

X ● **V85.5** **Driver of special construction vehicle injured in nontraffic accident**

X ● **V85.6** **Passenger of special construction vehicle injured in nontraffic accident**

X ● **V85.7** **Person on outside of special construction vehicle injured in nontraffic accident**

X ● **V85.9** **Unspecified occupant of special construction vehicle injured in nontraffic accident**
Special-construction-vehicle accident NOS

● **V86** **Occupant of special all-terrain or other off-road motor vehicle, injured in transport accident**

Excludes1	special all-terrain vehicle in stationary use or maintenance (W31.-)
	sport-utility vehicle (V50-V59)
	three-wheeled motor vehicle designed for on-road use (V30-V39)

The appropriate 7th character is to be added to each code from category V86

A	initial encounter
D	subsequent encounter
S	sequela

● **V86.0** **Driver of special all-terrain or other off-road motor vehicle injured in traffic accident**

X ● **V86.01** **Driver of ambulance or fire engine injured in traffic accident**

X ● **V86.02** **Driver of snowmobile injured in traffic accident**

X ● **V86.03** **Driver of dune buggy injured in traffic accident**

X ● **V86.04** **Driver of military vehicle injured in traffic accident**

X ● **V86.05** **Driver of 3- or 4-wheeled all-terrain vehicle (ATV) injured in traffic accident**

X ● **V86.06** **Driver of dirt bike or motor/cross bike injured in traffic accident**

X ● **V86.09** **Driver of other off-road special all-terrain or other off-road vehicle injured in traffic accident**
Driver of go cart injured in traffic accident
Driver of golf cart injured in traffic accident

● **V86.1** **Passenger of special all-terrain or other off-road motor vehicle injured in traffic accident**

X ● **V86.11** **Passenger of ambulance or fire engine injured in traffic accident**

X ● **V86.12** **Passenger of snowmobile injured in traffic accident**

X ● **V86.13** **Passenger of dune buggy injured in traffic accident**

X ● **V86.14** **Passenger of military vehicle injured in traffic accident**

X ● **V86.15** **Passenger of 3- or 4-wheeled all-terrain vehicle (ATV) injured in traffic accident**

X ● **V86.16** **Passenger of dirt bike or motor/cross bike injured in traffic accident**

X ● **V86.19** **Passenger of other off-road special all-terrain or other off-road off-road motor vehicle injured in traffic accident**
Passenger of go cart injured in traffic accident
Passenger of golf cart injured in traffic accident

● **V86.2** **Person on outside of special all-terrain or other off-road motor vehicle injured in traffic accident**

X ● **V86.21** **Person on outside of ambulance or fire engine injured in traffic accident**

X ● **V86.22** **Person on outside of snowmobile injured in traffic accident**

X ● **V86.23** **Person on outside of dune buggy injured in traffic accident**

X ● **V86.24** **Person on outside of military vehicle injured in traffic accident**

X ● **V86.25** **Person on outside of 3- or 4-wheeled all-terrain vehicle (ATV) injured in traffic accident**

X ● **V86.26** **Person on outside of dirt bike or motor/cross bike injured in traffic accident**

X ● **V86.29** **Person on outside of other special all-terrain or other off-road motor vehicle injured in traffic accident**
Person on outside of go cart in traffic accident
Person on outside of golf cart injured in traffic accident

● **V86.3** **Unspecified occupant of special all-terrain or other off-road motor vehicle injured in traffic accident**

X ● **V86.31** **Unspecified occupant of ambulance or fire engine injured in traffic accident**

X ● **V86.32** **Unspecified occupant of snowmobile injured in traffic accident**

X ● **V86.33** **Unspecified occupant of dune buggy injured in traffic accident**

X ● **V86.34** **Unspecified occupant of military vehicle injured in traffic accident**

X ● **V86.35** **Unspecified occupant of 3- or 4-wheeled all-terrain vehicle (ATV) injured in traffic accident**

X ● **V86.36** **Unspecified occupant of dirt bike or motor/cross bike injured in traffic accident**

X ● **V86.39** **Unspecified occupant of other special all-terrain or other off-road motor vehicle injured in traffic accident**
Unspecified occupant of go cart injured in traffic accident
Unspecified occupant of golf cart injured in traffic accident

▶ New   ⇒ Revised   ~~deleted~~ Deleted   Excludes 1   Excludes 2   Includes   Use additional   Code first   Code also   Key words

OGCR Official Guidelines   X Assign placeholder X   ● Use Additional Character(s)   ▷ Manifestation Code   🏷 Hierarchical Condition Category   Coding Clinic

● **V86.4**   Person injured while boarding or alighting from special all-terrain or other off-road motor vehicle

    X ● **V86.41**   Person injured while boarding or alighting from ambulance or fire engine

    X ● **V86.42**   Person injured while boarding or alighting from snowmobile

    X ● **V86.43**   Person injured while boarding or alighting from dune buggy

    X ● **V86.44**   Person injured while boarding or alighting from military vehicle

    X ● **V86.45**   Person injured while boarding or alighting from a 3- or 4-wheeled all-terrain vehicle (ATV)

    X ● **V86.46**   Person injured while boarding or alighting from a dirt bike or motor/cross bike

    X ● **V86.49**   Person injured while boarding or alighting from other special all-terrain or other off-road motor vehicle

       Person injured while boarding or alighting from go cart

       Person injured while boarding or alighting from golf cart

● **V86.5**   Driver of special all-terrain or other off-road motor vehicle injured in nontraffic accident

    X ● **V86.51**   Driver of ambulance or fire engine injured in nontraffic accident

    X ● **V86.52**   Driver of snowmobile injured in nontraffic accident

    X ● **V86.53**   Driver of dune buggy injured in nontraffic accident

    X ● **V86.54**   Driver of military vehicle injured in nontraffic accident

    X ● **V86.55**   Driver of 3- or 4-wheeled all-terrain vehicle (ATV) injured in nontraffic accident

    X ● **V86.56**   Driver of dirt bike or motor/cross bike injured in nontraffic accident

    X ● **V86.59**   Driver of other off-road special all-terrain or other off-road motor vehicle injured in nontraffic accident

       Driver of go cart injured in nontraffic accident

       Driver of golf cart injured in nontraffic accident

● **V86.6**   Passenger of special all-terrain or other off-road motor vehicle injured in nontraffic accident

    X ● **V86.61**   Passenger of ambulance or fire engine injured in nontraffic accident

    X ● **V86.62**   Passenger of snowmobile injured in nontraffic accident

    X ● **V86.63**   Passenger of dune buggy injured in nontraffic accident

    X ● **V86.64**   Passenger of military vehicle injured in nontraffic accident

    X ● **V86.65**   Passenger of 3- or 4-wheeled all-terrain vehicle (ATV) injured in nontraffic accident

    X ● **V86.66**   Passenger of dirt bike or motor/cross bike injured in nontraffic accident

    X ● **V86.69**   Passenger of other special all-terrain or other off-road vehicle injured in nontraffic accident

       Passenger of go cart injured in nontraffic accident

       Passenger of golf cart injured in nontraffic accident

● **V86.7**   Person on outside of special all-terrain or other off-road motor vehicle injured in nontraffic accident

    X ● **V86.71**   Person on outside of ambulance or fire engine injured in nontraffic accident

    X ● **V86.72**   Person on outside of snowmobile injured in nontraffic accident

    X ● **V86.73**   Person on outside of dune buggy injured in nontraffic accident

    X ● **V86.74**   Person on outside of military vehicle injured in nontraffic accident

    X ● **V86.75**   Person on outside of 3- or 4-wheeled all-terrain vehicle (ATV) injured in nontraffic accident

    X ● **V86.76**   Person on outside of dirt bike or motor/cross bike injured in nontraffic accident

    X ● **V86.79**   Person on outside of other special all-terrain or other off-road motor vehicles injured in nontraffic accident

       Person on outside of go cart injured in nontraffic accident

       Person on outside of golf cart injured in nontraffic accident

● **V86.9**   Unspecified occupant of special all-terrain or other off-road motor vehicle injured in nontraffic accident

    X ● **V86.91**   Unspecified occupant of ambulance or fire engine injured in nontraffic accident

    X ● **V86.92**   Unspecified occupant of snowmobile injured in nontraffic accident

    X ● **V86.93**   Unspecified occupant of dune buggy injured in nontraffic accident

    X ● **V86.94**   Unspecified occupant of military vehicle injured in nontraffic accident

    X ● **V86.95**   Unspecified occupant of 3- or 4-wheeled all-terrain vehicle (ATV) injured in nontraffic accident

    X ● **V86.96**   Unspecified occupant of dirt bike or motor/cross bike injured in nontraffic accident

    X ● **V86.99**   Unspecified occupant of other special all-terrain or other off-road motor vehicle injured in nontraffic accident

       Off-road motor-vehicle accident NOS

       Other motor-vehicle accident NOS

       Unspecified occupant of go cart injured in nontraffic accident

       Unspecified occupant of golf cart injured in nontraffic accident

       Unspecified occupant of race car injured in nontraffic accident

● **V87**   Traffic accident of specified type but victim's mode of transport unknown

    Excludes1   collision involving:

       pedal cycle (V10-V19)

       pedestrian (V01-V09)

    The appropriate 7th character is to be added to each code from category V87

A	initial encounter
D	subsequent encounter
S	sequela

    X ● **V87.0**   Person injured in collision between car and two- or three-wheeled powered vehicle (traffic)

    X ● **V87.1**   Person injured in collision between other motor vehicle and two- or three-wheeled motor vehicle (traffic)

    X ● **V87.2**   Person injured in collision between car and pick-up truck or van (traffic)

    X ● **V87.3**   Person injured in collision between car and bus (traffic)

    X ● **V87.4**   Person injured in collision between car and heavy transport vehicle (traffic)

    X ● **V87.5**   Person injured in collision between heavy transport vehicle and bus (traffic)

    X ● **V87.6**   Person injured in collision between railway train or railway vehicle and car (traffic)

    X ● **V87.7**   Person injured in collision between other specified motor vehicles (traffic)

    X ● **V87.8**   Person injured in other specified noncollision transport accidents involving motor vehicle (traffic)

    X ● **V87.9**   Person injured in other specified (collision) (noncollision) transport accidents involving nonmotor vehicle (traffic)

CHAPTER 20 (V00-Y99)

CHAPTER 20 (V00-Y99)

● **V88** **Nontraffic accident of specified type but victim's mode of transport unknown**

Excludes1 collision involving:
pedal cycle (V10-V19)
pedestrian (V01-V09)

The appropriate 7th character is to be added to each code from category V88

> A   initial encounter
> D   subsequent encounter
> S   sequela

X● **V88.0** **Person injured in collision between car and two- or three-wheeled motor vehicle, nontraffic**

X● **V88.1** **Person injured in collision between other motor vehicle and two- or three-wheeled motor vehicle, nontraffic**

X● **V88.2** **Person injured in collision between car and pick-up truck or van, nontraffic**

X● **V88.3** **Person injured in collision between car and bus, nontraffic**

X● **V88.4** **Person injured in collision between car and heavy transport vehicle, nontraffic**

X● **V88.5** **Person injured in collision between heavy transport vehicle and bus, nontraffic**

X● **V88.6** **Person injured in collision between railway train or railway vehicle and car, nontraffic**

X● **V88.7** **Person injured in collision between other specified motor vehicle, nontraffic**

X● **V88.8** **Person injured in other specified noncollision transport accidents involving motor vehicle, nontraffic**

X● **V88.9** **Person injured in other specified (collision) (noncollision) transport accidents involving nonmotor vehicle, nontraffic**

● **V89** **Motor- or nonmotor-vehicle accident, type of vehicle unspecified**

The appropriate 7th character is to be added to each code from category V89

> A   initial encounter
> D   subsequent encounter
> S   sequela

X● **V89.0** **Person injured in unspecified motor-vehicle accident, nontraffic**
Motor-vehicle accident NOS, nontraffic

X● **V89.1** **Person injured in unspecified nonmotor-vehicle accident, nontraffic**
Nonmotor-vehicle accident NOS (nontraffic)

X● **V89.2** **Person injured in unspecified motor-vehicle accident, traffic**
Motor-vehicle accident [MVA] NOS
Road (traffic) accident [RTA] NOS

X● **V89.3** **Person injured in unspecified nonmotor-vehicle accident, traffic**
Nonmotor-vehicle traffic accident NOS

X● **V89.9** **Person injured in unspecified vehicle accident**
Collision NOS

WATER TRANSPORT ACCIDENTS (V90-V94)

● **V90** **Drowning and submersion due to accident to watercraft**

Excludes1 civilian water transport accident involving military watercraft (V94.81-)
fall into water not from watercraft (W16.-)
military watercraft accident in military or war operations (Y36.0-, Y37.0-)
water-transport–related drowning or submersion without accident to watercraft (V92.-)

The appropriate 7th character is to be added to each code from category V90

> A   initial encounter
> D   subsequent encounter
> S   sequela

● **V90.0** **Drowning and submersion due to watercraft overturning**

X● **V90.00** **Drowning and submersion due to merchant ship overturning**

X● **V90.01** **Drowning and submersion due to passenger ship overturning**
Drowning and submersion due to ferry-boat overturning
Drowning and submersion due to liner overturning

X● **V90.02** **Drowning and submersion due to fishing boat overturning**

X● **V90.03** **Drowning and submersion due to other powered watercraft overturning**
Drowning and submersion due to hovercraft (on open water) overturning
Drowning and submersion due to jet ski overturning

X● **V90.04** **Drowning and submersion due to sailboat overturning**

X● **V90.05** **Drowning and submersion due to canoe or kayak overturning**

X● **V90.06** **Drowning and submersion due to (nonpowered) inflatable craft overturning**

X● **V90.08** **Drowning and submersion due to other unpowered watercraft overturning**
Drowning and submersion due to windsurfer overturning

X● **V90.09** **Drowning and submersion due to unspecified watercraft overturning**
Drowning and submersion due to boat NOS overturning
Drowning and submersion due to ship NOS overturning
Drowning and submersion due to watercraft NOS overturning

● **V90.1** **Drowning and submersion due to watercraft sinking**

X● **V90.10** **Drowning and submersion due to merchant ship sinking**

X● **V90.11** **Drowning and submersion due to passenger ship sinking**
Drowning and submersion due to ferry-boat sinking
Drowning and submersion due to liner sinking

X● **V90.12** **Drowning and submersion due to fishing boat sinking**

X● **V90.13** **Drowning and submersion due to other powered watercraft sinking**
Drowning and submersion due to hovercraft (on open water) sinking
Drowning and submersion due to jet ski sinking

▶ New   ➡ Revised   ~~deleted~~ Deleted   Excludes 1   Excludes 2   Includes   Use additional   Code first   Code also   Key words

OGCR Official Guidelines   X Assign placeholder X   ● Use Additional Character(s)   ▸ Manifestation Code   🏷 Hierarchical Condition Category   Coding Clinic

X ● **V90.14** **Drowning and submersion due to** sailboat sinking

X ● **V90.15** **Drowning and submersion due to** canoe or kayak sinking

X ● **V90.16** **Drowning and submersion due to** (nonpowered) inflatable craft sinking

X ● **V90.18** **Drowning and submersion due to** other unpowered watercraft sinking

X ● **V90.19** **Drowning and submersion due to** unspecified watercraft sinking
    Drowning and submersion due to boat NOS sinking
    Drowning and submersion due to ship NOS sinking
    Drowning and submersion due to watercraft NOS sinking

● **V90.2** **Drowning and submersion due to** falling or jumping from burning watercraft

X ● **V90.20** **Drowning and submersion due to falling or jumping from burning** merchant ship

X ● **V90.21** **Drowning and submersion due to falling or jumping from burning** passenger ship
    Drowning and submersion due to falling or jumping from burning ferry-boat
    Drowning and submersion due to falling or jumping from burning liner

X ● **V90.22** **Drowning and submersion due to falling or jumping from burning** fishing boat

X ● **V90.23** **Drowning and submersion due to falling or jumping from** other burning powered watercraft
    Drowning and submersion due to falling and jumping from burning hovercraft (on open water)
    Drowning and submersion due to falling and jumping from burning jet ski

X ● **V90.24** **Drowning and submersion due to falling or jumping from burning** sailboat

X ● **V90.25** **Drowning and submersion due to falling or jumping from burning** canoe or kayak

X ● **V90.26** **Drowning and submersion due to falling or jumping from burning** (nonpowered) inflatable craft

X ● **V90.27** **Drowning and submersion due to falling or jumping from burning** water-skis

X ● **V90.28** **Drowning and submersion due to falling or jumping from** other burning unpowered watercraft
    Drowning and submersion due to falling and jumping from burning surf-board
    Drowning and submersion due to falling and jumping from burning windsurfer

X ● **V90.29** **Drowning and submersion due to falling or jumping from** unspecified burning watercraft
    Drowning and submersion due to falling or jumping from burning boat NOS
    Drowning and submersion due to falling or jumping from burning ship NOS
    Drowning and submersion due to falling or jumping from burning watercraft NOS

● **V90.3** **Drowning and submersion due to** falling or jumping from crushed watercraft

X ● **V90.30** **Drowning and submersion due to falling or jumping from crushed** merchant ship

X ● **V90.31** **Drowning and submersion due to falling or jumping from crushed** passenger ship
    Drowning and submersion due to falling and jumping from crushed ferry-boat
    Drowning and submersion due to falling and jumping from crushed liner

X ● **V90.32** **Drowning and submersion due to falling or jumping from crushed** fishing boat

X ● **V90.33** **Drowning and submersion due to falling or jumping from** other crushed powered watercraft
    Drowning and submersion due to falling and jumping from crushed hovercraft
    Drowning and submersion due to falling and jumping from crushed jet ski

X ● **V90.34** **Drowning and submersion due to falling or jumping from crushed** sailboat

X ● **V90.35** **Drowning and submersion due to falling or jumping from crushed** canoe or kayak

X ● **V90.36** **Drowning and submersion due to falling or jumping from crushed** (nonpowered) inflatable craft

X ● **V90.37** **Drowning and submersion due to falling or jumping from crushed** water-skis

X ● **V90.38** **Drowning and submersion due to falling or jumping from** other crushed unpowered watercraft
    Drowning and submersion due to falling and jumping from crushed surf-board
    Drowning and submersion due to falling and jumping from crushed windsurfer

X ● **V90.39** **Drowning and submersion due to falling or jumping from crushed** unspecified watercraft
    Drowning and submersion due to falling and jumping from crushed boat NOS
    Drowning and submersion due to falling and jumping from crushed ship NOS
    Drowning and submersion due to falling and jumping from crushed watercraft NOS

● **V90.8** **Drowning and submersion due to** other accident to watercraft

X ● **V90.80** **Drowning and submersion due to other accident to** merchant ship

X ● **V90.81** **Drowning and submersion due to other accident to** passenger ship
    Drowning and submersion due to other accident to ferry-boat
    Drowning and submersion due to other accident to liner

X ● **V90.82** **Drowning and submersion due to other accident to** fishing boat

X ● **V90.83** **Drowning and submersion due to other accident to** other powered watercraft
    Drowning and submersion due to other accident to hovercraft (on open water)
    Drowning and submersion due to other accident to jet ski

X ● **V90.84** **Drowning and submersion due to other accident to** sailboat

X ● **V90.85** **Drowning and submersion due to other accident to** canoe or kayak

X ● **V90.86** **Drowning and submersion due to other accident to** (nonpowered) inflatable craft

X ● **V90.87** **Drowning and submersion due to other accident to** water-skis

X ● **V90.88** **Drowning and submersion due to other accident to** other unpowered watercraft
    Drowning and submersion due to other accident to surf-board
    Drowning and submersion due to other accident to windsurfer

X ● **V90.89** **Drowning and submersion due to other accident to** unspecified watercraft
    Drowning and submersion due to other accident to boat NOS
    Drowning and submersion due to other accident to ship NOS
    Drowning and submersion due to other accident to watercraft NOS

CHAPTER 20 (V00-Y99)

● **V91**   **Other injury due to accident to watercraft**

Includes   any injury except drowning and submersion as a result of an accident to watercraft

Excludes1   civilian water transport accident involving military watercraft (V94.81-)

military watercraft accident in military or war operations (Y36, Y37.-)

Excludes2   drowning and submersion due to accident to watercraft (V90.-)

The appropriate 7th character is to be added to each code from category V91

> A   initial encounter
> D   subsequent encounter
> S   sequela

● **V91.0**   **Burn due to watercraft on fire**

Excludes1   burn from localized fire or explosion on board ship without accident to watercraft (V93.-)

X● **V91.00**   Burn due to merchant ship on fire

X● **V91.01**   Burn due to passenger ship on fire
Burn due to ferry-boat on fire
Burn due to liner on fire

X● **V91.02**   Burn due to fishing boat on fire

X● **V91.03**   Burn due to other powered watercraft on fire
Burn due to hovercraft (on open water) on fire
Burn due to jet ski on fire

X● **V91.04**   Burn due to sailboat on fire

X● **V91.05**   Burn due to canoe or kayak on fire

X● **V91.06**   Burn due to (nonpowered) inflatable craft on fire

X● **V91.07**   Burn due to water-skis on fire

X● **V91.08**   Burn due to other unpowered watercraft on fire

X● **V91.09**   Burn due to unspecified watercraft on fire
Burn due to boat NOS on fire
Burn due to ship NOS on fire
Burn due to watercraft NOS on fire

● **V91.1**   **Crushed between watercraft and other watercraft or other object due to collision**
Crushed by lifeboat after abandoning ship in a collision
Note: Select the specified type of watercraft that the victim was on at the time of the collision.

X● **V91.10**   **Crushed between merchant ship and other watercraft or other object due to collision**

X● **V91.11**   **Crushed between passenger ship and other watercraft or other object due to collision**
Crushed between ferry-boat and other watercraft or other object due to collision
Crushed between liner and other watercraft or other object due to collision

X● **V91.12**   **Crushed between fishing boat and other watercraft or other object due to collision**

X● **V91.13**   **Crushed between other powered watercraft and other watercraft or other object due to collision**
Crushed between hovercraft (on open water) and other watercraft or other object due to collision
Crushed between jet ski and other watercraft or other object due to collision

X● **V91.14**   **Crushed between sailboat and other watercraft or other object due to collision**

X● **V91.15**   **Crushed between canoe or kayak and other watercraft or other object due to collision**

X● **V91.16**   **Crushed between (nonpowered) inflatable craft and other watercraft or other object due to collision**

X● **V91.18**   **Crushed between other unpowered watercraft and other watercraft or other object due to collision**
Crushed between surfboard and other watercraft or other object due to collision
Crushed between windsurfer and other watercraft or other object due to collision

X● **V91.19**   **Crushed between unspecified watercraft and other watercraft or other object due to collision**
Crushed between boat NOS and other watercraft or other object due to collision
Crushed between ship NOS and other watercraft or other object due to collision
Crushed between watercraft NOS and other watercraft or other object due to collision

● **V91.2**   **Fall due to collision between watercraft and other watercraft or other object**
Fall while remaining on watercraft after collision
Note: Select the specified type of watercraft that the victim was on at the time of the collision.

Excludes1   crushed between watercraft and other watercraft and other object due to collision (V91.1-)
drowning and submersion due to falling from crushed watercraft (V90.3-)

X● **V91.20**   **Fall due to collision between merchant ship and other watercraft or other object**

X● **V91.21**   **Fall due to collision between passenger ship and other watercraft or other object**
Fall due to collision between ferry-boat and other watercraft or other object
Fall due to collision between liner and other watercraft or other object

X● **V91.22**   **Fall due to collision between fishing boat and other watercraft or other object**

X● **V91.23**   **Fall due to collision between other powered watercraft and other watercraft or other object**
Fall due to collision between hovercraft (on open water) and other watercraft or other object
Fall due to collision between jet ski and other watercraft or other object

X● **V91.24**   **Fall due to collision between sailboat and other watercraft or other object**

X● **V91.25**   **Fall due to collision between canoe or kayak and other watercraft or other object**

X● **V91.26**   **Fall due to collision between (nonpowered) inflatable craft and other watercraft or other object**

X● **V91.29**   **Fall due to collision between unspecified watercraft and other watercraft or other object**
Fall due to collision between boat NOS and other watercraft or other object
Fall due to collision between ship NOS and other watercraft or other object
Fall due to collision between watercraft NOS and other watercraft or other object

● **V91.3**   **Hit or struck by falling object due to accident to watercraft**
Hit or struck by falling object (part of damaged watercraft or other object) after falling or jumping from damaged watercraft

Excludes2   drowning or submersion due to fall or jumping from damaged watercraft (V90.2-, V90.3-)

X● **V91.30**   **Hit or struck by falling object due to accident to merchant ship**

X● **V91.31**   **Hit or struck by falling object due to accident to passenger ship**
Hit or struck by falling object due to accident to ferry-boat
Hit or struck by falling object due to accident to liner

▶ New   ⇒ Revised   ~~deleted~~ Deleted   Excludes 1   Excludes 2   Includes   Use additional   Code first   Code also   Key words

OGCR Official Guidelines   X Assign placeholder X   ● Use Additional Character(s)   ▶ Manifestation Code   🅗🄲 Hierarchical Condition Category   **Coding Clinic**

X● **V91.32 Hit or struck by falling object due to accident to fishing boat**

X● **V91.33 Hit or struck by falling object due to accident to other powered watercraft**
　　Hit or struck by falling object due to accident to hovercraft (on open water)
　　Hit or struck by falling object due to accident to jet ski

X● **V91.34 Hit or struck by falling object due to accident to sailboat**

X● **V91.35 Hit or struck by falling object due to accident to canoe or kayak**

X● **V91.36 Hit or struck by falling object due to accident to (nonpowered) inflatable craft**

X● **V91.37 Hit or struck by falling object due to accident to water-skis**
　　Hit by water-skis after jumping off of waterskis

X● **V91.38 Hit or struck by falling object due to accident to other unpowered watercraft**
　　Hit or struck by surf-board after falling off damaged surf-board
　　Hit or struck by object after falling off damaged windsurfer

X● **V91.39 Hit or struck by falling object due to accident to unspecified watercraft**
　　Hit or struck by falling object due to accident to boat NOS
　　Hit or struck by falling object due to accident to ship NOS
　　Hit or struck by falling object due to accident to watercraft NOS

● **V91.8 Other injury due to other accident to watercraft**

X● **V91.80 Other injury due to other accident to merchant ship**

X● **V91.81 Other injury due to other accident to passenger ship**
　　Other injury due to other accident to ferry-boat
　　Other injury due to other accident to liner

X● **V91.82 Other injury due to other accident to fishing boat**

X● **V91.83 Other injury due to other accident to other powered watercraft**
　　Other injury due to other accident to hovercraft (on open water)
　　Other injury due to other accident to jet ski

X● **V91.84 Other injury due to other accident to sailboat**

X● **V91.85 Other injury due to other accident to canoe or kayak**

X● **V91.86 Other injury due to other accident to (nonpowered) inflatable craft**

X● **V91.87 Other injury due to other accident to water-skis**

X● **V91.88 Other injury due to other accident to other unpowered watercraft**
　　Other injury due to other accident to surf-board
　　Other injury due to other accident to windsurfer

X● **V91.89 Other injury due to other accident to unspecified watercraft**
　　Other injury due to other accident to boat NOS
　　Other injury due to other accident to ship NOS
　　Other injury due to other accident to watercraft NOS

● **V92 Drowning and submersion due to accident on board watercraft, without accident to watercraft**

Excludes1 civilian water transport accident involving military watercraft (V94.81-)
　　drowning or submersion due to accident to watercraft (V90-V91)
　　drowning or submersion of diver who voluntarily jumps from boat not involved in an accident (W16.711, W16.721)
　　fall into water without watercraft (W16.-)
　　military watercraft accident in military or war operations (Y36, Y37)

The appropriate 7th character is to be added to each code from category V92

A	initial encounter
D	subsequent encounter
S	sequela

● **V92.0 Drowning and submersion due to fall off watercraft**
　　Drowning and submersion due to fall from gangplank of watercraft
　　Drowning and submersion due to fall overboard watercraft

Excludes2 hitting head on object or bottom of body of water due to fall from watercraft (V94.0-)

X● **V92.00 Drowning and submersion due to fall off merchant ship**

X● **V92.01 Drowning and submersion due to fall off passenger ship**
　　Drowning and submersion due to fall off ferry-boat
　　Drowning and submersion due to fall off liner

X● **V92.02 Drowning and submersion due to fall off fishing boat**

X● **V92.03 Drowning and submersion due to fall off other powered watercraft**
　　Drowning and submersion due to fall off hovercraft (on open water)
　　Drowning and submersion due to fall off jet ski

X● **V92.04 Drowning and submersion due to fall off sailboat**

X● **V92.05 Drowning and submersion due to fall off canoe or kayak**

X● **V92.06 Drowning and submersion due to fall off (nonpowered) inflatable craft**

X● **V92.07 Drowning and submersion due to fall off water-skis**

Excludes1 drowning and submersion due to falling off burning water-skis (V90.27)
　　drowning and submersion due to falling off crushed water-skis (V90.37)
　　hit by boat while water-skiing NOS (V94.X)

X● **V92.08 Drowning and submersion due to fall off other unpowered watercraft**

Drowning and submersion due to fall off surf-board

Drowning and submersion due to fall off windsurfer

> **Excludes1** drowning and submersion due to fall off burning unpowered watercraft (V90.28)
>
> drowning and submersion due to fall off crushed unpowered watercraft (V90.38)
>
> drowning and submersion due to fall off damaged unpowered watercraft (V90.88)
>
> drowning and submersion due to rider of nonpowered watercraft being hit by other watercraft (V94.-)
>
> other injury due to rider of nonpowered watercraft being hit by other watercraft (V94.-)

X● **V92.09 Drowning and submersion due to fall off unspecified watercraft**

Drowning and submersion due to fall off boat NOS

Drowning and submersion due to fall off ship

Drowning and submersion due to fall off watercraft NOS

● **V92.1 Drowning and submersion due to being thrown overboard by motion of watercraft**

> **Excludes1** drowning and submersion due to fall off surf-board (V92.08)
>
> drowning and submersion due to fall off water-skis (V92.07)
>
> drowning and submersion due to fall off windsurfer (V92.08)

X● **V92.10 Drowning and submersion due to being thrown overboard by motion of merchant ship**

X● **V92.11 Drowning and submersion due to being thrown overboard by motion of passenger ship**

Drowning and submersion due to being thrown overboard by motion of ferry-boat

Drowning and submersion due to being thrown overboard by motion of liner

X● **V92.12 Drowning and submersion due to being thrown overboard by motion of fishing boat**

X● **V92.13 Drowning and submersion due to being thrown overboard by motion of other powered watercraft**

Drowning and submersion due to being thrown overboard by motion of hovercraft

X● **V92.14 Drowning and submersion due to being thrown overboard by motion of sailboat**

X● **V92.15 Drowning and submersion due to being thrown overboard by motion of canoe or kayak**

X● **V92.16 Drowning and submersion due to being thrown overboard by motion of (nonpowered) inflatable craft**

X● **V92.19 Drowning and submersion due to being thrown overboard by motion of unspecified watercraft**

Drowning and submersion due to being thrown overboard by motion of boat NOS

Drowning and submersion due to being thrown overboard by motion of ship NOS

Drowning and submersion due to being thrown overboard by motion of watercraft NOS

● **V92.2 Drowning and submersion due to being washed overboard from watercraft**

Code first any associated cataclysm (X37.0-)

X● **V92.20 Drowning and submersion due to being washed overboard from merchant ship**

X● **V92.21 Drowning and submersion due to being washed overboard from passenger ship**

Drowning and submersion due to being washed overboard from ferry-boat

Drowning and submersion due to being washed overboard from liner

X● **V92.22 Drowning and submersion due to being washed overboard from fishing boat**

X● **V92.23 Drowning and submersion due to being washed overboard from other powered watercraft**

Drowning and submersion due to being washed overboard from hovercraft (on open water)

Drowning and submersion due to being washed overboard from jet ski

X● **V92.24 Drowning and submersion due to being washed overboard from sailboat**

X● **V92.25 Drowning and submersion due to being washed overboard from canoe or kayak**

X● **V92.26 Drowning and submersion due to being washed overboard from (nonpowered) inflatable craft**

X● **V92.27 Drowning and submersion due to being washed overboard from water-skis**

> **Excludes1** drowning and submersion due to fall off water-skis (V92.07)

X● **V92.28 Drowning and submersion due to being washed overboard from other unpowered watercraft**

Drowning and submersion due to being washed overboard from surf-board

Drowning and submersion due to being washed overboard from windsurfer

X● **V92.29 Drowning and submersion due to being washed overboard from unspecified watercraft**

Drowning and submersion due to being washed overboard from boat NOS

Drowning and submersion due to being washed overboard from ship NOS

Drowning and submersion due to being washed overboard from watercraft NOS

● **V93 Other injury due to accident on board watercraft, without accident to watercraft**

> **Excludes1** civilian water transport accident involving military watercraft (V94.81-)
>
> other injury due to accident to watercraft (V91.-)
>
> military watercraft accident in military or war operations (Y36, Y37.-)

> **Excludes2** drowning and submersion due to accident on board watercraft, without accident to watercraft (V92.-)

The appropriate 7th character is to be added to each code from category V93

A	initial encounter
D	subsequent encounter
S	sequela

● **V93.0 Burn due to localized fire on board watercraft**

> **Excludes1** burn due to watercraft on fire (V91.0-)

X● **V93.00 Burn due to localized fire on board merchant vessel**

X● **V93.01 Burn due to localized fire on board passenger vessel**

Burn due to localized fire on board ferry-boat

Burn due to localized fire on board liner

▶ New　⇒ Revised　~~deleted~~ Deleted　Excludes 1　Excludes 2　Includes　Use additional　Code first　Code also　Key words

OGCR Official Guidelines　X Assign placeholder X　● Use Additional Character(s)　▷ Manifestation Code　🔧 Hierarchical Condition Category　Coding Clinic

X● **V93.02** Burn due to localized fire on board fishing boat
X● **V93.03** Burn due to localized fire on board other powered watercraft
　　　　　　Burn due to localized fire on board hovercraft
　　　　　　Burn due to localized fire on board jet ski
X● **V93.04** Burn due to localized fire on board sailboat
X● **V93.09** Burn due to localized fire on board unspecified watercraft
　　　　　　Burn due to localized fire on board boat NOS
　　　　　　Burn due to localized fire on board ship NOS
　　　　　　Burn due to localized fire on board watercraft NOS

●**V93.1** Other burn on board watercraft
　　　　Burn due to source other than fire on board watercraft
　　　　Excludes1 burn due to watercraft on fire (V91.0-)
X● **V93.10** Other burn on board merchant vessel
X● **V93.11** Other burn on board passenger vessel
　　　　　　Other burn on board ferry-boat
　　　　　　Other burn on board liner
X● **V93.12** Other burn on board fishing boat
X● **V93.13** Other burn on board other powered watercraft
　　　　　　Other burn on board hovercraft
　　　　　　Other burn on board jet ski
X● **V93.14** Other burn on board sailboat
X● **V93.19** Other burn on board unspecified watercraft
　　　　　　Other burn on board boat NOS
　　　　　　Other burn on board ship NOS
　　　　　　Other burn on board watercraft NOS

●**V93.2** Heat exposure on board watercraft
　　　　Excludes1 exposure to man-made heat not aboard watercraft (W92)
　　　　　　　　exposure to natural heat while on board watercraft (X30)
　　　　　　　　exposure to sunlight while on board watercraft (X32)
　　　　Excludes2 burn due to fire to board watercraft (V93.0-)
X● **V93.20** Heat exposure on board merchant ship
X● **V93.21** Heat exposure on board passenger ship
　　　　　　Heat exposure on board ferry-boat
　　　　　　Heat exposure on board liner
X● **V93.22** Heat exposure on board fishing boat
X● **V93.23** Heat exposure on board other powered watercraft
　　　　　　Heat exposure on board hovercraft
X● **V93.24** Heat exposure on board sailboat
X● **V93.29** Heat exposure on board unspecified watercraft
　　　　　　Heat exposure on board boat NOS
　　　　　　Heat exposure on board ship NOS
　　　　　　Heat exposure on board watercraft NOS

●**V93.3** Fall on board watercraft
　　　　Excludes1 fall due to collision of watercraft (V91.2-)
X● **V93.30** Fall on board merchant ship
X● **V93.31** Fall on board passenger ship
　　　　　　Fall on board ferry-boat
　　　　　　Fall on board liner
X● **V93.32** Fall on board fishing boat
X● **V93.33** Fall on board other powered watercraft
　　　　　　Fall on board hovercraft (on open water)
　　　　　　Fall on board jet ski
X● **V93.34** Fall on board sailboat
X● **V93.35** Fall on board canoe or kayak
X● **V93.36** Fall on board (nonpowered) inflatable craft
X● **V93.38** Fall on board other unpowered watercraft
X● **V93.39** Fall on board unspecified watercraft
　　　　　　Fall on board boat NOS
　　　　　　Fall on board ship NOS
　　　　　　Fall on board watercraft NOS

●**V93.4** Struck by falling object on board watercraft
　　　　Hit by falling object on board watercraft
　　　　Excludes1 struck by falling object due to accident to watercraft (V91.3)
X● **V93.40** Struck by falling object on merchant ship
X● **V93.41** Struck by falling object on passenger ship
　　　　　　Struck by falling object on ferry-boat
　　　　　　Struck by falling object on liner
X● **V93.42** Struck by falling object on fishing boat
X● **V93.43** Struck by falling object on other powered watercraft
　　　　　　Struck by falling object on hovercraft
X● **V93.44** Struck by falling object on sailboat
X● **V93.48** Struck by falling object on other unpowered watercraft
X● **V93.49** Struck by falling object on unspecified watercraft

●**V93.5** Explosion on board watercraft
　　　　Boiler explosion on steamship
　　　　Excludes2 fire on board watercraft (V93.0-)
X● **V93.50** Explosion on board merchant ship
X● **V93.51** Explosion on board passenger ship
　　　　　　Explosion on board ferry-boat
　　　　　　Explosion on board liner
X● **V93.52** Explosion on board fishing boat
X● **V93.53** Explosion on board other powered watercraft
　　　　　　Explosion on board hovercraft
　　　　　　Explosion on board jet ski
X● **V93.54** Explosion on board sailboat
X● **V93.59** Explosion on board unspecified watercraft
　　　　　　Explosion on board boat NOS
　　　　　　Explosion on board ship NOS
　　　　　　Explosion on board watercraft NOS

●**V93.6** Machinery accident on board watercraft
　　　　Excludes1 machinery explosion on board watercraft (V93.4-)
　　　　　　　　machinery fire on board watercraft (V93.0-)
X● **V93.60** Machinery accident on board merchant ship
X● **V93.61** Machinery accident on board passenger ship
　　　　　　Machinery accident on board ferry-boat
　　　　　　Machinery accident on board liner
X● **V93.62** Machinery accident on board fishing boat
X● **V93.63** Machinery accident on board other powered watercraft
　　　　　　Machinery accident on board hovercraft
X● **V93.64** Machinery accident on board sailboat
X● **V93.69** Machinery accident on board unspecified watercraft
　　　　　　Machinery accident on board boat NOS
　　　　　　Machinery accident on board ship NOS
　　　　　　Machinery accident on board watercraft NOS

●**V93.8** Other injury due to other accident on board watercraft
　　　　Accidental poisoning by gases or fumes on watercraft
X● **V93.80** Other injury due to other accident on board merchant ship
X● **V93.81** Other injury due to other accident on board passenger ship
　　　　　　Other injury due to other accident on board ferry-boat
　　　　　　Other injury due to other accident on board liner
X● **V93.82** Other injury due to other accident on board fishing boat

X ● **V93.83** **Other injury due to other accident on board other powered watercraft**
     Other injury due to other accident on board hovercraft
     Other injury due to other accident on board jet ski

X ● **V93.84** **Other injury due to other accident on board sailboat**

X ● **V93.85** **Other injury due to other accident on board canoe or kayak**

X ● **V93.86** **Other injury due to other accident on board (nonpowered) inflatable craft**

X ● **V93.87** **Other injury due to other accident on board water-skis**
     Hit or struck by object while waterskiing

X ● **V93.88** **Other injury due to other accident on board other unpowered watercraft**
     Hit or struck by object while surfing
     Hit or struck by object while on board windsurfer

X ● **V93.89** **Other injury due to other accident on board unspecified watercraft**
     Other injury due to other accident on board boat NOS
     Other injury due to other accident on board ship NOS
     Other injury due to other accident on board watercraft NOS

● **V94** **Other and unspecified water transport accidents**
     Excludes1   military watercraft accidents in military or war operations (Y36, Y37)

The appropriate 7th character is to be added to each code from category V94

A	initial encounter
D	subsequent encounter
S	sequela

X ● **V94.0** **Hitting object or bottom of body of water due to fall from watercraft**
     Excludes2   drowning and submersion due to fall from watercraft (V92.0-)

● **V94.1** **Bather struck by watercraft**
     Swimmer hit by watercraft

X ● **V94.11** **Bather struck by powered watercraft**

X ● **V94.12** **Bather struck by nonpowered watercraft**

● **V94.2** **Rider of nonpowered watercraft struck by other watercraft**

X ● **V94.21** **Rider of nonpowered watercraft struck by other nonpowered watercraft**
     Canoer hit by other nonpowered watercraft
     Surfer hit by other nonpowered watercraft
     Windsurfer hit by other nonpowered watercraft

X ● **V94.22** **Rider of nonpowered watercraft struck by powered watercraft**
     Canoer hit by motorboat
     Surfer hit by motorboat
     Windsurfer hit by motorboat

● **V94.3** **Injury to rider of (inflatable) watercraft being pulled behind other watercraft**

X ● **V94.31** **Injury to rider of (inflatable) recreational watercraft being pulled behind other watercraft**
     Injury to rider of inner-tube pulled behind motor boat

X ● **V94.32** **Injury to rider of non-recreational watercraft being pulled behind other watercraft**
     Injury to occupant of dingy being pulled behind boat or ship
     Injury to occupant of life-raft being pulled behind boat or ship

X ● **V94.4** **Injury to barefoot water-skier**
     Injury to person being pulled behind boat or ship

● **V94.8** **Other water transport accident**

● **V94.81** **Water transport accident involving military watercraft**

● **V94.810** **Civilian watercraft involved in water transport accident with military watercraft**
     Passenger on civilian watercraft injured due to accident with military watercraft

● **V94.811** **Civilian in water injured by military watercraft**

● **V94.818** **Other water transport accident involving military watercraft**

X ● **V94.89** **Other water transport accident**

X ● **V94.9** **Unspecified water transport accident**
     Water transport accident NOS

AIR AND SPACE TRANSPORT ACCIDENTS (V95-V97)

Excludes1   military aircraft accidents in military or war operations (Y36, Y37)

● **V95** **Accident to powered aircraft causing injury to occupant**

The appropriate 7th character is to be added to each code from category V95

A	initial encounter
D	subsequent encounter
S	sequela

● **V95.0** **Helicopter accident injuring occupant**

X ● **V95.00** **Unspecified helicopter accident injuring occupant**

X ● **V95.01** **Helicopter crash injuring occupant**

X ● **V95.02** **Forced landing of helicopter injuring occupant**

X ● **V95.03** **Helicopter collision injuring occupant**
     Helicopter collision with any object, fixed, movable or moving

X ● **V95.04** **Helicopter fire injuring occupant**

X ● **V95.05** **Helicopter explosion injuring occupant**

X ● **V95.09** **Other helicopter accident injuring occupant**

● **V95.1** **Ultralight, microlight or powered-glider accident injuring occupant**

X ● **V95.10** **Unspecified ultralight, microlight or powered-glider accident injuring occupant**

X ● **V95.11** **Ultralight, microlight or powered-glider crash injuring occupant**

X ● **V95.12** **Forced landing of ultralight, microlight or powered-glider injuring occupant**

X ● **V95.13** **Ultralight, microlight or powered-glider collision injuring occupant**
     Ultralight, microlight or powered-glider collision with any object, fixed, movable or moving

X ● **V95.14** **Ultralight, microlight or powered-glider fire injuring occupant**

X ● **V95.15** **Ultralight, microlight or powered-glider explosion injuring occupant**

X ● **V95.19** **Other ultralight, microlight or powered-glider accident injuring occupant**

▶ New   ⇢ Revised   ~~deleted~~ Deleted   Excludes 1   Excludes 2   Includes   Use additional   Code first   Code also   Key words
OGCR Official Guidelines   X Assign placeholder X   ● Use Additional Character(s)   ▶ Manifestation Code   Hierarchical Condition Category   Coding Clinic

● **V95.2 Other private fixed-wing aircraft accident injuring occupant**
   X● **V95.20** Unspecified accident to other private fixed-wing aircraft, injuring occupant
   X● **V95.21** Other private fixed-wing aircraft crash injuring occupant
   X● **V95.22** Forced landing of other private fixed-wing aircraft injuring occupant
   X● **V95.23** Other private fixed-wing aircraft collision injuring occupant
         Other private fixed-wing aircraft collision with any object, fixed, movable or moving
   X● **V95.24** Other private fixed-wing aircraft fire injuring occupant
   X● **V95.25** Other private fixed-wing aircraft explosion injuring occupant
   X● **V95.29** Other accident to other private fixed-wing aircraft injuring occupant

● **V95.3 Commercial fixed-wing aircraft accident injuring occupant**
   X● **V95.30** Unspecified accident to commercial fixed-wing aircraft injuring occupant
   X● **V95.31** Commercial fixed-wing aircraft crash injuring occupant
   X● **V95.32** Forced landing of commercial fixed-wing aircraft injuring occupant
   X● **V95.33** Commercial fixed-wing aircraft collision injuring occupant
         Commercial fixed-wing aircraft collision with any object, fixed, movable or moving
   X● **V95.34** Commercial fixed-wing aircraft fire injuring occupant
   X● **V95.35** Commercial fixed-wing aircraft explosion injuring occupant
   X● **V95.39** Other accident to commercial fixed-wing aircraft injuring occupant

● **V95.4 Spacecraft accident injuring occupant**
   X● **V95.40** Unspecified spacecraft accident injuring occupant
   X● **V95.41** Spacecraft crash injuring occupant
   X● **V95.42** Forced landing of spacecraft injuring occupant
   X● **V95.43** Spacecraft collision injuring occupant
         Spacecraft collision with any object, fixed, moveable or moving
   X● **V95.44** Spacecraft fire injuring occupant
   X● **V95.45** Spacecraft explosion injuring occupant
   X● **V95.49** Other spacecraft accident injuring occupant

X● **V95.8 Other powered aircraft accidents injuring occupant**
X● **V95.9 Unspecified aircraft accident injuring occupant**
    Aircraft accident NOS
    Air transport accident NOS

● **V96 Accident to nonpowered aircraft causing injury to occupant**
    The appropriate 7th character is to be added to each code from category V96

A	initial encounter
D	subsequent encounter
S	sequela

● **V96.0 Balloon accident injuring occupant**
   X● **V96.00** Unspecified balloon accident injuring occupant
   X● **V96.01** Balloon crash injuring occupant
   X● **V96.02** Forced landing of balloon injuring occupant
   X● **V96.03** Balloon collision injuring occupant
         Balloon collision with any object, fixed, moveable or moving
   X● **V96.04** Balloon fire injuring occupant
   X● **V96.05** Balloon explosion injuring occupant
   X● **V96.09** Other balloon accident injuring occupant

● **V96.1 Hang-glider accident injuring occupant**
   X● **V96.10** Unspecified hang-glider accident injuring occupant
   X● **V96.11** Hang-glider crash injuring occupant
   X● **V96.12** Forced landing of hang-glider injuring occupant
   X● **V96.13** Hang-glider collision injuring occupant
         Hang-glider collision with any object, fixed, moveable or moving
   X● **V96.14** Hang-glider fire injuring occupant
   X● **V96.15** Hang-glider explosion injuring occupant
   X● **V96.19** Other hang-glider accident injuring occupant

● **V96.2 Glider (nonpowered) accident injuring occupant**
   X● **V96.20** Unspecified glider (nonpowered) accident injuring occupant
   X● **V96.21** Glider (nonpowered) crash injuring occupant
   X● **V96.22** Forced landing of glider (nonpowered) injuring occupant
   X● **V96.23** Glider (nonpowered) collision injuring occupant
         Glider (nonpowered) collision with any object, fixed, moveable or moving
   X● **V96.24** Glider (nonpowered) fire injuring occupant
   X● **V96.25** Glider (nonpowered) explosion injuring occupant
   X● **V96.29** Other glider (nonpowered) accident injuring occupant

X● **V96.8 Other nonpowered-aircraft accidents injuring occupant**
    Kite carrying a person accident injuring occupant
X● **V96.9 Unspecified nonpowered-aircraft accident injuring occupant**
    Nonpowered-aircraft accident NOS

● **V97 Other specified air transport accidents**
    The appropriate 7th character is to be added to each code from category V97

A	initial encounter
D	subsequent encounter
S	sequela

X● **V97.0 Occupant of aircraft injured in other specified air transport accidents**
    Fall in, on or from aircraft in air transport accident
    Excludes1 accident while boarding or alighting aircraft (V97.1)
X● **V97.1 Person injured while boarding or alighting from aircraft**
● **V97.2 Parachutist accident**
   X● **V97.21** Parachutist entangled in object
         Parachutist landing in tree
   X● **V97.22** Parachutist injured on landing
   X● **V97.29** Other parachutist accident
● **V97.3 Person on ground injured in air transport accident**
   X● **V97.31** Hit by object falling from aircraft
         Hit by crashing aircraft
         Injured by aircraft hitting house
         Injured by aircraft hitting car
   X● **V97.32** Injured by rotating propeller
   X● **V97.33** Sucked into jet engine
   X● **V97.39** Other injury to person on ground due to air transport accident

CHAPTER 20 (V00-Y99)

● **V97.8** Other air transport accidents, not elsewhere classified

> **Excludes1** aircraft accident NOS (V95.9)
> exposure to changes in air pressure during ascent or descent (W94.-)

● **V97.81** Air transport accident involving military aircraft

● **V97.810** Civilian aircraft involved in air transport accident with military aircraft
> Passenger in civilian aircraft injured due to accident with military aircraft

● **V97.811** Civilian injured by military aircraft

● **V97.818** Other air transport accident involving military aircraft

X● **V97.89** Other air transport accidents, not elsewhere classified
> Injury from machinery on aircraft

OTHER AND UNSPECIFIED TRANSPORT ACCIDENTS (V98-V99)

> **Excludes1** vehicle accident, type of vehicle unspecified (V89.-)

● **V98** Other specified transport accidents

The appropriate 7th character is to be added to each code from category V98

A	initial encounter
D	subsequent encounter
S	sequela

X● **V98.0** Accident to, on or involving cable-car, not on rails
> Caught or dragged by cable-car, not on rails
> Fall or jump from cable-car, not on rails
> Object thrown from or in cable-car, not on rails

X● **V98.1** Accident to, on or involving land-yacht

X● **V98.2** Accident to, on or involving ice yacht

X● **V98.3** Accident to, on or involving ski lift
> Accident to, on or involving ski chair-lift
> Accident to, on or involving ski-lift with gondola

X● **V98.8** Other specified transport accidents

X● **V99** Unspecified transport accident

The appropriate 7th character is to be added to code V99

A	initial encounter
D	subsequent encounter
S	sequela

OTHER EXTERNAL CAUSES OF ACCIDENTAL INJURY (W00-X58)

SLIPPING, TRIPPING, STUMBLING AND FALLS (W00-W19)

> **Excludes1** assault involving a fall (Y01-Y02)
> fall from animal (V80.-)
> fall (in) (from) machinery (in operation) (W28-W31)
> fall (in) (from) transport vehicle (V01-V99)
> intentional self-harm involving a fall (X80-X81)

> **Excludes2** at risk for fall (history of fall) Z91.81
> fall (in) (from) burning building (X00.-)
> fall into fire (X00-X04, X08)

● **W00** Fall due to ice and snow

> **Includes** pedestrian on foot falling (slipping) on ice and snow

> **Excludes1** fall on (from) ice and snow involving pedestrian conveyance (V00.-)
> fall from stairs and steps not due to ice and snow (W10.-)

The appropriate 7th character is to be added to each code from category W00

A	initial encounter
D	subsequent encounter
S	sequela

X● **W00.0** Fall on same level due to ice and snow
> Coding Clinic: 2016, Q2, P5

X● **W00.1** Fall from stairs and steps due to ice and snow

X● **W00.2** Other fall from one level to another due to ice and snow

X● **W00.9** Unspecified fall due to ice and snow

● **W01** Fall on same level from slipping, tripping and stumbling

> **Includes** fall on moving sidewalk

> **Excludes1** fall due to bumping (striking) against object (W18.0-)
> fall in shower or bathtub (W18.2-)
> fall on same level NOS (W18.30)
> fall on same level from slipping, tripping and stumbling due to ice or snow (W00.0)
> fall off or from toilet (W18.1-)
> slipping, tripping and stumbling NOS (W18.40)
> slipping, tripping and stumbling without falling (W18.4-)

The appropriate 7th character is to be added to each code from category W01

A	initial encounter
D	subsequent encounter
S	sequela

X● **W01.0** Fall on same level from slipping, tripping and stumbling without subsequent striking against object
> Falling over animal

● **W01.1** Fall on same level from slipping, tripping and stumbling with subsequent striking against object

X● **W01.10** Fall on same level from slipping, tripping and stumbling with subsequent striking against unspecified object

● **W01.11** Fall on same level from slipping, tripping and stumbling with subsequent striking against sharp object

● **W01.110** Fall on same level from slipping, tripping and stumbling with subsequent striking against sharp glass

● **W01.111** Fall on same level from slipping, tripping and stumbling with subsequent striking against power tool or machine

● **W01.118** Fall on same level from slipping, tripping and stumbling with subsequent striking against other sharp object

● **W01.119** Fall on same level from slipping, tripping and stumbling with subsequent striking against unspecified sharp object

● **W01.19** Fall on same level from slipping, tripping and stumbling with subsequent striking against other object

     ● **W01.190** Fall on same level from slipping, tripping and stumbling with subsequent striking against furniture

     ● **W01.198** Fall on same level from slipping, tripping and stumbling with subsequent striking against other object

X ● **W03** Other fall on same level due to collision with another person
Fall due to non-transport collision with other person

> **Excludes1**   collision with another person without fall (W51)
> crushed or pushed by a crowd or human stampede (W52)
> fall involving pedestrian conveyance (V00-V09)
> fall due to ice or snow (W00)
> fall on same level NOS (W18.30)

The appropriate 7th character is to be added to code W03

A	initial encounter
D	subsequent encounter
S	sequela

Coding Clinic: 2015, Q1, P9-10; 2012, Q4, P108

X ● **W04** Fall while being carried or supported by other persons
Accidentally dropped while being carried
The appropriate 7th character is to be added to code W04

A	initial encounter
D	subsequent encounter
S	sequel

● **W05** Fall from non-moving wheelchair, nonmotorized scooter and motorized mobility scooter

> **Excludes1**   fall from moving wheelchair (powered) (V00.811)
> fall from moving motorized mobility scooter (V00.831)
> fall from nonmotorized scooter (V00.141)

The appropriate 7th character is to be added to each code from category W05

A	initial encounter
D	subsequent encounter
S	sequela

   X ● **W05.0**   Fall from non-moving wheelchair
        Coding Clinic: 2019, Q2, P27

   X ● **W05.1**   Fall from non-moving nonmotorized scooter

   X ● **W05.2**   Fall from non-moving motorized mobility scooter

X ● **W06** Fall from bed

The appropriate 7th character is to be added to code W06

A	initial encounter
D	subsequent encounter
S	sequela

X ● **W07** Fall from chair

The appropriate 7th character is to be added to code W07

A	initial encounter
D	subsequent encounter
S	sequela

X ● **W08** Fall from other furniture

The appropriate 7th character is to be added to code W08

A	initial encounter
D	subsequent encounter
S	sequela

● **W09** Fall on and from playground equipment

> **Excludes1**   fall involving recreational machinery (W31)

The appropriate 7th character is to be added to each code from category W09

A	initial encounter
D	subsequent encounter
S	sequela

X ● **W09.0** Fall on or from playground slide

X ● **W09.1** Fall from playground swing

X ● **W09.2** Fall on or from jungle gym

X ● **W09.8** Fall on or from other playground equipment

● **W10** Fall on and from stairs and steps

> **Excludes1**   fall from stairs and steps due to ice and snow (W00.1)

The appropriate 7th character is to be added to each code from category W10

A	initial encounter
D	subsequent encounter
S	sequela

X ● **W10.0** Fall (on) (from) escalator

X ● **W10.1** Fall (on) (from) sidewalk curb

X ● **W10.2** Fall (on) (from) incline
       Fall (on) (from) ramp

X ● **W10.8** Fall (on) (from) other stairs and steps

X ● **W10.9** Fall (on) (from) unspecified stairs and steps

X ● **W11** Fall on and from ladder

The appropriate 7th character is to be added to code W11

A	initial encounter
D	subsequent encounter
S	sequela

X ● **W12** Fall on and from scaffolding

The appropriate 7th character is to be added to code W12

A	initial encounter
D	subsequent encounter
S	sequela

● **W13** Fall from, out of or through building or structure

The appropriate 7th character is to be added to each code from category W13

A	initial encounter
D	subsequent encounter
S	sequela

X ● **W13.0** Fall from, out of or through balcony
       Fall from, out of or through railing

X ● **W13.1** Fall from, out of or through bridge

X ● **W13.2** Fall from, out of or through roof

X ● **W13.3** Fall through floor

X ● **W13.4** Fall from, out of or through window

> **Excludes2**   fall with subsequent striking against sharp glass (W01.110)

X ● **W13.8** Fall from, out of or through other building or structure
       Fall from, out of or through viaduct
       Fall from, out of or through wall
       Fall from, out of or through flag-pole

X ● **W13.9** Fall from, out of or through building, not otherwise specified

> **Excludes1**   collapse of a building or structure (W20.-)
> fall or jump from burning building or structure (X00.-)

CHAPTER 20 (V00-Y99)

X ● **W14 Fall from tree**

The appropriate 7th character is to be added to code W14

A	initial encounter
D	subsequent encounter
S	sequela

X ● **W15 Fall from cliff**

The appropriate 7th character is to be added to code W15

A	initial encounter
D	subsequent encounter
S	sequela

● **W16 Fall, jump or diving into water**

Excludes1 accidental non-watercraft drowning and
submersion not involving fall (W65-W74)
effects of air pressure from diving (W94.-)
fall into water from watercraft (V90-V94)
hitting an object or against bottom when falling
from watercraft (V94.0)

Excludes2 striking or hitting diving board (W21.4)

The appropriate 7th character is to be added to each code from
category W16

A	initial encounter
D	subsequent encounter
S	sequela

● **W16.0 Fall into swimming pool**
Fall into swimming pool NOS

Excludes1 fall into empty swimming pool (W17.3)

● **W16.01 Fall into swimming pool striking water surface**

● **W16.011 Fall into swimming pool striking
water surface causing drowning and
submersion**

Excludes1 drowning and
submersion while
in swimming
pool without fall
(W67)

● **W16.012 Fall into swimming pool striking
water surface causing other injury**

● **W16.02 Fall into swimming pool striking bottom**

● **W16.021 Fall into swimming pool striking
bottom causing drowning and
submersion**

Excludes1 drowning and
submersion while
in swimming
pool without fall
(W67)

● **W16.022 Fall into swimming pool striking
bottom causing other injury**

● **W16.03 Fall into swimming pool striking wall**

● **W16.031 Fall into swimming pool striking wall
causing drowning and submersion**

Excludes1 drowning and
submersion while
in swimming
pool without fall
(W67)

● **W16.032 Fall into swimming pool striking wall
causing other injury**

● **W16.1 Fall into natural body of water**
Fall into lake
Fall into open sea
Fall into river
Fall into stream

● **W16.11 Fall into natural body of water striking water
surface**

● **W16.111 Fall into natural body of water
striking water surface causing
drowning and submersion**

Excludes1 drowning and
submersion while
in natural body of
water without fall
(W69)

● **W16.112 Fall into natural body of water
striking water surface causing other
injury**

● **W16.12 Fall into natural body of water striking bottom**

● **W16.121 Fall into natural body of water
striking bottom causing drowning
and submersion**

Excludes1 drowning and
submersion while
in natural body of
water without fall
(W69)

● **W16.122 Fall into natural body of water
striking bottom causing other injury**

● **W16.13 Fall into natural body of water striking side**

● **W16.131 Fall into natural body of water
striking side causing drowning and
submersion**

Excludes1 drowning and
submersion while
in natural body of
water without fall
(W69)

● **W16.132 Fall into natural body of water
striking side causing other injury**

● **W16.2 Fall in (into) filled bathtub or bucket of water**

● **W16.21 Fall in (into) filled bathtub**

Excludes1 fall into empty bathtub (W18.2)

● **W16.211 Fall in (into) filled bathtub causing
drowning and submersion**

Excludes1 drowning and
submersion while
in filled bathtub
without fall
(W65)

● **W16.212 Fall in (into) filled bathtub causing
other injury**

● **W16.22 Fall in (into) bucket of water**

● **W16.221 Fall in (into) bucket of water causing
drowning and submersion**

● **W16.222 Fall in (into) bucket of water causing
other injury**

● **W16.3 Fall into other water**
  Fall into fountain
  Fall into reservoir

  ● **W16.31 Fall into other water striking water surface**

    ● **W16.311 Fall into other water striking water surface causing drowning and submersion**

      Excludes1 drowning and submersion while in other water without fall (W73)

    ● **W16.312 Fall into other water striking water surface causing other injury**

  ● **W16.32 Fall into other water striking bottom**

    ● **W16.321 Fall into other water striking bottom causing drowning and submersion**

      Excludes1 drowning and submersion while in other water without fall (W73)

    ● **W16.322 Fall into other water striking bottom causing other injury**

  ● **W16.33 Fall into other water striking wall**

    ● **W16.331 Fall into other water striking wall causing drowning and submersion**

      Excludes1 drowning and submersion while in other water without fall (W73)

    ● **W16.332 Fall into other water striking wall causing other injury**

● **W16.4 Fall into unspecified water**

  X ● **W16.41 Fall into unspecified water causing drowning and submersion**

  X ● **W16.42 Fall into unspecified water causing other injury**

● **W16.5 Jumping or diving into swimming pool**

  ● **W16.51 Jumping or diving into swimming pool striking water surface**

    ● **W16.511 Jumping or diving into swimming pool striking water surface causing drowning and submersion**

      Excludes1 drowning and submersion while in swimming pool without jumping or diving (W67)

    ● **W16.512 Jumping or diving into swimming pool striking water surface causing other injury**

  ● **W16.52 Jumping or diving into swimming pool striking bottom**

    ● **W16.521 Jumping or diving into swimming pool striking bottom causing drowning and submersion**

      Excludes1 drowning and submersion while in swimming pool without jumping or diving (W67)

    ● **W16.522 Jumping or diving into swimming pool striking bottom causing other injury**

● **W16.53 Jumping or diving into swimming pool striking wall**

  ● **W16.531 Jumping or diving into swimming pool striking wall causing drowning and submersion**

    Excludes1 drowning and submersion while in swimming pool without jumping or diving (W67)

  ● **W16.532 Jumping or diving into swimming pool striking wall causing other injury**

● **W16.6 Jumping or diving into natural body of water**
  Jumping or diving into lake
  Jumping or diving into open sea
  Jumping or diving into river
  Jumping or diving into stream

  ● **W16.61 Jumping or diving into natural body of water striking water surface**

    ● **W16.611 Jumping or diving into natural body of water striking water surface causing drowning and submersion**

      Excludes1 drowning and submersion while in natural body of water without jumping or diving (W69)

    ● **W16.612 Jumping or diving into natural body of water striking water surface causing other injury**

  ● **W16.62 Jumping or diving into natural body of water striking bottom**

    ● **W16.621 Jumping or diving into natural body of water striking bottom causing drowning and submersion**

      Excludes1 drowning and submersion while in natural body of water without jumping or diving (W69)

    ● **W16.622 Jumping or diving into natural body of water striking bottom causing other injury**

● **W16.7 Jumping or diving from boat**

  Excludes1 fall from boat into water - see watercraft accident (V90-V94)

  ● **W16.71 Jumping or diving from boat striking water surface**

    ● **W16.711 Jumping or diving from boat striking water surface causing drowning and submersion**

    ● **W16.712 Jumping or diving from boat striking water surface causing other injury**

  ● **W16.72 Jumping or diving from boat striking bottom**

    ● **W16.721 Jumping or diving from boat striking bottom causing drowning and submersion**

    ● **W16.722 Jumping or diving from boat striking bottom causing other injury**

CHAPTER 20 (V00-Y99)

● **W16.8 Jumping or diving into other water**
Jumping or diving into fountain
Jumping or diving into reservoir

  ● **W16.81 Jumping or diving into other water striking water surface**

    ● **W16.811 Jumping or diving into other water striking water surface causing drowning and submersion**

       Excludes1   drowning and submersion while in other water without jumping or diving (W73)

    ● **W16.812 Jumping or diving into other water striking water surface causing other injury**

  ● **W16.82 Jumping or diving into other water striking bottom**

    ● **W16.821 Jumping or diving into other water striking bottom causing drowning and submersion**

       Excludes1   drowning and submersion while in other water without jumping or diving (W73)

    ● **W16.822 Jumping or diving into other water striking bottom causing other injury**

  ● **W16.83 Jumping or diving into other water striking wall**

    ● **W16.831 Jumping or diving into other water striking wall causing drowning and submersion**

       Excludes1   drowning and submersion while in other water without jumping or diving (W73)

    ● **W16.832 Jumping or diving into other water striking wall causing other injury**

● **W16.9 Jumping or diving into unspecified water**

  X● **W16.91 Jumping or diving into unspecified water causing drowning and submersion**

  X● **W16.92 Jumping or diving into unspecified water causing other injury**

● **W17 Other fall from one level to another**
The appropriate 7th character is to be added to each code from category W17

A	initial encounter
D	subsequent encounter
S	sequela

X● **W17.0 Fall into well**

X● **W17.1 Fall into storm drain or manhole**

X● **W17.2 Fall into hole**
Fall into pit

X● **W17.3 Fall into empty swimming pool**
     Excludes1   fall into filled swimming pool (W16.0-)

X● **W17.4 Fall from dock**

● **W17.8 Other fall from one level to another**

  X● **W17.81 Fall down embankment (hill)**

  X● **W17.82 Fall from (out of) grocery cart**
Fall due to grocery cart tipping over

  X● **W17.89 Other fall from one level to another**
Fall from cherry picker
Fall from lifting device
Fall from mobile elevated work platform [MEWP]
Fall from sky lift
Coding Clinic: 2015, Q2, P6

● **W18 Other slipping, tripping and stumbling and falls**
The appropriate 7th character is to be added to each code from category W18

A	initial encounter
D	subsequent encounter
S	sequela

● **W18.0 Fall due to bumping against object**
Striking against object with subsequent fall
     Excludes1   fall on same level due to slipping, tripping, or stumbling with subsequent striking against object (W01.1-)

  X● **W18.00 Striking against unspecified object with subsequent fall**

  X● **W18.01 Striking against sports equipment with subsequent fall**

  X● **W18.02 Striking against glass with subsequent fall**

  X● **W18.09 Striking against other object with subsequent fall**

● **W18.1 Fall from or off toilet**

  X● **W18.11 Fall from or off toilet without subsequent striking against object**
Fall from (off) toilet NOS

  X● **W18.12 Fall from or off toilet with subsequent striking against object**

X● **W18.2 Fall in (into) shower or empty bathtub**
     Excludes1   fall in full bathtub causing drowning or submersion (W16.21-)

● **W18.3 Other and unspecified fall on same level**

  X● **W18.30 Fall on same level, unspecified**

  X● **W18.31 Fall on same level due to stepping on an object**
Fall on same level due to stepping on an animal
     Excludes1   slipping, tripping and stumbling without fall due to stepping on animal (W18.41)

  X● **W18.39 Other fall on same level**

● **W18.4 Slipping, tripping and stumbling without falling**
     Excludes1   collision with another person without fall (W51)

  X● **W18.40 Slipping, tripping and stumbling without falling, unspecified**

  X● **W18.41 Slipping, tripping and stumbling without falling due to stepping on object**
Slipping, tripping and stumbling without falling due to stepping on animal
     Excludes1   slipping, tripping and stumbling with fall due to stepping on animal (W18.31)

  X● **W18.42 Slipping, tripping and stumbling without falling due to stepping into hole or opening**

  X● **W18.43 Slipping, tripping and stumbling without falling due to stepping from one level to another**

  X● **W18.49 Other slipping, tripping and stumbling without falling**

X● **W19 Unspecified fall**
Accidental fall NOS
The appropriate 7th character is to be added to code W19

A	initial encounter
D	subsequent encounter
S	sequela

Coding Clinic: 2012, Q4, P95

▶ New   ⇒ Revised   ~~deleted~~ Deleted   Excludes 1   Excludes 2   Includes   Use additional   Code first   Code also   Key words
OGCR Official Guidelines   X Assign placeholder X   ● Use Additional Character(s)   ▶ Manifestation Code   Ⓗ Hierarchical Condition Category   Coding Clinic

EXPOSURE TO INANIMATE MECHANICAL FORCES (W20-W49)

Excludes1   assault (X92-Y09)
contact or collision with animals or persons (W50-W64)
exposure to inanimate mechanical forces involving military or war operations (Y36.-, Y37.-)
intentional self-harm (X71-X83)
Coding Clinic: 2016, Q4, P129

● **W20   Struck by thrown, projected or falling object**
Code first any associated:
cataclysm (X34-X39)
lightning strike (T75.00)
Excludes1   falling object in machinery accident (W24, W28-W31)
falling object in transport accident (V01-V99)
object set in motion by explosion (W35-W40)
object set in motion by firearm (W32-W34)
struck by thrown sports equipment (W21.-)

The appropriate 7th character is to be added to each code from category W20

A	initial encounter
D	subsequent encounter
S	sequela

X● **W20.0   Struck by falling object in cave-in**
Excludes2   asphyxiation due to cave-in (T71.21)
X● **W20.1   Struck by object due to collapse of building**
Excludes1   struck by object due to collapse of burning building (X00.2, X02.2)
X● **W20.8   Other cause of strike by thrown, projected or falling object**
Excludes1   struck by thrown sports equipment (W21.-)

● **W21   Striking against or struck by sports equipment**
Excludes1   assault with sports equipment (Y08.0-)
striking against or struck by sports equipment with subsequent fall (W18.01)

The appropriate 7th character is to be added to each code from category W21

A	initial encounter
D	subsequent encounter
S	sequela

● **W21.0   Struck by hit or thrown ball**
X● **W21.00   Struck by hit or thrown ball, unspecified type**
X● **W21.01   Struck by football**
X● **W21.02   Struck by soccer ball**
X● **W21.03   Struck by baseball**
X● **W21.04   Struck by golf ball**
X● **W21.05   Struck by basketball**
X● **W21.06   Struck by volleyball**
X● **W21.07   Struck by softball**
X● **W21.09   Struck by other hit or thrown ball**
● **W21.1   Struck by bat, racquet or club**
X● **W21.11   Struck by baseball bat**
X● **W21.12   Struck by tennis racquet**
X● **W21.13   Struck by golf club**
X● **W21.19   Struck by other bat, racquet or club**
● **W21.2   Struck by hockey stick or puck**
● **W21.21   Struck by hockey stick**
● **W21.210   Struck by ice hockey stick**
● **W21.211   Struck by field hockey stick**
● **W21.22   Struck by hockey puck**
● **W21.220   Struck by ice hockey puck**
● **W21.221   Struck by field hockey puck**

● **W21.3   Struck by sports foot wear**
X● **W21.31   Struck by shoe cleats**
Stepped on by shoe cleats
X● **W21.32   Struck by skate blades**
Skated over by skate blades
X● **W21.39   Struck by other sports foot wear**
X● **W21.4   Striking against diving board**
Use additional code for subsequent falling into water, if applicable (W16.-)
● **W21.8   Striking against or struck by other sports equipment**
X● **W21.81   Striking against or struck by football helmet**
X● **W21.89   Striking against or struck by other sports equipment**
X● **W21.9   Striking against or struck by unspecified sports equipment**

● **W22   Striking against or struck by other objects**
Excludes1   striking against or struck by object with subsequent fall (W18.09)

The appropriate 7th character is to be added to each code from category W22

A	initial encounter
D	subsequent encounter
S	sequela

● **W22.0   Striking against stationary object**
Excludes1   striking against stationary sports equipment (W21.8)
X● **W22.01   Walked into wall**
X● **W22.02   Walked into lamppost**
X● **W22.03   Walked into furniture**
● **W22.04   Striking against wall of swimming pool**
● **W22.041   Striking against wall of swimming pool causing drowning and submersion**
Excludes1   drowning and submersion while swimming without striking against wall (W67)
● **W22.042   Striking against wall of swimming pool causing other injury**
X● **W22.09   Striking against other stationary object**
● **W22.1   Striking against or struck by automobile airbag**
X● **W22.10   Striking against or struck by unspecified automobile airbag**
X● **W22.11   Striking against or struck by driver side automobile airbag**
X● **W22.12   Striking against or struck by front passenger side automobile airbag**
X● **W22.19   Striking against or struck by other automobile airbag**
X● **W22.8   Striking against or struck by other objects**
Striking against or struck by object NOS
Excludes1   struck by thrown, projected or falling object (W20.-)

● **W23   Caught, crushed, jammed or pinched in or between objects**

> **Excludes1**   injury caused by cutting or piercing instruments (W25-W27)
> injury caused by firearms malfunction (W32.1, W33.1-, W34.1-)
> injury caused by lifting and transmission devices (W24.-)
> injury caused by machinery (W28-W31)
> injury caused by nonpowered hand tools (W27.-)
> injury caused by transport vehicle being used as a means of transportation (V01-V99)
> injury caused by struck by thrown, projected or falling object (W20.-)

The appropriate 7th character is to be added to each code from category W23

> A   initial encounter
> D   subsequent encounter
> S   sequela

X● **W23.0   Caught, crushed, jammed, or pinched between moving objects**

X● **W23.1   Caught, crushed, jammed, or pinched between stationary objects**

● **W24   Contact with lifting and transmission devices, not elsewhere classified**

> **Excludes1**   transport accidents (V01-V99)

The appropriate 7th character is to be added to each code from category W24

> A   initial encounter
> D   subsequent encounter
> S   sequela

X● **W24.0   Contact with lifting devices, not elsewhere classified**
> Contact with chain hoist
> Contact with drive belt
> Contact with pulley (block)

X● **W24.1   Contact with transmission devices, not elsewhere classified**
> Contact with transmission belt or cable

X● **W25   Contact with sharp glass**

> *Code first any associated:*
> injury due to flying glass from explosion or firearm discharge (W32-W40)
> transport accident (V00-V99)

> **Excludes1**   fall on same level due to slipping, tripping and stumbling with subsequent striking against sharp glass (W01.110)
> striking against sharp glass with subsequent fall (W18.02)

> **Excludes2**   glass embedded in skin (W45)

The appropriate 7th character is to be added to code W25

> A   initial encounter
> D   subsequent encounter
> S   sequela

● **W26   Contact with other sharp objects**

> **Excludes2**   sharp object(s) embedded in skin (W45)

The appropriate 7th character is to be added to each code from category W26

> A   initial encounter
> D   subsequent encounter
> S   sequela

Coding Clinic: 2016, Q4, P73

X● **W26.0   Contact with knife**

> **Excludes1**   contact with electric knife (W29.1)

X● **W26.1   Contact with sword or dagger**

X● **W26.2   Contact with edge of stiff paper**
> Paper cut
> **Coding Clinic: 2016, Q4, P73**

X● **W26.8   Contact with other sharp object(s), not elsewhere classified**
> Contact with tin can lid
> **Coding Clinic: 2016, Q4, P73**

X● **W26.9   Contact with unspecified sharp object(s)**
> **Coding Clinic: 2016, Q4, P73**

● **W27   Contact with nonpowered hand tool**

The appropriate 7th character is to be added to each code from category W27

> A   initial encounter
> D   subsequent encounter
> S   sequela

X● **W27.0   Contact with workbench tool**
> Contact with auger
> Contact with axe
> Contact with chisel
> Contact with handsaw
> Contact with screwdriver

X● **W27.1   Contact with garden tool**
> Contact with hoe
> Contact with nonpowered lawn mower
> Contact with pitchfork
> Contact with rake

X● **W27.2   Contact with scissors**

X● **W27.3   Contact with needle (sewing)**

> **Excludes1**   contact with hypodermic needle (W46.-)

X● **W27.4   Contact with kitchen utensil**
> Contact with fork
> Contact with ice-pick
> Contact with can-opener NOS

X● **W27.5   Contact with paper-cutter**

X● **W27.8   Contact with other nonpowered hand tool**
> Contact with nonpowered sewing machine
> Contact with shovel

X● **W28   Contact with powered lawn mower**
> Powered lawn mower (commercial) (residential)

> **Excludes1**   contact with nonpowered lawn mower (W27.1)
> **Excludes2**   exposure to electric current (W86.-)

The appropriate 7th character is to be added to code W28

> A   initial encounter
> D   subsequent encounter
> S   sequela

● **W29   Contact with other powered hand tools and household machinery**

> **Excludes1**   contact with commercial machinery (W31.82)
> contact with hot household appliance (X15)
> contact with nonpowered hand tool (W27.-)
> exposure to electric current (W86)

The appropriate 7th character is to be added to each code from category W29

> A   initial encounter
> D   subsequent encounter
> S   sequela

X● **W29.0   Contact with powered kitchen appliance**
> Contact with blender
> Contact with can-opener
> Contact with garbage disposal
> Contact with mixer

X● **W29.1   Contact with electric knife**

X● **W29.2   Contact with other powered household machinery**
> Contact with electric fan
> Contact with powered dryer (clothes) (powered) (spin)
> Contact with washing-machine
> Contact with sewing machine

▶ New   ⇒ Revised   ~~deleted~~ Deleted   Excludes 1   Excludes 2   Includes   Use additional   Code first   Code also   Key words

OGCR Official Guidelines   X Assign placeholder X   ● Use Additional Character(s)   ▶ Manifestation Code   🅚 Hierarchical Condition Category   **Coding Clinic**

X● **W29.3   Contact with powered garden and outdoor hand tools and machinery**
     Contact with chainsaw
     Contact with edger
     Contact with garden cultivator (tiller)
     Contact with hedge trimmer
     Contact with other powered garden tool
     Excludes1   contact with powered lawn mower (W28)

X● **W29.4   Contact with nail gun**

X● **W29.8   Contact with other powered hand tools and household machinery**
     Contact with do-it-yourself tool NOS

● **W30   Contact with agricultural machinery**
     Includes   animal-powered farm machine
     Excludes1   agricultural transport vehicle accident (V01-V99)
         explosion of grain store (W40.8)
         exposure to electric current (W86.-)

The appropriate 7th character is to be added to each code from category W30

A	initial encounter
D	subsequent encounter
S	sequela

X● **W30.0   Contact with combine harvester**
     Contact with reaper
     Contact with thresher

X● **W30.1   Contact with power take-off devices (PTO)**

X● **W30.2   Contact with hay derrick**

X● **W30.3   Contact with grain storage elevator**
     Excludes1   explosion of grain store (W40.8)

● **W30.8   Contact with other specified agricultural machinery**

X● **W30.81   Contact with agricultural transport vehicle in stationary use**
     Contact with agricultural transport vehicle under repair, not on public roadway
     Excludes1   agricultural transport vehicle accident (V01-V99)

X● **W30.89   Contact with other specified agricultural machinery**

X● **W30.9   Contact with unspecified agricultural machinery**
     Contact with farm machinery NOS

● **W31   Contact with other and unspecified machinery**
     Excludes1   contact with agricultural machinery (W30.-)
         contact with machinery in transport under own power or being towed by a vehicle (V01-V99)
         exposure to electric current (W86)

The appropriate 7th character is to be added to each code from category W31

A	initial encounter
D	subsequent encounter
S	sequela

X● **W31.0   Contact with mining and earth-drilling machinery**
     Contact with bore or drill (land) (seabed)
     Contact with shaft hoist
     Contact with shaft lift
     Contact with undercutter

X● **W31.1   Contact with metalworking machines**
     Contact with abrasive wheel
     Contact with forging machine
     Contact with lathe
     Contact with mechanical shears
     Contact with metal drilling machine
     Contact with milling machine
     Contact with power press
     Contact with rolling-mill
     Contact with metal sawing machine

X● **W31.2   Contact with powered woodworking and forming machines**
     Contact with band saw
     Contact with bench saw
     Contact with circular saw
     Contact with molding machine
     Contact with overhead plane
     Contact with powered saw
     Contact with radial saw
     Contact with sander
     Excludes1   nonpowered woodworking tools (W27.0)

X● **W31.3   Contact with prime movers**
     Contact with gas turbine
     Contact with internal combustion engine
     Contact with steam engine
     Contact with water driven turbine

● **W31.8   Contact with other specified machinery**

X● **W31.81   Contact with recreational machinery**
     Contact with roller-coaster

X● **W31.82   Contact with other commercial machinery**
     Contact with commercial electric fan
     Contact with commercial kitchen appliances
     Contact with commercial powered dryer (clothes) (powered) (spin)
     Contact with commercial washing-machine
     Contact with commercial sewing machine
     Excludes1   contact with household machinery (W29.-)
         contact with powered lawn mower (W28)

X● **W31.83   Contact with special construction vehicle in stationary use**
     Contact with special construction vehicle under repair, not on public roadway
     Excludes1   special construction vehicle accident (V01-V99)

X● **W31.89   Contact with other specified machinery**

X● **W31.9   Contact with unspecified machinery**
     Contact with machinery NOS

● **W32   Accidental handgun discharge and malfunction**
     Includes   accidental discharge and malfunction of gun for single hand use
         accidental discharge and malfunction of pistol
         accidental discharge and malfunction of revolver
         handgun discharge and malfunction NOS
     Excludes1   accidental airgun discharge and malfunction (W34.010, W34.110)
         accidental BB gun discharge and malfunction (W34.010, W34.110)
         accidental pellet gun discharge and malfunction (W34.010, W34.110)
         accidental shotgun discharge and malfunction (W33.01, W33.11)
         assault by handgun discharge (X93)
         handgun discharge involving legal intervention (Y35.0-)
         handgun discharge involving military or war operations (Y36.4-)
         intentional self-harm by handgun discharge (X72)
         Very pistol discharge and malfunction (W34.09, W34.19)

The appropriate 7th character is to be added to each code from category W32

A	initial encounter
D	subsequent encounter
S	sequela

X● **W32.0   Accidental handgun discharge**

X● **W32.1   Accidental handgun malfunction**
     Injury due to explosion of handgun (parts)
     Injury due to malfunction of mechanism or component of handgun
     Injury due to recoil of handgun
     Powder burn from handgun

CHAPTER 20 (V00-Y99)

● **W33**   **Accidental rifle, shotgun and larger firearm discharge and malfunction**

     Includes   rifle, shotgun and larger firearm discharge and malfunction NOS

     Excludes1   accidental airgun discharge and malfunction (W34.010, W34.110)

           accidental BB gun discharge and malfunction (W34.010, W34.110)

           accidental handgun discharge and malfunction (W32.-)

           accidental pellet gun discharge and malfunction (W34.010, W34.110)

           assault by rifle, shotgun and larger firearm discharge (X94)

           firearm discharge involving legal intervention (Y35.0-)

           firearm discharge involving military or war operations (Y36.4-)

           intentional self-harm by rifle, shotgun and larger firearm discharge (X73)

The appropriate 7th character is to be added to each code from category W33

> A   initial encounter
> D   subsequent encounter
> S   sequela

● **W33.0**   **Accidental rifle, shotgun and larger firearm discharge**

   X● **W33.00**   **Accidental discharge of unspecified larger firearm**
        Discharge of unspecified larger firearm NOS

   X● **W33.01**   **Accidental discharge of shotgun**
        Discharge of shotgun NOS

   X● **W33.02**   **Accidental discharge of hunting rifle**
        Discharge of hunting rifle NOS

   X● **W33.03**   **Accidental discharge of machine gun**
        Discharge of machine gun NOS

   X● **W33.09**   **Accidental discharge of other larger firearm**
        Discharge of other larger firearm NOS

● **W33.1**   **Accidental rifle, shotgun and larger firearm malfunction**

       Injury due to explosion of rifle, shotgun and larger firearm (parts)

       Injury due to malfunction of mechanism or component of rifle, shotgun and larger firearm

       Injury due to piercing, cutting, crushing or pinching due to (by) slide trigger mechanism, scope or other gun part

       Injury due to recoil of rifle, shotgun and larger firearm

       Powder burn from rifle, shotgun and larger firearm

   X● **W33.10**   **Accidental malfunction of unspecified larger firearm**
        Malfunction of unspecified larger firearm NOS

   X● **W33.11**   **Accidental malfunction of shotgun**
        Malfunction of shotgun NOS

   X● **W33.12**   **Accidental malfunction of hunting rifle**
        Malfunction of hunting rifle NOS

   X● **W33.13**   **Accidental malfunction of machine gun**
        Malfunction of machine gun NOS

   X● **W33.19**   **Accidental malfunction of other larger firearm**
        Malfunction of other larger firearm NOS

● **W34**   **Accidental discharge and malfunction from other and unspecified firearms and guns**

The appropriate 7th character is to be added to each code from category W34

> A   initial encounter
> D   subsequent encounter
> S   sequela

● **W34.0**   **Accidental discharge from other and unspecified firearms and guns**

   X● **W34.00**   **Accidental discharge from unspecified firearms or gun**
        Discharge from firearm NOS
        Gunshot wound NOS
        Shot NOS
        Coding Clinic: 2015, Q1, P17

   ● **W34.01**   **Accidental discharge of gas, air or spring-operated guns**

     ● **W34.010**   **Accidental discharge of airgun**
          Accidental discharge of BB gun
          Accidental discharge of pellet gun

     ● **W34.011**   **Accidental discharge of paintball gun**
          Accidental injury due to paintball discharge

     ● **W34.018**   **Accidental discharge of other gas, air or spring-operated gun**

   X● **W34.09**   **Accidental discharge from other specified firearms**
        Accidental discharge from Very pistol [flare]

● **W34.1**   **Accidental malfunction from other and unspecified firearms and guns**

   X● **W34.10**   **Accidental malfunction from unspecified firearms or gun**
        Firearm malfunction NOS

   ● **W34.11**   **Accidental malfunction of gas, air or spring-operated guns**

     ● **W34.110**   **Accidental malfunction of airgun**
          Accidental malfunction of BB gun
          Accidental malfunction of pellet gun

     ● **W34.111**   **Accidental malfunction of paintball gun**
          Accidental injury due to paintball gun malfunction

     ● **W34.118**   **Accidental malfunction of other gas, air or spring-operated gun**

   X● **W34.19**   **Accidental malfunction from other specified firearms**
        Accidental malfunction from Very pistol [flare]

X● **W35**   **Explosion and rupture of boiler**

     Excludes1   explosion and rupture of boiler on watercraft (V93.4)

The appropriate 7th character is to be added to code W35

> A   initial encounter
> D   subsequent encounter
> S   sequela

● **W36**   **Explosion and rupture of gas cylinder**

The appropriate 7th character is to be added to each code from category W36

> A   initial encounter
> D   subsequent encounter
> S   sequela

   X● **W36.1**   **Explosion and rupture of aerosol can**
   X● **W36.2**   **Explosion and rupture of air tank**
   X● **W36.3**   **Explosion and rupture of pressurized-gas tank**
   X● **W36.8**   **Explosion and rupture of other gas cylinder**
   X● **W36.9**   **Explosion and rupture of unspecified gas cylinder**

▶ New   ⇒ Revised   ~~deleted~~ Deleted   Excludes 1   Excludes 2   Includes   Use additional   Code first   Code also   Key words

OGCR Official Guidelines   X Assign placeholder X   ● Use Additional Character(s)   ▶ Manifestation Code   HCC Hierarchical Condition Category   **Coding Clinic**

W37   Explosion and rupture of pressurized tire, pipe or hose

The appropriate 7th character is to be added to each code from category W37

A	initial encounter
D	subsequent encounter
S	sequela

X● **W37.0   Explosion of bicycle tire**

X● **W37.8   Explosion and rupture of other pressurized tire, pipe or hose**

X●**W38   Explosion and rupture of other specified pressurized devices**

The appropriate 7th character is to be added to code W38

A	initial encounter
D	subsequent encounter
S	sequela

X●**W39   Discharge of firework**

The appropriate 7th character is to be added to code W39

A	initial encounter
D	subsequent encounter
S	sequela

●**W40   Explosion of other materials**

Excludes1   assault by explosive material (X96)
explosion involving legal intervention (Y35.1-)
explosion involving military or war operations (Y36.0-, Y36.2-)
intentional self-harm by explosive material (X75)

The appropriate 7th character is to be added to each code from category W40

A	initial encounter
D	subsequent encounter
S	sequela

X● **W40.0   Explosion of blasting material**
Explosion of blasting cap
Explosion of detonator
Explosion of dynamite
Explosion of explosive (any) used in blasting operations

X● **W40.1   Explosion of explosive gases**
Explosion of acetylene
Explosion of butane
Explosion of coal gas
Explosion in mine NOS
Explosion of explosive gas
Explosion of fire damp
Explosion of gasoline fumes
Explosion of methane
Explosion of propane

X● **W40.8   Explosion of other specified explosive materials**
Explosion in dump NOS
Explosion in factory NOS
Explosion in grain store
Explosion in munitions

     Excludes1   explosion involving legal intervention (Y35.1-)
explosion involving military or war operations (Y36.0-, Y36.2-)

X● **W40.9   Explosion of unspecified explosive materials**
Explosion NOS

●**W42   Exposure to noise**

The appropriate 7th character is to be added to each code from category W42

A	initial encounter
D	subsequent encounter
S	sequela

X● **W42.0   Exposure to supersonic waves**

X● **W42.9   Exposure to other noise**
Exposure to sound waves NOS

●**W45   Foreign body or object entering through skin**

Includes   foreign body or object embedded in skin
nail embedded in skin

Excludes2   contact with hand tools (nonpowered) (powered) (W27-W29)
contact with other sharp object(s) (W26.-)
contact with sharp glass (W25.-)
struck by objects (W20-W22)

The appropriate 7th character is to be added to each code from category W45

A	initial encounter
D	subsequent encounter
S	sequela

X● **W45.0   Nail entering through skin**

X● **W45.8   Other foreign body or object entering through skin**
Splinter in skin NOS

●**W46   Contact with hypodermic needle**

The appropriate 7th character is to be added to each code from category W46

A	initial encounter
D	subsequent encounter
S	sequela

X● **W46.0   Contact with hypodermic needle**
Hypodermic needle stick NOS

X● **W46.1   Contact with contaminated hypodermic needle**

●**W49   Exposure to other inanimate mechanical forces**

Includes   exposure to abnormal gravitational [G] forces
exposure to inanimate mechanical forces NEC

Excludes1   exposure to inanimate mechanical forces involving military or war operations (Y36.-, Y37.-)

The appropriate 7th character is to be added to each code from category W49

A	initial encounter
D	subsequent encounter
S	sequela

●**W49.0   Item causing external constriction**

   X● **W49.01   Hair causing external constriction**

   X● **W49.02   String or thread causing external constriction**

   X● **W49.03   Rubber band causing external constriction**

   X● **W49.04   Ring or other jewelry causing external constriction**

   X● **W49.09   Other item causing external constriction**

X● **W49.9   Exposure to other inanimate mechanical forces**

CHAPTER 20 (V00-Y99)

EXPOSURE TO ANIMATE MECHANICAL FORCES (W50-W64)

Excludes1 toxic effect of contact with venomous animals and plants (T63.-)

● **W50 Accidental hit, strike, kick, twist, bite or scratch by another person**

Includes hit, strike, kick, twist, bite, or scratch by another person NOS

Excludes1 assault by bodily force (Y04)
struck by objects (W20-W22)

The appropriate 7th character is to be added to each code from category W50

A	initial encounter
D	subsequent encounter
S	sequela

X● **W50.0 Accidental hit or strike by another person**
Hit or strike by another person NOS

X● **W50.1 Accidental kick by another person**
Kick by another person NOS

X● **W50.2 Accidental twist by another person**
Twist by another person NOS
Coding Clinic: 2015, Q1, P8

X● **W50.3 Accidental bite by another person**
Human bite
Bite by another person NOS

X● **W50.4 Accidental scratch by another person**
Scratch by another person NOS

X● **W51 Accidental striking against or bumped into by another person**

Excludes1 assault by striking against or bumping into by another person (Y04.2)
fall due to collision with another person (W03)

The appropriate 7th character is to be added to code W51

A	initial encounter
D	subsequent encounter
S	sequela

X● **W52 Crushed, pushed or stepped on by crowd or human stampede**
Crushed, pushed or stepped on by crowd or human stampede with or without fall

The appropriate 7th character is to be added to code W52

A	initial encounter
D	subsequent encounter
S	sequela

● **W53 Contact with rodent**

Includes contact with saliva, feces or urine of rodent

The appropriate 7th character is to be added to each code from category W53

A	initial encounter
D	subsequent encounter
S	sequela

● **W53.0 Contact with mouse**
X● **W53.01 Bitten by mouse**
X● **W53.09 Other contact with mouse**
● **W53.1 Contact with rat**
X● **W53.11 Bitten by rat**
X● **W53.19 Other contact with rat**
● **W53.2 Contact with squirrel**
X● **W53.21 Bitten by squirrel**
X● **W53.29 Other contact with squirrel**
● **W53.8 Contact with other rodent**
X● **W53.81 Bitten by other rodent**
X● **W53.89 Other contact with other rodent**

● **W54 Contact with dog**

Includes contact with saliva, feces or urine of dog

The appropriate 7th character is to be added to each code from category W54

A	initial encounter
D	subsequent encounter
S	sequela

X● **W54.0 Bitten by dog**
X● **W54.1 Struck by dog**
Knocked over by dog
X● **W54.8 Other contact with dog**

● **W55 Contact with other mammals**

Includes contact with saliva, feces or urine of mammal

Excludes1 animal being ridden - see transport accidents
bitten or struck by dog (W54)
bitten or struck by rodent (W53.-)
contact with marine mammals (W56.X-)

The appropriate 7th character is to be added to each code from category W55

A	initial encounter
D	subsequent encounter
S	sequela

● **W55.0 Contact with cat**
X● **W55.01 Bitten by cat**
X● **W55.03 Scratched by cat**
X● **W55.09 Other contact with cat**
● **W55.1 Contact with horse**
X● **W55.11 Bitten by horse**
X● **W55.12 Struck by horse**
X● **W55.19 Other contact with horse**
● **W55.2 Contact with cow**
Contact with bull
X● **W55.21 Bitten by cow**
X● **W55.22 Struck by cow**
Gored by bull
X● **W55.29 Other contact with cow**
● **W55.3 Contact with other hoof stock**
Contact with goats
Contact with sheep
X● **W55.31 Bitten by other hoof stock**
X● **W55.32 Struck by other hoof stock**
Gored by goat
Gored by ram
X● **W55.39 Other contact with other hoof stock**
● **W55.4 Contact with pig**
X● **W55.41 Bitten by pig**
X● **W55.42 Struck by pig**
X● **W55.49 Other contact with pig**
● **W55.5 Contact with raccoon**
X● **W55.51 Bitten by raccoon**
X● **W55.52 Struck by raccoon**
X● **W55.59 Other contact with raccoon**
● **W55.8 Contact with other mammals**
X● **W55.81 Bitten by other mammals**
X● **W55.82 Struck by other mammals**
X● **W55.89 Other contact with other mammals**

▶ New   ⇒ Revised   ~~deleted~~ Deleted   Excludes 1   Excludes 2   Includes   Use additional   Code first   Code also   Key words
OGCR Official Guidelines   X Assign placeholder X   ● Use Additional Character(s)   ▶ Manifestation Code   🄷🄲🄲 Hierarchical Condition Category   Coding Clinic

● **W56   Contact with nonvenomous marine animal**

> **Excludes1**   contact with venomous marine animal (T63.-)
>
> The appropriate 7th character is to be added to each code from category W56
>
> | | |
> |---|---|
> | A | initial encounter |
> | D | subsequent encounter |
> | S | sequela |

   ● **W56.0   Contact with dolphin**
     X● **W56.01   Bitten by dolphin**
     X● **W56.02   Struck by dolphin**
     X● **W56.09   Other contact with dolphin**

   ● **W56.1   Contact with sea lion**
     X● **W56.11   Bitten by sea lion**
     X● **W56.12   Struck by sea lion**
     X● **W56.19   Other contact with sea lion**

   ● **W56.2   Contact with orca**
       Contact with killer whale
     X● **W56.21   Bitten by orca**
     X● **W56.22   Struck by orca**
     X● **W56.29   Other contact with orca**

   ● **W56.3   Contact with other marine mammals**
     X● **W56.31   Bitten by other marine mammals**
     X● **W56.32   Struck by other marine mammals**
     X● **W56.39   Other contact with other marine mammals**

   ● **W56.4   Contact with shark**
     X● **W56.41   Bitten by shark**
     X● **W56.42   Struck by shark**
     X● **W56.49   Other contact with shark**

   ● **W56.5   Contact with other fish**
     X● **W56.51   Bitten by other fish**
     X● **W56.52   Struck by other fish**
     X● **W56.59   Other contact with other fish**

   ● **W56.8   Contact with other nonvenomous marine animals**
     X● **W56.81   Bitten by other nonvenomous marine animals**
     X● **W56.82   Struck by other nonvenomous marine animals**
     X● **W56.89   Other contact with other nonvenomous marine animals**

X● **W57   Bitten or stung by nonvenomous insect and other nonvenomous arthropods**

> **Excludes1**   contact with venomous insects and arthropods (T63.2-, T63.3-, T63.4-)
>
> The appropriate 7th character is to be added to code W57
>
> | | |
> |---|---|
> | A | initial encounter |
> | D | subsequent encounter |
> | S | sequela |

● **W58   Contact with crocodile or alligator**

> The appropriate 7th character is to be added to each code from category W58
>
> | | |
> |---|---|
> | A | initial encounter |
> | D | subsequent encounter |
> | S | sequela |

   ● **W58.0   Contact with alligator**
     X● **W58.01   Bitten by alligator**
     X● **W58.02   Struck by alligator**
     X● **W58.03   Crushed by alligator**
     X● **W58.09   Other contact with alligator**

   ● **W58.1   Contact with crocodile**
     X● **W58.11   Bitten by crocodile**
     X● **W58.12   Struck by crocodile**
     X● **W58.13   Crushed by crocodile**
     X● **W58.19   Other contact with crocodile**

● **W59   Contact with other nonvenomous reptiles**

> **Excludes1**   contact with venomous reptile (T63.0-, T63.1-)
>
> The appropriate 7th character is to be added to each code from category W59
>
> | | |
> |---|---|
> | A | initial encounter |
> | D | subsequent encounter |
> | S | sequela |

   ● **W59.0   Contact with nonvenomous lizards**
     X● **W59.01   Bitten by nonvenomous lizards**
     X● **W59.02   Struck by nonvenomous lizards**
     X● **W59.09   Other contact with nonvenomous lizards**
       Exposure to nonvenomous lizards

   ● **W59.1   Contact with nonvenomous snakes**
     X● **W59.11   Bitten by nonvenomous snake**
     X● **W59.12   Struck by nonvenomous snake**
     X● **W59.13   Crushed by nonvenomous snake**
     X● **W59.19   Other contact with nonvenomous snake**

   ● **W59.2   Contact with turtles**
> **Excludes1**   contact with tortoises (W59.8-)

     X● **W59.21   Bitten by turtle**
     X● **W59.22   Struck by turtle**
     X● **W59.29   Other contact with turtle**
       Exposure to turtles

   ● **W59.8   Contact with other nonvenomous reptiles**
     X● **W59.81   Bitten by other nonvenomous reptiles**
     X● **W59.82   Struck by other nonvenomous reptiles**
     X● **W59.83   Crushed by other nonvenomous reptiles**
     X● **W59.89   Other contact with other nonvenomous reptiles**

X● **W60   Contact with nonvenomous plant thorns and spines and sharp leaves**

> **Excludes1**   contact with venomous plants (T63.X7-)
>
> The appropriate 7th character is to be added to code W60
>
> | | |
> |---|---|
> | A | initial encounter |
> | D | subsequent encounter |
> | S | sequela |

● **W61   Contact with birds (domestic) (wild)**

> **Includes**   contact with excreta of birds
>
> The appropriate 7th character is to be added to each code from category W61
>
> | | |
> |---|---|
> | A | initial encounter |
> | D | subsequent encounter |
> | S | sequela |

   ● **W61.0   Contact with parrot**
     X● **W61.01   Bitten by parrot**
     X● **W61.02   Struck by parrot**
     X● **W61.09   Other contact with parrot**
       Exposure to parrots

   ● **W61.1   Contact with macaw**
     X● **W61.11   Bitten by macaw**
     X● **W61.12   Struck by macaw**
     X● **W61.19   Other contact with macaw**
       Exposure to macaws

   ● **W61.2   Contact with other psittacines**
     X● **W61.21   Bitten by other psittacines**
     X● **W61.22   Struck by other psittacines**
     X● **W61.29   Other contact with other psittacines**
       Exposure to other psittacines

   ● **W61.3   Contact with chicken**
     X● **W61.32   Struck by chicken**
     X● **W61.33   Pecked by chicken**
     X● **W61.39   Other contact with chicken**
       Exposure to chickens

CHAPTER 20 (V00–Y99)

- **W61.4 Contact with turkey**
  - X● **W61.42 Struck by turkey**
  - X● **W61.43 Pecked by turkey**
  - X● **W61.49 Other contact with turkey**
- **W61.5 Contact with goose**
  - X● **W61.51 Bitten by goose**
  - X● **W61.52 Struck by goose**
  - X● **W61.59 Other contact with goose**
- **W61.6 Contact with duck**
  - X● **W61.61 Bitten by duck**
  - X● **W61.62 Struck by duck**
  - X● **W61.69 Other contact with duck**
- **W61.9 Contact with other birds**
  - X● **W61.91 Bitten by other birds**
  - X● **W61.92 Struck by other birds**
  - X● **W61.99 Other contact with other birds**
    - Contact with bird NOS

● **W62 Contact with nonvenomous amphibians**

> **Excludes1**   contact with venomous amphibians (T63.81-R63.83)

The appropriate 7th character is to be added to each code from category W62

A	initial encounter
D	subsequent encounter
S	sequela

- X● **W62.0 Contact with nonvenomous frogs**
- X● **W62.1 Contact with nonvenomous toads**
- X● **W62.9 Contact with other nonvenomous amphibians**

X● **W64 Exposure to other animate mechanical forces**

> **Includes**   exposure to nonvenomous animal NOS
> **Excludes1**   contact with venomous animal (T63.-)

The appropriate 7th character is to be added to code W64

A	initial encounter
D	subsequent encounter
S	sequela

ACCIDENTAL NON-TRANSPORT DROWNING AND SUBMERSION (W65-W74)

> **Excludes1**   accidental drowning and submersion due to fall into water (W16.-)
>   accidental drowning and submersion due to water transport accident (V90.-, V92.-)
> **Excludes2**   accidental drowning and submersion due to cataclysm (X34-X39)

X● **W65 Accidental drowning and submersion while in bathtub**

> **Excludes1**   accidental drowning and submersion due to fall in (into) bathtub (W16.211)

The appropriate 7th character is to be added to code W65

A	initial encounter
D	subsequent encounter
S	sequela

X● **W67 Accidental drowning and submersion while in swimming pool**

> **Excludes1**   accidental drowning and submersion due to fall into swimming pool (W16.011, W16.021, W16.031)
>   accidental drowning and submersion due to striking into wall of swimming pool (W22.041)

The appropriate 7th character is to be added to code W67

A	initial encounter
D	subsequent encounter
S	sequela

X● **W69 Accidental drowning and submersion while in natural water**
- Accidental drowning and submersion while in lake
- Accidental drowning and submersion while in open sea
- Accidental drowning and submersion while in river
- Accidental drowning and submersion while in stream

> **Excludes1**   accidental drowning and submersion due to fall into natural body of water (W16.111, W16.121, W16.131)

The appropriate 7th character is to be added to code W69

A	initial encounter
D	subsequent encounter
S	sequela

X● **W73 Other specified cause of accidental non-transport drowning and submersion**
- Accidental drowning and submersion while in quenching tank
- Accidental drowning and submersion while in reservoir

> **Excludes1**   accidental drowning and submersion due to fall into other water (W16.311, W16.321, W16.331)

The appropriate 7th character is to be added to code W73

A	initial encounter
D	subsequent encounter
S	sequela

X● **W74 Unspecified cause of accidental drowning and submersion**
- Drowning NOS

The appropriate 7th character is to be added to code W74

A	initial encounter
D	subsequent encounter
S	sequela

EXPOSURE TO ELECTRIC CURRENT, RADIATION AND EXTREME AMBIENT AIR TEMPERATURE AND PRESSURE (W85-W99)

> **Excludes1**   exposure to:
>   failure in dosage of radiation or temperature during surgical and medical care (Y63.2-Y63.5)
>   lightning (T75.0-)
>   natural cold (X31)
>   natural heat (X30)
>   natural radiation NOS (X39)
>   radiological procedure and radiotherapy (Y84.2)
>   sunlight (X32)

X● **W85 Exposure to electric transmission lines**
- Broken power line

The appropriate 7th character is to be added to code W85

A	initial encounter
D	subsequent encounter
S	sequela

● **W86 Exposure to other specified electric current**

The appropriate 7th character is to be added to each code from category W86

A	initial encounter
D	subsequent encounter
S	sequela

- X● **W86.0 Exposure to domestic wiring and appliances**
- X● **W86.1 Exposure to industrial wiring, appliances and electrical machinery**
  - Exposure to conductors
  - Exposure to control apparatus
  - Exposure to electrical equipment and machinery
  - Exposure to transformers

▶ New   ⇒ Revised   ~~deleted~~ Deleted   Excludes 1   Excludes 2   Includes   Use additional   Code first   Code also   Key words

OGCR Official Guidelines   X Assign placeholder X   ● Use Additional Character(s)   ▶ Manifestation Code   🦚 Hierarchical Condition Category   Coding Clinic

X● **W86.8 Exposure to other electric current**
> Exposure to wiring and appliances in or on farm (not farmhouse)
> Exposure to wiring and appliances outdoors
> Exposure to wiring and appliances in or on public building
> Exposure to wiring and appliances in or on residential institutions
> Exposure to wiring and appliances in or on schools

● **W88 Exposure to ionizing radiation**
> **Excludes1** exposure to sunlight (X32)
>
> The appropriate 7th character is to be added to each code from category W88
>
> | | |
> |---|---|
> | A | initial encounter |
> | D | subsequent encounter |
> | S | sequela |

X● **W88.0 Exposure to X-rays**
X● **W88.1 Exposure to radioactive isotopes**
X● **W88.8 Exposure to other ionizing radiation**

● **W89 Exposure to man-made visible and ultraviolet light**
> **Includes** exposure to welding light (arc)
> **Excludes1** exposure to sunlight (X32)
> ▶ **Excludes2** exposure to sunlight (X32)
>
> The appropriate 7th character is to be added to each code from category W89
>
> | | |
> |---|---|
> | A | initial encounter |
> | D | subsequent encounter |
> | S | sequela |

X● **W89.0 Exposure to welding light (arc)**
X● **W89.1 Exposure to tanning bed**
X● **W89.8 Exposure to other man-made visible and ultraviolet light**
X● **W89.9 Exposure to unspecified man-made visible and ultraviolet light**

● **W90 Exposure to other nonionizing radiation**
> **Excludes1** exposure to sunlight (X32)
> ▶ **Excludes2** exposure to sunlight (X32)
>
> The appropriate 7th character is to be added to each code from category W90
>
> | | |
> |---|---|
> | A | initial encounter |
> | D | subsequent encounter |
> | S | sequela |

X● **W90.0 Exposure to radiofrequency**
X● **W90.1 Exposure to infrared radiation**
X● **W90.2 Exposure to laser radiation**
X● **W90.8 Exposure to other nonionizing radiation**

X● **W92 Exposure to excessive heat of man-made origin**
> The appropriate 7th character is to be added to code W92
>
> | | |
> |---|---|
> | A | initial encounter |
> | D | subsequent encounter |
> | S | sequela |

● **W93 Exposure to excessive cold of man-made origin**
> The appropriate 7th character is to be added to each code from category W93
>
> | | |
> |---|---|
> | A | initial encounter |
> | D | subsequent encounter |
> | S | sequela |

● **W93.0 Contact with or inhalation of dry ice**
X● **W93.01 Contact with dry ice**
X● **W93.02 Inhalation of dry ice**

● **W93.1 Contact with or inhalation of liquid air**
X● **W93.11 Contact with liquid air**
> Contact with liquid hydrogen
> Contact with liquid nitrogen
X● **W93.12 Inhalation of liquid air**
> Inhalation of liquid hydrogen
> Inhalation of liquid nitrogen
X● **W93.2 Prolonged exposure in deep freeze unit or refrigerator**
X● **W93.8 Exposure to other excessive cold of man-made origin**

● **W94 Exposure to high and low air pressure and changes in air pressure**
> The appropriate 7th character is to be added to each code from category W94
>
> | | |
> |---|---|
> | A | initial encounter |
> | D | subsequent encounter |
> | S | sequela |

X● **W94.0 Exposure to prolonged high air pressure**
● **W94.1 Exposure to prolonged low air pressure**
X● **W94.11 Exposure to residence or prolonged visit at high altitude**
X● **W94.12 Exposure to other prolonged low air pressure**
● **W94.2 Exposure to rapid changes in air pressure during ascent**
X● **W94.21 Exposure to reduction in atmospheric pressure while surfacing from deep-water diving**
X● **W94.22 Exposure to reduction in atmospheric pressure while surfacing from underground**
X● **W94.23 Exposure to sudden change in air pressure in aircraft during ascent**
X● **W94.29 Exposure to other rapid changes in air pressure during ascent**
● **W94.3 Exposure to rapid changes in air pressure during descent**
X● **W94.31 Exposure to sudden change in air pressure in aircraft during descent**
X● **W94.32 Exposure to high air pressure from rapid descent in water**
X● **W94.39 Exposure to other rapid changes in air pressure during descent**

X● **W99 Exposure to other man-made environmental factors**
> The appropriate 7th character is to be added to code W99
>
> | | |
> |---|---|
> | A | initial encounter |
> | D | subsequent encounter |
> | S | sequela |

EXPOSURE TO SMOKE, FIRE AND FLAMES (X00-X08)

Excludes1 arson (X97)
Excludes2 explosions (W35-W40)
> lightning (T75.0-)
> transport accident (V01-V99)

● **X00 Exposure to uncontrolled fire in building or structure**
> **Includes** conflagration in building or structure
> *Code first any associated cataclysm*
> **Excludes2** exposure to ignition or melting of nightwear (X05)
>> exposure to ignition or melting of other clothing and apparel (X06.-)
>> exposure to other specified smoke, fire and flames (X08.-)
>
> The appropriate 7th character is to be added to each code from category X00
>
> | | |
> |---|---|
> | A | initial encounter |
> | D | subsequent encounter |
> | S | sequela |

X● **X00.0 Exposure to flames in uncontrolled fire in building or structure**
> Coding Clinic: 2016, Q2, P5-6; 2015, Q1, P19
X● **X00.1 Exposure to smoke in uncontrolled fire in building or structure**

CHAPTER 20 (V00–Y99)

X ● **X00.2** **Injury due to collapse** of burning building or structure in uncontrolled fire

> **Excludes1** injury due to collapse of building not on fire (W20.1)

X ● **X00.3** **Fall from** burning building or structure in uncontrolled fire

X ● **X00.4** **Hit by object** from burning building or structure in uncontrolled fire

X ● **X00.5** **Jump from** burning building or structure in uncontrolled fire

X ● **X00.8** **Other** exposure to uncontrolled fire in building or structure

● **X01** **Exposure to uncontrolled fire, not in building or structure**

> **Includes** exposure to forest fire

The appropriate 7th character is to be added to each code from category X01

A	initial encounter
D	subsequent encounter
S	sequela

X ● **X01.0** **Exposure to flames** in uncontrolled fire, not in building or structure

X ● **X01.1** **Exposure to smoke** in uncontrolled fire, not in building or structure

X ● **X01.3** **Fall due** to uncontrolled fire, not in building or structure

X ● **X01.4** **Hit by object** due to uncontrolled fire, not in building or structure

X ● **X01.8** **Other** exposure to uncontrolled fire, not in building or structure

● **X02** **Exposure to controlled fire in building or structure**

> **Includes** exposure to fire in fireplace exposure to fire in stove

The appropriate 7th character is to be added to each code from category X02

A	initial encounter
D	subsequent encounter
S	sequela

X ● **X02.0** **Exposure to flames** in controlled fire in building or structure

X ● **X02.1** **Exposure to smoke** in controlled fire in building or structure

X ● **X02.2** **Injury due to collapse** of burning building or structure in controlled fire

> **Excludes1** injury due to collapse of building not on fire (W20.1)

X ● **X02.3** **Fall from** burning building or structure in controlled fire

X ● **X02.4** **Hit by object** from burning building or structure in controlled fire

X ● **X02.5** **Jump from** burning building or structure in controlled fire

X ● **X02.8** **Other** exposure to controlled fire in building or structure

● **X03** **Exposure to controlled fire, not in building or structure**

> **Includes** exposure to bon fire exposure to camp fire exposure to trash fire

The appropriate 7th character is to be added to each code from category X03

A	initial encounter
D	subsequent encounter
S	sequela

X ● **X03.0** **Exposure to flames** in controlled fire, not in building or structure

> Coding Clinic: 2015, Q1, P19

X ● **X03.1** **Exposure to smoke** in controlled fire, not in building or structure

X ● **X03.3** **Fall due** to controlled fire, not in building or structure

X ● **X03.4** **Hit by object** due to controlled fire, not in building or structure

X ● **X03.8** **Other** exposure to controlled fire, not in building or structure

X ● **X04** **Exposure to ignition of highly flammable material**
> Exposure to ignition of gasoline
> Exposure to ignition of kerosene
> Exposure to ignition of petrol

> **Excludes2** exposure to ignition or melting of nightwear (X05)
> exposure to ignition or melting of other clothing and apparel (X06)

The appropriate 7th character is to be added to code X04

A	initial encounter
D	subsequent encounter
S	sequela

Coding Clinic: 2016, Q2, P4

X ● **X05** **Exposure to ignition or melting of nightwear**

> **Excludes2** exposure to uncontrolled fire in building or structure (X00.-)
> exposure to uncontrolled fire, not in building or structure (X01.-)
> exposure to controlled fire in building or structure (X02.-)
> exposure to controlled fire, not in building or structure (X03.-)
> exposure to ignition of highly flammable materials (X04.-)

The appropriate 7th character is to be added to code X05

A	initial encounter
D	subsequent encounter
S	sequela

● **X06** **Exposure to ignition or melting of other clothing and apparel**

> **Excludes2** exposure to uncontrolled fire in building or structure (X00.-)
> exposure to uncontrolled fire, not in building or structure (X01.-)
> exposure to controlled fire in building or structure (X02.-)
> exposure to controlled fire, not in building or structure (X03.-)
> exposure to ignition of highly flammable materials (X04.-)

The appropriate 7th character is to be added to each code from category X06

A	initial encounter
D	subsequent encounter
S	sequela

X ● **X06.0** **Exposure to ignition** of plastic jewelry

X ● **X06.1** **Exposure to melting** of plastic jewelry

X ● **X06.2** **Exposure to ignition** of other clothing and apparel

X ● **X06.3** **Exposure to melting** of other clothing and apparel

● **X08** **Exposure to other specified smoke, fire and flames**

The appropriate 7th character is to be added to each code from category X08

A	initial encounter
D	subsequent encounter
S	sequela

● **X08.0** **Exposure to bed fire**
> Exposure to mattress fire

X ● **X08.00** **Exposure to bed fire due to unspecified** burning material

X ● **X08.01** **Exposure to bed fire due to burning cigarette**
> Coding Clinic: 2015, Q1, P19

X ● **X08.09** **Exposure to bed fire due to other** burning material

---

▶ New   ⇒ Revised   ~~deleted~~ Deleted   Excludes 1   Excludes 2   Includes   Use additional   Code first   Code also   Key words

OGCR Official Guidelines   X Assign placeholder X   ● Use Additional Character(s)   ▶ Manifestation Code   ℞ℂ Hierarchical Condition Category   Coding Clinic

● X08.1   **Exposure to sofa fire**
    X ● **X08.10**   **Exposure to sofa fire due to unspecified burning material**
    X ● **X08.11**   **Exposure to sofa fire due to burning cigarette**
    X ● **X08.19**   **Exposure to sofa fire due to other burning material**

● X08.2   **Exposure to other furniture fire**
    X ● **X08.20**   **Exposure to other furniture fire due to unspecified burning material**
    X ● **X08.21**   **Exposure to other furniture fire due to burning cigarette**
    X ● **X08.29**   **Exposure to other furniture fire due to other burning material**

X ● **X08.8**   **Exposure to other specified smoke, fire and flames**

CONTACT WITH HEAT AND HOT SUBSTANCES (X10-X19)

Excludes1   exposure to excessive natural heat (X30)
               exposure to fire and flames (X00-X08)

● X10   **Contact with hot drinks, food, fats and cooking oils**
    The appropriate 7th character is to be added to each code from category X10

A	initial encounter
D	subsequent encounter
S	sequela

X ● **X10.0**   **Contact with hot drinks**
X ● **X10.1**   **Contact with hot food**
X ● **X10.2**   **Contact with fats and cooking oils**

● X11   **Contact with hot tap-water**
    Includes   contact with boiling tap-water
                 contact with boiling water NOS
    Excludes1   contact with water heated on stove (X12)
    The appropriate 7th character is to be added to each code from category X11

A	initial encounter
D	subsequent encounter
S	sequela

X ● **X11.0**   **Contact with hot water in bath or tub**
     Excludes1   contact with running hot water in bath or tub (X11.1)
X ● **X11.1**   **Contact with running hot water**
     Contact with hot water running out of hose
     Contact with hot water running out of tap
X ● **X11.8**   **Contact with other hot tap-water**
     Contact with hot water in bucket
     Contact with hot tap-water NOS

X ● X12   **Contact with other hot fluids**
    Contact with water heated on stove
    Excludes1   hot (liquid) metals (X18)
    The appropriate 7th character is to be added to code X12

A	initial encounter
D	subsequent encounter
S	sequela

● X13   **Contact with steam and other hot vapors**
    The appropriate 7th character is to be added to each code from category X13

A	initial encounter
D	subsequent encounter
S	sequela

X ● **X13.0**   **Inhalation of steam and other hot vapors**
X ● **X13.1**   **Other contact with steam and other hot vapors**

● X14   **Contact with hot air and other hot gases**
    The appropriate 7th character is to be added to each code from category X14

A	initial encounter
D	subsequent encounter
S	sequela

X ● **X14.0**   **Inhalation of hot air and gases**
X ● **X14.1**   **Other contact with hot air and other hot gases**

● X15   **Contact with hot household appliances**
    Excludes1   contact with heating appliances (X16)
                contact with powered household appliances (W29.-)
                exposure to controlled fire in building or structure due to household appliance (X02.8)
                exposure to household appliances electrical current (W86.0)
    The appropriate 7th character is to be added to each code from category X15

A	initial encounter
D	subsequent encounter
S	sequela

X ● **X15.0**   **Contact with hot stove (kitchen)**
X ● **X15.1**   **Contact with hot toaster**
X ● **X15.2**   **Contact with hotplate**
X ● **X15.3**   **Contact with hot saucepan or skillet**
X ● **X15.8**   **Contact with other hot household appliances**
     Contact with cooker
     Contact with kettle
     Contact with light bulbs

X ● X16   **Contact with hot heating appliances, radiators and pipes**
    Excludes1   contact with powered appliances (W29.-)
                exposure to controlled fire in building or structure due to appliance (X02.8)
                exposure to industrial appliances electrical current (W86.1)
    The appropriate 7th character is to be added to code X16

A	initial encounter
D	subsequent encounter
S	sequela

X ● X17   **Contact with hot engines, machinery and tools**
    Excludes1   contact with hot heating appliances, radiators and pipes (X16)
                contact with hot household appliances (X15)
    The appropriate 7th character is to be added to code X17

A	initial encounter
D	subsequent encounter
S	sequela

X ● X18   **Contact with other hot metals**
    Contact with liquid metal
    The appropriate 7th character is to be added to code X18

A	initial encounter
D	subsequent encounter
S	sequela

X ● X19   **Contact with other heat and hot substances**
    Excludes1   objects that are not normally hot, e.g., an object made hot by a house fire (X00-X08)
    The appropriate 7th character is to be added to code X19

A	initial encounter
D	subsequent encounter
S	sequela

CHAPTER 20 (V00-Y99)

EXPOSURE TO FORCES OF NATURE (X30-X39)

X ● **X30**   **Exposure to excessive natural heat**
     Exposure to excessive heat as the cause of sunstroke
     Exposure to heat NOS

     Excludes1   excessive heat of man-made origin (W92)
                exposure to man-made radiation (W89)
                exposure to sunlight (X32)
                exposure to tanning bed (W89)

     The appropriate 7th character is to be added to code X30

A	initial encounter
D	subsequent encounter
S	sequela

X ● **X31**   **Exposure to excessive natural cold**
     Excessive cold as the cause of chilblains NOS
     Excessive cold as the cause of immersion foot or hand
     Exposure to cold NOS
     Exposure to weather conditions

     Excludes1   cold of man-made origin (W93.-)
                contact with or inhalation of dry ice (W93.-)
                contact with or inhalation of liquefied gas (W93.-)

     The appropriate 7th character is to be added to code X31

A	initial encounter
D	subsequent encounter
S	sequela

X ● **X32**   **Exposure to sunlight**

     Excludes1   man-made radiation (tanning bed) (W89)

     Excludes2   radiation-related disorders of the skin and
                subcutaneous tissue (L55-L59)

     The appropriate 7th character is to be added to code X32

A	initial encounter
D	subsequent encounter
S	sequela

X ● **X34**   **Earthquake**

     Excludes2   tidal wave (tsunami) due to earthquake (X37.41)

     The appropriate 7th character is to be added to code X34

A	initial encounter
D	subsequent encounter
S	sequela

X ● **X35**   **Volcanic eruption**

     Excludes2   tidal wave (tsunami) due to volcanic eruption
                (X37.41)

     The appropriate 7th character is to be added to code X35

A	initial encounter
D	subsequent encounter
S	sequela

● **X36**   **Avalanche, landslide and other earth movements**

     Includes   victim of mudslide of cataclysmic nature

     Excludes1   earthquake (X34)

     Excludes2   transport accident involving collision with
                avalanche or landslide not in motion
                (V01-V99)

     The appropriate 7th character is to be added to each code from
         category X36

A	initial encounter
D	subsequent encounter
S	sequela

X ● **X36.0**   **Collapse of dam or man-made structure causing earth movement**

X ● **X36.1**   **Avalanche, landslide, or mudslide**

● **X37**   **Cataclysmic storm**
     The appropriate 7th character is to be added to each code from
         category X37

A	initial encounter
D	subsequent encounter
S	sequela

X ● **X37.0**   **Hurricane**
     Storm surge   Typhoon

X ● **X37.1**   **Tornado**
     Cyclone   Twister

X ● **X37.2**   **Blizzard (snow) (ice)**

X ● **X37.3**   **Dust storm**

● **X37.4**   **Tidalwave**

     X ● **X37.41**   **Tidal wave due to earthquake or volcanic eruption**
              Tidal wave NOS
              Tsunami

     X ● **X37.42**   **Tidal wave due to storm**

     X ● **X37.43**   **Tidal wave due to landslide**

X ● **X37.8**   **Other cataclysmic storms**
     Cloudburst
     Torrential rain

     Excludes2   flood (X38)

X ● **X37.9**   **Unspecified cataclysmic storm**
     Storm NOS

     Excludes1   collapse of dam or man-made structure
                causing earth movement (X36.0)

X ● **X38**   **Flood**
     Flood arising from remote storm
     Flood of cataclysmic nature arising from melting snow
     Flood resulting directly from storm

     Excludes1   collapse of dam or man-made structure causing
                earth movement (X36.0)
                tidal wave NOS (X37.41)
                tidal wave caused by storm (X37.42)

     The appropriate 7th character is to be added to code X38

A	initial encounter
D	subsequent encounter
S	sequela

● **X39**   **Exposure to other forces of nature**
     The appropriate 7th character is to be added to each code from
         category X39

A	initial encounter
D	subsequent encounter
S	sequela

● **X39.0**   **Exposure to natural radiation**

     Excludes1   contact with and (suspected) exposure to
                radon and other naturally occurring
                radiation (Z77.123)
                exposure to man-made radiation
                (W88-W90)
                exposure to sunlight (X32)

     X ● **X39.01**   **Exposure to radon**

     X ● **X39.08**   **Exposure to other natural radiation**

X ● **X39.8**   **Other exposure to forces of nature**

▶ New   ⇒ Revised   ~~deleted~~ Deleted   Excludes 1   Excludes 2   Includes   Use additional   Code first   Code also   Key words

OGCR Official Guidelines   X Assign placeholder X   ● Use Additional Character(s)   ▶ Manifestation Code   HCC Hierarchical Condition Category   **Coding Clinic**

OVEREXERTION AND STRENUOUS OR REPETITIVE MOVEMENTS (X50)

X50   Overexertion and strenuous or repetitive movements

The appropriate 7th character is to be added to each code from category X50

> A   initial encounter
> D   subsequent encounter
> S   sequela

Coding Clinic: 2016, Q4, P73-74

X X50.0   Overexertion from strenuous movement or load
Lifting heavy objects
Lifting weights
Coding Clinic: 2016, Q4, P74

X X50.1   Overexertion from prolonged static or awkward postures
Prolonged bending
Prolonged kneeling
Prolonged reaching
Prolonged sitting
Prolonged standing
Prolonged twisting
Static bending
Static kneeling
Static reaching
Static sitting
Static standing
Static twisting

X X50.3   Overexertion from repetitive movements
Use of hand as hammer

> **Excludes2**   Overuse from prolonged static or awkward postures (X50.1)

Coding Clinic: 2016, Q4, P74

X X50.9   Other and unspecified overexertion or strenuous movements or postures
Contact pressure
Contact stress

ACCIDENTAL EXPOSURE TO OTHER SPECIFIED FACTORS (X52, X58)

X X52   Prolonged stay in weightless environment
Weightlessness in spacecraft (simulator)

The appropriate 7th character is to be added to code X52

> A   initial encounter
> D   subsequent encounter
> S   sequela

X X58   Exposure to other specified factors
Accident NOS
Exposure NOS

The appropriate 7th character is to be added to code X58

> A   initial encounter
> D   subsequent encounter
> S   sequela

INTENTIONAL SELF-HARM (X71-X83)

Purposely self-inflicted injury
Suicide (attempted)

X71   Intentional self-harm by drowning and submersion

The appropriate 7th character is to be added to each code from category X71

> A   initial encounter
> D   subsequent encounter
> S   sequela

X X71.0   Intentional self-harm by drowning and submersion while in bathtub A, D, S 🦻

X X71.1   Intentional self-harm by drowning and submersion while in swimming pool A, D, S 🦻

X X71.2   Intentional self-harm by drowning and submersion after jump into swimming pool A, D, S 🦻

X X71.3   Intentional self-harm by drowning and submersion in natural water A, D, S 🦻

X X71.8   Other intentional self-harm by drowning and submersion A, D, S 🦻

X X71.9   Intentional self-harm by drowning and submersion, unspecified A, D, S 🦻

X X72   Intentional self-harm by handgun discharge A, D, S 🦻
Intentional self-harm by gun for single hand use
Intentional self-harm by pistol
Intentional self-harm by revolver

> **Excludes1**   Very pistol (X74.8)

The appropriate 7th character is to be added to code X72

> A   initial encounter
> D   subsequent encounter
> S   sequela

X73   Intentional self-harm by rifle, shotgun and larger firearm discharge

> **Excludes1**   airgun (X74.01)

The appropriate 7th character is to be added to each code from category X73

> A   initial encounter
> D   subsequent encounter
> S   sequela

X X73.0   Intentional self-harm by shotgun discharge A, D, S 🦻

X X73.1   Intentional self-harm by hunting rifle discharge A, D, S 🦻

X X73.2   Intentional self-harm by machine gun discharge A, D, S 🦻

X X73.8   Intentional self-harm by other larger firearm discharge A, D, S 🦻

X X73.9   Intentional self-harm by unspecified larger firearm discharge A, D, S 🦻

X74   Intentional self-harm by other and unspecified firearm and gun discharge

The appropriate 7th character is to be added to each code from category X74

> A   initial encounter
> D   subsequent encounter
> S   sequela

X74.0   Intentional self-harm by gas, air or spring-operated guns

X X74.01   Intentional self-harm by airgun A, D, S 🦻
Intentional self-harm by BB gun discharge
Intentional self-harm by pellet gun discharge

X X74.02   Intentional self-harm by paintball gun A, D, S 🦻

X X74.09   Intentional self-harm by other gas, air or spring-operated gun A, D, S 🦻

X X74.8   Intentional self-harm by other firearm discharge A, D, S 🦻
Intentional self-harm by Very pistol [flare] discharge

X X74.9   Intentional self-harm by unspecified firearm discharge A, D, S 🦻

X X75   Intentional self-harm by explosive material A, D, S 🦻

The appropriate 7th character is to be added to code X75

> A   initial encounter
> D   subsequent encounter
> S   sequela

X X76   Intentional self-harm by smoke, fire and flames A, D, S 🦻

The appropriate 7th character is to be added to code X76

> A   initial encounter
> D   subsequent encounter
> S   sequela

CHAPTER 20 (V00-Y99)

CHAPTER 20 (V00-Y99)

● **X77**   **Intentional self-harm by steam, hot vapors and hot objects**

The appropriate 7th character is to be added to each code from category X77

A	initial encounter
D	subsequent encounter
S	sequela

X● **X77.0**   Intentional self-harm by steam or hot vapors A, D, S 🐾

X● **X77.1**   Intentional self-harm by hot tap water A, D, S 🐾

X● **X77.2**   Intentional self-harm by other hot fluids A, D, S 🐾

X● **X77.3**   Intentional self-harm by hot household appliances A, D, S 🐾

X● **X77.8**   Intentional self-harm by other hot objects A, D, S 🐾

X● **X77.9**   Intentional self-harm by unspecified hot objects A, D, S 🐾

● **X78**   **Intentional self-harm by sharp object**

The appropriate 7th character is to be added to each code from category X78

A	initial encounter
D	subsequent encounter
S	sequela

X● **X78.0**   Intentional self-harm by sharp glass A, D, S 🐾

X● **X78.1**   Intentional self-harm by knife A, D, S 🐾

X● **X78.2**   Intentional self-harm by sword or dagger A, D, S 🐾

X● **X78.8**   Intentional self-harm by other sharp object A, D, S 🐾

X● **X78.9**   Intentional self-harm by unspecified sharp object A, D, S 🐾

X● **X79**   **Intentional self-harm by blunt object A, D, S 🐾**

The appropriate 7th character is to be added to code X79

A	initial encounter
D	subsequent encounter
S	sequela

X● **X80**   **Intentional self-harm by jumping from a high place A, D, S 🐾**

Intentional fall from one level to another

The appropriate 7th character is to be added to code X80

A	initial encounter
D	subsequent encounter
S	sequela

● **X81**   **Intentional self-harm by jumping or lying in front of moving object**

The appropriate 7th character is to be added to each code from category X81

A	initial encounter
D	subsequent encounter
S	sequela

X● **X81.0**   Intentional self-harm by jumping or lying in front of motor vehicle A, D, S 🐾

X● **X81.1**   Intentional self-harm by jumping or lying in front of (subway) train A, D, S 🐾

X● **X81.8**   Intentional self-harm by jumping or lying in front of other moving object A, D, S 🐾

● **X82**   **Intentional self-harm by crashing of motor vehicle**

The appropriate 7th character is to be added to each code from category X82

A	initial encounter
D	subsequent encounter
S	sequela

X● **X82.0**   Intentional collision of motor vehicle with other motor vehicle A, D, S 🐾

X● **X82.1**   Intentional collision of motor vehicle with train A, D, S 🐾

X● **X82.2**   Intentional collision of motor vehicle with tree A, D, S 🐾

X● **X82.8**   Other intentional self-harm by crashing of motor vehicle A, D, S 🐾

● **X83**   **Intentional self-harm by other specified means**

> **Excludes1**   intentional self-harm by poisoning or contact with toxic substance - see Table of Drugs and Chemicals

The appropriate 7th character is to be added to each code from category X83

A	initial encounter
D	subsequent encounter
S	sequela

X● **X83.0**   Intentional self-harm by crashing of aircraft A, D, S 🐾

X● **X83.1**   Intentional self-harm by electrocution A, D, S 🐾

X● **X83.2**   Intentional self-harm by exposure to extremes of cold A, D, S 🐾

X● **X83.8**   Intentional self-harm by other specified means A, D, S 🐾

ASSAULT (X92-Y09)

> **Includes**   homicide injuries inflicted by another person with intent to injure or kill, by any means

> **Excludes1**   injuries due to legal intervention (Y35.-)
> injuries due to operations of war (Y36.-)
> injuries due to terrorism (Y38.-)

● **X92**   **Assault by drowning and submersion**

The appropriate 7th character is to be added to each code from category X92

A	initial encounter
D	subsequent encounter
S	sequela

X● **X92.0**   Assault by drowning and submersion while in bathtub

X● **X92.1**   Assault by drowning and submersion while in swimming pool

X● **X92.2**   Assault by drowning and submersion after push into swimming pool

X● **X92.3**   Assault by drowning and submersion in natural water

X● **X92.8**   Other assault by drowning and submersion

X● **X92.9**   Assault by drowning and submersion, unspecified

X● **X93**   **Assault by handgun discharge**

Assault by discharge of gun for single hand use

Assault by discharge of pistol

Assault by discharge of revolver

> **Excludes1**   Very pistol (X95.8)

The appropriate 7th character is to be added to code X93

A	initial encounter
D	subsequent encounter
S	sequela

● **X94**   **Assault by rifle, shotgun and larger firearm discharge**

> **Excludes1**   airgun (X95.01)

The appropriate 7th character is to be added to each code from category X94

A	initial encounter
D	subsequent encounter
S	sequela

X● **X94.0**   Assault by shotgun

X● **X94.1**   Assault by hunting rifle

X● **X94.2**   Assault by machine gun

X● **X94.8**   Assault by other larger firearm discharge

X● **X94.9**   Assault by unspecified larger firearm discharge

▶ New   ⇒ Revised   ~~deleted~~ Deleted   Excludes 1   Excludes 2   Includes   Use additional   Code first   Code also   Key words

1524   OGCR Official Guidelines   X Assign placeholder X   ● Use Additional Character(s)   ▶ Manifestation Code   🐾 Hierarchical Condition Category   **Coding Clinic**

● **X95 Assault by other and unspecified firearm and gun discharge**

The appropriate 7th character is to be added to each code from category X95

> A initial encounter
> D subsequent encounter
> S sequela

● **X95.0 Assault by gas, air or spring-operated guns**

X● **X95.01 Assault by airgun discharge**
> Assault by BB gun discharge
> Assault by pellet gun discharge

X● **X95.02 Assault by paintball gun discharge**

X● **X95.09 Assault by other gas, air or spring-operated gun**

X● **X95.8 Assault by other firearm discharge**
> Assault by very pistol [flare] discharge

X● **X95.9 Assault by unspecified firearm discharge**
> Coding Clinic: 2016, Q3, P24

● **X96 Assault by explosive material**

> **Excludes1** incendiary device (X97)
> terrorism involving explosive material (Y38.2-)

The appropriate 7th character is to be added to each code from category X96

> A initial encounter
> D subsequent encounter
> S sequela

X● **X96.0 Assault by antipersonnel bomb**

> **Excludes1** antipersonnel bomb use in military or war (Y36.2-)

X● **X96.1 Assault by gasoline bomb**

X● **X96.2 Assault by letter bomb**

X● **X96.3 Assault by fertilizer bomb**

X● **X96.4 Assault by pipe bomb**

X● **X96.8 Assault by other specified explosive**

X● **X96.9 Assault by unspecified explosive**

X● **X97 Assault by smoke, fire and flames**
> Assault by arson
> Assault by cigarettes
> Assault by incendiary device

The appropriate 7th character is to be added to code X97

> A initial encounter
> D subsequent encounter
> S sequela

● **X98 Assault by steam, hot vapors and hot objects**

The appropriate 7th character is to be added to each code from category X98

> A initial encounter
> D subsequent encounter
> S sequela

X● **X98.0 Assault by steam or hot vapors**

X● **X98.1 Assault by hot tap water**

X● **X98.2 Assault by hot fluids**

X● **X98.3 Assault by hot household appliances**

X● **X98.8 Assault by other hot objects**

X● **X98.9 Assault by unspecified hot objects**

● **X99 Assault by sharp object**

> **Excludes1** assault by strike by sports equipment (Y08.0-)

The appropriate 7th character is to be added to each code from category X99

> A initial encounter
> D subsequent encounter
> S sequela

X● **X99.0 Assault by sharp glass**

X● **X99.1 Assault by knife**

X● **X99.2 Assault by sword or dagger**

X● **X99.8 Assault by other sharp object**

X● **X99.9 Assault by unspecified sharp object**
> Assault by stabbing NOS

X● **Y00 Assault by blunt object**

> **Excludes1** assault by strike by sports equipment (Y08.0)

The appropriate 7th character is to be added to code Y00

> A initial encounter
> D subsequent encounter
> S sequela

X● **Y01 Assault by pushing from high place**

The appropriate 7th character is to be added to code Y01

> A initial encounter
> D subsequent encounter
> S sequela

● **Y02 Assault by pushing or placing victim in front of moving object**

The appropriate 7th character is to be added to each code from category Y02

> A initial encounter
> D subsequent encounter
> S sequela

X● **Y02.0 Assault by pushing or placing victim in front of motor vehicle**

X● **Y02.1 Assault by pushing or placing victim in front of (subway) train**

X● **Y02.8 Assault by pushing or placing victim in front of other moving object**

● **Y03 Assault by crashing of motor vehicle**

The appropriate 7th character is to be added to each code from category Y03

> A initial encounter
> D subsequent encounter
> S sequela

X● **Y03.0 Assault by being hit or run over by motor vehicle**

X● **Y03.8 Other assault by crashing of motor vehicle**

● **Y04 Assault by bodily force**

> **Excludes1** assault by:
> submersion (X92.-)
> use of weapon (X93-X95, X99, Y00)

The appropriate 7th character is to be added to each code from category Y04

> A initial encounter
> D subsequent encounter
> S sequela

X● **Y04.0 Assault by unarmed brawl or fight**

X● **Y04.1 Assault by human bite**

X● **Y04.2 Assault by strike against or bumped into by another person**

X● **Y04.8 Assault by other bodily force**
> Assault by bodily force NOS

OGCR   Section I.C.19.f.

Adult and child abuse, neglect and other maltreatment

Sequence first the appropriate code from categories T74 or T76 for abuse, neglect and other maltreatment, followed by any accompanying mental health or injury code(s).

If the documentation in the medical record states abuse or neglect it is coded as confirmed (T74.-). It is coded as suspected if it is documented as suspected (T76.-).

For cases of confirmed abuse or neglect an external cause code from the assault section (X92-Y09) should be added to identify the cause of any physical injuries. A perpetrator code (Y07) should be added when the perpetrator of the abuse is known. For suspected cases of abuse or neglect, do not report external cause or perpetrator code.

If a suspected case of abuse, neglect or mistreatment is ruled out during an encounter code Z04.71, Encounter for examination and observation following alleged physical adult abuse, ruled out, or code Z04.72, Encounter for examination and observation following alleged adult rape, should be used, not a code from T76.

If a suspected case of alleged rape or sexual abuse is ruled out during an encounter code Z04.41, Encounter for examination and observation following alleged adult rape or code Z04.42, Encounter for examination and observation following alleged child rape should be used, not a code from T76.

● **Y07   Perpetrator of assault, maltreatment and neglect**

     Note: Codes from this category are for use only in cases of confirmed abuse (T74.-)

         Selection of the correct perpetrator code is based on the relationship between the perpetrator and the victim

     Includes   perpetrator of abandonment
                  perpetrator of emotional neglect
                  perpetrator of mental cruelty
                  perpetrator of physical abuse
                  perpetrator of physical neglect
                  perpetrator of sexual abuse
                  perpetrator of torture

     Coding Clinic: 2016, Q4, P129

● **Y07.0   Spouse or partner, perpetrator of maltreatment and neglect**

         Spouse or partner, perpetrator of maltreatment and neglect against spouse or partner

     Y07.01   **Husband**, perpetrator of maltreatment and neglect

     Y07.02   **Wife**, perpetrator of maltreatment and neglect

     Y07.03   **Male partner**, perpetrator of maltreatment and neglect

     Y07.04   **Female partner**, perpetrator of maltreatment and neglect

● **Y07.1   Parent (adoptive) (biological), perpetrator of maltreatment and neglect**

     Y07.11   **Biological father**, perpetrator of maltreatment and neglect

     Y07.12   **Biological mother**, perpetrator of maltreatment and neglect

     Y07.13   **Adoptive father**, perpetrator of maltreatment and neglect

     Y07.14   **Adoptive mother**, perpetrator of maltreatment and neglect

● **Y07.4   Other family member, perpetrator of maltreatment and neglect**

     ● Y07.41   **Sibling**, perpetrator of maltreatment and neglect

         Excludes 1   stepsibling, perpetrator of maltreatment and neglect (Y07.435, Y07.436)

         Y07.410   **Brother**, perpetrator of maltreatment and neglect

         Y07.411   **Sister**, perpetrator of maltreatment and neglect

● Y07.42   **Foster parent**, perpetrator of maltreatment and neglect

     Y07.420   **Foster father**, perpetrator of maltreatment and neglect

     Y07.421   **Foster mother**, perpetrator of maltreatment and neglect

● Y07.43   **Stepparent or stepsibling**, perpetrator of maltreatment and neglect

     Y07.430   **Stepfather**, perpetrator of maltreatment and neglect

     Y07.432   **Male friend of parent** (co-residing in household), perpetrator of maltreatment and neglect

     Y07.433   **Stepmother**, perpetrator of maltreatment and neglect

     Y07.434   **Female friend of parent** (co-residing in household), perpetrator of maltreatment and neglect

     Y07.435   **Stepbrother**, perpetrator or maltreatment and neglect

     Y07.436   **Stepsister**, perpetrator of maltreatment and neglect

● Y07.49   **Other family member**, perpetrator of maltreatment and neglect

     Y07.490   **Male cousin**, perpetrator of maltreatment and neglect

     Y07.491   **Female cousin**, perpetrator of maltreatment and neglect

     Y07.499   **Other family member**, perpetrator of maltreatment and neglect

● **Y07.5   Non-family member, perpetrator of maltreatment and neglect**

     Y07.50   **Unspecified non-family member**, perpetrator of maltreatment and neglect

     ● Y07.51   **Daycare provider**, perpetrator of maltreatment and neglect

         Y07.510   **At-home childcare provider**, perpetrator of maltreatment and neglect

         Y07.511   **Daycare center childcare provider**, perpetrator of maltreatment and neglect

         Y07.512   **At-home adultcare provider**, perpetrator of maltreatment and neglect

         Y07.513   **Adultcare center provider**, perpetrator of maltreatment and neglect

         Y07.519   **Unspecified daycare provider**, perpetrator of maltreatment and neglect

     ● Y07.52   **Healthcare provider**, perpetrator of maltreatment and neglect

         Y07.521   **Mental health provider**, perpetrator of maltreatment and neglect

         Y07.528   **Other therapist or healthcare provider**, perpetrator of maltreatment and neglect

             Nurse perpetrator of maltreatment and neglect
             Occupational therapist perpetrator of maltreatment and neglect
             Physical therapist perpetrator of maltreatment and neglect
             Speech therapist perpetrator of maltreatment and neglect

         Y07.529   **Unspecified healthcare provider**, perpetrator of maltreatment and neglect

Y07.53   **Teacher or instructor, perpetrator of maltreatment and neglect**
       Coach, perpetrator of maltreatment and neglect

Y07.59   **Other non-family member, perpetrator of maltreatment and neglect**

Y07.6   **Multiple perpetrators of maltreatment and neglect**

Y07.9   **Unspecified perpetrator of maltreatment and neglect**

● **Y08**   **Assault by other specified means**

The appropriate 7th character is to be added to each code from category Y08

A	initial encounter
D	subsequent encounter
S	sequela

● **Y08.0**   **Assault by strike by sport equipment**
   X● **Y08.01**   **Assault by strike by hockey stick**
   X● **Y08.02**   **Assault by strike by baseball bat**
   X● **Y08.09**   **Assault by strike by other specified type of sport equipment**

● **Y08.8**   **Assault by other specified means**
   X● **Y08.81**   **Assault by crashing of aircraft**
   X● **Y08.89**   **Assault by other specified means**

● **Y09**   **Assault by unspecified means**
   Assassination (attempted) NOS
   Homicide (attempted) NOS
   Manslaughter (attempted) NOS
   Murder (attempted) NOS

EVENT OF UNDETERMINED INTENT (Y21-Y33)

Undetermined intent is only for use when there is specific documentation in the record that the intent of the injury cannot be determined. If no such documentation is present, code to accidental (unintentional)

● **Y21**   **Drowning and submersion, undetermined intent**

The appropriate 7th character is to be added to each code from category Y21

A	initial encounter
D	subsequent encounter
S	sequela

X● **Y21.0**   **Drowning and submersion while in bathtub, undetermined intent**

X● **Y21.1**   **Drowning and submersion after fall into bathtub, undetermined intent**

X● **Y21.2**   **Drowning and submersion while in swimming pool, undetermined intent**

X● **Y21.3**   **Drowning and submersion after fall into swimming pool, undetermined intent**

X● **Y21.4**   **Drowning and submersion in natural water, undetermined intent**

X● **Y21.8**   **Other drowning and submersion, undetermined intent**

X● **Y21.9**   **Unspecified drowning and submersion, undetermined intent**

X● **Y22**   **Handgun discharge, undetermined intent**
   Discharge of gun for single hand use, undetermined intent
   Discharge of pistol, undetermined intent
   Discharge of revolver, undetermined intent

   Excludes2   very pistol (Y24.8)

   The appropriate 7th character is to be added to code Y22

A	initial encounter
D	subsequent encounter
S	sequela

● **Y23**   **Rifle, shotgun and larger firearm discharge, undetermined intent**

   Excludes2   airgun (Y24.0)

The appropriate 7th character is to be added to each code from category Y23

A	initial encounter
D	subsequent encounter
S	sequela

X● **Y23.0**   **Shotgun discharge, undetermined intent**
X● **Y23.1**   **Hunting rifle discharge, undetermined intent**
X● **Y23.2**   **Military firearm discharge, undetermined intent**
X● **Y23.3**   **Machine gun discharge, undetermined intent**
X● **Y23.8**   **Other larger firearm discharge, undetermined intent**
X● **Y23.9**   **Unspecified larger firearm discharge, undetermined intent**

● **Y24**   **Other and unspecified firearm discharge, undetermined intent**

The appropriate 7th character is to be added to each code from category Y24

A	initial encounter
D	subsequent encounter
S	sequela

X● **Y24.0**   **Airgun discharge, undetermined intent**
   BB gun discharge, undetermined intent
   Pellet gun discharge, undetermined intent

X● **Y24.8**   **Other firearm discharge, undetermined intent**
   Paintball gun discharge, undetermined intent
   Very pistol [flare] discharge, undetermined intent

X● **Y24.9**   **Unspecified firearm discharge, undetermined intent**

X● **Y25**   **Contact with explosive material, undetermined intent**

The appropriate 7th character is to be added to code Y25

A	initial encounter
D	subsequent encounter
S	sequela

X● **Y26**   **Exposure to smoke, fire and flames, undetermined intent**

The appropriate 7th character is to be added to code Y26

A	initial encounter
D	subsequent encounter
S	sequela

● **Y27**   **Contact with steam, hot vapors and hot objects, undetermined intent**

The appropriate 7th character is to be added to each code from category Y27

A	initial encounter
D	subsequent encounter
S	sequela

X● **Y27.0**   **Contact with steam and hot vapors, undetermined intent**
X● **Y27.1**   **Contact with hot tap water, undetermined intent**
X● **Y27.2**   **Contact with hot fluids, undetermined intent**
X● **Y27.3**   **Contact with hot household appliance, undetermined intent**
X● **Y27.8**   **Contact with other hot objects, undetermined intent**
X● **Y27.9**   **Contact with unspecified hot objects, undetermined intent**

● **Y28 Contact with sharp object, undetermined intent**

The appropriate 7th character is to be added to each code from category Y28

> A   initial encounter
> D   subsequent encounter
> S   sequela

X● **Y28.0 Contact with sharp glass, undetermined intent**
X● **Y28.1 Contact with knife, undetermined intent**
X● **Y28.2 Contact with sword or dagger, undetermined intent**
X● **Y28.8 Contact with other sharp object, undetermined intent**
X● **Y28.9 Contact with unspecified sharp object, undetermined intent**

X● **Y29 Contact with blunt object, undetermined intent**

The appropriate 7th character is to be added to code Y29

> A   initial encounter
> D   subsequent encounter
> S   sequela

X● **Y30 Falling, jumping or pushed from a high place, undetermined intent**

Victim falling from one level to another, undetermined intent

The appropriate 7th character is to be added to code Y30

> A   initial encounter
> D   subsequent encounter
> S   sequela

X● **Y31 Falling, lying or running before or into moving object, undetermined intent**

The appropriate 7th character is to be added to code Y31

> A   initial encounter
> D   subsequent encounter
> S   sequela

X● **Y32 Crashing of motor vehicle, undetermined intent**

The appropriate 7th character is to be added to code Y32

> A   initial encounter
> D   subsequent encounter
> S   sequela

X● **Y33 Other specified events, undetermined intent**

The appropriate 7th character is to be added to code Y33

> A   initial encounter
> D   subsequent encounter
> S   sequela

LEGAL INTERVENTION, OPERATIONS OF WAR, MILITARY OPERATIONS, AND TERRORISM (Y35-Y38)

● **Y35 Legal intervention**

> **Includes**   any injury sustained as a result of an encounter with any law enforcement official, serving in any capacity at the time of the encounter, whether on-duty or off-duty. Includes: injury to law enforcement official, suspect and bystander

The appropriate 7th character is to be added to each code from category Y35

> A   initial encounter
> D   subsequent encounter
> S   sequela

● **Y35.0 Legal intervention involving firearm discharge**

● **Y35.00 Legal intervention involving unspecified firearm discharge**

> Legal intervention involving gunshot wound
> Legal intervention involving shot NOS

● **Y35.001 Legal intervention involving unspecified firearm discharge, law enforcement official injured**
● **Y35.002 Legal intervention involving unspecified firearm discharge, bystander injured**
● **Y35.003 Legal intervention involving unspecified firearm discharge, suspect injured**
● **Y35.009 Legal intervention involving unspecified firearm discharge, unspecified person injured**

● **Y35.01 Legal intervention involving injury by machine gun**

● **Y35.011 Legal intervention involving injury by machine gun, law enforcement official injured**
● **Y35.012 Legal intervention involving injury by machine gun, bystander injured**
● **Y35.013 Legal intervention involving injury by machine gun, suspect injured**
● **Y35.019 Legal intervention involving injury by machine gun, unspecified person injured**

● **Y35.02 Legal intervention involving injury by handgun**

● **Y35.021 Legal intervention involving injury by handgun, law enforcement official injured**
● **Y35.022 Legal intervention involving injury by handgun, bystander injured**
● **Y35.023 Legal intervention involving injury by handgun, suspect injured**
● **Y35.029 Legal intervention involving injury by handgun, unspecified person injured**

● **Y35.03 Legal intervention involving injury by rifle pellet**

● **Y35.031 Legal intervention involving injury by rifle pellet, law enforcement official injured**
● **Y35.032 Legal intervention involving injury by rifle pellet, bystander injured**
● **Y35.033 Legal intervention involving injury by rifle pellet, suspect injured**
● **Y35.039 Legal intervention involving injury by rifle pellet, unspecified person injured**

● **Y35.04 Legal intervention involving injury by rubber bullet**

● **Y35.041 Legal intervention involving injury by rubber bullet, law enforcement official injured**
● **Y35.042 Legal intervention involving injury by rubber bullet, bystander injured**
● **Y35.043 Legal intervention involving injury by rubber bullet, suspect injured**
● **Y35.049 Legal intervention involving injury by rubber bullet, unspecified person injured**

● **Y35.09 Legal intervention involving other firearm discharge**

● **Y35.091 Legal intervention involving other firearm discharge, law enforcement official injured**
● **Y35.092 Legal intervention involving other firearm discharge, bystander injured**
● **Y35.093 Legal intervention involving other firearm discharge, suspect injured**
● **Y35.099 Legal intervention involving other firearm discharge, unspecified person injured**

▶ New   ⟹ Revised   ~~deleted~~ Deleted   Excludes 1   Excludes 2   Includes   Use additional   Code first   Code also   Key words

OGCR Official Guidelines   X Assign placeholder X   ● Use Additional Character(s)   ▶ Manifestation Code   🄗 Hierarchical Condition Category   **Coding Clinic**

- Y35.1 **Legal intervention involving** explosives
  - Y35.10 **Legal intervention involving** unspecified explosives
    - Y35.101 **Legal intervention involving unspecified explosives,** law enforcement official injured
    - Y35.102 **Legal intervention involving unspecified explosives,** bystander injured
    - Y35.103 **Legal intervention involving unspecified explosives,** suspect injured
    - Y35.109 **Legal intervention involving unspecified explosives, unspecified person injured**
  - Y35.11 **Legal intervention involving injury by** dynamite
    - Y35.111 **Legal intervention involving injury by dynamite,** law enforcement official injured
    - Y35.112 **Legal intervention involving injury by dynamite,** bystander injured
    - Y35.113 **Legal intervention involving injury by dynamite,** suspect injured
    - Y35.119 **Legal intervention involving injury by dynamite, unspecified person injured**
  - Y35.12 **Legal intervention involving injury by** explosive shell
    - Y35.121 **Legal intervention involving injury by explosive shell,** law enforcement official injured
    - Y35.122 **Legal intervention involving injury by explosive shell,** bystander injured
    - Y35.123 **Legal intervention involving injury by explosive shell,** suspect injured
    - Y35.129 **Legal intervention involving other explosives, unspecified person injured**
  - Y35.19 **Legal intervention involving** other explosives
    Legal intervention involving injury by grenade
    Legal intervention involving injury by mortar bomb
    - Y35.191 **Legal intervention involving other explosives,** law enforcement official injured
    - Y35.192 **Legal intervention involving other explosives,** bystander injured
    - Y35.193 **Legal intervention involving other explosives,** suspect injured
    - Y35.199 **Legal intervention involving other explosives, unspecified person injured**
- Y35.2 **Legal intervention involving** gas
  Legal intervention involving asphyxiation by gas
  Legal intervention involving poisoning by gas
  - Y35.20 **Legal intervention involving** unspecified gas
    - Y35.201 **Legal intervention involving unspecified gas,** law enforcement official injured
    - Y35.202 **Legal intervention involving unspecified gas,** bystander injured
    - Y35.203 **Legal intervention involving unspecified gas,** suspect injured
    - Y35.209 **Legal intervention involving unspecified gas, unspecified person injured**

- Y35.21 **Legal intervention involving injury by** tear gas
  - Y35.211 **Legal intervention involving injury by tear gas,** law enforcement official injured
  - Y35.212 **Legal intervention involving injury by tear gas,** bystander injured
  - Y35.213 **Legal intervention involving injury by tear gas,** suspect injured
  - Y35.219 **Legal intervention involving injury by tear gas, unspecified person injured**
- Y35.29 **Legal intervention involving** other gas
  - Y35.291 **Legal intervention involving other gas,** law enforcement official injured
  - Y35.292 **Legal intervention involving other gas,** bystander injured
  - Y35.293 **Legal intervention involving other gas,** suspect injured
  - Y35.299 **Legal intervention involving other gas, unspecified person injured**
- Y35.3 **Legal intervention involving** blunt objects
  Legal intervention involving being hit or struck by blunt object
  - Y35.30 **Legal intervention involving** unspecified blunt objects
    - Y35.301 **Legal intervention involving unspecified blunt objects,** law enforcement official injured
    - Y35.302 **Legal intervention involving unspecified blunt objects,** bystander injured
    - Y35.303 **Legal intervention involving unspecified blunt objects,** suspect injured
    - Y35.309 **Legal intervention involving unspecified blunt objects, unspecified person injured**
  - Y35.31 **Legal intervention involving** baton
    - Y35.311 **Legal intervention involving baton,** law enforcement official injured
    - Y35.312 **Legal intervention involving baton,** bystander injured
    - Y35.313 **Legal intervention involving baton,** suspect injured
    - Y35.319 **Legal intervention involving baton, unspecified person injured**
  - Y35.39 **Legal intervention involving** other blunt objects
    - Y35.391 **Legal intervention involving other blunt objects,** law enforcement official injured
    - Y35.392 **Legal intervention involving other blunt objects,** bystander injured
    - Y35.393 **Legal intervention involving other blunt objects,** suspect injured
    - Y35.399 **Legal intervention involving other blunt objects, unspecified person injured**
- Y35.4 **Legal intervention involving** sharp objects
  Legal intervention involving being cut by sharp objects
  Legal intervention involving being stabbed by sharp objects
  - Y35.40 **Legal intervention involving** unspecified sharp objects
    - Y35.401 **Legal intervention involving unspecified sharp objects,** law enforcement official injured
    - Y35.402 **Legal intervention involving unspecified sharp objects,** bystander injured

● Y35.403   Legal intervention involving unspecified sharp objects, suspect injured

● Y35.409   Legal intervention involving unspecified sharp objects, unspecified person injured

● Y35.41   Legal intervention involving bayonet

● Y35.411   Legal intervention involving bayonet, law enforcement official injured

● Y35.412   Legal intervention involving bayonet, bystander injured

● Y35.413   Legal intervention involving bayonet, suspect injured

● Y35.419   Legal intervention involving bayonet, unspecified person injured

● Y35.49   Legal intervention involving other sharp objects

● Y35.491   Legal intervention involving other sharp objects, law enforcement official injured

● Y35.492   Legal intervention involving other sharp objects, bystander injured

● Y35.493   Legal intervention involving other sharp objects, suspect injured

● Y35.499   Legal intervention involving other sharp objects, unspecified person injured

● Y35.8   Legal intervention involving other specified means

● Y35.81   Legal intervention involving manhandling

● Y35.811   Legal intervention involving manhandling, law enforcement official injured

● Y35.812   Legal intervention involving manhandling, bystander injured

● Y35.813   Legal intervention involving manhandling, suspect injured

● Y35.819   Legal intervention involving manhandling, unspecified person injured

● Y35.83   Legal intervention involving a conducted energy device
    Electroshock device (taser)
    Stun gun

● Y35.831   Legal intervention involving a conducted energy device, law enforcement official injured

● Y35.832   Legal intervention involving a conducted energy device, bystander injured

● Y35.833   Legal intervention involving a conducted energy device, suspect injured

● Y35.839   Legal intervention involving a conducted energy device, unspecified person injured

● Y35.89   Legal intervention involving other specified means

● Y35.891   Legal intervention involving other specified means, law enforcement official injured

● Y35.892   Legal intervention involving other specified means, bystander injured

● Y35.893   Legal intervention involving other specified means, suspect injured
    Coding Clinic: 2018, Q1, P5

● Y35.9   Legal intervention, means unspecified

X ● Y35.91   Legal intervention, means unspecified, law enforcement official injured

X ● Y35.92   Legal intervention, means unspecified, bystander injured

X ● Y35.93   Legal intervention, means unspecified, suspect injured

X ● Y35.99   Legal intervention, means unspecified, unspecified person injured

● Y36   Operations of war

Includes	injuries to military personnel and civilians caused by war, civil insurrection, and peacekeeping missions
Excludes 1	injury to military personnel occurring during peacetime military operations (Y37.-) military vehicles involved in transport accidents with non-military vehicle during peacetime (V09.01, V09.21, V19.81, V29.81, V39.81, V49.81, V59.81, V69.81, V79.81)

The appropriate 7th character is to be added to each code from category Y36

A   initial encounter
D   subsequent encounter
S   sequela

● Y36.0   War operations involving explosion of marine weapons
    Weapons and military watercraft

● Y36.00   War operations involving explosion of unspecified marine weapon
    War operations involving underwater blast NOS

● Y36.000   War operations involving explosion of unspecified marine weapon, military personnel

● Y36.001   War operations involving explosion of unspecified marine weapon, civilian

● Y36.01   War operations involving explosion of depth-charge

● Y36.010   War operations involving explosion of depth-charge, military personnel

● Y36.011   War operations involving explosion of depth-charge, civilian

● Y36.02   War operations involving explosion of marine mine
    War operations involving explosion of marine mine, at sea or in harbor

● Y36.020   War operations involving explosion of marine mine, military personnel

● Y36.021   War operations involving explosion of marine mine, civilian

● Y36.03   War operations involving explosion of sea-based artillery shell

● Y36.030   War operations involving explosion of sea-based artillery shell, military personnel

● Y36.031   War operations involving explosion of sea-based artillery shell, civilian

● Y36.04   War operations involving explosion of torpedo

● Y36.040   War operations involving explosion of torpedo, military personnel

● Y36.041   War operations involving explosion of torpedo, civilian

▶ New   ⇒ Revised   ~~deleted~~ Deleted   Excludes 1   Excludes 2   Includes   Use additional   Code first   Code also   Key words

OGCR Official Guidelines   X Assign placeholder X   ● Use Additional Character(s)   ▶ Manifestation Code   🐾 Hierarchical Condition Category   Coding Clinic

● Y36.05   War operations involving accidental detonation of onboard marine weapons
- ● Y36.050   War operations involving accidental detonation of onboard marine weapons, military personnel
- ● Y36.051   War operations involving accidental detonation of onboard marine weapons, civilian

● Y36.09   War operations involving explosion of other marine weapons
- ● Y36.090   War operations involving explosion of other marine weapons, military personnel
- ● Y36.091   War operations involving explosion of other marine weapons, civilian

● Y36.1   War operations involving destruction of aircraft

● Y36.10   War operations involving unspecified destruction of aircraft
- ● Y36.100   War operations involving unspecified destruction of aircraft, military personnel
- ● Y36.101   War operations involving unspecified destruction of aircraft, civilian

● Y36.11   War operations involving destruction of aircraft due to enemy fire or explosives
> War operations involving destruction of aircraft due to air to air missile
> War operations involving destruction of aircraft due to explosive placed on aircraft
> War operations involving destruction of aircraft due to rocket propelled grenade [RPG]
> War operations involving destruction of aircraft due to small arms fire
> War operations involving destruction of aircraft due to surface to air missile
- ● Y36.110   War operations involving destruction of aircraft due to enemy fire or explosives, military personnel
- ● Y36.111   War operations involving destruction of aircraft due to enemy fire or explosives, civilian

● Y36.12   War operations involving destruction of aircraft due to collision with other aircraft
- ● Y36.120   War operations involving destruction of aircraft due to collision with other aircraft, military personnel
- ● Y36.121   War operations involving destruction of aircraft due to collision with other aircraft, civilian

● Y36.13   War operations involving destruction of aircraft due to onboard fire
- ● Y36.130   War operations involving destruction of aircraft due to onboard fire, military personnel
- ● Y36.131   War operations involving destruction of aircraft due to onboard fire, civilian

● Y36.14   War operations involving destruction of aircraft due to accidental detonation of onboard munitions and explosives
- ● Y36.140   War operations involving destruction of aircraft due to accidental detonation of onboard munitions and explosives, military personnel
- ● Y36.141   War operations involving destruction of aircraft due to accidental detonation of onboard munitions and explosives, civilian

● Y36.19   War operations involving other destruction of aircraft
- ● Y36.190   War operations involving other destruction of aircraft, military personnel
- ● Y36.191   War operations involving other destruction of aircraft, civilian

● Y36.2   War operations involving other explosions and fragments

> **Excludes1**   war operations involving explosion of aircraft (Y36.1-)
> war operations involving explosion of marine weapons (Y36.0-)
> war operations involving explosion of nuclear weapons (Y36.5-)
> war operations involving explosion occurring after cessation of hostilities (Y36.8-)

● Y36.20   War operations involving unspecified explosion and fragments
> War operations involving air blast NOS
> War operations involving blast NOS
> War operations involving blast fragments NOS
> War operations involving blast wave NOS
> War operations involving blast wind NOS
> War operations involving explosion NOS
> War operations involving explosion of bomb NOS
- ● Y36.200   War operations involving unspecified explosion and fragments, military personnel
- ● Y36.201   War operations involving unspecified explosion and fragments, civilian

● Y36.21   War operations involving explosion of aerial bomb
- ● Y36.210   War operations involving explosion of aerial bomb, military personnel
- ● Y36.211   War operations involving explosion of aerial bomb, civilian

● Y36.22   War operations involving explosion of guided missile
- ● Y36.220   War operations involving explosion of guided missile, military personnel
- ● Y36.221   War operations involving explosion of guided missile, civilian

● Y36.23   War operations involving explosion of improvised explosive device [IED]
> War operations involving explosion of person-borne improvised explosive device [IED]
> War operations involving explosion of vehicle-borne improvised explosive device [IED]
> War operations involving explosion of roadside improvised explosive device [IED]
- ● Y36.230   War operations involving explosion of improvised explosive device [IED], military personnel
- ● Y36.231   War operations involving explosion of improvised explosive device [IED], civilian

● Y36.24   War operations involving explosion due to accidental detonation and discharge of own munitions or munitions launch device
- ● Y36.240   War operations involving explosion due to accidental detonation and discharge of own munitions or munitions launch device, military personnel
- ● Y36.241   War operations involving explosion due to accidental detonation and discharge of own munitions or munitions launch device, civilian

CHAPTER 20 (V00-Y99)

● **Y36.25   War operations involving fragments from munitions**

   ● Y36.250   War operations involving fragments from munitions, military personnel

   ● Y36.251   War operations involving fragments from munitions, civilian

● **Y36.26   War operations involving fragments of improvised explosive device [IED]**

   War operations involving fragments of person-borne improvised explosive device [IED]

   War operations involving fragments of vehicle-borne improvised explosive device [IED]

   War operations involving fragments of roadside improvised explosive device [IED]

   ● Y36.260   War operations involving fragments of improvised explosive device [IED], military personnel

   ● Y36.261   War operations involving fragments of improvised explosive device [IED], civilian

● **Y36.27   War operations involving fragments from weapons**

   ● Y36.270   War operations involving fragments from weapons, military personnel

   ● Y36.271   War operations involving fragments from weapons, civilian

● **Y36.29   War operations involving other explosions and fragments**

   War operations involving explosion of grenade

   War operations involving explosions of land mine

   War operations involving shrapnel NOS

   ● Y36.290   War operations involving other explosions and fragments, military personnel

   ● Y36.291   War operations involving other explosions and fragments, civilian

● **Y36.3   War operations involving fires, conflagrations and hot substances**

   War operations involving smoke, fumes, and heat from fires, conflagrations and hot substances

   Excludes1   war operations involving fires and conflagrations aboard military aircraft (Y36.1-)

       war operations involving fires and conflagrations aboard military watercraft (Y36.0-)

       war operations involving fires and conflagrations caused indirectly by conventional weapons (Y36.2-)

       war operations involving fires and thermal effects of nuclear weapons (Y36.53-)

   ● Y36.30   War operations involving unspecified fire, conflagration and hot substance

      ● Y36.300   War operations involving unspecified fire, conflagration and hot substance, military personnel

      ● Y36.301   War operations involving unspecified fire, conflagration and hot substance, civilian

   ● Y36.31   War operations involving gasoline bomb

      War operations involving incendiary bomb

      War operations involving petrol bomb

      ● Y36.310   War operations involving gasoline bomb, military personnel

      ● Y36.311   War operations involving gasoline bomb, civilian

● **Y36.32   War operations involving incendiary bullet**

   ● Y36.320   War operations involving incendiary bullet, military personnel

   ● Y36.321   War operations involving incendiary bullet, civilian

● **Y36.33   War operations involving flamethrower**

   ● Y36.330   War operations involving flamethrower, military personnel

   ● Y36.331   War operations involving flamethrower, civilian

● **Y36.39   War operations involving other fires, conflagrations and hot substances**

   ● Y36.390   War operations involving other fires, conflagrations and hot substances, military personnel

   ● Y36.391   War operations involving other fires, conflagrations and hot substances, civilian

● **Y36.4   War operations involving firearm discharge and other forms of conventional warfare**

   ● Y36.41   War operations involving rubber bullets

      ● Y36.410   War operations involving rubber bullets, military personnel

      ● Y36.411   War operations involving rubber bullets, civilian

   ● Y36.42   War operations involving firearms pellets

      ● Y36.420   War operations involving firearms pellets, military personnel

      ● Y36.421   War operations involving firearms pellets, civilian

   ● Y36.43   War operations involving other firearms discharge

      War operations involving bullets NOS

      Excludes1   war operations involving munitions fragments (Y36.25-)

         war operations involving incendiary bullets (Y36.32-)

      ● Y36.430   War operations involving other firearms discharge, military personnel

      ● Y36.431   War operations involving other firearms discharge, civilian

   ● Y36.44   War operations involving unarmed hand to hand combat

      Excludes1   war operations involving combat using blunt or piercing object (Y36.45-)

         war operations involving intentional restriction of air and airway (Y36.46-)

         war operations involving unintentional restriction of air and airway (Y36.47-)

      ● Y36.440   War operations involving unarmed hand to hand combat, military personnel

      ● Y36.441   War operations involving unarmed hand to hand combat, civilian

   ● Y36.45   War operations involving combat using blunt or piercing object

      ● Y36.450   War operations involving combat using blunt or piercing object, military personnel

      ● Y36.451   War operations involving combat using blunt or piercing object, civilian

●**Y36.46**   War operations involving intentional restriction of air and airway

    ●**Y36.460**   War operations involving intentional restriction of air and airway, military personnel

    ●**Y36.461**   War operations involving intentional restriction of air and airway, civilian

●**Y36.47**   War operations involving unintentional restriction of air and airway

    ●**Y36.470**   War operations involving unintentional restriction of air and airway, military personnel

    ●**Y36.471**   War operations involving unintentional restriction of air and airway, civilian

●**Y36.49**   War operations involving other forms of conventional warfare

    ●**Y36.490**   War operations involving other forms of conventional warfare, military personnel

    ●**Y36.491**   War operations involving other forms of conventional warfare, civilian

●**Y36.5**   War operations involving nuclear weapons
    War operations involving dirty bomb NOS

    ●**Y36.50**   War operations involving unspecified effect of nuclear weapon

      ●**Y36.500**   War operations involving unspecified effect of nuclear weapon, military personnel

      ●**Y36.501**   War operations involving unspecified effect of nuclear weapon, civilian

    ●**Y36.51**   War operations involving direct blast effect of nuclear weapon
      War operations involving blast pressure of nuclear weapon

      ●**Y36.510**   War operations involving direct blast effect of nuclear weapon, military personnel

      ●**Y36.511**   War operations involving direct blast effect of nuclear weapon, civilian

    ●**Y36.52**   War operations involving indirect blast effect of nuclear weapon
      War operations involving being thrown by blast of nuclear weapon
      War operations involving being struck or crushed by blast debris of nuclear weapon

      ●**Y36.520**   War operations involving indirect blast effect of nuclear weapon, military personnel

      ●**Y36.521**   War operations involving indirect blast effect of nuclear weapon, civilian

    ●**Y36.53**   War operations involving thermal radiation effect of nuclear weapon
      War operations involving direct heat from nuclear weapon
      War operation involving fireball effects from nuclear weapon

      ●**Y36.530**   War operations involving thermal radiation effect of nuclear weapon, military personnel

      ●**Y36.531**   War operations involving thermal radiation effect of nuclear weapon, civilian

●**Y36.54**   War operation involving nuclear radiation effects of nuclear weapon
    War operation involving acute radiation exposure from nuclear weapon
    War operation involving exposure to immediate ionizing radiation from nuclear weapon
    War operation involving fallout exposure from nuclear weapon
    War operation involving secondary effects of nuclear weapons

    ●**Y36.540**   War operation involving nuclear radiation effects of nuclear weapon, military personnel

    ●**Y36.541**   War operation involving nuclear radiation effects of nuclear weapon, civilian

●**Y36.59**   War operation involving other effects of nuclear weapons

    ●**Y36.590**   War operation involving other effects of nuclear weapons, military personnel

    ●**Y36.591**   War operation involving other effects of nuclear weapons, civilian

●**Y36.6**   War operations involving biological weapons

    ●**Y36.6X**   War operations involving biological weapons

      ●**Y36.6X0**   War operations involving biological weapons, military personnel

      ●**Y36.6X1**   War operations involving biological weapons, civilian

●**Y36.7**   War operations involving chemical weapons and other forms of unconventional warfare

    Excludes1   war operations involving incendiary devices (Y36.3-, Y36.5-)

    ●**Y36.7X**   War operations involving chemical weapons and other forms of unconventional warfare

      ●**Y36.7X0**   War operations involving chemical weapons and other forms of unconventional warfare, military personnel

      ●**Y36.7X1**   War operations involving chemical weapons and other forms of unconventional warfare, civilian

●**Y36.8**   War operations occurring after cessation of hostilities
    War operations classifiable to categories Y36.0-Y36.8 but occurring after cessation of hostilities

    ●**Y36.81**   Explosion of mine placed during war operations but exploding after cessation of hostilities

      ●**Y36.810**   Explosion of mine placed during war operations but exploding after cessation of hostilities, military personnel

      ●**Y36.811**   Explosion of mine placed during war operations but exploding after cessation of hostilities, civilian

    ●**Y36.82**   Explosion of bomb placed during war operations but exploding after cessation of hostilities

      ●**Y36.820**   Explosion of bomb placed during war operations but exploding after cessation of hostilities, military personnel

      ●**Y36.821**   Explosion of bomb placed during war operations but exploding after cessation of hostilities, civilian

CHAPTER 20 (V00-Y99)

● **Y36.88**   Other war operations occurring after cessation of hostilities

    ● **Y36.880**   Other war operations occurring after cessation of hostilities, military personnel

    ● **Y36.881**   Other war operations occurring after cessation of hostilities, civilian

● **Y36.89**   Unspecified war operations occurring after cessation of hostilities

    ● **Y36.890**   Unspecified war operations occurring after cessation of hostilities, military personnel

    ● **Y36.891**   Unspecified war operations occurring after cessation of hostilities, civilian

● **Y36.9**   Other and unspecified war operations

  X ● **Y36.90**   War operations, unspecified

  X ● **Y36.91**   War operations involving unspecified weapon of mass destruction [WMD]

  X ● **Y36.92**   War operations involving friendly fire

● **Y37**   **Military operations**

    Includes   Injuries to military personnel and civilians occurring during peacetime on military property and during routine military exercises and operations

    Excludes1   military aircraft involved in aircraft accident with civilian aircraft (V97.81-)

          military vehicles involved in transport accident with civilian vehicle (V09.01, V09.21, V19.81, V29.81, V39.81, V49.81, V59.81, V69.81, V79.81)

          military watercraft involved in water transport accident with civilian watercraft (V94.81-)

          war operations (Y36.-)

The appropriate 7th character is to be added to each code from category Y37

A	initial encounter
D	subsequent encounter
S	sequela

● **Y37.0**   Military operations involving explosion of marine weapons

    ● **Y37.00**   Military operations involving explosion of unspecified marine weapon

       Military operations involving underwater blast NOS

      ● **Y37.000**   Military operations involving explosion of unspecified marine weapon, military personnel

      ● **Y37.001**   Military operations involving explosion of unspecified marine weapon, civilian

    ● **Y37.01**   Military operations involving explosion of depth-charge

      ● **Y37.010**   Military operations involving explosion of depth-charge, military personnel

      ● **Y37.011**   Military operations involving explosion of depth-charge, civilian

    ● **Y37.02**   Military operations involving explosion of marine mine

       Military operations involving explosion of marine mine, at sea or in harbor

      ● **Y37.020**   Military operations involving explosion of marine mine, military personnel

      ● **Y37.021**   Military operations involving explosion of marine mine, civilian

● **Y37.03**   Military operations involving explosion of sea-based artillery shell

    ● **Y37.030**   Military operations involving explosion of sea-based artillery shell, military personnel

    ● **Y37.031**   Military operations involving explosion of sea-based artillery shell, civilian

● **Y37.04**   Military operations involving explosion of torpedo

    ● **Y37.040**   Military operations involving explosion of torpedo, military personnel

    ● **Y37.041**   Military operations involving explosion of torpedo, civilian

● **Y37.05**   Military operations involving accidental detonation of onboard marine weapons

    ● **Y37.050**   Military operations involving accidental detonation of onboard marine weapons, military personnel

    ● **Y37.051**   Military operations involving accidental detonation of onboard marine weapons, civilian

● **Y37.09**   Military operations involving explosion of other marine weapons

    ● **Y37.090**   Military operations involving explosion of other marine weapons, military personnel

    ● **Y37.091**   Military operations involving explosion of other marine weapons, civilian

● **Y37.1**   Military operations involving destruction of aircraft

    ● **Y37.10**   Military operations involving unspecified destruction of aircraft

      ● **Y37.100**   Military operations involving unspecified destruction of aircraft, military personnel

      ● **Y37.101**   Military operations involving unspecified destruction of aircraft, civilian

    ● **Y37.11**   Military operations involving destruction of aircraft due to enemy fire or explosives

       Military operations involving destruction of aircraft due to air to air missile

       Military operations involving destruction of aircraft due to explosive placed on aircraft

       Military operations involving destruction of aircraft due to rocket propelled grenade [RPG]

       Military operations involving destruction of aircraft due to small arms fire

       Military operations involving destruction of aircraft due to surface to air missile

      ● **Y37.110**   Military operations involving destruction of aircraft due to enemy fire or explosives, military personnel

      ● **Y37.111**   Military operations involving destruction of aircraft due to enemy fire or explosives, civilian

    ● **Y37.12**   Military operations involving destruction of aircraft due to collision with other aircraft

      ● **Y37.120**   Military operations involving destruction of aircraft due to collision with other aircraft, military personnel

      ● **Y37.121**   Military operations involving destruction of aircraft due to collision with other aircraft, civilian

● **Y37.13** **Military operations involving destruction of aircraft due to onboard fire**
   ● **Y37.130** **Military operations involving destruction of aircraft due to onboard fire, military personnel**
   ● **Y37.131** **Military operations involving destruction of aircraft due to onboard fire, civilian**
● **Y37.14** **Military operations involving destruction of aircraft due to accidental detonation of onboard munitions and explosives**
   ● **Y37.140** **Military operations involving destruction of aircraft due to accidental detonation of onboard munitions and explosives, military personnel**
   ● **Y37.141** **Military operations involving destruction of aircraft due to accidental detonation of onboard munitions and explosives, civilian**
● **Y37.19** **Military operations involving other destruction of aircraft**
   ● **Y37.190** **Military operations involving other destruction of aircraft, military personnel**
   ● **Y37.191** **Military operations involving other destruction of aircraft, civilian**
● **Y37.2** **Military operations involving other explosions and fragments**

   Excludes1   military operations involving explosion of aircraft (Y37.1-)
               military operations involving explosion of marine weapons (Y37.0-)
               military operations involving explosion of nuclear weapons (Y37.5-)

● **Y37.20** **Military operations involving unspecified explosion and fragments**
   Military operations involving air blast NOS
   Military operations involving blast NOS
   Military operations involving blast fragments NOS
   Military operations involving blast wave NOS
   Military operations involving blast wind NOS
   Military operations involving explosion NOS
   Military operations involving explosion of bomb NOS
   ● **Y37.200** **Military operations involving unspecified explosion and fragments, military personnel**
   ● **Y37.201** **Military operations involving unspecified explosion and fragments, civilian**
● **Y37.21** **Military operations involving explosion of aerial bomb**
   ● **Y37.210** **Military operations involving explosion of aerial bomb, military personnel**
   ● **Y37.211** **Military operations involving explosion of aerial bomb, civilian**
● **Y37.22** **Military operations involving explosion of guided missile**
   ● **Y37.220** **Military operations involving explosion of guided missile, military personnel**
   ● **Y37.221** **Military operations involving explosion of guided missile, civilian**

● **Y37.23** **Military operations involving explosion of improvised explosive device [IED]**
   Military operations involving explosion of person-borne improvised explosive device [IED]
   Military operations involving explosion of vehicle-borne improvised explosive device [IED]
   Military operations involving explosion of roadside improvised explosive device [IED]
   ● **Y37.230** **Military operations involving explosion of improvised explosive device [IED], military personnel**
   ● **Y37.231** **Military operations involving explosion of improvised explosive device [IED], civilian**
● **Y37.24** **Military operations involving explosion due to accidental detonation and discharge of own munitions or munitions launch device**
   ● **Y37.240** **Military operations involving explosion due to accidental detonation and discharge of own munitions or munitions launch device, military personnel**
   ● **Y37.241** **Military operations involving explosion due to accidental detonation and discharge of own munitions or munitions launch device, civilian**
● **Y37.25** **Military operations involving fragments from munitions**
   ● **Y37.250** **Military operations involving fragments from munitions, military personnel**
   ● **Y37.251** **Military operations involving fragments from munitions, civilian**
● **Y37.26** **Military operations involving fragments of improvised explosive device [IED]**
   Military operations involving fragments of person-borne improvised explosive device [IED]
   Military operations involving fragments of vehicle-borne improvised explosive device [IED]
   Military operations involving fragments of roadside improvised explosive device [IED]
   ● **Y37.260** **Military operations involving fragments of improvised explosive device [IED], military personnel**
   ● **Y37.261** **Military operations involving fragments of improvised explosive device [IED], civilian**
● **Y37.27** **Military operations involving fragments from weapons**
   ● **Y37.270** **Military operations involving fragments from weapons, military personnel**
   ● **Y37.271** **Military operations involving fragments from weapons, civilian**
● **Y37.29** **Military operations involving other explosions and fragments**
   Military operations involving explosion of grenade
   Military operations involving explosions of land mine
   Military operations involving shrapnel NOS
   ● **Y37.290** **Military operations involving other explosions and fragments, military personnel**
   ● **Y37.291** **Military operations involving other explosions and fragments, civilian**

CHAPTER 20 (V00-Y99)

● **Y37.3 Military operations involving fires, conflagrations and hot substances**

Military operations involving smoke, fumes, and heat from fires, conflagrations and hot substances

Excludes1 military operations involving fires and conflagrations aboard military aircraft (Y37.1-)
military operations involving fires and conflagrations aboard military watercraft (Y37.0-)
military operations involving fires and conflagrations caused indirectly by conventional weapons (Y37.2-)
military operations involving fires and thermal effects of nuclear weapons (Y36.53-)

● **Y37.30 Military operations involving unspecified fire, conflagration and hot substance**

● **Y37.300 Military operations involving unspecified fire, conflagration and hot substance, military personnel**

● **Y37.301 Military operations involving unspecified fire, conflagration and hot substance, civilian**

● **Y37.31 Military operations involving gasoline bomb**

Military operations involving incendiary bomb
Military operations involving petrol bomb

● **Y37.310 Military operations involving gasoline bomb, military personnel**

● **Y37.311 Military operations involving gasoline bomb, civilian**

● **Y37.32 Military operations involving incendiary bullet**

● **Y37.320 Military operations involving incendiary bullet, military personnel**

● **Y37.321 Military operations involving incendiary bullet, civilian**

● **Y37.33 Military operations involving flamethrower**

● **Y37.330 Military operations involving flamethrower, military personnel**

● **Y37.331 Military operations involving flamethrower, civilian**

● **Y37.39 Military operations involving other fires, conflagrations and hot substances**

● **Y37.390 Military operations involving other fires, conflagrations and hot substances, military personnel**

● **Y37.391 Military operations involving other fires, conflagrations and hot substances, civilian**

● **Y37.4 Military operations involving firearm discharge and other forms of conventional warfare**

● **Y37.41 Military operations involving rubber bullets**

● **Y37.410 Military operations involving rubber bullets, military personnel**

● **Y37.411 Military operations involving rubber bullets, civilian**

● **Y37.42 Military operations involving firearms pellets**

● **Y37.420 Military operations involving firearms pellets, military personnel**

● **Y37.421 Military operations involving firearms pellets, civilian**

● **Y37.43 Military operations involving other firearms discharge**

Military operations involving bullets NOS

Excludes1 military operations involving munitions fragments (Y37.25-)
military operations involving incendiary bullets (Y37.32-)

● **Y37.430 Military operations involving other firearms discharge, military personnel**

● **Y37.431 Military operations involving other firearms discharge, civilian**

● **Y37.44 Military operations involving unarmed hand to hand combat**

Excludes1 military operations involving combat using blunt or piercing object (Y37.45-)
military operations involving intentional restriction of air and airway (Y37.46-)
military operations involving unintentional restriction of air and airway (Y37.47-)

● **Y37.440 Military operations involving unarmed hand to hand combat, military personnel**

● **Y37.441 Military operations involving unarmed hand to hand combat, civilian**

● **Y37.45 Military operations involving combat using blunt or piercing object**

● **Y37.450 Military operations involving combat using blunt or piercing object, military personnel**

● **Y37.451 Military operations involving combat using blunt or piercing object, civilian**

● **Y37.46 Military operations involving intentional restriction of air and airway**

● **Y37.460 Military operations involving intentional restriction of air and airway, military personnel**

● **Y37.461 Military operations involving intentional restriction of air and airway, civilian**

● **Y37.47 Military operations involving unintentional restriction of air and airway**

● **Y37.470 Military operations involving unintentional restriction of air and airway, military personnel**

● **Y37.471 Military operations involving unintentional restriction of air and airway, civilian**

● **Y37.49 Military operations involving other forms of conventional warfare**

● **Y37.490 Military operations involving other forms of conventional warfare, military personnel**

● **Y37.491 Military operations involving other forms of conventional warfare, civilian**

● **Y37.5 Military operations involving nuclear weapons**

Military operation involving dirty bomb NOS

● **Y37.50 Military operations involving unspecified effect of nuclear weapon**

● **Y37.500 Military operations involving unspecified effect of nuclear weapon, military personnel**

● **Y37.501 Military operations involving unspecified effect of nuclear weapon, civilian**

● **Y37.51 Military operations involving direct blast effect of nuclear weapon**

Military operations involving blast pressure of nuclear weapon

● **Y37.510 Military operations involving direct blast effect of nuclear weapon, military personnel**

● **Y37.511 Military operations involving direct blast effect of nuclear weapon, civilian**

CHAPTER 20 (V00-Y99)

▶ New ⟫ Revised ~~deleted~~ Deleted Excludes 1 Excludes 2 Includes Use additional Code first Code also Key words
OGCR Official Guidelines X Assign placeholder X ● Use Additional Character(s) ▷ Manifestation Code ᴿᴄ Hierarchical Condition Category Coding Clinic

● **Y37.52** **Military operations involving indirect blast effect of nuclear weapon**
  Military operations involving being thrown by blast of nuclear weapon
  Military operations involving being struck or crushed by blast debris of nuclear weapon

 ● **Y37.520** **Military operations involving indirect blast effect of nuclear weapon, military personnel**

 ● **Y37.521** **Military operations involving indirect blast effect of nuclear weapon, civilian**

● **Y37.53** **Military operations involving thermal radiation effect of nuclear weapon**
  Military operations involving direct heat from nuclear weapon
  Military operation involving fireball effects from nuclear weapon

 ● **Y37.530** **Military operations involving thermal radiation effect of nuclear weapon, military personnel**

 ● **Y37.531** **Military operations involving thermal radiation effect of nuclear weapon, civilian**

● **Y37.54** **Military operation involving nuclear radiation effects of nuclear weapon**
  Military operation involving acute radiation exposure from nuclear weapon
  Military operation involving exposure to immediate ionizing radiation from nuclear weapon
  Military operation involving fallout exposure from nuclear weapon
  Military operation involving secondary effects of nuclear weapons

 ● **Y37.540** **Military operation involving nuclear radiation effects of nuclear weapon, military personnel**

 ● **Y37.541** **Military operation involving nuclear radiation effects of nuclear weapon, civilian**

● **Y37.59** **Military operation involving other effects of nuclear weapons**

 ● **Y37.590** **Military operation involving other effects of nuclear weapons, military personnel**

 ● **Y37.591** **Military operation involving other effects of nuclear weapons, civilian**

● **Y37.6** **Military operations involving biological weapons**

 ● **Y37.6X** **Military operations involving biological weapons**

  ● **Y37.6X0** **Military operations involving biological weapons, military personnel**

  ● **Y37.6X1** **Military operations involving biological weapons, civilian**

● **Y37.7** **Military operations involving chemical weapons and other forms of unconventional warfare**
  Excludes1 military operations involving incendiary devices (Y36.3-, Y36.5-)

 ● **Y37.7X** **Military operations involving chemical weapons and other forms of unconventional warfare**

  ● **Y37.7X0** **Military operations involving chemical weapons and other forms of unconventional warfare, military personnel**

  ● **Y37.7X1** **Military operations involving chemical weapons and other forms of unconventional warfare, civilian**

● **Y37.9** **Other and unspecified military operations**

 X ● **Y37.90** **Military operations, unspecified**

 X ● **Y37.91** **Military operations involving unspecified weapon of mass destruction [WMD]**

 X ● **Y37.92** **Military operations involving friendly fire**

● **Y38** **Terrorism**
 These codes are for use to identify injuries resulting from the unlawful use of force or violence against persons or property to intimidate or coerce a government, the civilian population, or any segment thereof, in furtherance of political or social objective
 Use additional code for place of occurrence (Y92.-)
 The appropriate 7th character is to be added to each code from category Y38

A	initial encounter
D	subsequent encounter
S	sequela

● **Y38.0** **Terrorism involving explosion of marine weapons**
  Terrorism involving depth-charge
  Terrorism involving marine mine
  Terrorism involving mine NOS, at sea or in harbor
  Terrorism involving sea-based artillery shell
  Terrorism involving torpedo
  Terrorism involving underwater blast

 ● **Y38.0X** **Terrorism involving explosion of marine weapons**

  ● **Y38.0X1** **Terrorism involving explosion of marine weapons, public safety official injured**

  ● **Y38.0X2** **Terrorism involving explosion of marine weapons, civilian injured**

  ● **Y38.0X3** **Terrorism involving explosion of marine weapons, terrorist injured**

● **Y38.1** **Terrorism involving destruction of aircraft**
  Terrorism involving aircraft burned
  Terrorism involving aircraft exploded
  Terrorism involving aircraft being shot down
  Terrorism involving aircraft used as a weapon

 ● **Y38.1X** **Terrorism involving destruction of aircraft**

  ● **Y38.1X1** **Terrorism involving destruction of aircraft, public safety official injured**

  ● **Y38.1X2** **Terrorism involving destruction of aircraft, civilian injured**

  ● **Y38.1X3** **Terrorism involving destruction of aircraft, terrorist injured**

● **Y38.2** **Terrorism involving other explosions and fragments**
  Terrorism involving antipersonnel (fragments) bomb
  Terrorism involving blast NOS
  Terrorism involving explosion NOS
  Terrorism involving explosion of breech block
  Terrorism involving explosion of cannon block
  Terrorism involving explosion (fragments) of artillery shell
  Terrorism involving explosion (fragments) of bomb
  Terrorism involving explosion (fragments) of grenade
  Terrorism involving explosion (fragments) of guided missile
  Terrorism involving explosion (fragments) of land mine
  Terrorism involving explosion of mortar bomb
  Terrorism involving explosion of munitions
  Terrorism involving explosion (fragments) of rocket
  Terrorism involving explosion (fragments) of shell
  Terrorism involving shrapnel
  Terrorism involving mine NOS, on land
  Excludes1 terrorism involving explosion of nuclear weapon (Y38.5)
   terrorism involving suicide bomber (Y38.81)

 ● **Y38.2X** **Terrorism involving other explosions and fragments**

  ● **Y38.2X1** **Terrorism involving other explosions and fragments, public safety official injured**

  ● **Y38.2X2** **Terrorism involving other explosions and fragments, civilian injured**

  ● **Y38.2X3** **Terrorism involving other explosions and fragments, terrorist injured**

● **Y38.3** **Terrorism involving fires, conflagration and hot substances**
Terrorism involving conflagration NOS
Terrorism involving fire NOS
Terrorism involving petrol bomb
Excludes1 terrorism involving fire or heat of nuclear weapon (Y38.5)

● **Y38.3X** **Terrorism involving fires, conflagration and hot substances**

● **Y38.3X1** Terrorism involving fires, conflagration and hot substances, public safety official injured

● **Y38.3X2** Terrorism involving fires, conflagration and hot substances, civilian injured

● **Y38.3X3** Terrorism involving fires, conflagration and hot substances, terrorist injured

● **Y38.4** **Terrorism involving firearms**
Terrorism involving carbine bullet
Terrorism involving machine gun bullet
Terrorism involving pellets (shotgun)
Terrorism involving pistol bullet
Terrorism involving rifle bullet
Terrorism involving rubber (rifle) bullet

● **Y38.4X** **Terrorism involving firearms**

● **Y38.4X1** Terrorism involving firearms, public safety official injured

● **Y38.4X2** Terrorism involving firearms, civilian injured

● **Y38.4X3** Terrorism involving firearms, terrorist injured

● **Y38.5** **Terrorism involving nuclear weapons**
Terrorism involving blast effects of nuclear weapon
Terrorism involving exposure to ionizing radiation from nuclear weapon
Terrorism involving fireball effect of nuclear weapon
Terrorism involving heat from nuclear weapon

● **Y38.5X** **Terrorism involving nuclear weapons**

● **Y38.5X1** Terrorism involving nuclear weapons, public safety official injured

● **Y38.5X2** Terrorism involving nuclear weapons, civilian injured

● **Y38.5X3** Terrorism involving nuclear weapons, terrorist injured

● **Y38.6** **Terrorism involving biological weapons**
Terrorism involving anthrax
Terrorism involving cholera
A serious, often deadly, infectious disease of the small intestine
Terrorism involving smallpox

● **Y38.6X** **Terrorism involving biological weapons**

● **Y38.6X1** Terrorism involving biological weapons, public safety official injured

● **Y38.6X2** Terrorism involving biological weapons, civilian injured

● **Y38.6X3** Terrorism involving biological weapons, terrorist injured

● **Y38.7** **Terrorism involving chemical weapons**
Terrorism involving gases, fumes, chemicals
Terrorism involving hydrogen cyanide
Terrorism involving phosgene
Terrorism involving sarin

● **Y38.7X** **Terrorism involving chemical weapons**

● **Y38.7X1** Terrorism involving chemical weapons, public safety official injured

● **Y38.7X2** Terrorism involving chemical weapons, civilian injured

● **Y38.7X3** Terrorism involving chemical weapons, terrorist injured

● **Y38.8** **Terrorism involving other and unspecified means**

● **Y38.80** **Terrorism involving unspecified means**
Terrorism NOS

● **Y38.81** **Terrorism involving suicide bomber**

● **Y38.811** Terrorism involving suicide bomber, public safety official injured

● **Y38.812** Terrorism involving suicide bomber, civilian injured

● **Y38.89** **Terrorism involving other means**
Terrorism involving drowning and submersion
Terrorism involving lasers
Terrorism involving piercing or stabbing instruments

● **Y38.891** Terrorism involving other means, public safety official injured

● **Y38.892** Terrorism involving other means, civilian injured

● **Y38.893** Terrorism involving other means, terrorist injured

● **Y38.9** **Terrorism, secondary effects**
Note: This code is for use to identify conditions occurring subsequent to a terrorist attack not those that are due to the initial terrorist attack.

● **Y38.9X** **Terrorism, secondary effects**

● **Y38.9X1** Terrorism, secondary effects, public safety official injured

● **Y38.9X2** Terrorism, secondary effects, civilian injured categories

COMPLICATIONS OF MEDICAL AND SURGICAL CARE (Y62-Y84)

Includes complications of medical devices surgical and medical procedures as the cause of abnormal reaction of the patient, or of later complication, without mention of misadventure at the time of the procedure

MISADVENTURES TO PATIENTS DURING SURGICAL AND MEDICAL CARE (Y62-Y69)

Excludes1 surgical and medical procedures as the cause of abnormal reaction of the patient, without mention of misadventure at the time of the procedure (Y83-Y84)

● **Y62** **Failure of sterile precautions during surgical and medical care**

Y62.0 Failure of sterile precautions during surgical operation

Y62.1 Failure of sterile precautions during infusion or transfusion

Y62.2 Failure of sterile precautions during kidney dialysis and other perfusion 🔥

Y62.3 Failure of sterile precautions during injection or immunization

Y62.4 Failure of sterile precautions during endoscopic examination

Y62.5 Failure of sterile precautions during heart catheterization

Y62.6 Failure of sterile precautions during aspiration, puncture and other catheterization

Y62.8 Failure of sterile precautions during other surgical and medical care

Y62.9 Failure of sterile precautions during unspecified surgical and medical care

● **Y63** **Failure in dosage during surgical and medical care**
Excludes2 accidental overdose of drug or wrong drug given in error (T36-T50)

Y63.0 Excessive amount of blood or other fluid given during transfusion or infusion

Y63.1 Incorrect dilution of fluid used during infusion

Y63.2 Overdose of radiation given during therapy

▶ New ➠ Revised ~~deleted~~ Deleted Excludes 1 Excludes 2 Includes Use additional Code first Code also Key words

1538 OGCR Official Guidelines X Assign placeholder X ● Use Additional Character(s) ▶ Manifestation Code 🔥 Hierarchical Condition Category **Coding Clinic**

Y63.3   Inadvertent exposure of patient to radiation during medical care

Y63.4   Failure in dosage in electroshock or insulin-shock therapy

Y63.5   Inappropriate temperature in local application and packing

Y63.6   Underdosing and nonadministration of necessary drug, medicament or biological substance

Y63.8   Failure in dosage during other surgical and medical care

Y63.9   Failure in dosage during unspecified surgical and medical care

● **Y64**   Contaminated medical or biological substances

Y64.0   Contaminated medical or biological substance, transfused or infused

Y64.1   Contaminated medical or biological substance, injected or used for immunization

Y64.8   Contaminated medical or biological substance administered by other means

Y64.9   Contaminated medical or biological substance administered by unspecified means
Administered contaminated medical or biological substance NOS

● **Y65**   Other misadventures during surgical and medical care

Y65.0   Mismatched blood in transfusion

Y65.1   Wrong fluid used in infusion

Y65.2   Failure in suture or ligature during surgical operation

Y65.3   Endotracheal tube wrongly placed during anesthetic procedure

Y65.4   Failure to introduce or to remove other tube or instrument

● **Y65.5**   Performance of wrong procedure (operation)

   ● **Y65.51**   Performance of wrong procedure (operation) on correct patient
Wrong device implanted into correct surgical site

     Excludes1   performance of correct procedure (operation) on wrong side or body part (Y65.53)

   ● **Y65.52**   Performance of procedure (operation) on patient not scheduled for surgery
Performance of procedure (operation) intended for another patient
Performance of procedure (operation) on wrong patient

   ● **Y65.53**   Performance of correct procedure (operation) on wrong side or body part
Performance of correct procedure (operation) on wrong side
Performance of correct procedure (operation) on wrong site

Y65.8   Other specified misadventures during surgical and medical care
Coding Clinic: 2019, Q2, P24

Y66   Nonadministration of surgical and medical care
Premature cessation of surgical and medical care

     Excludes1   DNR status (Z66)
palliative care (Z51.5)

Y69   Unspecified misadventure during surgical and medical care

---

MEDICAL DEVICES ASSOCIATED WITH ADVERSE INCIDENTS IN DIAGNOSTIC AND THERAPEUTIC USE (Y70-Y82)

Includes   breakdown or malfunction of medical devices (during use) (after implantation) (ongoing use)

Excludes2   later complications following use of medical devices without breakdown or malfunctioning of device (Y83-Y84)
misadventure to patients during surgical and medical care, classifiable to (Y62-Y69)
surgical and other medical procedures as the cause of abnormal reaction of the patient, or of later complication, without mention of misadventure at the time of the procedure (Y83-Y84)

● **Y70**   Anesthesiology devices associated with adverse incidents

Y70.0   Diagnostic and monitoring anesthesiology devices associated with adverse incidents

Y70.1   Therapeutic (nonsurgical) and rehabilitative anesthesiology devices associated with adverse incidents

Y70.2   Prosthetic and other implants, materials and accessory anesthesiology devices associated with adverse incidents

Y70.3   Surgical instruments, materials and anesthesiology devices (including sutures) associated with adverse incidents

Y70.8   Miscellaneous anesthesiology devices associated with adverse incidents, not elsewhere classified

● **Y71**   Cardiovascular devices associated with adverse incidents

Y71.0   Diagnostic and monitoring cardiovascular devices associated with adverse incidents

Y71.1   Therapeutic (nonsurgical) and rehabilitative cardiovascular devices associated with adverse incidents

Y71.2   Prosthetic and other implants, materials and accessory cardiovascular devices associated with adverse incidents

Y71.3   Surgical instruments, materials and cardiovascular devices (including sutures) associated with adverse incidents

Y71.8   Miscellaneous cardiovascular devices associated with adverse incidents, not elsewhere classified

● **Y72**   Otorhinolaryngological devices associated with adverse incidents

Y72.0   Diagnostic and monitoring otorhinolaryngological devices associated with adverse incidents

Y72.1   Therapeutic (nonsurgical) and rehabilitative otorhinolaryngological devices associated with adverse incidents

Y72.2   Prosthetic and other implants, materials and accessory otorhinolaryngological devices associated with adverse incidents

Y72.3   Surgical instruments, materials and otorhinolaryngological devices (including sutures) associated with adverse incidents

Y72.8   Miscellaneous otorhinolaryngological devices associated with adverse incidents, not elsewhere classified

● **Y73**   Gastroenterology and urology devices associated with adverse incidents

Y73.0   Diagnostic and monitoring gastroenterology and urology devices associated with adverse incidents

Y73.1   Therapeutic (nonsurgical) and rehabilitative gastroenterology and urology devices associated with adverse incidents

Y73.2   Prosthetic and other implants, materials and accessory gastroenterology and urology devices associated with adverse incidents

Y73.3 Surgical instruments, materials and gastroenterology and urology devices (including sutures) associated with adverse incidents

Y73.8 Miscellaneous gastroenterology and urology devices associated with adverse incidents, not elsewhere classified

● **Y74** General hospital and personal-use devices associated with adverse incidents

Y74.0 Diagnostic and monitoring general hospital and personal-use devices associated with adverse incidents

Y74.1 Therapeutic (nonsurgical) and rehabilitative general hospital and personal-use devices associated with adverse incidents

Y74.2 Prosthetic and other implants, materials and accessory general hospital and personal-use devices associated with adverse incidents

Y74.3 Surgical instruments, materials and general hospital and personal-use devices (including sutures) associated with adverse incidents

Y74.8 Miscellaneous general hospital and personal-use devices associated with adverse incidents, not elsewhere classified

● **Y75** Neurological devices associated with adverse incidents

Y75.0 Diagnostic and monitoring neurological devices associated with adverse incidents

Y75.1 Therapeutic (nonsurgical) and rehabilitative neurological devices associated with adverse incidents

Y75.2 Prosthetic and other implants, materials and neurological devices associated with adverse incidents

Y75.3 Surgical instruments, materials and neurological devices (including sutures) associated with adverse incidents

Y75.8 Miscellaneous neurological devices associated with adverse incidents, not elsewhere classified

● **Y76** Obstetric and gynecological devices associated with adverse incidents

Y76.0 Diagnostic and monitoring obstetric and gynecological devices associated with adverse incidents ♀

Y76.1 Therapeutic (nonsurgical) and rehabilitative obstetric and gynecological devices associated with adverse incidents ♀

Y76.2 Prosthetic and other implants, materials and accessory obstetric and gynecological devices associated with adverse incidents ♀

Y76.3 Surgical instruments, materials and obstetric and gynecological devices (including sutures) associated with adverse incidents ♀

Y76.8 Miscellaneous obstetric and gynecological devices associated with adverse incidents, not elsewhere classified ♀

● **Y77** Ophthalmic devices associated with adverse incidents

Y77.0 Diagnostic and monitoring ophthalmic devices associated with adverse incidents

● **Y77.1** Therapeutic (nonsurgical) and rehabilitative ophthalmic devices associated with adverse incidents

▶ **Y77.11** Contact lens associated with adverse incidents

▶Rigid gas permeable contact lens associated with adverse incidents

▶Soft (hydrophilic) contact lens associated with adverse incidents

▶ **Y77.19** Other therapeutic (nonsurgical) and rehabilitative ophthalmic devices associated with adverse incidents

Y77.2 Prosthetic and other implants, materials and accessory ophthalmic devices associated with adverse incidents

Y77.3 Surgical instruments, materials and ophthalmic devices (including sutures) associated with adverse incidents

Y77.8 Miscellaneous ophthalmic devices associated with adverse incidents, not elsewhere classified

● **Y78** Radiological devices associated with adverse incidents

Y78.0 Diagnostic and monitoring radiological devices associated with adverse incidents

Y78.1 Therapeutic (nonsurgical) and rehabilitative radiological devices associated with adverse incidents

Y78.2 Prosthetic and other implants, materials and accessory radiological devices associated with adverse incidents

Y78.3 Surgical instruments, materials and radiological devices (including sutures) associated with adverse incidents

Y78.8 Miscellaneous radiological devices associated with adverse incidents, not elsewhere classified

● **Y79** Orthopedic devices associated with adverse incidents

Y79.0 Diagnostic and monitoring orthopedic devices associated with adverse incidents

Y79.1 Therapeutic (nonsurgical) and rehabilitative orthopedic devices associated with adverse incidents

Y79.2 Prosthetic and other implants, materials and accessory orthopedic devices associated with adverse incidents

Y79.3 Surgical instruments, materials and orthopedic devices (including sutures) associated with adverse incidents

Y79.8 Miscellaneous orthopedic devices associated with adverse incidents, not elsewhere classified

● **Y80** Physical medicine devices associated with adverse incidents

Y80.0 Diagnostic and monitoring physical medicine devices associated with adverse incidents

Y80.1 Therapeutic (nonsurgical) and rehabilitative physical medicine devices associated with adverse incidents

Y80.2 Prosthetic and other implants, materials and accessory physical medicine devices associated with adverse incidents

Y80.3 Surgical instruments, materials and physical medicine devices (including sutures) associated with adverse incidents

Y80.8 Miscellaneous physical medicine devices associated with adverse incidents, not elsewhere classified

● **Y81** General- and plastic-surgery devices associated with adverse incidents

Y81.0 Diagnostic and monitoring general- and plastic-surgery devices associated with adverse incidents

Y81.1 Therapeutic (nonsurgical) and rehabilitative general- and plastic-surgery devices associated with adverse incidents

Y81.2 Prosthetic and other implants, materials and accessory general- and plastic-surgery devices associated with adverse incidents

Y81.3 Surgical instruments, materials and general- and plastic-surgery devices (including sutures) associated with adverse incidents

Y81.8 Miscellaneous general- and plastic-surgery devices associated with adverse incidents, not elsewhere classified

● **Y82** Other and unspecified medical devices associated with adverse incidents

Y82.8 Other medical devices associated with adverse incidents

Y82.9 Unspecified medical devices associated with adverse incidents

---

▶ New   ⇒ Revised   ~~deleted~~ Deleted   Excludes 1   Excludes 2   Includes   Use additional   Code first   Code also   Key words

1540   OGCR Official Guidelines   X Assign placeholder X   ● Use Additional Character(s)   ▶ Manifestation Code   🖭 Hierarchical Condition Category   Coding Clinic

SURGICAL AND OTHER MEDICAL PROCEDURES AS THE CAUSE OF ABNORMAL REACTION OF THE PATIENT, OR OF LATER COMPLICATION, WITHOUT MENTION OF MISADVENTURE AT THE TIME OF THE PROCEDURE (Y83-Y84)

> **Excludes1**   misadventures to patients during surgical and medical care, classifiable to (Y62-Y69)
>
> **Excludes2**   breakdown or malfunctioning of medical device (after implantation) (during procedure) (ongoing use) (Y70-Y82)

● **Y83**   **Surgical operation and other surgical procedures** as the cause of abnormal reaction of the patient, or of later complication, without mention of misadventure at the time of the procedure

   Y83.0   Surgical operation with transplant of whole organ as the cause of abnormal reaction of the patient, or of later complication, without mention of misadventure at the time of the procedure

   Y83.1   Surgical operation with implant of artificial internal device as the cause of abnormal reaction of the patient, or of later complication, without mention of misadventure at the time of the procedure

   Y83.2   Surgical operation with anastomosis, bypass or graft as the cause of abnormal reaction of the patient, or of later complication, without mention of misadventure at the time of the procedure

   Y83.3   Surgical operation with formation of external stoma as the cause of abnormal reaction of the patient, or of later complication, without mention of misadventure at the time of the procedure

   Y83.4   Other reconstructive surgery as the cause of abnormal reaction of the patient, or of later complication, without mention of misadventure at the time of the procedure

   Y83.5   Amputation of limb(s) as the cause of abnormal reaction of the patient, or of later complication, without mention of misadventure at the time of the procedure

   Y83.6   Removal of other organ (partial) (total) as the cause of abnormal reaction of the patient, or of later complication, without mention of misadventure at the time of the procedure

   Y83.8   Other surgical procedures as the cause of abnormal reaction of the patient, or of later complication, without mention of misadventure at the time of the procedure

   Y83.9   Surgical procedure, unspecified as the cause of abnormal reaction of the patient, or of later complication, without mention of misadventure at the time of the procedure

● **Y84**   **Other medical procedures** as the cause of abnormal reaction of the patient, or of later complication, without mention of misadventure at the time of the procedure

   Y84.0   Cardiac catheterization as the cause of abnormal reaction of the patient, or of later complication, without mention of misadventure at the time of the procedure

   Y84.1   Kidney dialysis as the cause of abnormal reaction of the patient, or of later complication, without mention of misadventure at the time of the procedure

   Y84.2   Radiological procedure and radiotherapy as the cause of abnormal reaction of the patient, or of later complication, without mention of misadventure at the time of the procedure
     Coding Clinic: 2019, Q1, P21; 2017, Q1, P34

   Y84.3   Shock therapy as the cause of abnormal reaction of the patient, or of later complication, without mention of misadventure at the time of the procedure

   Y84.4   Aspiration of fluid as the cause of abnormal reaction of the patient, or of later complication, without mention of misadventure at the time of the procedure

   Y84.5   Insertion of gastric or duodenal sound as the cause of abnormal reaction of the patient, or of later complication, without mention of misadventure at the time of the procedure

   Y84.6   Urinary catheterization as the cause of abnormal reaction of the patient, or of later complication, without mention of misadventure at the time of the procedure

   Y84.7   Blood-sampling as the cause of abnormal reaction of the patient, or of later complication, without mention of misadventure at the time of the procedure

   Y84.8   Other medical procedures as the cause of abnormal reaction of the patient, or of later complication, without mention of misadventure at the time of the procedure

   Y84.9   Medical procedure, unspecified as the cause of abnormal reaction of the patient, or of later complication, without mention of misadventure at the time of the procedure

SUPPLEMENTARY FACTORS RELATED TO CAUSES OF MORBIDITY CLASSIFIED ELSEWHERE (Y90-Y99)

Note: These categories may be used to provide supplementary information concerning causes of morbidity. They are not to be used for single-condition coding.

● **Y90**   **Evidence of alcohol involvement determined by blood alcohol level**
     Code first any associated alcohol related disorders (F10)

   Y90.0   Blood alcohol level of less than 20 mg/100 ml

   Y90.1   Blood alcohol level of 20-39 mg/100 ml

   Y90.2   Blood alcohol level of 40-59 mg/100 ml

   Y90.3   Blood alcohol level of 60-79 mg/100 ml

   Y90.4   Blood alcohol level of 80-99 mg/100 ml

   Y90.5   Blood alcohol level of 100-119 mg/100 ml

   Y90.6   Blood alcohol level of 120-199 mg/100 ml

   Y90.7   Blood alcohol level of 200-239 mg/100 ml

   Y90.8   Blood alcohol level of 240 mg/100 ml or more

   Y90.9   Presence of alcohol in blood, level not specified

OGCR Section I.C.20.b.

> Place of Occurrence Guideline
>
> Codes from category Y92, Place of occurrence of the external cause, are secondary codes for use after other external cause codes to identify the location of the patient at the time of injury or other condition.
>
> Generally, a place of occurrence code is assigned only once, at the initial encounter for treatment. However, in the rare instance that a new injury occurs during hospitalization, an additional place of occurrence code may be assigned. No 7th characters are used for Y92. Only one code from Y92 should be recorded on a medical record.
>
> Do not use place of occurrence code Y92.9 if the place is not stated or is not applicable.

● **Y92**   **Place of occurrence of the external cause**
     The following category is for use, when relevant, to identify the place of occurrence of the external cause. Use in conjunction with an activity code.
     Place of occurrence should be recorded only at the initial encounter for treatment

● **Y92.0**   **Non-institutional (private) residence** as the place of occurrence of the external cause

> **Excludes1**   abandoned or derelict house (Y92.89)
> home under construction but not yet occupied (Y92.6-)
> institutional place of residence (Y92.1-)

 ● **Y92.00**   Unspecified non-institutional (private) residence as the place of occurrence of the external cause

     Y92.000   Kitchen of unspecified non-institutional (private) residence as the place of occurrence of the external cause

     Y92.001   Dining room of unspecified non-institutional (private) residence as the place of occurrence of the external cause

CHAPTER 20 (V00-Y99)

⟹ Y92.002   **Bathroom** of unspecified non-institutional (private) residence as the place of occurrence of the external cause

Y92.003   **Bedroom** of unspecified non-institutional (private) residence as the place of occurrence of the external cause

Y92.007   **Garden or yard** of unspecified non-institutional (private) residence as the place of occurrence of the external cause

Y92.008   **Other place** in unspecified non-institutional (private) residence as the place of occurrence of the external cause

Y92.009   **Unspecified** place in unspecified non-institutional (private) residence as the place of occurrence of the external cause

> Home (NOS) as the place of occurrence of the external cause

● Y92.01   **Single-family non-institutional (private) house** as the place of occurrence of the external cause

> Farmhouse as the place of occurrence of the external cause

> **Excludes1**   barn (Y92.71)
> chicken coop or hen house (Y92.72)
> farm field (Y92.73)
> orchard (Y92.74)
> single family mobile home or trailer (Y92.02-)
> slaughter house (Y92.86)

Y92.010   **Kitchen** of single-family (private) house as the place of occurrence of the external cause

Y92.011   **Dining room** of single-family (private) house as the place of occurrence of the external cause

Y92.012   **Bathroom** of single-family (private) house as the place of occurrence of the external cause

Y92.013   **Bedroom** of single-family (private) house as the place of occurrence of the external cause

Y92.014   **Private driveway** to single-family (private) house as the place of occurrence of the external cause

Y92.015   **Private garage** of single-family (private) house as the place of occurrence of the external cause

Y92.016   **Swimming pool** in single-family (private) house or garden as the place of occurrence of the external cause

Y92.017   **Garden or yard** in single-family (private) house as the place of occurrence of the external cause

Y92.018   **Other place** in single-family (private) house as the place of occurrence of the external cause

Y92.019   **Unspecified** place in single-family (private) house as the place of occurrence of the external cause

● Y92.02   **Mobile home** as the place of occurrence of the external cause

Y92.020   **Kitchen** in mobile home as the place of occurrence of the external cause

Y92.021   **Dining room** in mobile home as the place of occurrence of the external cause

Y92.022   **Bathroom** in mobile home as the place of occurrence of the external cause

Y92.023   **Bedroom** in mobile home as the place of occurrence of the external cause

Y92.024   **Driveway** of mobile home as the place of occurrence of the external cause

Y92.025   **Garage** of mobile home as the place of occurrence of the external cause

Y92.026   **Swimming pool** of mobile home as the place of occurrence of the external cause

Y92.027   **Garden or yard** of mobile home as the place of occurrence of the external cause

Y92.028   **Other place** in mobile home as the place of occurrence of the external cause

Y92.029   **Unspecified** place in mobile home as the place of occurrence of the external cause

● Y92.03   **Apartment** as the place of occurrence of the external cause

> Condominium as the place of occurrence of the external cause
> Co-op apartment as the place of occurrence of the external cause

Y92.030   **Kitchen** in apartment as the place of occurrence of the external cause

Y92.031   **Bathroom** in apartment as the place of occurrence of the external cause

Y92.032   **Bedroom** in apartment as the place of occurrence of the external cause

Y92.038   **Other place** in apartment as the place of occurrence of the external cause

Y92.039   **Unspecified** place in apartment as the place of occurrence of the external cause

● Y92.04   **Boarding-house** as the place of occurrence of the external cause

Y92.040   **Kitchen** in boarding-house as the place of occurrence of the external cause

Y92.041   **Bathroom** in boarding-house as the place of occurrence of the external cause

Y92.042   **Bedroom** in boarding-house as the place of occurrence of the external cause

Y92.043   **Driveway** of boarding-house as the place of occurrence of the external cause

Y92.044   **Garage** of boarding-house as the place of occurrence of the external cause

Y92.045   **Swimming pool** of boarding-house as the place of occurrence of the external cause

Y92.046   **Garden or yard** of boarding-house as the place of occurrence of the external cause

Y92.048   **Other place** in boarding-house as the place of occurrence of the external cause

Y92.049   **Unspecified** place in boarding-house as the place of occurrence of the external cause

▶ New   ⟹ Revised   ~~deleted~~ Deleted   Excludes 1   Excludes 2   Includes   Use additional   Code first   Code also   Key words

OGCR Official Guidelines   X Assign placeholder X   ● Use Additional Character(s)   ▶ Manifestation Code   ℞ Hierarchical Condition Category   Coding Clinic

CHAPTER 20 (V00-Y99)

● **Y92.09**   **Other non-institutional residence** as the place of occurrence of the external cause

     Y92.090   **Kitchen** in other non-institutional residence as the place of occurrence of the external cause

     Y92.091   **Bathroom** in other non-institutional residence as the place of occurrence of the external cause

     Y92.092   **Bedroom** in other non-institutional residence as the place of occurrence of the external cause

     Y92.093   **Driveway** of other non-institutional residence as the place of occurrence of the external cause

     Y92.094   **Garage** of other non-institutional residence as the place of occurrence of the external cause

     Y92.095   **Swimming pool** of other non-institutional residence as the place of occurrence of the external cause

     Y92.096   **Garden or yard** of other non-institutional residence as the place of occurrence of the external cause

     Y92.098   **Other place** in other non-institutional residence as the place of occurrence of the external cause

     Y92.099   **Unspecified place** in other non-institutional residence as the place of occurrence of the external cause
         Coding Clinic: 2017, Q2, P10

● **Y92.1**   **Institutional (nonprivate) residence** as the place of occurrence of the external cause

     Y92.10   **Unspecified** residential institution as the place of occurrence of the external cause

   ● **Y92.11**   **Children's home and orphanage** as the place of occurrence of the external cause

     Y92.110   **Kitchen** in children's home and orphanage as the place of occurrence of the external cause

     Y92.111   **Bathroom** in children's home and orphanage as the place of occurrence of the external cause

     Y92.112   **Bedroom** in children's home and orphanage as the place of occurrence of the external cause

     Y92.113   **Driveway** of children's home and orphanage as the place of occurrence of the external cause

     Y92.114   **Garage** of children's home and orphanage as the place of occurrence of the external cause

     Y92.115   **Swimming pool** of children's home and orphanage as the place of occurrence of the external cause

     Y92.116   **Garden or yard** of children's home and orphanage as the place of occurrence of the external cause

     Y92.118   **Other place** in children's home and orphanage as the place of occurrence of the external cause

     Y92.119   **Unspecified** place in children's home and orphanage as the place of occurrence of the external cause

   ● **Y92.12**   **Nursing home** as the place of occurrence of the external cause

     Home for the sick as the place of occurrence of the external cause

     Hospice as the place of occurrence of the external cause

     Y92.120   **Kitchen** in nursing home as the place of occurrence of the external cause

     Y92.121   **Bathroom** in nursing home as the place of occurrence of the external cause

Y92.122   **Bedroom** in nursing home as the place of occurrence of the external cause

Y92.123   **Driveway** of nursing home as the place of occurrence of the external cause

Y92.124   **Garage** of nursing home as the place of occurrence of the external cause

Y92.125   **Swimming pool** of nursing home as the place of occurrence of the external cause

Y92.126   **Garden or yard** of nursing home as the place of occurrence of the external cause

Y92.128   **Other place** in nursing home as the place of occurrence of the external cause

Y92.129   **Unspecified** place in nursing home as the place of occurrence of the external cause
         Coding Clinic: 2017, Q2, P10

● **Y92.13**   **Military base** as the place of occurrence of the external cause

     Excludes1   military training grounds (Y92.83)

     Y92.130   **Kitchen** on military base as the place of occurrence of the external cause

     Y92.131   **Mess hall** on military base as the place of occurrence of the external cause

     Y92.133   **Barracks** on military base as the place of occurrence of the external cause

     Y92.135   **Garage** on military base as the place of occurrence of the external cause

     Y92.136   **Swimming pool** on military base as the place of occurrence of the external cause

     Y92.137   **Garden or yard** on military base as the place of occurrence of the external cause

     Y92.138   **Other place** on military base as the place of occurrence of the external cause

     Y92.139   **Unspecified** place military base as the place of occurrence of the external cause

● **Y92.14**   **Prison** as the place of occurrence of the external cause

     Y92.140   **Kitchen** in prison as the place of occurrence of the external cause

     Y92.141   **Dining room** in prison as the place of occurrence of the external cause

     Y92.142   **Bathroom** in prison as the place of occurrence of the external cause

     Y92.143   **Cell** of prison as the place of occurrence of the external cause

     Y92.146   **Swimming pool** of prison as the place of occurrence of the external cause

     Y92.147   **Courtyard** of prison as the place of occurrence of the external cause

     Y92.148   **Other place** in prison as the place of occurrence of the external cause

     Y92.149   **Unspecified** place in prison as the place of occurrence of the external cause

● **Y92.15**   **Reform school** as the place of occurrence of the external cause

     Y92.150   **Kitchen** in reform school as the place of occurrence of the external cause

     Y92.151   **Dining room** in reform school as the place of occurrence of the external cause

CHAPTER 20 (V00–Y99)

Y92.152   Bathroom in reform school as the place of occurrence of the external cause

Y92.153   Bedroom in reform school as the place of occurrence of the external cause

Y92.154   Driveway of reform school as the place of occurrence of the external cause

Y92.155   Garage of reform school as the place of occurrence of the external cause

Y92.156   Swimming pool of reform school as the place of occurrence of the external cause

Y92.157   Garden or yard of reform school as the place of occurrence of the external cause

Y92.158   Other place in reform school as the place of occurrence of the external cause

Y92.159   Unspecified place in reform school as the place of occurrence of the external cause

● Y92.16   School dormitory as the place of occurrence of the external cause

Excludes1   reform school as the place of occurrence of the external cause (Y92.15-)
school buildings and grounds as the place of occurrence of the external cause (Y92.2-)
school sports and athletic areas as the place of occurrence of the external cause (Y92.3-)

Y92.160   Kitchen in school dormitory as the place of occurrence of the external cause

Y92.161   Dining room in school dormitory as the place of occurrence of the external cause

Y92.162   Bathroom in school dormitory as the place of occurrence of the external cause

Y92.163   Bedroom in school dormitory as the place of occurrence of the external cause

Y92.168   Other place in school dormitory as the place of occurrence of the external cause

Y92.169   Unspecified place in school dormitory as the place of occurrence of the external cause

● Y92.19   Other specified residential institution as the place of occurrence of the external cause

Y92.190   Kitchen in other specified residential institution as the place of occurrence of the external cause

Y92.191   Dining room in other specified residential institution as the place of occurrence of the external cause

Y92.192   Bathroom in other specified residential institution as the place of occurrence of the external cause

Y92.193   Bedroom in other specified residential institution as the place of occurrence of the external cause

Y92.194   Driveway of other specified residential institution as the place of occurrence of the external cause

Y92.195   Garage of other specified residential institution as the place of occurrence of the external cause

Y92.196   Pool of other specified residential institution as the place of occurrence of the external cause

Y92.197   Garden or yard of other specified residential institution as the place of occurrence of the external cause

Y92.198   Other place in other specified residential institution as the place of occurrence of the external cause
Coding Clinic: 2017, Q2, P11

Y92.199   Unspecified place in other specified residential institution as the place of occurrence of the external cause
Coding Clinic: 2017, Q2, P10

● Y92.2   School, other institution and public administrative area as the place of occurrence of the external cause
Building and adjacent grounds used by the general public or by a particular group of the public

Excludes1   building under construction as the place of occurrence of the external cause (Y92.6)
residential institution as the place of occurrence of the external cause (Y92.1)
school dormitory as the place of occurrence of the external cause (Y92.16-)
sports and athletics area of schools as the place of occurrence of the external cause (Y92.3-)

● Y92.21   School (private) (public) (state) as the place of occurrence of the external cause

Y92.210   Daycare center as the place of occurrence of the external cause

Y92.211   Elementary school as the place of occurrence of the external cause
Kindergarten as the place of occurrence of the external cause

Y92.212   Middle school as the place of occurrence of the external cause

Y92.213   High school as the place of occurrence of the external cause
Coding Clinic: 2012, Q4, P108

Y92.214   College as the place of occurrence of the external cause
University as the place of occurrence of the external cause

Y92.215   Trade school as the place of occurrence of the external cause

Y92.218   Other school as the place of occurrence of the external cause

Y92.219   Unspecified school as the place of occurrence of the external cause

Y92.22   Religious institution as the place of occurrence of the external cause
Church as the place of occurrence of the external cause
Mosque as the place of occurrence of the external cause
Synagogue as the place of occurrence of the external cause

▶ New   ⇒ Revised   ~~deleted~~ Deleted   Excludes 1   Excludes 2   Includes   Use additional   Code first   Code also   Key words
OGCR Official Guidelines   X Assign placeholder X   ● Use Additional Character(s)   ▶ Manifestation Code   ⓗ Hierarchical Condition Category   Coding Clinic

● **Y92.23**   **Hospital** as the place of occurrence of the external cause

     Excludes1   ambulatory (outpatient) health services establishments (Y92.53-)
            home for the sick as the place of occurrence of the external cause (Y92.12-)
            hospice as the place of occurrence of the external cause (Y92.12-)
            nursing home as the place of occurrence of the external cause (Y92.12-)

     Y92.230   **Patient room** in hospital as the place of occurrence of the external cause

     Y92.231   **Patient bathroom** in hospital as the place of occurrence of the external cause

     Y92.232   **Corridor** of hospital as the place of occurrence of the external cause

     Y92.233   **Cafeteria** of hospital as the place of occurrence of the external cause

     Y92.234   **Operating room** of hospital as the place of occurrence of the external cause

     Y92.238   **Other place** in hospital as the place of occurrence of the external cause

     Y92.239   **Unspecified place** in hospital as the place of occurrence of the external cause

● **Y92.24**   **Public administrative building** as the place of occurrence of the external cause

     Y92.240   **Courthouse** as the place of occurrence of the external cause

     Y92.241   **Library** as the place of occurrence of the external cause

     Y92.242   **Post office** as the place of occurrence of the external cause

     Y92.243   **City hall** as the place of occurrence of the external cause

     Y92.248   **Other public administrative building** as the place of occurrence of the external cause

● **Y92.25**   **Cultural building** as the place of occurrence of the external cause

     Y92.250   **Art gallery** as the place of occurrence of the external cause

     Y92.251   **Museum** as the place of occurrence of the external cause

     Y92.252   **Music hall** as the place of occurrence of the external cause

     Y92.253   **Opera house** as the place of occurrence of the external cause

     Y92.254   **Theater (live)** as the place of occurrence of the external cause

     Y92.258   **Other cultural public building** as the place of occurrence of the external cause

  Y92.26   **Movie house or cinema** as the place of occurrence of the external cause

  Y92.29   **Other specified public building** as the place of occurrence of the external cause
       Assembly hall as the place of occurrence of the external cause
       Clubhouse as the place of occurrence of the external cause

● **Y92.3**   **Sports and athletics area** as the place of occurrence of the external cause

● **Y92.31**   **Athletic court** as the place of occurrence of the external cause

     Excludes1   tennis court in private home or garden (Y92.09)

     Y92.310   **Basketball court** as the place of occurrence of the external cause

     Y92.311   **Squash court** as the place of occurrence of the external cause

     Y92.312   **Tennis court** as the place of occurrence of the external cause

     Y92.318   **Other athletic court** as the place of occurrence of the external cause

● **Y92.32**   **Athletic field** as the place of occurrence of the external cause

     Y92.320   **Baseball field** as the place of occurrence of the external cause

     Y92.321   **Football field** as the place of occurrence of the external cause

     Y92.322   **Soccer field** as the place of occurrence of the external cause

     Y92.328   **Other athletic field** as the place of occurrence of the external cause
       Cricket field as the place of occurrence of the external cause
       Hockey field as the place of occurrence of the external cause

● **Y92.33**   **Skating rink** as the place of occurrence of the external cause

     Y92.330   **Ice skating rink (indoor) (outdoor)** as the place of occurrence of the external cause

     Y92.331   **Roller skating rink** as the place of occurrence of the external cause

  Y92.34   **Swimming pool (public)** as the place of occurrence of the external cause

     Excludes1   swimming pool in private home or garden (Y92.016)

  Y92.39   **Other specified sports and athletic area** as the place of occurrence of the external cause
       Golf-course as the place of occurrence of the external cause
       Gymnasium as the place of occurrence of the external cause
       Riding-school as the place of occurrence of the external cause
       Stadium as the place of occurrence of the external cause

● **Y92.4**   **Street, highway and other paved roadways** as the place of occurrence of the external cause

     Excludes1   private driveway of residence (Y92.014, Y92.024, Y92.043, Y92.093, Y92.113, Y92.123, Y92.154, Y92.194)

● **Y92.41**   **Street and highway** as the place of occurrence of the external cause

     Y92.410   **Unspecified street and highway** as the place of occurrence of the external cause
       Road NOS as the place of occurrence of the external cause

     Y92.411   **Interstate highway** as the place of occurrence of the external cause
       Freeway as the place of occurrence of the external cause
       Motorway as the place of occurrence of the external cause

     Y92.412   **Parkway** as the place of occurrence of the external cause

     Y92.413   **State road** as the place of occurrence of the external cause

Y92.414 Local residential or business street as the place of occurrence of the external cause

Y92.415 Exit ramp or entrance ramp of street or highway as the place of occurrence of the external cause

● **Y92.48** Other paved roadways as the place of occurrence of the external cause

Y92.480 Sidewalk as the place of occurrence of the external cause

Y92.481 Parking lot as the place of occurrence of the external cause

Y92.482 Bike path as the place of occurrence of the external cause

Y92.488 Other paved roadways as the place of occurrence of the external cause

● **Y92.5** Trade and service area as the place of occurrence of the external cause

> **Excludes1** garage in private home (Y92.015)
> schools and other public administration buildings (Y92.2-)

● **Y92.51** Private commercial establishments as the place of occurrence of the external cause

Y92.510 Bank as the place of occurrence of the external cause

Y92.511 Restaurant or café as the place of occurrence of the external cause

Y92.512 Supermarket, store or market as the place of occurrence of the external cause

Y92.513 Shop (commercial) as the place of occurrence of the external cause

● **Y92.52** Service areas as the place of occurrence of the external cause

Y92.520 Airport as the place of occurrence of the external cause

Y92.521 Bus station as the place of occurrence of the external cause

Y92.522 Railway station as the place of occurrence of the external cause

Y92.523 Highway rest stop as the place of occurrence of the external cause

Y92.524 Gas station as the place of occurrence of the external cause
> Petroleum station as the place of occurrence of the external cause
> Service station as the place of occurrence of the external cause

● **Y92.53** Ambulatory health services establishments as the place of occurrence of the external cause

Y92.530 Ambulatory surgery center as the place of occurrence of the external cause
> Outpatient surgery center, including that connected with a hospital as the place of occurrence of the external cause
> Same day surgery center, including that connected with a hospital as the place of occurrence of the external cause

Y92.531 Health care provider office as the place of occurrence of the external cause
> Physician office as the place of occurrence of the external cause

Y92.532 Urgent care center as the place of occurrence of the external cause

Y92.538 Other ambulatory health services establishments as the place of occurrence of the external cause
> Coding Clinic: 2019, Q1, P21

Y92.59 Other trade areas as the place of occurrence of the external cause
> Office building as the place of occurrence of the external cause
> Casino as the place of occurrence of the external cause
> Garage (commercial) as the place of occurrence of the external cause
> Hotel as the place of occurrence of the external cause
> Radio or television station as the place of occurrence of the external cause
> Shopping mall as the place of occurrence of the external cause
> Warehouse as the place of occurrence of the external cause

● **Y92.6** Industrial and construction area as the place of occurrence of the external cause

Y92.61 Building [any] under construction as the place of occurrence of the external cause

Y92.62 Dock or shipyard as the place of occurrence of the external cause
> Dockyard as the place of occurrence of the external cause
> Dry dock as the place of occurrence of the external cause
> Shipyard as the place of occurrence of the external cause

Y92.63 Factory as the place of occurrence of the external cause
> Factory building as the place of occurrence of the external cause
> Factory premises as the place of occurrence of the external cause
> Industrial yard as the place of occurrence of the external cause

Y92.64 Mine or pit as the place of occurrence of the external cause
> Mine as the place of occurrence of the external cause

Y92.65 Oil rig as the place of occurrence of the external cause
> Pit (coal) (gravel) (sand) as the place of occurrence of the external cause

Y92.69 Other specified industrial and construction area as the place of occurrence of the external cause
> Gasworks as the place of occurrence of the external cause
> Power-station (coal) (nuclear) (oil) as the place of occurrence of the external cause
> Tunnel under construction as the place of occurrence of the external cause
> Workshop as the place of occurrence of the external cause

● **Y92.7** Farm as the place of occurrence of the external cause
> Ranch as the place of occurrence of the external cause

> **Excludes1** farmhouse and home premises of farm (Y92.01-)

Y92.71 Barn as the place of occurrence of the external cause

Y92.72 Chicken coop as the place of occurrence of the external cause
> Hen house as the place of occurrence of the external cause

Y92.73 Farm field as the place of occurrence of the external cause

Y92.74 Orchard as the place of occurrence of the external cause

Y92.79 Other farm location as the place of occurrence of the external cause

▶ New   ⇒ Revised   ~~deleted~~ Deleted   Excludes 1   Excludes 2   Includes   Use additional   Code first   Code also   Key words

OGCR Official Guidelines   X Assign placeholder X   ● Use Additional Character(s)   ▶ Manifestation Code   ⬤ Hierarchical Condition Category   Coding Clinic

● **Y92.8**   **Other places** as the place of occurrence of the external cause
    ● **Y92.81**   **Transport vehicle** as the place of occurrence of the external cause
       Excludes1   transport accidents (V00-V99)
       Y92.810   **Car** as the place of occurrence of the external cause
       Y92.811   **Bus** as the place of occurrence of the external cause
       Y92.812   **Truck** as the place of occurrence of the external cause
       Y92.813   **Airplane** as the place of occurrence of the external cause
       Y92.814   **Boat** as the place of occurrence of the external cause
       Y92.815   **Train** as the place of occurrence of the external cause
       Y92.816   **Subway** car as the place of occurrence of the external cause
       Y92.818   **Other transport vehicle** as the place of occurrence of the external cause
    ● **Y92.82**   **Wilderness area**
       Y92.820   **Desert** as the place of occurrence of the external cause
       Y92.821   **Forest** as the place of occurrence of the external cause
       Y92.828   **Other wilderness area** as the place of occurrence of the external cause
          Swamp as the place of occurrence of the external cause
          Mountain as the place of occurrence of the external cause
          Marsh as the place of occurrence of the external cause
          Prairie as the place of occurrence of the external cause
    ● **Y92.83**   **Recreation area** as the place of occurrence of the external cause
       Y92.830   **Public park** as the place of occurrence of the external cause
       Y92.831   **Amusement park** as the place of occurrence of the external cause
       Y92.832   **Beach** as the place of occurrence of the external cause
          Seashore as the place of occurrence of the external cause
       Y92.833   **Campsite** as the place of occurrence of the external cause
       Y92.834   **Zoological garden (zoo)** as the place of occurrence of the external cause
       Y92.838   **Other recreation area** as the place of occurrence of the external cause
    Y92.84   **Military training ground** as the place of occurrence of the external cause
    Y92.85   **Railroad track** as the place of occurrence of the external cause
    Y92.86   **Slaughter house** as the place of occurrence of the external cause
    Y92.89   **Other specified places** as the place of occurrence of the external cause
       Derelict house as the place of occurrence of the external cause

OGCR   Section I.C.20.b.

Do not use place of occurrence code Y92.9 if the place is not stated or is not applicable.

Y92.9   **Unspecified** place or not applicable

OGCR   See Section I.C.20.c.

Activity Code

Assign a code from category Y93, Activity code, to describe the activity of the patient at the time the injury or other health condition occurred.

An activity code is used only once, at the initial encounter for treatment. Only one code from Y93 should be recorded on a medical record.

The activity codes are not applicable to poisonings, adverse effects, misadventures or sequela.

Do not assign Y93.9, Unspecified activity, if the activity is not stated.

A code from category Y93 is appropriate for use with external cause and intent codes if identifying the activity provides additional information about the event.

● **Y93**   **Activity codes**
    Note: Category Y93 is provided for use to indicate the activity of the person seeking healthcare for an injury or health condition, such as a heart attack while shoveling snow, which resulted from, or was contributed to, by the activity. These codes are appropriate for use for both acute injuries, such as those from Chapter 19, and conditions that are due to the long-term, cumulative effects of an activity, such as those from Chapter 13. They are also appropriate for use with external cause codes for cause and intent if identifying the activity provides additional information on the event. These codes should be used in conjunction with codes for external cause status (Y99) and place of occurrence (Y92).

    This section contains the following broad activity categories:
       Y93.0   Activities involving walking and running
       Y93.1   Activities involving water and water craft
       Y93.2   Activities involving ice and snow
       Y93.3   Activities involving climbing, rappelling, and jumping off
       Y93.4   Activities involving dancing and other rhythmic movement
       Y93.5   Activities involving other sports and athletics played individually
       Y93.6   Activities involving other sports and athletics played as a team or group
       Y93.7   Activities involving other specified sports and athletics
       Y93.A   Activities involving other cardiorespiratory exercise
       Y93.B   Activities involving other muscle strengthening exercises
       Y93.C   Activities involving computer technology and electronic devices
       Y93.D   Activities involving arts and handcrafts
       Y93.E   Activities involving personal hygiene and interior property and clothing maintenance
       Y93.F   Activities involving caregiving
       Y93.G   Activities involving food preparation, cooking and grilling
       Y93.H   Activities involving exterior property and land maintenance, building and construction
       Y93.I   Activities involving roller coasters and other types of external motion
       Y93.J   Activities involving playing musical instrument
       Y93.K   Activities involving animal care
       Y93.8   Activities, other specified
       Y93.9   Activity, unspecified

● **Y93.0**   **Activities involving walking and running**
    Excludes1   Activity, walking an animal (Y93.K1)
          Activity, walking or running on a treadmill (Y93.A1)
    Y93.01   **Activity, walking, marching and hiking**
       Activity, walking, marching and hiking on level or elevated terrain
       Excludes1   activity, mountain climbing (Y93.31)
    Y93.02   **Activity, running**

Y93.1 Activities involving water and water craft

> **Excludes1** activities involving ice (Y93.2-)

Y93.11 **Activity, swimming**

Y93.12 **Activity, springboard and platform diving**

Y93.13 **Activity, water polo**

Y93.14 **Activity, water aerobics and water exercise**

Y93.15 **Activity, underwater diving and snorkeling**
Activity, SCUBA diving

Y93.16 **Activity, rowing, canoeing, kayaking, rafting and tubing**
Activity, canoeing, kayaking, rafting and tubing in calm and turbulent water

Y93.17 **Activity, water skiing and wake boarding**

Y93.18 **Activity, surfing, windsurfing and boogie boarding**
Activity, water sliding

Y93.19 **Activity, other involving water and watercraft**
Activity involving water NOS
Activity, parasailing
Activity, water survival training and testing

Y93.2 Activities involving ice and snow

> **Excludes1** activity, shoveling ice and snow (Y93.H1)

Y93.21 **Activity, ice skating**
Activity, figure skating (singles) (pairs)
Activity, ice dancing

> **Excludes1** activity, ice hockey (Y93.22)

Y93.22 **Activity, ice hockey**

Y93.23 **Activity, snow (alpine) (downhill) skiing, snowboarding, sledding, tobogganing and snow tubing**

> **Excludes1** activity, cross country skiing (Y93.24)

Y93.24 **Activity, cross country skiing**
Activity, nordic skiing

Y93.29 **Activity, other activity involving ice and snow**
Activity, activity involving ice and snow NOS

Y93.3 Activities involving climbing, rappelling and jumping off

> **Excludes1** activity, hiking on level or elevated terrain (Y93.01)
> activity, jumping rope (Y93.56)
> activity, trampoline jumping (Y93.44)

Y93.31 **Activity, mountain climbing, rock climbing and wall climbing**

Y93.32 **Activity, rappelling**

Y93.33 **Activity, BASE jumping**
Activity, building, Antenna, Span, Earth jumping

Y93.34 **Activity, bungee jumping**

Y93.35 **Activity, hang gliding**

Y93.39 **Activity, other activity involving climbing, rappelling and jumping off**

Y93.4 Activities involving dancing and other rhythmic movement

> **Excludes1** activity, martial arts (Y93.75)

Y93.41 **Activity, dancing**
Coding Clinic: 2012, Q4, P108

Y93.42 **Activity, yoga**

Y93.43 **Activity, gymnastics**
Activity, rhythmic gymnastics

> **Excludes1** activity, trampolining (Y93.44)

Y93.44 **Activity, trampolining**

Y93.45 **Activity, cheerleading**

Y93.49 **Activity, other involving dancing and other rhythmic movements**

Y93.5 Activities involving other sports and athletics played individually

> **Excludes1** activity, dancing (Y93.41)
> activity, gymnastic (Y93.43)
> activity, trampolining (Y93.44)
> activity, yoga (Y93.42)

Y93.51 **Activity, roller skating (inline) and skateboarding**

Y93.52 **Activity, horseback riding**

Y93.53 **Activity, golf**

Y93.54 **Activity, bowling**

Y93.55 **Activity, bike riding**

Y93.56 **Activity, jumping rope**

Y93.57 **Activity, non-running track and field events**

> **Excludes1** activity, running (any form) (Y93.02)

Y93.59 **Activity, other involving other sports and athletics played individually**

> **Excludes1** activities involving climbing, rappelling, and jumping (Y93.3-)
> activities involving ice and snow (Y93.2-)
> activities involving walking and running (Y93.0-)
> activities involving water and watercraft (Y93.1-)

Y93.6 Activities involving other sports and athletics played as a team or group

> **Excludes1** activity, ice hockey (Y93.22)
> activity, water polo (Y93.13)

Y93.61 **Activity, American tackle football**
Activity, football NOS

Y93.62 **Activity, American flag or touch football**

Y93.63 **Activity, rugby**

Y93.64 **Activity, baseball**
Activity, softball

Y93.65 **Activity, lacrosse and field hockey**
Coding Clinic: 2015, Q1, P9

Y93.66 **Activity, soccer**

Y93.67 **Activity, basketball**
Coding Clinic: 2019, Q4, P18

Y93.68 **Activity, volleyball (beach) (court)**

Y93.6A **Activity, physical games generally associated with school recess, summer camp and children**
Activity, capture the flag
Activity, dodge ball
Activity, four square
Activity, kickball

Y93.69 **Activity, other involving other sports and athletics played as a team or group**
Cricket

Y93.7 Activities involving other specified sports and athletics

Y93.71 **Activity, boxing**

Y93.72 **Activity, wrestling**

Y93.73 **Activity, racquet and hand sports**
Activity, handball
Activity, racquetball
Activity, squash
Activity, tennis

Y93.74 **Activity, frisbee**
Activity, ultimate frisbee

Y93.75 **Activity, martial arts**
Activity, combatives

Y93.79 **Activity, other specified sports and athletics**

> **Excludes1** sports and athletics activities specified in categories Y93.0-Y93.6

▶ New   ⟹ Revised   ~~deleted~~ Deleted   Excludes 1   Excludes 2   Includes   Use additional   Code first   Code also   Key words

OGCR Official Guidelines   X Assign placeholder X   ● Use Additional Character(s)   ❱ Manifestation Code   ⬮ Hierarchical Condition Category   **Coding Clinic**

Y93.A   Activities involving other cardiorespiratory exercise
     Activities involving physical training

    Y93.A1   **Activity, exercise machines primarily for cardiorespiratory conditioning**
       Activity, elliptical and stepper machines
       Activity, stationary bike
       Activity, treadmill

    Y93.A2   **Activity, calisthenics**
       Activity, jumping jacks
       Activity, warm up and cool down

    Y93.A3   **Activity, aerobic and step exercise**

    Y93.A4   **Activity, circuit training**

    Y93.A5   **Activity, obstacle course**
       Activity, challenge course
       Activity, confidence course

    Y93.A6   **Activity, grass drills**
       Activity, guerilla drills

    Y93.A9   **Activity, other involving other cardiorespiratory exercise**
       Excludes1   activities involving cardiorespiratory exercise specified in categories Y93.0-Y93.7

Y93.B   Activity involving other muscle strengthening exercises

    Y93.B1   **Activity, exercise machines primarily for muscle strengthening**

    Y93.B2   **Activity, push-ups, pull-ups, sit-ups**

    Y93.B3   **Activity, free weights**
       Activity, barbells
       Activity, dumbbells

    Y93.B4   **Activity, pilates**

    Y93.B9   **Activity, other involving other muscle strengthening exercises**
       Excludes1   activities involving muscle strengthening specified in categories Y93.0-Y93.A

Y93.C   Activities involving computer technology and electronic devices
     Excludes1   activity, electronic musical keyboard or instruments (Y93.J-)

    Y93.C1   **Activity, computer keyboarding**
       Activity, electronic game playing using keyboard or other stationary device

    Y93.C2   **Activity, hand held interactive electronic device**
       Activity, cellular telephone and communication device
       Activity, electronic game playing using interactive device
       Excludes1   activity, electronic game playing using keyboard or other stationary device (Y93.C1)

    Y93.C9   **Activity, other involving computer technology and electronic devices**

Y93.D   Activities involving arts and handcrafts
     Excludes1   activities involving playing musical instrument (Y93.J-)

    Y93.D1   **Knitting and crocheting**

    Y93.D2   **Sewing**

    Y93.D3   **Furniture building and finishing**
       Furniture repair

    Y93.D9   **Activity, other involving arts and handcrafts**

Y93.E   Activities involving personal hygiene and interior property and clothing maintenance
     Excludes1   activities involving cooking and grilling (Y93.G-)
          activities involving exterior property and land maintenance, building and construction (Y93.H-)
          activity involving caregiving (Y93.F-)
          activity, dishwashing (Y93.G1)
          activity, food preparation (Y93.G1)
          activity, gardening (Y93.H2)

    Y93.E1   **Activity, personal bathing and showering**

    Y93.E2   **Activity, laundry**

    Y93.E3   **Activity, vacuuming**

    Y93.E4   **Activity, ironing**

    Y93.E5   **Activity, floor mopping and cleaning**

    Y93.E6   **Activity, residential relocation**
       Activity, packing up and unpacking involved in moving to a new residence

    Y93.E8   **Activity, other personal hygiene activity**

    Y93.E9   **Activity, other household maintenance**

Y93.F   Activities involving person providing caregiving
     Activity involving the provider of caregiving

    Y93.F1   **Activity, caregiving involving bathing**

    Y93.F2   **Activity, caregiving involving lifting**
       Coding Clinic: 2016, Q4, P74

    Y93.F9   **Activity, other caregiving**

Y93.G   Activities involving food preparation, cooking and grilling

    Y93.G1   **Activity, food preparation and clean up**
       Activity, dishwashing

    Y93.G2   **Activity, grilling and smoking food**

    Y93.G3   **Activity, cooking and baking**
       Activity, use of stove, oven and microwave oven

    Y93.G9   **Activity, other activity involving cooking and grilling**

Y93.H   Activities involving property and land maintenance, building and construction

    Y93.H1   **Activity, digging, shoveling and raking**
       Activity, dirt digging
       Activity, raking leaves
       Activity, snow shoveling

    Y93.H2   **Activity, gardening and landscaping**
       Activity, pruning, trimming shrubs, weeding

    Y93.H3   **Activity, building and construction**

    Y93.H9   **Activity, other activity involving property and land maintenance, building and construction**

Y93.I   Activities involving roller coasters and other types of external motion

    Y93.I1   **Activity, rollercoaster riding**

    Y93.I9   **Activity, other involving external motion**

Y93.J   Activities involving playing musical instrument
     Activity involving playing electric musical instrument

    Y93.J1   **Activity, piano playing**
       Activity, musical keyboard (electronic) playing

    Y93.J2   **Activity, drum and other percussion instrument playing**

    Y93.J3   **Activity, string instrument playing**

    Y93.J4   **Activity, winds and brass instrument playing**

CHAPTER 20 (V00-Y99)

● **Y93.K Activities involving animal care**
> **Excludes1** activity, horseback riding (Y93.52)

Y93.K1 Activity, walking an animal

Y93.K2 Activity, milking an animal

Y93.K3 Activity, grooming and shearing an animal

Y93.K9 Activity, other activity involving animal care

● **Y93.8 Other activity**
Coding Clinic: 2016, Q4, P74

Y93.81 Activity, refereeing a sports activity

Y93.82 Activity, spectator at an event

Y93.83 Activity, rough housing and horseplay
Coding Clinic: 2015, Q1, P8

Y93.84 Activity, sleeping

Y93.85 Activity, choking game
Activity, blackout game
Activity, fainting game
Activity, pass out game
Coding Clinic: 2016, Q4, P74-76

Y93.89 Activity, other specified

OGCR See Section I.C.20.c.

Do not assign Y93.9, Unspecified activity, if the activity is not stated.

● **Y93.9 Activity, unspecified**

Y95 Nosocomial condition

● **Y99 External cause status**
> **Note:** A single code from category Y99 should be used in conjunction with the external cause code(s) assigned to a record to indicate the status of the person at the time the event occurred.
Coding Clinic: 2016, Q4, P74

Y99.0 Civilian activity done for income or pay
Civilian activity done for financial or other compensation
> **Excludes1** military activity (Y99.1)
> volunteer activity (Y99.2)

Y99.1 Military activity
> **Excludes1** activity of off duty military personnel (Y99.8)

Y99.2 Volunteer activity
> **Excludes1** activity of child or other family member assisting in compensated work of other family member (Y99.8)

Y99.8 Other external cause status
Activity NEC
Activity of child or other family member assisting in compensated work of other family member
Hobby not done for income
Leisure activity
Off-duty activity of military personnel
Recreation or sport not for income or while a student
Student activity
> **Excludes1** civilian activity done for income or compensation (Y99.0)
> military activity (Y99.1)
Coding Clinic: 2012, Q4, P108

Y99.9 Unspecified external cause status

▶ New ⇒ Revised ~~deleted~~ Deleted Excludes 1 Excludes 2 Includes Use additional Code first Code also Key words
OGCR Official Guidelines X Assign placeholder X ● Use Additional Character(s) ▷ Manifestation Code ⚘ Hierarchical Condition Category Coding Clinic

CHAPTER 21

FACTORS INFLUENCING HEALTH STATUS AND CONTACT WITH HEALTH SERVICES (Z00-Z99)

OGCR Chapter-Specific Coding Guidelines

21. **Chapter 21: Factors influencing health status and contact with health services (Z00-Z99)**
   Note: The chapter specific guidelines provide additional information about the use of Z codes for specified encounters.

   a. Use of Z codes in any healthcare setting
   Z codes are for use in any healthcare setting. Z codes may be used as either a first-listed (principal diagnosis code in the inpatient setting) or secondary code, depending on the circumstances of the encounter. Certain Z codes may only be used as first-listed or principal diagnosis.

   b. Z Codes indicate a reason for an encounter
   Z codes are not procedure codes. A corresponding procedure code must accompany a Z code to describe any procedure performed.

   c. Categories of Z Codes

   1) Contact/Exposure
   Category Z20 indicates contact with, and suspected exposure to, communicable diseases. These codes are for patients who do not show any sign or symptom of a disease but are suspected to have been exposed to it by close personal contact with an infected individual or are in an area where a disease is epidemic.
   Category Z77, Other contact with and (suspected) exposures hazardous to health, indicates contact with and suspected exposures hazardous to health.
   Contact/exposure codes may be used as a first-listed code to explain an encounter for testing, or, more commonly, as a secondary code to identify a potential risk.

   2) Inoculations and vaccinations
   Code Z23 is for encounters for inoculations and vaccinations. It indicates that a patient is being seen to receive a prophylactic inoculation against a disease. Procedure codes are required to identify the actual administration of the injection and the type(s) of immunizations given. Code Z23 may be used as a secondary code if the inoculation is given as a routine part of preventive health care, such as a well-baby visit.

   3) Status
   Status codes indicate that a patient is either a carrier of a disease or has the sequelae or residual of a past disease or condition. This includes such things as the presence of prosthetic or mechanical devices resulting from past treatment. A status code is informative, because the status may affect the course of treatment and its outcome. A status code is distinct from a history code. The history code indicates that the patient no longer has the condition.
   A status code should not be used with a diagnosis code from one of the body system chapters, if the diagnosis code includes the information provided by the status code. For example, code Z94.1, Heart transplant status, should not be used with a code from subcategory T86.2, Complications of heart transplant. The status code does not provide additional information. The complication code indicates that the patient is a heart transplant patient.
   For encounters for weaning from a mechanical ventilator, assign a code from subcategory J96.1, Chronic respiratory failure, followed by code Z99.11, Dependence on respirator [ventilator] status.
   The status Z codes/categories are:
   Z14   Genetic carrier
           Genetic carrier status indicates that a person carries a gene, associated with a particular disease, which may be passed to offspring who may develop that disease. The person does not have the disease and is not at risk of developing the disease.
   Z15   Genetic susceptibility to disease Genetic susceptibility indicates that a person has a gene that increases the risk of that person developing the disease.
   Codes from category Z15 should not be used as principal or first-listed codes. If the patient has the condition to which he/she is susceptible, and that condition is the reason for the encounter, the code for the current condition should be sequenced first. If the patient is being seen for follow-up after completed treatment for this condition, and the condition no longer exists, a follow-up

code should be sequenced first, followed by the appropriate personal history and genetic susceptibility codes. If the purpose of the encounter is genetic counseling associated with procreative management, code Z31.5, Encounter for genetic counseling, should be assigned as the first-listed code, followed by a code from category Z15. Additional codes should be assigned for any applicable family or personal history.
   Z16   Resistance to antimicrobial drugs
           This code indicates that a patient has a condition that is resistant to antimicrobial drug treatment. Sequence the infection code first.
   Z17   Estrogen receptor status
   Z18   Retained foreign body fragments
   Z19   Hormone sensitivity malignancy status
   Z21   Asymptomatic HIV infection status This code indicates that a patient has tested positive for HIV but has manifested no signs or symptoms of the disease.
   Z22   Carrier of infectious disease Carrier status indicates that a person harbors the specific organisms of a disease without manifest symptoms and is capable of transmitting the infection.
   Z28.3   Underimmunization status
   Z33.1   Pregnant state, incidental This code is a secondary code only for use when the pregnancy is in no way complicating the reason for visit. Otherwise, a code from the obstetric chapter is required.
   Z66   Do not resuscitate
   This code may be used when it is documented by the provider that a patient is on do not resuscitate status at any time during the stay.
   Z67   Blood type
   Z68   Body mass index (BMI)
           BMI codes should only be assigned when the associated diagnosis (such as overweight or obesity) meets the definition of a reportable diagnosis (see Section III, Reporting Additional Diagnoses). Do not assign BMI codes during pregnancy. See Section I.B.14 for BMI documentation by clinicians other than the patient's provider.
   Z74.01 Bed confinement status
   Z76.82 Awaiting organ transplant status
   Z78   Other specified health status
           Code Z78.1, Physical restraint status, may be used when it is documented by the provider that a patient has been put in restraints during the current encounter. Please note that this code should not be reported when it is documented by the provider that a patient is temporarily restrained during a procedure.
   Z79   Long-term (current) drug therapy
           Codes from this category indicate a patient's continuous use of a prescribed drug (including such things as aspirin therapy) for the long-term treatment of a condition or for prophylactic use. It is not for use for patients who have addictions to drugs. This subcategory is not for use of medications for detoxification or maintenance programs to prevent withdrawal symptoms in patients with drug dependence (e.g., methadone maintenance for opiate dependence). Assign the appropriate code for the drug dependence instead.
           Assign a code from Z79 if the patient is receiving a medication for an extended period as a prophylactic measure (such as for the prevention of deep vein thrombosis) or as treatment of a chronic condition (such as arthritis) or a disease requiring a lengthy course of treatment (such as cancer). Do not assign a code from category Z79 for medication being administered for a brief period of time to treat an acute illness or injury (such as a course of antibiotics to treat acute bronchitis).
   Z88   Allergy status to drugs, medicaments and biological substances Except: Z88.9, Allergy status to unspecified drugs, medicaments and biological substances status
   Z89   Acquired absence of limb
   Z90   Acquired absence of organs, not elsewhere classified
   Z91.0- Allergy status, other than to drugs and biological substances
   Z92.82 Status post administration of tPA (rtPA) in a different facility within the last 24 hours prior to admission to a current facility Assign code Z92.82, Status post administration of tPA (rtPA) in a different facility within the last 24 hours prior to admission to current

facility, as a secondary diagnosis when a patient is received by transfer into a facility and documentation indicates they were administered tissue plasminogen activator (tPA) within the last 24 hours prior to admission to the current facility. This guideline applies even if the patient is still receiving the tPA at the time they are received into the current facility. The appropriate code for the condition for which the tPA was administered (such as cerebrovascular disease or myocardial infarction) should be assigned first. Code Z92.82 is only applicable to the receiving facility record and not to the transferring facility record.

Z93   Artificial opening status
Z94   Transplanted organ and tissue status
Z95   Presence of cardiac and vascular implants and grafts
Z96   Presence of other functional implants
Z97   Presence of other devices
Z98   Other postprocedural states

Assign code Z98.85, Transplanted organ removal status, to indicate that a transplanted organ has been previously removed. This code should not be assigned for the encounter in which the transplanted organ is removed. The complication necessitating removal of the transplant organ should be assigned for that encounter.

See Section I.C.19. for information on the coding of organ transplant complications.

Z99   Dependence on enabling machines and devices, not elsewhere classified

Note: Categories Z89-Z90 and Z93-Z99 are for use only if there are no complications or malfunctions of the organ or tissue replaced, the amputation site or the equipment on which the patient is dependent.

4) History (of)
There are two types of history Z codes, personal and family. Personal history codes explain a patient's past medical condition that no longer exists and is not receiving any treatment, but that has the potential for recurrence, and therefore may require continued monitoring.

Family history codes are for use when a patient has a family member(s) who has had a particular disease that causes the patient to be at higher risk of also contracting the disease.

Personal history codes may be used in conjunction with follow-up codes and family history codes may be used in conjunction with screening codes to explain the need for a test or procedure. History codes are also acceptable on any medical record regardless of the reason for visit. A history of an illness, even if no longer present, is important information that may alter the type of treatment ordered.

The history Z code categories are:
Z80   Family history of primary malignant neoplasm
Z81   Family history of mental and behavioral disorders
Z82   Family history of certain disabilities and chronic diseases (leading to disablement)
Z83   Family history of other specific disorders
Z84   Family history of other conditions
Z85   Personal history of malignant neoplasm
Z86   Personal history of certain other diseases
Z87   Personal history of other diseases and conditions
Z91.4-   Personal history of psychological trauma, not elsewhere classified
Z91.5   Personal history of self-harm
Z91.81   History of falling
Z91.82   Personal history of military deployment
Z92   Personal history of medical treatment Except: Z92.0, Personal history of contraception Except: Z92.82, Status post administration of tPA (rtPA) in a different facility within the last 24 hours prior to admission to a current facility

5) Screening
Screening is the testing for disease or disease precursors in seemingly well individuals so that early detection and treatment can be provided for those who test positive for the disease (e.g., screening mammogram).

The testing of a person to rule out or confirm a suspected diagnosis because the patient has some sign or symptom is a diagnostic examination, not a screening. In these cases, the sign or symptom is used to explain the reason for the test.

A screening code may be a first-listed code if the reason for the visit is specifically the screening exam. It may also be

used as an additional code if the screening is done during an office visit for other health problems. A screening code is not necessary if the screening is inherent to a routine examination, such as a pap smear done during a routine pelvic examination.

Should a condition be discovered during the screening then the code for the condition may be assigned as an additional diagnosis.

The Z code indicates that a screening exam is planned. A procedure code is required to confirm that the screening was performed.

The screening Z codes/categories:
Z11   Encounter for screening for infectious and parasitic diseases
Z12   Encounter for screening for malignant neoplasms
Z13   Encounter for screening for other diseases and disorders Except: Z13.9, Encounter for screening, unspecified
Z36   Encounter for antenatal screening for mother

6) Observation
There are three observation Z code categories. They are for use in very limited circumstances when a person is being observed for a suspected condition that is ruled out. The observation codes are not for use if an injury or illness or any signs or symptoms related to the suspected condition are present. In such cases the diagnosis/symptom code is used with the corresponding external cause code.

The observation codes are to be used as principal diagnosis only. The only exception to this is when the principal diagnosis is required to be a code from category Z38, Liveborn infants according to place of birth and type of delivery. Then a code from category Z05, Encounter for observation and evaluation of newborn for suspected diseases and conditions ruled out, is sequenced after the Z38 code. Additional codes may be used in addition to the observation code but only if they are unrelated to the suspected condition being observed.

Codes from subcategory Z03.7 Encounter for suspected maternal and fetal conditions ruled out, may either be used as a first-listed or as an additional code assignment depending on the case. They are for use in very limited circumstances on a maternal record when an encounter is for a suspected maternal or fetal condition that is ruled out during that encounter (for example, a maternal or fetal condition may be suspected due to an abnormal test result). These codes should not be used when the condition is confirmed. In those cases, the confirmed condition should be coded. In addition, these codes are not for use if an illness or any signs or symptoms related to the suspected condition or problem are present. In such cases the diagnosis/symptom code is used.

Additional codes may be used in addition to the code from subcategory Z03.7, but only if they are unrelated to the suspected condition being evaluated.

Codes from subcategory Z03.7 may not be used for encounters for antenatal screening of mother. *See Section I.C.21. Screening.*

For encounters for suspected fetal condition that are inconclusive following testing and evaluation, assign the appropriate code from category O35, O36, O40 or O41.

The observation Z code categories:
Z03   Encounter for medical observation for suspected diseases and conditions ruled out
Z04   Encounter for examination and observation for other reasons Except: Z04.9, Encounter for examination and observation for unspecified reason
Z05   Encounter for observation and evaluation of newborn for suspected diseases and conditions ruled out

7) Aftercare
Aftercare visit codes cover situations when the initial treatment of a disease has been performed and the patient requires continued care during the healing or recovery phase, or for the long-term consequences of the disease. The aftercare Z code should not be used if treatment is directed at a current, acute disease. The diagnosis code is to be used in these cases.

Exceptions to this rule are codes Z51.0, Encounter for antineoplastic radiation therapy, and codes from subcategory Z51.1, Encounter for antineoplastic chemotherapy and immunotherapy. These codes are to be first-listed, followed by the diagnosis code when a patient's encounter is solely to receive radiation therapy, chemotherapy, or immunotherapy for the treatment of a neoplasm. If the reason for the encounter is more than one type of antineoplastic therapy, code Z51.0 and a code from subcategory Z51.1 may be assigned together, in which case one of these codes would be reported as a secondary diagnosis.

The aftercare Z codes should also not be used for aftercare for injuries. For aftercare of an injury, assign the acute injury code with the appropriate 7th character (for subsequent encounter).

The aftercare codes are generally first-listed to explain the specific reason for the encounter. An aftercare code may be used as an additional code when some type of aftercare is provided in addition to the reason for admission and no diagnosis code is applicable. An example of this would be the closure of a colostomy during an encounter for treatment of another condition.

Aftercare codes should be used in conjunction with other aftercare codes or diagnosis codes to provide better detail on the specifics of an aftercare encounter visit, unless otherwise directed by the classification. Should a patient receive multiple types of antineoplastic therapy during the same encounter, code Z51.0, Encounter for antineoplastic radiation therapy, and codes from subcategory Z51.1, Encounter for antineoplastic chemotherapy and immunotherapy, may be used together on a record. The sequencing of multiple aftercare codes depends on the circumstances of the encounter.

Certain aftercare Z code categories need a secondary diagnosis code to describe the resolving condition or sequelae. For others, the condition is included in the code title.

Additional Z code aftercare category terms include fitting and adjustment, and attention to artificial openings.

Status Z codes may be used with aftercare Z codes to indicate the nature of the aftercare. For example code Z95.1, Presence of aortocoronary bypass graft, may be used with code Z48.812, Encounter for surgical aftercare following surgery on the circulatory system, to indicate the surgery for which the aftercare is being performed. A status code should not be used when the aftercare code indicates the type of status, such as using Z43.0, Encounter for attention to tracheostomy, with Z93.0, Tracheostomy status.

The aftercare Z category/codes:

Z42	Encounter for plastic and reconstructive surgery following medical procedure or healed injury
Z43	Encounter for attention to artificial openings
Z44	Encounter for fitting and adjustment of external prosthetic device
Z45	Encounter for adjustment and management of implanted device
Z46	Encounter for fitting and adjustment of other devices
Z47	Orthopedic aftercare
Z48	Encounter for other postprocedural aftercare
Z49	Encounter for care involving renal dialysis
Z51	Encounter for other aftercare and medical care

8) Follow-up

The follow-up codes are used to explain continuing surveillance following completed treatment of a disease, condition, or injury. They imply that the condition has been fully treated and no longer exists. They should not be confused with aftercare codes, or injury codes with a 7th character for subsequent encounter, that explain ongoing care of a healing condition or its sequelae. Follow-up codes may be used in conjunction with history codes to provide the full picture of the healed condition and its treatment. The follow-up code is sequenced first, followed by the history code.

A follow-up code may be used to explain multiple visits. Should a condition be found to have recurred on the follow-up visit, then the diagnosis code for the condition should be assigned in place of the follow-up code.

The follow-up Z code categories:

Z08	Encounter for follow-up examination after completed treatment for malignant neoplasm
Z09	Encounter for follow-up examination after completed treatment for conditions other than malignant neoplasm
Z39	Encounter for maternal postpartum care and examination

9) Donor

Codes in category Z52, Donors of organs and tissues, are used for living individuals who are donating blood or other body tissue.

These codes are only for individuals donating for others, not for self-donations. They are not used to identify cadaveric donations.

10) Counseling

Counseling Z codes are used when a patient or family member receives assistance in the aftermath of an illness or injury, or when support is required in coping with family or social problems.

The counseling Z codes/categories:

Z30.0-	Encounter for general counseling and advice on contraception
Z31.5	Encounter for procreative genetic counseling
Z31.6-	Encounter for general counseling and advice on procreation
Z32.2	Encounter for childbirth instruction
Z32.3	Encounter for childcare instruction
Z69	Encounter for mental health services for victim and perpetrator of abuse
Z70	Counseling related to sexual attitude, behavior and orientation
Z71	Persons encountering health services for other counseling and medical advice, not elsewhere classified
Z76.81	Expectant mother prebirth pediatrician visit

11) Encounters for Obstetrical and Reproductive Services

See Section I.C.15. Pregnancy, Childbirth, and the Puerperium, for further instruction on the use of these codes.

Z codes for pregnancy are for use in those circumstances when none of the problems or complications included in the codes from the Obstetrics chapter exist (a routine prenatal visit or postpartum care). Codes in category Z34, Encounter for supervision of normal pregnancy, are always first listed and are not to be used with any other code from the OB chapter.

Codes in category Z3A, Weeks of gestation, may be assigned to provide additional information about the pregnancy. Category Z3A codes should not be assigned for pregnancies with abortive outcomes (categories O00-O08), elective termination of pregnancy (code Z33.2), nor for postpartum conditions, as category Z3A is not applicable to these conditions. The date of the admission should be used to determine weeks of gestation for inpatient admissions that encompass more than one gestational week.

The outcome of delivery, category Z37, should be included on all maternal delivery records. It is always a secondary code. Codes in category Z37 should not be used on the newborn record.

Z codes for family planning (contraceptive) or procreative management and counseling should be included on an obstetric record either during the pregnancy or the postpartum stage, if applicable.

Z codes/categories for obstetrical and reproductive services:

Z30	Encounter for contraceptive management
Z31	Encounter for procreative management
Z32.2	Encounter for childbirth instruction
Z32.3	Encounter for childcare instruction
Z33	Pregnant state
Z34	Encounter for supervision of normal pregnancy
Z36	Encounter for antenatal screening of mother
Z3A	Weeks of gestation
Z37	Outcome of delivery
Z39	Encounter for maternal postpartum care and examination
Z76.81	Expectant mother prebirth pediatrician visit

12) Newborns and Infants

See Section I.C.16. Newborn (Perinatal) Guidelines, for further instruction on the use of these codes.

Newborn Z codes/categories:

Z76.1	Encounter for health supervision and care of foundling
Z00.1-	Encounter for routine child health examination
Z38	Liveborn infants according to place of birth and type of delivery

13) Routine and administrative examinations

The Z codes allow for the description of encounters for routine examinations, such as, a general check-up, or, examinations for administrative purposes, such as, a pre-employment physical. The codes are not to be used if the examination is for diagnosis of a suspected condition or for treatment purposes. In such cases the diagnosis code is used. During a routine exam, should a diagnosis or condition be discovered, it should be coded as an additional code. Pre-existing and chronic conditions and history codes may also be included as additional codes as long as the examination is for administrative purposes and not focused on any particular condition.

Some of the codes for routine health examinations distinguish between "with" and "without" abnormal findings. Code assignment depends on the information that is known at the time the encounter is being coded. For example, if no abnormal findings were found during the examination, but the encounter is being coded before test results are back, it is acceptable to assign the code for "without abnormal findings." When assigning a code for "with abnormal findings," additional code(s) should be assigned to identify the specific abnormal finding(s).

Pre-operative examination and pre-procedural laboratory examination Z codes are for use only in those situations when a patient is being cleared for a procedure or surgery and no treatment is given.

The Z codes/categories for routine and administrative examinations:

Z00	Encounter for general examination without complaint, suspected or reported diagnosis
Z01	Encounter for other special examination without complaint, suspected or reported diagnosis
Z02	Encounter for administrative examination Except: Z02.9, Encounter for administrative examinations, unspecified
Z32.0-	Encounter for pregnancy test

14) Miscellaneous Z codes
The miscellaneous Z codes capture a number of other health care encounters that do not fall into one of the other categories. Certain of these codes identify the reason for the encounter; others are for use as additional codes that provide useful information on circumstances that may affect a patient's care and treatment.

Prophylactic Organ Removal
For encounters specifically for prophylactic removal of an organ (such as prophylactic removal of breasts due to a genetic susceptibility to cancer or a family history of cancer), the principal or first-listed code should be a code from category Z40, Encounter for prophylactic surgery, followed by the appropriate codes to identify the associated risk factor (such as genetic susceptibility or family history).

If the patient has a malignancy of one site and is having prophylactic removal at another site to prevent either a new primary malignancy or metastatic disease, a code for the malignancy should also be assigned in addition to a code from subcategory Z40.0, Encounter for prophylactic surgery for risk factors related to malignant neoplasms. A Z40.0 code should not be assigned if the patient is having organ removal for treatment of a malignancy, such as the removal of the testes for the treatment of prostate cancer.

Miscellaneous Z codes/categories:

Z28	Immunization not carried out Except: Z28.3, Underimmunization status
Z29	Encounter for other prophylactic measures
Z40	Encounter for prophylactic surgery
Z41	Encounter for procedures for purposes other than remedying health state Except: Z41.9, Encounter for procedure for purposes other than remedying health state, unspecified
Z53	Persons encountering health services for specific procedures and treatment, not carried out
Z55	Problems related to education and literacy
Z56	Problems related to employment and unemployment
Z57	Occupational exposure to risk factors
Z58	Problems related to physical environment
Z59	Problems related to housing and economic circumstances
Z60	Problems related to social environment
Z62	Problems related to upbringing
Z63	Other problems related to primary support group, including family circumstances
Z64	Problems related to certain psychosocial circumstances
Z65	Problems related to other psychosocial circumstances
Z72	Problems related to lifestyle Note: These codes should be assigned only when the documentation specifies that the patient has an associated problem
Z73	Problems related to life management difficulty

Z74	Problems related to care provider dependency Except: Z74.01, Bed confinement status
Z75	Problems related to medical facilities and other health care
Z76.0	Encounter for issue of repeat prescription
Z76.3	Healthy person accompanying sick person
Z76.4	Other boarder to healthcare facility
Z76.5	Malingerer [conscious simulation]
Z91.1-	Patient's noncompliance with medical treatment and regimen
Z91.83	Wandering in diseases classified elsewhere
Z91.84-	Oral health risk factors
Z91.89	Other specified personal risk factors, not elsewhere classified

See Section I.B.14 for Z55-Z65 Persons with potential health hazards related to socioeconomic and psychosocial circumstances, documentation by clinicians other than the patient's provider.

15) Nonspecific Z codes
Certain Z codes are so non-specific, or potentially redundant with other codes in the classification, that there can be little justification for their use in the inpatient setting. Their use in the outpatient setting should be limited to those instances when there is no further documentation to permit more precise coding. Otherwise, any sign or symptom or any other reason for visit that is captured in another code should be used.

Nonspecific Z codes/categories:

Z02.9	Encounter for administrative examinations, unspecified
Z04.9	Encounter for examination and observation for unspecified reason
Z13.9	Encounter for screening, unspecified
Z41.9	Encounter for procedure for purposes other than remedying health state, unspecified
Z52.9	Donor of unspecified organ or tissue
Z86.59	Personal history of other mental and behavioral disorders
Z88.9	Allergy status to unspecified drugs, medicaments and biological substances status
Z92.0	Personal history of contraception

16) Z Codes That May Only Be Principal/First-Listed Diagnosis
The following Z codes/categories may only be reported as the principal/first-listed diagnosis, except when there are multiple encounters on the same day and the medical records for the encounters are combined:

Z00	Encounter for general examination without complaint, suspected or reported diagnosis Except: Z00.6
Z01	Encounter for other special examination without complaint, suspected or reported diagnosis
Z02	Encounter for administrative examination
Z03	Encounter for medical observation for suspected diseases and conditions ruled out
Z04	Encounter for examination and observation for other reasons
Z33.2	Encounter for elective termination of pregnancy
Z31.81	Encounter for male factor infertility in female patient
Z31.83	Encounter for assisted reproductive fertility procedure cycle
Z31.84	Encounter for fertility preservation procedure
Z34	Encounter for supervision of normal pregnancy
Z39	Encounter for maternal postpartum care and examination
Z38	Liveborn infants according to place of birth and type of delivery
Z40	Encounter for prophylactic surgery
Z42	Encounter for plastic and reconstructive surgery following medical procedure or healed injury
Z51.0	Encounter for antineoplastic radiation therapy
Z51.1-	Encounter for antineoplastic chemotherapy and immunotherapy
Z52	Donors of organs and tissues Except: Z52.9, Donor of unspecified organ or tissue
Z76.1	Encounter for health supervision and care of foundling
Z76.2	Encounter for health supervision and care of other healthy infant and child
Z99.12	Encounter for respirator [ventilator] dependence during power failure

CHAPTER 21

FACTORS INFLUENCING HEALTH STATUS AND CONTACT WITH HEALTH SERVICES (Z00-Z99)

Note: Z codes represent reasons for encounters. A corresponding procedure code must accompany a Z code if a procedure is performed. Categories Z00-Z99 are provided for occasions when circumstances other than a disease, injury or external cause classifiable to categories A00-Y89 are recorded as "diagnoses" or "problems." This can arise in two main ways:

(a) When a person who may or may not be sick encounters the health services for some specific purpose, such as to receive limited care or service for a current condition, to donate an organ or tissue, to receive prophylactic vaccination (immunization), or to discuss a problem which is in itself not a disease or injury.

(b) When some circumstance or problem is present which influences the person's health status but is not in itself a current illness or injury.

This chapter contains the following blocks:

Z00-Z13	Persons encountering health services for examination
Z14-Z15	Genetic carrier and genetic susceptibility to disease
Z16	Resistance to antimicrobial drugs
Z17	Estrogen receptor status
Z18	Retained foreign body fragments
Z19	Hormone sensitivity malignancy status
Z20-Z29	Persons with potential health hazards related to communicable diseases
Z30-Z39	Persons encountering health services in circumstances related to reproduction
Z40-Z53	Encounters for other specific health care
Z55-Z65	Persons with potential health hazards related to socioeconomic and psychosocial circumstances
Z66	Do not resuscitate status
Z67	Blood type
Z68	Body mass index (BMI)
Z69-Z76	Persons encountering health services in other circumstances
Z77-Z99	Persons with potential health hazards related to family and personal history and certain conditions influencing health status

PERSONS ENCOUNTERING HEALTH SERVICES FOR EXAMINATIONS (Z00-Z13)

Note: Nonspecific abnormal findings disclosed at the time of these examinations are classified to categories R70-R94.

Excludes1 examinations related to pregnancy and reproduction (Z30-Z36, Z39.-)

● **Z00   Encounter for general examination without complaint, suspected or reported diagnosis**

Excludes1 encounter for examination for administrative purposes (Z02.-)

Excludes2 encounter for pre-procedural examinations (Z01.81-)
special screening examinations (Z11-Z13)

● **Z00.0   Encounter for general adult medical examination**
Encounter for adult periodic examination (annual) (physical) and any associated laboratory and radiologic examinations

Excludes1 encounter for examination of sign or symptom - code to sign or symptom
general health check-up of infant or child (Z00.12.-)

Coding Clinic: 2016, Q4, P131

Z00.00   Encounter for general adult medical examination without abnormal findings   A
Encounter for adult health check-up NOS
Coding Clinic: 2017, Q4, P95; 2016, Q1, P37

Z00.01   Encounter for general adult medical examination with abnormal findings   A
Use additional code to identify abnormal findings
Coding Clinic: 2016, Q1, P36

● **Z00.1   Encounter for newborn, infant and child health examinations**

● **Z00.11   Newborn health examination**
Health check for child under 29 days old
Use additional code to identify any abnormal findings

Excludes1 health check for child over 28 days old (Z00.12-)

Z00.110   Health examination for newborn under 8 days old   N
Health check for newborn under 8 days old

Z00.111   Health examination for newborn 8 to 28 days old   N
Health check for newborn 8 to 28 days old
Newborn weight check

● **Z00.12   Encounter for routine child health examination**
Immunizations appropriate for age
Health check (routine) for child over 28 days old
Routine developmental screening of infant or child
Routine vision and hearing testing

Excludes1 health check for child under 29 days old (Z00.11-)
health supervision of foundling or other healthy infant or child (Z76.1-Z76.2)
newborn health examination (Z00.11-)

Z00.121   Encounter for routine child health examination with abnormal findings   P
Use additional code to identify abnormal findings
Coding Clinic: 2017, Q4, P95; 2016, Q1, P34-35

Z00.129   Encounter for routine child health examination without abnormal findings   P
Encounter for routine child health examination NOS
Coding Clinic: 2016, Q1, P34

Z00.2   Encounter for examination for period of rapid growth in childhood   P

Z00.3   Encounter for examination for adolescent development state   P
Encounter for puberty development state

Z00.5   Encounter for examination of potential donor of organ and tissue

Z00.6   Encounter for examination for normal comparison and control in clinical research program
Examination of participant or control in clinical research program

● **Z00.7   Encounter for examination for period of delayed growth in childhood**

Z00.70   Encounter for examination for period of delayed growth in childhood without abnormal findings   P

Z00.71   Encounter for examination for period of delayed growth in childhood with abnormal findings   P
Use additional code to identify abnormal findings

Z00.8   Encounter for other general examination
Encounter for health examination in population surveys

● **Z01   Encounter for other special examination without complaint, suspected or reported diagnosis**

Includes   routine examination of specific system

Note: Codes from category Z01 represent the reason for the encounter. A separate procedure code is required to identify any examinations or procedures performed.

Excludes1   encounter for examination for administrative purposes (Z02.-)
encounter for examination for suspected conditions, proven not to exist (Z03.-)
encounter for laboratory and radiologic examinations as a component of general medical examinations (Z00.0-)
encounter for laboratory, radiologic and imaging examinations for sign(s) and symptom(s) - code to the sign(s) or symptom(s)

Excludes2   screening examinations (Z11-Z13)

● **Z01.0   Encounter for examination of eyes and vision**

Excludes1   examination for driving license (Z02.4)

Z01.00   Encounter for examination of eyes and vision without abnormal findings
Encounter for examination of eyes and vision NOS

Z01.01   Encounter for examination of eyes and vision with abnormal findings
Use additional code to identify abnormal findings
Coding Clinic: 2016, Q4, P21

● **Z01.02   Encounter for examination of eyes and vision following failed vision screening**

Excludes1   examination for examination of eyes and vision with abnormal findings (Z01.01)
examination for examination of eyes and vision without abnormal findings (Z01.00)

● **Z01.020   Encounter for examination of eyes and vision following failed vision screening without abnormal findings**

● **Z01.021   Encounter for examination of eyes and vision following failed vision screening with abnormal findings**
Use additional code to identify abnormal findings

● **Z01.1   Encounter for examination of ears and hearing**

Z01.10   Encounter for examination of ears and hearing without abnormal findings
Encounter for examination of ears and hearing NOS
Coding Clinic: 2016, Q4, P25

● **Z01.11   Encounter for examination of ears and hearing with abnormal findings**
Coding Clinic: 2016, Q3, P18

Z01.110   Encounter for hearing examination following failed hearing screening
Coding Clinic: 2016, Q3, P18-19

Z01.118   Encounter for examination of ears and hearing with other abnormal findings
Use additional code to identify abnormal findings
Coding Clinic: 2016, Q3, P17

Z01.12   Encounter for hearing conservation and treatment

● **Z01.2   Encounter for dental examination and cleaning**

Z01.20   Encounter for dental examination and cleaning without abnormal findings
Encounter for dental examination and cleaning NOS

Z01.21   Encounter for dental examination and cleaning with abnormal findings
Use additional code to identify abnormal findings

● **Z01.3   Encounter for examination of blood pressure**

Z01.30   Encounter for examination of blood pressure without abnormal findings
Encounter for examination of blood pressure NOS

Z01.31   Encounter for examination of blood pressure with abnormal findings
Use additional code to identify abnormal findings

● **Z01.4   Encounter for gynecological examination**

Excludes2   pregnancy examination or test (Z32.0-)
routine examination for contraceptive maintenance (Z30.4-)

● **Z01.41   Encounter for routine gynecological examination**
Encounter for general gynecological examination with or without cervical smear
Encounter for gynecological examination (general) (routine) NOS
Encounter for pelvic examination (annual) (periodic)
Use additional code:
for screening for human papillomavirus, if applicable (Z11.51)
for screening vaginal pap smear, if applicable (Z12.72)
to identify acquired absence of uterus, if applicable (Z90.71-)

Excludes1   gynecologic examination status-post hysterectomy for malignant condition (Z08)
screening cervical pap smear not a part of a routine gynecological examination (Z12.4)

Z01.411   Encounter for gynecological examination (general) (routine) with abnormal findings ♀
Use additional code to identify any abnormal findings

Z01.419   Encounter for gynecological examination (general) (routine) without abnormal findings ♀

Z01.42   Encounter for cervical smear to confirm findings of recent normal smear following initial abnormal smear ♀

● **Z01.8   Encounter for other specified special examinations**

● **Z01.81   Encounter for preprocedural examinations**
Encounter for preoperative examinations
Encounter for radiological and imaging examinations as part of preprocedural examination

Z01.810   Encounter for preprocedural cardiovascular examination

Z01.811   Encounter for preprocedural respiratory examination

Z01.812   Encounter for preprocedural laboratory examination
Blood and urine tests prior to treatment or procedure

Z01.818   Encounter for other preprocedural examination
Encounter for preprocedural examination NOS
Encounter for examinations prior to antineoplastic chemotherapy

▶ New   ⇒ Revised   ~~deleted~~ Deleted   Excludes 1   Excludes 2   Includes   Use additional   Code first   Code also   Key words
OGCR Official Guidelines   X Assign placeholder X   ● Use Additional Character(s)   ▷ Manifestation Code   🐾 Hierarchical Condition Category   Coding Clinic

Z01.82   Encounter for allergy testing
> **Excludes1**   encounter for antibody response examination (Z01.84)

Z01.83   Encounter for blood typing
> Encounter for Rh typing

Z01.84   Encounter for antibody response examination
> Encounter for immunity status testing
> **Excludes1**   encounter for allergy testing (Z01.82)

Z01.89   Encounter for other specified special examinations

● **Z02   Encounter for administrative examination**

Z02.0   Encounter for examination for admission to educational institution
> Encounter for examination for admission to preschool (education)
> Encounter for examination for re-admission to school following illness or medical treatment

Z02.1   Encounter for pre-employment examination

Z02.2   Encounter for examination for admission to residential institution
> **Excludes1**   examination for admission to prison (Z02.89)

Z02.3   Encounter for examination for recruitment to armed forces

Z02.4   Encounter for examination for driving license

Z02.5   Encounter for examination for participation in sport
> **Excludes1**   blood-alcohol and blood-drug test (Z02.83)

Z02.6   Encounter for examination for insurance purposes

● **Z02.7   Encounter for issue of medical certificate**
> **Excludes1**   encounter for general medical examination (Z00-Z01, Z02.0-Z02.6, Z02.8-Z02.9)

Z02.71   Encounter for disability determination
> Encounter for issue of medical certificate of incapacity
> Encounter for issue of medical certificate of invalidity

Z02.79   Encounter for issue of other medical certificate

● **Z02.8   Encounter for other administrative examinations**

Z02.81   Encounter for paternity testing

Z02.82   Encounter for adoption services

Z02.83   Encounter for blood-alcohol and blood-drug test
> Use additional code for findings of alcohol or drugs in blood (R78.-)

Z02.89   Encounter for other administrative examinations
> Encounter for examination for admission to prison
> Encounter for examination for admission to summer camp
> Encounter for immigration examination
> Encounter for naturalization examination
> Encounter for premarital examination
> **Excludes1**   health supervision of foundling or other healthy infant or child (Z76.1-Z76.2)

Z02.9   Encounter for administrative examinations, unspecified

OGCR Section II.C.21.c.6.

Observation

There are three observation Z code categories. They are for use in very limited circumstances when a person is being observed for a suspected condition that is ruled out. The observation codes are not for use if an injury or illnesses or any signs or symptoms related to the suspected condition are present. In such cases the diagnosis/symptom code is used with the corresponding external cause code.

The observation codes are to be used as principal diagnosis only. The only exception to this is when the principal diagnosis is required to be a code from category Z38, Liveborn infants according to place of birth and type of delivery. Then a code from category Z05, Encounter for observation and evaluation of newborn for suspected diseases and conditions ruled out, is sequenced after the Z38 code. Additional codes may be used in addition to the observation code but only if they are unrelated to the suspected condition being observed.

Codes from subcategory Z03.7 Encounter for suspected maternal and fetal conditions ruled out, may either be used as a first listed or as an additional code assignment depending on the case. They are for use in very limited circumstances on a maternal record when an encounter is for a suspected maternal or fetal condition that is ruled out during that encounter (for example, a maternal or fetal condition may be suspected due to an abnormal test result). These codes should not be used when the condition is confirmed. In those cases, the confirmed condition should be coded. In addition, these codes are not for use if an illness or any signs or symptoms related to the suspected condition or problem are present. In such cases the diagnosis/symptom code is used.

Additional codes may be used in addition to the code from subcategory Z03.7, but only if they are unrelated to the suspected condition being evaluated.

Codes from subcategory Z03.7 may not be used for encounters for antenatal screening of mother. *See Section I.C.21. Screening.*

For encounters for suspected fetal condition that are inconclusive following testing and evaluation, assign the appropriate code from category O35, O36, O40 or O41.

The observation Z code categories:

Z03   Encounter for medical observation for suspected diseases and conditions ruled out

Z04   Encounter for examination and observation for other reasons
> Except: Z04.9, Encounter for examination and observation for unspecified reason

Z05   Encounter for observation and evaluation of newborn for suspected diseases and conditions ruled out

● **Z03   Encounter for medical observation for suspected diseases and conditions ruled out**
> This category is to be used when a person without a diagnosis is suspected of having an abnormal condition, without signs or symptoms, which requires study, but after examination and observation, is ruled out. This category is also for use for administrative and legal observation status.
> **Excludes1**   contact with and (suspected) exposures hazardous to health (Z77.-)
> encounter for observation and evaluation of newborn for suspected diseases and conditions ruled out (Z05.-)
> person with feared complaint in whom no diagnosis is made (Z71.1)
> signs or symptoms under study - code to signs or symptoms

Z03.6   Encounter for observation for suspected toxic effect from ingested substance ruled out
> Encounter for observation for suspected adverse effect from drug
> Encounter for observation for suspected poisoning

CHAPTER 21 (Z00-Z99)

● **Z03.7**   **Encounter for suspected maternal and fetal conditions ruled out**
Encounter for suspected maternal and fetal conditions not found

> **Excludes1**   known or suspected fetal anomalies affecting management of mother, not ruled out (O26.-, O35.-, O36.-, O40.-, O41.-)

Z03.71   **Encounter for suspected problem with amniotic cavity and membrane ruled out** ♀   **M**
Encounter for suspected oligohydramnios ruled out
Encounter for suspected polyhydramnios ruled out

Z03.72   **Encounter for suspected placental problem ruled out** ♀   **M**

Z03.73   **Encounter for suspected fetal anomaly ruled out** ♀   **M**
Coding Clinic: 2016, Q4, P6

Z03.74   **Encounter for suspected problem with fetal growth ruled out** ♀   **M**

Z03.75   **Encounter for suspected cervical shortening ruled out** ♀   **M**

Z03.79   **Encounter for other suspected maternal and fetal conditions ruled out** ♀   **M**
Coding Clinic: 2016, Q4, P7

● **Z03.8**   **Encounter for observation for other suspected diseases and conditions ruled out**

● **Z03.81**   **Encounter for observation for suspected exposure to biological agents ruled out**

Z03.810   **Encounter for observation for suspected exposure to anthrax ruled out**

Z03.818   **Encounter for observation for suspected exposure to other biological agents ruled out**

▶● **Z03.82** **Encounter for observation for suspected foreign body ruled out**

> ▶ **Excludes1**   retained foreign body (Z18.-)
> ▶ retained foreign body in eyelid (H02.81)
> ▶ residual foreign body in soft tissue (M79.5)

> ▶ **Excludes2**   confirmed foreign body ingestion or aspiration including:
> ▶ foreign body in alimentary tract (T18)
> ▶ foreign body in ear (T16)
> ▶ foreign body on external eye (T15)
> ▶ foreign body in respiratory tract (T17)

▶ **Z03.821**   **Encounter for observation for suspected ingested foreign body ruled out**

▶ **Z03.822**   **Encounter for observation for suspected aspirated (inhaled) foreign body ruled out**

▶ **Z03.823**   **Encounter for observation for suspected inserted (injected) foreign body ruled out**
> ▶ Encounter for observation for suspected inserted (injected) foreign body in eye ruled out
> ▶ Encounter for observation for suspected inserted (injected) foreign body in orifice ruled out
> ▶ Encounter for observation for suspected inserted (injected) foreign body in skin ruled out

Z03.89   **Encounter for observation for other suspected diseases and conditions ruled out**

● **Z04**   **Encounter for examination and observation for other reasons**

> **Includes**   encounter for examination for medicolegal reasons
> This category is to be used when a person without a diagnosis is suspected of having an abnormal condition, without signs or symptoms, which requires study, but after examination and observation, is ruled-out. This category is also for use for administrative and legal observation status.

Z04.1   **Encounter for examination and observation following transport accident**

> **Excludes1**   encounter for examination and observation following work accident (Z04.2)
Coding Clinic: 2019, Q2, P11

Z04.2   **Encounter for examination and observation following work accident**

Z04.3   **Encounter for examination and observation following other accident**

● **Z04.4**   **Encounter for examination and observation following alleged rape**
Encounter for examination and observation of victim following alleged rape
Encounter for examination and observation of victim following alleged sexual abuse
Coding Clinic: 2016, Q4, P129

Z04.41   **Encounter for examination and observation following alleged adult rape**   **A**
Suspected adult rape, ruled out
Suspected adult sexual abuse, ruled out

Z04.42   **Encounter for examination and observation following alleged child rape**   **P**
Suspected child rape, ruled out
Suspected child sexual abuse, ruled out

Z04.6   **Encounter for general psychiatric examination, requested by authority**

● **Z04.7**   **Encounter for examination and observation following alleged physical abuse**

Z04.71   **Encounter for examination and observation following alleged adult physical abuse**   **A**
Suspected adult physical abuse, ruled out

> **Excludes1**   confirmed case of adult physical abuse (T74.-)
> encounter for examination and observation following alleged adult sexual abuse (Z04.41)
> suspected case of adult physical abuse, not ruled out (T76.-)

Z04.72   **Encounter for examination and observation following alleged child physical abuse**   **P**
Suspected child physical abuse, ruled out

> **Excludes1**   confirmed case of child physical abuse (T74.-)
> encounter for examination and observation following alleged child sexual abuse (Z04.42)
> suspected case of child physical abuse, not ruled out (T76.-)

● **Z04.8**   **Encounter for examination and observation for other specified reasons**
Encounter for examination and observation for request for expert evidence

Z04.81   **Encounter for examination and observation of victim following forced sexual exploitation**

Z04.82   **Encounter for examination and observation of victim following forced labor exploitation**

Z04.89   **Encounter for examination and observation for other specified reasons**

Z04.9   **Encounter for examination and observation for unspecified reason**
Encounter for observation NOS

▶ New   ⇒ Revised   ~~deleted~~ Deleted   Excludes 1   Excludes 2   Includes   Use additional   Code first   Code also   Key words

   OGCR Official Guidelines   X Assign placeholder X   ● Use Additional Character(s)   ▷ Manifestation Code   🐾 Hierarchical Condition Category   Coding Clinic

● **Z05   Encounter for observation and evaluation of newborn for suspected diseases and conditions ruled out**

This category is to be used for newborns, within the neonatal period (the first 28 days of life), who are suspected of having an abnormal condition, but without signs or symptoms, and which, after examination and observation, is ruled out.

Coding Clinic: 2019, Q2, P11; 2016, Q4, P54, 77, 126-127, 130

Z05.0   Observation and evaluation of newborn for suspected cardiac condition ruled out   N

Z05.1   Observation and evaluation of newborn for suspected infectious condition ruled out   N

Coding Clinic: 2019, Q2, P11

Z05.2   Observation and evaluation of newborn for suspected neurological condition ruled out   N

Z05.3   Observation and evaluation of newborn for suspected respiratory condition ruled out   N

● **Z05.4   Observation and evaluation of newborn for suspected genetic, metabolic or immunologic condition ruled out**

    Z05.41   Observation and evaluation of newborn for suspected genetic condition ruled out   N

       Coding Clinic: 2016, Q4, P55

    Z05.42   Observation and evaluation of newborn for suspected metabolic condition ruled out   N

    Z05.43   Observation and evaluation of newborn for suspected immunologic condition ruled out   N

Z05.5   Observation and evaluation of newborn for suspected gastrointestinal condition ruled out   N

Z05.6   Observation and evaluation of newborn for suspected genitourinary condition ruled out   N

● **Z05.7   Observation and evaluation of newborn for suspected skin, subcutaneous, musculoskeletal and connective tissue condition ruled out**

    Z05.71   Observation and evaluation of newborn for suspected skin and subcutaneous tissue condition ruled out   N

    Z05.72   Observation and evaluation of newborn for suspected musculoskeletal condition ruled out   N

    Z05.73   Observation and evaluation of newborn for suspected connective tissue condition ruled out   N

Z05.8   Observation and evaluation of newborn for other specified suspected condition ruled out   N

Z05.9   Observation and evaluation of newborn for unspecified suspected condition ruled out   N

OGCR   See Section II.C.21.c.8.

> The follow-up codes are used to explain continuing surveillance following completed treatment of a disease, condition, or injury. They imply that the condition has been fully treated and no longer exists. They should not be confused with aftercare codes, or injury codes with 7th character "D," that explain ongoing care of a healing condition or its sequelae. Follow-up codes may be used in conjunction with history codes to provide the full picture of the healed condition and its treatment. The follow-up code is sequenced first, followed by the history code.
>
> A follow-up code may be used to explain multiple visits. Should a condition be found to have recurred on the follow-up visit, then the diagnosis code for the condition should be assigned in place of the follow-up code.
>
> The follow-up Z code categories:
>
> Z08   Encounter for follow-up examination after completed treatment for malignant neoplasm
>
> Z09   Encounter for follow-up examination after completed treatment for conditions other than malignant neoplasm
>
> Z39   Encounter for maternal postpartum care and examination

Z08   Encounter for follow-up examination after completed treatment for malignant neoplasm

Medical surveillance following completed treatment

Use additional code to identify any acquired absence of organs (Z90.-)

Use additional code to identify the personal history of malignant neoplasm (Z85.-)

Excludes1   aftercare following medical care (Z43-Z49, Z51)

Z09   Encounter for follow-up examination after completed treatment for conditions other than malignant neoplasm

Medical surveillance following completed treatment

Use additional code to identify any applicable history of disease code (Z86.-. Z87.-)

Excludes1   aftercare following medical care (Z43-Z49, Z51)
              surveillance of contraception (Z30.4-)
              surveillance of prosthetic and other medical devices (Z44-Z46)

Coding Clinic: 2017, Q1, P9; 2015, Q1, P8

OGCR   Section II.C.21.c.5.

> Screening
>
> Screening is the testing for disease or disease precursors in seemingly well individuals so that early detection and treatment can be provided for those who test positive for the disease (e.g., screening mammogram).
>
> The testing of a person to rule out or confirm a suspected diagnosis because the patient has some sign or symptom is a diagnostic examination, not a screening. In these cases, the sign or symptom is used to explain the reason for the test.
>
> A screening code may be a first listed code if the reason for the visit is specifically the screening exam. It may also be used as an additional code if the screening is done during an office visit for other health problems. A screening code is not necessary if the screening is inherent to a routine examination, such as a pap smear done during a routine pelvic examination.
>
> Should a condition be discovered during the screening then the code for the condition may be assigned as an additional diagnosis.
>
> The Z code indicates that a screening exam is planned. A procedure code is required to confirm that the screening was performed.
>
> The screening Z codes/categories:
>
> Z11   Encounter for screening for infectious and parasitic diseases
>
> Z12   Encounter for screening for malignant neoplasms
>
> Z13   Encounter for screening for other diseases and disorders
>   Except: Z13.9, Encounter for screening, unspecified
>
> Z36   Encounter for antenatal screening for mother

● **Z11   Encounter for screening for infectious and parasitic diseases**

Screening is the testing for disease or disease precursors in asymptomatic individuals so that early detection and treatment can be provided for those who test positive for the disease.

Excludes1   encounter for diagnostic examination - code to sign or symptom

Z11.0   Encounter for screening for intestinal infectious diseases

Encounter for screening for active tuberculosis disease

Z11.1   Encounter for screening for respiratory tuberculosis

Z11.2   Encounter for screening for other bacterial diseases

Z11.3   Encounter for screening for infections with a predominantly sexual mode of transmission

Excludes2   encounter for screening for human immunodeficiency virus [HIV] (Z11.4)
              encounter for screening for human papillomavirus (Z11.51)

Z11.4   Encounter for screening for human immunodeficiency virus [HIV]

● **Z11.5**   **Encounter for screening for other viral diseases**

> **Excludes2**   encounter for screening for viral intestinal disease (Z11.0)

     Z11.51   Encounter for screening for human papillomavirus (HPV)

     Z11.59   Encounter for screening for other viral diseases

Z11.6   **Encounter for screening for other protozoal diseases and helminthiases**

> *Diseases or infestations caused by parasitic worms*

> **Excludes2**   encounter for screening for protozoal intestinal disease (Z11.0)

Z11.7   **Encounter for testing for latent tuberculosis infection**

Z11.8   **Encounter for screening for other infectious and parasitic diseases**

> Encounter for screening for chlamydia
> Encounter for screening for rickettsial
> Encounter for screening for spirochetal
> Encounter for screening for mycoses

Z11.9   **Encounter for screening for infectious and parasitic diseases, unspecified**

● **Z12**   **Encounter for screening for malignant neoplasms**

> Screening is the testing for disease or disease precursors in asymptomatic individuals so that early detection and treatment can be provided for those who test positive for the disease.

> Use additional code to identify any family history of malignant neoplasm (Z80.-)

> **Excludes1**   encounter for diagnostic examination - code to sign or symptom

Z12.0   **Encounter for screening for malignant neoplasm of stomach**

● **Z12.1**   **Encounter for screening for malignant neoplasm of intestinal tract**

     Z12.10   Encounter for screening for malignant neoplasm of intestinal tract, unspecified

     Z12.11   Encounter for screening for malignant neoplasm of colon

> Encounter for screening colonoscopy NOS
> **Coding Clinic: 2018, Q1, P7; 2017, Q1, P8-9**

     Z12.12   Encounter for screening for malignant neoplasm of rectum

     Z12.13   Encounter for screening for malignant neoplasm of small intestine

Z12.2   **Encounter for screening for malignant neoplasm of respiratory organs**

● **Z12.3**   **Encounter for screening for malignant neoplasm of breast**

     Z12.31   Encounter for screening mammogram for malignant neoplasm of breast

> **Excludes1**   inconclusive mammogram (R92.2)
> **Coding Clinic: 2015, Q1, P24**

     Z12.39   Encounter for other screening for malignant neoplasm of breast

Z12.4   **Encounter for screening for malignant neoplasm of cervix ♀**

> Encounter for screening pap smear for malignant neoplasm of cervix

> **Excludes1**   when screening is part of general gynecological examination (Z01.4-)

> **Excludes2**   encounter for screening for human papillomavirus (Z11.51)

Z12.5   **Encounter for screening for malignant neoplasm of prostate ♂**

Z12.6   **Encounter for screening for malignant neoplasm of bladder**

● **Z12.7**   **Encounter for screening for malignant neoplasm of other genitourinary organs**

     Z12.71   Encounter for screening for malignant neoplasm of testis ♂

     Z12.72   Encounter for screening for malignant neoplasm of vagina ♀

> Vaginal pap smear status - post hysterectomy for non-malignant condition

> Use additional code to identify acquired absence of uterus (Z90.71-)

> **Excludes1**   vaginal pap smear status - post hysterectomy for malignant conditions (Z08)

     Z12.73   Encounter for screening for malignant neoplasm of ovary ♀

     Z12.79   Encounter for screening for malignant neoplasm of other genitourinary organs

● **Z12.8**   **Encounter for screening for malignant neoplasm of other sites**

     Z12.81   Encounter for screening for malignant neoplasm of oral cavity

     Z12.82   Encounter for screening for malignant neoplasm of nervous system

     Z12.83   Encounter for screening for malignant neoplasm of skin

     Z12.89   Encounter for screening for malignant neoplasm of other sites

Z12.9   **Encounter for screening for malignant neoplasm, site unspecified**

● **Z13**   **Encounter for screening for other diseases and disorders**

> Screening is the testing for disease or disease precursors in asymptomatic individuals so that early detection and treatment can be provided for those who test positive for the disease.

> **Excludes1**   encounter for diagnostic examination - code to sign or symptom

Z13.0   **Encounter for screening for diseases of the blood and blood-forming organs and certain disorders involving the immune mechanism**

Z13.1   **Encounter for screening for diabetes mellitus**

● **Z13.2**   **Encounter for screening for nutritional, metabolic and other endocrine disorders**

     Z13.21   Encounter for screening for nutritional disorder

     ● **Z13.22**   Encounter for screening for metabolic disorder

         Z13.220   Encounter for screening for lipoid disorders

> Encounter for screening for cholesterol level
> Encounter for screening for hypercholesterolemia
> Encounter for screening for hyperlipidemia

         Z13.228   Encounter for screening for other metabolic disorders

     Z13.29   Encounter for screening for other suspected endocrine disorder

> **Excludes1**   encounter for screening for diabetes mellitus (Z13.1)

● **Z13.3**   **Encounter for screening examination for mental health and behavioral disorders**

     Z13.30   Encounter for screening examination for mental health and behavioral disorders, unspecified

     Z13.31   Encounter for screening for depression

> Encounter for screening for depression, adult
> Encounter for screening for depression for child or adolescent

▶ New   ⇒ Revised   ~~deleted~~ Deleted   Excludes 1   Excludes 2   Includes   Use additional   Code first   Code also   Key words

OGCR Official Guidelines   **X** Assign placeholder X   ● Use Additional Character(s)   ▶ Manifestation Code   🝆 Hierarchical Condition Category   **Coding Clinic**

Z13.32   Encounter for screening for maternal depression ♀
   Encounter for screening for perinatal depression

Z13.39   Encounter for screening examination for other mental health and behavioral disorders
   Encounter for screening for alcoholism
   Encounter for screening for intellectual disabilities

● **Z13.4   Encounter for screening for certain developmental disorders in childhood**   P
   Encounter for development testing of infant or child
   Encounter for screening for developmental handicaps in early childhood

   Excludes2   encounter for routine child health examination (Z00.12-)

Z13.40   Encounter for screening for unspecified developmental delays

Z13.41   Encounter for autism screening

Z13.42   Encounter for screening for global developmental delays (milestones)
   Encounter for screening for developmental handicaps in early childhood

Z13.49   Encounter for screening for other developmental delays

Z13.5   Encounter for screening for eye and ear disorders

   Excludes2   encounter for general hearing examination (Z01.1-)
     encounter for general vision examination (Z01.0-)

   Coding Clinic: 2016, Q3, P17

Z13.6   Encounter for screening for cardiovascular disorders

● **Z13.7   Encounter for screening for genetic and chromosomal anomalies**

   Excludes1   genetic testing for procreative management (Z31.4-)

Z13.71   Encounter for nonprocreative screening for genetic disease carrier status

Z13.79   Encounter for other screening for genetic and chromosomal anomalies

● **Z13.8   Encounter for screening for other specified diseases and disorders**

   Excludes2   screening for malignant neoplasms (Z12.-)

● **Z13.81   Encounter for screening for digestive system disorders**

Z13.810   Encounter for screening for upper gastrointestinal disorder

Z13.811   Encounter for screening for lower gastrointestinal disorder

   Excludes1   encounter for screening for intestinal infectious disease (Z11.0)

Z13.818   Encounter for screening for other digestive system disorders

● **Z13.82   Encounter for screening for musculoskeletal disorder**

Z13.820   Encounter for screening for osteoporosis

Z13.828   Encounter for screening for other musculoskeletal disorder

Z13.83   Encounter for screening for respiratory disorder NEC

   Excludes1   encounter for screening for respiratory tuberculosis (Z11.1)

Z13.84   Encounter for screening for dental disorders

● **Z13.85   Encounter for screening for nervous system disorders**

Z13.850   Encounter for screening for traumatic brain injury

Z13.858   Encounter for screening for other nervous system disorders

Z13.88   Encounter for screening for disorder due to exposure to contaminants

   Excludes1   those exposed to contaminants without suspected disorders (Z57-Z77.-)

Z13.89   Encounter for screening for other disorder
   Encounter for screening for genitourinary disorders

Z13.9   Encounter for screening, unspecified

GENETIC CARRIER AND GENETIC SUSCEPTIBILITY TO DISEASE (Z14-Z15)

● **Z14   Genetic carrier**

● **Z14.0   Hemophilia A carrier**

Z14.01   Asymptomatic hemophilia A carrier

Z14.02   Symptomatic hemophilia A carrier

Z14.1   Cystic fibrosis carrier

Z14.8   Genetic carrier of other disease

● **Z15   Genetic susceptibility to disease**

   Excludes1   chromosomal anomalies (Q90-Q99)

   Includes   confirmed abnormal gene

   Use additional code, if applicable, for any associated family history of the disease (Z80-Z84)

● **Z15.0   Genetic susceptibility to malignant neoplasm**

   Code first if applicable, any current malignant neoplasm (C00-C75, C81-C96)

   Use additional code, if applicable, for any personal history of malignant neoplasm (Z85.-)

Z15.01   Genetic susceptibility to malignant neoplasm of breast

Z15.02   Genetic susceptibility to malignant neoplasm of ovary ♀

Z15.03   Genetic susceptibility to malignant neoplasm of prostate ♂

Z15.04   Genetic susceptibility to malignant neoplasm of endometrium ♀

Z15.09   Genetic susceptibility to other malignant neoplasm

● **Z15.8   Genetic susceptibility to other disease**

Z15.81   Genetic susceptibility to multiple endocrine neoplasia [MEN]

   Excludes1   multiple endocrine neoplasia [MEN] syndromes (E31.2-)

Z15.89   Genetic susceptibility to other disease

RESISTANCE TO ANTIMICROBIAL DRUGS (Z16)

● **Z16   Resistance to antimicrobial drugs**

   Note: The codes in this category are provided for use as additional codes to identify the resistance and non-responsiveness of a condition to antimicrobial drugs.

   Code first the infection

   Excludes1   Methicillin resistant Staphylococcus aureus infection (A49.02)
     Methicillin resistant Staphylococcus aureus pneumonia (J15.212)
     Sepsis due to Methicillin resistant Staphylococcus aureus (A41.02)

● **Z16.1   Resistance to beta lactam antibiotics**

Z16.10   Resistance to unspecified beta lactam antibiotics

Z16.11   Resistance to penicillins
   Resistance to amoxicillin
   Resistance to ampicillin

CHAPTER 21 (Z00-Z99)

Z16.12 Extended spectrum beta lactamase (ESBL) resistance

> **Excludes2** Methicillin resistant Staphylococcus aureus infection in diseases classified elsewhere (B95.62)

Z16.19 Resistance to other specified beta lactam antibiotics

Resistance to cephalosporins

● **Z16.2** Resistance to other antibiotics

Z16.20 Resistance to unspecified antibiotic

Resistance to antibiotics NOS

Z16.21 Resistance to vancomycin

Z16.22 Resistance to vancomycin related antibiotics

Z16.23 Resistance to quinolones and fluoroquinolones

Z16.24 Resistance to multiple antibiotics

Z16.29 Resistance to other single specified antibiotic

Resistance to aminoglycosides
Resistance to macrolides
Resistance to sulfonamides
Resistance to tetracyclines

● **Z16.3** Resistance to other antimicrobial drugs

> **Excludes1** resistance to antibiotics (Z16.1-, Z16.2-)

Z16.30 Resistance to unspecified antimicrobial drugs

Drug resistance NOS

Z16.31 Resistance to antiparasitic drug(s)

Resistance to quinine and related compounds

Z16.32 Resistance to antifungal drug(s)

Z16.33 Resistance to antiviral drug(s)

● **Z16.34** Resistance to antimycobacterial drug(s)

Resistance to tuberculostatics

Z16.341 Resistance to single antimycobacterial drug

Resistance to antimycobacterial drug NOS

Z16.342 Resistance to multiple antimycobacterial drugs

Z16.35 Resistance to multiple antimicrobial drugs

> **Excludes1** Resistance to multiple antibiotics only (Z16.24)

Z16.39 Resistance to other specified antimicrobial drug

ESTROGEN RECEPTOR STATUS (Z17)

● **Z17** Estrogen receptor status

Code first malignant neoplasm of breast (C50.-)

Z17.0 Estrogen receptor positive status [ER+]

Z17.1 Estrogen receptor negative status [ER-]

RETAINED FOREIGN BODY FRAGMENTS (Z18)

● **Z18** Retained foreign body fragments

> **Includes** embedded fragment (status)
> embedded splinter (status)
> retained foreign body status

> **Excludes1** artificial joint prosthesis status (Z96.6-)
> foreign body accidentally left during a procedure (T81.5-)
> foreign body entering through orifice (T15-T19)
> in situ cardiac device (Z95.-)
> organ or tissue replaced by means other than transplant (Z96.-, Z97.-)
> organ or tissue replaced by transplant (Z94.-)
> personal history of retained foreign body fully removed Z87.821
> superficial foreign body (non-embedded splinter) - code to superficial foreign body, by site

● **Z18.0** Retained radioactive fragments

Z18.01 Retained depleted uranium fragments

Z18.09 Other retained radioactive fragments

Other retained depleted isotope fragments
Retained nontherapeutic radioactive fragments

● **Z18.1** Retained metal fragments

> **Excludes1** retained radioactive metal fragments (Z18.01-Z18.09)

Z18.10 Retained metal fragments, unspecified

Retained metal fragment NOS

Z18.11 Retained magnetic metal fragments

Z18.12 Retained nonmagnetic metal fragments

Z18.2 Retained plastic fragments

Acrylics fragments
Diethylhexylphthalates fragments
Isocyanate fragments

● **Z18.3** Retained organic fragments

Z18.31 Retained animal quills or spines

Z18.32 Retained tooth

Z18.33 Retained wood fragments

Z18.39 Other retained organic fragments

● **Z18.8** Other specified retained foreign body

Z18.81 Retained glass fragments

Z18.83 Retained stone or crystalline fragments

Retained concrete or cement fragments

Z18.89 Other specified retained foreign body fragments

Coding Clinic: 2016, Q3, P24

Z18.9 Retained foreign body fragments, unspecified material

HORMONE SENSITIVITY MALIGNANCY STATUS (Z19)

● **Z19** Hormone sensitivity malignancy status

Code first malignant neoplasm —*see* Table of Neoplasms, by site, malignant

Coding Clinic: 2016, Q4, P129

Z19.1 Hormone sensitive malignancy status

Coding Clinic: 2016, Q4, P76

Z19.2 Hormone resistant malignancy status

Castrate resistant prostate malignancy status

Coding Clinic: 2016, Q4, P76

PERSONS WITH POTENTIAL HEALTH HAZARDS RELATED TO COMMUNICABLE DISEASES (Z20-Z29)

● **Z20** Contact with and (suspected) exposure to communicable diseases

> **Excludes1** carrier of infectious disease (Z22.-)
> diagnosed current infectious or parasitic disease - see Alphabetic Index

> **Excludes2** personal history of infectious and parasitic diseases (Z86.1-)

● **Z20.0** Contact with and (suspected) exposure to intestinal infectious diseases

Z20.01 Contact with and (suspected) exposure to intestinal infectious diseases due to Escherichia coli (E. coli)

Z20.09 Contact with and (suspected) exposure to other intestinal infectious diseases

Z20.1 Contact with and (suspected) exposure to tuberculosis

Z20.2 Contact with and (suspected) exposure to infections with a predominantly sexual mode of transmission

Z20.3 Contact with and (suspected) exposure to rabies

Z20.4 Contact with and (suspected) exposure to rubella

Z20.5 Contact with and (suspected) exposure to viral hepatitis

Z20.6 Contact with and (suspected) exposure to human immunodeficiency virus [HIV]

> **Excludes1** asymptomatic human immunodeficiency virus [HIV]
> HIV infection status (Z21)

Z20.7 Contact with and (suspected) exposure to pediculosis, acariasis and other infestations

- **Z20.8   Contact with and (suspected) exposure to other communicable diseases**
  - **Z20.81   Contact with and (suspected) exposure to other bacterial communicable diseases**
    - Z20.810   **Contact with and (suspected) exposure to anthrax**
    - Z20.811   **Contact with and (suspected) exposure to meningococcus**
    - Z20.818   **Contact with and (suspected) exposure to other bacterial communicable diseases**
  - **Z20.82   Contact with and (suspected) exposure to other viral communicable diseases**
    - Z20.820   **Contact with and (suspected) exposure to varicella**
    - Z20.821   **Contact with and (suspected) exposure to Zika virus**
    - Z20.828   **Contact with and (suspected) exposure to other viral communicable diseases**
      Coding Clinic: 2016, Q4, P6-7, 121
  - Z20.89   **Contact with and (suspected) exposure to other communicable diseases**
  - Z20.9   **Contact with and (suspected) exposure to unspecified communicable disease**

- Z21   **Asymptomatic human immunodeficiency virus [HIV] infection status** ⊛
  HIV positive NOS
  Code first Human immunodeficiency virus [HIV] disease complicating pregnancy, childbirth and the puerperium, if applicable (O98.7-)
  Excludes1   acquired immunodeficiency syndrome (B20)
  contact with human immunodeficiency virus [HIV] (Z20.6)
  exposure to human immunodeficiency virus [HIV] (Z20.6)
  human immunodeficiency virus [HIV] disease (B20)
  inconclusive laboratory evidence of human immunodeficiency virus [HIV] (R75)
  Coding Clinic: 2019, Q1, P10-11

- **Z22   Carrier of infectious disease**
  Includes   colonization status
  suspected carrier
  Excludes2   carrier of viral hepatitis (B18.-)
  - Z22.0   **Carrier of typhoid**
  - Z22.1   **Carrier of other intestinal infectious diseases**
  - Z22.2   **Carrier of diphtheria**
  - **Z22.3   Carrier of other specified bacterial diseases**
    - Z22.31   **Carrier of bacterial disease due to meningococci**
    - **Z22.32   Carrier of bacterial disease due to staphylococci**
      - Z22.321   **Carrier or suspected carrier of Methicillin susceptible Staphylococcus aureus**
        MSSA colonization
      - Z22.322   **Carrier or suspected carrier of Methicillin resistant Staphylococcus aureus**
        MRSA colonization
    - **Z22.33   Carrier of bacterial disease due to streptococci**
      - Z22.330   **Carrier of Group B streptococcus**
        Excludes1   Carrier of streptococcus group B (GBS) complicating pregnancy, childbirth and the puerperium (O99.82-)
      - Z22.338   **Carrier of other streptococcus**
    - Z22.39   **Carrier of other specified bacterial diseases**

- Z22.4   **Carrier of infections with a predominantly sexual mode of transmission**
- Z22.6   **Carrier of human T-lymphotropic virus type-1 [HTLV-1] infection**
- Z22.7   **Latent tuberculosis**
  Latent tuberculosis infection (LTBI)
  Excludes1   nonspecific reaction to cell mediated immunity measurement of gamma interferon antigen response without active tuberculosis (R76.12)
  nonspecific reaction to tuberculin skin test without active tuberculosis (R76.11)
- Z22.8   **Carrier of other infectious diseases**
- Z22.9   **Carrier of infectious disease, unspecified**

- Z23   **Encounter for immunization**
  Code first any routine childhood examination
  Note: Procedure codes are required to identify the types of immunizations given.

- **Z28   Immunization not carried out and underimmunization status**
  Includes   vaccination not carried out
  - **Z28.0   Immunization not carried out because of contraindication**
    - Z28.01   **Immunization not carried out because of acute illness of patient**
    - Z28.02   **Immunization not carried out because of chronic illness or condition of patient**
    - Z28.03   **Immunization not carried out because of immune compromised state of patient**
    - Z28.04   **Immunization not carried out because of patient allergy to vaccine or component**
    - Z28.09   **Immunization not carried out because of other contraindication**
  - Z28.1   **Immunization not carried out because of patient decision for reasons of belief or group pressure**
    Immunization not carried out because of religious belief
  - **Z28.2   Immunization not carried out because of patient decision for other and unspecified reason**
    - Z28.20   **Immunization not carried out because of patient decision for unspecified reason**
    - Z28.21   **Immunization not carried out because of patient refusal**
    - Z28.29   **Immunization not carried out because of patient decision for other reason**
  - Z28.3   **Underimmunization status**
    Delinquent immunization status
    Lapsed immunization schedule status
  - **Z28.8   Immunization not carried out for other reason**
    - Z28.81   **Immunization not carried out due to patient having had the disease**
    - Z28.82   **Immunization not carried out because of caregiver refusal**
      Immunization not carried out because of guardian refusal
      Immunization not carried out because of parent refusal
      Excludes1   immunization not carried out because of caregiver refusal because of religious belief (Z28.1)
    - Z28.83   **Immunization not carried out due to unavailability of vaccine**
      Delay in delivery of vaccine
      Lack of availability of vaccine
      Manufacturer delay of vaccine
    - Z28.89   **Immunization not carried out for other reason**
  - Z28.9   **Immunization not carried out for unspecified reason**

CHAPTER 21 (Z00-Z99)

CHAPTER 21 (Z00-Z99)

● **Z29**   **Encounter for other prophylactic measures**

     Excludes1   desensitization to allergens (Z51.6)
                      prophylactic surgery (Z40.-)
     Coding Clinic: 2016, Q4, P130

   ● **Z29.1**   **Encounter for prophylactic immunotherapy**
          Encounter for administration of immunoglobulin
          Coding Clinic: 2016, Q4, P78-79

     Z29.11   **Encounter for prophylactic immunotherapy for respiratory syncytial virus (RSV)**

     Z29.12   **Encounter for prophylactic antivenin**

     Z29.13   **Encounter for prophylactic Rho(D) immune globulin**
                Coding Clinic: 2019, Q3, P5

     Z29.14   **Encounter for prophylactic rabies immune globin**

   Z29.3   **Encounter for prophylactic fluoride administration**
       Coding Clinic: 2016, Q4, P79

   Z29.8   **Encounter for other specified prophylactic measures**
       Coding Clinic: 2016, Q4, P79

   Z29.9   **Encounter for prophylactic measures, unspecified**
       Coding Clinic: 2016, Q4, P79

PERSONS ENCOUNTERING HEALTH SERVICES IN CIRCUMSTANCES RELATED TO REPRODUCTION (Z30-Z39)

● **Z30**   **Encounter for contraceptive management**

   ● **Z30.0**   **Encounter for general counseling and advice on contraception**

     ● **Z30.01**   **Encounter for initial prescription of contraceptives**

          Excludes1   encounter for surveillance of contraceptives (Z30.4-)

       Z30.011   **Encounter for initial prescription of contraceptive pills** ♀

       Z30.012   **Encounter for prescription of emergency contraception** ♀
               Encounter for postcoital contraception

       Z30.013   **Encounter for initial prescription of injectable contraceptive** ♀

       Z30.014   **Encounter for initial prescription of intrauterine contraceptive device** ♀

          Excludes1   encounter for insertion of intrauterine contraceptive device (Z30.430, Z30.432)

       Z30.015   **Encounter for initial prescription of vaginal ring hormonal contraceptive** ♀
               Coding Clinic: 2016, Q4, P78

       Z30.016   **Encounter for initial prescription of transdermal patch hormonal contraceptive device**
               Coding Clinic: 2016, Q4, P78

       Z30.017   **Encounter for initial prescription of implantable subdermal contraceptive**
               Coding Clinic: 2016, Q4, P78

       Z30.018   **Encounter for initial prescription of other contraceptives** ♀
               Encounter for initial prescription of barrier contraception
               Encounter for initial prescription of diaphragm

       Z30.019   **Encounter for initial prescription of contraceptives, unspecified** ♀

     Z30.02   **Counseling and instruction in natural family planning to avoid pregnancy**

     Z30.09   **Encounter for other general counseling and advice on contraception**
          Encounter for family planning advice NOS

   Z30.2   **Encounter for sterilization**

   ● **Z30.4**   **Encounter for surveillance of contraceptives**

     Z30.40   **Encounter for surveillance of contraceptives, unspecified**

     Z30.41   **Encounter for surveillance of contraceptive pills** ♀
          Encounter for repeat prescription for contraceptive pill

     Z30.42   **Encounter for surveillance of injectable contraceptive** ♀

     ● **Z30.43**   **Encounter for surveillance of intrauterine contraceptive device**

       Z30.430   **Encounter for insertion of intrauterine contraceptive device** ♀

       Z30.431   **Encounter for routine checking of intrauterine contraceptive device** ♀

       Z30.432   **Encounter for removal of intrauterine contraceptive device** ♀

       Z30.433   **Encounter for removal and reinsertion of intrauterine contraceptive device** ♀
               Encounter for replacement of intrauterine contraceptive device

     Z30.44   **Encounter for surveillance of vaginal ring hormonal contraceptive device** ♀
          Coding Clinic: 2016, Q4, P78

     Z30.45   **Encounter for surveillance of transdermal patch hormonal contraceptive device** ♀
          Coding Clinic: 2016, Q4, P78

     Z30.46   **Encounter for surveillance of implantable subdermal contraceptive** ♀
          Encounter for checking, reinsertion or removal of implantable subdermal contraceptive
          Coding Clinic: 2016, Q4, P78

     Z30.49   **Encounter for surveillance of other contraceptives** ♀
          Encounter for surveillance of barrier contraception
          Encounter for surveillance of diaphragm

   Z30.8   **Encounter for other contraceptive management**
       Encounter for postvasectomy sperm count
       Encounter for routine examination for contraceptive maintenance

     Excludes1   sperm count following sterilization reversal (Z31.42)
                   sperm count for fertility testing (Z31.41)

   Z30.9   **Encounter for contraceptive management, unspecified**

● **Z31**   **Encounter for procreative management**

     Excludes1   complications associated with artificial fertilization (N98.-)
                   female infertility (N97.-)
                   male infertility (N46.-)

   Z31.0   **Encounter for reversal of previous sterilization**

   ● **Z31.4**   **Encounter for procreative investigation and testing**

     Excludes1   postvasectomy sperm count (Z30.8)

     Z31.41   **Encounter for fertility testing**
          Encounter for fallopian tube patency testing
          Encounter for sperm count for fertility testing

     Z31.42   **Aftercare following sterilization reversal**
          Sperm count following sterilization reversal

     ● **Z31.43**   **Encounter for genetic testing of female for procreative management**

          Use additional code for recurrent pregnancy loss, if applicable (N96, O26.2-)

          Excludes1   nonprocreative genetic testing (Z13.7-)

       Z31.430   **Encounter of female for testing for genetic disease carrier status for procreative management** ♀

       Z31.438   **Encounter for other genetic testing of female for procreative management** ♀

▶ New   ⟹ Revised   ~~deleted~~ Deleted   Excludes 1   Excludes 2   Includes   Use additional   Code first   Code also   Key words

OGCR Official Guidelines   X Assign placeholder X   ● Use Additional Character(s)   ▶ Manifestation Code   🝚 Hierarchical Condition Category   Coding Clinic

● **Z31.44**   Encounter for genetic testing of male for procreative management

> **Excludes1**   nonprocreative genetic testing (Z13.7-)

     Z31.440   Encounter of male for testing for genetic disease carrier status for procreative management ♂

     Z31.441   Encounter for testing of male partner of patient with recurrent pregnancy loss ♂   A

     Z31.448   Encounter for other genetic testing of male for procreative management ♂   A

Z31.49   Encounter for other procreative investigation and testing

Z31.5   Encounter for procreative genetic counseling

● **Z31.6**   Encounter for general counseling and advice on procreation

     Z31.61   Procreative counseling and advice using natural family planning

     Z31.62   Encounter for fertility preservation counseling
        Encounter for fertility preservation counseling prior to cancer therapy
        Encounter for fertility preservation counseling prior to surgical removal of gonads

     Z31.69   Encounter for other general counseling and advice on procreation

Z31.7   Encounter for procreative management and counseling for gestational carrier ♀

> **Excludes1**   pregnant state, gestational carrier (Z33.3)
> **Coding Clinic: 2016, Q4, P78**

● **Z31.8**   Encounter for other procreative management

     Z31.81   Encounter for male factor infertility in female patient ♀

     Z31.82   Encounter for Rh incompatibility status ♀
        Coding Clinic: 2015, Q3, P40

     Z31.83   Encounter for assisted reproductive fertility procedure cycle ♀
        Patient undergoing in vitro fertilization cycle
        Use additional code to identify the type of infertility

> **Excludes1**   pre-cycle diagnosis and testing - code to reason for encounter

     Z31.84   Encounter for fertility preservation procedure
        Encounter for fertility preservation procedure prior to cancer therapy
        Encounter for fertility preservation procedure prior to surgical removal of gonads

     Z31.89   Encounter for other procreative management

Z31.9   Encounter for procreative management, unspecified

● **Z32**   Encounter for pregnancy test and childbirth and childcare instruction

● **Z32.0**   Encounter for pregnancy test

     Z32.00   Encounter for pregnancy test, result unknown ♀
        Encounter for pregnancy test NOS

     Z32.01   Encounter for pregnancy test, result positive ♀   M

     Z32.02   Encounter for pregnancy test, result negative ♀

Z32.2   Encounter for childbirth instruction

Z32.3   Encounter for childcare instruction
     Encounter for prenatal or postpartum childcare instruction

| First trimester (0 to 14 weeks) | Second trimester (14 to 28 weeks) | Third trimester (28 weeks to delivery) |

Figure 21-1   Trimesters. (From Shiland, Betsy J. Medical Terminology & Anatomy for ICD-10 Coding, ed 2, Mosby, 2015)

● **Z33**   Pregnant state

     Z33.1   Pregnant state, incidental ♀   M
     ▸ Pregnancy NOS
        Pregnant state NOS

> **Excludes1**   complications of pregnancy (O00-O9A)
> pregnant state, gestational carrier (Z33.3)

     Z33.2   Encounter for elective termination of pregnancy ♀   M

> **Excludes1**   early fetal death with retention of dead fetus (O02.1)
> late fetal death (O36.4)
> spontaneous abortion (O03)
> **Coding Clinic: 2016, Q4, P130**

     Z33.3   Pregnant state, gestational carrier ♀

> **Excludes1**   encounter for procreative management and counseling for gestational carrier (Z31.7)
> **Coding Clinic: 2016, Q4, P78**

● **Z34**   Encounter for supervision of normal pregnancy

> **Excludes1**   any complication of pregnancy (O00-O9A)
> encounter for pregnancy test (Z32.0-)
> encounter for supervision of high risk pregnancy (O09.-)
> **Coding Clinic: 2016, Q4, P6**

● **Z34.0**   Encounter for supervision of normal first pregnancy

     Z34.00   Encounter for supervision of normal first pregnancy, unspecified trimester ♀   M

     Z34.01   Encounter for supervision of normal first pregnancy, first trimester ♀   M

     Z34.02   Encounter for supervision of normal first pregnancy, second trimester ♀   M

     Z34.03   Encounter for supervision of normal first pregnancy, third trimester ♀   M

● **Z34.8**   Encounter for supervision of other normal pregnancy

     Z34.80   Encounter for supervision of other normal pregnancy, unspecified trimester ♀   M

     Z34.81   Encounter for supervision of other normal pregnancy, first trimester ♀   M

     Z34.82   Encounter for supervision of other normal pregnancy, second trimester ♀   M

     Z34.83   Encounter for supervision of other normal pregnancy, third trimester ♀   M

● **Z34.9**   Encounter for supervision of normal pregnancy, unspecified

     Z34.90   Encounter for supervision of normal pregnancy, unspecified, unspecified trimester ♀   M

     Z34.91   Encounter for supervision of normal pregnancy, unspecified, first trimester ♀   M

     Z34.92   Encounter for supervision of normal pregnancy, unspecified, second trimester ♀   M

     Z34.93   Encounter for supervision of normal pregnancy, unspecified, third trimester ♀   M

CHAPTER 21 (Z00-Z99)

CHAPTER 21 (Z00-Z99)

● **Z36** **Encounter for antenatal screening of mother** ♀

Includes Encounter for placental sample (taken vaginally)

Screening is the testing for disease or disease precursors in asymptomatic individuals so that early detection and treatment can be provided for those who test positive for the disease.

Excludes1 diagnostic examination - code to sign or symptom

encounter for suspected maternal and fetal conditions ruled out (Z03.7-)

suspected fetal condition affecting management of pregnancy - code to condition in Chapter 15

Excludes2 abnormal findings on antenatal screening of mother (O28.-)

genetic counseling and testing (Z31.43-, Z31.5)

routine prenatal care (Z34)

Z36.0 **Encounter for antenatal screening for chromosomal anomalies** ♀ M

Z36.1 **Encounter for antenatal screening for raised alphafetoprotein level** ♀ M

Encounter for antenatal screening for elevated maternal serum alphafetoprotein level

Z36.2 **Encounter for other antenatal screening follow-up** ♀ M

Non-visualized anatomy on a previous scan

Z36.3 **Encounter for antenatal screening for malformations** ♀ M

Screening for a suspected anomaly

Z36.4 **Encounter for antenatal screening for fetal growth retardation** ♀ M

Intrauterine growth restriction (IUGR)/small-for-dates

Z36.5 **Encounter for antenatal screening for isoimmunization** ♀ M

● **Z36.8** **Encounter for other antenatal screening**

Z36.81 **Encounter for antenatal screening for hydrops fetalis** ♀ M

Z36.82 **Encounter for antenatal screening for nuchal translucency** ♀ M

Z36.83 **Encounter for fetal screening for congenital cardiac abnormalities** ♀ M

Z36.84 **Encounter for antenatal screening for fetal lung maturity** ♀ M

Z36.85 **Encounter for antenatal screening for Streptococcus B** ♀ M

Z36.86 **Encounter for antenatal screening for cervical length** ♀ M

Screening for risk of pre-term labor

Z36.87 **Encounter for antenatal screening for uncertain dates** ♀ M

Z36.88 **Encounter for antenatal screening for fetal macrosomia** ♀ M

Screening for large-for-dates

Z36.89 **Encounter for other specified antenatal screening** ♀ M

Z36.8A **Encounter for antenatal screening for other genetic defects** ♀ M

Z36.9 **Encounter for antenatal screening, unspecified** ♀ M

● **Z3A** **Weeks of gestation**

Note: Codes from category Z3A are for use, only on the maternal record, to indicate the weeks of gestation of the pregnancy, if known.

Code first complications of pregnancy, childbirth and the puerperium (O09-O9A)

Coding Clinic: 2016, Q4, P130; 2013, Q2, P33

● **Z3A.0** **Weeks of gestation of pregnancy, unspecified or less than 10 weeks**

Z3A.00 **Weeks of gestation of pregnancy not specified** ♀ M

Z3A.01 **Less than 8 weeks gestation of pregnancy** ♀ M

Z3A.08 **8 weeks gestation of pregnancy** ♀ M

Z3A.09 **9 weeks gestation of pregnancy** ♀ M

● **Z3A.1** **Weeks of gestation of pregnancy, weeks 10-19**

Z3A.10 **10 weeks gestation of pregnancy** ♀ M

Z3A.11 **11 weeks gestation of pregnancy** ♀ M

Z3A.12 **12 weeks gestation of pregnancy** ♀ M

Z3A.13 **13 weeks gestation of pregnancy** ♀ M

Z3A.14 **14 weeks gestation of pregnancy** ♀ M

Z3A.15 **15 weeks gestation of pregnancy** ♀ M

Z3A.16 **16 weeks gestation of pregnancy** ♀ M
Coding Clinic: 2016, Q4, P5

Z3A.17 **17 weeks gestation of pregnancy** ♀ M

Z3A.18 **18 weeks gestation of pregnancy** ♀ M
Coding Clinic: 2019, Q2, P11

Z3A.19 **19 weeks gestation of pregnancy** ♀ M

● **Z3A.2** **Weeks of gestation of pregnancy, weeks 20-29**

Z3A.20 **20 weeks gestation of pregnancy** ♀ M
Coding Clinic: 2016, Q4, P6

Z3A.21 **21 weeks gestation of pregnancy** ♀ M

Z3A.22 **22 weeks gestation of pregnancy** ♀ M
Coding Clinic: 2016, Q4, P6

Z3A.23 **23 weeks gestation of pregnancy** ♀ M

Z3A.24 **24 weeks gestation of pregnancy** ♀ M

Z3A.25 **25 weeks gestation of pregnancy** ♀ M

Z3A.26 **26 weeks gestation of pregnancy** ♀ M

Z3A.27 **27 weeks gestation of pregnancy** ♀ M

Z3A.28 **28 weeks gestation of pregnancy** ♀ M

Z3A.29 **29 weeks gestation of pregnancy** ♀ M

● **Z3A.3** **Weeks of gestation of pregnancy, weeks 30-39**

Z3A.30 **30 weeks gestation of pregnancy** ♀ M

Z3A.31 **31 weeks gestation of pregnancy** ♀ M

Z3A.32 **32 weeks gestation of pregnancy** ♀ M
Coding Clinic: 2016, Q4, P6

Z3A.33 **33 weeks gestation of pregnancy** ♀ M

Z3A.34 **34 weeks gestation of pregnancy** ♀ M

Z3A.35 **35 weeks gestation of pregnancy** ♀ M

Z3A.36 **36 weeks gestation of pregnancy** ♀ M

Z3A.37 **37 weeks gestation of pregnancy** ♀ M

Z3A.38 **38 weeks gestation of pregnancy** ♀ M
Coding Clinic: 2016, Q2, P34

Z3A.39 **39 weeks gestation of pregnancy** ♀ M

● **Z3A.4** **Weeks of gestation of pregnancy, weeks 40 or greater**

Z3A.40 **40 weeks gestation of pregnancy** ♀ M

Z3A.41 **41 weeks gestation of pregnancy** ♀ M

Z3A.42 **42 weeks gestation of pregnancy** ♀ M

Z3A.49 **Greater than 42 weeks gestation of pregnancy** ♀ M

● **Z37** **Outcome of delivery**

This category is intended for use as an additional code to identify the outcome of delivery on the mother's record. It is not for use on the newborn record.

Excludes1 stillbirth (P95)

Z37.0 **Single live birth** ♀ M
Coding Clinic: 2016, Q2, P34

Z37.1 **Single stillbirth** ♀ M

Z37.2 **Twins, both liveborn** ♀ M

Z37.3 **Twins, one liveborn and one stillborn** ♀ M

Z37.4 **Twins, both stillborn** ♀ M

● **Z37.5** **Other multiple births, all liveborn**

Z37.50 **Multiple births, unspecified, all liveborn** ♀ M

Z37.51 **Triplets, all liveborn** ♀ M

Z37.52 **Quadruplets, all liveborn** ♀ M

Z37.53 **Quintuplets, all liveborn** ♀ M

Z37.54 **Sextuplets, all liveborn** ♀ M

Z37.59 **Other multiple births, all liveborn** ♀ M

▶ New ⇒ Revised ~~deleted~~ Deleted | Excludes 1 | Excludes 2 | Includes | Use additional | Code first | Code also | Key words

OGCR Official Guidelines   X Assign placeholder X   ● Use Additional Character(s)   ▷ Manifestation Code   🐾 Hierarchical Condition Category   Coding Clinic

Z37.6   **Other multiple births, some liveborn**

     Z37.60   Multiple births, unspecified, some liveborn ♀   M

     Z37.61   Triplets, some liveborn ♀   M

     Z37.62   Quadruplets, some liveborn ♀   M

     Z37.63   Quintuplets, some liveborn ♀   M

     Z37.64   Sextuplets, some liveborn ♀   M

     Z37.69   Other multiple births, some liveborn ♀   M

Z37.7   **Other multiple births, all stillborn** ♀   M

Z37.9   **Outcome of delivery, unspecified** ♀   M
     Multiple birth NOS
     Single birth NOS

Z38   **Liveborn infants according to place of birth and type of delivery**
This category is for use as the principal code on the initial record of a newborn baby. It is to be used for the initial birth record only. It is not to be used on the mother's record.
Coding Clinic: 2017, Q2, P6-7; 2016, Q4, P126-127, 130; 2015, Q2, P15

Z38.0   **Single liveborn infant, born in hospital**
Single liveborn infant, born in birthing center or other health care facility
Coding Clinic: 2017, Q2, P5-7

     Z38.00   Single liveborn infant, delivered vaginally   N
       Coding Clinic: 2018, Q4, P26; 2016, Q4, P7, 55

     Z38.01   Single liveborn infant, delivered by cesarean   N
       Coding Clinic: 2017, Q2, P7; 2016, Q3, P18

Z38.1   **Single liveborn infant, born outside hospital**   N

Z38.2   **Single liveborn infant, unspecified as to place of birth**   N
     Single liveborn infant NOS

Z38.3   **Twin liveborn infant, born in hospital**

     Z38.30   Twin liveborn infant, delivered vaginally   N

     Z38.31   Twin liveborn infant, delivered by cesarean   N

Z38.4   **Twin liveborn infant, born outside hospital**   N

Z38.5   **Twin liveborn infant, unspecified as to place of birth**   N

Z38.6   **Other multiple liveborn infant, born in hospital**

     Z38.61   Triplet liveborn infant, delivered vaginally   N

     Z38.62   Triplet liveborn infant, delivered by cesarean   N

     Z38.63   Quadruplet liveborn infant, delivered vaginally   N

     Z38.64   Quadruplet liveborn infant, delivered by cesarean   N

     Z38.65   Quintuplet liveborn infant, delivered vaginally   N

     Z38.66   Quintuplet liveborn infant, delivered by cesarean   N

     Z38.68   Other multiple liveborn infant, delivered vaginally   N

     Z38.69   Other multiple liveborn infant, delivered by cesarean   N

Z38.7   **Other multiple liveborn infant, born outside hospital**   N

Z38.8   **Other multiple liveborn infant, unspecified as to place of birth**   N

Z39   **Encounter for maternal postpartum care and examination**

Z39.0   **Encounter for care and examination of mother immediately after delivery** ♀   M
Care and observation in uncomplicated cases when the delivery occurs outside a healthcare facility
     Excludes1   care for postpartum complication - see Alphabetic index

Z39.1   **Encounter for care and examination of lactating mother** ♀   M
Encounter for supervision of lactation
     Excludes1   disorders of lactation (O92.-)

Z39.2   **Encounter for routine postpartum follow-up** ♀   M

ENCOUNTERS FOR OTHER SPECIFIC HEALTH CARE (Z40-Z53)

Categories Z40-Z53 are intended for use to indicate a reason for care. They may be used for patients who have already been treated for a disease or injury, but who are receiving aftercare or prophylactic care, or care to consolidate the treatment, or to deal with a residual state

     Excludes2   follow-up examination for medical surveillance after treatment (Z08-Z09)

Z40   **Encounter for prophylactic surgery**
     Excludes1   organ donations (Z52.-)
       therapeutic organ removal - code to condition
Coding Clinic: 2016, Q4, P79

Z40.0   **Encounter for prophylactic surgery for risk factors related to malignant neoplasms**
Admission for prophylactic organ removal
Use additional code to identify risk factor

     Z40.00   Encounter for prophylactic removal of unspecified organ

     Z40.01   Encounter for prophylactic removal of breast

     Z40.02   Encounter for prophylactic removal of ovary(s) ♀
       Encounter for prophylactic removal of ovary(s) and fallopian tube(s)

     Z40.03   Encounter for prophylactic removal of fallopian tube(s) ♀

     Z40.09   Encounter for prophylactic removal of other organ

Z40.8   **Encounter for other prophylactic surgery**

Z40.9   **Encounter for prophylactic surgery, unspecified**

Z41   **Encounter for procedures for purposes other than remedying health state**

Z41.1   **Encounter for cosmetic surgery**
Encounter for cosmetic breast implant
Encounter for cosmetic procedure
     Excludes1   encounter for plastic and reconstructive surgery following medical procedure or healed injury (Z42.-)
       encounter for post-mastectomy breast implantation (Z42.1)

Z41.2   **Encounter for routine and ritual male circumcision** ♂

Z41.3   **Encounter for ear piercing**

Z41.8   **Encounter for other procedures for purposes other than remedying health state**

Z41.9   **Encounter for procedure for purposes other than remedying health state, unspecified**

Z42   **Encounter for plastic and reconstructive surgery following medical procedure or healed injury**
     Excludes1   encounter for cosmetic plastic surgery (Z41.1)
       encounter for plastic surgery for treatment of current injury - code to relevent injury

Z42.1   **Encounter for breast reconstruction following mastectomy**   A
     Excludes1   deformity and disproportion of reconstructed breast (N65.1-)

Z42.8   **Encounter for other plastic and reconstructive surgery following medical procedure or healed injury**
Coding Clinic: 2017, Q1, P42

CHAPTER 21 (Z00-Z99)

● **Z43 Encounter for attention to artificial openings**

    Includes   closure of artificial openings
                  passage of sounds or bougies through artificial openings
                  reforming artificial openings
                  removal of catheter from artificial openings
                  toilet or cleansing of artificial openings

    Excludes1   complications of external stoma (J95.0-, K94.-, N99.5-)

    Excludes2   fitting and adjustment of prosthetic and other devices (Z44-Z46)

    Z43.0   Encounter for attention to tracheostomy 🐾

    Z43.1   Encounter for attention to gastrostomy 🐾

           Excludes2   artificial opening status only, without need for care (Z93.-)

    Z43.2   Encounter for attention to ileostomy 🐾
           Coding Clinic: 2016, Q3, P5

    Z43.3   Encounter for attention to colostomy 🐾

    Z43.4   Encounter for attention to other artificial openings of digestive tract 🐾

    Z43.5   Encounter for attention to cystostomy 🐾

    Z43.6   Encounter for attention to other artificial openings of urinary tract 🐾
            Encounter for attention to nephrostomy
            Encounter for attention to ureterostomy
            Encounter for attention to urethrostomy

    Z43.7   Encounter for attention to artificial vagina

    Z43.8   Encounter for attention to other artificial openings 🐾

    Z43.9   Encounter for attention to unspecified artificial opening 🐾

● **Z44 Encounter for fitting and adjustment of external prosthetic device**

    Includes   removal or replacement of external prosthetic device

    Excludes1   malfunction or other complications of device - see Alphabetical Index presence of prosthetic device (Z97.-)

  ● **Z44.0**   Encounter for fitting and adjustment of artificial arm

    ● **Z44.00**   Encounter for fitting and adjustment of unspecified artificial arm

        Z44.001   Encounter for fitting and adjustment of unspecified right artificial arm

        Z44.002   Encounter for fitting and adjustment of unspecified left artificial arm

        Z44.009   Encounter for fitting and adjustment of unspecified artificial arm, unspecified arm

    ● **Z44.01**   Encounter for fitting and adjustment of complete artificial arm

        Z44.011   Encounter for fitting and adjustment of complete right artificial arm

        Z44.012   Encounter for fitting and adjustment of complete left artificial arm

        Z44.019   Encounter for fitting and adjustment of complete artificial arm, unspecified arm

    ● **Z44.02**   Encounter for fitting and adjustment of partial artificial arm

        Z44.021   Encounter for fitting and adjustment of partial artificial right arm

        Z44.022   Encounter for fitting and adjustment of partial artificial left arm

        Z44.029   Encounter for fitting and adjustment of partial artificial arm, unspecified arm

● **Z44.1**   Encounter for fitting and adjustment of artificial leg

  ● **Z44.10**   Encounter for fitting and adjustment of unspecified artificial leg

        Z44.101   Encounter for fitting and adjustment of unspecified right artificial leg 🐾

        Z44.102   Encounter for fitting and adjustment of unspecified left artificial leg 🐾

        Z44.109   Encounter for fitting and adjustment of unspecified artificial leg, unspecified leg 🐾

  ● **Z44.11**   Encounter for fitting and adjustment of complete artificial leg

        Z44.111   Encounter for fitting and adjustment of complete right artificial leg 🐾

        Z44.112   Encounter for fitting and adjustment of complete left artificial leg 🐾

        Z44.119   Encounter for fitting and adjustment of complete artificial leg, unspecified leg 🐾

  ● **Z44.12**   Encounter for fitting and adjustment of partial artificial leg

        Z44.121   Encounter for fitting and adjustment of partial artificial right leg 🐾

        Z44.122   Encounter for fitting and adjustment of partial artificial left leg 🐾

        Z44.129   Encounter for fitting and adjustment of partial artificial leg, unspecified leg 🐾

● **Z44.2**   Encounter for fitting and adjustment of artificial eye

    Excludes1   mechanical complication of ocular prosthesis (T85.3)

    Z44.20   Encounter for fitting and adjustment of artificial eye, unspecified

    Z44.21   Encounter for fitting and adjustment of artificial right eye

    Z44.22   Encounter for fitting and adjustment of artificial left eye

● **Z44.3**   Encounter for fitting and adjustment of external breast prosthesis

    Excludes1   complications of breast implant (T85.4-)
            encounter for adjustment or removal of breast implant (Z45.81-)
            encounter for initial breast implant insertion for cosmetic breast augmentation (Z41.1)
            encounter for breast reconstruction following mastectomy (Z42.1)

    Z44.30   Encounter for fitting and adjustment of external breast prosthesis, unspecified breast

    Z44.31   Encounter for fitting and adjustment of external right breast prosthesis

    Z44.32   Encounter for fitting and adjustment of external left breast prosthesis

  Z44.8   Encounter for fitting and adjustment of other external prosthetic devices

  Z44.9   Encounter for fitting and adjustment of unspecified external prosthetic device

▶ New   ⟩ Revised   ~~deleted~~ Deleted   Excludes 1   Excludes 2   Includes   Use additional   Code first   Code also   Key words
OGCR Official Guidelines   X Assign placeholder X   ● Use Additional Character(s)   ⟩ Manifestation Code   🐾 Hierarchical Condition Category   Coding Clinic

● **Z45**   **Encounter for adjustment and management of implanted device**

> **Includes**   removal or replacement of implanted device
>
> **Excludes1**   malfunction or other complications of device - see Alphabetical Index
>
> **Excludes2**   encounter for fitting and adjustment of non-implanted device (Z46.-)

● **Z45.0**   **Encounter for adjustment and management of cardiac device**

  ● **Z45.01**   **Encounter for adjustment and management of cardiac pacemaker**

> Encounter for adjustment and management of cardiac resynchronization therapy pacemaker (CRT-P)
>
> **Excludes1**   encounter for adjustment and management of automatic implantable cardiac defibrillator with synchronous cardiac pacemaker (Z45.02)

     Z45.010   **Encounter for checking and testing of cardiac pacemaker pulse generator [battery]**

> Encounter for replacing cardiac pacemaker pulse generator [battery]

     Z45.018   **Encounter for adjustment and management of other part of cardiac pacemaker**

> **Excludes1**   presence of other part of cardiac pacemaker (Z95.0)
>
> **Excludes2**   presence of prosthetic and other devices (Z95.1-Z95.5, Z95.811-Z97)

     Z45.02   **Encounter for adjustment and management of automatic implantable cardiac defibrillator**

> Encounter for adjustment and management of automatic implantable cardiac defibrillator with synchronous cardiac pacemaker
>
> Encounter for adjustment and management of cardiac resynchronization therapy defibrillator (CRT-D)

     Z45.09   **Encounter for adjustment and management of other cardiac device**

   Z45.1   **Encounter for adjustment and management of infusion pump**

   Z45.2   **Encounter for adjustment and management of vascular access device**

> Encounter for adjustment and management of vascular catheters
>
> **Excludes1**   encounter for adjustment and management of renal dialysis catheter (Z49.01)

● **Z45.3**   **Encounter for adjustment and management of implanted devices of the special senses**

     Z45.31   **Encounter for adjustment and management of implanted visual substitution device**

  ● **Z45.32**   **Encounter for adjustment and management of implanted hearing device**

> **Excludes1**   encounter for fitting and adjustment of hearing aide (Z46.1)

     Z45.320   **Encounter for adjustment and management of bone conduction device**

     Z45.321   **Encounter for adjustment and management of cochlear device**

     Z45.328   **Encounter for adjustment and management of other implanted hearing device**

● **Z45.4**   **Encounter for adjustment and management of implanted nervous system device**

     Z45.41   **Encounter for adjustment and management of cerebrospinal fluid drainage device**

> Encounter for adjustment and management of cerebral ventricular (communicating) shunt

     Z45.42   **Encounter for adjustment and management of neuropacemaker**

> Encounter for adjustment and management of brain neurostimulator
>
> Encounter for adjustment and management of gastric neurostimulator
>
> Encounter for adjustment and management of peripheral nerve neurostimulator
>
> Encounter for adjustment and management of sacral nerve neurostimulator
>
> Encounter for adjustment and management of spinal cord neurostimulator
>
> Encounter for adjustment and management of vagus nerve neurostimulator

     Z45.49   **Encounter for adjustment and management of other implanted nervous system device**

● **Z45.8**   **Encounter for adjustment and management of other implanted devices**

  ● **Z45.81**   **Encounter for adjustment or removal of breast implant**

> Encounter for elective implant exchange (different material) (different size)
>
> Encounter removal of tissue expander with or without synchronous insertion of permanent implant
>
> **Excludes1**   complications of breast implant (T85.4-)
>
>   encounter for initial breast implant insertion for cosmetic breast augmentation (Z41.1)
>
>   encounter for breast reconstruction following mastectomy (Z42.1)

     Z45.811   **Encounter for adjustment or removal of right breast implant**

     Z45.812   **Encounter for adjustment or removal of left breast implant**

     Z45.819   **Encounter for adjustment or removal of unspecified breast implant**

     Z45.82   **Encounter for adjustment or removal of myringotomy device (stent) (tube)**

     Z45.89   **Encounter for adjustment and management of other implanted devices**

   Z45.9   **Encounter for adjustment and management of unspecified implanted device**

● **Z46**   **Encounter for fitting and adjustment of other devices**

> **Includes**   removal or replacement of other device
>
> **Excludes1**   malfunction or other complications of device - see Alphabetical Index
>
> **Excludes2**   encounter for fitting and management of implanted devices (Z45.-)
>
>   issue of repeat prescription only (Z76.0)
>
>   presence of prosthetic and other devices (Z95-Z97)

   Z46.0   **Encounter for fitting and adjustment of spectacles and contact lenses**

   Z46.1   **Encounter for fitting and adjustment of hearing aid**

> **Excludes1**   encounter for adjustment and management of implanted hearing device (Z45.32-)

   Z46.2   **Encounter for fitting and adjustment of other devices related to nervous system and special senses**

> **Excludes2**   encounter for adjustment and management of implanted nervous system device (Z45.4-)
>
>   encounter for adjustment and management of implanted visual substitution device (Z45.31)

CHAPTER 21 (Z00-Z99)

Z46.3 Encounter for fitting and adjustment of dental prosthetic device
    Encounter for fitting and adjustment of dentures

Z46.4 Encounter for fitting and adjustment of orthodontic device

● **Z46.5** Encounter for fitting and adjustment of other gastrointestinal appliance and device
    Excludes1 encounter for attention to artificial openings of digestive tract (Z43.1-Z43.4)

    Z46.51 Encounter for fitting and adjustment of gastric lap band

    Z46.59 Encounter for fitting and adjustment of other gastrointestinal appliance and device

Z46.6 Encounter for fitting and adjustment of urinary device
    Excludes2 attention to artificial openings of urinary tract (Z43.5, Z43.6)

● **Z46.8** Encounter for fitting and adjustment of other specified devices

    Z46.81 Encounter for fitting and adjustment of insulin pump
        Encounter for insulin pump instruction and training
        Encounter for insulin pump titration

    Z46.82 Encounter for fitting and adjustment of non-vascular catheter

    Z46.89 Encounter for fitting and adjustment of other specified devices
        Encounter for fitting and adjustment of wheelchair

Z46.9 Encounter for fitting and adjustment of unspecified device

● **Z47** Orthopedic aftercare
    Excludes1 aftercare for healing fracture - code to fracture with 7th character D

Z47.1 Aftercare following joint replacement surgery
    Use additional code to identify the joint (Z96.6-)
    Coding Clinic: 2020, Q1, P23-24

Z47.2 Encounter for removal of internal fixation device
    Excludes1 encounter for adjustment of internal fixation device for fracture treatment - code to fracture with appropriate 7th character
        encounter for removal of external fixation device - code to fracture with 7th character D
        infection or inflammatory reaction to internal fixation device (T84.6-)
        mechanical complication of internal fixation device (T84.1-)

● **Z47.3** Aftercare following explantation of joint prosthesis
    Aftercare following explantation of joint prosthesis, staged procedure
    Encounter for joint prosthesis insertion following prior explantation of joint prosthesis
    Coding Clinic: 2020, Q1, P23; 2015, Q1, P17

    Z47.31 Aftercare following explantation of shoulder joint prosthesis
        Excludes1 acquired absence of shoulder joint following prior explantation of shoulder joint prosthesis (Z89.23-)
            shoulder joint prosthesis explantation status (Z89.23-)

    Z47.32 Aftercare following explantation of hip joint prosthesis
        Excludes1 acquired absence of hip joint following prior explantation of hip joint prosthesis (Z89.62-)
            hip joint prosthesis explantation status (Z89.62-)
        Coding Clinic: 2015, Q1, P17

    Z47.33 Aftercare following explantation of knee joint prosthesis
        Excludes1 acquired absence of knee joint following prior explantation of knee prosthesis (Z89.52-)
            knee joint prosthesis explantation status (Z89.52-)

● **Z47.8** Encounter for other orthopedic aftercare

    Z47.81 Encounter for orthopedic aftercare following surgical amputation
        Use additional code to identify the limb amputated (Z89.-)

    Z47.82 Encounter for orthopedic aftercare following scoliosis surgery

    Z47.89 Encounter for other orthopedic aftercare
        Coding Clinic: 2015, Q1, P8

● **Z48** Encounter for other postprocedural aftercare
    Excludes1 encounter for aftercare following injury - code to Injury, by site, with appropriate 7th character for subsequent encounter
        encounter for follow-up examination after completed treatment (Z08-Z09)
    Excludes2 encounter for attention to artificial openings (Z43.-)
        encounter for fitting and adjustment of prosthetic and other devices (Z44-Z46)

● **Z48.0** Encounter for attention to dressings, sutures and drains
    Excludes1 encounter for planned postprocedural wound closure (Z48.1)

    Z48.00 Encounter for change or removal of nonsurgical wound dressing
        Encounter for change or removal of wound dressing NOS

    Z48.01 Encounter for change or removal of surgical wound dressing
        Coding Clinic: 2019, Q2, P33; 2015, Q4, P38

    Z48.02 Encounter for removal of sutures
        Encounter for removal of staples
        Coding Clinic: 2015, Q1, P6

    Z48.03 Encounter for change or removal of drains

Z48.1 Encounter for planned postprocedural wound closure
    Excludes1 encounter for attention to dressings and sutures (Z48.0-)

● **Z48.2** Encounter for aftercare following organ transplant

    Z48.21 Encounter for aftercare following heart transplant 🔖

    Z48.22 Encounter for aftercare following kidney transplant

    Z48.23 Encounter for aftercare following liver transplant 🔖

    Z48.24 Encounter for aftercare following lung transplant 🔖

    ● **Z48.28** Encounter for aftercare following multiple organ transplant

        Z48.280 Encounter for aftercare following heart-lung transplant 🔖

        Z48.288 Encounter for aftercare following multiple organ transplant

    ● **Z48.29** Encounter for aftercare following other organ transplant

        Z48.290 Encounter for aftercare following bone marrow transplant 🔖

        Z48.298 Encounter for aftercare following other organ transplant

Z48.3 Aftercare following surgery for neoplasm
    Use additional code to identify the neoplasm

▶ New   ⇒ Revised   ~~deleted~~ Deleted   Excludes 1   Excludes 2   Includes   Use additional   Code first   Code also   Key words

OGCR Official Guidelines   X Assign placeholder X   ● Use Additional Character(s)   ▶ Manifestation Code   🔖 Hierarchical Condition Category   **Coding Clinic**

● **Z48.8 Encounter for other specified postprocedural aftercare**

    ● **Z48.81 Encounter for surgical aftercare following surgery on specified body systems**

       These codes identify the body system requiring aftercare. They are for use in conjunction with other aftercare codes to fully explain the aftercare encounter. The condition treated should also be coded if still present.

       Excludes1   aftercare for injury - code the injury with 7th character D

          aftercare following surgery for neoplasm (Z48.3)

       Excludes2   aftercare following organ transplant (Z48.2-)

          orthopedic aftercare (Z47.-)

       Z48.810   Encounter for surgical aftercare following surgery on the sense organs

       Z48.811   Encounter for surgical aftercare following surgery on the nervous system

          Excludes2   encounter for surgical aftercare following surgery on the sense organs (Z48.810)

       Z48.812   Encounter for surgical aftercare following surgery on the circulatory system

          Coding Clinic: 2012, Q4, P96

       Z48.813   Encounter for surgical aftercare following surgery on the respiratory system

          Coding Clinic: 2019, Q2, P33

       Z48.814   Encounter for surgical aftercare following surgery on the teeth or oral cavity

       Z48.815   Encounter for surgical aftercare following surgery on the digestive system

          Coding Clinic: 2015, Q4, P38

       Z48.816   Encounter for surgical aftercare following surgery on the genitourinary system

          Excludes1   encounter for aftercare following sterilization reversal (Z31.42)

       Z48.817   Encounter for surgical aftercare following surgery on the skin and subcutaneous tissue

          Coding Clinic: 2015, Q1, P6

    Z48.89   Encounter for other specified surgical aftercare

● **Z49 Encounter for care involving renal dialysis**

    Code also associated end stage renal disease (N18.6)

    ● **Z49.0 Preparatory care for renal dialysis**

       Encounter for dialysis instruction and training

       Z49.01   Encounter for fitting and adjustment of extracorporeal dialysis catheter 🎗

          Removal or replacement of renal dialysis catheter

          Toilet or cleansing of renal dialysis catheter

       Z49.02   Encounter for fitting and adjustment of peritoneal dialysis catheter 🎗

    ● **Z49.3 Encounter for adequacy testing for dialysis**

       Z49.31   Encounter for adequacy testing for hemodialysis 🎗

       Z49.32   Encounter for adequacy testing for peritoneal dialysis 🎗

          Encounter for peritoneal equilibration test

● **Z51 Encounter for other aftercare and medical care**

    Code also condition requiring care

    Excludes1   follow-up examination after treatment (Z08-Z09)

    Coding Clinic: 2017, Q1, P49; 2016, Q4, P130

    Z51.0   Encounter for antineoplastic radiation therapy

       Coding Clinic: 2017, Q4, P103

    ● Z51.1   Encounter for antineoplastic chemotherapy and immunotherapy

       Excludes2   encounter for chemotherapy and immunotherapy for nonneoplastic condition-code to condition

       Z51.11   Encounter for antineoplastic chemotherapy

          Coding Clinic: 2015, Q3, P19

       Z51.12   Encounter for antineoplastic immunotherapy

    Z51.5   Encounter for palliative care

       Coding Clinic: 2017, Q1, P48-49

    Z51.6   Encounter for desensitization to allergens

       Coding Clinic: 2016, Q4, P77-79

    ● Z51.8   Encounter for other specified aftercare

       Excludes1   holiday relief care (Z75.5)

       Z51.81   Encounter for therapeutic drug level monitoring

          Code also any long-term (current) drug therapy (Z79.-)

          Excludes1   encounter for blood-drug test for administrative or medicolegal reasons (Z02.83)

       Z51.89   Encounter for other specified aftercare

          Coding Clinic: 2012, Q4, P96-97

● **Z52 Donors of organs and tissues**

    Includes   autologous and other living donors

    Excludes1   cadaveric donor - omit code

       examination of potential donor (Z00.5)

    Coding Clinic: 2012, Q4, P100

    ● **Z52.0 Blood donor**

       ● Z52.00   Unspecified blood donor

          Z52.000   Unspecified donor, whole blood

          Z52.001   Unspecified donor, stem cells

          Z52.008   Unspecified donor, other blood

       ● Z52.01   Autologous blood donor

          Z52.010   Autologous donor, whole blood

          Z52.011   Autologous donor, stem cells

          Z52.018   Autologous donor, other blood

       ● Z52.09   Other blood donor

          Volunteer donor

          Z52.090   Other blood donor, whole blood

          Z52.091   Other blood donor, stem cells

          Z52.098   Other blood donor, other blood

    ● **Z52.1 Skin donor**

       Z52.10   Skin donor, unspecified

       Z52.11   Skin donor, autologous

       Z52.19   Skin donor, other

    ● **Z52.2 Bone donor**

       Z52.20   Bone donor, unspecified

       Z52.21   Bone donor, autologous

       Z52.29   Bone donor, other

    Z52.3   Bone marrow donor

    Z52.4   Kidney donor

    Z52.5   Cornea donor

    Z52.6   Liver donor

       Coding Clinic: 2012, Q4, P100

N Newborn Age: 0   **P** Pediatric Age: 0–17   **M** Maternity DX: 12–55   **A** Adult Age: 15–124   ♀ Females Only   ♂ Males Only

● **Z52.8   Donor of other specified organs or tissues**
  ● **Z52.81   Egg (Oocyte) donor**
        Z52.810   Egg (Oocyte) donor under age 35, anonymous recipient ♀
                  Egg donor under age 35 NOS
        Z52.811   Egg (Oocyte) donor under age 35, designated recipient ♀
        Z52.812   Egg (Oocyte) donor age 35 and over, anonymous recipient ♀
                  Egg donor age 35 and over NOS
        Z52.813   Egg (Oocyte) donor age 35 and over, designated recipient ♀
        Z52.819   Egg (Oocyte) donor, unspecified ♀
     Z52.89   Donor of other specified organs or tissues
  Z52.9   Donor of unspecified organ or tissue
          Donor NOS

● **Z53   Persons encountering health services for specific procedures and treatment, not carried out**
  ● **Z53.0   Procedure and treatment not carried out because of contraindication**
        Z53.01   Procedure and treatment not carried out due to patient smoking
        Z53.09   Procedure and treatment not carried out because of other contraindication
     Z53.1   Procedure and treatment not carried out because of patient's decision for reasons of belief and group pressure
  ● **Z53.2   Procedure and treatment not carried out because of patient's decision for other and unspecified reasons**
        Z53.20   Procedure and treatment not carried out because of patient's decision for unspecified reasons
        Z53.21   Procedure and treatment not carried out due to patient leaving prior to being seen by health care provider
        Z53.29   Procedure and treatment not carried out because of patient's decision for other reasons
  ● **Z53.3   Procedure converted to open procedure**
          Coding Clinic: 2016, Q4, P79
        Z53.31   Laparoscopic surgical procedure converted to open procedure
              Coding Clinic: 2016, Q4, P100
        Z53.32   Thoracoscopic surgical procedure converted to open procedure
        Z53.33   Arthroscopic surgical procedure converted to open procedure
        Z53.39   Other specified procedure converted to open procedure
     Z53.8   Procedure and treatment not carried out for other reasons
     Z53.9   Procedure and treatment not carried out, unspecified reason

PERSONS WITH POTENTIAL HEALTH HAZARDS RELATED TO SOCIOECONOMIC AND PSYCHOSOCIAL CIRCUMSTANCES (Z55-Z65)

● **Z55   Problems related to education and literacy**
     Excludes1   disorders of psychological development (F80-F89)
     Z55.0   Illiteracy and low-level literacy
     Z55.1   Schooling unavailable and unattainable
     Z55.2   Failed school examinations
     Z55.3   Underachievement in school
     Z55.4   Educational maladjustment and discord with teachers and classmates
     Z55.8   Other problems related to education and literacy
          Problems related to inadequate teaching
     Z55.9   Problems related to education and literacy, unspecified
          Academic problems NOS

● **Z56   Problems related to employment and unemployment**
     Excludes2   occupational exposure to risk factors (Z57.-)
                  problems related to housing and economic circumstances (Z59.-)
     Z56.0   Unemployment, unspecified
     Z56.1   Change of job
     Z56.2   Threat of job loss
     Z56.3   Stressful work schedule
     Z56.4   Discord with boss and workmates
     Z56.5   Uncongenial work environment
          Difficult conditions at work
     Z56.6   Other physical and mental strain related to work
  ● **Z56.8   Other problems related to employment**
        Z56.81   Sexual harassment on the job
        Z56.82   Military deployment status
                  Individual (civilian or military) currently deployed in theater or in support of military war, peacekeeping and humanitarian operations
        Z56.89   Other problems related to employment
     Z56.9   Unspecified problems related to employment
          Occupational problems NOS

● **Z57   Occupational exposure to risk factors**
     Z57.0   Occupational exposure to noise
     Z57.1   Occupational exposure to radiation
     Z57.2   Occupational exposure to dust
  ● **Z57.3   Occupational exposure to other air contaminants**
        Z57.31   Occupational exposure to environmental tobacco smoke
              Excludes2   exposure to environmental tobacco smoke (Z77.22)
        Z57.39   Occupational exposure to other air contaminants
     Z57.4   Occupational exposure to toxic agents in agriculture
          Occupational exposure to solids, liquids, gases or vapors in agriculture
     Z57.5   Occupational exposure to toxic agents in other industries
          Occupational exposure to solids, liquids, gases or vapors in other industries
     Z57.6   Occupational exposure to extreme temperature
     Z57.7   Occupational exposure to vibration
     Z57.8   Occupational exposure to other risk factors
     Z57.9   Occupational exposure to unspecified risk factor

● **Z59   Problems related to housing and economic circumstances**
     Excludes2   problems related to upbringing (Z62.-)
     Z59.0   Homelessness
     Z59.1   Inadequate housing
          Lack of heating
          Restriction of space
          Technical defects in home preventing adequate care
          Unsatisfactory surroundings
          Excludes1   problems related to the natural and physical environment (Z77.1-)
     Z59.2   Discord with neighbors, lodgers and landlord
     Z59.3   Problems related to living in residential institution
          Boarding-school resident
          Excludes1   institutional upbringing (Z62.2)
     Z59.4   Lack of adequate food and safe drinking water
          Inadequate drinking water supply
          Excludes1   effects of hunger (T73.0)
                      inappropriate diet or eating habits (Z72.4)
                      malnutrition (E40-E46)
     Z59.5   Extreme poverty
     Z59.6   Low income
     Z59.7   Insufficient social insurance and welfare support

A

▶ New   ▥ Revised   ~~deleted~~ Deleted   Excludes 1   Excludes 2   Includes   Use additional   Code first   Code also   Key words
OGCR Official Guidelines   X Assign placeholder X   ● Use Additional Character(s)   ▶ Manifestation Code   🅗 Hierarchical Condition Category   Coding Clinic

Z59.8   **Other problems related to housing and economic circumstances**
Foreclosure on loan
Isolated dwelling
Problems with creditors

Z59.9   **Problem related to housing and economic circumstances, unspecified**

● **Z60**   **Problems related to social environment**

Z60.0   **Problems of adjustment to life-cycle transitions**
Empty nest syndrome
Phase of life problem
Problem with adjustment to retirement [pension]

Z60.2   **Problems related to living alone**

Z60.3   **Acculturation difficulty**
Problem with migration
Problem with social transplantation

Z60.4   **Social exclusion and rejection**
Exclusion and rejection on the basis of personal characteristics, such as unusual physical appearance, illness or behavior.

    Excludes1   target of adverse discrimination such as for racial or religious reasons (Z60.5)

Z60.5   **Target of (perceived) adverse discrimination and persecution**

    Excludes1   social exclusion and rejection (Z60.4)

Z60.8   **Other problems related to social environment**

Z60.9   **Problem related to social environment, unspecified**

● **Z62**   **Problems related to upbringing**

    Includes   current and past negative life events in childhood
current and past problems of a child related to upbringing

    Excludes2   maltreatment syndrome (T74.-)
problems related to housing and economic circumstances (Z59.-)

Z62.0   **Inadequate parental supervision and control**

Z62.1   **Parental overprotection**

● **Z62.2**   **Upbringing away from parents**

    Excludes1   problems with boarding school (Z59.3)

   Z62.21   **Child in welfare custody**   P
Child in care of non-parental family member
Child in foster care

     Excludes2   problem for parent due to child in welfare custody (Z63.5)

   Z62.22   **Institutional upbringing**
Child living in orphanage or group home

   Z62.29   **Other upbringing away from parents**

Z62.3   **Hostility towards and scapegoating of child**   P

Z62.6   **Inappropriate (excessive) parental pressure**

● **Z62.8**   **Other specified problems related to upbringing**

   ● **Z62.81**   **Personal history of abuse in childhood**

     Z62.810   **Personal history of physical and sexual abuse in childhood**

       Excludes1   current child physical abuse (T74.12, T76.12)
current child sexual abuse (T74.22, T76.22)

     Z62.811   **Personal history of psychological abuse in childhood**

       Excludes1   current child psychological abuse (T74.32, T76.32)

     Z62.812   **Personal history of neglect in childhood**

       Excludes1   current child neglect (T74.02, T76.02)

     Z62.813   **Personal history of forced labor or sexual exploitation in childhood**

     Z62.819   **Personal history of unspecified abuse in childhood**

       Excludes1   current child abuse NOS (T74.92, T76.92)

   ● **Z62.82**   **Parent-child conflict**

     Z62.820   **Parent-biological child conflict**
Parent-child problem NOS

     Z62.821   **Parent-adopted child conflict**

     Z62.822   **Parent-foster child conflict**

   ● **Z62.89**   **Other specified problems related to upbringing**

     Z62.890   **Parent-child estrangement NEC**

     Z62.891   **Sibling rivalry**

     Z62.898   **Other specified problems related to upbringing**

Z62.9   **Problem related to upbringing, unspecified**

● **Z63**   **Other problems related to primary support group, including family circumstances**

    Excludes2   maltreatment syndrome (T74.-, T76)
parent-child problems (Z62.-)
problems related to negative life events in childhood (Z62.-)
problems related to upbringing (Z62.-)

Z63.0   **Problems in relationship with spouse or partner**
Relationship distress with spouse or intimate partner

    Excludes1   counseling for spousal or partner abuse problems (Z69.1)
counseling related to sexual attitude, behavior, and orientation (Z70.-)

Z63.1   **Problems in relationship with in-laws**

● **Z63.3**   **Absence of family member**

    Excludes1   absence of family member due to disappearance and death (Z63.4)
absence of family member due to separation and divorce (Z63.5)

   Z63.31   **Absence of family member due to military deployment**
Individual or family affected by other family member being on military deployment

     Excludes1   family disruption due to return of family member from military deployment (Z63.71)

   Z63.32   **Other absence of family member**

Z63.4   **Disappearance and death of family member**
Assumed death of family member
Bereavement

Z63.5   **Disruption of family by separation and divorce**
Marital estrangement

Z63.6   **Dependent relative needing care at home**

● **Z63.7**   **Other stressful life events affecting family and household**

   Z63.71   **Stress on family due to return of family member from military deployment**
Individual or family affected by family member having returned from military deployment (current or past conflict)

   Z63.72   **Alcoholism and drug addiction in family**

   Z63.79   **Other stressful life events affecting family and household**
Anxiety (normal) about sick person in family
Health problems within family
Ill or disturbed family member
Isolated family

N   Newborn Age: 0   **P**   Pediatric Age: 0–17   **M**   Maternity DX: 12–55   **A**   Adult Age: 15–124   ♀   Females Only   ♂   Males Only

Z63.8   **Other specified problems related to primary support group**
     Family discord NOS
     Family estrangement NOS
     High expressed emotional level within family
     Inadequate family support NOS
     Inadequate or distorted communication within family

Z63.9   **Problem related to primary support group, unspecified**
     Relationship disorder NOS

● **Z64**   **Problems related to certain psychosocial circumstances**

Z64.0   **Problems related to unwanted pregnancy ♀**

Z64.1   **Problems related to multiparity ♀**

Z64.4   **Discord with counselors**
     Discord with probation officer
     Discord with social worker

● **Z65**   **Problems related to other psychosocial circumstances**

Z65.0   **Conviction in civil and criminal proceedings without imprisonment**

Z65.1   **Imprisonment and other incarceration**

Z65.2   **Problems related to release from prison**

Z65.3   **Problems related to other legal circumstances**
     Arrest
     Child custody or support proceedings
     Litigation
     Prosecution

Z65.4   **Victim of crime and terrorism**
     Victim of torture

Z65.5   **Exposure to disaster, war and other hostilities**
     Excludes1   target of perceived discrimination or persecution (Z60.5)

Z65.8   **Other specified problems related to psychosocial circumstances**
     Religious or spiritual problem

Z65.9   **Problem related to unspecified psychosocial circumstances**

DO NOT RESUSCITATE STATUS (Z66)

Z66   **Do not resuscitate**
     DNR status

BLOOD TYPE (Z67)

● **Z67**   **Blood type**
     Coding Clinic: 2015, Q3, P40

● **Z67.1**   **Type A blood**
     Z67.10   Type A blood, Rh positive
     Z67.11   Type A blood, Rh negative

● **Z67.2**   **Type B blood**
     Z67.20   Type B blood, Rh positive
     Z67.21   Type B blood, Rh negative

● **Z67.3**   **Type AB blood**
     Z67.30   Type AB blood, Rh positive
     Z67.31   Type AB blood, Rh negative

● **Z67.4**   **Type O blood**
     Z67.40   Type O blood, Rh positive
     Z67.41   Type O blood, Rh negative

● **Z67.9**   **Unspecified blood type**
     Z67.90   Unspecified blood type, Rh positive
     Z67.91   Unspecified blood type, Rh negative
          Coding Clinic: 2015, Q3, P40

BODY MASS INDEX [BMI] (Z68)

OGCR Section I.B.14.

General Coding Guidelines

14. Documentation for BMI, Depth of Non-pressure ulcers, Pressure Ulcer Stages, Coma Scale, and NIH Stroke Scale

For the Body Mass Index (BMI), depth of non-pressure chronic ulcers, pressure ulcer stage, coma scale, and NIH stroke scale (NIHSS) codes, code assignment may be based on medical record documentation from clinicians who are not the patient's provider (i.e., physician or other qualified healthcare practitioner legally accountable for establishing the patient's diagnosis), since this information is typically documented by other clinicians involved in the care of the patient (e.g., a dietitian often documents the BMI, a nurse often documents the pressure ulcer stages, and an emergency medical technician often documents the coma scale). However, the associated diagnosis (such as overweight, obesity, acute stroke, or pressure ulcer) must be documented by the patient's provider. If there is conflicting medical record documentation, either from the same clinician or different clinicians, the patient's attending provider should be queried for clarification.

The BMI, coma scale, and NIHSS codes should only be reported as secondary diagnoses.

● **Z68**   **Body mass index [BMI]**
     Kilograms per meters squared
     Note: BMI adult codes are for use for persons 20 years of age or older.
          BMI pediatric codes are for use for persons 2-19 years of age.
          These percentiles are based on the growth charts published by the Centers for Disease Control and Prevention (CDC)
     Coding Clinic: 2018, Q4, P81; 2016, Q4, P129

➡ **Z68.1**   **Body mass index [BMI] 19.9 or less, adult**   A
          Coding Clinic: 2017, Q1, P39

➡● **Z68.2**   **Body mass index [BMI] 20-29, adult**
     ➡ **Z68.20**   Body mass index [BMI] 20.0-20.9, adult   A
     ➡ **Z68.21**   Body mass index [BMI] 21.0-21.9, adult   A
     ➡ **Z68.22**   Body mass index [BMI] 22.0-22.9, adult   A
     ➡ **Z68.23**   Body mass index [BMI] 23.0-23.9, adult   A
     ➡ **Z68.24**   Body mass index [BMI] 24.0-24.9, adult   A
     ➡ **Z68.25**   Body mass index [BMI] 25.0-25.9, adult   A
     ➡ **Z68.26**   Body mass index [BMI] 26.0-26.9, adult   A
     ➡ **Z68.27**   Body mass index [BMI] 27.0-27.9, adult   A
     ➡ **Z68.28**   Body mass index [BMI] 28.0-28.9, adult   A
     ➡ **Z68.29**   Body mass index [BMI] 29.0-29.9, adult   A

➡● **Z68.3**   **Body mass index [BMI] 30-39, adult**
     ➡ **Z68.30**   Body mass index [BMI] 30.0-30.9, adult   A
     ➡ **Z68.31**   Body mass index [BMI] 31.0-31.9, adult   A
     ➡ **Z68.32**   Body mass index [BMI] 32.0-32.9, adult   A
     ➡ **Z68.33**   Body mass index [BMI] 33.0-33.9, adult   A
     ➡ **Z68.34**   Body mass index [BMI] 34.0-34.9, adult   A
     ➡ **Z68.35**   Body mass index [BMI] 35.0-35.9, adult   A
     ➡ **Z68.36**   Body mass index [BMI] 36.0-36.9, adult   A
     ➡ **Z68.37**   Body mass index [BMI] 37.0-37.9, adult   A
     ➡ **Z68.38**   Body mass index [BMI] 38.0-38.9, adult   A
     ➡ **Z68.39**   Body mass index [BMI] 39.0-39.9, adult   A

➡● **Z68.4**   **Body mass index [BMI] 40 or greater, adult**
     ➡ **Z68.41**   Body mass index [BMI] 40.0-44.9, adult 🔖   A
     ➡ **Z68.42**   Body mass index [BMI] 45.0-49.9, adult 🔖   A
     ➡ **Z68.43**   Body mass index [BMI] 50.0-59.9, adult 🔖   A
     ➡ **Z68.44**   Body mass index [BMI] 60.0-69.9, adult 🔖   A
     ➡ **Z68.45**   Body mass index [BMI] 70 or greater, adult 🔖   A

▶ New   ➡ Revised   ~~deleted~~ Deleted   Excludes 1   Excludes 2   Includes   Use additional   Code first   Code also   Key words

OGCR Official Guidelines   X Assign placeholder X   ● Use Additional Character(s)   ▶ Manifestation Code   🔖 Hierarchical Condition Category   Coding Clinic

CHAPTER 21 (Z00-Z99)

⇒● **Z68.5**   **Body mass index [BMI] pediatric**
     Coding Clinic: 2018, Q4, P81

⇒   **Z68.51**   **Body mass index [BMI] pediatric, less than 5th percentile for age**
     Coding Clinic: 2018, Q4, P82

⇒   **Z68.52**   **Body mass index [BMI] pediatric, 5th percentile to less than 85th percentile for age**

⇒   **Z68.53**   **Body mass index [BMI] pediatric, 85th percentile to less than 95th percentile for age**

⇒   **Z68.54**   **Body mass index [BMI] pediatric, greater than or equal to 95th percentile for age**

PERSONS ENCOUNTERING HEALTH SERVICES IN OTHER CIRCUMSTANCES (Z69-Z76)

● **Z69**   **Encounter for mental health services for victim and perpetrator of abuse**

     Includes   counseling for victims and perpetrators of abuse

● **Z69.0**   **Encounter for mental health services for child abuse problems**

● **Z69.01**   **Encounter for mental health services for parental child abuse**

   Z69.010   **Encounter for mental health services for victim of parental child abuse**   P
     Encounter for mental health services for victim of child abuse by parent
     Encounter for mental health services for victim of child neglect by parent
     Encounter for mental health services for victim of child psychological abuse by parent
     Encounter for mental health services for victim of child sexual abuse by parent

   Z69.011   **Encounter for mental health services for perpetrator of parental child abuse**
     Encounter for mental health services for perpetrator of parental child neglect
     Encounter for mental health services for perpetrator of parental child psychological abuse
     Encounter for mental health services for perpetrator of parental child sexual abuse

     Excludes1   encounter for mental health services for non-parental child abuse (Z69.02-)

● **Z69.02**   **Encounter for mental health services for non-parental child abuse**

   Z69.020   **Encounter for mental health services for victim of non-parental child abuse**   P
     Encounter for mental health services for victim of non-parental child neglect
     Encounter for mental health services for victim of non-parental child psychological abuse
     Encounter for mental health services for victim of non-parental child sexual abuse

   Z69.021   **Encounter for mental health services for perpetrator of non- parental child abuse**
     Encounter for mental health services for perpetrator of non-parental child neglect
     Encounter for mental health services for perpetrator of non-parental child psychological abuse
     Encounter for mental health services for perpetrator of non-parental child sexual abuse

● **Z69.1**   **Encounter for mental health services for spousal or partner abuse problems**

   Z69.11   **Encounter for mental health services for victim of spousal or partner abuse**
     Encounter for mental health services for victim of spouse or partner neglect
     Encounter for mental health services for victim of spouse or partner psychological abuse
     Encounter for mental health services for victim of spouse or partner violence, physical

   Z69.12   **Encounter for mental health services for perpetrator of spousal or partner abuse**
     Encounter for mental health services for perpetrator of spouse or partner neglect
     Encounter for mental health services for perpetrator of spouse or partner psychological abuse
     Encounter for mental health services for perpetrator of spouse or partner violence, physical
     Encounter for mental health services for perpetrator of spouse or partner violence, sexual

● **Z69.8**   **Encounter for mental health services for victim or perpetrator of other abuse**

   Z69.81   **Encounter for mental health services for victim of other abuse**
     Encounter for mental health services for victim of non-spousal adult abuse
     Encounter for mental health services for victim of spouse or partner violence, sexual
     Encounter for rape victim counseling

   Z69.82   **Encounter for mental health services for perpetrator of other abuse**
     Encounter for mental health services for perpetrator of non-spousal adult abuse

● **Z70**   **Counseling related to sexual attitude, behavior and orientation**

     Includes   encounter for mental health services for sexual attitude, behavior and orientation

     Excludes2   contraceptive or procreative counseling (Z30-Z31)

Z70.0   **Counseling related to sexual attitude**

Z70.1   **Counseling related to patient's sexual behavior and orientation**
     Patient concerned regarding impotence
     Patient concerned regarding non-responsiveness
     Patient concerned regarding promiscuity
     Patient concerned regarding sexual orientation

Z70.2   **Counseling related to sexual behavior and orientation of third party**
     Advice sought regarding sexual behavior and orientation of child
     Advice sought regarding sexual behavior and orientation of partner
     Advice sought regarding sexual behavior and orientation of spouse

Z70.3   **Counseling related to combined concerns regarding sexual attitude, behavior and orientation**

Z70.8   **Other sex counseling**
     Encounter for sex education

Z70.9   **Sex counseling, unspecified**

● **Z71**   **Persons encountering health services for other counseling and medical advice, not elsewhere classified**

     Excludes2   contraceptive or procreation counseling (Z30-Z31)
         sex counseling (Z70.-)

Z71.0   **Person encountering health services to consult on behalf of another person**
     Person encountering health services to seek advice or treatment for non-attending third party

     Excludes2   anxiety (normal) about sick person in family (Z63.7)
         expectant (adoptive) parent(s) pre-birth pediatrician visit (Z76.81)

CHAPTER 21 (Z00-Z99)

CHAPTER 21 (Z00-Z99)

Z71.1   Person with feared health complaint in whom no diagnosis is made
> Person encountering health services with feared condition which was not demonstrated
> Person encountering health services in which problem was normal state
> "Worried well"
>> **Excludes1**   medical observation for suspected diseases and conditions proven not to exist (Z03.-)
>
> Coding Clinic: 2016, Q4, P7

Z71.2   Person consulting for explanation of examination or test findings

Z71.3   Dietary counseling and surveillance
> Use additional code for any associated underlying medical condition
> Use additional code to identify body mass index (BMI), if known (Z68.-)

● **Z71.4   Alcohol abuse counseling and surveillance**
> Use additional code for alcohol abuse or dependence (F10.-)

     Z71.41   Alcohol abuse counseling and surveillance of alcoholic

     Z71.42   Counseling for family member of alcoholic
> Counseling for significant other, partner, or friend of alcoholic

● **Z71.5   Drug abuse counseling and surveillance**
> Use additional code for drug abuse or dependence (F11-F16, F18-F19)

     Z71.51   Drug abuse counseling and surveillance of drug abuser

     Z71.52   Counseling for family member of drug abuser
> Counseling for significant other, partner, or friend of drug abuser

Z71.6   Tobacco abuse counseling
> Use additional code for nicotine dependence (F17.-)

Z71.7   Human immunodeficiency virus [HIV] counseling

● **Z71.8   Other specified counseling**
>> **Excludes2**   counseling for contraception (Z30.0-)

     Z71.81   Spiritual or religious counseling

     Z71.82   Exercise counseling

     Z71.83   Encounter for nonprocreative genetic counseling
>> **Excludes1**   counseling for procreative genetics (Z31.5)
>> counseling for procreative management (Z31.6)

     Z71.84   Encounter for health counseling related to travel
> Encounter for health risk and safety counseling for (international) travel
> Code also, if applicable, encounter for immunization (Z23)
>> **Excludes2**   encounter for administrative examination (Z02.-)
>> encounter for other special examination without complaint, suspected or reported diagnosis (Z01.-)

     Z71.89   Other specified counseling

Z71.9   Counseling, unspecified
> Encounter for medical advice NOS

● **Z72   Problems related to lifestyle**
>> **Excludes2**   problems related to life-management difficulty (Z73.-)
>> problems related to socioeconomic and psychosocial circumstances (Z55-Z65)
>
> Coding Clinic: 2016, Q4, P130

Z72.0   Tobacco use
> Tobacco use NOS
>> **Excludes1**   history of tobacco dependence (Z87.891)
>> nicotine dependence (F17.2-)
>> tobacco dependence (F17.2-)
>> tobacco use during pregnancy (O99.33-)

Z72.3   Lack of physical exercise

Z72.4   Inappropriate diet and eating habits
>> **Excludes1**   behavioral eating disorders of infancy or childhood (F98.2.-F98.3)
>> eating disorders (F50.-)
>> lack of adequate food (Z59.4)
>> malnutrition and other nutritional deficiencies (E40-E64)

● **Z72.5   High risk sexual behavior**
> Promiscuity
>> **Excludes1**   paraphilias (F65)

     Z72.51   High risk heterosexual behavior

     Z72.52   High risk homosexual behavior

     Z72.53   High risk bisexual behavior

Z72.6   Gambling and betting
>> **Excludes1**   compulsive or pathological gambling (F63.0)

● **Z72.8   Other problems related to lifestyle**

   ● **Z72.81   Antisocial behavior**
>> **Excludes1**   conduct disorders (F91.-)

     Z72.810   Child and adolescent antisocial behavior   P
> Antisocial behavior (child) (adolescent) without manifest psychiatric disorder
> Delinquency NOS
> Group delinquency
> Offenses in the context of gang membership
> Stealing in company with others
> Truancy from school

     Z72.811   Adult antisocial behavior   A
> Adult antisocial behavior without manifest psychiatric disorder

   ● **Z72.82   Problems related to sleep**

     Z72.820   Sleep deprivation
> Lack of adequate sleep
>> **Excludes1**   insomnia (G47.0-)

     Z72.821   Inadequate sleep hygiene
> Bad sleep habits
> Irregular sleep habits
> Unhealthy sleep wake schedule
>> **Excludes1**   insomnia (F51.0-, G47.0-)

     Z72.89   Other problems related to lifestyle
> Self-damaging behavior

Z72.9   Problem related to lifestyle, unspecified

● **Z73   Problems related to life management difficulty**
>> **Excludes2**   problems related to socioeconomic and psychosocial circumstances (Z55-Z65)

Z73.0   Burn-out

Z73.1   Type A behavior pattern

Z73.2   Lack of relaxation and leisure

Z73.3   Stress, not elsewhere classified
> Physical and mental strain NOS
>> **Excludes1**   stress related to employment or unemployment (Z56.-)

Z73.4 Inadequate social skills, not elsewhere classified

Z73.5 Social role conflict, not elsewhere classified

Z73.6 Limitation of activities due to disability

> **Excludes1** care-provider dependency (Z74.-)

● **Z73.8** Other problems related to life management difficulty

  ● **Z73.81** Behavioral insomnia of childhood

    Z73.810 Behavioral insomnia of childhood, sleep-onset association type P

    Z73.811 Behavioral insomnia of childhood, limit setting type P

    Z73.812 Behavioral insomnia of childhood, combined type P

    Z73.819 Behavioral insomnia of childhood, unspecified type P

  Z73.82 Dual sensory impairment

  Z73.89 Other problems related to life management difficulty

Z73.9 Problem related to life management difficulty, unspecified

● **Z74** Problems related to care provider dependency

> **Excludes2** dependence on enabling machines or devices NEC (Z99.-)

  ● **Z74.0** Reduced mobility

    Z74.01 Bed confinement status
      Bedridden

    Z74.09 Other reduced mobility
      Chairridden
      Reduced mobility NOS

>   **Excludes2** wheelchair dependence (Z99.3)

  Z74.1 Need for assistance with personal care

  Z74.2 Need for assistance at home and no other household member able to render care

  Z74.3 Need for continuous supervision

  Z74.8 Other problems related to care provider dependency

  Z74.9 Problem related to care provider dependency, unspecified

● **Z75** Problems related to medical facilities and other health care

  Z75.0 Medical services not available in home

>   **Excludes1** no other household member able to render care (Z74.2)

  Z75.1 Person awaiting admission to adequate facility elsewhere

  Z75.2 Other waiting period for investigation and treatment

  Z75.3 Unavailability and inaccessibility of health care facilities

>   **Excludes1** bed unavailable (Z75.1)

  Z75.4 Unavailability and inaccessibility of other helping agencies

  Z75.5 Holiday relief care

  Z75.8 Other problems related to medical facilities and other health care

  Z75.9 Unspecified problem related to medical facilities and other health care

● **Z76** Persons encountering health services in other circumstances

  Z76.0 Encounter for issue of repeat prescription
    Encounter for issue of repeat prescription for appliance
    Encounter for issue of repeat prescription for medicaments
    Encounter for issue of repeat prescription for spectacles

>   **Excludes2** issue of medical certificate (Z02.7)
>   repeat prescription for contraceptive (Z30.4-)

  Z76.1 Encounter for health supervision and care of foundling

Z76.2 Encounter for health supervision and care of other healthy infant and child P
  Encounter for medical or nursing care or supervision of healthy infant under circumstances such as adverse socioeconomic conditions at home
  Encounter for medical or nursing care or supervision of healthy infant under circumstances such as awaiting foster or adoptive placement
  Encounter for medical or nursing care or supervision of healthy infant under circumstances such as maternal illness
  Encounter for medical or nursing care or supervision of healthy infant under circumstances such as number of children at home preventing or interfering with normal care

Z76.3 Healthy person accompanying sick person

Z76.4 Other boarder to healthcare facility

> **Excludes1** homelessness (Z59.0)

Z76.5 Malingerer [conscious simulation]
  Person feigning illness (with obvious motivation)

> **Excludes1** factitious disorder (F68.1-, F68.A)
>   peregrinating patient (F68.1-)

● **Z76.8** Persons encountering health services in other specified circumstances

  Z76.81 Expectant parent(s) prebirth pediatrician visit
    Pre-adoption pediatrician visit for adoptive parent(s)

  Z76.82 Awaiting organ transplant status
    Patient waiting for organ availability

  Z76.89 Persons encountering health services in other specified circumstances
    Persons encountering health services NOS

PERSONS WITH POTENTIAL HEALTH HAZARDS RELATED TO FAMILY AND PERSONAL HISTORY AND CERTAIN CONDITIONS INFLUENCING HEALTH STATUS (Z77-Z99)

Code also any follow-up examination (Z08-Z09)

● **Z77** Other contact with and (suspected) exposures hazardous to health

> **Includes** contact with and (suspected) exposures to potential hazards to health

> **Excludes2** contact with and (suspected) exposure to communicable diseases (Z20.-)
>   exposure to (parental) (environmental) tobacco smoke in the perinatal period (P96.81)
>   newborn affected by noxious substances transmitted via placenta or breast milk (P04.-)
>   occupational exposure to risk factors (Z57.-)
>   retained foreign body (Z18.-)
>   retained foreign body fully removed (Z87.821)
>   toxic effects of substances chiefly nonmedicinal as to source (T51-T65)

● **Z77.0** Contact with and (suspected) exposure to hazardous, chiefly nonmedicinal, chemicals

  ● **Z77.01** Contact with and (suspected) exposure to hazardous metals

    Z77.010 Contact with and (suspected) exposure to arsenic

    Z77.011 Contact with and (suspected) exposure to lead

    Z77.012 Contact with and (suspected) exposure to uranium

>   **Excludes1** retained depleted uranium fragments (Z18.01)

    Z77.018 Contact with and (suspected) exposure to other hazardous metals
      Contact with and (suspected) exposure to chromium compounds
      Contact with and (suspected) exposure to nickel dust

CHAPTER 21 (Z00-Z99)

● **Z77.02** **Contact with and (suspected) exposure to hazardous aromatic compounds**

Z77.020 Contact with and (suspected) exposure to aromatic amines

Z77.021 Contact with and (suspected) exposure to benzene

Z77.028 Contact with and (suspected) exposure to other hazardous aromatic compounds
Aromatic dyes NOS
Polycyclic aromatic hydrocarbons

● **Z77.09** **Contact with and (suspected) exposure to other hazardous, chiefly nonmedicinal, chemicals**

Z77.090 Contact with and (suspected) exposure to asbestos

Z77.098 Contact with and (suspected) exposure to other hazardous, chiefly nonmedicinal, chemicals
Dyes NOS

● **Z77.1** **Contact with and (suspected) exposure to environmental pollution and hazards in the physical environment**

● **Z77.11** **Contact with and (suspected) exposure to environmental pollution**

Z77.110 Contact with and (suspected) exposure to air pollution

Z77.111 Contact with and (suspected) exposure to water pollution

Z77.112 Contact with and (suspected) exposure to soil pollution

Z77.118 Contact with and (suspected) exposure to other environmental pollution

● **Z77.12** **Contact with and (suspected) exposure to hazards in the physical environment**

Z77.120 Contact with and (suspected) exposure to mold (toxic)

Z77.121 Contact with and (suspected) exposure to harmful algae and algae toxins
Contact with and (suspected) exposure to (harmful) algae bloom NOS
Contact with and (suspected) exposure to blue-green algae bloom
Contact with and (suspected) exposure to brown tide
Contact with and (suspected) exposure to cyanobacteria bloom
Contact with and (suspected) exposure to Florida red tide
Contact with and (suspected) exposure to pfiesteria piscicida
Contact with and (suspected) exposure to red tide

Z77.122 Contact with and (suspected) exposure to noise

Z77.123 Contact with and (suspected) exposure to radon and other naturally occurring radiation

Excludes2 radiation exposure as the cause of a confirmed condition (W88-W90, X39.0-)
radiation sickness NOS (T66)

Z77.128 Contact with and (suspected) exposure to other hazards in the physical environment

● **Z77.2** **Contact with and (suspected) exposure to other hazardous substances**

Z77.21 Contact with and (suspected) exposure to potentially hazardous body fluids

Z77.22 Contact with and (suspected) exposure to environmental tobacco smoke (acute) (chronic)
Exposure to second hand tobacco smoke (acute) (chronic)
Passive smoking (acute) (chronic)

Excludes1 nicotine dependence (F17.-) tobacco use (Z72.0)

Excludes2 occupational exposure to environmental tobacco smoke (Z57.31)

Z77.29 Contact with and (suspected) exposure to other hazardous substances
Coding Clinic: 2016, Q2, P34

Z77.9 **Other contact with and (suspected) exposures hazardous to health**

● **Z78** **Other specified health status**

Excludes2 asymptomatic human immunodeficiency virus [HIV] infection status (Z21)
postprocedural status (Z93-Z99)
sex reassignment status (Z87.890)

Z78.0 **Asymptomatic menopausal state ♀**   A
Menopausal state NOS
Postmenopausal status NOS

Excludes2 symptomatic menopausal state (N95.1)

Z78.1 **Physical restraint status**

Excludes1 physical restraint due to a procedure - omit code

Z78.9 **Other specified health status**

● **Z79** **Long term (current) drug therapy**

Includes long term (current) drug use for prophylactic purposes

Code also any therapeutic drug level monitoring (Z51.81)

Excludes2 drug abuse and dependence (F11-F19)
drug use complicating pregnancy, childbirth, and the puerperium (O99.32-)
~~long term (current) use of oral antidiabetic drugs (Z79.84)~~
~~long term (current) use of oral hypoglycemic drugs (Z79.84)~~

● **Z79.0** **Long term (current) use of anticoagulants and antithrombotics/antiplatelets**

Excludes2 long term (current) use of aspirin (Z79.82)

Z79.01 **Long term (current) use of anticoagulants**

Z79.02 **Long term (current) use of antithrombotics/antiplatelets**

Z79.1 **Long term (current) use of non-steroidal anti-inflammatories (NSAID)**

Excludes2 long term (current) use of aspirin (Z79.82)

Z79.2 **Long term (current) use of antibiotics**

Z79.3 **Long term (current) use of hormonal contraceptives**
Long term (current) use of birth control pill or patch

Z79.4 **Long term (current) use of insulin** 🔗

▶ **Excludes1** long term (current) use of oral antidiabetic drugs (Z79.84)
▶ long term (current) use of oral hypoglycemic drugs (Z79.84)

● **Z79.5** **Long term (current) use of steroids**

Z79.51 **Long term (current) use of inhaled steroids**

Z79.52 **Long term (current) use of systemic steroids**

▶ New   ▮▶ Revised   ~~deleted~~ Deleted   Excludes 1   Excludes 2   Includes   Use additional   Code first   Code also   Key words

1578   OGCR Official Guidelines   X Assign placeholder X   ● Use Additional Character(s)   ▶ Manifestation Code   🔗 Hierarchical Condition Category   Coding Clinic

● **Z79.8   Other long term (current) drug therapy**
   ● **Z79.81   Long term (current) use of agents affecting estrogen receptors and estrogen levels**
      Code first, if applicable:
      malignant neoplasm of breast (C50.-)
      malignant neoplasm of prostate (C61)

      Use additional code, if applicable, to identify:
      estrogen receptor positive status (Z17.0)
      family history of breast cancer (Z80.3)
      genetic susceptibility to malignant neoplasm (cancer) (Z15.0-)
      personal history of breast cancer (Z85.3)
      personal history of prostate cancer (Z85.46)
      postmenopausal status (Z78.0)

      Excludes1   hormone replacement therapy (Z79.890)

     Z79.810   Long term (current) use of selective estrogen receptor modulators (SERMs)
       Long term (current) use of raloxifene (Evista)
       Long term (current) use of tamoxifen (Nolvadex)
       Long term (current) use of toremifene (Fareston)

     Z79.811   Long term (current) use of aromatase inhibitors
       Long term (current) use of anastrozole (Arimidex)
       Long term (current) use of exemestane (Aromasin)
       Long term (current) use of letrozole (Femara)

     Z79.818   Long term (current) use of other agents affecting estrogen receptors and estrogen levels
       Long term (current) use of estrogen receptor downregulators
       Long term (current) use of fulvestrant (Faslodex)
       Long term (current) use of gonadotropin-releasing hormone (GnRH) agonist
       Long term (current) use of goserelin acetate (Zoladex)
       Long term (current) use of leuprolide acetate (leuprorelin) (Lupron)
       Long term (current) use of megestrol acetate (Megace)

   Z79.82   Long term (current) use of aspirin

   Z79.83   Long term (current) use of bisphosphonates
     Coding Clinic: 2016, Q4, P42

   Z79.84   Long term (current) use of oral hypoglycemic drugs
     Long term (current) use of oral antidiabetic drugs
     Excludes2   long term (current) use of insulin (Z79.4)
     Coding Clinic: 2016, Q4, P76, 121-122, 126

   ● **Z79.89   Other long term (current) drug therapy**
     Z79.890   Hormone replacement therapy
     Z79.891   Long term (current) use of opiate analgesic
       Long term (current) use of methadone for pain management
       Excludes1   methodone use NOS (F11.9-)
         use of methodone for treatment of heroin addiction (F11.2-)

     Z79.899   Other long term (current) drug therapy
       Coding Clinic: 2015, Q4, P34, Q3, P21

● **Z80   Family history of primary malignant neoplasm**
   Z80.0   Family history of malignant neoplasm of digestive organs
     Conditions classifiable to C15-C26
     Coding Clinic: 2018, Q1, P7

   Z80.1   Family history of malignant neoplasm of trachea, bronchus and lung
     Conditions classifiable to C33-C34

   Z80.2   Family history of malignant neoplasm of other respiratory and intrathoracic organs
     Conditions classifiable to C30-C32, C37-C39

   Z80.3   Family history of malignant neoplasm of breast
     Conditions classifiable to C50.-

   ● **Z80.4   Family history of malignant neoplasm of genital organs**
     Conditions classifiable to C51-C63

     Z80.41   Family history of malignant neoplasm of ovary
     Z80.42   Family history of malignant neoplasm of prostate
     Z80.43   Family history of malignant neoplasm of testis
     Z80.49   Family history of malignant neoplasm of other genital organs

   ● **Z80.5   Family history of malignant neoplasm of urinary tract**
     Conditions classifiable to C64-C68

     Z80.51   Family history of malignant neoplasm of kidney
     Z80.52   Family history of malignant neoplasm of bladder
     Z80.59   Family history of malignant neoplasm of other urinary tract organ

   Z80.6   Family history of leukemia
     Conditions classifiable to C91-C95

   Z80.7   Family history of other malignant neoplasms of lymphoid, hematopoietic and related tissues
     Conditions classifiable to C81-C90, C96.-

   Z80.8   Family history of malignant neoplasm of other organs or systems
     Conditions classifiable to C00-C14, C40-C49, C69-C79

   Z80.9   Family history of malignant neoplasm, unspecified
     Conditions classifiable to C80.1

● **Z81   Family history of mental and behavioral disorders**
   Z81.0   Family history of intellectual disabilities
     Conditions classifiable to F70-F79

   Z81.1   Family history of alcohol abuse and dependence
     Conditions classifiable to F10.-

   Z81.2   Family history of tobacco abuse and dependence
     Conditions classifiable to F17.-

   Z81.3   Family history of other psychoactive substance abuse and dependence
     Conditions classifiable to F11-F16, F18-F19

   Z81.4   Family history of other substance abuse and dependence
     Conditions classifiable to F55

   Z81.8   Family history of other mental and behavioral disorders
     Conditions classifiable elsewhere in F01-F99

● **Z82   Family history of certain disabilities and chronic diseases (leading to disablement)**
   Z82.0   Family history of epilepsy and other diseases of the nervous system
     Conditions classifiable to G00-G99

   Z82.1   Family history of blindness and visual loss
     Conditions classifiable to H54.-

   Z82.2   Family history of deafness and hearing loss
     Conditions classifiable to H90-H91

   Z82.3   Family history of stroke
     Conditions classifiable to I60-I64

   ● **Z82.4   Family history of ischemic heart disease and other diseases of the circulatory system**
     Conditions classifiable to I00-I52, I65-I99

     Z82.41   Family history of sudden cardiac death
     Z82.49   Family history of ischemic heart disease and other diseases of the circulatory system

CHAPTER 21 (Z00-Z99)

CHAPTER 21 (Z00-Z99)

Z82.5   **Family history of asthma and other chronic lower respiratory diseases**
Conditions classifiable to J40-J47

     Excludes2   family history of other diseases of the respiratory system (Z83.6)

● **Z82.6**   **Family history of arthritis and other diseases of the musculoskeletal system and connective tissue**
Conditions classifiable to M00-M99

     Z82.61   **Family history of arthritis**

     Z82.62   **Family history of osteoporosis**

     Z82.69   **Family history of other diseases of the musculoskeletal system and connective tissue**

● **Z82.7**   **Family history of congenital malformations, deformations and chromosomal abnormalities**
Conditions classifiable to Q00-Q99

     Z82.71   **Family history of polycystic kidney**

     Z82.79   **Family history of other congenital malformations, deformations and chromosomal abnormalities**

Z82.8   **Family history of other disabilities and chronic diseases leading to disablement, not elsewhere classified**

● **Z83**   **Family history of other specific disorders**

     Excludes2   contact with and (suspected) exposure to communicable disease in the family (Z20.-)

Z83.0   **Family history of human immunodeficiency virus [HIV] disease**
Conditions classifiable to B20

Z83.1   **Family history of other infectious and parasitic diseases**
Conditions classifiable to A00-B19, B25-B94, B99

Z83.2   **Family history of diseases of the blood and blood-forming organs and certain disorders involving the immune mechanism**
Conditions classifiable to D50-D89

Z83.3   **Family history of diabetes mellitus**
Conditions classifiable to E08-E13

● **Z83.4**   **Family history of other endocrine, nutritional and metabolic diseases**
Conditions classifiable to E00-E07, E15-E88

     Z83.41   **Family history of multiple endocrine neoplasia [MEN] syndrome**

     Z83.42   **Family history of familial hypercholesterolemia**
           Coding Clinic: 2016, Q4, P77

    ● **Z83.43**   **Family history of other disorder of lipoprotein metabolism and other lipidemias**

         Z83.430   **Family history of elevated lipoprotein(a)**
              Family history of elevated Lp(a)

         Z83.438   **Family history of other disorder of lipoprotein metabolism and other lipidemia**
              Family history of familial combined hyperlipidemia

     Z83.49   **Family history of other endocrine, nutritional and metabolic diseases**

● **Z83.5**   **Family history of eye and ear disorders**

    ● **Z83.51**   **Family history of eye disorders**
Conditions classifiable to H00-H53, H55-H59

         Excludes2   family history of blindness and visual loss (Z82.1)

         Z83.511   **Family history of glaucoma**

         Z83.518   **Family history of other specified eye disorder**

     Z83.52   **Family history of ear disorders**
Conditions classifiable to H60-H83, H92-H95

         Excludes2   family history of deafness and hearing loss (Z82.2)

Z83.6   **Family history of other diseases of the respiratory system**
Conditions classifiable to J00-J39, J60-J99

     Excludes2   family history of asthma and other chronic lower respiratory diseases (Z82.5)

● **Z83.7**   **Family history of diseases of the digestive system**
Conditions classifiable to K00-K93

     Z83.71   **Family history of colonic polyps**

         Excludes2   family history of malignant neoplasm of digestive organs (Z80.0)

     Z83.79   **Family history of other diseases of the digestive system**

● **Z84**   **Family history of other conditions**

Z84.0   **Family history of diseases of the skin and subcutaneous tissue**
Conditions classifiable to L00-L99

Z84.1   **Family history of disorders of kidney and ureter**
Conditions classifiable to N00-N29

Z84.2   **Family history of other diseases of the genitourinary system**
Conditions classifiable to N30-N99
Coding Clinic: 2016, Q4, P77

Z84.3   **Family history of consanguinity**

● **Z84.8**   **Family history of other specified conditions**

     Z84.81   **Family history of carrier of genetic disease**

     Z84.82   **Family history of sudden infant death syndrome**
           Family history of SIDS

     Z84.89   **Family history of other specified conditions**

● **Z85**   **Personal history of malignant neoplasm**
Code first any follow-up examination after treatment of malignant neoplasm (Z08)

Use additional code to identify:
alcohol use and dependence (F10.-)
exposure to environmental tobacco smoke (Z77.22)
history of tobacco dependence (Z87.891)
occupational exposure to environmental tobacco smoke (Z57.31)
tobacco dependence (F17.-)
tobacco use (Z72.0)

     Excludes2   personal history of benign neoplasm (Z86.01-)
                personal history of carcinoma-in-situ (Z86.00-)

● **Z85.0**   **Personal history of malignant neoplasm of digestive organs**

     Z85.00   **Personal history of malignant neoplasm of unspecified digestive organ**

     Z85.01   **Personal history of malignant neoplasm of esophagus**
           Conditions classifiable to C15

    ● **Z85.02**   **Personal history of malignant neoplasm of stomach**

         Z85.020   **Personal history of malignant carcinoid tumor of stomach**
              Conditions classifiable to C7A.092

         Z85.028   **Personal history of other malignant neoplasm of stomach**
              Conditions classifiable to C16

    ● **Z85.03**   **Personal history of malignant neoplasm of large intestine**

         Z85.030   **Personal history of malignant carcinoid tumor of large intestine**
              Conditions classifiable to C7A.022-C7A.025, C7A.029

         Z85.038   **Personal history of other malignant neoplasm of large intestine**
              Conditions classifiable to C18

    ● **Z85.04**   **Personal history of malignant neoplasm of rectum, rectosigmoid junction, and anus**

         Z85.040   **Personal history of malignant carcinoid tumor of rectum**
              Conditions classifiable to C7A.026

         Z85.048   **Personal history of other malignant neoplasm of rectum, rectosigmoid junction, and anus**
              Conditions classifiable to C19-C21

▶ New   ⇒ Revised   ~~deleted~~ Deleted   Excludes 1   Excludes 2   Includes   Use additional   Code first   Code also   Key words

OGCR Official Guidelines   X Assign placeholder X   ● Use Additional Character(s)   ▷ Manifestation Code   ⦿ Hierarchical Condition Category   Coding Clinic

● Z85.05   Personal history of malignant neoplasm of liver
            Conditions classifiable to C22

● Z85.06   Personal history of malignant neoplasm of small intestine

   Z85.060   Personal history of malignant carcinoid tumor of small intestine
              Conditions classifiable to C7A.01-

   Z85.068   Personal history of other malignant neoplasm of small intestine
              Conditions classifiable to C17

● Z85.07   Personal history of malignant neoplasm of pancreas
            Conditions classifiable to C25

● Z85.09   Personal history of malignant neoplasm of other digestive organs

● Z85.1   Personal history of malignant neoplasm of trachea, bronchus and lung

● Z85.11   Personal history of malignant neoplasm of bronchus and lung

   Z85.110   Personal history of malignant carcinoid tumor of bronchus and lung
              Conditions classifiable to C7A.090

   Z85.118   Personal history of other malignant neoplasm of bronchus and lung
              Conditions classifiable to C34

● Z85.12   Personal history of malignant neoplasm of trachea
            Conditions classifiable to C33

● Z85.2   Personal history of malignant neoplasm of other respiratory and intrathoracic organs

   Z85.20   Personal history of malignant neoplasm of unspecified respiratory organ

   Z85.21   Personal history of malignant neoplasm of larynx
             Conditions classifiable to C32

   Z85.22   Personal history of malignant neoplasm of nasal cavities, middle ear, and accessory sinuses
             Conditions classifiable to C30-C31

● Z85.23   Personal history of malignant neoplasm of thymus

   Z85.230   Personal history of malignant carcinoid tumor of thymus
              Conditions classifiable to C7A.091

   Z85.238   Personal history of other malignant neoplasm of thymus
              Conditions classifiable to C37

   Z85.29   Personal history of malignant neoplasm of other respiratory and intrathoracic organs

● Z85.3   Personal history of malignant neoplasm of breast
            Conditions classifiable to C50.-

● Z85.4   Personal history of malignant neoplasm of genital organs
            Conditions classifiable to C51-C63

   Z85.40   Personal history of malignant neoplasm of unspecified female genital organ ♀

   Z85.41   Personal history of malignant neoplasm of cervix uteri ♀

   Z85.42   Personal history of malignant neoplasm of other parts of uterus ♀

   Z85.43   Personal history of malignant neoplasm of ovary ♀

   Z85.44   Personal history of malignant neoplasm of other female genital organs ♀

   Z85.45   Personal history of malignant neoplasm of unspecified male genital organ ♂

   Z85.46   Personal history of malignant neoplasm of prostate ♂

   Z85.47   Personal history of malignant neoplasm of testis ♂

   Z85.48   Personal history of malignant neoplasm of epididymis ♂

   Z85.49   Personal history of malignant neoplasm of other male genital organs ♂

● Z85.5   Personal history of malignant neoplasm of urinary tract
            Conditions classifiable to C64-C68

   Z85.50   Personal history of malignant neoplasm of unspecified urinary tract organ

   Z85.51   Personal history of malignant neoplasm of bladder

● Z85.52   Personal history of malignant neoplasm of kidney

   Excludes1   personal history of malignant neoplasm of renal pelvis (Z85.53)

   Z85.520   Personal history of malignant carcinoid tumor of kidney
              Conditions classifiable to C7A.093

   Z85.528   Personal history of other malignant neoplasm of kidney
              Conditions classifiable to C64

   Z85.53   Personal history of malignant neoplasm of renal pelvis

   Z85.54   Personal history of malignant neoplasm of ureter

   Z85.59   Personal history of malignant neoplasm of other urinary tract organ

   Z85.6   Personal history of leukemia
             Conditions classifiable to C91-C95

   Excludes1   leukemia in remission C91.0-C95.9 with 5th character 1

● Z85.7   Personal history of other malignant neoplasms of lymphoid, hematopoietic and related tissues

   Z85.71   Personal history of Hodgkin lymphoma
             Conditions classifiable to C81

   Z85.72   Personal history of non-Hodgkin lymphomas
             Conditions classifiable to C82-C85

   Z85.79   Personal history of other malignant neoplasms of lymphoid, hematopoietic and related tissues
             Conditions classifiable to C88-C90, C96

   Excludes1   multiple myeloma in remission (C90.01)
                plasma cell leukemia in remission (C90.11)
                plasmacytoma in remission (C90.21)

● Z85.8   Personal history of malignant neoplasms of other organs and systems
            Conditions classifiable to C00-C14, C40-C49, C69-C75, C7A.098, C76-C79

● Z85.81   Personal history of malignant neoplasm of lip, oral cavity, and pharynx
            ▶Conditions classifiable to C00-C14

   Z85.810   Personal history of malignant neoplasm of tongue

   Z85.818   Personal history of malignant neoplasm of other sites of lip, oral cavity, and pharynx

   Z85.819   Personal history of malignant neoplasm of unspecified site of lip, oral cavity, and pharynx

● Z85.82   Personal history of malignant neoplasm of skin

   Z85.820   Personal history of malignant melanoma of skin
              Conditions classifiable to C43

   Z85.821   Personal history of Merkel cell carcinoma
              Conditions classifiable to C4A

   Z85.828   Personal history of other malignant neoplasm of skin
              Conditions classifiable to C44

CHAPTER 21 (Z00-Z99)

● **Z85.83** **Personal history of malignant neoplasm of bone and soft tissue**
▶Conditions classifiable to C40-C41; C45-C49

Z85.830 **Personal history of malignant neoplasm of bone**

Z85.831 **Personal history of malignant neoplasm of soft tissue**

Excludes2 personal history of malignant neoplasm of skin (Z85.82-)

● **Z85.84** **Personal history of malignant neoplasm of eye and nervous tissue**
▶Conditions classifiable to C69-C72

Z85.840 **Personal history of malignant neoplasm of eye**

Z85.841 **Personal history of malignant neoplasm of brain**

Z85.848 **Personal history of malignant neoplasm of other parts of nervous tissue**

● **Z85.85** **Personal history of malignant neoplasm of endocrine glands**
▶Conditions classifiable to C73-C75

Z85.850 **Personal history of malignant neoplasm of thyroid**

Z85.858 **Personal history of malignant neoplasm of other endocrine glands**

Z85.89 **Personal history of malignant neoplasm of other organs and systems**
▶Conditions classifiable to C7A.098, C76, C77-C79

Z85.9 **Personal history of malignant neoplasm, unspecified**
Conditions classifiable to C7A.00, C80.1

● **Z86** **Personal history of certain other diseases**
Code first any follow-up examination after treatment (Z09)

● **Z86.0** **Personal history of in-situ and benign neoplasms and neoplasms of uncertain behavior**
Excludes2 personal history of malignant neoplasms (Z85.-)

● **Z86.00** **Personal history of in-situ neoplasm**
Conditions classifiable to D00-D09

Z86.000 **Personal history of in-situ neoplasm of breast**
Conditions classifiable to D05

Z86.001 **Personal history of in-situ neoplasm of cervix uteri ♀**
Conditions classifiable to D06
Personal history of cervical intraepithelial neoplasia III [CIN III]

Z86.002 **Personal history of in-situ neoplasm of other and unspecified genital organs**
Conditions classifiable to D07
Personal history of high-grade prostatic intraepithelial neoplasia III [HGPIN III]
Personal history of vaginal intraepithelial neoplasia III [VAIN III]
Personal history of vulvar intraepithelial neoplasia III [VIN III]

Z86.003 **Personal history of in-situ neoplasm of oral cavity, esophagus and stomach**
Conditions classifiable to D00

Z86.004 **Personal history of in-situ neoplasm of other and unspecified digestive organs**
Conditions classifiable to D01
Personal history of anal intraepithelial neoplasia (AIN III)

Z86.005 **Personal history of in-situ neoplasm of middle ear and respiratory system**
Conditions classifiable to D02

Z86.006 **Personal history of melanoma in-situ**
Conditions classifiable to D03
Excludes2 sites other than skin - code to personal history of in-situ neoplasm of the site

Z86.007 **Personal history of in-situ neoplasm of skin**
Conditions classifiable to D04
Personal history of carcinoma in situ of skin

Z86.008 **Personal history of in-situ neoplasm of other site**
Conditions classifiable to D09

● **Z86.01** **Personal history of benign neoplasm**
Coding Clinic: 2017, Q1, P14

Z86.010 **Personal history of colonic polyps**
Coding Clinic: 2017, Q1, P9, P14

Z86.011 **Personal history of benign neoplasm of the brain**

Z86.012 **Personal history of benign carcinoid tumor**

Z86.018 **Personal history of other benign neoplasm**
Coding Clinic: 2017, Q1, P14

Z86.03 **Personal history of neoplasm of uncertain behavior**

● **Z86.1** **Personal history of infectious and parasitic diseases**
Conditions classifiable to A00-B89, B99
Excludes1 personal history of infectious diseases specific to a body system sequelae of infectious and parasitic diseases (B90-B94)
Coding Clinic: 2016, Q4, P5

Z86.11 **Personal history of tuberculosis**

Z86.12 **Personal history of poliomyelitis**

Z86.13 **Personal history of malaria**

Z86.14 **Personal history of Methicillin resistant Staphylococcus aureus infection**
Personal history of MRSA infection

Z86.15 **Personal history of latent tuberculosis infection**

Z86.19 **Personal history of other infectious and parasitic diseases**

Z86.2 **Personal history of diseases of the blood and blood-forming organs and certain disorders involving the immune mechanism**
Conditions classifiable to D50-D89

● **Z86.3** **Personal history of endocrine, nutritional and metabolic diseases**
Conditions classifiable to E00-E88

Z86.31 **Personal history of diabetic foot ulcer**
Excludes2 current diabetic foot ulcer (E08.621, E09.621, E10.621, E11.621, E13.621)

Z86.32 **Personal history of gestational diabetes ♀**
Personal history of conditions classifiable to O24.4-
Excludes1 gestational diabetes mellitus in current pregnancy (O24.4-)

Z86.39 **Personal history of other endocrine, nutritional and metabolic disease**
Coding Clinic: 2020, Q1, P13

▶ New ⇒ Revised ~~deleted~~ Deleted | Excludes 1 | Excludes 2 | Includes | Use additional | Code first | Code also | Key words
OGCR Official Guidelines   X Assign placeholder X   ● Use Additional Character(s)   ▷ Manifestation Code   ⊗ Hierarchical Condition Category   Coding Clinic

● **Z86.5   Personal history of mental and behavioral disorders**
Conditions classifiable to F40-F59

  Z86.51   Personal history of combat and operational stress reaction   A

  Z86.59   Personal history of other mental and behavioral disorders

● **Z86.6   Personal history of diseases of the nervous system and sense organs**
Conditions classifiable to G00-G99, H00-H95

  Z86.61   Personal history of infections of the central nervous system
  Personal history of encephalitis
  Personal history of meningitis

  Z86.69   Personal history of other diseases of the nervous system and sense organs
  Coding Clinic: 2016, Q4, P25

● **Z86.7   Personal history of diseases of the circulatory system**
Conditions classifiable to I00-I99

  Excludes2   old myocardial infarction (I25.2)
  personal history of anaphylactic shock (Z87.892)
  postmyocardial infarction syndrome (I24.1)

  ● **Z86.71   Personal history of venous thrombosis and embolism**

    Z86.711   Personal history of pulmonary embolism

    Z86.718   Personal history of other venous thrombosis and embolism

  Z86.72   Personal history of thrombophlebitis

  Z86.73   Personal history of transient ischemic attack (TIA), and cerebral infarction without residual deficits
  Personal history of prolonged reversible ischemic neurological deficit (PRIND)
  Personal history of stroke NOS without residual deficits

    Excludes1   personal history of traumatic brain injury (Z87.820)
    sequelae of cerebrovascular disease (I69.-)
  Coding Clinic: 2012, Q4, P3

  Z86.74   Personal history of sudden cardiac arrest
  Personal history of sudden cardiac death successfully resuscitated

  Z86.79   Personal history of other diseases of the circulatory system
  Coding Clinic: 2020, Q1, P13

● **Z87   Personal history of other diseases and conditions**
Code first any follow-up examination after treatment (Z09)

  ● **Z87.0   Personal history of diseases of the respiratory system**
  Conditions classifiable to J00-J99

    Z87.01   Personal history of pneumonia (recurrent)

    Z87.09   Personal history of other diseases of the respiratory system

  ● **Z87.1   Personal history of diseases of the digestive system**
  Conditions classifiable to K00-K93

    Z87.11   Personal history of peptic ulcer disease

    Z87.19   Personal history of other diseases of the digestive system
    Coding Clinic: 2017, Q1, P14

  Z87.2   Personal history of diseases of the skin and subcutaneous tissue
  Conditions classifiable to L00-L99

    Excludes2   personal history of diabetic foot ulcer (Z86.31)

● **Z87.3   Personal history of diseases of the musculoskeletal system and connective tissue**
Conditions classifiable to M00-M99

  Excludes2   personal history of (healed) traumatic fracture (Z87.81)

  ● **Z87.31   Personal history of (healed) nontraumatic fracture**

    Z87.310   Personal history of (healed) osteoporosis fracture
    Personal history of (healed) fragility fracture
    Personal history of (healed) collapsed vertebra due to osteoporosis

    Z87.311   Personal history of (healed) other pathological fracture
    Personal history of (healed) collapsed vertebra NOS

      Excludes2   personal history of osteoporosis fracture (Z87.310)

    Z87.312   Personal history of (healed) stress fracture
    Personal history of (healed) fatigue fracture

  Z87.39   Personal history of other diseases of the musculoskeletal system and connective tissue

● **Z87.4   Personal history of diseases of genitourinary system**
Conditions classifiable to N00-N99

  ● **Z87.41   Personal history of dysplasia of the female genital tract**

    Excludes1   personal history of intraepithelial neoplasia III of female genital tract (Z86.001, Z86.008)
    personal history of malignant neoplasm of female genital tract (Z85.40-Z85.44)

    Z87.410   Personal history of cervical dysplasia ♀

    Z87.411   Personal history of vaginal dysplasia ♀

    Z87.412   Personal history of vulvar dysplasia ♀

  Z87.42   Personal history of other diseases of the female genital tract ♀

  ● **Z87.43   Personal history of diseases of male genital organs**

    Z87.430   Personal history of prostatic dysplasia ♂

      Excludes1   personal history of malignant neoplasm of prostate (Z85.46)

    Z87.438   Personal history of other diseases of male genital organs ♂

  ● **Z87.44   Personal history of diseases of urinary system**

    Excludes1   personal history of malignant neoplasm of cervix uteri (Z85.41)

    Z87.440   Personal history of urinary (tract) infections

    Z87.441   Personal history of nephrotic syndrome

    Z87.442   Personal history of urinary calculi
    Personal history of kidney stones

    Z87.448   Personal history of other diseases of urinary system

CHAPTER 21 (Z00-Z99)

● **Z87.5** **Personal history of complications of pregnancy, childbirth and the puerperium**
Conditions classifiable to O00-O9A
    Excludes2   recurrent pregnancy loss (N96)

  Z87.51   Personal history of pre-term labor ♀
      Excludes1 current pregnancy with history of pre-term labor (O09.21-)

  Z87.59   Personal history of other complications of pregnancy, childbirth and the puerperium ♀
      Personal history of trophoblastic disease

● **Z87.7** **Personal history of (corrected) congenital malformations**
Conditions classifiable to Q00-Q89 that have been repaired or corrected
    Excludes1 congenital malformations that have been partially corrected or repair but which still require medical treatment - code to condition
    Excludes2 other postprocedural states (Z98.-)
          personal history of medical treatment (Z92.-)
          presence of cardiac and vascular implants and grafts (Z95.-)
          presence of other devices (Z97.-)
          presence of other functional implants (Z96.-)
          transplanted organ and tissue status (Z94.-)

  ● **Z87.71** Personal history of (corrected) congenital malformations of genitourinary system
    Z87.710 Personal history of (corrected) hypospadias ♂
    Z87.718 Personal history of other specified (corrected) congenital malformations of genitourinary system

  ● **Z87.72** Personal history of (corrected) congenital malformations of nervous system and sense organs
    Z87.720 Personal history of (corrected) congenital malformations of eye
    Z87.721 Personal history of (corrected) congenital malformations of ear
    Z87.728 Personal history of other specified (corrected) congenital malformations of nervous system and sense organs

  ● **Z87.73** Personal history of (corrected) congenital malformations of digestive system
    Z87.730 Personal history of (corrected) cleft lip and palate
    Z87.738 Personal history of other specified (corrected) congenital malformations of digestive system

  Z87.74 Personal history of (corrected) congenital malformations of heart and circulatory system

  Z87.75 Personal history of (corrected) congenital malformations of respiratory system

  Z87.76 Personal history of (corrected) congenital malformations of integument, limbs and musculoskeletal system

  ● **Z87.79** Personal history of other (corrected) congenital malformations
    Z87.790 Personal history of (corrected) congenital malformations of face and neck
    Z87.798 Personal history of other (corrected) congenital malformations

● **Z87.8** **Personal history of other specified conditions**
    Excludes2 personal history of self harm (Z91.5)

  Z87.81 Personal history of (healed) traumatic fracture
    Excludes2 personal history of (healed) nontraumatic fracture (Z87.31-)

  ● **Z87.82** Personal history of other (healed) physical injury and trauma
    Conditions classifiable to S00-T88, except traumatic fractures
    Z87.820 Personal history of traumatic brain injury
      Excludes1 personal history of transient ischemic attack (TIA), and cerebral infarction without residual deficits (Z86.73)
    Z87.821 Personal history of retained foreign body fully removed
    Z87.828 Personal history of other (healed) physical injury and trauma

  ● **Z87.89** Personal history of other specified conditions
    Z87.890 Personal history of sex reassignment
    Z87.891 Personal history of nicotine dependence
      Excludes1 current nicotine dependence (F17.2-)
      Coding Clinic: 2017, Q2, P27
    Z87.892 Personal history of anaphylaxis
      Code also allergy status such as: allergy status to drugs, medicaments and biological substances (Z88.-)
      allergy status, other than to drugs and biological substances (Z91.0-)
    Z87.898 Personal history of other specified conditions
      Coding Clinic: 2013, Q1, P21

● **Z88** **Allergy status to drugs, medicaments and biological substances**
    Excludes2 allergy status, other than to drugs and biological substances (Z91.0-)

  Z88.0 Allergy status to penicillin
⇒ **Z88.1** Allergy status to other antibiotic agents
⇒ **Z88.2** Allergy status to sulfonamides
    Coding Clinic: 2015, Q3, P23
⇒ **Z88.3** Allergy status to other anti-infective agents
⇒ **Z88.4** Allergy status to anesthetic agent
⇒ **Z88.5** Allergy status to narcotic agent
⇒ **Z88.6** Allergy status to analgesic agent
⇒ **Z88.7** Allergy status to serum and vaccine
⇒ **Z88.8** Allergy status to other drugs, medicaments and biological substances
⇒ **Z88.9** Allergy status to unspecified drugs, medicaments and biological substances

▶ New   ⇒ Revised   ~~deleted~~ Deleted   Excludes 1   Excludes 2   Includes   Use additional   Code first   Code also   Key words
OGCR Official Guidelines   X Assign placeholder X   ● Use Additional Character(s)   ▌ Manifestation Code   ℞ Hierarchical Condition Category   Coding Clinic

● **Z89**   **Acquired absence of limb**

> **Includes**   amputation status
> postprocedural loss of limb
> post-traumatic loss of limb
>
> **Excludes1**   acquired deformities of limbs (M20-M21)
> congenital absence of limbs (Q71-Q73)

● **Z89.0**   **Acquired absence of thumb and other finger(s)**

  ● **Z89.01**   **Acquired absence of thumb**

    Z89.011   Acquired absence of right thumb

    Z89.012   Acquired absence of left thumb

    Z89.019   Acquired absence of unspecified thumb

  ● **Z89.02**   **Acquired absence of other finger(s)**

> **Excludes2**   acquired absence of thumb (Z89.01-)

    Z89.021   Acquired absence of right finger(s)

    Z89.022   Acquired absence of left finger(s)

    Z89.029   Acquired absence of unspecified finger(s)

● **Z89.1**   **Acquired absence of hand and wrist**

  ● **Z89.11**   **Acquired absence of hand**

    Z89.111   Acquired absence of right hand

    Z89.112   Acquired absence of left hand

    Z89.119   Acquired absence of unspecified hand

  ● **Z89.12**   **Acquired absence of wrist**
    Disarticulation at wrist

    Z89.121   Acquired absence of right wrist

    Z89.122   Acquired absence of left wrist

    Z89.129   Acquired absence of unspecified wrist

● **Z89.2**   **Acquired absence of upper limb above wrist**

  ● **Z89.20**   **Acquired absence of upper limb, unspecified level**

    Z89.201   Acquired absence of right upper limb, unspecified level

    Z89.202   Acquired absence of left upper limb, unspecified level

    Z89.209   Acquired absence of unspecified upper limb, unspecified level
      Acquired absence of arm NOS

  ● **Z89.21**   **Acquired absence of upper limb below elbow**

    Z89.211   Acquired absence of right upper limb below elbow

    Z89.212   Acquired absence of left upper limb below elbow

    Z89.219   Acquired absence of unspecified upper limb below elbow

  ● **Z89.22**   **Acquired absence of upper limb above elbow**
    Disarticulation at elbow

    Z89.221   Acquired absence of right upper limb above elbow

    Z89.222   Acquired absence of left upper limb above elbow

    Z89.229   Acquired absence of unspecified upper limb above elbow

  ● **Z89.23**   **Acquired absence of shoulder**
    Acquired absence of shoulder joint following explantation of shoulder joint prosthesis, with or without presence of antibiotic-impregnated cement spacer

    Z89.231   Acquired absence of right shoulder

    Z89.232   Acquired absence of left shoulder

    Z89.239   Acquired absence of unspecified shoulder

● **Z89.4**   **Acquired absence of toe(s), foot, and ankle**

  ● **Z89.41**   **Acquired absence of great toe**

    Z89.411   Acquired absence of right great toe 🦿

    Z89.412   Acquired absence of left great toe 🦿

    Z89.419   Acquired absence of unspecified great toe 🦿

  ● **Z89.42**   **Acquired absence of other toe(s)**

> **Excludes2**   acquired absence of great toe (Z89.41-)

    Z89.421   Acquired absence of other right toe(s) 🦿

    Z89.422   Acquired absence of other left toe(s) 🦿

    Z89.429   Acquired absence of other toe(s), unspecified side 🦿

  ● **Z89.43**   **Acquired absence of foot**

    Z89.431   Acquired absence of right foot 🦿

    Z89.432   Acquired absence of left foot 🦿

    Z89.439   Acquired absence of unspecified foot 🦿

  ● **Z89.44**   **Acquired absence of ankle**
    Disarticulation of ankle

    Z89.441   Acquired absence of right ankle 🦿

    Z89.442   Acquired absence of left ankle 🦿

    Z89.449   Acquired absence of unspecified ankle 🦿

● **Z89.5**   **Acquired absence of leg below knee**

  ● **Z89.51**   **Acquired absence of leg below knee**

    Z89.511   Acquired absence of right leg below knee 🦿

    Z89.512   Acquired absence of left leg below knee 🦿

    Z89.519   Acquired absence of unspecified leg below knee 🦿

  ● **Z89.52**   **Acquired absence of knee**
    Acquired absence of knee joint following explantation of knee joint prosthesis, with or without presence of antibiotic-impregnated cement spacer

    Z89.521   Acquired absence of right knee

    Z89.522   Acquired absence of left knee

    Z89.529   Acquired absence of unspecified knee

● **Z89.6**   **Acquired absence of leg above knee**

  ● **Z89.61**   **Acquired absence of leg above knee**
    Acquired absence of leg NOS
    Disarticulation at knee

    Z89.611   Acquired absence of right leg above knee 🦿

    Z89.612   Acquired absence of left leg above knee 🦿

    Z89.619   Acquired absence of unspecified leg above knee 🦿

  ● **Z89.62**   **Acquired absence of hip**
    Acquired absence of hip joint following explantation of hip joint prosthesis, with or without presence of antibiotic-impregnated cement spacer
    Disarticulation at hip

    Z89.621   Acquired absence of right hip joint

    Z89.622   Acquired absence of left hip joint

    Z89.629   Acquired absence of unspecified hip joint

Z89.9   **Acquired absence of limb, unspecified**

CHAPTER 21 (Z00-Z99)

● **Z90   Acquired absence of organs, not elsewhere classified**

> **Includes**   postprocedural or post-traumatic loss of body part NEC
>
> **Excludes1**   congenital absence - see Alphabetical Index
>
> **Excludes2**   postprocedural absence of endocrine glands (E89.-)

● **Z90.0   Acquired absence of part of head and neck**

   Z90.01   Acquired absence of eye

   Z90.02   Acquired absence of larynx

   Z90.09   Acquired absence of other part of head and neck

      Acquired absence of nose

> **Excludes2**   teeth (K08.1)

● **Z90.1   Acquired absence of breast and nipple**

   Z90.10   Acquired absence of unspecified breast and nipple

   Z90.11   Acquired absence of right breast and nipple

   Z90.12   Acquired absence of left breast and nipple

   Z90.13   Acquired absence of bilateral breasts and nipples

Z90.2   Acquired absence of lung [part of]

Z90.3   Acquired absence of stomach [part of]

● **Z90.4   Acquired absence of other specified parts of digestive tract**

   ● **Z90.41   Acquired absence of pancreas**

> Code also exocrine pancreatic insufficiency (K86.81)
>
> Use additional code to identify any associated:
> diabetes mellitus, postpancreatectomy (E13.-)
> insulin use (Z79.4)

     Z90.410   Acquired total absence of pancreas

        Acquired absence of pancreas NOS

     Z90.411   Acquired partial absence of pancreas

   Z90.49   Acquired absence of other specified parts of digestive tract

Z90.5   Acquired absence of kidney

Z90.6   Acquired absence of other parts of urinary tract

   Acquired absence of bladder

● **Z90.7   Acquired absence of genital organ(s)**

> **Excludes1**   personal history of sex reassignment (Z87.890)
>
> **Excludes2**   female genital mutilation status (N90.81-)

   ● **Z90.71   Acquired absence of cervix and uterus**

     Z90.710   Acquired absence of both cervix and uterus ♀

        Acquired absence of uterus NOS

        Status post total hysterectomy

     Z90.711   Acquired absence of uterus with remaining cervical stump ♀

        Status post partial hysterectomy with remaining cervical stump

     Z90.712   Acquired absence of cervix with remaining uterus ♀

   ● **Z90.72   Acquired absence of ovaries**

     Z90.721   Acquired absence of ovaries, unilateral ♀

     Z90.722   Acquired absence of ovaries, bilateral ♀

   Z90.79   Acquired absence of other genital organ(s)

● **Z90.8   Acquired absence of other organs**

   Z90.81   Acquired absence of spleen

   Z90.89   Acquired absence of other organs

● **Z91   Personal risk factors, not elsewhere classified**

> **Excludes2**   contact with and (suspected) exposures hazardous to health (Z77.-)
> exposure to pollution and other problems related to physical environment (Z77.1-)
> female genital mutilation status (N90.81-)
> occupational exposure to risk factors (Z57.-)
> personal history of physical injury and trauma (Z87.81, Z87.82-)

● **Z91.0   Allergy status, other than to drugs and biological substances**

> **Excludes2**   allergy status to drugs, medicaments, and biological substances (Z88.-)

   ● **Z91.01   Food allergy status**

> **Excludes2**   food additives allergy status (Z91.02)

     Z91.010   Allergy to peanuts

     Z91.011   Allergy to milk products

> **Excludes1**   lactose intolerance (E73.-)

     Z91.012   Allergy to eggs

     Z91.013   Allergy to seafood

        Allergy to shellfish

        Allergy to octopus or squid ink

     Z91.018   Allergy to other foods

        Allergy to nuts other than peanuts

   Z91.02   Food additives allergy status

   ● **Z91.03   Insect allergy status**

     Z91.030   Bee allergy status

     Z91.038   Other insect allergy status

   ● **Z91.04   Nonmedicinal substance allergy status**

     Z91.040   Latex allergy status

        Latex sensitivity status

     Z91.041   Radiographic dye allergy status

        Allergy status to contrast media used for diagnostic X-ray procedure

     Z91.048   Other nonmedicinal substance allergy status

   Z91.09   Other allergy status, other than to drugs and biological substances

● **Z91.1   Patient's noncompliance with medical treatment and regimen**

   Z91.11   Patient's noncompliance with dietary regimen

   ● **Z91.12   Patient's intentional underdosing of medication regimen**

> *Code first underdosing of medication (T36-T50) with fifth or sixth character 6*
>
> **Excludes1**   adverse effect of prescribed drug taken as directed - code to adverse effect
> poisoning (overdose) - code to poisoning

     Z91.120   Patient's intentional underdosing of medication regimen due to financial hardship

     Z91.128   Patient's intentional underdosing of medication regimen for other reason

▶ New   ⇒ Revised   ~~deleted~~ Deleted   Excludes 1   Excludes 2   Includes   Use additional   Code first   Code also   Key words

OGCR Official Guidelines   X Assign placeholder X   ● Use Additional Character(s)   ▌ Manifestation Code   🐾 Hierarchical Condition Category   Coding Clinic

● **Z91.13** Patient's unintentional underdosing of medication regimen

Code first underdosing of medication (T36–T50) with fifth or sixth character 6

Excludes1 adverse effect of prescribed drug taken as directed - code to adverse effect
poisoning (overdose) - code to poisoning

Z91.130 Patient's unintentional underdosing of medication regimen due to age-related debility

Z91.138 Patient's unintentional underdosing of medication regimen for other reason

Z91.14 Patient's other noncompliance with medication regimen
Patient's underdosing of medication NOS

Z91.15 Patient's noncompliance with renal dialysis 🔄

Z91.19 Patient's noncompliance with other medical treatment and regimen
Nonadherence to medical treatment

● **Z91.4** Personal history of psychological trauma, not elsewhere classified

● **Z91.41** Personal history of adult abuse

Excludes2 personal history of abuse in childhood (Z62.81-)

Z91.410 Personal history of adult physical and sexual abuse　A

Excludes1 current adult physical abuse (T74.11, T76.11)
current adult sexual abuse (T74.21, T76.11)

Z91.411 Personal history of adult psychological abuse　A

Z91.412 Personal history of adult neglect　A

Excludes1 current adult neglect (T74.01, T76.01)

Z91.419 Personal history of unspecified adult abuse　A

Z91.42 Personal history of forced labor or sexual exploitation

Z91.49 Other personal history of psychological trauma, not elsewhere classified

Z91.5 Personal history of self-harm
Personal history of parasuicide
Personal history of self-poisoning
Personal history of suicide attempt

● **Z91.8** Other specified personal risk factors, not elsewhere classified

Z91.81 History of falling
At risk for falling

Z91.82 Personal history of military deployment　A
Individual (civilian or military) with past history of military war, peacekeeping and humanitarian deployment (current or past conflict)
Returned from military deployment

▷ **Z91.83** *Wandering in diseases classified elsewhere*
Code first underlying disorder such as:
Alzheimer's disease (G30.-)
autism or pervasive developmental disorder (F84.-)
intellectual disabilities (F70-F79)
unspecified dementia with behavioral disturbance (F03.9-)

● **Z91.84** Oral health risk factors

Z91.841 Risk for dental caries, low

Z91.842 Risk for dental caries, moderate

Z91.843 Risk for dental caries, high

Z91.849 Unspecified risk for dental caries

Z91.89 Other specified personal risk factors, not elsewhere classified
Coding Clinic: 2017, Q1, P46

● **Z92** Personal history of medical treatment

Excludes2 postprocedural states (Z98.-)

Z92.0 Personal history of contraception

Excludes1 counseling or management of current contraceptive practices (Z30.-)
long term (current) use of contraception (Z79.3)
presence of (intrauterine) contraceptive device (Z97.5)

● **Z92.2** Personal history of drug therapy

Excludes2 long term (current) drug therapy (Z79.-)

Z92.21 Personal history of antineoplastic chemotherapy

Z92.22 Personal history of monoclonal drug therapy

Z92.23 Personal history of estrogen therapy

● **Z92.24** Personal history of steroid therapy

Z92.240 Personal history of inhaled steroid therapy

Z92.241 Personal history of systemic steroid therapy
Personal history of steroid therapy NOS

Z92.25 Personal history of immunosupression therapy

Excludes2 personal history of steroid therapy (Z92.24)

Z92.29 Personal history of other drug therapy

Z92.3 Personal history of irradiation
Personal history of exposure to therapeutic radiation

Excludes1 exposure to radiation in the physical environment (Z77.12)
occupational exposure to radiation (Z57.1)

● **Z92.8** Personal history of other medical treatment
Coding Clinic: 2016, Q4, P72

Z92.81 Personal history of extracorporeal membrane oxygenation (ECMO)

Z92.82 Status post administration of tPA (rtPA) in a different facility within the last 24 hours prior to admission to current facility

Code first condition requiring tPA administration, such as:
acute cerebral infarction (I63.-)
acute myocardial infarction (I21.-, I22.-)

Z92.83 Personal history of failed moderate sedation
Personal history of failed conscious sedation

Excludes2 failed moderate sedation during procedure (T88.52)

Z92.84 Personal history of unintended awareness under general anesthesia

Excludes2 unintended awareness under general anesthesia during procedure (T88.53)
Coding Clinic: 2016, Q4, P72, 77

Z92.89 Personal history of other medical treatment
Coding Clinic: 2020, Q1, P18

CHAPTER 21 (Z00-Z99)

Z93   Artificial opening status

> **Excludes1**   artificial openings requiring attention or management (Z43.-)
>
> complications of external stoma (J95.0-, K94.-, N99.5-)

    Z93.0   Tracheostomy status 🜲
    Z93.1   Gastrostomy status 🜲
    Z93.2   Ileostomy status 🜲
    Z93.3   Colostomy status 🜲
    Z93.4   Other artificial openings of gastrointestinal tract status 🜲

● Z93.5   Cystostomy status
        Z93.50   Unspecified cystostomy status 🜲
        Z93.51   Cutaneous-vesicostomy status 🜲
        Z93.52   Appendico-vesicostomy status 🜲
        Z93.59   Other cystostomy status 🜲

    Z93.6   Other artificial openings of urinary tract status 🜲
            Nephrostomy status
            Ureterostomy status
            Urethrostomy status

    Z93.8   Other artificial opening status 🜲
    Z93.9   Artificial opening status, unspecified 🜲

● **Z94   Transplanted organ and tissue status**

> **Includes**   organ or tissue replaced by heterogenous or homogenous transplant
>
> **Excludes1**   complications of transplanted organ or tissue - see Alphabetical Index
>
> **Excludes2**   presence of vascular grafts (Z95.-)

    Z94.0   Kidney transplant status
    Z94.1   Heart transplant status 🜲

> **Excludes1**   artificial heart status (Z95.812)
>
> heart-valve replacement status (Z95.2-Z95.4)

    Z94.2   Lung transplant status 🜲
    Z94.3   Heart and lungs transplant status 🜲
    Z94.4   Liver transplant status 🜲
    Z94.5   Skin transplant status
            Autogenous skin transplant status
    Z94.6   Bone transplant status
    Z94.7   Corneal transplant status

● Z94.8   Other transplanted organ and tissue status
        Z94.81   Bone marrow transplant status 🜲
        Z94.82   Intestine transplant status 🜲
        Z94.83   Pancreas transplant status 🜲
        Z94.84   Stem cells transplant status 🜲
        Z94.89   Other transplanted organ and tissue status

    Z94.9   Transplanted organ and tissue status, unspecified

● **Z95   Presence of cardiac and vascular implants and grafts**

> **Excludes2**   complications of cardiac and vascular devices, implants and grafts (T82.-)

    Z95.0   Presence of cardiac pacemaker
            Presence of cardiac resynchronization therapy (CRT-P) pacemaker

> **Excludes1**   adjustment or management of cardiac device (Z45.0-)
>
> adjustment or management of cardiac pacemaker (Z45.0)
>
> presence of automatic (implantable) cardiac defibrillator with synchronous cardiac pacemaker (Z95.810)

            Coding Clinic: 2019, Q1, P33

    Z95.1   Presence of aortocoronary bypass graft
            Presence of coronary artery bypass graft
    Z95.2   Presence of prosthetic heart valve
            Presence of heart valve NOS
    Z95.3   Presence of xenogenic heart valve

    Z95.4   Presence of other heart-valve replacement
    Z95.5   Presence of coronary angioplasty implant and graft

> **Excludes1**   coronary angioplasty status without implant and graft (Z98.61)

● Z95.8   Presence of other cardiac and vascular implants and grafts
    ● Z95.81   Presence of other cardiac implants and grafts
        Z95.810   Presence of automatic (implantable) cardiac defibrillator
                Presence of automatic (implantable) cardiac defribillator with synchronous cardiac pacemaker
                Presence of cardiac resynchronization therapy defibrillator (CRT-D)
                Presence of cardioverter-defibrillator (ICD)
        Z95.811   Presence of heart assist device 🜲
        Z95.812   Presence of fully implantable artificial heart 🜲
        Z95.818   Presence of other cardiac implants and grafts

    ● Z95.82   Presence of other vascular implants and grafts
        Z95.820   Peripheral vascular angioplasty status with implants and grafts

> **Excludes1**   peripheral vascular angioplasty without implant and graft (Z98.62)

        Z95.828   Presence of other vascular implants and grafts
                Presence of intravascular prosthesis NEC

    Z95.9   Presence of cardiac and vascular implant and graft, unspecified

● **Z96   Presence of other functional implants**

> **Excludes2**   complications of internal prosthetic devices, implants and grafts (T82-T85)
>
> fitting and adjustment of prosthetic and other devices (Z44-Z46)

    Z96.0   Presence of urogenital implants
    Z96.1   Presence of intraocular lens
            Presence of pseudophakia
● Z96.2   Presence of otological and audiological implants
        Z96.20   Presence of otological and audiological implant, unspecified
        Z96.21   Cochlear implant status
        Z96.22   Myringotomy tube(s) status
        Z96.29   Presence of other otological and audiological implants
                Presence of bone-conduction hearing device
                Presence of eustachian tube stent
                Stapes replacement
    Z96.3   Presence of artificial larynx
● Z96.4   Presence of endocrine implants
        Z96.41   Presence of insulin pump (external) (internal)
        Z96.49   Presence of other endocrine implants
    Z96.5   Presence of tooth-root and mandibular implants
● Z96.6   Presence of orthopedic joint implants
        Z96.60   Presence of unspecified orthopedic joint implant
    ● Z96.61   Presence of artificial shoulder joint
        Z96.611   Presence of right artificial shoulder joint
        Z96.612   Presence of left artificial shoulder joint
        Z96.619   Presence of unspecified artificial shoulder joint

▶ New   ⇒ Revised   ~~deleted~~ Deleted   Excludes 1   Excludes 2   Includes   Use additional   Code first   Code also   Key words

OGCR Official Guidelines   X Assign placeholder X   ● Use Additional Character(s)   ▌ Manifestation Code   🜲 Hierarchical Condition Category   Coding Clinic

● **Z96.62**   Presence of artificial elbow joint

     Z96.621   Presence of right artificial elbow joint

     Z96.622   Presence of left artificial elbow joint

     Z96.629   Presence of unspecified artificial elbow joint

● **Z96.63**   Presence of artificial wrist joint

     Z96.631   Presence of right artificial wrist joint

     Z96.632   Presence of left artificial wrist joint

     Z96.639   Presence of unspecified artificial wrist joint

● **Z96.64**   Presence of artificial hip joint

     Hip-joint replacement (partial) (total)

     Z96.641   Presence of right artificial hip joint
           Coding Clinic: 2016, Q3, P17

     Z96.642   Presence of left artificial hip joint
           Coding Clinic: 2015, Q1, P16

     Z96.643   Presence of artificial hip joint, bilateral

     Z96.649   Presence of unspecified artificial hip joint

● **Z96.65**   Presence of artificial knee joint

     Z96.651   Presence of right artificial knee joint

     Z96.652   Presence of left artificial knee joint
           Coding Clinic: 2019, Q3, P16

     Z96.653   Presence of artificial knee joint, bilateral

     Z96.659   Presence of unspecified artificial knee joint

● **Z96.66**   Presence of artificial ankle joint

     Z96.661   Presence of right artificial ankle joint

     Z96.662   Presence of left artificial ankle joint

     Z96.669   Presence of unspecified artificial ankle joint

● **Z96.69**   Presence of other orthopedic joint implants

     Z96.691   Finger-joint replacement of right hand

     Z96.692   Finger-joint replacement of left hand

     Z96.693   Finger-joint replacement, bilateral

     Z96.698   Presence of other orthopedic joint implants

Z96.7   Presence of other bone and tendon implants

     Presence of skull plate

● **Z96.8**   Presence of other specified functional implants

     Z96.81   Presence of artificial skin

     Z96.82   Presence of neurostimulator

         Presence of brain neurostimulator

         Presence of gastric neurostimulator

         Presence of peripheral nerve neurostimulator

         Presence of sacral nerve neurostimulator

         Presence of spinal cord neurostimulator

         Presence of vagus nerve neurostimulator

     Z96.89   Presence of other specified functional implants

Z96.9   Presence of functional implant, unspecified

● **Z97**   **Presence of other devices**

     Excludes2   fitting and adjustment of prosthetic and other devices (Z44-Z46)

                 presence of cerebrospinal fluid drainage device (Z98.2)

Z97.0   Presence of artificial eye

● **Z97.1**   Presence of artificial limb (complete) (partial)

     Z97.10   Presence of artificial limb (complete) (partial), unspecified

     Z97.11   Presence of artificial right arm (complete) (partial)

     Z97.12   Presence of artificial left arm (complete) (partial)

     Z97.13   Presence of artificial right leg (complete) (partial)

     Z97.14   Presence of artificial left leg (complete) (partial)

     Z97.15   Presence of artificial arms, bilateral (complete) (partial)

     Z97.16   Presence of artificial legs, bilateral (complete) (partial)

Z97.2   Presence of dental prosthetic device (complete) (partial)

     Presence of dentures (complete) (partial)

Z97.3   Presence of spectacles and contact lenses

Z97.4   Presence of external hearing-aid

Z97.5   Presence of (intrauterine) contraceptive device ♀

     Excludes1   checking, reinsertion or removal of implantable subdermal contraceptive (Z30.46)

                 checking, reinsertion or removal of intrauterine contraceptive device (Z30.43-)

Z97.8   Presence of other specified devices

● **Z98**   **Other postprocedural states**

     Excludes2   aftercare (Z43-Z49, Z51)

                 follow-up medical care (Z08-Z09)

                 postprocedural complication - see Alphabetical Index

Z98.0   Intestinal bypass and anastomosis status

     Excludes2   bariatric surgery status (Z98.84)

                 gastric bypass status (Z98.84)

                 obesity surgery status (Z98.84)

Z98.1   Arthrodesis status

Z98.2   Presence of cerebrospinal fluid drainage device

     Presence of CSF shunt

Z98.3   Post therapeutic collapse of lung status

     Code first underlying disease

● **Z98.4**   Cataract extraction status

     Use additional code to identify intraocular lens implant status (Z96.1)

     Excludes1   aphakia (H27.0)

     Z98.41   Cataract extraction status, right eye

     Z98.42   Cataract extraction status, left eye

     Z98.49   Cataract extraction status, unspecified eye

● **Z98.5**   Sterilization status

     Excludes1   female infertility (N97.-)

                 male infertility (N46.-)

     Z98.51   Tubal ligation status ♀

     Z98.52   Vasectomy status ♂   A

● **Z98.6**   Angioplasty status

     Z98.61   Coronary angioplasty status

         Excludes1   coronary angioplasty status with implant and graft (Z95.5)

     Z98.62   Peripheral vascular angioplasty status

         Excludes1   peripheral vascular angioplasty status with implant and graft (Z95.820)

● **Z98.8**   Other specified postprocedural states
     Coding Clinic: 2016, Q4, P76

     ● **Z98.81**   Dental procedure status

         Z98.810   Dental sealant status

         Z98.811   Dental restoration status

             Dental crown status

             Dental fillings status

         Z98.818   Other dental procedure status

     Z98.82   Breast implant status

         Excludes1   breast implant removal status (Z98.86)

     Z98.83   Filtering (vitreous) bleb after glaucoma surgery status

         Excludes1   inflammation (infection) of postprocedural bleb (H59.4-)

CHAPTER 21 (Z00-Z99)

Z98.84 **Bariatric surgery status**
Gastric banding status
Gastric bypass status for obesity
Obesity surgery status

> **Excludes1** bariatric surgery status complicating pregnancy, childbirth, or the puerperium (O99.84)

> **Excludes2** intestinal bypass and anastomosis status (Z98.0)

Coding Clinic: 2020, Q1, P12

Z98.85 **Transplanted organ removal status**
Transplanted organ previously removed due to complication, failure, rejection or infection

> **Excludes1** encounter for removal of transplanted organ - code to complication of transplanted organ (T86.-)

Z98.86 **Personal history of breast implant removal**

● **Z98.87** **Personal history of in utero procedure**

Z98.870 **Personal history of in utero procedure during pregnancy ♀**

> **Excludes2** complications from in utero procedure for current pregnancy (O35.7)
> supervision of current pregnancy with history of in utero procedure during previous pregnancy (O09.82-)

Z98.871 **Personal history of in utero procedure while a fetus**

● **Z98.89** **Other specified postprocedural states**
Coding Clinic: 2016, Q4, P76

Z98.890 **Other specified postprocedural states**
Personal history of surgery, not elsewhere classified

Z98.891 **History of uterine scar from previous surgery ♀**

> **Excludes1** Maternal care due to uterine scar from previous surgery (O34.2-)

Coding Clinic: 2016, Q4, P52, P76

● **Z99** **Dependence on enabling machines and devices, not elsewhere classified**

> **Excludes1** cardiac pacemaker status (Z95.0)

Coding Clinic: 2020, Q1, P11

Z99.0 **Dependence on aspirator**

● **Z99.1** **Dependence on respirator**
Dependence on ventilator

Z99.11 **Dependence on respirator [ventilator] status** 🅠
Coding Clinic: 2018, Q1, P14; 2015, Q1, P21

Z99.12 **Encounter for respirator [ventilator] dependence during power failure** 🅠

> **Excludes1** mechanical complication of respirator [ventilator] (J95.850)

Z99.2 **Dependence on renal dialysis** 🅠
Hemodialysis status
Peritoneal dialysis status
Presence of arteriovenous shunt for dialysis
Renal dialysis status NOS

> **Excludes1** encounter for fitting and adjustment of dialysis catheter (Z49.0-)

> **Excludes2** noncompliance with renal dialysis (Z91.15)

Coding Clinic: 2016, Q1, P13

Z99.3 **Dependence on wheelchair**
Wheelchair confinement status
Code first cause of dependence, such as:
muscular dystrophy (G71.0-)
obesity (E66.-)

● **Z99.8** **Dependence on other enabling machines and devices**

Z99.81 **Dependence on supplemental oxygen**
Dependence on long-term oxygen

Z99.89 **Dependence on other enabling machines and devices**
Dependence on machine or device NOS
Coding Clinic: 2020, Q1, P11

▶ New   ⇒ Revised   ~~deleted~~ Deleted   Excludes 1   Excludes 2   Includes   Use additional   Code first   Code also   Key words
OGCR Official Guidelines   X Assign placeholder X   ● Use Additional Character(s)   ▸ Manifestation Code   🅠 Hierarchical Condition Category   Coding Clinic

▶**CHAPTER 22**

  ▶**CODES FOR SPECIAL PURPOSES (U00–U85)**

    ▶**Note:** Codes from this chapter are for use on newborn records only, never on maternal records.

    ▶This chapter contains the following blocks:

▶	U00–U49 Provisional assignment of new diseases of uncertain etiology or emergency use

▶**PROVISIONAL ASSIGNMENT OF NEW DISEASES OF UNCERTAIN ETIOLOGY OR EMERGENCY USE (U00–U49)**

▶ **U07**   Emergency use of U07

  ▶ **U07.0**   **Vaping-related disorder**

    ▶Dabbing related lung damage

    ▶Dabbing related lung injury

    ▶E-cigarette, or vaping, product use associated lung injury [EVALI]

    ▶Electronic cigarette related lung damage

    ▶Electronic cigarette related lung injury

    ▶Use additional code to identify manifestations, such as:

      ▶abdominal pain (R10.84)

      ▶acute respiratory distress syndrome (J80)

      ▶diarrhea (R19.7)

      ▶drug-induced interstitial lung disorder (J70.4)

      ▶lipoid pneumonia (J69.1)

      ▶weight loss (R63.4)

▶ **U07.1**   **COVID-19**

  ▶Use additional code to identify pneumonia or other manifestations

  ▶ **Excludes1**   coronavirus infection, unspecified (B34.2)

    ▶coronavirus as the cause of diseases classified elsewhere (B97.2-)

    ▶pneumonia due to SARS-associated coronavirus (J12.81)